Weiss Ratings' Investment Research Guide to Stock Mutual Funds

Weiss Ratings' Investment Research Guide to Stock Mutual Funds

Winter 2017-18

GREY HOUSE PUBLISHING

Weiss Ratings
4400 Northcorp Parkway
Palm Beach Gardens, FL 33410
561-627-3300

WeissRatings
Independent. Unbiased. Accurate. Trusted.

Published by Grey House Publishing, Inc., located at 4919 Route 22, Amenia, NY 12501; telephone 518-789-8700. Grey House Publishing neither guarantees the accuracy of the data contained herein nor assumes any responsibility for errors, omissions or discrepancies. Grey House Publishing accepts no payment for listing; inclusion in the publication of any organization, agency, institution, publication, service or individual does not imply endorsement of the publisher.

Grey House Publishing

Edition #3, Winter 2017-18

ISBN: 978-1-68217-812-6

Contents

Terms and Conditions

This document is prepared strictly for the confidential use of our customer(s). It has been provided to you at your specific request. It is not directed to, or intended for distribution to or use by, any person or entity who is a citizen or resident of or located in any locality, state, country or other jurisdiction where such distribution, publication, availability or use would be contrary to law or regulation or which would subject Weiss Ratings, LLC or its affiliates to any registration or licensing requirement within such jurisdiction.

No part of the analysts' compensation was, is, or will be, directly or indirectly, related to the specific recommendations or views expressed in this research report.

This document is not intended for the direct or indirect solicitation of business. Weiss Ratings, LLC, and its affiliates disclaim any and all liability to any person or entity for any loss or damage caused, in whole or in part, by any error (negligent or otherwise) or other circumstances involved in, resulting from or relating to the procurement, compilation, analysis, interpretation, editing, transcribing, publishing and/or dissemination or transmittal of any information contained herein.

Weiss Ratings, LLC has not taken any steps to ensure that the securities or investment vehicle referred to in this report are suitable for any particular investor. The investment or services contained or referred to in this report may not be suitable for you and it is recommended that you consult an independent investment advisor if you are in doubt about such investments or investment services. Nothing in this report constitutes investment, legal, accounting or tax advice or a representation that any investment or strategy is suitable or appropriate to your individual circumstances or otherwise constitutes a personal recommendation to you.

The ratings and other opinions contained in this document must be construed solely as statements of opinion from Weiss Ratings, LLC, and not statements of fact. Each rating or opinion must be weighed solely as a factor in your choice of an institution and should not be construed as a recommendation to buy, sell or otherwise act with respect to the particular product or company involved.

Past performance should not be taken as an indication or guarantee of future performance, and no representation or warranty, expressed or implied, is made regarding future performance. Information, opinions and estimates contained in this report reflect a judgment at its original date of publication and are subject to change without notice. Weiss Ratings, LLC offers a notification service for rating changes on companies you specify. For more information visit WeissRatings.com or call 1-877-934-7778. The price, value and income from any of the securities or financial instruments mentioned in this report can fall as well as rise.

This document and the information contained herein is copyrighted by Weiss Ratings, LLC. Any copying, displaying, selling, distributing or otherwise delivering of this information or any part of this document to any other person or entity is prohibited without the express written consent of Weiss Ratings, LLC, with the exception of a reviewer or editor who may quote brief passages in connection with a review or a news story.

Date of Data Analyzed: December 31, 2017

Welcome to Weiss Ratings' Investment Research Guide to Stock Mutual Funds

With investing such a complex subject and the enormous popularity of mutual funds as a simple way to enter the markets it is no surprise that consumers need assistance. It is a complex subject and consumers want unbiased, independent guidance in helping them find a path to investing that is focused on their needs.

This is where Weiss Ratings comes in. We take all the data and process it, daily, to ensure that you receive not only the most up-to-date rating possible but also data that you may not easily find elsewhere. We publish this data in guides, and on our website so that you can feel empowered to make decisions about your investing future. Our focus is on balance and our ratings reflect this. No matter how strong a return has been if the level of risk taken is too high, in our opinion, then the overall rating will be reduced.

Weiss Ratings' Mission Statement

Weiss Ratings' mission is to empower consumers, professionals, and institutions with high quality advisory information for selecting or monitoring a financial services company or financial investment.

In doing so, Weiss Ratings will adhere to the highest ethical standards by maintaining our independent, unbiased outlook and approach for our customers.

Why rely on Weiss Ratings?

Weiss Ratings are fundamentally incomparable to nearly all other ratings available in America today. Here's why ...

Complete Independence

We are America's only 100% independent rating agency covering stocks, ETFs, mutual funds, insurance companies, banks, and credit unions; and our independence is grounded in a very critical difference in the way we do business: Unlike most other rating agencies,

- we never accept compensation from any company for its rating;
- we never allow companies to influence our analysis or conclusions (although they are always free to provide us with supplemental data that's not publicly available);
- we reserve the right to publish our ratings based exclusively on publicly available data;
- we never suppress publication of our ratings at a company's request; and
- we are always dedicated to providing our analysis and opinions with complete objectivity.

Dedication to End Users -- Investors and Consumers

Other rating agencies derive most of their revenues from the very same companies that they cover.

In contrast, our primary source of revenues is the end user – investors seeking the best combination of risk and reward, plus consumers seeking the best deals with the most safety.

Unmatched Accuracy and Performance

Our independence and objectivity help explain why the U.S. Government Accountability Office (GAO) concluded that Weiss was first in warning consumers about future insurance company failures three times more often than our closest competitor (A.M. Best) and why, in comparison to S&P or Moody's, there was no contest.

It's the reason why The New York Times wrote "Weiss was the first to warn of dangers and say so unambiguously."

And it's also why The Wall Street Journal was able to report that the Weiss Stock Ratings outperformed all Wall Street investment banks, brokers and independent research organizations in a third-party study of stock ratings.

Broader Coverage

While other rating agencies focus mostly on larger companies that can afford to pay them large fees, Weiss Ratings covers all companies, large or small, as long as they report sufficient data for us to analyze. This allows us to provide far broader coverage, including nearly all U.S.-traded stocks, ETFs and mutual funds plus nearly all U.S. banks, credit unions and insurance companies.

Overall ...

Weiss Ratings gives you more accuracy, more choices, and better wealth-building potential – all with stronger risk protection and safety.

How to Use This Guide

The purpose of the *Weiss Ratings' Investment Research Guide to Stock Mutual Funds* is to provide investors with a reliable source of investment ratings and analyses on a timely basis. We realize that past performance is an important factor to consider when making the decision to purchase shares in a mutual fund. The ratings and analyses in this Guide can make that evaluation easier when you are considering stock mutual funds. The rating for a particular fund indicates our opinion regarding that fund's past risk-adjusted performance.

When evaluating a specific mutual fund, we recommend you follow these steps:

Step 1 Confirm the fund name and ticker symbol. To ensure you evaluate the correct mutual fund, verify the fund's exact name and ticker symbol as it was given to you in its prospectus or appears on your account statement. Many funds have similar names, so you want to make sure the fund you look up is really the one you are interested in evaluating.

Step 2 Check the fund's Investment Rating. Turn to Section I, the *Weiss Ratings' Investment Research Guide to Stock Mutual Funds*, and locate the fund you are evaluating. This section contains all stock mutual funds analyzed by Weiss Ratings, including those that did not receive an Investment Rating. All funds are listed in alphabetical order by the name of the fund with the ticker symbol following the name for additional verification. Once you have located your specific fund, the fourth column after the ticker symbol under the Ratings header shows its overall Investment Rating. Turn to *About Weiss Investment Ratings* for information about what this rating means.

Step 3 Analyze the supporting data. In addition to the Weiss Mutual Fund Rating are some of the various measures we have used in rating the fund. Refer to the Section I introduction to see what each of these factors measures. In most cases, lower rated funds will have a low reward rating and/or a low risk rating (i.e., high volatility). Bear in mind, however, that the Weiss Mutual Fund Rating is the result of a complex proprietary computer-generated analysis which cannot be reproduced using only the data provided here.

Step 4 When looking to identify a mutual fund that achieves your specific investing goals, we recommend the following:

- **Check the listing of the Largest funds.** If your priority is to stick with large funds because you believe that the size of the fund matters then these funds should be looked at. In this listing of the 100 largest funds you can also be assured that the Weiss Mutual Fund Rating is just as important as for the smallest fund.

- **Check the listing of the Best All-Around funds.** If your priority is to achieve a balanced return with the amount of risk being taken then check out this listing. We have selected funds with better returns, lower expense and with a maximum initial investment of $5,000 or less required.

- **Check the listing of the Consistent Return Buy rated funds.** If your priority is to achieve a consistent return over at least a five-year period, including the last three months then check out this listing. We have selected the highest rated funds with excellent five-year returns with a size of invested assets to give them a substantial base. At the same time, we have looked for the smallest initial investment we could find.

- **Check the High Performance funds.** If your priority is to achieve the highest return, balanced with the amount of risk we have chosen the top mutual funds with the best financial performance. Not just "Buy" rated these funds have hit our demanding criteria of being in the top 25% of total returns for funds over a number of time-periods. Keep in mind that past performance alone is not always a guide to future performance.

- **Check the funds with Low Volatility.** On the other hand, if ultimate safety is your top priority, check out our list the top recommended mutual funds with the lowest volatility. These funds may have lower performance ratings than some other funds, but can provide a safe place for your savings.

- **Check out the Top-Rated Funds by Fund Type.** If you are looking to invest in a particular type of mutual fund turn to our listing of "Buy" rated Mutual Funds by Fund Type. There you will find the top mutual funds with the highest performance rating in each category.

Step 5 Refer back to Section I. Once you have identified a particular fund that interests you, refer back to Section I, the Index of Stock Mutual Funds, for a more thorough analysis.

If you are interested in contacting a provider, refer to the Index of Providers in the Appendix, where you will find the telephone number, address and website for all providers listed in this guide.

Step 6 Always remember:

- **Read our warnings and cautions.** In order to use Weiss Investment Ratings most effectively, we strongly recommend you consult the Important Warnings and Cautions. These are more than just "standard disclaimers." They are very important factors you should be aware of before using this guide.

- **Stay up to date.** Periodically review the latest Weiss Mutual Fund Ratings for the funds that you own to make sure they are still in line with your investment goals and level of risk tolerance. You can find more detailed information and receive automated updates on ratings through www.weissratings.com

Data Source: Weiss Ratings
Morningstar, Inc.

Date of data analyzed: December 31, 2017

About Weiss Investment Ratings

Weiss Investment Ratings of stocks, ETFs and mutual funds are in the same realm as "buy," "sell" and "hold" ratings. They are designed to help investors make more informed decisions with the goal of maximizing gains and minimizing risk. Safety is also an important consideration. The higher the rating, the more likely the investment will be profitable. But when using our investment ratings, you should always remember that, by definition, all investments involve some element of risk.

A Strong Buy
B Buy
C Hold or Avoid
D Sell
E Strong Sell

Our **Overall Rating** is measured on a scale from A to E based on each fund's risk and performance. The funds are analyzed using the latest daily data available and the quarterly filings with the SEC. Weiss takes thousands of pieces of fund data and, based on its own model, balances reward against the amount of risk to assign a rating. The results provide a simple and understandable opinion as to whether we think the fund is a BUY, SELL, or HOLD.

Our **Reward Rating** is based on the total return over a period of up to five years, including net asset value and price growth. The total return figure is stated net of the expenses and fees charged by the fund. Based on proprietary modeling the individual components of the risk and reward ratings are calculated and weighted and the final rating is generated.

Our **Risk Rating** includes the risk ratings of component stocks where applicable and also includes the financial stability of the fund, turnover where applicable, together with the level of volatility as measured by the fund's daily returns over a period of up to five years. Funds with greater stability are considered less risky and receive a higher risk rating. Funds with greater volatility are considered riskier, and will receive a lower risk rating. In addition to considering the fund's volatility, the risk rating also considers an assessment of the valuation and quality of a fund's holdings.

In order to help guarantee our objectivity, we reserve the right to publish ratings expressing our opinion of an investment reward and risk based exclusively on publicly available data and our own proprietary standards for safety. But when using our investment ratings, you should always remember that, by definition, all investments involve some element of risk.

Current Weiss Ratings Distribution of Stock Mutual Funds

as of December 31, 2017

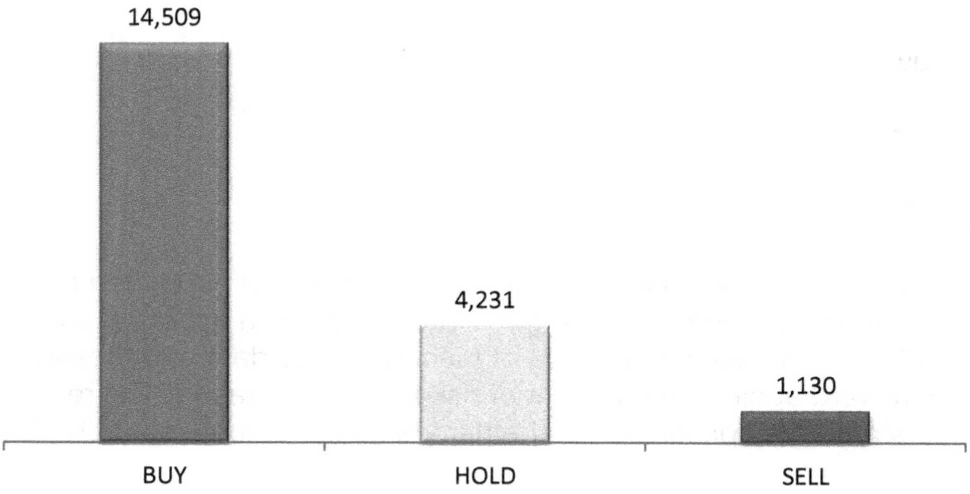

What Our Ratings Mean

Weiss Mutual Funds, Closed-End Funds, and Exchange Traded Funds Ratings represent a completely independent, unbiased opinion of funds—now, and in the future. The funds are analyzed using the latest daily data available and the quarterly filings with the SEC. Weiss takes thousands of pieces of fund data and, based on its own model, balances reward against the amount of risk to assign a rating. The results provide a simple and understandable opinion as to whether we think the fund is a BUY, SELL, or HOLD.

In order to help guarantee our objectivity, we reserve the right to publish ratings expressing our opinion of an investment reward and risk based exclusively on publicly available data and our own proprietary standards for safety. But when using our investment ratings, you should always remember that, by definition, all investments involve some element of risk.

Strong Buy

A **Excellent.** The fund has an excellent track record for maximizing performance while minimizing risk, thus delivering the best possible combination of total return on investment and reduced volatility. It has made the most of the recent economic environment to maximize risk-adjusted returns compared to other mutual funds. Although even the best funds can decline in a down market, our "A" rating can generally be considered the equivalent of a "Strong Buy".

Buy

B **Good.** The fund has a good track record for balancing performance with risk. Compared to other mutual funds, it has achieved above-average returns given the level of risk in its underlying investments. Although even good funds can decline in a down market, our "B" rating is considered the equivalent of a "Buy".

Hold or Avoid

C **Fair.** In the trade-off between performance and risk, the fund has a track record which is about average. It is neither significantly better nor significantly worse than most other funds. With some funds in this category, the total return may be better than average, but this can be misleading if the higher return was achieved with higher than average risk. With other funds, the risk may be lower than average, but the returns are also lower. Although funds can be driven higher or lower by general market trends, our "C" rating can generally be considered the equivalent of a "Hold" or "Avoid."

Sell

D **Weak.** The fund has underperformed the universe of other funds given the level of risk in its underlying investments, resulting in a weak risk-adjusted performance. Thus, its investment strategy and/or management has not been attuned to capitalize on the recent economic environment. Even weak funds can rise in an up market. However, our "D" rating can generally be considered equivalent to a "Sell."

Strong Sell

E **Very Weak.** The fund has significantly underperformed most other funds given the level of risk in its underlying investments, resulting in a very weak risk-adjusted performance. Thus, its investment strategy and/or management has done just the opposite of what was needed to maximize returns in the recent economic environment. Even some of the weakest funds can rise in certain market conditions. However, our "E" rating can generally be considered the equivalent of a "Strong Sell."

\+ The plus sign is an indication that the fund is in the upper third of the letter grade.

\- The minus sign is an indication that the fund is in the lower third of the letter grade.

U Unrated. The fund is unrated because it is too new to make a reliable assessment of its risk-adjusted performance. Typically, a fund must be established for at least one year before it is eligible to receive a Weiss Investment Rating.

Important Warnings & Cautions

1. A rating alone cannot tell the whole story. Please read the explanatory information contained here, in the section introductions and in the appendix. It is provided in order to give you an understanding of our rating methodology as well as to paint a more complete picture of a mutual fund's strengths and weaknesses.

2. Investment ratings shown in this directory were current as of the publication date. In the meantime, the rating may have been updated based on more recent data. Weiss Ratings offers a notification service for ratings changes on companies that you specify. For more information visit www.weissratings.com.

3. When deciding to invest in or sell holdings in a specific mutual fund, your decision must be based on a wide variety of factors in addition to the Weiss Mutual Fund Rating. These include any charges you may incur from switching funds, to what degree it meets your long-term planning needs, and what other choices are available to you. Weiss Ratings recommends that you should always consult an independent financial advisor over your investment decisions.

4. Weiss Mutual Fund Ratings represent our opinion of a mutual fund's past risk adjusted performance. As such, a high rating means we feel that the mutual fund has at least achieved above-average returns at the same time as it has balanced risk and returns. A high rating is not a guarantee that a fund will continue to perform well, nor is a low rating a prediction of continued weak performance. Any references to "Buy", "Hold", or "Sell" correlate with our opinion of a particular fund and Weiss Mutual Fund Ratings are not deemed to be a recommendation concerning the purchase or sale of any mutual fund.

5. All funds that have the same Weiss Investment Rating should be considered to be essentially equal from a risk/reward perspective. This is true regardless of any differences in the underlying numbers which might appear to indicate greater strengths.

6. Our rating standards are more consumer-oriented than those used by other rating agencies. We make more conservative assumptions about the amortization of loads and other fees as we attempt to identify those funds that have historically provided superior returns with only little or moderate risk.

7. We are an independent rating agency and do not depend on the cooperation of the managers operating the mutual funds we rate. Our data is obtained from a data aggregator. Data is input daily, as available, into our proprietary models where a complex series of algorithms provide us with ratings based on quantitative analysis. We do not grant mutual fund managers the right to stop or influence publication of the ratings. This policy stems from the fact that this Guide is designed for the information of the consumer.

Don't Lose Sight of "Real" Currency Moves Amid Digital Currency Debate!

By Mike Larson
Monday, January 29, 2018

The digital currency debate is really heating up!

* Heads of state, Treasury secretaries, central bankers, and major financiers all weighed in on cryptocurrencies at the World Economic Forum in Davos, Switzerland last week. Many were clearly skeptical about the role of Bitcoin and its competitors, and suggested stronger regulation was required.

* One of the larger crypto trading companies in Japan, Coincheck Inc., suspended withdrawals and most trading. That underscored another key risk – the risk cryptocurrency investors won't be able to easily get their money in AND out of the market when they want.

* And of course, we introduced our Weiss Cryptocurrency Ratings in an effort to bring some independent, objective guidance to the marketplace.

But as interesting and revolutionary as the DIGITAL currency marketplace is, you can't lose sight of what's going on in the REALcurrency market, either if you want to be a successful investor! One key recent development: The dollar is getting drubbed, plunging to its lowest level since 2014 last week.

Just look at this chart of the Dollar Index (DXY), an index that tracks how the greenback is performing against a basket of six major world currencies (with the euro most heavily weighted at 57.6%) ...

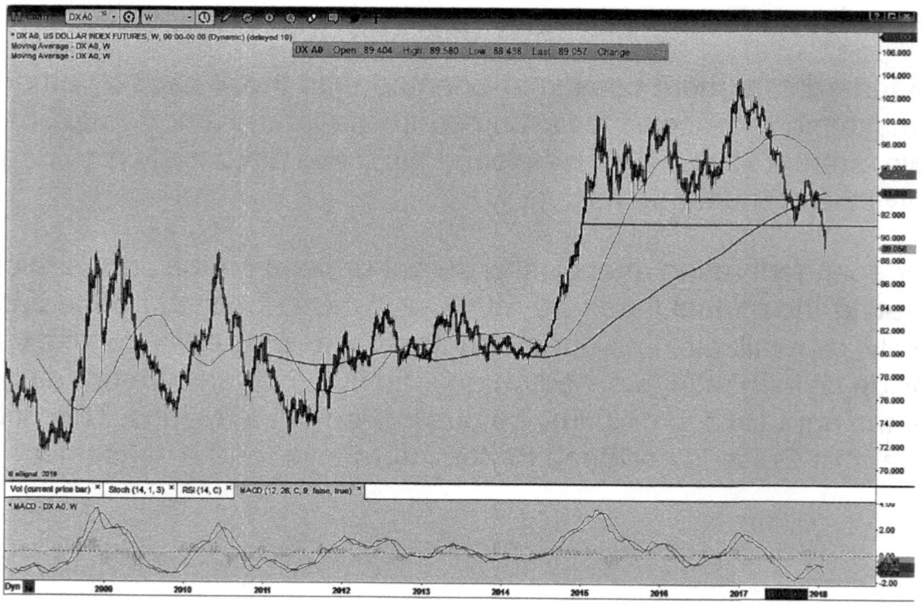

You can see that after a major rally in 2014, followed by a broadening top in 2015-2017, the DXY is now dropping like a rock. Some technical support remains in the 88 area, which corresponds with the previous tops in 2009 and 2010. But if that level gives way, the DXY could plunge all the way to the high 70s before finding firmer support.

The latest decline stems from comments Trump administration officials made in Davos. They seemed to tacitly endorse the dollar decline as a way to boost the U.S. manufacturing and export sectors, even as President Trump himself later attempted to walk that position back slightly.

Stronger economic growth in the eurozone is another factor. So are growing market expectations that foreign central banks will (eventually) start dialing back QE, just like the U.S. Federal Reserve already is.

Whatever the cause, the effect is clear: U.S.-traded ETFs, mutual funds, and American Depositary Receipts that track foreign stocks are benefitting. That's because as the dollar drops against foreign currencies, U.S.-based investors enjoy an extra "currency kicker" to their returns!

Consider this: I created a Weiss Ratings Mutual Fund Screener called Best Performing Mutual Funds in the Past Year with a few very simple criteria. I stipulated that it could only list funds with a Weiss Rating of "C-" (HOLD) or higher and that generated a positive return in the past year. It also had to exclude funds that use leverage to enhance profits.

Those criteria generated a list of more than 26,100 results, including multiple share classes of the same underlying fund. A quick review of the top 10 funds, as well as dozens that ranked just below them, showed that internationally focused funds are dominating the performing race. Have a look ...

Rating	Fund Name	Ticker	1-Year Total Return
C-	Morgan Stanley Institutional Fund, Inc. Asia Opportunity Portfolio Class IS	MSAYX	79.89%
C-	Morgan Stanley Institutional Fund, Inc. Asia Opportunity Portfolio Class I	MSAQX	79.71%
C-	Morgan Stanley Institutional Fund, Inc. Asia Opportunity Portfolio Class A	MSAUX	79.19%
C-	Morgan Stanley Institutional Fund, Inc. Asia Opportunity Portfolio Class C	MSA...	77.75%
B+	Neuberger Berman Greater China Equity Fund Institutional Class	NCEIX	76.86%
B+	Neuberger Berman Greater China Equity Fund Class A	NCEAX	76.26%
C	Quantified STF Fund Investor Class	QSTFX	75.82%
B+	Neuberger Berman Greater China Equity Fund Class C	NCECX	75.02%
C	Quantified STF Fund Advisor Class	QSTAX	74.72%
B+	Matthews China Fund Institutional Class	MICFX	69.40%

In first place is the Morgan Stanley International Fund Asia Opportunity Portfolio (MSAQX, Rated "C-"). Its top holdings include companies active in the Internet, education, hotel, and finance industries in China, Hong Kong, and elsewhere in Asia. Other China focused funds like the Neuberger Berman Greater China Equity Fund (NCEIX, Rated "B+") and Matthews China Fund (MICFX, Rated "B+") also dominated the Top 10.

Clearly, the dollar is oversold in the short term and we could see a bounce at any time. But the overall, longer-term trend is clear. Make sure you don't get so wrapped up in the digital currency debate that you miss out on profit opportunities the real currency market is creating – in foreign ETFs, foreign mutual funds, foreign stocks, and more!

Until next time,

Mike

Mike Larson is a Senior Analyst for Weiss Ratings. A graduate of Boston University, Mike Larson formerly worked at Bankrate.com and Bloomberg News, and is regularly featured on CNBC, CNN, Fox Business News and Bloomberg Television as well as many national radio programs. Due to the astonishing accuracy of his forecasts and warnings, Mike Larson is often quoted by the Washington Post, Chicago Tribune, Associated Press, Reuters, CNNMoney and many others.

Section I:
Index of Stock Mutual Funds

Investment Ratings and analysis of all rated and unrated Open End and Closed End Stock Mutual Funds. Funds are listed in alphabetical order.

Section I: Contents

This section contains Weiss Investment Ratings, key rating factors, and summary financial data for 20,000 stock mutual funds. Funds are listed in alphabetical order.

Left Pages

Fund Name

Describes the fund's assets, regions of investments and investment strategies. Many funds have similar names, so you want to make sure the fund you look up is really the one you are interested in evaluating. In many cases, the Fund Name indicates the Class of the fund.

The most common Classes are:

Class A: This class of Mutual Fund typically has a front-end sales load and a loaded fee structure. Although the fees for Class A may typically be lower, because they normally charge front end fees, your initial amount invested will be lower and your overall return will be affected. An annual asset based fee may well be levied, although this is typically lower than other classes.

Class B: This class of shares, instead of a front-end or back-end sales load normally charges fees called a contingent deferred sales charge (CDSC). This fee is paid if you sell the shares within a certain period of time and may well decline after each year. An annual asset based fee is likely to be levied. Often a Class B share will convert to Class A within a couple of years of reaching the end of the CDSC expiry at which point Class A fees will be initiated.

Class C: A C-share is a class of mutual fund with a level load. They typically don't have front-end loads, but do sometimes have back-end loads. They are usually around 1% but are sometimes eliminated after the shares are held for over a year. Annual asset based fees are normal for this class of share.

Class I: This class is sold to institutional shareholders. Also called Y-Shares, these have different fees and do not charge traditional loads.

Class R: R share funds, Also known as K shares, are for retirement accounts, and the R share class mutual funds are only available through employer-sponsored retirement plans. R share mutual funds do not have any loads, but they do have annual asset based fees typically of around 0.25% to 0.50%.

MARKET

Ticker Symbol

An arrangement of characters (usually letters) representing a particular security listed on an exchange or otherwise traded publicly. When a company issues securities to the public marketplace, it selects an available ticker symbol for its securities which investors use to place trade orders. Every listed security has a unique ticker symbol, facilitating the vast array of trade orders that flow through the financial markets every day. If a ticker symbol is not assigned to a particular fund, the International Securities Identification Number (ISIN) is displayed.

Traded On (Exchange)

The stock exchange on which the fund is listed. The core function of a stock exchange is to ensure fair and orderly trading, as well as efficient dissemination of price information. Exchanges such as: NYSE (New York Stock Exchange), AMEX (American Stock Exchange), NNM (NASDAQ National Market), and NASQ (NASDAQ Small Cap) give companies, governments and other groups a platform to sell securities to the investing public. NASDAQ CM is abbreviated as NAS in this table.

FUND TYPE, CATEGORY & OBJECTIVE

Fund Type

Describes the fund's assets, regions of investments and investment strategies.

Open End Fund

A type of mutual fund that does not have restrictions on the amount of shares the fund will issue. If demand is high enough, the fund will continue to issue shares no matter how many investors there are. Open-end funds also buy back shares when investors wish to sell.

Closed End Fund

They are launched through an Initial Public Offering in order to raise money and then trade in the open market just like a stock or an ETF. They only issue a set amount of shares and, although their value is also based on the Net Asset Value, the actual price of the fund is affected by supply and demand, allowing it to trade at prices above or below its real value.

Category

Identifies funds according to their actual investment styles as measured by their portfolio holdings. This categorization allows investors to spread their money around in a mix of funds with a variety of risk and return characteristics.

Prospectus Objective

Gives a general idea of a fund's overall investment approach and goals.

RATINGS

Overall Rating
The Weiss rating measured on a scale from A to E based on each fund's risk and performance. See the preceding section, "What Our Ratings Mean," for an explanation of each letter grade rating.

Reward Rating
This is based on the total return over a period of up to five years, including net asset value and price growth. The total return figure is stated net of the expenses and fees charged by the fund. Based on proprietary modeling the individual components of the risk and reward ratings are calculated and weighted and the final rating is generated.

Risk Rating
This is includes the risk ratings of component stocks where applicable and also includes the financial stability of the fund, turnover where applicable, together with the level of volatility as measured by the fund's daily returns over a period of up to five years. Funds with greater stability are considered less risky and receive a higher risk rating. Funds with greater volatility are considered riskier, and will receive a lower risk rating. In addition to considering the fund's volatility, the risk rating also considers an assessment of the valuation and quality of a fund's holdings.

Recent Upgrade/Downgrade
An "Up" or "Down" indicates that the Weiss Mutual Fund rating has changed since the publication of the last print edition. If a fund has had a rating change since September 30, 2017, the change is identified with an "Up" or "Down."

MINIMUMS

Open to New Investors
Indicates whether the fund accepts investments from those who are not existing investors. A "Y" in this column identifies that the fund accepts new investors. No data in this column indicates that the fund is closed to new investors. The fund may be closed to new investors because the fund's asset base is getting too large to effectively execute its investing style. Although, the fund may be closed, in most cases, existing investors are able to add to their holdings.

Minimum Initial Investment
The smallest investment amount a fund will accept to establish a new account. This amount could be $0 or any other number set by the fund.

Right Pages

MINIMUMS (continued)

Minimum Additional Investment
The smallest additional investment amount a fund will accept in an existing account.

TOTAL RETURNS

3-Month Total Return
The rate of return on an investment over three months that includes interest, capital gains, dividends and distributions realized.

6-Month Total Return
The rate of return on an investment over six months that includes interest, capital gains, dividends and distributions realized.

1-Year Total Return
The rate of return on an investment over one year that includes interest, capital gains, dividends and distributions realized.

3-Year Total Return
The rate of return on an investment over three years that includes interest, capital gains, dividends and distributions realized.

5-Year Total Return
The rate of return on an investment over five years that includes interest, capital gains, dividends and distributions realized.

PERFORMANCE

Dividend Yield (TTM)
Trailing twelve months dividends paid out relative to the share price. Expressed as a percentage and measures how much cash flow an investor is getting for each invested dollar. **Trailing Twelve Months (TTM)** is a representation of a fund's financial performance over the most recent 12 months. TTM uses the latest available financial data from a company's interim, quarterly or annual reports.

Expense Ratio
A measure of what it costs an investment company to operate a mutual fund. An expense ratio is determined through an annual calculation, where a fund's operating expenses are divided by the average dollar value of its assets under management. Operating expenses may include money spent on administration and management of the fund, advertising, etc. An expense ratio of 1 percent per annum means that each year 1 percent of the fund's total assets will be used to cover expenses.

3-Year Standard Deviation
A statistical measurement of dispersion about an average, which depicts how widely the returns varied over the past three years. Investors use the standard deviation of historical performance to try to predict the range of returns that are most likely for a given fund. When a fund has a high standard deviation, the predicted range of performance is wide, implying greater volatility. Standard deviation is most appropriate for measuring risk if it is for a fund that is an investor's only holding. The figure cannot be combined for more than one fund because the standard deviation for a portfolio of multiple funds is a function of not only the individual standard deviations, but also of the degree of correlation among the funds' returns. If a fund's returns follow a normal distribution, then approximately 68 percent of the time they will fall within one

standard deviation of the mean return for the fund, and 95 percent of the time within two standard deviations.

3-Year Beta

A three year measure of volatility, or systematic risk, of a security in comparison to the market as a whole. A beta of less than 1 means that the security will be less volatile than the market, a beta larger than 1 means more volatility. Beta value cannot be calculated if less than 24 months of pricing is available.

ASSETS

NAV (Net Asset Value)

A fund's price per share. The value is calculated by dividing the total value of all the securities in the portfolio, less any liabilities, by the number of fund shares outstanding.

Total Assets (MIL)

The total of all assets listed on the institution's balance sheet. This figure primarily consists of loans, investments, and fixed assets. Total Assets are displayed in millions.

ASSET ALLOCATION & TURNOVER

Asset Allocation

Indicates the percentage of assets in each category. Used as an investment strategy that attempts to balance risk versus reward by adjusting the percentage of each asset in an investment portfolio according to the investor's risk tolerance, goals and investment time frame. Allocation percentages may not add up to 100%. Negative values reflect short positions.

%Cash

The percentage of the fund's assets invested in short-term obligations, usually less than 90 days, that provide a return in the form of interest payments. This type of investment generally offers a low return compared to other investments but has a low risk level.

%Stocks

The percentage of the fund's assets invested in stock.

%Bonds

The percentage of the fund's assets invested in bonds. A bond is an unsecured debt security issued by companies, municipalities, states and sovereign governments to raise funds. When a company issues a bond it borrows money from the bondholder to boost the business, in exchange the bondholder receives the principal amount back plus the interest on the determined maturity date.

%Other

The percentage of the fund's assets invested in other financial instruments.

Turnover Ratio
The percentage of a mutual fund or other investment vehicle's holdings that have been replaced with other holdings in a given year. Generally, low turnover ratio is favorable, because high turnover equates to higher brokerage transaction fees, which reduce fund returns.

BULL & BEAR MARKETS

Last Bull Market Total Return
The fund's total return (the rate of return on an investment over a period of time that includes interest, capital gains, dividends and distributions realized) during the last market upswing. A **Bull Market** is a financial market condition in which prices are rising or are expected to rise. Bull markets are characterized by optimism, investor confidence and expectations that strong results will continue.

Last Bear Market Total Return
The fund's total return (the rate of return on an investment over a period of time that includes interest, capital gains, dividends and distributions realized) during the last market downturn. A **Bear Market** is a financial market condition in which the prices of securities are falling, investors anticipate losses, and selling of securities increases.

FEES

Front End Fee (%)
A commission or sales charge applied at the time of the initial purchase of an investment. The fee percentage is generally based on the amount of the investment. Larger investments, both initial and cumulative, generally receive percentage discounts based on the dollar value invested. Fees are displayed as a percent.

Back End Fee (%)
A fee that investors pay when withdrawing money from an investment within a specified number of years, usually five to 10 years. The back-end load is designed to discourage withdrawals and typically declines for each year that a shareholder remains in a fund. The fee is a percentage of the value of the share being sold. Fees are displayed as a percent.

Inception Date
The date on which the fund began its operations. The commencement date indicates when a fund began investing in the market. Many investors prefer funds with longer operating histories. Funds with longer histories have longer track records and can thereby provide investors with a more long-standing picture of their performance.

	MARKET		FUND TYPE, CATEGORY & OBJECTIVE		RATINGS				MINIMUMS	
Fund Name	Ticker Symbol	Traded On	Fund Type	Category and (Prospectus Objective)	Overall Rating	Reward Rating	Risk Rating	Recent Up/ Downgrade	Open to New Investors	Min Initial Investment
1290 Convertible Securities Fund Class A	TNFAX	NAS CM	Open End	Convertibles (Convertible Bond)	C	C	B	Up	Y	1,000
1290 Convertible Securities Fund Class I	TNFIX	NAS CM	Open End	Convertibles (Convertible Bond)	C	C+	B	Up	Y	1,000,000
1290 Convertible Securities Fund Class R	TNFRX	NAS CM	Open End	Convertibles (Convertible Bond)	C	C	B	Up	Y	0
1290 DoubleLine Dynamic Allocation Fund Class A	TNXAX	NAS CM	Open End	Cautious Alloc (Asset Alloc)	C-	C-	A	Up	Y	1,000
1290 DoubleLine Dynamic Allocation Fund Class I	TNVDX	NAS CM	Open End	Cautious Alloc (Asset Alloc)	C-	C-	A	Up	Y	1,000,000
1290 DoubleLine Dynamic Allocation Fund Class R	TNYRX	NAS CM	Open End	Cautious Alloc (Asset Alloc)	C-	D+	A	Up	Y	0
1290 GAMCO Small/Mid Cap Value Fund Class A	TNVAX	NAS CM	Open End	US Equity Small Cap (Growth)	C+	C+	B-	Down	Y	1,000
1290 GAMCO Small/Mid Cap Value Fund Class I	TNVIX	NAS CM	Open End	US Equity Small Cap (Growth)	C+	C+	B-	Down	Y	1,000,000
1290 GAMCO Small/Mid Cap Value Fund Class R	TNVRX	NAS CM	Open End	US Equity Small Cap (Growth)	B-	C+	B-	Up	Y	0
1290 GAMCO Small/Mid Cap Value Fund Class T	TNVCX	NAS CM	Open End	US Equity Small Cap (Growth)	B-	C+	B-	Up	Y	1,000
1290 Global Talents Fund Class A	TNYAX	NAS CM	Open End	Global Equity (Growth)	D+	C	B+	Up	Y	1,000
1290 Global Talents Fund Class I	TNYFX	NAS CM	Open End	Global Equity (Growth)	D+	C	B+	Up	Y	1,000,000
1290 Global Talents Fund Class R	TNTRX	NAS CM	Open End	Global Equity (Growth)	D+	C	B+	Up	Y	0
1290 Low Volatility Global Equity Fund Class I	TNZIX	NAS CM	Open End	Global Equity (Growth)	U	U	U		Y	1,000,000
1290 Multi-Alternative Strategies Fund Class A	TNMAX	NAS CM	Open End	Multialternative (Growth)	C	C	B	Up	Y	1,000
1290 Multi-Alternative Strategies Fund Class I	TNMIX	NAS CM	Open End	Multialternative (Growth)	C	C	B	Up	Y	1,000,000
1290 Multi-Alternative Strategies Fund Class R	TNMRX	NAS CM	Open End	Multialternative (Growth)	C	C	B	Up	Y	0
1290 Retirement 2020 Fund Class I	TNIIX	NAS CM	Open End	Target Date 2000-2020 (Asset Alloc)	U	U	U		Y	1,000,000
1290 Retirement 2025 Fund Class I	TNJIX	NAS CM	Open End	Target Date 2021-2045 (Asset Alloc)	U	U	U		Y	1,000,000
1290 Retirement 2030 Fund Class I	TNKIX	NAS CM	Open End	Target Date 2021-2045 (Asset Alloc)	U	U	U		Y	1,000,000
1290 Retirement 2035 Fund Class I	TNLIX	NAS CM	Open End	Target Date 2021-2045 (Asset Alloc)	U	U	U		Y	1,000,000
1290 Retirement 2040 Fund Class I	TNNIX	NAS CM	Open End	Target Date 2021-2045 (Asset Alloc)	U	U	U		Y	1,000,000
1290 Retirement 2045 Fund Class I	TNOIX	NAS CM	Open End	Target Date 2021-2045 (Asset Alloc)	U	U	U		Y	1,000,000
1290 Retirement 2050 Fund Class I	TNWIX	NAS CM	Open End	Target Date 2046+ (Asset Alloc)	U	U	U		Y	1,000,000
1290 Retirement 2055 Fund Class I	TNQIX	NAS CM	Open End	Target Date 2046+ (Asset Alloc)	U	U	U		Y	1,000,000
1290 Retirement 2060 Fund Class I	TNXIX	NAS CM	Open End	Target Date 2046+ (Asset Alloc)	U	U	U		Y	1,000,000
1290 SmartBeta Equity Fund Class A	TNBAX	NAS CM	Open End	Global Equity (Growth)	B-	C+	B	Up	Y	1,000
1290 SmartBeta Equity Fund Class I	TNBIX	NAS CM	Open End	Global Equity (Growth)	B-	C+	B	Up	Y	1,000,000
1290 SmartBeta Equity Fund Class R	TNBRX	NAS CM	Open End	Global Equity (Growth)	B-	C+	B	Up	Y	0
1290 SmartBeta Equity Fund Class T	TNBCX	NAS CM	Open End	Global Equity (Growth)	B-	C+	B	Up	Y	1,000
1290 VT Convertible Securities Portfolio Class IB	US29439V8616		Open End	Convertibles (Convertible Bond)	C+	C+	B-	Down	Y	0
1290 VT Convertible Securities Portfolio Class K	US29439V8533		Open End	Convertibles (Convertible Bond)	C+	C+	B-	Down	Y	0
1290 VT DoubleLine Dynamic Allocation Portfolio Class IB	US26884M6286		Open End	Moderate Alloc (Growth & Income)	C+	C+	B	Down	Y	0
1290 VT DoubleLine Dynamic Allocation Portfolio Class K	US26884M6104		Open End	Moderate Alloc (Growth & Income)	C+	C+	B	Down	Y	0
1290 VT Energy Portfolio Class IB	US29439V8384		Open End	Energy Sector Equity (Growth)	D+	D+	C-	Up	Y	0
1290 VT Energy Portfolio Class K	US29439V8202		Open End	Energy Sector Equity (Growth)	D+	D+	C-	Up	Y	0
1290 VT Equity Income Portfolio Class IA	US2689402442		Open End	US Equity Large Cap Value (Growth & Income)	B	B-	B	Up	Y	0
1290 VT Equity Income Portfolio Class IB	US29364E8012		Open End	US Equity Large Cap Value (Growth & Income)	B	B-	B	Up	Y	0
1290 VT Equity Income Portfolio Class K	US26883L7385		Open End	US Equity Large Cap Value (Growth & Income)	B	B-	B	Up	Y	0
1290 VT GAMCO Mergers & Acquisitions Portfolio Class IA	US2689545679		Open End	Market Neutral (Growth)	B	C+	A-	Up	Y	0
1290 VT GAMCO Mergers & Acquisitions Portfolio Class IB	US29364E7444		Open End	Market Neutral (Growth)	B	C+	A-	Up	Y	0
1290 VT GAMCO Mergers & Acquisitions Portfolio Class K	US26883L6478		Open End	Market Neutral (Growth)	B	C+	A-	Up	Y	0
1290 VT GAMCO Small Company Value Portfolio Class IA	US2689545596		Open End	US Equity Small Cap (Small Company)	B+	A-	B	Up	Y	0
1290 VT GAMCO Small Company Value Portfolio Class IB	US29364E2072		Open End	US Equity Small Cap (Small Company)	B+	A-	B	Up	Y	0
1290 VT GAMCO Small Company Value Portfolio Class K	US26883L6395		Open End	US Equity Small Cap (Small Company)	B+	A-	B	Up	Y	0
1290 VT Low Volatility Global Equity Portfolio Class IB	US29439V7964		Open End	Global Equity (Growth)	B	B-	B+		Y	0
1290 VT Low Volatility Global Equity Portfolio Class K	US29439V7881		Open End	Global Equity (Growth)	B	B-	B+		Y	0
1290 VT Micro Cap Portfolio Class IB	US29439V7543		Open End	US Equity Small Cap (Growth)	B	A-	C	Up	Y	0
1290 VT Micro Cap Portfolio Class K	US29439V7477		Open End	US Equity Small Cap (Growth)	B	A-	C	Up	Y	0
1290 VT Natural Resources Portfolio Class IB	US26884M5379		Open End	Natl Resources Sec Equity (Natl Res)	C	C	C	Up	Y	0
1290 VT Natural Resources Portfolio Class K	US26884M5296		Open End	Natl Resources Sec Equity (Natl Res)	C	C	C	Up	Y	0
1290 VT Real Estate Portfolio Class IB	US26884M5114		Open End	Real Estate Sector Equity (Real Estate)	B-	C+	B	Up	Y	0

★ Expanded analysis of this fund is included in Section II.

Min Additional Investment	TOTAL RETURNS 3-Month Total Return	6-Month Total Return	1-Year Total Return	3-Year Total Return	5-Year Total Return	PERFORMANCE Dividend Yield (TTM)	Expense Ratio	3-Yr Std Deviation	3-Year Beta	ASSETS NAV	Total Assets (MIL)	ASSET ALLOCATION & TURNOVER %Cash	%Stocks	%Bonds	%Other	Turnover Ratio	BULL & BEAR Last Bull Market Total Return	Last Bear Market Total Return	FEES Front End Fee (%)	Back End Fee (%)	Inception Date
50	1.43	4.71	13.48			1.46	1.3			10.64	23.6	3	2	0	0	32			4.50		Jul-15
	1.49	4.84	13.76			1.69	1.05			10.64	23.6	3	2	0	0	32					Jul-15
	1.36	4.57	13.19			1.22	1.55			10.64	23.6	3	2	0	0	32					Jul-15
50	2.87	4.08	9.86			0.76	1.25			10.7	61.4	15	22	62	1				5.50		Mar-16
	2.93	4.23	10.12			0.95	1			10.7	61.4	15	22	62	1						Mar-16
	2.80	3.92	9.49			0.58	1.5			10.7	61.4	15	22	62	1						Mar-16
50	2.92	11.46	19.29	36.74		0.11	1.25	12.54	0.98	13.15	25.9	4	96	0	0	76			5.50		Nov-14
	2.93	11.54	19.57	37.68		0.33	1	12.53	0.98	13.15	25.9	4	96	0	0	76					Nov-14
	2.78	11.26	19.00	35.71		0	1.5	12.6	0.99	13.1	25.9	4	96	0	0	76					Nov-14
50	2.92	11.53	19.56	37.66		0.33	1.25	12.54	0.98	13.15	25.9	4	96	0	0	76			2.50	1.00	Nov-14
50	6.08	10.81	24.25			0	1.25			12.91	26.8	3	97	0	1	11			5.50		Apr-16
	6.19	11.01	24.68			0.04	1			12.95	26.8	3	97	0	1	11					Apr-16
	6.01	10.67	24.01			0	1.5			12.86	26.8	3	97	0	1	11					Apr-16
	4.07	7.15					0.65			11.01	2.9	0	100	0	0						Feb-17
50	1.66	2.97	3.91			0.36	1.65			10.29	17.4	42	27	13	9	2			5.50		Jul-15
	1.71	3.02	4.16			0.6	1.4			10.28	17.4	42	27	13	9	2					Jul-15
	1.56	2.88	3.71			0.11	1.9			10.26	17.4	42	27	13	9	2					Jul-15
	2.92	5.53					0.65			10.66	2.7	3	57	39	0						Feb-17
	3.46	6.36					0.65			10.79	2.7	3	67	30	0						Feb-17
	3.73	6.84					0.65			10.87	2.7	3	74	23	0						Feb-17
	3.91	7.21					0.65			10.93	2.8	2	79	19	0						Feb-17
	4.19	7.70					0.65			10.99	2.8	2	83	15	0						Feb-17
	4.45	8.07					0.65			11.05	2.8	1	88	10	0						Feb-17
	4.54	8.35					0.65			11.1	2.8	1	93	6	0						Feb-17
	4.80	8.82					0.65			11.16	2.8	1	98	2	0						Feb-17
	4.90	8.92					0.65			11.18	2.8	0	100	0	0						Feb-17
50	5.12	9.50	21.28	28.57		0.88	1.15	8.8	0.8	12.28	15.4	1	99	0	0	27			5.50		Nov-14
	5.17	9.64	21.66	29.55		1.09	0.9	8.82	0.8	12.28	15.4	1	99	0	0	27					Nov-14
	5.13	9.33	21.10	27.56		0.66	1.4	8.79	0.8	12.28	15.4	1	99	0	0	27					Nov-14
50	5.26	9.64	21.66	29.55		1.09	1.15	8.82	0.8	12.28	15.4	1	99	0	0	27			2.50	1.00	Nov-14
	1.72	4.92	14.34	18.59		3.31	1.3	8.12	1.01		18.9	3	1	0	0	33					Oct-13
	1.79	5.08	14.64	19.50		3.54	1.05	8.14	1.01		18.9	3	1	0	0	33					Oct-13
	2.79	4.00	9.61	14.04	31.89	1.34	1.28	6.12	0.55		56.9	15	22	63	0	15					Aug-12
	2.86	4.16	9.88	14.89	33.54	1.57	1.03	6.12	0.55		56.9	15	22	63	0	15					Aug-12
	6.38	14.72	-1.88	-10.14		1.61	0.9	20.3	1.1		5.1	0	100	0	0	38					Oct-13
	6.47	14.80	-1.65	-9.48		1.88	0.65	20.34	1.1		5.1	0	100	0	0	38					Oct-13
	7.25	11.13	16.14	27.43	87.85	1.68	1	10.22	0.95		635.0	2	98	0	0	49	23.93	-17.76			Dec-04
	7.21	11.08	16.06	27.32	87.74	1.69	1	10.06	0.94		635.0	2	98	0	0	49	24.05	-17.91			Dec-98
	7.32	11.21	16.41	28.38	90.21	1.92	0.75	10.12	0.94		635.0	2	98	0	0	49	23.93	-17.75			Aug-11
	1.50	4.13	6.22	16.88	33.12	0.01	1.34	5.08	0.43		240.7	29	70	0	0	198	5.85	-5.42			Jun-07
	1.51	4.07	6.16	16.88	33.09	0.01	1.34	5.02	0.42		240.7	29	70	0	0	198	5.78	-5.53			May-03
	1.58	4.26	6.50	17.75	34.80	0.24	1.09	5.1	0.43		240.7	29	70	0	0	198	6.02	-5.51			Aug-11
	4.22	12.58	16.30	33.88	98.50	0.39	1.08	12.83	0.87		3,492	5	95	0	0	5	25.92	-23.09			Jul-07
	4.21	12.58	16.28	33.84	98.43	0.39	1.08	12.83	0.87		3,492	5	95	0	0	5	25.86	-23.19			Aug-88
	4.29	12.71	16.59	34.87	100.95	0.61	0.83	12.83	0.87		3,492	5	95	0	0	5	26.01	-23.16			Aug-11
	4.06	7.40	18.33	26.85		2.19	0.9	7.92	0.93		9.4	0	99	0	0	15					Oct-13
	4.14	7.57	18.62	27.82		2.41	0.65	7.91	0.93		9.4	0	99	0	0	15					Oct-13
	3.75	14.10	26.36	32.09		0	1.15	16.75	1.01		144.0	1	98	0	0	103					Apr-14
	3.80	14.11	26.56	32.91		0.13	0.9	16.78	1.01		144.0	1	98	0	0	103					Apr-14
	8.01	19.16	11.68	6.30		1.99	0.9	17.9	0.98		21.5	0	100	0	0	18					Feb-13
	8.13	19.28	11.94	7.08		2.23	0.65	17.91	0.98		21.5	0	100	0	0	18					Feb-13
	3.48	4.80	11.39	11.64		0.65	0.91	11.25	1.01		28.7	0	99	0	1	57					Feb-13

	MARKET			FUND TYPE, CATEGORY & OBJECTIVE	RATINGS					MINIMUMS
Fund Name	Ticker Symbol	Traded On	Fund Type	Category and (Prospectus Objective)	Overall Rating	Reward Rating	Risk Rating	Recent Up/ Downgrade	Open to New Investors	Min Initial Investment
1290 VT Real Estate Portfolio Class K	US26884M4950		Open End	Real Estate Sector Equity (Real Estate)	B-	C+	B	Up	Y	0
1290 VT Small Cap Value Portfolio Class IB	US29439V7709		Open End	US Equity Small Cap (Small Company)	B-	B-	B-	Up	Y	0
1290 VT Small Cap Value Portfolio Class K	US29439V7626		Open End	US Equity Small Cap (Small Company)	B-	B	B-	Up	Y	0
1290 VT SmartBeta Equity Portfolio Class IB	US29439V8046		Open End	Global Equity (Equity-Income)	B	B-	A-		Y	0
1290 VT SmartBeta Equity Portfolio Class K	US29439V8871		Open End	Global Equity (Equity-Income)	B-	B-	B	Down	Y	0
1290 VT Socially Responsible Portfolio Class IA	US2689404265		Open End	US Equity Large Cap Growth (Growth)	B	B-	B	Up	Y	0
1290 VT Socially Responsible Portfolio Class IB	US2689404182		Open End	US Equity Large Cap Growth (Growth)	B-	B-	B	Down	Y	0
13D Activist Fund Class A	DDDAX	NAS CM	Open End	US Equity Mid Cap (Growth)	B	B	B-	Up	Y	2,500
13D Activist Fund Class C	DDDCX	NAS CM	Open End	US Equity Mid Cap (Growth)	B	B	B-	Up	Y	2,500
13D Activist Fund Class I	DDDIX	NAS CM	Open End	US Equity Mid Cap (Growth)	B	B	B-	Up	Y	1,000,000
1789 Growth and Income Fund Class Class C	PSECX	NAS CM	Open End	Aggressive Alloc (Growth & Income)	B-	C	B		Y	2,000
1789 Growth and Income Fund Class P	PSEPX	NAS CM	Open End	Aggressive Alloc (Growth & Income)	B-	C	B	Down	Y	2,000
1919 Financial Services Fund Class A	SBFAX	NAS CM	Open End	Financials Sector Equity (Financial)	A-	A	B+	Up	Y	1,000
1919 Financial Services Fund Class C	SFSLX	NAS CM	Open End	Financials Sector Equity (Financial)	A-	A	B+	Up	Y	1,000
1919 Financial Services Fund Class I	LMRIX	NAS CM	Open End	Financials Sector Equity (Financial)	A-	A	B+	Up	Y	1,000,000
1919 Socially Responsive Balanced Fund Class A	SSIAX	NAS CM	Open End	Moderate Alloc (Balanced)	B-	C+	B	Down	Y	1,000
1919 Socially Responsive Balanced Fund Class B	SESIX	NAS CM	Open End	Moderate Alloc (Balanced)	B-	C+	B	Down		1,000
1919 Socially Responsive Balanced Fund Class C	SESLX	NAS CM	Open End	Moderate Alloc (Balanced)	B-	C+	B	Down	Y	1,000
1919 Socially Responsive Balanced Fund Class I	LMRNX	NAS CM	Open End	Moderate Alloc (Balanced)	B-	C+	B	Down	Y	1,000,000
361 Domestic Long/Short Equity Fund Class I	ADMZX	NAS CM	Open End	Long/Short Equity (Growth)	D+	C-	B	Up	Y	100,000
361 Domestic Long/Short Equity Fund Class Y	ADMWX	NAS CM	Open End	Long/Short Equity (Growth)	D+	C-	B	Up	Y	1,000,000
361 Domestic Long/Short Equity Fund Investor Class	ADMQX	NAS CM	Open End	Long/Short Equity (Growth)	D+	C-	B	Up	Y	2,500
361 Global Long/Short Equity Fund Class I	AGAZX	NAS CM	Open End	Long/Short Equity (Growth)	B	C+	B		Y	2,500
361 Global Long/Short Equity Fund Class Y	AGAWX	NAS CM	Open End	Long/Short Equity (Growth)	B	C+	A		Y	1,000,000
361 Global Long/Short Equity Fund Investor Class	AGAQX	NAS CM	Open End	Long/Short Equity (Growth)	B	C+	A-		Y	2,500
361 Global Managed Futures Strategy Fund Class I	AGFZX	NAS CM	Open End	Other Alternative (Growth)	B	C+	B+	Up	Y	100,000
361 Global Managed Futures Strategy Fund Investor Class	AGFQX	NAS CM	Open End	Other Alternative (Growth)	B	C+	B+	Up	Y	2,500
361 Macro Opportunity Fund Class I	AGMZX	NAS CM	Open End	Multialternative (Growth)	C+	C	C+	Up	Y	100,000
361 Macro Opportunity Fund Investor Class	AGMQX	NAS CM	Open End	Multialternative (Growth)	C	C	C+	Up	Y	2,500
361 Managed Futures Strategy Fund Class I	AMFZX	NAS CM	Open End	Other Alternative (Income)	C+	C	B	Up	Y	100,000
361 Managed Futures Strategy Fund Investor Class	AMFQX	NAS CM	Open End	Other Alternative (Income)	C+	C	B	Up	Y	2,500
361 U.S. Small Cap Equity Fund Class I	ASFZX	NAS CM	Open End	US Equity Small Cap (Small Company)	D-	D+	B+		Y	100,000
361 U.S. Small Cap Equity Fund Class Y	ASFWX	NAS CM	Open End	US Equity Small Cap (Small Company)	D-	D+	B+		Y	1,000,000
361 U.S. Small Cap Equity Fund Investor Class	ASFQX	NAS CM	Open End	US Equity Small Cap (Small Company)	D-	D+	B+		Y	2,500
7Twelve Balanced Portfolio Class 3	US66537U2134		Open End	Moderate Alloc (Balanced)	C+	C+	B-		Y	0
7Twelve Balanced Portfolio Class 4	US66537U6507		Open End	Moderate Alloc (Balanced)	C+	C+	B-		Y	0
AAM/Bahl & Gaynor Income Growth Fund Class A	AFNAX	NAS CM	Open End	US Equity Large Cap Blend (Equity-Income)	B-	B-	B	Down	Y	2,500
AAM/Bahl & Gaynor Income Growth Fund Class C	AFYCX	NAS CM	Open End	US Equity Large Cap Blend (Equity-Income)	B-	B-	B-	Down	Y	2,500
AAM/Bahl & Gaynor Income Growth Fund Class I	AFNIX	NAS CM	Open End	US Equity Large Cap Blend (Equity-Income)	B-	B-	B	Down	Y	25,000
AAMA Equity Fund	AMFEX	NAS CM	Open End	US Equity Large Cap Blend (Growth)	U	U	U		Y	10,000
Aasgard Dividend Growth Small & Mid-Cap Fund No Load Class	AADGX	NAS CM	Open End	US Equity Mid Cap (Growth & Income)	D+	C-	B+	Up	Y	2,500
AB All Market Alternative Return Portfolio Advisor Class	AARYX	NAS CM	Open End	Multialternative (Growth)	C-	D+	C	Down	Y	0
AB All Market Alternative Return Portfolio Class A	AARAX	NAS CM	Open End	Multialternative (Growth)	C-	D+	C	Down	Y	2,500
AB All Market Alternative Return Portfolio Class C	AARCX	NAS CM	Open End	Multialternative (Growth)	D+	D	C-	Down	Y	2,500
AB All Market Income Portfolio Advisor Class	MRKYX	NAS CM	Open End	Cautious Alloc (Growth)	B-	C	B	Up	Y	0
AB All Market Income Portfolio Class A	MRKAX	NAS CM	Open End	Cautious Alloc (Growth)	B-	C	B	Up	Y	2,500
AB All Market Income Portfolio Class C	MRKCX	NAS CM	Open End	Cautious Alloc (Growth)	B-	C	B	Up	Y	2,500
AB All Market Real Return Portfolio Advisor Class	AMTYX	NAS CM	Open End	Moderate Alloc (Growth & Income)	C	C	C	Up	Y	0
AB All Market Real Return Portfolio Class 1	AMTOX	NAS CM	Open End	Moderate Alloc (Growth & Income)	C	C	C	Up	Y	5,000
AB All Market Real Return Portfolio Class 2	AMTTX	NAS CM	Open End	Moderate Alloc (Growth & Income)	C	C	C	Up	Y	5,000,000
AB All Market Real Return Portfolio Class A	AMTAX	NAS CM	Open End	Moderate Alloc (Growth & Income)	C	C	C	Up	Y	2,500
AB All Market Real Return Portfolio Class C	ACMTX	NAS CM	Open End	Moderate Alloc (Growth & Income)	C	C	C	Up	Y	2,500

★Expanded analysis of this fund is included in Section II.

	TOTAL RETURNS					PERFORMANCE				ASSETS		ASSET ALLOCATION & TURNOVER					BULL & BEAR		FEES		
Min Additional Investment	3-Month Total Return	6-Month Total Return	1-Year Total Return	3-Year Total Return	5-Year Total Return	Dividend Yield (TTM)	Expense Ratio	3-Yr Std Deviation	3-Year Beta	NAV	Total Assets (MIL)	%Cash	%Stocks	%Bonds	%Other	Turnover Ratio	Last Bull Market Total Return	Last Bear Market Total Return	Front End Fee (%)	Back End Fee (%)	Inception Date
	3.53	4.94	11.72	12.47		0.87	0.66	11.27	1.02		28.7	0	99	0	1	57					Feb-13
	2.30	10.87	12.55	26.82		1.66	1.16	11.76	0.78		324.6	7	93	0	0	23					Apr-14
	2.26	10.82	12.73	27.68		1.89	0.91	11.79	0.78		324.6	7	93	0	0	23					Apr-14
	5.56	10.17	21.80	28.75		1.05	1.15	8.81	0.79		18.4	1	99	0	0	27					Oct-13
	5.64	10.34	22.08	29.71		1.26	0.9	8.83	0.79		18.4	1	99	0	0	27					Oct-13
	6.40	11.45	20.33	31.74	107.45	0.95	0.95	10.52	1		149.8	0	100	0	0	15	26.37	-16.45			Oct-02
	6.44	11.40	20.32	31.81	107.43	0.97	0.95	10.53	1		149.8	0	100	0	0	15	26.14	-16.45			Sep-99
500	10.58	11.03	23.44	29.97	108.15	0	1.76	13.74	1.11	21.69	329.7	12	88	0	0	119			5.75		Dec-11
500	10.38	10.60	22.51	27.03	101.03	0	2.51	13.74	1.1	21.66	329.7	12	88	0	0	119				1.00	Dec-12
	10.66	11.16	23.77	30.92	110.95	0	1.51	13.74	1.11	22.06	329.7	12	88	0	0	119					Dec-11
100	3.17	3.50	5.16	8.45	41.12	0.54	2.08	8.37	0.78	12.92	12.0	4	77	18	-2	5	17.41	-15.65		1.00	Jan-11
100	3.47	4.06	6.25	11.86	47.41	1.5	1.08	8.37	0.78	12.99	12.0	4	77	18	-2	5	17.41	-15.65			Aug-13
50	4.74	10.45	14.64	53.18	132.73	0.23	1.46	14.49	0.94	27.16	248.8	2	98	0	0	8	27.32	-18.69	5.75		Nov-98
50	4.57	10.03	13.81	50.06	124.99	0	2.19	14.48	0.94	25.12	248.8	2	98	0	0	8	26.7	-18.96		1.00	Nov-98
	4.82	10.55	14.95	54.84	137.23	0.49	1.18	14.49	0.94	27.42	248.8	2	98	0	0	8	27.5	-18.58			Mar-08
50	4.64	9.34	16.35	19.71	57.05	0.56	1.25	6.99	0.66	17.94	127.0	3	70	27	0	32	16.42	-10.86	5.75		Nov-92
50	4.45	8.94	15.32	16.63	49.56	0	2	7	0.67	17.48	127.0	3	70	27	0	32	15.7	-11.27		5.00	Jan-87
50	4.46	8.93	15.47	17.09	51.41	0.02	2	7.02	0.67	18.11	127.0	3	70	27	0	32	15.93	-11.09		1.00	May-93
	4.74	9.51	16.71	20.61	59.12	0.79	1	7	0.67	17.91	127.0	3	70	27	0	32	16.58	-10.71			Jul-08
	4.41	6.62	11.55			0.29	1.56			10.84	30.4	20	71	0	9						Mar-16
	4.41	6.61	11.53			0.39	1.41			10.85	30.4	20	71	0	9						Mar-16
	4.33	6.53	11.14			0.17	1.81			10.81	30.4	20	71	0	9						Mar-16
	2.54	7.40	15.24	24.65		0.61	1.49			11.65	567.6	17	69	0	14	229					Dec-14
	2.56	7.51	15.35	25.00		0.69	1.39			11.66	567.6	17	69	0	14	229					Dec-14
	2.51	7.39	14.94	23.62		0.27	1.79			11.63	567.6	17	69	0	14	229					Dec-14
	1.37	4.47	8.27	23.26		0	1.83	7.71	4.65	11.05	114.4	100	0	0	0	0					Feb-14
	1.29	4.23	7.96	22.25		0	2.08	7.65	5.98	10.93	114.4	100	0	0	0	0					Feb-14
	2.32	8.47	13.46	1.81		0	2.06	5.96	-7.05	10.11	11.6	3	94	5	-2	816					Jun-14
	2.24	8.32	13.22	1.10		0	2.31	6.02	-6.8	10.02	11.6	3	94	5	-2	816					Jun-14
	3.35	5.49	5.97	4.74	13.38	0	1.87	6.17	25.27	11.71	321.3	39	0	59	2	17					Dec-11
	3.31	5.38	5.67	3.96	11.98	0	2.12	6.21	24.31	11.54	321.3	39	0	59	2	17					Dec-11
	2.15	10.80	15.12				0.99			11.28	4.7	2	100	0	-2						Dec-16
	2.10	10.85	15.17				0.84			11.27	4.7	2	100	0	-2						Dec-16
	2.08	10.65	14.74				1.24			11.25	4.7	2	100	0	-2						Dec-16
	3.34	6.38	10.54	11.59	21.71	0.52	1.22	6.87	1.05	12.36	76.0	9	58	28	5	11					Apr-15
	3.22	6.22	10.34	11.06	21.14	0.34	1.42	6.82	1.04	12.47	76.0	9	58	28	5	11					Apr-12
500	6.77	10.80	19.26	30.56	84.21	1.5	1.24	9.01	0.85	16.77	557.3	3	97	0	0	22			5.50		Jul-12
500	6.55	10.41	18.40	27.69	76.93	0.86	1.99	8.98	0.84	16.65	557.3	3	97	0	0	22				1.00	Jan-13
5,000	6.82	10.93	19.50	31.61	86.47	1.73	0.99	9.03	0.85	16.81	557.3	3	97	0	0	22					Jul-12
	6.09	10.34					0.97			10.99	284.4	6	94	0	0						Jun-17
500	5.17	9.08	15.48			1.12	1.36			12.68	35.3	1	99	0	0	42					Apr-16
	-3.13	-4.63	-2.78			19.91	0.99			8.03	228.8	47	53	0	0	429					Mar-15
50	-3.14	-4.64	-2.91			19.69	1.24			8	228.8	47	53	0	0	429			4.25		Mar-15
50	-3.43	-5.06	-3.78			19.02	1.99			7.88	228.8	47	53	0	0	429				1.00	Mar-15
	1.85	4.53	11.21	23.21		6.31	0.74			10.25	95.4	7	32	46	6	94					Dec-14
50	1.69	4.41	10.88	22.22		6.11	0.99			10.23	95.4	7	32	46	6	94			4.25		Dec-14
50	1.60	4.04	10.08	19.60		5.34	1.74			10.24	95.4	7	32	46	6	94				1.00	Dec-14
	5.82	11.80	11.40	3.11	-8.83	2.36	1.07	12.6	0.64	8.98	1,230	5	71	23	0	119	13.47	-21.13			Mar-10
	5.72	11.65	11.24	2.63	-9.61	2.33	1.17	12.6	0.65	8.85	1,230	5	71	23	0	119	13.4	-21.25			Mar-10
	5.72	11.78	11.51	3.45	-8.39	2.5	0.92	12.54	0.64	9.04	1,230	5	71	23	0	119	13.52	-21.16			Mar-10
50	5.76	11.59	11.06	2.32	-10.06	2.13	1.32	12.66	0.65	9.02	1,230	5	71	23	0	119	13.35	-21.26	4.25		Mar-10
50	5.50	11.23	10.30	0.00	-13.31	1.33	2.07	12.57	0.64	9.03	1,230	5	71	23	0	119	12.89	-21.49		1.00	Mar-10

	MARKET			FUND TYPE, CATEGORY & OBJECTIVE	RATINGS					MINIMUMS
Fund Name	Ticker Symbol	Traded On	Fund Type	Category and (Prospectus Objective)	Overall Rating	Reward Rating	Risk Rating	Recent Up/ Downgrade	Open to New Investors	Min Initial Investment
AB All Market Real Return Portfolio Class I	AMTIX	NAS CM	Open End	Moderate Alloc (Growth & Income)	C	C	C	Up	Y	2,000,000
AB All Market Real Return Portfolio Class K	AMTKX	NAS CM	Open End	Moderate Alloc (Growth & Income)	C	C	C	Up	Y	0
AB All Market Real Return Portfolio Class R	AMTRX	NAS CM	Open End	Moderate Alloc (Growth & Income)	C	C	C	Up	Y	0
AB All Market Real Return Portfolio Class Z	AMTZX	NAS CM	Open End	Moderate Alloc (Growth & Income)	C	C	C	Up	Y	2,000,000
AB All Market Total Return Portfolio Advisor Class	ABWYX	NAS CM	Open End	Moderate Alloc (Balanced)	B-	C+	B	Down	Y	0
AB All Market Total Return Portfolio Class A	ABWAX	NAS CM	Open End	Moderate Alloc (Balanced)	B-	C+	B	Down	Y	2,500
AB All Market Total Return Portfolio Class B	ABWBX	NAS CM	Open End	Moderate Alloc (Balanced)	C+	C+	B	Down		2,500
AB All Market Total Return Portfolio Class C	ABWCX	NAS CM	Open End	Moderate Alloc (Balanced)	B-	C+	B+	Down	Y	2,500
AB All Market Total Return Portfolio Class I	ABWIX	NAS CM	Open End	Moderate Alloc (Balanced)	B-	C+	B	Down	Y	2,000,000
AB All Market Total Return Portfolio Class K	ABWKX	NAS CM	Open End	Moderate Alloc (Balanced)	B-	C+	B	Down	Y	0
AB All Market Total Return Portfolio Class R	ABWRX	NAS CM	Open End	Moderate Alloc (Balanced)	C+	C+	B	Down	Y	0
AB Asia ex-Japan Equity Portfolio Advisor Class	AXJYX	NAS CM	Open End	Asia ex-Japan Equity (Growth)	C	C	B+	Up	Y	0
AB Asia ex-Japan Equity Portfolio Class A	AXJAX	NAS CM	Open End	Asia ex-Japan Equity (Growth)	C	C	B+	Up	Y	2,500
AB Asia ex-Japan Equity Portfolio Class C	AXJCX	NAS CM	Open End	Asia ex-Japan Equity (Growth)	C	C	B+	Up	Y	2,500
AB Concentrated Growth Fund Advisor Class	WPSGX	NAS CM	Open End	US Equity Large Cap Growth (Growth)	B	B-	B		Y	0
AB Concentrated Growth Fund Class A	WPASX	NAS CM	Open End	US Equity Large Cap Growth (Growth)	B	B-	B		Y	2,500
AB Concentrated Growth Fund Class C	WPCSX	NAS CM	Open End	US Equity Large Cap Growth (Growth)	B-	B-	B-	Down	Y	2,500
AB Concentrated Growth Fund Class I	WPSIX	NAS CM	Open End	US Equity Large Cap Growth (Growth)	B	B-	B		Y	2,000,000
AB Concentrated Growth Fund Class K	WPSKX	NAS CM	Open End	US Equity Large Cap Growth (Growth)	B	B-	B		Y	0
AB Concentrated Growth Fund Class R	WPRSX	NAS CM	Open End	US Equity Large Cap Growth (Growth)	B	B-	B		Y	0
AB Concentrated Growth Fund Class Z	WPSZX	NAS CM	Open End	US Equity Large Cap Growth (Growth)	B	B-	B		Y	2,000,000
AB Concentrated International Growth Portfolio Advisor Cls	CIGYX	NAS CM	Open End	Global Equity Large Cap (Growth)	C+	C+	B-	Up	Y	0
AB Concentrated International Growth Portfolio Class A	CIAGX	NAS CM	Open End	Global Equity Large Cap (Growth)	C+	C+	B-	Up	Y	2,500
AB Concentrated International Growth Portfolio Class C	CICGX	NAS CM	Open End	Global Equity Large Cap (Growth)	C+	C+	B-	Up	Y	2,500
AB Conservative Wealth Strategy Advisor Class	ABPYX	NAS CM	Open End	Cautious Alloc (Balanced)	B	C	A-	Up	Y	0
AB Conservative Wealth Strategy Class A	ABPAX	NAS CM	Open End	Cautious Alloc (Balanced)	B	C	A-	Up	Y	2,500
AB Conservative Wealth Strategy Class B	ABPBX	NAS CM	Open End	Cautious Alloc (Balanced)	B-	C	B+	Up		2,500
AB Conservative Wealth Strategy Class C	ABPCX	NAS CM	Open End	Cautious Alloc (Balanced)	B-	C	B+	Up	Y	2,500
AB Conservative Wealth Strategy Class I	APWIX	NAS CM	Open End	Cautious Alloc (Balanced)	B-	C	B	Up	Y	2,000,000
AB Conservative Wealth Strategy Class K	APWKX	NAS CM	Open End	Cautious Alloc (Balanced)	B-	C	B	Up	Y	0
AB Conservative Wealth Strategy Class R	APPRX	NAS CM	Open End	Cautious Alloc (Balanced)	B-	C	B	Up	Y	0
AB Core Opportunities Fund Advisor Class	ADGYX	NAS CM	Open End	US Equity Large Cap Growth (Growth)	B	B	B+		Y	0
AB Core Opportunities Fund Class A	ADGAX	NAS CM	Open End	US Equity Large Cap Growth (Growth)	B	B	B+		Y	2,500
AB Core Opportunities Fund Class B	ADGBX	NAS CM	Open End	US Equity Large Cap Growth (Growth)	B	B	B+			2,500
AB Core Opportunities Fund Class C	ADGCX	NAS CM	Open End	US Equity Large Cap Growth (Growth)	B	B	B+		Y	2,500
AB Core Opportunities Fund Class I	ADGIX	NAS CM	Open End	US Equity Large Cap Growth (Growth)	B	B	B+		Y	2,000,000
AB Core Opportunities Fund Class K	ADGKX	NAS CM	Open End	US Equity Large Cap Growth (Growth)	B	B	B+		Y	0
AB Core Opportunities Fund Class R	ADGRX	NAS CM	Open End	US Equity Large Cap Growth (Growth)	B	B	B+		Y	0
AB Core Opportunities Fund Class Z	ADGZX	NAS CM	Open End	US Equity Large Cap Growth (Growth)	B	B	B+		Y	2,000,000
AB Credit Long/Short Portfolio Advisor Class	ALYSX	NAS CM	Open End	Other Alternative (Income)	C-	D+	C	Down	Y	0
AB Credit Long/Short Portfolio Class A	ALASX	NAS CM	Open End	Other Alternative (Income)	D+	D+	C	Down	Y	2,500
AB Credit Long/Short Portfolio Class C	ALCSX	NAS CM	Open End	Other Alternative (Income)	D+	D	C-	Down	Y	2,500
AB Discovery Growth Fund Advisor Class	CHCYX	NAS CM	Open End	US Equity Mid Cap (Growth)	B	A-	C+	Up	Y	0
AB Discovery Growth Fund Class A	CHCLX	NAS CM	Open End	US Equity Mid Cap (Growth)	B+	A-	B	Up	Y	2,500
AB Discovery Growth Fund Class B	CHCBX	NAS CM	Open End	US Equity Mid Cap (Growth)	B	B	B	Up		2,500
AB Discovery Growth Fund Class C	CHCCX	NAS CM	Open End	US Equity Mid Cap (Growth)	B	B+	B	Up	Y	2,500
AB Discovery Growth Fund Class I	CHCIX	NAS CM	Open End	US Equity Mid Cap (Growth)	B	A-	C+	Up	Y	2,000,000
AB Discovery Growth Fund Class K	CHCKX	NAS CM	Open End	US Equity Mid Cap (Growth)	B	A-	C+	Up	Y	0
AB Discovery Growth Fund Class R	CHCRX	NAS CM	Open End	US Equity Mid Cap (Growth)	B	B+	C+	Up	Y	0
AB Discovery Growth Fund Class Z	CHCZX	NAS CM	Open End	US Equity Mid Cap (Growth)	B+	A-	B	Up	Y	2,000,000
AB Discovery Value Fund Advisor Class	ABYSX	NAS CM	Open End	US Equity Mid Cap (Growth)	B	B+	B	Up	Y	0
AB Discovery Value Fund Class A	ABASX	NAS CM	Open End	US Equity Mid Cap (Growth)	B	B	B	Up	Y	2,500

★Expanded analysis of this fund is included in Section II.

	TOTAL RETURNS					PERFORMANCE				ASSETS		ASSET ALLOCATION & TURNOVER					BULL & BEAR		FEES		
Min Additional Investment	3-Month Total Return	6-Month Total Return	1-Year Total Return	3-Year Total Return	5-Year Total Return	Dividend Yield (TTM)	Expense Ratio	3-Yr Std Deviation	3-Year Beta	NAV	Total Assets (MIL)	%Cash	%Stocks	%Bonds	%Other	Turnover Ratio	Last Bull Market Total Return	Last Bear Market Total Return	Front End Fee (%)	Back End Fee (%)	Inception Date
	5.79	11.81	11.54	3.40	-8.53	2.52	0.93	12.59	0.64	8.91	1,230	5	71	23	0	119	13.49	-21.16			Mar-10
	5.63	11.53	10.99	2.16	-10.09	2.19	1.32	12.57	0.64	8.9	1,230	5	71	23	0	119	13.43	-21.26			Mar-10
	5.59	11.36	10.69	1.53	-11.21	2.01	1.57	12.62	0.65	8.9	1,230	5	71	23	0	119	13.19	-21.36			Mar-10
	5.80	11.82	11.55	3.47	-8.45	2.52	0.94	12.62	0.65	8.91	1,230	5	71	23	0	119	13.49	-21.16			Jan-14
	2.29	4.48	11.48	16.00	41.16	3.11	0.75	6.47	0.59	14.92	904.9	15	73	11	1	108	14.8	-14.55			Sep-03
50	2.20	4.33	11.21	15.14	39.22	2.9	1	6.51	0.6	14.83	904.9	15	73	11	1	108	14.64	-14.72	4.25		Sep-03
50	1.98	3.88	10.38	12.50	34.14	1.45	1.76	6.44	0.59	14.93	904.9	15	73	11	1	108	14.04	-14.91		4.00	Sep-03
50	2.04	3.98	10.41	12.57	34.22	2.19	1.75	6.46	0.59	14.77	904.9	15	73	11	1	108	14.22	-14.96		1.00	Sep-03
	2.23	4.36	11.38	15.85	40.90	3.1	0.75	6.45	0.59	15.07	904.9	15	73	11	1	108	14.84	-14.59			Mar-05
	2.15	4.29	11.10	14.75	38.69	2.77	1.07	6.5	0.59	14.79	904.9	15	73	11	1	108	14.63	-14.76			Mar-05
	2.09	4.09	10.73	13.71	36.53	2.5	1.39	6.48	0.59	14.78	904.9	15	73	11	1	108	14.46	-14.86			Feb-04
	7.34	12.28	40.18			1	1.15			13.13	6.4	0	100	0	0	78					Dec-15
50	7.32	12.18	39.87			0.91	1.4			13.08	6.4	0	100	0	0	78			4.25		Dec-15
50	7.11	11.80	38.75			0.16	2.15			13.04	6.4	0	100	0	0	78				1.00	Dec-15
	3.78	7.15	23.00	30.09	106.09	0	0.97	11.29	1.01	34.07	447.0	1	99	0	0	29	28.13	-11.36			Feb-94
50	3.72	7.03	22.70	29.16	103.66	0	1.22	11.27	1	33.75	447.0	1	99	0	0	29	27.95	-11.46	4.25		Feb-14
50	3.52	6.61	21.79	26.24	96.24	0	1.97	11.24	1	32.75	447.0	1	99	0	0	29	27.39	-11.73		1.00	Feb-14
	3.77	7.14	22.97	30.10	106.31	0	0.96	11.25	1	34.11	447.0	1	99	0	0	29	28.13	-11.36			Feb-14
	3.69	6.99	22.65	29.11	103.66	0	1.22	11.25	1	33.75	447.0	1	99	0	0	29	27.95	-11.46			Feb-14
	3.67	6.90	22.41	28.15	101.14	0	1.47	11.28	1.01	33.41	447.0	1	99	0	0	29	27.76	-11.55			Feb-14
	3.78	7.18	23.02	30.20	106.26	0	0.94	11.28	1.01	34.1	447.0	1	99	0	0	29	28.13	-11.36			Feb-14
	3.74	12.92	37.84			0.6	1.05			11.49	37.5	5	95	0	0	66					Apr-15
50	3.65	12.74	37.49			0.42	1.3			11.47	37.5	5	95	0	0	66			4.25		Apr-15
50	3.50	12.36	36.55			0	2.05			11.36	37.5	5	95	0	0	66				1.00	Apr-15
	1.98	3.91	8.55	11.97	24.92	2.56	1	3.59	0.27	12.18	232.0	18	48	33	1	86	8.1	-6.93			Sep-03
50	1.98	3.84	8.32	11.18	23.24	2.35	1.25	3.62	0.27	12.14	232.0	18	48	33	1	86	7.93	-7.09	4.25		Sep-03
50	1.73	3.34	7.41	8.58	18.70	0	2.03	3.62	0.27	12.41	232.0	18	48	33	1	86	7.5	-7.32		4.00	Sep-03
50	1.78	3.43	7.50	8.66	18.81	1.58	2.01	3.63	0.27	12.13	232.0	18	48	33	1	86	7.52	-7.31		1.00	Sep-03
	1.93	3.87	8.43	11.84	24.67	2.57	1.02	3.58	0.28	12.32	232.0	18	48	33	1	86	8.1	-6.97			Mar-05
	1.91	3.78	8.18	10.85	22.81	2.23	1.35	3.6	0.27	12.12	232.0	18	48	33	1	86	7.85	-7.12			Mar-05
	1.82	3.60	7.90	9.79	20.84	1.96	1.66	3.6	0.26	12.17	232.0	18	48	33	1	86	7.68	-7.26			Feb-04
	5.59	12.05	22.88	39.36	115.24	0.2	0.9	8.84	0.82	20.84	271.6	13	87	0	0	107	26.38	-16.08			Mar-10
50	5.54	11.89	22.52	38.23	112.34	0.09	1.15	8.82	0.82	20.26	271.6	13	87	0	0	107	26.23	-16.21	4.25		Dec-99
50	5.50	11.82	22.34	37.49	110.05	0	1.9	8.83	0.82	18.11	271.6	13	87	0	0	107	26.06	-16.33		4.00	Dec-99
50	5.35	11.50	21.67	35.29	104.92	0	1.9	8.81	0.82	17.05	271.6	13	87	0	0	107	25.62	-16.45		1.00	Dec-99
	5.62	12.12	22.96	39.47	115.55	0.22	0.9	8.82	0.82	21.09	271.6	13	87	0	0	107	26.37	-16.04			Mar-05
	5.54	11.89	22.50	38.25	112.65	0.06	1.15	8.82	0.82	20.44	271.6	13	87	0	0	107	26.22	-16.22			Mar-05
	5.46	11.77	22.26	37.26	109.95	0	1.4	8.83	0.82	19.6	271.6	13	87	0	0	107	26.05	-16.23			Nov-03
	5.66	12.15	23.05	39.66	115.38	0.24	0.85	8.84	0.82	21.13	271.6	13	87	0	0	107	26.23	-16.21			Oct-13
	-0.90	-2.30	-5.15	0.65		0	0.99	2.57	20.54	9.66	20.6	42	4	49	1	201					May-14
50	-1.01	-2.51	-5.47	-0.09		0	1.24	2.61	21.02	9.58	20.6	42	4	49	1	201			4.25		May-14
50	-1.04	-2.77	-6.06	-2.22		0	1.99	2.54	21.13	9.36	20.6	42	4	49	1	201				1.00	May-14
	9.00	15.43	32.70	38.03	101.89	0	0.76	13.77	1.02	11.58	2,141	1	99	0	0	70	31.52	-22.52			Oct-96
50	8.89	15.39	32.51	37.04	99.75	0	0.99	13.82	1.02	10.86	2,141	1	99	0	0	70	31.27	-22.64	4.25		Jul-38
50	8.61	14.80	31.34	33.72	91.42	0	1.8	13.78	1.02	6.91	2,141	1	99	0	0	70	30.6	-22.71		4.00	Mar-91
50	8.69	14.84	31.47	33.83	91.88	0	1.76	13.85	1.02	6.97	2,141	1	99	0	0	70	30.52	-22.82		1.00	May-93
	8.99	15.48	32.81	38.04	102.07	0	0.76	13.81	1.02	11.47	2,141	1	99	0	0	70	31.68	-22.49			Mar-05
	8.87	15.19	32.27	36.51	98.45	0	1.12	13.79	1.02	10.76	2,141	1	99	0	0	70	31.27	-22.53			Mar-05
	8.78	15.15	31.99	35.44	95.82	0	1.39	13.82	1.02	10.26	2,141	1	99	0	0	70	30.98	-22.66			Mar-05
	8.98	15.46	32.88	38.26	101.81	0	0.69	13.81	1.02	11.49	2,141	1	99	0	0	70	31.27	-22.64			May-14
	5.99	11.50	12.97	31.75	103.33	0.33	0.89	13.56	1.1	23.3	2,959	1	99	0	0	57	27.56	-26.49			Mar-01
50	5.92	11.36	12.70	30.76	100.48	0.15	1.15	13.54	1.1	22.78	2,959	1	99	0	0	57	27.33	-26.55	4.25		Mar-01

	MARKET		FUND TYPE, CATEGORY & OBJECTIVE		RATINGS				MINIMUMS	
Fund Name	Ticker Symbol	Traded On	Fund Type	Category and (Prospectus Objective)	Overall Rating	Reward Rating	Risk Rating	Recent Up/ Downgrade	Open to New Investors	Min Initial Investment
AB Discovery Value Fund Class B	ABBSX	NAS CM	Open End	US Equity Mid Cap (Growth)	B	B	B	Up		2,500
AB Discovery Value Fund Class C	ABCSX	NAS CM	Open End	US Equity Mid Cap (Growth)	B	B	B	Up	Y	2,500
AB Discovery Value Fund Class I	ABSIX	NAS CM	Open End	US Equity Mid Cap (Growth)	B	B+	B	Up	Y	2,000,000
AB Discovery Value Fund Class K	ABSKX	NAS CM	Open End	US Equity Mid Cap (Growth)	B	B	B	Up	Y	0
AB Discovery Value Fund Class R	ABSRX	NAS CM	Open End	US Equity Mid Cap (Growth)	B	B	B	Up	Y	0
AB Discovery Value Fund Class Z	ABSZX	NAS CM	Open End	US Equity Mid Cap (Growth)	B	B+	B	Up	Y	2,000,000
AB Emerging Markets Core Portfolio Advisor Class	EMPYX	NAS CM	Open End	Emerging Markets Equity (Div Emerging Mkts)	C	C+	B	Up	Y	0
AB Emerging Markets Core Portfolio Class A	EMPAX	NAS CM	Open End	Emerging Markets Equity (Div Emerging Mkts)	C	C+	B	Up	Y	2,500
AB Emerging Markets Core Portfolio Class C	EMPCX	NAS CM	Open End	Emerging Markets Equity (Div Emerging Mkts)	C	C+	B	Up	Y	2,500
AB Emerging Markets Multi-Asset Portfolio Advisor Class	ABYEX	NAS CM	Open End	Emerging Markets Equity (Multi-Asset Global)	B-	C+	B-		Y	0
AB Emerging Markets Multi-Asset Portfolio Class A	ABAEX	NAS CM	Open End	Emerging Markets Equity (Multi-Asset Global)	B-	C+	B-	Up	Y	2,500
AB Emerging Markets Multi-Asset Portfolio Class C	ABCEX	NAS CM	Open End	Emerging Markets Equity (Multi-Asset Global)	B-	C+	B-	Up	Y	2,500
AB Emerging Markets Multi-Asset Portfolio Class I	ABIEX	NAS CM	Open End	Emerging Markets Equity (Multi-Asset Global)	B-	C+	B-	Up	Y	2,000,000
AB Emerging Markets Multi-Asset Portfolio Class K	ABKEX	NAS CM	Open End	Emerging Markets Equity (Multi-Asset Global)	B-	C+	B-	Up	Y	0
AB Emerging Markets Multi-Asset Portfolio Class R	ABREX	NAS CM	Open End	Emerging Markets Equity (Multi-Asset Global)	B-	C+	B-	Up	Y	0
AB Emerging Markets Multi-Asset Portfolio Class Z	ABZEX	NAS CM	Open End	Emerging Markets Equity (Multi-Asset Global)	B-	C+	B-		Y	2,000,000
AB Emerging Markets Portfolio	SNEMX	NAS CM	Open End	Emerging Markets Equity (Div Emerging Mkts)	B-	B	C	Up	Y	5,000
AB Equity Income Fund Advisor Class	AUIYX	NAS CM	Open End	US Equity Large Cap Value (Equity-Income)	B-	B-	B-	Down	Y	0
AB Equity Income Fund Class A	AUIAX	NAS CM	Open End	US Equity Large Cap Value (Equity-Income)	B-	B-	B-	Down	Y	2,500
AB Equity Income Fund Class B	AUIBX	NAS CM	Open End	US Equity Large Cap Value (Equity-Income)	B-	C+	B	Down		2,500
AB Equity Income Fund Class C	AUICX	NAS CM	Open End	US Equity Large Cap Value (Equity-Income)	B-	C+	B-	Down	Y	2,500
AB Equity Income Fund Class I	AUIIX	NAS CM	Open End	US Equity Large Cap Value (Equity-Income)	B-	B-	B-	Down	Y	2,000,000
AB Equity Income Fund Class K	AUIKX	NAS CM	Open End	US Equity Large Cap Value (Equity-Income)	B-	B-	B-	Down	Y	0
AB Equity Income Fund Class R	AUIRX	NAS CM	Open End	US Equity Large Cap Value (Equity-Income)	B-	B-	B-	Down	Y	0
AB Equity Income Fund Class Z	AUIZX	NAS CM	Open End	US Equity Large Cap Value (Equity-Income)	B-	B-	B-	Down	Y	2,000,000
AB FlexFee Core Opportunities Portfolio Advisor Class	FFCYX	NAS CM	Open End	US Equity Large Cap Value (Growth)	U	U	U		Y	0
AB FlexFee Emerging Markets Growth Portfolio Advisor Class	FFEYX	NAS CM	Open End	Emerging Markets Equity (Div Emerging Mkts)	C+	B-	C	Up	Y	0
AB FlexFee Intl Strategic Core Portfolio Adv Cls	FFSYX	NAS CM	Open End	Global Equity Large Cap (Foreign Stock)	U	U	U		Y	0
AB FlexFee Large Cap Growth Portfolio Advisor Class	FFLYX	NAS CM	Open End	US Equity Large Cap Growth (Growth)	U	U	U		Y	0
AB FlexFee US Thematic Portfolio Advisor Class	FFTYX	NAS CM	Open End	US Equity Large Cap Blend (Growth)	U	U	U		Y	0
AB Global Core Equity Portfolio Advisor Class	GCEYX	NAS CM	Open End	Global Equity (World Stock)	C+	C+	B-	Down	Y	0
AB Global Core Equity Portfolio Class A	GCEAX	NAS CM	Open End	Global Equity (World Stock)	C+	C+	B-	Down	Y	2,500
AB Global Core Equity Portfolio Class C	GCECX	NAS CM	Open End	Global Equity (World Stock)	C+	C+	C+	Down	Y	2,500
AB Global Real Estate Investment Fund Advisor Class	ARSYX	NAS CM	Open End	Real Estate Sector Equity (Real Estate)	B-	C+	B		Y	0
AB Global Real Estate Investment Fund Class A	AREAX	NAS CM	Open End	Real Estate Sector Equity (Real Estate)	B-	C+	B		Y	2,500
AB Global Real Estate Investment Fund Class B	AREBX	NAS CM	Open End	Real Estate Sector Equity (Real Estate)	B-	C+	B	Up		2,500
AB Global Real Estate Investment Fund Class C	ARECX	NAS CM	Open End	Real Estate Sector Equity (Real Estate)	B-	C+	B	Up	Y	2,500
AB Global Real Estate Investment Fund Class I	AEEIX	NAS CM	Open End	Real Estate Sector Equity (Real Estate)	B-	C+	B		Y	2,000,000
AB Global Real Estate Investment Fund Class K	ARRKX	NAS CM	Open End	Real Estate Sector Equity (Real Estate)	B-	C+	B		Y	0
AB Global Real Estate Investment Fund Class R	ARRRX	NAS CM	Open End	Real Estate Sector Equity (Real Estate)	B-	C+	B	Up	Y	0
AB Global Real Estate Investment Fund II Class I	ARIIX	NAS CM	Open End	Real Estate Sector Equity (Real Estate)	B-	C+	B		Y	2,000,000
AB Global Risk Allocation Fund Class A	CABNX	NAS CM	Open End	Moderate Alloc (Asset Alloc)	B-	C+	B	Down	Y	2,500
AB Global Risk Allocation Fund Class Adv	CBSYX	NAS CM	Open End	Moderate Alloc (Asset Alloc)	C+	C+	B-	Down	Y	0
AB Global Risk Allocation Fund Class B	CABBX	NAS CM	Open End	Moderate Alloc (Asset Alloc)	B-	C+	B	Up		2,500
AB Global Risk Allocation Fund Class C	CBACX	NAS CM	Open End	Moderate Alloc (Asset Alloc)	C+	C+	C+	Down	Y	2,500
AB Global Risk Allocation Fund Class I	CABIX	NAS CM	Open End	Moderate Alloc (Asset Alloc)	C+	C+	B-	Down	Y	2,000,000
AB Global Risk Allocation Fund Class K	CBSKX	NAS CM	Open End	Moderate Alloc (Asset Alloc)	C+	C+	B-	Down	Y	0
AB Global Risk Allocation Fund Class R	CBSRX	NAS CM	Open End	Moderate Alloc (Asset Alloc)	C+	C+	B-	Down	Y	0
AB Growth Fund Advisor Class	AGRYX	NAS CM	Open End	US Equity Large Cap Growth (Growth)	A-	A-	A	Up	Y	0
AB Growth Fund Class A	AGRFX	NAS CM	Open End	US Equity Large Cap Growth (Growth)	A-	A-	A	Up	Y	2,500
AB Growth Fund Class B	AGBBX	NAS CM	Open End	US Equity Large Cap Growth (Growth)	A-	A-	A-	Up		2,500
AB Growth Fund Class C	AGRCX	NAS CM	Open End	US Equity Large Cap Growth (Growth)	A-	A-	A-	Up	Y	2,500

★ Expanded analysis of this fund is included in Section II.

	TOTAL RETURNS					PERFORMANCE				ASSETS		ASSET ALLOCATION & TURNOVER					BULL & BEAR		FEES		
Min Additional Investment	3-Month Total Return	6-Month Total Return	1-Year Total Return	3-Year Total Return	5-Year Total Return	Dividend Yield (TTM)	Expense Ratio	3-Yr Std Deviation	3-Year Beta	NAV	Total Assets (MIL)	%Cash	%Stocks	%Bonds	%Other	Turnover Ratio	Last Bull Market Total Return	Last Bear Market Total Return	Front End Fee (%)	Back End Fee (%)	Inception Date
50	5.93	11.35	12.56	30.33	99.72	0.01	1.92	13.56	1.1	21.38	2,959	1	99	0	0	57	27.24	-26.64		4.00	Mar-01
50	5.71	10.93	11.85	27.89	93.42	0	1.9	13.58	1.1	20.11	2,959	1	99	0	0	57	26.78	-26.8		1.00	Mar-01
	6.01	11.53	12.99	31.88	103.52	0.36	0.88	13.58	1.1	22.61	2,959	1	99	0	0	57	27.55	-26.49			Mar-05
	5.91	11.33	12.58	30.49	100.00	0.11	1.21	13.55	1.1	22.47	2,959	1	99	0	0	57	27.39	-26.59			Mar-05
	5.80	11.13	12.24	29.28	97.02	0	1.52	13.52	1.1	22.14	2,959	1	99	0	0	57	27.14	-26.66			Nov-03
	6.03	11.56	13.08	32.15	104.23	0.42	0.8	13.56	1.1	22.58	2,959	1	99	0	0	57	27.56	-26.49			Oct-13
	3.82	10.65	32.38			1.18	1.1			12.24	5.8	3	97	0	0	94					Sep-15
50	3.74	10.49	31.98			0.98	1.35			12.23	5.8	3	97	0	0	94			4.25		Sep-15
50	3.53	10.04	31.03			0.4	2.1			12.23	5.8	3	97	0	0	94				1.00	Sep-15
	3.98	7.67	20.59	26.80	18.15	4.15	0.99	10.98	0.65	9.95	119.8	0	74	25	1	118	14.59				Aug-11
50	3.90	7.54	20.36	25.81	16.46	3.92	1.24	10.92	0.65	9.93	119.8	0	74	25	1	118	14.48		4.25		Aug-11
50	3.74	7.13	19.35	22.94	12.33	3.38	1.99	10.99	0.65	9.89	119.8	0	74	25	1	118	14.03			1.00	Aug-11
	4.02	7.75	20.69	26.73	18.11	4.25	0.99	11.03	0.65	9.88	119.8	0	74	25	1	118	14.65				Aug-11
	3.99	7.60	20.32	25.82	16.66	3.91	1.24	11	0.65	9.9	119.8	0	74	25	1	118	14.47				Aug-11
	3.78	7.37	19.93	24.87	15.18	3.71	1.49	11.01	0.65	9.9	119.8	0	74	25	1	118	14.25				Aug-11
	3.99	7.82	20.78	26.82	18.19		0.99	11.03	0.65	9.89	119.8	0	74	25	1	118	14.65				Jul-17
	4.75	12.09	32.96	27.07	27.03	0.48	1.5	15.11	0.94	32.54	1,335	1	99	0	0	63	18.83	-30.43			Dec-95
	5.72	10.04	17.50	25.01	81.31	2.49	0.76	9.53	0.92	29.26	658.9	0	100	0	0	81	22.54	-15.94			Oct-96
50	5.65	9.91	17.22	24.02	78.74	2.29	1.01	9.51	0.92	28.99	658.9	0	100	0	0	81	22.35	-16.08	4.25		Oct-93
50	5.47	9.51	16.35	21.25	72.34	1.6	1.78	9.54	0.92	28.64	658.9	0	100	0	0	81	21.83	-16.32		4.00	Oct-93
50	5.43	9.48	16.31	21.29	72.43	1.6	1.76	9.52	0.92	28.62	658.9	0	100	0	0	81	21.83	-16.34		1.00	Oct-93
	5.71	10.05	17.45	24.97	81.20	2.5	0.76	9.52	0.92	28.92	658.9	0	100	0	0	81	22.56	-15.99			Mar-05
	5.63	9.86	17.07	23.71	78.25	2.19	1.09	9.51	0.92	28.98	658.9	0	100	0	0	81	22.32	-16.05			Mar-05
	5.54	9.70	16.73	22.62	75.57	1.92	1.38	9.53	0.92	28.85	658.9	0	100	0	0	81	22.14	-16.17			Mar-05
	5.74	10.11	17.57	25.32	81.52	2.59	0.66	9.53	0.92	28.91	658.9	0	100	0	0	81	22.35	-16.08			Oct-13
	5.67	12.04					0.6			11.05	1.1	14	86	0	0						Jun-17
	5.09	13.95	38.29	32.28		0.21	0.85	14.5	0.84	12.35	6.1	0	100	0	0	79					Nov-14
	4.41	8.51					0.65			10.7	3.2	0	100	0	0						Jun-17
	7.19	13.12					0.6			11.18	1.3	8	92	0	0						Jun-17
	6.93	12.32					0.6			11.11	1.1	5	95	0	0						Jun-17
	6.24	9.68	25.48	31.08		0.8	0.9	10.36	0.94	12.31	385.2	0	100	0	0	51					Nov-14
50	6.21	9.56	25.15	30.20		0.66	1.15	10.33	0.94	12.29	385.2	0	100	0	0	51			4.25		Nov-14
50	6.05	9.15	24.21	27.21		0.36	1.9	10.28	0.94	12.21	385.2	0	100	0	0	51				1.00	Nov-14
	3.54	5.82	13.66	16.27	43.22	2.52	1.03	10.09	0.67	14.41	148.8	0	99	0	0	83	24.86	-21.97			Sep-96
50	3.51	5.71	13.42	15.34	41.28	2.28	1.29	10.09	0.67	14.56	148.8	0	99	0	0	83	24.57	-22.02	4.25		Sep-96
50	3.30	5.31	12.51	12.66	35.85	1.59	2.09	10.1	0.67	14.39	148.8	0	99	0	0	83	24.03	-22.31		4.00	Sep-96
50	3.31	5.31	12.57	12.75	36.14	1.46	2.05	10.08	0.67	14.41	148.8	0	99	0	0	83	24.13	-22.34		1.00	Sep-96
	3.61	5.91	13.83	16.60	43.89	2.6	0.95	10.11	0.67	14.51	148.8	0	99	0	0	83	24.9	-21.9			Mar-05
	3.54	5.76	13.42	15.39	41.46	2.27	1.3	10.09	0.67	14.45	148.8	0	99	0	0	83	24.59	-22.03			Mar-05
	3.42	5.58	13.09	14.35	39.28	2.01	1.6	10.09	0.67	14.39	148.8	0	99	0	0	83	24.44	-22.17			Mar-05
	3.65	6.14	14.43	17.83	45.81	3.99	0.69	10.08	0.66	11.03	334.7	1	99	0	0	71	25.18	-21.42			Dec-97
50	3.64	6.58	11.78	15.14	24.13	5	1.31	6.3	0.45	16.42	282.0	11	25	63	0	79	19.34	-10.25	4.25		Jun-32
	3.70	6.67	12.05	15.95	25.76	5.19	1.06	6.26	0.45	16.54	282.0	11	25	63	0	79	19.53	-10.16			Oct-96
50	3.38	6.11	10.88	12.45	19.44	4.67	2.07	6.28	0.45	14.91	282.0	11	25	63	0	79	18.81	-10.52		4.00	Feb-91
50	3.45	6.17	10.94	12.52	19.61	4.8	2.06	6.29	0.44	15.07	282.0	11	25	63	0	79	18.84	-10.54		1.00	May-93
	3.71	6.75	12.14	16.48	26.67	5.37	0.89	6.26	0.44	16.52	282.0	11	25	63	0	79	19.6	-10.06			Mar-05
	3.61	6.55	11.69	15.02	23.96	4.94	1.33	6.29	0.45	16.38	282.0	11	25	63	0	79	19.31	-10.22			Mar-05
	3.53	6.35	11.37	13.95	22.08	4.53	1.64	6.28	0.44	16.31	282.0	11	25	63	0	79	19.13	-10.37			Nov-03
	7.89	13.51	34.18	47.68	129.94	0	1	10.81	0.96	79.66	847.7	7	93	0	0	54	27.83	-16.96			Oct-96
50	7.83	13.38	33.83	46.57	126.84	0	1.25	10.82	0.96	73.36	847.7	7	93	0	0	54	27.59	-17.06	4.25		Sep-90
50	7.62	12.93	32.80	43.09	117.98	0	2.01	10.8	0.96	38.96	847.7	7	93	0	0	54	27	-17.37		4.00	Oct-87
50	7.62	12.94	32.84	43.28	118.51	0	2.02	10.8	0.96	39.53	847.7	7	93	0	0	54	27.05	-17.3		1.00	Aug-93

	MARKET		FUND TYPE, CATEGORY & OBJECTIVE		RATINGS				MINIMUMS	
Fund Name	Ticker Symbol	Traded On	Fund Type	Category and (Prospectus Objective)	Overall Rating	Reward Rating	Risk Rating	Recent Up/ Downgrade	Open to New Investors	Min Initial Investment
AB Growth Fund Class I	AGFIX	NAS CM	Open End	US Equity Large Cap Growth (Growth)	A-	A-	A	Up	Y	2,000,000
AB Growth Fund Class K	AGFKX	NAS CM	Open End	US Equity Large Cap Growth (Growth)	A-	A-	A	Up	Y	0
AB Growth Fund Class R	AGFRX	NAS CM	Open End	US Equity Large Cap Growth (Growth)	A-	A-	A	Up	Y	0
AB International Growth Fund Advisor Class	AWPYX	NAS CM	Open End	Global Equity Large Cap (Foreign Stock)	B-	C+	B-	Up	Y	0
AB International Growth Fund Class A	AWPAX	NAS CM	Open End	Global Equity Large Cap (Foreign Stock)	B-	C+	B-	Up	Y	2,500
AB International Growth Fund Class B	AWPBX	NAS CM	Open End	Global Equity Large Cap (Foreign Stock)	C+	C+	B-	Up		2,500
AB International Growth Fund Class C	AWPCX	NAS CM	Open End	Global Equity Large Cap (Foreign Stock)	C+	C+	B-	Up	Y	2,500
AB International Growth Fund Class I	AWPIX	NAS CM	Open End	Global Equity Large Cap (Foreign Stock)	B-	B-	B-	Up	Y	2,000,000
AB International Growth Fund Class K	AWPKX	NAS CM	Open End	Global Equity Large Cap (Foreign Stock)	B-	C+	B-	Up	Y	0
AB International Growth Fund Class R	AWPRX	NAS CM	Open End	Global Equity Large Cap (Foreign Stock)	B-	C+	B-	Up	Y	0
AB International Portfolio	SIMTX	NAS CM	Open End	Global Equity Large Cap (Foreign Stock)	B	B-	B	Up	Y	10,000
AB International Portfolio Class A	AIZAX	NAS CM	Open End	Global Equity Large Cap (Foreign Stock)	B	B-	B	Up	Y	2,500
AB International Portfolio Class B	AIZBX	NAS CM	Open End	Global Equity Large Cap (Foreign Stock)	B-	C+	B	Up		2,500
AB International Portfolio Class C	AIZCX	NAS CM	Open End	Global Equity Large Cap (Foreign Stock)	B-	C+	B	Up	Y	2,500
AB International Small Cap Portfolio Advisor Class	IRCYX	NAS CM	Open End	Global Equity Mid/Small Cap (Small Company)	C-	C	B+	Up	Y	5,000
AB International Small Cap Portfolio Class Z	IRCZX	NAS CM	Open End	Global Equity Mid/Small Cap (Small Company)	C-	C	B+	Up	Y	2,000,000
AB International Strategic Core Portfolio Advisor Class	ISRYX	NAS CM	Open End	Global Equity Large Cap (Growth)	C	C+	B+	Up	Y	0
AB International Strategic Core Portfolio Class A	ISARX	NAS CM	Open End	Global Equity Large Cap (Growth)	C	C+	B+	Up	Y	2,500
AB International Strategic Core Portfolio Class C	ISCRX	NAS CM	Open End	Global Equity Large Cap (Growth)	C	C+	B	Up	Y	2,500
AB International Strategic Equities Portfolio Advisor Cls	STEYX	NAS CM	Open End	Global Equity Large Cap (Growth)	C-	C	B+	Up	Y	10,000
AB International Strategic Equities Portfolio Class Z	STEZX	NAS CM	Open End	Global Equity Large Cap (Growth)	C-	C	B+	Up	Y	2,000,000
AB International Value Fund Advisor Class	ABIYX	NAS CM	Open End	Global Equity Large Cap (Foreign Stock)	B	B-	B	Up	Y	0
AB International Value Fund Class A	ABIAX	NAS CM	Open End	Global Equity Large Cap (Foreign Stock)	B-	B-	B	Up	Y	2,500
AB International Value Fund Class B	ABIBX	NAS CM	Open End	Global Equity Large Cap (Foreign Stock)	B-	C+	B	Up		2,500
AB International Value Fund Class C	ABICX	NAS CM	Open End	Global Equity Large Cap (Foreign Stock)	B-	C+	B	Up	Y	2,500
AB International Value Fund Class I	AIVIX	NAS CM	Open End	Global Equity Large Cap (Foreign Stock)	B	B-	B	Up	Y	2,000,000
AB International Value Fund Class K	AIVKX	NAS CM	Open End	Global Equity Large Cap (Foreign Stock)	B-	B-	B	Up	Y	0
AB International Value Fund Class R	AIVRX	NAS CM	Open End	Global Equity Large Cap (Foreign Stock)	B-	B-	B	Up	Y	0
AB Large Cap Growth Fund Advisor Class	APGYX	NAS CM	Open End	US Equity Large Cap Growth (Growth)	A-	B+	A	Up	Y	0
AB Large Cap Growth Fund Class A	APGAX	NAS CM	Open End	US Equity Large Cap Growth (Growth)	A-	B+	A	Up	Y	2,500
AB Large Cap Growth Fund Class B	APGBX	NAS CM	Open End	US Equity Large Cap Growth (Growth)	B+	B+	A	Down		2,500
AB Large Cap Growth Fund Class C	APGCX	NAS CM	Open End	US Equity Large Cap Growth (Growth)	B+	B+	A	Down	Y	2,500
AB Large Cap Growth Fund Class I	ALLIX	NAS CM	Open End	US Equity Large Cap Growth (Growth)	A-	B+	A	Up	Y	2,000,000
AB Large Cap Growth Fund Class K	ALCKX	NAS CM	Open End	US Equity Large Cap Growth (Growth)	A-	B+	A	Up	Y	0
AB Large Cap Growth Fund Class R	ABPRX	NAS CM	Open End	US Equity Large Cap Growth (Growth)	A-	B+	A	Up	Y	0
AB Large Cap Growth Fund Class Z	APGZX	NAS CM	Open End	US Equity Large Cap Growth (Growth)	A-	B+	A	Up	Y	2,000,000
AB Multi-Manager Select 2010 Fund Advisor Class	TDBYX	NAS CM	Open End	Target Date 2000-2020 (Asset Alloc)	B-	C	B	Up	Y	0
AB Multi-Manager Select 2010 Fund Class A	TDBAX	NAS CM	Open End	Target Date 2000-2020 (Asset Alloc)	B-	C	B	Up	Y	2,500
AB Multi-Manager Select 2010 Fund Class C	TDBCX	NAS CM	Open End	Target Date 2000-2020 (Asset Alloc)	C+	C	B	Up	Y	2,500
AB Multi-Manager Select 2010 Fund Class I	TDIBX	NAS CM	Open End	Target Date 2000-2020 (Asset Alloc)	B-	C	B	Up	Y	2,000,000
AB Multi-Manager Select 2010 Fund Class K	TDBKX	NAS CM	Open End	Target Date 2000-2020 (Asset Alloc)	B-	C	B	Up	Y	0
AB Multi-Manager Select 2010 Fund Class R	TDBRX	NAS CM	Open End	Target Date 2000-2020 (Asset Alloc)	C+	C	B	Up	Y	0
AB Multi-Manager Select 2010 Fund Class Z	TDBZX	NAS CM	Open End	Target Date 2000-2020 (Asset Alloc)	B-	C	B	Up	Y	2,000,000
AB Multi-Manager Select 2015 Fund Advisor Class	TDCYX	NAS CM	Open End	Target Date 2000-2020 (Asset Alloc)	B-	C	B	Up	Y	0
AB Multi-Manager Select 2015 Fund Class A	TDCAX	NAS CM	Open End	Target Date 2000-2020 (Asset Alloc)	B-	C	B	Up	Y	2,500
AB Multi-Manager Select 2015 Fund Class C	TDCCX	NAS CM	Open End	Target Date 2000-2020 (Asset Alloc)	C+	C	B	Up	Y	2,500
AB Multi-Manager Select 2015 Fund Class I	TDCIX	NAS CM	Open End	Target Date 2000-2020 (Asset Alloc)	B-	C	B	Up	Y	2,000,000
AB Multi-Manager Select 2015 Fund Class K	TDCKX	NAS CM	Open End	Target Date 2000-2020 (Asset Alloc)	B-	C	B	Up	Y	0
AB Multi-Manager Select 2015 Fund Class R	TDCRX	NAS CM	Open End	Target Date 2000-2020 (Asset Alloc)	B-	C	B	Up	Y	0
AB Multi-Manager Select 2015 Fund Class Z	TDCZX	NAS CM	Open End	Target Date 2000-2020 (Asset Alloc)	B-	C	B	Up	Y	2,000,000
AB Multi-Manager Select 2020 Fund Advisor Class	TDDYX	NAS CM	Open End	Target Date 2000-2020 (Asset Alloc)	B-	C	B	Up	Y	0
AB Multi-Manager Select 2020 Fund Class A	TDDAX	NAS CM	Open End	Target Date 2000-2020 (Asset Alloc)	B-	C	B	Up	Y	2,500

★ Expanded analysis of this fund is included in Section II.

	TOTAL RETURNS					PERFORMANCE				ASSETS		ASSET ALLOCATION & TURNOVER					BULL & BEAR		FEES		
Min Additional Investment	3-Month Total Return	6-Month Total Return	1-Year Total Return	3-Year Total Return	5-Year Total Return	Dividend Yield (TTM)	Expense Ratio	3-Yr Std Deviation	3-Year Beta	NAV	Total Assets (MIL)	%Cash	%Stocks	%Bonds	%Other	Turnover Ratio	Last Bull Market Total Return	Last Bear Market Total Return	Front End Fee (%)	Back End Fee (%)	Inception Date
	7.93	13.59	34.36	48.20	131.39	0	0.85	10.81	0.96	79.28	847.7	7	93	0	0	54	27.99	-16.89			Mar-05
	7.81	13.35	33.79	46.56	127.32	0	1.27	10.8	0.96	75.22	847.7	7	93	0	0	54	27.8	-17.01			Mar-05
	7.72	13.17	33.37	45.15	123.75	0	1.58	10.81	0.96	71.63	847.7	7	93	0	0	54	27.49	-17.12			Mar-05
	2.79	9.95	34.87	22.81	40.24	0.75	1.18	13.07	0.98	19.88	313.0	6	94	0	0	27	20.35	-26.95			Oct-96
50	2.68	9.79	34.45	21.89	38.39	0.58	1.43	13.09	0.98	19.51	313.0	6	94	0	0	27	20.17	-27.04	4.25		Jun-94
50	2.49	9.39	33.35	18.90	32.99	0	2.26	13.08	0.98	17.23	313.0	6	94	0	0	27	19.53	-27.22		4.00	Jun-94
50	2.48	9.40	33.51	19.10	33.38	0	2.2	13.09	0.98	17.33	313.0	6	94	0	0	27	19.64	-27.24		1.00	Feb-95
	2.80	10.07	35.01	23.34	41.32	0.95	1.06	13.07	0.98	19.78	313.0	6	94	0	0	27	20.53	-26.89			Mar-05
	2.69	9.84	34.48	21.94	38.53	0.63	1.41	13.07	0.98	19.42	313.0	6	94	0	0	27	20.19	-27.03			Mar-05
	2.66	9.69	34.10	20.83	36.50	0.31	1.72	13.06	0.98	19.23	313.0	6	94	0	0	27	20	-27.12			Mar-05
	2.96	9.10	26.50	27.93	45.62	1.45	1.2	10.98	0.86	18.44	1,331	2	98	0	0	82	11.87	-25.54			Apr-99
50	2.95	9.12	26.49	27.95	44.50	1.47	1.2	10.98	0.86	18.14	1,331	2	98	0	0	82	11.22	-25.75	4.25		Jan-04
50	2.75	8.75	25.62	25.17	39.25	0.57	1.95	11	0.86	18.63	1,331	2	98	0	0	82	10.69	-25.97		4.00	Jan-04
50	2.74	8.71	25.54	25.10	39.28	0.75	1.95	10.96	0.86	18.33	1,331	2	98	0	0	82	10.8	-25.97		1.00	Jan-04
	4.71	12.78	32.14			1.19	1.1			12.82	1,129	2	98	0	0	65					Dec-15
	4.72	12.79	32.15			1.2	1.1			12.82	1,129	2	98	0	0	65					Dec-15
	4.20	8.16	24.61			0.8	0.95			11.81	52.2	1	99	0	0	64					Jul-15
50	4.18	8.05	24.26			0.68	1.2			11.8	52.2	1	99	0	0	64			4.25		Jul-15
50	3.92	7.60	23.28			0	1.95			11.76	52.2	1	99	0	0	64				1.00	Jul-15
	3.45	9.74	30.02			1.1	0.95			12.78	3,368	2	98	0	0	69					Dec-15
	3.52	9.82	29.96			1.1	0.95			12.8	3,368	2	98	0	0	69					Dec-15
	3.00	8.86	25.20	27.15	48.64	0.28	1.25	12.28	0.95	15.2	282.7	0	100	0	0	58	11.9	-27.85			Mar-01
50	2.93	8.69	24.82	26.21	46.58	0.14	1.5	12.25	0.95	14.86	282.7	0	100	0	0	58	11.74	-27.92	4.25		Mar-01
50	2.73	8.30	23.81	23.19	41.10	0	2.28	12.26	0.95	14.65	282.7	0	100	0	0	58	11.26	-28.22		4.00	Mar-01
50	2.73	8.29	23.92	23.40	41.40	0	2.25	12.27	0.95	14.59	282.7	0	100	0	0	58	11.31	-28.18		1.00	Mar-01
	3.06	8.98	25.36	28.01	50.41	0.45	0.97	12.25	0.95	14.83	282.7	0	100	0	0	58	12.01	-27.71			Mar-05
	2.98	8.76	24.95	26.38	47.22	0.22	1.4	12.27	0.95	14.82	282.7	0	100	0	0	58	11.7	-27.85			Mar-05
	2.87	8.53	24.48	25.19	44.92	0.03	1.71	12.31	0.96	14.75	282.7	0	100	0	0	58	11.52	-27.92			Nov-03
	7.05	12.70	31.66	49.01	139.38	0.1	0.75	10.28	0.91	51.89	5,860	10	90	0	0	60	27.52	-18.49			Oct-96
50	6.99	12.56	31.35	47.93	136.37	0	1	10.28	0.91	47.78	5,860	10	90	0	0	60	27.47	-18.59	4.25		Sep-92
50	6.77	12.11	30.32	44.48	127.07	0	1.8	10.27	0.91	35.69	5,860	10	90	0	0	60	26.74	-18.88		4.00	Sep-92
50	6.77	12.14	30.40	44.65	127.66	0	1.76	10.27	0.91	36.17	5,860	10	90	0	0	60	26.79	-18.86		1.00	May-93
	7.05	12.70	31.71	49.25	140.09	0.11	0.73	10.29	0.92	51.62	5,860	10	90	0	0	60	27.73	-18.45			Mar-05
	6.97	12.52	31.27	47.69	135.92	0	1.07	10.29	0.92	48.63	5,860	10	90	0	0	60	27.55	-18.59			Mar-05
	6.87	12.36	30.87	46.35	132.38	0	1.38	10.28	0.91	45.94	5,860	10	90	0	0	60	27.29	-18.65			Nov-03
	7.06	12.73	31.79	49.23	138.45	0.13	0.63	10.28	0.91	51.68	5,860	10	90	0	0	60	27.47	-18.59			Jun-15
	2.80	5.72	11.35	16.20		1.33	0.58			11.1	16.5	4	41	52	2	49					Dec-14
50	2.82	5.63	11.11	15.43		0.1	0.83			11.18	16.5	4	41	52	2	49			4.25		Dec-14
50	2.56	5.21	10.21	12.67		0	1.58			11.08	16.5	4	41	52	2	49				1.00	Dec-14
	2.88	5.72	11.33	16.20		2.48	0.58			10.58	16.5	4	41	52	2	49					Dec-14
	2.86	5.70	11.10	15.32		1.9	0.83			10.6	16.5	4	41	52	2	49					Dec-14
	2.70	5.45	10.84	14.59		1.69	1.08			10.62	16.5	4	41	52	2	49					Dec-14
	2.86	5.79	11.40	16.30		2.32	0.58			10.6	16.5	4	41	52	2	49					Dec-14
	3.25	6.45	12.70	18.51		2.06	0.58			11.02	43.8	4	46	46	3	38					Dec-14
50	3.14	6.37	12.38	17.60		1.6	0.83			10.88	43.8	4	46	46	3	38			4.25		Dec-14
50	2.93	5.99	11.60	14.95		1.16	1.58			10.84	43.8	4	46	46	3	38				1.00	Dec-14
	3.23	6.53	12.78	18.45		2.15	0.58			10.67	43.8	4	46	46	3	38					Dec-14
	3.15	6.35	12.49	17.66		1.82	0.83			10.66	43.8	4	46	46	3	38					Dec-14
	3.10	6.21	12.12	16.66		1.48	1.08			10.65	43.8	4	46	46	3	38					Dec-14
	3.21	6.41	12.66	18.38		2.2	0.58			10.63	43.8	4	46	46	3	38					Dec-14
	3.51	7.18	14.04	20.35		1.91	0.58			11.17	92.8	5	53	39	3	46					Dec-14
50	3.50	7.09	13.85	19.54		1.53	0.83			11.17	92.8	5	53	39	3	46			4.25		Dec-14

	MARKET			FUND TYPE, CATEGORY & OBJECTIVE	RATINGS					MINIMUMS
Fund Name	Ticker Symbol	Traded On	Fund Type	Category and (Prospectus Objective)	Overall Rating	Reward Rating	Risk Rating	Recent Up/ Downgrade	Open to New Investors	Min Initial Investment
AB Multi-Manager Select 2020 Fund Class C	TDDCX	NAS CM	Open End	Target Date 2000-2020 (Asset Alloc)	C+	C	B	Up	Y	2,500
AB Multi-Manager Select 2020 Fund Class I	TDDIX	NAS CM	Open End	Target Date 2000-2020 (Asset Alloc)	B-	C	B	Up	Y	2,000,000
AB Multi-Manager Select 2020 Fund Class K	TDDKX	NAS CM	Open End	Target Date 2000-2020 (Asset Alloc)	B-	C	B	Up	Y	0
AB Multi-Manager Select 2020 Fund Class R	TDDRX	NAS CM	Open End	Target Date 2000-2020 (Asset Alloc)	C+	C	B	Up	Y	0
AB Multi-Manager Select 2020 Fund Class Z	TDDZX	NAS CM	Open End	Target Date 2000-2020 (Asset Alloc)	B-	C	B	Up	Y	2,000,000
AB Multi-Manager Select 2025 Fund Advisor Class	TDGYX	NAS CM	Open End	Target Date 2021-2045 (Asset Alloc)	B-	C+	B	Up	Y	0
AB Multi-Manager Select 2025 Fund Class A	TDAGX	NAS CM	Open End	Target Date 2021-2045 (Asset Alloc)	B-	C+	B	Up	Y	2,500
AB Multi-Manager Select 2025 Fund Class C	TDCGX	NAS CM	Open End	Target Date 2021-2045 (Asset Alloc)	C+	C+	B	Down	Y	2,500
AB Multi-Manager Select 2025 Fund Class I	TDIGX	NAS CM	Open End	Target Date 2021-2045 (Asset Alloc)	B-	C+	B	Up	Y	2,000,000
AB Multi-Manager Select 2025 Fund Class K	TDGKX	NAS CM	Open End	Target Date 2021-2045 (Asset Alloc)	B-	C+	B	Up	Y	0
AB Multi-Manager Select 2025 Fund Class R	TDGRX	NAS CM	Open End	Target Date 2021-2045 (Asset Alloc)	B-	C+	B	Up	Y	0
AB Multi-Manager Select 2025 Fund Class Z	TDGZX	NAS CM	Open End	Target Date 2021-2045 (Asset Alloc)	B-	C+	B	Up	Y	2,000,000
AB Multi-Manager Select 2030 Fund Advisor Class	TDYHX	NAS CM	Open End	Target Date 2021-2045 (Asset Alloc)	B-	C+	B	Up	Y	0
AB Multi-Manager Select 2030 Fund Class A	TDHAX	NAS CM	Open End	Target Date 2021-2045 (Asset Alloc)	B-	C+	B	Up	Y	2,500
AB Multi-Manager Select 2030 Fund Class C	TDHCX	NAS CM	Open End	Target Date 2021-2045 (Asset Alloc)	B-	C+	B	Up	Y	2,500
AB Multi-Manager Select 2030 Fund Class I	TDIHX	NAS CM	Open End	Target Date 2021-2045 (Asset Alloc)	B-	C+	B	Up	Y	2,000,000
AB Multi-Manager Select 2030 Fund Class K	TDHKX	NAS CM	Open End	Target Date 2021-2045 (Asset Alloc)	B-	C+	B	Up	Y	0
AB Multi-Manager Select 2030 Fund Class R	TDHRX	NAS CM	Open End	Target Date 2021-2045 (Asset Alloc)	B-	C+	B	Up	Y	0
AB Multi-Manager Select 2030 Fund Class Z	TDHZX	NAS CM	Open End	Target Date 2021-2045 (Asset Alloc)	B-	C+	B	Up	Y	2,000,000
AB Multi-Manager Select 2035 Fund Advisor Class	TDMYX	NAS CM	Open End	Target Date 2021-2045 (Asset Alloc)	B-	C+	B	Up	Y	0
AB Multi-Manager Select 2035 Fund Class A	TDMAX	NAS CM	Open End	Target Date 2021-2045 (Asset Alloc)	B-	C+	B	Up	Y	2,500
AB Multi-Manager Select 2035 Fund Class C	TDMCX	NAS CM	Open End	Target Date 2021-2045 (Asset Alloc)	B-	C+	B	Up	Y	2,500
AB Multi-Manager Select 2035 Fund Class I	TDIMX	NAS CM	Open End	Target Date 2021-2045 (Asset Alloc)	B-	C+	B	Up	Y	2,000,000
AB Multi-Manager Select 2035 Fund Class K	TDMKX	NAS CM	Open End	Target Date 2021-2045 (Asset Alloc)	B-	C+	B	Up	Y	0
AB Multi-Manager Select 2035 Fund Class R	TDRMX	NAS CM	Open End	Target Date 2021-2045 (Asset Alloc)	B-	C+	B	Up	Y	0
AB Multi-Manager Select 2035 Fund Class Z	TDMZX	NAS CM	Open End	Target Date 2021-2045 (Asset Alloc)	B-	C+	B	Up	Y	2,000,000
AB Multi-Manager Select 2040 Fund Advisor Class	TDJYX	NAS CM	Open End	Target Date 2021-2045 (Asset Alloc)	B-	C+	B	Up	Y	0
AB Multi-Manager Select 2040 Fund Class A	TDJAX	NAS CM	Open End	Target Date 2021-2045 (Asset Alloc)	B-	C+	B	Up	Y	2,500
AB Multi-Manager Select 2040 Fund Class C	TDJCX	NAS CM	Open End	Target Date 2021-2045 (Asset Alloc)	B-	C+	B	Up	Y	2,500
AB Multi-Manager Select 2040 Fund Class I	TDJIX	NAS CM	Open End	Target Date 2021-2045 (Asset Alloc)	B-	C+	B	Up	Y	2,000,000
AB Multi-Manager Select 2040 Fund Class K	TDJKX	NAS CM	Open End	Target Date 2021-2045 (Asset Alloc)	B-	C+	B	Up	Y	0
AB Multi-Manager Select 2040 Fund Class R	TDJRX	NAS CM	Open End	Target Date 2021-2045 (Asset Alloc)	B-	C+	B	Up	Y	0
AB Multi-Manager Select 2040 Fund Class Z	TDJZX	NAS CM	Open End	Target Date 2021-2045 (Asset Alloc)	B-	C+	B	Up	Y	2,000,000
AB Multi-Manager Select 2045 Fund Advisor Class	TDNYX	NAS CM	Open End	Target Date 2021-2045 (Asset Alloc)	B-	C+	B	Up	Y	0
AB Multi-Manager Select 2045 Fund Class A	TDNAX	NAS CM	Open End	Target Date 2021-2045 (Asset Alloc)	B-	C+	B-	Up	Y	2,500
AB Multi-Manager Select 2045 Fund Class C	TDNCX	NAS CM	Open End	Target Date 2021-2045 (Asset Alloc)	C+	C+	B-	Down	Y	2,500
AB Multi-Manager Select 2045 Fund Class I	TDNIX	NAS CM	Open End	Target Date 2021-2045 (Asset Alloc)	B-	C+	B	Up	Y	2,000,000
AB Multi-Manager Select 2045 Fund Class K	TDNKX	NAS CM	Open End	Target Date 2021-2045 (Asset Alloc)	B-	C+	B	Up	Y	0
AB Multi-Manager Select 2045 Fund Class R	TDNRX	NAS CM	Open End	Target Date 2021-2045 (Asset Alloc)	B-	C+	B-	Up	Y	0
AB Multi-Manager Select 2045 Fund Class Z	TDNZX	NAS CM	Open End	Target Date 2021-2045 (Asset Alloc)	B-	C+	B	Up	Y	2,000,000
AB Multi-Manager Select 2050 Fund Advisor Class	TDLYX	NAS CM	Open End	Target Date 2046+ (Asset Alloc)	B-	C+	B-	Up	Y	0
AB Multi-Manager Select 2050 Fund Class A	TDLAX	NAS CM	Open End	Target Date 2046+ (Asset Alloc)	B-	C+	B-	Up	Y	2,500
AB Multi-Manager Select 2050 Fund Class C	TDCLX	NAS CM	Open End	Target Date 2046+ (Asset Alloc)	C+	C+	B-	Down	Y	2,500
AB Multi-Manager Select 2050 Fund Class I	TDLIX	NAS CM	Open End	Target Date 2046+ (Asset Alloc)	B-	C+	B-	Up	Y	2,000,000
AB Multi-Manager Select 2050 Fund Class K	TDLKX	NAS CM	Open End	Target Date 2046+ (Asset Alloc)	B-	C+	B-	Up	Y	0
AB Multi-Manager Select 2050 Fund Class R	TDLRX	NAS CM	Open End	Target Date 2046+ (Asset Alloc)	B-	C+	B-	Up	Y	0
AB Multi-Manager Select 2050 Fund Class Z	TDLZX	NAS CM	Open End	Target Date 2046+ (Asset Alloc)	B-	C+	B-	Up	Y	2,000,000
AB Multi-Manager Select 2055 Fund Advisor Class	TDPYX	NAS CM	Open End	Target Date 2046+ (Asset Alloc)	B-	C+	B-	Up	Y	0
AB Multi-Manager Select 2055 Fund Class A	TDAPX	NAS CM	Open End	Target Date 2046+ (Asset Alloc)	C+	C+	B-	Down	Y	2,500
AB Multi-Manager Select 2055 Fund Class C	TDCPX	NAS CM	Open End	Target Date 2046+ (Asset Alloc)	C+	C+	B-	Down	Y	2,500
AB Multi-Manager Select 2055 Fund Class I	TDIPX	NAS CM	Open End	Target Date 2046+ (Asset Alloc)	B-	C+	B-	Up	Y	2,000,000
AB Multi-Manager Select 2055 Fund Class K	TDPKX	NAS CM	Open End	Target Date 2046+ (Asset Alloc)	C+	C+	B-	Down	Y	0

★ Expanded analysis of this fund is included in Section II.

Min Additional Investment	TOTAL RETURNS: 3-Month Total Return	6-Month Total Return	1-Year Total Return	3-Year Total Return	5-Year Total Return	PERFORMANCE: Dividend Yield (TTM)	Expense Ratio	3-Yr Std Deviation	3-Year Beta	ASSETS: NAV	Total Assets (ML)	ASSET ALLOCATION & TURNOVER: %Cash	%Stocks	%Bonds	%Other	Turnover Ratio	BULL & BEAR: Last Bull Market Total Return	Last Bear Market Total Return	FEES: Front End Fee (%)	Back End Fee (%)	Inception Date
50	3.28	6.71	13.07	16.82		1.06	1.58			11.09	92.8	5	53	39	3	46				1.00	Dec-14
	3.54	7.10	13.98	20.29		1.94	0.58			11.22	92.8	5	53	39	3	46					Dec-14
	3.45	7.11	13.89	19.64		1.66	0.83			10.95	92.8	5	53	39	3	46					Dec-14
	3.39	6.95	13.51	18.62		1.23	1.08			10.93	92.8	5	53	39	3	46					Dec-14
	3.48	7.23	14.12	20.40		2	0.58			10.93	92.8	5	53	39	3	46					Dec-14
	4.00	8.11	16.26	23.37		1.8	0.58			11.5	145.9	4	61	30	4	41					Dec-14
50	3.95	7.97	15.90	22.35		1.29	0.83			11.49	145.9	4	61	30	4	41			4.25		Dec-14
50	3.66	7.53	15.07	19.71		1.02	1.58			11.41	145.9	4	61	30	4	41				1.00	Dec-14
	3.89	8.08	16.18	23.23		1.85	0.58			11.28	145.9	4	61	30	4	41					Dec-14
	3.90	7.91	15.89	22.37		1.58	0.83			11.25	145.9	4	61	30	4	41					Dec-14
	3.84	7.86	15.64	21.40		1.31	1.08			11.22	145.9	4	61	30	4	41					Dec-14
	3.92	8.11	16.22	23.24		1.92	0.58			11.24	145.9	4	61	30	4	41					Dec-14
	4.14	8.72	17.97	26.68		1.65	0.58			11.71	112.0	5	68	23	4	48					Dec-14
50	4.18	8.59	17.73	25.68		1.23	0.83			11.7	112.0	5	68	23	4	48			4.25		Dec-14
50	3.91	8.17	16.82	23.01		0.93	1.58			11.63	112.0	5	68	23	4	48				1.00	Dec-14
	4.12	8.70	18.02	26.68		1.7	0.58			11.48	112.0	5	68	23	4	48					Dec-14
	4.14	8.64	17.75	25.78		1.43	0.83			11.46	112.0	5	68	23	4	48					Dec-14
	4.10	8.41	17.40	24.82		1.08	1.08			11.44	112.0	5	68	23	4	48					Dec-14
	4.22	8.71	18.04	26.74		1.74	0.58			11.46	112.0	5	68	23	4	48					Dec-14
	4.57	9.64	20.14	29.03		1.39	0.58			12.02	103.7	5	77	14	4	38					Dec-14
50	4.43	9.42	19.83	28.01		0.88	0.83			11.98	103.7	5	77	14	4	38			4.25		Dec-14
50	4.35	9.04	18.99	25.19		0.66	1.58			11.92	103.7	5	77	14	4	38				1.00	Dec-14
	4.53	9.44	20.06	28.96		1.43	0.58			11.85	103.7	5	77	14	4	38					Dec-14
	4.46	9.38	19.80	28.09		1.18	0.83			11.71	103.7	5	77	14	4	38					Dec-14
	4.46	9.30	19.51	27.11		0.95	1.08			11.68	103.7	5	77	14	4	38					Dec-14
	4.54	9.54	20.19	29.04		1.49	0.58			11.71	103.7	5	77	14	4	38					Dec-14
	4.86	10.11	21.31	30.29		1.27	0.58			12.13	69.9	6	83	8	3	46					Dec-14
50	4.74	9.91	21.02	29.26		0.67	0.83			12.09	69.9	6	83	8	3	46			4.25		Dec-14
50	4.50	9.45	20.08	26.49		0.59	1.58			12.01	69.9	6	83	8	3	46				1.00	Dec-14
	4.82	10.01	21.26	30.26		1.31	0.58			11.88	69.9	6	83	8	3	46					Dec-14
	4.68	9.87	21.01	29.37		1.04	0.83			11.81	69.9	6	83	8	3	46					Dec-14
	4.69	9.81	20.76	28.46		0.87	1.08			11.79	69.9	6	83	8	3	46					Dec-14
	4.78	10.06	21.31	30.37		1.36	0.58			11.81	69.9	6	83	8	3	46					Dec-14
	4.88	10.15	21.74	30.62		1.05	0.58			12.35	58.9	5	86	6	3	39					Dec-14
50	4.83	10.13	21.48	29.79		0.52	0.83			12.28	58.9	5	86	6	3	39			4.25		Dec-14
50	4.60	9.73	20.63	26.89		0.29	1.58			12.27	58.9	5	86	6	3	39				1.00	Dec-14
	4.90	10.22	21.74	30.59		1.26	0.58			12.06	58.9	5	86	6	3	39					Dec-14
	4.83	10.07	21.48	29.73		1.02	0.83			11.96	58.9	5	86	6	3	39					Dec-14
	4.75	9.92	21.13	28.64		0.8	1.08			11.91	58.9	5	86	6	3	39					Dec-14
	4.92	10.26	21.78	30.58		1.31	0.58			11.95	58.9	5	86	6	3	39					Dec-14
	4.91	10.27	22.13	30.91		0.56	0.58			12.55	22.9	6	86	6	3	46					Dec-14
50	4.81	10.11	21.71	29.93		0	0.83			12.5	22.9	6	86	6	3	46			4.25		Dec-14
50	4.59	9.77	20.91	27.07		0	1.58			12.38	22.9	6	86	6	3	46				1.00	Dec-14
	4.84	10.24	22.05	30.97		1.25	0.58			12.16	22.9	6	86	6	3	46					Dec-14
	4.77	10.09	21.81	29.91		1.02	0.83			11.89	22.9	6	86	6	3	46					Dec-14
	4.75	9.99	21.51	29.06		0.92	1.08			11.87	22.9	6	86	6	3	46					Dec-14
	4.94	10.35	22.18	31.04		1.3	0.58			11.91	22.9	6	86	6	3	46					Dec-14
	4.96	10.27	22.11	30.23		0.29	0.58			12.56	27.6	5	86	6	3	40					Dec-14
50	4.87	10.15	21.78	29.23		0	0.83			12.41	27.6	5	86	6	3	40			4.25		Dec-14
50	4.69	9.77	20.86	26.41		0	1.58			12.31	27.6	5	86	6	3	40				1.00	Dec-14
	4.89	10.23	22.02	30.23		1.26	0.58			12.08	27.6	5	86	6	3	40					Dec-14
	4.76	10.11	21.69	29.22		1.03	0.83			11.93	27.6	5	86	6	3	40					Dec-14

	MARKET			FUND TYPE, CATEGORY & OBJECTIVE	RATINGS				MINIMUMS	
Fund Name	Ticker Symbol	Traded On	Fund Type	Category and (Prospectus Objective)	Overall Rating	Reward Rating	Risk Rating	Recent Up/ Downgrade	Open to New Investors	Min Initial Investment
AB Multi-Manager Select 2055 Fund Class R	TDPRX	NAS CM	Open End	Target Date 2046+ (Asset Alloc)	C+	C+	B-	Down	Y	0
AB Multi-Manager Select 2055 Fund Class Z	TDPZX	NAS CM	Open End	Target Date 2046+ (Asset Alloc)	B-	C+	B-	Up	Y	2,000,000
AB Multi-Manager Select Retmnt Allocation Fund Adv Cls	TDAYX	NAS CM	Open End	Target Date 2000-2020 (Asset Alloc)	C+	C	B	Up	Y	0
AB Multi-Manager Select Retirement Allocation Fund Class A	TDAAX	NAS CM	Open End	Target Date 2000-2020 (Asset Alloc)	C+	C	B	Up	Y	2,500
AB Multi-Manager Select Retirement Allocation Fund Class C	TDACX	NAS CM	Open End	Target Date 2000-2020 (Asset Alloc)	C+	C	B	Up	Y	2,500
AB Multi-Manager Select Retirement Allocation Fund Class I	TDAIX	NAS CM	Open End	Target Date 2000-2020 (Asset Alloc)	C+	C	B	Up	Y	2,000,000
AB Multi-Manager Select Retirement Allocation Fund Class K	TDAKX	NAS CM	Open End	Target Date 2000-2020 (Asset Alloc)	C+	C	B	Up	Y	0
AB Multi-Manager Select Retirement Allocation Fund Class R	TDARX	NAS CM	Open End	Target Date 2000-2020 (Asset Alloc)	C+	C	B	Up	Y	0
AB Multi-Manager Select Retirement Allocation Fund Class Z	TDAZX	NAS CM	Open End	Target Date 2000-2020 (Asset Alloc)	C+	C	B	Up	Y	2,000,000
AB Relative Value Fund Advisor Class	CBBYX	NAS CM	Open End	US Equity Large Cap Value (Growth & Income)	B	B	B		Y	0
AB Relative Value Fund Class A	CABDX	NAS CM	Open End	US Equity Large Cap Value (Growth & Income)	B	B	A-		Y	2,500
AB Relative Value Fund Class B	CBBDX	NAS CM	Open End	US Equity Large Cap Value (Growth & Income)	B-	B-	B	Down		2,500
AB Relative Value Fund Class C	CBBCX	NAS CM	Open End	US Equity Large Cap Value (Growth & Income)	B	B-	A-		Y	2,500
AB Relative Value Fund Class I	CBBIX	NAS CM	Open End	US Equity Large Cap Value (Growth & Income)	B	B	B+		Y	2,000,000
AB Relative Value Fund Class K	CBBKX	NAS CM	Open End	US Equity Large Cap Value (Growth & Income)	B	B	B		Y	0
AB Relative Value Fund Class R	CBBRX	NAS CM	Open End	US Equity Large Cap Value (Growth & Income)	B	B-	B		Y	0
AB Relative Value Fund Class Z	CBBZX	NAS CM	Open End	US Equity Large Cap Value (Growth & Income)	B	B	B+		Y	2,000,000
AB Select US Equity Portfolio Advisor Class	AUUYX	NAS CM	Open End	US Equity Large Cap Growth (Growth)	B	B	B		Y	0
AB Select US Equity Portfolio Class A	AUUAX	NAS CM	Open End	US Equity Large Cap Growth (Growth)	B	B	B		Y	2,500
AB Select US Equity Portfolio Class C	AUUCX	NAS CM	Open End	US Equity Large Cap Growth (Growth)	B-	B-	B	Down	Y	2,500
AB Select US Equity Portfolio Class I	AUUIX	NAS CM	Open End	US Equity Large Cap Growth (Growth)	B	B	B		Y	2,000,000
AB Select US Equity Portfolio Class K	AUUKX	NAS CM	Open End	US Equity Large Cap Growth (Growth)	B	B	B		Y	0
AB Select US Equity Portfolio Class R	AUURX	NAS CM	Open End	US Equity Large Cap Growth (Growth)	B	B	B		Y	0
AB Select US Long/Short Portfolio Advisor Class	ASYLX	NAS CM	Open End	Long/Short Equity (Growth)	B-	C+	B	Down	Y	0
AB Select US Long/Short Portfolio Class A	ASLAX	NAS CM	Open End	Long/Short Equity (Growth)	B-	C+	B	Down	Y	2,500
AB Select US Long/Short Portfolio Class C	ASCLX	NAS CM	Open End	Long/Short Equity (Growth)	B-	C+	B	Up	Y	2,500
AB Select US Long/Short Portfolio Class I	ASILX	NAS CM	Open End	Long/Short Equity (Growth)	B-	C+	B	Down	Y	2,000,000
AB Select US Long/Short Portfolio Class K	ASLKX	NAS CM	Open End	Long/Short Equity (Growth)	B-	C+	B	Down	Y	0
AB Select US Long/Short Portfolio Class R	ASRLX	NAS CM	Open End	Long/Short Equity (Growth)	B-	C+	B	Up	Y	0
AB Small Cap Core Portfolio Advisor Class	SCRYX	NAS CM	Open End	US Equity Small Cap (Small Company)	C-	C-	B+	Up	Y	5,000
AB Small Cap Core Portfolio Class Z	SCRZX	NAS CM	Open End	US Equity Small Cap (Small Company)	C-	C-	B+	Up	Y	2,000,000
AB Small Cap Growth Portfolio Advisor Class	QUAYX	NAS CM	Open End	US Equity Small Cap (Small Company)	B	A	C	Up		0
AB Small Cap Growth Portfolio Class A	QUASX	NAS CM	Open End	US Equity Small Cap (Small Company)	B+	A	B	Up		2,500
AB Small Cap Growth Portfolio Class B	QUABX	NAS CM	Open End	US Equity Small Cap (Small Company)	B	A-	C	Up		2,500
AB Small Cap Growth Portfolio Class C	QUACX	NAS CM	Open End	US Equity Small Cap (Small Company)	B+	A-	B-	Up		2,500
AB Small Cap Growth Portfolio Class I	QUAIX	NAS CM	Open End	US Equity Small Cap (Small Company)	B	A	C	Up		2,000,000
AB Small Cap Growth Portfolio Class K	QUAKX	NAS CM	Open End	US Equity Small Cap (Small Company)	B	A	C	Up		0
AB Small Cap Growth Portfolio Class R	QUARX	NAS CM	Open End	US Equity Small Cap (Small Company)	B	A	C	Up		0
AB Small Cap Growth Portfolio Class Z	QUAZX	NAS CM	Open End	US Equity Small Cap (Small Company)	B	A	C	Up	Y	2,000,000
AB Small Cap Value Portfolio Advisor Class	SCYVX	NAS CM	Open End	US Equity Small Cap (Small Company)	C+	C+	B-	Up	Y	0
AB Small Cap Value Portfolio Class A	SCAVX	NAS CM	Open End	US Equity Small Cap (Small Company)	C+	C+	B-	Up	Y	2,500
AB Small Cap Value Portfolio Class C	SCCVX	NAS CM	Open End	US Equity Small Cap (Small Company)	C+	C+	B-	Up	Y	2,500
AB Sustainable Global Thematic Fund Advisor Class	ATEYX	NAS CM	Open End	Global Equity (Growth)	B+	B+	B	Up	Y	0
AB Sustainable Global Thematic Fund Class A	ALTFX	NAS CM	Open End	Global Equity (Growth)	B+	B+	B	Up	Y	2,500
AB Sustainable Global Thematic Fund Class B	ATEBX	NAS CM	Open End	Global Equity (Growth)	B	B+	B	Up		2,500
AB Sustainable Global Thematic Fund Class C	ATECX	NAS CM	Open End	Global Equity (Growth)	B	B+	B	Up	Y	2,500
AB Sustainable Global Thematic Fund Class I	AGTIX	NAS CM	Open End	Global Equity (Growth)	B+	B+	B	Up	Y	2,000,000
AB Sustainable Global Thematic Fund Class K	ATEKX	NAS CM	Open End	Global Equity (Growth)	B+	B+	B	Up	Y	0
AB Sustainable Global Thematic Fund Class R	ATERX	NAS CM	Open End	Global Equity (Growth)	B+	B+	B	Up	Y	0
AB Tax-Managed All Market Income Portfolio Advisor Class	AGIYX	NAS CM	Open End	Cautious Alloc (Balanced)	B	C+	A-	Up	Y	0
AB Tax-Managed All Market Income Portfolio Class A	AGIAX	NAS CM	Open End	Cautious Alloc (Balanced)	B	C+	A-	Up	Y	2,500
AB Tax-Managed All Market Income Portfolio Class B	AGIBX	NAS CM	Open End	Cautious Alloc (Balanced)	B-	C	B+	Up		2,500

★Expanded analysis of this fund is included in Section II.

Min Additional Investment	TOTAL RETURNS: 3-Month Total Return	6-Month Total Return	1-Year Total Return	3-Year Total Return	5-Year Total Return	PERFORMANCE: Dividend Yield (TTM)	Expense Ratio	3-Yr Std Deviation	3-Year Beta	ASSETS: NAV	Total Assets (MIL)	ASSET ALLOCATION & TURNOVER: %Cash	%Stocks	%Bonds	%Other	Turnover Ratio	BULL & BEAR: Last Bull Market Total Return	Last Bear Market Total Return	FEES: Front End Fee (%)	Back End Fee (%)	Inception Date
	4.83	10.02	21.49	28.39		0.92	1.08			11.91	27.6	5	86	6	3	40					Dec-14
	4.92	10.36	22.05	30.31		1.3	0.58			11.95	27.6	5	86	6	3	40					Dec-14
	2.03	4.37	9.16	12.68		0	0.58			11.3	11.1	5	31	62	2	60					Dec-14
50	1.96	4.22	8.83	11.91		0	0.83			11.2	11.1	5	31	62	2	60			4.25		Dec-14
50	1.82	3.82	7.98	9.33		0	1.58			10.95	11.1	5	31	62	2	60				1.00	Dec-14
	2.14	4.29	9.00	12.65		2.07	0.58			10.76	11.1	5	31	62	2	60					Dec-14
	1.99	4.25	8.86	11.79		1.8	0.83			10.53	11.1	5	31	62	2	60					Dec-14
	1.95	4.11	8.61	10.93		1.46	1.08			10.49	11.1	5	31	62	2	60					Dec-14
	2.03	4.28	9.10	12.69		2.12	0.58			10.53	11.1	5	31	62	2	60					Dec-14
	6.29	12.59	19.05	33.45	100.82	1.71	0.65	9.76	0.9	5.88	1,811	15	85	0	0	72	26.83	-15.76			Oct-96
50	6.25	12.24	18.72	32.31	98.09	1.49	0.9	9.74	0.9	5.83	1,811	15	85	0	0	72	26.93	-16.07	4.25		Jul-32
50	5.92	11.88	17.71	29.34	91.09	0.69	1.65	9.75	0.9	5.86	1,811	15	85	0	0	72	25.94	-16.2		4.00	Feb-91
50	5.95	11.94	17.80	29.59	91.18	0.86	1.65	9.72	0.9	5.83	1,811	15	85	0	0	72	26.37	-16.39		1.00	May-93
	6.22	12.47	19.07	33.32	101.31	1.74	0.65	9.7	0.9	5.93	1,811	15	85	0	0	72	26.94	-15.84			Mar-05
	6.28	12.32	18.65	32.34	98.79	1.55	0.9	9.71	0.9	5.77	1,811	15	85	0	0	72	26.54	-15.89			Mar-05
	6.04	12.12	18.28	31.35	95.67	1.34	1.15	9.7	0.9	5.74	1,811	15	85	0	0	72	26.27	-15.97			Nov-03
	6.30	12.55	19.14	33.59	100.83	1.62	0.59	9.7	0.89	5.94	1,811	15	85	0	0	72	26.93	-16.07			Oct-13
	7.94	12.77	22.47	34.69	105.00	0.47	1.21	9.74	0.92	16.76	297.5	2	98	0	0	292					Dec-11
50	7.85	12.68	22.21	33.78	102.39	0	1.46	9.69	0.92	16.8	297.5	2	98	0	0	292			4.25		Dec-11
50	7.68	12.22	21.32	30.74	95.13	0	2.22	9.71	0.92	16	297.5	2	98	0	0	292				1.00	Dec-11
	7.95	12.83	22.56	34.81	104.99	0.47	1.2	9.69	0.92	16.6	297.5	2	98	0	0	292					Dec-11
	7.80	12.56	22.05	33.33	101.62	0.17	1.56	9.72	0.92	16.57	297.5	2	98	0	0	292					Dec-11
	7.74	12.45	21.76	32.57	99.71	0.09	1.75	9.71	0.92	16.43	297.5	2	98	0	0	292					Dec-11
	5.23	8.10	12.54	16.57	47.90	0	1.63	5.97	0.56	12.79	966.1	31	69	0	0	295					Dec-12
50	5.13	7.96	12.26	15.72	45.99	0	1.88	5.99	0.56	12.61	966.1	31	69	0	0	295			4.25		Dec-12
50	5.00	7.56	11.41	13.16	40.69	0	2.63	5.99	0.56	12.11	966.1	31	69	0	0	295				1.00	Dec-12
	5.30	8.17	12.61	16.83	48.23	0	1.59	6	0.56	12.82	966.1	31	69	0	0	295					Dec-12
	5.21	8.04	12.25	15.80	46.11	0	1.9	6.03	0.57	12.62	966.1	31	69	0	0	295					Dec-12
	5.12	7.89	12.04	14.93	44.30	0	2.15	5.97	0.56	12.45	966.1	31	69	0	0	295					Dec-12
	2.91	7.84	7.47			0.23	1.05			11.85	900.5	0	100	0	0	165					Dec-15
	2.94	7.79	7.42			0.26	1.05			11.84	900.5	0	100	0	0	165					Dec-15
	7.56	15.88	34.93	42.05	108.40	0	0.94	15.91	1.04	56.03	1,432	3	97	0	0	66	36.78	-24.26			Oct-96
50	7.49	15.71	34.60	41.01	105.74	0	1.19	15.91	1.04	51.56	1,432	3	97	0	0	66	36.59	-24.35	4.25		Feb-69
50	7.32	15.26	33.56	37.72	97.64	0	1.98	15.89	1.03	33.59	1,432	3	97	0	0	66	35.89	-24.58		4.00	Sep-90
50	7.31	15.29	33.61	37.86	98.20	0	1.95	15.9	1.03	34.06	1,432	3	97	0	0	66	35.96	-24.58		1.00	May-93
	7.56	15.86	34.90	42.25	109.16	0	0.93	15.92	1.04	55.79	1,432	3	97	0	0	66	36.91	-24.24			Mar-05
	7.50	15.72	34.54	41.01	106.02	0	1.22	15.92	1.04	52.8	1,432	3	97	0	0	66	36.62	-24.33			Mar-05
	7.39	15.49	34.09	39.62	102.70	0	1.53	15.91	1.04	50.1	1,432	3	97	0	0	66	36.37	-24.43			Mar-05
	7.60	15.90	35.03	42.34	107.68	0	0.83	15.9	1.03	55.94	1,432	3	97	0	0	66	36.59	-24.35			Jun-15
	3.91	9.13	8.97	37.39		0	1			13.35	271.1	3	97	0	0	51					Dec-14
50	3.87	8.96	8.70	36.33		0	1.25			13.24	271.1	3	97	0	0	51			4.25		Dec-14
50	3.63	8.56	7.88	33.33		0	2			12.94	271.1	3	97	0	0	51				1.00	Dec-14
	7.14	13.16	37.49	44.64	91.45	3.06	1.16	12.88	1.1	124.16	891.9	6	94	0	0	65	16.83	-29.75			Oct-96
50	7.07	13.02	37.15	43.55	88.89	2.97	1.41	12.88	1.1	117.38	891.9	6	94	0	0	65	16.62	-29.84	4.25		Mar-82
50	6.86	12.57	36.06	40.10	81.53	2.85	2.21	12.87	1.1	96.66	891.9	6	94	0	0	65	16.07	-30.07		4.00	May-93
50	6.87	12.58	36.09	40.28	81.93	3.04	2.19	12.87	1.1	97.25	891.9	6	94	0	0	65	16.13	-30.06		1.00	May-93
	7.19	13.26	37.74	45.61	93.70	3.19	0.94	12.88	1.1	124.52	891.9	6	94	0	0	65	17.1	-29.67			Mar-05
	7.08	13.03	37.20	44.00	90.31	3.05	1.33	12.87	1.1	119.92	891.9	6	94	0	0	65	16.85	-29.8			Mar-05
	7.01	12.89	36.82	42.70	87.39	2.88	1.64	12.87	1.1	116	891.9	6	94	0	0	65	16.65	-29.88			Nov-03
	1.59	4.57	11.26	13.67	31.91	1.55	0.74	4.37	0.2	12.89	128.4	2	37	55	0	85	11.17	-8.9			Sep-03
50	1.50	4.41	10.93	12.79	30.15	1.29	0.99	4.35	0.2	12.87	128.4	2	37	55	0	85	11.01	-9.06	4.25		May-92
50	1.43	4.08	10.16	10.28	25.41	0	1.74	4.38	0.2	13.17	128.4	2	37	55	0	85	10.64	-9.4		4.00	May-92

	MARKET			FUND TYPE, CATEGORY & OBJECTIVE	RATINGS					MINIMUMS
Fund Name	Ticker Symbol	Traded On	Fund Type	Category and (Prospectus Objective)	Overall Rating	Reward Rating	Risk Rating	Recent Up/ Downgrade	Open to New Investors	Min Initial Investment
AB Tax-Managed All Market Income Portfolio Class C	AGICX	NAS CM	Open End	Cautious Alloc (Balanced)	B-	C	B+	Up	Y	2,500
AB Tax-Managed International Portfolio	SNIVX	NAS CM	Open End	Global Equity Large Cap (Foreign Stock)	B	B-	B	Up	Y	10,000
AB Tax-Managed International Portfolio Class A	ABXAX	NAS CM	Open End	Global Equity Large Cap (Foreign Stock)	B	B-	B	Up	Y	2,500
AB Tax-Managed International Portfolio Class B	ABXBX	NAS CM	Open End	Global Equity Large Cap (Foreign Stock)	B-	C+	B	Up		2,500
AB Tax-Managed International Portfolio Class C	ABXCX	NAS CM	Open End	Global Equity Large Cap (Foreign Stock)	B-	C+	B	Up	Y	2,500
AB Tax-Managed Wealth Appreciation Strategy Advisor Class	ATWYX	NAS CM	Open End	Global Equity (Growth)	B-	B-	B-	Down	Y	0
AB Tax-Managed Wealth Appreciation Strategy Class A	ATWAX	NAS CM	Open End	Global Equity (Growth)	B-	B-	B-	Down	Y	2,500
AB Tax-Managed Wealth Appreciation Strategy Class B	ATWBX	NAS CM	Open End	Global Equity (Growth)	B-	C+	B-	Up		2,500
AB Tax-Managed Wealth Appreciation Strategy Class C	ATWCX	NAS CM	Open End	Global Equity (Growth)	B-	C+	B-	Up	Y	2,500
AB Value Fund Advisor Class	ABVYX	NAS CM	Open End	US Equity Large Cap Value (Growth)	B-	C+	B	Up	Y	0
AB Value Fund Class A	ABVAX	NAS CM	Open End	US Equity Large Cap Value (Growth)	B-	C+	B	Up	Y	2,500
AB Value Fund Class B	ABVBX	NAS CM	Open End	US Equity Large Cap Value (Growth)	B-	C+	B	Up		2,500
AB Value Fund Class C	ABVCX	NAS CM	Open End	US Equity Large Cap Value (Growth)	C+	C+	B-	Down	Y	2,500
AB Value Fund Class I	ABVIX	NAS CM	Open End	US Equity Large Cap Value (Growth)	B-	C+	B	Up	Y	2,000,000
AB Value Fund Class K	ABVKX	NAS CM	Open End	US Equity Large Cap Value (Growth)	B-	C+	B	Up	Y	0
AB Value Fund Class R	ABVRX	NAS CM	Open End	US Equity Large Cap Value (Growth)	B-	C+	B-	Up	Y	0
AB Wealth Appreciation Strategy Advisor Class	AWAYX	NAS CM	Open End	Global Equity (Growth)	B-	B-	B-	Down	Y	0
AB Wealth Appreciation Strategy Class A	AWAAX	NAS CM	Open End	Global Equity (Growth)	B-	B-	B-	Up	Y	2,500
AB Wealth Appreciation Strategy Class B	AWABX	NAS CM	Open End	Global Equity (Growth)	C+	C+	C+	Down		2,500
AB Wealth Appreciation Strategy Class C	AWACX	NAS CM	Open End	Global Equity (Growth)	C+	C+	C+	Down	Y	2,500
AB Wealth Appreciation Strategy Class I	AWAIX	NAS CM	Open End	Global Equity (Growth)	B-	B-	B-	Down	Y	2,000,000
AB Wealth Appreciation Strategy Class K	AWAKX	NAS CM	Open End	Global Equity (Growth)	B-	B-	B-	Up	Y	0
AB Wealth Appreciation Strategy Class R	AWARX	NAS CM	Open End	Global Equity (Growth)	B-	C+	B-	Up	Y	0
Abbey Capital Futures Strategy Fund Class A	ABYAX	NAS CM	Open End	Other Alternative (Growth)	C-	D+	C	Up	Y	2,500
Abbey Capital Futures Strategy Fund Class C	ABYCX	NAS CM	Open End	Other Alternative (Growth)	D+	D+	C-	Up	Y	2,500
Abbey Capital Futures Strategy Fund Class I	ABYIX	NAS CM	Open End	Other Alternative (Growth)	C-	D+	C	Up	Y	1,000,000
Aberdeen Asia Pacific (ex-Japan) Equity Fund Class A	APJAX	NAS CM	Open End	Asia ex-Japan Equity (Pacific Stock)	B-	B-	C	Up	Y	1,000
Aberdeen Asia Pacific (ex-Japan) Equity Fund Class C	APJCX	NAS CM	Open End	Asia ex-Japan Equity (Pacific Stock)	C+	B-	C	Up	Y	1,000
Aberdeen Asia Pacific (ex-Japan) Equity Fund Class R	APJRX	NAS CM	Open End	Asia ex-Japan Equity (Pacific Stock)	C+	B-	C	Up	Y	0
Aberdeen Asia Pacific (ex-Japan) Equity Fund Inst Cls	AAPIX	NAS CM	Open End	Asia ex-Japan Equity (Pacific Stock)	B-	B-	C	Up	Y	1,000,000
Aberdeen Asia Pacific (ex-Japan) Eq Fund Inst Serv Cls	AAPEX	NAS CM	Open End	Asia ex-Japan Equity (Pacific Stock)	B-	B-	C	Up	Y	1,000,000
Aberdeen Australia Equity Fund Inc	IAF	AMEX	Closed End	Other Equity (Pacific Stock)	C+	C+	C+	Up	Y	
Aberdeen Chile Fund Inc	CH	AMEX	Closed End	Other Equity (Foreign Stock)	B	A-	C	Up	Y	
Aberdeen China Opportunities Fund Class A	GOPAX	NAS CM	Open End	Greater China Equity (Growth)	B-	B-	C+	Up	Y	1,000
Aberdeen China Opportunities Fund Class C	GOPCX	NAS CM	Open End	Greater China Equity (Growth)	C+	B-	C+	Up	Y	1,000
Aberdeen China Opportunities Fund Class R	GOPRX	NAS CM	Open End	Greater China Equity (Growth)	C+	B-	C+	Up	Y	0
Aberdeen China Opportunities Fund Institutional Class	GOPIX	NAS CM	Open End	Greater China Equity (Growth)	B-	B-	C+	Up	Y	1,000,000
Aberdeen China Opp Fund Inst Service Cls	GOPSX	NAS CM	Open End	Greater China Equity (Growth)	B-	B-	C+	Up	Y	1,000,000
Aberdeen Diversified Alternatives Fund Class A	GASAX	NAS CM	Open End	Multialternative (Growth)	C+	C	B	Up	Y	1,000
Aberdeen Diversified Alternatives Fund Class C	GAMCX	NAS CM	Open End	Multialternative (Growth)	C	C	B-	Up	Y	1,000
Aberdeen Diversified Alternatives Fund Class I	GASIX	NAS CM	Open End	Multialternative (Growth)	C+	C	B	Up	Y	1,000,000
Aberdeen Diversified Alternatives Fund Class R	GASRX	NAS CM	Open End	Multialternative (Growth)	C	C	B-		Y	0
Aberdeen Diversified Income Fund Class A	GMAAX	NAS CM	Open End	Cautious Alloc (Growth & Income)	B-	C+	B	Down	Y	1,000
Aberdeen Diversified Income Fund Class C	GMACX	NAS CM	Open End	Cautious Alloc (Growth & Income)	C+	C+	B	Down	Y	1,000
Aberdeen Diversified Income Fund Class I	GMAIX	NAS CM	Open End	Cautious Alloc (Growth & Income)	B-	C+	B	Down	Y	1,000,000
Aberdeen Diversified Income Fund Cls Institutional Service	GAMSX	NAS CM	Open End	Cautious Alloc (Growth & Income)	B-	C+	B	Down	Y	1,000,000
Aberdeen Diversified Income Fund Class R	GMRRX	NAS CM	Open End	Cautious Alloc (Growth & Income)	C+	C+	B	Down	Y	0
Aberdeen Dynamic Allocation Fund Class A	GMMAX	NAS CM	Open End	Alloc (Growth & Income)	B-	C+	B+	Up	Y	1,000
Aberdeen Dynamic Allocation Fund Class C	GMMCX	NAS CM	Open End	Alloc (Growth & Income)	B-	C	B	Up	Y	1,000
Aberdeen Dynamic Allocation Fund Cls Institutional Service	GAASX	NAS CM	Open End	Alloc (Growth & Income)	C+	C+	B-	Up	Y	1,000,000
Aberdeen Dynamic Allocation Fund Class R	GAGRX	NAS CM	Open End	Alloc (Growth & Income)	B-	C+	B	Up	Y	0
Aberdeen Dynamic Allocation Fund Institutional Class	GMMIX	NAS CM	Open End	Alloc (Growth & Income)	C+	C+	B	Up	Y	1,000,000

★ Expanded analysis of this fund is included in Section II.

	TOTAL RETURNS					PERFORMANCE				ASSETS		ASSET ALLOCATION & TURNOVER					BULL & BEAR		FEES		
Min Additional Investment	3-Month Total Return	6-Month Total Return	1-Year Total Return	3-Year Total Return	5-Year Total Return	Dividend Yield (TTM)	Expense Ratio	3-Yr Std Deviation	3-Year Beta	NAV	Total Assets (MIL)	%Cash	%Stocks	%Bonds	%Other	Turnover Ratio	Last Bull Market Total Return	Last Bear Market Total Return	Front End Fee (%)	Back End Fee (%)	Inception Date
50	1.35	4.03	10.17	10.27	25.48	0.53	1.74	4.33	0.19	13.08	128.4	2	37	55	0	85	10.58	-9.36		1.00	Aug-93
	2.97	9.16	26.27	27.71	45.87	1.46	1.16	10.92	0.86	18.44	3,322	2	98	0	0	78	11.93	-25.47			Jun-92
50	3.00	9.16	26.31	27.79	45.28	1.51	1.2	10.95	0.86	18.18	3,322	2	98	0	0	78	11.07	-25.82	4.25		Jan-04
50	2.75	8.72	25.34	24.95	39.92	0.85	1.95	10.95	0.86	18.48	3,322	2	98	0	0	78	10.54	-26.05		4.00	Jan-04
50	2.79	8.75	25.28	24.86	39.95	0.78	1.95	10.95	0.86	18.38	3,322	2	98	0	0	78	10.61	-26.08		1.00	Jan-04
	5.81	11.22	23.05	27.72	73.90	1.8	0.76	9.54	0.88	16.18	726.5	1	99	0	0	112	20.88	-21.58			Sep-03
50	5.72	11.08	22.78	26.70	71.65	1.59	1.01	9.54	0.88	16.13	726.5	1	99	0	0	112	20.63	-21.66	4.25		Sep-03
50	5.52	10.65	21.84	23.87	65.27	0.79	1.77	9.53	0.88	16.06	726.5	1	99	0	0	112	20.12	-21.87		4.00	Sep-03
50	5.55	10.66	21.86	23.94	65.48	0.99	1.77	9.51	0.88	15.93	726.5	1	99	0	0	112	20.23	-21.92		1.00	Sep-03
	6.31	10.32	13.70	15.98	81.47	1.22	0.74	11.81	1.1	16.15	420.3	0	100	0	0	74	23.28	-21.22			Mar-01
50	6.15	10.10	13.39	14.99	78.86	0.99	0.99	11.8	1.1	16.14	420.3	0	100	0	0	74	23.02	-21.34	4.25		Mar-01
50	6.19	10.12	13.32	14.84	78.61	0.9	1.75	11.83	1.1	16.23	420.3	0	100	0	0	74	22.94	-21.37		4.00	Mar-01
50	6.02	9.69	12.51	12.49	72.53	0.36	1.74	11.78	1.09	16.18	420.3	0	100	0	0	74	22.54	-21.55		1.00	Mar-01
	6.27	10.25	13.73	16.05	81.88	1.27	0.69	11.74	1.09	16	420.3	0	100	0	0	74	23.31	-21.17			Mar-05
	6.12	10.06	13.25	14.60	78.12	0.95	1.11	11.79	1.09	15.86	420.3	0	100	0	0	74	23.12	-21.34			Mar-05
	6.10	9.93	12.93	13.63	75.44	0.59	1.43	11.82	1.1	16.04	420.3	0	100	0	0	74	22.88	-21.48			Nov-03
	5.78	11.07	21.95	26.01	66.60	2.9	0.78	9.42	0.87	16.29	1,383	1	99	0	0	111	20.85	-22.61			Sep-03
50	5.70	10.91	21.67	25.05	64.44	2.68	1.03	9.37	0.86	16.34	1,383	1	99	0	0	111	20.7	-22.72	4.25		Sep-03
50	5.52	10.48	20.71	22.26	58.34	1.64	1.82	9.36	0.86	16.56	1,383	1	99	0	0	111	20.21	-22.96		4.00	Sep-03
50	5.46	10.42	20.69	22.28	58.49	2.02	1.8	9.41	0.87	16.35	1,383	1	99	0	0	111	20.22	-22.94		1.00	Sep-03
	5.75	10.97	21.86	25.86	66.22	2.87	0.84	9.38	0.86	16.29	1,383	1	99	0	0	111	20.99	-22.68			Mar-05
	5.66	10.77	21.41	24.55	63.46	2.59	1.17	9.36	0.86	16.24	1,383	1	99	0	0	111	20.66	-22.72			Mar-05
	5.61	10.66	21.06	23.38	60.89	2.33	1.48	9.39	0.86	16.25	1,383	1	99	0	0	111	20.38	-22.84			Feb-04
100	5.09	5.57	-0.25	-0.11		0	2.04	8.49	-0.11	11.55	856.5	-143	83	139	21	0			5.75		Aug-14
100	4.98	5.17	-1.04	-2.25		0	2.79	8.51	-0.1	11.38	856.5	-143	83	139	21	0					Oct-15
1,000	5.16	5.64	-0.08	0.58		0	1.79	8.47	-0.1	11.61	856.5	-143	83	139	21	0					Jul-14
50	7.92	11.23	37.73	28.03	28.16	0	1.6	14.78	0.97	13.64	11.6	3	96	0	0	40	19.29	-19.27	5.75		Feb-12
50	7.77	10.86	36.64	25.47	23.68	0	2.31	14.85	0.98	13.41	11.6	3	96	0	0	40	18.81	-19.53		1.00	Feb-12
	7.94	11.18	37.44	27.28	26.56	0	1.81	14.8	0.98	13.58	11.6	3	96	0	0	40	19.16	-19.36			Feb-12
	8.02	11.39	38.03	28.90	29.68	0	1.31	14.83	0.98	13.72	11.6	3	96	0	0	40	19.4	-19.11			Nov-09
	8.02	11.40	37.81	28.89	29.45	0	1.35	14.78	0.97	13.7	11.6	3	96	0	0	40	19.41	-19.19			Nov-09
	6.18	7.67	18.91	20.11	10.77	1.73	1.32	13.88	0.87	6.52	146.7	0	98	2	0	15	20.95	-25.91			Dec-85
	8.06	25.29	39.73	42.09	-2.00	0	1.77	16.84	0.91	9.83	81.9	0	99	0	0	7	27.54	-27.7			Sep-89
50	9.00	11.77	35.84	27.44	19.82	0.85	1.98	14.16	0.69	23.25	13.6	1	99	0	0	16	19.76	-20.04	5.75		Jun-04
50	7.85	10.49	33.82	23.83	14.63	0	2.62	14.16	0.69	22.5	13.6	1	99	0	0	16	19.28	-20.29		1.00	Jun-04
	8.57	11.28	35.05	25.79	17.31	0.65	2.32	14.17	0.69	22.86	13.6	1	99	0	0	16	19.53	-20.17			Jun-04
	9.33	12.25	36.71	29.00	21.77	1.06	1.62	14.18	0.69	23.38	13.6	1	99	0	0	16	19.93	-19.97			Jun-04
	9.28	12.20	36.54	28.62	21.49	0.99	1.72	14.16	0.69	23.34	13.6	1	99	0	0	16	19.94	-19.94			Jun-04
50	1.77	3.27	4.61	1.11	17.71	0.76	2.47	3.13	15.4	13.03	41.2	39	26	27	2	36	15.7	-17.92	5.75		Jun-04
50	1.61	2.87	4.02	-0.70	13.84	0.12	2.97	3.14	15.59	12.51	41.2	39	26	27	2	36	15.2	-18.19		1.00	Jun-04
	1.94	3.49	5.05	2.32	19.60	1.05	1.97	3.15	13.94	13.17	41.2	39	26	27	2	36	15.84	-17.84			Jun-04
	1.70	3.10	4.30	0.31	15.93	0.49	2.67	3.12	14.79	12.91	41.2	39	26	27	2	36	15.35	-17.99			Jun-04
50	2.14	4.65	10.62	14.18	28.97	2.99	1.14	5.15	0.43	12.62	18.2	4	38	45	1	21	12.2	-12.06	5.75		Jun-04
50	1.98	4.26	9.91	11.85	24.45	2.29	1.81	5.17	0.42	12.35	18.2	4	38	45	1	21	11.83	-12.44		1.00	Jun-04
	2.22	4.81	11.02	15.33	30.93	3.24	0.81	5.17	0.42	12.62	18.2	4	38	45	1	21	12.48	-12.1			Jun-04
	2.24	4.85	11.00	15.30	30.91	3.29	0.81	5.19	0.42	12.6	18.2	4	38	45	1	21	12.48	-12.1			Jun-04
	2.21	4.62	10.50	13.24	26.72	2.76	1.48	5.22	0.42	12.53	18.2	4	38	45	1	21	11.93	-12.31			Jun-04
50	2.39	5.48	10.83	11.86	31.86	2.15	1.17	5.9	0.51	13.88	15.0	7	56	34	0	40	14.61	-14.96	5.75		Jun-04
50	2.26	5.12	10.12	9.61	27.31	1.49	1.84	5.94	0.51	13.61	15.0	7	56	34	0	40	14.14	-15.18		1.00	Jun-04
	2.49	5.61	11.16	12.85	33.78	2.48	0.84	5.92	0.51	13.81	15.0	7	56	34	0	40	14.61	-14.96			Jun-04
	2.31	5.22	10.40	10.56	29.21	1.82	1.53	5.91	0.51	13.8	15.0	7	56	34	0	40	14.48	-15.04			Jun-04
	2.48	5.60	11.12	12.92	33.88	2.35	0.84	5.9	0.51	13.85	15.0	7	56	34	0	40	14.85	-14.89			Jun-04

	MARKET			FUND TYPE, CATEGORY & OBJECTIVE	RATINGS				MINIMUMS	
Fund Name	Ticker Symbol	Traded On	Fund Type	Category and (Prospectus Objective)	Overall Rating	Reward Rating	Risk Rating	Recent Up/ Downgrade	Open to New Investors	Min Initial Investment
Aberdeen Emerging Markets Fund Class A	GEGAX	NAS CM	Open End	Emerging Markets Equity (Div Emerging Mkts)	C+	B-	C	Up		1,000
Aberdeen Emerging Markets Fund Class C	GEGCX	NAS CM	Open End	Emerging Markets Equity (Div Emerging Mkts)	C+	C+	C	Up		1,000
Aberdeen Emerging Markets Fund Class R	GEMRX	NAS CM	Open End	Emerging Markets Equity (Div Emerging Mkts)	C+	B-	C	Up		0
Aberdeen Emerging Markets Fund Institutional Class	ABEMX	NAS CM	Open End	Emerging Markets Equity (Div Emerging Mkts)	C+	B-	C	Up		1,000,000
Aberdeen Emerging Markets Fund Institutional Service Class	AEMSX	NAS CM	Open End	Emerging Markets Equity (Div Emerging Mkts)	C+	B-	C	Up		1,000,000
Aberdeen Emerging Mkts Smaller Company Opp Fund, Inc	ABE	AMEX	Closed End	Emerging Markets Equity (Comm)	C	C	C		Y	
Aberdeen Focused U.S. Equity Fund Class A	MLSAX	NAS CM	Open End	Long/Short Equity (Growth)	B-	C+	B	Up	Y	1,000
Aberdeen Focused U.S. Equity Fund Class C	MLSCX	NAS CM	Open End	Long/Short Equity (Growth)	B-	B-	B	Up	Y	1,000
Aberdeen Focused U.S. Equity Fund Class R	GLSRX	NAS CM	Open End	Long/Short Equity (Growth)	B-	C+	B	Up	Y	0
Aberdeen Focused U.S. Equity Fund Institutional Class	GGUIX	NAS CM	Open End	Long/Short Equity (Growth)	B-	C+	B	Up	Y	1,000,000
Aberdeen Focused U.S. Equity Fund Inst Service Cls	AELSX	NAS CM	Open End	Long/Short Equity (Growth)	B-	C+	B	Up	Y	1,000,000
Aberdeen Global Equity Fund Class A	GLLAX	NAS CM	Open End	Global Equity (World Stock)	C+	C+	C+	Up	Y	1,000
Aberdeen Global Equity Fund Class C	GLLCX	NAS CM	Open End	Global Equity (World Stock)	C+	C+	C+	Up	Y	1,000
Aberdeen Global Equity Fund Class R	GWLRX	NAS CM	Open End	Global Equity (World Stock)	C+	C+	C+	Up	Y	0
Aberdeen Global Equity Fund Institutional Class	GWLIX	NAS CM	Open End	Global Equity (World Stock)	C+	C+	C+	Up	Y	1,000,000
Aberdeen Global Equity Fund Institutional Service Class	GLLSX	NAS CM	Open End	Global Equity (World Stock)	C+	C+	C+	Up	Y	1,000,000
Aberdeen Greater China Fund	GCH	NYSE	Closed End	Greater China Equity (Pacific Stock)	B	B	C+	Up	Y	
Aberdeen Indonesia Fund Inc.	IF	AMEX	Closed End	Other Equity (Pacific Stock)	C-	C	C-	Down	Y	
Aberdeen International Equity Fund Class A	GIGAX	NAS CM	Open End	Global Equity Large Cap (Foreign Stock)	C+	C+	C	Up	Y	1,000
Aberdeen International Equity Fund Class C	GIGCX	NAS CM	Open End	Global Equity Large Cap (Foreign Stock)	C+	C+	C	Up	Y	1,000
Aberdeen International Equity Fund Class R	GIRRX	NAS CM	Open End	Global Equity Large Cap (Foreign Stock)	C+	C+	C	Up	Y	0
Aberdeen International Equity Fund Institutional Class	GIGIX	NAS CM	Open End	Global Equity Large Cap (Foreign Stock)	C+	C+	C+	Up	Y	1,000,000
Aberdeen Intl Equity Fund Inst Service Cls	GIGSX	NAS CM	Open End	Global Equity Large Cap (Foreign Stock)	C+	C+	C+	Up	Y	1,000,000
Aberdeen International Small Cap Fund Class A	WVCCX	NAS CM	Open End	Global Equity Mid/Small Cap (Small Company)	B	B	B	Up	Y	1,000
Aberdeen International Small Cap Fund Class C	CPVCX	NAS CM	Open End	Global Equity Mid/Small Cap (Small Company)	B	B	B	Up	Y	1,000
Aberdeen International Small Cap Fund Class R	WPVAX	NAS CM	Open End	Global Equity Mid/Small Cap (Small Company)	B	B	B	Up	Y	0
Aberdeen International Small Cap Fund Institutional Class	ABNIX	NAS CM	Open End	Global Equity Mid/Small Cap (Small Company)	B	B	B	Up	Y	1,000,000
Aberdeen Intl Small Cap Fund Inst Service Cls	AGISX	NAS CM	Open End	Global Equity Mid/Small Cap (Small Company)	B	B	B	Up	Y	1,000,000
Aberdeen Israel Fund Inc	ISL	AMEX	Closed End	Other Equity (Foreign Stock)	B-	C+	B-	Up	Y	
Aberdeen Japan Equity Fund, Inc.	JEQ	NYSE	Closed End	Japan Equity (Pacific Stock)	B+	A-	B	Up	Y	
Aberdeen Japanese Equities Fund Class A	AJEAX	NAS CM	Open End	Japan Equity (Foreign Stock)	C	C-	B+	Up	Y	1,000
Aberdeen Japanese Equities Fund Class C	AJECX	NAS CM	Open End	Japan Equity (Foreign Stock)	C	C-	B	Up	Y	1,000
Aberdeen Japanese Equities Fund Class R	AJERX	NAS CM	Open End	Japan Equity (Foreign Stock)	C	C-	B+	Up	Y	0
Aberdeen Japanese Equities Fund Institutional Class	AJEIX	NAS CM	Open End	Japan Equity (Foreign Stock)	C	C-	B+	Up	Y	1,000,000
Aberdeen Japanese Equities Fund Institutional Service Cls	AJESX	NAS CM	Open End	Japan Equity (Foreign Stock)	C	C-	B+	Up	Y	1,000,000
Aberdeen Latin America Equity Fund Inc	LAQ	AMEX	Closed End	Latin America Equity (Foreign Stock)	C	C	C		Y	
Aberdeen Select International Equity Fund Class A	BJBIX	NAS CM	Open End	Global Equity Large Cap (Foreign Stock)	C+	B-	C	Up	Y	1,000
Aberdeen Select International Equity Fund Class I	JIEIX	NAS CM	Open End	Global Equity Large Cap (Foreign Stock)	C+	B-	C	Up	Y	1,000,000
Aberdeen Select International Equity Fund II Class A	JETAX	NAS CM	Open End	Global Equity Large Cap (Foreign Stock)	C+	C+	C	Up	Y	1,000
Aberdeen Select International Equity Fund II Class I	JETIX	NAS CM	Open End	Global Equity Large Cap (Foreign Stock)	C+	C+	C+	Up	Y	1,000,000
Aberdeen Singapore Fund, Inc.	SGF	NYSE	Closed End	Other Equity (Pacific Stock)	C+	B-	C	Up	Y	
Aberdeen U.S. Mid Cap Equity Fund Class A	GUEAX	NAS CM	Open End	US Equity Mid Cap (Growth)	C-	C	B+	Up	Y	1,000
Aberdeen U.S. Mid Cap Equity Fund Class C	GUECX	NAS CM	Open End	US Equity Mid Cap (Growth)	C-	C	B+	Up	Y	1,000
Aberdeen U.S. Mid Cap Equity Fund Class R	GUERX	NAS CM	Open End	US Equity Mid Cap (Growth)	C-	C	B+	Up	Y	0
Aberdeen U.S. Mid Cap Equity Fund Institutional Class	GUEIX	NAS CM	Open End	US Equity Mid Cap (Growth)	C-	C	B+	Up	Y	1,000,000
Aberdeen U.S. Mid Cap Equity Fund Inst Service Cls	GUESX	NAS CM	Open End	US Equity Mid Cap (Growth)	C-	C	B+	Up	Y	1,000,000
Aberdeen U.S. Multi-Cap Equity Fund Class A	GXXAX	NAS CM	Open End	US Equity Large Cap Blend (Growth)	B-	B	B-	Down	Y	1,000
Aberdeen U.S. Multi-Cap Equity Fund Class C	GXXCX	NAS CM	Open End	US Equity Large Cap Blend (Growth)	B-	B-	C+	Down	Y	1,000
Aberdeen U.S. Multi-Cap Equity Fund Class R	GGLRX	NAS CM	Open End	US Equity Large Cap Blend (Growth)	B-	B-	B-	Down	Y	0
Aberdeen U.S. Multi-Cap Equity Fund Institutional Class	GGLIX	NAS CM	Open End	US Equity Large Cap Blend (Growth)	B-	B	B-	Down	Y	1,000,000
Aberdeen U.S. Multi-Cap Equity Fund Inst Service Cls	GXXIX	NAS CM	Open End	US Equity Large Cap Blend (Growth)	B-	B	B-	Down	Y	1,000,000
Aberdeen U.S. Small Cap Equity Fund Class A	GSXAX	NAS CM	Open End	US Equity Small Cap (Small Company)	A	A-	A	Up	Y	1,000

★Expanded analysis of this fund is included in Section II.

Min Additional Investment	3-Month Total Return	6-Month Total Return	1-Year Total Return	3-Year Total Return	5-Year Total Return	Dividend Yield (TTM)	Expense Ratio	3-Yr Std Deviation	3-Year Beta	NAV	Total Assets (MIL)	%Cash	%Stocks	%Bonds	%Other	Turnover Ratio	Last Bull Market Total Return	Last Bear Market Total Return	Front End Fee (%)	Back End Fee (%)	Inception Date
	TOTAL RETURNS					PERFORMANCE				ASSETS		ASSET ALLOCATION & TURNOVER					BULL & BEAR		FEES		
50	4.78	9.21	29.55	24.08	12.66	0.71	1.58	14.69	0.87	16.11	8,509	1	99	0	0	9	20.46	-18.14	5.75		May-12
50	4.66	8.91	28.93	21.81	9.20	0.18	2.1	14.73	0.87	15.99	8,509	1	99	0	0	9	19.94	-18.4		1.00	May-12
	4.75	9.14	29.34	23.07	10.98	0.61	1.74	14.73	0.87	15.99	8,509	1	99	0	0	9	20.29	-18.23			May-12
	4.92	9.41	30.24	25.58	14.74	0.99	1.1	14.73	0.87	16.14	8,509	1	99	0	0	9	20.64	-18.06			May-07
	4.88	9.38	29.94	24.83	13.57	0.87	1.25	14.72	0.87	16.14	8,509	1	99	0	0	9	20.48	-18.24			Nov-09
	2.70	6.04	24.15	12.05	-1.83	0.83		13.03	0.75	16.08	147.6	1	99	0	0	14	18.44	-13.04			Jun-92
50	5.99	7.65	12.81	13.91	27.60	0	1.27	6.06	0.53	6.64	25.5	0	100	0	0	36	8.51	-9.13	5.75		Oct-01
50	5.97	7.25	12.14	11.62	23.49	0	1.91	6.07	0.52	2.12	25.5	0	100	0	0	36	7.98	-9.42		1.00	Dec-97
	5.83	7.34	12.46	12.62	25.14	0	1.61	6.03	0.52	5.96	25.5	0	100	0	0	36	8.25	-9.11			Feb-04
	6.05	7.75	13.21	14.96	29.66	0	0.91	6.03	0.52	7.09	25.5	0	100	0	0	36	8.58	-9.02			Jun-04
	5.95	7.69	12.99	14.31	28.40	0	1.1	6.04	0.52	6.88	25.5	0	100	0	0	36	8.41	-9.03			Nov-09
50	4.66	8.25	24.01	16.03	31.09	0.6	1.57	10.85	0.92	13.87	42.8	1	99	0	0	22	19.07	-17.62	5.75		Aug-00
50	4.47	7.87	23.19	13.78	26.96	0.39	2.19	10.82	0.92	13.04	42.8	1	99	0	0	22	18.59	-17.84		1.00	Mar-01
	4.64	8.07	23.63	14.94	29.24	0.67	1.9	10.84	0.92	13.26	42.8	1	99	0	0	22	18.96	-17.62			Oct-03
	4.72	8.22	24.24	17.07	33.24	0.89	1.19	10.83	0.92	13.85	42.8	1	99	0	0	22	19.34	-17.48			Jun-04
	4.72	8.33	24.36	17.19	33.47	0.89	1.19	10.82	0.92	14.04	42.8	1	99	0	0	22	19.13	-17.62			Aug-00
	7.89	11.09	35.46	32.25	27.62	0.91	1.69	13.47	0.75	13.73	119.7	1	97	1	1	15	19.03	-27.82			Jul-92
	0.85	1.81	14.27	-4.69	-16.50	0.24		15.7	0.66	8.45	76.3	0	98	0	2	24	17.02	-8.1			Mar-90
50	5.46	8.39	26.91	14.63	20.52	1.1	1.42	12.5	0.96	15.33	532.5	4	96	0	0	28	17.09	-18.33	5.75		Aug-00
50	4.58	7.21	25.18	11.45	15.49	0.52	2.1	12.5	0.96	14.44	532.5	4	96	0	0	28	16.59	-18.58		1.00	Mar-01
	4.44	7.25	25.44	12.55	17.67	0.94	1.72	12.53	0.96	14.63	532.5	4	96	0	0	28	16.89	-18.38			Dec-03
	5.96	8.97	27.87	16.25	22.97	1.45	1.04	12.49	0.96	15.68	532.5	4	96	0	0	28	17.25	-18.22			Jun-04
	5.87	8.82	27.67	15.80	22.15	1.39	1.09	12.49	0.96	15.62	532.5	4	96	0	0	28	17.13	-18.18			Aug-00
50	5.65	15.11	31.75	34.63	50.86	0.44	1.64	10.76	0.83	31.49	79.5	1	96	0	2	36	19.46	-16.35	5.75		Sep-96
50	5.47	14.75	30.91	31.92	45.84	0	2.3	10.78	0.83	28.97	79.5	1	96	0	2	36	18.98	-16.6		1.00	Jul-01
	5.54	14.91	31.25	33.28	48.62	0.35	2.03	10.74	0.83	29.97	79.5	1	96	0	2	36	19.26	-16.46			Sep-96
	5.72	15.32	32.18	35.92	53.24	0.68	1.3	10.76	0.83	31.52	79.5	1	96	0	2	36	19.66	-16.22			Jul-09
	5.68	15.20	31.90	35.05	51.66	0.15	1.55	10.78	0.83	31.67	79.5	1	96	0	2	36	19.64	-16.24			Sep-09
	3.18	4.31	20.50	25.16	64.23	0		9.96	0.69	22.21	87.6	0	99	1	0	12	7.24	-22.78			Oct-92
	8.89	11.29	25.65	44.36	89.49	0.82		12.69	0.9	10.14	142.5	0	99	0	0	8	2.09	-7.35			Jul-92
50	7.63	10.21	23.10			0.22	1.25			12.25	1.6	2	98	0	0				5.75		Nov-15
50	7.54	9.86	22.22			0	2			12.13	1.6	2	98	0	0					1.00	Nov-15
	7.65	10.14	22.80			0	1.5			12.25	1.6	2	98	0	0						Nov-15
	7.81	10.48	23.50			0.31	1			12.29	1.6	2	98	0	0						Nov-15
	7.72	10.39	23.40			0.31	1			12.28	1.6	2	98	0	0						Nov-15
	-2.67	13.05	29.99	21.86	-11.19	1.06		24.14	0.95	29.16	210.7	0	97	0	1	11	23	-25.82			Jul-90
50	8.50	12.05	37.39	23.22	33.31	0.8	1.42	13.23	0.99	27.44	209.8	2	98	0	0	23	11.97	-28.37			Oct-93
	8.75	12.38	37.97	24.39	35.29	1	1.17	13.23	0.99	28.12	209.8	2	98	0	0	23	12.18	-28.31			Nov-99
50	4.29	7.40	29.42	16.05	25.37	1.31	1.5	12.8	0.97	11.91	93.0	2	98	0	0	23	12.98	-27.99			May-05
	4.39	7.60	29.80	17.09	27.10	1.54	1.27	12.78	0.97	11.9	93.0	2	98	0	0	23	13.22	-27.96			May-05
	6.94	10.16	33.52	12.82	11.88	0.16		14.78	0.85	13.63	102.8	1	98	1	1	11	19.85	-22.48			Jul-90
50	7.81	10.88	23.57			0.13	1.25			12.83	1.5	3	97	0	0				5.75		Feb-16
50	7.61	10.44	22.55			0	2			12.66	1.5	3	97	0	0					1.00	Feb-16
	7.71	10.70	23.18			0.05	1.5			12.78	1.5	3	97	0	0						Feb-16
	7.93	11.09	23.90			0.28	1			12.85	1.5	3	97	0	0						Feb-16
	7.94	11.09	23.90			0.28	1			12.85	1.5	3	97	0	0						Feb-16
50	7.08	10.16	20.57	27.16	78.51	0.1	1.19	10.48	0.98	12.41	373.2	2	98	0	0	63	23.59	-20.15	5.75		Jun-00
50	6.87	9.76	19.70	24.48	72.22	0	1.9	10.51	0.98	10.83	373.2	2	98	0	0	63	22.98	-20.27		1.00	Mar-01
	6.94	9.93	20.22	25.97	75.96	0	1.56	10.45	0.98	11.64	373.2	2	98	0	0	63	23.43	-20.16			Oct-03
	7.18	10.34	21.04	28.31	81.38	0.27	0.9	10.44	0.98	13.21	373.2	2	98	0	0	63	23.88	-20.07			Jun-04
	7.17	10.33	20.95	27.94	80.42	0.22	0.98	10.46	0.98	13.18	373.2	2	98	0	0	63	23.87	-20.15			Jun-00
50	3.44	9.46	11.02	46.89	128.77	0	1.3	11.69	0.76	36.65	2,025	3	97	0	0	32	32.36	-27.67	5.75		Nov-98

	MARKET			FUND TYPE, CATEGORY & OBJECTIVE	RATINGS					MINIMUMS
Fund Name	Ticker Symbol	Traded On	Fund Type	Category and (Prospectus Objective)	Overall Rating	Reward Rating	Risk Rating	Recent Up/ Downgrade	Open to New Investors	Min Initial Investment
Aberdeen U.S. Small Cap Equity Fund Class C	GSXCX	NAS CM	Open End	US Equity Small Cap (Small Company)	A-	A-	A	Up	Y	1,000
Aberdeen U.S. Small Cap Equity Fund Class R	GNSRX	NAS CM	Open End	US Equity Small Cap (Small Company)	A-	A-	A	Up	Y	0
Aberdeen U.S. Small Cap Equity Fund Institutional Class	GSCIX	NAS CM	Open End	US Equity Small Cap (Small Company)	A	A	A	Up	Y	1,000,000
Aberdeen U.S. Small Cap Equity Fund Inst Service Cls	GSXIX	NAS CM	Open End	US Equity Small Cap (Small Company)	A	A-	A	Up	Y	1,000,000
ABR Dynamic Blend Equity & Volatility Fund Inst Shares	ABRVX	NAS CM	Open End	Long/Short Equity (Growth)	C	C	B	Up	Y	100,000
ABR Dynamic Blend Equity & Volatility Fund Investor Shares	ABRTX	NAS CM	Open End	Long/Short Equity (Growth)	C	C	B	Up	Y	2,500
ABR Enhanced Short Volatility Fund Institutional Shares	ABRSX	NAS CM	Open End	Multialternative (Growth)	U	U	U			100,000
ABR Enhanced Short Volatility Fund Investor Shares	ABRJX	NAS CM	Open End	Multialternative (Growth)	U	U	U		Y	2,500
Absolute Capital Asset Allocator Fund Class A	AAMAX	NAS CM	Open End	Moderate Alloc (Growth & Income)	C-	C-	B+	Up	Y	2,500
Absolute Capital Asset Allocator Fund Institutional Class	AAMIX	NAS CM	Open End	Moderate Alloc (Growth & Income)	C-	C-	B+	Up	Y	100,000
Absolute Capital Asset Allocator Fund Investor Class	AAMCX	NAS CM	Open End	Moderate Alloc (Growth & Income)	C-	C-	B+	Up	Y	2,500
Absolute Capital Defender Fund Class A	ACMAX	NAS CM	Open End	Moderate Alloc (Growth & Income)	C-	C-	B+	Up	Y	2,500
Absolute Capital Defender Fund Institutional Class	ACMIX	NAS CM	Open End	Moderate Alloc (Growth & Income)	C-	C-	B+	Up	Y	100,000
Absolute Capital Defender Fund Investor Class	ACMDX	NAS CM	Open End	Moderate Alloc (Growth & Income)	C-	C-	B+	Up	Y	2,500
Absolute Capital Opportunities Fund Institutional Shares	CAPOX	NAS CM	Open End	Long/Short Equity (Growth)	C-	D+	A	Up	Y	25,000
Absolute Convertible Arbitrage Fund Institutional Shares	ARBIX	NAS CM	Open End	Multialternative (Convertible Bond)	U	U	U		Y	25,000
Absolute Strategies Fund Class R	ASFAX	NAS CM	Open End	Multialternative (Growth)	D	D-	D+	Down	Y	250,000
Absolute Strategies Fund Institutional Class	ASFIX	NAS CM	Open End	Multialternative (Growth)	D	D-	D+	Down	Y	25,000
AC Alternatives® Disciplined Long Short Fund A Class	ACDQX	NAS CM	Open End	US Equity Large Cap Growth (Growth)	B	C+	A-	Up	Y	2,500
AC Alternatives® Disciplined Long Short Fund C Class	ACDHX	NAS CM	Open End	US Equity Large Cap Growth (Growth)	B	C+	B+	Up	Y	2,500
AC Alternatives® Disciplined Long Short Fund I Class	ACDKX	NAS CM	Open End	US Equity Large Cap Growth (Growth)	B	C+	A-	Up	Y	5,000,000
AC Alternatives® Disciplined Long Short Fund Investor Cls	ACDJX	NAS CM	Open End	US Equity Large Cap Growth (Growth)	B	C+	A-	Up	Y	2,500
AC Alternatives® Disciplined Long Short Fund R Class	ACDWX	NAS CM	Open End	US Equity Large Cap Growth (Growth)	B	C+	A-	Up	Y	2,500
AC Alternatives® Equity Market Neutral Fund A Class	ALIAX	NAS CM	Open End	Market Neutral (Growth)	C	C-	C+	Up	Y	2,500
AC Alternatives® Equity Market Neutral Fund C Class	ALICX	NAS CM	Open End	Market Neutral (Growth)	C-	D+	C	Up	Y	2,500
AC Alternatives® Equity Market Neutral Fund I Class	ALISX	NAS CM	Open End	Market Neutral (Growth)	C+	C	B	Up	Y	5,000,000
AC Alternatives® Equity Market Neutral Fund Investor Class	ALHIX	NAS CM	Open End	Market Neutral (Growth)	C	C-	B-	Up	Y	2,500
AC Alternatives® Equity Market Neutral Fund R Class	ALIRX	NAS CM	Open End	Market Neutral (Growth)	C-	D+	C	Up	Y	2,500
AC Alternatives® Equity Market Neutral Fund R5 Class	ALIGX	NAS CM	Open End	Market Neutral (Growth)	C+	C	B	Up	Y	0
AC Alternatives® Equity Market Neutral Fund Y Class	ALYIX	NAS CM	Open End	Market Neutral (Growth)	C	C	B		Y	0
AC Alternatives® Income Fund A Class	ALNAX	NAS CM	Open End	Multialternative (Income)	C	C	B	Up	Y	2,500
AC Alternatives® Income Fund C Class	ALNHX	NAS CM	Open End	Multialternative (Income)	C	C	B	Up	Y	2,500
AC Alternatives® Income Fund I Class	ALNIX	NAS CM	Open End	Multialternative (Income)	C	C	B	Up	Y	5,000,000
AC Alternatives® Income Fund Investor Class	ALNNX	NAS CM	Open End	Multialternative (Income)	C	C	B	Up	Y	2,500
AC Alternatives® Income Fund R Class	ALNRX	NAS CM	Open End	Multialternative (Income)	C	C	B	Up	Y	2,500
AC Alternatives® Income Fund R6 Class	ALNDX	NAS CM	Open End	Multialternative (Income)	C	C	B	Up	Y	0
AC Alternatives® Income Fund Y Class	ALYNX	NAS CM	Open End	Multialternative (Income)	C	C	B	Up	Y	0
AC Alternatives® Long Short Fund A Class	ALEQX	NAS CM	Open End	Long/Short Equity (Growth)	C	C-	B+	Up	Y	2,500
AC Alternatives® Long Short Fund C Class	ALEHX	NAS CM	Open End	Long/Short Equity (Growth)	C	C-	B+	Up	Y	2,500
AC Alternatives® Long Short Fund I Class	ALEJX	NAS CM	Open End	Long/Short Equity (Growth)	C	C-	B+	Up	Y	5,000,000
AC Alternatives® Long Short Fund Investor Class	ALEVX	NAS CM	Open End	Long/Short Equity (Growth)	C	C-	B+	Up	Y	2,500
AC Alternatives® Long Short Fund R Class	ALEWX	NAS CM	Open End	Long/Short Equity (Growth)	C	C-	B+	Up	Y	2,500
AC Alternatives® Long Short Fund R6 Class	ALEDX	NAS CM	Open End	Long/Short Equity (Growth)	C	C-	B+	Up	Y	0
AC Alternatives® Long Short Fund Y Class	ALYEX	NAS CM	Open End	Long/Short Equity (Growth)	C	C-	B+	Up	Y	0
AC Alternatives® Market Neutral Value Fund A Class	ACVQX	NAS CM	Open End	Market Neutral (Growth)	C+	C	B	Up	Y	2,500
AC Alternatives® Market Neutral Value Fund C Class	ACVHX	NAS CM	Open End	Market Neutral (Growth)	C	C-	C	Up	Y	2,500
AC Alternatives® Market Neutral Value Fund I Class	ACVKX	NAS CM	Open End	Market Neutral (Growth)	B-	C	A-	Up		5,000,000
AC Alternatives® Market Neutral Value Fund Investor Class	ACVVX	NAS CM	Open End	Market Neutral (Growth)	C+	C	B	Up	Y	2,500
AC Alternatives® Market Neutral Value Fund R Class	ACVWX	NAS CM	Open End	Market Neutral (Growth)	C	C	B-	Up	Y	2,500
AC One China Fund Institutional Class	ACOIX	NAS CM	Open End	Greater China Equity (Growth)	B	A-	C+	Up	Y	25,000
Acadian Emerging Markets Portfolio Class I	AEMZX	NAS CM	Open End	Emerging Markets Equity (Growth)	B-	B	C	Up	Y	1,000,000
Acadian Emerging Markets Portfolio Class Y	AEMVX	NAS CM	Open End	Emerging Markets Equity (Growth)	B-	B	C	Up	Y	100,000

★Expanded analysis of this fund is included in Section II.

Min Additional Investment	TOTAL RETURNS 3-Month Total Return	6-Month Total Return	1-Year Total Return	3-Year Total Return	5-Year Total Return	PERFORMANCE Dividend Yield (TTM)	Expense Ratio	3-Yr Std Deviation	3-Year Beta	ASSETS NAV	Total Assets (ML)	ASSET ALLOCATION & TURNOVER %Cash	%Stocks	%Bonds	%Other	Turnover Ratio	BULL & BEAR Last Bull Market Total Return	Last Bear Market Total Return	FEES Front End Fee (%)	Back End Fee (%)	Inception Date
50	3.31	9.08	10.26	43.80	121.05	0	2.06	11.68	0.76	31.81	2,025	3	97	0	0	32	31.74	-27.81		1.00	Mar-01
	3.38	9.28	10.63	45.72	126.06	0	1.72	11.69	0.76	33.91	2,025	3	97	0	0	32	32.12	-27.65			Dec-03
	3.56	9.65	11.36	48.25	132.51	0	1.05	11.66	0.75	38.62	2,025	3	97	0	0	32	32.52	-27.53			Jun-04
	3.53	9.61	11.29	48.12	132.01	0	1.05	11.68	0.76	38.63	2,025	3	97	0	0	32	32.52	-27.53			Nov-98
	4.37	5.31	9.46			0	2			10.21	19.3	98	2	0	0	467					Aug-15
	4.40	5.34	9.29			0	2.25			10.16	19.3	98	2	0	0	467					Aug-15
	4.24						2.5			10.57	0.38	18	1	82	0						Oct-17
	3.93						2.75			10.57	0.38	18	1	82	0						Oct-17
100	3.45	7.02	11.38			0.37	2.16			11.07	18.0	21	65	10	0	144			5.75		Dec-15
	3.45	7.02	11.38			0.37	1.91			11.07	18.0	21	65	10	0	144					Dec-15
100	3.30	6.60	10.64			0.08	2.91			10.95	18.0	21	65	10	0	144					Dec-15
100	2.25	5.10	9.08			0.41	2.18			10.66	14.0	26	61	10	0	152			5.75		Dec-15
	2.25	5.10	9.08			0.41	1.93			10.66	14.0	26	61	10	0	152					Dec-15
100	2.08	4.75	8.32			0.12	2.93			10.54	14.0	26	61	10	0	152					Dec-15
	2.06	3.26	5.37			0	1.6			11.37	14.7	74	26	0	0	29					Dec-15
	0.89						1.6			10.19	19.9										Aug-17
100	-1.84	-5.00	-9.01	-8.83	-10.07	0	2.26	4.41	-0.34	7.97	312.2	68	14	1	0	72	0.27	1.74			Jul-05
	-1.66	-4.72	-8.41	-7.19	-7.52	0	1.96	4.45	-0.35	8.27	312.2	68	14	1	0	72	0.57	1.92			Jul-05
50	1.85	3.24	10.60	18.73	89.51	0	1.7	10.37	1.64	17.63	47.5	55	45	0	0	127			5.75		Oct-11
50	1.65	2.80	9.71	16.07	82.48	0	2.45	10.37	1.64	16.81	47.5	55	45	0	0	127				1.00	Oct-11
50	1.99	3.42	11.09	20.33	93.75	0.22	1.25	10.35	1.63	17.87	47.5	55	45	0	0	127					Oct-11
50	1.88	3.31	10.79	19.59	91.83	0.04	1.45	10.39	1.64	17.83	47.5	55	45	0	0	127					Oct-11
50	1.76	3.05	10.29	17.83	87.08	0	1.95	10.37	1.64	17.38	47.5	55	45	0	0	127					Oct-11
50	0.18	0.92	0.45	-1.88	5.60	0	1.63	2.78	-14.08	10.93	105.7	100	0	0	0	344	1.67	0.69	5.75		Sep-05
50	0.00	0.50	-0.19	-4.01	1.72	0	2.38	2.8	-13.72	10.05	105.7	100	0	0	0	344	1.22	0.4		1.00	Sep-05
50	0.26	1.14	0.96	-0.52	8.00	0	1.18	2.8	-13.56	11.47	105.7	100	0	0	0	344	1.92	0.87			Sep-05
50	0.17	0.99	0.71	-1.14	6.85	0	1.38	2.8	-12.08	11.22	105.7	100	0	0	0	344	1.84	0.78			Sep-05
50	0.09	0.75	0.28	-2.56	4.21	0	1.88	2.8	-12.8	10.63	105.7	100	0	0	0	344	1.49	0.59			Sep-05
	0.34	1.14	1.05	-0.43	8.09		1.18	2.8	-13.73	11.47	105.7	100	0	0	0	344	1.92	0.87			Apr-17
	0.26	1.14	0.96	-0.52	8.00		1.13	2.81	-12.81	11.47	105.7	100	0	0	0	344	1.92	0.87			Apr-17
50	0.85	2.38	5.30			1.71	2.23			9.8	257.7	10	20	62	7	98			5.75		Jul-15
50	0.54	1.88	4.53			0.98	2.98			9.75	257.7	10	20	62	7	98				1.00	Jul-15
50	0.98	2.63	5.78			2.16	1.78			9.8	257.7	10	20	62	7	98					Jul-15
50	0.92	2.52	5.68			1.96	1.98			9.8	257.7	10	20	62	7	98					Jul-15
50	0.78	2.25	5.15			1.47	2.48			9.79	257.7	10	20	62	7	98					Jul-15
	1.02	2.71	5.94			2.3	1.63			9.8	257.7	10	20	62	7	98					Jul-15
	1.02	2.71	5.92				1.63			9.8	257.7	10	20	62	7	98					Apr-17
50	0.72	4.92	9.37			0	2.43			10.76	48.8	59	41	0	0	410			5.75		Oct-15
50	0.45	4.49	8.44			0	3.18			10.59	48.8	59	41	0	0	410				1.00	Oct-15
50	0.81	5.17	9.81			0	1.98			10.86	48.8	59	41	0	0	410					Oct-15
50	0.72	4.99	9.53			0	2.18			10.81	48.8	59	41	0	0	410					Oct-15
50	0.63	4.74	8.99			0	2.68			10.7	48.8	59	41	0	0	410					Oct-15
	0.80	5.15	10.00			0	1.83			10.89	48.8	59	41	0	0	410					Oct-15
	0.80	5.15	10.00				1.83			10.89	48.8	59	41	0	0	410					Apr-17
50	0.86	1.15	1.45	8.18	12.80	0	1.92	2.17	-2.2	10.31	612.4	100	-7	0	0	374			5.75		Oct-11
50	0.60	0.81	0.70	5.82	8.68	0	2.67	2.21	-3.4	9.8	612.4	100	-7	0	0	374				1.00	Oct-11
	0.93	1.40	1.88	9.64	15.38	0	1.47	2.15	-3.04	10.62	612.4	100	-7	0	0	374					Oct-11
50	0.85	1.23	1.62	8.91	14.08	0	1.67	2.16	-2.84	10.47	612.4	100	-7	0	0	374					Oct-11
50	0.78	1.08	1.27	7.45	11.51	0	2.17	2.2	-2.67	10.14	612.4	100	-7	0	0	374					Oct-11
500	8.17	20.44	45.76	34.33	66.79	0.11	1.71	19.08	0.88	17.2	14.8	2	98	0	0						Jul-12
	6.38	14.83	37.90	28.55	26.76	1.56	1.19	15.38	0.96	22.38	1,164	1	99	0	0	31	18.16	-26.03			Oct-16
	6.19	14.44	37.64	28.38	26.59	1.56	1.29	15.37	0.96	22.35	1,164	1	99	0	0	31	18.16	-26.03			Oct-16

	MARKET			FUND TYPE, CATEGORY & OBJECTIVE	RATINGS				MINIMUMS	
Fund Name	Ticker Symbol	Traded On	Fund Type	Category and (Prospectus Objective)	Overall Rating	Reward Rating	Risk Rating	Recent Up/ Downgrade	Open to New Investors	Min Initial Investment
Acadian Emerging Markets Portfolio Investor Class	AEMGX	NAS CM	Open End	Emerging Markets Equity (Growth)	B-	B	C	Up		2,500
Access Flex Bear High Yield Fund Investor Class	AFBIX	NAS CM	Open End	Trading Tools (Corporate Bond - High Yield)	D	D	D		Y	15,000
Access Flex Bear High Yield Fund Service Class	AFBSX	NAS CM	Open End	Trading Tools (Corporate Bond - High Yield)	D	D	D		Y	15,000
ACM Dynamic Opportunity Fund Class A	ADOAX	NAS CM	Open End	Long/Short Equity (Growth)	C+	C	B	Up	Y	2,000
ACM Dynamic Opportunity Fund Class I	ADOIX	NAS CM	Open End	Long/Short Equity (Growth)	C+	C	B	Up	Y	100,000
ACM Dynamic Opportunity Fund Class I	IQRAX	NAS CM	Open End	Global Equity Large Cap (Foreign Stock)	D-	D+	B+		Y	5,000
ACM Dynamic Opportunity Fund Class I	IQRIX	NAS CM	Open End	Global Equity Large Cap (Foreign Stock)	D-	D+	B+		Y	10,000
ACR Multi-Strategy Quality Return (MQR) Fund Class A	MQRAX	NAS CM	Open End	Multialternative (Growth & Income)	B-	C	B	Up	Y	5,000
ACR Multi-Strategy Quality Return (MQR) Fund Class I	MQRIX	NAS CM	Open End	Multialternative (Growth & Income)	B-	C	B	Up	Y	10,000
Acuitas International Small Cap Fund Institutional Shares	AISCX	NAS CM	Open End	Global Equity Mid/Small Cap (Small Company)	B	B	B	Up	Y	100,000
Acuitas US Microcap Fund Institutional Shares	AFMCX	NAS CM	Open End	US Equity Small Cap (Small Company)	A-	A-	B	Up	Y	100,000
Adalta International Fund	ADAQX	NAS CM	Open End	Global Equity Mid/Small Cap (World Stock)	C+	C	B	Down	Y	2,500
Adams Diversified Equity Fund	ADX	NYSE	Closed End	US Equity Large Cap Blend (Growth & Income)	B	B	B-	Up	Y	
Adams Natural Resources Fund	PEO	NYSE	Closed End	Energy Sector Equity (Natl Res)	C	C	C		Y	
Adirondack Small Cap Fund	ADKSX	NAS CM	Open End	US Equity Small Cap (Small Company)	B	B	B	Up	Y	3,000
Advantus Dynamic Managed Volatility Fund Institutional Cls	VVMIX	NAS CM	Open End	Multialternative (Growth & Income)	C	C+	B	Up	Y	100,000
Advantus Managed Volatility Equity Fund Institutional Cls	VMEIX	NAS CM	Open End	Long/Short Equity (Growth & Income)	C	C+	B	Up	Y	100,000
Advantus Strategic Dividend Income Fund Inst Cls Shares	VSDIX	NAS CM	Open End	Aggressive Alloc (Equity-Income)	C+	C+	C	Down	Y	100,000
Advent Claymore Convertible Securities & Income Fund	AVK	NYSE	Closed End	Convertibles (Convertible Bond)	C+	C+	C	Up	Y	
Advent Claymore Convertible Securities & Income Fund II	AGC	NYSE	Closed End	Convertibles (Convertible Bond)	C+	C+	C+	Up	Y	
Advent/Claymore Enhanced Growth & Income Fund	LCM	NYSE	Closed End	Convertibles (Equity-Income)	C+	C+	B-	Up	Y	
AdvisorOne CLS Global Aggressive Equity Fund Class N	CLACX	NAS CM	Open End	Global Equity (Growth)	B-	B	C+	Down	Y	2,500
AdvisorOne CLS Global Diversified Equity Fund Class N	CLSAX	NAS CM	Open End	Global Equity (Growth)	C+	B-	C+	Down	Y	2,500
AdvisorOne CLS Growth and Income Fund Class N	CLERX	NAS CM	Open End	Cautious Alloc (Growth & Income)	B-	C+	B	Up	Y	2,500
AdvisorOne CLS International Equity Fund Class N	CLHAX	NAS CM	Open End	Global Equity Large Cap (Growth & Income)	B-	B-	B-	Up	Y	2,500
AdvisorOne CLS Shelter Fund Class N	CLSHX	NAS CM	Open End	Moderate Alloc (Income)	B-	B-	B-	Down	Y	2,500
Advisory Research All Cap Value Fund	ADVGX	NAS CM	Open End	US Equity Large Cap Blend (Growth)	B	B-	B	Up	Y	2,500
Advisory Research Emerging Markets Opportunities Fund	ADVMX	NAS CM	Open End	Emerging Markets Equity (Growth)	C+	C+	C+	Up	Y	2,500
Advisory Research Global Value Fund	ADVWX	NAS CM	Open End	Global Equity (World Stock)	C+	C+	C+	Down	Y	2,500
Advisory Research International Small Cap Value Fund Cls I	ADVLX	NAS CM	Open End	Global Equity Mid/Small Cap (Small Company)	B-	B	C+	Up	Y	500,000
Advy Research Intl Small Cap Value Fund Inv Cls	ADVIX	NAS CM	Open End	Global Equity Mid/Small Cap (Small Company)	B-	B	C+	Up	Y	2,500
Advisory Research MLP & Energy Income Fund Class A	INFRX	NAS CM	Open End	Energy Sector Equity (Natl Res)	D+	D+	D	Down	Y	2,500
Advisory Research MLP & Energy Income Fund Class C	INFFX	NAS CM	Open End	Energy Sector Equity (Natl Res)	D	D+	D	Down	Y	2,500
Advisory Research MLP & Energy Income Fund Class I	INFIX	NAS CM	Open End	Energy Sector Equity (Natl Res)	D+	D+	D	Down	Y	1,000,000
Advisory Research MLP & Energy Infrastructure Fund Class I	MLPPX	NAS CM	Open End	Energy Sector Equity (Natl Res)	D	D+	D	Down	Y	5,000,000
Advisory Research MLP & Equity Fund Class A	INFJX	NAS CM	Open End	Energy Sector Equity (Natl Res)	C-	D+	C-	Up	Y	2,500
Advisory Research MLP & Equity Fund Class C	INFKX	NAS CM	Open End	Energy Sector Equity (Natl Res)	C-	D+	C-	Up	Y	2,500
Advisory Research MLP & Equity Fund Class I	INFEX	NAS CM	Open End	Energy Sector Equity (Natl Res)	C-	D+	C-	Up	Y	1,000,000
Advisory Research Small Company Opportunities Fund	ADVSX	NAS CM	Open End	US Equity Small Cap (Growth)	B	B-	B	Up	Y	2,500
Aegis Value Fund	AVALX	NAS CM	Open End	US Equity Small Cap (Growth)	B	A-	C	Up	Y	1,000,000
Aegis Value Fund Class A	AVFAX	NAS CM	Open End	US Equity Small Cap (Growth)	B	B+	C	Up	Y	2,000
Affinity Small Cap Fund Class A	AISOX	NAS CM	Open End	US Equity Small Cap (Small Company)	C	C+	B-	Up	Y	2,500
Affinity Small Cap Fund Class C	AISPX	NAS CM	Open End	US Equity Small Cap (Small Company)	C	C+	B-	Up	Y	2,500
Affinity Small Cap Fund Class I	AISQX	NAS CM	Open End	US Equity Small Cap (Small Company)	C	C+	B-	Up	Y	100,000
AIG Active Allocation Fund Class A	FBAAX	NAS CM	Open End	Moderate Alloc (Asset Alloc)	B-	C+	B	Down	Y	500
AIG Active Allocation Fund Class B	FBABX	NAS CM	Open End	Moderate Alloc (Asset Alloc)	B-	C+	B	Down	Y	500
AIG Active Allocation Fund Class C	FBACX	NAS CM	Open End	Moderate Alloc (Asset Alloc)	B-	C+	B	Down	Y	500
AIG Active Allocation Fund Class I	US86704B8550		Open End	Moderate Alloc (Asset Alloc)	B-	C+	B	Down	Y	0
AIG Commodity Strategy Fund Class A	SUNAX	NAS CM	Open End	Commodities Broad Basket (Growth & Income)	D+	D	C-	Up	Y	500
AIG Commodity Strategy Fund Class C	SUNCX	NAS CM	Open End	Commodities Broad Basket (Growth & Income)	D+	D	C-	Up	Y	500
AIG Commodity Strategy Fund Class W	SUNWX	NAS CM	Open End	Commodities Broad Basket (Growth & Income)	C-	D+	C-	Up	Y	50,000
AIG ESG Dividend Fund A Shares	EDFAX	NAS CM	Open End	US Equity Large Cap Value (Growth & Income)	D-	D+	B+		Y	500

★Expanded analysis of this fund is included in Section II.

	TOTAL RETURNS					PERFORMANCE				ASSETS		ASSET ALLOCATION & TURNOVER					BULL & BEAR		FEES		
Min Additional Investment	3-Month Total Return	6-Month Total Return	1-Year Total Return	3-Year Total Return	5-Year Total Return	Dividend Yield (TTM)	Expense Ratio	3-Yr Std Deviation	3-Year Beta	NAV	Total Assets (MIL)	%Cash	%Stocks	%Bonds	%Other	Turnover Ratio	Last Bull Market Total Return	Last Bear Market Total Return	Front End Fee (%)	Back End Fee (%)	Inception Date
1,000	6.43	14.78	37.62	28.31	26.52	1.53	1.44	15.37	0.96	22.39	1,164	1	99	0	0	31	18.16	-26.03			Jun-93
	-1.19	-0.18	-4.50	-21.70	-39.23	0	1.78	4.61	-0.49	38.13	0.68	109	0	-9	0	650	-16.47	4.45			Apr-05
	-1.36	-0.23	-4.90	-23.44	-41.81	0	2.78	4.7	-0.48	33.95	0.68	109	0	-9	0	650	-17.09	3.84			Apr-05
500	3.20	7.72	17.58			0	2.08			17.72	63.3	32	67	0	0	481			5.75		Jan-15
500	3.24	7.86	17.85			0	1.83			17.82	63.3	32	67	0	0	481					Jan-15
100	0.49	5.05	10.94				1.41			11.01	63.3	45	55	0	0				5.75		Dec-16
100	0.46	5.12	11.11				1.26			11.01	63.3	45	55	0	0						Dec-16
100	5.95	9.37	13.23	17.07		0	1.46			11.39	94.8	23	49	23	5	14			5.75		Dec-14
100	6.01	9.52	13.49	17.67		0	1.26			11.44	94.8	23	49	23	5	14					Dec-14
	4.22	9.37	21.24	29.00		1.78	1.51	11.64	0.97	10.5	49.2	4	95	0	1	105					Jul-14
	1.51	9.02	10.25	36.91		0	1.71	13.22	0.8	13.23	99.9	3	97	0	0	50					Jul-14
1,000	-0.52	2.31	19.96	19.42	20.85	0.97	1.76	10.55	0.7	18.25	18.7	7	82	0	11	42	19.08	-21.55			Dec-93
	6.45	11.58	24.76	33.98	99.44	1.08		10.23	1	17.55	1,710	0	100	0	0	32	25.17	-19.08			Oct-29
	5.89	12.93	2.12	-1.68	12.50	1.65		16.89		23.26	633.0	0	99	0	1	19	23.17	-27			Jan-29
50	2.36	6.89	10.54	23.23	85.62	0	1.23	13.14	0.86	22.39	256.1	8	91	0	0	38	19.02	-21.93			Apr-05
1,000	5.38	9.31	17.53			1.52	0.6			12.05	38.6	19	61	20	0	0					Sep-15
1,000	4.22	7.48	16.68			2.01	0.72			12.14	38.0	10	85	4	0	0					Sep-15
1,000	0.36	0.99	5.18	8.10	43.78	1.92	0.96	9.53	0.51	10.97	80.8	0	76	13	0	74					Sep-12
	0.90	5.47	12.73	17.53	38.11	4.35	0	10.74		17.5	352.2	5	7	37	1	98	13.34	-20.22			Apr-03
	0.63	3.85	10.61	16.50	34.81	3.41		11.12		6.66	183.1	4	10	38	4	95	11.49	-26.3			May-07
	0.56	4.09	9.42	14.84	33.21	1.96	1.25	9.12		9.24	84.7	4	6	34	4	93	14.05	-20.34			Jan-05
250	5.91	11.28	24.51	34.62	81.31	1.14	1.63	11.07	1.01	15.69	172.1	2	97	0	1	32	25.94	-23.41			Oct-09
250	5.77	11.25	22.97	25.76	65.92	2.44	1.47	10.38	0.97	18.59	462.1	3	93	1	3	41	23.26	-22.36			Jul-97
250	3.18	6.58	12.18	15.95	32.66	1.73	1.54	5.52	0.49	11.36	462.0	2	43	50	3	45	14.46	-11.65			Jul-97
250	3.59	9.62	23.76	25.27	45.52	1.31	1.61	10.22	0.8	4.79	50.5	1	97	0	2	155	15.82	-13.74			Apr-06
250	6.27	11.12	20.88	28.41	78.37	0.76	1.35	9.12	0.81	14.56	171.1	2	98	0	0	147	0.16	-14.73			Dec-09
500	7.81	12.55	19.54	29.41	88.50	0.55	1.01	10.19	0.93	14.23	15.6	10	91	0	0	51	20.16	-16.92			Nov-09
500	4.57	8.45	25.04	23.57		1.8	1.35	13.82	0.83	10.78	33.0	3	95	0	2	32					Nov-13
500	3.90	7.17	16.62	23.34	57.06	0.98	1.1	10.12	0.91	11.85	11.2	4	94	0	1	23	19.84	-23.19			Jul-10
500	6.94	15.10	29.52	35.51	64.32	1.04	1.16	10.5	0.77	13.65	16.2	5	96	0	0	32	11.05	-20.2			Dec-13
500	6.88	15.03	29.44	35.44	64.02	1.01	1.19	10.49	0.77	13.65	16.2	5	96	0	0	32	11.05	-20.2			Mar-10
500	-1.83	0.11	-5.93	-18.84	10.57	8.18	1.4	20.32	0.93	8.84	871.8	2	74	20	0	65	18.71	-9.92	5.50		May-11
500	-2.01	-0.26	-6.62	-20.74	6.41	7.33	2.15	20.33	0.93	8.86	871.8	2	74	20	0	65	18.18	-10.21		1.00	Apr-12
100,000	-1.70	0.30	-5.60	-18.23	11.96	8.48	1.15	20.34	0.93	8.69	871.8	2	74	20	0	65	18.86	-9.83			Dec-10
500	-1.73	0.20	-5.91	-21.19	8.87	8.71	0.94	20.9	0.94	8.48	328.5	3	74	19	0	71	19.61	-10.42			Sep-10
500	-2.94	-0.13	-5.39			0.26	1.35			8.95	14.5	3	97	0	0	52			5.50		Aug-15
500	-3.10	-0.53	-6.23			0.08	2.1			8.97	14.5	3	97	0	0	52				1.00	Aug-15
100,000	-2.90	0.00	-5.25			0.39	1.1			8.96	14.5	3	97	0	0	52					Aug-15
500	1.04	7.30	4.86	22.56		0.53	1.11	12.39	0.83	11.71	7.4	7	94	0	0	52					Nov-13
250	21.65	21.43	17.37	52.40	56.29	1.34	1.5	28.29	0.89	19.66	118.0	0	100	0	0	37	24.09	-23.66			May-98
250	21.53	21.30	17.15	51.53	54.63	1.25	1.75	28.28	0.89	19.53	118.0	0	100	0	0	37	23.91	-23.74	3.75		Feb-14
500	6.91	16.07	20.79			0.05	1.75			12.16	9.2	4	96	0	0	64			5.75		Jul-15
500	6.75	15.71	20.00			0	2.5			11.96	9.2	4	96	0	0	64				1.00	Jul-15
1,000	7.07	16.31	21.14			0.2	1.5			12.22	9.2	4	96	0	0	64					Jul-15
100	3.52	7.38	14.49	19.55	52.99	1.34	1.73	7.02	0.66	17.67	155.3	2	64	30	3	29	12.11	-10.01	5.75		Nov-02
100	3.40	7.03	13.71	17.25	47.97	0.72	2.49	7.01	0.66	17.52	155.3	2	64	30	3	29	11.63	-10.25		4.00	Nov-02
100	3.40	7.03	13.74	17.35	48.23	0.73	2.37	7.03	0.66	17.59	155.3	2	64	30	3	29	11.6	-10.2		1.00	Nov-02
	3.56	7.34	14.43	19.49	52.85	1.32	3.21	7.04	0.67	17.71	155.3	2	64	30	3	29	12.09	-10.02			Feb-04
100	4.62	7.86	-0.49	-2.87	-13.95	0	1.72	9.77	0.23	7.34	38.0	55	0	6	39	50	-19.84	5.67	5.75		Nov-08
100	4.47	7.51	-1.26	-4.88	-16.64	0	2.37	9.72	0.24	7.05	38.0	55	0	6	39	50	-20.13	5.34		1.00	Nov-08
	4.63	7.98	-0.28	-2.25	-12.92	0	1.52	9.75	0.23	7.43	38.0	55	0	6	39	50	-19.81	5.75			Nov-08
100	5.73	7.50	13.65				1.25			16.32	26.4	0	100	0	0				5.75		Dec-16

	MARKET		FUND TYPE, CATEGORY & OBJECTIVE		RATINGS					MINIMUMS
Fund Name	Ticker Symbol	Traded On	Fund Type	Category and (Prospectus Objective)	Overall Rating	Reward Rating	Risk Rating	Recent Up/ Downgrade	Open to New Investors	Min Initial Investment
AIG ESG Dividend Fund C Shares	EDFCX	NAS CM	Open End	US Equity Large Cap Value (Growth & Income)	D-	D+	B+		Y	500
AIG ESG Dividend Fund W Shares	EDFWX	NAS CM	Open End	US Equity Large Cap Value (Growth & Income)	D-	D+	B+		Y	50,000
AIG Focused Alpha Large-Cap Fund Class A	SFLAX	NAS CM	Open End	US Equity Large Cap Growth (Growth)	B	A-	B-		Y	500
AIG Focused Alpha Large-Cap Fund Class C	SFLCX	NAS CM	Open End	US Equity Large Cap Growth (Growth)	B	B+	B-		Y	500
AIG Focused Alpha Large-Cap Fund Class W	SFLWX	NAS CM	Open End	US Equity Large Cap Growth (Growth)	B	A-	B-		Y	50,000
AIG Focused Dividend Strategy Fund Class A	FDSAX	NAS CM	Open End	US Equity Large Cap Value (Growth & Income)	B	B	B		Y	500
AIG Focused Dividend Strategy Fund Class B	FDSBX	NAS CM	Open End	US Equity Large Cap Value (Growth & Income)	B	B	B-		Y	500
AIG Focused Dividend Strategy Fund Class C	FDSTX	NAS CM	Open End	US Equity Large Cap Value (Growth & Income)	B	B	B-		Y	500
AIG Focused Dividend Strategy Fund Class W	FDSWX	NAS CM	Open End	US Equity Large Cap Value (Growth & Income)	B	B	B		Y	50,000
AIG Focused Multi-Cap Growth Fund Class A	FOCAX	NAS CM	Open End	US Equity Large Cap Growth (Growth)	A-	A	B+	Up	Y	500
AIG Focused Multi-Cap Growth Fund Class C	FOCCX	NAS CM	Open End	US Equity Large Cap Growth (Growth)	A-	A-	B+	Up	Y	500
AIG Focused Multi-Cap Growth Fund Class W	FOCWX	NAS CM	Open End	US Equity Large Cap Growth (Growth)	A-	A	B+	Up	Y	50,000
AIG Global Trends Fund A Share	GTFAX	NAS CM	Open End	Alloc (Growth)	B-	C	B+	Up	Y	500
AIG Global Trends Fund C Share	GTFCX	NAS CM	Open End	Alloc (Growth)	B-	C	B+	Up	Y	500
AIG Global Trends Fund W Share	GTFWX	NAS CM	Open End	Alloc (Growth)	C+	C	B	Up	Y	50,000
AIG Income Explorer Fund Class A	IEAAX	NAS CM	Open End	Alloc (Income)	B-	C+	B		Y	500
AIG Income Explorer Fund Class C	IEACX	NAS CM	Open End	Alloc (Income)	B-	C+	B		Y	500
AIG Income Explorer Fund Class W	IEAWX	NAS CM	Open End	Alloc (Income)	B-	C+	B		Y	50,000
AIG International Dividend Strategy Fund Class A	SIEAX	NAS CM	Open End	Global Equity Large Cap (Foreign Stock)	C	C	C	Up	Y	500
AIG International Dividend Strategy Fund Class C	SIETX	NAS CM	Open End	Global Equity Large Cap (Foreign Stock)	C	C	C-	Up	Y	500
AIG International Dividend Strategy Fund Class I	NAOIX	NAS CM	Open End	Global Equity Large Cap (Foreign Stock)	C	C	C	Up		0
AIG International Dividend Strategy Fund Class W	SIEWX	NAS CM	Open End	Global Equity Large Cap (Foreign Stock)	C	C	C	Up	Y	50,000
AIG Japan Fund Class A	SAESX	NAS CM	Open End	Japan Equity (Foreign Stock)	B+	A-	B	Up	Y	500
AIG Japan Fund Class C	SAJCX	NAS CM	Open End	Japan Equity (Foreign Stock)	B+	A-	B	Up	Y	500
AIG Japan Fund Class W	SAJWX	NAS CM	Open End	Japan Equity (Foreign Stock)	B+	A-	B	Up	Y	50,000
AIG Multi-Asset Allocation Fund Class A	FASAX	NAS CM	Open End	Moderate Alloc (Asset Alloc)	B-	C+	B-	Down	Y	500
AIG Multi-Asset Allocation Fund Class B	FMABX	NAS CM	Open End	Moderate Alloc (Asset Alloc)	B-	C+	B-	Down	Y	500
AIG Multi-Asset Allocation Fund Class C	FMATX	NAS CM	Open End	Moderate Alloc (Asset Alloc)	B-	C+	B-	Down	Y	500
AIG Multi-Asset Allocation Fund Class I	US86704F1049		Open End	Moderate Alloc (Asset Alloc)	B-	C+	B-	Down	Y	0
AIG Select Dividend Growth Fund Class A	SDVAX	NAS CM	Open End	US Equity Large Cap Value (Growth)	B	B	B	Up	Y	500
AIG Select Dividend Growth Fund Class C	SDVCX	NAS CM	Open End	US Equity Large Cap Value (Growth)	B	B	B	Up	Y	500
AIG Select Dividend Growth Fund Class W	SDVWX	NAS CM	Open End	US Equity Large Cap Value (Growth)	B	B	B	Up	Y	50,000
AIG Small-Cap Fund Class A	SASAX	NAS CM	Open End	US Equity Small Cap (Small Company)	A-	A	B	Up	Y	500
AIG Small-Cap Fund Class C	SASCX	NAS CM	Open End	US Equity Small Cap (Small Company)	A-	A	B	Up	Y	500
AIG Small-Cap Fund Class W	SASWX	NAS CM	Open End	US Equity Small Cap (Small Company)	B+	A	B-	Up	Y	50,000
AIG Strategic Value Fund Class A	SFVAX	NAS CM	Open End	US Equity Large Cap Value (Growth)	B-	B-	B	Down	Y	500
AIG Strategic Value Fund Class C	SFVTX	NAS CM	Open End	US Equity Large Cap Value (Growth)	B-	C+	B	Down	Y	500
AIG Strategic Value Fund Class W	SFVWX	NAS CM	Open End	US Equity Large Cap Value (Growth)	B-	B-	B	Down	Y	50,000
Akre Focus Fund Institutional Class	AKRIX	NAS CM	Open End	US Equity Large Cap Growth (Growth)	A-	A	B	Up	Y	250,000
Akre Focus Fund Retail Class	AKREX	NAS CM	Open End	US Equity Large Cap Growth (Growth)	B+	A	B	Up	Y	2,000
Akre Focus Fund Supra Institutional Class	AKRSX	NAS CM	Open End	US Equity Large Cap Growth (Growth)	A-	A	B	Up	Y	300,000,000
Al Frank Fund Class Advisor	VALAX	NAS CM	Open End	US Equity Large Cap Value (Growth)	B-	B-	B-	Down	Y	100,000
Al Frank Fund Class Investor	VALUX	NAS CM	Open End	US Equity Large Cap Value (Growth)	B-	B-	B-	Down	Y	1,000
Alambic Mid Cap Growth Plus Fund	ALMGX	NAS CM	Open End	US Equity Mid Cap (Growth)	D-	D+	B+		Y	50,000
Alambic Mid Cap Value Plus Fund	ALMVX	NAS CM	Open End	US Equity Mid Cap (Growth)	D-	D+	B+		Y	50,000
Alambic Small Cap Growth Plus Fund	ALGSX	NAS CM	Open End	US Equity Small Cap (Small Company)	C-	C	B+	Up	Y	50,000
Alambic Small Cap Value Plus Fund	ALAMX	NAS CM	Open End	US Equity Small Cap (Small Company)	C	C+	B	Up	Y	50,000
Alger Balanced Portfolio Class I-2	ABLOX	NAS CM	Open End	Moderate Alloc (Balanced)	B	B-	B		Y	500,000
Alger Capital Appreciation Focus Fund Class A	ALAFX	NAS CM	Open End	US Equity Large Cap Growth (Growth)	A-	A-	A-	Up	Y	1,000
Alger Capital Appreciation Focus Fund Class C	ALCFX	NAS CM	Open End	US Equity Large Cap Growth (Growth)	A-	A-	B+	Up	Y	1,000
Alger Capital Appreciation Focus Fund Class I	ALGRX	NAS CM	Open End	US Equity Large Cap Growth (Growth)	A-	A-	A-	Up	Y	0
Alger Capital Appreciation Focus Fund Class Y	ALGYX	NAS CM	Open End	US Equity Large Cap Growth (Growth)	A-	A-	A-	Up	Y	500,000

★ Expanded analysis of this fund is included in Section II.

	TOTAL RETURNS					PERFORMANCE				ASSETS		ASSET ALLOCATION & TURNOVER					BULL & BEAR		FEES		
Min Additional Investment	3-Month Total Return	6-Month Total Return	1-Year Total Return	3-Year Total Return	5-Year Total Return	Dividend Yield (TTM)	Expense Ratio	3-Yr Std Deviation	3-Year Beta	NAV	Total Assets (ML)	%Cash	%Stocks	%Bonds	%Other	Turnover Ratio	Last Bull Market Total Return	Last Bear Market Total Return	Front End Fee (%)	Back End Fee (%)	Inception Date
100	5.53	7.02	12.85				1.9			16.3	26.4	0	100	0	0					1.00	Dec-16
	5.71	7.55	13.85				1.05			16.32	26.4	0	100	0	0						Dec-16
100	4.23	13.47	30.88	34.71	121.91	0	1.67	10.15	0.91	29.79	651.4	4	96	0	0	38	26.75	-21.69	5.75		Dec-05
100	4.04	13.10	30.06	32.06	114.81	0	2.32	10.15	0.91	28.43	651.4	4	96	0	0	38	26.27	-21.9		1.00	Jan-12
	4.25	13.54	31.05	35.26	123.48	0	1.52	10.16	0.92	30.16	651.4	4	96	0	0	38	26.8	-21.69			Jan-12
100	7.46	13.58	20.24	36.12	112.44	2.72	1.05	10.65	0.92	18.75	14,853	1	99	0	0	60	22.05	-8.91	5.75		Jun-98
100	7.25	13.16	19.45	33.40	105.50	2.18	1.7	10.64	0.92	18.59	14,853	1	99	0	0	60	21.64	-9.16		4.00	Jun-98
100	7.26	13.17	19.46	33.45	105.59	2.17	1.7	10.66	0.92	18.58	14,853	1	99	0	0	60	21.57	-9.13		1.00	Jun-98
	7.52	13.71	20.48	36.97	114.39	2.94	0.85	10.66	0.92	18.73	14,853	1	99	0	0	60	22.05	-8.91			May-13
100	4.03	13.35	36.44	38.37	113.99	0	1.68	9.64	0.79	29.16	605.0	7	93	0	0	29	25.27	-19.96	5.75		Jul-05
100	3.90	12.99	35.54	35.71	107.01	0	2.33	9.64	0.79	27.77	605.0	7	93	0	0	29	24.77	-20.17		1.00	Jan-12
	4.11	13.48	36.68	39.20	115.82	0	1.51	9.65	0.79	29.57	605.0	7	93	0	0	29	25.26	-19.96			Jan-12
100	3.64	6.38	9.10	8.94	12.60	0	1.86	4.42	0.2	12.95	36.5	57	30	0	13	0	3.77		5.75		Jun-11
100	3.48	5.99	8.37	6.79	9.01	0	2.51	4.42	0.2	12.38	36.5	57	30	0	13	0	3.4			1.00	Jun-11
	3.74	6.53	9.38	9.64	13.86	0	1.66	4.43	0.2	13.15	36.5	57	30	0	13	0	3.89				Jun-11
100	1.77	4.57	14.90	23.12		3.6	2.27	7.58	0.6	15.93	44.7	-7	34	41	4	54			5.75		Jul-13
100	1.63	4.26	14.12	20.74		2.98	2.92	7.59	0.6	15.9	44.7	-7	34	41	4	54				1.00	Jul-13
	1.81	4.67	15.14	23.85		3.81	2.07	7.59	0.6	15.93	44.7	-7	34	41	4	54					Jul-13
100	1.15	3.20	17.74	4.86	-1.46	3.28	1.9	14.66	1.1	9.56	88.7	1	97	0	2	22	14.36	-25.34	5.75		Nov-96
100	0.92	2.77	16.97	2.79	-4.70	2.98	2.55	14.6	1.1	8.65	88.7	1	97	0	2	22	14.03	-25.67		1.00	Mar-97
	1.04	3.19	17.73	5.17	-0.86	3.32	1.8	14.65	1.1	9.67	88.7	1	97	0	2	22	14.43	-25.35			Nov-01
	1.19	3.29	17.97	5.38	-0.97	3.47	1.7	14.67	1.11	9.56	88.7	1	97	0	2	22	14.36	-25.34			Jan-15
100	7.33	12.28	29.58	41.04	79.16	0.42	1.9	13.84	0.96	8.6	31.4	3	97	0	0	115	9.29	-24.65	5.75		May-06
100	7.12	11.77	28.51	38.23	73.14	0.02	2.55	13.82	0.96	8.15	31.4	3	97	0	0	115	8.97	-24.97		1.00	May-06
	7.31	12.39	29.70	41.17	79.33		1.7	13.85	0.96	8.6	31.4	3	97	0	0	115	9.28	-24.65			Apr-17
100	4.03	8.04	13.80	19.92	54.97	1.11	1.76	7.6	0.72	18.36	274.7	9	63	21	5	18	5.77	-9.56	5.75		Nov-02
100	3.84	7.62	12.96	17.40	49.65	0.46	2.44	7.57	0.72	18.36	274.7	4	66	21	7	18	5.27	-9.76		4.00	Nov-02
100	3.85	7.63	13.04	17.60	50.08	0.53	2.4	7.57	0.72	18.34	274.7	9	63	21	5	18	5.33	-9.75		1.00	Nov-02
	4.04	7.93	13.68	19.65	54.46	1.07	3.3	7.56	0.72	18.35	274.7	9	63	21	5	18	5.68	-9.57			Aug-11
100	10.11	13.03	17.59	30.39		1.5	1.58	12.22	1.05	17.34	45.8	0	100	0	0	69			5.75		May-14
100	9.92	12.67	16.79	27.23		0.91	2.37	12.22	1.05	17.27	45.8	0	100	0	0	69				1.00	May-14
	10.12	13.15	17.75	30.49		1.61	1.52	12.24	1.05	17.29	45.8	0	100	0	0	69					May-14
100	1.90	11.29	17.73	43.10		0	1.72	13.86	0.96	18.51	59.7	3	97	0	0	67			5.75		Feb-14
100	1.69	10.89	16.93	40.22		0	2.37	13.88	0.96	17.95	59.7	3	97	0	0	67				1.00	Feb-14
	1.94	11.37	17.91	43.88		0	1.52	13.84	0.96	18.67	59.7	3	97	0	0	67					Feb-14
100	6.35	9.88	15.64	22.67	88.69	1.16	1.42	9.81	0.91	31.54	245.0	0	100	0	0	56	22.61	-19.32	5.75		Nov-99
100	6.20	9.53	14.90	20.25	82.58	0.68	2.08	9.81	0.91	29.24	245.0	0	100	0	0	56	22.11	-19.55		1.00	Nov-99
	6.46	9.95	15.71	22.75	88.81		1.26	9.8	0.91	31.54	245.0	0	100	0	0	56	22.61	-19.32			Apr-17
25,000	7.01	17.74	30.86	44.90	128.62	0	1.05	10.4	0.93	33.04	6,911	0	99	0	0	10	28.06	-5.89			Aug-09
250	6.91	17.59	30.48	43.72	125.72	0	1.33	10.4	0.93	32.41	6,911	0	99	0	0	10	27.84	-5.99			Aug-09
	7.00	17.78	30.94	45.16	129.03	0	0.96	10.42	0.94	33.1	6,911	0	99	0	0	10	28.06	-5.89			Aug-15
100	7.35	11.13	18.04	27.32	89.83	1.28	1.26	12.01	1.1	24.83	90.0	2	98	0	0	8	23.52	-22.48			May-06
100	7.29	10.98	17.75	26.36	87.46	1.07	1.51	12	1.09	24.79	90.0	2	98	0	0	8	23.35	-22.56			Jan-98
	6.49	10.69	21.25				0.85			12.05	1.1	1	99	0	0						Dec-16
	7.24	9.66	16.69				0.85			11.56	1.1	4	96	0	0						Dec-16
	4.30	10.24	17.00			0	0.95				2.9	4	96	0	0	199					Dec-15
	3.57	7.49	5.88			0.31	0.95				3.1	5	95	0	0	226					Sep-15
	4.28	7.38	15.44	26.40	62.26	1.68	0.96	6.54	0.59	17.2	47.4	1	73	26	0	4	13.27	-9.26			Sep-89
50	7.22	13.52	33.75	43.59	127.27	0	1.15	12.05	1.06	31.21	138.7	3	97	0	0	127	23.47	-16.92	5.25		Dec-12
50	7.00	13.05	32.70	40.35	118.84	0	1.9	12.01	1.05	30	138.7	3	97	0	0	127	22.94	-17.18		1.00	Dec-12
	7.22	13.53	33.71	43.80	128.31	0	1.15	12.03	1.06	31.36	138.7	3	97	0	0	127	23.65	-16.83			Nov-93
	7.35	13.82	34.14	44.27	129.06		0.65	12.05	1.06	31.84	138.7	3	97	0	0	127	23.65	-16.83			Mar-17

	MARKET			FUND TYPE, CATEGORY & OBJECTIVE	RATINGS				MINIMUMS	
Fund Name	Ticker Symbol	Traded On	Fund Type	Category and (Prospectus Objective)	Overall Rating	Reward Rating	Risk Rating	Recent Up/ Downgrade	Open to New Investors	Min Initial Investment
Alger Capital Appreciation Focus Fund Class Z	ALZFX	NAS CM	Open End	US Equity Large Cap Growth (Growth)	A-	A-	A-	Up	Y	500,000
Alger Capital Appreciation Fund Class A	ACAAX	NAS CM	Open End	US Equity Large Cap Growth (Aggr Growth)	B+	B+	A-	Up	Y	1,000
Alger Capital Appreciation Fund Class B	ACAPX	NAS CM	Open End	US Equity Large Cap Growth (Aggr Growth)	B+	B+	B+	Up		1,000
Alger Capital Appreciation Fund Class C	ALCCX	NAS CM	Open End	US Equity Large Cap Growth (Aggr Growth)	B+	B+	B+	Up	Y	1,000
Alger Capital Appreciation Fund Class Z	ACAZX	NAS CM	Open End	US Equity Large Cap Growth (Aggr Growth)	B+	B+	A-	Up	Y	500,000
Alger Capital Appreciation Institutional Fund Class I	ALARX	NAS CM	Open End	US Equity Large Cap Growth (Aggr Growth)	B+	B+	A-	Up	Y	0
Alger Capital Appreciation Institutional Fund Class R	ACARX	NAS CM	Open End	US Equity Large Cap Growth (Aggr Growth)	B+	B+	A-	Up	Y	0
Alger Capital Appreciation Institutional Fund Class Y	ACAYX	NAS CM	Open End	US Equity Large Cap Growth (Aggr Growth)	B+	B+	A-	Up	Y	500,000
Alger Capital Appreciation Institutional Fund Class Z-2	ACIZX	NAS CM	Open End	US Equity Large Cap Growth (Aggr Growth)	B+	B+	A-	Up	Y	500,000
Alger Capital Appreciation Portfolio Class I-2	ALVOX	NAS CM	Open End	US Equity Large Cap Growth (Aggr Growth)	B+	B+	A-	Up	Y	500,000
Alger Capital Appreciation Portfolio Class S	US0155448519		Open End	US Equity Large Cap Growth (Aggr Growth)	B+	B+	A-	Up	Y	0
Alger Dynamic Opportunities Fund Class A	SPEDX	NAS CM	Open End	Long/Short Equity (Growth)	B-	C+	B-	Up	Y	1,000
Alger Dynamic Opportunities Fund Class C	ADOCX	NAS CM	Open End	Long/Short Equity (Growth)	C+	C+	B-		Y	1,000
Alger Dynamic Opportunities Fund Class Z	ADOZX	NAS CM	Open End	Long/Short Equity (Growth)	B-	C+	B	Up	Y	500,000
Alger Emerging Markets Fund Class A	AAEMX	NAS CM	Open End	Emerging Markets Equity (Div Emerging Mkts)	B-	B	C+	Up	Y	1,000
Alger Emerging Markets Fund Class C	ACEMX	NAS CM	Open End	Emerging Markets Equity (Div Emerging Mkts)	B-	B-	C+	Up	Y	1,000
Alger Emerging Markets Fund Class I	AIEMX	NAS CM	Open End	Emerging Markets Equity (Div Emerging Mkts)	B-	B	C+	Up	Y	0
Alger Emerging Markets Fund Class Y	AYEMX	NAS CM	Open End	Emerging Markets Equity (Div Emerging Mkts)	B-	B	C+	Up	Y	500,000
Alger Emerging Markets Fund Class Y-2	AEMYX	NAS CM	Open End	Emerging Markets Equity (Div Emerging Mkts)	B-	B	C+	Up	Y	5,000,000
Alger Emerging Markets Fund Class Z	AZEMX	NAS CM	Open End	Emerging Markets Equity (Div Emerging Mkts)	B	B	C+	Up	Y	500,000
Alger Global Growth Fund Class A	CHUSX	NAS CM	Open End	Global Equity (Growth)	C+	B-	C+	Down	Y	1,000
Alger Global Growth Fund Class C	CHUCX	NAS CM	Open End	Global Equity (Growth)	C+	C+	C+	Down	Y	1,000
Alger Global Growth Fund Class I	AFGIX	NAS CM	Open End	Global Equity (Growth)	C+	B-	C+	Down	Y	0
Alger Global Growth Fund Class Z	AFGZX	NAS CM	Open End	Global Equity (Growth)	C+	B-	C+	Down	Y	500,000
Alger Growth & Income Fund Class A	ALBAX	NAS CM	Open End	US Equity Large Cap Blend (Growth & Income)	B	B-	B		Y	1,000
Alger Growth & Income Fund Class C	ALBCX	NAS CM	Open End	US Equity Large Cap Blend (Growth & Income)	B-	B-	B	Down	Y	1,000
Alger Growth & Income Fund Class Z	AGIZX	NAS CM	Open End	US Equity Large Cap Blend (Growth & Income)	B	B-	B		Y	500,000
Alger Growth & Income Portfolio I-2	AIGOX	NAS CM	Open End	US Equity Large Cap Blend (Equity-Income)	B-	B-	B	Down	Y	500,000
Alger Health Sciences Fund Class A	AHSAX	NAS CM	Open End	Healthcare Sector Equity (Health)	B-	B	C	Up	Y	1,000
Alger Health Sciences Fund Class C	AHSCX	NAS CM	Open End	Healthcare Sector Equity (Health)	B-	B	C	Up	Y	1,000
Alger Health Sciences Fund Class Z	AHSZX	NAS CM	Open End	Healthcare Sector Equity (Health)	B-	B+	C	Up	Y	500,000
Alger International Growth Fund Class A	ALGAX	NAS CM	Open End	Global Equity Large Cap (Growth)	B-	C+	B-	Up	Y	1,000
Alger International Growth Fund Class B	AFGPX	NAS CM	Open End	Global Equity Large Cap (Growth)	B-	C+	B-	Up		1,000
Alger International Growth Fund Class C	ALGCX	NAS CM	Open End	Global Equity Large Cap (Growth)	B-	C+	B-	Up	Y	1,000
Alger International Growth Fund Class I	AIGIX	NAS CM	Open End	Global Equity Large Cap (Growth)	B-	C+	B	Up	Y	0
Alger International Growth Fund Class Z	ALCZX	NAS CM	Open End	Global Equity Large Cap (Growth)	B-	C+	B	Up	Y	500,000
Alger Large Cap Growth Portfolio Class I-2	AAGOX	NAS CM	Open End	US Equity Large Cap Growth (Growth)	B	B	B	Up	Y	500,000
Alger Large Cap Growth Portfolio Class S	US0155448774		Open End	US Equity Large Cap Growth (Growth)	B	B	B	Up	Y	0
Alger Mid Cap Growth Fund Class A	AMGAX	NAS CM	Open End	US Equity Mid Cap (Growth)	B-	B	C	Up	Y	1,000
Alger Mid Cap Growth Fund Class B	AMCGX	NAS CM	Open End	US Equity Mid Cap (Growth)	B-	B	C	Up		1,000
Alger Mid Cap Growth Fund Class C	AMGCX	NAS CM	Open End	US Equity Mid Cap (Growth)	B-	B	C	Up	Y	1,000
Alger Mid Cap Growth Fund Class Z	AMCZX	NAS CM	Open End	US Equity Mid Cap (Growth)	B-	B	C	Up	Y	500,000
Alger Mid Cap Growth Institutional Fund Class I	ALMRX	NAS CM	Open End	US Equity Mid Cap (Growth)	B-	B	C	Up	Y	0
Alger Mid Cap Growth Institutional Fund Class R	AGIRX	NAS CM	Open End	US Equity Mid Cap (Growth)	B-	B	C	Up	Y	0
Alger Mid Cap Growth Portfolio Class I-2	AMGOX	NAS CM	Open End	US Equity Mid Cap (Growth)	B-	B	C	Up	Y	500,000
Alger Mid Cap Growth Portfolio Class S	US0155448857		Open End	US Equity Mid Cap (Growth)	B-	B	C	Up	Y	0
Alger MidCap Growth Institutional Fund Class Z-2	ALMZX	NAS CM	Open End	US Equity Mid Cap (Growth)	B-	B	C	Up	Y	500,000
Alger Responsible Investing Fund Class A	SPEGX	NAS CM	Open End	US Equity Large Cap Growth (Growth)	B	B	B-	Up	Y	1,000
Alger Responsible Investing Fund Class C	AGFCX	NAS CM	Open End	US Equity Large Cap Growth (Growth)	B	B	B-	Up	Y	1,000
Alger Responsible Investing Fund Class I	AGIFX	NAS CM	Open End	US Equity Large Cap Growth (Growth)	B	B	B-	Up	Y	0
Alger Responsible Investing Fund Class Z	ALGZX	NAS CM	Open End	US Equity Large Cap Growth (Growth)	B	B	B-	Up	Y	500,000
Alger SICAV - Alger Small Cap Focus Fund Class Y	AOFYX	NAS CM	Open End	US Equity Small Cap (Small Company)	B+	A	B	Up	Y	500,000

★ Expanded analysis of this fund is included in Section II.

	TOTAL RETURNS					PERFORMANCE				ASSETS		ASSET ALLOCATION & TURNOVER					BULL & BEAR		FEES		
Min Additional Investment	3-Month Total Return	6-Month Total Return	1-Year Total Return	3-Year Total Return	5-Year Total Return	Dividend Yield (TTM)	Expense Ratio	3-Yr Std Deviation	3-Year Beta	NAV	Total Assets (MIL)	%Cash	%Stocks	%Bonds	%Other	Turnover Ratio	Last Bull Market Total Return	Last Bear Market Total Return	Front End Fee (%)	Back End Fee (%)	Inception Date
	7.33	13.68	34.10	44.93	131.31	0	0.95	12.04	1.06	31.79	138.7	3	97	0	0	127	23.65	-16.83			Dec-12
50	6.48	12.58	31.22	38.79	117.60	0	1.22	11.89	1.06	24.66	2,859	0	99	0	0	104	26.89	-18.79	5.25		Dec-96
50	6.29	12.27	30.32	35.66	109.39	0	2.04	11.89	1.06	19.49	2,859	0	99	0	0	104	26.2	-19.1		5.00	Nov-93
50	6.31	12.21	30.30	35.70	109.55	0	1.98	11.92	1.06	19.59	2,859	0	99	0	0	104	26.31	-19.12		1.00	Jul-97
	6.57	12.82	31.68	40.24	121.29	0	0.89	11.94	1.06	25.28	2,859	0	99	0	0	104	27.05	-18.71			Dec-10
	6.56	12.48	31.01	38.83	117.75	0	1.12	11.82	1.05	32.42	3,685	0	99	0	0	95	27.22	-18.94			Nov-93
	6.47	12.24	30.47	36.85	112.60	0	1.61	11.82	1.05	29.08	3,685	0	99	0	0	95	26.87	-19.13			Jan-03
	6.67	12.73	31.38	39.22	118.37		0.75	11.83	1.05	32.53	3,685	0	99	0	0	95	27.22	-18.94			Mar-17
	6.66	12.68	31.44	39.39	118.63	0	0.95	11.82	1.05	32.56	3,685	0	99	0	0	95	27.22	-18.94			Oct-16
	6.37	12.30	30.88	38.65	119.13	0.15	0.94	11.8	1.05	82.64	532.1	0	99	0	0	90	27.25	-18.54			Jan-95
	6.47	12.31	30.73	37.73	116.46	0	1.21	11.81	1.05	79.13	532.1	0	99	0	0	90	26.98	-18.65			May-02
50	3.04	7.28	16.89	18.36	46.88	0	1.8	7.88	0.63	13.19	82.6	34	64	0	2	147	11.28	-14.77	5.25		Nov-09
50	2.82	6.79	16.02	15.64	41.47	0	2.55	7.9	0.63	12.39	82.6	34	64	0	2	147	10.75	-14.99		1.00	Dec-10
	3.05	7.36	17.25	19.38	49.00	0	1.49	7.88	0.63	13.48	82.6	34	64	0	2	147	11.47	-14.69			Dec-10
50	6.70	15.17	38.70	31.67	31.53	0	1.55	14.51	0.88	11.33	68.0	3	97	0	0	66	15.94	-27.73	5.25		Dec-10
50	6.43	14.70	37.65	28.65	26.61	0	2.3	14.47	0.87	10.87	68.0	3	97	0	0	66	15.27	-27.92		1.00	Dec-10
	6.64	15.16	38.68	31.54	31.40	0	1.55	14.52	0.88	11.26	68.0	3	97	0	0	66	15.73	-27.67			Dec-10
	6.73	15.41	39.48	32.62	32.47	0	1.05	14.56	0.88	11.34	68.0	3	97	0	0	66	15.73	-27.67			May-16
	6.81	15.51	39.43	32.72	32.57	0	0.99	14.54	0.88	11.31	68.0	3	97	0	0	66	15.73	-27.67			May-16
	6.70	15.34	39.08	32.97	33.27	0	1.25	14.5	0.88	11.38	68.0	3	97	0	0	66	15.73	-27.67			Feb-14
50	4.59	11.02	22.83	22.16	61.29	0.83	1.5	10.04	0.88	24.29	29.1	2	97	0	1	138	20.52	-29.36	5.25		Nov-03
50	4.40	10.59	21.89	19.40	55.35	0.25	2.25	10.03	0.88	23.06	29.1	2	97	0	1	138	20.04	-29.61		1.00	Mar-08
	4.68	11.17	23.16	22.97	62.95	4.21	1.25	10.07	0.88	23.55	29.1	2	97	0	1	138	20.52	-29.36			Jun-13
	4.71	11.26	23.34	23.81	64.87	0.95	1.09	10.04	0.88	24.75	29.1	2	97	0	1	138	20.52	-29.36			May-13
50	6.37	10.27	20.63	33.28	97.99	1.23	1.14	9.61	0.95	40.56	120.2	3	97	0	0	5	21.87	-12.88	5.25		Dec-96
50	6.18	9.86	19.71	30.28	90.57	0.58	1.88	9.6	0.94	40.04	120.2	3	97	0	0	5	21.37	-13.18		1.00	Jul-97
	6.46	10.45	21.00	34.38	100.50	1.49	0.87	9.61	0.94	40.58	120.2	3	97	0	0	5	21.92	-12.88			Mar-12
	6.57	10.59	21.32	33.74	100.16	1.51	1	9.69	0.95	21.02	39.0	1	99	0	0	7	22.6	-13.99			Nov-88
50	1.83	6.37	37.15	34.93	127.54	0	1.41	20.31	1.16	24.51	157.0	1	93	0	4	93	15.45	-12.93	5.25		May-02
50	1.62	5.97	36.11	31.80	119.07	0	2.18	20.28	1.15	19.54	157.0	1	93	0	4	93	14.86	-13.16		1.00	May-02
	1.91	6.61	37.74	35.03	127.71	0	0.99	20.29	1.16	24.48	157.0	1	93	0	4	93	15.45	-12.93			May-15
50	3.89	12.27	26.69	20.49	47.62	1.37	1.35	10.98	0.83	17.05	179.3	1	99	0	0	135	24.24	-16.67	5.25		Dec-96
50	3.71	11.78	25.80	17.90	42.55	1.02	2.06	10.95	0.82	14.85	179.3	1	99	0	0	135	23.65	-16.87		5.00	Nov-86
50	3.67	11.80	25.69	17.68	41.95	0.86	2.14	10.94	0.82	14.49	179.3	1	99	0	0	135	23.41	-16.91		1.00	Jul-97
	3.97	12.32	26.87	21.13	48.54	1.53	1.15	10.98	0.83	17.05	179.3	1	99	0	0	135	23.65	-16.87			May-13
	4.01	12.52	27.27	22.12	50.97	1.73	0.89	10.98	0.83	17.19	179.3	1	99	0	0	135	24.39	-16.58			Dec-10
	4.80	10.71	28.46	28.71	98.21	0	0.88	13.16	1.13	61.6	275.0	1	98	0	0	250	24.31	-16.7			Jan-89
	4.70	10.48	27.95	27.27	94.48	0	1.27	13.17	1.13	60.04	275.0	1	98	0	0	250	23.97	-16.83			May-02
50	6.03	11.78	29.77	27.84	90.79	0	1.33	12.61	1.08	13.68	187.0	4	94	0	1	99	28.29	-27.42	5.25		Dec-96
50	5.89	11.33	28.72	25.22	84.07	0	2.05	12.6	1.08	10.93	187.0	4	94	0	1	99	27.46	-27.61		5.00	May-93
50	5.76	11.37	28.70	24.73	83.12	0	2.16	12.58	1.08	10.8	187.0	4	94	0	1	99	27.36	-27.59		1.00	Jul-97
	6.06	11.87	29.97	28.48	88.87	0	1.05	12.6	1.08	13.78	187.0	4	94	0	1	99	27.46	-27.61			May-15
	5.88	11.64	29.54	28.97	96.71	0	1.25	12.83	1.1	29.33	111.1	5	92	0	2	96	27.32	-27.08			Nov-93
	5.73	11.36	28.83	26.83	91.47	0	1.82	12.85	1.1	26.94	111.1	5	92	0	2	96	26.93	-27.23			Jan-03
	6.18	11.99	29.79	28.42	92.69	0	0.99	12.67	1.09	25	141.5	6	92	0	1	119	27.61	-27.31			May-93
	6.03	11.66	29.18	26.74	88.83	0	1.44	12.66	1.09	23.64	141.5	6	92	0	1	119	27.36	-27.48			May-02
	5.94	11.78	29.84	29.33	97.25	0	1.05	12.84	1.1	29.41	111.1	5	92	0	2	96	27.32	-27.08			Oct-16
50	5.22	10.81	27.43	32.30	91.39	0	1.31	10.52	0.96	9.94	63.3	4	96	0	0	20	24.08	-17.34	5.25		Dec-00
50	4.92	10.27	26.28	29.17	83.90	0	2.09	10.51	0.95	9.08	63.3	4	96	0	0	20	23.32	-17.53		1.00	Sep-08
	5.21	10.71	27.33	32.21	91.39	0	1.28	10.52	0.96	9.92	63.3	4	96	0	0	20	24.13	-17.37			Sep-08
	5.29	11.07	27.96	33.00	92.39	0	0.9	10.53	0.96	10	63.3	4	96	0	0	20	24.08	-17.34			Oct-16
	4.56	9.29	29.23	41.56	104.72		0.9	14.52	0.87	15.56	617.1	1	99	0	0	76	29.53	-26.75			Feb-17

	MARKET		FUND TYPE, CATEGORY & OBJECTIVE		RATINGS				MINIMUMS	
Fund Name	Ticker Symbol	Traded On	Fund Type	Category and (Prospectus Objective)	Overall Rating	Reward Rating	Risk Rating	Recent Up/ Downgrade	Open to New Investors	Min Initial Investment
Alger Small Cap Focus Fund Class A	AOFAX	NAS CM	Open End	US Equity Small Cap (Small Company)	B+	A	B	Up	Y	1,000
Alger Small Cap Focus Fund Class C	AOFCX	NAS CM	Open End	US Equity Small Cap (Small Company)	B+	A-	B	Up	Y	1,000
Alger Small Cap Focus Fund Class I	AOFIX	NAS CM	Open End	US Equity Small Cap (Small Company)	B+	A	B	Up	Y	0
Alger Small Cap Focus Fund Class Z	AGOZX	NAS CM	Open End	US Equity Small Cap (Small Company)	B+	A	B	Up	Y	500,000
Alger Small Cap Growth Fund Class A	ALSAX	NAS CM	Open End	US Equity Small Cap (Small Company)	B	A-	C	Up	Y	1,000
Alger Small Cap Growth Fund Class B	ALSCX	NAS CM	Open End	US Equity Small Cap (Small Company)	B	A-	C	Up		1,000
Alger Small Cap Growth Fund Class C	AGSCX	NAS CM	Open End	US Equity Small Cap (Small Company)	B	B+	C	Up	Y	1,000
Alger Small Cap Growth Fund Class Z	ASCZX	NAS CM	Open End	US Equity Small Cap (Small Company)	B	A-	C	Up	Y	500,000
Alger Small Cap Growth Institutional Fund Class I	ALSRX	NAS CM	Open End	US Equity Small Cap (Small Company)	B	A-	C	Up	Y	0
Alger Small Cap Growth Institutional Fund Class R	ASIRX	NAS CM	Open End	US Equity Small Cap (Small Company)	B	A-	C	Up	Y	0
Alger Small Cap Growth Portfolio Class I-2	AASOX	NAS CM	Open End	US Equity Small Cap (Small Company)	B	A-	C	Up	Y	500,000
Alger SmallCap Growth Institutional Fund Class Z-2	AISZX	NAS CM	Open End	US Equity Small Cap (Small Company)	B	A-	C	Up	Y	500,000
Alger SMid Cap Focus Fund Class A	ALMAX	NAS CM	Open End	US Equity Mid Cap (Growth)	B+	A-	B	Up	Y	1,000
Alger SMid Cap Focus Fund Class C	ALMCX	NAS CM	Open End	US Equity Mid Cap (Growth)	B+	A-	B-	Up	Y	1,000
Alger SMid Cap Focus Fund Class I	ASIMX	NAS CM	Open End	US Equity Mid Cap (Growth)	B+	A-	B	Up	Y	0
Alger SMid Cap Focus Fund Class Y	ASYMX	NAS CM	Open End	US Equity Mid Cap (Growth)	B+	A-	B		Y	500,000
Alger SMid Cap Focus Fund Class Z	ASMZX	NAS CM	Open End	US Equity Mid Cap (Growth)	B+	A	B	Up	Y	500,000
Alger SMid Cap Focus Portfolio I-2	AAMOX	NAS CM	Open End	US Equity Mid Cap (Growth)	B	A-	C+	Up	Y	500,000
Alger Spectra Fund Class A	SPECX	NAS CM	Open End	US Equity Large Cap Growth (Growth)	B+	B+	A-	Up	Y	1,000
Alger Spectra Fund Class C	ASPCX	NAS CM	Open End	US Equity Large Cap Growth (Growth)	B+	B+	B+	Up	Y	1,000
Alger Spectra Fund Class I	ASPIX	NAS CM	Open End	US Equity Large Cap Growth (Growth)	B+	B+	A-	Up	Y	0
Alger Spectra Fund Class Z	ASPZX	NAS CM	Open End	US Equity Large Cap Growth (Growth)	B+	B+	A-	Up	Y	500,000
All Asset Growth – Alt 20 Portfolio Class IA	US26884M6930		Open End	Moderate Alloc (Growth & Income)	B-	C+	B-	Down	Y	0
All Asset Growth – Alt 20 Portfolio Class IB	US29364E3062		Open End	Moderate Alloc (Growth & Income)	B-	C+	B	Down	Y	0
All Asset Growth – Alt 20 Portfolio Class K	US26883L8037		Open End	Moderate Alloc (Growth & Income)	B-	C+	B-	Down	Y	0
All Terrain Opportunity Fund Class Institutional	TERIX	NAS CM	Open End	Multialternative (Growth)	C+	C	B	Up	Y	2,500
AllianzGI Best Styles Emerging Markets Equity Fund Class A	AABSX	NAS CM	Open End	Emerging Markets Equity (Div Emerging Mkts)	C+	C+	C	Up	Y	1,000
AllianzGI Best Styles Emerging Markets Equity Fund Class C	ACBSX	NAS CM	Open End	Emerging Markets Equity (Div Emerging Mkts)	C+	C+	C	Up	Y	1,000
AllianzGI Best Styles Emerging Markets Equity Fund Class P	ASMPX	NAS CM	Open End	Emerging Markets Equity (Div Emerging Mkts)	C+	C+	C	Up	Y	1,000,000
AllianzGI Best Styles Emerging Markets Equity Fund Cls R6	ABSTX	NAS CM	Open End	Emerging Markets Equity (Div Emerging Mkts)	C+	C+	C	Up	Y	0
AllianzGI Best Styles Emerging Mkts Equity Fund Inst Cls	AEMKX	NAS CM	Open End	Emerging Markets Equity (Div Emerging Mkts)	C+	C+	C	Up	Y	1,000,000
AllianzGI Best Styles Global Equity Fund Class A	ALLGX	NAS CM	Open End	Global Equity (World Stock)	B-	B-	C+	Down	Y	1,000
AllianzGI Best Styles Global Equity Fund Class C	ABSGX	NAS CM	Open End	Global Equity (World Stock)	B-	B-	C+	Down	Y	1,000
AllianzGI Best Styles Global Equity Fund Cls Institutional	ALLHX	NAS CM	Open End	Global Equity (World Stock)	B-	B-	B-	Down	Y	1,000,000
AllianzGI Best Styles Global Equity Fund Class P	ALGPX	NAS CM	Open End	Global Equity (World Stock)	B-	B-	B-	Down	Y	1,000,000
AllianzGI Best Styles Global Equity Fund Class R6	AGERX	NAS CM	Open End	Global Equity (World Stock)	B-	B-	B-	Down	Y	0
AllianzGI Best Styles International Equity Fund Class A	AXABX	NAS CM	Open End	Global Equity Large Cap (World Stock)	C+	C+	C+	Up	Y	1,000
AllianzGI Best Styles International Equity Fund Class C	AXCBX	NAS CM	Open End	Global Equity Large Cap (World Stock)	C+	C+	C+	Up	Y	1,000
AllianzGI Best Styles International Equity Fund Class P	ASQPX	NAS CM	Open End	Global Equity Large Cap (World Stock)	C+	C+	C+	Up	Y	1,000,000
AllianzGI Best Styles International Equity Fund Class R6	ASESX	NAS CM	Open End	Global Equity Large Cap (World Stock)	C+	C+	C+	Up	Y	0
AllianzGI Best Styles Intl Equity Fund Inst Cls	ASTYX	NAS CM	Open End	Global Equity Large Cap (World Stock)	C+	C+	C+	Up	Y	1,000,000
AllianzGI Best Styles U.S. Equity Fund Class A	AABUX	NAS CM	Open End	US Equity Large Cap Blend (Growth)	B-	C+	B-	Up	Y	1,000
AllianzGI Best Styles U.S. Equity Fund Class C	ACBUX	NAS CM	Open End	US Equity Large Cap Blend (Growth)	B-	C+	B-	Up	Y	1,000
AllianzGI Best Styles U.S. Equity Fund Class P	ALBPX	NAS CM	Open End	US Equity Large Cap Blend (Growth)	B-	C+	B-	Up	Y	1,000,000
AllianzGI Best Styles U.S. Equity Fund Class R6	ALSEX	NAS CM	Open End	US Equity Large Cap Blend (Growth)	B-	C+	B-	Up	Y	0
AllianzGI Best Styles U.S. Equity Fund Institutional Class	ABTLX	NAS CM	Open End	US Equity Large Cap Blend (Growth)	B-	C+	B-	Up	Y	1,000,000
AllianzGI Convertible & Income 2024 Target Term Fund	CBH	NYSE	Closed End	Convertibles (Convertible Bond)	U	U	U		Y	
AllianzGI Convertible & Income Fund	NCV	NYSE	Closed End	Convertibles (Convertible Bond)	C+	C+	C	Up	Y	
AllianzGI Convertible & Income Fund II	NCZ	NYSE	Closed End	Convertibles (Convertible Bond)	C+	C+	C	Up	Y	
AllianzGI Convertible Fund Administrative Class	ANNAX	NAS CM	Open End	Convertibles (Convertible Bond)	C+	C+	B-	Down		1,000,000
AllianzGI Convertible Fund Class A	ANZAX	NAS CM	Open End	Convertibles (Convertible Bond)	C+	C+	B-	Down		1,000
AllianzGI Convertible Fund Class C	ANZCX	NAS CM	Open End	Convertibles (Convertible Bond)	C+	C+	C+	Down		1,000

★ Expanded analysis of this fund is included in Section II.

	TOTAL RETURNS					PERFORMANCE				ASSETS		ASSET ALLOCATION & TURNOVER					BULL & BEAR		FEES		
Min Additional Investment	3-Month Total Return	6-Month Total Return	1-Year Total Return	3-Year Total Return	5-Year Total Return	Dividend Yield (TTM)	Expense Ratio	3-Yr Std Deviation	3-Year Beta	NAV	Total Assets (MIL)	%Cash	%Stocks	%Bonds	%Other	Turnover Ratio	Last Bull Market Total Return	Last Bear Market Total Return	Front End Fee (%)	Back End Fee (%)	Inception Date
50	4.52	9.11	28.87	40.98	102.65	0	1.2	14.52	0.87	15.01	617.1	1	99	0	0	76	29.43	-26.78	5.25		Mar-08
50	4.35	8.71	27.97	38.09	95.94	0	1.95	14.48	0.87	13.65	617.1	1	99	0	0	76	28.94	-27.04		1.00	Mar-08
	4.54	9.10	28.92	41.23	104.25	0	1.2	14.51	0.87	15.39	617.1	1	99	0	0	76	29.53	-26.75			Mar-08
	4.56	9.29	29.26	42.52	107.12	0	1.01	14.48	0.87	15.56	617.1	1	99	0	0	76	29.81	-26.74			Dec-10
50	4.55	11.67	28.29	29.88	78.12	0	1.38	14.12	0.9	8.43	128.0	1	98	0	1	55	29.93	-27.12	5.25		Dec-96
50	4.19	10.94	27.23	26.61	70.99	0	2.18	14.15	0.91	6.4	128.0	1	98	0	1	55	30.27	-27.23		5.00	Nov-86
50	4.32	11.11	27.25	26.58	70.91	0	2.22	14.25	0.91	6.21	128.0	1	98	0	1	55	28.25	-27.23		1.00	Jul-97
	4.45	11.67	28.63	31.08	80.97	0	0.99	14.17	0.91	8.62	128.0	1	98	0	1	55	29.35	-26.88			Dec-10
	4.74	11.94	28.42	32.16	81.81	0	1.28	14.29	0.92	20.26	213.5	1	96	0	1	55	29.01	-26.54			Nov-93
	4.62	11.69	27.72	30.22	77.43	0	1.8	14.25	0.91	17.12	213.5	1	96	0	1	55	28.65	-26.7			Jan-03
	4.36	11.59	28.73	31.38	81.96	0	1.01	14.03	0.9	24.15	202.3	1	97	0	1	61	28.64	-26.69			Sep-88
	4.82	12.11	28.80	32.80	82.68	0	0.99	14.3	0.92	20.36	213.5	1	96	0	1	55	29.01	-26.54			Aug-16
50	7.27	14.90	37.88	38.82	96.18	0	1.35	13.95	0.98	12	195.0	4	93	0	0	164	29.33	-26.1	5.25		May-02
50	7.17	14.41	36.89	35.62	88.71	0	2.15	13.88	0.97	8.59	195.0	4	93	0	0	164	28.69	-26.32		1.00	May-02
	7.37	15.03	37.90	38.78	96.17	0	1.47	13.91	0.97	12.29	195.0	4	93	0	0	164	29.31	-26.03			Aug-07
	7.53	15.08	38.10	39.04	96.50		0.87	13.95	0.98	12.3	195.0	4	93	0	0	164	29.33	-26.1			Aug-17
	7.42	15.08	38.39	40.19	99.49	0	1.01	13.96	0.98	12.63	195.0	4	93	0	0	164	29.61	-25.96			Dec-10
	7.86	15.35	36.90	40.62	100.12	0	0.99	12.96	0.89	2.27	4.9	3	93	0	0	187	29.55	-26			Jan-08
50	6.64	12.52	31.03	39.01	116.66	0	1.21	11.89	1.04	20.57	5,947	0	99	0	0	109	26.98	-18.83	5.25		Jul-69
50	6.48	12.10	30.00	35.88	108.59	0	1.97	11.89	1.04	18.93	5,947	0	99	0	0	109	26.41	-19.08		1.00	Sep-08
	6.62	12.50	31.04	39.04	116.71	0	1.19	11.87	1.04	20.77	5,947	0	99	0	0	109	26.99	-18.8			Sep-08
	6.74	12.73	31.46	40.40	120.09	0	0.89	11.9	1.05	21.05	5,947	0	99	0	0	109	27.09	-18.73			Dec-10
	4.10	7.86	15.90	21.14	44.26	1.14	1.33	7.41	0.67		344.2	4	69	21	5	11	15.39	-15.82			Oct-09
	4.14	8.47	15.91	21.15	44.29	1.14	1.33	7.41	0.68		344.2	4	69	21	5	11	15.28	-15.9			Aug-88
	4.21	8.55	16.14	22.01	46.06	1.36	1.08	7.39	0.67		344.2	4	69	21	5	11	15.28	-15.9			Aug-12
100	2.53	4.40	8.83	9.43		2.27	2.04	3.32	0.73	25.87	33.8	-7	28	84	-6	206			5.75		Nov-14
50	5.75	13.91	35.85	29.73		5.06	0.85			16.94	7.4	8	90	0	1	44			5.50		Apr-16
50	5.50	13.46	34.69	26.79		4.74	1.6			16.89	7.4	8	90	0	1	44				1.00	Apr-16
	5.75	13.94	36.00	30.04		4.98	0.7			17.02	7.4	8	90	0	1	44					Dec-14
	5.79	13.96	36.06	30.74		4.72	0.6			17.07	7.4	8	90	0	1	44					Dec-14
	5.76	13.96	36.04	30.41		5.05	0.6			16.98	7.4	8	90	0	1	44					Dec-14
50	4.48	10.58	24.35	28.14		0	0.7	10.27	0.95	17.16	617.7	1	96	0	3	81			5.50		Sep-14
50	4.25	10.14	23.46	25.69		0.95	1.4	10.24	0.95	16.85	617.7	1	96	0	3	81				1.00	Apr-16
	4.51	10.67	24.67	29.33		1.37	0.4	10.29	0.95	16.97	617.7	1	96	0	3	81					Sep-14
	4.48	10.59	24.53	28.96		1.22	0.5	10.25	0.95	17.14	617.7	1	96	0	3	81					Dec-14
	4.51	10.69	24.68	29.54		1.44	0.4	10.26	0.95	17.1	617.7	1	96	0	3	81					Dec-13
50	3.64	10.09	25.44	24.95		8.21	0.7			15.56	26.8	0	97	0	3	70			5.50		Apr-16
50	3.37	9.63	24.56	22.17		8.12	1.45			15.45	26.8	0	97	0	3	70				1.00	Apr-16
	3.58	10.09	25.61	25.30		8.22	0.55			15.57	26.8	0	97	0	3	70					Dec-14
	3.67	10.18	25.81	26.02		8.26	0.45			15.65	26.8	0	97	0	3	70					Dec-14
	3.64	10.21	25.74	25.65		8.23	0.45			15.61	26.8	0	97	0	3	70					Dec-14
50	6.74	12.22	23.73	33.38		1.19	0.65			18.7	123.0	1	98	0	1	55			5.50		Apr-16
50	6.60	11.81	22.83	30.51		1.14	1.4			18.34	123.0	1	98	0	1	55				1.00	Apr-16
	6.78	12.26	23.91	33.82		1.19	0.5			18.5	123.0	1	98	0	1	55					Dec-14
	6.82	12.39	24.06	34.60		1.2	0.4			18.64	123.0	1	98	0	1	55					Dec-14
	6.80	12.27	23.90	34.21		1.2	0.5			18.56	123.0	1	98	0	1	55					Dec-14
	0.80	2.06					2.64			9.79	178.4	3	0	57	0						Jun-17
	2.66	4.32	11.01	13.75	45.01	11.66		12.08	0.92	6.67	593.0	3	3	41	0	28	22.17	-19.06			Mar-03
	2.59	4.21	11.25	14.06	45.38	11.03		12.22	0.92	5.98	448.7	2	3	41	0	28	22.08	-19.17			Jul-03
	2.27	6.47	14.97	18.86	60.74	2.65	0.9	8.11	1	28.59	500.3	2	0	1	0	124	16.22	-17.14			Apr-10
50	2.22	6.39	14.80	18.47	59.97	2.19	0.99	8.12	1.01	28.86	500.3	2	0	1	0	124	16.19	-17.13	5.50		Apr-10
50	2.03	6.02	14.08	15.99	54.36	1.85	1.71	8.11	1	29.03	500.3	2	0	1	0	124	15.71	-17.42		1.00	Apr-10

Fund Name	MARKET Ticker Symbol	MARKET Traded On	FUND TYPE Fund Type	Category and (Prospectus Objective)	RATINGS Overall Rating	Reward Rating	Risk Rating	Recent Up/ Downgrade	Open to New Investors	MINIMUMS Min Initial Investment
AllianzGI Convertible Fund Class P	ANCMX	NAS CM	Open End	Convertibles (Convertible Bond)	C+	C+	B-	Down		1,000,000
AllianzGI Convertible Fund Class R	ANZRX	NAS CM	Open End	Convertibles (Convertible Bond)	C+	C+	C+	Down		0
AllianzGI Convertible Fund Institutional Class	ANNPX	NAS CM	Open End	Convertibles (Convertible Bond)	C+	C+	B-	Down		1,000,000
AllianzGI Diversified Income & Convertible Fund	ACV	NYSE	Closed End	Cautious Alloc (Convertible Bond)	C+	C+	B-	Up	Y	
AllianzGI Emerging Markets Consumer Fund Class A	AMMAX	NAS CM	Open End	Emerging Markets Equity (Growth)	C+	C+	C	Up	Y	1,000
AllianzGI Emerging Markets Consumer Fund Institutional Cls	AERIX	NAS CM	Open End	Emerging Markets Equity (Growth)	C+	C+	C	Up	Y	1,000,000
AllianzGI Emerging Markets Opportunities Fund Class A	AOTAX	NAS CM	Open End	Emerging Markets Equity (Div Emerging Mkts)	C+	B-	C	Up	Y	1,000
AllianzGI Emerging Markets Opportunities Fund Class C	AOTCX	NAS CM	Open End	Emerging Markets Equity (Div Emerging Mkts)	C+	B-	C	Up	Y	1,000
AllianzGI Emerging Markets Opportunities Fund Class P	AEMPX	NAS CM	Open End	Emerging Markets Equity (Div Emerging Mkts)	C+	B-	C	Up	Y	1,000,000
AllianzGI Emerging Mkts Opp Fund Inst Cls	AOTIX	NAS CM	Open End	Emerging Markets Equity (Div Emerging Mkts)	C+	B-	C	Up	Y	1,000,000
AllianzGI Emerging Markets Opportunities Fund R6	AEMOX	NAS CM	Open End	Emerging Markets Equity (Div Emerging Mkts)	C+	B-	C	Up	Y	0
AllianzGI Emerging Markets Small-Cap Fund Class A	ALMMX	NAS CM	Open End	Emerging Markets Equity (Small Company)	C+	C+	C	Up	Y	1,000
AllianzGI Emerging Mkts Small-Cap Fund Inst Cls	ALAIX	NAS CM	Open End	Emerging Markets Equity (Small Company)	C+	C+	C	Up	Y	1,000,000
AllianzGI Equity & Convertible Income Fund	NIE	NYSE	Closed End	Aggressive Alloc (Growth & Income)	B-	B-	B-	Up	Y	
AllianzGI Europe Equity Dividend Fund Class A	EEDFX	NAS CM	Open End	Europe Equity Large Cap (Europe Stock)	C+	C+	B-	Up	Y	1,000
AllianzGI Europe Equity Dividend Fund Class C	EEDCX	NAS CM	Open End	Europe Equity Large Cap (Europe Stock)	C+	C+	B-	Up	Y	1,000
AllianzGI Europe Equity Dividend Fund Class P	EEDPX	NAS CM	Open End	Europe Equity Large Cap (Europe Stock)	C+	C+	B-	Up	Y	1,000,000
AllianzGI Europe Equity Dividend Fund Institutional Class	EEDIX	NAS CM	Open End	Europe Equity Large Cap (Europe Stock)	C+	C+	B-	Up	Y	1,000,000
AllianzGI Focused Growth Fund Administrative Class	PGFAX	NAS CM	Open End	US Equity Large Cap Growth (Growth)	A-	A	A-	Up	Y	1,000,000
AllianzGI Focused Growth Fund Class A	PGWAX	NAS CM	Open End	US Equity Large Cap Growth (Growth)	A-	A	A-	Up	Y	1,000
AllianzGI Focused Growth Fund Class C	PGWCX	NAS CM	Open End	US Equity Large Cap Growth (Growth)	A-	A-	A-	Up	Y	1,000
AllianzGI Focused Growth Fund Class P	AOGPX	NAS CM	Open End	US Equity Large Cap Growth (Growth)	A-	A	A-	Up	Y	1,000,000
AllianzGI Focused Growth Fund Class R	PPGRX	NAS CM	Open End	US Equity Large Cap Growth (Growth)	A-	A-	A-	Up	Y	0
AllianzGI Focused Growth Fund Institutional Class	PGFIX	NAS CM	Open End	US Equity Large Cap Growth (Growth)	A-	A	A-	Up	Y	1,000,000
AllianzGI Focused Growth Fund R6	AFGFX	NAS CM	Open End	US Equity Large Cap Growth (Growth)	A-	A	A-	Up	Y	0
AllianzGI Global Allocation Fund Administrative Class	AGAMX	NAS CM	Open End	Alloc (Asset Alloc)	B-	C+	B+	Up	Y	1,000,000
AllianzGI Global Allocation Fund Class A	PALAX	NAS CM	Open End	Alloc (Asset Alloc)	B-	C+	B+	Up	Y	1,000
AllianzGI Global Allocation Fund Class C	PALCX	NAS CM	Open End	Alloc (Asset Alloc)	B-	C+	B	Up	Y	1,000
AllianzGI Global Allocation Fund Class P	AGAPX	NAS CM	Open End	Alloc (Asset Alloc)	B	C+	B+	Up	Y	1,000,000
AllianzGI Global Allocation Fund Class R	AGARX	NAS CM	Open End	Alloc (Asset Alloc)	B-	C+	B+	Up	Y	0
AllianzGI Global Allocation Fund Class R6	AGASX	NAS CM	Open End	Alloc (Asset Alloc)	B	C+	B+	Up	Y	0
AllianzGI Global Allocation Fund Institutional Class	PALLX	NAS CM	Open End	Alloc (Asset Alloc)	B-	C+	B+	Up	Y	1,000,000
AllianzGI Global Dynamic Allocation Fund Admin Cls	AGFAX	NAS CM	Open End	Moderate Alloc (Asset Alloc)	B-	C+	B	Up	Y	1,000,000
AllianzGI Global Dynamic Allocation Fund Class A	ASGAX	NAS CM	Open End	Moderate Alloc (Asset Alloc)	B-	C+	B	Up	Y	1,000
AllianzGI Global Dynamic Allocation Fund Class C	ASACX	NAS CM	Open End	Moderate Alloc (Asset Alloc)	B-	C+	B	Up	Y	1,000
AllianzGI Global Dynamic Allocation Fund Class P	AGSPX	NAS CM	Open End	Moderate Alloc (Asset Alloc)	B-	C+	B	Up	Y	1,000,000
AllianzGI Global Dynamic Allocation Fund Class R	ASFRX	NAS CM	Open End	Moderate Alloc (Asset Alloc)	B-	C+	B	Up	Y	0
AllianzGI Global Dynamic Allocation Fund Class R6	ADYFX	NAS CM	Open End	Moderate Alloc (Asset Alloc)	B-	C+	B+	Down	Y	0
AllianzGI Global Dynamic Allocation Fund Institutional Cls	AGAIX	NAS CM	Open End	Moderate Alloc (Asset Alloc)	B-	C+	B+	Down	Y	1,000,000
AllianzGI Global Fundamental Strategy Fund Class A	AZDAX	NAS CM	Open End	Alloc (Growth & Income)	B-	C+	B+	Up	Y	1,000
AllianzGI Global Fundamental Strategy Fund Class C	AZDCX	NAS CM	Open End	Alloc (Growth & Income)	B-	C	B	Up	Y	1,000
AllianzGI Global Fundamental Strategy Fund Class P	AZDPX	NAS CM	Open End	Alloc (Growth & Income)	B-	C+	B+	Up	Y	1,000,000
AllianzGI Global Fundamental Strategy Fund Inst Cls	AZDIX	NAS CM	Open End	Alloc (Growth & Income)	B-	C+	B+	Up	Y	1,000,000
AllianzGI Global Natural Resources Fund Class A	ARMAX	NAS CM	Open End	Natl Resources Sec Equity (Natl Res)	D+	D+	C-	Up	Y	1,000
AllianzGI Global Natural Resources Fund Class C	ARMCX	NAS CM	Open End	Natl Resources Sec Equity (Natl Res)	D+	D+	D+	Up	Y	1,000
AllianzGI Global Natural Resources Fund Class P	APGPX	NAS CM	Open End	Natl Resources Sec Equity (Natl Res)	C-	D+	C-	Up	Y	1,000,000
AllianzGI Global Natural Resources Fund Institutional Cls	RGLIX	NAS CM	Open End	Natl Resources Sec Equity (Natl Res)	C-	D+	C-	Up	Y	1,000,000
AllianzGI Global Small-Cap Fund Class A	RGSAX	NAS CM	Open End	Global Equity Mid/Small Cap (World Stock)	B	B	B	Up	Y	1,000
AllianzGI Global Small-Cap Fund Class C	RGSCX	NAS CM	Open End	Global Equity Mid/Small Cap (World Stock)	B	B-	B	Up	Y	1,000
AllianzGI Global Small-Cap Fund Class P	ARSPX	NAS CM	Open End	Global Equity Mid/Small Cap (World Stock)	B	B	B	Up	Y	1,000,000
AllianzGI Global Small-Cap Fund Institutional Class	DGSCX	NAS CM	Open End	Global Equity Mid/Small Cap (World Stock)	B	B	B	Up	Y	1,000,000
AllianzGI Global Sustainability Fund Class A	ASUAX	NAS CM	Open End	Global Equity (Growth)	B-	C+	B	Up	Y	1,000

★Expanded analysis of this fund is included in Section II.

Min Additional Investment	TOTAL RETURNS: 3-Month Total Return	6-Month Total Return	1-Year Total Return	3-Year Total Return	5-Year Total Return	PERFORMANCE: Dividend Yield (TTM)	Expense Ratio	3-Yr Std Deviation	3-Year Beta	ASSETS: NAV	Total Assets (MIL)	ASSET ALLOCATION & TURNOVER: %Cash	%Stocks	%Bonds	%Other	Turnover Ratio	BULL & BEAR: Last Bull Market Total Return	Last Bear Market Total Return	FEES: Front End Fee (%)	Back End Fee (%)	Inception Date
	2.30	6.55	15.18	19.51	62.05	2.83	0.73	8.1	1	28.3	500.3	2	0	1	0	124	16.31	-17.09			Jun-10
	2.13	6.30	14.48	17.14	56.87	1.96	1.43	8.11	1.01	29.85	500.3	2	0	1	0	124	16.04	-17.26			Apr-10
	2.30	6.58	15.22	19.66	62.60	2.79	0.67	8.1	1	28.55	500.3	2	0	1	0	124	16.38	-17.04			Apr-93
	4.02	8.00	17.77			0.41	2.69			22.77	234.8	3	25	21	0	196					May-15
50	7.42	12.12	35.88	20.95		0.7	1.56			16.04	46.0	3	96	0	1	122			5.50		Dec-14
	7.52	12.34	36.32	22.30		0.92	1.21			16.19	46.0	3	96	0	1	122					Dec-14
50	6.90	15.39	37.89	24.24	26.16	1.34	1.27	13.76	0.84	30.36	286.0	2	95	0	2	155	17.36	-29.08	5.50		Aug-06
50	6.67	14.96	36.85	21.51	21.53	0.39	2.02	13.77	0.84	29.96	286.0	2	95	0	2	155	16.9	-29.33		1.00	Aug-06
	6.95	15.53	38.25	25.20	27.76	1.5	1.02	13.78	0.84	29.78	286.0	2	95	0	2	155	17.55	-29.02			Jul-08
	6.99	15.61	38.36	25.59	28.41	1.43	0.92	13.78	0.84	30.51	286.0	2	95	0	2	155	17.57	-28.97			May-04
	7.00	15.62	38.45	25.68	28.51	1.66	0.87	13.77	0.84	30.35	286.0	2	95	0	2	155	17.57	-28.97			Dec-15
50	4.77	11.00	32.03	34.30		0	1.85			17.89	11.8	2	96	0	1	121			5.50		Dec-14
	4.92	11.27	32.55	35.75		2.43	1.5			17.68	11.8	2	96	0	1	121					Dec-14
	5.65	10.16	16.78	24.59	71.14	1.89	1.12	8.89		23.15	646.5	2	66	1	0	90	19.83	-17.24			Feb-07
50	1.61	8.47	22.08			3.79	1.2			16.23	10.1	1	99	0	0	71			5.50		Feb-15
50	1.38	7.98	21.12			2.81	1.95			16.29	10.1	1	99	0	0	71				1.00	Feb-15
	1.69	8.53	22.21			3.61	1.05			16.3	10.1	1	99	0	0	71					Feb-15
	1.69	8.60	22.37			3.41	0.95			16.4	10.1	1	99	0	0	71					Feb-15
	7.88	14.93	31.56	46.23	127.56	0	0.91	11.04	0.99	45.86	1,038	0	100	0	0	46	26.27	-16.8			Mar-99
50	7.84	14.87	31.45	45.81	126.38	0	0.99	11.04	0.99	52.85	1,038	0	100	0	0	46	26.22	-16.84	5.50		Oct-90
50	7.64	14.44	30.44	42.57	118.06	0	1.76	11.02	0.98	36.79	1,038	0	100	0	0	46	25.67	-17.12		1.00	Feb-84
	7.90	15.00	31.72	46.88	129.17	0	0.76	11.04	0.99	41.03	1,038	0	100	0	0	46	26.38	-16.74			Jul-08
	7.76	14.71	31.09	44.72	123.49	0	1.26	11.03	0.99	40.54	1,038	0	100	0	0	46	26.04	-16.92			Dec-02
	7.92	15.05	31.88	47.30	130.29	0	0.66	11.03	0.99	48.75	1,038	0	100	0	0	46	26.47	-16.72			Mar-99
	7.95	15.10	31.93	45.90	123.15	0	0.61	11.03	0.99	48.78	1,038	0	100	0	0	46	25.67	-17.12			Dec-15
	3.35	7.68	16.98	18.43	35.48	1.9	0.98	6.11	0.54	11.9	364.7	13	47	11	29	15	14.28	-15.46			May-09
50	3.35	7.60	16.89	18.28	35.31	1.62	1.03	6.1	0.54	11.6	364.7	13	47	11	29	15	14.17	-15.43	5.50		Sep-98
50	3.19	7.28	16.06	15.67	30.38	0.75	1.8	6.1	0.54	11.82	364.7	13	47	11	29	15	13.7	-15.77		1.00	Sep-98
	3.36	7.69	17.19	19.21	37.02	2.47	0.83	6.09	0.54	11.5	364.7	13	47	11	29	15	14.37	-15.4			May-09
	3.28	7.54	16.63	17.61	34.20	1.77	1.23	6.07	0.54	11.47	364.7	13	47	11	29	15	14	-15.59			May-09
	3.35	7.74	17.18	19.11	36.27	2.53	0.73	6.12	0.54	11.35	364.7	13	47	11	29	15	14.17	-15.43			Sep-15
	3.37	7.69	16.94	18.88	36.75	2.19	0.83	6.07	0.54	11.57	364.7	13	47	11	29	15	14.45	-15.37			Feb-99
	3.49	7.96	16.73	16.86	37.33	0	1.02	5.88	0.51	20.26	290.0	10	55	33	2	192	18.9	-20.72			Apr-09
50	3.54	8.01	16.80	16.91	37.33	0	1.02	5.9	0.51	20.31	290.0	10	55	33	2	192	18.85	-20.72	5.50		Apr-09
50	3.29	7.58	15.89	14.20	32.03	0	1.79	5.9	0.51	19.79	290.0	10	55	33	2	192	18.35	-20.96		1.00	Apr-09
	3.59	8.07	17.01	17.49	38.45	0.49	0.85	5.9	0.51	20.17	290.0	10	55	33	2	192	19	-20.66			Apr-09
	3.41	7.81	16.33	15.87	35.47	0	1.39	5.89	0.51	20.15	290.0	10	55	33	2	192	18.7	-20.81			Apr-09
	3.59	8.17	17.09	17.94	39.27	0.41	0.75	5.9	0.51	20.23	290.0	10	55	33	2	192	19.06	-20.61			Feb-16
	3.58	8.09	17.04	17.74	39.04	0.06	0.75	5.91	0.51	20.3	290.0	10	55	33	2	192	19.06	-20.61			Apr-09
50	0.57	4.28	9.77	13.38		2.07	1.12	5.56	85.55	15.39	17.2	14	44	38	4	49			5.50		Jul-13
50	0.43	3.94	8.97	10.85		1.81	1.87	5.58	85	15.4	17.2	14	44	38	4	49				1.00	Jul-13
	0.58	4.33	9.87	13.83		2.27	0.97	5.62	85.09	15.5	17.2	14	44	38	4	49					Jul-13
	0.61	4.42	10.01	14.24		2.15	0.87	5.6	83.06	15.56	17.2	14	44	38	4	49					Jul-13
50	7.73	15.32	-0.93	-2.77	2.70	0.87	1.42	18.69	1.11	15.85	24.4	0	96	0	4	108	19.53	-31.02	5.50		Mar-06
50	7.52	14.83	-1.65	-4.95	-1.03	0.03	2.17	18.67	1.1	14.86	24.4	0	96	0	4	108	19.06	-31.24		1.00	Mar-06
	7.75	15.39	-0.73	-2.08	4.00	0.99	1.17	18.68	1.11	16.12	24.4	0	96	0	4	108	19.7	-30.94			Jul-08
	7.77	15.48	-0.57	-1.80	4.51	0.84	1.07	18.7	1.1	16.25	24.4	0	96	0	4	108	19.82	-30.94			Jun-04
50	6.35	14.05	26.86	30.54	83.74	0	1.61	11.23	0.95	50.07	205.5	3	95	0	1	80	25.96	-23.75	5.50		Feb-02
50	6.15	13.63	25.92	27.64	77.00	0	2.36	11.22	0.95	44.13	205.5	3	95	0	1	80	25.42	-23.99		1.00	Feb-02
	6.43	14.20	27.19	31.53	86.09	0	1.36	11.23	0.95	53.1	205.5	3	95	0	1	80	26.13	-23.69			Jul-08
	6.45	14.26	27.32	31.93	87.00	0	1.26	11.23	0.95	53.5	205.5	3	95	0	1	80	26.21	-23.63			Dec-96
50	4.85	9.93	24.29	30.37		0.75	1.09			18.18	28.1	2	98	0	0	27			5.50		Dec-14

	MARKET			FUND TYPE, CATEGORY & OBJECTIVE	RATINGS					MINIMUMS
Fund Name	Ticker Symbol	Traded On	Fund Type	Category and (Prospectus Objective)	Overall Rating	Reward Rating	Risk Rating	Recent Up/ Downgrade	Open to New Investors	Min Initial Investment
AllianzGI Global Sustainability Fund Class P	ASTPX	NAS CM	Open End	Global Equity (Growth)	B-	C+	B	Up	Y	1,000,000
AllianzGI Global Sustainability Fund Institutional Class	ASTNX	NAS CM	Open End	Global Equity (Growth)	B-	C+	B	Up	Y	1,000,000
AllianzGI Global Water Fund Class A	AWTAX	NAS CM	Open End	Natl Resources Sec Equity (Natl Res)	B	B	B+	Up	Y	1,000
AllianzGI Global Water Fund Class C	AWTCX	NAS CM	Open End	Natl Resources Sec Equity (Natl Res)	B	B-	B	Up	Y	1,000
AllianzGI Global Water Fund Class P	AWTPX	NAS CM	Open End	Natl Resources Sec Equity (Natl Res)	B	B	B+	Up	Y	1,000,000
AllianzGI Global Water Fund Institutional Class	AWTIX	NAS CM	Open End	Natl Resources Sec Equity (Natl Res)	B	B	B+	Up	Y	1,000,000
AllianzGI Health Sciences Fund Class A	RAGHX	NAS CM	Open End	Healthcare Sector Equity (Health)	C+	C	B	Down	Y	1,000
AllianzGI Health Sciences Fund Class C	RCGHX	NAS CM	Open End	Healthcare Sector Equity (Health)	C+	C	B	Down	Y	1,000
AllianzGI Health Sciences Fund Institutional Class	HLHIX	NAS CM	Open End	Healthcare Sector Equity (Health)	C+	C	B	Down	Y	1,000,000
AllianzGI Income & Growth Fund Class A	AZNAX	NAS CM	Open End	Cautious Alloc (Growth & Income)	B-	C+	B	Down	Y	1,000
AllianzGI Income & Growth Fund Class C	AZNCX	NAS CM	Open End	Cautious Alloc (Growth & Income)	B-	C+	B-	Down	Y	1,000
AllianzGI Income & Growth Fund Class P	AIGPX	NAS CM	Open End	Cautious Alloc (Growth & Income)	B-	C+	B	Down	Y	1,000,000
AllianzGI Income & Growth Fund Class R	AIGRX	NAS CM	Open End	Cautious Alloc (Growth & Income)	B-	C+	B	Down	Y	0
AllianzGI Income & Growth Fund Institutional Class	AZNIX	NAS CM	Open End	Cautious Alloc (Growth & Income)	B-	C+	B	Down	Y	1,000,000
AllianzGI International Growth Fund Class A	AIGFX	NAS CM	Open End	Global Equity Large Cap (Growth)	B-	C+	B-	Up	Y	1,000
AllianzGI International Growth Fund Institutional Class	GLIIX	NAS CM	Open End	Global Equity Large Cap (Growth)	B-	C+	B-	Up	Y	1,000,000
AllianzGI International Small-Cap Fund Class A	AOPAX	NAS CM	Open End	Global Equity Mid/Small Cap (Foreign Stock)	B+	A-	B	Up	Y	1,000
AllianzGI International Small-Cap Fund Class C	AOPCX	NAS CM	Open End	Global Equity Mid/Small Cap (Foreign Stock)	B+	A-	B	Up	Y	1,000
AllianzGI International Small-Cap Fund Class P	ALOPX	NAS CM	Open End	Global Equity Mid/Small Cap (Foreign Stock)	B+	A-	B	Up	Y	1,000,000
AllianzGI International Small-Cap Fund Class R	ALORX	NAS CM	Open End	Global Equity Mid/Small Cap (Foreign Stock)	B+	A-	B	Up	Y	0
AllianzGI International Small-Cap Fund Class R6	AIISX	NAS CM	Open End	Global Equity Mid/Small Cap (Foreign Stock)	B+	A-	B	Up	Y	0
AllianzGI International Small-Cap Fund Institutional Class	ALOIX	NAS CM	Open End	Global Equity Mid/Small Cap (Foreign Stock)	B+	A-	B	Up	Y	1,000,000
AllianzGI Micro Cap Fund Class A	GMCAX	NAS CM	Open End	US Equity Small Cap (Growth)	B	B	B	Up	Y	1,000
AllianzGI Micro Cap Fund Class P	AAMPX	NAS CM	Open End	US Equity Small Cap (Growth)	B	B	B	Up	Y	1,000,000
AllianzGI Micro Cap Fund Institutional Class	AMCIX	NAS CM	Open End	US Equity Small Cap (Growth)	B	B	B	Up	Y	1,000,000
AllianzGI Mid-Cap Fund Administrative Class	DRMAX	NAS CM	Open End	US Equity Mid Cap (Growth)	B	B	B-		Y	1,000,000
AllianzGI Mid-Cap Fund Class A	RMDAX	NAS CM	Open End	US Equity Mid Cap (Growth)	B	B	B-	Up	Y	1,000
AllianzGI Mid-Cap Fund Class C	RMDCX	NAS CM	Open End	US Equity Mid Cap (Growth)	B	B	B	Up	Y	1,000
AllianzGI Mid-Cap Fund Class P	ARMPX	NAS CM	Open End	US Equity Mid Cap (Growth)	B	B+	B-		Y	1,000,000
AllianzGI Mid-Cap Fund Class R	PRMRX	NAS CM	Open End	US Equity Mid Cap (Growth)	B	B	B-	Up	Y	0
AllianzGI Mid-Cap Fund Institutional Class	DRMCX	NAS CM	Open End	US Equity Mid Cap (Growth)	B	B	B+		Y	1,000,000
AllianzGI NFJ Dividend Interest & Premium Strategy Fund	NFJ	NYSE	Closed End	Aggressive Alloc (Equity-Income)	C+	C+	B-	Up	Y	
AllianzGI NFJ Dividend Value Fund Administrative Class	ANDAX	NAS CM	Open End	US Equity Large Cap Value (Equity-Income)	B-	B-	C+	Down	Y	1,000,000
AllianzGI NFJ Dividend Value Fund Class A	PNEAX	NAS CM	Open End	US Equity Large Cap Value (Equity-Income)	B-	B-	C+	Down	Y	1,000
AllianzGI NFJ Dividend Value Fund Class C	PNECX	NAS CM	Open End	US Equity Large Cap Value (Equity-Income)	C+	C+	C+	Down	Y	1,000
AllianzGI NFJ Dividend Value Fund Class P	ADJPX	NAS CM	Open End	US Equity Large Cap Value (Equity-Income)	B-	B-	C+	Down	Y	1,000,000
AllianzGI NFJ Dividend Value Fund Class R	PNERX	NAS CM	Open End	US Equity Large Cap Value (Equity-Income)	C+	B-	C+	Down	Y	0
AllianzGI NFJ Dividend Value Fund Class R6	ANDVX	NAS CM	Open End	US Equity Large Cap Value (Equity-Income)	B-	B-	C+	Down	Y	0
AllianzGI NFJ Dividend Value Fund Institutional Class	NFJEX	NAS CM	Open End	US Equity Large Cap Value (Equity-Income)	B-	B-	C+	Down	Y	1,000,000
AllianzGI NFJ Emerging Markets Value Fund Class A	AZMAX	NAS CM	Open End	Emerging Markets Equity (Div Emerging Mkts)	B	B	C+	Up	Y	1,000
AllianzGI NFJ Emerging Markets Value Fund Class C	AZMCX	NAS CM	Open End	Emerging Markets Equity (Div Emerging Mkts)	B	B	C+	Up	Y	1,000
AllianzGI NFJ Emerging Markets Value Fund Class P	AZMPX	NAS CM	Open End	Emerging Markets Equity (Div Emerging Mkts)	B	B+	C+	Up	Y	1,000,000
AllianzGI NFJ Emerging Mkts Value Fund Inst Cls	AZMIX	NAS CM	Open End	Emerging Markets Equity (Div Emerging Mkts)	B	B+	C+	Up	Y	1,000,000
AllianzGI NFJ International Small-Cap Value Fund Class A	AJVAX	NAS CM	Open End	Global Equity Mid/Small Cap (Small Company)	B-	B-	B	Up	Y	1,000
AllianzGI NFJ International Small-Cap Value Fund Class C	AJVCX	NAS CM	Open End	Global Equity Mid/Small Cap (Small Company)	B-	C+	B	Up	Y	1,000
AllianzGI NFJ International Small-Cap Value Fund Class P	AJVPX	NAS CM	Open End	Global Equity Mid/Small Cap (Small Company)	B-	B-	B	Up	Y	1,000,000
AllianzGI NFJ International Small-Cap Value Fund Class R6	AJVSX	NAS CM	Open End	Global Equity Mid/Small Cap (Small Company)	B-	B-	B	Up	Y	0
AllianzGI NFJ Intl Small-Cap Value Fund Inst Cls	AJVIX	NAS CM	Open End	Global Equity Mid/Small Cap (Small Company)	B-	B-	B	Up	Y	1,000,000
AllianzGI NFJ International Value Fund Administrative Cls	AIVAX	NAS CM	Open End	Global Equity Large Cap (Foreign Stock)	C	C	C	Up	Y	1,000,000
AllianzGI NFJ International Value Fund Class A	AFJAX	NAS CM	Open End	Global Equity Large Cap (Foreign Stock)	C	C	C	Up	Y	1,000
AllianzGI NFJ International Value Fund Class C	AFJCX	NAS CM	Open End	Global Equity Large Cap (Foreign Stock)	C	C	C	Up	Y	1,000
AllianzGI NFJ International Value Fund Class P	AFVPX	NAS CM	Open End	Global Equity Large Cap (Foreign Stock)	C	C	C	Up	Y	1,000,000

★Expanded analysis of this fund is included in Section II.

Min Additional Investment	3-Month Total Return	6-Month Total Return	1-Year Total Return	3-Year Total Return	5-Year Total Return	Dividend Yield (TTM)	Expense Ratio	3-Yr Std Deviation	3-Year Beta	NAV	Total Assets (MIL)	%Cash	%Stocks	%Bonds	%Other	Turnover Ratio	Last Bull Market Total Return	Last Bear Market Total Return	Front End Fee (%)	Back End Fee (%)	Inception Date
	TOTAL RETURNS					PERFORMANCE				ASSETS		ASSET ALLOCATION & TURNOVER					BULL & BEAR		FEES		
	4.89	9.99	24.46	30.96		0.68	0.94			18.36	28.1	2	98	0	0	27					Dec-14
	4.87	10.03	24.51	31.28		0.82	0.84			18.38	28.1	2	98	0	0	27					Dec-14
50	3.90	9.34	22.30	27.87	59.45	0.29	1.27	9.73	0.76	15.67	668.5	5	95	0	0	29	22.07	-19.84	5.50		Mar-08
50	3.66	8.88	21.35	24.92	53.21	0	2.03	9.73	0.76	14.98	668.5	5	95	0	0	29	21.52	-20.17		1.00	Mar-08
	3.99	9.48	22.67	28.91	61.38	0.49	1.02	9.76	0.76	15.68	668.5	5	95	0	0	29	22.16	-19.78			Mar-08
	3.96	9.46	22.70	28.93	61.81	0.68	0.99	9.72	0.76	15.4	668.5	5	95	0	0	29	22.31	-19.8			Jul-08
50	-1.85	0.47	17.32	19.97	104.80	0	1.46	14.52	1.14	31.76	158.6	3	97	0	0	82	19.88	-14.96	5.50		Feb-02
50	-2.01	0.11	16.45	17.33	97.28	0	2.21	14.5	1.13	25.33	158.6	3	97	0	0	82	19.39	-15.23		1.00	Feb-02
	-1.74	0.65	17.74	21.25	106.98	0	1.11	14.52	1.14	32.11	158.6	3	97	0	0	82	19.88	-14.96			Dec-14
50	3.40	6.54	13.45	20.99	52.58	2.26	1.29	7.27	-0.36	11.48	3,426	2	36	31	0	159	16.01	-14.42	5.50		Feb-07
50	3.20	6.18	12.62	18.34	46.99	1.84	2.04	7.31	-0.36	10.63	3,426	2	36	31	0	159	15.4	-14.6		1.00	Feb-07
	3.47	6.70	13.79	21.90	54.41	2.42	1.04	7.33	-0.34	11.74	3,426	2	36	31	0	159	16.16	-14.31			Jul-08
	3.34	6.41	13.17	20.07	50.55	2.03	1.54	7.31	-0.34	11.48	3,426	2	36	31	0	159	15.82	-14.43			Feb-11
	3.47	6.69	13.86	22.25	55.15	2.48	0.94	7.3	-0.36	11.84	3,426	2	36	31	0	159	16.24	-14.26			Feb-07
50	4.95	13.65	38.69			0	1.05			18.02	19.4	1	98	0	1	18			5.50		Feb-15
	4.99	13.80	39.01			0.08	0.8			18.4	19.4	1	98	0	1	18					Feb-15
50	7.64	18.01	39.03	47.58	81.32	0.73	1.25	11.76	0.88	43.4	171.5	4	94	0	2	67	17.79	-24.53	5.50		Apr-10
50	7.39	17.52	37.89	44.18	74.54	0.59	2.08	11.77	0.88	42.18	171.5	4	94	0	2	67	17.25	-24.77		1.00	Apr-10
	7.66	18.09	39.22	48.26	82.81	0.79	1.1	11.78	0.88	43.32	171.5	4	94	0	2	67	17.93	-24.43			Dec-97
	7.55	17.83	38.58	46.32	78.95	0.75	1.59	11.77	0.88	42.31	171.5	4	94	0	2	67	17.58	-24.61			Apr-10
	7.72	18.19	39.40	48.75	83.67	0.78	1	11.78	0.88	44.88	171.5	4	94	0	2	67	18.03	-24.41			Feb-16
	7.68	18.13	39.28	48.54	83.42	0.77	1.07	11.79	0.88	44.9	171.5	4	94	0	2	67	18.03	-24.41			Dec-97
50	-0.19	5.95	14.47	31.63	101.48	0	1.62	16.88	0.93	14.94	32.3	1	99	0	0	32	38.87	-35.46	5.50		Dec-11
	-0.18	5.92	14.45	31.91	102.42	0	1.54	16.89	0.93	15.03	32.3	1	99	0	0	32	39	-35.45			Dec-10
	-0.25	5.96	14.45	31.83	102.40	0	1.54	16.88	0.93	15.11	32.3	1	99	0	0	32	39.08	-35.39			Jul-95
	6.00	10.57	24.83	36.59	106.14	0	1.03	12.34	1.07	3.98	314.1	1	99	0	0	77	25.65	-22.87			Feb-02
50	6.35	10.90	24.93	36.45	105.92	0	1.13	12.36	1.07	3.77	314.1	1	99	0	0	77	25.57	-22.65	5.50		Feb-02
50	5.92	10.24	23.82	33.02	97.71	0	1.88	12.34	1.07	3.14	314.1	1	99	0	0	77	24.86	-22.9		1.00	Feb-02
	6.35	10.92	25.27	37.44	108.61	0	0.88	12.41	1.07	4.27	314.1	1	99	0	0	77	25.84	-22.76			Apr-12
	6.14	10.74	24.21	35.41	103.35	0	1.38	12.46	1.08	3.71	314.1	1	99	0	0	77	25.56	-22.89			Dec-02
	6.06	10.84	25.11	37.58	109.29	0	0.78	12.32	1.07	4.29	314.1	1	99	0	0	77	25.91	-22.72			Nov-79
	3.63	6.12	9.15	9.41	36.78	0.5		7.79	0.89	14.74	1,412	1	71	1	0	39	18.3	-15.63			Feb-05
	6.53	11.34	15.80	21.55	76.23	1.97	0.84	10.96	1.02	15.42	2,687	0	100	0	0	41	21.46	-16.66			May-00
50	6.51	11.30	15.69	21.22	75.42	1.91	0.94	10.98	1.02	15.14	2,687	0	100	0	0	41	21.46	-16.79	5.50		Oct-01
50	6.32	10.91	14.84	18.48	68.94	1.21	1.69	11	1.02	15.3	2,687	0	100	0	0	41	20.89	-17		1.00	Oct-01
	6.60	11.49	15.99	22.12	77.53	2.11	0.69	10.98	1.02	15.26	2,687	0	100	0	0	41	21.65	-16.65			Jul-08
	6.46	11.18	15.44	20.30	73.23	1.69	1.19	11	1.02	15.09	2,687	0	100	0	0	41	21.26	-16.79			Dec-02
	6.65	11.53	16.20	22.66	78.71	2.24	0.54	10.98	1.02	15.22	2,687	0	100	0	0	41	21.71	-16.59			Dec-13
	6.61	11.47	16.08	22.44	78.36	2.17	0.59	11.03	1.02	15.25	2,687	0	100	0	0	41	21.71	-16.59			May-00
50	6.69	13.97	37.47	40.17	41.07	1.8	1.14	15.3	0.95	18.17	81.5	5	92	0	0	120			5.50		Dec-12
50	6.46	13.59	36.44	37.04	35.91	0.61	1.89	15.27	0.95	18.38	81.5	5	92	0	0	120				1.00	Dec-12
	6.70	14.07	37.69	40.94	42.28	2.37	0.98	15.26	0.95	18.14	81.5	5	92	0	0	120					Dec-12
	6.77	14.17	37.86	41.32	42.93	1.73	0.89	15.29	0.95	18.45	81.5	5	92	0	0	120					Dec-12
50	3.25	10.85	27.89	25.17	58.60	2.65	1.3	12.21	1	20.97	4.5	2	94	0	5	48			5.50		Jun-12
50	3.04	10.38	26.87	22.37	52.90	4.86	2.05	12.18	1	20.3	4.5	2	94	0	5	48				1.00	Jun-12
	3.32	10.95	28.19	25.85	59.92	6.16	1.05	12.2	1	20.29	4.5	2	94	0	5	48					Jun-12
	3.33	10.97	28.28	26.40	60.98	6.96	0.95	12.17	1	20.13	4.5	2	94	0	5	48					Sep-15
	3.31	10.99	28.20	26.19	60.72	4.75	1.01	12.21	1	20.94	4.5	2	94	0	5	48					Jun-12
	3.76	9.61	22.88	-0.74	4.96	2.07	1.2	13.07	1.04	19.83	396.4	0	98	0	2	63	19.41	-23.02			May-10
50	3.77	9.60	22.81	-1.01	4.48	1.98	1.3	13.08	1.04	19.77	396.4	0	98	0	2	63	19.39	-23.1	5.50		Apr-05
50	3.57	9.15	21.85	-3.21	0.62	1.33	2.05	13.08	1.04	19.43	396.4	0	98	0	2	63	18.78	-23.32		1.00	Apr-05
	3.81	9.69	23.02	-0.31	5.72	2.19	1.05	13.07	1.04	19.86	396.4	0	98	0	2	63	19.5	-22.98			Jul-08

	MARKET		FUND TYPE, CATEGORY & OBJECTIVE			RATINGS				MINIMUMS
Fund Name	Ticker Symbol	Traded On	Fund Type	Category and (Prospectus Objective)	Overall Rating	Reward Rating	Risk Rating	Recent Up/ Downgrade	Open to New Investors	Min Initial Investment
AllianzGI NFJ International Value Fund Class R	ANJRX	NAS CM	Open End	Global Equity Large Cap (Foreign Stock)	C	C	C	Up	Y	0
AllianzGI NFJ International Value Fund Class R6	ANAVX	NAS CM	Open End	Global Equity Large Cap (Foreign Stock)	C	C	C	Up	Y	0
AllianzGI NFJ International Value Fund Institutional Class	ANJIX	NAS CM	Open End	Global Equity Large Cap (Foreign Stock)	C	C	C	Up	Y	1,000,000
AllianzGI NFJ Large-Cap Value Fund Administrative Class	ALNFX	NAS CM	Open End	US Equity Large Cap Value (Growth & Income)	B-	B	C+	Down	Y	1,000,000
AllianzGI NFJ Large-Cap Value Fund Class A	PNBAX	NAS CM	Open End	US Equity Large Cap Value (Growth & Income)	B-	B	C+	Down	Y	1,000
AllianzGI NFJ Large-Cap Value Fund Class C	PNBCX	NAS CM	Open End	US Equity Large Cap Value (Growth & Income)	B-	B-	C+	Down	Y	1,000
AllianzGI NFJ Large-Cap Value Fund Class P	ALCPX	NAS CM	Open End	US Equity Large Cap Value (Growth & Income)	B-	B	C+	Down	Y	1,000,000
AllianzGI NFJ Large-Cap Value Fund Class R	ANLRX	NAS CM	Open End	US Equity Large Cap Value (Growth & Income)	B-	B-	C+	Down	Y	0
AllianzGI NFJ Large-Cap Value Fund Institutional Class	ANVIX	NAS CM	Open End	US Equity Large Cap Value (Growth & Income)	B-	B	C+	Down	Y	1,000,000
AllianzGI NFJ Mid-Cap Value Fund Administrative Class	PRAAX	NAS CM	Open End	US Equity Mid Cap (Growth & Income)	B	B	B-	Down	Y	1,000,000
AllianzGI NFJ Mid-Cap Value Fund Class A	PQNAX	NAS CM	Open End	US Equity Mid Cap (Growth & Income)	B	B	B-	Down	Y	1,000
AllianzGI NFJ Mid-Cap Value Fund Class C	PQNCX	NAS CM	Open End	US Equity Mid Cap (Growth & Income)	B	B	C+		Y	1,000
AllianzGI NFJ Mid-Cap Value Fund Class P	ANRPX	NAS CM	Open End	US Equity Mid Cap (Growth & Income)	B	B	B-	Down	Y	1,000,000
AllianzGI NFJ Mid-Cap Value Fund Class R	PRNRX	NAS CM	Open End	US Equity Mid Cap (Growth & Income)	B	B	B-	Down	Y	0
AllianzGI NFJ Mid-Cap Value Fund Institutional Class	PRNIX	NAS CM	Open End	US Equity Mid Cap (Growth & Income)	B	B	B-	Down	Y	1,000,000
AllianzGI NFJ Small-Cap Value Fund Administrative Class	PVADX	NAS CM	Open End	US Equity Small Cap (Small Company)	B-	B-	B-	Up		1,000,000
AllianzGI NFJ Small-Cap Value Fund Class A	PCVAX	NAS CM	Open End	US Equity Small Cap (Small Company)	B-	B-	B-	Up		1,000
AllianzGI NFJ Small-Cap Value Fund Class C	PCVCX	NAS CM	Open End	US Equity Small Cap (Small Company)	C+	C+	C+			1,000
AllianzGI NFJ Small-Cap Value Fund Class P	ASVPX	NAS CM	Open End	US Equity Small Cap (Small Company)	B-	B-	B-	Up		1,000,000
AllianzGI NFJ Small-Cap Value Fund Class R	PNVRX	NAS CM	Open End	US Equity Small Cap (Small Company)	B-	B-	B-	Up		0
AllianzGI NFJ Small-Cap Value Fund Class R6	ANFVX	NAS CM	Open End	US Equity Small Cap (Small Company)	B-	B-	B-	Up	Y	0
AllianzGI NFJ Small-Cap Value Fund Institutional Class	PSVIX	NAS CM	Open End	US Equity Small Cap (Small Company)	B-	B-	B-	Up		1,000,000
AllianzGI Retirement 2020 Fund Administrative Class	AGLMX	NAS CM	Open End	Target Date 2000-2020 (Asset Alloc)	B-	C+	B	Down	Y	1,000,000
AllianzGI Retirement 2020 Fund Class A	AGLAX	NAS CM	Open End	Target Date 2000-2020 (Asset Alloc)	B-	C+	B	Down	Y	1,000
AllianzGI Retirement 2020 Fund Class C	ABSCX	NAS CM	Open End	Target Date 2000-2020 (Asset Alloc)	B-	C+	B		Y	1,000
AllianzGI Retirement 2020 Fund Class P	AGLPX	NAS CM	Open End	Target Date 2000-2020 (Asset Alloc)	B-	C+	B+	Down	Y	1,000,000
AllianzGI Retirement 2020 Fund Class R	AGLRX	NAS CM	Open End	Target Date 2000-2020 (Asset Alloc)	B-	C+	B	Up	Y	0
AllianzGI Retirement 2020 Fund R6 Class	AGNIX	NAS CM	Open End	Target Date 2000-2020 (Asset Alloc)	B	C+	B+	Up	Y	0
AllianzGI Retirement 2025 Fund Administrative Class	GVDAX	NAS CM	Open End	Target Date 2021-2045 (Asset Alloc)	B-	C+	B	Down	Y	1,000,000
AllianzGI Retirement 2025 Fund Class A	GVSAX	NAS CM	Open End	Target Date 2021-2045 (Asset Alloc)	B-	C+	B	Down	Y	1,000
AllianzGI Retirement 2025 Fund Class P	GVSPX	NAS CM	Open End	Target Date 2021-2045 (Asset Alloc)	B-	C+	B	Down	Y	1,000,000
AllianzGI Retirement 2025 Fund Class R	GVSRX	NAS CM	Open End	Target Date 2021-2045 (Asset Alloc)	B-	C+	B	Down	Y	0
AllianzGI Retirement 2025 Fund R6 Class	GVSIX	NAS CM	Open End	Target Date 2021-2045 (Asset Alloc)	B-	C+	B	Down	Y	0
AllianzGI Retirement 2030 Fund Administrative Class	ABAMX	NAS CM	Open End	Target Date 2021-2045 (Asset Alloc)	B-	C+	B	Down	Y	1,000,000
AllianzGI Retirement 2030 Fund Class A	ABLAX	NAS CM	Open End	Target Date 2021-2045 (Asset Alloc)	B-	C+	B	Down	Y	1,000
AllianzGI Retirement 2030 Fund Class C	ABLCX	NAS CM	Open End	Target Date 2021-2045 (Asset Alloc)	B-	C+	B		Y	1,000
AllianzGI Retirement 2030 Fund Class P	ABLPX	NAS CM	Open End	Target Date 2021-2045 (Asset Alloc)	B-	C+	B	Down	Y	1,000,000
AllianzGI Retirement 2030 Fund Class R	ABLRX	NAS CM	Open End	Target Date 2021-2045 (Asset Alloc)	B-	C+	B	Down	Y	0
AllianzGI Retirement 2030 Fund R6 Class	ABLIX	NAS CM	Open End	Target Date 2021-2045 (Asset Alloc)	B-	B-	B	Down	Y	0
AllianzGI Retirement 2035 Fund Administrative Class	GVLAX	NAS CM	Open End	Target Date 2021-2045 (Asset Alloc)	B-	B-	B	Down	Y	1,000,000
AllianzGI Retirement 2035 Fund Class A	GVRAX	NAS CM	Open End	Target Date 2021-2045 (Asset Alloc)	B-	B-	B	Down	Y	1,000
AllianzGI Retirement 2035 Fund Class P	GVPAX	NAS CM	Open End	Target Date 2021-2045 (Asset Alloc)	B-	B-	B	Down	Y	1,000,000
AllianzGI Retirement 2035 Fund Class R	GVRRX	NAS CM	Open End	Target Date 2021-2045 (Asset Alloc)	B-	B-	B	Down	Y	0
AllianzGI Retirement 2035 Fund R6 Class	GVLIX	NAS CM	Open End	Target Date 2021-2045 (Asset Alloc)	B-	B-	B	Down	Y	0
AllianzGI Retirement 2040 Fund Administrative Class	AVAMX	NAS CM	Open End	Target Date 2021-2045 (Asset Alloc)	B-	B-	B-	Down	Y	1,000,000
AllianzGI Retirement 2040 Fund Class A	AVSAX	NAS CM	Open End	Target Date 2021-2045 (Asset Alloc)	B-	B-	B-	Down	Y	1,000
AllianzGI Retirement 2040 Fund Class C	AVSCX	NAS CM	Open End	Target Date 2021-2045 (Asset Alloc)	B-	B-	B-	Up	Y	1,000
AllianzGI Retirement 2040 Fund Class P	AVSPX	NAS CM	Open End	Target Date 2021-2045 (Asset Alloc)	B-	B-	B	Down	Y	1,000,000
AllianzGI Retirement 2040 Fund Class R	AVSRX	NAS CM	Open End	Target Date 2021-2045 (Asset Alloc)	B-	B-	B-	Down	Y	0
AllianzGI Retirement 2040 Fund R6 Class	AVTIX	NAS CM	Open End	Target Date 2021-2045 (Asset Alloc)	B-	B-	B	Down	Y	0
AllianzGI Retirement 2045 Fund Administrative Class	GBMAX	NAS CM	Open End	Target Date 2021-2045 (Asset Alloc)	B-	B-	B-	Down	Y	1,000,000
AllianzGI Retirement 2045 Fund Class A	GBVAX	NAS CM	Open End	Target Date 2021-2045 (Asset Alloc)	B-	B-	B-	Down	Y	1,000

★Expanded analysis of this fund is included in Section II.

	TOTAL RETURNS					PERFORMANCE				ASSETS		ASSET ALLOCATION & TURNOVER					BULL & BEAR		FEES		
Min Additional Investment	3-Month Total Return	6-Month Total Return	1-Year Total Return	3-Year Total Return	5-Year Total Return	Dividend Yield (TTM)	Expense Ratio	3-Yr Std Deviation	3-Year Beta	NAV	Total Assets (MIL)	%Cash	%Stocks	%Bonds	%Other	Turnover Ratio	Last Bull Market Total Return	Last Bear Market Total Return	Front End Fee (%)	Back End Fee (%)	Inception Date
	3.72	9.41	22.45	-1.76	3.12	1.79	1.55	13.06	1.04	19.77	396.4	0	98	0	2	63	19.18	-23.16			Nov-09
	3.86	9.78	23.21	0.12	6.45	2.14	0.9	13.09	1.04	19.89	396.4	0	98	0	2	63	19.61	-22.97			Dec-13
	3.86	9.75	23.15	-0.01	6.28	2.26	0.95	13.08	1.04	19.9	396.4	0	98	0	2	63	19.61	-22.97			Jan-03
	7.15	11.53	21.09	29.03	95.12	1.76	1.02	11.16	1.01	27.22	384.3	1	99	0	0	67	22.26	-16.73			Sep-06
50	7.11	11.46	20.94	28.61	94.08	1.68	1.12	11.14	1.01	26.85	384.3	1	99	0	0	67	22.14	-16.74	5.50		Jul-02
50	6.87	11.05	20.00	25.75	86.96	0.77	1.87	11.15	1.01	27.14	384.3	1	99	0	0	67	21.58	-17		1.00	Jul-02
	7.18	11.62	21.27	29.60	96.57	2.04	0.87	11.15	1.01	27.1	384.3	1	99	0	0	67	22.4	-16.7			Jul-08
	7.01	11.30	20.65	27.67	91.70	1.34	1.37	11.14	1.01	27.11	384.3	1	99	0	0	67	22	-16.86			Jan-06
	7.19	11.67	21.35	30.02	97.58	2.11	0.77	11.15	1.01	26.73	384.3	1	99	0	0	67	22.43	-16.6			May-00
	4.93	9.34	26.73	41.83	108.43	0.99	0.89	11.28	0.98	32.29	995.7	4	96	0	0	45	21.92	-19.79			Aug-98
50	4.90	9.27	26.61	41.44	107.30	0.98	0.99	11.27	0.98	31.32	995.7	4	96	0	0	45	21.85	-19.85	5.50		Feb-91
50	4.72	8.87	25.64	38.28	99.68	0.68	1.74	11.26	0.98	25.75	995.7	4	96	0	0	45	21.4	-20.16		1.00	Apr-88
	4.96	9.44	26.91	42.45	110.03	1.5	0.74	11.25	0.97	25.34	995.7	4	96	0	0	45	22.07	-19.75			Feb-11
	4.86	9.15	26.29	40.36	104.77	0.76	1.24	11.28	0.98	26.9	995.7	4	96	0	0	45	21.76	-19.96			Dec-02
	5.01	9.48	27.04	42.91	110.99	1.1	0.64	11.27	0.98	33.44	995.7	4	96	0	0	45	22.13	-19.75			Dec-97
	3.23	6.89	9.78	23.11	69.14	1.37	1.09	12.42	0.84	21.6	2,858	4	94	0	2	30	21.24	-18.44			Nov-95
50	3.19	6.84	9.67	22.55	67.85	1.21	1.19	12.43	0.84	21.67	2,858	4	94	0	2	30	21.12	-18.51	5.50		Jan-97
50	2.98	6.42	8.83	19.80	61.62	0.78	1.94	12.42	0.84	19.33	2,858	4	94	0	2	30	20.59	-18.75		1.00	Jan-97
	3.28	6.96	9.92	23.47	69.95	1.32	0.94	12.43	0.84	24.11	2,858	4	94	0	2	30	21.28	-18.41			Jul-08
	3.13	6.67	9.35	21.62	65.72	0.92	1.44	12.44	0.84	23.08	2,858	4	94	0	2	30	20.95	-18.6			Dec-02
	3.33	7.04	10.09	24.14	71.52	1.5	0.79	12.43	0.84	24.16	2,858	4	94	0	2	30	21.42	-18.39			Dec-13
	3.29	7.02	10.02	23.95	71.16	1.41	0.84	12.44	0.84	24.25	2,858	4	94	0	2	30	21.42	-18.39			Oct-91
	2.85	6.32	13.27	18.41	25.88	2.06	0.9	4.89	0.86	20.49	54.6	14	41	28	16	143	11.33	-9.3			Dec-08
50	2.86	6.30	13.23	18.31	25.66	2.23	0.95	4.91	0.86	20.36	54.6	14	41	28	16	143	11.36	-9.34	5.50		Dec-08
50	2.60	5.89	12.35	15.66	20.97	1.85	1.7	4.9	0.86	20.32	54.6	14	41	28	16	143	10.83	-9.6		1.00	Dec-08
	2.92	6.48	13.55	19.41	27.56	2.62	0.65	4.89	0.86	20.52	54.6	14	41	28	16	143	11.56	-9.25			Dec-08
	2.72	6.16	10.77	14.86	21.14	1.84	1.3	5.17	0.86	20.07	54.6	14	41	28	16	143	11.09	-9.43			Dec-08
	2.90	6.51	13.69	19.65	28.10	2.68	0.55	4.9	0.86	20.54	54.6	14	41	28	16	143	11.57	-9.24			Dec-08
	3.61	7.79	15.85	22.42	31.32	1.88	0.9	5.48	0.83	18.44	67.2	13	54	20	12	129					Dec-11
50	3.56	7.68	15.80	22.21	30.89	1.65	0.95	5.48	0.83	18.37	67.2	13	54	20	12	129			5.50		Dec-11
	3.69	7.94	16.15	23.39	33.02	2.41	0.65	5.49	0.83	18.34	67.2	13	54	20	12	129					Dec-11
	3.48	7.53	15.30	20.93	28.58	1.9	1.3	5.49	0.83	18.28	67.2	13	54	20	12	129					Dec-11
	3.71	7.95	16.30	23.76	33.65	2.46	0.55	5.5	0.83	18.37	67.2	13	54	20	12	129					Dec-11
	4.04	8.80	18.18	24.47	36.93	1.73	0.9	6.21	0.8	22.45	75.2	12	63	22	3	125	13.85	-13.85			Dec-08
50	3.99	8.78	18.12	24.24	36.59	1.52	0.95	6.21	0.8	22.17	75.2	12	63	22	3	125	13.84	-13.89	5.50		Dec-08
50	3.79	8.33	17.22	21.42	31.43	1.24	1.7	6.22	0.8	21.97	75.2	12	63	22	3	125	13.33	-14.12		1.00	Dec-08
	4.09	8.93	18.48	25.34	38.59	2.07	0.65	6.2	0.8	22.38	75.2	12	63	22	3	125	14	-13.75			Dec-08
	3.90	8.56	17.70	22.97	34.12	1.59	1.3	6.2	0.8	22.17	75.2	12	63	22	3	125	13.6	-13.98			Dec-08
	4.11	8.94	18.58	25.72	39.25	2.13	0.55	6.2	0.8	22.44	75.2	12	63	22	3	125	14.1	-13.74			Dec-08
	4.23	9.40	19.78	26.42	42.57	1.84	0.9	6.94	0.8	19.88	60.6	11	73	14	3	122					Dec-11
50	4.25	9.38	19.79	26.30	42.18	1.65	0.95	6.94	0.8	19.72	60.6	11	73	14	3	122			5.50		Dec-11
	4.32	9.54	20.11	27.42	44.40	2.09	0.65	6.95	0.8	19.79	60.6	11	73	14	3	122					Dec-11
	4.16	9.21	19.32	24.94	39.70	1.57	1.3	6.94	0.8	19.66	60.6	11	73	14	3	122					Dec-11
	4.36	9.62	20.26	27.84	45.13	2.18	0.55	6.95	0.8	19.82	60.6	11	73	14	3	122					Dec-11
	4.44	9.87	20.93	27.67	46.86	1.79	0.9	7.89	0.85	22.83	56.6	10	79	9	2	103	16.88	-19.19			Dec-08
50	4.45	9.83	20.88	27.53	46.51	1.5	0.95	7.89	0.85	22.84	56.6	10	79	9	2	103	16.89	-19.26	5.50		Dec-08
50	4.25	9.39	19.97	24.71	41.15	1.19	1.7	7.86	0.84	22.68	56.6	10	79	9	2	103	16.38	-19.5		1.00	Dec-08
	4.51	10.02	21.28	28.77	48.81	2.12	0.65	7.87	0.84	22.92	56.6	10	79	9	2	103	17.09	-19.16			Dec-08
	4.39	9.65	20.46	26.26	44.05	1.67	1.3	7.87	0.84	22.7	56.6	10	79	9	2	103	16.7	-19.33			Dec-08
	4.55	10.05	21.40	29.16	49.57	2.19	0.55	7.88	0.84	22.97	56.6	10	79	9	2	103	17.13	-19.11			Dec-08
	4.55	10.14	21.71	28.90	50.33	2.08	0.9	8.5	0.89	19.94	35.1	10	83	5	2	97					Dec-11
50	4.55	10.13	21.71	28.69	50.00	1.58	0.95	8.5	0.89	20.02	35.1	10	83	5	2	97			5.50		Dec-11

	MARKET			FUND TYPE, CATEGORY & OBJECTIVE	RATINGS					MINIMUMS
Fund Name	Ticker Symbol	Traded On	Fund Type	Category and (Prospectus Objective)	Overall Rating	Reward Rating	Risk Rating	Recent Up/ Downgrade	Open to New Investors	Min Initial Investment
AllianzGI Retirement 2045 Fund Class P	GBVPX	NAS CM	Open End	Target Date 2021-2045 (Asset Alloc)	B-	B-	B-	Down	Y	1,000,000
AllianzGI Retirement 2045 Fund Class R	GBVRX	NAS CM	Open End	Target Date 2021-2045 (Asset Alloc)	B-	B-	B-	Down	Y	0
AllianzGI Retirement 2045 Fund R6 Class	GBVIX	NAS CM	Open End	Target Date 2021-2045 (Asset Alloc)	B-	B-	B-	Down	Y	0
AllianzGI Retirement 2050 Fund Administrative Class	ANAMX	NAS CM	Open End	Target Date 2046+ (Asset Alloc)	B-	B-	B-	Down	Y	1,000,000
AllianzGI Retirement 2050 Fund Class A	ASNAX	NAS CM	Open End	Target Date 2046+ (Asset Alloc)	B-	B-	B-	Down	Y	1,000
AllianzGI Retirement 2050 Fund Class C	ASNCX	NAS CM	Open End	Target Date 2046+ (Asset Alloc)	B-	B-	B-	Down	Y	1,000
AllianzGI Retirement 2050 Fund Class P	ASNPX	NAS CM	Open End	Target Date 2046+ (Asset Alloc)	B-	B-	B-	Down	Y	1,000,000
AllianzGI Retirement 2050 Fund Class R	ASNRX	NAS CM	Open End	Target Date 2046+ (Asset Alloc)	B-	B-	B-	Down	Y	0
AllianzGI Retirement 2050 Fund R6 Class	ASNIX	NAS CM	Open End	Target Date 2046+ (Asset Alloc)	B-	B-	B-	Down	Y	0
AllianzGI Retirement 2055 Fund Administrative Class	GLRAX	NAS CM	Open End	Target Date 2046+ (Asset Alloc)	B-	B-	B-	Down	Y	1,000,000
AllianzGI Retirement 2055 Fund Class A	GLIAX	NAS CM	Open End	Target Date 2046+ (Asset Alloc)	B-	B-	B-	Down	Y	1,000
AllianzGI Retirement 2055 Fund Class P	GLIPX	NAS CM	Open End	Target Date 2046+ (Asset Alloc)	B-	B-	B-	Down	Y	1,000,000
AllianzGI Retirement 2055 Fund Class R	GLLRX	NAS CM	Open End	Target Date 2046+ (Asset Alloc)	B-	B-	B-	Down	Y	0
AllianzGI Retirement 2055 Fund R6 Class	GBLIX	NAS CM	Open End	Target Date 2046+ (Asset Alloc)	B-	B-	B-	Down	Y	0
AllianzGI Retirement Income Fund Administrative Class	ARAMX	NAS CM	Open End	Target Date 2000-2020 (Asset Alloc)	B-	C+	B	Down	Y	1,000,000
AllianzGI Retirement Income Fund Class A	AGRAX	NAS CM	Open End	Target Date 2000-2020 (Asset Alloc)	B-	C+	B+	Down	Y	1,000
AllianzGI Retirement Income Fund Class C	ARTCX	NAS CM	Open End	Target Date 2000-2020 (Asset Alloc)	B-	C+	B		Y	1,000
AllianzGI Retirement Income Fund Class P	AGRPX	NAS CM	Open End	Target Date 2000-2020 (Asset Alloc)	B-	C+	B+	Down	Y	1,000,000
AllianzGI Retirement Income Fund Class R	ASRRX	NAS CM	Open End	Target Date 2000-2020 (Asset Alloc)	B-	C+	B	Down	Y	0
AllianzGI Retirement Income Fund R6 Class	AVRIX	NAS CM	Open End	Target Date 2000-2020 (Asset Alloc)	B	C+	B+	Up	Y	0
AllianzGI Small-Cap Blend Fund Class A	AZBAX	NAS CM	Open End	US Equity Small Cap (Small Company)	B+	A-	B-	Up	Y	1,000
AllianzGI Small-Cap Blend Fund Class C	AZBCX	NAS CM	Open End	US Equity Small Cap (Small Company)	B	A-	C+	Up	Y	1,000
AllianzGI Small-Cap Blend Fund Class P	AZBPX	NAS CM	Open End	US Equity Small Cap (Small Company)	B+	A-	B-	Up	Y	1,000,000
AllianzGI Small-Cap Blend Fund Institutional Class	AZBIX	NAS CM	Open End	US Equity Small Cap (Small Company)	B+	A	B-	Up	Y	1,000,000
AllianzGI Structured Return Fund Class A	AZIAX	NAS CM	Open End	Long/Short Equity (Growth)	B	C	A-	Up	Y	1,000
AllianzGI Structured Return Fund Class C	AZICX	NAS CM	Open End	Long/Short Equity (Growth)	B-	C	A-	Up	Y	1,000
AllianzGI Structured Return Fund Class P	AZIPX	NAS CM	Open End	Long/Short Equity (Growth)	B	C	A-		Y	1,000,000
AllianzGI Structured Return Fund Class R6	AZIRX	NAS CM	Open End	Long/Short Equity (Growth)	B	C	A-		Y	0
AllianzGI Structured Return Fund Institutional Class	AZIIX	NAS CM	Open End	Long/Short Equity (Growth)	B	C	A-		Y	1,000,000
AllianzGI Technology Fund Administrative Class	DGTAX	NAS CM	Open End	Technology Sector Equity (Technology)	A	A+	B+	Up	Y	1,000,000
AllianzGI Technology Fund Class A	RAGTX	NAS CM	Open End	Technology Sector Equity (Technology)	A	A+	B+	Up	Y	1,000
AllianzGI Technology Fund Class C	RCGTX	NAS CM	Open End	Technology Sector Equity (Technology)	A	A+	B+	Up	Y	1,000
AllianzGI Technology Fund Class P	ARTPX	NAS CM	Open End	Technology Sector Equity (Technology)	A	A+	B+	Up	Y	1,000,000
AllianzGI Technology Fund Institutional Class	DRGTX	NAS CM	Open End	Technology Sector Equity (Technology)	A	A+	B+	Up	Y	1,000,000
AllianzGI U.S. Equity-Hedged Fund Class A	AZUAX	NAS CM	Open End	Long/Short Equity (Growth)	B-	C+	B	Down	Y	1,000
AllianzGI U.S. Equity-Hedged Fund Class C	AZUCX	NAS CM	Open End	Long/Short Equity (Growth)	C+	C+	B	Up	Y	1,000
AllianzGI U.S. Equity-Hedged Fund Class P	AZUPX	NAS CM	Open End	Long/Short Equity (Growth)	B-	C+	B	Down	Y	1,000,000
AllianzGI U.S. Equity-Hedged Fund Institutional Class	AZUIX	NAS CM	Open End	Long/Short Equity (Growth)	B-	C+	B	Down	Y	1,000,000
AllianzGI Ultra Micro Cap Fund Class A	GUCAX	NAS CM	Open End	US Equity Small Cap (Growth)	B-	B-	B-	Up		1,000
AllianzGI Ultra Micro Cap Fund Class P	AAUPX	NAS CM	Open End	US Equity Small Cap (Growth)	B-	B-	B-	Up		1,000,000
AllianzGI Ultra Micro Cap Fund Institutional Class	AUMIX	NAS CM	Open End	US Equity Small Cap (Growth)	B-	B-	B-	Up		1,000,000
Alpha Risk Tactical Rotation Fund Class C	ARSDX	NAS CM	Open End	Multialternative (Growth & Income)	D+	D	C-	Down	Y	1,000
Alpha Risk Tactical Rotation Fund Institutional Class	ARSAX	NAS CM	Open End	Multialternative (Growth & Income)	D+	D	C	Down	Y	1,000
AlphaCentric Asset Rotation Fund Class A	ROTAX	NAS CM	Open End	Moderate Alloc (Growth)	C+	C	C+	Up	Y	2,500
AlphaCentric Asset Rotation Fund Class C	ROTCX	NAS CM	Open End	Moderate Alloc (Growth)	C	C	C+	Up	Y	2,500
AlphaCentric Asset Rotation Fund Class I	ROTIX	NAS CM	Open End	Moderate Alloc (Growth)	C+	C	C+	Up	Y	2,500
AlphaCentric Global Innovations Fund Class A	GNXAX	NAS CM	Open End	Technology Sector Equity (Technology)	U	U	U		Y	2,500
AlphaCentric Global Innovations Fund Class C	GNXCX	NAS CM	Open End	Technology Sector Equity (Technology)	U	U	U		Y	2,500
AlphaCentric Global Innovations Fund Class I	GNXIX	NAS CM	Open End	Technology Sector Equity (Technology)	U	U	U		Y	2,500
AlphaCentric Hedged Market Opportunity Fund Class A	HMXAX	NAS CM	Open End	Long/Short Equity (Growth)	B	C	A-		Y	2,500
AlphaCentric Hedged Market Opportunity Fund Class C	HMXCX	NAS CM	Open End	Long/Short Equity (Growth)	B-	C	B+	Down	Y	2,500
AlphaCentric Hedged Market Opportunity Fund Class I	HMXIX	NAS CM	Open End	Long/Short Equity (Growth)	B	C+	A-		Y	2,500

★Expanded analysis of this fund is included in Section II.

	TOTAL RETURNS					PERFORMANCE				ASSETS		ASSET ALLOCATION & TURNOVER					BULL & BEAR		FEES		
Min Additional Investment	3-Month Total Return	6-Month Total Return	1-Year Total Return	3-Year Total Return	5-Year Total Return	Dividend Yield (TTM)	Expense Ratio	3-Yr Std Deviation	3-Year Beta	NAV	Total Assets (MIL)	%Cash	%Stocks	%Bonds	%Other	Turnover Ratio	Last Bull Market Total Return	Last Bear Market Total Return	Front End Fee (%)	Back End Fee (%)	Inception Date
	4.62	10.30	22.01	29.94	52.45	2.17	0.65	8.49	0.89	20.04	35.1	10	83	5	2	97					Dec-11
	4.40	9.91	21.19	27.34	47.43	1.72	1.3	8.48	0.89	19.86	35.1	10	83	5	2	97					Dec-11
	4.66	10.31	22.13	30.37	53.22	2.26	0.55	8.49	0.89	20.09	35.1	10	83	5	2	97					Dec-11
	4.57	10.19	21.82	28.86	51.46	2.02	0.9	8.79	0.91	22.28	34.4	10	83	4	2	94	18.31	-20.53			Dec-08
50	4.57	10.16	21.77	28.63	51.07	1.83	0.95	8.8	0.91	22.22	34.4	10	83	4	2	94	18.23	-20.51	5.50		Dec-08
50	4.38	9.76	20.84	25.83	45.52	1.46	1.7	8.77	0.91	21.9	34.4	10	83	4	2	94	17.77	-20.79		1.00	Dec-08
	4.64	10.33	22.10	29.84	53.37	2.24	0.65	8.78	0.91	22.37	34.4	10	83	4	2	94	18.45	-20.42			Dec-08
	4.49	9.97	21.28	27.24	48.36	1.78	1.3	8.78	0.91	22.25	34.4	10	83	4	2	94	18.07	-20.64			Dec-08
	4.63	10.35	22.19	30.20	54.04	2.31	0.55	8.77	0.91	22.45	34.4	10	83	4	2	94	18.57	-20.45			Dec-08
	4.53	10.22	21.78	28.32	51.21	1.69	0.9	8.8	0.91	19.24	16.3	11	83	4	2	76					Dec-11
50	4.52	10.16	21.66	28.21	50.84	1.59	0.95	8.79	0.91	19.19	16.3	11	83	4	2	76			5.50		Dec-11
	4.64	10.36	22.07	29.42	53.19	1.9	0.65	8.77	0.9	19.33	16.3	11	83	4	2	76					Dec-11
	4.45	9.96	21.23	26.91	48.29	1.46	1.3	8.77	0.9	19.16	16.3	11	83	4	2	76					Dec-11
	4.65	10.41	22.21	29.81	54.04	1.94	0.55	8.77	0.9	19.41	16.3	11	83	4	2	76					Dec-11
	1.87	3.13	9.66	15.41	21.61	5.49	0.9	4.6	0.82	18.57	50.7	3	33	60	2	151	9.73	-6.4			Dec-08
50	1.84	3.10	9.57	16.49	22.61	5.36	0.95	4.63	0.8	18.27	50.7	3	33	60	2	151	9.67	-6.41	5.50		Dec-08
50	1.64	2.72	8.76	13.89	18.10	3.99	1.7	4.64	0.8	18.27	50.7	3	33	60	2	151	9.22	-6.68		1.00	Dec-08
	1.95	3.28	9.91	17.55	24.48	5.8	0.65	4.63	0.8	18.46	50.7	3	33	60	2	151	9.85	-6.3			Dec-08
	1.77	2.89	9.15	15.23	20.43	4.35	1.3	4.63	0.8	19.07	50.7	3	33	60	2	151	9.52	-6.55			Dec-08
	1.96	3.34	10.03	17.89	25.10	6.03	0.55	4.64	0.81	18	50.7	3	33	60	2	151	9.96	-6.32			Dec-08
50	3.23	11.74	20.79	36.15		0.03	1.31	11.78	0.79	20.13	86.7	3	97	0	0	152			5.50		Jul-13
50	3.03	11.35	19.83	33.19		0	2.06	11.8	0.8	19.56	86.7	3	97	0	0	152				1.00	Jul-13
	3.30	11.87	21.02	37.22		0.05	1.06	11.8	0.79	20.29	86.7	3	97	0	0	152					Jul-13
	3.33	11.96	21.21	37.62		0.06	0.96	11.79	0.79	20.42	86.7	3	97	0	0	152					Jul-13
50	1.05	2.56	5.19	13.62	25.77	0.38	1.1	2.82	-4.46	15.83	581.7	16	84	0	0	680			5.50		Dec-12
50	0.89	2.19	4.40	11.09	21.01	0	1.9	2.85	-4.64	15.36	581.7	16	84	0	0	680				1.00	Dec-12
	1.16	2.67	5.44	14.25	26.79	0.72	0.89	2.84	-5.03	15.79	581.7	16	84	0	0	680					Dec-12
	1.17	2.75	5.57	14.53	27.36		0.79	2.83	-5.39	15.88	581.7	16	84	0	0	680					Dec-16
	1.10	2.73	5.47	14.41	27.24	0.36	0.81	2.83	-5.08	15.95	581.7	16	84	0	0	680					Dec-12
	7.78	18.85	46.83	60.13	166.29	0	1.35	14.85	0.99	64.77	1,600	3	97	0	0	128	16.28	-22.16			Mar-05
50	7.73	18.79	46.69	59.66	164.94	0	1.45	14.85	0.99	61.24	1,600	3	97	0	0	128	16.23	-22.19	5.50		Feb-02
50	7.55	18.34	45.62	56.09	155.22	0	2.2	14.85	0.99	47.49	1,600	3	97	0	0	128	15.71	-22.43		1.00	Feb-02
	7.81	18.94	47.07	60.86	168.30	0	1.2	14.86	0.99	67.53	1,600	3	97	0	0	128	16.38	-22.09			Jul-08
	7.83	19.00	47.21	61.33	169.66	0	1.1	14.85	0.99	68.65	1,600	3	97	0	0	128	16.43	-22.07			Dec-95
50	4.53	7.68	13.25	13.61	44.61	1.28	1.34	6.1	0.57	18.31	2.7	1	99	0	0	6			5.50		Dec-12
50	4.32	7.27	12.42	11.12	39.40	0.89	2.09	6.11	0.58	17.59	2.7	1	99	0	0	6				1.00	Dec-12
	4.56	7.74	13.38	14.11	45.71	2.19	1.19	6.08	0.57	18.05	2.7	1	99	0	0	6					Dec-12
	4.57	7.76	13.51	14.41	46.46	1.07	1.09	6.08	0.57	18.54	2.7	1	99	0	0	6					Dec-12
50	-1.22	3.86	10.69	15.93	81.35	0	2.01	16.33	0.9	17.84	35.9	2	98	0	0	33	40.07	-29.46	5.50		Dec-11
	-1.17	3.97	11.02	16.92	83.69	0	1.72	16.32	0.89	18.2	35.9	2	98	0	0	33	40	-29.36			Dec-10
	-1.15	4.02	11.01	16.81	83.45	0	1.69	16.3	0.89	18.25	35.9	2	98	0	0	33	40.23	-29.38			Jan-08
50	2.96	7.37	-4.34	-5.73	-7.01	0	2.69	5.77	0.24	9.03	2.0	13	87	0	0	152				1.00	Sep-12
50	3.17	7.89	-3.38	-2.73	-1.89	0	1.74	5.72	0.24	9.43	2.0	13	87	0	0	152					Sep-12
100	5.69	10.81	16.73	-0.76		2.34	1.62	6.7	0	9.62	12.8	4	94	0	1	691			5.75		Jul-14
100	5.59	10.35	15.83	-2.87		0.99	2.37	6.72	0	9.72	12.8	4	94	0	1	691					Jul-14
100	5.70	10.94	17.00	-0.02		2.88	1.37	6.73	0	9.59	12.8	4	94	0	1	691					Jul-14
100	5.36	22.41					1.75			12.03	16.7	6	94	0	0				5.75		May-17
100	5.20	22.04					2.5			11.98	16.7	6	94	0	0						May-17
100	5.44	22.61					1.5			12.05	16.7	6	94	0	0						May-17
100	1.14	2.16	5.02	17.41	49.20	0	2.3			18.63	20.5	52	0	48	0		15.65		5.75		Sep-16
100	0.93	1.74	4.31	14.85	43.79	0	3.05			18.47	20.5	52	0	48	0		15.15				Sep-16
100	1.24	2.32	5.28	18.38	51.19	0	2.05			18.7	20.5	52	0	48	0		15.82				Sep-16

	MARKET			FUND TYPE, CATEGORY & OBJECTIVE	RATINGS				MINIMUMS	
Fund Name	Ticker Symbol	Traded On	Fund Type	Category and (Prospectus Objective)	Overall Rating	Reward Rating	Risk Rating	Recent Up/ Downgrade	Open to New Investors	Min Initial Investment
AlphaCore Absolute Fund Institutional Class	GDAMX	NAS CM	Open End	Multialternative (Growth)	C+	C	B			25,000
AlphaCore Statistical Arbitrage Fund Institutional Class	STAKX	NAS CM	Open End	Market Neutral (Growth)	U	U	U		Y	500,000
AlphaMark Large Cap Growth Fund	AMLCX	NAS CM	Open End	US Equity Large Cap Blend (Growth)	B	B+	C+	Up	Y	1,000
AlphaOne Small Cap Opportunities Fund Institutional Class	AOMCX	NAS CM	Open End	US Equity Small Cap (Small Company)	B+	A-	B	Up	Y	100,000
AlphaOne Small Cap Opportunities Fund Investor Class	AOMAX	NAS CM	Open End	US Equity Small Cap (Small Company)	B+	A-	B	Up	Y	2,500
Alpine Dynamic Dividend Fund Class A Shares	ADAVX	NAS CM	Open End	Global Equity (Equity-Income)	B-	B-	C+	Up	Y	2,500
Alpine Dynamic Dividend Fund Institutional Class	ADVDX	NAS CM	Open End	Global Equity (Equity-Income)	B-	B-	C+	Up	Y	1,000,000
Alpine Financial Services Fund Class A Shares	ADAFX	NAS CM	Open End	Financials Sector Equity (Financial)	B+	A	B-	Up	Y	2,500
Alpine Financial Services Fund Institutional Class	ADFSX	NAS CM	Open End	Financials Sector Equity (Financial)	B+	A	B	Up		1,000,000
Alpine Global Dynamic Dividend Fund	AGD	NYSE	Closed End	Global Equity (World Stock)	B-	B-	C+	Up	Y	
Alpine Global Infrastructure Fund Class A shares	AIAFX	NAS CM	Open End	Other Sector Equity (Utility)	C+	B-	C+		Y	2,500
Alpine Global Infrastructure Fund Institutional Class	AIFRX	NAS CM	Open End	Other Sector Equity (Utility)	B-	B-	C+	Up	Y	1,000,000
Alpine Global Premier Property	AWP	NYSE	Closed End	Real Estate Sector Equity (Real Estate)	B-	B-	B	Up	Y	
Alpine International Real Estate Equity Fund Cls A shares	EGALX	NAS CM	Open End	Real Estate Sector Equity (Real Estate)	C+	C+	C+	Up	Y	2,500
Alpine Intl Real Estate Equity Fund Inst Cls	EGLRX	NAS CM	Open End	Real Estate Sector Equity (Real Estate)	C+	C+	C+	Up	Y	1,000,000
Alpine Realty Income & Growth Fund Class A shares	AIAGX	NAS CM	Open End	Real Estate Sector Equity (Real Estate)	B	B-	B	Up	Y	2,500
Alpine Realty Income and Growth Fund Institutional Class	AIGYX	NAS CM	Open End	Real Estate Sector Equity (Real Estate)	B	B-	B+	Up	Y	1,000,000
Alpine Rising Dividend Fund Class A Shares	AAADX	NAS CM	Open End	US Equity Large Cap Blend (Equity-Income)	B-	B-	C+	Down	Y	2,500
Alpine Rising Dividend Fund Institutional Class	AADDX	NAS CM	Open End	US Equity Large Cap Blend (Equity-Income)	B-	B-	C+	Down	Y	1,000,000
Alpine Small Cap Fund Class A Shares	ADIAX	NAS CM	Open End	US Equity Small Cap (Small Company)	B	B	B	Up	Y	2,500
Alpine Small Cap Fund Institutional Class	ADINX	NAS CM	Open End	US Equity Small Cap (Small Company)	B	B	B	Up		1,000,000
Alpine Total Dynamic Dividend Fund	AOD	NYSE	Closed End	Global Equity (World Stock)	B-	B-	C+	Up	Y	
ALPS | CoreCommod Mgmt CompleteCommodities Strat Cls C	JCRCX	NAS CM	Open End	Commodities Broad Basket (Growth & Income)	C-	C	D+	Up	Y	2,500
ALPS | CoreCommod Mgmt CompleteCommodities Strat Cls I	JCRIX	NAS CM	Open End	Commodities Broad Basket (Growth & Income)	C-	C	D+	Up	Y	100,000
ALPS | CoreCommod Mgmt CompleteCommodities Strat Cls Inv	JCRAX	NAS CM	Open End	Commodities Broad Basket (Growth & Income)	C-	C	D+	Up	Y	2,500
ALPS | Kotak India Growth Fund Class C	INFCX	NAS CM	Open End	India Equity (Foreign Stock)	B	B	B-	Up	Y	2,500
ALPS | Kotak India Growth Fund Class I	INDIX	NAS CM	Open End	India Equity (Foreign Stock)	B	B	B-	Up	Y	100,000
ALPS | Kotak India Growth Fund Class Investor	INDAX	NAS CM	Open End	India Equity (Foreign Stock)	B	B	B-	Up	Y	2,500
ALPS | Metis Global Micro Cap Value Fund Class C	METCX	NAS CM	Open End	Global Equity Mid/Small Cap (Growth & Income)	C-	C-	B+	Up	Y	2,500
ALPS | Metis Global Micro Cap Value Fund Class I	METIX	NAS CM	Open End	Global Equity Mid/Small Cap (Growth & Income)	C-	C-	B+	Up	Y	100,000
ALPS | Metis Global Micro Cap Value Fund Class Investor	METAX	NAS CM	Open End	Global Equity Mid/Small Cap (Growth & Income)	C-	C-	B+	Up	Y	2,500
ALPS | Red Rocks Listed Private Equity Fund Class C	LPFCX	NAS CM	Open End	Global Equity Mid/Small Cap (Growth & Income)	B	B	B	Up	Y	2,500
ALPS | Red Rocks Listed Private Equity Fund Class I	LPEIX	NAS CM	Open End	Global Equity Mid/Small Cap (Growth & Income)	B	B	C+	Up	Y	100,000
ALPS | Red Rocks Listed Private Equity Fund Class Investor	LPEFX	NAS CM	Open End	Global Equity Mid/Small Cap (Growth & Income)	B	B	C+	Up	Y	2,500
ALPS | Red Rocks Listed Private Equity Fund Class R	LPERX	NAS CM	Open End	Global Equity Mid/Small Cap (Growth & Income)	B-	B	C+	Up	Y	0
ALPS | WMC Research Value Fund Class C	AMWCX	NAS CM	Open End	US Equity Large Cap Blend (Growth)	B-	C+	B	Up	Y	2,500
ALPS | WMC Research Value Fund Class I	AMWIX	NAS CM	Open End	US Equity Large Cap Blend (Growth)	B	C+	B	Up	Y	100,000
ALPS | WMC Research Value Fund Class Investor	AMWYX	NAS CM	Open End	US Equity Large Cap Blend (Growth)	B-	C+	B	Down	Y	2,500
ALPS/Alerian MLP Infrastructure Index Fund Class C	ALRCX	NAS CM	Open End	Energy Sector Equity (Growth)	D	D	D	Down	Y	2,500
ALPS/Alerian MLP Infrastructure Index Fund Class I	ALRIX	NAS CM	Open End	Energy Sector Equity (Growth)	D	D	D	Down	Y	100,000
ALPS/Alerian MLP Infrastructure Index Fund Class Investor	ALERX	NAS CM	Open End	Energy Sector Equity (Growth)	D	D	D	Down	Y	2,500
ALPS/Red Rocks Listed Private Equity Portfolio Class I	US02110B7029		Open End	Global Equity Mid/Small Cap (Growth & Income)	C+	C+	C+	Down	Y	0
ALPS/Red Rocks Listed Private Equity Portfolio Class III	AVPEX	NAS CM	Open End	Global Equity Mid/Small Cap (Growth & Income)	C+	C+	C+	Down	Y	0
ALPS/Stadion Core ETF Portfolio Class I	US02110B1089		Open End	Moderate Alloc (Growth)	B-	C+	B-	Up	Y	0
ALPS/Stadion Core ETF Portfolio Class III	ALSTX	NAS CM	Open End	Moderate Alloc (Growth)	C+	C+	B-	Down	Y	0
ALPS/Stadion Tactical Growth Portfolio Class I	US02110B8845		Open End	Moderate Alloc (Growth)	C+	C	B	Up	Y	0
ALPS/Stadion Tactical Growth Portfolio Class III	ALSGX	NAS CM	Open End	Moderate Alloc (Growth)	C+	C	B	Up	Y	0
Altair Smaller Companies Fund	US74925K3427		Open End	US Equity Small Cap (Small Company)	C+	C+	C+	Down	Y	0
Altegris Futures Evolution Strategy Fund Class A	EVOAX	NAS CM	Open End	Other Alternative (Growth)	C+	C	B	Up	Y	2,500
Altegris Futures Evolution Strategy Fund Class C	EVOCX	NAS CM	Open End	Other Alternative (Growth)	C+	C	B-	Up	Y	5,000
Altegris Futures Evolution Strategy Fund Class I	EVOIX	NAS CM	Open End	Other Alternative (Growth)	C+	C	B	Up	Y	1,000,000
Altegris Futures Evolution Strategy Fund Class N	EVONX	NAS CM	Open End	Other Alternative (Growth)	C+	C	B	Up	Y	2,500

★ Expanded analysis of this fund is included in Section II.

	TOTAL RETURNS					PERFORMANCE				ASSETS		ASSET ALLOCATION & TURNOVER					BULL & BEAR		FEES		
Min Additional Investment	3-Month Total Return	6-Month Total Return	1-Year Total Return	3-Year Total Return	5-Year Total Return	Dividend Yield (TTM)	Expense Ratio	3-Yr Std Deviation	3-Year Beta	NAV	Total Assets (MIL)	%Cash	%Stocks	%Bonds	%Other	Turnover Ratio	Last Bull Market Total Return	Last Bear Market Total Return	Front End Fee (%)	Back End Fee (%)	Inception Date
100	0.45	1.62	0.87	3.80	49.61	0	1.64	10.85	1	9.44	34.9	36	39	20	4	283	14.92				Jul-11
100	-2.45						1.55			14.69	18.5	62	23	15	0						Aug-17
100	9.21	18.48	28.78	37.29	115.84	0.01	1.5	11.15	1.01	16.27	24.3	0	100	0	0	17	25.4	-19.86			Oct-08
10,000	0.10	6.68	8.74	39.69	101.07	0	1.3	16	1.05	13.93	175.4	4	96	0	0	27	21.81	-20.66			Mar-11
100	0.04	6.55	8.56	38.81	99.06	0	1.55	15.93	1.05	13.71	175.4	4	96	0	0	27	21.71	-20.76			Mar-11
	5.69	9.96	23.05	29.84	69.63	5.58	1.5	10.62	0.96	4.19	166.1	0	96	0	4	88	15.7	-29.18	5.50		Dec-11
	5.75	10.09	23.35	30.82	71.75	5.81	1.25	10.74	0.97	4.19	166.1	0	96	0	4	88	15.86	-29.11			Sep-03
	8.36	12.90	19.58	48.56	123.93	0.02	1.4	16.39	1	17.34	22.5	3	96	1	0	93	22.58	-28.26	5.50		Dec-11
	8.17	12.80	19.65	49.41	126.27	0.26	1.15	16.42	1	17.45	22.5	3	96	1	0	93	22.81	-28.19			Nov-05
	5.80	10.26	23.90	30.55	71.31	4.28	1.27	10.71	1	11.85	146.7	0	97	0	3	97	17.55	-31.09			Jul-06
	2.37	7.03	23.84	20.71	55.80	3.4	1.45	10.93	0.95	20.89	137.3	4	92	0	5	58	21.09	-20.76	5.50		Dec-11
	2.37	7.09	24.09	21.53	57.67	3.62	1.2	10.93	0.96	20.92	137.3	4	92	0	5	58	21.24	-20.68			Nov-08
	4.62	8.62	29.41	25.45	40.56	2.17		12.48	0.41	7.42	625.2	0	94	0	6	40	25.83	-27.66			Apr-07
	4.17	10.64	31.86	18.29	11.25	0	1.64	13.76	0.98	24.19	120.6	8	87	0	5	33	17.18	-31.63	5.50		Dec-11
	3.05	9.50	30.68	17.82	11.43	0.11	1.39	13.75	0.98	24.32	120.6	8	87	0	5	33	17.37	-31.56			Feb-89
	1.45	2.35	7.42	17.67	61.85	2.91	1.25	13.58	1	22.78	111.3	0	99	0	0	15	32.46	-18.03	5.50		Dec-11
	1.45	2.45	7.61	18.50	63.66	3.12	1	13.58	1	22.81	111.3	0	99	0	0	15	32.62	-17.95			Dec-98
	4.05	8.17	15.84	23.99	80.92	2.95	1.44	10.74	1.03	17.29	102.9	2	98	0	0	93	22.09	-17.58	5.50		Dec-11
	4.05	8.24	16.06	24.76	83.04	3.15	1.19	10.73	1.03	17.29	102.9	2	98	0	0	93	22.26	-17.5			Nov-08
	4.59	6.53	13.12	40.61	71.57	0	1.5	13.27	0.86	19.56	14.6	18	82	0	0	85	30.7	-21.25	5.50		Dec-11
	4.68	6.65	13.41	41.62	73.84	0	1.25	13.28	0.86	19.87	14.6	18	82	0	0	85	30.89	-21.17			Jul-06
	5.53	9.74	22.57	26.78	64.57	4.68	1.19	10.31	0.97	10.26	1,091	0	96	0	4	98	15.41	-27.89			Jan-07
	5.98	13.04	3.96	-8.26	-28.18	0	2.05	13.84	0.88	7.45	532.6	19	35	38	8	50	8.28	-22.61		1.00	Jun-10
	6.17	13.59	4.77	-5.77	-24.89	0.1	1.15	13.85	0.88	7.76	532.6	19	35	38	8	50	8.88	-22.3			Jun-10
	6.14	13.58	4.60	-6.44	-25.83	0.05	1.45	13.78	0.88	7.74	532.6	19	35	38	8	50	8.71	-22.44	5.50		Jun-10
	10.49	12.28	38.69	38.75	92.69	0	2.6	17.86	0.99	14.13	31.8	2	98	0	0	23	-0.04	-20.93		1.00	Feb-11
	10.78	12.86	40.17	42.92	102.59	0	1.6	17.86	0.99	15.21	31.8	2	98	0	0	23	0.44	-20.57			Feb-11
	10.75	12.71	39.73	41.69	99.31	0	2	17.87	0.99	14.84	31.8	2	98	0	0	23	0.19	-20.59	5.50		Feb-11
	3.19	6.41	13.96			0.85	2.71			11.77	31.2	0	100	0	1					1.00	Dec-15
	3.49	6.94	15.06			1.56	1.71			11.91	31.2	0	100	0	1						Dec-15
	3.34	6.69	14.59			1.12	2.11			11.9	31.2	0	100	0	1				5.50		Dec-15
	1.15	5.72	26.11	32.66	87.63	1.24	2.87	11.76	0.94	6.79	218.8	7	74	0	19	30	15.51	-31.03		1.00	Jun-10
	1.36	6.32	27.49	36.67	97.06	1.29	1.89	11.78	0.94	7.27	218.8	7	74	0	19	30	16.22	-30.75			Dec-07
	1.34	6.11	27.04	35.50	93.76	1.23	2.21	11.83	0.95	7.15	218.8	7	74	0	19	30	15.98	-30.74	5.50		Dec-07
	1.28	6.02	26.88	34.68	94.07	1.45	2.34	11.7	0.94	6.06	218.8	7	74	0	19	30	15.83	-30.87			Dec-07
	4.38	6.40	11.89	18.82	79.40	0.03	1.9	11.14	1.05	8.57	93.9	0	100	0	0	78	23.11	-20.76		1.00	Jun-10
	4.67	7.02	13.04	22.56	88.72	0.17	0.9	11.22	1.06	9.26	93.9	0	100	0	0	78	23.64	-20.43			Nov-98
	4.52	6.81	12.72	21.56	86.18	0.14	1.15	11.18	1.06	9	93.9	0	100	0	0	78	23.49	-20.48	5.50		Aug-71
	-2.16	-6.64	-10.38	-28.47	-12.50	8.72	1.85	19.38	0.97	6.03	43.0	0	100	0	0	63				1.00	Dec-12
	-1.77	-6.00	-9.41	-26.97	-9.57	8.4	0.85	19.35	0.97	6.27	43.0	0	100	0	0	63					Dec-12
	-1.96	-6.23	-9.68	-27.64	-10.79	8.53	1.25	19.37	0.97	6.17	43.0	0	100	0	0	63			5.50		Dec-12
	1.29	6.31	25.49	34.44		4.49	1.95	10.96	0.91	12.9	20.8	6	74	0	19	31					Oct-14
	1.17	6.14	24.95	33.27		0.59	2.3	10.96	0.91	13.5	20.8	6	74	0	19	31					Oct-14
	3.41	6.57	13.83	13.82		0	0.98	7.03	0.69	11.83	9.3	3	60	37	0	393					Apr-14
	3.38	6.38	13.57	12.92		0	1.33	6.89	0.69	12.09	9.3	3	60	37	0	393					Apr-14
	5.23	8.76	12.53			3.23	1.15			11.26	5.2	2	90	8	0	142					Apr-15
	5.27	8.61	12.18			0.24	1.5			11.59	5.2	2	90	8	0	142					Apr-15
	4.17	9.85	17.14	35.32		0	1.15	12.88	0.89	13.77	289.7	6	93	0	0	88					Oct-14
250	9.80	10.63	8.62	10.69	40.32	6.49	1.94	12.03	-9.73	10.31	607.8	8	22	69	2	77			5.75		Oct-11
250	9.75	10.24	7.87	8.41	35.32	5.9	2.69	12.02	-9.85	10.24	607.8	8	22	69	2	77				1.00	Feb-12
250	10.01	10.78	8.99	11.66	42.21	6.73	1.69	12	-8.63	10.3	607.8	8	22	69	2	77					Oct-11
250	9.92	10.64	8.62	10.78	40.49	6.5	1.94	12.01	-9.75	10.31	607.8	8	22	69	2	77					Oct-11

Fund Name	Ticker Symbol	Traded On	Fund Type	Category and (Prospectus Objective)	Overall Rating	Reward Rating	Risk Rating	Recent Up/ Downgrade	Open to New Investors	Min Initial Investment
	MARKET		FUND TYPE, CATEGORY & OBJECTIVE		RATINGS				MINIMUMS	
Altegris GSA Trend Strategy Fund Class A	TRNAX	NAS CM	Open End	Other Alternative (Growth)	D-	D+	C		Y	2,500
Altegris GSA Trend Strategy Fund Class I	TRNIX	NAS CM	Open End	Other Alternative (Growth)	D-	D+	C		Y	1,000,000
Altegris GSA Trend Strategy Fund Class N	TRNNX	NAS CM	Open End	Other Alternative (Growth)	D-	D+	C		Y	2,500
Altegris Managed Futures Strategy Fund Class A	MFTAX	NAS CM	Open End	Other Alternative (Growth)	C	C-	C	Up	Y	2,500
Altegris Managed Futures Strategy Fund Class C	MFTCX	NAS CM	Open End	Other Alternative (Growth)	C-	D+	C	Up	Y	5,000
Altegris Managed Futures Strategy Fund Class I	MFTIX	NAS CM	Open End	Other Alternative (Growth)	C	C-	C	Up	Y	1,000,000
Altegris Managed Futures Strategy Fund Class O	MFTOX	NAS CM	Open End	Other Alternative (Growth)	C	C-	C	Up	Y	2,500
Altegris Multi-Strategy Alternative Fund Class A	MULAX	NAS CM	Open End	Multialternative (Growth & Income)	C	C-	B	Up	Y	2,500
Altegris Multi-Strategy Alternative Fund Class I	MULIX	NAS CM	Open End	Multialternative (Growth & Income)	C+	C	B	Up	Y	1,000,000
Altegris Multi-Strategy Alternative Fund Class N	MULNX	NAS CM	Open End	Multialternative (Growth & Income)	C	C-	B	Up	Y	2,500
Altegris/AACA Opportunistic Real Estate Fund A	RAAAX	NAS CM	Open End	Real Estate Sector Equity (Real Estate)	B+	A-	B	Up	Y	2,500
Altegris/AACA Opportunistic Real Estate Fund I	RAAIX	NAS CM	Open End	Real Estate Sector Equity (Real Estate)	B+	A-	B	Up	Y	1,000,000
Altegris/AACA Opportunistic Real Estate Fund N	RAANX	NAS CM	Open End	Real Estate Sector Equity (Real Estate)	B+	A-	B	Up	Y	2,500
Alternative Strategies Fund Class A	LTAFX	NAS CM	Closed End	Multialternative (Growth)	C	C	C		Y	5,000
Alternative Strategies Fund Class C	LTCFX	NAS CM	Closed End	Multialternative (Growth)	C-	C-	C-	Up	Y	2,500
Amana Mutual Funds Trust Developing World Fund Inst	AMIDX	NAS CM	Open End	Emerging Markets Equity (Growth)	C	C	C	Up	Y	100,000
Amana Mutual Funds Trust Developing World Fund Investor	AMDWX	NAS CM	Open End	Emerging Markets Equity (Growth)	C	C	C	Up	Y	250
Amana Mutual Funds Trust Growth Fund Institutional	AMIGX	NAS CM	Open End	US Equity Large Cap Growth (Growth)	B	B+	B		Y	100,000
Amana Mutual Funds Trust Growth Fund Investor	AMAGX	NAS CM	Open End	US Equity Large Cap Growth (Growth)	B	B+	B		Y	250
Amana Mutual Funds Trust Income Fund Institutional	AMINX	NAS CM	Open End	US Equity Large Cap Blend (Equity-Income)	B-	B-	B-	Down	Y	100,000
Amana Mutual Funds Trust Income Fund Investor	AMANX	NAS CM	Open End	US Equity Large Cap Blend (Equity-Income)	B-	B-	B-	Down	Y	250
AmericaFirst Defensive Growth Fund Class A	DGQAX	NAS CM	Open End	Long/Short Equity (Growth)	D+	D	D+	Down	Y	1,000
AmericaFirst Defensive Growth Fund Class I	DGQIX	NAS CM	Open End	Long/Short Equity (Growth)	D+	D+	D+	Down	Y	1,000,000
AmericaFirst Defensive Growth Fund Class U	DGQUX	NAS CM	Open End	Long/Short Equity (Growth)	D	D	D	Down	Y	1,000
AmericaFirst Income Fund Class A	AFPAX	NAS CM	Open End	Moderate Alloc (Income)	C+	C	B-	Up	Y	1,000
AmericaFirst Income Fund Class I	AFPIX	NAS CM	Open End	Moderate Alloc (Income)	C+	C	B-	Up	Y	1,000,000
AmericaFirst Income Fund Class U	AFPUX	NAS CM	Open End	Moderate Alloc (Income)	C+	C	B-	Up	Y	1,000
AmericaFirst Large Cap Share Buyback Fund Class A	SBQAX	NAS CM	Open End	US Equity Large Cap Blend (Growth)	U	U	U		Y	1,000
AmericaFirst Large Cap Share Buyback Fund Class I	SBQIX	NAS CM	Open End	US Equity Large Cap Blend (Growth)	U	U	U		Y	1,000,000
AmericaFirst Large Cap Share Buyback Fund Class U	SBQUX	NAS CM	Open End	US Equity Large Cap Blend (Growth)	U	U	U		Y	1,000
AmericaFirst Quantitative Strategies Fund Class A	AFIAX	NAS CM	Open End	Moderate Alloc (Growth)	C+	C	C+	Down	Y	1,000
AmericaFirst Quantitative Strategies Fund Class C	AFISX	NAS CM	Open End	Moderate Alloc (Growth)	C+	C	C+	Down	Y	1,000
AmericaFirst Quantitative Strategies Fund Class I	AFIIX	NAS CM	Open End	Moderate Alloc (Growth)	C+	C	C+	Down	Y	1,000,000
AmericaFirst Seasonal Rotation Fund Class A	STQAX	NAS CM	Open End	Moderate Alloc (Growth)	C+	C	B-	Down	Y	1,000
AmericaFirst Seasonal Rotation Fund Class I	STQIX	NAS CM	Open End	Moderate Alloc (Growth)	C+	C+	B	Down	Y	1,000,000
AmericaFirst Seasonal Rotation Fund Class U	STQUX	NAS CM	Open End	Moderate Alloc (Growth)	C+	C	B-	Down	Y	1,000
AmericaFirst Tactical Alpha Fund Class A	ABRFX	NAS CM	Open End	Moderate Alloc (Growth)	C+	C	B-	Up	Y	1,000
AmericaFirst Tactical Alpha Fund Class I	ABRWX	NAS CM	Open End	Moderate Alloc (Growth)	C+	C	B		Y	1,000,000
AmericaFirst Tactical Alpha Fund Class U	ABRUX	NAS CM	Open End	Moderate Alloc (Growth)	C+	C	B-	Up	Y	1,000
American Beacon Acadian Emerg Mkts Managed Vol A Cls	ACDAX	NAS CM	Open End	Emerging Markets Equity (Div Emerging Mkts)	C+	C+	C	Up	Y	2,500
American Beacon Acadian Emerg Mkts Managed Vol C Cls	ACDCX	NAS CM	Open End	Emerging Markets Equity (Div Emerging Mkts)	C	C	C	Up	Y	1,000
American Beacon Acadian Emerg Mkts Managed Vol Inst Cls	ACDIX	NAS CM	Open End	Emerging Markets Equity (Div Emerging Mkts)	C+	C+	C	Up	Y	250,000
American Beacon Acadian Emerg Mkts Managed Vol Inv Cls	ACDPX	NAS CM	Open End	Emerging Markets Equity (Div Emerging Mkts)	C+	C+	C	Up	Y	2,500
American Beacon Acadian Emerg Mkts Managed Vol Y Cls	ACDYX	NAS CM	Open End	Emerging Markets Equity (Div Emerging Mkts)	C+	C+	C	Up	Y	100,000
American Beacon AHL Managed Futures Strategy Fund A Class	AHLAX	NAS CM	Open End	Other Alternative (Growth)	C	C	C	Up	Y	2,500
American Beacon AHL Managed Futures Strategy Fund C Class	AHLCX	NAS CM	Open End	Other Alternative (Growth)	C	C	C	Up	Y	1,000
American Beacon AHL Managed Futures Strategy Fund Inst Cls	AHLIX	NAS CM	Open End	Other Alternative (Growth)	C	C	C	Up	Y	250,000
American Beacon AHL Managed Futures Strategy Fund Inv Cls	AHLPX	NAS CM	Open End	Other Alternative (Growth)	C	C	C	Up	Y	2,500
American Beacon AHL Managed Futures Strategy Fund Y Class	AHLYX	NAS CM	Open End	Other Alternative (Growth)	C	C	C	Up	Y	100,000
American Beacon Alpha Quant Core Fund Institutional Class	AQCIX	NAS CM	Open End	US Equity Large Cap Blend (Growth)	U	U	U		Y	250,000
American Beacon Alpha Quant Core Fund Investor Class	AQCPX	NAS CM	Open End	US Equity Large Cap Blend (Growth)	U	U	U		Y	2,500
American Beacon Alpha Quant Core Fund Y Class	AQCYX	NAS CM	Open End	US Equity Large Cap Blend (Growth)	U	U	U		Y	100,000

★ Expanded analysis of this fund is included in Section II.

	TOTAL RETURNS					PERFORMANCE				ASSETS		ASSET ALLOCATION & TURNOVER					BULL & BEAR		FEES		
Min Additional Investment	3-Month Total Return	6-Month Total Return	1-Year Total Return	3-Year Total Return	5-Year Total Return	Dividend Yield (TTM)	Expense Ratio	3-Yr Std Deviation	3-Year Beta	NAV	Total Assets (MIL)	%Cash	%Stocks	%Bonds	%Other	Turnover Ratio	Last Bull Market Total Return	Last Bear Market Total Return	Front End Fee (%)	Back End Fee (%)	Inception Date
250	8.02	8.51	-3.10				1.85			9.69	57.6	53	0	41	6				5.75		Dec-16
250	8.24	8.84	-2.80				1.6			9.72	57.6	53	0	41	6						Dec-16
250	8.02	8.51	-3.10				1.85			9.69	57.6	53	0	41	6						Dec-16
250	3.90	4.28	0.70	3.97	7.54	7.8	1.9	8.64	-5.34		178.7	87	3	7	3	472	-3.12	-4.15	5.75		Aug-10
250	3.67	3.93	-0.12	1.62	3.50	7.2	2.65	8.61	-5.99		178.7	87	3	7	3	472	-3.54	-4.44		1.00	Feb-11
250	3.97	4.47	0.93	4.69	8.82	7.96	1.65	8.63	-4.85		178.7	87	3	7	3	472	-2.91	-4.05			Aug-10
250	3.90	4.41	0.70	4.10	7.48	7.7	1.9	8.62	-5.09		178.7	87	3	7	3	472	-3.05	-4.15			Mar-13
250	3.08	4.11	6.84	1.33		3.02	3.45	4.18	0.68	9.37	21.8	29	22	42	4	131			5.75		Feb-13
250	3.07	4.21	7.06	2.10		3.3	3.2	4.14	0.68	9.4	21.8	29	22	42	4	131					Feb-13
250	3.07	4.10	6.82	1.50		3.12	3.45	4.13	0.69	9.39	21.8	29	22	42	4	131					Feb-13
250	8.93	11.89	23.60	36.61	94.11	0	1.87	11.18	0.72	16.02	282.7	-1	101	0	0	60	32.88	-13.79	5.75		Jan-14
250	9.01	12.03	24.01	37.51	96.46	0	1.62	11.21	0.72	16.06	282.7	-1	101	0	0	60	33.08	-13.7			Jan-14
250	9.00	11.88	23.68	36.62	94.12	0	1.87	11.26	0.73	16.02	282.7	-1	101	0	0	60	32.88	-13.79			Jan-14
1,000	-0.38	-0.02	1.04	-2.47	11.45	7.97	3.74	7.92		7.66	--	0	91	7	2	21	11.01	-6.47	4.25		Sep-10
1,000	-2.35	-2.08	-1.31	-12.61	-0.12	5.78	4.49			7.48	--	0	91	7	2	21	11.01	-6.47		1.00	Jan-15
25	3.65	7.58	21.70	2.20	3.85	0.64	1.14	10.23	0.56	10.73	30.3	24	76	0	0	10	9.58	-12.31			Sep-13
25	3.56	7.40	21.39	1.33	2.58	0.24	1.35	10.29	0.56	10.7	30.3	24	76	0	0	10	9.58	-12.31			Sep-09
25	6.95	13.10	29.29	37.83	98.48	0.63	0.86	10.46	0.98	35.05	1,693	1	99	0	0	0	21.48	-15.64			Sep-13
25	6.89	12.96	28.97	36.93	96.48	0.53	1.1	10.47	0.98	34.96	1,693	1	99	0	0	0	21.48	-15.64			Feb-94
25	6.30	10.64	21.12	28.10	85.88	1.41	0.89	9.89	0.92	51.01	1,427	2	98	0	0	1	18.19	-15.52			Sep-13
25	6.43	10.69	21.05	27.36	84.24	1.07	1.13	9.88	0.92	51.18	1,427	2	98	0	0	1	18.19	-15.52			Jun-86
50	-0.19	-1.52	4.67	-10.29	22.23	0	2.66	8.47	0.5	10.3	22.2	11	89	0	0	341	13.1		5.00		May-11
50	-0.09	-1.27	5.32	-8.28	27.37	0	2.22	8.51	0.5	10.88	22.2	11	89	0	0	341	13.62				May-11
50	-0.30	-1.88	4.21	-11.69	18.97	0	3.23	8.48	0.5	9.9	22.2	11	89	0	0	341	12.72		2.50		May-11
50	3.33	2.78	8.84	5.48	16.81	6.02	2.61	8.12	-0.27	7.39	13.9	0	51	47	0	125	9.78	-16.27	4.00		Jul-10
50	3.46	3.12	9.68	8.06	21.37	6.13	1.81	8.14	-0.26	7.54	13.9	0	51	47	0	125	9.93	-16.02			Jul-10
50	3.14	2.42	8.21	3.80	13.82	5.28	3.11	8.17	-0.27	7.41	13.9	0	51	47	0	125	9.45	-16.41	2.00		Jul-10
50	5.51	9.42	12.04				2.21			11.15	2.6	6	94	0	0				5.00		Jan-17
50	5.67	9.77	12.84				1.5			11.23	2.6	6	94	0	0						Jan-17
50	5.34	9.15	11.54				2.95			11.1	2.6	6	94	0	0				2.50		Jan-17
50	10.20	12.54	18.40	8.54	34.53	2.71	2.32	7.85	0.6	6.37	11.0	0	81	19	0	340	12.94	-12.72	4.00		Sep-07
50	10.13	12.25	17.61	6.35	29.94	1	2.62	7.88	0.59	6.41	11.0	0	81	19	0	340	12.34	-12.97	1.00	1.00	Sep-07
50	10.40	12.38	18.11	7.99	33.84	3.22	1.87	7.8	0.59	6.26	11.0	0	81	19	0	340	12.94	-12.72			Dec-14
50	4.83	5.28	15.54	19.27		0	2.9	12.62	1.91	12.16	9.7	3	0	97	0	427			5.00		Oct-13
50	5.04	5.76	16.33	21.19		0	1.95	12.68	1.92	12.29	9.7	3	0	97	0	427					Oct-13
50	4.74	5.10	15.08	17.45		0	3.4	12.69	1.91	11.95	9.7	3	0	97	0	427			2.50		Oct-13
50	3.63	4.22	5.33	4.81	45.02	0	2.94	7.93	0.43	12.84	7.0	-1	91	9	0	355	8.9	-19.82	5.00		Feb-10
50	3.91	4.63	6.19	8.32	51.64	0	1.99	8.01	0.44	13.54	7.0	-1	91	9	0	355	9.17	-19.58			Jul-10
50	3.51	3.94	4.82	3.33	41.55	0	3.44	7.92	0.42	12.38	7.0	-1	91	9	0	355	8.64	-19.96	2.50		Feb-10
50	7.67	10.89	25.25	10.91		1.31	1.76	12.11	0.74	10.91	34.5	4	92	0	5	32			5.75		Sep-13
50	7.46	10.50	24.26	8.38		0.58	2.51	12.11	0.74	10.79	34.5	4	92	0	5	32				1.00	Sep-13
50	7.82	11.14	25.72	12.30		1.54	1.36	12.13	0.74	10.99	34.5	4	92	0	5	32					Sep-13
50	7.59	10.81	25.18	10.98		1.33	1.74	12.11	0.74	10.88	34.5	4	92	0	5	32					Sep-13
50	7.65	10.97	25.52	11.87		1.54	1.46	12.12	0.74	10.94	34.5	4	92	0	5	32					Sep-13
50	3.66	5.58	4.70	2.79		0	1.94	8.4	-32.72	10.42	513.6	13	21	59	7				5.75		Aug-14
50	3.55	5.30	4.04	0.61		0	2.69	8.38	-32.9	10.18	513.6	13	21	59	7					1.00	Aug-14
50	3.82	5.82	5.18	4.17		0	1.54	8.4	-32.41	10.55	513.6	13	21	59	7						Aug-14
50	3.67	5.69	4.77	2.92		0	1.92	8.4	-32.57	10.41	513.6	13	21	59	7						Aug-14
50	3.83	5.84	5.11	3.85		0	1.64	8.39	-33.13	10.51	513.6	13	21	59	7						Aug-14
50	7.36	13.47					0.7			11.44	2.3	0	98	2	0						Mar-17
50	7.19	13.19					1.08			11.4	2.3	0	98	2	0						Mar-17
50	7.37	13.37					0.8			11.43	2.3	0	98	2	0						Mar-17

Fund Name	MARKET Ticker Symbol	Traded On	FUND TYPE, CATEGORY & OBJECTIVE Fund Type	Category and (Prospectus Objective)	RATINGS Overall Rating	Reward Rating	Risk Rating	Recent Up/ Downgrade	MINIMUMS Open to New Investors	Min Initial Investment
American Beacon Alpha Quant Dividend Fund Inst Cls	AQDIX	NAS CM	Open End	US Equity Large Cap Value (Equity-Income)	U	U	U		Y	250,000
American Beacon Alpha Quant Dividend Fund Investor Class	AQDPX	NAS CM	Open End	US Equity Large Cap Value (Equity-Income)	U	U	U		Y	2,500
American Beacon Alpha Quant Dividend Fund Y Class	AQDYX	NAS CM	Open End	US Equity Large Cap Value (Equity-Income)	U	U	U		Y	100,000
American Beacon Alpha Quant Quality Fund Institutional Cls	AQQIX	NAS CM	Open End	US Equity Large Cap Blend (Growth)	U	U	U		Y	250,000
American Beacon Alpha Quant Quality Fund Investor Class	AQQPX	NAS CM	Open End	US Equity Large Cap Blend (Growth)	U	U	U		Y	2,500
American Beacon Alpha Quant Quality Fund Y Class	AQQYX	NAS CM	Open End	US Equity Large Cap Blend (Growth)	U	U	U		Y	100,000
American Beacon Alpha Quant Value Fund Institutional Class	AQVVX	NAS CM	Open End	US Equity Large Cap Value (Growth)	U	U	U		Y	250,000
American Beacon Alpha Quant Value Fund Investor Class	AQVPX	NAS CM	Open End	US Equity Large Cap Value (Growth)	U	U	U		Y	2,500
American Beacon Alpha Quant Value Fund Y Class	AQVYX	NAS CM	Open End	US Equity Large Cap Value (Growth)	U	U	U		Y	100,000
American Beacon ARK Transformational Innovation Inst Cls	ADNIX	NAS CM	Open End	Technology Sector Equity (World Stock)	U	U	U		Y	250,000
American Beacon ARK Transformational Innovation Inv Cls	ADNPX	NAS CM	Open End	Technology Sector Equity (World Stock)	U	U	U		Y	2,500
American Beacon ARK Transformational Innovation Fund Y Cls	ADNYX	NAS CM	Open End	Technology Sector Equity (World Stock)	U	U	U		Y	100,000
American Beacon Bahl & Gaynor Small Cap Growth Fund A Cls	GBSAX	NAS CM	Open End	US Equity Small Cap (Growth)	A-	A-	B	Up	Y	2,500
American Beacon Bahl & Gaynor Small Cap Growth Fund C Cls	GBSCX	NAS CM	Open End	US Equity Small Cap (Growth)	B+	A-	B	Up	Y	1,000
American Beacon Bahl & Gaynor Small Cap Growth Inst Cls	GBSIX	NAS CM	Open End	US Equity Small Cap (Growth)	A-	A	B	Up	Y	250,000
American Beacon Bahl & Gaynor Small Cap Growth Inv Cls	GBSPX	NAS CM	Open End	US Equity Small Cap (Growth)	A-	A-	B	Up	Y	2,500
American Beacon Bahl & Gaynor Small Cap Growth Fund Y Cls	GBSYX	NAS CM	Open End	US Equity Small Cap (Growth)	A-	A	B	Up	Y	100,000
American Beacon Balanced Fund Advisor Class	ABLSX	NAS CM	Open End	Moderate Alloc (Balanced)	B-	C+	B-	Down	Y	2,500
American Beacon Balanced Fund C Class	ABCCX	NAS CM	Open End	Moderate Alloc (Balanced)	B-	C+	B	Down	Y	1,000
American Beacon Balanced Fund Class A	ABFAX	NAS CM	Open End	Moderate Alloc (Balanced)	B-	C+	B-	Down	Y	2,500
American Beacon Balanced Fund Class Y	ACBYX	NAS CM	Open End	Moderate Alloc (Balanced)	B-	C+	B-	Down	Y	100,000
American Beacon Balanced Fund Institutional Class	AADBX	NAS CM	Open End	Moderate Alloc (Balanced)	B-	C+	B-	Down	Y	250,000
American Beacon Balanced Fund Investor Class	AABPX	NAS CM	Open End	Moderate Alloc (Balanced)	B-	C+	B-	Down	Y	2,500
American Beacon Bridgeway Large Cap Growth Fund A Class	BLYAX	NAS CM	Open End	US Equity Large Cap Growth (Growth)	B+	A-	B	Up	Y	2,500
American Beacon Bridgeway Large Cap Growth Fund C Class	BLYCX	NAS CM	Open End	US Equity Large Cap Growth (Growth)	B+	A-	B	Up	Y	1,000
American Beacon Bridgeway Large Cap Growth Fund Inst Cls	BRLGX	NAS CM	Open End	US Equity Large Cap Growth (Growth)	A-	A-	B	Up	Y	250,000
American Beacon Bridgeway Large Cap Growth Fund Inv Cls	BLYPX	NAS CM	Open End	US Equity Large Cap Growth (Growth)	B+	A-	B	Up	Y	2,500
American Beacon Bridgeway Large Cap Growth Fund Y Class	BLYYX	NAS CM	Open End	US Equity Large Cap Growth (Growth)	B+	A-	B	Up	Y	100,000
American Beacon Bridgeway Large Cap Value Fund A Class	BWLAX	NAS CM	Open End	US Equity Large Cap Value (Growth)	B	B	B	Up	Y	2,500
American Beacon Bridgeway Large Cap Value Fund C Class	BWLCX	NAS CM	Open End	US Equity Large Cap Value (Growth)	B	B-	B	Up	Y	1,000
American Beacon Bridgeway Large Cap Value Fund Inst Cls	BRLVX	NAS CM	Open End	US Equity Large Cap Value (Growth)	B	B	B+	Up	Y	250,000
American Beacon Bridgeway Large Cap Value Fund Inv Cls	BWLIX	NAS CM	Open End	US Equity Large Cap Value (Growth)	B	B	B	Up	Y	2,500
American Beacon Bridgeway Large Cap Value Fund R6 Class	BWLRX	NAS CM	Open End	US Equity Large Cap Value (Growth)	B	B	B	Up	Y	0
American Beacon Bridgeway Large Cap Value Fund Y Class	BWLYX	NAS CM	Open End	US Equity Large Cap Value (Growth)	B	B	B	Up	Y	100,000
American Beacon Grosvenor Long/Short Fund A Class	GSVAX	NAS CM	Open End	Long/Short Equity (Growth)	C	C	B	Up	Y	2,500
American Beacon Grosvenor Long/Short Fund C Class	GVRCX	NAS CM	Open End	Long/Short Equity (Growth)	C	C	B	Up	Y	1,000
American Beacon Grosvenor Long/Short Fund Inst Cls	GVRIX	NAS CM	Open End	Long/Short Equity (Growth)	C	C	B	Up	Y	250,000
American Beacon Grosvenor Long/Short Fund Investor Class	GVRPX	NAS CM	Open End	Long/Short Equity (Growth)	C	C	B	Up	Y	2,500
American Beacon Grosvenor Long/Short Fund Ultra Class	GVRUX	NAS CM	Open End	Long/Short Equity (Growth)	C	C-	B+		Y	350,000,000
American Beacon Grosvenor Long/Short Fund Y Class	GVRYX	NAS CM	Open End	Long/Short Equity (Growth)	C	C	B	Up	Y	100,000
American Beacon International Equity Fund Advisor Class	AAISX	NAS CM	Open End	Global Equity Large Cap (Foreign Stock)	B-	C+	B-	Up	Y	2,500
American Beacon International Equity Fund Class A	AIEAX	NAS CM	Open End	Global Equity Large Cap (Foreign Stock)	B-	C+	B-	Up	Y	2,500
American Beacon International Equity Fund Class C	AILCX	NAS CM	Open End	Global Equity Large Cap (Foreign Stock)	C+	C+	B-	Up	Y	1,000
American Beacon International Equity Fund Class R6	AAERX	NAS CM	Open End	Global Equity Large Cap (Foreign Stock)	B-	C+	B-	Up	Y	0
American Beacon International Equity Fund Class Y	ABEYX	NAS CM	Open End	Global Equity Large Cap (Foreign Stock)	B-	C+	B-	Up	Y	100,000
American Beacon Intl Equity Fund Inst Cls	AAIEX	NAS CM	Open End	Global Equity Large Cap (Foreign Stock)	B-	C+	B-	Up	Y	250,000
American Beacon International Equity Fund Investor Class	AAIPX	NAS CM	Open End	Global Equity Large Cap (Foreign Stock)	B-	C+	B-	Up	Y	2,500
American Beacon Ionic Strategic Arbitrage Fund Class A	IONAX	NAS CM	Open End	Market Neutral (Growth & Income)	C+	C-	B+	Up	Y	2,500
American Beacon Ionic Strategic Arbitrage Fund Class C	IONCX	NAS CM	Open End	Market Neutral (Growth & Income)	C-	D+	C+	Down	Y	1,000
American Beacon Ionic Strategic Arbitrage Fund Class Y	IONYX	NAS CM	Open End	Market Neutral (Growth & Income)	B-	C	A-	Up	Y	100,000
American Beacon Ionic Strategic Arbitrage Fund Inst Cls	IONIX	NAS CM	Open End	Market Neutral (Growth & Income)	C+	C	B	Up	Y	250,000
American Beacon Ionic Strategic Arbitrage Fund Inv Cls	IONPX	NAS CM	Open End	Market Neutral (Growth & Income)	C+	C	B+	Up	Y	2,500

★Expanded analysis of this fund is included in Section II.

Min Additional Investment	TOTAL RETURNS 3-Month Total Return	6-Month Total Return	1-Year Total Return	3-Year Total Return	5-Year Total Return	PERFORMANCE Dividend Yield (TTM)	Expense Ratio	3-Yr Std Deviation	3-Year Beta	ASSETS NAV	Total Assets (MIL)	ASSET ALLOCATION & TURNOVER %Cash	%Stocks	%Bonds	%Other	Turnover Ratio	BULL & BEAR Last Bull Market Total Return	Last Bear Market Total Return	FEES Front End Fee (%)	Back End Fee (%)	Inception Date
50	7.06	11.97					0.7			10.98	2.2	0	97	3	0	0					Mar-17
50	6.88	11.68					1.08			10.94	2.2	0	97	3	0	0					Mar-17
50	6.96	11.98					0.8			10.97	2.2	0	97	3	0	0					Mar-17
50	8.22	15.07					0.7			11.54	2.3	0	98	2	0						Mar-17
50	8.24	14.89					1.08			11.51	2.3	0	98	2	0						Mar-17
50	8.22	15.09					0.8			11.53	2.3	0	98	2	0						Mar-17
50	7.59	14.11					0.7			11.5	2.3	0	97	3	0						Mar-17
50	7.42	13.83					1.08			11.46	2.3	0	97	3	0						Mar-17
50	7.59	14.01					0.8			11.49	2.3	0	97	3	0						Mar-17
50	12.56	30.75	66.58				1			16.24	10.4	2	92	0	6						Jan-17
50	12.38	30.48	65.99				1.38			16.18	10.4	2	92	0	6						Jan-17
50	12.50	30.59	66.38				1.1			16.22	10.4	2	92	0	6						Jan-17
50	3.25	7.35	13.25	36.25		0.22	1.38	12.99	0.79	13.75	41.7	1	99	0	0	23			5.75		Jul-14
50	3.00	6.87	12.33	33.10		0.11	2.13	12.98	0.79	13.42	41.7	1	99	0	0	23				1.00	Jul-14
50	3.29	7.50	13.63	37.78		0.22	0.98	12.99	0.79	13.93	41.7	1	99	0	0	23					Jul-14
50	3.19	7.29	13.20	36.24		0.22	1.36	12.98	0.79	13.75	41.7	1	99	0	0	23					Jul-14
50	3.30	7.53	13.55	37.43		0.22	1.08	12.99	0.79	13.89	41.7	1	99	0	0	23					Jul-14
50	3.84	7.01	11.95	18.80	57.82	1.69	1.13	7.42	-0.74	15.84	356.1	2	66	32	0	16	17.92	-11.24			May-05
50	3.81	6.75	11.34	16.62	52.71	1.18	1.78	7.43	-0.75	15.09	356.1	2	66	32	0	16	17.42	-11.5		1.00	Sep-10
50	4.02	7.20	12.20	19.30	58.61	1.9	1.03	7.43	-0.74	14.92	356.1	2	66	32	0	16	17.9	-11.23	5.75		May-10
50	3.99	7.28	12.44	20.55	61.44	1.98	0.73	7.44	-0.74	16.88	356.1	2	66	32	0	16	18.05	-11.02			Mar-10
50	3.99	7.23	12.49	20.67	61.92	2.03	0.63	7.43	-0.75	16.79	356.1	2	66	32	0	16	18.24	-11.07			Jul-87
50	3.92	7.11	12.18	19.44	59.23	1.99	0.96	7.43	-0.75	14.94	356.1	2	66	32	0	16	18.06	-11.2			Aug-94
50	7.66	14.89	27.02	36.96	127.94	0.51	1.22	10.24	0.88	29.75	169.0	0	98	2	0		27.46	-20.06	5.75		Feb-16
50	8.06	15.11	26.79	34.65	120.79	0.52	1.97	10.24	0.88	29.53	169.0	0	98	2	0		26.91	-20.31		1.00	Feb-16
50	7.59	14.86	27.22	38.02	130.86	0.51	0.82	10.25	0.88	29.88	169.0	0	98	2	0		27.65	-19.98			Oct-03
50	7.45	14.63	26.74	37.01	129.17	0.51	1.2	10.23	0.88	29.65	169.0	0	98	2	0		27.65	-19.98			Feb-16
50	8.46	15.80	28.17	38.94	132.40	0.51	0.92	10.25	0.88	30.08	169.0	0	98	2	0		27.65	-19.98			Feb-16
50	7.55	11.40	15.43	30.18	108.90	0.85	1.12	10.21	0.96	28.31	4,683	2	98	0	0	56	23.47	-18.52	5.75		Feb-12
50	7.35	11.02	14.57	27.30	101.27	0.28	1.86	10.2	0.96	27.62	4,683	2	98	0	0	56	22.92	-18.77		1.00	Feb-12
50	7.66	11.63	15.89	31.64	113.03	1.17	0.73	10.22	0.96	28.57	4,683	2	98	0	0	56	23.76	-18.43			Oct-03
50	7.55	11.47	15.49	30.39	109.86	0.92	1.08	10.21	0.96	28.41	4,683	2	98	0	0	56	23.68	-18.43			Feb-12
50	7.61	11.59	15.84	31.58	112.94		0.71	10.21	0.96	28.55	4,683	2	98	0	0	56	23.76	-18.43			Apr-17
50	7.62	11.61	15.80	31.42	112.49	1.12	0.8	10.21	0.96	28.49	4,683	2	98	0	0	56	23.76	-18.43			Feb-12
50	4.00	7.07	12.01			0	2.51			10.71	19.1	27	77	-4	0	250			5.75		Oct-15
50	3.78	6.69	11.13			0	3.26			10.51	19.1	27	77	-4	0	250				1.00	Oct-15
50	4.15	7.40	12.52			0	2.11			10.82	19.1	27	77	-4	0	250					Oct-15
50	4.00	7.17	12.09			0	2.49			10.72	19.1	27	77	-4	0	250					Oct-15
50	4.14	7.39	12.51				2.04			10.82	19.1	27	77	-4	0	250					Nov-17
50	4.06	7.21	12.36			0	2.21			10.79	19.1	27	77	-4	0	250					Oct-15
50	4.47	10.12	24.31	20.63	40.37	1.6	1.2	11.86	0.95	21.21	3,140	5	93	0	2	25	14.67	-25.23			May-03
50	4.48	10.10	24.37	20.85	40.63	1.84	1.08	11.87	0.95	20.71	3,140	5	93	0	2	25	14.81	-25.2	5.75		May-10
50	4.27	9.68	23.46	18.15	35.47	1.64	1.86	11.86	0.95	20.09	3,140	5	93	0	2	25	14.31	-25.5		1.00	Sep-10
50	4.60	10.38	24.92	22.31	43.84		0.67	11.88	0.95	20.89	3,140	5	93	0	2	25	15.16	-25.12			Feb-17
50	4.53	10.26	24.76	21.98	42.95	1.91	0.78	11.87	0.95	21.68	3,140	5	93	0	2	25	15.09	-25.13			Aug-09
50	4.57	10.30	24.83	22.22	43.73	2.04	0.7	11.87	0.95	20.88	3,140	5	93	0	2	25	15.16	-25.12			Aug-91
50	4.45	10.11	24.39	20.94	41.07	1.78	1.07	11.87	0.95	20.72	3,140	5	93	0	2	25	14.86	-25.19			Aug-94
50	0.04	-0.17	-0.49	4.94		4.7	1.97			8.31	106.3	73	-31	18	4	436			4.75		Jun-15
50	-0.20	-0.65	-1.34	2.42		4.78	2.72			8.22	106.3	73	-31	18	4	436				1.00	Jun-15
50	0.05	-0.05	-0.25	5.86		4.66	1.67			8.36	106.3	73	-31	18	4	436					Jun-15
50	0.17	0.06	-0.09	6.00		4.66	1.57			8.37	106.3	73	-31	18	4	436					Jun-15
50	0.06	-0.15	-0.51	5.11		4.7	1.95			8.32	106.3	73	-31	18	4	436					Jun-15

Fund Name	MARKET Ticker Symbol	MARKET Traded On	FUND TYPE, CATEGORY & OBJECTIVE Fund Type	Category and (Prospectus Objective)	RATINGS Overall Rating	Reward Rating	Risk Rating	Recent Up/ Downgrade	Open to New Investors	MINIMUMS Min Initial Investment
American Beacon Large Cap Value Fund Advisor Class	AVASX	NAS CM	Open End	US Equity Large Cap Value (Growth & Income)	B-	B-	B	Up	Y	2,500
American Beacon Large Cap Value Fund Class A	ALVAX	NAS CM	Open End	US Equity Large Cap Value (Growth & Income)	B-	B-	B	Up	Y	2,500
American Beacon Large Cap Value Fund Class C	ALVCX	NAS CM	Open End	US Equity Large Cap Value (Growth & Income)	B-	B-	B-	Up	Y	1,000
American Beacon Large Cap Value Fund Class R6	AALRX	NAS CM	Open End	US Equity Large Cap Value (Growth & Income)	B-	B-	B	Down	Y	0
American Beacon Large Cap Value Fund Class Y	ABLYX	NAS CM	Open End	US Equity Large Cap Value (Growth & Income)	B-	B-	B	Down	Y	100,000
American Beacon Large Cap Value Fund Institutional Class	AADEX	NAS CM	Open End	US Equity Large Cap Value (Growth & Income)	B-	B-	B	Down	Y	250,000
American Beacon Large Cap Value Fund Investor Class	AAGPX	NAS CM	Open End	US Equity Large Cap Value (Growth & Income)	B-	B-	B	Up	Y	2,500
American Beacon Mid-Cap Value Fund Advisor Class	AMCSX	NAS CM	Open End	US Equity Mid Cap (Growth & Income)	B	B	B	Up	Y	2,500
American Beacon Mid-Cap Value Fund C Class	AMCCX	NAS CM	Open End	US Equity Mid Cap (Growth & Income)	B	B	B	Up	Y	1,000
American Beacon Mid-Cap Value Fund Class A	ABMAX	NAS CM	Open End	US Equity Mid Cap (Growth & Income)	B	B	B	Up	Y	2,500
American Beacon Mid-Cap Value Fund Class Y	ACMYX	NAS CM	Open End	US Equity Mid Cap (Growth & Income)	B	B	B	Up	Y	100,000
American Beacon Mid-Cap Value Fund Institutional Class	AACIX	NAS CM	Open End	US Equity Mid Cap (Growth & Income)	B	B	B	Up	Y	250,000
American Beacon Mid-Cap Value Fund Investor Class	AMPAX	NAS CM	Open End	US Equity Mid Cap (Growth & Income)	B	B	B	Up	Y	2,500
American Beacon Numeric Integrated Alpha Fund Inst Cls	NIAIX	NAS CM	Open End	Long/Short Equity (Growth)	D	D	C		Y	250,000
American Beacon Numeric Integrated Alpha Fund Investor Cls	NIAPX	NAS CM	Open End	Long/Short Equity (Growth)	D	D	C		Y	2,500
American Beacon Numeric Integrated Alpha Fund Ultra Class	NIAUX	NAS CM	Open End	Long/Short Equity (Growth)	D	D	C		Y	350,000,000
American Beacon Numeric Integrated Alpha Fund Y Class	NIAYX	NAS CM	Open End	Long/Short Equity (Growth)	D	D	C		Y	100,000
American Beacon SGA Global Growth Fund A Class	SGAAX	NAS CM	Open End	Global Equity (World Stock)	B+	B	A-	Up	Y	2,500
American Beacon SGA Global Growth Fund C Class	SGACX	NAS CM	Open End	Global Equity (World Stock)	B	B	A-	Up	Y	1,000
American Beacon SGA Global Growth Fund Institutional Class	SGAGX	NAS CM	Open End	Global Equity (World Stock)	B+	B	A-	Up	Y	250,000
American Beacon SGA Global Growth Fund Investor Class	SGAPX	NAS CM	Open End	Global Equity (World Stock)	B+	B	A-	Up	Y	2,500
American Beacon SGA Global Growth Fund Y Class	SGAYX	NAS CM	Open End	Global Equity (World Stock)	B+	B	A-	Up	Y	100,000
American Beacon Shapiro Equity Opp Fund Inst Cls	SHXIX	NAS CM	Open End	US Equity Large Cap Value (Growth)	U	U	U		Y	250,000
American Beacon Shapiro Equity Opp Fund Inv Cls	SHXPX	NAS CM	Open End	US Equity Large Cap Value (Growth)	U	U	U		Y	2,500
American Beacon Shapiro Equity Opportunities Fund Y Class	SHXYX	NAS CM	Open End	US Equity Large Cap Value (Growth)	U	U	U		Y	100,000
American Beacon Shapiro SMID Cap Equity Fund Inst Cls	SHDIX	NAS CM	Open End	US Equity Mid Cap (Growth)	U	U	U		Y	250,000
American Beacon Shapiro SMID Cap Equity Fund Investor Cls	SHDPX	NAS CM	Open End	US Equity Mid Cap (Growth)	U	U	U		Y	2,500
American Beacon Shapiro SMID Cap Equity Fund Y Class	SHDYX	NAS CM	Open End	US Equity Mid Cap (Growth)	U	U	U		Y	100,000
American Beacon Small Cap Value Fund Advisor Class	AASSX	NAS CM	Open End	US Equity Small Cap (Small Company)	B	B+	B	Up	Y	2,500
American Beacon Small Cap Value Fund C Class	ASVCX	NAS CM	Open End	US Equity Small Cap (Small Company)	B	B	B	Up	Y	1,000
American Beacon Small Cap Value Fund Class A	ABSAX	NAS CM	Open End	US Equity Small Cap (Small Company)	B	B+	B	Up	Y	2,500
American Beacon Small Cap Value Fund Class Institutional	AVFIX	NAS CM	Open End	US Equity Small Cap (Small Company)	B+	B+	B	Up	Y	250,000
American Beacon Small Cap Value Fund Class Y	ABSYX	NAS CM	Open End	US Equity Small Cap (Small Company)	B+	B+	B	Up	Y	100,000
American Beacon Small Cap Value Fund Investor Class	AVPAX	NAS CM	Open End	US Equity Small Cap (Small Company)	B	B+	B	Up	Y	2,500
American Beacon Small Cap Value Fund R6 Class	AASRX	NAS CM	Open End	US Equity Small Cap (Small Company)	B+	B+	B	Up	Y	0
American Beacon Stephens Mid-Cap Growth Fund A Class	SMFAX	NAS CM	Open End	US Equity Mid Cap (Growth)	B	B	C+	Up	Y	2,500
American Beacon Stephens Mid-Cap Growth Fund C Class	SMFCX	NAS CM	Open End	US Equity Mid Cap (Growth)	B-	B	C+	Down	Y	1,000
American Beacon Stephens Mid-Cap Growth Fund Inst Cls	SFMIX	NAS CM	Open End	US Equity Mid Cap (Growth)	B	B+	C+	Up	Y	250,000
American Beacon Stephens Mid-Cap Growth Fund Investor Cls	STMGX	NAS CM	Open End	US Equity Mid Cap (Growth)	B	B+	C+	Up	Y	2,500
American Beacon Stephens Mid-Cap Growth Fund Y Class	SMFYX	NAS CM	Open End	US Equity Mid Cap (Growth)	B	B+	C+	Up	Y	100,000
American Beacon Stephens Small Cap Growth Fund A Class	SPWAX	NAS CM	Open End	US Equity Small Cap (Growth)	B	B	B-	Up	Y	2,500
American Beacon Stephens Small Cap Growth Fund C Class	SPWCX	NAS CM	Open End	US Equity Small Cap (Growth)	C+	B-	C	Up	Y	1,000
American Beacon Stephens Small Cap Growth Fund Inst Cls	STSIX	NAS CM	Open End	US Equity Small Cap (Growth)	B	B	B	Up	Y	250,000
American Beacon Stephens Small Cap Growth Fund Inv Cls	STSGX	NAS CM	Open End	US Equity Small Cap (Growth)	B	B	B	Up	Y	2,500
American Beacon Stephens Small Cap Growth Fund Y Class	SPWYX	NAS CM	Open End	US Equity Small Cap (Growth)	B	B	B	Up	Y	100,000
American Beacon The London Company Income Eq Fund A Cls	ABCAX	NAS CM	Open End	US Equity Large Cap Value (Equity-Income)	B-	C+	B-	Down	Y	2,500
American Beacon The London Company Income Eq Fund C Cls	ABECX	NAS CM	Open End	US Equity Large Cap Value (Equity-Income)	B	C+	B+		Y	1,000
American Beacon The London Company Income Eq Fund Inst Cls	ABCIX	NAS CM	Open End	US Equity Large Cap Value (Equity-Income)	B-	C+	B	Down	Y	250,000
American Beacon The London Company Income Eq Fund Inv Cls	ABCVX	NAS CM	Open End	US Equity Large Cap Value (Equity-Income)	B	C+	B+		Y	2,500
American Beacon The London Company Income Eq Fund Y Cls	ABCYX	NAS CM	Open End	US Equity Large Cap Value (Equity-Income)	B-	C+	B	Down	Y	100,000
American Beacon Zebra Small Cap Equity Fund A Class	AZSAX	NAS CM	Open End	US Equity Small Cap (Small Company)	B+	A-	B	Up	Y	2,500
American Beacon Zebra Small Cap Equity Fund C Class	AZSCX	NAS CM	Open End	US Equity Small Cap (Small Company)	B+	A-	B	Up	Y	1,000

★ Expanded analysis of this fund is included in Section II.

Min Additional Investment	TOTAL RETURNS: 3-Month Total Return	6-Month Total Return	1-Year Total Return	3-Year Total Return	5-Year Total Return	PERFORMANCE: Dividend Yield (TTM)	Expense Ratio	3-Yr Std Deviation	3-Year Beta	ASSETS: NAV	Total Assets (MIL)	ASSET ALLOCATION & TURNOVER: %Cash	%Stocks	%Bonds	%Other	Turnover Ratio	BULL & BEAR: Last Bull Market Total Return	Last Bear Market Total Return	FEES: Front End Fee (%)	Back End Fee (%)	Inception Date
50	5.29	9.52	16.53	24.52	88.69	1.6	1.08	12.2	1.14	26.74	7,352	4	96	0	0	25	26.57	-19.73			May-05
50	5.35	9.62	16.67	24.92	89.34	1.77	0.98	12.2	1.14	26.76	7,352	4	96	0	0	25	26.46	-19.73	5.75		May-10
50	5.20	9.30	15.90	22.23	82.37	0.97	1.74	12.19	1.14	26.6	7,352	4	96	0	0	25	25.9	-19.94		1.00	Sep-10
50	5.41	9.78	17.07	26.31	93.26		0.58	12.21	1.14	29.14	7,352	4	96	0	0	25	26.84	-19.53			Feb-17
50	5.45	9.75	17.01	26.06	92.51	1.84	0.67	12.2	1.14	28.96	7,352	4	96	0	0	25	26.8	-19.59			Aug-09
50	5.41	9.78	17.07	26.30	93.25	1.89	0.6	12.2	1.14	29.15	7,352	4	96	0	0	25	26.84	-19.53			Jul-87
50	5.33	9.59	16.69	25.05	89.99	1.73	0.93	12.2	1.14	27.09	7,352	4	96	0	0	25	26.65	-19.68			Aug-94
50	5.60	9.62	17.08	29.80	100.13	0.83	1.41	12.79	1.17	17.08	692.1	5	95	0	0	27	29.35	-22.23			Jun-07
50	5.50	9.37	16.46	27.49	93.93	0.41	2.05	12.78	1.16	16.52	692.1	5	95	0	0	27	28.77	-22.49		1.00	Sep-10
50	5.62	9.71	17.29	30.38	101.37	0.95	1.27	12.8	1.17	17.05	692.1	5	95	0	0	27	29.29	-22.27	5.75		May-10
50	5.70	9.87	17.60	31.55	104.69	1.19	0.97	12.8	1.17	17.26	692.1	5	95	0	0	27	29.73	-22.16			Mar-10
50	5.73	9.92	17.72	31.86	105.55	1.24	0.9	12.79	1.17	17.4	692.1	5	95	0	0	27	29.7	-22.06			Nov-05
50	5.65	9.81	17.48	30.98	103.23	1.03	1.13	12.8	1.17	17.58	692.1	5	95	0	0	27	29.6	-22.18			Feb-06
50	-0.88	0.89	-0.79			0	1.97			9.91	175.7										Nov-16
50	-0.98	0.80	-1.07			0	2.35			9.88	175.7										Nov-16
50	-0.89	0.99	-0.59			0	1.87			9.91	175.7										Nov-16
50	-0.91	0.87	-0.84			0	2.07			9.9	175.7										Nov-16
50	8.67	11.92	32.69	47.91	82.64	0	1.39	12.7	1.09	18.42	39.7	3	97	0	0	32	25.45	-14.29	5.75		Oct-13
50	8.48	11.50	31.68	44.59	75.78	0	2.14	12.69	1.09	17.79	39.7	3	97	0	0	32	24.9	-14.56		1.00	Oct-13
50	8.80	12.20	33.25	49.73	86.19	0	0.99	12.7	1.1	18.78	39.7	3	97	0	0	32	25.63	-14.2			Dec-10
50	8.72	11.97	32.75	48.03	83.30	0	1.37	12.69	1.09	18.45	39.7	3	97	0	0	32	25.63	-14.2			Oct-13
50	8.78	12.13	33.11	49.28	85.36	0	1.09	12.7	1.1	18.69	39.7	3	97	0	0	32	25.63	-14.2			Oct-13
50	4.63						0.8			10.74	3.5	0	92	8	0						Sep-17
50	4.53						1.18			10.73	3.5	0	92	8	0						Sep-17
50	4.63						0.9			10.74	3.5	0	92	8	0						Sep-17
50	4.53						0.9			10.84	3.6	0	95	5	0						Sep-17
50	4.33						1.28			10.82	3.6	0	95	5	0						Sep-17
50	4.43						1			10.83	3.6	0	95	5	0						Sep-17
50	3.02	7.76	8.16	27.76	91.28	0.37	1.32	14.15	0.98	26.08	7,212	3	97	0	0	53	29.76	-26.52			May-03
50	2.98	7.50	7.57	25.42	85.05	0	1.97	14.14	0.98	24.97	7,212	3	97	0	0	53	29.06	-26.82		1.00	Sep-10
50	3.04	7.81	8.26	28.14	91.94	0.44	1.22	14.15	0.98	25.94	7,212	3	97	0	0	53	29.64	-26.58	5.75		May-10
50	3.15	8.01	8.67	29.63	96.06	0.73	0.84	14.15	0.98	27.41	7,212	3	97	0	0	53	30.14	-26.38			Dec-98
50	3.16	8.01	8.62	29.37	95.25	0.69	0.91	14.16	0.99	27.05	7,212	3	97	0	0	53	30.07	-26.4			Aug-09
50	3.06	7.82	8.34	28.41	92.81	0.5	1.15	14.15	0.98	26.41	7,212	3	97	0	0	53	29.92	-26.47			Feb-99
50	3.18	8.08	8.70	29.68	96.13		0.82	14.16	0.99	27.41	7,212	3	97	0	0	53	30.14	-26.38			Feb-17
50	5.90	11.54	27.89	32.79	85.71	0	1.4	12.05	1.01	19.08	98.3	0	100	0	0	22	27.32	-17.14	5.75		Feb-12
50	5.69	11.09	26.94	29.79	78.48	0	2.15	12.04	1.01	18.11	98.3	0	100	0	0	22	26.65	-17.4		1.00	Feb-12
50	5.96	11.70	28.35	34.37	89.58	0	1	12.04	1.01	22.45	98.3	0	100	0	0	22	27.52	-16.94			Aug-06
50	5.93	11.55	27.96	32.96	86.28	0	1.36	12.05	1.01	19.15	98.3	0	100	0	0	22	27.36	-17.06			Feb-06
50	5.94	11.66	28.26	33.97	88.51	0	1.1	12.04	1.01	22.34	98.3	0	100	0	0	22	27.38	-17.06			Feb-12
50	4.47	9.94	19.06	23.37	73.16	0	1.47	13.52	0.87	17.59	602.8	1	99	0	0	40	28.26	-21.96	5.75		Feb-12
50	4.32	9.58	18.19	20.57	66.77	0	2.24	13.51	0.87	16.74	602.8	1	99	0	0	40	27.76	-22.2		1.00	Feb-12
50	4.57	10.14	19.47	24.79	76.70	0	1.1	13.5	0.87	19.01	602.8	1	99	0	0	40	28.61	-21.74			Aug-06
50	4.54	10.04	19.22	23.78	74.45	0	1.36	13.52	0.87	17.77	602.8	1	99	0	0	40	28.49	-21.87			Dec-05
50	4.54	10.13	19.40	24.41	75.99	0	1.16	13.53	0.87	18.91	602.8	1	99	0	0	40	28.57	-21.87			Feb-12
50	5.37	7.48	14.05	23.57	86.18	1.6	1.14	9.09	0.81	17.02	1,173	4	96	0	0	14			5.75		May-12
50	5.16	7.00	13.18	20.85	79.38	0.91	1.88	9.09	0.81	16.9	1,173	4	96	0	0	14				1.00	May-12
50	5.49	7.62	14.48	24.97	90.09	1.95	0.78	9.09	0.81	17.18	1,173	4	96	0	0	14					May-12
50	5.37	7.42	14.07	23.68	87.03	1.66	1.07	9.08	0.81	17.11	1,173	4	96	0	0	14					May-12
50	5.44	7.63	14.37	24.72	89.37	1.89	0.83	9.09	0.81	17.09	1,173	4	96	0	0	14					May-12
50	0.93	6.67	9.08	32.74	100.68	0.98	1.3	13.41	0.89	16.22	56.1	3	97	0	0	77	25.07	-20.71	5.75		Jun-10
50	0.73	6.30	8.30	29.81	93.28	0.59	2.05	13.41	0.89	15.5	56.1	3	97	0	0	77	24.54	-20.96		1.00	Sep-10

	MARKET		FUND TYPE, CATEGORY & OBJECTIVE		RATINGS				MINIMUMS	
Fund Name	Ticker Symbol	Traded On	Fund Type	Category and (Prospectus Objective)	Overall Rating	Reward Rating	Risk Rating	Recent Up/ Downgrade	Open to New Investors	Min Initial Investment
American Beacon Zebra Small Cap Equity Fund Inst Cls	AZSIX	NAS CM	Open End	US Equity Small Cap (Small Company)	B+	A-	B	Up	Y	250,000
American Beacon Zebra Small Cap Equity Fund Investor Class	AZSPX	NAS CM	Open End	US Equity Small Cap (Small Company)	B+	A-	B	Up	Y	2,500
American Beacon Zebra Small Cap Equity Fund Y Class	AZSYX	NAS CM	Open End	US Equity Small Cap (Small Company)	B+	A-	B	Up	Y	100,000
American Century Adaptive All Cap Fund Advisor Class	ACMFX	NAS CM	Open End	US Equity Mid Cap (Growth)	B-	B	B-	Down	Y	2,500
American Century Adaptive All Cap Fund I Class	ACMHX	NAS CM	Open End	US Equity Mid Cap (Growth)	B	B	B-	Up	Y	5,000,000
American Century Adaptive All Cap Fund Investor Class	ACMNX	NAS CM	Open End	US Equity Mid Cap (Growth)	B	B	B-	Up	Y	2,500
American Century Adaptive All Cap Fund R Class	ACMEX	NAS CM	Open End	US Equity Mid Cap (Growth)	B-	B	B-	Down	Y	2,500
American Century Adaptive All Cap Fund R5 Class	ACMUX	NAS CM	Open End	US Equity Mid Cap (Growth)	B	B	B-	Up	Y	0
American Century Adaptive All Cap Fund R6 Class	ACMMX	NAS CM	Open End	US Equity Mid Cap (Growth)	B	B	B-	Up	Y	0
American Century Adaptive Equity Fund A CLASS	AVDAX	NAS CM	Open End	US Equity Large Cap Blend (Growth)	B	B	B-		Y	2,500
American Century Adaptive Equity Fund I Class	AVDIX	NAS CM	Open End	US Equity Large Cap Blend (Growth)	B	B	B-		Y	5,000,000
American Century Adaptive Equity Fund Investor Class	AMVIX	NAS CM	Open End	US Equity Large Cap Blend (Growth)	B	B	B-		Y	2,500
American Century Adaptive Equity Fund R CLASS	AVDRX	NAS CM	Open End	US Equity Large Cap Blend (Growth)	B	B	B-	Up	Y	2,500
American Century Adaptive Equity Fund R6 CLASS	AVDMX	NAS CM	Open End	US Equity Large Cap Blend (Growth)	B	B	B-		Y	0
American Century All Cap Growth Fund A Class	ACAQX	NAS CM	Open End	US Equity Large Cap Growth (Growth)	B	B	A-		Y	2,500
American Century All Cap Growth Fund C Class	ACAHX	NAS CM	Open End	US Equity Large Cap Growth (Growth)	B	B	A-		Y	2,500
American Century All Cap Growth Fund I Class	ACAJX	NAS CM	Open End	US Equity Large Cap Growth (Growth)	B	B	A-		Y	5,000,000
American Century All Cap Growth Fund Investor Class	TWGTX	NAS CM	Open End	US Equity Large Cap Growth (Growth)	B	B	A-		Y	2,500
American Century All Cap Growth Fund R Class	ACAWX	NAS CM	Open End	US Equity Large Cap Growth (Growth)	B	B	A-		Y	2,500
American Century Balanced Fund I Class	ABINX	NAS CM	Open End	Moderate Alloc (Balanced)	B-	C+	B	Up	Y	5,000,000
American Century Balanced Fund Investor Class	TWBIX	NAS CM	Open End	Moderate Alloc (Balanced)	B-	C+	B	Up	Y	2,500
American Century Balanced Fund R5 Class	ABGNX	NAS CM	Open End	Moderate Alloc (Balanced)	B-	C+	B	Up	Y	0
American Century Capital Value Fund Class A	ACCVX	NAS CM	Open End	US Equity Large Cap Value (Growth)	B-	C+	B	Down	Y	2,500
American Century Capital Value Fund I Class	ACPIX	NAS CM	Open End	US Equity Large Cap Value (Growth)	B-	B-	B	Down	Y	5,000,000
American Century Capital Value Fund Investor Class	ACTIX	NAS CM	Open End	US Equity Large Cap Value (Growth)	B-	B-	B	Down	Y	2,500
American Century Core Equity Plus Fund Class A	ACPQX	NAS CM	Open End	US Equity Large Cap Blend (Growth)	B-	B-	B-	Down	Y	2,500
American Century Core Equity Plus Fund Class C	ACPHX	NAS CM	Open End	US Equity Large Cap Blend (Growth)	B-	C+	B-	Down	Y	2,500
American Century Core Equity Plus Fund Class R	ACPWX	NAS CM	Open End	US Equity Large Cap Blend (Growth)	B-	B-	B-	Down	Y	2,500
American Century Core Equity Plus Fund I Class	ACPKX	NAS CM	Open End	US Equity Large Cap Blend (Growth)	B-	B-	B-	Down	Y	5,000,000
American Century Core Equity Plus Fund Investor Class	ACPVX	NAS CM	Open End	US Equity Large Cap Blend (Growth)	B-	B-	B-	Down	Y	2,500
American Century Disciplined Growth Fund Class A	ADCVX	NAS CM	Open End	US Equity Large Cap Growth (Growth)	B	B	B-		Y	2,500
American Century Disciplined Growth Fund Class C	ADCCX	NAS CM	Open End	US Equity Large Cap Growth (Growth)	B-	B	B-	Down	Y	2,500
American Century Disciplined Growth Fund Class R	ADRRX	NAS CM	Open End	US Equity Large Cap Growth (Growth)	B	B	B-		Y	2,500
American Century Disciplined Growth Fund Institutional Cls	ADCIX	NAS CM	Open End	US Equity Large Cap Growth (Growth)	B	B	B-		Y	5,000,000
American Century Disciplined Growth Fund Investor Class	ADSIX	NAS CM	Open End	US Equity Large Cap Growth (Growth)	B	B	B-		Y	2,500
American Century Disciplined Growth Fund R5 Class	ADGGX	NAS CM	Open End	US Equity Large Cap Growth (Growth)	B	B	B-		Y	0
American Century Disciplined Growth Fund Y Class	ADCYX	NAS CM	Open End	US Equity Large Cap Growth (Growth)	B	B	B-		Y	0
American Century Emerging Markets Fund A Class	AEMMX	NAS CM	Open End	Emerging Markets Equity (Div Emerging Mkts)	B+	A	C+	Up	Y	2,500
American Century Emerging Markets Fund C Class	ACECX	NAS CM	Open End	Emerging Markets Equity (Div Emerging Mkts)	B+	A	C+	Up	Y	2,500
American Century Emerging Markets Fund I Class	AMKIX	NAS CM	Open End	Emerging Markets Equity (Div Emerging Mkts)	B+	A	C+	Up	Y	5,000,000
American Century Emerging Markets Fund Investor Class	TWMIX	NAS CM	Open End	Emerging Markets Equity (Div Emerging Mkts)	B+	A	C+	Up	Y	2,500
American Century Emerging Markets Fund R Class	AEMRX	NAS CM	Open End	Emerging Markets Equity (Div Emerging Mkts)	B+	A	C+	Up	Y	2,500
American Century Emerging Markets Fund R5 Class	AEGMX	NAS CM	Open End	Emerging Markets Equity (Div Emerging Mkts)	B+	A	C+	Up	Y	0
American Century Emerging Markets Fund R6 Class	AEDMX	NAS CM	Open End	Emerging Markets Equity (Div Emerging Mkts)	B+	A	C+	Up	Y	0
American Century Emerging Markets Fund Y Class	AEYMX	NAS CM	Open End	Emerging Markets Equity (Div Emerging Mkts)	B+	A	C+	Up	Y	0
American Century Emerging Markets Small Cap Fund A Class	AECLX	NAS CM	Open End	Emerging Markets Equity (Div Emerging Mkts)	D+	C	B+	Up	Y	2,500
American Century Emerging Markets Small Cap Fund C Class	AECHX	NAS CM	Open End	Emerging Markets Equity (Div Emerging Mkts)	D+	C	B+	Up	Y	2,500
American Century Emerging Markets Small Cap Fund I Class	AECSX	NAS CM	Open End	Emerging Markets Equity (Div Emerging Mkts)	D+	C	B+	Up	Y	5,000,000
American Century Emerging Mkts Small Cap Fund Inv Cls	AECVX	NAS CM	Open End	Emerging Markets Equity (Div Emerging Mkts)	D+	C	B+	Up	Y	2,500
American Century Emerging Markets Small Cap Fund R Class	AECMX	NAS CM	Open End	Emerging Markets Equity (Div Emerging Mkts)	D+	C	B+	Up	Y	2,500
American Century Emerging Markets Small Cap Fund R6 Class	AECTX	NAS CM	Open End	Emerging Markets Equity (Div Emerging Mkts)	D+	C	B+	Up	Y	0
American Century Equity Growth Fund A Class	BEQAX	NAS CM	Open End	US Equity Large Cap Blend (Growth)	B-	B-	B-	Down	Y	2,500

★ Expanded analysis of this fund is included in Section II.

Min Additional Investment	TOTAL RETURNS: 3-Month Total Return	6-Month Total Return	1-Year Total Return	3-Year Total Return	5-Year Total Return	PERFORMANCE: Dividend Yield (TTM)	Expense Ratio	3-Yr Std Deviation	3-Year Beta	ASSETS: NAV	Total Assets (MIL)	ASSET ALLOCATION & TURNOVER: %Cash	%Stocks	%Bonds	%Other	Turnover Ratio	BULL & BEAR: Last Bull Market Total Return	Last Bear Market Total Return	FEES: Front End Fee (%)	Back End Fee (%)	Inception Date
50	0.99	6.89	9.52	34.32	104.94	0.97	0.9	13.42	0.9	16.32	56.1	3	97	0	0	77	25.45	-20.61			Jun-10
50	0.96	6.70	9.12	32.83	101.22	0.98	1.28	13.42	0.89	16.21	56.1	3	97	0	0	77	25.05	-20.64			Jun-10
50	1.04	6.89	9.45	33.99	104.07	0.97	1	13.41	0.89	16.46	56.1	3	97	0	0	77	25.38	-20.58			Jun-10
50	5.41	10.64	17.41	28.34	96.55	0.63	1.4	10.27	0.97	20.6	104.0	1	99	0	0	105	15.13	-12.51			May-06
50	5.50	10.91	17.93	30.03	100.88	1	0.95	10.27	0.97	20.94	104.0	1	99	0	0	105	15.39	-12.31			May-06
50	5.43	10.82	17.70	29.27	99.06	0.83	1.15	10.27	0.97	20.8	104.0	1	99	0	0	105	15.16	-12.31			May-06
50	5.30	10.49	17.08	27.28	94.00	0.42	1.65	10.26	0.97	20.35	104.0	1	99	0	0	105	14.89	-12.54			May-06
	5.54	10.95	17.97	30.08	100.95		0.95	10.27	0.97	20.96	104.0	1	99	0	0	105	15.39	-12.31			Apr-17
	5.55	11.00	18.13	30.25	101.22		0.8	10.27	0.97	21.18	104.0	1	99	0	0	105	15.39	-12.31			Dec-16
50	7.22	11.85	20.67	34.73	111.07		1.4	10.97	1.06	11.87	106.3	1	99	0	0	116	19.12	-14.01	5.75		Dec-16
	7.32	12.08	21.23	36.50	115.67	0.96	0.95	10.97	1.06	12.03	106.3	1	99	0	0	116	19.33	-13.69			Aug-00
50	7.28	12.05	20.96	35.73	113.70	0.81	1.15	10.97	1.06	11.76	106.3	1	99	0	0	116	19.3	-13.92			Nov-99
50	7.13	11.76	20.37	33.71	108.44		1.65	10.97	1.06	11.85	106.3	1	99	0	0	116	18.95	-14.1			Dec-16
	7.40	12.20	21.48	36.30	114.60		0.8	10.98	1.06	12.17	106.3	1	99	0	0	116	19.29	-13.92			Dec-16
50	6.55	9.78	24.58	34.81	95.32	0	1.25	10.97	0.99	32.35	1,136	1	99	0	0	49	27.59	-18.01	5.75		Sep-11
50	6.32	9.34	23.63	31.78	88.05	0	2	10.97	0.99	30.34	1,136	1	99	0	0	49	27.03	-18.26		1.00	Sep-11
50	6.66	10.02	25.13	36.62	99.75	0	0.8	10.96	0.99	33.57	1,136	1	99	0	0	49	27.91	-17.92			Sep-11
50	6.61	9.91	24.86	35.78	97.76	0	1	10.97	0.99	33.03	1,136	1	99	0	0	49	27.79	-17.92			Nov-83
50	6.49	9.64	24.24	33.77	92.92	0	1.5	10.98	0.99	31.67	1,136	1	99	0	0	49	27.43	-18.09			Sep-11
50	4.22	7.52	14.27	18.73	55.90	1.59	0.71	6.14	0.59	18.83	899.6	2	57	41	0	104	16.71	-8.1			May-00
50	4.11	7.36	14.05	17.97	54.30	1.41	0.91	6.16	0.59	18.82	899.6	2	57	41	0	104	16.6	-8.2			Oct-88
	4.22	7.53	14.27	18.21	54.61		0.71	6.17	0.59	18.83	899.6	2	57	41	0	104	16.6	-8.2			Apr-17
50	3.74	6.24	11.49	22.14	84.02	1.16	1.25	11.27	1.07	8.74	154.8	1	98	0	0	45	24.59	-17.53	5.75		May-03
50	3.74	6.45	11.81	23.57	88.06	1.57	0.8	11.23	1.07	8.77	154.8	1	98	0	0	45	24.86	-17.35			Mar-02
50	3.77	6.37	11.74	23.02	86.37	1.39	1	11.23	1.07	8.76	154.8	1	98	0	0	45	24.62	-17.35			Mar-99
50	6.66	11.22	19.15	23.08	93.98	0.13	1.55	9.77	0.93	15.35	195.4	1	99	0	0	111			5.75		Oct-11
50	6.41	10.76	18.23	20.25	86.69	0	2.3	9.8	0.94	14.92	195.4	1	99	0	0	111				1.00	Oct-11
50	6.55	11.05	18.83	22.05	91.52	0	1.8	9.79	0.94	15.26	195.4	1	99	0	0	111					Oct-11
50	6.69	11.40	19.61	24.63	98.26	0.54	1.1	9.75	0.93	15.35	195.4	1	99	0	0	111					Oct-11
50	6.65	11.28	19.32	23.85	96.28	0.35	1.3	9.78	0.93	15.36	195.4	1	99	0	0	111					Oct-11
50	6.05	12.42	25.75	32.36	106.43	0.32	1.27	10.36	0.94	22.65	768.9	1	99	0	0	124	27.89	-16.37	5.75		Sep-05
50	5.84	11.98	24.82	29.34	98.82	0	2.02	10.38	0.94	21.47	768.9	1	99	0	0	124	27.43	-16.69		1.00	Sep-07
50	5.95	12.26	25.42	31.32	103.76	0.21	1.52	10.38	0.94	22.29	768.9	1	99	0	0	124	27.76	-16.51			Sep-05
50	6.16	12.68	26.30	34.12	111.18	0.59	0.82	10.38	0.94	22.92	768.9	1	99	0	0	124	28.24	-16.26			Sep-05
50	6.09	12.58	26.06	33.30	109.05	0.42	1.02	10.39	0.94	22.82	768.9	1	99	0	0	124	28.09	-16.31			Sep-05
	6.16	12.67	26.28	34.09	111.15		0.82	10.38	0.94	22.93	768.9	1	99	0	0	124	28.24	-16.26			Apr-17
	6.15	12.67	26.29	34.10	111.16		0.77	10.38	0.94	22.93	768.9	1	99	0	0	124	28.24	-16.26			Apr-17
50	5.50	19.03	45.50	43.22	41.77	0.05	1.54	14.56	0.89	11.88	1,566	5	93	0	2	59	23.07	-30.25	5.75		May-99
50	5.41	18.73	44.56	40.28	36.70	0	2.29	14.57	0.89	10.9	1,566	5	93	0	2	59	22.5	-30.5		1.00	Dec-01
50	5.67	19.32	46.24	45.28	44.88	0.4	1.09	14.57	0.89	12.66	1,566	5	93	0	2	59	23.25	-30.07			Jan-99
50	5.65	19.24	45.85	44.29	43.50	0.25	1.29	14.56	0.89	12.33	1,566	5	93	0	2	59	23.13	-30.13			Sep-97
50	5.46	19.00	45.32	42.21	39.87	0	1.79	14.6	0.89	11.96	1,566	5	93	0	2	59	22.77	-30.35			Sep-07
	5.67	19.32	46.06	44.49	43.71		1.09	14.56	0.89	12.66	1,566	5	93	0	2	59	23.13	-30.13			Apr-17
	5.66	19.39	46.35	45.99	45.83	0.51	0.94	14.58	0.89	12.68	1,566	5	93	0	2	59	23.13	-30.13			Jul-13
	5.75	19.49	46.26	44.69	43.90		0.94	14.56	0.89	12.69	1,566	5	93	0	2	59	23.13	-30.13			Apr-17
50	6.26	19.09	37.96			0.45	1.91			14.07	11.6	7	91	0	2	51			5.75		Apr-16
50	6.01	18.69	37.03			0	2.66			14.08	11.6	7	91	0	2	51				1.00	Apr-16
50	6.42	19.44	38.75			0.79	1.46			14.06	11.6	7	91	0	2	51					Apr-16
50	6.29	19.20	38.34			0.64	1.66			14.06	11.6	7	91	0	2	51					Apr-16
50	6.15	18.88	37.71			0.27	2.16			14.08	11.6	7	91	0	2	51					Apr-16
	6.42	19.44	38.86			0.9	1.31			14.05	11.6	7	91	0	2	51					Apr-16
50	6.67	11.68	21.54	26.18	94.36	1.09	0.92	10.34	1.01	32.37	3,243	1	99	0	0	85	26.3	-15.82	5.75		Oct-97

	MARKET			FUND TYPE, CATEGORY & OBJECTIVE	RATINGS					MINIMUMS
Fund Name	Ticker Symbol	Traded On	Fund Type	Category and (Prospectus Objective)	Overall Rating	Reward Rating	Risk Rating	Recent Up/ Downgrade	Open to New Investors	Min Initial Investment
American Century Equity Growth Fund C Class	AEYCX	NAS CM	Open End	US Equity Large Cap Blend (Growth)	B-	B-	C+	Down	Y	2,500
American Century Equity Growth Fund I Class	AMEIX	NAS CM	Open End	US Equity Large Cap Blend (Growth)	B-	B-	B-	Down	Y	5,000,000
American Century Equity Growth Fund Investor Class	BEQGX	NAS CM	Open End	US Equity Large Cap Blend (Growth)	B-	B-	B-	Down	Y	2,500
American Century Equity Growth Fund R Class	AEYRX	NAS CM	Open End	US Equity Large Cap Blend (Growth)	B-	B-	C+	Down	Y	2,500
American Century Equity Growth Fund R5 Class	AEYGX	NAS CM	Open End	US Equity Large Cap Blend (Growth)	B-	B-	B-	Down	Y	0
American Century Equity Income Fund A Class	TWEAX	NAS CM	Open End	US Equity Large Cap Value (Equity-Income)	B	B-	B	Down	Y	2,500
American Century Equity Income Fund C Class	AEYIX	NAS CM	Open End	US Equity Large Cap Value (Equity-Income)	B	B-	B		Y	2,500
American Century Equity Income Fund I Class	ACIIX	NAS CM	Open End	US Equity Large Cap Value (Equity-Income)	B	B-	B	Down	Y	5,000,000
American Century Equity Income Fund Investor Class	TWEIX	NAS CM	Open End	US Equity Large Cap Value (Equity-Income)	B	B-	B	Down	Y	2,500
American Century Equity Income Fund R Class	AEURX	NAS CM	Open End	US Equity Large Cap Value (Equity-Income)	B	B-	B	Down	Y	2,500
American Century Equity Income Fund R5 Class	AEIUX	NAS CM	Open End	US Equity Large Cap Value (Equity-Income)	B	B-	B	Down	Y	0
American Century Equity Income Fund R6 Class	AEUDX	NAS CM	Open End	US Equity Large Cap Value (Equity-Income)	B	B-	B	Down	Y	0
American Century Equity Income Fund Y Class	AEIYX	NAS CM	Open End	US Equity Large Cap Value (Equity-Income)	B	B-	B	Down	Y	0
American Century Focused International Growth Fund A Class	AFCLX	NAS CM	Open End	Global Equity Large Cap (Growth)	D+	C	B-	Up	Y	2,500
American Century Focused International Growth Fund C Class	AFCHX	NAS CM	Open End	Global Equity Large Cap (Growth)	D+	C	B-	Up	Y	2,500
American Century Focused International Growth Fund I Class	AFCSX	NAS CM	Open End	Global Equity Large Cap (Growth)	D+	C	B-	Up	Y	5,000,000
American Century Focused Intl Growth Fund Inv Cls	AFCNX	NAS CM	Open End	Global Equity Large Cap (Growth)	D+	C	B-	Up	Y	2,500
American Century Focused International Growth Fund R Class	AFCWX	NAS CM	Open End	Global Equity Large Cap (Growth)	D+	C	B-	Up	Y	2,500
American Century Focused International Growth Fund R6 Cls	AFCMX	NAS CM	Open End	Global Equity Large Cap (Growth)	D+	C	B-	Up	Y	0
American Century Global Gold Fund A Class	ACGGX	NAS CM	Open End	Precious Metals Sector Equity (Precious Metals)	D+	C-	D	Down	Y	2,500
American Century Global Gold Fund C Class	AGYCX	NAS CM	Open End	Precious Metals Sector Equity (Precious Metals)	D+	C-	D	Down	Y	2,500
American Century Global Gold Fund I Class	AGGNX	NAS CM	Open End	Precious Metals Sector Equity (Precious Metals)	D+	C	D	Down	Y	5,000,000
American Century Global Gold Fund Investor Class	BGEIX	NAS CM	Open End	Precious Metals Sector Equity (Precious Metals)	D+	C-	D	Down	Y	2,500
American Century Global Gold Fund R Class	AGGWX	NAS CM	Open End	Precious Metals Sector Equity (Precious Metals)	D+	C-	D	Down	Y	2,500
American Century Global Growth Fund A Class	AGGRX	NAS CM	Open End	Global Equity (World Stock)	B	B-	B	Up	Y	2,500
American Century Global Growth Fund C Class	AGLCX	NAS CM	Open End	Global Equity (World Stock)	B	B-	B	Up	Y	2,500
American Century Global Growth Fund I Class	AGGIX	NAS CM	Open End	Global Equity (World Stock)	B	B	B	Up	Y	5,000,000
American Century Global Growth Fund Investor Class	TWGGX	NAS CM	Open End	Global Equity (World Stock)	B	B-	B	Up	Y	2,500
American Century Global Growth Fund R Class	AGORX	NAS CM	Open End	Global Equity (World Stock)	B	B-	B	Up	Y	2,500
American Century Global Growth Fund R5 Class	AGFGX	NAS CM	Open End	Global Equity (World Stock)	B	B-	B	Up	Y	0
American Century Global Growth Fund R6 Class	AGGDX	NAS CM	Open End	Global Equity (World Stock)	B	B	B	Up	Y	0
American Century Global Growth Fund Y Class	AGYGX	NAS CM	Open End	Global Equity (World Stock)	B	B-	B	Up	Y	0
American Century Global Real Estate Fund A Class	ARYMX	NAS CM	Open End	Real Estate Sector Equity (Real Estate)	B-	C+	B	Up	Y	2,500
American Century Global Real Estate Fund C Class	ARYTX	NAS CM	Open End	Real Estate Sector Equity (Real Estate)	C+	C	B	Up	Y	2,500
American Century Global Real Estate Fund I Class	ARYNX	NAS CM	Open End	Real Estate Sector Equity (Real Estate)	B-	C+	B	Up	Y	5,000,000
American Century Global Real Estate Fund Investor Class	ARYVX	NAS CM	Open End	Real Estate Sector Equity (Real Estate)	B-	C+	B	Up	Y	2,500
American Century Global Real Estate Fund R Class	ARYWX	NAS CM	Open End	Real Estate Sector Equity (Real Estate)	B-	C+	B	Up	Y	2,500
American Century Global Real Estate Fund R5 Class	ARYGX	NAS CM	Open End	Real Estate Sector Equity (Real Estate)	B-	C+	B	Up	Y	0
American Century Global Real Estate Fund R6 Class	ARYDX	NAS CM	Open End	Real Estate Sector Equity (Real Estate)	B-	C+	B	Up	Y	0
American Century Global Real Estate Fund Y Class	ARYYX	NAS CM	Open End	Real Estate Sector Equity (Real Estate)	B-	C+	B	Up	Y	0
American Century Global Small Cap Fund A Class	AGCLX	NAS CM	Open End	Global Equity Mid/Small Cap (Small Company)	D+	C	B+	Up	Y	2,500
American Century Global Small Cap Fund C Class	AGCHX	NAS CM	Open End	Global Equity Mid/Small Cap (Small Company)	D+	C	B+	Up	Y	2,500
American Century Global Small Cap Fund I Class	AGCSX	NAS CM	Open End	Global Equity Mid/Small Cap (Small Company)	D+	C	B+	Up	Y	5,000,000
American Century Global Small Cap Fund Investor Class	AGCVX	NAS CM	Open End	Global Equity Mid/Small Cap (Small Company)	D+	C	B+	Up	Y	2,500
American Century Global Small Cap Fund R Class	AGCWX	NAS CM	Open End	Global Equity Mid/Small Cap (Small Company)	D+	C	B+	Up	Y	2,500
American Century Global Small Cap Fund R6 Class	AGCTX	NAS CM	Open End	Global Equity Mid/Small Cap (Small Company)	D+	C	B+	Up	Y	0
American Century Growth Fund A Class	TCRAX	NAS CM	Open End	US Equity Large Cap Growth (Growth)	A-	B+	A-	Up	Y	2,500
American Century Growth Fund C Class	TWRCX	NAS CM	Open End	US Equity Large Cap Growth (Growth)	B	B	B		Y	2,500
American Century Growth Fund I Class	TWGIX	NAS CM	Open End	US Equity Large Cap Growth (Growth)	B+	B+	B	Up	Y	5,000,000
American Century Growth Fund Investor Class	TWCGX	NAS CM	Open End	US Equity Large Cap Growth (Growth)	A-	B+	A-	Up	Y	2,500
American Century Growth Fund R Class	AGWRX	NAS CM	Open End	US Equity Large Cap Growth (Growth)	B+	B+	B	Up	Y	2,500
American Century Growth Fund R5 Class	AGWUX	NAS CM	Open End	US Equity Large Cap Growth (Growth)	B+	B+	B	Up	Y	0

★Expanded analysis of this fund is included in Section II.

Min Additional Investment	TOTAL RETURNS: 3-Month Total Return	6-Month Total Return	1-Year Total Return	3-Year Total Return	5-Year Total Return	PERFORMANCE: Dividend Yield (TTM)	Expense Ratio	3-Yr Std Deviation	3-Year Beta	ASSETS: NAV	Total Assets (MIL)	ASSET ALLOCATION & TURNOVER: %Cash	%Stocks	%Bonds	%Other	Turnover Ratio	BULL & BEAR: Last Bull Market Total Return	Last Bear Market Total Return	FEES: Front End Fee (%)	Back End Fee (%)	Inception Date
50	6.45	11.28	20.64	23.33	87.24	0.42	1.67	10.3	1	32.08	3,243	1	99	0	0	85	25.75	-16.11		1.00	Jul-01
50	6.82	11.99	22.11	27.90	98.86	1.49	0.47	10.34	1.01	32.44	3,243	1	99	0	0	85	26.65	-15.69			Jan-98
50	6.73	11.85	21.85	27.13	96.86	1.31	0.67	10.32	1	32.41	3,243	1	99	0	0	85	26.49	-15.75			May-91
50	6.63	11.60	21.26	25.26	92.03	0.86	1.17	10.32	1	32.4	3,243	1	99	0	0	85	26.09	-15.92			Jul-05
	6.78	11.95	22.01	27.29	97.11		0.47	10.32	1	32.44	3,243	1	99	0	0	85	26.49	-15.75			Apr-17
50	3.74	7.25	13.05	34.16	82.65	1.43	1.18	7.25	0.63	8.91	12,660	3	79	0	1	93	16.61	-12.3	5.75		Mar-97
50	3.53	6.83	12.22	31.06	75.80	0.76	1.93	7.25	0.63	8.91	12,660	3	79	0	1	93	16.02	-12.51		1.00	Jul-01
	3.85	7.49	13.67	35.92	86.66	1.83	0.73	7.23	0.63	8.92	12,660	3	79	0	1	93	16.84	-11.97			Jul-98
50	3.69	7.38	13.33	35.15	84.93	1.66	0.93	7.27	0.64	8.91	12,660	3	79	0	1	93	16.75	-12.19			Aug-94
50	3.68	7.13	12.82	33.13	80.28	1.21	1.43	7.27	0.63	8.88	12,660	3	79	0	1	93	16.5	-12.32			Aug-03
	3.85	7.49	13.61	35.48	85.38		0.73	7.27	0.64	8.92	12,660	3	79	0	1	93	16.75	-12.19			Apr-17
	3.89	7.56	13.83	36.64	87.94	1.96	0.58	7.27	0.63	8.93	12,660	3	79	0	1	93	16.75	-12.19			Jul-13
	3.89	7.56	13.72	35.62	85.57		0.58	7.26	0.63	8.93	12,660	3	79	0	1	93	16.75	-12.19			Apr-17
50	4.75	15.46	32.82			0.4	1.49			12.99	9.7	7	89	0	0	47			5.75		Mar-16
50	4.54	15.08	31.93			0	2.24			12.89	9.7	7	89	0	0	47				1.00	Mar-16
50	4.90	15.80	33.46			0.74	1.04			13.04	9.7	7	89	0	0	47					Mar-16
50	4.83	15.63	33.26			0.59	1.24			13.02	9.7	7	89	0	0	47					Mar-16
50	4.68	15.39	32.61			0.21	1.74			12.97	9.7	7	89	0	0	47					Mar-16
	4.90	15.79	33.70			0.85	0.89			13.05	9.7	7	89	0	0	47					Mar-16
50	2.02	5.79	10.28	29.33	-42.96	9.91	0.92	40.2	0.16	8.58	378.0	0	97	0	2	27	-14.21	-15	5.75		May-98
50	1.85	5.51	9.58	26.64	-45.00	9.56	1.67	40.21	0.17	8.23	378.0	0	97	0	2	27	-14.57	-15.31		1.00	Sep-07
50	2.19	6.12	10.79	31.24	-41.61	10.07	0.47	40.17	0.16	8.83	378.0	0	97	0	2	27	-13.98	-14.85			Sep-07
50	2.10	6.06	10.61	30.41	-42.19	9.96	0.67	40.22	0.16	8.75	378.0	0	97	0	2	27	-14.09	-14.93			Aug-88
50	2.03	5.71	10.09	28.56	-43.60	9.74	1.17	40.2	0.17	8.51	378.0	0	97	0	2	27	-14.36	-15.11			Sep-07
50	3.73	9.88	27.32	27.02	72.69	0.21	1.33	11.37	1.03	11.85	552.9	1	98	0	1	57	24.86	-20.62	5.75		Feb-99
50	3.50	9.47	26.43	24.32	66.46	0.08	2.08	11.35	1.02	10.3	552.9	1	98	0	1	57	24.33	-20.9		1.00	Mar-02
50	3.87	10.20	27.91	28.91	76.75	0.29	0.88	11.33	1.02	12.46	552.9	1	98	0	1	57	25.37	-20.56			Aug-00
50	3.78	10.04	27.54	28.07	74.95	0.25	1.08	11.38	1.03	12.21	552.9	1	98	0	1	57	25.08	-20.55			Dec-98
50	3.70	9.75	26.96	26.19	70.62	0.17	1.58	11.35	1.03	11.68	552.9	1	98	0	1	57	24.8	-20.78			Jul-05
	3.87	10.11	27.76	28.29	75.25		0.88	11.38	1.03	12.45	552.9	1	98	0	1	57	25.08	-20.55			Apr-17
	3.85	10.22	28.02	29.34	77.57	0.31	0.73	11.38	1.03	12.52	552.9	1	98	0	1	57	25.08	-20.55			Jul-13
	3.85	10.22	27.88	28.41	75.41		0.73	11.39	1.03	12.52	552.9	1	98	0	1	57	25.08	-20.55			Apr-17
50	4.57	7.98	14.11	12.30	34.73	3.76	1.37	10.84	0.95	11.89	84.4	2	97	0	2	250	20.66	-17.3	5.75		Apr-11
50	4.31	7.53	13.23	9.77	29.69	3.09	2.12	10.87	0.96	11.9	84.4	2	97	0	2	250	20.14	-17.6		1.00	Apr-11
50	4.61	8.29	14.65	13.85	37.87	4.17	0.92	10.84	0.95	11.87	84.4	2	97	0	2	250	20.92	-17.1			Apr-11
50	4.57	8.16	14.41	13.16	36.47	3.99	1.12	10.87	0.96	11.88	84.4	2	97	0	2	250	20.82	-17.2			Apr-11
50	4.39	7.79	13.70	11.44	33.00	3.54	1.62	10.85	0.95	11.9	84.4	2	97	0	2	250	20.5	-17.4			Apr-11
	4.55	8.14	14.59	13.79	37.80		0.92	10.84	0.95	11.87	84.4	2	97	0	2	250	20.92	-17.09			Apr-17
	4.68	8.37	14.73	14.38	38.69	4.3	0.77	10.89	0.96	11.86	84.4	2	97	0	2	250	20.92	-17.09			Jul-13
	4.67	8.27	14.73	13.92	37.96		0.77	10.84	0.95	11.86	84.4	2	97	0	2	250	20.92	-17.1			Apr-17
50	7.21	16.84	38.58			0	1.76			14.24	14.7	1	96	0	3	95			5.75		Mar-16
50	7.08	16.45	37.59			0	2.51			14.05	14.7	1	96	0	3	95				1.00	Mar-16
50	7.31	17.14	39.18			0	1.31			14.36	14.7	1	96	0	3	95					Mar-16
50	7.33	17.02	38.98			0	1.51			14.31	14.7	1	96	0	3	95					Mar-16
50	7.17	16.74	38.29			0	2.01			14.18	14.7	1	96	0	3	95					Mar-16
	7.36	17.18	39.42			0	1.16			14.4	14.7	1	96	0	3	95					Mar-16
50	7.55	12.41	29.81	39.40	105.04	0.27	1.23	10.93	1	31.84	8,242	1	99	0	0	36	27.49	-17.33	5.75		Jun-97
50	7.36	11.99	28.87	36.30	97.46	0	1.98	10.93	1	30.49	8,242	1	99	0	0	36	26.94	-17.6		1.00	Mar-10
50	7.68	12.63	30.39	41.32	109.70	0.61	0.78	10.93	1	33.38	8,242	1	99	0	0	36	27.82	-17.17			Jun-97
50	7.60	12.52	30.08	40.44	107.55	0.46	0.98	10.94	1	32.82	8,242	1	99	0	0	36	27.64	-17.21			Jun-71
50	7.48	12.24	29.46	38.35	102.49	0.06	1.48	10.92	1	31.15	8,242	1	99	0	0	36	27.3	-17.42			Aug-03
	7.65	12.63	30.24	40.61	107.79		0.78	10.94	1	33.4	8,242	1	99	0	0	36	27.64	-17.21			Apr-17

	MARKET			FUND TYPE, CATEGORY & OBJECTIVE	RATINGS				MINIMUMS	
Fund Name	Ticker Symbol	Traded On	Fund Type	Category and (Prospectus Objective)	Overall Rating	Reward Rating	Risk Rating	Recent Up/ Downgrade	Open to New Investors	Min Initial Investment
American Century Growth Fund R6 Class	AGRDX	NAS CM	Open End	US Equity Large Cap Growth (Growth)	B+	B+	B	Up	Y	0
American Century Growth Fund Y Class	AGYWX	NAS CM	Open End	US Equity Large Cap Growth (Growth)	A-	B+	A-	Up	Y	0
American Century Heritage Fund A Class	ATHAX	NAS CM	Open End	US Equity Mid Cap (Growth)	B	B-	B	Up	Y	2,500
American Century Heritage Fund C Class	AHGCX	NAS CM	Open End	US Equity Mid Cap (Growth)	B	B-	B	Up	Y	2,500
American Century Heritage Fund I Class	ATHIX	NAS CM	Open End	US Equity Mid Cap (Growth)	B	B	B	Up	Y	5,000,000
American Century Heritage Fund Investor Class	TWHIX	NAS CM	Open End	US Equity Mid Cap (Growth)	B	B	B	Up	Y	2,500
American Century Heritage Fund R Class	ATHWX	NAS CM	Open End	US Equity Mid Cap (Growth)	B	B-	B	Up	Y	2,500
American Century Heritage Fund R5 Class	ATHGX	NAS CM	Open End	US Equity Mid Cap (Growth)	B	B	B	Up	Y	0
American Century Heritage Fund R6 Class	ATHDX	NAS CM	Open End	US Equity Mid Cap (Growth)	B	B	B	Up	Y	0
American Century Heritage Fund Y Class	ATHYX	NAS CM	Open End	US Equity Mid Cap (Growth)	B	B	B	Up	Y	0
American Century Income and Growth Fund C Class	ACGCX	NAS CM	Open End	US Equity Large Cap Value (Growth & Income)	B-	B-	C+	Down	Y	2,500
American Century Income and Growth Fund Class A	AMADX	NAS CM	Open End	US Equity Large Cap Value (Growth & Income)	B-	B-	C+	Down	Y	2,500
American Century Income and Growth Fund I Class	AMGIX	NAS CM	Open End	US Equity Large Cap Value (Growth & Income)	B-	B-	C+	Down	Y	5,000,000
American Century Income and Growth Fund Investor Class	BIGRX	NAS CM	Open End	US Equity Large Cap Value (Growth & Income)	B-	B-	C+	Down	Y	2,500
American Century Income and Growth Fund R Class	AICRX	NAS CM	Open End	US Equity Large Cap Value (Growth & Income)	B-	B-	C+	Down	Y	2,500
American Century Income and Growth Fund R5 Class	AICGX	NAS CM	Open End	US Equity Large Cap Value (Growth & Income)	B-	B-	C+	Down	Y	0
American Century International Core Equity Fund Class A	ACIQX	NAS CM	Open End	Global Equity Large Cap (Foreign Stock)	B-	C+	B-	Up	Y	2,500
American Century International Core Equity Fund Class C	ACIKX	NAS CM	Open End	Global Equity Large Cap (Foreign Stock)	C+	C+	C	Up	Y	2,500
American Century International Core Equity Fund Class R	ACIRX	NAS CM	Open End	Global Equity Large Cap (Foreign Stock)	C+	C+	C	Up	Y	2,500
American Century International Core Equity Fund I Class	ACIUX	NAS CM	Open End	Global Equity Large Cap (Foreign Stock)	C+	C+	C	Up	Y	5,000,000
American Century Intl Core Equity Fund Inv Cls	ACIMX	NAS CM	Open End	Global Equity Large Cap (Foreign Stock)	B-	C+	B-	Up	Y	2,500
American Century International Discovery Fund C Class	TWECX	NAS CM	Open End	Global Equity Mid/Small Cap (Foreign Stock)	B+	A-	B	Up	Y	10,000
American Century International Discovery Fund Class A	ACIDX	NAS CM	Open End	Global Equity Mid/Small Cap (Foreign Stock)	B+	A-	B	Up	Y	10,000
American Century International Discovery Fund I Class	TIDIX	NAS CM	Open End	Global Equity Mid/Small Cap (Foreign Stock)	B+	A-	B	Up	Y	5,000,000
American Century International Discovery Fund Investor Cls	TWEGX	NAS CM	Open End	Global Equity Mid/Small Cap (Foreign Stock)	B+	A-	B	Up	Y	10,000
American Century International Discovery Fund R Class	TWERX	NAS CM	Open End	Global Equity Mid/Small Cap (Foreign Stock)	B+	A-	B	Up	Y	10,000
American Century International Discovery Fund Y Class	AIYDX	NAS CM	Open End	Global Equity Mid/Small Cap (Foreign Stock)	B+	A-	B	Up	Y	0
American Century International Growth Fund A Class	TWGAX	NAS CM	Open End	Global Equity Large Cap (Foreign Stock)	B-	B-	B	Up	Y	2,500
American Century International Growth Fund C Class	AIWCX	NAS CM	Open End	Global Equity Large Cap (Foreign Stock)	B-	C+	B-	Up	Y	2,500
American Century International Growth Fund I Class	TGRIX	NAS CM	Open End	Global Equity Large Cap (Foreign Stock)	B-	B-	B	Up	Y	5,000,000
American Century International Growth Fund Investor Class	TWIEX	NAS CM	Open End	Global Equity Large Cap (Foreign Stock)	B-	B-	B	Up	Y	2,500
American Century International Growth Fund R Class	ATGRX	NAS CM	Open End	Global Equity Large Cap (Foreign Stock)	B-	B-	B	Up	Y	2,500
American Century International Growth Fund R5 Class	ATGGX	NAS CM	Open End	Global Equity Large Cap (Foreign Stock)	B-	B-	B	Up	Y	0
American Century International Growth Fund R6 Class	ATGDX	NAS CM	Open End	Global Equity Large Cap (Foreign Stock)	B	B-	B	Up	Y	0
American Century International Growth Fund Y Class	ATYGX	NAS CM	Open End	Global Equity Large Cap (Foreign Stock)	B-	B-	B	Up	Y	0
American Century International Opportunities Fund Class A	AIVOX	NAS CM	Open End	Global Equity Mid/Small Cap (Foreign Stock)	A-	A	B+	Up	Y	10,000
American Century International Opportunities Fund Class C	AIOCX	NAS CM	Open End	Global Equity Mid/Small Cap (Foreign Stock)	A-	A-	B+	Up	Y	10,000
American Century International Opportunities Fund Class R	AIORX	NAS CM	Open End	Global Equity Mid/Small Cap (Foreign Stock)	A-	A	B+	Up	Y	10,000
American Century International Opportunities Fund I Class	ACIOX	NAS CM	Open End	Global Equity Mid/Small Cap (Foreign Stock)	A-	A	B+	Up	Y	5,000,000
American Century Intl Opp Fund Inv Cls	AIOIX	NAS CM	Open End	Global Equity Mid/Small Cap (Foreign Stock)	A-	A	B+	Up	Y	10,000
American Century International Value Fund A Class	MEQAX	NAS CM	Open End	Global Equity Large Cap (Foreign Stock)	C+	C+	C	Up	Y	2,500
American Century International Value Fund C Class	ACCOX	NAS CM	Open End	Global Equity Large Cap (Foreign Stock)	C	C+	C		Y	2,500
American Century International Value Fund I Class	ACVUX	NAS CM	Open End	Global Equity Large Cap (Foreign Stock)	C+	C+	C	Up	Y	5,000,000
American Century International Value Fund Investor Class	ACEVX	NAS CM	Open End	Global Equity Large Cap (Foreign Stock)	C+	C+	C	Up	Y	2,500
American Century International Value Fund R Class	ACVRX	NAS CM	Open End	Global Equity Large Cap (Foreign Stock)	C+	C+	C	Up	Y	2,500
American Century International Value Fund R6 Class	ACVDX	NAS CM	Open End	Global Equity Large Cap (Foreign Stock)	C+	C+	C	Up	Y	0
American Century Inv Focused Dynamic Growth Fund Adv Cls	ACFDX	NAS CM	Open End	US Equity Large Cap Growth (Growth)	B+	A	B	Up	Y	2,500
American Century Inv Focused Dynamic Growth Fund I Cls	ACFSX	NAS CM	Open End	US Equity Large Cap Growth (Growth)	B+	A	B	Up	Y	5,000,000
American Century Inv Focused Dynamic Growth Fund Inv Cls	ACFOX	NAS CM	Open End	US Equity Large Cap Growth (Growth)	B+	A	B	Up	Y	2,500
American Century Inv Focused Dynamic Growth Fund R Cls	ACFCX	NAS CM	Open End	US Equity Large Cap Growth (Growth)	B+	A-	B	Up	Y	2,500
American Century Inv Focused Dynamic Growth Fund R6 Cls	ACFNX	NAS CM	Open End	US Equity Large Cap Growth (Growth)	B+	A	B	Up	Y	0
American Century Inv One Choice 2020 Port A Cls	ARBMX	NAS CM	Open End	Target Date 2000-2020 (Asset Alloc)	B-	C+	B	Up	Y	2,500

★ Expanded analysis of this fund is included in Section II.

Min Additional Investment	TOTAL RETURNS 3-Month Total Return	6-Month Total Return	1-Year Total Return	3-Year Total Return	5-Year Total Return	PERFORMANCE Dividend Yield (TTM)	Expense Ratio	3-Yr Std Deviation	3-Year Beta	ASSETS NAV	Total Assets (MIL)	ASSET ALLOCATION & TURNOVER %Cash	%Stocks	%Bonds	%Other	Turnover Ratio	BULL & BEAR Last Bull Market Total Return	Last Bear Market Total Return	FEES Front End Fee (%)	Back End Fee (%)	Inception Date
	7.73	12.71	30.58	41.95	110.80	0.73	0.63	10.94	1	33.34	8,242	1	99	0	0	36	27.64	-17.21			Jul-13
	7.71	12.72	30.39	40.77	108.03		0.63	10.95	1	33.38	8,242	1	99	0	0	36	27.64	-17.21			Apr-17
50	5.51	9.45	21.52	26.33	82.80	0	1.25	11.09	0.98	20.81	5,143	1	99	0	0	62	28.39	-21.45	5.75		Jul-97
50	5.27	8.98	20.59	23.53	75.99	0	2	11.08	0.98	16.79	5,143	1	99	0	0	62	27.86	-21.72		1.00	Jun-01
50	5.60	9.66	22.08	28.05	86.91	0	0.8	11.09	0.98	23.87	5,143	1	99	0	0	62	28.73	-21.3			Jun-97
50	5.57	9.57	21.84	27.28	85.01	0	1	11.11	0.98	22.48	5,143	1	99	0	0	62	28.57	-21.34			Nov-87
50	5.40	9.26	21.20	25.38	80.43	0	1.5	11.07	0.98	20.86	5,143	1	99	0	0	62	28.22	-21.53			Sep-07
	5.60	9.66	22.05	27.50	85.32		0.8	11.11	0.98	23.87	5,143	1	99	0	0	62	28.57	-21.34			Apr-17
	5.64	9.76	22.27	28.60	87.84	0	0.65	11.11	0.98	24.07	5,143	1	99	0	0	62	28.57	-21.34			Jul-13
	5.68	9.81	22.20	27.66	85.55		0.65	11.12	0.98	24.08	5,143	1	99	0	0	62	28.57	-21.34			Apr-17
50	6.62	11.95	19.39	24.10	90.76	1.2	1.67	10.28	0.99	39.18	2,228	1	99	0	0	81	24.37	-16.42		1.00	Jun-01
50	6.80	12.36	20.29	26.90	98.01	1.87	0.92	10.28	0.99	39.24	2,228	1	99	0	0	81	24.88	-16.15	5.75		Dec-97
50	6.94	12.65	20.86	28.66	102.61	2.26	0.47	10.28	0.99	39.35	2,228	1	99	0	0	81	25.19	-15.97			Jan-98
50	6.89	12.52	20.62	27.87	100.57	2.09	0.67	10.28	0.99	39.3	2,228	1	99	0	0	81	25.05	-16.07			Dec-90
50	6.75	12.23	20.00	25.96	95.62	1.64	1.17	10.27	0.99	39.29	2,228	1	99	0	0	81	24.71	-16.21			Aug-03
	6.94	12.62	20.80	28.06	100.87		0.47	10.28	0.99	39.35	2,228	1	99	0	0	81	25.05	-16.07			Apr-17
50	2.78	8.71	25.42	20.01	45.84	1.99	1.41	11.84	0.94	9.6	34.6	1	95	0	3	113	12.49	-23.88	5.75		Nov-06
50	2.56	8.17	24.41	17.13	40.21	1.38	2.16	11.76	0.93	9.57	34.6	1	95	0	3	113	12.04	-24.21		1.00	Nov-06
50	2.75	8.58	25.17	19.03	43.75	1.79	1.66	11.82	0.94	9.58	34.6	1	95	0	3	113	12.4	-24.03			Nov-06
50	2.92	8.97	26.02	21.52	48.81	2.35	0.96	11.71	0.93	9.59	34.6	1	95	0	3	113	12.81	-23.83			Nov-06
50	2.83	8.89	25.80	20.68	47.39	2.2	1.16	11.73	0.93	9.58	34.6	1	95	0	3	113	12.76	-23.86			Nov-06
50	6.57	18.66	39.02	36.90	65.72	0	2.65	12.31	0.95	16.21	550.8	2	95	0	3	139	17.78	-29.46		1.00	Mar-10
50	6.76	19.13	40.10	40.07	71.89	0	1.9	12.35	0.95	16.56	550.8	2	95	0	3	139	18.47	-29.32	5.75		Apr-98
50	6.91	19.46	40.73	41.93	75.94	0	1.45	12.3	0.95	17.31	550.8	2	95	0	3	139	18.79	-29.18			Jan-98
50	6.89	19.30	40.52	41.17	74.23	0	1.65	12.31	0.95	17.06	550.8	2	95	0	3	139	18.53	-29.25			Apr-94
50	6.75	19.06	39.84	38.99	69.87	0	2.15	12.33	0.95	16.74	550.8	2	95	0	3	139	18.25	-29.31			Mar-10
	6.97	19.51	40.83	41.47	74.60		1.3	12.32	0.95	17.33	550.8	2	95	0	3	139	18.53	-29.25			Apr-17
50	4.03	12.43	30.72	22.27	44.35	0.18	1.43	11.95	0.92	13.39	1,567	1	97	0	2	70	17.49	-24.4	5.75		Oct-96
50	3.77	11.89	29.74	19.53	38.95	0	2.18	11.91	0.92	13	1,567	1	97	0	2	70	17.03	-24.66		1.00	Jun-01
50	4.10	12.61	31.31	24.01	47.60	0.53	0.98	11.97	0.92	13.18	1,567	1	97	0	2	70	17.75	-24.29			Nov-97
50	4.10	12.47	31.03	23.25	46.03	0.38	1.18	11.99	0.92	13.27	1,567	1	97	0	2	70	17.57	-24.32			May-91
50	3.89	12.19	30.36	21.29	42.37	0	1.68	11.99	0.92	13.53	1,567	1	97	0	2	70	17.35	-24.49			Aug-03
	4.12	12.54	31.13	23.35	46.15		0.98	11.98	0.92	13.18	1,567	1	97	0	2	70	17.57	-24.32			Apr-17
	4.11	12.70	31.41	24.45	48.33	0.65	0.83	11.95	0.92	13.17	1,567	1	97	0	2	70	17.57	-24.32			Jul-13
	4.16	12.67	31.28	23.49	46.32		0.83	12	0.92	13.18	1,567	1	97	0	2	70	17.57	-24.32			Apr-17
50	7.80	18.98	44.76	50.00	82.44	0	1.79	11.66	0.86	11.15	190.1	0	95	0	5	130	24.18	-25.77	5.75		Mar-10
50	7.59	18.55	43.63	46.52	75.94	0	2.54	11.65	0.86	10.77	190.1	0	95	0	5	130	23.76	-26.18		1.00	Mar-10
50	7.78	18.85	44.36	48.87	80.16	0	2.04	11.67	0.86	11.06	190.1	0	95	0	5	130	23.99	-25.87			Mar-10
50	7.97	19.28	45.27	51.83	86.36	0.17	1.34	11.65	0.86	11.34	190.1	0	95	0	5	130	24.59	-25.77			Jan-03
50	7.92	19.13	45.04	51.06	84.76	0.03	1.54	11.67	0.86	11.23	190.1	0	95	0	5	130	24.4	-25.81			Jun-01
50	1.63	7.28	21.01	12.69	34.17	1.54	1.57	12.33	0.92	8.92	80.1	1	98	0	0	76	12.76	-23.17	5.75		Mar-97
50	1.38	6.84	20.13	10.28	29.18	1.04	2.32	12.24	0.91	8.85	80.1	1	98	0	0	76	12.4	-23.41		1.00	Apr-06
50	1.76	7.57	21.67	14.29	37.30	2.01	1.12	12.31	0.92	8.88	80.1	1	98	0	0	76	13.21	-23.09			Apr-06
50	1.72	7.40	21.27	13.61	35.73	1.8	1.32	12.33	0.92	8.88	80.1	1	98	0	0	76	12.95	-23.06			Apr-06
50	1.55	7.23	20.82	11.92	32.48	1.28	1.82	12.28	0.92	8.88	80.1	1	98	0	0	76	12.69	-23.25			Apr-06
	1.88	7.69	21.85	14.80	37.78	2.16	0.97	12.32	0.92	8.88	80.1	1	98	0	0	76	12.75	-23.17			Jul-13
50	5.32	13.67	34.25	34.83	110.71	0.66	1.27	11.74	1.01	21.95	28.9	3	97	0	0	21	17.84	-13.58			May-06
	5.40	13.94	34.83	36.62	115.31	0.98	0.82	11.75	1.01	22.22	28.9	3	97	0	0	21	18.19	-13.46			May-06
50	5.38	13.84	34.55	35.80	113.25	0.84	1.02	11.75	1.01	22.12	28.9	3	97	0	0	21	17.91	-13.5			May-06
50	5.27	13.56	33.88	33.72	107.88	0.47	1.52	11.75	1.01	21.77	28.9	3	97	0	0	21	17.67	-13.75			May-06
	5.48	14.02	35.01	36.81	115.60		0.67	11.75	1.01	22.52	28.9	3	97	0	0	21	18.19	-13.46			Dec-16
50	2.45	5.04	10.65	14.33	38.26	1.49	1.02	5.18	0.99	12.51	2,272	10	45	43	1	17	14.34	-9.29	5.75		May-08

Fund Name	MARKET Ticker Symbol	Traded On	FUND TYPE, CATEGORY & OBJECTIVE Fund Type	Category and (Prospectus Objective)	RATINGS Overall Rating	Reward Rating	Risk Rating	Recent Up/ Downgrade	Open to New Investors	MINIMUMS Min Initial Investment
American Century Inv One Choice 2020 Port C Cls	ARNCX	NAS CM	Open End	Target Date 2000-2020 (Asset Alloc)	B-	C+	B	Up	Y	2,500
American Century Inv One Choice 2020 Port I Cls	ARBSX	NAS CM	Open End	Target Date 2000-2020 (Asset Alloc)	B-	C+	B	Up	Y	5,000,000
American Century Inv One Choice 2020 Port Inv Cls	ARBVX	NAS CM	Open End	Target Date 2000-2020 (Asset Alloc)	B-	C+	B	Up	Y	2,500
American Century Inv One Choice 2020 Port R Cls	ARBRX	NAS CM	Open End	Target Date 2000-2020 (Asset Alloc)	B-	C+	B	Up	Y	2,500
American Century Inv One Choice 2020 Port R6 Cls	ARBDX	NAS CM	Open End	Target Date 2000-2020 (Asset Alloc)	B-	C+	B	Up	Y	0
American Century Inv One Choice 2025 Port A Cls	ARWAX	NAS CM	Open End	Target Date 2021-2045 (Asset Alloc)	B-	C+	B	Up	Y	2,500
American Century Inv One Choice 2025 Port C Cls	ARWCX	NAS CM	Open End	Target Date 2021-2045 (Asset Alloc)	B-	C+	B	Up	Y	2,500
American Century Inv One Choice 2025 Port I Cls	ARWFX	NAS CM	Open End	Target Date 2021-2045 (Asset Alloc)	B-	C+	B	Up	Y	5,000,000
American Century Inv One Choice 2025 Port Inv Cls	ARWIX	NAS CM	Open End	Target Date 2021-2045 (Asset Alloc)	B-	C+	B	Up	Y	2,500
American Century Inv One Choice 2025 Port R Cls	ARWRX	NAS CM	Open End	Target Date 2021-2045 (Asset Alloc)	B-	C+	B	Up	Y	2,500
American Century Inv One Choice 2025 Port R6 Cls	ARWDX	NAS CM	Open End	Target Date 2021-2045 (Asset Alloc)	B-	C+	B	Up	Y	0
American Century Inv One Choice 2030 Port A Cls	ARCMX	NAS CM	Open End	Target Date 2021-2045 (Asset Alloc)	B-	C+	B	Up	Y	2,500
American Century Inv One Choice 2030 Port C Cls	ARWOX	NAS CM	Open End	Target Date 2021-2045 (Asset Alloc)	B-	C+	B	Up	Y	2,500
American Century Inv One Choice 2030 Port I Cls	ARCSX	NAS CM	Open End	Target Date 2021-2045 (Asset Alloc)	B-	C+	B	Up	Y	5,000,000
American Century Inv One Choice 2030 Port Inv Cls	ARCVX	NAS CM	Open End	Target Date 2021-2045 (Asset Alloc)	B-	C+	B	Up	Y	2,500
American Century Inv One Choice 2030 Port R Cls	ARCRX	NAS CM	Open End	Target Date 2021-2045 (Asset Alloc)	B-	C+	B	Up	Y	2,500
American Century Inv One Choice 2030 Port R6 Cls	ARCUX	NAS CM	Open End	Target Date 2021-2045 (Asset Alloc)	B-	C+	B	Up	Y	0
American Century Inv One Choice 2035 Port A Cls	ARYAX	NAS CM	Open End	Target Date 2021-2045 (Asset Alloc)	B-	C+	B	Down	Y	2,500
American Century Inv One Choice 2035 Port C Cls	ARLCX	NAS CM	Open End	Target Date 2021-2045 (Asset Alloc)	B-	C+	B	Down	Y	2,500
American Century Inv One Choice 2035 Port I Cls	ARLIX	NAS CM	Open End	Target Date 2021-2045 (Asset Alloc)	B-	C+	B	Up	Y	5,000,000
American Century Inv One Choice 2035 Port Inv Cls	ARYIX	NAS CM	Open End	Target Date 2021-2045 (Asset Alloc)	B-	C+	B	Down	Y	2,500
American Century Inv One Choice 2035 Port R Cls	ARYRX	NAS CM	Open End	Target Date 2021-2045 (Asset Alloc)	B-	C+	B	Down	Y	2,500
American Century Inv One Choice 2035 Port R6 Cls	ARLDX	NAS CM	Open End	Target Date 2021-2045 (Asset Alloc)	B-	C+	B	Down	Y	0
American Century Inv One Choice 2040 Port A Cls	ARDMX	NAS CM	Open End	Target Date 2021-2045 (Asset Alloc)	B-	C+	B	Down	Y	2,500
American Century Inv One Choice 2040 Port C Cls	ARNOX	NAS CM	Open End	Target Date 2021-2045 (Asset Alloc)	B-	C+	B	Down	Y	2,500
American Century Inv One Choice 2040 Port I Cls	ARDSX	NAS CM	Open End	Target Date 2021-2045 (Asset Alloc)	B-	C+	B	Down	Y	5,000,000
American Century Inv One Choice 2040 Port Inv Cls	ARDVX	NAS CM	Open End	Target Date 2021-2045 (Asset Alloc)	B-	C+	B	Down	Y	2,500
American Century Inv One Choice 2040 Port R Cls	ARDRX	NAS CM	Open End	Target Date 2021-2045 (Asset Alloc)	B-	C+	B	Down	Y	2,500
American Century Inv One Choice 2040 Port R6 Cls	ARDUX	NAS CM	Open End	Target Date 2021-2045 (Asset Alloc)	B-	C+	B	Down	Y	0
American Century Inv One Choice 2045 Port A Cls	AROAX	NAS CM	Open End	Target Date 2021-2045 (Asset Alloc)	B-	C+	B	Down	Y	2,500
American Century Inv One Choice 2045 Port C Cls	AROCX	NAS CM	Open End	Target Date 2021-2045 (Asset Alloc)	B-	C+	B-	Down	Y	2,500
American Century Inv One Choice 2045 Port I Cls	AOOIX	NAS CM	Open End	Target Date 2021-2045 (Asset Alloc)	B-	B-	B	Down	Y	5,000,000
American Century Inv One Choice 2045 Port Inv Cls	AROIX	NAS CM	Open End	Target Date 2021-2045 (Asset Alloc)	B-	C+	B	Down	Y	2,500
American Century Inv One Choice 2045 Port R Cls	ARORX	NAS CM	Open End	Target Date 2021-2045 (Asset Alloc)	B-	C+	B	Down	Y	2,500
American Century Inv One Choice 2045 Port R6 Cls	ARDOX	NAS CM	Open End	Target Date 2021-2045 (Asset Alloc)	B-	B-	B	Down	Y	0
American Century Inv One Choice 2050 Port A Cls	ARFMX	NAS CM	Open End	Target Date 2046+ (Asset Alloc)	B-	B-	B	Down	Y	2,500
American Century Inv One Choice 2050 Port C Cls	ARFDX	NAS CM	Open End	Target Date 2046+ (Asset Alloc)	B-	C+	B-	Down	Y	2,500
American Century Inv One Choice 2050 Port I Cls	ARFSX	NAS CM	Open End	Target Date 2046+ (Asset Alloc)	B-	B-	B	Down	Y	5,000,000
American Century Inv One Choice 2050 Port Inv Cls	ARFVX	NAS CM	Open End	Target Date 2046+ (Asset Alloc)	B-	B-	B	Down	Y	2,500
American Century Inv One Choice 2050 Port R Cls	ARFWX	NAS CM	Open End	Target Date 2046+ (Asset Alloc)	B-	C+	B-	Down	Y	2,500
American Century Inv One Choice 2050 Port R6 Cls	ARFEX	NAS CM	Open End	Target Date 2046+ (Asset Alloc)	B-	B-	B	Down	Y	0
American Century Inv One Choice 2055 Port A Cls	AREMX	NAS CM	Open End	Target Date 2046+ (Asset Alloc)	B-	B-	B-	Down	Y	2,500
American Century Inv One Choice 2055 Port C Cls	AREFX	NAS CM	Open End	Target Date 2046+ (Asset Alloc)	B-	C+	B-	Down	Y	2,500
American Century Inv One Choice 2055 Port I Cls	ARENX	NAS CM	Open End	Target Date 2046+ (Asset Alloc)	B-	B-	B	Down	Y	5,000,000
American Century Inv One Choice 2055 Port Inv Cls	AREVX	NAS CM	Open End	Target Date 2046+ (Asset Alloc)	B-	B-	B-	Down	Y	2,500
American Century Inv One Choice 2055 Port R Cls	AREOX	NAS CM	Open End	Target Date 2046+ (Asset Alloc)	B-	B-	B-	Down	Y	2,500
American Century Inv One Choice 2055 Port R6 Cls	AREUX	NAS CM	Open End	Target Date 2046+ (Asset Alloc)	B-	B-	B	Down	Y	0
American Century Inv One Choice 2060 Port A Cls	ARGMX	NAS CM	Open End	Target Date 2046+ (Asset Alloc)	C	C+	B	Up	Y	2,500
American Century Inv One Choice 2060 Port C Cls	ARGHX	NAS CM	Open End	Target Date 2046+ (Asset Alloc)	C	C+	B	Up	Y	2,500
American Century Inv One Choice 2060 Port I Cls	ARGNX	NAS CM	Open End	Target Date 2046+ (Asset Alloc)	C	C+	B	Up	Y	5,000,000
American Century Inv One Choice 2060 Port Inv Cls	ARGVX	NAS CM	Open End	Target Date 2046+ (Asset Alloc)	C	C+	B	Up	Y	2,500
American Century Inv One Choice 2060 Port R Cls	ARGRX	NAS CM	Open End	Target Date 2046+ (Asset Alloc)	C	C+	B	Up	Y	2,500

★Expanded analysis of this fund is included in Section II.

	TOTAL RETURNS					PERFORMANCE				ASSETS		ASSET ALLOCATION & TURNOVER					BULL & BEAR		FEES		
Min Additional Investment	3-Month Total Return	6-Month Total Return	1-Year Total Return	3-Year Total Return	5-Year Total Return	Dividend Yield (TTM)	Expense Ratio	3-Yr Std Deviation	3-Year Beta	NAV	Total Assets (MIL)	%Cash	%Stocks	%Bonds	%Other	Turnover Ratio	Last Bull Market Total Return	Last Bear Market Total Return	Front End Fee (%)	Back End Fee (%)	Inception Date
50	2.32	4.66	9.86	11.81	33.23	0.28	1.77	5.19	1	12.55	2,272	10	45	43	1	17	13.83	-9.58		1.00	Mar-10
50	2.50	5.26	11.15	15.88	41.28	2.26	0.57	5.16	0.99	12.51	2,272	10	45	43	1	17	14.6	-9.18			May-08
50	2.54	5.22	10.92	15.19	39.98	1.92	0.77	5.14	0.99	12.52	2,272	10	45	43	1	17	14.49	-9.27			May-08
50	2.44	4.95	10.46	13.56	36.52	1.07	1.27	5.21	1	12.52	2,272	10	45	43	1	17	14.18	-9.48			May-08
	2.56	5.29	11.11	16.25	41.86	2.18	0.42	5.16	0.99	11.49	2,272	10	45	43	1	17	14.6	-9.18			Jul-13
50	2.80	5.71	11.98	16.05	42.53	1.4	1.04	5.6	0.94	14.86	3,307	8	50	40	1	16	15.49	-10.58	5.75		Aug-04
50	2.56	5.25	11.17	13.40	37.23	0.24	1.79	5.64	0.94	14.88	3,307	8	50	40	1	16	15.04	-10.9		1.00	Mar-10
50	2.85	5.90	12.49	17.55	45.81	2.16	0.59	5.63	0.94	14.85	3,307	8	50	40	1	16	15.77	-10.4			Aug-04
50	2.78	5.76	12.27	16.85	44.24	1.82	0.79	5.66	0.95	14.85	3,307	8	50	40	1	16	15.66	-10.49			Aug-04
50	2.68	5.53	11.71	15.11	40.67	0.98	1.29	5.61	0.94	14.85	3,307	8	50	40	1	16	15.32	-10.67			Aug-04
	2.87	5.91	12.56	17.91	46.62	2.09	0.44	5.62	0.94	11.79	3,307	8	50	40	1	16	15.77	-10.4			Jul-13
50	3.00	6.29	13.24	17.59	47.47	1.31	1.06	6.17	0.92	12.97	2,683	6	56	36	1	14	16.72	-11.99	5.75		May-08
50	2.84	5.87	12.32	14.97	41.92	0.17	1.81	6.15	0.92	13	2,683	6	56	36	1	14	16.2	-12.18		1.00	Mar-10
50	3.14	6.51	13.74	19.18	50.79	2.06	0.61	6.14	0.92	12.98	2,683	6	56	36	1	14	16.95	-11.69			May-08
50	3.09	6.46	13.50	18.45	49.38	1.73	0.81	6.14	0.92	12.99	2,683	6	56	36	1	14	16.85	-11.87			May-08
50	2.98	6.10	12.95	16.70	45.59	0.88	1.31	6.14	0.92	12.98	2,683	6	56	36	1	14	16.55	-12			May-08
	3.12	6.40	13.73	19.41	51.35	2.11	0.46	6.13	0.92	11.98	2,683	6	56	36	1	14	16.95	-11.69			Jul-13
50	3.30	6.88	14.42	19.10	52.71	1.26	1.09	6.7	0.91	16.21	2,806	6	62	30	1	17	18.09	-13.26	5.75		Aug-04
50	3.16	6.47	13.61	16.48	47.15	0.18	1.84	6.73	0.92	16.22	2,806	6	62	30	1	17	17.56	-13.51		1.00	Mar-10
50	3.45	7.08	14.93	20.72	56.27	2.01	0.64	6.73	0.92	16.22	2,806	6	62	30	1	17	18.38	-13.09			Aug-04
50	3.37	7.01	14.71	20.00	54.63	1.68	0.84	6.69	0.91	16.21	2,806	6	62	30	1	17	18.27	-13.17			Aug-04
50	3.30	6.74	14.13	18.21	50.89	0.84	1.34	6.7	0.91	16.22	2,806	6	62	30	1	17	17.92	-13.35			Aug-04
	3.43	7.11	14.92	21.13	57.09	2.03	0.49	6.74	0.92	12.19	2,806	6	62	30	1	17	18.38	-13.09			Jul-13
50	3.68	7.56	15.78	20.66	57.98	1.2	1.11	7.3	0.92	13.68	1,996	5	68	25	1	17	19.56	-14.62	5.75		May-08
50	3.42	7.06	14.87	17.91	52.00	0.14	1.86	7.27	0.92	13.67	1,996	5	68	25	1	17	19.08	-14.84		1.00	Mar-10
50	3.84	7.80	16.30	22.30	61.59	1.94	0.66	7.29	0.92	13.68	1,996	5	68	25	1	17	19.81	-14.42			May-08
50	3.71	7.66	16.07	21.56	59.96	1.61	0.86	7.31	0.93	13.68	1,996	5	68	25	1	17	19.7	-14.51			May-08
50	3.65	7.37	15.49	19.75	56.01	0.78	1.36	7.32	0.93	13.68	1,996	5	68	25	1	17	19.41	-14.65			May-08
	3.78	7.79	16.29	22.61	62.42	1.98	0.51	7.3	0.93	12.42	1,996	5	68	25	1	17	19.81	-14.42			Jul-13
50	4.06	8.19	17.21	22.41	62.91	1.12	1.15	7.88	0.95	17.18	2,007	2	74	21	2	16	20.44	-15.41	5.75		Aug-04
50	3.82	7.81	16.35	19.67	56.88	0.15	1.9	7.87	0.94	17.18	2,007	2	74	21	2	16	19.88	-15.65		1.00	Mar-10
50	4.10	8.41	17.72	24.05	66.56	1.86	0.7	7.87	0.94	17.19	2,007	2	74	21	2	16	20.81	-15.3			Aug-04
50	4.08	8.33	17.50	23.33	64.95	1.53	0.9	7.88	0.95	17.18	2,007	2	74	21	2	16	20.61	-15.39			Aug-04
50	2.75	6.83	15.59	20.10	59.00	0.71	1.4	7.88	0.95	17.19	2,007	2	74	21	2	16	20.26	-15.56			Aug-04
	4.20	8.53	17.84	24.60	67.55	1.91	0.55	7.91	0.95	12.59	2,007	2	74	21	2	16	20.81	-15.3			Jul-13
50	4.26	8.67	18.21	23.53	65.35	1.04	1.17	8.2	0.94	14.01	1,250	1	79	18	2	19	21.11	-15.98	5.75		May-08
50	4.05	8.29	17.32	20.75	59.37	0.06	1.92	8.18	0.94	14.02	1,250	1	79	18	2	19	20.51	-16.27		1.00	Mar-10
50	4.43	8.98	18.81	25.28	69.33	1.77	0.72	8.17	0.94	14.03	1,250	1	79	18	2	19	21.46	-15.85			May-08
50	4.37	8.93	18.58	24.55	67.56	1.45	0.92	8.16	0.94	14.02	1,250	1	79	18	2	19	21.27	-15.96			May-08
50	2.92	7.27	16.50	21.13	61.45	0.63	1.42	8.18	0.94	14.02	1,250	1	79	18	2	19	20.97	-16.17			May-08
	4.46	9.05	18.92	25.73	70.20	1.83	0.57	8.22	0.94	12.75	1,250	1	79	18	2	19	21.46	-15.85			Jul-13
50	3.05	7.65	17.30	22.69	65.47	0.94	1.17	8.44	0.93	15.01	651.1	1	81	16	2	11	21.38	-16.19	5.75		Mar-11
50	4.20	8.57	17.87	21.43	61.43	0.1	1.92	8.42	0.93	14.96	651.1	1	81	16	2	11	20.88	-16.4		1.00	Mar-11
50	4.52	9.25	19.28	25.90	71.46	1.67	0.72	8.44	0.93	15.02	651.1	1	81	16	2	11	21.74	-16			Mar-11
50	4.45	9.10	19.04	25.14	69.75	1.35	0.92	8.41	0.93	15.02	651.1	1	81	16	2	11	21.58	-16.1			Mar-11
50	3.12	7.58	17.03	21.80	63.68	0.53	1.42	8.45	0.93	15.03	651.1	1	81	16	2	11	21.29	-16.29			Mar-11
	4.52	9.28	19.35	26.32	72.31	1.77	0.57	8.45	0.93	13.03	651.1	1	81	16	2	11	21.74	-16			Jul-13
50	4.50	9.14	19.00			0.74	1.17			12.79	57.9	1	83	14	1	21			5.75		Sep-15
50	4.30	8.77	18.11			0	1.92			12.73	57.9	1	83	14	1	21				1.00	Sep-15
50	4.55	9.35	19.54			1.47	0.72			12.79	57.9	1	83	14	1	21					Sep-15
50	4.51	9.32	19.30			1.15	0.92			12.79	57.9	1	83	14	1	21					Sep-15
50	4.38	9.02	18.68			0.38	1.42			12.78	57.9	1	83	14	1	21					Sep-15

	MARKET		FUND TYPE, CATEGORY & OBJECTIVE		RATINGS					MINIMUMS
Fund Name	Ticker Symbol	Traded On	Fund Type	Category and (Prospectus Objective)	Overall Rating	Reward Rating	Risk Rating	Recent Up/ Downgrade	Open to New Investors	Min Initial Investment
American Century Inv One Choice 2060 Port R6 Cls	ARGDX	NAS CM	Open End	Target Date 2046+ (Asset Alloc)	C	C+	B	Up	Y	0
American Century Inv One Choice In Retmnt Port A Cls	ARTAX	NAS CM	Open End	Target Date 2000-2020 (Asset Alloc)	B-	C+	B	Up	Y	2,500
American Century Inv One Choice In Retmnt Port C Cls	ATTCX	NAS CM	Open End	Target Date 2000-2020 (Asset Alloc)	B-	C+	B	Up	Y	2,500
American Century Inv One Choice In Retmnt Port I Cls	ATTIX	NAS CM	Open End	Target Date 2000-2020 (Asset Alloc)	B-	C+	B	Up	Y	5,000,000
American Century Inv One Choice In Retmnt Port Inv Cls	ARTOX	NAS CM	Open End	Target Date 2000-2020 (Asset Alloc)	B-	C+	B	Up	Y	2,500
American Century Inv One Choice In Retmnt Port R Cls	ARSRX	NAS CM	Open End	Target Date 2000-2020 (Asset Alloc)	B-	C+	B	Up	Y	2,500
American Century Inv One Choice In Retmnt Port R6 Cls	ARDTX	NAS CM	Open End	Target Date 2000-2020 (Asset Alloc)	B-	C+	B	Up	Y	0
American Century Inv One Choice Port®: Aggressive Inv Cls	AOGIX	NAS CM	Open End	Aggressive Alloc (Asset Alloc)	B-	B-	B	Down	Y	2,500
American Century Inv One Choice Port®: Aggressive R Cls	AORYX	NAS CM	Open End	Aggressive Alloc (Asset Alloc)	B-	C+	B-	Down	Y	2,500
American Century Inv One Choice Port®: Cons Inv Cls	AOCIX	NAS CM	Open End	Cautious Alloc (Asset Alloc)	B	C+	A-	Up	Y	2,500
American Century Inv One Choice Port®: Conservative R Cls	AORSX	NAS CM	Open End	Cautious Alloc (Asset Alloc)	B	C+	A-	Up	Y	2,500
American Century Inv One Choice Port®: Moderate Inv Cls	AOMIX	NAS CM	Open End	Moderate Alloc (Asset Alloc)	B-	C+	B	Down	Y	2,500
American Century Inv One Choice Port®: Moderate R Cls	AORMX	NAS CM	Open End	Moderate Alloc (Asset Alloc)	B-	C+	B	Down	Y	2,500
American Century Inv One Choice Port®: Very Aggress Inv Cl	AOVIX	NAS CM	Open End	Aggressive Alloc (Asset Alloc)	B-	B-	B-	Down	Y	2,500
American Century Inv One Choice Port®: Very Aggress R Cls	AORVX	NAS CM	Open End	Aggressive Alloc (Asset Alloc)	B-	B-	B-	Down	Y	2,500
American Century Inv One Choice Port®: Very Cons Inv Cls	AONIX	NAS CM	Open End	Cautious Alloc (Asset Alloc)	B	C	A-	Up	Y	2,500
American Century Inv One Choice Port®: Very Cons R Cls	AORHX	NAS CM	Open End	Cautious Alloc (Asset Alloc)	B-	C	A-	Up	Y	2,500
American Century Large Company Value Fund A Class	ALPAX	NAS CM	Open End	US Equity Large Cap Value (Growth)	B-	C+	B	Down	Y	2,500
American Century Large Company Value Fund C Class	ALPCX	NAS CM	Open End	US Equity Large Cap Value (Growth)	B-	C+	B	Down	Y	2,500
American Century Large Company Value Fund I Class	ALVSX	NAS CM	Open End	US Equity Large Cap Value (Growth)	B-	B-	B	Down	Y	5,000,000
American Century Large Company Value Fund Investor Class	ALVIX	NAS CM	Open End	US Equity Large Cap Value (Growth)	B-	C+	B	Down	Y	2,500
American Century Large Company Value Fund R Class	ALVRX	NAS CM	Open End	US Equity Large Cap Value (Growth)	B-	C+	B	Down	Y	2,500
American Century Large Company Value Fund R5 Class	ALVGX	NAS CM	Open End	US Equity Large Cap Value (Growth)	B-	C+	B	Down	Y	0
American Century Large Company Value Fund R6 Class	ALVDX	NAS CM	Open End	US Equity Large Cap Value (Growth)	B-	B-	B	Down	Y	0
American Century Mid Cap Value Fund A Class	ACLAX	NAS CM	Open End	US Equity Mid Cap (Growth)	B	B-	B+			2,500
American Century Mid Cap Value Fund C Class	ACCLX	NAS CM	Open End	US Equity Mid Cap (Growth)	B	B-	B+			2,500
American Century Mid Cap Value Fund I Class	AVUAX	NAS CM	Open End	US Equity Mid Cap (Growth)	B	B-	B+			5,000,000
American Century Mid Cap Value Fund Investor Class	ACMVX	NAS CM	Open End	US Equity Mid Cap (Growth)	B	B-	B+			2,500
American Century Mid Cap Value Fund R Class	AMVRX	NAS CM	Open End	US Equity Mid Cap (Growth)	B	B-	B+			2,500
American Century Mid Cap Value Fund R5 Class	AMVGX	NAS CM	Open End	US Equity Mid Cap (Growth)	B	B-	B+		Y	0
American Century Mid Cap Value Fund R6 Class	AMDVX	NAS CM	Open End	US Equity Mid Cap (Growth)	B	B-	B+			0
American Century Mid Cap Value Fund Y Class	AMVYX	NAS CM	Open End	US Equity Mid Cap (Growth)	B	B-	B+			0
American Century Multi-Asset Income Fund A Class	AMJAX	NAS CM	Open End	Cautious Alloc (Growth & Income)	C+	C	B	Down	Y	2,500
American Century Multi-Asset Income Fund C Class	AMJCX	NAS CM	Open End	Cautious Alloc (Growth & Income)	C+	C	B	Up	Y	2,500
American Century Multi-Asset Income Fund I Class	AMJIX	NAS CM	Open End	Cautious Alloc (Growth & Income)	C+	C	B	Down	Y	5,000,000
American Century Multi-Asset Income Fund Investor Class	AMJVX	NAS CM	Open End	Cautious Alloc (Growth & Income)	C+	C	B	Down	Y	2,500
American Century Multi-Asset Income Fund R Class	AMJWX	NAS CM	Open End	Cautious Alloc (Growth & Income)	B-	C	B	Up	Y	2,500
American Century Multi-Asset Income Fund R5 Class	AMJGX	NAS CM	Open End	Cautious Alloc (Growth & Income)	C+	C	B	Down	Y	0
American Century Multi-Asset Income Fund R6 Class	AMJRX	NAS CM	Open End	Cautious Alloc (Growth & Income)	C+	C	B	Down	Y	0
American Century Multi-Asset Income Fund Y Class	AMJYX	NAS CM	Open End	Cautious Alloc (Growth & Income)	C+	C	B	Down	Y	0
American Century Multi-Asset Real Return Fund A Class	ASIDX	NAS CM	Open End	Cautious Alloc (Growth & Income)	C+	C	B-	Up	Y	2,500
American Century Multi-Asset Real Return Fund C Class	ASIZX	NAS CM	Open End	Cautious Alloc (Growth & Income)	C+	C	B-	Up	Y	2,500
American Century Multi-Asset Real Return Fund I Class	ASINX	NAS CM	Open End	Cautious Alloc (Growth & Income)	C+	C	B-	Up	Y	5,000,000
American Century Multi-Asset Real Return Fund Investor Cls	ASIOX	NAS CM	Open End	Cautious Alloc (Growth & Income)	C+	C	B-	Up	Y	2,500
American Century Multi-Asset Real Return Fund R Class	ASIUX	NAS CM	Open End	Cautious Alloc (Growth & Income)	C+	C	B-	Up	Y	2,500
American Century Multi-Asset Real Return Fund R5 Class	AMRUX	NAS CM	Open End	Cautious Alloc (Growth & Income)	C+	C	B-	Up	Y	0
American Century NT Core Equity Plus Fund G Class	ACNKX	NAS CM	Open End	US Equity Large Cap Blend (Growth)	B-	B-	B-	Down	Y	0
American Century NT Disciplined Growth Fund G Class	ANDGX	NAS CM	Open End	US Equity Large Cap Growth (Growth)	B-	C+	B-	Up		0
American Century NT Disciplined Growth Fund Investor Class	ANTDX	NAS CM	Open End	US Equity Large Cap Growth (Growth)	B-	C+	B-	Up	Y	0
American Century NT Emerging Markets Fund G Class	ACLKX	NAS CM	Open End	Emerging Markets Equity (Div Emerging Mkts)	B+	A	C+	Up	Y	0
American Century NT Equity Growth Fund G Class	ACLEX	NAS CM	Open End	US Equity Large Cap Blend (Growth)	B-	B-	B-	Down	Y	0
American Century NT Global Real Estate Fund G Class	ANRHX	NAS CM	Open End	Real Estate Sector Equity (Real Estate)	C+	C	B-	Up		0

★Expanded analysis of this fund is included in Section II.

	TOTAL RETURNS					PERFORMANCE				ASSETS		ASSET ALLOCATION & TURNOVER					BULL & BEAR		FEES		
Min Additional Investment	3-Month Total Return	6-Month Total Return	1-Year Total Return	3-Year Total Return	5-Year Total Return	Dividend Yield (TTM)	Expense Ratio	3-Yr Std Deviation	3-Year Beta	NAV	Total Assets (MIL)	%Cash	%Stocks	%Bonds	%Other	Turnover Ratio	Last Bull Market Total Return	Last Bear Market Total Return	Front End Fee (%)	Back End Fee (%)	Inception Date
	4.61	9.51	19.71			1.25	0.57			12.82	57.9	1	83	14	1	21					Sep-15
50	2.29	4.67	9.93	13.45	34.62	1.08	1.02	4.75	1.36	13.31	1,979	11	42	45	1	12	12.45	-7.3	5.75		Aug-04
50	2.17	4.37	9.14	10.96	29.74	0.39	1.77	4.79	1.37	13.28	1,979	11	42	45	1	12	11.94	-7.64		1.00	Mar-10
50	2.41	4.92	10.34	14.91	37.58	1.51	0.57	4.79	1.38	13.3	1,979	11	42	45	1	12	12.7	-7.09			Aug-04
50	2.35	4.81	10.21	14.22	36.22	1.32	0.77	4.81	1.38	13.3	1,979	11	42	45	1	12	12.69	-7.27			Aug-04
50	2.22	4.55	9.58	12.53	32.88	0.85	1.27	4.77	1.37	13.29	1,979	11	42	45	1	12	12.32	-7.42			Aug-04
	2.40	4.91	10.47	15.33	38.33	1.57	0.42	4.8	1.38	11.13	1,979	11	42	45	1	12	12.7	-7.09			Jul-13
50	4.27	8.95	19.13	24.96	64.72	1.22	0.99	8.27	0.77	16.91	1,282	2	77	18	1	18	20.63	-15.83			Sep-04
50	4.18	8.67	18.59	23.14	60.71	0.79	1.49	8.28	0.77	16.93	1,282	2	77	18	1	18	20.28	-16			Mar-15
50	2.51	5.16	11.08	15.23	36.96	1.45	0.81	4.94	0.44	13.77	1,269	8	45	46	1	12	12.42	-6.97			Sep-04
50	2.45	4.97	10.61	13.58	33.66	0.98	1.31	4.92	0.44	13.78	1,269	8	45	46	1	12	12.1	-7.17			Mar-15
50	3.52	7.24	15.43	20.32	51.58	1.38	0.9	6.73	0.62	15.85	1,933	5	63	30	1	15	17	-11.95			Sep-04
50	3.39	6.96	14.85	18.59	47.92	0.92	1.4	6.76	0.63	15.85	1,933	5	63	30	1	15	16.66	-12.13			Mar-15
50	5.13	10.72	22.77	29.12	79.62	0.75	1.05	9.95	0.94	18.29	306.4	1	97	0	2	11	23.75	-19.21			Sep-04
50	5.00	10.47	22.20	27.20	75.20	0.34	1.55	9.95	0.94	18.32	306.4	1	97	0	2	11	23.39	-19.38			Mar-15
50	1.59	3.12	6.45	10.97	22.77	1.47	0.7	3.2	0.26	12.06	454.3	8	25	66	1	13	8.03	-2.78			Sep-04
50	1.45	2.85	5.91	9.30	19.71	0.98	1.2	3.23	0.26	12.07	454.3	8	25	66	1	13	7.71	-2.98			Mar-15
50	3.56	5.96	10.73	21.09	82.95	1.87	1.08	11.17	1.06	10.21	851.6	0	98	0	0	68	24.5	-17.19	5.75		Oct-00
50	3.45	5.65	10.02	18.45	76.50	1.16	1.83	11.23	1.07	10.22	851.6	0	98	0	0	68	24.06	-17.51		1.00	Nov-01
50	3.69	6.21	11.22	22.71	87.29	2.3	0.63	11.19	1.06	10.22	851.6	0	98	0	0	68	24.98	-17.13			Aug-01
50	3.73	6.10	11.12	21.98	85.43	2.11	0.83	11.19	1.06	10.22	851.6	0	98	0	0	68	24.65	-17.22			Jul-99
50	3.49	5.82	10.45	20.16	80.84	1.63	1.33	11.22	1.07	10.22	851.6	0	98	0	0	68	24.36	-17.43			Aug-03
	3.69	6.21	11.16	22.03	85.51		0.63	11.2	1.06	10.22	851.6	0	98	0	0	68	24.65	-17.22			Apr-17
	3.73	6.29	11.39	23.27	88.15	2.44	0.48	11.22	1.07	10.22	851.6	0	98	0	0	68	24.65	-17.22			Jul-13
50	4.61	7.12	11.32	32.60	104.18	1.34	1.21	9.82	0.91	17.49	8,880	2	98	0	0	49	21.86	-17.25	5.75		Jan-05
50	4.38	6.70	10.47	29.56	96.70	0.7	1.96	9.8	0.91	17.32	8,880	2	98	0	0	49	21.21	-17.43		1.00	Mar-10
	4.72	7.41	11.79	34.40	108.91	1.75	0.76	9.83	0.91	17.53	8,880	2	98	0	0	49	22.16	-17.06			Aug-04
50	4.67	7.30	11.58	33.54	106.78	1.57	0.96	9.79	0.91	17.52	8,880	2	98	0	0	49	21.95	-17.14			Mar-04
50	4.49	7.00	11.01	31.53	101.65	1.11	1.46	9.81	0.91	17.44	8,880	2	98	0	0	49	21.57	-17.22			Jul-05
	4.72	7.35	11.73	33.73	107.06		0.76	9.8	0.91	17.53	8,880	2	98	0	0	49	21.95	-17.14			Apr-17
	4.71	7.43	11.96	34.93	110.02	1.89	0.61	9.82	0.91	17.52	8,880	2	98	0	0	49	21.95	-17.14			Jul-13
	4.76	7.43	11.84	33.87	107.28		0.61	9.8	0.91	17.53	8,880	2	98	0	0	49	21.95	-17.14			Apr-17
50	0.98	3.50	9.51	17.37		4.39	1.22			10.22	57.6	7	39	37	1	195			5.75		Dec-14
50	0.88	3.21	8.71	14.79		3.68	1.97			10.22	57.6	7	39	37	1	195				1.00	Dec-14
50	1.10	3.74	10.00	18.95		4.83	0.77			10.22	57.6	7	39	37	1	195					Dec-14
50	1.05	3.64	9.79	18.25		4.63	0.97			10.22	57.6	7	39	37	1	195					Dec-14
50	0.92	3.37	9.25	16.51		4.15	1.47			10.22	57.6	7	39	37	1	195					Dec-14
	1.10	3.84	9.99	18.94			0.77			10.23	57.6	7	39	37	1	195					Apr-17
	1.14	3.82	10.16	19.48		4.97	0.62			10.22	57.6	7	39	37	1	195					Dec-14
	1.24	3.92	10.16	19.48			0.62			10.23	57.6	7	39	37	1	195					Apr-17
50	3.08	6.26	10.46	6.70	0.83	0	1.18	4.86	0.76	10.34	14.1	3	50	43	4	173	5.91	-10.9	5.75		Apr-10
50	2.91	5.88	9.51	4.31	-2.94	0	1.93	4.8	0.74	9.9	14.1	3	50	43	4	173	5.5	-11.16		1.00	Apr-10
50	3.24	6.59	10.87	8.24	3.18	0	0.73	4.82	0.75	10.5	14.1	3	50	43	4	173	6.17	-10.69			Apr-10
50	3.26	6.52	10.70	7.51	2.09	0	0.93	4.88	0.76	10.44	14.1	3	50	43	4	173	6.11	-10.82			Apr-10
50	3.03	6.13	10.15	5.91	-0.48	0	1.43	4.86	0.75	10.2	14.1	3	50	43	4	173	5.81	-11.08			Apr-10
	3.24	6.59	10.87	8.24	3.18		0.73	4.82	0.74	10.5	14.1	3	50	43	4	173	6.17	-10.69			Apr-17
	6.93	11.86	20.00	24.77	98.36	0.5	0.01	9.76	0.93	16.6	623.9	1	99	0	0	111					Dec-11
	6.29	13.00	26.68			0.59	0.01			12.44	579.4	1	99	0	0	131					Mar-15
	6.07	12.48	25.99			0.42	1.02			12.44	579.4	1	99	0	0	131					Mar-15
	6.56	20.78	48.36	46.74	45.77	0.57	1.19	14.72	0.9	13.46	481.9	3	96	0	1	75	22.61	-29.91			May-06
	6.82	11.98	22.17	27.63	98.31	1.58	0.01	10.3	1	13.62	1,815	1	99	0	0	88	25.94	-15.43			May-06
	4.86	8.64	14.85			3.93	0.93			9.85	433.0	2	97	0	2	264					Mar-15

	MARKET			FUND TYPE, CATEGORY & OBJECTIVE	RATINGS				MINIMUMS	
Fund Name	Ticker Symbol	Traded On	Fund Type	Category and (Prospectus Objective)	Overall Rating	Reward Rating	Risk Rating	Recent Up/ Downgrade	Open to New Investors	Min Initial Investment
American Century NT Global Real Estate Fund Investor Class	ANREX	NAS CM	Open End	Real Estate Sector Equity (Real Estate)	C+	C	B-	Up		0
American Century NT Growth Fund G Class	ACLTX	NAS CM	Open End	US Equity Large Cap Growth (Growth)	B+	B+	B	Up	Y	0
American Century NT Heritage Fund G Class	ACLWX	NAS CM	Open End	US Equity Mid Cap (Growth)	B	B	B	Up	Y	0
American Century NT International Growth Fund G Class	ACLNX	NAS CM	Open End	Global Equity Large Cap (Foreign Stock)	B-	B-	B	Up	Y	0
American Century NT International Small-Mid Cap Fund G Cls	ANTMX	NAS CM	Open End	Global Equity Mid/Small Cap (Growth)	B-	C+	B-	Up		0
American Century NT Intl Small-Mid Cap Fund Inv Cls	ANTSX	NAS CM	Open End	Global Equity Mid/Small Cap (Growth)	B-	C+	B-	Up	Y	0
American Century NT International Value Fund G Class	ANTYX	NAS CM	Open End	Global Equity Large Cap (Growth)	C+	C+	C+	Up		0
American Century NT International Value Fund Investor Cls	ANTVX	NAS CM	Open End	Global Equity Large Cap (Growth)	C+	C+	C+	Up	Y	0
American Century NT Large Company Value Fund G Class	ACLLX	NAS CM	Open End	US Equity Large Cap Value (Growth)	B-	C+	B	Down	Y	0
American Century NT Mid Cap Value Fund G Class	ACLMX	NAS CM	Open End	US Equity Mid Cap (Growth)	B	B-	B+		Y	0
American Century NT Small Company Fund G Class	ACLOX	NAS CM	Open End	US Equity Small Cap (Small Company)	B	B	B	Up	Y	0
American Century Real Estate Fund A Class	AREEX	NAS CM	Open End	Real Estate Sector Equity (Real Estate)	B-	C+	B	Up	Y	2,500
American Century Real Estate Fund C Class	ARYCX	NAS CM	Open End	Real Estate Sector Equity (Real Estate)	B-	C+	B	Up	Y	2,500
American Century Real Estate Fund I Class	REAIX	NAS CM	Open End	Real Estate Sector Equity (Real Estate)	B-	C+	B	Up	Y	5,000,000
American Century Real Estate Fund Investor Class	REACX	NAS CM	Open End	Real Estate Sector Equity (Real Estate)	B-	C+	B	Up	Y	2,500
American Century Real Estate Fund R Class	AREWX	NAS CM	Open End	Real Estate Sector Equity (Real Estate)	B-	C+	B	Up	Y	2,500
American Century Real Estate Fund R5 Class	ARREX	NAS CM	Open End	Real Estate Sector Equity (Real Estate)	B-	C+	B	Up	Y	0
American Century Real Estate Fund R6 Class	AREDX	NAS CM	Open End	Real Estate Sector Equity (Real Estate)	B-	C+	B	Up	Y	0
American Century Real Estate Fund Y Class	ARYEX	NAS CM	Open End	Real Estate Sector Equity (Real Estate)	B-	C+	B	Up	Y	0
American Century Select Fund A Class	TWCAX	NAS CM	Open End	US Equity Large Cap Growth (Growth)	B+	B+	B	Up	Y	2,500
American Century Select Fund C Class	ACSLX	NAS CM	Open End	US Equity Large Cap Growth (Growth)	B	B	B	Down	Y	2,500
American Century Select Fund I Class	TWSIX	NAS CM	Open End	US Equity Large Cap Growth (Growth)	B+	B+	B	Up	Y	5,000,000
American Century Select Fund Investor Class	TWCIX	NAS CM	Open End	US Equity Large Cap Growth (Growth)	B+	B+	B	Up	Y	2,500
American Century Select Fund R Class	ASERX	NAS CM	Open End	US Equity Large Cap Growth (Growth)	B+	B+	B	Up	Y	2,500
American Century Select Fund R5 Class	ASLGX	NAS CM	Open End	US Equity Large Cap Growth (Growth)	B+	B+	B	Up	Y	0
American Century Select Fund R6 Class	ASDEX	NAS CM	Open End	US Equity Large Cap Growth (Growth)	B+	B+	B	Up	Y	0
American Century Select Fund Y Class	ASLWX	NAS CM	Open End	US Equity Large Cap Growth (Growth)	B+	B+	B	Up	Y	0
American Century Small Cap Growth Fund A Class	ANOAX	NAS CM	Open End	US Equity Small Cap (Small Company)	B	A-	C	Up	Y	2,500
American Century Small Cap Growth Fund C Class	ANOCX	NAS CM	Open End	US Equity Small Cap (Small Company)	B	A-	B-	Up	Y	2,500
American Century Small Cap Growth Fund I Class	ANONX	NAS CM	Open End	US Equity Small Cap (Small Company)	B	A-	C	Up	Y	5,000,000
American Century Small Cap Growth Fund Investor Class	ANOIX	NAS CM	Open End	US Equity Small Cap (Small Company)	B	A-	C	Up	Y	2,500
American Century Small Cap Growth Fund R Class	ANORX	NAS CM	Open End	US Equity Small Cap (Small Company)	B+	A-	B-	Up	Y	2,500
American Century Small Cap Growth Fund R5 Class	ANOGX	NAS CM	Open End	US Equity Small Cap (Small Company)	B	A-	C	Up	Y	0
American Century Small Cap Growth Fund R6 Class	ANODX	NAS CM	Open End	US Equity Small Cap (Small Company)	B	A-	C	Up	Y	0
American Century Small Cap Growth Fund Y Class	ANOYX	NAS CM	Open End	US Equity Small Cap (Small Company)	B	A-	C	Up	Y	0
American Century Small Cap Value Fund A Class	ACSCX	NAS CM	Open End	US Equity Small Cap (Small Company)	B	B+	B	Up		2,500
American Century Small Cap Value Fund C Class	ASVNX	NAS CM	Open End	US Equity Small Cap (Small Company)	B	B	B	Up		2,500
American Century Small Cap Value Fund I Class	ACVIX	NAS CM	Open End	US Equity Small Cap (Small Company)	B	B+	B	Up		5,000,000
American Century Small Cap Value Fund Investor Class	ASVIX	NAS CM	Open End	US Equity Small Cap (Small Company)	B	B+	B	Up		2,500
American Century Small Cap Value Fund R Class	ASVRX	NAS CM	Open End	US Equity Small Cap (Small Company)	B	B	B	Up		2,500
American Century Small Cap Value Fund R5 Class	ASVGX	NAS CM	Open End	US Equity Small Cap (Small Company)	B	B+	B	Up	Y	0
American Century Small Cap Value Fund R6 Class	ASVDX	NAS CM	Open End	US Equity Small Cap (Small Company)	B+	B+	B	Up		0
American Century Small Cap Value Fund Y Class	ASVYX	NAS CM	Open End	US Equity Small Cap (Small Company)	B	B+	B	Up		0
American Century Small Company Fund A Class	ASQAX	NAS CM	Open End	US Equity Small Cap (Small Company)	B	B	B	Up	Y	2,500
American Century Small Company Fund C Class	ASQCX	NAS CM	Open End	US Equity Small Cap (Small Company)	B-	B-	B	Up	Y	2,500
American Century Small Company Fund I Class	ASCQX	NAS CM	Open End	US Equity Small Cap (Small Company)	B	B	B	Up	Y	5,000,000
American Century Small Company Fund Investor Class	ASQIX	NAS CM	Open End	US Equity Small Cap (Small Company)	B	B	B	Up	Y	2,500
American Century Small Company Fund R Class	ASCRX	NAS CM	Open End	US Equity Small Cap (Small Company)	B	B	B	Up	Y	2,500
American Century Small Company Fund R5 Class	ASQGX	NAS CM	Open End	US Equity Small Cap (Small Company)	B	B	B	Up	Y	0
American Century Strategic Alloc: Aggressive Fund A Cls	ACVAX	NAS CM	Open End	Aggressive Alloc (Asset Alloc)	B-	B-	B-	Down	Y	2,500
American Century Strategic Alloc: Aggressive Fund C Cls	ASTAX	NAS CM	Open End	Aggressive Alloc (Asset Alloc)	B-	C+	B-	Down	Y	2,500
American Century Strategic Alloc: Aggressive Fund I Cls	AAAIX	NAS CM	Open End	Aggressive Alloc (Asset Alloc)	B-	B-	B-	Down	Y	5,000,000

★ Expanded analysis of this fund is included in Section II.

Min Additional Investment	3-Month Total Return	6-Month Total Return	1-Year Total Return	3-Year Total Return	5-Year Total Return	Dividend Yield (TTM)	Expense Ratio	3-Yr Std Deviation	3-Year Beta	NAV	Total Assets (MIL)	%Cash	%Stocks	%Bonds	%Other	Turnover Ratio	Last Bull Market Total Return	Last Bear Market Total Return	Front End Fee (%)	Back End Fee (%)	Inception Date
TOTAL RETURNS						PERFORMANCE				ASSETS		ASSET ALLOCATION & TURNOVER					BULL & BEAR		FEES		
	4.57	8.13	14.19			3.76	1.13			9.85	433.0	2	97	0	2	264					Mar-15
	7.93	13.18	30.81	41.01	110.05	0.6	0.78	11	1	17.3	1,371	1	99	0	0	60	26.98	-16.93			May-06
	5.77	10.04	22.44	28.52	85.97	0	0.8	11.09	0.98	13.97	832.8	1	99	0	0	73	27.07	-21.65			May-06
	4.29	13.29	31.82	24.04	47.93	0.71	0.98	11.81	0.9	12.28	1,041	1	95	0	4	69	17.51	-24.37			May-06
	7.07	17.52	37.19			0.13	1.27			13.03	249.6	2	96	0	2	138					Mar-15
	6.62	16.67	36.07			0	1.47			12.92	249.6	2	96	0	2	138					Mar-15
	1.92	8.10	22.33			2.7	1.11			10.31	953.8	1	96	0	3	81					Mar-15
	1.63	7.49	21.51			2.55	1.31			10.31	953.8	1	96	0	3	81					Mar-15
	3.93	6.59	11.54	21.70	85.37	2.3	0.01	11.29	1.07	11.56	2,016	0	99	0	0	79	24.8	-17.27			May-06
	4.91	7.71	12.08	34.84	109.97	1.85	0.01	9.82	0.91	13.56	1,096	1	99	0	0	60	22.16	-16.88			May-06
	3.01	8.27	11.31	24.65	94.78	0.49	0.01	14.3	0.99	9.63	460.8	0	100	0	0	118	28	-22.8			May-06
50	2.50	3.21	4.90	11.53	49.92	1.03	1.39	13.19	0.97	28.19	1,141	1	99	0	0	149	31.74	-14.81	5.75		Oct-98
50	2.30	2.82	4.12	9.04	44.42	0.86	2.14	13.18	0.97	27.48	1,141	1	99	0	0	149	31.18	-15.07		1.00	Sep-07
50	2.61	3.43	5.37	13.05	53.33	1.31	0.94	13.2	0.97	28.29	1,141	1	99	0	0	149	32.1	-14.62			Jun-97
50	2.56	3.33	5.18	12.37	51.84	1.14	1.14	13.2	0.97	28.22	1,141	1	99	0	0	149	31.98	-14.73			Sep-95
50	2.41	3.06	4.64	10.69	48.07	0.97	1.64	13.2	0.97	27.99	1,141	1	99	0	0	149	31.57	-14.9			Sep-07
	2.61	3.43	5.32	12.52	52.04		0.94	13.2	0.97	28.29	1,141	1	99	0	0	149	31.98	-14.73			Apr-17
	2.66	3.55	5.53	13.60	54.21	1.44	0.79	13.18	0.97	28.28	1,141	1	99	0	0	149	31.98	-14.73			Jul-13
	2.66	3.51	5.43	12.64	52.20		0.79	13.2	0.97	28.28	1,141	1	99	0	0	149	31.98	-14.73			Apr-17
50	6.44	13.29	28.57	44.00	112.13	0.09	1.22	10.74	0.97	68.72	2,939	0	99	0	1	16	27.76	-15.85	5.75		Aug-97
50	6.25	12.87	27.63	40.79	104.28	0	1.97	10.73	0.97	62.1	2,939	0	99	0	1	16	27.22	-16.11		1.00	Jan-03
50	6.56	13.54	29.15	45.95	116.94	0.44	0.77	10.74	0.97	71.19	2,939	0	99	0	1	16	28.12	-15.7			Mar-97
50	6.52	13.45	28.93	45.08	114.82	0.29	0.97	10.74	0.97	70.1	2,939	0	99	0	1	16	27.93	-15.75			Jun-71
50	6.38	13.16	28.28	42.92	109.47	0	1.47	10.74	0.97	68.3	2,939	0	99	0	1	16	27.59	-15.94			Jul-05
	6.56	13.54	29.08	45.25	115.06		0.77	10.74	0.97	71.23	2,939	0	99	0	1	16	27.93	-15.75			Apr-17
	6.62	13.64	29.35	46.62	118.15	0.56	0.62	10.74	0.97	71.13	2,939	0	99	0	1	16	27.93	-15.75			Jul-13
	6.62	13.64	29.22	45.42	115.31		0.62	10.74	0.97	71.2	2,939	0	99	0	1	16	27.93	-15.75			Apr-17
50	5.87	12.03	25.48	32.18	100.72	0	1.61	14.77	0.97	16.64	718.2	2	99	0	0	130	32.53	-28.79	5.75		Jan-03
50	5.71	11.62	24.62	29.26	93.35	0	2.36	14.75	0.97	15.25	718.2	2	99	0	0	130	32.14	-29.07		1.00	Jan-03
50	6.00	12.33	26.07	33.94	105.20	0	1.16	14.73	0.96	17.54	718.2	2	99	0	0	130	32.94	-28.69			May-07
50	5.94	12.25	25.84	33.15	103.21	0	1.36	14.77	0.97	17.18	718.2	2	99	0	0	130	32.79	-28.72			Jun-01
50	5.80	11.92	25.19	31.18	98.15	0	1.86	14.74	0.96	16.3	718.2	2	99	0	0	130	32.58	-28.92			Sep-07
	6.00	12.32	26.01	33.33	103.48		1.16	14.78	0.97	17.55	718.2	2	99	0	0	130	32.79	-28.72			Apr-17
	6.02	12.38	26.29	34.52	106.28	0	1.01	14.76	0.97	17.66	718.2	2	99	0	0	130	32.79	-28.72			Jul-13
	6.02	12.38	26.13	33.46	103.68		1.01	14.78	0.97	17.66	718.2	2	99	0	0	130	32.79	-28.72			Apr-17
50	2.66	6.88	9.90	33.16	91.69	0.04	1.5	14.56	0.99	8.64	1,646	3	96	0	0	90	25.33	-23.62	5.75		Dec-99
50	2.51	6.51	9.20	30.29	84.63	0	2.25	14.53	0.99	8.29	1,646	3	96	0	0	90	24.71	-23.83		1.00	Mar-10
50	2.73	7.06	10.39	35.11	96.05	0.39	1.05	14.5	0.99	8.81	1,646	3	96	0	0	90	25.69	-23.45			Oct-98
50	2.69	7.00	10.26	34.17	94.11	0.21	1.25	14.56	0.99	8.73	1,646	3	96	0	0	90	25.6	-23.55			Jul-98
50	2.63	6.86	9.72	32.30	89.38	0	1.75	14.54	0.99	8.61	1,646	3	96	0	0	90	25.21	-23.73			Mar-10
	2.83	7.16	10.46	34.42	94.47		1.05	14.52	0.99	8.82	1,646	3	96	0	0	90	25.6	-23.55			Apr-17
	2.77	7.14	10.55	35.57	96.98	0.52	0.9	14.54	0.99	8.81	1,646	3	96	0	0	90	25.6	-23.55			Jul-13
	2.87	7.25	10.58	34.56	94.68		0.9	14.52	0.99	8.82	1,646	3	96	0	0	90	25.6	-23.55			Apr-17
50	2.58	7.60	10.30	21.75	89.18	0.02	1.12	14.34	1	15.04	700.8	1	99	0	0	90	27.9	-23.14	5.75		Sep-00
50	2.40	7.13	9.51	18.97	82.22	0	1.87	14.3	0.99	14.5	700.8	1	99	0	0	90	27.39	-23.33		1.00	Mar-10
50	2.71	7.83	10.76	23.38	93.43	0.39	0.67	14.32	0.99	15.46	700.8	1	99	0	0	90	28.14	-22.94			Oct-99
50	2.65	7.71	10.58	22.67	91.48	0.21	0.87	14.29	0.99	15.39	700.8	1	99	0	0	90	27.96	-22.97			Jul-98
50	2.56	7.46	10.12	20.83	86.99	0	1.37	14.32	1	14.75	700.8	1	99	0	0	90	27.58	-23.1			Aug-03
	2.70	7.76	10.71	22.82	91.71		0.67	14.29	0.99	15.47	700.8	1	99	0	0	90	27.96	-22.97			Apr-17
50	4.30	8.75	18.91	23.57	60.48	0.95	1.36	8.38	0.79	8.38	976.0	2	76	20	2	82	20.32	-15.97	5.75		Oct-96
50	3.94	8.23	17.98	20.68	54.55	0.32	2.11	8.34	0.78	8.2	976.0	2	76	20	2	82	19.94	-16.31		1.00	Nov-01
50	4.35	8.99	19.31	25.17	64.11	1.35	0.91	8.28	0.78	8.25	976.0	2	76	20	2	82	20.79	-15.84			Aug-00

	MARKET			FUND TYPE, CATEGORY & OBJECTIVE	RATINGS					MINIMUMS
Fund Name	Ticker Symbol	Traded On	Fund Type	Category and (Prospectus Objective)	Overall Rating	Reward Rating	Risk Rating	Recent Up/ Downgrade	Open to New Investors	Min Initial Investment
American Century Strategic Alloc: Aggressive Fund Inv Cls	TWSAX	NAS CM	Open End	Aggressive Alloc (Asset Alloc)	B-	B-	B-	Down	Y	2,500
American Century Strategic Alloc: Aggressive Fund R Cls	AAARX	NAS CM	Open End	Aggressive Alloc (Asset Alloc)	B-	C+	B-	Down	Y	2,500
American Century Strategic Alloc: Aggressive Fund R5 Cls	ASAUX	NAS CM	Open End	Aggressive Alloc (Asset Alloc)	B-	B-	B-	Down	Y	0
American Century Strategic Alloc: Aggressive Fund R6 Cls	AAAUX	NAS CM	Open End	Aggressive Alloc (Asset Alloc)	B-	B-	B	Down	Y	0
American Century Strategic Alloc: Conservative Fund A Cls	ACCAX	NAS CM	Open End	Cautious Alloc (Asset Alloc)	B	C+	A-	Up	Y	2,500
American Century Strategic Alloc: Conservative Fund C Cls	AACCX	NAS CM	Open End	Cautious Alloc (Asset Alloc)	B-	C	B+	Up	Y	2,500
American Century Strategic Alloc: Conservative Fund I Cls	ACCIX	NAS CM	Open End	Cautious Alloc (Asset Alloc)	B-	C+	B	Up	Y	5,000,000
American Century Strat Alloc: Conservative Fund Inv Cls	TWSCX	NAS CM	Open End	Cautious Alloc (Asset Alloc)	B	C+	A-	Up	Y	2,500
American Century Strategic Alloc: Conservative Fund R Cls	AACRX	NAS CM	Open End	Cautious Alloc (Asset Alloc)	B	C+	A-	Up	Y	2,500
American Century Strategic Alloc: Conservative Fund R5 Cls	AACGX	NAS CM	Open End	Cautious Alloc (Asset Alloc)	B-	C+	B	Up	Y	0
American Century Strategic Alloc: Conservative Fund R6 Cls	AACDX	NAS CM	Open End	Cautious Alloc (Asset Alloc)	B-	C+	B	Up	Y	0
American Century Strategic Allocation: Moderate Fund A Cls	ACOAX	NAS CM	Open End	Moderate Alloc (Asset Alloc)	B	C+	B+	Up	Y	2,500
American Century Strategic Allocation: Moderate Fund C Cls	ASTCX	NAS CM	Open End	Moderate Alloc (Asset Alloc)	B-	C+	B	Down	Y	2,500
American Century Strategic Allocation: Moderate Fund I Cls	ASAMX	NAS CM	Open End	Moderate Alloc (Asset Alloc)	B-	C+	B	Down	Y	5,000,000
American Century Strategic Alloc: Moderate Fund Inv Cls	TWSMX	NAS CM	Open End	Moderate Alloc (Asset Alloc)	B-	C+	B	Down	Y	2,500
American Century Strategic Allocation: Moderate Fund R Cls	ASMRX	NAS CM	Open End	Moderate Alloc (Asset Alloc)	B-	C+	B	Down	Y	2,500
American Century Strategic Alloc: Moderate Fund R5 Cls	ASMUX	NAS CM	Open End	Moderate Alloc (Asset Alloc)	B-	C+	B	Down	Y	0
American Century Strategic Alloc: Moderate Fund R6 Cls	ASMDX	NAS CM	Open End	Moderate Alloc (Asset Alloc)	B-	C+	B	Down	Y	0
American Century Sustainable Equity Fund A Class	AFDAX	NAS CM	Open End	US Equity Large Cap Blend (Growth)	B	B	B-	Up	Y	2,500
American Century Sustainable Equity Fund C Class	AFDCX	NAS CM	Open End	US Equity Large Cap Blend (Growth)	B-	B-	B-	Down	Y	2,500
American Century Sustainable Equity Fund I Class	AFEIX	NAS CM	Open End	US Equity Large Cap Blend (Growth)	B	B	B-		Y	5,000,000
American Century Sustainable Equity Fund Investor Class	AFDIX	NAS CM	Open End	US Equity Large Cap Blend (Growth)	B	B	B-		Y	2,500
American Century Sustainable Equity Fund R Class	AFDRX	NAS CM	Open End	US Equity Large Cap Blend (Growth)	B	B	B-	Up	Y	2,500
American Century Sustainable Equity Fund R5 Class	AFDGX	NAS CM	Open End	US Equity Large Cap Blend (Growth)	B	B	B-	Up	Y	0
American Century Sustainable Equity Fund Y Class	AFYDX	NAS CM	Open End	US Equity Large Cap Blend (Growth)	B	B	B-	Up	Y	0
American Century Ultra® Fund A Class	TWUAX	NAS CM	Open End	US Equity Large Cap Growth (Growth)	B+	B+	B	Up	Y	2,500
American Century Ultra® Fund C Class	TWCCX	NAS CM	Open End	US Equity Large Cap Growth (Growth)	B+	B+	B	Up	Y	2,500
American Century Ultra® Fund I Class	TWUIX	NAS CM	Open End	US Equity Large Cap Growth (Growth)	B+	A-	B	Up	Y	5,000,000
American Century Ultra® Fund Investor Class	TWCUX	NAS CM	Open End	US Equity Large Cap Growth (Growth)	B+	A-	B	Up	Y	2,500
American Century Ultra® Fund R Class	AULRX	NAS CM	Open End	US Equity Large Cap Growth (Growth)	B+	B+	B	Up	Y	2,500
American Century Ultra® Fund R5 Class	AULGX	NAS CM	Open End	US Equity Large Cap Growth (Growth)	B+	A-	B	Up	Y	0
American Century Ultra® Fund R6 Class	AULDX	NAS CM	Open End	US Equity Large Cap Growth (Growth)	B+	A-	B	Up	Y	0
American Century Ultra® Fund Y Class	AULYX	NAS CM	Open End	US Equity Large Cap Growth (Growth)	B+	A-	B	Up	Y	0
American Century Utilities Fund Investor Class	BULIX	NAS CM	Open End	Utilities Sector Equity (Utility)	B-	C+	B		Y	2,500
American Century Value Fund A Class	TWADX	NAS CM	Open End	US Equity Large Cap Value (Growth)	B-	C+	B	Down	Y	2,500
American Century Value Fund C Class	ACLCX	NAS CM	Open End	US Equity Large Cap Value (Growth)	B-	C+	B		Y	2,500
American Century Value Fund I Class	AVLIX	NAS CM	Open End	US Equity Large Cap Value (Growth)	B-	C+	B	Down	Y	5,000,000
American Century Value Fund Investor Class	TWVLX	NAS CM	Open End	US Equity Large Cap Value (Growth)	B-	C+	B	Down	Y	2,500
American Century Value Fund R Class	AVURX	NAS CM	Open End	US Equity Large Cap Value (Growth)	B-	C+	B	Down	Y	2,500
American Century Value Fund R5 Class	AVUGX	NAS CM	Open End	US Equity Large Cap Value (Growth)	B-	C+	B	Down	Y	0
American Century Value Fund R6 Class	AVUDX	NAS CM	Open End	US Equity Large Cap Value (Growth)	B-	C+	B	Down	Y	0
American Century Value Fund Y Class	AVUYX	NAS CM	Open End	US Equity Large Cap Value (Growth)	B-	C+	B	Down	Y	0
American Funds 2010 Target Date Retirement Fund® Class A	AAATX	NAS CM	Open End	Target Date 2000-2020 (Asset Alloc)	B-	C+	B	Up	Y	250
American Funds 2010 Target Date Retirement Fund® Class C	CCATX	NAS CM	Open End	Target Date 2000-2020 (Asset Alloc)	B-	C+	B	Up	Y	250
American Funds 2010 Target Date Retirement Fund® Class F-1	FAATX	NAS CM	Open End	Target Date 2000-2020 (Asset Alloc)	B-	C+	B	Up	Y	250
American Funds 2010 Target Date Retirement Fund® Class F-2	FBATX	NAS CM	Open End	Target Date 2000-2020 (Asset Alloc)	B-	C+	B	Up	Y	250
American Funds 2010 Target Date Retirement Fund® Class F-3	DJTFX	NAS CM	Open End	Target Date 2000-2020 (Asset Alloc)	B-	C+	B	Up	Y	250
American Funds 2010 Target Date Retirement Fund® Class R-1	RAATX	NAS CM	Open End	Target Date 2000-2020 (Asset Alloc)	B-	C+	B	Up	Y	250
American Funds 2010 Target Date Retirement Fund® Class R-2	RBATX	NAS CM	Open End	Target Date 2000-2020 (Asset Alloc)	B-	C+	B+	Up	Y	250
American Funds 2010 Target Date Retirement Fund® Cls R-2E	RBEAX	NAS CM	Open End	Target Date 2000-2020 (Asset Alloc)	B-	C+	B	Up	Y	250
American Funds 2010 Target Date Retirement Fund® Class R-3	RCATX	NAS CM	Open End	Target Date 2000-2020 (Asset Alloc)	B-	C+	B	Up	Y	250
American Funds 2010 Target Date Retirement Fund® Class R-4	RDATX	NAS CM	Open End	Target Date 2000-2020 (Asset Alloc)	B-	C+	B	Up	Y	250

★ Expanded analysis of this fund is included in Section II.

	TOTAL RETURNS					PERFORMANCE				ASSETS		ASSET ALLOCATION & TURNOVER					BULL & BEAR		FEES		
Min Additional Investment	3-Month Total Return	6-Month Total Return	1-Year Total Return	3-Year Total Return	5-Year Total Return	Dividend Yield (TTM)	Expense Ratio	3-Yr Std Deviation	3-Year Beta	NAV	Total Assets (MIL)	%Cash	%Stocks	%Bonds	%Other	Turnover Ratio	Last Bull Market Total Return	Last Bear Market Total Return	Front End Fee (%)	Back End Fee (%)	Inception Date
50	4.36	8.84	19.23	24.40	62.64	1.17	1.11	8.3	0.78	8.31	976.0	2	76	20	2	82	20.54	-15.91			Feb-96
50	4.16	8.62	18.49	22.53	58.37	0.74	1.61	8.24	0.78	8.37	976.0	2	76	20	2	82	20.14	-15.97			Mar-05
	4.29	9.05	19.33	24.51	62.78		0.91	8.31	0.78	8.26	976.0	2	76	20	2	82	20.54	-15.91			Apr-17
	4.40	9.05	19.54	25.81	65.06	1.48	0.76	8.34	0.78	8.23	976.0	2	76	20	2	82	20.55	-15.91			Jul-13
50	2.35	4.92	10.36	13.41	32.90	1.01	1.25	4.86	0.44	5.77	521.5	4	43	50	2	87	12.11	-7.16	5.75		Oct-96
50	2.35	4.57	9.74	11.03	28.17	0.37	2	4.8	0.43	5.7	521.5	4	43	50	2	87	11.55	-7.33		1.00	Sep-04
50	2.65	5.16	11.04	15.08	36.05	1.43	0.8	4.86	0.44	5.78	521.5	4	43	50	2	87	12.33	-6.78			Aug-00
50	2.60	5.06	10.82	14.42	34.72	1.24	1	4.9	0.44	5.78	521.5	4	43	50	2	87	12.24	-7.04			Feb-96
50	2.29	4.61	10.10	12.51	31.20	0.77	1.5	4.81	0.44	5.76	521.5	4	43	50	2	87	11.98	-7.11			Mar-05
	2.65	5.15	10.96	14.56	34.89		0.8	4.89	0.44	5.79	521.5	4	43	50	2	87	12.24	-7.04			Apr-17
	2.69	5.24	11.20	15.58	36.84	1.57	0.65	4.81	0.44	5.78	521.5	4	43	50	2	87	12.24	-7.04			Jul-13
50	3.35	7.00	14.88	18.59	47.73	0.97	1.32	6.72	0.63	6.85	1,292	3	61	34	2	82	16.58	-12.04	5.75		Oct-96
50	3.33	6.65	14.18	16.16	42.49	0.41	2.07	6.79	0.64	6.79	1,292	3	61	34	2	82	16.12	-12.33		1.00	Oct-01
50	3.60	7.22	15.34	20.25	51.08	1.38	0.87	6.77	0.64	6.87	1,292	3	61	34	2	82	16.98	-11.97			Aug-00
50	3.56	7.12	15.13	19.54	49.59	1.2	1.07	6.73	0.63	6.87	1,292	3	61	34	2	82	16.87	-12.05			Feb-96
50	3.45	6.90	14.55	17.80	45.95	0.77	1.57	6.78	0.64	6.82	1,292	3	61	34	2	82	16.53	-12.29			Aug-03
	3.61	7.38	15.29	19.71	49.79		0.87	6.74	0.63	6.88	1,292	3	61	34	2	82	16.87	-12.05			Apr-17
	3.51	7.32	15.54	20.81	51.80	1.52	0.72	6.8	0.64	6.86	1,292	3	61	34	2	82	16.87	-12.05			Jul-13
50	8.60	13.95	25.51	32.45	103.21	0.75	1.25	10.26	0.99	27.7	231.4	1	99	0	0	71	25.8	-16.21	5.75		Nov-04
50	8.36	13.52	24.58	29.44	95.57	0.13	2	10.26	0.99	27.27	231.4	1	99	0	0	71	25.18	-16.43		1.00	Nov-04
50	8.73	14.19	26.05	34.24	107.68	1.11	0.8	10.25	0.99	27.78	231.4	1	99	0	0	71	26	-15.98			Jul-05
50	8.65	14.08	25.79	33.44	105.62	0.95	1	10.26	0.99	27.74	231.4	1	99	0	0	71	25.88	-16.06			Jul-05
50	8.52	13.81	25.20	31.42	100.53	0.55	1.5	10.26	0.99	27.6	231.4	1	99	0	0	71	25.47	-16.24			Jul-05
	8.75	14.21	25.89	32.84	103.81		0.8	10.27	0.99	27.8	231.4	1	99	0	0	71	25.8	-16.21			Apr-17
	8.78	14.33	26.02	32.99	104.03		0.65	10.28	0.99	27.8	231.4	1	99	0	0	71	25.8	-16.21			Apr-17
50	6.55	13.30	31.57	43.71	121.51	0.02	1.23	11.26	1.03	41.63	10,546	1	98	0	1	18	26.12	-15.65	5.75		Oct-96
50	6.32	12.88	30.58	40.49	113.26	0	1.98	11.24	1.02	35.55	10,546	1	98	0	1	18	25.52	-15.88		1.00	Oct-01
50	6.66	13.54	32.14	45.66	126.47	0.36	0.78	11.27	1.03	44.84	10,546	1	98	0	1	18	26.42	-15.46			Nov-96
50	6.59	13.45	31.89	44.77	124.23	0.22	0.98	11.26	1.03	43.42	10,546	1	98	0	1	18	26.29	-15.55			Nov-81
50	6.47	13.15	31.26	42.62	118.76	0	1.48	11.27	1.03	40.62	10,546	1	98	0	1	18	25.94	-15.73			Aug-03
	6.64	13.55	32.08	44.98	124.55		0.78	11.26	1.03	44.87	10,546	1	98	0	1	18	26.29	-15.55			Apr-17
	6.70	13.66	32.39	46.33	127.78	0.47	0.63	11.28	1.03	44.82	10,546	1	98	0	1	18	26.29	-15.55			Jul-13
	6.71	13.64	32.22	45.13	124.79		0.63	11.26	1.03	44.87	10,546	1	98	0	1	18	26.29	-15.55			Apr-17
50	-1.18	0.36	0.62	14.40	67.39	2.94	0.67	10.32	0.32	17.19	519.0	1	99	0	0	39	8.75	-4.69			Mar-93
50	4.17	7.08	8.20	22.69	84.99	1.2	1.23	10.59	1	8.92	3,321	3	96	0	0	46	22.51	-16.85	5.75		Oct-96
50	3.91	6.64	7.39	19.84	77.97	0.5	1.98	10.52	0.99	8.78	3,321	3	96	0	0	46	21.81	-17.01		1.00	Jun-01
	4.29	7.19	8.66	24.27	89.15	1.63	0.78	10.58	1	8.94	3,321	3	96	0	0	46	22.73	-16.63			Jul-97
50	4.24	7.09	8.46	23.45	86.97	1.44	0.98	10.48	0.99	8.92	3,321	3	96	0	0	46	22.41	-16.58			Sep-93
50	4.10	6.81	7.93	21.62	82.68	0.97	1.48	10.53	1	8.92	3,321	3	96	0	0	46	22.16	-16.79			Jul-05
	4.29	7.31	8.61	23.61	87.22		0.78	10.51	0.99	8.94	3,321	3	96	0	0	46	22.41	-16.58			Apr-17
	4.33	7.40	8.83	24.83	89.79	1.77	0.63	10.54	1	8.94	3,321	3	96	0	0	46	22.41	-16.58			Jul-13
	4.33	7.39	8.84	23.88	87.62		0.63	10.52	0.99	8.95	3,321	3	96	0	0	46	22.41	-16.58			Apr-17
50	2.13	4.72	9.97	16.02	39.67	1.58	0.72	4.82	1.05	10.91	2,764	4	42	51	3	14	11.3	-6.87	5.75		Feb-07
50	1.99	4.32	9.19	13.44	34.74	1.07	1.46	4.74	1.03	10.79	2,764	4	42	51	3	14	10.93	-7.13		1.00	Feb-14
50	2.07	4.66	9.93	15.96	39.79	1.73	0.71	4.83	1.05	10.86	2,764	4	42	51	3	14	11.41	-6.84			Feb-14
50	2.20	4.79	10.26	16.90	41.61	1.85	0.45	4.83	1.05	10.89	2,764	4	42	51	3	14	11.57	-6.74			Feb-14
50	2.18	4.85	10.32	17.07	41.81		0.35	4.8	1.04	10.9	2,764	4	42	51	3	14	11.57	-6.74			Jan-17
50	1.94	4.34	9.19	13.35	34.40	0.8	1.5	4.78	1.04	10.9	2,764	4	42	51	3	14	10.79	-7.21			Feb-07
50	2.00	4.33	9.20	13.61	34.81	0.94	1.45	4.79	1.04	10.8	2,764	4	42	51	3	14	11.02	-7.25			Feb-07
50	2.01	4.42	9.51	14.78	37.61	1.49	1.14	4.81	1.05	10.77	2,764	4	42	51	3	14	11.18	-6.97			Aug-14
50	2.00	4.50	9.67	14.87	37.41	1.36	1.03	4.82	1.05	10.85	2,764	4	42	51	3	14	11.11	-7			Feb-07
50	2.13	4.71	9.97	16.01	39.59	1.61	0.71	4.79	1.04	10.89	2,764	4	42	51	3	14	11.31	-6.87			Feb-07

	MARKET			FUND TYPE, CATEGORY & OBJECTIVE	RATINGS				MINIMUMS	
Fund Name	Ticker Symbol	Traded On	Fund Type	Category and (Prospectus Objective)	Overall Rating	Reward Rating	Risk Rating	Recent Up/ Downgrade	Open to New Investors	Min Initial Investment
American Funds 2010 Target Date Retirement Fund® Class R-5	REATX	NAS CM	Open End	Target Date 2000-2020 (Asset Alloc)	B-	C+	B	Up	Y	250
American Funds 2010 Target Date Retirement Fund® Cls R-5E	RHATX	NAS CM	Open End	Target Date 2000-2020 (Asset Alloc)	B-	C+	B	Up	Y	250
American Funds 2010 Target Date Retirement Fund® Class R-6	RFTTX	NAS CM	Open End	Target Date 2000-2020 (Asset Alloc)	B-	C+	B	Up	Y	250
American Funds 2015 Target Date Retirement Fund® Class A	AABTX	NAS CM	Open End	Target Date 2000-2020 (Asset Alloc)	B-	C+	B	Up	Y	250
American Funds 2015 Target Date Retirement Fund® Class C	CCBTX	NAS CM	Open End	Target Date 2000-2020 (Asset Alloc)	B-	C+	B	Up	Y	250
American Funds 2015 Target Date Retirement Fund® Class F-1	FAKTX	NAS CM	Open End	Target Date 2000-2020 (Asset Alloc)	B-	C+	B	Up	Y	250
American Funds 2015 Target Date Retirement Fund® Class F-2	FBBTX	NAS CM	Open End	Target Date 2000-2020 (Asset Alloc)	B-	C+	B	Up	Y	250
American Funds 2015 Target Date Retirement Fund® Class F-3	FDBTX	NAS CM	Open End	Target Date 2000-2020 (Asset Alloc)	B-	C+	B	Up	Y	250
American Funds 2015 Target Date Retirement Fund® Class R-1	RAJTX	NAS CM	Open End	Target Date 2000-2020 (Asset Alloc)	B	C+	B+	Up	Y	250
American Funds 2015 Target Date Retirement Fund® Class R-2	RBJTX	NAS CM	Open End	Target Date 2000-2020 (Asset Alloc)	B	C+	B+	Up	Y	250
American Funds 2015 Target Date Retirement Fund® Cls R-2E	RBEJX	NAS CM	Open End	Target Date 2000-2020 (Asset Alloc)	B	C+	A-	Up	Y	250
American Funds 2015 Target Date Retirement Fund® Class R-3	RCJTX	NAS CM	Open End	Target Date 2000-2020 (Asset Alloc)	B-	C+	B	Up	Y	250
American Funds 2015 Target Date Retirement Fund® Class R-4	RDBTX	NAS CM	Open End	Target Date 2000-2020 (Asset Alloc)	B-	C+	B	Up	Y	250
American Funds 2015 Target Date Retirement Fund® Class R-5	REJTX	NAS CM	Open End	Target Date 2000-2020 (Asset Alloc)	B-	C+	B	Up	Y	250
American Funds 2015 Target Date Retirement Fund® Cls R-5E	RHBTX	NAS CM	Open End	Target Date 2000-2020 (Asset Alloc)	B-	C+	B	Up	Y	250
American Funds 2015 Target Date Retirement Fund® Class R-6	RFJTX	NAS CM	Open End	Target Date 2000-2020 (Asset Alloc)	B-	C+	B	Up	Y	250
American Funds 2020 Target Date Retirement Fund® Class A	AACTX	NAS CM	Open End	Target Date 2000-2020 (Asset Alloc)	B-	C+	B	Up	Y	250
American Funds 2020 Target Date Retirement Fund® Class C	CCCTX	NAS CM	Open End	Target Date 2000-2020 (Asset Alloc)	B-	C+	B	Up	Y	250
American Funds 2020 Target Date Retirement Fund® Class F-1	FAOTX	NAS CM	Open End	Target Date 2000-2020 (Asset Alloc)	B-	C+	B	Up	Y	250
American Funds 2020 Target Date Retirement Fund® Class F-2	FBCTX	NAS CM	Open End	Target Date 2000-2020 (Asset Alloc)	B-	C+	B	Up	Y	250
American Funds 2020 Target Date Retirement Fund® Class F-3	FCCTX	NAS CM	Open End	Target Date 2000-2020 (Asset Alloc)	B-	C+	B	Up	Y	250
American Funds 2020 Target Date Retirement Fund® Class R-1	RACTX	NAS CM	Open End	Target Date 2000-2020 (Asset Alloc)	B-	C+	B	Up	Y	250
American Funds 2020 Target Date Retirement Fund® Class R-2	RBCTX	NAS CM	Open End	Target Date 2000-2020 (Asset Alloc)	B-	C+	B	Up	Y	250
American Funds 2020 Target Date Retirement Fund® Cls R-2E	RBEHX	NAS CM	Open End	Target Date 2000-2020 (Asset Alloc)	B-	C+	B	Up	Y	250
American Funds 2020 Target Date Retirement Fund® Class R-3	RCCTX	NAS CM	Open End	Target Date 2000-2020 (Asset Alloc)	B-	C+	B	Up	Y	250
American Funds 2020 Target Date Retirement Fund® Class R-4	RDCTX	NAS CM	Open End	Target Date 2000-2020 (Asset Alloc)	B-	C+	B	Up	Y	250
American Funds 2020 Target Date Retirement Fund® Class R-5	RECTX	NAS CM	Open End	Target Date 2000-2020 (Asset Alloc)	B-	C+	B	Up	Y	250
American Funds 2020 Target Date Retirement Fund® Cls R-5E	RHCTX	NAS CM	Open End	Target Date 2000-2020 (Asset Alloc)	B-	C+	B	Up	Y	250
American Funds 2020 Target Date Retirement Fund® Class R-6	RRCTX	NAS CM	Open End	Target Date 2000-2020 (Asset Alloc)	B-	C+	B	Up	Y	250
American Funds 2025 Target Date Retirement Fund® Class A	AADTX	NAS CM	Open End	Target Date 2021-2045 (Asset Alloc)	B-	C+	B	Up	Y	250
American Funds 2025 Target Date Retirement Fund® Class C	CCDTX	NAS CM	Open End	Target Date 2021-2045 (Asset Alloc)	B-	C+	B	Up	Y	250
American Funds 2025 Target Date Retirement Fund® Class F-1	FAPTX	NAS CM	Open End	Target Date 2021-2045 (Asset Alloc)	B-	C+	B	Up	Y	250
American Funds 2025 Target Date Retirement Fund® Class F-2	FBDTX	NAS CM	Open End	Target Date 2021-2045 (Asset Alloc)	B-	C+	B	Up	Y	250
American Funds 2025 Target Date Retirement Fund® Class F-3	FDDTX	NAS CM	Open End	Target Date 2021-2045 (Asset Alloc)	B-	C+	B	Up	Y	250
American Funds 2025 Target Date Retirement Fund® Class R-1	RADTX	NAS CM	Open End	Target Date 2021-2045 (Asset Alloc)	B-	C+	B	Up	Y	250
American Funds 2025 Target Date Retirement Fund® Class R-2	RBDTX	NAS CM	Open End	Target Date 2021-2045 (Asset Alloc)	B-	C+	B	Up	Y	250
American Funds 2025 Target Date Retirement Fund® Cls R-2E	RBEDX	NAS CM	Open End	Target Date 2021-2045 (Asset Alloc)	B-	C+	B	Up	Y	250
American Funds 2025 Target Date Retirement Fund® Class R-3	RCDTX	NAS CM	Open End	Target Date 2021-2045 (Asset Alloc)	B-	C+	B	Up	Y	250
American Funds 2025 Target Date Retirement Fund® Class R-4	RDDTX	NAS CM	Open End	Target Date 2021-2045 (Asset Alloc)	B-	C+	B	Up	Y	250
American Funds 2025 Target Date Retirement Fund® Class R-5	REDTX	NAS CM	Open End	Target Date 2021-2045 (Asset Alloc)	B-	C+	B	Up	Y	250
American Funds 2025 Target Date Retirement Fund® Cls R-5E	RHDTX	NAS CM	Open End	Target Date 2021-2045 (Asset Alloc)	B-	C+	B	Up	Y	250
American Funds 2025 Target Date Retirement Fund® Class R-6	RFDTX	NAS CM	Open End	Target Date 2021-2045 (Asset Alloc)	B-	C+	B	Up	Y	250
American Funds 2030 Target Date Retirement Fund® Class A	AAETX	NAS CM	Open End	Target Date 2021-2045 (Asset Alloc)	B-	B-	B	Down	Y	250
American Funds 2030 Target Date Retirement Fund® Class C	CCETX	NAS CM	Open End	Target Date 2021-2045 (Asset Alloc)	B-	C+	B	Down	Y	250
American Funds 2030 Target Date Retirement Fund® Class F-1	FAETX	NAS CM	Open End	Target Date 2021-2045 (Asset Alloc)	B-	B-	B	Down	Y	250
American Funds 2030 Target Date Retirement Fund® Class F-2	FBETX	NAS CM	Open End	Target Date 2021-2045 (Asset Alloc)	B-	B-	B	Down	Y	250
American Funds 2030 Target Date Retirement Fund® Class F-3	FCETX	NAS CM	Open End	Target Date 2021-2045 (Asset Alloc)	B-	B-	B	Down	Y	250
American Funds 2030 Target Date Retirement Fund® Class R-1	RAETX	NAS CM	Open End	Target Date 2021-2045 (Asset Alloc)	B-	C+	B	Down	Y	250
American Funds 2030 Target Date Retirement Fund® Class R-2	RBETX	NAS CM	Open End	Target Date 2021-2045 (Asset Alloc)	B-	C+	B	Down	Y	250
American Funds 2030 Target Date Retirement Fund® Cls R-2E	RBEEX	NAS CM	Open End	Target Date 2021-2045 (Asset Alloc)	B-	C+	B	Down	Y	250
American Funds 2030 Target Date Retirement Fund® Class R-3	RCETX	NAS CM	Open End	Target Date 2021-2045 (Asset Alloc)	B-	C+	B	Down	Y	250
American Funds 2030 Target Date Retirement Fund® Class R-4	RDETX	NAS CM	Open End	Target Date 2021-2045 (Asset Alloc)	B-	B-	B	Down	Y	250

★Expanded analysis of this fund is included in Section II.

	TOTAL RETURNS					PERFORMANCE				ASSETS		ASSET ALLOCATION & TURNOVER					BULL & BEAR		FEES		
Min Additional Investment	3-Month Total Return	6-Month Total Return	1-Year Total Return	3-Year Total Return	5-Year Total Return	Dividend Yield (TTM)	Expense Ratio	3-Yr Std Deviation	3-Year Beta	NAV	Total Assets (MIL)	%Cash	%Stocks	%Bonds	%Other	Turnover Ratio	Last Bull Market Total Return	Last Bear Market Total Return	Front End Fee (%)	Back End Fee (%)	Inception Date
50	2.20	4.86	10.31	17.06	41.80	1.86	0.41	4.82	1.05	10.96	2,764	4	42	51	3	14	11.57	-6.74			Feb-07
50	2.16	4.75	10.13	16.80	41.49	1.82	0.5	4.8	1.04	10.86	2,764	4	42	51	3	14	11.57	-6.74			Nov-15
50	2.17	4.84	10.40	17.18	42.13	1.9	0.35	4.84	1.05	10.93	2,764	4	42	51	3	14	11.54	-6.75			Jul-09
50	2.35	5.06	10.83	17.12	45.07	1.5	0.73	4.95	0.89	11.59	4,471	4	45	48	3	8	12.8	-8.97	5.75		Feb-07
50	2.19	4.76	9.98	14.53	39.92	0.96	1.46	4.96	0.89	11.46	4,471	4	45	48	3	8	12.31	-9.31		1.00	Feb-14
50	2.35	5.08	10.78	17.11	45.24	1.64	0.71	4.99	0.9	11.53	4,471	4	45	48	3	8	12.8	-9.02			Feb-14
50	2.43	5.23	11.12	18.09	47.15	1.75	0.44	4.99	0.9	11.58	4,471	4	45	48	3	8	12.97	-8.93			Feb-14
50	2.49	5.38	11.26	18.35	47.57		0.34	5	0.9	11.6	4,471	4	45	48	3	8	12.97	-8.93			Jan-17
50	2.16	4.64	9.98	14.46	39.53	0.81	1.49	4.94	0.89	11.43	4,471	4	45	48	3	8	12.31	-9.3			Feb-07
50	2.15	4.71	10.05	14.66	40.07	0.81	1.45	4.99	0.9	11.44	4,471	4	45	48	3	8	12.37	-9.3			Feb-07
50	2.26	4.91	10.34	15.95	43.09	1.46	1.14	4.94	0.88	11.44	4,471	4	45	48	3	8	12.57	-9.16			Aug-14
50	2.32	4.96	10.57	16.17	42.92	1.24	1.03	4.96	0.89	11.52	4,471	4	45	48	3	8	12.79	-9.23			Feb-07
50	2.28	5.09	10.77	17.11	45.13	1.52	0.71	4.94	0.89	11.57	4,471	4	45	48	3	8	12.95	-9.08			Feb-07
50	2.44	5.31	11.16	18.25	47.44	1.76	0.4	4.99	0.9	11.66	4,471	4	45	48	3	8	12.96	-8.93			Feb-07
50	2.42	5.24	11.04	17.95	47.07	1.74	0.49	4.96	0.89	11.54	4,471	4	45	48	3	8	12.97	-8.93			Nov-15
50	2.43	5.31	11.18	18.41	47.73	1.81	0.35	4.97	0.89	11.61	4,471	4	45	48	3	8	13.17	-8.95			Jul-09
50	2.68	5.80	12.45	19.21	51.93	1.18	0.74	5.57	0.87	12.56	11,839	4	49	44	3	5	14.79	-11.27	5.75		Feb-07
50	2.53	5.44	11.59	16.63	46.44	0.7	1.47	5.54	0.87	12.4	11,839	4	49	44	3	5	14.38	-11.49		1.00	Feb-14
50	2.72	5.77	12.36	19.17	51.93	1.29	0.73	5.56	0.87	12.49	11,839	4	49	44	3	5	14.88	-11.21			Feb-14
50	2.77	5.90	12.75	20.11	53.94	1.43	0.46	5.6	0.88	12.54	11,839	4	49	44	3	5	15.05	-11.12			Feb-14
50	2.76	5.96	12.89	20.44	54.31		0.36	5.57	0.87	12.56	11,839	4	49	44	3	5	15.05	-11.12			Jan-17
50	2.49	5.40	11.54	16.46	46.06	0.48	1.51	5.56	0.87	12.43	11,839	4	49	44	3	5	14.31	-11.51			Feb-07
50	2.55	5.38	11.63	16.69	46.74	0.54	1.47	5.56	0.87	12.38	11,839	4	49	44	3	5	14.36	-11.61			Feb-07
50	2.56	5.55	11.88	17.92	49.52	1.12	1.15	5.58	0.87	12.4	11,839	4	49	44	3	5	14.65	-11.34			Aug-14
50	2.64	5.62	12.12	18.14	49.61	0.94	1.04	5.57	0.87	12.47	11,839	4	49	44	3	5	14.66	-11.43			Feb-07
50	2.70	5.83	12.50	19.23	51.89	1.21	0.73	5.57	0.87	12.54	11,839	4	49	44	3	5	14.8	-11.27			Feb-07
50	2.84	5.95	12.85	20.39	54.25	1.43	0.42	5.56	0.87	12.64	11,839	4	49	44	3	5	15.05	-11.12			Feb-07
50	2.75	5.88	12.65	20.12	53.91	1.4	0.51	5.57	0.87	12.51	11,839	4	49	44	3	5	15.05	-11.12			Nov-15
50	2.83	5.94	12.86	20.53	54.65	1.47	0.37	5.59	0.88	12.6	11,839	4	49	44	3	5	15.02	-11.14			Jul-09
50	3.30	6.91	14.95	22.03	62.66	1.04	0.76	6.47	0.91	13.44	13,886	4	59	34	3	5	17.84	-14.43	5.75		Feb-07
50	3.14	6.56	14.05	19.36	56.64	0.58	1.49	6.47	0.91	13.25	13,886	4	59	34	3	5	17.43	-14.81		1.00	Feb-14
50	3.32	6.96	14.96	22.05	62.59	1.19	0.74	6.44	0.9	13.36	13,886	4	59	34	3	5	17.94	-14.54			Feb-14
50	3.38	7.08	15.14	22.96	64.64	1.27	0.48	6.48	0.91	13.42	13,886	4	59	34	3	5	18.11	-14.45			Feb-14
50	3.45	7.14	15.27	23.11	65.03		0.38	6.48	0.91	13.44	13,886	4	59	34	3	5	18.11	-14.45			Jan-17
50	3.14	6.48	13.95	19.20	56.35	0.39	1.53	6.45	0.9	13.26	13,886	4	59	34	3	5	17.36	-14.79			Feb-07
50	3.11	6.55	14.06	19.36	56.86	0.45	1.48	6.46	0.9	13.2	13,886	4	59	34	3	5	17.34	-14.72			Feb-07
50	3.18	6.67	14.41	20.70	60.01	0.99	1.18	6.45	0.9	13.26	13,886	4	59	34	3	5	17.7	-14.67			Aug-14
50	3.26	6.75	14.57	20.90	59.93	0.82	1.06	6.47	0.91	13.32	13,886	4	59	34	3	5	17.61	-14.6			Feb-07
50	3.31	6.93	14.90	22.04	62.61	1.07	0.75	6.46	0.9	13.41	13,886	4	59	34	3	5	17.87	-14.53			Feb-07
50	3.36	7.03	15.21	23.04	64.94	1.28	0.44	6.48	0.91	13.52	13,886	4	59	34	3	5	18.11	-14.45			Feb-07
50	3.36	6.99	15.15	22.80	64.62	1.25	0.53	6.47	0.91	13.39	13,886	4	59	34	3	5	18.11	-14.45			Nov-15
50	3.43	7.20	15.32	23.28	65.51	1.32	0.39	6.43	0.9	13.49	13,886	4	59	34	3	5	18.2	-14.4			Jul-09
50	4.04	8.39	18.10	26.15	71.56	0.93	0.76	7.77	1	14.42	14,786	3	70	23	3	3	19.04	-15.82	5.75		Feb-07
50	3.88	7.91	17.17	23.30	65.10	0.47	1.51	7.75	0.99	14.21	14,786	3	70	23	3	3	18.59	-16.01		1.00	Feb-14
50	4.03	8.32	17.99	26.02	71.36	1.08	0.76	7.72	0.99	14.32	14,786	3	70	23	3	3	19.1	-15.75			Feb-14
50	4.13	8.49	18.30	27.00	73.59	1.16	0.5	7.73	0.99	14.4	14,786	3	70	23	3	3	19.28	-15.66			Feb-14
50	4.12	8.47	18.43	27.32	74.11		0.4	7.74	0.99	14.41	14,786	3	70	23	3	3	19.28	-15.66			Jan-17
50	3.80	7.90	17.15	23.14	64.76	0.26	1.55	7.72	0.99	14.26	14,786	3	70	23	3	3	18.42	-16			Feb-07
50	3.84	7.97	17.18	23.40	65.36	0.36	1.5	7.72	0.99	14.16	14,786	3	70	23	3	3	18.53	-15.94			Feb-07
50	3.94	8.11	17.53	24.57	68.59	0.85	1.19	7.72	0.99	14.24	14,786	3	70	23	3	3	18.86	-15.87			Aug-14
50	3.93	8.17	17.67	24.93	68.64	0.7	1.08	7.72	0.99	14.29	14,786	3	70	23	3	3	18.79	-15.92			Feb-07
50	4.05	8.34	17.97	26.07	71.22	0.95	0.77	7.77	1	14.38	14,786	3	70	23	3	3	19.06	-15.74			Feb-07

	MARKET			FUND TYPE, CATEGORY & OBJECTIVE	RATINGS					MINIMUMS
Fund Name	Ticker Symbol	Traded On	Fund Type	Category and (Prospectus Objective)	Overall Rating	Reward Rating	Risk Rating	Recent Up/ Downgrade	Open to New Investors	Min Initial Investment
American Funds 2030 Target Date Retirement Fund® Class R-5	REETX	NAS CM	Open End	Target Date 2021-2045 (Asset Alloc)	B-	B-	B	Down	Y	250
American Funds 2030 Target Date Retirement Fund® Cls R-5E	RHETX	NAS CM	Open End	Target Date 2021-2045 (Asset Alloc)	B-	B-	B	Down	Y	250
American Funds 2030 Target Date Retirement Fund® Class R-6	RFETX	NAS CM	Open End	Target Date 2021-2045 (Asset Alloc)	B-	B-	B	Down	Y	250
American Funds 2035 Target Date Retirement Fund® Class A	AAFTX	NAS CM	Open End	Target Date 2021-2045 (Asset Alloc)	B-	B-	B	Down	Y	250
American Funds 2035 Target Date Retirement Fund® Class C	CCFTX	NAS CM	Open End	Target Date 2021-2045 (Asset Alloc)	B-	B-	B	Down	Y	250
American Funds 2035 Target Date Retirement Fund® Class F-1	FAQTX	NAS CM	Open End	Target Date 2021-2045 (Asset Alloc)	B-	B-	B	Down	Y	250
American Funds 2035 Target Date Retirement Fund® Class F-2	FBFTX	NAS CM	Open End	Target Date 2021-2045 (Asset Alloc)	B-	B-	B	Down	Y	250
American Funds 2035 Target Date Retirement Fund® Class F-3	FDFTX	NAS CM	Open End	Target Date 2021-2045 (Asset Alloc)	B-	B-	B	Down	Y	250
American Funds 2035 Target Date Retirement Fund® Class R-1	RAFTX	NAS CM	Open End	Target Date 2021-2045 (Asset Alloc)	B-	B-	B	Down	Y	250
American Funds 2035 Target Date Retirement Fund® Class R-2	RBFTX	NAS CM	Open End	Target Date 2021-2045 (Asset Alloc)	B-	B-	B	Down	Y	250
American Funds 2035 Target Date Retirement Fund® Cls R-2E	RBEFX	NAS CM	Open End	Target Date 2021-2045 (Asset Alloc)	B-	B-	B	Down	Y	250
American Funds 2035 Target Date Retirement Fund® Class R-3	RCFTX	NAS CM	Open End	Target Date 2021-2045 (Asset Alloc)	B-	B-	B	Down	Y	250
American Funds 2035 Target Date Retirement Fund® Class R-4	RDFTX	NAS CM	Open End	Target Date 2021-2045 (Asset Alloc)	B-	B-	B	Down	Y	250
American Funds 2035 Target Date Retirement Fund® Class R-5	REFTX	NAS CM	Open End	Target Date 2021-2045 (Asset Alloc)	B-	B-	B	Down	Y	250
American Funds 2035 Target Date Retirement Fund® Cls R-5E	RHFTX	NAS CM	Open End	Target Date 2021-2045 (Asset Alloc)	B-	B-	B	Down	Y	250
American Funds 2035 Target Date Retirement Fund® Class R-6	RFFTX	NAS CM	Open End	Target Date 2021-2045 (Asset Alloc)	B-	B-	B	Down	Y	250
American Funds 2040 Target Date Retirement Fund® Class A	AAGTX	NAS CM	Open End	Target Date 2021-2045 (Asset Alloc)	B-	B-	B	Down	Y	250
American Funds 2040 Target Date Retirement Fund® Class C	CCGTX	NAS CM	Open End	Target Date 2021-2045 (Asset Alloc)	B-	B-	B	Down	Y	250
American Funds 2040 Target Date Retirement Fund® Class F-1	FAUTX	NAS CM	Open End	Target Date 2021-2045 (Asset Alloc)	B-	B-	B	Down	Y	250
American Funds 2040 Target Date Retirement Fund® Class F-2	FBGTX	NAS CM	Open End	Target Date 2021-2045 (Asset Alloc)	B-	B-	B	Down	Y	250
American Funds 2040 Target Date Retirement Fund® Class F-3	FCGTX	NAS CM	Open End	Target Date 2021-2045 (Asset Alloc)	B-	B-	B	Down	Y	250
American Funds 2040 Target Date Retirement Fund® Class R-1	RAKTX	NAS CM	Open End	Target Date 2021-2045 (Asset Alloc)	B-	B-	B	Down	Y	250
American Funds 2040 Target Date Retirement Fund® Class R-2	RBKTX	NAS CM	Open End	Target Date 2021-2045 (Asset Alloc)	B-	B-	B	Down	Y	250
American Funds 2040 Target Date Retirement Fund® Cls R-2E	RBEKX	NAS CM	Open End	Target Date 2021-2045 (Asset Alloc)	B-	B-	B	Down	Y	250
American Funds 2040 Target Date Retirement Fund® Class R-3	RCKTX	NAS CM	Open End	Target Date 2021-2045 (Asset Alloc)	B-	B-	B	Down	Y	250
American Funds 2040 Target Date Retirement Fund® Class R-4	RDGTX	NAS CM	Open End	Target Date 2021-2045 (Asset Alloc)	B-	B-	B	Down	Y	250
American Funds 2040 Target Date Retirement Fund® Class R-5	REGTX	NAS CM	Open End	Target Date 2021-2045 (Asset Alloc)	B-	B-	B	Down	Y	250
American Funds 2040 Target Date Retirement Fund® Cls R-5E	RHGTX	NAS CM	Open End	Target Date 2021-2045 (Asset Alloc)	B-	B-	B	Down	Y	250
American Funds 2040 Target Date Retirement Fund® Class R-6	RFGTX	NAS CM	Open End	Target Date 2021-2045 (Asset Alloc)	B-	B-	B	Down	Y	250
American Funds 2045 Target Date Retirement Fund® Class A	AAHTX	NAS CM	Open End	Target Date 2021-2045 (Asset Alloc)	B-	B-	B	Down	Y	250
American Funds 2045 Target Date Retirement Fund® Class C	CCHTX	NAS CM	Open End	Target Date 2021-2045 (Asset Alloc)	B-	B-	B	Down	Y	250
American Funds 2045 Target Date Retirement Fund® Class F-1	FATTX	NAS CM	Open End	Target Date 2021-2045 (Asset Alloc)	B-	B-	B	Down	Y	250
American Funds 2045 Target Date Retirement Fund® Class F-2	FBHTX	NAS CM	Open End	Target Date 2021-2045 (Asset Alloc)	B-	B-	B	Down	Y	250
American Funds 2045 Target Date Retirement Fund® Class F-3	FCHTX	NAS CM	Open End	Target Date 2021-2045 (Asset Alloc)	B-	B-	B	Down	Y	250
American Funds 2045 Target Date Retirement Fund® Cls R-1	RAHTX	NAS CM	Open End	Target Date 2021-2045 (Asset Alloc)	B-	B-	B	Down	Y	250
American Funds 2045 Target Date Retirement Fund® Class R-2	RBHTX	NAS CM	Open End	Target Date 2021-2045 (Asset Alloc)	B-	B-	B	Down	Y	250
American Funds 2045 Target Date Retirement Fund® Cls R-2E	RBHHX	NAS CM	Open End	Target Date 2021-2045 (Asset Alloc)	B-	B-	B	Down	Y	250
American Funds 2045 Target Date Retirement Fund® Class R-3	RCHTX	NAS CM	Open End	Target Date 2021-2045 (Asset Alloc)	B-	B-	B	Down	Y	250
American Funds 2045 Target Date Retirement Fund® Class R-4	RDHTX	NAS CM	Open End	Target Date 2021-2045 (Asset Alloc)	B-	B-	B	Down	Y	250
American Funds 2045 Target Date Retirement Fund® Class R-5	REHTX	NAS CM	Open End	Target Date 2021-2045 (Asset Alloc)	B-	B-	B	Down	Y	250
American Funds 2045 Target Date Retirement Fund® Cls R-5E	RHHTX	NAS CM	Open End	Target Date 2021-2045 (Asset Alloc)	B-	B-	B	Down	Y	250
American Funds 2045 Target Date Retirement Fund® Class R-6	RFHTX	NAS CM	Open End	Target Date 2021-2045 (Asset Alloc)	B-	B-	B	Down	Y	250
American Funds 2050 Target Date Retirement Fund® Class A	AALTX	NAS CM	Open End	Target Date 2046+ (Asset Alloc)	B-	B-	B	Down	Y	250
American Funds 2050 Target Date Retirement Fund® Class C	CCITX	NAS CM	Open End	Target Date 2046+ (Asset Alloc)	B-	B-	B	Down	Y	250
American Funds 2050 Target Date Retirement Fund® Class F-1	FAITX	NAS CM	Open End	Target Date 2046+ (Asset Alloc)	B-	B-	B	Down	Y	250
American Funds 2050 Target Date Retirement Fund® Class F-2	FBITX	NAS CM	Open End	Target Date 2046+ (Asset Alloc)	B-	B-	B	Down	Y	250
American Funds 2050 Target Date Retirement Fund® Class F-3	DITFX	NAS CM	Open End	Target Date 2046+ (Asset Alloc)	B-	B-	B	Down	Y	250
American Funds 2050 Target Date Retirement Fund® Class R-1	RAITX	NAS CM	Open End	Target Date 2046+ (Asset Alloc)	B-	B-	B	Down	Y	250
American Funds 2050 Target Date Retirement Fund® Class R-2	RBITX	NAS CM	Open End	Target Date 2046+ (Asset Alloc)	B-	B-	B	Down	Y	250
American Funds 2050 Target Date Retirement Fund® Cls R-2E	RBHEX	NAS CM	Open End	Target Date 2046+ (Asset Alloc)	B-	B-	B	Down	Y	250
American Funds 2050 Target Date Retirement Fund® Class R-3	RCITX	NAS CM	Open End	Target Date 2046+ (Asset Alloc)	B-	B-	B	Down	Y	250
American Funds 2050 Target Date Retirement Fund® Class R-4	RDITX	NAS CM	Open End	Target Date 2046+ (Asset Alloc)	B-	B-	B	Down	Y	250

★ Expanded analysis of this fund is included in Section II.

Min Additional Investment	3-Month Total Return	6-Month Total Return	1-Year Total Return	3-Year Total Return	5-Year Total Return	Dividend Yield (TTM)	Expense Ratio	3-Yr Std Deviation	3-Year Beta	NAV	Total Assets (MIL)	%Cash	%Stocks	%Bonds	%Other	Turnover Ratio	Last Bull Market Total Return	Last Bear Market Total Return	Front End Fee (%)	Back End Fee (%)	Inception Date
	TOTAL RETURNS					PERFORMANCE				ASSETS		ASSET ALLOCATION & TURNOVER					BULL & BEAR		FEES		
50	4.11	8.51	18.33	27.22	73.96	1.16	0.46	7.75	0.99	14.51	14,786	3	70	23	3	3	19.28	-15.66			Feb-07
50	4.04	8.40	18.23	26.85	73.46	1.13	0.55	7.74	0.99	14.36	14,786	3	70	23	3	3	19.28	-15.66			Nov-15
50	4.11	8.53	18.39	27.32	74.24	1.2	0.41	7.74	0.99	14.45	14,786	3	70	23	3	3	19.26	-15.61			Jul-09
50	4.63	9.61	20.67	29.32	76.40	0.85	0.78	8.44	1.01	14.84	11,498	3	79	14	4	3	19.24	-16.2	5.75		Feb-07
50	4.41	9.15	19.78	26.42	69.85	0.38	1.52	8.46	1.01	14.63	11,498	3	79	14	4	3	18.66	-16.38		1.00	Feb-14
50	4.69	9.62	20.63	29.29	76.31	1.02	0.78	8.46	1.01	14.77	11,498	3	79	14	4	3	19.18	-16.12			Feb-14
50	4.72	9.70	20.95	30.23	78.55	1.07	0.51	8.47	1.02	14.83	11,498	3	79	14	4	3	19.35	-16.03			Feb-14
50	4.77	9.75	21.17	30.58	79.09		0.41	8.45	1.01	14.84	11,498	3	79	14	4	3	19.35	-16.03			Jan-17
50	4.45	9.15	19.75	26.27	69.50	0.18	1.55	8.44	1.01	14.56	11,498	3	79	14	4	3	18.66	-16.36			Feb-07
50	4.44	9.13	19.71	26.51	70.09	0.29	1.51	8.41	1.01	14.57	11,498	3	79	14	4	3	18.74	-16.41			Feb-07
50	4.55	9.37	20.17	27.90	73.60	0.77	1.21	8.44	1.01	14.64	11,498	3	79	14	4	3	18.94	-16.25			Aug-14
50	4.51	9.39	20.26	28.03	73.54	0.64	1.09	8.41	1.01	14.7	11,498	3	79	14	4	3	19.01	-16.29			Feb-07
50	4.63	9.55	20.63	29.23	76.23	0.87	0.78	8.42	1.01	14.8	11,498	3	79	14	4	3	19.13	-16.12			Feb-07
50	4.68	9.71	21.06	30.46	78.92	1.07	0.47	8.44	1.01	14.94	11,498	3	79	14	4	3	19.35	-16.03			Feb-07
50	4.63	9.62	20.89	30.22	78.60	1.03	0.56	8.42	1.01	14.79	11,498	3	79	14	4	3	19.35	-16.03			Nov-15
50	4.69	9.73	21.03	30.57	79.41	1.1	0.42	8.41	1.01	14.88	11,498	3	79	14	4	3	19.33	-15.98			Jul-09
50	4.90	10.09	21.61	30.54	78.97	0.82	0.8	8.67	0.99	15.2	10,103	3	82	11	4	2	19.45	-16.46	5.75		Feb-07
50	4.62	9.58	20.60	27.46	72.13	0.38	1.53	8.66	0.99	14.97	10,103	3	82	11	4	2	18.97	-16.73		1.00	Feb-14
50	4.90	10.04	21.62	30.43	78.75	0.95	0.78	8.65	0.99	15.12	10,103	3	82	11	4	2	19.49	-16.47			Feb-14
50	4.93	10.13	21.84	31.42	80.88	1.01	0.52	8.67	0.99	15.18	10,103	3	82	11	4	2	19.66	-16.38			Feb-14
50	4.98	10.25	21.94	31.61	81.36		0.43	8.62	0.98	15.2	10,103	3	82	11	4	2	19.66	-16.38			Jan-17
50	4.70	9.60	20.65	27.40	71.82	0.14	1.57	8.64	0.99	14.96	10,103	3	82	11	4	2	19.06	-16.78			Feb-07
50	4.64	9.63	20.71	27.69	72.42	0.26	1.52	8.68	0.99	14.91	10,103	3	82	11	4	2	19.07	-16.69			Feb-07
50	4.79	9.81	21.08	29.00	75.93	0.69	1.22	8.68	0.99	15.01	10,103	3	82	11	4	2	19.25	-16.59			Aug-14
50	4.79	9.81	21.23	29.27	75.90	0.59	1.11	8.69	0.99	15.06	10,103	3	82	11	4	2	19.32	-16.56			Feb-07
50	4.91	10.04	21.59	30.46	78.80	0.83	0.79	8.68	0.99	15.16	10,103	3	82	11	4	2	19.58	-16.48			Feb-07
50	4.97	10.20	21.92	31.58	81.33	1.03	0.48	8.62	0.98	15.3	10,103	3	82	11	4	2	19.66	-16.38			Feb-07
50	4.91	10.12	21.77	31.27	80.90	0.99	0.57	8.62	0.98	15.14	10,103	3	82	11	4	2	19.66	-16.38			Nov-15
50	4.97	10.21	21.97	31.78	81.93	1.06	0.43	8.66	0.99	15.25	10,103	3	82	11	4	2	19.64	-16.33			Jul-09
50	5.04	10.25	22.01	31.20	79.93	0.77	0.79	8.78	0.97	15.43	6,946	3	83	10	4	3	19.48	-16.5	5.75		Feb-07
50	4.75	9.81	21.09	28.13	73.20	0.33	1.53	8.82	0.98	15.19	6,946	3	83	10	4	3	19.13	-16.76		1.00	Feb-14
50	4.96	10.27	21.99	31.10	79.79	0.89	0.78	8.8	0.97	15.35	6,946	3	83	10	4	3	19.65	-16.5			Feb-14
50	5.07	10.42	22.29	32.09	82.03	0.96	0.52	8.8	0.97	15.43	6,946	3	83	10	4	3	19.82	-16.42			Feb-14
50	5.06	10.41	22.24	32.14	82.40		0.43	8.82	0.98	15.42	6,946	3	83	10	4	3	19.82	-16.42			Jan-17
50	4.80	9.79	21.08	28.09	72.81	0.05	1.57	8.79	0.97	15.17	6,946	3	83	10	4	3	18.93	-16.7			Feb-07
50	4.74	9.76	21.00	28.19	73.39	0.23	1.53	8.79	0.97	15.1	6,946	3	83	10	4	3	19.03	-16.73			Feb-07
50	4.87	9.99	21.40	29.66	77.00	0.64	1.22	8.82	0.98	15.22	6,946	3	83	10	4	3	19.4	-16.63			Aug-14
50	4.88	10.07	21.58	29.80	76.92	0.55	1.11	8.79	0.97	15.26	6,946	3	83	10	4	3	19.4	-16.61			Feb-07
50	4.98	10.20	21.98	31.10	79.68	0.77	0.79	8.78	0.97	15.39	6,946	3	83	10	4	3	19.5	-16.41			Feb-07
50	5.03	10.34	22.28	32.18	82.46	0.97	0.49	8.82	0.98	15.54	6,946	3	83	10	4	3	19.82	-16.42			Feb-07
50	5.07	10.36	22.27	31.93	82.12	0.94	0.58	8.81	0.98	15.37	6,946	3	83	10	4	3	19.82	-16.42			Nov-15
50	5.10	10.44	22.43	32.49	82.89	1	0.43	8.82	0.98	15.49	6,946	3	83	10	4	3	19.67	-16.37			Jul-09
50	5.06	10.31	22.17	31.42	80.33	0.74	0.8	8.85	0.96	15.1	5,563	3	84	9	4	2	19.41	-16.41	5.75		Feb-07
50	4.85	9.96	21.25	28.47	73.65	0.32	1.54	8.86	0.96	14.86	5,563	3	84	9	4	2	19.09	-16.78		1.00	Feb-14
50	5.05	10.32	22.15	31.33	80.31	0.86	0.79	8.85	0.96	15.02	5,563	3	84	9	4	2	19.61	-16.52			Feb-14
50	5.09	10.49	22.48	32.30	82.53	0.94	0.53	8.83	0.96	15.08	5,563	3	84	9	4	2	19.78	-16.43			Feb-14
50	5.21	10.61	22.57	32.57	83.02		0.43	8.84	0.96	15.11	5,563	3	84	9	4	2	19.78	-16.43			Jan-17
50	4.89	9.93	21.24	28.38	73.28	0.13	1.57	8.84	0.96	14.84	5,563	3	84	9	4	2	18.94	-16.73			Feb-07
50	4.82	9.94	21.26	28.49	73.85	0.2	1.53	8.82	0.96	14.83	5,563	3	84	9	4	2	18.99	-16.71			Feb-07
50	4.98	10.15	21.67	30.00	77.51	0.62	1.22	8.85	0.96	14.91	5,563	3	84	9	4	2	19.36	-16.64			Aug-14
50	4.98	10.13	21.72	30.09	77.20	0.52	1.11	8.83	0.96	14.95	5,563	3	84	9	4	2	19.32	-16.61			Feb-07
50	5.01	10.35	22.15	31.33	80.12	0.75	0.79	8.83	0.96	15.06	5,563	3	84	9	4	2	19.57	-16.43			Feb-07

	MARKET			FUND TYPE, CATEGORY & OBJECTIVE	RATINGS				MINIMUMS	
Fund Name	Ticker Symbol	Traded On	Fund Type	Category and (Prospectus Objective)	Overall Rating	Reward Rating	Risk Rating	Recent Up/ Downgrade	Open to New Investors	Min Initial Investment
American Funds 2050 Target Date Retirement Fund® Class R-5	REITX	NAS CM	Open End	Target Date 2046+ (Asset Alloc)	B-	B-	B	Down	Y	250
American Funds 2050 Target Date Retirement Fund® Cls R-5E	RHITX	NAS CM	Open End	Target Date 2046+ (Asset Alloc)	B-	B-	B	Down	Y	250
American Funds 2050 Target Date Retirement Fund® Class R-6	RFITX	NAS CM	Open End	Target Date 2046+ (Asset Alloc)	B-	B-	B	Down	Y	250
American Funds 2055 Target Date Retirement Fund® Class A	AAMTX	NAS CM	Open End	Target Date 2046+ (Asset Alloc)	B-	B-	B	Down	Y	250
American Funds 2055 Target Date Retirement Fund® Class C	CCJTX	NAS CM	Open End	Target Date 2046+ (Asset Alloc)	B-	B-	B	Down	Y	250
American Funds 2055 Target Date Retirement Fund® Class F-1	FAJTX	NAS CM	Open End	Target Date 2046+ (Asset Alloc)	B-	B-	B	Down	Y	250
American Funds 2055 Target Date Retirement Fund® Class F-2	FBJTX	NAS CM	Open End	Target Date 2046+ (Asset Alloc)	B-	B-	B	Down	Y	250
American Funds 2055 Target Date Retirement Fund® Class F-3	FCJTX	NAS CM	Open End	Target Date 2046+ (Asset Alloc)	B-	B-	B	Down	Y	250
American Funds 2055 Target Date Retirement Fund® Class R-1	RAMTX	NAS CM	Open End	Target Date 2046+ (Asset Alloc)	B-	B-	B	Down	Y	250
American Funds 2055 Target Date Retirement Fund® Class R-2	RBMTX	NAS CM	Open End	Target Date 2046+ (Asset Alloc)	B-	B-	B	Down	Y	250
American Funds 2055 Target Date Retirement Fund® Cls R-2E	RBEMX	NAS CM	Open End	Target Date 2046+ (Asset Alloc)	B-	B-	B	Down	Y	250
American Funds 2055 Target Date Retirement Fund® Class R-3	RCMTX	NAS CM	Open End	Target Date 2046+ (Asset Alloc)	B-	B-	B	Down	Y	250
American Funds 2055 Target Date Retirement Fund® Class R-4	RDJTX	NAS CM	Open End	Target Date 2046+ (Asset Alloc)	B-	B-	B	Down	Y	250
American Funds 2055 Target Date Retirement Fund® Class R-5	REKTX	NAS CM	Open End	Target Date 2046+ (Asset Alloc)	B-	B-	B	Down	Y	250
American Funds 2055 Target Date Retirement Fund® Cls R-5E	RHJTX	NAS CM	Open End	Target Date 2046+ (Asset Alloc)	B-	B-	B	Down	Y	250
American Funds 2055 Target Date Retirement Fund® Class R-6	RFKTX	NAS CM	Open End	Target Date 2046+ (Asset Alloc)	B-	B-	B	Down	Y	250
American Funds 2060 Target Date Retirement Fund® Class A	AANTX	NAS CM	Open End	Target Date 2046+ (Asset Alloc)	B-	C+	B	Up	Y	250
American Funds 2060 Target Date Retirement Fund® Class C	CCKTX	NAS CM	Open End	Target Date 2046+ (Asset Alloc)	B-	C+	B	Up	Y	250
American Funds 2060 Target Date Retirement Fund® Class F-1	FAWTX	NAS CM	Open End	Target Date 2046+ (Asset Alloc)	B-	C+	B	Up	Y	250
American Funds 2060 Target Date Retirement Fund® Class F-2	FBKTX	NAS CM	Open End	Target Date 2046+ (Asset Alloc)	B-	C+	B	Up	Y	250
American Funds 2060 Target Date Retirement Fund® Class F-3	FCKTX	NAS CM	Open End	Target Date 2046+ (Asset Alloc)	B-	C+	B	Up	Y	250
American Funds 2060 Target Date Retirement Fund® Class R-1	RANTX	NAS CM	Open End	Target Date 2046+ (Asset Alloc)	B-	C+	B	Up	Y	250
American Funds 2060 Target Date Retirement Fund® Class R-2	RBNTX	NAS CM	Open End	Target Date 2046+ (Asset Alloc)	B-	C+	B	Up	Y	250
American Funds 2060 Target Date Retirement Fund® Cls R-2E	RBENX	NAS CM	Open End	Target Date 2046+ (Asset Alloc)	B-	C+	B	Up	Y	250
American Funds 2060 Target Date Retirement Fund® Class R-3	RCNTX	NAS CM	Open End	Target Date 2046+ (Asset Alloc)	B-	C+	B	Up	Y	250
American Funds 2060 Target Date Retirement Fund® Class R-4	RDKTX	NAS CM	Open End	Target Date 2046+ (Asset Alloc)	B-	C+	B	Up	Y	250
American Funds 2060 Target Date Retirement Fund® Class R-5	REMTX	NAS CM	Open End	Target Date 2046+ (Asset Alloc)	B-	C+	B	Up	Y	250
American Funds 2060 Target Date Retirement Fund® Cls R-5E	RHKTX	NAS CM	Open End	Target Date 2046+ (Asset Alloc)	B-	C+	B	Up	Y	250
American Funds 2060 Target Date Retirement Fund® Class R-6	RFUTX	NAS CM	Open End	Target Date 2046+ (Asset Alloc)	B-	C+	B	Up	Y	250
American Funds AMCAP Fund® Class 529-A	CAFAX	NAS CM	Open End	US Equity Large Cap Growth (Growth)	B	B	B-	Up	Y	250
American Funds AMCAP Fund® Class 529-C	CAFCX	NAS CM	Open End	US Equity Large Cap Growth (Growth)	B-	B-	B-	Down	Y	250
American Funds AMCAP Fund® Class 529-E	CAFEX	NAS CM	Open End	US Equity Large Cap Growth (Growth)	B-	B	B-	Down	Y	250
American Funds AMCAP Fund® Class 529-F-1	CAFFX	NAS CM	Open End	US Equity Large Cap Growth (Growth)	B	B	B-	Up	Y	250
American Funds AMCAP Fund® Class A	AMCPX	NAS CM	Open End	US Equity Large Cap Growth (Growth)	B	B	B-	Up	Y	250
American Funds AMCAP Fund® Class C	AMPCX	NAS CM	Open End	US Equity Large Cap Growth (Growth)	B-	B-	B-	Down	Y	250
American Funds AMCAP Fund® Class F-1	AMPFX	NAS CM	Open End	US Equity Large Cap Growth (Growth)	B	B	B-	Up	Y	250
American Funds AMCAP Fund® Class F-2	AMCFX	NAS CM	Open End	US Equity Large Cap Growth (Growth)	B	B	B-	Up	Y	250
American Funds AMCAP Fund® Class F-3	FMACX	NAS CM	Open End	US Equity Large Cap Growth (Growth)	B	B	B-	Up	Y	250
American Funds AMCAP Fund® Class R-1	RAFAX	NAS CM	Open End	US Equity Large Cap Growth (Growth)	B-	B-	B-	Down	Y	250
American Funds AMCAP Fund® Class R-2	RAFBX	NAS CM	Open End	US Equity Large Cap Growth (Growth)	B-	B-	B-	Down	Y	250
American Funds AMCAP Fund® Class R-2E	RAEBX	NAS CM	Open End	US Equity Large Cap Growth (Growth)	B-	B	B-	Down	Y	250
American Funds AMCAP Fund® Class R-3	RAFCX	NAS CM	Open End	US Equity Large Cap Growth (Growth)	B-	B	B-	Down	Y	250
American Funds AMCAP Fund® Class R-4	RAFEX	NAS CM	Open End	US Equity Large Cap Growth (Growth)	B	B	B-	Up	Y	250
American Funds AMCAP Fund® Class R-5	RAFFX	NAS CM	Open End	US Equity Large Cap Growth (Growth)	B	B	B-	Up	Y	250
American Funds AMCAP Fund® Class R-5E	RAEFX	NAS CM	Open End	US Equity Large Cap Growth (Growth)	B	B	B-	Up	Y	250
American Funds AMCAP Fund® Class R-6	RAFGX	NAS CM	Open End	US Equity Large Cap Growth (Growth)	B	B	B-	Up	Y	250
★ American Funds American Balanced Fund® Class 529-A	CLBAX	NAS CM	Open End	Moderate Alloc (Balanced)	B	B-	A-		Y	250
★ American Funds American Balanced Fund® Class 529-C	CLBCX	NAS CM	Open End	Moderate Alloc (Balanced)	B	C+	B	Up	Y	250
★ American Funds American Balanced Fund® Class 529-E	CLBEX	NAS CM	Open End	Moderate Alloc (Balanced)	B	C+	A-		Y	250
★ American Funds American Balanced Fund® Class 529-F	CLBFX	NAS CM	Open End	Moderate Alloc (Balanced)	B	B-	A-		Y	250
★ American Funds American Balanced Fund® Class A	ABALX	NAS CM	Open End	Moderate Alloc (Balanced)	B	B-	A-		Y	250
★ American Funds American Balanced Fund® Class C	BALCX	NAS CM	Open End	Moderate Alloc (Balanced)	B	C+	B+	Up	Y	250

★Expanded analysis of this fund is included in Section II.

	TOTAL RETURNS					PERFORMANCE				ASSETS		ASSET ALLOCATION & TURNOVER					BULL & BEAR		FEES		
Min Additional Investment	3-Month Total Return	6-Month Total Return	1-Year Total Return	3-Year Total Return	5-Year Total Return	Dividend Yield (TTM)	Expense Ratio	3-Yr Std Deviation	3-Year Beta	NAV	Total Assets (MIL)	%Cash	%Stocks	%Bonds	%Other	Turnover Ratio	Last Bull Market Total Return	Last Bear Market Total Return	Front End Fee (%)	Back End Fee (%)	Inception Date
50	5.20	10.57	22.55	32.55	82.99	0.95	0.49	8.83	0.96	15.21	5,563	3	84	9	4	2	19.78	-16.43			Feb-07
50	5.07	10.48	22.40	32.24	82.57	0.92	0.58	8.82	0.96	15.05	5,563	3	84	9	4	2	19.78	-16.43			Nov-15
50	5.19	10.58	22.60	32.74	83.21	0.98	0.43	8.85	0.96	15.16	5,563	3	84	9	4	2	19.76	-16.38			Jul-09
50	5.07	10.39	22.18	31.41	80.37	0.68	0.82	8.83	0.95	18.8	2,616	3	84	9	4	3	19.55	-16.5	5.75		Feb-10
50	4.89	9.97	21.23	28.39	73.58	0.2	1.55	8.84	0.95	18.55	2,616	3	84	9	4	3	19.16	-16.79		1.00	Feb-14
50	5.09	10.37	22.14	31.29	80.30	0.78	0.8	8.81	0.95	18.71	2,616	3	84	9	4	3	19.68	-16.53			Feb-14
50	5.18	10.50	22.52	32.39	82.34	0.86	0.54	8.84	0.95	18.8	2,616	3	84	9	4	3	19.85	-16.44			Feb-14
50	5.18	10.55	22.63	32.71	83.13		0.44	8.86	0.95	18.81	2,616	3	84	9	4	3	19.85	-16.44			Jan-17
50	4.89	9.93	21.22	28.30	73.13	0.01	1.59	8.82	0.95	18.49	2,616	3	84	9	4	3	18.99	-16.81			Feb-10
50	4.86	9.96	21.25	28.50	73.72	0.16	1.54	8.84	0.95	18.48	2,616	3	84	9	4	3	19.07	-16.76			Feb-10
50	4.95	10.13	21.64	30.04	77.53	0.56	1.23	8.81	0.95	18.59	2,616	3	84	9	4	3	19.44	-16.65			Aug-14
50	4.96	10.20	21.79	30.09	77.09	0.48	1.12	8.83	0.95	18.63	2,616	3	84	9	4	3	19.31	-16.62			Feb-10
50	5.07	10.33	22.15	31.32	79.96	0.69	0.81	8.85	0.95	18.76	2,616	3	84	9	4	3	19.63	-16.57			Feb-10
50	5.16	10.50	22.52	32.50	82.76	0.88	0.5	8.82	0.95	18.92	2,616	3	84	9	4	3	19.71	-16.38			Feb-10
50	5.13	10.52	22.44	32.31	82.59	0.86	0.58	8.85	0.95	18.74	2,616	3	84	9	4	3	19.85	-16.44			Nov-15
50	5.14	10.54	22.62	32.70	83.12	0.91	0.45	8.86	0.95	18.94	2,616	3	84	9	4	3	19.85	-16.44			Feb-10
50	5.03	10.39	22.20			0.88	0.81			12.37	547.6	3	84	9	4	12			5.75		Mar-15
50	4.85	9.96	21.26			0.54	1.56			12.27	547.6	3	84	9	4	12				1.00	Mar-15
50	5.01	10.36	22.04			0.98	0.75			12.38	547.6	3	84	9	4	12					Mar-15
50	5.12	10.46	22.35			0.97	0.56			12.4	547.6	3	84	9	4	12					Mar-15
50	5.18	10.54	22.58				0.47			12.37	547.6	3	84	9	4	12					Jan-17
50	4.94	9.94	21.18			0.48	1.49			12.32	547.6	3	84	9	4	12					Mar-15
50	4.81	9.93	21.10			0.53	1.56			12.26	547.6	3	84	9	4	12					Mar-15
50	4.98	10.17	21.64			0.71	1.23			12.32	547.6	3	84	9	4	12					Mar-15
50	5.01	10.20	21.80			0.69	1.13			12.33	547.6	3	84	9	4	12					Mar-15
50	5.04	10.39	22.09			0.89	0.81			12.37	547.6	3	84	9	4	12					Mar-15
50	5.19	10.52	22.53			1.04	0.51			12.42	547.6	3	84	9	4	12					Mar-15
50	5.12	10.47	22.40			0.99	0.62			12.37	547.6	3	84	9	4	12					Nov-15
50	5.16	10.49	22.49			1.05	0.46			12.42	547.6	3	84	9	4	12					Mar-15
50	5.95	11.88	21.92	32.80	107.76	0.31	0.78	9.94	0.94	31.15	60,672	5	86	4	5	25	24.06	-15.79	5.75		Feb-02
50	5.77	11.48	20.99	29.80	99.89	0	1.54	9.93	0.94	28.03	60,672	5	86	4	5	25	23.46	-16.04		1.00	Feb-02
50	5.91	11.76	21.64	31.88	105.35	0.13	0.99	9.94	0.94	30.38	60,672	5	86	4	5	25	23.88	-15.91			Mar-02
50	6.01	12.00	22.19	33.64	109.99	0.48	0.55	9.94	0.94	31.38	60,672	5	86	4	5	25	24.2	-15.72			Sep-02
50	5.99	11.93	22.04	33.16	108.74	0.36	0.69	9.96	0.95	31.49	60,672	5	86	4	5	25	24.13	-15.76	5.75		May-67
50	5.77	11.50	21.07	29.99	100.47	0	1.49	9.94	0.94	27.87	60,672	5	86	4	5	25	23.51	-16.01		1.00	Mar-01
50	5.97	11.92	21.95	32.91	108.11	0.3	0.75	9.96	0.94	31.22	60,672	5	86	4	5	25	24.11	-15.77			Mar-01
50	6.04	12.06	22.26	33.98	110.92	0.55	0.48	9.94	0.94	31.67	60,672	5	86	4	5	25	24.27	-15.68			Aug-08
50	6.06	12.10	22.40	33.55	109.34		0.37	9.96	0.95	31.5	60,672	5	86	4	5	25	24.13	-15.76			Jan-17
50	5.76	11.47	21.06	30.02	100.69	0	1.47	9.94	0.94	28.63	60,672	5	86	4	5	25	23.54	-16.04			Jun-02
50	5.76	11.47	21.07	30.08	100.85	0	1.46	9.94	0.94	28.62	60,672	5	86	4	5	25	23.57	-16.02			May-02
50	5.86	11.67	21.45	31.53	105.01	0.29	1.16	9.95	0.94	31.2	60,672	5	86	4	5	25	23.87	-15.89			Aug-14
50	5.86	11.72	21.59	31.78	105.27	0.1	1.02	9.95	0.94	30.54	60,672	5	86	4	5	25	23.91	-15.87			Jun-02
50	5.94	11.90	21.97	33.00	108.43	0.35	0.72	9.93	0.94	31.21	60,672	5	86	4	5	25	24.13	-15.77			May-02
50	6.06	12.08	22.33	34.23	111.51	0.57	0.41	9.95	0.94	31.88	60,672	5	86	4	5	25	24.31	-15.68			May-02
50	5.98	11.98	22.26	33.54	109.33	0.45	0.52	9.95	0.94	31.52	60,672	5	86	4	5	25	24.13	-15.76			Nov-15
50	6.06	12.08	22.41	34.40	111.99	0.62	0.36	9.95	0.94	31.8	60,672	5	86	4	5	25	24.35	-15.61			May-09
50	4.51	8.25	15.42	26.49	69.97	1.48	0.68	6.48	0.62	27.11	123,185	3	59	36	2	79	17.38	-10.01	5.75		Feb-02
50	4.30	7.83	14.54	23.58	63.55	0.79	1.44	6.48	0.62	27.11	123,185	3	59	36	2	79	16.81	-10.27		1.00	Feb-02
50	4.44	8.08	15.10	25.55	67.90	1.27	0.91	6.46	0.62	27.09	123,185	3	59	36	2	79	17.24	-10.14			Mar-02
50	4.56	8.37	15.68	27.32	71.86	1.69	0.44	6.46	0.62	27.09	123,185	3	59	36	2	79	17.57	-9.91			Sep-02
50	4.51	8.27	15.47	26.76	70.72	1.55	0.6	6.46	0.62	27.15	123,185	3	59	36	2	79	17.46	-9.96	5.75		Jul-75
50	4.30	7.81	14.58	23.80	64.06	0.84	1.38	6.46	0.62	26.98	123,185	3	59	36	2	79	16.89	-10.23		1.00	Mar-01

			MARKET		FUND TYPE, CATEGORY & OBJECTIVE	RATINGS				MINIMUMS	
	Fund Name	Ticker Symbol	Traded On	Fund Type	Category and (Prospectus Objective)	Overall Rating	Reward Rating	Risk Rating	Recent Up/ Downgrade	Open to New Investors	Min Initial Investment
★	American Funds American Balanced Fund® Class F-1	BALFX	NAS CM	Open End	Moderate Alloc (Balanced)	B	B-	A-		Y	250
★	American Funds American Balanced Fund® Class F-2	AMBFX	NAS CM	Open End	Moderate Alloc (Balanced)	B	B-	A-		Y	250
★	American Funds American Balanced Fund® Class F-3	AFMBX	NAS CM	Open End	Moderate Alloc (Balanced)	B	B-	A-		Y	250
★	American Funds American Balanced Fund® Class R-1	RLBAX	NAS CM	Open End	Moderate Alloc (Balanced)	B	C+	B+	Up	Y	250
★	American Funds American Balanced Fund® Class R-2	RLBBX	NAS CM	Open End	Moderate Alloc (Balanced)	B	C+	B+	Up	Y	250
★	American Funds American Balanced Fund® Class R-2E	RAMHX	NAS CM	Open End	Moderate Alloc (Balanced)	B	C+	A-		Y	250
★	American Funds American Balanced Fund® Class R-3	RLBCX	NAS CM	Open End	Moderate Alloc (Balanced)	B	C+	A-		Y	250
★	American Funds American Balanced Fund® Class R-4	RLBEX	NAS CM	Open End	Moderate Alloc (Balanced)	B	B-	A-		Y	250
★	American Funds American Balanced Fund® Class R-5	RLBFX	NAS CM	Open End	Moderate Alloc (Balanced)	B	B-	A-		Y	250
★	American Funds American Balanced Fund® Class R-5E	RLEFX	NAS CM	Open End	Moderate Alloc (Balanced)	B	B-	A-		Y	250
★	American Funds American Balanced Fund® Class R-6	RLBGX	NAS CM	Open End	Moderate Alloc (Balanced)	B	B-	A-		Y	250
	American Funds American Mutual Fund® Class 529-A	CMLAX	NAS CM	Open End	US Equity Large Cap Value (Growth & Income)	B-	B-	B	Down	Y	250
	American Funds American Mutual Fund® Class 529-C	CMLCX	NAS CM	Open End	US Equity Large Cap Value (Growth & Income)	B-	B-	B-	Down	Y	250
	American Funds American Mutual Fund® Class 529-E	CMLEX	NAS CM	Open End	US Equity Large Cap Value (Growth & Income)	B-	B-	B	Down	Y	250
	American Funds American Mutual Fund® Class 529-F	CMLFX	NAS CM	Open End	US Equity Large Cap Value (Growth & Income)	B-	B-	B	Down	Y	250
	American Funds American Mutual Fund® Class A	AMRMX	NAS CM	Open End	US Equity Large Cap Value (Growth & Income)	B-	B-	B	Down	Y	250
	American Funds American Mutual Fund® Class C	AMFCX	NAS CM	Open End	US Equity Large Cap Value (Growth & Income)	B-	B-	B-	Down	Y	250
	American Funds American Mutual Fund® Class F-1	AMFFX	NAS CM	Open End	US Equity Large Cap Value (Growth & Income)	B-	B-	B	Down	Y	250
	American Funds American Mutual Fund® Class F-2	AMRFX	NAS CM	Open End	US Equity Large Cap Value (Growth & Income)	B-	B-	B	Down	Y	250
	American Funds American Mutual Fund® Class F-3	AFMFX	NAS CM	Open End	US Equity Large Cap Value (Growth & Income)	B-	B-	B	Down	Y	250
	American Funds American Mutual Fund® Class R-1	RMFAX	NAS CM	Open End	US Equity Large Cap Value (Growth & Income)	B-	B-	B-	Down	Y	250
	American Funds American Mutual Fund® Class R-2	RMFBX	NAS CM	Open End	US Equity Large Cap Value (Growth & Income)	B-	B-	B-	Down	Y	250
	American Funds American Mutual Fund® Class R-2E	RMEBX	NAS CM	Open End	US Equity Large Cap Value (Growth & Income)	B-	B-	B	Down	Y	250
	American Funds American Mutual Fund® Class R-3	RMFCX	NAS CM	Open End	US Equity Large Cap Value (Growth & Income)	B-	B-	B	Down	Y	250
	American Funds American Mutual Fund® Class R-4	RMFEX	NAS CM	Open End	US Equity Large Cap Value (Growth & Income)	B-	B-	B	Down	Y	250
	American Funds American Mutual Fund® Class R-5	RMFFX	NAS CM	Open End	US Equity Large Cap Value (Growth & Income)	B-	B-	B	Down	Y	250
	American Funds American Mutual Fund® Class R-5E	RMFHX	NAS CM	Open End	US Equity Large Cap Value (Growth & Income)	B-	B-	B	Down	Y	250
	American Funds American Mutual Fund® Class R-6	RMFGX	NAS CM	Open End	US Equity Large Cap Value (Growth & Income)	B-	B-	B	Down	Y	250
	American Funds Balanced Portfolio Class 529-A	CBAAX	NAS CM	Open End	Moderate Alloc (Balanced)	B-	C+	B	Up	Y	250
	American Funds Balanced Portfolio Class 529-C	CBPCX	NAS CM	Open End	Moderate Alloc (Balanced)	B-	C+	B	Up	Y	250
	American Funds Balanced Portfolio Class 529-E	CBAEX	NAS CM	Open End	Moderate Alloc (Balanced)	B-	C+	B	Up	Y	250
	American Funds Balanced Portfolio Class 529-F-1	CBAFX	NAS CM	Open End	Moderate Alloc (Balanced)	B-	C+	B	Up	Y	250
	American Funds Balanced Portfolio Class A	BLPAX	NAS CM	Open End	Moderate Alloc (Balanced)	B-	C+	B	Up	Y	250
	American Funds Balanced Portfolio Class C	BLPCX	NAS CM	Open End	Moderate Alloc (Balanced)	B-	C+	B	Up	Y	250
	American Funds Balanced Portfolio Class F-1	BLPFX	NAS CM	Open End	Moderate Alloc (Balanced)	B-	C+	B	Up	Y	250
	American Funds Balanced Portfolio Class F-2	BLPEX	NAS CM	Open End	Moderate Alloc (Balanced)	B-	C+	B	Up	Y	250
	American Funds Balanced Portfolio Class F-3	BLPDX	NAS CM	Open End	Moderate Alloc (Balanced)	B-	C+	B	Up	Y	250
	American Funds Balanced Portfolio Class R-1	RBAAX	NAS CM	Open End	Moderate Alloc (Balanced)	B	C+	A-	Up	Y	250
	American Funds Balanced Portfolio Class R-2	RBABX	NAS CM	Open End	Moderate Alloc (Balanced)	B-	C+	B	Up	Y	250
	American Funds Balanced Portfolio Class R-2E	RBBEX	NAS CM	Open End	Moderate Alloc (Balanced)	B-	C+	B	Up	Y	250
	American Funds Balanced Portfolio Class R-3	RBACX	NAS CM	Open End	Moderate Alloc (Balanced)	B-	C+	B	Up	Y	250
	American Funds Balanced Portfolio Class R-4	RBAEX	NAS CM	Open End	Moderate Alloc (Balanced)	B-	C+	B	Up	Y	250
	American Funds Balanced Portfolio Class R-5	RBAFX	NAS CM	Open End	Moderate Alloc (Balanced)	B-	C+	B	Up	Y	250
	American Funds Balanced Portfolio Class R-5E	RGPFX	NAS CM	Open End	Moderate Alloc (Balanced)	B	C+	A-	Up	Y	250
	American Funds Balanced Portfolio Class R-6	RBAGX	NAS CM	Open End	Moderate Alloc (Balanced)	B-	C+	B	Up	Y	250
★	American Funds Capital Income Builder® Class 529-A	CIRAX	NAS CM	Open End	Alloc (Equity-Income)	B-	C+	B	Down	Y	250
★	American Funds Capital Income Builder® Class 529-C	CIRCX	NAS CM	Open End	Alloc (Equity-Income)	B-	C+	B	Down	Y	250
★	American Funds Capital Income Builder® Class 529-E	CIREX	NAS CM	Open End	Alloc (Equity-Income)	B-	C+	B	Down	Y	250
★	American Funds Capital Income Builder® Class 529-F	CIRFX	NAS CM	Open End	Alloc (Equity-Income)	B-	C+	B	Down	Y	250
★	American Funds Capital Income Builder® Class A	CAIBX	NAS CM	Open End	Alloc (Equity-Income)	B-	C+	B	Down	Y	250
★	American Funds Capital Income Builder® Class C	CIBCX	NAS CM	Open End	Alloc (Equity-Income)	B-	C+	B	Down	Y	250
★	American Funds Capital Income Builder® Class F-1	CIBFX	NAS CM	Open End	Alloc (Equity-Income)	B-	C+	B	Down	Y	250

★Expanded analysis of this fund is included in Section II.

Min Additional Investment	3-Month Total Return	6-Month Total Return	1-Year Total Return	3-Year Total Return	5-Year Total Return	Dividend Yield (TTM)	Expense Ratio	3-Yr Std Deviation	3-Year Beta	NAV	Total Assets (MIL)	%Cash	%Stocks	%Bonds	%Other	Turnover Ratio	Last Bull Market Total Return	Last Bear Market Total Return	Front End Fee (%)	Back End Fee (%)	Inception Date
	TOTAL RETURNS					PERFORMANCE				ASSETS		ASSET ALLOCATION & TURNOVER					BULL & BEAR		FEES		
50	4.49	8.23	15.39	26.52	70.13	1.48	0.66	6.46	0.62	27.13	123,185	3	59	36	2	79	17.4	-9.96			Mar-01
50	4.56	8.33	15.69	27.47	72.31	1.72	0.39	6.48	0.62	27.13	123,185	3	59	36	2	79	17.66	-9.91			Aug-08
50	4.59	8.43	15.81	27.14	71.23		0.29	6.47	0.62	27.14	123,185	3	59	36	2	79	17.46	-9.96			Jan-17
50	4.29	7.80	14.55	23.76	64.01	0.81	1.38	6.46	0.62	26.96	123,185	3	59	36	2	79	16.93	-10.27			May-02
50	4.29	7.85	14.57	23.89	64.29	0.83	1.37	6.47	0.62	26.98	123,185	3	59	36	2	79	16.93	-10.26			May-02
50	4.39	7.98	14.88	25.42	68.00	1.13	1.08	6.43	0.61	27.05	123,185	3	59	36	2	79	17.22	-10.09			Aug-14
50	4.40	8.08	15.05	25.43	67.80	1.23	0.93	6.48	0.62	27.01	123,185	3	59	36	2	79	17.22	-10.05			Jun-02
50	4.50	8.21	15.43	26.57	70.25	1.51	0.64	6.46	0.62	27.1	123,185	3	59	36	2	79	17.41	-9.98			Jun-02
50	4.61	8.39	15.77	27.71	72.84	1.76	0.34	6.47	0.62	27.18	123,185	3	59	36	2	79	17.67	-9.88			May-02
50	4.56	8.39	15.70	27.14	71.24	1.74	0.42	6.46	0.62	27.12	123,185	3	59	36	2	79	17.46	-9.96			Nov-15
50	4.59	8.42	15.84	27.92	73.27	1.81	0.29	6.44	0.62	27.16	123,185	3	59	36	2	79	17.71	-9.86			May-09
50	5.05	10.20	17.59	28.87	89.52	1.75	0.7	8.94	0.86	40.71	48,494	2	91	2	4	18	19.79	-12.72	5.75		Feb-02
50	4.85	9.75	16.65	25.90	82.29	1.08	1.46	8.93	0.86	40.51	48,494	2	91	2	4	18	19.23	-13.01		1.00	Feb-02
50	5.00	10.04	17.29	27.93	87.28	1.54	0.93	8.94	0.86	40.55	48,494	2	91	2	4	18	19.56	-12.8			Mar-02
50	5.09	10.30	17.82	29.69	91.65	1.94	0.46	8.94	0.86	40.76	48,494	2	91	2	4	18	19.94	-12.65			Sep-02
50	5.05	10.21	17.67	29.21	90.44	1.81	0.6	8.94	0.86	40.8	48,494	2	91	2	4	18	19.85	-12.66	5.75		Feb-50
50	4.86	9.78	16.72	26.15	82.95	1.13	1.39	8.94	0.86	40.23	48,494	2	91	2	4	18	19.33	-13.01		1.00	Mar-01
50	5.05	10.17	17.57	28.89	89.71	1.74	0.67	8.94	0.86	40.63	48,494	2	91	2	4	18	19.86	-12.72			Mar-01
50	5.12	10.34	17.87	29.90	92.13	1.97	0.42	8.94	0.86	40.79	48,494	2	91	2	4	18	19.99	-12.61			Aug-08
50	5.13	10.37	17.98	29.55	90.95		0.3	8.94	0.86	40.78	48,494	2	91	2	4	18	19.85	-12.66			Jan-17
50	4.83	9.74	16.66	26.01	82.69	1.08	1.43	8.94	0.86	40.38	48,494	2	91	2	4	18	19.27	-12.96			Jun-02
50	4.85	9.78	16.72	26.12	82.93	1.12	1.41	8.94	0.86	40.34	48,494	2	91	2	4	18	19.33	-13.02			May-02
50	4.94	9.94	17.07	27.41	86.77	1.39	1.09	8.94	0.86	40.67	48,494	2	91	2	4	18	19.61	-12.79			Aug-14
50	4.97	10.03	17.22	27.79	87.01	1.5	0.97	8.93	0.86	40.49	48,494	2	91	2	4	18	19.6	-12.81			Jun-02
50	5.05	10.20	17.58	28.95	89.87	1.76	0.67	8.95	0.86	40.67	48,494	2	91	2	4	18	19.84	-12.71			Jun-02
50	5.11	10.34	17.93	30.14	92.71	2.02	0.36	8.95	0.86	40.8	48,494	2	91	2	4	18	20.05	-12.62			May-02
50	5.12	10.32	17.83	29.49	90.86	1.91	0.46	8.95	0.86	40.78	48,494	2	91	2	4	18	19.85	-12.66			Nov-15
50	5.15	10.39	17.99	30.32	93.23	2.07	0.3	8.95	0.86	40.81	48,494	2	91	2	4	18	20.03	-12.56			May-09
50	3.63	7.36	16.63	23.53	57.41	1.48	0.84	6.55	0.6	14.81	6,898	2	62	32	4	0			5.75		May-12
50	3.38	6.93	15.72	20.54	51.28	0.8	1.59	6.54	0.6	14.75	6,898	2	62	32	4	0				1.00	May-12
50	3.49	7.23	16.36	22.60	55.40	1.31	1.04	6.55	0.6	14.78	6,898	2	62	32	4	0					May-12
50	3.61	7.41	16.87	24.32	59.08	1.68	0.58	6.54	0.6	14.82	6,898	2	62	32	4	0					May-12
50	3.63	7.38	16.70	23.71	57.96	1.55	0.76	6.55	0.6	14.81	6,898	2	62	32	4	0			5.75		May-12
50	3.43	6.93	15.76	20.87	51.93	0.87	1.5	6.53	0.6	14.73	6,898	2	62	32	4	0				1.00	May-12
50	3.56	7.37	16.65	23.55	57.60	1.49	0.77	6.56	0.6	14.81	6,898	2	62	32	4	0					May-12
50	3.70	7.51	16.93	24.56	59.76	1.74	0.51	6.53	0.6	14.83	6,898	2	62	32	4	0					May-12
50	3.73	7.57	17.07	24.81	60.06		0.4	6.53	0.59	14.81	6,898	2	62	32	4	0					Jan-17
50	3.42	6.97	15.76	20.86	51.88	0.84	1.51	6.57	0.6	14.76	6,898	2	62	32	4	0					May-12
50	3.44	7.01	15.79	20.92	51.78	0.89	1.52	6.55	0.6	14.74	6,898	2	62	32	4	0					May-12
50	3.40	7.07	16.13	22.62	55.72	1.27	1.2	6.52	0.59	14.81	6,898	2	62	32	4	0					Aug-14
50	3.55	7.23	16.30	22.52	55.32	1.27	1.07	6.49	0.59	14.78	6,898	2	62	32	4	0					May-12
50	3.63	7.39	16.70	23.66	57.85	1.55	0.76	6.54	0.6	14.81	6,898	2	62	32	4	0					May-12
50	3.64	7.46	16.99	24.73	59.95	1.79	0.46	6.52	0.59	14.83	6,898	2	62	32	4	0					May-12
50	3.70	7.50	16.91	24.47	59.62	1.63	0.56	6.54	0.6	14.82	6,898	2	62	32	4	0					Nov-15
50	3.66	7.49	17.04	24.92	60.34	1.83	0.4	6.52	0.59	14.83	6,898	2	62	32	4	0					May-12
50	2.40	5.61	14.13	17.38	45.48	3.12	0.71	7.54	0.63	62.79	108,816	1	70	25	2	47	12.73	-10.01	5.75		Feb-02
50	2.20	5.22	13.26	14.71	39.96	2.39	1.46	7.54	0.63	62.86	108,816	1	70	25	2	47	12.2	-10.3		1.00	Feb-02
50	2.33	5.49	13.88	16.58	43.80	2.9	0.92	7.55	0.63	62.81	108,816	1	70	25	2	47	12.54	-10.09			Mar-02
50	2.45	5.74	14.40	18.17	47.13	3.34	0.46	7.55	0.63	62.8	108,816	1	70	25	2	47	12.84	-9.91			Sep-02
50	2.42	5.65	14.24	17.71	46.15	3.19	0.61	7.54	0.63	62.82	108,816	1	70	25	2	47	12.77	-9.97	5.75		Jul-87
50	2.20	5.24	13.32	14.91	40.40	2.42	1.4	7.54	0.63	62.9	108,816	1	70	25	2	47	12.25	-10.26		1.00	Mar-01
50	2.39	5.61	14.13	17.43	45.62	3.12	0.67	7.54	0.63	62.81	108,816	1	70	25	2	47	12.75	-9.97			Mar-01

	MARKET			FUND TYPE, CATEGORY & OBJECTIVE	RATINGS				MINIMUMS	
Fund Name	Ticker Symbol	Traded On	Fund Type	Category and (Prospectus Objective)	Overall Rating	Reward Rating	Risk Rating	Recent Up/ Downgrade	Open to New Investors	Min Initial Investment
★ American Funds Capital Income Builder® Class F-2	CAIFX	NAS CM	Open End	Alloc (Equity-Income)	B-	C+	B	Down	Y	250
★ American Funds Capital Income Builder® Class F-3	CFIHX	NAS CM	Open End	Alloc (Equity-Income)	B-	C+	B	Down	Y	250
★ American Funds Capital Income Builder® Class R-1	RIRAX	NAS CM	Open End	Alloc (Equity-Income)	B-	C+	B	Down	Y	250
★ American Funds Capital Income Builder® Class R-2	RIRBX	NAS CM	Open End	Alloc (Equity-Income)	B-	C+	B	Down	Y	250
★ American Funds Capital Income Builder® Class R-2E	RCEEX	NAS CM	Open End	Alloc (Equity-Income)	B-	C+	B	Down	Y	250
★ American Funds Capital Income Builder® Class R-3	RIRCX	NAS CM	Open End	Alloc (Equity-Income)	B-	C+	B	Down	Y	250
★ American Funds Capital Income Builder® Class R-4	RIREX	NAS CM	Open End	Alloc (Equity-Income)	B-	C+	B	Down	Y	250
★ American Funds Capital Income Builder® Class R-5	RIRFX	NAS CM	Open End	Alloc (Equity-Income)	B-	C+	B	Down	Y	250
★ American Funds Capital Income Builder® Class R-5E	RIRHX	NAS CM	Open End	Alloc (Equity-Income)	B-	C+	B	Down	Y	250
★ American Funds Capital Income Builder® Class R-6	RIRGX	NAS CM	Open End	Alloc (Equity-Income)	B-	C+	B	Down	Y	250
American Funds Capital World Growth & Inc Fund® Cls 529-A	CWIAX	NAS CM	Open End	Global Equity (Growth & Income)	B-	B-	B	Down	Y	250
American Funds Capital World Growth & Inc Fund® Cls 529-C	CWICX	NAS CM	Open End	Global Equity (Growth & Income)	B-	B-	B	Up	Y	250
American Funds Capital World Growth & Inc Fund® Cls 529-E	CWIEX	NAS CM	Open End	Global Equity (Growth & Income)	B-	B-	B	Down	Y	250
American Funds Capital World Growth & Inc Fund® Cls 529-F	CWIFX	NAS CM	Open End	Global Equity (Growth & Income)	B	B-	B	Up	Y	250
American Funds Capital World Growth & Income Fund® Cls A	CWGIX	NAS CM	Open End	Global Equity (Growth & Income)	B-	B-	B	Down	Y	250
American Funds Capital World Growth & Income Fund® Cls C	CWGCX	NAS CM	Open End	Global Equity (Growth & Income)	B-	B-	B	Up	Y	250
American Funds Capital World Growth & Income Fund® Cls F-1	CWGFX	NAS CM	Open End	Global Equity (Growth & Income)	B-	B-	B	Down	Y	250
American Funds Capital World Growth & Income Fund® Cls F-2	WGIFX	NAS CM	Open End	Global Equity (Growth & Income)	B	B-	B	Up	Y	250
American Funds Capital World Growth & Income Fund® Cls F-3	FWGIX	NAS CM	Open End	Global Equity (Growth & Income)	B	B-	B	Up	Y	250
American Funds Capital World Growth & Income Fund® Cls R-1	RWIAX	NAS CM	Open End	Global Equity (Growth & Income)	B-	B-	B	Up	Y	250
American Funds Capital World Growth & Income Fund® Cls R-2	RWIBX	NAS CM	Open End	Global Equity (Growth & Income)	B-	B-	B	Up	Y	250
American Funds Capital World Growth & Inc Fund® Cls R-2E	RWBEX	NAS CM	Open End	Global Equity (Growth & Income)	B-	B-	B	Down	Y	250
American Funds Capital World Growth & Income Fund® Cls R-3	RWICX	NAS CM	Open End	Global Equity (Growth & Income)	B-	B-	B	Down	Y	250
American Funds Capital World Growth & Income Fund® Cls R-4	RWIEX	NAS CM	Open End	Global Equity (Growth & Income)	B-	B-	B	Down	Y	250
American Funds Capital World Growth & Income Fund® Cls R-5	RWIFX	NAS CM	Open End	Global Equity (Growth & Income)	B	B-	B	Up	Y	250
American Funds Capital World Growth & Inc Fund® Cls R-5E	RWIHX	NAS CM	Open End	Global Equity (Growth & Income)	B	B-	B	Up	Y	250
American Funds Capital World Growth & Income Fund® Cls R-6	RWIGX	NAS CM	Open End	Global Equity (Growth & Income)	B	B-	B	Up	Y	250
American Funds College 2021 Fund Class 529-A	CTOAX	NAS CM	Open End	Cautious Alloc (Growth & Income)	B-	C	A-	Up	Y	250
American Funds College 2021 Fund Class 529-C	CTOCX	NAS CM	Open End	Cautious Alloc (Growth & Income)	B-	C	A-	Up	Y	250
American Funds College 2021 Fund Class 529-E	CTOEX	NAS CM	Open End	Cautious Alloc (Growth & Income)	B-	C	A-	Up	Y	250
American Funds College 2021 Fund Class 529F1	CTOFX	NAS CM	Open End	Cautious Alloc (Growth & Income)	B	C	A	Up	Y	250
American Funds College 2024 Fund Class 529-A	CFTAX	NAS CM	Open End	Cautious Alloc (Growth & Income)	B	C+	A-	Up	Y	250
American Funds College 2024 Fund Class 529-C	CTFCX	NAS CM	Open End	Cautious Alloc (Growth & Income)	B-	C	B	Up	Y	250
American Funds College 2024 Fund Class 529-E	CTFEX	NAS CM	Open End	Cautious Alloc (Growth & Income)	B-	C	B	Up	Y	250
American Funds College 2024 Fund Class 529F1	CTFFX	NAS CM	Open End	Cautious Alloc (Growth & Income)	B-	C+	B	Up	Y	250
American Funds College 2027 Fund Class 529-A	CSTAX	NAS CM	Open End	Moderate Alloc (Growth & Income)	B	C+	A-	Up	Y	250
American Funds College 2027 Fund Class 529-C	CTSCX	NAS CM	Open End	Moderate Alloc (Growth & Income)	B-	C+	B	Up	Y	250
American Funds College 2027 Fund Class 529-E	CTSEX	NAS CM	Open End	Moderate Alloc (Growth & Income)	B	C+	B+	Up	Y	250
American Funds College 2027 Fund Class 529F1	CTSFX	NAS CM	Open End	Moderate Alloc (Growth & Income)	B	C+	A-	Up	Y	250
American Funds College 2030 Fund Class 529-A	CTHAX	NAS CM	Open End	Aggressive Alloc (Growth & Income)	B-	C+	B	Up	Y	250
American Funds College 2030 Fund Class 529-C	CTYCX	NAS CM	Open End	Aggressive Alloc (Growth & Income)	B-	C+	B	Up	Y	250
American Funds College 2030 Fund Class 529-E	CTHEX	NAS CM	Open End	Aggressive Alloc (Growth & Income)	B-	C+	B	Up	Y	250
American Funds College 2030 Fund Class 529F1	CTHFX	NAS CM	Open End	Aggressive Alloc (Growth & Income)	B-	C+	B	Up	Y	250
American Funds College 2033 Fund Class 529-A	CTLAX	NAS CM	Open End	Aggressive Alloc (Growth & Income)	B-	C+	B	Up	Y	250
American Funds College 2033 Fund Class 529-C	CTLCX	NAS CM	Open End	Aggressive Alloc (Growth & Income)	B-	C+	B	Up	Y	250
American Funds College 2033 Fund Class 529-E	CTLEX	NAS CM	Open End	Aggressive Alloc (Growth & Income)	B-	C+	B	Up	Y	250
American Funds College 2033 Fund Class 529-F-1	CTLFX	NAS CM	Open End	Aggressive Alloc (Growth & Income)	B-	C+	B	Up	Y	250
American Funds Developing World Growth & Inc Cls 529-A	CDWAX	NAS CM	Open End	Emerging Markets Equity (Div Emerging Mkts)	C+	C+	C	Up	Y	250
American Funds Developing World Growth & Inc Cls 529-C	CDWCX	NAS CM	Open End	Emerging Markets Equity (Div Emerging Mkts)	C+	C+	C	Up	Y	250
American Funds Developing World Growth & Inc Cls 529-E	CDWEX	NAS CM	Open End	Emerging Markets Equity (Div Emerging Mkts)	C+	C+	C	Up	Y	250
American Funds Developing World Growth & Inc Cls 529-F-1	CDWFX	NAS CM	Open End	Emerging Markets Equity (Div Emerging Mkts)	C+	C+	C	Up	Y	250
American Funds Developing World Growth & Income Fund Cls A	DWGAX	NAS CM	Open End	Emerging Markets Equity (Div Emerging Mkts)	C+	C+	C	Up	Y	250

★ Expanded analysis of this fund is included in Section II.

Min Additional Investment	3-Month Total Return	6-Month Total Return	1-Year Total Return	3-Year Total Return	5-Year Total Return	Dividend Yield (TTM)	Expense Ratio	3-Yr Std Deviation	3-Year Beta	NAV	Total Assets (MIL)	%Cash	%Stocks	%Bonds	%Other	Turnover Ratio	Last Bull Market Total Return	Last Bear Market Total Return	Front End Fee (%)	Back End Fee (%)	Inception Date
	TOTAL RETURNS					PERFORMANCE				ASSETS		ASSET ALLOCATION & TURNOVER					BULL & BEAR		FEES		
50	2.46	5.76	14.44	18.36	47.54	3.37	0.4	7.55	0.63	62.77	108,816	1	70	25	2	47	12.92	-9.88			Aug-08
50	2.50	5.81	14.53	18.00	46.51		0.3	7.55	0.63	62.8	108,816	1	70	25	2	47	12.77	-9.97			Jan-17
50	2.20	5.22	13.29	14.88	40.40	2.42	1.4	7.54	0.63	62.84	108,816	1	70	25	2	47	12.24	-10.27			Jun-02
50	2.22	5.23	13.31	14.95	40.53	2.43	1.4	7.54	0.63	62.84	108,816	1	70	25	2	47	12.26	-10.27			May-02
50	2.29	5.39	13.67	16.09	43.17	2.77	1.11	7.53	0.63	62.6	108,816	1	70	25	2	47	12.54	-10.1			Aug-14
50	2.33	5.47	13.82	16.45	43.56	2.86	0.96	7.54	0.63	62.82	108,816	1	70	25	2	47	12.55	-10.1			Jun-02
50	2.40	5.63	14.14	17.50	45.76	3.14	0.65	7.55	0.63	62.79	108,816	1	70	25	2	47	12.73	-9.97			May-02
50	2.49	5.78	14.49	18.56	47.97	3.42	0.37	7.55	0.63	62.83	108,816	1	70	25	2	47	12.94	-9.85			May-02
50	2.45	5.75	14.40	17.99	46.50	3.38	0.46	7.54	0.63	62.74	108,816	1	70	25	2	47	12.77	-9.97			Nov-15
50	2.48	5.81	14.56	18.72	48.33	3.47	0.3	7.55	0.63	62.8	108,816	1	70	25	2	47	12.97	-9.85			May-09
50	5.05	10.30	24.60	28.68	69.68	1.92	0.88	10.08	0.93	50.94	97,411	1	94	1	4	35	17.87	-20.79	5.75		Feb-02
50	4.82	9.85	23.64	25.71	63.18	1.25	1.64	10.07	0.93	50.76	97,411	1	94	1	4	35	17.33	-21.07		1.00	Feb-02
50	4.97	10.17	24.30	27.80	67.74	1.73	1.09	10.07	0.93	50.87	97,411	1	94	1	4	35	17.67	-20.87			Mar-02
50	5.08	10.39	24.85	29.52	71.54	2.11	0.64	10.08	0.93	50.97	97,411	1	94	1	4	35	18.02	-20.74			Sep-02
50	5.06	10.32	24.67	28.98	70.39	1.97	0.8	10.07	0.93	51.11	97,411	1	94	1	4	35	17.92	-20.77	5.75		Mar-93
50	4.84	9.88	23.69	25.92	63.70	1.27	1.59	10.06	0.93	50.56	97,411	1	94	1	4	35	17.38	-21.02		1.00	Mar-01
50	5.04	10.29	24.61	28.81	70.01	1.93	0.83	10.08	0.93	51	97,411	1	94	1	4	35	17.93	-20.76			Mar-01
50	5.10	10.43	24.92	29.85	72.36	2.17	0.55	10.07	0.93	51.05	97,411	1	94	1	4	35	18.13	-20.7			Aug-08
50	5.13	10.50	25.03	29.35	70.88		0.45	10.08	0.93	51.09	97,411	1	94	1	4	35	17.92	-20.77			Jan-17
50	4.84	9.90	23.70	26.04	63.96	1.31	1.55	10.08	0.93	50.63	97,411	1	94	1	4	35	17.39	-21.01			Jun-02
50	4.84	9.89	23.70	26.08	64.14	1.32	1.54	10.06	0.93	50.49	97,411	1	94	1	4	35	17.42	-21.03			Jun-02
50	4.92	10.07	24.09	27.25	67.08	1.62	1.23	10.09	0.93	50.93	97,411	1	94	1	4	35	17.68	-20.88			Aug-14
50	4.97	10.14	24.29	27.76	67.73	1.7	1.1	10.07	0.93	50.77	97,411	1	94	1	4	35	17.72	-20.88			Jun-02
50	5.05	10.31	24.63	28.90	70.21	1.96	0.8	10.07	0.93	50.98	97,411	1	94	1	4	35	17.94	-20.77			Jun-02
50	5.11	10.47	25.01	30.07	72.77	2.22	0.5	10.08	0.93	51.11	97,411	1	94	1	4	35	18.14	-20.67			May-02
50	5.10	10.43	24.90	29.36	70.89	2.17	0.61	10.08	0.93	51.03	97,411	1	94	1	4	35	17.92	-20.77			Nov-15
50	5.13	10.50	25.07	30.24	73.22	2.26	0.45	10.07	0.93	51.1	97,411	1	94	1	4	35	18.17	-20.65			May-09
50	0.00	1.05	3.44	7.25	27.40	1.68	0.75	2.87	0.2	11.13	1,468	9	9	79	3	5			4.25		Sep-12
50	-0.13	0.67	2.70	4.78	22.56	1.06	1.49	2.86	0.2	11.04	1,468	9	9	79	3	5				1.00	Sep-12
50	-0.11	0.86	3.16	6.44	25.85	1.49	0.96	2.81	0.2	11.09	1,468	9	9	79	3	5					Sep-12
50	0.01	1.07	3.64	7.90	28.80	1.87	0.49	2.85	0.2	11.15	1,468	9	9	79	3	5					Sep-12
50	1.54	3.69	7.90	12.67	39.82	1.62	0.77	4.24	0.36	11.92	1,338	7	34	56	3	10			4.25		Sep-12
50	1.34	3.34	7.02	10.04	34.39	1.01	1.51	4.25	0.36	11.81	1,338	7	34	56	3	10				1.00	Sep-12
50	1.42	3.58	7.61	11.78	37.91	1.43	0.98	4.24	0.36	11.88	1,338	7	34	56	3	10					Sep-12
50	1.57	3.80	8.09	13.38	41.31	1.79	0.51	4.26	0.36	11.95	1,338	7	34	56	3	10					Sep-12
50	2.37	5.40	11.77	17.23	50.24	1.43	0.83	5.63	0.5	12.65	1,076	6	47	44	3	9			4.25		Sep-12
50	2.10	4.92	10.87	14.48	44.30	0.82	1.58	5.58	0.5	12.52	1,076	6	47	44	3	9				1.00	Sep-12
50	2.30	5.19	11.48	16.41	48.33	1.24	1.04	5.59	0.5	12.58	1,076	6	47	44	3	9					Sep-12
50	2.40	5.51	12.04	18.02	51.77	1.59	0.57	5.61	0.5	12.69	1,076	6	47	44	3	9					Sep-12
50	3.29	6.81	15.27	21.40	59.85	1.38	0.85	7.03	0.64	13.61	1,242	4	58	35	3	4			4.25		Sep-12
50	3.12	6.44	14.43	18.52	53.49	0.77	1.6	7.04	0.64	13.46	1,242	4	58	35	3	4				1.00	Sep-12
50	3.18	6.63	14.94	20.36	57.50	1.19	1.06	7.06	0.64	13.54	1,242	4	58	35	3	4					Sep-12
50	3.33	7.00	15.53	22.14	61.35	1.53	0.59	7.04	0.64	13.65	1,242	4	58	35	3	4					Sep-12
50	4.15	8.50	19.33			1.16	0.87			11.7	561.7	3	72	21	3				4.25		Mar-15
50	3.91	8.00	18.29			0.68	1.62			11.62	561.7	3	72	21	3					1.00	Mar-15
50	4.02	8.28	18.90			0.99	1.09			11.66	561.7	3	72	21	3						Mar-15
50	4.24	8.58	19.50			1.24	0.62			11.73	561.7	3	72	21	3						Mar-15
50	6.45	10.33	27.60	14.69		1.86	1.41	12.87	0.78	11.25	3,107	7	89	1	1	25			5.75		Feb-14
50	6.12	9.78	26.52	11.75		1.12	2.21	12.82	0.78	11.21	3,107	7	89	1	1	25				1.00	Feb-14
50	6.39	10.21	27.34	13.97		1.67	1.56	12.83	0.78	11.25	3,107	7	89	1	1	25					Feb-14
50	6.40	10.43	27.81	15.11		2.01	1.19	12.88	0.78	11.25	3,107	7	89	1	1	25					Feb-14
50	6.44	10.31	27.69	14.65		1.91	1.33	12.84	0.78	11.26	3,107	7	89	1	1	25			5.75		Feb-14

	MARKET			FUND TYPE, CATEGORY & OBJECTIVE	RATINGS					MINIMUMS
Fund Name	Ticker Symbol	Traded On	Fund Type	Category and (Prospectus Objective)	Overall Rating	Reward Rating	Risk Rating	Recent Up/ Downgrade	Open to New Investors	Min Initial Investment
American Funds Developing World Growth & Income Fund Cls C	DWGCX	NAS CM	Open End	Emerging Markets Equity (Div Emerging Mkts)	C+	C+	C	Up	Y	250
American Funds Developing World Growth & Inc Fund Cls F-1	DWGFX	NAS CM	Open End	Emerging Markets Equity (Div Emerging Mkts)	C+	C+	C	Up	Y	250
American Funds Developing World Growth & Inc Fund Cls F-2	DWGHX	NAS CM	Open End	Emerging Markets Equity (Div Emerging Mkts)	C+	C+	C	Up	Y	250
American Funds Developing World Growth & Inc Fund Cls F-3	FDWGX	NAS CM	Open End	Emerging Markets Equity (Div Emerging Mkts)	C+	C+	C	Up	Y	250
American Funds Developing World Growth & Inc Fund Cls R-1	RDWAX	NAS CM	Open End	Emerging Markets Equity (Div Emerging Mkts)	C+	C+	C	Up	Y	250
American Funds Developing World Growth & Inc Fund Cls R-2	RDWBX	NAS CM	Open End	Emerging Markets Equity (Div Emerging Mkts)	C+	C+	C	Up	Y	250
American Funds Developing World Growth & Inc Fund Cls R-2E	RDEGX	NAS CM	Open End	Emerging Markets Equity (Div Emerging Mkts)	C+	C+	C	Up	Y	250
American Funds Developing World Growth & Inc Fund Cls R-3	RDWCX	NAS CM	Open End	Emerging Markets Equity (Div Emerging Mkts)	C+	C+	C	Up	Y	250
American Funds Developing World Growth & Inc Fund Cls R-4	RDWEX	NAS CM	Open End	Emerging Markets Equity (Div Emerging Mkts)	C+	C+	C	Up	Y	250
American Funds Developing World Growth & Inc Fund Cls R-5	RDWFX	NAS CM	Open End	Emerging Markets Equity (Div Emerging Mkts)	C+	C+	C	Up	Y	250
American Funds Developing World Growth & Inc Fund Cls R-5E	RDWHX	NAS CM	Open End	Emerging Markets Equity (Div Emerging Mkts)	C+	C+	C	Up	Y	250
American Funds Developing World Growth & Inc Fund Cls R-6	RDWGX	NAS CM	Open End	Emerging Markets Equity (Div Emerging Mkts)	C+	C+	C	Up	Y	250
★ American Funds EuroPacific Growth Fund® Class 529-A	CEUAX	NAS CM	Open End	Global Equity Large Cap (Foreign Stock)	B	B	B	Up	Y	250
★ American Funds EuroPacific Growth Fund® Class 529-C	CEUCX	NAS CM	Open End	Global Equity Large Cap (Foreign Stock)	B-	B-	B	Up	Y	250
★ American Funds EuroPacific Growth Fund® Class 529-E	CEUEX	NAS CM	Open End	Global Equity Large Cap (Foreign Stock)	B	B	B	Up	Y	250
★ American Funds EuroPacific Growth Fund® Class 529-F-1	CEUFX	NAS CM	Open End	Global Equity Large Cap (Foreign Stock)	B	B	B	Up	Y	250
★ American Funds EuroPacific Growth Fund® Class A	AEPGX	NAS CM	Open End	Global Equity Large Cap (Foreign Stock)	B	B	B	Up	Y	250
★ American Funds EuroPacific Growth Fund® Class C	AEPCX	NAS CM	Open End	Global Equity Large Cap (Foreign Stock)	B-	B-	B	Up	Y	250
★ American Funds EuroPacific Growth Fund® Class F-1	AEGFX	NAS CM	Open End	Global Equity Large Cap (Foreign Stock)	B	B	B	Up	Y	250
★ American Funds EuroPacific Growth Fund® Class F-2	AEPFX	NAS CM	Open End	Global Equity Large Cap (Foreign Stock)	B	B	B	Up	Y	250
★ American Funds EuroPacific Growth Fund® Class F-3	FEUPX	NAS CM	Open End	Global Equity Large Cap (Foreign Stock)	B	B	B	Up	Y	250
★ American Funds EuroPacific Growth Fund® Class R-1	RERAX	NAS CM	Open End	Global Equity Large Cap (Foreign Stock)	B-	B-	B	Up	Y	250
★ American Funds EuroPacific Growth Fund® Class R-2	RERBX	NAS CM	Open End	Global Equity Large Cap (Foreign Stock)	B	B-	B	Up	Y	250
★ American Funds EuroPacific Growth Fund® Class R-2E	REEBX	NAS CM	Open End	Global Equity Large Cap (Foreign Stock)	B	B-	B	Up	Y	250
★ American Funds EuroPacific Growth Fund® Class R-3	RERCX	NAS CM	Open End	Global Equity Large Cap (Foreign Stock)	B	B	B	Up	Y	250
★ American Funds EuroPacific Growth Fund® Class R-4	REREX	NAS CM	Open End	Global Equity Large Cap (Foreign Stock)	B	B	B	Up	Y	250
★ American Funds EuroPacific Growth Fund® Class R-5	RERFX	NAS CM	Open End	Global Equity Large Cap (Foreign Stock)	B	B	B	Up	Y	250
★ American Funds EuroPacific Growth Fund® Class R-5E	RERHX	NAS CM	Open End	Global Equity Large Cap (Foreign Stock)	B	B	B	Up	Y	250
★ American Funds EuroPacific Growth Fund® Class R-6	RERGX	NAS CM	Open End	Global Equity Large Cap (Foreign Stock)	B	B	B	Up	Y	250
American Funds Fundamental Investors® Class 529-A	CFNAX	NAS CM	Open End	US Equity Large Cap Blend (Growth & Income)	B	B	B+	Down	Y	250
American Funds Fundamental Investors® Class 529-C	CFNCX	NAS CM	Open End	US Equity Large Cap Blend (Growth & Income)	B	B	B		Y	250
American Funds Fundamental Investors® Class 529-E	CFNEX	NAS CM	Open End	US Equity Large Cap Blend (Growth & Income)	B	B	B+	Down	Y	250
American Funds Fundamental Investors® Class 529-F-1	CFNFX	NAS CM	Open End	US Equity Large Cap Blend (Growth & Income)	B	B	B+	Down	Y	250
American Funds Fundamental Investors® Class A	ANCFX	NAS CM	Open End	US Equity Large Cap Blend (Growth & Income)	B	B	B+	Down	Y	250
American Funds Fundamental Investors® Class C	AFICX	NAS CM	Open End	US Equity Large Cap Blend (Growth & Income)	B	B	B+		Y	250
American Funds Fundamental Investors® Class F-1	AFIFX	NAS CM	Open End	US Equity Large Cap Blend (Growth & Income)	B	B	B+	Down	Y	250
American Funds Fundamental Investors® Class F-2	FINFX	NAS CM	Open End	US Equity Large Cap Blend (Growth & Income)	B	B	B+	Down	Y	250
American Funds Fundamental Investors® Class F-3	FUNFX	NAS CM	Open End	US Equity Large Cap Blend (Growth & Income)	B	B	B+	Down	Y	250
American Funds Fundamental Investors® Class R-1	RFNAX	NAS CM	Open End	US Equity Large Cap Blend (Growth & Income)	B	B	B		Y	250
American Funds Fundamental Investors® Class R-2	RFNBX	NAS CM	Open End	US Equity Large Cap Blend (Growth & Income)	B	B	B+		Y	250
American Funds Fundamental Investors® Class R-2E	RFEBX	NAS CM	Open End	US Equity Large Cap Blend (Growth & Income)	B	B	B+		Y	250
American Funds Fundamental Investors® Class R-3	RFNCX	NAS CM	Open End	US Equity Large Cap Blend (Growth & Income)	B	B	B+	Down	Y	250
American Funds Fundamental Investors® Class R-4	RFNEX	NAS CM	Open End	US Equity Large Cap Blend (Growth & Income)	B	B	B+	Down	Y	250
American Funds Fundamental Investors® Class R-5	RFNFX	NAS CM	Open End	US Equity Large Cap Blend (Growth & Income)	B	B	B+	Down	Y	250
American Funds Fundamental Investors® Class R-5E	RFNHX	NAS CM	Open End	US Equity Large Cap Blend (Growth & Income)	B	B	B+	Down	Y	250
American Funds Fundamental Investors® Class R-6	RFNGX	NAS CM	Open End	US Equity Large Cap Blend (Growth & Income)	B	B	B+	Down	Y	250
American Funds Global Balanced Fund Class 529-A	CBFAX	NAS CM	Open End	Alloc (Balanced)	B-	C+	B	Down	Y	250
American Funds Global Balanced Fund Class 529-C	CBFCX	NAS CM	Open End	Alloc (Balanced)	B-	C+	B	Up	Y	250
American Funds Global Balanced Fund Class 529-E	CBFEX	NAS CM	Open End	Alloc (Balanced)	B-	C+	B		Y	250
American Funds Global Balanced Fund Class 529-F-1	CBFFX	NAS CM	Open End	Alloc (Balanced)	B-	C+	B	Down	Y	250
American Funds Global Balanced Fund Class A	GBLAX	NAS CM	Open End	Alloc (Balanced)	B-	C+	B	Down	Y	250
American Funds Global Balanced Fund Class C	GBLCX	NAS CM	Open End	Alloc (Balanced)	B-	C+	B	Up	Y	250

★ Expanded analysis of this fund is included in Section II.

	TOTAL RETURNS					PERFORMANCE				ASSETS		ASSET ALLOCATION & TURNOVER					BULL & BEAR		FEES		
Min Additional Investment	3-Month Total Return	6-Month Total Return	1-Year Total Return	3-Year Total Return	5-Year Total Return	Dividend Yield (TTM)	Expense Ratio	3-Yr Std Deviation	3-Year Beta	NAV	Total Assets (MIL)	%Cash	%Stocks	%Bonds	%Other	Turnover Ratio	Last Bull Market Total Return	Last Bear Market Total Return	Front End Fee (%)	Back End Fee (%)	Inception Date
50	6.16	9.83	26.57	11.98		1.14	2.14	12.83	0.78	11.22	3,107	7	89	1	1	25				1.00	Feb-14
50	6.46	10.34	27.61	14.74		1.88	1.3	12.88	0.78	11.26	3,107	7	89	1	1	25					Feb-14
50	6.42	10.48	27.92	15.65		2.11	1.04	12.87	0.78	11.26	3,107	7	89	1	1	25					Feb-14
50	6.55	10.53	28.21	16.07			0.92	12.82	0.78	11.26	3,107	7	89	1	1	25					Jan-17
50	6.18	9.86	26.61	12.26		1.18	2.06	12.84	0.78	11.23	3,107	7	89	1	1	25					Feb-14
50	6.20	9.90	26.64	11.97		1.27	2.03	12.88	0.78	11.2	3,107	7	89	1	1	25					Feb-14
50	6.23	10.10	26.96	13.90		1.54	1.74	12.85	0.78	11.23	3,107	7	89	1	1	25					Aug-14
50	6.39	10.21	27.33	13.72		1.64	1.61	12.89	0.78	11.24	3,107	7	89	1	1	25					Feb-14
50	6.46	10.35	27.66	14.87		1.9	1.29	12.82	0.78	11.25	3,107	7	89	1	1	25					Feb-14
50	6.44	10.51	28.00	15.87		2.17	0.98	12.82	0.78	11.26	3,107	7	89	1	1	25					Feb-14
50	6.43	10.42	28.05	15.63		2.15	1.08	12.82	0.78	11.24	3,107	7	89	1	1	25					Nov-15
50	6.45	10.54	28.06	16.06		2.22	0.93	12.84	0.78	11.26	3,107	7	89	1	1	25					Feb-14
50	4.13	11.17	30.65	29.64	53.59	1.16	0.91	11.13	0.86	55.57	160,340	2	91	1	4	36	16.82	-24.05	5.75		Feb-02
50	3.93	10.72	29.64	26.62	47.69	0.4	1.68	11.13	0.86	54.47	160,340	2	91	1	4	36	16.27	-24.31		1.00	Feb-02
50	4.06	11.03	30.33	28.72	51.70	0.94	1.13	11.13	0.86	55.11	160,340	2	91	1	4	36	16.64	-24.14			Mar-02
50	4.19	11.29	30.92	30.47	55.24	1.38	0.68	11.14	0.86	55.53	160,340	2	91	1	4	36	16.95	-23.96			Sep-02
50	4.15	11.19	30.72	29.85	54.01	1.18	0.85	11.14	0.86	56.22	160,340	2	91	1	4	36	16.84	-24.03	5.75		Apr-84
50	3.94	10.76	29.70	26.82	48.12	0.33	1.63	11.14	0.86	55	160,340	2	91	1	4	36	16.33	-24.28		1.00	Mar-01
50	4.13	11.16	30.68	29.74	53.80	1.15	0.87	11.14	0.86	55.96	160,340	2	91	1	4	36	16.84	-24.04			Mar-01
50	4.19	11.30	31.02	30.79	55.88	1.46	0.6	11.14	0.86	56.04	160,340	2	91	1	4	36	17.03	-23.96			Aug-08
50	4.22	11.36	31.12	30.25	54.48		0.51	11.15	0.86	56.19	160,340	2	91	1	4	36	16.84	-24.03			Jan-17
50	3.94	10.76	29.70	26.90	48.23	0.49	1.61	11.13	0.86	54.14	160,340	2	91	1	4	36	16.33	-24.28			Jun-02
50	3.95	10.75	29.72	26.99	48.41	0.45	1.6	11.13	0.86	54.61	160,340	2	91	1	4	36	16.33	-24.29			May-02
50	4.01	10.92	30.13	28.29	51.14	1.04	1.28	11.12	0.86	55.39	160,340	2	91	1	4	36	16.59	-24.14			Aug-14
50	4.07	11.02	30.31	28.71	51.74	0.89	1.14	11.13	0.86	55.09	160,340	2	91	1	4	36	16.64	-24.13			May-02
50	4.13	11.19	30.70	29.84	54.00	1.21	0.85	11.14	0.86	55.09	160,340	2	91	1	4	36	16.84	-24.05			Jun-02
50	4.22	11.34	31.08	31.02	56.33	1.5	0.54	11.13	0.86	56.09	160,340	2	91	1	4	36	17.05	-23.93			May-02
50	4.19	11.29	30.98	30.34	54.59	1.57	0.62	11.15	0.86	55.82	160,340	2	91	1	4	36	16.84	-24.03			Nov-15
50	4.22	11.37	31.17	31.19	56.68	1.55	0.5	11.15	0.86	56.14	160,340	2	91	1	4	36	17.06	-23.91			May-09
50	6.63	12.16	23.27	41.99	107.87	1.26	0.7	10.3	1	62.12	95,399	2	95	1	2	24	23.6	-19.71	5.75		Feb-02
50	6.41	11.73	22.32	38.71	99.93	0.59	1.47	10.3	1	62.08	95,399	2	95	1	2	24	23.04	-19.97		1.00	Feb-02
50	6.55	12.03	22.96	40.98	105.44	1.06	0.93	10.31	1	62.06	95,399	2	95	1	2	24	23.44	-19.79			Mar-02
50	6.69	12.29	23.52	42.91	110.16	1.46	0.48	10.32	1	62.07	95,399	2	95	1	2	24	23.75	-19.63			Sep-02
50	6.65	12.21	23.37	42.35	108.82	1.32	0.62	10.31	1	62.21	95,399	2	95	1	2	24	23.66	-19.67	5.75		Aug-78
50	6.42	11.76	22.37	38.97	100.57	0.63	1.41	10.3	1	61.88	95,399	2	95	1	2	24	23.1	-19.96		1.00	Mar-01
50	6.61	12.15	23.27	42.03	108.11	1.26	0.68	10.3	1	62.17	95,399	2	95	1	2	24	23.66	-19.69			Mar-01
50	6.69	12.30	23.57	43.16	110.90	1.48	0.41	10.3	1	62.19	95,399	2	95	1	2	24	23.81	-19.6			Aug-08
50	6.71	12.36	23.67	42.70	109.33		0.32	10.32	1	62.19	95,399	2	95	1	2	24	23.66	-19.67			Jan-17
50	6.42	11.74	22.37	38.96	100.64	0.62	1.41	10.3	1	61.88	95,399	2	95	1	2	24	23.12	-19.93			Jun-02
50	6.42	11.76	22.39	39.06	100.93	0.63	1.39	10.3	1	61.86	95,399	2	95	1	2	24	23.1	-19.93			May-02
50	6.50	11.91	22.73	40.57	105.11	0.94	1.1	10.3	1	61.92	95,399	2	95	1	2	24	23.41	-19.78			Aug-14
50	6.55	12.01	22.93	40.88	105.22	1.02	0.96	10.31	1	62.05	95,399	2	95	1	2	24	23.43	-19.77			Jun-02
50	6.61	12.15	23.29	42.11	108.30	1.28	0.66	10.32	1	62.07	95,399	2	95	1	2	24	23.66	-19.69			Jul-02
50	6.71	12.34	23.67	43.41	111.48	1.54	0.35	10.3	1	62.25	95,399	2	95	1	2	24	23.86	-19.59			May-02
50	6.67	12.29	23.54	42.70	109.33	1.5	0.57	10.32	1	62.12	95,399	2	95	1	2	24	23.66	-19.67			Nov-15
50	6.71	12.37	23.72	43.62	111.98	1.58	0.31	10.31	1	62.22	95,399	2	95	1	2	24	23.9	-19.57			May-09
50	2.54	5.69	13.95	16.32	42.60	1.66	0.95	6.9	0.59	32.49	14,669	0	58	36	6	59	13.38	-12.19	5.75		Feb-11
50	2.35	5.30	13.04	13.57	37.06	0.94	1.72	6.89	0.59	32.39	14,669	0	58	36	6	59	12.81	-12.51		1.00	Feb-11
50	2.51	5.60	13.69	15.51	40.95	1.45	1.16	6.9	0.59	32.47	14,669	0	58	36	6	59	13.17	-12.28			Feb-11
50	2.59	5.80	14.18	17.02	44.06	1.87	0.72	6.88	0.59	32.5	14,669	0	58	36	6	59	13.44	-12.1			Feb-11
50	2.58	5.74	13.98	16.53	43.07	1.71	0.88	6.91	0.59	32.51	14,669	0	58	36	6	59	13.42	-12.22	5.75		Feb-11
50	2.36	5.31	13.10	13.81	37.50	0.98	1.65	6.88	0.59	32.44	14,669	0	58	36	6	59	12.86	-12.47		1.00	Feb-11

Fund Name	MARKET Ticker Symbol	Traded On	FUND TYPE, CATEGORY & OBJECTIVE Fund Type	Category and (Prospectus Objective)	RATINGS Overall Rating	Reward Rating	Risk Rating	Recent Up/ Downgrade	MINIMUMS Open to New Investors	Min Initial Investment
American Funds Global Balanced Fund Class F-1	GBLEX	NAS CM	Open End	Alloc (Balanced)	B-	C+	B	Down	Y	250
American Funds Global Balanced Fund Class F-2	GBLFX	NAS CM	Open End	Alloc (Balanced)	B-	C+	B	Down	Y	250
American Funds Global Balanced Fund Class F-3	GFBLX	NAS CM	Open End	Alloc (Balanced)	B-	C+	B	Down	Y	250
American Funds Global Balanced Fund Class R-1	RGBLX	NAS CM	Open End	Alloc (Balanced)	B-	C+	B	Up	Y	250
American Funds Global Balanced Fund Class R-2	RGBBX	NAS CM	Open End	Alloc (Balanced)	B-	C+	B	Up	Y	250
American Funds Global Balanced Fund Class R-2E	RGGHX	NAS CM	Open End	Alloc (Balanced)	B-	C+	B	Down	Y	250
American Funds Global Balanced Fund Class R-3	RGBCX	NAS CM	Open End	Alloc (Balanced)	B-	C+	B		Y	250
American Funds Global Balanced Fund Class R-4	RGBEX	NAS CM	Open End	Alloc (Balanced)	B-	C+	B	Down	Y	250
American Funds Global Balanced Fund Class R-5	RGBFX	NAS CM	Open End	Alloc (Balanced)	B-	C+	B	Down	Y	250
American Funds Global Balanced Fund Class R-5E	RGBHX	NAS CM	Open End	Alloc (Balanced)	B-	C+	B	Down	Y	250
American Funds Global Balanced Fund Class R-6	RGBGX	NAS CM	Open End	Alloc (Balanced)	B-	C+	B	Down	Y	250
American Funds Global Growth Portfolio Class 529-A	CPGAX	NAS CM	Open End	Global Equity (Foreign Stock)	B	B	B	Up	Y	250
American Funds Global Growth Portfolio Class 529-C	CPGCX	NAS CM	Open End	Global Equity (Foreign Stock)	B	B-	B	Up	Y	250
American Funds Global Growth Portfolio Class 529-E	CGGEX	NAS CM	Open End	Global Equity (Foreign Stock)	B	B-	B	Up	Y	250
American Funds Global Growth Portfolio Class 529-F-1	CGGFX	NAS CM	Open End	Global Equity (Foreign Stock)	B	B	B	Up	Y	250
American Funds Global Growth Portfolio Class A	PGGAX	NAS CM	Open End	Global Equity (Foreign Stock)	B	B	B	Up	Y	250
American Funds Global Growth Portfolio Class C	GGPCX	NAS CM	Open End	Global Equity (Foreign Stock)	B	B-	B	Up	Y	250
American Funds Global Growth Portfolio Class F-1	PGGFX	NAS CM	Open End	Global Equity (Foreign Stock)	B	B	B	Up	Y	250
American Funds Global Growth Portfolio Class F-2	PGWFX	NAS CM	Open End	Global Equity (Foreign Stock)	B	B	B	Up	Y	250
American Funds Global Growth Portfolio Class F-3	PGXFX	NAS CM	Open End	Global Equity (Foreign Stock)	B	B	B	Up	Y	250
American Funds Global Growth Portfolio Class R-1	RGGAX	NAS CM	Open End	Global Equity (Foreign Stock)	B	B-	B	Up	Y	250
American Funds Global Growth Portfolio Class R-2	RGGBX	NAS CM	Open End	Global Equity (Foreign Stock)	B	B-	B	Up	Y	250
American Funds Global Growth Portfolio Class R-2E	REBGX	NAS CM	Open End	Global Equity (Foreign Stock)	B	B	B	Up	Y	250
American Funds Global Growth Portfolio Class R-3	RGLCX	NAS CM	Open End	Global Equity (Foreign Stock)	B	B-	B	Up	Y	250
American Funds Global Growth Portfolio Class R-4	RGGEX	NAS CM	Open End	Global Equity (Foreign Stock)	B	B	B	Up	Y	250
American Funds Global Growth Portfolio Class R-5	RGGFX	NAS CM	Open End	Global Equity (Foreign Stock)	B	B	B	Up	Y	250
American Funds Global Growth Portfolio Class R-5E	RGTFX	NAS CM	Open End	Global Equity (Foreign Stock)	B	B	B	Up	Y	250
American Funds Global Growth Portfolio Class R-6	RGGGX	NAS CM	Open End	Global Equity (Foreign Stock)	B	B	B	Up	Y	250
American Funds Growth and Income Portfolio Class 529-A	CGNAX	NAS CM	Open End	Aggressive Alloc (Growth & Income)	B-	B-	B	Down	Y	250
American Funds Growth and Income Portfolio Class 529-C	CGNCX	NAS CM	Open End	Aggressive Alloc (Growth & Income)	B	C+	B+	Up	Y	250
American Funds Growth and Income Portfolio Class 529-E	CGNEX	NAS CM	Open End	Aggressive Alloc (Growth & Income)	B-	B-	B	Down	Y	250
American Funds Growth and Income Portfolio Class 529-F-1	CGNFX	NAS CM	Open End	Aggressive Alloc (Growth & Income)	B-	B-	B	Down	Y	250
American Funds Growth and Income Portfolio Class A	GAIOX	NAS CM	Open End	Aggressive Alloc (Growth & Income)	B	B-	B+	Up	Y	250
American Funds Growth and Income Portfolio Class C	GAITX	NAS CM	Open End	Aggressive Alloc (Growth & Income)	B-	C+	B	Down	Y	250
American Funds Growth and Income Portfolio Class F-1	GAIFX	NAS CM	Open End	Aggressive Alloc (Growth & Income)	B-	B-	B	Down	Y	250
American Funds Growth and Income Portfolio Class F-2	GAIEX	NAS CM	Open End	Aggressive Alloc (Growth & Income)	B-	B-	B	Down	Y	250
American Funds Growth and Income Portfolio Class F-3	GAIHX	NAS CM	Open End	Aggressive Alloc (Growth & Income)	B-	B-	B	Down	Y	250
American Funds Growth and Income Portfolio Class R-1	RGNAX	NAS CM	Open End	Aggressive Alloc (Growth & Income)	B	C+	B+	Up	Y	250
American Funds Growth and Income Portfolio Class R-2	RGNBX	NAS CM	Open End	Aggressive Alloc (Growth & Income)	B-	C+	B	Down	Y	250
American Funds Growth and Income Portfolio Class R-2E	RBEGX	NAS CM	Open End	Aggressive Alloc (Growth & Income)	B	B-	B+	Up	Y	250
American Funds Growth and Income Portfolio Class R-3	RAICX	NAS CM	Open End	Aggressive Alloc (Growth & Income)	B-	B-	B	Down	Y	250
American Funds Growth and Income Portfolio Class R-4	RGNEX	NAS CM	Open End	Aggressive Alloc (Growth & Income)	B-	B-	B	Down	Y	250
American Funds Growth and Income Portfolio Class R-5	RGNFX	NAS CM	Open End	Aggressive Alloc (Growth & Income)	B-	B-	B	Down	Y	250
American Funds Growth and Income Portfolio Class R-5E	RGQFX	NAS CM	Open End	Aggressive Alloc (Growth & Income)	B-	B-	B	Down	Y	250
American Funds Growth and Income Portfolio Class R-6	RGNGX	NAS CM	Open End	Aggressive Alloc (Growth & Income)	B-	B-	B	Down	Y	250
American Funds Growth Portfolio Class 529-A	CGPAX	NAS CM	Open End	US Equity Large Cap Growth (Growth)	B	B	B-	Up	Y	250
American Funds Growth Portfolio Class 529-C	CGPCX	NAS CM	Open End	US Equity Large Cap Growth (Growth)	B-	B-	B-	Down	Y	250
American Funds Growth Portfolio Class 529-E	CGPEX	NAS CM	Open End	US Equity Large Cap Growth (Growth)	B	B	B-	Up	Y	250
American Funds Growth Portfolio Class 529-F-1	CGPFX	NAS CM	Open End	US Equity Large Cap Growth (Growth)	B	B	B-	Up	Y	250
American Funds Growth Portfolio Class A	GWPAX	NAS CM	Open End	US Equity Large Cap Growth (Growth)	B	B	B-	Up	Y	250
American Funds Growth Portfolio Class C	GWPCX	NAS CM	Open End	US Equity Large Cap Growth (Growth)	B-	B-	B-	Down	Y	250
American Funds Growth Portfolio Class F-1	GWPFX	NAS CM	Open End	US Equity Large Cap Growth (Growth)	B	B	B-	Up	Y	250

★ Expanded analysis of this fund is included in Section II.

	TOTAL RETURNS					PERFORMANCE				ASSETS		ASSET ALLOCATION & TURNOVER					BULL & BEAR		FEES		
Min Additional Investment	3-Month Total Return	6-Month Total Return	1-Year Total Return	3-Year Total Return	5-Year Total Return	Dividend Yield (TTM)	Expense Ratio	3-Yr Std Deviation	3-Year Beta	NAV	Total Assets (MIL)	%Cash	%Stocks	%Bonds	%Other	Turnover Ratio	Last Bull Market Total Return	Last Bear Market Total Return	Front End Fee (%)	Back End Fee (%)	Inception Date
50	2.57	5.74	13.95	16.39	42.77	1.65	0.91	6.9	0.59	32.53	14,669	0	58	36	6	59	13.42	-12.2			Feb-11
50	2.63	5.89	14.26	17.30	44.64	1.91	0.65	6.91	0.59	32.53	14,669	0	58	36	6	59	13.53	-12.1			Feb-11
50	2.63	5.91	14.36	17.65	45.38		0.54	6.9	0.59	32.5	14,669	0	58	36	6	59	13.62	-12.07			Jan-17
50	2.36	5.30	13.08	14.00	38.52	0.95	1.64	6.89	0.59	32.47	14,669	0	58	36	6	59	12.9	-12.44			Feb-11
50	2.36	5.33	13.14	13.90	37.66	1	1.64	6.9	0.59	32.41	14,669	0	58	36	6	59	12.99	-12.43			Feb-11
50	2.46	5.49	13.46	15.46	41.16	1.33	1.4	6.87	0.59	32.48	14,669	0	58	36	6	59	13.22	-12.29			Aug-14
50	2.47	5.55	13.61	15.43	40.80	1.42	1.2	6.9	0.59	32.46	14,669	0	58	36	6	59	13.24	-12.3			Feb-11
50	2.58	5.73	13.97	16.45	42.98	1.7	0.9	6.9	0.59	32.51	14,669	0	58	36	6	59	13.44	-12.17			Feb-11
50	2.65	5.88	14.32	17.48	45.03	1.97	0.6	6.9	0.59	32.55	14,669	0	58	36	6	59	13.6	-12.08			Feb-11
50	2.64	5.90	14.35	17.34	45.00	1.94	0.7	6.88	0.59	32.5	14,669	0	58	36	6	59	13.62	-12.07			Nov-15
50	2.66	5.91	14.38	17.67	45.40	2.01	0.54	6.9	0.59	32.53	14,669	0	58	36	6	59	13.62	-12.07			Feb-11
50	5.21	11.14	28.53	33.00	73.93	0.78	0.94	10.42	0.95	16.7	2,670	2	93	1	4	2			5.75		May-12
50	5.03	10.69	27.53	29.80	67.03	0.03	1.7	10.45	0.95	16.52	2,670	2	93	1	4	2				1.00	May-12
50	5.14	10.97	28.24	31.90	71.58	0.58	1.16	10.46	0.95	16.63	2,670	2	93	1	4	2					May-12
50	5.31	11.29	28.84	33.77	75.62	0.92	0.7	10.46	0.95	16.75	2,670	2	93	1	4	2					May-12
50	5.22	11.14	28.61	33.20	74.43	0.81	0.88	10.43	0.95	16.72	2,670	2	93	1	4	2			5.75		May-12
50	4.98	10.72	27.66	30.13	67.74	0.22	1.62	10.47	0.95	16.51	2,670	2	93	1	4	2				1.00	May-12
50	5.21	11.13	28.56	33.04	73.91	0.75	0.89	10.43	0.95	16.74	2,670	2	93	1	4	2					May-12
50	5.29	11.26	28.95	34.08	76.30	0.98	0.62	10.45	0.95	16.77	2,670	2	93	1	4	2					May-12
50	5.32	11.37	29.00	34.33	76.76		0.52	10.46	0.96	16.73	2,670	2	93	1	4	2					Jan-17
50	5.02	10.73	27.66	30.11	67.62	0	1.63	10.46	0.95	16.58	2,670	2	93	1	4	2					May-12
50	5.07	10.76	27.66	30.12	67.60	0.29	1.64	10.47	0.96	16.47	2,670	2	93	1	4	2					May-12
50	5.10	10.86	28.02	32.57	72.60	0.93	1.35	10.44	0.95	16.63	2,670	2	93	1	4	2					Aug-14
50	5.17	11.00	28.19	31.88	71.41	0.58	1.19	10.44	0.95	16.63	2,670	2	93	1	4	2					May-12
50	5.20	11.14	28.62	33.07	74.15	0.82	0.88	10.47	0.96	16.7	2,670	2	93	1	4	2					May-12
50	5.30	11.25	28.93	34.27	76.67	1	0.58	10.46	0.96	16.84	2,670	2	93	1	4	2					May-12
50	5.30	11.30	28.99	34.05	76.39	0.87	0.68	10.46	0.95	16.69	2,670	2	93	1	4	2					Nov-15
50	5.27	11.34	29.02	34.45	77.07	1.03	0.52	10.43	0.95	16.87	2,670	2	93	1	4	2					May-12
50	4.57	8.69	18.98	26.31	65.79	1.66	0.82	7.99	0.73	15.13	7,736	2	77	17	3	0			5.75		May-12
50	4.41	8.33	18.05	23.35	59.36	0.97	1.57	7.98	0.73	15.07	7,736	2	77	17	3	0				1.00	May-12
50	4.57	8.63	18.73	25.37	63.63	1.44	1.03	8	0.73	15.11	7,736	2	77	17	3	0					May-12
50	4.70	8.87	19.29	27.07	67.50	1.84	0.57	8.01	0.73	15.15	7,736	2	77	17	3	0					May-12
50	4.65	8.78	19.12	26.57	66.49	1.71	0.75	8	0.73	15.14	7,736	2	77	17	3	0			5.75		May-12
50	4.44	8.39	18.17	23.73	59.98	1.04	1.49	7.98	0.73	15.06	7,736	2	77	17	3	0				1.00	May-12
50	4.64	8.76	19.07	26.39	65.94	1.66	0.76	7.98	0.73	15.14	7,736	2	77	17	3	0					May-12
50	4.71	8.90	19.34	27.39	68.17	1.89	0.5	7.96	0.73	15.16	7,736	2	77	17	3	0					May-12
50	4.74	8.97	19.48	27.67	68.65		0.39	8	0.73	15.14	7,736	2	77	17	3	0					Jan-17
50	4.44	8.36	18.21	23.66	59.98	1.01	1.5	8	0.73	15.09	7,736	2	77	17	3	0					May-12
50	4.38	8.34	18.13	23.60	59.73	1.06	1.51	7.99	0.73	15.04	7,736	2	77	17	3	0					May-12
50	4.53	8.52	18.49	25.48	64.01	1.34	1.19	7.98	0.73	15.11	7,736	2	77	17	3	0					Aug-14
50	4.50	8.56	18.65	25.27	63.42	1.43	1.06	7.99	0.73	15.09	7,736	2	77	17	3	0					May-12
50	4.57	8.70	19.02	26.40	66.14	1.69	0.75	7.99	0.73	15.13	7,736	2	77	17	3	0					May-12
50	4.71	8.99	19.46	27.64	68.62	1.94	0.45	8	0.73	15.19	7,736	2	77	17	3	0					May-12
50	4.72	8.94	19.44	27.35	68.23	1.91	0.55	8	0.73	15.13	7,736	2	77	17	3	0					Nov-15
50	4.67	8.95	19.46	27.77	68.93	1.98	0.39	8.02	0.74	15.16	7,736	2	77	17	3	0					May-12
50	5.94	11.58	25.03	35.39	89.49	0.76	0.88	9.93	0.92	18.06	5,887	3	91	2	4	0			5.75		May-12
50	5.69	11.14	24.03	32.15	81.89	0.23	1.65	9.96	0.92	17.81	5,887	3	91	2	4	0				1.00	May-12
50	5.87	11.48	24.77	34.37	86.80	0.56	1.1	9.98	0.93	17.96	5,887	3	91	2	4	0					May-12
50	5.99	11.67	25.33	36.17	91.16	0.89	0.64	9.97	0.93	18.11	5,887	3	91	2	4	0					May-12
50	5.96	11.59	25.11	35.70	90.09	0.8	0.81	9.94	0.92	18.08	5,887	3	91	2	4	0			5.75		May-12
50	5.75	11.21	24.17	32.49	82.70	0.22	1.56	9.98	0.93	17.83	5,887	3	91	2	4	0				1.00	May-12
50	5.92	11.62	25.08	35.37	89.47	0.74	0.83	9.95	0.92	18.07	5,887	3	91	2	4	0					May-12

	MARKET			FUND TYPE, CATEGORY & OBJECTIVE	RATINGS					MINIMUMS
Fund Name	Ticker Symbol	Traded On	Fund Type	Category and (Prospectus Objective)	Overall Rating	Reward Rating	Risk Rating	Recent Up/ Downgrade	Open to New Investors	Min Initial Investment
American Funds Growth Portfolio Class F-2	GWPEX	NAS CM	Open End	US Equity Large Cap Growth (Growth)	B	B	B-	Up	Y	250
American Funds Growth Portfolio Class F-3	GWPDX	NAS CM	Open End	US Equity Large Cap Growth (Growth)	B	B	B-	Up	Y	250
American Funds Growth Portfolio Class R-1	RGWAX	NAS CM	Open End	US Equity Large Cap Growth (Growth)	B-	B-	B-	Down	Y	250
American Funds Growth Portfolio Class R-2	RGWBX	NAS CM	Open End	US Equity Large Cap Growth (Growth)	B-	B-	B-	Down	Y	250
American Funds Growth Portfolio Class R-2E	RBGEX	NAS CM	Open End	US Equity Large Cap Growth (Growth)	B	B	B-	Up	Y	250
American Funds Growth Portfolio Class R-3	RGPCX	NAS CM	Open End	US Equity Large Cap Growth (Growth)	B	B	B-	Up	Y	250
American Funds Growth Portfolio Class R-4	RGWEX	NAS CM	Open End	US Equity Large Cap Growth (Growth)	B	B	B-	Up	Y	250
American Funds Growth Portfolio Class R-5	RGWFX	NAS CM	Open End	US Equity Large Cap Growth (Growth)	B	B	B-	Up	Y	250
American Funds Growth Portfolio Class R-5E	RGSFX	NAS CM	Open End	US Equity Large Cap Growth (Growth)	B	B	B-	Up	Y	250
American Funds Growth Portfolio Class R-6	RGWGX	NAS CM	Open End	US Equity Large Cap Growth (Growth)	B	B	B-	Up	Y	250
American Funds Income Portfolio Class 529-A	CIPAX	NAS CM	Open End	Moderate Alloc (Income)	B-	C+	B	Up	Y	250
American Funds Income Portfolio Class 529-C	CIPCX	NAS CM	Open End	Moderate Alloc (Income)	B-	C+	B	Up	Y	250
American Funds Income Portfolio Class 529-E	CIPEX	NAS CM	Open End	Moderate Alloc (Income)	B-	C+	B	Up	Y	250
American Funds Income Portfolio Class 529-F-1	CIPFX	NAS CM	Open End	Moderate Alloc (Income)	B-	C+	B	Up	Y	250
American Funds Income Portfolio Class A	INPAX	NAS CM	Open End	Moderate Alloc (Income)	B-	C+	B	Up	Y	250
American Funds Income Portfolio Class C	INPCX	NAS CM	Open End	Moderate Alloc (Income)	B-	C+	B	Up	Y	250
American Funds Income Portfolio Class F-1	INPFX	NAS CM	Open End	Moderate Alloc (Income)	B-	C+	B	Up	Y	250
American Funds Income Portfolio Class F-2	INPEX	NAS CM	Open End	Moderate Alloc (Income)	B-	C+	B	Up	Y	250
American Funds Income Portfolio Class F-3	INPDX	NAS CM	Open End	Moderate Alloc (Income)	B-	C+	B	Up	Y	250
American Funds Income Portfolio Class R-1	RNCAX	NAS CM	Open End	Moderate Alloc (Income)	B-	C+	B	Up	Y	250
American Funds Income Portfolio Class R-2	RINBX	NAS CM	Open End	Moderate Alloc (Income)	B-	C+	B	Up	Y	250
American Funds Income Portfolio Class R-2E	RNBEX	NAS CM	Open End	Moderate Alloc (Income)	B-	C+	B	Up	Y	250
American Funds Income Portfolio Class R-3	RNCCX	NAS CM	Open End	Moderate Alloc (Income)	B-	C+	B	Up	Y	250
American Funds Income Portfolio Class R-4	RINEX	NAS CM	Open End	Moderate Alloc (Income)	B-	C+	B	Up	Y	250
American Funds Income Portfolio Class R-5	RINFX	NAS CM	Open End	Moderate Alloc (Income)	B-	C+	B	Up	Y	250
American Funds Income Portfolio Class R-5E	RGOFX	NAS CM	Open End	Moderate Alloc (Income)	B-	C+	B	Up	Y	250
American Funds Income Portfolio Class R-6	RINGX	NAS CM	Open End	Moderate Alloc (Income)	B-	C+	B	Up	Y	250
American Funds Intl Growth & Income Fund Cls 529-A	CGIAX	NAS CM	Open End	Global Equity Large Cap (Foreign Stock)	C+	C+	C+	Up	Y	250
American Funds Intl Growth & Income Fund Cls 529-C	CIICX	NAS CM	Open End	Global Equity Large Cap (Foreign Stock)	C+	C+	C+	Up	Y	250
American Funds Intl Growth & Income Fund Cls 529-E	CGIEX	NAS CM	Open End	Global Equity Large Cap (Foreign Stock)	C+	C+	C+	Up	Y	250
American Funds Intl Growth & Income Fund Cls 529-F-1	CGIFX	NAS CM	Open End	Global Equity Large Cap (Foreign Stock)	C+	C+	C+	Up	Y	250
American Funds International Growth & Income Fund Cls A	IGAAX	NAS CM	Open End	Global Equity Large Cap (Foreign Stock)	C+	C+	C+	Up	Y	250
American Funds International Growth & Income Fund Cls C	IGICX	NAS CM	Open End	Global Equity Large Cap (Foreign Stock)	C+	C+	C+	Up	Y	250
American Funds International Growth & Income Fund Cls F-1	IGIFX	NAS CM	Open End	Global Equity Large Cap (Foreign Stock)	C+	C+	C+	Up	Y	250
American Funds International Growth & Income Fund Cls F-2	IGFFX	NAS CM	Open End	Global Equity Large Cap (Foreign Stock)	C+	C+	C+	Up	Y	250
American Funds International Growth & Income Fund Cls F-3	IGAIX	NAS CM	Open End	Global Equity Large Cap (Foreign Stock)	C+	C+	C+	Up	Y	250
American Funds International Growth & Income Fund Cls R-1	RIGAX	NAS CM	Open End	Global Equity Large Cap (Foreign Stock)	C+	C+	C+	Up	Y	250
American Funds International Growth & Income Fund Cls R-2	RIGBX	NAS CM	Open End	Global Equity Large Cap (Foreign Stock)	C+	C+	C+	Up	Y	250
American Funds International Growth & Income Fund Cls R-2E	RIIEX	NAS CM	Open End	Global Equity Large Cap (Foreign Stock)	C+	C+	C+	Up	Y	250
American Funds International Growth & Income Fund Cls R-3	RGICX	NAS CM	Open End	Global Equity Large Cap (Foreign Stock)	C+	C+	C+	Up	Y	250
American Funds International Growth & Income Fund Cls R-4	RIGEX	NAS CM	Open End	Global Equity Large Cap (Foreign Stock)	C+	C+	C+	Up	Y	250
American Funds International Growth & Income Fund Cls R-5	RIGFX	NAS CM	Open End	Global Equity Large Cap (Foreign Stock)	C+	C+	C+	Up	Y	250
American Funds International Growth & Income Fund Cls R-5E	RIGIX	NAS CM	Open End	Global Equity Large Cap (Foreign Stock)	C+	C+	C+	Up	Y	250
American Funds International Growth & Income Fund Cls R-6	RIGGX	NAS CM	Open End	Global Equity Large Cap (Foreign Stock)	C+	C+	C+	Up	Y	250
American Funds Investment Company of America® Class 529-A	CICAX	NAS CM	Open End	US Equity Large Cap Blend (Equity-Income)	B-	B-	B-	Down	Y	250
American Funds Investment Company of America® Class 529-C	CICCX	NAS CM	Open End	US Equity Large Cap Blend (Equity-Income)	B-	B-	B-	Down	Y	250
American Funds Investment Company of America® class 529-E	CICEX	NAS CM	Open End	US Equity Large Cap Blend (Equity-Income)	B-	B-	B-	Down	Y	250
American Funds Investment Company of America® class 529-F	CICFX	NAS CM	Open End	US Equity Large Cap Blend (Equity-Income)	B-	B-	B-	Down	Y	250
American Funds Investment Company of America® Class A	AIVSX	NAS CM	Open End	US Equity Large Cap Blend (Equity-Income)	B-	B-	B-	Down	Y	250
American Funds Investment Company of America® Class C	AICCX	NAS CM	Open End	US Equity Large Cap Blend (Equity-Income)	B-	B-	B-	Down	Y	250
American Funds Investment Company of America® Class F-1	AICFX	NAS CM	Open End	US Equity Large Cap Blend (Equity-Income)	B-	B-	B-	Down	Y	250
American Funds Investment Company of America® Class F-2	ICAFX	NAS CM	Open End	US Equity Large Cap Blend (Equity-Income)	B-	B-	B-	Down	Y	250

★ Expanded analysis of this fund is included in Section II.

	TOTAL RETURNS					PERFORMANCE				ASSETS		ASSET ALLOCATION & TURNOVER					BULL & BEAR		FEES		
Min Additional Investment	3-Month Total Return	6-Month Total Return	1-Year Total Return	3-Year Total Return	5-Year Total Return	Dividend Yield (TTM)	Expense Ratio	3-Yr Std Deviation	3-Year Beta	NAV	Total Assets (MIL)	%Cash	%Stocks	%Bonds	%Other	Turnover Ratio	Last Bull Market Total Return	Last Bear Market Total Return	Front End Fee (%)	Back End Fee (%)	Inception Date
50	5.97	11.70	25.35	36.41	91.87	0.94	0.57	9.96	0.92	18.13	5,887	3	91	2	4	0					May-12
50	6.07	11.82	25.58	36.84	92.57		0.46	9.98	0.93	18.09	5,887	3	91	2	4	0					Jan-17
50	5.75	11.18	24.16	32.47	82.56	0.14	1.57	9.95	0.92	17.91	5,887	3	91	2	4	0					May-12
50	5.74	11.20	24.16	32.43	82.40	0.27	1.58	9.96	0.92	17.82	5,887	3	91	2	4	0					May-12
50	5.78	11.34	24.49	34.20	86.82	0.66	1.25	9.93	0.92	17.9	5,887	3	91	2	4	0					Aug-14
50	5.84	11.44	24.70	34.24	86.59	0.59	1.13	9.97	0.93	17.98	5,887	3	91	2	4	0					May-12
50	5.95	11.59	25.06	35.55	89.73	0.77	0.82	9.97	0.93	18.05	5,887	3	91	2	4	0					May-12
50	5.98	11.76	25.45	36.70	92.37	0.98	0.52	9.98	0.93	18.2	5,887	3	91	2	4	0					May-12
50	6.00	11.76	25.49	36.49	92.08	0.84	0.63	9.96	0.92	18.04	5,887	3	91	2	4	0					Nov-15
50	5.98	11.77	25.49	36.86	92.89	1.01	0.47	9.98	0.93	18.16	5,887	3	91	2	4	0					May-12
50	2.36	5.51	11.42	18.59	43.36	2.81	0.76	5.66	0.49	12.7	4,631	3	54	39	3	8			5.75		May-12
50	2.18	5.05	10.58	15.97	37.98	2.13	1.5	5.7	0.5	12.66	4,631	3	54	39	3	8				1.00	May-12
50	2.36	5.37	11.15	17.89	41.72	2.61	0.96	5.64	0.49	12.7	4,631	3	54	39	3	8					May-12
50	2.42	5.63	11.65	19.51	44.93	3.03	0.5	5.69	0.5	12.71	4,631	3	54	39	3	8					May-12
50	2.45	5.54	11.56	18.96	43.89	2.87	0.7	5.71	0.5	12.71	4,631	3	54	39	3	8			5.75		May-12
50	2.24	5.13	10.70	16.22	38.48	2.18	1.42	5.66	0.5	12.65	4,631	3	54	39	3	8				1.00	May-12
50	2.36	5.51	11.42	18.81	43.58	2.83	0.69	5.69	0.5	12.71	4,631	3	54	39	3	8					May-12
50	2.43	5.65	11.70	19.72	45.54	3.08	0.43	5.64	0.49	12.72	4,631	3	54	39	3	8					May-12
50	2.47	5.72	11.93	19.97	46.04		0.32	5.69	0.5	12.7	4,631	3	54	39	3	8					Jan-17
50	2.22	5.19	10.73	16.25	38.50	2.16	1.43	5.67	0.5	12.67	4,631	3	54	39	3	8					May-12
50	2.24	5.13	10.70	16.21	38.34	2.2	1.45	5.68	0.5	12.66	4,631	3	54	39	3	8					May-12
50	2.24	5.26	10.93	18.38	42.59	2.46	1.13	5.67	0.5	12.7	4,631	3	54	39	3	8					Aug-14
50	2.36	5.37	11.16	17.81	41.57	2.61	0.99	5.68	0.5	12.69	4,631	3	54	39	3	8					May-12
50	2.45	5.52	11.46	18.92	43.85	2.87	0.68	5.68	0.5	12.71	4,631	3	54	39	3	8					May-12
50	2.45	5.68	11.85	19.88	45.93	3.13	0.38	5.68	0.5	12.73	4,631	3	54	39	3	8					May-12
50	2.52	5.65	11.80	19.74	45.76	3.07	0.48	5.67	0.5	12.7	4,631	3	54	39	3	8					Nov-15
50	2.46	5.71	11.82	20.07	46.20	3.18	0.33	5.68	0.5	12.72	4,631	3	54	39	3	8					May-12
50	3.87	9.96	26.00	17.27	35.81	1.88	1.01	10.53	0.83	34.94	13,868	1	91	1	6	37	12.97	-20.1	5.75		Oct-08
50	3.66	9.53	24.99	14.46	30.44	1.2	1.77	10.53	0.83	34.76	13,868	1	91	1	6	37	12.45	-20.37		1.00	Oct-08
50	3.82	9.85	25.71	16.47	34.19	1.7	1.19	10.53	0.83	34.93	13,868	1	91	1	6	37	12.82	-20.2			Oct-08
50	3.92	10.07	26.27	17.97	37.16	2.07	0.77	10.54	0.84	34.98	13,868	1	91	1	6	37	13.1	-20.03			Oct-08
50	3.88	9.97	26.07	17.47	36.26	1.93	0.93	10.54	0.83	34.98	13,868	1	91	1	6	37	13.02	-20.09	5.75		Oct-08
50	3.69	9.57	25.08	14.71	30.94	1.22	1.72	10.54	0.83	34.89	13,868	1	91	1	6	37	12.49	-20.37		1.00	Oct-08
50	3.86	9.97	26.03	17.31	35.94	1.87	0.97	10.55	0.84	35.01	13,868	1	91	1	6	37	13.02	-20.1			Oct-08
50	3.93	10.09	26.32	18.23	37.71	2.11	0.7	10.53	0.83	34.99	13,868	1	91	1	6	37	13.15	-20.01			Oct-08
50	3.97	10.19	26.46	18.37	37.87		0.58	10.54	0.83	34.97	13,868	1	91	1	6	37	13.15	-20.01			Jan-17
50	3.69	9.59	25.11	15.00	32.19	1.26	1.66	10.52	0.83	34.89	13,868	1	91	1	6	37	12.66	-20.25			Oct-08
50	3.70	9.59	25.15	14.66	30.79	1.28	1.68	10.54	0.83	34.8	13,868	1	91	1	6	37	12.46	-20.34			Oct-08
50	3.76	9.72	25.46	12.22	34.03	1.58	1.4	10.52	0.83	34.84	13,868	1	91	1	6	37	12.76	-20.21			Aug-14
50	3.80	9.82	25.66	16.32	33.96	1.66	1.25	10.53	0.83	34.91	13,868	1	91	1	6	37	12.76	-20.18			Oct-08
50	3.91	10.01	26.08	17.45	36.13	1.93	0.94	10.55	0.84	34.96	13,868	1	91	1	6	37	13.03	-20.08			Oct-08
50	3.96	10.14	26.44	18.49	38.19	2.18	0.63	10.54	0.83	35.16	13,868	1	91	1	6	37	13.2	-20			Oct-08
50	3.93	10.07	26.29	18.06	37.51	2.09	0.74	10.54	0.83	34.95	13,868	1	91	1	6	37	13.15	-20.01			Nov-15
50	3.97	10.19	26.50	18.66	38.52	2.23	0.58	10.54	0.83	34.98	13,868	1	91	1	6	37	13.2	-19.97			May-09
50	6.14	10.60	19.62	33.59	102.57	1.54	0.69	10.08	0.96	40.29	93,046	2	92	1	4	25	22.41	-17.26	5.75		Feb-02
50	5.94	10.17	18.70	30.55	94.94	0.87	1.45	10.07	0.96	40.19	93,046	2	92	1	4	25	21.82	-17.54		1.00	Feb-02
50	6.06	10.44	19.33	32.61	100.11	1.34	0.92	10.07	0.96	40.16	93,046	2	92	1	4	25	22.23	-17.38			Mar-02
50	6.20	10.71	19.87	34.46	104.79	1.74	0.46	10.07	0.96	40.24	93,046	2	92	1	4	25	22.56	-17.21			Sep-02
50	6.17	10.65	19.72	33.99	103.62	1.61	0.6	10.08	0.96	40.39	93,046	2	92	1	4	25	22.48	-17.24	5.75		Jan-34
50	5.97	10.20	18.77	30.81	95.58	0.92	1.39	10.06	0.96	39.98	93,046	2	92	1	4	25	21.89	-17.51		1.00	Mar-01
50	6.13	10.59	19.59	33.60	102.67	1.53	0.69	10.07	0.96	40.29	93,046	2	92	1	4	25	22.41	-17.24			Mar-01
50	6.22	10.75	19.93	34.69	105.45	1.76	0.41	10.08	0.96	40.37	93,046	2	92	1	4	25	22.62	-17.15			Aug-08

	MARKET		FUND TYPE, CATEGORY & OBJECTIVE		RATINGS				MINIMUMS	
Fund Name	Ticker Symbol	Traded On	Fund Type	Category and (Prospectus Objective)	Overall Rating	Reward Rating	Risk Rating	Recent Up/ Downgrade	Open to New Investors	Min Initial Investment
American Funds Investment Company of America® Class F-3	FFICX	NAS CM	Open End	US Equity Large Cap Blend (Equity-Income)	B-	B-	B-	Down	Y	250
American Funds Investment Company of America® Class R-1	RICAX	NAS CM	Open End	US Equity Large Cap Blend (Equity-Income)	B-	B-	B-	Down	Y	250
American Funds Investment Company of America® Class R-2	RICBX	NAS CM	Open End	US Equity Large Cap Blend (Equity-Income)	B-	B-	B-	Down	Y	250
American Funds Investment Company of America® Class R-2E	RIBEX	NAS CM	Open End	US Equity Large Cap Blend (Equity-Income)	B-	B-	B-	Down	Y	250
American Funds Investment Company of America® Class R-3	RICCX	NAS CM	Open End	US Equity Large Cap Blend (Equity-Income)	B-	B-	B-	Down	Y	250
American Funds Investment Company of America® Class R-4	RICEX	NAS CM	Open End	US Equity Large Cap Blend (Equity-Income)	B-	B-	B-	Down	Y	250
American Funds Investment Company of America® Class R-5	RICFX	NAS CM	Open End	US Equity Large Cap Blend (Equity-Income)	B-	B-	B-	Down	Y	250
American Funds Investment Company of America® Class R-5E	RICHX	NAS CM	Open End	US Equity Large Cap Blend (Equity-Income)	B-	B-	B-	Down	Y	250
American Funds Investment Company of America® Class R-6	RICGX	NAS CM	Open End	US Equity Large Cap Blend (Equity-Income)	B-	B-	B-	Down	Y	250
American Funds New Perspective Fund® Class 529-A	CNPAX	NAS CM	Open End	Global Equity (World Stock)	B+	B	A-	Up	Y	250
American Funds New Perspective Fund® Class 529-C	CNPCX	NAS CM	Open End	Global Equity (World Stock)	B	B	A-	Up	Y	250
American Funds New Perspective Fund® Class 529-E	CNPEX	NAS CM	Open End	Global Equity (World Stock)	B	B	A-	Up	Y	250
American Funds New Perspective Fund® Class 529-F	CNPFX	NAS CM	Open End	Global Equity (World Stock)	B+	B	A-	Up	Y	250
American Funds New Perspective Fund® Class A	ANWPX	NAS CM	Open End	Global Equity (World Stock)	B+	B	A-	Up	Y	250
American Funds New Perspective Fund® Class C	NPFCX	NAS CM	Open End	Global Equity (World Stock)	B	B	A-	Up	Y	250
American Funds New Perspective Fund® Class F-1	NPFFX	NAS CM	Open End	Global Equity (World Stock)	B+	B	A-	Up	Y	250
American Funds New Perspective Fund® Class F-2	ANWFX	NAS CM	Open End	Global Equity (World Stock)	B+	B	A-	Up	Y	250
American Funds New Perspective Fund® Class F-3	FNPFX	NAS CM	Open End	Global Equity (World Stock)	B+	B	A-	Up	Y	250
American Funds New Perspective Fund® Class R-1	RNPAX	NAS CM	Open End	Global Equity (World Stock)	B	B	A-	Up	Y	250
American Funds New Perspective Fund® Class R-2	RNPBX	NAS CM	Open End	Global Equity (World Stock)	B	B	A-	Up	Y	250
American Funds New Perspective Fund® Class R-2E	RPEBX	NAS CM	Open End	Global Equity (World Stock)	B	B	A-	Up	Y	250
American Funds New Perspective Fund® Class R-3	RNPCX	NAS CM	Open End	Global Equity (World Stock)	B	B	A-	Up	Y	250
American Funds New Perspective Fund® Class R-4	RNPEX	NAS CM	Open End	Global Equity (World Stock)	B+	B	A-	Up	Y	250
American Funds New Perspective Fund® Class R-5	RNPFX	NAS CM	Open End	Global Equity (World Stock)	B+	B	A-	Up	Y	250
American Funds New Perspective Fund® Class R-5E	RNPHX	NAS CM	Open End	Global Equity (World Stock)	B+	B	A-	Up	Y	250
American Funds New Perspective Fund® Class R-6	RNPGX	NAS CM	Open End	Global Equity (World Stock)	B+	B	A-	Up	Y	250
American Funds New World Fund® Class 529-A	CNWAX	NAS CM	Open End	Emerging Markets Equity (Div Emerging Mkts)	B-	B-	C+	Up	Y	250
American Funds New World Fund® Class 529-C	CNWCX	NAS CM	Open End	Emerging Markets Equity (Div Emerging Mkts)	C+	B-	C+	Up	Y	250
American Funds New World Fund® Class 529-E	CNWEX	NAS CM	Open End	Emerging Markets Equity (Div Emerging Mkts)	B-	B-	C+	Up	Y	250
American Funds New World Fund® Class 529-F	CNWFX	NAS CM	Open End	Emerging Markets Equity (Div Emerging Mkts)	B-	B-	C+	Up	Y	250
American Funds New World Fund® Class A	NEWFX	NAS CM	Open End	Emerging Markets Equity (Div Emerging Mkts)	B-	B-	C+	Up	Y	250
American Funds New World Fund® Class C	NEWCX	NAS CM	Open End	Emerging Markets Equity (Div Emerging Mkts)	C+	B-	C+	Up	Y	250
American Funds New World Fund® Class F-1	NWFFX	NAS CM	Open End	Emerging Markets Equity (Div Emerging Mkts)	B-	B-	C+	Up	Y	250
American Funds New World Fund® Class F-2	NFFFX	NAS CM	Open End	Emerging Markets Equity (Div Emerging Mkts)	B-	B-	C+	Up	Y	250
American Funds New World Fund® Class F-3	FNWFX	NAS CM	Open End	Emerging Markets Equity (Div Emerging Mkts)	B-	B-	C+	Up	Y	250
American Funds New World Fund® Class R-1	RNWAX	NAS CM	Open End	Emerging Markets Equity (Div Emerging Mkts)	C+	B-	C+	Up	Y	250
American Funds New World Fund® Class R-2	RNWBX	NAS CM	Open End	Emerging Markets Equity (Div Emerging Mkts)	C+	B-	C+	Up	Y	250
American Funds New World Fund® Class R-2E	RNEBX	NAS CM	Open End	Emerging Markets Equity (Div Emerging Mkts)	B-	B-	C+	Up	Y	250
American Funds New World Fund® Class R-3	RNWCX	NAS CM	Open End	Emerging Markets Equity (Div Emerging Mkts)	B-	B-	C+	Up	Y	250
American Funds New World Fund® Class R-4	RNWEX	NAS CM	Open End	Emerging Markets Equity (Div Emerging Mkts)	B-	B-	C+	Up	Y	250
American Funds New World Fund® Class R-5	RNWFX	NAS CM	Open End	Emerging Markets Equity (Div Emerging Mkts)	B-	B-	C+	Up	Y	250
American Funds New World Fund® Class R-5E	RNWHX	NAS CM	Open End	Emerging Markets Equity (Div Emerging Mkts)	B-	B-	C+	Up	Y	250
American Funds New World Fund® Class R-6	RNWGX	NAS CM	Open End	Emerging Markets Equity (Div Emerging Mkts)	B-	B-	C+	Up	Y	250
American Funds Retmnt Income Port - Conservative Cls A	NAARX	NAS CM	Open End	Cautious Alloc (Income)	C	C	A-	Up	Y	250
American Funds Retmnt Income Port - Conservative Cls C	NGCRX	NAS CM	Open End	Cautious Alloc (Income)	C	C	A-	Up	Y	250
American Funds Retmnt Income Port - Conservative Cls F-1	FAFWX	NAS CM	Open End	Cautious Alloc (Income)	C	C	B+	Up	Y	250
American Funds Retmnt Income Port - Conservative Cls F-2	FDFWX	NAS CM	Open End	Cautious Alloc (Income)	C	C	B+	Up	Y	250
American Funds Retmnt Income Port - Conservative Cls F-3	FICWX	NAS CM	Open End	Cautious Alloc (Income)	C	C	B+	Up	Y	250
American Funds Retmnt Income Port - Conservative Cls R-1	RARPX	NAS CM	Open End	Cautious Alloc (Income)	C	C	A-	Up	Y	250
American Funds Retmnt Income Port - Conservative Cls R-2	RDRPX	NAS CM	Open End	Cautious Alloc (Income)	C	C	A-	Up	Y	250
American Funds Retmnt Income Port - Conservative Cls R-2E	RGRPX	NAS CM	Open End	Cautious Alloc (Income)	C	C	A-	Up	Y	250
American Funds Retmnt Income Port - Conservative Cls R-3	RJRPX	NAS CM	Open End	Cautious Alloc (Income)	C	C	A-	Up	Y	250

★Expanded analysis of this fund is included in Section II.

Min Additional Investment	TOTAL RETURNS 3-Month Total Return	6-Month Total Return	1-Year Total Return	3-Year Total Return	5-Year Total Return	PERFORMANCE Dividend Yield (TTM)	Expense Ratio	3-Yr Std Deviation	3-Year Beta	ASSETS NAV	Total Assets (MIL)	ASSET ALLOCATION & TURNOVER %Cash	%Stocks	%Bonds	%Other	Turnover Ratio	BULL & BEAR Last Bull Market Total Return	Last Bear Market Total Return	FEES Front End Fee (%)	Back End Fee (%)	Inception Date
50	6.24	10.77	20.00	34.30	104.10		0.31	10.09	0.96	40.37	93,046	2	92	1	4	25	22.48	-17.24			Jan-17
50	5.95	10.19	18.73	30.74	95.51	0.9	1.4	10.06	0.96	40.07	93,046	2	92	1	4	25	21.91	-17.5			Jun-02
50	5.94	10.18	18.74	30.77	95.69	0.9	1.39	10.07	0.96	40.12	93,046	2	92	1	4	25	21.89	-17.52			May-02
50	6.03	10.37	19.13	32.15	99.62	1.22	1.09	10.08	0.96	40.28	93,046	2	92	1	4	25	22.23	-17.36			Aug-14
50	6.07	10.43	19.27	32.51	99.84	1.3	0.95	10.08	0.96	40.24	93,046	2	92	1	4	25	22.24	-17.36			Jun-02
50	6.16	10.61	19.63	33.75	103.03	1.57	0.64	10.07	0.96	40.28	93,046	2	92	1	4	25	22.41	-17.24			May-02
50	6.23	10.77	20.00	34.92	106.07	1.81	0.35	10.09	0.96	40.38	93,046	2	92	1	4	25	22.65	-17.13			May-02
50	6.21	10.70	19.89	34.30	104.10	1.74	0.43	10.08	0.96	40.36	93,046	2	92	1	4	25	22.48	-17.24			Nov-15
50	6.24	10.80	20.06	35.11	106.55	1.86	0.3	10.07	0.96	40.38	93,046	2	92	1	4	25	22.68	-17.13			May-09
50	4.55	10.18	28.78	37.07	82.54	0.57	0.84	10.59	0.96	42.65	76,532	1	93	0	5	28	20.66	-19.76	5.75		Feb-02
50	4.37	9.73	27.76	33.90	75.57	0	1.6	10.59	0.96	41.36	76,532	1	93	0	5	28	20.08	-20.01		1.00	Feb-02
50	4.51	10.07	28.47	36.12	80.39	0.39	1.06	10.61	0.96	42.25	76,532	1	93	0	5	28	20.46	-19.85			Mar-02
50	4.64	10.31	29.07	38.00	84.55	0.76	0.61	10.62	0.96	42.55	76,532	1	93	0	5	28	20.8	-19.68			Sep-02
50	4.59	10.23	28.89	37.43	83.35	0.62	0.75	10.61	0.96	43.16	76,532	1	93	0	5	28	20.71	-19.74	5.75		Mar-73
50	4.40	9.79	27.85	34.17	76.15	0	1.56	10.59	0.96	41.48	76,532	1	93	0	5	28	20.15	-20		1.00	Mar-01
50	4.57	10.20	28.77	37.15	82.75	0.58	0.83	10.59	0.96	42.89	76,532	1	93	0	5	28	20.71	-19.76			Mar-01
50	4.64	10.32	29.11	38.26	85.30	0.82	0.55	10.6	0.96	43.02	76,532	1	93	0	5	28	20.91	-19.65			Aug-08
50	4.66	10.38	29.25	37.82	83.86		0.45	10.62	0.96	43.15	76,532	1	93	0	5	28	20.71	-19.74			Jan-17
50	4.39	9.79	27.88	34.21	76.21	0	1.55	10.59	0.96	41.13	76,532	1	93	0	5	28	20.17	-19.99			Jun-02
50	4.40	9.80	27.89	34.25	76.35	0.01	1.55	10.6	0.96	41.53	76,532	1	93	0	5	28	20.16	-20			May-02
50	4.46	9.95	28.26	35.91	80.29	0.61	1.24	10.59	0.96	42.52	76,532	1	93	0	5	28	20.45	-19.86			Aug-14
50	4.49	10.03	28.45	36.02	80.24	0.37	1.09	10.6	0.96	42.2	76,532	1	93	0	5	28	20.51	-19.84			Jun-02
50	4.59	10.21	28.82	37.25	83.01	0.61	0.79	10.61	0.96	42.57	76,532	1	93	0	5	28	20.7	-19.76			May-02
50	4.67	10.38	29.21	38.51	85.77	0.84	0.49	10.6	0.96	43.11	76,532	1	93	0	5	28	20.9	-19.64			May-02
50	4.63	10.32	29.08	37.70	83.70	0.71	0.59	10.62	0.96	42.92	76,532	1	93	0	5	28	20.71	-19.74			Nov-15
50	4.67	10.41	29.29	38.69	86.23	0.88	0.45	10.59	0.96	43.17	76,532	1	93	0	5	28	20.94	-19.61			May-09
50	5.48	13.10	32.47	28.63	38.00	0.69	1.14	11.38	0.97	66.34	34,044	1	87	5	7	30	17.54	-21.94	5.75		Feb-02
50	5.26	12.64	31.40	25.58	32.62	0.09	1.92	11.38	0.97	64.85	34,044	1	87	5	7	30	16.99	-22.22		1.00	Feb-02
50	5.40	12.98	32.19	27.80	36.48	0.53	1.34	11.38	0.97	65.88	34,044	1	87	5	7	30	17.35	-22.03			Mar-02
50	5.53	13.23	32.74	29.43	39.42	0.85	0.93	11.39	0.97	66.3	34,044	1	87	5	7	30	17.68	-21.88			Sep-02
50	5.48	13.13	32.55	28.87	38.44	0.71	1.08	11.39	0.97	66.92	34,044	1	87	5	7	30	17.55	-21.93	5.75		Jun-99
50	5.28	12.67	31.47	25.77	32.98	0.08	1.88	11.38	0.97	64.69	34,044	1	87	5	7	30	17.03	-22.19		1.00	Mar-01
50	5.49	13.13	32.55	28.96	38.60	0.72	1.03	11.38	0.97	66.46	34,044	1	87	5	7	30	17.59	-21.93			Mar-01
50	5.57	13.28	32.91	29.99	40.47	0.98	0.76	11.38	0.97	66.74	34,044	1	87	5	7	30	17.78	-21.84			Aug-08
50	5.58	13.35	33.00	29.31	38.90		0.66	11.4	0.97	66.91	34,044	1	87	5	7	30	17.55	-21.92			Jan-17
50	5.27	12.67	31.51	25.90	33.24	0.14	1.83	11.38	0.97	64.87	34,044	1	87	5	7	30	17.03	-22.19			Jun-02
50	5.29	12.73	31.61	26.11	33.50	0.2	1.79	11.37	0.97	64.86	34,044	1	87	5	7	30	17.06	-22.18			Jun-02
50	5.38	12.91	32.02	27.50	36.05	0.75	1.45	11.37	0.97	66.16	34,044	1	87	5	7	30	17.31	-22.04			Aug-14
50	5.42	12.98	32.19	27.82	36.54	0.57	1.34	11.38	0.97	65.97	34,044	1	87	5	7	30	17.37	-22.04			Jun-02
50	5.50	13.15	32.59	29.05	38.78	0.82	1.01	11.39	0.97	66.52	34,044	1	87	5	7	30	17.61	-21.92			Oct-02
50	5.56	13.31	32.99	30.22	40.89	0.98	0.71	11.39	0.97	67.07	34,044	1	87	5	7	30	17.81	-21.82			May-02
50	5.54	13.26	32.85	29.39	38.99	1.07	0.8	11.4	0.97	66.31	34,044	1	87	5	7	30	17.55	-21.92			Nov-15
50	5.59	13.35	33.06	30.43	41.23	1.05	0.65	11.38	0.97	66.88	34,044	1	87	5	7	30	17.84	-21.8			May-09
50	1.74	4.00	8.88			2.09	0.68			11.04	452.4	5	38	54	3	0			5.75		Aug-15
50	1.47	3.63	8.09			1.45	1.38			11	452.4	5	38	54	3	0				1.00	Aug-15
50	1.73	4.06	8.93			2.04	0.69			11.05	452.4	5	38	54	3	0					Aug-15
50	1.80	4.09	9.18			2.26	0.45			11.05	452.4	5	38	54	3	0					Aug-15
50	1.82	4.23	9.28				0.36			11.05	452.4	5	38	54	3	0					Jan-17
50	1.48	3.60	8.09			1.3	1.46			11.04	452.4	5	38	54	3	0					Aug-15
50	1.58	3.69	8.31			1.59	1.47			11.04	452.4	5	38	54	3	0					Aug-15
50	1.84	4.13	9.22			2.24	1.19			11.06	452.4	5	38	54	3	0					Aug-15
50	1.65	3.80	8.52			1.76	0.98			11.05	452.4	5	38	54	3	0					Aug-15

	MARKET			FUND TYPE, CATEGORY & OBJECTIVE	RATINGS					MINIMUMS
Fund Name	Ticker Symbol	Traded On	Fund Type	Category and (Prospectus Objective)	Overall Rating	Reward Rating	Risk Rating	Recent Up/ Downgrade	Open to New Investors	Min Initial Investment
American Funds Retmnt Income Port - Conservative Cls R-4	RMRPX	NAS CM	Open End	Cautious Alloc (Income)	C	C	A-	Up	Y	250
American Funds Retmnt Income Port - Conservative Cls R-5	RQRPX	NAS CM	Open End	Cautious Alloc (Income)	C	C	A-	Up	Y	250
American Funds Retmnt Income Port - Conservative Cls R-5E	RROPX	NAS CM	Open End	Cautious Alloc (Income)	C	C	B+	Up	Y	250
American Funds Retmnt Income Port - Conservative Cls R-6	RTRPX	NAS CM	Open End	Cautious Alloc (Income)	C	C	B+	Up	Y	250
American Funds Retmnt Income Portfolio - Enhanced Cls A	NDARX	NAS CM	Open End	Moderate Alloc (Income)	C	C	A-	Up	Y	250
American Funds Retmnt Income Portfolio - Enhanced Cls C	NDCRX	NAS CM	Open End	Moderate Alloc (Income)	C	C	B+	Up	Y	250
American Funds Retmnt Income Portfolio - Enhanced Cls F-1	FCFWX	NAS CM	Open End	Moderate Alloc (Income)	C	C	A-	Up	Y	250
American Funds Retmnt Income Portfolio - Enhanced Cls F-2	FGFWX	NAS CM	Open End	Moderate Alloc (Income)	C	C+	A-	Up	Y	250
American Funds Retmnt Income Portfolio - Enhanced Cls F-3	FIEWX	NAS CM	Open End	Moderate Alloc (Income)	C	C+	B	Up	Y	250
American Funds Retmnt Income Portfolio - Enhanced Cls R-1	RCRPX	NAS CM	Open End	Moderate Alloc (Income)	C	C	A-	Up	Y	250
American Funds Retmnt Income Portfolio - Enhanced Cls R-2	RFRPX	NAS CM	Open End	Moderate Alloc (Income)	C	C	A-	Up	Y	250
American Funds Retmnt Income Portfolio - Enhanced Cls R-2E	RIRPX	NAS CM	Open End	Moderate Alloc (Income)	C	C+	A-	Up	Y	250
American Funds Retmnt Income Portfolio - Enhanced Cls R-3	RLRPX	NAS CM	Open End	Moderate Alloc (Income)	C	C	A-	Up	Y	250
American Funds Retmnt Income Portfolio - Enhanced Cls R-4	RPRPX	NAS CM	Open End	Moderate Alloc (Income)	C	C	A-	Up	Y	250
American Funds Retmnt Income Portfolio - Enhanced Cls R-5	RXRPX	NAS CM	Open End	Moderate Alloc (Income)	C	C+	A-	Up	Y	250
American Funds Retmnt Income Portfolio - Enhanced Cls R-5E	RRQPX	NAS CM	Open End	Moderate Alloc (Income)	C	C+	B	Up	Y	250
American Funds Retmnt Income Portfolio - Enhanced Cls R-6	RVRPX	NAS CM	Open End	Moderate Alloc (Income)	C	C+	A-	Up	Y	250
American Funds Retmnt Income Portfolio - Moderate Cls A	NBARX	NAS CM	Open End	Moderate Alloc (Income)	C	C	B+	Up	Y	250
American Funds Retmnt Income Portfolio - Moderate Cls C	NBCRX	NAS CM	Open End	Moderate Alloc (Income)	C	C	B+	Up	Y	250
American Funds Retmnt Income Portfolio - Moderate Cls F-1	FBFWX	NAS CM	Open End	Moderate Alloc (Income)	C	C	B+	Up	Y	250
American Funds Retmnt Income Portfolio - Moderate Cls F-2	FHFWX	NAS CM	Open End	Moderate Alloc (Income)	C	C	A-	Up	Y	250
American Funds Retmnt Income Portfolio - Moderate Cls F-3	FIMWX	NAS CM	Open End	Moderate Alloc (Income)	C	C	B	Up	Y	250
American Funds Retmnt Income Portfolio - Moderate Cls R-1	RBRPX	NAS CM	Open End	Moderate Alloc (Income)	C	C	B+	Up	Y	250
American Funds Retmnt Income Portfolio - Moderate Cls R-2	RERPX	NAS CM	Open End	Moderate Alloc (Income)	C	C	B+	Up	Y	250
American Funds Retmnt Income Portfolio - Moderate Cls R-2E	RHRPX	NAS CM	Open End	Moderate Alloc (Income)	C	C	B+	Up	Y	250
American Funds Retmnt Income Portfolio - Moderate Cls R-3	RKRPX	NAS CM	Open End	Moderate Alloc (Income)	C	C	B+	Up	Y	250
American Funds Retmnt Income Portfolio - Moderate Cls R-4	RNRPX	NAS CM	Open End	Moderate Alloc (Income)	C	C	B+	Up	Y	250
American Funds Retmnt Income Portfolio - Moderate Cls R-5	RRRPX	NAS CM	Open End	Moderate Alloc (Income)	C	C	B+	Up	Y	250
American Funds Retmnt Income Portfolio - Moderate Cls R-5E	RRPPX	NAS CM	Open End	Moderate Alloc (Income)	C	C	B	Up	Y	250
American Funds Retmnt Income Portfolio - Moderate Cls R-6	RURPX	NAS CM	Open End	Moderate Alloc (Income)	C	C	B+	Up	Y	250
American Funds SMALLCAP World Fund® Class 529-A	CSPAX	NAS CM	Open End	Global Equity Mid/Small Cap (Small Company)	B	B	B	Up	Y	250
American Funds SMALLCAP World Fund® Class 529-C	CSPCX	NAS CM	Open End	Global Equity Mid/Small Cap (Small Company)	B	B	B	Up	Y	250
American Funds SMALLCAP World Fund® Class 529-E	CSPEX	NAS CM	Open End	Global Equity Mid/Small Cap (Small Company)	B	B	B	Up	Y	250
American Funds SMALLCAP World Fund® Class 529-F	CSPFX	NAS CM	Open End	Global Equity Mid/Small Cap (Small Company)	B	B	B	Up	Y	250
American Funds SMALLCAP World Fund® Class A	SMCWX	NAS CM	Open End	Global Equity Mid/Small Cap (Small Company)	B	B	B	Up	Y	250
American Funds SMALLCAP World Fund® Class C	SCWCX	NAS CM	Open End	Global Equity Mid/Small Cap (Small Company)	B	B	B	Up	Y	250
American Funds SMALLCAP World Fund® Class F-1	SCWFX	NAS CM	Open End	Global Equity Mid/Small Cap (Small Company)	B	B	B	Up	Y	250
American Funds SMALLCAP World Fund® Class F-2	SMCFX	NAS CM	Open End	Global Equity Mid/Small Cap (Small Company)	B	B	B	Up	Y	250
American Funds SMALLCAP World Fund® Class F-3	SFCWX	NAS CM	Open End	Global Equity Mid/Small Cap (Small Company)	B	B	B	Up	Y	250
American Funds SMALLCAP World Fund® Class R-1	RSLAX	NAS CM	Open End	Global Equity Mid/Small Cap (Small Company)	B	B	B	Up	Y	250
American Funds SMALLCAP World Fund® Class R-2	RSLBX	NAS CM	Open End	Global Equity Mid/Small Cap (Small Company)	B	B	B	Up	Y	250
American Funds SMALLCAP World Fund® Class R-2E	RSEBX	NAS CM	Open End	Global Equity Mid/Small Cap (Small Company)	B	B	B	Up	Y	250
American Funds SMALLCAP World Fund® Class R-3	RSLCX	NAS CM	Open End	Global Equity Mid/Small Cap (Small Company)	B	B	B	Up	Y	250
American Funds SMALLCAP World Fund® Class R-4	RSLEX	NAS CM	Open End	Global Equity Mid/Small Cap (Small Company)	B	B	B	Up	Y	250
American Funds SMALLCAP World Fund® Class R-5	RSLFX	NAS CM	Open End	Global Equity Mid/Small Cap (Small Company)	B	B	B	Up	Y	250
American Funds SMALLCAP World Fund® Class R-5E	RSLDX	NAS CM	Open End	Global Equity Mid/Small Cap (Small Company)	B	B	B	Up	Y	250
American Funds SMALLCAP World Fund® Class R-6	RLLGX	NAS CM	Open End	Global Equity Mid/Small Cap (Small Company)	B	B	B	Up	Y	250
American Funds Tax-Advantaged Income Portfolio Class A	TAIAX	NAS CM	Open End	Cautious Alloc (Balanced)	B-	C+	B	Up	Y	250
American Funds Tax-Advantaged Income Portfolio Class C	TAICX	NAS CM	Open End	Cautious Alloc (Balanced)	B	C+	A-	Up	Y	250
American Funds TaxAdvantaged Income Portfolio Class F1	TAIFX	NAS CM	Open End	Cautious Alloc (Balanced)	B-	C+	B	Up	Y	250
American Funds TaxAdvantaged Income Portfolio Class F2	TXIFX	NAS CM	Open End	Cautious Alloc (Balanced)	B-	C+	B		Y	250
American Funds Tax-Advantaged Income Portfolio Class F-3	TYIFX	NAS CM	Open End	Cautious Alloc (Balanced)	B-	C+	B		Y	250

★ Expanded analysis of this fund is included in Section II.

Min Additional Investment	TOTAL RETURNS 3-Month Total Return	6-Month Total Return	1-Year Total Return	3-Year Total Return	5-Year Total Return	PERFORMANCE Dividend Yield (TTM)	Expense Ratio	3-Yr Std Deviation	3-Year Beta	ASSETS NAV	Total Assets (MIL)	ASSET ALLOCATION & TURNOVER %Cash	%Stocks	%Bonds	%Other	Turnover Ratio	BULL & BEAR Last Bull Market Total Return	Last Bear Market Total Return	FEES Front End Fee (%)	Back End Fee (%)	Inception Date
50	1.37	3.72	8.54			1.76	0.68			11.05	452.4	5	38	54	3	0					Aug-15
50	1.82	4.11	9.19			2.2	0.42			11.06	452.4	5	38	54	3	0					Aug-15
50	1.79	4.09	9.20			2.26	0.51			11.05	452.4	5	38	54	3	0					Nov-15
50	1.82	4.23	9.26			2.35	0.36			11.06	452.4	5	38	54	3	0					Aug-15
50	3.20	6.66	13.61			2.29	0.71			11.74	604.4	1	65	30	3	3			5.75		Aug-15
50	3.02	6.31	12.90			1.69	1.41			11.71	604.4	1	65	30	3	3				1.00	Aug-15
50	3.19	6.64	13.66			2.24	0.71			11.75	604.4	1	65	30	3	3					Aug-15
50	3.17	6.68	13.83			2.48	0.47			11.75	604.4	1	65	30	3	3					Aug-15
50	3.29	6.73	13.83				0.38			11.74	604.4	1	65	30	3	3					Jan-17
50	2.99	6.34	13.05			1.91	1.52			11.74	604.4	1	65	30	3	3					Aug-15
50	3.07	6.39	13.20			1.93	1.49			11.72	604.4	1	65	30	3	3					Aug-15
50	3.30	6.83	13.97			2.45	1.21			11.76	604.4	1	65	30	3	3					Aug-15
50	3.11	6.48	13.33			1.97	0.99			11.75	604.4	1	65	30	3	3					Aug-15
50	3.21	6.68	13.71			2.29	0.71			11.75	604.4	1	65	30	3	3					Aug-15
50	3.28	6.79	13.93			2.4	0.44			11.76	604.4	1	65	30	3	3					Aug-15
50	3.27	6.81	14.00			2.49	0.54			11.75	604.4	1	65	30	3	3					Nov-15
50	3.29	6.83	14.04			2.57	0.39			11.76	604.4	1	65	30	3	3					Aug-15
50	2.44	5.33	11.17			2.2	0.69			11.38	600.0	4	52	41	3	0			5.75		Aug-15
50	2.26	4.97	10.37			1.58	1.39			11.34	600.0	4	52	41	3	0				1.00	Aug-15
50	2.42	5.30	11.14			2.16	0.7			11.38	600.0	4	52	41	3	0					Aug-15
50	2.49	5.44	11.39			2.4	0.46			11.39	600.0	4	52	41	3	0					Aug-15
50	2.61	5.49	11.50				0.37			11.38	600.0	4	52	41	3	0					Jan-17
50	2.25	4.98	10.40			1.57	1.49			11.38	600.0	4	52	41	3	0					Aug-15
50	2.31	4.99	10.52			1.95	1.48			11.36	600.0	4	52	41	3	0					Aug-15
50	2.53	5.49	11.53			2.37	1.19			11.4	600.0	4	52	41	3	0					Aug-15
50	2.45	5.24	11.03			2.28	1.06			11.38	600.0	4	52	41	3	0					Aug-15
50	2.54	5.37	11.34			2.29	0.72			11.39	600.0	4	52	41	3	0					Aug-15
50	2.59	5.43	11.46			2.31	0.43			11.4	600.0	4	52	41	3	0					Aug-15
50	2.60	5.48	11.55			2.4	0.52			11.39	600.0	4	52	41	3	0					Nov-15
50	2.60	5.57	11.57			2.48	0.38			11.4	600.0	4	52	41	3	0					Aug-15
50	4.86	10.57	26.75	37.01	82.91	0.23	1.14	10.99	0.95	55.17	38,579	2	90	0	7	32	23.83	-24.43	5.75		Feb-02
50	4.65	10.14	25.75	33.83	75.84	0	1.91	10.99	0.95	50	38,579	2	90	0	7	32	23.27	-24.69		1.00	Feb-02
50	4.83	10.48	26.48	36.14	80.90	0.07	1.34	10.98	0.95	53.64	38,579	2	90	0	7	32	23.66	-24.53			Mar-02
50	4.92	10.70	26.99	37.87	84.82	0.39	0.91	11	0.95	55.8	38,579	2	90	0	7	32	24	-24.38			Sep-02
50	4.88	10.61	26.83	37.32	83.56	0.28	1.07	10.99	0.95	55.8	38,579	2	90	0	7	32	23.85	-24.41	5.75		Apr-90
50	4.68	10.17	25.84	34.07	76.39	0	1.86	10.98	0.95	49.09	38,579	2	90	0	7	32	23.33	-24.66		1.00	Mar-01
50	4.86	10.59	26.76	37.21	83.43	0.27	1.1	10.98	0.95	55.16	38,579	2	90	0	7	32	23.88	-24.41			Mar-01
50	4.95	10.76	27.16	38.39	86.03	0.5	0.81	11	0.95	56.51	38,579	2	90	0	7	32	24.12	-24.34			Aug-08
50	4.96	10.81	27.24	37.76	84.16		0.71	11	0.95	55.99	38,579	2	90	0	7	32	23.85	-24.41			Jan-17
50	4.70	10.18	25.86	34.23	76.81	0	1.83	10.98	0.95	50.66	38,579	2	90	0	7	32	23.34	-24.65			Jun-02
50	4.67	10.20	25.88	34.31	76.92	0	1.8	10.98	0.95	50.68	38,579	2	90	0	7	32	23.34	-24.67			May-02
50	4.77	10.36	26.27	35.94	80.82	0.12	1.5	10.99	0.95	55.38	38,579	2	90	0	7	32	23.6	-24.52			Aug-14
50	4.82	10.46	26.46	36.09	80.87	0.07	1.35	10.99	0.95	53.53	38,579	2	90	0	7	32	23.65	-24.51			Jun-02
50	4.88	10.62	26.84	37.38	83.81	0.29	1.04	10.99	0.95	55.36	38,579	2	90	0	7	32	23.93	-24.4			Jul-02
50	4.96	10.77	27.21	38.61	86.58	0.5	0.74	11	0.95	57.3	38,579	2	90	0	7	32	24.18	-24.32			May-02
50	4.94	10.72	27.09	37.83	84.25	0.6	0.84	10.99	0.95	55.78	38,579	2	90	0	7	32	23.85	-24.41			Nov-15
50	4.97	10.81	27.27	38.82	87.01	0.57	0.7	10.99	0.95	56.69	38,579	2	90	0	7	32	24.19	-24.3			May-09
50	3.43	6.98	14.24	21.53	50.22	2.4	0.78	4.82	0.42	13.6	1,756	2	47	50	2	0			3.75		May-12
50	3.17	6.55	13.36	18.95	44.92	1.76	1.49	4.84	0.43	13.52	1,756	2	47	50	2	0				1.00	May-12
50	3.37	6.92	14.20	21.56	50.32	2.43	0.76	4.82	0.43	13.59	1,756	2	47	50	2	0					May-12
50	3.43	7.04	14.41	22.55	52.15	2.61	0.5	4.88	0.43	13.61	1,756	2	47	50	2	0					May-12
50	3.46	7.10	14.54	22.68	52.32		0.39	4.88	0.43	13.6	1,756	2	47	50	2	0					Jan-17

	MARKET		FUND TYPE, CATEGORY & OBJECTIVE		RATINGS					MINIMUMS
Fund Name	Ticker Symbol	Traded On	Fund Type	Category and (Prospectus Objective)	Overall Rating	Reward Rating	Risk Rating	Recent Up/ Downgrade	Open to New Investors	Min Initial Investment
★ American Funds The Growth Fund of America® Class 529-A	CGFAX	NAS CM	Open End	US Equity Large Cap Growth (Growth)	B	B	B	Down	Y	250
★ American Funds The Growth Fund of America® Class 529-C	CGFCX	NAS CM	Open End	US Equity Large Cap Growth (Growth)	B	B	B		Y	250
★ American Funds The Growth Fund of America® Class 529-E	CGFEX	NAS CM	Open End	US Equity Large Cap Growth (Growth)	B	B	B	Down	Y	250
★ American Funds The Growth Fund of America® Class 529-F	CGFFX	NAS CM	Open End	US Equity Large Cap Growth (Growth)	B	B	B	Down	Y	250
★ American Funds The Growth Fund of America® Class A	AGTHX	NAS CM	Open End	US Equity Large Cap Growth (Growth)	B	B	B	Down	Y	250
★ American Funds The Growth Fund of America® Class C	GFACX	NAS CM	Open End	US Equity Large Cap Growth (Growth)	B	B	B		Y	250
★ American Funds The Growth Fund of America® Class F-1	GFAFX	NAS CM	Open End	US Equity Large Cap Growth (Growth)	B	B	B	Down	Y	250
★ American Funds The Growth Fund of America® Class F-2	GFFFX	NAS CM	Open End	US Equity Large Cap Growth (Growth)	B	B	B	Down	Y	250
★ American Funds The Growth Fund of America® Class F-3	GAFFX	NAS CM	Open End	US Equity Large Cap Growth (Growth)	B	B	B	Down	Y	250
★ American Funds The Growth Fund of America® Class R-1	RGAAX	NAS CM	Open End	US Equity Large Cap Growth (Growth)	B	B	B		Y	250
★ American Funds The Growth Fund of America® Class R-2	RGABX	NAS CM	Open End	US Equity Large Cap Growth (Growth)	B	B	B		Y	250
★ American Funds The Growth Fund of America® Class R-2E	RGEBX	NAS CM	Open End	US Equity Large Cap Growth (Growth)	B	B	B	Down	Y	250
★ American Funds The Growth Fund of America® Class R-3	RGACX	NAS CM	Open End	US Equity Large Cap Growth (Growth)	B	B	B	Down	Y	250
★ American Funds The Growth Fund of America® Class R-4	RGAEX	NAS CM	Open End	US Equity Large Cap Growth (Growth)	B	B	B	Down	Y	250
★ American Funds The Growth Fund of America® Class R-5	RGAFX	NAS CM	Open End	US Equity Large Cap Growth (Growth)	B	B	B	Down	Y	250
★ American Funds The Growth Fund of America® Class R-5E	RGAHX	NAS CM	Open End	US Equity Large Cap Growth (Growth)	B	B	B	Down	Y	250
★ American Funds The Growth Fund of America® Class R-6	RGAGX	NAS CM	Open End	US Equity Large Cap Growth (Growth)	B	B	B	Down	Y	250
★ American Funds The Income Fund of America® Class 529-A	CIMAX	NAS CM	Open End	Aggressive Alloc (Income)	B-	C+	B	Down	Y	250
★ American Funds The Income Fund of America® Class 529-C	CIMCX	NAS CM	Open End	Aggressive Alloc (Income)	B-	C+	B	Down	Y	250
★ American Funds The Income Fund of America® Class 529-E	CIMEX	NAS CM	Open End	Aggressive Alloc (Income)	B-	C+	B	Down	Y	250
★ American Funds The Income Fund of America® Class 529-F-1	CIMFX	NAS CM	Open End	Aggressive Alloc (Income)	B-	C+	B	Down	Y	250
★ American Funds The Income Fund of America® Class A	AMECX	NAS CM	Open End	Aggressive Alloc (Income)	B-	C+	B	Down	Y	250
★ American Funds The Income Fund of America® Class C	IFACX	NAS CM	Open End	Aggressive Alloc (Income)	B-	C+	B	Down	Y	250
★ American Funds The Income Fund of America® Class F-1	IFAFX	NAS CM	Open End	Aggressive Alloc (Income)	B-	C+	B	Down	Y	250
★ American Funds The Income Fund of America® Class F-2	AMEFX	NAS CM	Open End	Aggressive Alloc (Income)	B-	C+	B	Down	Y	250
★ American Funds The Income Fund of America® Class F-3	FIFAX	NAS CM	Open End	Aggressive Alloc (Income)	B-	C+	B	Down	Y	250
★ American Funds The Income Fund of America® Class R-1	RIDAX	NAS CM	Open End	Aggressive Alloc (Income)	B-	C+	B	Down	Y	250
★ American Funds The Income Fund of America® Class R-2	RIDBX	NAS CM	Open End	Aggressive Alloc (Income)	B-	C+	B	Down	Y	250
★ American Funds The Income Fund of America® Class R-2E	RIEBX	NAS CM	Open End	Aggressive Alloc (Income)	B-	C+	B	Down	Y	250
★ American Funds The Income Fund of America® Class R-3	RIDCX	NAS CM	Open End	Aggressive Alloc (Income)	B-	C+	B	Down	Y	250
★ American Funds The Income Fund of America® Class R-4	RIDEX	NAS CM	Open End	Aggressive Alloc (Income)	B-	C+	B	Down	Y	250
★ American Funds The Income Fund of America® Class R-5	RIDFX	NAS CM	Open End	Aggressive Alloc (Income)	B-	C+	B	Down	Y	250
★ American Funds The Income Fund of America® Class R-5E	RIDHX	NAS CM	Open End	Aggressive Alloc (Income)	B-	C+	B	Down	Y	250
★ American Funds The Income Fund of America® Class R-6	RIDGX	NAS CM	Open End	Aggressive Alloc (Income)	B-	C+	B	Down	Y	250
American Funds The New Economy Fund® Class 529-A	CNGAX	NAS CM	Open End	US Equity Large Cap Growth (Growth)	A-	A	B	Up	Y	250
American Funds The New Economy Fund® Class 529-C	CNGCX	NAS CM	Open End	US Equity Large Cap Growth (Growth)	B+	A-	B	Up	Y	250
American Funds The New Economy Fund® Class 529-E	CNGEX	NAS CM	Open End	US Equity Large Cap Growth (Growth)	A-	A	B	Up	Y	250
American Funds The New Economy Fund® Class 529-F	CNGFX	NAS CM	Open End	US Equity Large Cap Growth (Growth)	A-	A	B	Up	Y	250
American Funds The New Economy Fund® Class A	ANEFX	NAS CM	Open End	US Equity Large Cap Growth (Growth)	A-	A	B	Up	Y	250
American Funds The New Economy Fund® Class C	ANFCX	NAS CM	Open End	US Equity Large Cap Growth (Growth)	B+	A-	B	Up	Y	250
American Funds The New Economy Fund® Class F-1	ANFFX	NAS CM	Open End	US Equity Large Cap Growth (Growth)	A-	A	B	Up	Y	250
American Funds The New Economy Fund® Class F-2	NEFFX	NAS CM	Open End	US Equity Large Cap Growth (Growth)	A-	A	B	Up	Y	250
American Funds The New Economy Fund® Class F-3	FNEFX	NAS CM	Open End	US Equity Large Cap Growth (Growth)	A-	A	B	Up	Y	250
American Funds The New Economy Fund® Class R-1	RNGAX	NAS CM	Open End	US Equity Large Cap Growth (Growth)	B+	A-	B	Up	Y	250
American Funds The New Economy Fund® Class R-2	RNGBX	NAS CM	Open End	US Equity Large Cap Growth (Growth)	B+	A-	B	Up	Y	250
American Funds The New Economy Fund® Class R-2E	RNNEX	NAS CM	Open End	US Equity Large Cap Growth (Growth)	A-	A	B	Up	Y	250
American Funds The New Economy Fund® Class R-3	RNGCX	NAS CM	Open End	US Equity Large Cap Growth (Growth)	A-	A	B	Up	Y	250
American Funds The New Economy Fund® Class R-4	RNGEX	NAS CM	Open End	US Equity Large Cap Growth (Growth)	A-	A	B	Up	Y	250
American Funds The New Economy Fund® Class R-5	RNGFX	NAS CM	Open End	US Equity Large Cap Growth (Growth)	A-	A	B	Up	Y	250
American Funds The New Economy Fund® Class R-5E	RNGHX	NAS CM	Open End	US Equity Large Cap Growth (Growth)	A-	A	B	Up	Y	250
American Funds The New Economy Fund® Class R-6	RNGGX	NAS CM	Open End	US Equity Large Cap Growth (Growth)	A-	A	B	Up	Y	250
American Funds Washington Mutual Investors Fund Cls 529-A	CWMAX	NAS CM	Open End	US Equity Large Cap Value (Growth & Income)	B	B-	B		Y	250

★ Expanded analysis of this fund is included in Section II.

Min Additional Investment	TOTAL RETURNS 3-Month Total Return	6-Month Total Return	1-Year Total Return	3-Year Total Return	5-Year Total Return	PERFORMANCE Dividend Yield (TTM)	Expense Ratio	3-Yr Std Deviation	3-Year Beta	ASSETS NAV	Total Assets (MIL)	ASSET ALLOCATION & TURNOVER %Cash	%Stocks	%Bonds	%Other	Turnover Ratio	BULL & BEAR Last Bull Market Total Return	Last Bear Market Total Return	FEES Front End Fee (%)	Back End Fee (%)	Inception Date
50	6.88	12.25	26.05	42.84	113.34	0.41	0.72	10.67	0.99	49.03	176,790	4	91	2	2	25	24.13	-19.02	5.75		Feb-02
50	6.67	11.80	25.06	39.55	105.22	0	1.49	10.65	0.99	46.1	176,790	4	91	2	2	25	23.54	-19.3		1.00	Feb-02
50	6.81	12.10	25.73	41.80	110.72	0.23	0.94	10.66	0.99	48.55	176,790	4	91	2	2	25	23.94	-19.13			Mar-02
50	6.95	12.35	26.30	43.76	115.60	0.59	0.49	10.66	0.99	48.91	176,790	4	91	2	2	25	24.26	-18.95			Sep-02
50	6.91	12.27	26.13	43.20	114.21	0.46	0.64	10.66	0.99	49.54	176,790	4	91	2	2	25	24.15	-19.01	5.75		Nov-73
50	6.69	11.84	25.12	39.78	105.78	0	1.44	10.65	0.99	45.95	176,790	4	91	2	2	25	23.6	-19.27		1.00	Mar-01
50	6.90	12.25	26.07	42.94	113.65	0.42	0.7	10.66	0.99	49.22	176,790	4	91	2	2	25	24.17	-18.97			Mar-01
50	6.95	12.39	26.38	44.08	116.59	0.64	0.43	10.67	0.99	49.42	176,790	4	91	2	2	25	24.36	-18.91			Aug-08
50	6.98	12.45	26.47	43.57	114.77		0.33	10.66	0.99	49.53	176,790	4	91	2	2	25	24.15	-19.01			Jan-17
50	6.68	11.83	25.15	39.86	106.06	0	1.44	10.65	0.99	46.65	176,790	4	91	2	2	25	23.63	-19.26			Jun-02
50	6.71	11.85	25.16	40.01	106.50	0	1.42	10.66	0.99	47.13	176,790	4	91	2	2	25	23.64	-19.22			May-02
50	6.78	12.02	25.52	41.37	110.31	0.32	1.12	10.64	0.99	48.73	176,790	4	91	2	2	25	23.89	-19.13			Aug-14
50	6.83	12.09	25.70	41.77	110.79	0.19	0.98	10.66	0.99	48.63	176,790	4	91	2	2	25	23.96	-19.09			May-02
50	6.90	12.27	26.08	43.07	113.95	0.45	0.68	10.65	0.99	49.1	176,790	4	91	2	2	25	24.14	-19			May-02
50	6.97	12.43	26.43	44.33	117.12	0.66	0.38	10.66	0.99	49.49	176,790	4	91	2	2	25	24.39	-18.89			May-02
50	6.95	12.36	26.35	43.61	114.83	0.74	0.46	10.67	0.99	49.18	176,790	4	91	2	2	25	24.15	-19			Nov-15
50	7.00	12.45	26.52	44.54	117.67	0.71	0.33	10.67	0.99	49.56	176,790	4	91	2	2	25	24.41	-18.89			May-09
50	3.43	7.25	13.27	22.33	58.90	2.77	0.65	7.14	0.66	23.32	110,349	1	72	22	3	42	14.49	-10.13	5.75		Feb-02
50	3.24	6.86	12.40	19.51	52.84	2.05	1.41	7.12	0.66	23.25	110,349	1	72	22	3	42	13.96	-10.41		1.00	Feb-02
50	3.37	7.14	12.98	21.41	56.96	2.55	0.87	7.13	0.66	23.25	110,349	1	72	22	3	42	14.32	-10.21			Feb-02
50	3.48	7.37	13.52	23.12	60.64	2.98	0.41	7.11	0.66	23.31	110,349	1	72	22	3	42	14.61	-10.03			Sep-02
50	3.48	7.32	13.37	22.66	59.65	2.83	0.56	7.12	0.66	23.37	110,349	1	72	22	3	42	14.52	-10.07	5.75		Nov-73
50	3.27	6.88	12.48	19.76	53.37	2.11	1.35	7.13	0.66	23.08	110,349	1	72	22	3	42	13.95	-10.32		1.00	Mar-01
50	3.46	7.24	13.24	22.28	58.90	2.75	0.65	7.1	0.66	23.31	110,349	1	72	22	3	42	14.52	-10.11			Mar-01
50	3.53	7.41	13.57	23.25	60.99	2.99	0.39	7.14	0.66	23.35	110,349	1	72	22	3	42	14.63	-10			Aug-08
50	3.55	7.47	13.64	22.95	60.03		0.29	7.12	0.66	23.36	110,349	1	72	22	3	42	14.52	-10.07			Jan-17
50	3.24	6.87	12.42	19.65	53.20	2.07	1.39	7.13	0.66	23.23	110,349	1	72	22	3	42	14	-10.38			Jun-02
50	3.26	6.87	12.45	19.71	53.27	2.09	1.4	7.1	0.66	23.11	110,349	1	72	22	3	42	13.99	-10.37			May-02
50	3.31	7.02	12.75	20.87	56.44	2.39	1.09	7.09	0.66	23.31	110,349	1	72	22	3	42	14.28	-10.2			Aug-14
50	3.35	7.09	12.94	21.27	56.65	2.49	0.95	7.11	0.66	23.28	110,349	1	72	22	3	42	14.29	-10.22			Jun-02
50	3.47	7.29	13.31	22.38	59.04	2.77	0.64	7.11	0.66	23.33	110,349	1	72	22	3	42	14.43	-10.06			Jun-02
50	3.49	7.39	13.56	23.44	61.39	3.04	0.34	7.1	0.66	23.36	110,349	1	72	22	3	42	14.72	-9.97			May-02
50	3.48	7.35	13.46	22.85	59.89	2.95	0.44	7.12	0.66	23.34	110,349	1	72	22	3	42	14.52	-10.07			Nov-15
50	3.50	7.42	13.67	23.62	61.77	3.09	0.29	7.12	0.66	23.37	110,349	1	72	22	3	42	14.74	-9.94			May-09
50	5.50	14.41	34.29	41.36	115.98	0.15	0.9	11.6	0.98	44.18	18,784	2	89	1	8	25	24.2	-18.72	5.75		Feb-02
50	5.29	13.97	33.21	38.04	107.54	0	1.67	11.57	0.97	40.75	18,784	2	89	1	8	25	23.62	-18.98		1.00	Feb-02
50	5.45	14.29	33.97	40.32	113.30	0	1.12	11.58	0.97	43.56	18,784	2	89	1	8	25	24.01	-18.79			Mar-02
50	5.53	14.52	34.55	42.21	118.19	0.32	0.68	11.6	0.98	44.11	18,784	2	89	1	8	25	24.32	-18.63			Oct-02
50	5.52	14.44	34.37	41.69	116.77	0.19	0.82	11.59	0.98	44.63	18,784	2	89	1	8	25	24.23	-18.66	5.75		Dec-83
50	5.31	14.00	33.30	38.27	108.17	0	1.62	11.58	0.97	40.19	18,784	2	89	1	8	25	23.65	-18.94		1.00	Mar-01
50	5.48	14.41	34.28	41.44	116.24	0.12	0.85	11.58	0.97	44.76	18,784	2	89	1	8	25	24.25	-18.69			Mar-01
50	5.56	14.58	34.66	42.63	119.29	0.39	0.58	11.59	0.98	44.55	18,784	2	89	1	8	25	24.45	-18.61			Aug-08
50	5.58	14.62	34.78	42.12	117.42		0.47	11.61	0.98	44.63	18,784	2	89	1	8	25	24.23	-18.66			Jan-17
50	5.29	14.00	33.32	38.40	108.54	0	1.57	11.57	0.97	41.49	18,784	2	89	1	8	25	23.69	-18.94			Jun-02
50	5.31	14.00	33.31	38.40	108.63	0	1.59	11.56	0.97	41.74	18,784	2	89	1	8	25	23.73	-18.96			May-02
50	5.37	14.18	33.72	40.37	113.62	0.15	1.26	11.58	0.97	43.98	18,784	2	89	1	8	25	23.97	-18.79			Aug-14
50	5.42	14.24	33.90	40.29	113.24	0	1.13	11.59	0.98	43.63	18,784	2	89	1	8	25	24.03	-18.81			Jun-02
50	5.50	14.43	34.30	41.58	116.63	0.18	0.82	11.59	0.98	44.2	18,784	2	89	1	8	25	24.24	-18.66			Jul-02
50	5.59	14.60	34.74	42.89	119.89	0.42	0.52	11.6	0.98	44.84	18,784	2	89	1	8	25	24.45	-18.57			May-02
50	5.54	14.57	34.70	42.21	117.56	0.31	0.61	11.6	0.98	44.41	18,784	2	89	1	8	25	24.23	-18.66			Nov-15
50	5.61	14.65	34.79	43.08	120.41	0.48	0.47	11.59	0.98	44.68	18,784	2	89	1	8	25	24.49	-18.56			May-09
50	6.43	12.37	20.09	34.40	101.54	1.55	0.67	9.74	0.95	45.55	100,165	2	96	0	2	21	20.91	-12.56	5.75		Feb-02

	MARKET			FUND TYPE, CATEGORY & OBJECTIVE	RATINGS				MINIMUMS	
Fund Name	Ticker Symbol	Traded On	Fund Type	Category and (Prospectus Objective)	Overall Rating	Reward Rating	Risk Rating	Recent Up/ Downgrade	Open to New Investors	Min Initial Investment
American Funds Washington Mutual Investors Fund Cls 529-C	CWMCX	NAS CM	Open End	US Equity Large Cap Value (Growth & Income)	B-	B-	B	Down	Y	250
American Funds Washington Mutual Investors Fund Cls 529-E	CWMEX	NAS CM	Open End	US Equity Large Cap Value (Growth & Income)	B	B-	B		Y	250
American Funds Washington Mutual Invs Fund Cls 529-F-1	CWMFX	NAS CM	Open End	US Equity Large Cap Value (Growth & Income)	B	B	B		Y	250
American Funds Washington Mutual Investors Fund Class A	AWSHX	NAS CM	Open End	US Equity Large Cap Value (Growth & Income)	B	B-	B		Y	250
American Funds Washington Mutual Investors Fund Class C	WSHCX	NAS CM	Open End	US Equity Large Cap Value (Growth & Income)	B-	B-	B	Down	Y	250
American Funds Washington Mutual Investors Fund Class F-1	WSHFX	NAS CM	Open End	US Equity Large Cap Value (Growth & Income)	B	B-	B		Y	250
American Funds Washington Mutual Investors Fund Class F-2	WMFFX	NAS CM	Open End	US Equity Large Cap Value (Growth & Income)	B	B	B		Y	250
★ American Funds Washington Mutual Investors Fund Class F-3	FWMIX	NAS CM	Open End	US Equity Large Cap Value (Growth & Income)	B	B	B		Y	250
American Funds Washington Mutual Investors Fund Class R-1	RWMAX	NAS CM	Open End	US Equity Large Cap Value (Growth & Income)	B-	B-	B	Down	Y	250
American Funds Washington Mutual Investors Fund Class R-2	RWMBX	NAS CM	Open End	US Equity Large Cap Value (Growth & Income)	B-	B-	B	Down	Y	250
American Funds Washington Mutual Investors Fund Class R-2E	RWEBX	NAS CM	Open End	US Equity Large Cap Value (Growth & Income)	B-	B-	B	Down	Y	250
American Funds Washington Mutual Investors Fund Class R-3	RWMCX	NAS CM	Open End	US Equity Large Cap Value (Growth & Income)	B-	B-	B	Down	Y	250
American Funds Washington Mutual Investors Fund Class R-4	RWMEX	NAS CM	Open End	US Equity Large Cap Value (Growth & Income)	B	B-	B		Y	250
American Funds Washington Mutual Investors Fund Class R-5	RWMFX	NAS CM	Open End	US Equity Large Cap Value (Growth & Income)	B	B	B		Y	250
American Funds Washington Mutual Investors Fund Class R-5E	RWMHX	NAS CM	Open End	US Equity Large Cap Value (Growth & Income)	B	B	B		Y	250
American Funds Washington Mutual Investors Fund Class R-6	RWMGX	NAS CM	Open End	US Equity Large Cap Value (Growth & Income)	B	B	B		Y	250
American Growth Fund Series One Class A	AMRAX	NAS CM	Open End	US Equity Large Cap Growth (Growth)	B-	C+	B	Down	Y	0
American Growth Fund Series One Class B	AMRBX	NAS CM	Open End	US Equity Large Cap Growth (Growth)	B-	C+	B	Up	Y	0
American Growth Fund Series One Class C	AMRCX	NAS CM	Open End	US Equity Large Cap Growth (Growth)	B-	C+	B	Up	Y	0
American Growth Fund Series One Class D	AMRGX	NAS CM	Open End	US Equity Large Cap Growth (Growth)	B	B-	B	Up	Y	0
American Growth Fund Series Two Class E	AMREX	NAS CM	Open End	US Equity Large Cap Growth (Growth)	D-	D-	D-	Down	Y	0
American Growth Fund Series Two Class F	AMRHX	NAS CM	Open End	US Equity Large Cap Growth (Growth)	U	U	U		Y	0
American Independence Hillcrest Small Cap Value Fund Cls A	HLCAX	NAS CM	Open End	US Equity Small Cap (Small Company)	C-	C-	B	Up	Y	5,000
American Independence Hillcrest Small Cap Value Fund Cls C	HLCCX	NAS CM	Open End	US Equity Small Cap (Small Company)	C-	D+	B	Up	Y	5,000
American Independence Hillcrest Small Cap Value Inst Cls	HLCIX	NAS CM	Open End	US Equity Small Cap (Small Company)	C-	C-	B	Up	Y	3,000,000
American Independence JAForlines Global Tact Alloc Cls A	AARMX	NAS CM	Open End	Moderate Alloc (Growth)	B	C+	B+	Up	Y	5,000
American Independence JAForlines Global Tact Alloc Cls C	ACRMX	NAS CM	Open End	Moderate Alloc (Growth)	B	C+	B+	Up	Y	5,000
American Independence JAForlines Global Tact Alloc Inst Cl	RMAIX	NAS CM	Open End	Moderate Alloc (Growth)	B	C+	B+	Up	Y	3,000,000
American Trust Allegiance Fund	ATAFX	NAS CM	Open End	US Equity Large Cap Growth (World Stock)	B-	B-	C+	Up	Y	2,500
AMG Chicago Equity Partners Balanced Fund Class I	MBESX	NAS CM	Open End	Moderate Alloc (Balanced)	B	C+	B+	Up	Y	100,000
AMG Chicago Equity Partners Balanced Fund Class N	MBEAX	NAS CM	Open End	Moderate Alloc (Balanced)	B	C+	B+	Up	Y	2,000
AMG Chicago Equity Partners Balanced Fund Class Z	MBEYX	NAS CM	Open End	Moderate Alloc (Balanced)	B	C+	B+	Up	Y	5,000,000
AMG Chicago Equity Partners Small Cap Value Fund Class I	CESSX	NAS CM	Open End	US Equity Small Cap (Small Company)	C+	C+	B-	Up	Y	100,000
AMG Chicago Equity Partners Small Cap Value Fund Class N	CESVX	NAS CM	Open End	US Equity Small Cap (Small Company)	C+	C+	B-	Up	Y	2,000
AMG Chicago Equity Partners Small Cap Value Fund Class Z	CESIX	NAS CM	Open End	US Equity Small Cap (Small Company)	C+	C+	B-	Up	Y	5,000,000
AMG FQ Global Risk-Balanced Fund Class I	MMASX	NAS CM	Open End	Moderate Alloc (Growth & Income)	B-	C+	B	Up	Y	100,000
AMG FQ Global Risk-Balanced Fund Class N	MMAVX	NAS CM	Open End	Moderate Alloc (Growth & Income)	B-	C+	B	Up	Y	2,000
AMG FQ Global Risk-Balanced Fund Class Z	MMAFX	NAS CM	Open End	Moderate Alloc (Growth & Income)	B-	C+	B	Up	Y	5,000,000
AMG FQ Long-Short Equity Fund Class I	MEQFX	NAS CM	Open End	US Equity Large Cap Blend (Growth)	B-	B-	B	Down	Y	100,000
AMG FQ Long-Short Equity Fund Class N	FQUAX	NAS CM	Open End	US Equity Large Cap Blend (Growth)	B-	B-	B	Down	Y	2,000
AMG FQ Tax-Managed U.S. Equity Fund Class I	MFQTX	NAS CM	Open End	US Equity Large Cap Blend (Growth)	B-	B-	B-	Down	Y	100,000
AMG FQ Tax-Managed U.S. Equity Fund Class N	MFQAX	NAS CM	Open End	US Equity Large Cap Blend (Growth)	B-	B-	B-	Down	Y	2,000
AMG Frontier Small Cap Growth Fund Class I	MSSCX	NAS CM	Open End	US Equity Small Cap (Small Company)	B-	B	C	Up		100,000
AMG Frontier Small Cap Growth Fund Class N	MSSVX	NAS CM	Open End	US Equity Small Cap (Small Company)	C+	B	C	Up		2,000
AMG Frontier Small Cap Growth Fund Class Z	MSSYX	NAS CM	Open End	US Equity Small Cap (Small Company)	B-	B	C	Up		5,000,000
AMG GW&K Small Cap Core Fund Class I	GWEIX	NAS CM	Open End	US Equity Small Cap (Small Company)	A-	A-	B+	Up		100,000
AMG GW&K Small Cap Core Fund Class N	GWETX	NAS CM	Open End	US Equity Small Cap (Small Company)	B+	A-	B	Up		2,000
AMG GW&K Small Cap Core Fund Class Z	GWEZX	NAS CM	Open End	US Equity Small Cap (Small Company)	A-	A-	B	Up	Y	5,000,000
AMG GW&K Small/Mid Cap Fund Class I	GWGIX	NAS CM	Open End	US Equity Small Cap (Growth)	C	C+	B-	Up	Y	100,000
AMG GW&K Small/Mid Cap Fund Class N	GWGVX	NAS CM	Open End	US Equity Small Cap (Growth)	C	C+	B-	Up	Y	2,000
AMG GW&K Small/Mid Cap Fund Class Z	GWGZX	NAS CM	Open End	US Equity Small Cap (Growth)	C	C+	B-	Up	Y	5,000,000
AMG GW&K U.S. Small Cap Growth Fund Class I	ATSIX	NAS CM	Open End	US Equity Small Cap (Small Company)	B-	B	B-	Up	Y	100,000

★ Expanded analysis of this fund is included in Section II.

	TOTAL RETURNS					PERFORMANCE				ASSETS		ASSET ALLOCATION & TURNOVER					BULL & BEAR		FEES		
Min Additional Investment	3-Month Total Return	6-Month Total Return	1-Year Total Return	3-Year Total Return	5-Year Total Return	Dividend Yield (TTM)	Expense Ratio	3-Yr Std Deviation	3-Year Beta	NAV	Total Assets (MIL)	%Cash	%Stocks	%Bonds	%Other	Turnover Ratio	Last Bull Market Total Return	Last Bear Market Total Return	Front End Fee (%)	Back End Fee (%)	Inception Date
50	6.22	11.92	19.19	31.32	93.88	0.9	1.43	9.75	0.95	45.28	100,165	2	96	0	2	21	20.35	-12.85		1.00	Feb-02
50	6.37	12.24	19.80	33.44	99.08	1.35	0.9	9.76	0.95	45.3	100,165	2	96	0	2	21	20.76	-12.67			Mar-02
50	6.49	12.49	20.34	35.26	103.75	1.75	0.44	9.76	0.95	45.44	100,165	2	96	0	2	21	21.04	-12.48			Sep-02
50	6.45	12.40	20.19	34.75	102.42	1.62	0.58	9.76	0.95	45.65	100,165	2	96	0	2	21	20.97	-12.51	5.75		Jul-52
50	6.25	11.96	19.25	31.56	94.51	0.94	1.38	9.76	0.95	45.08	100,165	2	96	0	2	21	20.4	-12.8		1.00	Mar-01
50	6.42	12.34	20.06	34.39	101.62	1.54	0.67	9.76	0.95	45.48	100,165	2	96	0	2	21	20.97	-12.56			Mar-01
50	6.48	12.49	20.38	35.46	104.25	1.77	0.41	9.75	0.95	45.61	100,165	2	96	0	2	21	21.12	-12.44			Aug-08
50	6.52	12.56	20.48	35.08	102.91		0.3	9.76	0.95	45.63	100,165	2	96	0	2	21	20.97	-12.51			Jan-17
50	6.23	11.93	19.19	31.49	94.41	0.93	1.39	9.77	0.95	45.17	100,165	2	96	0	2	21	20.43	-12.83			May-02
50	6.26	11.95	19.21	31.60	94.73	0.94	1.39	9.75	0.95	45.02	100,165	2	96	0	2	21	20.48	-12.82			May-02
50	6.30	12.10	19.57	33.14	98.83	1.22	1.1	9.74	0.95	45.46	100,165	2	96	0	2	21	20.71	-12.64			Aug-14
50	6.36	12.20	19.73	33.26	98.80	1.31	0.95	9.76	0.95	45.27	100,165	2	96	0	2	21	20.78	-12.67			Jun-02
50	6.44	12.38	20.11	34.49	101.86	1.57	0.64	9.76	0.95	45.42	100,165	2	96	0	2	21	20.95	-12.54			May-02
50	6.51	12.53	20.46	35.69	104.91	1.82	0.35	9.76	0.95	45.63	100,165	2	96	0	2	21	21.19	-12.46			May-02
50	6.49	12.48	20.32	35.05	102.86	1.73	0.48	9.76	0.95	45.61	100,165	2	96	0	2	21	20.97	-12.51			Nov-15
50	6.52	12.55	20.53	35.89	105.35	1.86	0.3	9.76	0.95	45.67	100,165	2	96	0	2	21	21.2	-12.43			May-09
	4.00	8.80	12.82	20.69	78.96	0	6.37	12.83	1.2	5.19	17.2					15	28.44	-24.04	5.75		Mar-96
	4.21	8.53	12.37	18.35	73.15	0	7.07	12.94	1.22	4.45	17.2					15	28.86	-24.51		5.00	Mar-96
	3.99	8.59	12.18	18.18	72.65	0	7.07	13.02	1.22	4.42	17.2					15	27.83	-24.21		1.00	Mar-96
	4.15	9.10	13.37	21.63	81.84	0	6.07	12.75	1.2	5.51	17.2					15	29.07	-24.08	5.75		Jul-58
	25.87	14.46	-5.65	-15.25	8.17	0	14.53	18.6	0.53	4.67	0.55	0	88	0	12	151	19.5	-23.27	5.75		Feb-11
	5.94	3.21	2.27	12.07	34.68	0	7.57	11.46	0.96		0.90	3	97	0	0	0	19.06	-23.45		1.00	Feb-11
250	-0.99	2.59	-0.37			0.09	1.63			11.44	5.1	4	96	0	0				5.75		Dec-15
250	-1.16	2.29	-1.00			0	2.25			11.29	5.1	4	96	0	0					1.00	Dec-15
5,000	-0.97	2.76	-0.04			0.25	1.25			11.49	5.1	4	96	0	0						Dec-15
250	2.99	7.58	17.01	20.88		0.93	1.65	7.01	0.55	11.82	141.6	4	52	30	5	129			5.75		Sep-13
250	2.88	7.27	16.35	18.75		0.42	2.27	7.05	0.56	11.64	141.6	4	52	30	5	129				1.00	Sep-13
5,000	3.15	7.83	17.48	22.21		1.23	1.27	7	0.55	11.87	141.6	4	52	30	5	129					Sep-13
250	3.86	11.37	25.22	24.13	66.48	0	1.45	12.64	1.14	29.52	26.0	3	97	0	0	47	25.3	-18.59			Mar-97
100	4.65	8.03	15.71	23.37	61.94	0.76	0.94	5.96	0.56	17.19	199.6	1	65	33	0	119	15.06	-7.07			Nov-12
100	4.59	7.95	15.53	22.75	60.36	0.62	1.09	5.97	0.56	17.03	199.6	1	65	33	0	119	14.86	-7.11			Jan-97
1,000	4.68	8.15	15.89	23.72	62.45	0.85	0.84	5.98	0.56	17.19	199.6	1	65	33	0	119	15.06	-7.07			Jan-97
100	1.31	6.91	5.34	28.39		0.82	1.07			10.82	2.8	1	99	0	0	146					Dec-14
100	1.40	6.90	5.17	27.40		0.74	1.35			10.83	2.8	1	99	0	0	146					Dec-14
1,000	1.49	7.21	5.62	28.99		0.93	0.95			10.85	2.8	1	99	0	0	146					Dec-14
100	3.44	7.74	15.81	24.13	29.82	1.39	1.14	7.07	0.36	16.02	63.0	-62	83	68	10	71	10.59	-3.6			Jan-10
100	3.29	7.53	15.35	22.62	27.21	0.88	1.43	7.09	0.36	15.97	63.0	-62	83	68	10	71	10.39	-3.69			Jan-10
1,000	3.45	7.73	15.87	24.39	30.33	1.43	1.03	7.07	0.36	16.01	63.0	-62	83	68	10	71	10.69	-3.52			Nov-88
100	4.00	7.15	15.35	23.78	83.00	1.18	0.71	8.61	0.8	14.24	40.9	44	56	0	0	178	25.52	-16.37			Aug-92
100	3.83	6.83	14.93	22.61	80.44	0.84	1.04	8.62	0.8	14.24	40.9	44	56	0	0	178	25.36	-16.47			Mar-06
100	4.73	10.48	18.27	25.98	106.22	1.01	0.89	9.41	0.87	30.22	73.6	2	98	0	0	102	27.79	-18.69			Dec-00
100	4.65	10.33	17.97	25.03	103.71	0.78	1.14	9.4	0.87	30.28	73.6	2	98	0	0	102	27.55	-18.74			Mar-06
100	4.27	9.69	21.24	18.67	81.89	0	1.05	14.98	0.98	10.73	18.9	3	97	0	0	70	26.83	-26.8			Sep-97
100	4.20	9.55	20.88	17.77	79.41	0	1.3	14.98	0.98	10.46	18.9	3	97	0	0	70	26.59	-26.89			Dec-09
1,000	4.25	9.75	21.40	19.37	83.82	0	0.9	14.99	0.98	10.97	18.9	3	97	0	0	70	26.98	-26.72			Dec-09
100	4.64	10.02	20.78	37.66	105.52	0.32	0.95	11.91	0.8	28.42	544.7	2	98	0	0	19	25.63	-20.18			Jul-09
100	4.49	9.77	20.31	35.99	101.33	0	1.3	11.92	0.8	28.04	544.7	2	98	0	0	19	25.38	-20.38			Dec-96
1,000	4.65	10.02	20.79	36.53	102.13		0.9	11.93	0.8	28.42	544.7	2	98	0	0	19	25.38	-20.38			Feb-17
100	4.64	6.62	15.43			0.04	0.96			11.15	26.7	3	97	0	0	48					Jun-15
100	4.62	6.59	15.25				1.26			11.15	26.7	3	97	0	0	48					Feb-17
1,000	4.58	6.65	15.47				0.86			11.15	26.7	3	97	0	0	48					Feb-17
100	4.60	11.28	25.34	20.71	59.61	0	0.97	12.81	0.81	5.04	35.9	3	97	0	0	106	27.94	-24.27			Jan-05

	MARKET			FUND TYPE, CATEGORY & OBJECTIVE	RATINGS				MINIMUMS	
Fund Name	Ticker Symbol	Traded On	Fund Type	Category and (Prospectus Objective)	Overall Rating	Reward Rating	Risk Rating	Recent Up/ Downgrade	Open to New Investors	Min Initial Investment
AMG GW&K U.S. Small Cap Growth Fund Class N	ATASX	NAS CM	Open End	US Equity Small Cap (Small Company)	C+	B-	C	Up	Y	2,000
AMG GW&K U.S. Small Cap Growth Fund Class Z	ATAZX	NAS CM	Open End	US Equity Small Cap (Small Company)	C+	B	C	Up	Y	5,000,000
AMG Managers Brandywine Advisors Mid Cap Growth Fund Cls N	BWAFX	NAS CM	Open End	US Equity Mid Cap (Growth)	C+	B-	C	Up	Y	2,000
AMG Managers Brandywine Blue Fund Class I	BLUEX	NAS CM	Open End	US Equity Large Cap Growth (Growth)	B	A-	B-	Up	Y	2,000
AMG Managers Brandywine Fund Class I	BRWIX	NAS CM	Open End	US Equity Mid Cap (Growth)	B+	B+	B	Up	Y	2,000
AMG Managers Cadence Emerging Companies Fund - Class I	MECIX	NAS CM	Open End	US Equity Small Cap (Small Company)	A-	A	B+	Up	Y	100,000
AMG Managers Cadence Emerging Companies Fund - Class N	MECAX	NAS CM	Open End	US Equity Small Cap (Small Company)	A-	A	B+	Up	Y	2,000
AMG Managers Cadence Emerging Companies Fund - Class Z	MECZX	NAS CM	Open End	US Equity Small Cap (Small Company)	A-	A	B+	Up	Y	5,000,000
AMG Managers Cadence Mid Cap Fund - Class I	MCMYX	NAS CM	Open End	US Equity Mid Cap (Growth)	B	B	C+	Up	Y	100,000
AMG Managers Cadence Mid Cap Fund - Class N	MCMAX	NAS CM	Open End	US Equity Mid Cap (Growth)	B	B	C+	Up	Y	2,000
AMG Managers Cadence Mid Cap Fund - Class Z	MCMFX	NAS CM	Open End	US Equity Mid Cap (Growth)	B	B	C+	Up	Y	5,000,000
AMG Managers CenterSquare Real Estate Fund Class I	MRASX	NAS CM	Open End	Real Estate Sector Equity (Real Estate)	B	B-	B+	Up	Y	100,000
AMG Managers CenterSquare Real Estate Fund Class N	MRESX	NAS CM	Open End	Real Estate Sector Equity (Real Estate)	B	B-	B+	Up	Y	2,000
AMG Managers CenterSquare Real Estate Fund Class Z	MREZX	NAS CM	Open End	Real Estate Sector Equity (Real Estate)	B	B-	B+	Up	Y	5,000,000
AMG Managers Emerging Opportunities Fund Class I	MIMFX	NAS CM	Open End	US Equity Small Cap (Growth)	B+	A	B-	Up	Y	100,000
AMG Managers Emerging Opportunities Fund Class N	MMCFX	NAS CM	Open End	US Equity Small Cap (Growth)	B+	A	B-	Up	Y	2,000
AMG Managers Essex Small/Micro Cap Growth Fund - Class N	MBRSX	NAS CM	Open End	US Equity Small Cap (Growth)	B+	A-	B-	Up	Y	2,000
AMG Managers Fairpointe ESG Equity Fund Class I	AFFEX	NAS CM	Open End	US Equity Mid Cap (Growth)	C+	C+	C	Up	Y	100,000
AMG Managers Fairpointe ESG Equity Fund Class N	AFPTX	NAS CM	Open End	US Equity Mid Cap (Growth)	C+	C+	C	Up	Y	2,000
AMG Managers Fairpointe Mid Cap Fund Class I	ABMIX	NAS CM	Open End	US Equity Mid Cap (Growth)	B-	B-	C+	Up		100,000
AMG Managers Fairpointe Mid Cap Fund Class N	CHTTX	NAS CM	Open End	US Equity Mid Cap (Growth)	B-	B-	C+	Up		2,000
AMG Managers Fairpointe Mid Cap Fund Class Z	ABIZX	NAS CM	Open End	US Equity Mid Cap (Growth)	B-	B-	C+		Y	5,000,000
AMG Managers Guardian Capital Global Dividend Fund Class I	AGCDX	NAS CM	Open End	Global Equity (Growth & Income)	B-	C+	B-	Up	Y	100,000
AMG Managers Guardian Capital Global Dividend Fund Class N	AGCNX	NAS CM	Open End	Global Equity (Growth & Income)	B-	C+	B-	Up	Y	2,000
AMG Managers Lake Partners LASSO Alternatives Fund Class I	ALSOX	NAS CM	Open End	Multialternative (Asset Alloc)	C+	C	B	Up	Y	100,000
AMG Managers Lake Partners LASSO Alternatives Fund Class N	ALSNX	NAS CM	Open End	Multialternative (Asset Alloc)	C+	C	B	Up	Y	2,000
AMG Managers LMCG Small Cap Growth Fund Class I	ACWIX	NAS CM	Open End	US Equity Small Cap (Small Company)	C+	C+	C+	Up	Y	100,000
AMG Managers LMCG Small Cap Growth Fund Class N	ACWDX	NAS CM	Open End	US Equity Small Cap (Small Company)	C+	C+	C+	Up	Y	2,000
AMG Managers Montag & Caldwell Balanced Fund Class I	MOBIX	NAS CM	Open End	Moderate Alloc (Balanced)	B	C+	A-		Y	100,000
AMG Managers Montag & Caldwell Balanced Fund Class N	MOBAX	NAS CM	Open End	Moderate Alloc (Balanced)	B	C+	A-		Y	2,000
AMG Managers Montag & Caldwell Growth Fund Class I	MCGIX	NAS CM	Open End	US Equity Large Cap Growth (Growth)	B	B-	B+		Y	100,000
AMG Managers Montag & Caldwell Growth Fund Class N	MCGFX	NAS CM	Open End	US Equity Large Cap Growth (Growth)	B	B-	B+		Y	2,000
AMG Managers Montag & Caldwell Growth Fund Class R	MCRGX	NAS CM	Open End	US Equity Large Cap Growth (Growth)	B	B-	B+		Y	2,000
AMG Managers Montag & Caldwell Mid Cap Growth Fund Class I	AMMCX	NAS CM	Open End	US Equity Mid Cap (Growth & Income)	B	B-	B+	Up	Y	100,000
AMG Managers Montag & Caldwell Mid Cap Growth Fund Class N	AMCMX	NAS CM	Open End	US Equity Mid Cap (Growth & Income)	B	B-	B+	Up	Y	2,000
AMG Managers Pictet International Fund Class I	APCTX	NAS CM	Open End	Global Equity Large Cap (Growth)	B	B	B+	Up	Y	100,000
AMG Managers Pictet International Fund Class N	APINX	NAS CM	Open End	Global Equity Large Cap (Growth)	B	B	B+	Up	Y	2,000
AMG Managers Pictet International Fund Class Z	APCZX	NAS CM	Open End	Global Equity Large Cap (Growth)	B	B	B+		Y	5,000,000
AMG Managers Silvercrest Small Cap Fund Class I	ACRTX	NAS CM	Open End	US Equity Small Cap (Small Company)	B+	A-	B	Up	Y	100,000
AMG Managers Silvercrest Small Cap Fund Class N	ASCTX	NAS CM	Open End	US Equity Small Cap (Small Company)	B+	A-	B	Up	Y	2,000
AMG Managers Silvercrest Small Cap Fund Class Z	ACZTX	NAS CM	Open End	US Equity Small Cap (Small Company)	B+	A-	B		Y	5,000,000
AMG Managers Skyline Special Equities Fund Class I	SKSIX	NAS CM	Open End	US Equity Small Cap (Small Company)	B	B	B	Up	Y	100,000
AMG Managers Skyline Special Equities Fund Class N	SKSEX	NAS CM	Open End	US Equity Small Cap (Small Company)	B	B	B	Up		2,000
AMG Managers Skyline Special Equities Fund Class Z	SKSZX	NAS CM	Open End	US Equity Small Cap (Small Company)	B	B	B	Up	Y	5,000,000
AMG Managers Special Equity Fund Class I	MSEIX	NAS CM	Open End	US Equity Small Cap (Growth)	B+	A-	B	Up	Y	100,000
AMG Managers Special Equity Fund Class N	MGSEX	NAS CM	Open End	US Equity Small Cap (Growth)	B+	A-	B	Up	Y	2,000
AMG Managers Value Partners Asia Dividend Fund Class I	AAVPX	NAS CM	Open End	Asia ex-Japan Equity (Growth & Income)	C-	C	B+	Up	Y	100,000
AMG Managers Value Partners Asia Dividend Fund Class N	AVADX	NAS CM	Open End	Asia ex-Japan Equity (Growth & Income)	C-	C	B+	Up	Y	2,000
AMG Renaissance International Equity Fund Class I	RIESX	NAS CM	Open End	Global Equity Large Cap (World Stock)	B-	C+	B-	Up	Y	100,000
AMG Renaissance International Equity Fund Class N	RIEIX	NAS CM	Open End	Global Equity Large Cap (World Stock)	B-	C+	B-	Up	Y	2,000
AMG Renaissance International Equity Fund Class Z	RIELX	NAS CM	Open End	Global Equity Large Cap (World Stock)	B-	C+	B-	Up	Y	5,000,000
AMG Renaissance Large Cap Growth Fund Class I	MRLSX	NAS CM	Open End	US Equity Large Cap Growth (Growth)	B	B	B+		Y	100,000

★ Expanded analysis of this fund is included in Section II.

	TOTAL RETURNS					PERFORMANCE				ASSETS		ASSET ALLOCATION & TURNOVER					BULL & BEAR		FEES		
Min Additional Investment	3-Month Total Return	6-Month Total Return	1-Year Total Return	3-Year Total Return	5-Year Total Return	Dividend Yield (TTM)	Expense Ratio	3-Yr Std Deviation	3-Year Beta	NAV	Total Assets (MIL)	%Cash	%Stocks	%Bonds	%Other	Turnover Ratio	Last Bull Market Total Return	Last Bear Market Total Return	Front End Fee (%)	Back End Fee (%)	Inception Date
100	4.41	10.94	24.80	19.56	57.34	0	1.22	12.75	0.8	4.08	35.9	3	97	0	0	106	27.78	-24.36			Nov-00
1,000	4.60	11.28	25.22	19.95	57.85		0.9	12.77	0.81	5.04	35.9	3	97	0	0	106	27.78	-24.36			Feb-17
100	5.82	13.24	25.13	20.04	63.43	0	1.15	12.35	0.98	11.8	137.2	7	93	0	0	215	18.47	-29.17			Oct-00
100	4.77	12.50	27.85	33.95	98.51	0	1.2	10.21	0.88	47.87	179.7	9	91	0	0	167	22.79	-21.44			Jan-91
100	4.85	12.19	23.64	31.86	101.99	0	1.11	11.88	1.02	46.64	795.9	3	97	0	0	187	19.36	-28.92			Dec-85
100	1.28	13.88	22.40	62.90	141.22	0	0.97	14.12	0.74	58.4	100.4	2	98	0	0	90	36.59	-24.98			Jun-93
100	1.25	13.83	22.21	61.89	138.64	0	1.09	14.13	0.74	53.91	100.4	2	98	0	0	90	36.37	-25.07			Apr-96
1,000	1.30	13.92	22.46	62.98	141.34		0.89	14.13	0.74	58.43	100.4	2	98	0	0	90	36.59	-24.98			May-17
100	8.57	14.08	25.74	32.57	98.63	0.59	0.87	10.62	0.92	31.27	133.0	1	99	0	0	141	26	-19.81			Nov-94
100	8.50	13.95	25.46	31.86	97.03	0.44	1.1	10.61	0.92	30.25	133.0	1	99	0	0	141	25.93	-19.87			Jan-97
1,000	8.58	14.15	25.91	33.41	101.00	0.77	0.72	10.61	0.92	32.74	133.0	1	99	0	0	141	26.24	-19.77			Aug-91
100	3.59	4.34	5.53	16.77	61.14		0.92	13.47	0.99	10.43	304.6	0	100	0	0	65	30.76	-16.07			Feb-17
100	3.57	4.28	5.40	16.62	60.93	1.66	1.07	13.46	0.99	10.43	304.6	0	100	0	0	65	30.76	-16.07			Dec-97
1,000	3.72	4.49	5.59	16.84	61.23		0.82	13.46	0.99	10.43	304.6	0	100	0	0	65	30.76	-16.07			Feb-17
100	4.17	14.78	24.30	34.14	119.98	0	1.18	15.06	1.01	46.48	175.7	3	96	0	0	72	31.89	-25.16			Sep-11
100	4.11	14.66	24.01	33.18	117.36	0	1.43	15.05	1.01	45.91	175.7	3	96	0	0	72	31.86	-25.16			Jun-94
100	1.20	10.55	24.10	26.60	117.43	0	1.49	14.92	0.95	26.68	29.3	0	100	0	0	67	22.96	-27.95			Jun-02
100	6.78	9.12	18.50	27.11		0.82	0.9			12.23	7.1	8	92	0	0	31					Dec-14
100	6.78	9.02	18.23	26.25		0.12	1.15			12.31	7.1	8	92	0	0	31					Dec-14
100	5.38	6.24	11.79	23.92	102.80	0.51	0.87	15.86	1.26	43.79	4,200	5	95	0	0	24	27.42	-25.65			Jul-04
100	5.31	6.10	11.51	22.97	100.27	0.28	1.12	15.85	1.26	42.69	4,200	5	95	0	0	24	27.25	-25.74			Sep-94
1,000	5.38	6.17	11.59	23.06	100.40		0.79	15.85	1.26	43.76	4,200	5	95	0	0	24	27.25	-25.74			Sep-17
100	5.13	9.34	19.43	19.18		1.85	1.06	9.42	0.82	11.6	38.2	2	98	0	0	36					Apr-14
100	5.10	9.41	19.34	18.61		1.45	1.31	9.45	0.82	11.66	38.2	2	98	0	0	36					Apr-14
100	1.79	3.71	4.91	3.15	14.85	0	2.47	3.76	0.58	12.04	48.7	15	42	38	2	30	8.97	-9.5			Apr-09
100	1.74	3.59	4.63	2.44	13.47	0	2.72	3.76	0.58	11.98	48.7	15	42	38	2	30	8.84	-9.59			Mar-10
100	6.43	9.53	19.03	10.45	75.73	0	1.09	16.94	1.08	16.2	129.5	2	98	0	0	138	26.7	-30.21			Jun-11
100	6.33	9.32	18.68	9.64	73.61	0	1.35	16.93	1.08	15.94	129.5	2	98	0	0	138	26.5	-30.23			Nov-10
100	3.67	6.26	15.38	17.54	45.86	0.5	1.11	5.78	0.45	22.06	21.6	3	69	28	0	85	12.99	-5.84			Dec-98
100	3.63	6.24	15.24	17.25	45.19	0.43	1.36	5.78	0.45	22.15	21.6	3	69	28	0	85	12.86	-5.95			Nov-94
100	5.98	10.63	23.64	26.69	78.30	0.56	0.87	9.28	0.79	19.71	854.4	6	94	0	0	64	21.3	-11.61			Jun-96
100	5.96	10.52	23.34	25.81	76.21	0.17	1.12	9.29	0.8	19.64	854.4	6	94	0	0	64	21.06	-11.66			Nov-94
50	5.95	10.44	23.16	24.94	74.09	0.12	1.36	9.28	0.8	19.14	854.4	6	94	0	0	64	20.93	-11.77			Dec-02
100	8.95	12.70	23.47	28.79	81.15	0.46	1.01	10.25	0.87	11.36	9.8	7	93	0	0	39	26.16	-18			May-14
100	8.82	12.58	23.16	27.75	79.56	0.24	1.26	10.14	0.86	11.28	9.8	7	93	0	0	39	26.16	-18			Nov-07
100	3.64	7.71	27.46	38.93		1.14	1.01	11.57	0.9	11.32	2,055	1	99	0	0	38					Apr-14
100	3.51	7.56	27.11	37.68		0.59	1.26	11.55	0.9	11.31	2,055	1	99	0	0	38					Apr-14
1,000	3.63	7.70	27.45	38.92			0.94	11.57	0.9	11.29	2,055	1	99	0	0	38					Sep-17
100	3.53	9.14	10.54	36.52	101.93	0.18	1.16	14.58	0.99	18.42	279.9	4	96	0	0	32					Dec-11
100	3.44	8.99	10.26	35.48	99.27	0	1.41	14.62	0.99	18.26	279.9	4	96	0	0	32					Dec-11
1,000	3.54	9.16	10.55	36.54	101.95		1.09	14.58	0.99	18.41	279.9	4	96	0	0	32					Sep-17
100	0.90	6.80	8.57	22.64	100.34		1.03	15.12	1.02	44.06	1,333	11	89	0	0	34	32.76	-25.23			Feb-17
100	0.91	6.74	8.39	22.44	99.99	0	1.18	15.12	1.02	43.98	1,333	11	89	0	0	34	32.76	-25.23			Apr-87
1,000	0.97	6.87	8.62	22.70	100.42		0.93	15.12	1.02	44.08	1,333	11	89	0	0	34	32.76	-25.23			Feb-17
100	4.84	11.21	20.54	35.56	104.76	0	1.11	13.81	0.92	122.9	201.2	2	98	0	0	120	31.02	-23.36			May-04
100	4.78	11.07	20.25	34.56	102.97	0	1.36	13.8	0.91	119.45	201.2	2	98	0	0	120	30.69	-23.44			Jun-84
100	7.96	14.83	38.26			3.02	1.16			12.48	10.6	5	94	0	0						Dec-15
100	7.96	14.84	38.26			3.05	1.41			12.47	10.6	5	94	0	0						Dec-15
100	2.45	7.80	26.76	22.30		2.64	0.95	12.06	0.92	10.55	2.8	1	99	0	0	93					Jun-14
100	2.34	7.69	26.38	21.07		2.07	1.25	12.07	0.92	10.59	2.8	1	99	0	0	93					Jun-14
1,000	2.51	7.97	26.96	22.77		2.71	0.85	12.03	0.92	10.56	2.8	1	99	0	0	93					Jun-14
100	7.03	11.70	22.45	31.29	117.26	0.55	0.81	11.18	0.94	14.17	185.9	2	98	0	0	37	30	-21.99			Jun-09

	MARKET			FUND TYPE, CATEGORY & OBJECTIVE	RATINGS				MINIMUMS	
Fund Name	Ticker Symbol	Traded On	Fund Type	Category and (Prospectus Objective)	Overall Rating	Reward Rating	Risk Rating	Recent Up/ Downgrade	Open to New Investors	Min Initial Investment
AMG Renaissance Large Cap Growth Fund Class N	MRLTX	NAS CM	Open End	US Equity Large Cap Growth (Growth)	B	B	B+		Y	2,000
AMG Renaissance Large Cap Growth Fund Class Z	MRLIX	NAS CM	Open End	US Equity Large Cap Growth (Growth)	B	B	B+		Y	5,000,000
AMG River Road Dividend All Cap Value Fund Class I	ARIDX	NAS CM	Open End	US Equity Large Cap Value (Equity-Income)	B-	B-	B	Down		100,000
AMG River Road Dividend All Cap Value Fund Class N	ARDEX	NAS CM	Open End	US Equity Large Cap Value (Equity-Income)	B-	B-	B	Down		2,000
AMG River Road Dividend All Cap Value Fund Class Z	ARZDX	NAS CM	Open End	US Equity Large Cap Value (Equity-Income)	B-	B-	B		Y	5,000,000
AMG River Road Dividend All Cap Value Fund II Class I	ADIVX	NAS CM	Open End	US Equity Large Cap Value (Equity-Income)	B-	B-	B	Down	Y	100,000
AMG River Road Dividend All Cap Value Fund II Class N	ADVTX	NAS CM	Open End	US Equity Large Cap Value (Equity-Income)	B-	B-	B	Down	Y	2,000
AMG River Road Dividend All Cap Value Fund II Class Z	ADVZX	NAS CM	Open End	US Equity Large Cap Value (Equity-Income)	B-	B-	B		Y	5,000,000
AMG River Road Focused Absolute Value Fund Class I	AFAVX	NAS CM	Open End	US Equity Mid Cap (Growth)	C	C-	B	Up	Y	100,000
AMG River Road Focused Absolute Value Fund Class N	ARRFX	NAS CM	Open End	US Equity Mid Cap (Growth)	C	C-	B	Up	Y	2,000
AMG River Road Focused Absolute Value Fund Class Z	ARRZX	NAS CM	Open End	US Equity Mid Cap (Growth)	C	C-	B+		Y	5,000,000
AMG River Road Long-Short Fund Class I	ALSIX	NAS CM	Open End	Long/Short Equity (Growth & Income)	B	C+	A-	Up	Y	100,000
AMG River Road Long-Short Fund Class N	ARLSX	NAS CM	Open End	Long/Short Equity (Growth & Income)	B	C+	A-	Up	Y	2,000
AMG River Road Long-Short Fund Class Z	ARLZX	NAS CM	Open End	Long/Short Equity (Growth & Income)	B-	C+	B		Y	5,000,000
AMG River Road Small Cap Value Fund Class I	ARSIX	NAS CM	Open End	US Equity Small Cap (Small Company)	B	B	B+		Y	100,000
AMG River Road Small Cap Value Fund Class N	ARSVX	NAS CM	Open End	US Equity Small Cap (Small Company)	B	B	B+		Y	2,000
AMG River Road Small Cap Value Fund Class Z	ARZMX	NAS CM	Open End	US Equity Small Cap (Small Company)	B	B	B+		Y	5,000,000
AMG River Road Small-Mid Cap Value Fund Class I	ARIMX	NAS CM	Open End	US Equity Small Cap (Growth)	B	B	B		Y	100,000
AMG River Road Small-Mid Cap Value Fund Class N	ARSMX	NAS CM	Open End	US Equity Small Cap (Growth)	B	B	B		Y	2,000
AMG River Road Small-Mid Cap Value Fund Class Z	ARSZX	NAS CM	Open End	US Equity Small Cap (Growth)	B	B	B		Y	5,000,000
AMG SouthernSun Global Opportunities Fund Class I	SSOLX	NAS CM	Open End	Global Equity Mid/Small Cap (Growth)	D	C-	B		Y	100,000
AMG SouthernSun Global Opportunities Fund Class N	SSOVX	NAS CM	Open End	Global Equity Mid/Small Cap (Growth)	D	C-	B		Y	2,000
AMG SouthernSun Small Cap Fund Class I	SSSIX	NAS CM	Open End	US Equity Small Cap (Small Company)	C+	B-	C			100,000
AMG SouthernSun Small Cap Fund Class N	SSSFX	NAS CM	Open End	US Equity Small Cap (Small Company)	C+	B-	C			2,000
AMG SouthernSun U.S. Equity Fund Class C	SSECX	NAS CM	Open End	US Equity Mid Cap (Growth)	C+	C+	C+	Up	Y	2,000
AMG SouthernSun U.S. Equity Fund Class I	SSEIX	NAS CM	Open End	US Equity Mid Cap (Growth)	C+	C+	B-	Up	Y	100,000
AMG SouthernSun U.S. Equity Fund Class N	SSEFX	NAS CM	Open End	US Equity Mid Cap (Growth)	C+	C+	B-	Up	Y	2,000
AMG Systematic Mid Cap Value Fund Class I	SYIMX	NAS CM	Open End	US Equity Mid Cap (Growth)	B	B	B-	Up	Y	100,000
AMG Systematic Mid Cap Value Fund Class N	SYAMX	NAS CM	Open End	US Equity Mid Cap (Growth)	B-	B	B-	Up	Y	2,000
AMG TimesSquare Emerging Markets Small Cap Fund Class I	TQEIX	NAS CM	Open End	Emerging Markets Equity (Div Emerging Mkts)	D	D+	A-		Y	100,000
AMG TimesSquare Emerging Markets Small Cap Fund Class N	TQENX	NAS CM	Open End	Emerging Markets Equity (Div Emerging Mkts)	D-	D+	A-		Y	2,000
AMG TimesSquare Emerging Markets Small Cap Fund Class Z	TQEZX	NAS CM	Open End	Emerging Markets Equity (Div Emerging Mkts)	D	D+	A-		Y	5,000,000
AMG TimesSquare International Small Cap Fund Class I	TQTIX	NAS CM	Open End	Global Equity Mid/Small Cap (Small Company)	A-	A-	A	Up	Y	100,000
AMG TimesSquare International Small Cap Fund Class N	TCMPX	NAS CM	Open End	Global Equity Mid/Small Cap (Small Company)	A-	A-	A	Up	Y	2,000
AMG TimesSquare International Small Cap Fund Class Z	TCMIX	NAS CM	Open End	Global Equity Mid/Small Cap (Small Company)	A-	A-	A	Up	Y	5,000,000
AMG TimesSquare Mid Cap Growth Fund Class I	TQMIX	NAS CM	Open End	US Equity Mid Cap (Growth)	B	B	B-	Up	Y	100,000
AMG TimesSquare Mid Cap Growth Fund Class N	TMDPX	NAS CM	Open End	US Equity Mid Cap (Growth)	B-	B	B-	Down		2,000
AMG TimesSquare Mid Cap Growth Fund Class Z	TMDIX	NAS CM	Open End	US Equity Mid Cap (Growth)	B	B	B-	Up		5,000,000
AMG TimesSquare Small Cap Growth Fund Class I	TSQIX	NAS CM	Open End	US Equity Small Cap (Small Company)	B+	A-	B	Up	Y	100,000
AMG TimesSquare Small Cap Growth Fund Class N	TSCPX	NAS CM	Open End	US Equity Small Cap (Small Company)	B+	B+	B	Up		2,000
AMG TimesSquare Small Cap Growth Fund Class Z	TSCIX	NAS CM	Open End	US Equity Small Cap (Small Company)	B+	A-	B	Up		5,000,000
AMG Trilogy Emerging Markets Equity Fund Class I	TLESX	NAS CM	Open End	Emerging Markets Equity (Div Emerging Mkts)	B-	B	C	Up	Y	100,000
AMG Trilogy Emerging Markets Equity Fund Class N	TLEVX	NAS CM	Open End	Emerging Markets Equity (Div Emerging Mkts)	B-	B	C	Up	Y	2,000
AMG Trilogy Emerging Markets Equity Fund Class Z	TLEIX	NAS CM	Open End	Emerging Markets Equity (Div Emerging Mkts)	B-	B	C	Up	Y	5,000,000
AMG Trilogy Emerging Wealth Equity Fund Class I	TYWSX	NAS CM	Open End	Emerging Markets Equity (Div Emerging Mkts)	B-	B-	C+	Up	Y	100,000
AMG Trilogy Emerging Wealth Equity Fund Class N	TYWVX	NAS CM	Open End	Emerging Markets Equity (Div Emerging Mkts)	B-	B-	C+	Up	Y	2,000
AMG Trilogy Emerging Wealth Equity Fund Class Z	TYWIX	NAS CM	Open End	Emerging Markets Equity (Div Emerging Mkts)	B-	B-	C+	Up	Y	5,000,000
AMG Yacktman Focused Fund - Security Selection Only Cls I	YFSIX	NAS CM	Open End	US Equity Large Cap Blend (Growth & Income)	U	U	U		Y	100,000
AMG Yacktman Focused Fund - Security Selection Only Cls N	YFSNX	NAS CM	Open End	US Equity Large Cap Blend (Growth & Income)	U	U	U		Y	2,000
AMG Yacktman Focused Fund Class I	YAFIX	NAS CM	Open End	US Equity Large Cap Blend (Growth & Income)	B-	B-	B-	Down	Y	100,000
AMG Yacktman Focused Fund Class N	YAFFX	NAS CM	Open End	US Equity Large Cap Blend (Growth & Income)	B-	B-	B-	Down	Y	2,000
AMG Yacktman Fund Class I	YACKX	NAS CM	Open End	US Equity Large Cap Blend (Growth & Income)	B-	B-	B-	Down	Y	100,000

★ Expanded analysis of this fund is included in Section II.

Min Additional Investment	3-Month Total Return	6-Month Total Return	1-Year Total Return	3-Year Total Return	5-Year Total Return	Dividend Yield (TTM)	Expense Ratio	3-Yr Std Deviation	3-Year Beta	NAV	Total Assets (MIL)	%Cash	%Stocks	%Bonds	%Other	Turnover Ratio	Last Bull Market Total Return	Last Bear Market Total Return	Front End Fee (%)	Back End Fee (%)	Inception Date
	TOTAL RETURNS					PERFORMANCE				ASSETS		ASSET ALLOCATION & TURNOVER					BULL & BEAR		FEES		
100	6.96	11.50	22.03	29.95	113.45	0.35	1.06	11.17	0.94	14.03	185.9	2	98	0	0	37	29.82	-22.08			Jun-09
1,000	7.00	11.71	22.49	31.86	118.51	0.68	0.66	11.17	0.94	14	185.9	2	98	0	0	37	30.24	-21.97			Jun-09
100	3.87	6.13	9.05	24.08	83.83	1.67	0.85	9.82	0.89	12.51	949.8	3	97	0	0	47	17.73	-11.57			Jun-07
100	3.80	6.00	8.78	23.16	81.50	1.45	1.1	9.82	0.89	12.52	949.8	3	97	0	0	47	17.54	-11.64			Jun-05
1,000	3.89	6.09	8.87	23.26	81.65		0.79	9.82	0.89	12.51	949.8	3	97	0	0	47	17.54	-11.65			Sep-17
100	4.16	6.57	10.05	24.18	83.15	1.44	0.91	9.84	0.89	14.41	124.9	1	99	0	0	34					Jun-12
100	4.10	6.44	9.66	23.21	80.71	1.24	1.16	9.84	0.89	14.39	124.9	1	99	0	0	34					Jun-12
1,000	4.18	6.58	10.07	24.21	83.17		0.85	9.84	0.89	14.41	124.9	1	99	0	0	34					Sep-17
100	0.71	4.22	11.01			0.77	0.75			11.32	25.0	1	99	0	0						Nov-15
100	0.55	3.98	10.57			0.67	1			11.27	25.0	1	99	0	0						Nov-15
1,000	0.66	4.17	10.96				0.71			11.31	25.0	1	99	0	0						Sep-17
100	1.11	3.51	9.22	14.34	33.96	0	1.29	7.36	0.52	12.67	34.1	39	63	0	-1	298	8.54				Mar-13
100	1.04	3.38	8.87	13.42	32.32	0	1.54	7.38	0.53	12.51	34.1	39	63	0	-1	298	8.54				May-11
1,000	1.11	3.45	8.94	13.49	32.41		1.21	7.38	0.53	12.67	34.1	39	63	0	-1	298	8.54				Sep-17
100	3.25	4.75	12.02	40.48	87.75	0	1.16	11.57	0.75	13.21	319.7	7	93	0	0	57	22.16	-18.01			Dec-06
100	3.18	4.63	11.76	39.40	85.36	0	1.41	11.61	0.75	12.99	319.7	7	93	0	0	57	22.01	-18.1			Jun-05
1,000	3.28	4.73	11.86	39.53	85.54		1.07	11.61	0.75	13.2	319.7	7	93	0	0	57	22.01	-18.1			Sep-17
100	1.82	4.41	15.74	42.85	87.02	0.31	1.15	11.94	0.92	7.47	44.6	1	99	0	0	65	23.83	-17.5			Jun-07
100	1.77	4.28	15.34	41.83	84.69	0.1	1.4	11.92	0.91	7.33	44.6	1	99	0	0	65	23.53	-17.65			Mar-07
1,000	1.75	4.25	15.31	41.80	84.65		1.09	11.92	0.91	7.46	44.6	1	99	0	0	65	23.54	-17.65			Sep-17
100	1.68	10.08	16.92			0	1.32			11.78	2.9	18	82	0	0	32					Jul-16
100	1.60	9.82	16.54			0	1.57			11.73	2.9	18	82	0	0	32					Jul-16
100	1.10	7.21	18.34	17.65	65.37	0.2	0.97	16.08	0.98	26.45	364.9	7	93	0	0	21	33.84	-23.59			Sep-09
100	1.04	7.11	18.02	16.81	63.31	0	1.22	16.07	0.98	26.06	364.9	7	93	0	0	21	33.58	-23.67			Oct-03
100	1.61	4.92	9.57	11.17	55.40	0	1.96	13.64	1	13.85	793.0	5	95	0	0	18					Apr-12
100	1.82	5.40	10.66	14.48	63.27	0.35	0.96	13.64	1.01	14.35	793.0	5	95	0	0	18					Apr-12
100	1.78	5.30	10.40	13.68	61.31	0.12	1.21	13.6	1	14.34	793.0	5	95	0	0	18					Apr-12
100	7.95	14.19	15.11	28.43	86.04	2.04	0.87	13.76	1.25	15.66	89.9	2	98	0	0	146	29.1	-24.81			Dec-06
100	7.94	14.11	14.78	27.45	83.53	1.78	1.12	13.74	1.25	15.68	89.9	2	98	0	0	146	28.91	-24.83			Dec-06
100	9.70	16.10	32.85				1.35			12.35	6.6	1	97	0	0						Dec-16
100	9.59	15.89	32.44				1.65			12.33	6.6	1	97	0	0						Feb-17
1,000	9.70	16.10	32.85				1.25			12.35	6.6	1	97	0	0						Dec-16
100	4.61	12.31	38.83	55.85	98.98		1.15	11.95	0.91	17.08	578.9	2	98	0	0	58					Feb-17
100	4.58	12.19	38.62	54.71	97.19	0.4	1.3	11.96	0.91	16.99	578.9	2	98	0	0	58					Jan-13
1,000	4.56	12.25	38.85	55.88	99.01	0.46	1.05	11.95	0.91	17.08	578.9	2	98	0	0	58					Jan-13
100	5.96	10.58	22.57	31.76	94.19		1.14	10.52	0.92	18.86	2,108	2	98	0	0	47	30.1	-20.94			Feb-17
100	5.94	10.54	22.39	30.99	92.30	0	1.24	10.52	0.93	18.4	2,108	2	98	0	0	47	30.03	-21.05			Mar-05
1,000	5.96	10.63	22.63	31.82	94.28	0.04	1.04	10.52	0.92	18.87	2,108	2	98	0	0	47	30.1	-20.94			Mar-05
100	5.38	11.25	21.08	32.03	94.82		1.15	12.57	0.82	17.32	1,196	3	96	0	0	62	25.56	-21.5			Feb-17
100	5.32	11.13	20.87	31.32	92.91	0.16	1.25	12.56	0.82	16.9	1,196	3	96	0	0	62	25.36	-21.49			Jan-00
1,000	5.37	11.24	21.14	32.09	94.91	0.31	1.05	12.58	0.82	17.33	1,196	3	96	0	0	62	25.56	-21.5			Jan-00
100	5.89	16.91	38.10	31.27	21.97	0.86	1.07	15.39	0.94	10.33	132.6	2	98	0	0	33	15.56	-27.8			Mar-11
100	5.79	16.80	37.76	29.83	19.78	0.67	1.34	15.31	0.94	10.37	132.6	2	98	0	0	33	15.54	-27.87			Mar-12
1,000	6.05	17.03	38.53	31.85	22.76	0.94	0.94	15.36	0.94	10.28	132.6	2	98	0	0	33	15.58	-27.8			Mar-11
100	8.25	18.88	42.56			0.51	1.17			12.94	63.0	3	97	0	0	58					Mar-15
100	8.11	18.64	42.12			0.32	1.46			12.9	63.0	3	97	0	0	58					Mar-15
1,000	8.24	18.87	42.67			0.6	1.06			12.9	63.0	3	97	0	0	58					Mar-15
1,000	9.52	12.69	21.41				1.08			11.77	1.4	2	74	5	0						Jan-17
100	9.52	12.69	21.41				1.25			11.77	1.4	2	74	5	0						Jan-17
100	8.19	9.85	20.24	26.24	81.89	1.36	1.09	9.93	0.83	21.09	4,420	23	75	2	0	4	14.96	-9.39			Jul-12
100	8.11	9.77	20.03	25.57	80.32	1.2	1.27	9.93	0.83	21.13	4,420	23	75	2	0	4	14.96	-9.39			May-97
100	7.47	9.38	18.23	22.84	78.68	1.54	0.76	8.6	0.77	22.85	8,805	24	74	2	0	4	16.05	-10.2			Jul-92

Fund Name	MARKET Ticker Symbol	MARKET Traded On	FUND TYPE, CATEGORY & OBJECTIVE Fund Type	Category and (Prospectus Objective)	RATINGS Overall Rating	Reward Rating	Risk Rating	Recent Up/ Downgrade	Open to New Investors	MINIMUMS Min Initial Investment
AMG Yacktman Special Opportunities Fund Class I	YASSX	NAS CM	Open End	Global Equity Mid/Small Cap (Growth)	B	A	C	Up	Y	100,000
AMG Yacktman Special Opportunities Fund Class Z	YASLX	NAS CM	Open End	Global Equity Mid/Small Cap (Growth)	B	A	C	Up	Y	5,000,000
AMIDEX35 Israel Fund Class A	AMDAX	NAS CM	Open End	Other Equity (Foreign Stock)	D+	D+	C-	Down	Y	500
AMIDEX35 Israel Fund Class C	AMDCX	NAS CM	Open End	Other Equity (Foreign Stock)	D+	D+	C-	Down	Y	500
AMIDEX35 Israel Mutual Fund	AMDEX	NAS CM	Open End	Other Equity (Foreign Stock)	D+	D+	C-	Down	Y	500
Anchor Tactical Credit Strategies VP	US66538H8566		Open End	Other Alternative (Growth & Income)	D	D+	B+			0
Anchor Tactical Equity Strategies Fund Institutional Class	ATESX	NAS CM	Open End	Long/Short Equity (Growth & Income)	D	C-	B	Up	Y	2,000,000
Anchor Tactical Municipal Strategies Fund Inst Cls	ATMSX	NAS CM	Open End	Other Alternative (Municipal Bond - Natl)	D	D+	B-	Up	Y	2,000,000
Anchor Tactical Real Estate Fund Institutional Class	ARESX	NAS CM	Open End	Long/Short Equity (Real Estate)	D	D+	B	Up	Y	2,000,000
Ancora MicroCap Fund Class I	ANCIX	NAS CM	Open End	US Equity Small Cap (Small Company)	B+	A-	B	Up	Y	5,000
Ancora Special Opportunity Fund Class I	ANSIX	NAS CM	Open End	US Equity Small Cap (Growth & Income)	B	B	B	Up	Y	5,000
Ancora/Thelen Small-Mid Cap Fund Class I	AATIX	NAS CM	Open End	US Equity Small Cap (Growth & Income)	B-	B	C	Up	Y	5,000
Ancora/Thelen Small-Mid Cap Fund Class S	AATSX	NAS CM	Open End	US Equity Small Cap (Growth & Income)	B-	B	C	Up	Y	1,500,000
APEXcm Small/Mid Cap Growth Fund	APSGX	NAS CM	Open End	US Equity Mid Cap (Growth)	B-	B-	B	Up	Y	2,500
Appleseed Fund Institutional Share	APPIX	NAS CM	Open End	Alloc (Growth)	C+	C+	B-		Y	100,000
Appleseed Fund Investor Share	APPLX	NAS CM	Open End	Alloc (Growth)	C+	C+	B-		Y	2,500
AQR Alternative Risk Premia Fund Class I	QRPIX	NAS CM	Open End	Multialternative (Income)	U	U	U		Y	5,000,000
AQR Alternative Risk Premia Fund Class N	QRPNX	NAS CM	Open End	Multialternative (Income)	U	U	U		Y	1,000,000
AQR Alternative Risk Premia Fund Class R6	QRPRX	NAS CM	Open End	Multialternative (Income)	U	U	U		Y	100,000
AQR Diversified Arbitrage Fund Class I	ADAIX	NAS CM	Open End	Market Neutral (Growth & Income)	C+	C	B-	Up		5,000,000
AQR Diversified Arbitrage Fund Class N	ADANX	NAS CM	Open End	Market Neutral (Growth & Income)	C+	C	B-	Up		1,000,000
AQR Diversified Arbitrage Fund Class R6	QDARX	NAS CM	Open End	Market Neutral (Growth & Income)	C+	C	B-	Up	Y	100,000
AQR Emerging Defensive Style Fund Class I	AZEIX	NAS CM	Open End	Emerging Markets Equity (Div Emerging Mkts)	C	C+	C	Up	Y	5,000,000
AQR Emerging Defensive Style Fund Class N	AZENX	NAS CM	Open End	Emerging Markets Equity (Div Emerging Mkts)	C	C+	C	Up	Y	1,000,000
AQR Emerging Defensive Style Fund Class R6	AZERX	NAS CM	Open End	Emerging Markets Equity (Div Emerging Mkts)	C	C+	C	Up	Y	50,000,000
AQR Emerging Momentum Style Fund Class I	QEMLX	NAS CM	Open End	Emerging Markets Equity (Div Emerging Mkts)	C+	B-	C	Up	Y	5,000,000
AQR Emerging Momentum Style Fund Class N	QEMNX	NAS CM	Open End	Emerging Markets Equity (Div Emerging Mkts)	C+	B-	C	Up	Y	1,000,000
AQR Emerging Momentum Style Fund Class R6	QEMRX	NAS CM	Open End	Emerging Markets Equity (Div Emerging Mkts)	B-	B-	C	Up	Y	50,000,000
AQR Emerging Multi-Style Fund Class I	QEELX	NAS CM	Open End	Emerging Markets Equity (Div Emerging Mkts)	C+	B-	C	Up	Y	5,000,000
AQR Emerging Multi-Style Fund Class N	QEENX	NAS CM	Open End	Emerging Markets Equity (Div Emerging Mkts)	C+	B-	C	Up	Y	1,000,000
AQR Emerging Multi-Style Fund Class R6	QECRX	NAS CM	Open End	Emerging Markets Equity (Div Emerging Mkts)	C+	B-	C	Up	Y	50,000,000
AQR Emerging Relaxed Constraint Equity Fund Class I	QERIX	NAS CM	Open End	Emerging Markets Equity (Div Emerging Mkts)	D	D+	B+		Y	5,000,000
AQR Emerging Relaxed Constraint Equity Fund Class N	QERNX	NAS CM	Open End	Emerging Markets Equity (Div Emerging Mkts)	D	D+	B+		Y	1,000,000
AQR Emerging Relaxed Constraint Equity Fund Class R6	QERRX	NAS CM	Open End	Emerging Markets Equity (Div Emerging Mkts)	D	D+	B+		Y	100,000
AQR Equity Market Neutral Fund Class I	QMNIX	NAS CM	Open End	Market Neutral (Growth & Income)	B-	C	B+		Y	5,000,000
AQR Equity Market Neutral Fund Class N	QMNNX	NAS CM	Open End	Market Neutral (Growth & Income)	B-	C	B+		Y	1,000,000
AQR Equity Market Neutral Fund Class R6	QMNRX	NAS CM	Open End	Market Neutral (Growth & Income)	B-	C	B+		Y	100,000
AQR Global Equity Fund Class I	AQGIX	NAS CM	Open End	Global Equity (World Stock)	B	B	B-	Up	Y	5,000,000
AQR Global Equity Fund Class N	AQGNX	NAS CM	Open End	Global Equity (World Stock)	B	B	B-	Up	Y	1,000,000
AQR Global Equity Fund Class R6	AQGRX	NAS CM	Open End	Global Equity (World Stock)	B	B	B-	Up	Y	100,000
AQR Global Macro Fund Class I	QGMIX	NAS CM	Open End	Multialternative (Growth & Income)	D+	D	C	Up	Y	5,000,000
AQR Global Macro Fund Class N	QGMNX	NAS CM	Open End	Multialternative (Growth & Income)	D+	D	C	Up	Y	1,000,000
AQR Global Macro Fund Class R6	QGMRX	NAS CM	Open End	Multialternative (Growth & Income)	C-	D	C	Up	Y	100,000
AQR International Defensive Style Fund Class I	ANDIX	NAS CM	Open End	Global Equity Large Cap (Foreign Stock)	B-	C+	B	Up	Y	5,000,000
AQR International Defensive Style Fund Class N	ANDNX	NAS CM	Open End	Global Equity Large Cap (Foreign Stock)	B-	C+	B	Up	Y	1,000,000
AQR International Defensive Style Fund Class R6	ANDRX	NAS CM	Open End	Global Equity Large Cap (Foreign Stock)	B-	C+	B	Up	Y	50,000,000
AQR International Equity Fund Class I	AQIIX	NAS CM	Open End	Global Equity Large Cap (Foreign Stock)	B	B	B	Up	Y	5,000,000
AQR International Equity Fund Class N	AQINX	NAS CM	Open End	Global Equity Large Cap (Foreign Stock)	B	B	B	Up	Y	1,000,000
AQR International Equity Fund Class R6	AQIRX	NAS CM	Open End	Global Equity Large Cap (Foreign Stock)	B	B	B	Up	Y	100,000
AQR International Momentum Style Fund Class I	AIMOX	NAS CM	Open End	Global Equity Large Cap (Foreign Stock)	B-	C+	B	Up	Y	5,000,000
AQR International Momentum Style Fund Class N	AIONX	NAS CM	Open End	Global Equity Large Cap (Foreign Stock)	B-	C+	B	Up	Y	1,000,000
AQR International Momentum Style Fund Class R6	QIORX	NAS CM	Open End	Global Equity Large Cap (Foreign Stock)	B-	C+	B	Up	Y	50,000,000

★Expanded analysis of this fund is included in Section II.

Min Additional Investment	3-Month Total Return	6-Month Total Return	1-Year Total Return	3-Year Total Return	5-Year Total Return	Dividend Yield (TTM)	Expense Ratio	3-Yr Std Deviation	3-Year Beta	NAV	Total Assets (MIL)	%Cash	%Stocks	%Bonds	%Other	Turnover Ratio	Last Bull Market Total Return	Last Bear Market Total Return	Front End Fee (%)	Back End Fee (%)	Inception Date
TOTAL RETURNS						PERFORMANCE				ASSETS		ASSET ALLOCATION & TURNOVER					BULL & BEAR		FEES		
100	7.85	13.27	34.66	44.71		2.54	1.67	12.16	0.99	12.03	35.7	11	79	6	2	29					Jun-15
1,000	7.89	13.30	34.80	45.06		2.56	1.57	12.21	1	12.05	35.7	11	79	6	2	29					Jun-14
250	0.83	-1.27	10.80	-2.16	14.30	0	4.34	11.26		10.87	8.4	0	100	0	0	5	4.12	-28.81	5.50		Nov-99
250	0.67	-1.71	9.86	-4.35	10.02	0	5.09	11.31		7.46	8.4	0	100	0	0	5	3.57	-28.96		1.00	May-00
250	0.85	-1.32	10.76	-2.13	14.42	0	4.34	11.28		14.2	8.4	0	100	0	0	5	4.1	-28.74			Jun-99
	-0.29	0.77	1.57			0.87	2.69			9.81	4.2	2	2	96	0						Nov-16
5,000	6.45	7.82	17.05			0	2.29			11.09	69.3	2	98	0	0						Sep-16
5,000	0.56	1.73	2.25			0.57	2.49			9.79	62.3	0	0	100	0	366					Sep-16
5,000	3.50	6.10	6.21			0.31	2.75			10.02	104.9	5	95	0	0						Sep-16
1,000	0.30	6.49	17.99	25.97	102.72	0.17	1.61	13.53	0.76	14.09	21.9	11	89	0	0	14	17.82	-23.19			Sep-08
1,000	3.36	6.98	14.54	29.95	86.81	0	2.25	10.69	0.9	7.49	17.9	22	75	0	0	142	13.99	-18.5			Jan-04
1,000	4.57	8.38	18.49	24.56	78.40	0.12	1.34	12.12	0.92	15.55	88.9	5	95	0	0	80					Jan-13
1,000	5.17	9.07	19.45	26.15	80.69	0.09	1	12.14	0.93	15.85	88.9	5	95	0	0	80					Jun-15
100	8.60	14.02	26.60	26.30	89.81	0	1.05	13.83	1.01	20.32	277.1	5	95	0	0	55					Jun-12
	6.38	8.03	17.57	17.36	40.66	1.47	1.04	9.69	0.65	13.8	187.0	11	63	8	18	56	12.9	-11.65			Jan-11
	6.44	7.93	17.42	16.74	39.19	1.26	1.23	9.67	0.65	13.74	187.0	11	63	8	18	56	12.85	-11.74			Dec-06
	1.11						1.43			10.01	16.9										Sep-17
	1.11						1.68			10.01	16.9										Sep-17
	1.21						1.33			10.02	16.9										Sep-17
	0.88	1.20	5.91	8.33	4.64	6.87	1.33	3.42	-2.09	9.12	477.8	19	19	8	18	277	2.47	-0.53			Jan-09
	0.78	1.09	5.58	7.54	3.35	6.55	1.58	3.43	-1.54	9.12	477.8	19	19	8	18	277	2.35	-0.71			Jan-09
	0.98	1.29	6.02	8.60	4.95	6.99	1.23	3.42	-2.27	9.1	477.8	19	19	8	18	277	2.47	-0.53			Sep-14
	7.42	12.42	28.20	10.02	1.07	1.44	0.71	13.16	0.79	9.98	70.4	0	95	0	4	17					Jul-12
	7.27	12.26	27.90	9.24	0.00	1.22	0.96	13.12	0.79	10.23	70.4	0	95	0	4	17					Jul-12
	7.32	12.45	28.29	10.20	1.27	1.51	0.61	13.09	0.79	9.94	70.4	0	95	0	4	17					Sep-14
	9.24	22.75	44.25	27.21		1.16	0.72	15.76	0.97	11.39	13.4	0	98	0	1	121					May-14
	9.32	22.72	44.04	26.39		0.91	0.97	15.83	0.97	11.41	13.4	0	98	0	1	121					May-14
	9.31	22.82	44.30	27.48		1.2	0.62	15.74	0.97	11.4	13.4	0	98	0	1	121					Jul-14
	5.54	14.52	36.84	21.02		1.57	0.76	15.96	1	11.12	323.9	0	97	0	3	53					May-14
	5.52	14.30	36.44	20.22		1.4	1.01	15.92	0.99	11.12	323.9	0	97	0	3	53					May-14
	5.63	14.49	36.92	21.41		1.65	0.66	15.96	1	11.13	323.9	0	97	0	3	53					Jul-14
	7.79	16.51	37.34				1.2			13.51	26.3	0	82	9	8	114					Dec-16
	7.73	16.37	36.94				1.45			13.5	26.3	0	82	9	8	114					Dec-16
	7.75	16.57	37.40				1.1			13.51	26.3	0	82	9	8	114					Dec-16
	0.86	4.70	5.83	31.35		1.41	1.39	5.52	1.57	12.25	2,160	18	14	15	52	227					Oct-14
	0.75	4.50	5.55	30.28		1.11	1.66	5.58	2.63	12.21	2,160	18	14	15	52	227					Oct-14
	0.85	4.68	5.90	31.40		1.47	1.31	5.51	2.56	12.25	2,160	18	14	15	52	227					Oct-14
	5.40	12.76	25.44	36.55	85.28	1.81	0.81	9.42	0.86	8.92	244.6	2	90	0	7	88	19.51	-23.73			Jan-10
	5.22	12.61	25.02	35.30	82.73	1.65	1.06	9.32	0.86	8.88	244.6	2	90	0	7	88	19.23	-23.83			Dec-09
	5.39	12.82	25.57	37.05	86.01	2	0.71	9.36	0.86	8.99	244.6	2	90	0	7	88	19.23	-23.83			Jan-14
	-0.75	1.08	-3.38	-1.60		0	1.5	4.7	20.21	8.75	25.5	185	-2	-140	57	0					Apr-14
	-0.80	0.93	-3.67	-2.39		0	1.75	4.76	19.78	8.66	25.5	185	-2	-140	57	0					Apr-14
	-0.67	1.04	-3.41	-1.42		0	1.4	4.76	19.9	8.75	25.5	185	-2	-140	57	0					Sep-14
	3.45	7.25	21.60	23.17	44.63	1.21	0.56	9.5	0.71	13.42	194.9	0	96	0	3	3					Jul-12
	3.42	7.13	21.39	22.27	42.74	1.12	0.81	9.56	0.72	13.78	194.9	0	96	0	3	3					Jul-12
	3.47	7.27	21.74	23.51	45.08	1.27	0.46	9.46	0.71	13.4	194.9	0	96	0	3	3					Sep-14
	3.18	9.47	25.71	31.49	53.26	2.52	0.91	10.44	0.83	10.96	422.5	4	88	0	8	83	14.57	-28.03			Aug-09
	3.09	9.35	25.35	30.52	51.09	2.26	1.16	10.41	0.82	11.23	422.5	4	88	0	8	83	14.29	-28.13			Sep-09
	3.09	9.54	25.71	31.79	53.91	2.46	0.81	10.44	0.83	11.69	422.5	4	88	0	8	83	14.57	-28.03			Jan-14
	3.51	11.11	25.25	20.38	35.70	2.03	0.55	10.33	0.79	15.7	417.5	0	97	0	3	84	15.21	-26.89			Jul-09
	3.48	11.02	24.99	19.58	34.10	1.8	0.8	10.33	0.79	15.69	417.5	0	97	0	3	84	15.04	-26.97			Dec-12
	3.55	11.23	25.41	20.88	36.23	2.12	0.45	10.33	0.79	15.68	417.5	0	97	0	3	84	15.21	-26.89			Jul-14

	MARKET			FUND TYPE, CATEGORY & OBJECTIVE	RATINGS					MINIMUMS
Fund Name	Ticker Symbol	Traded On	Fund Type	Category and (Prospectus Objective)	Overall Rating	Reward Rating	Risk Rating	Recent Up/ Downgrade	Open to New Investors	Min Initial Investment
AQR International Multi-Style Fund Class I	QICLX	NAS CM	Open End	Global Equity Large Cap (Foreign Stock)	B-	C+	B-	Up	Y	5,000,000
AQR International Multi-Style Fund Class N	QICNX	NAS CM	Open End	Global Equity Large Cap (Foreign Stock)	C+	C+	B-	Up	Y	1,000,000
AQR International Multi-Style Fund Class R6	QICRX	NAS CM	Open End	Global Equity Large Cap (Foreign Stock)	B-	C+	B-	Up	Y	50,000,000
AQR International Relaxed Constraint Equity Fund Class I	QIRIX	NAS CM	Open End	Global Equity Large Cap (Foreign Stock)	D	D+	A-		Y	5,000,000
AQR International Relaxed Constraint Equity Fund Class N	QIRNX	NAS CM	Open End	Global Equity Large Cap (Foreign Stock)	D	D+	A-		Y	1,000,000
AQR International Relaxed Constraint Equity Fund Class R6	QIRRX	NAS CM	Open End	Global Equity Large Cap (Foreign Stock)	D	D+	A-		Y	100,000
AQR Large Cap Defensive Style Fund Class I	AUEIX	NAS CM	Open End	US Equity Large Cap Blend (Growth & Income)	B	B	B+	Down	Y	5,000,000
AQR Large Cap Defensive Style Fund Class N	AUENX	NAS CM	Open End	US Equity Large Cap Blend (Growth & Income)	B	B	B+	Down	Y	1,000,000
AQR Large Cap Defensive Style Fund Class R6	QUERX	NAS CM	Open End	US Equity Large Cap Blend (Growth & Income)	B	B	B+	Down	Y	50,000,000
AQR Large Cap Momentum Style Fund Class I	AMOMX	NAS CM	Open End	US Equity Large Cap Growth (Growth)	B	B	B	Up	Y	5,000,000
AQR Large Cap Momentum Style Fund Class N	AMONX	NAS CM	Open End	US Equity Large Cap Growth (Growth)	B	B	B	Up	Y	1,000,000
AQR Large Cap Momentum Style Fund Class R6	QMORX	NAS CM	Open End	US Equity Large Cap Growth (Growth)	B	B	B	Up	Y	50,000,000
AQR Large Cap Multi-Style Fund Class I	QCELX	NAS CM	Open End	US Equity Large Cap Blend (Growth)	B	B	B-	Up	Y	5,000,000
AQR Large Cap Multi-Style Fund Class N	QCENX	NAS CM	Open End	US Equity Large Cap Blend (Growth)	B	B	B-	Up	Y	1,000,000
AQR Large Cap Multi-Style Fund Class R6	QCERX	NAS CM	Open End	US Equity Large Cap Blend (Growth)	B	B	B-	Up	Y	50,000,000
AQR Large Cap Relaxed Constraint Equity Fund Class I	QLRIX	NAS CM	Open End	US Equity Large Cap Blend (Growth)	D	D+	A-		Y	5,000,000
AQR Large Cap Relaxed Constraint Equity Fund Class N	QLRNX	NAS CM	Open End	US Equity Large Cap Blend (Growth)	D	D+	A-		Y	1,000,000
AQR Large Cap Relaxed Constraint Equity Fund Class R6	QLRRX	NAS CM	Open End	US Equity Large Cap Blend (Growth)	D	D+	A-		Y	100,000
AQR Long-Short Equity Fund Class I	QLEIX	NAS CM	Open End	Long/Short Equity (Growth)	B+	B+	B+	Up	Y	5,000,000
AQR Long-Short Equity Fund Class N	QLENX	NAS CM	Open End	Long/Short Equity (Growth)	B+	B+	B+	Up	Y	1,000,000
AQR Long-Short Equity Fund Class R6	QLERX	NAS CM	Open End	Long/Short Equity (Growth)	B+	B+	B+	Up	Y	100,000
AQR Managed Futures Strategy Fund Class I	AQMIX	NAS CM	Open End	Other Alternative (Growth & Income)	D	D	D+	Down	Y	5,000,000
AQR Managed Futures Strategy Fund Class N	AQMNX	NAS CM	Open End	Other Alternative (Growth & Income)	D	D	D+	Down	Y	1,000,000
AQR Managed Futures Strategy Fund Class R6	AQMRX	NAS CM	Open End	Other Alternative (Growth & Income)	D	D	D+	Down	Y	100,000
AQR Managed Futures Strategy HV Fund Class I	QMHIX	NAS CM	Open End	Other Alternative (Growth & Income)	D	D	D	Down	Y	5,000,000
AQR Managed Futures Strategy HV Fund Class N	QMHNX	NAS CM	Open End	Other Alternative (Growth & Income)	D	D	D		Y	1,000,000
AQR Managed Futures Strategy HV Fund Class R6	QMHRX	NAS CM	Open End	Other Alternative (Growth & Income)	D	D	D	Down	Y	100,000
AQR Multi-Strategy Alternative Fund Class I	ASAIX	NAS CM	Open End	Multialternative (Growth & Income)	B	C	A-	Up		5,000,000
AQR Multi-Strategy Alternative Fund Class N	ASANX	NAS CM	Open End	Multialternative (Growth & Income)	B	C	A-	Up		1,000,000
AQR Multi-Strategy Alternative Fund Class R6	QSARX	NAS CM	Open End	Multialternative (Growth & Income)	B	C	A-	Up	Y	100,000
AQR Risk Parity Fund Class I	AQRIX	NAS CM	Open End	Moderate Alloc (Growth & Income)	C+	C+	B-			5,000,000
AQR Risk Parity Fund Class N	AQRNX	NAS CM	Open End	Moderate Alloc (Growth & Income)	C+	C+	C+			1,000,000
AQR Risk Parity Fund Class R6	AQRRX	NAS CM	Open End	Moderate Alloc (Growth & Income)	C+	C+	B-		Y	100,000
AQR Risk Parity II HV Fund Class I	QRHIX	NAS CM	Open End	Moderate Alloc (Growth & Income)	C+	C+	C+	Up	Y	5,000,000
AQR Risk Parity II HV Fund Class N	QRHNX	NAS CM	Open End	Moderate Alloc (Growth & Income)	C+	C+	C+	Up	Y	1,000,000
AQR Risk Parity II HV Fund Class R6	QRHRX	NAS CM	Open End	Moderate Alloc (Growth & Income)	C+	C+	C+	Up	Y	100,000
AQR Risk Parity II MV Fund Class I	QRMIX	NAS CM	Open End	Moderate Alloc (Growth & Income)	C+	C+	B-	Up	Y	5,000,000
AQR Risk Parity II MV Fund Class N	QRMNX	NAS CM	Open End	Moderate Alloc (Growth & Income)	C+	C	C+	Up	Y	1,000,000
AQR Risk Parity II MV Fund Class R6	QRMRX	NAS CM	Open End	Moderate Alloc (Growth & Income)	C+	C+	B-	Up	Y	100,000
AQR Risk-Balanced Commodities Strategy Fund Class I	ARCIX	NAS CM	Open End	Commodities Broad Basket (Income)	C	C	C	Up	Y	5,000,000
AQR Risk-Balanced Commodities Strategy Fund Class N	ARCNX	NAS CM	Open End	Commodities Broad Basket (Income)	C	C	C	Up	Y	1,000,000
AQR Risk-Balanced Commodities Strategy Fund Class R6	QRCRX	NAS CM	Open End	Commodities Broad Basket (Income)	C	C	C	Up	Y	100,000
AQR Small Cap Momentum Style Fund Class I	ASMOX	NAS CM	Open End	US Equity Small Cap (Small Company)	B	B+	B	Up	Y	5,000,000
AQR Small Cap Momentum Style Fund Class N	ASMNX	NAS CM	Open End	US Equity Small Cap (Small Company)	B	B+	B	Up	Y	1,000,000
AQR Small Cap Momentum Style Fund Class R6	QSMRX	NAS CM	Open End	US Equity Small Cap (Small Company)	B+	A-	B	Up	Y	50,000,000
AQR Small Cap Multi-Style Fund Class I	QSMLX	NAS CM	Open End	US Equity Small Cap (Small Company)	B	B+	B	Up	Y	5,000,000
AQR Small Cap Multi-Style Fund Class N	QSMNX	NAS CM	Open End	US Equity Small Cap (Small Company)	B	B	B	Up	Y	1,000,000
AQR Small Cap Multi-Style Fund Class R6	QSERX	NAS CM	Open End	US Equity Small Cap (Small Company)	B	B+	B	Up	Y	50,000,000
AQR Small Cap Relaxed Constraint Equity Fund Class I	QSRIX	NAS CM	Open End	US Equity Small Cap (Small Company)	D	D+	B		Y	5,000,000
AQR Small Cap Relaxed Constraint Equity Fund Class N	QSRNX	NAS CM	Open End	US Equity Small Cap (Small Company)	D	D+	B		Y	1,000,000
AQR Small Cap Relaxed Constraint Equity Fund Class R6	QSRRX	NAS CM	Open End	US Equity Small Cap (Small Company)	D	D+	B		Y	100,000
AQR Style Premia Alternative Fund Class I	QSPIX	NAS CM	Open End	Multialternative (Growth & Income)	B	B	B	Up		5,000,000

★Expanded analysis of this fund is included in Section II.

Min Additional Investment	3-Month Total Return	6-Month Total Return	1-Year Total Return	3-Year Total Return	5-Year Total Return	Dividend Yield (TTM)	Expense Ratio	3-Yr Std Deviation	3-Year Beta	NAV	Total Assets (MIL)	%Cash	%Stocks	%Bonds	%Other	Turnover Ratio	Last Bull Market Total Return	Last Bear Market Total Return	Front End Fee (%)	Back End Fee (%)	Inception Date
TOTAL RETURNS						PERFORMANCE				ASSETS		ASSET ALLOCATION & TURNOVER					BULL & BEAR		FEES		
	3.21	9.05	24.96	19.44		2.15	0.61	11.62	0.92	12.04	473.5	0	97	0	3	55					Mar-13
	3.08	8.93	24.62	18.55		1.97	0.86	11.58	0.92	12.03	473.5	0	97	0	3	55					Mar-13
	3.22	9.16	24.99	19.80		2.23	0.51	11.54	0.92	12.02	473.5	0	97	0	3	55					Jul-14
	2.55	10.98	28.92				0.98			12.98	30.0	1	98	0	1	162					Dec-16
	2.49	10.85	28.54				1.23			12.95	30.0	1	98	0	1	162					Dec-16
	2.57	11.00	29.05				0.88			12.99	30.0	1	98	0	1	162					Dec-16
	7.07	10.52	22.14	44.52	123.02	1.18	0.41	8.31	0.74	19.07	1,344	0	95	0	5	16					Jul-12
	6.95	10.35	21.75	43.39	120.08	1.02	0.66	8.31	0.74	19.04	1,344	0	95	0	5	16					Jul-12
	7.06	10.51	22.22	44.89	123.64	1.24	0.31	8.31	0.74	19.03	1,344	0	95	0	5	16					Sep-14
	6.93	13.26	23.87	32.05	102.08	1.29	0.4	9.74	0.9	21.56	1,045	0	97	0	3	88	27.52	-20.68			Jul-09
	6.87	13.15	23.57	31.10	99.60	1.07	0.65	9.72	0.9	21.58	1,045	0	97	0	3	88	27.34	-20.76			Dec-12
	6.99	13.34	23.99	32.43	102.79	1.38	0.3	9.72	0.89	21.51	1,045	0	97	0	3	88	27.52	-20.68			Jul-14
	7.02	13.12	24.25	31.19		1.04	0.45	10.41	0.99	17.66	1,886	0	97	0	3	61					Mar-13
	6.96	12.95	23.94	30.19		0.86	0.7	10.45	1	17.61	1,886	0	97	0	3	61					Mar-13
	7.04	13.15	24.37	31.61		1.15	0.35	10.42	1	17.65	1,886	0	97	0	3	61					Jul-14
	6.76	13.07	21.99				0.83			11.96	17.8	0	98	0	2	139					Dec-16
	6.73	12.94	21.62				1.08			11.98	17.8	0	98	0	2	139					Dec-16
	6.82	13.12	22.04				0.73			11.96	17.8	0	98	0	2	139					Dec-16
	3.17	9.76	15.72	49.22		1.59	1.38	6.46		13.88	5,573	20	41	15	25	247					Jul-13
	3.16	9.64	15.46	48.19		1.47	1.64	6.41		13.8	5,573	20	41	15	25	247					Jul-13
	3.23	9.81	15.85	49.72		1.63	1.29	6.44		13.91	5,573	20	41	15	25	247					Sep-14
	4.88	4.88	-0.96	-6.97	11.91	0.02	1.22	9.34	34.85	9.23	11,772	29	0	39	32	0	-4.01	-5.35			Jan-10
	4.71	4.71	-1.19	-7.68	10.32	0.02	1.49	9.28	34.35	9.1	11,772	29	0	39	32	0	-4.13	-5.36			Jan-10
	4.88	5.00	-0.85	-6.73	11.61	0.02	1.15	9.3	34.37	9.24	11,772	29	0	39	32	0	-4.13	-5.36			Sep-14
	7.15	7.15	-1.72	-11.65		0.01	1.68	13.84	50.32	9.14	759.4	24	0	41	35	0					Jul-13
	6.97	6.84	-2.05	-12.53		0.01	1.93	13.9	50.92	9.05	759.4	24	0	41	35	0					Jul-13
	7.01	7.14	-1.61	-11.51		0.01	1.58	13.91	50.88	9.15	759.4	24	0	41	35	0					Sep-14
	0.34	3.31	3.09	12.41	25.03	0.85	2.06	4.65	22.42	9.05	3,273	66	27	-120	89	261	1.9				Jul-11
	0.29	3.16	2.72	11.42	23.47	0.86	2.32	4.69	22.22	9	3,273	66	27	-120	89	261	1.84				Jul-11
	0.34	3.40	3.18	12.70	25.45	0.85	1.97	4.7	21.88	9.06	3,273	66	27	-120	89	261	1.9				Sep-14
	5.40	10.10	16.35	17.49	26.70	2.12	1.01	7.77		9.82	474.3	12	19	41	28	72	10.34	-6.49			Sep-10
	5.38	9.99	16.12	16.68	24.98	1.87	1.27	7.77		9.8	474.3	12	19	41	28	72	10.13	-6.6			Sep-10
	5.48	10.18	16.55	17.78	26.98	2.19	0.92	7.76		9.83	474.3	12	19	41	28	72	10.34	-6.49			Sep-14
	8.46	15.46	19.02	15.85	24.21	1.17	1.22	10.4		8.88	56.7	1	20	51	28	68					Nov-12
	8.24	15.10	18.51	14.63	22.29	0.95	1.47	10.43		8.85	56.7	1	20	51	28	68					Nov-12
	8.58	15.46	19.17	15.95	24.43	1.22	1.12	10.43		8.88	56.7	1	20	51	28	68					Sep-14
	5.54	9.91	12.36	12.18	18.19	0.87	1.02	6.95		9.26	81.1	7	17	47	29	58					Nov-12
	5.46	9.85	12.06	11.26	16.46	0.62	1.27	6.95		9.2	81.1	7	17	47	29	58					Nov-12
	5.54	10.03	12.48	12.39	18.50	0.96	0.92	6.97		9.26	81.1	7	17	47	29	58					Sep-14
	9.18	15.01	10.41	2.60	-26.55	4.59	1.08	13.8	0.86	6.9	195.0	15	0	9	76	0					Jul-12
	9.14	15.04	10.20	1.71	-27.53	4.47	1.33	13.7	0.86	6.81	195.0	15	0	9	76	0					Jul-12
	9.15	15.15	10.55	2.80	-26.31	4.63	0.98	13.81	0.86	6.92	195.0	15	0	9	76	0					Sep-14
	3.86	11.54	17.38	26.97	94.69	0.67	0.6	13.88	0.96	23.47	380.4	0	98	0	2	86	31.4	-26.17			Jul-09
	3.85	11.44	17.17	26.10	92.28	0	0.85	13.86	0.96	23.52	380.4	0	98	0	2	86	31.2	-26.25			Dec-12
	3.93	11.63	17.48	27.34	95.24	0.75	0.5	13.86	0.96	23.42	380.4	0	98	0	2	86	31.4	-26.17			Jul-14
	1.88	7.14	9.29	26.97		0.82	0.66	13.53	0.94	14.82	788.6	0	97	0	3	61					Mar-13
	1.85	6.99	9.07	25.99		0.63	0.91	13.52	0.94	14.79	788.6	0	97	0	3	61					Mar-13
	1.98	7.24	9.45	27.33		0.89	0.56	13.5	0.94	14.84	788.6	0	97	0	3	61					Jul-14
	1.10	8.10	5.27				1.03			10.36	3.4	0	98	0	1	124					Dec-16
	1.14	8.05	5.00				1.28			10.36	3.4	0	98	0	1	124					Dec-16
	1.18	8.18	5.35				0.93			10.36	3.4	0	98	0	1	124					Dec-16
	5.65	10.59	12.04	21.04		1.57	1.6	6.63	20.39	10.39	4,661	28	8	45	19	114					Oct-13

	MARKET			FUND TYPE, CATEGORY & OBJECTIVE	RATINGS				MINIMUMS	
Fund Name	Ticker Symbol	Traded On	Fund Type	Category and (Prospectus Objective)	Overall Rating	Reward Rating	Risk Rating	Recent Up/ Downgrade	Open to New Investors	Min Initial Investment
AQR Style Premia Alternative Fund Class N	QSPNX	NAS CM	Open End	Multialternative (Growth & Income)	B	B	B	Up		1,000,000
AQR Style Premia Alternative Fund Class R6	QSPRX	NAS CM	Open End	Multialternative (Growth & Income)	B	B	B	Up		100,000
AQR Style Premia Alternative LV Fund Class I	QSLIX	NAS CM	Open End	Multialternative (Growth & Income)	B-	C	B+	Up		5,000,000
AQR Style Premia Alternative LV Fund Class N	QSLNX	NAS CM	Open End	Multialternative (Growth & Income)	B-	C	B+	Up		1,000,000
AQR Style Premia Alternative LV Fund Class R6	QSLRX	NAS CM	Open End	Multialternative (Growth & Income)	B-	C	B+	Up		100,000
AQR TM Emerging Multi-Style Fund Class I	QTELX	NAS CM	Open End	Emerging Markets Equity (Div Emerging Mkts)	C+	C+	C	Up	Y	5,000,000
AQR TM Emerging Multi-Style Fund Class N	QTENX	NAS CM	Open End	Emerging Markets Equity (Div Emerging Mkts)	C+	C+	C	Up	Y	1,000,000
AQR TM Emerging Multi-Style Fund Class R6	QTERX	NAS CM	Open End	Emerging Markets Equity (Div Emerging Mkts)	C+	C+	C	Up	Y	50,000,000
AQR TM International Momentum Style Fund Class I	ATIMX	NAS CM	Open End	Global Equity Large Cap (Foreign Stock)	B-	C+	B	Up	Y	5,000,000
AQR TM International Momentum Style Fund Class N	ATNNX	NAS CM	Open End	Global Equity Large Cap (Foreign Stock)	B-	C+	B	Up	Y	1,000,000
AQR TM International Momentum Style Fund Class R6	QTIRX	NAS CM	Open End	Global Equity Large Cap (Foreign Stock)	B-	C+	B	Up	Y	50,000,000
AQR TM International Multi-Style Fund Class I	QIMLX	NAS CM	Open End	Global Equity Large Cap (Growth)	C+	C+	C+	Up	Y	5,000,000
AQR TM International Multi-Style Fund Class N	QIMNX	NAS CM	Open End	Global Equity Large Cap (Growth)	C+	C+	C+	Up	Y	1,000,000
AQR TM International Multi-Style Fund Class R6	QIMRX	NAS CM	Open End	Global Equity Large Cap (Growth)	C+	C+	B-	Up	Y	50,000,000
AQR TM Large Cap Momentum Style Fund Class I	ATMOX	NAS CM	Open End	US Equity Large Cap Growth (Growth)	B	B	B	Up	Y	5,000,000
AQR TM Large Cap Momentum Style Fund Class N	ATMNX	NAS CM	Open End	US Equity Large Cap Growth (Growth)	B	B	B	Up	Y	1,000,000
AQR TM Large Cap Momentum Style Fund Class R6	QTMRX	NAS CM	Open End	US Equity Large Cap Growth (Growth)	B	B	B	Up	Y	50,000,000
AQR TM Large Cap Multi-Style Fund Class I	QTLLX	NAS CM	Open End	US Equity Large Cap Blend (Growth)	B-	C+	B-	Up	Y	5,000,000
AQR TM Large Cap Multi-Style Fund Class N	QTLNX	NAS CM	Open End	US Equity Large Cap Blend (Growth)	B-	C+	B-	Up	Y	1,000,000
AQR TM Large Cap Multi-Style Fund Class R6	QTLRX	NAS CM	Open End	US Equity Large Cap Blend (Growth)	B-	C+	B-	Up	Y	50,000,000
AQR TM Small Cap Momentum Style Fund Class I	ATSMX	NAS CM	Open End	US Equity Small Cap (Small Company)	B+	A-	B	Up	Y	5,000,000
AQR TM Small Cap Momentum Style Fund Class N	ATSNX	NAS CM	Open End	US Equity Small Cap (Small Company)	B+	A-	B	Up	Y	1,000,000
AQR TM Small Cap Momentum Style Fund Class R6	QTSRX	NAS CM	Open End	US Equity Small Cap (Small Company)	B+	A-	B	Up	Y	50,000,000
AQR TM Small Cap Multi-Style Fund Class I	QSSLX	NAS CM	Open End	US Equity Small Cap (Small Company)	C+	C+	B-	Up	Y	5,000,000
AQR TM Small Cap Multi-Style Fund Class N	QSSNX	NAS CM	Open End	US Equity Small Cap (Small Company)	C+	C+	B-	Up	Y	1,000,000
AQR TM Small Cap Multi-Style Fund Class R6	QSSRX	NAS CM	Open End	US Equity Small Cap (Small Company)	C+	C+	B-	Up	Y	50,000,000
Aquila Three Peaks Opportunity Growth Fund Class A	ATGAX	NAS CM	Open End	US Equity Mid Cap (Growth)	B	C+	B+	Up	Y	1,000
Aquila Three Peaks Opportunity Growth Fund Class C	ATGCX	NAS CM	Open End	US Equity Mid Cap (Growth)	B	C+	B+	Up	Y	1,000
Aquila Three Peaks Opportunity Growth Fund Class Y	ATGYX	NAS CM	Open End	US Equity Mid Cap (Growth)	B	B-	B+	Up	Y	0
Aquila Three Peaks Opp Growth Fund Inst Cls	ATRIX	NAS CM	Open End	US Equity Mid Cap (Growth)	B	B-	B+	Up	Y	0
Arabesque Systematic USA Fund Institutional Class	ASUIX	NAS CM	Open End	Moderate Alloc (Growth)	U	U	U		Y	1,000,000
Arbitrage Credit Opportunities Fund Class C	ARCCX	NAS CM	Open End	Other Alternative (Growth & Income)	C	C	B-	Down	Y	2,000
Arbitrage Credit Opportunities Fund Class I	ACFIX	NAS CM	Open End	Other Alternative (Growth & Income)	B-	C	B+	Up	Y	100,000
Arbitrage Credit Opportunities Fund Class R	ARCFX	NAS CM	Open End	Other Alternative (Growth & Income)	C+	C	B	Up	Y	2,000
Archer Balanced Fund	ARCHX	NAS CM	Open End	Aggressive Alloc (Balanced)	B-	C+	B	Down	Y	2,500
Archer Dividend Growth Fund	ARDGX	NAS CM	Open End	US Equity Large Cap Blend (Equity-Income)	D	C-	B+	Up	Y	2,500
Archer Stock Fund	ARSKX	NAS CM	Open End	US Equity Mid Cap (Growth)	B-	C+	B	Up	Y	2,500
Ariel Appreciation Fund Institutional Class	CAAIX	NAS CM	Open End	US Equity Mid Cap (Growth)	B-	B-	B		Y	1,000,000
Ariel Appreciation Fund Investor Class	CAAPX	NAS CM	Open End	US Equity Mid Cap (Growth)	B-	C+	B		Y	1,000
Ariel Discovery Fund Institutional Class	ADYIX	NAS CM	Open End	US Equity Small Cap (Growth)	C	C+	C	Up	Y	1,000,000
Ariel Discovery Fund Investor Class	ARDFX	NAS CM	Open End	US Equity Small Cap (Growth)	C	C+	C	Up	Y	1,000
Ariel Focus Fund Institutional Class	AFOYX	NAS CM	Open End	US Equity Large Cap Value (Growth)	C+	C+	C+	Down	Y	1,000,000
Ariel Focus Fund Investor Class	ARFFX	NAS CM	Open End	US Equity Large Cap Value (Growth)	C+	C+	C+	Down	Y	1,000
Ariel Fund Institutional Class	ARAIX	NAS CM	Open End	US Equity Mid Cap (Growth)	B	B	B	Up	Y	1,000,000
Ariel Fund Investor Class	ARGFX	NAS CM	Open End	US Equity Mid Cap (Growth)	B	B	B	Up	Y	1,000
Ariel Global Fund Institutional Class	AGLYX	NAS CM	Open End	Global Equity (World Stock)	B	C+	B	Up	Y	1,000,000
Ariel Global Fund Investor Class	AGLOX	NAS CM	Open End	Global Equity (World Stock)	B-	C+	B		Y	1,000
Ariel International Fund Investor Class	AINTX	NAS CM	Open End	Global Equity Large Cap (Foreign Stock)	B-	C	B	Up	Y	1,000
Ariel International Institutional Class	AINIX	NAS CM	Open End	Global Equity Large Cap (Foreign Stock)	B-	C	B	Up	Y	1,000,000
Arin Large Cap Theta Fund Advisor Class	AVOAX	NAS CM	Open End	Long/Short Equity (Growth)	B-	C	B+	Up	Y	25,000
Arin Large Cap Theta Fund Institutional Class	AVOLX	NAS CM	Open End	Long/Short Equity (Growth)	B-	C	B+	Up	Y	25,000
Aristotle Core Equity Fund Class I Shares	ARSLX	NAS CM	Open End	US Equity Large Cap Blend (Growth)	U	U	U		Y	2,500

★ Expanded analysis of this fund is included in Section II.

	TOTAL RETURNS					PERFORMANCE				ASSETS		ASSET ALLOCATION & TURNOVER					BULL & BEAR		FEES		
Min Additional Investment	3-Month Total Return	6-Month Total Return	1-Year Total Return	3-Year Total Return	5-Year Total Return	Dividend Yield (TTM)	Expense Ratio	3-Yr Std Deviation	3-Year Beta	NAV	Total Assets (MIL)	%Cash	%Stocks	%Bonds	%Other	Turnover Ratio	Last Bull Market Total Return	Last Bear Market Total Return	Front End Fee (%)	Back End Fee (%)	Inception Date
	5.58	10.33	11.67	19.99		1.58	1.85	6.66	21.1	10.35	4,661	28	8	45	19	114					Oct-13
	5.72	10.54	12.10	21.27		1.57	1.5	6.62	19.86	10.41	4,661	28	8	45	19	114					Sep-14
	3.07	5.72	6.74	11.63		0.26	0.95	3.48	11.43	10.57	475.2	33	6	38	23	106					Sep-14
	2.98	5.54	6.45	10.73		0.26	1.2	3.47	12.53	10.53	475.2	33	6	38	23	106					Sep-14
	3.14	5.78	6.90	12.03		0.26	0.85	3.44	11.45	10.59	475.2	33	6	38	23	106					Sep-14
	5.33	14.38	37.15			1.88	0.77			11.53	358.4	0	97	0	2	51					Feb-15
	5.22	14.27	36.69			1.75	1.02			11.55	358.4	0	97	0	2	51					Feb-15
	5.40	14.45	37.21			1.93	0.67			11.54	358.4	0	97	0	2	51					Feb-15
	3.52	10.46	25.07	19.71	37.90	2.04	0.56	10.34	0.8	13.94	110.9	0	97	0	3	62					Jan-12
	3.49	10.37	24.83	19.10	36.39	1.94	0.81	10.37	0.8	13.87	110.9	0	97	0	3	62					Dec-12
	3.55	10.50	25.15	20.10	38.40	2.14	0.46	10.38	0.81	13.9	110.9	0	97	0	3	62					Jul-14
	3.58	9.57	25.52			1.71	0.61			11.29	183.2	0	96	0	3	52					Feb-15
	3.55	9.46	25.30			1.61	0.86			11.27	183.2	0	96	0	3	52					Feb-15
	3.67	9.65	25.70			1.76	0.51			11.31	183.2	0	96	0	3	52					Feb-15
	7.60	13.93	23.78	31.33	102.39	1.2	0.4	9.87	0.92	20.75	192.3	0	97	0	3	57					Jan-12
	7.47	13.75	23.40	30.49	100.16	1.06	0.65	9.89	0.92	20.66	192.3	0	97	0	3	57					Dec-12
	7.59	13.99	23.87	31.69	102.96	1.28	0.3	9.87	0.92	20.71	192.3	0	97	0	3	57					Jul-14
	7.16	13.35	24.58			0.97	0.46			12.81	246.1	0	98	0	2	77					Feb-15
	7.11	13.21	24.22			0.8	0.71			12.79	246.1	0	98	0	2	77					Feb-15
	7.25	13.43	24.78			1.01	0.36			12.82	246.1	0	98	0	2	77					Feb-15
	3.22	9.91	16.69	28.13	93.00	0.61	0.61	13.84	0.95	19.61	55.2	0	97	0	3	69					Jan-12
	3.14	9.74	16.40	27.39	90.87	0.48	0.86	13.86	0.95	19.5	55.2	0	97	0	3	69					Dec-12
	3.25	9.95	16.80	28.55	93.70	0.68	0.51	13.86	0.95	19.6	55.2	0	97	0	3	69					Jul-14
	1.86	7.30	9.41			0.88	0.67			11.93	30.9	0	98	0	2	92					Feb-15
	1.78	7.05	9.16			0.72	0.92			11.9	30.9	0	98	0	2	92					Feb-15
	1.86	7.38	9.58			0.93	0.57			11.95	30.9	0	98	0	2	92					Feb-15
	3.42	6.81	16.34	27.38	107.80	0	1.4	8.74	0.76	52.38	604.9	3	97	0	0	67	24.32	-20.94	4.25		Jul-94
	3.24	6.44	15.53	24.64	100.47	0	2.11	8.73	0.76	43.26	604.9	3	97	0	0	67	23.74	-21.19		1.00	May-96
	3.50	6.98	16.70	28.53	110.95	0	1.11	8.74	0.76	55.91	604.9	3	97	0	0	67	24.62	-20.89			May-96
	3.44	6.85	16.44	27.93	109.77	0	1.37	8.74	0.76	54.23	604.9	3	97	0	0	67	24.59	-20.84			Dec-05
	6.66	10.54					0.95			11.24	17.1	2	98	0	0						May-17
	0.09	0.00	0.38	2.32	7.25	2.2	2.27	1.79	0.02	9.61	53.6	31	-6	50	2	211				1.00	Oct-12
	0.24	0.51	1.35	5.38	12.50	3.34	1.27	1.76	0.03	9.6	53.6	31	-6	50	2	211					Oct-12
	0.16	0.26	0.99	4.43	11.08	2.95	1.52	1.79	0.01	9.64	53.6	31	-6	50	2	211					Oct-12
100	17.23	21.06	29.07	34.80	86.21	1.43	1.21	6.12	0.95	13.02	35.6	7	66	23	2	18	12.43	-10.69			Sep-05
100	5.03	8.20	9.85			2.8	0.98			21.84	14.6	4	96	0	0	31					Sep-16
100	5.46	12.82	19.49	20.21	81.12	0	1.4	12.76	1.17	47.08	15.8	1	98	0	0	74	23.1	-23.49			Mar-11
100	6.41	6.59	15.45	21.68	99.59	0.82	0.82	14.22	1.27	47.93	1,677	1	99	0	0	20	27.17	-24.84			Dec-11
100	6.34	6.43	15.09	20.53	96.42	0.56	1.12	14.22	1.26	47.88	1,677	1	99	0	0	20	27.05	-24.84			Dec-89
100	1.64	3.74	8.51	-1.92	24.56	0	1.08	16.58	1.01	11.09	38.4	4	96	0	0	39	29.83	-24.26			Dec-11
100	1.67	3.61	8.24	-2.55	22.96	0	1.33	16.56	1	10.9	38.4	4	96	0	0	39	29.7	-24.26			Jan-11
100	5.77	8.14	15.20	17.76	85.53	1.13	0.75	13.69	1.23	13.64	56.7	1	99	0	0	35	18.37	-17.3			Dec-11
100	5.73	8.02	14.96	16.97	83.35	0.92	1	13.66	1.23	13.67	56.7	1	99	0	0	35	18.26	-17.3			Jun-05
100	7.94	8.83	16.23	28.59	113.36	0.5	0.72	15.59	1.2	70.01	2,255	1	99	0	0	14	30.18	-31.05			Dec-11
100	7.86	8.68	15.88	27.46	110.21	0.25	1.02	15.58	1.2	69.98	2,255	1	99	0	0	14	30.05	-31.05			Nov-86
100	1.16	5.70	15.81	22.20	68.04	1.76	0.88	9.64	0.86	15.02	104.8	7	93	0	1	24					Dec-11
100	1.12	5.60	15.60	21.28	65.93	1.32	1.13	9.63	0.86	15.52	104.8	7	93	0	1	24					Dec-11
100	0.15	2.68	16.34	19.53	48.80	1.23	1.15	10.23	0.75	14	620.6	9	90	0	1	23					Dec-11
100	0.27	2.76	16.70	20.38	50.76	1.51	0.9	10.21	0.75	13.74	620.6	9	90	0	1	23					Dec-11
100	1.21	2.70	4.85	8.14		0	1.09	5.55	0.48	10.34	10.6	89	11	0	0	8					Sep-13
100	1.31	2.98	5.35	9.38		0	0.69	5.65	0.49	10.39	10.6	89	11	0	0	8					Aug-13
100	5.85	11.08					0.65			11.42	6.5	2	98	0	0						Mar-17

	MARKET		FUND TYPE, CATEGORY & OBJECTIVE		RATINGS				MINIMUMS	
Fund Name	Ticker Symbol	Traded On	Fund Type	Category and (Prospectus Objective)	Overall Rating	Reward Rating	Risk Rating	Recent Up/ Downgrade	Open to New Investors	Min Initial Investment
Aristotle International Equity Fund Class I	ARSFX	NAS CM	Open End	Global Equity Large Cap (World Stock)	B-	C+	B	Up	Y	2,500
Aristotle Small Cap Equity Fund Class I	ARSBX	NAS CM	Open End	US Equity Small Cap (Small Company)	C	C	B	Up	Y	2,500
Aristotle Value Equity Fund Class I	ARSQX	NAS CM	Open End	US Equity Large Cap Value (Growth)	D	C	A-	Up		2,500
Aristotle/Saul Global Opportunities Fund Class I	ARSOX	NAS CM	Open End	Alloc (Growth & Income)	B-	B-	B		Y	2,500
Arrow DWA Balanced Fund Class A	DWAFX	NAS CM	Open End	Alloc (Balanced)	B-	C	B	Up	Y	5,000
Arrow DWA Balanced Fund Class C	DWATX	NAS CM	Open End	Alloc (Balanced)	B-	C	B	Up	Y	5,000
Arrow DWA Balanced Fund Institutional Class	DWANX	NAS CM	Open End	Alloc (Balanced)	B-	C	B	Up	Y	1,000,000
Arrow DWA Tactical Fund Class A	DWTFX	NAS CM	Open End	Moderate Alloc (Growth)	B-	C+	B	Up	Y	5,000
Arrow DWA Tactical Fund Class C	DWTTX	NAS CM	Open End	Moderate Alloc (Growth)	B-	C+	B	Up	Y	5,000
Arrow DWA Tactical Fund Institutional Class	DWTNX	NAS CM	Open End	Moderate Alloc (Growth)	B-	C+	B	Up	Y	1,000,000
Arrow Managed Futures Strategy Fund Class A	MFTFX	NAS CM	Open End	Other Alternative (Growth)	C	C-	C	Up	Y	5,000
Arrow Managed Futures Strategy Fund Class C	MFTTX	NAS CM	Open End	Other Alternative (Growth)	C	C-	C	Up	Y	5,000
Arrow Managed Futures Strategy Fund Institutional Class	MFTNX	NAS CM	Open End	Other Alternative (Growth)	C	C	C	Up	Y	1,000,000
Artisan Developing World Fund Advisor Shares	APDYX	NAS CM	Open End	Emerging Markets Equity (Growth)	C	B-	B-	Up	Y	250,000
Artisan Developing World Fund Institutional Shares	APHYX	NAS CM	Open End	Emerging Markets Equity (Growth)	C	B-	B-	Up	Y	1,000,000
Artisan Developing World Fund Investor Shares	ARTYX	NAS CM	Open End	Emerging Markets Equity (Growth)	C	B-	B-	Up	Y	1,000
Artisan Emerging Markets Fund Institutional Class	APHEX	NAS CM	Open End	Emerging Markets Equity (Div Emerging Mkts)	B	A	C	Up	Y	1,000,000
Artisan Emerging Markets Fund Investor Class	ARTZX	NAS CM	Open End	Emerging Markets Equity (Div Emerging Mkts)	B	A	C	Up	Y	1,000
Artisan Global Discovery Fund Investor Shares	APFDX	NAS CM	Open End	Global Equity Large Cap (World Stock)	U	U	U		Y	1,000
Artisan Global Equity Fund Institutional Shares	APHHX	NAS CM	Open End	Global Equity (World Stock)	B	B	B	Up	Y	1,000,000
Artisan Global Equity Fund Investor Class	ARTHX	NAS CM	Open End	Global Equity (World Stock)	B	B	B	Up	Y	1,000
Artisan Global Opportunities Fund Advisor Class	APDRX	NAS CM	Open End	Global Equity (Growth)	B	B	B+	Down	Y	250,000
Artisan Global Opportunities Fund Institutional Class	APHRX	NAS CM	Open End	Global Equity (Growth)	B	B	A-	Down	Y	1,000,000
Artisan Global Opportunities Fund Investor Class	ARTRX	NAS CM	Open End	Global Equity (Growth)	B	B	B+	Down	Y	1,000
Artisan Global Value Fund Advisor Class	APDGX	NAS CM	Open End	Global Equity (World Stock)	B-	B	B-	Down		250,000
Artisan Global Value Fund Institutional Class	APHGX	NAS CM	Open End	Global Equity (World Stock)	B	B	B-	Up	Y	1,000,000
Artisan Global Value Fund Investor Class	ARTGX	NAS CM	Open End	Global Equity (World Stock)	B-	B	B-	Down	Y	1,000
Artisan International Fund Advisor Class	APDIX	NAS CM	Open End	Global Equity Large Cap (Foreign Stock)	C+	C+	B-	Up	Y	250,000
Artisan International Fund Institutional Class	APHIX	NAS CM	Open End	Global Equity Large Cap (Foreign Stock)	C+	C+	B-	Up	Y	1,000,000
Artisan International Fund Investor Class	ARTIX	NAS CM	Open End	Global Equity Large Cap (Foreign Stock)	C+	C+	B-	Up	Y	1,000
Artisan International Small Cap Fund Institutional Share	APHJX	NAS CM	Open End	Global Equity Mid/Small Cap (Small Company)	B-	B-	C	Up	Y	1,000,000
Artisan International Small Cap Fund Investor Share	ARTJX	NAS CM	Open End	Global Equity Mid/Small Cap (Small Company)	C+	B-	C	Up		1,000
Artisan International Value Fund Advisor Class	APDKX	NAS CM	Open End	Global Equity Large Cap (Foreign Stock)	B	B	B	Up		250,000
Artisan International Value Fund Institutional Class	APHKX	NAS CM	Open End	Global Equity Large Cap (Foreign Stock)	B	B	B	Up		1,000,000
Artisan International Value Fund Investor Class	ARTKX	NAS CM	Open End	Global Equity Large Cap (Foreign Stock)	B	B	B	Up		1,000
Artisan Mid Cap Fund Advisor Class	APDMX	NAS CM	Open End	US Equity Mid Cap (Growth)	B	B-	B	Up		250,000
Artisan Mid Cap Fund Institutional Class	APHMX	NAS CM	Open End	US Equity Mid Cap (Growth)	B	B-	B	Up		1,000,000
Artisan Mid Cap Fund Investor Class	ARTMX	NAS CM	Open End	US Equity Mid Cap (Growth)	B	B-	B	Up		1,000
Artisan Mid Cap Value Fund Advisor Class	APDQX	NAS CM	Open End	US Equity Mid Cap (Growth)	B-	B-	B-	Up		250,000
Artisan Mid Cap Value Fund Institutional Class	APHQX	NAS CM	Open End	US Equity Mid Cap (Growth)	B-	B-	B-	Up		1,000,000
Artisan Mid Cap Value Fund Investor Class	ARTQX	NAS CM	Open End	US Equity Mid Cap (Growth)	B-	B-	B-	Up		1,000
Artisan Small Cap Fund Advisor Shares	APDSX	NAS CM	Open End	US Equity Small Cap (Small Company)	B	B+	B	Up		250,000
Artisan Small Cap Fund Institutional Shares	APHSX	NAS CM	Open End	US Equity Small Cap (Small Company)	B	B+	B	Up		1,000,000
Artisan Small Cap Fund Investor Shares	ARTSX	NAS CM	Open End	US Equity Small Cap (Small Company)	B	B+	B	Up		1,000
Artisan Thematic Fund Investor Shares	ARTTX	NAS CM	Open End	US Equity Large Cap Blend (Growth)	U	U	U		Y	1,000
Artisan Value Fund Advisor Class	APDLX	NAS CM	Open End	US Equity Large Cap Value (Growth)	B	B	B-	Up	Y	250,000
Artisan Value Fund Institutional Class	APHLX	NAS CM	Open End	US Equity Large Cap Value (Growth)	B	B	B-	Up	Y	1,000,000
Artisan Value Fund Investor Class	ARTLX	NAS CM	Open End	US Equity Large Cap Value (Growth)	B	B	B-	Up	Y	1,000
Ascendant Deep Value Bond Fund Class A Shares	AEQAX	NAS CM	Open End	Convertibles (Growth & Income)	C	C-	B-	Up	Y	1,000
Ascendant Deep Value Bond Fund Class C Shares	AEQCX	NAS CM	Open End	Convertibles (Growth & Income)	C	C-	B-	Up	Y	1,000
Ascendant Deep Value Bond Fund Class I Shares	AEQIX	NAS CM	Open End	Convertibles (Growth & Income)	C	C	B-	Up	Y	1,000,000
Ashmore Emerging Markets Active Equity Fund Class A	EMQAX	NAS CM	Open End	Emerging Markets Equity (Div Emerging Mkts)	D	D+	B+		Y	1,000

★Expanded analysis of this fund is included in Section II.

Min Additional Investment	TOTAL RETURNS: 3-Month Total Return	6-Month Total Return	1-Year Total Return	3-Year Total Return	5-Year Total Return	PERFORMANCE: Dividend Yield (TTM)	Expense Ratio	3-Yr Std Deviation	3-Year Beta	ASSETS: NAV	Total Assets (MIL)	ASSET ALLOCATION & TURNOVER: %Cash	%Stocks	%Bonds	%Other	Turnover Ratio	BULL & BEAR: Last Bull Market Total Return	Last Bear Market Total Return	FEES: Front End Fee (%)	Back End Fee (%)	Inception Date
100	3.73	8.59	22.64	20.85		1.44	0.94	11.59	0.92	10.74	15.6	3	97	0	0	48					Mar-14
100	0.65	7.75	17.86			0	0.98			12.83	0.08	4	98	0	-1	18					Oct-15
100	6.33	10.84	22.15			0.22	0.78				8.5	3	98	0	0						Aug-16
100	4.55	7.66	15.28	28.02	42.68	0.37	1	9.15	0.75	13.29	106.0	9	87	0	0	39					Mar-12
250	5.21	8.08	12.84	9.72	32.52	0	1.83	6.54	0.46	12.91	110.8	4	58	28	6	169	11.7	-12.95	5.75		Aug-06
250	4.97	7.66	11.93	7.28	27.51	0	2.58	6.55	0.46	12.06	110.8	4	58	28	6	169	11.24	-13.28			Aug-06
	5.30	8.23	13.13	10.54	34.12	0	1.58	6.56	0.46	13.07	110.8	4	58	28	6	169	11.7	-12.95			Mar-12
250	5.00	9.92	16.04	13.88	56.52	1.45	1.85	7.94	0.65	10.48	188.5	1	99	0	0	206	6.21	-18.36	5.75		May-08
250	4.79	9.55	15.27	11.34	50.79	0.87	2.6	7.93	0.65	9.85	188.5	1	99	0	0	206	5.71	-18.59			May-08
	5.05	10.07	16.40	14.65	58.37	1.69	1.6	7.98	0.66	10.51	188.5	1	99	0	0	206	6.21	-18.36			Mar-12
250	23.71	19.88	19.08	12.23	16.35	8.27	1.39	17.12	-0.18	8.71	147.8	0	0	37	63	801	-9.17	-9.56	5.75		Apr-10
250	23.49	18.33	18.17	9.91	12.29	8.32	2.14	17.14	-0.18	8.36	147.8	0	0	37	63	801	-9.54	-9.88			Apr-10
	23.79	19.84	19.36	12.95	17.89	8.25	1.14	17.09	-0.17	8.81	147.8	0	0	37	63	801	-9.17	-9.56			Mar-12
	2.75	11.03	35.22			0.22	1.25			12.78	2,043	9	89	0	2	45					Jun-15
	2.80	11.07	35.35			0.28	1.15			12.8	2,043	9	89	0	2	45					Jun-15
	2.74	10.95	35.06			0.13	1.5			12.75	2,043	9	89	0	2	45					Jun-15
	8.32	17.49	39.91	42.05	32.01	0.49	1.5	16.63	1.02	16.71	53.9	2	95	0	0	26	14.53	-30.9			Jun-06
	8.32	17.44	39.94	42.23	31.34	0.53	1.5	16.61	1.02	16.79	53.9	2	95	0	0	26	14.33	-30.97			Jun-08
	4.22						1.5			10.69	14.7	7	93	0	0	2					Aug-17
	5.62	14.16	31.59	30.26	77.74	0	1.13	11.56	0.99	20.63	314.2	1	97	0	2	110	25.88	-20			Oct-15
	5.53	14.03	31.33	29.54	76.75	0	1.4	11.56	0.99	20.55	314.2	1	97	0	2	110	25.88	-20			Mar-10
	4.35	9.90	31.33	47.41	91.75	0	1.09	11.88	1	25.79	2,806	6	94	0	0	34	27.63	-19.86			Apr-15
	4.40	9.95	31.49	48.00	93.48	0	0.93	11.91	1	25.98	2,806	6	94	0	0	34	27.75	-19.92			Jul-11
	4.32	9.83	31.18	46.98	91.18	0	1.18	11.89	1	25.72	2,806	6	94	0	0	34	27.63	-19.86			Sep-08
	3.75	9.20	21.75	29.28	80.29	0.84	1.17	10.69	0.95	18.13	3,192	10	89	0	1	13	20.98	-14.73			Apr-15
	3.82	9.25	21.86	29.73	81.85	0.91	1.05	10.72	0.96	18.17	3,192	10	89	0	1	13	20.98	-14.73			Jul-12
	3.75	9.13	21.58	28.80	79.62	0.68	1.29	10.69	0.95	18.17	3,192	10	89	0	1	13	20.98	-14.73			Dec-07
	3.95	9.77	31.11	13.54	42.87	0.83	1.01	12.05	0.89	33.25	14,239	1	99	0	0	58	26.28	-24.17			Apr-15
	3.98	9.83	31.24	13.85	43.90	0.91	0.95	12.03	0.88	33.49	14,239	1	99	0	0	58	26.46	-24.11			Jul-97
	3.94	9.76	31.01	13.08	42.28	0.67	1.19	12.04	0.88	33.33	14,239	1	99	0	0	58	26.28	-24.17			Dec-95
	7.05	15.54	33.61	28.84	48.00	0	1.35	13.72	0.89	23.18	490.1	5	95	0	0	79	21.51	-23.82			Apr-16
	6.94	15.40	33.35	28.41	47.50	0	1.52	13.73	0.89	23.09	490.1	5	95	0	0	79	21.51	-23.82			Dec-01
	2.73	8.88	23.97	28.05	68.73	1.23	1.07	10.35	0.78	38.58	15,140	14	86	0	0	12	17.24	-19.88			Apr-15
	2.74	8.92	24.06	28.40	69.78	1.3	1.01	10.36	0.78	38.73	15,140	14	86	0	0	12	17.37	-19.81			Oct-06
	2.72	8.81	23.82	27.52	68.03	1.04	1.23	10.34	0.78	38.62	15,140	14	86	0	0	12	17.24	-19.88			Sep-02
	2.95	4.61	20.61	21.63	81.00	0	1.05	12.2	1.02	38.29	6,810	3	97	0	0	43	28.22	-16.53			Apr-15
	2.99	4.68	20.75	22.08	82.54	0	0.95	12.21	1.02	41.49	6,810	3	97	0	0	43	28.42	-16.43			Jul-00
	2.94	4.56	20.48	21.21	80.37	0	1.19	12.2	1.02	38.11	6,810	3	97	0	0	43	28.22	-16.53			Jun-97
	4.75	8.00	12.46	23.33	73.90	0.14	1.06	11.22	0.99	22.68	3,987	8	93	0	0	24	22.32	-17.02			Apr-15
	4.77	8.06	12.62	23.75	75.34	0.24	0.96	11.23	0.99	22.7	3,987	8	93	0	0	24	22.32	-17.02			Feb-12
	4.72	7.96	12.36	22.95	73.37	0.07	1.16	11.22	0.99	22.73	3,987	8	93	0	0	24	22.32	-17.02			Mar-01
	5.66	9.60	26.91	33.53	94.38		1.1	12.98	0.74	30.59	1,321	4	96	0	0	35	26.04	-16.87			Feb-17
	5.66	9.66	27.09	34.32	96.23	0	1.01	12.98	0.74	30.96	1,321	4	96	0	0	35	26.04	-16.87			May-12
	5.60	9.58	26.80	33.42	94.22	0	1.25	12.98	0.74	30.55	1,321	4	96	0	0	35	26.04	-16.87			Mar-95
	10.22	23.64					1.5			11.81	24.7	1	99	0	0	170					Apr-17
	5.42	10.43	16.10	35.38	83.10	0.6	0.84	13.8	1.1	14.49	629.7	5	91	0	0	44	22.54	-14.65			Apr-15
	5.49	10.48	16.23	35.76	84.67	0.73	0.78	13.79	1.1	14.52	629.7	5	91	0	0	44	22.65	-14.54			Jul-11
	5.41	10.40	15.98	34.91	82.46	0.35	0.97	13.84	1.11	14.56	629.7	5	91	0	0	44	22.54	-14.64			Mar-06
100	1.07	3.48	5.86	0.11	15.41	0.7	2.68	3.58	0.35	12.17	19.4	7	0	93	0	427			5.75		Oct-11
100	1.01	3.19	5.14	-2.00	11.41	0.46	3.43	3.56	0.35	11.95	19.4	7	0	93	0	427					Oct-11
25,000	1.18	3.67	6.19	0.91	16.89	0.82	2.43	3.58	0.35	12.15	19.4	7	0	93	0	427					Oct-11
50	6.49	17.67	37.92			0.39	1.27			11.99	18.1	11	89	0	0				5.25		Nov-16

Fund Name	Ticker Symbol	Traded On	Fund Type	Category and (Prospectus Objective)	Overall Rating	Reward Rating	Risk Rating	Recent Up/ Downgrade	Open to New Investors	Min Initial Investment
	MARKET		FUND TYPE, CATEGORY & OBJECTIVE		RATINGS				MINIMUMS	
Ashmore Emerging Markets Active Equity Fund Class C	EMQCX	NAS CM	Open End	Emerging Markets Equity (Div Emerging Mkts)	D	D+	B+		Y	1,000
Ashmore Emerging Mkts Active Equity Fund Inst Cls	EMQIX	NAS CM	Open End	Emerging Markets Equity (Div Emerging Mkts)	D	D+	B+		Y	1,000,000
Ashmore Emerging Markets Equity Fund Class A	EMEAX	NAS CM	Open End	Emerging Markets Equity (Growth)	B	A-	C	Up	Y	1,000
Ashmore Emerging Markets Equity Fund Class C	EMECX	NAS CM	Open End	Emerging Markets Equity (Growth)	B	B+	C	Up	Y	1,000
Ashmore Emerging Markets Equity Fund Institutional Class	EMFIX	NAS CM	Open End	Emerging Markets Equity (Growth)	B	A	C	Up	Y	1,000,000
Ashmore Emerging Markets Equity Opportunities Fund Class A	AEOAX	NAS CM	Open End	Emerging Markets Equity (Growth)	C	C	B+	Up	Y	1,000
Ashmore Emerging Markets Equity Opportunities Fund Class C	AEOCX	NAS CM	Open End	Emerging Markets Equity (Growth)	C	C	B+	Up	Y	1,000
Ashmore Emerging Mkts Equity Opp Fund Inst Cls	AEOIX	NAS CM	Open End	Emerging Markets Equity (Growth)	C	C	B+	Up		1,000,000
Ashmore Emerging Markets Frontier Equity Fund Class A	EFEAX	NAS CM	Open End	Emerging Markets Equity (Growth)	C+	B-	C		Y	1,000
Ashmore Emerging Markets Frontier Equity Fund Class C	EFECX	NAS CM	Open End	Emerging Markets Equity (Growth)	C+	B-	C		Y	1,000
Ashmore Emerging Mkts Frontier Equity Fund Inst Cls	EFEIX	NAS CM	Open End	Emerging Markets Equity (Growth)	C+	B-	C		Y	1,000,000
Ashmore Emerging Markets Small Cap Equity Fund Class A	ESSAX	NAS CM	Open End	Emerging Markets Equity (Small Company)	B	B	C+	Up	Y	1,000
Ashmore Emerging Markets Small Cap Equity Fund Class C	ESSCX	NAS CM	Open End	Emerging Markets Equity (Small Company)	B	B	C+	Up	Y	1,000
Ashmore Emerging Mkts Small Cap Equity Fund Inst Cls	ESCIX	NAS CM	Open End	Emerging Markets Equity (Small Company)	B	B	C+	Up		1,000,000
Asia Pacific Fund, Inc	APB	NYSE	Closed End	Asia ex-Japan Equity (Pacific Stock)	B	A-	B-	Up	Y	
Aspen Managed Futures Strategy Fund Class A	MFBPX	NAS CM	Open End	Other Alternative (Growth)	D	D	D+	Down	Y	2,500
Aspen Managed Futures Strategy Fund Class I	MFBTX	NAS CM	Open End	Other Alternative (Growth)	D	D	D+	Down	Y	100,000
Aspen Portfolio Strategy Fund Class A	ASPEX	NAS CM	Open End	Multialternative (Growth)	D-	D+	B+		Y	2,500
Aspen Portfolio Strategy Fund Class I	ASPNX	NAS CM	Open End	Multialternative (Growth)	D-	D+	B+		Y	100,000
Aspiration Flagship Fund	ASPFX	NAS CM	Open End	Multialternative (Growth)	C+	C	B	Up	Y	100
Aspiration Redwood Fund	REDWX	NAS CM	Open End	US Equity Large Cap Blend (Growth & Income)	C	C	B	Up	Y	100
Aspiriant Defensive Allocation Fund	RMDFX	NAS CM	Open End	Multialternative (Asset Alloc)	C	C-	A	Up	Y	0
Aspiriant Risk-Managed Equity Allocation Fund Adv Shares	RMEAX	NAS CM	Open End	Global Equity (World Stock)	B	B-	B+	Up	Y	0
Asset Management Fund Large Cap Equity Fund Class AMF	IICAX	NAS CM	Open End	US Equity Large Cap Blend (Growth)	B	B	B-		Y	2,500
Asset Management Fund Large Cap Equity Fund Class H	IICHX	NAS CM	Open End	US Equity Large Cap Blend (Growth)	B	B	B-		Y	3,000,000
Astor Dynamic Allocation Fund Class A	ASTLX	NAS CM	Open End	Moderate Alloc (Growth & Income)	B-	C+	B	Down	Y	5,000
Astor Dynamic Allocation Fund Class C	ASTZX	NAS CM	Open End	Moderate Alloc (Growth & Income)	B-	C+	B-	Down	Y	5,000
Astor Dynamic Allocation Fund Class I	ASTIX	NAS CM	Open End	Moderate Alloc (Growth & Income)	B-	C+	B	Down	Y	5,000
Astor Macro Alternative Fund Class I	GBLMX	NAS CM	Open End	Multialternative (Growth & Income)	C+	C	B	Up	Y	5,000
Astor Sector Allocation Fund Class A	ASPGX	NAS CM	Open End	Moderate Alloc (Growth)	C+	C+	C+	Down	Y	5,000
Astor Sector Allocation Fund Class C	CSPGX	NAS CM	Open End	Moderate Alloc (Growth)	C+	C+	C+	Down	Y	5,000
Astor Sector Allocation Fund Class I	STARX	NAS CM	Open End	Moderate Alloc (Growth)	C+	C+	C+	Down	Y	5,000
AT Disciplined Equity Fund Institutional Class	AWEIX	NAS CM	Open End	US Equity Large Cap Blend (World Stock)	B	B-	B+		Y	250,000
AT Income Opportunities Fund Institutional Class	AWIIX	NAS CM	Open End	Moderate Alloc (Income)	B-	C+	B-	Up	Y	250,000
AT Mid Cap Equity Fund Institutional Class	AWMIX	NAS CM	Open End	US Equity Mid Cap (Equity-Income)	B	B	B-	Up	Y	250,000
ATAC Inflation Rotation Fund Investor Class Shares	ATACX	NAS CM	Open End	Moderate Alloc (Growth & Income)	B+	A-	B+	Up	Y	2,500
Athena Value Fund Class A	ATVAX	NAS CM	Open End	US Equity Mid Cap (Growth)	C+	C	C+	Up	Y	2,500
Athena Value Fund Class I	ATVIX	NAS CM	Open End	US Equity Mid Cap (Growth)	C+	C	C+	Up	Y	100,000
ATM International Managed Volatility Portfolio Class K	US26883L8110		Open End	Global Equity Large Cap (Foreign Stock)	B-	C+	B	Up	Y	0
ATM Large Cap Managed Volatility Portfolio Class K	US26883L8789		Open End	US Equity Large Cap Blend (Growth)	B	B-	B		Y	0
ATM Mid Cap Managed Volatility Portfolio Class K	US26883L8524		Open End	US Equity Mid Cap (Growth)	B	B	B		Y	0
ATM Small Cap Managed Volatility Portfolio Class K	US26883L8375		Open End	US Equity Small Cap (Small Company)	B+	A-	B	Up	Y	0
Auer Growth Fund	AUERX	NAS CM	Open End	US Equity Small Cap (Growth)	C+	B-	C	Up	Y	2,000
Auxier Focus Fund Class A	AUXAX	NAS CM	Open End	US Equity Large Cap Value (Growth)	B-	C+	B	Down	Y	2,000
Auxier Focus Fund Class Investor	AUXFX	NAS CM	Open End	US Equity Large Cap Value (Growth)	B-	C+	B	Down	Y	5,000
Auxier Focus Fund Institutional	AUXIX	NAS CM	Open End	US Equity Large Cap Value (Growth)	B-	C+	B	Down	Y	1,000,000
Ave Maria Bond Fund	AVEFX	NAS CM	Open End	US Fixed Income (Govt Bond)	B	C	A+		Y	2,500
Ave Maria Growth Fund	AVEGX	NAS CM	Open End	US Equity Mid Cap (Growth)	B	B+	B-		Y	2,500
Ave Maria Rising Dividend Fund	AVEDX	NAS CM	Open End	US Equity Large Cap Blend (Growth & Income)	B-	B-	B	Down	Y	2,500
Ave Maria Value Fund	AVEMX	NAS CM	Open End	US Equity Mid Cap (Growth)	C+	C+	C+	Up	Y	2,500
Ave Maria World Equity Fund	AVEWX	NAS CM	Open End	Global Equity (World Stock)	B-	C+	B	Up	Y	2,500
Avenue Credit Strategies Fund Institutional Class Shares	ACSBX	NAS CM	Open End	Other Alternative (Growth & Income)	D+	D	C-	Up	Y	1,000,000

★Expanded analysis of this fund is included in Section II.

Min Additional Investment	TOTAL RETURNS 3-Month Total Return	6-Month Total Return	1-Year Total Return	3-Year Total Return	5-Year Total Return	PERFORMANCE Dividend Yield (TTM)	Expense Ratio	3-Yr Std Deviation	3-Year Beta	ASSETS NAV	Total Assets (MIL)	ASSET ALLOCATION & TURNOVER %Cash	%Stocks	%Bonds	%Other	Turnover Ratio	BULL & BEAR Last Bull Market Total Return	Last Bear Market Total Return	FEES Front End Fee (%)	Back End Fee (%)	Inception Date
50	6.34	17.36	37.20			0.34	2.02			11.93	18.1	11	89	0	0					1.00	Nov-16
5,000	6.44	17.69	38.19			0.39	1.02			12.01	18.1	11	89	0	0						Nov-16
50	8.35	18.83	45.81	36.19	28.73	1.28	1.42	18.22	1.08	11.61	10.1	2	97	0	1	119	17.55		5.25		Feb-12
50	8.18	18.49	44.80	33.29	24.20		2.17	18.16	1.08	11.17	10.1	2	97	0	1	119	17.18			1.00	Aug-12
5,000	8.53	18.98	46.23	37.31	30.51	1.4	1.17	18.18	1.08	11.21	10.1	2	97	0	1	119	17.86				Jun-11
50	5.77	14.24	37.54			1.27	1.58			10.86	7.5	2	90	3	1	15			5.25		Nov-15
50	5.67	13.91	36.79			1.18	2.33			10.72	7.5	2	90	3	1	15				1.00	Nov-15
5,000	5.83	14.20	37.67			1.29	1.33			10.91	7.5	2	90	3	1	15					Nov-15
50	4.79	9.23	28.68	27.42		1.66	1.77	11.08	0.83	9.42	89.1	1	97	0	0	76			5.25		May-14
50	4.44	8.79	27.77	24.32		1.18	2.52	11.08	0.83	9.23	89.1	1	97	0	0	76				1.00	May-14
5,000	4.83	9.37	29.01	28.53		1.6	1.52	11.08	0.83	10.85	89.1	1	97	0	0	76					Nov-13
50	4.52	10.11	28.73	34.57	32.21	1.81	1.77	15.58	0.99	10.42	40.1	3	96	0	0	104			5.25		Feb-12
50	4.35	9.86	27.90	31.51	27.14	1.47	2.52	15.57	1	11.02	40.1	3	96	0	0	104				1.00	Aug-12
5,000	4.59	10.21	28.89	35.59	33.79	1.47	1.52	15.56	0.99	13.36	40.1	3	96	0	0	104					Oct-11
	8.05	14.32	36.94	34.09	39.44	1.43		16.64	1	15.15	158.9	0	98	0	0	66	17.01	-27.6			May-87
	0.12	-0.86	-8.14	-11.31	1.64	1.31	1.62	7.2		8.01	121.2	71	25	-1	4	31	-11.56		5.50		Aug-11
	0.24	-0.72	-8.00	-11.06	2.76	0.97	1.29	7.15		8.16	121.2	71	25	-1	4	31	-11.26				Aug-11
	6.81	11.05	10.03				1.99			26.94	47.8	37	99	-39	4				5.50		Dec-16
	6.95	11.32	10.47				1.59			27	47.8	37	99	-39	4						Dec-16
1	1.76	3.07	5.05	4.62		0.58	1.49	3.25	0.29	10.27	11.3	27	35	33	4	14					Oct-14
1	1.52	8.19	21.87			1.54	0.51			12.5	46.5	2	98	0	0	132					Nov-15
	2.37	4.41	9.41			1.06	1.19			10.74	986.7	16	50	29	4	16					Dec-15
	5.58	8.88	21.77	26.27		1.45	0.51	7.86	0.7	13.22	1,004	5	93	0	2	89					Apr-13
100	6.84	11.31	20.55	33.35	89.29	0.89	1.46	9.51	0.88	8.45	47.4	3	97	0	0	76	19.21	-8.82			Jun-53
	6.78	11.29	20.64	33.89	90.52	1.1	1.21	9.51	0.88	8.41	47.4	3	97	0	0	76	19.3	-8.75			Feb-09
100	5.49	9.58	15.77	19.47	46.27	0.74	1.68	7.5	0.73	13.32	142.9	9	84	5	3	78	1.26	-11.49	4.75		Nov-11
100	5.34	9.16	14.90	16.80	40.86	0.35	2.43	7.51	0.73	12.85	142.9	9	84	5	3	78	0.88	-11.85		1.00	Mar-10
100	5.59	9.75	16.09	20.42	48.14	0.95	1.43	7.52	0.73	13.34	142.9	9	84	5	3	78	1.37	-11.4			Oct-09
100	4.68	6.56	7.05			1.57	1.95			10.61	4.0	2	72	19	6	114					Jun-15
100	5.70	9.92	16.29	16.09	63.87	0	1.82	9.68	0.9	17.53	79.8	4	92	5	0	82			4.75		Nov-11
100	5.50	9.40	15.29	13.47	57.76	0	2.57	9.67	0.89	16.79	79.8	4	92	5	0	82				1.00	Nov-11
100	5.71	9.89	16.44	16.92	65.39	0	1.57	9.68	0.9	17.68	79.8	4	92	5	0	82					Jan-14
	7.66	10.57	20.89	34.17	106.83	0.75	0.8	10.28	1	19.17	920.2	4	96	0	0	12	24.12	-13.59			Dec-05
	4.38	7.43	13.78	22.42		2.36	0.74	7.33	0.66	11.38	329.4	4	63	31	1	24					Jun-14
	6.75	11.20	20.87	29.19		0	0.89	10.44	0.91	13.9	540.7	4	96	0	0	23					Jun-14
100	4.72	15.89	26.93	40.42	46.59	0	1.96	13.97		32.17	109.3	2	0	98	0	2,270					Sep-12
100	5.29	5.71	6.03			1.39	1.51			9.96	11.5	2	98	0	0	94			5.75		May-15
100	5.24	5.77	6.30			1.61	1.26			9.96	11.5	2	98	0	0	94					May-15
	3.72	8.71	24.63	19.92	39.12	0.68	0.63	11.91	0.96		1,693	-1	100	0	0	4	7.44	-24.48			Aug-11
	6.98	11.78	21.09	33.96	105.70	1.3	0.59	10.06	1		3,662	0	100	0	0	10	19.21	-18.33			Aug-11
	6.67	10.12	15.73	32.98	98.91	0.88	0.6	11.05	1		205.1	-1	100	0	0	35	20.74	-24.54			Aug-11
	4.05	9.75	14.58	30.61	95.25	0.83	0.6	14.09	1		1,015	-1	101	0	0	29	20.25	-26.8			Aug-11
100	7.70	19.92	28.75	18.51	56.45	0	2.5	15	1.12	9.09	31.0	3	97	0	0	175	24.15	-33.72			Dec-07
50	5.63	7.20	17.39	22.82	66.37	0.6	1.25	8.54	0.82	22.67	253.6	5	94	0	0	5	15.61	-11.57	5.75		Jul-05
50	5.67	7.30	17.71	23.42	67.19	0.96	0.98	8.51	0.82	22.32	253.6	5	94	0	0	5	15.61	-11.63			Jul-99
	5.72	7.43	17.91	24.08	68.92	0.96	0.8	8.55	0.82	22.71	253.6	5	94	0	0	5	15.61	-11.63			May-12
	1.05	2.32	4.16	9.46	19.25	1.42	0.51	1.89	0.32	11.42	302.1	7	16	78	0	21	5.44	-1.83			May-03
	7.38	13.57	27.36	37.61	99.26	0.06	1.07	9.82	0.88	30.8	476.9	8	92	0	0	29	27.88	-19			May-03
	6.70	10.82	16.82	25.59	87.98	1.2	0.93	10.56	0.95	18.44	961.1	6	94	0	0	24	21.09	-16.05			May-05
	6.88	11.93	17.72	12.29	49.15	0	1.21	12.08	0.98	20.88	247.3	11	89	0	0	47	25.51	-19.84			May-01
	4.90	7.00	17.88	21.02	53.29	0.41	1.26	10.6	0.99	15.08	60.6	8	92	0	0	42	19.83	-23.8			Apr-10
	-0.81	0.41	-1.80	-11.12	-2.46	7.44	1.53	8.3	1.09	7.94	848.6	12	2	78	6	206					Jun-12

	MARKET			FUND TYPE, CATEGORY & OBJECTIVE	RATINGS					MINIMUMS
Fund Name	Ticker Symbol	Traded On	Fund Type	Category and (Prospectus Objective)	Overall Rating	Reward Rating	Risk Rating	Recent Up/ Downgrade	Open to New Investors	Min Initial Investment
Avenue Credit Strategies Fund Investor Class Shares	ACSAX	NAS CM	Open End	Other Alternative (Growth & Income)	D+	D	C-	Up	Y	5,000
Avondale Core Investment Fund	COREX	NAS CM	Open End	Moderate Alloc (Growth)	C-	D+	C		Y	5,000
AXA 2000 Managed Volatility Portfolio Class IB	US26884M8340		Open End	US Equity Small Cap (Growth)	B	B+	B	Up	Y	0
AXA 2000 Managed Volatility Portfolio Class K	US26883L8458		Open End	US Equity Small Cap (Growth)	B+	A-	B	Up	Y	0
AXA 400 Managed Volatility Portfolio Class IB	US26884M8001		Open End	US Equity Mid Cap (Growth)	B	B	B	Up	Y	0
AXA 400 Managed Volatility Portfolio Class K	US26883L8607		Open End	US Equity Mid Cap (Growth)	B	B	B		Y	0
AXA 500 Managed Volatility Portfolio Class IB	US26884M2061		Open End	US Equity Large Cap Blend (Growth)	B-	B-	B	Down	Y	0
AXA 500 Managed Volatility Portfolio Class K	US26883L8862		Open End	US Equity Large Cap Blend (Growth)	B	B-	B		Y	0
AXA Aggressive Allocation Portfolio Class K	US00247C5444		Open End	Aggressive Alloc (Asset Alloc)	B-	B-	B-	Down	Y	0
AXA Aggressive Strategy Portfolio Class IB	US26884M6443		Open End	Aggressive Alloc (Growth & Income)	B-	B-	B	Down	Y	0
AXA Balanced Strategy Fund Class IA	US2689543369		Open End	Moderate Alloc (Balanced)	B-	C+	B	Up	Y	0
AXA Balanced Strategy Fund Class IB	US2689543286		Open End	Moderate Alloc (Balanced)	B-	C+	B	Up	Y	0
AXA Charter Aggressive Growth Portfolio Class B	US00248T2078		Open End	Aggressive Alloc (Asset Alloc)	C+	C+	C+	Down	Y	0
AXA Charter Conservative Portfolio Class B	US00248T5048		Open End	Cautious Alloc (Asset Alloc)	B-	C	B+	Up	Y	0
AXA Charter Growth Portfolio Class B	US00248T8356		Open End	Moderate Alloc (Asset Alloc)	C+	C+	B-	Down	Y	0
AXA Charter Moderate Growth Portfolio Class B	US00248T6376		Open End	Moderate Alloc (Asset Alloc)	B-	C+	B	Down	Y	0
AXA Charter Moderate Portfolio Class B	US00248T5956		Open End	Cautious Alloc (Asset Alloc)	B-	C+	B	Up	Y	0
AXA Charter Small Cap Growth Portfolio Class A	US00247C5931		Open End	US Equity Small Cap (Small Company)	B	B+	C	Up	Y	0
AXA Charter Small Cap Growth Portfolio Class B	US29364E8764		Open End	US Equity Small Cap (Small Company)	B	B+	C	Up	Y	0
AXA Charter Small Cap Value Portfolio Class A	US2689406815		Open End	US Equity Small Cap (Small Company)	C+	B-	C+	Up	Y	0
AXA Charter Small Cap Value Portfolio Class B	US2689406732		Open End	US Equity Small Cap (Small Company)	C+	B-	C+	Up	Y	0
AXA Conservative Allocation Portfolio Class K	US00247C5857		Open End	Cautious Alloc (Asset Alloc)	B	C	A	Up	Y	0
AXA Conservative Growth Strategy Fund Class IB	US2689543443		Open End	Cautious Alloc (Growth & Income)	B-	C+	B	Up	Y	0
AXA Conservative Growth Strategy Fund Class IB	US2689543690		Open End	Cautious Alloc (Income)	B-	C	B+	Up	Y	0
AXA Conservative-Plus Allocation Portfolio Class K	US00247C5774		Open End	Cautious Alloc (Asset Alloc)	B-	C+	B	Up	Y	0
AXA Global Equity Managed Volatility Portfolio Class IA	US2689408894		Open End	Global Equity (World Stock)	B-	B-	B	Up	Y	0
AXA Global Equity Managed Volatility Portfolio Class IB	US2689407565		Open End	Global Equity (World Stock)	B-	B-	B	Up	Y	0
AXA Global Equity Managed Volatility Portfolio Class K	US26883L6213		Open End	Global Equity (World Stock)	B-	B-	C+	Up	Y	0
AXA Growth Strategy Fund Class IA	US2689542866		Open End	Aggressive Alloc (Growth & Income)	B-	C+	B	Up	Y	0
AXA Growth Strategy Fund Class IB	US2689542783		Open End	Aggressive Alloc (Growth & Income)	B-	C+	B	Up	Y	0
AXA International Core Managed Volatility Portfolio Cls IA	US2689404679		Open End	Global Equity Large Cap (Foreign Stock)	B-	C+	B-	Up	Y	0
AXA International Core Managed Volatility Portfolio Cls IB	US2689404596		Open End	Global Equity Large Cap (Foreign Stock)	B-	C+	B-	Up	Y	0
AXA International Core Managed Volatility Portfolio Cls K	US26883L6130		Open End	Global Equity Large Cap (Foreign Stock)	B-	C+	B-	Up	Y	0
AXA International Managed Volatility Portfolio Class IB	US26884M7680		Open End	Global Equity Large Cap (Foreign Stock)	B-	C+	B-	Up	Y	0
AXA International Managed Volatility Portfolio Class K	US26883L8292		Open End	Global Equity Large Cap (Foreign Stock)	B-	C+	B	Up	Y	0
AXA Intl Value Managed Volatility Portfolio Cls IA	US2689404000		Open End	Global Equity Large Cap (Growth & Income)	B-	C+	B-	Up	Y	0
AXA Intl Value Managed Volatility Portfolio Cls IB	US2689408142		Open End	Global Equity Large Cap (Growth & Income)	B-	C+	B-	Up	Y	0
AXA International Value Managed Volatility Portfolio Cls K	US26883L5892		Open End	Global Equity Large Cap (Growth & Income)	B-	C+	B-	Up	Y	0
AXA Large Cap Core Managed Volatility Portfolio Class IA	US2689405742		Open End	US Equity Large Cap Blend (Growth & Income)	B-	B-	B	Down	Y	0
AXA Large Cap Core Managed Volatility Portfolio Class IB	US2689405668		Open End	US Equity Large Cap Blend (Growth & Income)	B-	B-	B	Down	Y	0
AXA Large Cap Core Managed Volatility Portfolio Class K	US26883L5637		Open End	US Equity Large Cap Blend (Growth & Income)	B	B-	B		Y	0
AXA Large Cap Growth Managed Volatility Portfolio Class IA	US2689408068		Open End	US Equity Large Cap Growth (Growth)	B	B	B	Down	Y	0
AXA Large Cap Growth Managed Volatility Portfolio Class IB	US2689407649		Open End	US Equity Large Cap Growth (Growth)	B	B	B	Down	Y	0
AXA Large Cap Growth Managed Volatility Portfolio Class K	US26883L5488		Open End	US Equity Large Cap Growth (Growth)	B	B	B	Down	Y	0
AXA Large Cap Value Managed Volatility Portfolio Class IA	US2689407151		Open End	US Equity Large Cap Value (Growth)	B-	B-	B	Down	Y	0
AXA Large Cap Value Managed Volatility Portfolio Class IB	US2689406997		Open End	US Equity Large Cap Value (Growth)	B-	B-	B	Down	Y	0
AXA Large Cap Value Managed Volatility Portfolio Class K	US26883L5223		Open End	US Equity Large Cap Value (Growth)	B	B-	B	Up	Y	0
AXA Mid Cap Value Managed Volatility Portfolio Class IA	US2689408712		Open End	US Equity Mid Cap (Growth)	B	B-	B	Up	Y	0
AXA Mid Cap Value Managed Volatility Portfolio Class IB	US2689407490		Open End	US Equity Mid Cap (Growth)	B	B-	B	Up	Y	0
AXA Mid Cap Value Managed Volatility Portfolio Class K	US26883L4721		Open End	US Equity Mid Cap (Growth)	B	B-	B	Up	Y	0
AXA Moderate Allocation Portfolio Class K	US00247C5691		Open End	Moderate Alloc (Asset Alloc)	B-	C+	B	Up	Y	0
AXA Moderate Growth Strategy Fund Class IB	US2689542940		Open End	Moderate Alloc (Growth & Income)	B-	C+	B	Up	Y	0

★ Expanded analysis of this fund is included in Section II.

Min Additional Investment	TOTAL RETURNS					PERFORMANCE				ASSETS		ASSET ALLOCATION & TURNOVER					BULL & BEAR		FEES		
	3-Month Total Return	6-Month Total Return	1-Year Total Return	3-Year Total Return	5-Year Total Return	Dividend Yield (TTM)	Expense Ratio	3-Yr Std Deviation	3-Year Beta	NAV	Total Assets (MIL)	%Cash	%Stocks	%Bonds	%Other	Turnover Ratio	Last Bull Market Total Return	Last Bear Market Total Return	Front End Fee (%)	Back End Fee (%)	Inception Date
	-0.75	0.40	-1.93	-11.70	-3.64	7.18	1.78	8.31	1.09	7.95	848.6	12	2	78	6	206					Jun-12
100	0.20	0.20	0.10	-1.50		0	1.41	1.68	0.18	9.82	0.94	97	3	0	0	0					Nov-14
	4.01	9.65	14.34	29.76	92.20	0.58	0.85	14.13	1		3,529	-1	101	0	0	20	21.57	-26.42			Oct-09
	4.09	9.84	14.61	30.77	94.71	0.8	0.6	14.15	1		3,529	-1	101	0	0	20	21.62	-26.37			Aug-11
	6.59	9.96	15.39	32.28	96.02	0.61	0.85	11.08	1		714.3	-1	101	0	0	20	22.12	-24.27			Oct-09
	6.64	10.08	15.67	33.28	98.50	0.83	0.6	11.08	1		714.3	-1	101	0	0	20	22.24	-24.26			Aug-11
	6.94	11.66	20.82	33.16	103.43	0.98	0.83	10.12	1		8,905	0	100	0	0	4	20.15	-17.87			Oct-09
	7.04	11.82	21.15	34.20	105.98	1.19	0.58	10.12	1		8,905	0	100	0	0	4	20.39	-17.89			Aug-11
	5.29	9.94	19.50	27.02	73.69	1	0.94	9.49	0.92		3,568	1	92	8	0	5	16.87	-19.63			Dec-11
	4.58	8.46	15.83	23.82	66.61	0.83	1.07	8.25	0.8		3,516	1	82	18	0	20					Apr-12
	2.67	5.10	9.98	15.10	38.86	0.77	1.05	4.96	0.48		3,656	2	52	46	0	13	9.79	-10.08			Sep-09
	2.60	5.10	9.90	15.09	38.70	0.77	1.05	4.93	0.48		3,656	2	52	46	0	13	9.7	-10.23			Apr-09
	4.39	9.16	16.85	18.60		0.91	1.45	8.61	1.01		6.3	6	78	10	3	46					Oct-13
	1.47	3.51	7.95	10.93		1.86	1.25	3.77	0.85		31.3	6	23	62	1	11					Oct-13
	3.60	7.71	14.90	17.02		1.21	1.4	7.38	0.87		13.1	6	65	23	2	19					Oct-13
	2.93	6.31	12.93	15.84		1.55	1.35	6.07	0.96		24.0	7	52	35	2	17					Oct-13
	2.35	5.20	10.88	13.74		1.64	1.25	5.06	1.1		33.6	6	40	47	1	13					Oct-13
	6.62	12.28	25.09	28.19	89.86	0	1.45	15.09	1		97.2	2	98	0	0	3	21.33	-29.33			Jan-08
	6.61	12.24	25.18	28.20	90.01	0	1.45	15.06	1		97.2	2	98	0	0	3	21.4	-29.61			Dec-98
	2.85	11.24	11.17	20.26	68.15	1.1	1.45	14.15	0.95		172.3	6	94	0	0	11	25.06	-26.26			Oct-02
	2.85	11.23	11.17	20.25	68.09	1.1	1.45	14.15	0.95		172.3	6	94	0	0	11	25.01	-26.34			Jan-98
	1.03	2.22	5.29	8.31	17.14	1.17	0.75	2.14	0.17		1,219	4	21	75	0	12	4.81	-2.49			Aug-12
	2.00	3.99	8.03	12.41	30.62	0.8	1	3.87	0.37		1,605	2	41	56	0	12	7.95	-7.9			Apr-09
	0.74	1.83	4.30	6.79	14.98	0.78	0.95	2	0.16		1,605	4	21	75	0	14	4.59	-3.16			Apr-09
	2.28	4.35	9.26	13.67	31.48	1.1	0.85	4.01	0.38		1,391	3	41	56	0	11	8.26	-7.65			Dec-11
	5.54	10.99	26.15	27.79	60.39	0.75	1.15	10.8	1.01		2,365	0	100	0	0	15	14.93	-21.64			Oct-02
	5.55	11.01	26.14	27.77	60.44	0.75	1.15	10.78	1.01		2,365	0	100	0	0	15	14.79	-21.7			Aug-97
	5.60	11.11	26.44	28.73	62.39	0.95	0.9	10.76	1		2,365	0	100	0	0	15	15.03	-21.74			Aug-11
	3.97	7.38	13.84	20.87	56.96	0.81	1.06	7.11	0.69		5,165	1	72	27	0	15	13.3	-14.53			Sep-09
	3.91	7.31	13.84	20.86	56.91	0.81	1.06	7.13	0.7		5,165	1	72	27	0	15	13.2	-14.61			Apr-09
	3.80	9.24	26.32	19.03	34.24	0.23	1.08	12.1	0.98		1,755	0	100	0	0	14	12.58	-26.32			Mar-02
	3.80	9.33	26.41	19.12	34.32	0.23	1.08	12.12	0.98		1,755	0	100	0	0	14	12.57	-26.41			May-99
	3.93	9.45	26.78	20.02	36.05	0.43	0.83	12.11	0.98		1,755	0	100	0	0	14	12.71	-26.4			Aug-11
	3.60	8.51	24.30	19.08	37.33	1.03	0.87	11.92	0.97		2,290	-1	100	0	0	5	8.77	-24.13			Oct-09
	3.74	8.71	24.63	20.03	39.08	1.23	0.62	11.89	0.96		2,290	-1	100	0	0	5	8.94	-24.12			Aug-11
	3.05	7.91	23.59	18.14	33.99	0.39	1.02	12.37	1		1,031	-1	100	0	0	6	10.92	-25.08			Mar-02
	3.05	7.98	23.68	18.23	34.08	0.39	1.02	12.36	1		1,031	-1	100	0	0	6	10.87	-25.18			May-97
	3.13	8.05	23.90	19.05	35.71	0.59	0.77	12.38	1		1,031	-1	100	0	0	6	11.02	-25.17			Aug-11
	6.24	11.22	21.89	33.08	101.87	0.9	0.9	10.31	1.02		2,735	1	99	0	0	16	20.68	-18.74			Mar-02
	6.24	11.22	21.88	33.08	101.85	0.9	0.9	10.32	1.02		2,735	1	99	0	0	16	20.57	-18.87			Jan-99
	6.39	11.37	22.16	34.07	104.38	1.11	0.65	10.34	1.02		2,735	1	99	0	0	16	20.85	-18.86			Aug-11
	7.75	13.65	29.07	40.43	118.43	0.44	0.89	10.97	1.02		5,155	0	100	0	0	25	22.94	-16.94			Nov-98
	7.76	13.67	29.09	40.45	118.47	0.44	0.89	10.94	1.01		5,155	0	100	0	0	25	22.84	-17.28			May-97
	7.83	13.79	29.39	41.49	121.18	0.64	0.64	10.95	1.01		5,155	0	100	0	0	25	23	-17.24			Aug-11
	5.99	9.52	14.10	24.87	91.52	1.44	0.87	10.53	1.02		5,026	0	100	0	0	21	19.98	-19.71			May-01
	5.94	9.48	14.07	24.85	91.38	1.44	0.87	10.56	1.02		5,026	0	100	0	0	21	19.73	-19.76			Jan-98
	6.00	9.59	14.30	25.73	93.82	1.67	0.62	10.54	1.02		5,026	0	100	0	0	21	19.97	-19.82			Aug-11
	5.25	8.27	12.56	26.26	92.45	1.04	0.98	10.68	1.01		2,167	1	99	0	0	23	22.28	-23.74			Nov-98
	5.24	8.23	12.55	26.28	92.42	1.04	0.98	10.7	1.01		2,167	1	99	0	0	23	22.2	-23.94			May-97
	5.32	8.41	12.82	27.20	94.85	1.27	0.73	10.66	1.01		2,167	1	99	0	0	23	22.33	-23.94			Dec-11
	2.79	5.51	11.40	16.22	38.17	1.05	0.87	5.11	0.49		8,094	2	51	46	0	9	9.73	-10.25			Dec-11
	3.28	6.19	11.86	18.02	47.73	0.79	1.05	6.03	0.59		7,537	1	62	37	0	13	11.34	-12.31			Apr-09

	MARKET		FUND TYPE, CATEGORY & OBJECTIVE		RATINGS				MINIMUMS	
Fund Name	Ticker Symbol	Traded On	Fund Type	Category and (Prospectus Objective)	Overall Rating	Reward Rating	Risk Rating	Recent Up/ Downgrade	Open to New Investors	Min Initial Investment
AXA Moderate-Plus Allocation Portfolio Class K	US00247C5519		Open End	Aggressive Alloc (Asset Alloc)	B-	C+	B	Down	Y	0
AXA Premier VIP Aggressive Allocation Fund Class A	US00247C7184		Open End	Aggressive Alloc (Asset Alloc)	B-	B-	B-	Down	Y	0
AXA Premier VIP Aggressive Allocation Fund Class B	US00247C6921		Open End	Aggressive Alloc (Asset Alloc)	B-	B-	B-	Down	Y	0
AXA Premier VIP Conservative Allocation Fund Class A	US00247C7754		Open End	Cautious Alloc (Asset Alloc)	B	C	A	Up	Y	0
AXA Premier VIP Conservative Allocation Fund Class B	US00247C7671		Open End	Cautious Alloc (Asset Alloc)	B	C	A	Up	Y	0
AXA Premier VIP Conservative-Plus Allocation Fund Class A	US00247C7598		Open End	Cautious Alloc (Asset Alloc)	B-	C+	B	Up	Y	0
AXA Premier VIP Conservative-Plus Allocation Fund Class B	US00247C7424		Open End	Cautious Alloc (Asset Alloc)	B-	C+	B	Up	Y	0
AXA Premier VIP Moderate Allocation Fund Class A	US4049924974		Open End	Moderate Alloc (Asset Alloc)	B-	C+	B	Up	Y	0
AXA Premier VIP Moderate Allocation Fund Class B			Open End	Moderate Alloc (Asset Alloc)	B-	C+	B	Up	Y	0
AXA Premier VIP Moderate-Plus Allocation Fund Class A	US00247C7341		Open End	Aggressive Alloc (Asset Alloc)	B-	C+	B	Down	Y	0
AXA Premier VIP Moderate-Plus Allocation Fund Class B	US00247C7267		Open End	Aggressive Alloc (Asset Alloc)	B-	C+	B	Down	Y	0
AXA Target 2015 Allocation Fund Class B	US00247C6764		Open End	Target Date 2000-2020 (Asset Alloc)	B-	C+	B	Up	Y	0
AXA Target 2015 Allocation Portfolio Class K	US00247C4116		Open End	Target Date 2000-2020 (Asset Alloc)	B-	C+	B	Up	Y	0
AXA Target 2025 Allocation Fund Class B	US00247C6509		Open End	Target Date 2021-2045 (Asset Alloc)	B-	C+	B	Down	Y	0
AXA Target 2025 Allocation Portfolio Class K	US00247C3951		Open End	Target Date 2021-2045 (Asset Alloc)	B-	C+	B	Down	Y	0
AXA Target 2035 Allocation Fund Class B	US00247C6350		Open End	Target Date 2021-2045 (Asset Alloc)	B-	C+	B-	Down	Y	0
AXA Target 2035 Allocation Portfolio Class K	US00247C3878		Open End	Target Date 2021-2045 (Asset Alloc)	B-	B-	B	Down	Y	0
AXA Target 2045 Allocation Fund Class B	US00247C6194		Open End	Target Date 2021-2045 (Asset Alloc)	B-	B-	B-	Down	Y	0
AXA Target 2045 Allocation Portfolio Class K	US00247C3795		Open End	Target Date 2021-2045 (Asset Alloc)	B-	B-	B-	Down	Y	0
AXA Target 2055 Allocation Portfolio Class B	US00248T4397		Open End	Target Date 2046+ (Asset Alloc)	C+	C+	B-	Up	Y	0
AXA Target 2055 Allocation Portfolio Class K	US00248T4215		Open End	Target Date 2046+ (Asset Alloc)	C+	C+	B-	Up	Y	0
AXA/AB Dynamic Growth Portfolio Class IB	US29439V6719		Open End	Moderate Alloc (Growth)	B-	C	B	Up	Y	0
AXA/AB Dynamic Moderate Growth Portfolio Class IB	US26884M6518		Open End	Moderate Alloc (Growth)	B-	C+	B	Up	Y	0
AXA/AB Small Cap Growth Portfolio Class IA	US4049927035		Open End	US Equity Small Cap (Small Company)	B+	A-	B	Up	Y	0
AXA/AB Small Cap Growth Portfolio Class IB	US4049927118		Open End	US Equity Small Cap (Small Company)	B+	A-	B	Up	Y	0
AXA/AB Small Cap Growth Portfolio Class K	US26883L7617		Open End	US Equity Small Cap (Small Company)	B+	A-	B	Up	Y	0
AXA/ClearBridge Large Cap Growth Portfolio Class IA	US2689405338		Open End	US Equity Large Cap Growth (Growth)	B-	B-	B-	Down	Y	0
AXA/ClearBridge Large Cap Growth Portfolio Class IB	US2689405254		Open End	US Equity Large Cap Growth (Growth)	B	B-	B	Up	Y	0
AXA/ClearBridge Large Cap Growth Portfolio Class K	US26883L3657		Open End	US Equity Large Cap Growth (Growth)	B	B-	B	Up	Y	0
AXA/Franklin Balanced Managed Volatility Portfolio Cls IA	US2689548152		Open End	Moderate Alloc (Growth & Income)	B-	C+	B	Up	Y	0
AXA/Franklin Balanced Managed Volatility Portfolio Cls IB	US2689547998		Open End	Moderate Alloc (Growth & Income)	B-	C+	B	Up	Y	0
AXA/Franklin Balanced Managed Volatility Portfolio Class K	US26883L6544		Open End	Moderate Alloc (Growth & Income)	B-	C+	B	Up	Y	0
AXA/Franklin Small Cap Value Managed Vol Port Cls IA	US2689547816		Open End	US Equity Small Cap (Small Company)	B	B	B	Up	Y	0
AXA/Franklin Small Cap Value Managed Vol Port Cls IB	US2689547733		Open End	US Equity Small Cap (Small Company)	B	B	B	Up	Y	0
AXA/Franklin Small Cap Value Managed Vol Port Cls K	US26883L7534		Open End	US Equity Small Cap (Small Company)	B	B+	B	Up	Y	0
AXA/Franklin Templeton Alloc Managed Vol Port Cls IA	US2689545919		Open End	Aggressive Alloc (Growth & Income)	B-	C+	B-	Down	Y	0
AXA/Franklin Templeton Alloc Managed Vol Port Cls IB	US2689545836		Open End	Aggressive Alloc (Growth & Income)	B-	C+	B-	Down	Y	0
AXA/Goldman Sachs Strategic Allocation Portfolio Class IB	US29439V6149		Open End	Moderate Alloc (Asset Alloc)	B-	C	B	Up	Y	0
AXA/Invesco Strategic Allocation Portfolio Class IB	US29439V5729		Open End	Cautious Alloc (Asset Alloc)	C+	C	B	Up	Y	0
AXA/Janus Enterprise Portfolio Class IA	US2689401378		Open End	US Equity Mid Cap (Growth)	C+	C+	C+	Up	Y	0
AXA/Janus Enterprise Portfolio Class IB	US2689401295		Open End	US Equity Mid Cap (Growth)	C+	C+	C+	Up	Y	0
AXA/Janus Enterprise Portfolio Class K	US26883L4564		Open End	US Equity Mid Cap (Growth)	C+	C+	C+	Up	Y	0
AXA/Legg Mason Strategic Allocation Portfolio Class IB	US29439V5562		Open End	Moderate Alloc (Asset Alloc)	C-	C-	A-	Up	Y	0
AXA/Legg Mason Strategic Allocation Portfolio Class K	US29439V5497		Open End	Moderate Alloc (Asset Alloc)	C-	C-	A-	Up	Y	0
AXA/Loomis Sayles Growth Portfolio Class IA	US2689402368		Open End	US Equity Large Cap Growth (Growth)	A-	A-	A	Up	Y	0
AXA/Loomis Sayles Growth Portfolio Class IB	US29364E6032		Open End	US Equity Large Cap Growth (Growth)	A-	A-	A	Up	Y	0
AXA/Loomis Sayles Growth Portfolio Class K	US26883L4648		Open End	US Equity Large Cap Growth (Growth)	A-	A-	A	Up	Y	0
AXA/Morgan Stanley Small Cap Growth Portfolio Class IB	US29439V7394		Open End	US Equity Small Cap (Small Company)	B	B	B-	Up	Y	0
AXA/Morgan Stanley Small Cap Growth Portfolio Class K	US29439V7212		Open End	US Equity Small Cap (Small Company)	B	B+	B-	Up	Y	0
AXA/Mutual Large Cap Eq Managed Vol Port Cls IA	US2689547659		Open End	US Equity Large Cap Blend (Growth)	B-	B-	B-	Down	Y	0
AXA/Mutual Large Cap Eq Managed Vol Port Cls IB	US2689547576		Open End	US Equity Large Cap Blend (Growth)	B-	B-	B-	Down	Y	0
AXA/Mutual Large Cap Eq Managed Vol Port Cls K	US26883L4499		Open End	US Equity Large Cap Blend (Growth)	B-	B-	B-	Down	Y	0

★Expanded analysis of this fund is included in Section II.

	TOTAL RETURNS					PERFORMANCE				ASSETS		ASSET ALLOCATION & TURNOVER					BULL & BEAR		FEES		
Min Additional Investment	3-Month Total Return	6-Month Total Return	1-Year Total Return	3-Year Total Return	5-Year Total Return	Dividend Yield (TTM)	Expense Ratio	3-Yr Std Deviation	3-Year Beta	NAV	Total Assets (MIL)	%Cash	%Stocks	%Bonds	%Other	Turnover Ratio	Last Bull Market Total Return	Last Bear Market Total Return	Front End Fee (%)	Back End Fee (%)	Inception Date
	4.01	7.67	15.29	21.68	55.20	1	0.89	7.31	0.7		9,736	2	71	27	0	8	13.26	-15.11			Dec-11
	5.14	9.79	19.13	26.01	71.46	0.78	1.19	9.5	0.92		3,568	1	92	8	0	5	16.75	-19.63			Jul-03
	5.23	9.78	19.23	26.11	71.59	0.78	1.19	9.47	0.92		3,568	1	92	8	0	5	16.73	-19.74			Jul-03
	0.99	2.07	5.02	7.60	15.78	0.93	1	2.18	0.17		1,219	4	21	75	0	12	4.81	-2.49			Jul-03
	0.99	2.18	5.02	7.61	15.78	0.93	1	2.09	0.16		1,219	4	21	75	0	12	4.76	-2.49			Jul-03
	2.13	4.21	8.89	12.72	29.59	0.87	1.1	4.06	0.38		1,391	3	41	56	0	11	8.14	-7.65			Jul-03
	2.13	4.21	8.89	12.83	29.72	0.86	1.1	4.01	0.38		1,391	3	41	56	0	11	8.1	-7.66			Jul-03
	2.68	5.26	11.06	15.29	36.39	0.82	1.12	5.11	0.49		8,094	2	51	46	0	9	9.65	-10.25			Jan-86
	2.71	5.30	11.07	15.32	36.34	0.82	1.12	5.1	0.49		8,094	2	51	46	0	9	9.52	-10.39			Jul-98
	3.85	7.52	14.92	20.70	53.18	0.78	1.14	7.32	0.7		9,736	2	71	27	0	8	13.15	-15.11			Jul-03
	3.94	7.51	15.02	20.80	53.30	0.78	1.14	7.25	0.7		9,736	2	71	27	0	8	13.1	-15.12			Jul-03
	2.57	5.23	11.32	14.66	36.84	1.33	1.1	5.51	1.1		60.5	2	47	50	0	17	12.06	-12.43			Aug-06
	2.71	5.49	11.71	15.51	38.55	1.56	0.85	5.54	1.1		60.5	2	47	50	0	17	12.19	-12.43			Dec-11
	3.75	7.42	15.38	20.42	52.49	1.24	1.1	7.43	1.14		169.8	2	68	30	0	16	15.22	-15.58			Aug-06
	3.90	7.67	15.77	21.43	54.40	1.46	0.85	7.41	1.14		169.8	2	68	30	0	16	15.36	-15.58			Dec-11
	4.61	8.77	17.84	23.57	61.77	1.17	1.1	8.46	1.09		128.7	1	80	18	0	10	17.41	-17.66			Aug-06
	4.67	8.93	18.11	24.48	63.78	1.39	0.85	8.38	1.08		128.7	1	80	18	0	10	17.54	-17.66			Dec-11
	5.21	9.89	19.77	25.90	69.89	1.13	1.1	9.46	1.1		97.5	0	90	9	0	6	19.28	-19.65			Aug-06
	5.18	9.95	20.06	26.84	71.87	1.34	0.85	9.4	1.1		97.5	0	90	9	0	6	19.43	-19.65			Dec-11
	5.72	10.85	21.84			0.98	1.1				15.8	1	99	0	0	33					Apr-15
	5.86	11.09	22.23			1.19	0.85				15.8	1	99	0	0	33					Apr-15
	3.99	7.33	14.89			0.19	1.2				514.8	18	66	16	1	79					Apr-15
	3.35	6.35	12.98	15.59	43.45	0.27	1.13	5.94	0.56		2,779	13	59	28	0	34	10.55	-9.63			Feb-11
	6.84	13.03	23.11	33.51	97.13	0.28	0.95	13.52	0.9		2,071	0	100	0	0	37	29.97	-24.12			May-97
	6.81	13.04	23.09	33.49	97.19	0.28	0.95	13.55	0.9		2,071	0	100	0	0	37	29.83	-24.21			May-97
	6.87	13.11	23.31	34.47	99.53	0.49	0.7	13.59	0.9		2,071	0	100	0	0	37	30.04	-24.12			Aug-11
	7.70	13.38	25.51	27.20	90.34	0	1.04	11.3	1		365.0	1	99	0	0	78	32.07	-22.91			Oct-02
	7.57	13.23	25.49	27.10	90.15	0	1.04	11.34	1		365.0	1	99	0	0	78	32.05	-23.01			Jan-99
	7.66	13.46	25.79	28.15	92.77	0	0.79	11.36	1		365.0	1	99	0	0	78	32.05	-23.01			Aug-12
	2.40	5.46	9.95	16.98	44.80	2.28	1.05	5.9	0.54		1,284	11	48	38	0	24	11.3	-10.48			Sep-06
	2.40	5.46	9.95	16.98	44.64	2.28	1.05	5.84	0.54		1,284	11	48	38	0	24	11.29	-10.6			Sep-06
	2.55	5.62	10.32	17.86	46.65	2.51	0.8	5.93	0.55		1,284	11	48	38	0	24	11.43	-10.48			Aug-11
	5.02	10.18	12.09	29.67	87.36	0.29	1.1	13.3	0.91		306.9	2	98	0	0	23	24.27	-26.72			Sep-06
	5.07	10.17	12.07	29.63	87.19	0.29	1.1	13.31	0.91		306.9	2	98	0	0	23	24.36	-26.8			Sep-06
	5.15	10.32	12.35	30.64	89.70	0.52	0.85	13.31	0.91		306.9	2	98	0	0	23	24.4	-26.72			Aug-11
	3.95	7.36	14.95	21.21	61.32	1.42	1.25	8.63	0.83		1,275	5	81	13	0	4	15.06	-16.9			Apr-07
	3.95	7.36	14.95	21.21	61.32	1.42	1.25	8.63	0.83		1,275	5	81	13	0	4	14.94	-17.02			Apr-07
	2.85	5.23	10.70			0.23	1.25				443.1	-3	61	42	0	54					Apr-15
	2.24	4.50	9.96			0.04	1.25				225.4	0	50	50	0	378					Apr-15
	6.10	12.30	28.02	14.66	62.38	0	1.08	13.65	1.07		935.1	3	97	0	0	34	17.71	-21.43			Apr-05
	6.07	12.29	28.00	14.62	62.26	0	1.08	13.66	1.07		935.1	3	97	0	0	34	17.75	-21.58			Apr-05
	6.13	12.44	28.28	15.48	64.39	0	0.83	13.66	1.07		935.1	3	97	0	0	34	17.85	-21.43			Dec-11
	2.25	4.62	10.94			0.6	1.25				116.0	6	52	42	0	400					Feb-16
	2.75	3.66	10.69			0.8	1				121.6	6	51	42	0	400					Feb-16
	6.79	13.67	34.67	59.10	124.72	0.24	1.05	12.26	1.06		690.7	1	99	0	0	11	21.14	-11.82			Dec-04
	6.88	13.73	34.61	59.15	124.82	0.24	1.05	12.21	1.05		690.7	1	99	0	0	11	20.98	-11.81			Dec-98
	6.77	13.77	34.97	59.96	125.96	0.43	0.8	12.27	1.06		690.7	1	99	0	0	11	20.98	-11.8			Feb-15
	7.70	11.54	24.88	26.82		0	1.15	14.91	0.97		290.7	1	99	0	0	41					Apr-14
	7.84	11.75	25.17	27.89		0	0.9	14.96	0.97		290.7	1	99	0	0	41					Apr-14
	4.71	7.38	14.29	24.96	82.67	1.86	1.05	9.67	0.94		631.1	2	95	2	1	13	18.03	-18.14			Sep-06
	4.65	7.32	14.24	24.82	82.52	1.86	1.05	9.64	0.94		631.1	2	95	2	1	13	17.91	-18.18			Sep-06
	4.75	7.56	14.56	25.80	84.97	2.09	0.8	9.66	0.94		631.1	2	95	2	1	13	18.16	-18.14			Aug-11

	MARKET		FUND TYPE, CATEGORY & OBJECTIVE		RATINGS				MINIMUMS	
Fund Name	Ticker Symbol	Traded On	Fund Type	Category and (Prospectus Objective)	Overall Rating	Reward Rating	Risk Rating	Recent Up/ Downgrade	Open to New Investors	Min Initial Investment
AXA/Templeton Global Eq Managed Vol Port Cls IA	US2689546743		Open End	Global Equity (Growth)	C+	C+	C+	Up	Y	0
AXA/Templeton Global Eq Managed Vol Port Cls IB	US2689546669		Open End	Global Equity (Growth)	C+	C+	C+	Up	Y	0
AXA/Templeton Global Eq Managed Vol Port Cls K	US26883L3996		Open End	Global Equity (Growth)	C+	B-	C+	Up	Y	0
Azzad Ethical Fund	ADJEX	NAS CM	Open End	US Equity Mid Cap (Growth)	B-	C+	B	Up	Y	1,000
B. Riley Diversified Equity Fund Class A Shares	BRDAX	NAS CM	Open End	US Equity Small Cap (Growth)	B+	A-	B	Up	Y	0
B. Riley Diversified Equity Fund Institutional Cls Shares	BRDZX	NAS CM	Open End	US Equity Small Cap (Growth)	B+	A	B	Up	Y	0
Baillie Gifford The EAFE Choice Fund Class 2	BGCWX	NAS CM	Open End	Global Equity Large Cap (Foreign Stock)	B	B	B	Up	Y	25,000,000
Baillie Gifford The EAFE Choice Fund Class 3	BGCJX	NAS CM	Open End	Global Equity Large Cap (Foreign Stock)	B	B	B	Up	Y	100,000,000
Baillie Gifford The EAFE Choice Fund Class I	BGCSX	NAS CM	Open End	Global Equity Large Cap (Foreign Stock)	C+	C+	C	Up	Y	0
Baillie Gifford The EAFE Choice Fund Class K	BKGCX	NAS CM	Open End	Global Equity Large Cap (Foreign Stock)	C+	C+	C	Up	Y	25,000,000
Baillie Gifford The EAFE Fund Class 2	BGETX	NAS CM	Open End	Global Equity Large Cap (Foreign Stock)	B+	A	B-	Up	Y	25,000,000
Baillie Gifford The EAFE Fund Class 3	BGEUX	NAS CM	Open End	Global Equity Large Cap (Foreign Stock)	B+	A	B-	Up	Y	100,000,000
Baillie Gifford The EAFE Fund Class 4	BGEFX	NAS CM	Open End	Global Equity Large Cap (Foreign Stock)	B+	A	B-	Up	Y	200,000,000
Baillie Gifford The EAFE Fund Class 5	BGEVX	NAS CM	Open End	Global Equity Large Cap (Foreign Stock)	B+	A	B-	Up	Y	500,000,000
Baillie Gifford The EAFE Fund Class I	BGESX	NAS CM	Open End	Global Equity Large Cap (Foreign Stock)	C+	B	C	Up	Y	0
Baillie Gifford The EAFE Fund Class K	BGEKX	NAS CM	Open End	Global Equity Large Cap (Foreign Stock)	C+	B	C	Up	Y	25,000,000
Baillie Gifford The EAFE Pure Fund Class 2	BGPTX	NAS CM	Open End	Global Equity Large Cap (Foreign Stock)	B	B	B	Up	Y	25,000,000
Baillie Gifford The EAFE Pure Fund Class 3	US0568237848		Open End	Global Equity Large Cap (Foreign Stock)	B	B	B	Up	Y	100,000,000
Baillie Gifford The EAFE Pure Fund Class I	BSGPX	NAS CM	Open End	Global Equity Large Cap (Foreign Stock)	B	B	B	Up	Y	0
Baillie Gifford The EAFE Pure Fund Class K	BGPKX	NAS CM	Open End	Global Equity Large Cap (Foreign Stock)	B	B	B	Up	Y	25,000,000
Baillie Gifford The Emerging Markets Fund Class 2	BGEHX	NAS CM	Open End	Emerging Markets Equity (Div Emerging Mkts)	B	A	C	Up	Y	25,000,000
Baillie Gifford The Emerging Markets Fund Class 3	BGELX	NAS CM	Open End	Emerging Markets Equity (Div Emerging Mkts)	B	A	C	Up	Y	100,000,000
Baillie Gifford The Emerging Markets Fund Class 5	BGEDX	NAS CM	Open End	Emerging Markets Equity (Div Emerging Mkts)	B	A	C	Up	Y	500,000,000
Baillie Gifford The Emerging Markets Fund Class I	BGEGX	NAS CM	Open End	Emerging Markets Equity (Div Emerging Mkts)	D+	C-	D	Down	Y	0
Baillie Gifford The Emerging Markets Fund Class K	BGKEX	NAS CM	Open End	Emerging Markets Equity (Div Emerging Mkts)	D+	C-	D	Down	Y	25,000,000
Baillie Gifford The Global Alpha Equity Fund Class 2	BGATX	NAS CM	Open End	Global Equity (World Stock)	B+	A-	B-	Up	Y	25,000,000
Baillie Gifford The Global Alpha Equity Fund Class 3	BGAEX	NAS CM	Open End	Global Equity (World Stock)	B+	A	B-	Up	Y	100,000,000
Baillie Gifford The Global Alpha Equity Fund Class I	BGASX	NAS CM	Open End	Global Equity (World Stock)	B	B	C	Up	Y	0
Baillie Gifford The Global Alpha Equity Fund Class K	BGAKX	NAS CM	Open End	Global Equity (World Stock)	B	B	C	Up	Y	25,000,000
Baillie Gifford The International Equity Fund Class 2	BGITX	NAS CM	Open End	Global Equity Large Cap (Foreign Stock)	B	B+	B	Up	Y	25,000,000
Baillie Gifford The International Equity Fund Class 3	BGIFX	NAS CM	Open End	Global Equity Large Cap (Foreign Stock)	B	B+	B	Up	Y	100,000,000
Baillie Gifford The International Equity Fund Class 5	BGIVX	NAS CM	Open End	Global Equity Large Cap (Foreign Stock)	B	B+	B	Up	Y	500,000,000
Baillie Gifford The International Equity Fund Class I	BINSX	NAS CM	Open End	Global Equity Large Cap (Foreign Stock)	C+	B-	C	Up	Y	0
Baillie Gifford The International Equity Fund Class K	BGIKX	NAS CM	Open End	Global Equity Large Cap (Foreign Stock)	C+	B-	C	Up	Y	25,000,000
Baillie Gifford The Long Term Global Growth Eq Fund Cls 2	BGLTX	NAS CM	Open End	Global Equity (Growth)	A-	A+	B	Up	Y	25,000,000
Baillie Gifford The Long Term Global Growth Eq Fund Cls 4	BGLFX	NAS CM	Open End	Global Equity (Growth)	A-	A+	B	Up	Y	200,000,000
Baillie Gifford The Long Term Global Growth Eq Fund Cls I	BSGLX	NAS CM	Open End	Global Equity (Growth)	A-	A+	B	Up	Y	0
Baillie Gifford The Long Term Global Growth Eq Fund Cls K	BGLKX	NAS CM	Open End	Global Equity (Growth)	A-	A+	B	Up	Y	25,000,000
Baillie Gifford The U.S. Equity Growth Fund Class I	BGGSX	NAS CM	Open End	US Equity Large Cap Growth (Growth)	D-	D+	B+		Y	0
Baillie Gifford The U.S. Equity Growth Fund Class K	BGGKX	NAS CM	Open End	US Equity Large Cap Growth (Growth)	D-	D+	B+		Y	25,000,000
Baird LargeCap Fund Institutional Class	BHGIX	NAS CM	Open End	US Equity Large Cap Blend (Growth & Income)	B	B	B-		Y	25,000
Baird LargeCap Fund Investor Class	BHGSX	NAS CM	Open End	US Equity Large Cap Blend (Growth & Income)	B	B	B-	Up	Y	2,500
Baird MidCap Fund Institutional Class	BMDIX	NAS CM	Open End	US Equity Mid Cap (Growth)	B-	B	C+	Down	Y	25,000
Baird MidCap Fund Investor Class	BMDSX	NAS CM	Open End	US Equity Mid Cap (Growth)	B-	B-	C+	Down	Y	2,500
Baird Small/Mid Cap Value Fund Institutional Class	BMVIX	NAS CM	Open End	US Equity Small Cap (Growth)	C	C	B+	Up	Y	25,000
Baird Small/Mid Cap Value Fund Investor Class	BMVSX	NAS CM	Open End	US Equity Small Cap (Growth)	C	C	B+	Up	Y	2,500
Baird SmallCap Value Fund Institutional Class	BSVIX	NAS CM	Open End	US Equity Small Cap (Small Company)	B	B	B	Up	Y	25,000
Baird SmallCap Value Fund Investor Class	BSVSX	NAS CM	Open End	US Equity Small Cap (Small Company)	B	B	B	Up	Y	2,500
Balter Discretionary Global Macro Fund Institutional Class	BGMIX	NAS CM	Open End	Multialternative (Growth & Income)	D+	D	C-		Y	50,000
Balter Discretionary Global Macro Fund Investor Class	BGMVX	NAS CM	Open End	Multialternative (Growth & Income)	D+	D	C-		Y	5,000
Balter European L/S Small Cap Fund Institutional Class	BESMX	NAS CM	Open End	Long/Short Equity (Small Company)	B-	B	C+	Up	Y	50,000
Balter European L/S Small Cap Fund Investor Class	BESRX	NAS CM	Open End	Long/Short Equity (Small Company)	B-	B	C+	Up	Y	5,000

★ Expanded analysis of this fund is included in Section II.

Min Additional Investment	3-Month Total Return	6-Month Total Return	1-Year Total Return	3-Year Total Return	5-Year Total Return	Dividend Yield (TTM)	Expense Ratio	3-Yr Std Deviation	3-Year Beta	NAV	Total Assets (MIL)	%Cash	%Stocks	%Bonds	%Other	Turnover Ratio	Last Bull Market Total Return	Last Bear Market Total Return	Front End Fee (%)	Back End Fee (%)	Inception Date
	TOTAL RETURNS					PERFORMANCE				ASSETS		ASSET ALLOCATION & TURNOVER					BULL & BEAR		FEES		
	4.87	9.48	21.36	23.04	61.79	0.56	1.13	10.99	1.04		842.7	0	100	0	0	13	15.9	-21.5			Sep-06
	4.87	9.48	21.36	23.04	61.62	0.56	1.13	11	1.04		842.7	0	100	0	0	13	15.76	-21.53			Sep-06
	4.96	9.65	21.75	23.95	63.82	0.77	0.88	11.02	1.04		842.7	0	100	0	0	13	16.04	-21.5			Aug-11
50	6.12	10.25	23.21	18.08	76.26	0.07	0.99	11.31	0.99	13.32	75.3	3	97	0	0	108	25.95	-17.01			Dec-00
	2.33	7.76	21.07	37.49		0.36	1.5	15.41	0.91	14.02	22.4	0	100	0	0	202			5.75		Sep-14
	2.46	7.86	21.40	38.60		0.53	1.25	15.45	0.92	14.12	22.4	0	100	0	0	202					Feb-14
	4.55	9.74	31.28	34.15	58.27	0.98	0.65	12.75	0.97	16.1131	332.3	1	97	0	0	23	16.66	-16.58	0.21		Dec-09
	4.57	9.78	31.37	34.47	60.51	1.02	0.58	12.75	0.97	16.2626	332.3	1	97	0	0	23	16.66	-21.89	0.21		Jul-14
	4.94	10.14	31.70	16.01	36.87		0.8	12.75	0.97	16.0881	332.3	1	97	0	0	23	16.66	-21.89			Apr-17
	4.55	9.73	31.20	15.57	36.36		0.65	12.75	0.97	16.1029	332.3	1	97	0	0	23	16.66	-21.89			Apr-17
	2.90	16.50	46.09	42.56	74.24	0.45	0.61	15.95	1.19	14.3922	2,822	1	99	0	0	18	19.89	-24.92	0.21		Mar-08
	2.91	16.53	46.19	42.78	74.88	0.47	0.54	15.94	1.19	14.4206	2,822	1	99	0	0	18	19.93	-20.03	0.21		Apr-10
	2.92	16.55	46.23	42.75	74.48	0.55	0.51	15.95	1.19	14.4301	2,822	1	99	0	0	18	19.89	-24.92	0.21		Oct-13
	2.94	16.58	46.31	43.22	75.62	0.55	0.46	15.94	1.19	14.4582	2,822	1	99	0	0	18	19.89	-24.92	0.21		Jul-12
	2.88	16.51	45.98	15.87	41.63		0.76	15.95	1.19	14.3818	2,822	1	99	0	0	18	19.89	-24.92			Apr-17
	2.88	16.51	45.98	15.87	41.63		0.61	15.95	1.19	14.3818	2,822	1	99	0	0	18	19.89	-24.92			Apr-17
	3.76	8.60	28.58	33.45		1.12	0.66	12.48	0.96	12.0562	315.8	1	97	0	0	13			0.21		Apr-14
	3.78	8.64	28.65	33.52			0.59	12.48	0.96	12.1734	315.8	1	97	0	0	13			0.21		Mar-17
	3.82	8.71	28.59	29.57			0.81	12.48	0.96	12.0555	315.8	1	97	0	0	13					Apr-17
	3.82	8.71	28.59	29.57			0.66	12.48	0.96	12.0555	315.8	1	97	0	0	13					Apr-17
	7.51	20.43	53.02	46.05	54.52	0.61	0.87	16.7	0.96	22.8204	2,015	1	94	0	0	24	25.4	-27.56	0.20		Apr-15
	8.92	22.04	55.10	43.02	51.31	0.62	0.8	16.88	0.96	23.0019	2,015	1	94	0	0	24	25.4	-27.56	0.20		Apr-03
	7.55	20.52	53.25	46.53	55.02	0.65	0.71	16.7	0.96	23.5479	2,015	1	94	0	0	24	25.4	-27.56	0.20		Apr-15
	7.52	20.47	52.98	-58.03	-55.60		1.02	16.89	0.96	22.8021	2,015	1	94	0	0	24	25.4	-27.56			Apr-17
	7.50	20.43	52.92	-58.04	-55.61		0.87	16.88	0.96	22.7909	2,015	1	94	0	0	24	25.4	-27.56			Apr-17
	5.59	13.22	34.56	42.62	108.54	0.4	0.67	12.46	1.08	18.8538	786.7	2	96	0	0	20			0.15		Jan-13
	5.61	13.26	34.65	43.02	96.23	0.49	0.6	12.44	1.08	19.2158	786.7	2	96	0	0	20			0.15		Nov-11
	5.62	13.24	34.54	24.98	69.00		0.82	12.44	1.08	18.8367	786.7	2	96	0	0	20					Apr-17
	5.56	13.18	34.47	24.91	70.99		0.67	12.44	1.08	18.8247	786.7	2	96	0	0	20					Apr-17
	5.56	12.37	34.95	38.80	58.12	0.97	0.61	12.82	1	14.1969	2,100	1	99	0	0	12	19.51	-22.73	0.21		Feb-08
	5.58	12.41	35.05	39.12	58.74	1.04	0.54	12.81	1	14.373	2,100	1	99	0	0	12	19.56	-18.59	0.21		Sep-10
	5.60	12.46	35.16	39.45	62.32	1.06	0.46	12.81	1	14.8228	2,100	1	99	0	0	12	19.51	-22.73	0.21		Apr-14
	2.94	9.58	31.55	13.74	29.57		0.76	12.81	1	14.1903	2,100	1	99	0	0	12	19.51	-22.73			Apr-17
	2.89	9.52	31.48	13.69	29.51		0.61	12.81	1	14.1727	2,100	1	99	0	0	12	19.51	-22.73			Apr-17
	6.10	17.26	54.06	67.90		0	0.77	16.82	1.3	17.3341	198.3	2	98	0	0	15			0.10		Jun-14
	6.13	17.32	54.21	69.26		0	0.67	16.86	1.3	19.9887	198.3	2	98	0	0	15			0.10		Oct-15
	6.11	17.24	53.99	65.30			0.92	16.82	1.3	17.3399	198.3	2	98	0	0	15					Apr-17
	6.10	17.24	53.99	65.30			0.77	16.82	1.3	17.3405	198.3	2	98	0	0	15					Apr-17
	4.91	10.02	34.08				0.72			13.3888	1.3	0	100	0	0	3					Apr-17
	4.91	10.02	34.20				0.57			13.3862	1.3	0	100	0	0	3					Apr-17
	9.41	15.60	25.53	34.84	112.78	1.18	0.75	11.64	1.11		42.9	5	95	0	0	85	30.33	-18.42			Sep-00
100	9.32	15.40	25.08	33.69	110.11	0.65	1	11.72	1.12		42.9	5	95	0	0	85	30.19	-18.59			Sep-00
	5.51	9.31	26.88	28.28	82.69	0	0.83	10.74	0.92	19.16	1,397	3	97	0	0	57	32.5	-16.83			Dec-00
100	5.50	9.18	26.60	27.30	80.49	0	1.08	10.74	0.92	18.23	1,397	3	97	0	0	57	32.13	-16.86			Dec-00
	6.20	14.67	21.47			0.63	0.95			12.43	15.1	3	97	0	0	38					Nov-15
100	6.11	14.40	21.07			0.51	1.2			12.4	15.1	3	97	0	0	38					Nov-15
	5.58	14.26	18.04	28.10	84.33	0.97	1	11.16	0.62	16.99	35.1	3	97	0	0	49					May-12
100	5.52	14.16	17.78	27.16	82.10	0.62	1.25	11.14	0.62	16.97	35.1	3	97	0	0	49					May-12
500	-1.17	-3.00	-4.27			0	2.01			9.43	97.9	100	0	0	0						May-15
500	-1.28	-3.11	-4.59			0	2.31			9.38	97.9	100	0	0	0						May-15
500	5.46	7.86	25.02	24.61	62.29	0	2.32			11.27	71.6	25	75	0	0		12.13	-13.59			Dec-15
500	5.47	7.77	24.92	24.17	60.91	0	2.62			11.27	71.6	25	75	0	0		11.97	-13.68			Dec-15

Fund Name	MARKET Ticker Symbol	MARKET Traded On	FUND TYPE, CATEGORY & OBJECTIVE Fund Type	Category and (Prospectus Objective)	RATINGS Overall Rating	RATINGS Reward Rating	RATINGS Risk Rating	Recent Up/ Downgrade	Open to New Investors	MINIMUMS Min Initial Investment
Balter Invenomic Fund Institutional Class shares	BIVIX	NAS CM	Open End	Long/Short Equity (Growth)	U	U	U		Y	50,000
Balter Invenomic Fund Investor Class shares	BIVRX	NAS CM	Open End	Long/Short Equity (Growth)	U	U	U		Y	5,000
Balter L/S Small Cap Equity Fund Institutional Class	BEQIX	NAS CM	Open End	Long/Short Equity (Growth & Income)	B-	C+	B	Down	Y	50,000
Balter L/S Small Cap Equity Fund Investor Class	BEQRX	NAS CM	Open End	Long/Short Equity (Growth & Income)	B-	C+	B		Y	5,000
Bancroft Fund	BCV	AMEX	Closed End	Convertibles (Convertible Bond)	B	C+	B+	Up	Y	
Baron Asset Fund Class R6	BARUX	NAS CM	Open End	US Equity Mid Cap (Growth)	B	B	B-		Y	5,000,000
Baron Asset Fund Institutional Class	BARIX	NAS CM	Open End	US Equity Mid Cap (Growth)	B	B	B+	Down	Y	1,000,000
Baron Asset Fund Retail Class	BARAX	NAS CM	Open End	US Equity Mid Cap (Growth)	B	B	B		Y	2,000
Baron Discovery Fund Institutional Shares	BDFIX	NAS CM	Open End	US Equity Small Cap (Growth)	B	A	C	Up	Y	1,000,000
Baron Discovery Fund R6 Shares	BDFUX	NAS CM	Open End	US Equity Small Cap (Growth)	B	A	C	Up	Y	5,000,000
Baron Discovery Fund Retail Shares	BDFFX	NAS CM	Open End	US Equity Small Cap (Growth)	B	A	C	Up	Y	2,000
Baron Emerging Markets Fund Class R6	BEXUX	NAS CM	Open End	Emerging Markets Equity (Div Emerging Mkts)	B-	B	C	Up	Y	5,000,000
Baron Emerging Markets Fund Institutional Shares	BEXIX	NAS CM	Open End	Emerging Markets Equity (Div Emerging Mkts)	B-	B	C	Up	Y	1,000,000
Baron Emerging Markets Fund Retail Shares	BEXFX	NAS CM	Open End	Emerging Markets Equity (Div Emerging Mkts)	B-	B	C	Up	Y	2,000
Baron Energy and Resources Fund Institutional Shares	BENIX	NAS CM	Open End	Energy Sector Equity (Natl Res)	D	D	D	Down	Y	1,000,000
Baron Energy and Resources Fund R6 Shares	BENUX	NAS CM	Open End	Energy Sector Equity (Natl Res)	D	D	D	Down	Y	5,000,000
Baron Energy and Resources Fund Retail Shares	BENFX	NAS CM	Open End	Energy Sector Equity (Natl Res)	D	D	D	Down	Y	2,000
Baron Fifth Avenue Growth Fund Class R6	BFTUX	NAS CM	Open End	US Equity Large Cap Growth (Growth)	A-	A	B	Up	Y	5,000,000
Baron Fifth Avenue Growth Fund Institutional Class	BFTIX	NAS CM	Open End	US Equity Large Cap Growth (Growth)	A-	A	B	Up	Y	1,000,000
Baron Fifth Avenue Growth Fund Retail Class	BFTHX	NAS CM	Open End	US Equity Large Cap Growth (Growth)	A-	A	B	Up	Y	2,000
Baron Focused Growth Fund Institutional Shares	BFGIX	NAS CM	Open End	US Equity Mid Cap (Growth)	B	B	B	Up	Y	1,000,000
Baron Focused Growth Fund R6 Shares	BFGUX	NAS CM	Open End	US Equity Mid Cap (Growth)	B	B	B	Up	Y	5,000,000
Baron Focused Growth Fund Retail Shares	BFGFX	NAS CM	Open End	US Equity Mid Cap (Growth)	B	B	B	Up	Y	2,000
Baron Global Advantage Fund Institutional Shares	BGAIX	NAS CM	Open End	Global Equity (World Stock)	B+	A	B-	Up	Y	1,000,000
Baron Global Advantage Fund R6 Shares	BGLUX	NAS CM	Open End	Global Equity (World Stock)	B+	A	B-	Up	Y	5,000,000
Baron Global Advantage Fund Retail Shares	BGAFX	NAS CM	Open End	Global Equity (World Stock)	B+	A	B-	Up	Y	2,000
Baron Growth Fund Class R6	BGRUX	NAS CM	Open End	US Equity Mid Cap (Growth)	B	B	B	Up	Y	5,000,000
Baron Growth Fund Institutional Shares	BGRIX	NAS CM	Open End	US Equity Mid Cap (Growth)	B	B	B	Up	Y	1,000,000
Baron Growth Fund Retail Shares	BGRFX	NAS CM	Open End	US Equity Mid Cap (Growth)	B	B	B	Up	Y	2,000
Baron International Growth Fund Institutional Shares	BINIX	NAS CM	Open End	Global Equity Large Cap (Foreign Stock)	B+	A-	B	Up	Y	1,000,000
Baron International Growth Fund R6 Shares	BIGUX	NAS CM	Open End	Global Equity Large Cap (Foreign Stock)	B+	A-	B	Up	Y	5,000,000
Baron International Growth Fund Retail Shares	BIGFX	NAS CM	Open End	Global Equity Large Cap (Foreign Stock)	B+	B+	B	Up	Y	2,000
Baron Opportunity Fund Institutional Class	BIOIX	NAS CM	Open End	US Equity Mid Cap (Growth)	B	B	B	Up	Y	1,000,000
Baron Opportunity Fund R6 Shares	BIOUX	NAS CM	Open End	US Equity Mid Cap (Growth)	B	B	B	Up	Y	5,000,000
Baron Opportunity Fund Retail Class	BIOPX	NAS CM	Open End	US Equity Mid Cap (Growth)	B	B	B	Up	Y	2,000
Baron Partners Fund Institutional Shares	BPTIX	NAS CM	Open End	US Equity Mid Cap (Growth)	B	B	B	Up	Y	1,000,000
Baron Partners Fund R6 Shares	BPTUX	NAS CM	Open End	US Equity Mid Cap (Growth)	B	B	B-	Up	Y	5,000,000
Baron Partners Fund Retail Shares	BPTRX	NAS CM	Open End	US Equity Mid Cap (Growth)	B	B	B-	Up	Y	2,000
Baron Real Estate Fund Class R6	BREUX	NAS CM	Open End	Real Estate Sector Equity (Real Estate)	B-	B-	C+		Y	5,000,000
Baron Real Estate Fund Institutional Shares	BREIX	NAS CM	Open End	Real Estate Sector Equity (Real Estate)	B-	B-	B		Y	1,000,000
Baron Real Estate Fund Retail Shares	BREFX	NAS CM	Open End	Real Estate Sector Equity (Real Estate)	C+	B-	C+	Down	Y	2,000
Baron Small Cap Fund Class R6	BSCUX	NAS CM	Open End	US Equity Small Cap (Small Company)	B	B+	C	Up	Y	5,000,000
Baron Small Cap Fund Institutional Class	BSFIX	NAS CM	Open End	US Equity Small Cap (Small Company)	B	B+	C	Up	Y	1,000,000
Baron Small Cap Fund Retail Class	BSCFX	NAS CM	Open End	US Equity Small Cap (Small Company)	B	B	C	Up	Y	2,000
Barrett Growth Fund	BGRWX	NAS CM	Open End	US Equity Large Cap Growth (Growth)	B-	B-	B	Down	Y	2,500
Barrett Opportunity Fund	SAOPX	NAS CM	Open End	US Equity Large Cap Value (Growth)	B	B	B-		Y	1,000
Barrow Long/Short Opportunity Fund Institutional Class	BFSLX	NAS CM	Open End	Long/Short Equity (Growth)	D+	D	C	Down	Y	2,500
Barrow Value Opportunity Fund Institutional Class	BALIX	NAS CM	Open End	US Equity Mid Cap (Growth)	B	C+	B+	Up	Y	2,500
Baywood ValuePlus Fund Institutional Shares	BVPIX	NAS CM	Open End	US Equity Large Cap Value (Growth)	B-	B-	B-	Down	Y	100,000
Baywood ValuePlus Fund Investor Shares	BVPNX	NAS CM	Open End	US Equity Large Cap Value (Growth)	B-	B-	B-	Down	Y	2,500
BBH Core Select Fund Class N	BBTEX	NAS CM	Open End	US Equity Large Cap Blend (Growth)	B-	B-	B	Down		10,000
BBH Core Select Retail Class Shares	BBTRX	NAS CM	Open End	US Equity Large Cap Blend (Growth)	B-	C+	B	Down		5,000

★ Expanded analysis of this fund is included in Section II.

Min Additional Investment	TOTAL RETURNS 3-Month Total Return	6-Month Total Return	1-Year Total Return	3-Year Total Return	5-Year Total Return	PERFORMANCE Dividend Yield (TTM)	Expense Ratio	3-Yr Std Deviation	3-Year Beta	ASSETS NAV	Total Assets (MIL)	ASSET ALLOCATION & TURNOVER %Cash	%Stocks	%Bonds	%Other	Turnover Ratio	BULL & BEAR Last Bull Market Total Return	Last Bear Market Total Return	FEES Front End Fee (%)	Back End Fee (%)	Inception Date
500	6.88	7.95					2.32			10.74	30.1	71	28	0	0						Jun-17
500	6.79	7.75					2.67			10.72	30.1	71	28	0	0						Jun-17
500	3.00	7.16	15.61	24.51		0	1.77	6.84	0.4	11.4	170.7	49	52	0	-1						Dec-13
500	2.96	7.05	15.35	23.60			2.12	6.84	0.4	11.4	170.7	49	52	0	-1						Nov-17
	1.73	5.10	13.12	21.77	58.18	2.35		7.41	0.64	24.12	126.9	0	0	62	5	33	13.01	-15.33			Oct-71
	3.10	6.59	26.47	33.59	107.92	0	1.04	11.25	0.96	70.46	3,153	1	99	0	0	10	25.22	-19.8			Jan-16
	3.10	6.59	26.49	34.00	109.69	0	1.04	11.23	0.96	70.47	3,153	1	99	0	0	10	25.42	-19.7			May-09
	3.04	6.45	26.12	32.91	106.86	0	1.31	11.23	0.96	68.16	3,153	1	99	0	0	10	25.22	-19.8			Jun-87
	3.36	8.95	35.83	41.32		0.21	1.1	16.08	0.93	18.3	253.7	3	97	0	0	41					Sep-13
	3.38	8.97	35.85	41.33		0.22	1.09	16.08	0.93	18.3	253.7	3	97	0	0	41					Aug-16
	3.34	8.79	35.52	40.29		0.04	1.35	16.07	0.92	18.14	253.7	3	97	0	0	41					Sep-13
	6.15	16.96	40.58	30.50	57.01	0.47	1.13	12.8	0.82	15.38	4,592	6	91	0	3	25	14.8	-18.44			Jan-16
	6.16	16.88	40.62	30.41	56.91	0.47	1.13	12.82	0.82	15.37	4,592	6	91	0	3	25	14.8	-18.44			Dec-10
	6.09	16.76	40.33	29.35	54.91	0.24	1.38	12.81	0.82	15.33	4,592	6	91	0	3	25	14.71	-18.56			Dec-10
	5.32	5.97	-8.67	-19.93	-10.07	0.11	1.1	23.63	1.12	8.31	53.5	2	97	0	1	54					Dec-11
	5.32	6.11	-8.57	-19.93	-10.07	0.11	1.09	23.66	1.12	8.31	53.5	2	97	0	1	54					Aug-16
	5.26	5.93	-8.89	-20.47	-11.06	0.12	1.35	23.65	1.12	8.19	53.5	2	97	0	1	54					Dec-11
	6.01	12.74	41.02	46.12	119.36	0	0.75	14.26	1.21	25.92	199.5	1	99	0	0	14	32.62	-16.69			Jan-16
	6.01	12.75	40.96	46.54	120.98	0	0.75	14.23	1.21	25.91	199.5	1	99	0	0	14	32.86	-16.65			May-09
	5.94	12.59	40.64	45.37	118.25	0	1	14.24	1.21	25.47	199.5	1	99	0	0	14	32.62	-16.69			Apr-04
	2.66	5.95	26.58	24.41	63.78	0.01	1.1	12.67	0.79	15.66	194.5	3	93	0	0	14	22.73	-20.78			May-09
	2.66	6.01	26.66	23.98	62.45	0.01	1.1	12.66	0.79	15.67	194.5	3	93	0	0	14	22.62	-20.87			Aug-16
	2.58	5.83	26.35	23.52	61.84	0	1.35	12.66	0.79	15.38	194.5	3	93	0	0	14	22.62	-20.87			Jun-08
	9.88	18.67	49.81	45.98	103.28	0	0.9	16.02	1.33	20.78	40.1	4	96	0	0	21					Apr-12
	9.88	18.66	49.89	46.05	103.38	0	0.9	16.04	1.33	20.79	40.1	4	96	0	0	21					Aug-16
	9.82	18.49	49.59	45.13	101.16	0	1.15	16.05	1.34	20.57	40.1	4	96	0	0	21					Apr-12
	5.36	8.75	27.34	28.56	89.69	0	1.05	10.89	0.64	69.56	6,306	2	98	0	0	3	23.16	-19.29			Jan-16
	5.35	8.75	27.35	28.92	91.22	0	1.05	10.88	0.64	69.55	6,306	2	98	0	0	3	23.33	-19.2			May-09
	5.30	8.63	27.03	27.94	88.78	0	1.3	10.88	0.64	67.67	6,306	2	98	0	0	3	23.16	-19.29			Dec-94
	7.32	16.46	37.33	40.78	70.57	0	0.95	11.19	0.88	24.19	157.9	4	93	0	2	39	19.66	-22.84			May-09
	7.32	16.46	37.33	40.19	68.92	0	0.95	11.22	0.88	24.19	157.9	4	93	0	2	39	19.49	-22.93			Aug-16
	7.28	16.35	36.94	39.74	68.38	0	1.2	11.2	0.88	23.9	157.9	4	93	0	2	39	19.49	-22.93			Dec-08
	6.17	9.80	40.87	35.66	89.04	0	1.13	14.53	1.19	17.6	251.0	0	100	0	0	33	22.23	-19.91			May-09
	6.17	9.79	40.94	35.12	87.20	0	1.12	14.59	1.2	17.61	251.0	0	100	0	0	33	22.06	-20.01			Aug-16
	6.08	9.63	40.50	34.57	86.44	0	1.41	14.57	1.2	17	251.0	0	100	0	0	33	22.06	-20.01			Feb-00
	1.13	2.55	31.90	33.36	123.88	0	1.09	15.76	1.22	49.73	2,057	-21	121	0	0	16	29.72	-24.97			May-09
	1.13	2.55	31.87	32.78	121.72	0	1.09	15.76	1.22	49.73	2,057	-21	121	0	0	16	29.51	-25.06			Aug-16
	1.07	2.43	31.54	32.32	120.96	0	1.35	15.75	1.22	48.75	2,057	-21	121	0	0	16	29.51	-25.06			Apr-03
	9.68	13.53	31.41	22.57	87.36	0	1.07	13.94	1.1	30.01	1,071	4	96	0	0	56	39.39	-23.08			Jan-16
	9.69	13.53	31.41	22.56	87.34	0	1.07	13.94	1.1	30.01	1,071	4	96	0	0	56	39.39	-23.08			Dec-09
	9.60	13.32	31.04	21.59	84.88	0	1.33	13.93	1.1	29.58	1,071	4	96	0	0	56	39.23	-23.08			Dec-09
	5.25	9.99	27.40	32.41	90.09	0	1.06	12.2	0.76	29.34	4,299	6	94	0	0	29	28.61	-22.61			Jan-16
	5.25	9.98	27.44	32.77	91.55	0	1.06	12.18	0.76	29.35	4,299	6	94	0	0	29	28.77	-22.54			May-09
	5.18	9.84	27.13	31.76	89.15	0	1.32	12.18	0.76	28.34	4,299	6	94	0	0	29	28.61	-22.61			Sep-97
50	6.16	11.30	21.01	29.30	95.21	0.09	1.26	9.7	0.93	19.08	24.1	4	96	0	0	39	23.15	-17.81			Dec-98
50	3.20	8.67	20.57	36.18	84.45	0.85	1.28	10.76	0.95	29.98	66.8	2	98	0	0	1	21.35	-24.59			Feb-79
100	4.23	2.78	1.27	2.58		0	1.77	5.21	0.17	10.33	14.1	54	46	0	0	122					Aug-13
100	6.52	8.94	16.09	24.68	84.07	0.45	1.16	10.29	0.86	27.67	41.7	2	98	0	0	88	24.77	-20.16			Aug-13
	7.35	12.83	16.13	28.91	87.30	1.93	0.7	10.11		18.03	2.6	7	93	0	0	48	21.81	-15.33			Dec-13
100	7.32	12.69	15.85	27.87	85.41	1.72	0.95	10.09		17.95	2.6	7	93	0	0	48	21.81	-15.33			Dec-13
10,000	6.10	8.41	19.93	25.01	74.65	0.52	1	8.99	0.85	20.86	2,811	7	93	0	0	12	20.95	-11.49			Nov-98
250	6.07	8.25	19.64	24.11	72.61	0.64	1.23	9	0.85	10.73	2,811	7	93	0	0	12	20.83	-11.59			Mar-11

	MARKET			FUND TYPE, CATEGORY & OBJECTIVE	RATINGS				MINIMUMS	
Fund Name	Ticker Symbol	Traded On	Fund Type	Category and (Prospectus Objective)	Overall Rating	Reward Rating	Risk Rating	Recent Up/ Downgrade	Open to New Investors	Min Initial Investment
BBH Global Core Select Fund Class N Shares	BBGNX	NAS CM	Open End	Global Equity (Growth)	B	B-	B+	Up	Y	10,000
BBH Global Core Select Fund Retail Class Shares	BBGRX	NAS CM	Open End	Global Equity (Growth)	B	C+	B+	Up	Y	5,000
BBH Partner Fund - International Equity Cls Institutional	BBHLX	NAS CM	Open End	Global Equity Large Cap (Growth & Income)	B-	C+	B	Up	Y	10,000
Beacon Accelerated Return Strategy Fund Institutional Cls	BARLX	NAS CM	Open End	Long/Short Equity (Growth)	U	U	U		Y	1,000,000
Beacon Planned Return Strategy Fund Institutional Class	BPRLX	NAS CM	Open End	Long/Short Equity (Growth)	U	U	U		Y	1,000,000
Beck, Mack & Oliver Partners Fund	BMPEX	NAS CM	Open End	US Equity Large Cap Blend (Growth)	C+	C+	C		Y	2,500
Becker Value Equity Fund Institutional Class	BVEIX	NAS CM	Open End	US Equity Large Cap Value (Growth)	B-	B-	B	Down	Y	250,000
Becker Value Equity Fund Retail Class	BVEFX	NAS CM	Open End	US Equity Large Cap Value (Growth)	B-	B-	B	Down	Y	2,500
Beech Hill Total Return Fund Class A	BHTAX	NAS CM	Open End	Moderate Alloc (Growth & Income)	C+	B-	C	Down	Y	500
Beech Hill Total Return Fund Class C	BHTCX	NAS CM	Open End	Moderate Alloc (Growth & Income)	C+	C+	C	Down	Y	500
Berkshire Focus Fund	BFOCX	NAS CM	Open End	Technology Sector Equity (Technology)	A-	A	B	Up	Y	5,000
Bernstein International Small Cap Portfolio Class SCB	IRCSX	NAS CM	Open End	Global Equity Mid/Small Cap (Small Company)	C-	C	B+	Up	Y	5,000
Bernstein Intl Strategic Equities Portfolio Cls SCB	STESX	NAS CM	Open End	Global Equity Large Cap (Growth)	C-	C	B+	Up	Y	10,000
Bernstein Small Cap Core Portfolio Class SCB	SCRSX	NAS CM	Open End	US Equity Small Cap (Small Company)	C-	C-	B+	Up	Y	5,000
Bernzott US Small Cap Value Fund	BSCVX	NAS CM	Open End	US Equity Small Cap (Small Company)	B	A-	C+	Up	Y	25,000
Berwyn Fund	BERWX	NAS CM	Open End	US Equity Small Cap (Growth)	C+	B-	C	Up	Y	1,000
Berwyn Income Fund	BERIX	NAS CM	Open End	Cautious Alloc (Income)	B-	C	B+	Up	Y	1,000
BFS Equity Fund	BFSAX	NAS CM	Open End	US Equity Large Cap Growth (Growth)	B	B-	B	Up	Y	1,000
Biondo Focus Fund Investor Class	BFONX	NAS CM	Open End	US Equity Large Cap Growth (Growth)	C+	B	C	Up	Y	1,000
Biondo Growth Fund Class Investor	BIONX	NAS CM	Open End	US Equity Large Cap Growth (Growth)	C+	C+	C	Down	Y	1,000
Bishop Street Dividend Value Fund Class I	BSLIX	NAS CM	Open End	US Equity Large Cap Value (Equity-Income)	B	B	B		Y	1,000,000
Black Oak Emerging Technology Fund	BOGSX	NAS CM	Open End	Technology Sector Equity (Technology)	B	A-	B-	Up	Y	2,000
BlackRock 20/80 Target Allocation Fund Class K	BKCPX	NAS CM	Open End	Cautious Alloc (Asset Alloc)	B	C	A	Up	Y	5,000,000
BlackRock 20/80 Target Allocation Fund Inst Shares	BICPX	NAS CM	Open End	Cautious Alloc (Asset Alloc)	B	C	A	Up	Y	2,000,000
BlackRock 20/80 Target Allocation Fund Investor A Shares	BACPX	NAS CM	Open End	Cautious Alloc (Asset Alloc)	B	C	A	Up	Y	1,000
BlackRock 20/80 Target Allocation Fund Investor C Shares	BCCPX	NAS CM	Open End	Cautious Alloc (Asset Alloc)	B	C	A-	Up	Y	1,000
BlackRock 20/80 Target Allocation Fund R Shares	BRCPX	NAS CM	Open End	Cautious Alloc (Asset Alloc)	B	C	A	Up	Y	100
BlackRock 40/60 Target Allocation Fund Class K	BKMPX	NAS CM	Open End	Cautious Alloc (Asset Alloc)	B-	C+	B	Up	Y	5,000,000
BlackRock 40/60 Target Allocation Fund Class R Shares	BRMPX	NAS CM	Open End	Cautious Alloc (Asset Alloc)	B-	C+	B	Up	Y	100
BlackRock 40/60 Target Allocation Fund Institutional	BIMPX	NAS CM	Open End	Cautious Alloc (Asset Alloc)	B-	C+	B	Up	Y	2,000,000
BlackRock 40/60 Target Allocation Fund Investor A Shares	BAMPX	NAS CM	Open End	Cautious Alloc (Asset Alloc)	B-	C+	B	Up	Y	1,000
BlackRock 40/60 Target Allocation Fund Investor C Shares	BCMPX	NAS CM	Open End	Cautious Alloc (Asset Alloc)	B	C+	A-	Up	Y	1,000
BlackRock 60/40 Target Allocation Fund Class K	BKGPX	NAS CM	Open End	Moderate Alloc (Asset Alloc)	B-	C+	B	Down	Y	5,000,000
BlackRock 60/40 Target Allocation Fund Class R Shares	BRGPX	NAS CM	Open End	Moderate Alloc (Asset Alloc)	B-	C+	B	Down	Y	100
BlackRock 60/40 Target Allocation Fund Inst Shares	BIGPX	NAS CM	Open End	Moderate Alloc (Asset Alloc)	B-	C+	B	Down	Y	2,000,000
BlackRock 60/40 Target Allocation Fund Investor A Shares	BAGPX	NAS CM	Open End	Moderate Alloc (Asset Alloc)	B-	C+	B	Down	Y	1,000
BlackRock 60/40 Target Allocation Fund Investor C Shares	BCGPX	NAS CM	Open End	Moderate Alloc (Asset Alloc)	B-	C+	B	Down	Y	1,000
BlackRock 80/20 Target Allocation Fund Class A	BAAPX	NAS CM	Open End	Aggressive Alloc (Asset Alloc)	B-	C+	B-	Down	Y	1,000
BlackRock 80/20 Target Allocation Fund Class C	BCAPX	NAS CM	Open End	Aggressive Alloc (Asset Alloc)	B-	C+	B-	Down	Y	1,000
BlackRock 80/20 Target Allocation Fund Class Institutional	BIAPX	NAS CM	Open End	Aggressive Alloc (Asset Alloc)	B-	C+	B-	Down	Y	2,000,000
BlackRock 80/20 Target Allocation Fund Class K	BKAPX	NAS CM	Open End	Aggressive Alloc (Asset Alloc)	B-	C+	B-	Down	Y	5,000,000
BlackRock 80/20 Target Allocation Fund Class R	BRAPX	NAS CM	Open End	Aggressive Alloc (Asset Alloc)	B-	C+	B-	Down	Y	100
BlackRock Advantage Emerging Mkts Fund Inst Shares	BLSIX	NAS CM	Open End	Emerging Markets Equity (Div Emerging Mkts)	C+	C	B-	Up	Y	2,000,000
BlackRock Advantage Emerging Mkts Fund Inv A Shares	BLSAX	NAS CM	Open End	Emerging Markets Equity (Div Emerging Mkts)	C+	C	B-	Up	Y	1,000
BlackRock Advantage Emerging Mkts Fund Inv C Shares	BLSCX	NAS CM	Open End	Emerging Markets Equity (Div Emerging Mkts)	C	C	C+	Up	Y	1,000
BlackRock Advantage Global Fund Institutional Shares	MAGCX	NAS CM	Open End	Global Equity Mid/Small Cap (Growth)	C+	B-	C	Up	Y	2,000,000
BlackRock Advantage Global Fund Investor A Shares	MDGCX	NAS CM	Open End	Global Equity Mid/Small Cap (Growth)	C+	B-	C	Up	Y	1,000
BlackRock Advantage Global Fund Investor B Shares	MBGCX	NAS CM	Open End	Global Equity Mid/Small Cap (Growth)	C+	C+	C	Up		1,000
BlackRock Advantage Global Fund Investor C Shares	MCGCX	NAS CM	Open End	Global Equity Mid/Small Cap (Growth)	C+	B-	C	Up	Y	1,000
BlackRock Advantage Global Fund R Shares	MRGSX	NAS CM	Open End	Global Equity Mid/Small Cap (Growth)	C+	B-	C	Up	Y	100
BlackRock Advantage Intl Fund Inst Shares	BROIX	NAS CM	Open End	Global Equity Large Cap (World Stock)	B	B-	B	Up	Y	2,000,000
BlackRock Advantage International Fund Investor A Shares	BROAX	NAS CM	Open End	Global Equity Large Cap (World Stock)	B	B-	B	Up	Y	1,000

★ Expanded analysis of this fund is included in Section II.

Min Additional Investment	TOTAL RETURNS 3-Month Total Return	6-Month Total Return	1-Year Total Return	3-Year Total Return	5-Year Total Return	PERFORMANCE Dividend Yield (TTM)	Expense Ratio	3-Yr Std Deviation	3-Year Beta	ASSETS NAV	Total Assets (MIL)	ASSET ALLOCATION & TURNOVER %Cash	%Stocks	%Bonds	%Other	Turnover Ratio	BULL & BEAR Last Bull Market Total Return	Last Bear Market Total Return	FEES Front End Fee (%)	Back End Fee (%)	Inception Date
1,000	4.43	8.11	22.50	24.27		0.45	1.24	9.18	0.82	13.5	135.9	12	83	0	5	19					Mar-13
250	4.45	7.99	22.33	23.35		0.25	1.5	9.2	0.82	13.45	135.9	12	83	0	5	19					Apr-13
1,000	1.78	5.16	20.47	22.02	38.72	1.94	0.7	11.02	0.86	15.6	1,421	17	83	0	0	12	10.81	-16.63			Oct-02
1,000	3.51						1.37			10.37	139.0										Oct-17
1,000	1.71						1.32			10.19	353.3										Oct-17
1,000	5.04	11.46	17.76	9.55	30.34	0.91	1	14.32	1.18	11.67	38.3	0	100	0	0	26	25.7	-15.5			Dec-09
100	6.24	9.35	15.23	26.19	97.10	1.46	0.68	11.34	1.07	19.55	444.2	5	95	0	0	34	23.56	-18.53			Sep-11
100	6.24	9.30	15.14	25.75	95.41	1.37	0.78	11.31	1.07	19.49	444.2	5	95	0	0	34	23.48	-18.53			Nov-03
250	6.43	13.45	22.19	21.32	49.75	0.45	1.77	11.14	0.98	12.9	13.6	12	88	0	0	80	13.51	-13.01	4.00		Jan-11
250	6.26	13.05	21.31	18.65	44.28	0.14	2.52	11.11	0.98	12.56	13.6	12	88	0	0	80	12.93	-13.33			Jan-11
500	7.99	17.95	44.07	61.29	136.45	0	2.02	15.84	1.17	21.47	76.8	0	100	0	0	443	28.65	-13.33			Jul-97
	4.64	12.72	31.84			1.1	1.35			12.81	1,129	2	98	0	0	65					Dec-15
	3.44	9.67	29.72			1.05	1.2			12.77	3,368	2	98	0	0	69					Dec-15
	2.87	7.63	7.17			0.11	1.3			11.83	900.5	0	100	0	0	165					Dec-15
5,000	5.22	15.89	26.84	33.49	82.00	0.34	0.95	12.6	0.74	15.37	98.5	5	95	0	0	38					Sep-12
100	0.85	7.70	7.00	17.29	56.36	0	1.24	13.7	0.83	28.49	109.9	13	86	0	0		30.86	-24.84			May-84
100	1.13	1.37	3.91	9.02	31.46	1.6	0.68	3.27	0.15	13.42	1,657	15	22	49	0		9.27	-4.73			Sep-87
	6.89	10.81	20.97	30.00		0.38	1.25	9.63	0.93	14.47	29.9	2	98	0	0	48					Nov-13
100	3.37	9.34	31.37	16.19	118.19	0	2.23	20.12	1.6	16.75	28.5	-3	103	0	0	60	20.3	-28.76			Mar-10
100	3.34	9.72	24.13	13.94	72.40	0	1.52	14.76	1.28	15.12	32.7	4	96	0	0	36	20.1	-22			May-06
	6.92	11.46	20.47	35.42	100.35	1.43	1.05	9.32	0.84	16.05	42.5	2	98	0	0	17	23.24	-12.99			May-06
25	5.82	9.44	19.02	31.53	113.45	0.02	1.28	14.39	0.91	5.05	38.4	4	96	0	0	35	26.42	-28.69			Dec-00
	1.66	3.80	8.05	12.54	36.03	1.74	0.53	3.07	0.5	11.55	330.6	2	24	42	32	80	11.56	-8.23			Mar-16
	1.65	3.78	7.94	12.50	35.98	1.73	0.55	3.05	0.49	11.55	330.6	2	24	42	32	80	11.56	-8.23			Dec-06
50	1.58	3.56	7.56	11.35	33.48	1.49	0.89	3.05	0.5	11.42	330.6	2	24	42	32	80	11.38	-8.37	5.25		Dec-06
50	1.41	3.23	6.87	8.92	28.65	0.92	1.64	3.05	0.48	11.33	330.6	2	24	42	32	80	10.9	-8.69		1.00	Dec-06
	1.55	3.44	7.27	10.36	31.71	1.2	1.2	3.02	0.49	11.38	330.6	2	24	42	32	80	11.12	-8.42			Dec-06
	2.68	5.61	11.68	16.92	50.12	1.67	0.54	4.85	0.43	11.94	398.3	-1	45	54	1	74	15.09	-12.29			Mar-16
	2.52	5.30	11.13	15.17	46.29	1.29	1.06	4.83	0.43	11.81	398.3	-1	45	54	1	74	14.9	-12.51			Dec-06
	2.75	5.59	11.76	16.89	50.08	1.65	0.56	4.84	0.43	11.94	398.3	-1	45	54	1	74	15.09	-12.29			Dec-06
50	2.60	5.36	11.27	15.70	47.49	1.42	0.9	4.85	0.43	11.85	398.3	-1	45	54	1	74	14.97	-12.52	5.25		Dec-06
50	2.40	5.03	10.50	13.09	41.98	0.85	1.65	4.86	0.43	11.73	398.3	-1	45	54	1	74	14.45	-12.73		1.00	Dec-06
	2.87	6.41	13.72	18.04	59.18	1.56	0.49	6.71	0.6	13.28	524.3	-2	64	36	1	70	18.33	-16.38			Mar-16
	2.67	6.04	12.99	16.76	57.45	1.2	1.04	6.68	0.6	13.05	524.3	-2	64	36	1	70	18.33	-16.38			Dec-06
	2.85	6.31	13.61	18.74	61.80	1.55	0.51	6.64	0.6	13.28	524.3	-2	64	36	1	70	18.65	-16.12			Dec-06
50	2.79	6.23	13.26	17.53	58.92	1.37	0.85	6.68	0.6	13.09	524.3	-2	64	36	1	70	18.44	-16.35	5.25		Dec-06
50	3.56	6.77	13.52	15.96	54.64	0.83	1.6	6.67	0.6	12.84	524.3	-2	64	36	1	70	18.05	-16.55		1.00	Dec-06
50	4.77	8.87	17.02	21.35	73.33	1.29	0.81	8.59	0.78	12.46	306.2	0	80	16	4	59	22.4	-20.38	5.25		Dec-06
50	4.65	8.41	16.25	18.73	66.93	0.77	1.56	8.56	0.77	12.1	306.2	0	80	16	4	59	21.89	-20.68		1.00	Dec-06
	4.85	8.95	17.47	22.66	76.31	1.43	0.47	8.57	0.78	12.68	306.2	0	80	16	4	59	22.77	-20.35			Dec-06
	3.49	7.54	15.95	21.08	74.04	1.44	0.45	8.59	0.78	12.68	306.2	0	80	16	4	59	22.77	-20.35			Mar-16
	4.74	8.77	16.87	20.80	72.01	1.12	0.97	8.59	0.78	12.38	306.2	0	80	16	4	59	22.46	-20.53			Dec-06
	7.25	15.28	14.68	8.81	5.64	0	0.94	5.59	0.13	11.09	148.8	10	90	0	0	7					Oct-11
50	7.14	15.03	14.31	7.98	4.33	0	1.19	5.54	0.13	10.94	148.8	10	90	0	0	7			5.25		Oct-11
50	6.83	14.55	13.43	5.53	0.43	0	1.94	5.49	0.13	10.47	148.8	10	90	0	0	7				1.00	Oct-11
	5.41	13.04	23.88	25.72	76.33	0.97	0.71	12.58	1.07	21.75	757.8	3	97	0	0	59	20.43	-23.7			Oct-94
50	5.36	12.91	23.50	24.44	73.31	0.54	0.96	12.57	1.07	20.71	757.8	3	97	0	0	59	20.23	-23.79	5.25		Aug-94
50	5.92	12.10	22.66	21.40	65.89	0	1.71	12.55	1.07		757.8	3	97	0	0	59	19.47	-24.08		4.50	Aug-94
50	5.11	12.41	22.52	21.44	66.53	0	1.71	12.6	1.07	17.05	757.8	3	97	0	0	59	19.67	-24.07		1.00	Oct-94
	5.25	12.69	23.04	23.12	70.20	0.17	1.21	12.56	1.07	18.75	757.8	3	97	0	0	59	19.88	-23.93			Feb-03
	3.98	9.46	24.20	27.94	63.37	1.68	0.64	10.63	0.81	17.31	484.2	4	96	0	1	177	17.4	-23.79			Jan-06
50	3.86	9.32	23.76	26.89	61.17	1.47	0.89	10.64	0.81	17.14	484.2	4	96	0	1	177	17.21	-23.91	5.25		Jan-06

	MARKET		FUND TYPE, CATEGORY & OBJECTIVE		RATINGS					MINIMUMS
Fund Name	Ticker Symbol	Traded On	Fund Type	Category and (Prospectus Objective)	Overall Rating	Reward Rating	Risk Rating	Recent Up/ Downgrade	Open to New Investors	Min Initial Investment
BlackRock Advantage International Fund Investor C Shares	BROCX	NAS CM	Open End	Global Equity Large Cap (World Stock)	B-	B-	B	Up	Y	1,000
BlackRock Advantage International Fund R Shares	BGORX	NAS CM	Open End	Global Equity Large Cap (World Stock)	B-	B-	B	Up		100
BlackRock Advantage Large Cap Core Fund Inst Shares	MALRX	NAS CM	Open End	US Equity Large Cap Blend (Growth)	B	B	B-		Y	2,000,000
BlackRock Advantage Large Cap Core Fund Investor A Shares	MDLRX	NAS CM	Open End	US Equity Large Cap Blend (Growth)	B	B	B-		Y	1,000
BlackRock Advantage Large Cap Core Fund Investor B Shares	MBLRX	NAS CM	Open End	US Equity Large Cap Blend (Growth)	B	B	B-	Up		1,000
BlackRock Advantage Large Cap Core Fund Investor C Shares	MCLRX	NAS CM	Open End	US Equity Large Cap Blend (Growth)	B	B	B-	Up	Y	1,000
BlackRock Advantage Large Cap Core Fund R Shares	MRLRX	NAS CM	Open End	US Equity Large Cap Blend (Growth)	B	B	B-		Y	100
BlackRock Advantage Large Cap Core Fund Service Shares	MSLRX	NAS CM	Open End	US Equity Large Cap Blend (Growth)	B	B	B-		Y	5,000
BlackRock Advantage Large Cap Growth Fund Inst Shares	CMVIX	NAS CM	Open End	US Equity Large Cap Growth (Growth & Income)	B	B	B-		Y	2,000,000
BlackRock Advantage Large Cap Growth Fund Inv A Shares	BMCAX	NAS CM	Open End	US Equity Large Cap Growth (Growth & Income)	B	B	B-	Up	Y	1,000
BlackRock Advantage Large Cap Growth Fund Inv B Shares	BMCVX	NAS CM	Open End	US Equity Large Cap Growth (Growth & Income)	B	B	B-	Up		1,000
BlackRock Advantage Large Cap Growth Fund Inv C Shares	BMCCX	NAS CM	Open End	US Equity Large Cap Growth (Growth & Income)	B	B	B-	Up	Y	1,000
BlackRock Advantage Large Cap Growth Fund R Shares	BMCRX	NAS CM	Open End	US Equity Large Cap Growth (Growth & Income)	B	B	B-	Up		100
BlackRock Advantage Large Cap Growth Fund Service Shares	CMVSX	NAS CM	Open End	US Equity Large Cap Growth (Growth & Income)	B	B	B-	Up	Y	5,000
BlackRock Advantage Large Cap Value Fund Inst Shares	MALVX	NAS CM	Open End	US Equity Large Cap Value (Growth)	B	B	B+		Y	2,000,000
BlackRock Advantage Large Cap Value Fund Investor A Shares	MDLVX	NAS CM	Open End	US Equity Large Cap Value (Growth)	B	B	B	Up	Y	1,000
BlackRock Advantage Large Cap Value Fund Investor B Shares	MBLVX	NAS CM	Open End	US Equity Large Cap Value (Growth)	B	B-	B	Up		1,000
BlackRock Advantage Large Cap Value Fund Investor C Shares	MCLVX	NAS CM	Open End	US Equity Large Cap Value (Growth)	B	B-	B	Up	Y	1,000
BlackRock Advantage Large Cap Value Fund R Shares	MRLVX	NAS CM	Open End	US Equity Large Cap Value (Growth)	B	B	B	Up	Y	100
BlackRock Advantage Large Cap Value Fund Service Shares	MSLVX	NAS CM	Open End	US Equity Large Cap Value (Growth)	B	B	B	Up	Y	5,000
BlackRock Advantage Large Cap Value Retirement Fund	MKLVX	NAS CM	Open End	US Equity Large Cap Value (Growth)	B	B	B+			2,000,000
BlackRock Advantage Small Cap Core Fund Class K	BDSKX	NAS CM	Open End	US Equity Small Cap (Growth)	B+	B+	B	Up	Y	5,000,000
BlackRock Advantage Small Cap Core Fund Inst Shares	BDSIX	NAS CM	Open End	US Equity Small Cap (Growth)	B+	B+	B	Up	Y	2,000,000
BlackRock Advantage Small Cap Core Fund Investor A Shares	BDSAX	NAS CM	Open End	US Equity Small Cap (Growth)	B+	B+	B	Up	Y	1,000
BlackRock Advantage Small Cap Core Fund Investor C Shares	BDSCX	NAS CM	Open End	US Equity Small Cap (Growth)	B	B+	B	Up	Y	1,000
BlackRock Advantage Small Cap Growth Fund Inst Shares	PSGIX	NAS CM	Open End	US Equity Small Cap (Small Company)	B	B+	B	Up	Y	2,000,000
BlackRock Advantage Small Cap Growth Fund Inv A Shares	CSGEX	NAS CM	Open End	US Equity Small Cap (Small Company)	B	B	B	Up	Y	1,000
BlackRock Advantage Small Cap Growth Fund Inv C Shares	CGICX	NAS CM	Open End	US Equity Small Cap (Small Company)	B	B	B	Up	Y	1,000
BlackRock Advantage Small Cap Growth Fund Service Shares	PCGEX	NAS CM	Open End	US Equity Small Cap (Small Company)	B	B	B	Up	Y	5,000
BlackRock Advantage U.S. Total Mkt Fund Inst Shares	MASPX	NAS CM	Open End	US Equity Small Cap (Growth)	B	B	B	Up	Y	2,000,000
BlackRock Advantage U.S. Total Mkt Fund Inv A Shares	MDSPX	NAS CM	Open End	US Equity Small Cap (Growth)	B	B	B	Up	Y	1,000
BlackRock Advantage U.S. Total Mkt Fund Inv B Shares	MBSPX	NAS CM	Open End	US Equity Small Cap (Growth)	B-	B-	B-	Up		1,000
BlackRock Advantage U.S. Total Mkt Fund Inv C Shares	MCSPX	NAS CM	Open End	US Equity Small Cap (Growth)	B-	B	B-	Up	Y	1,000
BlackRock Advantage U.S. Total Market Fund R Shares	MRSPX	NAS CM	Open End	US Equity Small Cap (Growth)	B	B	B	Up	Y	100
BlackRock All-Cap Energy & Resources Portfolio Inst Cls	BACIX	NAS CM	Open End	Energy Sector Equity (Natl Res)	C	C	C-	Up	Y	2,000,000
BlackRock All-Cap Energy & Resources Portfolio Inv A Cls	BACAX	NAS CM	Open End	Energy Sector Equity (Natl Res)	C	C	C-	Up	Y	1,000
BlackRock All-Cap Energy & Resources Portfolio Inv B Cls	BACBX	NAS CM	Open End	Energy Sector Equity (Natl Res)	C-	C	C-			1,000
BlackRock All-Cap Energy & Resources Portfolio Inv C Cls	BACCX	NAS CM	Open End	Energy Sector Equity (Natl Res)	C-	C	C-		Y	1,000
BlackRock All-Cap Energy & Resources Portfolio Service Cls	BACSX	NAS CM	Open End	Energy Sector Equity (Natl Res)	C	C	C-	Up	Y	5,000
BlackRock Alternative Capital Strategies Fund Inst Shares	BIMBX	NAS CM	Open End	Multialternative (Growth & Income)	B-	C	B	Up	Y	2,000,000
BlackRock Alternative Capital Strategies Fund Inv A Shares	BAMBX	NAS CM	Open End	Multialternative (Growth & Income)	C+	C	B	Up	Y	1,000
BlackRock Alternative Capital Strategies Fund Inv C Shares	BMBCX	NAS CM	Open End	Multialternative (Growth & Income)	C+	C	B	Up	Y	1,000
BlackRock Asian Dragon Fund Class R	MRPCX	NAS CM	Open End	Asia Equity (Pacific Stock)	B-	B-	B-	Up	Y	100
BlackRock Asian Dragon Fund Institutional Shares	MAPCX	NAS CM	Open End	Asia Equity (Pacific Stock)	B-	B-	B-	Up	Y	2,000,000
BlackRock Asian Dragon Fund Investor A Shares	MDPCX	NAS CM	Open End	Asia Equity (Pacific Stock)	B-	B-	B-	Up	Y	1,000
BlackRock Asian Dragon Fund Investor C Shares	MCPCX	NAS CM	Open End	Asia Equity (Pacific Stock)	B-	B-	B-	Up	Y	1,000
BlackRock Balanced Capital Fund Institutional Shares	MACPX	NAS CM	Open End	Moderate Alloc (Balanced)	B-	B-	B	Down	Y	2,000,000
BlackRock Balanced Capital Fund Investor A Shares	MDCPX	NAS CM	Open End	Moderate Alloc (Balanced)	B-	C+	B	Down	Y	1,000
BlackRock Balanced Capital Fund Investor B Shares	MBCPX	NAS CM	Open End	Moderate Alloc (Balanced)	B-	C+	B	Up		1,000
BlackRock Balanced Capital Fund Investor C Shares	MCCPX	NAS CM	Open End	Moderate Alloc (Balanced)	B-	C+	B	Up	Y	1,000
BlackRock Balanced Capital Fund R Shares	MRBPX	NAS CM	Open End	Moderate Alloc (Balanced)	B-	C+	B	Up	Y	100
BlackRock Basic Value Fund Class K	MBVKX	NAS CM	Open End	US Equity Large Cap Value (Growth)	B-	C+	B-	Up	Y	5,000,000

★ Expanded analysis of this fund is included in Section II.

Min Additional Investment	3-Month Total Return	6-Month Total Return	1-Year Total Return	3-Year Total Return	5-Year Total Return	Dividend Yield (TTM)	Expense Ratio	3-Yr Std Deviation	3-Year Beta	NAV	Total Assets (MIL)	%Cash	%Stocks	%Bonds	%Other	Turnover Ratio	Last Bull Market Total Return	Last Bear Market Total Return	Front End Fee (%)	Back End Fee (%)	Inception Date
TOTAL RETURNS						PERFORMANCE				ASSETS		ASSET ALLOCATION & TURNOVER					BULL & BEAR		FEES		
50	3.69	8.88	22.86	23.92	54.75	0.82	1.64	10.63	0.81	16.55	484.2	4	96	0	1	177	16.66	-24.12		1.00	Jan-06
	3.80	9.14	23.44	25.53	58.16	1.15	1.14	10.63	0.81	17.13	484.2	4	96	0	1	177	16.99	-23.95			Sep-11
	5.73	11.51	22.09	33.90	105.98	0.81	0.48	11.49	1.1	16.38	1,696	1	99	0	0	130	25.5	-22.45			Dec-99
50	5.66	11.33	21.73	32.78	103.07	0.57	0.73	11.5	1.1	15.81	1,696	1	99	0	0	130	25.4	-22.5	5.25		Dec-99
50	6.12	10.52	20.37	29.68	95.56	0	1.48	11.49	1.1		1,697	1	99	0	0	130	24.74	-22.81		4.50	Dec-99
50	5.48	10.97	20.80	29.57	95.06	0	1.48	11.51	1.1	13.64	1,697	1	99	0	0	130	24.63	-22.77		1.00	Dec-99
	5.55	11.21	21.39	31.64	100.22	0.3	0.98	11.47	1.1	14.8	1,696	1	99	0	0	130	25.02	-22.64			Jan-03
	5.66	11.34	21.80	32.31	102.01	0	0.73	11.51	1.1	16.34	1,697	1	99	0	0	130	25.41	-22.58			Sep-07
	6.47	12.69	23.53	37.32	76.44	0.69	0.62	10.68	0.92	15.2	788.4	1	99	0	0	130	27.45	-24.3			Jun-93
50	6.42	12.59	23.13	35.95	73.67	0.46	0.87	10.62	0.92	14.57	788.8	1	99	0	0	130	27.26	-24.42	5.25		Aug-86
50	7.10	11.24	21.85	33.04	67.85	0	1.62	10.62	0.92		788.8	1	99	0	0	130	26.68	-24.73		4.50	Jan-99
50	6.26	12.17	22.27	32.92	67.12	0	1.62	10.67	0.92	12.46	788.4	1	99	0	0	130	26.66	-24.66		1.00	Jun-93
	6.28	12.42	22.71	34.53	70.70	0.23	1.12	10.66	0.92	15.08	788.8	1	99	0	0	130	26.99	-24.53			Jul-10
	6.32	12.49	23.02	35.95	73.63	0.45	0.87	10.67	0.92	14.95	788.4	1	99	0	0	130	27.22	-24.41			Jan-05
	5.29	10.73	17.54	30.17	99.06	1.19	0.54	11.67	1.09	29.26	675.8	1	99	0	0	137	23.97	-24.25			Dec-99
50	5.21	10.59	17.25	29.07	96.05	0.92	0.79	11.65	1.09	28.72	676.5	1	99	0	0	137	23.57	-24.28	5.25		Dec-99
50	5.53	10.14	15.90	26.03	88.26	0	1.54	11.65	1.09		676.5	1	99	0	0	137	23.17	-24.58		4.50	Dec-99
50	5.01	10.20	16.37	26.13	88.68	0.16	1.54	11.67	1.09	26.78	676.5	1	99	0	0	137	23.2	-24.53		1.00	Dec-99
	5.16	10.45	16.94	28.03	93.54	0.68	1.04	11.65	1.09	27.67	676.5	1	99	0	0	137	23.48	-24.35			Jan-03
	5.19	10.58	17.25	29.02	96.04	0.91	0.79	11.66	1.09	29.09	675.8	1	99	0	0	137	23.87	-24.25			Oct-06
	4.92	10.36	17.28	30.38	100.06	2.38	0.54	11.67	1.09	15.63	131.2	1	99	0	0	137	24.28	-24.05			Jan-08
	1.94	7.42	10.82	33.48		0.58	0.45	13.71	0.95	13.63	291.6	1	99	0	0	127					Mar-16
	1.92	7.47	10.78	33.42		0.56	0.5	13.67	0.94	13.63	291.6	1	99	0	0	127					Mar-13
50	1.88	7.29	10.52	32.44		0.36	0.75	13.68	0.94	13.58	291.6	1	99	0	0	127			5.25		Mar-13
50	1.66	6.88	9.72	29.40		0	1.5	13.67	0.94	13.39	291.6	1	99	0	0	127				1.00	Mar-13
	2.39	8.27	14.86	25.01	90.25	0.04	0.5	14.38	0.95	19.59	703.3	1	98	0	1	100	31.66	-26.86			Sep-93
50	2.32	8.12	14.61	23.98	87.58	0	0.75	14.4	0.95	15.15	703.3	1	98	0	1	100	31.4	-27.02	5.25		Sep-93
50	2.12	7.77	13.73	21.07	80.45	0	1.5	14.38	0.95	8.63	703.3	1	98	0	1	100	30.75	-27.24		1.00	Sep-96
	2.32	8.12	14.62	23.96	87.68	0	0.75	14.39	0.95	16.66	703.3	1	98	0	1	100	31.38	-26.93			Sep-93
	2.81	7.34	9.06	24.93	92.35	0	0.48	14.41	1.15	32.46	577.2	9	100	0	-8	68	27.59	-24.32			May-78
50	2.73	7.18	8.74	23.98	89.92	0	0.73	14.41	1.15	31.36	577.2	9	100	0	-8	68	27.37	-24.42	5.25		Oct-94
50	3.00	6.39	7.68	20.74	80.89	0	1.48	14.36	1.14		577.2	9	100	0	-8	68	26.66	-24.74		4.50	Oct-88
50	2.55	6.75	7.89	20.95	82.18	0	1.48	14.38	1.15	22.52	577.1	9	100	0	-8	68	26.69	-24.76		1.00	Oct-94
	2.69	7.08	8.44	22.91	87.06	0	0.98	14.41	1.15	24.74	577.1	9	100	0	-8	68	27.14	-24.57			Feb-03
	7.32	17.92	2.44	-8.39	-0.54	2.46	0.96	20.92	1.18	11.61	85.6	1	99	0	0	14	15.81	-33.62			Feb-05
50	7.24	17.78	2.05	-9.43	-2.50	2.01	1.38	20.89	1.17	11.32	85.6	1	99	0	0	14	15.46	-33.74	5.25		Feb-05
50	6.93	17.78	0.98	-12.16	-6.08	0	2.1	20.83	1.17		85.6	1	99	0	0	14	14.93	-33.92		4.50	Feb-05
50	7.14	17.40	1.43	-11.32	-5.96	1.22	2.1	20.89	1.17	10.81	85.6	1	99	0	0	14	14.99	-33.92		1.00	Feb-05
	7.30	17.81	2.14	-9.47	-2.40	2.03	1.38	20.88	1.17	11.38	85.6	1	99	0	0	14	15.54	-33.7			Feb-05
	2.50	5.33	9.89			1.9	0.97			10.14	28.6	-14	17	97	0	722					May-15
50	2.45	5.23	9.72			1.66	1.22			10.14	28.6	-14	17	97	0	722			4.00		May-15
50	2.19	4.81	8.86			0.66	1.97			10.15	28.6	-14	17	97	0	722				1.00	May-15
	6.93	11.14	27.52	27.10	51.62	0.78	1.66	12.87	0.78	13.07	238.0	-1	95	3	3	81	15.1	-23.98			Jan-03
	7.15	11.50	28.37	29.74	56.92	1.16	0.98	12.88	0.79	17.15	238.0	-1	95	3	3	81	15.64	-23.71			Sep-76
50	7.11	11.39	28.15	28.93	55.27	1	1.18	12.84	0.78	16.94	238.0	-1	95	3	3	81	15.46	-23.78	5.25		Oct-94
50	6.88	10.91	27.04	25.92	49.23	0.79	2	12.84	0.78	11.51	238.0	-1	95	3	3	81	14.88	-24.03		1.00	Oct-94
	3.39	7.15	14.61	24.14	68.41	1.46	0.6	6.93	0.67	22.7	1,071	6	59	34	0	109	16.19	-12.84			Nov-73
50	3.28	6.95	14.24	23.07	65.95	1.22	0.88	6.92	0.67	22.62	1,071	6	59	34	0	109	16.01	-12.99	5.25		Oct-94
50	1.94	4.15	10.36	16.15	53.48	0	2.15	6.86	0.66		1,071	6	59	34	0	109	15.22	-13.33		4.50	Oct-88
50	3.10	6.54	13.34	20.27	59.73	0.63	1.64	6.9	0.67	19.78	1,071	6	59	34	0	109	15.42	-13.22		1.00	Oct-94
	3.18	6.77	13.81	21.79	63.07	1.04	1.24	6.93	0.67	20.89	1,071	6	59	34	0	109	15.68	-13.13			Jan-03
	5.78	9.39	8.66	20.22	87.65	1.73	0.44	13.28	1.24	26.25	3,237	2	98	0	0	26	25.39	-21.05			Feb-15

	MARKET		FUND TYPE, CATEGORY & OBJECTIVE		RATINGS				MINIMUMS	
Fund Name	Ticker Symbol	Traded On	Fund Type	Category and (Prospectus Objective)	Overall Rating	Reward Rating	Risk Rating	Recent Up/ Downgrade	Open to New Investors	Min Initial Investment
BlackRock Basic Value Fund Institutional Shares	MABAX	NAS CM	Open End	US Equity Large Cap Value (Growth)	B-	C+	B-	Up	Y	2,000,000
BlackRock Basic Value Fund Investor A Shares	MDBAX	NAS CM	Open End	US Equity Large Cap Value (Growth)	C+	C+	B-	Up	Y	1,000
BlackRock Basic Value Fund Investor B Shares	MBBAX	NAS CM	Open End	US Equity Large Cap Value (Growth)	C+	C+	B-	Up		1,000
BlackRock Basic Value Fund Investor C Shares	MCBAX	NAS CM	Open End	US Equity Large Cap Value (Growth)	C+	C+	B-	Up	Y	1,000
BlackRock Basic Value Fund R Shares	MRBVX	NAS CM	Open End	US Equity Large Cap Value (Growth)	C+	C+	B-	Up	Y	100
BlackRock Capital Appreciation Fund Institutional Shares	MAFGX	NAS CM	Open End	US Equity Large Cap Growth (Growth)	B+	B+	B+	Up	Y	2,000,000
BlackRock Capital Appreciation Fund Investor A Shares	MDFGX	NAS CM	Open End	US Equity Large Cap Growth (Growth)	B+	B+	B+	Up	Y	1,000
BlackRock Capital Appreciation Fund Investor B Shares	MBFGX	NAS CM	Open End	US Equity Large Cap Growth (Growth)	B	B	B+	Up		1,000
BlackRock Capital Appreciation Fund Investor C Shares	MCFGX	NAS CM	Open End	US Equity Large Cap Growth (Growth)	B+	B+	B+	Up	Y	1,000
BlackRock Capital Appreciation Fund K Shares	BFGBX	NAS CM	Open End	US Equity Large Cap Growth (Growth)	B+	B+	B+	Up	Y	5,000,000
BlackRock Capital Appreciation Fund R Shares	MRFGX	NAS CM	Open End	US Equity Large Cap Growth (Growth)	B+	B+	B+	Up	Y	100
BlackRock Commodity Strategies Portfolio Inst Shares	BICSX	NAS CM	Open End	Commodities Broad Basket (Growth & Income)	C	C	C-	Up	Y	2,000,000
BlackRock Commodity Strategies Portfolio Investor A Shares	BCSAX	NAS CM	Open End	Commodities Broad Basket (Growth & Income)	C	C	C-	Up	Y	1,000
BlackRock Commodity Strategies Portfolio Investor C Shares	BCSCX	NAS CM	Open End	Commodities Broad Basket (Growth & Income)	C	C	D+	Up	Y	1,000
BlackRock Dynamic High Income Portfolio Class K	BDHKX	NAS CM	Open End	Alloc (Growth & Income)	C+	C+	B-	Down	Y	5,000,000
BlackRock Dynamic High Income Portfolio Institutional	BDHIX	NAS CM	Open End	Alloc (Growth & Income)	C+	C+	B-	Down	Y	2,000,000
BlackRock Dynamic High Income Portfolio Investor A	BDHAX	NAS CM	Open End	Alloc (Growth & Income)	C+	C+	B-	Down	Y	1,000
BlackRock Dynamic High Income Portfolio Investor C	BDHCX	NAS CM	Open End	Alloc (Growth & Income)	C+	C	B-	Down	Y	1,000
BlackRock Emerging Mkts Dividend Fund Inst Shares	BICHX	NAS CM	Open End	Emerging Markets Equity (Div Emerging Mkts)	B-	B	C	Up	Y	2,000,000
BlackRock Emerging Markets Dividend Fund Investor A Shares	BACHX	NAS CM	Open End	Emerging Markets Equity (Div Emerging Mkts)	C+	B-	C	Up	Y	1,000
BlackRock Emerging Markets Dividend Fund Investor C Shares	BCCHX	NAS CM	Open End	Emerging Markets Equity (Div Emerging Mkts)	C+	B-	C	Up	Y	1,000
BlackRock Emerging Markets Equity Strategies Fund Class K	BEFKX	NAS CM	Open End	Emerging Markets Equity (Div Emerging Mkts)	C-	C	B+	Up	Y	5,000,000
BlackRock Emerging Mkts Equity Strategies Fund Inst	BEFIX	NAS CM	Open End	Emerging Markets Equity (Div Emerging Mkts)	C-	C	B+	Up	Y	2,000,000
BlackRock Emerging Mkts Equity Strategies Fund Inv A	BEFAX	NAS CM	Open End	Emerging Markets Equity (Div Emerging Mkts)	C-	C	B+	Up	Y	1,000
BlackRock Emerging Mkts Equity Strategies Fund Inv C	BEFCX	NAS CM	Open End	Emerging Markets Equity (Div Emerging Mkts)	C-	C	B+	Up	Y	1,000
BlackRock Emerging Markets Fund Institutional Shares	MADCX	NAS CM	Open End	Emerging Markets Equity (Div Emerging Mkts)	C+	B-	C	Up	Y	2,000,000
BlackRock Emerging Markets Fund Investor A Shares	MDDCX	NAS CM	Open End	Emerging Markets Equity (Div Emerging Mkts)	C+	B-	C	Up	Y	1,000
BlackRock Emerging Markets Fund Investor C Shares	MCDCX	NAS CM	Open End	Emerging Markets Equity (Div Emerging Mkts)	C+	B-	C	Up	Y	1,000
BlackRock Energy & Resources Portfolio Inst Shares	SGLSX	NAS CM	Open End	Energy Sector Equity (Natl Res)	D	D	D	Down	Y	2,000,000
BlackRock Energy & Resources Portfolio Investor A Shares	SSGRX	NAS CM	Open End	Energy Sector Equity (Natl Res)	D	D	D	Down	Y	1,000
BlackRock Energy & Resources Portfolio Investor B Shares	SSGPX	NAS CM	Open End	Energy Sector Equity (Natl Res)	D	D	D	Down		1,000
BlackRock Energy & Resources Portfolio Investor C Shares	SSGDX	NAS CM	Open End	Energy Sector Equity (Natl Res)	D	D	D	Down	Y	1,000
BlackRock Energy & Resources Trust	BGR	NYSE	Closed End	Energy Sector Equity (Natl Res)	C	C	C	Up	Y	
BlackRock Enhanced Capital and Income Fund Inc	CII	NYSE	Closed End	US Equity Large Cap Blend (Equity-Income)	B	B	B	Up	Y	
BlackRock Enhanced Equity Dividend Fund	BDJ	NYSE	Closed End	US Equity Large Cap Value (Equity-Income)	B-	B-	B		Y	
BlackRock Enhanced Global Dividend Trust	BOE	NYSE	Closed End	Global Equity (World Stock)	B-	C+	B	Up	Y	
BlackRock Enhanced International Dividend Trust	BGY	NYSE	Closed End	Global Equity Large Cap (Foreign Stock)	B-	C+	B	Up	Y	
BlackRock Equity Dividend Fund Institutional Shares	MADVX	NAS CM	Open End	US Equity Large Cap Value (Equity-Income)	B	B	B		Y	2,000,000
BlackRock Equity Dividend Fund Investor A Shares	MDDVX	NAS CM	Open End	US Equity Large Cap Value (Equity-Income)	B	B	B		Y	1,000
BlackRock Equity Dividend Fund Investor B Shares	MBDVX	NAS CM	Open End	US Equity Large Cap Value (Equity-Income)	B	B	B			1,000
BlackRock Equity Dividend Fund Investor C Shares	MCDVX	NAS CM	Open End	US Equity Large Cap Value (Equity-Income)	B	B	B		Y	1,000
BlackRock Equity Dividend Fund Investor C1 Shares	BEDCX	NAS CM	Open End	US Equity Large Cap Value (Equity-Income)	B	B	B		Y	1,000
BlackRock Equity Dividend Fund K Shares	MKDVX	NAS CM	Open End	US Equity Large Cap Value (Equity-Income)	B	B	B		Y	5,000,000
BlackRock Equity Dividend Fund R Shares	MRDVX	NAS CM	Open End	US Equity Large Cap Value (Equity-Income)	B	B	B		Y	100
BlackRock Equity Dividend Fund Service Shares	MSDVX	NAS CM	Open End	US Equity Large Cap Value (Equity-Income)	B	B	B		Y	5,000
BlackRock EuroFund Class R Shares	MREFX	NAS CM	Open End	Europe Equity Large Cap (Europe Stock)	C+	C+	C	Up	Y	100
BlackRock EuroFund Institutional Shares	MAEFX	NAS CM	Open End	Europe Equity Large Cap (Europe Stock)	C+	C+	C+	Up	Y	2,000,000
BlackRock EuroFund Investor A Shares	MDEFX	NAS CM	Open End	Europe Equity Large Cap (Europe Stock)	C+	C+	C	Up	Y	1,000
BlackRock EuroFund Investor C Shares	MCEFX	NAS CM	Open End	Europe Equity Large Cap (Europe Stock)	C	C	C	Up	Y	1,000
BlackRock Event Driven Equity Fund Institutional Shares	BILPX	NAS CM	Open End	Market Neutral (Growth)	B-	C	A-	Up	Y	2,000,000
BlackRock Event Driven Equity Fund Investor A Shares	BALPX	NAS CM	Open End	Market Neutral (Growth)	B-	C	A-	Up	Y	1,000
BlackRock Event Driven Equity Fund Investor C Shares	BCLPX	NAS CM	Open End	Market Neutral (Growth)	B-	C	B+	Up	Y	1,000

★ Expanded analysis of this fund is included in Section II.

	TOTAL RETURNS					PERFORMANCE				ASSETS		ASSET ALLOCATION & TURNOVER					BULL & BEAR		FEES		
Min Additional Investment	3-Month Total Return	6-Month Total Return	1-Year Total Return	3-Year Total Return	5-Year Total Return	Dividend Yield (TTM)	Expense Ratio	3-Yr Std Deviation	3-Year Beta	NAV	Total Assets (MIL)	%Cash	%Stocks	%Bonds	%Other	Turnover Ratio	Last Bull Market Total Return	Last Bear Market Total Return	Front End Fee (%)	Back End Fee (%)	Inception Date
	5.75	9.32	8.58	19.83	87.04	1.64	0.54	13.26	1.23	26.25	3,237	2	98	0	0	26	25.39	-21.05			Jul-77
50	5.68	9.16	8.24	18.84	84.50	1.4	0.82	13.26	1.23	25.96	3,237	2	98	0	0	26	25.14	-21.16	5.25		Oct-94
50	5.89	8.12	6.06	14.73	74.48	0	2	13.25	1.23		3,237	2	98	0	0	26	24.42	-21.5		4.50	Oct-88
50	5.46	8.72	7.40	16.04	77.34	0.88	1.61	13.28	1.24	23.02	3,237	2	98	0	0	26	24.57	-21.43		1.00	Oct-94
	5.60	8.97	7.87	17.65	81.54	1.23	1.15	13.27	1.24	24.47	3,237	2	98	0	0	26	24.9	-21.28			Jan-03
	7.56	13.25	32.93	41.24	111.79	0	0.77	12.33	1.08	27.86	2,963	0	100	0	0	62	22.93	-20.41			Jun-10
50	7.49	13.07	32.58	40.05	108.87	0	1.08	12.32	1.08	25.87	2,963	0	100	0	0	62	22.7	-20.52	5.25		Dec-97
50	7.41	10.63	28.81	33.56	96.06	0	2.16	12.25	1.08		2,963	0	100	0	0	62	21.94	-20.76		4.50	Jan-99
50	7.26	12.60	31.51	36.69	100.61	0	1.89	12.33	1.08	19.4	2,963	0	100	0	0	62	22.11	-20.78		1.00	Dec-97
	7.63	13.33	33.19	41.82	112.93	0	0.67	12.34	1.08	28	2,963	0	100	0	0	62	22.96	-20.4			Dec-97
	7.42	12.94	32.25	38.94	106.10	0	1.35	12.31	1.08	21.57	2,963	0	100	0	0	62	22.47	-20.62			Jun-10
	5.71	12.05	8.27	-0.74	-19.29	0.91	1.03	14.13	0.94	7.98	212.1	27	50	9	10	96					Oct-11
50	5.71	11.96	8.01	-1.48	-20.14	0.73	1.28	14.1	0.93	7.91	212.1	27	50	9	10	96			5.25		Oct-11
50	5.37	11.53	7.15	-3.77	-23.13	0	2.03	14.08	0.93	7.64	212.1	27	50	9	10	96				1.00	Oct-11
	3.34	6.57	14.63	22.08		5.85	0.69	7.36	0.66	10.02	416.4	2	38	48	3	93					Mar-16
	3.33	6.44	14.46	22.00		5.8	0.74	7.38	0.66	10.01	416.4	2	38	48	3	93					Nov-14
50	3.26	6.41	14.29	21.19		5.56	0.99	7.36	0.66	10.02	416.4	2	38	48	3	93			5.25		Nov-14
50	3.07	6.02	13.45	18.37		4.83	1.74	7.36	0.66	10.01	416.4	2	38	48	3	93				1.00	Nov-14
	6.31	13.58	36.85	29.10	26.67	1.21	1.5	13.09	0.79	10.17	15.1	5	95	0	0	73	22.18	-31			Apr-11
50	6.32	13.44	36.70	28.35	25.26	1.01	1.75	13.04	0.79	10.14	15.1	5	95	0	0	73	22.01	-31.1	5.25		Apr-11
50	6.03	12.93	35.58	25.43	20.70	0.62	2.5	13.07	0.79	10.01	15.1	5	95	0	0	73	21.62	-31.3		1.00	Apr-11
	8.05	9.90	33.73			3.21	1.26			12.77	42.5	-1	101	0	0	161					Feb-16
	8.04	9.98	33.71			3.19	1.31			12.77	42.5	-1	101	0	0	161					Feb-16
50	7.95	9.72	33.29			3.02	1.56			12.76	42.5	-1	101	0	0	161			5.25		Feb-16
50	7.74	9.33	32.29			2.53	2.31			12.75	42.5	-1	101	0	0	161				1.00	Feb-16
	6.69	16.67	42.08	25.44	22.03	1.32	1.2	15.6	0.95	23.57	340.6	1	99	0	0	92	21.12	-24.75			Sep-89
50	6.59	16.45	41.65	23.81	19.59	1.06	1.68	15.58	0.94	22.74	340.6	1	99	0	0	92	20.83	-24.8	5.25		Oct-94
50	6.41	16.04	40.54	20.81	14.75	0.56	2.52	15.57	0.94	19.24	340.6	1	99	0	0	92	20.31	-25.09		1.00	Oct-94
	7.08	16.18	-5.87	-22.76	-32.67	0	1.07	27.15	1.03	21.56	183.9	0	100	0	0	12	20.21	-37.19			Jun-93
50	7.01	16.02	-6.16	-23.45	-33.67	0	1.38	27.16	1.03	18.5	183.9	0	100	0	0	12	19.98	-37.29	5.25		Mar-90
50	6.43	17.37	-7.67	-25.70	-36.19	0	2.1	27.14	1.02		184.0	0	100	0	0	12	19.48	-37.5		4.50	Jan-99
50	6.82	15.65	-6.80	-25.11	-36.07	0	2.1	27.13	1.02	13.02	184.0	0	100	0	0	12	19.48	-37.49		1.00	Jun-93
	6.65	15.71	3.12	-7.91	0.83	2.23	0	18.89		15.8262	452.2	1	99	0	0	73	24.05	-28.05			Dec-04
	5.83	11.39	21.15	35.43	82.80	0.85		9.2	0.88	17.1748	754.9	4	96	0	0	54	20.42	-12.11			Apr-04
	4.11	8.10	14.64	28.90	66.75	1.6		8.79		9.9658	1,862	0	100	0	0	33	19.32	-11.44			Aug-05
	2.68	4.00	16.36	18.84	41.62	0.89		9.48	0.85	13.2166	995.1	2	96	0	1	64	16.12	-19.89			May-05
	2.95	7.76	20.64	16.64	23.49	1.09		10.18		7.0803	764.4	4	94	0	1	74	14.51	-21.09			May-07
	5.40	9.73	16.75	34.20	87.32	1.6	0.73	10.21	0.97	22.77	21,757	4	96	0	0	29	21.49	-13.7			Nov-88
50	5.33	9.59	16.43	33.19	84.86	1.36	0.98	10.2	0.97	22.71	21,757	4	96	0	0	29	21.23	-13.78	5.25		Oct-94
50	5.64	8.98	15.24	29.71	77.94	0.31	1.76	10.19	0.96		21,757	4	96	0	0	29	20.7	-14.08		4.50	Nov-87
50	5.15	9.19	15.62	30.36	78.40	0.79	1.7	10.19	0.96	21.91	21,757	4	96	0	0	29	20.76	-14.1		1.00	Oct-94
50	5.17	9.28	15.80	31.06	80.11	0.72	1.51	10.2	0.97	21.93	21,757	4	96	0	0	29	20.88	-14.08		1.00	Sep-11
	5.43	9.80	16.92	32.78	81.59	1.71	0.6	10.24	0.97	22.76	21,757	4	96	0	0	29	20.7	-14.08			Mar-16
	5.21	9.39	16.04	31.90	82.00	1.08	1.3	10.21	0.97	22.88	21,757	4	96	0	0	29	21.07	-13.94			Jan-03
	5.32	9.61	16.47	33.14	84.60	1.39	0.93	10.21	0.97	22.7	21,757	4	96	0	0	29	21.34	-13.82			Oct-06
	-0.58	5.85	21.48	10.37	27.53	1.95	1.83	12.23	0.92	11.51	310.7	0	100	0	0	93	18.76	-29.14			Jan-03
	-0.40	6.26	22.42	12.67	32.01	1.92	1.1	12.23	0.92	15.52	310.7	0	100	0	0	93	19.34	-28.89			Oct-88
50	-0.50	6.16	22.08	11.92	30.55	1.7	1.32	12.18	0.92	15.23	310.7	0	100	0	0	93	19.28	-28.94	5.25		Oct-94
50	-0.63	5.71	21.20	9.35	25.47	1.61	2.13	12.19	0.92	10.72	310.7	0	100	0	0	93	18.66	-29.21		1.00	Oct-94
	-0.91	-0.07	7.14	8.78	63.27	0	1.54	6.66	-16.02	9.03	229.3	20	66	13	0	199	25.64	-22.09			Dec-07
50	-1.00	-0.25	6.86	7.99	61.04	0	1.81	6.68	-15.27	8.7	229.3	20	66	13	0	199	25.37	-22.16	5.25		Dec-07
50	-1.19	-0.60	6.15	5.64	55.35	0	2.55	6.69	-16.15	7.9	229.3	20	66	13	0	199	24.9	-22.38		1.00	Dec-07

	MARKET		FUND TYPE, CATEGORY & OBJECTIVE		RATINGS				MINIMUMS	
Fund Name	Ticker Symbol	Traded On	Fund Type	Category and (Prospectus Objective)	Overall Rating	Reward Rating	Risk Rating	Recent Up/ Downgrade	Open to New Investors	Min Initial Investment
BlackRock Exchange Portfolio BlackRock Shares	STSEX	NAS CM	Open End	US Equity Large Cap Blend (Growth)	B-	B-	B-	Down	Y	0
BlackRock Focus Growth Fund Institutional Shares	MAFOX	NAS CM	Open End	US Equity Large Cap Growth (Growth)	B	B+	B	Down	Y	2,000,000
BlackRock Focus Growth Fund Investor A Shares	MDFOX	NAS CM	Open End	US Equity Large Cap Growth (Growth)	B+	B	B+	Down	Y	1,000
BlackRock Focus Growth Fund Investor C Shares	MCFOX	NAS CM	Open End	US Equity Large Cap Growth (Growth)	B+	B	B+	Down	Y	1,000
BlackRock GA Disciplined Volatility Equity Fund	BGDVX	NAS CM	Open End	Global Equity Large Cap (Growth & Income)	U	U	U		Y	0
BlackRock GA Enhanced Equity Fund	BGEEX	NAS CM	Open End	Global Equity Large Cap (Growth & Income)	U	U	U		Y	0
BlackRock Global Allocation Fund, Inc. Class K	MKLOX	NAS CM	Open End	Alloc (Multi-Asset Global)	B-	C+	B	Down	Y	5,000,000
BlackRock Global Allocation Fund, Inc. Class R	MRLOX	NAS CM	Open End	Alloc (Multi-Asset Global)	B-	C+	B+	Down	Y	100
BlackRock Global Allocation Fund, Inc. Inst Shares	MALOX	NAS CM	Open End	Alloc (Multi-Asset Global)	B	C+	B+	Up	Y	2,000,000
BlackRock Global Allocation Fund, Inc. Investor A Shares	MDLOX	NAS CM	Open End	Alloc (Multi-Asset Global)	B-	C+	B+	Down	Y	1,000
BlackRock Global Allocation Fund, Inc. Investor B Shares	MBLOX	NAS CM	Open End	Alloc (Multi-Asset Global)	B-	C+	B+	Up		1,000
BlackRock Global Allocation Fund, Inc. Investor C Shares	MCLOX	NAS CM	Open End	Alloc (Multi-Asset Global)	B-	C+	B+	Down	Y	1,000
BlackRock Global Dividend Portfolio Class K	BKBDX	NAS CM	Open End	Global Equity (Equity-Income)	B	B-	A-		Y	5,000,000
BlackRock Global Dividend Portfolio Insitutional Shares	BIBDX	NAS CM	Open End	Global Equity (Equity-Income)	B	B-	A-		Y	2,000,000
BlackRock Global Dividend Portfolio Investor A Shares	BABDX	NAS CM	Open End	Global Equity (Equity-Income)	B	B-	B+		Y	1,000
BlackRock Global Dividend Portfolio Investor C Shares	BCBDX	NAS CM	Open End	Global Equity (Equity-Income)	B	C+	B+		Y	1,000
BlackRock Global Long/Short Credit Fund Class K	BDMKX	NAS CM	Open End	Other Alternative (Growth & Income)	C+	C	B	Up	Y	5,000,000
BlackRock Global Long/Short Credit Fund Inst Shares	BGCIX	NAS CM	Open End	Other Alternative (Growth & Income)	C+	C	B		Y	2,000,000
BlackRock Global Long/Short Credit Fund Investor A Shares	BGCAX	NAS CM	Open End	Other Alternative (Growth & Income)	C+	C	B		Y	1,000
BlackRock Global Long/Short Credit Fund Investor C Shares	BGCCX	NAS CM	Open End	Other Alternative (Growth & Income)	C+	C	B	Up	Y	1,000
BlackRock Global Long/Short Equity Fund Class K	BGCKX	NAS CM	Open End	Market Neutral (Growth & Income)	C+	C	B-	Up	Y	5,000,000
BlackRock Global Long/Short Equity Fund Inst Shares	BDMIX	NAS CM	Open End	Market Neutral (Growth & Income)	C+	C	B-	Up	Y	2,000,000
BlackRock Global Long/Short Equity Fund Investor A Shares	BDMAX	NAS CM	Open End	Market Neutral (Growth & Income)	C	C	C+	Up	Y	1,000
BlackRock Global Long/Short Equity Fund Investor C Shares	BDMCX	NAS CM	Open End	Market Neutral (Growth & Income)	C	C	C+	Up	Y	1,000
BlackRock Health Sciences Opportunities Portfolio Class K	SHSKX	NAS CM	Open End	Healthcare Sector Equity (Health)	B	B-	B		Y	5,000,000
BlackRock Health Sciences Opportunities Portfolio Class R	BHSRX	NAS CM	Open End	Healthcare Sector Equity (Health)	B	B-	B		Y	100
BlackRock Health Sciences Opp Portfolio Inst Shares	SHSSX	NAS CM	Open End	Healthcare Sector Equity (Health)	B	B-	B		Y	2,000,000
BlackRock Health Sciences Opp Portfolio Inv A Shares	SHSAX	NAS CM	Open End	Healthcare Sector Equity (Health)	B	B-	B		Y	1,000
BlackRock Health Sciences Opp Portfolio Inv B Shares	SHSPX	NAS CM	Open End	Healthcare Sector Equity (Health)	B	B-	B	Up		1,000
BlackRock Health Sciences Opp Portfolio Inv C Shares	SHSCX	NAS CM	Open End	Healthcare Sector Equity (Health)	B	B-	B	Up	Y	1,000
BlackRock Health Sciences Opp Portfolio Service Shares	SHISX	NAS CM	Open End	Healthcare Sector Equity (Health)	B	B-	B		Y	5,000
BlackRock Health Sciences Trust	BME	NYSE	Closed End	Healthcare Sector Equity (Health)	B	B-	B	Up	Y	
BlackRock High Equity Income Fund Institutional Shares	BMCIX	NAS CM	Open End	US Equity Large Cap Value (Growth)	B-	B-	B	Up	Y	2,000,000
BlackRock High Equity Income Fund Investor A Shares	BMEAX	NAS CM	Open End	US Equity Large Cap Value (Growth)	B-	B-	B	Up	Y	1,000
BlackRock High Equity Income Fund Investor B Shares	BRMBX	NAS CM	Open End	US Equity Large Cap Value (Growth)	B-	C+	B	Up	Y	1,000
BlackRock High Equity Income Fund Investor C Shares	BMECX	NAS CM	Open End	US Equity Large Cap Value (Growth)	B-	C+	B	Up	Y	1,000
BlackRock High Equity Income Fund Service Shares	BMCSX	NAS CM	Open End	US Equity Large Cap Value (Growth)	B-	B-	B	Up	Y	5,000
BlackRock Impact U.S. Equity Fund Class K	BIRKX	NAS CM	Open End	US Equity Large Cap Blend (Growth & Income)	C	C	B+	Up	Y	5,000,000
BlackRock Impact U.S. Equity Fund Institutional Shares	BIRIX	NAS CM	Open End	US Equity Large Cap Blend (Growth & Income)	C	C+	B	Up	Y	2,000,000
BlackRock Impact U.S. Equity Fund Investor A Shares	BIRAX	NAS CM	Open End	US Equity Large Cap Blend (Growth & Income)	C	C+	B	Up	Y	1,000
BlackRock Impact U.S. Equity Fund Investor C Shares	BIRCX	NAS CM	Open End	US Equity Large Cap Blend (Growth & Income)	C	C+	B	Up	Y	1,000
BlackRock International Dividend Fund Institutional Shares	BISIX	NAS CM	Open End	Global Equity Large Cap (Foreign Stock)	B-	C+	B	Up	Y	2,000,000
BlackRock International Dividend Fund Investor A Shares	BREAX	NAS CM	Open End	Global Equity Large Cap (Foreign Stock)	B-	C+	B	Up	Y	1,000
BlackRock International Dividend Fund Investor B Shares	BREBX	NAS CM	Open End	Global Equity Large Cap (Foreign Stock)	C+	C+	B	Up		1,000
BlackRock International Dividend Fund Investor C Shares	BRECX	NAS CM	Open End	Global Equity Large Cap (Foreign Stock)	C+	C+	B	Up	Y	1,000
BlackRock International Dividend Fund Service Shares	BRESX	NAS CM	Open End	Global Equity Large Cap (Foreign Stock)	B-	C+	B	Up	Y	5,000
BlackRock International Fund Class R Shares	BIFRX	NAS CM	Open End	Global Equity Large Cap (Foreign Stock)	B-	B-	B-	Up	Y	100
BlackRock International Fund Institutional Shares	MAILX	NAS CM	Open End	Global Equity Large Cap (Foreign Stock)	B-	B-	B	Up	Y	2,000,000
BlackRock International Fund Investor A Shares	MDILX	NAS CM	Open End	Global Equity Large Cap (Foreign Stock)	B-	B-	B	Up	Y	1,000
BlackRock International Fund Investor C Shares	MCILX	NAS CM	Open End	Global Equity Large Cap (Foreign Stock)	B-	C+	B-	Up	Y	1,000
BlackRock Large Cap Focus Growth Fund Institutional Shares	MALHX	NAS CM	Open End	US Equity Large Cap Growth (Growth)	B+	A-	B	Down	Y	2,000,000
BlackRock Large Cap Focus Growth Fund Investor A Shares	MDLHX	NAS CM	Open End	US Equity Large Cap Growth (Growth)	B+	B+	B	Down	Y	1,000

★Expanded analysis of this fund is included in Section II.

	TOTAL RETURNS					PERFORMANCE				ASSETS		ASSET ALLOCATION & TURNOVER					BULL & BEAR		FEES		
Min Additional Investment	3-Month Total Return	6-Month Total Return	1-Year Total Return	3-Year Total Return	5-Year Total Return	Dividend Yield (TTM)	Expense Ratio	3-Yr Std Deviation	3-Year Beta	NAV	Total Assets (MIL)	%Cash	%Stocks	%Bonds	%Other	Turnover Ratio	Last Bull Market Total Return	Last Bear Market Total Return	Front End Fee (%)	Back End Fee (%)	Inception Date
	4.92	8.88	15.23	26.34	82.48	1.72	0.62	9.32	0.87	1050.08	173.0	1	99	0	0	0	21.28	-15.14			Dec-76
	5.98	10.96	29.97	43.46	118.16	0	1.03	11.89	1.02	4.08	131.7	6	95	0	-4	63	21.27	-21.24			Mar-00
50	6.17	10.93	30.27	42.52	115.29	0	1.28	11.72	1.01	3.79	131.7	6	95	0	-4	63	21.33	-21.42	5.25		Mar-00
50	6.11	10.74	29.41	39.19	107.58	0	2.03	11.85	1.02	3.13	131.7	6	95	0	-4	63	20.13	-21.34		1.00	Mar-00
	3.93	6.98					0.5			10.48	5.3										Jun-17
	5.02	12.01					0.5			10.98	5.6										Jun-17
	2.46	5.55	13.70	17.01	38.79	1.38	0.71	6.37	0.59	19.8	38,826	7	53	32	5	131	11.67	-13.61			Jun-16
	2.29	5.19	12.94	14.75	34.44	0.65	1.39	6.39	0.59	18.76	38,829	7	53	32	5	131	11.19	-13.8			Jan-03
	2.46	5.52	13.60	16.85	38.60	1.25	0.8	6.36	0.59	19.81	38,826	7	53	32	5	131	11.67	-13.61			Feb-89
50	2.39	5.37	13.31	15.92	36.79	0.87	1.07	6.35	0.59	19.7	38,826	7	53	32	5	131	11.5	-13.7	5.25		Oct-94
50	2.48	4.41	12.36	12.51	31.20	0	1.9	6.35	0.59		38,829	7	53	32	5	131	10.97	-14		4.50	Feb-89
50	2.15	4.97	12.45	13.32	31.71	0.23	1.81	6.38	0.59	17.78	38,829	7	53	32	5	131	10.94	-13.97		1.00	Oct-94
	3.74	5.59	19.94	29.75	61.52	2.22	0.68	9.59	0.78	13.43	3,004	1	99	0	0	18	13.64	-9.67			Jun-16
	3.73	5.56	19.80	29.64	61.39	2.25	0.75	9.6	0.78	13.41	3,004	1	99	0	0	18	13.64	-9.67			Apr-08
50	3.68	5.45	19.53	28.57	59.29	1.99	1.02	9.61	0.78	13.37	3,004	1	99	0	0	18	13.49	-9.83	5.25		Apr-08
50	3.46	5.04	18.58	25.70	53.36	1.3	1.77	9.59	0.78	13.29	3,004	1	99	0	0	18	12.99	-10.1		1.00	Apr-08
	0.66	1.73	3.64	6.27	11.43	0	1.03	2.11	0.69	10.36	4,120	29	1	55	8	229	2.41				Mar-16
	0.58	1.65	3.46	6.09	11.24	0	1.1	2.1	1.94	10.35	4,120	29	1	55	8	229	2.41				Sep-11
50	0.52	1.50	3.21	5.29	9.70	0	1.37	2.06	1.27	10.34	4,120	29	1	55	8	229	2.21		4.00		Sep-11
50	0.39	1.19	2.51	2.97	5.75	0	2.11	2.07	1.26	10.17	4,120	29	1	55	8	229	1.9			1.00	Sep-11
	2.36	6.30	12.93	3.99	25.22	0	1.85	4.76	-19.62	12.14	701.6	90	9	0	1	34					Mar-16
	2.27	6.31	12.84	3.82	25.01	0	1.91	4.77	-20.44	12.12	701.6	90	9	0	1	34					Dec-12
50	2.12	6.10	12.57	3.01	23.36	0	2.16	4.7	-19.89	12	701.6	90	9	0	1	34			5.25		Dec-12
50	2.02	5.73	11.74	0.74	18.86	0	2.91	4.8	-19.59	11.61	701.6	90	9	0	1	34				1.00	Dec-12
	1.64	4.99	25.30	30.11	146.14	0	0.83	13.9	1.04	56.18	6,137	3	95	0	1	39	17.33	-12.6			Jun-16
	1.47	4.63	24.41	28.14	140.93	0	1.52	13.89	1.04	52.59	6,137	3	95	0	1	39	17.04	-12.69			Sep-11
	1.62	4.93	25.15	30.44	148.15	0	0.91	13.89	1.04	56.15	6,137	3	95	0	1	39	17.55	-12.49			Oct-00
50	1.56	4.80	24.81	29.37	144.73	0	1.19	13.89	1.04	53.64	6,137	3	95	0	1	39	17.33	-12.6	5.25		Dec-99
50	2.90	3.57	23.58	25.83	135.29	0	1.99	13.88	1.04		6,137	3	95	0	1	39	16.74	-12.86		4.50	Oct-00
50	1.36	4.42	23.90	26.60	135.99	0	1.91	13.89	1.04	47.29	6,137	3	95	0	1	39	16.8	-12.84		1.00	Oct-00
	1.53	4.78	24.79	29.35	144.62	0	1.18	13.89	1.04	53.83	6,137	3	95	0	1	39	17.33	-12.61			Jan-05
	2.16	5.07	22.68	28.73	123.25	0.19		12.6		35.8123	325.2	2	97	0	0	59	16.2	-12.29			Mar-05
	3.04	6.68	17.52	23.06	99.39	0.83	0.86	11	0.95	27.58	819.1	1	95	0	4	154	22.78	-24.74			May-98
50	2.96	6.53	17.21	21.75	95.68	0.33	1.11	11.01	0.95	23.72	819.3	1	95	0	4	154	22.44	-24.91	5.25		May-98
50	3.68	5.81	16.02	19.03	88.35	0	1.86	10.99	0.95		819.3	1	95	0	4	154	21.88	-25.13		4.50	May-98
50	2.79	6.15	16.35	19.07	88.43	0	1.86	11	0.95	16.16	819.1	1	95	0	4	154	21.92	-25.13		1.00	May-98
	2.99	6.53	17.18	21.76	95.66	0.27	1.11	11.01	0.95	25.1	819.3	1	95	0	4	154	22.45	-24.89			May-98
	6.59	11.96	21.53			1.25	0.5			12.92	49.7	1	99	0	0	82					Mar-16
	6.58	11.94	21.61			1.24	0.55			12.92	49.7	1	99	0	0	82					Oct-15
50	6.44	11.75	21.22			1.09	0.8			12.89	49.7	1	99	0	0	82			5.25		Oct-15
50	6.27	11.35	20.31			0.82	1.55			12.82	49.7	1	99	0	0	82				1.00	Oct-15
	1.94	4.80	16.71	16.81	29.06	4.13	0.85	11.09	0.83	31.12	423.4	1	98	0	1	130	15.7	-25.11			Sep-97
50	1.87	4.65	16.39	15.73	27.06	4.01	1.1	11.1	0.83	29.14	423.4	1	98	0	1	130	15.52	-25.22	5.25		Sep-97
50	1.38	2.31	15.32	11.18	21.19	1.33	1.85	11.1	0.83		423.4	1	98	0	1	130	14.96	-25.43		4.50	Sep-97
50	1.66	4.25	15.49	13.15	22.39	3.44	1.85	11.1	0.83	25.7	423.4	1	98	0	1	130	15.01	-25.46		1.00	Sep-97
	1.86	4.66	16.38	15.78	26.96	3.81	1.1	11.1	0.83	29.59	423.4	1	98	0	1	130	15.35	-25.23			Sep-97
	5.42	12.30	31.01	25.58	46.32	0.74	1.68	12.8	0.95	17.42	611.9	7	93	0	0	84	12.41	-24.44			Aug-11
	5.58	12.65	31.86	28.12	51.41	1.26	1	12.8	0.95	17.76	611.9	7	93	0	0	84	12.8	-24.27			Oct-98
50	5.46	12.48	31.31	26.67	48.54	1.03	1.38	12.77	0.95	17.39	611.9	7	93	0	0	84	12.65	-24.43	5.25		Oct-98
50	5.24	11.99	30.20	23.01	41.48	0.12	2.29	12.79	0.95	16.25	611.9	7	93	0	0	84	11.98	-24.68		1.00	Oct-98
	7.42	12.94	29.71	42.40	122.70	0.5	0.84	11.49	1.03	14.26	942.9	1	99	0	0	79	29.69	-20.51			Dec-99
50	7.34	12.71	29.35	41.11	119.45	0.23	1.13	11.44	1.03	13.4	942.9	1	99	0	0	79	29.37	-20.58	5.25		Dec-99

Fund Name	Ticker Symbol	Traded On	Fund Type	Category and (Prospectus Objective)	Overall Rating	Reward Rating	Risk Rating	Recent Up/ Downgrade	Open to New Investors	Min Initial Investment
	MARKET		FUND TYPE, CATEGORY & OBJECTIVE		RATINGS				MINIMUMS	
BlackRock Large Cap Focus Growth Fund Investor B Shares	MBLHX	NAS CM	Open End	US Equity Large Cap Growth (Growth)	B+	B+	B	Down		1,000
BlackRock Large Cap Focus Growth Fund Investor C Shares	MCLHX	NAS CM	Open End	US Equity Large Cap Growth (Growth)	B+	B+	B	Down	Y	1,000
BlackRock Large Cap Focus Growth Fund R Shares	MRLHX	NAS CM	Open End	US Equity Large Cap Growth (Growth)	B+	B+	B	Down	Y	100
BlackRock Large Cap Focus Growth Fund Service Shares	MSLHX	NAS CM	Open End	US Equity Large Cap Growth (Growth)	B+	A-	B	Down	Y	5,000
BlackRock Latin America Fund Institutional Shares	MALTX	NAS CM	Open End	Latin America Equity (Foreign Stock)	C	C	C		Y	2,000,000
BlackRock Latin America Fund Investor A Shares	MDLTX	NAS CM	Open End	Latin America Equity (Foreign Stock)	C	C	C		Y	1,000
BlackRock Latin America Fund Investor B Shares	MBLTX	NAS CM	Open End	Latin America Equity (Foreign Stock)	C	C-	C			1,000
BlackRock Latin America Fund Investor C Shares	MCLTX	NAS CM	Open End	Latin America Equity (Foreign Stock)	C	C	C		Y	1,000
BlackRock LifePath Dynamic 2060 Fund Class K Shares	LPDKX	NAS CM	Open End	Target Date 2046+ (Asset Alloc)	U	U	U		Y	5,000,000
BlackRock LifePath Dynamic 2060 Fund Class R Shares	LPDRX	NAS CM	Open End	Target Date 2046+ (Asset Alloc)	U	U	U		Y	100
BlackRock LifePath Dynamic 2060 Fund Institutional Shares	LPDIX	NAS CM	Open End	Target Date 2046+ (Asset Alloc)	U	U	U		Y	2,000,000
BlackRock LifePath Dynamic 2060 Fund Investor A Shares	LPDAX	NAS CM	Open End	Target Date 2046+ (Asset Alloc)	U	U	U		Y	1,000
BlackRock LifePath Dynamic 2060 Fund Investor C Shares	LPDCX	NAS CM	Open End	Target Date 2046+ (Asset Alloc)	U	U	U		Y	1,000
Blackrock Lifepath Smart Beta 2060 Fund Inst Shares	BIEGX	NAS CM	Open End	Target Date 2046+ (Asset Alloc)	U	U	U		Y	2,000,000
Blackrock Lifepath Smart Beta 2060 Fund Investor A Shares	BAPAX	NAS CM	Open End	Target Date 2046+ (Asset Alloc)	U	U	U		Y	1,000
Blackrock Lifepath Smart Beta 2060 Fund K Shares	BKJKX	NAS CM	Open End	Target Date 2046+ (Asset Alloc)	U	U	U		Y	5,000,000
Blackrock Lifepath Smart Beta 2060 Fund R Shares	BAPRX	NAS CM	Open End	Target Date 2046+ (Asset Alloc)	U	U	U		Y	100
BlackRock LifePath® Dynamic 2020 Fund Class K Shares	LPSCX	NAS CM	Open End	Target Date 2000-2020 (Asset Alloc)	B	C+	B+	Up	Y	5,000,000
BlackRock LifePath® Dynamic 2020 Fund Class R Shares	LPRMX	NAS CM	Open End	Target Date 2000-2020 (Asset Alloc)	B	C+	B+	Up	Y	100
BlackRock LifePath® Dynamic 2020 Fund Institutional Shares	STLCX	NAS CM	Open End	Target Date 2000-2020 (Asset Alloc)	B	C+	B+	Up	Y	2,000,000
BlackRock LifePath® Dynamic 2020 Fund Investor A Shares	LPRCX	NAS CM	Open End	Target Date 2000-2020 (Asset Alloc)	B-	C+	B	Up	Y	1,000
BlackRock LifePath® Dynamic 2020 Fund Investor C Shares	LPCMX	NAS CM	Open End	Target Date 2000-2020 (Asset Alloc)	B-	C+	B+	Up	Y	1,000
BlackRock LifePath® Dynamic 2025 Fund Class K Shares	LPBKX	NAS CM	Open End	Target Date 2021-2045 (Asset Alloc)	B-	C+	B	Up	Y	5,000,000
BlackRock LifePath® Dynamic 2025 Fund Class R Shares	LPBRX	NAS CM	Open End	Target Date 2021-2045 (Asset Alloc)	B	C+	B+	Up	Y	100
BlackRock LifePath® Dynamic 2025 Fund Institutional Shares	LPBIX	NAS CM	Open End	Target Date 2021-2045 (Asset Alloc)	B-	C+	B	Up	Y	2,000,000
BlackRock LifePath® Dynamic 2025 Fund Investor A Shares	LPBAX	NAS CM	Open End	Target Date 2021-2045 (Asset Alloc)	B-	C+	B	Up	Y	1,000
BlackRock LifePath® Dynamic 2025 Fund Investor C Shares	LPBCX	NAS CM	Open End	Target Date 2021-2045 (Asset Alloc)	B-	C+	B	Up	Y	1,000
BlackRock LifePath® Dynamic 2030 Fund Class K Shares	LPSDX	NAS CM	Open End	Target Date 2021-2045 (Asset Alloc)	B-	C+	B	Down	Y	5,000,000
BlackRock LifePath® Dynamic 2030 Fund Class R Shares	LPRNX	NAS CM	Open End	Target Date 2021-2045 (Asset Alloc)	B-	C+	B	Down	Y	100
BlackRock LifePath® Dynamic 2030 Fund Institutional Shares	STLDX	NAS CM	Open End	Target Date 2021-2045 (Asset Alloc)	B-	C+	B	Down	Y	2,000,000
BlackRock LifePath® Dynamic 2030 Fund Investor A Shares	LPRDX	NAS CM	Open End	Target Date 2021-2045 (Asset Alloc)	B-	C+	B	Down	Y	1,000
BlackRock LifePath® Dynamic 2030 Fund Investor C Shares	LPCNX	NAS CM	Open End	Target Date 2021-2045 (Asset Alloc)	B-	C+	B-	Down	Y	1,000
BlackRock LifePath® Dynamic 2035 Fund Class K Shares	LPJKX	NAS CM	Open End	Target Date 2021-2045 (Asset Alloc)	B-	B-	B-	Down	Y	5,000,000
BlackRock LifePath® Dynamic 2035 Fund Class R Shares	LPJRX	NAS CM	Open End	Target Date 2021-2045 (Asset Alloc)	B-	C+	B-	Down	Y	100
BlackRock LifePath® Dynamic 2035 Fund Institutional Shares	LPJIX	NAS CM	Open End	Target Date 2021-2045 (Asset Alloc)	B-	B-	B-	Down	Y	2,000,000
BlackRock LifePath® Dynamic 2035 Fund Investor A Shares	LPJAX	NAS CM	Open End	Target Date 2021-2045 (Asset Alloc)	B-	B-	B-	Down	Y	1,000
BlackRock LifePath® Dynamic 2035 Fund Investor C Shares	LPJCX	NAS CM	Open End	Target Date 2021-2045 (Asset Alloc)	B-	C+	B-	Down	Y	1,000
BlackRock LifePath® Dynamic 2040 Fund Class K Shares	LPSFX	NAS CM	Open End	Target Date 2021-2045 (Asset Alloc)	B-	B-	B-	Down	Y	5,000,000
BlackRock LifePath® Dynamic 2040 Fund Class R Shares	LPRKX	NAS CM	Open End	Target Date 2021-2045 (Asset Alloc)	B-	B-	B-	Down	Y	100
BlackRock LifePath® Dynamic 2040 Fund Institutional Shares	STLEX	NAS CM	Open End	Target Date 2021-2045 (Asset Alloc)	B-	B-	B-	Down	Y	2,000,000
BlackRock LifePath® Dynamic 2040 Fund Investor A Shares	LPREX	NAS CM	Open End	Target Date 2021-2045 (Asset Alloc)	B-	B-	B-	Down	Y	1,000
BlackRock LifePath® Dynamic 2040 Fund Investor C Shares	LPCKX	NAS CM	Open End	Target Date 2021-2045 (Asset Alloc)	B-	C+	B-	Down	Y	1,000
BlackRock LifePath® Dynamic 2045 Fund Class K Shares	LPHKX	NAS CM	Open End	Target Date 2021-2045 (Asset Alloc)	B-	B-	B-	Down	Y	5,000,000
BlackRock LifePath® Dynamic 2045 Fund Class R Shares	LPHRX	NAS CM	Open End	Target Date 2021-2045 (Asset Alloc)	B-	B-	B-	Down	Y	100
BlackRock LifePath® Dynamic 2045 Fund Institutional Shares	LPHIX	NAS CM	Open End	Target Date 2021-2045 (Asset Alloc)	B-	B-	B-	Down	Y	2,000,000
BlackRock LifePath® Dynamic 2045 Fund Investor A Shares	LPHAX	NAS CM	Open End	Target Date 2021-2045 (Asset Alloc)	B-	B-	B-	Down	Y	1,000
BlackRock LifePath® Dynamic 2045 Fund Investor C Shares	LPHCX	NAS CM	Open End	Target Date 2021-2045 (Asset Alloc)	B-	B-	B-	Down	Y	1,000
BlackRock LifePath® Dynamic 2050 Fund Class K Shares	LPSGX	NAS CM	Open End	Target Date 2046+ (Asset Alloc)	B-	B-	B-	Down	Y	5,000,000
BlackRock LifePath® Dynamic 2050 Fund Class R Shares	LPRPX	NAS CM	Open End	Target Date 2046+ (Asset Alloc)	B-	B-	B-	Down	Y	100
BlackRock LifePath® Dynamic 2050 Fund Institutional Shares	STLFX	NAS CM	Open End	Target Date 2046+ (Asset Alloc)	B-	B-	B-	Down	Y	2,000,000
BlackRock LifePath® Dynamic 2050 Fund Investor A Shares	LPRFX	NAS CM	Open End	Target Date 2046+ (Asset Alloc)	B-	B-	B-	Down	Y	1,000
BlackRock LifePath® Dynamic 2050 Porfolio Inv C Shares	LPCPX	NAS CM	Open End	Target Date 2046+ (Asset Alloc)	B-	B-	C+	Up	Y	1,000

★Expanded analysis of this fund is included in Section II.

	TOTAL RETURNS					PERFORMANCE				ASSETS		ASSET ALLOCATION & TURNOVER					BULL & BEAR		FEES		
Min Additional Investment	3-Month Total Return	6-Month Total Return	1-Year Total Return	3-Year Total Return	5-Year Total Return	Dividend Yield (TTM)	Expense Ratio	3-Yr Std Deviation	3-Year Beta	NAV	Total Assets (MIL)	%Cash	%Stocks	%Bonds	%Other	Turnover Ratio	Last Bull Market Total Return	Last Bear Market Total Return	Front End Fee (%)	Back End Fee (%)	Inception Date
50	8.32	11.49	27.69	37.56	111.54	0	1.95	11.44	1.03		942.9	1	99	0	0	79	28.75	-20.88		4.50	Dec-99
50	7.08	12.28	28.25	37.65	110.77	0	1.95	11.48	1.03	10.86	942.9	1	99	0	0	79	28.91	-20.89		1.00	Dec-99
	7.25	12.59	29.04	40.00	116.72	0.03	1.38	11.43	1.03	12.32	942.9	1	99	0	0	79	29.05	-20.64			Jan-03
	7.28	12.74	29.28	41.06	119.35	0.22	1.13	11.44	1.03	14.2	942.9	1	99	0	0	79	29.4	-20.53			Oct-06
	-1.54	15.24	28.19	11.07	-12.18	1.18	1.33	22.76	0.89	49.95	176.7	1	99	0	0	58	16.86	-28.94			Oct-94
50	-1.63	15.06	27.79	10.03	-13.47	0.93	1.65	22.76	0.89	49.36	176.7	1	99	0	0	58	16.71	-29.04	5.25		Sep-91
50	-1.68	13.56	25.49	5.31	-19.19	0	3.01	22.72	0.89		176.7	1	99	0	0	58	16.12	-29.29		4.50	Sep-91
50	-1.80	14.60	26.74	7.25	-17.03	0.3	2.51	22.74	0.89	45.11	176.7	1	99	0	0	58	16.16	-29.26		1.00	Oct-94
	5.85	10.93					0.45			11.02	2.2	7	91	2	1						May-17
	5.67	10.56					1.1			11.02	2.2	7	91	2	1						May-17
	5.81	10.83					0.65			11.02	2.2	7	91	2	1						May-17
50	5.73	10.70					0.9			11.02	2.2	7	91	2	1				5.25		May-17
50	4.95	9.58					1.7			11.02	2.2	7	91	2	1					1.00	May-17
	5.64	10.58					0.32			10.85	1.1	1	98	1	0						May-17
50	5.59	10.42					0.57			10.85	1.1	1	98	1	0				5.25		May-17
	5.66	10.60					0.22			10.85	1.1	1	98	1	0						May-17
	5.55	10.38					0.81			10.85	1.1	1	98	1	0						May-17
	3.22	6.64	13.60	18.75	39.35	1.53	0.46	5.35	0.48	15.94	370.7	-2	42	59	0	50	13.79	-9.73			May-08
	3.04	6.34	12.88	16.34	34.21	0.89	1.11	5.37	0.48	15.92	370.7	-2	42	59	0	50	13.24	-9.98			May-10
	3.21	6.57	13.37	17.91	37.43	1.31	0.66	5.36	0.48	16.01	370.7	-2	42	59	0	50	13.57	-9.84			Mar-94
50	3.08	6.43	13.04	16.97	35.64	1.23	0.91	5.36	0.48	14.75	370.7	-2	42	59	0	50	13.46	-9.95	5.25		Apr-01
50	2.91	6.02	12.15	14.29	30.56	0.4	1.71	5.36	0.48	15.79	370.7	-2	42	59	0	50	12.89	-10.17		1.00	May-10
	3.86	7.66	15.74	21.21	44.50	1.55	0.45	6.4	0.59	13.49	66.2	7	49	43	1	54	15.54	-11.81			Jun-10
	3.76	7.33	15.02	18.77	40.19	0.97	1.1	6.37	0.59	13.49	66.2	7	49	43	1	54	14.91	-12.12			Jun-10
	3.80	7.55	15.44	20.32	43.52	1.34	0.65	6.38	0.59	13.52	66.2	7	49	43	1	54	15.21	-11.94			Jun-10
50	3.80	7.50	15.21	19.46	41.74	1.13	0.9	6.36	0.59	13.5	66.2	7	49	43	1	54	15.19	-12.08	5.25		Jun-10
50	3.59	7.08	14.39	16.76	36.44	0.42	1.7	6.36	0.59	13.44	66.2	7	49	43	1	54	14.57	-12.3		1.00	Jun-10
	4.52	8.69	17.95	23.87	51.70	1.66	0.46	7.37	0.69	14.24	394.0	4	63	33	1	61	16.99	-13.44			May-08
	4.29	8.29	17.16	21.21	45.89	1.05	1.11	7.33	0.68	14.12	394.0	4	63	33	1	61	16.31	-13.77			May-10
	4.38	8.49	17.66	22.89	49.52	1.45	0.66	7.35	0.69	14.26	394.0	4	63	33	1	61	16.7	-13.6			Mar-94
50	4.41	8.37	17.42	22.03	47.66	1.31	0.91	7.38	0.69	13.72	394.0	4	63	33	1	61	16.46	-13.66	5.25		Apr-01
50	4.17	7.98	16.47	19.18	42.05	0.57	1.71	7.36	0.69	14.01	394.0	4	63	33	1	61	15.97	-13.88		1.00	May-10
	5.14	9.58	19.76	25.89	57.63	1.66	0.46	8.31	0.78	14.68	55.9	11	71	17	0	76	18.35	-14.97			Jun-10
	4.97	9.24	19.07	23.34	51.15	1.13	1.11	8.3	0.78	14.46	55.9	11	71	17	0	76	17.79	-15.3			Jun-10
	5.08	9.55	19.51	24.99	54.74	1.48	0.66	8.32	0.78	14.48	55.9	11	71	17	0	76	18.12	-15.05			Jun-10
50	5.01	9.41	19.29	24.12	52.99	1.29	0.91	8.32	0.79	14.46	55.9	11	71	17	0	76	18.01	-15.19	5.25		Jun-10
50	4.85	8.99	18.40	21.29	47.16	0.62	1.71	8.33	0.79	14.33	55.9	11	71	17	0	76	17.44	-15.49		1.00	Jun-10
	5.65	10.47	21.66	28.07	62.27	1.75	0.46	9.15	0.87	18.13	315.1	9	82	8	0	77	19.62	-16.41			May-08
	5.49	10.12	20.85	25.39	56.18	1.19	1.11	9.14	0.86	17.89	315.1	9	82	8	0	77	18.95	-16.75			May-10
	5.62	10.34	21.43	27.10	60.01	1.55	0.66	9.12	0.86	18.04	315.1	9	82	8	0	77	19.28	-16.57			Mar-94
50	5.56	10.23	21.17	26.21	58.03	1.5	0.91	9.15	0.87	16.53	315.1	9	82	8	0	77	19.09	-16.64	5.25		Apr-01
50	4.75	9.18	19.51	22.54	51.24	0.68	1.71	9.12	0.86	17.77	315.1	9	82	8	0	77	18.55	-16.93		1.00	May-10
	5.84	10.86	22.57	29.07	66.13	1.79	0.44	9.6	0.91	15.57	36.2	13	84	2	0	75	20.89	-17.74			Jun-10
	5.74	10.53	21.80	26.35	59.92	1.27	1.09	9.55	0.9	15.37	36.2	13	84	2	0	75	20.22	-18			Jun-10
	5.84	10.74	22.29	28.08	63.66	1.6	0.64	9.55	0.9	15.41	36.2	13	84	2	0	75	20.55	-17.81			Jun-10
50	5.77	10.67	22.04	27.17	61.79	1.41	0.89	9.55	0.9	15.4	36.2	13	84	2	0	75	20.38	-17.86	5.25		Jun-10
50	5.54	10.20	21.09	24.24	55.57	0.74	1.69	9.54	0.9	15.2	36.2	13	84	2	0	75	19.78	-18.11		1.00	Jun-10
	6.08	11.19	23.06	29.59	68.91	1.85	0.44	9.7	0.92	21.59	119.7	11	87	2	0	70	21.84	-18.93			Jun-08
	5.91	10.81	22.24	26.83	62.60	1.29	1.09	9.7	0.92	21.42	119.7	11	87	2	0	70	21.25	-19.21			May-10
	6.04	11.11	22.85	28.60	66.45	1.64	0.64	9.71	0.92	21.54	119.7	11	87	2	0	70	21.62	-19.03			Jun-08
50	5.95	10.90	22.47	27.65	64.45	1.46	0.89	9.69	0.92	21.47	119.7	11	87	2	0	70	21.41	-19.1	5.25		Jun-08
50	5.08	9.78	20.75	23.91	57.16	0.83	1.69	9.7	0.92	21.26	119.7	11	87	2	0	70	20.87	-19.36		1.00	May-10

	MARKET			FUND TYPE, CATEGORY & OBJECTIVE	RATINGS					MINIMUMS
Fund Name	Ticker Symbol	Traded On	Fund Type	Category and (Prospectus Objective)	Overall Rating	Reward Rating	Risk Rating	Recent Up/ Downgrade	Open to New Investors	Min Initial Investment
BlackRock LifePath® Dynamic 2055 Fund Class K Shares	LPVKX	NAS CM	Open End	Target Date 2046+ (Asset Alloc)	B-	B-	B-	Down	Y	5,000,000
BlackRock LifePath® Dynamic 2055 Fund Class R Shares	LPVRX	NAS CM	Open End	Target Date 2046+ (Asset Alloc)	B-	B-	B-	Down	Y	100
BlackRock LifePath® Dynamic 2055 Fund Institutional Shares	LPVIX	NAS CM	Open End	Target Date 2046+ (Asset Alloc)	B-	B-	B-	Down	Y	2,000,000
BlackRock LifePath® Dynamic 2055 Fund Investor A Shares	LPVAX	NAS CM	Open End	Target Date 2046+ (Asset Alloc)	B-	B-	B-	Down	Y	1,000
BlackRock LifePath® Dynamic 2055 Fund Investor C Shares	LPVCX	NAS CM	Open End	Target Date 2046+ (Asset Alloc)	B-	B-	C+	Up	Y	1,000
BlackRock LifePath® Dynamic Retirement Fund Class K Shares	LPSAX	NAS CM	Open End	Target Date 2000-2020 (Asset Alloc)	B	C+	A-	Up	Y	5,000,000
BlackRock LifePath® Dynamic Retirement Fund Class R Shares	LPRRX	NAS CM	Open End	Target Date 2000-2020 (Asset Alloc)	B	C+	B+	Up	Y	100
BlackRock LifePath® Dynamic Retmnt Fund Inst Shares	STLAX	NAS CM	Open End	Target Date 2000-2020 (Asset Alloc)	B	C+	A-	Up	Y	2,000,000
BlackRock LifePath® Dynamic Retmnt Fund Inv A Shares	LPRAX	NAS CM	Open End	Target Date 2000-2020 (Asset Alloc)	B	C+	B+	Up	Y	1,000
BlackRock LifePath® Dynamic Retmnt Fund Inv C Shares	LPCRX	NAS CM	Open End	Target Date 2000-2020 (Asset Alloc)	B-	C+	B+	Up	Y	1,000
BlackRock LifePath® Index 2020 Fund Class K Shares	LIMKX	NAS CM	Open End	Target Date 2000-2020 (Asset Alloc)	B	C+	A-	Up	Y	5,000,000
BlackRock LifePath® Index 2020 Fund Institutional Shares	LIQIX	NAS CM	Open End	Target Date 2000-2020 (Asset Alloc)	B-	C+	B	Up	Y	2,000,000
BlackRock LifePath® Index 2020 Fund Investor A Shares	LIQAX	NAS CM	Open End	Target Date 2000-2020 (Asset Alloc)	B-	C+	B	Up	Y	1,000
BlackRock LifePath® Index 2025 Fund Class K Shares	LIBKX	NAS CM	Open End	Target Date 2021-2045 (Asset Alloc)	B-	C+	B	Up	Y	5,000,000
BlackRock LifePath® Index 2025 Fund Institutional Shares	LIBIX	NAS CM	Open End	Target Date 2021-2045 (Asset Alloc)	B-	C+	B	Up	Y	2,000,000
BlackRock LifePath® Index 2025 Fund Investor A Shares	LILAX	NAS CM	Open End	Target Date 2021-2045 (Asset Alloc)	B-	C+	B	Up	Y	1,000
BlackRock LifePath® Index 2030 Fund Class K Shares	LINKX	NAS CM	Open End	Target Date 2021-2045 (Asset Alloc)	B-	C+	B	Down	Y	5,000,000
BlackRock LifePath® Index 2030 Fund Institutional Shares	LINIX	NAS CM	Open End	Target Date 2021-2045 (Asset Alloc)	B-	C+	B	Down	Y	2,000,000
BlackRock LifePath® Index 2030 Fund Investor A Shares	LINAX	NAS CM	Open End	Target Date 2021-2045 (Asset Alloc)	B-	C+	B	Down	Y	1,000
BlackRock LifePath® Index 2035 Fund Class K Shares	LIJKX	NAS CM	Open End	Target Date 2021-2045 (Asset Alloc)	B-	B-	B	Down	Y	5,000,000
BlackRock LifePath® Index 2035 Fund Institutional Shares	LIJIX	NAS CM	Open End	Target Date 2021-2045 (Asset Alloc)	B-	B-	B	Down	Y	2,000,000
BlackRock LifePath® Index 2035 Fund Investor A Shares	LIJAX	NAS CM	Open End	Target Date 2021-2045 (Asset Alloc)	B	C+	B+	Up	Y	1,000
BlackRock LifePath® Index 2040 Fund Class K Shares	LIKKX	NAS CM	Open End	Target Date 2021-2045 (Asset Alloc)	B-	B-	B-	Down	Y	5,000,000
BlackRock LifePath® Index 2040 Fund Institutional Shares	LIKIX	NAS CM	Open End	Target Date 2021-2045 (Asset Alloc)	B-	B-	B-	Down	Y	2,000,000
BlackRock LifePath® Index 2040 Fund Investor A Shares	LIKAX	NAS CM	Open End	Target Date 2021-2045 (Asset Alloc)	B-	B-	B-	Down	Y	1,000
BlackRock LifePath® Index 2045 Fund Class K Shares	LIHKX	NAS CM	Open End	Target Date 2021-2045 (Asset Alloc)	B-	B-	B-	Down	Y	5,000,000
BlackRock LifePath® Index 2045 Fund Institutional Shares	LIHIX	NAS CM	Open End	Target Date 2021-2045 (Asset Alloc)	B-	B-	B-	Down	Y	2,000,000
BlackRock LifePath® Index 2045 Fund Investor A Shares	LIHAX	NAS CM	Open End	Target Date 2021-2045 (Asset Alloc)	B-	B-	B-	Down	Y	1,000
BlackRock LifePath® Index 2050 Fund Class K Shares	LIPKX	NAS CM	Open End	Target Date 2046+ (Asset Alloc)	B-	B-	B-	Down	Y	5,000,000
BlackRock LifePath® Index 2050 Fund Institutional Shares	LIPIX	NAS CM	Open End	Target Date 2046+ (Asset Alloc)	B-	B-	B-	Down	Y	2,000,000
BlackRock LifePath® Index 2050 Fund Investor A Shares	LIPAX	NAS CM	Open End	Target Date 2046+ (Asset Alloc)	B-	B-	B-	Down	Y	1,000
BlackRock LifePath® Index 2055 Fund Class K Shares	LIVKX	NAS CM	Open End	Target Date 2046+ (Asset Alloc)	B-	B-	B-	Down	Y	5,000,000
BlackRock LifePath® Index 2055 Fund Institutional Shares	LIVIX	NAS CM	Open End	Target Date 2046+ (Asset Alloc)	B-	B-	B-	Down	Y	2,000,000
BlackRock LifePath® Index 2055 Fund Investor A Shares	LIVAX	NAS CM	Open End	Target Date 2046+ (Asset Alloc)	B-	B-	B-	Down	Y	1,000
BlackRock LifePath® Index 2060 Fund Class K	LIZKX	NAS CM	Open End	Target Date 2046+ (Asset Alloc)	C-	C	B+	Up	Y	5,000,000
BlackRock LifePath® Index 2060 Fund Institutional Shares	LIZIX	NAS CM	Open End	Target Date 2046+ (Asset Alloc)	C-	C	B+	Up	Y	2,000,000
BlackRock LifePath® Index 2060 Fund Investor A Shares	LIZAX	NAS CM	Open End	Target Date 2046+ (Asset Alloc)	C-	C	B+	Up	Y	1,000
BlackRock LifePath® Index Retirement Fund Class K Shares	LIRKX	NAS CM	Open End	Target Date 2000-2020 (Asset Alloc)	B	C+	A-	Up	Y	5,000,000
BlackRock LifePath® Index Retmnt Fund Inst Shares	LIRIX	NAS CM	Open End	Target Date 2000-2020 (Asset Alloc)	B	C+	A-	Up	Y	2,000,000
BlackRock LifePath® Index Retmnt Fund Inv A Shares	LIRAX	NAS CM	Open End	Target Date 2000-2020 (Asset Alloc)	B	C+	A-	Up	Y	1,000
BlackRock LifePath® Smart Beta 2020 Fund Class K	BIPCX	NAS CM	Open End	Target Date 2000-2020 (Asset Alloc)	B	C+	B+	Up	Y	5,000,000
BlackRock LifePath® Smart Beta 2020 Fund Class R Shares	BRPCX	NAS CM	Open End	Target Date 2000-2020 (Asset Alloc)	B-	C+	B	Up	Y	100
BlackRock LifePath® Smart Beta 2020 Fund Inst Shares	BLBIX	NAS CM	Open End	Target Date 2000-2020 (Asset Alloc)	B-	C+	B	Up	Y	2,000,000
BlackRock LifePath® Smart Beta 2020 Fund Investor A Shares	BAPCX	NAS CM	Open End	Target Date 2000-2020 (Asset Alloc)	B-	C+	B	Up	Y	1,000
BlackRock LifePath® Smart Beta 2025 Fund Class K	BIPDX	NAS CM	Open End	Target Date 2021-2045 (Asset Alloc)	B-	C+	B	Down	Y	5,000,000
BlackRock LifePath® Smart Beta 2025 Fund Class R Shares	BRPDX	NAS CM	Open End	Target Date 2021-2045 (Asset Alloc)	B-	C+	B	Down	Y	100
BlackRock LifePath® Smart Beta 2025 Fund Inst Shares	BLCIX	NAS CM	Open End	Target Date 2021-2045 (Asset Alloc)	B-	C+	B	Down	Y	2,000,000
BlackRock LifePath® Smart Beta 2025 Fund Investor A Shares	BAPDX	NAS CM	Open End	Target Date 2021-2045 (Asset Alloc)	B-	C+	B	Down	Y	1,000
BlackRock LifePath® Smart Beta 2030 Fund Class K	BIPEX	NAS CM	Open End	Target Date 2021-2045 (Asset Alloc)	B-	C+	B-	Down	Y	5,000,000
BlackRock LifePath® Smart Beta 2030 Fund Class R Shares	BRPEX	NAS CM	Open End	Target Date 2021-2045 (Asset Alloc)	B-	C+	B-	Down	Y	100
BlackRock LifePath® Smart Beta 2030 Fund Inst Shares	BLEIX	NAS CM	Open End	Target Date 2021-2045 (Asset Alloc)	B-	C+	B-	Down	Y	2,000,000
BlackRock LifePath® Smart Beta 2030 Fund Investor A Shares	BAPEX	NAS CM	Open End	Target Date 2021-2045 (Asset Alloc)	B-	C+	B-	Down	Y	1,000

★ Expanded analysis of this fund is included in Section II.

Min Additional Investment	3-Month Total Return	6-Month Total Return	1-Year Total Return	3-Year Total Return	5-Year Total Return	Dividend Yield (TTM)	Expense Ratio	3-Yr Std Deviation	3-Year Beta	NAV	Total Assets (MIL)	%Cash	%Stocks	%Bonds	%Other	Turnover Ratio	Last Bull Market Total Return	Last Bear Market Total Return	Front End Fee (%)	Back End Fee (%)	Inception Date
	TOTAL RETURNS					PERFORMANCE				ASSETS		ASSET ALLOCATION & TURNOVER					BULL & BEAR		FEES		
	5.98	11.09	22.79	29.23	70.90	1.73	0.43	9.68	0.92	16.06	19.1	13	84	2	1	80	22.39	-19.43			Jun-10
	5.82	10.77	21.95	26.45	63.95	1.23	1.08	9.72	0.92	15.8	19.1	13	84	2	1	80	21.77	-19.71			Jun-10
	5.93	10.98	22.57	28.27	68.00	1.56	0.63	9.69	0.92	15.86	19.1	13	84	2	1	80	22.22	-19.58			Jun-10
50	5.88	10.88	22.23	27.30	65.97	1.37	0.88	9.71	0.92	15.81	19.1	13	84	2	1	80	21.95	-19.65	5.25		Jun-10
50	5.05	9.78	20.59	23.65	58.73	0.76	1.68	9.69	0.92	15.63	19.1	13	84	2	1	80	21.4	-19.95		1.00	Jun-10
	2.77	5.91	11.86	17.04	32.11	1.45	0.46	4.34	0.34	10.96	139.2	-3	35	67	0	37	10.35	-5.11			May-08
	2.61	5.59	11.11	14.55	27.12	0.86	1.11	4.32	0.34	10.91	139.2	-3	35	67	0	37	9.82	-5.52			May-10
	2.70	5.77	11.67	16.13	30.23	1.22	0.66	4.32	0.34	11	139.2	-3	35	67	0	37	10.13	-5.29			Mar-94
50	2.69	5.67	11.39	15.37	28.72	1.2	0.91	4.35	0.32	9.72	139.2	-3	35	67	0	37	9.97	-5.36	5.25		Apr-01
50	2.54	5.26	10.47	12.75	23.76	0.34	1.71	4.34	0.34	10.87	139.2	-3	35	67	0	37	9.4	-5.61		1.00	May-10
	2.93	5.87	12.33	18.45	41.65	1.91	0.12	5.24	0.47	12.73	2,371	1	48	51	0	14	13.76				May-11
	2.92	5.75	12.28	18.26	41.31	1.86	0.17	5.23	0.47	12.73	2,371	1	48	51	0	14	13.74				May-11
50	2.85	5.62	12.02	17.45	39.64	1.64	0.42	5.25	0.47	12.71	2,371	1	48	51	0	14	13.5				May-11
	3.48	6.80	14.43	21.20	48.37	1.87	0.12	6.24	0.57	13.31	2,409	1	60	39	0	16	15.29				May-11
	3.47	6.86	14.37	21.01	48.05	1.82	0.17	6.22	0.57	13.31	2,409	1	60	39	0	16	15.39				May-11
50	3.32	6.64	14.02	20.08	46.23	1.6	0.42	6.22	0.57	13.29	2,409	1	60	39	0	16	15.17				May-11
	3.99	7.78	16.36	23.53	54.29	1.89	0.12	7.23	0.67	13.61	3,041	1	71	29	0	19	16.76				May-11
	3.97	7.75	16.29	23.32	53.86	1.84	0.17	7.25	0.68	13.62	3,041	1	71	29	0	19	16.86				May-11
50	3.90	7.61	16.00	22.44	52.14	1.61	0.42	7.22	0.67	13.62	3,041	1	71	29	0	19	16.6				May-11
	4.59	8.69	18.29	25.86	60.23	1.86	0.12	8.11	0.76	14.07	2,041	1	80	19	0	22	18.03				May-11
	4.50	8.65	18.21	25.64	59.83	1.82	0.17	8.15	0.77	14.08	2,041	1	80	19	0	22	18.02				May-11
50	4.44	8.46	17.89	24.62	57.66	1.6	0.42	8.17	0.77	14.04	2,041	1	80	19	0	22	17.77				May-11
	4.99	9.45	19.94	27.86	65.54	1.88	0.12	9	0.85	14.39	2,257	1	89	10	0	26	19.26				May-11
	4.98	9.43	19.89	27.65	65.14	1.84	0.17	8.99	0.85	14.39	2,257	1	89	10	0	26	19.37				May-11
50	4.84	9.31	19.55	26.62	63.02	1.62	0.42	9	0.85	14.36	2,257	1	89	10	0	26	19.11				May-11
	5.23	9.97	21.06	29.19	70.02	1.85	0.12	9.41	0.89	14.76	1,333	1	96	3	0	26	20.26				May-11
	5.22	9.95	21.02	29.01	69.53	1.81	0.17	9.42	0.89	14.75	1,333	1	96	3	0	26	20.24				May-11
50	5.24	9.83	20.76	28.06	67.52	1.6	0.42	9.41	0.89	14.73	1,333	1	96	3	0	26	20.12				May-11
	5.41	10.18	21.43	29.66	72.97	1.86	0.12	9.51	0.9	14.99	1,201	1	98	1	0	28	21.48				May-11
	5.39	10.15	21.37	29.45	72.56	1.82	0.17	9.51	0.9	14.99	1,201	1	98	1	0	28	21.59				May-11
50	5.34	10.04	21.13	28.53	70.43	1.61	0.42	9.49	0.9	14.96	1,201	1	98	1	0	28	21.33				May-11
	5.40	10.20	21.51	29.78	75.51	1.83	0.12	9.53	0.9	15.28	549.4	1	98	1	0	2	22.07				May-11
	5.32	10.10	21.37	29.50	74.99	1.79	0.17	9.54	0.9	15.27	549.4	1	98	1	0	2	22.04				May-11
50	5.26	9.99	21.05	28.59	72.82	1.58	0.42	9.53	0.9	15.24	549.4	1	98	1	0	2	21.79				May-11
	5.42	10.24	21.51			1.55	0.12			13.51	64.3	1	97	1	0	71					Feb-16
	5.33	10.13	21.37			1.52	0.17			13.5	64.3	1	97	1	0	71					Feb-16
50	5.27	10.03	21.06			1.35	0.42			13.48	64.3	1	97	1	0	71					Feb-16
	2.47	5.03	10.74	16.57	33.77	1.88	0.11	4.21	0.39	12.25	1,210	1	40	59	0	13	10.33				May-11
	2.46	5.09	10.68	16.36	33.55	1.83	0.16	4.22	0.41	12.26	1,210	1	40	59	0	13	10.42				May-11
50	2.39	4.96	10.42	15.56	31.94	1.6	0.41	4.22	0.4	12.25	1,210	1	40	59	0	13	10.18				May-11
	1.94	4.59	12.87	18.44	42.00	2.03	0.22	5.58	0.5	11	26.0	-1	55	45	0	30	15.03	-11.93			Apr-07
	1.76	4.26	12.21	16.41	37.78	1.42	0.81	5.64	0.51	10.84	26.0	-1	55	45	0	30	14.67	-12.25			Apr-07
	1.92	4.57	12.72	18.10	41.28	1.82	0.32	5.69	0.51	11.02	26.0	-1	55	45	0	30	15.03	-11.93			Nov-12
50	1.87	4.45	12.45	17.24	39.58	1.71	0.57	5.64	0.51	10.93	26.0	-1	55	45	0	30	14.84	-12.17	5.25		Apr-07
	3.08	6.25	15.62	21.11	49.22	1.77	0.21	6.72	0.62	11.12	31.0	0	68	32	0	36	16.26	-13.21			Apr-07
	2.93	5.95	14.98	19.02	44.78	1.28	0.8	6.72	0.62	10.97	31.0	0	68	32	0	36	15.77	-13.54			Apr-07
	3.08	6.15	15.52	20.69	48.43	1.7	0.31	6.7	0.62	11.1	31.0	0	68	32	0	36	16.26	-13.21			Nov-12
50	3.06	6.16	15.25	19.98	46.65	1.47	0.56	6.72	0.62	11.05	31.0	0	68	32	0	36	16	-13.45	5.25		Apr-07
	2.94	6.55	16.31	22.04	52.16	1.76	0.21	7.7	0.72	10.65	25.0	0	79	21	0	34	17.74	-15.16			Apr-07
	2.89	6.25	15.75	20.06	47.84	1.16	0.8	7.74	0.72	10.53	25.0	0	79	21	0	34	17.4	-15.5			Apr-07
	2.92	6.54	16.30	21.85	51.57	1.69	0.31	7.74	0.72	10.64	25.0	0	79	21	0	34	17.74	-15.16			Nov-12
50	2.83	6.38	15.98	20.90	49.62	1.45	0.56	7.75	0.72	10.56	25.0	0	79	21	0	34	17.61	-15.43	5.25		Apr-07

	MARKET		FUND TYPE, CATEGORY & OBJECTIVE		RATINGS					MINIMUMS
Fund Name	Ticker Symbol	Traded On	Fund Type	Category and (Prospectus Objective)	Overall Rating	Reward Rating	Risk Rating	Recent Up/ Downgrade	Open to New Investors	Min Initial Investment
BlackRock LifePath® Smart Beta 2035 Fund Class K	BIPGX	NAS CM	Open End	Target Date 2021-2045 (Asset Alloc)	B-	B-	B-	Down	Y	5,000,000
BlackRock LifePath® Smart Beta 2035 Fund Class R Shares	BRPGX	NAS CM	Open End	Target Date 2021-2045 (Asset Alloc)	B-	C+	B-	Down	Y	100
BlackRock LifePath® Smart Beta 2035 Fund Inst Shares	BLGIX	NAS CM	Open End	Target Date 2021-2045 (Asset Alloc)	B-	B-	B-	Down	Y	2,000,000
BlackRock LifePath® Smart Beta 2035 Fund Investor A Shares	BAPGX	NAS CM	Open End	Target Date 2021-2045 (Asset Alloc)	B-	C+	B-	Down	Y	1,000
BlackRock LifePath® Smart Beta 2040 Fund Class K	BIPHX	NAS CM	Open End	Target Date 2021-2045 (Asset Alloc)	B-	B-	B-	Down	Y	5,000,000
BlackRock LifePath® Smart Beta 2040 Fund Class R Shares	BRPHX	NAS CM	Open End	Target Date 2021-2045 (Asset Alloc)	C+	B-	C+	Down	Y	100
BlackRock LifePath® Smart Beta 2040 Fund Inst Shares	BLHIX	NAS CM	Open End	Target Date 2021-2045 (Asset Alloc)	B-	B-	B-	Down	Y	2,000,000
BlackRock LifePath® Smart Beta 2040 Fund Investor A Shares	BAPHX	NAS CM	Open End	Target Date 2021-2045 (Asset Alloc)	B-	B-	B-	Down	Y	1,000
BlackRock LifePath® Smart Beta 2045 Fund Class K	BIPJX	NAS CM	Open End	Target Date 2021-2045 (Asset Alloc)	B-	B-	C+	Down	Y	5,000,000
BlackRock LifePath® Smart Beta 2045 Fund Class R Shares	BRPJX	NAS CM	Open End	Target Date 2021-2045 (Asset Alloc)	C+	B-	C+	Down	Y	100
BlackRock LifePath® Smart Beta 2045 Fund Inst Shares	BLJIX	NAS CM	Open End	Target Date 2021-2045 (Asset Alloc)	B-	B-	C+	Down	Y	2,000,000
BlackRock LifePath® Smart Beta 2045 Fund Investor A Shares	BAPJX	NAS CM	Open End	Target Date 2021-2045 (Asset Alloc)	B-	B-	C+	Down	Y	1,000
BlackRock LifePath® Smart Beta 2050 Fund Class K	BIPKX	NAS CM	Open End	Target Date 2046+ (Asset Alloc)	B-	B-	C+	Down	Y	5,000,000
BlackRock LifePath® Smart Beta 2050 Fund Class R Shares	BRPKX	NAS CM	Open End	Target Date 2046+ (Asset Alloc)	C+	B-	C+	Down	Y	100
BlackRock LifePath® Smart Beta 2050 Fund Inst Shares	BLKIX	NAS CM	Open End	Target Date 2046+ (Asset Alloc)	B-	B-	C+	Down	Y	2,000,000
BlackRock LifePath® Smart Beta 2050 Fund Investor A Shares	BAPKX	NAS CM	Open End	Target Date 2046+ (Asset Alloc)	B-	B-	C+	Down	Y	1,000
BlackRock LifePath® Smart Beta 2055 Fund Class K Shares	BIPLX	NAS CM	Open End	Target Date 2046+ (Asset Alloc)	B-	B-	B-	Down	Y	5,000,000
BlackRock LifePath® Smart Beta 2055 Fund Class R Shares	BRPLX	NAS CM	Open End	Target Date 2046+ (Asset Alloc)	B-	B-	C+	Down	Y	100
BlackRock LifePath® Smart Beta 2055 Fund Inst Shares	BLLIX	NAS CM	Open End	Target Date 2046+ (Asset Alloc)	B-	B-	C+	Down	Y	2,000,000
BlackRock LifePath® Smart Beta 2055 Fund Investor A Shares	BAPLX	NAS CM	Open End	Target Date 2046+ (Asset Alloc)	B-	B-	C+	Down	Y	1,000
BlackRock LifePath® Smart Beta Retirement Fund Class K	BIPBX	NAS CM	Open End	Target Date 2000-2020 (Asset Alloc)	B-	C+	B	Up	Y	5,000,000
BlackRock LifePath® Smart Beta Retmnt Fund Cls R Shares	BRPBX	NAS CM	Open End	Target Date 2000-2020 (Asset Alloc)	C+	C+	B-		Y	100
BlackRock LifePath® Smart Beta Retmnt Fund Inst Shares	BLAIX	NAS CM	Open End	Target Date 2000-2020 (Asset Alloc)	B-	C+	B+	Up	Y	2,000,000
BlackRock LifePath® Smart Beta Retmnt Fund Inv A Shares	BAPBX	NAS CM	Open End	Target Date 2000-2020 (Asset Alloc)	B-	C+	B	Up	Y	1,000
BlackRock Long-Horizon Equity Fund Class R Shares	MREGX	NAS CM	Open End	Global Equity (World Stock)	B-	C+	B	Up	Y	100
BlackRock Long-Horizon Equity Fund Institutional Shares	MAEGX	NAS CM	Open End	Global Equity (World Stock)	B-	C+	B	Up	Y	2,000,000
BlackRock Long-Horizon Equity Fund Investor A Shares	MDEGX	NAS CM	Open End	Global Equity (World Stock)	B-	C+	B	Up	Y	1,000
BlackRock Long-Horizon Equity Fund Investor B Shares	MBEGX	NAS CM	Open End	Global Equity (World Stock)	C+	C+	B-	Up		1,000
BlackRock Long-Horizon Equity Fund Investor C Shares	MCEGX	NAS CM	Open End	Global Equity (World Stock)	C+	C+	B-	Up	Y	1,000
BlackRock Managed Income Fund Class K Shares	BLDRX	NAS CM	Open End	Cautious Alloc (Income)	B-	C+	B	Up	Y	5,000,000
BlackRock Managed Income Fund Institutional Shares	BLDIX	NAS CM	Open End	Cautious Alloc (Income)	B-	C+	B	Up	Y	2,000,000
BlackRock Managed Income Fund Investor A Shares	BLADX	NAS CM	Open End	Cautious Alloc (Income)	B-	C	B	Up	Y	1,000
BlackRock Managed Income Fund Investor C Shares	BMICX	NAS CM	Open End	Cautious Alloc (Income)	B-	C	B	Up	Y	1,000
BlackRock Mid Cap Dividend Fund Institutional Shares	MARFX	NAS CM	Open End	US Equity Mid Cap (Growth)	B-	B-	B	Up	Y	2,000,000
BlackRock Mid Cap Dividend Fund Investor A Shares	MDRFX	NAS CM	Open End	US Equity Mid Cap (Growth)	B-	B-	B	Up	Y	1,000
BlackRock Mid Cap Dividend Fund Investor C Shares	MCRFX	NAS CM	Open End	US Equity Mid Cap (Growth)	B-	C+	B-	Up	Y	1,000
BlackRock Mid Cap Dividend Fund R Shares	MRRFX	NAS CM	Open End	US Equity Mid Cap (Growth)	B-	C+	B-	Up	Y	100
BlackRock Mid-Cap Growth Equity Portfolio Class K	BMGKX	NAS CM	Open End	US Equity Mid Cap (Growth)	A-	A	B	Up	Y	5,000,000
BlackRock Mid-Cap Growth Equity Portfolio Class R	BMRRX	NAS CM	Open End	US Equity Mid Cap (Growth)	B+	A-	B	Up	Y	100
BlackRock Mid-Cap Growth Equity Portfolio Inst Shares	CMGIX	NAS CM	Open End	US Equity Mid Cap (Growth)	A-	A	B	Up	Y	2,000,000
BlackRock Mid-Cap Growth Equity Portfolio Inv A Shares	BMGAX	NAS CM	Open End	US Equity Mid Cap (Growth)	A-	A-	B	Up	Y	1,000
BlackRock Mid-Cap Growth Equity Portfolio Inv B Shares	BMGBX	NAS CM	Open End	US Equity Mid Cap (Growth)	B+	A-	B	Up		1,000
BlackRock Mid-Cap Growth Equity Portfolio Inv C Shares	BMGCX	NAS CM	Open End	US Equity Mid Cap (Growth)	B+	A-	B	Up	Y	1,000
BlackRock Mid-Cap Growth Equity Portfolio Service Shares	CMGSX	NAS CM	Open End	US Equity Mid Cap (Growth)	A-	A	B	Up	Y	5,000
BlackRock Multi-Asset Income Portfolio Class K	BKMIX	NAS CM	Open End	Moderate Alloc (Income)	B-	C+	B	Up	Y	5,000,000
BlackRock Multi-Asset Income Portfolio Inst Shares	BIICX	NAS CM	Open End	Moderate Alloc (Income)	B-	C+	B	Up	Y	2,000,000
BlackRock Multi-Asset Income Portfolio Investor A Shares	BAICX	NAS CM	Open End	Moderate Alloc (Income)	B-	C+	B	Up	Y	1,000
BlackRock Multi-Asset Income Portfolio Investor C Shares	BCICX	NAS CM	Open End	Moderate Alloc (Income)	B-	C	B	Up	Y	1,000
BlackRock Multi-Mgr Alternative Strat Fund Inst Shares	BMMNX	NAS CM	Open End	Multialternative (Growth & Income)	C+	C	B	Up	Y	2,000,000
BlackRock Multi-Mgr Alternative Strat Fund Inv A Shares	BMMAX	NAS CM	Open End	Multialternative (Growth & Income)	C	C	C+		Y	1,000
BlackRock Multi-Mgr Alternative Strat Fund Inv C Shares	BMMCX	NAS CM	Open End	Multialternative (Growth & Income)	C	C-	C	Up	Y	1,000
BlackRock Natural Resources Trust Institutional Shares	MAGRX	NAS CM	Open End	Energy Sector Equity (Natl Res)	C	C	C	Up	Y	2,000,000

★Expanded analysis of this fund is included in Section II.

	TOTAL RETURNS					PERFORMANCE				ASSETS		ASSET ALLOCATION & TURNOVER					BULL & BEAR		FEES		
Min Additional Investment	3-Month Total Return	6-Month Total Return	1-Year Total Return	3-Year Total Return	5-Year Total Return	Dividend Yield (TTM)	Expense Ratio	3-Yr Std Deviation	3-Year Beta	NAV	Total Assets (MIL)	%Cash	%Stocks	%Bonds	%Other	Turnover Ratio	Last Bull Market Total Return	Last Bear Market Total Return	Front End Fee (%)	Back End Fee (%)	Inception Date
	4.18	8.19	18.54	23.76	56.79	1.52	0.21	8.7	0.82	11.5	20.5	0	88	11	0	37	20.63	-18.23			Apr-07
	3.99	7.89	17.80	21.60	52.32	1.04	0.8	8.72	0.83	11.31	20.5	0	88	11	0	37	20.15	-18.47			Apr-07
	4.17	8.19	18.53	23.50	56.22	1.43	0.31	8.68	0.82	11.5	20.5	0	88	11	0	37	20.63	-18.23			Nov-12
50	4.03	7.99	18.05	22.45	54.17	1.21	0.56	8.69	0.82	11.41	20.5	0	88	11	0	37	20.26	-18.35	5.25		Apr-07
	4.40	8.86	18.64	24.48	60.11	1.36	0.21	9.62	0.92	11.22	16.2	1	95	4	0	35	20.73	-18.02			Apr-07
	5.04	9.28	18.65	23.23	56.42	0.79	0.8	9.58	0.91	11.08	16.2	1	95	4	0	35	20.22	-18.31			Apr-07
	4.48	8.83	18.49	24.19	59.31	1.27	0.31	9.58	0.91	11.22	16.2	1	95	4	0	35	20.73	-18.02			Nov-12
50	4.40	8.70	18.21	23.38	57.47	1.06	0.56	9.57	0.91	11.12	16.2	1	95	4	0	35	20.32	-18.24	5.25		Apr-07
	5.32	10.09	20.48	26.59	64.01	1.18	0.22	9.91	0.94	12.59	13.8	1	97	2	0	32	20.77	-17.98			Apr-07
	5.18	9.89	19.88	24.44	59.44	0.67	0.81	9.97	0.95	12.29	13.8	1	97	2	0	32	20.15	-18.19			Apr-07
	5.31	10.08	20.38	26.15	63.19	1.11	0.32	9.9	0.94	12.57	13.8	1	97	2	0	32	20.77	-17.98			Nov-12
50	5.24	9.90	20.02	25.27	61.12	0.91	0.57	9.98	0.95	12.39	13.8	1	97	2	0	32	20.49	-18.17	5.25		Apr-07
	5.42	10.35	20.64	26.69	66.26	1.25	0.22	10.07	0.96	11.76	15.0	1	98	1	0	36	20.77	-18.23			Apr-07
	5.27	10.09	19.83	24.43	61.33	0.75	0.81	10.07	0.96	11.56	15.0	1	98	1	0	36	20.2	-18.35			Apr-07
	5.40	10.24	20.29	26.22	65.26	1.18	0.32	10.08	0.96	11.73	15.0	1	98	1	0	36	20.77	-18.23			Nov-12
50	5.28	10.07	20.00	25.29	63.09	0.98	0.57	10.1	0.96	11.6	15.0	1	98	1	0	36	20.42	-18.28	5.25		Apr-07
	5.43	10.34	20.48	26.96		1.14	0.22	9.86	0.94	12.27	5.2	1	98	1	0	38					Feb-13
	5.29	10.06	19.74	24.81		0.76	0.81	9.86	0.94	12.14	5.2	1	98	1	0	38					Feb-13
	5.34	10.24	20.27	26.59		1.05	0.32	9.86	0.94	12.25	5.2	1	98	1	0	38					Feb-13
50	5.26	10.09	19.94	25.53		0.91	0.57	9.87	0.94	12.22	5.2	1	98	1	0	38			5.25		Feb-13
	2.13	4.27	11.38	16.19	36.01	2.18	0.21	4.57	0.29	10.73	15.9	-1	47	55	0	34	14.13	-10.94			Apr-07
	2.04	4.00	10.81	14.28	32.29	1.54	0.8	4.58	0.27	10.68	15.9	-1	47	55	0	34	13.65	-11.2			Apr-07
	1.99	4.12	11.22	15.92	35.54	2.14	0.31	4.56	0.27	10.72	15.9	-1	47	55	0	34	14.13	-10.94			Nov-12
50	2.07	4.13	10.95	15.08	33.85	1.85	0.56	4.59	0.28	10.66	15.9	-1	47	55	0	34	13.79	-11.1	5.25		Apr-07
	5.25	9.58	24.02	13.21	47.33	0.05	1.66	10.87	0.94	13.1	292.7	2	96	0	2	80	16.14	-19.71			Feb-07
	5.41	9.93	24.79	15.56	52.55	0.76	0.97	10.86	0.94	13.04	292.7	2	96	0	2	80	16.62	-19.49			Nov-05
50	5.39	9.75	24.48	14.65	50.40	0.51	1.23	10.86	0.94	13.04	292.7	2	96	0	2	80	16.39	-19.58	5.25		Nov-05
50	5.58	8.59	23.23	11.20	43.76	0	2.22	10.86	0.94		292.7	2	96	0	2	80	15.87	-19.88		4.50	Nov-05
50	5.14	9.34	23.44	12.02	44.75	0	2	10.85	0.94	12.95	292.7	2	96	0	2	80	15.81	-19.82		1.00	Nov-05
	1.18	2.48	5.44	14.43	14.73	3.34	0.44	3.06	0.79	10.05	168.5	1	11	83	0	74	5.09	15.72			Oct-07
	1.07	2.35	5.29	14.23	14.19	3.3	0.49	3.07	0.79	10.02	168.5	1	11	83	0	74	5.04	15.7			Oct-07
50	1.01	2.22	5.02	13.12	12.34	3.05	0.74	3.04	0.79	10.02	168.5	1	11	83	0	74	4.76	15.5	4.00		Oct-07
50	0.82	1.94	4.23	10.99	9.08	2.3	1.49	3.04	0.78	10.03	168.5	1	11	83	0	74	4.48	15.24		1.00	Oct-16
	4.90	7.77	8.81	23.36	81.24	1	0.85	12.62	1.15	18.3	443.4	1	99	0	0	93	26.67	-21.82			Feb-95
50	4.83	7.63	8.54	22.33	78.56	0.74	1.1	12.64	1.15	17.47	443.4	1	99	0	0	93	26.31	-21.87	5.25		Feb-95
50	4.68	7.28	7.73	19.46	71.60	0.3	1.85	12.62	1.15	13.95	443.4	1	99	0	0	93	25.69	-22.25		1.00	Feb-95
	4.73	7.47	8.19	21.19	75.85	0.56	1.35	12.63	1.15	15.16	443.4	1	99	0	0	93	26.02	-22.03			Feb-03
	5.46	11.29	34.81	47.89	136.83	0	0.98	12.35	0.99	22.58	1,021	1	97	0	1	59	25.85	-21.05			Mar-16
	5.31	10.91	33.89	45.06	129.83	0	1.65	12.36	0.99	19.36	1,021	1	97	0	1	59	25.37	-21.16			Oct-06
	5.41	11.19	34.66	47.55	136.28	0	1.11	12.35	0.99	22.54	1,021	1	97	0	1	59	25.85	-21.05			Dec-96
50	5.34	11.04	34.20	46.10	132.75	0	1.39	12.37	0.99	19.63	1,021	1	97	0	1	59	25.61	-21.19	5.25		Dec-96
50	6.09	9.94	33.04	42.73	124.49	0	2.16	12.34	0.99		1,021	1	97	0	1	59	24.99	-21.41		4.50	Dec-96
50	5.12	10.59	33.22	42.87	124.20	0	2.14	12.34	0.99	15.51	1,021	1	97	0	1	59	24.97	-21.39		1.00	Dec-96
	5.35	11.08	34.39	46.41	132.29	0	1.26	12.4	1	20.5	1,021	1	97	0	1	59	25.45	-21.18			Dec-96
	1.59	3.42	9.07	14.63	32.28		0.52	4.2	0.16	11.07	16,374	1	30	57	2	75	12.69	-6.99			Feb-17
	1.67	3.39	9.02	14.57	32.22	4.55	0.57	4.21	0.16	11.08	16,374	1	30	57	2	75	12.69	-6.98			Apr-08
50	1.61	3.26	8.75	13.72	30.58	4.3	0.82	4.18	0.16	11.07	16,374	1	30	57	2	75	12.36	-7.07	5.25		Apr-08
50	1.32	2.88	7.96	11.10	25.66	3.57	1.57	4.2	0.18	11.05	16,374	1	30	57	2	75	12.06	-7.45		1.00	Apr-08
	0.71	1.43	1.85	1.61		1.74	2.01	2.32	4.65	9.86	100.3	50	10	30	3	177					Aug-14
50	0.72	1.34	1.55	0.78		1.51	2.3	2.35	4.34	9.8	100.3	50	10	30	3	177			5.25		Aug-14
50	0.51	0.93	0.83	-1.38		0.34	3	2.33	4.52	9.71	100.3	50	10	30	3	177				1.00	Aug-14
	8.92	21.61	8.16	3.16	6.91	0.88	0.85	19.39	0.84	32.83	237.2	2	98	0	0	102	21.34	-30.69			Oct-88

Fund Name	MARKET Ticker Symbol	Traded On	FUND TYPE, CATEGORY & OBJECTIVE Fund Type	Category and (Prospectus Objective)	RATINGS Overall Rating	Reward Rating	Risk Rating	Recent Up/ Downgrade	MINIMUMS Open to New Investors	Min Initial Investment
BlackRock Natural Resources Trust Investor A Shares	MDGRX	NAS CM	Open End	Energy Sector Equity (Natl Res)	C	C	C	Up	Y	1,000
BlackRock Natural Resources Trust Investor B Shares	MBGRX	NAS CM	Open End	Energy Sector Equity (Natl Res)	C	C	C	Up		1,000
BlackRock Natural Resources Trust Investor C Shares	MCGRX	NAS CM	Open End	Energy Sector Equity (Natl Res)	C	C	C	Up	Y	1,000
BlackRock Real Estate Securities Fund Institutional Shares	BIREX	NAS CM	Open End	Real Estate Sector Equity (Real Estate)	B	C+	B+	Up	Y	2,000,000
BlackRock Real Estate Securities Fund Investor A Shares	BAREX	NAS CM	Open End	Real Estate Sector Equity (Real Estate)	B-	C+	B+		Y	1,000
BlackRock Real Estate Securities Fund Investor C Shares	BCREX	NAS CM	Open End	Real Estate Sector Equity (Real Estate)	B-	C+	B		Y	1,000
BlackRock Resources & Commodities Strategy Trust	BCX	NYSE	Closed End	Natl Resources Sec Equity (Growth & Income)	C	C+	C	Up	Y	
BlackRock Science & Technology Opp Portfolio Cls R Shares	BGSRX	NAS CM	Open End	Technology Sector Equity (Technology)	A	A+	B+	Up	Y	100
BlackRock Science & Technology Opp Portfolio Inst Shares	BGSIX	NAS CM	Open End	Technology Sector Equity (Technology)	A	A+	B+	Up	Y	2,000,000
BlackRock Science & Technology Opp Portfolio Inv A Shares	BGSAX	NAS CM	Open End	Technology Sector Equity (Technology)	A	A+	B+	Up	Y	1,000
BlackRock Science & Technology Opp Portfolio Inv C Shares	BGSCX	NAS CM	Open End	Technology Sector Equity (Technology)	A	A+	B+	Up	Y	1,000
BlackRock Science & Technology Opp Port Serv Shares	BSTSX	NAS CM	Open End	Technology Sector Equity (Technology)	A	A+	B+	Up	Y	5,000
BlackRock Science and Technology Trust	BST	NYSE	Closed End	Technology Sector Equity (Technology)	B	B-	B	Up	Y	
BlackRock Small Cap Growth Fund II Class R Shares	MRUSX	NAS CM	Open End	US Equity Small Cap (Small Company)	B	B	B	Up	Y	100
BlackRock Small Cap Growth Fund II Institutional Shares	MASWX	NAS CM	Open End	US Equity Small Cap (Small Company)	B	B	B	Up	Y	2,000,000
BlackRock Small Cap Growth Fund II Investor A Shares	MDSWX	NAS CM	Open End	US Equity Small Cap (Small Company)	B	B	B	Up	Y	1,000
BlackRock Small Cap Growth Fund II Investor C Shares	MCSWX	NAS CM	Open End	US Equity Small Cap (Small Company)	B	B	B	Up	Y	1,000
BlackRock Tactical Opportunities Fund Class K Shares	PBAKX	NAS CM	Open End	Moderate Alloc (Asset Alloc)	C+	C	B	Up	Y	5,000,000
BlackRock Tactical Opportunities Fund Institutional Shares	PBAIX	NAS CM	Open End	Moderate Alloc (Asset Alloc)	C+	C	B	Up	Y	2,000,000
BlackRock Tactical Opportunities Fund Investor A Shares	PCBAX	NAS CM	Open End	Moderate Alloc (Asset Alloc)	C+	C	B	Up	Y	1,000
BlackRock Tactical Opportunities Fund Investor B Shares	CBIBX	NAS CM	Open End	Moderate Alloc (Asset Alloc)	C+	C	B-	Up		1,000
BlackRock Tactical Opportunities Fund Investor C Shares	BRBCX	NAS CM	Open End	Moderate Alloc (Asset Alloc)	C+	C	B	Up	Y	1,000
BlackRock Tactical Opportunities Fund Service Shares	PCBSX	NAS CM	Open End	Moderate Alloc (Asset Alloc)	C+	C	B	Up	Y	5,000
BlackRock Total Emerging Markets Fund Institutional	BEEIX	NAS CM	Open End	Emerging Markets Equity (Growth & Income)	C+	C+	C+		Y	2,000,000
BlackRock Total Emerging Markets Fund Investor A	BEEAX	NAS CM	Open End	Emerging Markets Equity (Growth & Income)	C+	C+	C+		Y	1,000
BlackRock Total Emerging Markets Fund Investor C	BEECX	NAS CM	Open End	Emerging Markets Equity (Growth & Income)	C	C	C+	Down	Y	1,000
BlackRock Total Factor Fund Class K	BSTKX	NAS CM	Open End	Multialternative (Multi-Asset Global)	B-	C+	B	Down	Y	5,000,000
BlackRock Total Factor Fund Institutional Shares	BSTIX	NAS CM	Open End	Multialternative (Multi-Asset Global)	B-	C+	B	Down	Y	2,000,000
BlackRock Total Factor Fund Investor A Shares	BSTAX	NAS CM	Open End	Multialternative (Multi-Asset Global)	B-	C+	B	Up	Y	1,000
BlackRock Total Factor Fund Investor C Shares	BSTCX	NAS CM	Open End	Multialternative (Multi-Asset Global)	B-	C+	B	Up	Y	1,000
BlackRock Utilities, Infrastructure & Power Opp Trust	BUI	NYSE	Closed End	Utilities Sector Equity (Equity-Income)	C+	C+	C+	Up	Y	
Blackstone Alternative Multi-Strategy Fund Class D	BXMDX	NAS CM	Open End	Multialternative (Growth)	B-	C	A-	Up	Y	25,000
Blackstone Alternative Multi-Strategy Fund Class I	BXMIX	NAS CM	Open End	Multialternative (Growth)	B	C	A-	Up	Y	1,000,000
Blackstone Alternative Multi-Strategy Fund Class Y	BXMYX	NAS CM	Open End	Multialternative (Growth)	B	C	A-	Up	Y	0
Blue Chip Investor Fund	BCIFX	NAS CM	Open End	US Equity Large Cap Blend (Growth)	B	B-	B		Y	5,000
Blue Current Global Dividend Fund Institutional Class	BCGDX	NAS CM	Open End	Global Equity (Equity-Income)	C+	C+	B-	Down	Y	100,000
BMO Aggressive Allocation Fund Class I	BDSHX	NAS CM	Open End	Aggressive Alloc (Asset Alloc)	B-	B-	B-	Down	Y	1,000,000
BMO Aggressive Allocation Fund Class R3	BDSRX	NAS CM	Open End	Aggressive Alloc (Asset Alloc)	B-	B-	C+	Down	Y	0
BMO Aggressive Allocation Fund Class R6	BDSQX	NAS CM	Open End	Aggressive Alloc (Asset Alloc)	B-	B-	B-	Down	Y	0
BMO Aggressive Allocation Fund Class Y	BDSYX	NAS CM	Open End	Aggressive Alloc (Asset Alloc)	B-	B-	B-	Down	Y	1,000
BMO Alternative Strategies Fund Class A	BMATX	NAS CM	Open End	Multialternative (Growth)	C+	C	B	Up	Y	1,000
BMO Alternative Strategies Fund Class I	BMASX	NAS CM	Open End	Multialternative (Growth)	C+	C	B	Up	Y	1,000,000
BMO Balanced Allocation Fund Class I	BGRHX	NAS CM	Open End	Moderate Alloc (Balanced)	B-	C+	B	Down	Y	1,000,000
BMO Balanced Allocation Fund Class R3	BGRRX	NAS CM	Open End	Moderate Alloc (Balanced)	B-	C+	B	Down	Y	0
BMO Balanced Allocation Fund Class R6	BGRQX	NAS CM	Open End	Moderate Alloc (Balanced)	B-	C+	B	Down	Y	0
BMO Balanced Allocation Fund Class Y	BGRYX	NAS CM	Open End	Moderate Alloc (Balanced)	B-	C+	B	Down	Y	1,000
BMO Conservative Allocation Fund Class I	BDVIX	NAS CM	Open End	Cautious Alloc (Asset Alloc)	B-	C	B	Up	Y	1,000,000
BMO Conservative Allocation Fund Class R3	BDVRX	NAS CM	Open End	Cautious Alloc (Asset Alloc)	B-	C	B+	Up	Y	0
BMO Conservative Allocation Fund Class R6	BDVSX	NAS CM	Open End	Cautious Alloc (Asset Alloc)	B-	C	B	Up	Y	0
BMO Conservative Allocation Fund Class Y	BDVYX	NAS CM	Open End	Cautious Alloc (Asset Alloc)	B-	C	B+	Up	Y	1,000
BMO Disciplined International Equity Fund Class A	BDAQX	NAS CM	Open End	Global Equity Large Cap (Foreign Stock)	C	C+	B	Up	Y	1,000
BMO Disciplined International Equity Fund Class I	BDIQX	NAS CM	Open End	Global Equity Large Cap (Foreign Stock)	C	C+	B-	Up	Y	1,000,000

★Expanded analysis of this fund is included in Section II.

	TOTAL RETURNS					PERFORMANCE				ASSETS		ASSET ALLOCATION & TURNOVER					BULL & BEAR		FEES		
Min Additional Investment	3-Month Total Return	6-Month Total Return	1-Year Total Return	3-Year Total Return	5-Year Total Return	Dividend Yield (TTM)	Expense Ratio	3-Yr Std Deviation	3-Year Beta	NAV	Total Assets (ML)	%Cash	%Stocks	%Bonds	%Other	Turnover Ratio	Last Bull Market Total Return	Last Bear Market Total Return	Front End Fee (%)	Back End Fee (%)	Inception Date
50	8.85	21.47	7.88	2.33	5.49	0.66	1.13	19.38	0.84	31.19	237.2	2	98	0	0	102	21.16	-30.77	5.25		Oct-94
50	7.99	20.45	5.24	-1.90	-0.07	0	2.25	19.36	0.84		237.2	2	98	0	0	102	20.59	-30.99		4.50	Aug-85
50	8.63	20.96	7.00	-0.08	1.39	0.06	1.91	19.38	0.84	24.04	237.2	2	98	0	0	102	20.6	-30.99		1.00	Oct-94
	2.79	2.67	6.18	16.66	61.91	1.61	1.05	13.54	0.99	12.1	24.5	1	99	0	0	118					Sep-12
50	2.83	2.55	5.90	15.77	59.84	1.35	1.3	13.58	0.99	12.08	24.5	1	99	0	0	118			5.25		Sep-12
50	2.53	2.05	5.05	13.13	53.89	0.64	2.05	13.53	0.99	12	24.5	1	99	0	0	118				1.00	Sep-12
	8.21	19.40	15.05	11.70	7.22	1.99	1.1	16.58		10.6689	998.0	1	99	0	0	101	11.69	-19.42			Mar-11
	6.99	19.92	49.40	76.46	184.34	0	1.7	14.05	0.93	23.99	638.4	6	93	0	0	51	19.92	-21.5			Sep-08
	7.11	20.24	50.15	79.56	192.83	0	1.2	14.05	0.93	25.44	638.4	6	93	0	0	51	20.32	-21.36			May-00
50	7.02	20.06	49.72	77.96	188.10	0	1.45	14.04	0.93	23.68	638.4	6	93	0	0	51	19.97	-21.43	5.25		May-00
50	6.91	19.68	48.70	73.92	176.99	0	2.2	14.04	0.93	20.24	638.4	6	93	0	0	51	19.54	-21.78		1.00	May-00
	7.09	20.12	49.85	78.30	189.50	0	1.45	14.05	0.93	24.19	638.4	6	93	0	0	51	20.19	-21.36			May-00
	6.68	18.71	45.63	69.59		0.01	0.88	12.42	0.97	27.7807	625.1	0	98	0	0	74					Oct-14
	2.10	7.82	13.86	22.54	84.52	0.19	1.18	14.25	0.94	11.88	156.9	1	98	0	1	105	30.14	-27.53			Feb-03
	2.24	8.13	14.50	24.43	89.55	0.16	0.68	14.32	0.95	14.16	156.9	1	98	0	1	105	30.58	-27.32			Oct-99
50	2.15	7.96	14.22	23.53	86.69	0.17	0.93	14.35	0.95	13.22	156.9	1	98	0	1	105	30.37	-27.42	5.25		Oct-99
50	1.95	7.54	13.27	20.41	79.12	0.22	1.68	14.27	0.94	10.18	156.9	1	98	0	1	105	29.64	-27.68		1.00	Oct-99
	2.68	5.51	8.03	7.01	22.42	1.78	0.83	5.22	0.3	14.38	609.4	18	61	21	0	257	12.02	-13.09			Aug-16
	2.78	5.62	8.05	7.50	23.83	1.62	0.94	5.25	0.3	14.41	609.5	18	61	21	0	257	12.18	-12.99			Jun-93
50	2.65	5.42	7.71	6.56	21.91	1.32	1.27	5.21	0.3	14.32	609.4	18	61	21	0	257	12.02	-13.09	5.25		Dec-88
50	2.65	5.07	6.88	3.20	16.35	0	2.19	5.2	0.3		609.5	18	61	21	0	257	11.47	-13.41		4.50	Jan-99
50	2.47	5.01	6.93	4.34	17.80	0.59	1.96	5.23	0.3	13.92	609.4	18	61	21	0	257	11.54	-13.38		1.00	Jun-93
	2.72	5.50	7.78	6.64	21.90	1.39	1.22	5.24	0.3	14.33	609.5	18	61	21	0	257	12.04	-13.09			Jan-05
	1.89	8.19	21.15	21.36		0.96	0.93	11.71	0.68	10.53	439.4	-9	57	52	0	22					May-13
50	1.88	8.12	20.89	20.48		0.89	1.18	11.76	0.68	10.48	439.4	-9	57	52	0	22			5.25		May-13
50	1.68	7.65	19.93	17.83		0.51	1.93	11.74	0.68	10.42	439.4	-9	57	52	0	22				1.00	May-13
	4.20	5.75	10.23	14.62	22.59		0.61	6.41	0.46	10.19	38.8	64	13	23	0	73					Feb-17
	4.17	5.72	10.21	14.60	22.56	0.37	0.66	6.41	0.46	10.19	38.8	64	13	23	0	73					Dec-12
50	4.14	5.59	9.97	13.80	21.01	0.19	0.91	6.4	0.45	10.17	38.8	64	13	23	0	73			5.25		Dec-12
50	3.92	5.17	9.10	11.25	16.50	0	1.66	6.38	0.46	10.14	38.8	64	13	23	0	73				1.00	Dec-12
	2.18	5.52	16.64	15.80	53.00	2.49	1.15	9.46		21.1176	365.7	2	98	0	0	8					Nov-11
5,000	0.23	1.82	6.82	11.62		0.31	2.77	3.67	0.21	10.72	5,227	-13	29	42	38	237					Nov-14
200,000	0.22	1.99	7.19	12.49		0.42	2.52	3.68	0.21	10.73	5,227	-13	29	42	38	237					Jun-14
	0.31	2.00	7.23	12.95		0.53	2.42	3.71	0.21	10.65	5,227	-13	29	42	38	237					Jan-15
100	8.04	12.89	18.50	32.36	95.54	0.22	1.01	9.16	0.77	180.09	39.7	8	92	0	0	21	20.68	-15.99			Dec-01
	1.53	4.91	16.84	22.52		2.02	0.99	9.22	0.89	11.59	64.2	4	96	0	0	61					Sep-14
	5.65	10.52	22.01	27.40	80.91	1.2	0.76	10.11	0.98	9.46	185.0	3	95	1	2	33	23.49	-20.59			May-14
	5.56	10.21	21.40	25.53	76.41	0.79	1.26	10.16	0.98	9.47	185.0	3	95	1	2	33	23.13	-20.76			May-14
	5.67	10.53	22.14	27.97	81.88	1.35	0.61	10.14	0.98	9.45	185.0	3	95	1	2	33	23.49	-20.59			May-14
50	5.65	10.40	21.73	26.49	79.36	0.89	1.01	10.18	0.98	9.48	185.0	3	95	1	2	33	23.49	-20.59			May-14
50	0.08	1.49	4.23	8.03		0	2.05			10.14	88.2	32	44	5	18	251			5.00		Dec-14
	0.08	1.57	4.50	8.81		0	1.8			10.21	88.2	32	44	5	18	251					Dec-14
	3.65	7.15	14.80	19.52	50.48	1.95	0.83	6.95	0.66	9.13	381.7	6	61	31	2	35	16.31	-13.75			May-14
	3.50	6.79	14.15	17.70	46.68	1.4	1.33	6.95	0.66	9.15	381.7	6	61	31	2	35	15.97	-13.93			May-14
	3.65	7.04	14.92	20.01	51.23	2.1	0.68	7	0.66	9.12	381.7	6	61	31	2	35	16.31	-13.75			May-14
50	3.55	6.83	14.45	18.56	49.05	1.68	1.08	6.95	0.66	9.13	381.7	6	61	31	2	35	16.31	-13.75			May-14
	1.46	3.31	7.34	11.44	22.73	2.66	0.77	3.57	0.37	8.94	72.5	38	16	44	2	40	9.58	-5.34			May-14
	1.37	3.12	6.80	9.82	19.69	2.17	1.27	3.57	0.35	8.84	72.5	38	16	44	2	40	9.26	-5.54			May-14
	1.50	3.35	7.48	11.93	23.38	2.8	0.62	3.53	0.36	8.64	72.5	38	16	44	2	40	9.58	-5.34			May-14
50	1.46	3.21	7.12	10.64	21.67	2.34	1.02	3.55	0.36	8.66	72.5	38	16	44	2	40	9.58	-5.34			May-14
50	2.04	7.03	22.79			2.21	1.15			11.37	74.6	3	96	0	1	77			5.00		Sep-15
	2.05	7.04	23.03			2.46	0.9			11.37	74.6	3	96	0	1	77					Sep-15

	MARKET			FUND TYPE, CATEGORY & OBJECTIVE	RATINGS				MINIMUMS	
Fund Name	Ticker Symbol	Traded On	Fund Type	Category and (Prospectus Objective)	Overall Rating	Reward Rating	Risk Rating	Recent Up/ Downgrade	Open to New Investors	Min Initial Investment
BMO Dividend Income Fund Class A	BADIX	NAS CM	Open End	US Equity Large Cap Value (Equity-Income)	B-	B	B-	Down	Y	1,000
BMO Dividend Income Fund Class I	MDIVX	NAS CM	Open End	US Equity Large Cap Value (Equity-Income)	B	B	B-		Y	1,000,000
BMO Global Long/Short Equity Fund Class A	BGAQX	NAS CM	Open End	Long/Short Equity (Growth)	C	C+	B	Up	Y	1,000
BMO Global Long/Short Equity Fund Class I	BGIQX	NAS CM	Open End	Long/Short Equity (Growth)	C	C+	B	Up	Y	1,000,000
BMO Global Low Volatility Equity Fund Class A	BAEGX	NAS CM	Open End	Global Equity (World Stock)	B	C+	A-		Y	1,000
BMO Global Low Volatility Equity Fund Class I	BGLBX	NAS CM	Open End	Global Equity (World Stock)	B	C+	A-		Y	1,000,000
BMO Growth Allocation Fund Class I	BABHX	NAS CM	Open End	Aggressive Alloc (Asset Alloc)	B-	C+	B-	Down	Y	1,000,000
BMO Growth Allocation Fund Class R3	BABRX	NAS CM	Open End	Aggressive Alloc (Asset Alloc)	B-	C+	B-	Down	Y	0
BMO Growth Allocation Fund Class R6	BABQX	NAS CM	Open End	Aggressive Alloc (Asset Alloc)	B-	B-	B-	Down	Y	0
BMO Growth Allocation Fund Class Y	BABYX	NAS CM	Open End	Aggressive Alloc (Asset Alloc)	B-	C+	B-	Down	Y	1,000
BMO In-Retirement Fund Class R3	BTRRX	NAS CM	Open End	Target Date 2000-2020 (Asset Alloc)	B-	C+	B	Up	Y	0
BMO In-Retirement Fund Class R6	BTRTX	NAS CM	Open End	Target Date 2000-2020 (Asset Alloc)	B-	C+	B	Up	Y	0
BMO In-Retirement Fund Class Y	BTRYX	NAS CM	Open End	Target Date 2000-2020 (Asset Alloc)	B-	C+	B	Up	Y	1,000
BMO Large-Cap Growth Fund Class A	BALGX	NAS CM	Open End	US Equity Large Cap Growth (Growth)	B+	A-	B+	Up	Y	1,000
BMO Large-Cap Growth Fund Class I	MLCIX	NAS CM	Open End	US Equity Large Cap Growth (Growth)	B+	A-	B+	Up	Y	1,000,000
BMO Large-Cap Growth Fund Class R6	BLGRX	NAS CM	Open End	US Equity Large Cap Growth (Growth)	B+	A-	B+	Up	Y	0
BMO Large-Cap Growth Fund Class Y	MASTX	NAS CM	Open End	US Equity Large Cap Growth (Growth)	B+	A-	B+	Up	Y	1,000
BMO Large-Cap Value Fund Class A	BALVX	NAS CM	Open End	US Equity Large Cap Value (Growth)	B	B-	B	Up	Y	1,000
BMO Large-Cap Value Fund Class I	MLVIX	NAS CM	Open End	US Equity Large Cap Value (Growth)	B	B	B	Up	Y	1,000,000
BMO Large-Cap Value Fund Class R6	BLCRX	NAS CM	Open End	US Equity Large Cap Value (Growth)	B	B	B	Up	Y	0
BMO LGM Emerging Markets Equity Fund Class A	BAEMX	NAS CM	Open End	Emerging Markets Equity (Div Emerging Mkts)	C+	B-	C		Y	1,000
BMO LGM Emerging Markets Equity Fund Class I	MIEMX	NAS CM	Open End	Emerging Markets Equity (Div Emerging Mkts)	B-	B-	C	Up	Y	1,000,000
BMO LGM Frontier Markets Equity Fund Class Y	BLGFX	NAS CM	Closed End	Emerging Markets Equity (Growth)	C+	C+	C+	Up	Y	5,000
BMO Low Volatility Equity Fund Class A	BLVAX	NAS CM	Open End	US Equity Large Cap Value (Growth)	B	C+	A-		Y	1,000
BMO Low Volatility Equity Fund Class I	MLVEX	NAS CM	Open End	US Equity Large Cap Value (Growth)	B	C+	A-		Y	1,000,000
BMO Mid-Cap Growth Fund Class A	BGMAX	NAS CM	Open End	US Equity Mid Cap (Growth)	C+	B-	C	Up	Y	1,000
BMO Mid-Cap Growth Fund Class I	MRMIX	NAS CM	Open End	US Equity Mid Cap (Growth)	C+	B-	C	Up	Y	1,000,000
BMO Mid-Cap Growth Fund Class R6	BMGGX	NAS CM	Open End	US Equity Mid Cap (Growth)	C+	B-	C	Up	Y	0
BMO Mid-Cap Value Fund Class A	BAMCX	NAS CM	Open End	US Equity Mid Cap (Growth)	B-	B-	B	Up	Y	1,000
BMO Mid-Cap Value Fund Class I	MRVIX	NAS CM	Open End	US Equity Mid Cap (Growth)	B-	B-	B	Up	Y	1,000,000
BMO Mid-Cap Value Fund Class R3	BMVDX	NAS CM	Open End	US Equity Mid Cap (Growth)	B-	B-	B	Up	Y	0
BMO Mid-Cap Value Fund Class R6	BMVGX	NAS CM	Open End	US Equity Mid Cap (Growth)	B	B-	B	Up	Y	0
BMO Moderate Allocation Fund Class I	BMBHX	NAS CM	Open End	Cautious Alloc (Balanced)	B-	C+	B	Up	Y	1,000,000
BMO Moderate Allocation Fund Class R3	BMBQX	NAS CM	Open End	Cautious Alloc (Balanced)	B-	C+	B	Up	Y	0
BMO Moderate Allocation Fund Class R6	BMBTX	NAS CM	Open End	Cautious Alloc (Balanced)	B-	C+	B	Up	Y	0
BMO Moderate Allocation Fund Class Y	BMBYX	NAS CM	Open End	Cautious Alloc (Balanced)	B-	C+	B	Up	Y	1,000
BMO Pyrford International Stock Fund Class A	BPIAX	NAS CM	Open End	Global Equity Large Cap (Foreign Stock)	C+	C+	B-	Down	Y	1,000
BMO Pyrford International Stock Fund Class F3	BISBX	NAS CM	Open End	Global Equity Large Cap (Foreign Stock)	B-	C+	B-		Y	0
BMO Pyrford International Stock Fund Class I	MISNX	NAS CM	Open End	Global Equity Large Cap (Foreign Stock)	B-	C+	B-	Up	Y	1,000,000
BMO Pyrford International Stock Fund Class R6	BISGX	NAS CM	Open End	Global Equity Large Cap (Foreign Stock)	B-	C+	B-	Up	Y	0
BMO Pyrford International Stock Fund Class Y	MISYX	NAS CM	Open End	Global Equity Large Cap (Foreign Stock)	C+	C+	B-	Down	Y	1,000
BMO Small-Cap Core Fund Class A	BCCAX	NAS CM	Open End	US Equity Small Cap (Small Company)	A-	A	B	Up	Y	1,000
BMO Small-Cap Core Fund Class I	BSCNX	NAS CM	Open End	US Equity Small Cap (Small Company)	A-	A	B	Up	Y	1,000,000
BMO Small-Cap Growth Fund Class A	BSLAX	NAS CM	Open End	US Equity Small Cap (Small Company)	C+	B-	C	Up	Y	1,000
BMO Small-Cap Growth Fund Class I	MSGIX	NAS CM	Open End	US Equity Small Cap (Small Company)	C+	B-	C	Up	Y	1,000,000
BMO Small-Cap Value Fund Class A	BACVX	NAS CM	Open End	US Equity Small Cap (Small Company)	B	B	B	Up	Y	1,000
BMO Small-Cap Value Fund Class I	MRSNX	NAS CM	Open End	US Equity Small Cap (Small Company)	B	B+	B	Up	Y	1,000,000
BMO Small-Cap Value Fund Class R3	BSVDX	NAS CM	Open End	US Equity Small Cap (Small Company)	B	B	B	Up	Y	0
BMO Small-Cap Value Fund Class R6	BSVGX	NAS CM	Open End	US Equity Small Cap (Small Company)	B	B+	B	Up	Y	0
BMO Target Retirement 2015 Fund Class R3	BRTCX	NAS CM	Open End	Target Date 2000-2020 (Asset Alloc)	B-	C+	B	Up	Y	0
BMO Target Retirement 2015 Fund Class R6	BRTDX	NAS CM	Open End	Target Date 2000-2020 (Asset Alloc)	B-	C+	B	Up	Y	0
BMO Target Retirement 2015 Fund Class Y	BRTAX	NAS CM	Open End	Target Date 2000-2020 (Asset Alloc)	B-	C+	B	Up	Y	1,000

★Expanded analysis of this fund is included in Section II.

	TOTAL RETURNS					PERFORMANCE				ASSETS		ASSET ALLOCATION & TURNOVER					BULL & BEAR		FEES		
Min Additional Investment	3-Month Total Return	6-Month Total Return	1-Year Total Return	3-Year Total Return	5-Year Total Return	Dividend Yield (TTM)	Expense Ratio	3-Yr Std Deviation	3-Year Beta	NAV	Total Assets (MIL)	%Cash	%Stocks	%Bonds	%Other	Turnover Ratio	Last Bull Market Total Return	Last Bear Market Total Return	Front End Fee (%)	Back End Fee (%)	Inception Date
50	7.72	14.74	21.65	33.19	99.45	1.34	0.9	10.71	1	14.38	125.2	2	98	0	0	43			5.00		May-14
	7.81	14.92	21.90	34.20	102.01	2	0.65	10.71	1	14.33	125.2	2	98	0	0	43					Dec-11
50	2.06	6.58	14.01			0.33	1.64			12.33	11.7	38	60	0	2	42			5.00		Sep-15
	2.11	6.70	14.32			0.52	1.39			12.35	11.7	38	60	0	2	42					Sep-15
50	5.87	8.41	17.51	25.42		1.26	1.11	7.76	0.64	13.51	51.9	3	95	0	2	74			5.00		May-14
	5.87	8.57	17.76	26.20		1.41	0.86	7.79	0.64	13.54	51.9	3	95	0	2	74					Sep-13
	4.69	8.87	18.70	23.66	66.09	1.33	0.83	8.88	0.85	10.12	135.4	4	81	13	2	42	19.79	-17.51			May-14
	4.54	8.61	18.05	21.77	61.88	0.74	1.33	8.94	0.86	10.14	135.4	4	81	13	2	42	19.44	-17.68			May-14
	4.75	8.93	18.77	24.14	66.90	1.47	0.68	8.85	0.85	10.11	135.4	4	81	13	2	42	19.79	-17.51			May-14
50	4.58	8.76	18.33	22.66	64.52	1.06	1.08	8.89	0.86	10.13	135.4	4	81	13	2	42	19.79	-17.51			May-14
	1.97	4.17	9.10	12.81	30.93	1.9	1.21	4.51	1.08	8.94	15.2	5	36	56	2	26	14.25	-11.14			Aug-13
	2.29	4.61	9.96	15.15	35.32	2.72	0.56	4.51	1.08	8.88	15.2	5	36	56	2	26	14.59	-10.96			Aug-13
50	2.09	4.41	9.50	13.70	32.94	2.28	0.96	4.5	1.08	8.9	15.2	5	36	56	2	26	14.59	-10.96			Aug-13
50	7.15	13.16	27.96	45.69	127.46	0.37	1	10.92	1	17.94	380.3	1	99	0	0	75	27.44	-18.54	5.00		May-14
	7.22	13.32	28.34	46.78	131.16	0.67	0.75	10.9	1	18.09	380.3	1	99	0	0	75	27.79	-18.4			Jan-08
	7.29	13.45	28.56	46.90	130.17	0.82	0.6	10.93	1	18.11	380.3	1	99	0	0	75	27.62	-18.46			Dec-15
50	7.15	13.16	27.96	45.68	128.27	0.37	1	10.92	1	17.94	380.3	1	99	0	0	75	27.62	-18.46			Nov-92
50	7.64	13.73	19.97	28.55	100.84	0.95	1	10.56	0.98	16.19	360.4	1	99	0	0	62	24.1	-18.92	5.00		May-14
	7.70	13.85	20.31	29.56	103.47	1.22	0.75	10.55	0.98	16.2	360.4	1	99	0	0	62	24.29	-18.83			Jan-08
	7.72	13.92	20.49	29.93	104.06	1.35	0.6	10.56	0.98	16.2	360.4	1	99	0	0	62	24.29	-18.83			Dec-15
50	7.58	10.15	37.78	28.67	28.39	0.4	1.4	12.54	0.63	17.03	164.5	4	94	2	0	40	17.47	-27.38	5.00		May-14
	7.71	10.35	38.18	29.80	30.09	0.65	1.15	12.5	0.62	16.96	164.5	4	94	2	0	40	17.64	-27.31			Dec-08
100	7.51	8.04	23.06	21.16		0.68	2	9.42		10.93	--	4	94	2	0	31					Dec-13
50	6.15	7.12	12.67	24.06	86.94	1.36	0.91	7.46	0.62	14.73	161.5	1	98	0	0	56			5.00		May-14
	6.26	7.30	12.98	25.00	89.47	1.57	0.66	7.51	0.62	14.78	161.5	1	98	0	0	56					Sep-12
50	7.88	14.18	26.96	20.25	67.15	0.14	1.25	12.99	1.12	15.43	121.4	1	99	0	0	157	32.95	-25.77	5.00		May-14
	7.95	14.30	27.30	21.18	69.30	0.29	1	12.98	1.12	16.11	121.4	1	99	0	0	157	33.14	-25.69			Jan-08
	7.98	14.36	27.49	21.76	70.18	0.46	0.85	12.97	1.12	16.2	121.4	1	99	0	0	157	33.14	-25.69			May-14
50	7.05	10.86	14.44	24.85	97.92	0.51	1.23	12.21	1.11	12.52	219.2	2	98	0	0	139	26.82	-24.14	5.00		May-14
	7.16	11.00	14.70	25.80	100.44	1.15	0.98	12.22	1.11	12.44	219.2	2	98	0	0	139	27.01	-24.06			Jan-08
	6.97	10.72	14.12	23.82	95.28	0.4	1.48	12.23	1.11	12.42	219.2	2	98	0	0	139	26.64	-24.22			May-14
	7.19	11.11	14.82	26.27	101.36	1.33	0.83	12.23	1.11	12.44	219.2	2	98	0	0	139	27.01	-24.06			May-14
	2.60	5.19	11.02	15.52	36.10	2.37	0.77	5.18	0.11	9.76	113.2	9	41	48	2	39	12.87	-9.61			May-14
	2.45	4.93	10.51	13.75	32.65	1.89	1.27	5.15	0.11	9.77	113.2	9	41	48	2	39	12.55	-9.8			May-14
	2.60	5.29	11.24	16.03	36.82	2.53	0.62	5.24	0.1	9.74	113.2	9	41	48	2	39	12.87	-9.61			May-14
50	2.43	5.01	10.71	14.55	34.78	2.08	1.02	5.22	0.11	9.76	113.2	9	41	48	2	39	12.87	-9.61			May-14
50	3.16	5.62	18.18	15.44	34.93	1.82	1.19	10.05	0.76	13.71	678.3	4	94	0	2	33			5.00		May-14
	3.24	5.86	18.61	16.43	36.76		0.79	10.08	0.77	13.43	678.3	4	94	0	2	33					May-17
	3.26	5.80	18.55	16.36	36.68	2.01	0.94	10.07	0.76	13.43	678.3	4	94	0	2	33					Dec-11
	3.24	5.86	18.70	16.85	37.36	2.14	0.79	10.02	0.76	13.43	678.3	4	94	0	2	33					May-14
50	3.16	5.62	18.18	15.44	34.81	1.82	1.19	10.05	0.76	13.71	678.3	4	94	0	2	33					Dec-11
50	4.00	11.27	13.33	38.47		0.07	1.15	13.78	0.94	13.83	22.8	1	99	0	0	90			5.00		May-14
	4.04	11.42	13.57	39.50		0.25	0.9	13.8	0.94	13.92	22.8	1	99	0	0	90					Dec-13
50	4.09	9.49	20.08	17.56	70.63		1.17	15.89	1.03	17.93	146.6	2	98	0	0	197	34.81	-29.26	5.00		May-17
	4.21	9.71	20.47	18.53	72.90	0	0.92	15.89	1.03	18.64	146.6	2	98	0	0	197	35.01	-29.19			Jan-08
50	3.07	10.04	8.91	25.60	82.61	0.25	1.25	15.57	1.07	13.68	71.0	2	99	0	0	148	23.99	-22.15	5.00		May-14
	3.24	10.28	9.24	26.64	84.99	0.55	1	15.56	1.07	13.9	71.0	2	99	0	0	148	24.17	-22.07			Feb-11
	3.08	9.98	8.68	24.77	80.48	0.25	1.5	15.59	1.07	13.65	71.0	2	99	0	0	148	23.81	-22.23			May-14
	3.22	10.31	9.35	27.24	86.12	0.66	0.85	15.6	1.07	13.97	71.0	2	99	0	0	148	24.17	-22.07			May-14
	2.46	5.23	11.35	15.27		1.67	1.25	5.61	1.12	11.45	3.9	5	43	49	3	72					Dec-13
	2.68	5.62	12.14	17.57		2.24	0.6	5.58	1.11	11.5	3.9	5	43	49	3	72					Dec-13
50	2.55	5.32	11.54	16.08		1.81	1	5.61	1.12	11.5	3.9	5	43	49	3	72					Dec-13

	MARKET			FUND TYPE, CATEGORY & OBJECTIVE	RATINGS				MINIMUMS	
Fund Name	Ticker Symbol	Traded On	Fund Type	Category and (Prospectus Objective)	Overall Rating	Reward Rating	Risk Rating	Recent Up/ Downgrade	Open to New Investors	Min Initial Investment
BMO Target Retirement 2020 Fund Class R3	BTRFX	NAS CM	Open End	Target Date 2000-2020 (Asset Alloc)	B-	C+	B	Down	Y	0
BMO Target Retirement 2020 Fund Class R6	BTRGX	NAS CM	Open End	Target Date 2000-2020 (Asset Alloc)	B-	C+	B	Down	Y	0
BMO Target Retirement 2020 Fund Class Y	BTRDX	NAS CM	Open End	Target Date 2000-2020 (Asset Alloc)	B-	C+	B	Down	Y	1,000
BMO Target Retirement 2025 Fund Class R3	BRTGX	NAS CM	Open End	Target Date 2021-2045 (Asset Alloc)	B-	C+	B-	Down	Y	0
BMO Target Retirement 2025 Fund Class R6	BRTHX	NAS CM	Open End	Target Date 2021-2045 (Asset Alloc)	B-	C+	B	Down	Y	0
BMO Target Retirement 2025 Fund Class Y	BRTEX	NAS CM	Open End	Target Date 2021-2045 (Asset Alloc)	B-	C+	B	Down	Y	1,000
BMO Target Retirement 2030 Fund Class R3	BTRKX	NAS CM	Open End	Target Date 2021-2045 (Asset Alloc)	B-	C+	B-	Down	Y	0
BMO Target Retirement 2030 Fund Class R6	BTRLX	NAS CM	Open End	Target Date 2021-2045 (Asset Alloc)	B-	B-	B-	Down	Y	0
BMO Target Retirement 2030 Fund Class Y	BTRHX	NAS CM	Open End	Target Date 2021-2045 (Asset Alloc)	B-	C+	B-	Down	Y	1,000
BMO Target Retirement 2035 Fund Class R3	BRTKX	NAS CM	Open End	Target Date 2021-2045 (Asset Alloc)	B-	C+	B-	Down	Y	0
BMO Target Retirement 2035 Fund Class R6	BRTLX	NAS CM	Open End	Target Date 2021-2045 (Asset Alloc)	B-	B-	B-	Down	Y	0
BMO Target Retirement 2035 Fund Class Y	BRTIX	NAS CM	Open End	Target Date 2021-2045 (Asset Alloc)	B-	B-	B-	Down	Y	1,000
BMO Target Retirement 2040 Fund Class R3	BTRPX	NAS CM	Open End	Target Date 2021-2045 (Asset Alloc)	B-	B-	B-	Down	Y	0
BMO Target Retirement 2040 Fund Class R6	BTRQX	NAS CM	Open End	Target Date 2021-2045 (Asset Alloc)	B-	B-	B-	Down	Y	0
BMO Target Retirement 2040 Fund Class Y	BTRMX	NAS CM	Open End	Target Date 2021-2045 (Asset Alloc)	B-	B-	B-	Down	Y	1,000
BMO Target Retirement 2045 Fund Class R3	BRTPX	NAS CM	Open End	Target Date 2021-2045 (Asset Alloc)	B-	B-	B-	Down	Y	0
BMO Target Retirement 2045 Fund Class R6	BRTQX	NAS CM	Open End	Target Date 2021-2045 (Asset Alloc)	B-	B-	B-	Down	Y	0
BMO Target Retirement 2045 Fund Class Y	BRTMX	NAS CM	Open End	Target Date 2021-2045 (Asset Alloc)	B-	B-	B-	Down	Y	1,000
BMO Target Retirement 2050 Fund Class R3	BTRWX	NAS CM	Open End	Target Date 2046+ (Asset Alloc)	B-	B-	B-	Down	Y	0
BMO Target Retirement 2050 Fund Class R6	BTRZX	NAS CM	Open End	Target Date 2046+ (Asset Alloc)	B-	B-	B-	Down	Y	0
BMO Target Retirement 2050 Fund Class Y	BTRUX	NAS CM	Open End	Target Date 2046+ (Asset Alloc)	B-	B-	B-	Down	Y	1,000
BMO Target Retirement 2055 Fund Class R3	BRTTX	NAS CM	Open End	Target Date 2046+ (Asset Alloc)	B-	B-	B-	Down	Y	0
BMO Target Retirement 2055 Fund Class R6	BRTUX	NAS CM	Open End	Target Date 2046+ (Asset Alloc)	B-	B-	B-	Down	Y	0
BMO Target Retirement 2055 Fund Class Y	BRTRX	NAS CM	Open End	Target Date 2046+ (Asset Alloc)	B-	B-	B-	Down	Y	1,000
BMT Multi-Cap Fund Institutional Class	BMTMX	NAS CM	Open End	US Equity Large Cap Blend (Growth & Income)	U	U	U		Y	25,000
BNY Mellon Absolute Insight Multi-Strategy Fund Class A	MAJAX	NAS CM	Open End	Multialternative (Growth & Income)	C	D+	B	Up	Y	1,000
BNY Mellon Absolute Insight Multi-Strategy Fund Class C	MAJCX	NAS CM	Open End	Multialternative (Growth & Income)	C-	D+	C	Up	Y	1,000
BNY Mellon Absolute Insight Multi-Strategy Fund Class I	MAJIX	NAS CM	Open End	Multialternative (Growth & Income)	C	D+	B+	Up	Y	1,000
BNY Mellon Absolute Insight Multi-Strategy Fund Class Y	MAJYX	NAS CM	Open End	Multialternative (Growth & Income)	C	D+	B+	Up	Y	1,000,000
BNY Mellon Asset Allocation Fund Class M	MPBLX	NAS CM	Open End	Moderate Alloc (Balanced)	B-	C+	B	Down	Y	10,000
BNY Mellon Asset Allocation Fund Investor Class	MIBLX	NAS CM	Open End	Moderate Alloc (Balanced)	B-	C+	B	Down	Y	10,000
BNY Mellon Emerging Markets Fund Class Investor	MIEGX	NAS CM	Open End	Emerging Markets Equity (Div Emerging Mkts)	B-	B	C	Up	Y	10,000
BNY Mellon Emerging Markets Fund Class M	MEMKX	NAS CM	Open End	Emerging Markets Equity (Div Emerging Mkts)	B-	B	C	Up	Y	10,000
BNY Mellon Focused Equity Opportunities Fund Cls M Shares	MFOMX	NAS CM	Open End	US Equity Large Cap Growth (Growth)	B	A-	C+		Y	10,000
BNY Mellon Focused Equity Opp Fund Inv Shares	MFOIX	NAS CM	Open End	US Equity Large Cap Growth (Growth)	B	B+	C+		Y	10,000
BNY Mellon Income Stock Fund Class A	BMIAX	NAS CM	Open End	US Equity Large Cap Value (Equity-Income)	B	B-	B+		Y	1,000
BNY Mellon Income Stock Fund Class C	BMISX	NAS CM	Open End	US Equity Large Cap Value (Equity-Income)	B	B-	B		Y	1,000
BNY Mellon Income Stock Fund Class I	BMIIX	NAS CM	Open End	US Equity Large Cap Value (Equity-Income)	B	B-	B+		Y	1,000
BNY Mellon Income Stock Fund Class M	MPISX	NAS CM	Open End	US Equity Large Cap Value (Equity-Income)	B	B	B+		Y	10,000
BNY Mellon Income Stock Fund Class Y	BMIYX	NAS CM	Open End	US Equity Large Cap Value (Equity-Income)	B	B-	B+		Y	1,000,000
BNY Mellon Income Stock Fund Investor shares	MIISX	NAS CM	Open End	US Equity Large Cap Value (Equity-Income)	B	B-	B+		Y	10,000
BNY Mellon International Appreciation Fund Class M Shares	MPPMX	NAS CM	Open End	Global Equity Large Cap (Foreign Stock)	B-	C+	B	Up	Y	10,000
BNY Mellon International Appreciation Fund Investor Shares	MARIX	NAS CM	Open End	Global Equity Large Cap (Foreign Stock)	B-	C+	B	Up	Y	10,000
BNY Mellon International Equity Income Class M	MLIMX	NAS CM	Open End	Global Equity Large Cap (Foreign Stock)	C+	B-	C+	Up	Y	10,000
BNY Mellon International Equity Income Investor	MLIIX	NAS CM	Open End	Global Equity Large Cap (Foreign Stock)	C+	B-	C+	Up	Y	10,000
BNY Mellon International Fund Class Investor	MIINX	NAS CM	Open End	Global Equity Large Cap (Foreign Stock)	B-	B-	B	Up	Y	10,000
BNY Mellon International Fund Class M	MPITX	NAS CM	Open End	Global Equity Large Cap (Foreign Stock)	B-	B-	B	Up	Y	10,000
BNY Mellon Large Cap Mkt Opp Fund Cls Investment	MMOIX	NAS CM	Open End	US Equity Large Cap Growth (Growth)	B	B	B-		Y	10,000
BNY Mellon Large Cap Market Opportunities Fund Class M	MMOMX	NAS CM	Open End	US Equity Large Cap Growth (Growth)	B	B	B-		Y	10,000
BNY Mellon Large Cap Stock Fund Class Investor	MILCX	NAS CM	Open End	US Equity Large Cap Blend (Growth)	B-	B-	B-	Down	Y	10,000
BNY Mellon Large Cap Stock Fund Class M	MPLCX	NAS CM	Open End	US Equity Large Cap Blend (Growth)	B-	B	B-	Down	Y	10,000
BNY Mellon Mid Cap Multi-Strategy Fund Class Investor	MIMSX	NAS CM	Open End	US Equity Mid Cap (Growth)	B-	B-	C+	Down	Y	10,000

★Expanded analysis of this fund is included in Section II.

Min Additional Investment	TOTAL RETURNS: 3-Month Total Return	6-Month Total Return	1-Year Total Return	3-Year Total Return	5-Year Total Return	PERFORMANCE: Dividend Yield (TTM)	Expense Ratio	3-Yr Std Deviation	3-Year Beta	ASSETS: NAV	Total Assets (MIL)	ASSET ALLOCATION & TURNOVER: %Cash	%Stocks	%Bonds	%Other	Turnover Ratio	BULL & BEAR: Last Bull Market Total Return	Last Bear Market Total Return	FEES: Front End Fee (%)	Back End Fee (%)	Inception Date
	3.45	6.55	14.29	18.39	47.17	1.38	1.28	6.59	1.14	10.35	82.7	5	61	32	2	23	18.09	-15.28			Aug-13
	3.59	6.89	15.01	20.71	51.96	2.01	0.63	6.62	1.14	10.3	82.7	5	61	32	2	23	18.44	-15.1			Aug-13
50	3.46	6.67	14.54	19.19	49.31	1.61	1.03	6.59	1.14	10.31	82.7	5	61	32	2	23	18.44	-15.1			Aug-13
	3.94	7.52	16.58	20.43		1.2	1.28	7.44	1.14	12.04	22.2	5	70	23	2	31					Dec-13
	3.97	7.70	17.12	22.60		1.71	0.63	7.44	1.14	11.93	22.2	5	70	23	2	31					Dec-13
50	3.87	7.52	16.64	21.22		1.32	1.03	7.45	1.14	11.89	22.2	5	70	23	2	31					Dec-13
	4.28	8.06	17.97	21.80	59.98	0.99	1.34	8.12	1.13	11.67	96.7	4	78	16	2	25	20.78	-18.12			Aug-13
	4.42	8.38	18.77	24.15	65.10	1.59	0.69	8.15	1.13	11.62	96.7	4	78	16	2	25	21.13	-17.95			Aug-13
50	4.32	8.19	18.23	22.74	62.29	1.21	1.09	8.11	1.13	11.64	96.7	4	78	16	2	25	21.13	-17.95			Aug-13
	4.61	8.66	19.46	23.15		0.95	1.31	8.79	1.13	11.76	13.1	4	84	10	2	32					Dec-13
	4.79	9.07	20.25	25.68		1.44	0.66	8.78	1.13	11.71	13.1	4	84	10	2	32					Dec-13
50	4.68	8.89	19.67	24.09		1.12	1.06	8.75	1.12	11.67	13.1	4	84	10	2	32					Dec-13
	4.77	9.03	20.29	23.92	67.68	0.76	1.33	9.26	1.12	11.29	54.9	4	88	7	2	24	22.06	-19.37			Aug-13
	4.95	9.40	21.07	26.41	73.14	1.43	0.68	9.31	1.13	11.22	54.9	4	88	7	2	24	22.42	-19.2			Aug-13
50	4.93	9.20	20.62	24.88	70.19	1.05	1.08	9.29	1.12	11.24	54.9	4	88	7	2	24	22.42	-19.2			Aug-13
	4.85	9.09	20.51	24.48		0.88	1.3	9.28	1.08	12.12	7.8	4	88	6	2	31					Dec-13
	5.08	9.47	21.36	26.90		1.37	0.65	9.31	1.08	12.03	7.8	4	88	6	2	31					Dec-13
50	4.97	9.30	20.80	25.46		1.02	1.05	9.26	1.08	11.99	7.8	4	88	6	2	31					Dec-13
	4.83	9.13	20.46	24.38	68.85	0.82	1.33	9.27	1.03	12.26	40.6	4	89	6	2	27	22.33	-16.49			Aug-13
	4.53	8.99	20.73	26.29	72.89	1.43	0.68	9.31	1.04	12.23	40.6	4	89	6	2	27	22.33	-19.17			Aug-13
50	4.92	9.31	20.76	25.29	70.70	0.97	1.08	9.28	1.04	12.25	40.6	4	89	6	2	27	22.33	-19.17			Aug-13
	4.91	9.18	20.42	24.63		0.85	1.32	9.24	0.87	12.27	8.1	4	88	6	2	56					Dec-13
	5.05	9.54	21.15	26.98		1.26	0.67	9.17	0.86	12.37	8.1	4	88	6	2	56					Dec-13
50	4.87	9.29	20.59	25.48		0.88	1.07	9.24	0.87	12.37	8.1	4	88	6	2	56					Dec-13
5,000	4.04						1.01			10.74	137.1	8	92	0	0						Aug-17
100	0.63	1.27	1.93			0	1.75			12.59	284.8	77	-9	23	8				5.75		Dec-15
100	0.31	0.80	1.13			0	2.5			12.38	284.8	77	-9	23	8					1.00	Dec-15
100	0.69	1.42	2.23			0	1.5			12.6	284.8	77	-9	23	8						Dec-15
	0.69	1.42	2.24			0	1.5			12.6	284.8	77	-9	23	8						Dec-15
100	3.90	8.07	16.30	20.78	49.93	1.54	0.87	7.12	1.12	12.61	484.7	5	71	23	0	27	14.29	-15.02			Oct-00
100	3.83	7.97	15.91	19.98	48.12	1.31	1.12	7.08	1.12	12.7	484.7	5	71	23	0	27	14.13	-15.1			Jul-01
100	8.43	18.72	42.30	30.58	22.89	0.42	1.7	15.79	0.97	12.32	976.5	2	98	0	0	92	17.61	-28.36			Jul-01
100	8.41	18.75	42.59	31.47	24.42	0.6	1.45	15.74	0.97	11.98	976.5	2	98	0	0	92	17.81	-28.35			Oct-00
100	8.77	13.24	32.65	47.92	127.26	0.94	0.87	12.47	1.16	16.78	537.0	1	99	0	0	62	26.33	-23.1			Sep-09
100	8.68	13.06	32.35	46.83	124.27	0.78	1.12	12.46	1.16	16.63	537.0	1	99	0	0	62	26.16	-23.06			Sep-09
100	6.64	9.72	15.03	33.81	103.84	1.68	1.15	10.29	0.99	9.37	1,278	2	97	0	0	53	21.61	-16.11	5.75		May-16
100	6.34	9.21	14.01	30.72	96.18	1.05	1.85	10.3	1	9.35	1,278	2	97	0	0	53	21.09	-16.37		1.00	May-16
100	6.60	9.73	15.05	34.18	104.41	1.9	0.86	10.31	1	9.36	1,278	2	97	0	0	53	21.61	-16.11			May-16
100	6.60	9.75	15.07	34.22	104.46	1.9	0.81	10.33	1	9.36	1,278	2	97	0	0	53	21.61	-16.11			Oct-00
	6.72	9.75	15.20	34.20	104.44	1.9	0.86	10.31	1	9.36	1,278	2	97	0	0	53	21.61	-16.11			May-16
100	6.57	9.62	14.85	33.35	101.98	1.66	1.06	10.31	1	9.47	1,278	2	97	0	0	53	21.47	-16.18			Jul-01
100	3.64	8.85	23.78	23.11	42.51	2.25	0.92	11.59	0.93	14.43	80.9	1	99	0	0	4	13.38	-24.32			Apr-97
100	3.58	8.76	23.50	22.13	40.66	1.75	1.17	11.61	0.93	14.32	80.9	1	99	0	0	4	13.2	-24.41			Apr-97
100	4.57	13.09	26.79	25.63	28.78	2.86	1.09	11.92	0.92	14.95	383.8	1	99	0	0	46					Dec-11
100	4.50	12.92	25.78	24.21	26.39	2.12	1.34	11.9	0.92	15.11	383.8	1	99	0	0	46					Dec-11
100	3.92	11.02	27.72	25.71	48.99	1.32	1.28	12.6	0.99	14.76	1,153	1	99	0	0	82	11.44	-25.09			Jul-01
100	4.00	11.16	27.96	26.67	50.80	1.62	1.03	12.66	1	13.84	1,153	1	99	0	0	82	11.54	-25.04			Oct-00
100	7.57	11.44	24.15	36.63	100.84	0.76	1.26	10.86	1.06	12.12	72.7	2	98	0	0	30	24.32	-19.56			Jul-10
100	7.58	11.58	23.91	37.74	103.48	1.26	1.02	10.82	1.05	11.96	72.7	2	98	0	0	30	23.47	-19.48			Jul-10
100	6.60	12.21	21.66	29.48	94.84	0.75	1.08	10.4	1.02	6.06	307.8	1	99	0	0	46	23.29	-21.27			Jul-01
100	6.49	12.34	21.75	30.43	97.15	0.97	0.83	10.41	1.02	6.05	307.8	1	99	0	0	46	23.46	-21.21			Oct-00
100	5.29	9.36	18.38	26.84	94.50	0.41	1.15	11.05	1.04	17.04	3,092	2	98	0	0	63	24.69	-26.78			Jul-01

	MARKET			FUND TYPE, CATEGORY & OBJECTIVE	RATINGS				MINIMUMS	
Fund Name	Ticker Symbol	Traded On	Fund Type	Category and (Prospectus Objective)	Overall Rating	Reward Rating	Risk Rating	Recent Up/ Downgrade	Open to New Investors	Min Initial Investment
BNY Mellon Mid Cap Multi-Strategy Fund Class M	MPMCX	NAS CM	Open End	US Equity Mid Cap (Growth)	B-	B	C+	Down	Y	10,000
BNY Mellon Small Cap Multi-Strategy Fund Class Investor	MISCX	NAS CM	Open End	US Equity Small Cap (Small Company)	B	B+	B	Up	Y	10,000
BNY Mellon Small Cap Multi-Strategy Fund Class M	MPSSX	NAS CM	Open End	US Equity Small Cap (Small Company)	B	B+	B	Up	Y	10,000
BNY Mellon Small/Mid Cap Multi-Strategy Fund Cls M Shares	MMCMX	NAS CM	Open End	US Equity Small Cap (Growth)	B	B+	B	Up	Y	10,000
BNY Mellon Small/Mid Cap Multi-Strategy Fund Inv Shares	MMCIX	NAS CM	Open End	US Equity Small Cap (Growth)	B	B	B	Up	Y	10,000
BNY Mellon Tax-Sensitive Large Cap Multi-Strat Cls Inv	MTSIX	NAS CM	Open End	US Equity Large Cap Blend (Growth)	B	B	B-		Y	10,000
BNY Mellon Tax-Sensitive Large Cap Multi-Strat Fund Cls M	MTSMX	NAS CM	Open End	US Equity Large Cap Blend (Growth)	B	B	B-		Y	10,000
Bogle Investment Mgmt Small Cap Growth Fund Inst Cls	BOGIX	NAS CM	Open End	US Equity Small Cap (Small Company)	B	B+	B-	Up	Y	10,000
Boston Common International Fund	BCAIX	NAS CM	Open End	Global Equity Large Cap (Foreign Stock)	B-	C+	B-	Up	Y	100,000
Boston Common U.S. Equity Fund	BCAMX	NAS CM	Open End	US Equity Large Cap Growth (Growth)	B	B-	B		Y	100,000
Boston Partners All Cap Value Fund Institutional Class	BPAIX	NAS CM	Open End	US Equity Large Cap Value (Growth & Income)	B	B	B-		Y	100,000
Boston Partners All Cap Value Fund Investor Class	BPAVX	NAS CM	Open End	US Equity Large Cap Value (Growth & Income)	B	B	B+	Up	Y	2,500
Boston Partners Emerging Markets Fund Institutional Class	BPEMX	NAS CM	Open End	Emerging Markets Equity (Div Emerging Mkts)	U	U	U		Y	100,000
Boston Partners Emerging Mkts Long/Short Fund Inst Cls	BELSX	NAS CM	Open End	Long/Short Equity (Div Emerging Mkts)	C+	C+	B-	Up	Y	100,000
Boston Partners Global Equity Institutional Class	BPGIX	NAS CM	Open End	Global Equity (World Stock)	B-	B-	B-	Down	Y	100,000
Boston Partners Global Long/Short Fund Institutional Class	BGLSX	NAS CM	Open End	Long/Short Equity (World Stock)	B	C+	A-	Up	Y	100,000
Boston Partners Global Long/Short Fund Investor Class	BGRSX	NAS CM	Open End	Long/Short Equity (World Stock)	B	C	A-	Up	Y	2,500
Boston Partners Long/Short Equity Fund Institutional Class	BPLSX	NAS CM	Open End	Long/Short Equity (Growth)	B	C+	B+	Up		100,000
Boston Partners Long/Short Equity Fund Investor Class	BPLEX	NAS CM	Open End	Long/Short Equity (Growth)	B	C+	B+	Up		2,500
Boston Partners Long/Short Research Fund Institutional Cls	BPIRX	NAS CM	Open End	Long/Short Equity (Growth & Income)	B	C+	A+	Up		100,000
Boston Partners Long/Short Research Fund Investor Class	BPRRX	NAS CM	Open End	Long/Short Equity (Growth & Income)	B	C+	A+	Up		2,500
Boston Partners Small Cap Value Fund II Institutional Cls	BPSIX	NAS CM	Open End	US Equity Small Cap (Small Company)	B	B+	B	Up	Y	100,000
Boston Partners Small Cap Value Fund II Investor Class	BPSCX	NAS CM	Open End	US Equity Small Cap (Small Company)	B	B+	B	Up	Y	2,500
Boston Trust Asset Management Fund	BTBFX	NAS CM	Open End	Aggressive Alloc (Asset Alloc)	B	B-	A-		Y	100,000
Boston Trust Equity Fund	BTEFX	NAS CM	Open End	US Equity Large Cap Blend (Growth)	B	B-	B		Y	100,000
Boston Trust Midcap Fund	BTMFX	NAS CM	Open End	US Equity Mid Cap (Growth)	B	B	B+		Y	100,000
Boston Trust Small Cap Fund	BOSOX	NAS CM	Open End	US Equity Small Cap (Small Company)	B+	B+	B	Up		100,000
Boston Trust SMID Cap Fund	BTSMX	NAS CM	Open End	US Equity Small Cap (Growth)	B	B	B		Y	1,000,000
Boulder Growth & Income Fund	BIF	NYSE	Closed End	US Equity Large Cap Value (Growth & Income)	B-	B-	C+	Down	Y	
Boyar Value Fund	BOYAX	NAS CM	Open End	US Equity Large Cap Blend (Growth)	B-	C+	B	Down	Y	5,000
BP Capital TwinLine Energy Fund Class A	BPEAX	NAS CM	Open End	Energy Sector Equity (Natl Res)	C-	C	C-	Up	Y	3,000
BP Capital TwinLine Energy Fund Class I	BPEIX	NAS CM	Open End	Energy Sector Equity (Natl Res)	C-	C	C-	Up	Y	250,000
BP Capital TwinLine MLP Fund Class A	BPMAX	NAS CM	Open End	Energy Sector Equity (Natl Res)	D	D+	D	Down	Y	3,000
BP Capital TwinLine MLP Fund Class I	BPMIX	NAS CM	Open End	Energy Sector Equity (Natl Res)	D	D+	D	Down	Y	250,000
Brandes Emerging Markets Value Fund Class A	BEMAX	NAS CM	Open End	Emerging Markets Equity (Div Emerging Mkts)	C	C+	C	Down	Y	2,500
Brandes Emerging Markets Value Fund Class C	BEMCX	NAS CM	Open End	Emerging Markets Equity (Div Emerging Mkts)	C	C+	C		Y	2,500
Brandes Emerging Markets Value Fund Class I	BEMIX	NAS CM	Open End	Emerging Markets Equity (Div Emerging Mkts)	C	C+	C	Down	Y	100,000
Brandes Emerging Markets Value Fund Class R6	BEMRX	NAS CM	Open End	Emerging Markets Equity (Div Emerging Mkts)	C	C+	C	Down	Y	0
Brandes Global Equity Fund Class A	BGEAX	NAS CM	Open End	Global Equity (World Stock)	B-	C+	B	Up	Y	2,500
Brandes Global Equity Fund Class C	BGVCX	NAS CM	Open End	Global Equity (World Stock)	B-	C+	B	Up	Y	2,500
Brandes Global Equity Fund Class I	BGVIX	NAS CM	Open End	Global Equity (World Stock)	B-	C+	B	Up	Y	100,000
Brandes Global Equity Income Fund Class A	BGIAX	NAS CM	Open End	Global Equity (World Stock)	C+	C+	B-	Down	Y	2,500
Brandes Global Equity Income Fund Class C	BGICX	NAS CM	Open End	Global Equity (World Stock)	C+	C+	B-	Down	Y	2,500
Brandes Global Equity Income Fund Class I	BGIIX	NAS CM	Open End	Global Equity (World Stock)	C+	C+	B-	Down	Y	100,000
Brandes Global Opportunities Value Fund Class A	BGOAX	NAS CM	Open End	Global Equity Large Cap (World Stock)	C+	C+	C+	Up	Y	2,500
Brandes Global Opportunities Value Fund Class C	BGOCX	NAS CM	Open End	Global Equity Large Cap (World Stock)	C+	C+	C+	Up	Y	2,500
Brandes Global Opportunities Value Fund Class I	BGOIX	NAS CM	Open End	Global Equity Large Cap (World Stock)	C+	C+	C+	Up	Y	100,000
Brandes International Equity Fund A	BIEAX	NAS CM	Open End	Global Equity Large Cap (Foreign Stock)	B-	C+	B	Up	Y	2,500
Brandes International Equity Fund Class C	BIECX	NAS CM	Open End	Global Equity Large Cap (Foreign Stock)	B-	C+	B	Up	Y	2,500
Brandes International Equity Fund Class I	BIIEX	NAS CM	Open End	Global Equity Large Cap (Foreign Stock)	B-	C+	B	Up	Y	100,000
Brandes International Equity Fund Class R6	BIERX	NAS CM	Open End	Global Equity Large Cap (Foreign Stock)	B-	C+	B	Up	Y	0
Brandes International Small Cap Equity Fund Class A	BISAX	NAS CM	Open End	Global Equity Mid/Small Cap (Small Company)	B	C	A		Y	2,500

★Expanded analysis of this fund is included in Section II.

Min Additional Investment	TOTAL RETURNS					PERFORMANCE				ASSETS		ASSET ALLOCATION & TURNOVER					BULL & BEAR		FEES		
	3-Month Total Return	6-Month Total Return	1-Year Total Return	3-Year Total Return	5-Year Total Return	Dividend Yield (TTM)	Expense Ratio	3-Yr Std Deviation	3-Year Beta	NAV	Total Assets (MIL)	%Cash	%Stocks	%Bonds	%Other	Turnover Ratio	Last Bull Market Total Return	Last Bear Market Total Return	Front End Fee (%)	Back End Fee (%)	Inception Date
100	5.36	9.57	18.67	27.79	96.82	0.58	0.9	11.07	1.04	17.32	3,092	2	98	0	0	63	24.94	-26.68			Oct-00
100	6.15	11.01	18.18	33.95	101.51	0	1.3	15.18	1.05	19.16	582.9	3	97	0	0	76	28.54	-28.02			Jul-01
100	6.19	11.13	18.45	34.95	103.95	0	1.05	15.17	1.05	20.06	582.9	3	97	0	0	76	28.7	-27.91			Oct-00
100	6.56	11.20	19.91	34.36	96.89	0.06	0.95	12.88	1.02	14.59	355.3	2	98	0	0	79	20.64	-27.58			Sep-09
100	6.57	11.12	19.68	33.24	94.21	0	1.2	12.87	1.02	14.37	355.3	2	98	0	0	79	20.51	-27.7			Sep-09
100	7.21	11.57	22.17	35.38	102.88	1.06	1.15	10.46	1.03	16.7	363.0	2	98	0	0	24	23.53	-19.18			Jul-10
100	7.29	11.67	22.45	36.38	102.25	1.22	0.9	10.44	1.03	16.3	363.0	2	98	0	0	24	23.7	-18.5			Jul-10
250	3.69	13.83	17.06	28.59	99.36	0	1.25	16.38	1.06	31.23	110.2	2	98	0	0	366	30.94	-26.8			Oct-99
1,000	3.03	7.86	26.38	22.06	39.65	1.29	1.12	12.36	0.98	30.69	228.6	2	96	0	0	33	16.53	-22.76			Dec-10
1,000	5.28	9.80	20.64	31.48	92.91	0.7	1	9.66	0.93	42.65	35.1	3	97	0	0	22					Apr-12
5,000	4.85	9.24	17.85	35.34	116.76	0.97	0.8	11.57	1.06	26.52	1,981	5	95	0	0	27	26.87	-19.9			Jul-02
100	4.85	9.13	17.63	34.38	114.42	0.78	1.05	11.56	1.06	26.4	1,981	5	95	0	0	27	26.86	-20.08			Jul-02
5,000	3.96						1.1			10.35	5.8										Oct-17
5,000	2.83	8.76	24.78			6.67	2			11.73	57.6	54	58	0	-12	184					Feb-15
5,000	5.80	9.62	20.37	30.74	83.68	1.6	0.95	10.52	0.97	18.41	640.3	4	96	0	0	83					Dec-11
5,000	3.32	5.15	7.55	16.72		0.2	1.74	4.94	0.39	11.82	1,054	56	42	0	-1	109					Dec-13
100	3.16	5.01	7.22	15.75		0.12	1.99	4.89	0.39	11.72	1,054	56	42	0	-1	109					Apr-14
5,000	2.76	7.07	2.76	24.04	41.08	0	2.46	9.19	0.31	22.28	963.5	36	66	-2	0	63	14.44	-4.16			Nov-98
100	2.69	6.93	2.54	23.09	39.34	0	2.71	9.19	0.31	20.55	963.5	36	66	-2	0	63	14.29	-4.23			Nov-98
5,000	3.78	6.17	10.09	14.98	47.47	0	1.41	6.44	0.59	17.01	6,833	55	45	0	0	54	16.97	-10.52			Sep-10
100	3.72	6.03	9.79	14.13	45.59	0	1.66	6.43	0.59	16.7	6,833	55	45	0	0	54	16.71	-10.54			Nov-10
5,000	3.14	7.63	9.78	31.18	89.36	0.76	1.1	13.37	0.93	26.26	577.9	4	96	0	0	24	28.54	-23.52			Jul-98
100	3.06	7.48	9.50	30.19	87.09	0.59	1.35	13.36	0.93	25.15	577.9	4	96	0	0	24	28.32	-23.65			Jul-98
1,000	5.85	8.45	16.22	26.80	69.25	0.94	0.95	6.9	0.66	46.88	490.8	2	80	18	0	8	17.32	-10.2			Dec-95
1,000	7.88	11.30	20.66	32.09	89.68	0.79	0.96	9.08	0.87	23.63	134.0	0	100	0	0	7	23.51	-15.69			Oct-03
1,000	7.91	10.43	20.01	32.85	95.61	0.68	1	9.57	0.87	17.26	62.1	1	99	0	0	15	25.44	-18.01			Sep-07
1,000	5.34	8.32	12.25	32.15	77.60	0.82	1	12.15	0.81	14.73	370.8	1	99	0	0	52	25.71	-21.85			Dec-05
1,000	8.12	9.90	18.38	37.39	92.02	0.91	0.75	11.64	0.91	15.79	55.8	1	99	0	0	23					Nov-11
	8.48	13.45	22.22	28.84	86.63	0.68	2.28	10.12	0.89	13.01	1,357	12	91	-4	1	9	12.85	-14.28			Dec-72
1,000	6.50	8.38	15.47	22.71	82.20	0.12	1.8	9.6	0.89	26.54	26.7	11	89	0	0	4	26.55	-16.94	5.00		May-98
100	9.55	15.01	1.89	9.15		0	1.89	23.64	1.36	20.99	145.2	2	98	0	0	83			5.75		Dec-13
	9.64	15.14	2.17	10.12		0	1.6	23.65	1.36	21.14	145.2	2	98	0	0	83					Dec-13
100	-0.81	-2.07	-4.96	-16.94		7.1	1.75	18.74	1.15	14.89	99.1	5	94	0	0	139			5.75		Dec-13
	-0.74	-1.99	-4.74	-16.31		7.03	1.49	18.76	1.16	15.05	99.1	5	94	0	0	139					Dec-13
500	2.57	11.47	25.69	25.14	20.91	1.55	1.37	19.16	1.11	9.67	1,727	2	88	0	1	24	18.6	-26.15	5.75		Jan-11
500	2.40	10.99	24.76	22.31	16.63	0.59	2.12	19.1	1.11	9.63	1,727	2	88	0	1	24	18.22	-26.28		1.00	Jan-13
500	2.62	11.54	25.98	25.99	22.49	1.73	1.12	19.16	1.11	9.71	1,727	2	88	0	1	24	18.74	-26.05			Jan-11
0	2.73	11.78	26.26	26.47	22.95	1.77	0.97	19.19	1.11	9.74	1,727	2	88	0	1	24	18.74	-26.05			Jul-16
500	3.46	6.96	15.92	20.71	61.89	1.68	1.25	10.48	0.92	24.61	69.4	4	96	0	0	17	12.46	-19.09	5.75		Jan-11
500	3.25	6.56	15.05	18.03	56.09	0.96	2	10.47	0.92	24.46	69.4	4	96	0	0	17	12.09	-19.25		1.00	Jan-13
500	3.53	7.09	16.21	21.63	63.96	1.86	1	10.5	0.92	24.77	69.4	4	96	0	0	17	12.58	-19			Oct-08
500	2.29	6.74	19.56	39.13		0.3	1.25			12.28	1.0	0	95	0	0	13			5.75		Dec-14
500	1.95	6.67	16.55	33.10		1.22	2			11.76	1.0	0	95	0	0	13				1.00	Dec-14
500	2.12	6.62	17.17	36.13		2.22	1			11.65	1.0	0	95	0	0	13					Dec-14
500	2.43	5.64	15.03	26.41		1.32	1.4			11.75	32.6	7	93	0	0	11			5.75		Dec-14
500	1.27	4.21	13.15	22.39		0.66	2.15			11.72	32.6	7	93	0	0	11				1.00	Dec-14
500	2.58	5.85	15.39	26.87		1.5	1.15			11.74	32.6	7	93	0	0	11					Dec-14
500	1.71	5.83	14.88	21.45	47.88	3.11	1.18	12.11	0.92	17.78	625.5	7	93	0	0	34	7.81	-20.63	5.75		Jan-11
500	1.56	5.46	14.03	18.76	42.51	2.62	1.93	12.09	0.92	17.57	625.5	7	93	0	0	34	7.48	-20.99		1.00	Jan-13
500	1.76	5.93	15.13	22.16	49.26	3.23	1	12.13	0.92	17.83	625.5	7	93	0	0	34	7.95	-20.74			Jan-97
0	1.82	5.98	15.27	22.57	49.77	3.26	0.82	12.13	0.92	17.88	625.5	7	93	0	0	34	7.95	-20.74			Feb-16
500	1.09	2.55	11.45	29.06	61.35	2.34	1.32	10.71	0.81		1,759	10	89	0	1	21	10.55	-20.13	5.75		Jan-12

	MARKET			FUND TYPE, CATEGORY & OBJECTIVE	RATINGS				MINIMUMS	
Fund Name	Ticker Symbol	Traded On	Fund Type	Category and (Prospectus Objective)	Overall Rating	Reward Rating	Risk Rating	Recent Up/ Downgrade	Open to New Investors	Min Initial Investment
Brandes International Small Cap Equity Fund Class C	BINCX	NAS CM	Open End	Global Equity Mid/Small Cap (Small Company)	B	C	A	Up	Y	2,500
Brandes International Small Cap Equity Fund Class I	BISMX	NAS CM	Open End	Global Equity Mid/Small Cap (Small Company)	B	C	A		Y	100,000
Brandes International Small Cap Equity Fund Class R6	BISRX	NAS CM	Open End	Global Equity Mid/Small Cap (Small Company)	B	C	A		Y	0
Bread & Butter Fund	BABFX	NAS CM	Open End	US Equity Large Cap Value (Growth)	C+	C+	B-		Y	3,000
Bretton Fund	BRTNX	NAS CM	Open End	US Equity Large Cap Blend (Growth)	B-	C+	B		Y	5,000
Bridge Builder International Equity Fund	BBIEX	NAS CM	Open End	Global Equity Large Cap (Foreign Stock)	C	C+	B	Up	Y	0
Bridge Builder Large Cap Growth Fund	BBGLX	NAS CM	Open End	US Equity Large Cap Growth (Growth)	B-	C+	B	Up	Y	0
Bridge Builder Large Cap Value Fund	BBVLX	NAS CM	Open End	US Equity Large Cap Value (Growth)	B-	C+	B	Up	Y	0
Bridge Builder Small/Mid Cap Growth Fund	BBGSX	NAS CM	Open End	US Equity Mid Cap (Growth)	C+	C+	B-	Up	Y	0
Bridge Builder Small/Mid Cap Value Fund	BBVSX	NAS CM	Open End	US Equity Mid Cap (Growth)	C+	C+	B-	Up	Y	0
Bridges Investment Fund	BRGIX	NAS CM	Open End	US Equity Large Cap Growth (Growth & Income)	B-	B-	B-	Down	Y	1,000
Bridgeway Aggressive Investors 1 Fund	BRAGX	NAS CM	Open End	US Equity Mid Cap (Aggr Growth)	B	B	B-	Up	Y	2,000
Bridgeway Blue Chip 35 Index Fund	BRLIX	NAS CM	Open End	US Equity Large Cap Blend (Growth & Income)	B	B-	B+		Y	2,000
Bridgeway Managed Volatility Fund	BRBPX	NAS CM	Open End	Long/Short Equity (Balanced)	B-	C	B	Up	Y	2,000
Bridgeway Omni Small-Cap Value Fund Class N	BOSVX	NAS CM	Open End	US Equity Small Cap (Small Company)	B+	A-	B-	Up	Y	0
Bridgeway Omni Tax-Managed Small-Cap Value Fund Class N	BOTSX	NAS CM	Open End	US Equity Small Cap (Small Company)	B+	A-	B-	Up	Y	0
Bridgeway Small Cap Growth Fund	BRSGX	NAS CM	Open End	US Equity Small Cap (Small Company)	A-	A	B+	Up	Y	2,000
Bridgeway Small Cap Value Fund	BRSVX	NAS CM	Open End	US Equity Small Cap (Small Company)	B	B	B-	Up	Y	2,000
Bridgeway Small-Cap Momentum Fund Class N	BRSMX	NAS CM	Open End	US Equity Small Cap (Small Company)	B+	A-	B	Up	Y	2,000
Bridgeway Ultra Small Company Fund	BRUSX	NAS CM	Open End	US Equity Small Cap (Small Company)	C	C	C	Up		2,000
Bridgeway Ultra Small Company Market Fund	BRSIX	NAS CM	Open End	US Equity Small Cap (Small Company)	B	B	B-	Up	Y	2,000
Bright Rock Mid Cap Growth Fund Institutional Class	BQMGX	NAS CM	Open End	US Equity Mid Cap (Growth)	B+	B+	B+	Up	Y	100,000
Bright Rock Mid Cap Growth Fund Investor Class	BQMIX	NAS CM	Open End	US Equity Mid Cap (Growth)	B+	B+	B+	Up	Y	5,000
Bright Rock Quality Large Cap Fund Institutional Class	BQLCX	NAS CM	Open End	US Equity Large Cap Blend (Growth)	B	C+	B+		Y	100,000
Bright Rock Quality Large Cap Fund Investor Class	BQLIX	NAS CM	Open End	US Equity Large Cap Blend (Growth)	B	C+	B+		Y	5,000
Broadview Opportunity Fund	BVAOX	NAS CM	Open End	US Equity Small Cap (Growth)	B-	C+	B-	Up	Y	1,000
Brookfield Global Listed Infrastructure Fund Class A	BGLAX	NAS CM	Open End	Other Sector Equity (Growth & Income)	C	C	C-		Y	1,000
Brookfield Global Listed Infrastructure Fund Class C	BGLCX	NAS CM	Open End	Other Sector Equity (Growth & Income)	C	C	C-		Y	1,000
Brookfield Global Listed Infrastructure Fund Class I	BGLIX	NAS CM	Open End	Other Sector Equity (Growth & Income)	C	C	C-		Y	1,000,000
Brookfield Global Listed Infrastructure Fund Class Y	BGLYX	NAS CM	Open End	Other Sector Equity (Growth & Income)	C	C	C-		Y	1,000
Brookfield Global Listed Infrastructure Income Fund	INF	NYSE	Closed End	Global Equity (Growth & Income)	C-	C	D+		Y	
Brookfield Global Listed Real Estate Fund Class A	BLRAX	NAS CM	Open End	Real Estate Sector Equity (Real Estate)	B-	C+	B	Up	Y	1,000
Brookfield Global Listed Real Estate Fund Class C	BLRCX	NAS CM	Open End	Real Estate Sector Equity (Real Estate)	B-	C	B	Up	Y	1,000
Brookfield Global Listed Real Estate Fund Class I	BLRIX	NAS CM	Open End	Real Estate Sector Equity (Real Estate)	B-	C+	B		Y	1,000,000
Brookfield Global Listed Real Estate Fund Class Y	BLRYX	NAS CM	Open End	Real Estate Sector Equity (Real Estate)	B-	C+	B		Y	1,000
Brookfield Real Assets Securities Fund Class A	RASAX	NAS CM	Open End	Aggressive Alloc (Growth & Income)	C	C	C+		Y	1,000
Brookfield Real Assets Securities Fund Class C	RASCX	NAS CM	Open End	Aggressive Alloc (Growth & Income)	C	C	C		Y	1,000
Brookfield Real Assets Securities Fund Class I	RASIX	NAS CM	Open End	Aggressive Alloc (Growth & Income)	C	C	C+		Y	1,000,000
Brookfield Real Assets Securities Fund Class Y	RASYX	NAS CM	Open End	Aggressive Alloc (Growth & Income)	C	C	C+		Y	1,000
Brookfield U.S. Listed Real Estate Fund Class A	BRUAX	NAS CM	Open End	Real Estate Sector Equity (Real Estate)	C	C	C+	Down	Y	1,000
Brookfield U.S. Listed Real Estate Fund Class C	BRUCX	NAS CM	Open End	Real Estate Sector Equity (Real Estate)	C	C	C	Down	Y	1,000
Brookfield U.S. Listed Real Estate Fund Class I	BRUIX	NAS CM	Open End	Real Estate Sector Equity (Real Estate)	C+	C	B-		Y	1,000,000
Brookfield U.S. Listed Real Estate Fund Class Y	BRUYX	NAS CM	Open End	Real Estate Sector Equity (Real Estate)	C+	C	B-		Y	1,000
Brown Advy - Macquarie Asia New Stars Fund Inst Shares	BAFNX	NAS CM	Open End	Asia ex-Japan Equity (Foreign Stock)	C	C	C	Up	Y	1,000,000
Brown Advy - Macquarie Asia New Stars Fund Inv Shares	BIANX	NAS CM	Open End	Asia ex-Japan Equity (Foreign Stock)	C	C	C	Up	Y	100
Brown Advy - WMC Japan Alpha Opp Fund Adv Shares	BAJAX	NAS CM	Open End	Japan Equity (Growth)	B	B	B-	Up	Y	100
Brown Advy - WMC Japan Alpha Opp Fund Inst Shares	BAFJX	NAS CM	Open End	Japan Equity (Growth)	B	B	B-	Up	Y	1,000,000
Brown Advy - WMC Japan Alpha Opp Fund Inv Shares	BIAJX	NAS CM	Open End	Japan Equity (Growth)	B	B	B-	Up	Y	100
Brown Advisory Equity Income Fund Advisor Shares	BADAX	NAS CM	Open End	US Equity Large Cap Blend (Equity-Income)	B-	B-	B-	Down	Y	100
Brown Advisory Equity Income Fund Inst Shares	BAFDX	NAS CM	Open End	US Equity Large Cap Blend (Equity-Income)	B-	B-	B-	Down	Y	1,000,000
Brown Advisory Equity Income Fund Investor Shares	BIADX	NAS CM	Open End	US Equity Large Cap Blend (Equity-Income)	B-	B-	B-	Down	Y	100
Brown Advisory Flexible Equity Fund Advisor Shares	BAFAX	NAS CM	Open End	US Equity Large Cap Growth (Growth)	B	B	B-	Up	Y	100

★ Expanded analysis of this fund is included in Section II.

	TOTAL RETURNS					PERFORMANCE				ASSETS		ASSET ALLOCATION & TURNOVER					BULL & BEAR		FEES		
Min Additional Investment	3-Month Total Return	6-Month Total Return	1-Year Total Return	3-Year Total Return	5-Year Total Return	Dividend Yield (TTM)	Expense Ratio	3-Yr Std Deviation	3-Year Beta	NAV	Total Assets (MIL)	%Cash	%Stocks	%Bonds	%Other	Turnover Ratio	Last Bull Market Total Return	Last Bear Market Total Return	Front End Fee (%)	Back End Fee (%)	Inception Date
500	-2.41	-1.43	6.71	22.12	50.60	1.88	2.06	10.69	0.81	13.22	1,759	10	89	0	1	21	10.1	-20.3		1.00	Jan-13
500	1.16	2.65	11.78	29.95	63.26	2.51	1.13	10.72	0.81		1,759	10	89	0	1	21	10.65	-20.05			Feb-12
0	1.16	2.67	11.82	29.84	62.33	2.55	1	10.72	0.81		1,759	10	89	0	1	21	11.66	-20.05			Jun-16
500	3.00	6.51	11.26	7.74	33.70	0	2.03	7.91	0.65	14.41	1.6	36	62	0	0	19	8.98	-13.06			Oct-05
100	11.44	16.93	18.18	21.52	72.38	0	1.5	11.25	0.92	30.87	29.4	8	92	0	0	16	33.1	-11.72			Sep-10
	4.34	9.52	26.69			1.12	0.43			11.89	6,425	5	95	0	0						Jul-15
	5.86	10.61	25.32			0.74	0.29			12.72	5,110	4	96	0	0						Apr-15
	5.25	9.04	17.18			1.54	0.31			12.22	6,001	5	95	0	0						Apr-15
	6.36	10.24	21.45			0.3	0.44			12.53	2,968	6	94	0	0						Apr-15
	4.31	8.80	12.64			0.73	0.54			11.99	3,738	3	97	0	0						Apr-15
	5.66	10.72	21.98	29.81	94.09	0.39	0.84	11.15	0.99	60.57	143.3	5	95	0	0	11	27.75	-16.09			Jul-63
100	7.66	13.51	18.44	26.59	113.07	0.48	1.66	13.35	1.15	75.33	239.9	2	97	0	1	153	30.5	-30.95			Aug-94
100	7.29	11.60	18.42	35.43	104.00	2.08	0.15	10.44		14.57	571.4	0	100	0	0	17	24.19	-13.18			Jul-97
100	2.72	4.66	8.17	10.50	28.67	0.38	0.94	3.76	0.32	15.39	33.6	37	63	0	0	50	14.01	-10.64			Jun-01
	3.42	9.86	6.00	32.62	98.81	0.83	0.6	16.02	1.1	18.66	811.1	0	100	0	0	23	30.35				Aug-11
	2.99	9.15	5.51	33.51	97.31	0.73	0.6	15.82	1.09	17.9	736.1	1	99	0	0	23	28.33	-26.06			Dec-10
100	4.11	11.22	19.62	44.96	135.70	0.27	0.94	14.15	0.9	27.66	49.8	2	98	0	0	136	34.51	-27.76			Oct-03
100	2.82	7.83	7.10	22.01	76.71	0.91	0.94	15.03	1.03	26.53	64.0	0	99	1	0	77	30.06	-24.02			Oct-03
100	3.90	10.52	16.99	31.98	84.56	0.88	0.93	12.06	0.81	12.99	5.8	0	100	0	0	208	31.49	-25.09			May-10
100	-0.05	2.70	3.88	-0.92	57.10	1.1	1.48	16.47		30.24	96.9	2	98	0	0	113	35.36	-30			Aug-94
100	2.22	9.00	12.47	25.46	102.01	0.86	0.87	14.85		14.26	367.9	0	99	1	0	31	30.64	-26			Jul-97
5,000	9.35	14.29	22.15	39.21	89.41	0.05	1.2	9.84	0.78	17.21	65.8	1	99	0	0	30	23.25	-23.4			May-10
1,000	9.25	14.13	21.78	38.17	90.94	0.02	1.45	9.85	0.78	17.62	65.8	1	99	0	0	30	23.45	-23.48			Jan-12
5,000	7.43	10.59	16.31	25.47	86.09	1.14	0.89	9.15	0.85	16.62	234.2	1	99	0	0	60	26.86	-15.8			May-10
1,000	7.31	10.39	15.86	24.38	85.18	0.66	1.14	9.11	0.84	16.99	234.2	1	99	0	0	60	26.96	-15.88			Jan-12
100	3.64	6.54	8.90	17.47	78.40	0	1.27	12.76	0.98	34.53	613.4	10	90	0	0	53	28.21	-24.46			Dec-96
100	-0.46	1.49	10.52	-0.37	33.98	3.67	1.35	11.78	1.06	12.73	238.7	0	100	0	0	100			4.75		Dec-11
100	-0.69	1.10	9.62	-2.64	28.91	2.97	2.1	11.76	1.06	12.58	238.7	0	100	0	0	100				1.00	Apr-12
	-0.46	1.56	10.70	0.30	35.55	3.91	1.1	11.75	1.06	12.76	238.7	0	100	0	0	100					Nov-11
100	-0.39	1.64	10.79	0.44	35.69	3.92	1.1	11.75	1.06	12.76	238.7	0	100	0	0	100					Nov-11
	-0.48	1.93	13.74	-13.58	14.50	1.71	2.41	18.59		14.79	207.8	0	99	1	0	93	28.6				Aug-11
100	3.73	4.71	9.83	13.34	45.08	3.35	1.2	11.41	1.01	13.34	1,942	0	99	0	1	88			4.75		Apr-12
100	3.61	4.32	9.07	10.91	39.83	2.65	1.95	11.44	1.01	13.28	1,942	0	99	0	1	88				1.00	Apr-12
	3.81	4.85	10.12	14.19	46.79	3.61	0.95	11.4	1.01	13.35	1,942	0	99	0	1	88					Nov-11
100	3.88	4.93	10.20	14.26	46.98	3.6	0.95	11.4	1.01	13.37	1,942	0	99	0	1	88					Nov-11
100	1.04	2.56	9.73	6.10		3.58	1.35	9.79	0.74	9.39	76.7	0	87	10	0	119			4.75		Nov-14
100	0.90	2.29	8.94	4.08		2.81	2.1	9.82	0.74	9.41	76.7	0	87	10	0	119				1.00	Nov-14
	1.12	2.58	9.65	6.19		3.93	1.1	9.78	0.73	9.29	76.7	0	87	10	0	119					Nov-14
100	1.11	2.47	9.64	6.29		3.93	1.1	9.77	0.73	9.3	76.7	0	87	10	0	119					Nov-14
100	0.54	0.52	2.73	3.97		2.69	1.2	13.69	0.98	10.27	24.5	0	100	0	0	111			4.75		Dec-13
100	0.42	0.20	1.94	1.82		2.16	1.95	13.6	0.98	10.25	24.5	0	100	0	0	111				1.00	Dec-13
	0.61	0.65	2.99	4.79		2.86	0.95	13.68	0.98	10.21	24.5	0	100	0	0	111					Dec-13
100	0.71	0.74	3.18	5.16		2.85	0.95	13.61	0.98	10.25	24.5	0	100	0	0	111					Dec-13
100	8.27	10.57	33.09	16.76		0	1.57	14.33	0.89	10.88	271.8	5	95	0	1						Nov-14
100	8.19	10.50	32.95	16.22		0	1.72	14.34	0.89	10.84	271.8	5	95	0	1						Nov-14
100	8.36	13.98	27.98	25.43		0	1.55	16.31	0.94	11.32	1,138	4	96	0	0						Mar-14
100	8.35	14.12	28.38	26.81		0	1.15	16.28	0.94	11.45	1,138	4	96	0	0						Mar-14
100	8.39	14.08	28.27	26.30		0	1.3	16.33	0.94	11.4	1,138	4	96	0	0						Mar-14
100	6.46	9.95	19.97	22.63	75.67	1.32	1.17	8.87	0.84	14.59	119.0	4	96	0	0						Dec-11
100	6.55	10.22	20.49	24.05	79.20	1.67	0.77	8.82	0.84	14.62	119.0	4	96	0	0						Oct-12
100	6.51	10.07	20.23	23.50	77.70	1.53	0.92	8.85	0.84	14.61	119.0	4	96	0	0						Dec-11
100	7.16	12.43	23.74	29.56	101.96	0	1.14	11.41	1.07	20.77	451.1	4	96	0	0		26.39	-15.49			Jan-07

	MARKET		FUND TYPE, CATEGORY & OBJECTIVE		RATINGS					MINIMUMS
Fund Name	Ticker Symbol	Traded On	Fund Type	Category and (Prospectus Objective)	Overall Rating	Reward Rating	Risk Rating	Recent Up/ Downgrade	Open to New Investors	Min Initial Investment
Brown Advisory Flexible Equity Fund Institutional Shares	BAFFX	NAS CM	Open End	US Equity Large Cap Growth (Growth)	B	B	B-		Y	1,000,000
Brown Advisory Flexible Equity Fund Investor Shares	BIAFX	NAS CM	Open End	US Equity Large Cap Growth (Growth)	B	B	B-		Y	100
Brown Advisory Global Leaders Fund Investor Shares	BIALX	NAS CM	Open End	Global Equity (World Stock)	C	C+	B+	Up	Y	100
Brown Advisory Growth Equity Fund Advisor Shares	BAGAX	NAS CM	Open End	US Equity Large Cap Growth (Growth)	B+	B	A-	Up	Y	100
Brown Advisory Growth Equity Fund Institutional Shares	BAFGX	NAS CM	Open End	US Equity Large Cap Growth (Growth)	B+	B+	A-	Up	Y	1,000,000
Brown Advisory Growth Equity Fund Investor Shares	BIAGX	NAS CM	Open End	US Equity Large Cap Growth (Growth)	B+	B	A-	Up	Y	100
Brown Advisory Mid-Cap Growth Fund Investor Class	BMIDX	NAS CM	Open End	US Equity Small Cap (Growth)	U	U	U		Y	100
Brown Advy Small-Cap Fundamental Value Fund Adv Shares	BAUAX	NAS CM	Open End	US Equity Small Cap (Small Company)	B	B	B	Up	Y	100
Brown Advy Small-Cap Fundamental Value Fund Inst Shares	BAUUX	NAS CM	Open End	US Equity Small Cap (Small Company)	B	B	B	Up	Y	1,000,000
Brown Advy Small-Cap Fundamental Value Fund Inv Shares	BIAUX	NAS CM	Open End	US Equity Small Cap (Small Company)	B	B	B	Up	Y	100
Brown Advisory Small-Cap Growth Fund Advisor Shares	BASAX	NAS CM	Open End	US Equity Small Cap (Small Company)	B	B	B+	Up	Y	100
Brown Advisory Small-Cap Growth Fund Institutional Shares	BAFSX	NAS CM	Open End	US Equity Small Cap (Small Company)	B	B	B+	Up	Y	1,000,000
Brown Advisory Small-Cap Growth Fund Investor Shares	BIASX	NAS CM	Open End	US Equity Small Cap (Small Company)	B	B	B+	Up	Y	100
Brown Advy Somerset Emerging Mkts Fund Adv Shares	BAQAX	NAS CM	Open End	Emerging Markets Equity (Div Emerging Mkts)	C+	B-	C+	Up	Y	100
Brown Advy Somerset Emerging Mkts Fund Inst Shares	BAFQX	NAS CM	Open End	Emerging Markets Equity (Div Emerging Mkts)	C+	B-	C+	Up	Y	1,000,000
Brown Advy Somerset Emerging Mkts Fund Inv Shares	BIAQX	NAS CM	Open End	Emerging Markets Equity (Div Emerging Mkts)	C+	B-	C+	Up	Y	100
Brown Advisory Sustainable Growth Fund Advisor Shares	BAWAX	NAS CM	Open End	US Equity Large Cap Growth (Growth)	A-	A-	A-	Up	Y	100
Brown Advy Sustainable Growth Fund Inst Shares	BAFWX	NAS CM	Open End	US Equity Large Cap Growth (Growth)	B+	A-	B	Up	Y	1,000,000
Brown Advisory Sustainable Growth Fund Investor Shares	BIAWX	NAS CM	Open End	US Equity Large Cap Growth (Growth)	A-	A-	A-	Up	Y	100
Brown Advy WMC Strategic European Equity Fund Adv Shares	BAHAX	NAS CM	Open End	Europe Equity Large Cap (Europe Stock)	B	B	B	Up	Y	100
Brown Advy WMC Strategic European Equity Fund Inst Shares	BAFHX	NAS CM	Open End	Europe Equity Large Cap (Europe Stock)	B	B	B	Up	Y	1,000,000
Brown Advy WMC Strategic European Equity Fund Inv Shares	BIAHX	NAS CM	Open End	Europe Equity Large Cap (Europe Stock)	B	B	B	Up	Y	100
Brown Capital Mgmt Intl Equity Fund Inst Shares	BCISX	NAS CM	Open End	Global Equity Large Cap (Foreign Stock)	B-	C+	B	Up	Y	500,000
Brown Capital Mgmt Intl Equity Fund Inv Shares	BCIIX	NAS CM	Open End	Global Equity Large Cap (Foreign Stock)	B-	C+	B	Up	Y	5,000
Brown Capital Mgmt Intl Small Company Fund Inst Shares	BCSFX	NAS CM	Open End	Global Equity Mid/Small Cap (Small Company)	C	C+	B	Up	Y	500,000
Brown Capital Mgmt Intl Small Company Fund Inv Shares	BCSVX	NAS CM	Open End	Global Equity Mid/Small Cap (Small Company)	C	C+	B	Up	Y	5,000
Brown Capital Mgmt Mid Company Fund Inst Shares	BCMIX	NAS CM	Open End	US Equity Mid Cap (Growth)	C+	C+	B-	Up	Y	500,000
Brown Capital Management Mid Company Fund Investor Shares	BCMSX	NAS CM	Open End	US Equity Mid Cap (Growth)	C	C+	C		Y	5,000
Brown Capital Mgmt Small Company Fund Inst Shares	BCSSX	NAS CM	Open End	US Equity Small Cap (Small Company)	A-	A	B+	Up		500,000
Brown Capital Mgmt Small Company Fund Inv Shares	BCSIX	NAS CM	Open End	US Equity Small Cap (Small Company)	A-	A	B+	Up		5,000
Bruce Fund	BRUFX	NAS CM	Open End	Moderate Alloc (Growth)	B	C+	A		Y	1,000
Buffalo Discovery Fund	BUFTX	NAS CM	Open End	US Equity Mid Cap (Growth)	B+	B	B+	Up	Y	2,500
Buffalo Dividend Focus Fund	BUFDX	NAS CM	Open End	US Equity Large Cap Blend (Equity-Income)	B	B-	B+		Y	2,500
Buffalo Emerging Opportunities Fund	BUFOX	NAS CM	Open End	US Equity Small Cap (Growth)	B	A-	C	Up		2,500
Buffalo Flexible Income Fund	BUFBX	NAS CM	Open End	Aggressive Alloc (Balanced)	B-	C+	B	Down	Y	2,500
Buffalo Growth Fund	BUFGX	NAS CM	Open End	US Equity Large Cap Growth (Growth)	B	B	B+	Up	Y	2,500
Buffalo International Fund	BUFIX	NAS CM	Open End	Global Equity Large Cap (Foreign Stock)	B	B	B	Up	Y	2,500
Buffalo Large Cap Fund	BUFEX	NAS CM	Open End	US Equity Large Cap Growth (Growth)	B+	B	A-	Up	Y	2,500
Buffalo Mid Cap Fund	BUFMX	NAS CM	Open End	US Equity Mid Cap (Growth)	B-	C+	B	Up	Y	2,500
Buffalo Small Cap Fund	BUFSX	NAS CM	Open End	US Equity Small Cap (Small Company)	B	B+	B-	Up		2,500
Bullfinch Greater Western New York Series	BWNYX	NAS CM	Open End	US Equity Mid Cap (Growth)	B-	C+	B	Up	Y	2,500
Calamos Convertible & High Income Fund	CHY	NAS CM	Closed End	Convertibles (Convertible Bond)	C+	C+	C+		Y	
Calamos Convertible Fund Class A	CCVIX	NAS CM	Open End	Convertibles (Convertible Bond)	C+	C+	C+	Down	Y	2,500
Calamos Convertible Fund Class C	CCVCX	NAS CM	Open End	Convertibles (Convertible Bond)	C+	C+	C+	Down	Y	2,500
Calamos Convertible Fund Class R	CCVRX	NAS CM	Open End	Convertibles (Convertible Bond)	C+	C+	C+	Down	Y	0
Calamos Convertible Fund Class T	CCVTX	NAS CM	Open End	Convertibles (Convertible Bond)	C+	C+	B-	Down	Y	0
Calamos Convertible Fund Institutional Class	CICVX	NAS CM	Open End	Convertibles (Convertible Bond)	C+	C+	C+	Down	Y	1,000,000
Calamos Convertible Opportunities and Income Fund	CHI	NAS CM	Closed End	Convertibles (Convertible Bond)	C+	C+	C+		Y	
Calamos Dividend Growth Fund Class A	CADVX	NAS CM	Open End	US Equity Large Cap Value (Equity-Income)	B-	B-	B-	Down	Y	2,500
Calamos Dividend Growth Fund Class C	CCDVX	NAS CM	Open End	US Equity Large Cap Value (Equity-Income)	B-	B-	B-	Down	Y	2,500
Calamos Dividend Growth Fund Class I	CIDVX	NAS CM	Open End	US Equity Large Cap Value (Equity-Income)	B-	B-	B-	Down	Y	1,000,000
Calamos Dividend Growth Fund Class T	CTDVX	NAS CM	Open End	US Equity Large Cap Value (Equity-Income)	B-	C+	B-	Down	Y	0

★Expanded analysis of this fund is included in Section II.

Min Additional Investment	TOTAL RETURNS 3-Month Total Return	6-Month Total Return	1-Year Total Return	3-Year Total Return	5-Year Total Return	PERFORMANCE Dividend Yield (TTM)	Expense Ratio	3-Yr Std Deviation	3-Year Beta	ASSETS NAV	Total Assets (MIL)	ASSET ALLOCATION & TURNOVER %Cash	%Stocks	%Bonds	%Other	Turnover Ratio	BULL & BEAR Last Bull Market Total Return	Last Bear Market Total Return	FEES Front End Fee (%)	Back End Fee (%)	Inception Date
100	7.28	12.66	24.27	31.14	105.89	0	0.74	11.41	1.07	20.76	451.1	4	96	0	0		26.58	-15.41			Oct-12
100	7.30	12.58	24.12	30.60	104.43	0	0.89	11.42	1.07	20.74	451.1	4	96	0	0		26.58	-15.41			Nov-06
100	7.59	13.48	33.99			0.14	0.85			13.04	48.8	3	97	0	0	35					Jul-15
100	7.79	12.83	30.12	33.16	86.01	0	1.12	11.56	1	19.81	1,953	3	97	0	0		30.1	-18.48			May-06
100	7.92	13.09	30.56	34.69	89.71	0	0.72	11.58	1	20.98	1,953	3	97	0	0		30.27	-18.41			Oct-12
100	7.89	12.98	30.43	34.07	88.29	0	0.87	11.56	1	20.8	1,953	3	97	0	0		30.27	-18.41			Jun-99
100	0.78						0.86			10.28	3.6										Oct-17
100	4.30	9.18	11.88	27.10	92.14	0	1.56	12.4	0.84	28.34	1,335	5	95	0	0		22.45	-20.6			Jul-11
100	4.39	9.40	12.34	28.63	96.15	0.31	1.16	12.38	0.84	28.45	1,335	5	95	0	0		22.64	-20.57			Oct-12
100	4.36	9.33	12.19	28.11	94.68	0.19	1.31	12.4	0.84	28.44	1,335	5	95	0	0		22.64	-20.57			Dec-08
100	1.49	7.09	16.57	36.46	95.91	0	1.39	12.23	0.76	17.78	754.9	7	93	0	0		28.16	-24.49			Apr-06
100	1.58	7.30	17.10	38.14	99.82	0	0.99	12.25	0.77	37.07	754.9	7	93	0	0		28.37	-24.3			Sep-02
100	1.51	7.21	16.91	37.46	98.37	0	1.14	12.22	0.76	18.57	754.9	7	93	0	0		28.34	-24.33			Jun-99
100	3.14	11.24	32.43	20.63	15.58	0.62	1.57	11.98	0.7	11.27	649.4	5	95	0	0						Dec-12
100	3.35	11.59	33.04	22.22	18.17	1.02	1.17	12.03	0.7	11.24	649.4	5	95	0	0						Dec-12
100	3.30	11.44	32.76	21.65	17.24	0.91	1.32	12.01	0.7	11.22	649.4	5	95	0	0						Dec-12
100	6.86	11.70	27.60	50.18	116.76	0	1.14	10.81	0.94	20.36	499.2	3	97	0	0						Jun-12
100	6.96	11.93	28.10	52.05	121.23	0	0.74	10.78	0.93	20.85	499.2	3	97	0	0						Jun-12
100	6.92	11.82	27.89	51.28	119.44	0	0.89	10.8	0.94	20.65	499.2	3	97	0	0						Jun-12
100	2.52	7.74	32.11	35.45		0.81	1.49	11.57	0.84	12.8	1,305	1	96	0	2						Oct-13
100	2.62	7.99	32.65	37.12		1	1.09	11.56	0.84	12.9	1,305	1	96	0	2						Oct-13
100	2.58	7.86	32.35	36.45		0.92	1.24	11.57	0.84	12.89	1,305	1	96	0	2						Oct-13
500	4.84	8.00	23.88	25.05	57.78	1.71	1.01	10.63	0.82	14.19	38.4	1	97	0	2	2	16.67	-25.21			Aug-14
500	4.76	7.84	23.61	24.14	56.41	1.52	1.26	10.67	0.82	14.18	38.4	1	97	0	2	2	16.67	-25.21			May-99
500	7.20	14.58	37.30			0	1.26			14.77	22.3	4	96	0	0	11					Sep-15
500	7.17	14.41	36.98			0	1.51			14.68	22.3	4	96	0	0	11					Sep-15
500	7.63	8.92	19.57	8.96	53.50	0	0.91	11.85	0.99	11.26	20.4	2	98	0	0	45	22.97	-20.78			Dec-11
500	7.54	8.77	19.33	8.19	51.29	0	1.16	11.87	0.99	10.85	20.4	2	98	0	0	45	22.91	-20.78			Sep-02
500	5.45	9.56	29.16	52.37	136.95	0	1.09	14.17	0.82	90.59	4,256	3	97	0	0	14	22.99	-18.77			Dec-11
500	5.40	9.44	28.90	51.45	134.59	0	1.29	14.17	0.82	89.26	4,256	3	97	0	0	14	22.89	-18.77			Jul-92
500	2.67	4.52	12.46	19.97	63.85	1.78	0.71	6.04	0.36	525.14	578.8	12	56	26	0	5	13.69	-10.34			Mar-68
100	4.44	10.40	25.43	38.63	115.76	0	1.03	10.28	0.87	24.22	1,662	3	97	0	0	51	31.74	-19.13			Apr-01
100	6.46	9.29	18.01	31.45	98.65	1.11	0.96	9.47	0.9	16.66	63.3	5	94	0	0	26					Dec-12
100	1.32	8.22	27.18	27.87	95.25	0	1.49	16.07	0.97	15.62	92.9	8	92	0	0	95	40.57	-20.94			May-04
100	5.49	11.36	13.20	21.12	48.59	2.31	1.01	8.59		15.6	748.2	0	84	9	0	1	14.47	-6.69			Aug-94
100	6.14	9.66	22.81	30.92	98.49	0.61	0.92	9.7	0.87	29.13	235.9	1	99	0	0	18	26.47	-18.13			May-95
100	2.49	7.73	29.33	32.28	56.20	0.81	1.05	11.42	0.88	14.91	252.7	12	88	0	0	4	19.39	-23.5			Sep-07
100	6.54	9.55	24.86	41.76	117.63	0.42	0.96	10.14	0.89	29.03	72.5	4	96	0	0	41	22.39	-19.57			May-95
100	3.88	6.28	13.65	19.01	66.70	0	1.02	11.23	0.94	13.61	191.3	5	95	0	0	51	23.82	-19.97			Dec-01
100	3.80	9.01	27.07	28.62	76.97	0	1.02	14.09	0.9	14.66	569.9	2	98	0	0	45	35.67	-25.5			Apr-98
250	2.43	4.04	5.06	9.72	65.10	0	1.56	10.2		21.57	0.73	15	85	0	0	0	18.17	-15.81			Dec-97
	1.27	5.03	14.08	15.04	41.15	5.93	1.23	9.5	-0.36	11.64	859.6	2	3	39	0	34	13.61	-8.91			May-03
50	2.06	4.95	14.32	14.26	46.51	1.72	1.15	8.1	1	17.66	597.8	4	7	0	0	56	7.83	-13.85	2.25		Jun-85
50	1.88	4.60	13.43	11.71	41.08	1.11	1.9	8.07	1	17.49	597.8	4	7	0	0	56	7.33	-14.1		1.00	Jul-96
	2.06	4.90	14.11	13.43	44.69	1.5	1.4	8.1	1	17.6	597.8	4	7	0	0	56	7.68	-13.95			Mar-07
	1.65	5.33	14.79	15.24	45.46		1.15	8.07	1		596.5	2	7	6	0	44	7.83	-13.85	2.50		Feb-17
	2.17	5.14	14.61	15.14	48.40	2.16	0.9	8.07	1	15.85	597.8	4	7	0	0	56	7.93	-13.73			Jun-97
	1.43	5.08	14.28	15.61	43.44	5.9	1.44	9.37	0.8	11.05	787.1	3	2	39	0	90	13.27	-9.01			Jun-02
50	6.23	10.85	20.93	31.31		0.38	1.34	9.58	0.93	12.17	25.5	1	99	0	0	15			4.75		Aug-13
50	5.97	10.39	19.99	28.38		0.17	2.09	9.54	0.92	11.96	25.5	1	99	0	0	15				1.00	Aug-13
	6.22	10.92	21.13	32.26		0.83	1.09	9.54	0.92	12.15	25.5	1	99	0	0	15					Aug-13
	3.69	7.94	21.58	27.56			1.34	9.47	0.91		25.1	0	100	0	0	12			2.50		Feb-17

	MARKET		FUND TYPE, CATEGORY & OBJECTIVE		RATINGS					MINIMUMS
Fund Name	Ticker Symbol	Traded On	Fund Type	Category and (Prospectus Objective)	Overall Rating	Reward Rating	Risk Rating	Recent Up/ Downgrade	Open to New Investors	Min Initial Investment
Calamos Dynamic Convertible and Income Fund	CCD	NAS CM	Closed End	Convertibles (Convertible Bond)	C+	C+	B-	Up	Y	
Calamos Emerging Market Equity Fund Class A	CEGAX	NAS CM	Open End	Emerging Markets Equity (Div Emerging Mkts)	C+	C+	C	Up	Y	2,500
Calamos Emerging Market Equity Fund Class C	CEGCX	NAS CM	Open End	Emerging Markets Equity (Div Emerging Mkts)	C+	C+	C	Up	Y	2,500
Calamos Emerging Market Equity Fund Class I	CIEIX	NAS CM	Open End	Emerging Markets Equity (Div Emerging Mkts)	C+	B-	C	Up	Y	1,000,000
Calamos Emerging Market Equity Fund Class T	CEGTX	NAS CM	Open End	Emerging Markets Equity (Div Emerging Mkts)	C+	C+	C	Up	Y	0
Calamos Evolving World Growth Fund Class A	CNWGX	NAS CM	Open End	Emerging Markets Equity (Growth)	C+	C+	C	Up	Y	2,500
Calamos Evolving World Growth Fund Class C	CNWDX	NAS CM	Open End	Emerging Markets Equity (Growth)	C+	C+	C	Up	Y	2,500
Calamos Evolving World Growth Fund Class I	CNWIX	NAS CM	Open End	Emerging Markets Equity (Growth)	C+	C+	C	Up	Y	1,000,000
Calamos Evolving World Growth Fund Class R	CNWRX	NAS CM	Open End	Emerging Markets Equity (Growth)	C+	C+	C	Up	Y	0
Calamos Evolving World Growth Fund Class T	CNWTX	NAS CM	Open End	Emerging Markets Equity (Growth)	C+	C+	C+	Up	Y	0
Calamos Global Convertible Fund Class A	CAGCX	NAS CM	Open End	Convertibles (Growth & Income)	C+	C	B	Up	Y	2,500
Calamos Global Convertible Fund Class C	CCGCX	NAS CM	Open End	Convertibles (Growth & Income)	C+	C	B	Up	Y	2,500
Calamos Global Convertible Fund Class I	CXGCX	NAS CM	Open End	Convertibles (Growth & Income)	C+	C	B	Up	Y	1,000,000
Calamos Global Convertible Fund Class R	CRGCX	NAS CM	Open End	Convertibles (Growth & Income)	C+	C	B	Up	Y	0
Calamos Global Convertible Fund Class T	CTGCX	NAS CM	Open End	Convertibles (Growth & Income)	C+	C	B	Up	Y	0
Calamos Global Dynamic Income Fund	CHW	NAS CM	Closed End	Alloc (Multi-Asset Global)	B-	B-	B	Up	Y	
Calamos Global Equity Fund Class A	CAGEX	NAS CM	Open End	Global Equity (World Stock)	B+	B+	B+	Up	Y	2,500
Calamos Global Equity Fund Class C	CCGEX	NAS CM	Open End	Global Equity (World Stock)	B	B	B	Up	Y	2,500
Calamos Global Equity Fund Class R	CRGEX	NAS CM	Open End	Global Equity (World Stock)	B	B	B	Up	Y	0
Calamos Global Equity Fund Class T	CTGEX	NAS CM	Open End	Global Equity (World Stock)	B	B-	B+	Up	Y	0
Calamos Global Equity Fund Institutional Class	CIGEX	NAS CM	Open End	Global Equity (World Stock)	B+	B+	B+	Up	Y	1,000,000
Calamos Global Growth & Income Fund Class A	CVLOX	NAS CM	Open End	Alloc (Multi-Asset Global)	B	C+	B+	Up	Y	2,500
Calamos Global Growth & Income Fund Class C	CVLCX	NAS CM	Open End	Alloc (Multi-Asset Global)	B-	C+	B+	Up	Y	2,500
Calamos Global Growth & Income Fund Class I	CGCIX	NAS CM	Open End	Alloc (Multi-Asset Global)	B	C+	B+	Up	Y	1,000,000
Calamos Global Growth & Income Fund Class R	CVLRX	NAS CM	Open End	Alloc (Multi-Asset Global)	B	C+	B+	Up	Y	0
Calamos Global Growth & Income Fund Class T	CVLTX	NAS CM	Open End	Alloc (Multi-Asset Global)	B	C+	B+	Up	Y	0
Calamos Global Total Return Fund	CGO	NAS CM	Closed End	Alloc (Multi-Asset Global)	B	B-	B	Up	Y	
Calamos Growth & Income Fund Class A	CVTRX	NAS CM	Open End	Aggressive Alloc (Growth & Income)	B	B-	B+		Y	2,500
Calamos Growth & Income Fund Class C	CVTCX	NAS CM	Open End	Aggressive Alloc (Growth & Income)	B-	C+	B	Down	Y	2,500
Calamos Growth & Income Fund Class R	CGNRX	NAS CM	Open End	Aggressive Alloc (Growth & Income)	B	C+	B		Y	0
Calamos Growth & Income Fund Class T	CVTTX	NAS CM	Open End	Aggressive Alloc (Growth & Income)	B	C+	B+		Y	0
Calamos Growth & Income Fund Institutional Class	CGIIX	NAS CM	Open End	Aggressive Alloc (Growth & Income)	B	B-	B+		Y	1,000,000
Calamos Growth Fund Class A	CVGRX	NAS CM	Open End	US Equity Large Cap Growth (Growth)	B	B-	B+	Up	Y	2,500
Calamos Growth Fund Class C	CVGCX	NAS CM	Open End	US Equity Large Cap Growth (Growth)	B-	C+	B	Up	Y	2,500
Calamos Growth Fund Class R	CGRRX	NAS CM	Open End	US Equity Large Cap Growth (Growth)	B	B-	B	Up	Y	0
Calamos Growth Fund Class T	CVGTX	NAS CM	Open End	US Equity Large Cap Growth (Growth)	B	C+	B+	Up	Y	0
Calamos Growth Fund Institutional Class	CGRIX	NAS CM	Open End	US Equity Large Cap Growth (Growth)	B	B-	B+	Up	Y	1,000,000
Calamos Hedged Equity Income Fund Class A	CAHEX	NAS CM	Open End	Long/Short Equity (Income)	C+	C	B	Down	Y	2,500
Calamos Hedged Equity Income Fund Class C	CCHEX	NAS CM	Open End	Long/Short Equity (Income)	C+	C	B	Down	Y	2,500
Calamos Hedged Equity Income Fund Class I	CIHEX	NAS CM	Open End	Long/Short Equity (Income)	B-	C	B	Up	Y	1,000,000
Calamos Hedged Equity Income Fund Class T	CAHTX	NAS CM	Open End	Long/Short Equity (Income)	C+	C	B	Down	Y	0
Calamos International Growth Fund Class A	CIGRX	NAS CM	Open End	Global Equity Large Cap (Foreign Stock)	B	B	B	Up	Y	2,500
Calamos International Growth Fund Class C	CIGCX	NAS CM	Open End	Global Equity Large Cap (Foreign Stock)	B	B-	B	Up	Y	2,500
Calamos International Growth Fund Class R	CIGFX	NAS CM	Open End	Global Equity Large Cap (Foreign Stock)	B	B	B	Up	Y	0
Calamos International Growth Fund Class T	CITGX	NAS CM	Open End	Global Equity Large Cap (Foreign Stock)	B-	B-	B	Up	Y	0
Calamos International Growth Fund Institutional Class	CIGIX	NAS CM	Open End	Global Equity Large Cap (Foreign Stock)	B	B	B	Up	Y	1,000,000
Calamos Market Neutral Income Class T	CVSTX	NAS CM	Open End	Market Neutral (Income)	B-	C	B+	Up	Y	0
Calamos Market Neutral Income Fund Class A	CVSIX	NAS CM	Open End	Market Neutral (Income)	B-	C	B+		Y	2,500
Calamos Market Neutral Income Fund Class C	CVSCX	NAS CM	Open End	Market Neutral (Income)	B-	C	B	Up	Y	2,500
Calamos Market Neutral Income Fund Class R	CVSRX	NAS CM	Open End	Market Neutral (Income)	B-	C	B	Up	Y	0
Calamos Market Neutral Income Fund Institutional Class	CMNIX	NAS CM	Open End	Market Neutral (Income)	B-	C	B+		Y	1,000,000
Calamos Opportunistic Value Fund Class A	CVAAX	NAS CM	Open End	US Equity Large Cap Value (Growth)	B-	B-	B-	Down	Y	2,500

★ Expanded analysis of this fund is included in Section II.

	TOTAL RETURNS					PERFORMANCE				ASSETS		ASSET ALLOCATION & TURNOVER					BULL & BEAR		FEES		
Min Additional Investment	3-Month Total Return	6-Month Total Return	1-Year Total Return	3-Year Total Return	5-Year Total Return	Dividend Yield (TTM)	Expense Ratio	3-Yr Std Deviation	3-Year Beta	NAV	Total Assets (MIL)	%Cash	%Stocks	%Bonds	%Other	Turnover Ratio	Last Bull Market Total Return	Last Bear Market Total Return	Front End Fee (%)	Back End Fee (%)	Inception Date
	1.97	5.54	16.60			5.19	1.82			20.54	509.6	4	2	16	0	40					Mar-15
50	5.81	16.68	38.83	17.57		0	1.68	14.75	0.89	10.88	17.1	2	98	0	0	104			4.75		Dec-13
50	5.64	16.24	37.90	15.11		0	2.44	14.75	0.89	10.66	17.1	2	98	0	0	104				1.00	Dec-13
	5.84	16.80	39.06	18.50		0	1.43	14.74	0.89	10.9	17.1	2	98	0	0	104					Dec-13
	5.02	16.89	20.85	11.01			1.68	14.68	0.89		16.7	0	95	0	4	75			2.50		Feb-17
50	5.33	16.07	36.55	18.98	22.14	0	1.64	12.72	0.75	15.25	302.4	2	79	1	4	105	14.02	-21.47	4.75		Aug-08
50	5.18	15.64	35.55	16.30	17.66	0	2.39	12.73	0.75	14.41	302.4	2	79	1	4	105	13.57	-21.73		1.00	Aug-08
	5.44	16.28	36.97	19.80	23.73	0	1.39	12.72	0.75	15.33	302.4	2	79	1	4	105	14.2	-21.38			Aug-08
	5.31	15.94	36.32	18.03	20.68	0	1.89	12.74	0.75	15.05	302.4	2	79	1	4	105	13.85	-21.54			Aug-08
	5.02	15.01	20.21	12.88	18.54		1.64	12.65	0.75		319.5	1	78	1	7	87	14.04	-21.46	2.50		Feb-17
50	1.45	4.68	14.10	16.44		0.95	1.36			10.9	109.5	7	0	22	8	52			2.25		Dec-14
50	1.27	4.31	13.30	13.92		0.67	2.11			10.8	109.5	7	0	22	8	52				1.00	Dec-14
	1.51	4.80	14.44	17.34		1.33	1.11			10.9	109.5	7	0	22	8	52					Dec-14
	1.18	4.29	13.59	15.28		0.89	1.6			10.84	109.5	7	0	22	8	52					Dec-14
	1.75	6.08	13.51				1.36				102.2	3	1	19	8	38			2.50		Feb-17
	4.12	9.62	24.47	28.54	54.35	5.09	4.28	11.98		9.16	545.2	4	47	18	5	29	20.49	-19.85			Jun-07
50	6.88	15.95	34.41	38.77	70.50	0	1.38	12.36	1.08	14.72	134.5	2	96	0	2	102	18.61	-17.65	4.75		Mar-07
50	6.67	15.48	33.34	35.62	64.13	0	2.13	12.33	1.08	13.42	134.5	2	96	0	2	102	18.02	-17.93		1.00	Mar-07
	6.88	15.82	34.06	37.73	68.48	0	1.63	12.37	1.08	14.25	134.5	2	96	0	2	102	18.34	-17.73			Mar-07
	5.36	14.32	25.74	35.21	62.47		1.38	12.29	1.08		127.9	1	96	0	3	65	18.5	-17.58	2.50		Feb-17
	6.99	16.12	34.75	39.83	72.70	0	1.13	12.38	1.08	15.04	134.5	2	96	0	2	102	18.68	-17.49			Mar-07
50	4.81	9.49	20.05	21.11	41.07	0.07	1.46	8.57	0.78	9.47	226.2	1	53	3	10	100	9.27	-12.54	4.75		Sep-96
50	4.66	9.10	19.06	18.34	35.84	0	2.21	8.56	0.78	8.43	226.2	1	53	3	10	100	8.86	-12.79		1.00	Sep-96
	4.89	9.69	20.33	22.05	42.84	0.4	1.21	8.58	0.78	9.74	226.2	1	53	3	10	100	9.5	-12.42			Sep-97
	4.78	9.43	19.81	20.15	39.32	0.01	1.71	8.61	0.78	9.3	226.2	1	53	3	10	100	9.11	-12.56			Mar-07
	3.07	7.96	15.22	19.46	37.31		1.46	8.47	0.77		219.5	1	54	5	10	58	9.28	-12.54	2.50		Feb-17
	5.63	11.60	24.72	27.90	50.87	6.24	1.61	11.55		13.42	114.4	1	52	13	4	114	14.42	-15.73			Oct-05
50	4.68	8.16	16.37	25.80	60.73	2.4	1.12	8.27	0.81	32.05	2,078	4	70	7	0	32	13.12	-13.74	4.75		Sep-88
50	4.46	7.71	15.49	22.87	54.65	1.68	1.87	8.3	0.81	32.22	2,078	4	70	7	0	32	12.64	-13.99		1.00	Aug-96
	4.58	8.00	16.03	24.87	58.73	2.2	1.37	8.26	0.81	31.78	2,078	4	70	7	0	32	12.92	-13.8			Mar-07
	2.33	5.92	15.84	26.56	54.83		1.12	8.27	0.81		2,051	2	70	9	0	24	13.12	-13.74	2.50		Feb-17
	4.73	8.28	16.64	26.67	62.69	2.71	0.87	8.3	0.81	30.82	2,078	4	70	7	0	32	13.28	-13.63			Sep-97
50	6.58	10.97	26.59	26.57	87.90	0	1.35	10.67	0.96	32.48	1,686	3	97	0	0	104	22.83	-22.64	4.75		Sep-90
50	6.38	10.54	25.65	23.74	80.98	0	2.1	10.66	0.96	20.71	1,686	3	97	0	0	104	22.3	-22.88		1.00	Sep-96
	6.52	10.79	26.29	25.60	85.55	0	1.6	10.68	0.96	30.36	1,686	3	97	0	0	104	22.66	-22.71			Mar-07
	2.54	7.48	20.87	27.09	77.58		1.35	10.75	0.97		1,669	4	96	0	0	90	22.83	-22.64	2.50		Feb-17
	6.65	11.07	26.90	27.50	90.25	0	1.1	10.67	0.96	42.52	1,686	3	97	0	0	104	23.01	-22.55			Sep-97
50	2.21	3.78	8.01	14.18		0.52	1.23			10.99	13.0	1	99	0	0	49			4.75		Dec-14
50	2.05	3.40	7.25	11.68		0.25	1.98			10.92	13.0	1	99	0	0	49				1.00	Dec-14
	2.37	3.91	8.37	15.14		1.01	0.98			10.98	13.0	1	99	0	0	49					Dec-14
	1.05	2.56	7.95				1.23				13.0	1	99	0	0	20			2.50		Feb-17
50	6.93	17.74	39.18	33.76	45.01	0	1.38	12.44	0.96	21.4	293.9	1	95	0	5	100	16.77	-19.95	4.75		Mar-05
50	6.78	17.32	38.22	30.86	39.65	0	2.13	12.44	0.96	19.49	293.9	1	95	0	5	100	16.29	-20.17		1.00	Mar-05
	6.90	17.60	38.89	32.79	43.26	0	1.63	12.45	0.96	20.88	293.9	1	95	0	5	100	16.66	-20.02			Mar-07
	6.49	17.10	26.87	27.38	40.22		1.38	12.35	0.96		274.1	1	95	0	4	69	16.78	-19.93	2.50		Feb-17
	7.02	17.85	39.57	34.78	46.80	0	1.13	12.46	0.96	21.88	293.9	1	95	0	5	100	16.95	-19.84			Mar-05
	0.44	1.63	4.34	10.54	18.53		1.08	3.09	-0.13		4,634	34	17	4	1	38	8.39	-4.51	2.50		Feb-17
50	1.07	1.82	4.56	10.36	19.71	0.97	1.08	3.09	-0.14	13.23	4,780	33	16	3	1	81	8.39	-4.51	2.25		Sep-90
50	0.86	1.41	3.80	7.86	15.35	0.25	1.83	3.05	-0.14	13.45	4,780	33	16	3	1	81	7.93	-4.84		1.00	Feb-00
	1.00	1.68	4.31	9.58	18.26	0.74	1.33	3.11	-0.15	13.18	4,780	33	16	3	1	81	8.21	-4.64			Mar-07
	1.07	1.90	4.73	11.09	21.21	1.24	0.83	3.11	-0.15	13.07	4,780	33	16	3	1	81	8.52	-4.42			May-00
50	6.86	12.08	17.14	24.24	71.13	0.61	1.12	10	0.96	15.3	53.4	1	99	0	0	105	17.76	-17.42	4.75		Jan-02

	MARKET			FUND TYPE, CATEGORY & OBJECTIVE	RATINGS					MINIMUMS
Fund Name	Ticker Symbol	Traded On	Fund Type	Category and (Prospectus Objective)	Overall Rating	Reward Rating	Risk Rating	Recent Up/ Downgrade	Open to New Investors	Min Initial Investment
Calamos Opportunistic Value Fund Class C	CVACX	NAS CM	Open End	US Equity Large Cap Value (Growth)	B-	C+	B-	Down	Y	2,500
Calamos Opportunistic Value Fund Class R	CVARX	NAS CM	Open End	US Equity Large Cap Value (Growth)	B-	C+	B-	Down	Y	0
Calamos Opportunistic Value Fund Class T	CVATX	NAS CM	Open End	US Equity Large Cap Value (Growth)	C+	C+	B-	Down	Y	0
Calamos Opportunistic Value Fund Institutional Class	CVAIX	NAS CM	Open End	US Equity Large Cap Value (Growth)	B-	B-	B-	Down	Y	1,000,000
Calamos Phineus Long/Short Fund Class A	CPLSX	NAS CM	Open End	Long/Short Equity (Growth & Income)	B	C+	A-	Up	Y	2,500
Calamos Phineus Long/Short Fund Class C	CPCLX	NAS CM	Open End	Long/Short Equity (Growth & Income)	B	C+	A-	Up	Y	2,500
Calamos Phineus Long/Short Fund Class I	CPLIX	NAS CM	Open End	Long/Short Equity (Growth & Income)	B	C+	A-	Up	Y	1,000,000
Calamos Phineus Long/Short Fund Class T	CPLTX	NAS CM	Open End	Long/Short Equity (Growth & Income)	B	C+	A-	Up	Y	0
Calamos Strategic Total Return Fund	CSQ	NAS CM	Closed End	Moderate Alloc (Growth & Income)	B-	B	B-		Y	
Calamos® Growth & Income Portfolio	US1281161000		Open End	Aggressive Alloc (Growth & Income)	B	C+	B+	Up	Y	0
Caldwell & Orkin Market Opportunity Fund	COAGX	NAS CM	Open End	Long/Short Equity (Asset Alloc)	D+	D	C	Down	Y	25,000
Calvert Aggressive Allocation Fund Class A	CAAAX	NAS CM	Open End	Aggressive Alloc (Asset Alloc)	B-	B-	B	Down	Y	1,000
Calvert Aggressive Allocation Fund Class C	CAACX	NAS CM	Open End	Aggressive Alloc (Asset Alloc)	B-	B-	B-	Down	Y	1,000
Calvert Balanced Fund Class A	CSIFX	NAS CM	Open End	Moderate Alloc (Balanced)	B-	C+	B	Down	Y	1,000
Calvert Balanced Fund Class C	CSGCX	NAS CM	Open End	Moderate Alloc (Balanced)	C+	C+	B	Down	Y	1,000
Calvert Balanced Fund Class I	CBAIX	NAS CM	Open End	Moderate Alloc (Balanced)	B-	C+	B	Down	Y	250,000
Calvert Conservative Allocation Fund Class A	CCLAX	NAS CM	Open End	Cautious Alloc (Asset Alloc)	B-	C+	B	Up	Y	1,000
Calvert Conservative Allocation Fund Class C	CALCX	NAS CM	Open End	Cautious Alloc (Asset Alloc)	B-	C+	B	Up	Y	1,000
Calvert Conservative Allocation Fund Class I	CFAIX	NAS CM	Open End	Cautious Alloc (Asset Alloc)	B-	C+	B	Down	Y	250,000
Calvert Emerging Markets Equity Fund Class A	CVMAX	NAS CM	Open End	Emerging Markets Equity (Div Emerging Mkts)	B	A	C+	Up	Y	1,000
Calvert Emerging Markets Equity Fund Class C	CVMCX	NAS CM	Open End	Emerging Markets Equity (Div Emerging Mkts)	B	A-	C	Up	Y	1,000
Calvert Emerging Markets Equity Fund Class I	CVMIX	NAS CM	Open End	Emerging Markets Equity (Div Emerging Mkts)	B	A	C+	Up	Y	250,000
Calvert Equity Fund Class A	CSIEX	NAS CM	Open End	US Equity Large Cap Growth (Growth)	B+	B	A	Up	Y	1,000
Calvert Equity Fund Class C	CSECX	NAS CM	Open End	US Equity Large Cap Growth (Growth)	B	B-	A		Y	1,000
Calvert Equity Fund Class I	CEYIX	NAS CM	Open End	US Equity Large Cap Growth (Growth)	B+	B	A	Up	Y	250,000
Calvert Equity Fund Class R6	CEYRX	NAS CM	Open End	US Equity Large Cap Growth (Growth)	B+	B	A		Y	1,000,000
Calvert Equity Fund Class Y	CIEYX	NAS CM	Open End	US Equity Large Cap Growth (Growth)	B	B	A		Y	250,000
Calvert Global Energy Solutions Fund Class A	CGAEX	NAS CM	Open End	Global Equity Mid/Small Cap (Natl Res)	C+	C+	C+	Up	Y	1,000
Calvert Global Energy Solutions Fund Class C	CGACX	NAS CM	Open End	Global Equity Mid/Small Cap (Natl Res)	C+	C+	C+	Up	Y	5,000
Calvert Global Energy Solutions Fund Class I	CAEIX	NAS CM	Open End	Global Equity Mid/Small Cap (Natl Res)	C+	C+	C+	Up	Y	250,000
Calvert Global Energy Solutions Fund Class Y	CGAYX	NAS CM	Open End	Global Equity Mid/Small Cap (Natl Res)	C+	C+	C+	Up	Y	2,000
Calvert Global Water Fund Class A	CFWAX	NAS CM	Open End	Natl Resources Sec Equity (Natl Res)	C+	C+	C+	Up	Y	1,000
Calvert Global Water Fund Class C	CFWCX	NAS CM	Open End	Natl Resources Sec Equity (Natl Res)	C+	C+	C+	Up	Y	5,000
Calvert Global Water Fund Class I	CFWIX	NAS CM	Open End	Natl Resources Sec Equity (Natl Res)	C+	C+	C+	Up	Y	250,000
Calvert Global Water Fund Class Y	CFWYX	NAS CM	Open End	Natl Resources Sec Equity (Natl Res)	C+	C+	C+	Up	Y	2,000
Calvert International Equity Fund Class A	CWVGX	NAS CM	Open End	Global Equity Large Cap (Foreign Stock)	C+	C+	B-	Up	Y	1,000
Calvert International Equity Fund Class C	CWVCX	NAS CM	Open End	Global Equity Large Cap (Foreign Stock)	C+	C+	B-	Up	Y	1,000
Calvert International Equity Fund Class I	CWVIX	NAS CM	Open End	Global Equity Large Cap (Foreign Stock)	B-	C+	B	Up	Y	250,000
Calvert International Opportunities Fund Class A	CIOAX	NAS CM	Open End	Global Equity Mid/Small Cap (Foreign Stock)	B+	A-	B	Up	Y	1,000
Calvert International Opportunities Fund Class C	COICX	NAS CM	Open End	Global Equity Mid/Small Cap (Foreign Stock)	B	B+	B	Up	Y	1,000
Calvert International Opportunities Fund Class I	COIIX	NAS CM	Open End	Global Equity Mid/Small Cap (Foreign Stock)	B+	A-	B	Up	Y	250,000
Calvert International Responsible Index Fund Class A	CDHAX	NAS CM	Open End	Global Equity Large Cap (Growth & Income)	C	C	B	Up	Y	5,000
Calvert International Responsible Index Fund Class I	CDHIX	NAS CM	Open End	Global Equity Large Cap (Growth & Income)	C	C	B	Up	Y	100,000
Calvert Mid-Cap Fund Class A	CCAFX	NAS CM	Open End	US Equity Mid Cap (Growth)	B-	C+	B	Up	Y	1,000
Calvert Mid-Cap Fund Class C	CCACX	NAS CM	Open End	US Equity Mid Cap (Growth)	C+	C+	B	Up	Y	1,000
Calvert Mid-Cap Fund Class I	CCPIX	NAS CM	Open End	US Equity Mid Cap (Growth)	B-	C+	B	Up	Y	250,000
Calvert Moderate Allocation Fund Class A	CMAAX	NAS CM	Open End	Moderate Alloc (Asset Alloc)	B-	C+	B	Down	Y	1,000
Calvert Moderate Allocation Fund Class C	CMACX	NAS CM	Open End	Moderate Alloc (Asset Alloc)	B-	C+	B	Down	Y	1,000
Calvert Small-Cap Fund Class A	CCVAX	NAS CM	Open End	US Equity Small Cap (Small Company)	B	B	B+	Up	Y	1,000
Calvert Small-Cap Fund Class C	CSCCX	NAS CM	Open End	US Equity Small Cap (Small Company)	B	B	B	Up	Y	1,000
Calvert Small-Cap Fund Class I	CSVIX	NAS CM	Open End	US Equity Small Cap (Small Company)	B+	B	B+	Up	Y	250,000
Calvert US Large Cap Core Responsible Index Fund Class A	CSXAX	NAS CM	Open End	US Equity Large Cap Blend (Growth)	B	B-	B		Y	5,000

★ Expanded analysis of this fund is included in Section II.

	TOTAL RETURNS					PERFORMANCE				ASSETS		ASSET ALLOCATION & TURNOVER					BULL & BEAR		FEES		
Min Additional Investment	3-Month Total Return	6-Month Total Return	1-Year Total Return	3-Year Total Return	5-Year Total Return	Dividend Yield (TTM)	Expense Ratio	3-Yr Std Deviation	3-Year Beta	NAV	Total Assets (MIL)	%Cash	%Stocks	%Bonds	%Other	Turnover Ratio	Last Bull Market Total Return	Last Bear Market Total Return	Front End Fee (%)	Back End Fee (%)	Inception Date
50	6.71	11.63	16.27	21.45	64.87	0.05	1.87	9.98	0.96	13.8	53.4	1	99	0	0	105	17.26	-17.67		1.00	Jan-02
	6.81	11.95	16.90	23.26	68.97	0.42	1.37	9.97	0.96	15.1	53.4	1	99	0	0	105	17.49	-17.45			Mar-07
	4.43	8.11	20.26	21.10	62.66		1.12	9.84	0.93		51.7	0	100	0	0	41	17.76	-17.42	2.50		Feb-17
	6.98	12.22	17.49	25.21	73.35	0.82	0.87	10.01	0.96	15.7	53.4	1	99	0	0	105	17.91	-17.29			Mar-02
50	2.03	2.44	8.89	20.92	60.78	0	2.26			12.48	497.6	72	28	0	0	168	17.37	-14.1	4.75		Apr-16
50	1.89	2.14	8.07	18.14	54.77	0	3.01			12.32	497.6	72	28	0	0	168	16.86	-14.37		1.00	Apr-16
	2.18	2.68	9.21	22.02	63.06	0	2.01			12.55	497.6	72	28	0	0	168	17.54	-14.01			Apr-16
	0.08	2.49	15.30	25.22	57.38		2.26				381.7	59	40	0	0	178	17.37	-14.1	2.50		Feb-17
	5.13	9.87	20.97	34.40	86.11	5.4	1.91	11.65		12.89	2,001	2	64	17	0	31	21.72	-18.83			Mar-04
	4.60	7.71	15.51	23.19	56.22	1.93	1.58	8.14	0.79	15.54	26.9	5	67	6	0	29	13.26	-14.75			May-99
100	1.42	1.92	0.93	-5.15	6.82	0	1.5	5.71	-0.12	20.6	84.4	79	21	1	0	500	4.52	0.4			Aug-92
	4.83	9.25	20.25	27.99	76.35	1.69	0.98	9.06	0.86	20.13	141.2	1	84	11	4	55	19.06	-17.54	4.75		Jun-05
	4.67	8.84	19.41	24.71	67.95	1.81	1.73	9.1	0.86	17.32	141.2	1	84	11	4	55	18.2	-18.03		1.00	Jun-05
	3.97	6.21	11.52	16.02	51.67	1.37	0.94	6.57	0.64	31.65	672.8	2	60	37	1	128	16.64	-8.24	4.75		Oct-82
	3.75	5.77	10.65	13.24	45.72	0.69	1.69	6.56	0.63	30.65	672.8	2	60	37	1	128	16.07	-8.55		1.00	Mar-94
	4.07	6.39	11.94	17.40	55.02	1.7	0.62	6.56	0.63	32.23	672.8	2	60	37	1	128	17.01	-8.03			Feb-99
	2.18	4.15	9.64	15.00	34.41	2	1	3.61	0.13	17.14	186.3	3	30	52	14	46	9	-3.06	4.75		Apr-05
	1.96	3.76	8.81	12.12	28.53	1.18	1.75	3.63	0.13	16.94	186.3	3	30	52	14	46	8.35	-3.58		1.00	Apr-05
	2.18	4.31	9.90	15.54	35.04	2.39	0.65	3.63	0.13	17.12	186.3	3	30	52	14	46	9.01	-3.06			May-16
	6.66	16.12	44.19	41.12	56.93	0.39	1.27	13.38	0.8	17.39	255.1	3	95	0	2	36			4.75		Oct-12
	6.48	15.64	43.16	37.86	50.35	0.1	2.02	13.41	0.8	17.08	255.1	3	95	0	2	36				1.00	Oct-12
	6.77	16.30	44.71	42.60	59.73	0.61	0.92	13.44	0.8	17.55	255.1	3	95	0	2	36					Oct-12
	6.97	11.66	25.78	32.34	96.47	0.11	1.09	9.48	0.86	42.89	2,222	3	95	1	1	29	21.82	-16	4.75		Aug-87
	6.74	11.22	24.83	29.29	89.26	0	1.84	9.47	0.86	25.25	2,222	3	95	1	1	29	21.28	-16.24		1.00	Mar-94
	7.03	11.83	26.24	33.94	100.98	0.48	0.72	9.47	0.86	49.3	2,222	3	95	1	1	29	22.18	-15.79			Nov-99
	7.00	11.69	25.82	32.38	96.52		0.72	9.48	0.86	49.28	2,222	3	95	1	1	29	21.82	-16			Oct-17
250	6.59	10.36	23.14	35.59	94.75	0.42	0.78	9.48	0.86		2,222	3	95	1	1	29	22.12	-15.86			Oct-08
	5.24	12.56	29.41	15.69	39.84	0.83	1.3	15.08		7.52	88.8	0	94	2	4	133	1.97	-38.7	4.75		May-07
	5.16	12.13	28.32	12.88	33.64	0.16	2.05	15.1		7.07	88.8	0	94	2	4	133	1.35	-38.88		1.00	Jul-07
	5.26	12.62	29.63	16.99	42.71	1.41	0.95	15		7.62	88.8	0	94	2	4	133	2.09	-38.5			May-07
250	2.55	9.01	24.05	12.85	38.69	0.99	1.05	15.02			88.8	0	94	2	4	133	2.18	-38.5			Jul-11
	4.07	9.29	18.87	17.43	48.16	0	1.28	13.01		20.54	470.5	0	98	0	1	34	22.02	-19.03	4.75		Sep-08
	3.79	8.85	17.91	14.77	42.63	0	2.03	13.01		18.91	470.5	0	98	0	1	34	21.31	-19.37		1.00	Sep-08
	4.15	9.49	19.30	18.92	50.91	0	0.93	13.04		20.64	470.5	0	98	0	1	34	22.02	-19.03			Jan-14
250	4.79	7.12	14.75	19.83	50.76	0	1.03	13.04			470.5	0	98	0	1	34	22.26	-19			Sep-08
	4.37	8.03	21.25	15.27	33.27	2.3	1.33	11.25	0.89	17.59	188.9	1	97	2	1	138	15.08	-23.31	4.75		Jul-92
	4.19	7.63	20.43	12.68	27.92	1.76	2.08	11.27	0.89	15.14	188.9	1	97	2	1	138	14.52	-23.54		1.00	Mar-94
	4.42	8.22	21.70	16.69	36.84	2.73	0.96	11.26	0.89	18.73	188.9	1	97	2	1	138	15.59	-23.07			Feb-99
	5.67	14.56	37.90	40.25	73.21	2.04	1.43	12.04	0.97	18.52	173.3	3	93	0	4	158	18.79	-23.46	4.75		May-07
	5.52	14.13	36.88	36.65	65.87	0.89	2.26	12	0.96	18.14	173.3	3	93	0	4	158	18.16	-23.74		1.00	Jul-07
	5.79	14.77	38.50	41.94	76.95	2.89	1.16	12.03	0.97	18.15	173.3	3	93	0	4	158	19.03	-23.25			May-07
	3.37	8.34	24.88			1.82	0.63			23.57	55.3	1	94	0	5	26			4.75		Oct-15
	3.47	8.50	25.30			1.62	0.28			23.8	55.3	1	94	0	5	26					Oct-15
	4.07	6.20	11.70	13.27	61.89	0.44	1.21	10.67	0.9	31.52	247.7	0	98	0	2	162	29.64	-23.97	4.75		Oct-94
	3.87	5.76	10.87	10.65	55.75	0	1.96	10.64	0.9	22.42	247.7	0	98	0	2	162	29.03	-24.26		1.00	Oct-94
	4.17	6.40	12.14	14.81	66.11	0.76	0.85	10.66	0.9	36.96	247.7	0	98	0	2	162	30.15	-23.74			Feb-99
	3.63	6.90	15.07	21.63	55.13	1.78	1	6.76	0.64	19.14	273.4	2	60	29	8	45	14.73	-11.62	4.75		Apr-05
	3.49	6.50	14.25	18.93	49.55	1.71	1.75	6.79	0.64	18.26	273.4	2	60	29	8	45	14.19	-11.86		1.00	Apr-05
	5.31	8.56	13.19	33.22	107.09	0	1.29	12.04	0.8	23.64	259.7	1	99	0	0	137	21.5	-23.67	4.75		Oct-04
	5.12	8.13	12.33	30.23	99.30	0	2.04	12.04	0.8	20.46	259.7	1	99	0	0	137	20.77	-23.95		1.00	Apr-05
	5.42	8.78	13.69	35.07	112.62	0.32	0.91	12.03	0.8	25.47	259.7	1	99	0	0	137	22.03	-23.41			Apr-05
	6.07	10.29	20.73	32.89	108.41	0.95	0.54	10.55	0.99	22.23	1,027	0	100	0	0	31	26.34	-15.85	4.75		Jun-00

	MARKET			FUND TYPE, CATEGORY & OBJECTIVE	RATINGS				MINIMUMS	
Fund Name	Ticker Symbol	Traded On	Fund Type	Category and (Prospectus Objective)	Overall Rating	Reward Rating	Risk Rating	Recent Up/ Downgrade	Open to New Investors	Min Initial Investment
Calvert US Large Cap Core Responsible Index Fund Class C	CSXCX	NAS CM	Open End	US Equity Large Cap Blend (Growth)	B-	B-	B-	Down	Y	5,000
Calvert US Large Cap Core Responsible Index Fund Class I	CISIX	NAS CM	Open End	US Equity Large Cap Blend (Growth)	B	B	B		Y	100,000
Calvert US Large Cap Core Responsible Index Fund Class R6	CSXRX	NAS CM	Open End	US Equity Large Cap Blend (Growth)	B	B	B		Y	1,000,000
Calvert US Large Cap Core Responsible Index Fund Class Y	CISYX	NAS CM	Open End	US Equity Large Cap Blend (Growth)	B-	B-	B	Down	Y	10,000
Calvert US Large Cap Growth Responsible Index Fund Class A	CGJAX	NAS CM	Open End	US Equity Large Cap Growth (Growth)	C	C+	B+	Up	Y	5,000
Calvert US Large Cap Growth Responsible Index Fund Class I	CGJIX	NAS CM	Open End	US Equity Large Cap Growth (Growth)	C	C+	B	Up	Y	100,000
Calvert US Large Cap Value Responsible Index Fund Class A	CFJAX	NAS CM	Open End	US Equity Large Cap Value (Growth)	C	C+	B	Up	Y	5,000
Calvert US Large Cap Value Responsible Index Fund Class I	CFJIX	NAS CM	Open End	US Equity Large Cap Value (Growth)	C	C+	B	Up	Y	100,000
Calvert US Mid Cap Core Responsible Index Fund Class A	CMJAX	NAS CM	Open End	US Equity Mid Cap (Growth & Income)	C	C	B	Up	Y	5,000
Calvert US Mid Cap Core Responsible Index Fund Class I	CMJIX	NAS CM	Open End	US Equity Mid Cap (Growth & Income)	C	C	B	Up	Y	100,000
Cambiar Global Equity Fund Investor Class	CAMGX	NAS CM	Open End	Global Equity (World Stock)	B-	C+	B-	Up	Y	2,500
Cambiar Global Ultra Focus Fund Investor Class	CAMAX	NAS CM	Open End	Global Equity (World Stock)	B-	C+	B	Up	Y	2,500
Cambiar International Equity Fund Investor Class	CAMIX	NAS CM	Open End	Global Equity Large Cap (Foreign Stock)	B	B-	B	Up	Y	2,500
Cambiar International Equity Institutional	CAMYX	NAS CM	Open End	Global Equity Large Cap (Foreign Stock)	B-	B-	B-	Up	Y	5,000,000
Cambiar International Small Cap Fund Institutional Class	CAMFX	NAS CM	Open End	Global Equity Mid/Small Cap (Small Company)	B-	C+	B-	Up	Y	500,000
Cambiar Opportunity Fund Class Institutional	CAMWX	NAS CM	Open End	US Equity Large Cap Blend (Growth & Income)	B	B	B+	Up	Y	5,000,000
Cambiar Opportunity Fund Class Investor	CAMOX	NAS CM	Open End	US Equity Large Cap Blend (Growth & Income)	B	B-	B+	Up	Y	2,500
Cambiar Small Cap Fund Class Investor	CAMSX	NAS CM	Open End	US Equity Small Cap (Small Company)	C	C+	C			2,500
Cambiar Small Cap Institutional Class	CAMZX	NAS CM	Open End	US Equity Small Cap (Small Company)	C	C+	C		Y	5,000,000
Cambiar SMID Fund Institutional Class	CAMUX	NAS CM	Open End	US Equity Mid Cap (Growth)	B-	C+	B	Up	Y	5,000,000
Cambiar SMID Fund Investor Class Shares	CAMMX	NAS CM	Open End	US Equity Mid Cap (Growth)	B-	C+	B	Up	Y	2,500
Camelot Excalibur Small Cap Income Fund Class A	CEXAX	NAS CM	Open End	US Equity Small Cap (Income)	C+	C+	C	Up	Y	2,500
Camelot Excalibur Small Cap Income Fund Class C	CEXCX	NAS CM	Open End	US Equity Small Cap (Income)	C	C	C		Y	2,500
Camelot Excalibur Small Cap Income Fund Class I	CEXIX	NAS CM	Open End	US Equity Small Cap (Income)	C+	C+	C	Up	Y	100,000
Camelot Premium Return Fund Class A	CPRFX	NAS CM	Open End	Long/Short Equity (Income)	C+	C+	C+	Up	Y	2,500
Camelot Premium Return Fund Class C	CPRCX	NAS CM	Open End	Long/Short Equity (Income)	C+	C	C+	Up	Y	2,500
Camelot Premium Return Fund Class I	CPRIX	NAS CM	Open End	Long/Short Equity (Income)	C+	C+	C+		Y	100,000
Campbell Dynamic Trend Fund Institutional Shares	CDRTX	NAS CM	Open End	Other Alternative (Growth)	C-	D+	C	Up	Y	2,500
Campbell Multi-Asset Carry Fund Institutional Shares	CCRYX	NAS CM	Open End	Other Alternative (Growth & Income)	D+	D	C-	Up	Y	2,500
CAN SLIM Select Growth Fund	CANGX	NAS CM	Open End	Aggressive Alloc (Growth)	B-	B-	B-	Down	Y	2,500
Cane Alternative Strategies Fund Class A	CDMAX	NAS CM	Open End	Multialternative (Growth)	D	D	C-	Down	Y	2,500
Cane Alternative Strategies Fund Class C	CDMCX	NAS CM	Open End	Multialternative (Growth)	D	D	C-	Down	Y	2,500
Cane Alternative Strategies Fund Class I	CDMIX	NAS CM	Open End	Multialternative (Growth)	D	D	C	Down	Y	500,000
Canterbury Portfolio Thermostat Fund Class I Shares	CAPTX	NAS CM	Open End	Alloc (Growth)	D	C-	B+		Y	5,000
Capital Advisors Growth Fund Investor Class	CIAOX	NAS CM	Open End	US Equity Large Cap Growth (Growth)	B-	C+	B-		Y	5,000
Capital Emerging Markets Growth Fund, Inc.	EMRGX	NAS CM	Open End	Emerging Markets Equity (Div Emerging Mkts)	B-	B	C	Up	Y	1,000,000
Capital Group Emerging Markets Growth Fund, Inc. Class F-3	EMGEX	NAS CM	Open End	Emerging Markets Equity (Div Emerging Mkts)	B-	B	C		Y	1,000,000
Capital Group Emerging Markets Growth Fund, Inc. Class R-6	REFGX	NAS CM	Open End	Emerging Markets Equity (Div Emerging Mkts)	B-	B	C		Y	1,000,000
Capital Group Emerging Mkts Total Opp Fund Cls F-2	CTPFX	NAS CM	Open End	Emerging Markets Equity (Div Emerging Mkts)	C+	C+	C+		Y	1,000,000
Capital Group Emerging Mkts Total Opp Fund Cls F-3	ETPFX	NAS CM	Open End	Emerging Markets Equity (Div Emerging Mkts)	C+	C+	C+		Y	1,000,000
Capital Group Emerging Mkts Total Opp Fund Cls R-6	REPGX	NAS CM	Open End	Emerging Markets Equity (Div Emerging Mkts)	C+	C+	C+		Y	1,000,000
Capital Group Global Equity Fund	CGLOX	NAS CM	Open End	Global Equity (World Stock)	B	B	B	Up	Y	25,000
Capital Group International Equity Fund	CNUSX	NAS CM	Open End	Global Equity Large Cap (Foreign Stock)	B	B-	B	Up	Y	25,000
Capital Group U.S. Equity Fund	CUSEX	NAS CM	Open End	US Equity Large Cap Growth (Growth)	B-	B-	B	Down	Y	25,000
Capital Management Mid Cap Fund Class Institutional	CMEIX	NAS CM	Open End	US Equity Mid Cap (Growth)	B+	B	A-	Up	Y	25,000
Capital Management Mid Cap Fund Class Investor	CMCIX	NAS CM	Open End	US Equity Mid Cap (Growth)	B	B	B+		Y	1,000
Capital Management Small Cap Fund Class Institutional	CMSSX	NAS CM	Open End	US Equity Small Cap (Small Company)	C	C	C	Down	Y	25,000
Capital Management Small Cap Fund Class Investor	CMSVX	NAS CM	Open End	US Equity Small Cap (Small Company)	C	C	C	Down	Y	1,000
Cardinal Small Cap Value Fund Institutional Class	CCMSX	NAS CM	Open End	US Equity Small Cap (Small Company)	B+	A-	B	Up	Y	1,000,000
Carillon ClariVest Capital Appreciation Fund Class A	HRCPX	NAS CM	Open End	US Equity Large Cap Growth (Growth)	A-	A	B	Up	Y	1,000
Carillon ClariVest Capital Appreciation Fund Class C	HRCCX	NAS CM	Open End	US Equity Large Cap Growth (Growth)	A-	A-	B	Up	Y	1,000
Carillon ClariVest Capital Appreciation Fund Class I	HRCIX	NAS CM	Open End	US Equity Large Cap Growth (Growth)	A-	A	B	Up	Y	1,000,000

★Expanded analysis of this fund is included in Section II.

Min Additional Investment	3-Month Total Return	6-Month Total Return	1-Year Total Return	3-Year Total Return	5-Year Total Return	Dividend Yield (TTM)	Expense Ratio	3-Yr Std Deviation	3-Year Beta	NAV	Total Assets (MIL)	%Cash	%Stocks	%Bonds	%Other	Turnover Ratio	Last Bull Market Total Return	Last Bear Market Total Return	Front End Fee (%)	Back End Fee (%)	Inception Date
TOTAL RETURNS						PERFORMANCE				ASSETS		ASSET ALLOCATION & TURNOVER					BULL & BEAR		FEES		
	5.84	9.82	19.81	29.89	100.28	0.26	1.29	10.53	0.99	20.99	1,027	0	100	0	0	31	25.63	-16.21		1.00	Jun-00
	6.15	10.48	21.18	34.41	113.15	1.3	0.19	10.58	1	22.74	1,027	0	100	0	0	31	26.73	-15.7			Jun-00
	6.10	10.43	21.12	34.35	113.05		0.19	10.57	1	22.73	1,027	0	100	0	0	31	26.73	-15.7			Oct-17
250	6.85	9.28	18.73	35.37	105.29	1.25	0.29	10.56	1		1,027	0	100	0	0	31	26.73	-15.7			Jul-12
	6.33	11.27	26.98			0.62	0.57			25.37	49.9	0	100	0	0	75			4.75		Jun-15
	6.39	11.45	27.39			0.89	0.22			25.46	49.9	0	100	0	0	75					Jun-15
	5.69	9.05	14.70			1.47	0.57			22.82	126.3	0	100	0	0	73			4.75		Jun-15
	5.79	9.29	15.15			1.77	0.22			22.9	126.3	0	100	0	0	73					Jun-15
	5.88	8.91	18.70			0.61	0.57			25.17	42.1	0	100	0	0	63			4.75		Oct-15
	5.99	9.15	19.14			0.71	0.22			25.31	42.1	0	100	0	0	63					Oct-15
100	5.08	12.38	17.97	25.31	69.43	0.56	1.1	10.56	0.94	13.25	14.4	4	96	0	0	60					Nov-11
100	0.86	5.23	6.47	18.72	87.81	0.22	1.35	16.86	1.26	19.84	110.2	3	95	0	1	72	18.06	-39.93			Aug-07
100	3.73	11.25	21.25	28.16	51.44	1.41	1.06	10.68	0.82	28.42	3,618	5	95	0	0	57	20.24	-24.08			Sep-02
	3.77	11.35	21.38	28.67	52.69	1.48	0.95	10.7	0.82	28.48	3,618	5	95	0	0	57	20.24	-24.08			Nov-12
	6.02	11.25	33.75	40.17		0.9	1.15	10.8	0.87	12.43	2.1	5	95	0	0	49					Nov-14
	4.55	10.11	15.01	31.42	94.43	1.63	0.8	11.92	1.07	23.76	347.9	1	99	0	0	46	20.51	-26.56			Nov-05
100	4.53	10.04	14.78	30.50	92.12	1.41	1.05	11.91	1.07	23.85	347.9	1	99	0	0	46	20.27	-26.59			Jun-98
100	3.13	8.10	3.99	8.99	52.88	0	1.3	16.64	1.09	19.08	294.6	2	98	0	0	54	34.37	-26.92			Aug-04
	3.14	8.10	4.14	9.65	54.62	0	1.05	16.63	1.08	19.52	294.6	2	98	0	0	54	34.51	-26.83			Oct-08
	3.74	6.36	11.79	21.82	93.36	0.52	0.95	13.05	0.97	16.79	34.2	7	93	0	0	48	36.76				Nov-14
100	3.78	6.40	11.76	21.64	93.18	0.48	1	13.09	0.97	16.8	34.2	7	93	0	0	48	36.76				May-11
50	3.76	4.69	6.84	13.76		3.65	2.16	12.74	0.7	8.56	11.7	22	59	10	1	25			5.75		Dec-13
50	2.07	-1.37	5.96	3.19		2.98	2.91	12.46	0.69		11.6	18	63	10	1	23					Dec-13
50	3.74	4.73	6.64	13.54			1.91	12.79	0.71	8.52	11.7	22	59	10	1	25					Dec-16
50	2.05	3.16	6.26	14.18	44.71	2.73	2.45	12.68	1.01	9.83	59.7	25	52	16	0	32	23.95	-17.18	5.75		Dec-10
50	1.99	2.90	5.59	11.72	39.46	1.99	3.2	12.7	1.01	9.78	59.7	25	52	16	0	32	23.39	-17.41			Dec-10
50	2.24	3.42	6.65	14.61	45.24		2.2	12.67	1.01	9.84	59.7	25	52	16	0	32	23.95	-17.18			Dec-16
500	3.15	4.32	3.38	-6.75		0	1.25			9	9.3	-10	24	86	0	0					Dec-14
500	1.03	-1.52	-0.60			0.47	1.25			8.5	14.7	27	4	69	0	0					Dec-15
100	6.85	11.39	20.35	23.60	79.37	0.17	1.42	9.06	0.84	14.18	62.4	4	65	31	0	242	11.02	-15.78			Sep-05
500	0.41	0.00	-1.60	-8.72	22.73	0	2.5	4.51	-0.04	9.69	19.7	68	19	0	13	26	4.51	-5.82	4.75		Aug-14
500	0.11	-0.73	-2.80	-11.80	16.74	0	3.25	4.51	-0.04	9.27	19.7	68	19	0	13	26	4.06	-6.11		1.00	Aug-14
500	0.51	0.10	-1.29	-8.04	24.29	0	2.25	4.48	-0.04	9.77	19.7	68	19	0	13	26	4.66	-5.72			Aug-14
1,000	3.93	7.43	13.01			0.66	1.75			11.29	22.8	6	69	11	7						Aug-16
250	3.24	6.49	14.97	21.08	80.44	0.19	1.03	10.75	1.02	25.68	52.4	11	89	0	0	40	19.24	-12.82			Dec-99
	8.72	16.27	41.30	31.04	24.01	0.84	0.88	16.04	0.99	8.44	2,645	4	91	0	3	46	15.53	-28.15			May-86
	8.71	16.27	41.29	31.03	24.00		0.93	16.04	0.99	8.44	2,645	4	91	0	3	46	15.53	-28.15			Sep-17
	8.67	16.22	41.23	30.97	23.94		0.93	16.04	0.99	8.44	2,645	4	91	0	3	46	15.53	-28.15			Sep-17
	3.80	8.20	18.79	14.67	7.11	0	1.12	9.36	0.58	11.72	142.3	10	44	45	0	51					Jan-12
	3.82	8.21	18.81	14.69	7.12		1	9.36	0.58	11.72	142.3	10	44	45	0	51					Sep-17
	3.82	8.21	18.81	14.69	7.12		1	9.36	0.58	11.72	142.3	10	44	45	0	51					Sep-17
	5.36	10.74	27.73	30.39	74.27	1.2	0.65	9.82	0.9	15.31	588.6	3	94	0	3	36	18.7	-18.86			Apr-11
	3.97	9.86	30.15	25.53	44.59	1.27	0.65	10.91	0.83	13.76	1,604	2	90	0	7	21	15.85	-20.01			Apr-11
	4.37	8.55	20.60	33.87	94.09	1.26	0.43	9.61	0.93	22.42	239.9	5	95	0	0	31	21.94	-17.63			Apr-11
500	7.75	13.36	18.44	36.34	96.63	0	1.53	10.49	0.92	24.04	22.0	0	90	10	0	39	21.85	-21.51			Jan-95
500	7.55	12.90	17.51	33.28	89.76	0	2.28	10.48	0.92	18.4	22.0	0	90	10	0	39	21.33	-21.72	3.00		Apr-95
500	2.16	3.61	2.21	4.30	40.88	0	1.53	11.98	0.76	20.99	15.1	0	92	8	0	47	18.08	-17.58			Jan-99
500	2.06	3.40	1.90	3.24	38.50	0	2.28	11.97	0.76	19.55	15.1	0	92	8	0	47	17.85	-17.66	3.00		Jan-99
	4.65	10.47	13.77	35.54		0.33	1	11.61	0.77	12.81	54.9	5	95	0	0	72					Apr-14
	7.47	15.14	31.43	46.01	124.21	0.05	1.23	10.7	0.98	42	399.6	0	100	0	0	35	27.77	-17.63	4.75		Dec-85
	7.26	14.68	30.37	42.63	115.83	0	2	10.69	0.98	30.65	399.6	0	100	0	0	35	27.28	-17.84		1.00	Apr-95
	7.58	15.35	31.84	47.37	127.70	0.24	0.92	10.7	0.98	44.03	399.6	0	100	0	0	35	28.02	-17.48			Mar-06

	MARKET		FUND TYPE, CATEGORY & OBJECTIVE		RATINGS					MINIMUMS
Fund Name	Ticker Symbol	Traded On	Fund Type	Category and (Prospectus Objective)	Overall Rating	Reward Rating	Risk Rating	Recent Up/ Downgrade	Open to New Investors	Min Initial Investment
Carillon ClariVest Capital Appreciation Fund Class R3	HRCLX	NAS CM	Open End	US Equity Large Cap Growth (Growth)	A-	A	B	Up	Y	0
Carillon ClariVest Capital Appreciation Fund Class R5	HRCMX	NAS CM	Open End	US Equity Large Cap Growth (Growth)	A-	A	B	Up	Y	0
Carillon ClariVest Capital Appreciation Fund Class R6	HRCUX	NAS CM	Open End	US Equity Large Cap Growth (Growth)	A-	A	B	Up	Y	0
Carillon ClariVest Capital Appreciation Fund Class Y	HRCYX	NAS CM	Open End	US Equity Large Cap Growth (Growth)	A-	A	B		Y	1,000
Carillon ClariVest International Stock Fund Class A	EISAX	NAS CM	Open End	Global Equity Large Cap (Foreign Stock)	B	B	B	Up	Y	1,000
Carillon ClariVest International Stock Fund Class C	EISDX	NAS CM	Open End	Global Equity Large Cap (Foreign Stock)	B-	B-	B-	Up	Y	1,000
Carillon ClariVest International Stock Fund Class I	EISIX	NAS CM	Open End	Global Equity Large Cap (Foreign Stock)	B	B	B-	Up	Y	100,000
Carillon ClariVest International Stock Fund Class R-3	EISRX	NAS CM	Open End	Global Equity Large Cap (Foreign Stock)	B	B-	B	Up	Y	0
Carillon ClariVest International Stock Fund Class R-5	EISSX	NAS CM	Open End	Global Equity Large Cap (Foreign Stock)	B	B	B	Up	Y	0
Carillon ClariVest International Stock Fund Class R-6	EISVX	NAS CM	Open End	Global Equity Large Cap (Foreign Stock)	B	B	B-	Up	Y	0
Carillon Clarivest International Stock Fund Class Y	EISYX	NAS CM	Open End	Global Equity Large Cap (Foreign Stock)	B	B	B		Y	1,000
Carillon Cougar Tactical Allocation Fund Class A	ETAFX	NAS CM	Open End	Moderate Alloc (Growth & Income)	C-	C-	A-	Up	Y	1,000
Carillon Cougar Tactical Allocation Fund Class C	ETDFX	NAS CM	Open End	Moderate Alloc (Growth & Income)	C-	C-	A-	Up	Y	1,000
Carillon Cougar Tactical Allocation Fund Class I	ETIFX	NAS CM	Open End	Moderate Alloc (Growth & Income)	C-	C-	A-	Up	Y	100,000
Carillon Cougar Tactical Allocation Fund Class R-3	ETRFX	NAS CM	Open End	Moderate Alloc (Growth & Income)	C-	C-	A-	Up	Y	0
Carillon Cougar Tactical Allocation Fund Class R-5	ETSFX	NAS CM	Open End	Moderate Alloc (Growth & Income)	C-	C-	A-	Up	Y	0
Carillon Cougar Tactical Allocation Fund Class R-6	ETUFX	NAS CM	Open End	Moderate Alloc (Growth & Income)	C-	C-	A-	Up	Y	0
Carillon Cougar Tactical Allocation Fund Class Y	ETYFX	NAS CM	Open End	Moderate Alloc (Growth & Income)	C-	C-	A-		Y	1,000
Carillon Eagle Growth & Income Fund Class A	HRCVX	NAS CM	Open End	US Equity Large Cap Value (Growth & Income)	B-	B-	B-	Down	Y	1,000
Carillon Eagle Growth & Income Fund Class C	HIGCX	NAS CM	Open End	US Equity Large Cap Value (Growth & Income)	B-	B-	B-	Down	Y	1,000
Carillon Eagle Growth & Income Fund Class I	HIGJX	NAS CM	Open End	US Equity Large Cap Value (Growth & Income)	B-	B-	B-	Down	Y	100,000
Carillon Eagle Growth & Income Fund Class R3	HIGRX	NAS CM	Open End	US Equity Large Cap Value (Growth & Income)	B-	B-	B-	Down	Y	0
Carillon Eagle Growth & Income Fund Class R5	HIGSX	NAS CM	Open End	US Equity Large Cap Value (Growth & Income)	B-	B-	B-	Down	Y	0
Carillon Eagle Growth & Income Fund Class R6	HIGUX	NAS CM	Open End	US Equity Large Cap Value (Growth & Income)	B-	B-	B-	Down	Y	0
Carillon Eagle Growth & Income Fund Class Y	HIGYX	NAS CM	Open End	US Equity Large Cap Value (Growth & Income)	B-	B-	B-		Y	1,000
Carillon Eagle Mid Cap Growth Fund Class A	HAGAX	NAS CM	Open End	US Equity Mid Cap (Growth)	B+	A	C+	Up	Y	1,000
Carillon Eagle Mid Cap Growth Fund Class C	HAGCX	NAS CM	Open End	US Equity Mid Cap (Growth)	B	A-	C+	Up	Y	1,000
Carillon Eagle Mid Cap Growth Fund Class I	HAGIX	NAS CM	Open End	US Equity Mid Cap (Growth)	B+	A	B-	Up	Y	100,000
Carillon Eagle Mid Cap Growth Fund Class R3	HAREX	NAS CM	Open End	US Equity Mid Cap (Growth)	B	A-	C+	Down	Y	0
Carillon Eagle Mid Cap Growth Fund Class R5	HARSX	NAS CM	Open End	US Equity Mid Cap (Growth)	B+	A	B-	Up	Y	0
Carillon Eagle Mid Cap Growth Fund Class R6	HRAUX	NAS CM	Open End	US Equity Mid Cap (Growth)	B+	A	B-	Up	Y	0
Carillon Eagle Mid Cap Growth Fund Class Y	HRAYX	NAS CM	Open End	US Equity Mid Cap (Growth)	B+	A	C+		Y	1,000
Carillon Eagle Mid Cap Stock Fund Class A	HMCAX	NAS CM	Open End	US Equity Mid Cap (Growth)	B	B-	B	Up	Y	1,000
Carillon Eagle Mid Cap Stock Fund Class C	HMCCX	NAS CM	Open End	US Equity Mid Cap (Growth)	B	B-	B	Up	Y	1,000
Carillon Eagle Mid Cap Stock Fund Class I	HMCJX	NAS CM	Open End	US Equity Mid Cap (Growth)	B-	B	C+	Down	Y	100,000
Carillon Eagle Mid Cap Stock Fund Class R3	HMRRX	NAS CM	Open End	US Equity Mid Cap (Growth)	B-	B-	C+		Y	0
Carillon Eagle Mid Cap Stock Fund Class R5	HMRSX	NAS CM	Open End	US Equity Mid Cap (Growth)	B-	B	C+	Down	Y	0
Carillon Eagle Mid Cap Stock Fund Class R6	HMRUX	NAS CM	Open End	US Equity Mid Cap (Growth)	B-	B	C+	Down	Y	0
Carillon Eagle Mid Cap Stock Fund Class Y	HMRYX	NAS CM	Open End	US Equity Mid Cap (Growth)	B	B-	B		Y	1,000
Carillon Eagle Small Cap Growth Fund Class A	HRSCX	NAS CM	Open End	US Equity Small Cap (Small Company)	B	B+	B	Up	Y	1,000
Carillon Eagle Small Cap Growth Fund Class C	HSCCX	NAS CM	Open End	US Equity Small Cap (Small Company)	B	B+	B	Up	Y	1,000
Carillon Eagle Small Cap Growth Fund Class I	HSIIX	NAS CM	Open End	US Equity Small Cap (Small Company)	B	B+	B	Up	Y	100,000
Carillon Eagle Small Cap Growth Fund Class R3	HSRRX	NAS CM	Open End	US Equity Small Cap (Small Company)	B	B+	B	Up	Y	0
Carillon Eagle Small Cap Growth Fund Class R5	HSRSX	NAS CM	Open End	US Equity Small Cap (Small Company)	B	B+	B	Up	Y	0
Carillon Eagle Small Cap Growth Fund Class R6	HSRUX	NAS CM	Open End	US Equity Small Cap (Small Company)	B	B+	B	Up	Y	0
Carillon Eagle Small Cap Growth Fund Class Y	HSRYX	NAS CM	Open End	US Equity Small Cap (Small Company)	B	B+	B		Y	1,000
Carillon Eagle Smaller Company Fund Class A	EGEAX	NAS CM	Open End	US Equity Small Cap (Small Company)	B	B	B	Up	Y	1,000
Carillon Eagle Smaller Company Fund Class C	EGECX	NAS CM	Open End	US Equity Small Cap (Small Company)	B	B	B	Up	Y	1,000
Carillon Eagle Smaller Company Fund Class I	EGEIX	NAS CM	Open End	US Equity Small Cap (Small Company)	B	B+	B	Up	Y	100,000
Carillon Eagle Smaller Company Fund Class R3	EGERX	NAS CM	Open End	US Equity Small Cap (Small Company)	B	B	B	Up	Y	0
Carillon Eagle Smaller Company Fund Class R5	EGESX	NAS CM	Open End	US Equity Small Cap (Small Company)	B	B+	B	Up	Y	0
Carillon Eagle Smaller Company Fund Class R6	EGEUX	NAS CM	Open End	US Equity Small Cap (Small Company)	B	B+	B	Up	Y	0

★ Expanded analysis of this fund is included in Section II.

	TOTAL RETURNS					PERFORMANCE				ASSETS		ASSET ALLOCATION & TURNOVER					BULL & BEAR		FEES		
Min Additional Investment	3-Month Total Return	6-Month Total Return	1-Year Total Return	3-Year Total Return	5-Year Total Return	Dividend Yield (TTM)	Expense Ratio	3-Yr Std Deviation	3-Year Beta	NAV	Total Assets (MIL)	%Cash	%Stocks	%Bonds	%Other	Turnover Ratio	Last Bull Market Total Return	Last Bear Market Total Return	Front End Fee (%)	Back End Fee (%)	Inception Date
	7.37	14.94	30.98	44.61	120.53	0	1.5	10.7	0.98	40.38	399.6	0	100	0	0	35	27.51	-17.69			Sep-07
	7.56	15.33	31.88	47.37	127.55	0.27	0.9	10.71	0.98	43.91	399.6	0	100	0	0	35	27.99	-17.48			Oct-06
	7.58	15.35	31.93	47.16	125.98	0.39	0.85	10.74	0.98	43.68	399.6	0	100	0	0	35	27.77	-17.63			Jul-15
	7.50	15.17	31.46	46.04	124.26		1.25	10.7	0.98	43.95	399.6	0	100	0	0	35	27.77	-17.63			Nov-17
	4.99	11.47	27.08	29.50		1	1.45	11.7	0.92	18.94	19.4	4	95	0	1	100			4.75		Feb-13
	4.81	11.09	26.21	26.48		0.87	2.2	11.69	0.92	18.63	19.4	4	95	0	1	100				1.00	Feb-13
	5.03	11.64	27.56	31.17		1.83	1.15	11.69	0.92	18.89	19.4	4	95	0	1	100					Feb-13
	4.91	11.32	26.81	28.86		1.74	1.7	11.74	0.93	18.78	19.4	4	95	0	1	100					Feb-13
	5.04	11.60	27.42	31.04		1.83	1.15	11.69	0.92	18.91	19.4	4	95	0	1	100					Feb-13
	5.08	11.68	27.65	31.51		1.89	1.05	11.71	0.92	18.93	19.4	4	95	0	1	100					Feb-13
	5.04	11.57	27.36	30.56			1.45	11.71	0.92	18.88	19.4	4	95	0	1	100					Nov-17
	3.96	7.77	12.10			0.23	1.31			16.07	17.5	5	66	29	0	66			4.75		Dec-15
	3.72	7.35	11.24			0	2.06			15.94	17.5	5	66	29	0	66				1.00	Dec-15
	4.01	7.88	12.44			0.49	1.01			16.05	17.5	5	66	29	0	66					Dec-15
	3.87	7.61	11.86			0	1.56			16.06	17.5	5	66	29	0	66					Dec-15
	4.09	7.97	12.46			0.49	1.01			16.07	17.5	5	66	29	0	66					Dec-15
	4.03	7.97	12.52			0.52	0.91			16.07	17.5	5	66	29	0	66					Dec-15
	4.00	7.87	12.28				1.31			16.04	17.5	5	66	29	0	66					Nov-17
	7.75	11.37	20.13	28.99	86.11	1.5	1.01	10.1	0.96	21.04	625.0	0	98	0	2	15	20.65	-14.29	4.75		Dec-86
	7.57	10.95	19.22	26.12	79.26	0.9	1.77	10.1	0.96	20.16	625.0	0	98	0	2	15	20.06	-14.53		1.00	Apr-95
	7.90	11.56	20.47	30.11	88.70	1.76	0.79	10.08	0.96	20.99	625.0	0	98	0	2	15	20.84	-14.11			Mar-09
	7.69	11.18	19.73	27.79	82.94	1.23	1.32	10.05	0.96	20.96	625.0	0	98	0	2	15	20.39	-14.34			Sep-09
	7.82	11.52	20.42	29.45	87.83	1.76	0.75	10.15	0.97	21.01	625.0	0	98	0	2	15	20.74	-14.26			Dec-09
	7.89	11.58	20.57	30.13	89.19	1.84	0.67	10.01	0.95	20.94	625.0	0	98	0	2	15	20.82	-14.35			Aug-11
	7.84	11.45	20.22	29.09	86.25		1.01	10.1	0.96	20.99	625.0	0	98	0	2	15	20.65	-14.29			Nov-17
	6.87	12.12	29.90	40.61	117.87	0	1.12	12.24	1.08	56.49	2,495	2	98	0	0	34	27.97	-24.05	4.75		Aug-98
	6.66	11.72	28.98	37.61	110.20	0	1.83	12.24	1.08	45.39	2,495	2	98	0	0	34	27.54	-24.25		1.00	Aug-98
	6.94	12.30	30.35	42.01	121.55	0	0.82	12.25	1.08	59.48	2,495	2	98	0	0	34	28.25	-23.91			Jun-06
	6.80	11.95	29.54	39.46	114.84	0	1.41	12.25	1.08	54.88	2,495	2	98	0	0	34	27.8	-24.13			Jan-09
	6.94	12.27	30.31	41.84	121.24	0.01	0.83	12.24	1.08	59.32	2,495	2	98	0	0	34	28.23	-23.89			Dec-09
	6.97	12.34	30.43	42.46	122.68	0.02	0.72	12.25	1.08	59.82	2,495	2	98	0	0	34	28.3	-24.02			Aug-11
	6.85	12.10	29.88	40.59	117.84		1.08	12.24	1.08	59.46	2,495	2	98	0	0	34	27.97	-24.05			Nov-17
	5.68	9.84	19.59	28.05	78.47	0	1.24	10.63	0.97	28.38	267.0	2	98	0	0	44	24.14	-22.98	4.75		Nov-97
	5.46	9.39	18.65	25.17	71.84	0	1.99	10.61	0.97	20.6	267.0	2	98	0	0	44	23.62	-23.16		1.00	Nov-97
	5.74	9.98	19.95	29.27	81.05	0	0.95	10.64	0.97	30.09	267.0	2	98	0	0	44	24.41	-22.84			Jun-06
	5.58	9.67	19.28	26.86	75.75	0	1.5	10.62	0.97	27.16	267.0	2	98	0	0	44	23.85	-23.02			Aug-06
	5.77	9.99	19.94	29.22	81.83	0	0.95	10.64	0.97	30.28	267.0	2	98	0	0	44	24.34	-22.87			Oct-06
	5.78	10.06	20.06	29.63	82.16	0	0.85	10.62	0.97	30.42	267.0	2	98	0	0	44	24.31	-23			Aug-11
	5.69	9.86	19.60	28.06	78.49		1.25	10.63	0.97	30.08	267.0	2	98	0	0	44	24.14	-22.98			Nov-17
	5.92	10.01	22.82	33.17	92.91	0	1.1	14.01	0.91	59.6	5,195	3	97	0	0	32	26.49	-21.84	4.75		May-93
	5.73	9.66	21.98	30.39	86.23	0	1.8	14.02	0.91	44.24	5,195	3	97	0	0	32	26	-22.08		1.00	Apr-95
	6.02	10.24	23.27	34.53	96.10	0	0.81	14.01	0.91	62.61	5,195	3	97	0	0	32	26.35	-21.72			Jun-06
	5.86	9.89	22.51	32.18	90.36	0	1.34	14	0.91	57.72	5,195	3	97	0	0	32	26.3	-21.79			Sep-06
	6.03	10.24	23.29	34.60	96.26	0	0.78	14.02	0.91	62.89	5,195	3	97	0	0	32	26.68	-21.71			Oct-06
	6.05	10.29	23.40	35.02	97.37	0	0.67	14.01	0.91	63.38	5,195	3	97	0	0	32	26.79	-21.84			Aug-11
	5.95	10.04	22.86	33.22	92.97		1.1	14.01	0.91	62.6	5,195	3	97	0	0	32	26.49	-21.84			Nov-17
	5.81	10.19	19.31	31.28	83.55	0	1.25	11.61	0.9	14.01	47.0	3	97	0	0	46	24.49	-21.64	4.75		Nov-08
	5.63	9.76	18.46	28.40	76.93	0	2	11.6	0.9	12.04	47.0	3	97	0	0	46	23.97	-21.98		1.00	Nov-08
	5.90	10.33	19.71	33.60	88.64	0	0.95	11.69	0.91	15.2	47.0	3	97	0	0	46	24.78	-21.53			Mar-09
	5.75	10.06	19.06	30.29	81.00	0	1.5	11.61	0.9	13.43	47.0	3	97	0	0	46	24.5	-21.88			Dec-09
	5.91	10.40	19.74	32.99	87.55	0	0.95	11.6	0.9	15	47.0	3	97	0	0	46	24.84	-21.54			Dec-09
	5.95	10.41	19.88	33.47	88.29	0	0.85	11.62	0.9	15.09	47.0	3	97	0	0	46	24.79	-21.62			Aug-11

	MARKET			FUND TYPE, CATEGORY & OBJECTIVE	RATINGS				MINIMUMS	
Fund Name	Ticker Symbol	Traded On	Fund Type	Category and (Prospectus Objective)	Overall Rating	Reward Rating	Risk Rating	Recent Up/ Downgrade	Open to New Investors	Min Initial Investment
Carillon Eagle Smaller Company Fund Class Y	EGEYX	NAS CM	Open End	US Equity Small Cap (Small Company)	B	B	B		Y	1,000
Carillon Scout International Fund Class A	CSIGX	NAS CM	Open End	Global Equity Large Cap (Foreign Stock)	B-	B-	B-		Y	1,000
Carillon Scout International Fund Class C	CSIHX	NAS CM	Open End	Global Equity Large Cap (Foreign Stock)	B-	B-	B-		Y	1,000
Carillon Scout International Fund Class I	UMBWX	NAS CM	Open End	Global Equity Large Cap (Foreign Stock)	B-	B-	B-	Up	Y	100,000
Carillon Scout International Fund Class R-3	CSIQX	NAS CM	Open End	Global Equity Large Cap (Foreign Stock)	B-	B-	B-		Y	0
Carillon Scout International Fund Class R-5	CSIUX	NAS CM	Open End	Global Equity Large Cap (Foreign Stock)	B-	B-	B-		Y	0
Carillon Scout International Fund Class R-6	CSIWX	NAS CM	Open End	Global Equity Large Cap (Foreign Stock)	B-	B-	B-		Y	0
Carillon Scout International Fund Class Y	CSIZX	NAS CM	Open End	Global Equity Large Cap (Foreign Stock)	B-	B-	B-		Y	1,000
Carillon Scout Mid Cap Fund Class A	CSMEX	NAS CM	Open End	US Equity Mid Cap (Growth)	B+	A	B-		Y	1,000
Carillon Scout Mid Cap Fund Class C	CSMFX	NAS CM	Open End	US Equity Mid Cap (Growth)	B+	A	B-		Y	1,000
Carillon Scout Mid Cap Fund Class I	UMBMX	NAS CM	Open End	US Equity Mid Cap (Growth)	B+	A	B-	Up	Y	100,000
Carillon Scout Mid Cap Fund Class R-3	CSMRX	NAS CM	Open End	US Equity Mid Cap (Growth)	B+	A	B-		Y	0
Carillon Scout Mid Cap Fund Class R-5	CSMSX	NAS CM	Open End	US Equity Mid Cap (Growth)	B+	A	B-		Y	0
Carillon Scout Mid Cap Fund Class R-6	CSMUX	NAS CM	Open End	US Equity Mid Cap (Growth)	B+	A	B-		Y	0
Carillon Scout Mid Cap Fund Class Y	CSMZX	NAS CM	Open End	US Equity Mid Cap (Growth)	B+	A	B-		Y	1,000
Carillon Scout Small Cap Fund Class A	CSSAX	NAS CM	Open End	US Equity Small Cap (Small Company)	B+	A	C+		Y	1,000
Carillon Scout Small Cap Fund Class C	CSSJX	NAS CM	Open End	US Equity Small Cap (Small Company)	B+	A	C+		Y	1,000
Carillon Scout Small Cap Fund Class I	UMBHX	NAS CM	Open End	US Equity Small Cap (Small Company)	B+	A	C+	Up	Y	100,000
Carillon Scout Small Cap Fund Class R-3	CSSQX	NAS CM	Open End	US Equity Small Cap (Small Company)	B+	A	C+		Y	0
Carillon Scout Small Cap Fund Class R-5	CSSSX	NAS CM	Open End	US Equity Small Cap (Small Company)	B+	A	C+		Y	0
Carillon Scout Small Cap Fund Class R-6	CSSVX	NAS CM	Open End	US Equity Small Cap (Small Company)	B+	A	C+		Y	0
Carillon Scout Small Cap Fund Class Y	CSSWX	NAS CM	Open End	US Equity Small Cap (Small Company)	B+	A	C+		Y	1,000
Castle Focus Fund Class C	CASTX	NAS CM	Open End	US Equity Large Cap Value (Growth)	B-	C+	B	Down	Y	2,000
Castle Focus Fund Class Investor	MOATX	NAS CM	Open End	US Equity Large Cap Value (Growth)	B	C+	B+		Y	4,000
Castlemaine Emerging Markets Opportunities Fund	CNEMX	NAS CM	Open End	Long/Short Equity (Div Emerging Mkts)	C-	D+	C	Up	Y	1,000,000
Castlemaine Event Driven Fund	CNEVX	NAS CM	Open End	Market Neutral (Growth & Income)	C-	D+	B-	Up	Y	1,000,000
Castlemaine Long/Short Fund	CNLSX	NAS CM	Open End	Long/Short Equity (Growth)	C-	D+	C	Up	Y	1,000,000
Castlemaine Market Neutral Fund	CNMNX	NAS CM	Open End	Market Neutral (Growth & Income)	C-	C-	B+	Up	Y	1,000,000
Castlemaine Multi-Strategy Fund	CNMSX	NAS CM	Open End	Multialternative (Growth & Income)	C-	D+	B	Up	Y	1,000,000
Catalyst Buyback Strategy Fund Class A	BUYAX	NAS CM	Open End	US Equity Mid Cap (Growth)	B	B	B-	Up	Y	2,500
Catalyst Buyback Strategy Fund Class C	BUYCX	NAS CM	Open End	US Equity Mid Cap (Growth)	B	B	B-	Up	Y	2,500
Catalyst Buyback Strategy Fund Class I	BUYIX	NAS CM	Open End	US Equity Mid Cap (Growth)	B	B	B-	Up	Y	2,500
Catalyst Dynamic Alpha Fund Class A	CPEAX	NAS CM	Open End	US Equity Large Cap Growth (Growth)	B+	A	B	Up	Y	2,500
Catalyst Dynamic Alpha Fund Class C	CPECX	NAS CM	Open End	US Equity Large Cap Growth (Growth)	B+	A	B-	Up	Y	2,500
Catalyst Dynamic Alpha Fund Class I	CPEIX	NAS CM	Open End	US Equity Large Cap Growth (Growth)	A-	A	B	Up	Y	2,500
Catalyst Hedged Commodity Strategy Fund Class A	CFHAX	NAS CM	Open End	Commodities Broad Basket (Growth)	C	C	B	Up	Y	2,500
Catalyst Hedged Commodity Strategy Fund Class C	CFHCX	NAS CM	Open End	Commodities Broad Basket (Growth)	C	C	B	Up	Y	2,500
Catalyst Hedged Commodity Strategy Fund Class I	CFHIX	NAS CM	Open End	Commodities Broad Basket (Growth)	C	C	B	Up	Y	2,500
Catalyst Hedged Futures Strategy Fund Class A	HFXAX	NAS CM	Open End	Long/Short Equity (Growth)	D	D-	D		Y	2,500
Catalyst Hedged Futures Strategy Fund Class C	HFXCX	NAS CM	Open End	Long/Short Equity (Growth)	D	D-	D		Y	2,500
Catalyst Hedged Futures Strategy Fund Class I	HFXIX	NAS CM	Open End	Long/Short Equity (Growth)	D	D-	D		Y	2,500
Catalyst Insider Buying Fund Class A	INSAX	NAS CM	Open End	US Equity Large Cap Growth (Growth)	C+	C+	C	Down	Y	2,500
Catalyst Insider Buying Fund Class C	INSCX	NAS CM	Open End	US Equity Large Cap Growth (Growth)	C+	C+	C+	Up	Y	2,500
Catalyst Insider Buying Fund Class I	INSIX	NAS CM	Open End	US Equity Large Cap Growth (Growth)	C+	C+	C+	Down	Y	2,500
Catalyst Insider Long/Short Fund Class A	CIAAX	NAS CM	Open End	Long/Short Equity (Growth)	D+	D+	C-	Down	Y	2,500
Catalyst Insider Long/Short Fund Class C	CIACX	NAS CM	Open End	Long/Short Equity (Growth)	D+	D+	D+		Y	2,500
Catalyst Insider Long/Short Fund Class I	CIAIX	NAS CM	Open End	Long/Short Equity (Growth)	D+	D+	C-	Down	Y	2,500
Catalyst IPOx Allocation Fund Class A	OIPAX	NAS CM	Open End	US Equity Mid Cap (Growth)	C	C+	B-	Up	Y	2,500
Catalyst IPOx Allocation Fund Class C	OIPCX	NAS CM	Open End	US Equity Mid Cap (Growth)	C	C+	B-	Up	Y	2,500
Catalyst IPOx Allocation Fund Class I	OIPIX	NAS CM	Open End	US Equity Mid Cap (Growth)	C	C+	B-	Up	Y	2,500
Catalyst Macro Strategy Fund Class A	MCXAX	NAS CM	Open End	Multialternative (Growth & Income)	C	C	C-	Up	Y	2,500
Catalyst Macro Strategy Fund Class C	MCXCX	NAS CM	Open End	Multialternative (Growth & Income)	C	C	C-	Up	Y	2,500

★ Expanded analysis of this fund is included in Section II.

	TOTAL RETURNS					PERFORMANCE				ASSETS		ASSET ALLOCATION & TURNOVER					BULL & BEAR		FEES		
Min Additional Investment	3-Month Total Return	6-Month Total Return	1-Year Total Return	3-Year Total Return	5-Year Total Return	Dividend Yield (TTM)	Expense Ratio	3-Yr Std Deviation	3-Year Beta	NAV	Total Assets (MIL)	%Cash	%Stocks	%Bonds	%Other	Turnover Ratio	Last Bull Market Total Return	Last Bear Market Total Return	Front End Fee (%)	Back End Fee (%)	Inception Date
	5.80	10.18	19.30	31.27	83.54		1.25	11.61	0.9	15.2	47.0	3	97	0	0	46	24.49	-21.64			Nov-17
	3.36	9.66	23.11	24.15	36.24		1.36	11.34	0.89	21.47	1,147	2	98	0	0	20	18.96	-24.31	4.75		Nov-17
	3.18	9.27	22.22	21.42	31.27		2.11	11.33	0.89	21.47	1,147	2	98	0	0	20	18.45	-24.55		1.00	Nov-17
	3.40	9.78	23.39	25.03	37.86	1.45	1.06	11.34	0.89	21.47	1,147	2	98	0	0	20	19.13	-24.23			Sep-93
	3.28	9.51	22.80	23.21	34.54		1.61	11.34	0.89	21.47	1,147	2	98	0	0	20	18.79	-24.39			Nov-17
	3.43	9.80	23.42	25.05	37.89		1.06	11.34	0.89	21.47	1,147	2	98	0	0	20	19.13	-24.23			Nov-17
	3.43	9.80	23.42	25.05	37.89		0.96	11.34	0.89	21.47	1,147	2	98	0	0	20	19.13	-24.23			Nov-17
	3.36	9.66	23.11	24.15	36.24		1.36	11.34	0.89	21.47	1,147	2	98	0	0	20	18.96	-24.31			Nov-17
	7.41	13.45	23.76	46.45	114.87		1.33	10.2	0.92	19.01	1,790	1	100	0	0	87	21.67	-15.77	4.75		Nov-17
	7.21	13.03	22.84	43.21	107.01		2.08	10.2	0.92	19.01	1,790	1	100	0	0	87	21.15	-16.03		1.00	Nov-17
	7.44	13.55	24.02	47.46	117.39	0.35	1.03	10.2	0.92	19.01	1,790	1	100	0	0	87	21.84	-15.68			Oct-06
	7.31	13.27	23.41	45.31	112.14		1.58	10.2	0.92	19.01	1,790	1	100	0	0	87	21.5	-15.85			Nov-17
	7.46	13.57	24.04	47.48	117.42		1.03	10.2	0.92	19.01	1,790	1	100	0	0	87	21.84	-15.68			Nov-17
	7.46	13.57	24.04	47.48	117.42		0.93	10.2	0.92	19.01	1,790	1	100	0	0	87	21.84	-15.68			Nov-17
	7.41	13.45	23.76	46.44	114.86		1.33	10.2	0.92	19.01	1,790	1	100	0	0	87	21.67	-15.77			Nov-17
	6.18	14.15	31.52	47.05	117.47		1.25	13.71	0.87	27.91	280.9	0	99	0	1	25	30.22	-26.66	4.75		Nov-17
	6.02	13.76	30.58	43.84	109.58		2	13.7	0.87	27.89	280.9	0	99	0	1	25	29.66	-26.89		1.00	Nov-17
	6.26	14.31	31.87	48.17	120.23	0	1.04	13.71	0.87	27.92	280.9	0	99	0	1	25	30.41	-26.59			Nov-86
	6.14	14.03	31.22	45.98	114.83		1.5	13.7	0.87	27.9	280.9	0	99	0	1	25	30.03	-26.74			Nov-17
	6.26	14.31	31.87	48.17	120.23		0.95	13.71	0.87	27.92	280.9	0	99	0	1	25	30.41	-26.59			Nov-17
	6.26	14.31	31.87	48.17	120.23		0.85	13.71	0.87	27.92	280.9	0	99	0	1	25	30.41	-26.59			Nov-17
	6.18	14.15	31.52	47.05	117.47		1.25	13.71	0.87	27.91	280.9	0	99	0	1	25	30.22	-26.66			Nov-17
100	1.27	3.67	11.54	17.10	45.45	0	2.41	6.36	0.5	20.85	194.1	35	66	0	0	48	9.12	-6.12		1.00	Jun-10
100	1.52	4.16	12.70	20.68	52.95	0.11	1.41	6.35	0.49	22.19	194.1	35	66	0	0	48	9.8	-5.69			Jun-10
	0.88	4.95	10.24			0	1.59			10.19	1.3	6	93	0	1	166					Dec-15
	1.88	1.24	3.57			0	1.53			10.73	1.4	13	85	0	2	317					Dec-15
	3.84	4.36	3.33			0	1.58			10.53	1.2	18	80	0	2	207					Dec-15
	4.38	7.21	10.81			0	1.62				1.4	27	68	4	0	110					Dec-15
	1.86	3.22	5.42			0	1.65			10.8	1.1	6	73	19	1	8					Dec-15
50	2.35	9.20	19.63	36.27		0.19	1.5	11.48	0.96	10.66	9.6	2	98	0	0	734			5.75		Dec-13
50	2.16	8.75	18.77	33.23		0	2.25	11.49	0.96	10.4	9.6	2	98	0	0	734					Dec-13
50	2.42	9.24	19.86	37.28		0.41	1.25	11.46	0.96	10.72	9.6	2	98	0	0	734					Dec-13
50	8.29	14.47	26.87	44.71	147.63	0	1.36	12.46	0.96	21.97	353.5	3	97	0	0	95			5.75		Dec-11
50	8.13	14.06	25.92	41.52	138.50	0	2.11	12.45	0.96	20.92	353.5	3	97	0	0	95					Dec-11
50	8.39	14.64	27.19	45.89	149.63	0	1.11	12.5	0.96	22.15	353.5	3	97	0	0	95					Jun-14
50	1.83	2.11	8.65			0.98	2.52			11.04	105.4	15	20	53	13	19			5.75		Sep-15
50	1.66	1.76	7.81			0.75	3.27			10.94	105.4	15	20	53	13	19					Sep-15
50	1.81	2.18	8.80			1.06	2.27			11.06	105.4	15	20	53	13	19					Sep-15
50	-4.86	-6.85	-22.73	-11.43	-7.07	0	2.29	12.23	-0.41	8.02	1,552	29	0	66	5	54	6.12	8.52	5.75		Aug-13
50	-5.14	-7.30	-23.36	-13.50	-10.55	0	3.04	12.23	-0.4	7.74	1,552	29	0	66	5	54	5.65	8.18			Aug-13
50	-4.92	-6.89	-22.63	-10.88	-6.23	0	2.04	12.26	-0.41	8.1	1,552	29	0	66	5	54	6.12	8.52			Aug-13
50	6.85	8.92	17.02	10.35	71.59	0	1.5	11.02	0.99	16.84	59.4	1	99	0	0	160	22.83		5.75		Jul-11
50	6.65	8.52	16.16	7.96	65.32	0	2.25	11	0.98	16.67	59.4	1	99	0	0	160	22.26				Jul-11
50	6.92	9.05	17.34	11.27	73.29	0	1.25	11.04	0.99	16.98	59.4	1	99	0	0	160	22.83				Jun-14
50	3.44	2.66	4.22	-8.20	1.55	0	1.78	11.44	0.38	9.62	2.7	20	80	0	0	121			5.75		Apr-12
50	3.24	2.32	3.35	-10.37	-1.81	0	2.53	11.41	0.38	9.24	2.7	20	80	0	0	121					Apr-12
50	3.51	2.74	4.40	-7.42	2.60	0	1.53	11.41	0.38	9.72	2.7	20	80	0	0	121					Jun-14
50	5.79	11.20	22.06			0	2.18			13.82	1.3	10	90	0	0	151			5.75		Sep-15
50	5.58	10.72	21.15			0	2.93			13.57	1.3	10	90	0	0	151					Sep-15
50	5.85	11.33	22.26			0	1.93			13.88	1.3	10	90	0	0	151					Sep-15
50	14.01	20.26	24.56	18.06		0	2.03	21.18	1.3	10.09	24.6	66	28	7	0	188			5.75		Mar-14
50	13.86	19.75	23.78	16.30		0	2.78	21.21	1.3	9.94	24.6	66	28	7	0	188					Mar-14

	MARKET			FUND TYPE, CATEGORY & OBJECTIVE	RATINGS				MINIMUMS	
Fund Name	Ticker Symbol	Traded On	Fund Type	Category and (Prospectus Objective)	Overall Rating	Reward Rating	Risk Rating	Recent Up/ Downgrade	Open to New Investors	Min Initial Investment
Catalyst Macro Strategy Fund Class I	MCXIX	NAS CM	Open End	Multialternative (Growth & Income)	C	C	C-	Up	Y	2,500
Catalyst MLP & Infrastructure Fund Class A	MLXAX	NAS CM	Open End	Energy Sector Equity (Growth & Income)	D+	D+	D	Down	Y	2,500
Catalyst MLP & Infrastructure Fund Class C	MLXCX	NAS CM	Open End	Energy Sector Equity (Growth & Income)	D+	D+	D	Down	Y	2,500
Catalyst MLP & Infrastructure Fund Class I	MLXIX	NAS CM	Open End	Energy Sector Equity (Growth & Income)	D+	D+	D	Down	Y	2,500
Catalyst Multi-Strategy Fund Class A	ACXAX	NAS CM	Open End	Other Alternative (Growth)	D+	D	C-	Down	Y	2,500
Catalyst Multi-Strategy Fund Class C	ACXCX	NAS CM	Open End	Other Alternative (Growth)	D	D	C-	Down	Y	2,500
Catalyst Multi-Strategy Fund Class I	ACXIX	NAS CM	Open End	Other Alternative (Growth)	D+	D	C-	Down	Y	2,500
Catalyst Small Cap Insider Buying Fund Class A	CTVAX	NAS CM	Open End	US Equity Small Cap (Growth)	C	C	C		Y	2,500
Catalyst Small Cap Insider Buying Fund Class C	CTVCX	NAS CM	Open End	US Equity Small Cap (Growth)	C	C	C		Y	2,500
Catalyst Small Cap Insider Buying Fund Class I	CTVIX	NAS CM	Open End	US Equity Small Cap (Growth)	C	C	C		Y	2,500
Catalyst Systematic Alpha Fund Class A	ATRAX	NAS CM	Open End	Long/Short Equity (Growth & Income)	D+	D	C		Y	2,500
Catalyst Systematic Alpha Fund Class C	ATRCX	NAS CM	Open End	Long/Short Equity (Growth & Income)	D+	D	C		Y	2,500
Catalyst Systematic Alpha Fund Class I	ATRFX	NAS CM	Open End	Long/Short Equity (Growth & Income)	D+	D	C		Y	2,500
Catalyst Time Value Trading Fund Class A	TVTAX	NAS CM	Open End	Other Alternative (Growth)	C	C	C	Up	Y	2,500
Catalyst Time Value Trading Fund Class C	TVTCX	NAS CM	Open End	Other Alternative (Growth)	C	C	C	Up	Y	2,500
Catalyst Time Value Trading Fund Class I	TVTIX	NAS CM	Open End	Other Alternative (Growth)	C	C	C	Up	Y	2,500
Catalyst/Exceed Defined Risk Fund Class A	CLPAX	NAS CM	Open End	US Equity Mid Cap (Growth)	C	C	C+		Y	2,500
Catalyst/Exceed Defined Risk Fund Class C	CLPCX	NAS CM	Open End	US Equity Mid Cap (Growth)	C	C	C+		Y	2,500
Catalyst/Exceed Defined Risk Fund Class I	CLPFX	NAS CM	Open End	US Equity Mid Cap (Growth)	C	C	C+		Y	2,500
Catalyst/Exceed Defined Shield Fund Class A	SHIEX	NAS CM	Open End	Long/Short Equity (Income)	B-	C	B	Up	Y	2,500
Catalyst/Exceed Defined Shield Fund Class C	SHINX	NAS CM	Open End	Long/Short Equity (Income)	B-	C	B		Y	2,500
Catalyst/Exceed Defined Shield Fund Class I	SHIIX	NAS CM	Open End	Long/Short Equity (Income)	B-	C	B	Up	Y	2,500
Catalyst/Groesbeck Growth of Income Class A	CGGAX	NAS CM	Open End	US Equity Large Cap Blend (Equity-Income)	C+	B-	C	Down	Y	2,500
Catalyst/Groesbeck Growth of Income Class C	CGGCX	NAS CM	Open End	US Equity Large Cap Blend (Equity-Income)	C+	C+	C	Down	Y	2,500
Catalyst/Groesbeck Growth of Income Fund Class I	CGGIX	NAS CM	Open End	US Equity Large Cap Blend (Equity-Income)	C+	B-	C	Down	Y	2,500
Catalyst/Lyons Tactical Allocation Fund Class A	CLTAX	NAS CM	Open End	US Equity Large Cap Blend (Asset Alloc)	B	C+	B		Y	2,500
Catalyst/Lyons Tactical Allocation Fund Class C	CLTCX	NAS CM	Open End	US Equity Large Cap Blend (Asset Alloc)	B-	C+	B	Down	Y	2,500
Catalyst/Lyons Tactical Allocation Fund Class I	CLTIX	NAS CM	Open End	US Equity Large Cap Blend (Asset Alloc)	B	B-	B		Y	2,500
Catalyst/MAP Global Balanced Fund Class A	TRXAX	NAS CM	Open End	Alloc (Multi-Asset Global)	B	C+	A-		Y	2,500
Catalyst/MAP Global Balanced Fund Class C	TRXCX	NAS CM	Open End	Alloc (Multi-Asset Global)	B-	C	B+	Down	Y	2,500
Catalyst/MAP Global Balanced Fund Class I	TRXIX	NAS CM	Open End	Alloc (Multi-Asset Global)	B	C+	A-		Y	2,500
Catalyst/MAP Global Equity Fund Class A	CAXAX	NAS CM	Open End	Global Equity (World Stock)	B-	B-	B		Y	2,500
Catalyst/MAP Global Equity Fund Class C	CAXCX	NAS CM	Open End	Global Equity (World Stock)	B-	C+	B		Y	2,500
Catalyst/MAP Global Equity Fund Class I	CAXIX	NAS CM	Open End	Global Equity (World Stock)	B	B-	B	Up	Y	2,500
Catalyst/Millburn Hedge Strategy Fund Class A	MBXAX	NAS CM	Open End	Multialternative (Growth & Income)	B	B	B+	Up	Y	2,500
Catalyst/Millburn Hedge Strategy Fund Class C	MBXCX	NAS CM	Open End	Multialternative (Growth & Income)	B	B	B+	Up	Y	2,500
Catalyst/Millburn Hedge Strategy Fund Class I	MBXIX	NAS CM	Open End	Multialternative (Growth & Income)	B+	B	B+	Up	Y	2,500
Catalyst/SMH Total Return Income Fund Class A	TRIFX	NAS CM	Open End	Moderate Alloc (Growth & Income)	C	C	C		Y	2,500
Catalyst/SMH Total Return Income Fund Class C	TRICX	NAS CM	Open End	Moderate Alloc (Growth & Income)	C	C	C		Y	2,500
Catalyst/SMH Total Return Income Fund Class I	TRIIX	NAS CM	Open End	Moderate Alloc (Growth & Income)	C	C	C		Y	2,500
Causeway Emerging Markets Fund Class Institutional	CEMIX	NAS CM	Open End	Emerging Markets Equity (Div Emerging Mkts)	B-	B	C	Up	Y	1,000,000
Causeway Emerging Markets Fund Investor Class	CEMVX	NAS CM	Open End	Emerging Markets Equity (Div Emerging Mkts)	B-	B	C	Up	Y	5,000
Causeway Global Absolute Return Fund Institutional Class	CGAIX	NAS CM	Open End	Market Neutral (Growth)	C-	D+	C	Up	Y	1,000,000
Causeway Global Absolute Return Fund Investor Class	CGAVX	NAS CM	Open End	Market Neutral (Growth)	C-	D+	C	Up	Y	5,000
Causeway Global Value Fund Institutional Class	CGVIX	NAS CM	Open End	Global Equity (Growth & Income)	C+	C+	B-	Down	Y	1,000,000
Causeway Global Value Fund Investor	CGVVX	NAS CM	Open End	Global Equity (Growth & Income)	C+	C+	C+	Down	Y	5,000
Causeway Intl Opp Fund Inst Cls	CIOIX	NAS CM	Open End	Global Equity Large Cap (Foreign Stock)	B-	B-	B-	Up	Y	1,000,000
Causeway International Opportunities Fund Investor Class	CIOVX	NAS CM	Open End	Global Equity Large Cap (Foreign Stock)	B-	B-	B-	Up	Y	5,000
Causeway International Small Cap Fund Institutional Class	CIISX	NAS CM	Open End	Global Equity Mid/Small Cap (Small Company)	B-	C+	B-	Up	Y	1,000,000
Causeway International Small Cap Fund Investor Class	CVISX	NAS CM	Open End	Global Equity Mid/Small Cap (Small Company)	B-	C+	B-	Up	Y	5,000
Causeway International Value Fund Class Institutional	CIVIX	NAS CM	Open End	Global Equity Large Cap (Foreign Stock)	B-	C+	B-	Up	Y	1,000,000
Causeway International Value Fund Class Investor	CIVVX	NAS CM	Open End	Global Equity Large Cap (Foreign Stock)	B-	C+	B-	Up	Y	5,000

★ Expanded analysis of this fund is included in Section II.

Min Additional Investment	3-Month Total Return	6-Month Total Return	1-Year Total Return	3-Year Total Return	5-Year Total Return	Dividend Yield (TTM)	Expense Ratio	3-Yr Std Deviation	3-Year Beta	NAV	Total Assets (MIL)	%Cash	%Stocks	%Bonds	%Other	Turnover Ratio	Last Bull Market Total Return	Last Bear Market Total Return	Front End Fee (%)	Back End Fee (%)	Inception Date
TOTAL RETURNS						PERFORMANCE				ASSETS		ASSET ALLOCATION & TURNOVER					BULL & BEAR		FEES		
50	14.15	20.37	24.96	18.88		0	1.78	21.22	1.3	10.16	24.6	66	28	7	0	188					Mar-14
50	-1.98	-2.55	-14.02	-23.72		11.88	1.65			5.79	147.5	0	100	0	0	32			5.75		Dec-14
50	-2.16	-2.90	-14.62	-25.21		11.05	2.4			5.79	147.5	0	100	0	0	32					Dec-14
50	-1.92	-2.43	-13.80	-23.11		12.15	1.4			5.8	147.5	0	100	0	0	32					Dec-14
50	4.14	0.13	1.36	0.96	7.06	0.14	2.46			14.81	8.2	91	9	0	0	0	-0.73	-4.41	5.75		Aug-15
50	3.99	-0.27	0.62	-1.35	3.05	0	3.21			14.57	8.2	91	9	0	0	0	-1.16	-4.71			Aug-15
50	4.21	0.20	1.64	1.73	8.41	0.71	2.21			14.82	8.2	91	9	0	0	0	-0.59	-4.31			Aug-15
50	1.52	9.81	9.34	-3.87	43.38	0.58	1.78	17.09	1	15.33	17.0	2	98	0	0	228	22	-32.88	5.75		Jul-06
50	1.38	9.41	8.60	-6.03	38.16	0	2.53	17.03	1	14.64	17.0	2	98	0	0	228	21.47	-33.09			Jul-06
50	1.64	9.91	9.60	-3.16	45.24	0.93	1.53	17.07	1	15.41	17.0	2	98	0	0	228	22.12	-32.76			Mar-09
50	2.63	2.96	1.77	0.32		0.1	2.49	6.41	0.28	9.73	2.4	44	26	26	3	17			5.75		Jul-14
50	2.36	2.47	0.84	-2.19		0	3.24	6.39	0.28	9.53	2.4	44	26	26	3	17					Jul-14
50	2.64	3.08	1.99	0.68		0.91	2.24	6.37	0.28	9.69	2.4	44	26	26	3	17					Jul-14
50	-0.35	2.89	7.70	1.86		0	2.3	10.83	0.49	8.53	3.8	102	-2	0	0	0			5.75		Nov-14
50	-0.47	2.46	6.95	-0.40		0	3.05	10.81	0.49	8.31	3.8	102	-2	0	0	0					Nov-14
50	-0.34	2.99	7.91	2.64		0	2.05	10.87	0.49	8.59	3.8	102	-2	0	0	0					Nov-14
50	1.65	3.89	8.19	-1.41		0	1.53	11.72		9.92	11.2	9	5	85	0	292			5.75		Dec-13
50	1.48	3.57	7.41	-3.81		0	2.28	11.69		9.56	11.2	9	5	85	0	292					Dec-13
50	1.70	4.03	8.55	-0.80		0	1.28	11.69		9.98	11.2	9	5	85	0	292					Jun-14
50	4.69	8.18	14.33			0.31	1.45			10.16	28.9	28	7	66	0	89			5.75		Apr-15
50	4.02	7.57	13.76				2.2			10.1	28.9	28	7	66	0	89					Sep-17
50	3.90	7.45	13.63			0.42	1.2			10.2	28.9	28	7	66	0	89					Apr-15
50	6.01	10.96	22.46	17.54	73.36	1.17	1.36	12.26	1.11	9.93	7.4	0	100	0	0	48	20.64	-11.11	5.75		Dec-09
50	5.88	10.55	21.63	14.95	66.99	0.92	2.11	12.29	1.11	9.66	7.4	0	100	0	0	48	20.12	-11.35			Dec-09
50	6.14	11.15	23.00	18.80	76.07	1.24	1.11	12.31	1.12	9.99	7.4	0	100	0	0	48	20.78	-11			Nov-10
50	8.64	12.22	16.70	24.53	96.86	1.19	1.5	10.99		16.23	83.1	0	100	0	0	95			5.75		Jul-12
50	8.51	11.85	15.89	21.87	89.85	0.46	2.25	11.02		16.03	83.1	0	100	0	0	95					Jul-12
50	8.69	12.35	16.99	25.58	98.61	1.5	1.25	11.02		16.2	83.1	0	100	0	0	95					Jun-14
50	3.01	3.92	11.12	10.53	32.67	1.55	1.55	5.8	0.5	12.16	23.3	11	53	33	1	50	9.18		5.75		Jul-11
50	2.77	3.46	10.27	7.46	27.68	0.98	2.3	5.83	0.5	12.05	23.3	11	53	33	1	50	8.79				Jul-11
50	3.00	4.08	11.43	11.46	33.94	1.81	1.25	5.82	0.5	12.17	23.3	11	53	33	1	50	9.18				Jun-14
50	2.49	4.60	17.08	25.98	54.47	0.92	1.57	9.26	0.78	14.78	39.9	7	90	0	3	26	12.94		5.75		Jul-11
50	2.31	4.23	16.11	23.13	48.69	0.33	2.32	9.26	0.78	14.62	39.9	7	90	0	3	26	12.41				Jul-11
50	2.54	4.80	17.30	27.41	56.38	1.12	1.27	9.22	0.77	14.75	39.9	7	90	0	3	26	12.94				Jun-14
50	4.12	9.43	13.66	35.81	72.26	1.07	2.25			31.59	3,561	26	54	20	0	4	7.6	-17.85	5.75		Dec-15
50	3.94	9.01	12.82	32.69	65.82	0.85	3			31.18	3,561	26	54	20	0	4	7.13	-18.11			Dec-15
50	4.18	9.54	13.96	36.81	74.39	1.15	2			31.71	3,561	26	54	20	0	4	7.76	-17.77			Dec-15
50	-1.93	3.83	12.64	8.21	11.63	6.08	3.85	14.28	0.94	4.49	22.4	2	48	42	0	32	13.64	-19.62	5.75		May-08
50	-1.90	3.46	11.83	5.84	7.55	5.36	4.6	14.26	0.94	4.49	22.4	2	48	42	0	32	13.16	-19.87			May-08
50	-1.87	3.99	12.96	8.84	12.70	6.35	3.6	14.22	0.94	4.48	22.4	2	48	42	0	32	13.64	-19.62			Jul-13
	7.21	16.88	39.58	28.08	28.75	1.15	1.18	15.92	1	14.17	4,614	3	92	0	0	50	21	-27.43			Mar-07
	7.16	16.68	39.27	27.12	27.21	0.97	1.43	15.9	1	14.28	4,614	3	92	0	0	50	20.84	-27.41			Mar-07
	0.88	3.87	-8.16	-2.71	8.91	12.09	1.55	7.75	-38.31	9.11	46.0	96	0	0	4		4.4	-0.67			Jan-11
	0.89	3.79	-8.32	-3.39	7.38	11.86	1.8	7.74	-38.89	9.03	46.0	96	0	0	4		4.25	-0.77			Jan-11
	6.68	11.13	20.12	20.57	67.42	1.18	1.04	10.93	0.97	12.04	118.8	1	93	0	0	55	21.6	-22.83			Apr-08
	6.42	10.79	19.58	19.36	65.05	1.04	1.29	10.93	0.97	11.99	118.8	1	93	0	0	55	21.47	-22.88			Jan-11
	5.61	13.21	29.57	23.49	42.39	3.11	1.07	11.57	0.91	14.58	144.0	3	89	0	1	62	19.13	-26.14			Dec-09
	5.64	13.13	29.38	22.54	40.56	2.96	1.32	11.58	0.91	14.49	144.0	3	89	0	1	62	18.97	-26.26			Dec-09
	4.52	15.32	34.72	45.70		2.11	1.33	12.46	0.99	13.06	12.4	2	97	0	1	91					Oct-14
	4.52	15.23	34.49	44.78		1.91	1.58	12.35	0.98	13.07	12.4	2	97	0	1	91					Oct-14
	5.12	12.35	27.18	23.36	45.88	1.57	0.91	11.46	0.9	17.32	8,499	2	91	0	0	35	18.76	-25.79			Oct-01
	5.23	12.39	27.07	22.58	44.33	1.36	1.16	11.45	0.9	17.21	8,499	2	91	0	0	35	18.61	-25.94			Oct-01

	MARKET		FUND TYPE, CATEGORY & OBJECTIVE		RATINGS				MINIMUMS	
Fund Name	Ticker Symbol	Traded On	Fund Type	Category and (Prospectus Objective)	Overall Rating	Reward Rating	Risk Rating	Recent Up/ Downgrade	Open to New Investors	Min Initial Investment
Cavalier Dynamic Growth Fund C Class	CADYX	NAS CM	Open End	Moderate Alloc (Growth)	B-	C+	B	Up	Y	1,000
Cavalier Dynamic Growth Fund Institutional Class	CDYGX	NAS CM	Open End	Moderate Alloc (Growth)	B-	C+	B-	Down	Y	1,000
Cavalier Fundamental Growth Fund C Class	CFGAX	NAS CM	Open End	US Equity Mid Cap (Growth)	B	B+	C+	Up	Y	1,000
Cavalier Fundamental Growth Fund Institutional Class	CAFGX	NAS CM	Open End	US Equity Mid Cap (Growth)	B	A-	C+	Up	Y	1,000
Cavalier Global Opportunities Fund C Class	CATDX	NAS CM	Open End	Moderate Alloc (Growth)	B-	B-	C+	Up	Y	1,000
Cavalier Global Opportunities Fund Institutional Class	CATEX	NAS CM	Open End	Moderate Alloc (Growth)	B-	B	C+	Down	Y	1,000
Cavalier Multi Strategist Fund C Class	CMSYX	NAS CM	Open End	Aggressive Alloc (Growth & Income)	B-	C+	B	Up	Y	1,000
Cavalier Multi Strategist Fund Institutional Class	CMSFX	NAS CM	Open End	Aggressive Alloc (Growth & Income)	B-	C+	B	Down	Y	1,000
Cavalier Tactical Rotation Fund C Class	CATOX	NAS CM	Open End	Moderate Alloc (Growth)	C+	C+	B-	Down	Y	1,000
Cavalier Tactical Rotation Fund Institutional Class	CTROX	NAS CM	Open End	Moderate Alloc (Growth)	B-	C+	B-	Down	Y	1,000
Cavanal Hill Active Core Fund Class A	AABAX	NAS CM	Open End	Moderate Alloc (Balanced)	B-	C+	B	Up	Y	0
Cavanal Hill Active Core Fund Class C	AACBX	NAS CM	Open End	Moderate Alloc (Balanced)	B-	C+	B	Up	Y	0
Cavanal Hill Active Core Fund Institutional Class	AIBLX	NAS CM	Open End	Moderate Alloc (Balanced)	B-	C+	B	Up	Y	1,000
Cavanal Hill Active Core Fund Investor Class	APBAX	NAS CM	Open End	Moderate Alloc (Balanced)	B-	C+	B	Up	Y	100
Cavanal Hill Opportunistic Fund Class A	AAOPX	NAS CM	Open End	Aggressive Alloc (Growth)	B-	C+	B	Up	Y	0
Cavanal Hill Opportunistic Fund Class C	AACOX	NAS CM	Open End	Aggressive Alloc (Growth)	B-	C+	B+	Up	Y	0
Cavanal Hill Opportunistic Fund Institutional	AIOPX	NAS CM	Open End	Aggressive Alloc (Growth)	B-	C+	B	Up	Y	1,000
Cavanal Hill Opportunistic Fund Investor	APOPX	NAS CM	Open End	Aggressive Alloc (Growth)	B-	C+	B	Up	Y	100
Cavanal Hill World Energy Fund A	AAWEX	NAS CM	Open End	Energy Sector Equity (Growth & Income)	C-	D+	C	Up	Y	0
Cavanal Hill World Energy Fund C	ACWEX	NAS CM	Open End	Energy Sector Equity (Growth & Income)	C-	D+	C	Up	Y	0
Cavanal Hill World Energy Fund Institutional	AIWEX	NAS CM	Open End	Energy Sector Equity (Growth & Income)	C-	D+	C	Up	Y	1,000
Cavanal Hill World Energy Fund Investor	APWEX	NAS CM	Open End	Energy Sector Equity (Growth & Income)	C-	D+	C	Up	Y	100
Cavanal Mid Cap Core Equity Fund Class A	AAWVX	NAS CM	Open End	US Equity Mid Cap (Growth & Income)	D-	D+	B+		Y	0
Cavanal Mid Cap Core Equity Fund Class C	ACWVX	NAS CM	Open End	US Equity Mid Cap (Growth & Income)	D-	D+	B+		Y	0
Cavanal Mid Cap Core Equity Fund Institutional Shares	AIWVX	NAS CM	Open End	US Equity Mid Cap (Growth & Income)	D-	D+	B+		Y	1,000
Cavanal Mid Cap Core Equity Fund Investor Shares	APWVX	NAS CM	Open End	US Equity Mid Cap (Growth & Income)	D-	D+	B+		Y	100
CBOE Vest Defined Distribution Strategy Fund Cls A Shares	VDDAX	NAS CM	Open End	Long/Short Equity (Growth)	D	D+	C+		Y	1,000
CBOE Vest Defined Distribution Strategy Fund Cls C Shares	VDDCX	NAS CM	Open End	Long/Short Equity (Growth)	D	D+	C		Y	1,000
CBOE Vest Defined Distribution Strat Fund Cls Inst Shares	VDDIX	NAS CM	Open End	Long/Short Equity (Growth)	D	D+	B-	Up	Y	100,000
CBOE Vest Defined Distribution Strat Fund Cls Inv Shares	VDDLX	NAS CM	Open End	Long/Short Equity (Growth)	D	D+	C+		Y	1,000
CBOE Vest S&P 500 Div Aristocrats Target Income Fund Cls A	KNGAX	NAS CM	Open End	Long/Short Equity (Growth & Income)	U	U	U		Y	1,000
CBOE Vest S&P 500 Div Aristocrats Target Income Fund Cls C	KNGCX	NAS CM	Open End	Long/Short Equity (Growth & Income)	U	U	U		Y	1,000
CBOE Vest S&P 500 Div Aristocrats Target Income Inst Cls	KNGIX	NAS CM	Open End	Long/Short Equity (Growth & Income)	U	U	U		Y	100,000
CBOE Vest S&P 500 Div Aristocrats Target Income Inv Cls	KNGLX	NAS CM	Open End	Long/Short Equity (Growth & Income)	U	U	U		Y	1,000
CBOE Vest S&P 500® Buffer Protect Strat Cls Inst Shares	BUIGX	NAS CM	Open End	Long/Short Equity (Growth & Income)	D	C-	A-	Up	Y	100,000
CBOE Vest S&P 500® Buffer Protect Strat Cls Inv Shares	BUMGX	NAS CM	Open End	Long/Short Equity (Growth & Income)	D	C-	B+	Up	Y	1,000
CBOE Vest S&P 500® Enhanced Growth Strat Fund Cls A Shares	ENGAX	NAS CM	Open End	Long/Short Equity (Growth & Income)	D-	D+	A		Y	1,000
CBOE Vest S&P 500® Enhanced Growth Strat Inst Cls Shares	ENGIX	NAS CM	Open End	Long/Short Equity (Growth & Income)	D-	D+	A		Y	100,000
CBOE Vest S&P 500® Enhanced Growth Strat Inv Cls Shares	ENGLX	NAS CM	Open End	Long/Short Equity (Growth & Income)	D-	D+	A		Y	1,000
CBRE Clarion Global Real Estate Income Fund	IGR	NYSE	Closed End	Real Estate Sector Equity (Real Estate)	C+	C	B-	Up	Y	
CCA Aggressive Return Fund Institutional Class Shares	RSKIX	NAS CM	Open End	Alloc (Growth)	C+	C+	C+	Up	Y	100,000
CCM Alternative Income Fund Institutional Shares	CCMNX	NAS CM	Open End	Multialternative (Income)	C+	C	B		Y	1,000
Cedar Ridge Unconstrained Credit Fund Institutional Class	CRUMX	NAS CM	Open End	Other Alternative (Growth & Income)	C	C	B-	Down	Y	1,000,000
Cedar Ridge Unconstrained Credit Fund Investor Class	CRUPX	NAS CM	Open End	Other Alternative (Growth & Income)	C	C	C+	Down	Y	2,500
Centaur Total Return Fund	TILDX	NAS CM	Open End	Moderate Alloc (Growth & Income)	B-	C+	B	Down	Y	1,500
Center Coast MLP & Infrastructure Fund	CEN	NYSE	Closed End	Energy Sector Equity (Growth & Income)	D	D	D	Down	Y	
Center Coast MLP Focus Fund Class A	CCCAX	NAS CM	Open End	Energy Sector Equity (Growth & Income)	D	D	D	Down	Y	2,500
Center Coast MLP Focus Fund Class C	CCCCX	NAS CM	Open End	Energy Sector Equity (Growth & Income)	D	D	D	Down	Y	2,500
Center Coast MLP Focus Fund Institutional Class	CCCNX	NAS CM	Open End	Energy Sector Equity (Growth & Income)	D	D	D	Down	Y	1,000,000
Centerstone International Fund Class A	CSIAX	NAS CM	Open End	Global Equity Large Cap (Growth)	D+	C-	B	Up	Y	2,500
Centerstone International Fund Class C	CSINX	NAS CM	Open End	Global Equity Large Cap (Growth)	D+	C-	B	Up	Y	2,500
Centerstone International Fund Class I	CINTX	NAS CM	Open End	Global Equity Large Cap (Growth)	D+	C-	B	Up	Y	100,000

★Expanded analysis of this fund is included in Section II.

	TOTAL RETURNS					PERFORMANCE				ASSETS		ASSET ALLOCATION & TURNOVER					BULL & BEAR		FEES		
Min Additional Investment	3-Month Total Return	6-Month Total Return	1-Year Total Return	3-Year Total Return	5-Year Total Return	Dividend Yield (TTM)	Expense Ratio	3-Yr Std Deviation	3-Year Beta	NAV	Total Assets (MIL)	%Cash	%Stocks	%Bonds	%Other	Turnover Ratio	Last Bull Market Total Return	Last Bear Market Total Return	Front End Fee (%)	Back End Fee (%)	Inception Date
50	0.42	2.20	14.78	17.59	49.03	0	2.3	10.12	0.78	9.85	21.3	5	95	0	0	160	14.17	-17.38		1.00	Feb-11
50	0.67	2.73	15.89	21.26	56.61	0	1.3	10.11	0.78	10.53	21.3	5	95	0	0	160	14.58	-17.03			Oct-09
50	2.34	16.86	29.99	28.39		0.13	2.25	12.02	0.76	14.53	84.3	4	96	0	0	136				1.00	Nov-13
50	2.61	17.43	31.26	32.31		0.13	1.25	11.98	0.76	14.98	84.3	4	96	0	0	136					Oct-13
50	7.27	13.74	26.33	29.43	71.36	0.16	2.72	9.34	0.66	16.19	30.5	3	97	0	0	440				1.00	Sep-12
50	7.56	14.39	27.63	33.54	80.91	0.16	1.72	9.37	0.67	16.74	30.5	3	97	0	0	440					Sep-12
50	5.66	9.11	16.10	14.37	43.27	0	2.62	7.1	0.64	12.83	10.9	1	91	4	5	190				1.00	Sep-12
50	5.84	9.60	17.17	17.64	50.52	0	1.62	7.12	0.65	13.36	10.9	1	91	4	5	190					Sep-12
50	5.07	8.04	15.68	16.14	51.22	0	2.39	8.66	0.81	13.33	117.9	4	96	0	0	167				1.00	Sep-12
50	5.34	8.54	16.90	19.59	60.62	0	1.39	8.67	0.81	13.88	117.9	4	96	0	0	167					Sep-12
	4.03	6.58	12.07	17.61	48.03	1.21	1.03	5.18	0.49	13.63	54.3	3	57	39	0	55	14.07	-9.37	2.00		May-11
	3.81	6.04	11.21	14.97	42.67	0.49	1.78	5.16	0.49	13.63	54.3	3	57	39	0	55	13.57	-9.6		1.00	Dec-14
	4.07	6.68	12.36	18.52	50.09	1.43	0.78	5.22	0.49	13.71	54.3	3	57	39	0	55	14.25	-9.25			Dec-05
	4.02	6.48	12.03	17.83	48.42	1.2	1.03	5.26	0.5	13.67	54.3	3	57	39	0	55	14.06	-9.32			Jun-95
	3.27	5.63	11.84	17.53	54.09	0.06	1.64	7.83	0.58	14.97	47.7	4	82	13	0	227	26.03		2.00		Sep-11
	3.08	5.20	10.96	14.98	48.45	0	2.42	7.83	0.58	14.64	47.7	4	82	13	0	227	25.51			1.00	Dec-14
	3.39	5.81	12.12	18.55	56.13	0.23	1.39	7.83	0.58	15.08	47.7	4	82	13	0	227	26.25				Sep-11
	3.34	5.63	11.86	17.52	53.65	0.05	1.68	7.81	0.58	14.92	47.7	4	82	13	0	227	26.14				Sep-11
	7.39	14.20	-1.89	0.15		0.66	1.26	16.44	0.88	9.37	59.0	2	94	4	0	103			2.00		Feb-14
	7.15	13.70	-2.56	-1.94		0.07	2.01	16.45	0.88	9.29	59.0	2	94	4	0	103				1.00	Feb-14
	7.45	14.24	-1.59	1.07		0.85	1.01	16.48	0.88	9.39	59.0	2	94	4	0	103					Feb-14
	7.36	14.16	-1.94	0.13		0.62	1.33	16.42	0.88	9.37	59.0	2	94	4	0	103					Feb-14
	5.66	7.87	13.38				1.06			11.3	2.7	3	97	0	0	45			2.00		Dec-16
	4.98	6.08	11.60				1.81			11.16	2.7	3	97	0	0	45				1.00	Dec-16
	5.79	8.01	13.35				0.81			11.24	2.7	3	97	0	0	45					Dec-16
	5.69	7.92	13.26				1.06			11.23	2.7	3	97	0	0	45					Dec-16
100	-2.20	-0.82	-0.86				1.5			9.63	51.2	101	-1	0	0				5.75		Feb-17
100	-2.22	-1.13	-1.63			0	2.25			9.55	51.2	101	-1	0	0					1.00	Nov-16
100	-1.99	-0.61	-0.62			0	1.25			9.66	51.2	101	-1	0	0						Sep-16
100	-2.10	-0.71	-0.92			0	1.5			9.63	51.2	101	-1	0	0						Nov-16
100	7.44						1.2			10.79	9.4	3	97	0	0				5.75		Sep-17
100	7.24						1.95			10.78	9.4	3	97	0	0						Sep-17
100	7.58						0.95			10.8	9.4	3	97	0	0						Sep-17
100	7.35						1.2			10.78	9.4	3	97	0	0						Sep-17
100	3.34	5.05	11.85			0	0.95			11.42	12.6	0	93	7	0						Aug-16
100	3.35	4.97	11.66				1.2			11.39	12.6	0	93	7	0						Dec-16
100	4.25	7.79	18.54				1.2			11.75	38.1	0	100	0	0				5.75		Jan-17
100	4.51	8.05	19.17				0.95			11.81	38.1	0	100	0	0						Dec-16
100	4.43	7.87	18.84				1.2			11.78	38.1	0	100	0	0						Jan-17
	3.66	6.65	11.29	6.25	28.94	2.24	0	11.77	1.05	8.99	1,035	0	88	0	-12	67	21.71	-15.27			Feb-04
100	4.62	9.26	19.64	9.93	34.04	0.36	1.13	8.58	0.86	12.17	36.0	7	74	17	1	520					Dec-12
	1.04	2.70	5.01	6.15		4.86	1.6	3.62	0.6	9.56	32.7	-149	78	25	11	47					May-13
100	-1.66	-1.13	3.30	6.77		2.55	1.41	3.85	0.92	10.53	89.9	15	0	77	4	70					Dec-13
100	-1.62	-1.16	3.05	6.00		2.3	1.66	3.81	0.89	10.53	89.9	15	0	77	4	70					Dec-13
100	2.89	7.34	13.52	19.79	52.76	0	2.06	6.17	0.53	12.91	25.6	55	44	0	1	127	16.62	-15.4			Mar-05
	-3.79	-3.93	-8.57	-26.96		0	2.45	26.43		9.84	204.0	0	132	0	-32	62					Sep-13
100	-2.74	-4.54	-6.79	-17.06	7.91	9.73	1.5	16.51	0.97	7.31	2,545	1	99	0	0	60	10.68	-4.49	5.75		Dec-10
100	-2.94	-4.86	-7.48	-18.91	4.03	10.46	2.25	16.45	0.96	6.79	2,545	1	99	0	0	60	10.14	-4.8		1.00	Dec-10
100,000	-2.70	-4.47	-6.57	-16.43	9.33	9.55	1.25	16.48	0.96	7.44	2,545	1	99	0	0	60	10.8	-4.4			Dec-10
100	2.71	5.83	19.19			0.49	1.37			12	122.9	3	75	17	5				5.00		May-16
100	2.55	5.51	18.42			0.45	2.12			11.92	122.9	3	75	17	5					1.00	May-16
100	2.79	6.00	19.60			0.53	1.12			12.01	122.9	3	75	17	5						May-16

	MARKET		FUND TYPE, CATEGORY & OBJECTIVE		RATINGS				MINIMUMS	
Fund Name	Ticker Symbol	Traded On	Fund Type	Category and (Prospectus Objective)	Overall Rating	Reward Rating	Risk Rating	Recent Up/ Downgrade	Open to New Investors	Min Initial Investment
Centerstone Investors Fund Class A	CETAX	NAS CM	Open End	Alloc (Growth & Income)	D+	C-	B	Up	Y	2,500
Centerstone Investors Fund Class C	CENNX	NAS CM	Open End	Alloc (Growth & Income)	D+	C-	B	Up	Y	2,500
Centerstone Investors Fund Class I	CENTX	NAS CM	Open End	Alloc (Growth & Income)	D+	C-	B	Up	Y	100,000
Central Securities Corporation	CET	AMEX	Closed End	US Equity Large Cap Blend (Growth & Income)	B+	A	B	Up	Y	
Centre Active U.S. Tax Exempt Fund Institutional Class	DHBIX	NAS CM	Open End	Other Alternative (Municipal Bond - Natl)	C	C	C+		Y	1,000,000
Centre Active U.S. Tax Exempt Fund Investor Class	DHBRX	NAS CM	Open End	Other Alternative (Municipal Bond - Natl)	C	C	C		Y	5,000
Centre Active U.S. Treasury Fund Institutional Class	DHTUX	NAS CM	Open End	Other Alternative (Govt Bond - Treasury)	C	C-	C		Y	1,000,000
Centre Active U.S. Treasury Fund Investor Class	DHTRX	NAS CM	Open End	Other Alternative (Govt Bond - Treasury)	C-	C-	C		Y	5,000
Centre American Select Equity Fund Institutional Class	DHANX	NAS CM	Open End	US Equity Large Cap Growth (Growth)	B	B-	A		Y	1,000,000
Centre American Select Equity Fund Investor Class	DHAMX	NAS CM	Open End	US Equity Large Cap Growth (Growth)	B	B-	A		Y	5,000
CG Core Total Return Fund Institutional Class	CGBNX	NAS CM	Open End	Aggressive Alloc (Growth)	B-	B	C+	Up	Y	100,000
CGM Focus Fund	CGMFX	NAS CM	Open End	US Equity Large Cap Blend (Growth)	B	A-	B-	Up	Y	2,500
CGM Mutual Fund	LOMMX	NAS CM	Open End	Aggressive Alloc (Balanced)	B-	B-	B	Up	Y	2,500
CGM Realty Fund	CGMRX	NAS CM	Open End	Real Estate Sector Equity (Real Estate)	B+	A-	B	Up	Y	2,500
Chadwick & D'Amato Fund	CDFFX	NAS CM	Open End	Moderate Alloc (Growth)	C	C	C+	Up	Y	250
Champlain Emerging Markets Fund Advisor Shares	CIPDX	NAS CM	Open End	Emerging Markets Equity (Div Emerging Mkts)	C+	C+	C	Up	Y	10,000
Champlain Mid Cap Fund Advisor Class	CIPMX	NAS CM	Open End	US Equity Mid Cap (Growth)	B	B	B-		Y	10,000
Champlain Mid Cap Fund Institutional Class	CIPIX	NAS CM	Open End	US Equity Mid Cap (Growth)	B	B	B-		Y	1,000,000
Champlain Small Company Fund Class Advisor	CIPSX	NAS CM	Open End	US Equity Small Cap (Small Company)	B	B	B	Up		10,000
Champlain Small Company Fund Institutional Class	CIPNX	NAS CM	Open End	US Equity Small Cap (Small Company)	B	B	B	Up	Y	1,000,000
Chartwell Mid Cap Value Fund	BERCX	NAS CM	Open End	US Equity Large Cap Value (Growth)	B-	B	C	Up	Y	1,000
Chartwell Small Cap Growth Fund	CWSGX	NAS CM	Open End	US Equity Small Cap (Small Company)	U	U	U		Y	1,000
Chartwell Small Cap Value Fund	CWSIX	NAS CM	Open End	US Equity Small Cap (Small Company)	B	B+	B	Up	Y	1,000
Chase Growth Fund Class Institutional	CHAIX	NAS CM	Open End	US Equity Large Cap Growth (Growth)	B	B	B+		Y	1,000,000
Chase Growth Fund Class N Shares	CHASX	NAS CM	Open End	US Equity Large Cap Growth (Growth)	B	B	B+		Y	2,000
Chase Mid Cap Growth Fund Class N	CHAMX	NAS CM	Open End	US Equity Mid Cap (Growth)	B	B	B	Up	Y	2,000
Chase Mid Cap Growth Fund Institutional Class	CHIMX	NAS CM	Open End	US Equity Mid Cap (Growth)	B	B	B	Up	Y	1,000,000
Chautauqua Global Growth Fund Institutional Class	CCGIX	NAS CM	Open End	Global Equity (Growth)	D+	C	B+	Up	Y	25,000
Chautauqua Global Growth Fund Investor Class	CCGSX	NAS CM	Open End	Global Equity (Growth)	D+	C	B+	Up	Y	2,500
Chautauqua International Growth Fund Institutional Class	CCWIX	NAS CM	Open End	Global Equity Large Cap (Growth)	D+	C	B-	Up	Y	25,000
Chautauqua International Growth Fund Investor Class	CCWSX	NAS CM	Open End	Global Equity Large Cap (Growth)	D+	C	B-	Up	Y	2,500
Chesapeake Growth Fund	CHCGX	NAS CM	Open End	US Equity Large Cap Growth (Growth)	B	B	B	Up	Y	2,500
CHILTON STRATEGIC EUROPEAN EQUITIES FUND	CHEUX	NAS CM	Open End	Europe Equity Large Cap (Europe Stock)	D	D+	B+		Y	10,000,000
China Fund, Inc.	CHN	NYSE	Closed End	Greater China Equity (Pacific Stock)	B	A-	C+	Up	Y	
Chiron Capital Allocation Fund Class I	CCAPX	NAS CM	Open End	Alloc (Growth & Income)	C	C-	B+	Up	Y	100,000
Chiron SMid Opportunities Fund Class I Shares	CSMOX	NAS CM	Open End	Global Equity Mid/Small Cap (Growth)	U	U	U		Y	100,000
Chou Income Fund	CHOIX	NAS CM	Open End	Alloc (Income)	C	C-	C		Y	5,000
Chou Opportunity Fund	CHOEX	NAS CM	Open End	Moderate Alloc (Growth)	D+	D+	D+	Up	Y	5,000
Christopher Weil & Company Core Investment Fund	CWCFX	NAS CM	Open End	US Equity Large Cap Growth (Growth)	C+	C+	C+	Down	Y	3,500
City National Rochdale Dividend & Income Fund Class N	RIMHX	NAS CM	Open End	US Equity Large Cap Value (Equity-Income)	B	C+	A		Y	0
City National Rochdale Emerging Markets Fund Class N	RIMIX	NAS CM	Open End	Emerging Markets Equity (Div Emerging Mkts)	B+	A	C+	Up	Y	0
City National Rochdale Emerging Markets Fund Class Y	CNRYX	NAS CM	Open End	Emerging Markets Equity (Div Emerging Mkts)	B+	A	C+	Up	Y	0
City National Rochdale Select Strategies Fund Class 1	US17801L1089		Closed End	Other Sector Equity (Growth & Income)	U	U	U		Y	1,000,000
City National Rochdale U.S. Core Equity Fund Cls Inst	CNRUX	NAS CM	Open End	US Equity Large Cap Growth (Growth)	B	B	B		Y	1,000,000
City National Rochdale U.S. Core Equity Fund Class N	CNRWX	NAS CM	Open End	US Equity Large Cap Growth (Growth)	B	B	B		Y	0
City National Rochdale U.S. Core Equity Fund Cls Servicing	CNRVX	NAS CM	Open End	US Equity Large Cap Growth (Growth)	B	B	B		Y	0
Clarkston Founders Fund Institutional Class	CIMDX	NAS CM	Open End	US Equity Mid Cap (Growth)	U	U	U		Y	10,000
Clarkston Fund Institutional Class	CILGX	NAS CM	Open End	US Equity Large Cap Blend (Growth)	D+	C-	A-	Up	Y	10,000
Clarkston Partners Fund Founders Class	CFSMX	NAS CM	Open End	US Equity Mid Cap (Growth)	C	C+	B	Up	Y	100,000,000
Clarkston Partners Fund Institutional Class	CISMX	NAS CM	Open End	US Equity Mid Cap (Growth)	C	C+	B	Up	Y	25,000
Clarkston Select Fund Institutional Class	CIDDX	NAS CM	Open End	US Equity Mid Cap (Equity-Income)	U	U	U		Y	10,000
ClearBridge Aggressive Growth Fund Class A	SHRAX	NAS CM	Open End	US Equity Large Cap Growth (Aggr Growth)	B-	C+	B	Up	Y	1,000

★ Expanded analysis of this fund is included in Section II.

	TOTAL RETURNS					PERFORMANCE				ASSETS		ASSET ALLOCATION & TURNOVER					BULL & BEAR		FEES		
Min Additional Investment	3-Month Total Return	6-Month Total Return	1-Year Total Return	3-Year Total Return	5-Year Total Return	Dividend Yield (TTM)	Expense Ratio	3-Yr Std Deviation	3-Year Beta	NAV	Total Assets (MIL)	%Cash	%Stocks	%Bonds	%Other	Turnover Ratio	Last Bull Market Total Return	Last Bear Market Total Return	Front End Fee (%)	Back End Fee (%)	Inception Date
100	3.16	5.39	13.49			0.43	1.38			11.56	224.2	4	69	22	5				5.00		May-16
100	2.98	4.94	12.70			0.45	2.13			11.5	224.2	4	69	22	5					1.00	May-16
100	3.30	5.62	13.93			0.46	1.13			11.6	224.2	4	69	22	5						May-16
	8.32	12.67	25.01	44.70	92.83	0.81		9.57	0.77	32.86	805.6	7	93	0	0	9	13.02	-18.34			Oct-29
10,000	0.33	0.85	2.76	4.16	5.03	2.16	0.7	2.62	0.72	9.94	22.5	12	0	88	0	9	3.76	4.47			Oct-10
1,000	0.27	0.72	2.49	3.41	4.42	1.9	0.95	2.6	0.72	10	22.5	12	0	88	0	9	3.71	4.37			Feb-90
10,000	0.22	0.54	1.11	1.66		3.89	0.6	3.14	0.75	9.78	49.5	90	0	10	0	4					Jan-14
1,000	0.05	0.31	0.86	0.80		3.65	0.85	3.1	0.74	9.71	49.5	90	0	10	0	4					Jan-14
10,000	6.59	11.73	25.43	31.00	84.95	2.08	0.95	7.77	0.67	12.3	130.0	1	99	0	0	81					Jan-14
1,000	6.48	11.71	25.19	30.51	84.07	1.79	1.05	7.82	0.68	12.29	130.0	1	99	0	0	81					Dec-11
100	7.16	13.67	32.11	29.30		0.53	1.02	11.38	-1.58	13.8	6.5	4	89	2	0	155					Dec-13
50	3.73	14.23	24.82	30.40	87.19	0	1.2	19.19	1.48	53.35	994.8	1	153	-55	0	334	20.04	-27.53			Sep-97
50	5.68	11.65	16.91	21.98	58.35	0.19	1.17	12	0.91	31.02	412.4	1	74	25	0	436	20.61	-18.89			Nov-29
50	12.96	20.97	32.64	31.60	80.39	0.48	0.99	15.55	1.16	32.19	990.3	1	99	0	0	241	33.35	-22.49			May-94
50	8.10	11.09	13.11	3.86	22.77	0	2.9	9.31	1.75	11.97	78.6	-6	87	17	2	27	6.45	-14.6			Jun-10
	10.26	16.11	39.58	17.99		0.36	1.5	13.33	0.71	10.36	3.6	6	94	0	0	37					Sep-14
	5.98	7.89	19.21	41.50	113.87	0	1.17	10.54	0.93	17.1	1,902	3	97	0	0	33	24.79	-18.44			Jun-08
	6.09	8.03	19.50	42.54	116.43	0.05	0.93	10.57	0.94	17.38	1,902	3	97	0	0	33	24.94	-18.28			Jan-11
	1.86	5.24	10.57	38.67	101.65	0	1.3	13.17	0.88	19.9	1,530	8	91	0	0	40	23.71	-18.95			Nov-04
	1.94	5.38	10.81	39.18	102.38	0	1.05	13.17	0.88	19.98	1,530	8	91	0	0	40	23.71	-18.95			Aug-16
100	6.92	13.63	16.86	26.55	77.71	1.27	1.07	13.63	1.16	15.76	24.2	8	92	0	0		25.94	-18.66			May-02
100	6.01	11.19					1.05			11.15	11.1	3	94	0	3						Jun-17
100	4.85	9.96	8.91	27.01	91.96	0.43	1.05	13.92	0.95	19.66	172.9	2	99	0	0	22					Mar-12
1,000	5.06	12.10	24.77	32.82	106.13	0	1.08	9.4	0.83	13.36	78.9	3	97	0	0	83	24.59	-15.76			Jan-07
250	5.02	11.99	24.52	32.07	103.92	0	1.23	9.43	0.83	12.82	78.9	3	97	0	0	83	24.41	-15.88			Dec-97
250	9.39	16.44	23.43	35.41	94.22	0	1.33	12.24	1.06	39.07	22.7	3	97	0	0	148	23.2	-15.13			Aug-02
1,000	9.44	16.51	23.58	36.15	96.27	0	1.18	12.23	1.06	39.83	22.7	3	97	0	0	148	23.23	-15.13			Feb-12
	6.26	15.24	37.75			0	0.95			13.43	18.3	8	92	0	0						Apr-16
100	6.12	15.13	37.28			0	1.2			13.37	18.3	8	92	0	0						Apr-16
	5.55	16.51	36.11			0	0.95			12.59	73.6	9	91	0	0						Apr-16
100	5.51	16.28	35.86			0	1.2			12.57	73.6	9	91	0	0						Apr-16
500	6.96	11.37	23.65	34.71	98.43	0	2.12	11.84	1.1	31.63	33.6	5	95	0	0	79	29.22	-22.85			Sep-97
	-1.27	0.74	5.65			0	1.77			10.83	513.0	0	95	0	-1						Nov-16
	8.08	16.71	37.82	31.80	61.91	1.99	0	18.57	1.05	23.4328	368.7	2	97	1	0	52	6.12	-24.29			Jul-92
	2.40	6.19	15.30			0.41	1.15			12.36	1,483	17	65	17	1						Nov-15
	1.85						1.2			10.47	5.1										Oct-17
500	-4.81	-5.17	-4.54	0.38	18.57	6.44	1.2	13.12	1.51	7.17	17.0	35	11	32	0	22	10.07	-11.18			Jul-10
500	16.93	13.71	15.28	-15.07	18.57	8.18	1.2	17.92	0.96	9.86	66.0	22	54	24	0	18	16.23	-25.64			Jul-10
100	3.44	6.53	18.33	17.88	76.69	0	1.24	10.8	0.96	14.4	38.0	11	89	0	0	21					Dec-11
	3.37	3.52	7.76	22.64	67.73	2.69	1.14	7.75	0.54	40.3	259.8	0	96	0	0	15	14.73	-8.54			Jun-99
	5.42	15.34	43.29	42.78	73.74	0.13	1.63	14.58	0.79	51.96	1,669	10	89	0	1	24					Dec-11
	5.50	15.48	43.61	43.30	74.37	0.19	1.38	14.59	0.79	52.08	1,669	10	89	0	1	24					Jun-16
	28.13						0.97			9.61	--	100	0	0	0						Jul-17
	7.19	12.43	25.60	36.24	111.70	0.98	0.52	10.08	0.95	16.7	274.6	0	100	0	0	25					Dec-12
	7.06	12.14	24.96	34.22	104.88	0.58	1.02	10.06	0.94	16.52	274.6	0	100	0	0	25					Dec-12
	7.12	12.33	25.30	35.23	107.60	0.78	0.77	10.11	0.95	16.55	274.6	0	100	0	0	25					Dec-12
	4.55	7.17	11.13				0.95			11.08	26.8	32	68	0	0	4					Jan-17
	4.66	6.90	11.37			0.81	0.7			11.84	30.5	16	84	0	0	5					Apr-16
	4.36	9.03	13.03			0.45	0.85			12.76	722.2	30	70	0	0	13					Sep-15
	4.33	9.01	12.82			0.42	1			12.73	722.2	30	70	0	0	13					Sep-15
	4.08	7.72	10.76				0.7			10.86	15.2	17	83	0	0	3					Jan-17
50	3.20	5.74	14.27	14.53	94.79	0.31	1.12	13	1.05	203.41	11,391	0	100	0	0	1	28.57	-19.64	5.75		Oct-83

	MARKET			FUND TYPE, CATEGORY & OBJECTIVE	RATINGS				MINIMUMS	
Fund Name	Ticker Symbol	Traded On	Fund Type	Category and (Prospectus Objective)	Overall Rating	Reward Rating	Risk Rating	Recent Up/ Downgrade	Open to New Investors	Min Initial Investment
ClearBridge Aggressive Growth Fund Class B	SAGBX	NAS CM	Open End	US Equity Large Cap Growth (Aggr Growth)	C+	C+	B-	Down		1,000
ClearBridge Aggressive Growth Fund Class C	SAGCX	NAS CM	Open End	US Equity Large Cap Growth (Aggr Growth)	C+	C+	B-	Down	Y	1,000
ClearBridge Aggressive Growth Fund Class FI	LMPFX	NAS CM	Open End	US Equity Large Cap Growth (Aggr Growth)	B-	C+	B	Up	Y	0
ClearBridge Aggressive Growth Fund Class I	SAGYX	NAS CM	Open End	US Equity Large Cap Growth (Aggr Growth)	B-	C+	B	Up	Y	1,000,000
ClearBridge Aggressive Growth Fund Class IS	LSIFX	NAS CM	Open End	US Equity Large Cap Growth (Aggr Growth)	B-	C+	B	Up	Y	1,000,000
ClearBridge Aggressive Growth Fund Class R	LMPRX	NAS CM	Open End	US Equity Large Cap Growth (Aggr Growth)	C+	C+	B-	Down	Y	0
ClearBridge All Cap Value Fund Class A	SHFVX	NAS CM	Open End	US Equity Large Cap Value (Growth)	B	B	B-	Up	Y	1,000
ClearBridge All Cap Value Fund Class B	SFVBX	NAS CM	Open End	US Equity Large Cap Value (Growth)	B-	B-	B-	Up		1,000
ClearBridge All Cap Value Fund Class C	SFVCX	NAS CM	Open End	US Equity Large Cap Value (Growth)	B-	B-	B-	Down	Y	1,000
ClearBridge All Cap Value Fund Class I	SFVYX	NAS CM	Open End	US Equity Large Cap Value (Growth)	B	B	B-	Up	Y	1,000,000
ClearBridge All Cap Value Fund Class IS	LSISX	NAS CM	Open End	US Equity Large Cap Value (Growth)	B	B	B-		Y	1,000,000
ClearBridge American Energy MLP Fund	CBA	NYSE	Closed End	Energy Sector Equity (Equity-Income)	D	D	D	Down	Y	
ClearBridge Appreciation Fund Class A	SHAPX	NAS CM	Open End	US Equity Large Cap Blend (Growth)	B	B-	B+		Y	1,000
ClearBridge Appreciation Fund Class B	SAPBX	NAS CM	Open End	US Equity Large Cap Blend (Growth)	B-	B-	B	Down		1,000
ClearBridge Appreciation Fund Class C	SAPCX	NAS CM	Open End	US Equity Large Cap Blend (Growth)	B-	B-	B	Down	Y	1,000
ClearBridge Appreciation Fund Class FI	LMPIX	NAS CM	Open End	US Equity Large Cap Blend (Growth)	B	B-	B+		Y	0
ClearBridge Appreciation Fund Class I	SAPYX	NAS CM	Open End	US Equity Large Cap Blend (Growth)	B	B-	B+		Y	1,000,000
ClearBridge Appreciation Fund Class IS	LMESX	NAS CM	Open End	US Equity Large Cap Blend (Growth)	B	B-	B+		Y	1,000,000
ClearBridge Appreciation Fund Class R	LMPPX	NAS CM	Open End	US Equity Large Cap Blend (Growth)	B	B-	B		Y	0
ClearBridge Dividend Strategy Fund Class 1	LCBOX	NAS CM	Open End	US Equity Large Cap Blend (Equity-Income)	B-	B-	B	Down	Y	0
ClearBridge Dividend Strategy Fund Class A	SOPAX	NAS CM	Open End	US Equity Large Cap Blend (Equity-Income)	B-	B-	B	Down	Y	1,000
ClearBridge Dividend Strategy Fund Class B	SOPTX	NAS CM	Open End	US Equity Large Cap Blend (Equity-Income)	B-	B-	B-	Down		1,000
ClearBridge Dividend Strategy Fund Class C	SBPLX	NAS CM	Open End	US Equity Large Cap Blend (Equity-Income)	B-	B-	B-	Down	Y	1,000
ClearBridge Dividend Strategy Fund Class FI	LBRIX	NAS CM	Open End	US Equity Large Cap Blend (Equity-Income)	B-	B-	B	Down	Y	0
ClearBridge Dividend Strategy Fund Class I	SOPYX	NAS CM	Open End	US Equity Large Cap Blend (Equity-Income)	B-	B-	B	Down	Y	1,000,000
ClearBridge Dividend Strategy Fund Class IS	LCBEX	NAS CM	Open End	US Equity Large Cap Blend (Equity-Income)	B-	B-	B	Down	Y	1,000,000
ClearBridge Dividend Strategy Fund Class R	LMMRX	NAS CM	Open End	US Equity Large Cap Blend (Equity-Income)	B-	B-	B-	Down	Y	0
ClearBridge Energy MLP & Infrastructure Fund Class A	LCPAX	NAS CM	Open End	Energy Sector Equity (Growth & Income)	D	D+	D	Down	Y	1,000
ClearBridge Energy MLP & Infrastructure Fund Class C	LCPCX	NAS CM	Open End	Energy Sector Equity (Growth & Income)	D	D+	D	Down	Y	1,000
ClearBridge Energy MLP & Infrastructure Fund Class I	LCPIX	NAS CM	Open End	Energy Sector Equity (Growth & Income)	D	D+	D	Down	Y	1,000,000
ClearBridge Energy MLP & Infrastructure Fund Class IS	LCPSX	NAS CM	Open End	Energy Sector Equity (Growth & Income)	D	D+	D	Down	Y	1,000,000
ClearBridge Energy MLP Fund	CEM	NYSE	Closed End	Energy Sector Equity (Natl Res)	D	D	D	Down	Y	
ClearBridge Energy MLP Opportunity Fund	EMO	NYSE	Closed End	Energy Sector Equity (Natl Res)	D	D	D	Down	Y	
ClearBridge Energy MLP Total Return Fund Inc	CTR	NYSE	Closed End	Energy Sector Equity (Growth & Income)	D	D	D	Down	Y	
ClearBridge Global Health Care Innovations Fund Class A	CGALX	NAS CM	Open End	Healthcare Sector Equity (Health)	D+	C-	B-	Up	Y	1,000
ClearBridge Global Health Care Innovations Fund Class I	CGIHX	NAS CM	Open End	Healthcare Sector Equity (Health)	D+	C-	B-	Up	Y	1,000,000
ClearBridge Global Health Care Innovations Fund Class IS	CGSLX	NAS CM	Open End	Healthcare Sector Equity (Health)	D+	C-	B-	Up	Y	1,000,000
ClearBridge International Growth Fund Class A	LGGAX	NAS CM	Open End	Global Equity Large Cap (Growth)	B	B	B	Up	Y	1,000
ClearBridge International Growth Fund Class C	LMGTX	NAS CM	Open End	Global Equity Large Cap (Growth)	B	B	B	Up	Y	1,000
ClearBridge International Growth Fund Class FI	LMGFX	NAS CM	Open End	Global Equity Large Cap (Growth)	B	B	B	Up	Y	0
ClearBridge International Growth Fund Class I	LMGNX	NAS CM	Open End	Global Equity Large Cap (Growth)	B	B	B	Up	Y	1,000,000
ClearBridge International Growth Fund Class R	LMGRX	NAS CM	Open End	Global Equity Large Cap (Growth)	B	B	B	Up	Y	0
ClearBridge International Small Cap Fund Class A	LCOAX	NAS CM	Open End	Global Equity Mid/Small Cap (Small Company)	B	B	B	Up	Y	1,000
ClearBridge International Small Cap Fund Class A2	LCRNX	NAS CM	Open End	Global Equity Mid/Small Cap (Small Company)	B	B	B	Up	Y	1,000
ClearBridge International Small Cap Fund Class C	LCOCX	NAS CM	Open End	Global Equity Mid/Small Cap (Small Company)	B	B	B	Up	Y	1,000
ClearBridge International Small Cap Fund Class I	LCOIX	NAS CM	Open End	Global Equity Mid/Small Cap (Small Company)	B	B	B	Up	Y	1,000,000
ClearBridge International Small Cap Fund Class IS	CBISX	NAS CM	Open End	Global Equity Mid/Small Cap (Small Company)	B	B	B	Up	Y	1,000,000
ClearBridge International Value Fund Class A	SBIEX	NAS CM	Open End	Global Equity Large Cap (Foreign Stock)	B-	C+	B-	Up	Y	1,000
ClearBridge International Value Fund Class C	SBICX	NAS CM	Open End	Global Equity Large Cap (Foreign Stock)	C+	C+	B-	Up	Y	1,000
ClearBridge International Value Fund Class I	SBIYX	NAS CM	Open End	Global Equity Large Cap (Foreign Stock)	B-	C+	B-	Up	Y	1,000,000
ClearBridge International Value Fund Class IS	LSIUX	NAS CM	Open End	Global Equity Large Cap (Foreign Stock)	C+	C+	C+	Up	Y	1,000,000
ClearBridge International Value Fund Class R	LIORX	NAS CM	Open End	Global Equity Large Cap (Foreign Stock)	C+	C+	C	Up	Y	0

★ Expanded analysis of this fund is included in Section II.

Min Additional Investment	TOTAL RETURNS 3-Month Total Return	6-Month Total Return	1-Year Total Return	3-Year Total Return	5-Year Total Return	PERFORMANCE Dividend Yield (TTM)	Expense Ratio	3-Yr Std Deviation	3-Year Beta	ASSETS NAV	Total Assets (MIL)	ASSET ALLOCATION & TURNOVER %Cash	%Stocks	%Bonds	%Other	Turnover Ratio	BULL & BEAR Last Bull Market Total Return	Last Bear Market Total Return	FEES Front End Fee (%)	Back End Fee (%)	Inception Date
50	2.91	5.15	12.99	10.84	84.80	0	2.26	12.98	1.05	154.97	11,391	0	100	0	0	1	27.83	-19.95		5.00	Nov-92
50	3.02	5.37	13.47	12.14	88.15	0	1.83	12.99	1.05	163.3	11,391	0	100	0	0	1	28.09	-19.85		1.00	May-93
	3.19	5.73	14.28	14.52	94.73	0.25	1.1	13	1.05	204.42	11,391	0	100	0	0	1	28.55	-19.64			Apr-07
	3.28	5.92	14.63	15.59	97.90	0.49	0.81	13	1.05	224.25	11,391	0	100	0	0	1	28.88	-19.49			Jan-96
	3.31	5.96	14.73	15.98	99.02	0.61	0.71	13	1.05	226.57	11,391	0	100	0	0	1	28.97	-19.45			Aug-08
	3.12	5.59	13.93	13.51	92.16	0.03	1.42	13	1.05	199.11	11,391	0	100	0	0	1	28.42	-19.71			Dec-06
50	5.46	9.39	17.11	28.89	85.85	0.8	1.18	13.12	1.21	14.54	1,887	3	97	0	0	24	24.75	-24.3	5.75		Nov-81
50	4.60	8.08	14.86	23.10	73.64	0	2.85	13.04	1.21	12.19	1,887	3	97	0	0	24	24.05	-24.65		5.00	Nov-92
50	5.26	8.93	16.28	26.33	79.68	0.35	1.9	13.08	1.21	12.56	1,887	3	97	0	0	24	24.44	-24.56		1.00	Aug-93
	5.55	9.54	17.54	30.45	89.61	1.08	0.8	13.13	1.22	15.42	1,887	3	97	0	0	24	25.15	-24.21			Jan-96
	5.60	9.53	17.27	29.06	86.09		0.7	13.12	1.21	15.41	1,887	3	97	0	0	24	24.75	-24.3			Feb-14
	-3.73	-6.21	-11.01	-38.61		7.31	1.82	30.49		8.6421	481.0	1	99	0	0	25					Jun-13
50	6.50	10.50	19.51	30.94	92.21	0.84	1	9.68	0.95	23.6	6,159	5	95	0	0	7	23.36	-15.31	5.75		Mar-70
50	6.19	9.79	18.05	26.38	81.43	0	2.21	9.68	0.95	22.45	6,159	5	95	0	0	7	22.51	-15.76		5.00	Nov-92
50	6.33	10.07	18.65	28.19	85.50	0.27	1.71	9.68	0.95	22.78	6,159	5	95	0	0	7	22.75	-15.53		1.00	Feb-93
	6.47	10.44	19.46	30.89	92.08	0.86	1.01	9.66	0.94	23.72	6,159	5	95	0	0	7	23.28	-15.29			Dec-08
	6.55	10.62	19.80	32.05	95.14	1.09	0.7	9.7	0.95	23.43	6,159	5	95	0	0	7	23.57	-15.18			Jan-96
	6.65	10.70	19.98	32.52	96.12	1.17	0.6	9.68	0.95	23.5	6,159	5	95	0	0	7	23.64	-15.15			Aug-08
	6.43	10.30	19.16	29.74	89.30	0.58	1.3	9.69	0.95	23.56	6,159	5	95	0	0	7	23.22	-15.45			Dec-06
	5.70	10.17	19.44	30.46	90.17	1.28	0.82	9.12	0.86	23.53	6,226	6	93	0	1	9	21.12	-11.4			Apr-11
50	5.68	10.02	19.12	29.41	87.73	1.04	1.09	9.12	0.86	23.52	6,226	6	93	0	1	9	20.98	-11.51	5.75		Nov-92
50	5.40	9.44	17.86	25.83	79.84	0.13	2.16	9.1	0.86	23.15	6,226	6	93	0	1	9	20.47	-11.7		5.00	Sep-85
50	5.50	9.65	18.30	26.75	81.33	0.41	1.78	9.14	0.86	23.19	6,226	6	93	0	1	9	20.4	-11.71		1.00	Jun-98
	5.63	9.96	19.01	29.27	86.62	0.97	1.15	9.1	0.86	23.49	6,226	6	93	0	1	9	20.47	-11.7			May-13
	5.73	10.18	19.44	30.54	90.66	1.25	0.8	9.14	0.86	24.13	6,226	6	93	0	1	9	21.24	-11.34			Feb-96
	5.79	10.22	19.60	30.91	90.43	1.34	0.7	9.12	0.86	24.16	6,226	6	93	0	1	9	20.47	-11.7			Apr-13
	5.56	9.79	18.75	28.47	85.20	0.92	1.32	9.12	0.86	23.37	6,226	6	93	0	1	9	20.6	-11.7			Feb-12
50	-0.47	0.00	-4.19	-20.05		0.59	1.61	21.77	1	9.44	15.0	1	99	0	0	37			5.75		Oct-13
50	-0.63	-0.42	-4.96	-21.89		0.48	2.36	21.74	0.99	9.38	15.0	1	99	0	0	37				1.00	Oct-13
	-0.43	0.10	-4.05	-19.40		0.81	1.26	21.78	0.99	9.38	15.0	1	99	0	0	37					Aug-13
	-0.43	0.13	-3.99	-19.32		0.86	1.16	21.82	1	9.37	15.0	1	99	0	0	37					Aug-13
	4.23	2.18	-1.00	-30.49	2.03	3.38	14.09	22.33	1.12	15.4306	973.7	1	99	0	0	24	18.61	-8.58			Jun-10
	-0.08	-2.11	-6.73	-35.35	-6.94	0.79	14.87	24.84		12.2206	354.7	0	100	0	0	23	23.46				Jun-11
	-1.47	-2.42	-5.48	-31.82	-4.52	0	14.21	25.8		12.508	458.5	1	99	0	0	22					Jun-12
50	-3.60	1.35	19.01			0.22	1.26			11.05	4.6	6	88	0	0	20			5.75		Mar-16
	-3.51	1.61	19.54			0.38	0.91			11.05	4.6	6	88	0	0	20					Mar-16
	-3.54	1.59	19.51			0.4	0.81			11.04	4.6	6	88	0	0	20					Mar-16
50	3.67	12.70	36.10	29.00	82.35	0.3	1.15	12.59	0.96	42.65	228.4	2	97	0	1	89	25.63	-17.54	5.75		Feb-09
50	3.45	12.26	35.08	26.15	75.71	0	1.9	12.59	0.96	40.08	228.4	2	97	0	1	89	25.05	-17.8		1.00	Apr-95
	3.66	12.69	36.10	29.02	82.38	0.23	1.15	12.6	0.96	44.47	228.4	2	97	0	1	89	25.65	-17.57			Jan-04
	3.70	12.81	36.41	29.95	84.65	0.41	0.9	12.61	0.96	46.01	228.4	2	97	0	1	89	25.83	-17.48			Mar-04
	3.59	12.55	35.79	28.02	80.04	0.21	1.4	12.6	0.96	43.21	228.4	2	97	0	1	89	25.47	-17.65			Dec-06
50	5.97	13.87	32.27	37.51	69.68	1.55	1.43	11.52	0.92	18.99	181.4	3	94	0	3	41	15.5	-20.9	5.75		Oct-10
50	5.94	13.75	31.98	36.64	68.53	1.51	1.63	11.52	0.92	18.88	181.4	3	94	0	3	41	15.5	-20.89	5.75		Aug-14
50	5.79	13.46	31.28	34.49	63.37	0.86	2.18	11.48	0.92	18.77	181.4	3	94	0	3	41	14.99	-21.1		1.00	Oct-10
	6.08	14.03	32.63	38.74	71.97	1.77	1.08	11.53	0.92	19.12	181.4	3	94	0	3	41	15.67	-20.81			Oct-10
	6.09	14.11	32.79	39.16	72.49	1.88	0.98	11.53	0.92	19.13	181.4	3	94	0	3	41	15.67	-20.81			May-15
50	2.54	7.90	23.23	21.88	37.96	1.25	1.26	12.08	0.94	11.82	327.2	1	99	0	0	32	14.2	-21.48	5.75		Feb-86
50	2.38	7.57	22.39	19.25	33.01	1.24	2.01	12.12	0.95	9.72	327.2	1	99	0	0	32	13.64	-21.68		1.00	Jan-93
	2.72	8.18	23.68	23.33	40.61	1.56	0.91	12.09	0.94	11.63	327.2	1	99	0	0	32	14.57	-21.35			Dec-06
	2.68	8.11	23.74	23.64	41.25	1.59	0.81	12.1	0.95	11.86	327.2	1	99	0	0	32	14.47	-21.3			Aug-08
	2.49	7.81	22.90	21.07	36.38	1.39	1.51	12.06	0.94	11.72	327.2	1	99	0	0	32	14.03	-21.56			Jan-14

	MARKET			FUND TYPE, CATEGORY & OBJECTIVE	RATINGS					MINIMUMS
Fund Name	Ticker Symbol	Traded On	Fund Type	Category and (Prospectus Objective)	Overall Rating	Reward Rating	Risk Rating	Recent Up/ Downgrade	Open to New Investors	Min Initial Investment
ClearBridge Large Cap Growth Fund Class A	SBLGX	NAS CM	Open End	US Equity Large Cap Growth (Growth)	B	B	B+	Down	Y	1,000
ClearBridge Large Cap Growth Fund Class C	SLCCX	NAS CM	Open End	US Equity Large Cap Growth (Growth)	B	B	B	Down	Y	1,000
ClearBridge Large Cap Growth Fund Class I	SBLYX	NAS CM	Open End	US Equity Large Cap Growth (Growth)	B	B	B+	Down	Y	1,000,000
ClearBridge Large Cap Growth Fund Class IS	LSITX	NAS CM	Open End	US Equity Large Cap Growth (Growth)	B	B	B+	Down	Y	1,000,000
ClearBridge Large Cap Growth Fund Class O	LCMMX	NAS CM	Open End	US Equity Large Cap Growth (Growth)	B	B	B+	Down	Y	0
ClearBridge Large Cap Growth Fund Class R	LMPLX	NAS CM	Open End	US Equity Large Cap Growth (Growth)	B	B	B+	Down	Y	0
ClearBridge Large Cap Value Fund Class 1	LCLIX	NAS CM	Open End	US Equity Large Cap Value (Growth & Income)	B-	B-	B-	Down	Y	0
ClearBridge Large Cap Value Fund Class A	SINAX	NAS CM	Open End	US Equity Large Cap Value (Growth & Income)	B	C+	B	Up	Y	1,000
ClearBridge Large Cap Value Fund Class A2	LIVVX	NAS CM	Open End	US Equity Large Cap Value (Growth & Income)	B-	C+	B-	Down	Y	1,000
ClearBridge Large Cap Value Fund Class C	SINOX	NAS CM	Open End	US Equity Large Cap Value (Growth & Income)	B-	C+	B	Down	Y	1,000
ClearBridge Large Cap Value Fund Class I	SAIFX	NAS CM	Open End	US Equity Large Cap Value (Growth & Income)	B	B-	B		Y	1,000,000
ClearBridge Large Cap Value Fund Class IS	LMLSX	NAS CM	Open End	US Equity Large Cap Value (Growth & Income)	B-	B-	B-	Down	Y	1,000,000
ClearBridge Large Cap Value Fund Class R	LCBVX	NAS CM	Open End	US Equity Large Cap Value (Growth & Income)	B-	C+	B-	Down	Y	0
ClearBridge Mid Cap Fund Class 1	SMCPX	NAS CM	Open End	US Equity Mid Cap (Growth)	B	B-	B+	Up		0
ClearBridge Mid Cap Fund Class A	SBMAX	NAS CM	Open End	US Equity Mid Cap (Growth)	B	B-	B+	Up	Y	1,000
ClearBridge Mid Cap Fund Class C	SBMLX	NAS CM	Open End	US Equity Mid Cap (Growth)	B	C+	B	Up	Y	1,000
ClearBridge Mid Cap Fund Class I	SMBYX	NAS CM	Open End	US Equity Mid Cap (Growth)	B	B-	B+	Up	Y	1,000,000
ClearBridge Mid Cap Fund Class IS	LSIRX	NAS CM	Open End	US Equity Mid Cap (Growth)	B	B-	B+	Up	Y	1,000,000
ClearBridge Mid Cap Fund Class R	LMREX	NAS CM	Open End	US Equity Mid Cap (Growth)	B	B-	B+	Up	Y	0
ClearBridge Mid Cap Growth Fund Class A	LBGAX	NAS CM	Open End	US Equity Mid Cap (Growth)	B	B-	B	Up	Y	1,000
ClearBridge Mid Cap Growth Fund Class A2	LCBGX	NAS CM	Open End	US Equity Mid Cap (Growth)	B-	B-	B	Up	Y	1,000
ClearBridge Mid Cap Growth Fund Class C	LBGCX	NAS CM	Open End	US Equity Mid Cap (Growth)	B-	C+	B	Up	Y	1,000
ClearBridge Mid Cap Growth Fund Class I	LBGIX	NAS CM	Open End	US Equity Mid Cap (Growth)	B	B-	B	Up	Y	1,000,000
ClearBridge Mid Cap Growth Fund Class IS	LCMIX	NAS CM	Open End	US Equity Mid Cap (Growth)	B	B-	B	Up	Y	1,000,000
ClearBridge Mid Cap Growth Fund Class R	LCMRX	NAS CM	Open End	US Equity Mid Cap (Growth)	B-	B-	B	Up	Y	0
ClearBridge Real Estate Opportunities Fund Class I	CRENX	NAS CM	Open End	Real Estate Sector Equity (Real Estate)	B-	C+	B	Up	Y	1,000,000
ClearBridge Real Estate Opportunities Fund Class O	CREOX	NAS CM	Open End	Real Estate Sector Equity (Real Estate)	B-	C+	B	Up	Y	0
ClearBridge Select Fund Class A	LCLAX	NAS CM	Open End	US Equity Mid Cap (Growth)	B+	A	B	Up	Y	1,000
ClearBridge Select Fund Class C	LCLCX	NAS CM	Open End	US Equity Mid Cap (Growth)	B+	A-	B	Up	Y	1,000
ClearBridge Select Fund Class FI	LCBSX	NAS CM	Open End	US Equity Mid Cap (Growth)	B+	A	B	Up	Y	0
ClearBridge Select Fund Class I	LBFIX	NAS CM	Open End	US Equity Mid Cap (Growth)	B+	A	B	Up	Y	1,000,000
ClearBridge Select Fund Class IS	LCSSX	NAS CM	Open End	US Equity Mid Cap (Growth)	B+	A	B	Up	Y	1,000,000
ClearBridge Small Cap Fund Class A	LMSAX	NAS CM	Open End	US Equity Small Cap (Small Company)	B	B	B	Up	Y	1,000
ClearBridge Small Cap Fund Class A2	LBRTX	NAS CM	Open End	US Equity Small Cap (Small Company)	B	B	B	Up	Y	1,000
ClearBridge Small Cap Fund Class C	LMASX	NAS CM	Open End	US Equity Small Cap (Small Company)	B	B	B	Up	Y	1,000
ClearBridge Small Cap Fund Class FI	LGASX	NAS CM	Open End	US Equity Small Cap (Small Company)	B	B	B	Up	Y	0
ClearBridge Small Cap Fund Class I	LMNSX	NAS CM	Open End	US Equity Small Cap (Small Company)	B	B	B		Y	1,000,000
ClearBridge Small Cap Fund Class IS	LISGX	NAS CM	Open End	US Equity Small Cap (Small Company)	B	B	B		Y	1,000,000
ClearBridge Small Cap Fund Class R	LMARX	NAS CM	Open End	US Equity Small Cap (Small Company)	B	B	B	Up	Y	0
ClearBridge Small Cap Growth Fund Class 1	LMPMX	NAS CM	Open End	US Equity Small Cap (Small Company)	B	B+	B	Up		0
ClearBridge Small Cap Growth Fund Class A	SASMX	NAS CM	Open End	US Equity Small Cap (Small Company)	B	B	B	Up		1,000
ClearBridge Small Cap Growth Fund Class C	SCSMX	NAS CM	Open End	US Equity Small Cap (Small Company)	B	B	B-	Up		1,000
ClearBridge Small Cap Growth Fund Class FI	LMPSX	NAS CM	Open End	US Equity Small Cap (Small Company)	B	B	B	Up		0
ClearBridge Small Cap Growth Fund Class I	SBPYX	NAS CM	Open End	US Equity Small Cap (Small Company)	B	B+	B	Up		1,000,000
ClearBridge Small Cap Growth Fund Class IS	LMOIX	NAS CM	Open End	US Equity Small Cap (Small Company)	B	B+	B	Up		1,000,000
ClearBridge Small Cap Growth Fund Class R	LMPOX	NAS CM	Open End	US Equity Small Cap (Small Company)	B	B	B	Up		0
ClearBridge Small Cap Value Fund Class A	SBVAX	NAS CM	Open End	US Equity Small Cap (Small Company)	B	B	B-	Up	Y	1,000
ClearBridge Small Cap Value Fund Class C	SBVLX	NAS CM	Open End	US Equity Small Cap (Small Company)	B-	B-	C+	Up	Y	1,000
ClearBridge Small Cap Value Fund Class I	SMCYX	NAS CM	Open End	US Equity Small Cap (Small Company)	B	B	B-	Up	Y	1,000,000
ClearBridge Small Cap Value Fund Class IS	LCBIX	NAS CM	Open End	US Equity Small Cap (Small Company)	B	B	B-	Up	Y	1,000,000
ClearBridge Sustainability Leaders Fund Class A	CLSUX	NAS CM	Open End	US Equity Large Cap Growth (Growth)	C+	C+	B-	Up	Y	1,000
ClearBridge Sustainability Leaders Fund Class FI	LCSTX	NAS CM	Open End	US Equity Large Cap Growth (Growth)	C+	C+	B-	Up	Y	0

★Expanded analysis of this fund is included in Section II.

	TOTAL RETURNS					PERFORMANCE				ASSETS		ASSET ALLOCATION & TURNOVER					BULL & BEAR		FEES		
Min Additional Investment	3-Month Total Return	6-Month Total Return	1-Year Total Return	3-Year Total Return	5-Year Total Return	Dividend Yield (TTM)	Expense Ratio	3-Yr Std Deviation	3-Year Beta	NAV	Total Assets (MIL)	%Cash	%Stocks	%Bonds	%Other	Turnover Ratio	Last Bull Market Total Return	Last Bear Market Total Return	Front End Fee (%)	Back End Fee (%)	Inception Date
50	6.96	12.51	25.04	44.44	130.50	0.06	1.06	10.14	0.91	40.64	9,321	1	99	0	0	13	24.63	-15.48	5.75		Aug-97
50	6.76	12.11	24.13	41.30	122.16	0	1.8	10.12	0.91	32.8	9,321	1	99	0	0	13	24.09	-15.77		1.00	Aug-97
	7.03	12.68	25.42	45.82	134.54	0.25	0.75	10.14	0.91	44.99	9,321	1	99	0	0	13	24.87	-15.4			Oct-97
	7.07	12.75	25.53	46.11	134.71	0.28	0.69	10.13	0.91	45.02	9,321	1	99	0	0	13	24.63	-15.48			Mar-13
50	7.05	12.73	25.47	45.95	132.94	0.25	0.75	10.14	0.91	45.02	9,321	1	99	0	0	13	24.63	-15.48			Dec-14
	6.87	12.37	24.66	43.29	127.07	0.05	1.33	10.13	0.91	39.08	9,321	1	99	0	0	13	24.39	-15.61			Dec-06
	4.70	7.06	14.38	24.40	87.91	1.34	0.69	10.47	0.99	33.21	1,746	4	96	0	0	5	26.33	-16.62			Aug-13
50	4.64	6.94	14.12	23.64	85.91	1.14	0.87	10.48	0.99	33.22	1,746	4	96	0	0	5	26.12	-16.74	5.75		Jan-95
50	4.61	6.88	13.99	23.07	84.60	1.02	1.07	10.49	0.99	33.2	1,746	4	96	0	0	5	26.14	-16.71	5.75		Aug-13
50	4.43	6.54	13.24	20.84	78.83	0.46	1.65	10.47	0.99	32.27	1,746	4	96	0	0	5	25.55	-17		1.00	Jan-95
	4.72	7.10	14.44	24.74	88.81	1.41	0.58	10.46	0.99	33.16	1,746	4	96	0	0	5	26.33	-16.62			May-58
	4.73	7.13	14.51	25.01	89.20	1.47	0.51	10.49	0.99	33.17	1,746	4	96	0	0	5	26.33	-16.62			Oct-13
	4.52	6.77	13.66	21.80	82.25	0.89	1.1	10.44	0.98	33.24	1,746	4	96	0	0	5	25.96	-16.79			Dec-13
	3.56	6.29	13.07	25.15	89.76	0.38	0.86	11.51	1.04	34.86	2,414	2	98	0	0	32	33.24	-24.44			Sep-00
50	3.48	6.13	12.71	23.95	87.49	0.13	1.18	11.49	1.04	33.43	2,414	2	98	0	0	32	33.05	-24.52	5.75		Sep-98
50	3.28	5.72	11.90	21.36	80.94	0	1.9	11.48	1.04	26.78	2,414	2	98	0	0	32	32.45	-24.72		1.00	Sep-98
	3.54	6.29	13.06	25.23	90.83	0.4	0.85	11.49	1.04	37.06	2,414	2	98	0	0	32	33.31	-24.38			Dec-98
	3.58	6.36	13.21	25.61	91.77	0.46	0.75	11.5	1.04	37.4	2,414	2	98	0	0	32	33.31	-24.36			Aug-08
	3.38	5.99	12.40	22.99	85.12	0	1.44	11.49	1.04	32.64	2,414	2	98	0	0	32	32.74	-24.63			Sep-08
50	8.07	11.65	22.65	24.55	87.29	0	1.2	13.19	1.15	28.33	102.7	1	99	0	0	25	41.94	-25.1	5.75		Aug-10
50	7.99	11.50	22.42	23.79	85.75	0	1.4	13.2	1.15	28.08	102.7	1	99	0	0	25	42	-25.15	5.75		Dec-13
50	7.82	11.19	21.67	21.61	80.18	0	1.95	13.19	1.15	26.71	102.7	1	99	0	0	25	41.44	-25.4		1.00	Aug-10
	8.15	11.79	22.99	25.61	89.77	0	0.85	13.18	1.15	28.89	102.7	1	99	0	0	25	42.2	-25.07			Aug-10
	8.14	11.78	23.08	25.69	89.90	0	0.75	13.19	1.15	28.91	102.7	1	99	0	0	25	42.2	-25.07			Sep-13
	7.95	11.40	22.26	23.32	84.35	0	1.45	13.2	1.15	27.92	102.7	1	99	0	0	25	41.79	-25.23			Sep-13
	3.12	3.75	2.82	14.71	55.08	2.77	0.99	12.75	0.92	9.04	35.5	1	99	0	0	28	24	-13.03			Nov-16
50	3.25	3.95	3.10	14.86	55.28	2.56	1.09	12.72	0.92	9.08	35.5	1	99	0	0	28	24	-13.03			Jul-02
50	8.46	13.46	38.69	37.25	138.93	0	1.52	15.59	1.29	20.25	28.7	8	92	0	0	38			5.75		Sep-13
50	8.26	12.97	37.43	34.13	129.67	0	2.27	15.58	1.29	19.54	28.7	8	92	0	0	38				1.00	Sep-13
	8.41	13.41	38.55	37.11	137.48	0	1.52	15.58	1.29	20.23	28.7	8	92	0	0	38					Nov-12
	8.49	13.50	38.93	38.47	142.24	0	1.17	15.63	1.3	20.69	28.7	8	92	0	0	38					Nov-12
	8.51	13.53	39.04	38.75	142.29	0	1.07	15.61	1.29	20.65	28.7	8	92	0	0	38					Nov-12
50	2.27	4.97	11.86	35.66	103.67	0	1.26	13.4	0.91	40.61	1,053	2	98	0	0	35	27.53	-30.24	5.75		Feb-09
50	2.21	4.88	11.63	34.79	99.66	0	1.87	13.39	0.91	40.31	1,053	2	98	0	0	35	26.97	-30.49	5.75		Aug-14
50	2.08	4.57	10.99	32.49	95.78	0	2.05	13.37	0.91	38.5	1,053	2	98	0	0	35	26.97	-30.49		1.00	Dec-85
	2.23	4.86	11.63	35.13	101.61	0	1.31	13.4	0.91	57.88	1,053	2	98	0	0	35	27.47	-30.3			Jul-04
	2.33	5.08	12.10	36.54	105.77	0	1.03	13.4	0.91	60.59	1,053	2	98	0	0	35	27.74	-30.19			Dec-94
	2.36	4.86	11.30	32.85	96.32		0.95	13.37	0.91	60.62	1,053	2	98	0	0	35	26.97	-30.49			Sep-17
	2.19	4.80	11.63	34.32	99.81	0	1.65	13.39	0.91	56.63	1,053	2	98	0	0	35	27.2	-30.37			Dec-06
	6.16	11.83	25.16	25.78	93.73	0	1.05	15.24	0.98	33.57	3,038	1	99	0	0	9	37.5	-22.6			Mar-07
50	6.11	11.76	24.95	25.00	92.33	0	1.24	15.25	0.98	32.81	3,038	1	99	0	0	9	37.33	-22.7	5.75		Jul-98
50	5.95	11.35	24.04	22.37	85.56	0	1.95	15.22	0.97	26.56	3,038	1	99	0	0	9	36.54	-22.98		1.00	Jul-98
	6.11	11.76	24.96	25.09	92.52	0	1.18	15.24	0.98	33	3,038	1	99	0	0	9	37.29	-22.66			Dec-07
	6.20	11.92	25.28	26.18	95.52	0	0.9	15.22	0.97	34.93	3,038	1	99	0	0	9	37.71	-22.53			Nov-04
	6.23	11.98	25.47	26.70	96.72	0	0.78	15.26	0.98	35.26	3,038	1	99	0	0	9	37.72	-22.54			Aug-08
	6.02	11.61	24.59	24.05	90.02	0	1.47	15.23	0.97	32.04	3,038	1	99	0	0	9	37.16	-22.72			Dec-06
50	3.92	8.12	10.54	23.29	72.80	0	1.36	15.76	1.08	19.9	181.6	1	99	0	0	48	28.46	-26.96	5.75		Feb-99
50	3.71	7.69	9.70	20.64	66.73	0	2.07	15.77	1.08	15.51	181.6	1	99	0	0	48	27.83	-27.24		1.00	Feb-99
	4.00	8.25	10.85	24.57	75.76	0	0.99	15.76	1.08	21.53	181.6	1	99	0	0	48	28.62	-26.83			Apr-03
	4.03	8.32	11.02	24.94	76.20	0	0.89	15.78	1.08	21.58	181.6	1	99	0	0	48	28.46	-26.96			May-13
50	7.16	10.80	20.98			0.3	1.2			12.3	8.3	2	98	0	0	18			5.75		Nov-15
	7.10	10.84	21.13			0.57	1.2			12.33	8.3	2	98	0	0	18					Mar-15

	MARKET		FUND TYPE, CATEGORY & OBJECTIVE		RATINGS				MINIMUMS	
Fund Name	Ticker Symbol	Traded On	Fund Type	Category and (Prospectus Objective)	Overall Rating	Reward Rating	Risk Rating	Recent Up/ Downgrade	Open to New Investors	Min Initial Investment
ClearBridge Sustainability Leaders Fund Class I	LCISX	NAS CM	Open End	US Equity Large Cap Growth (Growth)	B-	C+	B	Up	Y	1,000,000
ClearBridge Sustainability Leaders Fund Class IS	LCILX	NAS CM	Open End	US Equity Large Cap Growth (Growth)	B-	C+	B	Up	Y	1,000,000
ClearBridge Tactical Dividend Income Fund Class A	CFLGX	NAS CM	Open End	US Equity Mid Cap (Equity-Income)	C	C	C	Down	Y	1,000
ClearBridge Tactical Dividend Income Fund Class A2	LBDAX	NAS CM	Open End	US Equity Mid Cap (Equity-Income)	C	C	C	Down	Y	1,000
ClearBridge Tactical Dividend Income Fund Class C	SMDLX	NAS CM	Open End	US Equity Mid Cap (Equity-Income)	C	C	C		Y	1,000
ClearBridge Tactical Dividend Income Fund Class I	LADIX	NAS CM	Open End	US Equity Mid Cap (Equity-Income)	C	C	C	Down	Y	1,000,000
ClearBridge Tactical Dividend Income Fund Class IS	LCBDX	NAS CM	Open End	US Equity Mid Cap (Equity-Income)	C	C	C	Down	Y	1,000,000
ClearBridge Value Trust Class A	LGVAX	NAS CM	Open End	US Equity Large Cap Blend (Growth)	B-	B-	B		Y	1,000
ClearBridge Value Trust Class C	LMVTX	NAS CM	Open End	US Equity Large Cap Blend (Growth)	B-	C+	B-	Up	Y	1,000
ClearBridge Value Trust Class FI	LMVFX	NAS CM	Open End	US Equity Large Cap Blend (Growth)	B-	B-	B		Y	0
ClearBridge Value Trust Class I	LMNVX	NAS CM	Open End	US Equity Large Cap Blend (Growth)	B-	B-	B	Down	Y	1,000,000
ClearBridge Value Trust Class R	LMVRX	NAS CM	Open End	US Equity Large Cap Blend (Growth)	B-	C+	B-		Y	0
ClearTrack 2015 Fund Class R1	TCFTX	NAS CM	Open End	Target Date 2000-2020 (Growth & Income)	C+	C	B	Up	Y	0
ClearTrack 2015 Fund Class R6	TDKTX	NAS CM	Open End	Target Date 2000-2020 (Growth & Income)	B-	C	B	Up	Y	0
ClearTrack 2020 Fund Class R1	TCHTX	NAS CM	Open End	Target Date 2000-2020 (Growth & Income)	B-	C	B	Up	Y	0
ClearTrack 2020 Fund Class R6	TCSUX	NAS CM	Open End	Target Date 2000-2020 (Growth & Income)	C+	C	B	Up	Y	0
ClearTrack 2025 Fund Class R1	TDITX	NAS CM	Open End	Target Date 2021-2045 (Growth & Income)	C+	C	B	Up	Y	0
ClearTrack 2025 Fund Class R6	TDOTX	NAS CM	Open End	Target Date 2021-2045 (Growth & Income)	B-	C	B	Up	Y	0
ClearTrack 2030 Fund Class R1	TDFTX	NAS CM	Open End	Target Date 2021-2045 (Growth & Income)	B-	C	B	Up	Y	0
ClearTrack 2030 Fund Class R6	TDHTX	NAS CM	Open End	Target Date 2021-2045 (Growth & Income)	B-	C	B	Up	Y	0
ClearTrack 2035 Fund Class R1	TCETX	NAS CM	Open End	Target Date 2021-2045 (Growth & Income)	B-	C+	B	Up	Y	0
ClearTrack 2035 Fund Class R6	TCHDX	NAS CM	Open End	Target Date 2021-2045 (Growth & Income)	B-	C+	B	Up	Y	0
ClearTrack 2040 Fund Class R1	TCRTX	NAS CM	Open End	Target Date 2021-2045 (Growth & Income)	C+	C+	B	Up	Y	0
ClearTrack 2040 Fund Class R6	TCKTX	NAS CM	Open End	Target Date 2021-2045 (Growth & Income)	B-	C+	B	Up	Y	0
ClearTrack 2045 Fund Class R1	TCPTX	NAS CM	Open End	Target Date 2021-2045 (Growth & Income)	C+	C+	B-	Up	Y	0
ClearTrack 2045 Fund Class R6	TCOTX	NAS CM	Open End	Target Date 2021-2045 (Growth & Income)	C+	C+	B-	Up	Y	0
ClearTrack 2050 Fund Class R1	TRNTX	NAS CM	Open End	Target Date 2046+ (Growth & Income)	C+	C+	B-	Up	Y	0
ClearTrack 2050 Fund Class R6	TCMTX	NAS CM	Open End	Target Date 2046+ (Growth & Income)	C+	C+	B-	Up	Y	0
ClearTrack 2055 Fund Class R1	TCTOX	NAS CM	Open End	Target Date 2046+ (Growth & Income)	U	U	U		Y	0
ClearTrack 2055 Fund Class R6	TCTSX	NAS CM	Open End	Target Date 2046+ (Growth & Income)	U	U	U		Y	0
ClearTrack 2060 Fund Class R1	TCSOX	NAS CM	Open End	Target Date 2046+ (Growth & Income)	U	U	U		Y	0
ClearTrack 2060 Fund Class R6	TCSSX	NAS CM	Open End	Target Date 2046+ (Growth & Income)	U	U	U		Y	0
ClearTrack Retirement Income Fund Class R1	TCITX	NAS CM	Open End	Target Date 2000-2020 (Growth & Income)	C+	C	B	Up	Y	0
ClearTrack Retirement Income Fund Class R6	TCJTX	NAS CM	Open End	Target Date 2000-2020 (Growth & Income)	B-	C	B	Up	Y	0
Clifford Capital Partners Fund Institutional Class	CLIFX	NAS CM	Open End	US Equity Mid Cap (Growth)	B-	B	B-	Down	Y	100,000
Clifford Capital Partners Fund Investor Class	CLFFX	NAS CM	Open End	US Equity Mid Cap (Growth)	B-	B	B-		Y	2,500
Clipper Fund	CFIMX	NAS CM	Open End	US Equity Large Cap Blend (Growth)	B	B	B+	Up	Y	2,500
Clough China Fund Class C	CHNCX	NAS CM	Open End	Greater China Equity (Foreign Stock)	B	B	C+	Up	Y	2,500
Clough China Fund Class I	CHNIX	NAS CM	Open End	Greater China Equity (Foreign Stock)	B	A-	C+	Up	Y	100,000
Clough China Fund Class Investor	CHNAX	NAS CM	Open End	Greater China Equity (Foreign Stock)	B	A-	C+	Up	Y	2,500
Clough Global Dividend and Income Fund	GLV	AMEX	Closed End	Moderate Alloc (Multi-Asset Global)	B-	C+	B	Up	Y	
Clough Global Equity Fund	GLQ	AMEX	Closed End	Global Equity (World Stock)	B-	C+	B-	Up	Y	
Clough Global Long/Short Fund Class C	CLOCX	NAS CM	Open End	Long/Short Equity (Growth)	C+	C	B-	Up	Y	2,500
Clough Global Long/Short Fund Class I	CLOIX	NAS CM	Open End	Long/Short Equity (Growth)	C+	C	B-	Up	Y	1,000,000
Clough Global Long/Short Fund Investor Class	CLOAX	NAS CM	Open End	Long/Short Equity (Growth)	C+	C	B-	Up	Y	2,500
Clough Global Opportunities Fund	GLO	AMEX	Closed End	Moderate Alloc (Multi-Asset Global)	B-	C+	B	Up	Y	
CM Advisors Fund	CMAFX	NAS CM	Open End	US Equity Mid Cap (Growth)	C	C	C	Up	Y	2,500
CM Advisors Small Cap Value Fund	CMOVX	NAS CM	Open End	US Equity Small Cap (Small Company)	C	C+	C-	Up	Y	2,500
CMG Mauldin Solutions Core Fund Class A Shares	GEFAX	NAS CM	Open End	Global Equity (Growth)	C+	C	B-	Up	Y	5,000
CMG Mauldin Solutions Core Fund Class I Shares	GEFIX	NAS CM	Open End	Global Equity (Growth)	C+	C	B-	Up	Y	15,000
CMG Tactical All Asset Strategy Fund Class A Shares	CMGQX	NAS CM	Open End	Multialternative (Growth)	D+	D+	B	Up	Y	5,000
CMG Tactical All Asset Strategy Fund Class I Shares	CMGHX	NAS CM	Open End	Multialternative (Growth)	D+	D+	B	Up	Y	15,000

★ Expanded analysis of this fund is included in Section II.

Min Additional Investment	TOTAL RETURNS 3-Month Total Return	6-Month Total Return	1-Year Total Return	3-Year Total Return	5-Year Total Return	PERFORMANCE Dividend Yield (TTM)	Expense Ratio	3-Yr Std Deviation	3-Year Beta	ASSETS NAV	Total Assets (MIL)	ASSET ALLOCATION & TURNOVER %Cash	%Stocks	%Bonds	%Other	Turnover Ratio	BULL & BEAR Last Bull Market Total Return	Last Bear Market Total Return	FEES Front End Fee (%)	Back End Fee (%)	Inception Date
	7.25	10.98	21.47			0.64	0.85			12.37	8.3	2	98	0	0	18					Mar-15
	7.23	11.05	21.53			0.66	0.75			12.39	8.3	2	98	0	0	18					Mar-15
50	1.76	1.93	6.67	1.75	42.70	5.07	1.77	10.35	1.09	16.81	511.7	1	91	0	1	20	20.51	-21.45	5.75		Oct-90
50	1.74	1.87	6.61	1.36	41.93	5.02	1.93	10.35	1.09	16.76	511.7	1	91	0	1	20	20.51	-21.45	5.75		Jun-13
50	1.54	1.51	5.88	-0.52	37.44	4.57	2.51	10.35	1.09	15.98	511.7	1	91	0	1	20	20.11	-21.74		1.00	Sep-00
	1.81	2.03	6.97	2.52	44.51	5.32	1.51	10.36	1.09	16.93	511.7	1	91	0	1	20	20.77	-21.42			May-08
	1.83	2.06	7.02	2.56	44.40	5.35	1.5	10.33	1.08	16.93	511.7	1	91	0	1	20	20.51	-21.45			May-13
50	3.74	7.26	14.59	23.15	98.46	0.83	1.07	13.54	1.24	81.46	2,407	3	97	0	0	45	24	-18.11	5.75		Feb-09
50	3.56	6.86	13.75	20.53	91.30	0.09	1.77	13.52	1.24	79.97	2,407	3	97	0	0	45	23.44	-18.4		0.95	Apr-82
	3.72	7.20	14.48	22.87	97.74	0.51	1.15	13.54	1.24	92.68	2,407	3	97	0	0	45	23.99	-18.16			Mar-01
	3.79	7.37	14.83	24.00	100.63	0.81	0.8	13.54	1.24	95.64	2,407	3	97	0	0	45	24.12	-18			Dec-94
	3.63	7.04	14.20	21.86	94.62	0.32	1.4	13.53	1.24	91.44	2,407	3	97	0	0	45	23.66	-18.29			Dec-06
	2.45	4.94	10.73			1.1	1.2			10.59	52.5	3	48	48	1	43					Mar-15
	2.65	5.32	11.43			1.54	0.55			10.64	52.5	3	48	48	1	43					Mar-15
	2.82	5.50	11.75			1.03	1.2			10.74	77.3	4	53	43	1	42					Mar-15
	2.97	5.82	12.50			1.43	0.55			10.8	77.3	4	53	43	1	42					Mar-15
	3.05	6.05	12.84			0.98	1.2			11.1	91.2	3	59	37	1	3					Mar-15
	3.21	6.29	13.58			1.34	0.55			11.16	91.2	3	59	37	1	3					Mar-15
	3.38	6.63	14.02			0.93	1.2			11.3	70.7	2	64	33	1	0					Mar-15
	3.55	6.97	14.65			1.3	0.55			11.37	70.7	2	64	33	1	0					Mar-15
	3.90	7.51	16.00			1.05	1.2			11.55	71.5	2	74	23	1	0					Mar-15
	4.06	7.93	16.83			1.41	0.55			11.63	71.5	2	74	23	1	0					Mar-15
	4.40	8.39	17.82			1.06	1.2			11.72	61.8	3	82	15	0	2					Mar-15
	4.54	8.76	18.56			1.41	0.55			11.84	61.8	3	82	15	0	2					Mar-15
	4.78	9.21	19.19			0.98	1.2			11.93	39.4	2	90	7	0	2					Mar-15
	5.02	9.61	20.00			1.35	0.55			12.01	39.4	2	90	7	0	2					Mar-15
	4.86	9.39	19.37			0.91	1.2			12.01	30.3	2	91	6	0	0					Mar-15
	5.09	9.68	20.16			1.25	0.55			12.09	30.3	2	91	6	0	0					Mar-15
	4.99	7.35					1.2			10.89	0.54	2	92	6	0						Jul-17
	5.20	7.57					0.55			10.89	0.54	2	92	6	0						Jul-17
	4.99	7.35					1.2			10.89	0.54	2	92	6	0						Jul-17
	5.20	7.57					0.55			10.89	0.54	2	92	6	0						Jul-17
	1.58	3.44	7.59			1.12	1.2			10.53	97.7	4	32	63	1						Mar-15
	1.76	3.80	8.35			1.51	0.55			10.6	97.7	4	32	63	1						Mar-15
1,000	5.47	9.03	10.35	33.57		0.48	0.9	12.89	1.08	14.72	13.4	16	84	0	0	34					Jan-14
100	5.46	8.88	10.12	32.73		0.38	1.1	12.91	1.08	14.68	13.4	16	84	0	0	34					Jan-14
25	5.75	10.14	17.68	43.51	111.88	1.06	0.72	11.99	1.06	120.46	1,170	5	95	0	0	33	18.57	-13.97			Feb-84
	6.74	17.67	39.98	22.75	44.96	0	2.7	17.76	0.84	26.57	61.0	6	94	0	1	126	15.17	-24.44		1.00	Dec-05
	7.02	18.28	41.46	26.90	53.10	0.21	1.7	17.77	0.84	28.66	61.0	6	94	0	1	126	15.84	-24.13			Dec-05
	6.95	18.16	41.08	25.57	50.58	0.07	1.95	17.77	0.84	28	61.0	6	94	0	1	126	15.69	-24.21	5.50		Dec-05
	3.37	5.70	19.33	12.07	43.06	1.36	0	9.38	1.16	14.59	103.0	-31	59	69	-1	205	18.09	-20.89			Jul-04
	5.32	10.58	27.83	14.97	50.64	0.45	0	10.96	0.61	14.4681	160.1	-14	98	12	1	182	18.62	-21.92			Apr-05
	5.22	9.93	18.77	8.90		0	2.77			11.07	33.0	37	61	1	1	261				1.00	Sep-15
	5.52	10.38	20.02	11.70		0	1.77			11.27	33.0	37	61	1	1	261					Sep-15
	5.36	10.24	19.55	10.70		0	2.12			11.19	33.0	37	61	1	1	261			5.50		Sep-15
	5.46	9.78	23.79	12.79	43.73	0.26	0	9.77		12.12	389.6	-29	77	52	-2	191	17.81	-21.16			Apr-06
	5.72	14.04	-1.32	7.41	18.24	0.57	1.44	19.59	1.32	12.75	50.0	1	99	0	0	17	22.33	-16.79			May-03
	5.14	21.02	-1.41	12.33	32.44	0.66	1.27	25.71	1.37	11.86	47.3	3	97	0	0	28	25.51	-22.22			Apr-11
1,000	3.52	5.98	14.00	3.60		0	2	6.56	0.53	11.01	66.6	3	66	26	5	248			5.75		May-13
1,000	3.40	6.04	14.14	4.20		0	1.75	6.52	0.53	11.04	66.6	3	66	26	5	248					May-13
1,000	1.67	3.72	7.74			0.26	1.83			10.42	69.3	3	81	9	8				5.75		Apr-16
1,000	1.75	3.79	8.02			0.34	1.58			10.43	69.3	3	81	9	8						Apr-16

	MARKET		FUND TYPE, CATEGORY & OBJECTIVE		RATINGS				MINIMUMS	
Fund Name	Ticker Symbol	Traded On	Fund Type	Category and (Prospectus Objective)	Overall Rating	Reward Rating	Risk Rating	Recent Up/ Downgrade	Open to New Investors	Min Initial Investment
Cognios Large Cap Growth Fund Institutional Class	COGEX	NAS CM	Open End	US Equity Large Cap Growth (Growth)	D	D+	B+		Y	100,000
Cognios Large Cap Growth Fund Investor Class	COGGX	NAS CM	Open End	US Equity Large Cap Growth (Growth)	D	D+	B+		Y	1,000
Cognios Large Cap Value Fund Institutional Class	COGVX	NAS CM	Open End	US Equity Large Cap Value (Growth)	D	D+	A-		Y	100,000
Cognios Large Cap Value Fund Investor Class	COGLX	NAS CM	Open End	US Equity Large Cap Value (Growth)	D	D+	A-		Y	1,000
Cognios Market Neutral Large Cap Fund Institutional Class	COGIX	NAS CM	Open End	Market Neutral (Growth)	C	C-	B-	Down	Y	100,000
Cognios Market Neutral Large Cap Fund Investor Class	COGMX	NAS CM	Open End	Market Neutral (Growth)	C	C-	B-	Up	Y	1,000
Cohen & Steers Active Commodities Strat Fund, Inc. Cls A	CDFAX	NAS CM	Open End	Commodities Broad Basket (Growth & Income)	D	D	D	Up	Y	0
Cohen & Steers Active Commodities Strat Fund, Inc. Cls C	CDFCX	NAS CM	Open End	Commodities Broad Basket (Growth & Income)	D	D	D	Up	Y	0
Cohen & Steers Active Commodities Strat Fund, Inc. Cls I	CDFIX	NAS CM	Open End	Commodities Broad Basket (Growth & Income)	D	D	D	Up	Y	100,000
Cohen & Steers Active Commodities Strat Fund, Inc. Cls R	CDFRX	NAS CM	Open End	Commodities Broad Basket (Growth & Income)	D	D	D	Up	Y	0
Cohen & Steers Active Commodities Strat Fund, Inc. Cls Z	CDFZX	NAS CM	Open End	Commodities Broad Basket (Growth & Income)	D	D	D	Up	Y	0
Cohen & Steers Closed-End Opportunity Fund	FOF	NYSE	Closed End	Moderate Alloc (Growth & Income)	C+	C+	C+	Up	Y	
Cohen & Steers Dividend Value Fund , Inc.Class A	DVFAX	NAS CM	Open End	US Equity Large Cap Blend (Equity-Income)	B-	B-	B	Down	Y	0
Cohen & Steers Dividend Value Fund , Inc.Class C	DVFCX	NAS CM	Open End	US Equity Large Cap Blend (Equity-Income)	B-	B-	B	Down	Y	0
Cohen & Steers Dividend Value Fund , Inc.Cls Institutional	DVFIX	NAS CM	Open End	US Equity Large Cap Blend (Equity-Income)	B	B-	B	Up	Y	100,000
Cohen & Steers Dividend Value Fund, Inc. Class R	DVFRX	NAS CM	Open End	US Equity Large Cap Blend (Equity-Income)	B-	B-	B	Down	Y	0
Cohen & Steers Dividend Value Fund, Inc. Class Z	DVFZX	NAS CM	Open End	US Equity Large Cap Blend (Equity-Income)	B	B-	B	Up	Y	0
Cohen & Steers Global Income Builder Inc	INB	NYSE	Closed End	Global Equity (World Stock)	C+	C+	C+	Up	Y	
Cohen & Steers Global Infrastructure Fund, Inc. Class A	CSUAX	NAS CM	Open End	Other Sector Equity (Utility)	B-	C+	B-		Y	0
Cohen & Steers Global Infrastructure Fund, Inc. Class C	CSUCX	NAS CM	Open End	Other Sector Equity (Utility)	C+	C+	C+	Down	Y	0
Cohen & Steers Global Infrastructure Fund, Inc. Class I	CSUIX	NAS CM	Open End	Other Sector Equity (Utility)	B-	C+	B-		Y	100,000
Cohen & Steers Global Infrastructure Fund, Inc. Class R	CSURX	NAS CM	Open End	Other Sector Equity (Utility)	C+	C+	B-	Down	Y	0
Cohen & Steers Global Infrastructure Fund, Inc. Class Z	CSUZX	NAS CM	Open End	Other Sector Equity (Utility)	B-	C+	B-		Y	0
Cohen & Steers Global Realty Shares, Inc. Class A	CSFAX	NAS CM	Open End	Real Estate Sector Equity (Real Estate)	B-	C+	B		Y	0
Cohen & Steers Global Realty Shares, Inc. Class C	CSFCX	NAS CM	Open End	Real Estate Sector Equity (Real Estate)	B-	C+	B		Y	0
Cohen & Steers Global Realty Shares, Inc. Class I	CSSPX	NAS CM	Open End	Real Estate Sector Equity (Real Estate)	B-	C+	B		Y	100,000
Cohen & Steers Global Realty Shares, Inc. Class R	GRSRX	NAS CM	Open End	Real Estate Sector Equity (Real Estate)	B-	C+	B		Y	0
Cohen & Steers Global Realty Shares, Inc. Class Z	CSFZX	NAS CM	Open End	Real Estate Sector Equity (Real Estate)	B-	C+	B		Y	0
Cohen & Steers Infrastructure Fund	UTF	NYSE	Closed End	Other Sector Equity (Utility)	B-	B-	C+	Up	Y	
Cohen & Steers Institutional Global Realty Shares	GRSIX	NAS CM	Open End	Real Estate Sector Equity (Real Estate)	B-	C+	B		Y	1,000,000
Cohen & Steers Institutional Realty Shares	CSRIX	NAS CM	Open End	Real Estate Sector Equity (Real Estate)	B	C+	B+	Up	Y	1,000,000
Cohen & Steers International Realty Fund Class A	IRFAX	NAS CM	Open End	Real Estate Sector Equity (Real Estate)	B-	C+	B	Up	Y	0
Cohen & Steers International Realty Fund Class C	IRFCX	NAS CM	Open End	Real Estate Sector Equity (Real Estate)	B-	C+	B	Up	Y	0
Cohen & Steers International Realty Fund Class I	IRFIX	NAS CM	Open End	Real Estate Sector Equity (Real Estate)	B-	C+	B	Up	Y	100,000
Cohen & Steers International Realty Fund Class R	IRFRX	NAS CM	Open End	Real Estate Sector Equity (Real Estate)	B-	C+	B	Up	Y	0
Cohen & Steers International Realty Fund Class Z	IRFZX	NAS CM	Open End	Real Estate Sector Equity (Real Estate)	B-	C+	B	Up	Y	0
Cohen & Steers Limited Dur Preferred & Income Fund, Inc	LDP	NYSE	Closed End	US Fixed Income (Growth & Income)	B	B-	A+	Up	Y	
Cohen & Steers Low Duration Preferred & Income Fund Cls A	LPXAX	NAS CM	Open End	US Fixed Income (Income)	C	D+	A-	Up	Y	0
Cohen & Steers Low Duration Preferred & Income Fund Cls C	LPXCX	NAS CM	Open End	US Fixed Income (Income)	C	D+	A-	Up	Y	0
Cohen & Steers Low Duration Preferred & Income Fund Cls I	LPXIX	NAS CM	Open End	US Fixed Income (Income)	C	D+	A-	Up	Y	100,000
Cohen & Steers Low Duration Preferred & Income Fund Cls R	LPXRX	NAS CM	Open End	US Fixed Income (Income)	C	D+	A-	Up	Y	0
Cohen & Steers Low Duration Preferred & Income Fund Cls Z	LPXZX	NAS CM	Open End	US Fixed Income (Income)	C	D+	A-	Up	Y	0
Cohen & Steers MLP & Energy Opportunity Fund, Inc. Class A	MLOAX	NAS CM	Open End	Energy Sector Equity (Growth & Income)	C-	C-	D	Down	Y	0
Cohen & Steers MLP & Energy Opportunity Fund, Inc. Class C	MLOCX	NAS CM	Open End	Energy Sector Equity (Growth & Income)	D+	C-	D	Down	Y	0
Cohen & Steers MLP & Energy Opportunity Fund, Inc. Class I	MLOIX	NAS CM	Open End	Energy Sector Equity (Growth & Income)	C-	C	D	Down	Y	100,000
Cohen & Steers MLP & Energy Opportunity Fund, Inc. Class R	MLORX	NAS CM	Open End	Energy Sector Equity (Growth & Income)	D+	C-	D	Down	Y	0
Cohen & Steers MLP & Energy Opportunity Fund, Inc. Class Z	MLOZX	NAS CM	Open End	Energy Sector Equity (Growth & Income)	C-	C	D	Down	Y	0
Cohen & Steers MLP Income & Energy Opportunity Fund, Inc.	MIE	NYSE	Closed End	Energy Sector Equity (Natl Res)	D	D	D	Down	Y	
Cohen & Steers Preferred Sec & Income Fund, Inc. Cls A	CPXAX	NAS CM	Open End	US Fixed Income (Growth & Income)	B	C+	A+	Up	Y	0
Cohen & Steers Preferred Sec & Income Fund, Inc. Cls C	CPXCX	NAS CM	Open End	US Fixed Income (Growth & Income)	B	C+	A+	Up	Y	0
Cohen & Steers Preferred Sec & Income Fund, Inc. Cls F	CPXFX	NAS CM	Open End	US Fixed Income (Growth & Income)	B	C+	A+	Up	Y	0
Cohen & Steers Preferred Sec & Income Fund, Inc. Cls I	CPXIX	NAS CM	Open End	US Fixed Income (Growth & Income)	B	C+	A+	Up	Y	100,000

★ Expanded analysis of this fund is included in Section II.

	TOTAL RETURNS					PERFORMANCE				ASSETS		ASSET ALLOCATION & TURNOVER					BULL & BEAR		FEES		
Min Additional Investment	3-Month Total Return	6-Month Total Return	1-Year Total Return	3-Year Total Return	5-Year Total Return	Dividend Yield (TTM)	Expense Ratio	3-Yr Std Deviation	3-Year Beta	NAV	Total Assets (MIL)	%Cash	%Stocks	%Bonds	%Other	Turnover Ratio	Last Bull Market Total Return	Last Bear Market Total Return	Front End Fee (%)	Back End Fee (%)	Inception Date
	9.01	14.46	25.81			0.1	0.9			11.75	5.9	4	96	0	0						Oct-16
	8.96	14.31	25.53			0.06	1.15			11.73	5.9	4	96	0	0						Oct-16
	7.44	10.42	16.24			0.07	0.85			9.94	24.1	2	98	0	0						Oct-16
	7.37	10.35	16.05			0.02	1.1			9.94	24.1	2	98	0	0						Oct-16
	6.67	7.12	5.22	10.34	23.47	0	1.71	7.84	0.09	10.07	63.2	64	36	0	0	277					Dec-12
	6.65	6.99	4.96	9.53	22.00	0	1.96	7.85	0.1	9.94	63.2	64	36	0	0	277					Dec-12
	3.61	5.12	-4.96	-23.67		0	1.26	13.55	1.02	5.74	8.5	97	0	3	0				4.50		May-14
	3.48	4.83	-5.36	-24.69		0	1.66	13.58	1.02	5.64	8.5	97	0	3	0					1.00	May-14
	3.56	5.25	-4.59	-22.94		0	0.91	13.5	1.02	5.81	8.5	97	0	3	0						May-14
	3.44	4.96	-5.14	-24.16		0	1.41	13.53	1.02	5.71	8.5	97	0	3	0						Oct-14
	3.75	5.25	-4.59	-22.94		0	0.91	13.5	1.02	5.81	8.5	97	0	3	0						May-14
	2.57	5.73	16.20	22.61	51.36	3.38	0.95	9.43		14.02	373.3	-14	59	45	4	36	16.36	-15.09			Nov-06
	7.73	11.19	17.59	27.39	94.81	0.89	1	11	1.05	15.29	195.2	2	98	0	0	70	23.83	-16.83	4.50		Aug-05
	7.58	10.81	16.90	25.02	88.60	0.32	1.65	10.98	1.04	15.19	195.2	2	98	0	0	70	23.32	-17.04		1.00	Aug-05
	7.87	11.44	18.06	28.79	98.36	1.2	0.65	11	1.04	15.32	195.2	2	98	0	0	70	24.14	-16.67			Aug-05
	7.75	11.09	17.48	26.87	93.49	0.79	1.15	11	1.04	15.31	195.2	2	98	0	0	70	23.78	-16.85			Oct-14
	7.80	11.36	17.98	28.70	98.23	1.2	0.65	10.99	1.04	15.31	195.2	2	98	0	0	70	24.14	-16.67			Oct-14
	4.50	8.14	18.97	20.39	51.91	1.41	1.8	9.06	0.75	10.75	247.4	0	92	2	2	78	25.08	-18.44			Jul-07
	3.49	5.62	18.89	17.01	57.38	1.87	1.35	9.88	0.98	19.14	252.9	2	98	0	0	89	10.4	-8.09	4.50		May-04
	3.34	5.31	18.18	14.79	52.41	1.24	2	9.87	0.98	19.1	252.9	2	98	0	0	89	9.96	-8.35		1.00	May-04
	3.58	5.81	19.29	18.14	59.91	2.14	1	9.89	0.98	19.2	252.9	2	98	0	0	89	10.57	-7.97			May-04
	3.49	5.56	18.69	16.54	56.17	1.74	1.5	9.87	0.98	19.18	252.9	2	98	0	0	89	10.25	-8.16			Oct-14
	3.58	5.81	19.29	18.29	60.18	2.16	1	9.87	0.98	19.2	252.9	2	98	0	0	89	10.57	-7.97			Oct-14
	3.82	5.21	12.53	17.66	41.60	3.63	1.3	10.83	0.96	53.63	579.3	3	97	0	0	104	23.3	-22.25	4.50		Sep-04
	3.66	4.88	11.82	15.39	37.09	2.97	1.95	10.84	0.96	53.31	579.3	3	97	0	0	104	22.87	-22.47		1.00	Sep-04
	3.90	5.41	12.95	18.90	44.06	3.94	0.95	10.84	0.96	53.87	579.3	3	97	0	0	104	23.55	-22.12			May-97
	3.78	5.15	12.36	17.35	40.76	3.45	1.45	10.85	0.96	54.01	579.3	3	97	0	0	104	23.19	-22.28			Oct-14
	3.93	5.42	12.95	18.93	44.09	3.94	0.95	10.84	0.96	53.88	579.3	3	97	0	0	104	23.55	-22.12			Oct-14
	3.06	6.25	24.63	22.83	77.82	2.91	0	11.9	0.74	25.53	2,239	1	81	3	4	51	19.25	-15.27			Mar-04
10,000	3.86	5.38	12.93	18.92	44.44	4	1	10.86	0.96	27.07	482.3	1	98	0	0	100	23.5	-22.06			Aug-06
10,000	3.02	3.12	7.44	17.93	63.14	2.94	0.75	12.98	0.96	43.31	2,827	2	98	0	0	79	30.16	-17.69			Feb-00
	6.00	10.29	23.02	19.67	30.23	5.24	1.35	11.25	0.98	12.02	638.2	0	95	0	4	68	16.95	-23.02	4.50		Mar-05
	5.88	10.01	22.27	17.43	26.12	4.54	2	11.26	0.98	11.92	638.2	0	95	0	4	68	16.46	-23.23		1.00	Mar-05
	6.06	10.52	23.39	20.97	32.48	5.53	1	11.27	0.98	12.09	638.2	0	95	0	4	68	17.1	-22.92			Mar-05
	5.95	10.20	22.77	19.65	29.73	5.15	1.5	11.21	0.97	12.12	638.2	0	95	0	4	68	16.76	-23.08			Oct-15
	6.06	10.52	23.39	21.08	32.60	5.53	1	11.22	0.98	12.09	638.2	0	95	0	4	68	17.11	-22.92			Oct-15
	1.57	3.79	14.85	31.89	56.20	5.09	1.8	5.75	0.87	27.16	787.1	1	0	35	7	48					Jul-12
	0.68	1.80	6.28			3.64	0.9			10.15	779.9	5	0	37	8	52			2.00		Nov-15
	0.40	1.45	5.54			3.04	1.55			10.13	779.9	5	0	37	8	52				1.00	Nov-15
	0.75	1.96	6.64			4	0.55			10.15	779.9	5	0	37	8	52					Nov-15
	0.47	1.64	6.03			3.41	1.05			10.15	779.9	5	0	37	8	52					Nov-15
	0.75	1.96	6.64			4	0.55			10.15	779.9	5	0	37	8	52					Nov-15
	0.50	1.87	-0.01	-17.18		3.53	1.46	19.18	1.02	8.35	102.6	3	97	0	0	59			4.50		Dec-13
	0.34	1.42	-0.68	-18.85		2.85	2.11	19.18	1.02	8.32	102.6	3	97	0	0	59				1.00	Dec-13
	0.69	2.04	0.44	-16.28		3.89	1.11	19.19	1.02	8.37	102.6	3	97	0	0	59					Dec-13
	0.58	1.81	-0.13	-17.56		3.41	1.61	19.15	1.02	8.36	102.6	3	97	0	0	59					Oct-14
	0.57	2.04	0.32	-16.38		3.9	1.11	19.22	1.02	8.36	102.6	3	97	0	0	59					Dec-13
	-1.82	-3.67	-7.50	-36.59		0.08	2.53	29.41		10.66	270.9	1	91	2	0	54					Mar-13
	0.97	2.66	11.04	22.42	40.12	4.97	1.18	4	0.92	14.14	7,962	3	0	31	5	51	11.95	-5	3.75		May-10
	0.81	2.34	10.30	20.00	35.66	4.36	1.83	3.99	0.92	14.06	7,962	3	0	31	5	51	11.49	-5.26		1.00	May-10
	0.99	2.77	11.31	23.54	42.48		0.83	4	0.92	14.16	7,962	3	0	31	5	51	12.14	-4.87			Apr-17
	1.05	2.82	11.36	23.59	42.54	5.28	0.85	3.99	0.92	14.17	7,962	3	0	31	5	51	12.14	-4.87			May-10

	MARKET			FUND TYPE, CATEGORY & OBJECTIVE	RATINGS					MINIMUMS
Fund Name	Ticker Symbol	Traded On	Fund Type	Category and (Prospectus Objective)	Overall Rating	Reward Rating	Risk Rating	Recent Up/ Downgrade	Open to New Investors	Min Initial Investment
Cohen & Steers Preferred Sec & Income Fund, Inc. Cls R	CPRRX	NAS CM	Open End	US Fixed Income (Growth & Income)	B	C+	A+	Up	Y	0
Cohen & Steers Preferred Sec & Income Fund, Inc. Cls Z	CPXZX	NAS CM	Open End	US Fixed Income (Growth & Income)	B	C+	A+	Up	Y	0
Cohen & Steers Quality Income Realty Fund	RQI	NYSE	Closed End	Real Estate Sector Equity (Real Estate)	B	B-	B	Up	Y	
Cohen & Steers Real Assets Fund Inc Class A	RAPAX	NAS CM	Open End	Alloc (Asset Alloc)	C	C	C	Up	Y	0
Cohen & Steers Real Assets Fund Inc Class C	RAPCX	NAS CM	Open End	Alloc (Asset Alloc)	C	C	C	Up	Y	0
Cohen & Steers Real Assets Fund Inc Class I	RAPIX	NAS CM	Open End	Alloc (Asset Alloc)	C	C	C	Up	Y	100,000
Cohen & Steers Real Assets Fund Inc Class R	RAPRX	NAS CM	Open End	Alloc (Asset Alloc)	C	C	C	Up	Y	0
Cohen & Steers Real Assets Fund Inc Class Z	RAPZX	NAS CM	Open End	Alloc (Asset Alloc)	C	C	C	Up	Y	0
Cohen & Steers Real Estate Securities Fund, Inc. Class A	CSEIX	NAS CM	Open End	Real Estate Sector Equity (Real Estate)	B	B-	B+	Up	Y	0
Cohen & Steers Real Estate Securities Fund, Inc. Class C	CSCIX	NAS CM	Open End	Real Estate Sector Equity (Real Estate)	B	C+	B+	Up	Y	0
Cohen & Steers Real Estate Securities Fund, Inc. Class F	CREFX	NAS CM	Open End	Real Estate Sector Equity (Real Estate)	B	B-	B+	Up	Y	0
Cohen & Steers Real Estate Securities Fund, Inc. Cls Inst	CSDIX	NAS CM	Open End	Real Estate Sector Equity (Real Estate)	B	B-	B+		Y	100,000
Cohen & Steers Real Estate Securities Fund, Inc. Class R	CIRRX	NAS CM	Open End	Real Estate Sector Equity (Real Estate)	B	B-	B+	Up	Y	0
Cohen & Steers Real Estate Securities Fund, Inc. Class Z	CSZIX	NAS CM	Open End	Real Estate Sector Equity (Real Estate)	B	B-	B+		Y	0
Cohen & Steers Realty Shares Fund	CSRSX	NAS CM	Open End	Real Estate Sector Equity (Real Estate)	B	C+	B+	Up	Y	10,000
Cohen & Steers REIT & Preferred Income Fund	RNP	NYSE	Closed End	Moderate Alloc (Income)	B	B-	A-	Up	Y	
Cohen & Steers Select Preferred and Income Fund	PSF	NYSE	Closed End	US Fixed Income (Growth)	B	B-	A+	Up	Y	
Cohen & Steers Total Return Realty	RFI	NYSE	Closed End	Real Estate Sector Equity (Real Estate)	B	C+	A-	Up	Y	
Coho Relative Value Equity Fund Advisor Class	COHOX	NAS CM	Open End	US Equity Large Cap Blend (Equity-Income)	B-	B-	B-	Down	Y	5,000
Coho Relative Value Equity Fund Institutional Class	COHIX	NAS CM	Open End	US Equity Large Cap Blend (Equity-Income)	B-	B-	B-	Down	Y	1,000,000
Collins Long/Short Credit Fund Class A	CLCAX	NAS CM	Open End	Other Alternative (Growth & Income)	C+	C	B	Up	Y	2,500
Collins Long/Short Credit Fund Institutional Class	CCLIX	NAS CM	Open End	Other Alternative (Growth & Income)	C+	C	B	Up	Y	1,000,000
Columbia Acorn Emerging Markets Fund Advisor Class	CAERX	NAS CM	Open End	Emerging Markets Equity (Div Emerging Mkts)	C	C+	C	Up		2,000
Columbia Acorn Emerging Markets Fund Class A	CAGAX	NAS CM	Open End	Emerging Markets Equity (Div Emerging Mkts)	C	C+	C	Up		2,000
Columbia Acorn Emerging Markets Fund Class C	CGMCX	NAS CM	Open End	Emerging Markets Equity (Div Emerging Mkts)	C	C	C	Up		2,000
Columbia Acorn Emerging Markets Fund Institutional 2 Class	CANRX	NAS CM	Open End	Emerging Markets Equity (Div Emerging Mkts)	C	C+	C	Up		0
Columbia Acorn Emerging Markets Fund Institutional 3 Class	CPHRX	NAS CM	Open End	Emerging Markets Equity (Div Emerging Mkts)	C	C+	C	Up		1,000,000
Columbia Acorn Emerging Markets Fund Institutional Class	CEFZX	NAS CM	Open End	Emerging Markets Equity (Div Emerging Mkts)	C	C+	C	Up		2,000
Columbia Acorn European Fund Advisor Class	CLOFX	NAS CM	Open End	Europe Equity Large Cap (Europe Stock)	B+	A-	B	Up	Y	2,000
Columbia Acorn European Fund Class A	CAEAX	NAS CM	Open End	Europe Equity Large Cap (Europe Stock)	B+	A-	B	Up	Y	2,000
Columbia Acorn European Fund Class C	CAECX	NAS CM	Open End	Europe Equity Large Cap (Europe Stock)	B+	B+	B	Up	Y	2,000
Columbia Acorn European Fund Institutional 2 Class	CAEEX	NAS CM	Open End	Europe Equity Large Cap (Europe Stock)	B+	A-	B	Up	Y	0
Columbia Acorn European Fund Institutional 3 Class	CAEYX	NAS CM	Open End	Europe Equity Large Cap (Europe Stock)	B+	A-	B	Up	Y	1,000,000
Columbia Acorn European Fund Institutional Class	CAEZX	NAS CM	Open End	Europe Equity Large Cap (Europe Stock)	B+	A-	B	Up	Y	2,000
Columbia Acorn Fund Advisor Class	CEARX	NAS CM	Open End	US Equity Mid Cap (Growth)	B	B+	C+	Up	Y	2,000
Columbia Acorn Fund Class A	LACAX	NAS CM	Open End	US Equity Mid Cap (Growth)	B	B+	C+	Up	Y	2,000
Columbia Acorn Fund Class C	LIACX	NAS CM	Open End	US Equity Mid Cap (Growth)	B	B	C+	Up	Y	2,000
Columbia Acorn Fund Institutional 2 Class	CRBRX	NAS CM	Open End	US Equity Mid Cap (Growth)	B	B+	C+	Up	Y	0
Columbia Acorn Fund Institutional 3 Class	CRBYX	NAS CM	Open End	US Equity Mid Cap (Growth)	B	B+	C+	Up	Y	1,000,000
Columbia Acorn Fund Institutional Class	ACRNX	NAS CM	Open End	US Equity Mid Cap (Growth)	B	B+	C+	Up	Y	2,000
Columbia Acorn International Fund Advisor Class	CCIRX	NAS CM	Open End	Global Equity Mid/Small Cap (Foreign Stock)	B-	B-	B	Up	Y	2,000
Columbia Acorn International Fund Class A	LAIAX	NAS CM	Open End	Global Equity Mid/Small Cap (Foreign Stock)	B-	B-	B	Up	Y	2,000
Columbia Acorn International Fund Class C	LAICX	NAS CM	Open End	Global Equity Mid/Small Cap (Foreign Stock)	B-	C+	B	Up	Y	2,000
Columbia Acorn International Fund Class R	CACRX	NAS CM	Open End	Global Equity Mid/Small Cap (Foreign Stock)	B-	C+	B	Up	Y	0
Columbia Acorn International Fund Institutional 2 Class	CAIRX	NAS CM	Open End	Global Equity Mid/Small Cap (Foreign Stock)	B-	B-	B	Up	Y	0
Columbia Acorn International Fund Institutional 3 Class	CCYIX	NAS CM	Open End	Global Equity Mid/Small Cap (Foreign Stock)	B-	B-	B	Up	Y	1,000,000
Columbia Acorn International Fund Institutional Class	ACINX	NAS CM	Open End	Global Equity Mid/Small Cap (Foreign Stock)	B-	B-	B	Up	Y	2,000
Columbia Acorn International Select Fund Advisor Class	CILRX	NAS CM	Open End	Global Equity Large Cap (Foreign Stock)	B	B	B	Up	Y	2,000
Columbia Acorn International Select Fund Class A	LAFAX	NAS CM	Open End	Global Equity Large Cap (Foreign Stock)	B	B	B	Up	Y	2,000
Columbia Acorn International Select Fund Class C	LFFCX	NAS CM	Open End	Global Equity Large Cap (Foreign Stock)	B-	B-	B	Up	Y	2,000
Columbia Acorn Intl Select Fund Inst 2 Cls	CRIRX	NAS CM	Open End	Global Equity Large Cap (Foreign Stock)	B	B	B	Up	Y	0
Columbia Acorn Intl Select Fund Inst 3 Cls	CSIRX	NAS CM	Open End	Global Equity Large Cap (Foreign Stock)	B	B	B	Up	Y	1,000,000

★ Expanded analysis of this fund is included in Section II.

Min Additional Investment	TOTAL RETURNS 3-Month Total Return	6-Month Total Return	1-Year Total Return	3-Year Total Return	5-Year Total Return	PERFORMANCE Dividend Yield (TTM)	Expense Ratio	3-Yr Std Deviation	3-Year Beta	ASSETS NAV	Total Assets (MIL)	ASSET ALLOCATION & TURNOVER %Cash	%Stocks	%Bonds	%Other	Turnover Ratio	BULL & BEAR Last Bull Market Total Return	Last Bear Market Total Return	FEES Front End Fee (%)	Back End Fee (%)	Inception Date
	0.93	2.58	10.85	21.83	39.02	4.81	1.33	3.99	0.92	14.15	7,962	3	0	31	5	51	11.82	-5.07			Oct-14
	1.06	2.84	11.41	23.66	42.52	5.31	0.83	4.01	0.92	14.16	7,962	3	0	31	5	51	12.14	-4.87			Oct-14
	2.82	3.35	8.68	21.90	76.79	1.91	0	14.38	1.12	13.59	1,496	1	81	2	0	33	38.4	-20.97			Feb-02
	3.82	6.83	6.32	1.56	-0.83	2.46	1.16	8.66	0.55	9.14	156.2	9	53	6	29	118			4.50		Jan-12
	3.65	6.42	5.48	-0.64	-4.18	1.75	1.81	8.67	0.56	9.12	156.2	9	53	6	29	118				1.00	Jan-12
	3.84	6.96	6.61	2.44	0.72	2.76	0.81	8.72	0.56	9.16	156.2	9	53	6	29	118					Jan-12
	3.67	6.53	5.98	0.95	-1.74	2.29	1.31	8.67	0.56	9.22	156.2	9	53	6	29	118					Jan-12
	3.85	6.86	6.50	2.44	0.41	2.76	0.81	8.66	0.56	9.14	156.2	9	53	6	29	118					Jan-12
	2.80	3.41	7.78	22.77	73.98	2.77	1.19	12.53	0.93	14.82	4,350	0	100	0	0	83	29.76	-17.17	4.50		Sep-97
	2.62	3.05	7.07	20.32	68.39	2.42	1.84	12.53	0.93	13.44	4,350	0	100	0	0	83	29.31	-17.39		1.00	Jan-98
	2.88	3.63	7.97	22.99	74.30		0.84	12.53	0.93	15.59	4,350	0	100	0	0	83	29.76	-17.17			Apr-17
	2.86	3.51	8.08	23.71	76.32	2.86	0.91	12.54	0.93	15.59	4,350	0	100	0	0	83	30.12	-17.04			Jul-98
	2.77	3.32	7.62	22.21	72.46	2.52	1.34	12.54	0.93	15.55	4,350	0	100	0	0	83	29.57	-17.25			Oct-14
	2.81	3.56	8.17	23.95	75.93	2.93	0.84	12.56	0.93	15.59	4,350	0	100	0	0	83	29.76	-17.17			Oct-14
500	2.96	2.94	7.08	16.93	61.17	2.74	0.96	13.05	0.97	64.44	4,656	1	99	0	0	78	30.18	-17.67			Jul-91
	2.17	3.53	11.97	27.64	73.69	4.18	0	10.17	0.78	22.8	1,091	3	49	13	1	46	30.51	-16.63			Jun-03
	1.71	3.87	15.91	31.61	57.75	5.74	2.08	5.11		27.79	335.1	1	0	30	7	51	17.33	-8.29			Nov-10
	2.40	2.93	7.87	18.37	58.81	1.97	0	10.95	0.86	13.41	352.6	0	81	1	0	36	26.34	-14.98			Sep-93
100	7.57	10.92	18.30	27.24		1.28	0.95	9.48	0.84	14.4	566.3	3	97	0	0						Aug-13
100	7.64	11.07	18.44	27.67		1.35	0.8	9.51	0.85	14.42	566.3	3	97	0	0						May-14
100	-0.03	-0.40	0.61			3.63	1.77			9.65	118.9	50	0	45	1	87			5.00		Feb-15
1,000	0.04	-0.27	0.93			3.18	1.52			9.73	118.9	50	0	45	1	87					Feb-15
	8.60	12.06	34.87	7.83	16.55	0.5	1.31	14.1	0.89	13.38	104.1	0	98	0	2	43	23.41				Nov-12
	8.52	11.91	34.55	6.97	14.91	0.28	1.56	14.1	0.89	13.24	104.1	0	98	0	2	43	22.96		5.75		Aug-11
	8.36	11.49	33.57	4.57	10.72	0	2.31	14.09	0.89	13.09	104.1	0	98	0	2	43	22.53			1.00	Aug-11
	8.51	12.06	35.01	8.06	16.75	0.58	1.2	14.13	0.89	13.38	104.1	0	98	0	2	43	23.41				Nov-12
	8.59	12.07	35.13	8.22	17.02	0.6	1.15	14.12	0.89	13.27	104.1	0	98	0	2	43	23.41				Jun-13
	8.57	12.05	34.92	7.72	16.30	0.49	1.31	14.12	0.89	13.29	104.1	0	98	0	2	43	23.41				Aug-11
	4.51	11.80	38.28	39.36	75.00	0.98	1.2	13.14	0.9	19.36	96.6	0	98	0	2	40	19.84				Jun-14
	4.44	11.65	37.89	38.26	72.81	0.79	1.45	13.12	0.89	19.27	96.6	0	98	0	2	40	19.51		5.75		Aug-11
	4.29	11.21	36.95	35.17	66.42	0.15	2.2	13.08	0.89	19.12	96.6	0	98	0	2	40	19.08			1.00	Aug-11
	4.55	11.81	38.32	39.46	74.99	1	1.13	13.08	0.89	19.46	96.6	0	98	0	2	40	19.84				Nov-12
	4.54	11.84	38.44	39.42	75.02		1.08	13.09	0.89	19.17	96.6	0	98	0	2	40	19.84				Mar-17
	4.54	11.81	38.34	39.32	74.90	0.98	1.2	13.1	0.89	19.27	96.6	0	98	0	2	40	19.84				Aug-11
	5.99	11.41	25.19	34.74	82.18	0	0.86	12.03	0.89	16.06	4,848	0	100	0	0	85	26.21	-22.11			Nov-12
	5.90	11.26	24.91	33.97	80.17	0	1.11	12.01	0.89	12.92	4,848	0	100	0	0	85	25.97	-22.19	5.75		Oct-00
	5.70	10.77	23.88	30.96	73.70	0	1.86	12.02	0.89	6.58	4,848	0	100	0	0	85	25.45	-22.46		1.00	Oct-00
	6.00	11.44	25.20	35.10	82.93	0	0.84	12.03	0.89	16.2	4,848	0	100	0	0	85	26.21	-22.11			Nov-12
	6.02	11.55	25.31	35.39	83.49	0	0.79	12.02	0.89	16.34	4,848	0	100	0	0	85	26.21	-22.11			Nov-12
	6.04	11.47	25.23	35.10	82.76	0	0.86	12.03	0.89	15.39	4,848	0	100	0	0	85	26.21	-22.11			Jun-70
	6.32	11.51	32.21	27.08	50.28	1.24	1.01	10.95	0.87	46.95	4,936	0	100	0	0	46	17.63	-21.34			Nov-12
	6.27	11.38	31.90	26.28	48.67	1.1	1.26	10.96	0.87	46.51	4,936	0	100	0	0	46	17.36	-21.45	5.75		Oct-00
	6.07	10.94	30.92	23.46	43.18	0.56	2.01	10.96	0.87	44.57	4,936	0	100	0	0	46	16.84	-21.68		1.00	Oct-00
	6.20	11.22	31.57	25.06	46.10	0.83	1.51	10.96	0.87	46.51	4,936	0	100	0	0	46	17.13	-21.49			Aug-11
	6.34	11.54	32.27	27.41	51.00	1.34	0.95	10.96	0.87	46.54	4,936	0	100	0	0	46	17.66	-21.34			Aug-11
	6.36	11.57	32.35	27.60	51.37	1.37	0.9	10.95	0.87	46.95	4,936	0	100	0	0	46	17.63	-21.34			Nov-12
	6.34	11.52	32.23	27.26	50.71	1.3	1.01	10.96	0.87	46.57	4,936	0	100	0	0	46	17.63	-21.34			Sep-92
	6.81	12.77	35.66	35.12	46.95	0.66	1.15	11.33	0.8	29.46	129.4	0	100	0	0	49	15.68	-18.46			Nov-12
	6.76	12.62	35.30	34.08	45.06	0.48	1.4	11.34	0.81	28.89	129.4	0	100	0	0	49	15.46	-18.58	5.75		Oct-00
	6.58	12.20	34.31	31.06	39.58	0	2.15	11.33	0.81	26.85	129.4	0	100	0	0	49	14.94	-18.85		1.00	Oct-00
	6.84	12.76	35.72	35.40	47.44	0.71	1.08	11.35	0.81	29.44	129.4	0	100	0	0	49	15.68	-18.46			Nov-12
	6.86	12.82	35.81	35.62	47.81	0.76	1.03	11.35	0.81	29.42	129.4	0	100	0	0	49	15.68	-18.46			Nov-12

	MARKET			FUND TYPE, CATEGORY & OBJECTIVE	RATINGS					MINIMUMS
Fund Name	Ticker Symbol	Traded On	Fund Type	Category and (Prospectus Objective)	Overall Rating	Reward Rating	Risk Rating	Recent Up/ Downgrade	Open to New Investors	Min Initial Investment
Columbia Acorn International Select Fund Institutional Cls	ACFFX	NAS CM	Open End	Global Equity Large Cap (Foreign Stock)	B	B	B	Up	Y	2,000
Columbia Acorn Select Fund Advisor Class	CSSRX	NAS CM	Open End	US Equity Mid Cap (Growth)	B+	A-	B-	Up	Y	2,000
Columbia Acorn Select Fund Class A	LTFAX	NAS CM	Open End	US Equity Mid Cap (Growth)	B	A-	B-	Up	Y	2,000
Columbia Acorn Select Fund Class C	LTFCX	NAS CM	Open End	US Equity Mid Cap (Growth)	B	B+	B-	Up	Y	2,000
Columbia Acorn Select Fund Institutional 2 Class	CSLRX	NAS CM	Open End	US Equity Mid Cap (Growth)	B+	A-	B-	Up	Y	0
Columbia Acorn Select Fund Institutional 3 Class	CSLYX	NAS CM	Open End	US Equity Mid Cap (Growth)	B+	A-	B-	Up	Y	1,000,000
Columbia Acorn Select Fund Institutional Class	ACTWX	NAS CM	Open End	US Equity Mid Cap (Growth)	B+	A-	B-	Up	Y	2,000
Columbia Acorn USA Fund Advisor Class	CUSAX	NAS CM	Open End	US Equity Small Cap (Growth)	B	B+	B	Up	Y	2,000
Columbia Acorn USA Fund Class A	LAUAX	NAS CM	Open End	US Equity Small Cap (Growth)	B	B+	B	Up	Y	2,000
Columbia Acorn USA Fund Class C	LAUCX	NAS CM	Open End	US Equity Small Cap (Growth)	B	B	B	Up	Y	2,000
Columbia Acorn USA Fund Institutional 2 Class	CYSRX	NAS CM	Open End	US Equity Small Cap (Growth)	B	B+	B	Up	Y	0
Columbia Acorn USA Fund Institutional 3 Class	CUSYX	NAS CM	Open End	US Equity Small Cap (Growth)	B	B+	B	Up	Y	1,000,000
Columbia Acorn USA Fund Institutional Class	AUSAX	NAS CM	Open End	US Equity Small Cap (Growth)	B	B+	B	Up	Y	2,000
Columbia Adaptive Retirement 2020 Fund Advisor Class	CARGX	NAS CM	Open End	Target Date 2000-2020 (Asset Alloc)	U	U	U		Y	2,000
Columbia Adaptive Retirement 2020 Fund Institutional 3 Cls	CARHX	NAS CM	Open End	Target Date 2000-2020 (Asset Alloc)	U	U	U		Y	1,000,000
Columbia Adaptive Retirement 2030 Fund Advisor Class	CARLX	NAS CM	Open End	Target Date 2021-2045 (Asset Alloc)	U	U	U		Y	2,000
Columbia Adaptive Retirement 2030 Fund Institutional 3 Cls	CARMX	NAS CM	Open End	Target Date 2021-2045 (Asset Alloc)	U	U	U		Y	1,000,000
Columbia Adaptive Retirement 2040 Fund Advisor Class	CAROX	NAS CM	Open End	Target Date 2021-2045 (Asset Alloc)	U	U	U		Y	2,000
Columbia Adaptive Retirement 2040 Fund Institutional 3 Cls	CARQX	NAS CM	Open End	Target Date 2021-2045 (Asset Alloc)	U	U	U		Y	1,000,000
Columbia Adaptive Retirement 2050 Fund Advisor Class	CARSX	NAS CM	Open End	Target Date 2046+ (Asset Alloc)	U	U	U		Y	2,000
Columbia Adaptive Retirement 2050 Fund Institutional 3 Cls	CARUX	NAS CM	Open End	Target Date 2046+ (Asset Alloc)	U	U	U		Y	1,000,000
Columbia Adaptive Retirement 2060 Fund Advisor Class	CARKX	NAS CM	Open End	Target Date 2046+ (Asset Alloc)	U	U	U		Y	2,000
Columbia Adaptive Retirement 2060 Fund Institutional 3 Cls	CARVX	NAS CM	Open End	Target Date 2046+ (Asset Alloc)	U	U	U		Y	1,000,000
Columbia Adaptive Risk Allocation Fund Advisor Class	CARRX	NAS CM	Open End	Moderate Alloc (Growth & Income)	B-	C+	B	Down	Y	2,000
Columbia Adaptive Risk Allocation Fund Class A	CRAAX	NAS CM	Open End	Moderate Alloc (Growth & Income)	B-	C+	B	Down	Y	2,000
Columbia Adaptive Risk Allocation Fund Class C	CRACX	NAS CM	Open End	Moderate Alloc (Growth & Income)	B-	C+	B		Y	2,000
Columbia Adaptive Risk Allocation Fund Class K	CRFRX	NAS CM	Open End	Moderate Alloc (Growth & Income)	B-	C+	B	Down		0
Columbia Adaptive Risk Allocation Fund Class R	CRKRX	NAS CM	Open End	Moderate Alloc (Growth & Income)	B-	C+	B		Y	0
Columbia Adaptive Risk Allocation Fund Class T	CRAWX	NAS CM	Open End	Moderate Alloc (Growth & Income)	B-	C+	B	Down	Y	2,000
Columbia Adaptive Risk Allocation Fund Institutional 2 Cls	CRDRX	NAS CM	Open End	Moderate Alloc (Growth & Income)	B-	C+	B	Down	Y	0
Columbia Adaptive Risk Allocation Fund Institutional 3 Cls	CARYX	NAS CM	Open End	Moderate Alloc (Growth & Income)	B-	C+	B	Down	Y	1,000,000
Columbia Adaptive Risk Allocation Fund Institutional Class	CRAZX	NAS CM	Open End	Moderate Alloc (Growth & Income)	B-	C+	B	Down	Y	2,000
Columbia Alternative Beta Fund Advisor Class	CLFUX	NAS CM	Open End	Multialternative (Growth & Income)	C	C	C+	Up	Y	2,000
Columbia Alternative Beta Fund Class A	CLAAX	NAS CM	Open End	Multialternative (Growth & Income)	C	C	C	Up	Y	2,000
Columbia Alternative Beta Fund Class C	CLABX	NAS CM	Open End	Multialternative (Growth & Income)	C	C	C	Up	Y	2,000
Columbia Alternative Beta Fund Class R	CRRLX	NAS CM	Open End	Multialternative (Growth & Income)	C	C	C	Up	Y	0
Columbia Alternative Beta Fund Class T	CLAWX	NAS CM	Open End	Multialternative (Growth & Income)	C	C	C	Up	Y	2,000
Columbia Alternative Beta Fund Institutional 2 Class	CLIVX	NAS CM	Open End	Multialternative (Growth & Income)	C	C	C+	Up	Y	0
Columbia Alternative Beta Fund Institutional 3 Class	CLAYX	NAS CM	Open End	Multialternative (Growth & Income)	C	C	C+	Up	Y	1,000,000
Columbia Alternative Beta Fund Institutional Class	CLAZX	NAS CM	Open End	Multialternative (Growth & Income)	C	C	C+	Up	Y	2,000
Columbia Asia Pacific ex-Japan Fund Class A	CAJAX	NAS CM	Open End	Asia ex-Japan Equity (Pacific Stock)	B	B+	C+	Up	Y	2,000
Columbia Asia Pacific ex-Japan Fund Class C	CAJCX	NAS CM	Open End	Asia ex-Japan Equity (Pacific Stock)	B-	B	C+	Up	Y	2,000
Columbia Asia Pacific ex-Japan Fund Class R	CAJRX	NAS CM	Open End	Asia ex-Japan Equity (Pacific Stock)	B	B	C+	Up	Y	0
Columbia Asia Pacific ex-Japan Fund Institutional 2 Class	TAPRX	NAS CM	Open End	Asia ex-Japan Equity (Pacific Stock)	B	B+	C+	Up	Y	100,000
Columbia Asia Pacific ex-Japan Fund Institutional 3 Class	CAPYX	NAS CM	Open End	Asia ex-Japan Equity (Pacific Stock)	B	B+	C+	Up	Y	0
Columbia Asia Pacific ex-Japan Fund Institutional Class	CAJZX	NAS CM	Open End	Asia ex-Japan Equity (Pacific Stock)	B	B+	C+	Up	Y	2,000
Columbia Balanced Fund Advisor Class	CBDRX	NAS CM	Open End	Moderate Alloc (Balanced)	B	C+	A-		Y	0
Columbia Balanced Fund Class A	CBLAX	NAS CM	Open End	Moderate Alloc (Balanced)	B	C+	B+		Y	2,000
Columbia Balanced Fund Class C	CBLCX	NAS CM	Open End	Moderate Alloc (Balanced)	B-	C+	B	Down	Y	2,000
Columbia Balanced Fund Class K	CLRFX	NAS CM	Open End	Moderate Alloc (Balanced)	B	C+	B+			0
Columbia Balanced Fund Class R	CBLRX	NAS CM	Open End	Moderate Alloc (Balanced)	B-	C+	B	Down	Y	0
Columbia Balanced Fund Class T	CBDTX	NAS CM	Open End	Moderate Alloc (Balanced)	B	C+	B+		Y	2,000

★ Expanded analysis of this fund is included in Section II.

	TOTAL RETURNS					PERFORMANCE				ASSETS		ASSET ALLOCATION & TURNOVER					BULL & BEAR		FEES		
Min Additional Investment	3-Month Total Return	6-Month Total Return	1-Year Total Return	3-Year Total Return	5-Year Total Return	Dividend Yield (TTM)	Expense Ratio	3-Yr Std Deviation	3-Year Beta	NAV	Total Assets (MIL)	%Cash	%Stocks	%Bonds	%Other	Turnover Ratio	Last Bull Market Total Return	Last Bear Market Total Return	Front End Fee (%)	Back End Fee (%)	Inception Date
	6.86	12.78	35.70	35.23	47.17	0.69	1.15	11.34	0.81	29.25	129.4	0	100	0	0	49	15.68	-18.46			Nov-98
	7.93	13.36	26.70	39.75	96.85	0	0.93	11.86	0.84	17.19	314.9	0	100	0	0	75	26.43	-27.19			Nov-12
	7.85	13.13	26.33	38.69	94.31	0	1.18	11.9	0.84	14.61	314.9	0	100	0	0	75	26.17	-27.28	5.75		Oct-00
	7.69	12.68	25.39	35.67	87.35	0	1.93	11.91	0.85	9.59	314.9	0	100	0	0	75	25.66	-27.53		1.00	Oct-00
	7.96	13.35	26.71	40.09	97.51	0	0.87	11.88	0.84	17.28	314.9	0	100	0	0	75	26.43	-27.19			Nov-12
	7.95	13.37	26.78	40.25	98.01	0	0.82	11.92	0.85	17.43	314.9	0	100	0	0	75	26.43	-27.19			Nov-12
	7.92	13.33	26.58	39.81	97.01	0	0.93	11.87	0.84	16.54	314.9	0	100	0	0	75	26.43	-27.19			Nov-98
	2.54	7.14	19.42	32.03	86.51	0	1.17	13.48	0.88	16.08	334.0	0	100	0	0	98	27.79	-24.71			Nov-12
	2.48	7.07	19.13	31.13	84.17	0	1.42	13.49	0.88	12.48	334.0	0	100	0	0	98	27.6	-24.83	5.75		Oct-00
	2.32	6.68	18.30	28.45	77.92	0	2.17	13.47	0.88	6.56	334.0	0	100	0	0	98	27.06	-25.05		1.00	Oct-00
	2.59	7.27	19.56	32.54	87.43	0	1.08	13.52	0.88	16.21	334.0	0	100	0	0	98	27.79	-24.71			Nov-12
	2.62	7.26	19.59	32.74	87.88	0	1.03	13.5	0.88	16.36	334.0	0	100	0	0	98	27.79	-24.71			Nov-12
	2.55	7.19	19.43	32.15	86.54	0	1.17	13.51	0.88	15.21	334.0	0	100	0	0	98	27.79	-24.71			Sep-96
	0.80						0.68			10.15	5.1	6	6	8	81						Oct-17
	0.80						0.5			10.15	5.1	6	6	8	81						Oct-17
	1.15						0.68			10.2	10.2	7	6	8	80						Oct-17
	1.15						0.5			10.2	10.2	7	6	8	80						Oct-17
	1.54						0.68			10.25	1.0	5	6	8	81						Oct-17
	1.54						0.5			10.25	1.0	5	6	8	81						Oct-17
	1.66						0.68			10.28	1.0	5	6	8	81						Oct-17
	1.66						0.5			10.28	1.0	5	6	8	81						Oct-17
	1.68						0.68			10.28	1.0	5	6	8	81						Oct-17
	1.68						0.5			10.28	1.0	5	6	8	81						Oct-17
	5.03	7.16	13.31	18.18	23.81	1.13	0.88	5.79		10.86	2,643	66	7	26	0	396					Oct-14
	4.93	6.97	13.05	17.30	22.15	0.92	1.13	5.78		10.76	2,643	66	7	26	0	396			5.75		Jun-12
	4.80	6.59	12.26	14.79	17.65	0.27	1.88	5.76		10.41	2,643	66	7	26	0	396				1.00	Jun-12
	5.01	7.05	13.12	17.59	22.71	1	1.13	5.77		10.79	2,643	66	7	26	0	396					Jun-12
	4.98	6.94	12.85	16.48	20.77	0.7	1.38	5.78		10.66	2,643	66	7	26	0	396					Jun-12
	5.02	6.96	13.03	17.38	22.36	0.91	1.13	5.78		10.78	2,643	66	7	26	0	396			2.50		Jun-12
	5.01	7.03	13.28	18.32	24.10	1.18	0.88	5.77		10.87	2,643	66	7	26	0	396					Jun-12
	5.07	7.09	13.43	18.56	24.11	1.24	0.83	5.76		10.89	2,643	66	7	26	0	396					Oct-14
	5.03	7.06	13.31	18.18	23.70	1.13	0.88	5.72		10.85	2,643	66	7	26	0	396					Jun-12
	1.60	4.79	6.41			0.54	1.06			9.45	680.4	100	0	0	0	71					Jan-15
	1.61	4.70	6.21			0.43	1.31			9.42	680.4	100	0	0	0	71			5.75		Jan-15
	1.43	4.33	5.37			0.13	2.06			9.32	680.4	100	0	0	0	71				1.00	Jan-15
	1.53	4.63	5.91			0.33	1.56			9.38	680.4	100	0	0	0	71					Jan-15
	1.62	4.72	6.22			0.44	1.31			9.41	680.4	100	0	0	0	71			2.50		Jan-15
	1.68	4.88	6.61			0.57	0.93			9.46	680.4	100	0	0	0	71					Jan-15
	1.70	5.00	6.73			0.59	0.87			9.48	680.4	100	0	0	0	71					Jan-15
	1.63	4.83	6.56			0.54	1.06			9.44	680.4	100	0	0	0	71					Jan-15
	9.52	17.53	43.32	34.87	49.81	0.7	1.59	13.92	0.94	14.18	38.8	4	96	0	0	20	20.03	-27.16	5.75		Sep-10
	9.41	17.16	42.16	31.81	44.17	0.17	2.34	13.89	0.94	14.03	38.8	4	96	0	0	20	19.33	-27.47		1.00	Sep-10
	9.52	17.42	42.90	33.84	47.85	0.52	1.84	13.93	0.94	14.07	38.8	4	96	0	0	20	19.76	-27.31			Sep-10
	9.74	17.82	43.69	36.29	52.51	0.95	1.25	13.88	0.93	14.23	38.8	4	96	0	0	20	20.13	-26.99			Jul-09
	9.64	17.80	43.67	36.27	52.49		1.2	13.87	0.93	14.07	38.8	4	96	0	0	20	20.13	-26.99			Mar-17
	9.59	17.69	43.49	35.83	51.58	0.87	1.34	13.89	0.94	14.18	38.8	4	96	0	0	20	20.04	-27.19			Sep-10
	3.49	6.46	14.29	23.19	67.50	1.22	0.75	6.23		41.69	7,468	6	62	32	0	63	17.17	-10.86			Nov-12
	3.43	6.32	14.00	22.27	65.40	1	1	6.24		41.39	7,468	6	62	32	0	63	16.98	-10.92	5.75		Nov-02
	3.24	5.91	13.16	19.58	59.32	0.3	1.75	6.23		41.3	7,468	6	62	32	0	63	16.51	-11.22		1.00	Oct-03
	3.42	6.34	14.05	22.54	66.10	1.07	0.96	6.23		41.3	7,468	6	62	32	0	63	17.03	-10.89			Mar-11
	3.36	6.19	13.72	21.36	63.39	0.76	1.25	6.24		41.4	7,468	6	62	32	0	63	16.85	-11.01			Sep-10
	3.46	6.35	14.01	22.30	65.41		1	6.25		41.39	7,468	6	62	32	0	63	17	-10.95	2.50		Apr-17

	MARKET			FUND TYPE, CATEGORY & OBJECTIVE	RATINGS				MINIMUMS	
Fund Name	Ticker Symbol	Traded On	Fund Type	Category and (Prospectus Objective)	Overall Rating	Reward Rating	Risk Rating	Recent Up/ Downgrade	Open to New Investors	Min Initial Investment
Columbia Balanced Fund Institutional 2 Class	CLREX	NAS CM	Open End	Moderate Alloc (Balanced)	B	C+	A-		Y	100,000
Columbia Balanced Fund Institutional 3 Class	CBDYX	NAS CM	Open End	Moderate Alloc (Balanced)	B	C+	A-		Y	0
Columbia Balanced Fund Institutional Class	CBALX	NAS CM	Open End	Moderate Alloc (Balanced)	B	C+	A-		Y	2,000
Columbia Capital Allocation Aggressive Portfolio Adv Cls	CPDAX	NAS CM	Open End	Aggressive Alloc (Growth & Income)	B-	B-	B	Down	Y	2,000
Columbia Capital Allocation Aggressive Portfolio Class A	AXBAX	NAS CM	Open End	Aggressive Alloc (Growth & Income)	B-	B-	B	Down	Y	2,000
Columbia Capital Allocation Aggressive Portfolio Class C	RBGCX	NAS CM	Open End	Aggressive Alloc (Growth & Income)	B-	B-	B	Down	Y	2,000
Columbia Capital Allocation Aggressive Portfolio Class K	CAGRX	NAS CM	Open End	Aggressive Alloc (Growth & Income)	B-	B-	B	Down		0
Columbia Capital Allocation Aggressive Portfolio Class R	CPARX	NAS CM	Open End	Aggressive Alloc (Growth & Income)	B-	B-	B	Down	Y	0
Columbia Capital Alloc Aggressive Port Inst 2 Cls	CPANX	NAS CM	Open End	Aggressive Alloc (Growth & Income)	B-	B-	B	Down	Y	0
Columbia Capital Alloc Aggressive Port Inst 3 Cls	CPDIX	NAS CM	Open End	Aggressive Alloc (Growth & Income)	B-	B-	B	Down	Y	1,000,000
Columbia Capital Allocation Aggressive Portfolio Inst Cls	CPAZX	NAS CM	Open End	Aggressive Alloc (Growth & Income)	B-	B-	B	Down	Y	2,000
Columbia Capital Allocation Conservative Portfolio Adv Cls	CPCYX	NAS CM	Open End	Cautious Alloc (Growth & Income)	B	C	A-	Up	Y	2,000
Columbia Capital Allocation Conservative Portfolio Class A	ABDAX	NAS CM	Open End	Cautious Alloc (Growth & Income)	B	C	A-	Up	Y	2,000
Columbia Capital Allocation Conservative Portfolio Class C	RPCCX	NAS CM	Open End	Cautious Alloc (Growth & Income)	B-	C	A-	Up	Y	2,000
Columbia Capital Allocation Conservative Portfolio Class K	CPVRX	NAS CM	Open End	Cautious Alloc (Growth & Income)	B	C	A-	Up		0
Columbia Capital Allocation Conservative Portfolio Class R	CBVRX	NAS CM	Open End	Cautious Alloc (Growth & Income)	B	C	A-	Up	Y	0
Columbia Capital Alloc Conservative Port Inst 2 Cls	CPAOX	NAS CM	Open End	Cautious Alloc (Growth & Income)	B	C	A-	Up	Y	0
Columbia Capital Alloc Conservative Port Inst 3 Cls	CPDHX	NAS CM	Open End	Cautious Alloc (Growth & Income)	B	C	A-	Up	Y	1,000,000
Columbia Capital Alloc Conservative Port Inst Cls	CBVZX	NAS CM	Open End	Cautious Alloc (Growth & Income)	B	C	A-	Up	Y	2,000
Columbia Capital Alloc Moderate Aggressive Port Adv Cls	CGBRX	NAS CM	Open End	Moderate Alloc (Growth & Income)	B-	B-	B	Down	Y	2,000
Columbia Capital Alloc Moderate Aggressive Port Cls A	NBIAX	NAS CM	Open End	Moderate Alloc (Growth & Income)	B-	B-	B	Down	Y	2,000
Columbia Capital Alloc Moderate Aggressive Port Cls C	NBICX	NAS CM	Open End	Moderate Alloc (Growth & Income)	B-	C+	B	Down	Y	2,000
Columbia Capital Alloc Moderate Aggressive Port Cls K	CAMKX	NAS CM	Open End	Moderate Alloc (Growth & Income)	B-	B-	B	Down		0
Columbia Capital Alloc Moderate Aggressive Port Cls R	CLBRX	NAS CM	Open End	Moderate Alloc (Growth & Income)	B-	C+	B	Down	Y	0
Columbia Capital Alloc Moderate Aggressive Port Cls V	CGGTX	NAS CM	Open End	Moderate Alloc (Growth & Income)	B-	B-	B	Down		2,000
Columbia Capital Alloc Moderate Aggressive Port Inst 2 Cls	CLHRX	NAS CM	Open End	Moderate Alloc (Growth & Income)	B-	B-	B	Down	Y	0
Columbia Capital Alloc Moderate Aggressive Port Inst 3 Cls	CPHNX	NAS CM	Open End	Moderate Alloc (Growth & Income)	B-	B-	B	Down	Y	1,000,000
Columbia Capital Alloc Moderate Aggressive Port Inst Cls	NBGPX	NAS CM	Open End	Moderate Alloc (Growth & Income)	B-	B-	B	Down	Y	2,000
Columbia Capital Alloc Moderate Conservative Port Adv Cls	CHWRX	NAS CM	Open End	Cautious Alloc (Growth & Income)	B-	C+	B	Up	Y	2,000
Columbia Capital Alloc Moderate Conservative Port Cls A	NLGAX	NAS CM	Open End	Cautious Alloc (Growth & Income)	B	C+	A-	Up	Y	2,000
Columbia Capital Alloc Moderate Conservative Port Cls C	NIICX	NAS CM	Open End	Cautious Alloc (Growth & Income)	B	C+	A-	Up	Y	2,000
Columbia Capital Alloc Moderate Conservative Port Cls K	CCAKX	NAS CM	Open End	Cautious Alloc (Growth & Income)	B-	C+	B	Up		0
Columbia Capital Alloc Moderate Conservative Port Cls R	CLIRX	NAS CM	Open End	Cautious Alloc (Growth & Income)	B-	C+	B	Up	Y	0
Columbia Capital Alloc Mod Conservative Port Inst 2 Cls	CLRRX	NAS CM	Open End	Cautious Alloc (Growth & Income)	B	C+	A-	Up	Y	0
Columbia Capital Alloc Mod Conservative Port Inst 3 Cls	CPDGX	NAS CM	Open End	Cautious Alloc (Growth & Income)	B-	C+	B	Up	Y	1,000,000
Columbia Capital Alloc Moderate Conservative Port Inst Cls	NIPAX	NAS CM	Open End	Cautious Alloc (Growth & Income)	B	C+	A-	Up	Y	2,000
Columbia Capital Allocation Moderate Portfolio Advisor Cls	CPCZX	NAS CM	Open End	Cautious Alloc (Growth & Income)	B-	C+	B	Up	Y	2,000
Columbia Capital Allocation Moderate Portfolio Class A	ABUAX	NAS CM	Open End	Cautious Alloc (Growth & Income)	B	C+	A-	Up	Y	2,000
Columbia Capital Allocation Moderate Portfolio Class C	AMTCX	NAS CM	Open End	Cautious Alloc (Growth & Income)	B-	C+	B	Up	Y	2,000
Columbia Capital Allocation Moderate Portfolio Class K	CBRRX	NAS CM	Open End	Cautious Alloc (Growth & Income)	B-	C+	B	Up		0
Columbia Capital Allocation Moderate Portfolio Class R	CBMRX	NAS CM	Open End	Cautious Alloc (Growth & Income)	B-	C+	B	Up	Y	0
Columbia Capital Allocation Moderate Portfolio Inst 2 Cls	CPAMX	NAS CM	Open End	Cautious Alloc (Growth & Income)	B-	C+	B	Up	Y	0
Columbia Capital Allocation Moderate Portfolio Inst 3 Cls	CPDMX	NAS CM	Open End	Cautious Alloc (Growth & Income)	B-	C+	B	Up	Y	1,000,000
Columbia Capital Allocation Moderate Portfolio Inst Cls	CBMZX	NAS CM	Open End	Cautious Alloc (Growth & Income)	B-	C+	B	Up	Y	2,000
Columbia Commodity Strategy Fund Advisor Class	CCOMX	NAS CM	Open End	Commodities Broad Basket ()	D+	C-	D+	Up	Y	2,000
Columbia Commodity Strategy Fund Class A	CCSAX	NAS CM	Open End	Commodities Broad Basket ()	D+	C-	D+	Up	Y	2,000
Columbia Commodity Strategy Fund Class C	CCSCX	NAS CM	Open End	Commodities Broad Basket ()	D+	D+	D	Up	Y	2,000
Columbia Commodity Strategy Fund Class R	CCSRX	NAS CM	Open End	Commodities Broad Basket ()	D+	C-	D+	Up	Y	0
Columbia Commodity Strategy Fund Class T	CCSWX	NAS CM	Open End	Commodities Broad Basket ()	D+	C-	D+	Up	Y	2,000
Columbia Commodity Strategy Fund Institutional 2 Class	CADLX	NAS CM	Open End	Commodities Broad Basket ()	D+	C-	D+	Up	Y	0
Columbia Commodity Strategy Fund Institutional 3 Class	CCFYX	NAS CM	Open End	Commodities Broad Basket ()	C-	C-	D+	Up	Y	1,000,000
Columbia Commodity Strategy Fund Institutional Class	CCSZX	NAS CM	Open End	Commodities Broad Basket ()	D+	C-	D+	Up	Y	2,000

★Expanded analysis of this fund is included in Section II.

	TOTAL RETURNS					PERFORMANCE				ASSETS		ASSET ALLOCATION & TURNOVER					BULL & BEAR		FEES		
Min Additional Investment	3-Month Total Return	6-Month Total Return	1-Year Total Return	3-Year Total Return	5-Year Total Return	Dividend Yield (TTM)	Expense Ratio	3-Yr Std Deviation	3-Year Beta	NAV	Total Assets (MIL)	%Cash	%Stocks	%Bonds	%Other	Turnover Ratio	Last Bull Market Total Return	Last Bear Market Total Return	Front End Fee (%)	Back End Fee (%)	Inception Date
	3.51	6.46	14.34	23.50	68.33	1.29	0.71	6.24		41.33	7,468	6	62	32	0	63	17.24	-10.8			Mar-11
	3.51	6.48	14.38	23.68	68.74	1.33	0.66	6.24		41.69	7,468	6	62	32	0	63	17.17	-10.86			Nov-12
	3.50	6.46	14.28	23.20	67.47	1.23	0.75	6.25		41.31	7,468	6	62	32	0	63	17.17	-10.86			Oct-91
	5.25	10.72	22.54	30.39	73.19	1.19	0.97	8.6		13.17	748.6	14	74	12	0	12	18.6	-16.33			Jun-13
	5.24	10.53	22.31	29.49	71.15	0.98	1.22	8.64		13.43	748.6	14	74	12	0	12	18.6	-16.45	5.75		Mar-04
	5.00	10.16	21.28	26.56	64.77	0.43	1.97	8.63		13.12	748.6	14	74	12	0	12	18.07	-16.71		1.00	Mar-04
	5.26	10.62	22.38	29.73	71.90	1.03	1.17	8.63		13.47	748.6	14	74	12	0	12	18.6	-16.33			Mar-04
	5.22	10.46	22.04	28.56	69.07	0.8	1.47	8.64		13.33	748.6	14	74	12	0	12	18.23	-16.42			Sep-10
	5.29	10.67	22.60	30.63	73.88	1.24	0.92	8.6		13.16	748.6	14	74	12	0	12	18.6	-16.33			Jun-13
	5.34	10.73	22.77	30.93	74.32	1.28	0.86	8.65		13.16	748.6	14	74	12	0	12	18.6	-16.33			Jun-13
	5.25	10.63	22.57	30.42	73.23	1.17	0.97	8.63		13.37	748.6	14	74	12	0	12	18.66	-16.3			Sep-10
	1.66	3.55	8.15	12.13	23.23	1.93	0.79	3.43		10.23	256.0	19	23	57	0	24	7.67	-4.18			Jun-13
	1.59	3.50	7.94	11.33	21.94	1.69	1.04	3.42		10.3	256.0	19	23	57	0	24	7.51	-4.15	4.75		Mar-04
	1.41	3.03	7.07	8.80	17.42	0.97	1.79	3.4		10.24	256.0	19	23	57	0	24	7.16	-4.52		1.00	Mar-04
	1.61	3.56	7.96	11.54	22.42	1.75	1.01	3.35		10.19	256.0	19	23	57	0	24	7.67	-4.18			Mar-04
	1.53	3.27	7.57	10.40	20.44	1.45	1.29	3.39		10.29	256.0	19	23	57	0	24	7.47	-4.36			Sep-10
	1.67	3.67	8.19	12.34	23.73	1.98	0.76	3.38		10.23	256.0	19	23	57	0	24	7.67	-4.18			Jun-13
	1.69	3.60	8.15	12.39	23.88	2.03	0.7	3.4		10.21	256.0	19	23	57	0	24	7.67	-4.18			Jun-13
	1.66	3.63	8.10	12.17	23.46	1.93	0.79	3.44		10.29	256.0	19	23	57	0	24	7.64	-4.11			Sep-10
	4.30	8.82	18.81	26.42	60.18	1.44	0.91	7.26		13.09	2,241	19	57	24	0	9	16.18	-13.32			Nov-12
	4.27	8.76	18.58	25.49	58.08	1.23	1.16	7.28		12.99	2,241	19	57	24	0	9	16.02	-13.43	5.75		Oct-96
	4.07	8.31	17.62	22.68	52.37	0.68	1.91	7.23		13.02	2,241	19	57	24	0	9	15.5	-13.7		1.00	Oct-96
	4.31	8.77	18.69	25.68	58.83	1.31	1.1	7.27		12.93	2,241	19	57	24	0	9	16.18	-13.32			Feb-13
	4.21	8.64	18.31	24.58	56.19	1.01	1.41	7.28		12.98	2,241	19	57	24	0	9	15.9	-13.55			Jan-06
	4.27	8.76	18.58	25.49	58.07	1.23	1.16	7.28		12.99	2,241	19	57	24	0	9	16	-13.45	5.75		Mar-11
	4.32	8.86	18.90	26.67	60.86	1.5	0.85	7.29		13.08	2,241	19	57	24	0	9	16.18	-13.32			Nov-12
	4.43	8.92	19.01	26.93	61.22	1.58	0.8	7.3		12.8	2,241	19	57	24	0	9	16.18	-13.32			Jun-13
	4.35	8.83	18.82	26.39	60.06	1.45	0.91	7.23		12.96	2,241	19	57	24	0	9	16.18	-13.32			Oct-96
	2.46	5.23	11.35	16.52	34.73	1.91	0.79	4.59		11.08	598.1	16	35	47	0	18	10.83	-6.19			Nov-12
	2.37	5.05	10.97	15.60	32.98	1.66	1.04	4.56		11.18	598.1	16	35	47	0	18	10.69	-6.34	5.75		Oct-96
	2.21	4.73	10.19	13.12	28.13	0.97	1.79	4.58		11.03	598.1	16	35	47	0	18	10.18	-6.59		1.00	Oct-96
	2.42	5.06	10.98	15.77	33.43	1.72	1.01	4.56		11	598.1	16	35	47	0	18	10.83	-6.19			Feb-13
	2.31	4.91	10.78	14.72	31.35	1.42	1.29	4.55		11.2	598.1	16	35	47	0	18	10.54	-6.45			Jan-06
	2.47	5.16	11.29	16.61	35.11	1.95	0.76	4.54		11.07	598.1	16	35	47	0	18	10.83	-6.19			Nov-12
	2.42	5.25	11.28	16.76	35.49	2.02	0.72	4.56		10.93	598.1	16	35	47	0	18	10.83	-6.19			Jun-13
	2.38	5.16	11.20	16.38	34.59	1.92	0.79	4.54		11.02	598.1	16	35	47	0	18	10.83	-6.19			Oct-96
	3.39	7.00	15.13	22.33	48.84	1.97	0.83	5.8		11.51	1,600	13	46	39	0	10	13.28	-10.4			Jun-13
	3.37	6.87	14.86	21.47	47.13	1.72	1.08	5.85		11.65	1,600	13	46	39	0	10	13.26	-10.44	5.75		Mar-04
	3.11	6.53	14.02	18.71	41.69	1.04	1.83	5.8		11.56	1,600	13	46	39	0	10	12.82	-10.75		1.00	Mar-04
	3.29	6.81	14.82	21.57	47.59	1.76	1.04	5.83		11.63	1,600	13	46	39	0	10	13.28	-10.4			Mar-04
	3.31	6.76	14.62	20.51	45.32	1.49	1.33	5.78		11.62	1,600	13	46	39	0	10	13.03	-10.49			Sep-10
	3.39	7.02	15.18	22.41	49.38	2.01	0.79	5.84		11.5	1,600	13	46	39	0	10	13.28	-10.4			Jun-13
	3.41	6.95	15.24	22.67	49.80	2.06	0.74	5.81		11.5	1,600	13	46	39	0	10	13.28	-10.4			Jun-13
	3.35	7.02	15.17	22.30	49.06	1.95	0.83	5.79		11.63	1,600	13	46	39	0	10	13.3	-10.31			Sep-10
	4.48	7.43	1.69	-14.05	-38.81	0	0.85	13.33	1.02	5.71	507.2	84	0	16	0	0	8.14				Mar-13
	4.46	7.47	1.44	-14.74	-39.48	0	1.1	13.39	1.02	5.61	507.2	84	0	16	0	0	8.14		5.75		Jun-12
	4.46	6.95	0.74	-16.58	-41.71	0	1.85	13.43	1.03	5.38	507.2	84	0	16	0	0	7.67			1.00	Jun-12
	4.53	7.17	1.28	-15.44	-40.28	0	1.35	13.36	1.02	5.53	507.2	84	0	16	0	0	7.98				Jun-12
	4.46	7.47	1.44	-14.61	-39.48	0	1.1	13.37	1.02	5.61	507.2	84	0	16	0	0	8.14		2.50		Jul-11
	4.50	7.44	1.72	-13.98	-38.79	0	0.79	13.37	1.02	5.73	507.2	84	0	16	0	0	8.14				Jan-14
	4.72	7.65	1.93	-13.77	-38.77	0	0.73	13.39	1.02	5.75	507.2	84	0	16	0	0	8.14				Oct-14
	4.52	7.49	1.71	-14.26	-38.84	0	0.85	13.35	1.02	5.67	507.2	84	0	16	0	0	8.14				Jun-12

	MARKET			FUND TYPE, CATEGORY & OBJECTIVE	RATINGS					MINIMUMS
Fund Name	Ticker Symbol	Traded On	Fund Type	Category and (Prospectus Objective)	Overall Rating	Reward Rating	Risk Rating	Recent Up/ Downgrade	Open to New Investors	Min Initial Investment
Columbia Contrarian Core Fund Advisor Class	CORRX	NAS CM	Open End	US Equity Large Cap Blend (Growth & Income)	B	B-	B+		Y	0
Columbia Contrarian Core Fund Class A	LCCAX	NAS CM	Open End	US Equity Large Cap Blend (Growth & Income)	B	B-	B+		Y	2,000
Columbia Contrarian Core Fund Class C	LCCCX	NAS CM	Open End	US Equity Large Cap Blend (Growth & Income)	B-	B-	B	Down	Y	2,000
Columbia Contrarian Core Fund Class K	CCRFX	NAS CM	Open End	US Equity Large Cap Blend (Growth & Income)	B	B-	B+			0
Columbia Contrarian Core Fund Class R	CCCRX	NAS CM	Open End	US Equity Large Cap Blend (Growth & Income)	B	B-	B		Y	0
Columbia Contrarian Core Fund Class T	CTRWX	NAS CM	Open End	US Equity Large Cap Blend (Growth & Income)	B	B-	B+		Y	2,000
Columbia Contrarian Core Fund Class V	SGIEX	NAS CM	Open End	US Equity Large Cap Blend (Growth & Income)	B	B-	B+			2,000
Columbia Contrarian Core Fund Institutional 2 Class	COFRX	NAS CM	Open End	US Equity Large Cap Blend (Growth & Income)	B	B-	B+	Down	Y	100,000
Columbia Contrarian Core Fund Institutional 3 Class	COFYX	NAS CM	Open End	US Equity Large Cap Blend (Growth & Income)	B	B-	B+	Down	Y	0
Columbia Contrarian Core Fund Institutional Class	SMGIX	NAS CM	Open End	US Equity Large Cap Blend (Growth & Income)	B	B-	B+		Y	2,000
Columbia Convertible Securities Fund Advisor Class	COVRX	NAS CM	Open End	Convertibles (Convertible Bond)	C+	B-	C+	Down	Y	2,000
Columbia Convertible Securities Fund Class A	PACIX	NAS CM	Open End	Convertibles (Convertible Bond)	C+	C+	C+	Down	Y	2,000
Columbia Convertible Securities Fund Class C	PHIKX	NAS CM	Open End	Convertibles (Convertible Bond)	C+	C+	C+	Down	Y	2,000
Columbia Convertible Securities Fund Class R	CVBRX	NAS CM	Open End	Convertibles (Convertible Bond)	C+	C+	C+	Down	Y	0
Columbia Convertible Securities Fund Class T	CVBWX	NAS CM	Open End	Convertibles (Convertible Bond)	C+	C+	C+	Down	Y	2,000
Columbia Convertible Securities Fund Institutional 2 Class	COCRX	NAS CM	Open End	Convertibles (Convertible Bond)	C+	B-	C+	Down	Y	0
Columbia Convertible Securities Fund Institutional 3 Class	CSFYX	NAS CM	Open End	Convertibles (Convertible Bond)	C+	B-	C+	Down	Y	1,000,000
Columbia Convertible Securities Fund Institutional Class	NCIAX	NAS CM	Open End	Convertibles (Convertible Bond)	C+	B-	C+	Down	Y	2,000
Columbia Disciplined Core Fund Advisor Class	CLCQX	NAS CM	Open End	US Equity Large Cap Blend (Growth)	B	B	B		Y	0
Columbia Disciplined Core Fund Class A	AQEAX	NAS CM	Open End	US Equity Large Cap Blend (Growth)	B	B	B		Y	2,000
Columbia Disciplined Core Fund Class C	RDCEX	NAS CM	Open End	US Equity Large Cap Blend (Growth)	B-	B-	B-	Down	Y	2,000
Columbia Disciplined Core Fund Class K	RQEYX	NAS CM	Open End	US Equity Large Cap Blend (Growth)	B	B	B			0
Columbia Disciplined Core Fund Class R	CLQRX	NAS CM	Open End	US Equity Large Cap Blend (Growth)	B	B	B	Up	Y	0
Columbia Disciplined Core Fund Class T	RDEWX	NAS CM	Open End	US Equity Large Cap Blend (Growth)	B	B	B		Y	2,000
Columbia Disciplined Core Fund Institutional 2 Class	RSIPX	NAS CM	Open End	US Equity Large Cap Blend (Growth)	B	B	B		Y	100,000
Columbia Disciplined Core Fund Institutional 3 Class	CCQYX	NAS CM	Open End	US Equity Large Cap Blend (Growth)	B	B	B		Y	0
Columbia Disciplined Core Fund Institutional Class	CCRZX	NAS CM	Open End	US Equity Large Cap Blend (Growth)	B	B	B		Y	2,000
Columbia Disciplined Growth Fund Advisor Class	CGQFX	NAS CM	Open End	US Equity Large Cap Growth (Growth)	B+	B+	B	Up	Y	0
Columbia Disciplined Growth Fund Class A	RDLAX	NAS CM	Open End	US Equity Large Cap Growth (Growth)	B+	B+	B	Up	Y	2,000
Columbia Disciplined Growth Fund Class C	RDLCX	NAS CM	Open End	US Equity Large Cap Growth (Growth)	B	B	B	Down	Y	2,000
Columbia Disciplined Growth Fund Class K	RDLFX	NAS CM	Open End	US Equity Large Cap Growth (Growth)	B+	B+	B	Up		0
Columbia Disciplined Growth Fund Class R	CGQRX	NAS CM	Open End	US Equity Large Cap Growth (Growth)	B+	B+	B	Up	Y	0
Columbia Disciplined Growth Fund Class T	RDLWX	NAS CM	Open End	US Equity Large Cap Growth (Growth)	B+	B+	B	Up	Y	2,000
Columbia Disciplined Growth Fund Institutional 2 Class	CQURX	NAS CM	Open End	US Equity Large Cap Growth (Growth)	B+	B+	B	Up	Y	100,000
Columbia Disciplined Growth Fund Institutional 3 Class	CGQYX	NAS CM	Open End	US Equity Large Cap Growth (Growth)	B+	B+	B	Up	Y	0
Columbia Disciplined Growth Fund Institutional Class	CLQZX	NAS CM	Open End	US Equity Large Cap Growth (Growth)	B+	B+	B	Up	Y	2,000
Columbia Disciplined Small Core Fund Advisor Class	CFFRX	NAS CM	Open End	US Equity Small Cap (Small Company)	B-	C+	B-	Up	Y	0
Columbia Disciplined Small Core Fund Class A	LSMAX	NAS CM	Open End	US Equity Small Cap (Small Company)	B-	C+	B-	Up	Y	2,000
Columbia Disciplined Small Core Fund Class C	LSMCX	NAS CM	Open End	US Equity Small Cap (Small Company)	C+	C+	B-	Up	Y	2,000
Columbia Disciplined Small Core Fund Class T	CSCWX	NAS CM	Open End	US Equity Small Cap (Small Company)	B-	C+	B-	Up	Y	2,000
Columbia Disciplined Small Core Fund Class V	SSCEX	NAS CM	Open End	US Equity Small Cap (Small Company)	B-	C+	B-	Up		2,000
Columbia Disciplined Small Core Fund Institutional 2 Class	CLLRX	NAS CM	Open End	US Equity Small Cap (Small Company)	B-	C+	B-	Up	Y	100,000
Columbia Disciplined Small Core Fund Institutional 3 Class	CPFRX	NAS CM	Open End	US Equity Small Cap (Small Company)	B-	C+	B-	Up	Y	0
Columbia Disciplined Small Core Fund Institutional Class	SMCEX	NAS CM	Open End	US Equity Small Cap (Small Company)	B-	C+	B-	Up	Y	2,000
Columbia Disciplined Value Fund Advisor Class	COLEX	NAS CM	Open End	US Equity Large Cap Value (Growth)	B	B-	B	Up	Y	0
Columbia Disciplined Value Fund Class A	RLCAX	NAS CM	Open End	US Equity Large Cap Value (Growth)	B	B-	B	Up	Y	2,000
Columbia Disciplined Value Fund Class C	RDCCX	NAS CM	Open End	US Equity Large Cap Value (Growth)	B-	B-	B	Down	Y	2,000
Columbia Disciplined Value Fund Class K	RLCYX	NAS CM	Open End	US Equity Large Cap Value (Growth)	B	B-	B	Up		0
Columbia Disciplined Value Fund Class R	RLCOX	NAS CM	Open End	US Equity Large Cap Value (Growth)	B	B-	B	Up	Y	0
Columbia Disciplined Value Fund Class T	RLCWX	NAS CM	Open End	US Equity Large Cap Value (Growth)	B	B-	B	Up	Y	2,000
Columbia Disciplined Value Fund Class V	CVQTX	NAS CM	Open End	US Equity Large Cap Value (Growth)	B	B-	B	Up		2,000
Columbia Disciplined Value Fund Institutional 2 Class	COLVX	NAS CM	Open End	US Equity Large Cap Value (Growth)	B	B-	B	Up	Y	100,000

★ Expanded analysis of this fund is included in Section II.

	TOTAL RETURNS					PERFORMANCE				ASSETS		ASSET ALLOCATION & TURNOVER					BULL & BEAR		FEES		
Min Additional Investment	3-Month Total Return	6-Month Total Return	1-Year Total Return	3-Year Total Return	5-Year Total Return	Dividend Yield (TTM)	Expense Ratio	3-Yr Std Deviation	3-Year Beta	NAV	Total Assets (MIL)	%Cash	%Stocks	%Bonds	%Other	Turnover Ratio	Last Bull Market Total Return	Last Bear Market Total Return	Front End Fee (%)	Back End Fee (%)	Inception Date
	5.38	9.75	21.70	34.92	112.36	0.74	0.81	10.09	0.97	26.3	11,572	3	97	0	0	52	26.12	-18.05			Nov-12
	5.32	9.61	21.42	33.90	109.65	0.56	1.06	10.1	0.97	25.69	11,572	3	97	0	0	52	25.96	-18.19	5.75		Oct-98
	5.10	9.20	20.49	30.89	101.91	0	1.81	10.08	0.97	23.33	11,572	3	97	0	0	52	25.37	-18.44		1.00	Dec-02
	5.33	9.64	21.49	34.34	110.96	0.65	0.97	10.09	0.97	25.85	11,572	3	97	0	0	52	25.96	-18.11			Mar-11
	5.23	9.43	21.11	32.90	107.10	0.36	1.31	10.09	0.97	25.72	11,572	3	97	0	0	52	25.79	-18.25			Sep-10
	5.27	9.57	21.38	33.86	109.59	0.56	1.06	10.1	0.97	25.68	11,572	3	97	0	0	52	25.86	-18.13	2.50		Sep-10
	5.32	9.57	21.39	33.90	109.44	0.56	1.06	10.1	0.97	25.44	11,572	3	97	0	0	52	25.84	-18.14	5.75		Feb-93
	5.41	9.77	21.79	35.36	113.67	0.83	0.72	10.09	0.97	26.27	11,572	3	97	0	0	52	26.12	-18.05			Nov-12
	5.41	9.81	21.88	35.53	114.23	0.87	0.67	10.11	0.97	26.28	11,572	3	97	0	0	52	26.12	-18.05			Nov-12
	5.35	9.74	21.69	34.89	112.29	0.75	0.81	10.1	0.97	25.86	11,572	3	97	0	0	52	26.12	-18.05			Dec-92
	1.48	6.46	15.39	22.62	67.85	3.11	0.88	9.07	1.14	20.1	820.6	5	5	0	1	72	15.05	-16.72			Nov-12
	1.43	6.33	15.07	21.67	65.73	2.91	1.13	9.11	1.15	19.91	820.6	5	5	0	1	72	15.05	-16.72	5.75		Sep-87
	1.24	5.95	14.25	18.96	59.55	2.22	1.88	9.08	1.14	19.86	820.6	5	5	0	1	72	14.57	-16.97		1.00	Oct-96
	1.36	6.20	14.79	20.78	63.62	2.68	1.38	9.08	1.14	19.9	820.6	5	5	0	1	72	14.97	-16.81			Nov-11
	1.43	6.35	15.05	21.70	65.63	2.92	1.13	9.1	1.14	19.85	820.6	5	5	0	1	72	15.05	-16.72	2.50		Nov-11
	1.55	6.56	15.50	22.99	68.76	3.19	0.8	9.07	1.14	20.08	820.6	5	5	0	1	72	15.05	-16.72			Nov-12
	1.55	6.54	15.55	23.18	67.86	3.21	0.75	9.11	1.15	20.23	820.6	5	5	0	1	72	15.05	-16.72			Oct-14
	1.49	6.51	15.39	22.63	67.79	3.13	0.88	9.1	1.14	19.94	820.6	5	5	0	1	72	15.26	-16.66			May-99
	7.81	13.94	24.45	34.23	113.00	1.23	0.76	10.47	1.02	12.05	4,356	1	99	0	0	72	27.51	-14.71			Mar-13
	7.63	13.71	24.06	33.24	110.48	1.05	1.01	10.44	1.02	11.94	4,356	1	99	0	0	72	27.42	-14.62	5.75		Apr-03
	7.42	13.32	23.13	30.19	102.70	0.48	1.76	10.46	1.02	11.72	4,356	1	99	0	0	72	26.85	-14.84		1.00	Apr-03
	7.65	13.79	24.09	33.45	111.38	1.11	0.96	10.47	1.02	12.01	4,356	1	99	0	0	72	27.52	-14.71			Apr-03
	7.67	13.67	23.79	32.18	107.73	0.86	1.26	10.49	1.02	11.94	4,356	1	99	0	0	72	27.29	-14.78			Dec-06
	7.67	13.72	24.00	33.11	110.42	1.05	1.01	10.52	1.02	12.02	4,356	1	99	0	0	72	27.29	-14.54	2.50		Dec-06
	7.73	13.90	24.47	34.42	114.04	1.3	0.71	10.52	1.02	11.96	4,356	1	99	0	0	72	27.68	-14.42			Dec-06
	7.74	13.99	24.53	34.45	112.97	1.33	0.66	10.5	1.02	12.01	4,356	1	99	0	0	72	27.51	-14.71			Jun-15
	7.75	13.90	24.44	34.13	113.21	1.24	0.76	10.5	1.02	12	4,356	1	99	0	0	72	27.71	-14.69			Sep-10
	7.36	14.41	29.46	44.52	133.33	0.6	0.94	10.94	1	9.35	542.0	2	98	0	0	81	28.09	-15.85			Jun-15
	7.37	14.35	29.19	43.64	131.23	0.41	1.19	10.96	1	9.3	542.0	2	98	0	0	81	27.97	-15.89	5.75		May-07
	7.22	13.95	28.18	40.41	122.72	0	1.94	11.01	1	8.94	542.0	2	98	0	0	81	27.45	-16.17		1.00	May-07
	7.35	14.32	29.31	44.27	132.92	0.55	1.11	10.95	1	9.48	542.0	2	98	0	0	81	28.09	-15.85			May-07
	7.33	14.17	28.93	42.61	128.15	0.23	1.44	10.95	1	9.34	542.0	2	98	0	0	81	27.82	-16			May-07
	7.33	14.27	29.14	43.51	130.68	0.41	1.19	10.98	1	9.36	542.0	2	98	0	0	81	27.93	-15.85	2.50		Aug-08
	7.41	14.47	29.61	45.16	135.72	0.67	0.86	10.96	1	9.69	542.0	2	98	0	0	81	28.09	-15.85			Nov-12
	7.40	14.49	29.68	45.11	134.28	0.72	0.81	10.98	1	9.46	542.0	2	98	0	0	81	28.09	-15.85			Jun-15
	7.34	14.37	29.52	44.62	134.08	0.6	0.94	11	1	9.38	542.0	2	98	0	0	81	28.11	-15.8			Sep-10
	3.00	6.18	6.51	14.25	59.45	0.39	1.14	14.16	0.97	8.55	215.3	2	98	0	0	87	26.3	-23.61			Nov-12
	3.01	6.12	6.36	13.40	57.55	0.21	1.39	14.14	0.97	7.43	215.3	2	98	0	0	87	26.06	-23.6	5.75		Nov-98
	2.78	5.67	5.47	10.85	51.72	0	2.14	14.15	0.97	3.93	215.3	2	98	0	0	87	25.53	-23.86		1.00	Nov-02
	3.01	6.12	6.36	13.47	57.56	0.21	1.39	14.17	0.97	7.43	215.3	2	98	0	0	87	26.06	-23.6	2.50		Sep-10
	2.92	6.06	6.32	13.39	57.32	0.22	1.39	14.14	0.97	6.96	215.3	2	98	0	0	87	26.06	-23.65	5.75		Feb-93
	3.07	6.23	6.67	14.68	60.82	0.47	1	14.16	0.97	8.62	215.3	2	98	0	0	87	26.3	-23.61			Nov-12
	3.08	6.21	6.65	14.84	61.09	0.5	0.95	14.17	0.97	8.72	215.3	2	98	0	0	87	26.3	-23.61			Nov-12
	2.94	6.08	6.53	14.21	59.41	0.39	1.14	14.18	0.97	8.34	215.3	2	98	0	0	87	26.3	-23.61			Dec-92
	6.80	12.22	17.98	27.75	102.55	1.5	0.9	10.75	1.02	10.68	853.1	1	99	0	0	78	25.31	-18.51			Jun-15
	6.81	12.17	17.74	26.94	100.65	1.32	1.15	10.74	1.02	10.6	853.1	1	99	0	0	78	25.11	-18.56	5.75		Aug-08
	6.52	11.68	16.87	24.05	93.25	0.75	1.9	10.7	1.02	10.36	853.1	1	99	0	0	78	24.6	-18.93		1.00	Aug-08
	6.88	12.22	17.87	27.36	101.93	1.41	1.02	10.73	1.02	10.66	853.1	1	99	0	0	78	25.31	-18.51			Aug-08
	6.64	11.89	17.43	25.84	98.29	1.12	1.4	10.73	1.02	10.62	853.1	1	99	0	0	78	24.85	-18.66			Aug-08
	6.76	12.10	17.63	26.76	100.61	1.31	1.15	10.76	1.02	10.66	853.1	1	99	0	0	78	25.09	-18.54	2.50		Aug-08
	6.83	12.10	17.80	26.87	100.58	1.32	1.15	10.76	1.02	10.57	853.1	1	99	0	0	78	25.19	-18.58	5.75		Mar-11
	6.90	12.34	18.12	27.93	102.83	1.6	0.77	10.73	1.02	10.66	853.1	1	99	0	0	78	25.31	-18.51			Jun-15

	MARKET			FUND TYPE, CATEGORY & OBJECTIVE	RATINGS				MINIMUMS	
Fund Name	Ticker Symbol	Traded On	Fund Type	Category and (Prospectus Objective)	Overall Rating	Reward Rating	Risk Rating	Recent Up/ Downgrade	Open to New Investors	Min Initial Investment
Columbia Disciplined Value Fund Institutional 3 Class	COLYX	NAS CM	Open End	US Equity Large Cap Value (Growth)	B	B-	B	Up	Y	0
Columbia Disciplined Value Fund Institutional Class	CVQZX	NAS CM	Open End	US Equity Large Cap Value (Growth)	B	B-	B	Up	Y	2,000
Columbia Diversified Absolute Return Fund Advisor Class	CDUFX	NAS CM	Open End	Multialternative (Growth & Income)	C-	C-	C		Y	0
Columbia Diversified Absolute Return Fund Class A	CDUAX	NAS CM	Open End	Multialternative (Growth & Income)	C-	D+	C		Y	2,000
Columbia Diversified Absolute Return Fund Class C	CDUCX	NAS CM	Open End	Multialternative (Growth & Income)	C-	D+	C	Up	Y	2,000
Columbia Diversified Absolute Return Fund Class T	CDUWX	NAS CM	Open End	Multialternative (Growth & Income)	C	C-	C		Y	2,000
Columbia Diversified Absolute Return Fund Inst 2 Cls	CDUGX	NAS CM	Open End	Multialternative (Growth & Income)	C-	C-	C	Down	Y	100,000
Columbia Diversified Absolute Return Fund Inst 3 Cls	CDAYX	NAS CM	Open End	Multialternative (Growth & Income)	C-	C-	C	Down	Y	1,000,000
Columbia Diversified Absolute Return Fund Inst Cls	CDUZX	NAS CM	Open End	Multialternative (Growth & Income)	C-	C-	C	Down	Y	2,000
Columbia Diversified Equity Income Fund Advisor Class	RDERX	NAS CM	Open End	US Equity Large Cap Value (Equity-Income)	B	B	B-	Up	Y	2,000
Columbia Diversified Equity Income Fund Class A	INDZX	NAS CM	Open End	US Equity Large Cap Value (Equity-Income)	B	B	B	Up	Y	2,000
Columbia Diversified Equity Income Fund Class C	ADECX	NAS CM	Open End	US Equity Large Cap Value (Equity-Income)	B-	B-	B-	Down	Y	2,000
Columbia Diversified Equity Income Fund Class K	IDQYX	NAS CM	Open End	US Equity Large Cap Value (Equity-Income)	B	B	B	Up		0
Columbia Diversified Equity Income Fund Class R	RDEIX	NAS CM	Open End	US Equity Large Cap Value (Equity-Income)	B-	B-	B-	Down	Y	0
Columbia Diversified Equity Income Fund Class T	CDEWX	NAS CM	Open End	US Equity Large Cap Value (Equity-Income)	B-	B	B-	Down	Y	2,000
Columbia Diversified Equity Income Fund Inst 2 Cls	RSEDX	NAS CM	Open End	US Equity Large Cap Value (Equity-Income)	B	B	B-	Up	Y	0
Columbia Diversified Equity Income Fund Inst 3 Cls	CDEYX	NAS CM	Open End	US Equity Large Cap Value (Equity-Income)	B	B	B-	Up	Y	1,000,000
Columbia Diversified Equity Income Fund Institutional Cls	CDVZX	NAS CM	Open End	US Equity Large Cap Value (Equity-Income)	B	B	B	Up	Y	2,000
Columbia Dividend Income Fund Advisor Class	CVIRX	NAS CM	Open End	US Equity Large Cap Value (Equity-Income)	B	B	B		Y	2,000
Columbia Dividend Income Fund Class A	LBSAX	NAS CM	Open End	US Equity Large Cap Value (Equity-Income)	B	B	B		Y	2,000
Columbia Dividend Income Fund Class C	LBSCX	NAS CM	Open End	US Equity Large Cap Value (Equity-Income)	B-	B-	B	Down	Y	2,000
Columbia Dividend Income Fund Class R	CDIRX	NAS CM	Open End	US Equity Large Cap Value (Equity-Income)	B	B-	B		Y	0
Columbia Dividend Income Fund Class T	CDVWX	NAS CM	Open End	US Equity Large Cap Value (Equity-Income)	B	B	B		Y	2,000
Columbia Dividend Income Fund Class V	GEQAX	NAS CM	Open End	US Equity Large Cap Value (Equity-Income)	B	B	B			2,000
Columbia Dividend Income Fund Institutional 2 Class	CDDRX	NAS CM	Open End	US Equity Large Cap Value (Equity-Income)	B	B	B		Y	0
Columbia Dividend Income Fund Institutional 3 Class	CDDYX	NAS CM	Open End	US Equity Large Cap Value (Equity-Income)	B	B	B		Y	1,000,000
Columbia Dividend Income Fund Institutional Class	GSFTX	NAS CM	Open End	US Equity Large Cap Value (Equity-Income)	B	B	B		Y	2,000
Columbia Dividend Opportunity Fund Advisor Class	CDORX	NAS CM	Open End	US Equity Large Cap Value (Equity-Income)	B-	B-	B	Down	Y	2,000
Columbia Dividend Opportunity Fund Class A	INUTX	NAS CM	Open End	US Equity Large Cap Value (Equity-Income)	B-	C+	B	Down	Y	2,000
Columbia Dividend Opportunity Fund Class C	ACUIX	NAS CM	Open End	US Equity Large Cap Value (Equity-Income)	B-	C+	B	Down	Y	2,000
Columbia Dividend Opportunity Fund Class K	RSORX	NAS CM	Open End	US Equity Large Cap Value (Equity-Income)	B-	C+	B	Down		0
Columbia Dividend Opportunity Fund Class R	RSOOX	NAS CM	Open End	US Equity Large Cap Value (Equity-Income)	B-	C+	B	Down	Y	0
Columbia Dividend Opportunity Fund Class T	CDOWX	NAS CM	Open End	US Equity Large Cap Value (Equity-Income)	B-	C+	B	Down	Y	2,000
Columbia Dividend Opportunity Fund Institutional 2 Class	RSDFX	NAS CM	Open End	US Equity Large Cap Value (Equity-Income)	B-	B-	B	Down	Y	0
Columbia Dividend Opportunity Fund Institutional 3 Class	CDOYX	NAS CM	Open End	US Equity Large Cap Value (Equity-Income)	B-	B-	B	Down	Y	1,000,000
Columbia Dividend Opportunity Fund Institutional Class	CDOZX	NAS CM	Open End	US Equity Large Cap Value (Equity-Income)	B-	B-	B	Down	Y	2,000
Columbia Emerging Markets Fund Advisor Class	CEMHX	NAS CM	Open End	Emerging Markets Equity (Div Emerging Mkts)	B	A-	C	Up	Y	0
Columbia Emerging Markets Fund Class A	EEMAX	NAS CM	Open End	Emerging Markets Equity (Div Emerging Mkts)	B	A-	C	Up	Y	2,000
Columbia Emerging Markets Fund Class C	EEMCX	NAS CM	Open End	Emerging Markets Equity (Div Emerging Mkts)	B	B+	C	Up	Y	2,000
Columbia Emerging Markets Fund Class K	CEKMX	NAS CM	Open End	Emerging Markets Equity (Div Emerging Mkts)	B	A-	C	Up		0
Columbia Emerging Markets Fund Class R	CEMRX	NAS CM	Open End	Emerging Markets Equity (Div Emerging Mkts)	B	B+	C	Up	Y	0
Columbia Emerging Markets Fund Class T	CEMWX	NAS CM	Open End	Emerging Markets Equity (Div Emerging Mkts)	B	A-	C	Up	Y	2,000
Columbia Emerging Markets Fund Institutional 2 Class	CEKRX	NAS CM	Open End	Emerging Markets Equity (Div Emerging Mkts)	B	A	C	Up	Y	100,000
Columbia Emerging Markets Fund Institutional 3 Class	CEKYX	NAS CM	Open End	Emerging Markets Equity (Div Emerging Mkts)	B	A	C	Up	Y	0
Columbia Emerging Markets Fund Institutional Class	UMEMX	NAS CM	Open End	Emerging Markets Equity (Div Emerging Mkts)	B	A-	C	Up	Y	2,000
Columbia European Equity Fund Advisor Class	CADJX	NAS CM	Open End	Europe Equity Large Cap (Europe Stock)	B-	B-	C+	Up	Y	0
Columbia European Equity Fund Class A	AXEAX	NAS CM	Open End	Europe Equity Large Cap (Europe Stock)	C+	C+	C+	Up	Y	2,000
Columbia European Equity Fund Class C	REECX	NAS CM	Open End	Europe Equity Large Cap (Europe Stock)	C+	C+	C+	Up	Y	2,000
Columbia European Equity Fund Class K	CEQRX	NAS CM	Open End	Europe Equity Large Cap (Europe Stock)	C+	B-	C+	Up		0
Columbia European Equity Fund Class T	CEEWX	NAS CM	Open End	Europe Equity Large Cap (Europe Stock)	C+	B-	C+	Up	Y	2,000
Columbia European Equity Fund Institutional 2 Class	CADKX	NAS CM	Open End	Europe Equity Large Cap (Europe Stock)	B-	B-	C+	Up	Y	100,000
Columbia European Equity Fund Institutional 3 Class	CEEUX	NAS CM	Open End	Europe Equity Large Cap (Europe Stock)	B-	B-	C+	Up	Y	0

★ Expanded analysis of this fund is included in Section II.

	TOTAL RETURNS					PERFORMANCE				ASSETS		ASSET ALLOCATION & TURNOVER					BULL & BEAR		FEES		
Min Additional Investment	3-Month Total Return	6-Month Total Return	1-Year Total Return	3-Year Total Return	5-Year Total Return	Dividend Yield (TTM)	Expense Ratio	3-Yr Std Deviation	3-Year Beta	NAV	Total Assets (MIL)	%Cash	%Stocks	%Bonds	%Other	Turnover Ratio	Last Bull Market Total Return	Last Bear Market Total Return	Front End Fee (%)	Back End Fee (%)	Inception Date
	6.94	12.37	18.26	28.20	103.25	1.62	0.71	10.77	1.03	10.68	853.1	1	99	0	0	78	25.31	-18.51			Jun-15
	6.89	12.21	18.08	27.85	103.15	1.5	0.9	10.77	1.03	10.69	853.1	1	99	0	0	78	25.18	-18.47			Sep-10
	0.62	0.83	2.55			0	1.4			9.63	78.2	77	2	11	4	135					Feb-15
	0.52	0.63	2.35			0	1.65			9.57	78.2	77	2	11	4	135			5.75		Feb-15
	0.32	0.32	1.62			0	2.4			9.39	78.2	77	2	11	4	135				1.00	Feb-15
	0.61	0.72	4.27			0	1.65			9.76	78.2	77	2	11	4	135			2.50		Feb-15
	0.62	0.83	2.87			0	1.3			9.67	78.2	77	2	11	4	135					Feb-15
	0.62	0.83	3.19				1.25			9.65	78.2	77	2	11	4	135					Mar-17
	0.51	0.72	3.08			0	1.4			9.68	78.2	77	2	11	4	135					Feb-15
	5.79	9.95	16.87	30.20	95.73	1.27	0.77	10.6	1.01	14.53	2,419	2	98	0	0	31	22.71	-21.68			Dec-06
	5.72	9.81	16.65	29.30	93.37	1.05	1.02	10.59	1.01	14.55	2,419	2	98	0	0	31	22.75	-21.6	5.75		Oct-90
	5.53	9.42	15.74	26.42	86.20	0.39	1.77	10.59	1.01	14.52	2,419	2	98	0	0	31	22.22	-21.88		1.00	Jun-00
	5.73	9.84	16.63	29.51	94.13	1.11	0.96	10.58	1.01	14.55	2,419	2	98	0	0	31	22.83	-21.5			Mar-95
	5.69	9.74	16.39	28.35	91.05	0.83	1.27	10.62	1.02	14.46	2,419	2	98	0	0	31	22.47	-21.62			Dec-06
	5.70	9.77	16.50	29.05	93.00	1.03	1.02	10.59	1.01	14.57	2,419	2	98	0	0	31	22.63	-21.49	2.50		Dec-06
	5.80	9.98	17.01	30.58	96.76	1.33	0.71	10.57	1.01	14.55	2,419	2	98	0	0	31	22.99	-21.39			Dec-06
	5.82	10.04	17.04	30.71	97.33	1.36	0.67	10.6	1.01	14.7	2,419	2	98	0	0	31	22.75	-21.6			Nov-12
	5.79	9.96	16.88	30.22	95.64	1.27	0.77	10.57	1.01	14.52	2,419	2	98	0	0	31	22.95	-21.47			Sep-10
	6.92	11.61	20.80	36.29	102.48	1.65	0.73	9.33	0.88	22.41	11,269	2	98	0	0	16	22.72	-12.43			Nov-12
	6.87	11.41	20.46	35.27	99.78	1.46	0.98	9.33	0.88	22.04	11,269	2	98	0	0	16	22.59	-12.56	5.75		Nov-02
	6.63	11.03	19.52	32.24	92.52	0.84	1.73	9.33	0.88	21.37	11,269	2	98	0	0	16	22.07	-12.84		1.00	Nov-02
	6.80	11.31	20.15	34.31	97.47	1.25	1.23	9.34	0.88	22.06	11,269	2	98	0	0	16	22.42	-12.66			Mar-08
	6.87	11.47	20.47	35.29	99.75	1.46	0.98	9.3	0.88	22.03	11,269	2	98	0	0	16	22.6	-12.55	2.50		Sep-10
	6.87	11.46	20.45	35.24	99.64	1.46	0.98	9.33	0.88	22.05	11,269	2	98	0	0	16	22.54	-12.51	5.75		Mar-98
	6.95	11.61	20.88	36.82	103.72	1.75	0.64	9.34	0.88	22.39	11,269	2	98	0	0	16	22.72	-12.43			Nov-12
	6.95	11.66	20.95	37.02	104.27	1.78	0.59	9.31	0.88	22.42	11,269	2	98	0	0	16	22.72	-12.43			Nov-12
	6.93	11.59	20.74	36.32	102.42	1.68	0.73	9.33	0.88	22.06	11,269	2	98	0	0	16	22.72	-12.43			Mar-98
	5.57	8.87	14.55	25.85	78.52	3.73	0.73	9.5	1	9.86	3,781	0	98	0	0	65	21.26	-14.28			Nov-12
	5.49	8.79	14.29	24.85	76.40	3.56	0.98	9.56	1.01	9.69	3,781	0	98	0	0	65	21.26	-14.28	5.75		Aug-88
	5.41	8.45	13.50	22.19	70.08	2.92	1.73	9.57	1.01	9.49	3,781	0	98	0	0	65	20.88	-14.6		1.00	Jun-00
	5.58	8.87	14.39	25.26	77.37	3.6	0.92	9.56	1.01	9.75	3,781	0	98	0	0	65	21.4	-14.17			Mar-95
	5.53	8.65	14.01	24.06	74.23	3.33	1.23	9.56	1.01	9.69	3,781	0	98	0	0	65	21.09	-14.31			Aug-08
	5.59	8.77	14.26	24.94	76.35	3.55	0.98	9.54	1.01	9.71	3,781	0	98	0	0	65	21.31	-14.28	2.50		Dec-06
	5.64	8.89	14.55	26.19	79.57	3.83	0.67	9.5	1	9.75	3,781	0	98	0	0	65	21.58	-14.17			Aug-08
	5.69	9.02	14.75	26.40	79.93	3.82	0.62	9.55	1.01	9.89	3,781	0	98	0	0	65	21.26	-14.28			Nov-12
	5.53	8.88	14.51	25.80	78.65	3.77	0.73	9.57	1.01	9.73	3,781	0	98	0	0	65	21.5	-14.22			Sep-10
	7.12	19.41	46.81	39.89	35.77	0	1.36	14.16	0.84	13.9	1,455	1	98	0	1	51	18.23	-25.72			Mar-13
	7.11	19.23	46.52	38.80	34.12	0	1.61	14.13	0.84	13.68	1,455	1	98	0	1	51	18.01	-25.8	5.75		Sep-07
	6.84	18.80	45.50	35.74	29.11	0	2.36	14.14	0.84	12.95	1,455	1	98	0	1	51	17.51	-25.97		1.00	Sep-07
	7.11	19.36	46.66	39.39	35.18	0	1.49	14.16	0.84	13.75	1,455	1	98	0	1	51	18.23	-25.72			Feb-13
	7.04	19.11	46.16	37.81	32.41	0	1.86	14.18	0.84	13.52	1,455	1	98	0	1	51	18.04	-25.83			Sep-10
	7.02	19.24	46.40	38.83	33.99	0	1.61	14.15	0.84	13.67	1,455	1	98	0	1	51	18.01	-25.8	2.50		Sep-10
	7.17	19.56	47.03	40.52	36.81	0	1.24	14.13	0.84	13.89	1,455	1	98	0	1	51	18.23	-25.72			Nov-12
	7.16	19.49	47.08	40.73	37.18	0	1.19	14.14	0.84	13.95	1,455	1	98	0	1	51	18.23	-25.72			Nov-12
	7.17	19.45	46.94	39.97	35.82	0	1.36	14.16	0.84	13.81	1,455	1	98	0	1	51	18.23	-25.72			Jan-98
	1.37	9.13	25.80	19.27	44.00	1.93	1.1	12.44	0.93	7.28	402.0	1	98	0	1	55	17.93	-25.49			Jan-14
	1.45	9.03	25.61	18.47	42.39	1.7	1.35	12.34	0.92	7.32	402.0	1	98	0	1	55	17.48	-25.56	5.75		Jun-00
	1.18	8.63	24.77	15.82	37.19	1.09	2.1	12.41	0.92	7.15	402.0	1	98	0	1	55	16.8	-25.72		1.00	Jun-00
	1.51	9.13	25.81	18.76	43.24	1.8	1.27	12.38	0.92	7.29	402.0	1	98	0	1	55	17.93	-25.49			Jun-00
	1.46	9.08	25.75	18.46	42.70	1.71	1.35	12.45	0.92	7.29	402.0	1	98	0	1	55	17.76	-25.56	2.50		Jun-12
	1.43	9.14	26.11	19.68	44.74	2	1.02	12.38	0.92	7.33	402.0	1	98	0	1	55	17.93	-25.49			Jan-14
	1.51	9.29	26.14	19.41	44.02	2.11	0.95	12.39	0.92	7.14	402.0	1	98	0	1	55	17.93	-25.48			Mar-16

	MARKET		FUND TYPE, CATEGORY & OBJECTIVE		RATINGS					MINIMUMS
Fund Name	Ticker Symbol	Traded On	Fund Type	Category and (Prospectus Objective)	Overall Rating	Reward Rating	Risk Rating	Recent Up/ Downgrade	Open to New Investors	Min Initial Investment
Columbia European Equity Fund Institutional Class	CEEZX	NAS CM	Open End	Europe Equity Large Cap (Europe Stock)	B-	B-	C+	Up	Y	2,000
Columbia Flexible Capital Income Fund Advisor Class	CFCRX	NAS CM	Open End	Moderate Alloc (Income)	B-	B-	B-	Down	Y	2,000
Columbia Flexible Capital Income Fund Class A	CFIAX	NAS CM	Open End	Moderate Alloc (Income)	B-	B-	B-	Up	Y	2,000
Columbia Flexible Capital Income Fund Class C	CFIGX	NAS CM	Open End	Moderate Alloc (Income)	C+	C+	C+	Down	Y	2,000
Columbia Flexible Capital Income Fund Class R	CFIRX	NAS CM	Open End	Moderate Alloc (Income)	B-	B-	B-	Up	Y	0
Columbia Flexible Capital Income Fund Class T	CFIWX	NAS CM	Open End	Moderate Alloc (Income)	B-	B-	B-	Down	Y	2,000
Columbia Flexible Capital Income Fund Institutional 2 Cls	CFXRX	NAS CM	Open End	Moderate Alloc (Income)	B-	B-	B-	Down	Y	0
Columbia Flexible Capital Income Fund Institutional 3 Cls	CFCYX	NAS CM	Open End	Moderate Alloc (Income)	B-	B-	B-	Down	Y	1,000,000
Columbia Flexible Capital Income Fund Institutional Class	CFIZX	NAS CM	Open End	Moderate Alloc (Income)	B-	B-	B-	Down	Y	2,000
Columbia Global Dividend Opportunity Fund Advisor Class	CGOLX	NAS CM	Open End	Global Equity (Equity-Income)	C+	C+	C+		Y	0
Columbia Global Dividend Opportunity Fund Class A	CSVAX	NAS CM	Open End	Global Equity (Equity-Income)	C+	C+	C+		Y	2,000
Columbia Global Dividend Opportunity Fund Class C	CSRCX	NAS CM	Open End	Global Equity (Equity-Income)	C+	C+	C+	Up	Y	2,000
Columbia Global Dividend Opportunity Fund Class R	CSGRX	NAS CM	Open End	Global Equity (Equity-Income)	C+	C+	C+		Y	0
Columbia Global Dividend Opportunity Fund Class T	CTVWX	NAS CM	Open End	Global Equity (Equity-Income)	C+	C+	C+		Y	2,000
Columbia Global Dividend Opp Fund Inst 2 Cls	CADPX	NAS CM	Open End	Global Equity (Equity-Income)	C+	C+	B-	Down	Y	100,000
Columbia Global Dividend Opp Fund Inst 3 Cls	CLSYX	NAS CM	Open End	Global Equity (Equity-Income)	C+	C+	B-	Down	Y	0
Columbia Global Dividend Opp Fund Inst Cls	CSVFX	NAS CM	Open End	Global Equity (Equity-Income)	C+	C+	C+		Y	2,000
Columbia Global Energy & Natural Resources Fund Adv Cls	CENRX	NAS CM	Open End	Natl Resources Sec Equity (Natl Res)	C	C	C	Up	Y	0
Columbia Global Energy And Natural Resources Fund Class A	EENAX	NAS CM	Open End	Natl Resources Sec Equity (Natl Res)	C	C	C	Up	Y	2,000
Columbia Global Energy And Natural Resources Fund Class C	EENCX	NAS CM	Open End	Natl Resources Sec Equity (Natl Res)	C	C	C	Up	Y	2,000
Columbia Global Energy And Natural Resources Fund Class K	CEGFX	NAS CM	Open End	Natl Resources Sec Equity (Natl Res)	C	C	C	Up		0
Columbia Global Energy And Natural Resources Fund Class R	CETRX	NAS CM	Open End	Natl Resources Sec Equity (Natl Res)	C	C	C	Up	Y	0
Columbia Global Energy & Natural Resources Fund Inst 2 Cls	CNRRX	NAS CM	Open End	Natl Resources Sec Equity (Natl Res)	C	C	C	Up	Y	100,000
Columbia Global Energy & Natural Resources Fund Inst 3 Cls	CGEYX	NAS CM	Open End	Natl Resources Sec Equity (Natl Res)	C	C	C	Up	Y	0
Columbia Global Energy & Natural Resources Fund Inst Cls	UMESX	NAS CM	Open End	Natl Resources Sec Equity (Natl Res)	C	C	C	Up	Y	2,000
Columbia Global Equity Value Fund Advisor Class	RSEVX	NAS CM	Open End	Global Equity (Growth & Income)	C+	B-	C+	Down	Y	2,000
Columbia Global Equity Value Fund Class A	IEVAX	NAS CM	Open End	Global Equity (Growth & Income)	C+	B-	C+	Down	Y	2,000
Columbia Global Equity Value Fund Class C	REVCX	NAS CM	Open End	Global Equity (Growth & Income)	C+	C+	C+		Y	2,000
Columbia Global Equity Value Fund Class K	AEVYX	NAS CM	Open End	Global Equity (Growth & Income)	C+	B-	C+	Down		0
Columbia Global Equity Value Fund Class R	REVRX	NAS CM	Open End	Global Equity (Growth & Income)	C+	C+	C+	Down	Y	0
Columbia Global Equity Value Fund Class T	CEVWX	NAS CM	Open End	Global Equity (Growth & Income)	C+	B-	C+	Down	Y	2,000
Columbia Global Equity Value Fund Institutional 2 Class	RSEYX	NAS CM	Open End	Global Equity (Growth & Income)	C+	B-	C+	Down	Y	0
Columbia Global Equity Value Fund Institutional 3 Class	CEVYX	NAS CM	Open End	Global Equity (Growth & Income)	C+	B-	C+	Down	Y	1,000,000
Columbia Global Equity Value Fund Institutional Class	CEVZX	NAS CM	Open End	Global Equity (Growth & Income)	C+	B-	C+	Down	Y	2,000
Columbia Global Infrastructure Fund Advisor Class	CRRIX	NAS CM	Open End	Other Sector Equity (Utility)	C+	C+	C+	Down	Y	2,000
Columbia Global Infrastructure Fund Class A	RRIAX	NAS CM	Open End	Other Sector Equity (Utility)	C+	C+	C+	Down	Y	2,000
Columbia Global Infrastructure Fund Class C	RRICX	NAS CM	Open End	Other Sector Equity (Utility)	C+	C+	C+	Down	Y	2,000
Columbia Global Infrastructure Fund Class K	RRIYX	NAS CM	Open End	Other Sector Equity (Utility)	C+	C+	C+	Down		0
Columbia Global Infrastructure Fund Class R	RRIRX	NAS CM	Open End	Other Sector Equity (Utility)	C+	C+	C+	Down	Y	0
Columbia Global Infrastructure Fund Institutional 2 Class	RRIZX	NAS CM	Open End	Other Sector Equity (Utility)	C+	C+	C+	Down	Y	0
Columbia Global Infrastructure Fund Institutional 3 Class	CGLYX	NAS CM	Open End	Other Sector Equity (Utility)	C+	C+	C+	Down	Y	1,000,000
Columbia Global Infrastructure Fund Institutional Class	CRIZX	NAS CM	Open End	Other Sector Equity (Utility)	C+	C+	C+	Down	Y	2,000
Columbia Global Opportunities Fund Advisor Class	CSDRX	NAS CM	Open End	Alloc (Growth & Income)	B	C+	B+	Up	Y	0
Columbia Global Opportunities Fund Class A	IMRFX	NAS CM	Open End	Alloc (Growth & Income)	B	C+	B+	Up	Y	2,000
Columbia Global Opportunities Fund Class C	RSSCX	NAS CM	Open End	Alloc (Growth & Income)	B-	C+	B+	Down	Y	2,000
Columbia Global Opportunities Fund Class K	IDRYX	NAS CM	Open End	Alloc (Growth & Income)	B	C+	B+	Up		0
Columbia Global Opportunities Fund Class R	CSARX	NAS CM	Open End	Alloc (Growth & Income)	B	C+	B+	Up	Y	0
Columbia Global Opportunities Fund Class T	CGOPX	NAS CM	Open End	Alloc (Growth & Income)	B	C+	B+	Up	Y	2,000
Columbia Global Opportunities Fund Institutional 2 Class	CLNRX	NAS CM	Open End	Alloc (Growth & Income)	B	C+	B+	Up	Y	100,000
Columbia Global Opportunities Fund Institutional 3 Class	CGOYX	NAS CM	Open End	Alloc (Growth & Income)	B	C+	B+	Up	Y	0
Columbia Global Opportunities Fund Institutional Class	CSAZX	NAS CM	Open End	Alloc (Growth & Income)	B	C+	B+	Up	Y	2,000
Columbia Global Strategic Equity Fund Advisor Class	CWPRX	NAS CM	Open End	Global Equity (Growth)	B-	B	B-	Down	Y	2,000

★ Expanded analysis of this fund is included in Section II.

	TOTAL RETURNS					PERFORMANCE				ASSETS		ASSET ALLOCATION & TURNOVER					BULL & BEAR		FEES		
Min Additional Investment	3-Month Total Return	6-Month Total Return	1-Year Total Return	3-Year Total Return	5-Year Total Return	Dividend Yield (TTM)	Expense Ratio	3-Yr Std Deviation	3-Year Beta	NAV	Total Assets (MIL)	%Cash	%Stocks	%Bonds	%Other	Turnover Ratio	Last Bull Market Total Return	Last Bear Market Total Return	Front End Fee (%)	Back End Fee (%)	Inception Date
	1.50	9.12	25.98	19.22	44.27	1.91	1.1	12.42	0.92	7.29	402.0	1	98	0	1	55	17.46	-25.37			Sep-10
	2.62	6.89	13.63	26.20	57.14	4.28	0.9	8.55		13.11	552.5	1	37	28	1	71	19.03				Nov-12
	2.57	6.81	13.46	25.36	55.27	4.08	1.15	8.55		13.02	552.5	1	37	28	1	71	18.79		5.75		Jul-11
	2.39	6.36	12.60	22.51	49.44	3.4	1.9	8.54		12.95	552.5	1	37	28	1	71	18.35			1.00	Jul-11
	2.51	6.59	13.09	24.34	53.19	3.85	1.4	8.52		13.01	552.5	1	37	28	1	71	18.64				Jul-11
	2.57	6.72	13.37	25.27	55.10	4.09	1.15	8.55		13.02	552.5	1	37	28	1	71	18.89		2.50		Jul-11
	2.62	6.90	13.66	26.53	57.61	4.32	0.86	8.53		13.12	552.5	1	37	28	1	71	19.03				Nov-12
	2.59	6.88	13.80	26.36	57.29		0.81	8.54		12.96	552.5	1	37	28	1	71	19.03				Mar-17
	2.64	6.86	13.65	26.20	57.09	4.31	0.9	8.54		13.01	552.5	1	37	28	1	71	19.03				Jul-11
	4.75	8.39	20.15	17.87	44.96	3.17	1.1	9.81	0.95	19.58	611.4	2	98	0	0	43	23.48	-24.42			Mar-13
	4.73	8.27	19.83	17.01	43.18	2.97	1.35	9.78	0.95	19.43	611.4	2	98	0	0	43	23.3	-24.49	5.75		Nov-02
	4.49	7.86	18.90	14.43	37.92	2.43	2.1	9.79	0.95	18.22	611.4	2	98	0	0	43	22.76	-24.76		1.00	Oct-03
	4.61	8.15	19.56	16.16	41.45	2.74	1.6	9.8	0.95	19.41	611.4	2	98	0	0	43	23.09	-24.58			Sep-10
	4.67	8.28	19.84	17.12	43.47	2.97	1.35	9.82	0.95	19.42	611.4	2	98	0	0	43	23.19	-24.43	2.50		Sep-10
	4.83	8.47	20.35	18.46	45.91	3.33	0.96	9.81	0.95	19.44	611.4	2	98	0	0	43	23.48	-24.42			Jan-14
	4.78	8.49	20.37	18.62	46.69	3.36	0.91	9.82	0.95	19.47	611.4	2	98	0	0	43	23.58	-24.42			Jul-09
	4.78	8.44	20.12	17.89	44.98	3.18	1.1	9.81	0.95	19.49	611.4	2	98	0	0	43	23.48	-24.42			Nov-00
	7.58	17.02	12.83	10.52	15.79	1.83	1.1	16.25		20.37	240.1	1	99	0	0	19	17.6	-30.41			Nov-12
	7.50	16.85	12.48	9.63	14.30	1.68	1.35	16.24		19.78	240.1	1	99	0	0	19	17.43	-30.51	5.75		Sep-07
	7.30	16.40	11.67	7.25	10.11	1.12	2.1	16.23		18.74	240.1	1	99	0	0	19	16.95	-30.71		1.00	Sep-07
	7.52	16.94	12.67	10.16	15.26	1.77	1.2	16.26		19.97	240.1	1	99	0	0	19	17.51	-30.45			Mar-11
	7.46	16.75	12.28	8.87	12.93	1.48	1.6	16.26		19.66	240.1	1	99	0	0	19	17.31	-30.58			Sep-10
	7.65	17.10	12.99	11.07	16.75	1.95	0.95	16.22		20.46	240.1	1	99	0	0	19	17.6	-30.41			Nov-12
	7.64	17.15	12.98	10.70	15.96		0.9	16.26		19.84	240.1	1	99	0	0	19	17.6	-30.41			Mar-17
	7.61	17.03	12.82	10.54	15.80	1.86	1.1	16.26		20.02	240.1	1	99	0	0	19	17.6	-30.41			Dec-92
	5.25	11.12	22.11	21.90	75.30	1.99	0.93	11.08	1.03	14.27	859.5	1	99	0	0	36	23.23	-22.35			Dec-06
	5.20	11.03	21.91	21.00	73.17	1.78	1.18	11.05	1.02	14.22	859.5	1	99	0	0	36	23.23	-22.28	5.75		Mar-95
	4.99	10.58	20.89	18.36	66.70	1.14	1.93	11.06	1.02	14.07	859.5	1	99	0	0	36	22.74	-22.55		1.00	Jun-00
	5.20	11.03	21.93	21.44	74.23	1.86	1.07	11.06	1.02	14.27	859.5	1	99	0	0	36	23.36	-22.28			Mar-95
	5.22	10.91	21.55	20.13	71.06	1.56	1.43	11.08	1.03	14.2	859.5	1	99	0	0	36	23.09	-22.35			Dec-06
	5.25	11.04	21.85	21.06	73.17	1.78	1.18	11.06	1.02	14.32	859.5	1	99	0	0	36	23.09	-22.34	2.50		Dec-06
	5.30	11.23	22.25	22.36	76.22	2.09	0.82	11.05	1.02	14.2	859.5	1	99	0	0	36	23.56	-22.15			Dec-06
	5.36	11.20	22.33	22.61	76.88	2.18	0.79	11.05	1.02	13.86	859.5	1	99	0	0	36	23.36	-22.28			Feb-13
	5.26	11.16	22.19	21.97	75.27	1.99	0.93	11.08	1.03	14.23	859.5	1	99	0	0	36	23.5	-22.2			Sep-10
	3.03	7.60	17.31	13.49	77.98	2.29	0.96	9.5	0.71	13.54	270.2	4	86	6	1	60	30.31	-32.66			Mar-13
	2.96	7.41	17.07	12.59	75.62	2.15	1.21	9.51	0.71	13.17	270.2	4	86	6	1	60	29.97	-32.77	5.75		Feb-09
	3.09	7.60	17.38	12.99	73.48	2.52	1.96	9.49	0.71	12.28	270.2	4	86	6	1	60	29.39	-32.96		1.00	Feb-09
	2.97	7.47	17.08	12.89	76.35	2.21	1.15	9.52	0.71	13.26	270.2	4	86	6	1	60	30.12	-32.73			Feb-09
	2.87	7.28	16.72	11.78	73.40	1.99	1.46	9.47	0.71	12.8	270.2	4	86	6	1	60	29.81	-32.82			Feb-09
	2.99	7.60	17.38	13.74	78.54	2.38	0.9	9.49	0.71	13.43	270.2	4	86	6	1	60	30.31	-32.66			Feb-09
	3.06	7.69	17.40	13.75	78.57		0.84	9.48	0.71	13.39	270.2	4	86	6	1	60	30.31	-32.66			Mar-17
	3.06	7.59	17.37	13.45	77.79	2.31	0.96	9.49	0.71	13.43	270.2	4	86	6	1	60	30.14	-32.66			Sep-10
	3.98	8.56	18.42	23.47	42.64	2.56	0.95	6.42		13.82	628.7	24	59	17	0	103	17.09	-11.78			Nov-12
	3.93	8.45	18.17	22.62	41.08	2.37	1.2	6.41		13.72	628.7	24	59	17	0	103	17.09	-11.78	5.75		Jan-85
	3.68	7.99	17.28	19.85	35.84	1.79	1.95	6.38		13.23	628.7	24	59	17	0	103	16.71	-12.2		1.00	Jun-00
	3.92	8.50	18.18	22.92	41.81	2.43	1.15	6.43		13.78	628.7	24	59	17	0	103	17.26	-11.69			Mar-95
	3.82	8.29	17.88	21.62	39.15	2.18	1.45	6.44		13.58	628.7	24	59	17	0	103	16.99	-11.9			Dec-06
	3.95	8.49	18.16	22.41	40.72	2.38	1.2	6.4		13.66	628.7	24	59	17	0	103	17.09	-11.78	2.50		Jun-14
	4.05	8.61	18.54	23.89	43.65	2.61	0.9	6.43		13.87	628.7	24	59	17	0	103	17.09	-11.78			Nov-12
	3.99	8.57	18.37	22.83	41.32		0.85	6.42		13.8	628.7	24	59	17	0	103	17.09	-11.78			Mar-17
	3.99	8.58	18.47	23.53	42.93	2.56	0.95	6.41		13.79	628.7	24	59	17	0	103	17.38	-11.72			Sep-10
	5.77	12.57	27.86	31.50	82.65	0.95	1.02	10.15	0.94	16.22	690.5	2	94	0	0	54	22.64	-19.97			Nov-12

Fund Name	Ticker Symbol	MARKET Traded On	Fund Type	FUND TYPE, CATEGORY & OBJECTIVE Category and (Prospectus Objective)	RATINGS Overall Rating	Reward Rating	Risk Rating	Recent Up/ Downgrade	Open to New Investors	MINIMUMS Min Initial Investment
Columbia Global Strategic Equity Fund Class A	NLGIX	NAS CM	Open End	Global Equity (Growth)	B	B-	B	Up	Y	2,000
Columbia Global Strategic Equity Fund Class C	NLGCX	NAS CM	Open End	Global Equity (Growth)	B	B-	B	Up	Y	2,000
Columbia Global Strategic Equity Fund Class K	CGRUX	NAS CM	Open End	Global Equity (Growth)	B-	B-	B-	Down		0
Columbia Global Strategic Equity Fund Class R	CLGRX	NAS CM	Open End	Global Equity (Growth)	B-	B-	C+	Down	Y	0
Columbia Global Strategic Equity Fund Institutional 2 Cls	CGPRX	NAS CM	Open End	Global Equity (Growth)	B	B	B	Up	Y	0
Columbia Global Strategic Equity Fund Institutional 3 Cls	CGSYX	NAS CM	Open End	Global Equity (Growth)	B-	B	B-	Down	Y	1,000,000
Columbia Global Strategic Equity Fund Institutional Class	NGPAX	NAS CM	Open End	Global Equity (Growth)	B	B	B	Up	Y	2,000
Columbia Global Technology Growth Fund Advisor Class	CTYRX	NAS CM	Open End	Technology Sector Equity (Technology)	A-	A+	B		Y	0
Columbia Global Technology Growth Fund Class A	CTCAX	NAS CM	Open End	Technology Sector Equity (Technology)	A-	A+	B		Y	2,000
Columbia Global Technology Growth Fund Class C	CTHCX	NAS CM	Open End	Technology Sector Equity (Technology)	A-	A+	B		Y	2,000
Columbia Global Technology Growth Fund Institutional 2 Cls	CTHRX	NAS CM	Open End	Technology Sector Equity (Technology)	A-	A+	B		Y	100,000
Columbia Global Technology Growth Fund Institutional 3 Cls	CGTUX	NAS CM	Open End	Technology Sector Equity (Technology)	A-	A+	B		Y	0
Columbia Global Technology Growth Fund Institutional Class	CMTFX	NAS CM	Open End	Technology Sector Equity (Technology)	A-	A+	B		Y	2,000
Columbia Greater China Fund Advisor Class	CGCHX	NAS CM	Open End	Greater China Equity (Pacific Stock)	B+	A	C+	Up	Y	0
Columbia Greater China Fund Class A	NGCAX	NAS CM	Open End	Greater China Equity (Pacific Stock)	B+	A	C+	Up	Y	2,000
Columbia Greater China Fund Class C	NGCCX	NAS CM	Open End	Greater China Equity (Pacific Stock)	B+	A	C+	Up	Y	2,000
Columbia Greater China Fund Class T	CGCWX	NAS CM	Open End	Greater China Equity (Pacific Stock)	B+	A	C+	Up	Y	2,000
Columbia Greater China Fund Institutional 2 Class	CGCRX	NAS CM	Open End	Greater China Equity (Pacific Stock)	B+	A	C+	Up	Y	100,000
Columbia Greater China Fund Institutional 3 Class	CGCYX	NAS CM	Open End	Greater China Equity (Pacific Stock)	B+	A	C+	Up	Y	0
Columbia Greater China Fund Institutional Class	LNGZX	NAS CM	Open End	Greater China Equity (Pacific Stock)	B+	A	C+	Up	Y	2,000
Columbia Income Builder Fund Advisor Class	CNMRX	NAS CM	Open End	Cautious Alloc (Growth & Income)	B-	C+	B	Down	Y	2,000
Columbia Income Builder Fund Class A	RBBAX	NAS CM	Open End	Cautious Alloc (Growth & Income)	B-	C+	B	Down	Y	2,000
Columbia Income Builder Fund Class C	RBBCX	NAS CM	Open End	Cautious Alloc (Growth & Income)	B-	C+	B		Y	2,000
Columbia Income Builder Fund Class K	CIPRX	NAS CM	Open End	Cautious Alloc (Growth & Income)	B-	C+	B	Down		0
Columbia Income Builder Fund Class R	CBURX	NAS CM	Open End	Cautious Alloc (Growth & Income)	B-	C+	B	Down	Y	0
Columbia Income Builder Fund Class T	CINDX	NAS CM	Open End	Cautious Alloc (Growth & Income)	B-	C+	B	Up	Y	2,000
Columbia Income Builder Fund Institutional 2 Class	CKKRX	NAS CM	Open End	Cautious Alloc (Growth & Income)	B-	C+	B	Down	Y	0
Columbia Income Builder Fund Institutional 3 Class	CIBYX	NAS CM	Open End	Cautious Alloc (Growth & Income)	B-	C+	B	Down	Y	1,000,000
Columbia Income Builder Fund Institutional Class	CBUZX	NAS CM	Open End	Cautious Alloc (Growth & Income)	B-	C+	B	Down	Y	2,000
Columbia Large Cap Enhanced Core Fund Advisor Class	CECFX	NAS CM	Open End	US Equity Large Cap Blend (Growth)	B	B	B-		Y	2,000
Columbia Large Cap Enhanced Core Fund Class A	NMIAX	NAS CM	Open End	US Equity Large Cap Blend (Growth)	B	B	B-		Y	2,000
Columbia Large Cap Enhanced Core Fund Class R	CCERX	NAS CM	Open End	US Equity Large Cap Blend (Growth)	B	B	B-		Y	0
Columbia Large Cap Enhanced Core Fund Institutional 2 Cls	CLNCX	NAS CM	Open End	US Equity Large Cap Blend (Growth)	B	B	B		Y	0
Columbia Large Cap Enhanced Core Fund Institutional 3 Cls	CECYX	NAS CM	Open End	US Equity Large Cap Blend (Growth)	B	B	B		Y	1,000,000
Columbia Large Cap Enhanced Core Fund Institutional Class	NMIMX	NAS CM	Open End	US Equity Large Cap Blend (Growth)	B	B	B-		Y	2,000
Columbia Large Cap Growth Fund Advisor Class	CCGRX	NAS CM	Open End	US Equity Large Cap Growth (Growth)	B	B	B	Down	Y	0
Columbia Large Cap Growth Fund Class A	LEGAX	NAS CM	Open End	US Equity Large Cap Growth (Growth)	B	B	B+	Down	Y	2,000
Columbia Large Cap Growth Fund Class C	LEGCX	NAS CM	Open End	US Equity Large Cap Growth (Growth)	B	B	B+	Down	Y	2,000
Columbia Large Cap Growth Fund Class E	CLGEX	NAS CM	Open End	US Equity Large Cap Growth (Growth)	B	B	B+	Down		0
Columbia Large Cap Growth Fund Class K	CLRUX	NAS CM	Open End	US Equity Large Cap Growth (Growth)	B	B	B+	Down		0
Columbia Large Cap Growth Fund Class R	CGWRX	NAS CM	Open End	US Equity Large Cap Growth (Growth)	B	B	B	Down	Y	0
Columbia Large Cap Growth Fund Class T	CLGWX	NAS CM	Open End	US Equity Large Cap Growth (Growth)	B	B	B+	Down	Y	2,000
Columbia Large Cap Growth Fund Class V	GAEGX	NAS CM	Open End	US Equity Large Cap Growth (Growth)	B	B	B+	Down		2,000
Columbia Large Cap Growth Fund III Advisor Class	CSFRX	NAS CM	Open End	US Equity Large Cap Growth (Growth)	B	B	B	Down	Y	2,000
Columbia Large Cap Growth Fund III Class A	NFEAX	NAS CM	Open End	US Equity Large Cap Growth (Growth)	B	B	B	Down	Y	2,000
Columbia Large Cap Growth Fund III Class C	NFECX	NAS CM	Open End	US Equity Large Cap Growth (Growth)	B	B	B	Up	Y	2,000
Columbia Large Cap Growth Fund III Class R	CLGPX	NAS CM	Open End	US Equity Large Cap Growth (Growth)	B	B	B		Y	0
Columbia Large Cap Growth Fund III Class T	CLCPX	NAS CM	Open End	US Equity Large Cap Growth (Growth)	B	B	B-	Down	Y	2,000
Columbia Large Cap Growth Fund III Institutional 2 Class	CADRX	NAS CM	Open End	US Equity Large Cap Growth (Growth)	B	B	B-	Down	Y	0
Columbia Large Cap Growth Fund III Institutional 3 Class	CLRYX	NAS CM	Open End	US Equity Large Cap Growth (Growth)	B	B	B-	Down	Y	1,000,000
Columbia Large Cap Growth Fund III Institutional Class	NFEPX	NAS CM	Open End	US Equity Large Cap Growth (Growth)	B	B	B+	Down	Y	2,000
Columbia Large Cap Growth Fund Institutional 2 Class	CLWFX	NAS CM	Open End	US Equity Large Cap Growth (Growth)	B	B	B+	Down	Y	100,000

★ Expanded analysis of this fund is included in Section II.

	TOTAL RETURNS					PERFORMANCE				ASSETS		ASSET ALLOCATION & TURNOVER					BULL & BEAR		FEES		
Min Additional Investment	3-Month Total Return	6-Month Total Return	1-Year Total Return	3-Year Total Return	5-Year Total Return	Dividend Yield (TTM)	Expense Ratio	3-Yr Std Deviation	3-Year Beta	NAV	Total Assets (MIL)	%Cash	%Stocks	%Bonds	%Other	Turnover Ratio	Last Bull Market Total Return	Last Bear Market Total Return	Front End Fee (%)	Back End Fee (%)	Inception Date
	5.71	12.41	27.46	30.55	80.55	0.89	1.27	10.18	0.94	15.53	690.5	2	94	0	0	54	22.46	-20.02	5.75		Oct-96
	5.44	12.01	26.58	27.73	73.85	0.79	2.02	10.18	0.94	13.3	690.5	2	94	0	0	54	22.04	-20.28		1.00	Oct-96
	5.72	12.48	27.57	30.95	81.42	0.89	1.22	10.17	0.94	15.93	690.5	2	94	0	0	54	22.6	-20.05			Mar-11
	5.61	12.34	27.20	29.65	78.24	0.8	1.52	10.14	0.93	15.28	690.5	2	94	0	0	54	22.29	-20.11			Jan-06
	5.72	12.58	27.88	31.90	83.84	0.98	0.97	10.16	0.94	16.24	690.5	2	94	0	0	54	22.64	-19.97			Nov-12
	5.74	12.60	27.86	31.67	82.91		0.92	10.16	0.94	16.05	690.5	2	94	0	0	54	22.64	-19.97			Mar-17
	5.80	12.63	27.81	31.61	82.83	0.97	1.02	10.16	0.94	15.97	690.5	2	94	0	0	54	22.64	-19.97			Oct-96
	7.13	18.52	43.36	77.35	212.73	0	1.09	13.9	0.94	31.78	953.1	1	99	0	0	40	21.6	-24.74			Nov-12
	7.06	18.32	42.93	75.99	208.86	0	1.34	13.88	0.94	30.22	953.1	1	99	0	0	40	21.42	-24.83	5.75		Nov-02
	6.84	17.90	41.94	72.20	197.42	0	2.09	13.88	0.94	27.25	953.1	1	99	0	0	40	20.81	-25		1.00	Oct-03
	7.15	18.55	43.46	77.99	214.79	0	1.01	13.88	0.94	31.97	953.1	1	99	0	0	40	21.6	-24.74			Nov-12
	7.14	18.55	43.51	77.76	213.44	0	0.96	13.88	0.94	32.04	953.1	1	99	0	0	40	21.6	-24.74			Mar-16
	7.12	18.49	43.32	77.34	212.70	0	1.09	13.89	0.95	31.37	953.1	1	99	0	0	40	21.6	-24.74			Nov-00
	11.96	27.33	61.03	51.06	84.89	0	1.37	18.93	0.86	56.43	130.0	1	99	0	0	35	19.85	-32.11			Mar-13
	11.89	27.19	60.65	49.98	82.63	0	1.62	18.93	0.86	51.12	130.0	1	99	0	0	35	19.68	-32.2	5.75		May-97
	11.69	26.70	59.45	46.62	75.91	0	2.37	18.9	0.86	47.38	130.0	1	99	0	0	35	19.16	-32.41		1.00	May-97
	11.91	27.19	60.61	49.90	82.78	0	1.62	18.92	0.86	51.11	130.0	1	99	0	0	35	19.68	-32.18	2.50		Jun-12
	11.99	27.41	61.20	51.68	86.21	0	1.23	18.94	0.86	56.56	130.0	1	99	0	0	35	19.85	-32.11			Nov-12
	12.02	27.45	61.23	51.28	85.16		1.18	18.93	0.86	55.13	130.0	1	99	0	0	35	19.85	-32.11			Mar-17
	11.99	27.36	61.05	51.12	84.96	0	1.37	18.93	0.86	55.42	130.0	1	99	0	0	35	19.85	-32.11			May-97
	1.47	3.63	7.84	16.56	31.20	3.51	0.76	4.52		12.05	1,253	4	20	70	1	22	11.63	-5.92			Nov-12
	1.32	3.51	7.50	15.65	29.65	3.27	1.01	4.53		12.01	1,253	4	20	70	1	22	11.59	-5.93	4.75		Feb-06
	1.21	3.11	6.76	13.12	24.89	2.53	1.76	4.54		12.06	1,253	4	20	70	1	22	11.08	-6.2		1.00	Feb-06
	1.41	3.52	7.54	16.00	30.09	3.32	0.99	4.52		12.03	1,253	4	20	70	1	22	11.63	-5.92			Feb-06
	1.33	3.36	7.28	14.80	27.99	3.01	1.26	4.51		12.08	1,253	4	20	70	1	22	11.53	-6.01			Sep-10
	1.31	3.50	7.48	15.59	29.07	3.25	1.01	4.52		12	1,253	4	20	70	1	22	11.47	-6.02	2.50		Jun-14
	1.47	3.64	7.85	16.70	31.60	3.53	0.74	4.53		12.06	1,253	4	20	70	1	22	11.63	-5.92			Nov-12
	1.48	3.75	7.86	16.35	30.47		0.7	4.53		12.05	1,253	4	20	70	1	22	11.63	-5.92			Mar-17
	1.47	3.73	7.86	16.61	31.27	3.51	0.76	4.52		12.02	1,253	4	20	70	1	22	11.87	-5.83			Sep-10
	7.58	13.71	24.33	34.94	116.46	1.33	0.64	10.49	1.03	24.39	404.8	1	99	0	0	79	26.02	-15.15			Jul-15
	7.54	13.61	24.12	33.98	113.65	1.12	0.89	10.46	1.03	24.68	404.8	1	99	0	0	79	25.89	-15.23			Jul-96
	7.47	13.41	23.76	32.96	110.88	0.93	1.14	10.45	1.03	24.64	404.8	1	99	0	0	79	25.7	-15.35			Jan-06
	7.65	13.81	24.50	35.35	117.26	1.39	0.57	10.49	1.03	24.52	404.8	1	99	0	0	79	26.03	-15.16			Jun-14
	7.63	13.81	24.52	35.53	117.74	1.42	0.52	10.48	1.03	24.61	404.8	1	99	0	0	79	26.03	-15.13			Jul-09
	7.64	13.73	24.41	34.96	116.50	1.32	0.64	10.47	1.03	24.62	404.8	1	99	0	0	79	26.03	-15.15			Jul-96
	4.34	9.37	27.95	39.97	114.29	0.35	0.83	12.44	1.1	42.05	3,657	3	97	0	0	29	26.92	-18.6			Nov-12
	4.27	9.23	27.61	38.96	111.51	0.17	1.08	12.44	1.1	39.69	3,657	3	97	0	0	29	26.97	-18.59	5.75		Oct-98
	4.08	8.81	26.66	35.88	103.71	0	1.83	12.42	1.1	33.36	3,657	3	97	0	0	29	26.33	-18.82		1.00	Nov-02
	4.26	9.19	27.52	38.55	110.47	0.1	1.18	12.44	1.1	39.53	3,657	3	97	0	0	29	26.87	-18.59	4.50		Sep-06
	4.31	9.28	27.74	39.43	112.82	0.24	1	12.43	1.1	41.01	3,657	3	97	0	0	29	27.05	-18.49			Mar-11
	4.22	9.10	27.34	37.94	109.00	0	1.33	12.44	1.1	39.42	3,657	3	97	0	0	29	26.74	-18.69			Sep-10
	4.29	9.24	27.62	38.95	111.70	0.17	1.08	12.44	1.1	39.77	3,657	3	97	0	0	29	26.93	-18.55	2.50		Sep-10
	4.28	9.23	27.64	38.95	111.35	0.18	1.08	12.46	1.1	39.34	3,657	3	97	0	0	29	26.92	-18.6	5.75		Dec-90
	4.33	9.33	27.87	32.18	109.95	0	0.86	12.02	1.06	19.38	1,765	1	99	0	0	29	27.72	-17.52			Nov-12
	4.29	9.24	27.57	31.25	107.46	0	1.11	12.02	1.06	17.53	1,765	1	99	0	0	29	27.54	-17.58	5.75		Dec-97
	4.05	8.78	26.58	28.37	99.79	0	1.86	11.99	1.06	12.58	1,765	1	99	0	0	29	26.98	-17.88		1.00	Dec-97
	4.23	9.08	27.31	30.32	104.92	0	1.36	12.02	1.06	17.68	1,765	1	99	0	0	29	27.35	-17.69			Oct-16
	4.24	9.20	27.67	31.28	107.46	0	1.11	12.02	1.06	17.7	1,765	1	99	0	0	29	27.53	-17.6	2.50		Oct-16
	4.35	9.42	28.05	32.70	111.00	0	0.78	12.02	1.06	19.55	1,765	1	99	0	0	29	27.72	-17.52			Dec-13
	4.35	9.42	28.05	32.39	110.26		0.75	12.02	1.06	18.9	1,765	1	99	0	0	29	27.71	-17.52			Mar-17
	4.34	9.37	27.94	32.28	110.08	0	0.86	12.02	1.06	18.84	1,765	1	99	0	0	29	27.72	-17.52			Dec-97
	4.37	9.42	28.06	40.42	115.43	0.43	0.75	12.45	1.1	41.19	3,657	3	97	0	0	29	27.27	-18.44			Mar-11

	MARKET			FUND TYPE, CATEGORY & OBJECTIVE	RATINGS				MINIMUMS	
Fund Name	Ticker Symbol	Traded On	Fund Type	Category and (Prospectus Objective)	Overall Rating	Reward Rating	Risk Rating	Recent Up/ Downgrade	Open to New Investors	Min Initial Investment
Columbia Large Cap Growth Fund Institutional 3 Class	CGFYX	NAS CM	Open End	US Equity Large Cap Growth (Growth)	B	B	B+	Down	Y	0
Columbia Large Cap Growth Fund Institutional Class	GEGTX	NAS CM	Open End	US Equity Large Cap Growth (Growth)	B	B	B+	Down	Y	2,000
Columbia Large Cap Index Fund Class A	NEIAX	NAS CM	Open End	US Equity Large Cap Blend (Growth & Income)	B	B	B		Y	2,000
Columbia Large Cap Index Fund Institutional 2 Class	CLXRX	NAS CM	Open End	US Equity Large Cap Blend (Growth & Income)	B	B	B		Y	0
Columbia Large Cap Index Fund Institutional 3 Class	CLPYX	NAS CM	Open End	US Equity Large Cap Blend (Growth & Income)	B	B	B		Y	1,000,000
Columbia Large Cap Index Fund Institutional Class	NINDX	NAS CM	Open End	US Equity Large Cap Blend (Growth & Income)	B	B	B		Y	2,000
Columbia Mid Cap Growth Fund Advisor Class	CPGRX	NAS CM	Open End	US Equity Mid Cap (Growth)	B	B	B	Up	Y	0
Columbia Mid Cap Growth Fund Class A	CBSAX	NAS CM	Open End	US Equity Mid Cap (Growth)	B	B	B+	Up	Y	2,000
Columbia Mid Cap Growth Fund Class C	CMCCX	NAS CM	Open End	US Equity Mid Cap (Growth)	B	B-	B	Up	Y	2,000
Columbia Mid Cap Growth Fund Class K	CMCKX	NAS CM	Open End	US Equity Mid Cap (Growth)	B	B	B	Up		0
Columbia Mid Cap Growth Fund Class R	CMGRX	NAS CM	Open End	US Equity Mid Cap (Growth)	B	B	B	Up	Y	0
Columbia Mid Cap Growth Fund Class T	CMRWX	NAS CM	Open End	US Equity Mid Cap (Growth)	B	B	B	Up	Y	2,000
Columbia Mid Cap Growth Fund Class V	CBSTX	NAS CM	Open End	US Equity Mid Cap (Growth)	B	B	B	Up		2,000
Columbia Mid Cap Growth Fund Institutional 2 Class	CMGVX	NAS CM	Open End	US Equity Mid Cap (Growth)	B	B	B	Up	Y	100,000
Columbia Mid Cap Growth Fund Institutional 3 Class	CMGYX	NAS CM	Open End	US Equity Mid Cap (Growth)	B	B	B	Up	Y	0
Columbia Mid Cap Growth Fund Institutional Class	CLSPX	NAS CM	Open End	US Equity Mid Cap (Growth)	B	B	B+	Up	Y	2,000
Columbia Mid Cap Index Fund Class A	NTIAX	NAS CM	Open End	US Equity Mid Cap (Growth & Income)	B	B	B		Y	2,000
Columbia Mid Cap Index Fund Institutional 2 Class	CPXRX	NAS CM	Open End	US Equity Mid Cap (Growth & Income)	B	B	B		Y	0
Columbia Mid Cap Index Fund Institutional 3 Class	CMDYX	NAS CM	Open End	US Equity Mid Cap (Growth & Income)	B	B	B		Y	1,000,000
Columbia Mid Cap Index Fund Institutional Class	NMPAX	NAS CM	Open End	US Equity Mid Cap (Growth & Income)	B	B	B		Y	2,000
Columbia Mid Cap Value Fund Advisor Class	CFDRX	NAS CM	Open End	US Equity Mid Cap (Growth)	B-	C+	B	Down	Y	2,000
Columbia Mid Cap Value Fund Class A	CMUAX	NAS CM	Open End	US Equity Mid Cap (Growth)	B-	C+	B		Y	2,000
Columbia Mid Cap Value Fund Class C	CMUCX	NAS CM	Open End	US Equity Mid Cap (Growth)	B-	C+	B	Up	Y	2,000
Columbia Mid Cap Value Fund Class K	CMUFX	NAS CM	Open End	US Equity Mid Cap (Growth)	B-	C+	B	Down		0
Columbia Mid Cap Value Fund Class R	CMVRX	NAS CM	Open End	US Equity Mid Cap (Growth)	B-	C+	B		Y	0
Columbia Mid Cap Value Fund Class T	CMUWX	NAS CM	Open End	US Equity Mid Cap (Growth)	B-	C+	B		Y	2,000
Columbia Mid Cap Value Fund Institutional 2 Class	CVERX	NAS CM	Open End	US Equity Mid Cap (Growth)	B-	C+	B	Down	Y	0
Columbia Mid Cap Value Fund Institutional 3 Class	CMVYX	NAS CM	Open End	US Equity Mid Cap (Growth)	B-	C+	B	Down	Y	1,000,000
Columbia Mid Cap Value Fund Institutional Class	NAMAX	NAS CM	Open End	US Equity Mid Cap (Growth)	B-	C+	B	Down	Y	2,000
Columbia Multi-Asset Income Fund Advisor Class	CLNFX	NAS CM	Open End	Cautious Alloc (Asset Alloc)	C+	C	B	Up	Y	2,000
Columbia Multi-Asset Income Fund Class A	CLNAX	NAS CM	Open End	Cautious Alloc (Asset Alloc)	B-	C	B	Up	Y	2,000
Columbia Multi-Asset Income Fund Class C	CLCNX	NAS CM	Open End	Cautious Alloc (Asset Alloc)	C+	C	B	Up	Y	2,000
Columbia Multi-Asset Income Fund Class T	CLNWX	NAS CM	Open End	Cautious Alloc (Asset Alloc)	B-	C	B	Up	Y	2,000
Columbia Multi-Asset Income Fund Institutional 2 Class	CLNVX	NAS CM	Open End	Cautious Alloc (Asset Alloc)	C+	C	B	Up	Y	0
Columbia Multi-Asset Income Fund Institutional 3 Class	CMUYX	NAS CM	Open End	Cautious Alloc (Asset Alloc)	B-	C	B	Up	Y	1,000,000
Columbia Multi-Asset Income Fund Institutional Class	CLNZX	NAS CM	Open End	Cautious Alloc (Asset Alloc)	C+	C	B	Up	Y	2,000
Columbia Overseas Value Fund Advisor Class	COSVX	NAS CM	Open End	Global Equity Large Cap (Foreign Stock)	B	B	B-	Up	Y	2,000
Columbia Overseas Value Fund Class A	COAVX	NAS CM	Open End	Global Equity Large Cap (Foreign Stock)	B	B	B-	Up	Y	2,000
Columbia Overseas Value Fund Class C	COCVX	NAS CM	Open End	Global Equity Large Cap (Foreign Stock)	B	B	B-	Up	Y	2,000
Columbia Overseas Value Fund Class K	COKVX	NAS CM	Open End	Global Equity Large Cap (Foreign Stock)	B	B	B-	Up		0
Columbia Overseas Value Fund Class R	COVUX	NAS CM	Open End	Global Equity Large Cap (Foreign Stock)	B	B	B-	Up		0
Columbia Overseas Value Fund Class T	COVWX	NAS CM	Open End	Global Equity Large Cap (Foreign Stock)	B	B	B-	Up	Y	2,000
Columbia Overseas Value Fund Institutional 2 Class	COSSX	NAS CM	Open End	Global Equity Large Cap (Foreign Stock)	B	B	B-	Up	Y	0
Columbia Overseas Value Fund Institutional 3 Class	COSYX	NAS CM	Open End	Global Equity Large Cap (Foreign Stock)	B	B	B-	Up	Y	1,000,000
Columbia Overseas Value Fund Institutional Class	COSZX	NAS CM	Open End	Global Equity Large Cap (Foreign Stock)	B	B	B-	Up		2,000
Columbia Pacific/Asia Fund Advisor Class	CPRAX	NAS CM	Open End	Asia Equity (Pacific Stock)	B+	A	B	Up	Y	2,000
Columbia Pacific/Asia Fund Class A	CASAX	NAS CM	Open End	Asia Equity (Pacific Stock)	B+	A	B	Up	Y	2,000
Columbia Pacific/Asia Fund Class C	CASCX	NAS CM	Open End	Asia Equity (Pacific Stock)	B+	A	B	Up	Y	2,000
Columbia Pacific/Asia Fund Class T	CPAWX	NAS CM	Open End	Asia Equity (Pacific Stock)	B+	A	B	Up	Y	2,000
Columbia Pacific/Asia Fund Institutional 3 Class	CPAYX	NAS CM	Open End	Asia Equity (Pacific Stock)	B+	A	B	Up	Y	1,000,000
Columbia Pacific/Asia Fund Institutional Class	USPAX	NAS CM	Open End	Asia Equity (Pacific Stock)	B+	A	B	Up	Y	2,000
Columbia Real Estate Equity Fund Advisor Class	CRERX	NAS CM	Open End	Real Estate Sector Equity (Real Estate)	B-	C+	B+		Y	2,000

★ Expanded analysis of this fund is included in Section II.

Min Additional Investment	3-Month Total Return	6-Month Total Return	1-Year Total Return	3-Year Total Return	5-Year Total Return	Dividend Yield (TTM)	Expense Ratio	3-Yr Std Deviation	3-Year Beta	NAV	Total Assets (MIL)	%Cash	%Stocks	%Bonds	%Other	Turnover Ratio	Last Bull Market Total Return	Last Bear Market Total Return	Front End Fee (%)	Back End Fee (%)	Inception Date
	TOTAL RETURNS					PERFORMANCE				ASSETS		ASSET ALLOCATION & TURNOVER					BULL & BEAR		FEES		
	4.37	9.44	28.11	40.64	116.04	0.46	0.71	12.44	1.1	41.28	3,657	3	97	0	0	29	27.29	-18.44			Jul-09
	4.34	9.37	27.97	39.99	114.14	0.35	0.83	12.43	1.1	41.17	3,657	3	97	0	0	29	27.14	-18.52			Dec-90
	6.52	11.19	21.29	35.11	107.08	1.46	0.45	10.1	1	49.55	3,855	1	99	0	0	4	24.76	-16.39			Oct-95
	6.60	11.32	21.59	36.12	109.67	1.63	0.2	10.09	1	50.48	3,855	1	99	0	0	4	25	-16.32			Nov-12
	6.57	11.31	21.58	36.08	109.62		0.2	10.1	1	49.07	3,855	1	99	0	0	4	25	-16.32			Mar-17
	6.59	11.32	21.60	36.10	109.66	1.65	0.2	10.11	1	49.79	3,855	1	99	0	0	4	25	-16.32			Dec-93
	5.00	9.97	22.93	31.29	89.01	0	0.95	10.99	0.97	27.96	1,916	3	97	0	0	119	24.31	-23.02			Nov-12
	4.93	9.86	22.62	30.32	86.89	0	1.2	10.99	0.97	25.46	1,916	3	97	0	0	119	24.14	-23.12	5.75		Nov-02
	4.74	9.44	21.69	27.41	80.00	0	1.95	10.98	0.97	21.3	1,916	3	97	0	0	119	23.55	-23.37		1.00	Oct-03
	4.95	9.88	22.76	30.74	88.10	0	1.11	10.98	0.97	27.08	1,916	3	97	0	0	119	24.31	-23.02			Feb-13
	4.86	9.72	22.29	29.33	84.63	0	1.45	10.96	0.97	24.45	1,916	3	97	0	0	119	23.95	-23.18			Jan-13
	4.93	9.86	22.62	30.32	86.85	0	1.2	10.99	0.97	25.46	1,916	3	97	0	0	119	24.13	-23.11	2.50		Sep-10
	4.95	9.85	22.61	30.32	86.70	0	1.2	10.98	0.97	25.36	1,916	3	97	0	0	119	24.08	-23.14	5.75		Nov-02
	5.00	10.02	23.02	31.70	90.25	0	0.86	10.99	0.97	27.36	1,916	3	97	0	0	119	24.46	-23.01			Mar-11
	5.05	10.07	23.12	31.99	90.90	0	0.81	10.98	0.97	27.37	1,916	3	97	0	0	119	24.34	-23.01			Jul-09
	4.99	9.98	22.88	31.24	89.21	0	0.95	10.98	0.97	27.15	1,916	3	97	0	0	119	24.31	-23.02			Nov-85
	6.15	9.44	15.68	33.99	99.85	0.84	0.45	11.05	1	16.55	4,925	1	99	0	0	18	27.52	-22.66			May-00
	6.20	9.57	15.99	35.00	102.49	1.02	0.2	11.03	1	16.8	4,925	1	99	0	0	18	27.76	-22.6			Nov-12
	6.17	9.53	15.96	34.95	102.23		0.2	11.08	1	16.19	4,925	1	99	0	0	18	27.76	-22.6			Mar-17
	6.20	9.57	15.96	34.96	102.24	1.04	0.2	11.07	1	16.47	4,925	1	99	0	0	18	27.76	-22.6			Mar-00
	5.62	7.69	13.53	21.96	90.94	0.93	0.92	10.51	0.97	14.07	2,351	4	96	0	0	33	26.28	-23.12			Nov-12
	5.64	7.62	13.33	21.10	88.54	0.74	1.17	10.55	0.98	13.67	2,351	4	96	0	0	33	26.15	-23.19	5.75		Nov-01
	5.46	7.19	12.51	18.44	81.64	0.24	1.92	10.52	0.98	12.68	2,351	4	96	0	0	33	25.62	-23.44		1.00	Nov-01
	5.57	7.58	13.42	21.63	89.81	0.87	1.06	10.56	0.98	13.73	2,351	4	96	0	0	33	26.35	-23.21			Mar-11
	5.53	7.44	13.01	20.20	86.26	0.52	1.42	10.53	0.98	13.62	2,351	4	96	0	0	33	26.03	-23.32			Jan-06
	5.64	7.62	13.33	21.10	88.55	0.74	1.17	10.55	0.98	13.67	2,351	4	96	0	0	33	26.15	-23.23	2.50		Sep-10
	5.65	7.75	13.67	22.44	92.18	1.04	0.81	10.52	0.97	14.07	2,351	4	96	0	0	33	26.28	-23.12			Nov-12
	5.68	7.77	13.80	22.66	92.65	1.1	0.76	10.51	0.97	13.66	2,351	4	96	0	0	33	26.39	-23.11			Jul-09
	5.63	7.74	13.57	22.03	90.94	0.95	0.92	10.52	0.98	13.7	2,351	4	96	0	0	33	26.28	-23.12			Nov-01
	1.60	3.41	9.18			5.02	0.74			9.87	136.6	14	15	59	0	69					Mar-15
	1.54	3.39	8.91			4.77	0.99			9.87	136.6	14	15	59	0	69			4.75		Mar-15
	1.45	3.00	8.21			4.03	1.74			9.88	136.6	14	15	59	0	69				1.00	Mar-15
	1.64	3.39	8.91			4.78	0.99			9.88	136.6	14	15	59	0	69			2.50		Mar-15
	1.71	3.54	9.23			5.07	0.71			9.88	136.6	14	15	59	0	69					Mar-15
	1.73	3.57	9.28				0.65			9.86	136.6	14	15	59	0	69					Mar-17
	1.70	3.52	9.18			5.01	0.74			9.88	136.6	14	15	59	0	69					Mar-15
	4.01	12.82	30.04	36.29	59.07	1.55	1.15	11.53	0.84	10.29	945.5	1	99	0	0	89	13.32	-22.47			Jul-15
	4.00	12.68	29.68	35.24	57.27	1.39	1.4	11.48	0.84	10.32	945.5	1	99	0	0	89	13.15	-22.55	5.75		Feb-13
	3.71	12.21	28.79	32.32	51.37	0.92	2.15	11.55	0.84	10.27	945.5	1	99	0	0	89	12.66	-22.79		1.00	Feb-13
	4.00	12.79	29.94	36.16	58.70	1.53	1.23	11.52	0.84	10.33	945.5	1	99	0	0	89	13.32	-22.47			Feb-13
	3.88	12.54	29.34	34.19	55.06	1.26	1.65	11.53	0.84	10.08	945.5	1	99	0	0	89	12.99	-22.63			Mar-16
	3.89	12.57	29.57	35.14	57.03	1.39	1.4	11.53	0.84	10.3	945.5	1	99	0	0	89	13.27	-22.59	2.50		Mar-11
	4.02	12.84	30.22	36.79	59.65	1.7	0.98	11.53	0.84	10.28	945.5	1	99	0	0	89	13.32	-22.47			Jul-15
	4.06	12.87	30.23	36.95	59.84	1.71	0.95	11.57	0.84	10.29	945.5	1	99	0	0	89	13.32	-22.47			Jul-15
	3.99	12.77	30.05	36.20	58.96	1.55	1.15	11.53	0.84	10.33	945.5	1	99	0	0	89	13.32	-22.47			Mar-08
	9.18	18.11	41.99	48.57	67.83	0.13	1.25	12.16	0.86	11.58	233.1	5	95	0	0	80	12.63	-18.67			Mar-13
	9.10	17.99	41.71	47.40	66.03	0	1.5	12.23	0.86	11.51	233.1	5	95	0	0	80	12.44	-18.85	5.75		Mar-08
	8.92	17.55	40.62	44.18	59.93	0	2.25	12.19	0.86	11.3	233.1	5	95	0	0	80	11.85	-19.02		1.00	Mar-08
	9.05	17.93	41.64	47.40	65.99	0	1.5	12.16	0.86	11.5	233.1	5	95	0	0	80	12.47	-18.76	2.50		Jun-12
	9.19	18.23	41.99	48.59	68.11		1.09	12.16	0.86	11.43	233.1	5	95	0	0	80	12.63	-18.67			Mar-17
	9.21	18.16	41.94	48.54	68.05	0.13	1.25	12.17	0.86	11.56	233.1	5	95	0	0	80	12.63	-18.67			Dec-92
	1.40	1.65	5.36	14.22	51.61	1.92	1.01	13.11	0.98	14.32	365.2	0	100	0	0	36	30.84	-16.56			Nov-12

	MARKET			FUND TYPE, CATEGORY & OBJECTIVE	RATINGS					MINIMUMS
Fund Name	Ticker Symbol	Traded On	Fund Type	Category and (Prospectus Objective)	Overall Rating	Reward Rating	Risk Rating	Recent Up/ Downgrade	Open to New Investors	Min Initial Investment
Columbia Real Estate Equity Fund Class A	CREAX	NAS CM	Open End	Real Estate Sector Equity (Real Estate)	B-	C+	B+		Y	2,000
Columbia Real Estate Equity Fund Class C	CRECX	NAS CM	Open End	Real Estate Sector Equity (Real Estate)	B-	C+	B		Y	2,000
Columbia Real Estate Equity Fund Class K	CRRFX	NAS CM	Open End	Real Estate Sector Equity (Real Estate)	B-	C+	B+			0
Columbia Real Estate Equity Fund Class R	CRSRX	NAS CM	Open End	Real Estate Sector Equity (Real Estate)	B-	C+	B		Y	0
Columbia Real Estate Equity Fund Class T	CREWX	NAS CM	Open End	Real Estate Sector Equity (Real Estate)	B-	C+	B+		Y	2,000
Columbia Real Estate Equity Fund Institutional 2 Class	CRRVX	NAS CM	Open End	Real Estate Sector Equity (Real Estate)	B-	C+	B+		Y	0
Columbia Real Estate Equity Fund Institutional 3 Class	CREYX	NAS CM	Open End	Real Estate Sector Equity (Real Estate)	B-	C+	B+		Y	1,000,000
Columbia Real Estate Equity Fund Institutional Class	CREEX	NAS CM	Open End	Real Estate Sector Equity (Real Estate)	B-	C+	B+		Y	2,000
Columbia Select Global Equity Fund Class A	IGLGX	NAS CM	Open End	Global Equity (World Stock)	B	B	B+	Up	Y	2,000
Columbia Select Global Equity Fund Class C	RGCEX	NAS CM	Open End	Global Equity (World Stock)	B	B-	B	Up	Y	2,000
Columbia Select Global Equity Fund Class K	IDGYX	NAS CM	Open End	Global Equity (World Stock)	B	B	B+	Up		0
Columbia Select Global Equity Fund Class R	CGERX	NAS CM	Open End	Global Equity (World Stock)	B	B	B+	Up	Y	0
Columbia Select Global Equity Fund Class T	CGEWX	NAS CM	Open End	Global Equity (World Stock)	B	B	B+	Up	Y	2,000
Columbia Select Global Equity Fund Institutional 2 Class	RGERX	NAS CM	Open End	Global Equity (World Stock)	B	B	B+	Up	Y	100,000
Columbia Select Global Equity Fund Institutional 3 Class	CSEYX	NAS CM	Open End	Global Equity (World Stock)	B	B	B+	Up	Y	0
Columbia Select Global Equity Fund Institutional Class	CGEZX	NAS CM	Open End	Global Equity (World Stock)	B	B	B+	Up	Y	2,000
Columbia Select Global Growth Fund Advisor Class	CADHX	NAS CM	Open End	Global Equity (World Stock)	B	B	B	Up	Y	2,000
Columbia Select Global Growth Fund Class A	COGAX	NAS CM	Open End	Global Equity (World Stock)	B	B-	B	Up	Y	2,000
Columbia Select Global Growth Fund Class C	COGCX	NAS CM	Open End	Global Equity (World Stock)	B-	B-	B	Up	Y	2,000
Columbia Select Global Growth Fund Class R	COGRX	NAS CM	Open End	Global Equity (World Stock)	B	B-	B	Up	Y	0
Columbia Select Global Growth Fund Institutional 2 Class	CADIX	NAS CM	Open End	Global Equity (World Stock)	B	B	B	Up	Y	0
Columbia Select Global Growth Fund Institutional 3 Class	CGGYX	NAS CM	Open End	Global Equity (World Stock)	B	B-	B	Up	Y	1,000,000
Columbia Select Global Growth Fund Institutional Class	COGZX	NAS CM	Open End	Global Equity (World Stock)	B	B-	B	Up	Y	2,000
Columbia Select International Equity Fund Advisor Class	CQYRX	NAS CM	Open End	Global Equity Large Cap (Foreign Stock)	C+	C+	C+	Up	Y	2,000
Columbia Select International Equity Fund Class A	NIIAX	NAS CM	Open End	Global Equity Large Cap (Foreign Stock)	C+	C+	C+	Up	Y	2,000
Columbia Select International Equity Fund Class C	NITRX	NAS CM	Open End	Global Equity Large Cap (Foreign Stock)	C+	C+	C+	Up	Y	2,000
Columbia Select International Equity Fund Class K	CMEFX	NAS CM	Open End	Global Equity Large Cap (Foreign Stock)	C+	C+	C+	Up		0
Columbia Select International Equity Fund Class R	CIERX	NAS CM	Open End	Global Equity Large Cap (Foreign Stock)	C+	C+	C+	Up	Y	0
Columbia Select International Equity Fund Class T	CMAWX	NAS CM	Open End	Global Equity Large Cap (Foreign Stock)	C+	C+	C+	Up	Y	2,000
Columbia Select Intl Equity Fund Inst 2 Cls	CQQRX	NAS CM	Open End	Global Equity Large Cap (Foreign Stock)	C+	C+	C+	Up	Y	0
Columbia Select Intl Equity Fund Inst 3 Cls	CMIYX	NAS CM	Open End	Global Equity Large Cap (Foreign Stock)	C+	C+	C+	Up	Y	1,000,000
Columbia Select Intl Equity Fund Inst Cls	NIEQX	NAS CM	Open End	Global Equity Large Cap (Foreign Stock)	C+	C+	C+	Up	Y	2,000
Columbia Select Large Cap Equity Fund Advisor Class	CLSRX	NAS CM	Open End	US Equity Large Cap Blend (Growth)	B	B	B+	Down	Y	2,000
Columbia Select Large Cap Equity Fund Class A	NSGAX	NAS CM	Open End	US Equity Large Cap Blend (Growth)	B	B	B+	Down	Y	2,000
Columbia Select Large Cap Equity Fund Class C	NSGCX	NAS CM	Open End	US Equity Large Cap Blend (Growth)	B	B	B	Down	Y	2,000
Columbia Select Large Cap Equity Fund Class T	CLCWX	NAS CM	Open End	US Equity Large Cap Blend (Growth)	B	B	B+	Down	Y	2,000
Columbia Select Large Cap Equity Fund Institutional 2 Cls	CLCRX	NAS CM	Open End	US Equity Large Cap Blend (Growth)	B	B	B+	Down	Y	0
Columbia Select Large Cap Equity Fund Institutional 3 Cls	CLEYX	NAS CM	Open End	US Equity Large Cap Blend (Growth)	B	B	B+	Down	Y	1,000,000
Columbia Select Large Cap Equity Fund Institutional Class	NSEPX	NAS CM	Open End	US Equity Large Cap Blend (Growth)	B	B	B+	Down	Y	2,000
Columbia Select Large Cap Growth Fund Advisor Class	CSRRX	NAS CM	Open End	US Equity Large Cap Growth (World Stock)	B	B-	B	Up	Y	2,000
Columbia Select Large Cap Growth Fund Class A	ELGAX	NAS CM	Open End	US Equity Large Cap Growth (World Stock)	B	B-	B	Up	Y	2,000
Columbia Select Large Cap Growth Fund Class C	ELGCX	NAS CM	Open End	US Equity Large Cap Growth (World Stock)	B-	B-	B	Down	Y	2,000
Columbia Select Large Cap Growth Fund Class R	URLGX	NAS CM	Open End	US Equity Large Cap Growth (World Stock)	B-	B-	B	Down	Y	0
Columbia Select Large Cap Growth Fund Class T	CSLWX	NAS CM	Open End	US Equity Large Cap Growth (World Stock)	B	B-	B	Up	Y	2,000
Columbia Select Large Cap Growth Fund Institutional 2 Cls	CGTRX	NAS CM	Open End	US Equity Large Cap Growth (World Stock)	B	B	B	Up	Y	0
Columbia Select Large Cap Growth Fund Institutional 3 Cls	CCWRX	NAS CM	Open End	US Equity Large Cap Growth (World Stock)	B	B	B	Up	Y	1,000,000
Columbia Select Large Cap Growth Fund Institutional Class	UMLGX	NAS CM	Open End	US Equity Large Cap Growth (World Stock)	B	B-	B	Up	Y	2,000
Columbia Select Large-Cap Value Fund Advisor Class	CSERX	NAS CM	Open End	US Equity Large Cap Value (Growth)	B	B	B-	Up	Y	2,000
Columbia Select Large-Cap Value Fund Class A	SLVAX	NAS CM	Open End	US Equity Large Cap Value (Growth)	B	B	B-	Up	Y	2,000
Columbia Select Large-Cap Value Fund Class C	SVLCX	NAS CM	Open End	US Equity Large Cap Value (Growth)	B	B	C+	Up	Y	2,000
Columbia Select Large-Cap Value Fund Class K	SLVTX	NAS CM	Open End	US Equity Large Cap Value (Growth)	B	B	C+	Up		0
Columbia Select Large-Cap Value Fund Class R	SLVRX	NAS CM	Open End	US Equity Large Cap Value (Growth)	B	B	B-	Up	Y	0

★Expanded analysis of this fund is included in Section II.

Min Additional Investment	TOTAL RETURNS: 3-Month Total Return	6-Month Total Return	1-Year Total Return	3-Year Total Return	5-Year Total Return	PERFORMANCE: Dividend Yield (TTM)	Expense Ratio	3-Yr Std Deviation	3-Year Beta	ASSETS: NAV	Total Assets (MIL)	ASSET ALLOCATION & TURNOVER: %Cash	%Stocks	%Bonds	%Other	Turnover Ratio	BULL & BEAR: Last Bull Market Total Return	Last Bear Market Total Return	FEES: Front End Fee (%)	Back End Fee (%)	Inception Date
	1.30	1.49	5.06	13.29	49.65	1.72	1.26	13.1	0.98	14.02	365.2	0	100	0	0	36	30.64	-16.43	5.75		Nov-02
	1.11	1.10	4.28	10.76	44.20	1	2.01	13.12	0.98	14.02	365.2	0	100	0	0	36	29.98	-16.7		1.00	Oct-03
	1.33	1.55	5.19	13.80	50.82	1.85	1.13	13.11	0.98	14.07	365.2	0	100	0	0	36	30.75	-16.42			Mar-11
	1.24	1.36	4.80	12.52	47.82	1.48	1.51	13.14	0.98	14.01	365.2	0	100	0	0	36	30.43	-16.54			Sep-10
	1.30	1.49	5.06	13.28	49.61	1.72	1.26	13.1	0.98	14.03	365.2	0	100	0	0	36	30.61	-16.42	2.50		Sep-10
	1.40	1.69	5.48	14.64	52.62	2.1	0.88	13.14	0.98	14.01	365.2	0	100	0	0	36	30.94	-16.29			Mar-11
	1.40	1.70	5.51	14.39	51.82		0.82	13.15	0.98	14.15	365.2	0	100	0	0	36	30.84	-16.56			Mar-17
	1.36	1.61	5.31	14.18	51.53	1.95	1.01	13.15	0.98	14.05	365.2	0	100	0	0	36	30.84	-16.56			Apr-94
	5.06	8.41	32.22	32.09	73.66	0	1.39	11.56	0.96	12.89	421.8	2	98	0	0	66	21.71	-23.01	5.75		May-90
	4.84	7.97	31.26	29.06	67.11	0	2.14	11.54	0.96	11.51	421.8	2	98	0	0	66	21.29	-23.29		1.00	Jun-00
	5.12	8.43	32.30	32.45	74.99	0	1.26	11.5	0.95	13.03	421.8	2	98	0	0	66	21.88	-23.06			Mar-95
	4.99	8.25	31.91	30.99	71.30	0	1.64	11.52	0.95	12.86	421.8	2	98	0	0	66	21.65	-23.18			Dec-06
	5.04	8.37	32.19	31.80	73.37	0	1.39	11.49	0.95	12.94	421.8	2	98	0	0	66	21.81	-23.05	2.50		Dec-06
	5.12	8.50	32.65	33.46	77.25	0	1.01	11.46	0.95	13.08	421.8	2	98	0	0	66	22.05	-23.06			Dec-06
	5.15	8.56	32.58	32.45	74.13		0.96	11.56	0.96	12.94	421.8	2	98	0	0	66	21.71	-23.01			Mar-17
	5.14	8.53	32.56	32.98	75.75	0	1.14	11.55	0.96	13.03	421.8	2	98	0	0	66	21.93	-23.09			Sep-10
	4.26	8.90	33.99	26.95	87.72	0	1.12	13.67	1.12	15.41	64.6	0	100	0	0	27	29.82	-23.61			Jan-14
	4.14	8.71	33.65	26.00	85.38	0	1.37	13.64	1.11	15.09	64.6	0	100	0	0	27	29.56	-23.56	5.75		Apr-08
	3.96	8.33	32.58	23.18	78.50	0	2.12	13.63	1.11	14.16	64.6	0	100	0	0	27	29.03	-23.88		1.00	Apr-08
	4.08	8.59	33.27	25.12	83.12	0	1.62	13.66	1.12	14.78	64.6	0	100	0	0	27	29.33	-23.69			Apr-08
	4.18	8.87	33.99	27.25	88.17	0	1.1	13.64	1.11	15.45	64.6	0	100	0	0	27	29.82	-23.61			Jan-14
	4.22	8.89	34.06	27.00	87.81		1.05	13.68	1.12	15.3	64.6	0	100	0	0	27	29.82	-23.61			Mar-17
	4.19	8.82	34.00	26.94	87.71	0	1.12	13.68	1.12	15.41	64.6	0	100	0	0	27	29.82	-23.61			Apr-08
	4.29	11.52	27.63	20.07	31.91	1.77	1.15	12.5	0.98	15.29	328.7	0	98	0	2	103	19.81	-25.11			Nov-12
	4.27	11.46	27.34	19.20	30.37	1.59	1.4	12.47	0.98	14.87	328.7	0	98	0	2	103	19.58	-25.21	5.75		Jun-92
	4.07	11.00	26.25	16.47	25.55	1.12	2.15	12.46	0.98	13.01	328.7	0	98	0	2	103	19.12	-25.42		1.00	Jun-92
	4.33	11.54	27.45	19.76	31.43	1.68	1.28	12.5	0.98	15.17	328.7	0	98	0	2	103	19.61	-25.11			Mar-11
	4.16	11.23	26.90	18.32	28.71	1.4	1.65	12.48	0.98	14.75	328.7	0	98	0	2	103	19.42	-25.3			Jan-06
	4.27	11.46	27.22	19.18	30.36	1.59	1.4	12.51	0.98	14.87	328.7	0	98	0	2	103	19.58	-25.21	2.50		Sep-10
	4.34	11.62	27.72	20.68	32.99	1.86	1.03	12.49	0.98	15.36	328.7	0	98	0	2	103	19.81	-25.11			Nov-12
	4.35	11.66	27.87	20.78	33.47	1.91	0.98	12.5	0.98	15.32	328.7	0	98	0	2	103	19.87	-25.01			Mar-11
	4.32	11.60	27.61	20.11	32.03	1.76	1.15	12.49	0.98	15.2	328.7	0	98	0	2	103	19.81	-25.11			Dec-91
	6.41	11.82	24.53	40.94	111.57		0.9	10.44	1.02	14.44	671.4	3	97	0	0	67	25.74	-18.09			Jul-17
	6.27	11.72	24.17	39.96	108.95	0.77	1.15	10.44	1.02	14.6	671.4	3	97	0	0	67	25.49	-18.14	5.75		Aug-99
	6.02	11.22	23.26	36.73	101.23	0.25	1.9	10.44	1.02	13.45	671.4	3	97	0	0	67	24.97	-18.4		1.00	Aug-99
	6.29	11.73	24.20	39.90	108.97	0.77	1.15	10.46	1.02	14.59	671.4	3	97	0	0	67	25.51	-18.19	2.50		Sep-10
	6.33	11.82	24.48	41.26	112.43	1.02	0.87	10.46	1.02	14.88	671.4	3	97	0	0	67	25.74	-18.09			Nov-12
	6.42	11.89	24.71	41.13	111.86		0.81	10.45	1.02	14.29	671.4	3	97	0	0	67	25.74	-18.09			Mar-17
	6.38	11.86	24.58	40.99	111.64	0.97	0.9	10.43	1.02	14.49	671.4	3	97	0	0	67	25.74	-18.09			Oct-98
	5.24	9.13	35.46	32.79	113.34	0	0.81	15.72	1.26	17.01	4,164	0	100	0	0	35	26.34	-18.55			Nov-12
	5.16	9.00	35.12	31.85	110.77	0	1.06	15.69	1.25	16.05	4,164	0	100	0	0	35	26.13	-18.62	5.75		Sep-07
	4.94	8.58	34.04	28.86	102.93	0	1.81	15.67	1.25	14.39	4,164	0	100	0	0	35	25.66	-18.85		1.00	Sep-07
	5.09	8.80	34.74	30.80	108.15	0	1.31	15.71	1.26	15.05	4,164	0	100	0	0	35	26.05	-18.69			Dec-04
	5.17	8.93	35.05	31.78	110.64	0	1.06	15.7	1.25	16.04	4,164	0	100	0	0	35	26.13	-18.62	2.50		Sep-10
	5.23	9.16	35.55	33.24	114.77	0	0.7	15.73	1.26	17.09	4,164	0	100	0	0	35	26.34	-18.55			Nov-12
	5.27	9.16	35.53	33.38	115.32	0	0.66	15.7	1.26	17.26	4,164	0	100	0	0	35	26.34	-18.55			Nov-12
	5.20	9.13	35.41	32.77	113.40	0	0.81	15.69	1.26	16.53	4,164	0	100	0	0	35	26.34	-18.55			Oct-97
	7.86	13.50	20.36	35.78	114.14	1.06	0.9	12.64	1.2	27.55	1,001	3	97	0	0	8	28.43	-22.6			Nov-12
	7.77	13.37	20.05	34.75	111.37	0.92	1.15	12.62	1.2	26.23	1,001	3	97	0	0	8	28.43	-22.6	5.75		Apr-97
	7.58	12.94	19.20	31.80	103.59	0.38	1.9	12.61	1.2	24.09	1,001	3	97	0	0	8	27.85	-22.85		1.00	May-99
	7.80	13.40	20.18	35.15	112.48	0.96	1.08	12.62	1.2	27.08	1,001	3	97	0	0	8	28.56	-22.59			Aug-09
	7.68	13.18	19.75	33.73	108.72	0.74	1.4	12.61	1.2	25.83	1,001	3	97	0	0	8	28.24	-22.66			Apr-03

	MARKET			FUND TYPE, CATEGORY & OBJECTIVE	RATINGS				MINIMUMS	
Fund Name	Ticker Symbol	Traded On	Fund Type	Category and (Prospectus Objective)	Overall Rating	Reward Rating	Risk Rating	Recent Up/ Downgrade	Open to New Investors	Min Initial Investment
Columbia Select Large-Cap Value Fund Class T	CSVWX	NAS CM	Open End	US Equity Large Cap Value (Growth)	B	B	C+	Up	Y	2,000
Columbia Select Large-Cap Value Fund Institutional 2 Class	SLVIX	NAS CM	Open End	US Equity Large Cap Value (Growth)	B	B	B-	Up	Y	0
Columbia Select Large-Cap Value Fund Institutional 3 Class	CSRYX	NAS CM	Open End	US Equity Large Cap Value (Growth)	B	B	C+	Up	Y	1,000,000
Columbia Select Large-Cap Value Fund Institutional Class	CSVZX	NAS CM	Open End	US Equity Large Cap Value (Growth)	B	B	B-	Up	Y	2,000
Columbia Select Smaller-Cap Value Fund Advisor Class	CSPRX	NAS CM	Open End	US Equity Small Cap (Small Company)	B	B	B	Up	Y	2,000
Columbia Select Smaller-Cap Value Fund Class A	SSCVX	NAS CM	Open End	US Equity Small Cap (Small Company)	B	B	B	Up	Y	2,000
Columbia Select Smaller-Cap Value Fund Class C	SVMCX	NAS CM	Open End	US Equity Small Cap (Small Company)	B-	B-	B	Up	Y	2,000
Columbia Select Smaller-Cap Value Fund Class K	SSLRX	NAS CM	Open End	US Equity Small Cap (Small Company)	B	B	B	Up		0
Columbia Select Smaller-Cap Value Fund Class R	SSVRX	NAS CM	Open End	US Equity Small Cap (Small Company)	B	B	B	Up	Y	0
Columbia Select Smaller-Cap Value Fund Institutional 2 Cls	SSVIX	NAS CM	Open End	US Equity Small Cap (Small Company)	B	B	B	Up	Y	0
Columbia Select Smaller-Cap Value Fund Institutional 3 Cls	CSSYX	NAS CM	Open End	US Equity Small Cap (Small Company)	B	B	B	Up	Y	1,000,000
Columbia Select Smaller-Cap Value Fund Institutional Class	CSSZX	NAS CM	Open End	US Equity Small Cap (Small Company)	B	B	B	Up	Y	2,000
Columbia Seligman Communications & Information Adv Cls	SCIOX	NAS CM	Open End	Technology Sector Equity (Technology)	A	A+	B+	Up	Y	2,000
Columbia Seligman Communications & Information Fund Cls A	SLMCX	NAS CM	Open End	Technology Sector Equity (Technology)	A	A+	B+	Up	Y	2,000
Columbia Seligman Communications & Information Fund Cls C	SCICX	NAS CM	Open End	Technology Sector Equity (Technology)	A	A+	B+	Up	Y	2,000
Columbia Seligman Communications & Information Fund Cls K	SCIFX	NAS CM	Open End	Technology Sector Equity (Technology)	A	A+	B+	Up		0
Columbia Seligman Communications & Information Fund Cls R	SCIRX	NAS CM	Open End	Technology Sector Equity (Technology)	A	A+	B+	Up	Y	0
Columbia Seligman Communications & Information Fund Cls T	CITTX	NAS CM	Open End	Technology Sector Equity (Technology)	A	A+	B+	Up	Y	2,000
Columbia Seligman Communications & Information Inst 2 Cls	SCMIX	NAS CM	Open End	Technology Sector Equity (Technology)	A	A+	B+	Up	Y	0
Columbia Seligman Communications & Information Inst 3 Cls	CCOYX	NAS CM	Open End	Technology Sector Equity (Technology)	A	A+	B+	Up	Y	1,000,000
Columbia Seligman Communications & Information Inst Cls	CCIZX	NAS CM	Open End	Technology Sector Equity (Technology)	A	A+	B+	Up	Y	2,000
Columbia Seligman Global Technology Fund Advisor Class	CCHRX	NAS CM	Open End	Technology Sector Equity (Technology)	A	A+	B+	Up	Y	0
Columbia Seligman Global Technology Fund Class A	SHGTX	NAS CM	Open End	Technology Sector Equity (Technology)	A	A+	B+	Up	Y	2,000
Columbia Seligman Global Technology Fund Class C	SHTCX	NAS CM	Open End	Technology Sector Equity (Technology)	A	A+	B+	Up	Y	2,000
Columbia Seligman Global Technology Fund Class K	SGTSX	NAS CM	Open End	Technology Sector Equity (Technology)	A	A+	B+	Up		0
Columbia Seligman Global Technology Fund Class R	SGTRX	NAS CM	Open End	Technology Sector Equity (Technology)	A	A+	B+	Up	Y	0
Columbia Seligman Global Technology Fund Inst 2 Cls	SGTTX	NAS CM	Open End	Technology Sector Equity (Technology)	A	A+	B+	Up	Y	100,000
Columbia Seligman Global Technology Fund Inst 3 Cls	CGTYX	NAS CM	Open End	Technology Sector Equity (Technology)	A	A+	B+	Up	Y	0
Columbia Seligman Global Technology Fund Institutional Cls	CSGZX	NAS CM	Open End	Technology Sector Equity (Technology)	A	A+	B+	Up	Y	2,000
Columbia Seligman Premium Technology Growth Fund	STK	NYSE	Closed End	Technology Sector Equity (Technology)	A	A+	B+	Up	Y	
Columbia Small Cap Growth Fund I Advisor Class	CHHRX	NAS CM	Open End	US Equity Small Cap (Small Company)	B+	A	B-	Up		0
Columbia Small Cap Growth Fund I Class A	CGOAX	NAS CM	Open End	US Equity Small Cap (Small Company)	B+	A	B-	Up		5,000
Columbia Small Cap Growth Fund I Class C	CGOCX	NAS CM	Open End	US Equity Small Cap (Small Company)	B+	A	B-	Up		5,000
Columbia Small Cap Growth Fund I Class K	CSCKX	NAS CM	Open End	US Equity Small Cap (Small Company)	B+	A	B-	Up		0
Columbia Small Cap Growth Fund I Class R	CCRIX	NAS CM	Open End	US Equity Small Cap (Small Company)	B+	A	B-	Up		0
Columbia Small Cap Growth Fund I Institutional 2 Class	CSCRX	NAS CM	Open End	US Equity Small Cap (Small Company)	B+	A	B-	Up		100,000
Columbia Small Cap Growth Fund I Institutional 3 Class	CSGYX	NAS CM	Open End	US Equity Small Cap (Small Company)	B+	A	B-	Up		0
Columbia Small Cap Growth Fund I Institutional Class	CMSCX	NAS CM	Open End	US Equity Small Cap (Small Company)	B+	A	B-	Up		2,000
Columbia Small Cap Index Fund Class A	NMSAX	NAS CM	Open End	US Equity Small Cap (Small Company)	B+	A-	B	Up	Y	2,000
Columbia Small Cap Index Fund Class K	CIDUX	NAS CM	Open End	US Equity Small Cap (Small Company)	B+	A-	B	Up		0
Columbia Small Cap Index Fund Class T	CSMWX	NAS CM	Open End	US Equity Small Cap (Small Company)	B+	A-	B	Up	Y	2,000
Columbia Small Cap Index Fund Institutional 2 Class	CXXRX	NAS CM	Open End	US Equity Small Cap (Small Company)	A-	A-	B	Up	Y	0
Columbia Small Cap Index Fund Institutional 3 Class	CSPYX	NAS CM	Open End	US Equity Small Cap (Small Company)	A-	A-	B	Up	Y	1,000,000
Columbia Small Cap Index Fund Institutional Class	NMSCX	NAS CM	Open End	US Equity Small Cap (Small Company)	A-	A-	B	Up	Y	2,000
Columbia Small Cap Value Fund I Advisor Class	CVVRX	NAS CM	Open End	US Equity Small Cap (Small Company)	B+	A	B	Up	Y	2,000
Columbia Small Cap Value Fund I Class A	CSMIX	NAS CM	Open End	US Equity Small Cap (Small Company)	B+	A	B	Up	Y	2,000
Columbia Small Cap Value Fund I Class C	CSSCX	NAS CM	Open End	US Equity Small Cap (Small Company)	B+	A	B	Up	Y	2,000
Columbia Small Cap Value Fund I Class R	CSVRX	NAS CM	Open End	US Equity Small Cap (Small Company)	B+	A	B	Up	Y	0
Columbia Small Cap Value Fund I Institutional 2 Class	CUURX	NAS CM	Open End	US Equity Small Cap (Small Company)	B+	A	B	Up	Y	0
Columbia Small Cap Value Fund I Institutional 3 Class	CSVYX	NAS CM	Open End	US Equity Small Cap (Small Company)	B+	A	B	Up	Y	1,000,000
Columbia Small Cap Value Fund I Institutional Class	CSCZX	NAS CM	Open End	US Equity Small Cap (Small Company)	B+	A	B	Up	Y	2,000
Columbia Small Cap Value Fund II Advisor Class	CLURX	NAS CM	Open End	US Equity Small Cap (Growth)	B+	A-	B	Up		0

★ Expanded analysis of this fund is included in Section II.

Min Additional Investment	TOTAL RETURNS 3-Month Total Return	6-Month Total Return	1-Year Total Return	3-Year Total Return	5-Year Total Return	PERFORMANCE Dividend Yield (TTM)	Expense Ratio	3-Yr Std Deviation	3-Year Beta	ASSETS NAV	Total Assets (MIL)	ASSET ALLOCATION & TURNOVER %Cash	%Stocks	%Bonds	%Other	Turnover Ratio	BULL & BEAR Last Bull Market Total Return	Last Bear Market Total Return	FEES Front End Fee (%)	Back End Fee (%)	Inception Date
	7.78	13.32	20.04	34.70	111.07	0.92	1.15	12.61	1.2	26.06	1,001	3	97	0	0	8	28.44	-22.59	2.50		Sep-10
	7.84	13.50	20.44	36.13	115.02	1.14	0.83	12.62	1.2	27.2	1,001	3	97	0	0	8	28.72	-22.47			Nov-01
	7.84	13.55	20.49	36.38	114.12	1.15	0.78	12.62	1.2	27.61	1,001	3	97	0	0	8	28.43	-22.6			Oct-14
	7.84	13.51	20.36	35.80	114.06	1.07	0.9	12.61	1.2	27.2	1,001	3	97	0	0	8	28.6	-22.5			Sep-10
	3.23	7.35	12.89	22.49	97.46	0	1.05	14.66	0.93	20.96	688.0	1	99	0	0	24	30.9	-27.67			Nov-12
	3.13	7.17	12.59	21.56	95.01	0	1.3	14.68	0.93	18.05	688.0	1	99	0	0	24	30.9	-27.67	5.75		Apr-97
	3.00	6.83	11.74	18.88	87.88	0	2.05	14.66	0.93	13.09	688.0	1	99	0	0	24	30.38	-27.96		1.00	May-99
	3.19	7.22	12.64	21.99	96.32	0	1.21	14.67	0.93	20.3	688.0	1	99	0	0	24	31.12	-27.59			Aug-09
	3.11	7.10	12.33	20.69	92.64	0	1.55	14.68	0.93	16.9	688.0	1	99	0	0	24	30.67	-27.73			Apr-03
	3.24	7.37	12.92	22.90	98.81	0	0.96	14.68	0.93	20.9	688.0	1	99	0	0	24	31.34	-27.57			Nov-01
	3.23	7.39	12.99	23.15	97.48	0	0.91	14.68	0.93	21.58	688.0	1	99	0	0	24	30.9	-27.67			Oct-14
	3.23	7.31	12.87	22.48	97.48	0	1.05	14.68	0.93	20.63	688.0	1	99	0	0	24	31.06	-27.58			Sep-10
	3.01	13.26	34.37	68.94	171.04	0	1.02	15.13	0.9	68.62	6,150	2	98	0	0	54	27.03	-17.5			Aug-09
	2.94	13.12	34.05	67.68	167.69	0	1.27	15.13	0.9	70.78	6,150	2	98	0	0	54	27.09	-17.47	5.75		Jun-83
	2.76	12.69	33.03	63.94	157.83	0	2.02	15.12	0.9	48.99	6,150	2	98	0	0	54	26.54	-17.72		1.00	May-99
	2.97	13.14	34.11	68.17	169.17	0	1.22	15.12	0.9	75.87	6,150	2	98	0	0	54	27.22	-17.42			Aug-09
	2.89	12.98	33.70	66.45	164.40	0	1.52	15.13	0.9	67.43	6,150	2	98	0	0	54	26.92	-17.56			Apr-03
	2.94	13.09	34.01	67.63	167.61		1.27	15.13	0.9	71.09	6,150	2	98	0	0	54	27.09	-17.47	2.50		Apr-17
	3.02	13.27	34.43	69.42	172.57	0	0.97	15.14	0.9	77.3	6,150	2	98	0	0	54	27.39	-17.33			Nov-01
	3.04	13.31	34.40	68.11	168.38		0.93	15.13	0.9	76.67	6,150	2	98	0	0	54	27.09	-17.47			Mar-17
	3.01	13.25	34.38	68.94	171.05	0	1.02	15.13	0.9	77	6,150	2	98	0	0	54	27.3	-17.35			Sep-10
	3.11	13.40	34.82	72.36	179.46	0	1.12	15.03	0.91	40.62	1,210	3	97	0	0	55	25.4	-17.78			Nov-12
	3.04	13.26	34.49	71.03	175.92	0	1.37	15.05	0.91	39.31	1,210	3	97	0	0	55	25.4	-17.78	5.75		May-94
	2.86	12.84	33.46	67.28	165.83	0	2.12	15.03	0.91	30.46	1,210	3	97	0	0	55	24.8	-18.05		1.00	May-99
	3.04	13.29	34.55	71.60	177.83	0	1.29	15.04	0.91	39.75	1,210	3	97	0	0	55	25.6	-17.71			Aug-09
	3.00	13.12	34.14	69.81	172.65	0	1.62	15.04	0.91	37.91	1,210	3	97	0	0	55	25.19	-17.87			Apr-03
	3.12	13.45	34.88	72.91	181.51	0	1.04	15.05	0.92	40.2	1,210	3	97	0	0	55	25.53	-17.63			Aug-09
	3.20	13.51	34.90	71.55	176.76		1	15.05	0.92	39.97	1,210	3	97	0	0	55	25.4	-17.78			Mar-17
	3.13	13.43	34.81	72.39	179.47	0	1.12	15.04	0.91	40.01	1,210	3	97	0	0	55	25.6	-17.67			Sep-10
	2.34	12.60	32.90	65.14	144.31	0	1.26	14.62	0.84	20.83	339.9	1	99	0	0	61	24.5	-19.47			Nov-09
	5.27	12.93	28.70	50.29	104.93	0	1.1	13.62	0.88	20.29	474.3	2	98	0	0	174	27.57	-28.38			Nov-12
	5.21	12.78	28.43	49.23	102.42	0	1.35	13.64	0.89	18.21	474.3	2	98	0	0	174	27.42	-28.46	5.75		Nov-05
	5.01	12.36	27.40	45.88	94.86	0	2.1	13.64	0.89	14.88	474.3	2	98	0	0	174	26.87	-28.7		1.00	Nov-05
	5.21	12.83	28.53	49.76	103.77	0	1.27	13.65	0.89	19.16	474.3	2	98	0	0	174	27.57	-28.38			Feb-13
	5.09	12.63	28.04	48.06	99.84	0	1.6	13.62	0.88	17.84	474.3	2	98	0	0	174	27.24	-28.56			Sep-10
	5.32	13.03	28.91	50.91	106.85	0	1.02	13.63	0.89	19.51	474.3	2	98	0	0	174	27.57	-28.38			Feb-13
	5.31	13.01	28.93	51.11	106.76	0	0.97	13.64	0.89	19.71	474.3	2	98	0	0	174	27.72	-28.33			Jul-09
	5.27	12.94	28.76	50.34	104.90	0	1.1	13.63	0.88	19.31	474.3	2	98	0	0	174	27.57	-28.38			Oct-96
	3.87	9.92	12.80	37.51	108.94	0.66	0.45	13.81	1	24.71	4,151	1	99	0	0	18	29.24	-22.15			Oct-96
	3.81	9.88	12.80	37.41	108.83	0.66	0.45	13.81	1	24.8	4,151	1	99	0	0	18	29.23	-22.15			Mar-11
	3.82	9.88	12.79	37.47	108.96	0.66	0.45	13.82	1	24.47	4,151	1	99	0	0	18	29.28	-22.16	2.50		Jun-14
	3.89	10.05	13.09	38.53	111.68	0.83	0.2	13.79	1	25.37	4,151	1	99	0	0	18	29.47	-22.08			Nov-12
	3.89	10.06	13.15	38.58	111.66		0.2	13.79	1	24.26	4,151	1	99	0	0	18	29.47	-22.08			Mar-17
	3.88	10.04	13.09	38.51	111.55	0.85	0.2	13.8	1	24.84	4,151	1	99	0	0	18	29.47	-22.08			Oct-96
	3.09	11.10	14.20	40.95	100.59	0.39	1.07	16.08	1.11	47.77	648.8	2	98	0	0	50	23.34	-23.99			Nov-12
	3.04	10.97	13.91	39.86	97.96	0.31	1.32	16.06	1.11	41.8	648.8	2	98	0	0	50	23.34	-23.99	5.75		Jul-86
	2.85	10.55	13.05	36.76	90.69	0	2.07	16.06	1.11	28.36	648.8	2	98	0	0	50	22.8	-24.25		1.00	Jan-96
	2.97	10.81	13.61	38.84	95.56	0.18	1.57	16.07	1.11	41.73	648.8	2	98	0	0	50	23.2	-24.04			Sep-10
	3.12	11.15	14.32	41.53	101.95	0.46	0.95	16.08	1.11	47.76	648.8	2	98	0	0	50	23.34	-23.99			Nov-12
	3.11	11.18	14.36	41.74	102.43	0.5	0.9	16.09	1.11	46.6	648.8	2	98	0	0	50	23.68	-23.87			Jul-09
	3.09	11.09	14.17	40.93	100.48	0.4	1.07	16.08	1.11	46.41	648.8	2	98	0	0	50	23.54	-23.93			Jul-95
	3.36	9.32	10.88	32.08	99.30	0.21	1.02	13.51	0.93	18.37	1,661	2	98	0	0	58	30.6	-26.75			Nov-12

	MARKET		FUND TYPE, CATEGORY & OBJECTIVE		RATINGS				MINIMUMS	
Fund Name	Ticker Symbol	Traded On	Fund Type	Category and (Prospectus Objective)	Overall Rating	Reward Rating	Risk Rating	Recent Up/ Downgrade	Open to New Investors	Min Initial Investment
Columbia Small Cap Value Fund II Class A	COVAX	NAS CM	Open End	US Equity Small Cap (Growth)	B+	B+	B	Up		2,000
Columbia Small Cap Value Fund II Class C	COVCX	NAS CM	Open End	US Equity Small Cap (Growth)	B	B	B	Up		2,000
Columbia Small Cap Value Fund II Class R	CCTRX	NAS CM	Open End	US Equity Small Cap (Growth)	B	B+	B	Up		0
Columbia Small Cap Value Fund II Institutional 2 Class	CRRRX	NAS CM	Open End	US Equity Small Cap (Growth)	B+	A-	B	Up		100,000
Columbia Small Cap Value Fund II Institutional 3 Class	CRRYX	NAS CM	Open End	US Equity Small Cap (Growth)	B+	A-	B	Up		0
Columbia Small Cap Value Fund II Institutional Class	NSVAX	NAS CM	Open End	US Equity Small Cap (Growth)	B+	A-	B	Up		2,000
Columbia Small/Mid Cap Value Fund Advisor Class	RMCRX	NAS CM	Open End	US Equity Small Cap (Growth)	B	B	B	Up	Y	2,000
Columbia Small/Mid Cap Value Fund Class A	AMVAX	NAS CM	Open End	US Equity Small Cap (Growth)	B-	B-	B	Up	Y	2,000
Columbia Small/Mid Cap Value Fund Class C	AMVCX	NAS CM	Open End	US Equity Small Cap (Growth)	B-	B-	B-	Up	Y	2,000
Columbia Small/Mid Cap Value Fund Class K	RMCVX	NAS CM	Open End	US Equity Small Cap (Growth)	B-	B-	B	Up		0
Columbia Small/Mid Cap Value Fund Class R	RMVTX	NAS CM	Open End	US Equity Small Cap (Growth)	B-	B-	B	Up	Y	0
Columbia Small/Mid Cap Value Fund Class T	CVOWX	NAS CM	Open End	US Equity Small Cap (Growth)	B-	B-	B	Up	Y	2,000
Columbia Small/Mid Cap Value Fund Institutional 2 Class	RSCMX	NAS CM	Open End	US Equity Small Cap (Growth)	B	B	B	Up	Y	0
Columbia Small/Mid Cap Value Fund Institutional 3 Class	CPHPX	NAS CM	Open End	US Equity Small Cap (Growth)	B	B	B	Up	Y	1,000,000
Columbia Small/Mid Cap Value Fund Institutional Class	CMOZX	NAS CM	Open End	US Equity Small Cap (Growth)	B	B-	B	Up	Y	2,000
Columbia Thermostat Fund Advisor Class	CTORX	NAS CM	Open End	Cautious Alloc (Growth)	B	C	A	Up	Y	2,000
Columbia Thermostat Fund Class A	CTFAX	NAS CM	Open End	Cautious Alloc (Growth)	B	C	A-	Up	Y	2,000
Columbia Thermostat Fund Class C	CTFDX	NAS CM	Open End	Cautious Alloc (Growth)	B-	C	A-	Up	Y	2,000
Columbia Thermostat Fund Institutional 2 Class	CQTRX	NAS CM	Open End	Cautious Alloc (Growth)	B	C	A	Up	Y	0
Columbia Thermostat Fund Institutional 3 Class	CYYYX	NAS CM	Open End	Cautious Alloc (Growth)	B	C	A	Up	Y	1,000,000
Columbia Thermostat Fund Institutional Class	COTZX	NAS CM	Open End	Cautious Alloc (Growth)	B	C	A	Up	Y	2,000
Commerce Growth Fund	CFGRX	NAS CM	Open End	US Equity Large Cap Growth (Growth)	B	B	B+	Down	Y	1,000
Commerce MidCap Growth Fund	CFAGX	NAS CM	Open End	US Equity Mid Cap (Growth)	B	B	B		Y	1,000
Commerce Value Fund	CFVLX	NAS CM	Open End	US Equity Large Cap Value (Growth & Income)	B	B-	B+		Y	1,000
Commonwealth Africa Fund	CAFRX	NAS CM	Open End	Other Equity (Foreign Stock)	C	C	C	Up	Y	200
Commonwealth Australia/New Zealand Fund	CNZLX	NAS CM	Open End	Other Equity (Foreign Stock)	C	C	C+	Down	Y	200
Commonwealth Global Fund	CNGLX	NAS CM	Open End	Global Equity (World Stock)	C+	C+	C+	Up	Y	200
Commonwealth Japan Fund	CNJFX	NAS CM	Open End	Japan Equity (Pacific Stock)	A-	B+	A	Up	Y	200
Commonwealth Real Estate Securities Fund	CNREX	NAS CM	Open End	Real Estate Sector Equity (Real Estate)	C+	C+	C+	Down	Y	200
Comstock Capital Value Fund AAA Class	COMVX	NAS CM	Open End	Other Alternative (Multi-Asset Global)	D-	D-	D-		Y	1,000
Comstock Capital Value Fund Class A	DRCVX	NAS CM	Open End	Other Alternative (Multi-Asset Global)	D-	D-	D-		Y	1,000
Comstock Capital Value Fund Class C	CPCCX	NAS CM	Open End	Other Alternative (Multi-Asset Global)	D-	D-	D-		Y	1,000
Comstock Capital Value Fund Class I	CPCRX	NAS CM	Open End	Other Alternative (Multi-Asset Global)	D-	D-	D-		Y	500,000
Concorde Wealth Management Fund	CONWX	NAS CM	Open End	US Equity Large Cap Blend (Growth)	C+	C	C+	Down	Y	500
Conductor Global Equity Value Fund Class A	RAALX	NAS CM	Open End	Global Equity Mid/Small Cap (Growth & Income)	B+	A	B-	Up	Y	2,500
Conductor Global Equity Value Fund Class C	RACLX	NAS CM	Open End	Global Equity Mid/Small Cap (Growth & Income)	B	A-	B-	Up	Y	2,500
Conductor Global Equity Value Fund Class I	RAILX	NAS CM	Open End	Global Equity Mid/Small Cap (Growth & Income)	B+	A	B-	Up	Y	100,000
Conductor Global Equity Value Fund Class Y	RAYLX	NAS CM	Open End	Global Equity Mid/Small Cap (Growth & Income)	B+	A	B-	Up	Y	10,000,000
Conestoga Small Cap Fund Investors Class	CCASX	NAS CM	Open End	US Equity Small Cap (Small Company)	A-	A	B	Up	Y	2,500
Conestoga Small Cap Institutional Class	CCALX	NAS CM	Open End	US Equity Small Cap (Small Company)	A-	A	B	Up	Y	250,000
Conestoga SMid Cap Fund Institutional Class	CCSGX	NAS CM	Open End	US Equity Small Cap (Small Company)	B+	A	B-	Up	Y	250,000
Conestoga SMid Cap Fund Investors Class	CCSMX	NAS CM	Open End	US Equity Small Cap (Small Company)	B+	A	B-	Up	Y	2,500
Congress All Cap Opportunity Fund Institutional Class	IACOX	NAS CM	Open End	US Equity Mid Cap (Growth)	B	B+	B	Up	Y	500,000
Congress All Cap Opportunity Fund Retail Class	CACOX	NAS CM	Open End	US Equity Mid Cap (Growth)	B	B	B	Up	Y	2,000
Congress Large Cap Growth Fund Institutional Class	CMLIX	NAS CM	Open End	US Equity Large Cap Growth (Growth)	B+	B	A	Up	Y	500,000
Congress Large Cap Growth Fund Retail Class	CAMLX	NAS CM	Open End	US Equity Large Cap Growth (Growth)	B	B	B		Y	2,000
Congress Mid Cap Growth Fund Institutional Class	IMIDX	NAS CM	Open End	US Equity Mid Cap (Growth)	B	B	B-		Y	500,000
Congress Mid Cap Growth Fund Retail Class	CMIDX	NAS CM	Open End	US Equity Mid Cap (Growth)	B	B	B+		Y	2,000
Congress Small Cap Growth Fund Institutional Class	CSMCX	NAS CM	Open End	US Equity Small Cap (Small Company)	B	B	B	Up	Y	500,000
Congress Small Cap Growth Fund Retail Class	CSMVX	NAS CM	Open End	US Equity Small Cap (Small Company)	B	B	B-	Up	Y	2,000
Consulting Group Emerging Markets Equity Fund	TEMUX	NAS CM	Open End	Emerging Markets Equity (Div Emerging Mkts)	B-	B	C	Up	Y	100
Consulting Group International Equity Fund	TIEUX	NAS CM	Open End	Global Equity Large Cap (Foreign Stock)	B-	B-	B	Up	Y	100

★ Expanded analysis of this fund is included in Section II.

	TOTAL RETURNS					PERFORMANCE				ASSETS		ASSET ALLOCATION & TURNOVER					BULL & BEAR		FEES		
Min Additional Investment	3-Month Total Return	6-Month Total Return	1-Year Total Return	3-Year Total Return	5-Year Total Return	Dividend Yield (TTM)	Expense Ratio	3-Yr Std Deviation	3-Year Beta	NAV	Total Assets (MIL)	%Cash	%Stocks	%Bonds	%Other	Turnover Ratio	Last Bull Market Total Return	Last Bear Market Total Return	Front End Fee (%)	Back End Fee (%)	Inception Date
	3.33	9.19	10.62	31.16	96.89	0.06	1.27	13.5	0.93	17.72	1,661	2	98	0	0	58	30.37	-26.81	5.75		May-02
	3.09	8.78	9.82	28.21	89.60	0	2.02	13.47	0.93	15.61	1,661	2	98	0	0	58	29.81	-27.06		1.00	May-02
	3.29	9.12	10.38	30.23	94.43	0	1.52	13.51	0.93	17.45	1,661	2	98	0	0	58	30.17	-26.94			Jan-06
	3.42	9.43	11.06	32.74	100.82	0.3	0.9	13.48	0.93	18.4	1,661	2	98	0	0	58	30.6	-26.75			Nov-12
	3.45	9.50	11.19	32.96	101.41	0.33	0.85	13.46	0.93	18.46	1,661	2	98	0	0	58	30.6	-26.75			Nov-12
	3.37	9.33	10.94	32.13	99.40	0.22	1.02	13.51	0.93	17.98	1,661	2	98	0	0	58	30.6	-26.75			May-02
	3.42	9.63	12.97	23.75	83.01	0.4	0.99	13.06	1.06	10.17	849.2	2	98	0	0	57	26.05	-25.37			Dec-06
	3.38	9.50	12.73	22.85	80.70	0.22	1.24	13.11	1.07	10.14	849.2	2	98	0	0	57	26.16	-25.37	5.75		Feb-02
	3.28	9.11	11.90	20.12	73.99	0	1.99	13.06	1.06	9.1	849.2	2	98	0	0	57	25.44	-25.57		1.00	Feb-02
	3.39	9.55	12.86	23.26	81.94	0.3	1.14	13.08	1.07	10.26	849.2	2	98	0	0	57	26.19	-25.34			Feb-02
	3.32	9.46	12.51	22.02	78.42	0.02	1.49	13.12	1.07	9.93	849.2	2	98	0	0	57	25.82	-25.35			Dec-06
	3.37	9.53	12.84	23.01	80.83	0.21	1.24	13.07	1.06	10.25	849.2	2	98	0	0	57	26.05	-25.31	2.50		Dec-06
	3.52	9.75	13.15	24.29	84.19	0.48	0.89	13.14	1.07	10.34	849.2	2	98	0	0	57	26.45	-25.2			Dec-06
	3.50	9.71	13.16	24.26	84.10	0.52	0.85	13.05	1.06	10.17	849.2	2	98	0	0	57	26.19	-25.34			Jun-13
	3.54	9.71	13.09	23.89	82.97	0.39	0.99	13.1	1.07	10.43	849.2	2	98	0	0	57	26.3	-25.22			Sep-10
	0.70	2.14	5.49	10.73	28.76	1.97	0.76	3.16	0.25	14.5	886.5	2	15	81	0	95	17.07	-7.98			Nov-12
	0.65	2.01	5.18	9.89	27.10	1.72	1.01	3.17	0.25	14.63	886.5	2	15	81	0	95	16.87	-8.12	5.75		Mar-03
	0.51	1.73	4.47	7.45	22.54	1.02	1.76	3.15	0.25	14.74	886.5	2	15	81	0	95	16.39	-8.37		1.00	Mar-03
	0.72	2.23	5.50	10.76	28.92	1.98	0.74	3.15	0.25	14.52	886.5	2	15	81	0	95	17.07	-7.98			Nov-12
	0.77	2.29	5.63	10.94	29.24	2.03	0.69	3.18	0.26	14.5	886.5	2	15	81	0	95	17.07	-7.98			Nov-12
	0.77	2.23	5.52	10.78	28.83	1.98	0.76	3.17	0.25	14.43	886.5	2	15	81	0	95	17.06	-7.98			Sep-02
250	7.12	11.85	27.54	44.76	121.43	0.68	0.83	9.88	0.9	32.57	120.9	1	99	0	0	37	28.21	-18.01			Dec-94
250	6.85	10.71	23.36	37.44	104.86	0.42	0.88	8.96	0.78	39.5	156.4	2	98	0	0	39	25.41	-22.12			Dec-94
250	6.17	11.05	12.86	31.94	96.90	2.48	0.71	9.95	0.92	31.49	254.9	0	100	0	0	41	20.42	-11.81			Mar-97
	20.67	23.43	33.21	13.44	4.71	0.55	1.95	19.21	0.98	10.72	3.0	7	92	1	0	13					Nov-11
	4.04	3.27	16.09	26.33	34.25	2.29	2.84	14.1	0.7	13.85	21.1	2	95	0	0	26	17.71	-13.04			Nov-91
	3.61	6.54	15.60	7.91	28.92	0	2.93	10.3	0.89	15.78	16.4	2	98	0	0	45	15.79	-23.14			Dec-02
	7.85	10.25	20.60	31.78	50.18	0	1.77	9.84	0.67	3.98	5.9	4	96	0	0	4	-0.72	-0.35			Jul-89
	4.36	5.91	14.60	18.01	52.46	0	2.95	10.27	0.6	17.12	11.6	6	93	0	0	12	27.57	-22.53			Jan-04
	-6.64	-10.86	-20.51	-38.95	-65.10	0	1.91	12.6	-1.19	4.92	26.0	90	-34	41	2	196	-25	21.95			Dec-08
	-6.66	-10.90	-20.58	-39.13	-64.99	0	1.91	12.58	-1.19	4.9	26.0	90	-34	41	2	196	-25.37	22.56	5.75		Oct-85
	-6.78	-11.06	-20.96	-40.16	-66.19	0	2.66	12.56	-1.19	4.26	26.0	90	-34	41	2	196	-26.22	22.81		1.00	Aug-95
	-6.67	-10.65	-20.41	-38.43	-64.57	0	1.66	12.62	-1.19	5.03	26.0	90	-34	41	2	196	-25.24	22.42			Aug-95
100	1.92	4.12	7.16	6.12	49.71	0	1.87	9.19	0.81	15.04	20.5	12	52	33	3	40	21.96	-21.31			Dec-87
500	7.17	15.68	28.55	46.12		0	2.19	9.52	0.78	14.32	83.4	4	96	0	0	123			5.75	1.00	Apr-14
500	6.91	15.24	27.55	42.89		0	2.94	9.58	0.78	14.15	83.4	4	96	0	0	123				1.00	Sep-15
1,000	7.16	15.87	28.90	47.15		0	1.94	9.58	0.78	14.4	83.4	4	96	0	0	123					Dec-13
1,000	7.41	16.16	29.59	48.46		0	1.29	9.61	0.79	14.53	83.4	4	96	0	0	123					Apr-16
	3.60	13.70	28.44	57.85	121.56	0	1.1	13.71	0.86	48.95	1,552	9	91	0	0	24	23.86	-17.95			Oct-02
	3.67	13.84	28.74	58.88	123.14	0	0.9	13.72	0.86	49.34	1,552	9	91	0	0	24	23.86	-17.95			Aug-14
	6.99	14.41	34.39	48.05		0	0.9	13.08	0.95	13.65	28.0	6	94	0	0	24					Dec-14
	6.88	14.25	34.10	47.02		0	1.15	13.1	0.95	13.54	28.0	6	94	0	0	24					Jan-14
	6.09	12.59	21.71	30.89	95.51	0.38	1.01	13.48	1.14	18.78	27.7	6	94	0	0	68					Oct-12
	6.03	12.38	21.37	29.83	92.84	0.26	1.26	13.47	1.14	18.73	27.7	6	94	0	0	68					Oct-12
	6.22	11.43	27.88	37.81	113.51	0.41	0.74	10.24	0.93	27.23	288.4	0	100	0	0	44	26.32	-17.33			Mar-28
	6.17	11.70	25.21	31.94	90.53	0.42	0.99	10.02	0.94	27.22	4.6	1	99	0	0	33	26.52	-15.34			Mar-09
	3.38	5.52	15.91	30.47	102.47	0.16	0.84	10.74	0.96	18.84	964.9	2	98	0	0	18					Oct-12
	3.31	5.41	15.58	29.38	100.19	0.01	1.09	10.68	0.96	18.69	964.9	2	98	0	0	18					Oct-12
	4.48	10.07	22.30	26.60	74.15	0	1.27	15.13	0.98	26.11	78.2	4	96	0	0	82	30.88	-24.24			Dec-99
	4.41	9.90	22.03	25.49	71.60	0	1.52	15.12	0.98	24.12	78.2	4	96	0	0	82	30.6	-24.32			Feb-00
	7.14	16.56	39.16	34.92	22.63	0.82	0.86	14.34	0.88	16.22	504.4	3	97	0	0	27	18.84	-27.03			Apr-94
	4.00	10.53	27.14	25.45	38.10	2.2	0.64	11.1	0.89	12.98	1,330	2	98	0	0	27	17.9	-25.51			Nov-91

Fund Name	Ticker Symbol	Traded On	Fund Type	Category and (Prospectus Objective)	Overall Rating	Reward Rating	Risk Rating	Recent Up/ Downgrade	Open to New Investors	Min Initial Investment
Consulting Group Large Cap Equity Fund	TLGUX	NAS CM	Open End	US Equity Large Cap Growth (Growth)	B-	B-	B	Down	Y	100
Consulting Group Small-Mid Cap Equity Fund	TSGUX	NAS CM	Open End	US Equity Small Cap (Small Company)	B-	B-	B-	Up	Y	100
Context Macro Opportunities Fund Institutional Shares	CMOTX	NAS CM	Open End	Multialternative (Growth & Income)	C-	D+	C		Y	10,000
Context Macro Opportunities Fund Investor Shares	CMOFX	NAS CM	Open End	Multialternative (Growth & Income)	C-	D+	C	Up	Y	2,000
Context Strategic Global Equity Fund Institutional Share	CGPGX	NAS CM	Open End	Global Equity (Growth)	D	D+	A		Y	10,000
Convergence Core Plus Fund Institutional Class	MARNX	NAS CM	Open End	US Equity Large Cap Blend (Growth)	B	B	A-	Up	Y	15,000
Convergence Market Neutral Fund Institutional Class	CPMNX	NAS CM	Open End	Market Neutral (Growth & Income)	C-	D+	B+	Up	Y	15,000
Convergence Opportunities Fund Institutional Class	CIPOX	NAS CM	Open End	US Equity Small Cap (Growth)	B+	A-	B	Up	Y	15,000
Copeland Intl Risk Managed Div Growth Fund Cls A Shares	IDVGX	NAS CM	Open End	Global Equity Large Cap (Growth & Income)	C+	C+	B-	Up	Y	2,500
Copeland Intl Risk Managed Div Growth Fund Cls C Shares	IDVCX	NAS CM	Open End	Global Equity Large Cap (Growth & Income)	C+	C+	C+	Up	Y	2,500
Copeland Intl Risk Managed Div Growth Fund Cls I Shares	IDVIX	NAS CM	Open End	Global Equity Large Cap (Growth & Income)	C+	C+	B-	Up	Y	25,000
Copeland Risk Managed Dividend Growth Fund Class A Shares	CDGRX	NAS CM	Open End	US Equity Large Cap Blend (Growth & Income)	B-	C+	B	Up	Y	1,000
Copeland Risk Managed Dividend Growth Fund Class C Shares	CDCRX	NAS CM	Open End	US Equity Large Cap Blend (Growth & Income)	B-	C+	B	Up	Y	1,000
Copeland Risk Managed Dividend Growth Fund Class I Shares	CDIVX	NAS CM	Open End	US Equity Large Cap Blend (Growth & Income)	C+	C+	C+	Down	Y	25,000
Copeland SMID Cap Dividend Growth Fund Class I Shares	CSMDX	NAS CM	Open End	US Equity Mid Cap (Equity-Income)	U	U	U		Y	5,000
Copley Fund	COPLX	NAS CM	Open End	US Equity Large Cap Value (Equity-Income)	B	B	B		Y	1,000
CornerCap Balanced Fund	CBLFX	NAS CM	Open End	Moderate Alloc (Balanced)	B-	C+	B	Down	Y	2,000
CornerCap Large/Mid-Cap Value Fund	CMCRX	NAS CM	Open End	US Equity Large Cap Value (Growth)	B-	B-	C+	Down	Y	2,000
CornerCap Small-Cap Value Fund Institutional Shares	CSCJX	NAS CM	Open End	US Equity Small Cap (Small Company)	B+	A-	B	Up	Y	1,000,000
CornerCap Small-Cap Value Fund Investor Shares	CSCVX	NAS CM	Open End	US Equity Small Cap (Small Company)	B+	A-	B	Up	Y	2,000
Cornerstone Advs Global Public Equity Fund Inst Shares	CAGLX	NAS CM	Open End	Global Equity (Growth)	B-	B	B-	Down	Y	2,000
Cornerstone Advs Income Opp Fund Inst Shares	CAIOX	NAS CM	Open End	Moderate Alloc (Income)	C	C	C		Y	2,000
Cornerstone Advs Public Alternatives Fund Inst Shares	CAALX	NAS CM	Open End	Multialternative (Growth & Income)	B-	C	B+	Up	Y	2,000
Cornerstone Advisors Real Assets Fund Institutional Shares	CAREX	NAS CM	Open End	Cautious Alloc (Real Estate)	C-	C	D+	Up	Y	2,000
Cornerstone Strategic Value Fund	CLM	AMEX	Closed End	US Equity Large Cap Blend (Growth)	B	B+	C+	Up	Y	
Cornerstone Total Return Fund Inc	CRF	AMEX	Closed End	US Equity Large Cap Blend (Growth)	B+	A-	B	Up	Y	
Cortina Small Cap Growth Fund	CRSGX	NAS CM	Open End	US Equity Small Cap (Small Company)	B	B	B	Up	Y	25,000
Cortina Small Cap Value Fund Institutional Class	CRSVX	NAS CM	Open End	US Equity Small Cap (Small Company)	B-	B-	B-	Up	Y	25,000
Cortina Small Cap Value Fund Investor Class	CISVX	NAS CM	Open End	US Equity Small Cap (Small Company)	C+	C+	B-	Up	Y	2,500
Counterpoint Long-Short Equity Fund Class A Shares	CPQAX	NAS CM	Open End	Long/Short Equity (Growth)	U	U	U		Y	5,000
Counterpoint Long-Short Equity Fund Class C Shares	CPQCX	NAS CM	Open End	Long/Short Equity (Growth)	U	U	U		Y	5,000
Counterpoint Long-Short Equity Fund Class I Shares	CPQIX	NAS CM	Open End	Long/Short Equity (Growth)	U	U	U		Y	100,000
Counterpoint Tactical Equity Fund Class A	CPAEX	NAS CM	Open End	Long/Short Equity (Growth)	C	C-	B	Up	Y	5,000
Counterpoint Tactical Equity Fund Class C	CPCEX	NAS CM	Open End	Long/Short Equity (Growth)	C	C-	B	Up	Y	5,000
Counterpoint Tactical Equity Fund Class I	CPIEX	NAS CM	Open End	Long/Short Equity (Growth)	C	C-	B	Up	Y	100,000
Cove Street Capital Small Cap Value Fund Inst Cls Shares	CSCAX	NAS CM	Open End	US Equity Small Cap (Small Company)	B-	C+	B	Up	Y	10,000
Crawford Dividend Growth Fund Class C	CDGCX	NAS CM	Open End	US Equity Large Cap Blend (Growth)	C+	C+	B-	Down	Y	2,500
Crawford Dividend Growth Fund Class Institutional	CDGIX	NAS CM	Open End	US Equity Large Cap Blend (Growth)	C+	B-	C+	Down	Y	10,000
Crawford Dividend Opportunity Fund	CDOFX	NAS CM	Open End	US Equity Small Cap (Small Company)	A-	A	B	Up	Y	10,000
Crawford Dividend Opportunity Fund Class C	CDOCX	NAS CM	Open End	US Equity Small Cap (Small Company)	B+	A-	B	Up	Y	2,500
Crawford Dividend Yield Fund	CDYLX	NAS CM	Open End	US Equity Large Cap Value (Equity-Income)	C+	C	B	Up	Y	10,000
Crawford Multi-Asset Income Fund	CMALX	NAS CM	Open End	Moderate Alloc (Multi-Asset Global)	U	U	U		Y	10,000
Credit Suisse Commodity Access Strategy Fund Class A	CRCAX	NAS CM	Open End	Commodities Broad Basket (Growth & Income)	C-	C-	D	Up	Y	2,500
Credit Suisse Commodity Access Strategy Fund Class C	CRCCX	NAS CM	Open End	Commodities Broad Basket (Growth & Income)	D+	C-	D	Up	Y	2,500
Credit Suisse Commodity Access Strategy Fund Class I	CRCIX	NAS CM	Open End	Commodities Broad Basket (Growth & Income)	C-	C-	D	Up	Y	250,000
Credit Suisse Commodity Return Strategy Fund Class A	CRSAX	NAS CM	Open End	Commodities Broad Basket (Growth & Income)	D+	C-	D+	Up	Y	2,500
Credit Suisse Commodity Return Strategy Fund Class C	CRSCX	NAS CM	Open End	Commodities Broad Basket (Growth & Income)	D+	C-	D	Up	Y	2,500
Credit Suisse Commodity Return Strategy Fund Class I	CRSOX	NAS CM	Open End	Commodities Broad Basket (Growth & Income)	D+	C-	D+	Up	Y	250,000
Credit Suisse Managed Futures Strategy Fund Class A	CSAAX	NAS CM	Open End	Other Alternative (Growth & Income)	C-	C-	C	Down	Y	2,500
Credit Suisse Managed Futures Strategy Fund Class C	CSACX	NAS CM	Open End	Other Alternative (Growth & Income)	C-	D+	C	Up	Y	2,500
Credit Suisse Managed Futures Strategy Fund Class I	CSAIX	NAS CM	Open End	Other Alternative (Growth & Income)	C	C-	C	Up	Y	250,000
Credit Suisse Multialternative Strategy Fund Cls A Shares	CSQAX	NAS CM	Open End	Multialternative (Growth & Income)	B-	C	A-	Up	Y	2,500

★Expanded analysis of this fund is included in Section II.

Min Additional Investment	3-Month Total Return	6-Month Total Return	1-Year Total Return	3-Year Total Return	5-Year Total Return	Dividend Yield (TTM)	Expense Ratio	3-Yr Std Deviation	3-Year Beta	NAV	Total Assets (MIL)	%Cash	%Stocks	%Bonds	%Other	Turnover Ratio	Last Bull Market Total Return	Last Bear Market Total Return	Front End Fee (%)	Back End Fee (%)	Inception Date
	TOTAL RETURNS					PERFORMANCE				ASSETS		ASSET ALLOCATION & TURNOVER					BULL & BEAR		FEES		
	6.14	10.58	20.48	31.71	102.05	1.3	0.48	10.88	1.05	19.42	1,788	2	98	0	0	18	26.95	-18.39			Nov-91
	5.50	10.60	19.65	20.23	91.77	0.27	0.68	14.67	1.14	20.77	744.0	3	97	0	0	34	29.1	-28.08			Nov-91
	-0.10	0.10	-1.52	-0.15		0.56	1.99				102.2	152	0	-59	2	230					Aug-15
200	-0.10	-0.10	-1.84			0.34	2.24				102.2	152	0	-59	2	230					Jan-16
	4.72	7.91	15.67			0	1.29				22.5	-34	104	28	2						Oct-16
5,000	6.90	13.96	17.79	30.73	95.78	0.81	1.31	10.92	0.98	18.73	128.6	31	69	0	0	261	29.8	-19.56			Dec-09
5,000	2.46	5.25	3.44			0	1.52			10.81	22.6	77	23	0	0	218					Jan-16
5,000	2.11	10.10	10.81	26.82		0	1.36	12.9	0.83	12.11	68.9	31	69	0	0	316					Nov-13
500	3.03	8.89	24.09	12.32	25.69	0.49	1.65	7.82	0.47	12.33	21.3	3	97	0	0	180			5.75		Dec-12
500	2.89	8.44	23.15	9.72	21.13	0	2.4	7.79	0.47	12.03	21.3	3	97	0	0	180					Dec-12
500	3.09	8.96	24.31	12.62	26.37	0.89	1.5	7.85	0.48	12.29	21.3	3	97	0	0	180					Dec-12
500	7.45	9.80	19.56	13.19	66.94	0.61	1.51	8.24	0.59	13.9	175.2	0	100	0	0	201	11.01	-7.83	5.75		Dec-10
500	7.26	9.41	18.64	10.66	60.77	0	2.26	8.21	0.59	13.61	175.2	0	100	0	0	201	10.57	-8.12			Jan-12
500	7.49	9.85	19.78	13.72	68.47	0.93	1.36	8.21	0.59	13.79	175.2	0	100	0	0	201	11.01	-7.83			Mar-13
500	5.55	9.72					0.95			11.03	0.62	1	99	0	0						Feb-17
100	2.25	6.33	9.67	22.65	69.40	0	6.99	8.17	0.38	88.41	86.6	-35	135	0	0	0	11.69	-3.17			Sep-78
250	4.22	7.87	13.51	17.67	60.02	1.28	1.02	7.66		14.63	35.8	6	61	33	0	60	13.73	-13.29			May-97
250	7.26	13.29	21.55	23.95	99.77	0.74	1	12.36	1.14	13.5	30.7	3	97	0	0	129	21.27	-22.98			Jul-00
	2.44	8.62	8.04	34.90	113.08	0.44	1	14.37	0.99	15.74	119.6	0	100	0	0	129	27.64	-28.03			Dec-15
250	2.31	8.42	7.71	34.02	111.69	0.16	1.3	14.36	0.99	15.72	119.6	0	100	0	0	129	27.64	-28.03			Sep-92
	4.80	10.91	25.05	32.94	79.24	0.84	0.95	9.98	0.92	13.99	1,113	2	98	0	1	49					Aug-12
	0.42	2.56	6.15	3.20	20.74	4.57	0.96	10	0.76	9.36	215.2	6	22	46	0	35					Aug-12
	1.90	4.73	4.84	8.15	17.49	0.49	1.57	3.55	-0.04	9.89	562.6	57	21	13	9	92					Aug-12
	3.47	6.10	3.16	-5.96	-7.46	3.48	0.92	10.2	0.61	8.03	204.9	12	34	32	23	36					Aug-12
	6.26	12.14	24.01	30.35	129.49	2.11	2.01	10.05	0.94	13.55	592.2	2	95	2	0	88	20.6	-13.67			Jun-87
	6.35	12.55	22.73	37.61	147.55	1.49	1.84	8.95	0.84	13.18	291.6	1	98	1	0	64	23.98	-14.67			May-73
	0.76	3.56	14.12	30.76	79.31	0	1.1	14.5	0.91	16.28	26.7	2	98	0	0	88	30.91				Sep-11
	2.98	7.01	9.79	18.08	74.04	0.15	1.1	13.83	0.93	20.46	45.9	1	99	0	0	89	28.51				Sep-11
	2.95	6.85	9.53	17.15	71.91	0.01	1.35	13.83	0.93	20.3	45.9	1	99	0	0	89	28.32				Apr-14
250	0.19						1.99			15.19	13.1								5.75		Oct-17
250	0.11						2.74			15.16	13.1										Oct-17
1,000	0.24						1.74			15.19	13.1										Oct-17
250	2.98	9.07	13.90			0	2.01			15.33	17.8	55	44	0	1	369			5.75		Nov-15
250	2.83	8.71	13.09			0	2.76			15.08	17.8	55	44	0	1	369					Nov-15
10,000	3.03	9.17	14.13			0	1.76			15.41	17.8	55	44	0	1	369					Nov-15
100	1.71	3.03	5.73	18.32	64.28	0	1.24	14.07	0.84	36.02	147.1	13	87	0	0	48	42.49	-19.74			Oct-01
	5.15	8.26	12.94	18.19	63.16	0.43	1.98	10.06	0.93	10.54	39.2	2	98	0	0	13	21.9	-17.15		1.00	Jan-04
	5.38	8.83	14.08	21.75	71.50	1.28	0.98	10.07	0.93	10.63	39.2	2	98	0	0	13	22.61	-16.77			Jan-04
	4.18	9.80	13.93	40.26	108.78	1.03	1.05	11.09	0.74	42.42	185.7	3	97	0	0	31					Sep-12
	3.90	9.24	12.78	36.10	98.60	0.36	2.05	11.09	0.74	42.27	185.7	3	97	0	0	31				1.00	Apr-15
	2.85	4.25	6.98	17.92		2.75	1.01	9.17	0.78	27.22	11.7	3	97	0	0	43					Nov-14
0	-0.33						1			24.79	23.1	19	39	12	0						Sep-17
100	7.18	18.26	3.19	-17.97	-37.01	0	1.15	19.39	1.04	5.55	34.0	9	0	68	22	137			4.75		Sep-12
100	6.99	17.78	2.49	-19.77	-39.30	0	1.9	19.36	1.04	5.37	34.0	9	0	68	22	137				1.00	Sep-12
100,000	7.37	18.34	3.42	-17.38	-36.27	0	0.9	19.32	1.04	5.61	34.0	9	0	68	22	137					Sep-12
100	4.25	6.68	1.52	-16.21	-36.57	0	1.04	12.74	0.98	4.91	3,431	6	0	75	18	151	0.15	-19.96	4.75		Dec-04
100	3.90	6.25	0.79	-17.99	-38.86	0	1.79	12.81	0.98	4.62	3,431	6	0	75	18	151	-0.34	-20.12		1.00	Dec-04
100,000	4.42	7.02	1.74	-15.57	-35.76	0	0.79	12.82	0.98	5.02	3,431	6	0	75	18	151	0.27	-19.82			Dec-04
100	3.40	5.66	-1.57	5.74	30.98	0	1.55	9.48	0.98	10.64	327.9	27	19	54	1				5.25		Sep-12
100	3.11	5.23	-2.47	3.29	25.97	0	2.3	9.55	0.99	10.26	327.9	27	19	54	1					1.00	Sep-12
100,000	3.47	5.72	-1.47	6.44	32.38	0	1.3	9.54	0.99	10.72	327.9	27	19	54	1						Sep-12
100	1.70	3.49	3.59	5.61	15.17	0.11	1.11	3.6	0.92	10.1	104.0	26	21	48	5	1,021			5.25		Mar-12

	MARKET		FUND TYPE, CATEGORY & OBJECTIVE		RATINGS				MINIMUMS	
Fund Name	Ticker Symbol	Traded On	Fund Type	Category and (Prospectus Objective)	Overall Rating	Reward Rating	Risk Rating	Recent Up/ Downgrade	Open to New Investors	Min Initial Investment
Credit Suisse Multialternative Strategy Fund Cls C Shares	CSQCX	NAS CM	Open End	Multialternative (Growth & Income)	B-	C	B+	Up	Y	2,500
Credit Suisse Multialternative Strategy Fund Cls I Shares	CSQIX	NAS CM	Open End	Multialternative (Growth & Income)	B-	C	A-	Up	Y	250,000
Credit Suisse Trust Commodity Return Strategy Portfolio	CCRSX	NAS CM	Open End	Commodities Broad Basket (Growth & Income)	D+	C-	D+	Up	Y	0
CRM All Cap Value Fund Class Institutional	CRIEX	NAS CM	Open End	US Equity Large Cap Blend (Growth)	B	B	B-	Up	Y	1,000,000
CRM All Cap Value Fund Class Investor	CRMEX	NAS CM	Open End	US Equity Large Cap Blend (Growth)	B	B	B-	Up	Y	2,500
CRM International Opportunity Fund Institutional Class	CRIIX	NAS CM	Open End	Global Equity Large Cap (Foreign Stock)	B	B	A	Up	Y	1,000,000
CRM International Opportunity Fund Investor Class	CRMIX	NAS CM	Open End	Global Equity Large Cap (Foreign Stock)	B	B	A	Up	Y	2,500
CRM Large Cap Opportunity Fund Institutional Class	CRIGX	NAS CM	Open End	US Equity Large Cap Blend (Growth)	B	B	B+	Up	Y	1,000,000
CRM Large Cap Opportunity Fund Investor Class	CRMGX	NAS CM	Open End	US Equity Large Cap Blend (Growth)	B	B	B	Up	Y	2,500
CRM Long/Short Opportunities Fund Institutional Shares	CRIHX	NAS CM	Open End	Long/Short Equity (Growth)	D	D+	B	Up	Y	100,000,000
CRM Mid Cap Value Fund Class Institutional	CRIMX	NAS CM	Open End	US Equity Mid Cap (Growth & Income)	B	B	B-	Up	Y	1,000,000
CRM Mid Cap Value Fund Class Investor	CRMMX	NAS CM	Open End	US Equity Mid Cap (Growth & Income)	B	B	B-	Up	Y	2,500
CRM Small Cap Value Fund Class Institutional	CRISX	NAS CM	Open End	US Equity Small Cap (Small Company)	B+	A	B	Up	Y	1,000,000
CRM Small Cap Value Fund Class Investor	CRMSX	NAS CM	Open End	US Equity Small Cap (Small Company)	B+	A-	B	Up	Y	2,500
CRM Small/Mid Cap Value Fund Class Institutional	CRIAX	NAS CM	Open End	US Equity Mid Cap (Growth)	B-	B-	B-	Up	Y	1,000,000
CRM Small/Mid Cap Value Fund Class Investor	CRMAX	NAS CM	Open End	US Equity Mid Cap (Growth)	B-	B-	B-	Up	Y	2,500
Cross Shore Discovery Fund Institutional Shares	US22757Y1047		Closed End	Long/Short Equity (Growth)	C+	C	B-	Up	Y	50,000
Crow Point Defined Risk Global Eq Income Fund Cls A Shares	CGHAX	NAS CM	Open End	Long/Short Equity (Equity-Income)	C+	C	B-	Up	Y	500
Crow Point Defined Risk Global Eq Income Fund Cls I Shares	CGHIX	NAS CM	Open End	Long/Short Equity (Equity-Income)	C+	C	B-	Up	Y	100,000
Cullen Emerging Markets High Dividend Fund Class C	CEMGX	NAS CM	Open End	Emerging Markets Equity (Div Emerging Mkts)	C+	C+	C	Up	Y	1,000
Cullen Emerging Markets High Dividend Fund Class I	CEMFX	NAS CM	Open End	Emerging Markets Equity (Div Emerging Mkts)	C+	B-	C	Up	Y	1,000,000
Cullen Emerging Markets High Dividend Fund Retail Class	CEMDX	NAS CM	Open End	Emerging Markets Equity (Div Emerging Mkts)	C+	C+	C	Up	Y	1,000
Cullen Enhanced Equity Income Fund Class C	ENHCX	NAS CM	Open End	Long/Short Equity (Equity-Income)	C	C-	B+	Up	Y	1,000
Cullen Enhanced Equity Income Fund Class I	ENHNX	NAS CM	Open End	Long/Short Equity (Equity-Income)	C	C-	B+	Up	Y	1,000,000
Cullen Enhanced Equity Income Fund Retail Class	ENHRX	NAS CM	Open End	Long/Short Equity (Equity-Income)	C-	C-	B+	Up	Y	1,000
Cullen High Dividend Equity Fund Class C	CHVCX	NAS CM	Open End	US Equity Large Cap Value (Equity-Income)	B-	B-	B	Down	Y	1,000
Cullen High Dividend Equity Fund Class Institutional	CHDVX	NAS CM	Open End	US Equity Large Cap Value (Equity-Income)	B-	B-	B	Down	Y	1,000,000
Cullen High Dividend Equity Fund Class R1	CHDRX	NAS CM	Open End	US Equity Large Cap Value (Equity-Income)	B-	B-	B	Down	Y	0
Cullen High Dividend Equity Fund Class R2	CHDPX	NAS CM	Open End	US Equity Large Cap Value (Equity-Income)	B-	B-	B	Down	Y	0
Cullen High Dividend Equity Fund Retail Class	CHDEX	NAS CM	Open End	US Equity Large Cap Value (Equity-Income)	B-	B-	B	Down	Y	1,000
Cullen International High Dividend Fund Class C	CIHCX	NAS CM	Open End	Global Equity Large Cap (Equity-Income)	C+	C+	B-	Up	Y	1,000
Cullen International High Dividend Fund Cls Institutional	CIHIX	NAS CM	Open End	Global Equity Large Cap (Equity-Income)	B-	C+	B	Up	Y	1,000,000
Cullen International High Dividend Fund Class R1	CIHRX	NAS CM	Open End	Global Equity Large Cap (Equity-Income)	C+	C+	B-	Up	Y	0
Cullen International High Dividend Fund Class R2	CIHPX	NAS CM	Open End	Global Equity Large Cap (Equity-Income)	C+	C+	B	Up	Y	0
Cullen International High Dividend Fund Retail Class	CIHDX	NAS CM	Open End	Global Equity Large Cap (Equity-Income)	C+	C+	B	Up	Y	1,000
Cullen Small Cap Value Fund Class C	CUSCX	NAS CM	Open End	US Equity Small Cap (Small Company)	C+	C	C+	Up	Y	1,000
Cullen Small Cap Value Fund Class I	CUSIX	NAS CM	Open End	US Equity Small Cap (Small Company)	C+	C+	C+	Up	Y	1,000,000
Cullen Small Cap Value Fund Class Retail Class	CUSRX	NAS CM	Open End	US Equity Small Cap (Small Company)	C+	C+	C+	Up	Y	1,000
Cullen Value Fund Class C	CVLFX	NAS CM	Open End	US Equity Large Cap Value (Growth & Income)	B-	B-	B-	Down	Y	1,000
Cullen Value Fund Class I	CVLVX	NAS CM	Open End	US Equity Large Cap Value (Growth & Income)	B-	B-	B-	Down	Y	1,000,000
Cullen Value Fund Retail Class	CVLEX	NAS CM	Open End	US Equity Large Cap Value (Growth & Income)	B-	B-	B-	Down	Y	1,000
Cushing MLP Total Return Fund	SRV	NYSE	Closed End	Energy Sector Equity (Natl Res)	D	D	D	Down	Y	
Cutler Emerging Markets Fund	CUTDX	NAS CM	Open End	Emerging Markets Equity (Div Emerging Mkts)	C	C+	B-	Up	Y	2,500
Cutler Equity Fund	CALEX	NAS CM	Open End	US Equity Large Cap Value (Growth)	B-	B-	B	Down	Y	2,500
CVR Dynamic Allocation Fund Institutional Shares	CVRAX	NAS CM	Open End	Moderate Alloc (Growth)	C+	C	B-	Up	Y	100,000
Dana Large Cap Equity Fund Institutional Class	DLCIX	NAS CM	Open End	US Equity Large Cap Blend (Growth)	B	B	B-	Up	Y	1,000,000
Dana Large Cap Equity Fund Investor Class	DLCEX	NAS CM	Open End	US Equity Large Cap Blend (Growth)	B	B	B-	Up	Y	1,000
Dana Small Cap Equity Fund Institutional Class	DSCIX	NAS CM	Open End	US Equity Small Cap (Small Company)	C	C-	B	Up	Y	1,000,000
Dana Small Cap Equity Fund Investor Class	DSCEX	NAS CM	Open End	US Equity Small Cap (Small Company)	C	C-	B	Up	Y	1,000
Davenport Balanced Income Fund	DBALX	NAS CM	Open End	Moderate Alloc (Growth & Income)	C-	C-	A-	Up	Y	5,000
Davenport Core Fund	DAVPX	NAS CM	Open End	US Equity Large Cap Growth (Growth)	B-	B-	B	Down	Y	5,000
Davenport Equity Opportunities Fund	DEOPX	NAS CM	Open End	US Equity Mid Cap (Growth)	B-	B-	B		Y	5,000

★ Expanded analysis of this fund is included in Section II.

Min Additional Investment	TOTAL RETURNS 3-Month Total Return	6-Month Total Return	1-Year Total Return	3-Year Total Return	5-Year Total Return	PERFORMANCE Dividend Yield (TTM)	Expense Ratio	3-Yr Std Deviation	3-Year Beta	ASSETS NAV	Total Assets (MIL)	ASSET ALLOCATION & TURNOVER %Cash	%Stocks	%Bonds	%Other	Turnover Ratio	BULL & BEAR Last Bull Market Total Return	Last Bear Market Total Return	FEES Front End Fee (%)	Back End Fee (%)	Inception Date
100	1.45	3.19	2.88	3.28	10.95	0	1.86	3.57	0.91	9.77	104.0	26	21	48	5	1,021				1.00	Mar-12
100,000	1.68	3.66	3.86	6.31	16.64	0.34	0.86	3.59	0.91	10.18	104.0	26	21	48	5	1,021					Mar-12
	4.13	6.61	1.51	-16.10	-36.57	9.94	1.05	12.82	0.98	4.03	393.7	7	0	75	18	113	0.14	-20.01			Feb-06
	5.35	9.39	18.87	34.80	87.82	0.53	1.26	10.46	0.91	8.8	23.1	4	96	0	0	91	22.69	-24.53			Oct-06
50	5.32	9.30	18.63	34.00	85.78	0.32	1.51	10.51	0.92	8.66	23.1	4	96	0	0	91	22.47	-24.64			Oct-06
	4.28	9.56	25.77	35.53	40.47	0.91	1.26	10.91	0.79	14.09	14.3	7	93	0	0	80	20.96	-27.48			Dec-08
50	4.20	9.43	25.50	34.49	38.81	0.71	1.51	10.89	0.79	14.03	14.3	7	93	0	0	80	20.85	-27.56			Dec-08
	5.50	9.91	17.35	30.42	91.88	0.83	0.66	10.79	0.97	9.62	99.5	5	95	0	0	111	24.29	-19.48			Dec-05
50	5.46	9.77	17.08	29.48	89.49	0.62	0.91	10.76	0.97	9.61	99.5	5	95	0	0	111	24.14	-19.6			Dec-05
	-0.05	0.92	4.48			0	1.37			10.32	495.6	11	90	0	0	319					Aug-16
	5.45	9.55	19.36	34.32	94.74	0.14	0.95	10.66	0.93	21.8	519.2	4	96	0	0	74	22.72	-23.07			Jan-98
50	5.40	9.40	19.05	33.54	92.74	0.01	1.16	10.67	0.94	20.97	519.2	4	96	0	0	74	22.57	-23.15			Sep-00
	3.58	11.54	14.63	38.89	105.32	0.5	0.92	13.62	0.93	19.79	465.4	5	95	0	0	91	22.11	-28.05			Jan-98
50	3.51	11.36	14.33	37.90	103.04	0.38	1.16	13.63	0.94	17.18	465.4	5	95	0	0	91	21.96	-28.11			Sep-95
	5.59	9.44	14.47	23.49	76.30	2.04	0.94	12.01	0.94	12.56	307.3	4	96	0	0	76	30.84	-24.3			Sep-04
50	5.57	9.34	14.21	22.72	74.44	1.86	1.15	12.04	0.95	12.26	307.3	4	96	0	0	76	30.65	-24.34			Sep-04
5,000	2.17	5.32	17.60			0.77	6.83				--										Jan-15
250	3.74	6.73	10.52	6.82	12.50	2.16	1.26	5.55	0.41	8.86	13.2	56	54	28	-40	101			2.25		Jun-12
	3.71	6.74	10.78	7.71	13.78	2.33	1.01	5.54	0.41	8.93	13.2	56	54	28	-40	101					Apr-13
100	5.89	10.35	28.54	19.48	20.68	3.09	2.01	12.78	0.78	11.41	362.3	3	93	0	3						Aug-12
100	6.05	10.93	29.80	23.17	27.13	3.84	1.01	12.82	0.79	11.59	362.3	3	93	0	3						Aug-12
100	6.03	10.77	29.44	22.04	25.31	3.65	1.26	12.78	0.78	11.52	362.3	3	93	0	3						Aug-12
100	0.88	3.52	9.62			6.06	1.77			10.64	37.1	3	97	0	0						Dec-15
100	1.10	3.98	10.68			6.79	0.77			10.67	37.1	3	97	0	0						Dec-15
100	1.05	3.89	10.37			6.57	1.02			10.62	37.1	3	97	0	0						Dec-15
100	3.82	7.13	15.68	24.71	72.88	1.29	1.75	9.57	0.87	18.24	1,882	1	99	0	0		16.51	-8.75			Oct-04
100	4.08	7.88	17.12	28.52	81.73	2.07	0.75	9.6	0.87	18.42	1,882	1	99	0	0		17.19	-8.42			Oct-04
	3.90	7.50	16.26	25.69	74.99	1.67	1.5	9.61	0.87	16.02	1,882	1	99	0	0		16.74	-8.76			Mar-10
	3.98	7.67	16.52	26.60	76.72	1.84	1.25	9.6	0.87	16.22	1,882	1	99	0	0		16.93	-8.6			Mar-10
100	4.02	7.76	16.77	27.53	79.31	1.84	1	9.59	0.87	18.41	1,882	1	99	0	0		17.04	-8.5			Aug-03
100	1.53	4.03	16.89	11.61	17.53	2.43	2.01	10.32	0.8	10.54	251.4	3	95	0	2		13.35	-21.05			Dec-05
100	1.77	4.59	17.99	14.95	23.63	3.35	1.01	10.29	0.8	10.65	251.4	3	95	0	2		14.02	-20.74			Dec-05
	1.53	4.16	17.16	12.53	19.14	2.26	1.73	10.29	0.8	12.24	251.4	3	95	0	2		13.53	-21			Mar-10
	1.69	4.31	17.47	13.50	20.85	2.51	1.48	10.27	0.79	12.16	251.4	3	95	0	2		13.7	-20.88			Mar-10
100	1.72	4.39	17.72	14.06	21.99	3.14	1.26	10.31	0.8	10.57	251.4	3	95	0	2		13.84	-20.92			Dec-05
100	0.83	1.91	0.76	9.03	30.95	0	2.03	16.72	1.22	10.96	3.9	2	98	0	0		27.04	-23.39			Oct-09
100	1.06	2.42	1.77	12.42	37.19	0	1.03	16.69	1.22	12.02	3.9	2	98	0	0		27.82	-23.13			Oct-09
100	1.01	2.24	1.51	11.45	35.83	0	1.28	16.69	1.22	11.76	3.9	2	98	0	0		27.55	-23.24			Oct-09
100	4.53	8.98	16.76	27.84	82.18	0.57	1.77	9.65	0.89	15.63	34.2	2	98	0	0						Aug-12
100	4.78	9.51	17.91	31.72	91.50	1.48	0.77	9.68	0.9	15.64	34.2	2	98	0	0						Aug-12
100	4.72	9.37	17.60	30.71	89.31	1.24	1.02	9.68	0.89	15.65	34.2	2	98	0	0						Aug-12
	-1.86	-2.40	-12.97	-36.80	-31.45	0	2.84	28.9		12.79	81.0	0	98	0	2	98	13.32	-18.12			Aug-07
	6.15	10.55	25.62			0.55	1.64			10.33	14.1	5	95	0	0	15					Jul-15
	10.02	14.47	17.82	30.66	89.45	1.36	1.14	10.06	0.93	20.64	157.6	2	98	0	0	5	21.06	-12.97			Dec-92
	4.01	5.05	10.14	8.28		0.05	1.65	9.05	1.36	11.34	23.7	10	90	0	0	108					Dec-13
1,000	7.47	13.99	27.42	32.69	105.82	1.33	0.73	10.25	0.97	22.83	192.6	1	99	0	0	69	24.45	-18.04			Oct-13
250	7.44	13.89	27.09	31.69	103.44	1.12	0.98	10.26	0.97	22.84	192.6	1	99	0	0	69	24.45	-18.04			Mar-10
1,000	4.40	9.70	11.58			0.13	0.95			11.68	21.5	1	99	0	0						Nov-15
250	4.30	9.51	11.30			0.07	1.2			11.62	21.5	1	99	0	0						Nov-15
	3.87	6.79	11.11			1.39	1.13			11.71	115.4	4	59	37	0	16					Dec-15
	4.89	8.30	19.86	29.58	93.68	0.5	0.9	9.76	0.94	23.18	455.0	1	99	0	0	23	25.41	-16.22			Jan-98
	3.67	11.26	20.78	21.26	84.97	0	0.92	11.2	0.96	18.07	403.0	1	99	0	0	23	28.2	-17.1			Dec-10

Fund Name	Ticker Symbol	Traded On	Fund Type	Category and (Prospectus Objective)	Overall Rating	Reward Rating	Risk Rating	Recent Up/ Downgrade	Open to New Investors	Min Initial Investment
	MARKET		FUND TYPE, CATEGORY & OBJECTIVE		RATINGS				MINIMUMS	
Davenport Small Cap Focus Fund	DSCPX	NAS CM	Open End	US Equity Small Cap (Small Company)	C+	C+	C+	Up	Y	5,000
Davenport Value & Income Fund	DVIPX	NAS CM	Open End	US Equity Large Cap Value (Growth & Income)	B-	B-	B-	Down	Y	5,000
Davidson Multi-Cap Equity Fund Class A	DFMAX	NAS CM	Open End	US Equity Large Cap Blend (Growth)	B	C+	B	Up	Y	2,500
Davidson Multi-Cap Equity Fund Class I	DFMIX	NAS CM	Open End	US Equity Large Cap Blend (Growth)	B	C+	B+	Up	Y	250,000
Davis Appreciation & Income Fund Class A	RPFCX	NAS CM	Open End	Aggressive Alloc (Growth & Income)	C+	C+	C	Down	Y	1,000
Davis Appreciation & Income Fund Class C	DCSCX	NAS CM	Open End	Aggressive Alloc (Growth & Income)	C+	C+	C	Up	Y	1,000
Davis Appreciation & Income Fund Class Y	DCSYX	NAS CM	Open End	Aggressive Alloc (Growth & Income)	C+	C+	C	Down	Y	5,000,000
Davis Financial Fund Class A	RPFGX	NAS CM	Open End	Financials Sector Equity (Financial)	B+	B	B+	Up	Y	1,000
Davis Financial Fund Class C	DFFCX	NAS CM	Open End	Financials Sector Equity (Financial)	B	B	B+		Y	1,000
Davis Financial Fund Class Y	DVFYX	NAS CM	Open End	Financials Sector Equity (Financial)	B+	B	B+	Up	Y	5,000,000
Davis Global Fund Class A	DGFAX	NAS CM	Open End	Global Equity (World Stock)	B+	A	B-	Up	Y	1,000
Davis Global Fund Class C	DGFCX	NAS CM	Open End	Global Equity (World Stock)	A-	A	B	Up	Y	1,000
Davis Global Fund Class Y	DGFYX	NAS CM	Open End	Global Equity (World Stock)	B+	A	B-	Up	Y	5,000,000
Davis International Fund Class A	DILAX	NAS CM	Open End	Global Equity Large Cap (Foreign Stock)	B	B+	B	Up	Y	1,000
Davis International Fund Class C	DILCX	NAS CM	Open End	Global Equity Large Cap (Foreign Stock)	B	B	B-	Up	Y	1,000
Davis International Fund Class Y	DILYX	NAS CM	Open End	Global Equity Large Cap (Foreign Stock)	B+	A-	B	Up	Y	5,000,000
Davis New York Venture Fund Class A	NYVTX	NAS CM	Open End	US Equity Large Cap Blend (Growth)	B	B	B	Up	Y	1,000
Davis New York Venture Fund Class B	NYVBX	NAS CM	Open End	US Equity Large Cap Blend (Growth)	B	B	B	Up	Y	1,000
Davis New York Venture Fund Class C	NYVCX	NAS CM	Open End	US Equity Large Cap Blend (Growth)	B	B	B	Up	Y	1,000
Davis New York Venture Fund Class R	NYVRX	NAS CM	Open End	US Equity Large Cap Blend (Growth)	B	B	B	Up	Y	500,000
Davis New York Venture Fund Class T	DNVTX	NAS CM	Open End	US Equity Large Cap Blend (Growth)	B	B	B		Y	1,000
Davis New York Venture Fund Class Y	DNVYX	NAS CM	Open End	US Equity Large Cap Blend (Growth)	B	B	B	Up	Y	5,000,000
Davis Opportunity Fund Class A	RPEAX	NAS CM	Open End	US Equity Large Cap Growth (Growth)	B+	B+	A-	Up	Y	1,000
Davis Opportunity Fund Class C	DGOCX	NAS CM	Open End	US Equity Large Cap Growth (Growth)	B+	B+	A-	Up	Y	1,000
Davis Opportunity Fund Class Y	DGOYX	NAS CM	Open End	US Equity Large Cap Growth (Growth)	B+	B+	A-	Up	Y	5,000,000
Davis Real Estate Fund Class A	RPFRX	NAS CM	Open End	Real Estate Sector Equity (Real Estate)	B	B-	B	Up	Y	1,000
Davis Real Estate Fund Class C	DRECX	NAS CM	Open End	Real Estate Sector Equity (Real Estate)	B	B-	B	Up	Y	1,000
Davis Real Estate Fund Class Y	DREYX	NAS CM	Open End	Real Estate Sector Equity (Real Estate)	B	B-	B	Up	Y	5,000,000
Day Hagan Hedged Strategy Fund Class A	DHJAX	NAS CM	Open End	Long/Short Equity (Growth)	B	C	A-	Up	Y	1,000
Day Hagan Hedged Strategy Fund Class C	DHJCX	NAS CM	Open End	Long/Short Equity (Growth)	B	C	A-	Up	Y	1,000
Day Hagan Hedged Strategy Fund Class I	DHJIX	NAS CM	Open End	Long/Short Equity (Growth)	B	C	A-	Up	Y	1,000
Day Hagan Logix Tactical Dividend Fund Class A	DHQAX	NAS CM	Open End	US Equity Large Cap Value (Equity-Income)	B	C+	B+	Up	Y	1,000
Day Hagan Logix Tactical Dividend Fund Class C	DHQCX	NAS CM	Open End	US Equity Large Cap Value (Equity-Income)	B-	C+	B+	Up	Y	1,000
Day Hagan Logix Tactical Dividend Fund Class I	DHQIX	NAS CM	Open End	US Equity Large Cap Value (Equity-Income)	B	C+	B+	Up	Y	1,000
Day Hagan Tactical Allocation Fund Class A	DHAAX	NAS CM	Open End	Moderate Alloc (Growth)	B-	C	B	Up	Y	1,000
Day Hagan Tactical Allocation Fund Class C	DHACX	NAS CM	Open End	Moderate Alloc (Growth)	C+	C	B	Up	Y	1,000
Day Hagan Tactical Allocation Fund Class I	DHAIX	NAS CM	Open End	Moderate Alloc (Growth)	B-	C	B	Up	Y	1,000
Dean Mid Cap Value Fund	DALCX	NAS CM	Open End	US Equity Mid Cap (Growth & Income)	B	B	B+		Y	1,000
Dean Small Cap Value Fund	DASCX	NAS CM	Open End	US Equity Small Cap (Small Company)	B	B	B	Up	Y	1,000
Dearborn Partners Rising Dividend Fund Class A Shares	DRDAX	NAS CM	Open End	US Equity Large Cap Blend (Equity-Income)	B-	B-	B-	Down	Y	5,000
Dearborn Partners Rising Dividend Fund Class C Shares	DRDCX	NAS CM	Open End	US Equity Large Cap Blend (Equity-Income)	B-	C+	B-	Down	Y	5,000
Dearborn Partners Rising Dividend Fund Class I Shares	DRDIX	NAS CM	Open End	US Equity Large Cap Blend (Equity-Income)	B-	B-	B-	Down	Y	500,000
Delaware Emerging Markets Fund Class A	DEMAX	NAS CM	Open End	Emerging Markets Equity (Div Emerging Mkts)	B	A-	C	Up	Y	1,000
Delaware Emerging Markets Fund Class C	DEMCX	NAS CM	Open End	Emerging Markets Equity (Div Emerging Mkts)	B	B+	C	Up	Y	1,000
Delaware Emerging Markets Fund Class R	DEMRX	NAS CM	Open End	Emerging Markets Equity (Div Emerging Mkts)	B	A-	C	Up	Y	0
Delaware Emerging Markets Fund Class R6	DEMZX	NAS CM	Open End	Emerging Markets Equity (Div Emerging Mkts)	B	A-	C	Up	Y	0
Delaware Emerging Markets Fund Institutional Class	DEMIX	NAS CM	Open End	Emerging Markets Equity (Div Emerging Mkts)	B	A-	C	Up	Y	0
Delaware Enhanced Global Dividend & Income	DEX	NYSE	Closed End	Alloc (World Stock)	B-	B-	B-	Up	Y	
Delaware Foundation Conservative Allocation Class A	DFIAX	NAS CM	Open End	Cautious Alloc (Asset Alloc)	B	C+	B+	Up	Y	1,000
Delaware Foundation Conservative Allocation Class C	DFICX	NAS CM	Open End	Cautious Alloc (Asset Alloc)	B-	C	B	Up	Y	1,000
Delaware Foundation Conservative Allocation Class R	DFIRX	NAS CM	Open End	Cautious Alloc (Asset Alloc)	B-	C+	B	Up	Y	0
Delaware Foundation Conservative Allocation Inst Cls	DFIIX	NAS CM	Open End	Cautious Alloc (Asset Alloc)	B-	C+	B	Up	Y	0

★ Expanded analysis of this fund is included in Section II.

	TOTAL RETURNS					PERFORMANCE				ASSETS		ASSET ALLOCATION & TURNOVER					BULL & BEAR		FEES		
Min Additional Investment	3-Month Total Return	6-Month Total Return	1-Year Total Return	3-Year Total Return	5-Year Total Return	Dividend Yield (TTM)	Expense Ratio	3-Yr Std Deviation	3-Year Beta	NAV	Total Assets (MIL)	%Cash	%Stocks	%Bonds	%Other	Turnover Ratio	Last Bull Market Total Return	Last Bear Market Total Return	Front End Fee (%)	Back End Fee (%)	Inception Date
	5.78	12.41	19.87	38.11		0	1.06			13.42	98.4	6	94	0	0	37					Dec-14
	6.58	11.15	18.22	31.04	95.93	1.68	0.89	8.96	0.83	17.55	648.5	4	96	0	0	26	24.33	-12.73			Dec-10
	5.20	6.41	13.18	23.86	87.27	0.16	1.15	11.23	1.05	25.23	117.6	3	97	0	0	28	24.11	-19.3	5.00		Aug-08
	5.27	6.60	13.49	24.84	89.27	0.4	0.9	11.23	1.06	25.25	117.6	3	97	0	0	28	24.1	-19.3			Oct-13
25	4.59	8.56	16.34	13.25	57.19	0.96	0.91	12.15	1	39.8	199.6	2	71	25	0	109	19.19	-21.6	4.75		May-92
25	4.39	8.14	15.48	10.55	50.90	0.3	1.75	12.12	0.99	39.94	199.6	2	71	25	0	109	18.62	-21.88		1.00	Aug-97
25	4.68	8.73	16.75	14.10	58.89	1.27	0.7	12.16	1	39.98	199.6	2	71	25	0	109	19.25	-21.52			Nov-96
25	6.31	10.55	19.26	38.19	109.97	0.55	0.92	12.44	1.04	51.94	1,332	10	90	0	0	17	21.19	-19.77	4.75		May-91
25	6.10	10.11	18.37	34.82	101.12	0	1.74	12.44	1.04	43.27	1,332	10	90	0	0	17	20.56	-20.06		1.00	Aug-97
25	6.36	10.68	19.56	39.05	111.99	0.69	0.72	12.46	1.04	53.5	1,332	10	90	0	0	17	21.38	-19.73			Mar-97
25	7.05	16.77	33.33	50.61	111.25	0	0.97	12.45	1.04	26.24	999.6	6	93	0	0	53	18.49	-26.01	4.75		Dec-04
25	6.83	16.29	32.31	47.10	102.36	0	1.77	12.43	1.04	24.69	999.6	6	93	0	0	53	17.97	-26.34		1.00	Dec-04
25	7.07	16.86	33.59	51.67	113.87	0	0.72	12.41	1.04	26.3	999.6	6	93	0	0	53	18.77	-25.93			Jul-07
25	4.67	16.07	38.08	36.85	62.56	0.02	1.04	14.9	1.09	13.31	200.7	4	96	0	0	47	19.25	-31.52	4.75		Dec-06
25	4.34	15.42	36.61	32.46	54.04	0	2.14	14.93	1.08	12.5	200.7	4	96	0	0	47	18.78	-32.94		1.00	Dec-06
25	4.70	16.13	38.43	38.00	65.33	0.21	0.78	14.91	1.08	13.14	200.7	4	96	0	0	47	19.67	-32.5			Dec-09
25	7.22	12.17	22.14	39.97	105.19	0.62	0.89	12.33	1.11	34.25	11,581	4	96	0	0	12	22.99	-20.21	4.75		Feb-69
25	7.00	11.68	20.97	35.98	95.66	0.04	1.87	12.31	1.11	30.22	11,581	4	96	0	0	12	22.37	-20.54		4.00	Dec-94
25	7.04	11.78	21.21	36.76	97.34	0.14	1.66	12.32	1.11	31.11	11,581	4	96	0	0	12	22.43	-20.47		1.00	Dec-94
25	7.15	12.05	21.80	38.76	102.18	0.38	1.18	12.33	1.11	34.37	11,581	4	96	0	0	12	22.74	-20.33			Aug-03
25	7.20	12.16	22.12	39.91	105.07		1	12.33	1.11	34.27	11,581	4	96	0	0	12	22.98	-20.21	2.50		Jun-17
25	7.29	12.34	22.47	41.05	107.74	0.84	0.63	12.33	1.11	35	11,581	4	96	0	0	12	23.2	-20.14			Oct-96
25	5.74	11.67	23.09	47.82	129.69	0	0.95	12.35	1.06	37.01	661.6	5	93	0	2	61	17.27	-18.33	4.75		Dec-94
25	5.54	11.27	22.16	44.39	120.79	0	1.75	12.35	1.06	30.36	661.6	5	93	0	2	61	16.75	-18.65		1.00	Aug-97
25	5.80	11.82	23.41	48.91	132.45	0	0.71	12.34	1.06	38.77	661.6	5	93	0	2	61	17.45	-18.28			Sep-97
25	2.90	5.33	8.30	19.16	53.20	1.36	0.93	12.52	0.66	39.7	206.0	3	97	0	0	53	30.03	-14.3	4.75		Jan-94
25	2.68	4.90	7.40	16.10	46.63	0.56	1.82	12.49	0.66	39.69	206.0	3	97	0	0	53	29.42	-14.63		1.00	Aug-97
25	2.94	5.44	8.56	19.92	54.82	1.58	0.73	12.5	0.66	40.25	206.0	3	97	0	0	53	30.2	-14.2			Nov-96
50	1.36	4.27	7.44	28.59			2.25			10.34	27.0	98	2	0	0				5.75		Jan-17
50	1.46	4.28	7.27	26.41			3			10.33	27.0	98	2	0	0						Jan-17
50	1.56	4.38	7.47	29.28			2			10.34	27.0	98	2	0	0						Jan-17
50	6.02	8.32	10.12	17.95		0.66	1.65	8.41	0.71	11.47	135.8	18	75	6	0	72			5.75		Jul-14
50	5.76	7.85	9.30	15.34		0.12	2.4	8.48	0.71	11.25	135.8	18	75	6	0	72					Jul-14
50	6.08	8.34	10.30	18.76		0.91	1.4	8.4	0.7	11.5	135.8	18	75	6	0	72					Jul-14
50	2.72	5.55	8.25	7.85	29.39	0	1.8	6.26	0.56	11.45	29.1	30	59	11	0	176	13.11	-13.95	5.75		Oct-09
50	2.51	5.13	7.47	5.49	24.69	0	2.55	6.25	0.56	10.73	29.1	30	59	11	0	176	12.69	-14.18			Oct-09
50	2.89	5.70	8.58	8.84	30.82	0	1.55	6.27	0.56	11.5	29.1	30	59	11	0	176	13.11	-13.95			Jul-14
	6.42	9.76	15.11	32.79	97.90	0.38	1.1	9.34	0.85	20.47	31.9	2	98	0	0	57	31.17	-23.86			May-97
	1.55	3.76	3.70	25.49	86.89	1	1.15	13.53	0.92	14.9	335.1	5	95	0	0	154	32.71	-25.81			May-97
500	3.84	7.23	14.75	20.85		1.3	1.35	9.11	0.8	14.37	214.0	1	99	0	0	5			5.00		Apr-13
500	3.65	6.84	13.87	18.09		0.6	2.1	9.07	0.8	14.32	214.0	1	99	0	0	5				1.00	Apr-13
500	3.89	7.35	15.03	21.72		1.55	1.1	9.12	0.8	14.39	214.0	1	99	0	0	5					Apr-13
100	2.51	16.23	41.61	43.26	51.24	0.51	1.7	20.33	1.23	20.17	4,736	0	100	0	-1	25	17.15	-30.41	5.75		Jun-96
100	2.34	15.78	40.58	40.08	45.66	0.06	2.45	20.33	1.23	18.84	4,736	0	100	0	-1	25	16.61	-30.66		1.00	Jun-96
	2.46	16.08	41.32	42.18	49.33	0.34	1.95	20.26	1.22	20.33	4,736	0	100	0	-1	25	16.94	-30.5			Aug-09
	2.59	16.39	42.17	44.59	53.36	0.74	1.32	20.3	1.22	20.28	4,736	0	100	0	-1	25	17.27	-30.33			May-16
	2.56	16.31	41.97	44.35	53.11	0.68	1.45	20.28	1.22	20.29	4,736	0	100	0	-1	25	17.27	-30.33			Jun-96
	2.38	7.02	18.58	25.43	50.76	2.47	0	10.61		13.16	207.2	-37	70	47	2	54	16.65	-16.68			Jun-07
100	1.92	4.54	9.84	14.02	30.15	2.01	1.15	4.23	0.19	9.69	81.3	16	39	46	-3	161	10.51	-7.69	5.75		Dec-97
100	1.82	4.24	9.12	11.46	25.41	1.31	1.9	4.22	0.19	9.72	81.3	16	39	46	-3	161	10.07	-7.93		1.00	Dec-97
	1.85	4.52	9.70	13.19	28.67	1.78	1.4	4.28	0.18	9.69	81.3	16	39	46	-3	161	10.36	-7.72			Jun-03
	1.97	4.65	10.09	14.84	31.83	2.24	0.9	4.28	0.2	9.71	81.3	16	39	46	-3	161	10.73	-7.56			Dec-97

Fund Name	MARKET Ticker Symbol	Traded On	FUND TYPE, CATEGORY & OBJECTIVE Fund Type	Category and (Prospectus Objective)	RATINGS Overall Rating	Reward Rating	Risk Rating	Recent Up/ Downgrade	MINIMUMS Open to New Investors	Min Initial Investment
Delaware Foundation Moderate Allocation Class A	DFBAX	NAS CM	Open End	Moderate Alloc (Asset Alloc)	B-	C+	B	Up	Y	1,000
Delaware Foundation Moderate Allocation Class C	DFBCX	NAS CM	Open End	Moderate Alloc (Asset Alloc)	B-	C+	B	Up	Y	1,000
Delaware Foundation Moderate Allocation Class R	DFBRX	NAS CM	Open End	Moderate Alloc (Asset Alloc)	B-	C+	B+	Up	Y	0
Delaware Foundation Moderate Allocation Institutional Cls	DFFIX	NAS CM	Open End	Moderate Alloc (Asset Alloc)	B-	C+	B	Up	Y	0
Delaware Global Real Estate Opportunities Fund Class A	DGRPX	NAS CM	Open End	Real Estate Sector Equity (Real Estate)	B-	C	B	Up	Y	1,000
Delaware Global Real Estate Opportunities Fund Class C	DLPCX	NAS CM	Open End	Real Estate Sector Equity (Real Estate)	B-	C	B	Up	Y	1,000
Delaware Global Real Estate Opportunities Fund Class R	DLPRX	NAS CM	Open End	Real Estate Sector Equity (Real Estate)	B-	C	B	Up	Y	0
Delaware Global Real Estate Opp Fund Inst Cls	DGROX	NAS CM	Open End	Real Estate Sector Equity (Real Estate)	B-	C+	B		Y	0
Delaware Global Value Fund Class A	DABAX	NAS CM	Open End	Global Equity (World Stock)	C+	C+	C+	Down	Y	1,000
Delaware Global Value Fund Class C	DABCX	NAS CM	Open End	Global Equity (World Stock)	C+	C+	C+	Down	Y	1,000
Delaware Global Value Fund Institutional Class	DABIX	NAS CM	Open End	Global Equity (World Stock)	C+	C+	C+	Down	Y	0
Delaware Healthcare Fund Class A	DLHAX	NAS CM	Open End	Healthcare Sector Equity (Health)	A-	A-	B+	Up	Y	1,000
Delaware Healthcare Fund Class C	DLHCX	NAS CM	Open End	Healthcare Sector Equity (Health)	B+	A-	B+	Up	Y	1,000
Delaware Healthcare Fund Class I	DLHIX	NAS CM	Open End	Healthcare Sector Equity (Health)	A-	A-	B+	Up	Y	0
Delaware Healthcare Fund Class R	DLRHX	NAS CM	Open End	Healthcare Sector Equity (Health)	A-	A-	B+	Up	Y	0
Delaware International Small Cap Fund Class A	DGGAX	NAS CM	Open End	Global Equity Mid/Small Cap (Small Company)	B+	A	B	Up	Y	1,000
Delaware International Small Cap Fund Class C	DGGCX	NAS CM	Open End	Global Equity Mid/Small Cap (Small Company)	B+	A	B	Up	Y	1,000
Delaware International Small Cap Fund Class R	DGGRX	NAS CM	Open End	Global Equity Mid/Small Cap (Small Company)	B+	A	B	Up	Y	0
Delaware International Small Cap Fund Class R6	DGRRX	NAS CM	Open End	Global Equity Mid/Small Cap (Small Company)	B+	A	B	Up	Y	0
Delaware International Small Cap Fund Institutional Class	DGGIX	NAS CM	Open End	Global Equity Mid/Small Cap (Small Company)	B+	A	B	Up	Y	0
Delaware International Value Equity Fund Class A	DEGIX	NAS CM	Open End	Global Equity Large Cap (Foreign Stock)	B	B-	B	Up	Y	1,000
Delaware International Value Equity Fund Class C	DEGCX	NAS CM	Open End	Global Equity Large Cap (Foreign Stock)	B-	C+	B	Up	Y	1,000
Delaware International Value Equity Fund Class R	DIVRX	NAS CM	Open End	Global Equity Large Cap (Foreign Stock)	B-	B-	B	Up	Y	0
Delaware International Value Equity Fund Institutional Cls	DEQIX	NAS CM	Open End	Global Equity Large Cap (Foreign Stock)	B	B-	B	Up	Y	0
Delaware Investments Dividend and Income Fund	DDF	NYSE	Closed End	Moderate Alloc (Income)	B-	B-	B	Up	Y	
Delaware Mid Cap Value Fund Class A	DLMAX	NAS CM	Open End	US Equity Mid Cap (Growth)	B+	B+	B+	Up	Y	1,000
Delaware Mid Cap Value Fund Class C	DLMCX	NAS CM	Open End	US Equity Mid Cap (Growth)	B	B	B	Up	Y	1,000
Delaware Mid Cap Value Fund Class R	DLMRX	NAS CM	Open End	US Equity Mid Cap (Growth)	B	B	B		Y	0
Delaware Mid Cap Value Fund Institutional Class	DLMIX	NAS CM	Open End	US Equity Mid Cap (Growth)	B+	B+	B+	Up	Y	0
Delaware REIT Fund Class A	DPREX	NAS CM	Open End	Real Estate Sector Equity (Real Estate)	C+	C	B-		Y	1,000
Delaware REIT Fund Class C	DPRCX	NAS CM	Open End	Real Estate Sector Equity (Real Estate)	C	C	C	Down	Y	1,000
Delaware REIT Fund Class R	DPRRX	NAS CM	Open End	Real Estate Sector Equity (Real Estate)	C	C	C+	Down	Y	0
Delaware REIT Fund Class R6	DPRDX	NAS CM	Open End	Real Estate Sector Equity (Real Estate)	C	C	C+	Down	Y	0
Delaware REIT Fund Institutional Class	DPRSX	NAS CM	Open End	Real Estate Sector Equity (Real Estate)	C+	C	B		Y	0
Delaware Select Growth Fund Class A	DVEAX	NAS CM	Open End	US Equity Large Cap Growth (Growth)	B-	B-	B	Up		1,000
Delaware Select Growth Fund Class C	DVECX	NAS CM	Open End	US Equity Large Cap Growth (Growth)	B-	C+	B	Up		1,000
Delaware Select Growth Fund Class R	DFSRX	NAS CM	Open End	US Equity Large Cap Growth (Growth)	B-	B-	B	Up		0
Delaware Select Growth Fund Institutional Class	VAGGX	NAS CM	Open End	US Equity Large Cap Growth (Growth)	B	B-	B	Up		0
Delaware Small Cap Core Fund Class A	DCCAX	NAS CM	Open End	US Equity Small Cap (Small Company)	B+	A-	B	Up	Y	1,000
Delaware Small Cap Core Fund Class C	DCCCX	NAS CM	Open End	US Equity Small Cap (Small Company)	B+	A-	B	Up	Y	1,000
Delaware Small Cap Core Fund Class R	DCCRX	NAS CM	Open End	US Equity Small Cap (Small Company)	B+	A-	B	Up	Y	0
Delaware Small Cap Core Fund Class R6	DCZRX	NAS CM	Open End	US Equity Small Cap (Small Company)	B+	A-	B	Up	Y	0
Delaware Small Cap Core Fund Institutional Class	DCCIX	NAS CM	Open End	US Equity Small Cap (Small Company)	B+	A-	B	Up	Y	0
Delaware Small Cap Growth Fund Class A	DSGDX	NAS CM	Open End	US Equity Small Cap (Small Company)	D	C-	B-		Y	1,000
Delaware Small Cap Growth Fund Class C	DSGEX	NAS CM	Open End	US Equity Small Cap (Small Company)	D	C-	B-		Y	1,000
Delaware Small Cap Growth Fund Class R	DSGFX	NAS CM	Open End	US Equity Small Cap (Small Company)	D	C-	B-		Y	0
Delaware Small Cap Growth Fund Institutional Class	DSGGX	NAS CM	Open End	US Equity Small Cap (Small Company)	D	C	B-		Y	0
Delaware Small Cap Value Fund Class A	DEVLX	NAS CM	Open End	US Equity Small Cap (Small Company)	B+	A-	B	Up	Y	1,000
Delaware Small Cap Value Fund Class C	DEVCX	NAS CM	Open End	US Equity Small Cap (Small Company)	B	B+	B	Up	Y	1,000
Delaware Small Cap Value Fund Class R	DVLRX	NAS CM	Open End	US Equity Small Cap (Small Company)	B	B+	B	Up	Y	0
Delaware Small Cap Value Fund Class R6	DVZRX	NAS CM	Open End	US Equity Small Cap (Small Company)	B+	A-	B	Up	Y	0
Delaware Small Cap Value Fund Institutional Class	DEVIX	NAS CM	Open End	US Equity Small Cap (Small Company)	B+	A-	B	Up	Y	0

★Expanded analysis of this fund is included in Section II.

Min Additional Investment	3-Month Total Return	6-Month Total Return	1-Year Total Return	3-Year Total Return	5-Year Total Return	Dividend Yield (TTM)	Expense Ratio	3-Yr Std Deviation	3-Year Beta	NAV	Total Assets (MIL)	%Cash	%Stocks	%Bonds	%Other	Turnover Ratio	Last Bull Market Total Return	Last Bear Market Total Return	Front End Fee (%)	Back End Fee (%)	Inception Date
	TOTAL RETURNS					PERFORMANCE				ASSETS		ASSET ALLOCATION & TURNOVER					BULL & BEAR		FEES		
100	2.09	5.83	12.74	17.32	40.89	2.1	1.14	6.1	0.56	11.62	264.7	11	57	33	-2	133	13.94	-12.33	5.75		Dec-97
100	1.90	5.43	11.89	14.69	35.64	1.4	1.9	6.04	0.55	11.62	264.7	11	57	33	-2	133	13.3	-12.53		1.00	Dec-97
	2.03	5.71	12.50	16.38	38.94	1.87	1.4	6.07	0.56	11.57	264.7	11	57	33	-2	133	13.72	-12.4			Jun-03
	2.24	5.95	13.09	18.14	42.56	2.31	0.9	6.07	0.56	11.63	264.7	11	57	33	-2	133	14.08	-12.23			Dec-97
100	3.06	3.20	8.64	10.86	37.31	2.67	1.4	10.4	0.93	7.65	61.4	9	90	0	1	193	23.47	-18.05	5.75		Jan-07
100	2.99	2.94	7.83	8.54	32.24	1.82	2.15	10.44	0.93	7.65	61.4	9	90	0	1	193	22.8	-18.19		1.00	Sep-12
	3.13	3.20	8.37	10.20	35.60	2.42	1.65	10.49	0.94	7.65	61.4	9	90	0	1	193	23.16	-18.02			Sep-12
	3.25	3.46	8.91	11.85	39.05	2.92	1.15	10.47	0.94	7.65	61.4	9	90	0	1	193	23.52	-17.85			Jan-07
100	3.77	7.68	16.76	19.43	54.33	1.5	1.55	11.18	1.02	13.28	19.5	2	98	0	0	12	16.93	-23.65	5.75		Dec-97
100	3.61	7.35	15.88	16.77	48.75	0.91	2.3	11.18	1.02	13.05	19.5	2	98	0	0	12	16.26	-23.89		1.00	Sep-01
	3.84	7.82	17.07	20.33	56.30	1.7	1.3	11.13	1.02	13.32	19.5	2	98	0	0	12	17.04	-23.58			Dec-97
100	1.26	10.85	31.95	39.84	151.76	0.73	1.38	13.7	0.92	22.39	443.2	1	98	0	1	29	25.09	-17.52	5.75		Sep-07
100	1.10	10.46	31.02	36.75	142.51	0.18	2.13	13.69	0.92	21.42	443.2	1	98	0	1	29	24.53	-17.75		1.00	Jan-10
	1.36	10.95	32.32	40.89	154.93	0.91	1.13	13.68	0.92	22.48	443.2	1	98	0	1	29	25.19	-17.43			Sep-07
	1.23	10.72	31.64	38.84	148.66	0.54	1.63	13.68	0.92	22.15	443.2	1	98	0	1	29	24.84	-17.57			Jan-10
100	5.47	21.65	46.76	43.23	83.47	0	1.38	13.76	0.99	7.92	31.7	4	96	0	0	66	24.07	-16.78	5.75		Dec-08
100	5.19	21.12	45.70	39.87	76.56	0	2.13	13.77	0.99	6.71	31.7	4	96	0	0	66	23.49	-17.02		1.00	Dec-10
	5.33	21.47	46.40	41.99	81.04	0	1.63	13.77	0.99	7.52	31.7	4	96	0	0	66	23.79	-16.86			Dec-10
	5.60	21.89	47.31	44.40	85.89		1	13.77	0.99	8.29	31.7	4	96	0	0	66	24.17	-16.69			Jun-17
	5.61	21.75	47.14	44.24	85.68	0	1.13	13.76	0.99	8.28	31.7	4	96	0	0	66	24.17	-16.69			Dec-08
100	2.07	7.53	22.39	28.03	45.69	1.71	1.36	11.72	0.92	15.63	319.9	4	96	0	0	13	13.33	-28.13	5.75		Oct-91
100	1.86	7.12	21.53	25.12	40.26	1.15	2.11	11.71	0.92	15.42	319.9	4	96	0	0	13	12.83	-28.32		1.00	Nov-95
	2.03	7.44	22.15	27.06	43.90	1.52	1.61	11.69	0.92	15.6	319.9	4	96	0	0	13	13.1	-28.14			Jun-03
	2.10	7.69	22.68	28.96	47.56	1.91	1.11	11.68	0.92	15.68	319.9	4	96	0	0	13	13.56	-28.03			Nov-92
	4.22	8.70	13.48	28.05	85.28	2.9	0	11.18	1.02	11.92	92.9	-39	90	37	2	47	26.24	-16.29			Mar-93
100	6.61	11.78	16.83	36.78	93.57	0.43	1.25	12.45	1.11	6.38	13.0	0	100	0	0	49	29.21	-25.14	5.75		Feb-08
100	6.31	11.23	15.73	33.40	86.11	0	2	12.41	1.11	5.95	13.0	0	100	0	0	49	28.6	-25.39		1.00	Jul-08
	6.56	11.73	16.58	35.68	91.01	0.25	1.5	12.46	1.12	6.38	13.0	0	100	0	0	49	28.51	-25.21			Jul-08
	6.68	12.04	17.10	37.50	95.68	0.63	1	12.38	1.11	6.38	13.0	0	100	0	0	49	29.34	-25.02			Feb-08
100	1.39	0.00	0.99	8.02	45.32	1.48	1.33	12.89	0.96	11.38	126.8	3	96	0	1	111	31.18	-15.36	5.75		Dec-95
100	1.14	-0.46	0.17	5.56	39.93	0.91	2.08	12.86	0.96	11.31	126.8	3	96	0	1	111	30.52	-15.55		1.00	Nov-97
	1.31	-0.24	0.62	7.17	43.48	1.29	1.58	12.89	0.96	11.36	126.8	3	96	0	1	111	30.79	-15.38			Jun-03
	1.56	0.17	1.37	8.62	46.13	1.78	0.93	12.9	0.96	11.44	126.8	3	96	0	1	111	31.18	-15.36			Aug-16
	1.47	0.05	1.16	8.77	47.16	1.66	1.08	12.86	0.96	11.43	126.8	3	96	0	1	111	31.28	-15.22			Nov-97
100	3.13	11.67	22.19	18.44	70.55	0	1.25	11.75	0.94	37.77	387.2	2	98	0	0	33	25.98	-11.97	5.75		May-94
100	2.93	11.22	21.27	15.80	64.26	0	2	11.74	0.94	26.7	387.2	2	98	0	0	33	25.42	-12.23		1.00	May-94
	3.07	11.52	21.91	17.56	68.42	0	1.5	11.75	0.94	35.52	387.2	2	98	0	0	33	25.77	-12.06			Jun-03
	3.18	11.82	22.52	19.33	72.72	0	1	11.75	0.94	41.1	387.2	2	98	0	0	33	26.14	-11.87			Aug-97
100	2.63	8.67	13.92	32.11	109.89	0	1.24	13.57	0.94	23.58	2,828	3	98	0	-1	43	32.16	-24.22	5.75		Dec-98
100	2.45	8.30	13.06	29.23	102.12	0	1.99	13.56	0.94	21.23	2,828	3	98	0	-1	43	31.5	-24.48		1.00	Aug-05
	2.54	8.52	13.65	31.13	107.26	0	1.49	13.57	0.94	22.85	2,828	3	98	0	-1	43	31.82	-24.25			Aug-05
	1.80	7.92	13.32	32.22	111.08	0.14	0.82	13.56	0.94	24.11	2,828	3	98	0	-1	43	32.2	-24.14			May-16
	2.72	8.86	14.20	33.13	112.53	0.06	0.99	13.57	0.94	24.11	2,828	3	98	0	-1	43	32.2	-24.14			Dec-98
100	19.39	23.34	34.47			0	1.3			11.15	7.2	0	100	0	0	145			5.75		Jun-16
100	19.18	22.78	33.33			0	2.05			11.01	7.2	0	100	0	0	145				1.00	Jun-16
	19.37	23.20	34.05			0	1.55			11.1	7.2	0	100	0	0	145					Jun-16
	19.43	23.50	34.61			0	1.05			11.19	7.2	0	100	0	0	145					Jun-16
100	5.07	8.80	11.69	35.62	94.61	0.46	1.24	14.01	0.95	65.94	4,547	1	99	0	0	19	28.26	-22.44	5.75		Jun-87
100	4.87	8.40	10.85	32.59	87.45	0.03	1.99	14	0.95	54.74	4,547	1	99	0	0	19	27.67	-22.67		1.00	Nov-95
	5.01	8.68	11.43	34.60	92.19	0.3	1.49	14	0.95	64.01	4,547	1	99	0	0	19	28.08	-22.52			Jun-03
	5.17	9.04	12.19	36.53	95.92	0.72	0.77	14.03	0.95	69.5	4,547	1	99	0	0	19	28.26	-22.44			May-16
	5.14	8.94	11.99	36.65	97.06	0.61	0.99	14	0.95	69.49	4,547	1	99	0	0	19	28.44	-22.37			Nov-92

	MARKET		FUND TYPE, CATEGORY & OBJECTIVE		RATINGS					MINIMUMS
Fund Name	Ticker Symbol	Traded On	Fund Type	Category and (Prospectus Objective)	Overall Rating	Reward Rating	Risk Rating	Recent Up/ Downgrade	Open to New Investors	Min Initial Investment
Delaware Smid Cap Growth Fund Class A	DFCIX	NAS CM	Open End	US Equity Mid Cap (Growth)	B+	B+	B	Up		1,000
Delaware Smid Cap Growth Fund Class C	DEEVX	NAS CM	Open End	US Equity Mid Cap (Growth)	B	B	B	Up		1,000
Delaware Smid Cap Growth Fund Class R	DFRIX	NAS CM	Open End	US Equity Mid Cap (Growth)	B	B+	B	Up		0
Delaware Smid Cap Growth Fund Class R6	DFZRX	NAS CM	Open End	US Equity Mid Cap (Growth)	B+	A-	B	Up		0
Delaware Smid Cap Growth Fund Institutional Class	DFDIX	NAS CM	Open End	US Equity Mid Cap (Growth)	B+	A-	B	Up		0
Delaware U.S. Growth Fund Class A	DUGAX	NAS CM	Open End	US Equity Large Cap Growth (Growth)	B	B	A-	Up	Y	1,000
Delaware U.S. Growth Fund Class C	DEUCX	NAS CM	Open End	US Equity Large Cap Growth (Growth)	B	B	B	Up	Y	1,000
Delaware U.S. Growth Fund Class R	DEURX	NAS CM	Open End	US Equity Large Cap Growth (Growth)	B	B	B+	Up	Y	0
Delaware U.S. Growth Fund Class R6	DUZRX	NAS CM	Open End	US Equity Large Cap Growth (Growth)	B	B	A-	Up	Y	0
Delaware U.S. Growth Fund Institutional Class	DEUIX	NAS CM	Open End	US Equity Large Cap Growth (Growth)	B	B	A-	Up	Y	0
Delaware Value® Fund Class A	DDVAX	NAS CM	Open End	US Equity Large Cap Value (Growth)	B	B-	B+			1,000
Delaware Value® Fund Class C	DDVCX	NAS CM	Open End	US Equity Large Cap Value (Growth)	B	C+	B			1,000
Delaware Value® Fund Class R	DDVRX	NAS CM	Open End	US Equity Large Cap Value (Growth)	B	B-	B		Y	0
Delaware Value® Fund Class R6	DDZRX	NAS CM	Open End	US Equity Large Cap Value (Growth)	B	B-	B+		Y	0
Delaware Value® Fund Institutional Class	DDVIX	NAS CM	Open End	US Equity Large Cap Value (Growth)	B	B-	B+			0
Delaware Wealth Builder Fund Class A	DDIAX	NAS CM	Open End	Moderate Alloc (Equity-Income)	B-	C+	B	Down	Y	1,000
Delaware Wealth Builder Fund Class C	DDICX	NAS CM	Open End	Moderate Alloc (Equity-Income)	C+	C+	B	Down	Y	1,000
Delaware Wealth Builder Fund Class R	DDDRX	NAS CM	Open End	Moderate Alloc (Equity-Income)	B-	C+	B	Down	Y	0
Delaware Wealth Builder Fund Institutional Class	DDIIX	NAS CM	Open End	Moderate Alloc (Equity-Income)	B-	C+	B	Down	Y	0
Destinations Equity Income Fund Class I	DGEFX	NAS CM	Open End	US Equity Large Cap Value (Income)	U	U	U		Y	0
Destinations International Equity Fund Class I	DIEFX	NAS CM	Open End	Global Equity Large Cap (Foreign Stock)	U	U	U		Y	0
Destinations Large Cap Equity Fund Class I	DLCFX	NAS CM	Open End	US Equity Large Cap Blend (Growth)	U	U	U		Y	0
Destinations Multi Strategy Alternatives Fund Class I	DMSFX	NAS CM	Open End	Multialternative (Growth)	U	U	U		Y	0
Destinations Real Assets Fund Class I	DRAFX	NAS CM	Open End	Alloc (Growth)	U	U	U		Y	0
Destinations Small-Mid Cap Equity Fund Class I	DSMFX	NAS CM	Open End	US Equity Mid Cap (Growth)	U	U	U		Y	0
Destra Flaherty & Crumrine Preferred & Income Fund Cls A	DPIAX	NAS CM	Open End	US Fixed Income (Income)	B	C+	A+	Up	Y	2,500
Destra Flaherty & Crumrine Preferred & Income Fund Cls C	DPICX	NAS CM	Open End	US Fixed Income (Income)	B	C+	A+	Up	Y	2,500
Destra Flaherty & Crumrine Preferred & Income Fund Cls I	DPIIX	NAS CM	Open End	US Fixed Income (Income)	B	C+	A+	Up	Y	100,000
Destra Wolverine Dynamic Asset Fund Class A	DWAAX	NAS CM	Open End	Multialternative (Growth & Income)	C	C	B	Up	Y	2,500
Destra Wolverine Dynamic Asset Fund Class C	DWACX	NAS CM	Open End	Multialternative (Growth & Income)	C	C	B	Up	Y	2,500
Destra Wolverine Dynamic Asset Fund Class I	DWAIX	NAS CM	Open End	Multialternative (Growth & Income)	C	C	B	Up	Y	100,000
Deutsche Capital Growth Fund Class A	SDGAX	NAS CM	Open End	US Equity Large Cap Growth (Growth)	B	B	B	Down	Y	1,000
Deutsche Capital Growth Fund Class C	SDGCX	NAS CM	Open End	US Equity Large Cap Growth (Growth)	B	B	B	Down	Y	1,000
Deutsche Capital Growth Fund Class R	SDGRX	NAS CM	Open End	US Equity Large Cap Growth (Growth)	B	B	B	Down	Y	0
Deutsche Capital Growth Fund Class R6	SDGZX	NAS CM	Open End	US Equity Large Cap Growth (Growth)	B	B	B	Down	Y	0
Deutsche Capital Growth Fund Class S	SCGSX	NAS CM	Open End	US Equity Large Cap Growth (Growth)	B	B	B	Down	Y	2,500
Deutsche Capital Growth Fund Institutional Class	SDGTX	NAS CM	Open End	US Equity Large Cap Growth (Growth)	B	B	B	Down	Y	1,000,000
Deutsche Communications Fund Class A	TISHX	NAS CM	Open End	Communications Sector Equity (Comm)	B-	C+	B+		Y	1,000
Deutsche Communications Fund Class C	FTICX	NAS CM	Open End	Communications Sector Equity (Comm)	B-	C+	B		Y	1,000
Deutsche Communications Fund Institutional Class	FLICX	NAS CM	Open End	Communications Sector Equity (Comm)	B-	C+	B+		Y	1,000,000
Deutsche Core Equity Fund Class A	SUWAX	NAS CM	Open End	US Equity Large Cap Blend (Growth & Income)	B	B	B		Y	1,000
Deutsche Core Equity Fund Class C	SUWCX	NAS CM	Open End	US Equity Large Cap Blend (Growth & Income)	B	B	B	Up	Y	1,000
Deutsche Core Equity Fund Class R	SUWTX	NAS CM	Open End	US Equity Large Cap Blend (Growth & Income)	B	B	B	Up	Y	0
Deutsche Core Equity Fund Class R6	SUWZX	NAS CM	Open End	US Equity Large Cap Blend (Growth & Income)	B	B	B		Y	0
Deutsche Core Equity Fund Class S	SCDGX	NAS CM	Open End	US Equity Large Cap Blend (Growth & Income)	B	B	B		Y	2,500
Deutsche Core Equity Fund Class T	SUWUX	NAS CM	Open End	US Equity Large Cap Blend (Growth & Income)	B	B	B		Y	1,000
Deutsche Core Equity Fund Institutional Class	SUWIX	NAS CM	Open End	US Equity Large Cap Blend (Growth & Income)	B	B	B		Y	1,000,000
Deutsche CROCI® Equity Dividend Fund Class A	KDHAX	NAS CM	Open End	US Equity Large Cap Value (Growth & Income)	B-	B	C+	Down	Y	1,000
Deutsche CROCI® Equity Dividend Fund Class C	KDHCX	NAS CM	Open End	US Equity Large Cap Value (Growth & Income)	B-	B-	C+	Down	Y	1,000
Deutsche CROCI® Equity Dividend Fund Class R	KDHRX	NAS CM	Open End	US Equity Large Cap Value (Growth & Income)	B-	B	C+	Down	Y	0
Deutsche CROCI® Equity Dividend Fund Class R6	KDHTX	NAS CM	Open End	US Equity Large Cap Value (Growth & Income)	B-	B	C+	Down	Y	0
Deutsche CROCI® Equity Dividend Fund Class S	KDHSX	NAS CM	Open End	US Equity Large Cap Value (Growth & Income)	B-	B	C+	Down	Y	2,500

★ Expanded analysis of this fund is included in Section II.

	TOTAL RETURNS					PERFORMANCE				ASSETS		ASSET ALLOCATION & TURNOVER					BULL & BEAR		FEES		
Min Additional Investment	3-Month Total Return	6-Month Total Return	1-Year Total Return	3-Year Total Return	5-Year Total Return	Dividend Yield (TTM)	Expense Ratio	3-Yr Std Deviation	3-Year Beta	NAV	Total Assets (MIL)	%Cash	%Stocks	%Bonds	%Other	Turnover Ratio	Last Bull Market Total Return	Last Bear Market Total Return	Front End Fee (%)	Back End Fee (%)	Inception Date
100	17.92	21.66	35.13	37.41	102.61	0	1.21	12.99	0.79	21.91	960.3	0	100	0	0	159	25.49	-15.71	5.75		Mar-86
100	17.70	21.19	34.14	34.35	95.11	0	1.96	12.99	0.79	11.11	960.3	0	100	0	0	159	25.02	-15.97		1.00	Nov-95
	17.81	21.51	34.77	36.33	100.00	0	1.46	12.97	0.79	20.18	960.3	0	100	0	0	159	25.35	-15.81			Jun-03
	18.03	21.84	35.60	38.16	103.71	0.1	0.84	13	0.79	29.46	960.3	0	100	0	0	159	25.49	-15.71			May-16
	17.99	21.76	35.45	38.41	105.04	0.02	0.96	12.99	0.79	29.44	960.3	0	100	0	0	159	25.7	-15.63			Nov-92
100	3.00	11.89	27.88	25.91	94.42	0	1.05	11.68	0.95	23.69	3,031	2	98	0	0	22	28.08	-12.42	5.75		Dec-93
100	2.79	11.47	26.92	23.10	87.25	0	1.8	11.72	0.95	20.48	3,031	2	98	0	0	22	27.54	-12.7		1.00	May-94
	2.96	11.77	27.54	24.98	91.99	0	1.3	11.69	0.95	22.7	3,031	2	98	0	0	22	27.9	-12.53			Jun-03
	2.66	11.67	27.82	26.15	94.79	0.22	0.66	11.7	0.95	25.84	3,031	2	98	0	0	22	28.08	-12.42			May-16
	3.10	12.07	28.23	26.84	96.86	0.14	0.8	11.71	0.95	25.82	3,031	2	98	0	0	22	28.24	-12.3			Feb-94
100	5.39	10.37	13.36	27.63	97.36	1.31	0.97	10.09	0.93	21.48	12,711	1	99	0	0	9	24.12	-14.44	5.75		Sep-98
100	5.21	9.98	12.50	24.81	90.10	0.63	1.72	10.08	0.92	21.44	12,711	1	99	0	0	9	23.58	-14.67		1.00	May-02
	5.32	10.24	13.09	26.69	94.79	1.08	1.22	10.09	0.92	21.47	12,711	1	99	0	0	9	23.97	-14.54			Sep-05
	4.50	9.54	12.71	27.62	98.18	1.64	0.62	10.08	0.92	21.48	12,711	1	99	0	0	9	24.27	-14.34			May-16
	5.45	10.50	13.64	28.64	99.76	1.53	0.72	10.07	0.92	21.48	12,711	1	99	0	0	9	24.27	-14.34			Sep-98
100	2.37	4.74	9.13	15.19	51.20	2.43	1.1	6.56		14.71	685.8	7	58	19	2	102	16.5	-13.26	5.75		Dec-96
100	2.20	4.36	8.32	12.63	45.57	1.69	1.85	6.54		14.73	685.8	7	58	19	2	102	15.99	-13.61		1.00	Oct-03
	2.32	4.62	8.86	14.34	49.34	2.18	1.35	6.56		14.71	685.8	7	58	19	2	102	16.44	-13.44			Oct-03
	2.44	4.87	9.40	16.05	53.09	2.67	0.85	6.56		14.71	685.8	7	58	19	2	102	16.8	-13.26			Dec-96
	4.59	7.73					0.88			10.58	366.8	3	97	0	0						Mar-17
	5.28	10.41					1.05			11.69	1,349	4	96	0	0						Mar-17
	5.40	9.75					0.79			11.36	2,775	3	97	0	0						Mar-17
	0.78	1.35					1.32			10.09	1,006	37	14	42	2						Mar-17
	0.05	9.09					1.09			9.97	197.6	6	94	0	0						Mar-17
	4.40	7.50					0.98			11.13	617.3	4	96	0	0						Mar-17
	0.73	2.04	11.56	23.72	39.19	4.13	1.47	4.02		18.53	270.2	0	3	15	1	18	9.94	-1.1	4.50		Apr-11
	0.55	1.66	10.76	20.96	34.16	3.39	2.21	4.01		18.61	270.2	0	3	15	1	18	9.5	-1.43		1.00	Nov-11
	0.80	2.18	11.87	24.95	41.61	4.39	1.2	4.04		18.47	270.2	0	3	15	1	18	10.17	-1.02			Apr-11
	2.18	6.66	12.77			2.29	2.17			11.21	58.5	2	96	0	2	250			4.50		Oct-15
	2.11	6.41	12.09			1.64	2.92			11.12	58.5	2	96	0	2	250				1.00	Oct-15
	2.18	6.66	12.89			2.51	1.92			11.21	58.5	2	96	0	2	250					Oct-15
50	5.89	10.61	25.93	39.93	116.65	0.19	0.97	11.46	1.04	77.03	1,521	0	98	1	0	17	27.04	-19.54	5.75		Jun-01
50	5.65	10.07	24.83	36.45	107.92	0	1.79	11.45	1.04	66.57	1,521	0	98	1	0	17	26.49	-19.8		1.00	Jun-01
	5.76	10.36	25.41	38.26	112.38	0	1.37	11.46	1.04	76.04	1,521	0	98	1	0	17	26.94	-19.42			Nov-03
	5.96	10.77	26.33	40.82	119.23	0.43	0.67	11.47	1.04	77.41	1,521	0	98	1	0	17	27.23	-19.43			Aug-14
50	5.96	10.73	26.26	41.01	119.43	0.4	0.71	11.46	1.04	77.75	1,521	0	98	1	0	17	27.23	-19.43			Jul-00
	5.94	10.78	26.20	40.98	119.48	0.41	0.7	11.46	1.04	77.65	1,521	0	98	1	0	17	27.28	-19.41			Aug-02
50	1.45	5.04	8.32	20.21	59.84	3.73	1.61	11.4	0.84	26.96	101.8	0	97	2	0	13	14.44	-15.27	5.75		Jan-84
50	1.29	4.64	7.53	17.54	53.98	3.01	2.36	11.39	0.84	24.77	101.8	0	97	2	0	13	13.96	-15.53		1.00	Oct-98
	1.53	5.19	8.57	21.08	61.94	3.97	1.36	11.38	0.84	27.52	101.8	0	97	2	0	13	14.49	-15.28			Jun-98
50	6.41	11.53	21.12	38.48	116.70	0.85	0.88	10.91	1.06	27.31	3,680	0	99	1	0	47	23.53	-19.32	5.75		Aug-99
50	6.22	11.15	20.21	35.33	108.61	0.19	1.64	10.89	1.06	26.13	3,680	0	99	1	0	47	22.93	-19.57		1.00	Dec-00
	6.30	11.34	20.65	36.98	111.69	0.52	1.26	10.9	1.06	27.57	3,680	0	99	1	0	47	23.34	-19.4			May-12
	6.48	11.74	21.57	39.72	120.20	1.18	0.5	10.88	1.06	27.62	3,680	0	99	1	0	47	23.7	-19.24			Aug-14
50	6.47	11.70	21.45	39.67	119.94	1.11	0.58	10.9	1.06	27.59	3,680	0	99	1	0	47	23.7	-19.24			May-29
50	6.39	11.45	21.02	38.49	116.99		0.9	10.89	1.06	27.3	3,680	0	99	1	0	47	23.52	-19.32	2.50		Jun-17
	6.46	11.69	21.48	39.76	120.42	1.13	0.56	10.9	1.06	27.64	3,680	0	99	1	0	47	23.81	-19.16			Aug-02
50	5.11	9.40	19.24	30.59	86.95	1.62	1.04	10.93	1	57.51	1,134	0	99	1	0	55	25.04	-19.47	5.75		Mar-88
50	4.93	9.01	18.35	27.69	80.06	0.93	1.79	10.9	1	57.37	1,134	0	99	1	0	55	24.44	-19.73		1.00	Sep-95
	5.06	9.26	18.94	29.62	84.64	1.39	1.29	10.92	1	57.39	1,134	0	99	1	0	55	24.8	-19.54			Oct-03
	5.21	9.61	19.67	31.63	88.44	1.88	0.72	10.92	1	57.55	1,134	0	99	1	0	55	25.04	-19.47			Mar-15
50	5.20	9.56	19.54	31.58	89.32	1.84	0.79	10.93	1	57.51	1,134	0	99	1	0	55	25.24	-19.43			Feb-05

Fund Name	Ticker Symbol	Traded On	Fund Type	Category and (Prospectus Objective)	Overall Rating	Reward Rating	Risk Rating	Recent Up/ Downgrade	Open to New Investors	Min Initial Investment
	MARKET			FUND TYPE, CATEGORY & OBJECTIVE	RATINGS				MINIMUMS	
Deutsche CROCI® Equity Dividend Fund Class T	KDHUX	NAS CM	Open End	US Equity Large Cap Value (Growth & Income)	B-	B	C+	Down	Y	1,000
Deutsche CROCI® Equity Dividend Fund Institutional Class	KDHIX	NAS CM	Open End	US Equity Large Cap Value (Growth & Income)	B-	B	C+	Down	Y	1,000,000
Deutsche CROCI® International Fund Class A	SUIAX	NAS CM	Open End	Global Equity Large Cap (Foreign Stock)	C+	C+	C+	Up	Y	1,000
Deutsche CROCI® International Fund Class C	SUICX	NAS CM	Open End	Global Equity Large Cap (Foreign Stock)	C+	C+	C+	Up	Y	1,000
Deutsche CROCI® International Fund Class R6	SUIRX	NAS CM	Open End	Global Equity Large Cap (Foreign Stock)	C+	C+	C+	Up	Y	0
Deutsche CROCI® International Fund Class S	SCINX	NAS CM	Open End	Global Equity Large Cap (Foreign Stock)	C+	C+	C+	Up	Y	2,500
Deutsche CROCI® International Fund Class T	SUITX	NAS CM	Open End	Global Equity Large Cap (Foreign Stock)	C+	C+	C+	Up	Y	1,000
Deutsche CROCI® International Fund Institutional Class	SUIIX	NAS CM	Open End	Global Equity Large Cap (Foreign Stock)	C+	C+	C+	Up	Y	1,000,000
Deutsche CROCI® Sector Opportunities Fund Class A	DSOAX	NAS CM	Open End	Global Equity (Growth)	C+	C+	C+	Down	Y	1,000
Deutsche CROCI® Sector Opportunities Fund Class C	DSOCX	NAS CM	Open End	Global Equity (Growth)	C+	C+	C+	Down	Y	1,000
Deutsche CROCI® Sector Opportunities Fund Class S	DSOSX	NAS CM	Open End	Global Equity (Growth)	C+	C+	C+	Down	Y	2,500
Deutsche CROCI® Sector Opp Fund Inst Cls	DSOIX	NAS CM	Open End	Global Equity (Growth)	C+	C+	C+	Down	Y	1,000,000
Deutsche CROCI® U.S. Fund Class A	DCUAX	NAS CM	Open End	US Equity Large Cap Value (Growth)	C+	C+	B-	Up	Y	1,000
Deutsche CROCI® U.S. Fund Class C	DCUCX	NAS CM	Open End	US Equity Large Cap Value (Growth)	C+	C+	C+	Up	Y	1,000
Deutsche CROCI® U.S. Fund Class R	DCUTX	NAS CM	Open End	US Equity Large Cap Value (Growth)	C+	C+	B-	Up	Y	0
Deutsche CROCI® U.S. Fund Class R6	DCURX	NAS CM	Open End	US Equity Large Cap Value (Growth)	C+	C+	B-	Up	Y	0
Deutsche CROCI® U.S. Fund Class S	DCUSX	NAS CM	Open End	US Equity Large Cap Value (Growth)	C+	C+	B-	Up	Y	2,500
Deutsche CROCI® U.S. Fund Class T	DCUUX	NAS CM	Open End	US Equity Large Cap Value (Growth)	C+	C+	B-	Up	Y	1,000
Deutsche CROCI® U.S. Fund Institutional Class	DCUIX	NAS CM	Open End	US Equity Large Cap Value (Growth)	C+	C+	B-	Up	Y	1,000,000
Deutsche EAFE Equity Index Fund Institutional Class	BTAEX	NAS CM	Open End	Global Equity Large Cap (Foreign Stock)	B-	B-	B	Up	Y	1,000,000
Deutsche Emerging Markets Equity Fund Class A	SEKAX	NAS CM	Open End	Emerging Markets Equity (Div Emerging Mkts)	B-	B	C	Up	Y	1,000
Deutsche Emerging Markets Equity Fund Class C	SEKCX	NAS CM	Open End	Emerging Markets Equity (Div Emerging Mkts)	B-	B	C	Up	Y	1,000
Deutsche Emerging Markets Equity Fund Class S	SEMGX	NAS CM	Open End	Emerging Markets Equity (Div Emerging Mkts)	B-	B	C	Up	Y	2,500
Deutsche Emerging Markets Equity Fund Class T	SEKTX	NAS CM	Open End	Emerging Markets Equity (Div Emerging Mkts)	B-	B	C	Up	Y	1,000
Deutsche Emerging Markets Equity Fund Institutional Class	SEKIX	NAS CM	Open End	Emerging Markets Equity (Div Emerging Mkts)	B-	B	C	Up	Y	1,000,000
Deutsche Enhanced Commodity Strategy Fund Class A	SKNRX	NAS CM	Open End	Commodities Broad Basket (Growth & Income)	C-	C-	C-	Up	Y	1,000
Deutsche Enhanced Commodity Strategy Fund Class C	SKCRX	NAS CM	Open End	Commodities Broad Basket (Growth & Income)	D+	D+	C-	Up	Y	1,000
Deutsche Enhanced Commodity Strategy Fund Class R6	SKRRX	NAS CM	Open End	Commodities Broad Basket (Growth & Income)	C-	C-	C-	Up	Y	0
Deutsche Enhanced Commodity Strategy Fund Class S	SKSRX	NAS CM	Open End	Commodities Broad Basket (Growth & Income)	C-	C-	C-	Up	Y	2,500
Deutsche Enhanced Commodity Strategy Fund Class T	SKSTX	NAS CM	Open End	Commodities Broad Basket (Growth & Income)	C-	C-	C-	Up	Y	1,000
Deutsche Enhanced Commodity Strategy Fund Inst Cls	SKIRX	NAS CM	Open End	Commodities Broad Basket (Growth & Income)	C-	C-	C-	Up	Y	1,000,000
Deutsche Equity 500 Index Fund Class R6	BTIRX	NAS CM	Open End	US Equity Large Cap Blend (Growth)	B	B	B		Y	0
Deutsche Equity 500 Index Fund Class S	BTIEX	NAS CM	Open End	US Equity Large Cap Blend (Growth)	B	B	B		Y	2,500
Deutsche Equity 500 Index Fund Institutional Class	BTIIX	NAS CM	Open End	US Equity Large Cap Blend (Growth)	B	B	B		Y	1,000,000
Deutsche European Equity Fund Class A	DURAX	NAS CM	Open End	Europe Equity Large Cap (Europe Stock)	C+	C+	C+	Up	Y	1,000
Deutsche European Equity Fund Class C	DURCX	NAS CM	Open End	Europe Equity Large Cap (Europe Stock)	C+	C+	C+	Up	Y	1,000
Deutsche European Equity Fund Class S	DURSX	NAS CM	Open End	Europe Equity Large Cap (Europe Stock)	C+	C+	C+	Up	Y	2,500
Deutsche European Equity Fund Institutional Class	DURIX	NAS CM	Open End	Europe Equity Large Cap (Europe Stock)	C+	C+	C+	Up	Y	1,000,000
Deutsche Global Income Builder Fund Class A	KTRAX	NAS CM	Open End	Alloc (Balanced)	B-	C+	B-	Up	Y	1,000
Deutsche Global Income Builder Fund Class C	KTRCX	NAS CM	Open End	Alloc (Balanced)	C+	C+	B-	Down	Y	1,000
Deutsche Global Income Builder Fund Class R6	KTRZX	NAS CM	Open End	Alloc (Balanced)	B-	C+	B-		Y	0
Deutsche Global Income Builder Fund Class S	KTRSX	NAS CM	Open End	Alloc (Balanced)	B-	C+	B-		Y	2,500
Deutsche Global Income Builder Fund Institutional Class	KTRIX	NAS CM	Open End	Alloc (Balanced)	B-	C+	B-		Y	1,000,000
Deutsche Global Infrastructure Fund Class A	TOLLX	NAS CM	Open End	Other Sector Equity (Growth & Income)	C	C	C	Down	Y	1,000
Deutsche Global Infrastructure Fund Class C	TOLCX	NAS CM	Open End	Other Sector Equity (Growth & Income)	C	C	C		Y	1,000
Deutsche Global Infrastructure Fund Class R6	TOLZX	NAS CM	Open End	Other Sector Equity (Growth & Income)	C+	C+	C+		Y	0
Deutsche Global Infrastructure Fund Class S	TOLSX	NAS CM	Open End	Other Sector Equity (Growth & Income)	C	C+	C	Down	Y	2,500
Deutsche Global Infrastructure Fund Class T	TOLTX	NAS CM	Open End	Other Sector Equity (Growth & Income)	C	C+	C	Down	Y	1,000
Deutsche Global Infrastructure Fund Institutional Class	TOLIX	NAS CM	Open End	Other Sector Equity (Growth & Income)	C	C+	C	Down	Y	1,000,000
Deutsche Global Macro Fund Class A	DBISX	NAS CM	Open End	Multialternative (World Stock)	B-	C+	B	Up	Y	1,000
Deutsche Global Macro Fund Class C	DBICX	NAS CM	Open End	Multialternative (World Stock)	B-	C+	B	Up	Y	1,000
Deutsche Global Macro Fund Class R	DBITX	NAS CM	Open End	Multialternative (World Stock)	B-	C+	B	Up	Y	0

★ Expanded analysis of this fund is included in Section II.

Min Additional Investment	TOTAL RETURNS 3-Month Total Return	6-Month Total Return	1-Year Total Return	3-Year Total Return	5-Year Total Return	PERFORMANCE Dividend Yield (TTM)	Expense Ratio	3-Yr Std Deviation	3-Year Beta	ASSETS NAV	Total Assets (MIL)	ASSET ALLOCATION & TURNOVER %Cash	%Stocks	%Bonds	%Other	Turnover Ratio	BULL & BEAR Last Bull Market Total Return	Last Bear Market Total Return	FEES Front End Fee (%)	Back End Fee (%)	Inception Date
50	5.13	9.42	19.26	30.58	86.90		1.04	10.93	1	57.51	1,134	0	99	1	0	55	25.03	-19.47	2.50		Jun-17
	5.19	9.55	19.56	31.59	89.48	1.84	0.79	10.92	1	57.53	1,134	0	99	1	0	55	25.28	-19.35			Aug-02
50	2.47	6.31	21.73	16.00	40.81	2.91	1.13	11.35	0.77	48.58	1,108	0	95	1	2	67	16.71	-26.25	5.75		Aug-99
50	2.27	5.87	20.73	13.39	35.47	2.27	1.92	11.34	0.77	48.33	1,108	0	95	1	2	67	16.14	-26.49		1.00	Dec-00
	2.57	6.49	22.17	17.16	43.01	3.25	0.75	11.34	0.77	48.41	1,108	0	95	1	2	67	16.9	-26.15			Dec-14
50	2.54	6.41	22.00	16.79	42.56	3.1	0.9	11.36	0.77	48.75	1,108	0	95	1	2	67	16.9	-26.15			Jun-53
50	2.44	6.21	21.62	15.85	40.70		1.18	11.36	0.77	48.56	1,108	0	95	1	2	67	16.73	-26.22	2.50		Jun-17
	2.55	6.44	22.08	17.03	43.10	3.18	0.83	11.35	0.77	48.51	1,108	0	95	1	2	67	17.04	-26.13			Dec-00
50	0.00	3.84	14.06	10.04		1	1.34	11.17	0.87	9.77	71.9	0	100	0	0	67			5.75		Jun-14
50	-0.17	3.48	13.20	7.55		0.35	2.09	11.14	0.87	9.76	71.9	0	100	0	0	67				1.00	Jun-14
50	0.04	3.89	14.23	10.55		1.13	1.14	11.2	0.87	9.77	71.9	0	100	0	0	67					Jun-14
	0.14	4.00	14.35	10.89		1.22	1.07	11.19	0.87	9.77	71.9	0	100	0	0	67					Jun-14
50	4.76	9.55	21.58			0.05	1.04			11.5	930.9	0	100	0	0	100			5.75		Apr-15
50	4.57	9.21	20.73			0	1.76			11.41	930.9	0	100	0	0	100				1.00	Apr-15
	4.72	9.41	21.31				1.29			11.51	930.9	0	100	0	0	100					Dec-16
	4.85	9.74	22.13			0.25	0.59			11.5	930.9	0	100	0	0	100					Apr-15
50	4.88	9.77	22.06			0.17	0.69			11.5	930.9	0	100	0	0	100					Apr-15
50	4.68	9.47	21.57				1.04			11.5	930.9	0	100	0	0	100			2.50		Jun-17
	4.80	9.69	21.96			0.25	0.69			11.49	930.9	0	100	0	0	100					Apr-15
	4.08	9.63	25.44	24.57	44.61	3.22	0.33	11.72	0.95	6.58	60.6	0	92	0	8	51	13.17	-23.36			Jan-96
50	8.72	18.06	37.38	31.86	28.82	0.22	1.15	15.16	0.94	20.39	89.1	0	93	5	2	72	18.07	-29.96	5.75		May-01
50	8.56	17.66	36.39	28.97	24.08	0	1.9	15.14	0.94	18.25	89.1	0	93	5	2	72	17.49	-30.17		1.00	May-01
50	8.74	18.13	37.70	32.79	30.36	0.41	0.98	15.22	0.95	20.65	89.1	0	93	5	2	72	18.16	-29.85			May-96
50	8.72	18.06	37.44	31.88	28.82		1.65	15.22	0.95	20.39	89.1	0	93	5	2	72	17.99	-29.92	2.50		Jun-17
	8.77	18.18	37.77	32.86	30.41	0.41	0.9	15.2	0.94	20.63	89.1	0	93	5	2	72	18.35	-29.8			Mar-08
50	4.38	8.16	1.22	-7.93	-19.70	3.34	1.35	9.34	0.69	11.76	2,786	2	0	96	3	52	1.28	-20.13	5.75		Feb-05
50	4.24	7.85	0.47	-9.92	-22.71	3.1	2.1	9.38	0.69	10.57	2,786	2	0	96	3	52	0.94	-20.35		1.00	Feb-05
	4.50	8.43	1.57	-6.94	-18.46	3.72	0.95	9.38	0.69	11.94	2,786	2	0	96	3	52	1.36	-19.91			Jun-16
50	4.47	8.26	1.40	-7.34	-19.01	3.54	1.15	9.37	0.69	11.91	2,786	2	0	96	3	52	1.3	-19.91			Feb-05
50	4.37	8.15	1.17	-7.79	-19.61		1.35	9.37	0.69	11.76	2,786	2	0	96	3	52	1.21	-20	2.50		Jun-17
	4.49	8.40	1.54	-7.00	-18.51	3.67	0.99	9.38	0.69	11.95	2,786	2	0	96	3	52	1.36	-19.91			Feb-05
	6.56	11.30	21.46	35.74	108.71		0.24	10.08	1	220.83	774.5	0	98	2	0	3	25	-16.32			Mar-17
50	6.55	11.26	21.41	35.55	108.18	1.57	0.29	10.08	1	217.91	774.5	0	98	2	0	3	24.96	-16.35			Dec-92
	6.57	11.28	21.47	35.75	108.73	1.62	0.24	10.08	1	220.85	774.5	0	98	2	0	3	25	-16.32			Dec-92
50	1.80	9.06	25.40	25.73		0	1.12	13.03	0.83	12.39	49.2	4	90	0	7	51			5.75		Nov-14
50	1.58	8.65	24.41	22.90		0	1.87	13.03	0.83	12.18	49.2	4	90	0	7	51				1.00	Nov-14
50	1.80	9.23	25.58	26.11		0	0.92	13.07	0.83	12.42	49.2	4	90	0	7	51					Nov-14
	1.88	9.29	25.73	26.60		0	0.87	13.05	0.83	12.46	49.2	4	90	0	7	51					Nov-14
50	3.99	8.41	16.30	20.49	41.15	2.62	0.94	7.08	1.42	9.58	839.0	2	49	38	5	123	14.01	-12.47	5.75		Mar-64
50	3.78	7.98	15.50	17.77	35.59	1.88	1.74	7.12	1.43	9.58	839.0	2	49	38	5	123	13.44	-12.84		1.00	May-94
	4.08	8.62	16.81	21.37	42.16	2.88	0.69	7.1	1.43	9.56	839.0	2	49	38	5	123	14.01	-12.47			Aug-14
50	4.04	8.52	16.54	21.23	42.59	2.82	0.73	7.13	1.43	9.58	839.0	2	49	38	5	123	14.13	-12.47			Mar-05
	3.95	8.44	16.60	21.39	42.67	2.84	0.71	7.07	1.42	9.56	839.0	2	49	38	5	123	14.08	-12.49			Jul-95
50	0.98	3.22	13.22	3.88	47.68	1.76	1.39	9.6	0.58	15.03	3,346	0	97	1	2	86	14.29	-3.71	5.75		Jun-08
50	0.86	2.86	12.44	1.54	42.21	1.04	2.15	9.58	0.58	14.85	3,346	0	97	1	2	86	13.8	-4.09		1.00	Jun-08
	1.14	3.42	13.65	4.87	50.11	2.07	1.18	9.6	0.58	14.99	3,346	0	97	1	2	86	14.56	-3.63			Aug-14
50	1.04	3.29	13.45	4.45	49.03	1.96	1.18	9.62	0.59	14.97	3,346	0	97	1	2	86	14.58	-3.72			Jun-08
50	1.04	3.22	13.28	3.97	47.99		1.43	9.59	0.58	15.04	3,346	0	97	1	2	86	14.4	-3.73	2.50		Jun-17
	1.12	3.38	13.60	4.79	49.91	2.04	1.11	9.59	0.58	14.97	3,346	0	97	1	2	86	14.56	-3.63			Jun-08
50	0.20	0.71	13.33	16.27	40.72	0	1.02	9.68	2.55	9.86	19.1	2	38	50	9	42	12.04	-23.13	5.75		Feb-01
50	0.10	0.43	12.62	13.86	35.64	0	1.77	9.67	3.81	9.28	19.1	2	38	50	9	42	11.56	-23.42		1.00	Feb-01
	0.21	0.63	13.07	15.41	39.09	0	1.27	9.75	3.77	9.51	19.1	2	38	50	9	42	12.13	-23.27			Jul-03

	MARKET		FUND TYPE, CATEGORY & OBJECTIVE		RATINGS				MINIMUMS	
Fund Name	Ticker Symbol	Traded On	Fund Type	Category and (Prospectus Objective)	Overall Rating	Reward Rating	Risk Rating	Recent Up/ Downgrade	Open to New Investors	Min Initial Investment
Deutsche Global Macro Fund Class S	DBIVX	NAS CM	Open End	Multialternative (World Stock)	B-	C+	B	Up	Y	2,500
Deutsche Global Macro Fund Institutional Class	MGINX	NAS CM	Open End	Multialternative (World Stock)	B-	C+	B	Up	Y	1,000,000
Deutsche Global Real Estate Securities Fund Class A	RRGAX	NAS CM	Open End	Real Estate Sector Equity (Real Estate)	B-	C+	B	Up	Y	1,000
Deutsche Global Real Estate Securities Fund Class C	RRGCX	NAS CM	Open End	Real Estate Sector Equity (Real Estate)	B-	C	B	Up	Y	1,000
Deutsche Global Real Estate Securities Fund Class S	RRGTX	NAS CM	Open End	Real Estate Sector Equity (Real Estate)	B-	C+	B	Up	Y	2,500
Deutsche Global Real Estate Securities Fund Class T	RRGUX	NAS CM	Open End	Real Estate Sector Equity (Real Estate)	B-	C+	B		Y	1,000
Deutsche Global Real Estate Securities Fund Inst Cls	RRGIX	NAS CM	Open End	Real Estate Sector Equity (Real Estate)	B-	C+	B		Y	1,000,000
Deutsche Global Real Estate Securities Fund R6	RRGRX	NAS CM	Open End	Real Estate Sector Equity (Real Estate)	B-	C+	B		Y	0
Deutsche Global Small Cap Fund Class A	KGDAX	NAS CM	Open End	Global Equity Mid/Small Cap (World Stock)	C+	C+	C+	Up	Y	1,000
Deutsche Global Small Cap Fund Class C	KGDCX	NAS CM	Open End	Global Equity Mid/Small Cap (World Stock)	C+	C+	C+	Up	Y	1,000
Deutsche Global Small Cap Fund Class R6	KGDZX	NAS CM	Open End	Global Equity Mid/Small Cap (World Stock)	C+	C+	C+	Up	Y	0
Deutsche Global Small Cap Fund Class S	SGSCX	NAS CM	Open End	Global Equity Mid/Small Cap (World Stock)	C+	C+	C+	Up	Y	2,500
Deutsche Global Small Cap Fund Class T	KGDTX	NAS CM	Open End	Global Equity Mid/Small Cap (World Stock)	C+	C+	C+		Y	1,000
Deutsche Global Small Cap Fund Institutional Class	KGDIX	NAS CM	Open End	Global Equity Mid/Small Cap (World Stock)	C+	C+	C+	Up	Y	1,000,000
Deutsche Health and Wellness Fund Class A	SUHAX	NAS CM	Open End	Healthcare Sector Equity (Health)	B-	C+	B	Up	Y	1,000
Deutsche Health and Wellness Fund Class C	SUHCX	NAS CM	Open End	Healthcare Sector Equity (Health)	C+	C+	B-	Up	Y	1,000
Deutsche Health and Wellness Fund Class S	SCHLX	NAS CM	Open End	Healthcare Sector Equity (Health)	B-	C+	B	Up	Y	2,500
Deutsche Health and Wellness Fund Institutional Class	SUHIX	NAS CM	Open End	Healthcare Sector Equity (Health)	B-	C+	B	Up	Y	1,000,000
Deutsche International Growth Fund - Class A	SGQAX	NAS CM	Open End	Global Equity Large Cap (World Stock)	B-	C+	B	Up	Y	1,000
Deutsche International Growth Fund - Class C	SGQCX	NAS CM	Open End	Global Equity Large Cap (World Stock)	B-	C+	B	Up	Y	1,000
Deutsche International Growth Fund - Class Institutional	SGQIX	NAS CM	Open End	Global Equity Large Cap (World Stock)	B-	B-	B	Up	Y	1,000,000
Deutsche International Growth Fund - Class R	SGQRX	NAS CM	Open End	Global Equity Large Cap (World Stock)	B-	C+	B	Up	Y	0
Deutsche International Growth Fund - Class R6	SGQTX	NAS CM	Open End	Global Equity Large Cap (World Stock)	B-	B-	B	Up	Y	0
Deutsche International Growth Fund - Class S	SCOBX	NAS CM	Open End	Global Equity Large Cap (World Stock)	B-	B-	B	Up	Y	2,500
Deutsche Large Cap Focus Growth Fund Class A	SGGAX	NAS CM	Open End	US Equity Large Cap Growth (Growth)	B	B	B		Y	1,000
Deutsche Large Cap Focus Growth Fund Class C	SGGCX	NAS CM	Open End	US Equity Large Cap Growth (Growth)	B	B-	B		Y	1,000
Deutsche Large Cap Focus Growth Fund Class S	SCQGX	NAS CM	Open End	US Equity Large Cap Growth (Growth)	B	B	B		Y	2,500
Deutsche Large Cap Focus Growth Fund Institutional Class	SGGIX	NAS CM	Open End	US Equity Large Cap Growth (Growth)	B	B	B		Y	1,000,000
Deutsche Latin America Equity Fund Class A	SLANX	NAS CM	Open End	Latin America Equity (Foreign Stock)	C	C	C	Up	Y	1,000
Deutsche Latin America Equity Fund Class C	SLAPX	NAS CM	Open End	Latin America Equity (Foreign Stock)	C	C	C	Up	Y	1,000
Deutsche Latin America Equity Fund Class S	SLAFX	NAS CM	Open End	Latin America Equity (Foreign Stock)	C	C	C	Up	Y	2,500
Deutsche Latin America Equity Fund Institutional Class	SLARX	NAS CM	Open End	Latin America Equity (Foreign Stock)	C	C	C	Up	Y	1,000,000
Deutsche Mid Cap Value Fund Class A	MIDVX	NAS CM	Open End	US Equity Mid Cap (Growth)	B	C+	B	Up	Y	1,000
Deutsche Mid Cap Value Fund Class C	MIDZX	NAS CM	Open End	US Equity Mid Cap (Growth)	B-	C+	B	Up	Y	1,000
Deutsche Mid Cap Value Fund Class R	MIDQX	NAS CM	Open End	US Equity Mid Cap (Growth)	B	C+	B	Up	Y	0
Deutsche Mid Cap Value Fund Class R6	MIDUX	NAS CM	Open End	US Equity Mid Cap (Growth)	B	B-	B	Up	Y	0
Deutsche Mid Cap Value Fund Class S	MIDTX	NAS CM	Open End	US Equity Mid Cap (Growth)	B	B-	B	Up	Y	2,500
Deutsche Mid Cap Value Fund Institutional Class	MIDIX	NAS CM	Open End	US Equity Mid Cap (Growth)	B	B-	B	Up	Y	1,000,000
Deutsche MLP & Energy Infrastructure Fund Class A	DMPAX	NAS CM	Open End	Energy Sector Equity (Growth & Income)	D	D+	D	Down	Y	1,000
Deutsche MLP & Energy Infrastructure Fund Class C	DMPCX	NAS CM	Open End	Energy Sector Equity (Growth & Income)	D	D+	D	Down	Y	1,000
Deutsche MLP & Energy Infrastructure Fund Class S	DMPSX	NAS CM	Open End	Energy Sector Equity (Growth & Income)	D	D+	D	Down	Y	2,500
Deutsche MLP & Energy Infrastructure Fund Inst Cls	DMPIX	NAS CM	Open End	Energy Sector Equity (Growth & Income)	D	D+	D	Down	Y	1,000,000
Deutsche Multi-Asset Conservative Allocation Fund - Cls A	SPDAX	NAS CM	Open End	Cautious Alloc (Asset Alloc)	B-	C+	B	Up	Y	1,000
Deutsche Multi-Asset Conservative Allocation Fund - Cls C	SPDCX	NAS CM	Open End	Cautious Alloc (Asset Alloc)	B-	C	B+	Up	Y	1,000
Deutsche Multi-Asset Conservative Allocation Fund - Cls S	SPBAX	NAS CM	Open End	Cautious Alloc (Asset Alloc)	B-	C+	B	Up	Y	2,500
Deutsche Multi-Asset Global Allocation Fund - Class A	SUPAX	NAS CM	Open End	Alloc (Asset Alloc)	B-	C+	B	Up	Y	1,000
Deutsche Multi-Asset Global Allocation Fund - Class C	SUPCX	NAS CM	Open End	Alloc (Asset Alloc)	B-	C	B	Up	Y	1,000
Deutsche Multi-Asset Global Allocation Fund - Class S	SPGRX	NAS CM	Open End	Alloc (Asset Alloc)	B-	C+	B	Up	Y	2,500
Deutsche Multi-Asset Moderate Allocation Fund - Class A	PLUSX	NAS CM	Open End	Moderate Alloc (Asset Alloc)	B-	C+	B	Up	Y	1,000
Deutsche Multi-Asset Moderate Allocation Fund - Class C	PLSCX	NAS CM	Open End	Moderate Alloc (Asset Alloc)	C+	C+	B	Up	Y	1,000
Deutsche Multi-Asset Moderate Allocation Fund - Class S	PPLSX	NAS CM	Open End	Moderate Alloc (Asset Alloc)	B-	C+	B	Up	Y	2,500
Deutsche Real Assets Fund Class A	AAAAX	NAS CM	Open End	Alloc (Growth & Income)	C+	C	C+	Up	Y	1,000

★ Expanded analysis of this fund is included in Section II.

Min Additional Investment	TOTAL RETURNS: 3-Month Total Return	6-Month Total Return	1-Year Total Return	3-Year Total Return	5-Year Total Return	PERFORMANCE: Dividend Yield (TTM)	Expense Ratio	3-Yr Std Deviation	3-Year Beta	ASSETS: NAV	Total Assets (MIL)	ASSET ALLOCATION & TURNOVER: %Cash	%Stocks	%Bonds	%Other	Turnover Ratio	BULL & BEAR: Last Bull Market Total Return	Last Bear Market Total Return	FEES: Front End Fee (%)	Back End Fee (%)	Inception Date
50	0.20	0.83	13.56	17.01	42.03	0	0.82	9.73	2.78	9.63	19.1	2	38	50	9	42	12.28	-23.07			Feb-05
	0.31	0.94	13.64	17.23	42.41	0	0.77	9.74	4.2	9.66	19.1	2	38	50	9	42	12.17	-23.01			May-95
50	4.41	5.92	11.33	13.64	38.03	3.94	1.2	10.71	0.61	9.25	860.0	0	91	1	8	118	23.44	-20.42	5.75		Jul-06
50	4.14	5.41	10.39	10.86	32.69	3.22	1.95	10.71	0.61	9.3	860.0	0	91	1	8	118	23.06	-20.66		1.00	Jul-06
50	4.40	5.91	11.46	13.55	38.43	4.1	1.05	10.72	0.61	9.22	860.0	0	91	1	8	118	23.97	-20.34			Jul-06
50	4.40	5.90	11.44	13.63	38.36		1.2	10.71	0.61	9.24	860.0	0	91	1	8	118	23.57	-20.37	2.50		Jun-17
	4.47	5.98	11.65	14.42	40.02	4.2	0.95	10.71	0.61	9.22	860.0	0	91	1	8	118	23.75	-20.29			Jul-06
	4.37	5.87	11.54	14.30	39.87	4.09	0.95	10.7	0.61	9.22	860.0	0	91	1	8	118	23.76	-20.29			Nov-16
50	3.57	8.85	19.40	21.66	58.25	0	1.43	11.78	1.03	37.01	396.9	0	92	3	5	31	17.08	-21.04	5.75		Apr-98
50	3.41	8.46	18.54	18.96	52.44	0	2.19	11.78	1.03	30.05	396.9	0	92	3	5	31	16.59	-21.29		1.00	Apr-98
	3.70	9.13	19.88	22.87	60.78	0	1	11.8	1.03	39.2	396.9	0	92	3	5	31	17.28	-20.96			Aug-14
50	3.66	9.01	19.72	22.61	60.35	0	1.12	11.79	1.03	39.13	396.9	0	92	3	5	31	17.28	-20.96			Sep-91
50	3.57	8.85	19.39	21.66	58.32		1.41	11.78	1.03	37.01	396.9	0	92	3	5	31	17.11	-21.05	2.50		Jun-17
	3.68	9.06	19.73	22.71	60.69	0	1.11	11.8	1.03	39.16	396.9	0	92	3	5	31	17.34	-20.91			Aug-08
50	-0.67	2.05	19.01	12.81	113.75	0.01	1.37	14.55	1.01	35.12	303.5	0	96	4	0	35	22.12	-13.76	5.75		Dec-00
50	-0.84	1.67	18.16	10.33	105.94	0	2.12	14.55	1	27.61	303.5	0	96	4	0	35	21.69	-14.05		1.00	Dec-00
50	-0.60	2.18	19.34	13.71	116.53	0.22	1.08	14.56	1.01	37.59	303.5	0	96	4	0	35	22.31	-13.64			Mar-98
	-0.61	2.19	19.30	13.68	116.47	0.23	1.07	14.55	1.01	39.12	303.5	0	96	4	0	35	22.27	-13.63			Dec-00
50	3.02	8.14	25.10	22.15	53.73	0	1.24	10.55	0.76	35.18	629.2	2	96	0	2	68	17.09	-26.06	5.75		Jun-01
50	2.81	7.71	24.17	19.40	48.01	0	1.97	10.57	0.76	33.23	629.2	2	96	0	2	68	16.59	-26.27		1.00	Jun-01
	3.12	8.33	25.54	23.22	55.87	0.14	0.82	10.57	0.76	35.15	629.2	2	96	0	2	68	17.29	-25.96			Aug-08
	2.94	7.97	24.77	21.18	51.71	0	1.52	10.55	0.76	34.95	629.2	2	96	0	2	68	16.92	-26.21			Nov-03
	3.11	8.29	25.46	23.06	55.64	0.12	1.02	10.56	0.76	35.14	629.2	2	96	0	2	68	17.28	-25.93			Jun-16
50	3.10	8.28	25.45	23.09	55.68	0.12	0.93	10.56	0.76	35.14	629.2	2	96	0	2	68	17.28	-25.93			Jul-86
50	4.59	8.07	24.80	39.63	110.00	0	1.25	11.85	1.05	43.16	239.1	0	98	2	0	30	27.75	-20.05	5.75		Aug-99
50	4.41	7.68	23.88	36.52	102.30	0	1.99	11.83	1.04	36.6	239.1	0	98	2	0	30	27.15	-20.29		1.00	Dec-00
50	4.68	8.23	25.11	40.71	112.68	0.14	0.98	11.85	1.05	44.96	239.1	0	98	2	0	30	27.88	-19.97			May-91
	4.69	8.25	25.11	40.72	112.84	0.15	0.98	11.84	1.05	45.56	239.1	0	98	2	0	30	27.96	-19.96			Dec-00
50	2.10	23.32	32.13	18.02	-1.91	1.29	1.73	25.22	0.98	25.87	282.2	0	95	1	4	108	19.41	-27.73	5.75		May-01
50	1.93	22.86	31.16	15.40	-5.48	0.69	2.48	25.18	0.98	24.56	282.2	0	95	1	4	108	18.9	-27.97		1.00	May-01
50	2.20	23.50	32.46	18.90	-0.61	1.49	1.48	25.2	0.98	25.83	282.2	0	95	1	4	108	19.62	-27.65			Dec-92
	2.20	23.49	32.51	18.94	-0.57	1.49	1.48	25.23	0.98	25.84	282.2	0	95	1	4	108	19.62	-27.65			Feb-15
50	4.93	9.13	12.75	26.81	96.21	0.81	1.23	11.41	0.98	18.75	324.8	0	97	3	0	62	22.23	-23.69	5.75		Aug-05
50	4.74	8.68	11.85	23.93	88.85	0.12	2	11.39	0.98	18.3	324.8	0	97	3	0	62	21.68	-23.86		1.00	Aug-05
	4.89	8.98	12.47	25.82	93.85	0.55	1.5	11.42	0.98	18.75	324.8	0	97	3	0	62	22.2	-23.79			Mar-11
	5.00	9.27	13.10	27.99	99.08	1.12	0.88	11.43	0.98	18.69	324.8	0	97	3	0	62	22.47	-23.59			Aug-14
50	4.98	9.24	13.00	27.72	98.61	1.01	1	11.46	0.98	18.71	324.8	0	97	3	0	62	22.35	-23.61			Aug-05
	5.01	9.27	13.03	27.78	98.65	1.04	0.97	11.4	0.98	18.72	324.8	0	97	3	0	62	22.47	-23.59			Aug-05
50	-0.46	-2.27	-3.57			3	1.65			7.37	11.5	1	99	0	0	233			5.75		Feb-15
50	-0.64	-2.77	-4.30			2.18	2.4			7.37	11.5	1	99	0	0	233				1.00	Feb-15
50	-0.29	-2.20	-3.31			3.16	1.5			7.37	11.5	1	99	0	0	233					Feb-15
	-0.26	-2.15	-3.20			3.27	1.4			7.38	11.5	1	99	0	0	233					Feb-15
50	2.21	5.23	10.62	11.97	30.67	1.67	1.15	4.93	1.23	13.18	94.5	3	25	65	1	5	13.32	-12.24	5.75		Dec-00
50	2.02	4.75	9.79	9.55	25.95	0.96	1.9	4.9	1.22	13.18	94.5	3	25	65	1	5	12.89	-12.49		1.00	Dec-00
50	2.20	5.29	10.92	12.83	32.38	1.91	0.9	4.91	1.22	13.15	94.5	3	25	65	1	5	13.59	-12.15			Nov-96
50	2.83	7.05	16.56	11.34	34.41	2.79	1.15	6.87	1.38	16.15	100.7	2	51	39	3	11	15.11	-14.19	5.75		Dec-00
50	2.63	6.61	15.73	8.83	29.44	2.12	1.9	6.86	1.39	16.1	100.7	2	51	39	3	11	14.63	-14.5		1.00	Dec-00
50	2.89	7.12	16.86	12.13	36.06	3.01	0.9	6.89	1.39	16.14	100.7	2	51	39	3	11	15.29	-14.11			Nov-96
50	3.56	7.20	13.80	14.62	46.16	1.44	1.15	6.66	1.32	9.82	32.0	2	50	42	1	9	18.5	-18.49	5.75		Nov-04
50	3.40	6.83	12.91	12.14	40.80	0.76	1.9	6.67	1.32	9.84	32.0	2	50	42	1	9	18.06	-18.72		1.00	Nov-04
50	3.62	7.38	13.98	15.42	47.96	1.66	0.9	6.7	1.33	9.8	32.0	2	50	42	1	9	18.78	-18.39			Nov-04
50	3.88	7.13	14.67	7.10	12.21	1.21	1.22	6.27	0.36	9.56	374.2	4	62	12	22	222	8.11	-11.22	5.75		Jul-07

	MARKET		FUND TYPE, CATEGORY & OBJECTIVE		RATINGS					MINIMUMS
Fund Name	Ticker Symbol	Traded On	Fund Type	Category and (Prospectus Objective)	Overall Rating	Reward Rating	Risk Rating	Recent Up/ Downgrade	Open to New Investors	Min Initial Investment
Deutsche Real Assets Fund Class C	AAAPX	NAS CM	Open End	Alloc (Growth & Income)	C+	C	C+	Up	Y	1,000
Deutsche Real Assets Fund Class Institutional	AAAZX	NAS CM	Open End	Alloc (Growth & Income)	C+	C	C+	Up	Y	1,000,000
Deutsche Real Assets Fund Class R	AAAQX	NAS CM	Open End	Alloc (Growth & Income)	C+	C	C+	Up	Y	0
Deutsche Real Assets Fund Class R6	AAAVX	NAS CM	Open End	Alloc (Growth & Income)	C+	C	C+	Up	Y	0
Deutsche Real Assets Fund Class S	AAASX	NAS CM	Open End	Alloc (Growth & Income)	C+	C	C+	Up	Y	2,500
Deutsche Real Assets Fund T	AAAWX	NAS CM	Open End	Alloc (Growth & Income)	C+	C	C+	Up	Y	1,000
Deutsche Real Estate Securities Fund Class A	RRRAX	NAS CM	Open End	Real Estate Sector Equity (Real Estate)	B-	C+	B		Y	1,000
Deutsche Real Estate Securities Fund Class C	RRRCX	NAS CM	Open End	Real Estate Sector Equity (Real Estate)	B-	C+	B		Y	1,000
Deutsche Real Estate Securities Fund Class R	RRRSX	NAS CM	Open End	Real Estate Sector Equity (Real Estate)	B-	C+	B		Y	0
Deutsche Real Estate Securities Fund Class R6	RRRZX	NAS CM	Open End	Real Estate Sector Equity (Real Estate)	B-	C+	B		Y	0
Deutsche Real Estate Securities Fund Class S	RRREX	NAS CM	Open End	Real Estate Sector Equity (Real Estate)	B-	C+	B		Y	2,500
Deutsche Real Estate Securities Fund Class T	RRRTX	NAS CM	Open End	Real Estate Sector Equity (Real Estate)	B-	C+	B		Y	1,000
Deutsche Real Estate Securities Fund Institutional Class	RRRRX	NAS CM	Open End	Real Estate Sector Equity (Real Estate)	B-	C+	B		Y	1,000,000
Deutsche S&P 500 Index Fund Class A	SXPAX	NAS CM	Open End	US Equity Large Cap Blend (Growth & Income)	B	B	B		Y	1,000
Deutsche S&P 500 Index Fund Class C	SXPCX	NAS CM	Open End	US Equity Large Cap Blend (Growth & Income)	B-	B-	B	Down	Y	1,000
Deutsche S&P 500 Index Fund Class R6	SXPRX	NAS CM	Open End	US Equity Large Cap Blend (Growth & Income)	B	B	B		Y	0
Deutsche S&P 500 Index Fund Class S	SCPIX	NAS CM	Open End	US Equity Large Cap Blend (Growth & Income)	B	B	B		Y	2,500
Deutsche Science and Technology Fund Class A	KTCAX	NAS CM	Open End	Technology Sector Equity (Technology)	A-	A	B	Up	Y	1,000
Deutsche Science and Technology Fund Class C	KTCCX	NAS CM	Open End	Technology Sector Equity (Technology)	A-	A	B	Up	Y	1,000
Deutsche Science and Technology Fund Class S	KTCSX	NAS CM	Open End	Technology Sector Equity (Technology)	A-	A	B	Up	Y	2,500
Deutsche Science and Technology Fund Institutional Class	KTCIX	NAS CM	Open End	Technology Sector Equity (Technology)	A-	A	B	Up	Y	1,000,000
Deutsche Small Cap Core Fund Class A	SZCAX	NAS CM	Open End	US Equity Small Cap (Small Company)	B	B	B	Up	Y	1,000
Deutsche Small Cap Core Fund Class C	SZCCX	NAS CM	Open End	US Equity Small Cap (Small Company)	B	B	B	Up	Y	1,000
Deutsche Small Cap Core Fund Class R6	SZCRX	NAS CM	Open End	US Equity Small Cap (Small Company)	B	B	B	Up	Y	0
Deutsche Small Cap Core Fund Class S	SSLCX	NAS CM	Open End	US Equity Small Cap (Small Company)	B	B	B+	Up	Y	2,500
Deutsche Small Cap Core Fund Class T	SZCTX	NAS CM	Open End	US Equity Small Cap (Small Company)	B	B	B	Up	Y	1,000
Deutsche Small Cap Core Fund Institutional Class	SZCIX	NAS CM	Open End	US Equity Small Cap (Small Company)	B	B	B	Up	Y	1,000,000
Deutsche Small Cap Growth Fund Class A	SSDAX	NAS CM	Open End	US Equity Small Cap (Small Company)	B	B	B	Up	Y	1,000
Deutsche Small Cap Growth Fund Class C	SSDCX	NAS CM	Open End	US Equity Small Cap (Small Company)	B	B	B	Up	Y	1,000
Deutsche Small Cap Growth Fund Class R	SSDGX	NAS CM	Open End	US Equity Small Cap (Small Company)	B	B	B	Up	Y	0
Deutsche Small Cap Growth Fund Class R6	SSDZX	NAS CM	Open End	US Equity Small Cap (Small Company)	B	B+	B	Up	Y	0
Deutsche Small Cap Growth Fund Class S	SSDSX	NAS CM	Open End	US Equity Small Cap (Small Company)	B	B+	B	Up	Y	2,500
Deutsche Small Cap Growth Fund Institutional Class	SSDIX	NAS CM	Open End	US Equity Small Cap (Small Company)	B	B+	B	Up	Y	1,000,000
Deutsche Small Cap Value Fund Class A	KDSAX	NAS CM	Open End	US Equity Small Cap (Small Company)	B	B-	B	Up	Y	1,000
Deutsche Small Cap Value Fund Class C	KDSCX	NAS CM	Open End	US Equity Small Cap (Small Company)	B-	B-	B-	Up	Y	1,000
Deutsche Small Cap Value Fund Class R6	KDSZX	NAS CM	Open End	US Equity Small Cap (Small Company)	B	B	B	Up	Y	0
Deutsche Small Cap Value Fund Class S	KDSSX	NAS CM	Open End	US Equity Small Cap (Small Company)	B	B	B	Up	Y	2,500
Deutsche Small Cap Value Fund Institutional Class	KDSIX	NAS CM	Open End	US Equity Small Cap (Small Company)	B	B	B	Up	Y	1,000,000
Deutsche U.S. Multi-Factor Fund Class R6	DMFRX	NAS CM	Open End	US Equity Large Cap Blend (Growth)	U	U	U		Y	0
Deutsche U.S. Multi-Factor Fund Institutional Class	DMFJX	NAS CM	Open End	US Equity Large Cap Blend (Growth)	U	U	U		Y	1,000,000
Deutsche World Dividend Fund Class A	SERAX	NAS CM	Open End	Global Equity (Growth & Income)	C+	C+	C+		Y	1,000
Deutsche World Dividend Fund Class C	SERCX	NAS CM	Open End	Global Equity (Growth & Income)	C+	C	C+	Up	Y	1,000
Deutsche World Dividend Fund Class R6	SERZX	NAS CM	Open End	Global Equity (Growth & Income)	C+	C+	C+		Y	0
Deutsche World Dividend Fund Class S	SCGEX	NAS CM	Open End	Global Equity (Growth & Income)	C+	C+	C+		Y	2,500
Deutsche World Dividend Fund Class T	SERTX	NAS CM	Open End	Global Equity (Growth & Income)	C+	C+	C+		Y	1,000
Deutsche World Dividend Fund Institutional Class	SERNX	NAS CM	Open End	Global Equity (Growth & Income)	C+	C+	C+		Y	1,000,000
DF Dent Midcap Growth Fund Institutional Shares	DFMGX	NAS CM	Open End	US Equity Mid Cap (Growth)	A-	A-	B+		Y	500,000
DF Dent Midcap Growth Fund Investor Shares	DFDMX	NAS CM	Open End	US Equity Mid Cap (Growth)	A-	A-	B+	Up	Y	2,500
DF Dent Premier Growth Fund Investor Shares	DFDPX	NAS CM	Open End	US Equity Mid Cap (Growth)	A-	A-	B+	Up	Y	2,500
DF Dent Small Cap Growth Fund Institutional Shares	DFSGX	NAS CM	Open End	US Equity Small Cap (Small Company)	U	U	U		Y	500,000
DF Dent Small Cap Growth Fund Investor Shares	DFDSX	NAS CM	Open End	US Equity Small Cap (Small Company)	B	B	B	Up	Y	2,500
DFA Asia Pacific Small Company Portfolio Institutional Cls	DFRSX	NAS CM	Open End	Asia ex-Japan Equity (Pacific Stock)	B-	B	B-	Up	Y	0

★ Expanded analysis of this fund is included in Section II.

Min Additional Investment	TOTAL RETURNS: 3-Month Total Return	6-Month Total Return	1-Year Total Return	3-Year Total Return	5-Year Total Return	PERFORMANCE: Dividend Yield (TTM)	Expense Ratio	3-Yr Std Deviation	3-Year Beta	ASSETS: NAV	Total Assets (MIL)	ASSET ALLOCATION & TURNOVER: %Cash	%Stocks	%Bonds	%Other	Turnover Ratio	BULL & BEAR: Last Bull Market Total Return	Last Bear Market Total Return	FEES: Front End Fee (%)	Back End Fee (%)	Inception Date
50	3.59	6.62	13.69	4.59	8.07	0.85	1.97	6.33	0.37	9.5	374.2	4	62	12	22	222	7.68	-11.47		1.00	Jul-07
	3.90	7.16	14.97	8.06	14.10	1.5	0.95	6.28	0.37	9.48	374.2	4	62	12	22	222	8.3	-11.14			Jul-07
	3.66	6.88	14.29	6.24	11.23	0.98	1.47	6.27	0.37	9.62	374.2	4	62	12	22	222	8.07	-11.34			Jun-11
	3.79	7.16	14.98	8.05	14.09	1.49	0.95	6.31	0.37	9.48	374.2	4	62	12	22	222	8.3	-11.14			Nov-14
50	3.92	7.19	14.83	7.51	13.06	1.36	1.07	6.33	0.38	9.48	374.2	4	62	12	22	222	8.17	-11.04			Jul-07
50	3.77	7.01	14.66	7.23	12.67		1.22	6.29	0.37	9.55	374.2	4	62	12	22	222	8.14	-11.23	2.50		Jun-17
50	2.30	2.94	6.11	14.31	53.60	2.53	0.98	13.38	0.53	20.39	1,371	0	100	0	0	153	31.9	-17.25	5.75		Sep-02
50	2.15	2.60	5.42	11.99	48.40	1.91	1.66	13.35	0.53	20.65	1,371	0	100	0	0	153	31.29	-17.46		1.00	Sep-02
	2.22	2.77	5.76	13.19	51.15	2.24	1.3	13.36	0.53	20.39	1,371	0	100	0	0	153	31.38	-17.16			Oct-03
	2.48	3.19	6.61	15.93	56.92	2.95	0.53	13.35	0.53	20.37	1,371	0	100	0	0	153	32.04	-17.07			Aug-14
50	2.41	3.12	6.42	15.29	55.60	2.79	0.71	13.36	0.53	20.52	1,371	0	100	0	0	153	32.05	-17.12			May-05
50	2.35	2.98	6.21	14.62	54.34		0.93	13.36	0.53	20.4	1,371	0	100	0	0	153	31.85	-17.16	2.50		Jun-17
	2.40	3.13	6.49	15.50	56.31	2.86	0.63	13.37	0.53	20.36	1,371	0	100	0	0	153	32.04	-17.07			Dec-99
50	6.48	11.09	21.09	34.28	104.92	1.36	0.6	10.11	1	30.5	1,011	0	98	2	0	3	24.74	-16.5	4.50		Feb-05
50	6.27	10.68	20.19	31.51	97.85	0.74	1.31	10.08	1	30.43	1,011	0	98	2	0	3	24.19	-16.73		1.00	Feb-05
	6.54	11.25	21.36	35.63	108.54		0.28	10.08	1	30.55	1,011	0	98	2	0	3	25	-16.32			Mar-17
50	6.54	11.22	21.37	35.38	107.77	1.6	0.33	10.09	1	30.56	1,011	0	98	2	0	3	24.86	-16.34			Aug-97
50	6.62	14.53	35.78	50.29	117.61	0	0.99	13.92	1.16	21.43	800.2	0	99	1	0	171	28.57	-16.76	5.75		Sep-48
50	6.35	14.00	34.51	46.22	107.94	0	1.89	13.97	1.16	14.75	800.2	0	99	1	0	171	28.02	-17.09		1.00	May-94
50	6.69	14.62	35.92	50.93	119.04	0	0.84	13.94	1.16	21.68	800.2	0	99	1	0	171	28.66	-16.73			Dec-04
	6.65	14.64	35.97	51.25	120.04	0	0.74	13.91	1.15	23.33	800.2	0	99	1	0	171	28.86	-16.63			Aug-02
50	3.74	6.43	11.44	34.75	100.40	0.34	1.09	12.94	0.88	29.8	171.6	0	97	3	0	62	30.92	-25.39	5.75		Jun-01
50	3.52	6.07	10.59	31.76	93.07	0	1.84	12.95	0.88	25.02	171.6	0	97	3	0	62	30.36	-25.67		1.00	Jun-01
	3.79	6.58	11.71	35.84	103.00	0.61	0.79	12.96	0.88	31.1	171.6	0	97	3	0	62	31.13	-25.3			Jun-16
50	3.78	6.53	11.66	35.76	102.88	0.54	0.89	12.96	0.88	31.12	171.6	0	97	3	0	62	31.13	-25.3			Jul-00
50	3.74	6.44	11.42	34.79	100.43		1.09	12.96	0.88	29.76	171.6	0	97	3	0	62	30.94	-25.37	2.50		Jun-17
	3.78	6.57	11.70	35.83	102.98	0.61	0.84	12.96	0.88	31.08	171.6	0	97	3	0	62	31.13	-25.3			Jun-16
50	4.51	11.20	20.78	27.18	92.80	0	1.17	14.59	0.95	33.58	461.4	0	97	2	0	32	26.14	-21.27	5.75		Jun-02
50	4.29	10.77	19.85	24.34	85.66	0	1.92	14.59	0.95	28.48	461.4	0	97	2	0	32	25.53	-21.46		1.00	Jun-02
	4.40	11.02	20.40	26.11	90.37	0	1.42	14.6	0.95	33	461.4	0	97	2	0	32	25.95	-21.35			May-12
	4.56	11.34	21.06	28.07	94.44	0	0.92	14.6	0.96	33.89	461.4	0	97	2	0	32	26.14	-21.27			Aug-14
50	4.56	11.34	21.04	28.11	95.15	0	0.92	14.6	0.95	35.07	461.4	0	97	2	0	32	26.27	-21.18			Dec-04
	4.56	11.32	21.04	28.24	95.76	0	0.92	14.6	0.95	35.52	461.4	0	97	2	0	32	26.41	-21.08			Dec-04
50	1.99	8.66	9.17	17.01	62.90	0	1.25	14.38	0.97	25.77	356.1	0	98	2	0	29	26.78	-27.1	5.75		May-92
50	1.78	8.21	8.31	14.39	56.90	0	2	14.37	0.97	20.35	356.1	0	98	2	0	29	26.26	-27.31		1.00	Sep-95
	2.07	8.85	9.61	18.18	64.75	0.3	0.9	14.4	0.97	26.41	356.1	0	98	2	0	29	26.78	-27.1			Aug-14
50	2.05	8.76	9.43	17.91	64.83	0.11	0.97	14.4	0.97	26.23	356.1	0	98	2	0	29	26.88	-27.04			Feb-05
	2.07	8.78	9.49	18.16	65.79	0.25	0.9	14.37	0.97	26.41	356.1	0	98	2	0	29	27.1	-26.95			Aug-02
	6.38	10.42					0.3			11.09	280.9	3	97	0	0						May-17
	6.38	10.42					0.35			11.09	280.9	3	97	0	0						May-17
50	1.34	1.71	8.66	12.12	42.56	1.3	1.08	9.4	0.88	30.6	247.7	0	85	15	0	33	13.79	-15.61	5.75		Mar-01
50	1.15	1.32	7.82	9.64	37.37	0.62	1.83	9.38	0.88	30.36	247.7	0	85	15	0	33	13.34	-15.86		1.00	Mar-01
	1.43	1.88	8.98	13.02	44.26	1.56	0.78	9.41	0.88	30.63	247.7	0	85	15	0	33	13.95	-15.56			Aug-14
50	1.40	1.83	8.89	12.92	44.13	1.54	0.88	9.4	0.88	30.64	247.7	0	85	15	0	33	13.95	-15.56			Oct-94
50	1.34	1.71	8.61	12.08	42.34		1.08	9.4	0.88	30.6	247.7	0	85	15	0	33	13.78	-15.65	2.50		Jun-17
	1.42	1.86	8.91	13.03	44.58	1.55	0.83	9.4	0.88	30.89	247.7	0	85	15	0	33	14.05	-15.49			Mar-05
0	6.85	13.00	31.21	37.05	103.93		0.85	11.83	0.97	20.37	41.6	4	96	0	0	31	30.1				Nov-17
500	6.85	13.00	31.21	37.05	103.93	0	0.98	11.83	0.97	20.37	41.6	4	96	0	0	31	30.11				Jul-11
500	6.18	12.91	31.83	36.18	97.16	0	1.1	11.88	1.07	29.03	158.7	0	100	0	0	13	28.2	-18.87			Jul-01
0	2.13	7.75	15.57	30.73			0.95			14.32	8.6	1	99	0	0	45					Nov-17
500	3.31	7.75	15.57	28.64		0	1.05	12.42	0.73	14.32	8.6	1	99	0	0	45					Nov-13
	7.19	11.71	25.16	32.97	25.68	3.14	0.54	14.78	0.98	23.87	335.7	1	98	0	1	9	23.19	-27.94			Jan-93

	MARKET			FUND TYPE, CATEGORY & OBJECTIVE	RATINGS				MINIMUMS	
Fund Name	Ticker Symbol	Traded On	Fund Type	Category and (Prospectus Objective)	Overall Rating	Reward Rating	Risk Rating	Recent Up/ Downgrade	Open to New Investors	Min Initial Investment
DFA Commodity Strategy Portfolio Institutional Cls Shares	DCMSX	NAS CM	Open End	Commodities Broad Basket (Growth & Income)	C-	C-	D+	Up	Y	0
DFA Continental Small Company Portfolio Institutional Cls	DFCSX	NAS CM	Open End	Europe Equity Large Cap (Europe Stock)	B+	B+	A	Up	Y	0
DFA CSTG&E International Social Core Equity Portfolio	DFCCX	NAS CM	Open End	Global Equity Large Cap (Growth)	B-	B	C+	Up		0
DFA CSTG&E U.S. Social Core Equity 2 Portfolio	DFCUX	NAS CM	Open End	US Equity Mid Cap (Growth)	B	B	B	Up		0
DFA Emerging Mkts Core Equity Portfolio Inst Cls	DFCEX	NAS CM	Open End	Emerging Markets Equity (Div Emerging Mkts)	B-	B	C	Up	Y	0
DFA Emerging Markets Portfolio II	DFETX	NAS CM	Open End	Emerging Markets Equity (Div Emerging Mkts)	B-	B	C	Up		0
DFA Emerging Markets Portfolio Institutional Class	DFEMX	NAS CM	Open End	Emerging Markets Equity (Div Emerging Mkts)	B-	B	C	Up	Y	0
DFA Emerging Markets Small Cap Portfolio Institutional Cls	DEMSX	NAS CM	Open End	Emerging Markets Equity (Div Emerging Mkts)	B	B	C+	Up	Y	0
DFA Emerging Markets Social Core Portfolio	DFESX	NAS CM	Open End	Emerging Markets Equity (Growth)	B-	B	C	Up	Y	0
DFA Emerging Markets Value Portfolio Class R2	DFEPX	NAS CM	Open End	Emerging Markets Equity (Div Emerging Mkts)	C+	B-	C	Up	Y	0
DFA Emerging Markets Value Portfolio Institutional Class	DFEVX	NAS CM	Open End	Emerging Markets Equity (Div Emerging Mkts)	C+	B	C	Up	Y	0
DFA Enhanced U.S. Large Company Portfolio Inst Cls	DFELX	NAS CM	Open End	US Equity Large Cap Blend (Growth)	B	B	B		Y	0
DFA Global Allocation 25/75 Portfolio Class R2	DFGPX	NAS CM	Open End	Cautious Alloc (Growth & Income)	B-	C	B	Up	Y	0
DFA Global Allocation 25/75 Portfolio Institutional Class	DGTSX	NAS CM	Open End	Cautious Alloc (Growth & Income)	B-	C	B	Up	Y	0
DFA Global Allocation 60/40 Portfolio Class R2	DFPRX	NAS CM	Open End	Moderate Alloc (Growth & Income)	B-	C+	B	Up	Y	0
DFA Global Allocation 60/40 Portfolio Institutional Class	DGSIX	NAS CM	Open End	Moderate Alloc (Growth & Income)	B-	C+	B	Up	Y	0
DFA Global Equity Portfolio Class Retirement 2	DGERX	NAS CM	Open End	Global Equity (World Stock)	B-	B	C+	Down	Y	0
DFA Global Equity Portfolio Institutional Class	DGEIX	NAS CM	Open End	Global Equity (World Stock)	B-	B	C+	Down	Y	0
DFA Global Real Estate Securities Portfolio	DFGEX	NAS CM	Open End	Real Estate Sector Equity (Real Estate)	B-	C+	B		Y	0
DFA Global Small Company Portfolio Institutional Class	DGLIX	NAS CM	Open End	Global Equity Mid/Small Cap (Small Company)	U	U	U		Y	0
DFA International Core Equity Portfolio Institutional Cls	DFIEX	NAS CM	Open End	Global Equity Large Cap (Growth)	B	B	B	Up	Y	0
DFA Intl High Relative Profitability Portfolio Inst Cls	DIHRX	NAS CM	Open End	Global Equity Large Cap (Foreign Stock)	U	U	U		Y	0
DFA International Large Cap Growth Portfolio	DILRX	NAS CM	Open End	Global Equity Large Cap (Growth)	B-	B-	B	Up	Y	0
DFA Intl Real Estate Securities Portfolio Inst Cls	DFITX	NAS CM	Open End	Real Estate Sector Equity (Real Estate)	C+	C	B-	Up	Y	0
DFA International Small Cap Growth Portfolio	DISMX	NAS CM	Open End	Global Equity Mid/Small Cap (Small Company)	A-	B+	A-	Up	Y	0
DFA Intl Small Cap Value Portfolio Inst Cls	DISVX	NAS CM	Open End	Global Equity Mid/Small Cap (Foreign Stock)	B	B	B-	Up	Y	0
DFA Intl Small Company Portfolio Inst Cls	DFISX	NAS CM	Open End	Global Equity Mid/Small Cap (Foreign Stock)	B+	B	B+	Up	Y	0
DFA Intl Social Core Equity Portfolio Inst Cls Shares	DSCLX	NAS CM	Open End	Global Equity Large Cap (Growth)	B-	B	C+	Up	Y	0
DFA International Sustainability Core 1 Portfolio	DFSPX	NAS CM	Open End	Global Equity Large Cap (Growth)	B	B-	B	Up	Y	0
DFA International Value Portfolio Class R2	DFIPX	NAS CM	Open End	Global Equity Large Cap (Foreign Stock)	B-	B-	B-	Up	Y	0
DFA International Value Portfolio II	DIVTX	NAS CM	Open End	Global Equity Large Cap (Foreign Stock)	C+	B-	C	Up		0
DFA International Value Portfolio III	DFVIX	NAS CM	Open End	Global Equity Large Cap (Foreign Stock)	C+	B-	C	Up		0
DFA International Value Portfolio Institutional Class	DFIVX	NAS CM	Open End	Global Equity Large Cap (Foreign Stock)	C+	B-	C	Up	Y	0
DFA Intl Vector Equity Portfolio Inst Cls	DFVQX	NAS CM	Open End	Global Equity Mid/Small Cap (Foreign Stock)	B	B	C+	Up	Y	0
DFA Japanese Small Company Portfolio Institutional Class	DFJSX	NAS CM	Open End	Japan Equity (Pacific Stock)	A	A	A-	Up	Y	0
DFA Large Cap International Portfolio Institutional Class	DFALX	NAS CM	Open End	Global Equity Large Cap (Foreign Stock)	B-	B-	B	Up	Y	0
DFA Real Estate Securities Portfolio Institutional Class	DFREX	NAS CM	Open End	Real Estate Sector Equity (Real Estate)	B	C+	B+	Up	Y	0
DFA Selectively Hedged Global Eq Port Inst Cls Shares	DSHGX	NAS CM	Open End	Global Equity (Growth)	B-	B	C+	Down	Y	0
DFA T.A. U.S. Core Equity 2 Portfolio Institutional Class	DFTCX	NAS CM	Open End	US Equity Mid Cap (Growth & Income)	B	B	B	Up	Y	0
DFA T.A. World ex U.S. Core Equity Portfolio Inst Cls	DFTWX	NAS CM	Open End	Global Equity Large Cap (Equity-Income)	B	B	B-	Up	Y	0
DFA Tax Managed International Value Portfolio	DTMIX	NAS CM	Open End	Global Equity Large Cap (World Stock)	B-	B-	B-	Up	Y	0
DFA Tax Managed U.S. Equity Portfolio	DTMEX	NAS CM	Open End	US Equity Large Cap Blend (Growth)	B	B	B		Y	0
DFA Tax Managed U.S. Small Cap Portfolio	DFTSX	NAS CM	Open End	US Equity Small Cap (Small Company)	B+	A-	B	Up	Y	0
DFA Tax-Managed U.S. Marketwide Value Portfolio	DTMMX	NAS CM	Open End	US Equity Large Cap Value (Growth)	B	B	B	Up	Y	0
DFA Tax-Managed U.S. Marketwide Value Portfolio II	DFMVX	NAS CM	Open End	US Equity Large Cap Value (Growth)	B	B	B	Up		0
DFA Tax-Managed U.S. Targeted Value Portfolio	DTMVX	NAS CM	Open End	US Equity Small Cap (Growth)	B+	B+	B	Up	Y	0
DFA U.S. Core Equity 1 Portfolio Institutional Class	DFEOX	NAS CM	Open End	US Equity Large Cap Blend (Growth)	B	B	B-		Y	0
DFA U.S. Core Equity II Portfolio Institutional Class	DFQTX	NAS CM	Open End	US Equity Mid Cap (Growth)	B	B	B-	Up	Y	0
DFA U.S. Large Cap Equity Portfolio Institutional Class	DUSQX	NAS CM	Open End	US Equity Large Cap Blend (Growth)	B	B	B-		Y	0
DFA U.S. Large Cap Growth Portfolio Institutional Class	DUSLX	NAS CM	Open End	US Equity Large Cap Growth (Growth)	B	B	B		Y	0
DFA U.S. Large Cap Growth Portfolio Institutional Class	DFCVX	NAS CM	Open End	US Equity Large Cap Value (Growth)	B	B	B	Up		0
DFA U.S. Large Cap Value III Portfolio	DFUVX	NAS CM	Open End	US Equity Large Cap Value (Growth)	B	B	B	Up		0

★ Expanded analysis of this fund is included in Section II.

	TOTAL RETURNS					PERFORMANCE				ASSETS		ASSET ALLOCATION & TURNOVER					BULL & BEAR		FEES		
Min Additional Investment	3-Month Total Return	6-Month Total Return	1-Year Total Return	3-Year Total Return	5-Year Total Return	Dividend Yield (TTM)	Expense Ratio	3-Yr Std Deviation	3-Year Beta	NAV	Total Assets (MIL)	%Cash	%Stocks	%Bonds	%Other	Turnover Ratio	Last Bull Market Total Return	Last Bear Market Total Return	Front End Fee (%)	Back End Fee (%)	Inception Date
	4.36	7.11	2.72	-12.36	-30.91	1.35	0.33	12.77	0.98	5.96	1,696	4	0	73	23	159	1.22	-19.69			Nov-10
	2.09	9.74	35.13	58.44	106.46	1.5	0.54	12.84	0.93	28.59	649.7	1	96	0	3	13	12.65	-32.88			Apr-88
	4.47	11.90	27.49	31.87	52.92	2.22	0.55	11.81	0.96	10.28	98.0	0	97	0	2	5	13.07	-24.62			Aug-07
	7.21	12.86	18.64	34.42	101.80	1.42	0.32	11.63	1.08	17.58	105.8	0	100	0	0	16	27.21	-22.43			Aug-07
	7.70	14.75	36.55	30.83	27.64	1.75	0.53	15.22	0.95	23.22	27,437	1	99	0	0	21	17.58	-27.36			Apr-05
	7.22	14.14	36.73	29.81	25.56	1.81	0.34	15.15	0.95	29.13	83.9	1	97	0	1	4	17.67	-25.69			Aug-97
	7.21	14.08	36.57	29.03	24.25	1.67	0.48	15.16	0.95	30.47	6,686	1	97	0	1	4	17.5	-25.72			Apr-94
	8.58	15.17	35.25	37.46	40.66	2.08	0.72	14.97	0.91	23.87	7,375	1	99	0	0	11	17.6	-27.08			Mar-98
	7.33	14.72	37.30	31.53	27.23	1.82	0.56	15.36	0.96	14.91	1,368	0	98	0	1	12	17.75	-28.06			Aug-06
	7.82	13.78	33.45	29.44	19.97	1.6	0.81	17.48	1.08	31.02	19,105	1	99	0	0	22	15.62	-31.19			Jan-08
	7.91	13.91	33.76	30.36	21.47	1.73	0.56	17.5	1.08	31.22	19,105	1	99	0	0	22	15.79	-31.13			Apr-98
	6.21	10.91	21.43	36.64	112.54	0.84	0.15	10.15	1	12.94	353.2	-2	51	50	0	119	25.36	-16.11			Jul-96
	1.79	3.27	6.35	10.62	19.67	1.31	0.5	2.67	0.23	13.44	854.9	5	25	67	3		6.72	-4.87			Dec-03
	1.81	3.43	6.63	11.45	21.63	1.51	0.25	2.64	0.23	13.48	854.9	5	25	67	3		6.86	-4.66			Dec-03
	3.87	7.11	13.79	20.92	46.79	1.51	0.53	6.36	0.59	18.19	3,926	5	59	33	2		14.3	-13.95			Dec-03
	3.99	7.25	14.03	21.78	48.54	1.71	0.28	6.38	0.59	18.09	3,926	5	59	33	2		14.43	-13.82			Dec-03
	6.59	11.72	21.87	32.23	81.84	1.48	0.55	10.34	0.96	23.39	6,535	1	98	0	1		22.08	-23.11			Dec-03
	6.62	11.84	22.15	33.26	84.19	1.66	0.3	10.35	0.96	23.25	6,535	1	98	0	1		22.24	-23.04			Dec-03
	3.71	5.25	9.20	15.66	47.67	4.27	0.24	11.39	0.99	10.95	7,025	1	98	0	1	2	24.88	-17.23			Jun-08
	4.75	10.99	15.96				0.49			11.68	17.0	1	94	0	5						Jan-17
	4.69	11.94	28.05	34.03	58.13	2.25	0.3	11.54	0.94	14.54	25,849	1	97	0	2	2	13.83	-25.04			Sep-05
	3.69	9.26					0.35			10.87	77.3	2	93	0	5						May-17
	3.26	8.19	26.42	25.22	49.44	1.96	0.3	10.56	0.88	13.19	328.9	0	99	0	1	20					Dec-12
	6.12	8.45	15.38	13.89	31.01	7.71	0.28	10.84	0.96	5.2	5,762	1	96	0	3	1	16.43	-18.78			Mar-07
	5.01	12.57	34.64	50.33	84.79	1.74	0.55	11.11	0.92	15.92	181.2	0	97	0	3	29					Dec-12
	3.83	11.72	27.97	43.42	82.85	1.19	0.68	11.98	0.99	22.97	16,235	1	99	0	0	19	15.02	-26.05			Dec-94
	4.60	11.90	30.24	45.68	76.15	1.52	0.53	11.03	0.93	21.27	13,645	2	95	0	3	0	14.45	-23.33			Sep-96
	4.47	11.91	27.65	34.09	54.99	2.23	0.37	11.72	0.95	13.99	845.5	2	94	0	4	8					Nov-12
	3.85	9.90	27.25	29.92	52.26	2.15	0.38	11.51	0.94	11.05	794.8	1	96	0	3	24	13.64	-24.43			Mar-08
	5.41	14.09	25.80	26.41	46.92	2.7	0.68	13.76	1.08	20.44	9,950	1	96	0	3	15	10.52	-26.96			Apr-08
	5.55	14.39	26.17	28.03	50.18	6.38	0.27	13.73	1.08	5.22	13.3	1	96	0	3	15	10.78	-26.79			Aug-94
	5.48	14.25	26.22	27.88	49.94	2.97	0.24	13.72	1.08	17.36	2,560	1	96	0	3	15	10.8	-26.8			Feb-95
	5.42	14.17	26.08	27.34	48.70	2.9	0.43	13.72	1.08	20.49	9,950	1	96	0	3	15	10.67	-26.87			Feb-94
	4.84	12.60	28.94	37.25	62.34	2.06	0.49	11.73	0.95	13.57	2,555	1	98	0	1	4	13.54	-25.81			Aug-08
	8.34	16.69	35.68	68.83	106.82	1.48	0.54	9.67	0.87	29.14	664.3	0	99	0	1	16	2.72	3.5			Jan-86
	4.10	9.99	25.36	24.96	45.41	2.45	0.23	11.41	0.94	23.93	4,774	1	96	0	3	10	13.7	-23.5			Jul-91
	2.05	3.13	5.71	16.35	58.99	2.38	0.18	13.44	0.99	35.3	8,586	1	99	0	0	3	31	-16.08			Jan-93
	6.60	11.75	22.65	33.56	76.76	1.8	0.35	10.32	0.94	16.65	412.1	18	81	0	1						Nov-11
	6.54	11.60	18.81	33.48	106.72	1.41	0.24	11.06	1.04	18.12	8,570	0	100	0	0	7	26.95	-22.02			Oct-07
	5.53	12.80	30.50	33.18	49.86	2.13	0.37	11.86	0.96	11.87	3,447	0	97	0	2	7	14.78	-25.97			Mar-08
	5.34	13.99	25.94	26.73	46.66	2.57	0.53	13.77	1.08	16.87	3,968	1	96	0	3	18	11.09	-26.97			Apr-99
	6.55	11.44	21.43	36.11	110.10	1.55	0.22	10.29	1	29.02	3,414	0	100	0	0	4	25.16	-17.4			Sep-01
	3.92	9.89	11.87	32.98	103.76	0.76	0.52	13.54	0.94	44.07	3,026	0	100	0	0	10	28.4	-24.63			Dec-98
	6.54	11.01	17.00	31.95	109.67	1.63	0.37	11.72	1.1	30.92	5,038	0	100	0	0	5	26.68	-23.77			Dec-98
	6.56	11.06	17.15	32.48	111.16	1.74	0.22	11.71	1.1	28.8	1,882	0	100	0	0	5	26.71	-23.72			Dec-98
	4.29	10.07	11.07	32.01	103.63	0.9	0.44	13.78	0.95	37.53	4,885	0	100	0	0	20	29.3	-26.56			Dec-98
	6.90	12.06	20.89	35.62	110.27	1.52	0.19	10.65	1.03	22.78	21,603	1	99	0	0	4	26.31	-20.17			Sep-05
	6.66	11.82	18.93	33.17	106.11	1.43	0.22	11.19	1.06	21.56	23,310	1	99	0	0	4	27.11	-21.99			Sep-05
	7.28	12.20	22.08	35.36		1.59	0.18	10.39	1.02	16.63	1,268	0	100	0	0	12					Jun-13
	8.74	13.87	25.53	38.59	113.73	1.53	0.2	10.15	0.92	19.17	1,747	0	100	0	0	14					Dec-12
	7.49	12.52	19.13	35.56	116.21	1.91	0.15	12.03	1.14	18.72	1,747	1	99	0	0	15	26.06	-23.92			Aug-94
	7.50	12.51	19.10	35.65	116.47	1.84	0.13	12.05	1.15	27.01	3,849	1	99	0	0	15	26.07	-23.96			Feb-95

	MARKET			FUND TYPE, CATEGORY & OBJECTIVE	RATINGS				MINIMUMS	
Fund Name	Ticker Symbol	Traded On	Fund Type	Category and (Prospectus Objective)	Overall Rating	Reward Rating	Risk Rating	Recent Up/ Downgrade	Open to New Investors	Min Initial Investment
DFA U.S. Large Cap Value Portfolio Institutional Class	DFLVX	NAS CM	Open End	US Equity Large Cap Value (Growth & Income)	B	B	B	Up	Y	0
DFA U.S. Large Company Portfolio	DFUSX	NAS CM	Open End	US Equity Large Cap Blend (Growth & Income)	B	B	B		Y	0
DFA U.S. Micro Cap Portfolio Institutional Class	DFSCX	NAS CM	Open End	US Equity Small Cap (Small Company)	B+	A-	B	Up	Y	0
DFA U.S. Small Cap Growth Portfolio Institutional Class	DSCGX	NAS CM	Open End	US Equity Small Cap (Small Company)	B+	A-	B	Up	Y	0
DFA U.S. Small Cap Portfolio Institutional Class	DFSTX	NAS CM	Open End	US Equity Small Cap (Small Company)	B+	A-	B	Up	Y	0
DFA U.S. Small Cap Value Portfolio Institutional Class	DFSVX	NAS CM	Open End	US Equity Small Cap (Small Company)	B	B	B-	Up	Y	0
DFA U.S. Social Core Equity 2 Portfolio	DFUEX	NAS CM	Open End	US Equity Mid Cap (Growth)	B	B	C+	Up	Y	0
DFA U.S. Sustainability Core 1 Portfolio	DFSIX	NAS CM	Open End	US Equity Large Cap Blend (Growth)	B	B	B-		Y	0
DFA U.S. Targeted Value Portfolio Class R1	DFTVX	NAS CM	Open End	US Equity Small Cap (Growth & Income)	B	B	B	Up	Y	0
DFA U.S. Targeted Value Portfolio Class R2	DFTPX	NAS CM	Open End	US Equity Small Cap (Growth & Income)	B	B	B-	Up	Y	0
DFA U.S. Targeted Value Portfolio Institutional Class	DFFVX	NAS CM	Open End	US Equity Small Cap (Growth & Income)	B	B	B	Up	Y	0
DFA U.S. Vector Equity Portfolio Institutional Class	DFVEX	NAS CM	Open End	US Equity Mid Cap (Growth)	B	B	B	Up	Y	0
DFA United Kingdom Small Company Portfolio Inst Cls	DFUKX	NAS CM	Open End	Other Equity (Europe Stock)	C+	B	C	Up	Y	0
DFA US High Relative Profitability Portfolio Inst Cls	DURPX	NAS CM	Open End	US Equity Large Cap Blend (Growth)	U	U	U		Y	0
DFA World Core Equity Portfolio Institutional Class	DREIX	NAS CM	Open End	Global Equity (Growth)	B-	B	C+	Down	Y	0
DFA World ex U.S. Core Equity Portfolio Inst Cls Shares	DFWIX	NAS CM	Open End	Global Equity Large Cap (World Stock)	B	B	B-	Up	Y	0
DFA World ex U.S. Targeted Value Portfolio Inst Cls Shares	DWUSX	NAS CM	Open End	Global Equity Mid/Small Cap (Foreign Stock)	B	B	B	Up	Y	0
DFA World ex U.S. Value Port Institution Class	DFWVX	NAS CM	Open End	Global Equity Large Cap (Foreign Stock)	C+	B-	C	Up	Y	0
DGHM All-Cap Value Fund Class C	DGACX	NAS CM	Open End	US Equity Large Cap Value (Growth)	B-	C+	B-	Up	Y	1,000
DGHM All-Cap Value Fund Institutional Class	DGAIX	NAS CM	Open End	US Equity Large Cap Value (Growth)	B-	C+	B-	Up	Y	100,000
DGHM All-Cap Value Fund Investor Class	DGHMX	NAS CM	Open End	US Equity Large Cap Value (Growth)	B-	C+	B-	Up	Y	2,500
DGHM MicroCap Value Fund Institutional Class	DGMIX	NAS CM	Open End	US Equity Small Cap (Growth)	B+	A	B-	Up	Y	100,000
DGHM MicroCap Value Fund Investor Class	DGMMX	NAS CM	Open End	US Equity Small Cap (Growth)	B+	A	B-	Up	Y	2,500
DGHM V2000 SmallCap Value Fund Institutional Class	DGIVX	NAS CM	Open End	US Equity Small Cap (Small Company)	B	B	B	Up	Y	100,000
DGHM V2000 SmallCap Value Fund Investor Class	DGSMX	NAS CM	Open End	US Equity Small Cap (Small Company)	B	B	B	Up	Y	2,500
Diamond Hill All Cap Select Fund Class A	DHTAX	NAS CM	Open End	US Equity Large Cap Blend (Growth)	B	B	B	Up	Y	2,500
Diamond Hill All Cap Select Fund Class C	DHTCX	NAS CM	Open End	US Equity Large Cap Blend (Growth)	B	B-	B	Up	Y	2,500
Diamond Hill All Cap Select Fund Class I	DHLTX	NAS CM	Open End	US Equity Large Cap Blend (Growth)	B	B	B	Up	Y	2,500
Diamond Hill All Cap Select Fund Class Y	DHTYX	NAS CM	Open End	US Equity Large Cap Blend (Growth)	B	B	B	Up	Y	500,000
Diamond Hill Financial Long Short Fund Class A	BANCX	NAS CM	Open End	Financials Sector Equity (Financial)	B	B	B	Up	Y	2,500
Diamond Hill Financial Long Short Fund Class C	BSGCX	NAS CM	Open End	Financials Sector Equity (Financial)	B	B	B	Up	Y	2,500
Diamond Hill Financial Long Short Fund Class I	DHFSX	NAS CM	Open End	Financials Sector Equity (Financial)	B	B	B	Up	Y	2,500
Diamond Hill Large Cap Fund Class A	DHLAX	NAS CM	Open End	US Equity Large Cap Value (Growth)	B	B	B-		Y	2,500
Diamond Hill Large Cap Fund Class C	DHLCX	NAS CM	Open End	US Equity Large Cap Value (Growth)	B-	B-	B-	Down	Y	2,500
Diamond Hill Large Cap Fund Class I	DHLRX	NAS CM	Open End	US Equity Large Cap Value (Growth)	B	B	B-		Y	2,500
Diamond Hill Large Cap Fund Class Y	DHLYX	NAS CM	Open End	US Equity Large Cap Value (Growth)	B	B	B-		Y	500,000
Diamond Hill Long Short Fund Class A	DIAMX	NAS CM	Open End	Long/Short Equity (Growth)	B-	C+	B+			2,500
Diamond Hill Long Short Fund Class C	DHFCX	NAS CM	Open End	Long/Short Equity (Growth)	B-	C	B			2,500
Diamond Hill Long Short Fund Class I	DHLSX	NAS CM	Open End	Long/Short Equity (Growth)	B-	C+	B+			2,500
Diamond Hill Long-Short Fund Class Y	DIAYX	NAS CM	Open End	Long/Short Equity (Growth)	B-	C+	B+			500,000
Diamond Hill Mid Cap Fund Class A	DHPAX	NAS CM	Open End	US Equity Mid Cap (Growth)	B	B-	A-		Y	2,500
Diamond Hill Mid Cap Fund Class I	DHPIX	NAS CM	Open End	US Equity Mid Cap (Growth)	B	B-	A-		Y	2,500
Diamond Hill Mid Cap Fund Class Y	DHPYX	NAS CM	Open End	US Equity Mid Cap (Growth)	B	B-	A-		Y	500,000
Diamond Hill Research Opportunities Fund Class A	DHROX	NAS CM	Open End	Long/Short Equity (Growth)	B-	C+	B	Up	Y	2,500
Diamond Hill Research Opportunities Fund Class C	DROCX	NAS CM	Open End	Long/Short Equity (Growth)	B-	C+	B	Up	Y	2,500
Diamond Hill Research Opportunities Fund Class I	DROIX	NAS CM	Open End	Long/Short Equity (Growth)	B-	C+	B	Up	Y	2,500
Diamond Hill Research Opportunities Fund Class Y	DROYX	NAS CM	Open End	Long/Short Equity (Growth)	B-	C+	B	Up	Y	500,000
Diamond Hill Small Cap Fund Class A	DHSCX	NAS CM	Open End	US Equity Small Cap (Small Company)	B-	C+	B	Up	Y	5,000
Diamond Hill Small Cap Fund Class C	DHSMX	NAS CM	Open End	US Equity Small Cap (Small Company)	B-	C+	B	Up	Y	5,000
Diamond Hill Small Cap Fund Class I	DHSIX	NAS CM	Open End	US Equity Small Cap (Small Company)	B-	C+	B	Up		5,000
Diamond Hill Small Cap Fund Class Y	DHSYX	NAS CM	Open End	US Equity Small Cap (Small Company)	B-	C+	B	Up	Y	500,000
Diamond Hill Small Mid Cap Fund Class A	DHMAX	NAS CM	Open End	US Equity Mid Cap (Growth)	B	B-	A-	Up		2,500

★Expanded analysis of this fund is included in Section II.

Min Additional Investment	TOTAL RETURNS 3-Month Total Return	6-Month Total Return	1-Year Total Return	3-Year Total Return	5-Year Total Return	PERFORMANCE Dividend Yield (TTM)	Expense Ratio	3-Yr Std Deviation	3-Year Beta	ASSETS NAV	Total Assets (MIL)	ASSET ALLOCATION & TURNOVER %Cash	%Stocks	%Bonds	%Other	Turnover Ratio	BULL & BEAR Last Bull Market Total Return	Last Bear Market Total Return	FEES Front End Fee (%)	Back End Fee (%)	Inception Date
	7.46	12.42	18.96	35.07	114.95	1.7	0.27	12.05	1.14	39.12	24,727	1	99	0	0	15	25.91	-23.99			Feb-93
	6.60	11.36	21.73	36.66	110.85	1.88	0.08	10.09	1	20.71	8,252	0	100	0	0	9	25.07	-16.26			Sep-99
	2.70	9.42	11.17	33.92	105.34	0.66	0.52	14.36	0.98	22.03	6,474	1	99	0	0	15	28.05	-23.94			Dec-81
	5.31	10.28	16.20	33.02	103.70	0.73	0.4	12.88	0.83	18.67	528.9	0	100	0	0	47					Dec-12
	3.79	9.42	11.52	32.21	101.97	0.9	0.37	13.55	0.94	35.94	17,435	1	99	0	0	10	28.39	-24.71			Mar-92
	3.12	9.28	7.21	25.79	91.08	0.72	0.52	15.22	1.06	37.92	15,503	1	99	0	0	19	29.63	-27.77			Mar-93
	7.02	12.11	18.98	32.42	101.47	1.32	0.28	11.58	1.08	16.08	997.7	1	99	0	0	17	27.54	-22.88			Oct-07
	6.89	11.93	21.35	35.23	109.63	1.34	0.25	10.7	1.03	21.11	1,249	0	100	0	0	26	26.54	-20.08			Mar-08
	4.44	9.91	9.50	29.60	96.21	0.91	0.47	14.75	1.02	24.88	11,043	1	99	0	0	28	29.1	-27.48			Jan-08
	4.40	9.85	9.31	29.04	94.52	0.8	0.62	14.74	1.02	24.75	11,043	1	99	0	0	28	28.99	-27.49			Jun-08
	4.50	9.99	9.58	30.01	97.03	0.98	0.37	14.74	1.02	24.89	11,043	1	99	0	0	28	29.16	-27.42			Feb-00
	5.39	10.78	14.63	30.64	100.42	1.13	0.32	12.74	1.11	19.17	4,856	0	100	0	0	10	28.02	-24.76			Dec-05
	4.69	12.29	28.40	22.33	62.36	2.76	0.59	15.61	0.92	31.15	44.5	0	100	0	0	17	26.84	-22.75			Mar-86
	10.03	15.62					0.25			11.68	169.5	1	99	0	0						May-17
	6.67	12.26	25.08	34.26	82.08	1.8	0.35	10.39	0.97	16.57	637.1	1	98	0	1						Mar-12
	5.50	12.76	30.12	32.76		2.16	0.39	11.96	0.96	12.49	2,863	0	97	0	3	1					Apr-13
	5.13	12.79	31.52	41.91	64.51	1.81	0.76	12.75	1.06	15.25	474.6	0	95	0	4	28					Nov-12
	5.95	13.92	28.21	29.67	44.93	1.89	0.53	13.57	1.07	12.98	248.9	1	97	0	2		12.05	-27.79			Aug-10
500	4.93	7.72	9.66	17.08	76.25	1.57	2.1	12.16	1.12	7.1	10.8	0	100	0	0	56	19.83	-21.77		1.00	Jun-07
500	5.26	8.29	10.84	20.85	85.74	2.37	1.1	12.12	1.11	8	10.8	0	100	0	0	56	20.54	-21.38			Jul-10
500	5.05	7.96	10.38	19.32	82.32	1.86	1.5	12.1	1.11	7.95	10.8	0	100	0	0	56	20.35	-21.53			Jun-07
500	-0.11	8.08	15.40	52.43	125.51	0.25	1.19			12.47	24.7	7	91	0	0		30.68	-20.37			May-16
500	-0.21	7.89	15.01	50.94	122.20	0	1.5			12.49	24.7	7	91	0	0		30.49	-20.45			Jul-16
500	4.13	8.77	8.19	27.36	77.62	0.51	0.98	12.68	0.87	13.69	57.2	3	96	0	1	36	24.11	-22.25			Jun-10
500	4.02	8.54	7.76	25.75	74.02	0.45	1.4	12.63	0.86	12.95	57.2	3	96	0	1	36	23.93	-22.19			Jun-10
	7.95	12.82	19.92	28.37	110.06	0	1.18	12.1	0.97	16.01	159.3	2	96	2	0	70	20.28	-18.47	5.00		Dec-05
	7.77	12.42	19.07	25.44	102.24	0	1.93	12.1	0.97	15.11	159.3	2	96	2	0	70	19.79	-18.8		1.00	Dec-05
	8.00	12.99	20.33	29.50	112.88	0.08	0.88	12.08	0.97	16.11	159.3	2	96	2	0	70	20.38	-18.38			Dec-05
	8.05	13.11	20.45	29.85	114.30	0.17	0.78	12.07	0.96	16.14	159.3	2	96	2	0	70	20.49	-18.38			Dec-11
	3.52	6.47	11.57	25.53	89.50	0	1.43	15.26	1.1	24.67	34.3	19	81	0	0	34	28.66	-23.6	5.00		Aug-97
	3.29	6.07	10.76	22.70	82.36	0	2.18	15.23	1.1	22.54	34.3	19	81	0	0	34	28.19	-23.88		1.00	Jun-99
	3.57	6.65	11.90	26.56	92.02	0	1.13	15.24	1.1	24.74	34.3	19	81	0	0	34	28.97	-23.52			Dec-06
	5.61	9.62	19.94	34.18	106.79	0.84	0.98	11.51	1.1	26.45	5,748	2	98	0	0	23	23.39	-17.08	5.00		Jun-01
	5.43	9.23	19.03	31.19	99.18	0.37	1.73	11.49	1.09	25.07	5,748	2	98	0	0	23	22.87	-17.32		1.00	Sep-01
	5.72	9.84	20.30	35.36	109.60	1.07	0.68	11.52	1.1	26.62	5,748	2	98	0	0	23	23.59	-17.01			Jan-05
	5.74	9.86	20.41	35.83	110.95	1.15	0.58	11.5	1.1	26.64	5,748	2	98	0	0	23	23.59	-17.08			Dec-11
	2.80	2.16	5.64	13.83	52.23	0	1.4	8.59	0.74	25.76	4,767	40	58	2	0	45	16.96	-12.08	5.00		Jun-00
	2.59	1.75	4.82	11.26	46.59	0	2.15	8.6	0.74	23.04	4,767	40	58	2	0	45	16.5	-12.37		1.00	Feb-01
	2.91	2.33	5.99	14.82	54.33	0	1.1	8.6	0.74	26.39	4,767	40	58	2	0	45	17.17	-12.05			Jan-05
	2.92	2.37	6.06	15.15	55.28	0	1	8.59	0.74	26.49	4,767	40	58	2	0	45	17.14	-12.08			Dec-11
	3.70	6.00	10.13	29.64		0.13	1.09	9.7	0.86	13.66	120.0	7	91	2	0	17			5.00		Dec-13
	3.80	6.09	10.47	30.84		0.37	0.79	9.68	0.86	13.7	120.0	7	91	2	0	17					Dec-13
	3.78	6.15	10.51	31.12		0.4	0.69	9.68	0.86	13.73	120.0	7	91	2	0	17					Dec-13
	5.91	4.68	12.98	16.70	68.28	0	1.43	10.6	0.82	23.56	67.3	19	79	2	0	67	21.14	-10.28	5.00		Dec-11
	5.69	4.21	12.12	14.05	62.02	0	2.18	10.62	0.82	22.4	67.3	19	79	2	0	67	20.59	-10.69		1.00	Dec-11
	6.03	4.80	13.34	17.69	70.54	0	1.13	10.61	0.82	23.83	67.3	19	79	2	0	67	21.24	-10.22			Dec-11
	6.06	4.88	13.47	18.11	71.70	0	1.03	10.58	0.82	23.88	67.3	19	79	2	0	67	21.34	-10.17			Dec-11
	3.79	8.78	10.61	20.70	80.54	0	1.3	9.56	0.63	35.62	1,511	10	87	4	0	15	18.93	-21.7	5.00		Dec-00
	3.57	8.40	9.80	18.02	73.92	0	2.05	9.55	0.63	30.98	1,511	10	87	4	0	15	18.45	-21.96		1.00	Feb-01
	3.85	8.97	10.94	21.76	83.02	0.19	1	9.56	0.63	36.15	1,511	10	87	4	0	15	19.08	-21.6			Apr-05
	3.90	9.02	11.05	22.14	84.15	0.26	0.9	9.57	0.63	36.17	1,511	10	87	4	0	15	19.08	-21.7			Dec-11
	2.12	4.73	8.34	27.85	98.30	0.05	1.24	10.15	0.78	22.24	2,535	8	91	2	0	17	22.16	-21.36	5.00		Dec-05

	MARKET			FUND TYPE, CATEGORY & OBJECTIVE	RATINGS					MINIMUMS
Fund Name	Ticker Symbol	Traded On	Fund Type	Category and (Prospectus Objective)	Overall Rating	Reward Rating	Risk Rating	Recent Up/ Downgrade	Open to New Investors	Min Initial Investment
Diamond Hill Small Mid Cap Fund Class C	DHMCX	NAS CM	Open End	US Equity Mid Cap (Growth)	B	C+	A-	Up		2,500
Diamond Hill Small Mid Cap Fund Class I	DHMIX	NAS CM	Open End	US Equity Mid Cap (Growth)	B	B-	A-	Up		2,500
Diamond Hill Small-Mid Cap Fund Class Y	DHMYX	NAS CM	Open End	US Equity Mid Cap (Growth)	B	B-	A-	Up		500,000
Dimensional 2005 Target Date Retmnt Income Fund Inst Cls	DRIMX	NAS CM	Open End	Target Date 2000-2020 (Asset Alloc)	C	D+	A	Up	Y	0
Dimensional 2010 Target Date Retmnt Income Fund Inst Cls	DRIBX	NAS CM	Open End	Target Date 2000-2020 (Asset Alloc)	C	D+	A-	Up	Y	0
Dimensional 2015 Target Date Retmnt Income Fund Inst Cls	DRIQX	NAS CM	Open End	Target Date 2000-2020 (Asset Alloc)	C	D+	B+	Up	Y	0
Dimensional 2020 Target Date Retmnt Income Fund Inst Cls	DRIRX	NAS CM	Open End	Target Date 2000-2020 (Asset Alloc)	C	D+	B+	Up	Y	0
Dimensional 2025 Target Date Retmnt Income Fund Inst Cls	DRIUX	NAS CM	Open End	Target Date 2021-2045 (Asset Alloc)	C	C-	B+	Up	Y	0
Dimensional 2030 Target Date Retmnt Income Fund Inst Cls	DRIWX	NAS CM	Open End	Target Date 2021-2045 (Asset Alloc)	C	C-	B+	Up	Y	0
Dimensional 2035 Target Date Retmnt Income Fund Inst Cls	DRIGX	NAS CM	Open End	Target Date 2021-2045 (Asset Alloc)	C	C-	B+	Up	Y	0
Dimensional 2040 Target Date Retmnt Income Fund Inst Cls	DRIHX	NAS CM	Open End	Target Date 2021-2045 (Asset Alloc)	C	C	B+	Up	Y	0
Dimensional 2045 Target Date Retmnt Income Fund Inst Cls	DRIIX	NAS CM	Open End	Target Date 2021-2045 (Asset Alloc)	C	C	B+	Up	Y	0
Dimensional 2050 Target Date Retmnt Income Fund Inst Cls	DRIJX	NAS CM	Open End	Target Date 2046+ (Asset Alloc)	C	C	B+	Up	Y	0
Dimensional 2055 Target Date Retmnt Income Fund Inst Cls	DRIKX	NAS CM	Open End	Target Date 2046+ (Asset Alloc)	C	C	B+	Up	Y	0
Dimensional 2060 Target Date Retmnt Income Fund Inst Cls	DRILX	NAS CM	Open End	Target Date 2046+ (Asset Alloc)	C	C	B+	Up	Y	0
Dimensional Retirement Income Fund Institutional Class	TDIFX	NAS CM	Open End	Target Date 2000-2020 (Asset Alloc)	C	D+	A	Up	Y	0
Dinosaur Lisanti Small Cap Growth Fund	ASCGX	NAS CM	Open End	US Equity Small Cap (Small Company)	B	A-	C+	Up	Y	2,000
Direxion Hilton Tactical Income Fund Class A	HCYAX	NAS CM	Open End	Moderate Alloc (Growth & Income)	B-	C+	B	Down	Y	2,500
Direxion Hilton Tactical Income Fund Class C	HCYCX	NAS CM	Open End	Moderate Alloc (Growth & Income)	B-	C+	B	Down	Y	2,500
Direxion Hilton Tactical Income Fund Institutional Class	HCYIX	NAS CM	Open End	Moderate Alloc (Growth & Income)	B-	C+	B	Down	Y	50,000
Direxion Indexed Commodity Strategy Fund Class A	DXCTX	NAS CM	Open End	Commodities Broad Basket (Growth)	D	D	D		Y	2,500
Direxion Indexed Commodity Strategy Fund Class C	DXSCX	NAS CM	Open End	Commodities Broad Basket (Growth)	D	D	D		Y	2,500
Direxion Indexed Commodity Strategy Fund Institutional Cls	DXCIX	NAS CM	Open End	Commodities Broad Basket (Growth)	D	D	D+		Y	5,000,000
Direxion Indexed CVT Strategy Fund	DXCBX	NAS CM	Open End	Convertibles (Growth & Income)	C+	C+	C+	Down	Y	25,000
Direxion Monthly 25+ Year Treasury Bear 1.35X Fund Inv Cls	DXSTX	NAS CM	Open End	Trading Tools (Growth & Income)	D	D	D+	Down	Y	25,000
Direxion Monthly 25+ Year Treasury Bull 1.35X Fund Inv Cls	DXLTX	NAS CM	Open End	Trading Tools (Growth & Income)	D+	D+	C-	Up	Y	25,000
Direxion Monthly 7-10 Year Treasury Bear 2X Fund	DXKSX	NAS CM	Open End	Trading Tools (Growth)	D	D	D+	Down	Y	25,000
Direxion Monthly 7-10 Year Treasury Bull 2X Fund	DXKLX	NAS CM	Open End	Trading Tools (Growth)	C-	D+	C-	Down	Y	25,000
Direxion Monthly Emerging Markets Bull 2X Fund	DXELX	NAS CM	Open End	Trading Tools (Div Emerging Mkts)	B	A	C-	Up	Y	25,000
Direxion Monthly High Yield Bull 1.2X Fund Investor Class	DXHYX	NAS CM	Open End	Trading Tools (Growth & Income)	C-	D+	A-	Up	Y	25,000
Direxion Monthly NASDAQ-100 Bull 2X Fund Investor Class	DXQLX	NAS CM	Open End	Trading Tools (Growth)	A-	A+	B-	Up	Y	25,000
Direxion Monthly NASDAQ-100® Bear 1.25X Fund	DXNSX	NAS CM	Open End	Trading Tools (Growth & Income)	D-	D	D-	Down	Y	25,000
Direxion Monthly NASDAQ-100® Bull 1.25X Fund	DXNLX	NAS CM	Open End	Trading Tools (Growth & Income)	D+	C	B+	Up	Y	25,000
Direxion Monthly S&P 500 Bear 2X Fund Investor Class	DXSSX	NAS CM	Open End	Other Alternative (Growth)	D-	D-	D-	Down	Y	25,000
Direxion Monthly S&P 500 Bull 2X Fund Investor Class	DXSLX	NAS CM	Open End	Trading Tools (Growth)	B+	A+	C+	Down	Y	25,000
Direxion Monthly Small Cap Bear 2X Fund	DXRSX	NAS CM	Open End	Other Alternative (Small Company)	E+	E+	E+	Down	Y	25,000
Direxion Monthly Small Cap Bull 2X Fund	DXRLX	NAS CM	Open End	Trading Tools (Small Company)	B+	A+	C	Up	Y	25,000
Dividend and Income Fund	DNI	NYSE	Closed End	Moderate Alloc (Income)	C+	B-	C+	Up	Y	
DNP Select Income Fund	DNP	NYSE	Closed End	Utilities Sector Equity (Utility)	B-	B	C+	Down	Y	
Dodge & Cox Balanced Fund	DODBX	NAS CM	Open End	Moderate Alloc (Balanced)	B	B-	B+	Up	Y	2,500
Dodge & Cox Global Stock Fund	DODWX	NAS CM	Open End	Global Equity (World Stock)	B-	B	C	Up	Y	2,500
Dodge & Cox International Stock Fund	DODFX	NAS CM	Open End	Global Equity Large Cap (Foreign Stock)	C+	C+	C+	Up		2,500
Dodge & Cox Stock Fund	DODGX	NAS CM	Open End	US Equity Large Cap Value (Growth & Income)	B	B	B	Up	Y	2,500
Domini Impact Equity Fund A Shares	DSEPX	NAS CM	Open End	US Equity Large Cap Blend (Growth)	B-	C+	B	Down	Y	2,500
Domini Impact Equity Fund Institutional Shares	DIEQX	NAS CM	Open End	US Equity Large Cap Blend (Growth)	B-	C+	B	Down	Y	500,000
Domini Impact Equity Fund Investor Shares	DSEFX	NAS CM	Open End	US Equity Large Cap Blend (Growth)	B-	C+	B	Down	Y	2,500
Domini Impact Equity Fund R Shares	DSFRX	NAS CM	Open End	US Equity Large Cap Blend (Growth)	C+	C+	C+	Down	Y	0
Domini Impact International Equity Fund A Shares	DOMAX	NAS CM	Open End	Global Equity Large Cap (Foreign Stock)	B	B	B	Up	Y	2,500
Domini Impact Intl Equity Fund Inst Shares	DOMOX	NAS CM	Open End	Global Equity Large Cap (Foreign Stock)	B	B	B	Up	Y	500,000
Domini Impact International Equity Fund Investor Shares	DOMIX	NAS CM	Open End	Global Equity Large Cap (Foreign Stock)	B	B-	B	Up	Y	2,500
DoubleLine Multi-Asset Growth Fund Class A	DMLAX	NAS CM	Open End	Moderate Alloc (Asset Alloc)	B-	C+	B	Down	Y	2,000
DoubleLine Multi-Asset Growth Fund Class I	DMLIX	NAS CM	Open End	Moderate Alloc (Asset Alloc)	B-	C+	B	Down	Y	100,000

★ Expanded analysis of this fund is included in Section II.

	TOTAL RETURNS					PERFORMANCE				ASSETS		ASSET ALLOCATION & TURNOVER					BULL & BEAR		FEES		
Min Additional Investment	3-Month Total Return	6-Month Total Return	1-Year Total Return	3-Year Total Return	5-Year Total Return	Dividend Yield (TTM)	Expense Ratio	3-Yr Std Deviation	3-Year Beta	NAV	Total Assets (MIL)	%Cash	%Stocks	%Bonds	%Other	Turnover Ratio	Last Bull Market Total Return	Last Bear Market Total Return	Front End Fee (%)	Back End Fee (%)	Inception Date
	1.92	4.34	7.49	24.95	90.96	0	1.99	10.14	0.78	20.39	2,535	8	91	2	0	17	21.57	-21.58		1.00	Dec-05
	2.23	4.90	8.63	28.95	100.98	0.29	0.94	10.15	0.78	22.45	2,535	8	91	2	0	17	22.32	-21.19			Dec-05
	2.22	4.94	8.76	29.43	102.26	0.36	0.84	10.16	0.78	22.49	2,535	8	91	2	0	17	22.41	-21.19			Dec-11
	2.37	3.86	7.24			1.77	0.21			10.62	4.7	2	22	75	2						Nov-15
	2.97	4.62	8.36			1.92	0.21			10.8	14.9	0	25	74	0						Nov-15
	3.52	5.28	9.07			1.97	0.21			10.92	32.7	0	25	75	0						Nov-15
	4.34	6.57	11.14			1.99	0.23			11.22	88.8	2	30	68	0						Nov-15
	5.39	8.30	14.40			1.93	0.25			11.6	105.9	0	43	56	1						Nov-15
	5.75	9.10	16.81			1.83	0.26			11.84	97.9	0	57	42	1						Nov-15
	5.39	9.16	18.23			1.65	0.28			11.93	76.0	2	70	27	2						Nov-15
	5.53	9.81	20.48			1.61	0.28			12.21	58.3	1	83	14	2						Nov-15
	6.25	11.00	22.65			1.64	0.29			12.46	39.8	1	93	5	1						Nov-15
	6.28	11.06	22.77			1.67	0.29			12.41	35.3	1	93	5	1						Nov-15
	6.28	11.06	22.62			1.69	0.29			12.4	11.7	1	93	5	1						Nov-15
	6.14	11.02	22.67			1.48	0.29			12.44	8.5	2	92	4	1						Nov-15
	2.04	3.42	6.40			1.31	0.22			10.58	12.5	3	20	75	3						Nov-15
250	6.66	13.27	27.78	36.38	118.31	0	1.8	15.64	0.97	18.81	14.4	3	97	0	0	268	28.34	-26.35			Feb-04
100	2.28	4.73	8.32	17.98		2.76	1.52	4.21	0.03	16.76	107.7	-2	47	24	1	61			5.50		Sep-13
100	2.10	4.36	7.55	15.38		2.07	2.27	4.21	0.02	16.75	107.7	-2	47	24	1	61				1.00	Jun-15
100	2.34	4.85	8.63	18.90		2.99	1.27	4.23	0.03	16.79	107.7	-2	47	24	1	61					Sep-13
100	4.94	2.11	-8.35	-16.58	-27.90	5.23	1.42	6.9	0.99	13.68	19.1	95	0	0	5		-8.1	-25.44	5.50		Jun-08
100	4.70	1.73	-9.06	-18.47	-30.56	4.53	2.17	6.85	0.99	13.03	19.1	95	0	0	5		-8.39	-25.65		1.00	Mar-10
100	4.97	2.12	-8.11	-15.95	-27.00	5.72	1.17	6.86	0.99	13.87	19.1	95	0	0	5		-7.94	-25.38			May-09
500	3.04	6.57	13.06	18.02		0.36	1.63	8.37		46.91	2.0	32	0	19	49						Feb-14
500	-4.04	-4.64	-12.53			0	1.23			16.92	1.2	239	0	0	-139	0					Nov-15
500	2.95	2.46	10.01			0	1.24			21.46	93.4	43	0	57	0	0					Nov-15
500	0.51	-0.33	-5.45	-16.30	-24.55	0	1.5	10.71		29.31	5.5	304	0	0	-204	0	-5.35	-26.38			May-04
500	-0.91	-0.66	2.73	2.00	0.87	0	1.51	10.69		34.61	13.8	33	0	0	67	0	0.48	27.98			Mar-05
500	12.86	30.85	80.88	39.75	8.68	0	1.5	30.93		60.18	9.7	33	67	0	0	0	38.08	-53.83			Nov-05
500	-0.09	1.37	5.66			3.54	1.76			23.94	146.9	17	0	69	14	362					Feb-16
500	13.69	26.66	68.62	107.40	452.81	0	1.5	27.14		106.54	207.6	32	56	0	11	0	58.38	-21.33			May-06
500	-8.42	-14.97	-30.68			0	1.28			12.12	0.08	241	-141	0	0	0					Mar-16
500	8.43	15.97	39.04			0	1.32			28.67	22.8	44	56	0	0	0					Mar-16
500	-11.92	-19.06	-32.51	-51.90	-81.76	0	1.51	20.02		14.26	7.1	292	-192	0	0	0	-40.11	37.8			May-06
500	12.46	21.49	42.67	66.33	274.16	0	1.49	20.15		135.95	91.9	33	67	0	0	0	51.62	-31.44			May-06
500	-6.19	-16.77	-25.50	-55.14	-83.53	0	1.52	28.16		15.13	4.6	283	-183	0	0	0	-45.71	64.81			Dec-99
500	5.90	16.92	27.05	54.12	223.35	0	1.51	28.23		76.97	20.4	32	68	0	0	0	58.24	-45.76			Feb-99
	9.66	14.23	23.04	24.29	75.43	1.19	0	12.09	1.08	16.78	177.4	13	84	0	0	35	30.97	-15.77			Jun-98
	0.19	3.71	10.91	19.60	81.52	2.43	1.86	12.73	0.8	9.7175	2,902	-34	118	14	1	16	14.71	-0.93			Jan-87
100	3.61	6.86	12.59	26.70	80.37	2.04	0.53	8.73	0.8	107	16,335	2	65	27	0	24	19.12	-16.16			Jun-31
100	3.44	9.55	21.51	29.74	88.86	0.98	0.63	13.02	1.16	13.86	9,241	2	98	0	0	25	19.6	-24.32			May-08
100	1.20	8.23	23.94	18.13	52.16	1.82	0.64	14.55	1.1	46.32	64,913	1	99	0	0	17	14.7	-25.68			May-01
100	5.74	10.78	18.32	35.77	116.29	1.52	0.52	12.82	1.16	203.61	69,876	1	99	0	0	16	24.41	-21.54			Jan-65
100	4.77	9.53	15.44	17.79	83.06	3.74	1.12	10.9	1.03	5.08	892.2	1	98	0	1	85	24.71	-16.11	4.75		Nov-08
	4.90	9.69	15.79	19.18	86.60	1.28	0.74	10.82	1.02	23.56	892.2	1	98	0	1	85	24.99	-15.93			Nov-08
100	4.80	9.50	15.41	17.96	83.20	0.39	1.09	10.83	1.02	47.11	892.2	1	98	0	1	85	24.68	-16.07			Jun-91
	5.07	9.81	15.84	19.17	86.19	4.93	0.8	10.87	1.02	3.67	892.2	1	98	0	1	85	24.93	-15.93			Nov-03
100	2.75	7.35	24.45	29.55	60.84	1.23	1.5	11.6	0.9	9.4	1,226	2	95	0	3	85	12.02	-24.4	4.75		Nov-08
	2.85	7.58	24.78	31.17	63.97	1.78	1.04	11.62	0.91	8.9	1,226	2	95	0	3	85	11.95	-24.46			Nov-12
100	2.85	7.45	24.60	29.61	60.83	1.34	1.43	11.65	0.91	8.93	1,226	2	95	0	3	85	11.95	-24.46			Dec-06
100	1.88	4.84	13.73	21.45	29.74	2.1	1.57	6.16	0.52	9.57	212.7	14	45	35	6	59	1.71	-0.06	4.25		Dec-10
100	2.03	5.05	14.06	22.58	31.46	2.32	1.32	6.15	0.52	9.61	212.7	14	45	35	6	59	1.72	0.03			Dec-10

	MARKET			FUND TYPE, CATEGORY & OBJECTIVE	RATINGS					MINIMUMS
Fund Name	Ticker Symbol	Traded On	Fund Type	Category and (Prospectus Objective)	Overall Rating	Reward Rating	Risk Rating	Recent Up/ Downgrade	Open to New Investors	Min Initial Investment
DoubleLine Shiller Enhanced CAPE® Class I	DSEEX	NAS CM	Open End	US Equity Large Cap Value (Growth)	B	B	B+	Down	Y	100,000
DoubleLine Shiller Enhanced CAPE® Class N	DSENX	NAS CM	Open End	US Equity Large Cap Value (Growth)	B	B	B+	Down	Y	2,000
DoubleLine Shiller Enhanced International CAPE® Class I	DSEUX	NAS CM	Open End	Europe Equity Large Cap (Growth & Income)	D-	D+	B+		Y	100,000
DoubleLine Shiller Enhanced International CAPE® Class N	DLEUX	NAS CM	Open End	Europe Equity Large Cap (Growth & Income)	D-	D+	B+		Y	2,000
DoubleLine Strategic Commodity Fund Class I	DBCMX	NAS CM	Open End	Commodities Broad Basket (Growth)	C	C	C+	Up	Y	100,000
DoubleLine Strategic Commodity Fund Class N	DLCMX	NAS CM	Open End	Commodities Broad Basket (Growth)	C	C	C+	Up	Y	2,000
Dreyfus Active MidCap Fund Class A	DNLDX	NAS CM	Open End	US Equity Mid Cap (Growth)	B	B-	B+	Up	Y	1,000
Dreyfus Active MidCap Fund Class C	DNLCX	NAS CM	Open End	US Equity Mid Cap (Growth)	B	B-	B+	Up	Y	1,000
Dreyfus Active MidCap Fund Class I	DNLRX	NAS CM	Open End	US Equity Mid Cap (Growth)	B	B	B+	Up	Y	1,000
Dreyfus Active MidCap Fund Class Y	DNLYX	NAS CM	Open End	US Equity Mid Cap (Growth)	B	B	B+	Up	Y	1,000,000
Dreyfus Alternative Diversifier Strategies Fund Class A	DRNAX	NAS CM	Open End	Multialternative (Growth)	C	C	C	Up	Y	1,000
Dreyfus Alternative Diversifier Strategies Fund Class C	DRNCX	NAS CM	Open End	Multialternative (Growth)	C	C	C	Up	Y	1,000
Dreyfus Alternative Diversifier Strategies Fund Class I	DRNIX	NAS CM	Open End	Multialternative (Growth)	C	C	B-		Y	1,000
Dreyfus Alternative Diversifier Strategies Fund Class Y	DRYNX	NAS CM	Open End	Multialternative (Growth)	C	C	B-		Y	1,000,000
Dreyfus Appreciation Fund, Inc. Class I	DGIGX	NAS CM	Open End	US Equity Large Cap Blend (Growth)	B-	B	B-	Down	Y	1,000
Dreyfus Appreciation Fund, Inc. Class Investor	DGAGX	NAS CM	Open End	US Equity Large Cap Blend (Growth)	B-	B-	B-	Down	Y	2,500
Dreyfus Appreciation Fund, Inc. Class Y	DGYGX	NAS CM	Open End	US Equity Large Cap Blend (Growth)	B-	B-	B-	Down	Y	1,000,000
Dreyfus Balanced Opportunity Fund Class A	DBOAX	NAS CM	Open End	Moderate Alloc (Balanced)	B	C+	A-	Up	Y	1,000
Dreyfus Balanced Opportunity Fund Class C	DBOCX	NAS CM	Open End	Moderate Alloc (Balanced)	B	C+	A-	Up	Y	1,000
Dreyfus Balanced Opportunity Fund Class I	DBORX	NAS CM	Open End	Moderate Alloc (Balanced)	B-	C+	B	Down	Y	1,000
Dreyfus Balanced Opportunity Fund Class J	THPBX	NAS CM	Open End	Moderate Alloc (Balanced)	B	C+	A-	Up		1,000
Dreyfus Balanced Opportunity Fund Class Y	DBOYX	NAS CM	Open End	Moderate Alloc (Balanced)	B-	C+	B	Down	Y	1,000,000
Dreyfus Balanced Opportunity Fund Class Z	DBOZX	NAS CM	Open End	Moderate Alloc (Balanced)	B	C+	A-	Up		1,000
Dreyfus Core Equity Fund Class A	DLTSX	NAS CM	Open End	US Equity Large Cap Blend (Growth)	B-	B-	B-	Down	Y	1,000
Dreyfus Core Equity Fund Class C	DPECX	NAS CM	Open End	US Equity Large Cap Blend (Growth)	B-	B-	B-	Down	Y	1,000
Dreyfus Core Equity Fund Class I	DPERX	NAS CM	Open End	US Equity Large Cap Blend (Growth)	B-	B-	B-	Down	Y	1,000
Dreyfus Disciplined Stock Fund	DDSTX	NAS CM	Open End	US Equity Large Cap Blend (Growth & Income)	B	B-	A-		Y	2,500
Dreyfus Diversified Emerging Markets Fund Class A	DBEAX	NAS CM	Open End	Emerging Markets Equity (Div Emerging Mkts)	B-	B	C	Up	Y	1,000
Dreyfus Diversified Emerging Markets Fund Class C	DBECX	NAS CM	Open End	Emerging Markets Equity (Div Emerging Mkts)	C+	B-	C	Up	Y	1,000
Dreyfus Diversified Emerging Markets Fund Class I	SBCEX	NAS CM	Open End	Emerging Markets Equity (Div Emerging Mkts)	B-	B	C	Up	Y	1,000
Dreyfus Diversified Emerging Markets Fund Class Y	SBYEX	NAS CM	Open End	Emerging Markets Equity (Div Emerging Mkts)	B-	B	C	Up	Y	1,000,000
Dreyfus Diversified International Fund Class A	DFPAX	NAS CM	Open End	Global Equity Large Cap (Foreign Stock)	B-	B-	B	Up	Y	1,000
Dreyfus Diversified International Fund Class C	DFPCX	NAS CM	Open End	Global Equity Large Cap (Foreign Stock)	B-	C+	B	Up	Y	1,000
Dreyfus Diversified International Fund Class I	DFPIX	NAS CM	Open End	Global Equity Large Cap (Foreign Stock)	B	B-	B	Up	Y	1,000
Dreyfus Diversified International Fund Class Y	DDIFX	NAS CM	Open End	Global Equity Large Cap (Foreign Stock)	B	B-	B	Up	Y	1,000,000
Dreyfus Dynamic Total Return Fund Class A	AVGAX	NAS CM	Open End	Multialternative (Growth)	B-	C	B	Up	Y	1,000
Dreyfus Dynamic Total Return Fund Class C	AVGCX	NAS CM	Open End	Multialternative (Growth)	C+	C	B	Up	Y	1,000
Dreyfus Dynamic Total Return Fund Class I	AVGRX	NAS CM	Open End	Multialternative (Growth)	B-	C	B	Up	Y	1,000
Dreyfus Dynamic Total Return Fund Class Y	AVGYX	NAS CM	Open End	Multialternative (Growth)	B-	C	B	Up	Y	1,000,000
Dreyfus Emerging Markets Fund Class A	DRFMX	NAS CM	Open End	Emerging Markets Equity (Div Emerging Mkts)	C+	C+	C	Up	Y	1,000
Dreyfus Emerging Markets Fund Class C	DCPEX	NAS CM	Open End	Emerging Markets Equity (Div Emerging Mkts)	C	C+	C	Down	Y	1,000
Dreyfus Emerging Markets Fund Class I	DRPEX	NAS CM	Open End	Emerging Markets Equity (Div Emerging Mkts)	C+	C+	C	Up	Y	1,000
Dreyfus Emerging Markets Fund Class Y	DYPEX	NAS CM	Open End	Emerging Markets Equity (Div Emerging Mkts)	C+	B-	C		Y	1,000,000
Dreyfus Equity Income Fund Class A	DQIAX	NAS CM	Open End	US Equity Large Cap Value (Equity-Income)	B	B-	B		Y	1,000
Dreyfus Equity Income Fund Class C	DQICX	NAS CM	Open End	US Equity Large Cap Value (Equity-Income)	B-	B-	B-	Down	Y	1,000
Dreyfus Equity Income Fund Class I	DQIRX	NAS CM	Open End	US Equity Large Cap Value (Equity-Income)	B-	B-	B-	Down	Y	1,000
Dreyfus Equity Income Fund Class Y	DQIYX	NAS CM	Open End	US Equity Large Cap Value (Equity-Income)	B-	B-	B-	Down	Y	1,000,000
Dreyfus Fund Incorporated	DREVX	NAS CM	Open End	US Equity Large Cap Growth (Growth & Income)	B	B-	B		Y	2,500
Dreyfus Global Emerging Markets Fund Class A	DGEAX	NAS CM	Open End	Emerging Markets Equity (Growth)	B-	B	C	Up	Y	1,000
Dreyfus Global Emerging Markets Fund Class C	DGECX	NAS CM	Open End	Emerging Markets Equity (Growth)	B-	B	C	Up	Y	1,000
Dreyfus Global Emerging Markets Fund Class I	DGIEX	NAS CM	Open End	Emerging Markets Equity (Growth)	B-	B	C	Up	Y	1,000
Dreyfus Global Emerging Markets Fund Class Y	DGEYX	NAS CM	Open End	Emerging Markets Equity (Growth)	B-	B	C	Up	Y	1,000,000

★Expanded analysis of this fund is included in Section II.

	TOTAL RETURNS					PERFORMANCE				ASSETS		ASSET ALLOCATION & TURNOVER					BULL & BEAR		FEES		
Min Additional Investment	3-Month Total Return	6-Month Total Return	1-Year Total Return	3-Year Total Return	5-Year Total Return	Dividend Yield (TTM)	Expense Ratio	3-Yr Std Deviation	3-Year Beta	NAV	Total Assets (MIL)	%Cash	%Stocks	%Bonds	%Other	Turnover Ratio	Last Bull Market Total Return	Last Bear Market Total Return	Front End Fee (%)	Back End Fee (%)	Inception Date
100	5.68	8.67	21.59	51.30		1.94	0.58	10.96		15.27	4,743	4	41	43	11	68					Oct-13
100	5.62	8.54	21.32	50.24		1.72	0.83	10.95		15.26	4,743	4	41	43	11	68					Oct-13
100	-0.68	6.69	20.62				0.66			11.58	124.1	17	39	44	0						Dec-16
100	-0.72	6.59	20.39				0.91			11.58	124.1	17	39	44	0						Dec-16
100	5.22	12.64	3.71			0	1.17			10.07	32.7	76	0	0	24	0					May-15
100	5.15	12.61	3.52			0	1.42			10	32.7	76	0	0	24	0					May-15
100	7.23	10.59	16.63	27.78	103.99	0.44	1.14	10.87	0.99	62.37	661.8	0	100	0	0	60	26.46	-24.02	5.75		Jan-85
100	7.01	10.14	15.65	24.56	95.53	0	1.99	10.88	1	57.44	661.8	0	100	0	0	60	25.84	-24.26		1.00	Nov-02
100	7.29	10.73	16.90	28.58	106.10	0.83	0.94	10.87	0.99	62.64	661.8	0	100	0	0	60	26.63	-24.03			Nov-02
	7.31	10.74	16.93	28.70	105.46	0.98	0.78	10.88	1	62.58	661.8	0	100	0	0	60	26.46	-24.02			Sep-15
100	1.80	2.95	4.73	1.61		0.08	2.46	3.71	0.25	12.69	477.8	27	59	6	7	20			5.75		Mar-14
100	1.36	2.35	3.70	-0.55		0	3.1	3.72	0.25	12.61	477.8	27	59	6	7	20				1.00	Mar-14
100	1.94	3.17	5.12	2.74		0.51	2.03	3.66	0.24	12.69	477.8	27	59	6	7	20					Mar-14
	1.93	3.16	5.19	3.15		0.56	1.96	3.71	0.24	12.73	477.8	27	59	6	7	20					Mar-14
100	7.45	12.19	26.90	31.44	77.07	1.29	0.67	9.95	0.94	35.89	2,003	1	99	0	0	6	21.88	-12.48			Aug-16
100	7.42	12.08	26.64	31.07	76.57	1.05	0.94	9.94	0.94	36.07	2,003	1	99	0	0	6	21.88	-12.48			Jan-84
	7.49	12.24	27.03	32.38	79.17	1.32	0.65	9.94	0.94	35.96	2,003	1	99	0	0	6	21.88	-12.48			Jul-13
100	3.67	6.31	10.57	20.12	59.09	0.99	1.2	7.29	0.7	22.81	323.0	14	62	25	0	106	16.41	-14.42	5.75		Jan-04
100	4.33	6.76	10.68	18.39	54.45	0.29	1.95	7.28	0.69	22.91	323.0	14	62	25	0	106	15.86	-14.72		1.00	Jan-04
100	3.53	6.21	10.61	20.74	60.64	1.2	0.95	7.3	0.7	22.84	323.0	14	62	25	0	106	16.61	-14.34			Jan-04
100	3.48	6.21	10.61	20.73	60.63	1.19	0.95	7.29	0.7	22.84	323.0	14	62	25	0	106	16.52	-14.4			Mar-87
	5.00	7.77	11.95	22.19	62.92	1.19	0.95	7.29	0.7		323.0	14	62	25	0	106	16.52	-14.4			Sep-16
100	3.55	6.25	10.62	20.54	60.13	1.14	1.02	7.3	0.7	22.71	323.0	14	62	25	0	106	16.25	-14.41			Dec-04
100	7.50	11.99	26.20	29.59	73.14	0.67	1.35	10.1	0.96	17.85	182.0	1	99	0	0	3	21.68	-12.71	5.75		Sep-98
100	7.31	11.55	25.28	26.81	66.92	0.12	2.1	10.1	0.96	17.31	182.0	1	99	0	0	3	21.13	-12.95		1.00	Apr-02
100	7.56	12.11	26.48	30.40	75.08	0.85	1.1	10.11	0.96	18.44	182.0	1	99	0	0	3	21.87	-12.58			Apr-02
100	6.97	10.81	19.06	35.32	95.69	0.85	1	11.15	1.08	36.57	615.6	2	98	0	0	49	23.16	-21.03			Dec-87
100	7.40	15.02	39.18	29.06	29.15	0.06	1.9	14.88	0.92	25.79	234.0	2	98	0	0	50	17.59	-29.11	5.75		Mar-09
100	7.08	14.39	37.85	25.80	23.98	0	2.74	14.84	0.92	24.47	234.0	2	98	0	0	50	17.03	-29.32		1.00	Mar-09
100	7.50	15.28	39.76	30.68	31.50	0.33	1.62	14.89	0.92	25.67	234.0	2	98	0	0	50	18.1	-28.91			Jul-06
	7.53	15.31	39.82	30.98	32.00	0.39	1.52	14.88	0.92	25.7	234.0	2	98	0	0	50	18.1	-28.91			Jan-14
100	4.70	10.93	27.45	25.70	40.93	0.82	1.3	11.36	0.9	13.47	894.8	2	98	0	0	11	14.28	-23.25	5.75		Dec-07
100	4.54	10.50	26.47	23.06	35.68	0	2.05	11.33	0.9	13.46	894.8	2	98	0	0	11	13.84	-23.36		1.00	Dec-07
100	4.84	11.16	27.82	27.10	43.22	1.12	0.96	11.33	0.9	13.47	894.8	2	98	0	0	11	14.48	-23.14			Dec-07
	4.81	11.13	27.91	27.15	43.29	1.19	0.95	11.36	0.9	13.45	894.8	2	98	0	0	11	14.48	-23.14			Oct-15
100	2.14	3.79	7.42	6.86	33.00	0	1.44	6.35	0.48	15.8	1,564	36	31	33	0	11	11.65	-11.38	5.75		May-06
100	1.95	3.45	6.64	4.49	28.25	0	2.19	6.36	0.48	14.72	1,564	36	31	33	0	11	11.16	-11.59		1.00	May-06
100	2.20	3.95	7.70	7.69	34.79	0	1.19	6.36	0.48	16.22	1,564	36	31	33	0	11	11.91	-11.21			May-06
	2.21	4.01	7.76	7.96	34.87	0	1.16	6.36	0.48	16.23	1,564	36	31	33	0	11	11.91	-11.21			Jul-13
100	4.59	9.97	27.27	25.99	15.99	0.6	2	18.59	1.15	11.22	146.3	1	99	0	0	80	14.43	-28.08	5.75		Jun-96
100	4.24	9.41	26.17	22.93	11.57	0.01	2.75	18.58	1.14	11.04	146.3	1	99	0	0	80	13.87	-28.36		1.00	Nov-02
100	4.51	10.04	27.51	26.61	17.32	0.82	1.75	18.61	1.15	11.51	146.3	1	99	0	0	80	14.6	-28.04			Nov-02
	4.54	10.01	27.54	27.42	18.18	0.96	1.75	18.54	1.14	11.22	146.3	1	99	0	0	80	14.43	-28.08			Jul-13
100	5.91	10.13	16.98	30.08	94.55	2.17	1.03	8.93	0.82	18.99	372.6	0	100	0	0	62	19.91	-10.25	5.75		Jul-06
100	5.72	9.72	16.15	27.26	87.43	1.29	1.78	8.91	0.82	18.76	372.6	0	100	0	0	62	19.34	-10.54		1.00	Jul-06
100	5.99	10.33	17.36	31.12	97.06	2.59	0.78	8.88	0.82	19.03	372.6	0	100	0	0	62	20.07	-10.13			Jul-06
	5.97	10.30	17.71	31.69	97.50	2.57	0.78	8.92	0.82	19.07	372.6	0	100	0	0	62	20.07	-10.13			Jul-13
100	6.62	10.87	20.11	30.13	94.02	0.85	0.76	10.4	1	11.55	1,234	3	97	0	0	69	24.21	-20.24			May-51
100	8.95	15.54	45.58	34.89		0	1.25	15.76	0.85	18.71	296.5	5	95	0	0	51			5.75		Feb-14
100	8.74	15.06	44.53	31.89		0	2	15.77	0.85	18.23	296.5	5	95	0	0	51				1.00	Feb-14
100	8.98	15.60	46.01	35.76		0.03	1	15.77	0.85	18.81	296.5	5	95	0	0	51					Feb-14
	9.00	15.60	45.95	35.94		0.03	1	15.79	0.85	18.89	296.5	5	95	0	0	51					Feb-14

	MARKET			FUND TYPE, CATEGORY & OBJECTIVE	RATINGS				MINIMUMS	
Fund Name	Ticker Symbol	Traded On	Fund Type	Category and (Prospectus Objective)	Overall Rating	Reward Rating	Risk Rating	Recent Up/ Downgrade	Open to New Investors	Min Initial Investment
Dreyfus Global Equity Income Fund Class Y	DEQYX	NAS CM	Open End	Global Equity (Equity-Income)	B	B-	A		Y	1,000,000
Dreyfus Global Equity Income Fund Fund Class A	DEQAX	NAS CM	Open End	Global Equity (Equity-Income)	B	B-	A		Y	1,000
Dreyfus Global Equity Income Fund Fund Class C	DEQCX	NAS CM	Open End	Global Equity (Equity-Income)	B	B-	A-		Y	1,000
Dreyfus Global Equity Income Fund Fund Class I	DQEIX	NAS CM	Open End	Global Equity (Equity-Income)	B	B-	A		Y	1,000
Dreyfus Global Infrastructure Fund Class A	DGANX	NAS CM	Open End	Other Sector Equity ()	C+	C+	C+	Up	Y	1,000
Dreyfus Global Infrastructure Fund Class C	DGCNX	NAS CM	Open End	Other Sector Equity ()	C+	C+	C+	Up	Y	1,000
Dreyfus Global Infrastructure Fund Class I	DIGNX	NAS CM	Open End	Other Sector Equity ()	C+	C+	C+	Up	Y	1,000
Dreyfus Global Infrastructure Fund Class Y	DYGNX	NAS CM	Open End	Other Sector Equity ()	C+	C+	C+	Up	Y	1,000,000
Dreyfus Global Real Estate Securities Fund Class A	DRLAX	NAS CM	Open End	Real Estate Sector Equity (Real Estate)	B-	C+	B		Y	1,000
Dreyfus Global Real Estate Securities Fund Class C	DGBCX	NAS CM	Open End	Real Estate Sector Equity (Real Estate)	B-	C+	B	Up	Y	1,000
Dreyfus Global Real Estate Securities Fund Class I	DRLIX	NAS CM	Open End	Real Estate Sector Equity (Real Estate)	B-	C+	B		Y	1,000
Dreyfus Global Real Estate Securities Fund Class Y	DRLYX	NAS CM	Open End	Real Estate Sector Equity (Real Estate)	B-	C+	B		Y	1,000,000
Dreyfus Global Real Return Fund Class A	DRRAX	NAS CM	Open End	Multialternative (Growth & Income)	C	C	C	Down	Y	1,000
Dreyfus Global Real Return Fund Class C	DRRCX	NAS CM	Open End	Multialternative (Growth & Income)	C	C	C	Up	Y	1,000
Dreyfus Global Real Return Fund Class I	DRRIX	NAS CM	Open End	Multialternative (Growth & Income)	C	C	C+	Down	Y	1,000
Dreyfus Global Real Return Fund Class Y	DRRYX	NAS CM	Open End	Multialternative (Growth & Income)	C	C	C+	Down	Y	1,000,000
Dreyfus Global Stock Fund Class A	DGLAX	NAS CM	Open End	Global Equity (World Stock)	B	B-	B+	Up		1,000
Dreyfus Global Stock Fund Class C	DGLCX	NAS CM	Open End	Global Equity (World Stock)	B	B-	B	Up		1,000
Dreyfus Global Stock Fund Class I	DGLRX	NAS CM	Open End	Global Equity (World Stock)	B	B-	B+	Up		1,000
Dreyfus Global Stock Fund Class Y	DGLYX	NAS CM	Open End	Global Equity (World Stock)	B	B-	B+	Up		1,000,000
Dreyfus Growth and Income Fund	DGRIX	NAS CM	Open End	US Equity Large Cap Growth (Growth & Income)	B-	B	B-	Down	Y	2,500
Dreyfus Institutional S&P 500 Stock Index Fund Class I	DSPIX	NAS CM	Open End	US Equity Large Cap Blend (Growth & Income)	B	B	B		Y	1,000
Dreyfus International Equity Fund Class A	DIEAX	NAS CM	Open End	Global Equity Large Cap (Foreign Stock)	B-	B-	B	Up	Y	1,000
Dreyfus International Equity Fund Class C	DIECX	NAS CM	Open End	Global Equity Large Cap (Foreign Stock)	B-	B-	B	Up	Y	1,000
Dreyfus International Equity Fund Class I	DIERX	NAS CM	Open End	Global Equity Large Cap (Foreign Stock)	B	B-	B	Up	Y	1,000
Dreyfus International Equity Fund Class Y	DIEYX	NAS CM	Open End	Global Equity Large Cap (Foreign Stock)	B	B-	B	Up	Y	1,000,000
Dreyfus International Small Cap Fund Class A	DYAPX	NAS CM	Open End	Global Equity Mid/Small Cap (Small Company)	C+	C+	B-	Down	Y	1,000
Dreyfus International Small Cap Fund Class C	DYCPX	NAS CM	Open End	Global Equity Mid/Small Cap (Small Company)	C+	C+	B-	Up	Y	1,000
Dreyfus International Small Cap Fund Class I	DYIPX	NAS CM	Open End	Global Equity Mid/Small Cap (Small Company)	C+	C+	B-	Down	Y	1,000
Dreyfus International Small Cap Fund Class Y	DYYPX	NAS CM	Open End	Global Equity Mid/Small Cap (Small Company)	C+	C+	B-	Down	Y	1,000,000
Dreyfus International Stock Fund Class A	DISAX	NAS CM	Open End	Global Equity Large Cap (Foreign Stock)	B	B	B	Up		1,000
Dreyfus International Stock Fund Class C	DISCX	NAS CM	Open End	Global Equity Large Cap (Foreign Stock)	B-	B-	B	Up		1,000
Dreyfus International Stock Fund Class I	DISRX	NAS CM	Open End	Global Equity Large Cap (Foreign Stock)	B	B	B	Up		1,000
Dreyfus International Stock Fund Class Y	DISYX	NAS CM	Open End	Global Equity Large Cap (Foreign Stock)	B	B	B	Up		1,000,000
Dreyfus International Stock Index Fund Class I	DINIX	NAS CM	Open End	Global Equity Large Cap (Foreign Stock)	B-	B-	B	Up	Y	1,000
Dreyfus International Stock Index Fund Investor Shares	DIISX	NAS CM	Open End	Global Equity Large Cap (Foreign Stock)	B-	B-	B	Up	Y	2,500
Dreyfus Large Cap Equity Fund Class A	DLQAX	NAS CM	Open End	US Equity Large Cap Growth (Growth)	B	B	B-		Y	1,000
Dreyfus Large Cap Equity Fund Class C	DEYCX	NAS CM	Open End	US Equity Large Cap Growth (Growth)	B	B	B-		Y	1,000
Dreyfus Large Cap Equity Fund Class I	DLQIX	NAS CM	Open End	US Equity Large Cap Growth (Growth)	B	B	B-		Y	1,000
Dreyfus Large Cap Equity Fund Class Y	DLACX	NAS CM	Open End	US Equity Large Cap Growth (Growth)	B	B	B-		Y	1,000,000
Dreyfus Large Cap Growth Fund Class A	DAPAX	NAS CM	Open End	US Equity Large Cap Growth (Growth)	B	B+	B-	Down	Y	1,000
Dreyfus Large Cap Growth Fund Class C	DGTCX	NAS CM	Open End	US Equity Large Cap Growth (Growth)	B	B	B-	Down	Y	1,000
Dreyfus Large Cap Growth Fund Class I	DAPIX	NAS CM	Open End	US Equity Large Cap Growth (Growth)	B	B+	B-	Down	Y	1,000
Dreyfus Large Cap Growth Fund Class Y	DLCGX	NAS CM	Open End	US Equity Large Cap Growth (Growth)	B	B+	B-	Down	Y	1,000,000
Dreyfus Mid Cap Index Fund Class I	DMIDX	NAS CM	Open End	US Equity Mid Cap (Growth)	B	B	B		Y	1,000
Dreyfus Mid Cap Index Fund Investor Shares	PESPX	NAS CM	Open End	US Equity Mid Cap (Growth)	B	B	B		Y	2,500
Dreyfus Mid-Cap Growth Fund Class A	FRSDX	NAS CM	Open End	US Equity Mid Cap (Growth)	B-	B	C+	Up	Y	1,000
Dreyfus Mid-Cap Growth Fund Class C	FRSCX	NAS CM	Open End	US Equity Mid Cap (Growth)	B-	B-	C+	Up	Y	1,000
Dreyfus Mid-Cap Growth Fund Class F	FRSPX	NAS CM	Open End	US Equity Mid Cap (Growth)	B-	B	C+	Down		1,000
Dreyfus Mid-Cap Growth Fund Class I	FRSRX	NAS CM	Open End	US Equity Mid Cap (Growth)	B-	B	C+	Down	Y	1,000
Dreyfus Natural Resources Fund Class A	DNLAX	NAS CM	Open End	Natl Resources Sec Equity (Natl Res)	C	C+	C	Up	Y	1,000
Dreyfus Natural Resources Fund Class C	DLDCX	NAS CM	Open End	Natl Resources Sec Equity (Natl Res)	C	C+	C	Up	Y	1,000

★Expanded analysis of this fund is included in Section II.

	TOTAL RETURNS					PERFORMANCE				ASSETS		ASSET ALLOCATION & TURNOVER					BULL & BEAR		FEES		
Min Additional Investment	3-Month Total Return	6-Month Total Return	1-Year Total Return	3-Year Total Return	5-Year Total Return	Dividend Yield (TTM)	Expense Ratio	3-Yr Std Deviation	3-Year Beta	NAV	Total Assets (MIL)	%Cash	%Stocks	%Bonds	%Other	Turnover Ratio	Last Bull Market Total Return	Last Bear Market Total Return	Front End Fee (%)	Back End Fee (%)	Inception Date
	3.83	6.55	18.21	32.97	61.23	2.46	0.84	8.97	0.68	13.08	457.4	2	98	0	1	28	15.19	-13.17			Jul-13
100	3.75	6.35	17.83	31.59	58.68	1.87	1.17	8.92	0.68	13.71	457.4	2	98	0	1	28	15.07	-13.24	5.75		Oct-07
100	3.53	5.94	16.94	28.71	52.92	0.76	1.92	8.94	0.68	14.13	457.4	2	98	0	1	28	14.62	-13.51		1.00	Oct-07
100	3.84	6.55	18.17	32.68	60.86	2.37	0.91	8.95	0.68	13.1	457.4	2	98	0	1	28	15.19	-13.17			Oct-07
100	2.31	4.27	19.05			1.45	1.3			13.15	27.7	1	99	0	0	91			5.75		Mar-15
100	1.99	3.75	18.01			0.62	2.05			13.19	27.7	1	99	0	0	91				1.00	Mar-15
100	2.31	4.33	19.23			1.87	1.05			13.1	27.7	1	99	0	0	91					Mar-15
	2.31	4.33	19.23			1.87	1.05			13.1	27.7	1	99	0	0	91					Mar-15
100	3.85	6.05	11.09	14.13	37.13	3.89	1.3	11.19	1.01	9.15	763.2	0	98	0	2	61	23.96	-19.19	5.75		Dec-06
100	3.53	5.53	10.13	11.51	32.20	3.19	2.05	11.18	1.01	9	763.2	0	98	0	2	61	23.33	-19.33		1.00	Sep-08
100	3.88	6.11	11.22	14.96	39.05	4.22	1.03	11.25	1.01	9.01	763.2	0	98	0	2	61	24.04	-18.93			Dec-06
	3.92	6.15	11.39	15.16	39.13	4.23	1.01	11.16	1.01	9.02	763.2	0	98	0	2	61	24.04	-18.93			Jul-13
100	0.57	0.29	3.84	5.67	17.97	2.67	1.15	5.23	28.32	14.34	1,575	7	52	39	2	57	4.04	-7.18	5.75		May-10
100	0.50	0.00	3.17	3.44	13.73	2.19	1.9	5.26	29.74	13.99	1,575	7	52	39	2	57	3.55	-7.45		1.00	May-10
100	0.73	0.52	4.28	6.64	19.74	2.86	0.88	5.2	30.46	14.37	1,575	7	52	39	2	57	4.16	-7.09			May-10
	0.72	0.58	4.34	6.83	19.97	2.89	0.81	5.23	29.57	14.38	1,575	7	52	39	2	57	4.16	-7.09			Jul-13
100	5.19	9.41	23.04	29.13	59.33	0.42	1.22	9.45	0.86	20.11	1,297	2	98	0	0	12	18.95	-14.07	5.75		Dec-06
100	5.75	9.77	22.99	27.14	54.50	0	1.99	9.44	0.86	19.61	1,297	2	98	0	0	12	18.43	-14.36		1.00	Dec-06
100	5.03	9.35	23.11	29.99	61.45	0.69	0.91	9.42	0.86	20.37	1,297	2	98	0	0	12	19.25	-13.98			Dec-06
	4.98	9.30	23.15	30.05	61.46	0.72	0.89	9.43	0.86	20.34	1,297	2	98	0	0	12	19.25	-13.98			Jul-13
100	7.22	11.29	19.64	31.91	103.62	0.75	0.93	11.02	1.07	21.21	907.0	1	99	0	0	52	26.25	-20.41			Dec-91
100	6.57	11.31	21.58	36.06	109.68	1.63	0.2	10.08	1	53.49	2,623	1	99	0	0	5	25.01	-16.31			Sep-93
100	3.95	11.18	27.99	26.68	53.62	1.54	1.12	12.49	0.98	40.45	722.6	1	99	0	0	90	16.52	-24.88	5.75		Dec-88
100	3.76	10.74	26.99	23.77	47.76	0.82	1.9	12.47	0.98	40.97	722.6	1	99	0	0	90	16.03	-25.13		1.00	Dec-88
100	4.02	11.32	28.34	27.29	54.71	1.43	0.85	12.52	0.98	41.06	722.6	1	99	0	0	90	16.37	-24.83			Dec-88
	4.03	11.33	28.35	27.23	54.64	1.43	0.85	12.52	0.98	41.04	722.6	1	99	0	0	90	16.37	-24.83			Jun-15
100	5.34	14.53	33.98			1.15	1.4			16.94	904.5	1	99	0	0	118			5.75		Jan-15
100	5.16	14.09	33.16			0.6	2.12			16.89	904.5	1	99	0	0	118				1.00	Jan-15
100	5.48	14.65	34.57			1.35	1.12			16.96	904.5	1	99	0	0	118					Jan-15
	5.44	14.68	34.40			1.38	1.09			16.95	904.5	1	99	0	0	118					Jan-15
100	4.51	9.51	26.51	29.98	36.35	0.68	1.27	11.12	0.84	18.62	4,096	3	97	0	0	11	15.67	-18.47	5.75		Dec-06
100	4.36	9.13	25.68	27.07	31.36	0	2.04	11.13	0.84	18.4	4,096	3	97	0	0	11	15.19	-18.75		1.00	Dec-06
100	4.57	9.67	27.00	31.29	38.75	0.98	0.94	11.16	0.84	18.69	4,096	3	97	0	0	11	15.93	-18.4			Dec-06
	4.59	9.75	26.99	31.44	37.45	1.02	0.91	11.13	0.84	18.48	4,096	3	97	0	0	11	15.93	-18.4			Jul-13
100	3.88	9.32	24.71	23.66	43.11	2.53	0.39	11.72	0.95	17.91	621.1	2	98	0	0	6	13.19	-23.39			Aug-16
100	3.80	9.18	24.46	23.22	42.60	2.35	0.6	11.72	0.95	17.93	621.1	2	98	0	0	6	13.19	-23.39			Jun-97
100	7.58	12.15	24.55	40.37	110.98	0.56	1.11	11	1.06	20.43	612.2	0	100	0	0	46	25.84	-20.37	5.75		Aug-92
100	7.36	11.78	23.71	37.26	103.19	0	1.9	10.99	1.05	20.66	612.2	0	100	0	0	46	25.05	-20.59		1.00	Sep-08
100	7.67	12.34	24.94	41.68	114.49	0.75	0.76	11.02	1.06	21.57	612.2	0	100	0	0	46	26.1	-20.16			Apr-97
	7.66	12.39	25.04	41.45	112.61	0.81	0.76	11.01	1.06	21.56	612.2	0	100	0	0	46	25.84	-20.37			Oct-15
100	7.12	12.01	28.43	40.44	124.60	0.45	1.15	11.45	1.04	11.87	58.9	0	100	0	0	41	23.17	-18.81	5.75		Dec-86
100	6.95	11.61	27.55	37.39	116.79	0	1.9	11.47	1.05	11.41	58.9	0	100	0	0	41	22.83	-19.24		1.00	Sep-08
100	7.25	12.20	28.77	41.60	127.85	0.5	0.9	11.47	1.05	12.24	58.9	0	100	0	0	41	23.39	-18.73			Apr-97
	7.25	12.20	28.77	41.46	126.22	0.5	0.9	11.42	1.04	12.24	58.9	0	100	0	0	41	23.17	-18.81			Oct-15
100	6.21	9.57	15.98	34.41	100.59	1.12	0.25	11.06	1	37.13	3,851	1	99	0	0	22	27.56	-22.73			Aug-16
100	6.12	9.42	15.67	33.99	99.96	0.87	0.5	11.06	1	37.23	3,851	1	99	0	0	22	27.56	-22.73			Jun-91
100	3.86	10.31	25.33	27.23	88.84	0	1.37	11.27	0.98	9.06	145.5	3	97	0	0	88	26.29	-16.72	5.75		Dec-99
100	3.59	9.82	24.28	24.35	81.83	0	2.14	11.21	0.98	7.52	145.5	3	97	0	0	88	25.74	-17.14		1.00	Dec-99
100	3.99	10.48	25.63	28.20	90.97	0	1.16	11.26	0.98	9.56	145.5	3	97	0	0	88	26.5	-16.86			Sep-61
100	3.89	10.37	25.68	28.25	90.94	0	1.14	11.28	0.98	9.54	145.5	3	97	0	0	88	26.61	-16.77			Dec-99
100	7.10	18.33	13.69	11.01	31.15	1.18	1.35	15.38	0.93	32.04	336.2	1	99	0	0	94	16.04	-27.19	5.75		Oct-03
100	6.96	17.95	12.91	8.66	26.42	0.67	2.1	15.36	0.93	29.63	336.2	1	99	0	0	94	15.53	-27.44		1.00	Oct-03

	MARKET			FUND TYPE, CATEGORY & OBJECTIVE	RATINGS					MINIMUMS
Fund Name	Ticker Symbol	Traded On	Fund Type	Category and (Prospectus Objective)	Overall Rating	Reward Rating	Risk Rating	Recent Up/ Downgrade	Open to New Investors	Min Initial Investment
Dreyfus Natural Resources Fund Class I	DLDRX	NAS CM	Open End	Natl Resources Sec Equity (Natl Res)	C	C+	C	Up	Y	1,000
Dreyfus Natural Resources Fund Class Y	DLDYX	NAS CM	Open End	Natl Resources Sec Equity (Natl Res)	C	C+	C	Up	Y	1,000,000
Dreyfus Opportunistic Midcap Value Fund Class A	DMCVX	NAS CM	Open End	US Equity Mid Cap (Growth & Income)	B-	C+	B-	Up	Y	1,000
Dreyfus Opportunistic Midcap Value Fund Class C	DVLCX	NAS CM	Open End	US Equity Mid Cap (Growth & Income)	C+	C+	B-	Up	Y	1,000
Dreyfus Opportunistic Midcap Value Fund Class I	DVLIX	NAS CM	Open End	US Equity Mid Cap (Growth & Income)	B-	B-	B-	Up	Y	1,000
Dreyfus Opportunistic Midcap Value Fund Class Y	DMCYX	NAS CM	Open End	US Equity Mid Cap (Growth & Income)	B-	B-	B-	Up	Y	1,000,000
Dreyfus Opportunistic Small Cap Fund Class I	DOPIX	NAS CM	Open End	US Equity Small Cap (Small Company)	B+	A-	B	Up	Y	1,000
Dreyfus Opportunistic Small Cap Fund Class Y	DSCYX	NAS CM	Open End	US Equity Small Cap (Small Company)	B+	A-	B	Up		1,000,000
Dreyfus Opportunistic Small Cap Fund Investor Class	DSCVX	NAS CM	Open End	US Equity Small Cap (Small Company)	B	A-	B	Up		2,500
Dreyfus Research Growth Fund, Inc. Class A	DWOAX	NAS CM	Open End	US Equity Large Cap Growth (Growth)	B	B	B		Y	1,000
Dreyfus Research Growth Fund, Inc. Class C	DWOCX	NAS CM	Open End	US Equity Large Cap Growth (Growth)	B	B-	A-		Y	1,000
Dreyfus Research Growth Fund, Inc. Class I	DWOIX	NAS CM	Open End	US Equity Large Cap Growth (Growth)	B	B	B		Y	1,000
Dreyfus Research Growth Fund, Inc. Class Y	DRYQX	NAS CM	Open End	US Equity Large Cap Growth (Growth)	B	B	B		Y	1,000,000
Dreyfus Research Growth Fund, Inc. Class Z	DREQX	NAS CM	Open End	US Equity Large Cap Growth (Growth)	B	B	A-			1,000
Dreyfus S&P 500 Index Fund	PEOPX	NAS CM	Open End	US Equity Large Cap Blend (Growth & Income)	B	B	B		Y	2,500
Dreyfus Select Managers Long/Short Fund Class A	DBNAX	NAS CM	Open End	Long/Short Equity (Growth)	C+	C	B	Up	Y	1,000
Dreyfus Select Managers Long/Short Fund Class C	DBNCX	NAS CM	Open End	Long/Short Equity (Growth)	C	C	C		Y	1,000
Dreyfus Select Managers Long/Short Fund Class I	DBNIX	NAS CM	Open End	Long/Short Equity (Growth)	B-	C	B+	Up	Y	1,000
Dreyfus Select Managers Long/Short Fund Class Y	DBNYX	NAS CM	Open End	Long/Short Equity (Growth)	B-	C	B+	Up	Y	1,000,000
Dreyfus Select Managers Small Cap Growth Fund Class A	DSGAX	NAS CM	Open End	US Equity Small Cap (Small Company)	B	B+	C	Up	Y	1,000
Dreyfus Select Managers Small Cap Growth Fund Class C	DSGCX	NAS CM	Open End	US Equity Small Cap (Small Company)	B-	B	C	Up	Y	1,000
Dreyfus Select Managers Small Cap Growth Fund Class I	DSGIX	NAS CM	Open End	US Equity Small Cap (Small Company)	B	B+	C	Up	Y	1,000
Dreyfus Select Managers Small Cap Growth Fund Class Y	DSGYX	NAS CM	Open End	US Equity Small Cap (Small Company)	B	B+	C	Up	Y	1,000,000
Dreyfus Select Managers Small Cap Value Fund Class A	DMVAX	NAS CM	Open End	US Equity Small Cap (Small Company)	B	B	B	Up	Y	1,000
Dreyfus Select Managers Small Cap Value Fund Class C	DMECX	NAS CM	Open End	US Equity Small Cap (Small Company)	B	B	B-	Up	Y	1,000
Dreyfus Select Managers Small Cap Value Fund Class I	DMVIX	NAS CM	Open End	US Equity Small Cap (Small Company)	B	B	B	Up	Y	1,000
Dreyfus Select Managers Small Cap Value Fund Class Y	DMVYX	NAS CM	Open End	US Equity Small Cap (Small Company)	B	B	B	Up	Y	1,000,000
Dreyfus Small Cap Equity Fund Class A	DSEAX	NAS CM	Open End	US Equity Mid Cap (Small Company)	B	B-	B	Up	Y	1,000
Dreyfus Small Cap Equity Fund Class C	DSECX	NAS CM	Open End	US Equity Mid Cap (Small Company)	B-	C+	B	Up	Y	1,000
Dreyfus Small Cap Equity Fund Class I	DSERX	NAS CM	Open End	US Equity Mid Cap (Small Company)	B	B-	B	Up	Y	1,000
Dreyfus Small Cap Stock Index Fund Class I	DISIX	NAS CM	Open End	US Equity Small Cap (Small Company)	B+	A-	B	Up	Y	1,000
Dreyfus Small Cap Stock Index Fund Investor Shares	DISSX	NAS CM	Open End	US Equity Small Cap (Small Company)	B+	A-	B	Up	Y	2,500
Dreyfus Strategic Beta Emerging Markets Equity Fund Cls A	DOFAX	NAS CM	Open End	Emerging Markets Equity (Growth)	B-	B	C	Up	Y	1,000
Dreyfus Strategic Beta Emerging Markets Equity Fund Cls C	DOFCX	NAS CM	Open End	Emerging Markets Equity (Growth)	B-	B	C	Up	Y	1,000
Dreyfus Strategic Beta Emerging Markets Equity Fund Cls I	DOFIX	NAS CM	Open End	Emerging Markets Equity (Growth)	B-	B	C	Up	Y	1,000
Dreyfus Strategic Beta Emerging Markets Equity Fund Cls Y	DOFYX	NAS CM	Open End	Emerging Markets Equity (Growth)	B-	B	C	Up	Y	1,000,000
Dreyfus Strategic Value Fund Class A	DAGVX	NAS CM	Open End	US Equity Large Cap Value (Growth)	B	B	B	Up	Y	1,000
Dreyfus Strategic Value Fund Class C	DCGVX	NAS CM	Open End	US Equity Large Cap Value (Growth)	B	B-	B	Up	Y	1,000
Dreyfus Strategic Value Fund Class I	DRGVX	NAS CM	Open End	US Equity Large Cap Value (Growth)	B	B	B	Up	Y	1,000
Dreyfus Strategic Value Fund Class Y	DRGYX	NAS CM	Open End	US Equity Large Cap Value (Growth)	B	B	B	Up	Y	1,000,000
Dreyfus Structured Midcap Fund Class A	DPSAX	NAS CM	Open End	US Equity Mid Cap (Growth)	B	B	B	Up	Y	1,000
Dreyfus Structured Midcap Fund Class C	DPSCX	NAS CM	Open End	US Equity Mid Cap (Growth)	B	B-	B	Up	Y	1,000
Dreyfus Structured Midcap Fund Class I	DPSRX	NAS CM	Open End	US Equity Mid Cap (Growth)	B	B	B	Up	Y	1,000
Dreyfus Structured MidCap Fund Class Y	DPSYX	NAS CM	Open End	US Equity Mid Cap (Growth)	B	B	B	Up	Y	1,000,000
Dreyfus Sustainable U.S. Equity Fund Class A	DTCAX	NAS CM	Open End	US Equity Large Cap Blend (Growth)	B-	B-	B-	Down	Y	1,000
Dreyfus Sustainable U.S. Equity Fund Class C	DTCCX	NAS CM	Open End	US Equity Large Cap Blend (Growth)	C+	C+	C+	Down	Y	1,000
Dreyfus Sustainable U.S. Equity Fund Class I	DRTCX	NAS CM	Open End	US Equity Large Cap Blend (Growth)	B-	B-	B-	Down	Y	1,000
Dreyfus Sustainable U.S. Equity Fund Class Y	DTCYX	NAS CM	Open End	US Equity Large Cap Blend (Growth)	B-	B-	B-	Down	Y	1,000,000
Dreyfus Sustainable U.S. Equity Fund Class Z	DRTHX	NAS CM	Open End	US Equity Large Cap Blend (Growth)	B-	B-	B-	Down		1,000
Dreyfus Tax Managed Growth Fund Class A	DTMGX	NAS CM	Open End	US Equity Large Cap Blend (Growth)	B-	B-	B-	Down	Y	1,000
Dreyfus Tax Managed Growth Fund Class C	DPTAX	NAS CM	Open End	US Equity Large Cap Blend (Growth)	B-	B-	B-	Down	Y	1,000
Dreyfus Tax Managed Growth Fund Class I	DPTRX	NAS CM	Open End	US Equity Large Cap Blend (Growth)	B-	B-	B-	Down	Y	1,000

★ Expanded analysis of this fund is included in Section II.

	TOTAL RETURNS					PERFORMANCE				ASSETS		ASSET ALLOCATION & TURNOVER					BULL & BEAR		FEES		
Min Additional Investment	3-Month Total Return	6-Month Total Return	1-Year Total Return	3-Year Total Return	5-Year Total Return	Dividend Yield (TTM)	Expense Ratio	3-Yr Std Deviation	3-Year Beta	NAV	Total Assets (MIL)	%Cash	%Stocks	%Bonds	%Other	Turnover Ratio	Last Bull Market Total Return	Last Bear Market Total Return	Front End Fee (%)	Back End Fee (%)	Inception Date
100	7.22	18.53	14.05	11.95	32.90	1.35	1.1	15.39	0.93	32.92	336.2	1	99	0	0	94	16.23	-27.17			Oct-03
	7.25	18.63	14.15	12.19	33.19	1.39	0.98	15.39	0.92	32.92	336.2	1	99	0	0	94	16.23	-27.17			Sep-15
100	6.60	11.33	15.62	20.56	89.02	0.02	1.21	13.9	1.2	33.43	1,106	0	100	0	0	105	29.55	-27.85	5.75		Sep-95
100	6.42	10.90	14.78	17.93	82.09	0	1.94	13.9	1.2	29.3	1,106	0	100	0	0	105	28.98	-28.12		1.00	May-08
100	6.71	11.52	15.97	21.64	91.66	0.32	0.9	13.9	1.2	33.21	1,106	0	100	0	0	105	29.73	-27.82			May-08
	6.73	11.54	16.08	22.00	92.70	0.43	0.78	13.9	1.2	33.26	1,106	0	100	0	0	105	29.55	-27.85			Jul-13
100	8.55	13.64	24.40	40.05	115.13	0	0.84	18.05	1.2	36.82	1,092	2	97	0	1	85	37.59	-34.06			Sep-16
	8.61	13.77	24.50	40.12	115.24	0	0.8	18.04	1.2	36.84	1,092	2	97	0	1	85	37.59	-34.06			Sep-16
100	8.52	13.59	24.18	39.72	114.62	0	1.11	18.04	1.2	36.72	1,092	2	97	0	1	85	37.59	-34.06			Dec-93
100	6.57	10.56	23.44	32.42	99.14	0.12	1.03	10.84	0.98	15.18	1,845	2	98	0	0	63	26.02	-19.28	5.75		Sep-08
100	6.43	10.24	22.66	29.54	91.85	0	1.78	10.88	0.99	14.02	1,845	2	98	0	0	63	25.41	-19.56		1.00	Sep-08
100	6.66	10.71	23.80	33.50	101.84	0.43	0.78	10.87	0.99	15.21	1,845	2	98	0	0	63	26.26	-19.19			Sep-08
	6.69	10.68	23.77	33.74	102.24	0.56	0.78	10.87	0.99	15.18	1,845	2	98	0	0	63	26.03	-19.14			Jul-13
100	6.66	10.65	23.70	33.28	101.31	0.32	0.88	10.88	0.99	15.46	1,845	2	98	0	0	63	26.03	-19.14			Feb-72
100	6.52	11.16	21.24	34.83	106.54	1.44	0.5	10.1	1	54.05	2,716	1	100	0	0	4	24.76	-16.43			Jan-90
100	0.31	1.19	3.94	3.52		0	2.25	3.44	0.47	12.5	458.6	-1	83	10	9	369			5.75		Mar-14
100	0.07	0.73	3.10	1.14		0	3	3.41	0.47	12.15	458.6	-1	83	10	9	369				1.00	Mar-14
100	0.30	1.26	4.15	4.41		0	2	3.44	0.47	12.64	458.6	-1	83	10	9	369					Mar-14
	0.38	1.26	4.15	4.49		0	2	3.41	0.46	12.65	458.6	-1	83	10	9	369					Mar-14
100	4.85	11.81	24.59	27.31	86.22	0	1.29	14.09	0.93	26.31	744.6	0	100	0	0	138	23.72	-20.42	5.75		Jul-10
100	4.68	11.40	23.67	24.44	79.39	0	2.05	14.1	0.93	24.58	744.6	0	100	0	0	138	23.29	-20.71		1.00	Jul-10
100	4.95	12.00	24.96	28.45	89.10	0	1.03	14.1	0.93	27.03	744.6	0	100	0	0	138	23.98	-20.32			Jul-10
	4.95	12.00	25.01	28.56	89.21	0	0.96	14.12	0.94	27.03	744.6	0	100	0	0	138	23.98	-20.32			Jul-13
100	2.76	9.01	12.09	24.85	83.46	0.28	1.3	14.21	0.98	24.7	964.7	0	100	0	0	67	27.65	-25.62	5.75		Dec-08
100	2.55	8.57	11.26	22.17	76.87	0	2.05	14.2	0.98	22.77	964.7	0	100	0	0	67	27.09	-25.78		1.00	Dec-08
100	2.64	8.99	12.26	25.80	86.09	0.48	0.99	14.21	0.98	25.11	964.7	0	100	0	0	67	27.88	-25.43			Dec-08
	2.60	8.96	12.23	25.86	86.10	0.52	0.95	14.2	0.98	25.08	964.7	0	100	0	0	67	27.88	-25.43			Jul-13
100	5.63	8.37	12.50	24.85	84.27	0	1.39	11.74	0.94	24.67	47.3	1	99	0	0	57	29.77	-26.29	5.75		Feb-00
100	5.39	7.87	11.53	21.75	76.71	0	2.22	11.69	0.93	19.52	47.3	1	99	0	0	57	29.14	-26.52		1.00	Feb-00
100	5.64	8.43	12.73	25.71	86.41	0	1.16	11.75	0.94	26.27	47.3	1	99	0	0	57	29.94	-26.18			Feb-00
100	3.85	9.91	12.66	37.73	109.94	0.97	0.26	13.77	1	31.47	2,469	1	99	0	0	24	29.55	-22.16			Aug-16
100	3.78	9.81	12.40	37.29	109.27	0.78	0.5	13.78	1	31.52	2,469	1	99	0	0	24	29.55	-22.16			Jun-97
100	5.54	11.78	30.72	29.27		1.63	1	16.08	1.01	13.94	19.5	1	98	0	0	80			5.75		Sep-14
100	5.37	11.44	29.42	26.14		0.68	1.75	16.09	1.01	13.97	19.5	1	98	0	0	80				1.00	Sep-14
100	5.64	11.97	30.60	29.86		1.7	0.75	16.08	1	13.93	19.5	1	98	0	0	80					Sep-14
	5.64	11.96	30.69	29.83		1.7	0.75	16.09	1.01	13.94	19.5	1	98	0	0	80					Sep-14
100	7.52	11.64	14.84	31.21	105.23	1.11	0.93	12.24	1.14	40.09	1,905	0	100	0	0	96	25.74	-24.52	5.75		Sep-95
100	7.31	11.22	13.97	28.27	97.68	0.54	1.68	12.23	1.14	37.43	1,905	0	100	0	0	96	25.19	-24.76		1.00	May-01
100	7.58	11.78	15.13	32.19	107.82	1.26	0.68	12.22	1.14	40.16	1,905	0	100	0	0	96	25.87	-24.41			May-01
	7.62	11.82	15.16	32.23	107.59	1.26	0.64	12.23	1.14	40.17	1,905	0	100	0	0	96	25.74	-24.52			Jul-13
100	7.75	10.40	17.07	29.05	98.80	0.64	1.25	11.4	1.01	31.42	219.7	0	100	0	0	63	29.54	-23.16	5.75		Jun-01
100	7.53	9.96	16.17	26.22	91.56	0.12	1.99	11.42	1.01	27.53	219.7	0	100	0	0	63	29.03	-23.38		1.00	Jun-01
100	7.78	10.51	17.34	30.02	101.22	0.97	1	11.41	1.01	32.07	219.7	0	100	0	0	63	29.67	-23.09			Jun-01
	7.84	10.62	17.49	30.55	102.35	1.19	0.87	11.41	1.01	32	219.7	0	100	0	0	63	29.67	-23.09			Jul-13
100	2.72	7.01	14.95	20.72	87.24	0.75	0.95	10.32	1	11.07	321.0	3	97	0	0	130	24.29	-16.69	5.75		Aug-99
100	2.44	6.52	14.03	17.92	80.05	0.23	1.7	10.29	0.99	9.39	321.0	3	97	0	0	130	23.79	-16.95		1.00	Aug-99
100	2.69	7.12	15.26	21.80	90.11	1.01	0.7	10.31	1	11.33	321.0	3	97	0	0	130	24.45	-16.52			Aug-99
	2.63	7.06	15.30	21.58	89.32	1.04	0.7	10.33	1	11.31	321.0	3	97	0	0	130	24.43	-16.63			Sep-16
100	2.66	7.02	15.16	21.43	89.09	0.91	0.76	10.35	1	11.33	321.0	3	97	0	0	130	24.43	-16.63			Mar-72
100	7.23	11.57	25.48	27.75	70.02	0.76	1.35	9.87	0.93	29.36	181.8	2	98	0	0	11	21.5	-11.03	5.75		Nov-97
100	7.04	11.20	24.52	24.94	63.74	0.15	2.1	9.86	0.93	27.68	181.8	2	98	0	0	11	20.96	-11.36		1.00	Nov-97
100	7.31	11.76	25.79	28.71	72.12	0.98	1.1	9.86	0.93	29.41	181.8	2	98	0	0	11	21.71	-10.96			May-04

		MARKET		FUND TYPE, CATEGORY & OBJECTIVE	RATINGS				MINIMUMS	
Fund Name	Ticker Symbol	Traded On	Fund Type	Category and (Prospectus Objective)	Overall Rating	Reward Rating	Risk Rating	Recent Up/ Downgrade	Open to New Investors	Min Initial Investment
Dreyfus Technology Growth Fund Class A	DTGRX	NAS CM	Open End	Technology Sector Equity (Technology)	A-	A	B+	Up	Y	1,000
Dreyfus Technology Growth Fund Class C	DTGCX	NAS CM	Open End	Technology Sector Equity (Technology)	A-	A	B+	Up	Y	1,000
Dreyfus Technology Growth Fund Class I	DGVRX	NAS CM	Open End	Technology Sector Equity (Technology)	A	A	B+	Up	Y	1,000
Dreyfus Technology Growth Fund Class Y	DTEYX	NAS CM	Open End	Technology Sector Equity (Technology)	A	A	B+	Up	Y	1,000,000
Dreyfus Total Emerging Markets Fund Class A	DTMAX	NAS CM	Open End	Emerging Markets Equity (Div Emerging Mkts)	B	B	C	Up	Y	1,000
Dreyfus Total Emerging Markets Fund Class C	DTMCX	NAS CM	Open End	Emerging Markets Equity (Div Emerging Mkts)	B-	B	C	Up	Y	1,000
Dreyfus Total Emerging Markets Fund Class I	DTEIX	NAS CM	Open End	Emerging Markets Equity (Div Emerging Mkts)	B	B+	C	Up	Y	1,000
Dreyfus Total Emerging Markets Fund Class Y	DTMYX	NAS CM	Open End	Emerging Markets Equity (Div Emerging Mkts)	B	B+	C	Up	Y	1,000,000
Dreyfus U.S. Equity Fund Class A	DPUAX	NAS CM	Open End	US Equity Large Cap Growth (Growth & Income)	B	B	B-			1,000
Dreyfus U.S. Equity Fund Class C	DPUCX	NAS CM	Open End	US Equity Large Cap Growth (Growth & Income)	B	B	B-			1,000
Dreyfus U.S. Equity Fund Class I	DPUIX	NAS CM	Open End	US Equity Large Cap Growth (Growth & Income)	B	B	B-			1,000
Dreyfus U.S. Equity Fund Class Y	DPUYX	NAS CM	Open End	US Equity Large Cap Growth (Growth & Income)	B	B	B-			1,000,000
Dreyfus Worldwide Growth Fund Class A	PGROX	NAS CM	Open End	Global Equity (World Stock)	B	B	B		Y	1,000
Dreyfus Worldwide Growth Fund Class C	PGRCX	NAS CM	Open End	Global Equity (World Stock)	B	B-	B	Up	Y	1,000
Dreyfus Worldwide Growth Fund Class I	DPWRX	NAS CM	Open End	Global Equity (World Stock)	B	B	B		Y	1,000
Dreyfus Worldwide Growth Fund Class Y	DPRIX	NAS CM	Open End	Global Equity (World Stock)	B	B	B-		Y	1,000,000
Dreyfus/Newton International Equity Fund Class A	NIEAX	NAS CM	Open End	Global Equity Large Cap (Foreign Stock)	B-	C+	B	Up	Y	1,000
Dreyfus/Newton International Equity Fund Class C	NIECX	NAS CM	Open End	Global Equity Large Cap (Foreign Stock)	B-	C+	B	Up	Y	1,000
Dreyfus/Newton International Equity Fund Class I	SNIEX	NAS CM	Open End	Global Equity Large Cap (Foreign Stock)	B-	C+	B	Up	Y	1,000
Dreyfus/Newton International Equity Fund Class Y	NIEYX	NAS CM	Open End	Global Equity Large Cap (Foreign Stock)	B-	C+	B	Up	Y	1,000,000
Dreyfus/The Boston Company Small Cap Growth Fund Class I	SSETX	NAS CM	Open End	US Equity Small Cap (Small Company)	B+	A-	B	Up	Y	1,000
Dreyfus/The Boston Company Small Cap Growth Fund Class Y	SSYGX	NAS CM	Open End	US Equity Small Cap (Small Company)	B+	A-	B	Up	Y	1,000,000
Dreyfus/The Boston Company Small Cap Value Fund Class A	RUDAX	NAS CM	Open End	US Equity Small Cap (Small Company)	B	B	B	Up	Y	1,000
Dreyfus/The Boston Company Small Cap Value Fund Class C	BOSCX	NAS CM	Open End	US Equity Small Cap (Small Company)	B	B	B	Up	Y	1,000
Dreyfus/The Boston Company Small Cap Value Fund Class I	STSVX	NAS CM	Open End	US Equity Small Cap (Small Company)	B	B	B	Up		1,000
Dreyfus/The Boston Company Small Cap Value Fund Class Y	BOSYX	NAS CM	Open End	US Equity Small Cap (Small Company)	B	B	B	Up	Y	1,000,000
Dreyfus/The Boston Company Small/Mid Cap Growth Fund Cls A	DBMAX	NAS CM	Open End	US Equity Mid Cap (Growth)	B	A-	C+	Up	Y	1,000
Dreyfus/The Boston Company Small/Mid Cap Growth Fund Cls C	DBMCX	NAS CM	Open End	US Equity Mid Cap (Growth)	B	B+	C+	Up	Y	1,000
Dreyfus/The Boston Company Small/Mid Cap Growth Fund Cls I	SDSCX	NAS CM	Open End	US Equity Mid Cap (Growth)	B+	A-	B	Up	Y	1,000
Dreyfus/The Boston Company Small/Mid Cap Growth Fund Cls Y	DBMYX	NAS CM	Open End	US Equity Mid Cap (Growth)	B	A-	C+	Up	Y	1,000,000
Driehaus Active Income Fund	LCMAX	NAS CM	Open End	Other Alternative (Income)	C+	C	B+	Up		25,000
Driehaus Emerging Markets Growth Fund Institutional Class	DIEMX	NAS CM	Open End	Emerging Markets Equity (Div Emerging Mkts)	B-	B	C+	Up	Y	500,000
Driehaus Emerging Markets Growth Fund Investor Class	DREGX	NAS CM	Open End	Emerging Markets Equity (Div Emerging Mkts)	B-	B	C+	Up	Y	10,000
Driehaus Emerging Markets Small Cap Growth Fund	DRESX	NAS CM	Open End	Emerging Markets Equity (Div Emerging Mkts)	C+	C+	C+	Up	Y	10,000
Driehaus Event Driven Fund	DEVDX	NAS CM	Open End	Multialternative (Growth)	C+	C	B	Up	Y	10,000
Driehaus Frontier Emerging Markets Fund	DRFRX	NAS CM	Open End	Emerging Markets Equity (Div Emerging Mkts)	C+	C+	B-	Up	Y	250,000
Driehaus International Small Cap Growth Fund	DRIOX	NAS CM	Open End	Global Equity Mid/Small Cap (Small Company)	A-	A	B	Up		10,000
Driehaus Micro Cap Growth Fund	DMCRX	NAS CM	Open End	US Equity Small Cap (Growth)	B+	A	C+	Up	Y	10,000
Driehaus Multi-Asset Growth Economies Fund	DMAGX	NAS CM	Open End	Multialternative (Multi-Asset Global)	U	U	U		Y	10,000
Driehaus Small Cap Growth Fund Institutional Class	DNSMX	NAS CM	Open End	US Equity Small Cap (Small Company)	U	U	U		Y	500,000
Driehaus Small Cap Growth Fund Investor Class	DVSMX	NAS CM	Open End	US Equity Small Cap (Small Company)	U	U	U		Y	10,000
Duff & Phelps Global Utility Income	DPG	NYSE	Closed End	Utilities Sector Equity (Utility)	C-	C-	D+	Down	Y	
Duff & Phelps Select Energy MLP Fund Inc.	DSE	NYSE	Closed End	Energy Sector Equity (Growth)	D	D	D	Down	Y	
DUNDAS International Equity Growth Fund Institutional Cls	DUNIX	NAS CM	Open End	Global Equity Large Cap (Growth)	D+	D+	C	Up	Y	100,000
Dunham Alternative Dividend Fund Class A	DADHX	NAS CM	Open End	Long/Short Equity (Equity-Income)	D	D+	C+	Up	Y	5,000
Dunham Alternative Dividend Fund Class C	DCDHX	NAS CM	Open End	Long/Short Equity (Equity-Income)	D	D	C	Up	Y	5,000
Dunham Alternative Dividend Fund Class N	DNDHX	NAS CM	Open End	Long/Short Equity (Equity-Income)	D	D+	C+	Up	Y	100,000
Dunham Appreciation & Income Fund Class A	DAAIX	NAS CM	Open End	Convertibles (Growth & Income)	C+	C	B	Up	Y	5,000
Dunham Appreciation & Income Fund Class C	DCAIX	NAS CM	Open End	Convertibles (Growth & Income)	C+	C	B	Up	Y	5,000
Dunham Appreciation & Income Fund Class N	DNAIX	NAS CM	Open End	Convertibles (Growth & Income)	C+	C	B	Up	Y	100,000
Dunham Dynamic Macro Fund Class A	DAAVX	NAS CM	Open End	Multialternative (Growth & Income)	C+	C	B	Up	Y	5,000
Dunham Dynamic Macro Fund Class C	DCAVX	NAS CM	Open End	Multialternative (Growth & Income)	C+	C	B	Up	Y	5,000

★ Expanded analysis of this fund is included in Section II.

	TOTAL RETURNS					PERFORMANCE				ASSETS		ASSET ALLOCATION & TURNOVER					BULL & BEAR		FEES		
Min Additional Investment	3-Month Total Return	6-Month Total Return	1-Year Total Return	3-Year Total Return	5-Year Total Return	Dividend Yield (TTM)	Expense Ratio	3-Yr Std Deviation	3-Year Beta	NAV	Total Assets (MIL)	%Cash	%Stocks	%Bonds	%Other	Turnover Ratio	Last Bull Market Total Return	Last Bear Market Total Return	Front End Fee (%)	Back End Fee (%)	Inception Date
100	7.10	17.12	42.54	56.21	127.51	0	1.28	14.58	1.2	48.99	304.3	1	99	0	0	58	28.02	-19.56	5.75		Oct-97
100	6.90	16.68	41.42	52.47	118.41	0	2.1	14.57	1.2	37.89	304.3	1	99	0	0	58	27.42	-19.82		1.00	Apr-99
100	7.18	17.28	42.92	57.43	130.38	0	1.03	14.59	1.2	54.12	304.3	1	99	0	0	58	28.28	-19.42			Apr-99
	7.19	17.34	43.07	56.96	128.60	0	0.87	14.6	1.2	54.21	304.3	1	99	0	0	58	28.02	-19.56			Sep-16
100	8.79	18.19	42.36	40.68	32.77	1.08	1.6	13.36	0.8	14.89	116.5	2	79	19	0	80	17.34	-21.05	5.75		Mar-11
100	8.58	17.72	41.26	37.59	27.88	0.52	2.35	13.34	0.8	14.65	116.5	2	79	19	0	80	16.91	-21.31		1.00	Mar-11
100	8.85	18.38	42.71	41.87	34.54	1.24	1.32	13.37	0.8	14.95	116.5	2	79	19	0	80	17.46	-20.98			Mar-11
	8.92	18.36	42.78	42.03	34.80	1.22	1.32	13.38	0.8	14.97	116.5	2	79	19	0	80	17.46	-20.97			Jul-13
100	6.73	11.18	24.24	34.37	84.77	0.45	1.15	9.22	0.87	18.88	549.2	1	99	0	0	5	21.89	-14.14	5.75		May-08
100	6.74	10.96	23.49	31.57	78.12	0	1.9	9.21	0.87	17.74	549.2	1	99	0	0	5	21.31	-14.47		1.00	May-08
100	6.39	10.92	24.11	35.18	87.28	0.65	0.83	9.22	0.87	18.92	549.2	1	99	0	0	5	22.24	-14.04			May-08
	6.39	10.93	24.13	35.23	87.45	0.68	0.8	9.23	0.87	18.91	549.2	1	99	0	0	5	22.24	-14.04			Jul-13
100	5.70	9.78	27.03	31.94	67.71	0.97	1.19	10.22	0.88	53.52	669.7	1	99	0	0	6	22.22	-14.2	5.75		Jul-93
100	5.51	9.37	26.11	29.06	61.60	0.38	1.93	10.23	0.88	47.14	669.7	1	99	0	0	6	21.65	-14.45		1.00	Jun-95
100	5.79	9.93	27.37	33.01	69.94	1.35	0.92	10.23	0.88	53.81	669.7	1	99	0	0	6	22.36	-14.12			Mar-96
	5.82	9.97	27.50	33.35	70.40	1.49	0.86	10.23	0.88	53.76	669.7	1	99	0	0	6	22.22	-14.2			Jul-13
100	6.43	11.94	28.42	21.74	40.60	0.8	1.07	11	0.84	22.69	1,214	2	98	0	0	38	14.64	-21.92	5.75		Mar-08
100	6.24	11.48	27.44	18.76	35.20	0.07	1.82	11	0.84	22.21	1,214	2	98	0	0	38	14.1	-22.16		1.00	Mar-08
100	6.47	12.03	28.68	22.62	42.54	1.1	0.82	11.03	0.84	22.46	1,214	2	98	0	0	38	14.82	-21.85			Dec-05
	6.47	12.05	28.72	22.78	42.94	1.15	0.81	11.03	0.84	22.36	1,214	2	98	0	0	38	14.82	-21.85			Jul-13
100	4.32	10.87	20.63	37.06	110.75	0	1	15.46	1	28.75	6.7	4	96	0	0	126	27.02	-22.93			Dec-96
	4.39	11.00	20.77	37.31	111.17	0	1	15.45	1	28.82	6.7	4	96	0	0	126	27.02	-22.93			Jul-13
100	4.78	8.35	10.21	28.88	85.09	0.33	1.37	13.5	0.93	22.31	210.2	0	100	0	0	77	33.58	-24.81	5.75		Aug-16
100	4.53	7.82	9.13	25.70	77.84	0.23	2.13	13.47	0.93	22.06	210.2	0	100	0	0	77	33	-25.05		1.00	Aug-16
100	4.84	8.49	10.52	29.39	85.82	0.36	1	13.5	0.93	22.38	210.2	0	100	0	0	77	33.58	-24.82			Feb-00
	4.84	8.50	10.58	29.34	85.75	0.39	1	13.49	0.93	22.46	210.2	0	100	0	0	77	33.58	-24.82			Aug-16
100	5.08	11.36	26.09	35.22	101.56	0	1.04	12.15	0.88	19.06	1,225	5	96	0	0	68	30.85	-18.14	5.75		Mar-09
100	4.89	10.95	25.18	32.12	93.63	0	1.83	12.14	0.88	17.02	1,225	5	96	0	0	68	30.17	-18.46		1.00	Mar-09
100	5.18	11.56	26.52	36.33	104.25	0	0.79	12.12	0.87	19.7	1,225	5	96	0	0	68	31.14	-18.05			Aug-90
	5.21	11.56	26.58	36.77	105.11	0	0.68	12.12	0.87	19.8	1,225	5	96	0	0	68	31.14	-18.04			Jul-13
5,000	1.11	-0.11	0.58	5.11	7.41	3.44	0.8	3.51	19.96	9.86	1,677	0	3	66	17	115	7.14	-9.07			Nov-05
	7.52	19.36	42.61	34.88	40.27		1.22	12.92	0.78	39.61	1,730	5	94	0	0	232	16.09	-22.2			Jul-17
2,000	7.48	19.28	42.52	34.79	40.18	0.28	1.47	12.92	0.78	39.64	1,730	5	94	0	0	232	16.09	-22.2			Dec-97
2,000	6.52	16.00	33.30	8.64	29.14	0.12	1.75	11.55	0.62	14.21	244.7	8	91	0	0	240	12.29	-18.03			Aug-11
2,000	1.12	-0.27	4.35	9.44		1.18	1.44	7.66	0.33	10.79	160.5	0	44	18	36	246					Aug-13
50,000	6.95	8.26	20.04			0.48	2.01			10.86	45.0	6	92	0	2	90					May-15
2,000	5.65	15.65	41.44	48.20	86.83	0	1.72	11.15	0.84	11.39	321.6	4	96	0	0	151	12.58	-22.35			Sep-07
2,000	4.41	13.94	24.30	46.38	160.88	0	1.48	18.97	1.02	14.44	333.7	1	98	0	0	180	33.09	-35.11			Nov-13
2,000	5.16	14.07					1.77			11.54	27.1	0	75	15	9						Apr-17
	7.81						0.95			11.63	44.3										Aug-17
2,000	7.72						1.2			11.62	44.3										Aug-17
	1.12	0.52	3.97	-8.60	36.32	1.87	2.26	14.38		17.58	676.7	-33	133	0	0	53	10.48				Jul-11
	-2.92	-6.64	-14.95	-45.46		0	2.25	33.51	1.68	5.84	144.6	4	150	0	-53	28					Jun-14
	0.00	0.00	0.00			0	0.65			10	0.00	3	97	0	0						Mar-16
100	1.82	0.63	-0.35			4.79	1.97			11.48	37.3	4	93	1	1				5.75		Aug-16
100	1.60	0.22	-1.13			4.03	2.72			11.47	37.3	4	93	1	1						Aug-16
	1.87	0.73	-0.12			4.9	1.72			11.49	37.3	4	93	1	1						Aug-16
100	4.94	9.61	11.27	8.59	37.27	2.58	1.63	8.04	0.89	8.7	19.2	8	0	0	0	96	11.8	-14.49	5.75		Jan-07
100	4.64	9.00	10.40	6.05	31.93	2.07	2.38	8	0.89	8.52	19.2	8	0	0	0	96	11.34	-14.86			Dec-04
	4.93	9.59	11.52	9.30	38.84	2.83	1.38	7.99	0.88	8.7	19.2	8	0	0	0	96	11.87	-14.45			Dec-04
100	1.81	2.84	7.89	3.48	7.47	0	2.03	6.37	1.13	10.11	44.6	52	39	10	0	54	11.03	-7.88	5.75		Apr-10
100	1.56	2.42	7.05	1.14	3.43	0	2.78	6.36	1.13	9.71	44.6	52	39	10	0	54	10.62	-8.13			Apr-10

	MARKET			FUND TYPE, CATEGORY & OBJECTIVE	RATINGS				MINIMUMS	
Fund Name	Ticker Symbol	Traded On	Fund Type	Category and (Prospectus Objective)	Overall Rating	Reward Rating	Risk Rating	Recent Up/ Downgrade	Open to New Investors	Min Initial Investment
Dunham Dynamic Macro Fund Class N	DNAVX	NAS CM	Open End	Multialternative (Growth & Income)	C+	C	B	Up	Y	100,000
Dunham Emerging Markets Stock Fund Class A	DAEMX	NAS CM	Open End	Emerging Markets Equity (Div Emerging Mkts)	C	C+	C		Y	5,000
Dunham Emerging Markets Stock Fund Class C	DCEMX	NAS CM	Open End	Emerging Markets Equity (Div Emerging Mkts)	C	C	C		Y	5,000
Dunham Emerging Markets Stock Fund Class N	DNEMX	NAS CM	Open End	Emerging Markets Equity (Div Emerging Mkts)	C	C+	C		Y	100,000
Dunham Focused Large Cap Growth Fund Class A	DAFGX	NAS CM	Open End	US Equity Large Cap Growth (Growth)	B	B	B		Y	5,000
Dunham Focused Large Cap Growth Fund Class C	DCFGX	NAS CM	Open End	US Equity Large Cap Growth (Growth)	B	B	B		Y	5,000
Dunham Focused Large Cap Growth Fund Class N	DNFGX	NAS CM	Open End	US Equity Large Cap Growth (Growth)	B	B	B		Y	100,000
Dunham International Stock Fund Class A	DAINX	NAS CM	Open End	Global Equity Large Cap (Foreign Stock)	B-	C+	B-	Up	Y	5,000
Dunham International Stock Fund Class C	DCINX	NAS CM	Open End	Global Equity Large Cap (Foreign Stock)	B-	C+	B-	Up	Y	5,000
Dunham International Stock Fund Class N	DNINX	NAS CM	Open End	Global Equity Large Cap (Foreign Stock)	B-	C+	B-	Up	Y	100,000
Dunham Large Cap Value Fund Class A	DALVX	NAS CM	Open End	US Equity Large Cap Value (Growth & Income)	B-	C+	B	Down	Y	5,000
Dunham Large Cap Value Fund Class C	DCLVX	NAS CM	Open End	US Equity Large Cap Value (Growth & Income)	B-	C+	B	Down	Y	5,000
Dunham Large Cap Value Fund Class N	DNLVX	NAS CM	Open End	US Equity Large Cap Value (Growth & Income)	B	B-	B	Up	Y	100,000
Dunham Monthly Distribution Fund Class A	DAMDX	NAS CM	Open End	Multialternative (Growth)	B-	C	B	Up	Y	5,000
Dunham Monthly Distribution Fund Class C	DCMDX	NAS CM	Open End	Multialternative (Growth)	C+	C	B	Up	Y	5,000
Dunham Monthly Distribution Fund Class N	DNMDX	NAS CM	Open End	Multialternative (Growth)	C+	C	B	Down	Y	100,000
Dunham Real Estate Stock Fund Class A	DAREX	NAS CM	Open End	Real Estate Sector Equity (Real Estate)	B-	C+	B		Y	5,000
Dunham Real Estate Stock Fund Class C	DCREX	NAS CM	Open End	Real Estate Sector Equity (Real Estate)	B-	C	B		Y	5,000
Dunham Real Estate Stock Fund Class N	DNREX	NAS CM	Open End	Real Estate Sector Equity (Real Estate)	B-	C+	B		Y	100,000
Dunham Small Cap Growth Fund Class A	DADGX	NAS CM	Open End	US Equity Small Cap (Small Company)	B+	A-	B	Up	Y	5,000
Dunham Small Cap Growth Fund Class C	DCDGX	NAS CM	Open End	US Equity Small Cap (Small Company)	B+	A-	B	Up	Y	5,000
Dunham Small Cap Growth Fund Class N	DNDGX	NAS CM	Open End	US Equity Small Cap (Small Company)	B+	A-	B	Up	Y	100,000
Dunham Small Cap Value Fund Class A	DASVX	NAS CM	Open End	US Equity Small Cap (Small Company)	B	B+	B	Up	Y	5,000
Dunham Small Cap Value Fund Class C	DCSVX	NAS CM	Open End	US Equity Small Cap (Small Company)	B	B	B	Up	Y	5,000
Dunham Small Cap Value Fund Class N	DNSVX	NAS CM	Open End	US Equity Small Cap (Small Company)	B	B+	B	Up	Y	100,000
DuPont Capital Emerging Markets Fund Class I	DCMEX	NAS CM	Open End	Emerging Markets Equity (Div Emerging Mkts)	C+	B-	C	Up	Y	1,000,000
Dynamic International Opportunity Fund Class I	ICCIX	NAS CM	Open End	Alloc (Growth)	C+	C+	C+	Down	Y	100,000
Dynamic International Opportunity Fund Class N	ICCNX	NAS CM	Open End	Alloc (Growth)	C+	C+	C+	Down	Y	5,000
Dynamic U.S. Opportunity Fund Class I	ICSIX	NAS CM	Open End	Moderate Alloc (Growth)	B-	B-	B	Down	Y	100,000
Dynamic U.S. Opportunity Fund Class N	ICSNX	NAS CM	Open End	Moderate Alloc (Growth)	B-	B-	B	Down	Y	5,000
Eagle Capital Growth Fund, Inc.	GRF	AMEX	Closed End	US Equity Large Cap Blend (Growth)	B+	B+	B+	Up	Y	
Eagle Growth and Income Opportunities Fund	EGIF	NYSE	Closed End	Cautious Alloc (Growth & Income)	C	C	B	Up	Y	
Eagle MLP Strategy Fund Class A Shares	EGLAX	NAS CM	Open End	Energy Sector Equity (Growth & Income)	D	D	D	Down	Y	2,500
Eagle MLP Strategy Fund Class C Shares	EGLCX	NAS CM	Open End	Energy Sector Equity (Growth & Income)	D	D	D	Down	Y	2,500
Eagle MLP Strategy Fund Class I Shares	EGLIX	NAS CM	Open End	Energy Sector Equity (Growth & Income)	D	D	D	Down	Y	100,000
EAS Crow Point Alternatives Fund Class A	EASAX	NAS CM	Open End	Multialternative (Growth)	C+	C	B	Up	Y	500
EAS Crow Point Alternatives Fund Class C	EASYX	NAS CM	Open End	Multialternative (Growth)	C+	C	B	Up	Y	2,500
EAS Crow Point Alternatives Fund Class I	EASIX	NAS CM	Open End	Multialternative (Growth)	C+	C	B	Up	Y	500,000
Eaton Vance Atlanta Capital Focused Growth Fund Class C	EAGCX	NAS CM	Open End	US Equity Large Cap Growth (Growth)	B	B	B		Y	1,000
Eaton Vance Atlanta Capital Select Equity Fund Class A	ESEAX	NAS CM	Open End	US Equity Large Cap Growth (Growth)	B	B	B+		Y	1,000
Eaton Vance Atlanta Capital Select Equity Fund Class C	ESECX	NAS CM	Open End	US Equity Large Cap Growth (Growth)	B	B-	B+		Y	1,000
Eaton Vance Atlanta Capital Select Equity Fund Class I	ESEIX	NAS CM	Open End	US Equity Large Cap Growth (Growth)	B	B	B+		Y	250,000
Eaton Vance Atlanta Capital Select Equity Fund Class R6	ESERX	NAS CM	Open End	US Equity Large Cap Growth (Growth)	B+	B	A+	Up	Y	1,000,000
Eaton Vance Atlanta Capital SMID-Cap Fund Class A	EAASX	NAS CM	Open End	US Equity Mid Cap (Growth)	B+	A-	B+	Up		1,000
Eaton Vance Atlanta Capital SMID-Cap Fund Class C	ECASX	NAS CM	Open End	US Equity Mid Cap (Growth)	B+	A-	B+	Up		1,000
Eaton Vance Atlanta Capital SMID-Cap Fund Class I	EISMX	NAS CM	Open End	US Equity Mid Cap (Growth)	A-	A-	B+	Up		250,000
Eaton Vance Atlanta Capital SMID-Cap Fund Class R	ERSMX	NAS CM	Open End	US Equity Mid Cap (Growth)	B+	A-	B+	Up		1,000
Eaton Vance Atlanta Capital SMID-Cap Fund Class R6	ERASX	NAS CM	Open End	US Equity Mid Cap (Growth)	A-	A-	B+	Up	Y	1,000,000
Eaton Vance Balanced Fund Class A	EVIFX	NAS CM	Open End	Moderate Alloc (Balanced)	B	C+	A+	Up	Y	1,000
Eaton Vance Balanced Fund Class B	EMIFX	NAS CM	Open End	Moderate Alloc (Balanced)	B-	C+	B	Up		1,000
Eaton Vance Balanced Fund Class C	ECIFX	NAS CM	Open End	Moderate Alloc (Balanced)	B	C+	A	Up	Y	1,000
Eaton Vance Balanced Fund Class I	EIIFX	NAS CM	Open End	Moderate Alloc (Balanced)	B	C+	A-	Up	Y	250,000

★ Expanded analysis of this fund is included in Section II.

Min Additional Investment	TOTAL RETURNS 3-Month Total Return	6-Month Total Return	1-Year Total Return	3-Year Total Return	5-Year Total Return	PERFORMANCE Dividend Yield (TTM)	Expense Ratio	3-Yr Std Deviation	3-Year Beta	ASSETS NAV	Total Assets (MIL)	ASSET ALLOCATION & TURNOVER %Cash	%Stocks	%Bonds	%Other	Turnover Ratio	BULL & BEAR Last Bull Market Total Return	Last Bear Market Total Return	FEES Front End Fee (%)	Back End Fee (%)	Inception Date
	1.80	2.83	8.08	4.20	8.79	0	1.78	6.36	1.12	10.16	44.6	52	39	10	0	54	11.16	-7.66			Apr-10
100	3.44	12.03	33.41	19.04	13.51	1.36	1.55	14.81	0.89	15.67	61.9	2	98	0	0	97	17.38	-30.64	5.75		Jan-07
100	3.32	11.66	32.45	16.49	9.23	1	2.3	14.78	0.89	14.88	61.9	2	98	0	0	97	16.84	-30.86			Dec-04
	3.52	12.22	33.75	20.02	14.86	1.52	1.3	14.82	0.89	16.01	61.9	2	98	0	0	97	17.55	-30.57			Dec-04
100	3.56	7.14	26.09	29.10	84.91	0	1.45	13.46	1.13	19	77.4	1	99	0	0	29			5.75		Dec-11
100	3.38	6.75	25.18	26.26	78.22	0	2.2	13.5	1.13	18.16	77.4	1	99	0	0	29					Dec-11
	3.56	7.27	26.42	30.09	87.33	0	1.2	13.47	1.13	19.29	77.4	1	99	0	0	29					Dec-11
100	4.42	10.07	25.36	22.16	44.35	0	1.88	11.99	0.92	16.97	112.9	1	99	0	1	143	10.23	-23.55	5.75		Jan-07
100	4.25	9.62	24.38	19.43	39.00	0	2.63	11.99	0.92	16.18	112.9	1	99	0	1	143	9.73	-23.78			Dec-04
	4.47	10.15	25.61	23.08	46.12	0	1.63	11.95	0.92	17.06	112.9	1	99	0	1	143	10.32	-23.42			Dec-04
100	6.31	10.86	14.90	23.20	78.92	1.3	1.18	10.64	1.01	14.55	73.0	2	98	0	0	59	20.64	-18.41	5.75		Jan-07
100	6.08	10.40	14.05	20.47	72.31	0.84	1.93	10.59	1	13.96	73.0	2	98	0	0	59	20.1	-18.71			Dec-04
	6.42	11.03	15.25	24.12	81.28	1.49	0.93	10.65	1.01	14.6	73.0	2	98	0	0	59	20.79	-18.38			Dec-04
100	-0.29	1.13	4.08	4.78	14.28	0	1.87	4.18	1	35.22	287.0	46	51	3	0	208	8.51	-6.3	5.75		Aug-08
100	-0.46	0.76	3.30	2.42	10.08	0	2.62	4.18	1	28.65	287.0	46	51	3	0	208	8.02	-6.59			Aug-08
	-0.60	0.89	3.95	5.18	15.33	0	1.62	4.17	1	36.21	287.0	46	51	3	0	208	8.68	-6.21			Sep-08
100	2.02	2.67	3.99	10.47	52.29	1.35	1.46	13.16	1.06	15.94	44.0	2	98	0	0	110	30.67	-17.85	5.75		Jan-07
100	1.81	2.29	3.19	7.93	46.69	1.14	2.21	13.17	1.06	15.09	44.0	2	98	0	0	110	30.05	-18.11			Dec-04
	2.11	2.83	4.23	11.29	54.32	1.91	1.21	13.18	1.06	15.8	44.0	2	98	0	0	110	30.83	-17.75			Dec-04
100	6.31	15.22	29.77	34.20	107.81	0	1.49	13.99	0.88	17.41	35.5	3	96	0	0	181	26.93	-27.77	5.75		Jan-07
100	6.10	14.72	28.75	31.25	100.15	0	2.24	13.97	0.88	14.43	35.5	3	96	0	0	181	26.35	-27.98			Dec-04
	6.34	15.30	30.03	35.22	110.37	0	1.24	13.97	0.88	18.14	35.5	3	96	0	0	181	27.13	-27.73			Dec-04
100	2.94	9.67	8.72	26.35	85.48	0.38	1.73	13.98	0.97	15.83	30.9	0	100	0	0	129	23.31	-20.51	5.75		Jan-07
100	2.80	9.28	7.94	23.62	78.70	0	2.48	13.98	0.97	14.15	30.9	0	100	0	0	129	22.84	-20.72			Dec-04
	3.02	9.75	8.95	27.36	87.72	0.53	1.48	13.98	0.97	15.97	30.9	0	100	0	0	129	23.42	-20.38			Dec-04
100,000	7.60	15.78	35.98	28.04	5.17	1.12	1.29	14.56	0.91	9.43	34.5	2	98	0	0	28	19.01	-24.54			Dec-10
	4.81	11.52	23.55	25.20	24.50	0.77	1.68	8.86	0.66	11.83	115.6	1	90	4	0	120					Dec-11
1,000	4.81	11.43	23.34	24.40	22.96	0.57	1.93	8.95	0.67	11.83	115.6	1	90	4	0	120					Dec-11
	3.75	7.00	15.17	31.21	30.72	0.47	1.41	5.71	0.42	12.35	68.3	0	98	2	0	298					Dec-11
1,000	3.73	6.98	14.95	30.33	29.38	0.28	1.66	5.7	0.41	12.37	68.3	0	98	2	0	298					Dec-11
	2.17	6.35	13.30	27.23	80.19	2.29	1.61	9.25	0.85	8.8181	32.5	0	91	9	0	22	18.24	-14.07			Jul-90
	2.81	3.13	8.90			5.09	2.71			19.65	139.0	-32	69	30	6	19					Jun-15
100	0.10	0.39	-9.58	-29.21	0.11	7.35	1.65	24.18	1.13	7.5	656.8	1	91	0	8	31			5.75		Sep-12
100	-0.11	0.01	-10.31	-30.79	-3.59	6.48	2.4	24.19	1.13	7.47	656.8	1	91	0	8	31					Feb-13
100	0.17	0.54	-9.32	-28.62	1.34	7.67	1.4	24.2	1.13	7.51	656.8	1	91	0	8	31					Sep-12
500	1.55	3.04	7.02	2.59	12.96	0	4.51	3.6	0.9	9.14	23.3	29	63	9	-1	138	4.85	-11.44	5.50		Aug-08
500	1.83	3.13	6.72	0.81	9.29	0	5.26	3.54	0.91	8.89	23.3	29	63	9	-1	138	4.36	-11.71		1.00	Aug-08
	1.43	3.02	7.21	3.28	14.23	0	4.26	3.52	0.88	9.21	23.3	29	63	9	-1	138	5.05	-11.37			Aug-08
	6.61	12.52	26.09	30.25	81.50	0	1.96	11.11	1	8.96	30.7	2	98	0	0	28	23.38	-18.36		1.00	May-11
	4.95	7.58	19.48	28.51	88.60	0	1.05	9.5	0.89	20.64	378.4	4	96	0	0	14			5.75		Jan-12
	4.76	7.20	18.59	25.65	81.74	0	1.8	9.56	0.89	19.88	378.4	4	96	0	0	14				1.00	Mar-13
	4.98	7.70	19.72	29.44	90.96	0	0.8	9.56	0.89	20.91	378.4	4	96	0	0	14					Jan-12
	5.03	7.75	19.71	29.44	90.95		0.75	9.57	0.89	20.92	378.4	4	96	0	0	14					Feb-17
	8.87	12.63	24.41	49.69	117.69	0	1.21	10.88	0.79	30.5	11,256	6	94	0	0	11	29.89	-19.15	5.75		Nov-03
	8.72	12.23	23.51	46.39	109.73	0	1.96	10.88	0.79	28.38	11,256	6	94	0	0	11	29.31	-19.38		1.00	Oct-09
	8.96	12.78	24.73	50.85	120.48	0	0.96	10.89	0.79	33.61	11,256	6	94	0	0	11	30.09	-19.02			Apr-02
	8.82	12.50	24.11	48.63	115.11	0	1.46	10.89	0.79	29.79	11,256	6	94	0	0	11	29.72	-19.17			Aug-09
	8.99	12.84	24.83	51.27	121.26	0	0.87	10.89	0.79	33.74	11,256	6	94	0	0	11	30.09	-19.02			Jul-14
	4.15	6.63	13.52	21.18	63.58	1.44	0.98	5.79	0.54	9.11	841.4	0	62	38	0	11	15.59	-10.59	5.75		Apr-32
	3.94	6.19	12.59	18.45	57.45	0.69	1.73	5.83	0.54	9.13	841.4	0	62	38	0	11	15.15	-10.94		5.00	Nov-93
	3.82	6.08	12.63	18.48	57.40	0.74	1.73	5.83	0.54	9.14	841.4	0	62	38	0	11	15.09	-10.9		1.00	Nov-93
	4.21	6.77	13.80	22.05	65.57	1.67	0.73	5.85	0.55	9.11	841.4	0	62	38	0	11	15.59	-10.59			Sep-12

	MARKET			FUND TYPE, CATEGORY & OBJECTIVE	RATINGS					MINIMUMS
Fund Name	Ticker Symbol	Traded On	Fund Type	Category and (Prospectus Objective)	Overall Rating	Reward Rating	Risk Rating	Recent Up/ Downgrade	Open to New Investors	Min Initial Investment
Eaton Vance Balanced Fund Class R	ERIFX	NAS CM	Open End	Moderate Alloc (Balanced)	B	C+	B+	Up	Y	1,000
Eaton Vance Balanced Fund Class R6	ESIFX	NAS CM	Open End	Moderate Alloc (Balanced)	B	C+	A-	Up	Y	1,000,000
Eaton Vance Commodity Strategy Fund Class A	EACSX	NAS CM	Open End	Commodities Broad Basket (Growth)	C-	C-	D+	Up	Y	1,000
Eaton Vance Commodity Strategy Fund Class C	ECCSX	NAS CM	Open End	Commodities Broad Basket (Growth)	C-	C-	D+	Up	Y	1,000
Eaton Vance Commodity Strategy Fund Class I	EICSX	NAS CM	Open End	Commodities Broad Basket (Growth)	C-	C-	D+	Up	Y	250,000
Eaton Vance Dividend Builder Fund Class A	EVTMX	NAS CM	Open End	US Equity Large Cap Blend (Equity-Income)	B-	B-	B	Down	Y	1,000
Eaton Vance Dividend Builder Fund Class C	ECTMX	NAS CM	Open End	US Equity Large Cap Blend (Equity-Income)	B-	B-	B	Down	Y	1,000
Eaton Vance Dividend Builder Fund Class I	EIUTX	NAS CM	Open End	US Equity Large Cap Blend (Equity-Income)	B-	B-	B	Down	Y	250,000
Eaton Vance Emerging & Frontier Countries Eq Fund Cls A	EACOX	NAS CM	Open End	Emerging Markets Equity (Growth & Income)	C+	C+	C	Up	Y	1,000
Eaton Vance Emerging & Frontier Countries Eq Fund Cls I	EICOX	NAS CM	Open End	Emerging Markets Equity (Growth & Income)	C+	C+	C	Up	Y	250,000
Eaton Vance Enhanced Equity Income Fund	EOI	NYSE	Closed End	Long/Short Equity (Equity-Income)	B-	B-	B	Up	Y	
Eaton Vance Enhanced Equity Income Fund II	EOS	NYSE	Closed End	Long/Short Equity (Equity-Income)	B	B-	A-	Up	Y	
Eaton Vance Focused Global Opportunities Fund Class I	EFGIX	NAS CM	Open End	Global Equity (World Stock)	C-	C	B+	Up	Y	250,000
Eaton Vance Focused Growth Opportunities Fund Class A	EAFGX	NAS CM	Open End	US Equity Large Cap Growth (Growth)	B	B	B		Y	1,000
Eaton Vance Focused Growth Opportunities Fund Class C	ECFGX	NAS CM	Open End	US Equity Large Cap Growth (Growth)	B	B	B+		Y	1,000
Eaton Vance Focused Growth Opportunities Fund Class I	EIFGX	NAS CM	Open End	US Equity Large Cap Growth (Growth)	B	B	B		Y	250,000
Eaton Vance Focused International Opportunities Fund Cls I	EFIIX	NAS CM	Open End	Global Equity Large Cap (Foreign Stock)	C-	C	B	Up	Y	250,000
Eaton Vance Focused Value Opportunities Fund Class A	EAFVX	NAS CM	Open End	US Equity Large Cap Value (Growth & Income)	B-	B-	B-	Down	Y	1,000
Eaton Vance Focused Value Opportunities Fund Class C	ECFVX	NAS CM	Open End	US Equity Large Cap Value (Growth & Income)	B-	C+	B	Down	Y	1,000
Eaton Vance Focused Value Opportunities Fund Class I	EIFVX	NAS CM	Open End	US Equity Large Cap Value (Growth & Income)	B	B-	B	Up	Y	250,000
Eaton Vance Global Income Builder Fund Class A	EDIAX	NAS CM	Open End	Alloc (Growth & Income)	B-	C+	B	Down	Y	1,000
Eaton Vance Global Income Builder Fund Class C	EDICX	NAS CM	Open End	Alloc (Growth & Income)	B-	C+	B	Down	Y	1,000
Eaton Vance Global Income Builder Fund Class I	EDIIX	NAS CM	Open End	Alloc (Growth & Income)	B-	C+	B	Down	Y	250,000
Eaton Vance Global Income Builder Fund Class R	EDIRX	NAS CM	Open End	Alloc (Growth & Income)	B-	C+	B	Down	Y	1,000
Eaton Vance Global Small-Cap Fund Class A	EAVSX	NAS CM	Open End	Global Equity (Small Company)	C+	B-	C+	Down	Y	1,000
Eaton Vance Global Small-Cap Fund Class C	ECVSX	NAS CM	Open End	Global Equity (Small Company)	C+	B-	C	Down	Y	1,000
Eaton Vance Global Small-Cap Fund Class I	EIVSX	NAS CM	Open End	Global Equity (Small Company)	C+	B-	C+	Down	Y	250,000
Eaton Vance Greater China Growth Fund Class A	EVCGX	NAS CM	Open End	Greater China Equity (Foreign Stock)	B+	A	C+	Up	Y	1,000
Eaton Vance Greater China Growth Fund Class C	ECCGX	NAS CM	Open End	Greater China Equity (Foreign Stock)	B	A	C+	Up	Y	1,000
Eaton Vance Greater China Growth Fund Class I	EICGX	NAS CM	Open End	Greater China Equity (Foreign Stock)	B+	A	C+	Up	Y	250,000
Eaton Vance Greater India Fund Class A	ETGIX	NAS CM	Open End	India Equity (Foreign Stock)	B	B	B-	Up	Y	1,000
Eaton Vance Greater India Fund Class B	EMGIX	NAS CM	Open End	India Equity (Foreign Stock)	B	B	C+	Up		1,000
Eaton Vance Greater India Fund Class C	ECGIX	NAS CM	Open End	India Equity (Foreign Stock)	B	B	C+	Up	Y	1,000
Eaton Vance Greater India Fund Class I	EGIIX	NAS CM	Open End	India Equity (Foreign Stock)	B	B	B-	Up	Y	250,000
Eaton Vance Growth Fund Class A	EALCX	NAS CM	Open End	US Equity Large Cap Growth (Growth & Income)	B	B	A-		Y	1,000
Eaton Vance Growth Fund Class C	ECLCX	NAS CM	Open End	US Equity Large Cap Growth (Growth & Income)	B	B	B+		Y	1,000
Eaton Vance Growth Fund Class I	ELCIX	NAS CM	Open End	US Equity Large Cap Growth (Growth & Income)	B	B	A-		Y	250,000
Eaton Vance Growth Fund Class R	ELCRX	NAS CM	Open End	US Equity Large Cap Growth (Growth & Income)	B	B	A-		Y	1,000
Eaton Vance Hedged Stock Fund Class A	EROAX	NAS CM	Open End	Long/Short Equity (Growth & Income)	B-	C	B	Down	Y	1,000
Eaton Vance Hedged Stock Fund Class C	EROCX	NAS CM	Open End	Long/Short Equity (Growth & Income)	C+	C	B	Down	Y	1,000
Eaton Vance Hedged Stock Fund Class I	EROIX	NAS CM	Open End	Long/Short Equity (Growth & Income)	B-	C	B+	Down	Y	250,000
Eaton Vance Hexavest Global Equity Fund Class A	EHGAX	NAS CM	Open End	Global Equity (World Stock)	B-	B-	B-	Down	Y	1,000
Eaton Vance Hexavest Global Equity Fund Class C	EHGCX	NAS CM	Open End	Global Equity (World Stock)	B-	C+	B-	Down	Y	1,000
Eaton Vance Hexavest Global Equity Fund Class I	EHGIX	NAS CM	Open End	Global Equity (World Stock)	B-	B-	B-	Down	Y	250,000
Eaton Vance Hexavest International Equity Fund Class A	EHIAX	NAS CM	Open End	Global Equity Large Cap (Foreign Stock)	B-	C+	B	Up	Y	1,000
Eaton Vance Hexavest International Equity Fund Class I	EHIIX	NAS CM	Open End	Global Equity Large Cap (Foreign Stock)	B-	C+	B	Up	Y	250,000
Eaton Vance International Small-Cap Fund Class A	EILAX	NAS CM	Open End	Global Equity Mid/Small Cap (Small Company)	C	C	B+	Up	Y	1,000
Eaton Vance International Small-Cap Fund Class I	EILIX	NAS CM	Open End	Global Equity Mid/Small Cap (Small Company)	C	C	B+	Up	Y	250,000
Eaton Vance Large-Cap Value Fund Class A	EHSTX	NAS CM	Open End	US Equity Large Cap Value (Growth & Income)	B-	C+	B	Down	Y	1,000
Eaton Vance Large-Cap Value Fund Class C	ECSTX	NAS CM	Open End	US Equity Large Cap Value (Growth & Income)	B-	C+	B	Down	Y	1,000
Eaton Vance Large-Cap Value Fund Class I	EILVX	NAS CM	Open End	US Equity Large Cap Value (Growth & Income)	B	C+	B	Up	Y	250,000
Eaton Vance Large-Cap Value Fund Class R	ERSTX	NAS CM	Open End	US Equity Large Cap Value (Growth & Income)	B-	C+	B	Down	Y	1,000

★Expanded analysis of this fund is included in Section II.

Min Additional Investment	TOTAL RETURNS 3-Month Total Return	6-Month Total Return	1-Year Total Return	3-Year Total Return	5-Year Total Return	PERFORMANCE Dividend Yield (TTM)	Expense Ratio	3-Yr Std Deviation	3-Year Beta	ASSETS NAV	Total Assets (MIL)	ASSET ALLOCATION & TURNOVER %Cash	%Stocks	%Bonds	%Other	Turnover Ratio	BULL & BEAR Last Bull Market Total Return	Last Bear Market Total Return	FEES Front End Fee (%)	Back End Fee (%)	Inception Date
	4.14	6.45	13.21	20.39	61.69	1.35	1.23	5.83	0.54	9.09	841.4	0	62	38	0	11	15.42	-10.69			May-16
	4.23	6.68	13.74	21.69	64.26	1.74	0.69	5.82	0.54	9.11	841.4	0	62	38	0	11	15.59	-10.59			May-16
	4.65	7.41	4.84	-11.14	-33.85	1.76	1.37	12.79	0.97	5.45	22.2	26	2	67	5		0.2	-20.19	4.75		Apr-10
	4.52	7.14	4.32	-12.92	-36.18	0.95	2.12	12.7	0.97	5.32	22.2	26	2	67	5		-0.22	-20.45		1.00	Apr-10
	4.75	7.50	5.33	-10.43	-32.97	1.98	1.12	12.63	0.96	5.45	22.2	26	2	67	5		0.3	-20.09			Apr-10
	7.33	11.88	18.88	32.21	90.17	1.66	1.04	9.05	0.87	14.55	991.8	0	99	0	1	97	21.45	-14.62	5.75		Dec-81
	7.08	11.39	17.89	29.19	83.23	0.98	1.79	9.02	0.87	14.62	991.8	0	99	0	1	97	20.96	-14.86		1.00	Nov-93
	7.33	11.95	19.11	33.15	92.54	1.88	0.79	9.06	0.87	14.53	991.8	0	99	0	1	97	21.76	-14.54			Jun-05
	7.37	12.15	31.21	23.41		0.27	1.65	11.91	0.71	11.35	165.9	8	90	0	3	40			5.75		Nov-14
	7.45	12.22	31.40	24.22		0.46	1.4	11.92	0.71	11.38	165.9	8	90	0	3	40					Nov-14
	6.19	9.64	19.36	26.64	79.30	0.67	0	9.2	0.88	15.1	585.2	1	99	0	0	76	20.33	-15.99			Oct-04
	5.16	8.99	23.82	33.75	94.37	0.01	0	10.63	0.94	15.77	746.3	0	99	0	1	58	21.06	-14.18			Jan-05
	3.78	9.07	20.85			0.69	0.96			11.55	4.2	1	99	0	0						Dec-15
	6.86	10.02	25.15	36.51	113.51	0.04	1.05	11.83	1.04	20.38	203.6	1	99	0	0	71	24.57	-20.66	5.75		Mar-11
	6.70	9.59	24.26	33.45	105.70	0	1.8	11.85	1.04	19.41	203.6	1	99	0	0	71	24.07	-20.97		1.00	Mar-11
	6.95	10.13	25.44	37.50	116.14	0.29	0.8	11.84	1.04	20.61	203.6	1	99	0	0	71	24.8	-20.56			Mar-11
	3.90	9.22	24.66			1.19	1.03			11.54	4.1	1	99	0	0						Dec-15
	8.57	12.36	20.12	27.23	89.93	1.11	1.05	9.68	0.88	16.65	66.3	1	99	0	0	87	24.39	-19.9	5.75		Mar-11
	8.41	11.94	19.29	24.51	82.99	0.74	1.8	9.64	0.88	16.42	66.3	1	99	0	0	87	23.86	-20.13		1.00	Mar-11
	8.64	12.50	20.42	28.24	92.46	1.34	0.8	9.67	0.88	16.67	66.3	1	99	0	0	87	24.69	-19.9			Mar-11
	3.14	5.74	16.18	22.91	58.62	3.56	1.31	8.49	0.78	9.17	358.6	3	58	25	8	143	17.63	-18.79	5.75		Nov-05
	2.98	5.40	15.34	20.29	52.91	2.88	2.06	8.44	0.78	9.08	358.6	3	58	25	8	143	17.1	-19.06		1.00	Nov-05
	3.21	5.88	16.52	24.01	60.83	3.82	1.06	8.49	0.78	9.16	358.6	3	58	25	8	143	17.79	-18.71			Jan-06
	3.18	5.60	15.91	22.11	56.85	3.32	1.56	8.52	0.79	9.15	358.6	3	58	25	8	143	17.52	-18.89			Jan-06
	4.58	10.09	23.07	21.91	69.61	0.88	1.4	10.21	0.86	15.02	19.1	1	97	0	2	99	24.58	-22.99	5.75		Jun-02
	4.36	9.66	22.17	19.25	63.43	0.38	2.15	10.21	0.86	13.25	19.1	1	97	0	2	99	23.99	-23.17		1.00	Jul-02
	4.65	10.18	23.37	22.83	71.73	1.07	1.15	10.24	0.86	15.39	19.1	1	97	0	2	99	24.79	-22.85			Oct-09
	10.93	20.46	49.38	44.69	68.54	0.65	1.85	16.07	0.92	25.35	103.8	2	97	0	1	14	19.98	-28.27	5.75		Oct-92
	10.72	20.02	48.31	41.66	62.75	0.54	2.55	16.05	0.92	23.94	103.8	2	97	0	1	14	19.56	-28.52		1.00	Dec-93
	10.98	20.63	49.85	45.98	71.03	0.71	1.55	16.09	0.92	25.53	103.8	2	97	0	1	14	20.22	-28.21			Oct-09
	11.08	14.70	44.79	42.18	78.90	0.94	1.72	17.58	0.98	36.83	264.3	1	93	0	7	91	-1.83	-23.33	5.75		May-94
	10.89	14.28	43.78	39.20	72.73	0.6	2.42	17.57	0.98	32.29	264.3	1	93	0	7	91	-2.25	-23.53		5.00	May-94
	10.91	14.31	43.81	39.23	72.77	0.61	2.42	17.58	0.98	32.05	264.3	1	93	0	7	91	-2.25	-23.56		1.00	Jul-06
	11.19	14.88	45.22	43.43	81.57	1.16	1.42	17.58	0.98	37.52	264.3	1	93	0	7	91	-1.67	-23.23			Oct-09
	6.10	9.85	25.41	36.16	116.32	0.1	1.05	11.42	1.02	26.65	335.0	2	98	0	0	60	23.11	-17.76	5.75		Sep-02
	5.85	9.40	24.45	33.06	108.28	0	1.8	11.41	1.02	22.87	335.0	2	98	0	0	60	22.57	-17.97		1.00	Sep-02
	6.14	9.97	25.71	37.15	119.01	0.33	0.8	11.41	1.02	27.34	335.0	2	98	0	0	60	23.36	-17.66			May-07
	6.03	9.72	25.12	35.17	113.58	0	1.3	11.44	1.02	26.09	335.0	2	98	0	0	60	22.95	-17.83			Aug-09
	2.77	4.20	9.63	12.12	37.67	0.74	1.15	5.67	0.52	8.97	41.0	0	100	0	0	130	6	-7.51	5.75		Feb-08
	2.65	3.85	8.82	9.62	32.62	0	1.9	5.62	0.51	8.88	41.0	0	100	0	0	130	5.61	-7.75		1.00	Feb-08
	2.81	4.22	9.78	12.90	39.35	0.99	0.9	5.68	0.52	8.98	41.0	0	100	0	0	130	6.13	-7.42			Feb-08
	4.18	7.06	14.47	26.10	63.01	0.42	1.15	8.11	0.7	12.83	106.1	16	80	0	4	109			5.75		Aug-12
	3.99	6.72	13.67	23.38	57.08		1.9	8.13	0.7	12.79	106.1	16	80	0	4	109				1.00	Dec-16
	4.26	7.30	14.81	27.13	65.10	0.59	0.9	8.14	0.7	12.85	106.1	16	80	0	4	109					Aug-12
	1.84	4.67	16.63	17.75	34.03	1.54	1.15	9.66	0.75	11.8	8.0	12	84	0	4	107			5.75		Aug-12
	1.89	4.89	17.06	18.76	35.69	1.73	0.9	9.63	0.75	11.84	8.0	12	84	0	4	107					Aug-12
	5.31	13.73	36.86			1.67	1.4			13.2	15.8	3	92	0	5				5.75		Dec-15
	5.40	13.91	37.19			1.85	1.15			13.23	15.8	3	92	0	5						Dec-15
	6.71	10.27	14.80	23.11	81.27	1.2	1.06	9.88	0.93	19.52	2,198	1	99	0	0	94	22.42	-18.96	5.75		Sep-31
	6.50	9.89	13.96	20.38	74.59	0.47	1.81	9.9	0.93	19.54	2,198	1	99	0	0	94	21.88	-19.2		1.00	Nov-94
	6.76	10.37	15.09	24.01	83.54	1.42	0.81	9.89	0.93	19.59	2,198	1	99	0	0	94	22.65	-18.9			Dec-04
	6.61	10.10	14.49	22.19	78.95	0.96	1.31	9.89	0.93	19.46	2,198	1	99	0	0	94	22.3	-19.05			Feb-04

	MARKET		FUND TYPE, CATEGORY & OBJECTIVE		RATINGS					MINIMUMS
Fund Name	Ticker Symbol	Traded On	Fund Type	Category and (Prospectus Objective)	Overall Rating	Reward Rating	Risk Rating	Recent Up/ Downgrade	Open to New Investors	Min Initial Investment
Eaton Vance Large-Cap Value Fund Class R6	ERLVX	NAS CM	Open End	US Equity Large Cap Value (Growth & Income)	B	C+	B	Up	Y	1,000,000
Eaton Vance Multi-Strategy All Market Fund Class A	EAAMX	NAS CM	Open End	Alloc (Income)	B-	C+	B	Up	Y	1,000
Eaton Vance Multi-Strategy All Market Fund Class C	ECAMX	NAS CM	Open End	Alloc (Income)	B-	C+	B+	Up	Y	1,000
Eaton Vance Multi-Strategy All Market Fund Class I	EIAMX	NAS CM	Open End	Alloc (Income)	B-	C+	B	Up	Y	250,000
Eaton Vance Real Estate Fund Class A	EAREX	NAS CM	Open End	Real Estate Sector Equity (Real Estate)	B-	C+	B		Y	1,000
Eaton Vance Real Estate Fund Class I	EIREX	NAS CM	Open End	Real Estate Sector Equity (Real Estate)	B-	C+	B		Y	250,000
Eaton Vance Richard Bernstein All Asset Strat Fund Cls A	EARAX	NAS CM	Open End	Moderate Alloc (Asset Alloc)	B-	C+	B	Up	Y	1,000
Eaton Vance Richard Bernstein All Asset Strat Fund Cls C	ECRAX	NAS CM	Open End	Moderate Alloc (Asset Alloc)	B-	C+	B	Up	Y	1,000
Eaton Vance Richard Bernstein All Asset Strat Fund Cls I	EIRAX	NAS CM	Open End	Moderate Alloc (Asset Alloc)	B-	C+	B	Up	Y	250,000
Eaton Vance Richard Bernstein Equity Strategy Fund Class A	ERBAX	NAS CM	Open End	Global Equity (Growth)	B-	B-	B-	Down	Y	1,000
Eaton Vance Richard Bernstein Equity Strategy Fund Class C	ERBCX	NAS CM	Open End	Global Equity (Growth)	B-	B-	B-	Down	Y	1,000
Eaton Vance Richard Bernstein Equity Strategy Fund Class I	ERBIX	NAS CM	Open End	Global Equity (Growth)	B-	B-	B-	Down	Y	250,000
Eaton Vance Risk-Managed Diversified Equity Income Fund	ETJ	NYSE	Closed End	Long/Short Equity (Equity-Income)	B-	C	B	Up	Y	
Eaton Vance Small-Cap Fund Class A	ETEGX	NAS CM	Open End	US Equity Small Cap (Small Company)	B	B	B	Up	Y	1,000
Eaton Vance Small-Cap Fund Class C	ECSMX	NAS CM	Open End	US Equity Small Cap (Small Company)	B	B	B	Up	Y	1,000
Eaton Vance Small-Cap Fund Class I	EISGX	NAS CM	Open End	US Equity Small Cap (Small Company)	B	B	B	Up	Y	250,000
Eaton Vance Small-Cap Fund Class R	ERSGX	NAS CM	Open End	US Equity Small Cap (Small Company)	B	B	B	Up	Y	1,000
Eaton Vance Special Equities Fund Class A	EVSEX	NAS CM	Open End	US Equity Mid Cap (Growth)	B	B	B	Up	Y	1,000
Eaton Vance Special Equities Fund Class C	ECSEX	NAS CM	Open End	US Equity Mid Cap (Growth)	B	B-	B	Up	Y	1,000
Eaton Vance Special Equities Fund Class I	EISEX	NAS CM	Open End	US Equity Mid Cap (Growth)	B	B	B	Up	Y	250,000
Eaton Vance Stock Fund Class A	EAERX	NAS CM	Open End	US Equity Large Cap Blend (Growth)	B	B-	B+		Y	1,000
Eaton Vance Stock Fund Class C	ECERX	NAS CM	Open End	US Equity Large Cap Blend (Growth)	B	B-	B+	Up	Y	1,000
Eaton Vance Stock Fund Institutional Class	EIERX	NAS CM	Open End	US Equity Large Cap Blend (Growth)	B	B-	B+		Y	250,000
Eaton Vance Tax-Advantaged Bond & Options Strategies Fund	EXD	NYSE	Closed End	Multialternative (Growth)	C-	D+	C	Down	Y	
Eaton Vance Tax-Advantaged Dividend Income Fund	EVT	NYSE	Closed End	Aggressive Alloc (Equity-Income)	B	B-	B+	Up	Y	
Eaton Vance Tax-Advantaged Global Dividend Income Fund	ETG	NYSE	Closed End	Alloc (World Stock)	B	B-	B	Up	Y	
Eaton Vance Tax-Advantaged Global Dividend Opp Fund	ETO	NYSE	Closed End	Alloc (World Stock)	B	B-	B+	Up	Y	
Eaton Vance Tax-Managed Buy-Write Income Fund	ETB	NYSE	Closed End	Long/Short Equity (Equity-Income)	B	B-	B+	Up	Y	
Eaton Vance Tax-Managed Buy-Write Opportunities Fund	ETV	NYSE	Closed End	Long/Short Equity (Equity-Income)	B	B-	B+	Up	Y	
Eaton Vance Tax-Managed Diversified Equity Income Fund	ETY	NYSE	Closed End	Long/Short Equity (Equity-Income)	B	B-	B+	Up	Y	
Eaton Vance Tax-Managed Equity Asset Allocation Fund Cls A	EAEAX	NAS CM	Open End	Aggressive Alloc (Asset Alloc)	B-	B-	B	Down	Y	1,000
Eaton Vance Tax-Managed Equity Asset Allocation Fund Cls B	EBEAX	NAS CM	Open End	Aggressive Alloc (Asset Alloc)	B-	B-	B	Down		1,000
Eaton Vance Tax-Managed Equity Asset Allocation Fund Cls C	ECEAX	NAS CM	Open End	Aggressive Alloc (Asset Alloc)	B-	B-	B	Down	Y	1,000
Eaton Vance Tax-Managed Equity Asset Allocation Fund Cls I	EIEAX	NAS CM	Open End	Aggressive Alloc (Asset Alloc)	B-	B-	B	Down	Y	250,000
Eaton Vance Tax-Managed Global Buy-Write Opp Fund	ETW	NYSE	Closed End	Long/Short Equity (World Stock)	B	C+	A	Up	Y	
Eaton Vance Tax-Managed Global Diversified Eq Income Fund	EXG	NYSE	Closed End	Long/Short Equity (World Stock)	B	C+	A-	Up	Y	
Eaton Vance Tax-Managed Global Dividend Income Fund Cls A	EADIX	NAS CM	Open End	Global Equity (Equity-Income)	B-	C+	B	Down	Y	1,000
Eaton Vance Tax-Managed Global Dividend Income Fund Cls B	EBDIX	NAS CM	Open End	Global Equity (Equity-Income)	B	C+	B+	Up		1,000
Eaton Vance Tax-Managed Global Dividend Income Fund Cls C	ECDIX	NAS CM	Open End	Global Equity (Equity-Income)	B-	C+	B-	Down	Y	1,000
Eaton Vance Tax-Managed Global Dividend Income Fund Cls I	EIDIX	NAS CM	Open End	Global Equity (Equity-Income)	B-	C+	B	Down	Y	250,000
Eaton Vance Tax-Managed Global Small-Cap Fund Class A	ESVAX	NAS CM	Open End	Global Equity (Small Company)	C+	B-	C+	Down	Y	1,000
Eaton Vance Tax-Managed Global Small-Cap Fund Class C	ESVCX	NAS CM	Open End	Global Equity (Small Company)	C+	B-	C	Down	Y	1,000
Eaton Vance Tax-Managed Global Small-Cap Fund Class I	ESVIX	NAS CM	Open End	Global Equity (Small Company)	C+	B-	C+	Down	Y	250,000
Eaton Vance Tax-Managed Growth 1.0 Fund	CAPEX	NAS CM	Open End	US Equity Large Cap Blend (Growth)	B	B	B			0
Eaton Vance Tax-Managed Growth 1.1 Fund Class A	ETTGX	NAS CM	Open End	US Equity Large Cap Blend (Growth)	B	B	B			1,000
Eaton Vance Tax-Managed Growth 1.1 Fund Class B	EMTGX	NAS CM	Open End	US Equity Large Cap Blend (Growth)	B	B-	B			1,000
Eaton Vance Tax-Managed Growth 1.1 Fund Class C	ECTGX	NAS CM	Open End	US Equity Large Cap Blend (Growth)	B	B-	B			1,000
Eaton Vance Tax-Managed Growth 1.1 Fund Class I	EITMX	NAS CM	Open End	US Equity Large Cap Blend (Growth)	B	B	B			250,000
Eaton Vance Tax-Managed Growth 1.2 Fund Class A	EXTGX	NAS CM	Open End	US Equity Large Cap Blend (Growth)	B	B	B		Y	1,000
Eaton Vance Tax-Managed Growth 1.2 Fund Class B	EYTGX	NAS CM	Open End	US Equity Large Cap Blend (Growth)	B	B-	B			1,000
Eaton Vance Tax-Managed Growth 1.2 Fund Class C	EZTGX	NAS CM	Open End	US Equity Large Cap Blend (Growth)	B	B-	B		Y	1,000
Eaton Vance Tax-Managed Growth 1.2 Fund Institutional Cls	EITGX	NAS CM	Open End	US Equity Large Cap Blend (Growth)	B	B	B		Y	250,000

★ Expanded analysis of this fund is included in Section II.

Min Additional Investment	TOTAL RETURNS: 3-Month Total Return	6-Month Total Return	1-Year Total Return	3-Year Total Return	5-Year Total Return	PERFORMANCE: Dividend Yield (TTM)	Expense Ratio	3-Yr Std Deviation	3-Year Beta	ASSETS: NAV	Total Assets (MIL)	ASSET ALLOCATION & TURNOVER: %Cash	%Stocks	%Bonds	%Other	Turnover Ratio	BULL & BEAR: Last Bull Market Total Return	Last Bear Market Total Return	FEES: Front End Fee (%)	Back End Fee (%)	Inception Date
	6.78	10.48	15.24	24.40	83.39	1.5	0.71	9.87	0.93	19.61	2,198	1	99	0	0	94	22.42	-18.96			Jul-14
	2.64	5.06	11.29	18.42	23.80	1.84	1.45	4.94	0.63	10.83	39.1	11	45	36	9	49			4.75		Oct-11
	2.46	4.67	10.50	15.74	19.16	1.13	2.2	4.95	0.62	10.79	39.1	11	45	36	9	49				1.00	Oct-11
	2.71	5.11	11.60	19.25	25.22	2.09	1.2	4.94	0.63	10.81	39.1	11	45	36	9	49					Oct-11
	2.13	3.09	3.92	14.25	54.51	1.46	1.25	13.06	0.96	13.93	49.7	2	98	0	0	52	30.05	-15.13	5.75		Jun-10
	2.26	3.30	4.23	15.13	56.47	1.73	1	13.09	0.96	13.93	49.7	2	98	0	0	52	30.31	-15.04			Apr-06
	3.80	7.73	14.70	20.71	42.66	0.42	1.33	6.04	0.05	14.76	657.1	14	60	25	1	41	8.78		5.75		Sep-11
	3.55	7.32	13.88	18.09	37.35	0	2.08	6.04	0.05	14.52	657.1	14	60	25	1	41	8.24			1.00	Sep-11
	3.82	7.88	15.00	21.64	44.45	0.64	1.08	6.03	0.05	14.81	657.1	14	60	25	1	41	8.9				Sep-11
	5.51	11.10	20.70	30.43	77.09	0.66	1.26	9.29	0.81	17.09	965.6	17	81	0	3	24	14.98	-19.58	5.75		Oct-10
	5.31	10.70	19.82	27.51	70.58	0.01	2.01	9.29	0.81	16.94	965.6	17	81	0	3	24	14.43	-19.86		1.00	Oct-10
	5.53	11.24	20.92	31.39	79.24	0.88	1.01	9.35	0.82	17.09	965.6	17	81	0	3	24	15.04	-19.48			Oct-10
	3.84	5.30	11.01	11.83	37.58	7.02	0	6.2	0.56	10.08	638.6	1	99	0	0	79	4.44	-7.59			Jul-07
	4.66	8.92	14.90	32.17	90.56	0	1.35	11.75	0.79	13.15	81.5	0	100	0	0	76	22.87	-25.29	5.75		Jan-97
	4.48	8.60	14.10	29.22	83.63	0	2.1	11.72	0.78	11.11	81.5	0	100	0	0	76	22.28	-25.5		1.00	May-02
	4.74	9.10	15.17	33.17	92.98	0	1.1	11.75	0.79	14.45	81.5	0	100	0	0	76	23.04	-25.22			Sep-08
	4.58	8.82	14.64	31.17	88.32	0	1.6	11.74	0.78	12.67	81.5	0	100	0	0	76	22.64	-25.34			Aug-09
	4.51	8.34	15.37	28.17	82.45	0	1.35	11	0.85	22.7	46.3	1	99	0	0	67	20.17	-21.21	5.75		Apr-68
	4.29	7.90	14.45	25.28	75.72	0	2.1	10.97	0.85	20.23	46.3	1	99	0	0	67	19.66	-21.46		1.00	Nov-94
	4.55	8.45	15.63	29.08	84.78	0	1.1	10.98	0.85	23.17	46.3	1	99	0	0	67	20.46	-21.21			Jul-11
	6.39	9.98	19.90	32.47	102.57	0.84	0.98	9.48	0.92	17.49	103.1	0	100	0	0	118	24.34	-17.85	5.75		Nov-01
	6.19	9.56	18.94	29.48	94.97	0.26	1.73	9.47	0.92	17.1	103.1	0	100	0	0	118	23.72	-18		1.00	Oct-09
	6.47	10.07	20.14	33.46	105.00	1.05	0.73	9.49	0.92	17.49	103.1	0	100	0	0	118	24.46	-17.7			Sep-08
	-3.98	-3.68	-1.34	5.15	-0.96	0.8	1.45	6.27	1.08	11.45	114.1	3	0	97	0	46	6.04	3.98			Jun-10
	6.70	10.59	17.71	31.34	85.48	3.71	0	9.58	0.88	23.86	1,712	0	72	5	1	91	24.75	-20.14			Sep-03
	4.91	7.81	24.66	28.98	78.80	3.58	1.28	11.26	1.03	18.56	1,399	2	79	3	1	197	22.96	-22.78			Jan-04
	4.90	8.71	24.83	32.68	77.79	1.66	0	11.64	1.08	24.93	359.2	0	78	4	1	60	23.17	-24.56			Apr-04
	2.63	6.41	14.37	27.29	67.47	0.92	0	7.3	0.68	16.35	407.8	0	100	0	0	6	23.82	-11.79			Apr-05
	4.48	9.34	17.06	32.10	74.96	0.6	0	7.36	0.69	15.01	974.3	0	100	0	0	4	24.22	-10.74			Jun-05
	5.87	8.98	17.99	28.97	75.27	0.74	1.2	8.4	0.79	12.35	1,829	1	99	0	0	86	19.44	-17.62			Nov-06
	6.07	10.17	19.14	28.37	83.40	0.79	1.34	9.1	0.88	20.15	488.5	1	88	1	1	6	23.58	-20.16	5.75		Mar-02
	5.87	9.74	18.27	25.50	76.61	0	2.1	9.08	0.88	19.05	488.5	1	88	1	1	6	22.99	-20.48		5.00	Mar-02
	5.86	9.72	18.21	25.48	76.68	0.23	2.09	9.08	0.88	18.76	488.5	1	88	1	1	6	23.1	-20.49		1.00	Mar-02
	6.11	10.27	19.47	29.03	84.34	1	1.09	9.09	0.88	20.1	488.5	1	88	1	1	6	23.58	-20.16			Sep-15
	3.01	7.54	19.33	26.36	54.03	1.16	0	8	0.7	11.59	1,234	0	98	0	2	8	19.27	-15.04			Sep-05
	3.43	6.31	18.15	23.38	50.92	0.93	1.2	8.51	0.78	9.48	2,837	0	98	0	2	65	18.16	-20			Feb-07
	4.54	7.29	20.01	25.01	58.52	3.42	1.18	9.28	0.86	12.8	774.9	2	92	2	1	134	16.63	-16.68	5.75		May-03
	4.35	6.91	19.14	22.16	52.66	2.71	1.93	9.21	0.85	12.77	774.9	2	92	2	1	134	16.16	-16.9		5.00	May-03
	4.36	7.01	19.15	22.20	52.73	2.72	1.93	9.2	0.85	12.77	774.9	2	92	2	1	134	16.16	-16.98		1.00	May-03
	4.68	7.50	20.47	26.03	60.57	3.66	0.93	9.28	0.86	12.82	774.9	2	92	2	1	134	16.91	-16.59			Aug-07
	4.66	10.13	23.19	22.54	80.93	0	1.4	10.43	0.88	14.18	24.6	1	96	0	2	92	24.36	-21.24	5.75		Mar-02
	4.57	9.71	22.33	19.83	74.39	0	2.15	10.43	0.88	11.08	24.6	1	96	0	2	92	23.83	-21.48		1.00	Mar-02
	4.83	10.28	23.51	23.56	83.32	0	1.15	10.41	0.88	14.64	24.6	1	96	0	2	92	24.55	-21.11			Oct-09
	7.66	12.44	22.72	35.82	107.57	1.23		10.38	1.02	1146.13	970.3	1	98	0	1	1	24.9	-16.06			Mar-66
	7.57	12.26	22.34	34.58	104.39	0.88	0.81	10.39	1.02	51.3	1,604	1	98	0	1	1	24.66	-16.17	5.75		Mar-96
	7.37	11.85	21.42	31.56	96.79	0.12	1.56	10.39	1.02	50.49	1,604	1	98	0	1	1	24.15	-16.48		5.00	Mar-96
	7.39	11.86	21.45	31.58	96.84	0.41	1.56	10.39	1.02	46.1	1,604	1	98	0	1	1	24.11	-16.43		1.00	Aug-96
	7.66	12.43	22.67	35.57	106.97	1.16	0.56	10.39	1.02	47.92	1,604	1	98	0	1	1	24.89	-16.12			Jul-99
	7.51	12.18	22.15	33.97	102.73	0.75	0.97	10.4	1.02	23.06	768.8	1	98	0	1	1	24.45	-16.2	5.75		Feb-01
	7.31	11.76	21.22	30.97	95.25	0	1.72	10.35	1.02	22.9	768.8	1	98	0	1	1	23.94	-16.53		5.00	Feb-01
	7.33	11.76	21.23	30.96	95.23	0.18	1.72	10.37	1.02	22.46	768.8	1	98	0	1	1	23.96	-16.53		1.00	Feb-01
	7.59	12.30	22.43	34.98	105.20	0.95	0.72	10.44	1.03	23.11	768.8	1	98	0	1	1	24.72	-16.16			Feb-01

	MARKET		FUND TYPE, CATEGORY & OBJECTIVE		RATINGS				MINIMUMS	
Fund Name	Ticker Symbol	Traded On	Fund Type	Category and (Prospectus Objective)	Overall Rating	Reward Rating	Risk Rating	Recent Up/ Downgrade	Open to New Investors	Min Initial Investment
Eaton Vance Tax-Managed Multi-Cap Growth Fund Class A	EACPX	NAS CM	Open End	US Equity Large Cap Growth (Growth)	B	B	B	Up	Y	1,000
Eaton Vance Tax-Managed Multi-Cap Growth Fund Class C	ECCPX	NAS CM	Open End	US Equity Large Cap Growth (Growth)	B	B	B+	Up	Y	1,000
Eaton Vance Tax-Managed Small-Cap Fund Class A	ETMGX	NAS CM	Open End	US Equity Small Cap (Small Company)	B	B	B	Up	Y	1,000
Eaton Vance Tax-Managed Small-Cap Fund Class C	ECMGX	NAS CM	Open End	US Equity Small Cap (Small Company)	B	B	B	Up	Y	1,000
Eaton Vance Tax-Managed Small-Cap Fund Class I	EIMGX	NAS CM	Open End	US Equity Small Cap (Small Company)	B	B+	B	Up	Y	250,000
Eaton Vance Tax-Managed Value Fund Class A	EATVX	NAS CM	Open End	US Equity Large Cap Value (Growth)	B-	B-	B-	Down	Y	1,000
Eaton Vance Tax-Managed Value Fund Class C	ECTVX	NAS CM	Open End	US Equity Large Cap Value (Growth)	B-	C+	B	Down	Y	1,000
Eaton Vance Tax-Managed Value Fund Class I	EITVX	NAS CM	Open End	US Equity Large Cap Value (Growth)	B	B-	B	Up	Y	250,000
Eaton Vance Worldwide Health Sciences Fund Class A	ETHSX	NAS CM	Open End	Healthcare Sector Equity (Health)	C	C	C	Down	Y	1,000
Eaton Vance Worldwide Health Sciences Fund Class B	EMHSX	NAS CM	Open End	Healthcare Sector Equity (Health)	C	C	C	Down		1,000
Eaton Vance Worldwide Health Sciences Fund Class C	ECHSX	NAS CM	Open End	Healthcare Sector Equity (Health)	C	C	C	Down	Y	1,000
Eaton Vance Worldwide Health Sciences Fund Class I	EIHSX	NAS CM	Open End	Healthcare Sector Equity (Health)	C+	C	C+	Down	Y	250,000
Eaton Vance Worldwide Health Sciences Fund Class R	ERHSX	NAS CM	Open End	Healthcare Sector Equity (Health)	C	C	C	Down	Y	1,000
Eaton Vance-Atlanta Capital Focused Growth Fund Class A	EAALX	NAS CM	Open End	US Equity Large Cap Growth (Growth)	B	B	B		Y	1,000
Eaton Vance-Atlanta Capital Focused Growth Fund Class I	EILGX	NAS CM	Open End	US Equity Large Cap Growth (Growth)	B	B	B		Y	250,000
Edgar Lomax Value Fund	LOMAX	NAS CM	Open End	US Equity Large Cap Value (Growth & Income)	B-	B-	B	Down	Y	2,500
Edgewood Growth Fund Class Institutional	EGFIX	NAS CM	Open End	US Equity Large Cap Growth (Growth)	B+	B+	A-	Up	Y	100,000
Edgewood Growth Fund Retail Class	EGFFX	NAS CM	Open End	US Equity Large Cap Growth (Growth)	B+	B	A-	Up	Y	3,000
EIC Value Fund Class A	EICVX	NAS CM	Open End	US Equity Large Cap Value (Growth)	B-	C+	B	Down	Y	2,500
EIC Value Fund Class C	EICCX	NAS CM	Open End	US Equity Large Cap Value (Growth)	B-	C+	B-	Down	Y	2,500
EIC Value Fund Institutional Class	EICIX	NAS CM	Open End	US Equity Large Cap Value (Growth)	B-	C+	B	Down	Y	100,000
EIP Growth and Income Fund Class I	EIPIX	NAS CM	Open End	Energy Sector Equity (Natl Res)	C-	C-	D+	Down	Y	1,000,000
EIP Growth and Income Fund Investor Class	EIPFX	NAS CM	Open End	Energy Sector Equity (Natl Res)	C-	C-	D+	Down	Y	2,500
Elfun Diversified Fund	ELDFX	NAS CM	Open End	Moderate Alloc (Asset Alloc)	B	C+	B+	Up	Y	500
Elfun International Equity Fund	EGLBX	NAS CM	Open End	Global Equity Large Cap (World Stock)	B-	C+	B-	Up	Y	500
Elfun Trusts	ELFNX	NAS CM	Open End	US Equity Large Cap Growth (Growth)	B	B	B+		Y	500
Ellsworth Growth and Income Fund Ltd	ECF	AMEX	Closed End	Convertibles (Convertible Bond)	B-	C+	B	Up	Y	
Emerald Banking and Finance Fund Class A	HSSAX	NAS CM	Open End	Financials Sector Equity (Financial)	A-	A	B	Up	Y	2,000
Emerald Banking and Finance Fund Class C	HSSCX	NAS CM	Open End	Financials Sector Equity (Financial)	A-	A	B	Up	Y	2,000
Emerald Banking and Finance Fund Institutional Class	HSSIX	NAS CM	Open End	Financials Sector Equity (Financial)	A-	A	B	Up	Y	1,000,000
Emerald Banking and Finance Fund Investor Class	FFBFX	NAS CM	Open End	Financials Sector Equity (Financial)	A-	A	B	Up	Y	2,000
Emerald Growth Fund Class A	HSPGX	NAS CM	Open End	US Equity Small Cap (Growth)	B+	A-	B	Up	Y	2,000
Emerald Growth Fund Class C	HSPCX	NAS CM	Open End	US Equity Small Cap (Growth)	B	A-	C+	Up	Y	2,000
Emerald Growth Fund Institutional Class	FGROX	NAS CM	Open End	US Equity Small Cap (Growth)	B	A	C+	Up	Y	1,000,000
Emerald Growth Fund Investor Class	FFGRX	NAS CM	Open End	US Equity Small Cap (Growth)	B	A-	C+	Up	Y	2,000
Emerald Insights Fund Class A	EFCAX	NAS CM	Open End	US Equity Mid Cap (Growth)	B-	B-	B	Up	Y	2,000
Emerald Insights Fund Class C	EFCCX	NAS CM	Open End	US Equity Mid Cap (Growth)	B-	B-	B-	Up	Y	2,000
Emerald Insights Fund Institutional Class	EFCIX	NAS CM	Open End	US Equity Mid Cap (Growth)	B	B-	B	Up	Y	1,000,000
Emerald Insights Fund Investor Class	EFCNX	NAS CM	Open End	US Equity Mid Cap (Growth)	B-	B-	B	Up	Y	2,000
Emerald Small Cap Value Fund Class A	ELASX	NAS CM	Open End	US Equity Small Cap (Small Company)	A-	A	B	Up	Y	2,000
Emerald Small Cap Value Fund Class C	ELCSX	NAS CM	Open End	US Equity Small Cap (Small Company)	B+	A-	B	Up	Y	2,000
Emerald Small Cap Value Fund Institutional Class	LSRYX	NAS CM	Open End	US Equity Small Cap (Small Company)	A-	A	B	Up	Y	1,000,000
Emerald Small Cap Value Fund Investor Class	LSRIX	NAS CM	Open End	US Equity Small Cap (Small Company)	A-	A	B	Up	Y	2,000
Empiric 2500 Fund Class A	EMCAX	NAS CM	Open End	US Equity Small Cap (Growth)	C+	C+	C+	Up	Y	2,500
Empiric 2500 Fund Class C	EMCCX	NAS CM	Open End	US Equity Small Cap (Growth)	C+	C+	C+	Up	Y	2,500
Ensemble Fund	ENSBX	NAS CM	Open End	US Equity Large Cap Growth (Growth)	C	C	B	Up	Y	5,000
Entrepreneur U.S. Small Cap Fund Institutional Class	IMPAX	NAS CM	Open End	US Equity Small Cap (Growth & Income)	B	A-	C	Up	Y	2,500
Entrepreneur US Large Cap Fund Institutional Class	IMPLX	NAS CM	Open End	US Equity Large Cap Growth (Growth)	B+	B+	B	Up	Y	2,500
EntrepreneurShares Global Fund Institutional Class	ENTIX	NAS CM	Open End	Global Equity Large Cap (Growth)	B	B+	B-	Up	Y	2,500
EnTrustPermal Alternative Core Fund Class A	LPTAX	NAS CM	Open End	Multialternative (Asset Alloc)	C+	C	B		Y	1,000
EnTrustPermal Alternative Core Fund Class C	LPTCX	NAS CM	Open End	Multialternative (Asset Alloc)	C	C	C	Down	Y	1,000
EnTrustPermal Alternative Core Fund Class FI	LPTFX	NAS CM	Open End	Multialternative (Asset Alloc)	C+	C	B		Y	0

★ Expanded analysis of this fund is included in Section II.

	TOTAL RETURNS					PERFORMANCE				ASSETS		ASSET ALLOCATION & TURNOVER					BULL & BEAR		FEES		
Min Additional Investment	3-Month Total Return	6-Month Total Return	1-Year Total Return	3-Year Total Return	5-Year Total Return	Dividend Yield (TTM)	Expense Ratio	3-Yr Std Deviation	3-Year Beta	NAV	Total Assets (MIL)	%Cash	%Stocks	%Bonds	%Other	Turnover Ratio	Last Bull Market Total Return	Last Bear Market Total Return	Front End Fee (%)	Back End Fee (%)	Inception Date
	6.07	11.15	25.78	34.17	97.52	0	1.4	11.99	1.07	26.88	82.6	1	99	0	0	33	28.91	-20.68	5.75		Jun-00
	5.89	10.75	24.88	31.18	90.26	0	2.15	12	1.07	23.34	82.6	1	99	0	0	33	28.25	-20.89		1.00	Jul-00
	4.67	9.07	15.19	31.75	89.39	0	1.22	11.65	0.78	25.31	121.7	1	99	0	0	66	23.05	-25.12	5.75		Sep-97
	4.46	8.63	14.34	28.79	82.43	0	1.97	11.63	0.78	20.71	121.7	1	99	0	0	66	22.5	-25.35		1.00	Sep-97
	4.75	9.21	15.48	32.77	91.75	0	0.97	11.66	0.78	25.98	121.7	1	99	0	0	66	23.3	-25.06			Oct-09
	8.17	12.12	17.65	24.98	86.88	0.95	1.21	9.59	0.9	26.45	599.2	0	100	0	0	45	22.94	-18.28	5.75		Dec-99
	7.96	11.69	16.76	22.20	80.05	0.37	1.96	9.58	0.9	25.44	599.2	0	100	0	0	45	22.39	-18.51		1.00	Jan-00
	8.20	12.26	17.93	25.80	89.16	1.17	0.96	9.57	0.9	26.31	599.2	0	100	0	0	45	23.09	-18.19			Nov-07
	-1.58	0.94	16.23	6.61	99.72	0	1.39	14.5	1.14	10.3	1,092	0	98	0	2	36	17.5	-9.67	5.75		Jul-85
	-1.82	0.55	15.37	4.27	92.24	0	2.14	14.44	1.14	10.51	1,092	0	98	0	2	36	17.04	-10.05		5.00	Sep-96
	-1.84	0.55	15.41	4.23	92.32	0	2.14	14.39	1.14	10.41	1,092	0	98	0	2	36	17.04	-10.05		1.00	Jan-98
	-1.63	1.01	16.55	7.40	102.15	0	1.14	14.49	1.14	10.55	1,092	0	98	0	2	36	17.76	-9.63			Oct-09
	-1.75	0.79	15.93	5.77	97.05	0	1.64	14.45	1.14	10.98	1,092	0	98	0	2	36	17.37	-9.77			Sep-03
	6.77	12.99	27.09	33.17	88.51	0	1.21	11.14	1	9.52	30.7	2	98	0	0	28	23.95	-18.17	5.75		Nov-03
	6.87	13.17	27.43	34.28	90.93	0.2	0.96	11.15	1	8.41	30.7	2	98	0	0	28	24.24	-18.15			Apr-02
100	7.56	13.68	19.48	31.02	103.63	1.81	0.7	9.98	0.92	14.86	85.2	1	99	0	0	56	17.73	-10.29			Dec-97
	3.89	9.56	34.81	54.66	147.26	0	1	12.87	1.12	29.56	11,115	2	98	0	0	31	25.3	-11.91			Feb-06
	3.74	9.32	34.27	52.83	144.18	0	1.39	12.89	1.12	28.5	11,115	2	98	0	0	31	25.71	-12.38			Feb-06
250	6.63	9.66	14.15	18.64	67.53	0.76	1.25	8.13	0.74	14.6	253.7	16	84	0	0	29	17.06	-8.6	5.50		May-11
250	6.48	9.23	13.27	16.04	61.45	0.01	2	8.15	0.74	14.42	253.7	16	84	0	0	29	16.54	-8.9		1.00	Jul-11
	6.69	9.78	14.41	19.56	69.63	1.11	1	8.16	0.74	14.63	253.7	16	84	0	0	29	17.2	-8.5			Apr-11
	-0.79	0.17	-0.68	-10.31	31.22	2.43	2.04	9.91	0.54	15.44	45.8	44	52	0	5	53	21.83	-6.29			Aug-06
100	-0.89	-0.09	-1.11	-11.17	29.32	2.16	2.44	9.91	0.54	15.42	45.8	44	52	0	5	53	21.65	-6.39			Oct-16
	3.75	7.42	15.40	19.50	48.71	1.73	0.47	7.02	0.65	18.6	211.4	4	63	32	0	116	15.87	-13.76			Jan-88
	4.37	9.43	22.98	20.60	38.54	1.8	0.38	12.88	1.04	22.68	235.8	0	99	1	0	33	16.45	-25.88			Jan-88
	5.00	10.70	25.61	34.12	110.46	1.13	0.18	12.23	1.15	60.36	2,772	0	96	4	0	15	28.83	-17.03			May-35
	2.46	4.41	12.66	19.52	58.44	1.2	0	7.94		10.32	133.4	11	21	0	1	32	13.78	-14.73			Jun-86
100	4.52	10.20	12.57	64.83	157.44	0	1.43	16.96	0.97	45.41	515.7	1	98	0	1	36	30.66	-20.17	4.75		Feb-97
100	4.36	9.84	11.82	61.62	149.21	0	2.08	16.96	0.97	40.38	515.7	1	98	0	1	36	30.18	-20.29		1.00	Jul-00
	4.62	10.35	12.92	66.38	161.67	0	1.14	16.98	0.97	46.28	515.7	1	98	0	1	36	30.66	-20.17			Mar-12
100	4.51	10.15	12.57	64.83	157.31	0	1.48	16.96	0.97	43.43	515.7	1	98	0	1	36	30.94	-19.98			Mar-10
100	7.87	14.70	27.71	42.42	132.96	0	1.08	15.14	0.96	26.45	1,180	2	98	0	0	54	38.81	-26.92	4.75		Oct-92
100	7.66	14.30	26.86	39.64	125.51	0	1.73	15.14	0.96	22.62	1,180	2	98	0	0	54	38.25	-27.13		1.00	Jul-00
	7.96	14.84	28.11	43.75	136.63	0	0.77	15.16	0.96	27.39	1,180	2	98	0	0	54	39.01	-26.81			Oct-08
100	7.85	14.66	27.66	42.26	132.53	0	1.13	15.16	0.96	26.35	1,180	2	98	0	0	54	38.76	-26.94			May-11
100	6.97	11.03	22.54	25.53		0	1.35	14.13	1.22	12.88	11.0	1	99	0	0	75			4.75		Aug-14
100	6.79	10.55	21.80	22.99		0	2	14.11	1.22	12.57	11.0	1	99	0	0	75				1.00	Aug-14
	7.00	11.12	22.89	26.60		0	1.05	14.04	1.21	12.99	11.0	1	99	0	0	75					Aug-14
100	7.00	10.97	22.51	25.26		0	1.4	14.08	1.21	12.84	11.0	1	99	0	0	75					Aug-14
100	3.59	11.68	13.50	37.05	94.76	0	1.36	14.44	0.98	10.37	8.7	3	97	0	0	66			4.75		Jun-15
100	3.39	11.31	12.71	34.42	89.50	0	2.01	14.45	0.98	10.09	8.7	3	97	0	0	66				1.00	Jun-15
	3.68	11.87	13.82	38.41	98.07	0	1.01	14.46	0.98	10.5	8.7	3	97	0	0	66					Oct-12
100	3.64	11.74	13.63	37.71	96.02	0	1.26	14.42	0.97	10.38	8.7	3	97	0	0	66					Oct-12
50	7.32	11.09	21.81	15.81	82.17	0	1.98	14.47	1.02	39.25	25.7	0	100	0	0	150	19.8	-23.98	5.75		Nov-95
50	7.09	10.69	20.91	13.19	75.36	0	2.73	14.48	1.02	35.61	25.7	0	100	0	0	150	19.31	-24.22			Oct-05
100	7.32	10.61	21.23			0.48	1			12.45	18.9	1	99	0	0						Nov-15
	2.61	9.69	23.77	36.70		0.13	0.85	13.33	0.9	12.65	133.6	2	98	0	0	53					Dec-13
	8.83	13.75	27.39	39.76		0.43	0.75	9.78	0.92	13.04	109.5	2	98	0	0	43					Jun-14
	7.32	13.25	30.13	43.44	83.45	0	1.7	10.44	0.92	15.34	39.2	3	97	0	0	65	21.77	-24.83			Nov-10
50	-0.21	-1.05	2.02	5.40	24.18	0.14	1.69	3.71	0.27	14.06	366.5	50	39	4	8	85	9.81	-12.34	5.75		Apr-09
50	-0.42	-1.48	1.23	3.08	19.52	0	2.44	3.73	0.27	13.93	366.5	50	39	4	8	85	9.4	-12.62		1.00	Apr-09
	-0.20	-1.10	2.03	5.41	24.17	0.18	1.69	3.74	0.27	14.35	366.5	50	39	4	8	85	9.82	-12.35			Apr-09

Fund Name	MARKET Ticker Symbol	Traded On	FUND TYPE, CATEGORY & OBJECTIVE Fund Type	Category and (Prospectus Objective)	RATINGS Overall Rating	Reward Rating	Risk Rating	Recent Up/ Downgrade	Open to New Investors	MINIMUMS Min Initial Investment
EnTrustPermal Alternative Core Fund Class I	LPTIX	NAS CM	Open End	Multialternative (Asset Alloc)	B-	C	B+	Up	Y	1,000,000
EnTrustPermal Alternative Core Fund Class IS	LPTSX	NAS CM	Open End	Multialternative (Asset Alloc)	B-	C	B+	Up	Y	1,000,000
EP Emerging Markets Small Companies Fund Class A	EPASX	NAS CM	Open End	Emerging Markets Equity (Small Company)	C+	C+	C	Up	Y	2,500
EP Emerging Markets Small Companies Fund Class I	EPEIX	NAS CM	Open End	Emerging Markets Equity (Small Company)	C+	C+	C	Up	Y	15,000
Epiphany Faith and Family Values Fund Class A	EPVNX	NAS CM	Open End	US Equity Large Cap Blend (Growth)	C+	B-	C+	Down	Y	1,000
Epiphany Faith and Family Values Fund Class I	EPVCX	NAS CM	Open End	US Equity Large Cap Blend (Growth)	C+	B-	C+	Down	Y	100,000
Epoch Global Equity Shareholder Fund Advisor Class	TDGIX	NAS CM	Open End	Global Equity (Equity-Income)	B-	C+	B		Y	100,000
Epoch Global Equity Shareholder Fund Institutional Class	TDGEX	NAS CM	Open End	Global Equity (Equity-Income)	B-	C+	B		Y	1,000,000
Epoch U.S. Small-Mid Cap Equity Fund Advisor Class	TDUAX	NAS CM	Open End	US Equity Small Cap (Growth)	B	B	B	Up	Y	100,000
Epoch U.S. Small-Mid Cap Equity Fund Institutional Class	TDUSX	NAS CM	Open End	US Equity Small Cap (Growth)	B	B	B	Up	Y	1,000,000
EQ/BlackRock Basic Value Equity Portfolio Class IA	US2689408555		Open End	US Equity Large Cap Value (Growth & Income)	C+	C+	B-	Up	Y	0
EQ/BlackRock Basic Value Equity Portfolio Class IB	US2689407235		Open End	US Equity Large Cap Value (Growth & Income)	C+	C+	B-	Up	Y	0
EQ/BlackRock Basic Value Equity Portfolio Class K	US26883L7468		Open End	US Equity Large Cap Value (Growth & Income)	C+	C+	B-	Up	Y	0
EQ/Capital Guardian Research Portfolio Class IA	US2689404422		Open End	US Equity Large Cap Growth (Growth)	B	B	B-		Y	0
EQ/Capital Guardian Research Portfolio Class IB	US2689404349		Open End	US Equity Large Cap Growth (Growth)	B	B	B-		Y	0
EQ/Capital Guardian Research Portfolio Class K	US26883L7120		Open End	US Equity Large Cap Growth (Growth)	B	B	B-		Y	0
EQ/Common Stock Index Portfolio Class IA	US4049925054		Open End	US Equity Large Cap Blend (Growth)	B-	B-	B-	Down	Y	0
EQ/Common Stock Index Portfolio Class IB	US4049925138		Open End	US Equity Large Cap Blend (Growth)	B-	B-	B-	Down	Y	0
EQ/Emerging Markets Equity PLUS Portfolio Class IB	US26884M5783		Open End	Emerging Markets Equity (Div Emerging Mkts)	C+	B-	C	Up	Y	0
EQ/Emerging Markets Equity PLUS Portfolio Class K	US26884M5601		Open End	Emerging Markets Equity (Div Emerging Mkts)	C+	B-	C	Up	Y	0
EQ/Equity 500 Index Portfolio Class IA	US4049925476		Open End	US Equity Large Cap Blend (Growth & Income)	B	B-	B		Y	0
EQ/Equity 500 Index Portfolio Class IB	US4049925542		Open End	US Equity Large Cap Blend (Growth & Income)	B	B-	B		Y	0
EQ/Equity 500 Index Portfolio Class K	US26883L6700		Open End	US Equity Large Cap Blend (Growth & Income)	B	B	B		Y	0
EQ/International Equity Index Portfolio Class IA Shares	US4049926615		Open End	Global Equity Large Cap (Foreign Stock)	B-	B-	B	Up	Y	0
EQ/International Equity Index Portfolio Class IB Shares	US4049926797		Open End	Global Equity Large Cap (Foreign Stock)	C+	B-	C+	Up	Y	0
EQ/International Equity Index Portfolio Class K	US26883L5975		Open End	Global Equity Large Cap (Foreign Stock)	C+	B-	C+	Up	Y	0
EQ/Invesco Comstock Portfolio Class IA	US2689401527		Open End	US Equity Large Cap Value (Growth & Income)	B	B	B-	Up	Y	0
EQ/Invesco Comstock Portfolio Class IB	US2689401451		Open End	US Equity Large Cap Value (Growth & Income)	B	B	B-	Up	Y	0
EQ/Invesco Comstock Portfolio Class K	US26883L3731		Open End	US Equity Large Cap Value (Growth & Income)	B	B	B-	Up	Y	0
EQ/JPMorgan Value Opportunities Portfolio Class IA	US2689403010		Open End	US Equity Large Cap Value (Growth & Income)	B	B	B		Y	0
EQ/JPMorgan Value Opportunities Portfolio Class IB	US2689408225		Open End	US Equity Large Cap Value (Growth & Income)	B	B	B		Y	0
EQ/JPMorgan Value Opportunities Portfolio Class K	US26883L5710		Open End	US Equity Large Cap Value (Growth & Income)	B	B	B		Y	0
EQ/Large Cap Growth Index Portfolio Class IA	US2689405171		Open End	US Equity Large Cap Growth (Growth)	B+	B+	B+	Up	Y	0
EQ/Large Cap Growth Index Portfolio Class IB	US2689404919		Open End	US Equity Large Cap Growth (Growth)	B+	B+	B+	Up	Y	0
EQ/Large Cap Growth Index Portfolio Class K	US26883L5553		Open End	US Equity Large Cap Growth (Growth)	B+	B+	B+	Up	Y	0
EQ/Large Cap Value Index Portfolio Class IA	US2689547089		Open End	US Equity Large Cap Value (Growth & Income)	B-	B-	B	Down	Y	0
EQ/Large Cap Value Index Portfolio Class IB	US2689548079		Open End	US Equity Large Cap Value (Growth & Income)	B-	B-	B	Down	Y	0
EQ/Large Cap Value Index Portfolio Class K	US26883L5306		Open End	US Equity Large Cap Value (Growth & Income)	B-	B-	B	Down	Y	0
EQ/MFS International Growth Portfolio Class IA	US2689544359		Open End	Global Equity Large Cap (Foreign Stock)	B	B	B	Up	Y	0
EQ/MFS International Growth Portfolio Class IB	US29364E4052		Open End	Global Equity Large Cap (Foreign Stock)	B	B	B	Up	Y	0
EQ/MFS International Growth Portfolio Class K	US26883L4986		Open End	Global Equity Large Cap (Foreign Stock)	B	B	B	Up	Y	0
EQ/Mid Cap Index Portfolio Class IA	US2689403192		Open End	US Equity Mid Cap (Growth)	B	B	B		Y	0
EQ/Mid Cap Index Portfolio Class IB	US2689402939		Open End	US Equity Mid Cap (Growth)	B	B	B		Y	0
EQ/Mid Cap Index Portfolio Class K	US26883L4804		Open End	US Equity Mid Cap (Growth)	B	B	B		Y	0
EQ/Oppenheimer Global Portfolio Class IA	US2689547402		Open End	Global Equity (Growth)	B	B+	C+	Up	Y	0
EQ/Oppenheimer Global Portfolio Class IB	US2689547329		Open End	Global Equity (Growth)	B	B+	B	Up	Y	0
EQ/Small Company Index Class K	US26883L4234		Open End	US Equity Small Cap (Growth)	B+	A-	B	Up	Y	0
EQ/Small Company Index Portfolio Class IA	US2689406401		Open End	US Equity Small Cap (Growth)	B+	A-	B	Up	Y	0
EQ/Small Company Index Portfolio Class IB	US2689406328		Open End	US Equity Small Cap (Growth)	B+	B+	B	Up	Y	0
EQ/T. Rowe Price Growth Stock Portfolio Class IA	US2689545752		Open End	US Equity Large Cap Growth (Growth)	B+	B+	B	Down	Y	0
EQ/T. Rowe Price Growth Stock Portfolio Class IB	US29364E1082		Open End	US Equity Large Cap Growth (Growth)	B+	B+	B	Down	Y	0
EQ/T. Rowe Price Growth Stock Portfolio Class K	US26883L4150		Open End	US Equity Large Cap Growth (Growth)	B+	B+	B	Down	Y	0

★ Expanded analysis of this fund is included in Section II.

	TOTAL RETURNS					PERFORMANCE				ASSETS		ASSET ALLOCATION & TURNOVER					BULL & BEAR		FEES		
Min Additional Investment	3-Month Total Return	6-Month Total Return	1-Year Total Return	3-Year Total Return	5-Year Total Return	Dividend Yield (TTM)	Expense Ratio	3-Yr Std Deviation	3-Year Beta	NAV	Total Assets (MIL)	%Cash	%Stocks	%Bonds	%Other	Turnover Ratio	Last Bull Market Total Return	Last Bear Market Total Return	Front End Fee (%)	Back End Fee (%)	Inception Date
	-0.14	-0.91	2.29	6.24	25.72	0.7	1.44	3.74	0.26	14.04	366.5	50	39	4	8	85	9.93	-12.22			Apr-09
	-0.21	-1.04	2.18	6.18	25.63	0.76	1.44	3.75	0.27	14.23	366.5	50	39	4	8	85	9.93	-12.22			Apr-09
250	12.05	13.98	34.37	24.29	37.15	0	1.75	12.74	0.7	13.97	73.7	3	97	0	0	79	25.19	-25.04	4.50		Dec-10
2,500	12.14	14.14	34.67	25.29	38.69	0	1.5	12.74	0.7	14.15	73.7	3	97	0	0	79	25.19	-25.04			Jul-13
250	7.68	13.20	22.64	21.66	84.87	0.58	1.5	10.28	0.98	12.05	20.8	2	98	0	0	63	21.56	-17.79	5.00		Jan-07
250	7.67	13.23	22.43	19.71	79.09	0.1	1.25	10.24	0.98	11.74	20.8	2	98	0	0	63	21.19	-18.04		1.00	Feb-08
	3.32	6.93	16.68	18.28		1.98	1.25	9.15	0.73	11.81	9.6	1	99	0	0	54					Mar-13
	3.33	6.94	16.69	18.32		1.99	1	9.18	0.73	11.81	9.6	1	99	0	0	54					Mar-13
	7.18	9.16	16.23	27.33		0.23	1.25	12.84	1.01	13.35	101.7	1	99	0	0	77					May-13
	7.17	9.15	16.25	27.35		0.25	1	12.83	1.01	13.35	101.7	1	99	0	0	77					May-13
	6.18	9.84	8.28	18.78	84.47	1.31	0.95	13.24	1.23		1,778	1	99	0	0	34	25.06	-20.93			Oct-02
	6.21	9.86	8.30	18.78	84.47	1.31	0.95	13.22	1.23		1,778	1	99	0	0	34	24.98	-20.97			May-97
	6.25	10.00	8.58	19.67	86.79	1.55	0.7	13.22	1.23		1,778	1	99	0	0	34	25.15	-20.98			Aug-11
	4.32	11.18	25.37	37.40	106.78	0.68	0.97	11.22	1.06		413.9	2	98	0	0	20	25.53	-15.82			Mar-02
	4.31	11.16	25.34	37.42	106.71	0.68	0.97	11.25	1.06		413.9	2	98	0	0	20	25.3	-15.88			May-99
	4.41	11.32	25.72	38.44	108.93	0.89	0.72	11.24	1.06		413.9	2	98	0	0	20	25.3	-15.88			Oct-13
	6.79	11.60	20.57	33.23	104.10	1.27	0.71	10.18	0.99		5,955	0	100	0	0	3	25.31	-17.73			Jan-76
	6.80	11.60	20.58	33.22	104.06	1.28	0.71	10.17	0.99		5,955	0	100	0	0	3	25.16	-17.79			Oct-96
	5.91	14.06	32.78	19.90		0.62	1.37	15.34	0.96		55.9	1	98	0	0	16					Feb-13
	5.95	14.20	33.26	20.79		0.81	1.12	15.39	0.96		55.9	1	98	0	0	16					Feb-13
	7.02	11.79	21.09	34.36	106.13	1.32	0.61	10.06	1		5,594	0	100	0	0	5	24.62	-16.32			Mar-94
	7.03	11.80	21.09	34.34	106.06	1.32	0.61	10.08	1		5,594	0	100	0	0	5	24.62	-16.45			May-97
	7.09	11.94	21.42	35.27	108.57	1.53	0.36	10.07	1		5,594	0	100	0	0	5	24.72	-16.32			Aug-11
	3.50	8.86	23.50	20.80	40.24	2.27	0.79	12.22			1,841	0	100	0	0	8	10.93	-23.48			Apr-95
	3.45	8.78	23.51	20.81	40.28	2.26	0.79	12.26			1,841	0	100	0	0	8	10.76	-23.45			May-97
	3.42	8.89	23.81	21.59	42.05	2.47	0.54	12.23			1,841	0	100	0	0	8	10.93	-23.48			Aug-11
	7.93	14.53	18.28	28.94	95.20	1.9	1	13.11	1.22		232.9	5	95	0	0	18	24.84	-19.97			Apr-05
	7.92	14.52	18.27	28.83	95.11	1.9	1	13.12	1.22		232.9	5	95	0	0	18	24.79	-20.07			Apr-05
	8.00	14.68	18.60	29.88	97.24	2.13	0.75	13.12	1.22		232.9	5	95	0	0	18	24.84	-19.97			Oct-13
	7.80	11.62	18.04	39.06	122.03	0.78	0.99	12.57	1.11		665.9	2	98	0	0	188	25.6	-21.77			Oct-02
	7.78	11.65	18.05	38.94	121.89	0.78	0.99	12.57	1.11		665.9	2	98	0	0	188	25.5	-21.83			May-97
	7.89	11.76	18.37	40.10	124.81	1	0.74	12.59	1.12		665.9	2	98	0	0	188	25.53	-21.83			Dec-11
	8.28	14.64	29.10	42.70	119.33	0.78	0.73	10.78	1		1,412	0	100	0	0	13	26.23	-15.4			May-99
	8.23	14.59	29.06	42.73	119.25	0.78	0.73	10.76	1		1,412	0	100	0	0	13	26.1	-15.52			May-99
	8.29	14.80	29.38	43.74	122.08	0.98	0.48	10.77	1		1,412	0	100	0	0	13	26.36	-15.4			Aug-11
	5.64	8.97	13.26	24.67	90.28	1.68	0.73	10.35	1		670.8	0	100	0	0	18	24.01	-19.07			Oct-05
	5.66	8.88	13.30	24.60	90.39	1.68	0.73	10.31	1		670.8	0	100	0	0	18	24.01	-19.13			Oct-05
	5.69	9.03	13.59	25.41	91.41	1.92	0.48	10.32	1		670.8	0	100	0	0	18	24	-19.06			Aug-11
	5.46	10.17	32.03	32.91	46.40	0.77	1.2	11.58	0.94		1,546	1	99	0	0	20	20.24	-21.73			Sep-08
	5.45	10.29	32.14	33.02	46.51	0.77	1.2	11.57	0.94		1,546	1	99	0	0	20	20.31	-21.84			Nov-94
	5.44	10.27	32.33	33.88	48.22	0.96	0.95	11.52	0.93		1,546	1	99	0	0	20	20.43	-21.84			Aug-11
	6.71	10.12	15.66	33.35	98.56	0.87	0.72	11.06	1		2,031	0	100	0	0	20	27.64	-22.75			Mar-02
	6.67	10.06	15.60	33.22	98.53	0.87	0.72	11.07	1		2,031	0	100	0	0	20	27.45	-22.77			Sep-00
	6.75	10.23	16.00	34.34	101.25	1.1	0.47	11.06	1		2,031	0	100	0	0	20	27.64	-22.83			Aug-11
	7.52	13.73	35.98	38.49	82.47	0.47	1.2	12.92	1.13		271.8	3	97	0	1	18	17.8	-22.94			Aug-06
	7.52	13.74	36.00	38.52	82.38	0.47	1.2	12.95	1.13		271.8	3	97	0	1	18	17.77	-23.04			Aug-06
	4.06	9.88	14.79	31.64	96.83	1.12	0.38	14.05	0.99		1,203	0	100	0	0	15	27.51	-24.88			Aug-11
	3.98	9.70	14.42	30.65	94.38	0.9	0.63	14.02	0.99		1,203	0	100	0	0	15	27.38	-24.87			Mar-02
	3.97	9.70	14.50	30.62	94.49	0.9	0.63	14.05	0.99		1,203	0	100	0	0	15	27.32	-24.89			Jan-98
	6.71	12.52	33.20	48.17	129.11	0	1.05	12.21	1.07		1,349	1	99	0	0	44	30.92	-16.9			May-07
	6.72	12.53	33.20	48.18	129.07	0	1.05	12.23	1.08		1,349	1	99	0	0	44	30.77	-16.96			Aug-88
	6.77	12.65	33.50	49.27	131.99	0	0.8	12.22	1.08		1,349	1	99	0	0	44	30.88	-16.96			Dec-11

Fund Name	MARKET Ticker Symbol	MARKET Traded On	FUND TYPE, CATEGORY & OBJECTIVE Fund Type	Category and (Prospectus Objective)	RATINGS Overall Rating	Reward Rating	Risk Rating	Recent Up/ Downgrade	MINIMUMS Open to New Investors	Min Initial Investment
EQ/UBS Growth and Income Portfolio Class IB	US29364E7022		Open End	US Equity Large Cap Blend (Growth & Income)	B-	B-	C+	Down	Y	0
Equinox Aspect Core Diversified Strategy Fund Class A	EQAAX	NAS CM	Open End	Other Alternative (Growth)	C-	D+	C	Up	Y	2,500
Equinox Aspect Core Diversified Strategy Fund Class C	EQACX	NAS CM	Open End	Other Alternative (Growth)	D+	D	C	Up	Y	2,500
Equinox Aspect Core Diversified Strategy Fund Class I	EQAIX	NAS CM	Open End	Other Alternative (Growth)	C-	D+	C	Up	Y	100,000
Equinox BH-DG Strategy Fund Class I	EBHIX	NAS CM	Open End	Other Alternative (Growth)	C+	C	B-	Up	Y	25,000
Equinox Campbell Strategy Fund Class A	EBSAX	NAS CM	Open End	Other Alternative (Growth)	D+	D	D+	Up	Y	2,500
Equinox Campbell Strategy Fund Class C	EBSCX	NAS CM	Open End	Other Alternative (Growth)	D	D	D+	Down	Y	2,500
Equinox Campbell Strategy Fund Class I	EBSIX	NAS CM	Open End	Other Alternative (Growth)	D+	D	D+	Up	Y	100,000
Equinox Campbell Strategy Fund Class P	EBSPX	NAS CM	Open End	Other Alternative (Growth)	D+	D	D+	Up	Y	2,500
Equinox Chesapeake Strategy Fund Class A	ECHAX	NAS CM	Open End	Other Alternative (Growth)	C	C	C		Y	2,500
Equinox Chesapeake Strategy Fund Class C	ECHCX	NAS CM	Open End	Other Alternative (Growth)	C	C	C		Y	2,500
Equinox Chesapeake Strategy Fund Class I	EQCHX	NAS CM	Open End	Other Alternative (Growth)	C+	C	C+	Up	Y	100,000
Equinox Crabel Strategy Fund Class I	EQCRX	NAS CM	Open End	Other Alternative (Growth)	D	D	C-		Y	25,000
Equinox EquityHedge U.S. Strategy Fund Class A Shares	EEHAX	NAS CM	Open End	Long/Short Equity (Growth)	B-	B-	B-	Down	Y	2,500
Equinox EquityHedge U.S. Strategy Fund Class C Shares	EEHCX	NAS CM	Open End	Long/Short Equity (Growth)	B	C+	B+		Y	2,500
Equinox EquityHedge U.S. Strategy Fund Class I Shares	EEHIX	NAS CM	Open End	Long/Short Equity (Growth)	B-	B-	B-	Down	Y	1,000,000
Equinox IPM Systematic Macro Fund Class I	EQIPX	NAS CM	Open End	Other Alternative (Growth)	C	C	C+	Up	Y	200,000,000
Equinox MutualHedge Futures Strategy Fund - Class A	MHFAX	NAS CM	Open End	Other Alternative (Growth)	C-	C-	C-	Down	Y	2,500
Equinox MutualHedge Futures Strategy Fund - Class C	MHFCX	NAS CM	Open End	Other Alternative (Growth)	D+	D+	C-	Down	Y	2,500
Equinox MutualHedge Futures Strategy Fund - Class I	MHFIX	NAS CM	Open End	Other Alternative (Growth)	C-	C-	C-	Down	Y	1,000,000
Equinox Systematica Macro Fund Class I	EBCIX	NAS CM	Open End	Other Alternative (Growth)	D	D	D+	Down	Y	25,000
Equity Hedge A	JAHAX	NAS CM	Open End	Long/Short Equity (Growth)	U	U	U		Y	2,500
EquityCompass Quality Dividend Fund Class A	QDVAX	NAS CM	Open End	US Equity Large Cap Value (Equity-Income)	B-	B-	B-	Down	Y	1,000
EquityCompass Quality Dividend Fund Class C	QDVCX	NAS CM	Open End	US Equity Large Cap Value (Equity-Income)	B-	C+	B-	Down	Y	1,000
EquityCompass Quality Dividend Fund Institutional Class	QDVIX	NAS CM	Open End	US Equity Large Cap Value (Equity-Income)	B-	B-	B-	Down	Y	1,000,000
Essential 40 Stock Fund Class I	ESSIX	NAS CM	Open End	Long/Short Equity (Growth)	C+	C	B	Up	Y	10,000
Essex Environmental Opportunities Fund Institutional Class	GEOSX	NAS CM	Open End	Global Equity Large Cap (Growth)	U	U	U		Y	100,000
Essex Environmental Opportunities Fund Investor Class	EEOFX	NAS CM	Open End	Global Equity Large Cap (Growth)	U	U	U		Y	2,000
EuroPac Gold Fund Class A	EPGFX	NAS CM	Open End	Precious Metals Sector Equity (Precious Metals)	C	C	C-		Y	2,500
EuroPac International Dividend Income Fund Class A	EPDPX	NAS CM	Open End	Global Equity Large Cap (Equity-Income)	C	C	C-	Up	Y	2,500
EuroPac International Dividend Income Fund Class I	EPDIX	NAS CM	Open End	Global Equity Large Cap (Equity-Income)	C	C	C-	Up	Y	15,000
EuroPac International Value Fund Class A	EPIVX	NAS CM	Open End	Global Equity Large Cap (Foreign Stock)	C-	C	D+	Down	Y	2,500
EuroPac International Value Fund Class I	EPVIX	NAS CM	Open End	Global Equity Large Cap (Foreign Stock)	C-	C	D+	Down	Y	15,000
E-Valuator Aggressive RMS Fund R4 Class Shares	EVFGX	NAS CM	Open End	Aggressive Alloc (Aggr Growth)	B-	B	B-	Down	Y	10,000
E-Valuator Aggressive RMS Fund Service Class Shares	EVAGX	NAS CM	Open End	Aggressive Alloc (Aggr Growth)	B-	B	B-	Down	Y	10,000
E-Valuator Conservative RMS Fund R4 Class	EVFCX	NAS CM	Open End	Cautious Alloc (Growth & Income)	B-	C+	B	Up	Y	10,000
E-Valuator Conservative RMS Fund Service Class	EVCLX	NAS CM	Open End	Cautious Alloc (Growth & Income)	B-	C+	B	Up	Y	10,000
E-Valuator Growth RMS Fund R4 Class Shares	EVGRX	NAS CM	Open End	Aggressive Alloc (Growth)	B-	B-	B-	Down	Y	10,000
E-Valuator Growth RMS Fund Service Class Shares	EVGLX	NAS CM	Open End	Aggressive Alloc (Growth)	B-	B-	B-	Down	Y	10,000
E-Valuator Moderate RMS Fund R4 Class Shares	EVFMX	NAS CM	Open End	Moderate Alloc (Growth & Income)	B-	C+	B	Up	Y	10,000
E-Valuator Moderate RMS Fund Service Class Shares	EVMLX	NAS CM	Open End	Moderate Alloc (Growth & Income)	B-	C+	B	Up	Y	10,000
E-Valuator Tactically Managed RMS Fund R4 Class	EVFTX	NAS CM	Open End	Moderate Alloc (Growth & Income)	C+	C+	B-	Up	Y	10,000
E-Valuator Tactically Managed RMS Fund Service Class	EVTTX	NAS CM	Open End	Moderate Alloc (Growth & Income)	C+	C+	B-	Up	Y	10,000
E-Valuator Very Conservative RMS Fund R4 Class	EVVCX	NAS CM	Open End	Cautious Alloc (Growth & Income)	B-	C	B	Up	Y	10,000
E-Valuator Very Conservative RMS Fund Service Class	EVVLX	NAS CM	Open End	Cautious Alloc (Growth & Income)	B-	C	A-	Up	Y	10,000
Eventide Gilead Class A	ETAGX	NAS CM	Open End	US Equity Mid Cap (Growth)	B	A-	C	Up	Y	1,000
Eventide Gilead Class C	ETCGX	NAS CM	Open End	US Equity Mid Cap (Growth)	B	B+	C	Up	Y	1,000
Eventide Gilead Class I	ETILX	NAS CM	Open End	US Equity Mid Cap (Growth)	B	A-	C	Up	Y	100,000
Eventide Gilead Class N	ETGLX	NAS CM	Open End	US Equity Mid Cap (Growth)	B	A-	B-	Up	Y	1,000
Eventide Global Dividend Opportunities Fund Class A Shares	ETADX	NAS CM	Open End	Global Equity Large Cap (Growth & Income)	U	U	U		Y	100,000
Eventide Global Dividend Opportunities Fund Class C Shares	ETCDX	NAS CM	Open End	Global Equity Large Cap (Growth & Income)	U	U	U		Y	1,000
Eventide Global Dividend Opportunities Fund Class I Shares	ETIDX	NAS CM	Open End	Global Equity Large Cap (Growth & Income)	U	U	U		Y	1,000

★ Expanded analysis of this fund is included in Section II.

	TOTAL RETURNS					PERFORMANCE				ASSETS		ASSET ALLOCATION & TURNOVER					BULL & BEAR		FEES		
Min Additional Investment	3-Month Total Return	6-Month Total Return	1-Year Total Return	3-Year Total Return	5-Year Total Return	Dividend Yield (TTM)	Expense Ratio	3-Yr Std Deviation	3-Year Beta	NAV	Total Assets (MIL)	%Cash	%Stocks	%Bonds	%Other	Turnover Ratio	Last Bull Market Total Return	Last Bear Market Total Return	Front End Fee (%)	Back End Fee (%)	Inception Date
	5.18	9.54	21.52	30.91	109.98	0.66	1.05	12.21	1.11		112.4	1	99	0	0	61	24.88	-19.25			Dec-98
500	5.05	6.43	1.56	-1.60		0.78	1.7	7.63	-0.14	9.76	36.2	66	0	32	2	0			5.75		Aug-15
500	4.82	5.98	0.73	-3.97		0.86	2.45	7.6	-0.14	9.56	36.2	66	0	32	2	0				1.00	Aug-15
	5.06	6.56	1.77	-1.14		1.23	1.45	7.62	-0.13	9.74	36.2	66	0	32	2	0					Nov-14
	6.11	9.80	5.36	9.10		0	1.1	11.06	-0.17	11.98	0.08	80	0	0	20	0					Dec-13
500	7.37	7.83	3.82	-11.42		0	1.15	11.49	-0.05	10.05	378.2	42	0	38	20	0			5.75		Mar-13
500	7.10	7.33	3.04	-13.35		0	1.9	11.42	-0.06	9.8	378.2	42	0	38	20	0				1.00	Feb-14
	7.52	7.97	4.10	-10.68		0	0.9	11.48	-0.06	10.15	378.2	42	0	38	20	0					Mar-13
	7.41	7.87	4.10	-10.76		0	0.9	11.46	-0.06	10.14	378.2	42	0	38	20	0					Mar-13
500	8.25	9.46	14.80	10.98	67.27	0	2.1	14.36	1.55	12.72	80.8	53	0	43	4	0			5.75		Aug-15
500	8.03	9.06	13.93	8.61	61.27	0	2.85	14.32	1.54	12.51	80.8	53	0	43	4	0				1.00	Aug-15
	8.29	9.58	15.10	11.87	69.45	0	1.85	14.31	1.54	12.8	80.8	53	0	43	4	0					Sep-12
	-0.72	-0.24	-8.37	-7.30		6.01	1.1	7.38	0.05	8.21	1.7	21	0	57	22	0					Mar-13
500	5.41	8.87	15.44	25.33		2.28	1.45	8.31	0.65	10.36	10.6	54	0	49	-4	0			5.75		Sep-13
500	5.31	8.57	14.51	22.55		2.06	2.2	8.32	0.66	9.96	10.6	54	0	49	-4	0					Sep-13
	5.46	9.00	15.53	26.18		2.49	1.2	8.32	0.66	10.45	10.6	54	0	49	-4	0					Sep-13
	-2.82	-2.25	0.90			0	1.89			9.99	448.6	60	0	30	10	0					Jul-15
500	0.37	-1.82	-4.37	2.79	8.87	2.98	2.02	10.69	-0.11	8.08	259.6	37	0	42	21	78	-3.62	-0.18	5.75		Dec-09
500	0.25	-2.14	-5.12	0.54	4.94	2.25	2.77	10.68	-0.11	7.77	259.6	37	0	42	21	78	-3.98	-0.56		1.00	Dec-09
	0.49	-1.56	-4.11	3.67	10.42	3.23	1.77	10.7	-0.11	8.16	259.6	37	0	42	21	78	-3.47	-0.19			May-11
	6.16	3.89	0.73	-1.90		11.17	0.79	12	-0.12	8.26	1.2	77	0	0	23	0					Jun-14
	3.32						2.16			10.61	2.8	17	65	15	1				5.75		Aug-17
100	4.62	8.52	13.75	22.42		2.16	1.24	9.04	0.75	13.13	75.5	0	100	0	0	44			5.75		Sep-13
100	4.49	8.16	12.93	19.75		1.45	1.99	9.05	0.75	13.19	75.5	0	100	0	0	44				1.00	Oct-13
	4.76	8.74	14.12	22.89		2.4	0.99	9.04	0.75	13.14	75.5	0	100	0	0	44					Oct-16
1,000	8.08	8.99	11.57	4.85		1.05	0.7	5.74			6.4	27	73	0	0	48					Jun-14
	-1.43						1.19			10.32	5.6	6	94	0	0						Sep-17
	-1.52						1.44			10.32	5.6	6	94	0	0						Sep-17
250	-2.20	5.61	12.66	43.56		18.06	1.52	37.98		8.88	73.2	2	95	0	3	21			4.50		Jul-13
250	0.63	5.28	15.52	-2.35	5.38	2.53	1.5	12.94	0.77	8.44	66.0	7	94	0	-1	25	14.6	-17.58	4.50		Jan-14
2,000	0.70	5.41	15.80	-1.53	6.68	2.75	1.25	12.97	0.77	8.44	66.0	7	94	0	-1	25	14.77	-17.49			Jan-14
250	1.76	5.51	15.09	-0.29	-11.49	1.36	1.75	18.35	0.92	7.86	65.3	9	92	0	-2	40	15.52	-23.6	4.50		Apr-10
2,500	1.82	5.63	15.35	0.44	-10.56	1.58	1.5	18.33	0.91	7.87	65.3	9	92	0	-2	40	15.52	-23.6			Jul-13
100	4.44	9.88	18.52	26.19	71.55	0.09	1.25	9.35	0.89	11.67	71.2	3	92	3	2	145					Feb-12
100	5.53	11.12	20.09	27.94	73.93	0.37	0.89	9.34	0.89	11.64	71.2	3	92	3	2	145					May-16
100	2.44	4.96	9.52	12.75	30.67	0.56	1.22	4.02	0.18	10.61	55.9	0	31	58	1	143					Feb-12
100	2.47	5.09	9.87	13.28	31.29	0.79	0.85	4.02	0.17	10.59	55.9	0	31	58	1	143					May-16
100	5.13	9.94	18.71	25.58	68.60	0.23	1.22	8.65	0.83	11.37	226.6	3	81	11	1	125					Feb-12
100	5.17	10.07	19.08	26.13	69.34	0.5	0.85	8.65	0.83	11.32	226.6	3	81	11	1	125					May-16
100	4.25	8.39	15.83	20.97	51.82	0.45	1.2	6.74	0.64	11.2	165.9	2	66	24	1	138					Feb-12
100	4.35	8.60	16.26	21.62	52.63	0.68	0.83	6.75	0.64	11.18	165.9	2	66	24	1	138					May-16
100	3.26	6.64	11.66	13.18	33.63	0.42	1.67				16.2	9	59	23	8	158					May-16
100	3.27	6.86	11.91	14.15	35.45	1.01	1.28			10.57	16.2	9	59	23	8	158					May-16
100	1.40	3.26	6.45	8.21	15.92	0.46	1.22			10.36	16.4	0	16	77	1	190					May-16
100	1.47	3.33	6.73	9.09	17.46	0.65	0.86			10.37	16.4	0	16	77	1	190					May-16
50	7.25	14.18	32.80	30.86	140.31	0	1.46	16.21	1.29	34.13	1,522	8	92	0	0	26	34.76	-25.45	5.75		Oct-09
50	7.06	13.72	31.76	27.92	131.28	0	2.21	16.19	1.29	31.98	1,522	8	92	0	0	26	34.18	-25.69		1.00	Oct-09
50	7.34	14.32	33.09	31.82	143.39	0	1.21	16.21	1.3	34.79	1,522	8	92	0	0	26	34.81	-25.38			Feb-10
50	7.29	14.20	32.85	31.06	140.98	0	1.41	16.21	1.29	34.25	1,522	8	92	0	0	26	34.72	-25.43			Jul-08
50	2.50						0.97			10.21	2.5								5.75		Sep-17
50	2.31						1.22			10.22	2.5								5.75		Sep-17
50	2.52						1.97			10.21	2.5										Sep-17

	MARKET		FUND TYPE, CATEGORY & OBJECTIVE		RATINGS				MINIMUMS	
Fund Name	Ticker Symbol	Traded On	Fund Type	Category and (Prospectus Objective)	Overall Rating	Reward Rating	Risk Rating	Recent Up/ Downgrade	Open to New Investors	Min Initial Investment
Eventide Global Dividend Opportunities Fund Class N Shares	ETNDX	NAS CM	Open End	Global Equity Large Cap (Growth & Income)	U	U	U		Y	1,000
Eventide Healthcare & Life Sciences Fund Class A Shares	ETAHX	NAS CM	Open End	Healthcare Sector Equity (Health)	B	A-	C	Up	Y	1,000
Eventide Healthcare & Life Sciences Fund CLASS C SHARES	ETCHX	NAS CM	Open End	Healthcare Sector Equity (Health)	B	A-	C	Up	Y	1,000
Eventide Healthcare & Life Sciences Fund CLASS I SHARES	ETIHX	NAS CM	Open End	Healthcare Sector Equity (Health)	B	A-	C	Up	Y	100,000
Eventide Healthcare & Life Sciences Fund CLASS N SHARES	ETNHX	NAS CM	Open End	Healthcare Sector Equity (Health)	B	A-	C	Up	Y	1,000
Eventide Multi-Asset Income Fund Class A	ETAMX	NAS CM	Open End	Alloc (Income)	C	C	B	Up	Y	1,000
Eventide Multi-Asset Income Fund Class C	ETCMX	NAS CM	Open End	Alloc (Income)	C	C	B	Up	Y	1,000
Eventide Multi-Asset Income Fund Class I	ETIMX	NAS CM	Open End	Alloc (Income)	C	C+	B	Up	Y	100,000
Eventide Multi-Asset Income Fund Class N	ETNMX	NAS CM	Open End	Alloc (Income)	C	C	B	Up	Y	1,000
Evercore Equity Fund	EWMCX	NAS CM	Open End	US Equity Large Cap Growth (Growth)	B-	B	B-	Down	Y	1,000
Evermore Global Value Fund Institutional Class	EVGIX	NAS CM	Open End	Global Equity Mid/Small Cap (World Stock)	B	B	B+		Y	1,000,000
Evermore Global Value Fund Investor Class	EVGBX	NAS CM	Open End	Global Equity Mid/Small Cap (World Stock)	B	B	B+		Y	5,000
Fairholme Allocation Fund	FAAFX	NAS CM	Open End	Moderate Alloc (Asset Alloc)	D	D	D	Down		10,000
Fairholme Fund	FAIRX	NAS CM	Open End	US Equity Large Cap Value (Growth)	C	C-	C	Up	Y	10,000
Fallen Angels Income Fund	FAINX	NAS CM	Open End	Aggressive Alloc (Income)	B-	C+	B-	Down	Y	10,000
FAM Equity-Income Fund Investor Class	FAMEX	NAS CM	Open End	US Equity Mid Cap (Equity-Income)	B	B	B+		Y	500
FAM Small Cap Fund Institutional Class	FAMDX	NAS CM	Open End	US Equity Small Cap (Small Company)	B	B	B+	Up	Y	500,000
FAM Small Cap Fund Investor Class	FAMFX	NAS CM	Open End	US Equity Small Cap (Small Company)	B	B	B+	Up	Y	500
FAM Value Fund Institutional Class	FAMWX	NAS CM	Open End	US Equity Mid Cap (Growth)	B	B	B+			500,000
FAM Value Fund Investor Class	FAMVX	NAS CM	Open End	US Equity Mid Cap (Growth)	B	B	B+		Y	500
FBP Appreciation & Income Opportunities Fund	FBPBX	NAS CM	Open End	Aggressive Alloc (Growth & Income)	C+	C+	B-	Down	Y	5,000
FBP Equity & Dividend Plus Fund	FBPEX	NAS CM	Open End	US Equity Large Cap Value (Equity-Income)	C+	C+	C+	Down	Y	5,000
FDP BlackRock Capital Appreciation Fund Inst Shares	MADDX	NAS CM	Open End	US Equity Large Cap Growth (Growth)	B	B-	B	Up	Y	2,000,000
FDP BlackRock Capital Appreciation Fund Investor A Shares	MDDDX	NAS CM	Open End	US Equity Large Cap Growth (Growth)	B	B-	B	Up	Y	1,000
FDP BlackRock Capital Appreciation Fund Investor C Shares	MCDDX	NAS CM	Open End	US Equity Large Cap Growth (Growth)	B-	C+	B	Down	Y	1,000
FDP BlackRock Equity Dividend Fund Institutional Shares	MAVVX	NAS CM	Open End	US Equity Large Cap Value (Growth & Income)	B-	B	B-	Up	Y	2,000,000
FDP BlackRock Equity Dividend Fund Investor A Shares	MDVVX	NAS CM	Open End	US Equity Large Cap Value (Growth & Income)	B-	B-	B-	Up	Y	1,000
FDP BlackRock Equity Dividend Fund Investor C Shares	MCVVX	NAS CM	Open End	US Equity Large Cap Value (Growth & Income)	B-	B-	B-	Up	Y	1,000
FDP BlackRock International Fund Institutional Shares	MAIQX	NAS CM	Open End	Global Equity Large Cap (Growth)	B-	C+	B-	Up	Y	2,000,000
FDP BlackRock International Fund Investor A Shares	MDIQX	NAS CM	Open End	Global Equity Large Cap (Growth)	B-	C+	B-	Up	Y	1,000
FDP BlackRock International Fund Investor C Shares	MCIQX	NAS CM	Open End	Global Equity Large Cap (Growth)	B-	C+	B-	Up	Y	1,000
Federated Absolute Return Fund Class A Shares	FMAAX	NAS CM	Open End	Market Neutral (Growth)	C-	D+	C	Up	Y	1,500
Federated Absolute Return Fund Class B Shares	FMBBX	NAS CM	Open End	Market Neutral (Growth)	D+	D+	C			1,500
Federated Absolute Return Fund Class C Shares	FMRCX	NAS CM	Open End	Market Neutral (Growth)	D+	D+	C		Y	1,500
Federated Absolute Return Fund Class Institutional Shares	FMIIX	NAS CM	Open End	Market Neutral (Growth)	C-	D+	C	Up	Y	1,000,000
Federated Capital Income Fund Class A Shares	CAPAX	NAS CM	Open End	Cautious Alloc (Income)	C+	C+	B-		Y	1,500
Federated Capital Income Fund Class B Shares	CAPBX	NAS CM	Open End	Cautious Alloc (Income)	C+	C	B-		Y	1,500
Federated Capital Income Fund Class C Shares	CAPCX	NAS CM	Open End	Cautious Alloc (Income)	C+	C	B-		Y	1,500
Federated Capital Income Fund Class F Shares	CAPFX	NAS CM	Open End	Cautious Alloc (Income)	C+	C+	B-		Y	1,500
Federated Capital Income Fund Class R	CAPRX	NAS CM	Open End	Cautious Alloc (Income)	C+	C	B-		Y	0
Federated Capital Income Fund Institutional Class	CAPSX	NAS CM	Open End	Cautious Alloc (Income)	C+	C+	B-		Y	1,000,000
Federated Clover Small Value Fund Class A	VSFAX	NAS CM	Open End	US Equity Small Cap (Small Company)	B	B	B	Up	Y	1,500
Federated Clover Small Value Fund Class C	VSFCX	NAS CM	Open End	US Equity Small Cap (Small Company)	B	B-	B	Up	Y	1,500
Federated Clover Small Value Fund Class R	VSFRX	NAS CM	Open End	US Equity Small Cap (Small Company)	B	B	B	Up	Y	0
Federated Clover Small Value Fund Class R6	VSFSX	NAS CM	Open End	US Equity Small Cap (Small Company)	B	B	B	Up	Y	0
Federated Clover Small Value Fund Institutional Shares	VSFIX	NAS CM	Open End	US Equity Small Cap (Small Company)	B	B	B	Up	Y	1,000,000
Federated Equity Advantage Fund Class A	FEKAX	NAS CM	Open End	US Equity Small Cap (Growth)	C-	C-	B+	Up	Y	1,500
Federated Equity Advantage Fund Institutional Shares	FEKIX	NAS CM	Open End	US Equity Small Cap (Growth)	C-	C-	B+	Up	Y	1,000,000
Federated Equity Income Fund, Inc. Class A Shares	LEIFX	NAS CM	Open End	US Equity Large Cap Value (Equity-Income)	B-	C+	B	Up	Y	1,500
Federated Equity Income Fund, Inc. Class B Shares	LEIBX	NAS CM	Open End	US Equity Large Cap Value (Equity-Income)	B-	C+	B	Up	Y	1,500
Federated Equity Income Fund, Inc. Class C Shares	LEICX	NAS CM	Open End	US Equity Large Cap Value (Equity-Income)	B-	C+	B	Up	Y	1,500
Federated Equity Income Fund, Inc. Class F Shares	LFEIX	NAS CM	Open End	US Equity Large Cap Value (Equity-Income)	B-	C+	B	Up	Y	1,500

★Expanded analysis of this fund is included in Section II.

Min Additional Investment	TOTAL RETURNS: 3-Month Total Return	6-Month Total Return	1-Year Total Return	3-Year Total Return	5-Year Total Return	PERFORMANCE: Dividend Yield (TTM)	Expense Ratio	3-Yr Std Deviation	3-Year Beta	ASSETS: NAV	Total Assets (MIL)	ASSET ALLOCATION & TURNOVER: %Cash	%Stocks	%Bonds	%Other	Turnover Ratio	BULL & BEAR: Last Bull Market Total Return	Last Bear Market Total Return	FEES: Front End Fee (%)	Back End Fee (%)	Inception Date
50	2.48						1.17			10.21	2.5										Sep-17
50	4.76	24.11	45.51	41.13	194.31	0	1.6	29.9	1.76	28.57	437.8	7	93	0	0	27			5.75		Dec-12
50	4.56	23.60	44.39	37.99	183.61	0	2.35	29.88	1.76	27.51	437.8	7	93	0	0	27				1.00	Dec-12
50	4.81	24.26	45.83	42.17	198.04	0	1.35	29.9	1.76	28.94	437.8	7	93	0	0	27					Dec-12
50	4.78	24.12	45.57	41.34	195.32	0	1.55	29.9	1.76	28.67	437.8	7	93	0	0	27					Dec-12
50	1.19	3.52	11.72			2.99	1.51			11.14	91.8	9	55	25	1	38			5.75		Jul-15
50	0.98	3.23	10.93			2.33	2.26			11.12	91.8	9	55	25	1	38					Jul-15
50	1.23	3.63	11.97			3.23	1.26			11.14	91.8	9	55	25	1	38					Jul-15
50	1.20	3.55	11.78			3.05	1.46			11.14	91.8	9	55	25	1	38					Jul-15
100	8.33	12.83	25.34	27.80	109.50	0.15	1.01	11.3	1.07	17.32	142.3	4	96	0	0	23	27.59	-16.78			Dec-45
100	-0.95	7.58	19.00	51.54	98.35	0.21	1.25	11.38	0.62	15.2	580.1	4	93	0	2	59	14.04	-30.04			Dec-09
100	-1.02	7.42	18.72	50.42	95.99	0.21	1.5	11.39	0.62	15.08	580.1	4	93	0	2	59	13.96	-30.06			Dec-09
1,000	0.43	4.17	-5.86	-7.67	23.99	2.14	1.01	21.76	-2.67	7.98	114.2	22	42	8	0	14	36.73	-25.6			Dec-10
1,000	0.42	6.73	-5.95	3.97	40.22	2	1.03	23.86	1.13	20.14	1,876	19	32	16	0	19	29.98	-30.59			Dec-99
1,000	4.93	6.89	13.67	20.02	54.87	0.75	2.2	8.6	1.26	11.74	10.4	10	67	10	2	15	15.53	-11.01			Nov-06
50	4.19	7.64	12.63	34.74	93.10	0.69	1.27	9.48	0.78	30.11	225.3	6	94	0	0	26	24.27	-14.37			Apr-96
	1.64	4.31	4.66	25.42	89.50	0	1.18	13.42	0.83	18.26	162.4	7	93	0	0	26					Jan-16
50	1.63	4.25	4.55	25.08	88.98	0	1.38	13.4	0.83	18.21	162.4	7	93	0	0	26					Mar-12
	6.47	11.10	17.16	32.13	103.02		0.99	10.14	0.9	73.64	1,262	9	91	0	0	4	24.48	-18.36			Jan-17
50	6.43	11.03	17.00	31.95	102.73	0	1.19	10.14	0.9	73.52	1,262	9	91	0	0	4	24.48	-18.36			Jan-87
	5.11	8.11	11.47	17.30	62.20	2.01	1.16	10.18	0.92	19.26	34.7	11	74	15	0	18	17.91	-18.08			Jul-89
	5.07	9.71	12.40	22.04	77.34	1.89	1.25	10.76	0.97	26.29	27.1	3	97	0	0	19	21.78	-25.25			Jul-93
	5.71	8.77	24.24	24.83	87.66	0	0.95	10.92	0.98	15.86	88.3	1	99	0	0	48	28.44	-18.23			Jul-05
50	5.63	8.62	23.99	23.94	85.29	0	1.2	10.93	0.98	15.27	88.3	1	99	0	0	48	28.28	-18.26	5.25		Jul-05
50	5.40	8.13	22.95	20.99	78.30	0	1.97	10.93	0.98	13.54	88.3	1	99	0	0	48	27.63	-18.5		1.00	Jul-05
	5.97	12.28	16.00	26.22	90.49	1.49	0.89	13.2	1.23	16.39	89.9	4	96	0	0	14	24.77	-19.79			Jul-05
50	5.87	12.09	15.71	25.30	88.02	1.32	1.14	13.18	1.23	16.22	89.9	4	96	0	0	14	24.69	-19.93	5.25		Jul-05
50	5.73	11.71	14.88	22.51	81.07	0.81	1.91	13.18	1.23	15.86	89.9	4	96	0	0	14	24.03	-20.16		1.00	Jul-05
	5.68	10.50	28.53	23.49	38.34	1.29	1.15	11.72	0.91	14.14	102.5	0	96	0	4	30	13.56	-22.03			Jul-05
50	5.63	10.39	28.32	22.54	36.58	1.14	1.4	11.7	0.91	14.05	102.5	0	96	0	4	30	13.39	-22.13	5.25		Jul-05
50	5.42	9.98	27.29	19.76	31.57	0	2.16	11.68	0.91	13.99	102.5	0	96	0	4	30	12.85	-22.4		1.00	Jul-05
100	2.96	3.18	5.59	-1.33	9.26	0	1.34	4.43	8.8	9.88	138.6	25	125	-61	12	118	-0.98	-0.5	5.50		Dec-00
100	2.87	2.87	4.88	-3.49	5.27	0	2.09	4.44	9.35	9.66	138.6	25	125	-61	12	118	-1.33	-0.81		5.50	Dec-00
100	2.78	2.78	4.79	-3.51	5.19	0	2.09	4.47	9.17	9.61	138.6	25	125	-61	12	118	-1.44	-0.81		1.00	Dec-00
	3.10	3.31	5.92	-0.57	10.69	0	1.09	4.46	8.78	9.98	138.6	25	125	-61	12	118	-0.79	-0.4			Jun-07
100	2.93	6.13	10.04	10.87	29.23	3.9	0.9	5.94	0.52	8.13	1,801	1	41	38	14	71	12.28	-7.23	5.50		May-88
100	2.86	5.71	9.18	8.35	24.56	3.15	1.66	5.99	0.53	8.15	1,801	1	41	38	14	71	11.76	-7.51		5.50	Sep-94
100	2.73	5.72	9.20	8.36	24.48	3.16	1.66	5.98	0.52	8.13	1,801	1	41	38	14	71	11.78	-7.51		1.00	Apr-93
100	2.93	5.99	10.04	10.72	29.22	3.89	0.91	6	0.53	8.12	1,801	1	41	38	14	71	12.29	-7.23	1.00		May-96
	2.85	5.99	9.79	10.19	28.01	3.69	1.15	5.95	0.52	8.14	1,801	1	41	38	14	71	11.96	-7.42			Jun-13
	3.00	6.25	10.30	11.70	30.81	4.14	0.65	5.94	0.52	8.14	1,801	1	41	38	14	71	12.43	-7.23			Mar-12
100	3.91	9.90	12.14	26.25	83.28	0.46	1.27	12.65	0.87	25.93	630.1	2	98	0	0	66	24.65	-24.87	5.50		Feb-96
100	3.68	9.49	11.26	23.42	76.51	0	2.02	12.67	0.87	24.68	630.1	2	98	0	0	66	24.16	-25.13		1.00	Feb-96
	3.86	9.85	12.08	25.99	82.28	0.47	1.41	12.66	0.87	25.51	630.1	2	98	0	0	66	24.5	-24.96			Dec-10
	4.01	10.08	12.49	26.82	84.11	0.69	0.95	12.66	0.87	25.9	630.1	2	98	0	0	66	24.65	-24.87			Mar-16
	3.95	10.07	12.39	27.18	85.57	0.67	1.02	12.67	0.87	26	630.1	2	98	0	0	66	24.83	-24.77			Mar-09
100	5.73	11.21	17.76			0	1.23			14.04	3.3	1	99	0	0	82			5.50		Feb-16
	5.79	11.34	18.07			0	0.98			14.09	3.3	1	99	0	0	82					Feb-16
100	6.87	11.42	16.05	18.78	73.40	1.84	1.14	10.46	0.98	25.31	1,174	4	93	3	0	133	21.84	-12.19	5.50		Dec-86
100	6.68	11.01	15.19	15.97	66.72	1.12	1.95	10.45	0.98	25.23	1,174	4	93	3	0	133	21.24	-12.46		5.50	Sep-94
100	6.68	11.02	15.16	16.07	66.91	1.14	1.9	10.44	0.98	25.26	1,174	4	93	3	0	133	21.29	-12.5		1.00	May-93
100	6.80	11.32	15.81	17.90	71.33	1.62	1.39	10.45	0.98	25.33	1,174	4	93	3	0	133	21.62	-12.3	1.00		Nov-93

	MARKET		FUND TYPE, CATEGORY & OBJECTIVE		RATINGS				MINIMUMS	
Fund Name	Ticker Symbol	Traded On	Fund Type	Category and (Prospectus Objective)	Overall Rating	Reward Rating	Risk Rating	Recent Up/ Downgrade	Open to New Investors	Min Initial Investment
Federated Equity Income Fund, Inc. Class R Shares	FDERX	NAS CM	Open End	US Equity Large Cap Value (Equity-Income)	B-	C+	B	Up	Y	0
Federated Equity Income Fund, Inc. Institutional Shares	LEISX	NAS CM	Open End	US Equity Large Cap Value (Equity-Income)	B-	C+	B	Up	Y	1,000,000
Federated Global Allocation Fund Class A Shares	FSTBX	NAS CM	Open End	Alloc (Asset Alloc)	B-	C+	B	Up	Y	1,500
Federated Global Allocation Fund Class B Shares	FSBBX	NAS CM	Open End	Alloc (Asset Alloc)	B-	C+	B	Up	Y	1,500
Federated Global Allocation Fund Class C Shares	FSBCX	NAS CM	Open End	Alloc (Asset Alloc)	B-	C+	B	Up	Y	1,500
Federated Global Allocation Fund Class R Shares	FSBKX	NAS CM	Open End	Alloc (Asset Alloc)	B-	C+	B	Up	Y	0
Federated Global Allocation Fund Class R6	FSBLX	NAS CM	Open End	Alloc (Asset Alloc)	B-	C+	B	Up	Y	0
Federated Global Allocation Fund Institutional Shares	SBFIX	NAS CM	Open End	Alloc (Asset Alloc)	B-	C+	B	Up	Y	1,000,000
Federated Global Strategic Value Div Fund Cls A Shares	GVDSX	NAS CM	Open End	Global Equity (Equity-Income)	U	U	U		Y	1,500
Federated Global Strategic Value Div Fund Cls C Shares	GVDCX	NAS CM	Open End	Global Equity (Equity-Income)	U	U	U		Y	1,500
Federated Global Strategic Value Div Fund Cls R6 Shares	GVDLX	NAS CM	Open End	Global Equity (Equity-Income)	U	U	U		Y	0
Federated Global Strategic Value Dividend Fund Inst Shares	GVDIX	NAS CM	Open End	Global Equity (Equity-Income)	U	U	U		Y	1,000,000
Federated International Dividend Strategy Portfolio	FIDPX	NAS CM	Open End	Global Equity Large Cap (Equity-Income)	C	C	C		Y	0
Federated International Leaders Fund Class A Shares	FGFAX	NAS CM	Open End	Global Equity Large Cap (World Stock)	C+	B-	C	Up	Y	1,500
Federated International Leaders Fund Class B Shares	FGFBX	NAS CM	Open End	Global Equity Large Cap (World Stock)	C+	C+	C	Up	Y	1,500
Federated International Leaders Fund Class C Shares	FGFCX	NAS CM	Open End	Global Equity Large Cap (World Stock)	C+	C+	C	Up	Y	1,500
Federated International Leaders Fund Class R	FGFRX	NAS CM	Open End	Global Equity Large Cap (World Stock)	C+	B-	C	Up	Y	0
Federated International Leaders Fund Class R6 Shares	FGRSX	NAS CM	Open End	Global Equity Large Cap (World Stock)	C+	B-	C	Up	Y	0
Federated International Leaders Fund Institutional Class	FGFLX	NAS CM	Open End	Global Equity Large Cap (World Stock)	C+	B-	C	Up	Y	1,000,000
Federated International Small-Mid Company Fund Class A	ISCAX	NAS CM	Open End	Global Equity Mid/Small Cap (Growth)	B	B	B	Up	Y	1,500
Federated International Small-Mid Company Fund Class B	ISCBX	NAS CM	Open End	Global Equity Mid/Small Cap (Growth)	B	B	B-	Up		1,500
Federated International Small-Mid Company Fund Class C	ISCCX	NAS CM	Open End	Global Equity Mid/Small Cap (Growth)	B	B	B-	Up	Y	1,500
Federated Intl Small-Mid Company Fund Inst Cls	ISCIX	NAS CM	Open End	Global Equity Mid/Small Cap (Growth)	B	B	B	Up	Y	1,000,000
Federated Intl Strategic Value Dividend Fund Cls A Shares	IVFAX	NAS CM	Open End	Global Equity Large Cap (Growth & Income)	C	C	C		Y	1,500
Federated Intl Strategic Value Dividend Fund Cls C Shares	IVFCX	NAS CM	Open End	Global Equity Large Cap (Growth & Income)	C	C	C		Y	1,500
Federated Intl Strategic Value Dividend Fund Cls R6 Shares	IVFLX	NAS CM	Open End	Global Equity Large Cap (Growth & Income)	C	C	C		Y	0
Federated Intl Strategic Value Dividend Fund Inst Shares	IVFIX	NAS CM	Open End	Global Equity Large Cap (Growth & Income)	C	C	C		Y	1,000,000
Federated Kaufmann Fund Class A Shares	KAUAX	NAS CM	Open End	US Equity Mid Cap (Aggr Growth)	B	B	B	Up	Y	1,500
Federated Kaufmann Fund Class B Shares	KAUBX	NAS CM	Open End	US Equity Mid Cap (Aggr Growth)	B	B	B	Up	Y	1,500
Federated Kaufmann Fund Class C Shares	KAUCX	NAS CM	Open End	US Equity Mid Cap (Aggr Growth)	B	B	B	Up	Y	1,500
Federated Kaufmann Fund Class R Shares	KAUFX	NAS CM	Open End	US Equity Mid Cap (Aggr Growth)	B	B+	B	Up	Y	0
Federated Kaufmann Fund Institutional Shares	KAUIX	NAS CM	Open End	US Equity Mid Cap (Aggr Growth)	B	B+	C+	Up	Y	1,000,000
Federated Kaufmann Large Cap Fund Class A	KLCAX	NAS CM	Open End	US Equity Large Cap Growth (Growth)	B-	B	B-	Down	Y	1,500
Federated Kaufmann Large Cap Fund Class C	KLCCX	NAS CM	Open End	US Equity Large Cap Growth (Growth)	B-	B	C+	Down	Y	1,500
Federated Kaufmann Large Cap Fund Class R Shares	KLCKX	NAS CM	Open End	US Equity Large Cap Growth (Growth)	B-	B	B-	Down	Y	0
Federated Kaufmann Large Cap Fund Class R6	KLCSX	NAS CM	Open End	US Equity Large Cap Growth (Growth)	B-	B	B-	Down	Y	0
Federated Kaufmann Large Cap Fund Institutional Shares	KLCIX	NAS CM	Open End	US Equity Large Cap Growth (Growth)	B-	B	B-	Down	Y	1,000,000
Federated Kaufmann Small Cap Fund Class A Shares	FKASX	NAS CM	Open End	US Equity Small Cap (Small Company)	B+	A	B-	Up	Y	1,500
Federated Kaufmann Small Cap Fund Class B Shares	FKBSX	NAS CM	Open End	US Equity Small Cap (Small Company)	B+	A	B-	Up	Y	1,500
Federated Kaufmann Small Cap Fund Class C Shares	FKCSX	NAS CM	Open End	US Equity Small Cap (Small Company)	B+	A	B-	Up	Y	1,500
Federated Kaufmann Small Cap Fund Class R Shares	FKKSX	NAS CM	Open End	US Equity Small Cap (Small Company)	B+	A	B-	Up	Y	0
Federated Kaufmann Small Cap Fund Class R6 Shares	FKALX	NAS CM	Open End	US Equity Small Cap (Small Company)	B+	A	B-		Y	0
Federated Kaufmann Small Cap Fund Institutional Shares	FKAIX	NAS CM	Open End	US Equity Small Cap (Small Company)	B+	A	B-	Up	Y	1,000,000
Federated Max-Cap Index Fund Class C Shares	MXCCX	NAS CM	Open End	US Equity Large Cap Blend (Growth & Income)	B-	B-	B	Down	Y	1,500
Federated Max-Cap Index Fund Class R Shares	FMXKX	NAS CM	Open End	US Equity Large Cap Blend (Growth & Income)	B	B-	B		Y	0
Federated Max-Cap Index Fund Institutional Shares	FISPX	NAS CM	Open End	US Equity Large Cap Blend (Growth & Income)	B	B	B		Y	1,000,000
Federated Max-Cap Index Fund Service Shares	FMXSX	NAS CM	Open End	US Equity Large Cap Blend (Growth & Income)	B	B	B		Y	1,000,000
Federated MDT All Cap Core Fund Class A Shares	QAACX	NAS CM	Open End	US Equity Large Cap Value (Growth)	B	B	B	Up	Y	1,500
Federated MDT All Cap Core Fund Class C Shares	QCACX	NAS CM	Open End	US Equity Large Cap Value (Growth)	B	B-	B	Up	Y	1,500
Federated MDT All Cap Core Fund Class R6 Shares	QKACX	NAS CM	Open End	US Equity Large Cap Value (Growth)	B-	B	C+	Down	Y	0
Federated MDT All Cap Core Fund Institutional Shares	QIACX	NAS CM	Open End	US Equity Large Cap Value (Growth)	B-	B	C+	Down	Y	1,000,000
Federated MDT Balanced Fund Class A Shares	QABGX	NAS CM	Open End	Moderate Alloc (Balanced)	B-	C+	B	Down	Y	1,500

★ Expanded analysis of this fund is included in Section II.

	TOTAL RETURNS					PERFORMANCE				ASSETS		ASSET ALLOCATION & TURNOVER					BULL & BEAR		FEES		
Min Additional Investment	3-Month Total Return	6-Month Total Return	1-Year Total Return	3-Year Total Return	5-Year Total Return	Dividend Yield (TTM)	Expense Ratio	3-Yr Std Deviation	3-Year Beta	NAV	Total Assets (MIL)	%Cash	%Stocks	%Bonds	%Other	Turnover Ratio	Last Bull Market Total Return	Last Bear Market Total Return	Front End Fee (%)	Back End Fee (%)	Inception Date
	6.83	11.33	15.86	18.16	71.97	1.69	1.35	10.46	0.98	25.31	1,174	4	93	3	0	133	21.49	-12.37			Jan-13
	6.94	11.56	16.34	19.65	75.59	2.06	0.88	10.46	0.98	25.3	1,174	4	93	3	0	133	21.79	-12.19			Mar-12
100	3.67	8.15	17.05	14.88	43.47	1.56	1.17	7.39	0.66	20.16	426.1	4	64	25	8	105	14.66	-13.4	5.50		Dec-68
100	3.45	7.69	16.04	12.08	37.68	0.84	1.98	7.38	0.65	19.67	426.1	4	64	25	8	105	14.15	-13.7		5.50	Aug-96
100	3.42	7.75	16.12	12.29	38.08	0.91	1.92	7.38	0.65	19.6	426.1	4	64	25	8	105	14.21	-13.69		1.00	Apr-93
	3.53	7.92	16.48	13.40	40.44	1.25	1.6	7.39	0.66	20.02	426.1	4	64	25	8	105	14.41	-13.54			Apr-03
	3.75	8.31	17.33	15.33	44.03	1.85	0.86	7.4	0.66	20.16	426.1	4	64	25	8	105	14.66	-13.4			Jun-16
	3.73	8.31	17.35	15.91	45.50	1.86	0.88	7.37	0.65	20.27	426.1	4	64	25	8	105	14.91	-13.29			Jun-09
100	3.17	6.24	14.83				1.11			5.47	1.7	2	97	0	0	23			5.50		Jan-17
100	2.99	5.88	14.33				1.86			5.47	1.7	2	97	0	0	23				1.00	Jan-17
	3.23	6.36	15.05				0.85			5.47	1.7	2	97	0	0	23					Jan-17
	3.22	6.36	15.04				0.86			5.47	1.7	2	97	0	0	23					Jan-17
	-1.13	1.28	13.54			4.47	0.01			8.65	112.0	2	98	0	0	30					Feb-15
100	3.65	10.23	27.97	20.80	49.77	1.69	1.25	13.6	1.05	37.39	2,004	10	90	0	0	34	23.27	-29.47	5.50		Sep-98
100	3.43	9.82	26.96	18.08	44.20	1.18	2	13.58	1.05	34.89	2,004	10	90	0	0	34	22.71	-29.69		5.50	Sep-98
100	3.45	9.81	26.98	18.13	44.26	1.08	2	13.58	1.05	34.78	2,004	10	90	0	0	34	22.69	-29.7		1.00	Sep-98
	3.59	10.14	27.74	20.17	48.25	1.61	1.44	13.59	1.05	37.19	2,004	10	90	0	0	34	22.91	-29.62			Jun-13
	3.71	10.41	28.34	21.93	51.80	1.98	0.94	13.6	1.05	37.37	2,004	10	90	0	0	34	23.27	-29.47			Aug-13
	3.73	10.39	28.29	21.75	51.68	1.94	0.99	13.59	1.05	37.42	2,004	10	90	0	0	34	23.38	-29.36			Jun-10
100	5.75	14.41	34.69	35.07	58.86	0	1.85	13.32	1.06	40.01	166.6	1	99	0	0	39	24.17	-29.35	5.50		Feb-96
100	5.54	13.98	33.61	31.89	52.66	0	2.65	13.31	1.06	31.13	166.6	1	99	0	0	39	23.62	-29.6		5.50	Feb-96
100	5.54	13.96	33.61	31.89	52.68	0	2.65	13.31	1.06	31.09	166.6	1	99	0	0	39	23.6	-29.58		1.00	Feb-96
	5.82	14.54	34.95	35.89	60.51	0	1.65	13.31	1.06	40.86	166.6	1	99	0	0	39	24.25	-29.28			Mar-08
100	0.13	2.11	14.35	5.91	16.43	3.8	1.11	10.76	0.7	3.77	772.8	1	98	0	0	27	12.4	-15.92	5.50		Jun-08
100	0.00	1.79	13.68	3.58	12.12	3.14	1.86	10.65	0.7	3.74	772.8	1	98	0	0	27	12.02	-16.27		1.00	Jun-08
	-0.06	2.24	14.64	6.37	17.48		0.85	10.64	0.7	3.77	772.8	1	98	0	0	27	12.84	-15.82			Jan-17
	-0.06	2.24	14.63	6.37	17.47	4.05	0.86	10.64	0.7	3.77	772.8	1	98	0	0	27	12.84	-15.82			Jun-08
100	5.41	11.60	27.73	39.04	117.63	0	2	13.95	1.14	5.59	5,697	17	81	0	2	47	26.19	-25.63	5.50		Apr-01
100	5.37	11.31	27.26	36.97	111.91	0	2.55	13.94	1.13	4.65	5,697	17	81	0	2	47	25.85	-25.71		5.50	Apr-01
100	5.39	11.34	27.32	36.79	111.71	0	2.55	13.96	1.14	4.64	5,697	17	81	0	2	47	25.84	-25.71		1.00	Apr-01
	5.40	11.57	27.68	38.96	117.34	0	2	13.93	1.14	5.6	5,697	17	81	0	2	47	26.2	-25.63			Feb-86
	5.73	11.91	28.51	39.87	118.76		1.55	13.94	1.14	5.64	5,697	17	81	0	2	47	26.2	-25.63			Dec-16
100	4.53	8.24	23.26	31.72	105.93	0	1.09	10.91	0.94	23.47	3,311	7	93	0	0	44	33.29	-20.36	5.50		Dec-07
100	4.36	7.88	22.29	28.72	97.89	0	1.87	10.9	0.94	21.73	3,311	7	93	0	0	44	32.74	-20.65		1.00	Dec-07
	4.40	8.06	22.77	30.20	101.82	0	1.48	10.91	0.94	22.48	3,311	7	93	0	0	44	33.04	-20.53			Dec-07
	4.60	8.46	23.62	33.00	108.99	0	0.78	10.9	0.94	24.06	3,311	7	93	0	0	44	33.54	-20.28			Dec-13
	4.57	8.38	23.57	32.74	108.48	0	0.84	10.9	0.94	24	3,311	7	93	0	0	44	33.54	-20.28			Dec-07
100	8.39	16.87	37.87	53.52	132.02	0	1.36	16.02	1	32.17	860.2	10	88	0	2	46	40.09	-29.15	5.50		Dec-02
100	8.21	16.47	37.07	51.00	125.61	0	2.03	16.03	1	27.86	860.2	10	88	0	2	46	39.64	-29.33		5.50	Dec-02
100	8.25	16.51	37.06	50.98	125.69	0	1.99	16.01	1	27.87	860.2	10	88	0	2	46	39.64	-29.33		1.00	Dec-02
	8.39	16.87	37.90	53.75	132.70	0	1.36	16.04	1	32.3	860.2	10	88	0	2	46	40.07	-29.14			Nov-05
	8.49	16.97	37.99	53.65	132.22		0.89	16.02	1	32.21	860.2	10	88	0	2	46	40.09	-29.15			Sep-17
	8.52	17.13	38.45	54.90	134.11	0	0.9	16.02	1	32.48	860.2	10	88	0	2	46	40.09	-29.15			Dec-15
100	6.31	10.80	20.38	31.79	99.39	0.5	1.44	10.12	1	12.52	439.0	0	100	0	0	31	24.02	-16.73		1.00	Nov-97
	6.40	11.00	20.82	33.15	102.68	0.73	1.11	10.12	1	12.7	439.0	0	100	0	0	31	24.17	-16.62			Apr-03
	6.68	11.46	21.72	36.20	110.41	1.3	0.36	10.13	1	12.85	439.0	0	100	0	0	31	24.68	-16.3			Jul-90
	6.59	11.32	21.32	34.96	107.18	1.06	0.66	10.11	1	12.71	439.0	0	100	0	0	31	24.54	-16.5			Sep-93
100	6.71	13.52	20.72	28.03	108.21	0.7	1.39	11.14	1.05	27.46	145.7	2	98	0	0	77	26.21	-23.03	5.50		Feb-03
100	6.49	13.10	19.86	25.13	100.34	0.14	2.14	11.16	1.05	26.07	145.7	2	98	0	0	77	25.66	-23.3		1.00	Sep-05
	6.80	13.69	21.15	27.56	105.54	0	1.08	11.18	1.05	27.3	145.7	2	98	0	0	77	25.95	-23.23			Dec-06
	6.76	13.67	21.06	29.13	111.19	0.93	1.09	11.17	1.05	27.74	145.7	2	98	0	0	77	26.53	-23.02			Oct-02
100	4.13	8.50	13.86	17.50	58.20	1.42	1.33	6.7	0.63	18.64	140.3	2	63	33	1	82	15.91	-14.77	5.50		Sep-05

	MARKET			FUND TYPE, CATEGORY & OBJECTIVE	RATINGS				MINIMUMS	
Fund Name	Ticker Symbol	Traded On	Fund Type	Category and (Prospectus Objective)	Overall Rating	Reward Rating	Risk Rating	Recent Up/ Downgrade	Open to New Investors	Min Initial Investment
Federated MDT Balanced Fund Class C Shares	QCBGX	NAS CM	Open End	Moderate Alloc (Balanced)	B-	C+	B	Down	Y	1,500
Federated MDT Balanced Fund Class R6 Shares	QKBGX	NAS CM	Open End	Moderate Alloc (Balanced)	B-	C+	B	Down	Y	0
Federated MDT Balanced Fund Institutional Shares	QIBGX	NAS CM	Open End	Moderate Alloc (Balanced)	B-	C+	B	Down	Y	1,000,000
Federated MDT Large Cap Growth Fund Class A Shares	QALGX	NAS CM	Open End	US Equity Large Cap Blend (Growth)	B-	B-	C+		Y	1,500
Federated MDT Large Cap Growth Fund Class B Shares	QBLGX	NAS CM	Open End	US Equity Large Cap Blend (Growth)	B-	B-	C+	Up	Y	1,500
Federated MDT Large Cap Growth Fund Class C Shares	QCLGX	NAS CM	Open End	US Equity Large Cap Blend (Growth)	B-	B-	C+	Up	Y	1,500
Federated MDT Large Cap Growth Fund Institutional Shares	QILGX	NAS CM	Open End	US Equity Large Cap Blend (Growth)	B-	B	C+		Y	1,000,000
Federated MDT Large Cap Value Fund Class A	FSTRX	NAS CM	Open End	US Equity Large Cap Value (Growth & Income)	B-	B-	B	Down	Y	1,500
Federated MDT Large Cap Value Fund Class R6	FSTLX	NAS CM	Open End	US Equity Large Cap Value (Growth & Income)	B	B-	B	Up	Y	0
Federated MDT Large Cap Value Fund Institutional Shares	FMSTX	NAS CM	Open End	US Equity Large Cap Value (Growth & Income)	B	B-	B	Up	Y	1,000,000
Federated MDT Large Cap Value Fund Service Shares	FSTKX	NAS CM	Open End	US Equity Large Cap Value (Growth & Income)	B-	B-	B	Down	Y	1,000,000
Federated MDT Mid Cap Growth Fund Class A Shares	FGSAX	NAS CM	Open End	US Equity Mid Cap (Growth)	B	B	B	Up	Y	1,500
Federated MDT Mid Cap Growth Fund Class B Shares	FGSBX	NAS CM	Open End	US Equity Mid Cap (Growth)	B	B	B	Up		1,500
Federated MDT Mid Cap Growth Fund Class C Shares	FGSCX	NAS CM	Open End	US Equity Mid Cap (Growth)	B	B	B	Up	Y	1,500
Federated MDT Mid Cap Growth Fund Class R6 Shares	FGSKX	NAS CM	Open End	US Equity Mid Cap (Growth)	B	B	B	Up	Y	0
Federated MDT Mid Cap Growth Fund Institutional Shares	FGSIX	NAS CM	Open End	US Equity Mid Cap (Growth)	B	B	B	Up	Y	1,000,000
Federated MDT Small Cap Core Fund Class A Shares	QASCX	NAS CM	Open End	US Equity Small Cap (Small Company)	A-	A	B	Up	Y	1,500
Federated MDT Small Cap Core Fund Class C Shares	QCSCX	NAS CM	Open End	US Equity Small Cap (Small Company)	A-	A	B	Up	Y	1,500
Federated MDT Small Cap Core Fund Class R6	QLSCX	NAS CM	Open End	US Equity Small Cap (Small Company)	A-	A	B	Up	Y	0
Federated MDT Small Cap Core Fund Institutional Shares	QISCX	NAS CM	Open End	US Equity Small Cap (Small Company)	A-	A	B	Up	Y	1,000,000
Federated MDT Small Cap Growth Fund Class A Shares	QASGX	NAS CM	Open End	US Equity Small Cap (Small Company)	A-	A	B	Up	Y	1,500
Federated MDT Small Cap Growth Fund Class B Shares	QBSGX	NAS CM	Open End	US Equity Small Cap (Small Company)	A-	A	B	Up		1,500
Federated MDT Small Cap Growth Fund Class C Shares	QCSGX	NAS CM	Open End	US Equity Small Cap (Small Company)	A-	A	B	Up	Y	1,500
Federated MDT Small Cap Growth Fund Class R6	QLSGX	NAS CM	Open End	US Equity Small Cap (Small Company)	A-	A	B	Up	Y	0
Federated MDT Small Cap Growth Fund Institutional Shares	QISGX	NAS CM	Open End	US Equity Small Cap (Small Company)	A-	A	B	Up	Y	1,000,000
Federated Mid-Cap Index Fund Class R6 Shares	FMCLX	NAS CM	Open End	US Equity Mid Cap (Growth & Income)	B	B	B		Y	0
Federated Mid-Cap Index Fund Institutional Shares	FMCRX	NAS CM	Open End	US Equity Mid Cap (Growth & Income)	B	B	B		Y	1,000,000
Federated Mid-Cap Index Fund Service Shares	FMDCX	NAS CM	Open End	US Equity Mid Cap (Growth & Income)	B	B	B		Y	1,000,000
Federated Muni and Stock Advantage Fund Class A Shares	FMUAX	NAS CM	Open End	Cautious Alloc (Income)	B-	C+	B	Up	Y	1,500
Federated Muni and Stock Advantage Fund Class B Shares	FMNBX	NAS CM	Open End	Cautious Alloc (Income)	B-	C+	B	Up	Y	1,500
Federated Muni and Stock Advantage Fund Class C Shares	FMUCX	NAS CM	Open End	Cautious Alloc (Income)	B-	C+	B	Up	Y	1,500
Federated Muni and Stock Advantage Fund Class F Shares	FMUFX	NAS CM	Open End	Cautious Alloc (Income)	B-	C+	B	Up	Y	1,500
Federated Muni & Stock Advantage Fund Institutional Shares	FMUIX	NAS CM	Open End	Cautious Alloc (Income)	B-	C+	B	Up	Y	1,000,000
Federated Prudent Bear Fund Class A Shares	BEARX	NAS CM	Open End	Other Alternative (Growth)	D-	D-	D	Down	Y	1,500
Federated Prudent Bear Fund Class C Shares	PBRCX	NAS CM	Open End	Other Alternative (Growth)	D-	D-	D	Down	Y	1,500
Federated Prudent Bear Fund Institutional Shares	PBRIX	NAS CM	Open End	Other Alternative (Growth)	D-	D-	D	Down	Y	1,000,000
Federated Strategic Value Dividend Fund Class A Shares	SVAAX	NAS CM	Open End	US Equity Large Cap Value (Equity-Income)	B	B-	A	Up	Y	1,500
Federated Strategic Value Dividend Fund Class C Shares	SVACX	NAS CM	Open End	US Equity Large Cap Value (Equity-Income)	B	C+	A	Up	Y	1,500
Federated Strategic Value Dividend Fund Class R6	SVALX	NAS CM	Open End	US Equity Large Cap Value (Equity-Income)	B	B-	A	Up	Y	0
Federated Strategic Value Dividend Fund Inst Shares	SVAIX	NAS CM	Open End	US Equity Large Cap Value (Equity-Income)	B	B-	A	Up	Y	1,000,000
Fidelity Advisor Asset Manager® 20% Fund Class A	FTAWX	NAS CM	Open End	Cautious Alloc (Asset Alloc)	B	C	A-	Up	Y	2,500
Fidelity Advisor Asset Manager® 20% Fund Class C	FTCWX	NAS CM	Open End	Cautious Alloc (Asset Alloc)	B-	C	A-	Up	Y	2,500
Fidelity Advisor Asset Manager® 20% Fund Class M	FTDWX	NAS CM	Open End	Cautious Alloc (Asset Alloc)	B	C	A-	Up	Y	2,500
Fidelity Advisor Asset Manager® 20% Fund I Class	FTIWX	NAS CM	Open End	Cautious Alloc (Asset Alloc)	B	C	A-	Up	Y	2,500
Fidelity Advisor Asset Manager® 30% Fund Class A	FTAAX	NAS CM	Open End	Cautious Alloc (Asset Alloc)	B	C+	A-	Up	Y	2,500
Fidelity Advisor Asset Manager® 30% Fund Class C	FCANX	NAS CM	Open End	Cautious Alloc (Asset Alloc)	B	C	A-	Up	Y	2,500
Fidelity Advisor Asset Manager® 30% Fund Class M	FTTNX	NAS CM	Open End	Cautious Alloc (Asset Alloc)	B	C+	A-	Up	Y	2,500
Fidelity Advisor Asset Manager® 30% Fund I Class	FTINX	NAS CM	Open End	Cautious Alloc (Asset Alloc)	B	C+	A-	Up	Y	2,500
Fidelity Advisor Asset Manager® 40% Fund Class A	FFNAX	NAS CM	Open End	Cautious Alloc (Asset Alloc)	B-	C+	B	Up	Y	2,500
Fidelity Advisor Asset Manager® 40% Fund Class C	FFNCX	NAS CM	Open End	Cautious Alloc (Asset Alloc)	B	C+	B+	Up	Y	2,500
Fidelity Advisor Asset Manager® 40% Fund Class M	FFNTX	NAS CM	Open End	Cautious Alloc (Asset Alloc)	B-	C+	B	Up	Y	2,500
Fidelity Advisor Asset Manager® 40% Fund I Class	FFNIX	NAS CM	Open End	Cautious Alloc (Asset Alloc)	B-	C+	B	Up	Y	2,500

★ Expanded analysis of this fund is included in Section II.

Min Additional Investment	3-Month Total Return	6-Month Total Return	1-Year Total Return	3-Year Total Return	5-Year Total Return	Dividend Yield (TTM)	Expense Ratio	3-Yr Std Deviation	3-Year Beta	NAV	Total Assets (MIL)	%Cash	%Stocks	%Bonds	%Other	Turnover Ratio	Last Bull Market Total Return	Last Bear Market Total Return	Front End Fee (%)	Back End Fee (%)	Inception Date
	TOTAL RETURNS					PERFORMANCE				ASSETS		ASSET ALLOCATION & TURNOVER					BULL & BEAR		FEES		
100	3.94	8.11	12.98	14.92	52.30	0.77	2.08	6.7	0.63	18.46	140.3	2	63	33	1	82	15.31	-15.04		1.00	Sep-05
	4.22	8.65	14.15	17.42	57.27	1.33	1.07	6.71	0.63	18.64	140.3	2	63	33	1	82	15.54	-14.96			Dec-06
	4.21	8.62	14.11	18.41	60.12	1.64	1.08	6.71	0.63	18.67	140.3	2	63	33	1	82	16.02	-14.73			Oct-02
100	7.77	14.51	25.05	26.46	101.48	0	1.51	11.1	0.98	18.18	88.4	2	98	0	0	104	26.31	-18.77	5.50		Sep-05
100	7.50	14.02	24.05	23.62	93.98	0	2.26	11.12	0.98	16.66	88.4	2	98	0	0	104	25.7	-18.93		5.50	Mar-07
100	7.51	14.06	24.11	23.66	94.04	0	2.26	11.1	0.98	16.22	88.4	2	98	0	0	104	25.68	-19.05		1.00	Sep-05
	7.81	14.63	25.31	27.43	104.16	0	1.26	11.12	0.98	18.91	88.4	2	98	0	0	104	26.39	-18.65			Sep-05
100	6.69	10.97	14.23	23.75	103.67	1.27	0.99	11.44	1.08		733.5	2	98	0	0	99	30.17	-22.29	5.50		May-14
	6.22	10.44	14.43	23.92	103.36	1.52	0.7	11.46	1.08	28.18	733.5	2	98	0	0	99	30.17	-22.29			Jun-16
	6.17	10.42	14.36	24.26	104.72	1.46	0.77	11.44	1.08	28.17	733.5	2	98	0	0	99	30.31	-22.23			Jan-10
	6.15	10.29	14.11	23.46	102.61	1.26	0.99	11.46	1.08	28.19	733.5	2	98	0	0	99	30.17	-22.29			Mar-82
100	8.74	13.98	24.41	29.11	110.73	0.03	1.23	12.41	1.02	39.47	324.9	2	98	0	0	109	18.77	-22.71	5.50		Aug-84
100	8.53	13.52	23.48	26.22	103.00	0	1.98	12.4	1.02	27.28	324.9	2	98	0	0	109	18.25	-22.95		5.50	Aug-95
100	8.55	13.59	23.52	26.30	103.08	0	1.98	12.39	1.02	27.98	324.9	2	98	0	0	109	18.23	-22.93		1.00	Aug-95
	8.80	14.13	24.72	28.52	107.79	0	0.97	12.43	1.03	37.11	324.9	2	98	0	0	109	18.43	-22.85			Dec-06
	8.83	14.15	24.74	30.09	113.39	0.23	0.98	12.41	1.02	40.47	324.9	2	98	0	0	109	18.95	-22.61			Jan-10
100	2.86	9.85	15.29	49.15	130.17	0	1.14	15.69	1.06	19.35	347.9	3	97	0	0	91	29.52	-29.24	5.50		Sep-05
100	2.67	9.48	14.45	45.85	122.00	0	1.89	15.71	1.06	17.29	347.9	3	97	0	0	91	28.98	-29.45		1.00	Sep-05
	2.99	10.04	15.63	50.40	133.32	0.03	0.88	15.76	1.07	20.02	347.9	3	97	0	0	91	29.79	-29.17			Jun-16
	2.94	9.98	15.57	50.32	133.20	0.03	0.89	15.76	1.07	20.01	347.9	3	97	0	0	91	29.79	-29.17			Sep-05
100	4.20	11.56	24.75	53.65	128.04	0	1.14	15.35	0.99	22.65	290.2	3	97	0	0	118	33.43	-27.18	5.50		Sep-05
100	4.02	11.15	23.82	50.16	119.66	0	1.89	15.33	0.98	20.85	290.2	3	97	0	0	118	32.83	-27.42		5.50	Mar-08
100	4.00	11.14	23.81	50.19	119.56	0	1.89	15.34	0.99	20.18	290.2	3	97	0	0	118	32.78	-27.4		1.00	Sep-05
	4.27	11.67	25.05	54.70	130.73	0	0.88	15.35	0.99	23.52	290.2	3	97	0	0	118	33.54	-27.1			Jun-16
	4.27	11.71	25.04	54.77	130.83	0	0.89	15.35	0.99	23.53	290.2	3	97	0	0	118	33.54	-27.1			Sep-05
	6.18	9.48	15.87	34.19	100.70	0.88	0.3	11.03	1	24.61	831.1	3	97	0	0	35	27.57	-22.72			Oct-16
	6.19	9.50	15.89	34.78	102.53	0.88	0.31	11.05	1	24.59	831.1	3	97	0	0	35	27.59	-22.72			Jan-12
	6.11	9.33	15.56	33.75	100.04	0.67	0.56	11.03	1	24.61	831.1	3	97	0	0	35	27.57	-22.72			Nov-92
100	3.90	7.12	11.08	16.39	36.86	2.17	1	4.15	0.13	13.64	1,609	0	46	54	0	71	10.89	-0.53	5.50		Sep-03
100	3.71	6.64	10.26	13.82	31.86	1.46	1.75	4.13	0.13	13.63	1,609	0	46	54	0	71	10.4	-0.84		5.50	Sep-03
100	3.71	6.72	10.26	13.83	31.89	1.46	1.75	4.14	0.12	13.63	1,609	0	46	54	0	71	10.4	-0.84		1.00	Sep-03
100	3.90	7.12	11.08	16.40	36.86	2.17	1	4.15	0.13	13.64	1,609	0	46	54	0	71	10.89	-0.53	1.00		May-07
	3.96	7.26	11.36	17.36	38.56	2.41	0.75	4.17	0.14	13.64	1,609	0	46	54	0	71	11.04	-0.42			Dec-10
100	-4.05	-8.71	-15.75	-30.00	-57.92	0	0.22	9.25	-0.82	15.61	199.1	118	-187	169	0	315	-21.68	16.08	5.50		Dec-95
100	-4.29	-9.09	-16.41	-31.68	-59.53	0	0.97	9	-0.79	13.8	199.1	118	-187	169	0	315	-21.9	15.53		1.00	Feb-99
	-4.08	-8.64	-15.60	-29.42	-57.46	0	0.02	9.06	-0.8	15.95	199.1	118	-187	169	0	315	-21.55	15.97			Dec-08
100	3.13	5.89	14.73	29.65	78.88	3.21	1.06	9.3	0.54	6.12	14,186	1	99	0	0	19	11.47	-4.1	5.50		Mar-05
100	2.92	5.48	13.84	26.73	72.20	2.5	1.81	9.4	0.55	6.13	14,186	1	99	0	0	19	10.98	-4.39		1.00	Mar-05
	3.18	6.00	15.15	30.50	81.03	3.45	0.79	9.39	0.55	6.15	14,186	1	99	0	0	19	11.82	-4.2			Jun-16
	3.18	5.99	15.13	30.47	80.99	3.43	0.81	9.38	0.55	6.15	14,186	1	99	0	0	19	11.82	-4.2			Mar-05
	1.46	3.02	6.65	10.49	20.68	1.2	0.85	2.9	0.4	13.41	5,055	28	20	47	5	22	6.39	-3.36	5.75		Oct-06
	1.28	2.65	5.87	8.05	16.25	0.46	1.6	2.89	0.4	13.34	5,055	28	20	47	5	22	5.86	-3.57		1.00	Oct-06
	1.45	2.94	6.36	9.64	19.15	0.93	1.11	2.88	0.4	13.39	5,055	28	20	47	5	22	6.24	-3.46	3.50		Oct-06
	1.48	3.18	6.92	11.38	22.30	1.44	0.57	2.9	0.41	13.42	5,055	28	20	47	5	22	6.54	-3.16			Oct-06
	2.03	4.16	9.17	13.90	28.94	1.17	0.86	3.83	0.34	11.1	1,294	18	30	47	5	24	8.46	-5.69	5.75		Oct-07
	1.79	3.72	8.22	11.20	24.05	0.48	1.62	3.83	0.35	11.03	1,294	18	30	47	5	24	8.01	-5.99		1.00	Oct-07
	1.86	3.91	8.80	12.85	27.07	0.94	1.12	3.81	0.33	11.08	1,294	18	30	47	5	24	8.3	-5.78	3.50		Oct-07
	2.03	4.21	9.33	14.66	30.36	1.4	0.63	3.78	0.34	11.09	1,294	18	30	47	5	24	8.71	-5.59			Oct-07
	2.58	5.19	11.41	16.73	36.72	1.07	0.86	4.73	0.24	11.71	1,498	13	40	42	6	20	10.56	-8.19	5.75		Oct-07
	2.36	4.78	10.63	14.05	31.44	0.37	1.63	4.7	0.25	11.67	1,498	13	40	42	6	20	10.01	-8.45		1.00	Oct-07
	2.44	4.98	11.05	15.79	34.80	0.84	1.14	4.74	0.24	11.69	1,498	13	40	42	6	20	10.36	-8.25	3.50		Oct-07
	2.63	5.31	11.74	17.67	38.39	1.35	0.58	4.72	0.25	11.7	1,498	13	40	42	6	20	10.75	-8.13			Oct-07

	MARKET		FUND TYPE, CATEGORY & OBJECTIVE		RATINGS					MINIMUMS
Fund Name	Ticker Symbol	Traded On	Fund Type	Category and (Prospectus Objective)	Overall Rating	Reward Rating	Risk Rating	Recent Up/ Downgrade	Open to New Investors	Min Initial Investment
Fidelity Advisor Asset Manager® 50% Fund Class A	FFAMX	NAS CM	Open End	Cautious Alloc (Asset Alloc)	B-	C+	B	Up	Y	2,500
Fidelity Advisor Asset Manager® 50% Fund Class C	FFCMX	NAS CM	Open End	Cautious Alloc (Asset Alloc)	B-	C+	B	Up	Y	2,500
Fidelity Advisor Asset Manager® 50% Fund Class M	FFTMX	NAS CM	Open End	Cautious Alloc (Asset Alloc)	B-	C+	B	Up	Y	2,500
Fidelity Advisor Asset Manager® 50% Fund I Class	FFIMX	NAS CM	Open End	Cautious Alloc (Asset Alloc)	B	C+	A-	Up	Y	2,500
Fidelity Advisor Asset Manager® 60% Fund Class A	FSAAX	NAS CM	Open End	Moderate Alloc (Asset Alloc)	B-	C+	B	Down	Y	2,500
Fidelity Advisor Asset Manager® 60% Fund Class C	FSCNX	NAS CM	Open End	Moderate Alloc (Asset Alloc)	B-	C+	B	Down	Y	2,500
Fidelity Advisor Asset Manager® 60% Fund Class M	FSATX	NAS CM	Open End	Moderate Alloc (Asset Alloc)	B-	C+	B	Down	Y	2,500
Fidelity Advisor Asset Manager® 60% Fund I Class	FSNIX	NAS CM	Open End	Moderate Alloc (Asset Alloc)	B-	C+	B	Down	Y	2,500
Fidelity Advisor Asset Manager® 70% Fund Class A	FAASX	NAS CM	Open End	Moderate Alloc (Asset Alloc)	B-	C+	B	Down	Y	2,500
Fidelity Advisor Asset Manager® 70% Fund Class C	FCASX	NAS CM	Open End	Moderate Alloc (Asset Alloc)	B-	C+	B-	Down	Y	2,500
Fidelity Advisor Asset Manager® 70% Fund Class M	FTASX	NAS CM	Open End	Moderate Alloc (Asset Alloc)	B-	C+	B	Down	Y	2,500
Fidelity Advisor Asset Manager® 70% Fund I Class	FAAIX	NAS CM	Open End	Moderate Alloc (Asset Alloc)	B-	B-	B	Down	Y	2,500
Fidelity Advisor Asset Manager® 85% Fund Class A	FEYAX	NAS CM	Open End	Aggressive Alloc (Asset Alloc)	B-	B-	B-	Down	Y	2,500
Fidelity Advisor Asset Manager® 85% Fund Class C	FEYCX	NAS CM	Open End	Aggressive Alloc (Asset Alloc)	B-	B-	B-	Down	Y	2,500
Fidelity Advisor Asset Manager® 85% Fund Class M	FEYTX	NAS CM	Open End	Aggressive Alloc (Asset Alloc)	B-	B-	B-	Down	Y	2,500
Fidelity Advisor Asset Manager® 85% Fund I Class	FEYIX	NAS CM	Open End	Aggressive Alloc (Asset Alloc)	B-	B-	B-	Down	Y	2,500
Fidelity Advisor Freedom® 2005 Fund Class A	FFAVX	NAS CM	Open End	Target Date 2000-2020 (Asset Alloc)	B	C+	A-	Up	Y	2,500
Fidelity Advisor Freedom® 2005 Fund Class C	FCFVX	NAS CM	Open End	Target Date 2000-2020 (Asset Alloc)	B-	C+	B+	Up	Y	2,500
Fidelity Advisor Freedom® 2005 Fund Class I	FFIVX	NAS CM	Open End	Target Date 2000-2020 (Asset Alloc)	B-	C+	B	Up	Y	2,500
Fidelity Advisor Freedom® 2005 Fund Class M	FFTVX	NAS CM	Open End	Target Date 2000-2020 (Asset Alloc)	B	C+	A-	Up	Y	2,500
Fidelity Advisor Freedom® 2005 Fund Class Z6	FYGLX	NAS CM	Open End	Target Date 2000-2020 (Asset Alloc)	B-	C+	B	Up	Y	0
Fidelity Advisor Freedom® 2010 Fund Class A	FACFX	NAS CM	Open End	Target Date 2000-2020 (Asset Alloc)	B-	C+	B	Up	Y	2,500
Fidelity Advisor Freedom® 2010 Fund Class C	FCFCX	NAS CM	Open End	Target Date 2000-2020 (Asset Alloc)	B	C+	B+	Up	Y	2,500
Fidelity Advisor Freedom® 2010 Fund Class I	FCIFX	NAS CM	Open End	Target Date 2000-2020 (Asset Alloc)	B-	C+	B	Up	Y	2,500
Fidelity Advisor Freedom® 2010 Fund Class M	FCFTX	NAS CM	Open End	Target Date 2000-2020 (Asset Alloc)	B-	C+	B	Up	Y	2,500
Fidelity Advisor Freedom® 2010 Fund Class Z6	FUGLX	NAS CM	Open End	Target Date 2000-2020 (Asset Alloc)	B-	C+	B	Up	Y	0
Fidelity Advisor Freedom® 2015 Fund Class A	FFVAX	NAS CM	Open End	Target Date 2000-2020 (Asset Alloc)	B-	C+	B	Up	Y	2,500
Fidelity Advisor Freedom® 2015 Fund Class C	FFVCX	NAS CM	Open End	Target Date 2000-2020 (Asset Alloc)	B	C+	B+	Up	Y	2,500
Fidelity Advisor Freedom® 2015 Fund Class I	FFVIX	NAS CM	Open End	Target Date 2000-2020 (Asset Alloc)	B-	C+	B	Up	Y	2,500
Fidelity Advisor Freedom® 2015 Fund Class M	FFVTX	NAS CM	Open End	Target Date 2000-2020 (Asset Alloc)	B-	C+	B	Up	Y	2,500
Fidelity Advisor Freedom® 2015 Fund Class Z6	FIGLX	NAS CM	Open End	Target Date 2000-2020 (Asset Alloc)	B	C+	A-	Up	Y	0
Fidelity Advisor Freedom® 2020 Fund Class A	FDAFX	NAS CM	Open End	Target Date 2000-2020 (Asset Alloc)	B-	C+	B	Down	Y	2,500
Fidelity Advisor Freedom® 2020 Fund Class C	FDCFX	NAS CM	Open End	Target Date 2000-2020 (Asset Alloc)	B	C+	B+	Up	Y	2,500
Fidelity Advisor Freedom® 2020 Fund Class I	FDIFX	NAS CM	Open End	Target Date 2000-2020 (Asset Alloc)	B	C+	B+	Up	Y	2,500
Fidelity Advisor Freedom® 2020 Fund Class M	FDTFX	NAS CM	Open End	Target Date 2000-2020 (Asset Alloc)	B-	C+	B	Up	Y	2,500
Fidelity Advisor Freedom® 2020 Fund Class Z6	FOGLX	NAS CM	Open End	Target Date 2000-2020 (Asset Alloc)	B-	C+	B	Up	Y	0
Fidelity Advisor Freedom® 2025 Fund Class A	FATWX	NAS CM	Open End	Target Date 2021-2045 (Asset Alloc)	B-	C+	B	Down	Y	2,500
Fidelity Advisor Freedom® 2025 Fund Class C	FCTWX	NAS CM	Open End	Target Date 2021-2045 (Asset Alloc)	B-	C+	B	Down	Y	2,500
Fidelity Advisor Freedom® 2025 Fund Class I	FITWX	NAS CM	Open End	Target Date 2021-2045 (Asset Alloc)	B-	C+	B	Down	Y	2,500
Fidelity Advisor Freedom® 2025 Fund Class M	FTTWX	NAS CM	Open End	Target Date 2021-2045 (Asset Alloc)	B-	C+	B	Down	Y	2,500
Fidelity Advisor Freedom® 2025 Fund Class Z6	FPGLX	NAS CM	Open End	Target Date 2021-2045 (Asset Alloc)	B-	C+	B	Down	Y	0
Fidelity Advisor Freedom® 2030 Fund Class A	FAFEX	NAS CM	Open End	Target Date 2021-2045 (Asset Alloc)	B-	B-	B-	Down	Y	2,500
Fidelity Advisor Freedom® 2030 Fund Class C	FCFEX	NAS CM	Open End	Target Date 2021-2045 (Asset Alloc)	B-	C+	B-	Down	Y	2,500
Fidelity Advisor Freedom® 2030 Fund Class I	FEFIX	NAS CM	Open End	Target Date 2021-2045 (Asset Alloc)	B-	B-	B	Down	Y	2,500
Fidelity Advisor Freedom® 2030 Fund Class M	FTFEX	NAS CM	Open End	Target Date 2021-2045 (Asset Alloc)	B-	B-	B-	Down	Y	2,500
Fidelity Advisor Freedom® 2030 Fund Class Z6	FDGLX	NAS CM	Open End	Target Date 2021-2045 (Asset Alloc)	B-	B-	B	Down	Y	0
Fidelity Advisor Freedom® 2035 Fund Class A	FATHX	NAS CM	Open End	Target Date 2021-2045 (Asset Alloc)	B-	B-	B-	Down	Y	2,500
Fidelity Advisor Freedom® 2035 Fund Class C	FCTHX	NAS CM	Open End	Target Date 2021-2045 (Asset Alloc)	B-	B-	B-	Down	Y	2,500
Fidelity Advisor Freedom® 2035 Fund Class I	FITHX	NAS CM	Open End	Target Date 2021-2045 (Asset Alloc)	B-	B-	B-	Down	Y	2,500
Fidelity Advisor Freedom® 2035 Fund Class M	FTTHX	NAS CM	Open End	Target Date 2021-2045 (Asset Alloc)	B-	B-	B-	Down	Y	2,500
Fidelity Advisor Freedom® 2035 Fund Class Z6	FHGLX	NAS CM	Open End	Target Date 2021-2045 (Asset Alloc)	B-	B-	B-	Down	Y	0
Fidelity Advisor Freedom® 2040 Fund Class A	FAFFX	NAS CM	Open End	Target Date 2021-2045 (Asset Alloc)	B-	B-	B-	Down	Y	2,500

★ Expanded analysis of this fund is included in Section II.

Min Additional Investment	TOTAL RETURNS 3-Month Total Return	6-Month Total Return	1-Year Total Return	3-Year Total Return	5-Year Total Return	PERFORMANCE Dividend Yield (TTM)	Expense Ratio	3-Yr Std Deviation	3-Year Beta	ASSETS NAV	Total Assets (MIL)	ASSET ALLOCATION & TURNOVER %Cash	%Stocks	%Bonds	%Other	Turnover Ratio	BULL & BEAR Last Bull Market Total Return	Last Bear Market Total Return	FEES Front End Fee (%)	Back End Fee (%)	Inception Date
	3.11	6.25	13.75	19.33	44.11	1	0.98	5.69	0.52	18.21	8,756	8	50	36	6	20	12.36	-10.68	5.75		Oct-06
	2.91	5.82	12.84	16.64	38.76	0.34	1.74	5.7	0.52	18.1	8,756	8	50	36	6	20	11.89	-11		1.00	Oct-06
	3.04	6.12	13.41	18.42	42.21	0.78	1.23	5.7	0.52	18.2	8,756	8	50	36	6	20	12.24	-10.79	3.50		Oct-06
	3.20	6.41	14.05	20.33	46.04	1.25	0.7	5.69	0.52	18.24	8,756	8	50	36	6	20	12.49	-10.57			Oct-06
	3.57	7.28	15.99	22.03	51.61	0.9	1.05	6.67	0.62	12.53	2,053	3	60	31	5	18	14.27	-13.18	5.75		Oct-07
	3.41	6.83	15.13	19.18	45.86	0.31	1.8	6.69	0.62	12.35	2,053	3	60	31	5	18	13.88	-13.47		1.00	Oct-07
	3.61	7.17	15.81	21.07	49.79	0.7	1.3	6.67	0.61	12.48	2,053	3	60	31	5	18	14.1	-13.31	3.50		Oct-07
	3.65	7.35	16.33	23.00	53.72	1.18	0.77	6.66	0.61	12.57	2,053	3	60	31	5	18	14.5	-13.14			Oct-07
	4.20	8.29	18.35	24.68	59.58	0.86	1.04	7.63	0.71	22.39	5,190	2	71	22	5	19	16.33	-15.83	5.75		Sep-08
	4.00	7.91	17.46	21.85	53.69	0.23	1.79	7.64	0.71	22.32	5,190	2	71	22	5	19	15.73	-16.06		1.00	Sep-08
	4.13	8.21	18.08	23.75	57.52	0.65	1.29	7.63	0.71	22.41	5,190	2	71	22	5	19	16.13	-15.9	3.50		Sep-08
	4.25	8.47	18.65	25.69	61.78	1.14	0.76	7.61	0.71	22.41	5,190	2	71	22	5	19	16.5	-15.68			Sep-08
	4.98	9.83	21.83	28.56	72.53	0.63	1.06	9.09	0.86	19.38	2,147	3	84	9	4	23	19.07	-19.41	5.75		Oct-06
	4.78	9.42	20.93	25.64	66.05	0.04	1.81	9.08	0.86	19.09	2,147	3	84	9	4	23	18.63	-19.67		1.00	Oct-06
	4.88	9.70	21.53	27.49	70.09	0.35	1.33	9.09	0.86	19.29	2,147	3	84	9	4	23	18.8	-19.41	3.50		Oct-06
	5.07	10.01	22.24	29.75	75.08	0.8	0.78	9.07	0.86	19.48	2,147	3	84	9	4	23	19.21	-19.26			Oct-06
	2.06	4.36	10.02	14.93	29.64	1.38	0.74	4.43	0.23	12	204.3	22	34	44	0	32	9.71	-8.46	5.75		Nov-03
	1.79	4.01	9.24	12.31	24.80	0.65	1.49	4.39	0.24	12	204.3	22	34	44	0	32	9.3	-8.83		1.00	Nov-03
	2.09	4.47	10.36	15.76	31.26	1.61	0.49	4.42	0.22	12.07	204.3	22	34	44	0	32	9.94	-8.44			Nov-03
	1.98	4.29	9.78	14.05	27.97	1.14	0.99	4.44	0.23	11.99	204.3	22	34	44	0	32	9.58	-8.6	3.50		Nov-03
	2.17	4.55	10.44	15.84	31.36		0.38	4.42	0.22	12.06	204.3	22	34	44	0	32	9.94	-8.44			Jun-17
	2.44	5.16	11.86	17.31	36.56	1.41	0.78	5.23	0.14	12.49	493.9	18	43	39	0	26	11.88	-10.37	5.75		Jul-03
	2.31	4.89	11.05	14.76	31.65	0.75	1.53	5.26	0.13	12.39	493.9	18	43	39	0	26	11.3	-10.63		1.00	Jul-03
	2.51	5.39	12.24	18.24	38.38	1.66	0.53	5.27	0.14	12.54	493.9	18	43	39	0	26	12.04	-10.34			Jul-03
	2.38	5.02	11.56	16.45	34.92	1.18	1.03	5.26	0.15	12.45	493.9	18	43	39	0	26	11.69	-10.47	3.50		Jul-03
	2.58	5.46	12.32	18.32	38.47		0.4	5.27	0.14	12.53	493.9	18	43	39	0	26	12.04	-10.34			Jun-17
	2.94	6.07	13.78	19.76	40.88	1.36	0.83	6	0.55	12.66	1,172	15	51	33	0	22	12.12	-10.57	5.75		Nov-03
	2.68	5.66	12.92	17.12	35.68	0.7	1.58	6.03	0.55	12.57	1,172	15	51	33	0	22	11.66	-10.94		1.00	Nov-03
	2.90	6.16	13.99	20.57	42.63	1.59	0.58	6.04	0.56	12.75	1,172	15	51	33	0	22	12.34	-10.55			Nov-03
	2.85	5.90	13.45	18.84	39.13	1.14	1.08	6	0.55	12.64	1,172	15	51	33	0	22	12	-10.72	3.50		Nov-03
	2.99	6.25	14.08	20.66	42.74		0.42	6.04	0.56	12.73	1,172	15	51	33	0	22	12.34	-10.55			Jun-17
	3.19	6.64	14.96	21.34	44.94	1.33	0.87	6.58	0.61	13.79	2,567	12	58	30	0	19	13.69	-12.61	5.75		Jul-03
	2.97	6.20	14.17	18.58	39.60	0.68	1.62	6.55	0.61	13.7	2,567	12	58	30	0	19	13.21	-12.87		1.00	Jul-03
	3.23	6.73	15.25	22.22	46.66	1.55	0.62	6.58	0.61	13.89	2,567	12	58	30	0	19	13.91	-12.56			Jul-03
	3.08	6.45	14.69	20.37	43.07	1.11	1.12	6.58	0.61	13.79	2,567	12	58	30	0	19	13.55	-12.68	3.50		Jul-03
	3.28	6.85	15.38	22.37	46.83		0.44	6.58	0.61	13.87	2,567	12	58	30	0	19	13.91	-12.56			Jun-17
	3.53	7.17	16.25	22.72	51.65	1.28	0.91	7.27	0.68	13.82	3,049	10	64	26	0	20	15.67	-14.98	5.75		Nov-03
	3.25	6.69	15.26	19.95	45.98	0.68	1.66	7.26	0.68	13.64	3,049	10	64	26	0	20	15.16	-15.19		1.00	Nov-03
	3.58	7.26	16.51	23.67	53.45	1.48	0.66	7.27	0.68	13.93	3,049	10	64	26	0	20	15.87	-14.91			Nov-03
	3.43	6.98	15.95	21.80	49.74	1.05	1.16	7.26	0.68	13.85	3,049	10	64	26	0	20	15.51	-15.09	3.50		Nov-03
	3.54	7.38	16.64	23.80	53.62		0.45	7.28	0.68	13.91	3,049	10	64	26	0	20	15.87	-14.91			Jun-17
	4.09	8.36	18.96	26.16	58.14	1.17	0.95	8.64	0.82	15.03	2,989	6	76	18	0	18	16.33	-15.82	5.75		Jul-03
	3.97	8.00	18.16	23.40	52.33	0.65	1.7	8.6	0.81	14.82	2,989	6	76	18	0	18	15.81	-16.06		1.00	Jul-03
	4.16	8.47	19.27	27.09	60.17	1.37	0.7	8.58	0.81	15.11	2,989	6	76	18	0	18	16.46	-15.7			Jul-03
	4.01	8.22	18.70	25.25	56.23	0.95	1.2	8.62	0.82	14.97	2,989	6	76	18	0	18	16.13	-15.85	3.50		Jul-03
	4.23	8.62	19.44	27.27	60.40		0.47	8.58	0.81	15.09	2,989	6	76	18	0	18	16.46	-15.7			Jun-17
	4.63	9.36	21.19	28.78	65.42	1.05	1	9.37	0.89	14.72	2,395	5	87	7	0	18	18.1	-18.06	5.75		Nov-03
	4.46	8.91	20.23	25.86	59.28	0.63	1.75	9.38	0.89	14.38	2,395	5	87	7	0	18	17.47	-18.29		1.00	Nov-03
	4.70	9.47	21.49	29.74	67.52	1.2	0.75	9.41	0.89	14.81	2,395	5	87	7	0	18	18.21	-17.93			Nov-03
	4.67	9.21	20.94	27.85	63.43	0.9	1.25	9.4	0.89	14.61	2,395	5	87	7	0	18	17.84	-18.13	3.50		Nov-03
	4.85	9.63	21.66	29.92	67.76		0.49	9.4	0.89	14.8	2,395	5	87	7	0	18	18.21	-17.93			Jun-17
	4.74	9.44	21.33	28.99	66.17	1.05	1	9.4	0.89	15.76	2,167	5	89	6	0	18	18.24	-18.29	5.75		Jul-03

	MARKET			FUND TYPE, CATEGORY & OBJECTIVE	RATINGS					MINIMUMS
Fund Name	Ticker Symbol	Traded On	Fund Type	Category and (Prospectus Objective)	Overall Rating	Reward Rating	Risk Rating	Recent Up/ Downgrade	Open to New Investors	Min Initial Investment
Fidelity Advisor Freedom® 2040 Fund Class C	FCFFX	NAS CM	Open End	Target Date 2021-2045 (Asset Alloc)	B-	B-	B-	Down	Y	2,500
Fidelity Advisor Freedom® 2040 Fund Class I	FIFFX	NAS CM	Open End	Target Date 2021-2045 (Asset Alloc)	B-	B-	B-	Down	Y	2,500
Fidelity Advisor Freedom® 2040 Fund Class M	FTFFX	NAS CM	Open End	Target Date 2021-2045 (Asset Alloc)	B-	B-	B-	Down	Y	2,500
Fidelity Advisor Freedom® 2040 Fund Class Z6	FKGLX	NAS CM	Open End	Target Date 2021-2045 (Asset Alloc)	B-	B-	B-	Down	Y	0
Fidelity Advisor Freedom® 2045 Fund Class A	FFFZX	NAS CM	Open End	Target Date 2021-2045 (Asset Alloc)	B-	B-	B-	Down	Y	2,500
Fidelity Advisor Freedom® 2045 Fund Class C	FFFJX	NAS CM	Open End	Target Date 2021-2045 (Asset Alloc)	B-	B-	B-	Down	Y	2,500
Fidelity Advisor Freedom® 2045 Fund Class I	FFFIX	NAS CM	Open End	Target Date 2021-2045 (Asset Alloc)	B-	B-	B-	Down	Y	2,500
Fidelity Advisor Freedom® 2045 Fund Class M	FFFTX	NAS CM	Open End	Target Date 2021-2045 (Asset Alloc)	B-	B-	B-	Down	Y	2,500
Fidelity Advisor Freedom® 2045 Fund Class Z6	FCGLX	NAS CM	Open End	Target Date 2021-2045 (Asset Alloc)	B-	B-	B-	Down	Y	0
Fidelity Advisor Freedom® 2050 Fund Class A	FFFLX	NAS CM	Open End	Target Date 2046+ (Asset Alloc)	B-	B-	B-	Down	Y	2,500
Fidelity Advisor Freedom® 2050 Fund Class C	FFFYX	NAS CM	Open End	Target Date 2046+ (Asset Alloc)	B-	B-	B-	Down	Y	2,500
Fidelity Advisor Freedom® 2050 Fund Class I	FFFPX	NAS CM	Open End	Target Date 2046+ (Asset Alloc)	B-	B-	B-	Down	Y	2,500
Fidelity Advisor Freedom® 2050 Fund Class M	FFFQX	NAS CM	Open End	Target Date 2046+ (Asset Alloc)	B-	B-	B-	Down	Y	2,500
Fidelity Advisor Freedom® 2050 Fund Class Z6	FVGLX	NAS CM	Open End	Target Date 2046+ (Asset Alloc)	B-	B-	B-	Down	Y	0
Fidelity Advisor Freedom® 2055 Fund Class A	FHFAX	NAS CM	Open End	Target Date 2046+ (Asset Alloc)	B-	B-	B-	Down	Y	2,500
Fidelity Advisor Freedom® 2055 Fund Class C	FHFCX	NAS CM	Open End	Target Date 2046+ (Asset Alloc)	B-	B-	B-	Down	Y	2,500
Fidelity Advisor Freedom® 2055 Fund Class I	FHFIX	NAS CM	Open End	Target Date 2046+ (Asset Alloc)	B-	B-	B-	Down	Y	2,500
Fidelity Advisor Freedom® 2055 Fund Class M	FHFTX	NAS CM	Open End	Target Date 2046+ (Asset Alloc)	B-	B-	B-	Down	Y	2,500
Fidelity Advisor Freedom® 2055 Fund Class Z6	FBGLX	NAS CM	Open End	Target Date 2046+ (Asset Alloc)	B-	B-	B-	Down	Y	0
Fidelity Advisor Freedom® 2060 Fund Class A	FDKPX	NAS CM	Open End	Target Date 2046+ (Asset Alloc)	B-	B-	B-	Up	Y	2,500
Fidelity Advisor Freedom® 2060 Fund Class C	FDKSX	NAS CM	Open End	Target Date 2046+ (Asset Alloc)	B-	B-	B-	Up	Y	2,500
Fidelity Advisor Freedom® 2060 Fund Class I	FDKQX	NAS CM	Open End	Target Date 2046+ (Asset Alloc)	B-	B-	B-	Up	Y	2,500
Fidelity Advisor Freedom® 2060 Fund Class M	FDKTX	NAS CM	Open End	Target Date 2046+ (Asset Alloc)	B-	B-	B-	Up	Y	2,500
Fidelity Advisor Freedom® 2060 Fund Class Z6	FNGLX	NAS CM	Open End	Target Date 2046+ (Asset Alloc)	B-	B-	B-		Y	0
Fidelity Advisor Freedom® Income Fund Class A	FAFAX	NAS CM	Open End	Target Date 2000-2020 (Asset Alloc)	B	C	A-	Up	Y	2,500
Fidelity Advisor Freedom® Income Fund Class C	FCAFX	NAS CM	Open End	Target Date 2000-2020 (Asset Alloc)	B-	C	A-	Up	Y	2,500
Fidelity Advisor Freedom® Income Fund Class I	FIAFX	NAS CM	Open End	Target Date 2000-2020 (Asset Alloc)	B	C	A-	Up	Y	2,500
Fidelity Advisor Freedom® Income Fund Class M	FTAFX	NAS CM	Open End	Target Date 2000-2020 (Asset Alloc)	B	C	A-	Up	Y	2,500
Fidelity Advisor Freedom® Income Fund Class Z6	FEGLX	NAS CM	Open End	Target Date 2000-2020 (Asset Alloc)	B-	C	B	Up	Y	0
Fidelity Advisor Managed Retirement 2005 Fund Class A	FIOAX	NAS CM	Open End	Cautious Alloc (Asset Alloc)	B-	C+	B	Up	Y	2,500
Fidelity Advisor Managed Retirement 2005 Fund Class C	FIOCX	NAS CM	Open End	Cautious Alloc (Asset Alloc)	B-	C	B	Up	Y	2,500
Fidelity Advisor Managed Retirement 2005 Fund Class I	FIOIX	NAS CM	Open End	Cautious Alloc (Asset Alloc)	B-	C+	B	Up	Y	2,500
Fidelity Advisor Managed Retirement 2005 Fund Class M	FIOTX	NAS CM	Open End	Cautious Alloc (Asset Alloc)	B-	C+	B	Up	Y	2,500
Fidelity Advisor Managed Retirement 2010 Fund Class A	FRQAX	NAS CM	Open End	Moderate Alloc (Asset Alloc)	B-	C+	B	Up	Y	2,500
Fidelity Advisor Managed Retirement 2010 Fund Class C	FRQCX	NAS CM	Open End	Moderate Alloc (Asset Alloc)	B-	C+	B	Up	Y	2,500
Fidelity Advisor Managed Retirement 2010 Fund Class I	FRQIX	NAS CM	Open End	Moderate Alloc (Asset Alloc)	B-	C+	B	Up	Y	2,500
Fidelity Advisor Managed Retirement 2010 Fund Class M	FRQTX	NAS CM	Open End	Moderate Alloc (Asset Alloc)	B-	C+	B	Up	Y	2,500
Fidelity Advisor Managed Retirement 2015 Fund Class A	FARSX	NAS CM	Open End	Moderate Alloc (Asset Alloc)	B-	C+	B	Up	Y	2,500
Fidelity Advisor Managed Retirement 2015 Fund Class C	FCRSX	NAS CM	Open End	Moderate Alloc (Asset Alloc)	B-	C+	B	Up	Y	2,500
Fidelity Advisor Managed Retirement 2015 Fund Class I	FRASX	NAS CM	Open End	Moderate Alloc (Asset Alloc)	B-	C+	B	Up	Y	2,500
Fidelity Advisor Managed Retirement 2015 Fund Class M	FTRSX	NAS CM	Open End	Moderate Alloc (Asset Alloc)	B-	C+	B	Up	Y	2,500
Fidelity Advisor Managed Retirement 2020 Fund Class A	FARVX	NAS CM	Open End	Moderate Alloc (Asset Alloc)	B-	C+	B	Up	Y	2,500
Fidelity Advisor Managed Retirement 2020 Fund Class C	FCRVX	NAS CM	Open End	Moderate Alloc (Asset Alloc)	B-	C+	B	Up	Y	2,500
Fidelity Advisor Managed Retirement 2020 Fund Class I	FIIVX	NAS CM	Open End	Moderate Alloc (Asset Alloc)	B-	C+	B	Up	Y	2,500
Fidelity Advisor Managed Retirement 2020 Fund Class M	FTRVX	NAS CM	Open End	Moderate Alloc (Asset Alloc)	B-	C+	B	Up	Y	2,500
Fidelity Advisor Managed Retirement 2025 Fund Class A	FARFX	NAS CM	Open End	Moderate Alloc (Asset Alloc)	B-	C+	B	Up	Y	2,500
Fidelity Advisor Managed Retirement 2025 Fund Class C	FCRFX	NAS CM	Open End	Moderate Alloc (Asset Alloc)	B-	C+	B	Up	Y	2,500
Fidelity Advisor Managed Retirement 2025 Fund Class M	FITTX	NAS CM	Open End	Moderate Alloc (Asset Alloc)	B-	C+	B	Up	Y	2,500
Fidelity Advisor Managed Retirement 2025 Fund I Class	FIRFX	NAS CM	Open End	Moderate Alloc (Asset Alloc)	B-	C+	B	Up	Y	2,500
Fidelity Advisor Managed Retirement Income Fund Class A	FRAMX	NAS CM	Open End	Cautious Alloc (Asset Alloc)	B-	C	B	Up	Y	2,500
Fidelity Advisor Managed Retirement Income Fund Class C	FRCMX	NAS CM	Open End	Cautious Alloc (Asset Alloc)	B-	C	A-	Up	Y	2,500
Fidelity Advisor Managed Retirement Income Fund Class I	FRIMX	NAS CM	Open End	Cautious Alloc (Asset Alloc)	B-	C	B	Up	Y	2,500

★Expanded analysis of this fund is included in Section II.

	TOTAL RETURNS					PERFORMANCE				ASSETS		ASSET ALLOCATION & TURNOVER					BULL & BEAR		FEES		
Min Additional Investment	3-Month Total Return	6-Month Total Return	1-Year Total Return	3-Year Total Return	5-Year Total Return	Dividend Yield (TTM)	Expense Ratio	3-Yr Std Deviation	3-Year Beta	NAV	Total Assets (MIL)	%Cash	%Stocks	%Bonds	%Other	Turnover Ratio	Last Bull Market Total Return	Last Bear Market Total Return	Front End Fee (%)	Back End Fee (%)	Inception Date
	4.60	9.12	20.50	26.17	60.10	0.62	1.75	9.38	0.89	15.43	2,167	5	89	6	0	18	17.8	-18.55		1.00	Jul-03
	4.81	9.56	21.64	29.94	68.25	1.2	0.75	9.38	0.89	15.84	2,167	5	89	6	0	18	18.47	-18.25			Jul-03
	4.66	9.31	21.02	28.00	64.06	0.9	1.25	9.4	0.89	15.7	2,167	5	89	6	0	18	18.15	-18.38	3.50		Jul-03
	4.92	9.82	21.93	30.25	68.65		0.49	9.38	0.89	15.82	2,167	5	89	6	0	18	18.47	-18.25			Jun-17
	4.73	9.54	21.32	29.02	67.12	1.04	1	9.38	0.89	12.27	1,328	5	89	6	0	22	18.77	-18.87	5.75		Jun-06
	4.48	8.99	20.42	26.12	60.99	0.62	1.75	9.37	0.89	12.05	1,328	5	89	6	0	22	18.28	-19.16		1.00	Jun-06
	4.77	9.55	21.65	29.92	69.22	1.19	0.75	9.38	0.89	12.33	1,328	5	89	6	0	22	18.89	-18.75			Jun-06
	4.70	9.36	21.04	28.01	65.10	0.91	1.25	9.41	0.89	12.18	1,328	5	89	6	0	22	18.59	-18.9	3.50		Jun-06
	4.90	9.78	21.91	30.19	69.57		0.49	9.38	0.89	12.32	1,328	5	89	6	0	22	18.89	-18.75			Jun-17
	4.77	9.51	21.35	29.06	67.61	1.04	1	9.38	0.89	12.23	1,051	5	89	6	0	25	19.44	-19.73	5.75		Jun-06
	4.60	9.13	20.42	26.15	61.47	0.61	1.75	9.35	0.89	12.06	1,051	5	89	6	0	25	18.92	-20.01		1.00	Jun-06
	4.87	9.68	21.64	29.99	69.75	1.18	0.75	9.36	0.89	12.3	1,051	5	89	6	0	25	19.57	-19.68			Jun-06
	4.63	9.30	20.99	28.00	65.44	0.9	1.25	9.37	0.89	12.17	1,051	5	89	6	0	25	19.28	-19.85	3.50		Jun-06
	4.89	9.79	21.77	30.12	69.91		0.49	9.36	0.89	12.28	1,051	5	89	6	0	25	19.57	-19.68			Jun-17
	4.76	9.52	21.36	29.03	68.70	1.01	1	9.37	0.89	13.44	506.8	5	89	6	0	24	19.79		5.75		Jun-11
	4.53	9.07	20.35	26.10	62.43	0.61	1.75	9.37	0.89	13.34	506.8	5	89	6	0	24	19.29			1.00	Jun-11
	4.81	9.63	21.61	29.99	70.87	1.16	0.75	9.39	0.89	13.48	506.8	5	89	6	0	24	19.92				Jun-11
	4.64	9.33	21.01	28.08	66.60	0.88	1.25	9.38	0.89	13.38	506.8	5	89	6	0	24	19.47		3.50		Jun-11
	4.83	9.74	21.73	30.12	71.04		0.49	9.4	0.89	13.46	506.8	5	89	6	0	24	19.92				Jun-17
	4.81	9.53	21.34	28.98		0.96	1	9.37	0.89		77.0	5	89	6	0	32			5.75		Aug-14
	4.49	9.09	20.41	26.10		0.5	1.75	9.36	0.89		77.0	5	89	6	0	32				1.00	Aug-14
	4.78	9.67	21.65	30.00		1.09	0.75	9.39	0.89		77.0	5	89	6	0	32					Aug-14
	4.67	9.39	21.01	28.08		0.84	1.25	9.4	0.89	11.92	77.0	5	89	6	0	32			3.50		Aug-14
	4.90	9.80	21.79	30.15			0.49	9.39	0.89	11.94	77.0	5	89	6	0	32					Jun-17
	1.56	3.44	7.80	11.93	21.16	1.2	0.72	3.27	0.35	11.1	215.3	27	24	49	0	38	6.14	-3.86	5.75		Jul-03
	1.30	2.99	6.90	9.38	16.59	0.48	1.47	3.28	0.36	11.07	215.3	27	24	49	0	38	5.7	-4.17		1.00	Jul-03
	1.55	3.49	8.04	12.82	22.67	1.42	0.47	3.26	0.35	11.13	215.3	27	24	49	0	38	6.27	-3.76			Jul-03
	1.48	3.30	7.53	11.10	19.65	0.95	0.97	3.23	0.35	11.09	215.3	27	24	49	0	38	6.02	-3.97	3.50		Jul-03
	1.53	3.52	8.06	12.85	22.71		0.37	3.26	0.36	11.12	215.3	27	24	49	0	38	6.27	-3.76			Jun-17
	1.74	3.84	8.63	14.38	38.34	1.14	0.74	4.72	-0.02	58.97	8.4	25	27	47	0	136	12.54	-10.62	5.75		Aug-07
	1.56	3.47	7.83	11.82	33.28	0.49	1.49	4.72	-0.02	58.71	8.4	25	27	47	0	136	12.03	-10.89		1.00	Aug-07
	1.80	3.97	8.89	15.23	40.09	1.4	0.49	4.72	-0.02	58.95	8.4	25	27	47	0	136	12.69	-10.51			Aug-07
	1.68	3.73	8.35	13.51	36.65	0.93	0.99	4.73	-0.02	59.01	8.4	25	27	47	0	136	12.36	-10.7	3.50		Aug-07
	2.13	4.62	10.33	16.72	43.48	1.13	0.78	5.4	-0.1	56.85	10.9	21	35	44	0	117	13.37	-11.54	5.75		Aug-07
	1.97	4.24	9.53	14.15	38.23	0.55	1.53	5.4	-0.1	56.45	10.9	21	35	44	0	117	12.9	-11.82		1.00	Aug-07
	2.20	4.76	10.63	17.61	45.31	1.34	0.53	5.4	-0.1	56.85	10.9	21	35	44	0	117	13.56	-11.45			Aug-07
	2.09	4.50	10.08	15.87	41.70	0.91	1.03	5.41	-0.1	56.98	10.9	21	35	44	0	117	13.16	-11.63	3.50		Aug-07
	2.54	5.39	11.76	18.48	47.17	1.08	0.83	5.83	-0.15	53.85	4.8	17	42	40	0	106	13.99	-12.31	5.75		Aug-07
	2.35	5.00	10.93	15.84	41.74	0.57	1.58	5.82	-0.14	53.67	4.8	17	42	40	0	106	13.5	-12.59		1.00	Aug-07
	2.62	5.53	12.04	19.38	49.01	1.32	0.58	5.83	-0.15	53.83	4.8	17	42	40	0	106	14.16	-12.22			Aug-07
	2.47	5.26	11.53	17.59	45.34	0.78	1.08	5.82	-0.14	53.95	4.8	17	42	40	0	106	13.82	-12.4	3.50		Aug-07
	2.93	6.09	13.01	19.92	50.39	1.1	0.87	6.16	0.58	52.2	4.0	14	50	36	0	115	14.75	-13.24	5.75		Dec-07
	2.73	5.69	12.15	17.24	44.85	0.56	1.62	6.16	0.58	51.69	4.0	14	50	36	0	115	14.27	-13.51		1.00	Dec-07
	3.00	6.24	13.31	20.84	52.32	1.24	0.62	6.18	0.58	52.2	4.0	14	50	36	0	115	14.92	-13.13			Dec-07
	2.88	5.97	12.73	19.02	48.55	0.84	1.12	6.16	0.58	52.17	4.0	14	50	36	0	115	14.58	-13.31	3.50		Dec-07
	3.15	6.50	13.94	21.02	53.94	1.03	0.91	6.56	0.62	53.83	20.8	11	54	34	0	108	15.66	-14.13	5.75		Dec-07
	2.94	6.10	13.10	18.34	48.29	0.58	1.66	6.56	0.62	53.31	20.8	11	54	34	0	108	15.15	-14.39		1.00	Dec-07
	3.07	6.36	13.65	20.13	52.04	0.84	1.16	6.55	0.62	53.84	20.8	11	54	34	0	108	15.47	-14.22	3.50		Dec-07
	3.21	6.65	14.23	21.96	55.93	1.25	0.66	6.56	0.62	53.93	20.8	11	54	34	0	108	15.8	-14.03			Dec-07
	1.57	3.50	6.81	11.25	30.30	1.14	0.72	3.47	0.12	57.89	10.9	27	24	49	0	111	11.21	-9.16	5.75		Aug-07
	1.38	3.11	6.00	8.78	25.52	0.49	1.47	3.47	0.12	57.75	10.9	27	24	49	0	111	10.71	-9.45		1.00	Aug-07
	1.64	3.65	7.08	12.10	31.96	1.35	0.47	3.47	0.12	57.85	10.9	27	24	49	0	111	11.36	-9.05			Aug-07

Fund Name	Ticker Symbol	Traded On	Fund Type	Category and (Prospectus Objective)	Overall Rating	Reward Rating	Risk Rating	Recent Up/ Downgrade	Open to New Investors	Min Initial Investment
	MARKET			FUND TYPE, CATEGORY & OBJECTIVE	RATINGS				MINIMUMS	
Fidelity Advisor Managed Retirement Income Fund Class M	FRTMX	NAS CM	Open End	Cautious Alloc (Asset Alloc)	B-	C	B	Up	Y	2,500
Fidelity Advisor Simplicity RMD 2005 Fund Class A	FARPX	NAS CM	Open End	Moderate Alloc (Asset Alloc)	B-	C+	B	Up	Y	2,500
Fidelity Advisor Simplicity RMD 2005 Fund Class C	FCRPX	NAS CM	Open End	Moderate Alloc (Asset Alloc)	B-	C+	B	Up	Y	2,500
Fidelity Advisor Simplicity RMD 2005 Fund Class I	FRAPX	NAS CM	Open End	Moderate Alloc (Asset Alloc)	B-	C+	B	Up	Y	2,500
Fidelity Advisor Simplicity RMD 2005 Fund Class M	FTRPX	NAS CM	Open End	Moderate Alloc (Asset Alloc)	B-	C+	B	Up	Y	2,500
Fidelity Advisor Simplicity RMD 2010 Fund Class A	FIARX	NAS CM	Open End	Moderate Alloc (Asset Alloc)	B-	C+	B	Up	Y	2,500
Fidelity Advisor Simplicity RMD 2010 Fund Class C	FICRX	NAS CM	Open End	Moderate Alloc (Asset Alloc)	B-	C+	B	Up	Y	2,500
Fidelity Advisor Simplicity RMD 2010 Fund Class I	FIIRX	NAS CM	Open End	Moderate Alloc (Asset Alloc)	B-	C+	B	Up	Y	2,500
Fidelity Advisor Simplicity RMD 2010 Fund Class M	FTIRX	NAS CM	Open End	Moderate Alloc (Asset Alloc)	B-	C+	B	Up	Y	2,500
Fidelity Advisor Simplicity RMD 2015 Fund Class A	FURAX	NAS CM	Open End	Moderate Alloc (Asset Alloc)	B-	C+	B	Up	Y	2,500
Fidelity Advisor Simplicity RMD 2015 Fund Class C	FURCX	NAS CM	Open End	Moderate Alloc (Asset Alloc)	B-	C+	B	Up	Y	2,500
Fidelity Advisor Simplicity RMD 2015 Fund Class I	FURIX	NAS CM	Open End	Moderate Alloc (Asset Alloc)	B-	C+	B	Up	Y	2,500
Fidelity Advisor Simplicity RMD 2015 Fund Class M	FURTX	NAS CM	Open End	Moderate Alloc (Asset Alloc)	B-	C+	B	Up	Y	2,500
Fidelity Advisor Simplicity RMD 2020 Fund Class A	FARWX	NAS CM	Open End	Moderate Alloc (Asset Alloc)	B-	C+	B	Up	Y	2,500
Fidelity Advisor Simplicity RMD 2020 Fund Class C	FCRWX	NAS CM	Open End	Moderate Alloc (Asset Alloc)	B-	C+	B	Up	Y	2,500
Fidelity Advisor Simplicity RMD 2020 Fund Class I	FIIWX	NAS CM	Open End	Moderate Alloc (Asset Alloc)	B-	C+	B	Up	Y	2,500
Fidelity Advisor Simplicity RMD 2020 Fund Class M	FTRWX	NAS CM	Open End	Moderate Alloc (Asset Alloc)	B-	C+	B	Up	Y	2,500
Fidelity Advisor Simplicity RMD Income Fund Class A	FRNAX	NAS CM	Open End	Cautious Alloc (Asset Alloc)	B-	C+	B	Up	Y	2,500
Fidelity Advisor Simplicity RMD Income Fund Class C	FRNCX	NAS CM	Open End	Cautious Alloc (Asset Alloc)	B-	C	B	Up	Y	2,500
Fidelity Advisor Simplicity RMD Income Fund Class I	FRNIX	NAS CM	Open End	Cautious Alloc (Asset Alloc)	B-	C+	B	Up	Y	2,500
Fidelity Advisor Simplicity RMD Income Fund Class M	FRNTX	NAS CM	Open End	Cautious Alloc (Asset Alloc)	B-	C	B	Up	Y	2,500
Fidelity Advisor® Balanced Fund Class A	FABLX	NAS CM	Open End	Moderate Alloc (Balanced)	B-	C+	B	Down	Y	2,500
Fidelity Advisor® Balanced Fund Class C	FABCX	NAS CM	Open End	Moderate Alloc (Balanced)	B-	C+	B	Down	Y	2,500
Fidelity Advisor® Balanced Fund Class M	FAIGX	NAS CM	Open End	Moderate Alloc (Balanced)	B-	C+	B	Down	Y	2,500
Fidelity Advisor® Balanced Fund Class Z	FZAAX	NAS CM	Open End	Moderate Alloc (Balanced)	B-	B-	B	Down	Y	0
Fidelity Advisor® Balanced Fund I Class	FAIOX	NAS CM	Open End	Moderate Alloc (Balanced)	B-	B-	B	Down	Y	2,500
Fidelity Advisor® Biotechnology Fund Class A	FBTAX	NAS CM	Open End	Healthcare Sector Equity (Health)	C	C	C		Y	2,500
Fidelity Advisor® Biotechnology Fund Class C	FBTCX	NAS CM	Open End	Healthcare Sector Equity (Health)	C	C-	C		Y	2,500
Fidelity Advisor® Biotechnology Fund Class M	FBTTX	NAS CM	Open End	Healthcare Sector Equity (Health)	C	C	C		Y	2,500
Fidelity Advisor® Biotechnology Fund I Class	FBTIX	NAS CM	Open End	Healthcare Sector Equity (Health)	C	C	C	Down	Y	2,500
Fidelity Advisor® Canada Fund Class A	FACNX	NAS CM	Open End	Other Equity (Foreign Stock)	C	C+	C		Y	2,500
Fidelity Advisor® Canada Fund Class C	FCCNX	NAS CM	Open End	Other Equity (Foreign Stock)	C	C+	C		Y	2,500
Fidelity Advisor® Canada Fund Class M	FTCNX	NAS CM	Open End	Other Equity (Foreign Stock)	C	C+	C		Y	2,500
Fidelity Advisor® Canada Fund I Class	FICCX	NAS CM	Open End	Other Equity (Foreign Stock)	C+	C+	C	Up	Y	2,500
Fidelity Advisor® Capital Development Fund Class A	FDTTX	NAS CM	Open End	US Equity Large Cap Blend (World Stock)	B	B	B	Up	Y	0
Fidelity Advisor® Capital Development Fund Class C	FDECX	NAS CM	Open End	US Equity Large Cap Blend (World Stock)	B-	B-	B	Down	Y	2,500
Fidelity Advisor® Capital Development Fund Class M	FDTZX	NAS CM	Open End	US Equity Large Cap Blend (World Stock)	B-	B	C+	Down	Y	2,500
Fidelity Advisor® Capital Development Fund Class O	FDETX	NAS CM	Open End	US Equity Large Cap Blend (World Stock)	B	B	B	Up		0
Fidelity Advisor® Capital Development Fund I Class	FDEIX	NAS CM	Open End	US Equity Large Cap Blend (World Stock)	B	B	B	Up	Y	2,500
Fidelity Advisor® China Region Fund Class A	FHKAX	NAS CM	Open End	Greater China Equity (Pacific Stock)	B	A	C	Up	Y	2,500
Fidelity Advisor® China Region Fund Class C	FCHKX	NAS CM	Open End	Greater China Equity (Pacific Stock)	B	A-	C	Up	Y	2,500
Fidelity Advisor® China Region Fund Class M	FHKTX	NAS CM	Open End	Greater China Equity (Pacific Stock)	B	A	C	Up	Y	2,500
Fidelity Advisor® China Region Fund I Class	FHKIX	NAS CM	Open End	Greater China Equity (Pacific Stock)	B	A	C	Up	Y	2,500
Fidelity Advisor® Communications Equipment Fund Class A	FDMAX	NAS CM	Open End	Technology Sector Equity (Comm)	B-	B-	B-	Up	Y	2,500
Fidelity Advisor® Communications Equipment Fund Class C	FDMCX	NAS CM	Open End	Technology Sector Equity (Comm)	C+	C+	B-		Y	2,500
Fidelity Advisor® Communications Equipment Fund Class M	FDMTX	NAS CM	Open End	Technology Sector Equity (Comm)	B-	B-	B-	Up	Y	2,500
Fidelity Advisor® Communications Equipment Fund I Class	FDMIX	NAS CM	Open End	Technology Sector Equity (Comm)	B-	B-	B-	Up	Y	2,500
Fidelity Advisor® Consumer Discretionary Fund Class A	FCNAX	NAS CM	Open End	Consumer Goods Sec Equity ()	B	B	A-	Up	Y	2,500
Fidelity Advisor® Consumer Discretionary Fund Class C	FCECX	NAS CM	Open End	Consumer Goods Sec Equity ()	B	B-	A-	Up	Y	2,500
Fidelity Advisor® Consumer Discretionary Fund Class M	FACPX	NAS CM	Open End	Consumer Goods Sec Equity ()	B	B	A-	Up	Y	2,500
Fidelity Advisor® Consumer Discretionary Fund I Class	FCNIX	NAS CM	Open End	Consumer Goods Sec Equity ()	B	B	A-	Up	Y	2,500
Fidelity Advisor® Consumer Staples Fund Class A	FDAGX	NAS CM	Open End	Consumer Goods Sec Equity ()	C	C	C+	Down	Y	2,500

★ Expanded analysis of this fund is included in Section II.

	TOTAL RETURNS					PERFORMANCE				ASSETS		ASSET ALLOCATION & TURNOVER					BULL & BEAR		FEES		
Min Additional Investment	3-Month Total Return	6-Month Total Return	1-Year Total Return	3-Year Total Return	5-Year Total Return	Dividend Yield (TTM)	Expense Ratio	3-Yr Std Deviation	3-Year Beta	NAV	Total Assets (MIL)	%Cash	%Stocks	%Bonds	%Other	Turnover Ratio	Last Bull Market Total Return	Last Bear Market Total Return	Front End Fee (%)	Back End Fee (%)	Inception Date
	1.50	3.37	6.54	10.41	28.74	0.9	0.97	3.47	0.12	57.94	10.9	27	24	49	0	111	11.04	-9.25	3.50		Aug-07
	1.76	3.89	9.16	15.28	40.76	1.14	0.74	5.11	-0.06	58.33	19.4	25	27	47	0	102	12.98	-11.11	5.75		Aug-07
	1.57	3.49	8.34	12.70	35.56	0.49	1.49	5.12	-0.06	58.05	19.4	25	27	47	0	102	12.5	-11.38		1.00	Aug-07
	1.81	4.00	9.40	16.13	42.52	1.38	0.49	5.11	-0.06	58.28	19.4	25	27	47	0	102	13.15	-11.01			Aug-07
	1.69	3.75	8.88	14.42	39.00	0.94	0.99	5.11	-0.06	58.29	19.4	25	27	47	0	102	12.81	-11.19	3.50		Aug-07
	2.19	4.72	10.76	17.32	45.10	1.1	0.78	5.62	-0.12	53.42	6.5	21	36	43	0	128	13.67	-11.9	5.75		Aug-07
	2.01	4.33	9.92	14.68	39.74	0.55	1.53	5.62	-0.12	53.11	6.5	21	36	43	0	128	13.18	-12.18		1.00	Aug-07
	2.26	4.84	11.01	18.18	46.90	1.33	0.53	5.62	-0.12	53.42	6.5	21	36	43	0	128	13.84	-11.8			Aug-07
	2.13	4.59	10.46	16.41	43.28	0.89	1.03	5.63	-0.12	53.46	6.5	21	36	43	0	128	13.49	-12	3.50		Aug-07
	2.66	5.60	12.23	19.05	48.56	1.03	0.83	5.99	-0.16	58.91	9.5	17	45	38	0	115	14.3	-12.73	5.75		Aug-07
	2.47	5.22	11.41	16.40	43.10	0.56	1.58	5.99	-0.17	58.37	9.5	17	45	38	0	115	13.8	-13		1.00	Aug-07
	2.71	5.75	12.52	20.05	50.67	1.34	0.58	5.98	-0.16	58.97	9.5	17	45	38	0	115	14.46	-12.64			Aug-07
	2.59	5.48	11.95	18.13	46.72	0.83	1.08	6	-0.17	58.86	9.5	17	45	38	0	115	14.14	-12.82	3.50		Aug-07
	3.12	6.48	13.67	20.68	52.31	1.01	0.87	6.36	0.6	59.34	14.0	14	53	32	0	118	15.28	-13.79	5.75		Dec-07
	2.92	6.06	12.81	17.98	46.70	0.56	1.62	6.36	0.6	58.71	14.0	14	53	32	0	118	14.77	-14.07		1.00	Dec-07
	3.19	6.58	13.94	21.56	54.21	1.28	0.62	6.36	0.6	59.24	14.0	14	53	32	0	118	15.46	-13.71			Dec-07
	3.05	6.33	13.38	19.76	50.43	0.81	1.12	6.35	0.6	59.4	14.0	14	53	32	0	118	15.1	-13.88	3.50		Dec-07
	1.55	3.50	7.61	12.81	34.69	1.14	0.72	4.18	0.04	57.92	11.8	27	24	49	0	128	12.04	-9.99	5.75		Aug-07
	1.38	3.11	6.82	10.29	29.72	0.49	1.47	4.18	0.04	57.69	11.8	27	24	49	0	128	11.53	-10.27		1.00	Aug-07
	1.64	3.63	7.89	13.66	36.38	1.36	0.47	4.18	0.04	57.91	11.8	27	24	49	0	128	12.18	-9.89			Aug-07
	1.51	3.39	7.37	11.98	33.03	0.91	0.97	4.17	0.04	57.92	11.8	27	24	49	0	128	11.87	-10.07	3.50		Aug-07
	3.49	7.04	16.08	23.45	65.73	1.17	0.89	7.3	0.7	20.85	2,879	4	65	28	2	86	15.64	-10.52	5.75		Sep-96
	3.31	6.65	15.23	20.68	59.56	0.43	1.64	7.28	0.7	20.72	2,879	4	65	28	2	86	15.09	-10.79		1.00	Nov-97
	3.46	6.91	15.78	22.56	63.79	0.92	1.13	7.28	0.7	21.09	2,879	4	65	28	2	86	15.46	-10.6	3.50		Jan-87
	3.57	7.21	16.50	24.89	68.33	1.5	0.5	7.28	0.7	21.24	2,879	4	65	28	2	86	15.46	-10.6			Aug-13
	3.55	7.16	16.35	24.39	67.87	1.38	0.63	7.29	0.7	21.24	2,879	4	65	28	2	86	15.74	-10.37			Jul-95
	-4.92	5.23	25.80	6.90	138.29	0	1.05	27.63	1.48	25.11	2,595	1	97	0	0	30	37.41	-12.02	5.75		Dec-00
	-5.10	4.82	24.81	4.50	129.57	0	1.79	27.59	1.48	21.73	2,595	1	97	0	0	30	36.71	-12.21		1.00	Dec-00
	-4.98	5.07	25.36	5.88	134.67	0	1.38	27.62	1.48	23.82	2,595	1	97	0	0	30	37.05	-12.02	3.50		Dec-00
	-4.87	5.36	26.15	7.79	141.64	0	0.78	27.65	1.48	26.53	2,595	1	97	0	0	30	37.53	-11.86			Dec-00
	2.65	10.74	14.06	8.63	24.67	0.84	1.48	12.93	0.89	54.51	1,208	2	98	0	0	44	12.65	-23.87	5.75		May-07
	2.46	10.33	13.22	6.28	20.16	0.2	2.21	12.92	0.88	53.43	1,208	2	98	0	0	44	12.15	-24.11		1.00	May-07
	2.55	10.58	13.72	7.67	22.82	0.63	1.77	12.92	0.88	54.32	1,208	2	98	0	0	44	12.48	-23.97	3.50		May-07
	2.74	10.94	14.47	9.77	26.74	1.21	1.14	12.93	0.89	54.55	1,208	2	98	0	0	44	12.85	-23.78			May-07
	5.77	10.35	17.73	31.60	94.65	1.02	0.88	12.48	1.16	15.99	3,223	1	99	0	0	31	20.37	-19.55	5.75		Apr-99
	5.56	9.91	16.63	27.80	85.22	0.47	1.85	12.47	1.16	15.08	3,223	1	99	0	0	31	19.75	-19.8		1.00	Jul-05
	5.70	10.12	17.11	29.47	89.42	0.66	1.42	12.46	1.16	15.6	3,223	1	99	0	0	31	20.04	-19.72	3.50		Jul-05
	5.87	10.58	18.12	32.81	97.57	1.22	0.59	12.46	1.16	16.53	3,223	1	99	0	0	31	20.58	-19.41			Dec-85
	5.91	10.53	17.96	32.20	96.14	1.14	0.74	12.46	1.16	16.61	3,223	1	99	0	0	31	20.33	-19.48			Jul-05
	9.88	19.97	51.45	37.48	75.38	0.52	1.33	22.02	1.24	35.59	1,442	0	99	0	0	70	17.55	-27.15	5.75		May-08
	9.68	19.51	50.36	34.40	68.99	0	2.07	22	1.24	34.78	1,442	0	99	0	0	70	17	-27.38		1.00	May-08
	9.81	19.75	50.93	36.03	72.61	0.32	1.67	22.02	1.24	35.47	1,442	0	99	0	0	70	17.34	-27.23	3.50		May-08
	9.96	20.13	51.91	38.73	78.39	0.8	1	22.02	1.24	35.72	1,442	0	99	0	0	70	17.75	-27.06			May-08
	5.01	5.94	10.94	17.21	73.90	0.36	1.78	15.75	1.31	13.73	14.6	1	99	0	0	71	14.21	-32.37	5.75		Dec-00
	4.80	5.58	10.18	14.68	67.54	0	2.55	15.71	1.3	12.12	14.6	1	99	0	0	71	13.65	-32.57		1.00	Dec-00
	4.98	5.86	10.70	16.42	71.67	0.16	2.11	15.74	1.3	13.22	14.6	1	99	0	0	71	14.09	-32.52	3.50		Dec-00
	5.09	6.14	11.28	18.14	76.03	0.52	1.46	15.75	1.31	14.27	14.6	1	99	0	0	71	14.44	-32.35			Dec-00
	10.87	11.51	21.77	31.34	106.74	0.37	1.1	10.99	0.96	25.28	274.2	0	100	0	0	47	31.4	-16.55	5.75		Sep-96
	10.68	11.16	20.95	28.41	98.99	0	1.85	11	0.96	20.61	274.2	0	100	0	0	47	30.89	-16.85		1.00	Nov-97
	10.81	11.39	21.45	30.20	103.75	0.33	1.39	10.98	0.96	23.66	274.2	0	100	0	0	47	31.17	-16.65	3.50		Sep-96
	10.97	11.69	22.18	32.40	109.68	0.52	0.83	11.01	0.96	27.21	274.2	0	100	0	0	47	31.72	-16.44			Sep-96
	3.54	0.03	11.75	15.80	63.89	1.38	1.04	9.98	0.59	91.73	2,453	1	99	0	0	56	17.63	-6.73	5.75		Dec-06

Fund Name	MARKET Ticker Symbol	Traded On	FUND TYPE, CATEGORY & OBJECTIVE Fund Type	Category and (Prospectus Objective)	RATINGS Overall Rating	Reward Rating	Risk Rating	Recent Up/ Downgrade	Open to New Investors	MINIMUMS Min Initial Investment
Fidelity Advisor® Consumer Staples Fund Class C	FDCGX	NAS CM	Open End	Consumer Goods Sec Equity ()	C	C	C	Down	Y	2,500
Fidelity Advisor® Consumer Staples Fund Class M	FDTGX	NAS CM	Open End	Consumer Goods Sec Equity ()	C	C	C	Down	Y	2,500
Fidelity Advisor® Consumer Staples Fund I Class	FDIGX	NAS CM	Open End	Consumer Goods Sec Equity ()	C	C	B-	Down	Y	2,500
Fidelity Advisor® Convertible Securities Fund Class A	FACVX	NAS CM	Open End	Convertibles (Convertible Bond)	C+	C	C+	Up	Y	2,500
Fidelity Advisor® Convertible Securities Fund Class C	FCCVX	NAS CM	Open End	Convertibles (Convertible Bond)	C	C	C+	Down	Y	2,500
Fidelity Advisor® Convertible Securities Fund Class M	FTCVX	NAS CM	Open End	Convertibles (Convertible Bond)	C+	C	C+	Up	Y	2,500
Fidelity Advisor® Convertible Securities Fund I Class	FICVX	NAS CM	Open End	Convertibles (Convertible Bond)	C+	C	C+	Up	Y	2,500
Fidelity Advisor® Diversified International Fund Class A	FDVAX	NAS CM	Open End	Global Equity Large Cap (Foreign Stock)	B	B-	B	Up	Y	2,500
Fidelity Advisor® Diversified International Fund Class C	FADCX	NAS CM	Open End	Global Equity Large Cap (Foreign Stock)	B-	C+	B	Up	Y	2,500
Fidelity Advisor® Diversified International Fund Class M	FADIX	NAS CM	Open End	Global Equity Large Cap (Foreign Stock)	B	B-	B	Up	Y	2,500
Fidelity Advisor® Diversified International Fund Class Z	FZABX	NAS CM	Open End	Global Equity Large Cap (Foreign Stock)	B	B-	B	Up	Y	0
Fidelity Advisor® Diversified International Fund I Class	FDVIX	NAS CM	Open End	Global Equity Large Cap (Foreign Stock)	B	B-	B	Up	Y	2,500
Fidelity Advisor® Diversified Stock Fund Class A	FDTOX	NAS CM	Open End	US Equity Large Cap Blend (World Stock)	B-	B	C+	Down	Y	0
Fidelity Advisor® Diversified Stock Fund Class C	FDTCX	NAS CM	Open End	US Equity Large Cap Blend (World Stock)	B-	B-	B-	Down	Y	2,500
Fidelity Advisor® Diversified Stock Fund Class M	FDTEX	NAS CM	Open End	US Equity Large Cap Blend (World Stock)	B-	B-	B	Down	Y	2,500
Fidelity Advisor® Diversified Stock Fund Class O	FDESX	NAS CM	Open End	US Equity Large Cap Blend (World Stock)	B-	B	C+	Down		0
Fidelity Advisor® Diversified Stock Fund Class Z	FZACX	NAS CM	Open End	US Equity Large Cap Blend (World Stock)	B-	B	C+	Down	Y	0
Fidelity Advisor® Diversified Stock Fund I Class	FDTIX	NAS CM	Open End	US Equity Large Cap Blend (World Stock)	B-	B	C+	Down	Y	2,500
Fidelity Advisor® Dividend Growth Fund Class A	FADAX	NAS CM	Open End	US Equity Large Cap Blend (Growth)	B-	B-	B-	Down	Y	2,500
Fidelity Advisor® Dividend Growth Fund Class C	FDGCX	NAS CM	Open End	US Equity Large Cap Blend (Growth)	B-	C+	B-	Down	Y	2,500
Fidelity Advisor® Dividend Growth Fund Class M	FDGTX	NAS CM	Open End	US Equity Large Cap Blend (Growth)	B-	B-	B-	Down	Y	2,500
Fidelity Advisor® Dividend Growth Fund Class Z	FZADX	NAS CM	Open End	US Equity Large Cap Blend (Growth)	B-	B-	B-	Down	Y	0
Fidelity Advisor® Dividend Growth Fund I Class	FDGIX	NAS CM	Open End	US Equity Large Cap Blend (Growth)	B-	B-	B-	Down	Y	2,500
Fidelity Advisor® Emerging Asia Fund Class A	FEAAX	NAS CM	Open End	Asia ex-Japan Equity (Pacific Stock)	B+	A	C+	Up	Y	2,500
Fidelity Advisor® Emerging Asia Fund Class C	FERCX	NAS CM	Open End	Asia ex-Japan Equity (Pacific Stock)	B+	A	C+	Up	Y	2,500
Fidelity Advisor® Emerging Asia Fund Class M	FEATX	NAS CM	Open End	Asia ex-Japan Equity (Pacific Stock)	B+	A	C+	Up	Y	2,500
Fidelity Advisor® Emerging Asia Fund I Class	FERIX	NAS CM	Open End	Asia ex-Japan Equity (Pacific Stock)	B+	A	C+	Up	Y	2,500
Fidelity Advisor® Emerg Eur, Mid East, Afr (EMEA) Cls A	FMEAX	NAS CM	Open End	Emerging Markets Equity (Foreign Stock)	C+	B-	C	Up	Y	2,500
Fidelity Advisor® Emerg Eur, Mid East, Afr (EMEA) Cls C	FEMCX	NAS CM	Open End	Emerging Markets Equity (Foreign Stock)	C+	C+	C	Up	Y	2,500
Fidelity Advisor® Emerg Eur, Mid East, Afr (EMEA) Cls M	FEMTX	NAS CM	Open End	Emerging Markets Equity (Foreign Stock)	C+	B-	C	Up	Y	2,500
Fidelity Advisor® Emerg Eur, Mid East, Afr (EMEA) I Cls	FIEMX	NAS CM	Open End	Emerging Markets Equity (Foreign Stock)	C+	B-	C	Up	Y	2,500
Fidelity Advisor® Emerging Markets Discovery Fund Class A	FEDAX	NAS CM	Open End	Emerging Markets Equity (Div Emerging Mkts)	B	B	C+	Up	Y	2,500
Fidelity Advisor® Emerging Markets Discovery Fund Class C	FEDGX	NAS CM	Open End	Emerging Markets Equity (Div Emerging Mkts)	B-	B	C+	Up	Y	2,500
Fidelity Advisor® Emerging Markets Discovery Fund Class M	FEDTX	NAS CM	Open End	Emerging Markets Equity (Div Emerging Mkts)	B	B	C+	Up	Y	2,500
Fidelity Advisor® Emerging Markets Discovery Fund I Class	FEDIX	NAS CM	Open End	Emerging Markets Equity (Div Emerging Mkts)	B	B	B-	Up	Y	2,500
Fidelity Advisor® Emerging Markets Fund Class A	FAMKX	NAS CM	Open End	Emerging Markets Equity (Div Emerging Mkts)	B	B	C	Up	Y	2,500
Fidelity Advisor® Emerging Markets Fund Class C	FMCKX	NAS CM	Open End	Emerging Markets Equity (Div Emerging Mkts)	B-	B	C	Up	Y	2,500
Fidelity Advisor® Emerging Markets Fund Class M	FTMKX	NAS CM	Open End	Emerging Markets Equity (Div Emerging Mkts)	B	B	C	Up	Y	2,500
Fidelity Advisor® Emerging Markets Fund Class Z	FZAEX	NAS CM	Open End	Emerging Markets Equity (Div Emerging Mkts)	B	B+	C	Up	Y	0
Fidelity Advisor® Emerging Markets Fund I Class	FIMKX	NAS CM	Open End	Emerging Markets Equity (Div Emerging Mkts)	B	B+	C	Up	Y	2,500
Fidelity Advisor® Energy Fund Class A	FANAX	NAS CM	Open End	Energy Sector Equity (Natl Res)	C-	D+	C-	Up	Y	2,500
Fidelity Advisor® Energy Fund Class C	FNRCX	NAS CM	Open End	Energy Sector Equity (Natl Res)	D+	D+	C-	Up	Y	2,500
Fidelity Advisor® Energy Fund Class M	FAGNX	NAS CM	Open End	Energy Sector Equity (Natl Res)	C-	D+	C-	Up	Y	2,500
Fidelity Advisor® Energy Fund I Class	FANIX	NAS CM	Open End	Energy Sector Equity (Natl Res)	C-	D+	C-	Up	Y	2,500
Fidelity Advisor® Equity Growth Fund Class A	EPGAX	NAS CM	Open End	US Equity Large Cap Growth (Growth)	A-	B+	A-	Up	Y	2,500
Fidelity Advisor® Equity Growth Fund Class C	EPGCX	NAS CM	Open End	US Equity Large Cap Growth (Growth)	B+	B+	A-	Up	Y	2,500
Fidelity Advisor® Equity Growth Fund Class M	FAEGX	NAS CM	Open End	US Equity Large Cap Growth (Growth)	A-	B+	A-	Up	Y	2,500
Fidelity Advisor® Equity Growth Fund Class Z	FZAFX	NAS CM	Open End	US Equity Large Cap Growth (Growth)	A-	A-	A-	Up	Y	0
Fidelity Advisor® Equity Growth Fund I Class	EQPGX	NAS CM	Open End	US Equity Large Cap Growth (Growth)	A-	A-	A-	Up	Y	2,500
Fidelity Advisor® Equity Income Fund Class A	FEIAX	NAS CM	Open End	US Equity Large Cap Value (Equity-Income)	B-	B-	B	Down	Y	2,500
Fidelity Advisor® Equity Income Fund Class C	FEICX	NAS CM	Open End	US Equity Large Cap Value (Equity-Income)	B-	C+	B	Down	Y	2,500
Fidelity Advisor® Equity Income Fund Class M	FEIRX	NAS CM	Open End	US Equity Large Cap Value (Equity-Income)	B-	C+	B	Down	Y	2,500

★Expanded analysis of this fund is included in Section II.

	TOTAL RETURNS					PERFORMANCE				ASSETS		ASSET ALLOCATION & TURNOVER					BULL & BEAR		FEES		
Min Additional Investment	3-Month Total Return	6-Month Total Return	1-Year Total Return	3-Year Total Return	5-Year Total Return	Dividend Yield (TTM)	Expense Ratio	3-Yr Std Deviation	3-Year Beta	NAV	Total Assets (MIL)	%Cash	%Stocks	%Bonds	%Other	Turnover Ratio	Last Bull Market Total Return	Last Bear Market Total Return	Front End Fee (%)	Back End Fee (%)	Inception Date
	3.34	-0.33	10.92	13.22	57.86	0.76	1.8	9.98	0.59	89.5	2,453	1	99	0	0	56	17.12	-7.02		1.00	Dec-06
	3.47	-0.10	11.45	14.84	61.67	1.17	1.32	9.98	0.59	90.96	2,453	1	99	0	0	56	17.43	-6.84	3.50		Dec-06
	3.60	0.16	12.05	16.72	66.04	1.66	0.78	9.99	0.59	92.32	2,453	1	99	0	0	56	17.78	-6.64			Dec-06
	2.33	4.27	9.30	4.09	42.55	2.46	0.73	9.2	1.1	27.87	1,528	7	8	3	0	112	15.92	-19.86	5.75		Feb-09
	2.15	3.89	8.52	1.77	37.21	1.74	1.5	9.22	1.11	27.73	1,528	7	8	3	0	112	15.33	-20.1		1.00	Feb-09
	2.25	4.12	9.01	3.20	40.51	2.3	1.04	9.21	1.1	27.86	1,528	7	8	3	0	112	15.68	-19.96	3.50		Feb-09
	2.38	4.43	9.63	4.95	44.42	2.73	0.47	9.2	1.1	27.92	1,528	7	8	3	0	112	16.03	-19.79			Feb-09
	3.75	9.05	26.56	27.19	56.86	0.79	1.23	11.35	0.89	23.66	2,266	2	98	0	0	44	16.95	-24.67	5.75		Dec-98
	3.56	8.60	25.62	24.37	51.09	0.14	1.98	11.32	0.89	22.72	2,266	2	98	0	0	44	16.4	-24.85		1.00	Dec-98
	3.68	8.88	26.17	26.18	54.81	0.55	1.49	11.32	0.88	23.52	2,266	2	98	0	0	44	16.78	-24.72	3.50		Dec-98
	3.85	9.26	27.06	28.86	60.25	1.16	0.79	11.32	0.88	23.98	2,266	2	98	0	0	44	17.13	-24.56			Aug-13
	3.80	9.16	26.87	28.20	59.12	1.03	0.94	11.34	0.89	24.01	2,266	2	98	0	0	44	17.13	-24.56			Dec-98
	6.13	11.53	18.91	29.81	97.25	1.14	0.84	11.36	1.06	24.75	2,130	0	100	0	0	77	26.62	-18.31	5.75		Apr-99
	5.84	10.99	17.77	26.23	88.10	0.47	1.77	11.38	1.06	24.02	2,130	0	100	0	0	77	26.01	-18.66		1.00	Jul-05
	6.03	11.33	18.45	28.31	93.13	0.85	1.23	11.36	1.06	24.57	2,130	0	100	0	0	77	26.32	-18.45	3.50		Jul-05
	6.23	11.76	19.32	31.20	100.47	1.38	0.49	11.37	1.06	25.4	2,130	0	100	0	0	77	26.92	-18.22			Jul-70
	6.16	11.69	19.22	31.04	100.21	1.32	0.52	11.37	1.06	26.01	2,130	0	100	0	0	77	26.92	-18.22			Aug-13
	6.16	11.65	19.11	30.62	98.96	1.2	0.64	11.38	1.06	26.27	2,130	0	100	0	0	77	26.67	-18.24			Jul-05
	7.46	11.64	19.65	26.36	90.04	1.02	0.9	9.8	0.96	17.46	1,087	5	95	0	0	31	27.21	-24.67	5.75		Dec-98
	7.23	11.25	18.70	23.51	83.11	0.42	1.66	9.77	0.95	16.56	1,087	5	95	0	0	31	26.7	-24.88		1.00	Dec-98
	7.35	11.43	19.32	25.39	87.77	0.81	1.14	9.75	0.95	17.38	1,087	5	95	0	0	31	26.97	-24.7	3.50		Dec-98
	7.53	11.81	20.07	27.87	93.66	1.24	0.49	9.77	0.95	18.66	1,087	5	95	0	0	31	27.48	-24.61			Aug-13
	7.45	11.73	19.90	27.24	92.32	1.15	0.67	9.77	0.95	18.39	1,087	5	95	0	0	31	27.48	-24.61			Dec-98
	10.26	16.90	46.75	41.62	58.05	0.61	1.42	15.46	1.01	41.09	314.6	3	97	0	0	43	18.38	-25.51	5.75		Mar-94
	10.07	16.47	45.68	38.51	52.27	0.21	2.16	15.45	1.01	37.4	314.6	3	97	0	0	43	17.88	-25.76		1.00	Jun-99
	10.18	16.76	46.30	40.30	55.66	0.46	1.72	15.46	1.01	39.94	314.6	3	97	0	0	43	18.2	-25.6	3.50		Jun-99
	10.36	17.08	47.16	42.92	60.46	0.74	1.11	15.47	1.01	42.31	314.6	3	97	0	0	43	18.62	-25.43			Jun-99
	13.02	20.54	24.84	34.31	22.04	0.87	1.69	17.07	0.89	10.35	102.3	0	97	0	0	47	19.71	-26.75	5.75		May-08
	12.93	19.97	23.98	31.20	17.34	0.34	2.47	17.03	0.88	10.34	102.3	0	97	0	0	47	19.19	-26.96		1.00	May-08
	13.04	20.33	24.63	33.32	20.33	0.71	2	17.02	0.88	10.33	102.3	0	97	0	0	47	19.6	-26.8	3.50		May-08
	13.22	20.75	25.35	35.85	24.15	1.11	1.31	17.03	0.88	10.34	102.3	0	97	0	0	47	20.01	-26.67			May-08
	6.44	13.39	37.21	37.42	31.66	0.43	1.7	13.4	0.89	15.29	427.1	4	95	0	0	60			5.75		Nov-11
	6.15	12.93	36.11	34.38	26.79	0.03	2.45	13.4	0.89	14.93	427.1	4	95	0	0	60				1.00	Nov-11
	6.34	13.24	36.81	36.38	30.00	0.29	1.95	13.42	0.89	15.23	427.1	4	95	0	0	60			3.50		Nov-11
	6.49	13.55	37.55	38.50	33.46	0.67	1.45	13.38	0.89	15.39	427.1	4	95	0	0	60					Nov-11
	8.21	17.90	46.78	34.85	42.52	0.02	1.51	13.7	0.8	30.18	644.2	4	96	0	0	86	16.5	-28.44	5.75		Mar-04
	7.99	17.43	45.62	31.80	37.21	0	2.26	13.7	0.8	28.76	644.2	4	96	0	0	86	16.03	-28.7		1.00	Mar-04
	8.12	17.72	46.33	33.73	40.65	0	1.77	13.7	0.8	29.96	644.2	4	96	0	0	86	16.32	-28.55	3.50		Mar-04
	8.32	18.16	47.45	36.82	45.96	0.45	1.01	13.72	0.8	30.26	644.2	4	96	0	0	86	16.69	-28.35			Aug-13
	8.27	18.10	47.28	36.28	45.01	0.32	1.16	13.72	0.81	30.3	644.2	4	96	0	0	86	16.69	-28.35			Mar-04
	10.01	17.68	-2.85	1.88	13.21	0	1.09	21.46	1.1	34.43	890.2	0	100	0	0	90	21.69	-31.01	5.75		Sep-96
	9.78	17.23	-3.56	-0.33	9.13	0	1.82	21.46	1.1	31.69	890.2	0	100	0	0	90	21.18	-31.2		1.00	Nov-97
	9.93	17.49	-3.14	1.06	11.83	0	1.36	21.46	1.1	35.25	890.2	0	100	0	0	90	21.56	-31.07	3.50		Dec-87
	10.07	17.85	-2.59	2.71	14.76	0.22	0.81	21.47	1.1	36.25	890.2	0	100	0	0	90	21.97	-30.93			Jul-95
	5.16	12.07	34.84	43.34	121.69	0	1.05	10.94	0.94	109.2	3,134	2	97	0	0	60	27.7	-18.21	5.75		Sep-96
	4.96	11.63	33.81	40.09	113.47	0	1.81	10.94	0.94	93.57	3,134	2	97	0	0	60	27.16	-18.45		1.00	Nov-97
	5.10	11.94	34.53	42.37	119.33	0	1.28	10.94	0.94	107.37	3,134	2	97	0	0	60	27.56	-18.25	3.50		Sep-92
	5.26	12.28	35.37	45.11	126.20	0	0.64	10.95	0.94	120.12	3,134	2	97	0	0	60	27.95	-18.08			Aug-13
	5.23	12.21	35.20	44.51	124.88	0	0.78	10.95	0.94	119.45	3,134	2	97	0	0	60	27.95	-18.08			Nov-83
	4.77	7.99	12.29	25.08	76.71	1.78	1	9.96	0.93	32.38	1,949	1	99	0	0	36	22.43	-17.86	5.75		Sep-96
	4.56	7.56	11.44	22.22	70.06	1.06	1.77	9.94	0.93	32.62	1,949	1	99	0	0	36	21.89	-18.14		1.00	Nov-97
	4.69	7.84	12.02	24.19	74.68	1.52	1.23	9.95	0.93	33.1	1,949	1	99	0	0	36	22.3	-17.93	3.50		Sep-92

Fund Name	Ticker Symbol	Traded On	Fund Type	Category and (Prospectus Objective)	Overall Rating	Reward Rating	Risk Rating	Recent Up/ Downgrade	Open to New Investors	Min Initial Investment
Fidelity Advisor® Equity Income Fund Class Z	FZAGX	NAS CM	Open End	US Equity Large Cap Value (Equity-Income)	B-	B-	B	Down	Y	0
Fidelity Advisor® Equity Income Fund I Class	EQPIX	NAS CM	Open End	US Equity Large Cap Value (Equity-Income)	B-	B-	B	Down	Y	2,500
Fidelity Advisor® Equity Value Fund Class A	FAVAX	NAS CM	Open End	US Equity Large Cap Value (Growth)	B	B-	B	Up	Y	2,500
Fidelity Advisor® Equity Value Fund Class C	FAVCX	NAS CM	Open End	US Equity Large Cap Value (Growth)	B-	C+	B	Down	Y	2,500
Fidelity Advisor® Equity Value Fund Class M	FAVTX	NAS CM	Open End	US Equity Large Cap Value (Growth)	B-	C+	B	Down	Y	2,500
Fidelity Advisor® Equity Value Fund Class Z	FAEVX	NAS CM	Open End	US Equity Large Cap Value (Growth)	B	B-	B	Up	Y	0
Fidelity Advisor® Equity Value Fund I Class	FAIVX	NAS CM	Open End	US Equity Large Cap Value (Growth)	B	B-	B	Up	Y	2,500
Fidelity Advisor® Europe Fund Class A	FHJUX	NAS CM	Open End	Europe Equity Large Cap (Europe Stock)	B	B	B	Up	Y	2,500
Fidelity Advisor® Europe Fund Class C	FHJTX	NAS CM	Open End	Europe Equity Large Cap (Europe Stock)	B-	B-	B	Up	Y	2,500
Fidelity Advisor® Europe Fund Class M	FHJVX	NAS CM	Open End	Europe Equity Large Cap (Europe Stock)	B	B-	B	Up	Y	2,500
Fidelity Advisor® Europe Fund I Class	FHJMX	NAS CM	Open End	Europe Equity Large Cap (Europe Stock)	B	B	B	Up	Y	2,500
Fidelity Advisor® Event Driven Opportunities Fund Class A	FCHSX	NAS CM	Open End	US Equity Small Cap (Growth)	B	B	B		Y	2,500
Fidelity Advisor® Event Driven Opportunities Fund Class C	FATJX	NAS CM	Open End	US Equity Small Cap (Growth)	B	B	B	Up	Y	2,500
Fidelity Advisor® Event Driven Opportunities Fund Class M	FJPDX	NAS CM	Open End	US Equity Small Cap (Growth)	B	B	B	Up	Y	2,500
Fidelity Advisor® Event Driven Opportunities Fund I Class	FMRMX	NAS CM	Open End	US Equity Small Cap (Growth)	B	B	B		Y	2,500
Fidelity Advisor® Financial Services Fund Class A	FAFDX	NAS CM	Open End	Financials Sector Equity (Financial)	B+	A-	B	Up	Y	2,500
Fidelity Advisor® Financial Services Fund Class C	FAFCX	NAS CM	Open End	Financials Sector Equity (Financial)	B	B+	B		Y	2,500
Fidelity Advisor® Financial Services Fund Class M	FAFSX	NAS CM	Open End	Financials Sector Equity (Financial)	B	A-	B		Y	2,500
Fidelity Advisor® Financial Services Fund I Class	FFSIX	NAS CM	Open End	Financials Sector Equity (Financial)	B+	A-	B	Up	Y	2,500
Fidelity Advisor® Global Balanced Fund Class A	FGLAX	NAS CM	Open End	Alloc (Multi-Asset Global)	B-	C+	B	Up	Y	2,500
Fidelity Advisor® Global Balanced Fund Class C	FGLCX	NAS CM	Open End	Alloc (Multi-Asset Global)	B-	C+	B	Up	Y	2,500
Fidelity Advisor® Global Balanced Fund Class I	FGLIX	NAS CM	Open End	Alloc (Multi-Asset Global)	B-	C+	B	Up	Y	2,500
Fidelity Advisor® Global Balanced Fund Class M	FGLTX	NAS CM	Open End	Alloc (Multi-Asset Global)	B-	C+	B	Up	Y	2,500
Fidelity Advisor® Global Capital Appreciation Fund Class A	FGEAX	NAS CM	Open End	Global Equity Mid/Small Cap (World Stock)	B	B	B	Up	Y	2,500
Fidelity Advisor® Global Capital Appreciation Fund Class C	FEUCX	NAS CM	Open End	Global Equity Mid/Small Cap (World Stock)	B	B	B	Up	Y	2,500
Fidelity Advisor® Global Capital Appreciation Fund Class M	FGETX	NAS CM	Open End	Global Equity Mid/Small Cap (World Stock)	B	B	B	Up	Y	2,500
Fidelity Advisor® Global Capital Appreciation Fund I Class	FEUIX	NAS CM	Open End	Global Equity Mid/Small Cap (World Stock)	B	B	B	Up	Y	2,500
Fidelity Advisor® Global Commodity Stock Fund Class A	FFGAX	NAS CM	Open End	Natl Resources Sec Equity (Growth)	C	C+	C	Up	Y	2,500
Fidelity Advisor® Global Commodity Stock Fund Class C	FCGCX	NAS CM	Open End	Natl Resources Sec Equity (Growth)	C	C	C	Up	Y	2,500
Fidelity Advisor® Global Commodity Stock Fund Class M	FFGTX	NAS CM	Open End	Natl Resources Sec Equity (Growth)	C	C	C	Up	Y	2,500
Fidelity Advisor® Global Commodity Stock Fund I Class	FFGIX	NAS CM	Open End	Natl Resources Sec Equity (Growth)	C	C+	C	Up	Y	2,500
Fidelity Advisor® Global Equity Income Fund Class A	FBLYX	NAS CM	Open End	Global Equity (Equity-Income)	B-	B-	B	Down	Y	2,500
Fidelity Advisor® Global Equity Income Fund Class C	FGTNX	NAS CM	Open End	Global Equity (Equity-Income)	B	C+	B+	Up	Y	2,500
Fidelity Advisor® Global Equity Income Fund Class M	FGABX	NAS CM	Open End	Global Equity (Equity-Income)	B	B-	B+	Up	Y	2,500
Fidelity Advisor® Global Equity Income Fund I Class	FBUSX	NAS CM	Open End	Global Equity (Equity-Income)	B	B-	B+	Up	Y	2,500
Fidelity Advisor® Global Real Estate Fund Class A	FWRAX	NAS CM	Open End	Real Estate Sector Equity (Real Estate)	D	C-	B-		Y	2,500
Fidelity Advisor® Global Real Estate Fund Class C	FWRCX	NAS CM	Open End	Real Estate Sector Equity (Real Estate)	D	C-	B-		Y	2,500
Fidelity Advisor® Global Real Estate Fund Class I	FWRIX	NAS CM	Open End	Real Estate Sector Equity (Real Estate)	D	C-	B-		Y	2,500
Fidelity Advisor® Global Real Estate Fund Class M	FWRTX	NAS CM	Open End	Real Estate Sector Equity (Real Estate)	D	C-	B-		Y	2,500
Fidelity Advisor® Global Strategies Fund Class A	FDASX	NAS CM	Open End	Alloc (Growth & Income)	B	C+	B+	Up	Y	2,500
Fidelity Advisor® Global Strategies Fund Class C	FDCSX	NAS CM	Open End	Alloc (Growth & Income)	B	C+	B+	Up	Y	2,500
Fidelity Advisor® Global Strategies Fund Class M	FDTSX	NAS CM	Open End	Alloc (Growth & Income)	B	C+	B+	Up	Y	2,500
Fidelity Advisor® Global Strategies Fund I Class	FDYIX	NAS CM	Open End	Alloc (Growth & Income)	B	C+	B+	Up	Y	2,500
Fidelity Advisor® Growth & Income Fund Class A	FGIRX	NAS CM	Open End	US Equity Large Cap Blend (Growth & Income)	B	B-	B	Up	Y	2,500
Fidelity Advisor® Growth & Income Fund Class C	FGIUX	NAS CM	Open End	US Equity Large Cap Blend (Growth & Income)	B-	B-	B	Down	Y	2,500
Fidelity Advisor® Growth & Income Fund Class M	FGITX	NAS CM	Open End	US Equity Large Cap Blend (Growth & Income)	B	B-	B	Up	Y	2,500
Fidelity Advisor® Growth & Income Fund Class Z	FGIZX	NAS CM	Open End	US Equity Large Cap Blend (Growth & Income)	B	B	B	Up	Y	0
Fidelity Advisor® Growth & Income Fund I Class	FGIOX	NAS CM	Open End	US Equity Large Cap Blend (Growth & Income)	B	B	B	Up	Y	2,500
Fidelity Advisor® Growth Opportunities Fund Class A	FAGAX	NAS CM	Open End	US Equity Large Cap Growth (Growth)	B+	B+	B+	Up	Y	2,500
Fidelity Advisor® Growth Opportunities Fund Class C	FACGX	NAS CM	Open End	US Equity Large Cap Growth (Growth)	B+	B	B+	Up	Y	2,500
Fidelity Advisor® Growth Opportunities Fund Class M	FAGOX	NAS CM	Open End	US Equity Large Cap Growth (Growth)	B+	B+	B+	Up	Y	2,500
Fidelity Advisor® Growth Opportunities Fund Class Z	FZAHX	NAS CM	Open End	US Equity Large Cap Growth (Growth)	B+	B+	B+	Up	Y	0

★Expanded analysis of this fund is included in Section II.

	TOTAL RETURNS					PERFORMANCE				ASSETS		ASSET ALLOCATION & TURNOVER					BULL & BEAR		FEES		
Min Additional Investment	3-Month Total Return	6-Month Total Return	1-Year Total Return	3-Year Total Return	5-Year Total Return	Dividend Yield (TTM)	Expense Ratio	3-Yr Std Deviation	3-Year Beta	NAV	Total Assets (MIL)	%Cash	%Stocks	%Bonds	%Other	Turnover Ratio	Last Bull Market Total Return	Last Bear Market Total Return	Front End Fee (%)	Back End Fee (%)	Inception Date
	4.87	8.19	12.74	26.64	80.14	2.08	0.59	9.95	0.93	33.8	1,949	1	99	0	0	36	22.63	-17.78			Aug-13
	4.83	8.14	12.57	26.05	78.98	1.92	0.74	9.95	0.93	33.83	1,949	1	99	0	0	36	22.63	-17.78			Apr-83
	4.87	7.28	13.79	23.08	93.42	0.7	1.19	9.87	0.91	18.98	283.1	5	95	0	0	46	25.73	-21.17	5.75		May-01
	4.64	6.87	12.89	20.26	86.19	0.13	1.96	9.88	0.91	18.59	283.1	5	95	0	0	46	25.12	-21.4		1.00	May-01
	4.81	7.16	13.46	22.11	91.05	0.47	1.46	9.87	0.91	18.99	283.1	5	95	0	0	46	25.51	-21.21	3.50		May-01
	4.92	7.52	14.19	24.28	96.57		0.77	9.86	0.91	19.26	283.1	5	95	0	0	46	25.89	-21.1			Feb-17
	4.93	7.47	14.07	24.15	96.37	0.9	0.91	9.86	0.91	19.26	283.1	5	95	0	0	46	25.89	-21.1			May-01
	3.80	8.99	28.78	25.48	48.27	0.52	1.39	13.38	0.97	42.33	1,263	-2	97	0	3	62	17.82	-29.4	5.75		Mar-14
	3.59	8.56	27.74	22.51	42.64	0	2.18	13.36	0.97	42.18	1,263	-2	97	0	3	62	17.31	-29.62		1.00	Mar-14
	3.71	8.82	28.40	24.36	46.21	0.21	1.7	13.37	0.97	42.41	1,263	-2	97	0	3	62	17.65	-29.48	3.50		Mar-14
	3.86	9.16	29.20	26.81	50.76	0.95	1.01	13.39	0.97	42.3	1,263	-2	97	0	3	62	17.99	-29.33			Mar-14
	4.41	6.47	17.45	39.43		0	1.55	14.67	1.23	13.68	33.4	9	91	0	0	120			5.75		Dec-13
	4.22	6.16	16.61	36.34		0	2.3	14.7	1.24	13.48	33.4	9	91	0	0	120				1.00	Dec-13
	4.32	6.39	17.13	38.43		0	1.8	14.68	1.23	13.63	33.4	9	91	0	0	120			3.50		Dec-13
	4.47	6.60	17.72	40.47		0	1.3	14.68	1.23	13.74	33.4	9	91	0	0	120					Dec-13
	8.56	14.38	20.54	35.60	104.75	0.18	1.12	13.99	1.13	21.87	431.7	2	98	0	0	81	29.79	-28.14	5.75		Sep-96
	8.39	13.99	19.63	32.58	97.33	0.01	1.87	14.01	1.13	20.53	431.7	2	98	0	0	81	29.09	-28.3		1.00	Nov-97
	8.50	14.21	20.23	34.43	101.87	0.09	1.4	13.99	1.13	21.66	431.7	2	98	0	0	81	29.58	-28.27	3.50		Sep-96
	8.64	14.53	20.90	36.85	108.05	0.27	0.84	14.01	1.13	22.47	431.7	2	98	0	0	81	29.87	-28.02			Sep-96
	4.40	8.67	19.57	18.41	37.09	0.02	1.3	7.28	0.6	24.72	485.0	2	61	36	2	155	12.05	-13.02	5.75		Feb-09
	4.17	8.17	18.61	15.48	31.61	0	2.11	7.29	0.61	23.9	485.0	2	61	36	2	155	11.56	-13.32		1.00	Feb-09
	4.48	8.82	19.94	19.41	38.99	0.06	1.01	7.29	0.61	24.97	485.0	2	61	36	2	155	12.21	-12.93			Feb-09
	4.32	8.49	19.23	17.40	35.20	0	1.58	7.27	0.6	24.48	485.0	2	61	36	2	155	11.92	-13.1	3.50		Feb-09
	5.60	13.87	30.24	37.69	99.95	0	1.45	10.25	0.9	18.32	140.8	0	98	0	0	137	14.64	-23.04	5.75		Dec-98
	5.36	13.41	29.23	34.58	92.58	0	2.2	10.23	0.9	15.78	140.8	0	98	0	0	137	14.16	-23.31		1.00	Dec-98
	5.49	13.68	29.88	36.61	97.41	0	1.71	10.23	0.9	17.49	140.8	0	98	0	0	137	14.45	-23.1	3.50		Dec-98
	5.62	13.97	30.61	38.72	102.73	0	1.21	10.26	0.9	19.25	140.8	0	98	0	0	137	14.83	-22.93			Dec-98
	7.77	19.46	18.19	10.38	-2.19	0.62	1.38	18.46	1.26	13.19	541.6	1	99	0	0	81	14.17	-29.68	5.75		Mar-09
	7.52	19.02	17.32	7.86	-5.79	0.1	2.13	18.4	1.26	13.09	541.6	1	99	0	0	81	13.66	-29.92		1.00	Mar-09
	7.68	19.37	17.89	9.41	-3.51	0.4	1.65	18.43	1.25	13.19	541.6	1	99	0	0	81	14.04	-29.79	3.50		Mar-09
	7.80	19.66	18.60	11.44	-0.64	0.93	1.01	18.42	1.26	13.18	541.6	1	99	0	0	81	14.35	-29.62			Mar-09
	5.67	10.30	21.29	27.30	70.86	0.87	1.45	8.73	0.8	14.83	18.4	4	95	0	0	43			5.75		May-12
	5.48	9.90	20.46	24.52	64.60	0.2	2.2	8.77	0.8	14.77	18.4	4	95	0	0	43				1.00	May-12
	5.58	10.08	20.96	26.30	68.68	0.65	1.7	8.71	0.8	14.82	18.4	4	95	0	0	43			3.50		May-12
	5.75	10.42	21.58	28.29	72.94	1.08	1.2	8.74	0.8	14.85	18.4	4	95	0	0	43					May-12
	3.74	6.43	12.76			0.72	1.4			9.96	2.9	4	95	0	1	59			5.75		Aug-16
	3.59	6.07	11.92			0.49	2.15			9.96	2.9	4	95	0	1	59				1.00	Aug-16
	3.85	6.65	13.11			0.81	1.15			9.97	2.9	4	95	0	1	59					Aug-16
	3.69	6.39	12.49			0.63	1.65			9.96	2.9	4	95	0	1	59			3.50		Aug-16
	4.59	8.56	19.01	24.41	40.41	1	1.35	6.51	0.59	9.32	174.9	8	64	28	1	38	13.23	-16.09	5.75		Oct-07
	4.42	7.99	18.18	21.58	35.31	0.56	2.1	6.55	0.6	9.16	174.9	8	64	28	1	38	12.76	-16.41		1.00	Oct-07
	4.46	8.33	18.67	23.43	38.67	0.83	1.6	6.5	0.59	9.28	174.9	8	64	28	1	38	12.98	-16.13	3.50		Oct-07
	4.61	8.56	19.36	25.28	42.25	1.23	1.1	6.52	0.59	9.35	174.9	8	64	28	1	38	13.36	-16.05			Oct-07
	6.00	10.19	16.57	30.11	94.85	1.33	0.99	11.77	1.11	28.38	596.1	0	99	0	0	31	26.76	-16.92	5.75		Dec-96
	5.78	9.74	15.63	27.14	87.65	0.83	1.74	11.79	1.11	26.67	596.1	0	99	0	0	31	26.24	-17.2		1.00	Nov-97
	5.92	10.03	16.23	29.09	92.49	1.12	1.24	11.79	1.11	28.41	596.1	0	99	0	0	31	26.6	-17.03	3.50		Dec-96
	6.09	10.41	16.98	31.29	98.07		0.57	11.8	1.11	28.92	596.1	0	99	0	0	31	27.01	-16.8			Feb-17
	6.06	10.32	16.84	31.13	97.83	1.48	0.73	11.8	1.11	28.93	596.1	0	99	0	0	31	27.01	-16.8			Dec-96
	6.53	12.05	34.68	40.21	120.16	0	0.86	12.82	1.14	64.73	3,029	1	98	0	0	66	28.41	-16.24	5.75		Sep-96
	6.33	11.63	33.65	37.11	112.09	0	1.61	12.82	1.14	56.84	3,029	1	98	0	0	66	27.87	-16.49		1.00	Nov-97
	6.46	11.92	34.36	39.26	117.71	0	1.09	12.83	1.14	64.37	3,029	1	98	0	0	66	28.27	-16.3	3.50		Nov-87
	6.64	12.28	35.21	41.95	123.88	0	0.45	12.84	1.14	69.64	3,029	1	98	0	0	66	28.27	-16.3			Aug-13

	MARKET			FUND TYPE, CATEGORY & OBJECTIVE	RATINGS				MINIMUMS	
Fund Name	Ticker Symbol	Traded On	Fund Type	Category and (Prospectus Objective)	Overall Rating	Reward Rating	Risk Rating	Recent Up/ Downgrade	Open to New Investors	Min Initial Investment
Fidelity Advisor® Growth Opportunities Fund I Class	FAGCX	NAS CM	Open End	US Equity Large Cap Growth (Growth)	B+	B+	B+	Up	Y	2,500
Fidelity Advisor® Health Care Fund Class A	FACDX	NAS CM	Open End	Healthcare Sector Equity (Health)	B-	C+	B-		Y	2,500
Fidelity Advisor® Health Care Fund Class C	FHCCX	NAS CM	Open End	Healthcare Sector Equity (Health)	B-	C+	B-	Up	Y	2,500
Fidelity Advisor® Health Care Fund Class M	FACTX	NAS CM	Open End	Healthcare Sector Equity (Health)	B-	C+	B-		Y	2,500
Fidelity Advisor® Health Care Fund I Class	FHCIX	NAS CM	Open End	Healthcare Sector Equity (Health)	B-	C+	B		Y	2,500
Fidelity Advisor® Industrials Fund Class A	FCLAX	NAS CM	Open End	Industrials Sector Equity ()	B	B	B		Y	2,500
Fidelity Advisor® Industrials Fund Class C	FCLCX	NAS CM	Open End	Industrials Sector Equity ()	B	B	B		Y	2,500
Fidelity Advisor® Industrials Fund Class M	FCLTX	NAS CM	Open End	Industrials Sector Equity ()	B	B	B		Y	2,500
Fidelity Advisor® Industrials Fund I Class	FCLIX	NAS CM	Open End	Industrials Sector Equity ()	B	B+	B		Y	2,500
Fidelity Advisor® Intl Capital Appreciation Fund Cls A	FCPAX	NAS CM	Open End	Global Equity Large Cap (Foreign Stock)	B	B	B	Up	Y	2,500
Fidelity Advisor® Intl Capital Appreciation Fund Cls C	FCPCX	NAS CM	Open End	Global Equity Large Cap (Foreign Stock)	B	B	B	Up	Y	2,500
Fidelity Advisor® Intl Capital Appreciation Fund Cls M	FIATX	NAS CM	Open End	Global Equity Large Cap (Foreign Stock)	B	B	B	Up	Y	2,500
Fidelity Advisor® Intl Capital Appreciation Fund Cls Z	FIDZX	NAS CM	Open End	Global Equity Large Cap (Foreign Stock)	B	B	B	Up	Y	0
Fidelity Advisor® Intl Capital Appreciation Fund I Cls	FCPIX	NAS CM	Open End	Global Equity Large Cap (Foreign Stock)	B	B	B	Up	Y	2,500
Fidelity Advisor® International Discovery Fund Class A	FAIDX	NAS CM	Open End	Global Equity Large Cap (Foreign Stock)	B	B-	B	Up	Y	2,500
Fidelity Advisor® International Discovery Fund Class C	FCADX	NAS CM	Open End	Global Equity Large Cap (Foreign Stock)	B-	B-	B	Up	Y	2,500
Fidelity Advisor® International Discovery Fund Class I	FIADX	NAS CM	Open End	Global Equity Large Cap (Foreign Stock)	B	B	B	Up	Y	2,500
Fidelity Advisor® International Discovery Fund Class M	FTADX	NAS CM	Open End	Global Equity Large Cap (Foreign Stock)	B	B-	B	Up	Y	2,500
Fidelity Advisor® International Discovery Fund Class Z	FZAIX	NAS CM	Open End	Global Equity Large Cap (Foreign Stock)	B	B	B	Up	Y	0
Fidelity Advisor® International Growth Fund Class A	FIAGX	NAS CM	Open End	Global Equity Large Cap (Foreign Stock)	B	B-	B	Up	Y	2,500
Fidelity Advisor® International Growth Fund Class C	FIGCX	NAS CM	Open End	Global Equity Large Cap (Foreign Stock)	B-	C+	B	Up	Y	2,500
Fidelity Advisor® International Growth Fund Class M	FITGX	NAS CM	Open End	Global Equity Large Cap (Foreign Stock)	B	B-	B	Up	Y	2,500
Fidelity Advisor® International Growth Fund Class Z	FZAJX	NAS CM	Open End	Global Equity Large Cap (Foreign Stock)	B	B-	B	Up	Y	0
Fidelity Advisor® International Growth Fund I Class	FIIIX	NAS CM	Open End	Global Equity Large Cap (Foreign Stock)	B	B-	B	Up	Y	2,500
Fidelity Advisor® International Real Estate Fund Class A	FIRAX	NAS CM	Open End	Real Estate Sector Equity (Real Estate)	B	B-	B	Up	Y	2,500
Fidelity Advisor® International Real Estate Fund Class C	FIRCX	NAS CM	Open End	Real Estate Sector Equity (Real Estate)	B-	C+	B	Up	Y	2,500
Fidelity Advisor® International Real Estate Fund Class I	FIRIX	NAS CM	Open End	Real Estate Sector Equity (Real Estate)	B	B-	B	Up	Y	2,500
Fidelity Advisor® International Real Estate Fund Class M	FIRTX	NAS CM	Open End	Real Estate Sector Equity (Real Estate)	B	C+	B	Up	Y	2,500
Fidelity Advisor® International Small Cap Fund Class A	FIASX	NAS CM	Open End	Global Equity Mid/Small Cap (Foreign Stock)	B+	B+	B+	Up	Y	2,500
Fidelity Advisor® International Small Cap Fund Class C	FICSX	NAS CM	Open End	Global Equity Mid/Small Cap (Foreign Stock)	B+	B+	B+	Up	Y	2,500
Fidelity Advisor® International Small Cap Fund Class I	FIXIX	NAS CM	Open End	Global Equity Mid/Small Cap (Foreign Stock)	B+	B+	A-	Up	Y	2,500
Fidelity Advisor® International Small Cap Fund Class M	FTISX	NAS CM	Open End	Global Equity Mid/Small Cap (Foreign Stock)	B+	B+	B+	Up	Y	2,500
Fidelity Advisor® Intl Small Cap Opp Fund Cls A	FOPAX	NAS CM	Open End	Global Equity Mid/Small Cap (Small Company)	A-	B+	A	Up	Y	2,500
Fidelity Advisor® Intl Small Cap Opp Fund Cls C	FOPCX	NAS CM	Open End	Global Equity Mid/Small Cap (Small Company)	B+	B	A	Up	Y	2,500
Fidelity Advisor® Intl Small Cap Opp Fund Cls M	FOPTX	NAS CM	Open End	Global Equity Mid/Small Cap (Small Company)	A-	B+	A	Up	Y	2,500
Fidelity Advisor® Intl Small Cap Opp Fund I Cls	FOPIX	NAS CM	Open End	Global Equity Mid/Small Cap (Small Company)	A-	B+	A	Up	Y	2,500
Fidelity Advisor® International Value Fund Class A	FIVMX	NAS CM	Open End	Global Equity Large Cap (Foreign Stock)	B-	C+	B	Up	Y	2,500
Fidelity Advisor® International Value Fund Class C	FIVOX	NAS CM	Open End	Global Equity Large Cap (Foreign Stock)	C+	C+	B-	Up	Y	2,500
Fidelity Advisor® International Value Fund Class M	FIVPX	NAS CM	Open End	Global Equity Large Cap (Foreign Stock)	B-	C+	B	Up	Y	2,500
Fidelity Advisor® International Value Fund I Class	FIVQX	NAS CM	Open End	Global Equity Large Cap (Foreign Stock)	C+	C+	C+	Up	Y	2,500
Fidelity Advisor® Japan Fund Class A	FPJAX	NAS CM	Open End	Japan Equity (Pacific Stock)	B+	A-	B	Up	Y	2,500
Fidelity Advisor® Japan Fund Class C	FJPCX	NAS CM	Open End	Japan Equity (Pacific Stock)	B+	A-	B	Up	Y	2,500
Fidelity Advisor® Japan Fund Class I	FJPIX	NAS CM	Open End	Japan Equity (Pacific Stock)	B+	A-	B	Up	Y	2,500
Fidelity Advisor® Japan Fund Class M	FJPTX	NAS CM	Open End	Japan Equity (Pacific Stock)	B+	A-	B	Up	Y	2,500
Fidelity Advisor® Large Cap Fund Class A	FALAX	NAS CM	Open End	US Equity Large Cap Blend (Growth)	B	B	B	Up	Y	2,500
Fidelity Advisor® Large Cap Fund Class C	FLCCX	NAS CM	Open End	US Equity Large Cap Blend (Growth)	B-	B-	B	Down	Y	2,500
Fidelity Advisor® Large Cap Fund Class M	FALGX	NAS CM	Open End	US Equity Large Cap Blend (Growth)	B	B	B	Up	Y	2,500
Fidelity Advisor® Large Cap Fund Class Z	FIDLX	NAS CM	Open End	US Equity Large Cap Blend (Growth)	B	B	B	Up	Y	0
Fidelity Advisor® Large Cap Fund I Class	FALIX	NAS CM	Open End	US Equity Large Cap Blend (Growth)	B	B	B	Up	Y	2,500
Fidelity Advisor® Latin America Fund Class A	FLFAX	NAS CM	Open End	Latin America Equity (Foreign Stock)	C	C	C		Y	2,500
Fidelity Advisor® Latin America Fund Class C	FLFCX	NAS CM	Open End	Latin America Equity (Foreign Stock)	C	C	C		Y	2,500
Fidelity Advisor® Latin America Fund Class I	FLFIX	NAS CM	Open End	Latin America Equity (Foreign Stock)	C	C	C		Y	2,500

★ Expanded analysis of this fund is included in Section II.

Min Additional Investment	TOTAL RETURNS 3-Month Total Return	6-Month Total Return	1-Year Total Return	3-Year Total Return	5-Year Total Return	PERFORMANCE Dividend Yield (TTM)	Expense Ratio	3-Yr Std Deviation	3-Year Beta	ASSETS NAV	Total Assets (MIL)	ASSET ALLOCATION & TURNOVER %Cash	%Stocks	%Bonds	%Other	Turnover Ratio	BULL & BEAR Last Bull Market Total Return	Last Bear Market Total Return	FEES Front End Fee (%)	Back End Fee (%)	Inception Date
	6.60	12.21	35.05	41.40	123.24	0	0.58	12.84	1.14	69.23	3,029	1	98	0	0	66	28.66	-16.12			Jul-95
	-1.08	2.52	24.09	17.30	145.95	0	1.04	15.48	1	42.65	2,734	3	96	0	0	64	22.31	-14.88	5.75		Sep-96
	-1.29	2.11	23.11	14.67	136.86	0	1.79	15.47	1	34.35	2,734	3	96	0	0	64	21.77	-15.12		1.00	Nov-97
	-1.16	2.38	23.72	16.36	142.68	0	1.31	15.47	1	39.95	2,734	3	96	0	0	64	22.11	-14.97	3.50		Sep-96
	-1.03	2.63	24.37	18.22	149.17	0	0.78	15.48	1	46.23	2,734	3	96	0	0	64	22.47	-14.75			Sep-96
	8.01	13.34	19.55	33.87	102.95	0.35	1.06	12.87	1.12	41.91	865.8	1	99	0	0	57	30.66	-26.12	5.75		Sep-96
	7.82	12.91	18.65	30.85	95.43	0	1.82	12.86	1.12	37.61	865.8	1	99	0	0	57	30.15	-26.35		1.00	Nov-97
	7.94	13.21	19.23	32.86	100.35	0.18	1.33	12.86	1.12	41.01	865.8	1	99	0	0	57	30.52	-26.2	3.50		Sep-96
	8.09	13.49	19.87	34.95	105.73	0.55	0.8	12.86	1.12	44.02	865.8	1	99	0	0	57	30.9	-26.02			Sep-96
	5.71	12.51	35.49	33.97	68.95	0.08	1.45	10.93	0.79	19.76	1,134	4	96	0	0	155	26.59	-26.03	5.75		Nov-97
	5.49	12.05	34.46	30.93	62.60	0	2.2	10.92	0.79	17.48	1,134	4	96	0	0	155	26	-26.27		1.00	Nov-97
	5.64	12.28	35.10	32.96	66.81	0	1.7	10.93	0.79	19.28	1,134	4	96	0	0	155	26.41	-26.11	3.50		Nov-97
	5.80	12.68	36.03	35.21	71.26		1.05	10.97	0.79	21.08	1,134	4	96	0	0	155	26.79	-25.95			Feb-17
	5.78	12.61	35.87	35.05	71.05	0.28	1.2	10.97	0.79	21.07	1,134	4	96	0	0	155	26.79	-25.95			Nov-97
	3.90	11.41	31.24	28.34	52.24	1	1.35	11.43	0.88	45.41	10,832	4	96	0	0	42	15.39	-24.59	5.75		Jan-05
	3.70	10.98	30.27	25.45	46.59	0.29	2.1	11.43	0.88	44.94	10,832	4	96	0	0	42	14.86	-24.82		1.00	Jan-05
	4.00	11.60	31.69	29.68	54.85	1.28	1	11.45	0.88	45.55	10,832	4	96	0	0	42	15.62	-24.5			Jan-05
	3.83	11.28	30.94	27.43	50.43	0.79	1.58	11.44	0.88	45.18	10,832	4	96	0	0	42	15.21	-24.68	3.50		Jan-05
	4.03	11.67	31.88	30.22	55.81	1.41	0.86	11.44	0.88	45.5	10,832	4	96	0	0	42	15.57	-24.47			Aug-13
	4.33	8.39	29.18	28.44	53.38	0.76	1.27	10.87	0.88	13.61	2,366	2	98	0	0	22	21.26	-22.04	5.75		Nov-07
	4.19	7.97	28.22	25.51	47.54	0.12	2.07	10.83	0.88	13.4	2,366	2	98	0	0	22	20.69	-22.32		1.00	Nov-07
	4.29	8.27	28.85	27.27	51.12	0.52	1.61	10.84	0.88	13.6	2,366	2	98	0	0	22	21.11	-22.15	3.50		Nov-07
	4.47	8.67	29.85	30.18	56.74	1.1	0.85	10.82	0.87	13.67	2,366	2	98	0	0	22	21.45	-21.99			Aug-13
	4.44	8.56	29.62	29.60	55.81	1	0.98	10.85	0.88	13.66	2,366	2	98	0	0	22	21.45	-21.99			Nov-07
	6.17	10.25	26.47	25.40	48.33	1.43	1.35	10.24	0.72	11.53	490.3	6	93	0	1	55	19.51	-25.3	5.75		Apr-07
	6.00	9.78	25.46	22.62	42.89	0.83	2.09	10.24	0.72	11.28	490.3	6	93	0	1	55	18.94	-25.48		1.00	Apr-07
	6.23	10.44	26.94	26.81	50.76	1.92	0.95	10.24	0.72	11.57	490.3	6	93	0	1	55	19.66	-25.17			Apr-07
	6.10	10.06	26.13	24.31	46.19	1.22	1.65	10.25	0.72	11.45	490.3	6	93	0	1	55	19.29	-25.29	3.50		Apr-07
	5.45	12.05	32.52	51.56	94.30	0.92	1.61	10.06	0.82	29.4	1,803	5	93	0	1	29	14.13	-21.69	5.75		May-03
	5.24	11.62	31.46	48.09	87.10	0.28	2.4	10.04	0.82	28.42	1,803	5	93	0	1	29	13.54	-21.9		1.00	May-03
	5.51	12.19	32.85	53.00	97.74	1.21	1.31	10.07	0.82	30.09	1,803	5	93	0	1	29	14.38	-21.6			May-03
	5.37	11.89	32.10	50.19	91.65	0.63	1.9	10.04	0.82	29.28	1,803	5	93	0	1	29	13.92	-21.77	3.50		May-03
	6.76	12.49	35.28	46.22	81.26	0.62	1.45	10.19	0.82	19.15	1,149	5	95	0	0	11	19.76	-20.48	5.75		Aug-05
	6.56	12.02	34.16	42.80	74.55	0	2.26	10.17	0.82	18.56	1,149	5	95	0	0	11	19.13	-20.73		1.00	Aug-05
	6.68	12.32	34.90	44.92	78.78	0.29	1.77	10.2	0.82	19.02	1,149	5	95	0	0	11	19.51	-20.55	3.50		Aug-05
	6.83	12.63	35.66	47.62	84.10	0.91	1.16	10.17	0.82	19.31	1,149	5	95	0	0	11	19.79	-20.37			Aug-05
	2.08	6.70	19.29	17.38	33.65	1.82	1.4	10.68	0.78	9.08	554.5	0	99	0	0	50	10.82	-27.71	5.75		May-06
	1.86	6.24	18.35	14.62	28.63	1.18	2.17	10.71	0.78	9.08	554.5	0	99	0	0	50	10.27	-27.98		1.00	May-06
	1.89	6.50	18.94	16.29	31.76	1.56	1.7	10.69	0.78	9.08	554.5	0	99	0	0	50	10.76	-27.85	3.50		May-06
	2.01	6.74	19.48	18.18	35.24	2.08	1.17	10.71	0.78	9.07	554.5	0	99	0	0	50	11.06	-27.65			May-06
	8.92	12.47	29.85	43.17	62.94	0.38	1.08	11.92	0.88	15.43	405.1	1	99	0	0	15	5.64	-10.39	5.75		Dec-10
	8.69	12.03	28.86	40.03	57.22	0	1.81	11.91	0.88	15.31	405.1	1	99	0	0	15	5.22	-10.7		1.00	Dec-10
	8.95	12.57	30.16	44.42	65.69	0.7	0.77	11.89	0.88	15.41	405.1	1	99	0	0	15	5.9	-10.28			Dec-10
	8.85	12.24	29.37	41.62	60.31	0.06	1.44	11.91	0.88	15.43	405.1	1	99	0	0	15	5.43	-10.49	3.50		Dec-10
	5.95	10.85	18.17	31.64	106.87	0.95	0.92	12.53	1.16	33.26	1,387	0	100	0	0	28	27.79	-19.28	5.75		Sep-96
	5.75	10.39	17.24	28.64	99.13	0.47	1.67	12.52	1.16	30.19	1,387	0	100	0	0	28	27.23	-19.57		1.00	Nov-97
	5.88	10.68	17.86	30.60	104.19	0.73	1.18	12.52	1.16	33.21	1,387	0	100	0	0	28	27.6	-19.37	3.50		Feb-96
	6.04	11.05	18.62	32.84	109.93		0.51	12.52	1.16	34.76	1,387	0	100	0	0	28	28	-19.17			Feb-17
	6.02	11.00	18.50	32.70	109.71	1.1	0.65	12.52	1.16	34.77	1,387	0	100	0	0	28	28	-19.17			Feb-96
	-4.51	14.09	30.07	8.56	-24.51	1.74	1.4	22.81	0.88	24.59	609.7	1	99	0	0	108	18.57	-24.85	5.75		Sep-10
	-4.71	13.66	29.14	6.11	-27.30	1.13	2.15	22.81	0.88	24.94	609.7	1	99	0	0	108	18.06	-25.09		1.00	Sep-10
	-4.44	14.27	30.54	9.66	-23.21	1.99	1.07	22.84	0.88	24.44	609.7	1	99	0	0	108	18.8	-24.76			Sep-10

	MARKET		FUND TYPE, CATEGORY & OBJECTIVE		RATINGS					MINIMUMS
Fund Name	Ticker Symbol	Traded On	Fund Type	Category and (Prospectus Objective)	Overall Rating	Reward Rating	Risk Rating	Recent Up/ Downgrade	Open to New Investors	Min Initial Investment
Fidelity Advisor® Latin America Fund Class M	FLFTX	NAS CM	Open End	Latin America Equity (Foreign Stock)	C	C	C		Y	2,500
Fidelity Advisor® Leveraged Company Stock Fund Class A	FLSAX	NAS CM	Open End	US Equity Mid Cap (Growth)	B-	C+	B	Up	Y	10,000
Fidelity Advisor® Leveraged Company Stock Fund Class C	FLSCX	NAS CM	Open End	US Equity Mid Cap (Growth)	B-	C+	B-	Up	Y	10,000
Fidelity Advisor® Leveraged Company Stock Fund Class M	FLSTX	NAS CM	Open End	US Equity Mid Cap (Growth)	B-	C+	B-	Up	Y	10,000
Fidelity Advisor® Leveraged Company Stock Fund Class Z	FZAKX	NAS CM	Open End	US Equity Mid Cap (Growth)	B-	C+	B	Up	Y	0
Fidelity Advisor® Leveraged Company Stock Fund I Class	FLVIX	NAS CM	Open End	US Equity Mid Cap (Growth)	B-	C+	B	Up	Y	10,000
Fidelity Advisor® Materials Fund Class A	FMFAX	NAS CM	Open End	Natl Resources Sec Equity (Natl Res)	B-	B	C+	Up	Y	2,500
Fidelity Advisor® Materials Fund Class C	FMFCX	NAS CM	Open End	Natl Resources Sec Equity (Natl Res)	B-	B-	C+	Up	Y	2,500
Fidelity Advisor® Materials Fund Class I	FMFEX	NAS CM	Open End	Natl Resources Sec Equity (Natl Res)	B-	B	C+	Up	Y	2,500
Fidelity Advisor® Materials Fund Class M	FMFTX	NAS CM	Open End	Natl Resources Sec Equity (Natl Res)	B-	B	C+	Up	Y	2,500
Fidelity Advisor® Mega Cap Stock Fund Class A	FGTAX	NAS CM	Open End	US Equity Large Cap Blend (Growth)	B-	B-	B-	Down	Y	2,500
Fidelity Advisor® Mega Cap Stock Fund Class C	FGRCX	NAS CM	Open End	US Equity Large Cap Blend (Growth)	B-	B-	B-	Down	Y	2,500
Fidelity Advisor® Mega Cap Stock Fund Class I	FTRIX	NAS CM	Open End	US Equity Large Cap Blend (Growth)	B-	B-	B-	Down	Y	2,500
Fidelity Advisor® Mega Cap Stock Fund Class M	FTGRX	NAS CM	Open End	US Equity Large Cap Blend (Growth)	B-	B-	B-	Down	Y	2,500
Fidelity Advisor® Mega Cap Stock Fund Class Z	FZALX	NAS CM	Open End	US Equity Large Cap Blend (Growth)	B-	B	B-	Down	Y	0
Fidelity Advisor® Mid Cap II Fund Class A	FIIAX	NAS CM	Open End	US Equity Mid Cap (Growth)	B	B	B	Up	Y	2,500
Fidelity Advisor® Mid Cap II Fund Class C	FIICX	NAS CM	Open End	US Equity Mid Cap (Growth)	B	B	B	Up	Y	2,500
Fidelity Advisor® Mid Cap II Fund Class I	FIIMX	NAS CM	Open End	US Equity Mid Cap (Growth)	B	B	B	Up	Y	2,500
Fidelity Advisor® Mid Cap II Fund Class M	FITIX	NAS CM	Open End	US Equity Mid Cap (Growth)	B	B	B	Up	Y	2,500
Fidelity Advisor® Mid Cap II Fund Class Z	FZAMX	NAS CM	Open End	US Equity Mid Cap (Growth)	B	B	B-	Up	Y	0
Fidelity Advisor® Mid Cap Value Fund Class A	FMPAX	NAS CM	Open End	US Equity Mid Cap (Growth)	B-	B-	B		Y	2,500
Fidelity Advisor® Mid Cap Value Fund Class C	FMPEX	NAS CM	Open End	US Equity Mid Cap (Growth)	B-	C+	B	Up	Y	2,500
Fidelity Advisor® Mid Cap Value Fund Class I	FMPOX	NAS CM	Open End	US Equity Mid Cap (Growth)	B-	B-	B	Down	Y	2,500
Fidelity Advisor® Mid Cap Value Fund Class M	FMPTX	NAS CM	Open End	US Equity Mid Cap (Growth)	B-	B-	B	Up	Y	2,500
Fidelity Advisor® Mid Cap Value Fund Class Z	FIDFX	NAS CM	Open End	US Equity Mid Cap (Growth)	B-	B-	B	Down	Y	0
Fidelity Advisor® Multi-Asset Income Fund Class A	FWATX	NAS CM	Open End	Cautious Alloc (Income)	C	C	B	Up	Y	2,500
Fidelity Advisor® Multi-Asset Income Fund Class C	FWBTX	NAS CM	Open End	Cautious Alloc (Income)	C	C	B	Up	Y	2,500
Fidelity Advisor® Multi-Asset Income Fund Class I	FAYZX	NAS CM	Open End	Cautious Alloc (Income)	C	C	B	Up	Y	2,500
Fidelity Advisor® Multi-Asset Income Fund Class M	FAZYX	NAS CM	Open End	Cautious Alloc (Income)	C	C	B	Up	Y	2,500
Fidelity Advisor® New Insights Fund Class A	FNIAX	NAS CM	Open End	US Equity Large Cap Growth (Growth)	B	B	B	Up	Y	2,500
Fidelity Advisor® New Insights Fund Class C	FNICX	NAS CM	Open End	US Equity Large Cap Growth (Growth)	B	B	B	Up	Y	2,500
Fidelity Advisor® New Insights Fund Class I	FINSX	NAS CM	Open End	US Equity Large Cap Growth (Growth)	B	B	B	Down	Y	2,500
Fidelity Advisor® New Insights Fund Class M	FNITX	NAS CM	Open End	US Equity Large Cap Growth (Growth)	B	B	B	Up	Y	2,500
Fidelity Advisor® New Insights Fund Class Z	FZANX	NAS CM	Open End	US Equity Large Cap Growth (Growth)	B	B	B	Down	Y	0
Fidelity Advisor® Overseas Fund Class A	FAOAX	NAS CM	Open End	Global Equity Large Cap (Foreign Stock)	B-	B-	B	Up	Y	2,500
Fidelity Advisor® Overseas Fund Class C	FAOCX	NAS CM	Open End	Global Equity Large Cap (Foreign Stock)	B-	C+	B	Up	Y	2,500
Fidelity Advisor® Overseas Fund Class I	FAOIX	NAS CM	Open End	Global Equity Large Cap (Foreign Stock)	B	B-	B	Up	Y	2,500
Fidelity Advisor® Overseas Fund Class M	FAERX	NAS CM	Open End	Global Equity Large Cap (Foreign Stock)	B-	B-	B	Up	Y	2,500
Fidelity Advisor® Overseas Fund Class Z	FAOSX	NAS CM	Open End	Global Equity Large Cap (Foreign Stock)	B-	B-	B	Up	Y	0
Fidelity Advisor® Real Estate Fund Class A	FHEAX	NAS CM	Open End	Real Estate Sector Equity (Real Estate)	B-	C+	B		Y	2,500
Fidelity Advisor® Real Estate Fund Class C	FHECX	NAS CM	Open End	Real Estate Sector Equity (Real Estate)	C+	C	B	Down	Y	2,500
Fidelity Advisor® Real Estate Fund Class M	FHETX	NAS CM	Open End	Real Estate Sector Equity (Real Estate)	B-	C+	B		Y	2,500
Fidelity Advisor® Real Estate Fund I Class	FHEIX	NAS CM	Open End	Real Estate Sector Equity (Real Estate)	B-	C+	B+		Y	2,500
Fidelity Advisor® Real Estate Income Fund Class A	FRINX	NAS CM	Open End	Real Estate Sector Equity (Real Estate)	B	C+	A-	Up	Y	2,500
Fidelity Advisor® Real Estate Income Fund Class C	FRIOX	NAS CM	Open End	Real Estate Sector Equity (Real Estate)	B	C+	A-	Up	Y	2,500
Fidelity Advisor® Real Estate Income Fund Class I	FRIRX	NAS CM	Open End	Real Estate Sector Equity (Real Estate)	B	C+	A	Up	Y	2,500
Fidelity Advisor® Real Estate Income Fund Class M	FRIQX	NAS CM	Open End	Real Estate Sector Equity (Real Estate)	B	C+	A-	Up	Y	2,500
Fidelity Advisor® Semiconductors Fund Class A	FELAX	NAS CM	Open End	Technology Sector Equity (Technology)	A-	A+	B	Up	Y	2,500
Fidelity Advisor® Semiconductors Fund Class C	FELCX	NAS CM	Open End	Technology Sector Equity (Technology)	A-	A+	B	Up	Y	2,500
Fidelity Advisor® Semiconductors Fund Class I	FELIX	NAS CM	Open End	Technology Sector Equity (Technology)	A-	A+	B	Up	Y	2,500
Fidelity Advisor® Semiconductors Fund Class M	FELTX	NAS CM	Open End	Technology Sector Equity (Technology)	A-	A+	B	Up	Y	2,500
Fidelity Advisor® Series Equity Growth Fund	FMFMX	NAS CM	Open End	US Equity Large Cap Growth (Growth)	A-	A-	A-	Up	Y	0

★Expanded analysis of this fund is included in Section II.

Min Additional Investment	3-Month Total Return	6-Month Total Return	1-Year Total Return	3-Year Total Return	5-Year Total Return	Dividend Yield (TTM)	Expense Ratio	3-Yr Std Deviation	3-Year Beta	NAV	Total Assets (MIL)	%Cash	%Stocks	%Bonds	%Other	Turnover Ratio	Last Bull Market Total Return	Last Bear Market Total Return	Front End Fee (%)	Back End Fee (%)	Inception Date
	TOTAL RETURNS					PERFORMANCE				ASSETS		ASSET ALLOCATION & TURNOVER					BULL & BEAR		FEES		
	-4.55	13.96	29.75	7.66	-25.54	1.5	1.68	22.83	0.88	24.67	609.7	1	99	0	0	108	18.39	-24.94	3.50		Sep-10
	5.51	9.37	17.32	19.50	76.85	0.64	1.08	13.04	1.14	43.37	2,243	2	96	2	0	68	33.44	-30.13	5.75		Dec-00
	5.33	8.96	16.46	16.84	70.35	0.08	1.83	13.03	1.14	38.84	2,243	2	96	2	0	68	32.9	-30.36		1.00	Dec-00
	5.46	9.23	17.02	18.64	74.73	0.45	1.32	13.03	1.14	42	2,243	2	96	2	0	68	33.29	-30.21	3.50		Dec-00
	5.63	9.59	17.78	20.93	80.22	1.02	0.68	13.04	1.14	44.29	2,243	2	96	2	0	68	33.65	-30.05			Aug-13
	5.58	9.52	17.63	20.43	79.19	0.9	0.81	13.04	1.14	44.3	2,243	2	96	2	0	68	33.65	-30.05			Dec-00
	6.86	14.53	25.85	26.72	58.02	0.79	1.08	15.87	1.33	90.59	1,888	1	99	0	0	49	29.81	-28.36	5.75		Dec-06
	6.67	14.10	24.92	23.91	52.21	0.25	1.83	15.86	1.33	87.66	1,888	1	99	0	0	49	29.24	-28.58		1.00	Dec-06
	6.94	14.70	26.20	27.80	60.28	1.02	0.79	15.87	1.33	90.79	1,888	1	99	0	0	49	30.02	-28.26			Dec-06
	6.79	14.38	25.49	25.57	55.65	0.58	1.39	15.87	1.33	89.92	1,888	1	99	0	0	49	29.59	-28.45	3.50		Dec-06
	5.70	10.15	17.49	29.65	96.39	1.26	0.94	11.68	1.12	17.27	2,556	0	99	0	0	25	27.98	-16.12	5.75		Feb-08
	5.52	9.80	16.62	26.80	89.39	0.61	1.69	11.68	1.12	17.03	2,556	0	99	0	0	25	27.47	-16.36		1.00	Feb-08
	5.77	10.29	17.77	30.75	99.30	1.49	0.67	11.68	1.12	17.44	2,556	0	99	0	0	25	28.13	-15.99			Feb-08
	5.69	10.07	17.20	28.69	94.16	1.04	1.2	11.68	1.12	17.27	2,556	0	99	0	0	25	27.81	-16.15	3.50		Feb-08
	5.87	10.45	17.96	31.28	100.58	1.64	0.53	11.67	1.12	17.36	2,556	0	99	0	0	25	28.24	-16.02			Aug-13
	6.18	10.65	20.25	30.67	92.62	0.19	1.07	11.68	1.02	20.94	2,632	0	99	0	0	29	18.04	-20.5	5.75		Aug-04
	5.89	10.20	19.26	27.64	85.30	0	1.83	11.67	1.02	18.7	2,632	0	99	0	0	29	17.59	-20.75		1.00	Aug-04
	6.20	10.80	20.55	31.75	95.09	0.39	0.77	11.66	1.02	21.57	2,632	0	99	0	0	29	18.25	-20.44			Aug-04
	6.06	10.53	19.90	29.70	90.36	0.01	1.3	11.67	1.02	20.43	2,632	0	99	0	0	29	17.92	-20.54	3.50		Aug-04
	6.24	10.89	20.71	32.30	96.45	0.52	0.64	11.68	1.02	21.57	2,632	0	99	0	0	29	18.25	-20.44			Aug-13
	7.98	10.69	16.66	23.31	104.12	0.96	1.01	10.64	0.97	26.26	3,256	1	99	0	0	83	26.62	-23.2	5.75		Feb-07
	7.74	10.29	15.76	20.53	96.55	0.41	1.76	10.63	0.97	25.42	3,256	1	99	0	0	83	26.09	-23.46		1.00	Feb-07
	8.04	10.83	16.96	24.33	107.00	1.18	0.73	10.64	0.97	26.39	3,256	1	99	0	0	83	26.87	-23.14			Feb-07
	7.88	10.52	16.32	22.24	101.31	0.78	1.29	10.65	0.97	26.15	3,256	1	99	0	0	83	26.46	-23.3	3.50		Feb-07
	8.08	10.91	17.14	24.51	107.56		0.59	10.63	0.97	26.38	3,256	1	99	0	0	83	26.86	-23.1			Feb-17
	2.79	3.54	5.91			2.53	1.11			10.41	46.7	13	28	54	0	239			4.00		Sep-15
	2.64	3.20	5.17			1.82	1.86			10.41	46.7	13	28	54	0	239				1.00	Sep-15
	2.85	3.66	6.17			2.77	0.86			10.41	46.7	13	28	54	0	239					Sep-15
	2.79	3.54	5.91			2.53	1.11			10.41	46.7	13	28	54	0	239			4.00		Sep-15
	6.60	12.54	28.02	38.20	105.01	0.1	0.89	10.02	0.93	31.39	28,060	3	95	0	0	42	23.44	-14.48	5.75		Jul-03
	6.37	12.10	27.03	35.14	97.45	0	1.64	10.04	0.93	27.64	28,060	3	95	0	0	42	22.95	-14.76		1.00	Jul-03
	6.64	12.67	28.34	39.28	107.61	0.32	0.63	10.06	0.93	32.04	28,060	3	95	0	0	42	23.6	-14.38			Jul-03
	6.53	12.42	27.69	37.21	102.51	0	1.14	10.05	0.93	30.4	28,060	3	95	0	0	42	23.24	-14.56	3.50		Jul-03
	6.68	12.77	28.53	39.84	108.85	0.42	0.5	10.04	0.93	32.07	28,060	3	95	0	0	42	23.6	-14.38			Aug-13
	3.54	9.30	29.64	26.43	53.09	0.78	1.36	12.24	0.95	24.85	669.4	2	98	0	0	42	18	-27.57	5.75		Sep-96
	3.30	8.85	28.56	23.37	47.15	0.04	2.16	12.23	0.95	24.17	669.4	2	98	0	0	42	17.5	-27.8		1.00	Nov-97
	3.58	9.44	30.03	27.63	55.60	1.11	1.04	12.22	0.95	25.35	669.4	2	98	0	0	42	18.27	-27.46			Jul-95
	3.46	9.14	29.35	25.64	51.61	0.57	1.56	12.23	0.95	25.54	669.4	2	98	0	0	42	17.91	-27.64	3.50		Apr-90
	3.64	9.50	30.05	26.32	52.43		0.91	12.26	0.96	25.34	669.4	2	98	0	0	42	17.91	-27.64			Feb-17
	1.66	1.57	3.57	10.86	49.84	1.34	1.09	13.26	0.6	21.8	803.9	1	99	0	0	69	33.56	-18.89	5.75		Sep-02
	1.43	1.19	2.75	8.31	44.24	0.78	1.86	13.24	0.6	21.32	803.9	1	99	0	0	69	33.01	-19.18		1.00	Sep-02
	1.59	1.48	3.34	10.10	48.20	1.11	1.33	13.27	0.59	21.79	803.9	1	99	0	0	69	33.32	-18.99	3.50		Sep-02
	1.71	1.70	3.85	11.68	51.78	1.6	0.82	13.26	0.6	21.99	803.9	1	99	0	0	69	33.74	-18.8			Sep-02
	0.33	1.61	7.03	18.95	39.82	3.8	1.03	4.72	0.25	11.93	5,468	6	31	37	0	22	14.08	-6.48	4.00		Apr-10
	0.16	1.26	6.22	16.25	34.67	3.05	1.78	4.64	0.25	11.83	5,468	6	31	37	0	22	13.59	-6.74		1.00	Apr-10
	0.43	1.78	7.33	19.91	41.66	4.06	0.76	4.67	0.25	11.95	5,468	6	31	37	0	22	14.22	-6.38			Apr-10
	0.41	1.68	7.01	18.84	39.60	3.78	1.06	4.68	0.25	11.94	5,468	6	31	37	0	22	14.05	-6.49	4.00		Apr-10
	11.28	21.72	34.24	81.11	251.97	0.17	1.17	17.39	1.26	23.33	280.4	5	95	0	0	99	22.97	-23.47	5.75		Dec-00
	11.03	21.29	33.17	76.93	238.87	0	1.95	17.32	1.26	20.46	280.4	5	95	0	0	99	22.22	-23.63		1.00	Dec-00
	11.36	21.90	34.65	82.85	257.00	0.32	0.88	17.33	1.26	24.47	280.4	5	95	0	0	99	23.06	-23.39			Dec-00
	11.21	21.54	33.77	79.28	246.65	0	1.53	17.35	1.26	22.43	280.4	5	95	0	0	99	22.69	-23.57	3.50		Dec-00
	5.75	13.12	36.69	46.42		0.09	0	11.26	0.97	13.04	935.3	0	100	0	0	60					Jun-14

	MARKET			FUND TYPE, CATEGORY & OBJECTIVE	RATINGS				MINIMUMS	
Fund Name	Ticker Symbol	Traded On	Fund Type	Category and (Prospectus Objective)	Overall Rating	Reward Rating	Risk Rating	Recent Up/ Downgrade	Open to New Investors	Min Initial Investment
Fidelity Advisor® Series Equity-Income Fund	FLMLX	NAS CM	Open End	US Equity Large Cap Value (Equity-Income)	B-	B-	B	Down	Y	0
Fidelity Advisor® Series Growth & Income Fund	FMALX	NAS CM	Open End	US Equity Large Cap Blend (Growth & Income)	B	B	B	Up	Y	0
Fidelity Advisor® Series Growth Opportunities Fund	FAOFX	NAS CM	Open End	US Equity Large Cap Growth (World Stock)	B+	B+	B+	Up	Y	0
Fidelity Advisor® Series Opportunistic Insights Fund	FAMGX	NAS CM	Open End	US Equity Large Cap Growth (Growth)	A-	A	A-	Up	Y	0
Fidelity Advisor® Series Small Cap Fund	FSSFX	NAS CM	Open End	US Equity Small Cap (Small Company)	B	B-	B	Up	Y	0
Fidelity Advisor® Ser Stock Selector Large Cap Value Fund	FMMLX	NAS CM	Open End	US Equity Large Cap Value (Growth)	B-	B-	B	Down	Y	0
Fidelity Advisor® Small Cap Fund Class A	FSCDX	NAS CM	Open End	US Equity Small Cap (Small Company)	B-	B-	B	Up	Y	2,500
Fidelity Advisor® Small Cap Fund Class C	FSCEX	NAS CM	Open End	US Equity Small Cap (Small Company)	B-	C+	B	Up	Y	2,500
Fidelity Advisor® Small Cap Fund Class M	FSCTX	NAS CM	Open End	US Equity Small Cap (Small Company)	B-	B-	B	Up	Y	2,500
Fidelity Advisor® Small Cap Fund Class Z	FZAOX	NAS CM	Open End	US Equity Small Cap (Small Company)	B	B-	B	Up	Y	0
Fidelity Advisor® Small Cap Fund I Class	FSCIX	NAS CM	Open End	US Equity Small Cap (Small Company)	B	B-	B	Up	Y	2,500
Fidelity Advisor® Small Cap Growth Fund Class A	FCAGX	NAS CM	Open End	US Equity Small Cap (Small Company)	A-	A	B	Up	Y	2,500
Fidelity Advisor® Small Cap Growth Fund Class C	FCCGX	NAS CM	Open End	US Equity Small Cap (Small Company)	B+	A	B	Up	Y	2,500
Fidelity Advisor® Small Cap Growth Fund Class M	FCTGX	NAS CM	Open End	US Equity Small Cap (Small Company)	B+	A	B	Up	Y	2,500
Fidelity Advisor® Small Cap Growth Fund Class Z	FIDGX	NAS CM	Open End	US Equity Small Cap (Small Company)	A-	A	B	Up	Y	0
Fidelity Advisor® Small Cap Growth Fund I Class	FCIGX	NAS CM	Open End	US Equity Small Cap (Small Company)	A-	A	B	Up	Y	2,500
Fidelity Advisor® Small Cap Value Fund Class A	FCVAX	NAS CM	Open End	US Equity Small Cap (Small Company)	A-	B+	A-	Up		2,500
Fidelity Advisor® Small Cap Value Fund Class C	FCVCX	NAS CM	Open End	US Equity Small Cap (Small Company)	B+	B	B+	Up		2,500
Fidelity Advisor® Small Cap Value Fund Class I	FCVIX	NAS CM	Open End	US Equity Small Cap (Small Company)	A-	B+	A-	Up		2,500
Fidelity Advisor® Small Cap Value Fund Class M	FCVTX	NAS CM	Open End	US Equity Small Cap (Small Company)	B+	B+	A-	Up		2,500
Fidelity Advisor® Stock Selector All Cap Fund Class A	FMAMX	NAS CM	Open End	US Equity Large Cap Growth (Growth)	B	B	B-	Up	Y	2,500
Fidelity Advisor® Stock Selector All Cap Fund Class C	FLACX	NAS CM	Open End	US Equity Large Cap Growth (Growth)	B-	B	C+	Down	Y	2,500
Fidelity Advisor® Stock Selector All Cap Fund Class K	FSSKX	NAS CM	Open End	US Equity Large Cap Growth (Growth)	B	B	B-		Y	0
Fidelity Advisor® Stock Selector All Cap Fund Class M	FSJHX	NAS CM	Open End	US Equity Large Cap Growth (Growth)	B	B	B-	Up	Y	2,500
Fidelity Advisor® Stock Selector All Cap Fund Class Z	FZAPX	NAS CM	Open End	US Equity Large Cap Growth (Growth)	B	B	B-		Y	0
Fidelity Advisor® Stock Selector All Cap Fund I Class	FBRNX	NAS CM	Open End	US Equity Large Cap Growth (Growth)	B	B	B-	Up	Y	2,500
Fidelity Advisor® Stock Selector Large Cap Value Cls A	FLUAX	NAS CM	Open End	US Equity Large Cap Value (Growth)	B-	B-	B	Down	Y	2,500
Fidelity Advisor® Stock Selector Large Cap Value Cls C	FLUEX	NAS CM	Open End	US Equity Large Cap Value (Growth)	B-	C+	B	Down	Y	2,500
Fidelity Advisor® Stock Selector Large Cap Value Cls I	FLUIX	NAS CM	Open End	US Equity Large Cap Value (Growth)	B-	B-	B	Down	Y	2,500
Fidelity Advisor® Stock Selector Large Cap Value Cls M	FLUTX	NAS CM	Open End	US Equity Large Cap Value (Growth)	B-	C+	B	Down	Y	2,500
Fidelity Advisor® Stock Selector Large Cap Value Cls Z	FSCZX	NAS CM	Open End	US Equity Large Cap Value (Growth)	B-	B-	B	Down	Y	0
Fidelity Advisor® Stock Selector Mid Cap Fund	FSSMX	NAS CM	Open End	US Equity Mid Cap (Growth)	B-	B	C+	Down	Y	2,500
Fidelity Advisor® Stock Selector Mid Cap Fund Class A	FMCDX	NAS CM	Open End	US Equity Mid Cap (Growth)	B-	B	C+	Down	Y	2,500
Fidelity Advisor® Stock Selector Mid Cap Fund Class C	FMCEX	NAS CM	Open End	US Equity Mid Cap (Growth)	B-	B-	C+	Up	Y	2,500
Fidelity Advisor® Stock Selector Mid Cap Fund Class M	FMCAX	NAS CM	Open End	US Equity Mid Cap (Growth)	B-	B-	C+	Up	Y	2,500
Fidelity Advisor® Stock Selector Mid Cap Fund Class Z	FSLZX	NAS CM	Open End	US Equity Mid Cap (Growth)	B-	B	C+	Down	Y	0
Fidelity Advisor® Stock Selector Mid Cap Fund I Class	FMCCX	NAS CM	Open End	US Equity Mid Cap (Growth)	B-	B	C+	Down	Y	2,500
Fidelity Advisor® Stock Selector Small Cap Fund Class A	FCDAX	NAS CM	Open End	US Equity Small Cap (Small Company)	B	B	B	Up	Y	2,500
Fidelity Advisor® Stock Selector Small Cap Fund Class C	FCDCX	NAS CM	Open End	US Equity Small Cap (Small Company)	B	B	B	Up	Y	2,500
Fidelity Advisor® Stock Selector Small Cap Fund Class M	FCDTX	NAS CM	Open End	US Equity Small Cap (Small Company)	B	B	B	Up	Y	2,500
Fidelity Advisor® Stock Selector Small Cap Fund Class Z	FSSZX	NAS CM	Open End	US Equity Small Cap (Small Company)	B	B	B	Up	Y	0
Fidelity Advisor® Stock Selector Small Cap Fund I Class	FCDIX	NAS CM	Open End	US Equity Small Cap (Small Company)	B	B	B	Up	Y	2,500
Fidelity Advisor® Strategic Dividend & Income® Fund Cls A	FASDX	NAS CM	Open End	Aggressive Alloc (Equity-Income)	B-	C+	B	Down	Y	2,500
Fidelity Advisor® Strategic Dividend & Income® Fund Cls C	FCSDX	NAS CM	Open End	Aggressive Alloc (Equity-Income)	B-	C+	B	Down	Y	2,500
Fidelity Advisor® Strategic Dividend & Income® Fund Cls M	FTSDX	NAS CM	Open End	Aggressive Alloc (Equity-Income)	B-	C+	B	Down	Y	2,500
Fidelity Advisor® Strategic Dividend & Income® Fund I Cls	FSIDX	NAS CM	Open End	Aggressive Alloc (Equity-Income)	B-	B-	B	Down	Y	2,500
Fidelity Advisor® Strategic Real Return Fund Class A	FSRAX	NAS CM	Open End	Cautious Alloc (Growth & Income)	C	C	C+		Y	2,500
Fidelity Advisor® Strategic Real Return Fund Class C	FCSRX	NAS CM	Open End	Cautious Alloc (Growth & Income)	C	C-	C	Up	Y	2,500
Fidelity Advisor® Strategic Real Return Fund Class M	FSRTX	NAS CM	Open End	Cautious Alloc (Growth & Income)	C	C	C+		Y	2,500
Fidelity Advisor® Strategic Real Return Fund I Class	FSIRX	NAS CM	Open End	Cautious Alloc (Growth & Income)	C	C	B-		Y	2,500
Fidelity Advisor® Technology Fund Class A	FADTX	NAS CM	Open End	Technology Sector Equity (Technology)	A	A+	B+	Up	Y	2,500
Fidelity Advisor® Technology Fund Class C	FTHCX	NAS CM	Open End	Technology Sector Equity (Technology)	A	A+	B+	Up	Y	2,500

★ Expanded analysis of this fund is included in Section II.

Min Additional Investment	TOTAL RETURNS 3-Month Total Return	6-Month Total Return	1-Year Total Return	3-Year Total Return	5-Year Total Return	PERFORMANCE Dividend Yield (TTM)	Expense Ratio	3-Yr Std Deviation	3-Year Beta	ASSETS NAV	Total Assets (MIL)	ASSET ALLOCATION & TURNOVER %Cash	%Stocks	%Bonds	%Other	Turnover Ratio	BULL & BEAR Last Bull Market Total Return	Last Bear Market Total Return	FEES Front End Fee (%)	Back End Fee (%)	Inception Date
	5.11	7.32	11.61	26.11	83.24	1.79	0.05	10.15	0.95	12.94	1,128	6	94	0	0	39					Dec-12
	6.24	10.75	17.32	31.51	96.51	1.51	0.01	11.78	1.11	15.53	1,751	1	99	0	0	58					Dec-12
	7.10	12.95	35.48	42.85		0.26	0.01	12.78	1.13	12.74	619.6	2	97	0	0	67					Nov-13
	6.92	13.73	34.51	45.60	133.03	0	0.01	11.09	0.92	17.46	870.9	2	96	0	0	41					Dec-12
	3.60	7.99	14.50	21.91		0.75	0.01	11.48	0.78	11.91	463.9	7	93	0	0	90					Nov-13
	4.14	7.82	11.83	22.36	88.74	1.35	0	10.26	0.98	13.11	1,134	5	95	0	0	48					Dec-12
	3.40	7.45	13.77	21.04	85.71	0.26	1.32	11.48	0.78	25.81	2,630	5	95	0	0	81	22.24	-23.87	5.75		Sep-98
	3.21	7.05	12.92	18.32	78.87	0	2.08	11.48	0.78	19.47	2,630	5	95	0	0	81	21.72	-24.14		1.00	Sep-98
	3.33	7.30	13.50	20.21	83.62	0.09	1.55	11.49	0.78	23.88	2,630	5	95	0	0	81	22.05	-23.93	3.50		Sep-98
	3.53	7.66	14.26	22.57	89.50	0.62	0.89	11.49	0.78	28.29	2,630	5	95	0	0	81	22.43	-23.78			Aug-13
	3.49	7.59	14.08	22.05	88.33	0.47	1.05	11.48	0.78	28.31	2,630	5	95	0	0	81	22.43	-23.78			Sep-98
	4.92	14.01	28.63	49.56	128.48	0	1.36	12.27	0.79	23.78	3,744	1	99	0	0	140	26.2	-24.61	5.75		Nov-04
	4.69	13.56	27.61	46.08	119.82	0	2.12	12.26	0.79	21.37	3,744	1	99	0	0	140	25.64	-24.84		1.00	Nov-04
	4.83	13.88	28.29	48.31	125.32	0	1.63	12.27	0.79	23.07	3,744	1	99	0	0	140	25.99	-24.7	3.50		Nov-04
	5.01	14.26	29.17	50.98	132.17		0.91	12.26	0.79	24.81	3,744	1	99	0	0	140	26.42	-24.47			Feb-17
	4.95	14.15	28.98	50.79	131.78	0	1.07	12.27	0.79	24.79	3,744	1	99	0	0	140	26.46	-24.53			Nov-04
	6.32	9.20	11.98	31.83	96.68	0.9	1.24	10.57	0.7	19.97	3,612	1	97	0	1	26	30.67	-23.75	5.75		Nov-04
	6.09	8.79	11.10	28.82	89.24	0.32	2	10.52	0.7	18.25	3,612	1	97	0	1	26	30.11	-23.96		1.00	Nov-04
	6.36	9.35	12.26	32.90	99.22	1.14	0.98	10.55	0.7	20.32	3,612	1	97	0	1	26	30.88	-23.59			Nov-04
	6.21	9.01	11.66	30.81	94.18	0.72	1.49	10.54	0.7	19.51	3,612	1	97	0	1	26	30.48	-23.76	3.50		Nov-04
	5.71	11.27	24.86	34.88	104.43	0.37	0.95	10.67	1.03	44	8,710	2	98	0	0	9	24.58	-21.21	5.75		Oct-12
	5.53	10.84	23.91	31.83	96.69	0	1.72	10.65	1.03	43.7	8,710	2	98	0	0	9	24.04	-21.45		1.00	Oct-12
	5.83	11.49	25.37	36.59	108.86	0.71	0.54	10.66	1.03	43.94	8,710	2	98	0	0	9	24.82	-21.05			May-08
	5.65	11.13	24.55	33.85	101.80	0.16	1.21	10.66	1.03	44.01	8,710	2	98	0	0	9	24.4	-21.29	3.50		Oct-12
	5.83	11.50	25.35	36.60	108.70	0.72	0.54	10.66	1.03	43.84	8,710	2	98	0	0	9	24.76	-21.12			Aug-13
	5.79	11.43	25.20	36.00	107.24	0.6	0.68	10.67	1.03	43.97	8,710	2	98	0	0	9	24.76	-21.12			Oct-12
	4.11	8.07	11.94	23.16	88.34	0.97	1.06	9.92	0.95	20.58	1,153	5	95	0	0	51	24.72	-20.26	5.75		Feb-07
	3.95	7.61	11.05	20.17	80.80	0.37	1.88	9.9	0.95	20.16	1,153	5	95	0	0	51	24.24	-20.47		1.00	Feb-07
	4.24	8.19	12.24	24.15	90.80	1.19	0.85	9.92	0.95	20.6	1,153	5	95	0	0	51	24.94	-20.2			Feb-07
	4.04	7.90	11.63	21.96	85.44	0.67	1.4	9.91	0.95	20.56	1,153	5	95	0	0	51	24.56	-20.33	3.50		Feb-07
	4.23	8.29	12.41	24.38	91.36		0.63	9.94	0.95	20.61	1,153	5	95	0	0	51	24.88	-20.13			Feb-17
	4.98	9.80	20.12	27.57	88.58	0.62	0.64	11.27	0.97	39.96	2,551	3	97	0	0	98	27.84	-21.01			Jun-12
	4.92	9.72	19.89	26.73	86.51	0.48	0.88	11.27	0.97	38.34	2,551	3	97	0	0	98	27.57	-21.09	5.75		Sep-96
	4.73	9.30	19.02	23.87	79.65	0	1.63	11.27	0.97	35.06	2,551	3	97	0	0	98	27.12	-21.37		1.00	Nov-97
	4.87	9.58	19.58	25.80	84.36	0.27	1.12	11.27	0.97	38.57	2,551	3	97	0	0	98	27.51	-21.18	3.50		Feb-96
	5.01	9.91	20.35	27.71	88.87		0.47	11.28	0.97	40.02	2,551	3	97	0	0	98	27.84	-21.01			Feb-17
	4.97	9.84	20.18	27.53	88.60	0.66	0.64	11.28	0.97	40.03	2,551	3	97	0	0	98	27.84	-21.01			Feb-96
	3.76	9.38	11.33	26.72	82.23	0.23	1.16	12.15	0.84	25.96	1,608	3	97	0	0	62	27.27	-25.51	5.75		May-07
	3.55	8.93	10.47	23.65	75.02	0	1.98	12.12	0.84	23.97	1,608	3	97	0	0	62	26.69	-25.73		1.00	May-07
	3.65	9.19	10.96	25.41	79.20	0	1.51	12.14	0.84	25.3	1,608	3	97	0	0	62	27.1	-25.6	3.50		May-07
	3.88	9.66	11.84	27.93	84.95		0.72	12.15	0.84	26.52	1,608	3	97	0	0	62	27.46	-25.4			Feb-17
	3.85	9.59	11.72	27.87	84.97	0.41	0.87	12.13	0.84	26.54	1,608	3	97	0	0	62	27.74	-25.45			May-07
	3.90	6.45	11.90	23.01	66.20	2.4	1.05	7.12	0.65	15.16	5,260	7	64	2	0	60	18.9	-11.67	5.75		Dec-03
	3.71	6.07	11.13	20.29	59.99	1.72	1.81	7.05	0.65	15.1	5,260	7	64	2	0	60	18.35	-11.94		1.00	Dec-03
	3.84	6.25	11.66	22.04	64.04	2.18	1.3	7.07	0.65	15.15	5,260	7	64	2	0	60	18.79	-11.74	3.50		Dec-03
	3.96	6.57	12.19	24.00	68.39	2.66	0.79	7.08	0.65	15.21	5,260	7	64	2	0	60	19.11	-11.51			Dec-03
	2.14	3.50	3.76	3.84	2.68	1.85	1.1	4.45	0.64	8.86	717.8	1	10	32	53	24	8.3	-7.81	4.00		Sep-05
	2.00	3.15	3.02	1.44	-1.18	1.12	1.86	4.48	0.64	8.78	717.8	1	10	32	53	24	7.76	-8.14		1.00	Sep-05
	2.14	3.60	3.78	3.81	2.54	1.86	1.13	4.49	0.66	8.87	717.8	1	10	32	53	24	8.29	-7.9	4.00		Sep-05
	2.18	3.72	4.10	4.67	3.91	2.17	0.82	4.5	0.64	8.87	717.8	1	10	32	53	24	8.47	-7.75			Sep-05
	6.14	16.98	49.35	77.27	164.04	0	1.07	15.2	1.21	53.54	1,815	1	97	0	0	73	25.54	-21.71	5.75		Sep-96
	5.94	16.54	48.21	73.28	154.36	0	1.83	15.18	1.21	45.59	1,815	1	97	0	0	73	25.05	-21.99		1.00	Nov-97

Fund Name	Ticker Symbol	Traded On	Fund Type	Category and (Prospectus Objective)	Overall Rating	Reward Rating	Risk Rating	Recent Up/ Downgrade	Open to New Investors	Min Initial Investment
	MARKET		FUND TYPE, CATEGORY & OBJECTIVE		RATINGS				MINIMUMS	
Fidelity Advisor® Technology Fund Class M	FATEX	NAS CM	Open End	Technology Sector Equity (Technology)	A	A+	B+	Up	Y	2,500
Fidelity Advisor® Technology Fund I Class	FATIX	NAS CM	Open End	Technology Sector Equity (Technology)	A	A+	B+	Up	Y	2,500
Fidelity Advisor® Telecommunications Fund Class A	FTUAX	NAS CM	Open End	Communications Sector Equity (Comm)	C+	C	B		Y	2,500
Fidelity Advisor® Telecommunications Fund Class C	FTUCX	NAS CM	Open End	Communications Sector Equity (Comm)	C+	C	B		Y	2,500
Fidelity Advisor® Telecommunications Fund Class M	FTUTX	NAS CM	Open End	Communications Sector Equity (Comm)	C+	C	B		Y	2,500
Fidelity Advisor® Telecommunications Fund I Class	FTUIX	NAS CM	Open End	Communications Sector Equity (Comm)	C+	C	B		Y	2,500
Fidelity Advisor® Total Emerging Markets Fund Class A	FTEDX	NAS CM	Open End	Emerging Markets Equity (Div Emerging Mkts)	B-	B	B-	Up	Y	2,500
Fidelity Advisor® Total Emerging Markets Fund Class C	FTEFX	NAS CM	Open End	Emerging Markets Equity (Div Emerging Mkts)	B-	B-	B-	Up	Y	2,500
Fidelity Advisor® Total Emerging Markets Fund Class M	FTEHX	NAS CM	Open End	Emerging Markets Equity (Div Emerging Mkts)	B-	B-	B-	Up	Y	2,500
Fidelity Advisor® Total Emerging Markets Fund I Class	FTEJX	NAS CM	Open End	Emerging Markets Equity (Div Emerging Mkts)	B	B	B-	Up	Y	2,500
Fidelity Advisor® Total International Equity Fund Class A	FTAEX	NAS CM	Open End	Global Equity Large Cap (Foreign Stock)	B-	B-	B	Up	Y	2,500
Fidelity Advisor® Total International Equity Fund Class C	FTCEX	NAS CM	Open End	Global Equity Large Cap (Foreign Stock)	B-	B-	B	Up	Y	2,500
Fidelity Advisor® Total International Equity Fund Class M	FTTEX	NAS CM	Open End	Global Equity Large Cap (Foreign Stock)	B-	B-	B	Up	Y	2,500
Fidelity Advisor® Total International Equity Fund Class Z	FIEZX	NAS CM	Open End	Global Equity Large Cap (Foreign Stock)	B	B-	B	Up	Y	0
Fidelity Advisor® Total International Equity Fund I Class	FTEIX	NAS CM	Open End	Global Equity Large Cap (Foreign Stock)	B	B-	B	Up	Y	2,500
Fidelity Advisor® Utilities Fund Class A	FUGAX	NAS CM	Open End	Utilities Sector Equity (Utility)	B-	B	C+	Down	Y	2,500
Fidelity Advisor® Utilities Fund Class C	FUGCX	NAS CM	Open End	Utilities Sector Equity (Utility)	B-	B	C+	Down	Y	2,500
Fidelity Advisor® Utilities Fund Class M	FAUFX	NAS CM	Open End	Utilities Sector Equity (Utility)	B-	B	C+	Down	Y	2,500
Fidelity Advisor® Utilities Fund I Class	FUGIX	NAS CM	Open End	Utilities Sector Equity (Utility)	B-	B	C+	Down	Y	2,500
Fidelity Advisor® Value Fund Class A	FAVFX	NAS CM	Open End	US Equity Mid Cap (Growth)	C+	B-	C+	Down	Y	2,500
Fidelity Advisor® Value Fund Class C	FCVFX	NAS CM	Open End	US Equity Mid Cap (Growth)	B-	C+	B	Up	Y	2,500
Fidelity Advisor® Value Fund Class M	FTVFX	NAS CM	Open End	US Equity Mid Cap (Growth)	C+	C+	C+	Down	Y	2,500
Fidelity Advisor® Value Fund Class Z	FVLZX	NAS CM	Open End	US Equity Mid Cap (Growth)	C+	B-	C+	Down	Y	0
Fidelity Advisor® Value Fund I Class	FVIFX	NAS CM	Open End	US Equity Mid Cap (Growth)	C+	B-	C+	Down	Y	2,500
Fidelity Advisor® Value Leaders Fund Class A	FVLAX	NAS CM	Open End	US Equity Large Cap Value (Growth)	B	C+	B	Up	Y	2,500
Fidelity Advisor® Value Leaders Fund Class C	FVLCX	NAS CM	Open End	US Equity Large Cap Value (Growth)	B-	C+	B	Down	Y	2,500
Fidelity Advisor® Value Leaders Fund Class M	FVLTX	NAS CM	Open End	US Equity Large Cap Value (Growth)	B-	C+	B	Down	Y	2,500
Fidelity Advisor® Value Leaders Fund I Class	FVLIX	NAS CM	Open End	US Equity Large Cap Value (Growth)	B	C+	B	Up	Y	2,500
Fidelity Advisor® Value Strategies Fund Class A	FSOAX	NAS CM	Open End	US Equity Large Cap Value (Growth)	B	B-	B	Up	Y	2,500
Fidelity Advisor® Value Strategies Fund Class C	FVCSX	NAS CM	Open End	US Equity Large Cap Value (Growth)	B-	B-	B	Up	Y	2,500
Fidelity Advisor® Value Strategies Fund Class I	FASOX	NAS CM	Open End	US Equity Large Cap Value (Growth)	B	B-	B	Up	Y	2,500
Fidelity Advisor® Value Strategies Fund Class K	FVSKX	NAS CM	Open End	US Equity Large Cap Value (Growth)	B	B-	B	Up	Y	0
Fidelity Advisor® Value Strategies Fund Class M	FASPX	NAS CM	Open End	US Equity Large Cap Value (Growth)	B	B-	B	Up	Y	2,500
Fidelity Advisor® Worldwide Fund Class A	FWAFX	NAS CM	Open End	Global Equity (World Stock)	B	B	B	Up	Y	2,500
Fidelity Advisor® Worldwide Fund Class C	FWCFX	NAS CM	Open End	Global Equity (World Stock)	B	B-	B	Up	Y	2,500
Fidelity Advisor® Worldwide Fund Class M	FWTFX	NAS CM	Open End	Global Equity (World Stock)	B	B-	B	Up	Y	2,500
Fidelity Advisor® Worldwide Fund I Class	FWIFX	NAS CM	Open End	Global Equity (World Stock)	B	B	B	Up	Y	2,500
Fidelity Asset Manager® 20% Fund	FASIX	NAS CM	Open End	Cautious Alloc (Asset Alloc)	B	C	A-	Up	Y	2,500
Fidelity Asset Manager® 30% Fund	FTANX	NAS CM	Open End	Cautious Alloc (Asset Alloc)	B	C+	A-	Up	Y	2,500
Fidelity Asset Manager® 40% Fund	FFANX	NAS CM	Open End	Cautious Alloc (Asset Alloc)	B-	C+	B	Up	Y	2,500
Fidelity Asset Manager® 50% Fund	FASMX	NAS CM	Open End	Cautious Alloc (Asset Alloc)	B	C+	A-	Up	Y	2,500
Fidelity Asset Manager® 60% Fund	FSANX	NAS CM	Open End	Moderate Alloc (Asset Alloc)	B-	C+	B	Down	Y	2,500
Fidelity Asset Manager® 70% Fund	FASGX	NAS CM	Open End	Moderate Alloc (Asset Alloc)	B-	B-	B	Down	Y	2,500
Fidelity Asset Manager® 85% Fund	FAMRX	NAS CM	Open End	Aggressive Alloc (Asset Alloc)	B-	B-	B-	Down	Y	2,500
Fidelity Flex Freedom 2005 Fund	FERNX	NAS CM	Open End	Target Date 2000-2020 (Asset Alloc)	U	U	U		Y	0
Fidelity Flex Freedom 2010 Fund	FISNX	NAS CM	Open End	Target Date 2000-2020 (Asset Alloc)	U	U	U		Y	0
Fidelity Flex Freedom 2015 Fund	FILSX	NAS CM	Open End	Target Date 2000-2020 (Asset Alloc)	U	U	U		Y	0
Fidelity Flex Freedom 2020 Fund	FULSX	NAS CM	Open End	Target Date 2000-2020 (Asset Alloc)	U	U	U		Y	0
Fidelity Flex Freedom 2025 Fund	FELSX	NAS CM	Open End	Target Date 2021-2045 (Asset Alloc)	U	U	U		Y	0
Fidelity Flex Freedom 2030 Fund	FVLSX	NAS CM	Open End	Target Date 2021-2045 (Asset Alloc)	U	U	U		Y	0
Fidelity Flex Freedom 2035 Fund	FJLSX	NAS CM	Open End	Target Date 2021-2045 (Asset Alloc)	U	U	U		Y	0
Fidelity Flex Freedom 2040 Fund	FCLSX	NAS CM	Open End	Target Date 2021-2045 (Asset Alloc)	U	U	U		Y	0

★ Expanded analysis of this fund is included in Section II.

	TOTAL RETURNS					PERFORMANCE				ASSETS		ASSET ALLOCATION & TURNOVER					BULL & BEAR		FEES		
Min Additional Investment	3-Month Total Return	6-Month Total Return	1-Year Total Return	3-Year Total Return	5-Year Total Return	Dividend Yield (TTM)	Expense Ratio	3-Yr Std Deviation	3-Year Beta	NAV	Total Assets (MIL)	%Cash	%Stocks	%Bonds	%Other	Turnover Ratio	Last Bull Market Total Return	Last Bear Market Total Return	Front End Fee (%)	Back End Fee (%)	Inception Date
	6.07	16.82	48.94	75.88	160.61	0	1.33	15.18	1.21	50.83	1,815	1	97	0	0	73	25.39	-21.81	3.50		Sep-96
	6.23	17.14	49.76	78.92	168.19	0	0.77	15.19	1.21	57.44	1,815	1	97	0	0	73	25.84	-21.64			Sep-96
	1.06	3.72	1.36	25.63	60.20	1.65	1.14	11.08	0.74	58.63	399.3	0	100	0	0	105	12.09	-16.68	5.75		Dec-06
	0.86	3.34	0.62	22.88	54.54	1.05	1.88	11.06	0.74	58.39	399.3	0	100	0	0	105	11.61	-16.93		1.00	Dec-06
	0.96	3.53	1.00	24.39	57.67	1.18	1.46	11.08	0.74	58.38	399.3	0	100	0	0	105	11.89	-16.77	3.50		Dec-06
	1.13	3.89	1.68	26.89	62.72	1.94	0.8	11.08	0.74	58.77	399.3	0	100	0	0	105	12.27	-16.59			Dec-06
	5.15	12.29	29.33	34.59	32.53	0.89	1.65	11.16	0.68	13.54	749.9	3	71	25	0	57			5.75		Nov-11
	4.91	11.92	28.31	31.59	27.57	0.42	2.4	11.15	0.68	13.47	749.9	3	71	25	0	57				1.00	Nov-11
	5.01	12.06	28.81	33.35	30.76	0.63	1.9	11.16	0.68	13.55	749.9	3	71	25	0	57			3.50		Nov-11
	5.13	12.44	29.63	35.54	34.23	1.01	1.41	11.2	0.69	13.53	749.9	3	71	25	0	57					Nov-11
	4.95	10.84	30.06	28.57	42.79	0.88	1.45	10.73	0.84	9.29	119.1	1	99	0	0	66	16.31	-25.3	5.75		Nov-07
	4.78	10.41	29.01	25.71	37.69	0.24	2.2	10.76	0.84	9.32	119.1	1	99	0	0	66	15.86	-25.58		1.00	Nov-07
	4.83	10.69	29.64	27.58	41.07	0.69	1.7	10.73	0.84	9.33	119.1	1	99	0	0	66	16.22	-25.33	3.50		Nov-07
	5.05	11.08	30.37	29.58	44.76		1.04	10.72	0.84	9.28	119.1	1	99	0	0	66	16.52	-25.24			Feb-17
	4.95	10.97	30.27	29.48	44.65	1.05	1.2	10.72	0.84	9.26	119.1	1	99	0	0	66	16.52	-25.24			Nov-07
	0.56	5.42	17.30	16.71	74.99	1.55	1.12	11.28	0.33	29.04	326.0	0	100	0	0	37	11.31	-2.6	5.75		Sep-96
	0.38	5.02	16.45	14.10	68.59	0.95	1.87	11.29	0.33	28.49	326.0	0	100	0	0	37	10.85	-2.87		1.00	Nov-97
	0.49	5.24	16.94	15.66	72.44	1.29	1.41	11.28	0.33	29.12	326.0	0	100	0	0	37	11.17	-2.66	3.50		Sep-96
	0.64	5.55	17.64	17.73	77.55	1.72	0.85	11.27	0.33	29.61	326.0	0	100	0	0	37	11.53	-2.47			Sep-96
	4.43	7.49	14.99	22.85	91.23	0.53	1.24	11.25	1.04	25.54	112.2	3	97	0	0	77	26.59	-24.82	5.75		Dec-03
	4.17	7.03	14.04	19.95	83.95	0	2.03	11.25	1.04	24.35	112.2	3	97	0	0	77	25.93	-24.98		1.00	Dec-03
	4.35	7.35	14.67	21.89	88.74	0.35	1.52	11.24	1.04	25.33	112.2	3	97	0	0	77	26.37	-24.86	3.50		Dec-03
	4.49	7.69	15.37	23.97	94.01		0.8	11.27	1.04	25.74	112.2	3	97	0	0	77	26.72	-24.68			Feb-17
	4.48	7.64	15.32	23.91	93.91	0.78	0.94	11.27	1.04	25.76	112.2	3	97	0	0	77	26.72	-24.68			Dec-03
	5.54	7.85	14.41	22.54	90.67	0.4	1.47	10.61	0.96	19.62	34.1	5	95	0	0	63	20.66	-23.85	5.75		Jun-03
	5.29	7.42	13.56	19.72	83.67	0	2.29	10.65	0.96	19.09	34.1	5	95	0	0	63	20.11	-24.09		1.00	Jun-03
	5.45	7.69	14.10	21.55	88.27	0.21	1.77	10.66	0.96	19.69	34.1	5	95	0	0	63	20.4	-23.89	3.50		Jun-03
	5.59	8.00	14.71	23.43	93.17	0.61	1.18	10.65	0.96	19.74	34.1	5	95	0	0	63	20.81	-23.77			Jun-03
	4.99	8.85	18.85	26.95	80.03	1.2	0.86	12.05	1.06	36.18	1,118	3	97	0	0	121	29.06	-26.82	5.75		Sep-96
	4.78	8.40	17.91	24.03	73.24	0.71	1.63	12.05	1.06	31.5	1,118	3	97	0	0	121	28.48	-27.07		1.00	Aug-01
	5.07	8.97	19.14	27.88	82.31	1.33	0.61	12.07	1.06	39.52	1,118	3	97	0	0	121	29.28	-26.75			Jul-95
	5.10	9.03	19.30	28.55	83.92	1.38	0.44	12.07	1.06	42.02	1,118	3	97	0	0	121	29.39	-26.68			May-08
	4.95	8.71	18.59	26.11	78.12	0.95	1.08	12.06	1.06	38.08	1,118	3	97	0	0	121	28.89	-26.87	3.50		Aug-86
	6.00	13.14	29.11	31.18	76.10	0.44	1.22	10.54	0.93	26.14	1,761	2	98	0	0	5	19.17	-20.04	5.75		Feb-09
	5.85	12.72	28.15	28.19	69.48	0	2.01	10.54	0.93	25.58	1,761	2	98	0	0	5	18.68	-20.29		1.00	Feb-09
	5.94	12.98	28.73	30.03	73.58	0.11	1.53	10.55	0.93	26.03	1,761	2	98	0	0	5	19.01	-20.17	3.50		Feb-09
	6.13	13.31	29.53	32.33	78.60	0.66	0.99	10.54	0.92	26.29	1,761	2	98	0	0	5	19.32	-19.93			Feb-09
	1.57	3.21	6.97	11.59	22.63	1.49	0.53	2.94	0.4	13.43	5,055	28	20	47	5	22	6.57	-3.23			Oct-92
	2.06	4.27	9.43	14.90	30.78	1.49	0.55	3.8	0.34	11.09	1,294	18	30	47	5	24	8.75	-5.56			Oct-07
	2.65	5.34	11.77	17.80	38.65	1.37	0.56	4.72	0.25	11.7	1,498	13	40	42	6	20	10.77	-8.03			Oct-07
	3.15	6.37	14.06	20.44	46.35	1.28	0.67	5.69	0.52	18.27	8,756	8	50	36	6	20	12.59	-10.58			Dec-88
	3.70	7.40	16.40	23.15	54.00	1.19	0.73	6.63	0.61	12.56	2,053	3	60	31	5	18	14.49	-13.04			Oct-07
	4.24	8.46	18.70	25.76	62.03	1.11	0.73	7.64	0.71	22.4	5,190	2	71	22	5	19	16.54	-15.69			Dec-91
	5.07	10.00	22.26	29.74	75.23	0.87	0.75	9.08	0.86	19.53	2,147	3	84	9	4	23	19.23	-19.22			Sep-99
	2.24	4.91					0			10.24	0.10	22	34	44	0						Jun-17
	2.73	5.82					0			10.31	0.10	18	42	39	0						Jun-17
	3.20	6.61					0			10.37	0.11	15	51	33	0						Jun-17
	3.51	7.35					0			10.42	0.11	12	57	30	0						Jun-17
	3.91	7.97					0			10.47	0.11	10	63	26	0						Jun-17
	4.55	9.28					0			10.56	0.11	6	76	18	0						Jun-17
	5.14	10.32					0			10.65	0.11	5	87	7	0						Jun-17
	5.25	10.54					0			10.67	0.11	5	89	6	0						Jun-17

Fund Name	Ticker Symbol	Traded On	Fund Type	Category and (Prospectus Objective)	Overall Rating	Reward Rating	Risk Rating	Recent Up/ Downgrade	Open to New Investors	Min Initial Investment
Fidelity Flex Freedom 2045 Fund	FOLSX	NAS CM	Open End	Target Date 2021-2045 (Asset Alloc)	U	U	U		Y	0
Fidelity Flex Freedom 2050 Fund	FYLSX	NAS CM	Open End	Target Date 2046+ (Asset Alloc)	U	U	U		Y	0
Fidelity Flex Freedom 2055 Fund	FQLSX	NAS CM	Open End	Target Date 2046+ (Asset Alloc)	U	U	U		Y	0
Fidelity Flex Freedom 2060 Fund	FWLSX	NAS CM	Open End	Target Date 2046+ (Asset Alloc)	U	U	U		Y	0
Fidelity Flex Freedom Income Fund	FTLSX	NAS CM	Open End	Target Date 2000-2020 (Asset Alloc)	U	U	U		Y	0
Fidelity Freedom® 2005 Fund	FFFVX	NAS CM	Open End	Target Date 2000-2020 (Asset Alloc)	B-	C+	B	Up	Y	2,500
Fidelity Freedom® 2005 Fund Class K6	FITKX	NAS CM	Open End	Target Date 2000-2020 (Asset Alloc)	B-	C+	B	Up	Y	0
Fidelity Freedom® 2010 Fund	FFFCX	NAS CM	Open End	Target Date 2000-2020 (Asset Alloc)	B-	C+	B	Up	Y	2,500
Fidelity Freedom® 2010 Fund Class K6	FOTKX	NAS CM	Open End	Target Date 2000-2020 (Asset Alloc)	B-	C+	B	Up	Y	0
Fidelity Freedom® 2015 Fund	FFVFX	NAS CM	Open End	Target Date 2000-2020 (Asset Alloc)	B-	C+	B	Up	Y	2,500
Fidelity Freedom® 2015 Fund Class K6	FPTKX	NAS CM	Open End	Target Date 2000-2020 (Asset Alloc)	B-	C+	B	Up	Y	0
Fidelity Freedom® 2020 Fund	FFFDX	NAS CM	Open End	Target Date 2000-2020 (Asset Alloc)	B-	C+	B	Down	Y	2,500
Fidelity Freedom® 2020 Fund Class K6	FATKX	NAS CM	Open End	Target Date 2000-2020 (Asset Alloc)	B	C+	A-		Y	0
Fidelity Freedom® 2025 Fund	FFTWX	NAS CM	Open End	Target Date 2021-2045 (Asset Alloc)	B-	C+	B	Down	Y	2,500
Fidelity Freedom® 2025 Fund Class K6	FDTKX	NAS CM	Open End	Target Date 2021-2045 (Asset Alloc)	B-	C+	B	Down	Y	0
Fidelity Freedom® 2030 Fund	FFFEX	NAS CM	Open End	Target Date 2021-2045 (Asset Alloc)	B-	B-	B	Down	Y	2,500
Fidelity Freedom® 2030 Fund Class K6	FGTKX	NAS CM	Open End	Target Date 2021-2045 (Asset Alloc)	B-	B-	B	Down	Y	0
Fidelity Freedom® 2035 Fund	FFTHX	NAS CM	Open End	Target Date 2021-2045 (Asset Alloc)	B-	B-	B-	Down	Y	2,500
Fidelity Freedom® 2035 Fund Class K6	FWTKX	NAS CM	Open End	Target Date 2021-2045 (Asset Alloc)	B-	B-	B-	Down	Y	0
Fidelity Freedom® 2040 Fund	FFFFX	NAS CM	Open End	Target Date 2021-2045 (Asset Alloc)	B-	B-	B-	Down	Y	2,500
Fidelity Freedom® 2040 Fund Class K6	FHTKX	NAS CM	Open End	Target Date 2021-2045 (Asset Alloc)	B-	B-	B-	Down	Y	0
Fidelity Freedom® 2045 Fund	FFFGX	NAS CM	Open End	Target Date 2021-2045 (Asset Alloc)	B-	B-	B-	Down	Y	2,500
Fidelity Freedom® 2045 Fund Class K6	FJTKX	NAS CM	Open End	Target Date 2021-2045 (Asset Alloc)	B-	B-	B-	Down	Y	0
Fidelity Freedom® 2050 Fund	FFFHX	NAS CM	Open End	Target Date 2046+ (Asset Alloc)	B-	B-	B-	Down	Y	2,500
Fidelity Freedom® 2050 Fund Class K6	FZTKX	NAS CM	Open End	Target Date 2046+ (Asset Alloc)	B-	B-	B-	Down	Y	0
Fidelity Freedom® 2055 Fund	FDEEX	NAS CM	Open End	Target Date 2046+ (Asset Alloc)	B-	B-	B-	Down	Y	2,500
Fidelity Freedom® 2055 Fund Class K6	FCTKX	NAS CM	Open End	Target Date 2046+ (Asset Alloc)	B-	B-	B-	Down	Y	0
Fidelity Freedom® 2060 Fund	FDKVX	NAS CM	Open End	Target Date 2046+ (Asset Alloc)	B-	B-	B-	Up	Y	2,500
Fidelity Freedom® 2060 Fund Class K6	FVTKX	NAS CM	Open End	Target Date 2046+ (Asset Alloc)	B-	B-	B-		Y	0
Fidelity Freedom® Income Fund	FFFAX	NAS CM	Open End	Target Date 2000-2020 (Asset Alloc)	B	C+	A-	Up	Y	2,500
Fidelity Freedom® Income Fund Class K6	FYTKX	NAS CM	Open End	Target Date 2000-2020 (Asset Alloc)	B-	C+	B	Up	Y	0
Fidelity Freedom® Index 2005 Fund Inst Premium Cls	FFGFX	NAS CM	Open End	Target Date 2000-2020 (Asset Alloc)	B-	C+	B	Up	Y	0
Fidelity Freedom® Index 2005 Fund Investor Class	FJIFX	NAS CM	Open End	Target Date 2000-2020 (Asset Alloc)	B-	C+	B	Up	Y	2,500
Fidelity Freedom® Index 2010 Fund Inst Premium Cls	FFWTX	NAS CM	Open End	Target Date 2000-2020 (Asset Alloc)	B-	C+	B	Up	Y	0
Fidelity Freedom® Index 2010 Fund Investor Class	FKIFX	NAS CM	Open End	Target Date 2000-2020 (Asset Alloc)	B-	C+	B	Up	Y	2,500
Fidelity Freedom® Index 2015 Fund Inst Premium Cls	FIWFX	NAS CM	Open End	Target Date 2000-2020 (Asset Alloc)	B-	C+	B	Up	Y	0
Fidelity Freedom® Index 2015 Fund Investor Class	FLIFX	NAS CM	Open End	Target Date 2000-2020 (Asset Alloc)	B-	C+	B	Up	Y	2,500
Fidelity Freedom® Index 2020 Fund Inst Premium Cls	FIWTX	NAS CM	Open End	Target Date 2000-2020 (Asset Alloc)	B-	C+	B	Up	Y	0
Fidelity Freedom® Index 2020 Fund Investor Class	FPIFX	NAS CM	Open End	Target Date 2000-2020 (Asset Alloc)	B-	C+	B	Up	Y	2,500
Fidelity Freedom® Index 2025 Fund Inst Premium Cls	FFEDX	NAS CM	Open End	Target Date 2021-2045 (Asset Alloc)	B-	C+	B	Up	Y	0
Fidelity Freedom® Index 2025 Fund Investor Class	FQIFX	NAS CM	Open End	Target Date 2021-2045 (Asset Alloc)	B-	C+	B	Up	Y	2,500
Fidelity Freedom® Index 2030 Fund Inst Premium Cls	FFEGX	NAS CM	Open End	Target Date 2021-2045 (Asset Alloc)	B-	B-	B	Down	Y	0
Fidelity Freedom® Index 2030 Fund Investor Class	FXIFX	NAS CM	Open End	Target Date 2021-2045 (Asset Alloc)	B-	B-	B	Down	Y	2,500
Fidelity Freedom® Index 2035 Fund Inst Premium Cls	FFEZX	NAS CM	Open End	Target Date 2021-2045 (Asset Alloc)	B-	B-	B-	Down	Y	0
Fidelity Freedom® Index 2035 Fund Investor Class	FIHFX	NAS CM	Open End	Target Date 2021-2045 (Asset Alloc)	B-	B-	B-	Down	Y	2,500
Fidelity Freedom® Index 2040 Fund Inst Premium Cls	FFIZX	NAS CM	Open End	Target Date 2021-2045 (Asset Alloc)	B-	B-	B-	Down	Y	0
Fidelity Freedom® Index 2040 Fund Investor Class	FBIFX	NAS CM	Open End	Target Date 2021-2045 (Asset Alloc)	B-	B-	B-	Down	Y	2,500
Fidelity Freedom® Index 2045 Fund Inst Premium Cls	FFOLX	NAS CM	Open End	Target Date 2021-2045 (Asset Alloc)	B-	B-	B-	Down	Y	0
Fidelity Freedom® Index 2045 Fund Investor Class	FIOFX	NAS CM	Open End	Target Date 2021-2045 (Asset Alloc)	B-	B-	B-	Down	Y	2,500
Fidelity Freedom® Index 2050 Fund Inst Premium Cls	FFOPX	NAS CM	Open End	Target Date 2046+ (Asset Alloc)	B-	B-	B-	Down	Y	0
Fidelity Freedom® Index 2050 Fund Investor Class	FIPFX	NAS CM	Open End	Target Date 2046+ (Asset Alloc)	B-	B-	B-	Down	Y	2,500
Fidelity Freedom® Index 2055 Fund Inst Premium Cls	FFLDX	NAS CM	Open End	Target Date 2046+ (Asset Alloc)	B-	B-	B-	Down	Y	0

★Expanded analysis of this fund is included in Section II.

Min Additional Investment	TOTAL RETURNS 3-Month Total Return	6-Month Total Return	1-Year Total Return	3-Year Total Return	5-Year Total Return	PERFORMANCE Dividend Yield (TTM)	Expense Ratio	3-Yr Std Deviation	3-Year Beta	ASSETS NAV	Total Assets (MIL)	ASSET ALLOCATION & TURNOVER %Cash	%Stocks	%Bonds	%Other	Turnover Ratio	BULL & BEAR Last Bull Market Total Return	Last Bear Market Total Return	FEES Front End Fee (%)	Back End Fee (%)	Inception Date
	5.27	10.56					0			10.67	0.11	5	89	6	0						Jun-17
	5.25	10.54					0			10.67	0.11	5	89	6	0						Jun-17
	5.26	10.55					0			10.67	0.11	5	89	6	0						Jun-17
	5.25	10.54					0			10.67	0.11	5	89	6	0						Jun-17
	1.74	3.81					0			10.16	0.10	27	24	48	0						Jun-17
	2.17	4.65	10.47	16.32	32.31	1.57	0.49	4.44	0.23	12.56	1,036	22	34	44	0	38	9.87	-8.45			Nov-03
	2.18	4.67	10.48	16.33	32.33		0.38	4.43	0.23	12.55	1,036	22	34	44	0	38	9.87	-8.45			Jun-17
	2.65	5.59	12.47	18.97	39.90	1.57	0.53	5.29	0.14	16.06	6,777	18	42	39	0	24	12.02	-10.33			Oct-96
	2.67	5.61	12.49	18.99	39.92		0.4	5.29	0.14	16.03	6,777	18	42	39	0	24	12.02	-10.33			Jun-17
	3.07	6.40	14.28	21.52	44.29	1.54	0.58	6.04	0.55	13.38	10,472	15	51	34	0	22	12.21	-10.53			Nov-03
	3.18	6.52	14.40	21.65	44.45		0.42	6.04	0.55	13.37	10,472	15	51	34	0	22	12.21	-10.53			Jun-17
	3.39	7.02	15.64	23.18	48.71	1.51	0.62	6.62	0.61	16.57	30,350	12	57	30	0	20	13.9	-12.61			Oct-96
	3.48	7.12	15.74	23.28	48.84		0.44	6.63	0.61	16.56	30,350	12	57	30	0	20	13.9	-12.61			Jun-17
	3.71	7.56	16.81	24.77	55.68	1.44	0.66	7.34	0.69	14.4	26,834	10	63	26	0	22	15.83	-14.91			Nov-03
	3.78	7.70	16.97	24.94	55.88		0.45	7.34	0.69	14.4	26,834	10	63	26	0	22	15.83	-14.91			Jun-17
	4.40	8.86	19.81	28.55	62.95	1.33	0.7	8.69	0.82	18.06	31,461	6	76	18	0	21	16.47	-15.8			Oct-96
	4.45	9.03	20.00	28.75	63.20		0.47	8.7	0.82	18.05	31,461	6	76	18	0	21	16.47	-15.8			Jun-17
	4.99	9.93	22.00	31.36	70.65	1.2	0.75	9.5	0.9	15.24	21,304	5	87	7	0	20	18.28	-18.08			Nov-03
	5.09	10.10	22.19	31.56	70.92		0.49	9.51	0.9	15.23	21,304	5	87	7	0	20	18.28	-18.08			Jun-17
	5.04	10.08	22.25	31.69	71.67	1.2	0.75	9.5	0.9	10.7	22,091	5	89	6	0	19	18.43	-18.4			Sep-00
	5.18	10.23	22.41	31.86	71.90		0.49	9.5	0.9	10.69	22,091	5	89	6	0	19	18.44	-18.4			Jun-17
	5.07	10.00	22.20	31.59	72.34	1.19	0.75	9.49	0.9	12.12	12,978	5	89	6	0	19	18.94	-18.96			Jun-06
	5.14	10.26	22.50	31.90	72.76		0.49	9.5	0.9	12.11	12,978	5	89	6	0	19	18.94	-18.96			Jun-17
	5.05	10.04	22.28	31.64	72.79	1.18	0.75	9.51	0.9	12.19	10,884	5	89	6	0	19	19.66	-19.85			Jun-06
	5.20	10.30	22.56	31.95	73.20		0.49	9.52	0.9	12.18	10,884	5	89	6	0	19	19.66	-19.85			Jun-17
	5.11	10.12	22.31	31.62	74.09	1.15	0.75	9.46	0.9	13.74	4,031	5	89	6	0	18	19.84				Jun-11
	5.10	10.20	22.39	31.71	74.21		0.49	9.47	0.9	13.72	4,031	5	89	6	0	18	19.84				Jun-17
	5.01	10.00	22.10	31.42		1.06	0.75	9.45	0.9		633.6	5	89	6	0	18					Aug-14
	5.20	10.20	22.33	31.66			0.49	9.45	0.9	12.23	633.6	5	89	6	0	18					Jun-17
	1.68	3.71	8.21	13.27	23.42	1.37	0.47	3.28	0.35	11.78	3,795	27	24	49	0	36	6.35	-3.87			Oct-96
	1.73	3.72	8.22	13.28	23.44		0.37	3.28	0.35	11.77	3,795	27	24	49	0	36	6.35	-3.87			Jun-17
	2.19	4.30	8.93	13.44	27.37	1.53	0.1	3.77	0.23	13.45	103.9	25	33	42	1	52	8.59	-6.91			Jun-15
	2.17	4.27	8.89	13.29	27.21	1.48	0.15	3.75	0.23	13.45	103.9	25	33	42	1	52	8.59	-6.91			Oct-09
	2.61	5.20	10.72	16.07	34.51	1.58	0.1	4.56	0.15	14.35	532.8	19	42	38	1	36	10.69	-8.56			Jun-15
	2.65	5.17	10.67	15.87	34.29	1.53	0.15	4.6	0.16	14.35	532.8	19	42	38	1	36	10.69	-8.56			Oct-09
	3.11	6.11	12.66	18.62	39.10	1.63	0.1	5.4	0.5	15.02	1,160	14	51	35	1	29	10.94	-8.79			Jun-15
	3.14	6.08	12.60	18.42	38.87	1.58	0.15	5.44	0.51	15.03	1,160	14	51	35	1	29	10.94	-8.79			Oct-09
	3.52	6.76	13.95	20.36	43.19	1.65	0.1	6	0.56	15.8	3,828	10	57	32	1	20	12.38	-10.57			Jun-15
	3.42	6.72	13.89	20.16	42.95	1.59	0.15	6.02	0.57	15.8	3,828	10	57	32	1	20	12.38	-10.57			Oct-09
	3.81	7.33	15.19	22.07	50.25	1.68	0.1	6.72	0.64	16.79	3,390	7	63	30	1	18	14.27	-12.7			Jun-15
	3.78	7.37	15.14	21.88	50.02	1.63	0.15	6.69	0.63	16.79	3,390	7	63	30	1	18	14.27	-12.7			Oct-09
	4.48	8.70	18.03	25.77	57.39	1.7	0.1	8.15	0.78	17.69	4,182	2	75	22	1	13	14.8	-13.49			Jun-15
	4.51	8.67	18.04	25.64	57.24	1.65	0.15	8.13	0.78	17.7	4,182	2	75	22	1	13	14.8	-13.49			Oct-09
	5.17	9.89	20.39	28.93	65.42	1.64	0.1	8.99	0.87	18.76	2,663	2	86	11	1	13	16.63	-15.72			Jun-15
	5.19	9.85	20.34	28.74	65.18	1.6	0.15	9.02	0.87	18.76	2,663	2	86	11	1	13	16.63	-15.72			Oct-09
	5.21	10.03	20.56	29.13	66.19	1.67	0.1	9	0.87	18.89	2,941	2	88	10	1	13	16.69	-15.89			Jun-15
	5.24	9.99	20.57	28.98	66.01	1.62	0.15	8.98	0.86	18.9	2,941	2	88	10	1	13	16.69	-15.89			Oct-09
	5.23	10.01	20.56	29.08	66.92	1.68	0.1	9	0.87	19.04	1,748	2	88	10	1	15	16.99	-16.31			Jun-15
	5.26	9.98	20.58	28.97	66.77	1.63	0.15	9.02	0.87	19.04	1,748	2	88	10	1	15	16.99	-16.31			Oct-09
	5.22	10.03	20.60	29.13	67.46	1.75	0.1	9.03	0.87	19.12	1,623	2	88	10	1	19	17.57	-17.18			Jun-15
	5.24	10.00	20.53	28.92	67.18	1.71	0.15	9.01	0.87	19.13	1,623	2	88	10	1	19	17.57	-17.18			Oct-09
	5.20	10.01	20.56	28.96	68.55	1.92	0.1	8.99	0.86	15.12	560.5	2	88	10	1	33	17.86				Jun-15

	MARKET			FUND TYPE, CATEGORY & OBJECTIVE	RATINGS					MINIMUMS
Fund Name	Ticker Symbol	Traded On	Fund Type	Category and (Prospectus Objective)	Overall Rating	Reward Rating	Risk Rating	Recent Up/ Downgrade	Open to New Investors	Min Initial Investment
Fidelity Freedom® Index 2055 Fund Investor Class	FDEWX	NAS CM	Open End	Target Date 2046+ (Asset Alloc)	B-	B-	B-	Down	Y	2,500
Fidelity Freedom® Index 2060 Fund Inst Premium Cls	FFLEX	NAS CM	Open End	Target Date 2046+ (Asset Alloc)	B-	B-	B-	Up	Y	0
Fidelity Freedom® Index 2060 Fund Investor Class	FDKLX	NAS CM	Open End	Target Date 2046+ (Asset Alloc)	B-	B-	B-	Up	Y	2,500
Fidelity Freedom® Index Income Fund Inst Premium Cls	FFGZX	NAS CM	Open End	Target Date 2000-2020 (Asset Alloc)	B	C	A	Up	Y	0
Fidelity Freedom® Index Income Fund Investor Class	FIKFX	NAS CM	Open End	Target Date 2000-2020 (Asset Alloc)	B	C	A	Up	Y	2,500
Fidelity Managed Retirement 2005 Fund	FIROX	NAS CM	Open End	Cautious Alloc (Asset Alloc)	B-	C+	B	Up	Y	2,500
Fidelity Managed Retirement 2010 Fund	FIRQX	NAS CM	Open End	Moderate Alloc (Asset Alloc)	B-	C+	B	Up	Y	2,500
Fidelity Managed Retirement 2015 Fund	FIRSX	NAS CM	Open End	Moderate Alloc (Asset Alloc)	B-	C+	B	Up	Y	2,500
Fidelity Managed Retirement 2020 Fund	FIRVX	NAS CM	Open End	Moderate Alloc (Asset Alloc)	B-	C+	B	Up	Y	2,500
Fidelity Managed Retirement 2025 Fund	FIXRX	NAS CM	Open End	Moderate Alloc (Asset Alloc)	B-	C+	B	Up	Y	2,500
Fidelity Managed Retirement Income Fund	FIRMX	NAS CM	Open End	Cautious Alloc (Asset Alloc)	B-	C	B	Up	Y	2,500
Fidelity Select Advisor® Gold Fund Class A	FGDAX	NAS CM	Open End	Precious Metals Sector Equity (Precious Metals)	D+	C-	D	Down	Y	2,500
Fidelity Select Advisor® Gold Fund Class C	FGDCX	NAS CM	Open End	Precious Metals Sector Equity (Precious Metals)	D+	C-	D	Down	Y	2,500
Fidelity Select Advisor® Gold Fund Class I	FGDIX	NAS CM	Open End	Precious Metals Sector Equity (Precious Metals)	C-	C	D	Down	Y	2,500
Fidelity Select Advisor® Gold Fund Class M	FGDTX	NAS CM	Open End	Precious Metals Sector Equity (Precious Metals)	D+	C-	D	Down	Y	2,500
Fidelity Simplicity RMD 2005 Fund	FIRPX	NAS CM	Open End	Moderate Alloc (Asset Alloc)	B-	C+	B	Up	Y	2,500
Fidelity Simplicity RMD 2010 Fund	FIRRX	NAS CM	Open End	Moderate Alloc (Asset Alloc)	B-	C+	B	Up	Y	2,500
Fidelity Simplicity RMD 2015 Fund	FIRUX	NAS CM	Open End	Moderate Alloc (Asset Alloc)	B-	C+	B	Up	Y	2,500
Fidelity Simplicity RMD 2020 Fund	FIRWX	NAS CM	Open End	Moderate Alloc (Asset Alloc)	B-	C+	B	Up	Y	2,500
Fidelity Simplicity RMD Income Fund	FIRNX	NAS CM	Open End	Cautious Alloc (Asset Alloc)	B-	C+	B	Up	Y	2,500
Fidelity® 500 Index Fund Institutional Class	FXSIX	NAS CM	Open End	US Equity Large Cap Blend (Growth & Income)	B	B	B		Y	5,000,000
Fidelity® 500 Index Fund Institutional Premium Class	FXAIX	NAS CM	Open End	US Equity Large Cap Blend (Growth & Income)	B	B	B		Y	200,000,000
★ Fidelity® 500 Index Fund Investor Class	FUSEX	NAS CM	Open End	US Equity Large Cap Blend (Growth & Income)	B	B	B		Y	2,500
★ Fidelity® 500 Index Fund Premium Class	FUSVX	NAS CM	Open End	US Equity Large Cap Blend (Growth & Income)	B	B	B		Y	10,000
Fidelity® Balanced Fund	FBALX	NAS CM	Open End	Moderate Alloc (Balanced)	B-	B-	B	Down	Y	2,500
Fidelity® Balanced Fund Class K	FBAKX	NAS CM	Open End	Moderate Alloc (Balanced)	B-	B-	B	Down	Y	0
Fidelity® Blue Chip Growth Fund	FBGRX	NAS CM	Open End	US Equity Large Cap Growth (Growth)	A-	A	B+	Up	Y	2,500
Fidelity® Blue Chip Growth Fund Class K	FBGKX	NAS CM	Open End	US Equity Large Cap Growth (Growth)	A-	A	B+	Up	Y	0
Fidelity® Blue Chip Growth K6 Fund	FBCGX	NAS CM	Open End	US Equity Large Cap Growth (World Stock)	U	U	U		Y	0
Fidelity® Blue Chip Value Fund	FBCVX	NAS CM	Open End	US Equity Large Cap Value (Growth)	B	B-	B	Up	Y	2,500
Fidelity® Canada Fund	FICDX	NAS CM	Open End	Other Equity (Foreign Stock)	C+	C+	C	Up	Y	2,500
Fidelity® Capital Appreciation Fund	FDCAX	NAS CM	Open End	US Equity Large Cap Growth (Aggr Growth)	B-	B	B-	Down	Y	2,500
Fidelity® Capital Appreciation Fund Class K	FCAKX	NAS CM	Open End	US Equity Large Cap Growth (Aggr Growth)	B-	B	B-	Down	Y	0
Fidelity® China Region Fund	FHKCX	NAS CM	Open End	Greater China Equity (Pacific Stock)	B	A	C	Up	Y	2,500
Fidelity® Commodity Strategy Fund	FYHTX	NAS CM	Open End	Commodities Broad Basket (Growth & Income)	U	U	U		Y	0
Fidelity® Commodity Strategy Fund Class F	FIHTX	NAS CM	Open End	Commodities Broad Basket (Growth & Income)	U	U	U		Y	0
★ Fidelity® Contrafund® Fund	FCNTX	NAS CM	Open End	US Equity Large Cap Growth (Growth)	A-	A-	A-	Up	Y	2,500
★ Fidelity® Contrafund® Fund Class K	FCNKX	NAS CM	Open End	US Equity Large Cap Growth (Growth)	A-	A-	A-	Up	Y	0
Fidelity® Contrafund® K6	FLCNX	NAS CM	Open End	US Equity Large Cap Growth (World Stock)	U	U	U		Y	0
Fidelity® Convertible Securities Fund	FCVSX	NAS CM	Open End	Convertibles (Convertible Bond)	C+	C	C+	Up	Y	2,500
Fidelity® Disciplined Equity Fund	FDEQX	NAS CM	Open End	US Equity Large Cap Blend (Growth)	B-	B-	B-	Down	Y	2,500
Fidelity® Disciplined Equity Fund Class K	FDEKX	NAS CM	Open End	US Equity Large Cap Blend (Growth)	B-	B-	B-	Down	Y	0
Fidelity® Diversified International Fund	FDIVX	NAS CM	Open End	Global Equity Large Cap (Foreign Stock)	B-	B-	B	Up	Y	2,500
Fidelity® Diversified International Fund Class K	FDIKX	NAS CM	Open End	Global Equity Large Cap (Foreign Stock)	B-	B-	B	Up	Y	0
Fidelity® Diversified International K6 Fund	FKIDX	NAS CM	Open End	Global Equity Large Cap (Foreign Stock)	U	U	U		Y	0
Fidelity® Dividend Growth Fund	FDGFX	NAS CM	Open End	US Equity Large Cap Blend (Equity-Income)	B-	B-	B-	Down	Y	2,500
Fidelity® Dividend Growth Fund Class K	FDGKX	NAS CM	Open End	US Equity Large Cap Blend (Equity-Income)	B-	B-	B-	Down	Y	0
Fidelity® Emerging Asia Fund	FSEAX	NAS CM	Open End	Asia ex-Japan Equity (Pacific Stock)	B+	A	C+	Up	Y	2,500
Fidelity® Emerging Europe, Middle East, Africa (EMEA) Fund	FEMEX	NAS CM	Open End	Emerging Markets Equity (Foreign Stock)	C+	B-	C	Up	Y	2,500
Fidelity® Emerging Markets Discovery Fund	FEDDX	NAS CM	Open End	Emerging Markets Equity (Div Emerging Mkts)	B	B	C+	Up	Y	2,500
Fidelity® Emerging Markets Fund	FEMKX	NAS CM	Open End	Emerging Markets Equity (Div Emerging Mkts)	B	B+	C	Up	Y	2,500
Fidelity® Emerging Markets Fund Class K	FKEMX	NAS CM	Open End	Emerging Markets Equity (Div Emerging Mkts)	B	B+	C	Up	Y	0

★ Expanded analysis of this fund is included in Section II.

Min Additional Investment	3-Month Total Return	6-Month Total Return	1-Year Total Return	3-Year Total Return	5-Year Total Return	Dividend Yield (TTM)	Expense Ratio	3-Yr Std Deviation	3-Year Beta	NAV	Total Assets (MIL)	%Cash	%Stocks	%Bonds	%Other	Turnover Ratio	Last Bull Market Total Return	Last Bear Market Total Return	Front End Fee (%)	Back End Fee (%)	Inception Date
	TOTAL RETURNS					PERFORMANCE				ASSETS		ASSET ALLOCATION & TURNOVER					BULL & BEAR		FEES		
	5.17	9.98	20.52	28.86	68.41	1.9	0.15	8.99	0.86	15.11	560.5	2	88	10	1	33	17.86				Jun-11
	5.24	9.95	20.62	29.05		1.8	0.1	9.02	0.87	12.31	119.0	2	88	10	1	41					Jun-15
	5.22	10.02	20.57	28.92		1.77	0.15	9.04	0.87		119.0	2	88	10	1	41					Aug-14
	1.65	3.28	6.72	10.36	18.54	1.59	0.1	2.59	0.34	11.94	282.8	31	23	45	1	52	5.06	-2.57			Jun-15
	1.54	3.15	6.65	10.18	18.36	1.53	0.15	2.53	0.33	11.95	282.8	31	23	45	1	52	5.06	-2.57			Oct-09
	1.80	3.99	8.91	15.24	40.11	1.37	0.49	4.73	-0.02	58.98	8.4	25	27	47	0	136	12.69	-10.51			Aug-07
	2.20	4.75	10.62	17.60	45.30	1.34	0.53	5.41	-0.1	56.85	10.9	21	35	44	0	117	13.56	-11.45			Aug-07
	2.63	5.54	12.05	19.39	49.03	1.31	0.58	5.84	-0.14	53.83	4.8	17	42	40	0	106	14.16	-12.22			Aug-07
	2.99	6.24	13.29	20.82	52.32	1.25	0.62	6.17	0.58	52.2	4.0	14	50	36	0	115	14.92	-13.13			Dec-07
	3.21	6.64	14.23	21.96	55.89	1.24	0.66	6.56	0.62	53.86	20.8	11	54	34	0	108	15.83	-14.05			Dec-07
	1.61	3.63	7.07	12.07	31.95	1.36	0.47	3.46	0.12	57.85	10.9	27	24	49	0	111	11.36	-9.07			Aug-07
	0.00	2.42	8.28	29.82	-40.88	0	1.16	37.18	-0.27	20.25	1,337	0	93	0	6	28	-15.15	-13.71	5.75		Dec-06
	-0.21	2.04	7.54	27.13	-42.97	0	1.85	37.15	-0.26	18.99	1,337	0	93	0	6	28	-15.51	-13.97		1.00	Dec-06
	0.04	2.56	8.58	31.10	-39.91	0	0.84	37.2	-0.27	20.76	1,337	0	93	0	6	28	-14.99	-13.58			Dec-06
	-0.05	2.26	7.94	28.76	-41.70	0	1.46	37.17	-0.26	19.87	1,337	0	93	0	6	28	-15.3	-13.82	3.50		Dec-06
	1.82	4.01	9.43	16.14	42.52	1.38	0.49	5.11	-0.06	58.28	19.4	25	27	47	0	102	13.15	-11.01			Aug-07
	2.27	4.85	11.02	18.19	46.91	1.33	0.53	5.63	-0.12	53.42	6.5	21	36	43	0	128	13.84	-11.8			Aug-07
	2.72	5.74	12.51	19.93	50.45	1.3	0.58	5.99	-0.17	58.88	9.5	17	45	38	0	115	14.46	-12.64			Aug-07
	3.18	6.59	13.93	21.55	54.20	1.24	0.62	6.36	0.6	59.26	14.0	14	53	32	0	118	15.46	-13.69			Dec-07
	1.63	3.63	7.90	13.67	36.39	1.36	0.47	4.18	0.04	57.91	11.8	27	24	49	0	128	12.18	-9.89			Aug-07
	6.63	11.41	21.78	36.75	111.39	1.79	0.03	10.09	1	93.45	136,827	0	100	0	0	5	25.05	-16.26			May-11
	6.64	11.41	21.81	36.85	111.60	1.81	0.02	10.09	1	93.45	136,827	0	100	0	0	5	25.1	-16.26			May-11
	6.62	11.38	21.72	36.52	110.78	1.74	0.09	10.09	1	93.44	136,827	0	100	0	0	5	25.04	-16.29			Feb-88
	6.63	11.40	21.79	36.73	111.29	1.78	0.04	10.09	1	93.45	136,827	0	100	0	0	5	25.06	-16.29			Oct-05
	3.60	7.27	16.50	24.47	68.39	1.47	0.55	7.22	0.69	23.73	32,486	3	66	28	2	91	15.77	-10.4			Nov-86
	3.64	7.34	16.60	24.81	69.20	1.55	0.46	7.24	0.7	23.73	32,486	3	66	28	2	91	15.82	-10.32			May-08
	7.13	13.93	36.06	45.94	140.23	0.12	0.7	12.06	1.05	87.76	23,260	0	98	0	0	43	26.11	-17.2			Dec-87
	7.16	14.00	36.20	46.45	141.69	0.21	0.59	12.06	1.05	87.86	23,260	0	98	0	0	43	26.2	-17.11			May-08
	7.38	14.60					0.45			11.4	630.8	1	99	0	0						May-17
	5.68	8.10	14.87	24.23	95.69	0.98	0.79	10.63	0.95	19.6	393.4	5	95	0	0	32	20.64	-23.89			Jun-03
	2.72	10.93	14.42	9.65	26.58	1.12	1.17	12.94	0.89	54.66	1,208	2	98	0	0	44	12.86	-23.78			Nov-87
	5.86	13.09	23.94	29.09	99.75	0.98	0.61	11.86	1.06	35.2	7,390	2	98	0	0	129	27.89	-16.97			Nov-86
	5.87	13.14	24.06	29.53	100.86	1.07	0.5	11.84	1.06	35.26	7,390	2	98	0	0	129	28.02	-16.91			May-08
	9.98	20.18	51.92	38.75	78.25	0.77	1.02	22.02	1.24	35.98	1,442	0	99	0	0	70	17.74	-27.07			Nov-95
	4.37	6.84					0.6			10.56	797.1	50	0	0	50	0					May-17
	4.30	6.74					0.4			10.56	797.1	50	0	0	50	0					May-17
	6.74	13.25	32.26	44.32	117.69	0.22	0.68	10.12	0.9	122.47	124,619	2	96	0	0	41	24.33	-14.42			May-67
	6.77	13.31	32.38	44.75	118.81	0.3	0.58	10.12	0.9	122.39	124,619	2	96	0	0	41	24.41	-14.38			May-08
	7.02	13.65					0.45			11.36	1,313	4	96	0	0						May-17
	2.40	4.41	9.65	4.99	44.59	2.75	0.45	9.21	1.1	27.96	1,528	7	8	3	0	112	16.06	-19.75			Jan-87
	6.55	11.59	21.53	28.01	101.40	1.22	0.68	10.04	0.97	38.79	1,402	1	99	0	0	179	24.88	-21.87			Dec-88
	6.55	11.62	21.65	28.40	102.41	1.3	0.57	10.04	0.97	38.72	1,402	1	99	0	0	179	25.04	-21.86			May-08
	3.67	8.92	26.65	25.37	53.71	0.92	1.05	11.43	0.89	40.02	19,405	4	96	0	0	2	16.78	-24.53			Dec-91
	3.70	8.98	26.79	25.86	54.69	1.03	0.92	11.43	0.89	39.93	19,405	4	96	0	0	2	16.84	-24.48			May-08
	3.93	9.26					0.6			10.84	679.7	4	96	0	0						May-17
	7.54	11.86	20.13	27.88	93.61	1.42	0.52	9.83	0.96	32.83	7,560	4	96	0	0	43	27.42	-24.6			Apr-93
	7.53	11.89	20.24	28.28	94.72	1.52	0.41	9.84	0.96	32.78	7,560	4	96	0	0	43	27.51	-24.51			May-08
	10.30	16.76	46.36	42.05	59.73	0.77	1.16	15.27	1	45.04	1,266	2	98	0	0	77	18.63	-25.38			Apr-93
	13.21	20.60	25.19	35.36	23.41	1.04	1.46	17.05	0.88	10.35	102.3	0	97	0	0	47	19.87	-26.67			May-08
	6.49	13.57	37.63	38.56	33.39	0.6	1.45	13.4	0.89	15.36	427.1	4	95	0	0	60					Nov-11
	8.40	18.29	47.67	36.98	46.06	0.47	1.01	13.7	0.8	32.75	5,082	2	98	0	0	79	16.52	-28.26			Nov-90
	8.42	18.38	47.89	37.67	47.42	0.59	0.84	13.71	0.8	32.76	5,082	2	98	0	0	79	16.68	-28.19			May-08

	MARKET		FUND TYPE, CATEGORY & OBJECTIVE		RATINGS				MINIMUMS	
Fund Name	Ticker Symbol	Traded On	Fund Type	Category and (Prospectus Objective)	Overall Rating	Reward Rating	Risk Rating	Recent Up/ Downgrade	Open to New Investors	Min Initial Investment
Fidelity® Emerging Markets Index Fund Institutional Class	FPMIX	NAS CM	Open End	Emerging Markets Equity (Div Emerging Mkts)	B-	B	C	Up	Y	5,000,000
Fidelity® Emerging Mkts Index Fund Inst Premium Cls	FPADX	NAS CM	Open End	Emerging Markets Equity (Div Emerging Mkts)	B-	B	C	Up	Y	100,000,000
Fidelity® Emerging Markets Index Fund Investor Class	FPEMX	NAS CM	Open End	Emerging Markets Equity (Div Emerging Mkts)	B-	B	C	Up	Y	2,500
Fidelity® Emerging Markets Index Fund Premium Class	FPMAX	NAS CM	Open End	Emerging Markets Equity (Div Emerging Mkts)	B-	B	C	Up	Y	10,000
Fidelity® Equity Dividend Income Fund	FEQTX	NAS CM	Open End	US Equity Large Cap Value (Equity-Income)	B	B-	B		Y	2,500
Fidelity® Equity Dividend Income Fund Class K	FETKX	NAS CM	Open End	US Equity Large Cap Value (Equity-Income)	B	B-	B		Y	0
Fidelity® Equity-Income Fund	FEQIX	NAS CM	Open End	US Equity Large Cap Value (Equity-Income)	B-	B-	B	Down	Y	2,500
Fidelity® Equity-Income Fund Class K	FEIKX	NAS CM	Open End	US Equity Large Cap Value (Equity-Income)	B-	B-	B	Down	Y	0
Fidelity® Europe Fund	FIEUX	NAS CM	Open End	Europe Equity Large Cap (Europe Stock)	B	B	B	Up	Y	2,500
Fidelity® Event Driven Opportunities Fund	FARNX	NAS CM	Open End	US Equity Small Cap (Growth)	B	B	B		Y	2,500
Fidelity® Export and Multinational Fund	FEXPX	NAS CM	Open End	US Equity Large Cap Blend (Growth)	B	B-	B+		Y	2,500
Fidelity® Export and Multinational Fund Class K	FEXKX	NAS CM	Open End	US Equity Large Cap Blend (Growth)	B	B-	B+		Y	0
Fidelity® Extended Mkt Index Fund Inst Premium Cls	FSMAX	NAS CM	Open End	US Equity Mid Cap (Growth & Income)	B	B	B	Up	Y	100,000,000
Fidelity® Extended Market Index Fund Investor Class	FSEMX	NAS CM	Open End	US Equity Mid Cap (Growth & Income)	B	B	B	Up	Y	2,500
Fidelity® Extended Market Index Fund Premium Class	FSEVX	NAS CM	Open End	US Equity Mid Cap (Growth & Income)	B	B	B	Up	Y	10,000
Fidelity® Flex 500 Index Fund	FDFIX	NAS CM	Open End	US Equity Large Cap Blend (Growth & Income)	U	U	U		Y	0
Fidelity® Flex International Fund	FULTX	NAS CM	Open End	Global Equity Large Cap (Foreign Stock)	U	U	U		Y	0
Fidelity® Flex International Index Fund	FITFX	NAS CM	Open End	Global Equity Large Cap (Foreign Stock)	U	U	U		Y	0
Fidelity® Flex Intrinsic Opportunities Fund	FFNPX	NAS CM	Open End	US Equity Large Cap Blend (Growth)	U	U	U		Y	0
Fidelity® Flex Large Cap Growth Fund	FLCLX	NAS CM	Open End	US Equity Large Cap Growth (Growth)	U	U	U		Y	0
Fidelity® Flex Large Cap Value Fund	FVCLX	NAS CM	Open End	US Equity Large Cap Value (Growth)	U	U	U		Y	0
Fidelity® Flex Mid Cap Index Fund	FLAPX	NAS CM	Open End	US Equity Mid Cap (Growth & Income)	U	U	U		Y	0
Fidelity® Flex Mid Cap Value Fund	FFMVX	NAS CM	Open End	US Equity Mid Cap (Growth)	U	U	U		Y	0
Fidelity® Flex Opportunistic Insights Fund	FFPIX	NAS CM	Open End	US Equity Large Cap Blend (Growth)	U	U	U		Y	0
Fidelity® Flex Real Estate Fund	FFERX	NAS CM	Open End	Real Estate Sector Equity (Real Estate)	U	U	U		Y	0
Fidelity® Flex Small Cap Fund	FCUTX	NAS CM	Open End	US Equity Small Cap (Small Company)	U	U	U		Y	0
Fidelity® Flex Small Cap Index Fund	FLXSX	NAS CM	Open End	US Equity Small Cap (Small Company)	U	U	U		Y	0
Fidelity® Focused Stock Fund	FTQGX	NAS CM	Open End	US Equity Large Cap Growth (Growth)	B+	B+	B	Up	Y	2,500
Fidelity® Four-in-One Index Fund	FFNOX	NAS CM	Open End	Aggressive Alloc (Asset Alloc)	B-	B-	B	Down	Y	2,500
Fidelity® Fund	FFIDX	NAS CM	Open End	US Equity Large Cap Growth (Growth)	B	B	B	Up	Y	2,500
Fidelity® Fund Class K	FFDKX	NAS CM	Open End	US Equity Large Cap Growth (Growth)	B	B	B	Up	Y	0
Fidelity® Global Balanced Fund	FGBLX	NAS CM	Open End	Alloc (Multi-Asset Global)	B-	C+	B	Up	Y	2,500
Fidelity® Global Commodity Stock Fund	FFGCX	NAS CM	Open End	Natl Resources Sec Equity (Growth)	C	C+	C	Up	Y	2,500
Fidelity® Global Equity Income Fund	FGILX	NAS CM	Open End	Global Equity (Equity-Income)	B-	B-	B-	Down	Y	2,500
Fidelity® Global ex U.S. Index Fund Institutional Class	FSGSX	NAS CM	Open End	Global Equity Large Cap (Foreign Stock)	B-	B-	B-	Up	Y	5,000,000
Fidelity® Global ex U.S. Index Fund Inst Premium Cls	FSGGX	NAS CM	Open End	Global Equity Large Cap (Foreign Stock)	B-	B-	B-	Up	Y	100,000,000
Fidelity® Global ex U.S. Index Fund Investor Class	FSGUX	NAS CM	Open End	Global Equity Large Cap (Foreign Stock)	B-	B-	B-	Up	Y	2,500
Fidelity® Global ex U.S. Index Fund Premium Class	FSGDX	NAS CM	Open End	Global Equity Large Cap (Foreign Stock)	B-	B-	B-	Up	Y	10,000
Fidelity® Global Strategies Fund	FDYSX	NAS CM	Open End	Alloc (Growth & Income)	B	C+	B+	Up	Y	2,500
Fidelity® Growth & Income Portfolio	FGRIX	NAS CM	Open End	US Equity Large Cap Blend (Growth & Income)	B	B	B	Up	Y	2,500
Fidelity® Growth & Income Portfolio Class K	FGIKX	NAS CM	Open End	US Equity Large Cap Blend (Growth & Income)	B-	B	B-	Down	Y	0
Fidelity® Growth Company	FDGRX	NAS CM	Open End	US Equity Large Cap Growth (Growth)	A-	A	B	Up		2,500
Fidelity® Growth Company Fund Class K	FGCKX	NAS CM	Open End	US Equity Large Cap Growth (Growth)	A-	A	B	Up		0
Fidelity® Growth Discovery Fund	FDSVX	NAS CM	Open End	US Equity Large Cap Growth (Growth)	A-	B+	A-	Up	Y	2,500
Fidelity® Growth Discovery Fund Class K	FGDKX	NAS CM	Open End	US Equity Large Cap Growth (Growth)	A-	B+	A-	Up	Y	0
Fidelity® Growth Strategies Fund	FDEGX	NAS CM	Open End	US Equity Mid Cap (Aggr Growth)	B	B	B+	Up	Y	2,500
Fidelity® Growth Strategies Fund Class K	FAGKX	NAS CM	Open End	US Equity Mid Cap (Aggr Growth)	B	B	B+	Up	Y	0
Fidelity® Growth Strategies K6 Fund	FSKGX	NAS CM	Open End	US Equity Mid Cap (World Stock)	U	U	U		Y	0
Fidelity® Independence Fund	FDFFX	NAS CM	Open End	US Equity Large Cap Growth (Growth)	C+	B-	C+	Up	Y	2,500
Fidelity® Independence Fund Class K	FDFKX	NAS CM	Open End	US Equity Large Cap Growth (Growth)	B-	B-	C+	Up	Y	0
Fidelity® International Capital Appreciation Fund	FIVFX	NAS CM	Open End	Global Equity Large Cap (Foreign Stock)	B	B	B	Up	Y	2,500
Fidelity® International Capital Appreciation K6 Fund	FAPCX	NAS CM	Open End	Global Equity Large Cap (Foreign Stock)	U	U	U		Y	0

★Expanded analysis of this fund is included in Section II.

Min Additional Investment	TOTAL RETURNS 3-Month Total Return	6-Month Total Return	1-Year Total Return	3-Year Total Return	5-Year Total Return	PERFORMANCE Dividend Yield (TTM)	Expense Ratio	3-Yr Std Deviation	3-Year Beta	ASSETS NAV	Total Assets (MIL)	ASSET ALLOCATION & TURNOVER %Cash	%Stocks	%Bonds	%Other	Turnover Ratio	BULL & BEAR Last Bull Market Total Return	Last Bear Market Total Return	FEES Front End Fee (%)	Back End Fee (%)	Inception Date
	7.30	15.72	37.45	29.06	24.48	1.26	0.1	15.59	0.98	11.42	1,412	2	98	0	0	4	15.83				Sep-11
	7.32	15.75	37.64	29.15	24.65	1.27	0.08	15.63	0.98	11.42	1,412	2	98	0	0	4	15.83				Sep-11
	7.20	15.64	37.23	28.23	23.35	1.12	0.29	15.64	0.99	11.41	1,412	2	98	0	0	4	15.6				Sep-11
	7.27	15.71	37.45	28.78	24.16	1.24	0.13	15.65	0.99	11.41	1,412	2	98	0	0	4	15.72				Sep-11
	5.39	9.18	14.09	27.60	88.20	2.06	0.72	9.52	0.89	27.77	5,588	2	98	0	0	55	25.87	-22.33			Aug-90
	5.44	9.22	14.20	28.00	89.18	2.16	0.61	9.52	0.89	27.77	5,588	2	98	0	0	55	26.02	-22.3			May-08
	5.09	8.30	13.35	27.25	80.47	2.18	0.67	9.9	0.92	60.7	7,267	3	97	0	0	36	23.58	-22.28			May-66
	5.13	8.35	13.46	27.68	81.53	2.28	0.56	9.9	0.92	60.66	7,267	3	97	0	0	36	23.7	-22.23			May-08
	3.87	9.17	29.18	26.69	50.55	0.89	1.07	13.38	0.97	42.33	1,263	-2	97	0	3	62	17.99	-29.33			Oct-86
	4.68	6.98	18.62	42.49		0.22	1.11	14.72	1.23	13.96	447.0	11	89	0	0	117					Dec-13
	7.70	11.70	20.92	32.76	88.20	0.85	0.76	9.64	0.92	22.21	1,805	4	96	0	0	109	22.88	-18.47			Oct-94
	7.71	11.77	21.07	33.22	89.40	0.97	0.64	9.62	0.92	22.16	1,805	4	96	0	0	109	22.96	-18.39			May-08
	4.87	10.11	18.22	31.76	101.30	1.16	0.05	12.25	1	62.03	21,493	0	100	0	0	12	28.68	-23.57			Sep-11
	4.85	10.08	18.14	31.56	100.84	1.11	0.1	12.26	1	62.05	21,493	0	100	0	0	12	28.64	-23.57			Nov-97
	4.85	10.09	18.18	31.68	101.14	1.14	0.07	12.26	1	62.05	21,493	0	100	0	0	12	28.71	-23.57			Oct-05
	6.70	11.43					0			11.38	16.3	3	97	0	0						Mar-17
	5.09	11.06					0			12.21	28.1	2	98	0	0						Mar-17
	4.73	10.97					0			11.9	7.6	2	98	0	0						Mar-17
	6.75	11.95					0			11.74	17.8	6	94	0	0						Mar-17
	7.33	14.43					0			12.41	12.7	1	99	0	0						Mar-17
	4.50	8.58					0			10.78	9.5	9	91	0	0						Mar-17
	6.05	9.72					0			11.35	7.1	0	100	0	0	1					Mar-17
	4.44	7.81					0			10.89	3.2	1	99	0	0						Mar-17
	7.15	14.25					0			12.19	14.2	2	98	0	0						Mar-17
	1.50	2.38					0			10.25	0.27	1	99	0	0	9					Mar-17
	5.62	10.47					0			10.95	0.55	1	99	0	0						Mar-17
	3.32	9.25					0			11.34	5.5	0	100	0	0						Mar-17
	8.32	16.72	31.22	36.15	102.63	0.42	0.62	11.21	0.94	22.65	1,755	0	100	0	0	141	24.8	-17.3			Nov-96
	4.79	9.13	19.27	28.48	74.01	1.81	0.11	8.56		44.45	5,671	0	85	15	0	10	18.88	-16.03			Jun-99
	6.81	13.42	23.81	32.95	98.71	0.87	0.52	10.17	0.96	45.23	4,666	2	98	0	0	82	22.11	-18.42			Apr-30
	6.86	13.48	23.94	33.37	99.86	0.96	0.41	10.16	0.96	45.21	4,666	2	98	0	0	82	22.21	-18.36			May-08
	4.49	8.82	19.90	19.38	39.06	0.06	1.02	7.29	0.61	25.06	485.0	2	61	36	2	155	12.21	-12.92			Feb-93
	7.73	19.58	18.42	11.13	-1.04	0.83	1.13	18.44	1.26	13.18	541.6	1	99	0	0	81	14.28	-29.62			Mar-09
	5.95	10.67	22.05	28.47	73.87	1.14	1.18	8.78	0.8	14.49	82.4	3	96	0	0	40					May-12
	4.74	11.04	27.37	25.26	38.60	1.63	0.08	11.67	0.95	13.54	3,166	2	98	0	0	9	14.5				Sep-11
	4.68	10.97	27.39	25.35	38.79	1.65	0.06	11.66	0.94	13.54	3,166	2	98	0	0	9	14.5				Sep-11
	4.73	11.03	27.25	24.91	37.96	1.56	0.17	11.73	0.95	13.54	3,166	2	98	0	0	9	14.39				Sep-11
	4.72	11.02	27.34	25.19	38.38	1.61	0.1	11.68	0.95	13.54	3,166	2	98	0	0	9	14.5				Sep-11
	4.72	8.57	19.37	25.29	42.27	1.23	1.1	6.54	0.6	9.35	174.9	8	64	28	1	38	13.36	-16.05			Oct-07
	6.11	10.34	16.88	31.39	98.09	1.54	0.63	11.79	1.11	37.87	7,343	0	99	0	0	37	26.97	-16.93			Dec-85
	6.14	10.45	17.03	31.86	99.38	1.65	0.52	11.77	1.11	37.84	7,343	0	99	0	0	37	27.08	-16.85			May-08
	6.89	14.98	36.76	55.41	151.40	0.05	0.77	13.23	1.16	178.65	41,677	0	98	0	0	25	29.31	-16.92			Jan-83
	6.92	15.04	36.90	55.88	152.77	0.12	0.66	13.23	1.16	178.62	41,677	0	98	0	0	25	29.42	-16.87			May-08
	5.17	11.96	34.69	44.29	125.66	0.15	0.66	10.98	0.95	32.56	1,725	5	95	0	0	65	27.37	-17.56			Mar-98
	5.19	12.01	34.83	44.81	127.12	0.24	0.54	10.97	0.94	32.57	1,725	5	95	0	0	65	27.5	-17.53			May-08
	6.71	10.03	21.49	27.93	105.10	0.45	0.89	9.72	0.85	41.12	2,728	1	99	0	0	63	21.89	-23.67			Dec-90
	6.73	10.09	21.68	28.50	106.91	0.56	0.73	9.74	0.85	41.4	2,728	1	99	0	0	63	22.05	-23.56			May-08
	6.79	9.99					0.45			11.01	80.5	2	98	0	0						May-17
	6.44	13.01	26.41	24.73	100.56	0.42	0.54	13.05	1.14	37.28	3,919	2	98	0	0	76	27.89	-25.49			Mar-83
	6.50	13.09	26.53	25.08	101.55	0.49	0.45	13.07	1.14	37.3	3,919	2	98	0	0	76	27.98	-25.42			May-08
	5.84	12.75	36.24	35.55	72.16	0.51	1.14	10.96	0.79	21.06	2,158	2	98	0	0	167	26.68	-25.87			Nov-94
	5.60	13.17					0.65			11.33	191.9	3	97	0	0						May-17

	MARKET		FUND TYPE, CATEGORY & OBJECTIVE		RATINGS				MINIMUMS	
Fund Name	Ticker Symbol	Traded On	Fund Type	Category and (Prospectus Objective)	Overall Rating	Reward Rating	Risk Rating	Recent Up/ Downgrade	Open to New Investors	Min Initial Investment
Fidelity® International Discovery Fund	FIGRX	NAS CM	Open End	Global Equity Large Cap (Foreign Stock)	B	B	B	Up	Y	2,500
Fidelity® International Discovery Fund Class K	FIDKX	NAS CM	Open End	Global Equity Large Cap (Foreign Stock)	B	B	B	Up	Y	0
Fidelity® International Enhanced Index Fund	FIENX	NAS CM	Open End	Global Equity Large Cap (Growth)	B-	B	C+	Up	Y	2,500
Fidelity® International Growth Fund	FIGFX	NAS CM	Open End	Global Equity Large Cap (Foreign Stock)	B	B-	B	Up	Y	2,500
Fidelity® International Index Fund Institutional Class	FSPNX	NAS CM	Open End	Global Equity Large Cap (Foreign Stock)	B-	B-	B	Up	Y	5,000,000
Fidelity® Intl Index Fund Inst Premium Cls	FSPSX	NAS CM	Open End	Global Equity Large Cap (Foreign Stock)	B-	B-	B	Up	Y	100,000,000
Fidelity® International Index Fund Investor Class	FSIIX	NAS CM	Open End	Global Equity Large Cap (Foreign Stock)	B-	C+	B	Up	Y	2,500
Fidelity® International Index Fund Premium Class	FSIVX	NAS CM	Open End	Global Equity Large Cap (Foreign Stock)	B-	B-	B	Up	Y	10,000
Fidelity® International Real Estate Fund	FIREX	NAS CM	Open End	Real Estate Sector Equity (Real Estate)	B	B-	B	Up	Y	2,500
Fidelity® International Small Cap Fund	FISMX	NAS CM	Open End	Global Equity Mid/Small Cap (Foreign Stock)	B+	B+	A-	Up	Y	2,500
Fidelity® International Small Cap Opportunities Fund	FSCOX	NAS CM	Open End	Global Equity Mid/Small Cap (Small Company)	A-	B+	A	Up	Y	2,500
Fidelity® International Value Fund	FIVLX	NAS CM	Open End	Global Equity Large Cap (Foreign Stock)	B-	C+	B	Up	Y	2,500
Fidelity® Intl Sustainability Idx Fd Institutional Class	FNIDX	NAS CM	Open End	Global Equity Large Cap (Growth & Income)	U	U	U		Y	5,000,000
Fidelity® Intl Sustainability Idx Fd Investor Class	FNIYX	NAS CM	Open End	Global Equity Large Cap (Growth & Income)	U	U	U		Y	2,500
Fidelity® Intl Sustainability Idx Fd Premium Class	FNIRX	NAS CM	Open End	Global Equity Large Cap (Growth & Income)	U	U	U		Y	10,000
Fidelity® Japan Fund	FJPNX	NAS CM	Open End	Japan Equity (Pacific Stock)	B+	A-	B	Up	Y	2,500
Fidelity® Japan Smaller Companies Fund	FJSCX	NAS CM	Open End	Japan Equity (Pacific Stock)	A	A	A	Up	Y	2,500
Fidelity® Large Cap Core Enhanced Index Fund	FLCEX	NAS CM	Open End	US Equity Large Cap Blend (Growth)	B	B	B-		Y	2,500
Fidelity® Large Cap Growth Enhanced Index Fund	FLGEX	NAS CM	Open End	US Equity Large Cap Growth (Growth)	B+	B+	B+	Up	Y	2,500
Fidelity® Large Cap Growth Index Fund Institutional Class	FSWIX	NAS CM	Open End	US Equity Large Cap Growth (Growth)	D+	C	B+	Up	Y	5,000,000
Fidelity® Large Cap Growth Index Fund Inst Premium Cls	FSPGX	NAS CM	Open End	US Equity Large Cap Growth (Growth)	D+	C	B+	Up	Y	100,000,000
Fidelity® Large Cap Growth Index Fund Investor Class	FSUIX	NAS CM	Open End	US Equity Large Cap Growth (Growth)	D+	C	B+	Up	Y	2,500
Fidelity® Large Cap Growth Index Fund Premium Class	FSUPX	NAS CM	Open End	US Equity Large Cap Growth (Growth)	D+	C	B+	Up	Y	10,000
Fidelity® Large Cap Stock Fund	FLCSX	NAS CM	Open End	US Equity Large Cap Blend (Growth)	B	B	B	Up	Y	2,500
Fidelity® Large Cap Stock K6 Fund	FCLKX	NAS CM	Open End	US Equity Large Cap Blend (World Stock)	U	U	U		Y	0
Fidelity® Large Cap Value Enhanced Index Fund	FLVEX	NAS CM	Open End	US Equity Large Cap Value (Growth)	B	B-	B		Y	2,500
Fidelity® Large Cap Value Index Fund Institutional Class	FLCMX	NAS CM	Open End	US Equity Large Cap Value (Growth)	D+	C-	B+	Up	Y	5,000,000
Fidelity® Large Cap Value Index Fund Inst Premium Cls	FLCOX	NAS CM	Open End	US Equity Large Cap Value (Growth)	D+	C-	B+	Up	Y	100,000,000
Fidelity® Large Cap Value Index Fund Investor Class	FLCDX	NAS CM	Open End	US Equity Large Cap Value (Growth)	D+	C-	B+	Up	Y	2,500
Fidelity® Large Cap Value Index Fund Premium Class	FLCHX	NAS CM	Open End	US Equity Large Cap Value (Growth)	D+	C-	B+	Up	Y	10,000
Fidelity® Latin America Fund	FLATX	NAS CM	Open End	Latin America Equity (Foreign Stock)	C	C	C		Y	2,500
Fidelity® Leveraged Company Stock Fund	FLVCX	NAS CM	Open End	US Equity Mid Cap (Growth)	B-	C+	B-	Up	Y	10,000
Fidelity® Leveraged Company Stock Fund Class K	FLCKX	NAS CM	Open End	US Equity Mid Cap (Growth)	B-	C+	B	Up	Y	0
Fidelity® Iex Mid Cap Growth Fund	FFMGX	NAS CM	Open End	US Equity Mid Cap (Growth)	U	U	U		Y	0
Fidelity® Low-Priced Stock Fund	FLPSX	NAS CM	Open End	US Equity Mid Cap (Growth)	B-	B-	B	Down	Y	2,500
Fidelity® Low-Priced Stock Fund Class K	FLPKX	NAS CM	Open End	US Equity Mid Cap (Growth)	B-	B-	B	Down	Y	0
Fidelity® Low-Priced Stock K6 Fund	FLKSX	NAS CM	Open End	US Equity Mid Cap (World Stock)	U	U	U		Y	0
Fidelity® Magellan® Fund Class K	FMGKX	NAS CM	Open End	US Equity Large Cap Growth (Growth)	B	B+	B		Y	0
Fidelity® Mega Cap Stock Fund	FGRTX	NAS CM	Open End	US Equity Large Cap Blend (Growth)	B-	B-	B-	Down	Y	2,500
Fidelity® Mid Cap Enhanced Index Fund	FMEIX	NAS CM	Open End	US Equity Mid Cap (Growth)	B	B	B	Up	Y	2,500
Fidelity® Mid Cap Index Fund Institutional Class	FSTPX	NAS CM	Open End	US Equity Mid Cap (Growth)	B-	B	B-	Down	Y	5,000,000
Fidelity® Mid Cap Index Fund Institutional Premium Class	FSMDX	NAS CM	Open End	US Equity Mid Cap (Growth)	B-	B	B-	Down	Y	100,000,000
Fidelity® Mid Cap Index Fund Investor Class	FSCLX	NAS CM	Open End	US Equity Mid Cap (Growth)	B-	B	B-	Down	Y	2,500
Fidelity® Mid Cap Index Fund Premium Class	FSCKX	NAS CM	Open End	US Equity Mid Cap (Growth)	B-	B	B-	Down	Y	10,000
Fidelity® Mid Cap Value Fund	FSMVX	NAS CM	Open End	US Equity Mid Cap (Growth)	B-	B-	B	Down	Y	2,500
Fidelity® Mid Cap Value K6 Fund	FCMVX	NAS CM	Open End	US Equity Mid Cap (World Stock)	U	U	U		Y	0
Fidelity® Mid-Cap Stock Fund	FMCSX	NAS CM	Open End	US Equity Mid Cap (Growth)	B-	B	B-	Down	Y	2,500
Fidelity® Mid-Cap Stock Fund Class K	FKMCX	NAS CM	Open End	US Equity Mid Cap (Growth)	B-	B	B-	Down	Y	0
Fidelity® NASDAQ Composite Index® Fund	FNCMX	NAS CM	Open End	US Equity Large Cap Growth (Growth)	B+	A-	B	Down	Y	2,500
Fidelity® New Millennium Fund®	FMILX	NAS CM	Open End	US Equity Large Cap Growth (Aggr Growth)	B	B	B-	Up	Y	2,500
Fidelity® Nordic Fund	FNORX	NAS CM	Open End	Other Equity (Europe Stock)	B	B-	B	Up	Y	2,500
Fidelity® OTC Portfolio	FOCPX	NAS CM	Open End	US Equity Large Cap Growth (Growth)	A-	A	B	Up	Y	2,500

★Expanded analysis of this fund is included in Section II.

Min Additional Investment	TOTAL RETURNS 3-Month Total Return	6-Month Total Return	1-Year Total Return	3-Year Total Return	5-Year Total Return	PERFORMANCE Dividend Yield (TTM)	Expense Ratio	3-Yr Std Deviation	3-Year Beta	ASSETS NAV	Total Assets (MIL)	ASSET ALLOCATION & TURNOVER %Cash	%Stocks	%Bonds	%Other	Turnover Ratio	BULL & BEAR Last Bull Market Total Return	Last Bear Market Total Return	FEES Front End Fee (%)	Back End Fee (%)	Inception Date
	3.99	11.60	31.70	29.72	54.92	1.29	1	11.44	0.88	45.66	10,832	4	96	0	0	42	15.57	-24.47			Dec-86
	4.03	11.65	31.85	30.18	55.96	1.41	0.86	11.44	0.88	45.53	10,832	4	96	0	0	42	15.72	-24.43			May-08
	3.60	10.61	27.58	31.29	57.58	1.88	0.59	11.46	0.92	10.14	925.2	4	96	0	0	70	12.73	-22.44			Dec-07
	4.43	8.54	29.56	29.61	55.63	0.97	0.99	10.82	0.87	13.69	2,366	2	98	0	0	22	21.42	-21.89			Nov-07
	3.93	9.36	25.33	25.52	46.77	2.33	0.05	11.5	0.93	43.18	20,829	1	98	0	0	2	13.1	-23.02			Sep-11
	3.94	9.39	25.37	25.56	46.84	2.34	0.05	11.5	0.93	43.18	20,829	1	98	0	0	2	13.11	-23.02			Sep-11
	3.93	9.32	25.22	25.05	45.83	2.22	0.16	11.5	0.93	43.18	20,829	1	98	0	0	2	13.08	-23.02			Nov-97
	3.95	9.37	25.35	25.41	46.48	2.31	0.06	11.49	0.93	43.18	20,829	1	98	0	0	2	13.14	-23.02			Oct-05
	6.24	10.30	26.69	26.20	50.03	1.62	1.12	10.22	0.72	11.65	490.3	6	93	0	1	55	19.61	-25.14			Sep-04
	5.54	12.19	32.90	52.85	97.10	1.12	1.34	10.07	0.82	29.9	1,803	5	93	0	1	29	14.26	-21.6			Sep-02
	6.89	12.68	35.68	47.58	84.12	0.87	1.17	10.18	0.82	19.34	1,149	5	95	0	0	11	19.79	-20.38			Aug-05
	2.13	6.87	19.64	18.60	36.00	2.17	1.03	10.78	0.79	9.06	554.5	0	99	0	0	50	11.04	-27.71			May-06
	4.69	10.65					0.2				20.4	4	96	0	0						May-17
	4.62	10.57					0.3				20.4	4	96	0	0						May-17
	4.65	10.61					0.25				20.4	4	96	0	0						May-17
	8.96	12.58	30.15	44.34	65.50	0.71	0.78	11.91	0.88	15.45	405.1	1	99	0	0	15	5.77	-10.28			Sep-92
	9.23	17.50	35.70	67.60	138.95	0.85	0.96	9.36	0.68	18.96	770.3	3	97	0	0	30	5.37	-6.41			Nov-95
	7.65	13.27	21.65	32.81	108.03	1.44	0.39	10.13	0.99	14.66	590.2	1	99	0	0	88	24.34	-15.12			Apr-07
	8.75	15.48	27.13	40.67	122.39	1.01	0.39	10.57	0.97	18.93	1,010	0	100	0	0	110	26.38	-15.12			Apr-07
	7.88	14.17	30.11			0.48	0.04			13.39	783.3	1	99	0	0	17					Jun-16
	7.88	14.17	30.12			0.49	0.04			13.39	783.3	1	99	0	0	17					Jun-16
	7.80	14.08	29.93			0.35	0.17			13.39	783.3	1	99	0	0	17					Jun-16
	7.87	14.16	30.09			0.47	0.05			13.39	783.3	1	99	0	0	17					Jun-16
	5.94	10.77	18.14	32.38	108.30	1	0.62	12.54	1.16	33.46	5,287	2	98	0	0	32	28.09	-19.28			Jun-95
	6.02	10.85					0.45			11.13	61.2	1	99	0	0						May-17
	6.61	11.36	15.88	28.71	102.28	1.72	0.39	10.59	1.01	13.2	3,362	0	99	0	0	93	23.45	-17.48			Apr-07
	5.35	8.58	13.77			0.9	0.04			12.17	844.7	1	99	0	0	23					Jun-16
	5.35	8.58	13.78			0.91	0.04			12.17	844.7	1	99	0	0	23					Jun-16
	5.36	8.60	13.62			0.76	0.17			12.17	844.7	1	99	0	0	23					Jun-16
	5.34	8.57	13.76			0.89	0.05			12.17	844.7	1	99	0	0	23					Jun-16
	-4.47	14.22	30.47	9.44	-23.43	1.94	1.14	22.84	0.88	24.48	609.7	1	99	0	0	108	18.79	-24.75			Apr-93
	5.77	11.69	21.02	20.83	77.29	0.4	0.8	13.48	1.18	33.46	3,092	2	98	0	0	100	33.13	-30.1			Dec-00
	5.81	11.73	21.14	21.26	78.35	0.49	0.68	13.49	1.18	33.53	3,092	2	98	0	0	100	33.31	-30.07			May-08
	6.67	10.08					0			11.26	0.71	1	99	0	0						Mar-17
	6.63	11.99	20.66	30.03	91.20	1.26	0.68	8.89	0.55	54.52	39,445	11	89	0	0	8	23.38	-17.6			Dec-89
	6.67	12.04	20.79	30.41	92.16	1.34	0.58	8.88	0.55	54.47	39,445	11	89	0	0	8	23.49	-17.56			May-08
	6.53	12.24					0.5			11.22	898.3	16	84	0	0						May-17
	6.91	14.08	26.62	37.80	118.95	0.6	0.59	10.94	1.05	104.41	16,929	1	98	0	0	51	24.34	-24.22			May-08
	5.78	10.29	17.77	30.72	99.24	1.43	0.68	11.7	1.12	17.43	2,556	0	99	0	0	25	28.24	-16.02			Dec-98
	7.59	11.35	18.40	29.78	110.76	1.22	0.59	10.51	0.98	15.65	1,270	0	99	0	0	94	25.54	-21.49			Dec-07
	6.07	9.72	18.45	30.33	103.85	1.14	0.04	10.5	1	20.98	5,324	1	99	0	0	14	26.43				Sep-11
	6.07	9.72	18.46	30.40	104.04	1.16	0.04	10.49	1	20.98	5,324	1	99	0	0	14	26.44				Sep-11
	6.00	9.65	18.26	29.74	102.22	1.03	0.17	10.53	1	20.95	5,324	1	99	0	0	14	26.2				Sep-11
	6.07	9.77	18.44	30.28	103.68	1.13	0.05	10.52	1	20.98	5,324	1	99	0	0	14	26.32				Sep-11
	8.06	10.87	17.00	24.35	107.30	1.16	0.73	10.62	0.97	26.61	3,256	1	99	0	0	83	26.86	-23.1			Nov-01
	8.12	11.10					0.45			11.18	43.9	1	99	0	0						May-17
	5.02	9.85	18.67	31.21	100.13	0.51	0.58	9.92	0.85	38.22	8,227	7	93	0	0	27	23.35	-18.77			Mar-94
	5.06	9.93	18.79	31.64	101.32	0.61	0.46	9.92	0.85	38.23	8,227	7	93	0	0	27	23.46	-18.71			May-08
	6.39	12.79	29.24	48.86	145.36	0.71	0.3	12.55	1	90.63	4,896	2	98	0	0	4	26.87	-15.56			Sep-03
	6.13	12.03	20.05	32.63	99.19	0.96	0.54	10.78	1.01	39.79	3,289	3	97	0	0	44	22.93	-15.37			Dec-92
	2.99	4.15	23.65	33.75	92.03	1.2	0.99	12.04		53.29	344.8	0	99	0	1	63	20.95	-31.79			Nov-95
	6.01	12.19	38.59	57.31	176.34	0	0.81	15.03	1.13	109.85	17,435	0	97	0	0	71	19.51	-17.41			Dec-84

	MARKET		FUND TYPE, CATEGORY & OBJECTIVE		RATINGS					MINIMUMS
Fund Name	Ticker Symbol	Traded On	Fund Type	Category and (Prospectus Objective)	Overall Rating	Reward Rating	Risk Rating	Recent Up/ Downgrade	Open to New Investors	Min Initial Investment
Fidelity® OTC Portfolio Class K	FOCKX	NAS CM	Open End	US Equity Large Cap Growth (Growth)	A-	A	B	Up	Y	0
Fidelity® Overseas Fund	FOSFX	NAS CM	Open End	Global Equity Large Cap (Foreign Stock)	B	B	A-	Up	Y	2,500
Fidelity® Overseas Fund Class K	FOSKX	NAS CM	Open End	Global Equity Large Cap (Foreign Stock)	B	B	A-	Up	Y	0
Fidelity® Pacific Basin Fund	FPBFX	NAS CM	Open End	Asia Equity (Pacific Stock)	A-	A	B	Up	Y	2,500
Fidelity® Puritan® Fund	FPURX	NAS CM	Open End	Moderate Alloc (Growth & Income)	B-	B-	B	Down	Y	2,500
Fidelity® Puritan® Fund Class K	FPUKX	NAS CM	Open End	Moderate Alloc (Growth & Income)	B-	B-	B	Down	Y	0
Fidelity® Real Estate Income Fund	FRIFX	NAS CM	Open End	Real Estate Sector Equity (Real Estate)	B	C+	A	Up	Y	2,500
Fidelity® Real Estate Index Fund Institutional Class	FSRNX	NAS CM	Open End	Real Estate Sector Equity (Real Estate)	B-	C+	B+		Y	5,000,000
Fidelity® Real Estate Index Fund Investor Class	FRXIX	NAS CM	Open End	Real Estate Sector Equity (Real Estate)	B-	C+	B+		Y	2,500
Fidelity® Real Estate Index Fund Premium Class	FSRVX	NAS CM	Open End	Real Estate Sector Equity (Real Estate)	B-	C+	B+		Y	10,000
Fidelity® Real Estate Investment Portfolio	FRESX	NAS CM	Open End	Real Estate Sector Equity (Real Estate)	B	C+	B+		Y	2,500
Fidelity® SAI Emerging Markets Index Fund	FERGX	NAS CM	Open End	Emerging Markets Equity (Div Emerging Mkts)	C-	C	B+	Up	Y	0
Fidelity® SAI International Index Fund	FIONX	NAS CM	Open End	Global Equity Large Cap (Foreign Stock)	C-	C	B+	Up	Y	0
Fidelity® SAI International Minimum Volatility Index Fund	FSKLX	NAS CM	Open End	Global Equity Large Cap (Foreign Stock)	B-	C+	B	Up	Y	0
Fidelity® SAI Real Estate Index Fund	FESIX	NAS CM	Open End	Real Estate Sector Equity (Real Estate)	C-	D+	C+	Up	Y	0
Fidelity® SAI Small-Mid Cap 500 Index Fund	FZFLX	NAS CM	Open End	US Equity Mid Cap (Growth)	C	C+	B	Up	Y	0
Fidelity® SAI U.S. Large Cap Index Fund	FLCPX	NAS CM	Open End	US Equity Large Cap Blend (Growth)	C-	C	B+	Up	Y	0
Fidelity® SAI U.S. Minimum Volatility Index Fund	FSUVX	NAS CM	Open End	US Equity Large Cap Blend (Growth)	B-	C+	B+	Up	Y	0
Fidelity® SAI U.S. Momentum Index Fund	FUMIX	NAS CM	Open End	US Equity Large Cap Growth (Growth & Income)	U	U	U		Y	0
Fidelity® SAI U.S. Quality Index Fund	FUQIX	NAS CM	Open End	US Equity Large Cap Growth (Growth)	C	C+	B	Up	Y	0
Fidelity® Select Automotive Portfolio	FSAVX	NAS CM	Open End	Consumer Goods Sec Equity ()	B-	B-	C+	Up	Y	2,500
Fidelity® Select Banking Portfolio	FSRBX	NAS CM	Open End	Financials Sector Equity (Financial)	B+	A	B-	Up	Y	2,500
Fidelity® Select Biotechnology Portfolio	FBIOX	NAS CM	Open End	Healthcare Sector Equity (Health)	C	C	C	Up	Y	2,500
Fidelity® Select Brokerage & Invmt Mgmt Portfolio	FSLBX	NAS CM	Open End	Financials Sector Equity (Financial)	B	B	C+	Up	Y	2,500
Fidelity® Select Chemicals Portfolio	FSCHX	NAS CM	Open End	Natl Resources Sec Equity (Natl Res)	B+	A	C+	Up	Y	2,500
Fidelity® Select Communications Equip Portfolio	FSDCX	NAS CM	Open End	Technology Sector Equity (Comm)	B-	B-	B-	Up	Y	2,500
Fidelity® Select Computers Portfolio	FDCPX	NAS CM	Open End	Technology Sector Equity (Technology)	B	A	C+	Up	Y	2,500
Fidelity® Select Construction & Housing Portfolio	FSHOX	NAS CM	Open End	US Equity Mid Cap ()	A-	A-	B+	Up	Y	2,500
Fidelity® Select Consumer Discretionary Portfolio	FSCPX	NAS CM	Open End	Consumer Goods Sec Equity ()	B	B	A-	Up	Y	2,500
Fidelity® Select Consumer Finance Portfolio	FSVLX	NAS CM	Open End	Financials Sector Equity (Financial)	B	B+	B	Up	Y	2,500
Fidelity® Select Consumer Staples Portfolio	FDFAX	NAS CM	Open End	Consumer Goods Sec Equity ()	C	C	B-	Down	Y	2,500
Fidelity® Select Defense & Aerospace Portfolio	FSDAX	NAS CM	Open End	Industrials Sector Equity ()	B+	A+	C+	Up	Y	2,500
Fidelity® Select Energy Portfolio	FSENX	NAS CM	Open End	Energy Sector Equity (Natl Res)	C-	C-	C-	Up	Y	2,500
Fidelity® Select Energy Service Portfolio	FSESX	NAS CM	Open End	Energy Sector Equity (Natl Res)	D	D+	D		Y	2,500
Fidelity® Select Envir and Alt Energy Portfolio	FSLEX	NAS CM	Open End	Industrials Sector Equity ()	B+	A-	B	Up	Y	2,500
Fidelity® Select Financial Services Portfolio	FIDSX	NAS CM	Open End	Financials Sector Equity (Financial)	B+	A-	B	Up	Y	2,500
Fidelity® Select Gold Portfolio	FSAGX	NAS CM	Open End	Precious Metals Sector Equity (Precious Metals)	C-	C	D	Down	Y	2,500
Fidelity® Select Health Care Portfolio	FSPHX	NAS CM	Open End	Healthcare Sector Equity (Health)	C+	C+	B-	Down	Y	2,500
Fidelity® Select Health Care Services Portfolio	FSHCX	NAS CM	Open End	Healthcare Sector Equity (Health)	B	B-	B		Y	2,500
Fidelity® Select Industrial Equipment Portfolio	FSCGX	NAS CM	Open End	Industrials Sector Equity ()	A-	A-	B+	Up	Y	2,500
Fidelity® Select Industrials Portfolio	FCYIX	NAS CM	Open End	Industrials Sector Equity ()	B	B+	B		Y	2,500
Fidelity® Select Insurance Portfolio	FSPCX	NAS CM	Open End	Financials Sector Equity (Financial)	B+	B+	A-	Up	Y	2,500
Fidelity® Select IT Services Portfolio	FBSOX	NAS CM	Open End	Technology Sector Equity (Technology)	A-	A	B	Up	Y	2,500
Fidelity® Select Leisure Portfolio	FDLSX	NAS CM	Open End	Consumer Goods Sec Equity ()	B+	B+	A-	Up	Y	2,500
Fidelity® Select Materials Portfolio	FSDPX	NAS CM	Open End	Natl Resources Sec Equity (Natl Res)	B-	B	C+	Up	Y	2,500
Fidelity® Select Medical Equipment and Systems Portfolio	FSMEX	NAS CM	Open End	Healthcare Sector Equity (Health)	B	B	B		Y	2,500
Fidelity® Select Multimedia Portfolio	FBMPX	NAS CM	Open End	Consumer Goods Sec Equity ()	C+	C	B	Down	Y	2,500
Fidelity® Select Natural Gas Portfolio	FSNGX	NAS CM	Open End	Energy Sector Equity (Natl Res)	D	D+	D	Down	Y	2,500
Fidelity® Select Natural Resources Portfolio	FNARX	NAS CM	Open End	Energy Sector Equity (Natl Res)	C-	D+	C-	Up	Y	2,500
Fidelity® Select Pharmaceuticals Portfolio	FPHAX	NAS CM	Open End	Healthcare Sector Equity (Health)	C-	C-	C-	Down	Y	2,500
Fidelity® Select Portfolios Air Transportation Portfolio	FSAIX	NAS CM	Open End	Industrials Sector Equity ()	A-	A	B	Up	Y	2,500
Fidelity® Select Retailing Portfolio	FSRPX	NAS CM	Open End	Consumer Goods Sec Equity ()	A-	A-	A-	Up	Y	2,500

★Expanded analysis of this fund is included in Section II.

	TOTAL RETURNS					PERFORMANCE				ASSETS		ASSET ALLOCATION & TURNOVER					BULL & BEAR		FEES		
Min Additional Investment	3-Month Total Return	6-Month Total Return	1-Year Total Return	3-Year Total Return	5-Year Total Return	Dividend Yield (TTM)	Expense Ratio	3-Yr Std Deviation	3-Year Beta	NAV	Total Assets (MIL)	%Cash	%Stocks	%Bonds	%Other	Turnover Ratio	Last Bull Market Total Return	Last Bear Market Total Return	Front End Fee (%)	Back End Fee (%)	Inception Date
	6.04	12.26	38.75	57.84	177.99	0	0.7	15.03	1.13	111.27	17,435	0	97	0	0	71	19.61	-17.37			May-08
	3.35	9.30	29.64	38.13	70.58	1.43	1.03	11.37	0.89	50.7	8,058	3	97	0	0	33	21.23	-27.53			Dec-84
	3.38	9.36	29.80	38.66	71.75	1.53	0.91	11.37	0.89	50.58	8,058	3	97	0	0	33	21.35	-27.48			May-08
	10.10	16.83	40.06	52.55	97.65	0.47	1.19	11.44	0.8	35.48	998.8	2	98	0	0	30	14.83	-21.34			Oct-86
	4.59	9.25	18.74	26.22	70.91	1.25	0.55	7.21	0.68	23.42	27,421	2	70	29	0	45	16.96	-11.82			Apr-47
	4.63	9.32	18.85	26.60	71.82	1.33	0.46	7.19	0.68	23.41	27,421	2	70	29	0	45	17.07	-11.75			May-08
	0.43	1.77	7.29	19.80	41.41	4.03	0.78	4.68	0.25	11.99	5,468	6	31	37	0	22	14.26	-6.41			Feb-03
	1.94	2.34	3.74	13.61	55.69	2.46	0.07	13.52	1	15.58	1,080	0	100	0	0	8	31.16				Sep-11
	1.96	2.31	3.58	13.02	54.56	2.27	0.23	13.5	0.99	15.57	1,080	0	100	0	0	8	31.02				Sep-11
	2.00	2.39	3.72	13.53	55.66	2.44	0.09	13.55	1	15.58	1,080	0	100	0	0	8	31.15				Sep-11
	1.27	2.04	4.27	17.17	59.24	1.73	0.76	13.45	0.58	41.8	4,277	3	97	0	0	15	33.4	-16.94			Nov-86
	7.29	15.70	37.60			0.84	0.08			14.97	3,252	2	98	0	0	16					Jan-16
	3.92	9.30	25.03			0.93	0.05			12.41	6,583	0	100	0	0	1					Jan-16
	4.48	7.60	21.40			1.97	0.2			10.98	1,903	3	97	0	0	22					May-15
	1.99	2.31	3.72			2.51	0.07			10.98	99.6	1	99	0	0	6					Feb-16
	6.68	11.01	18.40			0.89	0.15			12.24	1,746	1	99	0	0	22					Aug-15
	6.62	11.37	21.74			1.23	0.02			14.28	10,148	1	99	0	0	17					Feb-16
	5.26	8.87	18.91			1.88	0.15			12.52	936.6	0	100	0	0	37					May-15
	7.83	15.11					0.15			12.16	1,984	0	99	0	1	47					Feb-17
	8.81	13.89	25.75			1.44	0.15			13.23	6,213	0	100	0	0	31					Oct-15
	4.38	15.45	23.95	16.49	79.48	0.96	0.96	17.14	1.35	37.1	61.6	1	99	0	0	83	24.96	-33.09			Jun-86
	6.37	10.79	12.67	42.36	117.72	0.7	0.79	19.16	1.2	35.37	798.9	1	99	0	0	34	39.28	-25.92			Jun-86
	-4.38	5.41	27.86	11.16	152.03	0	0.75	28.7	1.57	219.41	8,774	1	97	0	0	28	36.69	-12.52			Dec-85
	9.16	16.21	29.93	24.43	98.77	1	0.82	19.21	1.52	81.76	441.5	1	99	0	0	146	24.31	-30.13			Jul-85
	6.02	17.24	31.75	46.09	103.76	0.9	0.8	16.37	1.36	178.31	1,890	1	99	0	0	85	39.76	-26.7			Jul-85
	5.26	6.43	11.65	19.00	79.95	1.04	0.88	15.8	1.31	36	189.8	0	100	0	0	38	15.37	-31.85			Jun-90
	8.68	14.80	33.74	32.14	105.61	0.76	0.81	16.99	1.38	88.87	543.3	0	100	0	0	49	33.79	-20.42			Jul-85
	10.65	14.54	26.13	41.69	102.63	0.61	0.8	13.07	0.96	64.87	355.6	1	99	0	0	87	49.73	-23.37			Sep-86
	11.02	11.85	22.07	33.90	112.98	0.67	0.76	11.45	1.01	41.45	717.5	0	100	0	0	39	31.52	-16.18			Jun-90
	8.45	16.10	23.10	32.84	93.34	1.4	0.94	14.33	1.06	16.21	98.2	1	99	0	0	44	30.31	-15.88			Dec-85
	3.61	0.17	12.06	16.76	66.16	1.63	0.76	9.98	0.59	92.5	2,453	1	99	0	0	56	17.81	-6.63			Jul-85
	6.49	21.19	34.21	62.36	153.73	0.58	0.79	12.86	1.01	166.95	2,421	1	99	0	0	24	24.46	-15.39			May-84
	9.98	17.73	-2.63	3.00	14.93	0.46	0.79	21.54	1.1	44.69	1,908	1	99	0	0	93	21.86	-30.86			Jul-81
	2.24	10.50	-12.68	-12.66	-12.70	0.5	0.85	26.3	1.14	45.34	410.4	0	100	0	0	96	23.26	-36.39			Dec-85
	7.52	10.16	25.24	42.85	102.03	0.59	0.94	12.77	1.12	26.42	182.9	2	98	0	0	82	13.34	-29.03			Jun-89
	8.67	14.58	20.94	36.60	106.55	0.88	0.77	14.05	1.14	114.22	1,211	1	99	0	0	84	29.62	-28.26			Dec-81
	0.09	2.56	8.62	31.05	-40.00	0	0.84	37.18	-0.26	20.77	1,337	0	93	0	6	28	-15.04	-13.6			Dec-85
	-1.45	2.12	24.01	17.46	148.47	0.1	0.74	15.88	1.02	223.76	6,863	2	97	0	0	49	23.29	-14.87			Jul-81
	6.85	5.60	24.34	33.91	130.16	0.13	0.78	12.97	0.73	89.89	807.5	2	98	0	0	26	25.93	-17.59			Jun-86
	6.42	13.07	19.71	36.89	88.00	0.74	0.83	12.57	1.12	43.99	171.8	0	100	0	0	166	35.93	-28.46			Sep-86
	8.14	13.59	20.07	34.84	104.98	0.63	0.77	12.84	1.12	36.79	883.6	0	100	0	0	62	30.71	-26.07			Mar-97
	4.18	7.30	15.38	39.47	125.71	0.97	0.8	11.97	1.01	79.5	372.2	3	97	0	0	16	26.56	-22.51			Dec-85
	8.57	17.88	34.24	58.75	162.98	0.24	0.79	12.78	1.12	54.48	2,076	1	99	0	0	27	30.74	-17.3			Feb-98
	9.79	11.60	29.05	41.48	121.72	0.88	0.8	11.09	0.8	166.01	521.9	0	100	0	0	23	34.21	-12.07			May-84
	6.94	14.69	26.21	27.74	60.16	1.01	0.81	15.88	1.33	90.97	1,888	1	99	0	0	49	30.02	-28.27			Sep-86
	1.11	0.24	26.57	46.29	168.59	0	0.76	13.74	0.8	43.88	4,013	2	97	0	0	55	14.18	-15.89			Apr-98
	2.41	3.31	12.58	19.56	93.88	0.31	0.82	15.15	1.22	79.49	535.8	0	100	0	0	33	30.76	-22.5			Jun-86
	1.77	6.94	-15.64	-21.10	-12.57	0.52	0.87	28.05	1.36	23.96	301.8	0	100	0	0	76	18.45	-27.97			Apr-93
	9.99	17.30	-0.10	1.38	7.56	0.35	0.84	20.85	1.09	30.1	940.4	1	99	0	0	84	18.12	-30.94			Mar-97
	-2.24	-1.42	10.68	-0.15	77.50	1.1	0.8	13.76	0.84	18.56	804.4	0	100	0	0	77	19.93	-10.42			Jun-01
	7.79	14.57	24.32	35.95	167.32	0.36	0.85	13.46	0.92	84.29	396.1	3	97	0	0	106	22.07	-18.05			Dec-85
	13.11	15.72	25.82	55.57	155.67	0.11	0.78	11.15	0.92	133.17	1,923	1	99	0	0	17	30.64	-8.42			Dec-85

	MARKET			FUND TYPE, CATEGORY & OBJECTIVE	RATINGS				MINIMUMS	
Fund Name	Ticker Symbol	Traded On	Fund Type	Category and (Prospectus Objective)	Overall Rating	Reward Rating	Risk Rating	Recent Up/ Downgrade	Open to New Investors	Min Initial Investment
Fidelity® Select Semiconductors Portfolio	FSELX	NAS CM	Open End	Technology Sector Equity (Utility)	A-	A+	B	Up	Y	2,500
Fidelity® Select Software & IT Services Portfolio	FSCSX	NAS CM	Open End	Technology Sector Equity (Technology)	A	A	A-	Up	Y	2,500
Fidelity® Select Technology Portfolio	FSPTX	NAS CM	Open End	Technology Sector Equity (Technology)	A	A+	B+	Up	Y	2,500
Fidelity® Select Telecommunications Portfolio	FSTCX	NAS CM	Open End	Communications Sector Equity (Comm)	C+	C	B		Y	2,500
Fidelity® Select Transportation Portfolio	FSRFX	NAS CM	Open End	Industrials Sector Equity ()	B	B+	C+	Up	Y	2,500
Fidelity® Select Utilities Portfolio	FSUTX	NAS CM	Open End	Utilities Sector Equity (Utility)	B-	B	C+	Down	Y	2,500
Fidelity® Select Wireless Portfolio	FWRLX	NAS CM	Open End	Communications Sector Equity (Comm)	B-	B	C+	Up	Y	2,500
Fidelity® Series 100 Index Fund	FOHIX	NAS CM	Open End	US Equity Large Cap Blend (Growth & Income)	B	B	B+		Y	0
Fidelity® Series 1000 Value Index Fund	FIOOX	NAS CM	Open End	US Equity Large Cap Value (Equity-Income)	B	B-	B		Y	0
Fidelity® Series All-Sector Equity Fund	FSAEX	NAS CM	Open End	US Equity Large Cap Growth (Growth)	B-	B-	B-	Down		0
Fidelity® Series Blue Chip Growth Fund	FSBDX	NAS CM	Open End	US Equity Large Cap Growth (Growth)	A-	A	B+	Up	Y	0
Fidelity® Series Canada Fund	FCNSX	NAS CM	Open End	Global Equity (Growth)	U	U	U		Y	0
Fidelity® Series Commodity Strategy Fund	FCSSX	NAS CM	Open End	Commodities Broad Basket (Growth)	D+	C-	D+	Up		0
Fidelity® Series Emerging Markets Fund	FEMSX	NAS CM	Open End	Emerging Markets Equity (Div Emerging Mkts)	B	B	C	Up		0
Fidelity® Series Global ex U.S. Index Fund	FSGEX	NAS CM	Open End	Global Equity Large Cap (Foreign Stock)	B-	B-	B-	Up	Y	0
Fidelity® Series Growth & Income Fund	FGLGX	NAS CM	Open End	US Equity Large Cap Blend (Growth & Income)	B	B	B	Up	Y	0
Fidelity® Series Growth Company Fund	FCGSX	NAS CM	Open End	US Equity Large Cap Growth (Growth)	A-	A	B	Up	Y	0
Fidelity® Series International Growth Fund	FIGSX	NAS CM	Open End	Global Equity Large Cap (Foreign Stock)	B	B-	B	Up		0
Fidelity® Series International Small Cap Fund	FSTSX	NAS CM	Open End	Global Equity Mid/Small Cap (Small Company)	B+	B+	A-	Up		0
Fidelity® Series International Value Fund	FINVX	NAS CM	Open End	Global Equity Large Cap (Foreign Stock)	C+	C+	C+	Up		0
Fidelity® Series Intrinsic Opportunities Fund	FDMLX	NAS CM	Open End	US Equity Mid Cap (Growth)	B	B	B	Up	Y	0
Fidelity® Series Opportunistic Insights Fund	FVWSX	NAS CM	Open End	US Equity Large Cap Growth (Growth)	A-	A-	A-	Up	Y	0
Fidelity® Series Real Estate Equity Fund	FREDX	NAS CM	Open End	Real Estate Sector Equity (Real Estate)	B-	C+	B+			0
Fidelity® Series Real Estate Income Fund	FSREX	NAS CM	Open End	Real Estate Sector Equity (Real Estate)	B	C+	A+	Up		0
Fidelity® Series Small Cap Discovery Fund	FJACX	NAS CM	Open End	US Equity Small Cap (Small Company)	B	B	B	Up	Y	0
Fidelity® Series Small Cap Opportunities Fund	FSOPX	NAS CM	Open End	US Equity Small Cap (Small Company)	B	B	B	Up		0
Fidelity® Series Stock Selector Large Cap Value Fund	FBLEX	NAS CM	Open End	US Equity Large Cap Value (Growth)	B-	B-	B	Down	Y	0
Fidelity® Series Value Discovery Fund	FNKLX	NAS CM	Open End	US Equity Large Cap Value (Equity-Income)	B-	B-	B	Down	Y	0
Fidelity® Small Cap Discovery Fund	FSCRX	NAS CM	Open End	US Equity Small Cap (Small Company)	B	B	B	Up		2,500
Fidelity® Small Cap Enhanced Index Fund	FCPEX	NAS CM	Open End	US Equity Small Cap (Growth)	B	B	B	Up	Y	2,500
Fidelity® Small Cap Growth Fund	FCPGX	NAS CM	Open End	US Equity Small Cap (Small Company)	A-	A	B	Up	Y	2,500
Fidelity® Small Cap Growth K6 Fund	FOCSX	NAS CM	Open End	US Equity Small Cap (Small Company)	U	U	U		Y	0
Fidelity® Small Cap Index Fund Institutional Class	FSSSX	NAS CM	Open End	US Equity Small Cap (Small Company)	B+	A-	B	Up	Y	5,000,000
Fidelity® Small Cap Index Fund Institutional Premium Class	FSSNX	NAS CM	Open End	US Equity Small Cap (Small Company)	B+	A-	B	Up	Y	100,000,000
Fidelity® Small Cap Index Fund Investor Class	FSSPX	NAS CM	Open End	US Equity Small Cap (Small Company)	B+	A-	B	Up	Y	2,500
Fidelity® Small Cap Index Fund Premium Class	FSSVX	NAS CM	Open End	US Equity Small Cap (Small Company)	B+	A-	B	Up	Y	10,000
Fidelity® Small Cap Stock Fund	FSLCX	NAS CM	Open End	US Equity Small Cap (Small Company)	B	B	B+	Up	Y	2,500
Fidelity® Small Cap Stock K6 Fund	FKICX	NAS CM	Open End	US Equity Small Cap (Small Company)	U	U	U		Y	0
Fidelity® Small Cap Value Fund	FCPVX	NAS CM	Open End	US Equity Small Cap (Small Company)	A-	B+	A-	Up		2,500
Fidelity® Stock Selector All Cap Fund	FDSSX	NAS CM	Open End	US Equity Large Cap Growth (Growth)	B	B	B-	Up	Y	2,500
Fidelity® Stock Selector Large Cap Value Fund	FSLVX	NAS CM	Open End	US Equity Large Cap Value (Growth)	B-	B-	B	Down	Y	2,500
Fidelity® Stock Selector Small Cap Fund	FDSCX	NAS CM	Open End	US Equity Small Cap (Small Company)	B	B	B	Up	Y	2,500
Fidelity® Strategic Dividend & Income® Fund	FSDIX	NAS CM	Open End	Aggressive Alloc (Equity-Income)	B-	B-	B	Down	Y	2,500
Fidelity® Strategic Real Return Fund	FSRRX	NAS CM	Open End	Cautious Alloc (Growth & Income)	C	C	B-		Y	2,500
Fidelity® Telecom and Utilities Fund	FIUIX	NAS CM	Open End	Utilities Sector Equity (Utility)	B-	B-	C+	Down	Y	2,500
Fidelity® Total Emerging Markets Fund	FTEMX	NAS CM	Open End	Emerging Markets Equity (Div Emerging Mkts)	B	B	B-	Up	Y	2,500
Fidelity® Total International Equity Fund	FTIEX	NAS CM	Open End	Global Equity Large Cap (Foreign Stock)	B	B-	B	Up	Y	2,500
Fidelity® Total International Index Fund Institutional Cls	FTIUX	NAS CM	Open End	Global Equity Large Cap (Foreign Stock)	D+	C	B	Up	Y	5,000,000
Fidelity® Total Intl Index Fund Inst Premium Cls	FTIHX	NAS CM	Open End	Global Equity Large Cap (Foreign Stock)	D+	C	B	Up	Y	100,000,000
Fidelity® Total International Index Fund Investor Class	FTIGX	NAS CM	Open End	Global Equity Large Cap (Foreign Stock)	D+	C	B	Up	Y	2,500
Fidelity® Total International Index Fund Premium Class	FTIPX	NAS CM	Open End	Global Equity Large Cap (Foreign Stock)	D+	C	B	Up	Y	10,000
Fidelity® Total Market Index Fund Class F	FFSMX	NAS CM	Open End	US Equity Large Cap Blend (Growth & Income)	B	B	B		Y	0

★ Expanded analysis of this fund is included in Section II.

	TOTAL RETURNS					PERFORMANCE				ASSETS		ASSET ALLOCATION & TURNOVER					BULL & BEAR		FEES		
Min Additional Investment	3-Month Total Return	6-Month Total Return	1-Year Total Return	3-Year Total Return	5-Year Total Return	Dividend Yield (TTM)	Expense Ratio	3-Yr Std Deviation	3-Year Beta	NAV	Total Assets (MIL)	%Cash	%Stocks	%Bonds	%Other	Turnover Ratio	Last Bull Market Total Return	Last Bear Market Total Return	Front End Fee (%)	Back End Fee (%)	Inception Date
	11.47	22.21	35.05	82.03	259.80	0.67	0.77	17.38	1.25	111.73	3,591	5	95	0	0	110	23.03	-22.9			Jul-85
	9.22	16.74	38.52	67.77	180.01	0	0.76	14.59	1.19	165.7	4,976	4	96	0	0	44	30.74	-15.42			Jul-85
	6.30	17.22	49.86	78.73	168.20	0.04	0.77	15.12	1.2	178.74	6,508	2	97	0	0	82	25.83	-21.57			Jul-81
	1.13	3.88	1.69	26.90	62.91	1.96	0.8	11.08	0.74	58.92	399.3	0	100	0	0	105	12.29	-16.57			Jul-85
	7.59	14.26	22.19	24.84	153.45	0.48	0.83	15.72	1.05	104.28	539.3	3	97	0	0	104	26.05	-23.34			Sep-86
	0.75	5.64	17.95	17.95	78.27	1.95	0.79	11.26	0.33	79.77	820.7	0	100	0	0	70	11.56	-2.42			Dec-81
	5.45	10.35	25.01	32.48	78.72	0.9	0.87	12.3	0.96	10.12	273.8	-1	101	0	0	98	11.91	-15.61			Sep-00
	6.98	11.98	22.00	37.90	107.92	1.86	0	10.5	1	17.36	3,541	0	100	0	0	4	25.39	-14.92			Mar-07
	5.37	8.57	13.68	26.64		1.42	0	10.34	1	12.73	3,903	0	100	0	0	16					Nov-13
	5.49	10.02	21.49	33.49	106.18	1.12	0	10.48	1.03	12.68	6,378	2	98	0	0	43	23.46	-18.65			Oct-08
	6.94	13.78	35.93	46.57		0.25	0.01	12.02	1.05	13.84	5,885	0	96	0	0	47					Nov-13
	3.47						0			10.89	1,483	3	97	0	0	3					Aug-17
	4.42	6.82	0.91	-17.50	-37.84	0.15	0.05	13.14	1.01	5.44	3,988	95	0	3	2	0	0.78	-20.53			Oct-09
	7.03	16.78	40.43	36.20	36.14	0.91	0.01	14.6	0.91	21.41	15,789	1	99	0	0	45	20.8	-28.26			Dec-08
	4.74	11.00	27.47	25.26	38.55	2.01	0.06	11.69	0.95	13.24	5,095	3	97	0	0	1	14.17	-24.16			Sep-09
	6.19	10.74	17.36	31.69	96.66	1.63	0	11.75	1.11	15.75	13,377	1	99	0	0	54					Dec-12
	7.06	15.33	37.52	56.42		0.08	0	13.19	1.16	16.63	11,616	0	98	0	0	20					Nov-13
	4.88	9.36	30.21	30.36	56.09	0.96	0.01	10.84	0.88	16.15	14,950	1	99	0	0	26	21.28	-22.34			Dec-09
	6.83	12.74	34.45	43.42	77.12	0.81	0.01	10.49	0.85	17.97	3,669	1	99	0	0	21	19.73	-20.86			Dec-09
	2.42	7.41	20.42	19.27	37.06	2.04	0.01	10.77	0.79	10.69	14,909	0	99	0	0	45	11.11	-27.58			Dec-09
	6.87	12.10	24.36	40.70	117.37	1.16	0.01	9.3	0.84	18.11	13,638	8	92	0	0	35					Dec-12
	6.81	13.73	33.03	43.13	129.47	0.02	0	10.62	0.9	17.33	6,392	2	95	0	0	40					Dec-12
	1.92	2.09	4.39	12.37	53.12	1.68	0	13.24	0.59	12.81	1,275	1	99	0	0	64					Oct-11
	0.73	2.32	7.44	18.73	38.94	4.81	0	3.49	0.17	10.92	908.2	3	16	50	0	24					Oct-11
	5.10	7.61	9.58	23.07		0.72	0	12.54	0.84	12.52	1,744	2	97	0	0	24					Nov-13
	3.94	9.74	12.01	27.62	80.78	0.39	0	12.15	0.84	14.03	5,762	4	96	0	0	58	27.07	-25.36			Mar-07
	4.57	8.32	12.38	22.48	88.79	1.23	0	10.21	0.98	13.01	9,963	5	95	0	0	54					Dec-12
	5.05	7.20	11.51	25.92	83.10	1.9	0.05	10.13	0.95	13.36	7,072	5	94	0	0	42					Dec-12
	4.15	5.73	7.91	20.76	84.04	0.6	0.87	12.57	0.84	29.91	5,176	3	97	0	0	18	33.13	-24.35			Sep-00
	2.90	6.60	7.22	28.21	93.19	0.66	0.64	14.12	0.97	14.02	844.9	1	99	0	0	76	29.29	-23.49			Dec-07
	5.01	14.19	29.00	50.78	131.86	0	1.09	12.26	0.79	24.73	3,744	1	99	0	0	140	26.43	-24.47			Nov-04
	5.16	14.26					0.6			11.61	208.1	3	97	0	0						May-17
	3.32	9.28	14.83	32.81	99.53	1	0.04	14.13	1	20.32	4,095	1	99	0	0	11	27.54				Sep-11
	3.38	9.28	14.85	32.89	99.72	1.02	0.04	14.12	1	20.32	4,095	1	99	0	0	11	27.55				Sep-11
	3.36	9.22	14.70	32.28	98.03	0.89	0.17	14.12	1	20.3	4,095	1	99	0	0	11	27.44				Sep-11
	3.37	9.28	14.82	32.76	99.37	0.99	0.05	14.14	1	20.32	4,095	1	99	0	0	11	27.42				Sep-11
	5.46	9.46	13.84	30.68	85.83	0.06	1.02	11.49	0.78	19.61	1,718	2	98	0	0	48	26.12	-32.43			Mar-98
	5.43	9.47					0.6			11.06	58.8	1	99	0	0						May-17
	6.37	9.35	12.25	32.84	99.24	1.13	0.99	10.51	0.7	20.32	3,612	1	97	0	1	26	30.92	-23.61			Nov-04
	5.81	11.45	25.26	36.23	107.85	0.64	0.63	10.66	1.03	43.94	8,710	2	98	0	0	9	24.76	-21.12			Sep-90
	4.24	8.22	12.33	24.28	91.21	1.2	0.77	9.93	0.95	20.72	1,153	5	95	0	0	51	24.88	-20.13			Nov-01
	3.87	9.59	11.73	27.80	84.76	0.42	0.89	12.15	0.84	26.46	1,608	3	97	0	0	62	27.46	-25.4			Jun-93
	3.96	6.57	12.16	23.98	68.43	2.65	0.78	7.08	0.65	15.24	5,260	7	64	2	0	60	19.05	-11.48			Dec-03
	2.18	3.71	4.07	4.63	4.10	2.14	0.83	4.49	0.65	8.89	717.8	1	10	32	53	24	8.48	-7.72			Sep-05
	1.75	6.25	11.98	22.33	71.22	2.44	0.57	9.91	0.54	26.13	1,009	1	99	0	0	41	12.28	-5.75			Nov-87
	5.20	12.42	29.59	35.43	34.19	0.99	1.4	11.16	0.68	13.55	749.9	3	71	25	0	57					Nov-11
	4.90	10.91	30.29	29.63	45.23	1.15	1.11	10.78	0.84	9.31	119.1	1	99	0	0	66	16.46	-25.18			Nov-07
	4.93	11.34	27.60			0.31	0.08			12.53	693.0	1	99	0	0	1					Jun-16
	4.95	11.36	27.62			0.32	0.06			12.53	693.0	1	99	0	0	1					Jun-16
	4.92	11.24	27.48			0.26	0.17			12.53	693.0	1	99	0	0	1					Jun-16
	5.00	11.32	27.57			0.3	0.1			12.53	693.0	1	99	0	0	1					Jun-16
	6.32	11.19	21.17	35.83	109.47	1.53	0.02	10.25	1	76.37	48,089	0	100	0	0	4	25.77	-17.7			Sep-09

	MARKET		FUND TYPE, CATEGORY & OBJECTIVE		RATINGS				MINIMUMS	
Fund Name	Ticker Symbol	Traded On	Fund Type	Category and (Prospectus Objective)	Overall Rating	Reward Rating	Risk Rating	Recent Up/ Downgrade	Open to New Investors	Min Initial Investment
Fidelity® Total Market Index Fund Institutional Class	FSKTX	NAS CM	Open End	US Equity Large Cap Blend (Growth & Income)	B	B	B		Y	5,000,000
Fidelity® Total Mkt Index Fund Inst Premium Cls	FSKAX	NAS CM	Open End	US Equity Large Cap Blend (Growth & Income)	B	B	B		Y	100,000,000
Fidelity® Total Market Index Fund Investor Class	FSTMX	NAS CM	Open End	US Equity Large Cap Blend (Growth & Income)	B	B	B		Y	2,500
Fidelity® Total Market Index Fund Premium Class	FSTVX	NAS CM	Open End	US Equity Large Cap Blend (Growth & Income)	B	B	B		Y	10,000
Fidelity® Trend Fund	FTRNX	NAS CM	Open End	US Equity Large Cap Growth (Growth)	A-	B+	A-	Up	Y	2,500
Fidelity® US Sustainability Index Fund Institutional Class	FITLX	NAS CM	Open End	US Equity Large Cap Blend (Growth & Income)	U	U	U		Y	5,000,000
Fidelity® US Sustainability Index Fund Investor Class	FENSX	NAS CM	Open End	US Equity Large Cap Blend (Growth & Income)	U	U	U		Y	2,500
Fidelity® US Sustainability Index Fund Premium Class	FPNSX	NAS CM	Open End	US Equity Large Cap Blend (Growth & Income)	U	U	U		Y	10,000
Fidelity® Value Discovery Fund	FVDFX	NAS CM	Open End	US Equity Large Cap Value (Growth)	B	B-	B	Up	Y	2,500
Fidelity® Value Discovery Fund Class K	FVDKX	NAS CM	Open End	US Equity Large Cap Value (Growth)	B	B-	B	Up	Y	0
Fidelity® Value Discovery K6 Fund	FDVKX	NAS CM	Open End	US Equity Large Cap Value (World Stock)	U	U	U		Y	0
Fidelity® Value Fund	FDVLX	NAS CM	Open End	US Equity Mid Cap (Growth)	C+	B-	C+	Down	Y	2,500
Fidelity® Value Fund Class K	FVLKX	NAS CM	Open End	US Equity Mid Cap (Growth)	C+	B-	C+	Down	Y	0
Fidelity® Value Strategies Fund	FSLSX	NAS CM	Open End	US Equity Large Cap Value (Growth)	B	B-	B	Up	Y	2,500
Fidelity® Worldwide Fund	FWWFX	NAS CM	Open End	Global Equity (World Stock)	B	B	B	Up	Y	2,500
Fiduciary/Claymore MLP Opportunity Fund	FMO	NYSE	Closed End	Energy Sector Equity (Natl Res)	D	D	D	Down	Y	
Fiera Capital Diversified Alternatives Fund Inst Cls	FCAIX	NAS CM	Open End	Multialternative (Income)	C-	C-	C	Down	Y	10,000
Fiera Capital Diversified Alternatives Fund Investor Class	FCARX	NAS CM	Open End	Multialternative (Income)	C-	C-	C	Down	Y	2,000
Fiera Capital Global Equity Focused Fund Institutional Cls	FCGIX	NAS CM	Open End	Global Equity Large Cap (Growth)	U	U	U		Y	1,000,000
Fiera Capital Global Equity Focused Fund Investor Class	FCGEX	NAS CM	Open End	Global Equity Large Cap (Growth)	U	U	U		Y	1,000
FIERA CAPITAL INTERNATIONAL EQUITY FUND Class Z	FCIWX	NAS CM	Open End	Global Equity Large Cap (Foreign Stock)	U	U	U		Y	100,000,000
FIERA CAPITAL INTERNATIONAL EQUITY FUND Institutional Cls	FCIUX	NAS CM	Open End	Global Equity Large Cap (Foreign Stock)	U	U	U		Y	1,000,000
FIERA CAPITAL INTERNATIONAL EQUITY FUND Investor Class	FCIRX	NAS CM	Open End	Global Equity Large Cap (Foreign Stock)	U	U	U		Y	1,000
First Eagle Fund of America Class A	FEFAX	NAS CM	Open End	US Equity Mid Cap (Growth)	B-	C+	B	Up	Y	2,500
First Eagle Fund of America Class C	FEAMX	NAS CM	Open End	US Equity Mid Cap (Growth)	B-	C+	B-	Up	Y	2,500
First Eagle Fund of America Class I	FEAIX	NAS CM	Open End	US Equity Mid Cap (Growth)	B-	C+	B	Up	Y	1,000,000
First Eagle Fund of America Class R6	FEFRX	NAS CM	Open End	US Equity Mid Cap (Growth)	B-	C+	B	Up	Y	0
First Eagle Fund of America Class Y	FEAFX	NAS CM	Open End	US Equity Mid Cap (Growth)	B-	C+	B	Up		2,500
First Eagle Global Fund Class A	SGENX	NAS CM	Open End	Alloc (Multi-Asset Global)	B	C+	B+		Y	2,500
First Eagle Global Fund Class C	FESGX	NAS CM	Open End	Alloc (Multi-Asset Global)	B	C+	B+		Y	2,500
First Eagle Global Fund Class I	SGIIX	NAS CM	Open End	Alloc (Multi-Asset Global)	B	C+	B+		Y	1,000,000
First Eagle Global Fund Class R6	FEGRX	NAS CM	Open End	Alloc (Multi-Asset Global)	B	C+	B+		Y	0
First Eagle Global Income Builder Fund Class A	FEBAX	NAS CM	Open End	Alloc (Multi-Asset Global)	B-	C+	B	Down	Y	2,500
First Eagle Global Income Builder Fund Class C	FEBCX	NAS CM	Open End	Alloc (Multi-Asset Global)	B-	C+	B		Y	2,500
First Eagle Global Income Builder Fund Class I	FEBIX	NAS CM	Open End	Alloc (Multi-Asset Global)	B-	C+	B	Down	Y	1,000,000
First Eagle Global Income Builder Fund Class R6	FEBRX	NAS CM	Open End	Alloc (Multi-Asset Global)	B-	C+	B	Down	Y	0
First Eagle Gold Fund Class A	SGGDX	NAS CM	Open End	Precious Metals Sector Equity (Precious Metals)	D+	C-	D	Down	Y	2,500
First Eagle Gold Fund Class C	FEGOX	NAS CM	Open End	Precious Metals Sector Equity (Precious Metals)	D+	C-	D	Down	Y	2,500
First Eagle Gold Fund Class I	FEGIX	NAS CM	Open End	Precious Metals Sector Equity (Precious Metals)	D+	C-	D	Down	Y	1,000,000
First Eagle Gold Fund Class R6	FEURX	NAS CM	Open End	Precious Metals Sector Equity (Precious Metals)	D+	C-	D	Down	Y	0
First Eagle Overseas Fund Class A	SGOVX	NAS CM	Open End	Global Equity Large Cap (Foreign Stock)	B-	C+	B+			2,500
First Eagle Overseas Fund Class C	FESOX	NAS CM	Open End	Global Equity Large Cap (Foreign Stock)	B-	C+	B			2,500
First Eagle Overseas Fund Class I	SGOIX	NAS CM	Open End	Global Equity Large Cap (Foreign Stock)	B	C+	B+	Up		1,000,000
First Eagle Overseas Fund Class R6	FEORX	NAS CM	Open End	Global Equity Large Cap (Foreign Stock)	B-	C+	B+			0
First Eagle U.S. Value Fund Class A	FEVAX	NAS CM	Open End	US Equity Large Cap Blend (Growth)	B-	C+	B	Down	Y	2,500
First Eagle U.S. Value Fund Class C	FEVCX	NAS CM	Open End	US Equity Large Cap Blend (Growth)	B-	C+	B	Down	Y	2,500
First Eagle U.S. Value Fund Class I	FEVIX	NAS CM	Open End	US Equity Large Cap Blend (Growth)	B-	C+	B	Down	Y	1,000,000
First Eagle U.S. Value Fund Class R6	FEVRX	NAS CM	Open End	US Equity Large Cap Blend (Growth)	B-	C+	B	Down	Y	0
First Investors Balanced Income Fund Advisor Class	FBIKX	NAS CM	Open End	Cautious Alloc (Balanced)	C	C	B+	Up	Y	1,000
First Investors Balanced Income Fund Class A	FBIJX	NAS CM	Open End	Cautious Alloc (Balanced)	C	C	B	Up	Y	1,000
First Investors Balanced Income Fund Institutional Class	FBILX	NAS CM	Open End	Cautious Alloc (Balanced)	C	C	B+	Up	Y	2,000,000
First Investors Covered Call Strategy Fund Class A	FRCCX	NAS CM	Open End	Long/Short Equity (Growth)	D+	C-	A-	Up	Y	1,000

★ Expanded analysis of this fund is included in Section II.

Min Additional Investment	TOTAL RETURNS: 3-Month Total Return	6-Month Total Return	1-Year Total Return	3-Year Total Return	5-Year Total Return	PERFORMANCE: Dividend Yield (TTM)	Expense Ratio	3-Yr Std Deviation	3-Year Beta	ASSETS: NAV	Total Assets (MIL)	ASSET ALLOCATION & TURNOVER: %Cash	%Stocks	%Bonds	%Other	Turnover Ratio	BULL & BEAR: Last Bull Market Total Return	Last Bear Market Total Return	FEES: Front End Fee (%)	Back End Fee (%)	Inception Date
	6.32	11.18	21.15	35.79	109.34	1.51	0.03	10.25	1	76.36	48,089	0	100	0	0	4	25.75	-17.7			Sep-11
	6.33	11.19	21.18	35.85	109.47	1.53	0.02	10.26	1	76.35	48,089	0	100	0	0	4	25.77	-17.7			Sep-11
	6.30	11.15	21.08	35.57	108.77	1.47	0.09	10.25	1	76.37	48,089	0	100	0	0	4	25.73	-17.7			Nov-97
	6.33	11.19	21.14	35.77	109.27	1.5	0.04	10.25	1	76.37	48,089	0	100	0	0	4	25.77	-17.7			Oct-05
	6.81	13.32	29.41	41.57	120.59	0.34	0.74	11.13	1	99.59	1,787	0	99	0	0	129	24.13	-16.98			Jun-58
	6.73	11.88					0.11				21.7	2	98	0	0						May-17
	6.66	11.81					0.21				21.7	2	98	0	0						May-17
	6.71	11.86					0.14				21.7	2	98	0	0						May-17
	4.93	7.40	14.17	24.48	97.58	1	0.75	9.82	0.9	28.93	3,690	5	95	0	0	32	26.09	-21.01			Dec-02
	4.94	7.47	14.28	24.97	99.06	1.05	0.63	9.8	0.9	28.94	3,690	5	95	0	0	32	26.21	-20.96			May-08
	5.01	7.49					0.45			10.85	325.5	8	92	0	0	0					May-17
	4.56	7.80	15.66	24.43	95.52	1.09	0.67	11.32	1.04	121.14	8,707	2	98	0	0	73	26.86	-24.68			Dec-78
	4.58	7.85	15.77	24.83	96.61	1.18	0.55	11.32	1.04	121.22	8,707	2	98	0	0	73	26.95	-24.63			May-08
	5.07	8.97	19.17	28.03	82.58	1.27	0.56	12.07	1.06	42.08	1,118	3	97	0	0	121	29.28	-26.76			Dec-83
	6.09	13.32	29.54	32.43	78.87	0.7	0.91	10.54	0.93	26.41	1,761	2	98	0	0	5	19.45	-19.94			May-90
	7.30	3.93	-2.84	-27.69	4.90	0	11.57	24.04	1.58	13.16	411.2	0	100	0	0	24	18.53	-11.03			Dec-04
	0.20	-0.51	-0.41	-3.26		0	2.57	5.31	-20.29	9.59	53.7	57	26	19	-2						Jul-14
	0.21	-0.62	-0.62	-3.85		0	2.92	5.25	-19.76	9.51	53.7	57	26	19	-2						Jul-14
100	6.23	11.44					0.9			11.55	11.5	0	100	0	0						Apr-17
100	6.16	11.38					1.15			11.55	11.5	0	100	0	0						Apr-17
	3.30						0.8			10.33	149.1										Sep-17
	3.20						1			10.32	149.1										Sep-17
100	3.10						1.25			10.31	149.1										Sep-17
100	3.44	10.62	21.77	14.28	69.04	0.16	1.3	12.27	1.03	35.4	2,240	1	99	0	0	55	26.66	-19.88	5.00		Nov-98
100	3.25	10.20	20.82	11.72	62.77	0	2.06	12.25	1.03	28.1	2,240	1	99	0	0	55	26.11	-20.13		1.00	Mar-98
100	3.51	10.78	22.14	15.33	71.34	0.42	1.01	12.27	1.03	36.39	2,240	1	99	0	0	55	26.68	-19.92			Mar-13
	3.51	10.75	22.03	14.51	69.40		0.96	12.29	1.03	36.38	2,240	1	99	0	0	55	26.68	-19.92			Mar-17
100	3.44	10.60	21.77	14.26	69.03	0.19	1.31	12.29	1.03	36.31	2,240	1	99	0	0	55	26.68	-19.92			Apr-87
100	3.21	6.02	13.48	23.52	49.33	0.33	1.1	7.59	0.65	59.06	57,793	20	71	1	7	12	12.73	-11.43	5.00		Apr-70
100	3.02	5.62	12.62	20.76	43.79	0	1.86	7.57	0.65	57.05	57,793	20	71	1	7	12	12.23	-11.69		1.00	Jun-00
100	3.27	6.16	13.77	24.51	51.28	0.55	0.84	7.57	0.65	59.31	57,793	20	71	1	7	12	12.88	-11.32			Jul-98
	3.30	6.18	13.75	23.81	49.68		0.8	7.59	0.65	59.31	57,793	20	71	1	7	12	12.73	-11.43			Mar-17
100	2.18	4.47	12.95	21.11	38.47	2.79	1.18	7.11		12.13	1,418	7	55	33	4	30			5.00		May-12
100	2.08	4.09	12.14	18.44	33.35	1.95	1.94	7.13		12.1	1,418	7	55	33	4	30				1.00	May-12
100	2.24	4.61	13.27	22.09	40.12	3.07	0.92	7.15		12.1	1,418	7	55	33	4	30					May-12
	2.34	4.63	13.54	22.38	40.46		0.88	7.15		12.1	1,418	7	55	33	4	30					Mar-17
100	-0.23	0.53	8.11	18.90	-36.84	0	1.27	31.74	0.1	16.92	1,162	2	74	0	23	16	-11.18	-11.27	5.00		Aug-93
100	-0.37	0.12	7.36	16.07	-39.27	0	2.04	31.75	0.1	15.74	1,162	2	74	0	23	16	-11.55	-11.55		1.00	May-03
100	-0.17	0.63	8.44	19.91	-35.96	0	0.98	31.75	0.1	17.34	1,162	2	74	0	23	16	-11.07	-11.16			May-03
	-0.11	0.69	8.51	19.34	-36.60		0.86	31.74	0.1	17.36	1,162	2	74	0	23	16	-11.18	-11.27			Mar-17
100	1.94	4.39	14.05	22.54	37.14	1	1.14	8.44	0.59	24.69	18,411	20	70	2	8	9	7.98	-11.71	5.00		Aug-93
100	1.73	4.02	13.22	19.81	32.11	0.35	1.89	8.46	0.59	23.76	18,411	20	70	2	8	9	7.52	-11.97		1.00	Jun-00
100	2.00	4.53	14.36	23.54	38.92	1.22	0.87	8.43	0.59	25.22	18,411	20	70	2	8	9	8.14	-11.62			Jul-98
	2.02	4.59	14.33	22.84	37.48		0.81	8.44	0.59	25.22	18,411	20	70	2	8	9	7.98	-11.71			Mar-17
100	4.45	7.74	12.79	21.72	57.06	0.15	1.09	8.17	0.73	20.09	2,151	16	74	1	9	11	16.9	-10.31	5.00		Sep-01
100	4.26	7.33	11.88	18.96	51.14	0	1.85	8.17	0.73	19.34	2,151	16	74	1	9	11	16.42	-10.58		1.00	Sep-01
100	4.49	7.83	13.04	22.71	59.04	0.37	0.82	8.16	0.73	20.39	2,151	16	74	1	9	11	17.08	-10.2			Sep-01
	4.48	7.87	13.02	22.70	59.02		0.77	8.16	0.73	20.39	2,151	16	74	1	9	11	17.08	-10.2			Mar-17
	3.42	5.35	9.47			2.3	0.82			11.25	49.5	10	39	51	0	51					Oct-15
	3.27	5.16	8.92			2.15	1.15			11.19	49.5	10	39	51	0	51			4.00		Oct-15
	3.45	5.42	9.40			2.42	0.69			11.24	49.5	10	39	51	0	51					Oct-15
	3.86	6.54	10.93			0.96	1.3			11.59	316.5	1	99	0	0	121			5.75		Apr-16

	MARKET		FUND TYPE, CATEGORY & OBJECTIVE		RATINGS					MINIMUMS
Fund Name	Ticker Symbol	Traded On	Fund Type	Category and (Prospectus Objective)	Overall Rating	Reward Rating	Risk Rating	Recent Up/ Downgrade	Open to New Investors	Min Initial Investment
First Investors Covered Call Strategy Fund Class Advisor	FRCDX	NAS CM	Open End	Long/Short Equity (Growth)	D+	C-	A	Up	Y	1,000
First Invs Covered Call Strategy Fund Cls Inst	FRCEX	NAS CM	Open End	Long/Short Equity (Growth)	D+	C-	A-	Up	Y	2,000,000
First Investors Equity Income Fund Advisor Class	FIUUX	NAS CM	Open End	US Equity Large Cap Value (Growth & Income)	B-	B-	B-	Down	Y	1,000
First Investors Equity Income Fund Class A	FIUTX	NAS CM	Open End	US Equity Large Cap Value (Growth & Income)	B-	B-	B-	Down	Y	1,000
First Investors Equity Income Fund Class B	FIUBX	NAS CM	Open End	US Equity Large Cap Value (Growth & Income)	B-	C+	B-	Down	Y	1,000
First Investors Equity Income Fund Institutional Class	FIUVX	NAS CM	Open End	US Equity Large Cap Value (Growth & Income)	B-	B-	B-	Down	Y	2,000,000
First Investors Global Fund Advisor Class	FIITX	NAS CM	Open End	Global Equity (World Stock)	B-	B	B-	Down	Y	1,000
First Investors Global Fund Class A	FIISX	NAS CM	Open End	Global Equity (World Stock)	B-	B-	B-	Up	Y	1,000
First Investors Global Fund Class B	FIBGX	NAS CM	Open End	Global Equity (World Stock)	B-	B-	B-	Up	Y	1,000
First Investors Global Fund Institutional Class	FIIUX	NAS CM	Open End	Global Equity (World Stock)	B-	B	B-	Down	Y	2,000,000
First Investors Growth and Income Fund Advisor Class	FGIPX	NAS CM	Open End	US Equity Large Cap Blend (Growth & Income)	B-	B-	B	Down	Y	1,000
First Investors Growth and Income Fund Class A	FGINX	NAS CM	Open End	US Equity Large Cap Blend (Growth & Income)	B-	B-	B	Down	Y	1,000
First Investors Growth and Income Fund Class B	FGIBX	NAS CM	Open End	US Equity Large Cap Blend (Growth & Income)	B-	C+	B	Up	Y	1,000
First Investors Growth and Income Fund Institutional Class	FGIQX	NAS CM	Open End	US Equity Large Cap Blend (Growth & Income)	B-	B-	B	Down	Y	2,000,000
First Invs Hedged U.S. Equity Opp Fund A Cls	FHEJX	NAS CM	Open End	Long/Short Equity (Growth)	D	C-	B		Y	1,000
First Invs Hedged U.S. Equity Opp Fund Adv Cls	FHEKX	NAS CM	Open End	Long/Short Equity (Growth)	D	C-	B		Y	1,000
First Invs Hedged U.S. Equity Opp Fund Inst Cls	FHELX	NAS CM	Open End	Long/Short Equity (Growth)	D	C-	B		Y	2,000,000
First Investors International Fund Advisor Class	FIIPX	NAS CM	Open End	Global Equity Large Cap (Foreign Stock)	B	B	B	Up	Y	1,000
First Investors International Fund Class A	FIINX	NAS CM	Open End	Global Equity Large Cap (Foreign Stock)	B	B-	B	Up	Y	1,000
First Investors International Fund Class B	FIIOX	NAS CM	Open End	Global Equity Large Cap (Foreign Stock)	B-	C+	B	Up	Y	1,000
First Investors International Fund Institutional Class	FIIQX	NAS CM	Open End	Global Equity Large Cap (Foreign Stock)	B	B	B	Up	Y	2,000,000
First Investors Long Short Fund Advisor Class	FRLDX	NAS CM	Open End	Long/Short Equity (Growth)	D	D+	A-		Y	1,000
First Investors Long Short Fund Class A	FRLBX	NAS CM	Open End	Long/Short Equity (Growth)	D	D+	B+		Y	1,000
First Investors Long Short Fund Institutional Class	FRLIX	NAS CM	Open End	Long/Short Equity (Growth)	D	D+	A-		Y	2,000,000
First Investors Opportunity Fund Advisor Class	FIVUX	NAS CM	Open End	US Equity Mid Cap (Growth)	B	B-	B	Up	Y	1,000
First Investors Opportunity Fund Class A	FIUSX	NAS CM	Open End	US Equity Mid Cap (Growth)	B-	B-	B	Up	Y	1,000
First Investors Opportunity Fund Class B	FIMBX	NAS CM	Open End	US Equity Mid Cap (Growth)	B-	C+	B	Up	Y	1,000
First Investors Opportunity Fund Institutional Class	FIVVX	NAS CM	Open End	US Equity Mid Cap (Growth)	B	B-	B	Up	Y	2,000,000
First Investors Real Estate Fund Advisor Class	FIRGX	NAS CM	Open End	Real Estate Sector Equity (Real Estate)	C	C	C		Y	1,000
First Investors Real Estate Fund Class A	FIRDX	NAS CM	Open End	Real Estate Sector Equity (Real Estate)	C	C	C		Y	1,000
First Investors Real Estate Fund Institutional Class	FIRHX	NAS CM	Open End	Real Estate Sector Equity (Real Estate)	C	C	C		Y	2,000,000
First Investors Select Growth Fund Advisor Class	FICHX	NAS CM	Open End	US Equity Large Cap Growth (Growth)	A-	A	B	Up	Y	1,000
First Investors Select Growth Fund Class A	FICGX	NAS CM	Open End	US Equity Large Cap Growth (Growth)	A-	A-	B	Up	Y	1,000
First Investors Select Growth Fund Class B	FIGBX	NAS CM	Open End	US Equity Large Cap Growth (Growth)	B+	B+	B	Up	Y	1,000
First Investors Select Growth Fund Institutional Class	FICIX	NAS CM	Open End	US Equity Large Cap Growth (Growth)	A-	A	B	Up	Y	2,000,000
First Investors Special Situations Class A	FISSX	NAS CM	Open End	US Equity Small Cap (Aggr Growth)	B	B+	B	Up	Y	1,000
First Investors Special Situations Class B	FISBX	NAS CM	Open End	US Equity Small Cap (Aggr Growth)	B	B	B	Up	Y	1,000
First Investors Special Situations Fund Advisor Class	FISTX	NAS CM	Open End	US Equity Small Cap (Aggr Growth)	B+	B+	B	Up	Y	1,000
First Investors Special Situations Fund Institutional Cls	FISUX	NAS CM	Open End	US Equity Small Cap (Aggr Growth)	B+	B+	B	Up	Y	2,000,000
First Investors Total Return Fund Advisor Class	FITUX	NAS CM	Open End	Moderate Alloc (Asset Alloc)	B-	C+	B	Up	Y	1,000
First Investors Total Return Fund Institutional Class	FITVX	NAS CM	Open End	Moderate Alloc (Asset Alloc)	B-	C+	B	Up	Y	2,000,000
First Investors Total Return Series Class A	FITRX	NAS CM	Open End	Moderate Alloc (Asset Alloc)	B-	C+	B	Up	Y	1,000
First Investors Total Return Series Class B	FBTRX	NAS CM	Open End	Moderate Alloc (Asset Alloc)	B-	C+	B+	Up	Y	1,000
First State Global Listed Infrastructure Fund Class I	FLIIX	NAS CM	Open End	Other Sector Equity ()	U	U	U		Y	1,000,000
First Trust AQA Equity Fund Class A	AQAAX	NAS CM	Open End	US Equity Mid Cap (Growth)	C	C	B+	Up	Y	2,500
First Trust AQA Equity Fund Class C	AQACX	NAS CM	Open End	US Equity Mid Cap (Growth)	C	C	B+	Up	Y	2,500
First Trust AQA Equity Fund Class I	AQAIX	NAS CM	Open End	US Equity Mid Cap (Growth)	C	C	B+	Up	Y	1,000,000
First Trust Dynamic Europe Equity Income	FDEU	NYSE	Closed End	Europe Equity Large Cap (Equity-Income)	C	C	B	Up	Y	
First Trust Energy Income and Growth Fund	FEN	AMEX	Closed End	Energy Sector Equity (Natl Res)	D+	C-	D	Down	Y	
First Trust Energy Infrastructure Fund	FIF	NYSE	Closed End	Energy Sector Equity (Equity-Income)	C-	C	D+	Down	Y	
First Trust Enhanced Equity Income Fund	FFA	NYSE	Closed End	US Equity Large Cap Blend (Equity-Income)	B-	B-	B-	Up	Y	
First Trust Intermediate Duration Preferred & Income Fund	FPF	NYSE	Closed End	US Fixed Income (Income)	B	B-	A+	Up	Y	

★ Expanded analysis of this fund is included in Section II.

	TOTAL RETURNS					PERFORMANCE				ASSETS		ASSET ALLOCATION & TURNOVER					BULL & BEAR		FEES		
Min Additional Investment	3-Month Total Return	6-Month Total Return	1-Year Total Return	3-Year Total Return	5-Year Total Return	Dividend Yield (TTM)	Expense Ratio	3-Yr Std Deviation	3-Year Beta	NAV	Total Assets (MIL)	%Cash	%Stocks	%Bonds	%Other	Turnover Ratio	Last Bull Market Total Return	Last Bear Market Total Return	Front End Fee (%)	Back End Fee (%)	Inception Date
	3.92	6.77	11.40			1.33	0.97			11.57	316.5	1	99	0	0	121					Apr-16
	3.97	6.86	11.57			1.47	0.84			11.59	316.5	1	99	0	0	121					Apr-16
	5.28	9.31	15.52	28.13	83.84	1.86	0.86	9.4	0.91	10.93	664.4	3	95	0	0	15	23.06	-17.75			Apr-13
	5.14	9.12	15.06	26.65	81.19	1.88	1.23	9.33	0.91	10.86	664.4	3	95	0	0	15	23.06	-17.75	5.75		Feb-93
	5.04	8.67	14.09	23.57	73.98	1.04	2.08	9.38	0.91	10.64	664.4	3	95	0	0	15	22.5	-17.97		4.00	Jan-95
	5.32	9.35	15.49	28.22	84.55	2.7	0.79	9.37	0.91	10.88	664.4	3	95	0	0	15	23.06	-17.75			Apr-13
	5.13	8.84	24.23	28.67	73.65	0.2	1.1	11.02	1	8.55	602.5	3	97	0	0	117	21.79	-22.62			Apr-13
	5.03	8.56	23.73	26.97	70.84	0.12	1.52	11.03	1	8.36	602.5	3	97	0	0	117	21.79	-22.62	5.75		Nov-81
	4.70	8.18	22.66	23.87	63.98	0.02	2.32	11.09	1.01	6.49	602.5	3	97	0	0	117	21.15	-22.79		4.00	Jan-95
	5.12	8.82	24.12	28.61	74.33	0.21	1.06	11.07	1.01	8.59	602.5	3	97	0	0	117	21.79	-22.62			Apr-13
	6.74	10.50	18.51	24.92	89.77	1.86	0.78	11.18	1.06	24	1,948	1	98	0	0	16	29.31	-18.78			Apr-13
	6.66	10.27	18.07	23.49	86.52	1.44	1.17	11.19	1.06	23.83	1,948	1	98	0	0	16	29.31	-18.78	5.75		Oct-93
	6.44	9.84	17.17	20.66	79.44	0.57	1.95	11.16	1.06	22.03	1,948	1	98	0	0	16	28.87	-19.06		4.00	Jan-95
	6.78	10.51	18.53	25.01	90.06	1.78	0.75	11.2	1.06	23.93	1,948	1	98	0	0	16	29.31	-18.78			Apr-13
	3.71	5.07	12.26			0	1.75			11.17	86.2	8	92	0	0	75			5.75		Aug-16
	3.79	5.25	12.65			0.02	1.42			11.22	86.2	8	92	0	0	75					Aug-16
	3.88	5.34	12.85			0.02	1.31			11.24	86.2	8	92	0	0	75					Aug-16
	4.72	8.54	32.21	29.36	41.36	0.48	1.24	11.04	0.76	16.64	371.0	3	94	0	1	38	19.65	-14.2			Apr-13
	4.64	8.37	31.68	27.87	39.14	0.42	1.61	11.05	0.76	16.39	371.0	3	94	0	1	38	19.65	-14.2	5.75		Jun-06
	4.37	7.83	30.51	24.68	33.45	0.3	2.45	11.01	0.76	15.27	371.0	3	94	0	1	38	19.21	-14.44		4.00	Jun-06
	4.74	8.55	32.35	29.78	42.47	0.53	1.12	11.07	0.77	16.68	371.0	3	94	0	1	38	19.65	-14.2			Apr-13
	1.24	2.31	5.90				1.67			10.59	55.8	71	30	0	0	89					Dec-16
	1.24	2.22	5.60				1.95			10.56	55.8	71	30	0	0	89			5.75		Dec-16
	1.24	2.31	6.00				1.54			10.6	55.8	71	30	0	0	89					Dec-16
	5.49	9.61	19.00	26.50	98.39	0.53	0.94	11.33	0.97	42.38	1,147	4	96	0	0	32	29.41	-20.87			Apr-13
	5.42	9.48	18.66	25.41	95.90	0.49	1.23	11.33	0.97	41.64	1,147	4	96	0	0	32	29.41	-20.87	5.75		Aug-92
	5.21	9.04	17.76	22.55	88.51	0.5	2	11.35	0.97	32.03	1,147	4	96	0	0	32	28.87	-21.11		4.00	Jan-95
	5.54	9.70	19.14	27.02	99.74	0.56	0.8	11.33	0.97	42.31	1,147	4	96	0	0	32	29.41	-20.87			Apr-13
	4.87	2.08	1.26			1.85	1.12			9.59	123.3	3	97	0	0	17					Apr-15
	4.78	2.01	1.01			1.32	1.45			9.58	123.3	3	97	0	0	17			5.75		Apr-15
	4.90	2.14	1.46			1.95	1			9.58	123.3	3	97	0	0	17					Apr-15
	8.15	17.05	32.66	41.29	118.51	0.29	0.86	10.47	0.91	12.14	574.3	1	99	0	0	58	26.78	-16.53			Apr-13
	8.00	16.73	32.15	39.59	114.88	0.21	1.27	10.48	0.91	11.93	574.3	1	99	0	0	58	26.78	-16.53	5.75		Oct-00
	7.84	16.42	31.16	36.41	106.75	0.12	2.03	10.48	0.91	9.91	574.3	1	99	0	0	58	26.34	-16.85		4.00	Oct-00
	8.20	17.06	32.72	41.45	119.67	0.3	0.83	10.52	0.92	12.21	574.3	1	99	0	0	58	26.78	-16.53			Apr-13
	5.28	10.34	17.66	33.58	87.83	0.48	1.35	12.27	0.84	31.95	720.6	1	99	0	0	27	24.96	-19.73	5.75		Sep-90
	5.07	9.91	16.75	30.42	80.44	0.51	2.16	12.25	0.84	23.92	720.6	1	99	0	0	27	24.52	-19.98		4.00	Jan-95
	5.34	10.54	18.02	34.81	90.17	0.53	1.05	12.26	0.84	32.26	720.6	1	99	0	0	27	24.96	-19.73			Apr-13
	5.37	10.61	18.17	35.35	91.75	0.55	0.91	12.26	0.84	32.46	720.6	1	99	0	0	27	24.96	-19.73			Apr-13
	4.27	6.72	12.06	17.10	51.48	1.81	0.82	6.56	0.62	20.36	939.1	6	60	31	3	39	19.07	-10.59			Apr-13
	4.26	6.71	12.09	17.14	52.03	1.76	0.77	6.6	0.62	20.43	939.1	6	60	31	3	39	19.07	-10.59			Apr-13
	4.14	6.47	11.64	15.74	49.19	1.55	1.19	6.58	0.62	20.25	939.1	6	60	31	3	39	19.07	-10.59	5.75		Apr-90
	3.97	6.11	10.83	13.09	43.56	0.81	1.96	6.58	0.62	19.92	939.1	6	60	31	3	39	18.5	-10.79		4.00	Jan-95
	0.23	3.78					1.09			10.43	6.4	1	99	0	0						Feb-17
50	9.33	16.89	26.19			0	1.6			28.13	45.0	0	100	0	0	57			5.50		Nov-15
50	9.11	16.43	25.25			0	2.35			27.69	45.0	0	100	0	0	57				1.00	Nov-15
	9.40	17.05	26.51			0	1.35			28.04	45.0	0	100	0	0	57					Nov-15
	2.12	8.04	22.10			5	1.99			19.87	340.2	9	121	-30	0	41					Sep-15
	7.97	8.55	6.47	-13.94	31.53	2.55	13.3	15.28	0.74	25.45	440.5	1	99	0	0	54	21	-8.85			Jun-04
	-0.78	1.22	-0.19	-11.95	41.31	1.76		14.91		18.81	328.9	2	98	0	0	72	23.94				Sep-11
	3.53	6.75	16.02	24.22	72.87	0.54	0	9.58	1.41	16.51	333.6	0	98	0	0	32	24.69	-16.94			Aug-04
	1.52	4.10	15.89	32.64		7.5	1.92	5.05		24.88	1,523	-44	0	61	0	50					May-13

	MARKET			FUND TYPE, CATEGORY & OBJECTIVE	RATINGS				MINIMUMS	
Fund Name	Ticker Symbol	Traded On	Fund Type	Category and (Prospectus Objective)	Overall Rating	Reward Rating	Risk Rating	Recent Up/ Downgrade	Open to New Investors	Min Initial Investment
First Trust MLP and Energy Income Fund Common	FEI	NYSE	Closed End	Energy Sector Equity (Growth & Income)	D+	C-	D	Down	Y	
First Trust New Opps MLP & Energy Fund	FPL	NYSE	Closed End	Energy Sector Equity (Income)	D+	C-	D	Down	Y	
First Trust Preferred Securities and Income Fund Class A	FPEAX	NAS CM	Open End	US Fixed Income (Income)	B	C+	A+		Y	2,500
First Trust Preferred Securities and Income Fund Class C	FPECX	NAS CM	Open End	US Fixed Income (Income)	B	C+	A+		Y	2,500
First Trust Preferred Securities and Income Fund Class F	FPEFX	NAS CM	Open End	US Fixed Income (Income)	B	C+	A		Y	2,500
First Trust Preferred Securities and Income Fund Class I	FPEIX	NAS CM	Open End	US Fixed Income (Income)	B	C+	A+		Y	1,000,000
First Trust Preferred Securities and Income Fund Class R3	FPERX	NAS CM	Open End	US Fixed Income (Income)	B	C+	A+		Y	0
First Trust Special Finance & Financial Opportunities Fund	FGB	NYSE	Closed End	Financials Sector Equity (Financial)	C	C	C	Down	Y	
First Trust/Aberdeen Emerging Opportunity Fund	FEO	NYSE	Closed End	Emerging Markets Equity (Multi-Asset Global)	C+	C+	C+	Up	Y	
First Trust/Confluence Small Cap Value Fund Class A	FOVAX	NAS CM	Open End	US Equity Small Cap (Small Company)	B+	A-	B+	Up	Y	2,500
First Trust/Confluence Small Cap Value Fund Class C	FOVCX	NAS CM	Open End	US Equity Small Cap (Small Company)	B	B+	B	Up	Y	2,500
First Trust/Confluence Small Cap Value Fund Class I	FOVIX	NAS CM	Open End	US Equity Small Cap (Small Company)	B+	A-	B+	Up	Y	1,000,000
Firsthand Alternative Energy Fund	ALTEX	NAS CM	Open End	Technology Sector Equity (Natl Res)	C	C+	C	Up	Y	2,000
Firsthand Technology Opportunities Fund	TEFQX	NAS CM	Open End	Technology Sector Equity (Technology)	A-	A+	B	Up	Y	2,000
Flaherty & Crumrine Dynamic Preferred and Income Fund	DFP	NYSE	Closed End	US Fixed Income (Growth & Income)	B	B-	A+	Up	Y	
Flaherty & Crumrine Preferred Income Fund	PFD	NYSE	Closed End	US Fixed Income (Income)	B	B-	A	Up	Y	
Flaherty & Crumrine Preferred Income Opportunity Fund	PFO	NYSE	Closed End	US Fixed Income (Income)	B	B-	A	Up	Y	
Flaherty & Crumrine Preferred Securities Income Fund	FFC	NYSE	Closed End	US Fixed Income (Income)	B	B-	A	Up	Y	
Flaherty & CrumrineTotal Return Fund	FLC	NYSE	Closed End	US Fixed Income (Income)	B	B-	A	Up	Y	
FMC Select Fund	FMSLX	NAS CM	Open End	US Equity Large Cap Growth (Growth)	B-	C+	B	Down	Y	10,000
FMC Strategic Value Fund	FMSVX	NAS CM	Open End	US Equity Small Cap (Growth)	C-	C-	C-	Down	Y	10,000
FMI Common Stock Fund	FMIMX	NAS CM	Open End	US Equity Mid Cap (Growth)	B	B-	B	Up		1,000
FMI Common Stock Fund Institutional Class	FMIUX	NAS CM	Open End	US Equity Mid Cap (Growth)	B-	B	C+	Down	Y	100,000
FMI International Fund	FMIJX	NAS CM	Open End	Global Equity Large Cap (Foreign Stock)	B	B-	B+	Up	Y	2,500
FMI International Fund Institutional Class	FMIYX	NAS CM	Open End	Global Equity Large Cap (Foreign Stock)	B	B-	B+	Up	Y	100,000
FMI Large Cap Fund	FMIHX	NAS CM	Open End	US Equity Large Cap Blend (Growth)	B-	B-	B-	Down		1,000
FMI Large Cap Fund Institutional Class	FMIQX	NAS CM	Open End	US Equity Large Cap Blend (Growth)	B-	B-	B-	Down	Y	100,000
Footprints Discover Value Fund Class A Shares	DAVAX	NAS CM	Open End	Aggressive Alloc (Growth & Income)	D	D+	D		Y	10,000
Forester Discovery Fund	INTLX	NAS CM	Open End	Global Equity Large Cap (Growth)	C+	C	B	Up	Y	2,500
Forester Value Fund Class I	FVILX	NAS CM	Open End	Long/Short Equity (Growth)	D	D	C-	Down	Y	25,000
Forester Value Fund Class N	FVALX	NAS CM	Open End	Long/Short Equity (Growth)	D	D	C-	Down	Y	2,500
Forester Value Fund Class R	FVRLX	NAS CM	Open End	Long/Short Equity (Growth)	D	D	D+	Down	Y	2,500
FormulaFolios US Equity Fund Institutional Class	FFILX	NAS CM	Open End	US Equity Large Cap Blend (Growth)	C-	C-	B+	Up	Y	50,000
FormulaFolios US Equity Fund Investor Class	FFIOX	NAS CM	Open End	US Equity Large Cap Blend (Growth)	C-	C-	B+	Up	Y	2,000
FormulaFolios US Equity Portfolio Class 1	US66538F5382		Open End	US Equity Large Cap Blend (Growth)	C	C-	B	Up	Y	0
Fort Pitt Capital Total Return Fund	FPCGX	NAS CM	Open End	US Equity Large Cap Blend (Growth & Income)	B	B	B		Y	2,500
Foundry Partners Fundamental Small Cap Value Fund Inst Cls	DRISX	NAS CM	Open End	US Equity Small Cap (Small Company)	B	B+	B	Up	Y	100,000
Foundry Partners Fundamental Small Cap Value Fund Inv Cls	DRSVX	NAS CM	Open End	US Equity Small Cap (Small Company)	B	B+	B	Up	Y	2,500
Foxby Corp	FXBY	OTC BB	Closed End	US Equity Large Cap Blend (Multi-Asset Global)	C+	C+	C+	Up	Y	
FPA Capital Fund	FPPTX	NAS CM	Open End	US Equity Mid Cap (Growth)	C-	C-	C			1,500
FPA Crescent Fund	FPACX	NAS CM	Open End	Moderate Alloc (Growth)	B	C+	B+	Up	Y	1,500
FPA International Value Fund	FPIVX	NAS CM	Open End	Global Equity Mid/Small Cap (Foreign Stock)	B-	B	C+	Up	Y	1,500
FPA Paramount Fund	FPRAX	NAS CM	Open End	Global Equity (Growth & Income)	B	B	C+	Up	Y	1,500
FPA U.S. Value Fund	FPPFX	NAS CM	Open End	US Equity Large Cap Blend (Growth & Income)	C+	C	B			1,500
Frank Value Fund Class C	FNKCX	NAS CM	Open End	US Equity Mid Cap (Growth)	D+	D	C-	Down	Y	1,500
Frank Value Fund Institutional Class	FNKIX	NAS CM	Open End	US Equity Mid Cap (Growth)	D+	D+	C	Down	Y	1,000,000
Frank Value Fund Investor Class	FRNKX	NAS CM	Open End	US Equity Mid Cap (Growth)	D+	D	C	Down	Y	1,500
Franklin Balance Sheet Investment Fund Advisor Class	FBSAX	NAS CM	Open End	US Equity Mid Cap (Growth & Income)	C+	B-	C+	Down	Y	100,000
Franklin Balance Sheet Investment Fund Class A	FRBSX	NAS CM	Open End	US Equity Mid Cap (Growth & Income)	C+	B-	C+		Y	1,000
Franklin Balance Sheet Investment Fund Class C	FCBSX	NAS CM	Open End	US Equity Mid Cap (Growth & Income)	C+	B-	C+	Up	Y	1,000
Franklin Balance Sheet Investment Fund Class R	FBSRX	NAS CM	Open End	US Equity Mid Cap (Growth & Income)	C+	B-	C+		Y	1,000
Franklin Balance Sheet Investment Fund Class R6	FBSIX	NAS CM	Open End	US Equity Mid Cap (Growth & Income)	C+	B-	C+	Down	Y	1,000,000

★ Expanded analysis of this fund is included in Section II.

	TOTAL RETURNS					PERFORMANCE				ASSETS		ASSET ALLOCATION & TURNOVER					BULL & BEAR		FEES		
Min Additional Investment	3-Month Total Return	6-Month Total Return	1-Year Total Return	3-Year Total Return	5-Year Total Return	Dividend Yield (TTM)	Expense Ratio	3-Yr Std Deviation	3-Year Beta	NAV	Total Assets (MIL)	%Cash	%Stocks	%Bonds	%Other	Turnover Ratio	Last Bull Market Total Return	Last Bear Market Total Return	Front End Fee (%)	Back End Fee (%)	Inception Date
	1.30	2.19	0.91	-18.05	12.90	0	2.17	15.62		14.63	645.6	4	96	0	0	68					Nov-12
	-1.81	-0.79	-1.70	-22.80		0	2.14	18.68	0.89	11.89	284.9	2	98	0	0	68					Mar-14
50	1.37	3.15	11.16	23.67	31.18	5.14	1.4	3.35	0.71	22.28	254.2	1	0	37	0	71	10.93	-0.58	4.50		Feb-11
50	1.23	2.85	10.41	21.05	26.48	4.39	2.15	3.33	0.71	22.34	254.2	1	0	37	0	71	10.54	-0.69		1.00	Feb-11
50	1.43	3.35	11.40	24.25	31.94	5.18	1.3	3.37	0.72	22.52	254.2	1	0	37	0	71	11.86	-0.78			Mar-11
	1.47	3.35	11.53	24.71	33.05	5.36	1.15	3.36	0.72	22.39	254.2	1	0	37	0	71	11.22	-0.77			Jan-11
	1.27	2.98	10.80	22.60	29.41	4.91	1.65	3.37	0.71	22.24	254.2	1	0	37	0	71	10.95	-1.01			Mar-11
	-5.82	-6.75	0.25	17.42	28.67	10.51	0	16.47		6.31	92.1	0	94	0	5	13	23.9	-19.82			May-07
	1.92	5.77	19.82	22.49	10.97	2.98	1.3	11.89		17.9	91.6	1	43	56	0	53	17.62	-12.83			Aug-06
50	6.07	11.91	18.95	37.60	89.96	0	1.78	11.43	0.71	33.83	17.5	12	88	0	0	15	20.82	-19.31	5.50		Feb-11
50	5.96	11.62	18.17	34.14	82.43	0	2.53	11.32	0.7	30.69	17.5	12	88	0	0	15	19.21	-19.27		1.00	Mar-11
	6.17	12.09	18.71	37.18	92.11	0	1.53	11.31	0.7	34.46	17.5	12	88	0	0	15	21.44	-17.27			Jan-11
50	4.44	8.47	27.34	4.12	104.75	0	1.98	15.48	1.14	6.72	5.8	6	94	0	0	10	-7.15	-40.74			Oct-07
50	9.91	22.90	55.45	70.57	151.90	0	1.85	15.53	1.09	9.98	122.6	4	96	0	0	18	12.06	-17.98			Sep-99
	0.96	2.61	16.74	33.95		7.3	1.75	5.74		26.27	503.7	0	3	24	1	19					May-13
	1.01	2.65	16.19	30.89	58.77	7.2		5.04	0.91	14.33	160.1	0	4	24	0	16	15.34	-3.4			Jan-91
	1.06	2.68	16.20	30.92	58.78	7.35		4.93	0.89	11.93	149.4	1	3	24	1	16	15.81	-3.38			Feb-92
	1.16	2.89	17.18	32.10	62.68	7.37	0	5.11	0.88	20.33	899.7	0	2	25	2	13	15.7	-3.31			Jan-03
	1.14	2.85	16.74	30.89	59.56	7.23	0	5	1	21.66	216.0	0	2	25	2	14	14.55	-2.76			Aug-03
1,000	5.70	6.30	16.10	12.68	59.28	0.4	0.99	8.69	0.77	27.83	228.1	1	99	0	0	32	21.42	-16.91			May-95
1,000	0.18	0.39	1.74	-8.53	19.34	0	1.22	12.65	0.78	19.82	96.0	11	89	0	0	42	28.59	-30.22			Aug-98
100	3.15	7.51	13.77	26.37	81.33	0	1.04	11.25	0.73	26.58	1,099	20	80	0	0	26	26.95	-17.61			Dec-81
100	3.18	7.58	13.87	26.51	81.53	0.02	0.94	11.26	0.73	26.6	1,099	20	80	0	0	26	26.95	-17.61			Oct-16
100	2.69	5.52	15.44	30.65	72.84	2.65	0.94	7.17		33.94	8,143	18	80	0	0	26	20.22	-13.71			Dec-10
1,000	2.73	5.62	15.58	30.84	73.09	2.67	0.8	7.17		33.97	8,143	18	80	0	0	26	20.22	-13.71			Oct-16
100	6.01	9.83	19.18	31.14	96.40	0.94	0.84	9.88	0.91	21.5	6,570	9	91	0	0	16	22.61	-15.37			Dec-01
100	6.00	9.87	19.29	31.24	96.54	0.96	0.72	9.87	0.91	21.47	6,570	9	91	0	0	16	22.61	-15.37			Oct-16
100	5.95	13.10	-9.96	-24.83	-36.03	0.48	2	27.93	1.19	5.87	6.7	4	95	0	0	37			5.75		Dec-12
100	0.51	3.37	12.07	8.47	17.09	0.56	1.37	6.2	0.41	14.33	4.6	19	79	0	2	13	5.19	-10.05			Sep-99
100	0.90	0.11	-1.61	-10.82	1.07	1.07	1	3.91	0	11.29	38.9	24	76	0	0	13	1.81	-5.27			Jun-09
100	0.77	-0.03	-1.88	-11.60	-0.17	0.43	1.26	3.89	0	11.02	38.9	24	76	0	0	13	1.58	-5.43			Sep-99
100	0.67	-0.11	-2.08	-11.97	-0.60	0.09	1.51	3.91	0	11.38	38.9	24	76	0	0	13	2.06	-5.55			Dec-10
500	4.73	8.20	14.07			0.15	1.25			10.84	248.4	20	80	0	0						Dec-15
500	4.45	7.57	15.42			0.15	2.25			10.63	248.4	20	80	0	0						Dec-15
	4.10	7.55	11.30			0	2.18			9.14	0.22	21	79	0	0						Nov-15
100	7.02	13.79	21.91	38.86	97.96	0.76	1.25	10.46	0.98	26.09	71.6	2	98	0	0	5	18.3	-11.79			Dec-01
1,000	2.76	5.79	7.81	31.65	96.49	0.71	1.19	12.86	0.88	23.89	198.5	5	95	0	0	13	26.71	-26.84			Aug-07
1,000	2.68	5.68	7.53	30.67	94.35	0.49	1.44	12.87	0.88	23.8	198.5	5	95	0	0	13	26.69	-27			Dec-03
	10.20	12.18	15.49	16.88	55.72	0.22	0	12.31	0.76	3.13	8.1	7	90	0	0	58	26.82	-8.37			Oct-99
100	1.83	-0.11	-5.11	-4.22	19.06	0.11	0.8	14.04	0.84	34.33	431.4	15	64	17	4	23	22.18	-22.15			Jul-84
100	2.90	4.85	10.38	18.63	56.13	0.98	1.07	7.44	0.67	34.69	17,529	15	57	27	1	35	15.46	-11.58			Jun-93
100	2.58	9.14	27.11	30.44	39.34	2.55	1.28	11.13	0.81	15.45	262.8	36	63	0	1	93					Dec-11
100	4.59	11.00	27.23	35.22	66.36	0.79	1.29	11.8	1.03	22.2	179.3	12	79	0	10	72	28.82	-24.14			Jun-84
100	2.27	1.79	9.52	2.71	59.64	0.46	1.11	11.96	0.82	9.91	86.9	10	88	0	2	115	28.85	-24.83			Apr-84
100	-2.82	-1.76	-3.46	-8.33	34.49	0	2.29	5.61	0.33	11.69	23.4	24	38	38	0	61	22.49	-14.66			Sep-10
500	-2.55	-1.33	-2.55	-5.56	41.38	0	1.29	5.62	0.33	12.58	23.4	24	38	38	0	61	23.07	-14.44			Nov-10
100	-2.66	-1.42	-2.81	-6.24	39.57	0	1.54	5.64	0.33	12.43	23.4	24	38	38	0	61	22.93	-14.43			Jul-04
	5.87	10.24	12.71	22.57	73.57	0.62	0.68	12.74	1.11	40.54	1,031	15	84	0	0	30	23.74	-22.59			Mar-01
	5.84	10.13	12.43	21.68	71.44	0.41	0.93	12.74	1.11	39.25	1,031	15	84	0	0	30	23.56	-22.67	5.75		Apr-90
	5.61	9.70	11.58	18.98	65.10	0	1.68	12.73	1.11	37.62	1,031	15	84	0	0	30	23.05	-22.92		1.00	Mar-01
	5.77	9.99	12.14	20.78	69.32	0.21	1.18	12.74	1.11	39.39	1,031	15	84	0	0	30	23.42	-22.76			Jan-02
	5.91	10.31	12.83	23.12	74.44	0.62	0.52	12.73	1.11	40.44	1,031	15	84	0	0	30	23.56	-22.67			May-13

Fund Name	MARKET Ticker Symbol	Traded On	FUND TYPE, CATEGORY & OBJECTIVE Fund Type	Category and (Prospectus Objective)	RATINGS Overall Rating	Reward Rating	Risk Rating	Recent Up/ Downgrade	Open to New Investors	MINIMUMS Min Initial Investment
Franklin Balanced Fund Advisor Class	FBFZX	NAS CM	Open End	Moderate Alloc (Balanced)	B-	C+	B	Up	Y	100,000
Franklin Balanced Fund Class A	FBLAX	NAS CM	Open End	Moderate Alloc (Balanced)	B-	C+	B	Up	Y	1,000
Franklin Balanced Fund Class C	FBMCX	NAS CM	Open End	Moderate Alloc (Balanced)	B-	C+	B	Down	Y	1,000
Franklin Balanced Fund Class R	US3536126663		Open End	Moderate Alloc (Balanced)	B-	C+	B+	Down	Y	1,000
Franklin Balanced Fund Class R6	FBFRX	NAS CM	Open End	Moderate Alloc (Balanced)	B-	C+	B	Up	Y	1,000,000
Franklin Biotechnology Discovery Fund Advisor Class	FTDZX	NAS CM	Open End	Healthcare Sector Equity (Health)	C	C-	C			100,000
Franklin Biotechnology Discovery Fund Class A	FBDIX	NAS CM	Open End	Healthcare Sector Equity (Health)	C	C-	C			1,000
Franklin Biotechnology Discovery Fund Class C	FBTDX	NAS CM	Open End	Healthcare Sector Equity (Health)	C	C-	C			1,000
Franklin Biotechnology Discovery Fund Class R6	FRBRX	NAS CM	Open End	Healthcare Sector Equity (Health)	C	C-	C			1,000,000
Franklin Conservative Allocation Fund Advisor Class	FTCZX	NAS CM	Open End	Cautious Alloc (Asset Alloc)	B-	C+	B	Up	Y	0
Franklin Conservative Allocation Fund Class A	FTCIX	NAS CM	Open End	Cautious Alloc (Asset Alloc)	B-	C+	B	Up	Y	1,000
Franklin Conservative Allocation Fund Class C	FTCCX	NAS CM	Open End	Cautious Alloc (Asset Alloc)	C+	C	B	Up	Y	1,000
Franklin Conservative Allocation Fund Class R	FTCRX	NAS CM	Open End	Cautious Alloc (Asset Alloc)	C+	C+	B	Up	Y	1,000
Franklin Conservative Allocation Fund Class R6	US35472P4303		Open End	Cautious Alloc (Asset Alloc)	B-	C+	B	Up	Y	1,000,000
Franklin Convertible Securities Fund Advisor Class	FCSZX	NAS CM	Open End	Convertibles (Convertible Bond)	B	B-	B+	Up	Y	100,000
Franklin Convertible Securities Fund Class A	FISCX	NAS CM	Open End	Convertibles (Convertible Bond)	B	B-	B+	Up	Y	1,000
Franklin Convertible Securities Fund Class C	FROTX	NAS CM	Open End	Convertibles (Convertible Bond)	B	B-	B+	Up	Y	1,000
Franklin Convertible Securities Fund Class R6	FCSKX	NAS CM	Open End	Convertibles (Convertible Bond)	B	B-	B+	Up	Y	1,000,000
Franklin Corefolio Allocation Fund Advisor Class	FCAZX	NAS CM	Open End	Aggressive Alloc (Growth)	B-	B-	B-	Down	Y	0
Franklin Corefolio Allocation Fund Class A	FTCOX	NAS CM	Open End	Aggressive Alloc (Growth)	B-	B-	B-	Down	Y	1,000
Franklin Corefolio Allocation Fund Class C	FTCLX	NAS CM	Open End	Aggressive Alloc (Growth)	B-	B-	B-	Down	Y	1,000
Franklin Corefolio Allocation Fund Class R	US35472P7520		Open End	Aggressive Alloc (Growth)	B-	B-	B-	Down	Y	1,000
Franklin Corefolio Allocation Fund Class R6	FTLQX	NAS CM	Open End	Aggressive Alloc (Growth)	B-	B-	B-		Y	0
Franklin DynaTech Fund Advisor Class	FDYZX	NAS CM	Open End	US Equity Large Cap Growth (Technology)	A-	A	B+	Up	Y	100,000
Franklin DynaTech Fund Class A	FKDNX	NAS CM	Open End	US Equity Large Cap Growth (Technology)	A-	A	B+	Up	Y	1,000
Franklin DynaTech Fund Class C	FDYNX	NAS CM	Open End	US Equity Large Cap Growth (Technology)	A-	A	B+	Up	Y	1,000
Franklin DynaTech Fund Class R	FDNRX	NAS CM	Open End	US Equity Large Cap Growth (Technology)	A-	A	B+	Up	Y	1,000
Franklin DynaTech Fund Class R6	FDTRX	NAS CM	Open End	US Equity Large Cap Growth (Technology)	A-	A	B+	Up	Y	1,000,000
Franklin Equity Income Fund Advisor Class	FEIFX	NAS CM	Open End	US Equity Large Cap Value (Equity-Income)	B-	B-	B	Down	Y	100,000
Franklin Equity Income Fund Class A	FISEX	NAS CM	Open End	US Equity Large Cap Value (Equity-Income)	B-	B-	B	Down	Y	1,000
Franklin Equity Income Fund Class C	FRETX	NAS CM	Open End	US Equity Large Cap Value (Equity-Income)	B-	B-	B	Down	Y	1,000
Franklin Equity Income Fund Class R	FREIX	NAS CM	Open End	US Equity Large Cap Value (Equity-Income)	B-	B-	B	Down	Y	1,000
Franklin Equity Income Fund Class R6	FEIQX	NAS CM	Open End	US Equity Large Cap Value (Equity-Income)	B-	B-	B	Down	Y	1,000,000
Franklin Focused Core Equity Fund Class A	FCEQX	NAS CM	Open End	US Equity Large Cap Blend (Growth)	B-	C+	B	Up	Y	1,000
Franklin Focused Core Equity Fund Class Adv	FCEZX	NAS CM	Open End	US Equity Large Cap Blend (Growth)	B-	C+	B	Up	Y	100,000
Franklin Focused Core Equity Fund Class C	FCEDX	NAS CM	Open End	US Equity Large Cap Blend (Growth)	C+	C+	B	Down	Y	1,000
Franklin Focused Core Equity Fund Class R	FCERX	NAS CM	Open End	US Equity Large Cap Blend (Growth)	B-	C+	B	Up	Y	1,000
Franklin Focused Core Equity Fund Class R6	FEFCX	NAS CM	Open End	US Equity Large Cap Blend (Growth)	B-	C+	B	Up	Y	1,000,000
Franklin Founding Funds Allocation Fund Advisor Class	FFAAX	NAS CM	Open End	Aggressive Alloc (Asset Alloc)	C+	C+	C+	Down	Y	0
Franklin Founding Funds Allocation Fund Class A	FFALX	NAS CM	Open End	Aggressive Alloc (Asset Alloc)	B-	C+	B-	Up	Y	1,000
Franklin Founding Funds Allocation Fund Class C	FFACX	NAS CM	Open End	Aggressive Alloc (Asset Alloc)	C+	C+	B-	Down	Y	1,000
Franklin Founding Funds Allocation Fund Class R	FFARX	NAS CM	Open End	Aggressive Alloc (Asset Alloc)	C+	C+	C+	Down	Y	1,000
Franklin Founding Funds Allocation Fund Class R6	FFAQX	NAS CM	Open End	Aggressive Alloc (Asset Alloc)	B-	C+	B		Y	0
Franklin Global Listed Infrastructure Fund Advisor Class	FLGZX	NAS CM	Open End	Other Sector Equity (World Stock)	B-	B-	C+		Y	100,000
Franklin Global Listed Infrastructure Fund Class A	FLGIX	NAS CM	Open End	Other Sector Equity (World Stock)	B-	B-	C+	Up	Y	1,000
Franklin Global Listed Infrastructure Fund Class C	US3535336156		Open End	Other Sector Equity (World Stock)	C+	B-	C+	Down	Y	1,000
Franklin Global Listed Infrastructure Fund Class R	US3535335992		Open End	Other Sector Equity (World Stock)	B-	B-	C+	Up	Y	1,000
Franklin Global Listed Infrastructure Fund Class R6	US3535335810		Open End	Other Sector Equity (World Stock)	B-	B-	B-		Y	1,000,000
Franklin Global Real Estate Fund Advisor Class	FVGRX	NAS CM	Open End	Real Estate Sector Equity (Real Estate)	B-	C+	B	Up	Y	100,000
Franklin Global Real Estate Fund Class A	FGRRX	NAS CM	Open End	Real Estate Sector Equity (Real Estate)	B-	C	B	Up	Y	1,000
Franklin Global Real Estate Fund Class C	FCGRX	NAS CM	Open End	Real Estate Sector Equity (Real Estate)	C+	C	B	Up	Y	1,000
Franklin Global Real Estate Fund Class R6	FGGRX	NAS CM	Open End	Real Estate Sector Equity (Real Estate)	B-	C+	B	Up	Y	1,000,000

★Expanded analysis of this fund is included in Section II.

	TOTAL RETURNS					PERFORMANCE				ASSETS		ASSET ALLOCATION & TURNOVER					BULL & BEAR		FEES		
Min Additional Investment	3-Month Total Return	6-Month Total Return	1-Year Total Return	3-Year Total Return	5-Year Total Return	Dividend Yield (TTM)	Expense Ratio	3-Yr Std Deviation	3-Year Beta	NAV	Total Assets (MIL)	%Cash	%Stocks	%Bonds	%Other	Turnover Ratio	Last Bull Market Total Return	Last Bear Market Total Return	Front End Fee (%)	Back End Fee (%)	Inception Date
	2.79	6.46	9.84	19.49	48.07	3.08	0.77	6.81	0.63	12.37	3,540	6	54	32	0	46	17.01	-10.75			Jul-06
	2.65	6.26	9.51	18.52	45.91	2.86	1.02	6.82	0.63	12.34	3,540	6	54	32	0	46	16.72	-10.79	5.75		Jul-06
	2.49	5.92	8.78	15.91	40.81	2.17	1.77	6.82	0.63	12.23	3,540	6	54	32	0	46	16.39	-11.14		1.00	Jul-06
	2.58	6.11	9.30	17.63	44.30	2.61	1.27	6.79	0.63	12.37	3,540	6	54	32	0	46	16.68	-10.95			Jul-06
	2.81	6.51	9.95	19.73	48.92	3.18	0.67	6.82	0.63	12.37	3,529	6	54	32	0	46	17.01	-10.75			May-13
	-5.49	3.33	19.10	4.62	140.96	1.33	0.79	25.36	1.06	153.75	1,374	2	97	0	0	34	34.31	-15.49			Sep-09
	-5.55	3.20	18.80	3.86	137.82	1.13	1.04	25.35	1.06	150.37	1,374	2	97	0	0	34	34.08	-15.59	5.75		Sep-97
	-5.73	2.81	17.91	1.58	129.16	0.87	1.79	25.34	1.05	146.21	1,374	2	97	0	0	34	33.5	-15.85		1.00	Mar-14
	-5.42	3.44	19.31	5.13	142.47	1.46	0.63	25.36	1.06	154.83	1,374	2	97	0	0	34	34.08	-15.59			May-13
	1.87	4.63	10.87	13.50	31.26	1.39	0.99	5.4	0.5	14.86	1,380	9	41	47	3	35	9.18	-8.27			Dec-05
	1.80	4.48	10.58	12.59	29.55	1.13	1.24	5.37	0.49	14.86	1,380	9	41	47	3	35	8.96	-8.38	5.75		Dec-96
	1.61	4.07	9.80	10.10	24.78	0.42	1.98	5.35	0.49	14.57	1,380	9	41	47	3	35	8.55	-8.65		1.00	Dec-96
	1.71	4.34	10.25	11.69	27.92	0.9	1.49	5.36	0.49	14.8	1,380	9	41	47	3	35	8.87	-8.52			Jan-02
	1.91	4.62	10.99	13.71	31.62	1.47	0.89	5.36	0.49	14.84	1,380	9	41	47	3	35	8.96	-8.38			May-13
	2.06	6.61	18.23	28.46	68.29	2.45	0.61	7.81	0.95	19.48	2,694	4	5	1	0	28	14.92	-18.31			May-08
	2.03	6.51	17.93	27.54	66.24	2.22	0.86	7.79	0.94	19.49	2,694	4	5	1	0	28	14.77	-18.37	5.75		Apr-87
	1.85	6.08	17.07	24.73	60.15	1.57	1.61	7.79	0.95	19.21	2,694	4	5	1	0	28	14.19	-18.65		1.00	Oct-95
	2.14	6.69	18.31	28.93	68.60	2.53	0.5	7.79	0.95	19.59	2,694	4	5	1	0	28	14.77	-18.37			Mar-14
	4.16	8.01	20.40	27.82	82.94	1.06	0.79	10.44	0.98	19.71	781.0	3	94	1	2	0	22	-18.79			Aug-03
	4.12	7.87	20.06	26.85	80.53	0.84	1.04	10.44	0.98	19.68	781.0	3	94	1	2	0	21.81	-18.92	5.75		Aug-03
	3.89	7.46	19.19	24.04	74.03	0.22	1.79	10.44	0.99	19.43	781.0	3	94	1	2	0	21.38	-19.14		1.00	Aug-03
	4.04	7.73	19.78	25.95	78.51	0.64	1.29	10.44	0.99	19.68	781.0	3	94	1	2	0	21.64	-18.94			Aug-03
	4.25	8.10	20.49	27.92	83.09		0.66	10.44	0.98	19.7	781.0	3	94	1	2	0	22	-18.79			Aug-17
	5.52	13.58	39.67	53.03	136.26	0	0.66	13.28	1.13	67.2	4,467	2	98	0	0	20	25.88	-16.77			May-08
	5.44	13.44	39.30	51.86	133.26	0	0.91	13.27	1.13	65.39	4,467	2	98	0	0	20	25.66	-16.83	5.75		Jan-68
	5.26	13.01	38.27	48.49	124.70	0	1.66	13.26	1.12	55.15	4,467	2	98	0	0	20	25.11	-17.09		1.00	Sep-96
	5.39	13.29	38.96	50.73	130.40	0	1.16	13.27	1.13	63.67	4,467	2	98	0	0	20	25.5	-16.92			Dec-08
	5.57	13.68	39.88	53.79	137.71	0	0.49	13.28	1.13	67.75	4,467	2	98	0	0	20	25.66	-16.83			May-13
	5.60	10.07	16.25	28.34	85.91	2.43	0.63	9.12	0.89	25.17	2,157	5	87	1	2	50	21.33	-15.46			May-08
	5.49	9.89	15.95	27.36	83.57	2.2	0.88	9.14	0.89	25.13	2,157	5	87	1	2	50	21.18	-15.56	5.75		Mar-88
	5.27	9.49	15.07	24.55	76.81	1.55	1.63	9.11	0.89	24.95	2,157	5	87	1	2	50	20.64	-15.8		1.00	Oct-95
	5.41	9.79	15.68	26.46	81.26	2	1.12	9.11	0.89	25.13	2,157	5	87	1	2	50	20.93	-15.6			Aug-02
	5.62	10.12	16.41	28.86	86.79	2.52	0.5	9.13	0.89	25.17	2,189	5	87	1	2	50	21.18	-15.56			May-13
	4.19	6.17	12.06	14.46	85.66	0	1.25	12.31	1.09	16.16	97.8	0	99	0	1	17	23.47	-20.77	5.75		Dec-07
	4.32	6.28	12.40	15.35	88.23	0	1	12.34	1.09	16.4	97.8	0	99	0	1	17	23.73	-20.63			Dec-07
	4.07	5.80	11.26	11.96	79.35	0	2	12.27	1.08	15.31	97.8	0	99	0	1	17	23.22	-21		1.00	Dec-07
	4.18	6.12	11.92	13.88	84.03	0	1.42	12.34	1.09	15.95	97.8	0	99	0	1	17	23.56	-20.87			Dec-07
	4.30	6.39	12.50	15.84	89.38	0	0.84	12.33	1.09	16.46	97.8	0	99	0	1	17	23.73	-20.63			May-13
	1.98	4.57	11.57	18.68	54.30	3.09	0.75	9.76	0.88	14.63	4,731	5	74	15	4	0	17.19	-17.38			Aug-03
	1.85	4.38	11.20	17.72	52.35	2.86	1	9.75	0.88	14.54	4,731	5	74	15	4	0	16.91	-17.42	5.75		Aug-03
	1.74	4.09	10.43	15.15	46.87	2.18	1.75	9.71	0.88	14.33	4,731	5	74	15	4	0	16.36	-17.66		1.00	Aug-03
	1.82	4.28	10.96	16.88	50.47	2.55	1.25	9.71	0.88	14.58	4,731	5	74	15	4	0	16.88	-17.59			Aug-03
	1.99	4.58	11.58	18.69	54.32		0.64	9.76	0.88	14.63	4,731	5	74	15	4	0	17.19	-17.38			Aug-17
	2.75	5.85	23.59	22.10		1.69	1.15	11.08	1.04	13.87	67.7	0	99	0	1	72					Sep-13
	2.74	5.81	23.25	21.11		1.46	1.4	11.04	1.04	13.85	67.7	0	99	0	1	72			5.75		Sep-13
	2.52	5.40	22.35	18.50		0.89	2.15	11.08	1.04	13.77	67.7	0	99	0	1	72				1.00	Sep-13
	2.66	5.65	23.00	20.33		1.27	1.65	11.05	1.04	13.84	67.7	0	99	0	1	72					Sep-13
	2.84	6.04	23.87	22.71		1.8	0.98	11.06	1.04	13.88	67.7	0	99	0	1	72					Sep-13
	3.64	5.15	10.74	11.37	33.84	1.77	1.15	11	0.99	9.34	147.7	1	98	0	1	28	23.76	-18.85			Jun-06
	3.60	5.00	10.48	10.49	31.92	1.67	1.4	11.04	1	9.31	147.7	1	98	0	1	28	23.67	-19.03	5.75		Jun-06
	3.38	4.56	9.57	8.11	27.23	1.39	2.15	11.09	1	9.16	147.7	1	98	0	1	28	23.1	-19.29		1.00	Jun-06
	3.69	5.19	10.92	11.90	34.69	1.84	1.01	11	0.99	9.33	147.7	1	98	0	1	28	23.75	-18.85			May-13

	MARKET			FUND TYPE, CATEGORY & OBJECTIVE	RATINGS				MINIMUMS	
Fund Name	Ticker Symbol	Traded On	Fund Type	Category and (Prospectus Objective)	Overall Rating	Reward Rating	Risk Rating	Recent Up/ Downgrade	Open to New Investors	Min Initial Investment
Franklin Gold and Precious Metals Fund Advisor Class	FGADX	NAS CM	Open End	Precious Metals Sector Equity (Precious Metals)	D+	C	D	Down	Y	100,000
Franklin Gold and Precious Metals Fund Class A	FKRCX	NAS CM	Open End	Precious Metals Sector Equity (Precious Metals)	D+	C	D	Down	Y	1,000
Franklin Gold and Precious Metals Fund Class C	FRGOX	NAS CM	Open End	Precious Metals Sector Equity (Precious Metals)	D+	C	D	Down	Y	1,000
Franklin Gold and Precious Metals Fund Class R6	FGPMX	NAS CM	Open End	Precious Metals Sector Equity (Precious Metals)	D+	C	D	Down	Y	1,000,000
Franklin Growth Allocation Fund Advisor Class	FGTZX	NAS CM	Open End	Aggressive Alloc (Asset Alloc)	B-	B-	B-	Down	Y	0
Franklin Growth Allocation Fund Class A	FGTIX	NAS CM	Open End	Aggressive Alloc (Asset Alloc)	B-	C+	B-	Down	Y	1,000
Franklin Growth Allocation Fund Class C	FTGTX	NAS CM	Open End	Aggressive Alloc (Asset Alloc)	B-	C+	B-	Down	Y	1,000
Franklin Growth Allocation Fund Class R	FGTRX	NAS CM	Open End	Aggressive Alloc (Asset Alloc)	B-	C+	B-	Down	Y	1,000
Franklin Growth Allocation Fund Class R6	US35472P4147		Open End	Aggressive Alloc (Asset Alloc)	B-	B-	B-	Down	Y	1,000,000
Franklin Growth Fund Advisor Class	FCGAX	NAS CM	Open End	US Equity Large Cap Growth (Growth)	B	B	B	Down	Y	100,000
Franklin Growth Opportunities Fund Advisor Class	FRAAX	NAS CM	Open End	US Equity Large Cap Growth (Aggr Growth)	B	B	B+	Up	Y	100,000
Franklin Growth Opportunities Fund Class A	FGRAX	NAS CM	Open End	US Equity Large Cap Growth (Aggr Growth)	B	B	B+	Up	Y	1,000
Franklin Growth Opportunities Fund Class C	FKACX	NAS CM	Open End	US Equity Large Cap Growth (Aggr Growth)	B	B	B	Up	Y	1,000
Franklin Growth Opportunities Fund Class R	FKARX	NAS CM	Open End	US Equity Large Cap Growth (Aggr Growth)	B	B	B+	Up	Y	1,000
Franklin Growth Opportunities Fund Class R6	FOPPX	NAS CM	Open End	US Equity Large Cap Growth (Aggr Growth)	B	B	B+	Up	Y	1,000,000
Franklin Growth Series Class A	FKGRX	NAS CM	Open End	US Equity Large Cap Growth (Growth)	B	B	B	Down	Y	1,000
Franklin Growth Series Class C	FRGSX	NAS CM	Open End	US Equity Large Cap Growth (Growth)	B	B	B	Down	Y	1,000
Franklin Growth Series Class R	FGSRX	NAS CM	Open End	US Equity Large Cap Growth (Growth)	B	B	B	Down	Y	1,000
Franklin Growth Series Class R6	FIFRX	NAS CM	Open End	US Equity Large Cap Growth (Growth)	B	B	B	Down	Y	1,000,000
Franklin Income Fund Advisor Class	FRIAX	NAS CM	Open End	Cautious Alloc (Balanced)	C+	C+	C+	Down	Y	100,000
Franklin Income Fund Class A	FKINX	NAS CM	Open End	Cautious Alloc (Balanced)	C+	C+	C+	Down	Y	1,000
Franklin Income Fund Class R6	FNCFX	NAS CM	Open End	Cautious Alloc (Balanced)	C+	C+	C+		Y	1,000,000
Franklin Income Series Class C	FCISX	NAS CM	Open End	Cautious Alloc (Balanced)	C+	C+	C+		Y	1,000
Franklin Income Series Class R	FISRX	NAS CM	Open End	Cautious Alloc (Balanced)	C+	C+	C+		Y	1,000
Franklin India Growth Fund Advisor Class	FIGZX	NAS CM	Open End	India Equity (Foreign Stock)	B	B	B-	Up	Y	100,000
Franklin India Growth Fund Class A	FINGX	NAS CM	Open End	India Equity (Foreign Stock)	B	B	B-	Up	Y	1,000
Franklin India Growth Fund Class C	FINDX	NAS CM	Open End	India Equity (Foreign Stock)	B-	B	B-	Down	Y	1,000
Franklin India Growth Fund Class R6	US35361F7336		Open End	India Equity (Foreign Stock)	B	B	B-	Up	Y	1,000,000
Franklin International Growth Fund Class A	FNGAX	NAS CM	Open End	Global Equity Large Cap (Foreign Stock)	B+	A-	B	Up	Y	1,000
Franklin International Growth Fund Class Adv	FNGZX	NAS CM	Open End	Global Equity Large Cap (Foreign Stock)	B+	A-	B	Up	Y	100,000
Franklin International Growth Fund Class C	US3535337220		Open End	Global Equity Large Cap (Foreign Stock)	B	B+	B	Up	Y	1,000
Franklin International Growth Fund Class R	US3535337147		Open End	Global Equity Large Cap (Foreign Stock)	B+	A-	B	Up	Y	1,000
Franklin International Growth Fund Class R6	FILRX	NAS CM	Open End	Global Equity Large Cap (Foreign Stock)	B+	A-	B	Up	Y	1,000,000
Franklin International Small Cap Growth Fund Advisor Class	FKSCX	NAS CM	Open End	Global Equity Mid/Small Cap (Small Company)	B+	B+	B	Up		100,000
Franklin International Small Cap Growth Fund Class A	FINAX	NAS CM	Open End	Global Equity Mid/Small Cap (Small Company)	B+	B+	B	Up		1,000
Franklin International Small Cap Growth Fund Class C	FCSMX	NAS CM	Open End	Global Equity Mid/Small Cap (Small Company)	B	B+	B	Up		1,000
Franklin International Small Cap Growth Fund Class R	FISDX	NAS CM	Open End	Global Equity Mid/Small Cap (Small Company)	B+	B+	B	Up		1,000
Franklin International Small Cap Growth Fund Class R6	FCAPX	NAS CM	Open End	Global Equity Mid/Small Cap (Small Company)	B+	B+	B	Up		1,000,000
Franklin K2 Alternative Strategies Fund Advisor Class	FABZX	NAS CM	Open End	Multialternative (Growth)	C+	C	B	Up	Y	100,000
Franklin K2 Alternative Strategies Fund Class A	FAAAX	NAS CM	Open End	Multialternative (Growth)	C+	C	B	Up	Y	1,000
Franklin K2 Alternative Strategies Fund Class C	FASCX	NAS CM	Open End	Multialternative (Growth)	C+	C	B		Y	1,000
Franklin K2 Alternative Strategies Fund Class R	FSKKX	NAS CM	Open End	Multialternative (Growth)	C+	C	B	Up	Y	1,000
Franklin K2 Alternative Strategies Fund Class R6	FASRX	NAS CM	Open End	Multialternative (Growth)	C+	C	B	Up	Y	1,000,000
Franklin K2 Global Macro Opportunities Fund Advisor Class	FKMZX	NAS CM	Open End	Multialternative (Growth)	D	D	C-		Y	100,000
Franklin K2 Global Macro Opportunities Fund Class A	FKMAX	NAS CM	Open End	Multialternative (Growth)	D	D	C-		Y	1,000
Franklin K2 Global Macro Opportunities Fund Class C	FKMDX	NAS CM	Open End	Multialternative (Growth)	D	D	C-		Y	1,000
Franklin K2 Global Macro Opportunities Fund Class R	FKMRX	NAS CM	Open End	Multialternative (Growth)	D	D	C-		Y	1,000
Franklin K2 Global Macro Opportunities Fund Class R6	FKMQX	NAS CM	Open End	Multialternative (Growth)	D	D	C-		Y	1,000,000
Franklin K2 Long Short Credit Fund Advisor Class	FKLZX	NAS CM	Open End	Other Alternative (Income)	C	C	B+	Up	Y	100,000
Franklin K2 Long Short Credit Fund Class A	FKLSX	NAS CM	Open End	Other Alternative (Income)	C	C	B+	Up	Y	1,000
Franklin K2 Long Short Credit Fund Class C	FKLCX	NAS CM	Open End	Other Alternative (Income)	C	C	B+	Up	Y	1,000
Franklin K2 Long Short Credit Fund Class R	FKLRX	NAS CM	Open End	Other Alternative (Income)	C	C	B+	Up	Y	1,000

★Expanded analysis of this fund is included in Section II.

	TOTAL RETURNS					PERFORMANCE				ASSETS		ASSET ALLOCATION & TURNOVER					BULL & BEAR		FEES		
Min Additional Investment	3-Month Total Return	6-Month Total Return	1-Year Total Return	3-Year Total Return	5-Year Total Return	Dividend Yield (TTM)	Expense Ratio	3-Yr Std Deviation	3-Year Beta	NAV	Total Assets (MIL)	%Cash	%Stocks	%Bonds	%Other	Turnover Ratio	Last Bull Market Total Return	Last Bear Market Total Return	Front End Fee (%)	Back End Fee (%)	Inception Date
	1.08	-3.86	0.05	22.09	-41.41	8.95	0.73	37.16	0.85	16.6	961.3	3	96	0	1	14	-11.69	-21.06			Dec-96
	1.03	-3.96	-0.12	21.18	-42.13	9.34	0.98	37.16	0.85	15.68	961.3	3	96	0	1	14	-11.8	-21.14	5.75		May-69
	0.76	-4.35	-0.95	18.45	-44.26	9.35	1.73	37.13	0.85	14.49	961.3	3	96	0	1	14	-12.2	-21.37		1.00	May-95
	1.11	-3.73	0.33	23.13	-40.64	9.14	0.55	37.19	0.85	16.72	961.3	3	96	0	1	14	-11.8	-21.14			May-13
	3.89	8.48	19.76	24.10	60.84	1.32	1.07	8.21	0.76	19.42	1,334	6	80	12	2	30	15.13	-15			Dec-05
	3.82	8.32	19.44	23.17	58.85	1.11	1.32	8.18	0.76	19.34	1,334	6	80	12	2	30	14.97	-15.05	5.75		Dec-96
	3.60	7.95	18.55	20.40	52.95	0.5	2.06	8.2	0.76	18.81	1,334	6	80	12	2	30	14.42	-15.31		1.00	Dec-96
	3.73	8.23	19.16	22.24	56.84	0.87	1.57	8.22	0.76	19.1	1,334	6	80	12	2	30	14.75	-15.1			Jan-02
	3.89	8.53	19.89	24.60	61.64	1.45	0.92	8.23	0.76	19.4	1,334	6	80	12	2	30	14.97	-15.05			May-13
	6.10	11.74	27.13	39.97	114.02	0.61	0.63	9.79	0.93	94.65	14,695	2	98	0	0	6	24.31	-15.87			Dec-96
	5.48	10.97	29.02	32.33	105.52	0	0.79	12.11	1.04	38.84	3,750	0	99	0	1	48	27.59	-19.9			Jun-99
	5.40	10.80	28.67	31.24	102.67	0	1.04	12.1	1.04	36.27	3,750	0	99	0	1	48	27.33	-19.97	5.75		Jun-99
	5.21	10.38	27.70	28.34	95.39	0	1.79	12.1	1.04	30.79	3,750	0	99	0	1	48	26.83	-20.17		1.00	Jun-99
	5.34	10.66	28.36	30.32	100.41	0	1.29	12.1	1.04	34.75	3,750	0	99	0	1	48	27.21	-20.03			Jan-02
	5.56	11.09	29.26	33.08	107.28	0	0.58	12.12	1.05	39.23	3,750	0	99	0	1	48	27.59	-19.9			May-13
	6.04	11.61	26.82	38.92	111.37	0.4	0.88	9.78	0.93	94.51	14,695	2	98	0	0	6	24.16	-15.97	5.75		Apr-48
	5.85	11.19	25.88	35.82	103.57	0	1.63	9.78	0.93	86.91	14,695	2	98	0	0	6	23.6	-16.24		1.00	May-95
	5.98	11.46	26.49	37.87	108.73	0.21	1.13	9.78	0.93	94.17	14,695	2	98	0	0	6	23.96	-16.06			Jan-02
	6.16	11.85	27.35	40.66	115.51	0.72	0.46	9.79	0.93	94.54	14,695	2	98	0	0	6	24.16	-15.97			May-13
	0.88	4.42	8.61	15.86	40.19	5.22	0.46	8.32	0.7	2.36	82,341	6	45	39	1	34	13.7	-11.64			Dec-96
	0.84	4.31	8.41	15.73	38.84	5.06	0.61	8.42	0.7	2.38	82,341	6	45	39	1	34	14.05	-11.64	4.25		Aug-48
	0.90	4.45	8.67	16.09	39.85	5.27	0.38	8.32	0.7	2.36	82,341	6	45	39	1	34	14.04	-11.64			May-13
	0.70	3.99	8.21	13.78	35.46	4.5	1.11	8.18	0.68	2.41	82,341	6	45	39	1	34	13.6	-11.73		1.00	May-95
	0.77	4.21	8.17	14.31	36.53	4.79	0.96	8.39	0.7	2.34	82,341	6	45	39	1	34	13.44	-11.48			Jan-02
	11.26	11.48	36.49	34.53	84.64	0	1.4	16.48	0.9	16.39	156.5	0	3	0	96	22	-2.06	-18.36			Jan-08
	11.13	11.28	36.17	33.52	81.99	0	1.65	16.51	0.9	15.97	156.5	0	3	0	96	22	-2.08	-18.51	5.75		Jan-08
	10.86	10.86	35.11	30.52	75.46	0	2.4	16.46	0.9	14.91	156.5	0	3	0	96	22	-2.48	-18.71		1.00	Jan-08
	11.46	11.75	36.98	35.35	86.27	0	1.19	16.5	0.9	16.52	156.5	0	3	0	96	22	-2.06	-18.36			May-13
	6.19	15.65	36.80	38.46	47.79	0.4	1.26	12.69	0.97	14.47	307.2	3	95	0	0	29	20.88	-25.04	5.75		Jun-08
	6.23	15.82	37.03	39.55	49.91	0.67	1.01	12.74	0.97	14.47	307.2	3	95	0	0	29	21.13	-24.97			Jun-08
	5.93	15.22	35.71	35.45	42.48	0	2.01	12.69	0.97	14	307.2	3	95	0	0	29	20.34	-25.23		1.00	Jun-08
	6.09	15.56	36.37	37.50	46.19	0.08	1.51	12.68	0.97	14.4	307.2	3	95	0	0	29	20.66	-25.09			Jun-08
	6.23	15.91	37.24	40.36	50.92	0.89	0.78	12.7	0.97	14.47	307.2	3	95	0	0	29	21.13	-24.97			May-13
	1.72	10.64	34.49	39.18	70.89	0.94	1.14	12.64	0.93	20.17	1,480	1	91	0	8	22	14.21	-20.17			Oct-02
	1.67	10.45	34.16	38.20	68.78	0.76	1.38	12.63	0.93	20.14	1,480	1	91	0	8	22	14.02	-20.32	5.75		May-08
	1.48	10.04	33.19	35.03	62.62	0.1	2.14	12.64	0.93	19.96	1,480	1	91	0	8	22	13.53	-20.52		1.00	May-08
	1.63	10.34	33.89	37.14	66.65	0.5	1.64	12.64	0.93	20.22	1,480	1	91	0	8	22	13.85	-20.34			May-08
	1.75	10.62	34.61	39.75	71.97	1.13	0.99	12.65	0.93	20.15	1,480	1	91	0	8	22	14.21	-20.17			May-13
	2.01	2.74	6.84	8.98		0.73	1.98	3.51	0.88	11.33	1,083	33	22	29	3	209					Oct-13
	1.92	2.56	6.57	8.13		0.43	2.23	3.5	0.88	11.32	1,083	33	22	29	3	209			5.75		Oct-13
	1.71	2.17	5.71	5.82		0	2.98	3.53	0.88	11.22	1,083	33	22	29	3	209				1.00	Oct-13
	1.82	2.37	6.16	6.85		0.46	2.48	3.65	0.9	11.36	1,083	33	22	29	3	209					Oct-13
	1.91	2.73	6.83	9.23		0.82	1.88	3.43	0.87	11.33	1,083	33	22	29	3	209					Oct-13
	1.86	1.53	-2.00			0.64	2.01			9.28	23.4	54	26	19	0	240					Jul-16
	1.75	1.42	-2.21			0.63	2.26			9.26	23.4	54	26	19	0	240			5.75		Jul-16
	1.55	0.99	-2.96			0.48	3.01			9.16	23.4	54	26	19	0	240				1.00	Jul-16
	1.76	1.42	-2.21			0.64	2.51			9.25	23.4	54	26	19	0	240					Jul-16
	1.86	1.53	-2.00			0.65	2.01			9.28	23.4	54	26	19	0	240					Jul-16
	1.41	2.47	4.96			2.94	1.98			10.42	85.4	15	1	81	1	318					Sep-15
	1.39	2.45	4.84			2.93	2.23			10.42	85.4	15	1	81	1	318			5.75		Sep-15
	1.22	2.10	3.90			2.64	2.98			10.3	85.4	15	1	81	1	318				1.00	Sep-15
	1.32	2.29	4.49			2.93	2.48			10.34	85.4	15	1	81	1	318					Sep-15

	MARKET		FUND TYPE, CATEGORY & OBJECTIVE		RATINGS					MINIMUMS
Fund Name	Ticker Symbol	Traded On	Fund Type	Category and (Prospectus Objective)	Overall Rating	Reward Rating	Risk Rating	Recent Up/ Downgrade	Open to New Investors	Min Initial Investment
Franklin K2 Long Short Credit Fund Class R6	FKLQX	NAS CM	Open End	Other Alternative (Income)	C	C	B+	Up	Y	1,000,000
Franklin LifeSmart™ 2020 Retmnt Target Fund Adv Cls	FLROX	NAS CM	Open End	Target Date 2000-2020 (Asset Alloc)	C+	C+	B	Up	Y	100,000
Franklin LifeSmart™ 2020 Retirement Target Fund Class A	FLRMX	NAS CM	Open End	Target Date 2000-2020 (Asset Alloc)	C+	C+	B	Up	Y	1,000
Franklin LifeSmart™ 2020 Retirement Target Fund Class C	FLRQX	NAS CM	Open End	Target Date 2000-2020 (Asset Alloc)	C+	C	B-	Up	Y	1,000
Franklin LifeSmart™ 2020 Retirement Target Fund Class R	FLRVX	NAS CM	Open End	Target Date 2000-2020 (Asset Alloc)	C+	C+	B-	Up	Y	1,000
Franklin LifeSmart™ 2020 Retirement Target Fund Class R6	FRTSX	NAS CM	Open End	Target Date 2000-2020 (Asset Alloc)	C+	C+	B	Up	Y	1,000,000
Franklin LifeSmart™ 2025 Retmnt Target Fund Adv Cls	FLRFX	NAS CM	Open End	Target Date 2021-2045 (Asset Alloc)	B-	C+	B-	Down	Y	100,000
Franklin LifeSmart™ 2025 Retirement Target Fund Class A	FTRTX	NAS CM	Open End	Target Date 2021-2045 (Asset Alloc)	C+	C+	B-	Down	Y	1,000
Franklin LifeSmart™ 2025 Retirement Target Fund Class C	FTTCX	NAS CM	Open End	Target Date 2021-2045 (Asset Alloc)	B-	C+	B	Up	Y	1,000
Franklin LifeSmart™ 2025 Retirement Target Fund Class R	FRELX	NAS CM	Open End	Target Date 2021-2045 (Asset Alloc)	C+	C+	B-	Down	Y	1,000
Franklin LifeSmart™ 2025 Retirement Target Fund Class R6	FTLMX	NAS CM	Open End	Target Date 2021-2045 (Asset Alloc)	B-	C+	B-	Down	Y	1,000,000
Franklin LifeSmart™ 2030 Retmnt Target Fund Adv Cls	FLRZX	NAS CM	Open End	Target Date 2021-2045 (Asset Alloc)	B	C+	B+	Up	Y	100,000
Franklin LifeSmart™ 2030 Retirement Target Fund Class A	FLRSX	NAS CM	Open End	Target Date 2021-2045 (Asset Alloc)	B-	C+	B-	Down	Y	1,000
Franklin LifeSmart™ 2030 Retirement Target Fund Class C	FLRTX	NAS CM	Open End	Target Date 2021-2045 (Asset Alloc)	B-	C+	B	Up	Y	1,000
Franklin LifeSmart™ 2030 Retirement Target Fund Class R	FLRWX	NAS CM	Open End	Target Date 2021-2045 (Asset Alloc)	C+	C+	B-	Down	Y	1,000
Franklin LifeSmart™ 2030 Retirement Target Fund Class R6	FLERX	NAS CM	Open End	Target Date 2021-2045 (Asset Alloc)	B-	C+	B-	Down	Y	1,000,000
Franklin LifeSmart™ 2035 Retmnt Target Fund Adv Cls	FLRHX	NAS CM	Open End	Target Date 2021-2045 (Asset Alloc)	B-	C+	B-	Down	Y	100,000
Franklin LifeSmart™ 2035 Retirement Target Fund Class A	FRTAX	NAS CM	Open End	Target Date 2021-2045 (Asset Alloc)	B-	C+	B-	Up	Y	1,000
Franklin LifeSmart™ 2035 Retirement Target Fund Class C	FTRCX	NAS CM	Open End	Target Date 2021-2045 (Asset Alloc)	C+	C+	B-	Down	Y	1,000
Franklin LifeSmart™ 2035 Retirement Target Fund Class R	FLRGX	NAS CM	Open End	Target Date 2021-2045 (Asset Alloc)	B-	C+	B-	Up	Y	1,000
Franklin LifeSmart™ 2035 Retirement Target Fund Class R6	FMTLX	NAS CM	Open End	Target Date 2021-2045 (Asset Alloc)	B-	C+	B-	Down	Y	1,000,000
Franklin LifeSmart™ 2040 Retmnt Target Fund Adv Cls	FLSHX	NAS CM	Open End	Target Date 2021-2045 (Asset Alloc)	B	C+	B+	Up	Y	100,000
Franklin LifeSmart™ 2040 Retirement Target Fund Class A	FLADX	NAS CM	Open End	Target Date 2021-2045 (Asset Alloc)	B-	C+	B-	Up	Y	1,000
Franklin LifeSmart™ 2040 Retirement Target Fund Class C	FLOLX	NAS CM	Open End	Target Date 2021-2045 (Asset Alloc)	C+	C+	B-	Down	Y	1,000
Franklin LifeSmart™ 2040 Retirement Target Fund Class R	FLSGX	NAS CM	Open End	Target Date 2021-2045 (Asset Alloc)	C+	C+	B-	Down	Y	1,000
Franklin LifeSmart™ 2040 Retirement Target Fund Class R6	FLREX	NAS CM	Open End	Target Date 2021-2045 (Asset Alloc)	B	C+	B+	Up	Y	1,000,000
Franklin LifeSmart™ 2045 Retmnt Target Fund Adv Cls	FLRLX	NAS CM	Open End	Target Date 2021-2045 (Asset Alloc)	B-	C+	B-	Up	Y	100,000
Franklin LifeSmart™ 2045 Retirement Target Fund Class A	FTTAX	NAS CM	Open End	Target Date 2021-2045 (Asset Alloc)	B-	C+	B-	Up	Y	1,000
Franklin LifeSmart™ 2045 Retirement Target Fund Class C	FLRIX	NAS CM	Open End	Target Date 2021-2045 (Asset Alloc)	B-	C+	B	Up	Y	1,000
Franklin LifeSmart™ 2045 Retirement Target Fund Class R	FLRJX	NAS CM	Open End	Target Date 2021-2045 (Asset Alloc)	B-	C+	B-	Up	Y	1,000
Franklin LifeSmart™ 2045 Retirement Target Fund Class R6	FMLTX	NAS CM	Open End	Target Date 2021-2045 (Asset Alloc)	B-	C+	B-	Down	Y	1,000,000
Franklin LifeSmart™ 2050 Retmnt Target Fund Adv Cls	FLSOX	NAS CM	Open End	Target Date 2046+ (Asset Alloc)	B-	C+	B-	Down	Y	100,000
Franklin LifeSmart™ 2050 Retirement Target Fund Class A	FLSJX	NAS CM	Open End	Target Date 2046+ (Asset Alloc)	B-	C+	B-	Down	Y	1,000
Franklin LifeSmart™ 2050 Retirement Target Fund Class C	FLSKX	NAS CM	Open End	Target Date 2046+ (Asset Alloc)	C+	C+	B-	Down	Y	1,000
Franklin LifeSmart™ 2050 Retirement Target Fund Class R	FLSNX	NAS CM	Open End	Target Date 2046+ (Asset Alloc)	B-	C+	B-	Up	Y	1,000
Franklin LifeSmart™ 2050 Retirement Target Fund Class R6	FRLEX	NAS CM	Open End	Target Date 2046+ (Asset Alloc)	B-	C+	B-	Down	Y	1,000,000
Franklin LifeSmart™ 2055 Retmnt Target Fund Adv Cls	FLTKX	NAS CM	Open End	Target Date 2046+ (Asset Alloc)	B-	C+	B	Up	Y	100,000
Franklin LifeSmart™ 2055 Retirement Target Fund Class A	FLTFX	NAS CM	Open End	Target Date 2046+ (Asset Alloc)	C+	C+	B	Up	Y	1,000
Franklin LifeSmart™ 2055 Retirement Target Fund Class C	FLTNX	NAS CM	Open End	Target Date 2046+ (Asset Alloc)	C+	C+	B	Up	Y	1,000
Franklin LifeSmart™ 2055 Retirement Target Fund Class R	FLSBX	NAS CM	Open End	Target Date 2046+ (Asset Alloc)	B-	C+	B	Up	Y	1,000
Franklin LifeSmart™ 2055 Retirement Target Fund Class R6	FLSZX	NAS CM	Open End	Target Date 2046+ (Asset Alloc)	C+	C+	B	Up	Y	1,000,000
Franklin LifeSmart™ Retirement Income Fund Advisor Class	FLRDX	NAS CM	Open End	Target Date 2000-2020 (Asset Alloc)	C+	C	B	Down	Y	100,000
Franklin LifeSmart™ Retirement Income Fund Class A	FTRAX	NAS CM	Open End	Target Date 2000-2020 (Asset Alloc)	C+	C	B	Down	Y	1,000
Franklin LifeSmart™ Retirement Income Fund Class C	FRTCX	NAS CM	Open End	Target Date 2000-2020 (Asset Alloc)	C+	C	B	Down	Y	1,000
Franklin LifeSmart™ Retirement Income Fund Class R	FBRLX	NAS CM	Open End	Target Date 2000-2020 (Asset Alloc)	C+	C	B	Down	Y	1,000
Franklin LifeSmart™ Retirement Income Fund Class R6	FLMTX	NAS CM	Open End	Target Date 2000-2020 (Asset Alloc)	C+	C	B	Down	Y	1,000,000
Franklin MicroCap Value Fund Advisor Class	FVRMX	NAS CM	Open End	US Equity Small Cap (Growth & Income)	B	B	B-	Up		100,000
Franklin MicroCap Value Fund Class A	FRMCX	NAS CM	Open End	US Equity Small Cap (Growth & Income)	B	B	C+	Up		1,000
Franklin MicroCap Value Fund Class R6	FMCVX	NAS CM	Open End	US Equity Small Cap (Growth & Income)	B	B	B-	Up		1,000,000
Franklin Moderate Allocation Fund Advisor Class	FMTZX	NAS CM	Open End	Moderate Alloc (Asset Alloc)	B-	C+	B	Down	Y	0
Franklin Moderate Allocation Fund Class A	FMTIX	NAS CM	Open End	Moderate Alloc (Asset Alloc)	B-	C+	B	Down	Y	1,000
Franklin Moderate Allocation Fund Class C	FTMTX	NAS CM	Open End	Moderate Alloc (Asset Alloc)	B-	C+	B	Down	Y	1,000

★ Expanded analysis of this fund is included in Section II.

	TOTAL RETURNS					PERFORMANCE				ASSETS		ASSET ALLOCATION & TURNOVER					BULL & BEAR		FEES		
Min Additional Investment	3-Month Total Return	6-Month Total Return	1-Year Total Return	3-Year Total Return	5-Year Total Return	Dividend Yield (TTM)	Expense Ratio	3-Yr Std Deviation	3-Year Beta	NAV	Total Assets (MIL)	%Cash	%Stocks	%Bonds	%Other	Turnover Ratio	Last Bull Market Total Return	Last Bear Market Total Return	Front End Fee (%)	Back End Fee (%)	Inception Date
	1.42	2.58	4.97			2.95	1.97			10.42	85.4	15	1	81	1	318					Sep-15
	2.22	5.08	11.87	13.00		1.71	0.7	6.53	0.6	11.79	36.6	9	46	43	2	87					Jul-13
	2.15	4.95	11.52	12.10		1.48	0.95	6.53	0.6	11.76	36.6	9	46	43	2	87			5.75		Jul-13
	1.94	4.57	10.69	9.61		0.79	1.7	6.54	0.6	11.69	36.6	9	46	43	2	87				1.00	Jul-13
	2.16	4.81	11.25	11.22		1.14	1.2	6.56	0.6	11.75	36.6	9	46	43	2	87					Jul-13
	2.23	5.11	11.92	13.16		1.75	0.65	6.52	0.6	11.79	36.6	9	46	43	2	87					Jul-13
	3.06	6.67	15.29	16.38	48.96	1.63	0.72	7.49	0.69	13	129.3	7	61	30	2	84	14.09	-14.21			Aug-06
	2.99	6.50	14.95	15.42	46.84	1.4	0.97	7.46	0.68	12.97	129.3	7	61	30	2	84	13.92	-14.36	5.75		Aug-06
	2.82	6.17	14.06	12.92	41.66	0.71	1.72	7.5	0.69	12.77	129.3	7	61	30	2	84	13.46	-14.64		1.00	Aug-06
	3.00	6.44	14.73	14.71	45.41	1.1	1.22	7.46	0.69	12.93	129.3	7	61	30	2	84	13.79	-14.48			Aug-06
	3.07	6.71	15.33	16.53	49.27	1.68	0.67	7.48	0.69	13.01	129.3	7	61	30	2	84	14.09	-14.21			May-13
	3.47	7.47	16.97	18.39		2.1	0.74	7.98	0.73	12.73	45.7	7	69	22	2	82					Jul-13
	3.41	7.40	16.72	17.53		1.73	0.99	7.96	0.73	12.7	45.7	7	69	22	2	82			5.75		Jul-13
	3.23	7.00	15.89	15.01		0.74	1.74	8	0.74	12.56	45.7	7	69	22	2	82				1.00	Jul-13
	3.34	7.25	16.38	16.65		1.29	1.24	8.03	0.74	12.68	45.7	7	69	22	2	82					Jul-13
	3.48	7.51	17.01	18.61		2.17	0.69	7.98	0.73	12.74	45.7	7	69	22	2	82					Jul-13
	3.71	7.94	18.23	19.57	56.45	1.49	0.74	8.32	0.76	13.81	115.1	6	74	18	2	77	15.05	-15.26			Aug-06
	3.57	7.83	17.93	18.61	54.22	1.3	0.99	8.34	0.77	13.7	115.1	6	74	18	2	77	14.82	-15.34	5.75		Aug-06
	3.43	7.38	17.09	15.96	48.81	0.69	1.74	8.27	0.76	13.4	115.1	6	74	18	2	77	14.38	-15.66		1.00	Aug-06
	3.59	7.70	17.70	17.79	52.62	1.17	1.24	8.31	0.76	13.69	115.1	6	74	18	2	77	14.67	-15.52			Aug-06
	3.76	8.00	18.31	19.71	56.89	1.54	0.69	8.34	0.77	13.8	115.1	6	74	18	2	77	15.05	-15.26			May-13
	3.83	8.23	18.87	19.99		1.31	0.75	8.53	0.78	13.1	36.5	6	77	16	1	72					Jul-13
	3.76	8.10	18.50	18.95		1.26	1	8.51	0.78	13.03	36.5	6	77	16	1	72			5.75		Jul-13
	3.56	7.71	17.62	16.47		1.1	1.75	8.48	0.78	12.83	36.5	6	77	16	1	72				1.00	Jul-13
	3.80	7.99	18.30	18.34		1.21	1.25	8.52	0.78	13.02	36.5	6	77	16	1	72					Jul-13
	3.87	8.27	18.91	20.16		1.32	0.7	8.5	0.78	13.11	36.5	6	77	16	1	72					Jul-13
	3.87	8.34	19.03	20.38	58.69	1.46	0.76	8.54	0.78	13.88	79.3	6	78	15	1	76	15.24	-15.51			Aug-06
	3.81	8.23	18.71	19.40	56.65	1.29	1.01	8.56	0.79	13.78	79.3	6	78	15	1	76	15.01	-15.58	5.75		Aug-06
	3.65	7.78	17.92	16.82	51.09	0.69	1.76	8.54	0.78	13.44	79.3	6	78	15	1	76	14.53	-15.86		1.00	Aug-06
	3.74	8.10	18.43	18.54	54.87	1.11	1.26	8.55	0.79	13.72	79.3	6	78	15	1	76	14.73	-15.7			Aug-06
	3.93	8.39	19.10	20.58	59.18	1.52	0.71	8.54	0.78	13.88	79.3	6	78	15	1	76	15.24	-15.51			May-13
	3.97	8.42	19.19	21.08		1.43	0.75	8.6	0.79	13.26	30.9	6	78	14	1	90					Jul-13
	3.85	8.23	18.96	20.22		1.27	1	8.56	0.78	13.19	30.9	6	78	14	1	90			5.75		Jul-13
	3.70	7.87	18.02	17.53		0.72	1.75	8.57	0.79	13.11	30.9	6	78	14	1	90				1.00	Jul-13
	3.84	8.15	18.67	19.31		1.1	1.25	8.58	0.79	13.19	30.9	6	78	14	1	90					Jul-13
	3.93	8.46	19.35	21.25		1.47	0.7	8.59	0.79	13.26	30.9	6	78	14	1	90					Jul-13
	3.90	8.40	19.16			1.22	0.75			11.06	9.2	6	80	13	1	93					May-15
	3.99	8.40	19.05			1.05	1			11.05	9.2	6	80	13	1	93			5.75		May-15
	3.72	7.98	18.10			0.77	1.75			10.92	9.2	6	80	13	1	93				1.00	May-15
	3.82	8.14	18.68			0.99	1.25			11.01	9.2	6	80	13	1	93					May-15
	4.04	8.55	19.32			1.26	0.7			11.06	9.2	6	80	13	1	93					May-15
	0.49	1.91	5.08	8.07	26.91	4.1	0.6	5.15	0.45	11.09	59.3	5	18	64	3	150	10.99	-10.34			Aug-06
	0.43	1.87	4.83	7.29	25.22	3.86	0.85	5.17	0.45	11.05	59.3	5	18	64	3	150	10.86	-10.5	5.75		Aug-06
	0.24	1.50	4.07	4.96	20.82	3.13	1.59	5.11	0.45	10.92	59.3	5	18	64	3	150	10.38	-10.73		1.00	Aug-06
	0.27	1.65	4.57	6.41	23.72	3.61	1.1	5.13	0.45	11	59.3	5	18	64	3	150	10.67	-10.53			Aug-06
	0.51	1.93	5.14	8.24	27.21	4.15	0.55	5.14	0.45	11.1	59.3	5	18	64	3	150	10.99	-10.34			May-13
	4.48	11.50	8.48	29.53	74.43	0.47	0.95	14.81	0.94	34.15	345.2	3	97	0	0	12	19.05	-15.8			Nov-05
	4.39	11.35	8.22	28.57	72.31	0.27	1.19	14.82	0.94	33.98	345.2	3	97	0	0	12	18.86	-15.88	5.75		Dec-95
	4.49	11.57	8.60	30.08	75.35	0.58	0.81	14.81	0.94	34.29	345.2	3	97	0	0	12	18.86	-15.88			May-13
	2.85	6.55	15.19	18.86	43.79	1.37	1.02	6.73	0.62	16.12	2,173	7	61	29	2	29	11.49	-10.8			Dec-05
	2.83	6.40	14.98	17.92	41.95	1.15	1.27	6.73	0.62	16.11	2,173	7	61	29	2	29	11.27	-10.85	5.75		Dec-96
	2.65	6.06	14.09	15.38	36.82	0.49	2.01	6.72	0.62	15.67	2,173	7	61	29	2	29	10.8	-11.15		1.00	Dec-96

Fund Name	Ticker Symbol	Traded On	Fund Type	Category and (Prospectus Objective)	Overall Rating	Reward Rating	Risk Rating	Recent Up/ Downgrade	Open to New Investors	Min Initial Investment
	MARKET		FUND TYPE, CATEGORY & OBJECTIVE		RATINGS				MINIMUMS	
Franklin Moderate Allocation Fund Class R	FTMRX	NAS CM	Open End	Moderate Alloc (Asset Alloc)	B-	C+	B	Down	Y	1,000
Franklin Moderate Allocation Fund Class R6	US35472P4220		Open End	Moderate Alloc (Asset Alloc)	B-	C+	B	Down	Y	1,000,000
Franklin Mutual Beacon Fund Class A	TEBIX	NAS CM	Open End	Aggressive Alloc (Growth & Income)	B-	B-	B		Y	1,000
Franklin Mutual Beacon Fund Class C	TEMEX	NAS CM	Open End	Aggressive Alloc (Growth & Income)	B-	C+	B	Up	Y	1,000
Franklin Mutual Beacon Fund Class R	US3540268584		Open End	Aggressive Alloc (Growth & Income)	B-	B-	B		Y	1,000
Franklin Mutual Beacon Fund Class R6	FMBRX	NAS CM	Open End	Aggressive Alloc (Growth & Income)	B-	B-	B		Y	1,000,000
Franklin Mutual Beacon Fund Class Z	BEGRX	NAS CM	Open End	Aggressive Alloc (Growth & Income)	B-	B-	B		Y	100,000
Franklin Mutual European Fund Class A	TEMIX	NAS CM	Open End	Europe Equity Large Cap (Europe Stock)	C+	C+	B-	Up	Y	1,000
Franklin Mutual European Fund Class C	TEURX	NAS CM	Open End	Europe Equity Large Cap (Europe Stock)	C+	C+	B-	Up	Y	1,000
Franklin Mutual European Fund Class R	FMURX	NAS CM	Open End	Europe Equity Large Cap (Europe Stock)	C+	C+	B-	Up	Y	1,000
Franklin Mutual European Fund Class R6	FMEUX	NAS CM	Open End	Europe Equity Large Cap (Europe Stock)	B-	C+	B	Up	Y	1,000,000
Franklin Mutual European Fund Class Z	MEURX	NAS CM	Open End	Europe Equity Large Cap (Europe Stock)	C+	C+	B	Up	Y	100,000
Franklin Mutual Financial Services Fund Class A	TFSIX	NAS CM	Open End	Financials Sector Equity (Financial)	B	B	B+	Up	Y	1,000
Franklin Mutual Financial Services Fund Class C	TMFSX	NAS CM	Open End	Financials Sector Equity (Financial)	B	B-	B+	Up	Y	1,000
Franklin Mutual Financial Services Fund Class R6	FMFVX	NAS CM	Open End	Financials Sector Equity (Financial)	B	B	B+	Up	Y	1,000,000
Franklin Mutual Financial Services Fund Class Z	TEFAX	NAS CM	Open End	Financials Sector Equity (Financial)	B	B	B+	Up	Y	100,000
Franklin Mutual Global Discovery Fund Class A	TEDIX	NAS CM	Open End	Global Equity (World Stock)	B-	C+	B	Up	Y	1,000
Franklin Mutual Global Discovery Fund Class C	TEDSX	NAS CM	Open End	Global Equity (World Stock)	B-	C+	B	Up	Y	1,000
Franklin Mutual Global Discovery Fund Class R	TEDRX	NAS CM	Open End	Global Equity (World Stock)	B-	C+	B	Up	Y	1,000
Franklin Mutual Global Discovery Fund Class R6	FMDRX	NAS CM	Open End	Global Equity (World Stock)	B-	C+	B	Up	Y	1,000,000
Franklin Mutual Global Discovery Fund Class Z	MDISX	NAS CM	Open End	Global Equity (World Stock)	B-	C+	B	Up	Y	100,000
Franklin Mutual International Fund Class A	FMIAX	NAS CM	Open End	Global Equity Large Cap (Foreign Stock)	C+	C+	C	Up	Y	1,000
Franklin Mutual International Fund Class C	FCMIX	NAS CM	Open End	Global Equity Large Cap (Foreign Stock)	C+	C+	C	Up	Y	1,000
Franklin Mutual International Fund Class R	FRMIX	NAS CM	Open End	Global Equity Large Cap (Foreign Stock)	C+	C+	C	Up	Y	1,000
Franklin Mutual International Fund Class R6	FIMFX	NAS CM	Open End	Global Equity Large Cap (Foreign Stock)	C+	C+	C+	Up	Y	1,000,000
Franklin Mutual International Fund Class Z	FMIZX	NAS CM	Open End	Global Equity Large Cap (Foreign Stock)	C+	C+	C	Up	Y	100,000
Franklin Mutual Quest Fund Class A	TEQIX	NAS CM	Open End	Alloc (World Stock)	B-	C+	B	Up	Y	1,000
Franklin Mutual Quest Fund Class C	TEMQX	NAS CM	Open End	Alloc (World Stock)	B-	C+	B	Up	Y	1,000
Franklin Mutual Quest Fund Class R	FMQSX	NAS CM	Open End	Alloc (World Stock)	B-	C+	B	Up	Y	1,000
Franklin Mutual Quest Fund Class R6	FMQRX	NAS CM	Open End	Alloc (World Stock)	B-	C+	B	Down	Y	1,000,000
Franklin Mutual Quest Fund Class Z	MQIFX	NAS CM	Open End	Alloc (World Stock)	B-	C+	B	Down	Y	100,000
Franklin Mutual Shares Fund Class A	TESIX	NAS CM	Open End	Aggressive Alloc (Growth & Income)	B-	C+	B	Down	Y	1,000
Franklin Mutual Shares Fund Class C	TEMTX	NAS CM	Open End	Aggressive Alloc (Growth & Income)	B-	C+	B	Down	Y	1,000
Franklin Mutual Shares Fund Class R	TESRX	NAS CM	Open End	Aggressive Alloc (Growth & Income)	B-	C+	B	Down	Y	1,000
Franklin Mutual Shares Fund Class R6	FMSHX	NAS CM	Open End	Aggressive Alloc (Growth & Income)	B-	C+	B		Y	1,000,000
Franklin Mutual Shares Fund Class Z	MUTHX	NAS CM	Open End	Aggressive Alloc (Growth & Income)	B-	C+	B	Down	Y	100,000
Franklin Natural Resources Fund Advisor Class	FNRAX	NAS CM	Open End	Natl Resources Sec Equity (Natl Res)	D+	C-	D+	Up	Y	100,000
Franklin Natural Resources Fund Class A	FRNRX	NAS CM	Open End	Natl Resources Sec Equity (Natl Res)	D+	C-	D+	Up	Y	1,000
Franklin Natural Resources Fund Class C	FNCRX	NAS CM	Open End	Natl Resources Sec Equity (Natl Res)	D+	C-	D+	Up	Y	1,000
Franklin Natural Resources Fund Class R6	FNCSX	NAS CM	Open End	Natl Resources Sec Equity (Natl Res)	C-	C-	D+	Up	Y	1,000,000
Franklin NextStep Conservative Fund Advisor Class	FNCVX	NAS CM	Open End	Cautious Alloc (Growth & Income)	C-	D+	A	Up	Y	100,000
Franklin NextStep Conservative Fund Class A	FNCAX	NAS CM	Open End	Cautious Alloc (Growth & Income)	C-	D+	A-	Up	Y	1,000
Franklin NextStep Conservative Fund Class C	FNCDX	NAS CM	Open End	Cautious Alloc (Growth & Income)	C-	D+	A-	Up	Y	1,000
Franklin NextStep Growth Fund Advisor Class	FNGVX	NAS CM	Open End	Aggressive Alloc (Growth)	C-	C-	A-	Up	Y	100,000
Franklin NextStep Growth Fund Class A	FNGBX	NAS CM	Open End	Aggressive Alloc (Growth)	C-	C-	B+	Up	Y	1,000
Franklin NextStep Growth Fund Class C	FNGCX	NAS CM	Open End	Aggressive Alloc (Growth)	C-	C-	B+	Up	Y	1,000
Franklin NextStep Moderate Fund Advisor Class	FNMZX	NAS CM	Open End	Moderate Alloc (Growth & Income)	C-	C-	A	Up	Y	100,000
Franklin NextStep Moderate Fund Class A	FNMDX	NAS CM	Open End	Moderate Alloc (Growth & Income)	C-	C-	A-	Up	Y	1,000
Franklin NextStep Moderate Fund Class C	FNMFX	NAS CM	Open End	Moderate Alloc (Growth & Income)	C-	C-	A-	Up	Y	1,000
Franklin Pelagos Commodities Strategy Fund Advisor Class	FSLPX	NAS CM	Open End	Commodities Broad Basket (Growth & Income)	D+	C-	D+	Up	Y	100,000
Franklin Pelagos Commodities Strategy Fund Class A	FLSQX	NAS CM	Open End	Commodities Broad Basket (Growth & Income)	D+	C-	D+	Up	Y	1,000
Franklin Pelagos Commodities Strategy Fund Class C	FLSVX	NAS CM	Open End	Commodities Broad Basket (Growth & Income)	D+	D+	D+	Up	Y	1,000

★ Expanded analysis of this fund is included in Section II.

Min Additional Investment	TOTAL RETURNS 3-Month Total Return	6-Month Total Return	1-Year Total Return	3-Year Total Return	5-Year Total Return	PERFORMANCE Dividend Yield (TTM)	Expense Ratio	3-Yr Std Deviation	3-Year Beta	ASSETS NAV	Total Assets (MIL)	ASSET ALLOCATION & TURNOVER %Cash	%Stocks	%Bonds	%Other	Turnover Ratio	BULL & BEAR Last Bull Market Total Return	Last Bear Market Total Return	FEES Front End Fee (%)	Back End Fee (%)	Inception Date
	2.79	6.31	14.68	17.09	40.24	0.89	1.52	6.73	0.62	16.08	2,173	7	61	29	2	29	11.18	-11			Jan-02
	2.96	6.59	15.39	19.23	44.38	1.49	0.92	6.78	0.63	16.11	2,173	7	61	29	2	29	11.27	-10.85			May-13
	2.92	5.02	14.09	25.71	75.05	1.98	1.05	10.48	0.94	16.47	4,013	4	84	2	3	31	19.49	-17.25	5.75		Jun-62
	2.69	4.63	13.24	22.90	68.71	1.33	1.8	10.46	0.94	16.34	4,013	4	84	2	3	31	19.03	-17.49		1.00	Jun-62
	2.81	4.88	13.76	24.81	72.98	1.81	1.3	10.48	0.94	16.28	4,013	4	84	2	3	31	19.34	-17.3			Oct-09
	2.98	5.13	14.41	26.97	78.04	2.26	0.71	10.49	0.94	16.6	4,013	4	84	2	3	31	19.64	-17.12			May-13
	2.96	5.18	14.39	26.71	77.45	2.18	0.8	10.49	0.94	16.61	4,013	4	84	2	3	31	19.64	-17.12			Jun-62
	0.29	2.91	10.14	13.34	37.85	2.24	1.31	11.37		20.33	2,582	9	84	2	0	16	14.29	-20.79	5.75		Jul-96
	0.09	2.51	9.36	10.85	32.97	1.47	2.06	11.38		20.38	2,582	9	84	2	0	16	13.84	-21.02		1.00	Jul-96
	0.24	2.80	9.92	12.59	36.37	1.91	1.56	11.37		19.97	2,582	9	84	2	0	16	14.14	-20.83			Oct-09
	0.36	3.10	10.63	14.81	40.81	2.6	0.89	11.36		20.91	2,582	9	84	2	0	16	14.46	-20.67			May-13
	0.35	3.04	10.45	14.25	39.86	2.44	1.06	11.37		20.93	2,582	9	84	2	0	16	14.46	-20.67			Jul-96
	3.47	7.50	13.34	36.17	91.75	1.01	1.38	11.35	0.77	24.2	705.2	9	88	2	1	35	14.8	-19.82	5.75		Aug-97
	3.31	7.10	12.49	33.15	84.94	0.4	2.13	11.34	0.77	24.08	705.2	9	88	2	1	35	14.41	-20.08		1.00	Aug-97
	3.58	7.73	13.76	37.81	95.62	1.34	0.96	11.35	0.77	24.3	705.2	9	88	2	1	35	14.97	-19.72			May-13
	3.56	7.65	13.61	37.26	94.33	1.21	1.13	11.36	0.77	24.14	705.2	9	88	2	1	35	14.97	-19.72			Aug-97
	0.99	2.80	9.56	18.34	57.78	1.85	1.24	9.58	0.86	31.8	21,893	3	90	2	3	17	16.82	-17.26	5.75		Dec-92
	0.82	2.43	8.77	15.78	52.20	1.18	1.99	9.59	0.86	31.44	21,893	3	90	2	3	17	16.31	-17.49		1.00	Dec-92
	0.96	2.70	9.30	17.53	56.06	1.66	1.49	9.58	0.86	31.37	21,893	3	90	2	3	17	16.66	-17.33			Jan-02
	1.09	2.99	9.97	19.77	61.08	2.17	0.85	9.58	0.86	32.41	21,893	3	90	2	3	17	17.01	-17.14			May-13
	1.06	2.96	9.84	19.29	59.98	2.04	0.99	9.58	0.86	32.42	21,893	3	90	2	3	17	17.01	-17.14			Dec-92
	1.03	4.49	13.66	17.32	37.70	1.47	1.42	10.79		15.89	223.9	9	88	1	0	25	16.29	-21.14	5.75		May-09
	0.87	4.13	12.78	14.78	32.87	0.78	2.17	10.79		15.69	223.9	9	88	1	0	25	15.83	-21.37		1.00	May-09
	1.02	4.44	13.42	16.60	36.28	1.31	1.67	10.81		15.8	223.9	9	88	1	0	25	16.21	-21.21			May-09
	1.16	4.74	14.10	18.78	40.57	1.85	1.01	10.82		15.97	223.9	9	88	1	0	25	16.52	-21.07			May-13
	1.11	4.69	13.98	18.29	39.63	1.7	1.17	10.8		15.96	223.9	9	88	1	0	25	16.52	-21.07			May-09
	1.53	4.09	6.94	16.48	52.62	5.73	1.04	7.6	0.63	15.66	5,279	9	59	25	7	44	15.46	-14.94	5.75		Sep-80
	1.34	3.68	6.16	13.89	47.23	5.15	1.79	7.55	0.63	15.39	5,279	9	59	25	7	44	15.05	-15.18		1.00	Sep-80
	1.51	3.98	6.72	15.66	50.98	5.54	1.29	7.57	0.63	15.45	5,279	9	59	25	7	44	15.38	-15.01			May-09
	1.59	4.25	7.27	17.63	55.13	5.96	0.71	7.57	0.63	15.86	5,279	9	59	25	7	44	15.7	-14.82			May-13
	1.64	4.23	7.25	17.41	54.75	5.89	0.79	7.59	0.63	15.88	5,279	9	59	25	7	44	15.7	-14.82			Sep-80
	1.94	2.73	8.20	19.12	66.38	1.9	1.05	9.52	0.87	28.35	15,462	6	86	4	4	21	19.91	-17.62	5.75		Jul-49
	1.75	2.34	7.37	16.48	60.43	1.26	1.8	9.49	0.87	28.04	15,462	6	86	4	4	21	19.46	-17.9		1.00	Jul-49
	1.88	2.61	7.95	18.29	64.54	1.66	1.3	9.51	0.87	28.21	15,462	6	86	4	4	21	19.82	-17.73			Jan-02
	2.06	2.91	8.60	20.50	69.56	2.22	0.68	9.49	0.87	28.61	15,462	6	86	4	4	21	20.12	-17.51			May-13
	2.02	2.87	8.49	20.08	68.64	2.12	0.8	9.5	0.87	28.63	15,462	6	86	4	4	21	20.12	-17.51			Jul-49
	7.06	16.40	0.53	-2.41	-11.40	1.33	0.81	23.13	1.19	28.72	513.0	0	98	0	1	30	19.87	-32.51			Dec-96
	7.04	16.29	0.32	-3.14	-12.62	1.09	1.06	23.12	1.19	26.98	513.0	0	98	0	1	30	19.65	-32.6	5.75		Jun-95
	6.78	15.77	-0.45	-5.27	-15.75	0.55	1.81	23.11	1.18	26.27	513.0	0	98	0	1	30	19.18	-32.8		1.00	Sep-05
	7.22	16.64	0.88	-1.47	-10.51	1.38	0.57	23.13	1.19	28.7	513.0	0	98	0	1	30	19.65	-32.6			Sep-13
	1.32	3.33	7.27			1.65	0.78			10.92	3.4	8	25	63	3	103					Jun-16
	1.21	3.24	7.05			1.38	1.03			10.93	3.4	8	25	63	3	103			5.75		Feb-16
	1.00	2.81	6.22			0.71	1.78			10.88	3.4	8	25	63	3	103				1.00	Feb-16
	4.22	8.69	16.26			1.05	0.98			12.37	7.5	4	76	18	1	87					Jun-16
	4.22	8.62	16.09			0.88	1.23			12.36	7.5	4	76	18	1	87			5.75		Feb-16
	3.96	8.15	15.22			0.44	1.98			12.27	7.5	4	76	18	1	87				1.00	Feb-16
	3.33	7.05	13.60			1.01	0.93			12	15.6	5	62	32	1	76					Jun-16
	3.34	6.99	13.45			0.87	1.18			11.99	15.6	5	62	32	1	76			5.75		Feb-16
	3.06	6.49	12.45			0.5	1.93			11.9	15.6	5	62	32	1	76				1.00	Feb-16
	4.34	7.34	1.05	-12.15	-33.00	0	0.95	12.9	0.98	6.72	129.2	34	23	43	0	42					Dec-11
	4.45	7.35	0.76	-12.63	-33.79	0	1.2	12.88	0.98	6.57	129.2	34	23	43	0	42			5.75		Jan-14
	4.24	6.86	0.15	-14.59	-36.22	0	1.95	12.9	0.98	6.38	129.2	34	23	43	0	42				1.00	Jan-14

	MARKET		FUND TYPE, CATEGORY & OBJECTIVE		RATINGS					MINIMUMS
Fund Name	Ticker Symbol	Traded On	Fund Type	Category and (Prospectus Objective)	Overall Rating	Reward Rating	Risk Rating	Recent Up/ Downgrade	Open to New Investors	Min Initial Investment
Franklin Pelagos Commodities Strategy Fund Class R	FLSWX	NAS CM	Open End	Commodities Broad Basket (Growth & Income)	D+	D+	D+	Up	Y	1,000
Franklin Pelagos Commodities Strategy Fund Class R6	FPELX	NAS CM	Open End	Commodities Broad Basket (Growth & Income)	C-	C-	D+	Up	Y	1,000,000
Franklin Real Estate Securities Fund Advisor Class	FRLAX	NAS CM	Open End	Real Estate Sector Equity (Real Estate)	B-	C+	B	Up	Y	100,000
Franklin Real Estate Securities Fund Class A	FREEX	NAS CM	Open End	Real Estate Sector Equity (Real Estate)	B-	C+	B	Up	Y	1,000
Franklin Real Estate Securities Fund Class C	FRRSX	NAS CM	Open End	Real Estate Sector Equity (Real Estate)	B-	C+	B	Up	Y	1,000
Franklin Real Estate Securities Fund Class R6	FSERX	NAS CM	Open End	Real Estate Sector Equity (Real Estate)	B-	C+	B	Up	Y	1,000,000
Franklin Rising Dividends Fund Advisor Class	FRDAX	NAS CM	Open End	US Equity Large Cap Blend (Equity-Income)	B	B	B-		Y	100,000
Franklin Rising Dividends Fund Class A	FRDPX	NAS CM	Open End	US Equity Large Cap Blend (Equity-Income)	B	B	B-		Y	1,000
Franklin Rising Dividends Fund Class C	FRDTX	NAS CM	Open End	US Equity Large Cap Blend (Equity-Income)	B-	B-	B-	Down	Y	1,000
Franklin Rising Dividends Fund Class R	FRDRX	NAS CM	Open End	US Equity Large Cap Blend (Equity-Income)	B-	B	B-	Down	Y	1,000
Franklin Rising Dividends Fund R6 Class	FRISX	NAS CM	Open End	US Equity Large Cap Blend (Equity-Income)	B	B	B-		Y	1,000,000
Franklin Small Cap Growth Fund Advisor Class	FSSAX	NAS CM	Open End	US Equity Small Cap (Small Company)	B	B	B-	Up		100,000
Franklin Small Cap Growth Fund Class A	FSGRX	NAS CM	Open End	US Equity Small Cap (Small Company)	B	B	B-	Up		1,000
Franklin Small Cap Growth Fund Class C	FCSGX	NAS CM	Open End	US Equity Small Cap (Small Company)	B-	B	B-	Up		1,000
Franklin Small Cap Growth Fund Class R	FSSRX	NAS CM	Open End	US Equity Small Cap (Small Company)	B	B	B-	Up		1,000
Franklin Small Cap Growth Fund Class R6	FSMLX	NAS CM	Open End	US Equity Small Cap (Small Company)	B	B	B-	Up		1,000,000
Franklin Small Cap Value Fund Advisor Class	FVADX	NAS CM	Open End	US Equity Small Cap (Small Company)	B	B	B	Up	Y	100,000
Franklin Small Cap Value Fund Class A	FRVLX	NAS CM	Open End	US Equity Small Cap (Small Company)	B	B	B	Up	Y	1,000
Franklin Small Cap Value Fund Class C	FRVFX	NAS CM	Open End	US Equity Small Cap (Small Company)	B	B	B-	Up	Y	1,000
Franklin Small Cap Value Fund Class R	FVFRX	NAS CM	Open End	US Equity Small Cap (Small Company)	B	B	B-	Up	Y	1,000
Franklin Small Cap Value Fund Class R6	FRCSX	NAS CM	Open End	US Equity Small Cap (Small Company)	B	B+	B	Up	Y	1,000,000
Franklin Small-Mid Cap Growth Fund Advisor Class	FSGAX	NAS CM	Open End	US Equity Mid Cap (Growth)	B	B-	B	Up	Y	100,000
Franklin Small-Mid Cap Growth Fund Class A	FRSGX	NAS CM	Open End	US Equity Mid Cap (Growth)	B	B-	B	Up	Y	1,000
Franklin Small-Mid Cap Growth Fund Class C	FRSIX	NAS CM	Open End	US Equity Mid Cap (Growth)	B-	C+	B	Up	Y	1,000
Franklin Small-Mid Cap Growth Fund Class R	FSMRX	NAS CM	Open End	US Equity Mid Cap (Growth)	B-	B-	B	Up	Y	1,000
Franklin Small-Mid Cap Growth Fund Class R6	FMGGX	NAS CM	Open End	US Equity Mid Cap (Growth)	B	B	B	Up	Y	1,000,000
Franklin Universal Trust	FT	NYSE	Closed End	Moderate Alloc (Balanced)	C+	B-	C+	Up	Y	
Franklin Utilities Advisor Class	FRUAX	NAS CM	Open End	Utilities Sector Equity (Utility)	B	B-	B		Y	100,000
Franklin Utilities Class A	FKUTX	NAS CM	Open End	Utilities Sector Equity (Utility)	B	B-	B		Y	1,000
Franklin Utilities Class C	FRUSX	NAS CM	Open End	Utilities Sector Equity (Utility)	B-	B-	B	Down	Y	1,000
Franklin Utilities Class R	FRURX	NAS CM	Open End	Utilities Sector Equity (Utility)	B-	B-	B	Down	Y	1,000
Franklin Utilities Fund Class R6	FUFRX	NAS CM	Open End	Utilities Sector Equity (Utility)	B	B-	B		Y	1,000,000
Free Market International Equity Fund Institutional Class	FMNEX	NAS CM	Open End	Global Equity Mid/Small Cap (Foreign Stock)	B-	B	C	Up	Y	0
Friess Small Cap Growth Fund Institutional Class	SCGFX	NAS CM	Open End	US Equity Small Cap (Small Company)	U	U	U		Y	100,000
Friess Small Cap Growth Fund Investor Class	SCGNX	NAS CM	Open End	US Equity Small Cap (Small Company)	U	U	U		Y	2,000
Frontier MFG Core Infrastructure Fund Institutional Class	FMGIX	NAS CM	Open End	Other Sector Equity (Utility)	B	B-	B		Y	100,000
Frontier MFG Core Infrastructure Fund Service Class	FCIVX	NAS CM	Open End	Other Sector Equity (Utility)	B	B-	B		Y	10,000
Frontier MFG Global Equity Fund Institutional Class	FMGEX	NAS CM	Open End	US Equity Large Cap Growth (World Stock)	B	B	B+	Up		1,000,000
Frontier MFG Global Plus Fund Institutional Class	FMGPX	NAS CM	Open End	US Equity Large Cap Blend (Growth)	B-	C+	B	Up	Y	1,000,000
Frontier MFG Global Plus Fund Service Class	FMPSX	NAS CM	Open End	US Equity Large Cap Blend (Growth)	B-	C+	B	Up	Y	10,000
Frontier Phocas Small Cap Value Fund Institutional Class	FPSVX	NAS CM	Open End	US Equity Small Cap (Small Company)	B	B	B	Up	Y	100,000
Frontier Phocas Small Cap Value Fund Service Class	FPVSX	NAS CM	Open End	US Equity Small Cap (Small Company)	B	B	B	Up	Y	10,000
Frontier Silk Invest New Horizons Fund Institutional Class	FSNHX	NAS CM	Open End	Emerging Markets Equity (Growth)	D+	C	B-	Up		100,000
Frontier Silk Invest New Horizons Fund Service Class	FNHSX	NAS CM	Open End	Emerging Markets Equity (Growth)	D+	C	B-	Up		10,000
Frontier Timpani Small Cap Growth Fund Class Y	FTSYX	NAS CM	Open End	US Equity Small Cap (Small Company)	B	A-	B-	Up	Y	1,000
Frontier Timpani Small Cap Growth Fund Institutional Class	FTSGX	NAS CM	Open End	US Equity Small Cap (Small Company)	B	A-	B-	Up	Y	100,000
Frontier Timpani Small Cap Growth Fund Service Class	FTSCX	NAS CM	Open End	US Equity Small Cap (Small Company)	B	A-	B-	Up	Y	10,000
Frost Growth Equity Fund Class Institutional	FICEX	NAS CM	Open End	US Equity Large Cap Growth (Growth)	B	B+	B	Down	Y	1,000,000
Frost Growth Equity Fund Investor Class Shares	FACEX	NAS CM	Open End	US Equity Large Cap Growth (Growth)	B	B	B	Down	Y	2,500
Frost Mid Cap Equity Fund Class Institutional	FIKSX	NAS CM	Open End	US Equity Mid Cap (Growth)	B-	B-	C+	Up	Y	1,000,000
Frost Mid Cap Equity Fund Investor Class Shares	FAKSX	NAS CM	Open End	US Equity Mid Cap (Growth)	B-	B-	C+	Up	Y	2,500
Frost Value Equity Fund Class Institutional	FIDVX	NAS CM	Open End	US Equity Large Cap Value (Growth & Income)	B	B	B-	Up	Y	1,000,000

★ Expanded analysis of this fund is included in Section II.

	TOTAL RETURNS					PERFORMANCE				ASSETS		ASSET ALLOCATION & TURNOVER					BULL & BEAR		FEES		
Min Additional Investment	3-Month Total Return	6-Month Total Return	1-Year Total Return	3-Year Total Return	5-Year Total Return	Dividend Yield (TTM)	Expense Ratio	3-Yr Std Deviation	3-Year Beta	NAV	Total Assets (MIL)	%Cash	%Stocks	%Bonds	%Other	Turnover Ratio	Last Bull Market Total Return	Last Bear Market Total Return	Front End Fee (%)	Back End Fee (%)	Inception Date
	4.48	7.23	0.61	-13.18	-34.47	0	1.45	12.91	0.98	6.52	129.2	34	23	43	0	42					Jan-14
	4.66	7.70	1.33	-11.41	-32.41	0	0.63	12.9	0.98	6.68	129.2	34	23	43	0	42					Jan-14
	1.89	2.04	4.17	12.15	53.92	2.15	0.75	13.43	0.99	21.21	412.0	0	99	0	0	40	31.06	-15.37			Dec-96
	1.80	1.91	3.94	11.32	51.97	2.02	1	13.44	0.99	21	412.0	0	99	0	0	40	30.88	-15.5	5.75		Jan-94
	1.61	1.53	3.14	8.80	46.34	1.6	1.75	13.45	0.99	20.13	412.0	0	99	0	0	40	30.32	-15.77		1.00	May-95
	1.99	2.21	4.45	12.88	55.36	2.29	0.55	13.45	0.99	21.22	412.0	0	99	0	0	40	30.88	-15.5			May-13
	6.77	12.02	20.59	32.44	93.39	1.5	0.66	10.1	0.96	61.09	19,377	0	99	0	1	3	19.77	-11.85			Oct-05
	6.70	11.89	20.28	31.46	90.96	1.28	0.91	10.09	0.96	61.16	19,377	0	99	0	1	3	19.56	-11.92	5.75		Jan-87
	6.51	11.46	19.40	28.53	83.90	0.65	1.66	10.09	0.96	60.08	19,377	0	99	0	1	3	19.04	-12.19		1.00	May-95
	6.64	11.73	19.98	30.48	88.54	1.05	1.16	10.1	0.96	60.97	19,377	0	99	0	1	3	19.41	-12.03			Jan-02
	6.82	12.11	20.78	33.05	94.48	1.62	0.52	10.09	0.96	61.09	19,377	0	99	0	1	3	19.56	-11.92			May-13
	7.02	12.77	21.28	25.59	106.70	0	0.85	16.49	1.06	23.52	2,662	0	97	0	3	30	27.59	-22.43			May-00
	6.91	12.61	20.93	24.62	103.89	0	1.1	16.5	1.06	22	2,662	0	97	0	3	30	27.38	-22.58	5.75		May-00
	6.73	12.21	20.06	21.84	96.59	0	1.85	16.51	1.06	18.61	2,662	0	97	0	3	30	26.86	-22.71		1.00	May-00
	6.89	12.45	20.69	23.75	101.58	0	1.35	16.52	1.06	20.99	2,662	0	97	0	3	30	27.21	-22.57			Jan-02
	7.04	12.89	21.51	26.45	108.72	0	0.63	16.52	1.06	23.76	2,662	0	97	0	3	30	27.59	-22.43			May-13
	6.04	10.95	10.95	32.22	84.31	0.4	0.86	13.2	0.87	58.5	2,633	3	97	1	0	42	31.95	-25.56			Dec-96
	5.96	10.76	10.62	31.14	81.69	0.2	1.11	13.2	0.87	55.84	2,633	3	97	1	0	42	31.72	-25.66	5.75		Mar-96
	5.76	10.37	9.81	28.28	75.22	0	1.86	13.19	0.87	49.63	2,633	3	97	1	0	42	31.18	-25.88		1.00	Sep-96
	5.88	10.62	10.36	30.19	79.67	0	1.36	13.2	0.87	55.3	2,633	3	97	1	0	42	31.58	-25.72			Aug-02
	6.07	11.02	11.11	33.04	85.90	0.53	0.64	13.21	0.87	58.37	2,633	3	97	1	0	42	31.72	-25.66			May-13
	5.20	9.67	21.81	24.58	90.90	0	0.7	11.45	0.99	38.47	3,617	2	97	0	1	35	28.26	-23.82			Dec-96
	5.13	9.51	21.52	23.66	88.48	0	0.95	11.44	0.99	35.31	3,617	2	97	0	1	35	28.06	-23.89	5.75		Feb-92
	4.93	9.06	20.56	20.83	81.47	0	1.7	11.44	0.99	25.36	3,617	2	97	0	1	35	27.51	-24.15		1.00	Oct-95
	5.07	9.39	21.24	22.72	86.15	0	1.2	11.43	0.99	32.48	3,617	2	97	0	1	35	27.89	-23.99			Feb-92
	5.34	9.88	22.21	25.56	92.80	0	0.48	11.45	0.99	39.02	3,617	2	97	0	1	35	28.06	-23.89			May-13
	1.04	3.75	10.52	19.15	44.94	4.59	0	8.37	1.13	8.16	210.1	-27	43	82	1	23	14.7	-5.23			Sep-88
	-0.13	2.52	10.76	19.30	75.26	2.5	0.58	11.47	0.88	18.84	6,788	0	99	1	0	1	11.53	1.68			Dec-96
	-0.11	2.46	10.56	18.78	73.95	2.39	0.73	11.5	0.88	18.7	6,788	0	99	1	0	1	11.43	1.61	4.25		Sep-48
	-0.29	2.17	10.02	16.98	69.67	1.95	1.23	11.45	0.88	18.6	6,788	0	99	1	0	1	11.04	1.46		1.00	May-95
	-0.20	2.30	10.22	17.54	70.91	2.08	1.08	11.47	0.88	18.63	6,788	0	99	1	0	1	11.19	1.45			Jan-02
	-0.05	2.63	10.87	19.69	76.07	2.6	0.47	11.48	0.88	18.84	6,788	0	99	1	0	1	11.43	1.61			May-13
	4.80	12.39	27.73	33.76	56.21	1.61	1.14	12.21	0.98	11.41	2,294	1	92	0	6	2	13.6	-26.31			Dec-07
100	7.11	12.91					1.35			22.4	94.2	0	97	3	0						May-17
100	7.07	12.76					1.6			22.37	94.2	0	97	3	0						May-17
1,000	1.85	4.35	20.24	25.20	67.15	2.98	0.71	10.45	0.4	16.25	276.5	0	94	2	1	39					Jan-12
1,000	1.76	4.24	20.17	25.10	67.02	2.93	0.86	10.44	0.4	16.25	276.5	0	94	2	1	39					Jul-16
1,000	6.30	10.55	24.40	33.64	86.35	0.72	0.83	9.47	0.84	18.36	1,218	0	91	9	0	30					Dec-11
1,000	6.21	10.18	24.48			0.13	0.83			12.39	439.1	0	90	10	0	31					Mar-15
1,000	6.10	10.08	24.36			0.12	0.98			12.39	439.1	0	90	10	0	31					May-16
1,000	2.67	8.60	8.16	26.27	103.03	0.71	0.95	13.43	0.92	38.8	62.5	1	99	0	0	53	24.34	-24.48			Sep-06
1,000	2.53	8.49	7.89	25.99	102.59	0.74	1.1	13.45	0.93	38.7	62.5	1	99	0	0	53	24.35	-24.48			Jul-16
1,000	4.08	5.51	18.09			0.26	1.86			10.99	60.1	3	89	5	2	25					May-16
1,000	4.03	5.47	17.92			0.22	2.01			10.99	60.1	3	89	5	2	25					May-16
50	7.67	14.23	35.59	29.85	105.60	0	1.5	16.21	0.99	21.18	55.6	2	98	0	0	179	35.81	-27.94			Jan-14
1,000	7.76	14.41	36.13	31.39	109.24	0	1.1	16.19	0.99	21.51	55.6	2	98	0	0	179	36.01	-27.87			Mar-11
1,000	7.76	14.41	36.13	31.39	109.24	0	1.25	16.19	0.99	21.51	55.6	2	98	0	0	179	36.01	-27.87			Jul-16
	7.27	12.42	30.69	38.64	109.31	0.13	0.64	11.51	1.04	12.64	310.8	3	97	0	0	16	25.26	-17.1			Apr-08
500	7.17	12.29	30.39	37.56	106.64	0	0.89	11.5	1.03	12.49	310.8	3	97	0	0	16	25.08	-17.12			Jun-08
	8.32	14.03	22.74	30.35	83.70	0	1.21	13.74	1.2	9.76	13.3	6	93	0	0	38	27.46	-24.14			Apr-08
500	8.31	14.10	22.80	29.78	82.19	0	1.47	13.87	1.21	9.62	13.3	6	93	0	0	38	27.33	-24.22			Feb-12
	4.77	9.89	19.47	29.27	97.06	1.36	0.65	11.74	1.04	9.11	112.3	3	97	0	0	35	16.86	-17.9			Apr-08

	MARKET			FUND TYPE, CATEGORY & OBJECTIVE	RATINGS				MINIMUMS	
Fund Name	Ticker Symbol	Traded On	Fund Type	Category and (Prospectus Objective)	Overall Rating	Reward Rating	Risk Rating	Recent Up/ Downgrade	Open to New Investors	Min Initial Investment
Frost Value Equity Fund Investor Class Shares	FADVX	NAS CM	Open End	US Equity Large Cap Value (Growth & Income)	B	B	B-	Up	Y	2,500
FS Energy Total Return Fund A	US3026822086		Closed End	Natl Resources Sec Equity (Natl Res)	U	U	U		Y	2,500
FS Energy Total Return Fund I	US3026821096		Closed End	Natl Resources Sec Equity (Natl Res)	U	U	U		Y	1,000,000
FS Multi-Strategy Alternatives Fund Class A	FSMMX	NAS CM	Open End	Multialternative (Growth & Income)	U	U	U		Y	2,500
FS Multi-Strategy Alternatives Fund Class I	FSMSX	NAS CM	Open End	Multialternative (Growth & Income)	U	U	U		Y	1,000,000
Fulcrum Diversified Absolute Return Fund Institutional Cls	FARIX	NAS CM	Open End	Multialternative (Growth & Income)	C	C	B	Up	Y	1,000,000
Fulcrum Diversified Absolute Return Fund Super Inst Cls	FARYX	NAS CM	Open End	Multialternative (Growth & Income)	C	C	B	Up	Y	25,000,000
FundX Aggressive Upgrader Fund	HOTFX	NAS CM	Open End	US Equity Large Cap Growth (Growth)	B-	C+	B	Up	Y	1,000
FundX Conservative Upgrader Fund	RELAX	NAS CM	Open End	Moderate Alloc (Growth & Income)	B-	C+	B	Up	Y	1,000
FundX Sustainable Impact Fund	SRIFX	NAS CM	Open End	Alloc (Growth)	U	U	U		Y	1,000
FundX Tactical Upgrader Fund	TACTX	NAS CM	Open End	Long/Short Equity (Growth)	B-	C+	B+	Down	Y	1,000
FundX Upgrader Fund	FUNDX	NAS CM	Open End	Aggressive Alloc (Growth)	B	C+	B	Up	Y	1,000
Gabelli ABC Fund Class Advisor	GADVX	NAS CM	Open End	Market Neutral (Growth & Income)	B-	C	A	Up	Y	10,000
Gabelli ABC Fund Class Class AAA	GABCX	NAS CM	Open End	Market Neutral (Growth & Income)	B	C	A	Up	Y	10,000
Gabelli Asset Fund Class A	GATAX	NAS CM	Open End	US Equity Large Cap Blend (Growth)	B-	B-	C+	Down	Y	1,000
Gabelli Asset Fund Class AAA	GABAX	NAS CM	Open End	US Equity Large Cap Blend (Growth)	B-	B-	C+	Down	Y	1,000
Gabelli Asset Fund Class C	GATCX	NAS CM	Open End	US Equity Large Cap Blend (Growth)	C+	B-	C+	Down	Y	1,000
Gabelli Asset Fund Class I	GABIX	NAS CM	Open End	US Equity Large Cap Blend (Growth)	B-	B-	C+	Down	Y	500,000
Gabelli Asset Fund T	GALTX	NAS CM	Open End	US Equity Large Cap Blend (Growth)	B-	B-	C+	Down	Y	1,000
Gabelli Convertible & Income Securities	GCV	NYSE	Closed End	Aggressive Alloc (Convertible Bond)	C+	C+	C+	Up	Y	
Gabelli Dividend & Income Trust	GDV	NYSE	Closed End	US Equity Large Cap Value (Equity-Income)	C+	B-	C+		Y	
Gabelli Dividend Growth Fund Class A	GBCAX	NAS CM	Open End	US Equity Large Cap Blend (Growth)	C+	C+	C+	Down	Y	1,000
Gabelli Dividend Growth Fund Class AAA	GABBX	NAS CM	Open End	US Equity Large Cap Blend (Growth)	B-	C+	B-	Up	Y	1,000
Gabelli Dividend Growth Fund Class C	GBCCX	NAS CM	Open End	US Equity Large Cap Blend (Growth)	C+	C+	B-	Down	Y	1,000
Gabelli Dividend Growth Fund Class Institutional	GBCIX	NAS CM	Open End	US Equity Large Cap Blend (Growth)	C+	C+	C+	Down	Y	100,000
Gabelli Enterprise Mergers and Acquisitions Fund Class A	EMAAX	NAS CM	Open End	Market Neutral (Aggr Growth)	B	C+	A-	Up	Y	1,000
Gabelli Enterprise Mergers and Acquisitions Fund Class AAA	EAAAX	NAS CM	Open End	Market Neutral (Aggr Growth)	B	C+	A-	Up	Y	1,000
Gabelli Enterprise Mergers and Acquisitions Fund Class C	EMACX	NAS CM	Open End	Market Neutral (Aggr Growth)	B	C+	A-	Up	Y	1,000
Gabelli Enterprise Mergers and Acquisitions Fund Class Y	EMAYX	NAS CM	Open End	Market Neutral (Aggr Growth)	B-	C+	B	Up	Y	500,000
Gabelli Enterprise Mergers and Acquisitions Fund T	EMATX	NAS CM	Open End	Market Neutral (Aggr Growth)	B	C+	A-	Up	Y	1,000
Gabelli Equity Income Fund Class A	GCAEX	NAS CM	Open End	US Equity Large Cap Blend (Equity-Income)	C+	C+	C+	Down	Y	1,000
Gabelli Equity Income Fund Class AAA	GABEX	NAS CM	Open End	US Equity Large Cap Blend (Equity-Income)	C+	C+	C+	Down	Y	1,000
Gabelli Equity Income Fund Class C	GCCEX	NAS CM	Open End	US Equity Large Cap Blend (Equity-Income)	C+	C+	C+	Down	Y	1,000
Gabelli Equity Income Fund Class Institutional	GCIEX	NAS CM	Open End	US Equity Large Cap Blend (Equity-Income)	C+	C+	B-	Down	Y	500,000
Gabelli Equity Income Fund T	GCTEX	NAS CM	Open End	US Equity Large Cap Blend (Equity-Income)	C+	C+	C+	Down	Y	1,000
Gabelli Equity Trust	GAB	NYSE	Closed End	US Equity Large Cap Blend (Growth)	B	B	C+	Up	Y	
Gabelli ESG Fund Class A	SRIAX	NAS CM	Open End	US Equity Large Cap Blend (Growth)	B	C+	B+	Up	Y	1,000
Gabelli ESG Fund Class AAA	SRIGX	NAS CM	Open End	US Equity Large Cap Blend (Growth)	B	C+	B+	Up	Y	1,000
Gabelli ESG Fund Class C	SRICX	NAS CM	Open End	US Equity Large Cap Blend (Growth)	B	C+	B+	Up	Y	1,000
Gabelli ESG Fund Class I	SRIDX	NAS CM	Open End	US Equity Large Cap Blend (Growth)	B	C+	B+	Up	Y	100,000
Gabelli Focus Five Fund Class A	GWSAX	NAS CM	Open End	US Equity Mid Cap (Growth)	C	C-	C		Y	1,000
Gabelli Focus Five Fund Class AAA	GWSVX	NAS CM	Open End	US Equity Mid Cap (Growth)	C	C-	C		Y	1,000
Gabelli Focus Five Fund Class C	GWSCX	NAS CM	Open End	US Equity Mid Cap (Growth)	C-	C-	C	Down	Y	1,000
Gabelli Focus Five Fund Class Institutional	GWSIX	NAS CM	Open End	US Equity Mid Cap (Growth)	C	C	C		Y	500,000
Gabelli Focus Five Fund T	GWSTX	NAS CM	Open End	US Equity Mid Cap (Growth)	C	C-	C		Y	1,000
Gabelli Global Content & Connectivity Fund Class A	GTCAX	NAS CM	Open End	Communications Sector Equity (Comm)	B-	C+	B	Up	Y	1,000
Gabelli Global Content & Connectivity Fund Class AAA	GABTX	NAS CM	Open End	Communications Sector Equity (Comm)	B-	C+	B	Up	Y	1,000
Gabelli Global Content & Connectivity Fund Class C	GTCCX	NAS CM	Open End	Communications Sector Equity (Comm)	B-	C	B	Up	Y	1,000
Gabelli Global Content & Connectivity Fund Cls Inst	GTTIX	NAS CM	Open End	Communications Sector Equity (Comm)	B-	C+	B	Up	Y	100,000
Gabelli Global Deal Fund	GDL	NYSE	Closed End	US Equity Mid Cap (Income)	B	C	A+	Up	Y	
Gabelli Global Rising Income and Dividend Fund Class A	GAGAX	NAS CM	Open End	Moderate Alloc (Growth & Income)	B-	B-	B	Down	Y	1,000
Gabelli Global Rising Income and Dividend Fund Class C	GACCX	NAS CM	Open End	Moderate Alloc (Growth & Income)	B-	B-	B	Down	Y	1,000

★ Expanded analysis of this fund is included in Section II.

	TOTAL RETURNS					PERFORMANCE				ASSETS		ASSET ALLOCATION & TURNOVER					BULL & BEAR		FEES		
Min Additional Investment	3-Month Total Return	6-Month Total Return	1-Year Total Return	3-Year Total Return	5-Year Total Return	Dividend Yield (TTM)	Expense Ratio	3-Yr Std Deviation	3-Year Beta	NAV	Total Assets (MIL)	%Cash	%Stocks	%Bonds	%Other	Turnover Ratio	Last Bull Market Total Return	Last Bear Market Total Return	Front End Fee (%)	Back End Fee (%)	Inception Date
500	4.71	9.78	19.20	28.36	94.55	1.14	0.9	11.73	1.04	9.1	112.3	3	97	0	0	35	16.57	-17.98			Jun-08
100	0.58	5.69					2.43			11.99	--								5.75		May-17
	0.71	5.87					2.18			12	--										Mar-17
100	1.40	0.91					0.75			10.18	48.0								5.75		May-17
0	1.44	0.98					0.5			10.19	48.0										May-17
100	1.06	2.31	1.79			0.39	1.2			9.61	179.1	37	33	27	2	4					Jul-15
1,000	1.06	2.42	1.89			0.39	1.07			9.62	179.1	37	33	27	2	4					Jul-15
100	5.00	11.42	14.91	15.94	61.64	0.25	1.87	11.49	1.03	65.27	44.1	0	99	0	0	186	21.18	-22.16			Jul-02
100	2.69	6.96	10.97	17.65	49.85	1.32	1.84	6.69	0.63	41.49	59.7	0	66	31	1	129	13.22	-14.31			Jul-02
100	4.83	10.83					1.83			28.85	12.0	5	94	0	1	27					Mar-17
100	-0.60	3.98	8.14	18.37	32.09	0.31	1.63	9.39	0.87	24.79	42.1	35	65	0	0	396	7.36	-3.7			Feb-08
100	4.22	10.42	15.35	21.10	74.09	0.44	1.79	10.62	1	59.96	225.3	1	97	0	1	172	20.73	-20.95			Nov-01
	0.43	0.82	2.02	7.04	13.38	0.47	0.85	1.58	0.12	10.27	1,429	40	31	28	0	287	4.98	-3.36			May-07
	0.42	0.81	2.20	7.69	14.74	0.7	0.6	1.62	0.12	10.38	1,429	40	31	28	0	287	5.06	-3.14			May-93
	5.37	9.87	20.17	25.07	77.85	0.59	1.36	10.44	0.99	58.36	2,698	0	100	0	0	3	21.92	-18.99	5.75		Dec-03
	5.36	9.88	20.16	25.06	77.85	0.6	1.36	10.43	0.99	58.97	2,698	0	100	0	0	3	21.9	-18.98			Mar-86
	5.18	9.47	19.27	22.29	71.32	0	2.11	10.43	0.99	54.28	2,698	0	100	0	0	3	21.4	-19.26		1.00	Dec-03
	5.44	10.02	20.48	26.02	80.09	0.82	1.11	10.43	0.99	58.85	2,698	0	100	0	0	3	22.11	-18.92			Jan-08
	5.40	9.92	20.20	25.10	77.91		1.36	10.43	0.99	58.91	2,698	0	100	0	0	3	21.9	-18.98	2.50		Jul-17
	1.99	5.92	14.15	16.69	50.53	1.06	1.8	9.86	0.91	5.57	80.0	8	23	1	0	71	15.12	-13.56			Mar-95
	6.06	11.03	19.19	25.44	89.19	2.99	1.38	12.28	1.17	25.12	2,040	1	97	1	0	16	23.87	-20.51			Nov-03
	2.41	6.38	12.14	16.20	67.14	0.37	2	12.51	1.17	17.19	29.0	3	97	0	0	14	23.76	-19.33	5.75		Dec-03
	2.39	6.35	12.10	16.20	67.13	0.36	2	12.5	1.17	17.23	29.0	3	97	0	0	14	23.85	-19.39			Aug-99
	2.24	5.97	11.31	13.63	61.04	0	2.75	12.51	1.17	15.79	29.0	3	97	0	0	14	23.35	-19.6		1.00	Dec-03
	2.70	6.96	13.25	18.19	70.75	0.74	1	12.53	1.17	17.33	29.0	3	97	0	0	14	24.05	-19.3			Jun-04
	0.63	2.29	5.10	14.56	32.74	0	1.72	5.29	0.44	14.7	168.1	21	74	5	0	151	7.24	-6.66	5.75		Feb-01
	0.62	2.39	5.32	15.27	34.07	0	1.52	5.32	0.44	14.93	168.1	21	74	5	0	151	7.41	-6.47			Feb-10
	0.47	2.04	4.54	12.72	29.12	0	2.27	5.26	0.43	13.48	168.1	21	74	5	0	151	6.9	-6.81		1.00	Feb-01
	0.72	2.54	5.60	16.18	35.73	0	1.27	5.25	0.43	15.7	168.1	21	74	5	0	151	7.54	-6.44			Feb-01
	0.63	2.43	5.36	15.33	34.06		1.52	5.26	0.43	14.72	168.1	21	74	5	0	151	7.39	-6.54	2.50		Jun-17
	4.21	7.65	15.10	20.40	70.87	0.36	1.39	10.03	0.96	23.38	1,419	0	100	0	0	1	20.6	-16.28	5.75		Dec-03
	4.23	7.66	15.12	20.45	70.98	0.35	1.39	10.03	0.96	23.5	1,419	0	100	0	0	1	20.66	-16.34			Jan-92
	4.05	7.24	14.28	17.77	64.71	0.41	2.14	10.03	0.96	19.64	1,419	0	100	0	0	1	20.14	-16.59		1.00	Dec-03
	4.28	7.75	15.38	21.31	73.09	0.34	1.14	10.03	0.96	24.46	1,419	0	100	0	0	1	20.9	-16.28			Jan-08
	4.18	7.61	15.07	20.40	70.91		1.39	10.03	0.96	23.49	1,419	0	100	0	0	1	20.66	-16.34	2.50		Jul-17
	3.09	9.82	21.95	27.80	94.83	0.36	0	12.15	1.15	6.47	1,583	0	100	0	0	13	29.69	-25.03			Aug-86
	2.82	5.27	13.23	19.84	63.01	0.21	1.25	9.44	0.8	15.93	66.9	3	97	0	0	18	12.75	-28.47	5.75		Jun-07
	2.88	5.33	13.29	19.90	63.05	0.22	1.25	9.47	0.8	15.95	66.9	3	97	0	0	18	12.84	-28.52			Jun-07
	2.66	4.94	12.43	17.22	57.07	0	2	9.42	0.79	14.78	66.9	3	97	0	0	18	12.35	-28.78		1.00	Jun-07
	2.96	5.43	13.52	20.74	65.05	0.46	1	9.41	0.8	16.27	66.9	3	97	0	0	18	13	-28.43			Jun-07
	0.17	3.76	17.07	3.00	43.09	0	1.42	14.57	0.79	14.71	150.5	7	92	1	0	77	28.83	-27.79	5.75		Dec-02
	0.17	3.72	17.08	2.96	43.15	0	1.42	14.56	0.79	14.56	150.5	7	92	1	0	77	28.71	-27.84			Dec-02
	0.04	3.37	16.18	0.73	37.86	0	2.17	14.55	0.79	12.67	150.5	7	92	1	0	77	28.21	-28.05		1.00	Dec-02
	0.24	3.90	17.35	3.72	44.92	0	1.17	14.54	0.79	14.98	150.5	7	92	1	0	77	28.91	-27.77			Jan-08
	0.17	3.76	17.07	3.01	43.10		1.42	14.58	0.79	14.56	150.5	7	92	1	0	77	28.83	-27.79	2.50		Jul-17
	1.94	4.59	13.38	12.61	40.96	0.39	1.65	11.38	0.83	21.94	96.1	0	100	0	0	9	9.44	-18.57	5.75		Mar-00
	1.91	4.57	13.38	12.74	41.16	1.19	1.65	11.36	0.83	21.77	96.1	0	100	0	0	9	9.46	-18.6			Nov-93
	1.71	4.18	12.53	10.26	35.96	0.41	2.4	11.36	0.83	21.08	96.1	0	100	0	0	9	9.02	-18.84		1.00	Jun-00
	2.17	5.03	14.19	14.18	43.63	1.44	1	11.37	0.83	21.75	96.1	0	100	0	0	9	9.61	-18.51			Jan-08
	0.60	1.03	2.49	11.96	20.60	0	0	3.14		11.59	212.6	32	56	12	0	284	5.36	-5.81			Jan-07
	3.81	7.57	20.93	27.67	49.12	0.8	1.61	6.6	0.59	27.26	68.7	28	70	0	0	52	2.97	-11.32	5.75		May-01
	3.60	7.13	19.97	24.78	41.99	0.47	2.36	6.58	0.58	22.93	68.7	28	70	0	0	52	2.6	-11.58		1.00	Nov-01

Fund Name	Ticker Symbol	Traded On	Fund Type	Category and (Prospectus Objective)	Overall Rating	Reward Rating	Risk Rating	Recent Up/ Downgrade	Open to New Investors	Min Initial Investment
	MARKET		FUND TYPE, CATEGORY & OBJECTIVE		RATINGS				MINIMUMS	
Gabelli Global Rising Income and Dividend Fund Class I	GAGIX	NAS CM	Open End	Moderate Alloc (Growth & Income)	B	B-	B	Up	Y	100,000
Gabelli Global Utility & Income Trust	GLU	AMEX	Closed End	Utilities Sector Equity (Utility)	B-	C+	B	Up	Y	
Gabelli Go Anywhere Trust	GGO	AMEX	Closed End	US Equity Large Cap Blend (Equity-Income)	D	D	D-		Y	
Gabelli Gold Fund Class A	GLDAX	NAS CM	Open End	Precious Metals Sector Equity (Precious Metals)	D+	C-	D	Down	Y	1,000
Gabelli Gold Fund Class AAA	GOLDX	NAS CM	Open End	Precious Metals Sector Equity (Precious Metals)	D+	C-	D	Down	Y	1,000
Gabelli Gold Fund Class C	GLDCX	NAS CM	Open End	Precious Metals Sector Equity (Precious Metals)	D+	C-	D	Down	Y	1,000
Gabelli Gold Fund Class I	GLDIX	NAS CM	Open End	Precious Metals Sector Equity (Precious Metals)	D+	C-	D	Down	Y	500,000
Gabelli Gold Fund Class T	GLDTX	NAS CM	Open End	Precious Metals Sector Equity (Precious Metals)	D+	C-	D	Down	Y	1,000
Gabelli Healthcare & WellnessRx Trust	GRX	NYSE	Closed End	Healthcare Sector Equity (Health)	C	C	C		Y	
Gabelli International Small Cap Fund Class A	GOCAX	NAS CM	Open End	Global Equity (World Stock)	B	B-	B	Up	Y	1,000
Gabelli International Small Cap Fund Class AAA	GABOX	NAS CM	Open End	Global Equity (World Stock)	B	B-	B	Up	Y	1,000
Gabelli International Small Cap Fund Class C	GGLCX	NAS CM	Open End	Global Equity (World Stock)	B-	C+	B	Up	Y	1,000
Gabelli International Small Cap Fund Class Institutional	GLOIX	NAS CM	Open End	Global Equity (World Stock)	B	B-	B	Up	Y	500,000
Gabelli Small Cap Growth Fund Class A	GCASX	NAS CM	Open End	US Equity Small Cap (Small Company)	B	B	B-	Up	Y	1,000
Gabelli Small Cap Growth Fund Class AAA	GABSX	NAS CM	Open End	US Equity Small Cap (Small Company)	B	B	B-	Up	Y	1,000
Gabelli Small Cap Growth Fund Class C	GCCSX	NAS CM	Open End	US Equity Small Cap (Small Company)	B	B	C+	Up	Y	1,000
Gabelli Small Cap Growth Fund Class I	GACIX	NAS CM	Open End	US Equity Small Cap (Small Company)	B	B+	B-	Up	Y	500,000
Gabelli Small Cap Growth Fund T	GATIX	NAS CM	Open End	US Equity Small Cap (Small Company)	B	B	B-		Y	1,000
Gabelli Utilities Fund Class A	GAUAX	NAS CM	Open End	Utilities Sector Equity (Utility)	B-	C+	B-	Down	Y	1,000
Gabelli Utilities Fund Class AAA	GABUX	NAS CM	Open End	Utilities Sector Equity (Utility)	B-	C+	B-	Down	Y	1,000
Gabelli Utilities Fund Class C	GAUCX	NAS CM	Open End	Utilities Sector Equity (Utility)	C+	C+	B-	Down	Y	1,000
Gabelli Utilities Fund Class Institutional	GAUIX	NAS CM	Open End	Utilities Sector Equity (Utility)	B-	B-	B-	Down	Y	500,000
Gabelli Utilities Fund T	GAUTX	NAS CM	Open End	Utilities Sector Equity (Utility)	B-	C+	B-		Y	1,000
Gabelli Utility Trust	GUT	NYSE	Closed End	Utilities Sector Equity (Utility)	B	B-	B	Up	Y	
Gabelli Value 25 Fund Class A	GABVX	NAS CM	Open End	US Equity Mid Cap (Growth)	C+	C+	B-	Down	Y	1,000
Gabelli Value 25 Fund Class AAA	GVCAX	NAS CM	Open End	US Equity Mid Cap (Growth)	C+	C+	B-	Down	Y	1,000
Gabelli Value 25 Fund Class C	GVCCX	NAS CM	Open End	US Equity Mid Cap (Growth)	C+	C+	B-	Down	Y	1,000
Gabelli Value 25 Fund Class I	GVCIX	NAS CM	Open End	US Equity Mid Cap (Growth)	C+	C+	B-	Down	Y	100,000
Gabelli Value 25 Fund Class T	GVCTX	NAS CM	Open End	US Equity Mid Cap (Growth)	C+	C+	B-	Down	Y	1,000
GAMCO Global Gold, Natural Resources & Income Trust	GGN	AMEX	Closed End	Natl Resources Sec Equity (Natl Res)	C	C	C-	Up	Y	
GAMCO Global Growth Fund Class A	GGGAX	NAS CM	Open End	Global Equity (World Stock)	B	B-	B	Up	Y	1,000
GAMCO Global Growth Fund Class AAA	GICPX	NAS CM	Open End	Global Equity (World Stock)	B	B-	B	Up	Y	1,000
GAMCO Global Growth Fund Class C	GGGCX	NAS CM	Open End	Global Equity (World Stock)	B	B-	B	Up	Y	1,000
GAMCO Global Growth Fund Class Institutional	GGGIX	NAS CM	Open End	Global Equity (World Stock)	B	B	B	Up	Y	500,000
GAMCO Global Telecommunications Fund T	GGTTX	NAS CM	Open End	Communications Sector Equity (Comm)	B-	C+	B	Up	Y	1,000
GAMCO Growth Fund Class A	GGCAX	NAS CM	Open End	US Equity Large Cap Growth (Growth)	A-	B+	A-	Up	Y	1,000
GAMCO Growth Fund Class AAA	GABGX	NAS CM	Open End	US Equity Large Cap Growth (Growth)	A-	B+	A-	Up	Y	1,000
GAMCO Growth Fund Class C	GGCCX	NAS CM	Open End	US Equity Large Cap Growth (Growth)	B+	B+	A-	Up	Y	1,000
GAMCO Growth Fund Class I	GGCIX	NAS CM	Open End	US Equity Large Cap Growth (Growth)	A-	B+	A-	Up	Y	500,000
GAMCO Growth Fund Class T	GGGTX	NAS CM	Open End	US Equity Large Cap Growth (Growth)	B+	B+	B		Y	1,000
GAMCO International Growth Fund Class A	GAIGX	NAS CM	Open End	Global Equity Large Cap (Foreign Stock)	B-	C+	B-	Up	Y	1,000
GAMCO International Growth Fund Class AAA	GIGRX	NAS CM	Open End	Global Equity Large Cap (Foreign Stock)	B-	C+	B-	Up	Y	1,000
GAMCO International Growth Fund Class C	GCIGX	NAS CM	Open End	Global Equity Large Cap (Foreign Stock)	B-	C+	B-	Up	Y	1,000
GAMCO International Growth Fund Class I	GIIGX	NAS CM	Open End	Global Equity Large Cap (Foreign Stock)	B-	B-	B	Up	Y	500,000
GAMCO Mathers Fund Class AAA	MATRX	NAS CM	Open End	Other Alternative (Asset Alloc)	D	D-	D	Up	Y	1,000
GAMCO Natural Resources Gold & Income Trust	GNT	NYSE	Closed End	Natl Resources Sec Equity (Natl Res)	C	C	C-	Up	Y	
Gateway Equity Call Premium Fund Class A	GCPAX	NAS CM	Open End	Long/Short Equity (Growth & Income)	B-	C	B+	Down	Y	2,500
Gateway Equity Call Premium Fund Class C	GCPCX	NAS CM	Open End	Long/Short Equity (Growth & Income)	B-	C	B+		Y	2,500
Gateway Equity Call Premium Fund Class N	GCPNX	NAS CM	Open End	Long/Short Equity (Growth & Income)	B-	C	B+	Down	Y	1,000,000
Gateway Equity Call Premium Fund Class Y	GCPYX	NAS CM	Open End	Long/Short Equity (Growth & Income)	B-	C	B+	Down	Y	100,000
Gateway Fund Class A Shares	GATEX	NAS CM	Open End	Long/Short Equity (Growth & Income)	B	C+	A-	Up	Y	2,500
Gateway Fund Class C Shares	GTECX	NAS CM	Open End	Long/Short Equity (Growth & Income)	B-	C+	B+	Down	Y	2,500

★Expanded analysis of this fund is included in Section II.

Min Additional Investment	TOTAL RETURNS: 3-Month Total Return	6-Month Total Return	1-Year Total Return	3-Year Total Return	5-Year Total Return	PERFORMANCE: Dividend Yield (TTM)	Expense Ratio	3-Yr Std Deviation	3-Year Beta	ASSETS: NAV	Total Assets (MIL)	ASSET ALLOCATION & TURNOVER: %Cash	%Stocks	%Bonds	%Other	Turnover Ratio	BULL & BEAR: Last Bull Market Total Return	Last Bear Market Total Return	FEES: Front End Fee (%)	Back End Fee (%)	Inception Date
	4.00	7.91	21.68	29.23	51.76	1.14	1	6.6	0.59	27.35	68.7	28	70	0	0	52	3.37	-11.16			Jan-08
	3.52	7.08	19.59	20.23	46.94	1.63	1.37	12.98	0.57	22.43	93.7	12	85	3	0	22	8.72	-9.68			May-04
	3.55	6.84	8.94			0	8.45			20.3	32.3	29	60	11	0	102					Nov-16
	-0.13	-0.92	6.20	34.09	-33.94	2.2	1.51	39.04	-0.19	13.8	297.9	1	99	0	0	14	-12.15	-12.23	5.75		Dec-02
	-0.13	-0.92	6.22	34.01	-33.96	2.16	1.51	39.12	-0.19	13.78	297.9	1	99	0	0	14	-12.39	-12.26			Jul-94
	-0.39	-1.31	5.38	31.08	-36.38	1.77	2.26	39.05	-0.19	12.73	297.9	1	99	0	0	14	-12.73	-12.53		1.00	Dec-02
	-0.07	-0.77	6.46	35.20	-33.08	2.4	1.26	39.08	-0.19	14.04	297.9	1	99	0	0	14	-12.26	-12.14			Jan-08
	-0.13	-0.91	6.22	34.01	-33.96		1.51	39.11	-0.19	13.76	297.9	1	99	0	0	14	-12.39	-12.26	2.50		Jul-17
	3.15	0.38	13.10	13.10	73.06	0	1.99	11.35	0.81	11.75	231.4	6	94	0	0	32	24.65	-11.96			Jun-07
	6.47	11.24	27.73	28.23	53.86	0.93	2.01	10.75	0.91	18.44	11.1	3	97	0	0	4	19.58	-22.66	5.75		Mar-00
	6.70	11.60	28.08	28.62	54.38	0.98	1	10.75	0.92	18.55	11.1	3	97	0	0	4	19.58	-22.63			May-98
	6.28	10.86	26.78	26.00	48.91	0.93	2.76	10.75	0.92	17.26	11.1	3	97	0	0	4	19.05	-22.88		1.00	Nov-01
	6.75	11.81	29.02	31.28	58.73	1.26	1	10.77	0.92	18.93	11.1	3	97	0	0	4	19.74	-22.56			Jan-08
	4.34	11.87	18.94	33.44	92.14	0	1.39	11.48	0.78	57.99	3,861	0	100	0	0	4	22.6	-20.98	5.75		Dec-03
	4.34	11.88	18.95	33.45	92.17	0	1.39	11.49	0.78	58.02	3,861	0	100	0	0	4	22.56	-20.95			Oct-91
	4.14	11.46	18.07	30.47	85.10	0	2.14	11.49	0.78	51.05	3,861	0	100	0	0	4	22.07	-21.2		1.00	Dec-03
	4.40	12.00	19.22	34.44	94.53	0	1.14	11.5	0.78	59.34	3,861	0	100	0	0	4	22.76	-20.88			Jan-08
	4.31	11.84	18.91	33.40	92.11		1.39	11.49	0.78	58	3,861	0	100	0	0	4	22.56	-20.95	2.50		Jul-17
	0.61	3.25	8.78	15.39	54.80	1.04	1.38	9.04	0.52	9.37	2,327	3	96	1	0	4	9.98	-8.66	5.75		Dec-02
	0.73	3.41	8.92	15.61	54.97	1.06	1.38	9	0.52	9.23	2,327	3	96	1	0	4	9.89	-8.69			Aug-99
	0.56	2.91	8.04	12.84	48.99	1.47	2.13	9.03	0.52	6.58	2,327	3	96	1	0	4	9.49	-9.01		1.00	Dec-02
	0.80	3.48	9.11	16.38	56.74	1.01	1.13	9.04	0.51	9.65	2,327	3	96	1	0	4	10.13	-8.63			Jan-08
	0.62	3.30	8.81	15.49	54.81		1.38	9	0.52	9.22	2,327	3	96	1	0	4	9.89	-8.69	2.50		Jul-17
	1.23	3.84	9.27	18.47	68.01	1.28	1.45	10.5	0.74	5.34	247.0	13	84	3	0	22	15.37	-8.1			Jul-99
	1.87	4.31	12.78	12.82	56.54	0.4	1.4	11.47	1.02	15.48	445.9	1	99	0	0	2	20.93	-19.68	5.75		Sep-89
	1.83	4.28	12.71	12.76	56.48	0.4	1.4	11.49	1.02	15.41	445.9	1	99	0	0	2	20.97	-19.65			Apr-10
	1.63	3.88	11.82	10.22	50.79	0	2.15	11.46	1.02	12.12	445.9	1	99	0	0	2	20.39	-19.89		1.00	Mar-00
	1.97	4.54	13.19	13.83	58.86	0.66	1	11.48	1.02	15.45	445.9	1	99	0	0	2	21.2	-19.58			Jan-08
	1.82	4.27	12.73	12.77	56.47		1.4	11.47	1.02	15.45	445.9	1	99	0	0	2	20.93	-19.68	2.50		Jul-17
	2.45	4.34	7.06	7.94	-21.93	1.79	1.31	17.83	0.46	5.46	725.3	12	82	5	0	198	8.91	-22.1			Mar-05
	6.36	12.18	28.97	27.96	75.03	0.38	1.72	11.02	0.99	33.41	89.0	1	99	0	0	63	29.71	-22.46	5.75		Mar-00
	6.39	12.18	29.01	27.97	74.99	0.37	1.72	11.03	0.99	33.42	89.0	1	99	0	0	63	29.66	-22.43			Feb-94
	6.17	11.75	28.04	25.07	68.52	0	2.47	11.03	0.99	28.73	89.0	1	99	0	0	63	29.13	-22.68		1.00	Mar-00
	6.53	12.53	29.84	30.60	79.82	0.95	1	11.04	0.99	33.9	89.0	1	99	0	0	63	29.85	-22.33			Jan-08
	1.91	4.62	13.43	12.79	41.22		1.65	11.36	0.83	21.75	96.1	0	100	0	0	9	9.46	-18.6	2.50		Jul-17
	8.33	13.17	29.50	38.81	109.72	0	1.44	11.76	1.07	56.76	615.7	1	99	0	0	52	29.46	-19.86	5.75		Dec-03
	8.32	13.16	29.49	38.80	109.68	0	1.44	11.75	1.07	56.74	615.7	1	99	0	0	52	29.44	-19.86			Apr-87
	8.11	12.73	28.53	35.70	101.92	0	2.19	11.75	1.07	50.02	615.7	1	99	0	0	52	28.94	-20.14		1.00	Dec-03
	8.38	13.30	29.83	39.82	112.34	0	1.19	11.76	1.07	57.87	615.7	1	99	0	0	52	29.64	-19.8			Jan-08
	8.32	13.14	29.47	38.77	109.65		1.44	11.75	1.07	56.73	615.7	1	99	0	0	52	29.44	-19.86	2.50		Jul-17
	6.08	10.63	29.32	21.41	31.17	1.26	2.07	12.03	0.88	24.65	25.1	0	100	0	0	9	18.65	-20.89	5.75		Jul-01
	6.04	10.59	29.29	21.39	31.08	1.3	2.07	12.01	0.88	24.15	25.1	0	100	0	0	9	18.61	-20.88			Jun-95
	5.89	10.25	28.37	18.71	26.36	0.7	2.82	12.01	0.88	21.92	25.1	0	100	0	0	9	18.09	-21.13		1.00	Dec-00
	6.35	11.24	30.78	25.50	36.70	2.2	1	12.04	0.88	24.45	25.1	0	100	0	0	9	18.84	-20.79			Jan-08
	-1.96	-3.66	-14.67	-28.05	-44.32	0	2.24	7.95	-0.75	5	8.6	124	-24	0	0	0	-6.43	0.6			Aug-65
	1.87	4.49	8.30	9.90	-11.53	1.4	1.18	16.84		7.11	146.1	5	94	0	0	183	9.02	-23.88			Jan-11
50	2.68	5.76	11.80	24.34		0.84	1.2	5.59	0.89	12.08	84.4	3	97	0	0	24			5.75		Sep-14
50	2.46	5.35	10.95	21.57		0.21	1.95	5.57	0.89	12.05	84.4	3	97	0	0	24				1.00	Sep-14
	2.81	5.97	12.25	25.29			0.9	5.59	0.89	12.09	84.4	3	97	0	0	24					May-17
50	2.80	6.04	12.21	25.25		1.05	0.95	5.6	0.89	12.09	84.4	3	97	0	0	24					Sep-14
50	1.97	4.48	9.66	17.81	32.99	1.19	0.94	4.01	0.37	33.47	8,434	2	98	0	0	14	8.86	-6.02	5.75		Dec-77
50	1.80	4.12	8.85	15.14	28.01	0.46	1.7	4.03	0.37	33.32	8,434	2	98	0	0	14	8.38	-6.3		1.00	Feb-08

	MARKET			FUND TYPE, CATEGORY & OBJECTIVE	RATINGS				MINIMUMS	
Fund Name	Ticker Symbol	Traded On	Fund Type	Category and (Prospectus Objective)	Overall Rating	Reward Rating	Risk Rating	Recent Up/ Downgrade	Open to New Investors	Min Initial Investment
Gateway Fund Class N	GTENX	NAS CM	Open End	Long/Short Equity (Growth & Income)	B	C+	A-		Y	1,000,000
Gateway Fund Class Y Shares	GTEYX	NAS CM	Open End	Long/Short Equity (Growth & Income)	B	C+	A-	Up	Y	100,000
Gator Focus Fund Institutional Shares	GFFIX	NAS CM	Open End	US Equity Small Cap (Small Company)	C	C	C		Y	100,000
Gator Focus Fund Investor Shares	GFFAX	NAS CM	Open End	US Equity Small Cap (Small Company)	C	C	C		Y	5,000
GE RSP U.S. Equity Fund	GESSX	NAS CM	Open End	US Equity Large Cap Blend (Growth)	B-	B-	B-	Down	Y	0
General American Investors Co. Inc.	GAM	NYSE	Closed End	US Equity Large Cap Blend (Growth)	B-	C+	B	Up	Y	
Geneva Advisors All Cap Growth Fund Class Institutional	GNVIX	NAS CM	Open End	US Equity Large Cap Growth (Growth)	A-	A-	B+	Up	Y	100,000
Geneva Advisors All Cap Growth Fund Class Retail	GNVRX	NAS CM	Open End	US Equity Large Cap Growth (Growth)	B+	A-	B+	Up	Y	1,000
Geneva Advisors Equity Income Fund Class I	GNEIX	NAS CM	Open End	US Equity Large Cap Growth (Equity-Income)	C+	B-	C+	Down	Y	100,000
Geneva Advisors Equity Income Fund Class R	GNERX	NAS CM	Open End	US Equity Large Cap Growth (Equity-Income)	C+	B-	C+	Down	Y	1,000
George Putnam Balanced Fund Class A	PGEOX	NAS CM	Open End	Moderate Alloc (Balanced)	B-	C+	B	Down	Y	0
George Putnam Balanced Fund Class B	PGEBX	NAS CM	Open End	Moderate Alloc (Balanced)	B-	C+	B	Down	Y	0
George Putnam Balanced Fund Class C	PGPCX	NAS CM	Open End	Moderate Alloc (Balanced)	B-	C+	B	Down	Y	0
George Putnam Balanced Fund Class M	PGEMX	NAS CM	Open End	Moderate Alloc (Balanced)	B-	C+	B	Down	Y	0
George Putnam Balanced Fund Class R	PGPRX	NAS CM	Open End	Moderate Alloc (Balanced)	B-	C+	B	Down	Y	0
George Putnam Balanced Fund Class R5	PGELX	NAS CM	Open End	Moderate Alloc (Balanced)	B-	C+	B	Down	Y	0
George Putnam Balanced Fund Class R6	PGEJX	NAS CM	Open End	Moderate Alloc (Balanced)	B-	C+	B	Down	Y	0
George Putnam Balanced Fund Class Y	PGEYX	NAS CM	Open End	Moderate Alloc (Balanced)	B-	C+	B	Down	Y	0
Gerstein Fisher Multi-Factor Global Real Estate Sec Fund	GFMRX	NAS CM	Open End	Real Estate Sector Equity (Equity-Income)	B-	C+	B		Y	250
Gerstein Fisher Multi-Factor Growth Equity Fund	GFMGX	NAS CM	Open End	US Equity Large Cap Growth (Growth)	B+	B	B+	Up	Y	250
Gerstein Fisher Multi-Factor Intl Growth Equity Fund	GFIGX	NAS CM	Open End	Global Equity Large Cap (Foreign Stock)	B	B	B	Up	Y	250
Glenmede Equity Income Portfolio	GEQIX	NAS CM	Open End	US Equity Large Cap Value (Growth & Income)	D-	D+	A-		Y	0
Glenmede Fund International Portfolio	GTCIX	NAS CM	Open End	Global Equity Large Cap (Foreign Stock)	B-	C+	B	Up	Y	0
Glenmede Fund Large Cap Value Portfolio	GTMEX	NAS CM	Open End	US Equity Large Cap Value (Growth)	B	B	B	Up	Y	0
Glenmede Global Secured Options Portfolio	NOVIX	NAS CM	Open End	Long/Short Equity (Growth)	C+	C	B	Up	Y	0
Glenmede Large Cap Core Portfolio	GTLOX	NAS CM	Open End	US Equity Large Cap Blend (Growth)	B	B	B		Y	0
Glenmede Large Cap Core Portfolio Institutional Shares	GTLIX	NAS CM	Open End	US Equity Large Cap Blend (Growth)	B	B	B		Y	10,000,000
Glenmede Large Cap Growth Fund Institutional Shares	GTILX	NAS CM	Open End	US Equity Large Cap Growth (Growth)	B+	A-	B+	Up	Y	10,000,000
Glenmede Large Cap Growth Portfolio	GTLLX	NAS CM	Open End	US Equity Large Cap Growth (Growth)	B+	A-	B+	Up	Y	0
Glenmede Long/Short Portfolio	GTAPX	NAS CM	Open End	Long/Short Equity (Equity-Income)	B	C+	A-	Up	Y	0
Glenmede Mid Cap Equity Portfolio Advisor Shares	GMQAX	NAS CM	Open End	US Equity Mid Cap (Growth & Income)	C+	C	C+	Up	Y	0
Glenmede Responsible ESG U.S. Equity Portfolio	RESGX	NAS CM	Open End	US Equity Large Cap Blend (Growth)	C-	C	B+	Up	Y	0
Glenmede Secured Options Portfolio	GTSOX	NAS CM	Open End	Long/Short Equity (Growth)	B	C+	B+	Up	Y	0
Glenmede Secured Options Portfolio Institutional Class	GLSOX	NAS CM	Open End	Long/Short Equity (Growth)	B	C+	B+	Up	Y	10,000,000
Glenmede Small Cap Equity Portfolio Class Advisor	GTCSX	NAS CM	Open End	US Equity Small Cap (Small Company)	B+	B+	B	Up	Y	0
Glenmede Small Cap Equity Portfolio Institutional Class	GTSCX	NAS CM	Open End	US Equity Small Cap (Small Company)	B+	A-	B	Up	Y	10,000,000
Glenmede Strategic Equity Portfolio	GTCEX	NAS CM	Open End	US Equity Large Cap Blend (Growth)	B	B	B		Y	0
Glenmede Total Market Portfolio	GTTMX	NAS CM	Open End	US Equity Mid Cap (Growth)	B+	B+	B	Up	Y	0
Glenmede Women in Leadership U.S. Equity Portfolio	GWILX	NAS CM	Open End	US Equity Large Cap Blend (Growth)	C-	C	B+	Up	Y	0
Global IPO Fund	IPOSX	NAS CM	Open End	US Equity Mid Cap (Growth)	C+	C+	C+		Y	5,000
Global Strategic Income Fund Class A	VEEEX	NAS CM	Open End	Europe Equity Large Cap (Growth)	B-	C	B	Up	Y	2,500
GMO Alpha Only Fund Class III	GGHEX	NAS CM	Open End	Market Neutral (World Stock)	C	C	C	Down	Y	10,000,000
GMO Alpha Only Fund Class IV	GAPOX	NAS CM	Open End	Market Neutral (World Stock)	C	C	C	Down	Y	250,000,000
GMO Benchmark-Free Allocation Fund Class III	GBMFX	NAS CM	Open End	Alloc (Asset Alloc)	B-	C+	B	Up	Y	10,000,000
GMO Benchmark-Free Allocation Fund Class IV	GBMBX	NAS CM	Open End	Alloc (Asset Alloc)	B-	C+	B	Up	Y	250,000,000
GMO Benchmark-Free Allocation Fund Class MF	US3620148052		Open End	Alloc (Asset Alloc)	B-	C+	B	Up	Y	0
GMO Benchmark-Free Allocation Series Fund Class R6	GBMRX	NAS CM	Open End	Alloc (Growth)	B-	C+	B	Up	Y	10,000,000
GMO Benchmark-Free Fund Class III	GBFFX	NAS CM	Open End	Alloc (Income)	B-	C+	B	Up	Y	10,000,000
GMO Climate Change Fund Class III	GCCHX	NAS CM	Open End	Global Equity (Growth & Income)	U	U	U		Y	10,000,000
GMO Emerging Domestic Opportunities Fund Class II	GEDTX	NAS CM	Open End	Emerging Markets Equity (Div Emerging Mkts)	B-	B	B-	Up	Y	10,000,000
GMO Emerging Domestic Opportunities Fund Class III	GEDSX	NAS CM	Open End	Emerging Markets Equity (Div Emerging Mkts)	B-	B	B-	Up	Y	50,000,000
GMO Emerging Domestic Opportunities Fund Class IV	GEDIX	NAS CM	Open End	Emerging Markets Equity (Div Emerging Mkts)	B-	B	B-	Up	Y	250,000,000

★ Expanded analysis of this fund is included in Section II.

Min Additional Investment	TOTAL RETURNS: 3-Month Total Return	6-Month Total Return	1-Year Total Return	3-Year Total Return	5-Year Total Return	PERFORMANCE: Dividend Yield (TTM)	Expense Ratio	3-Yr Std Deviation	3-Year Beta	ASSETS: NAV	Total Assets (MIL)	ASSET ALLOCATION & TURNOVER: %Cash	%Stocks	%Bonds	%Other	Turnover Ratio	BULL & BEAR: Last Bull Market Total Return	Last Bear Market Total Return	FEES: Front End Fee (%)	Back End Fee (%)	Inception Date
	2.05	4.67	9.83	18.00	33.20		0.65	4.01	0.37	33.46	8,434	2	98	0	0	14	8.86	-6.02			May-17
50	2.03	4.65	9.93	18.67	34.62	1.42	0.7	4.02	0.37	33.46	8,434	2	98	0	0	14	9.03	-5.94			Feb-08
2,000	7.18	12.85	16.13	0.67		0.89	1.49	16	1	12.27	3.1	1	99	0	0	32					Apr-13
1,000	7.07	12.67	15.87	-0.06		0.67	1.74	15.98	1	12.18	3.1	1	99	0	0	32					Apr-13
	4.57	9.01	20.49	28.62	102.25	1.49	0.15	11.38	1.1	52.45	5,503	2	98	0	0	38	26.59	-18.59			Jun-67
	2.91	7.51	16.61	21.85	74.37	1.12	1.17	11.2	1.05	40.39	1,064	16	97	0	4	20	28.81	-21.86			Feb-27
1,000	7.17	11.84	32.05	37.98	85.77	0	1.1	12.33	1.04	27.81	155.2	1	99	0	0	36	22.31	-18.71			Sep-07
100	7.06	11.66	31.60	36.53	82.47	0	1.45	12.33	1.04	26.6	155.2	1	99	0	0	36	22.08	-18.8			Sep-07
1,000	4.93	8.61	20.61	20.23	70.39	0.78	1.1	10.75	1.02	37.21	111.4	4	96	0	0	17	22.72	-13.1			Apr-10
100	4.83	8.43	20.21	18.95	67.41	0.54	1.45	10.77	1.02	37.05	111.4	4	96	0	0	17	22.54	-13.24			Apr-10
	3.61	7.05	15.02	22.04	61.04	1.11	1.01	6.84	0.66	20.01	1,234	2	60	37	0	204	15.42	-10.52	5.75		Nov-37
	3.39	6.60	14.19	19.29	55.13	0.39	1.76	6.83	0.66	19.79	1,234	2	60	37	0	204	14.96	-10.85		5.00	Apr-92
	3.38	6.64	14.16	19.29	55.10	0.41	1.76	6.85	0.66	19.87	1,234	2	60	37	0	204	14.89	-10.84		1.00	Jul-99
	3.42	6.72	14.44	20.18	57.09	0.66	1.51	6.84	0.66	19.73	1,234	2	60	37	0	204	15.06	-10.73	3.50		Dec-94
	3.52	6.91	14.73	21.12	59.07	0.88	1.26	6.86	0.66	19.95	1,234	2	60	37	0	204	15.23	-10.66			Jan-03
	3.64	7.19	15.37	23.04	62.80	1.03	0.74	6.86	0.66	20.16	1,234	2	60	37	0	204	15.42	-10.52			Dec-13
	3.64	7.17	15.45	23.35	63.39	1.46	0.64	6.85	0.66	20.08	1,234	2	60	37	0	204	15.42	-10.52			Dec-13
	3.65	7.16	15.30	22.93	63.09	1.34	0.76	6.86	0.66	20.08	1,234	2	60	37	0	204	15.61	-10.52			Mar-94
	2.55	4.01	10.20	17.15		2.61	1	10.57	0.94	11.17	135.4	0	98	0	1	20					Apr-13
	5.81	12.24	22.95	32.92	111.18	0.46	0.99	10.75	0.94	21.55	307.2	0	100	0	0	22	27.2	-16.81			Jan-10
	4.66	11.65	32.12	30.26	66.05	0.81	1.11	12.46	0.98	15.97	239.6	1	97	0	1	36					Jan-12
	6.65	10.71	18.25				0.85			11.54	14.3	0	99	0	1						Dec-16
	3.55	7.80	22.43	21.47	34.07	1.68	1	11.06	0.88	15.4	464.5	0	99	0	1	121	15.1	-27.66			Nov-88
	6.76	11.08	15.84	30.16	100.18	1.92	0.91	12.12	1.13	11.07	77.5	0	100	0	0	110	25.47	-26.53			Jan-93
	3.82	5.60	13.03	10.89	20.22	0.6	0.99	9.43	0.82	10.74	10.8	4	96	0	0	70					Sep-12
	7.45	13.71	24.76	39.45	129.39	0.8	0.88	10.46	1.01	28.2	2,775	1	99	0	0	111	27	-18.36			Feb-04
	7.51	13.81	25.01	40.02	130.34	0.97	0.68	10.47	1.01	28.21	2,775	1	99	0	0	111	27	-18.36			Dec-15
	7.85	15.10	28.08	41.96	140.27	0.62	0.68	10.6	0.95	32.32	4,017	0	100	0	0	88	27.67	-18.42			Nov-15
	7.79	14.98	27.81	41.35	139.23	0.45	0.88	10.6	0.95	32.31	4,017	0	100	0	0	88	27.67	-18.42			Feb-04
	2.75	5.57	8.78	15.80	39.81	0	1.17	4.66	0.33	13.06	304.3	68	32	0	0	98	9.12	-5.03			Sep-06
	6.27	7.96	12.36	16.31		0.33	1	12.11	1.06	12.16	15.1	4	96	0	0	84					Sep-14
	6.69	12.83	22.84			0.6	1			14.17	14.3	0	100	0	0	65					Dec-15
	0.79	2.40	5.94	19.53	46.47	0	0.85	6.61	1.03	12.03	818.8	22	78	0	0	1,108	20.5	-10.31			Jun-10
	0.86	2.55	6.18	19.83	46.84	0	0.65	6.61	1.03	12.06	818.8	22	78	0	0	1,108	20.5	-10.31			Nov-16
	5.10	9.44	15.74	31.56	106.38	0.06	0.91	14.24	0.99	30.1	3,588	3	97	0	0	58	26.67	-23.64			Mar-91
	5.14	9.53	15.98	32.36	108.45	0.09	0.71	14.24	0.99	31.57	3,588	3	97	0	0	58	26.83	-23.56			Jan-98
	6.96	12.41	25.92	41.27	113.93	0.71	0.84	10.29	0.89	24.34	213.6	1	99	0	0	22	27.14	-18.32			Jul-89
	8.82	13.94	22.85	36.40	120.77	0.21	1.25	10.83	0.99	19.32	79.9	0	99	0	1	88	23.72	-21.03			Dec-06
	7.22	12.25	23.18			0.79	1			13.61	12.8	0	100	0	0	81					Dec-15
100	4.61	9.35	20.02	8.58	65.77	0	2.51	14.98	1.07	15.85	6.8	3	97	0	0	119	18.61	-27.61			Dec-97
50	1.63	3.58	12.69	13.95	20.47	0	2.6	9.68		26.41	12.6	0	93	0	0	35	5.28	-29.49	5.75		Feb-96
	0.04	0.79	6.23	2.74	-2.36	1.83	0.68	4.15	6.91	21.58	230.4	2	89	7	0	22	-2.6	6.05			Jul-94
	0.09	0.79	6.28	2.87	-2.14	1.85	0.62	4.14	6.11	21.59	230.4	2	89	7	0	22	-2.59	6.04			Mar-06
	2.74	5.05	13.04	11.66	26.08	1.57	0.94	6.19	0.74	27.43	13,414	9	40	38	11	7	8.53	-3.99	0.20		Jul-03
	2.73	5.03	13.06	11.80	26.40	1.63	0.89	6.18	0.74	27.42	13,414	10	42	39	8	7	8.53	-3.99	0.20		Dec-12
	2.73	5.02	13.09	11.85	26.47	1.62	0.88	6.19	0.74	27.44	13,414	10	42	39	8	7	8.53	-3.99	0.20		Mar-12
	2.70	5.01	12.88	11.29	25.26	1.51	0.99	6.14	0.74	10.59	323.0	9	40	38	11	34	8.53	-3.99	0.18		Jan-13
	3.74	6.82	17.05	19.20	31.41	2.35	0.32	7.85	1.07	20.65	4,381	8	50	39	1	83	6.56		0.25		Jun-11
	4.50	17.95					0.76			24.08	19.2	2	90	2	1						Apr-17
	8.15	15.80	37.46	31.94	35.98	1.98	1.19	11.34	0.65	28.45	2,355	1	74	2	20	227	19.53	-17.93	0.80		Mar-11
	8.15	15.84	37.51	32.15	36.41	2.02	1.12	11.36	0.65	28.45	2,355	1	74	2	20	227	19.53	-17.93	0.80		Jun-12
	8.21	15.89	37.67	32.39	36.78	2.04	1.08	11.37	0.65	28.47	2,355	1	74	2	20	227	19.53	-17.93	0.80		May-12

	MARKET			FUND TYPE, CATEGORY & OBJECTIVE	RATINGS				MINIMUMS	
Fund Name	Ticker Symbol	Traded On	Fund Type	Category and (Prospectus Objective)	Overall Rating	Reward Rating	Risk Rating	Recent Up/ Downgrade	Open to New Investors	Min Initial Investment
GMO Emerging Domestic Opportunities Fund Class V	GEDOX	NAS CM	Open End	Emerging Markets Equity (Div Emerging Mkts)	B-	B	B-	Up	Y	500,000,000
GMO Emerging Markets Fund Class II	GMEMX	NAS CM	Open End	Emerging Markets Equity (Div Emerging Mkts)	C+	B-	C	Up	Y	10,000,000
GMO Emerging Markets Fund Class III	GMOEX	NAS CM	Open End	Emerging Markets Equity (Div Emerging Mkts)	B-	B-	C	Up	Y	50,000,000
GMO Emerging Markets Fund Class IV	GMEFX	NAS CM	Open End	Emerging Markets Equity (Div Emerging Mkts)	B-	B-	C	Up	Y	250,000,000
GMO Emerging Markets Fund Class V	GEMVX	NAS CM	Open End	Emerging Markets Equity (Div Emerging Mkts)	B-	B	C	Up	Y	500,000,000
GMO Emerging Markets Fund Class VI	GEMMX	NAS CM	Open End	Emerging Markets Equity (Div Emerging Mkts)	B-	B	C	Up	Y	750,000,000
GMO Emerging Markets Series Fund Class R6	GECRX	NAS CM	Open End	Emerging Markets Equity (Div Emerging Mkts)	B-	B	C	Up	Y	10,000,000
GMO Foreign Small Companies Fund Class III	GMFSX	NAS CM	Open End	Global Equity Mid/Small Cap (Foreign Stock)	B	B	B	Up	Y	10,000,000
GMO Foreign Small Companies Fund Class IV	GFSFX	NAS CM	Open End	Global Equity Mid/Small Cap (Foreign Stock)	B	B	B	Up	Y	250,000,000
GMO Global Asset Allocation Fund Class III	GMWAX	NAS CM	Open End	Alloc (Asset Alloc)	B-	C+	B	Up	Y	10,000,000
GMO Global Asset Allocation Series Fund Class R6	GATRX	NAS CM	Open End	Alloc (Multi-Asset Global)	B-	C+	B	Up	Y	10,000,000
GMO Global Developed Equity Allocation Fund Class III	GWOAX	NAS CM	Open End	Global Equity (Asset Alloc)	C+	B-	C+	Down	Y	10,000,000
GMO Global Equity Allocation Fund Class III	GMGEX	NAS CM	Open End	Global Equity (World Stock)	B-	B-	B-	Up	Y	10,000,000
GMO Global Equity Allocation Series Fund Class R6	GGASX	NAS CM	Open End	Global Equity (World Stock)	C+	B-	C+	Down	Y	10,000,000
GMO Implementation Fund	GIMFX	NAS CM	Open End	Alloc (Growth)	B-	C+	B	Up	Y	10,000,000
GMO International Developed Equity Allocation Fund Cls III	GIOTX	NAS CM	Open End	Global Equity Large Cap (Growth & Income)	B-	C+	B-	Up	Y	10,000,000
GMO Intl Developed Equity Allocation Series Fund Cls R6	GIDRX	NAS CM	Open End	Global Equity Large Cap (Growth & Income)	C+	C+	C	Up	Y	10,000,000
GMO International Equity Allocation Fund Class III	GIEAX	NAS CM	Open End	Global Equity Large Cap (Foreign Stock)	B-	B-	B-	Up	Y	10,000,000
GMO International Equity Allocation Series Fund Class R6	GEARX	NAS CM	Open End	Global Equity Large Cap (Foreign Stock)	B-	B-	B-	Up	Y	10,000,000
GMO International Equity Fund Class II	GMICX	NAS CM	Open End	Global Equity Large Cap (Foreign Stock)	B-	C+	B-	Up	Y	10,000,000
GMO International Equity Fund Class III	GMOIX	NAS CM	Open End	Global Equity Large Cap (Foreign Stock)	B-	C+	B-	Up	Y	35,000,000
GMO International Equity Fund Class IV	GMCFX	NAS CM	Open End	Global Equity Large Cap (Foreign Stock)	B-	C+	B-	Up	Y	250,000,000
GMO International Large/Mid Cap Equity Fund Class III	GMIEX	NAS CM	Open End	Global Equity Large Cap (Foreign Stock)	C+	C+	B-	Up	Y	10,000,000
GMO International Large/Mid Cap Equity Fund Class IV	GMIRX	NAS CM	Open End	Global Equity Large Cap (Foreign Stock)	B-	C+	B-	Up	Y	250,000,000
GMO International Small Companies Fund Class III	GMISX	NAS CM	Open End	Global Equity Mid/Small Cap (Foreign Stock)	B	B	B	Up	Y	10,000,000
GMO Quality Fund Class III	GQETX	NAS CM	Open End	US Equity Large Cap Blend (Growth)	B+	B	A-	Up	Y	10,000,000
GMO Quality Fund Class IV	GQEFX	NAS CM	Open End	US Equity Large Cap Blend (Growth)	B+	B	A-		Y	250,000,000
GMO Quality Fund Class V	GQLFX	NAS CM	Open End	US Equity Large Cap Blend (Growth)	B+	B	A-		Y	500,000,000
GMO Quality Fund Class VI	GQLOX	NAS CM	Open End	US Equity Large Cap Blend (Growth)	B+	B	A-		Y	750,000,000
GMO Resources Fund Class III	GOFIX	NAS CM	Open End	Natl Resources Sec Equity (Natl Res)	B-	B	C	Up	Y	10,000,000
GMO Resources Fund Class IV	GOVIX	NAS CM	Open End	Natl Resources Sec Equity (Natl Res)	B-	B	C	Up	Y	250,000,000
GMO Risk Premium Fund Class III	GMRPX	NAS CM	Open End	Alloc (Growth)	B	B-	B+	Up	Y	10,000,000
GMO Risk Premium Fund Class VI	GMOKX	NAS CM	Open End	Alloc (Growth)	B	B-	B+	Up	Y	750,000,000
GMO SGM Major Markets Fund Class III	GSMFX	NAS CM	Open End	Multialternative (Growth & Income)	B-	C	B	Up	Y	10,000,000
GMO SGM Major Markets Fund Class IV	GSMJX	NAS CM	Open End	Multialternative (Growth & Income)	B-	C	B	Up	Y	250,000,000
GMO SGM Major Markets Fund Class VI	GSMHX	NAS CM	Open End	Multialternative (Growth & Income)	B-	C	B	Up	Y	750,000,000
GMO Special Opportunities Fund Class VI	GSOFX	NAS CM	Open End	Multialternative (Income)	A-	B	A	Up	Y	750,000,000
GMO Strategic Opportunities Allocation Fund Class III	GBATX	NAS CM	Open End	Alloc (Growth)	B-	C+	B	Up	Y	10,000,000
GMO Tax-Managed International Equities Fund Class III	GTMIX	NAS CM	Open End	Global Equity Large Cap (Foreign Stock)	B-	C+	B-	Up	Y	10,000,000
GMO U.S. Equity Allocation Fund Class III	GMUEX	NAS CM	Open End	US Equity Large Cap Blend (Growth & Income)	B	B	B+		Y	10,000,000
GMO U.S. Equity Allocation Fund Class IV	GMRTX	NAS CM	Open End	US Equity Large Cap Blend (Growth & Income)	B	B	B+		Y	250,000,000
GMO U.S. Equity Allocation Fund Class V	GMEQX	NAS CM	Open End	US Equity Large Cap Blend (Growth & Income)	B	B	B		Y	500,000,000
GMO U.S. Equity Allocation Fund Class VI	GMCQX	NAS CM	Open End	US Equity Large Cap Blend (Growth & Income)	B	B	B		Y	750,000,000
Goehring & Rozencwajg Resources Fund Institutional Class	GRHIX	NAS CM	Open End	Natl Resources Sec Equity (Natl Res)	D-	D+	D+		Y	100,000
Goehring & Rozencwajg Resources Fund Retail Class	GRHAX	NAS CM	Open End	Natl Resources Sec Equity (Natl Res)	D-	D+	D+		Y	3,000
Goldman Sachs Absolute Return Multi-Asset Fund Class A	GARDX	NAS CM	Open End	Multialternative (Multi-Asset Global)	C	C-	B	Up	Y	1,000
Goldman Sachs Absolute Return Multi-Asset Fund Class C	GAREX	NAS CM	Open End	Multialternative (Multi-Asset Global)	C	C-	B-	Up	Y	1,000
Goldman Sachs Absolute Return Multi-Asset Fund Class R	GARRX	NAS CM	Open End	Multialternative (Multi-Asset Global)	C	C-	B	Up	Y	0
Goldman Sachs Absolute Return Multi-Asset Fund Class R6	GARNX	NAS CM	Open End	Multialternative (Multi-Asset Global)	C	C	B+	Up	Y	5,000,000
Goldman Sachs Absolute Return Multi-Asset Fund Inst Cls	GARFX	NAS CM	Open End	Multialternative (Multi-Asset Global)	C	C	B+	Up	Y	1,000,000
Goldman Sachs Absolute Return Multi-Asset Fund Inv Cls	GARMX	NAS CM	Open End	Multialternative (Multi-Asset Global)	C	C	B	Up	Y	0
Goldman Sachs Absolute Return Tracker Fund Class A	GARTX	NAS CM	Open End	Multialternative (Income)	B-	C	B	Up	Y	1,000

★ Expanded analysis of this fund is included in Section II.

	TOTAL RETURNS					PERFORMANCE				ASSETS		ASSET ALLOCATION & TURNOVER					BULL & BEAR		FEES		
Min Additional Investment	3-Month Total Return	6-Month Total Return	1-Year Total Return	3-Year Total Return	5-Year Total Return	Dividend Yield (TTM)	Expense Ratio	3-Yr Std Deviation	3-Year Beta	NAV	Total Assets (MIL)	%Cash	%Stocks	%Bonds	%Other	Turnover Ratio	Last Bull Market Total Return	Last Bear Market Total Return	Front End Fee (%)	Back End Fee (%)	Inception Date
	8.20	15.90	37.65	32.50	36.77	2.1	1.06	11.36	0.65	28.43	2,355	1	74	2	20	227	19.53	-17.93	0.80		Mar-11
	6.72	10.54	31.96	28.52	14.90	2.01	0.99	16.28	1.02	34.98	5,203	1	92	1	3		15	-26.5	0.80		Nov-96
	6.74	10.58	32.04	28.83	15.21	2.03	0.94	16.38	1.02	35.07	5,203	1	92	1	3		15.02	-26.49	0.80		Dec-93
	6.75	10.59	32.08	28.89	15.40	2.14	0.89	16.34	1.02	34.73	5,203	1	92	1	3		15.12	-26.53	0.80		Jan-98
	6.73	10.60	32.12	29.03	15.66	2.15	0.84	16.34	1.02	34.63	5,203	1	92	1	3		15.21	-26.51	0.80		Aug-03
	6.76	10.66	32.22	29.20	15.90	2.19	0.81	16.38	1.02	34.72	5,203	1	92	1	3		15.11	-26.45	0.80		Jun-03
	6.68	10.49	32.94	32.65	18.90	0.98	0.99	16.28	1.01	10.47	15.8	1	91	1	5	11	15.02	-26.49			May-14
	7.80	13.37	28.16	35.79	58.60	3.1	0.76	11.19	0.92	15.57	256.6	2	95	0	2	49	14.2	-24.16	0.50		Jan-95
	7.84	13.42	28.30	36.09	58.95	3.16	0.71	11.16	0.92	15.53	256.6	2	95	0	2	49	14.3	-24.18	0.50		Jun-02
	3.38	6.63	15.72	16.70	34.31	2.07	0.58	6.79		33.12	2,501	7	55	36	1	19	9.19	-7.89	0.15		Oct-96
	3.32	6.52	15.42	16.10	33.18	2	0.63	6.72		9.71	193.3	4	52	31	13	2	9.19	-7.89	0.14		Jul-12
	5.65	11.40	25.63	27.61	62.24	2.8	0.59	10.61	0.98	22.66	500.1	6	97	1	-4	29	15.22	-14.19	0.08		Jun-05
	5.82	11.21	26.39	27.74	55.98	2.69	0.68	11.05	1.01	26.46	2,494	1	96	1	1	27	14.76	-15.64	0.18		Nov-96
	5.69	10.94	25.80	26.69	54.05	2.59	0.73	10.95	1	11.22	5.9	0	94	0	5	14	14.76	-15.64	0.19		Sep-12
	2.98	5.50	14.08	12.41	36.49	2.28	0.05	6.99	0.78	13.89	11,384	8	48	33	9	142			0.20		Mar-12
	4.31	11.16	26.38	21.30	44.17	3.33	0.68	11.73	0.92	17.27	671.7	0	97	0	2	10	10.37	-20.32	0.08		Jun-06
	4.24	10.96	26.00	20.90	43.68	3.23	0.73	11.61	0.91	11.18	12.9	0	95	0	3	3	10.37	-20.32	0.08		Jan-15
	5.02	11.03	27.79	23.52	37.19	2.92	0.78	12.29	0.98	32.18	1,076	0	95	0	2	7	11.58	-21.86	0.25		Oct-96
	4.96	10.94	27.37	23.08	36.40	2.82	0.83	12.16	0.96	10.52	253.6	0	94	0	3	3	11.36	-21.86	0.27		Mar-12
	4.04	11.14	25.60	19.79	41.64	3.37	0.72	11.66	0.92	23.66	5,428	0	96	0	2	27	7.37	-21.82			Sep-96
	4.05	11.19	25.72	20.05	42.11	3.39	0.65	11.66	0.92	23.95	5,428	0	96	0	2	27	7.42	-21.79			Mar-87
	4.10	11.25	25.81	20.33	42.62	3.47	0.59	11.64	0.92	23.91	5,428	0	96	0	2	27	7.4	-21.75			Jan-98
	5.02	11.42	24.92	19.01	40.35	2.62	0.54	11.64	0.92	26.37	80.4	1	92	1	3	26	10.12	-21.22			Jan-02
	5.06	11.49	25.03	19.25	40.84	2.69	0.48	11.65	0.92	26.32	80.4	1	92	1	3	26	10.14	-21.21			Jun-03
	7.63	15.12	31.22	36.35	68.55	5.24	0.78	12.08	1	19.79	19.6	2	96	0	0	159	12.38	-22.93	0.50		Oct-91
	7.58	10.97	29.06	42.27	105.01	1.36	0.48	9.76	0.87	24.44	8,453	1	97	2	0	29	20.44	-6.85			Feb-04
	7.60	10.94	29.06	42.45	105.50	1.39	0.44	9.8	0.88	24.47	8,453	1	97	2	0	29	20.46	-6.79			Feb-04
	7.62	10.99	29.11	42.58	105.80	1.43	0.42	9.82	0.88	24.48	8,453	1	97	2	0	29	20.54	-6.83			Dec-06
	7.64	11.03	29.18	42.72	106.06	1.45	0.39	9.82	0.88	24.44	8,453	1	97	2	0	29	20.52	-6.78			Dec-06
	8.56	27.73	28.19	43.29	25.26	4.15	0.77	22.68	1.14	20.24	228.2	1	84	1	1	29			0.30		Dec-11
	8.58	27.77	28.31	43.47	25.48	4.2	0.72	22.66	1.14	20.17	228.2	1	84	1	1	29			0.30		Mar-13
	1.66	4.72	12.85	32.96	45.15	0	0.61	7.3	0.57	27.57	150.4	40	0	54	6	0			0.15		Dec-12
	1.66	4.78	12.94	33.31	45.80	0	0.51	7.33	0.58	27.71	150.4	40	0	54	6	0			0.15		Nov-12
	0.09	1.05	3.88	8.63	19.52	2	1.01	6.6	43.2	32.04	1,482	35	0	65	0	15					Oct-11
	0.12	1.08	3.96	8.72	19.62	2.39	0.96	6.6	43.02	31.93	1,482	35	0	65	0	15					Oct-16
	0.09	1.08	3.99	8.84	19.75	2.37	0.92	6.62	42.9	31.95	1,482	35	0	65	0	15					Dec-15
	9.07	13.75	32.22	41.28		1.06	1.27	9.7	-0.74	24.42	1,025	13	76	10	1	87			0.50		Jul-14
	4.25	8.24	19.30	20.88	49.81	2.34	0.52	8.14		21.89	1,937	4	67	26	1	28	12.17	-9.79	0.20		May-05
	4.11	12.31	28.44	20.50	42.10	1.88	0.68	12.23	0.96	17.01	110.9	1	93	0	3	47	9.87	-21.34			Jul-98
	4.76	10.58	16.67	31.98	91.57	1.13	0.46	10.74	1.03	15.4	1,528	1	99	0	0	66	21.75	-10.31			Sep-85
	6.36	12.25	18.42	34.28	95.00	0.94	0.41	10.71	1.02	15.41	1,528	1	99	0	0	66	21.75	-10.31			Jan-98
	4.71	10.52	16.63	31.99	91.58	1.24	0.4	10.73	1.03	15.33	1,528	1	99	0	0	66	21.75	-10.31			Aug-16
	4.66	10.49	16.61	32.21	92.16	1.24	0.37	10.72	1.03	15.29	1,528	1	99	0	0	66	21.81	-10.24			Jun-03
	10.20	22.96	-0.15				0.93			9.92	21.1	0	99	1	0						Dec-16
	10.00	22.77	-0.55				1.26			9.88	21.1	0	99	1	0						Dec-16
50	0.45	1.78	4.11			0.93	1.48			9.97	29.9	47	29	24	0	38			5.50		Sep-15
50	0.30	1.32	3.22			0.16	2.24			9.92	29.9	47	29	24	0	38				1.00	Sep-15
	0.40	1.63	3.85			0.65	1.74			9.97	29.9	47	29	24	0	38					Sep-15
	0.61	2.04	4.59			1.31	1.06			10	29.9	47	29	24	0	38					Sep-15
	0.49	1.92	4.47			1.28	1.08			9.99	29.9	47	29	24	0	38					Sep-15
	0.44	1.87	4.31			1.13	1.23			9.99	29.9	47	29	24	0	38					Sep-15
50	1.84	3.81	6.92	8.71	21.31	0	1.18	3.63	0.94	9.31	1,621	77	18	3	1	130	3.94	-8.3	5.50		May-08

	MARKET		FUND TYPE, CATEGORY & OBJECTIVE		RATINGS				MINIMUMS	
Fund Name	Ticker Symbol	Traded On	Fund Type	Category and (Prospectus Objective)	Overall Rating	Reward Rating	Risk Rating	Recent Up/ Downgrade	Open to New Investors	Min Initial Investment
Goldman Sachs Absolute Return Tracker Fund Class C	GCRTX	NAS CM	Open End	Multialternative (Income)	C+	C	B	Up	Y	1,000
Goldman Sachs Absolute Return Tracker Fund Class R	GRRTX	NAS CM	Open End	Multialternative (Income)	C+	C	B	Up	Y	0
Goldman Sachs Absolute Return Tracker Fund Class R6	GARUX	NAS CM	Open End	Multialternative (Income)	B-	C	B	Up	Y	5,000,000
Goldman Sachs Absolute Return Tracker Fund Inst Cls	GJRTX	NAS CM	Open End	Multialternative (Income)	B-	C	B	Up	Y	1,000,000
Goldman Sachs Absolute Return Tracker Fund Investor Class	GSRTX	NAS CM	Open End	Multialternative (Income)	B-	C	B	Up	Y	0
Goldman Sachs Alternative Premia Fund Class A	GDAFX	NAS CM	Open End	Moderate Alloc (Growth)	C+	C+	B-	Up	Y	1,000
Goldman Sachs Alternative Premia Fund Class C	GDCFX	NAS CM	Open End	Moderate Alloc (Growth)	C+	C	B-	Up	Y	1,000
Goldman Sachs Alternative Premia Fund Class R	GDRFX	NAS CM	Open End	Moderate Alloc (Growth)	C+	C+	B-	Up	Y	0
Goldman Sachs Alternative Premia Fund Class R6	GDHUX	NAS CM	Open End	Moderate Alloc (Growth)	C+	C+	B-	Up	Y	5,000,000
Goldman Sachs Alternative Premia Fund Institutional Class	GDIFX	NAS CM	Open End	Moderate Alloc (Growth)	C+	C+	B-	Up	Y	1,000,000
Goldman Sachs Alternative Premia Fund Investor Class	GDHFX	NAS CM	Open End	Moderate Alloc (Growth)	C+	C+	B-	Up	Y	0
Goldman Sachs Asia Equity Fund Class A	GSAGX	NAS CM	Open End	Asia ex-Japan Equity (Pacific Stock)	B+	A	B	Up	Y	1,000
Goldman Sachs Asia Equity Fund Class C	GSACX	NAS CM	Open End	Asia ex-Japan Equity (Pacific Stock)	B+	A	B	Up	Y	1,000
Goldman Sachs Asia Equity Fund Institutional Class	GSAIX	NAS CM	Open End	Asia ex-Japan Equity (Pacific Stock)	B+	A	B	Up	Y	1,000,000
Goldman Sachs Asia Equity Fund Investor Class	GSAEX	NAS CM	Open End	Asia ex-Japan Equity (Pacific Stock)	B+	A	B	Up	Y	0
Goldman Sachs Balanced Strategy Portfolio Class A	GIPAX	NAS CM	Open End	Moderate Alloc (Asset Alloc)	B	C+	B+	Up	Y	1,000
Goldman Sachs Balanced Strategy Portfolio Class C	GIPCX	NAS CM	Open End	Moderate Alloc (Asset Alloc)	B-	C+	B+	Up	Y	1,000
Goldman Sachs Balanced Strategy Portfolio Class R	GIPRX	NAS CM	Open End	Moderate Alloc (Asset Alloc)	B-	C+	B+	Up	Y	0
Goldman Sachs Balanced Strategy Portfolio Class R6	GIPUX	NAS CM	Open End	Moderate Alloc (Asset Alloc)	B-	C+	B	Up	Y	5,000,000
Goldman Sachs Balanced Strategy Portfolio Inst Cls	GIPIX	NAS CM	Open End	Moderate Alloc (Asset Alloc)	B-	C+	B	Up	Y	1,000,000
Goldman Sachs Balanced Strategy Portfolio Investor Class	GIPTX	NAS CM	Open End	Moderate Alloc (Asset Alloc)	B	C+	B+	Up	Y	0
Goldman Sachs Balanced Strategy Portfolio Service Class	GIPSX	NAS CM	Open End	Moderate Alloc (Asset Alloc)	B	C+	B+	Up	Y	0
Goldman Sachs Blue Chip Fund Class A	GAGVX	NAS CM	Open End	US Equity Large Cap Growth (Growth)	C+	C+	B-	Down	Y	1,000
Goldman Sachs Blue Chip Fund Class C	GCGVX	NAS CM	Open End	US Equity Large Cap Growth (Growth)	B-	C+	B	Down	Y	1,000
Goldman Sachs Blue Chip Fund Class R	GRGVX	NAS CM	Open End	US Equity Large Cap Growth (Growth)	B-	C+	B	Down	Y	0
Goldman Sachs Blue Chip Fund Class R6	GDEUX	NAS CM	Open End	US Equity Large Cap Growth (Growth)	B-	C+	B	Down	Y	5,000,000
Goldman Sachs Blue Chip Fund Institutional Class	GINGX	NAS CM	Open End	US Equity Large Cap Growth (Growth)	B-	C+	B-	Down	Y	1,000,000
Goldman Sachs Blue Chip Fund Investor Class	GIRGX	NAS CM	Open End	US Equity Large Cap Growth (Growth)	B-	C+	B	Down	Y	0
Goldman Sachs Capital Growth Fund Class A	GSCGX	NAS CM	Open End	US Equity Large Cap Growth (Growth)	B	B	B+	Down	Y	1,000
Goldman Sachs Capital Growth Fund Class C	GSPCX	NAS CM	Open End	US Equity Large Cap Growth (Growth)	B	B	B+		Y	1,000
Goldman Sachs Capital Growth Fund Class R	GSPRX	NAS CM	Open End	US Equity Large Cap Growth (Growth)	B	B	B+	Down	Y	0
Goldman Sachs Capital Growth Fund Class R6	GSPUX	NAS CM	Open End	US Equity Large Cap Growth (Growth)	B	B	B-	Down	Y	5,000,000
Goldman Sachs Capital Growth Fund Institutional Class	GSPIX	NAS CM	Open End	US Equity Large Cap Growth (Growth)	B+	B	B+	Up	Y	1,000,000
Goldman Sachs Capital Growth Fund Investor Class	GSPTX	NAS CM	Open End	US Equity Large Cap Growth (Growth)	B+	B	B+	Up	Y	0
Goldman Sachs Capital Growth Fund Service Class	GSPSX	NAS CM	Open End	US Equity Large Cap Growth (Growth)	B	B	B+	Down	Y	0
Goldman Sachs Commodity Strategy Fund Class A	GSCAX	NAS CM	Open End	Commodities Broad Basket (Growth & Income)	D	D+	D		Y	1,000
Goldman Sachs Commodity Strategy Fund Class C	GSCCX	NAS CM	Open End	Commodities Broad Basket (Growth & Income)	D	D+	D		Y	1,000
Goldman Sachs Commodity Strategy Fund Class R	GCCRX	NAS CM	Open End	Commodities Broad Basket (Growth & Income)	D	D+	D		Y	0
Goldman Sachs Commodity Strategy Fund Class R6	GCCUX	NAS CM	Open End	Commodities Broad Basket (Growth & Income)	D+	D+	D	Up	Y	5,000,000
Goldman Sachs Commodity Strategy Fund Institutional Class	GCCIX	NAS CM	Open End	Commodities Broad Basket (Growth & Income)	D+	D+	D	Up	Y	1,000,000
Goldman Sachs Commodity Strategy Fund Investor Class	GCCTX	NAS CM	Open End	Commodities Broad Basket (Growth & Income)	D	D+	D		Y	0
Goldman Sachs Concentrated Growth Fund Class A	GCGAX	NAS CM	Open End	US Equity Large Cap Growth (Growth)	B	B	B+	Up	Y	1,000
Goldman Sachs Concentrated Growth Fund Class C	GCGCX	NAS CM	Open End	US Equity Large Cap Growth (Growth)	B	B-	B	Up	Y	1,000
Goldman Sachs Concentrated Growth Fund Class R	GGCRX	NAS CM	Open End	US Equity Large Cap Growth (Growth)	B	B	B+	Up	Y	0
Goldman Sachs Concentrated Growth Fund Class R6	GCGUX	NAS CM	Open End	US Equity Large Cap Growth (Growth)	B	B	B+		Y	5,000,000
Goldman Sachs Concentrated Growth Fund Institutional Class	GCRIX	NAS CM	Open End	US Equity Large Cap Growth (Growth)	B	B	B+		Y	1,000,000
Goldman Sachs Concentrated Growth Fund Investor Class	GGCTX	NAS CM	Open End	US Equity Large Cap Growth (Growth)	B	B	B+		Y	0
Goldman Sachs Emerging Markets Equity Fund Class A	GEMAX	NAS CM	Open End	Emerging Markets Equity (Div Emerging Mkts)	B+	A	C+	Up	Y	1,000
Goldman Sachs Emerging Markets Equity Fund Class C	GEMCX	NAS CM	Open End	Emerging Markets Equity (Div Emerging Mkts)	B	A-	C+	Up	Y	1,000
Goldman Sachs Emerging Markets Equity Fund Class R6	GEMUX	NAS CM	Open End	Emerging Markets Equity (Div Emerging Mkts)	B+	A	C+	Up	Y	5,000,000
Goldman Sachs Emerging Mkts Equity Fund Inst Cls	GEMIX	NAS CM	Open End	Emerging Markets Equity (Div Emerging Mkts)	B+	A	C+	Up	Y	1,000,000
Goldman Sachs Emerging Markets Equity Fund Investor Class	GIRMX	NAS CM	Open End	Emerging Markets Equity (Div Emerging Mkts)	B+	A	C+	Up	Y	0

★Expanded analysis of this fund is included in Section II.

	TOTAL RETURNS					PERFORMANCE				ASSETS		ASSET ALLOCATION & TURNOVER					BULL & BEAR		FEES		
Min Additional Investment	3-Month Total Return	6-Month Total Return	1-Year Total Return	3-Year Total Return	5-Year Total Return	Dividend Yield (TTM)	Expense Ratio	3-Yr Std Deviation	3-Year Beta	NAV	Total Assets (MIL)	%Cash	%Stocks	%Bonds	%Other	Turnover Ratio	Last Bull Market Total Return	Last Bear Market Total Return	Front End Fee (%)	Back End Fee (%)	Inception Date
50	1.64	3.40	6.10	6.31	16.78	0	1.93	3.63	0.93	8.61	1,621	77	18	3	1	130	3.56	-8.59		1.00	May-08
	1.89	3.80	6.74	7.97	19.86	0	1.43	3.61	0.93	9.08	1,621	77	18	3	1	130	3.85	-8.46			May-08
	1.95	3.98	7.36	9.93	23.71	0.24	0.75	3.62	0.93	9.57	1,621	77	18	3	1	130	4.12	-8.11			Jul-15
	1.93	3.96	7.45	9.96	23.75	0.22	0.77	3.61	0.93	9.58	1,621	77	18	3	1	130	4.12	-8.11			May-08
	1.91	3.96	7.24	9.61	22.88	0.13	0.93	3.61	0.93	9.5	1,621	77	18	3	1	130	4.02	-8.15			May-08
50	6.01	9.25	14.16	11.94	21.60	0	1.24	6.12	2.65	8.91	156.6	91	0	0	9	272	6.63	-9.79	5.50		Jan-10
50	5.93	8.91	13.36	9.57	17.17	0	1.99	6.09	1.77	8.37	156.6	91	0	0	9	272	6.16	-10.15		1.00	Jan-10
	5.96	9.14	13.89	11.17	20.07	0	1.49	6.07	3.23	8.75	156.6	91	0	0	9	272	6.4	-9.91			Jan-10
	6.02	9.41	14.48	13.18	23.96	0	0.82	6.1	2.53	9.05	156.6	91	0	0	9	272	6.84	-9.73			Jul-15
	6.12	9.51	14.58	13.25	24.04	0	0.84	6.08	2.69	9.07	156.6	91	0	0	9	272	6.84	-9.73			Jan-10
	6.17	9.48	14.47	12.85	23.15	0	0.99	6.08	2.97	9.02	156.6	91	0	0	9	272	6.76	-9.67			Jan-10
50	11.45	22.92	51.59	49.90	59.78	0	1.55	13.87	0.87	29.1	86.3	1	99	0	0	111	16.51	-24.58	5.50		Jul-94
50	11.24	22.42	50.39	46.54	53.83	0	2.3	13.84	0.87	26.52	86.3	1	99	0	0	111	16.02	-24.83		1.00	Aug-97
	11.57	23.15	52.15	51.71	62.97	0	1.15	13.85	0.87	30.8	86.3	1	99	0	0	111	16.8	-24.46			Feb-96
	11.52	23.06	51.97	51.01	61.28	0	1.3	13.88	0.87	30.64	86.3	1	99	0	0	111	16.51	-24.58			Feb-14
50	2.48	5.61	11.19	15.34	29.15	1.28	1.36	4.6		11.55	500.3	13	37	37	12	76	9.18	-10.04	5.50		Jan-98
50	2.29	5.18	10.29	12.77	24.37	0.49	2.11	4.59		11.55	500.3	13	37	37	12	76	8.54	-10.3		1.00	Jan-98
	2.34	5.42	10.81	14.64	27.80	1.09	1.61	4.54		11.5	500.3	13	37	37	12	76	8.87	-10.09			Nov-07
	2.59	5.74	11.53	16.76	31.79	1.67	0.94	4.55		11.55	500.3	13	37	37	12	76	9.39	-9.92			Jul-15
	2.59	5.83	11.63	16.74	31.77	1.67	0.96	4.54		11.55	500.3	13	37	37	12	76	9.39	-9.92			Jan-98
	2.56	5.67	11.41	16.18	30.70	1.53	1.11	4.56		11.5	500.3	13	37	37	12	76	9.25	-9.92			Nov-07
	2.51	5.57	11.03	15.88	29.44	1.17	1.46	4.41		11.68	500.3	13	37	37	12	76	9.09	-10.06			Jan-98
50	5.11	6.96	18.49	20.04	84.40	0.45	1.03	11.35	1.08	12.71	6.1	7	93	0	0	77	24.63	-19.85	5.50		Nov-09
50	4.85	6.53	17.51	17.37	77.60	0	1.78	11.3	1.08	12.22	6.1	7	93	0	0	77	24.03	-20.08		1.00	Nov-09
	4.99	6.83	18.13	19.17	82.07	0	1.28	11.35	1.08	12.79	6.1	7	93	0	0	77	24.38	-19.87			Nov-09
	5.11	7.09	18.83	21.51	88.07	0.87	0.67	11.35	1.08	12.77	6.1	7	93	0	0	77	24.99	-19.72			Jul-15
	5.10	7.15	18.82	21.46	87.99	0.86	0.67	11.36	1.08	12.77	6.1	7	93	0	0	77	24.99	-19.72			Nov-09
	5.13	7.11	18.68	20.86	86.63	0.67	0.78	11.35	1.08	12.78	6.1	7	93	0	0	77	24.69	-19.69			Nov-09
50	7.17	12.42	31.80	35.80	108.85	0.04	1.15	11.81	1.08	28.7	967.6	1	99	0	0	48	29.04	-16.71	5.50		Apr-90
50	6.95	11.99	30.81	32.72	101.06	0	1.9	11.81	1.08	21.33	967.6	1	99	0	0	48	28.41	-16.94		1.00	Aug-97
	7.10	12.28	31.44	34.72	106.20	0	1.4	11.8	1.08	27.68	967.6	1	99	0	0	48	28.82	-16.8			Nov-07
	7.28	12.66	32.32	37.16	110.95	0.34	0.74	11.81	1.08	31.52	967.6	1	99	0	0	48	29.04	-16.71			Jul-15
	7.26	12.64	32.29	37.40	113.05	0.33	0.75	11.82	1.08	31.53	967.6	1	99	0	0	48	29.33	-16.56			Aug-97
	7.24	12.58	32.13	36.78	111.42	0.26	0.9	11.82	1.08	29.07	967.6	1	99	0	0	48	29.18	-16.6			Nov-07
	7.17	12.39	31.70	35.40	107.79	0	1.25	11.79	1.08	27.72	967.6	1	99	0	0	48	28.9	-16.7			Aug-97
50	9.14	16.48	3.94	-22.23	-46.57	0.47	0.96	18.68	0.92	11.49	364.8	59	0	41	0	145	13.53	-22.9	4.50		Mar-07
50	8.91	16.06	3.15	-23.92	-48.46	0	1.71	18.59	0.91	10.92	364.8	59	0	41	0	145	13.16	-23.23		1.00	Mar-07
	9.02	16.25	3.59	-22.85	-47.20	0.26	1.2	18.7	0.92	11.31	364.8	59	0	41	0	145	13.29	-22.99			Nov-07
	9.15	16.62	4.28	-21.26	-45.53	0.81	0.6	18.56	0.91	11.62	364.8	59	0	41	0	145	13.69	-22.76			Jul-15
	9.23	16.72	4.26	-21.31	-45.57	0.79	0.62	18.6	0.91	11.61	364.8	59	0	41	0	145	13.69	-22.76			Mar-07
	9.07	16.54	4.07	-21.66	-45.90	0.69	0.71	18.62	0.91	11.61	364.8	59	0	41	0	145	13.79	-22.83			Nov-07
50	6.02	9.95	27.42	27.50	89.71	0.16	1.19	11.65	1.04	16.58	156.6	2	98	0	0	54	27.81	-16.84	5.50		Sep-02
50	5.80	9.47	26.48	24.61	82.76	0	1.95	11.68	1.04	13.69	156.6	2	98	0	0	54	27.28	-17.1		1.00	Sep-02
	5.93	9.78	27.06	26.48	87.36	0	1.45	11.63	1.04	16.05	156.6	2	98	0	0	54	27.72	-16.97			Nov-07
	6.14	10.09	27.86	29.04	93.52	0.51	0.81	11.66	1.04	17.63	156.6	2	98	0	0	54	28.16	-16.72			Jul-15
	6.12	10.13	27.91	29.04	93.53	0.5	0.82	11.66	1.04	17.64	156.6	2	98	0	0	54	28.16	-16.72			Sep-02
	6.10	10.10	27.82	28.55	92.26	0.42	0.94	11.66	1.04	16.84	156.6	2	98	0	0	54	27.98	-16.73			Nov-07
50	9.26	20.62	47.63	45.32	43.82	0.51	1.66	13.86	0.84	22.02	927.6	0	98	0	0	92	15.21	-26.38	5.50		Dec-97
50	9.05	20.16	46.56	42.14	38.56	0	2.41	13.88	0.84	19.78	927.6	0	98	0	0	92	14.58	-26.57		1.00	Dec-97
	9.36	20.88	48.34	47.26	46.80	0.78	1.24	13.87	0.84	23.65	927.6	0	98	0	0	92	15.47	-26.27			Jul-15
	9.39	20.91	48.31	47.15	46.69	0.76	1.26	13.88	0.84	23.55	927.6	0	98	0	0	92	15.47	-26.27			Dec-97
	9.35	20.78	48.10	46.40	45.59	0.74	1.41	13.88	0.84	23.38	927.6	0	98	0	0	92	15.27	-26.3			Aug-10

	MARKET			FUND TYPE, CATEGORY & OBJECTIVE	RATINGS				MINIMUMS	
Fund Name	Ticker Symbol	Traded On	Fund Type	Category and (Prospectus Objective)	Overall Rating	Reward Rating	Risk Rating	Recent Up/ Downgrade	Open to New Investors	Min Initial Investment
Goldman Sachs Emerging Markets Equity Fund Service Class	GEMSX	NAS CM	Open End	Emerging Markets Equity (Div Emerging Mkts)	B+	A	C+	Up	Y	0
Goldman Sachs Emerging Markets Equity Insights Fund Cls A	GERAX	NAS CM	Open End	Emerging Markets Equity (Div Emerging Mkts)	B	A-	C+	Up	Y	1,000
Goldman Sachs Emerging Markets Equity Insights Fund Cls C	GERCX	NAS CM	Open End	Emerging Markets Equity (Div Emerging Mkts)	B	B+	C+	Up	Y	1,000
Goldman Sachs Emerging Markets Equity Insights Fund Cls R	GRRPX	NAS CM	Open End	Emerging Markets Equity (Div Emerging Mkts)	B	A-	C+	Up	Y	0
Goldman Sachs Emerging Markets Equity Insights Fund Cls R6	GERUX	NAS CM	Open End	Emerging Markets Equity (Div Emerging Mkts)	B+	A	C+	Up	Y	5,000,000
Goldman Sachs Emerging Mkts Equity Insights Fund Intl	GERIX	NAS CM	Open End	Emerging Markets Equity (Div Emerging Mkts)	B+	A	C+	Up	Y	1,000,000
Goldman Sachs Emerging Mkts Equity Insights Fund Inv Cls	GIRPX	NAS CM	Open End	Emerging Markets Equity (Div Emerging Mkts)	B+	A	C+	Up	Y	0
Goldman Sachs Enhanced Div Global Eq Port Cls A	GADGX	NAS CM	Open End	Global Equity Large Cap (Growth & Income)	B-	C+	B-	Down	Y	1,000
Goldman Sachs Enhanced Div Global Eq Port Cls Inst	GIDGX	NAS CM	Open End	Global Equity Large Cap (Growth & Income)	B-	C+	B-	Up	Y	1,000,000
Goldman Sachs Equity Growth Strategy Portfolio Class A	GAPAX	NAS CM	Open End	Global Equity (Growth)	B	B	B-	Up	Y	1,000
Goldman Sachs Equity Growth Strategy Portfolio Class C	GAXCX	NAS CM	Open End	Global Equity (Growth)	B-	B-	B-	Down	Y	1,000
Goldman Sachs Equity Growth Strategy Portfolio Class R	GAPRX	NAS CM	Open End	Global Equity (Growth)	B	B	B-	Up	Y	0
Goldman Sachs Equity Growth Strategy Portfolio Class R6	GAPUX	NAS CM	Open End	Global Equity (Growth)	B	B	B-	Up	Y	5,000,000
Goldman Sachs Equity Growth Strategy Portfolio Inst Cls	GAPIX	NAS CM	Open End	Global Equity (Growth)	B	B	B-	Up	Y	1,000,000
Goldman Sachs Equity Growth Strategy Portfolio Inv Cls	GAPTX	NAS CM	Open End	Global Equity (Growth)	B	B	B-	Up	Y	0
Goldman Sachs Equity Growth Strategy Portfolio Service Cls	GAPSX	NAS CM	Open End	Global Equity (Growth)	B	B	B-	Up	Y	0
Goldman Sachs Equity Income Fund Class A	GSGRX	NAS CM	Open End	US Equity Large Cap Value (Growth & Income)	B-	C+	B	Up	Y	1,000
Goldman Sachs Equity Income Fund Class C	GSGCX	NAS CM	Open End	US Equity Large Cap Value (Growth & Income)	B-	C+	B	Up	Y	1,000
Goldman Sachs Equity Income Fund Class R	GRGRX	NAS CM	Open End	US Equity Large Cap Value (Growth & Income)	B-	C+	B	Up	Y	0
Goldman Sachs Equity Income Fund Class R6	GRGUX	NAS CM	Open End	US Equity Large Cap Value (Growth & Income)	B-	C+	B		Y	5,000,000
Goldman Sachs Equity Income Fund Institutional Class	GSIIX	NAS CM	Open End	US Equity Large Cap Value (Growth & Income)	B-	C+	B	Down	Y	1,000,000
Goldman Sachs Equity Income Fund Investor Class	GRGTX	NAS CM	Open End	US Equity Large Cap Value (Growth & Income)	B-	C+	B		Y	0
Goldman Sachs Equity Income Fund Service Class	GSGSX	NAS CM	Open End	US Equity Large Cap Value (Growth & Income)	B-	C+	B	Up	Y	0
Goldman Sachs Flexible Cap Fund Class A	GALLX	NAS CM	Open End	US Equity Large Cap Growth (Growth)	B	B	B+		Y	1,000
Goldman Sachs Flexible Cap Fund Class C	GCLLX	NAS CM	Open End	US Equity Large Cap Growth (Growth)	B	B	B+	Up	Y	1,000
Goldman Sachs Flexible Cap Fund Class R	GRLLX	NAS CM	Open End	US Equity Large Cap Growth (Growth)	B	B	B+		Y	0
Goldman Sachs Flexible Cap Fund Class R6	GFCUX	NAS CM	Open End	US Equity Large Cap Growth (Growth)	B	B	B+	Down	Y	5,000,000
Goldman Sachs Flexible Cap Fund Institutional Class	GILLX	NAS CM	Open End	US Equity Large Cap Growth (Growth)	B	B	B+	Down	Y	1,000,000
Goldman Sachs Flexible Cap Fund Investor Class	GSLLX	NAS CM	Open End	US Equity Large Cap Growth (Growth)	B	B	B+	Down	Y	0
Goldman Sachs Focused International Equity Fund Class A	GSIFX	NAS CM	Open End	Global Equity Large Cap (Foreign Stock)	B-	C+	B	Up	Y	1,000
Goldman Sachs Focused International Equity Fund Class C	GSICX	NAS CM	Open End	Global Equity Large Cap (Foreign Stock)	B-	C+	B-	Up	Y	1,000
Goldman Sachs Focused International Equity Fund Class R6	GSIWX	NAS CM	Open End	Global Equity Large Cap (Foreign Stock)	B-	C+	B	Up	Y	5,000,000
Goldman Sachs Focused Intl Equity Fund Inst Cls	GSIEX	NAS CM	Open End	Global Equity Large Cap (Foreign Stock)	B-	C+	B	Up	Y	1,000,000
Goldman Sachs Focused Intl Equity Fund Inv Cls	GIRNX	NAS CM	Open End	Global Equity Large Cap (Foreign Stock)	B-	C+	B	Up	Y	0
Goldman Sachs Focused Intl Equity Fund Service Cls	GSISX	NAS CM	Open End	Global Equity Large Cap (Foreign Stock)	B-	C+	B	Up	Y	0
Goldman Sachs Focused Value Fund Class A	GFVAX	NAS CM	Open End	US Equity Large Cap Value (Growth)	C	C+	B	Up	Y	1,000
Goldman Sachs Focused Value Fund Class C	GFVCX	NAS CM	Open End	US Equity Large Cap Value (Growth)	C	C+	B	Up	Y	1,000
Goldman Sachs Focused Value Fund Class R	GFVRX	NAS CM	Open End	US Equity Large Cap Value (Growth)	C	C+	B	Up	Y	0
Goldman Sachs Focused Value Fund Class R6	GFVUX	NAS CM	Open End	US Equity Large Cap Value (Growth)	C	C+	B	Up	Y	5,000,000
Goldman Sachs Focused Value Fund Institutional Class	GFVSX	NAS CM	Open End	US Equity Large Cap Value (Growth)	C	C+	B	Up	Y	1,000,000
Goldman Sachs Focused Value Fund Investor Class	GFVIX	NAS CM	Open End	US Equity Large Cap Value (Growth)	C	C+	B	Up	Y	0
Goldman Sachs Global Infrastructure Fund Class A	GGIAX	NAS CM	Open End	Other Sector Equity (Utility)	D	C-	B-		Y	1,000
Goldman Sachs Global Infrastructure Fund Class C	GGICX	NAS CM	Open End	Other Sector Equity (Utility)	D	C-	B-		Y	1,000
Goldman Sachs Global Infrastructure Fund Class R	GGIEX	NAS CM	Open End	Other Sector Equity (Utility)	D	C-	B-		Y	0
Goldman Sachs Global Infrastructure Fund Class R6	GGIJX	NAS CM	Open End	Other Sector Equity (Utility)	D	C-	B-		Y	5,000,000
Goldman Sachs Global Infrastructure Fund Institutional Cls	GGIDX	NAS CM	Open End	Other Sector Equity (Utility)	D	C-	B-		Y	1,000,000
Goldman Sachs Global Infrastructure Fund Investor Class	GGINX	NAS CM	Open End	Other Sector Equity (Utility)	D	C-	B-		Y	0
Goldman Sachs Global Real Estate Securities Fund Class A	GARGX	NAS CM	Open End	Real Estate Sector Equity (Real Estate)	C	C	B-	Up	Y	1,000
Goldman Sachs Global Real Estate Securities Fund Class C	GARKX	NAS CM	Open End	Real Estate Sector Equity (Real Estate)	C	C	B-	Up	Y	1,000
Goldman Sachs Global Real Estate Securities Fund Class R	GARHX	NAS CM	Open End	Real Estate Sector Equity (Real Estate)	C	C	B-	Up	Y	0
Goldman Sachs Global Real Estate Securities Fund Class R6	GARVX	NAS CM	Open End	Real Estate Sector Equity (Real Estate)	C	C	B-	Up	Y	5,000,000
Goldman Sachs Global Real Estate Securities Fund Inst Cls	GARSX	NAS CM	Open End	Real Estate Sector Equity (Real Estate)	C	C	B-	Up	Y	1,000,000

★ Expanded analysis of this fund is included in Section II.

	TOTAL RETURNS					PERFORMANCE				ASSETS		ASSET ALLOCATION & TURNOVER					BULL & BEAR		FEES		
Min Additional Investment	3-Month Total Return	6-Month Total Return	1-Year Total Return	3-Year Total Return	5-Year Total Return	Dividend Yield (TTM)	Expense Ratio	3-Yr Std Deviation	3-Year Beta	NAV	Total Assets (MIL)	%Cash	%Stocks	%Bonds	%Other	Turnover Ratio	Last Bull Market Total Return	Last Bear Market Total Return	Front End Fee (%)	Back End Fee (%)	Inception Date
	9.26	20.58	47.49	44.95	43.09	0.54	1.76	13.87	0.84	21.29	927.6	0	98	0	0	92	15.1	-26.44			Dec-97
50	5.20	17.19	38.76	38.93	33.23	0.76	1.52	15.32	0.95	10.75	1,721	0	100	0	0	216	21.4	-26.76	5.50		Oct-07
50	4.97	16.71	37.72	35.78	28.31	0.25	2.27	15.32	0.95	10.64	1,721	0	100	0	0	216	20.93	-27.03		1.00	Oct-07
	5.09	16.97	38.43	37.90	31.72	0.61	1.77	15.34	0.95	10.63	1,721	0	100	0	0	216	21.33	-26.84			Feb-14
	5.25	17.37	39.17	40.58	35.78	1.01	1.13	15.3	0.95	10.72	1,721	0	100	0	0	216	21.69	-26.68			Jul-15
	5.33	17.33	39.27	40.59	35.79	0.99	1.15	15.34	0.95	10.73	1,721	0	100	0	0	216	21.69	-26.68			Oct-07
	5.29	17.30	39.09	40.15	34.97	0.92	1.27	15.27	0.95	10.72	1,721	0	100	0	0	216	21.62	-26.78			Aug-10
50	3.41	7.73	14.67	22.50	56.11	2	1.37	9.05		12.07	674.5	0	88	0	10	8	18.56	-17.16	5.50		Apr-08
	3.57	7.89	15.17	23.99	59.37	2.32	0.97	9.01		12.17	674.5	0	88	0	10	8	18.71	-16.94			Apr-08
50	5.31	12.39	25.96	34.74	75.00	0.94	1.37	10.06	0.94	18.84	370.4	6	91	0	2	39	20.38	-22.16	5.50		Jan-98
50	5.10	11.94	25.07	31.75	68.64	0.36	2.12	10.08	0.94	18.01	370.4	6	91	0	2	39	19.74	-22.39		1.00	Jan-98
	5.27	12.22	25.70	33.66	72.86	0.83	1.62	10.07	0.94	18.69	370.4	6	91	0	2	39	20.16	-22.24			Nov-07
	5.41	12.61	26.53	36.36	78.63	1.26	0.95	10.11	0.94	19.04	370.4	6	91	0	2	39	20.61	-22.06			Jul-15
	5.43	12.63	26.47	36.33	78.60	1.26	0.97	10.07	0.94	19.01	370.4	6	91	0	2	39	20.61	-22.06			Jan-98
	5.38	12.50	26.35	35.76	77.32	1.17	1.12	10.09	0.94	18.58	370.4	6	91	0	2	39	20.43	-22.02			Nov-07
	5.27	12.33	25.79	34.22	74.15	0.86	1.47	10.07	0.94	18.75	370.4	6	91	0	2	39	20.22	-22.15			Jan-98
50	4.02	6.89	10.36	19.96	81.42	1.58	1.14	10.64	1.01	37.29	396.3	1	99	0	0	43	23.99	-21.81	5.50		Feb-93
50	3.81	6.48	9.54	17.27	74.72	0.93	1.89	10.66	1.01	35.55	396.3	1	99	0	0	43	23.46	-22.04		1.00	Aug-97
	3.96	6.74	10.11	19.05	79.13	1.35	1.39	10.65	1.01	37.11	396.3	1	99	0	0	43	23.75	-21.84			Nov-07
	4.11	7.11	10.81	21.15	83.21	1.93	0.74	10.65	1.01	37.9	396.3	1	99	0	0	43	23.99	-21.81			Jul-15
	4.11	7.08	10.80	21.39	84.99	1.93	0.74	10.66	1.01	37.9	396.3	1	99	0	0	43	24.29	-21.68			Jun-96
	4.09	7.02	10.64	20.84	83.64	1.84	0.89	10.65	1.01	37.22	396.3	1	99	0	0	43	24.15	-21.72			Nov-07
	4.00	6.84	10.28	19.60	80.50	1.19	1.24	10.65	1.01	37.42	396.3	1	99	0	0	43	23.89	-21.82			Feb-93
50	6.32	12.91	32.93	36.56	111.73	0	0.95	11.36	1.04	11.57	20.3	1	99	0	0	47	28.53	-19.12	5.50		Jan-08
50	6.09	12.48	31.93	33.49	103.80	0	1.7	11.38	1.04	10.1	20.3	1	99	0	0	47	27.95	-19.38		1.00	Jan-08
	6.26	12.73	32.47	35.48	109.21	0	1.2	11.36	1.04	11.11	20.3	1	99	0	0	47	28.3	-19.24			Jan-08
	6.46	13.16	33.41	38.12	115.89	0	0.58	11.38	1.04	12.41	20.3	1	99	0	0	47	28.79	-19			Jul-15
	6.48	13.18	33.43	38.14	115.92	0	0.59	11.38	1.04	12.41	20.3	1	99	0	0	47	28.79	-19			Jan-08
	6.39	13.04	33.23	37.55	114.29	0	0.7	11.37	1.04	12.18	20.3	1	99	0	0	47	28.62	-19.01			Jan-08
50	5.09	9.34	25.29	23.14	39.53	2.26	1.3	12.97	1.04	20.28	186.0	0	100	0	0	78	13.07	-24.91	5.50		Dec-92
50	4.89	8.94	24.40	20.44	34.42	1.87	2.05	12.98	1.04	18.82	186.0	0	100	0	0	78	12.6	-25.14		1.00	Aug-97
	5.19	9.59	25.86	23.83	40.04	2.6	0.89	12.98	1.04	20.61	186.0	0	100	0	0	78	13.1	-24.98			Feb-16
	5.22	9.63	25.82	24.61	42.39	2.59	0.9	13	1.04	20.62	186.0	0	100	0	0	78	13.42	-24.83			Feb-96
	5.17	9.53	25.62	24.10	41.31	2.44	1.05	13.01	1.04	20.61	186.0	0	100	0	0	78	13.25	-24.85			Aug-10
	5.08	9.33	25.19	22.72	38.78	0	1.41	12.96	1.03	21.22	186.0	0	100	0	0	78	13.1	-24.98			Dec-92
50	2.55	4.84	12.48			0.97	1.13			10.79	5.3	2	97	0	2	126			5.50		Jul-15
50	2.37	4.48	11.68			0.28	1.88			10.79	5.3	2	97	0	2	126				1.00	Jul-15
	2.46	4.66	12.28			0.69	1.38			10.8	5.3	2	97	0	2	126					Jul-15
	2.70	5.07	13.02			1.23	0.71			10.82	5.3	2	97	0	2	126					Jul-15
	2.60	4.98	12.91			1.21	0.73			10.81	5.3	2	97	0	2	126					Jul-15
	2.55	4.93	12.76			1.09	0.88			10.81	5.3	2	97	0	2	126					Jul-15
50	1.22	3.95	12.28			1.57	1.39			10.85	221.3	1	99	0	0	59			5.50		Jun-16
50	1.02	3.54	11.45			0.93	2.14			10.84	221.3	1	99	0	0	59				1.00	Jun-16
	1.15	3.81	11.99			1.33	1.64			10.85	221.3	1	99	0	0	59					Jun-16
	1.33	4.17	12.74			1.94	0.97			10.85	221.3	1	99	0	0	59					Jun-16
	1.33	4.17	12.72			1.93	0.99			10.85	221.3	1	99	0	0	59					Jun-16
	1.29	4.09	12.55			1.79	1.14			10.85	221.3	1	99	0	0	59					Jun-16
50	3.45	5.27	8.49			2.8	1.4			10.64	333.9	0	98	0	2	60			5.50		Aug-15
50	3.23	4.88	7.71			2.07	2.15			10.64	333.9	0	98	0	2	60				1.00	Aug-15
	3.38	5.16	8.26			2.51	1.65			10.65	333.9	0	98	0	2	60					Aug-15
	3.56	5.52	8.96			3.12	0.98			10.66	333.9	0	98	0	2	60					Aug-15
	3.55	5.52	8.95			3.11	1			10.66	333.9	0	98	0	2	60					Aug-15

	MARKET		FUND TYPE, CATEGORY & OBJECTIVE		RATINGS				MINIMUMS	
Fund Name	Ticker Symbol	Traded On	Fund Type	Category and (Prospectus Objective)	Overall Rating	Reward Rating	Risk Rating	Recent Up/ Downgrade	Open to New Investors	Min Initial Investment
Goldman Sachs Global Real Estate Securities Fund Inv Cls	GARJX	NAS CM	Open End	Real Estate Sector Equity (Real Estate)	C	C	B-	Up	Y	0
Goldman Sachs GQG Partners Intl Opp Fund Cls A Shares	GSIHX	NAS CM	Open End	Global Equity Large Cap (Foreign Stock)	D	D+	B+		Y	1,000
Goldman Sachs GQG Partners Intl Opp Fund Cls C Shares	GSILX	NAS CM	Open End	Global Equity Large Cap (Foreign Stock)	D	D+	B+		Y	1,000
Goldman Sachs GQG Partners Intl Opp Fund Cls IR Shares	GSINX	NAS CM	Open End	Global Equity Large Cap (Foreign Stock)	D	D+	B+		Y	0
Goldman Sachs GQG Partners Intl Opp Fund Cls R Shares	GSIQX	NAS CM	Open End	Global Equity Large Cap (Foreign Stock)	D	D+	B+		Y	0
Goldman Sachs GQG Partners Intl Opp Fund Cls R6 Shares	GSIYX	NAS CM	Open End	Global Equity Large Cap (Foreign Stock)	D	D+	B+		Y	5,000,000
Goldman Sachs GQG Partners Intl Opp Fund Inst Shares	GSIMX	NAS CM	Open End	Global Equity Large Cap (Foreign Stock)	D	D+	B+		Y	1,000,000
Goldman Sachs Growth and Income Strategy Portfolio Class A	GOIAX	NAS CM	Open End	Moderate Alloc (Growth & Income)	B-	C+	B	Up	Y	1,000
Goldman Sachs Growth and Income Strategy Portfolio Class C	GOICX	NAS CM	Open End	Moderate Alloc (Growth & Income)	B-	C+	B	Up	Y	1,000
Goldman Sachs Growth and Income Strategy Portfolio Class R	GPIRX	NAS CM	Open End	Moderate Alloc (Growth & Income)	B-	C+	B	Up	Y	0
Goldman Sachs Growth & Income Strategy Portfolio Cls R6	GOIUX	NAS CM	Open End	Moderate Alloc (Growth & Income)	B-	C+	B	Up	Y	5,000,000
Goldman Sachs Growth & Income Strategy Portfolio Inst Cls	GOIIX	NAS CM	Open End	Moderate Alloc (Growth & Income)	B-	C+	B	Up	Y	1,000,000
Goldman Sachs Growth & Income Strategy Portfolio Inv Cls	GPITX	NAS CM	Open End	Moderate Alloc (Growth & Income)	B-	C+	B	Up	Y	0
Goldman Sachs Growth & Inc Strategy Port Serv Cls	GOISX	NAS CM	Open End	Moderate Alloc (Growth & Income)	B-	C+	B	Up	Y	0
Goldman Sachs Growth Opportunities Fund Class A	GGOAX	NAS CM	Open End	US Equity Mid Cap (Growth)	B-	B-	B	Up	Y	1,000
Goldman Sachs Growth Opportunities Fund Class C	GGOCX	NAS CM	Open End	US Equity Mid Cap (Growth)	B-	C+	B-	Up	Y	1,000
Goldman Sachs Growth Opportunities Fund Class R	GGORX	NAS CM	Open End	US Equity Mid Cap (Growth)	B-	B-	B	Up	Y	0
Goldman Sachs Growth Opportunities Fund Class R6	GGOUX	NAS CM	Open End	US Equity Mid Cap (Growth)	B-	B-	B	Up	Y	5,000,000
Goldman Sachs Growth Opportunities Fund Institutional Cls	GGOIX	NAS CM	Open End	US Equity Mid Cap (Growth)	B-	B-	B	Up	Y	1,000,000
Goldman Sachs Growth Opportunities Fund Investor Class	GGOTX	NAS CM	Open End	US Equity Mid Cap (Growth)	B-	B-	B	Up	Y	0
Goldman Sachs Growth Opportunities Fund Service Class	GGOSX	NAS CM	Open End	US Equity Mid Cap (Growth)	B-	B-	B	Up	Y	0
Goldman Sachs Growth Strategy Portfolio Class A	GGSAX	NAS CM	Open End	Alloc (Growth & Income)	B-	B-	B-	Down	Y	1,000
Goldman Sachs Growth Strategy Portfolio Class C	GGSCX	NAS CM	Open End	Alloc (Growth & Income)	B-	B-	B-	Down	Y	1,000
Goldman Sachs Growth Strategy Portfolio Class R	GGSRX	NAS CM	Open End	Alloc (Growth & Income)	B-	B-	B-	Down	Y	0
Goldman Sachs Growth Strategy Portfolio Class R6	GGSUX	NAS CM	Open End	Alloc (Growth & Income)	B-	B-	B-	Down	Y	5,000,000
Goldman Sachs Growth Strategy Portfolio Institutional Cls	GGSIX	NAS CM	Open End	Alloc (Growth & Income)	B-	B-	B-	Down	Y	1,000,000
Goldman Sachs Growth Strategy Portfolio Investor Class	GGSTX	NAS CM	Open End	Alloc (Growth & Income)	B-	B-	B-	Down	Y	0
Goldman Sachs Growth Strategy Portfolio Service Class	GGSSX	NAS CM	Open End	Alloc (Growth & Income)	B-	B-	B-	Down	Y	0
Goldman Sachs Income Builder Fund Class A	GSBFX	NAS CM	Open End	Cautious Alloc (Balanced)	C+	C+	B		Y	1,000
Goldman Sachs Income Builder Fund Class C	GSBCX	NAS CM	Open End	Cautious Alloc (Balanced)	C+	C	B	Up	Y	1,000
Goldman Sachs Income Builder Fund Class R6	GSBUX	NAS CM	Open End	Cautious Alloc (Balanced)	B-	C+	B	Up	Y	5,000,000
Goldman Sachs Income Builder Fund Institutional Class	GSBIX	NAS CM	Open End	Cautious Alloc (Balanced)	B-	C+	B	Up	Y	1,000,000
Goldman Sachs Income Builder Fund Investor Class	GKIRX	NAS CM	Open End	Cautious Alloc (Balanced)	B-	C+	B	Up	Y	0
Goldman Sachs Intl Equity Dividend & Premium Fund Cls A	GIDAX	NAS CM	Open End	Global Equity Large Cap (Foreign Stock)	C+	C+	B-	Up	Y	1,000
Goldman Sachs Intl Equity Dividend & Premium Fund Cls C	GIDCX	NAS CM	Open End	Global Equity Large Cap (Foreign Stock)	C+	C+	C+	Up	Y	1,000
Goldman Sachs Intl Equity Dividend & Premium Fund Inst Cls	GIDHX	NAS CM	Open End	Global Equity Large Cap (Foreign Stock)	C+	C+	B-	Up	Y	1,000,000
Goldman Sachs Intl Equity Dividend & Premium Fund Inv Cls	GIRVX	NAS CM	Open End	Global Equity Large Cap (Foreign Stock)	C+	C+	B-	Up	Y	0
Goldman Sachs International Equity Insights Fund Class A	GCIAX	NAS CM	Open End	Global Equity Large Cap (Foreign Stock)	B	B	B+	Up	Y	1,000
Goldman Sachs International Equity Insights Fund Class C	GCICX	NAS CM	Open End	Global Equity Large Cap (Foreign Stock)	B	B	B	Up	Y	1,000
Goldman Sachs International Equity Insights Fund Class R	GCIRX	NAS CM	Open End	Global Equity Large Cap (Foreign Stock)	B	B	B-	Up	Y	0
Goldman Sachs International Equity Insights Fund Class R6	GCIUX	NAS CM	Open End	Global Equity Large Cap (Foreign Stock)	B	B+	B-	Up	Y	5,000,000
Goldman Sachs International Equity Insights Fund Class S	GCISX	NAS CM	Open End	Global Equity Large Cap (Foreign Stock)	B	B	B+	Up	Y	0
Goldman Sachs Intl Equity Insights Fund Inst Cls	GCIIX	NAS CM	Open End	Global Equity Large Cap (Foreign Stock)	B+	B+	B+	Up	Y	1,000,000
Goldman Sachs Intl Equity Insights Fund Inv Cls	GCITX	NAS CM	Open End	Global Equity Large Cap (Foreign Stock)	B	B	B-	Up	Y	0
Goldman Sachs Intl Real Estate Securities Fund Cls A	GIRAX	NAS CM	Open End	Real Estate Sector Equity (Real Estate)	C+	C	B	Up	Y	1,000
Goldman Sachs Intl Real Estate Securities Fund Cls C	GIRCX	NAS CM	Open End	Real Estate Sector Equity (Real Estate)	C+	C	B	Up	Y	1,000
Goldman Sachs Intl Real Estate Securities Fund Cls R6	GIRUX	NAS CM	Open End	Real Estate Sector Equity (Real Estate)	B-	C+	B	Up	Y	5,000,000
Goldman Sachs Intl Real Estate Securities Fund Inst Cls	GIRIX	NAS CM	Open End	Real Estate Sector Equity (Real Estate)	B-	C+	B	Up	Y	1,000,000
Goldman Sachs Intl Real Estate Securities Fund Inv Cls	GIRTX	NAS CM	Open End	Real Estate Sector Equity (Real Estate)	B-	C+	B	Up	Y	0
Goldman Sachs International Small Cap Insights Fund Cls A	GICAX	NAS CM	Open End	Global Equity Mid/Small Cap (Small Company)	A-	B+	A-	Up	Y	1,000
Goldman Sachs International Small Cap Insights Fund Cls C	GICCX	NAS CM	Open End	Global Equity Mid/Small Cap (Small Company)	A-	B+	A-	Up	Y	1,000
Goldman Sachs International Small Cap Insights Fund Cls R6	GICUX	NAS CM	Open End	Global Equity Mid/Small Cap (Small Company)	A-	A-	A	Up	Y	5,000,000

★ Expanded analysis of this fund is included in Section II.

Min Additional Investment	3-Month Total Return	6-Month Total Return	1-Year Total Return	3-Year Total Return	5-Year Total Return	Dividend Yield (TTM)	Expense Ratio	3-Yr Std Deviation	3-Year Beta	NAV	Total Assets (MIL)	%Cash	%Stocks	%Bonds	%Other	Turnover Ratio	Last Bull Market Total Return	Last Bear Market Total Return	Front End Fee (%)	Back End Fee (%)	Inception Date
TOTAL RETURNS						PERFORMANCE				ASSETS		ASSET ALLOCATION & TURNOVER					BULL & BEAR		FEES		
	3.42	5.34	8.79			2.97	1.15			10.65	333.9	0	98	0	2	60					Aug-15
50	4.25	11.80	31.24				1.3			12.98	527.9	4	94	0	2				5.50		Dec-16
50	4.03	11.32	30.23				2.05			12.88	527.9	4	94	0	2					1.00	Dec-16
	4.37	11.92	31.49				1.05			12.99	527.9	4	94	0	2						Dec-16
	4.18	11.64	30.83				1.55			12.94	527.9	4	94	0	2						Dec-16
	4.41	12.04	31.75				0.88			13.01	527.9	4	94	0	2						Dec-16
	4.41	12.04	31.75				0.9			13.01	527.9	4	94	0	2						Dec-16
50	3.55	8.02	16.19	21.71	42.72	1.33	1.37	6.33		13.81	960.0	12	57	18	12	67	12.63	-14.19	5.50		Jan-98
50	3.28	7.54	15.31	18.92	37.36	0.68	2.12	6.32		13.49	960.0	12	57	18	12	67	12.21	-14.51		1.00	Jan-98
	3.43	7.78	15.82	20.65	40.84	1.16	1.62	6.36		13.7	960.0	12	57	18	12	67	12.44	-14.26			Nov-07
	3.65	8.22	16.70	23.13	45.50	1.71	0.95	6.31		13.85	960.0	12	57	18	12	67	12.92	-14.05			Jul-15
	3.65	8.22	16.59	23.11	45.47	1.7	0.97	6.29		13.85	960.0	12	57	18	12	67	12.93	-14.05			Jan-98
	3.56	8.12	16.39	22.58	44.46	1.58	1.12	6.3		13.74	960.0	12	57	18	12	67	12.72	-14.1			Nov-07
	3.45	7.90	16.02	21.23	41.97	1.24	1.47	6.32		13.77	960.0	12	57	18	12	67	12.61	-14.27			Jan-98
50	5.68	10.58	26.80	20.05	80.20	0	1.32	11.16	0.96	21.09	2,590	2	98	0	0	61	32.76	-23.27	5.50		May-99
50	5.50	10.15	25.84	17.38	73.62	0	2.07	11.16	0.96	14.58	2,590	2	98	0	0	61	32.18	-23.52		1.00	May-99
	5.55	10.38	26.41	19.11	77.93	0	1.57	11.16	0.96	20.14	2,590	2	98	0	0	61	32.52	-23.34			Nov-07
	5.72	10.74	27.23	21.40	83.71	0	0.93	11.17	0.97	24.97	2,590	2	98	0	0	61	33.06	-23.12			Jul-15
	5.77	10.75	27.20	21.37	83.67	0	0.95	11.17	0.96	24.96	2,590	2	98	0	0	61	33.06	-23.12			May-99
	5.70	10.73	27.06	20.96	82.46	0	1.07	11.18	0.97	22.11	2,590	2	98	0	0	61	32.95	-23.18			Nov-07
	5.60	10.51	26.61	19.58	79.08	0	1.45	11.16	0.96	20.09	2,590	2	98	0	0	61	32.68	-23.29			May-99
50	4.48	10.38	21.02	27.96	57.81	0.77	1.38	8.13		15.83	892.1	9	78	-1	12	59	16.41	-18.94	5.50		Jan-98
50	4.25	9.88	20.08	25.06	51.86	0.11	2.13	8.13		15.81	892.1	9	78	-1	12	59	15.94	-19.24		1.00	Jan-98
	4.39	10.22	20.67	26.92	55.75	0.62	1.63	8.12		15.42	892.1	9	78	-1	12	59	16.21	-19.05			Nov-07
	4.53	10.51	21.50	29.53	60.89	1.13	0.96	8.17		15.81	892.1	9	78	-1	12	59	16.71	-18.87			Jul-15
	4.55	10.60	21.52	29.51	60.87	1.13	0.98	8.17		15.81	892.1	9	78	-1	12	59	16.71	-18.87			Jan-98
	4.51	10.50	21.30	28.90	59.78	1.02	1.13	8.12		15.59	892.1	9	78	-1	12	59	16.58	-18.84			Nov-07
	4.45	10.30	20.88	27.55	57.08	0.72	1.48	8.14		15.77	892.1	9	78	-1	12	59	16.24	-18.92			Jan-98
50	1.31	3.21	7.93	13.26	38.03	3.71	0.99	6.02	0.51	22.81	2,039	1	37	49	7	80	15.11	-8.38	5.50		Oct-94
50	1.10	2.79	7.14	10.71	32.94	3.04	1.74	6.02	0.51	22.43	2,039	1	37	49	7	80	14.58	-8.66		1.00	Aug-97
	1.38	3.39	8.38	14.35	39.36	4.03	0.59	6.05	0.52	23.29	2,039	1	37	49	7	80	15.11	-8.38			Jul-15
	1.38	3.39	8.37	14.57	40.79	4.02	0.59	6.05	0.52	23.29	2,039	1	37	49	7	80	15.38	-8.21			Aug-97
	1.35	3.32	8.20	14.11	39.76	3.9	0.74	6.05	0.52	23.23	2,039	1	37	49	7	80	15.29	-8.3			Aug-10
50	2.51	7.84	23.36	17.40	30.81	2.12	1.37	10.85	0.86	7.76	410.7	1	99	0	0	18	10.36	-22.18	5.50		Jan-08
50	2.29	7.31	22.49	14.74	25.94	1.64	2.12	10.83	0.86	7.48	410.7	1	99	0	0	18	9.86	-22.43		1.00	Jan-08
	2.54	7.92	23.84	18.79	33.29	2.55	0.97	10.82	0.86	7.62	410.7	1	99	0	0	18	10.56	-22.04			Jan-08
	2.51	7.87	23.58	18.24	32.28	2.46	1.12	10.78	0.85	7.6	410.7	1	99	0	0	18	10.55	-22.12			Aug-10
50	3.78	10.99	29.13	41.04	62.72	1.76	1.19	10.9	0.87	13.25	1,482	2	96	0	3	176	14.25	-26.49	5.50		Aug-97
50	3.60	10.49	28.08	37.80	56.71	1.27	1.94	10.87	0.87	12.97	1,482	2	96	0	3	176	13.73	-26.71		1.00	Aug-97
	3.72	10.85	28.76	39.92	60.71	1.85	1.44	10.91	0.87	12.9	1,482	2	96	0	3	176	14.06	-26.55			Nov-07
	3.93	11.21	29.69	42.58	66.03	1.99	0.84	10.86	0.87	13.59	1,482	2	96	0	3	176	14.44	-26.34			Jul-15
	3.75	10.88	28.92	40.47	61.75	1.62	1.35	10.88	0.87	13.38	1,482	2	96	0	3	176	14.14	-26.5			Aug-97
	3.91	11.19	29.65	42.58	66.03	1.97	0.85	10.89	0.87	13.6	1,482	2	96	0	3	176	14.44	-26.34			Aug-97
	3.91	11.17	29.48	41.96	64.70	2.03	0.94	10.9	0.87	12.99	1,482	2	96	0	3	176	14.28	-26.41			Nov-07
50	5.66	8.25	17.90	12.59	21.89	4.64	1.39	11.2	0.96	6.48	125.5	0	97	0	3	41	19.52	-24.4	5.50		Jul-06
50	5.68	7.92	17.23	10.14	17.68	3.8	2.14	11.16	0.96	6.5	125.5	0	97	0	3	41	18.77	-24.43		1.00	Jul-06
	5.94	8.44	18.49	13.82	24.45	5.21	0.97	11.14	0.96	6.26	125.5	0	97	0	3	41	19.76	-24.22			Jul-15
	5.75	8.43	18.46	13.77	24.39	5.19	0.99	11.09	0.96	6.26	125.5	0	97	0	3	41	19.76	-24.22			Jul-06
	5.78	8.39	18.29	13.51	23.67	4.93	1.14	11.19	0.96	6.43	125.5	0	97	0	3	41	19.56	-24.21			Nov-07
50	4.84	13.09	32.53	47.92	85.77	1.83	1.3	10.58	0.88	12.76	2,617	1	97	0	2	140	13.89	-21.91	5.50		Sep-07
50	4.68	12.65	31.68	44.62	78.92	1.28	2.05	10.57	0.88	12.35	2,617	1	97	0	2	140	13.47	-22.11		1.00	Sep-07
	4.97	13.28	33.20	50.00	90.01	2.17	0.88	10.61	0.88	12.78	2,617	1	97	0	2	140	14.26	-21.81			Jul-15

	MARKET			FUND TYPE, CATEGORY & OBJECTIVE	RATINGS					MINIMUMS
Fund Name	Ticker Symbol	Traded On	Fund Type	Category and (Prospectus Objective)	Overall Rating	Reward Rating	Risk Rating	Recent Up/ Downgrade	Open to New Investors	Min Initial Investment
Goldman Sachs Intl Small Cap Insights Fund Inst Cls	GICIX	NAS CM	Open End	Global Equity Mid/Small Cap (Small Company)	A-	A-	A	Up	Y	1,000,000
Goldman Sachs Intl Small Cap Insights Fund Inv Cls	GIRLX	NAS CM	Open End	Global Equity Mid/Small Cap (Small Company)	A-	A-	A	Up	Y	0
Goldman Sachs International Tax-Managed Equity Fund Cls A	GATMX	NAS CM	Open End	Global Equity Large Cap (Foreign Stock)	B	B	B	Up	Y	1,000
Goldman Sachs International Tax-Managed Equity Fund Cls C	GCTMX	NAS CM	Open End	Global Equity Large Cap (Foreign Stock)	B	B	B	Up	Y	1,000
Goldman Sachs Intl Tax-Managed Equity Fund Inst Cls	GHTMX	NAS CM	Open End	Global Equity Large Cap (Foreign Stock)	B	B	B	Up	Y	1,000,000
Goldman Sachs Intl Tax-Managed Equity Fund Inv Cls	GITRX	NAS CM	Open End	Global Equity Large Cap (Foreign Stock)	B	B	B	Up	Y	0
Goldman Sachs Large Cap Growth Insights Fund Class A	GLCGX	NAS CM	Open End	US Equity Large Cap Growth (Growth & Income)	B+	A-	B	Up	Y	1,000
Goldman Sachs Large Cap Growth Insights Fund Class C	GLCCX	NAS CM	Open End	US Equity Large Cap Growth (Growth & Income)	B+	B+	B	Up	Y	1,000
Goldman Sachs Large Cap Growth Insights Fund Class R	GLCRX	NAS CM	Open End	US Equity Large Cap Growth (Growth & Income)	B+	B+	B	Up	Y	0
Goldman Sachs Large Cap Growth Insights Fund Class R6	GLCUX	NAS CM	Open End	US Equity Large Cap Growth (Growth & Income)	B+	A-	B	Up	Y	5,000,000
Goldman Sachs Large Cap Growth Insights Fund Inst Cls	GCGIX	NAS CM	Open End	US Equity Large Cap Growth (Growth & Income)	B+	A-	B	Up	Y	1,000,000
Goldman Sachs Large Cap Growth Insights Fund Investor Cls	GLCTX	NAS CM	Open End	US Equity Large Cap Growth (Growth & Income)	B+	A-	B	Up	Y	0
Goldman Sachs Large Cap Growth Insights Fund Service Class	GSCLX	NAS CM	Open End	US Equity Large Cap Growth (Growth & Income)	B+	B+	B	Up	Y	0
Goldman Sachs Large Cap Value Fund Class A	GSLAX	NAS CM	Open End	US Equity Large Cap Value (Growth)	B-	C+	B	Up	Y	1,000
Goldman Sachs Large Cap Value Fund Class C	GSVCX	NAS CM	Open End	US Equity Large Cap Value (Growth)	C+	C+	B	Down	Y	1,000
Goldman Sachs Large Cap Value Fund Class R	GSVRX	NAS CM	Open End	US Equity Large Cap Value (Growth)	B-	C+	B	Up	Y	0
Goldman Sachs Large Cap Value Fund Class R6	GSVUX	NAS CM	Open End	US Equity Large Cap Value (Growth)	B-	C+	B	Up	Y	5,000,000
Goldman Sachs Large Cap Value Fund Institutional Class	GSLIX	NAS CM	Open End	US Equity Large Cap Value (Growth)	B-	C+	B	Up	Y	1,000,000
Goldman Sachs Large Cap Value Fund Investor Class	GSVTX	NAS CM	Open End	US Equity Large Cap Value (Growth)	B-	C+	B	Up	Y	0
Goldman Sachs Large Cap Value Fund Service Class	GSVSX	NAS CM	Open End	US Equity Large Cap Value (Growth)	B-	C+	B	Up	Y	0
Goldman Sachs Large Cap Value Insights Fund Class A	GCVAX	NAS CM	Open End	US Equity Large Cap Value (Growth & Income)	B	B	B	Up	Y	1,000
Goldman Sachs Large Cap Value Insights Fund Class C	GCVCX	NAS CM	Open End	US Equity Large Cap Value (Growth & Income)	B-	B-	B-	Down	Y	1,000
Goldman Sachs Large Cap Value Insights Fund Class R	GCVRX	NAS CM	Open End	US Equity Large Cap Value (Growth & Income)	B	B	B-	Up	Y	0
Goldman Sachs Large Cap Value Insights Fund Class R6	GCVUX	NAS CM	Open End	US Equity Large Cap Value (Growth & Income)	B	B	B-	Up	Y	5,000,000
Goldman Sachs Large Cap Value Insights Fund Inst Cls	GCVIX	NAS CM	Open End	US Equity Large Cap Value (Growth & Income)	B	B	B-	Up	Y	1,000,000
Goldman Sachs Large Cap Value Insights Fund Investor Class	GCVTX	NAS CM	Open End	US Equity Large Cap Value (Growth & Income)	B	B	B-	Up	Y	0
Goldman Sachs Large Cap Value Insights Fund Service Class	GCLSX	NAS CM	Open End	US Equity Large Cap Value (Growth & Income)	B	B	B	Up	Y	0
Goldman Sachs Long Short Credit Strat Fund Inst Shares	GSAWX	NAS CM	Open End	Other Alternative (Growth & Income)	B-	C	A-	Up	Y	1,000,000
Goldman Sachs Managed Futures Strategy Fund Class A	GMSAX	NAS CM	Open End	Other Alternative (Growth & Income)	C+	C	B	Up	Y	1,000
Goldman Sachs Managed Futures Strategy Fund Class C	GMSCX	NAS CM	Open End	Other Alternative (Growth & Income)	C	C	C+		Y	1,000
Goldman Sachs Managed Futures Strategy Fund Class R	GFFRX	NAS CM	Open End	Other Alternative (Growth & Income)	C+	C	B	Up	Y	0
Goldman Sachs Managed Futures Strategy Fund Inst Cls	GMSSX	NAS CM	Open End	Other Alternative (Growth & Income)	B-	C	B	Up	Y	1,000,000
Goldman Sachs Managed Futures Strategy Fund Investor Class	GFIRX	NAS CM	Open End	Other Alternative (Growth & Income)	C+	C	B		Y	0
Goldman Sachs Mid Cap Value Fund Class A	GCMAX	NAS CM	Open End	US Equity Mid Cap (Growth)	C+	C+	B-	Down	Y	1,000
Goldman Sachs Mid Cap Value Fund Class C	GCMCX	NAS CM	Open End	US Equity Mid Cap (Growth)	C+	C+	B-	Down	Y	1,000
Goldman Sachs Mid Cap Value Fund Class R	GCMRX	NAS CM	Open End	US Equity Mid Cap (Growth)	C+	C+	B-	Down	Y	0
Goldman Sachs Mid Cap Value Fund Class R6	GCMUX	NAS CM	Open End	US Equity Mid Cap (Growth)	C+	C+	B-	Down	Y	5,000,000
Goldman Sachs Mid Cap Value Fund Institutional Class	GSMCX	NAS CM	Open End	US Equity Mid Cap (Growth)	C+	C+	B-	Down	Y	1,000,000
Goldman Sachs Mid Cap Value Fund Investor Class	GCMTX	NAS CM	Open End	US Equity Mid Cap (Growth)	C+	C+	B-	Down	Y	0
Goldman Sachs Mid Cap Value Fund Service Class	GSMSX	NAS CM	Open End	US Equity Mid Cap (Growth)	C+	C+	B-	Down	Y	0
Goldman Sachs MLP & Energy Fund Class A Shares	GLEAX	NAS CM	Open End	Energy Sector Equity (Growth & Income)	U	U	U		Y	1,000
Goldman Sachs MLP & Energy Fund Class C Shares	GLECX	NAS CM	Open End	Energy Sector Equity (Growth & Income)	U	U	U		Y	1,000
Goldman Sachs MLP & Energy Fund Class R Shares	GLERX	NAS CM	Open End	Energy Sector Equity (Growth & Income)	U	U	U		Y	0
Goldman Sachs MLP & Energy Fund Class R6 Shares	GLESX	NAS CM	Open End	Energy Sector Equity (Growth & Income)	U	U	U		Y	5,000,000
Goldman Sachs MLP & Energy Fund Institutional Shares	GLEPX	NAS CM	Open End	Energy Sector Equity (Growth & Income)	U	U	U		Y	1,000,000
Goldman Sachs MLP & Energy Fund Investor Shares	GLEIX	NAS CM	Open End	Energy Sector Equity (Growth & Income)	U	U	U		Y	0
Goldman Sachs MLP and Energy Renaissance Fund	GER	NYSE	Closed End	Energy Sector Equity (Income)	D	D	D	Down	Y	
Goldman Sachs MLP Energy Infrastructure Fund Class A	GLPAX	NAS CM	Open End	Energy Sector Equity (Growth & Income)	D	D	D	Down	Y	1,000
Goldman Sachs MLP Energy Infrastructure Fund Class C	GLPCX	NAS CM	Open End	Energy Sector Equity (Growth & Income)	D	D	D	Down	Y	1,000
Goldman Sachs MLP Energy Infrastructure Fund Class R	GLPRX	NAS CM	Open End	Energy Sector Equity (Growth & Income)	D	D	D	Down	Y	0
Goldman Sachs MLP Energy Infrastructure Fund Inst Cls	GMLPX	NAS CM	Open End	Energy Sector Equity (Growth & Income)	D	D	D	Down	Y	1,000,000
Goldman Sachs MLP Energy Infrastructure Fund Investor Cls	GLPIX	NAS CM	Open End	Energy Sector Equity (Growth & Income)	D	D	D	Down	Y	0

★ Expanded analysis of this fund is included in Section II.

Min Additional Investment	TOTAL RETURNS: 3-Month Total Return	6-Month Total Return	1-Year Total Return	3-Year Total Return	5-Year Total Return	PERFORMANCE: Dividend Yield (TTM)	Expense Ratio	3-Yr Std Deviation	3-Year Beta	ASSETS: NAV	Total Assets (MIL)	ASSET ALLOCATION & TURNOVER: %Cash	%Stocks	%Bonds	%Other	Turnover Ratio	BULL & BEAR: Last Bull Market Total Return	Last Bear Market Total Return	FEES: Front End Fee (%)	Back End Fee (%)	Inception Date
	4.88	13.30	33.02	49.57	89.46	2.14	0.9	10.6	0.88	12.75	2,617	1	97	0	2	140	14.26	-21.81			Sep-07
	4.82	13.18	32.85	49.00	88.11	2.07	1.05	10.62	0.88	12.69	2,617	1	97	0	2	140	14.13	-21.83			Aug-10
50	4.09	10.96	28.85	34.49	57.27	1.2	1.3	10.57	0.84	10.93	622.3	0	100	0	0	125	13.01	-23.8	5.50		Jan-08
50	3.84	10.47	27.85	31.44	51.44	0.66	2.05	10.47	0.83	10.59	622.3	0	100	0	0	125	12.4	-24.03		1.00	Jan-08
	4.17	11.19	29.42	35.99	60.58	1.46	0.9	10.5	0.83	10.85	622.3	0	100	0	0	125	13.19	-23.54			Jan-08
	4.16	11.03	29.09	35.29	59.11	1.32	1.05	10.52	0.83	10.92	622.3	0	100	0	0	125	13.11	-23.66			Aug-10
50	7.07	14.13	29.20	41.65	132.46	0.36	0.95	10.99	1.01	29.95	1,944	3	97	0	0	254	25.85	-15.13	5.50		May-97
50	6.86	13.70	28.25	38.55	123.95	0	1.7	10.94	1	26.96	1,944	3	97	0	0	254	25.41	-15.44		1.00	Aug-97
	6.99	13.97	28.90	40.64	129.57	0.26	1.2	10.98	1.01	29.28	1,944	3	97	0	0	254	25.75	-15.2			Nov-07
	7.15	14.38	29.73	43.42	137.23	0.62	0.55	10.96	1.01	30.91	1,944	3	97	0	0	254	26.23	-14.94			Jul-15
	7.16	14.39	29.73	43.39	137.19	0.59	0.56	10.97	1.01	30.93	1,944	3	97	0	0	254	26.23	-14.94			May-97
	7.13	14.28	29.51	42.73	135.31	0.57	0.7	10.99	1.01	29.54	1,944	3	97	0	0	254	26.14	-15.08			Nov-07
	7.00	14.04	29.06	41.28	131.36	0.43	1.06	10.97	1.01	29.47	1,944	3	97	0	0	254	25.84	-15.13			May-97
50	2.79	3.90	9.32	14.91	75.59	1.55	1.12	11.62	1.09	15.64	852.6	1	99	0	0	124	24.17	-22.56	5.50		Dec-99
50	2.64	3.55	8.58	12.35	69.15	1.04	1.87	11.64	1.09	14.91	852.6	1	99	0	0	124	23.74	-22.89		1.00	Dec-99
	2.73	3.81	9.08	14.05	73.41	1.36	1.37	11.67	1.09	15.23	852.6	1	99	0	0	124	24.07	-22.65			Nov-07
	2.85	4.12	9.95	16.49	79.41	1.96	0.77	11.64	1.09	16.09	852.6	1	99	0	0	124	24.53	-22.49			Jul-15
	2.87	4.09	9.73	16.17	78.93	1.93	0.79	11.64	1.09	15.76	852.6	1	99	0	0	124	24.53	-22.49			Dec-99
	2.84	4.07	9.62	15.74	77.67	1.75	0.87	11.67	1.1	15.62	852.6	1	99	0	0	124	24.46	-22.54			Nov-07
	2.75	3.81	9.19	14.46	74.48	1.42	1.29	11.65	1.09	15.53	852.6	1	99	0	0	124	24.27	-22.67			Dec-99
50	5.74	11.36	18.94	30.75	105.42	1.4	0.95	11.19	1.06	21.93	395.4	3	97	0	0	229	23.01	-17.41	5.50		Dec-98
50	5.55	11.00	18.10	27.89	97.91	0.76	1.7	11.18	1.06	21.75	395.4	3	97	0	0	229	22.54	-17.67		1.00	Dec-98
	5.67	11.19	18.67	29.75	102.93	1.26	1.2	11.17	1.06	21.8	395.4	3	97	0	0	229	22.87	-17.51			Nov-07
	5.87	11.61	19.46	32.34	109.57	1.78	0.55	11.22	1.06	21.9	395.4	3	97	0	0	229	23.39	-17.32			Jul-15
	5.86	11.60	19.43	32.36	109.59	1.77	0.56	11.18	1.06	21.91	395.4	3	97	0	0	229	23.39	-17.32			Dec-98
	5.84	11.50	19.28	31.75	108.09	1.65	0.7	11.18	1.06	21.86	395.4	3	97	0	0	229	23.22	-17.31			Nov-07
	5.69	11.31	18.81	30.34	104.50	1.32	1.06	11.2	1.06	22.02	395.4	3	97	0	0	229	22.96	-17.46			Dec-98
	-0.19	0.16	2.60	7.21	10.03	3.6	1.13	2.9	6.67	9.27	215.3	19	0	72	8	266	9.86	-2.61			Jun-09
50	2.28	2.79	2.28	11.43	3.01	0	1.69	8.02	19.64	10.3	261.4	75	0	2	23	529			5.50		Feb-12
50	2.06	2.38	1.44	8.95	-0.88	0	2.45	8.02	20.95	9.88	261.4	75	0	2	23	529				1.00	Feb-12
	2.21	2.72	2.11	10.69	1.78	0	1.95	7.94	20.54	10.16	261.4	75	0	2	23	529					Feb-12
	2.43	3.03	2.73	12.84	5.09	0.11	1.3	8	20.23	10.52	261.4	75	0	2	23	529					Feb-12
	2.35	2.95	2.55	12.35	4.41	0	1.45	7.94	19.72	10.44	261.4	75	0	2	23	529					Feb-12
50	4.79	6.43	10.66	12.05	72.44	0.93	1.16	11.14	1.03	35.2	2,439	2	98	0	0	124	23.76	-22.25	5.50		Aug-97
50	4.64	6.06	9.86	9.60	66.13	0.42	1.91	11.14	1.03	31.49	2,439	2	98	0	0	124	23.2	-22.49		1.00	Aug-97
	4.75	6.29	10.41	11.23	70.35	0.82	1.41	11.14	1.03	34.2	2,439	2	98	0	0	124	23.57	-22.34			Jan-09
	4.91	6.65	11.11	13.45	76.03	1.38	0.74	11.15	1.04	35.51	2,439	2	98	0	0	124	24	-22.12			Jul-15
	4.93	6.65	11.13	13.41	75.98	1.36	0.76	11.15	1.04	35.53	2,439	2	98	0	0	124	24	-22.12			Aug-95
	4.87	6.58	10.95	12.90	74.67	1.26	0.91	11.15	1.04	34.44	2,439	2	98	0	0	124	23.92	-22.19			Nov-07
	4.80	6.39	10.56	11.73	71.60	0.82	1.26	11.16	1.04	34.52	2,439	2	98	0	0	124	23.67	-22.28			Jul-97
50	1.78						1.49			10.11	2.9								5.50		Sep-17
50	1.67						2.24			10.11	2.9									1.00	Sep-17
	1.75						1.74			10.11	2.9										Sep-17
	1.94						1.09			10.12	2.9										Sep-17
	1.94						1.1			10.12	2.9										Sep-17
	1.82						1.24			10.11	2.9										Sep-17
	-4.08	-7.06	-11.76	-40.43		0	2.44	34.83	1.69	6.4558	478.7	1	99	0	0	64					Sep-14
50	0.83	-0.85	-6.83	-25.88		6.44	1.45	20.52	1.02	7.25	2,116	3	97	0	0	104			5.50		Mar-13
50	0.58	-1.29	-7.57	-27.58		6.71	2.2	20.52	1.02	6.96	2,116	3	97	0	0	104				1.00	Mar-13
	0.84	-0.99	-7.04	-26.47		6.54	1.7	20.48	1.02	7.15	2,116	3	97	0	0	104					Mar-13
	0.95	-0.57	-6.47	-25.01		6.31	1.05	20.5	1.02	7.41	2,116	3	97	0	0	104					Mar-13
	0.96	-0.70	-6.63	-25.36		6.36	1.2	20.52	1.02	7.35	2,116	3	97	0	0	104					Mar-13

	MARKET			FUND TYPE, CATEGORY & OBJECTIVE	RATINGS				MINIMUMS	
Fund Name	Ticker Symbol	Traded On	Fund Type	Category and (Prospectus Objective)	Overall Rating	Reward Rating	Risk Rating	Recent Up/ Downgrade	Open to New Investors	Min Initial Investment
Goldman Sachs MLP Income Opportunities Fund	GMZ	NYSE	Closed End	Energy Sector Equity (Income)	D	D	D	Down	Y	
Goldman Sachs Multi-Manager Alternatives Fund Cls A Shares	GMAMX	NAS CM	Open End	Multialternative (Growth)	C	C-	C		Y	1,000
Goldman Sachs Multi-Manager Alternatives Fund Cls C Shares	GMCMX	NAS CM	Open End	Multialternative (Growth)	D+	D+	C	Down	Y	1,000
Goldman Sachs Multi-Mgr Alternatives Fund Cls IR Shares	GIMMX	NAS CM	Open End	Multialternative (Growth)	C	C	C		Y	0
Goldman Sachs Multi-Manager Alternatives Fund Cls R Shares	GRMMX	NAS CM	Open End	Multialternative (Growth)	C-	C-	C	Down	Y	0
Goldman Sachs Multi-Manager Alternatives Fund Inst Shares	GSMMX	NAS CM	Open End	Multialternative (Growth)	C	C	C		Y	1,000,000
Goldman Sachs N-11 Equity Fund Class A	GSYAX	NAS CM	Open End	Emerging Markets Equity (Growth)	C	C	C	Up		1,000
Goldman Sachs N-11 Equity Fund Class C	GSYCX	NAS CM	Open End	Emerging Markets Equity (Growth)	C	C	C-	Up		1,000
Goldman Sachs N-11 Equity Fund Institutional Class	GSYIX	NAS CM	Open End	Emerging Markets Equity (Growth)	C	C	C	Up		1,000,000
Goldman Sachs N-11 Equity Fund Investor Class	GSYRX	NAS CM	Open End	Emerging Markets Equity (Growth)	C	C	C	Up		0
Goldman Sachs Real Estate Securities Fund Class A	GREAX	NAS CM	Open End	Real Estate Sector Equity (Real Estate)	B-	C	B	Up	Y	1,000
Goldman Sachs Real Estate Securities Fund Class C	GRECX	NAS CM	Open End	Real Estate Sector Equity (Real Estate)	C+	C	B-		Y	1,000
Goldman Sachs Real Estate Securities Fund Class R	GRERX	NAS CM	Open End	Real Estate Sector Equity (Real Estate)	B-	C	B	Up	Y	0
Goldman Sachs Real Estate Securities Fund Class R6	GREUX	NAS CM	Open End	Real Estate Sector Equity (Real Estate)	B-	C+	B+	Up	Y	5,000,000
Goldman Sachs Real Estate Securities Fund Inst Cls	GREIX	NAS CM	Open End	Real Estate Sector Equity (Real Estate)	B-	C+	B+	Up	Y	1,000,000
Goldman Sachs Real Estate Securities Fund Investor Class	GRETX	NAS CM	Open End	Real Estate Sector Equity (Real Estate)	B-	C+	B+	Up	Y	0
Goldman Sachs Real Estate Securities Fund Service Class	GRESX	NAS CM	Open End	Real Estate Sector Equity (Real Estate)	B-	C	B	Up	Y	0
Goldman Sachs Rising Dividend Growth Fund Class A	GSRAX	NAS CM	Open End	US Equity Large Cap Growth (Equity-Income)	B-	C+	B	Up	Y	1,000
Goldman Sachs Rising Dividend Growth Fund Class C	GSRCX	NAS CM	Open End	US Equity Large Cap Growth (Equity-Income)	C+	C+	B-	Down	Y	1,000
Goldman Sachs Rising Dividend Growth Fund Class R	GSRRX	NAS CM	Open End	US Equity Large Cap Growth (Equity-Income)	B-	C+	B	Up	Y	0
Goldman Sachs Rising Dividend Growth Fund Inst Cls	GSRLX	NAS CM	Open End	US Equity Large Cap Growth (Equity-Income)	B-	C+	B	Up	Y	1,000,000
Goldman Sachs Rising Dividend Growth Fund Investor Class	GSRIX	NAS CM	Open End	US Equity Large Cap Growth (Equity-Income)	B-	C+	B	Up	Y	0
Goldman Sachs Satellite Strategies Fund Class R6	GXSUX	NAS CM	Open End	Alloc (Growth)	B-	C+	B	Up	Y	5,000,000
Goldman Sachs Satellite Strategies Portfolio Class A	GXSAX	NAS CM	Open End	Alloc (Growth)	B-	C+	B	Up	Y	1,000
Goldman Sachs Satellite Strategies Portfolio Class C	GXSCX	NAS CM	Open End	Alloc (Growth)	C+	C+	B-		Y	1,000
Goldman Sachs Satellite Strategies Portfolio Class R	GXSRX	NAS CM	Open End	Alloc (Growth)	B-	C+	B	Up	Y	0
Goldman Sachs Satellite Strategies Portfolio Inst Cls	GXSIX	NAS CM	Open End	Alloc (Growth)	B-	C+	B	Up	Y	1,000,000
Goldman Sachs Satellite Strategies Portfolio Investor Cls	GXSTX	NAS CM	Open End	Alloc (Growth)	B-	C+	B	Up	Y	0
Goldman Sachs Satellite Strategies Portfolio Service Class	GXSSX	NAS CM	Open End	Alloc (Growth)	B-	C+	B	Up	Y	0
Goldman Sachs Small Cap Equity Insights Fund Class A	GCSAX	NAS CM	Open End	US Equity Small Cap (Small Company)	B+	A-	B	Up	Y	1,000
Goldman Sachs Small Cap Equity Insights Fund Class C	GCSCX	NAS CM	Open End	US Equity Small Cap (Small Company)	B+	A-	B	Up	Y	1,000
Goldman Sachs Small Cap Equity Insights Fund Class R	GDSRX	NAS CM	Open End	US Equity Small Cap (Small Company)	B+	A-	B	Up	Y	0
Goldman Sachs Small Cap Equity Insights Fund Class R6	GCSUX	NAS CM	Open End	US Equity Small Cap (Small Company)	B+	A-	B	Up	Y	5,000,000
Goldman Sachs Small Cap Equity Insights Fund Inst Cls	GCSIX	NAS CM	Open End	US Equity Small Cap (Small Company)	B+	A-	B	Up	Y	1,000,000
Goldman Sachs Small Cap Equity Insights Fund Investor Cls	GDSTX	NAS CM	Open End	US Equity Small Cap (Small Company)	B+	A-	B	Up	Y	0
Goldman Sachs Small Cap Equity Insights Fund Service Class	GCSSX	NAS CM	Open End	US Equity Small Cap (Small Company)	B+	A-	B	Up	Y	0
Goldman Sachs Small Cap Growth Insights Fund Class A	GSAOX	NAS CM	Open End	US Equity Small Cap (Small Company)	B+	A-	B	Up	Y	1,000
Goldman Sachs Small Cap Growth Insights Fund Class C	GSCOX	NAS CM	Open End	US Equity Small Cap (Small Company)	B+	A-	B	Up	Y	1,000
Goldman Sachs Small Cap Growth Insights Fund Class R	GSROX	NAS CM	Open End	US Equity Small Cap (Small Company)	B+	A-	B	Up	Y	0
Goldman Sachs Small Cap Growth Insights Fund Class R6	GINUX	NAS CM	Open End	US Equity Small Cap (Small Company)	B+	A-	B	Up	Y	5,000,000
Goldman Sachs Small Cap Growth Insights Fund Inst Cls	GSIOX	NAS CM	Open End	US Equity Small Cap (Small Company)	B+	A-	B	Up	Y	1,000,000
Goldman Sachs Small Cap Growth Insights Fund Investor Cls	GSTOX	NAS CM	Open End	US Equity Small Cap (Small Company)	B+	A-	B	Up	Y	0
Goldman Sachs Small Cap Value Fund Class A	GSSMX	NAS CM	Open End	US Equity Small Cap (Small Company)	B	B+	B	Up		1,000
Goldman Sachs Small Cap Value Fund Class C	GSSCX	NAS CM	Open End	US Equity Small Cap (Small Company)	B	B	B	Up		1,000
Goldman Sachs Small Cap Value Fund Class R	GSQRX	NAS CM	Open End	US Equity Small Cap (Small Company)	B	B	B	Up		0
Goldman Sachs Small Cap Value Fund Class R6	GSSUX	NAS CM	Open End	US Equity Small Cap (Small Company)	B	B+	B	Up	Y	5,000,000
Goldman Sachs Small Cap Value Fund Institutional Class	GSSIX	NAS CM	Open End	US Equity Small Cap (Small Company)	B	B+	B	Up		1,000,000
Goldman Sachs Small Cap Value Fund Investor Class	GSQTX	NAS CM	Open End	US Equity Small Cap (Small Company)	B	B+	B	Up		0
Goldman Sachs Small Cap Value Fund Service Class	GSSSX	NAS CM	Open End	US Equity Small Cap (Small Company)	B	B	B	Up		0
Goldman Sachs Small Cap Value Insights Fund Class A	GSATX	NAS CM	Open End	US Equity Small Cap (Small Company)	B+	A-	B	Up	Y	1,000
Goldman Sachs Small Cap Value Insights Fund Class C	GSCTX	NAS CM	Open End	US Equity Small Cap (Small Company)	B	A-	B	Up	Y	1,000
Goldman Sachs Small Cap Value Insights Fund Class R	GTTRX	NAS CM	Open End	US Equity Small Cap (Small Company)	B+	A-	B	Up	Y	0

★ Expanded analysis of this fund is included in Section II.

	TOTAL RETURNS					PERFORMANCE				ASSETS		ASSET ALLOCATION & TURNOVER					BULL & BEAR		FEES		
Min Additional Investment	3-Month Total Return	6-Month Total Return	1-Year Total Return	3-Year Total Return	5-Year Total Return	Dividend Yield (TTM)	Expense Ratio	3-Yr Std Deviation	3-Year Beta	NAV	Total Assets (MIL)	%Cash	%Stocks	%Bonds	%Other	Turnover Ratio	Last Bull Market Total Return	Last Bear Market Total Return	Front End Fee (%)	Back End Fee (%)	Inception Date
	-0.27	-1.10	-6.29	-32.13		0	1.75	29.54	1.46	9.398	390.2	3	97	0	0	83					Nov-13
50	0.09	0.78	-0.38	-1.53		1.38	2.38	4.37	7.81	10.23	932.9	54	16	21	7	73			5.50		Apr-13
50	-0.09	0.40	-1.18	-3.82		0.44	3.13	4.39	7.5	10	932.9	54	16	21	7	73				1.00	Apr-13
	0.19	0.98	-0.19	-0.83		1.84	2.14	4.4	6.41	10.26	932.9	54	16	21	7	73					Apr-13
	0.09	0.69	-0.68	-2.33		1.04	2.63	4.34	7.21	10.16	932.9	54	16	21	7	73					Apr-13
	0.19	0.98	0.00	-0.39		1.97	1.98	4.36	7.41	10.3	932.9	54	16	21	7	73					Apr-13
50	4.62	7.10	27.39	-1.32	-3.96	0	1.75	12.77		10.42	79.3	0	100	0	0	27	12.8	-19.89	5.50		Feb-11
50	4.50	6.74	26.52	-3.48	-7.43	0	2.5	12.76		9.97	79.3	0	100	0	0	27	12.3	-20.18		1.00	Feb-11
	4.81	7.38	28.02	-0.08	-1.96	0.03	1.34	12.76		10.49	79.3	0	100	0	0	27	13.11	-19.78			Feb-11
	4.74	7.31	27.86	-0.53	-2.68	0	1.49	12.77		10.47	79.3	0	100	0	0	27	13.01	-19.8			Feb-11
50	1.38	2.13	2.10	9.29	48.59	1.77	1.31	12.94	0.97	15.53	294.2	0	100	0	0	31	32.45	-16.14	5.50		Jul-98
50	1.19	1.77	1.37	6.87	43.11	1.16	2.06	12.95	0.97	14.88	294.2	0	100	0	0	31	31.82	-16.4		1.00	Jul-98
	1.33	2.03	1.92	8.50	46.81	1.55	1.56	12.95	0.97	15.39	294.2	0	100	0	0	31	32.29	-16.24			Nov-07
	1.51	2.41	2.59	10.70	51.67	2.11	0.89	12.96	0.97	15.98	294.2	0	100	0	0	31	32.76	-15.97			Jul-15
	1.51	2.35	2.57	10.65	51.61	2.09	0.91	12.96	0.97	15.98	294.2	0	100	0	0	31	32.76	-15.97			Jul-98
	1.49	2.31	2.41	10.17	50.50	2	1.06	12.97	0.97	15.65	294.2	0	100	0	0	31	32.57	-16.11			Nov-07
	1.37	2.08	2.07	9.01	47.89	1.68	1.41	12.95	0.97	15.65	294.2	0	100	0	0	31	32.37	-16.16			Jul-98
50	7.28	12.01	17.98	16.30	71.48	1.85	1.14	10.17	0.95	19.79	1,955	2	98	0	0	16	19.34	-12.36	5.50		Mar-04
50	7.11	11.35	16.89	13.51	64.87	0.97	1.89	10.14	0.95	19.96	1,955	2	98	0	0	16	19	-12.46		1.00	Apr-05
	7.25	11.43	17.26	14.98	68.77	1.3	1.39	10.14	0.95	19.75	1,955	2	98	0	0	16	19.2	-12.45			Feb-12
	7.44	11.81	18.05	17.30	74.34	1.84	0.74	10.18	0.96	20.31	1,955	2	98	0	0	16	19.65	-12.11			Mar-07
	7.37	11.69	17.86	16.74	72.96	1.71	0.89	10.14	0.95	20.29	1,955	2	98	0	0	16	19.44	-12.36			Feb-12
	2.62	6.85	14.66	18.12	22.89	3.47	1.03	7.45		8.43	681.4	3	58	35	2	22	14.57	-13.5			Jul-15
50	2.62	6.72	14.28	16.70	20.41	3.03	1.45	7.41		8.45	681.4	3	58	35	2	22	14.18	-13.56	5.50		Mar-07
50	2.43	6.34	13.36	14.02	15.90	2.33	2.2	7.47		8.4	681.4	3	58	35	2	22	13.84	-13.95		1.00	Mar-07
	2.56	6.62	13.94	15.82	18.92	2.84	1.7	7.42		8.41	681.4	3	58	35	2	22	14.24	-13.69			Nov-07
	2.74	6.97	14.79	18.08	22.83	3.45	1.05	7.48		8.43	681.4	3	58	35	2	22	14.57	-13.5			Mar-07
	2.70	6.89	14.62	17.53	21.90	3.3	1.2	7.45		8.43	681.4	3	58	35	2	22	14.49	-13.55			Nov-07
	2.48	6.54	14.05	16.22	19.83	2.95	1.55	7.39		8.43	681.4	3	58	35	2	22	14.19	-13.64			Aug-08
50	3.07	9.88	11.39	32.46	95.35	0.24	1.23	13.98	0.97	25.12	308.2	3	97	0	0	144	27.47	-22.81	5.50		Aug-97
50	2.92	9.47	10.58	29.53	88.23	0	1.98	13.96	0.96	21.84	308.2	3	97	0	0	144	27.01	-23.11		1.00	Aug-97
	3.01	9.75	11.14	31.46	93.06	0.1	1.48	14	0.97	24.63	308.2	3	97	0	0	144	27.31	-22.95			Nov-07
	3.18	10.14	11.89	34.13	99.51	0.55	0.83	14.01	0.97	26.04	308.2	3	97	0	0	144	27.8	-22.71			Jul-15
	3.16	10.12	11.82	34.03	99.36	0.54	0.84	14	0.97	26.04	308.2	3	97	0	0	144	27.8	-22.71			Aug-97
	3.13	9.99	11.67	33.48	97.94	0.52	0.98	13.99	0.97	24.95	308.2	3	97	0	0	144	27.64	-22.73			Nov-07
	3.08	9.84	11.28	32.06	94.52	0.15	1.34	14.02	0.97	24.76	308.2	3	97	0	0	144	27.37	-22.87			Aug-97
50	3.78	11.74	18.00	33.24	101.31	0	1.19	14.18	0.93	35.74	615.7	3	97	0	0	139	28.92	-23.35	5.50		Jun-07
50	3.60	11.34	17.12	30.31	93.90	0	1.94	14.2	0.93	27.99	615.7	3	97	0	0	139	28.34	-23.61		1.00	Jun-07
	3.70	11.60	17.68	32.22	98.74	0	1.44	14.19	0.93	34.52	615.7	3	97	0	0	139	28.74	-23.46			Nov-07
	3.86	11.93	18.43	34.85	105.32	0.18	0.83	14.18	0.93	41.68	615.7	3	97	0	0	139	29.19	-23.22			Jul-15
	3.86	11.93	18.41	34.79	105.24	0.17	0.84	14.19	0.93	41.67	615.7	3	97	0	0	139	29.19	-23.22			Jun-07
	3.84	11.88	18.27	34.24	103.79	0.17	0.94	14.19	0.93	36.56	615.7	3	97	0	0	139	29.15	-23.29			Nov-07
50	3.90	10.04	11.88	29.67	96.79	0.35	1.37	13.14	0.91	56.27	7,002	0	100	0	0	68	30.56	-22.84	5.50		Oct-92
50	3.73	9.62	11.06	26.79	89.59	0	2.12	13.13	0.91	42.78	7,002	0	100	0	0	68	29.99	-23.08		1.00	Aug-97
	3.84	9.89	11.60	28.70	94.34	0.17	1.62	13.13	0.91	55.15	7,002	0	100	0	0	68	30.39	-22.93			Nov-07
	4.03	10.27	12.37	31.00	98.81	0.64	0.95	13.14	0.91	60.71	7,002	0	100	0	0	68	30.56	-22.84			Jul-15
	4.01	10.26	12.34	31.23	100.78	0.62	0.97	13.14	0.91	60.73	7,002	0	100	0	0	68	30.88	-22.71			Aug-97
	3.98	10.18	12.15	30.63	99.27	0.55	1.12	13.14	0.91	55.82	7,002	0	100	0	0	68	30.78	-22.76			Nov-07
	3.89	9.98	11.78	29.27	95.84	0.28	1.47	13.12	0.91	54.55	7,002	0	100	0	0	68	30.51	-22.9			Aug-97
50	2.57	8.27	7.09	31.88	89.15	0.52	1.23	14.27	1	42.21	190.0	1	99	0	0	129	25.72	-21.91	5.50		Jun-07
50	2.39	7.87	6.28	28.96	82.14	0.21	1.98	14.27	1	30.48	190.0	1	99	0	0	129	25.15	-22.14		1.00	Jun-07
	2.50	8.14	6.82	30.89	86.73	0.4	1.48	14.28	1	41.63	190.0	1	99	0	0	129	25.5	-21.97			Nov-07

Fund Name	Ticker Symbol	Traded On	Fund Type	Category and (Prospectus Objective)	Overall Rating	Reward Rating	Risk Rating	Recent Up/ Downgrade	Open to New Investors	Min Initial Investment
	MARKET		FUND TYPE, CATEGORY & OBJECTIVE		RATINGS				MINIMUMS	
Goldman Sachs Small Cap Value Insights Fund Class R6	GTTUX	NAS CM	Open End	US Equity Small Cap (Small Company)	B+	A-	B	Up	Y	5,000,000
Goldman Sachs Small Cap Value Insights Fund Inst Cls	GSITX	NAS CM	Open End	US Equity Small Cap (Small Company)	B+	A-	B	Up	Y	1,000,000
Goldman Sachs Small Cap Value Insights Fund Investor Class	GTTTX	NAS CM	Open End	US Equity Small Cap (Small Company)	B+	A-	B	Up	Y	0
Goldman Sachs Small/Mid Cap Growth Fund Class A	GSMAX	NAS CM	Open End	US Equity Mid Cap (Growth)	B	B	B	Up	Y	1,000
Goldman Sachs Small/Mid Cap Growth Fund Class C	GSMGX	NAS CM	Open End	US Equity Mid Cap (Growth)	B	B-	B	Up	Y	1,000
Goldman Sachs Small/Mid Cap Growth Fund Class R	GTMRX	NAS CM	Open End	US Equity Mid Cap (Growth)	B	B	B	Up	Y	0
Goldman Sachs Small/Mid Cap Growth Fund Class R6	GTMUX	NAS CM	Open End	US Equity Mid Cap (Growth)	B	B	B	Up	Y	5,000,000
Goldman Sachs Small/Mid Cap Growth Fund Institutional Cls	GSMYX	NAS CM	Open End	US Equity Mid Cap (Growth)	B	B	B	Up	Y	1,000,000
Goldman Sachs Small/Mid Cap Growth Fund Investor Class	GTMTX	NAS CM	Open End	US Equity Mid Cap (Growth)	B	B	B	Up	Y	0
Goldman Sachs Small/Mid Cap Growth Fund Service Class	GSMQX	NAS CM	Open End	US Equity Mid Cap (Growth)	B	B	B	Up	Y	0
Goldman Sachs Small/Mid Cap Value Fund Class A	GMVAX	NAS CM	Open End	US Equity Mid Cap (Growth)	B-	B-	B	Up	Y	1,000
Goldman Sachs Small/Mid Cap Value Fund Class C	GMVCX	NAS CM	Open End	US Equity Mid Cap (Growth)	B-	B-	B	Up	Y	1,000
Goldman Sachs Small/Mid Cap Value Fund Class R	GMVRX	NAS CM	Open End	US Equity Mid Cap (Growth)	B-	B-	B	Up	Y	0
Goldman Sachs Small/Mid Cap Value Fund Class R6	GMCUX	NAS CM	Open End	US Equity Mid Cap (Growth)	B	B-	B	Up	Y	5,000,000
Goldman Sachs Small/Mid Cap Value Fund Institutional Class	GSMVX	NAS CM	Open End	US Equity Mid Cap (Growth)	B	B-	B	Up	Y	1,000,000
Goldman Sachs Small/Mid Cap Value Fund Investor Class	GMVIX	NAS CM	Open End	US Equity Mid Cap (Growth)	B	B-	B	Up	Y	0
Goldman Sachs Strategic Growth Fund Class A	GGRAX	NAS CM	Open End	US Equity Large Cap Growth (Growth)	B+	B	A-	Up	Y	1,000
Goldman Sachs Strategic Growth Fund Class C	GGRCX	NAS CM	Open End	US Equity Large Cap Growth (Growth)	B+	B	A-	Up	Y	1,000
Goldman Sachs Strategic Growth Fund Class R	GSTRX	NAS CM	Open End	US Equity Large Cap Growth (Growth)	B+	B	A-	Up	Y	0
Goldman Sachs Strategic Growth Fund Class R6	GGRUX	NAS CM	Open End	US Equity Large Cap Growth (Growth)	B+	B	A-	Up	Y	5,000,000
Goldman Sachs Strategic Growth Fund Institutional Class	GSTIX	NAS CM	Open End	US Equity Large Cap Growth (Growth)	B+	B	A-	Up	Y	1,000,000
Goldman Sachs Strategic Growth Fund Investor Class	GSTTX	NAS CM	Open End	US Equity Large Cap Growth (Growth)	B+	B	A-	Up	Y	0
Goldman Sachs Strategic Growth Fund Service Class	GSTSX	NAS CM	Open End	US Equity Large Cap Growth (Growth)	B+	B	A-	Up	Y	0
Goldman Sachs Strategic International Equity Fund Class A	GSAKX	NAS CM	Open End	Global Equity Large Cap (Foreign Stock)	B-	C+	B	Up	Y	1,000
Goldman Sachs Strategic International Equity Fund Class C	GSCKX	NAS CM	Open End	Global Equity Large Cap (Foreign Stock)	B-	C+	B-	Up	Y	1,000
Goldman Sachs Strategic Intl Equity Fund Cls Inst	GSIKX	NAS CM	Open End	Global Equity Large Cap (Foreign Stock)	B-	C+	B	Up	Y	1,000,000
Goldman Sachs Strategic International Equity Fund Class R	GSRKX	NAS CM	Open End	Global Equity Large Cap (Foreign Stock)	B-	C+	B	Up	Y	0
Goldman Sachs Strategic International Equity Fund Class R6	GSUKX	NAS CM	Open End	Global Equity Large Cap (Foreign Stock)	B-	C+	B	Up	Y	5,000,000
Goldman Sachs Strategic Intl Equity Fund Inv Cls	GSTKX	NAS CM	Open End	Global Equity Large Cap (Foreign Stock)	B-	C+	B	Up	Y	0
Goldman Sachs Target Date 2020 Portfolio Class A Shares	GTAHX	NAS CM	Open End	Target Date 2000-2020 (Asset Alloc)	B	C+	A-	Up	Y	1,000
Goldman Sachs Target Date 2020 Portfolio Cls Inst Shares	GTIHX	NAS CM	Open End	Target Date 2000-2020 (Asset Alloc)	B-	C+	B	Up	Y	1,000,000
Goldman Sachs Target Date 2020 Portfolio Class IR Shares	GTMHX	NAS CM	Open End	Target Date 2000-2020 (Asset Alloc)	B-	C+	B	Up	Y	0
Goldman Sachs Target Date 2020 Portfolio Class R Shares	GTRHX	NAS CM	Open End	Target Date 2000-2020 (Asset Alloc)	B	C	A-	Up	Y	0
Goldman Sachs Target Date 2020 Portfolio Class R6 Shares	GTZHX	NAS CM	Open End	Target Date 2000-2020 (Asset Alloc)	B	C+	A-	Up	Y	5,000,000
Goldman Sachs Target Date 2020 Port Cls Serv Shares	GTVHX	NAS CM	Open End	Target Date 2000-2020 (Asset Alloc)	B-	C+	B	Up	Y	0
Goldman Sachs Target Date 2025 Portfolio Class A Shares	GTADX	NAS CM	Open End	Target Date 2021-2045 (Asset Alloc)	D	C-	B+	Up	Y	1,000
Goldman Sachs Target Date 2025 Portfolio Cls Inst Shares	GTIFX	NAS CM	Open End	Target Date 2021-2045 (Asset Alloc)	D	C-	B+	Up	Y	1,000,000
Goldman Sachs Target Date 2025 Portfolio Class IR Shares	GTMFX	NAS CM	Open End	Target Date 2021-2045 (Asset Alloc)	D	C-	B+	Up	Y	0
Goldman Sachs Target Date 2025 Portfolio Class R Shares	GTRDX	NAS CM	Open End	Target Date 2021-2045 (Asset Alloc)	D	C-	B+	Up	Y	0
Goldman Sachs Target Date 2025 Portfolio Class R6 Shares	GTZFX	NAS CM	Open End	Target Date 2021-2045 (Asset Alloc)	D	C-	B+	Up	Y	5,000,000
Goldman Sachs Target Date 2025 Port Cls Serv Shares	GTVFX	NAS CM	Open End	Target Date 2021-2045 (Asset Alloc)	D	C-	B+	Up	Y	0
Goldman Sachs Target Date 2030 Portfolio Class A Shares	GTAJX	NAS CM	Open End	Target Date 2021-2045 (Asset Alloc)	B-	C+	B	Up	Y	1,000
Goldman Sachs Target Date 2030 Portfolio Cls Inst Shares	GTIJX	NAS CM	Open End	Target Date 2021-2045 (Asset Alloc)	B-	C+	B	Up	Y	1,000,000
Goldman Sachs Target Date 2030 Portfolio Class IR Shares	GTMJX	NAS CM	Open End	Target Date 2021-2045 (Asset Alloc)	B-	C+	B	Up	Y	0
Goldman Sachs Target Date 2030 Portfolio Class R Shares	GTRJX	NAS CM	Open End	Target Date 2021-2045 (Asset Alloc)	B-	C+	B	Up	Y	0
Goldman Sachs Target Date 2030 Portfolio Class R6 Shares	GTZJX	NAS CM	Open End	Target Date 2021-2045 (Asset Alloc)	B-	C+	B	Up	Y	5,000,000
Goldman Sachs Target Date 2030 Port Cls Serv Shares	GTVJX	NAS CM	Open End	Target Date 2021-2045 (Asset Alloc)	B-	C+	B	Up	Y	0
Goldman Sachs Target Date 2035 Portfolio Class A Shares	GTALX	NAS CM	Open End	Target Date 2021-2045 (Asset Alloc)	D	C-	B+	Up	Y	1,000
Goldman Sachs Target Date 2035 Portfolio Cls Inst Shares	GTIOX	NAS CM	Open End	Target Date 2021-2045 (Asset Alloc)	D	C-	B+	Up	Y	1,000,000
Goldman Sachs Target Date 2035 Portfolio Class IR Shares	GTMPX	NAS CM	Open End	Target Date 2021-2045 (Asset Alloc)	D	C-	B+	Up	Y	0
Goldman Sachs Target Date 2035 Portfolio Class R Shares	GTROX	NAS CM	Open End	Target Date 2021-2045 (Asset Alloc)	D	C-	B+	Up	Y	0
Goldman Sachs Target Date 2035 Portfolio Class R6 Shares	GTZLX	NAS CM	Open End	Target Date 2021-2045 (Asset Alloc)	D	C-	B+	Up	Y	5,000,000

★ Expanded analysis of this fund is included in Section II.

	TOTAL RETURNS					PERFORMANCE				ASSETS		ASSET ALLOCATION & TURNOVER					BULL & BEAR		FEES		
Min Additional Investment	3-Month Total Return	6-Month Total Return	1-Year Total Return	3-Year Total Return	5-Year Total Return	Dividend Yield (TTM)	Expense Ratio	3-Yr Std Deviation	3-Year Beta	NAV	Total Assets (MIL)	%Cash	%Stocks	%Bonds	%Other	Turnover Ratio	Last Bull Market Total Return	Last Bear Market Total Return	Front End Fee (%)	Back End Fee (%)	Inception Date
	2.68	8.49	7.51	33.49	92.97	0.65	0.83	14.28	1	55.41	190.0	1	99	0	0	129	25.99	-21.77			Jul-15
	2.67	8.49	7.50	33.46	92.93	0.66	0.84	14.28	1	55.42	190.0	1	99	0	0	129	25.99	-21.77			Jun-07
	2.64	8.42	7.35	32.87	91.53	0.8	0.98	14.27	1	42.01	190.0	1	99	0	0	129	25.86	-21.81			Nov-07
50	5.10	10.94	27.73	25.13	92.43	0	1.31	12.83	0.92	20.86	2,352	3	97	0	0	60	30.83	-22.87	5.50		Jun-05
50	4.93	10.57	26.82	22.37	85.31	0	2.06	12.84	0.92	18.04	2,352	3	97	0	0	60	30.26	-23.06		1.00	Jun-05
	5.03	10.83	27.48	24.24	90.01	0	1.56	12.81	0.91	20.15	2,352	3	97	0	0	60	30.61	-22.93			Nov-07
	5.20	11.18	28.25	26.67	96.32	0	0.92	12.84	0.92	22.29	2,352	3	97	0	0	60	31.11	-22.76			Jul-15
	5.20	11.19	28.27	26.63	96.24	0	0.93	12.84	0.92	22.28	2,352	3	97	0	0	60	31.11	-22.76			Jun-05
	5.12	11.07	28.05	26.06	94.81	0	1.06	12.84	0.92	21.61	2,352	3	97	0	0	60	31	-22.73			Nov-07
	5.09	10.90	27.62	24.72	91.43	0	1.43	12.86	0.92	20.34	2,352	3	97	0	0	60	30.75	-22.91			Jun-05
50	6.70	11.18	14.90	26.51		0.54	1.26	11.6	0.94	13.19	123.3	2	98	0	0	108			5.50		Jan-14
50	6.58	10.79	14.07	23.93		0.18	2.01	11.5	0.94	12.99	123.3	2	98	0	0	108				1.00	Jan-14
	6.68	11.08	14.61	25.70		0.24	1.52	11.55	0.94	13.19	123.3	2	98	0	0	108					Jan-14
	6.89	11.43	15.40	28.45		0.8	0.88	11.56	0.94	13.32	123.3	2	98	0	0	108					Jul-15
	6.80	11.42	15.30	28.32		0.8	0.87	11.58	0.94	13.31	123.3	2	98	0	0	108					Jan-14
	6.82	11.37	15.26	27.60		0.6	1.01	11.59	0.94	13.26	123.3	2	98	0	0	108					Jan-14
50	6.94	11.87	30.29	34.88	107.23	0.25	1.15	11.52	1.05	11.82	281.5	1	99	0	0	54	27.24	-15.7	5.50		May-99
50	6.80	11.46	29.31	31.85	99.60	0	1.9	11.53	1.05	9.29	281.5	1	99	0	0	54	26.6	-15.87		1.00	May-99
	6.87	11.80	29.99	33.92	105.00	0.33	1.4	11.51	1.05	11.55	281.5	1	99	0	0	54	27	-15.73			Jan-09
	7.01	12.12	30.72	36.41	111.35	0.54	0.76	11.51	1.05	12.7	281.5	1	99	0	0	54	27.41	-15.5			Jul-15
	7.07	12.18	30.89	36.52	111.53	0.53	0.75	11.51	1.04	12.72	281.5	1	99	0	0	54	27.41	-15.5			May-99
	7.01	12.04	30.52	35.82	109.72	0.43	0.9	11.55	1.05	12.7	281.5	1	99	0	0	54	27.33	-15.71			Jan-09
	6.91	11.79	30.09	34.47	106.19	0.28	1.25	11.52	1.05	11.69	281.5	1	99	0	0	54	27.16	-15.65			May-99
50	3.81	9.06	26.04	22.13	41.28	1.62	1.3	12.11	0.96	14.69	63.2	0	100	0	0	68	14.25	-23.75	5.50		Jun-07
50	3.57	8.64	25.06	19.45	36.00	1.13	2.05	12.1	0.96	13.2	63.2	0	100	0	0	68	13.72	-23.95		1.00	Jun-07
	3.90	9.27	26.53	23.58	44.13	1.89	0.9	12.14	0.96	15.36	63.2	0	100	0	0	68	14.54	-23.64			Jun-07
	3.81	8.94	25.76	21.30	39.55	1.47	1.55	12.12	0.96	14.79	63.2	0	100	0	0	68	14.2	-23.85			Nov-07
	3.93	9.31	26.48	23.56	44.10	1.9	0.88	12.11	0.96	15.35	63.2	0	100	0	0	68	14.54	-23.64			Feb-16
	3.88	9.28	26.42	23.19	43.14	1.86	1.05	12.15	0.96	14.68	63.2	0	100	0	0	68	14.47	-23.62			Nov-07
50	1.81	3.58	7.88	12.71	34.54	1.55	0.91	3.48	0.62	9.31	48.0	6	30	65	0	189	10.84	-8.21	5.50		Aug-16
	2.03	3.90	8.43	13.92	36.66	1.67	0.51	3.47	0.62	9.33	48.0	6	30	65	0	189	11	-8.11			Aug-16
	2.00	3.88	8.30	13.72	36.42	1.63	0.66	3.49	0.62	9.32	48.0	6	30	65	0	189	11	-8.11			Aug-16
	1.85	3.51	7.70	12.07	33.11	1.47	1.16	3.48	0.62	9.32	48.0	6	30	65	0	189	10.68	-8.3			Aug-16
	2.03	3.90	8.44	13.93	36.67	1.68	0.49	3.5	0.62	9.33	48.0	6	30	65	0	189	11	-8.11			Oct-07
	1.87	3.53	7.83	12.73	34.56	1.52	1.01	3.48	0.62	9.32	48.0	6	30	65	0	189	10.84	-8.21			Aug-16
50	2.81	5.27	11.01			0.7	0.91			10.74	11.5	6	46	48	0	167			5.50		Aug-16
	2.89	5.35	11.41			0.73	0.51			10.72	11.5	6	46	48	0	167					Aug-16
	2.88	5.33	11.28			0.68	0.66			10.71	11.5	6	46	48	0	167					Aug-16
	2.75	5.11	10.73			0.52	1.16			10.72	11.5	6	46	48	0	167					Aug-16
	2.92	5.38	11.44			0.73	0.49			10.72	11.5	6	46	48	0	167					Aug-16
	2.80	5.16	10.89			0.57	1.01			10.72	11.5	6	46	48	0	167					Aug-16
50	3.26	6.03	12.89	19.00	51.26	1.68	0.91	5.52	0.82	9.44	77.7	6	55	39	0	143	13.11	-10.52	5.50		Aug-16
	3.51	6.39	13.48	20.35	53.73	1.74	0.51	5.52	0.82	9.47	77.7	6	55	39	0	143	13.28	-10.43			Aug-16
	3.39	6.27	13.24	20.04	53.34	1.7	0.66	5.51	0.82	9.45	77.7	6	55	39	0	143	13.28	-10.43			Aug-16
	3.24	5.92	12.64	18.20	49.50	1.55	1.16	5.52	0.82	9.44	77.7	6	55	39	0	143	12.95	-10.61			Aug-16
	3.41	6.29	13.37	20.25	53.60	1.75	0.49	5.52	0.82	9.46	77.7	6	55	39	0	143	13.28	-10.43			Oct-07
	3.27	6.04	12.89	19.02	51.28	1.59	1.01	5.51	0.82	9.46	77.7	6	55	39	0	143	13.11	-10.52			Aug-16
50	3.64	6.66	13.93			0.63	0.91			11.04	12.2	6	60	34	0	137			5.50		Aug-16
	3.73	6.84	14.34			0.75	0.51			11.04	12.2	6	60	34	0	137					Aug-16
	3.62	6.73	14.12			0.71	0.66			11.02	12.2	6	60	34	0	137					Aug-16
	3.58	6.50	13.66			0.55	1.16			11.04	12.2	6	60	34	0	137					Aug-16
	3.67	6.87	14.38			0.75	0.49			11.04	12.2	6	60	34	0	137					Aug-16

	MARKET			FUND TYPE, CATEGORY & OBJECTIVE	RATINGS				MINIMUMS	
Fund Name	Ticker Symbol	Traded On	Fund Type	Category and (Prospectus Objective)	Overall Rating	Reward Rating	Risk Rating	Recent Up/ Downgrade	Open to New Investors	Min Initial Investment
Goldman Sachs Target Date 2035 Port Cls Serv Shares	GTVOX	NAS CM	Open End	Target Date 2021-2045 (Asset Alloc)	D	C-	B+	Up	Y	0
Goldman Sachs Target Date 2040 Portfolio Class A Shares	GTAMX	NAS CM	Open End	Target Date 2021-2045 (Asset Alloc)	B-	C+	B	Up	Y	1,000
Goldman Sachs Target Date 2040 Portfolio Cls Inst Shares	GTIMX	NAS CM	Open End	Target Date 2021-2045 (Asset Alloc)	B-	C+	B	Up	Y	1,000,000
Goldman Sachs Target Date 2040 Portfolio Class IR Shares	GTMMX	NAS CM	Open End	Target Date 2021-2045 (Asset Alloc)	B-	C+	B	Up	Y	0
Goldman Sachs Target Date 2040 Portfolio Class R Shares	GTRMX	NAS CM	Open End	Target Date 2021-2045 (Asset Alloc)	B-	C+	B	Up	Y	0
Goldman Sachs Target Date 2040 Portfolio Class R6 Shares	GTZMX	NAS CM	Open End	Target Date 2021-2045 (Asset Alloc)	B-	C+	B	Up	Y	5,000,000
Goldman Sachs Target Date 2040 Port Cls Serv Shares	GTVMX	NAS CM	Open End	Target Date 2021-2045 (Asset Alloc)	B-	C+	B	Up	Y	0
Goldman Sachs Target Date 2045 Portfolio Class A Shares	GTAQX	NAS CM	Open End	Target Date 2021-2045 (Asset Alloc)	D	C-	B+	Up	Y	1,000
Goldman Sachs Target Date 2045 Portfolio Cls Inst Shares	GTIQX	NAS CM	Open End	Target Date 2021-2045 (Asset Alloc)	D	C-	B+	Up	Y	1,000,000
Goldman Sachs Target Date 2045 Portfolio Class IR Shares	GTMQX	NAS CM	Open End	Target Date 2021-2045 (Asset Alloc)	D	C-	B+	Up	Y	0
Goldman Sachs Target Date 2045 Portfolio Class R Shares	GTREX	NAS CM	Open End	Target Date 2021-2045 (Asset Alloc)	D	C-	B+	Up	Y	0
Goldman Sachs Target Date 2045 Portfolio Class R6 Shares	GTZQX	NAS CM	Open End	Target Date 2021-2045 (Asset Alloc)	D	C-	B+	Up	Y	5,000,000
Goldman Sachs Target Date 2045 Port Cls Serv Shares	GTVEX	NAS CM	Open End	Target Date 2021-2045 (Asset Alloc)	D	C-	B+	Up	Y	0
Goldman Sachs Target Date 2050 Portfolio Class A Shares	GTASX	NAS CM	Open End	Target Date 2046+ (Asset Alloc)	B-	B-	B	Down	Y	1,000
Goldman Sachs Target Date 2050 Portfolio Cls Inst Shares	GTIPX	NAS CM	Open End	Target Date 2046+ (Asset Alloc)	B-	B-	B	Down	Y	1,000,000
Goldman Sachs Target Date 2050 Portfolio Class IR Shares	GTMAX	NAS CM	Open End	Target Date 2046+ (Asset Alloc)	B-	B-	B	Down	Y	0
Goldman Sachs Target Date 2050 Portfolio Class R Shares	GTRSX	NAS CM	Open End	Target Date 2046+ (Asset Alloc)	B-	B-	B	Down	Y	0
Goldman Sachs Target Date 2050 Portfolio Class R6 Shares	GTZSX	NAS CM	Open End	Target Date 2046+ (Asset Alloc)	B-	B-	B	Down	Y	5,000,000
Goldman Sachs Target Date 2050 Port Cls Serv Shares	GTVSX	NAS CM	Open End	Target Date 2046+ (Asset Alloc)	B-	B-	B	Down	Y	0
Goldman Sachs Target Date 2055 Portfolio Class A Shares	GTANX	NAS CM	Open End	Target Date 2046+ (Asset Alloc)	D	C-	B+	Up	Y	1,000
Goldman Sachs Target Date 2055 Portfolio Cls Inst Shares	GTIWX	NAS CM	Open End	Target Date 2046+ (Asset Alloc)	D	C	B+	Up	Y	1,000,000
Goldman Sachs Target Date 2055 Portfolio Class IR Shares	GTMWX	NAS CM	Open End	Target Date 2046+ (Asset Alloc)	D	C	B+	Up	Y	0
Goldman Sachs Target Date 2055 Portfolio Class R Shares	GTRZX	NAS CM	Open End	Target Date 2046+ (Asset Alloc)	D	C-	B+	Up	Y	0
Goldman Sachs Target Date 2055 Portfolio Class R6 Shares	GTZWX	NAS CM	Open End	Target Date 2046+ (Asset Alloc)	D	C	B+	Up	Y	5,000,000
Goldman Sachs Target Date 2055 Port Cls Serv Shares	GTVIX	NAS CM	Open End	Target Date 2046+ (Asset Alloc)	D	C-	B+	Up	Y	0
Goldman Sachs Tax-Advantaged Global Equity Portfolio Cls A	TAGGX	NAS CM	Open End	Aggressive Alloc (Growth)	B-	B-	B-	Down	Y	1,000
Goldman Sachs Tax-Advantaged Global Eq Port Inst Cls	TIGGX	NAS CM	Open End	Aggressive Alloc (Growth)	B-	B-	B-	Down	Y	1,000,000
Goldman Sachs Technology Opportunities Fund Class A	GITAX	NAS CM	Open End	Technology Sector Equity (Technology)	A-	A	B+	Up	Y	1,000
Goldman Sachs Technology Opportunities Fund Class C	GITCX	NAS CM	Open End	Technology Sector Equity (Technology)	A-	A	B+	Up	Y	1,000
Goldman Sachs Technology Opp Fund Inst Cls	GITIX	NAS CM	Open End	Technology Sector Equity (Technology)	A-	A	B+	Up	Y	1,000,000
Goldman Sachs Technology Opportunities Fund Investor Class	GISTX	NAS CM	Open End	Technology Sector Equity (Technology)	A-	A	B+	Up	Y	0
Goldman Sachs Technology Opportunities Fund Service Class	GITSX	NAS CM	Open End	Technology Sector Equity (Technology)	A-	A	B+	Up	Y	0
Goldman Sachs U.S. Equity Dividend & Premium Fund Cls A	GSPAX	NAS CM	Open End	US Equity Large Cap Blend (Equity-Income)	B	B-	B		Y	1,000
Goldman Sachs U.S. Equity Dividend & Premium Fund Cls C	GSPQX	NAS CM	Open End	US Equity Large Cap Blend (Equity-Income)	B-	B-	B	Down	Y	1,000
Goldman Sachs U.S. Equity Dividend & Premium Fund Inst Cls	GSPKX	NAS CM	Open End	US Equity Large Cap Blend (Equity-Income)	B	B-	B+		Y	1,000,000
Goldman Sachs U.S. Equity Dividend & Premium Fund Inv Cls	GVIRX	NAS CM	Open End	US Equity Large Cap Blend (Equity-Income)	B	B-	B+		Y	0
Goldman Sachs U.S. Equity Insights Fund Class A	GSSQX	NAS CM	Open End	US Equity Large Cap Blend (Growth)	B	B	B-		Y	1,000
Goldman Sachs U.S. Equity Insights Fund Class C	GSUSX	NAS CM	Open End	US Equity Large Cap Blend (Growth)	B	B	B-	Up	Y	1,000
Goldman Sachs U.S. Equity Insights Fund Class R	GSURX	NAS CM	Open End	US Equity Large Cap Blend (Growth)	B	B	B-		Y	0
Goldman Sachs U.S. Equity Insights Fund Class R6	GSEUX	NAS CM	Open End	US Equity Large Cap Blend (Growth)	B	B	B-		Y	5,000,000
Goldman Sachs U.S. Equity Insights Fund Institutional Cls	GSELX	NAS CM	Open End	US Equity Large Cap Blend (Growth)	B	B	B-		Y	1,000,000
Goldman Sachs U.S. Equity Insights Fund Investor Class	GSUTX	NAS CM	Open End	US Equity Large Cap Blend (Growth)	B	B	B-		Y	0
Goldman Sachs U.S. Equity Insights Fund Service Class	GSESX	NAS CM	Open End	US Equity Large Cap Blend (Growth)	B	B	B-		Y	0
Goldman Sachs U.S. Tax-Managed Equity Fund Class A	GCTAX	NAS CM	Open End	US Equity Large Cap Blend (Growth)	B	B	B-	Up	Y	1,000
Goldman Sachs U.S. Tax-Managed Equity Fund Class C	GCTCX	NAS CM	Open End	US Equity Large Cap Blend (Growth)	B-	B-	B-	Down	Y	1,000
Goldman Sachs U.S. Tax-Managed Equity Fund Inst Cls	GCTIX	NAS CM	Open End	US Equity Large Cap Blend (Growth)	B	B	B-		Y	1,000,000
Goldman Sachs U.S. Tax-Managed Equity Fund Investor Class	GQIRX	NAS CM	Open End	US Equity Large Cap Blend (Growth)	B	B	B-		Y	0
Goldman Sachs U.S. Tax-Managed Equity Fund Service Class	GCTSX	NAS CM	Open End	US Equity Large Cap Blend (Growth)	B	B	B-	Up	Y	0
Golub Group Equity Fund	GGEFX	NAS CM	Open End	US Equity Large Cap Blend (Growth)	B	B-	A-	Up	Y	1,000
Good Harbor Tactical Core US Fund Class A Shares	GHUAX	NAS CM	Open End	Moderate Alloc (Growth & Income)	C+	C+	B-	Up	Y	2,500
Good Harbor Tactical Core US Fund Class C Shares	GHUCX	NAS CM	Open End	Moderate Alloc (Growth & Income)	C+	C	C+	Up	Y	2,500
Good Harbor Tactical Core US Fund Class I Shares	GHUIX	NAS CM	Open End	Moderate Alloc (Growth & Income)	C+	C+	B-	Up	Y	5,000,000

★ Expanded analysis of this fund is included in Section II.

	TOTAL RETURNS					PERFORMANCE				ASSETS		ASSET ALLOCATION & TURNOVER					BULL & BEAR		FEES		
Min Additional Investment	3-Month Total Return	6-Month Total Return	1-Year Total Return	3-Year Total Return	5-Year Total Return	Dividend Yield (TTM)	Expense Ratio	3-Yr Std Deviation	3-Year Beta	NAV	Total Assets (MIL)	%Cash	%Stocks	%Bonds	%Other	Turnover Ratio	Last Bull Market Total Return	Last Bear Market Total Return	Front End Fee (%)	Back End Fee (%)	Inception Date
	3.64	6.56	13.82			0.6	1.01			11.04	12.2	6	60	34	0	137					Aug-16
50	3.91	7.16	14.94	22.18	60.19	1.7	0.91	6.5	0.82	9.22	50.6	6	65	29	0	142	14.7	-12.34	5.50		Aug-16
	4.05	7.41	15.44	23.24	62.39	1.8	0.51	6.5	0.82	9.24	50.6	6	65	29	0	142	14.86	-12.25			Aug-16
	3.91	7.16	15.17	23.02	62.10	1.76	0.66	6.5	0.82	9.22	50.6	6	65	29	0	142	14.86	-12.25			Aug-16
	3.82	6.97	14.61	21.21	58.13	1.61	1.16	6.49	0.82	9.21	50.6	6	65	29	0	142	14.53	-12.43			Aug-16
	3.94	7.29	15.43	23.24	62.39	1.8	0.49	6.5	0.82	9.24	50.6	6	65	29	0	142	14.87	-12.25			Oct-07
	3.93	7.08	14.85	22.02	59.98	1.65	1.01	6.48	0.82	9.23	50.6	6	65	29	0	142	14.7	-12.34			Aug-16
50	4.21	7.68	15.95			0.64	0.91			11.24	12.2	6	69	25	0	143			5.50		Aug-16
	4.31	7.88	16.38			0.76	0.51			11.26	12.2	6	69	25	0	143					Aug-16
	4.20	7.67	16.15			0.71	0.66			11.24	12.2	6	69	25	0	143					Aug-16
	4.12	7.49	15.64			0.56	1.16			11.24	12.2	6	69	25	0	143					Aug-16
	4.25	7.82	16.31			0.76	0.49			11.25	12.2	6	69	25	0	143					Aug-16
	4.13	7.60	15.75			0.61	1.01			11.25	12.2	6	69	25	0	143					Aug-16
50	4.38	8.12	16.95	25.06	69.06	1.64	0.91	7.55	0.86	10.33	28.8	5	74	21	0	139	16.55	-14.31	5.50		Aug-16
	4.51	8.35	17.43	26.27	71.58	1.76	0.51	7.56	0.87	10.36	28.8	5	74	21	0	139	16.72	-14.22			Aug-16
	4.50	8.34	17.30	26.07	71.31	1.72	0.66	7.55	0.86	10.35	28.8	5	74	21	0	139	16.72	-14.22			Aug-16
	4.41	8.06	16.66	24.13	66.93	1.57	1.16	7.55	0.86	10.35	28.8	5	74	21	0	139	16.38	-14.4			Aug-16
	4.52	8.36	17.44	26.29	71.60	1.76	0.49	7.56	0.87	10.36	28.8	5	74	21	0	139	16.72	-14.22			Jan-11
	4.36	8.10	16.82	24.88	68.81	1.62	1.01	7.55	0.86	10.35	28.8	5	74	21	0	139	16.55	-14.31			Aug-16
50	4.77	8.69	17.85			0.68	0.91			11.45	12.3	6	79	16	0	182			5.50		Aug-16
	4.86	8.87	18.37			0.78	0.51			11.47	12.3	6	79	16	0	182					Aug-16
	4.84	8.86	18.24			0.73	0.66			11.46	12.3	6	79	16	0	182					Aug-16
	4.76	8.60	17.64			0.58	1.16			11.43	12.3	6	79	16	0	182					Aug-16
	4.79	8.90	18.30			0.78	0.49			11.46	12.3	6	79	16	0	182					Aug-16
	4.67	8.59	17.74			0.63	1.01			11.46	12.3	6	79	16	0	182					Aug-16
50	4.51	9.50	18.61	25.60	72.47	0.56	1.36	9.64		15.68	2,400	0	89	0	11	8	20.27	-18.45	5.50		Apr-08
	4.62	9.71	19.14	27.17	75.99	0.95	0.96	9.65		15.59	2,400	0	89	0	11	8	20.64	-18.36			Apr-08
50	6.52	14.47	38.02	56.33	127.58	0	1.39	14.87	1	22.8	473.5	0	100	0	0	19	31.43	-23.64	5.50		Oct-99
50	6.34	14.08	36.98	52.83	119.24	0	2.14	14.83	1	18.93	473.5	0	100	0	0	19	30.8	-23.91		1.00	Oct-99
	6.61	14.72	38.53	58.15	132.17	0	0.99	14.85	1	25.08	473.5	0	100	0	0	19	31.64	-23.46			Oct-99
	6.57	14.64	38.35	57.39	130.43	0	1.14	14.86	1	24.74	473.5	0	100	0	0	19	31.52	-23.54			Sep-10
	6.51	14.44	37.87	55.84	126.39	0	1.49	14.89	1	22.36	473.5	0	100	0	0	19	31.32	-23.62			Oct-99
50	4.61	8.51	14.82	31.27	84.38	1.39	1.15	8.65	0.85	13.15	3,487	0	100	0	0	23	21.66	-13.02	5.50		Aug-05
50	4.42	8.13	13.98	28.33	77.77	0.78	1.9	8.67	0.85	13.1	3,487	0	100	0	0	23	21.16	-13.36		1.00	Aug-05
	4.72	8.74	15.30	32.76	88.30	1.73	0.76	8.68	0.85	13.12	3,487	0	100	0	0	23	21.91	-12.86			Aug-05
	4.68	8.67	15.17	32.24	86.76	1.64	0.9	8.7	0.85	13.13	3,487	0	100	0	0	23	21.83	-13			Aug-10
50	5.78	12.12	23.44	33.72	115.64	0.58	0.95	10.57	1.03	46.64	689.6	3	97	0	0	213	23.35	-15.33	5.50		May-91
50	5.60	11.73	22.53	30.75	107.74	0.03	1.7	10.57	1.03	42.1	689.6	3	97	0	0	213	22.83	-15.61		1.00	Aug-97
	5.73	11.98	23.12	32.69	112.92	0.44	1.2	10.58	1.03	45.78	689.6	3	97	0	0	213	23.14	-15.42			Nov-07
	5.90	12.36	23.94	34.96	117.19	0.9	0.55	10.58	1.03	48	689.6	3	97	0	0	213	23.27	-15.37			Jul-15
	5.90	12.35	23.93	35.31	119.99	0.87	0.56	10.57	1.03	48.03	689.6	3	97	0	0	213	23.65	-15.24			Jun-95
	5.86	12.27	23.75	34.73	118.36	0.86	0.7	10.58	1.03	46.01	689.6	3	97	0	0	213	23.56	-15.27			Nov-07
	5.75	12.07	23.30	33.29	114.51	0.59	1.06	10.57	1.03	46.38	689.6	3	97	0	0	213	23.27	-15.37			May-91
50	5.87	10.94	19.87	29.10	107.89	0.48	1.17	10.79	1.04	22.37	1,456	1	99	0	0	118	24.65	-16.69	5.50		Apr-00
50	5.67	10.50	18.92	26.23	100.27	0	1.92	10.79	1.04	21.24	1,456	1	99	0	0	118	24.03	-16.95		1.00	Apr-00
	5.98	11.13	20.29	30.69	112.08	0.8	0.77	10.82	1.04	22.71	1,456	1	99	0	0	118	24.85	-16.49			Apr-00
	5.94	11.09	20.14	30.10	110.53	0.72	0.92	10.82	1.04	22.7	1,456	1	99	0	0	118	24.63	-16.49			Aug-10
	5.85	10.89	19.70	28.73	106.84	0.12	1.27	10.8	1.04	22.51	1,456	1	99	0	0	118	24.48	-16.74			Apr-00
	2.52	3.70	12.52	25.21	84.45	0.22	1.26	11.42	1.07	18.22	59.5	15	85	0	0	27	23.87	-13.47			Apr-09
250	3.44	2.93	6.16	10.74	6.56	0	1.53	6.89	0.42	10.51	72.6	30	70	0	0	566			5.75		Dec-12
250	3.36	2.63	5.41	8.22	2.65	0	2.28	6.86	0.42	10.13	72.6	30	70	0	0	566				1.00	Jan-13
10,000	3.50	3.10	6.40	11.52	7.87	0	1.28	6.94	0.42	10.64	72.6	30	70	0	0	566					Dec-12

Fund Name	Ticker Symbol	Traded On	Fund Type	Category and (Prospectus Objective)	Overall Rating	Reward Rating	Risk Rating	Recent Up/ Downgrade	Open to New Investors	Min Initial Investment
	MARKET		FUND TYPE, CATEGORY & OBJECTIVE		RATINGS				MINIMUMS	
Good Harbor Tactical Select Fund Class A	GHSAX	NAS CM	Open End	Moderate Alloc (Growth & Income)	C+	C+	C+		Y	2,500
Good Harbor Tactical Select Fund Class C	GHSCX	NAS CM	Open End	Moderate Alloc (Growth & Income)	C+	C+	C+		Y	2,500
Good Harbor Tactical Select Fund Class I	GHSIX	NAS CM	Open End	Moderate Alloc (Growth & Income)	C+	C+	C+	Down	Y	5,000,000
GoodHaven Fund	GOODX	NAS CM	Open End	US Equity Mid Cap (Growth)	C	C	C	Up	Y	10,000
Goodwood SMID Long/Short Fund Advisor Class	GAMAX	NAS CM	Open End	Long/Short Equity (Growth)	D	D	D	Down	Y	2,500
Goodwood SMID Long/Short Fund Institutional Class	GAMIX	NAS CM	Open End	Long/Short Equity (Growth)	D	D	D	Down	Y	100,000
Gotham Absolute 500 Core Fund Institutional Class	GACFX	NAS CM	Open End	Long/Short Equity (Growth)	D	C-	B+		Y	250,000
Gotham Absolute 500 Fund Institutional Class	GFIVX	NAS CM	Open End	Long/Short Equity (Growth)	B-	C+	B		Y	250,000
Gotham Absolute Return Fund Institutional Class Shares	GARIX	NAS CM	Open End	Long/Short Equity (Growth)	C+	C	B-		Y	250,000
Gotham Defensive Long 500 Fund Institutional Class	GDLFX	NAS CM	Open End	Long/Short Equity (Growth)	D	C	B		Y	250,000
Gotham Defensive Long Fund Institutional Class	GDLIX	NAS CM	Open End	Long/Short Equity (Growth)	D	C-	B		Y	250,000
Gotham Enhanced 500 Core Fund Institutional Class	GECFX	NAS CM	Open End	US Equity Large Cap Blend (Growth)	D	C	B		Y	250,000
Gotham Enhanced 500 Fund Institutional Class	GENFX	NAS CM	Open End	US Equity Large Cap Blend (Growth)	B-	C+	B-	Up	Y	250,000
Gotham Enhanced Return Fund Institutional Class Shares	GENIX	NAS CM	Open End	US Equity Mid Cap (Growth)	C+	C+	C+		Y	250,000
Gotham Enhanced S&P 500 Index Fund Institutional Class	GSPFX	NAS CM	Open End	US Equity Large Cap Blend (Growth)	D-	D+	A		Y	250,000
Gotham Hedged Core Fund Institutional Class	GCHDX	NAS CM	Open End	Long/Short Equity (Growth)	D	C-	B+		Y	250,000
Gotham Hedged Plus Fund Institutional Class	GHPLX	NAS CM	Open End	Long/Short Equity (Growth & Income)	D+	C-	B+	Up	Y	250,000
Gotham Index Core Fund Institutional Class	GCIDX	NAS CM	Open End	US Equity Large Cap Blend (Growth)	D	C	B		Y	250,000
Gotham Index Plus Fund Institutional Class	GINDX	NAS CM	Open End	US Equity Large Cap Blend (Growth)	B-	C+	B	Up	Y	250,000
Gotham Institutional Value Fund Institutional Class	GINVX	NAS CM	Open End	US Equity Large Cap Value (Growth)	C-	C	B+	Up	Y	5,000,000
Gotham Master Long Fund Institutional Class Shares	GMLFX	NAS CM	Open End	Long/Short Equity (Growth)	U	U	U		Y	250,000
Gotham Master Neutral Fund Institutional Class Shares	GMNFX	NAS CM	Open End	Market Neutral (Growth)	U	U	U		Y	250,000
Gotham Neutral 500 Fund Institutional Class	GONFX	NAS CM	Open End	Market Neutral (Growth)	D	D+	B		Y	250,000
Gotham Neutral Fund Institutional Class	GONIX	NAS CM	Open End	Market Neutral (Growth)	C	C-	C+	Up	Y	250,000
Gotham Short Strategies Fund Institutional Shares	GSSFX	NAS CM	Open End	Long/Short Equity (Growth & Income)	U	U	U		Y	250,000
Gotham Total Return Fund Institutional Class	GTRFX	NAS CM	Open End	Long/Short Equity (Growth)	B-	C+	B	Up	Y	250,000
Government Street Equity Fund	GVEQX	NAS CM	Open End	US Equity Large Cap Growth (Growth)	B-	B-	B	Down	Y	5,000
Government Street Mid-Cap Fund	GVMCX	NAS CM	Open End	US Equity Mid Cap (Growth)	B	B	B		Y	5,000
GQG Partners Emerging Mkts Equity Fund Inst Shares	GQGIX	NAS CM	Open End	Emerging Markets Equity (Div Emerging Mkts)	D-	D+	B+		Y	500,000
GQG Partners Emerging Markets Equity Fund Investor Shares	GQGPX	NAS CM	Open End	Emerging Markets Equity (Div Emerging Mkts)	D-	D+	B+		Y	2,500
GQG Partners Emerging Markets Equity Fund R6 Shares	GQGRX	NAS CM	Open End	Emerging Markets Equity (Div Emerging Mkts)	D-	D+	B+		Y	0
Grandeur Peak Emerging Mkts Opp Fund Inst Cls	GPEIX	NAS CM	Open End	Emerging Markets Equity (Div Emerging Mkts)	B-	B-	B-	Up		2,000
Grandeur Peak Emerging Mkts Opp Fund Inv Cls	GPEOX	NAS CM	Open End	Emerging Markets Equity (Div Emerging Mkts)	B-	B-	B-	Up		2,000
Grandeur Peak Global Micro Cap Fund Institutional Class	GPMCX	NAS CM	Open End	Global Equity Mid/Small Cap (Growth)	C	C	B+	Up		2,000
Grandeur Peak Global Opportunities Fund Institutional Cls	GPGIX	NAS CM	Open End	Global Equity Mid/Small Cap (World Stock)	B+	B+	B	Up		2,000
Grandeur Peak Global Opportunities Fund Investor Class	GPGOX	NAS CM	Open End	Global Equity Mid/Small Cap (World Stock)	B+	B+	B	Up		2,000
Grandeur Peak Global Reach Fund Institutional Class	GPRIX	NAS CM	Open End	Global Equity Mid/Small Cap (World Stock)	B	B	B	Up		2,000
Grandeur Peak Global Reach Fund Investor Class	GPROX	NAS CM	Open End	Global Equity Mid/Small Cap (World Stock)	B	B	B	Up		2,000
Grandeur Peak Global Stalwarts Fund Institutional Class	GGSYX	NAS CM	Open End	Global Equity Mid/Small Cap (World Stock)	C	C+	B+	Up	Y	2,000
Grandeur Peak Global Stalwarts Fund Investor Class	GGSOX	NAS CM	Open End	Global Equity Mid/Small Cap (World Stock)	C	C+	B+	Up	Y	2,000
Grandeur Peak Intl Opp Fund Inst Cls	GPIIX	NAS CM	Open End	Global Equity Mid/Small Cap (Foreign Stock)	B+	A-	B	Up		2,000
Grandeur Peak Intl Opp Fund Inv Cls	GPIOX	NAS CM	Open End	Global Equity Mid/Small Cap (Foreign Stock)	B+	A-	B	Up		2,000
Grandeur Peak Intl Stalwarts Fund Inst Cls	GISYX	NAS CM	Open End	Global Equity Large Cap (Foreign Stock)	C	C+	B+	Up	Y	2,000
Grandeur Peak International Stalwarts Fund Investor Class	GISOX	NAS CM	Open End	Global Equity Large Cap (Foreign Stock)	C	C+	B+	Up	Y	2,000
Grant Park Absolute Return Fund Class A	GPHAX	NAS CM	Open End	Market Neutral (Growth & Income)	B-	C+	B	Up	Y	2,500
Grant Park Absolute Return Fund Class C	GPHCX	NAS CM	Open End	Market Neutral (Growth & Income)	B-	C+	B	Up	Y	2,500
Grant Park Absolute Return Fund Class I	GPHIX	NAS CM	Open End	Market Neutral (Growth & Income)	B-	C+	B	Up	Y	25,000
Grant Park Absolute Return Fund Class N	GPHNX	NAS CM	Open End	Market Neutral (Growth & Income)	B-	C+	B	Up	Y	2,500
Grant Park Multi Alternative Strategies Fund Class A	GPAAX	NAS CM	Open End	Multialternative (Growth)	C+	C	B	Up	Y	2,500
Grant Park Multi Alternative Strategies Fund Class C	GPACX	NAS CM	Open End	Multialternative (Growth)	C+	C	B	Up	Y	2,500
Grant Park Multi Alternative Strategies Fund Class I	GPAIX	NAS CM	Open End	Multialternative (Growth)	C+	C	B	Up	Y	100,000
Grant Park Multi Alternative Strategies Fund Class N	GPANX	NAS CM	Open End	Multialternative (Growth)	C+	C	B	Up	Y	2,500

★ Expanded analysis of this fund is included in Section II.

Min Additional Investment	TOTAL RETURNS 3-Month Total Return	6-Month Total Return	1-Year Total Return	3-Year Total Return	5-Year Total Return	PERFORMANCE Dividend Yield (TTM)	Expense Ratio	3-Yr Std Deviation	3-Year Beta	ASSETS NAV	Total Assets (MIL)	ASSET ALLOCATION & TURNOVER %Cash	%Stocks	%Bonds	%Other	Turnover Ratio	BULL & BEAR Last Bull Market Total Return	Last Bear Market Total Return	FEES Front End Fee (%)	Back End Fee (%)	Inception Date
250	3.81	6.77	14.99	17.33		0	1.79	5.2	0.13	11.02	8.7	-2	102	0	0	310			5.75		Aug-15
250	3.67	6.46	14.15	15.19		0	2.54	5.19	0.13	10.89	8.7	-2	102	0	0	310				1.00	Aug-15
10,000	3.93	6.98	15.29	18.31		0	1.54	5.23	0.13	11.02	8.7	-2	102	0	0	310					May-14
1,000	3.95	8.28	3.95	1.80	12.27	0	1.1	12.4	0.69	24.19	208.4	0	97	1	2	8	17.74	-6.06			Apr-11
100	4.03	1.47	-6.03	-16.58	-31.53	0	1.95	20.22	1.01	8.25	21.5	35	65	0	0	439	16.44	-15.82	4.50		Jan-10
100	4.02	1.52	-5.87	-15.54	-29.63	0	1.7	20.18	1.01	8.01	21.5	35	65	0	0	439	16.44	-15.82			Jul-14
5,000	6.75	11.32	15.19			0	1.15			11.8	2.3	39	61	0	0	245					Sep-16
5,000	8.32	14.38	16.52	21.11		0	1.5	11.18	1.5	12.21	12.2	40	60	0	0	204					Jul-14
5,000	4.87	7.89	10.00	5.61	52.87	0	2.15	7.04	1.03	14.62	966.7	40	60	0	0	238					Aug-12
5,000	9.65	16.94	22.64			0	1.5			12.76	8.5	1	99	0	0	259					Sep-16
5,000	7.57	10.21	12.22			0	2.15			11.45	2.3	0	100	0	0	263					Sep-16
5,000	9.58	16.14	23.89			0	1.15			12.79	2.6	1	99	0	0	237					Sep-16
5,000	11.40	19.85	25.73	37.22		0.25	1.5			12.8	27.0	1	99	0	0	193					Dec-14
5,000	8.88	13.87	18.21	17.24		0	2.15	11.4	1.01	14.75	922.6	1	99	0	0	196					May-13
5,000	8.42	15.75	25.01				0.5			12.08	3.1	0	100	0	0	268					Dec-16
5,000	6.48	11.08	15.55			0	0.85			11.89	2.4	39	61	0	0	249					Sep-16
5,000	9.18	15.55	16.85			0.9	1.16			12.22	2.5	40	60	0	0	183					Mar-16
5,000	9.79	17.03	25.06			0	0.85			13.06	2.6	0	100	0	0	232					Sep-16
5,000	11.88	20.71	26.05			0.4	1.15			14.48	227.9	2	98	0	0	204					Mar-15
10,000	8.15	13.62	22.17			1.98	0.95			11.84	2.8	-1	101	0	0	169					Dec-15
5,000	9.71	17.00					1.2			11.47	1.2	1	99	0	0						Apr-17
5,000	2.38	4.88					1.36			10.17	4.1	69	23	8	0						Apr-17
5,000	5.35	9.73	8.68			0	1.5			11.29	3.7	77	23	0	0	202					Sep-16
5,000	2.54	3.45	0.67	-4.54		0	2.15	4.63	-0.37	10.49	498.1	75	25	0	0	261					Aug-13
5,000	-2.43	-2.14					1.35			9.8	13.9	4	96	0	0	165					Jul-17
5,000	8.98	15.45	18.93			0.04	1.51			12.6	19.9	20	80	0	0	27					Mar-15
	6.01	11.63	22.69	28.73	86.05	0.87	0.87	10.1	0.98	75.28	64.8	2	98	0	0	20	23.42	-16.33			Jun-91
	4.54	8.66	19.53	36.20	97.17	0.53	1.1	9.13	0.77	26.34	50.6	6	94	0	0	14	22.13	-18.81			Nov-03
	5.41	15.69	32.00				1.08			13.26	446.1	4	94	0	2	45					Dec-16
100	5.34	15.54	31.60				1.33			13.23	446.1	4	94	0	2	45					Dec-16
	5.41	15.69	32.00				1.08			13.26	446.1	4	94	0	2	45					Dec-16
	8.41	10.87	28.33	30.49		0.45	1.55	12.37	0.85	13.19	449.2	0	98	0	2	42					Dec-13
	8.33	10.80	27.97	29.55		0.32	1.8	12.42	0.85	13.13	449.2	0	98	0	2	42					Dec-13
	7.12	13.66	31.48			0.17	2			13.35	41.4	1	98	0	1	37					Oct-15
	7.70	14.06	32.95	43.98	110.02	0.11	1.37	10.29	0.89	4.03	797.8	2	97	0	1	30					Oct-11
	7.68	13.81	32.48	42.65	107.13	0	1.62	10.42	0.9	3.98	797.8	2	97	0	1	30					Oct-11
	7.33	13.24	30.77	40.74		0.23	1.29	10.64	0.92	16.82	358.5	2	97	0	1	42					Jun-13
	7.28	13.21	30.50	39.63		0.11	1.54	10.63	0.91	16.78	358.5	2	97	0	1	42					Jun-13
	6.38	13.89	31.58			0.17	1.1			14.78	155.9	3	95	0	2	32					Sep-15
	6.26	13.71	31.19			0.07	1.35			14.71	155.9	3	95	0	2	32					Sep-15
	7.84	14.74	38.81	47.04	102.40	0.51	1.37	11.23	0.94	4.16	893.4	4	95	0	1	30					Oct-11
	7.72	14.65	38.39	46.11	100.65	0.39	1.62	11.3	0.94	4.14	893.4	4	95	0	1	30					Oct-11
	6.18	14.95	36.85			0.35	1.02			15.25	454.5	5	94	0	2	37					Sep-15
	6.19	14.82	36.48			0.22	1.27			15.23	454.5	5	94	0	2	37					Sep-15
100	6.41	6.41	16.26			0	2.09			11.08	29.7	29	0	69	0	0			5.75		Apr-15
100	6.37	6.17	15.40			0	2.84			10.83	29.7	29	0	69	0	0					Apr-15
1,000	6.58	6.58	16.51			0	1.84			11.14	29.7	29	0	69	0	0					Apr-15
100	6.52	6.52	16.29			0	2.09			11.07	29.7	29	0	69	0	0					Apr-15
100	7.90	9.12	12.10	9.05		1.56	2.05	8.44	5.54	11.32	290.5	26	20	51	2	51			5.75		Dec-13
100	7.64	8.68	11.24	6.62		1.12	2.8	8.42	5.5	11.11	290.5	26	20	51	2	51					Dec-13
1,000	7.94	9.27	12.34	9.90		1.74	1.8	8.46	5.57	11.39	290.5	26	20	51	2	51					Dec-13
100	7.88	9.11	12.07	9.08		1.56	2.06	8.41	5.53	11.34	290.5	26	20	51	2	51					Dec-13

	MARKET			FUND TYPE, CATEGORY & OBJECTIVE	RATINGS				MINIMUMS	
Fund Name	Ticker Symbol	Traded On	Fund Type	Category and (Prospectus Objective)	Overall Rating	Reward Rating	Risk Rating	Recent Up/ Downgrade	Open to New Investors	Min Initial Investment
Great Lakes Disciplined Equity Fund Institutional Class	GLDNX	NAS CM	Open End	US Equity Large Cap Blend (Growth & Income)	B	B	B		Y	1,000
Great Lakes Disciplined Intl Smaller Company Fund Inst Cls	GLISX	NAS CM	Open End	Global Equity Mid/Small Cap (Small Company)	C-	C	B+	Up	Y	100,000
Great Lakes Large Cap Value Fund Institutional Cls Shares	GLLIX	NAS CM	Open End	US Equity Large Cap Value (Growth & Income)	B	B	B-		Y	1,000
Great Lakes Small Cap Opportunity Fund Institutional Class	GLSIX	NAS CM	Open End	US Equity Small Cap (Small Company)	C+	B-	C+		Y	100,000
Great Lakes Small Cap Opportunity Fund Investor Class	GLSCX	NAS CM	Open End	US Equity Small Cap (Small Company)	C+	C+	C+		Y	1,000
Great-West Aggressive Profile Fund Class L	MXEPX	NAS CM	Open End	Aggressive Alloc (Aggr Growth)	B-	B-	B-	Down	Y	0
Great-West Aggressive Profile Fund Institutional Class	MXGTX	NAS CM	Open End	Aggressive Alloc (Aggr Growth)	B-	B-	B-	Down	Y	0
Great-West Aggressive Profile Fund Investor Class	MXAPX	NAS CM	Open End	Aggressive Alloc (Aggr Growth)	B-	B-	B-	Down	Y	0
Great-West Ariel Mid Cap Value Fund Class L	MXAMX	NAS CM	Open End	US Equity Mid Cap (Growth)	B-	C+	B		Y	0
Great-West Ariel Mid Cap Value Fund Institutional Class	MXOAX	NAS CM	Open End	US Equity Mid Cap (Growth)	B-	B-	B		Y	0
Great-West Ariel Mid Cap Value Fund Investor Class	MXMCX	NAS CM	Open End	US Equity Mid Cap (Growth)	B-	B-	B		Y	0
Great-West Conservative Profile Fund Class L	MXIPX	NAS CM	Open End	Cautious Alloc (Growth)	B-	C	B	Up	Y	0
Great-West Conservative Profile Fund Institutional Class	MXKVX	NAS CM	Open End	Cautious Alloc (Growth)	B-	C+	B	Up	Y	0
Great-West Conservative Profile Fund Investor Class	MXCPX	NAS CM	Open End	Cautious Alloc (Growth)	B-	C+	B	Up	Y	0
Great-West Goldman Sachs Mid Cap Value Fund Inst Cls	MXKJX	NAS CM	Open End	US Equity Mid Cap (Growth)	B	B	B		Y	0
Great-West Goldman Sachs Mid Cap Value Fund Investor Class	MXMVX	NAS CM	Open End	US Equity Mid Cap (Growth)	B	B	B		Y	0
Great-West International Index Fund Institutional Class	MXPBX	NAS CM	Open End	Global Equity Large Cap (Growth)	B-	C+	B	Up	Y	0
Great-West International Index Fund Investor Class	MXINX	NAS CM	Open End	Global Equity Large Cap (Growth)	B-	C+	B	Up	Y	0
Great-West Invesco Small Cap Value Fund Institutional Cls	MXMYX	NAS CM	Open End	US Equity Small Cap (Small Company)	B	B	B	Up	Y	0
Great-West Invesco Small Cap Value Fund Investor Class	MXSVX	NAS CM	Open End	US Equity Small Cap (Small Company)	B	B	B-	Up	Y	0
Great-West Lifetime 2015 Fund Class L	MXABX	NAS CM	Open End	Target Date 2000-2020 (Asset Alloc)	B-	C+	B	Up	Y	0
Great-West Lifetime 2020 Fund Class L	MXAJX	NAS CM	Open End	Target Date 2000-2020 (Asset Alloc)	D+	C-	A	Up	Y	0
Great-West Lifetime 2020 Fund Institutional Class	MXAKX	NAS CM	Open End	Target Date 2000-2020 (Asset Alloc)	D+	C-	A	Up	Y	0
Great-West Lifetime 2020 Fund Investor Class	MXAGX	NAS CM	Open End	Target Date 2000-2020 (Asset Alloc)	D+	C-	A	Up	Y	0
Great-West Lifetime 2020 Fund Service Class	MXAHX	NAS CM	Open End	Target Date 2000-2020 (Asset Alloc)	D+	C-	A	Up	Y	0
Great-West Lifetime 2025 Fund Class L	MXANX	NAS CM	Open End	Target Date 2021-2045 (Asset Alloc)	B-	C+	B	Down	Y	0
Great-West Lifetime 2030 Fund Class L	MXAWX	NAS CM	Open End	Target Date 2021-2045 (Asset Alloc)	D+	C-	A-	Up	Y	0
Great-West Lifetime 2030 Fund Institutional Class	MXAYX	NAS CM	Open End	Target Date 2021-2045 (Asset Alloc)	D+	C-	A-	Up	Y	0
Great-West Lifetime 2030 Fund Investor Class	MXATX	NAS CM	Open End	Target Date 2021-2045 (Asset Alloc)	D+	C-	A-	Up	Y	0
Great-West Lifetime 2030 Fund Service Class	MXAUX	NAS CM	Open End	Target Date 2021-2045 (Asset Alloc)	D+	C-	A-	Up	Y	0
Great-West Lifetime 2035 Fund Class L	MXAZX	NAS CM	Open End	Target Date 2021-2045 (Asset Alloc)	B-	B-	B-	Down	Y	0
Great-West Lifetime 2040 Fund Class L	MXBFX	NAS CM	Open End	Target Date 2021-2045 (Asset Alloc)	D+	C	B+	Up	Y	0
Great-West Lifetime 2040 Fund Institutional Class	MXBGX	NAS CM	Open End	Target Date 2021-2045 (Asset Alloc)	D+	C	B+	Up	Y	0
Great-West Lifetime 2040 Fund Investor Class	MXBDX	NAS CM	Open End	Target Date 2021-2045 (Asset Alloc)	D+	C	B+	Up	Y	0
Great-West Lifetime 2040 Fund Service Class	MXBEX	NAS CM	Open End	Target Date 2021-2045 (Asset Alloc)	D+	C	B+	Up	Y	0
Great-West Lifetime 2045 Fund Class L	MXBHX	NAS CM	Open End	Target Date 2021-2045 (Asset Alloc)	B-	B-	B-	Down	Y	0
Great-West Lifetime 2050 Fund Class L	MXBRX	NAS CM	Open End	Target Date 2046+ (Asset Alloc)	D+	C	B+	Up	Y	0
Great-West Lifetime 2050 Fund Institutional Class	MXBSX	NAS CM	Open End	Target Date 2046+ (Asset Alloc)	D+	C	B+	Up	Y	0
Great-West Lifetime 2050 Fund Investor Class	MXBOX	NAS CM	Open End	Target Date 2046+ (Asset Alloc)	D+	C	B+	Up	Y	0
Great-West Lifetime 2050 Fund Service Class	MXBQX	NAS CM	Open End	Target Date 2046+ (Asset Alloc)	D+	C	B+	Up	Y	0
Great-West Lifetime 2055 Fund Class L	MXBTX	NAS CM	Open End	Target Date 2046+ (Asset Alloc)	B-	B-	B-	Down	Y	0
Great-West Lifetime Conservative 2015 Fund Inst Cls	MXMAX	NAS CM	Open End	Target Date 2000-2020 (Asset Alloc)	B-	C+	B	Up	Y	0
Great-West Lifetime Conservative 2015 Fund Investor Class	MXLTX	NAS CM	Open End	Target Date 2000-2020 (Asset Alloc)	B-	C+	B	Up	Y	0
Great-West Lifetime Conservative 2015 Fund Service Class	MXLUX	NAS CM	Open End	Target Date 2000-2020 (Asset Alloc)	B-	C+	B	Up	Y	0
Great-West Lifetime Conservative 2020 Fund Inst Cls	MXAFX	NAS CM	Open End	Target Date 2000-2020 (Asset Alloc)	D+	C-	A	Up	Y	0
Great-West Lifetime Conservative 2020 Fund Investor Class	MXACX	NAS CM	Open End	Target Date 2000-2020 (Asset Alloc)	D+	C-	A	Up	Y	0
Great-West Lifetime Conservative 2020 Fund Service Class	MXAEX	NAS CM	Open End	Target Date 2000-2020 (Asset Alloc)	D+	C-	A	Up	Y	0
Great-West Lifetime Conservative 2025 Fund Inst Cls	MXOZX	NAS CM	Open End	Target Date 2021-2045 (Asset Alloc)	B-	C+	B	Up	Y	0
Great-West Lifetime Conservative 2025 Fund Investor Class	MXALX	NAS CM	Open End	Target Date 2021-2045 (Asset Alloc)	B-	C+	B	Up	Y	0
Great-West Lifetime Conservative 2025 Fund Service Class	MXBLX	NAS CM	Open End	Target Date 2021-2045 (Asset Alloc)	B-	C+	B	Up	Y	0
Great-West Lifetime Conservative 2030 Fund Inst Cls	MXARX	NAS CM	Open End	Target Date 2021-2045 (Asset Alloc)	D+	C-	A	Up	Y	0
Great-West Lifetime Conservative 2030 Fund Investor Class	MXAOX	NAS CM	Open End	Target Date 2021-2045 (Asset Alloc)	D+	C-	A	Up	Y	0

★ Expanded analysis of this fund is included in Section II.

Min Additional Investment	3-Month Total Return	6-Month Total Return	1-Year Total Return	3-Year Total Return	5-Year Total Return	Dividend Yield (TTM)	Expense Ratio	3-Yr Std Deviation	3-Year Beta	NAV	Total Assets (MIL)	%Cash	%Stocks	%Bonds	%Other	Turnover Ratio	Last Bull Market Total Return	Last Bear Market Total Return	Front End Fee (%)	Back End Fee (%)	Inception Date
	TOTAL RETURNS					PERFORMANCE				ASSETS		ASSET ALLOCATION & TURNOVER					BULL & BEAR		FEES		
100	7.94	11.33	18.56	32.82	107.70	1.11	0.85	10.15	0.97	15.48	48.0	1	99	0	0	114	24.88	-15.07			Jun-09
100	4.25	8.34	24.51			0.47	1.46			12.41	29.3	5	92	0	0	107					Dec-15
100	5.10	10.56	18.30	33.87	101.79	1.3	0.86	10.58	1	15.11	54.0	4	96	0	0	48					Sep-12
100	7.41	8.14	9.51	20.65	82.71	0.53	0.86	14.34	0.91	17.69	78.6	8	92	0	0	106	32.89	-25.15			Dec-08
200	7.42	8.04	9.30	19.75	80.55	0.32	1.11	14.32	0.91	17.42	78.6	8	92	0	0	106	32.63	-25.24			Dec-08
	5.81	10.23	20.68	30.86	87.35	0.53	1.42	9.57	0.92		803.2	1	97	0	1	30	22.53	-20.54			Jul-11
	5.88	10.46	21.30	33.02	91.46	0.83	0.82	9.58	0.92		803.2	1	97	0	1	30	22.87	-20.6			May-15
	5.83	10.39	20.93	31.82	89.73	0.86	1.17	9.55	0.92		803.2	1	97	0	1	30	22.87	-20.6			Sep-99
	6.77	7.29	14.76	20.11	96.31	0	1.3	13.92	1.23		170.8	1	99	0	0	20	27.14	-25.26			Dec-13
	6.95	7.53	15.43	22.57	100.69	0	0.7	13.93	1.23		170.8	1	99	0	0	20	27.33	-25.18			May-15
	6.35	6.95	15.00	20.59	97.45	1.32	1.05	13.73	1.2		170.8	1	99	0	0	20	27.33	-25.18			Jan-94
	1.61	3.15	7.16	11.79	26.90	1.26	1.05	3.75	0.15		719.4	28	30	38	3	21	9.23	-6.55			Jul-11
	1.70	3.46	7.73	13.72	29.86	1.59	0.45	3.81	0.15		719.4	28	30	38	3	21	9.36	-6.52			May-15
	1.76	3.30	7.52	12.62	28.61	1.61	0.8	3.83	0.15		719.4	28	30	38	3	21	9.36	-6.52			Sep-99
	7.89	12.03	17.80	35.25	116.60	4.3	0.8	10.91	1.02		628.1	0	100	0	0	219	25.02	-20.47			May-15
	7.74	11.71	17.33	33.79	114.25	2.95	1.15	10.88	1.02		628.1	0	100	0	0	219	25.02	-20.47			May-08
	3.74	9.07	25.50	23.29	43.74	2.11	0.32	11.46	0.93		965.4	1	94	0	5	7	12.78	-23.41			May-15
	3.65	8.91	24.97	22.31	42.59	1.39	0.67	11.5	0.93		965.4	1	94	0	5	7	12.78	-23.41			Jan-11
	2.19	8.77	7.88	23.83	88.05	0.79	0.83	14.65	1		79.5	0	100	0	0	72	27.26	-24.54			May-15
	2.10	8.61	7.49	22.67	86.29	0	1.18	14.65	1		79.5	0	100	0	0	72	27.26	-24.53			May-08
	2.55	4.96	10.93	16.20	39.45	2.12	1.12	5.35	1.07		1,014	12	44	42	2	33	15.71	-12.44			Apr-16
	2.84	5.53	12.33			1.66	1.13				101.5	9	50	39	2	36					Apr-16
	3.01	5.83	12.80			1.99	0.53				101.5	9	50	39	2	36					Apr-16
	2.93	5.70	12.53			1.92	0.88				101.5	9	50	39	2	36					Apr-16
	2.89	5.63	12.40			1.83	0.98				101.5	9	50	39	2	36					Apr-16
	3.33	6.42	13.91	19.78	53.90	2.23	1.16	6.99	1.07		1,864	7	58	33	2	27	19.37	-16.99			Apr-16
	3.86	7.46	16.12			1.55	1.17				92.4	5	68	25	2	17					Apr-16
	4.12	7.74	16.78			1.85	0.57				92.4	5	68	25	2	17					Apr-16
	3.93	7.51	16.26			1.76	0.92				92.4	5	68	25	2	17					Apr-16
	3.91	7.56	16.33			1.69	1.02				92.4	5	68	25	2	17					Apr-16
	4.48	8.51	18.16	24.78	67.31	1.9	1.19	8.75	1.02		1,703	3	78	16	2	25	21.42	-19.31			Apr-16
	4.83	8.84	19.40			1.68	1.2				58.1	2	85	10	2	40					Apr-16
	4.99	9.23	19.97			2	0.6				58.1	2	85	10	2	40					Apr-16
	4.88	9.08	19.60			2.75	0.95				58.1	2	85	10	2	40					Apr-16
	4.87	8.95	19.52			1.83	1.05				58.1	2	85	10	2	40					Apr-16
	5.00	9.56	20.22	27.11	69.53	1.69	1.21	9.3	0.98		968.7	2	89	7	2	23	21.45	-19.73			Apr-16
	5.03	9.50	20.52			1.42	1.21				33.9	2	89	7	2	17					Apr-16
	5.14	9.91	21.34			1.71	0.61				33.9	2	89	7	2	17					Apr-16
	5.07	9.66	20.77			1.71	0.96				33.9	2	89	7	2	17					Apr-16
	5.09	9.70	20.73			1.52	1.06				33.9	2	89	7	2	17					Apr-16
	4.99	9.67	20.62	27.05	68.30	2.07	1.21	9.37	0.97		366.6	2	90	6	2	20	21.28	-19.88			Apr-16
	2.04	3.53	9.02	14.84	29.66	2.57	0.5	4	1.01		109.8	15	29	54	2	21	11.61	-7.71			May-15
	1.85	3.77	8.47	13.70	28.47	1.86	0.85	3.98	1.01		109.8	15	29	54	2	21	11.61	-7.71			May-09
	1.78	3.69	8.35	13.38	27.85	1.7	0.95	4	1.02		109.8	15	29	54	2	21	11.57	-7.79			May-09
	2.21	4.44	9.96			2.07	0.52				3.3	13	33	51	2	46					Apr-16
	2.12	4.25	9.56			1.69	0.87				3.3	13	33	51	2	46					Apr-16
	2.06	4.20	9.49			1.84	0.97				3.3	13	33	51	2	46					Apr-16
	2.56	4.49	11.25	17.79	39.08	3.17	0.54	4.99	1.02		219.4	10	39	48	2	24	14.4	-11.38			May-15
	2.39	4.83	10.74	16.53	37.79	1.73	0.89	5	1.03		219.4	10	39	48	2	24	14.4	-11.38			May-09
	2.33	4.76	10.65	16.16	37.17	1.61	0.99	4.96	1.02		219.4	10	39	48	2	24	14.38	-11.46			May-09
	3.03	5.86	12.91			2.61	0.55				5.5	8	47	42	2	193					Apr-16
	2.87	5.68	12.53			2.41	0.9				5.5	8	47	42	2	193					Apr-16

	MARKET		FUND TYPE, CATEGORY & OBJECTIVE		RATINGS				MINIMUMS	
Fund Name	Ticker Symbol	Traded On	Fund Type	Category and (Prospectus Objective)	Overall Rating	Reward Rating	Risk Rating	Recent Up/ Downgrade	Open to New Investors	Min Initial Investment
Great-West Lifetime Conservative 2030 Fund Service Class	MXAQX	NAS CM	Open End	Target Date 2021-2045 (Asset Alloc)	D+	C-	A	Up	Y	0
Great-West Lifetime Conservative 2035 Fund Inst Cls	MXRCX	NAS CM	Open End	Target Date 2021-2045 (Asset Alloc)	B-	C+	B	Down	Y	0
Great-West Lifetime Conservative 2035 Fund Investor Class	MXGLX	NAS CM	Open End	Target Date 2021-2045 (Asset Alloc)	B-	C+	B	Down	Y	0
Great-West Lifetime Conservative 2035 Fund Service Class	MXHLX	NAS CM	Open End	Target Date 2021-2045 (Asset Alloc)	B-	C+	B	Down	Y	0
Great-West Lifetime Conservative 2040 Fund Inst Cls	MXBCX	NAS CM	Open End	Target Date 2021-2045 (Asset Alloc)	D+	C-	A-	Up	Y	0
Great-West Lifetime Conservative 2040 Fund Investor Class	MXBAX	NAS CM	Open End	Target Date 2021-2045 (Asset Alloc)	D+	C-	A-	Up	Y	0
Great-West Lifetime Conservative 2040 Fund Service Class	MXBBX	NAS CM	Open End	Target Date 2021-2045 (Asset Alloc)	D+	C-	A-	Up	Y	0
Great-West Lifetime Conservative 2045 Fund Inst Cls	MXUCX	NAS CM	Open End	Target Date 2021-2045 (Asset Alloc)	B-	B-	B	Down	Y	0
Great-West Lifetime Conservative 2045 Fund Investor Class	MXMLX	NAS CM	Open End	Target Date 2021-2045 (Asset Alloc)	B-	B-	B-	Down	Y	0
Great-West Lifetime Conservative 2045 Fund Service Class	MXNLX	NAS CM	Open End	Target Date 2021-2045 (Asset Alloc)	B-	B-	B-	Down	Y	0
Great-West Lifetime Conservative 2050 Fund Inst Cls	MXBNX	NAS CM	Open End	Target Date 2046+ (Asset Alloc)	D+	C	A-	Up	Y	0
Great-West Lifetime Conservative 2050 Fund Investor Class	MXBKX	NAS CM	Open End	Target Date 2046+ (Asset Alloc)	D+	C	A-	Up	Y	0
Great-West Lifetime Conservative 2050 Fund Service Class	MXBMX	NAS CM	Open End	Target Date 2046+ (Asset Alloc)	D+	C	A-	Up	Y	0
Great-West Lifetime Conservative 2055 Fund Inst Cls	MXXFX	NAS CM	Open End	Target Date 2046+ (Asset Alloc)	B-	B-	B-	Down	Y	0
Great-West Lifetime Conservative 2055 Fund Investor Class	MXSLX	NAS CM	Open End	Target Date 2046+ (Asset Alloc)	B-	B-	B-	Down	Y	0
Great-West Lifetime Conservative 2055 Fund Service Class	MXTLX	NAS CM	Open End	Target Date 2046+ (Asset Alloc)	B-	B-	B-	Down	Y	0
Great-West Loomis Sayles Small Cap Value Fund Inst Cls	MXTFX	NAS CM	Open End	US Equity Small Cap (Small Company)	B+	A-	B	Up	Y	0
Great-West Loomis Sayles Small Cap Value Fund Investor Cls	MXLSX	NAS CM	Open End	US Equity Small Cap (Small Company)	B+	A-	B	Up	Y	0
Great-West MFS International Growth Fund Institutional Cls	MXHTX	NAS CM	Open End	Global Equity Large Cap (Foreign Stock)	B-	B-	B	Up	Y	0
Great-West MFS International Growth Fund Investor Class	MXIGX	NAS CM	Open End	Global Equity Large Cap (Foreign Stock)	B-	B-	B	Up	Y	0
Great-West MFS International Value Fund Class L	MXMIX	NAS CM	Open End	Global Equity Large Cap (Foreign Stock)	B	B	B+		Y	0
Great-West MFS International Value Fund Institutional Cls	MXJVX	NAS CM	Open End	Global Equity Large Cap (Foreign Stock)	B+	B	A-	Up	Y	0
Great-West MFS International Value Fund Investor Class	MXIVX	NAS CM	Open End	Global Equity Large Cap (Foreign Stock)	B	B	B+		Y	0
Great-West Moderate Profile Fund Class L	MXGPX	NAS CM	Open End	Moderate Alloc (Growth)	B-	C+	B	Up	Y	0
Great-West Moderate Profile Fund Institutional Class	MXITX	NAS CM	Open End	Moderate Alloc (Growth)	B-	C+	B	Up	Y	0
Great-West Moderate Profile Fund Investor Class	MXMPX	NAS CM	Open End	Moderate Alloc (Growth)	B-	C+	B	Up	Y	0
Great-West Moderately Aggressive Profile Fund Class L	MXFPX	NAS CM	Open End	Aggressive Alloc (Aggr Growth)	B-	C+	B	Down	Y	0
Great-West Moderately Aggressive Profile Fund Inst Cls	MXHRX	NAS CM	Open End	Aggressive Alloc (Aggr Growth)	B-	B-	B	Down	Y	0
Great-West Moderately Aggressive Profile Fund Investor Cls	MXBPX	NAS CM	Open End	Aggressive Alloc (Aggr Growth)	B-	C+	B	Down	Y	0
Great-West Moderately Conservative Profile Fund Class L	MXHPX	NAS CM	Open End	Cautious Alloc (Growth & Income)	B-	C+	B	Up	Y	0
Great-West Moderately Conservative Profile Fund Inst Cls	MXJUX	NAS CM	Open End	Cautious Alloc (Growth & Income)	B-	C+	B	Up	Y	0
Great-West Moderately Conservative Profile Fund Inv Cls	MXDPX	NAS CM	Open End	Cautious Alloc (Growth & Income)	B-	C+	B	Up	Y	0
Great-West Multi-Manager Large Cap Growth Fund Inst Cls	MXGSX	NAS CM	Open End	US Equity Large Cap Growth (Growth)	B	B	B	Down	Y	0
Great-West Multi-Manager Large Cap Growth Fund Inv Cls	MXLGX	NAS CM	Open End	US Equity Large Cap Growth (Growth)	B	B	B	Down	Y	0
Great-West Multi-Manager Small Cap Growth Fund Inst Cls	MXMSX	NAS CM	Open End	US Equity Small Cap (Small Company)	C	C+	B-	Up	Y	0
Great-West Multi-Manager Small Cap Growth Fund Inv Cls	MXMTX	NAS CM	Open End	US Equity Small Cap (Small Company)	C	C+	B-	Up	Y	0
Great-West Putnam Equity Income Fund Institutional Class	MXQCX	NAS CM	Open End	US Equity Large Cap Value (Growth & Income)	B-	B-	B-	Down	Y	0
Great-West Putnam Equity Income Fund Investor Class	MXQIX	NAS CM	Open End	US Equity Large Cap Value (Growth & Income)	B-	B-	B-	Down	Y	0
Great-West Real Estate Index Fund Institutional Class	MXSFX	NAS CM	Open End	Real Estate Sector Equity (Real Estate)	B-	C+	B+	Up	Y	0
Great-West Real Estate Index Fund Investor Class	MXREX	NAS CM	Open End	Real Estate Sector Equity (Real Estate)	B-	C+	B+	Up	Y	0
Great-West S&P 500® Index Fund Class L	MXVJX	NAS CM	Open End	US Equity Large Cap Blend (Growth)	B	B-	B		Y	0
Great-West S&P 500® Index Fund Institutional Class	MXKWX	NAS CM	Open End	US Equity Large Cap Blend (Growth)	B	B	B		Y	0
Great-West S&P 500® Index Fund Investor Class	MXVIX	NAS CM	Open End	US Equity Large Cap Blend (Growth)	B	B	B		Y	0
Great-West S&P Mid Cap 400® Index Fund Class L	MXBUX	NAS CM	Open End	US Equity Mid Cap (Growth)	B	B	B	Up	Y	0
Great-West S&P Mid Cap 400® Index Fund Institutional Class	MXNZX	NAS CM	Open End	US Equity Mid Cap (Growth)	B	B	B		Y	0
Great-West S&P Mid Cap 400® Index Fund Investor Class	MXMDX	NAS CM	Open End	US Equity Mid Cap (Growth)	B	B	B		Y	0
Great-West S&P Small Cap 600® Index Fund Class L	MXNSX	NAS CM	Open End	US Equity Small Cap (Small Company)	B+	A-	B	Up	Y	0
Great-West S&P Small Cap 600® Index Fund Institutional Cls	MXERX	NAS CM	Open End	US Equity Small Cap (Small Company)	A-	A-	B	Up	Y	0
Great-West S&P Small Cap 600® Index Fund Investor Class	MXISX	NAS CM	Open End	US Equity Small Cap (Small Company)	B+	A-	B	Up	Y	0
Great-West SecureFoundation® Balanced ETF Fund Class A	SFBPX	NAS CM	Open End	Moderate Alloc (Balanced)	B-	C+	B	Up	Y	10,000
Great-West SecureFoundation® Balanced Fund Class L	MXLDX	NAS CM	Open End	Moderate Alloc (Balanced)	B-	C+	B	Up	Y	0
Great-West SecureFoundation® Balanced Fund Inst Cls	MXCJX	NAS CM	Open End	Moderate Alloc (Balanced)	B-	C+	B	Up	Y	0

★Expanded analysis of this fund is included in Section II.

	TOTAL RETURNS					PERFORMANCE				ASSETS		ASSET ALLOCATION & TURNOVER					BULL & BEAR		FEES		
Min Additional Investment	3-Month Total Return	6-Month Total Return	1-Year Total Return	3-Year Total Return	5-Year Total Return	Dividend Yield (TTM)	Expense Ratio	3-Yr Std Deviation	3-Year Beta	NAV	Total Assets (MIL)	%Cash	%Stocks	%Bonds	%Other	Turnover Ratio	Last Bull Market Total Return	Last Bear Market Total Return	Front End Fee (%)	Back End Fee (%)	Inception Date
	2.85	5.63	12.40			2.19	1				5.5	8	47	42	2	193					Apr-16
	3.62	6.05	14.96	22.25	53.90	3.25	0.58	6.67	1.01		185.7	5	57	35	2	25	18.02	-15.61			May-15
	3.37	6.66	14.50	21.12	52.67	1.54	0.93	6.69	1.01		185.7	5	57	35	2	25	18.02	-15.61			May-09
	3.35	6.64	14.43	20.85	51.96	1.4	1.03	6.7	1.02		185.7	5	57	35	2	25	18.02	-15.63			May-09
	4.03	7.84	16.99			1.78	0.58				2.6	4	68	24	4	6					Apr-16
	3.93	7.69	16.63			1.51	0.93				2.6	4	68	24	4	6					Apr-16
	3.92	7.71	16.61			1.62	1.03				2.6	4	68	24	4	6					Apr-16
	4.52	8.75	18.62	26.71	64.65	3.1	0.61	8.13	0.98		114.9	3	76	19	2	28	19.56	-17.5			May-15
	4.36	8.46	18.23	25.48	63.04	1.3	0.96	8.18	0.99		114.9	3	76	19	2	28	19.55	-17.5			May-09
	4.36	8.47	18.21	25.16	62.27	1.2	1.06	8.14	0.98		114.9	3	76	19	2	28	19.46	-17.51			May-09
	4.61	9.04	19.49			3.14	0.6				1.3	2	80	14	3	130					Apr-16
	4.55	8.89	19.04			2.99	0.95				1.3	2	80	14	3	130					Apr-16
	4.60	8.88	18.97			2.53	1.05				1.3	2	80	14	3	130					Apr-16
	4.82	9.30	19.97	27.75	65.48	3.05	0.62	8.53	0.97		44.5	2	82	14	2	40	19.61	-17.92			May-15
	4.65	9.03	19.46	26.53	63.90	1.36	0.97	8.54	0.97		44.5	2	82	14	2	40	19.61	-17.92			May-09
	4.63	9.01	19.40	26.18	63.15	1.22	1.07	8.55	0.97		44.5	2	82	14	2	40	19.55	-17.94			May-09
	3.67	10.45	10.47	33.70	94.63	0.66	0.74	13.76	0.94		227.4	0	100	0	0	31	29.28	-23.68			May-15
	3.53	10.24	10.04	32.38	92.70	0.07	1.09	13.75	0.94		227.4	0	100	0	0	31	29.28	-23.68			Nov-94
	3.30	7.41	27.41	25.26	43.78	1.19	0.85	11.58	0.92		371.4	1	98	0	2	27	18.55	-23.16			May-15
	3.29	7.28	26.98	24.58	43.00	0.2	1.2	11.58	0.92		371.4	1	98	0	2	27	18.55	-23.16			May-03
	5.58	8.91	26.36	36.82	79.44	0.04	1.32	9.78	0.7		1,285	3	93	0	2	22	13	-13.43			Apr-13
	5.71	9.14	27.08	39.34	83.83	1.52	0.71	9.8	0.71		1,285	3	93	0	2	22	13.16	-13.34			May-15
	5.65	9.05	26.68	38.10	82.20	0.9	1.07	9.76	0.71		1,285	3	93	0	2	22	13.16	-13.34			Dec-93
	3.43	6.17	12.75	19.87	50.24	0.82	1.19	6.2	-0.12		1,583	20	58	19	2	26	14.64	-12.65			Jul-11
	3.49	6.43	13.39	21.79	53.49	1.17	0.59	6.18	-0.14		1,583	20	58	19	2	26	14.83	-12.51			May-15
	3.45	6.29	13.09	20.70	52.12	1.24	0.94	6.25	-0.14		1,583	20	58	19	2	26	14.83	-12.51			Sep-99
	4.16	7.34	15.29	23.31	61.70	0.87	1.28	7.27	-0.26		739.5	12	71	14	2	30	17.48	-15.28			Jul-11
	4.29	7.70	15.98	25.34	65.19	1.23	0.68	7.29	-0.25		739.5	12	71	14	2	30	17.63	-15.29			May-15
	4.18	7.56	15.54	24.25	63.75	1.11	1.03	7.25	-0.24		739.5	12	71	14	2	30	17.62	-15.29			Sep-99
	2.49	4.65	9.97	15.76	38.16	1.18	1.1	4.92	0		388.6	27	44	26	2	25	12.01	-9.69			Jul-11
	2.59	4.92	10.58	17.66	41.12	1.63	0.5	4.98	-0.01		388.6	27	44	26	2	25	12.09	-9.54			May-15
	2.55	4.81	10.19	16.65	39.91	1.46	0.85	4.94	-0.01		388.6	27	44	26	2	25	12.09	-9.54			Sep-99
	6.94	12.19	30.36	40.72	110.81	0.44	0.65	10.96	0.99		907.8	3	97	0	0	48	25.1	-20.34			May-15
	6.86	11.88	29.88	38.67	107.74	0.08	1	10.92	0.99		907.8	3	97	0	0	48	25.1	-20.34			May-03
	5.58	12.22	22.24			0	0.84				59.7	0	99	0	0	91					Sep-15
	5.44	11.90	21.82			0	1.19				59.7	0	99	0	0	91					Sep-15
	6.79	12.19	19.26	29.78	97.87	1.57	0.75	9.95	0.94		649.3	0	97	0	2	25	25.67				May-15
	6.76	12.00	18.90	28.40	95.77	0.47	1.1	10	0.94		649.3	0	97	0	2	25	25.67				Jun-11
	2.04	2.15	4.91	12.34	52.35	2.51	0.35	13.49	1		329.3	0	100	0	0	23					May-15
	1.89	1.89	4.42	11.16	50.75	1.4	0.7	13.49	1		329.3	0	100	0	0	23					Nov-12
	7.01	11.74	20.94	33.50	104.05	1.03	0.81	10.06	1		3,261	0	100	0	0	7	24.52	-16.47			Jul-11
	7.18	12.08	21.64	35.69	108.57	2.58	0.19	10.09	1		3,261	0	100	0	0	7	24.66	-16.44			May-15
	7.06	11.91	21.24	34.47	106.69	0.77	0.54	10.1	1		3,261	0	100	0	0	7	24.66	-16.44			Sep-03
	6.67	10.13	15.55	32.64	97.40		0.8	11.02	1		853.7	1	99	0	0	30	27.15	-22.8			Apr-17
	6.81	10.43	16.25	34.98	101.89	1.57	0.2	11.03	1		853.7	1	99	0	0	30	27.34	-22.72			May-15
	6.70	10.17	15.81	33.60	99.82	0.51	0.55	11.03	1		853.7	1	99	0	0	30	27.34	-22.72			Jan-11
	4.51	10.65	12.81	36.80	107.49	0.47	0.81	13.79	1		973.2	0	100	0	0	26	28.85	-22.22			Aug-11
	4.69	11.00	13.53	39.12	112.06	1.7	0.21	13.81	1		973.2	0	100	0	0	26	29.16	-22.2			May-15
	4.61	10.83	13.15	37.87	110.15	0.85	0.56	13.85	1		973.2	0	100	0	0	26	29.15	-22.2			Dec-93
500	3.68	7.06	13.68	21.82	52.07	1.8	0.61	6.13	0.58		46.3	3	61	36	0	14			5.00		Jan-12
	3.56	6.66	12.71	20.31	50.07	1.73	0.88	5.88	0.56		691.4	5	59	34	1	11	14.7	-11.21			Jan-11
	3.76	6.93	13.48	22.47	53.52	2.75	0.28	5.86	0.56		691.4	5	59	34	1	11	14.83	-11.15			May-15

	MARKET			FUND TYPE, CATEGORY & OBJECTIVE	RATINGS				MINIMUMS	
Fund Name	Ticker Symbol	Traded On	Fund Type	Category and (Prospectus Objective)	Overall Rating	Reward Rating	Risk Rating	Recent Up/ Downgrade	Open to New Investors	Min Initial Investment
Great-West SecureFoundation® Balanced Fund Investor Class	MXSBX	NAS CM	Open End	Moderate Alloc (Balanced)	B-	C+	B	Up	Y	0
Great-West SecureFoundation® Balanced Fund Service Class	MXSHX	NAS CM	Open End	Moderate Alloc (Balanced)	B-	C+	B	Up	Y	0
Great-West SecureFoundation® Lifetime 2015 Fund Class L	MXLEX	NAS CM	Open End	Target Date 2000-2020 (Asset Alloc)	B-	C+	B	Up	Y	0
Great-West SecureFoundation® Lifetime 2015 Fund Inv Cls	MXSJX	NAS CM	Open End	Target Date 2000-2020 (Asset Alloc)	B-	C+	B	Up	Y	0
Great-West SecureFoundation® Lifetime 2015 Fund Serv Cls	MXSKX	NAS CM	Open End	Target Date 2000-2020 (Asset Alloc)	B-	C+	B	Up	Y	0
Great-West SecureFoundation® Lifetime 2020 Fund Class L	MXLFX	NAS CM	Open End	Target Date 2000-2020 (Asset Alloc)	B-	C+	B	Up	Y	0
Great-West SecureFoundation® Lifetime 2020 Fund Inv Cls	MXSMX	NAS CM	Open End	Target Date 2000-2020 (Asset Alloc)	B-	C+	B	Up	Y	0
Great-West SecureFoundation® Lifetime 2020 Fund Serv Cls	MXSPX	NAS CM	Open End	Target Date 2000-2020 (Asset Alloc)	B-	C+	B	Up	Y	0
Great-West SecureFoundation® Lifetime 2025 Fund Class L	MXLHX	NAS CM	Open End	Target Date 2021-2045 (Asset Alloc)	B-	C+	B	Up	Y	0
Great-West SecureFoundation® Lifetime 2025 Fund Inv Cls	MXSNX	NAS CM	Open End	Target Date 2021-2045 (Asset Alloc)	B-	C+	B	Up	Y	0
Great-West SecureFoundation® Lifetime 2025 Fund Serv Cls	MXSOX	NAS CM	Open End	Target Date 2021-2045 (Asset Alloc)	B-	C+	B	Up	Y	0
Great-West SecureFoundation® Lifetime 2030 Fund Class L	MXLIX	NAS CM	Open End	Target Date 2021-2045 (Asset Alloc)	B-	C+	B	Down	Y	0
Great-West SecureFoundation® Lifetime 2030 Fund Inv Cls	MXSQX	NAS CM	Open End	Target Date 2021-2045 (Asset Alloc)	B-	C+	B	Down	Y	0
Great-West SecureFoundation® Lifetime 2030 Fund Serv Cls	MXASX	NAS CM	Open End	Target Date 2021-2045 (Asset Alloc)	B-	C+	B	Down	Y	0
Great-West SecureFoundation® Lifetime 2035 Fund Class L	MXLJX	NAS CM	Open End	Target Date 2021-2045 (Asset Alloc)	B-	B-	B	Down	Y	0
Great-West SecureFoundation® Lifetime 2035 Fund Inv Cls	MXSRX	NAS CM	Open End	Target Date 2021-2045 (Asset Alloc)	B-	B-	B	Down	Y	0
Great-West SecureFoundation® Lifetime 2035 Fund Serv Cls	MXSSX	NAS CM	Open End	Target Date 2021-2045 (Asset Alloc)	B-	B-	B	Down	Y	0
Great-West SecureFoundation® Lifetime 2040 Fund Class L	MXLKX	NAS CM	Open End	Target Date 2021-2045 (Asset Alloc)	B-	B-	B-	Down	Y	0
Great-West SecureFoundation® Lifetime 2040 Fund Inv Cls	MXDSX	NAS CM	Open End	Target Date 2021-2045 (Asset Alloc)	B-	B-	B-	Down	Y	0
Great-West SecureFoundation® Lifetime 2040 Fund Serv Cls	MXESX	NAS CM	Open End	Target Date 2021-2045 (Asset Alloc)	B-	B-	B-	Down	Y	0
Great-West SecureFoundation® Lifetime 2045 Fund Class L	MXLNX	NAS CM	Open End	Target Date 2021-2045 (Asset Alloc)	B-	B-	B-	Down	Y	0
Great-West SecureFoundation® Lifetime 2045 Fund Inv Cls	MXSTX	NAS CM	Open End	Target Date 2021-2045 (Asset Alloc)	B-	B-	B-	Down	Y	0
Great-West SecureFoundation® Lifetime 2045 Fund Serv Cls	MXSWX	NAS CM	Open End	Target Date 2021-2045 (Asset Alloc)	B-	B-	B-	Down	Y	0
Great-West SecureFoundation® Lifetime 2050 Fund Class L	MXLOX	NAS CM	Open End	Target Date 2046+ (Asset Alloc)	B-	B-	B-	Down	Y	0
Great-West SecureFoundation® Lifetime 2050 Fund Inv Cls	MXFSX	NAS CM	Open End	Target Date 2046+ (Asset Alloc)	B-	B-	B-	Down	Y	0
Great-West SecureFoundation® Lifetime 2050 Fund Serv Cls	MXHSX	NAS CM	Open End	Target Date 2046+ (Asset Alloc)	B-	B-	B-	Down	Y	0
Great-West SecureFoundation® Lifetime 2055 Fund Class L	MXLPX	NAS CM	Open End	Target Date 2046+ (Asset Alloc)	B-	B-	B-	Down	Y	0
Great-West SecureFoundation® Lifetime 2055 Fund Inv Cls	MXSYX	NAS CM	Open End	Target Date 2046+ (Asset Alloc)	B-	B-	B-	Down	Y	0
Great-West SecureFoundation® Lifetime 2055 Fund Serv Cls	MXSZX	NAS CM	Open End	Target Date 2046+ (Asset Alloc)	B-	B-	B-	Down	Y	0
Great-West T. Rowe Price Equity Income Fund Class L	MXTQX	NAS CM	Open End	US Equity Large Cap Value (Equity-Income)	B-	B-	B-	Down	Y	0
Great-West T. Rowe Price Equity Income Fund Inst Cls	MXVHX	NAS CM	Open End	US Equity Large Cap Value (Equity-Income)	B-	B	C+	Down	Y	0
Great-West T. Rowe Price Equity Income Fund Investor Class	MXEQX	NAS CM	Open End	US Equity Large Cap Value (Equity-Income)	B-	B	B-	Down	Y	0
Great-West T. Rowe Price Mid Cap Growth Fund Class L	MXTMX	NAS CM	Open End	US Equity Mid Cap (Growth)	B	B	B	Down	Y	0
Great-West T. Rowe Price Mid Cap Growth Fund Inst Cls	MXYKX	NAS CM	Open End	US Equity Mid Cap (Growth)	B	B	B	Down	Y	0
Great-West T. Rowe Price Mid Cap Growth Fund Investor Cls	MXMGX	NAS CM	Open End	US Equity Mid Cap (Growth)	B	B	B	Down	Y	0
Green Century Balanced Fund	GCBLX	NAS CM	Open End	Moderate Alloc (Balanced)	B-	C+	B	Down	Y	2,500
Green Century Equity Fund	GCEQX	NAS CM	Open End	US Equity Large Cap Growth (Growth & Income)	B	B	B		Y	2,500
Green Century MSCI Intl Index Fund Individual Inv	GCINX	NAS CM	Open End	Global Equity Large Cap (Growth & Income)	D	C	B		Y	2,500
Green Century MSCI International Index Fund Institutional	GCIFX	NAS CM	Open End	Global Equity Large Cap (Growth & Income)	D	C	B		Y	250,000
Green Owl Intrinsic Value Fund	GOWLX	NAS CM	Open End	US Equity Large Cap Blend (Growth)	B	B	B-	Up	Y	2,500
Greenspring Fund	GRSPX	NAS CM	Open End	Moderate Alloc (Growth)	B-	C+	B-	Up	Y	5,000
Griffin Institutional Access Real Estate Fund Class A	GIREX	NAS CM	Closed End	Real Estate Sector Equity (Real Estate)	B	C+	A+	Up	Y	2,500
Griffin Institutional Access Real Estate Fund Class C	US39822J2015		Closed End	Real Estate Sector Equity (Real Estate)	B	C+	A+	Up	Y	2,500
Griffin Institutional Access Real Estate Fund Class I	US39822J3005		Closed End	Real Estate Sector Equity (Real Estate)	B	C+	A+	Up	Y	1,000,000
Griffin Institutional Access Real Estate Fund Class L	US39822J4094		Closed End	Real Estate Sector Equity (Real Estate)	B	C+	A+	Up	Y	2,500
Griffin Institutional Access Real Estate Fund Class M	US39822J5083		Closed End	Real Estate Sector Equity (Real Estate)	B	C+	A+	Up	Y	25,000
Grizzly Short Fund	GRZZX	NAS CM	Open End	Other Alternative (Growth)	D-	D-	D-	Down	Y	10,000
Guggenheim Alpha Opportunity Fund Class A	SAOAX	NAS CM	Open End	Long/Short Equity (Growth)	B-	C+	B	Up	Y	2,500
Guggenheim Alpha Opportunity Fund Class C	SAOCX	NAS CM	Open End	Long/Short Equity (Growth)	B-	C+	B	Up	Y	2,500
Guggenheim Alpha Opportunity Fund Class P	SAOSX	NAS CM	Open End	Long/Short Equity (Growth)	B-	C+	B	Up	Y	0
Guggenheim Alpha Opportunity Fund Institutional Class	SAOIX	NAS CM	Open End	Long/Short Equity (Growth)	B-	C+	B	Up	Y	2,000,000
Guggenheim Directional Allocation Fund Class A	TVRAX	NAS CM	Open End	US Equity Large Cap Growth (Growth & Income)	B-	B-	B-	Down	Y	2,500

★ Expanded analysis of this fund is included in Section II.

	TOTAL RETURNS					PERFORMANCE				ASSETS		ASSET ALLOCATION & TURNOVER					BULL & BEAR		FEES		
Min Additional Investment	3-Month Total Return	6-Month Total Return	1-Year Total Return	3-Year Total Return	5-Year Total Return	Dividend Yield (TTM)	Expense Ratio	3-Yr Std Deviation	3-Year Beta	NAV	Total Assets (MIL)	%Cash	%Stocks	%Bonds	%Other	Turnover Ratio	Last Bull Market Total Return	Last Bear Market Total Return	Front End Fee (%)	Back End Fee (%)	Inception Date
	3.63	6.78	13.10	21.23	51.97	1.61	0.63	5.92	0.56		691.4	5	59	34	1	11	14.83	-11.15			Nov-09
	3.55	6.74	12.91	20.95	51.27	1.41	0.73	5.87	0.56		691.4	5	59	34	1	11	14.75	-11.2			Nov-09
	3.31	6.19	12.68	18.98	45.55	1.72	0.9	5.46			102.6	7	55	37	1	28	13.32	-10.85			Jan-11
	3.26	6.30	12.81	19.73	47.22	1.79	0.65	5.45			102.6	7	55	37	1	28	13.58	-10.73			Nov-09
	3.27	6.17	12.72	19.32	46.53	1.57	0.75	5.43			102.6	7	55	37	1	28	13.53	-10.8			Nov-09
	2.08	5.00	11.34	17.46	43.77	1.51	0.9	5.47			81.0	7	55	37	1	21	13.61	-10.68			Jan-11
	1.85	4.86	11.37	18.03	45.20	1.76	0.65	5.45			81.0	7	55	37	1	21	13.72	-10.65			Jan-11
	3.68	6.74	13.28	19.90	47.08	1.65	0.75	5.48			81.0	7	55	37	1	21	13.58	-10.67			Jan-11
	3.24	6.20	12.66	18.71	47.78	1.73	0.9	5.51			82.8	7	55	37	1	23	14.73	-13.44			Jan-11
	3.21	6.21	12.82	19.62	49.54	1.8	0.65	5.52			82.8	7	55	37	1	23	14.96	-13.38			Nov-09
	3.27	6.24	12.82	19.27	48.85	1.62	0.75	5.51			82.8	7	55	37	1	23	14.9	-13.44			Nov-09
	2.42	5.79	12.98	19.48	53.41	1.43	0.92	6.63			111.4	5	62	32	1	18	17.24	-15.82			Jan-11
	2.14	5.54	12.85	19.90	54.59	1.75	0.67	6.65			111.4	5	62	32	1	18	17.23	-15.79			Jan-11
	2.29	5.68	12.91	19.73	54.11	1.55	0.77	6.66			111.4	5	62	32	1	18	17.14	-15.8			Jan-11
	4.30	8.29	16.71	24.41	63.49	1.97	0.94	7.84			69.8	3	73	23	1	26	18.87	-17.68			Jan-11
	4.34	8.38	16.87	24.74	64.65	1.76	0.69	7.83			69.8	3	73	23	1	26	18.91	-17.67			Nov-09
	4.26	8.26	16.76	24.31	63.67	1.55	0.79	7.82			69.8	3	73	23	1	26	18.81	-17.72			Nov-09
	3.24	7.63	16.89	25.15	66.59	1.67	0.95	8.64			86.2	2	83	15	1	15	19.64	-18.52			Jan-11
	3.20	7.63	16.89	25.14	66.56	1.71	0.7	8.65			86.2	2	83	15	1	15	19.74	-18.59			Jan-11
	3.34	7.77	16.92	24.95	66.13	1.53	0.8	8.61			86.2	2	83	15	1	15	19.64	-18.6			Jan-11
	5.11	9.81	19.58	27.88	69.91	1.63	0.96	9.06			32.8	1	88	10	1	27	19.93	-18.98			Jan-11
	5.10	9.92	19.80	28.39	70.86	1.54	0.71	9.03			32.8	1	88	10	1	27	19.91	-18.99			Nov-09
	5.12	9.88	19.78	27.99	69.91	1.79	0.81	9.04			32.8	1	88	10	1	27	19.93	-18.98			Nov-09
	5.17	10.04	20.05	28.44	70.18	1.61	0.96	9.13			23.6	1	89	8	1	13	19.91	-19.19			Jan-11
	3.50	8.30	18.33	26.69	67.77	1.69	0.71	9.18			23.6	1	89	8	1	13	20.02	-19.26			Jan-11
	5.18	10.08	20.12	28.33	69.72	1.56	0.81	9.19			23.6	1	89	8	1	13	19.93	-19.27			Jan-11
	8.08	13.19	23.70	32.18	74.15	1.98	0.96	9.23			8.6	1	90	8	1	32	19.94	-19.44			Jan-11
	7.62	12.72	23.25	31.72	73.46	1.73	0.71	9.24			8.6	1	90	8	1	32	19.93	-19.41			Nov-09
	5.19	10.17	20.38	28.32	68.62	1.5	0.81	9.26			8.6	1	90	8	1	32	19.91	-19.47			Nov-09
	6.01	10.75	16.02	26.09	79.90	1.88	1.07	11.14	1.04		899.5	1	97	0	0	26	23.48	-18.28			Jul-11
	6.10	11.09	16.68	28.46	84.69	2.78	0.47	11.16	1.04		899.5	1	97	0	0	26	23.65	-18.26			May-15
	6.07	10.91	16.40	27.32	83.06	0.55	0.82	11.12	1.04		899.5	1	97	0	0	26	23.65	-18.26			Nov-94
	4.74	9.41	24.33	38.53	118.22	0.51	1.27	10.8	0.87		1,401	6	94	0	1	42	24.83	-20.36			Aug-11
	4.98	9.85	25.10	40.99	123.41	0.37	0.67	10.81	0.87		1,401	6	94	0	1	42	25.03	-20.33			May-15
	4.86	9.63	24.70	39.70	121.37	0.28	1.02	10.81	0.87		1,401	6	94	0	1	42	25.03	-20.33			Jul-97
100	2.95	5.18	12.78	16.51	57.33	0.13	1.48	7.8	0.72	26.3	240.0	4	65	31	0	26	16.74	-11.72			Mar-92
100	5.88	10.35	21.95	32.43	105.86	0.52	1.25	10.4		40.81	241.0	0	100	0	0	17	22.48	-15.2			Sep-95
100	3.35	8.53	23.85			0.87	1.28			11.82	37.0	1	90	0	2						Sep-16
100	3.45	8.64	24.13			1.01	0.98			11.82	37.0	1	90	0	2						Sep-16
	5.45	10.88	17.11	29.42	90.12	0.3	1.12	13.02	1.13	19.42	84.5	2	98	0	0	21					Dec-11
100	3.90	5.14	7.81	20.79	41.29	1.32	1.03	8.18	0.65	24.32	277.2	10	67	23	0	48	11.67	-10.02			Jul-83
100	2.23	3.58	6.46	22.19		5.19	1.91	1.94		26.82	--	4	96	0	0	29			5.75		Jun-14
100	2.01	3.20	5.71	20.15		5.22	2.66			26.36	--	4	96	0	0	29				1.00	Aug-15
100	2.26	3.69	6.73	22.88		5.19	1.66			26.98	--	4	96	0	0	29					Aug-15
	2.11	3.51	6.38	22.10			2.16			26.79	--	4	96	0	0	29			4.25		Apr-17
10,000	2.08	3.31	5.94	21.51		5.21	2.41			26.67	--	4	96	0	0	29					Nov-16
100	-5.95	-9.98	-19.84	-28.47	-54.42	0	1.67	14.56	-1.24	5.05	204.5	216	-116	0	0	0	-26.88	30.16			Jun-00
100	4.50	6.96	7.48	14.90	70.67	0	1.76	5.68	-7.53	20.61	222.8	3	102	0	-5	92	30.85	-24.46	4.75		Jul-03
100	4.24	6.55	6.67	12.32	64.35	0	2.51	5.67	-8.24	17.97	222.8	3	102	0	-5	92	30.2	-24.66		1.00	Jul-03
	4.44	6.98	7.71	15.38	71.38	0	1.52	5.66	-7.69	20.69	222.8	3	102	0	-5	92	30.85	-24.46			May-15
	4.65	7.29	8.15	16.56	74.00	0	1.28	5.69	-7.08	29.81	222.8	3	102	0	-5	92	30.96	-24.37			Nov-08
100	6.00	10.75	23.02	32.02	89.46	0	1.5	10.26		16.78	706.4	0	100	0	0	89			4.75		Jun-12

	MARKET			FUND TYPE, CATEGORY & OBJECTIVE	RATINGS				MINIMUMS	
Fund Name	Ticker Symbol	Traded On	Fund Type	Category and (Prospectus Objective)	Overall Rating	Reward Rating	Risk Rating	Recent Up/ Downgrade	Open to New Investors	Min Initial Investment
Guggenheim Directional Allocation Fund Class C	TVRCX	NAS CM	Open End	US Equity Large Cap Growth (Growth & Income)	B-	B-	B-		Y	2,500
Guggenheim Directional Allocation Fund Class I	TVRIX	NAS CM	Open End	US Equity Large Cap Growth (Growth & Income)	B-	B	B-	Down	Y	2,000,000
Guggenheim Directional Allocation Fund Class P	TVFRX	NAS CM	Open End	US Equity Large Cap Growth (Growth & Income)	B-	B	B-	Down	Y	0
Guggenheim Diversified Income Fund Class A	GUDAX	NAS CM	Open End	Alloc (Income)	C-	D+	A	Up	Y	2,500
Guggenheim Diversified Income Fund Class C	GUDCX	NAS CM	Open End	Alloc (Income)	C-	D+	A	Up	Y	2,500
Guggenheim Diversified Income Fund Class P	GUDPX	NAS CM	Open End	Alloc (Income)	C-	D+	A	Up	Y	0
Guggenheim Diversified Income Fund Institutional	GUDIX	NAS CM	Open End	Alloc (Income)	C-	D+	A	Up	Y	2,000,000
Guggenheim Enhanced Equity Income	GPM	NYSE	Closed End	US Equity Large Cap Blend (Growth & Income)	B	B	B	Up	Y	
Guggenheim Event Driven & Distressed Strategies Fund A Cls	RYDOX	NAS CM	Open End	Multialternative (Growth)	C+	C	B	Up	Y	2,500
Guggenheim Event Driven & Distressed Strategies Fund C Cls	RYDQX	NAS CM	Open End	Multialternative (Growth)	C+	C	B	Up	Y	2,500
Guggenheim Event Driven & Distressed Strategies Fund Cls P	RYDSX	NAS CM	Open End	Multialternative (Growth)	C+	C	B	Up	Y	0
Guggenheim Event Driven & Distressed Strategies Fund I Cls	RYDTX	NAS CM	Open End	Multialternative (Growth)	C+	C	B	Up	Y	2,000,000
Guggenheim Large Cap Value Fund Class A	SECIX	NAS CM	Open End	US Equity Large Cap Value (Growth)	B	B	B	Up	Y	2,500
Guggenheim Large Cap Value Fund Class C	SEGIX	NAS CM	Open End	US Equity Large Cap Value (Growth)	B-	B-	B-	Down	Y	2,500
Guggenheim Large Cap Value Fund Class Institutional	GILCX	NAS CM	Open End	US Equity Large Cap Value (Growth)	B	B	B		Y	2,000,000
Guggenheim Large Cap Value Fund Class P	SEGPX	NAS CM	Open End	US Equity Large Cap Value (Growth)	B	B	B	Up	Y	0
Guggenheim Long Short Equity Fund Class A	RYAMX	NAS CM	Open End	Long/Short Equity (Growth)	B-	C+	B+	Up	Y	2,500
Guggenheim Long Short Equity Fund Class C	RYISX	NAS CM	Open End	Long/Short Equity (Growth)	B-	C+	B	Up	Y	2,500
Guggenheim Long Short Equity Fund Class P	RYSRX	NAS CM	Open End	Long/Short Equity (Growth)	B-	C+	B+	Up	Y	0
Guggenheim Long Short Equity Fund Institutional Cls Shares	RYQTX	NAS CM	Open End	Long/Short Equity (Growth)	B-	C+	B+	Up	Y	2,000,000
Guggenheim Managed Futures Strategy Fund Class P	RYMFX	NAS CM	Open End	Other Alternative (Growth & Income)	D+	D+	C-	Up	Y	0
Guggenheim Market Neutral Real Estate Fund Class A	GUMAX	NAS CM	Open End	Market Neutral (Real Estate)	C-	D+	B+	Up	Y	2,500
Guggenheim Market Neutral Real Estate Fund Class C	GUMCX	NAS CM	Open End	Market Neutral (Real Estate)	C-	D+	B+	Up	Y	2,500
Guggenheim Market Neutral Real Estate Fund Class P	GUMPX	NAS CM	Open End	Market Neutral (Real Estate)	C-	D+	B+	Up	Y	0
Guggenheim Market Neutral Real Estate Fund Institutional	GUMNX	NAS CM	Open End	Market Neutral (Real Estate)	C-	D+	B+	Up	Y	2,000,000
Guggenheim Mid Cap Value Fund Class A	SEVAX	NAS CM	Open End	US Equity Small Cap (Growth)	B	B	B-	Up	Y	2,500
Guggenheim Mid Cap Value Fund Class C	SEVSX	NAS CM	Open End	US Equity Small Cap (Growth)	B-	B	C+		Y	2,500
Guggenheim Mid Cap Value Fund Class P	SEVPX	NAS CM	Open End	US Equity Small Cap (Growth)	B	B	B-	Up	Y	0
Guggenheim Mid Cap Value Institutional Fund	SVUIX	NAS CM	Open End	US Equity Small Cap (Growth)	B	B	B	Up	Y	2,000,000
Guggenheim Multi-Hedge Strategies Fund Class A	RYMQX	NAS CM	Open End	Multialternative (Growth)	C+	C	B	Up	Y	2,500
Guggenheim Multi-Hedge Strategies Fund Class C	RYMRX	NAS CM	Open End	Multialternative (Growth)	C	C	B	Up	Y	2,500
Guggenheim Multi-Hedge Strategies Fund Class I	RYIMX	NAS CM	Open End	Multialternative (Growth)	C+	C	B	Up	Y	2,000,000
Guggenheim Multi-Hedge Strategies Fund Class P	RYMSX	NAS CM	Open End	Multialternative (Growth)	C+	C	B	Up	Y	0
Guggenheim RBP® Dividend Fund Class A	TVEAX	NAS CM	Open End	US Equity Mid Cap (Growth & Income)	B	B-	B		Y	2,500
Guggenheim RBP® Dividend Fund Class C	TVECX	NAS CM	Open End	US Equity Mid Cap (Growth & Income)	B	B-	B	Up	Y	2,500
Guggenheim RBP® Dividend Fund Class I	TVEIX	NAS CM	Open End	US Equity Mid Cap (Growth & Income)	B	B	B		Y	2,000,000
Guggenheim RBP® Dividend Fund Class P	TVEFX	NAS CM	Open End	US Equity Mid Cap (Growth & Income)	B	B-	B		Y	0
Guggenheim RBP® Large-Cap Defensive Fund Class A	TVDAX	NAS CM	Open End	US Equity Large Cap Growth (Growth & Income)	B-	B-	B	Down	Y	2,500
Guggenheim RBP® Large-Cap Defensive Fund Class C	TVDCX	NAS CM	Open End	US Equity Large Cap Growth (Growth & Income)	B-	B-	B-	Down	Y	2,500
Guggenheim RBP® Large-Cap Defensive Fund Class I	TVIDX	NAS CM	Open End	US Equity Large Cap Growth (Growth & Income)	B-	B-	B	Down	Y	2,000,000
Guggenheim RBP® Large-Cap Defensive Fund Class P	TVFDX	NAS CM	Open End	US Equity Large Cap Growth (Growth & Income)	B-	B-	B	Down	Y	0
Guggenheim RBP® Large-Cap Market Fund Class A	TVMAX	NAS CM	Open End	US Equity Large Cap Growth (Growth & Income)	B-	B	B-	Down	Y	2,500
Guggenheim RBP® Large-Cap Market Fund Class C	TVMCX	NAS CM	Open End	US Equity Large Cap Growth (Growth & Income)	B-	B-	B-	Down	Y	2,500
Guggenheim RBP® Large-Cap Market Fund Class I	TVIMX	NAS CM	Open End	US Equity Large Cap Growth (Growth & Income)	B	B	B-	Up	Y	2,000,000
Guggenheim RBP® Large-Cap Market Fund Class P	TVFMX	NAS CM	Open End	US Equity Large Cap Growth (Growth & Income)	B-	B-	B-	Down	Y	0
Guggenheim RBP® Large-Cap Value Fund Class A	TVVAX	NAS CM	Open End	US Equity Mid Cap (Growth & Income)	B-	B-	B-	Down	Y	2,500
Guggenheim RBP® Large-Cap Value Fund Class C	TVVCX	NAS CM	Open End	US Equity Mid Cap (Growth & Income)	B-	B-	B	Down	Y	2,500
Guggenheim RBP® Large-Cap Value Fund Class I	TVVIX	NAS CM	Open End	US Equity Mid Cap (Growth & Income)	B-	B-	B-	Down	Y	2,000,000
Guggenheim RBP® Large-Cap Value Fund Class P	TVVFX	NAS CM	Open End	US Equity Mid Cap (Growth & Income)	B-	B-	B-	Down	Y	0
Guggenheim Risk Managed Real Estate Fund Class A	GURAX	NAS CM	Open End	Real Estate Sector Equity (Real Estate)	B	B-	A-	Up	Y	2,500
Guggenheim Risk Managed Real Estate Fund Class C	GURCX	NAS CM	Open End	Real Estate Sector Equity (Real Estate)	B	C+	B+	Up	Y	2,500
Guggenheim Risk Managed Real Estate Fund Class P	GURPX	NAS CM	Open End	Real Estate Sector Equity (Real Estate)	B	B-	A-	Up	Y	0

★ Expanded analysis of this fund is included in Section II.

Min Additional Investment	TOTAL RETURNS 3-Month Total Return	6-Month Total Return	1-Year Total Return	3-Year Total Return	5-Year Total Return	PERFORMANCE Dividend Yield (TTM)	Expense Ratio	3-Yr Std Deviation	3-Year Beta	ASSETS NAV	Total Assets (MIL)	ASSET ALLOCATION & TURNOVER %Cash	%Stocks	%Bonds	%Other	Turnover Ratio	BULL & BEAR Last Bull Market Total Return	Last Bear Market Total Return	FEES Front End Fee (%)	Back End Fee (%)	Inception Date
100	5.82	10.36	22.20	29.33	83.41	0	2.1	10.28		16.18	706.4	0	100	0	0	89				1.00	Jun-12
	6.14	10.95	23.44	33.35	92.79	0	1.1	10.25		17.11	706.4	0	100	0	0	89					Jun-12
	6.03	10.77	23.06	32.23	90.31	0	1.35	10.29		16.86	706.4	0	100	0	0	89					Jun-12
100	0.56	2.50	6.91			3.32	1.36				6.1	7	24	67	0	44			4.00		Jan-16
100	-0.86	0.69	4.67			2.58	2.11			27.23	6.1	7	24	67	0	44				1.00	Jan-16
	0.56	2.49	6.86			3.27	1.39				6.1	7	24	67	0	44					Jan-16
	0.64	2.59	7.12			3.51	1.13				6.1	7	24	67	0	44					Jan-16
	6.24	10.72	20.46	35.79	76.45	1.3	0	10.23	0.98	9.02	438.1	0	100	0	0	143	27.79	-15.02			Aug-05
	1.70	4.07	6.02	11.11	20.78	3.19	1.96	5.53	0.46	26.9	6.7	23	22	10	45	47	11.17	-12.87	4.75		Jun-10
	1.46	3.64	5.20	8.60	16.27	3.4	2.7	5.52	0.46	25.16	6.7	23	22	10	45	47	10.68	-13.13		1.00	Jun-10
	1.66	4.03	5.98	11.07	20.73	3.19	1.96	5.53	0.46	26.89	6.7	23	22	10	45	47	11.17	-12.87			Jun-10
	1.74	4.17	6.25	11.90	22.20	3.13	1.71	5.54	0.46	27.47	6.7	23	22	10	45	47	11.3	-12.74			Jun-10
100	6.74	10.84	15.28	30.84	91.45	1.15	1.17	11.1	1.06	46.31	68.2	3	97	0	0	40	25.11	-22.16	4.75		Aug-44
100	6.52	10.43	14.37	27.84	84.35	0.61	1.92	11.1	1.06	42.65	68.2	3	97	0	0	40	24.56	-22.42		1.00	Jan-99
	6.79	10.99	15.52	31.74	93.53	2.18	0.92	11.11	1.06	45.78	68.2	3	97	0	0	40	25.11	-22.16			Jun-13
	6.73	10.84	15.23	30.93	91.58	1.12	1.17	11.12	1.06	46.24	68.2	3	97	0	0	40	25.11	-22.16			May-15
	6.29	11.09	14.87	15.96	42.19	0	1.67	5.85	0.37	18.23	33.3	5	96	0	0	223	11.81	-19.05	4.75		Mar-04
	6.03	10.60	13.95	13.31	36.80	0	2.42	5.84	0.36	16.17	33.3	5	96	0	0	223	11.34	-19.32		1.00	Mar-02
	6.27	10.98	14.82	15.91	42.03	0	1.67	5.83	0.36	18.28	33.3	5	96	0	0	223	11.77	-19.06			Mar-02
	6.34	11.17	15.08	16.89	43.92	0	1.43	5.82	0.37	18.61	33.3	5	96	0	0	223	11.85	-19.06			Nov-11
	3.89	8.72	7.67	-9.52	4.16	4.86	1.88	9.72	-28.85	19.24	51.5	35	3	30	33	16	-8.56	-7.81			Mar-07
100	2.31	2.47	6.53			0	1.64			25.71	5.6	7	92	0	1	145			4.75		Feb-16
100	2.19	2.15	5.82			0	2.38			25.36	5.6	7	92	0	1	145				1.00	Feb-16
	2.31	2.47	6.53			0	1.66			25.7	5.6	7	92	0	1	145					Feb-16
	2.38	2.57	6.79			0	1.39			25.83	5.6	7	92	0	1	145					Feb-16
100	4.54	10.18	13.32	31.51	80.72	0.99	1.4	11.92	0.95	34.39	514.6	3	97	0	0	55	20.97	-24.15	4.75		May-97
100	4.35	9.73	12.47	28.50	74.03	0.67	2.12	11.92	0.95	24.89	514.6	3	97	0	0	55	20.43	-24.39		1.00	Jan-99
	4.57	10.18	13.35	31.22	80.33	1.28	1.23	11.94	0.95	34.16	514.6	3	97	0	0	55	20.97	-24.15			May-15
	4.55	9.98	13.23	33.01	83.33	4.08	1.14	11.77	0.94	10.9	79.7	4	96	0	0	72	21.3	-24.35			Jul-08
	2.72	3.35	3.48	4.20	10.71	0.15	1.61	2.97	0.08	24.92	78.1	66	12	12	9	123	0.33	1.48	4.75		Sep-05
	2.53	2.95	2.71	1.86	6.60	0.16	2.36	2.99	0.08	22.68	78.1	66	12	12	9	123	-0.06	1.17		1.00	Sep-05
	2.79	3.50	3.75	4.97	12.07	0.14	1.36	2.98	0.08	25.42	78.1	66	12	12	9	123	0.51	1.61			May-10
	2.67	3.35	3.48	4.15	10.65	0.14	1.61	3	0.08	24.93	78.1	66	12	12	9	123	0.38	1.48			Sep-05
100	7.11	11.60	18.81	29.01	84.92	1.29	1.2	9.61		12.07	18.9	0	99	0	0	251	23.01	-16.3	4.75		Apr-11
100	6.91	11.18	17.88	26.38	78.98	0.66	1.95	9.66		12.06	18.9	0	99	0	0	251	22.6	-16.49		1.00	Apr-11
	7.21	11.72	19.10	30.30	88.23	1.76	0.95	9.62		11.8	18.9	0	99	0	0	251	23.27	-16.11			Feb-11
	7.16	11.59	18.83	29.34	85.90	1.39	1.2	9.6		12.2	18.9	0	99	0	0	251	23.2	-16.29			Apr-11
100	6.78	12.71	24.06	29.60	89.73	0.18	1.2	8.53		11.2	22.1	1	99	0	0	107	21.97	-11.62	4.75		Apr-10
100	6.59	12.34	23.04	26.89	83.64	0	1.95	8.54		10.95	22.1	1	99	0	0	107	21.47	-11.71		1.00	Apr-11
	6.84	12.88	24.33	30.88	93.17	0.49	0.95	8.52		11.58	22.1	1	99	0	0	107	22.23	-11.43			Feb-11
	6.78	12.77	24.08	29.91	90.82	0	1.2	8.56		11.49	22.1	1	99	0	0	107	22.01	-11.52			Apr-10
100	6.25	10.53	22.91	32.33	96.07	0	1.2	10.96		10.89	20.5	1	99	0	0	98	22.92	-16.87	4.75		Apr-10
100	6.00	10.11	22.00	29.72	89.62	0	1.95	10.88		10.46	20.5	1	99	0	0	98	22.56	-17.06		1.00	Apr-11
	6.29	10.66	23.15	33.72	99.44	0	0.95	10.88		11.48	20.5	1	99	0	0	98	23.22	-16.87			Feb-11
	6.18	10.44	22.84	32.54	96.98	0	1.2	10.94		11.19	20.5	1	99	0	0	98	23.05	-16.96			Apr-10
100	5.68	10.13	16.81	26.22	91.93	1.93	1.2	9.69		10.6	4.1	0	98	0	1	132	26.25	-18.86	4.75		Apr-11
100	5.45	9.65	15.90	23.20	85.19	0.69	1.95	9.72		10.58	4.1	0	98	0	1	132	25.79	-19.15		1.00	Apr-11
	5.78	10.30	17.16	27.34	95.31	0.85	0.95	9.74		10.75	4.1	0	98	0	1	132	26.61	-18.85			Feb-11
	5.65	10.11	16.79	26.36	92.51	0	1.2	9.7		10.67	4.1	0	98	0	1	132	26.3	-18.86			Apr-11
100	-1.07	0.08	5.65	18.29		1.8	1.3	10.92	0.79	29.38	144.9	14	85	0	0	85			4.75		Mar-14
100	-1.15	-0.24	4.98	15.76		1.25	2.05	10.91	0.79	29.19	144.9	14	85	0	0	85				1.00	Mar-14
	-1.07	0.02	5.64	18.29		1.79	1.3	10.93	0.79	29.53	144.9	14	85	0	0	85					May-15

	MARKET		FUND TYPE, CATEGORY & OBJECTIVE		RATINGS					MINIMUMS
Fund Name	Ticker Symbol	Traded On	Fund Type	Category and (Prospectus Objective)	Overall Rating	Reward Rating	Risk Rating	Recent Up/ Downgrade	Open to New Investors	Min Initial Investment
Guggenheim Risk Managed Real Estate Fund Institutional	GURIX	NAS CM	Open End	Real Estate Sector Equity (Real Estate)	B	B-	A-	Up	Y	2,000,000
Guggenheim Series Trust Managed Futures Strat Fund Cls A	RYMTX	NAS CM	Open End	Other Alternative (Growth & Income)	D+	D+	C-	Up	Y	2,500
Guggenheim Series Trust Managed Futures Strat Fund Cls C	RYMZX	NAS CM	Open End	Other Alternative (Growth & Income)	D+	D+	C-	Up	Y	2,500
Guggenheim Series Trust Managed Futures Strat Fund Cls I	RYIFX	NAS CM	Open End	Other Alternative (Growth & Income)	D+	D+	C-	Up	Y	2,000,000
Guggenheim Small Cap Value Fund Class A	SSUAX	NAS CM	Open End	US Equity Small Cap (Small Company)	B-	B-	B-	Up	Y	2,500
Guggenheim Small Cap Value Fund Class C	SSVCX	NAS CM	Open End	US Equity Small Cap (Small Company)	B-	B-	B-	Up	Y	2,500
Guggenheim Small Cap Value Fund Class P	SSUPX	NAS CM	Open End	US Equity Small Cap (Small Company)	B-	B-	B-	Up	Y	0
Guggenheim Small Cap Value Institutional Fund	SSUIX	NAS CM	Open End	US Equity Small Cap (Small Company)	B-	B-	B-	Up	Y	2,000,000
Guggenheim StylePlus - Large Core Fund Class A	SECEX	NAS CM	Open End	US Equity Large Cap Blend (Growth)	B	B	B		Y	2,500
Guggenheim StylePlus - Large Core Fund Class C	SFECX	NAS CM	Open End	US Equity Large Cap Blend (Growth)	B-	B-	B	Down	Y	2,500
Guggenheim StylePlus - Large Core Fund Class P	SFEPX	NAS CM	Open End	US Equity Large Cap Blend (Growth)	B	B	B		Y	0
Guggenheim StylePlus - Large Core Fund Institutional	GILIX	NAS CM	Open End	US Equity Large Cap Blend (Growth)	B	B	B		Y	2,000,000
Guggenheim StylePlus - Mid Growth Fund Class A	SECUX	NAS CM	Open End	US Equity Mid Cap (Growth)	B	B	B-	Up	Y	2,500
Guggenheim StylePlus - Mid Growth Fund Class C	SUFCX	NAS CM	Open End	US Equity Mid Cap (Growth)	B-	B	C+	Down	Y	2,500
Guggenheim StylePlus - Mid Growth Fund Class P	SEUPX	NAS CM	Open End	US Equity Mid Cap (Growth)	B	B	B-	Up	Y	0
Guggenheim StylePlus - Mid Growth Fund Institutional	GIUIX	NAS CM	Open End	US Equity Mid Cap (Growth)	B	B	B-	Up	Y	2,000,000
Guggenheim World Equity Income Fund Class A	SEQAX	NAS CM	Open End	Global Equity (World Stock)	B-	C+	B	Down	Y	2,500
Guggenheim World Equity Income Fund Class C	SFGCX	NAS CM	Open End	Global Equity (World Stock)	B-	C+	B	Down	Y	2,500
Guggenheim World Equity Income Fund Class P	SEQPX	NAS CM	Open End	Global Equity (World Stock)	B-	C+	B	Down	Y	0
Guggenheim World Equity Income Fund Institutional Class	SEWIX	NAS CM	Open End	Global Equity (World Stock)	B-	C+	B	Down	Y	2,000,000
GuideMark® Emerging Markets Fund Service Shares	GMLVX	NAS CM	Open End	Emerging Markets Equity (Div Emerging Mkts)	B+	A	B-	Up	Y	0
GuideMark® Large Cap Core Fund Institutional Shares	GILGX	NAS CM	Open End	US Equity Large Cap Growth (Growth)	B	B	B	Up	Y	0
GuideMark® Large Cap Core Fund Service Shares	GMLGX	NAS CM	Open End	US Equity Large Cap Growth (Growth)	B-	B-	B	Down	Y	0
GuideMark® Small/Mid Cap Core Fund Institutional Shares	GISMX	NAS CM	Open End	US Equity Small Cap (Growth)	C+	C+	B-	Down	Y	0
GuideMark® Small/Mid Cap Core Fund Service Shares	GMSMX	NAS CM	Open End	US Equity Small Cap (Growth)	B	B	B	Up	Y	0
GuideMark® World ex-US Fund Institutional Shares	GIWEX	NAS CM	Open End	Global Equity Large Cap (Foreign Stock)	B-	B-	B-	Up	Y	0
GuideMark® World ex-US Fund Service Shares	GMWEX	NAS CM	Open End	Global Equity Large Cap (Foreign Stock)	B-	C+	B-	Up	Y	0
GuidePath® Absolute Return Allocation Fund Inst Shares	GIARX	NAS CM	Open End	Cautious Alloc (Asset Alloc)	B-	C+	B	Down	Y	0
GuidePath® Absolute Return Allocation Fund Service Shares	GPARX	NAS CM	Open End	Cautious Alloc (Asset Alloc)	B-	C	B	Up	Y	0
GuidePath® Conservative Allocation Fund Inst Shares	GITTX	NAS CM	Open End	Aggressive Alloc (Asset Alloc)	B-	C	B	Up	Y	0
GuidePath® Conservative Allocation Fund Service Shares	GPTCX	NAS CM	Open End	Aggressive Alloc (Asset Alloc)	B-	C	B	Up	Y	0
GuidePath® Growth Allocation Fund Institutional Shares	GISRX	NAS CM	Open End	Global Equity (Asset Alloc)	C+	B-	C+	Down	Y	0
GuidePath® Growth Allocation Fund Service Shares	GPSTX	NAS CM	Open End	Global Equity (Asset Alloc)	B-	B-	B	Up	Y	0
GuidePath® Managed Futures Strategy Fund Inst Shares	GIFMX	NAS CM	Open End	Other Alternative (Growth & Income)	C-	D+	C-	Up	Y	0
GuidePath® Managed Futures Strategy Fund Service Shares	GPMFX	NAS CM	Open End	Other Alternative (Growth & Income)	C-	D+	C-	Up	Y	0
GuidePath® Multi-Asset Income Alloc Fund Serv Shares	GPMIX	NAS CM	Open End	Alloc (Multi-Asset Global)	B-	C+	B		Y	0
GuidePath® Tactical Allocation Fund Institutional Shares	GITUX	NAS CM	Open End	Moderate Alloc (Balanced)	C+	C+	B-	Down	Y	0
GuidePath® Tactical Allocation Fund Service Shares	GPTUX	NAS CM	Open End	Moderate Alloc (Balanced)	C+	C+	B-	Up	Y	0
GuideStone Funds Aggressive Allocation Fund Inst Cls	GAGYX	NAS CM	Open End	Global Equity (Asset Alloc)	B-	B-	C+	Down	Y	1,000,000
GuideStone Funds Aggressive Allocation Fund Investor Class	GGBZX	NAS CM	Open End	Global Equity (Asset Alloc)	B-	B-	C+	Down	Y	1,000
GuideStone Funds Balanced Allocation Fund Inst Cls	GBAYX	NAS CM	Open End	Cautious Alloc (Balanced)	B-	C+	B	Up	Y	1,000,000
GuideStone Funds Balanced Allocation Fund Investor Class	GGIZX	NAS CM	Open End	Cautious Alloc (Balanced)	B-	C+	B	Up	Y	1,000
GuideStone Funds Conservative Allocation Fund Inst Cls	GCAYX	NAS CM	Open End	Cautious Alloc (Asset Alloc)	B-	C	B	Up	Y	1,000,000
GuideStone Funds Conservative Allocation Fund Investor Cls	GFIZX	NAS CM	Open End	Cautious Alloc (Asset Alloc)	B-	C	B	Up	Y	1,000
GuideStone Funds Defensive Mkt Strategies Fund Inst Cls	GDMYX	NAS CM	Open End	Moderate Alloc (Growth)	B	B-	A-	Up	Y	1,000,000
GuideStone Funds Defensive Mkt Strategies Fund Inv Cls	GDMZX	NAS CM	Open End	Moderate Alloc (Growth)	B	B-	A-	Up	Y	1,000
GuideStone Funds Emerging Mkts Equity Fund Inst Cls	GEMYX	NAS CM	Open End	Emerging Markets Equity (Div Emerging Mkts)	C+	B-	C	Up	Y	1,000,000
GuideStone Funds Emerging Markets Equity Fund Investor Cls	GEMZX	NAS CM	Open End	Emerging Markets Equity (Div Emerging Mkts)	C+	B-	C	Up	Y	1,000
GuideStone Funds Equity Index Fund Institutional Class	GEQYX	NAS CM	Open End	US Equity Large Cap Blend (Growth)	B	B	B		Y	1,000,000
GuideStone Funds Equity Index Fund Investor Class	GEQZX	NAS CM	Open End	US Equity Large Cap Blend (Growth)	B	B	B		Y	1,000
GuideStone Funds Global Real Estate Sec Fund Inst Cls	GREYX	NAS CM	Open End	Real Estate Sector Equity (Real Estate)	B-	C+	B		Y	1,000,000
GuideStone Funds Global Real Estate Sec Fund Inv Cls	GREZX	NAS CM	Open End	Real Estate Sector Equity (Real Estate)	B-	C+	B		Y	1,000

★ Expanded analysis of this fund is included in Section II.

Min Additional Investment	3-Month Total Return	6-Month Total Return	1-Year Total Return	3-Year Total Return	5-Year Total Return	Dividend Yield (TTM)	Expense Ratio	3-Yr Std Deviation	3-Year Beta	NAV	Total Assets (MIL)	%Cash	%Stocks	%Bonds	%Other	Turnover Ratio	Last Bull Market Total Return	Last Bear Market Total Return	Front End Fee (%)	Back End Fee (%)	Inception Date
	TOTAL RETURNS					PERFORMANCE				ASSETS		ASSET ALLOCATION & TURNOVER					BULL & BEAR		FEES		
	-1.09	0.06	5.87	19.23		2.01	1.02	10.93	0.79	29.71	144.9	14	85	0	0	85					Mar-14
	3.90	8.68	7.40	-9.74	3.90	4.87	1.85	9.72	-27.85	19.19	51.5	35	3	30	33	16	-8.56	-7.81	4.75		Mar-07
	3.69	8.27	6.64	-11.75	0.05	5.32	2.62	9.71	-28.4	17.49	51.5	35	3	30	33	16	-8.98	-8.06		1.00	Mar-07
	3.98	8.89	7.69	-9.07	5.17	4.77	1.62	9.74	-27.78	19.62	51.5	35	3	30	33	16	-8.44	-7.71			May-10
100	0.99	3.96	3.48	19.94	65.15	0.53	1.32	12.7	0.87	14.78	21.3	1	99	0	0	48	29.9	-25.87	4.75		Jul-08
100	0.76	3.55	2.67	17.23	58.90	0	2.07	12.7	0.87	13.65	21.3	1	99	0	0	48	29.45	-26.13		1.00	Jul-08
	0.96	3.93	3.45	19.93	65.03	0.44	1.32	12.75	0.87	14.94	21.3	1	99	0	0	48	29.97	-25.88			May-15
	1.09	4.10	3.74	20.89	67.18	0.8	1.07	12.74	0.87	13.5	21.3	1	99	0	0	48	30.16	-25.8			Jul-08
100	6.81	11.54	21.94	37.70	108.63	0.6	1.4	10.26	1.02	22.7	223.2	13	21	36	29	30	25.4	-20.65	4.75		Sep-62
100	6.58	11.08	20.92	34.05	99.22	0	2.34	10.27	1.02	16.98	223.2	13	21	36	29	30	24.78	-20.88		1.00	Jan-99
	6.78	11.50	21.93	37.23	107.92	0.73	1.28	10.3	1.02	22.5	223.2	13	21	36	29	30	25.4	-20.65			May-15
	6.94	11.74	22.32	39.42	111.30	0.87	1.06	10.4	1.03	22.54	223.2	13	21	36	29	30	25.4	-20.65			Mar-12
100	6.44	11.67	24.14	32.25	97.66	0.48	1.52	11.18	1.01	44.64	88.4	12	24	37	27	43	27.97	-20.55	4.75		Sep-69
100	6.24	11.23	23.10	28.94	89.08	0	2.41	11.17	1.01	32.35	88.4	12	24	37	27	43	27.41	-20.83		1.00	Jan-99
	6.41	11.61	24.02	31.66	96.78	0.67	1.44	11.13	1	44.2	88.4	12	24	37	27	43	27.97	-20.55			May-15
	6.55	11.88	24.51	32.75	98.50	0.62	1.53	11.18	1.01	44.68	88.4	12	24	37	27	43	28.04	-20.55			Mar-12
100	4.00	8.63	14.70	23.46	57.16	2.28	1.24	7.72	0.68	15.4	91.4	1	99	0	0	94	10.26	-21.2	4.75		Oct-93
100	3.77	8.18	13.79	20.62	51.32	1.76	1.99	7.75	0.68	13.2	91.4	1	99	0	0	94	9.84	-21.48		1.00	Jan-99
	3.92	8.60	14.65	24.38	58.34	2.09	1.23	7.71	0.68	15.64	91.4	1	99	0	0	94	10.26	-21.2			May-15
	4.07	8.76	14.98	24.31	59.30	2.47	0.98	7.72	0.68	15.3	91.4	1	99	0	0	94	9.6	-21.2			May-11
	6.42	15.91	38.26	34.98	104.63	0.26	1.7	13.23	0.68	16.51	111.1	1	99	0	0	60	24.33	-20.72			Jun-01
	7.29	12.23	21.34	31.43	98.29	1.01	0.66	9.87	0.93	17.72	302.6	1	99	0	0	90	27.51	-20.05			Apr-11
	7.13	12.00	20.67	29.17	92.70	0.58	1.23	9.85	0.93	17.49	302.6	1	99	0	0	90	27.12	-20.34			Jun-01
	0.00	-0.10	5.18	15.42	77.23	0.65	0.92	11.51	0.88	18.88	54.9	1	99	0	0	42	32.72	-26.85			Apr-11
	4.47	8.90	14.37	23.92	87.94	0.24	1.5	11.92	0.95	14.87	54.9	1	99	0	0	42	32.37	-27.1			Jun-01
	4.04	10.54	27.64	23.35	37.87	1.62	0.83	11.15	0.9	9.74	200.7	1	99	0	0	61	16.23	-25.48			Apr-11
	3.81	9.22	25.93	20.11	32.68	1.5	1.43	11.14	0.9	9.5	200.7	1	99	0	0	61	15.98	-25.6			Jun-01
	0.47	1.82	5.04	14.64	18.67	3.76	1.22	2.6	18.22	10.41	245.8	8	6	85	1	42	2.96	-2			Sep-12
	0.34	1.49	4.49	12.56	15.14	3.04	1.82	2.51	17.54	10.44	245.8	8	6	85	1	42	2.96	-2			Apr-11
	2.43	5.27	12.21	9.39	34.47	0	0.76	6.86	1.67	9.66	241.6	4	43	52	1	44	16.12	-15.9			Sep-12
	2.33	4.85	11.56	7.37	30.35	0	1.35	6.87	1.68	9.61	241.6	4	43	52	1	44	16.12	-15.9			Apr-11
	5.14	11.02	22.65	24.73	58.60	1.49	0.75	9.65	1.17	11.61	553.9	2	98	0	0	43	20.31	-21.29			Sep-12
	4.97	10.70	21.91	22.63	53.96	1.07	1.34	9.66	1.17	11.55	553.9	2	98	0	0	43	20.31	-21.3			Apr-11
	5.10	7.98	5.59			0	1.34			9.06	101.8	-21	72	39	11	0					Jan-16
	4.84	7.74	4.96			0	1.94			8.95	101.8	-21	72	39	11	0					Jan-16
	1.97	3.84	9.73	13.47	26.79	2.53	1.61	5.43	0.91	10.9	120.3	2	50	40	1	61					Aug-12
	5.67	10.51	19.51	17.03	38.75	1.05	0.65	6.58	0.72	11.08	262.7	-8	95	13	0	337	9.48	-13.5			Sep-12
	5.49	10.17	18.88	14.93	34.69	0.89	1.24	6.58	0.72	11.05	262.7	-8	95	13	0	337	9.48	-13.5			Apr-11
	5.28	11.51	25.88	29.94	75.30	0	0.95	10.84	0.99	12.28	1,049	5	94	0	1	2	22.89	-20.59			Nov-15
100	5.26	11.42	25.48	29.28	74.41	0	1.21	10.83	0.99	12.24	1,049	5	94	0	1	2	22.89	-20.59			Aug-01
	2.74	5.88	12.56	16.28	33.88	0.88	0.77	5.65	0.2	12.16	1,604	7	44	44	3	4	12.39	-9.11			Nov-15
100	2.67	5.81	12.30	15.68	33.19	0.65	1.02	5.64	0.21	12.16	1,604	7	44	44	3	4	12.39	-9.11			Aug-01
	1.45	3.43	7.33	10.69	16.94	1.31	0.7	3.28	-0.22	11.47	514.5	13	25	56	4	5	6.69	-4.15			Nov-15
100	1.42	3.31	7.10	10.17	16.39	1.08	0.97	3.27	-0.28	11.47	514.5	13	25	56	4	5	6.69	-4.15			Aug-01
	3.32	6.22	12.73	28.21	70.68	0.68	0.69	5.49	0.53	12.68	964.8	11	47	14	1	78	12.25				Sep-11
100	3.25	5.98	12.34	27.12	68.41	0.47	0.97	5.52	0.53	12.68	964.8	11	47	14	1	78	12.06				Sep-11
	6.09	14.39	35.79	24.63		1.35	1.33	16.34	1.02	11	475.4	5	89	0	2	54					Oct-13
100	6.09	14.29	35.36	23.76		1.19	1.58	16.34	1.02	11	475.4	5	89	0	2	54					Oct-13
	6.77	11.74	21.96	36.70	110.68	1.47	0.17	10.17	1.01	29.43	962.8	3	97	0	0	3	24.73	-15.18			Aug-01
100	6.74	11.62	21.65	35.58	108.46	1.26	0.43	10.19	1.01	29.45	962.8	3	97	0	0	3	24.71	-15.33			Aug-01
	4.34	5.88	11.04	14.57	38.44	3.83	0.88	10.52	0.95	9.69	227.5	2	97	0	1	130	32.34	-17.74			Apr-15
100	4.20	5.73	10.72	13.85	37.57	3.54	1.17	10.55	0.95	9.72	227.5	2	97	0	1	130	32.34	-17.74			Dec-06

Fund Name	Ticker Symbol	Traded On	Fund Type	Category and (Prospectus Objective)	Overall Rating	Reward Rating	Risk Rating	Recent Up/ Downgrade	Open to New Investors	Min Initial Investment
	MARKET			FUND TYPE, CATEGORY & OBJECTIVE	RATINGS					MINIMUMS
GuideStone Funds Growth Allocation Fund Institutional Cls	GGRYX	NAS CM	Open End	Aggressive Alloc (Asset Alloc)	B-	C+	B-	Down	Y	1,000,000
GuideStone Funds Growth Allocation Fund Investor Class	GCOZX	NAS CM	Open End	Aggressive Alloc (Asset Alloc)	B-	C+	B-	Down	Y	1,000
GuideStone Funds Growth Equity Fund Institutional Class	GGEYX	NAS CM	Open End	US Equity Large Cap Growth (Growth)	B+	B+	B+	Up	Y	1,000,000
GuideStone Funds Growth Equity Fund Investor Class	GGEZX	NAS CM	Open End	US Equity Large Cap Growth (Growth)	B+	B+	B+	Up	Y	1,000
GuideStone Funds Intl Equity Fund Inst Cls	GIEYX	NAS CM	Open End	Global Equity Large Cap (Foreign Stock)	B	B	B	Up	Y	1,000,000
GuideStone Funds International Equity Fund Investor Class	GIEZX	NAS CM	Open End	Global Equity Large Cap (Foreign Stock)	B	B	B	Up	Y	1,000
GuideStone Funds Intl Equity Index Fund Inst Cls	GIIYX	NAS CM	Open End	Global Equity Large Cap (Foreign Stock)	C	C+	B-	Up	Y	1,000,000
GuideStone Funds MyDestination 2015 Fund Institutional	GMTYX	NAS CM	Open End	Target Date 2000-2020 (Asset Alloc)	B-	C+	B	Up	Y	1,000,000
GuideStone Funds MyDestination 2015 Fund Investor Class	GMTZX	NAS CM	Open End	Target Date 2000-2020 (Asset Alloc)	B-	C+	B	Up	Y	1,000
GuideStone Funds MyDestination 2025 Fund Institutional	GMWYX	NAS CM	Open End	Target Date 2021-2045 (Asset Alloc)	B-	C+	B	Down	Y	1,000,000
GuideStone Funds MyDestination 2025 Fund Investor Class	GMWZX	NAS CM	Open End	Target Date 2021-2045 (Asset Alloc)	B-	C+	B	Down	Y	1,000
GuideStone Funds MyDestination 2035 Fund Institutional	GMHYX	NAS CM	Open End	Target Date 2021-2045 (Asset Alloc)	B-	C+	B-	Down	Y	1,000,000
GuideStone Funds MyDestination 2035 Fund Investor Class	GMHZX	NAS CM	Open End	Target Date 2021-2045 (Asset Alloc)	B-	C+	B-	Down	Y	1,000
GuideStone Funds MyDestination 2045 Fund Institutional	GMYYX	NAS CM	Open End	Target Date 2021-2045 (Asset Alloc)	C+	B-	C+	Down	Y	1,000,000
GuideStone Funds MyDestination 2045 Fund Investor Class	GMFZX	NAS CM	Open End	Target Date 2021-2045 (Asset Alloc)	C+	B-	C+	Down	Y	1,000
GuideStone Funds MyDestination 2055 Fund Institutional	GMGYX	NAS CM	Open End	Target Date 2046+ (Asset Alloc)	C+	B-	C+	Down	Y	1,000,000
GuideStone Funds MyDestination 2055 Fund Investor Class	GMGZX	NAS CM	Open End	Target Date 2046+ (Asset Alloc)	C+	B-	C+	Down	Y	1,000
GuideStone Funds Small Cap Equity Fund Institutional Class	GSCYX	NAS CM	Open End	US Equity Small Cap (Small Company)	B	B	B	Up	Y	1,000,000
GuideStone Funds Small Cap Equity Fund Investor Class	GSCZX	NAS CM	Open End	US Equity Small Cap (Small Company)	B	B	B	Up	Y	1,000
GuideStone Funds Strategic Alternatives Fund Institutional	GFSYX	NAS CM	Open End	Multialternative (Income)	U	U	U		Y	1,000,000
GuideStone Funds Strategic Alternatives Fund Investor	GFSZX	NAS CM	Open End	Multialternative (Income)	U	U	U		Y	1,000
GuideStone Funds Value Equity Fund Institutional Class	GVEYX	NAS CM	Open End	US Equity Large Cap Value (Growth)	B	B-	B	Up	Y	1,000,000
GuideStone Funds Value Equity Fund Investor Class	GVEZX	NAS CM	Open End	US Equity Large Cap Value (Growth)	B-	B-	B	Down	Y	1,000
Guinness Atkinson Alternative Energy Fund	GAAEX	NAS CM	Open End	Global Equity Mid/Small Cap (Growth)	C-	C-	C-	Up	Y	5,000
Guinness Atkinson Asia Focus Fund	IASMX	NAS CM	Open End	Asia ex-Japan Equity (Pacific Stock)	B	A	C+	Up	Y	5,000
Guinness Atkinson Asia Pacific Dividend Builder Fund	GAADX	NAS CM	Open End	Asia ex-Japan Equity (Growth & Income)	B+	A	B-	Up	Y	5,000
Guinness Atkinson China And Hong Kong Fund	ICHKX	NAS CM	Open End	Greater China Equity (Pacific Stock)	B	A	C+	Up	Y	5,000
Guinness Atkinson Dividend Builder Fund	GAINX	NAS CM	Open End	Global Equity (Equity-Income)	B-	C+	B	Down	Y	10,000
Guinness Atkinson Global Energy Fund	GAGEX	NAS CM	Open End	Energy Sector Equity (Growth)	C-	C-	C-	Up	Y	5,000
Guinness Atkinson™ Global Innovators Fund Inst Cls	GINNX	NAS CM	Open End	US Equity Large Cap Blend (Growth)	B+	A	C+	Up	Y	100,000
Guinness Atkinson™ Global Innovators Fund Investor Class	IWIRX	NAS CM	Open End	US Equity Large Cap Blend (Growth)	B+	A	C+	Up	Y	5,000
Hamlin High Dividend Equity Fund Institutional Cls Shares	HHDFX	NAS CM	Open End	US Equity Large Cap Value (Equity-Income)	B-	B-	B		Y	100,000
Hamlin High Dividend Equity Fund Investor Class Shares	HHDVX	NAS CM	Open End	US Equity Large Cap Value (Equity-Income)	B-	C+	B		Y	2,500
Hancock Horizon Burkenroad Small Cap Fund Class D	HYBUX	NAS CM	Open End	US Equity Small Cap (Small Company)	B	B	B	Up	Y	1,000
Hancock Horizon Burkenroad Small Cap Fund Inst Cls	HIBUX	NAS CM	Open End	US Equity Small Cap (Small Company)	B	B	B	Up	Y	1,000
Hancock Horizon Burkenroad Small Cap Fund Investor Class	HHBUX	NAS CM	Open End	US Equity Small Cap (Small Company)	B	B	B	Up	Y	1,000
Hancock Horizon Diversified Income Fund Class C	HHICX	NAS CM	Open End	Moderate Alloc (Income)	C	C	C		Y	1,000
Hancock Horizon Diversified Income Fund Institutional Cls	HHIIX	NAS CM	Open End	Moderate Alloc (Income)	C	C	C+		Y	1,000
Hancock Horizon Diversified Income Fund Investor Class	HHIAX	NAS CM	Open End	Moderate Alloc (Income)	C	C	C+		Y	1,000
Hancock Horizon Diversified International Fund Class C	HHDCX	NAS CM	Open End	Global Equity Large Cap (Foreign Stock)	C+	C+	C+	Up	Y	1,000
Hancock Horizon Diversified Intl Fund Inst Cls	HHDTX	NAS CM	Open End	Global Equity Large Cap (Foreign Stock)	C+	B-	C+	Up	Y	1,000
Hancock Horizon Diversified Intl Fund Inv Cls	HHDAX	NAS CM	Open End	Global Equity Large Cap (Foreign Stock)	C+	B-	C+	Up	Y	1,000
Hancock Horizon Dynamic Asset Allocation Fund Class C	HDACX	NAS CM	Open End	Alloc (Asset Alloc)	C+	C	B	Up	Y	1,000
Hancock Horizon Dynamic Asset Allocation Fund Inst Cls	HDAIX	NAS CM	Open End	Alloc (Asset Alloc)	C+	C	B	Up	Y	1,000
Hancock Horizon Dynamic Asset Allocation Fund Investor Cls	HDAAX	NAS CM	Open End	Alloc (Asset Alloc)	C+	C	B	Up	Y	1,000
Hancock Horizon International Small Cap Fund Class C	HICCX	NAS CM	Open End	Global Equity Mid/Small Cap (Small Company)	C+	C+	B-	Up	Y	1,000
Hancock Horizon Intl Small Cap Fund Inst Cls	HICIX	NAS CM	Open End	Global Equity Mid/Small Cap (Small Company)	C+	C+	B-	Up	Y	1,000
Hancock Horizon International Small Cap Fund Investor Cls	HISAX	NAS CM	Open End	Global Equity Mid/Small Cap (Small Company)	C+	C+	B-	Up	Y	1,000
Hancock Horizon Microcap Fund Class C	HMICX	NAS CM	Open End	US Equity Small Cap (Growth)	B-	C+	B	Up	Y	1,000
Hancock Horizon Microcap Fund Institutional Class	HMIIX	NAS CM	Open End	US Equity Small Cap (Growth)	B-	C+	B	Up	Y	1,000
Hancock Horizon Microcap Fund Investor Class	HMIAX	NAS CM	Open End	US Equity Small Cap (Growth)	B-	C+	B	Up	Y	1,000
Hancock Horizon Quantitative Long/Short Fund Class C	HHQCX	NAS CM	Open End	Long/Short Equity (Growth)	B-	C	B+	Up	Y	1,000

★Expanded analysis of this fund is included in Section II.

Min Additional Investment	TOTAL RETURNS: 3-Month Total Return	6-Month Total Return	1-Year Total Return	3-Year Total Return	5-Year Total Return	PERFORMANCE: Dividend Yield (TTM)	Expense Ratio	3-Yr Std Deviation	3-Year Beta	ASSETS: NAV	Total Assets (MIL)	ASSET ALLOCATION & TURNOVER: %Cash	%Stocks	%Bonds	%Other	Turnover Ratio	BULL & BEAR: Last Bull Market Total Return	Last Bear Market Total Return	FEES: Front End Fee (%)	Back End Fee (%)	Inception Date
	4.04	8.72	18.93	22.16	51.50	0.87	0.87	8.36	-0.12	12.43	1,243	7	70	21	2	4	18.14	-15.45			Nov-15
100	3.98	8.58	18.58	21.49	50.67	0.66	1.13	8.36	-0.12	12.42	1,243	7	70	21	2	4	18.14	-15.45			Aug-01
	6.46	12.61	32.43	37.45	110.07	0.06	0.73	12.21	1.07	25.18	1,734	3	96	0	0	24	29.39	-15.81			Aug-01
100	6.35	12.46	32.06	36.31	107.45	0	0.99	12.21	1.07	25.11	1,734	3	96	0	0	24	29.28	-15.89			Aug-01
	3.49	11.24	29.84	30.25	48.14	1.6	0.81	11.63	0.93	15.72	1,604	4	93	0	1	33	14.34	-24.88			Aug-01
100	3.38	11.04	29.50	29.10	46.18	1.4	1.08	11.6	0.93	15.74	1,604	4	93	0	1	33	14.16	-24.98			Aug-01
	3.82	9.27	24.68			2.06	0.58			10.76	184.5	5	93	0	0	6					Jun-15
	2.37	5.40	11.81	16.73	35.28		0.74	5.03		10.37	622.1	7	41	45	3	16	13.61	-10.19			May-17
100	2.43	5.26	11.66	16.58	35.10	1.29	0.96	5.02		10.38	622.1	7	41	45	3	16	13.61	-10.19			Dec-06
	3.28	7.00	15.07	20.11	45.68		0.81	6.65		10.25	1,083	5	55	32	2	17	17.36	-13.96			May-17
100	3.23	6.85	14.91	19.95	45.48	1.12	1.05	6.65		10.26	1,083	5	55	32	2	17	17.36	-13.96			Dec-06
	4.32	8.93	18.80	22.40	55.79		0.83	8.96		9.95	636.7	5	72	20	2	16	21.8	-18.61			May-17
100	4.20	8.80	18.53	22.13	55.45	0.72	1.06	8.96		9.95	636.7	5	72	20	2	16	21.81	-18.61			Dec-06
	4.84	10.13	21.15	24.54	60.89		0.85	9.99		9.6	478.1	5	83	11	1	16	22.89	-20.1			May-17
100	4.83	10.01	20.89	24.27	60.54	0.46	1.07	9.99		9.6	478.1	5	83	11	1	16	22.89	-20.1			Dec-06
	5.12	10.48	21.86	25.76	62.19		0.92	10.1		13.45	110.9	5	87	7	1	27					May-17
100	5.08	10.45	21.72	25.62	62.00	0.97	1.12	10.1		13.45	110.9	5	87	7	1	27					Dec-11
	4.68	10.40	12.98	24.24	84.03	0.33	1	13.88	0.97	18.36	556.8	4	95	0	0	77	28.84	-23.72			Aug-01
100	4.62	10.21	12.66	23.34	81.86	0.13	1.27	13.88	0.97	18.37	556.8	4	95	0	0	77	28.87	-23.82			Aug-01
	0.10	1.40					1.13			10.07	331.4	24	15	57	4						Jun-17
100	0.00	1.30					1.42			10.07	331.4	24	15	57	4						Jun-17
	6.12	10.11	15.54	26.04	94.51	1.53	0.59	11.21	1.07	22.76	1,503	3	97	0	0	36	26.16	-19.81			Aug-01
100	6.07	10.01	15.24	25.10	92.03	1.31	0.86	11.18	1.06	22.78	1,503	3	97	0	0	36	26.12	-19.92			Aug-01
250	2.33	10.54	20.67	-11.17	24.14	0	1.98	18.22	0.76	3.02	10.6	2	98	0	0	64	-9.66	-48.34			Mar-06
250	11.38	19.81	47.09	42.24	31.38	1	1.98	16.94	1.03	22.59	19.8	1	99	0	0	38	17.13	-31.5			Apr-96
250	7.82	14.43	36.70	41.88	52.63	2.85	1.1	13.29	0.82	17.85	7.4	2	98	0	0	31	20.78	-22.54			Mar-06
250	10.74	20.30	48.85	42.17	49.75	0.95	1.67	19.73	1.03	26.55	78.4	1	99	0	0	28	23.33	-34.42			Jun-94
1,000	5.70	8.01	21.33	24.15	71.84	2.59	0.68	9.78	0.85	18.09	9.0	0	99	0	0	22					Mar-12
250	5.85	16.67	-1.05	-8.42	-6.26	1.2	1.45	22.14	1.22	22.71	31.5	-1	101	0	0	15	18.1	-34.12			Jun-04
5,000	6.31	15.71	35.06	42.59	138.54	0.76	0.99	13.11	1.14	45.09	225.4	2	98	0	0	31	24.44	-21.04			Dec-15
250	6.24	15.55	34.74	41.86	137.33	0.69	1.24	13.09	1.13	44.98	225.4	2	98	0	0	31	24.44	-21.04			Dec-98
	5.50	9.97	14.85	24.54	88.98	2.47	1.01	10.6	0.93	23.46	891.0	11	89	0	0	42					Mar-12
	5.37	9.79	14.38	23.06	84.21	2.11	1.39	10.62	0.93	23.49	891.0	11	89	0	0	42					Mar-12
100	4.46	10.47	10.09	29.51	83.23	0	1.64	13.66	0.9	65.34	718.3	3	97	0	0	38	28.67	-19.79			Dec-01
100	4.71	10.88	10.75	31.15	86.48	0	1.14	13.67	0.9	68.11	718.3	3	97	0	0	38	28.86	-19.7			May-16
100	4.54	10.62	10.37	30.48	85.54	0	1.39	13.66	0.9	67.88	718.3	3	97	0	0	38	28.86	-19.7	5.25		Dec-01
100	0.07	0.62	3.99	0.44	9.54	3.63	2.06	5.68	0.5	13.19	55.0	2	34	47	0						Sep-12
100	0.25	1.13	5.02	3.48	15.11	4.62	1.06	5.69	0.51	13.24	55.0	2	34	47	0						Sep-12
100	0.26	1.08	4.76	2.77	13.84	4.37	1.31	5.7	0.51	13.23	55.0	2	34	47	0				4.25		Sep-12
100	3.84	10.51	27.01	18.09	24.14	0.11	2.24	12.78	1.02	24.59	280.0	3	97	0	0	29	12.23	-25.05			Sep-08
100	4.12	11.06	28.30	21.70	30.53	0.93	1.24	12.81	1.02	25.23	280.0	3	97	0	0	29	12.96	-24.76			Sep-08
100	4.06	10.91	28.00	20.67	28.75	0.61	1.49	12.79	1.02	25.25	280.0	3	97	0	0	29	12.75	-24.8	5.25		Sep-08
100	3.28	5.89	10.99			0	2.68			15.88	5.3	9	60	30	0						May-15
100	3.50	6.43	12.04			0.64	1.68			15.98	5.3	9	60	30	0						May-15
100	3.49	6.36	11.82			0.36	1.93			15.98	5.3	9	60	30	0				5.25		May-15
100	5.98	15.48	33.47			0.43	2.56			17.94	16.4	14	86	0	1						May-15
100	6.03	15.54	33.79			1.2	1.56			17.97	16.4	14	86	0	1						May-15
100	6.01	15.47	33.55			0.95	1.81			17.98	16.4	14	86	0	1				5.25		May-15
100	1.72	7.67	9.03			0	2.5			18.62	14.2	3	97	0	0						May-15
100	1.95	8.20	10.10			0.22	1.5			19.07	14.2	3	97	0	0						May-15
100	1.85	8.05	9.83			0	1.75			18.99	14.2	3	97	0	0				5.25		May-15
100	2.52	4.47	6.55	7.55	46.97	0	2.11	5.53	0.44	17.33	158.7	39	61	0	0	126	20.3	-20.43			Sep-08

	MARKET		FUND TYPE, CATEGORY & OBJECTIVE		RATINGS				MINIMUMS	
Fund Name	Ticker Symbol	Traded On	Fund Type	Category and (Prospectus Objective)	Overall Rating	Reward Rating	Risk Rating	Recent Up/ Downgrade	Open to New Investors	Min Initial Investment
Hancock Horizon Quantitative Long/Short Fund Inst Cls	HHQTX	NAS CM	Open End	Long/Short Equity (Growth)	B	C	A+	Up	Y	1,000
Hancock Horizon Quantitative Long/Short Fund Investor Cls	HHQAX	NAS CM	Open End	Long/Short Equity (Growth)	B	C	A	Up	Y	1,000
Hancock Horizon U.S. Small Cap Fund Class C	HHSCX	NAS CM	Open End	US Equity Small Cap (Small Company)	B	B-	B	Up	Y	1,000
Hancock Horizon U.S. Small Cap Fund Institutional Class	HSCIX	NAS CM	Open End	US Equity Small Cap (Small Company)	B	B	B	Up	Y	1,000
Hancock Horizon U.S. Small Cap Fund Investor Class	HSCAX	NAS CM	Open End	US Equity Small Cap (Small Company)	B	B	B	Up	Y	1,000
Hanlon Tactical Dividend and Momentum Fund Class A	HTDAX	NAS CM	Open End	Moderate Alloc (Growth & Income)	C	C	B-	Up	Y	2,500
Hanlon Tactical Dividend and Momentum Fund Class C	HTDCX	NAS CM	Open End	Moderate Alloc (Growth & Income)	C	C	B-	Up	Y	2,500
Hanlon Tactical Dividend and Momentum Fund Class I	HTDIX	NAS CM	Open End	Moderate Alloc (Growth & Income)	C	C	B-	Up	Y	100,000
Hanlon Tactical Dividend and Momentum Fund Class R	HTDRX	NAS CM	Open End	Moderate Alloc (Growth & Income)	C	C	B-	Up	Y	2,500
Harbor Capital Appreciation Fund Administrative Class	HRCAX	NAS CM	Open End	US Equity Large Cap Growth (Growth)	A-	A	B+	Up	Y	50,000
Harbor Capital Appreciation Fund Institutional Class	HACAX	NAS CM	Open End	US Equity Large Cap Growth (Growth)	A-	A	B+	Up	Y	50,000
Harbor Capital Appreciation Fund Investor Class	HCAIX	NAS CM	Open End	US Equity Large Cap Growth (Growth)	A-	A	B+	Up	Y	2,500
Harbor Capital Appreciation Fund Retirement Class	HNACX	NAS CM	Open End	US Equity Large Cap Growth (Growth)	A-	A	B+	Up	Y	1,000,000
Harbor Commodity Real Return Strategy Fund Admin Cls	HCMRX	NAS CM	Open End	Commodities Broad Basket (Growth)	C-	C-	D+	Up	Y	50,000
Harbor Commodity Real Return Strategy Fund Inst Cls	HACMX	NAS CM	Open End	Commodities Broad Basket (Growth)	C-	C-	D+	Up	Y	1,000
Harbor Convertible Securities Fund Administrative Class	HRCSX	NAS CM	Open End	Convertibles (Convertible Bond)	B-	C+	B	Up	Y	50,000
Harbor Convertible Securities Fund Institutional Class	HACSX	NAS CM	Open End	Convertibles (Convertible Bond)	B	C+	A-	Up	Y	1,000
Harbor Convertible Securities Fund Investor Class	HICSX	NAS CM	Open End	Convertibles (Convertible Bond)	B	C	A-	Up	Y	2,500
Harbor Convertible Securities Fund Retirement Class	HNCVX	NAS CM	Open End	Convertibles (Convertible Bond)	B	C+	A-	Up	Y	1,000,000
Harbor Diversified Intl All Cap Fund Admin Cls	HRIDX	NAS CM	Open End	Global Equity Large Cap (Growth)	C	C	B	Up	Y	50,000
Harbor Diversified Intl All Cap Fund Inst Cls	HAIDX	NAS CM	Open End	Global Equity Large Cap (Growth)	C	C	B	Up	Y	50,000
Harbor Diversified International All Cap Fund Investor Cls	HIIDX	NAS CM	Open End	Global Equity Large Cap (Growth)	C	C	B	Up	Y	2,500
Harbor Diversified Intl All Cap Fund Retmnt Cls	HNIDX	NAS CM	Open End	Global Equity Large Cap (Growth)	C	C	B+	Up	Y	1,000,000
Harbor Emerging Markets Equity Fund Administrative Class	HREMX	NAS CM	Open End	Emerging Markets Equity (Growth)	C+	B-	C	Up	Y	50,000
Harbor Emerging Markets Equity Fund Institutional Class	HAEMX	NAS CM	Open End	Emerging Markets Equity (Growth)	C+	B-	C	Up	Y	50,000
Harbor Emerging Markets Equity Fund Investor Class	HIEEX	NAS CM	Open End	Emerging Markets Equity (Growth)	C+	B-	C	Up	Y	2,500
Harbor Emerging Markets Equity Fund Retirement Class	HNEMX	NAS CM	Open End	Emerging Markets Equity (Growth)	C+	B-	C	Up	Y	1,000,000
Harbor Global Leaders Fund Administrative Class	HRGAX	NAS CM	Open End	Global Equity (World Stock)	B	B-	B	Up	Y	50,000
Harbor Global Leaders Fund Institutional Class	HGGAX	NAS CM	Open End	Global Equity (World Stock)	B	B-	B	Up	Y	50,000
Harbor Global Leaders Fund Investor Class	HGGIX	NAS CM	Open End	Global Equity (World Stock)	B	B-	B	Up	Y	2,500
Harbor Global Leaders Fund Retirement Class	HNGIX	NAS CM	Open End	Global Equity (World Stock)	B	B-	B	Up	Y	1,000,000
Harbor International Fund Administrative Class	HRINX	NAS CM	Open End	Global Equity Large Cap (Foreign Stock)	C+	C+	B-	Up	Y	50,000
Harbor International Fund Institutional Class	HAINX	NAS CM	Open End	Global Equity Large Cap (Foreign Stock)	B-	C+	B-	Up	Y	50,000
Harbor International Fund Investor Class	HIINX	NAS CM	Open End	Global Equity Large Cap (Foreign Stock)	C+	C+	B-	Up	Y	2,500
Harbor International Fund Retirement Class	HNINX	NAS CM	Open End	Global Equity Large Cap (Foreign Stock)	B-	C+	B-	Up	Y	1,000,000
Harbor International Growth Fund Administrative Class	HRIGX	NAS CM	Open End	Global Equity Large Cap (Foreign Stock)	B	B	B	Up	Y	50,000
Harbor International Growth Fund Institutional Class	HAIGX	NAS CM	Open End	Global Equity Large Cap (Foreign Stock)	B	B	B	Up	Y	50,000
Harbor International Growth Fund Investor Class	HIIGX	NAS CM	Open End	Global Equity Large Cap (Foreign Stock)	B	B	B	Up	Y	2,500
Harbor International Growth Fund Retirement Class	HNGFX	NAS CM	Open End	Global Equity Large Cap (Foreign Stock)	B	B	B	Up	Y	1,000,000
Harbor International Small Cap Fund Administrative Class	HRISX	NAS CM	Open End	Global Equity Mid/Small Cap (Small Company)	C-	C	B+	Up	Y	50,000
Harbor International Small Cap Fund Institutional Class	HAISX	NAS CM	Open End	Global Equity Mid/Small Cap (Small Company)	C-	C	B+	Up	Y	50,000
Harbor International Small Cap Fund Investor Class	HIISX	NAS CM	Open End	Global Equity Mid/Small Cap (Small Company)	C-	C	B+	Up	Y	2,500
Harbor International Small Cap Fund Retirement Class	HNISX	NAS CM	Open End	Global Equity Mid/Small Cap (Small Company)	C-	C	B+	Up	Y	1,000,000
Harbor Large Cap Value Fund Administrative Class	HRLVX	NAS CM	Open End	US Equity Large Cap Blend (Growth & Income)	B	B	B		Y	50,000
Harbor Large Cap Value Fund Institutional Class	HAVLX	NAS CM	Open End	US Equity Large Cap Blend (Growth & Income)	B	B	B		Y	50,000
Harbor Large Cap Value Fund Investor Class	HILVX	NAS CM	Open End	US Equity Large Cap Blend (Growth & Income)	B	B	B		Y	2,500
Harbor Large Cap Value Fund Retirement Class	HNLVX	NAS CM	Open End	US Equity Large Cap Blend (Growth & Income)	B	B	B		Y	1,000,000
Harbor Mid Cap Growth Fund Administrative Class	HRMGX	NAS CM	Open End	US Equity Mid Cap (Growth)	B+	B+	B	Up	Y	50,000
Harbor Mid Cap Growth Fund Institutional Class	HAMGX	NAS CM	Open End	US Equity Mid Cap (Growth)	B+	A-	B	Up	Y	50,000
Harbor Mid Cap Growth Fund Investor Class	HIMGX	NAS CM	Open End	US Equity Mid Cap (Growth)	B	B+	B	Up	Y	2,500
Harbor Mid Cap Growth Fund Retirement Class	HNMGX	NAS CM	Open End	US Equity Mid Cap (Growth)	B+	A-	B	Up	Y	1,000,000
Harbor Mid Cap Value Fund Administrative Class	HRMVX	NAS CM	Open End	US Equity Mid Cap (Growth & Income)	B-	B-	B	Up	Y	50,000

★ Expanded analysis of this fund is included in Section II.

Min Additional Investment	3-Month Total Return	6-Month Total Return	1-Year Total Return	3-Year Total Return	5-Year Total Return	Dividend Yield (TTM)	Expense Ratio	3-Yr Std Deviation	3-Year Beta	NAV	Total Assets (MIL)	%Cash	%Stocks	%Bonds	%Other	Turnover Ratio	Last Bull Market Total Return	Last Bear Market Total Return	Front End Fee (%)	Back End Fee (%)	Inception Date
	TOTAL RETURNS					PERFORMANCE				ASSETS		ASSET ALLOCATION & TURNOVER					BULL & BEAR		FEES		
100	2.79	5.00	7.66	10.82	54.39	0	1.1	5.52	0.44	19.31	158.7	39	61	0	0	126	21.02	-20.09			Sep-08
100	3.02	5.17	7.66	10.32	52.93	0	1.37	5.56	0.44	18.89	158.7	39	61	0	0	126	20.79	-20.15	5.25		Sep-08
100	2.52	8.46	3.88	24.81		0	2.1	13.35	0.88	18.71	32.6	0	100	0	0						Dec-13
100	2.76	8.98	4.89	28.68		0.57	1.1	13.35	0.88	19.26	32.6	0	100	0	0						Dec-13
100	2.73	8.85	4.63	27.74		0.34	1.35	13.32	0.88	19.17	32.6	0	100	0	0				5.25		Dec-13
500	6.25	9.51	14.43			0	1.6			10.67	176.6	7	93	0	0	384			5.75		Sep-15
500	6.19	9.18	13.69			0.62	2.35			10.46	176.6	7	93	0	0	384				1.00	Sep-15
500	6.40	9.81	14.81			1.14	1.35			10.54	176.6	7	93	0	0	384					Sep-15
500	6.32	9.52	14.39			0.66	1.75			10.53	176.6	7	93	0	0	384					Sep-15
	7.15	16.31	36.25	47.65	128.51	0	0.9	12.7	1.11	68.24	29,337	2	98	0	0	34	26.75	-13.86			Nov-02
	7.21	16.46	36.59	48.76	131.38	0.08	0.65	12.7	1.11	69.44	29,337	2	98	0	0	34	26.94	-13.77			Dec-87
	7.11	16.23	36.08	47.11	127.12	0	1.02	12.7	1.11	66.99	29,337	2	98	0	0	34	26.67	-13.9			Nov-02
	7.23	16.50	36.68	48.90	131.60	0.12	0.57	12.7	1.11	69.41	29,337	2	98	0	0	34	26.94	-13.77			Mar-16
	3.27	6.81	0.69	-15.89	-41.20	0.9	1.19	14.59	1.11	3.65	50.6	2	0	75	23	1,069	5.75	-19.86			Sep-08
	3.32	6.92	1.02	-15.37	-40.53	1.15	0.94	14.51	1.1	3.66	50.6	2	0	75	23	1,069	5.97	-19.74			Sep-08
	0.80	2.37	7.97	12.95	30.12	1.28	0.98	5.45	0.64	10.24	114.5	2	0	1	1	102	9				May-11
	0.96	2.59	8.24	13.79	31.72	1.53	0.73	5.41	0.63	10.25	114.5	2	0	1	1	102	9.01				May-11
	0.76	2.30	7.86	12.47	29.26	1.18	1.1	5.4	0.63	10.23	114.5	2	0	1	1	102	8.83				May-11
	0.88	2.53	8.33	13.81	31.76	1.6	0.65	5.44	0.64	10.24	114.5	2	0	1	1	102	9.01				Mar-16
	3.53	8.80	24.28			0.88	1.1			11.59	350.1	5	92	0	2						Nov-15
	3.58	8.94	24.56			1.1	0.85			11.59	350.1	5	92	0	2						Nov-15
	3.41	8.70	23.99			1.09	1.22			11.53	350.1	5	92	0	2						Nov-15
	3.57	8.94	24.55			1.14	0.77			11.58	350.1	5	92	0	2						Mar-16
	4.00	12.10	32.62	19.73		0.71	1.4	17.45	1.09	10.86	56.6	2	93	0	5	49					Nov-13
	4.14	12.23	33.05	20.61		0.88	1.15	17.42	1.08	10.87	56.6	2	93	0	5	49					Nov-13
	3.98	11.98	32.51	19.23		0.64	1.52	17.43	1.08	10.85	56.6	2	93	0	5	49					Nov-13
	4.11	12.20	33.01	20.66		0.93	1.07	17.42	1.08	10.86	56.6	2	93	0	5	49					Mar-16
	5.83	10.99	31.09	26.70	88.52	0	1.15	11.74	0.95	23.79	47.8	1	99	0	0	76	30.3	-24.36			Mar-09
	5.92	11.14	31.43	27.68	90.95	0	0.9	11.74	0.95	24.15	47.8	1	99	0	0	76	30.5	-24.26			Mar-09
	5.81	10.97	30.90	26.29	87.49	0	1.27	11.73	0.95	23.53	47.8	1	99	0	0	76	30.23	-24.4			Mar-09
	5.90	11.16	31.50	27.81	91.14	0	0.82	11.74	0.96	24.16	47.8	1	99	0	0	76	30.5	-24.27			Mar-16
	2.10	5.72	22.57	17.11	28.87	1.4	0.97	12.6	0.99	67.39	31,937	0	94	0	6	14	21.26	-25.72			Nov-02
	2.18	5.87	22.89	18.00	30.51	1.65	0.72	12.6	0.99	67.52	31,937	0	94	0	6	14	21.44	-25.64			Dec-87
	2.08	5.67	22.44	16.68	28.11	1.28	1.09	12.6	0.99	66.98	31,937	0	94	0	6	14	21.18	-25.77			Nov-02
	2.20	5.91	22.98	18.12	30.64	1.71	0.64	12.6	0.99	67.48	31,937	0	94	0	6	14	21.44	-25.64			Mar-16
	4.34	9.27	30.77	32.05	45.95	0.84	1.1	12.85	0.98	15.81	403.4	1	97	0	2	19	20.83	-24.48			Nov-02
	4.44	9.44	31.06	33.11	47.88	1.05	0.85	12.84	0.98	15.81	403.4	1	97	0	2	19	20.95	-24.4			Nov-93
	4.33	9.21	30.63	31.61	45.13	0.73	1.22	12.81	0.98	15.74	403.4	1	97	0	2	19	20.75	-24.55			Nov-02
	4.50	9.51	31.34	33.37	48.16	1.1	0.77	12.84	0.98	15.82	403.4	1	97	0	2	19	20.95	-24.4			Mar-16
	5.56	13.60	37.34			0.7	1.2			14.17	48.1	5	95	0	1						Feb-16
	5.57	13.68	37.66			0.87	0.95			14.17	48.1	5	95	0	1						Feb-16
	5.54	13.49	37.21			0.6	1.32			14.17	48.1	5	95	0	1						Feb-16
	5.63	13.74	37.86			0.91	0.87			14.17	48.1	5	95	0	1						Feb-16
	5.88	10.30	21.93	44.51	113.16	0.75	0.93	10.97	1.01	14.94	805.0	3	97	0	0	34	24	-17.07			Nov-02
	5.96	10.37	22.30	45.79	115.88	0.86	0.68	10.96	1.01	14.93	805.0	3	97	0	0	34	24.11	-16.95			Dec-87
	5.86	10.30	21.85	44.23	111.98	0.56	1.05	10.94	1.01	15.08	805.0	3	97	0	0	34	23.95	-17.16			Nov-02
	6.00	10.49	22.38	46.10	116.34	0.92	0.6	10.97	1.01	14.93	805.0	3	97	0	0	34	24.11	-16.95			Mar-16
	5.91	10.34	31.89	32.88	95.72	0	1.12	13.37	1.12	9.87	420.8	4	96	0	0	84	24.15	-24.07			Nov-02
	5.96	10.43	32.23	33.84	98.23	0	0.87	13.36	1.12	10.31	420.8	4	96	0	0	84	24.36	-23.98			Nov-00
	5.85	10.28	31.67	32.38	94.62	0	1.24	13.36	1.12	9.59	420.8	4	96	0	0	84	24.01	-24.11			Nov-02
	6.04	10.51	32.31	34.07	98.57	0	0.79	13.37	1.12	10.33	420.8	4	96	0	0	84	24.36	-23.98			Mar-16
	5.58	8.66	11.67	23.27	108.21	1.25	1.11	11.9	1.08	23.74	1,015	0	99	0	1	18	29.22	-25.19			Nov-02

	MARKET			FUND TYPE, CATEGORY & OBJECTIVE	RATINGS					MINIMUMS
Fund Name	Ticker Symbol	Traded On	Fund Type	Category and (Prospectus Objective)	Overall Rating	Reward Rating	Risk Rating	Recent Up/ Downgrade	Open to New Investors	Min Initial Investment
Harbor Mid Cap Value Fund Institutional Class	HAMVX	NAS CM	Open End	US Equity Mid Cap (Growth & Income)	B	B-	B	Up	Y	50,000
Harbor Mid Cap Value Fund Investor Class	HIMVX	NAS CM	Open End	US Equity Mid Cap (Growth & Income)	B-	B-	B	Up	Y	2,500
Harbor Mid Cap Value Fund Retirement Class	HNMVX	NAS CM	Open End	US Equity Mid Cap (Growth & Income)	B	B-	B	Up	Y	1,000,000
Harbor Small Cap Growth Fund Administrative Class	HRSGX	NAS CM	Open End	US Equity Small Cap (Small Company)	B	B	B	Up		50,000
Harbor Small Cap Growth Fund Institutional Class	HASGX	NAS CM	Open End	US Equity Small Cap (Small Company)	B	B	B	Up		50,000
Harbor Small Cap Growth Fund Investor Class	HISGX	NAS CM	Open End	US Equity Small Cap (Small Company)	B	B	B-	Up		2,500
Harbor Small Cap Growth Fund Retirement Class	HNSGX	NAS CM	Open End	US Equity Small Cap (Small Company)	B	B+	C	Up	Y	1,000,000
Harbor Small Cap Growth Opp Fund Admin Cls	HRSOX	NAS CM	Open End	US Equity Small Cap (Small Company)	B-	B-	B	Up	Y	50,000
Harbor Small Cap Growth Opp Fund Inst Cls	HASOX	NAS CM	Open End	US Equity Small Cap (Small Company)	B-	B-	B	Up	Y	50,000
Harbor Small Cap Growth Opportunities Fund Investor Class	HISOX	NAS CM	Open End	US Equity Small Cap (Small Company)	B-	B-	B	Up	Y	2,500
Harbor Small Cap Growth Opportunities Fund Retirement Cls	HNSOX	NAS CM	Open End	US Equity Small Cap (Small Company)	B-	B-	B	Up	Y	1,000,000
Harbor Small Cap Value Fund Administrative Class	HSVRX	NAS CM	Open End	US Equity Small Cap (Small Company)	A-	A	B	Up	Y	50,000
Harbor Small Cap Value Fund Institutional Class	HASCX	NAS CM	Open End	US Equity Small Cap (Small Company)	A-	A	B	Up	Y	50,000
Harbor Small Cap Value Fund Investor Class	HISVX	NAS CM	Open End	US Equity Small Cap (Small Company)	A-	A	B	Up	Y	2,500
Harbor Small Cap Value Fund Retirement Class	HNVRX	NAS CM	Open End	US Equity Small Cap (Small Company)	A-	A	B	Up	Y	1,000,000
Harbor Small Cap Value Opp Fund Admin Cls	HSAVX	NAS CM	Open End	US Equity Small Cap (Small Company)	U	U	U		Y	50,000
Harbor Small Cap Value Opp Fund Inst Cls	HSOVX	NAS CM	Open End	US Equity Small Cap (Small Company)	U	U	U		Y	50,000
Harbor Small Cap Value Opportunities Fund Investor Class	HSIVX	NAS CM	Open End	US Equity Small Cap (Small Company)	U	U	U		Y	2,500
Harbor Small Cap Value Opportunities Fund Retirement Class	HSRVX	NAS CM	Open End	US Equity Small Cap (Small Company)	U	U	U		Y	1,000,000
Harbor Strategic Growth Fund Administrative Class	HSRGX	NAS CM	Open End	US Equity Large Cap Growth (Growth)	B	B-	A		Y	50,000
Harbor Strategic Growth Fund Institutional Class	MVSGX	NAS CM	Open End	US Equity Large Cap Growth (Growth)	B	B	B+		Y	50,000
Harbor Strategic Growth Fund Investor Class	HISWX	NAS CM	Open End	US Equity Large Cap Growth (Growth)	B	B-	B+		Y	2,500
Harbor Strategic Growth Fund Retirement Class	HNGSX	NAS CM	Open End	US Equity Large Cap Growth (Growth)	B	B	B+		Y	1,000,000
Harbor Target Retirement 2015 Fund Institutional Class	HARGX	NAS CM	Open End	Target Date 2000-2020 (Asset Alloc)	B	C+	A-	Up	Y	1,000
Harbor Target Retirement 2020 Fund Institutional Class	HARJX	NAS CM	Open End	Target Date 2000-2020 (Asset Alloc)	B	C+	B+	Up	Y	1,000
Harbor Target Retirement 2025 Fund Institutional Class	HARMX	NAS CM	Open End	Target Date 2021-2045 (Asset Alloc)	B-	C+	B	Up	Y	1,000
Harbor Target Retirement 2030 Fund Institutional Class	HARPX	NAS CM	Open End	Target Date 2021-2045 (Asset Alloc)	B	C+	B+	Up	Y	1,000
Harbor Target Retirement 2035 Fund Institutional Class	HARUX	NAS CM	Open End	Target Date 2021-2045 (Asset Alloc)	B-	C+	B-	Down	Y	1,000
Harbor Target Retirement 2040 Fund Institutional Class	HARYX	NAS CM	Open End	Target Date 2021-2045 (Asset Alloc)	B	C+	B+	Up	Y	1,000
Harbor Target Retirement 2045 Fund Institutional Class	HACCX	NAS CM	Open End	Target Date 2021-2045 (Asset Alloc)	B-	B-	B-	Down	Y	1,000
Harbor Target Retirement 2050 Fund Institutional Class	HAFFX	NAS CM	Open End	Target Date 2046+ (Asset Alloc)	B-	B-	B-	Down	Y	1,000
Harbor Target Retirement 2055 Fund Institutional Class	HATRX	NAS CM	Open End	Target Date 2046+ (Asset Alloc)	C+	C+	B-	Down	Y	1,000
Harbor Target Retirement Income Fund Institutional Class	HARAX	NAS CM	Open End	Target Date 2000-2020 (Asset Alloc)	B	C	A-	Up	Y	1,000
Harding Loevner Emerging Markets Portfolio Advisor Class	HLEMX	NAS CM	Open End	Emerging Markets Equity (Div Emerging Mkts)	B-	B	C	Up	Y	5,000
Harding Loevner Emerging Mkts Research Portfolio Inst Cls	HLREX	NAS CM	Open End	Emerging Markets Equity (Div Emerging Mkts)	D-	D+	B+		Y	100,000
Harding Loevner Emerging Mkts Research Portfolio Inv Cls	HLENX	NAS CM	Open End	Emerging Markets Equity (Div Emerging Mkts)	D-	D+	B+		Y	5,000
Harding Loevner Frontier Emerging Mkts Fund Inst Cls	HLFMX	NAS CM	Open End	Emerging Markets Equity (Div Emerging Mkts)	C	C	C	Up	Y	100,000
Harding Loevner Frontier Emerging Mkts Fund Inst Cls II	HLFFX	NAS CM	Open End	Emerging Markets Equity (Div Emerging Mkts)	C	C	C	Up	Y	10,000,000
Harding Loevner Frontier Emerging Mkts Fund Inv Cls	HLMOX	NAS CM	Open End	Emerging Markets Equity (Div Emerging Mkts)	C	C	C	Up	Y	5,000
Harding Loevner Global Equity Portfolio Advisor Class	HLMGX	NAS CM	Open End	Global Equity (World Stock)	B	B	B+	Up	Y	5,000
Harding Loevner Global Equity Portfolio Institutional Cls	HLMVX	NAS CM	Open End	Global Equity (World Stock)	B	B	B+	Up	Y	100,000
Harding Loevner Global Equity Portfolio Inst Cls Z	HLGZX	NAS CM	Open End	Global Equity (World Stock)	B	B	B+		Y	10,000,000
Harding Loevner Global Equity Research Portfolio Inst Cls	HLRGX	NAS CM	Open End	Global Equity (World Stock)	D-	D+	A		Y	100,000
Harding Loevner Global Equity Research Portfolio Inv Cls	HLGNX	NAS CM	Open End	Global Equity (World Stock)	D-	D+	A		Y	5,000
Harding Loevner Inst Emerging Mkts Portfolio Cls I	HLMEX	NAS CM	Open End	Emerging Markets Equity (Div Emerging Mkts)	B-	B	C	Up	Y	500,000
Harding Loevner Inst Emerging Mkts Portfolio Cls II	HLEEX	NAS CM	Open End	Emerging Markets Equity (Div Emerging Mkts)	B-	B	C	Up		25,000,000
Harding Loevner Intl Equity Portfolio Inst Cls	HLMIX	NAS CM	Open End	Global Equity Large Cap (Foreign Stock)	B	B	B-	Up	Y	100,000
Harding Loevner Intl Equity Portfolio Inst Cls Z	HLIZX	NAS CM	Open End	Global Equity Large Cap (Foreign Stock)	B	B	B-	Up	Y	10,000,000
Harding Loevner Intl Equity Portfolio Inv Cls	HLMNX	NAS CM	Open End	Global Equity Large Cap (Foreign Stock)	B	B	B-	Up	Y	5,000
Harding Loevner Intl Equity Research Portfolio Inst Cls	HLIRX	NAS CM	Open End	Global Equity Large Cap (Foreign Stock)	C	C	B+	Up	Y	100,000
Harding Loevner Intl Equity Research Portfolio Inv Cls	HLINX	NAS CM	Open End	Global Equity Large Cap (Foreign Stock)	C	C	B+	Up	Y	5,000
Harding Loevner Intl Small Companies Portfolio Inst	HLMRX	NAS CM	Open End	Global Equity Mid/Small Cap (Small Company)	B	B	B	Up	Y	100,000

★ Expanded analysis of this fund is included in Section II.

Min Additional Investment	TOTAL RETURNS: 3-Month Total Return	6-Month Total Return	1-Year Total Return	3-Year Total Return	5-Year Total Return	PERFORMANCE: Dividend Yield (TTM)	Expense Ratio	3-Yr Std Deviation	3-Year Beta	ASSETS: NAV	Total Assets (MIL)	ASSET ALLOCATION & TURNOVER: %Cash	%Stocks	%Bonds	%Other	Turnover Ratio	BULL & BEAR: Last Bull Market Total Return	Last Bear Market Total Return	FEES: Front End Fee (%)	Back End Fee (%)	Inception Date
	5.66	8.81	11.95	24.23	110.84	1.45	0.86	11.91	1.08	23.54	1,015	0	99	0	1	18	29.4	-25.11			Mar-02
	5.54	8.60	11.54	22.87	107.00	1.13	1.23	11.91	1.08	23.53	1,015	0	99	0	1	18	29.01	-25.19			Nov-02
	5.64	8.84	12.03	24.32	110.99	1.49	0.78	11.92	1.08	23.53	1,015	0	99	0	1	18	29.4	-25.11			Mar-16
	6.89	11.19	23.93	28.52	106.36	0	1.11	14.68	0.96	13.47	732.1	2	98	0	0	89	27.76	-28.65			Nov-02
	6.96	11.31	24.60	29.95	109.36	0	0.86	14.67	0.96	14.41	732.1	2	98	0	0	89	27.84	-28.58			Nov-00
	6.88	11.10	24.18	28.44	105.60	0	1.23	14.69	0.96	12.88	732.1	2	98	0	0	89	27.51	-28.69			Nov-02
	7.03	11.38	24.74	30.09	109.58	0	0.78	14.68	0.96	14.44	732.1	2	98	0	0	89	27.84	-28.58			Mar-16
	3.14	3.97	17.28	23.11		0	1.15	16.76	1.07	12.17	299.5	3	97	0	0	85					Feb-14
	3.21	4.12	17.61	23.44		0	0.9	16.77	1.07	12.23	299.5	3	97	0	0	85					Feb-14
	3.18	3.93	17.28	22.00		0	1.27	16.78	1.07	12.04	299.5	3	97	0	0	85					Feb-14
	3.29	4.20	17.70	23.63		0	0.82	16.76	1.07	12.25	299.5	3	97	0	0	85					Mar-16
	6.43	13.87	21.29	42.50	112.79	0.15	1.12	13.15	0.85	36.14	1,241	3	97	0	0	10	27.37	-22.55			Nov-02
	6.52	14.00	21.60	43.59	115.58	0.3	0.87	13.15	0.85	36.3	1,241	3	97	0	0	10	27.63	-22.5			Dec-01
	6.40	13.81	21.18	41.98	111.61	0.04	1.24	13.16	0.85	35.44	1,241	3	97	0	0	10	27.36	-22.6			Nov-02
	6.56	14.07	21.71	43.75	115.82	0.34	0.79	13.15	0.85	36.31	1,241	3	97	0	0	10	27.63	-22.49			Mar-16
	0.68	4.84					1.13			10.35	25.5	4	96	0	0						Aug-17
	0.78	4.95					0.88			10.35	25.5	4	96	0	0						Aug-17
	0.73	4.79					1.25			10.35	25.5	4	96	0	0						Aug-17
	0.81	4.98					0.8			10.35	25.5	4	96	0	0						Aug-17
	6.30	10.04	24.88	33.68	105.24		0.95	9.49	0.84	19.07	59.5	5	95	0	0	21					Mar-17
	6.44	10.23	25.25	34.75	107.91	0.55	0.7	9.5	0.84	19.08	59.5	5	95	0	0	21					Nov-11
	6.31	10.04	24.89	33.69	105.25		1.07	9.5	0.84	19.06	59.5	5	95	0	0	21					Mar-17
	6.47	10.27	25.36	34.87	108.09		0.62	9.5	0.84	19.09	59.5	5	95	0	0	21					Mar-17
	1.60	3.98	9.50	14.04	26.27	2.58	0.62	4.35	0.32	10.8	6.2	14	24	59	2	32	12.53	-8.97			Jan-09
	2.02	4.79	11.69	16.91	31.61	2.43	0.66	5.26	0.19	9.74	27.7	9	34	55	2	33	13.74	-10.39			Jan-09
	2.31	5.39	13.14	18.52	35.61	2.17	0.69	5.86	0.1	12.58	21.2	5	40	54	2	25	15.02	-12.6			Jan-09
	2.65	6.01	14.68	20.16	41.24	2.14	0.7	6.67	-0.03	9.12	28.9	4	47	46	2	31	16.84	-14.82			Jan-09
	3.10	6.93	16.87	22.53	48.50	1.87	0.72	7.45	-0.14	14.37	15.3	4	58	37	2	26	18.84	-16.83			Jan-09
	3.60	7.71	18.90	24.89	56.37	1.69	0.74	8.26	-0.24	9.21	25.2	3	67	28	2	30	20.48	-18.97			Jan-09
	4.13	8.56	20.95	27.10	63.56	1.35	0.75	9.2	-0.37	15.32	10.1	3	76	20	1	24	22.07	-20.81			Jan-09
	4.54	9.46	22.92	29.38	70.73	1.16	0.77	10.11	-0.49	10.28	23.3	2	85	11	1	24	23.07	-21.52			Jan-09
	4.84	9.90	24.08	30.66		0.99	0.78	10.37	-0.49	11.99	2.8	2	90	6	1	33					Nov-14
	1.37	3.46	8.41	13.07	21.40	2.9	0.61	3.71	0.42	9.12	14.1	15	20	63	2	26	9.94	-5.08			Jan-09
	5.69	13.34	35.22	32.41	36.67	0.46	1.42	14.16	0.87	59.23	4,057	2	98	0	0	26	21.64	-24.08			Nov-98
	5.90	14.27	34.53				1.3			12.59	6.5	1	95	0	3						Dec-16
	5.83	14.11	34.22				1.55			12.56	6.5	1	95	0	3						Dec-16
	5.31	11.58	25.08	3.25	28.86	0.84	1.64	10.77	0.81	8.82	471.4					47	10	-19.66			May-08
	5.31	11.62	25.38	3.50	29.16		1.35	10.78	0.81	8.81	471.4					47	10	-19.66			Mar-17
	5.21	11.38	24.60	1.93	26.16	0.43	2	10.72	0.8	8.78	471.4					47	9.87	-19.81			Dec-10
	6.63	11.99	31.84	40.06	80.37	0.1	1.19	11.18	1.02	37.17	823.7	2	98	0	0	24	21.34	-18.51			Nov-96
	6.65	12.09	32.14	41.10	82.69	0.31	0.92	11.18	1.02	37.18	823.7	2	98	0	0	24	21.52	-18.41			Nov-09
0	6.65	12.03	31.88	40.11	80.43		0.9	11.18	1.02	37.15	823.7	2	98	0	0	24	21.34	-18.52			Aug-17
	7.06	12.33	28.24				0.9			12.26	6.0	2	97	0	0						Dec-16
	6.99	12.17	27.94				1.15			12.23	6.0	2	97	0	0						Dec-16
	5.69	13.37	35.32	32.70	36.92	0.47	1.29	14.04	0.86	22.61	4,891	2	98	0	0	20	22.32	-24.13			Oct-05
	5.85	13.55	35.78	33.66	38.03	0.91	1.13	14.08	0.87	22.61	4,891	2	98	0	0	20	22.32	-24.13			Mar-14
	4.51	10.76	29.90	33.89	52.50	0.77	0.83	12.46	0.96	22.78	12,226	4	96	0	0	22	17.02	-22.16			May-94
	3.69	9.99	28.99	32.95	51.43		0.9	12.46	0.96	22.77	12,226	4	96	0	0	22	17.02	-22.16			Jul-17
	4.46	10.62	29.43	32.59	50.06	0.51	1.14	12.42	0.96	22.75	12,226	4	96	0	0	22	16.77	-22.32			Sep-05
	5.92	11.30	29.57			1.27	0.9			12.83	10.7	2	97	0	1						Dec-15
	5.95	11.27	29.24			1.27	1.15			12.77	10.7	2	97	0	1						Dec-15
	4.84	11.02	34.66	40.64	69.74	0.9	1.15	10.46	0.81	17.12	204.6	5	94	0	0	49	19.45	-23.15			Jun-11

	MARKET		FUND TYPE, CATEGORY & OBJECTIVE		RATINGS				MINIMUMS	
Fund Name	Ticker Symbol	Traded On	Fund Type	Category and (Prospectus Objective)	Overall Rating	Reward Rating	Risk Rating	Recent Up/ Downgrade	Open to New Investors	Min Initial Investment
Harding Loevner Intl Small Companies Portfolio Inv	HLMSX	NAS CM	Open End	Global Equity Mid/Small Cap (Small Company)	B	B	B	Up	Y	5,000
Hartford Balanced Fund Class A	ITTAX	NAS CM	Open End	Moderate Alloc (Balanced)	B-	C+	B	Down	Y	2,000
Hartford Balanced Fund Class C	HAFCX	NAS CM	Open End	Moderate Alloc (Balanced)	B-	C+	B	Down	Y	2,000
Hartford Balanced Fund Class I	ITTIX	NAS CM	Open End	Moderate Alloc (Balanced)	B-	C+	B	Down	Y	2,000
Hartford Balanced Fund Class R3	ITTRX	NAS CM	Open End	Moderate Alloc (Balanced)	B-	C+	B	Down	Y	0
Hartford Balanced Fund Class R4	ITTSX	NAS CM	Open End	Moderate Alloc (Balanced)	B-	C+	B	Down	Y	0
Hartford Balanced Fund Class R5	ITTTX	NAS CM	Open End	Moderate Alloc (Balanced)	B-	C+	B	Down	Y	0
Hartford Balanced Fund Class Y	IHAYX	NAS CM	Open End	Moderate Alloc (Balanced)	B-	C+	B	Down	Y	250,000
Hartford Balanced HLS Fund Class IA	HADAX	NAS CM	Open End	Moderate Alloc (Asset Alloc)	B-	C+	B	Down	Y	0
Hartford Balanced HLS Fund Class IB	HAIBX	NAS CM	Open End	Moderate Alloc (Asset Alloc)	B-	C+	B	Down	Y	0
Hartford Capital Appreciation HLS Fund Class IA	HIACX	NAS CM	Open End	US Equity Large Cap Blend (Growth)	B-	B-	B-	Down	Y	0
Hartford Capital Appreciation HLS Fund Class IB	HIBCX	NAS CM	Open End	US Equity Large Cap Blend (Growth)	B-	B-	B-	Down	Y	0
Hartford Capital Appreciation HLS Fund Class IC	HCPCX	NAS CM	Open End	US Equity Large Cap Blend (Growth)	B-	B-	B-	Down	Y	0
Hartford Checks and Balances Fund Class A	HCKAX	NAS CM	Open End	Moderate Alloc (Growth & Income)	B-	C+	B	Up	Y	2,000
Hartford Checks and Balances Fund Class C	HCKCX	NAS CM	Open End	Moderate Alloc (Growth & Income)	B-	C+	B	Up	Y	2,000
Hartford Checks and Balances Fund Class F	HCKFX	NAS CM	Open End	Moderate Alloc (Growth & Income)	B-	C+	B	Up	Y	1,000,000
Hartford Checks and Balances Fund Class I	HCKIX	NAS CM	Open End	Moderate Alloc (Growth & Income)	B-	C+	B	Up	Y	2,000
Hartford Checks and Balances Fund Class R3	HCKRX	NAS CM	Open End	Moderate Alloc (Growth & Income)	B-	C+	B	Up	Y	0
Hartford Checks and Balances Fund Class R4	HCKSX	NAS CM	Open End	Moderate Alloc (Growth & Income)	B-	C+	B	Up	Y	0
Hartford Checks and Balances Fund Class R5	HCKTX	NAS CM	Open End	Moderate Alloc (Growth & Income)	B-	C+	B	Up	Y	0
Hartford Conservative Allocation Fund Class A	HCVAX	NAS CM	Open End	Alloc (Asset Alloc)	B-	C	B	Up	Y	2,000
Hartford Conservative Allocation Fund Class C	HCVCX	NAS CM	Open End	Alloc (Asset Alloc)	C+	C	B	Up	Y	2,000
Hartford Conservative Allocation Fund Class F	HCVFX	NAS CM	Open End	Alloc (Asset Alloc)	B-	C	B	Up	Y	1,000,000
Hartford Conservative Allocation Fund Class I	HCVIX	NAS CM	Open End	Alloc (Asset Alloc)	C+	C	B	Down	Y	2,000
Hartford Conservative Allocation Fund Class R3	HCVRX	NAS CM	Open End	Alloc (Asset Alloc)	B-	C	B	Up	Y	0
Hartford Conservative Allocation Fund Class R4	HCVSX	NAS CM	Open End	Alloc (Asset Alloc)	C+	C	B	Down	Y	0
Hartford Conservative Allocation Fund Class R5	HCVTX	NAS CM	Open End	Alloc (Asset Alloc)	B-	C	B	Up	Y	0
Hartford Core Equity Fund Class A	HAIAX	NAS CM	Open End	US Equity Large Cap Growth (Growth)	B	B-	B+		Y	2,000
Hartford Core Equity Fund Class C	HGICX	NAS CM	Open End	US Equity Large Cap Growth (Growth)	B	B-	B+		Y	2,000
Hartford Core Equity Fund Class F	HGIFX	NAS CM	Open End	US Equity Large Cap Growth (Growth)	B	B	B+		Y	1,000,000
Hartford Core Equity Fund Class I	HGIIX	NAS CM	Open End	US Equity Large Cap Growth (Growth)	B	B	B+		Y	2,000
Hartford Core Equity Fund Class R3	HGIRX	NAS CM	Open End	US Equity Large Cap Growth (Growth)	B	B-	A		Y	0
Hartford Core Equity Fund Class R4	HGISX	NAS CM	Open End	US Equity Large Cap Growth (Growth)	B	B-	B+		Y	0
Hartford Core Equity Fund Class R5	HGITX	NAS CM	Open End	US Equity Large Cap Growth (Growth)	B	B	B+		Y	0
Hartford Core Equity Fund Class R6	HAITX	NAS CM	Open End	US Equity Large Cap Growth (Growth)	B	B	B+		Y	0
Hartford Core Equity Fund Class Y	HGIYX	NAS CM	Open End	US Equity Large Cap Growth (Growth)	B	B	B+		Y	250,000
Hartford Disciplined Equity HLS Fund Class IA	HIAGX	NAS CM	Open End	US Equity Large Cap Growth (Growth)	B	B	B+		Y	0
Hartford Disciplined Equity HLS Fund Class IB	HBGIX	NAS CM	Open End	US Equity Large Cap Growth (Growth)	B	B-	B+		Y	0
Hartford Dividend and Growth HLS Fund Class IA	HIADX	NAS CM	Open End	US Equity Large Cap Value (Growth & Income)	B	B	B-		Y	0
Hartford Dividend and Growth HLS Fund Class IB	HDGBX	NAS CM	Open End	US Equity Large Cap Value (Growth & Income)	B	B	B-		Y	0
Hartford Emerging Markets Equity Fund Class A	HERAX	NAS CM	Open End	Emerging Markets Equity (Div Emerging Mkts)	B	B	C	Up	Y	2,000
Hartford Emerging Markets Equity Fund Class C	HERCX	NAS CM	Open End	Emerging Markets Equity (Div Emerging Mkts)	B-	B	C	Up	Y	2,000
Hartford Emerging Markets Equity Fund Class F	HERFX	NAS CM	Open End	Emerging Markets Equity (Div Emerging Mkts)	B	B+	C+	Up	Y	1,000,000
Hartford Emerging Markets Equity Fund Class I	HERIX	NAS CM	Open End	Emerging Markets Equity (Div Emerging Mkts)	B	B+	C+	Up	Y	2,000
Hartford Emerging Markets Equity Fund Class R3	HERRX	NAS CM	Open End	Emerging Markets Equity (Div Emerging Mkts)	B	B	C	Up	Y	0
Hartford Emerging Markets Equity Fund Class R4	HERSX	NAS CM	Open End	Emerging Markets Equity (Div Emerging Mkts)	B	B	C+	Up	Y	0
Hartford Emerging Markets Equity Fund Class R5	HERTX	NAS CM	Open End	Emerging Markets Equity (Div Emerging Mkts)	B	B	C+	Up	Y	0
Hartford Emerging Markets Equity Fund Class Y	HERYX	NAS CM	Open End	Emerging Markets Equity (Div Emerging Mkts)	B	B+	C+	Up	Y	250,000
Hartford Environmental Opportunities Fund Class A	HEOMX	NAS CM	Open End	Global Equity Mid/Small Cap (Growth & Income)	C-	C	B+	Up	Y	5,000
Hartford Environmental Opportunities Fund Class C	HEONX	NAS CM	Open End	Global Equity Mid/Small Cap (Growth & Income)	C-	C	B+	Up	Y	5,000
Hartford Environmental Opportunities Fund Class F	HEOFX	NAS CM	Open End	Global Equity Mid/Small Cap (Growth & Income)	C-	C	B+	Up	Y	1,000,000
Hartford Environmental Opportunities Fund Class I	HEOIX	NAS CM	Open End	Global Equity Mid/Small Cap (Growth & Income)	C-	C	B+	Up	Y	5,000

★ Expanded analysis of this fund is included in Section II.

	TOTAL RETURNS					PERFORMANCE				ASSETS		ASSET ALLOCATION & TURNOVER					BULL & BEAR		FEES		
Min Additional Investment	3-Month Total Return	6-Month Total Return	1-Year Total Return	3-Year Total Return	5-Year Total Return	Dividend Yield (TTM)	Expense Ratio	3-Yr Std Deviation	3-Year Beta	NAV	Total Assets (MIL)	%Cash	%Stocks	%Bonds	%Other	Turnover Ratio	Last Bull Market Total Return	Last Bear Market Total Return	Front End Fee (%)	Back End Fee (%)	Inception Date
	4.84	10.93	34.41	39.61	67.74	0.84	1.4	10.42	0.8	17.01	204.6	5	94	0	0	49	19.32	-23.23			Mar-07
50	4.43	7.66	15.12	20.40	61.26	1.16	1.14	7.14		24.18	954.9	3	66	32	0	26	17.84	-12.15	5.50		Jul-96
50	4.25	7.28	14.30	17.87	55.68	0.5	1.84	7.16		24.18	954.9	3	66	32	0	26	17.32	-12.42		1.00	Jul-98
50	4.52	7.83	15.38	21.51	64.15	1.36	0.84	7.14		24.17	954.9	3	66	32	0	26	18.17	-11.99			Mar-15
	4.32	7.50	14.74	19.40	59.13	0.86	1.4	7.15		24.42	954.9	3	66	32	0	26	17.76	-12.28			Dec-06
	4.42	7.65	15.08	20.48	61.53	1.17	1.1	7.16		24.47	954.9	3	66	32	0	26	17.82	-12.16			Dec-06
	4.50	7.80	15.48	21.59	64.08	1.42	0.8	7.15		24.5	954.9	3	66	32	0	26	18.14	-12.02			Dec-06
	4.55	7.87	15.49	21.81	64.55	1.48	0.79	7.17		24.51	954.9	3	66	32	0	26	18.17	-11.99			Jul-96
	4.67	8.36	15.59	22.06	65.04	1.86	0.66	6.74	0.65	31.02	2,368	0	67	32	1	25	18.53	-12.11			Mar-83
	4.61	8.26	15.29	21.14	63.01	1.61	0.91	6.74	0.65	31.48	2,368	0	67	32	1	25	18.36	-12.2			Apr-98
	4.98	8.74	22.13	29.27	97.66	1.05	0.68	11.38	1.08	48.16	5,083	1	97	0	1	103	24.25	-24.7			Apr-84
	4.90	8.57	21.81	28.28	95.17	0.85	0.93	11.38	1.08	47.48	5,083	1	97	0	1	103	24.07	-24.77			Apr-98
	4.83	8.44	21.50	27.32	93.43	0.7	1.18	11.39	1.08	47.76	5,083	1	97	0	1	103	24.07	-24.77			Apr-14
50	0.70	3.24	11.12	18.31	59.49	1.12	1	7.1		9.47	1,722	2	65	32	0	8	16.22	-13.83	5.50		May-07
50	0.71	3.12	10.51	15.87	53.83	0.42	1.75	7.12		9.41	1,722	2	65	32	0	8	15.7	-14.12		1.00	May-07
	0.69	2.98	10.48	17.63	58.58		0.65	7.1		9.48	1,722	2	65	32	0	8	16.22	-13.83			Feb-17
50	0.69	3.31	11.19	18.98	61.18	1.34	0.78	7.18		9.48	1,722	2	65	32	0	8	16.36	-13.8			Feb-08
	0.70	3.13	10.72	17.13	56.75	0.79	1.35	7.14		9.43	1,722	2	65	32	0	8	16.06	-14.07			Aug-08
	0.70	3.23	10.98	18.16	59.04	1.07	1.06	7.13		9.44	1,722	2	65	32	0	8	16.22	-13.95			Aug-08
	0.69	3.31	11.32	19.20	61.49	1.35	0.75	7.11		9.48	1,722	2	65	32	0	8	16.36	-13.79			Aug-08
50	-0.57	1.55	6.85	7.37	8.79	1.24	1.19	4.43		10.44	127.7	3	39	56	1	80	11.49	-8.16	5.50		May-04
50	0.09	1.97	6.83	5.74	5.62	0.5	1.94	4.46		10.32	127.7	3	39	56	1	80	10.98	-8.42		1.00	May-04
	-0.76	1.45	6.75	7.26	8.68		0.84	4.45		10.44	127.7	3	39	56	1	80	11.49	-8.16			Feb-17
50	-0.76	1.45	6.85	7.86	9.99	1.51	0.94	4.41		10.44	127.7	3	39	56	1	80	11.76	-8.04			Aug-06
	-0.28	1.75	6.85	6.80	7.57	1.06	1.44	4.44		10.44	127.7	3	39	56	1	80	11.29	-8.28			Dec-06
	-0.66	1.45	6.74	7.33	8.81	1.29	1.14	4.37		10.44	127.7	3	39	56	1	80	11.48	-8.1			Dec-06
	-0.85	1.35	6.84	7.95	10.16	1.58	0.84	4.43		10.46	127.7	3	39	56	1	80	11.63	-8.04			Dec-06
50	7.68	10.68	21.75	35.30	116.04	0.42	0.8	9.06	0.86	28.83	3,288	2	99	0	0	33	23.64	-16.17	5.50		Apr-98
50	7.43	10.25	20.80	32.31	108.43	0.07	1.55	9.06	0.86	26.46	3,288	2	99	0	0	33	23.11	-16.48		1.00	Jul-98
	7.73	10.84	22.12	36.65	120.41		0.43	9.08	0.86	28.84	3,288	2	99	0	0	33	24.04	-16.03			Feb-17
50	7.73	10.84	22.01	36.37	119.96	0.64	0.55	9.07	0.86	28.85	3,288	2	99	0	0	33	24.04	-16.03			Mar-15
	7.57	10.49	21.34	34.04	113.36	0.33	1.1	9.08	0.86	29.25	3,288	2	99	0	0	33	23.55	-16.3			Dec-06
	7.63	10.62	21.64	35.26	116.53	0.46	0.8	9.05	0.86	29.65	3,288	2	99	0	0	33	23.75	-16.16			Dec-06
	7.71	10.80	22.02	36.43	119.82	0.65	0.5	9.06	0.86	29.05	3,288	2	99	0	0	33	23.98	-16.04			Dec-06
	7.76	10.88	22.16	36.65	120.41	0.69	0.43	9.07	0.86	29.16	3,288	2	99	0	0	33	24.04	-16.03			Mar-15
	7.73	10.81	22.08	36.60	120.33	0.69	0.48	9.08	0.86	29.16	3,288	2	99	0	0	33	24.04	-16.03			Apr-98
	7.69	10.69	21.91	36.38	120.70	0.63	0.78	9.3	0.89	15.43	702.5	0	100	0	0	33	24.3	-16.35			May-98
	7.59	10.55	21.63	35.34	117.96	0.41	1.03	9.25	0.88	15.27	702.5	0	100	0	0	33	24.12	-16.44			May-98
	6.07	10.69	18.35	32.99	102.99	1.59	0.68	10.45	1.02	23.95	3,619	0	99	0	1	20	22.82	-17.47			Mar-94
	6.07	10.57	18.10	32.02	100.50	1.39	0.93	10.42	1.01	23.85	3,619	0	99	0	1	20	22.64	-17.55			Apr-98
50	5.44	15.96	41.43	34.80	32.13	0.76	1.46	16.23	1.01	9.97	86.3	3	96	0	1	97	17.63		5.50		May-11
50	5.38	15.61	40.40	32.05	27.67	0.33	2.21	16.19	1.01	9.79	86.3	3	96	0	1	97	17.08			1.00	May-11
	5.58	16.26	42.06	36.60	35.01		0.99	16.27	1.01	9.89	86.3	3	96	0	1	97	17.8				Feb-17
50	5.62	16.19	41.81	36.36	34.77	1.04	1.21	16.26	1.01	9.94	86.3	3	96	0	1	97	17.8				May-11
	5.44	15.84	41.08	33.96	30.78	0	1.71	16.2	1.01	9.98	86.3	3	96	0	1	97	17.33				May-11
	5.48	16.08	41.42	34.89	32.47	0	1.46	16.27	1.01	10.03	86.3	3	96	0	1	97	17.59				May-11
	5.67	16.30	42.09	35.64	33.97	0.93	1.16	16.25	1.01	9.9	86.3	3	96	0	1	97	17.76				May-11
	5.61	16.32	42.01	36.73	35.19	1.1	1.11	16.19	1.01	9.93	86.3	3	96	0	1	97	17.8				May-11
50	2.40	7.40	21.66			0.84	1.31			12.51	39.1	3	97	0	0				5.50		Feb-16
50	2.39	7.48	21.56			0.33	2.06			12.5	39.1	3	97	0	0					1.00	Feb-16
	2.49	7.65	21.93				0.91			12.56	39.1	3	97	0	0						Feb-17
50	2.44	7.51	21.87			0.98	1.06			12.48	39.1	3	97	0	0						Feb-16

	MARKET			FUND TYPE, CATEGORY & OBJECTIVE	RATINGS				MINIMUMS	
Fund Name	Ticker Symbol	Traded On	Fund Type	Category and (Prospectus Objective)	Overall Rating	Reward Rating	Risk Rating	Recent Up/ Downgrade	Open to New Investors	Min Initial Investment
Hartford Environmental Opportunities Fund Class R3	HEORX	NAS CM	Open End	Global Equity Mid/Small Cap (Growth & Income)	C-	C	B+	Up	Y	0
Hartford Environmental Opportunities Fund Class R4	HEOSX	NAS CM	Open End	Global Equity Mid/Small Cap (Growth & Income)	C-	C	B+	Up	Y	0
Hartford Environmental Opportunities Fund Class R5	HEOTX	NAS CM	Open End	Global Equity Mid/Small Cap (Growth & Income)	C-	C	B+	Up	Y	0
Hartford Environmental Opportunities Fund Class R6	HEOVX	NAS CM	Open End	Global Equity Mid/Small Cap (Growth & Income)	C-	C	B+	Up	Y	0
Hartford Environmental Opportunities Fund Class Y	HEOYX	NAS CM	Open End	Global Equity Mid/Small Cap (Growth & Income)	C-	C	B+	Up	Y	250,000
Hartford Global All-Asset Fund Class C	HLACX	NAS CM	Open End	Alloc (Asset Alloc)	B-	C+	B	Down	Y	5,000
Hartford Global All-Asset Fund Class F	HLAFX	NAS CM	Open End	Alloc (Asset Alloc)	B-	C+	B	Down	Y	1,000,000
Hartford Global All-Asset Fund Class I	HLAIX	NAS CM	Open End	Alloc (Asset Alloc)	B	C+	B+	Up	Y	5,000
Hartford Global All-Asset Fund Class R3	HLARX	NAS CM	Open End	Alloc (Asset Alloc)	B-	C+	B	Down	Y	0
Hartford Global All-Asset Fund Class R4	HLASX	NAS CM	Open End	Alloc (Asset Alloc)	B	C+	B+	Up	Y	0
Hartford Global All-Asset Fund Class R5	HLATX	NAS CM	Open End	Alloc (Asset Alloc)	B	C+	B+	Up	Y	0
Hartford Global Capital Appreciation Fund Class A	HCTAX	NAS CM	Open End	Global Equity (Growth)	C+	C+	C+	Down	Y	2,000
Hartford Global Capital Appreciation Fund Class C	HFCCX	NAS CM	Open End	Global Equity (Growth)	B-	C+	B	Up	Y	2,000
Hartford Global Capital Appreciation Fund Class F	HCTFX	NAS CM	Open End	Global Equity (Growth)	C+	C+	C+	Down	Y	1,000,000
Hartford Global Capital Appreciation Fund Class I	HCTIX	NAS CM	Open End	Global Equity (Growth)	C+	C+	C+	Down	Y	2,000
Hartford Global Capital Appreciation Fund Class R3	HCTRX	NAS CM	Open End	Global Equity (Growth)	B-	C+	B	Up	Y	0
Hartford Global Capital Appreciation Fund Class R4	HCTSX	NAS CM	Open End	Global Equity (Growth)	C+	C+	C+	Down	Y	0
Hartford Global Capital Appreciation Fund Class R5	HCTTX	NAS CM	Open End	Global Equity (Growth)	C+	C+	C+	Down	Y	0
Hartford Global Capital Appreciation Fund Class Y	HCTYX	NAS CM	Open End	Global Equity (Growth)	C+	C+	C+	Down	Y	250,000
Hartford Global Equity Income Fund Class A	HLEAX	NAS CM	Open End	Global Equity (Equity-Income)	C+	B-	C+	Down	Y	2,000
Hartford Global Equity Income Fund Class C	HLECX	NAS CM	Open End	Global Equity (Equity-Income)	C+	C+	C+	Down	Y	2,000
Hartford Global Equity Income Fund Class F	HLEFX	NAS CM	Open End	Global Equity (Equity-Income)	B-	B-	C+	Up	Y	1,000,000
Hartford Global Equity Income Fund Class I	HLEJX	NAS CM	Open End	Global Equity (Equity-Income)	C+	B-	C+	Down	Y	2,000
Hartford Global Equity Income Fund Class R3	HLERX	NAS CM	Open End	Global Equity (Equity-Income)	C+	B-	C+	Down	Y	0
Hartford Global Equity Income Fund Class R4	HLESX	NAS CM	Open End	Global Equity (Equity-Income)	C+	B-	C+	Down	Y	0
Hartford Global Equity Income Fund Class R5	HLETX	NAS CM	Open End	Global Equity (Equity-Income)	B-	B-	C+	Up	Y	0
Hartford Global Equity Income Fund Class Y	HLEYX	NAS CM	Open End	Global Equity (Equity-Income)	B-	B-	C+	Up	Y	250,000
Hartford Global Growth HLS Fund Class IA	HIALX	NAS CM	Open End	Global Equity (World Stock)	B+	B+	A-	Up	Y	0
Hartford Global Growth HLS Fund Class IB	HBGLX	NAS CM	Open End	Global Equity (World Stock)	B+	B+	A-	Up	Y	0
Hartford Global Impact Fund Class A	HGXAX	NAS CM	Open End	Global Equity Mid/Small Cap (World Stock)	U	U	U		Y	5,000
Hartford Global Impact Fund Class C	HGXCX	NAS CM	Open End	Global Equity Mid/Small Cap (World Stock)	U	U	U		Y	5,000
Hartford Global Impact Fund Class F	HGXFX	NAS CM	Open End	Global Equity Mid/Small Cap (World Stock)	U	U	U		Y	1,000,000
Hartford Global Impact Fund Class I	HGXIX	NAS CM	Open End	Global Equity Mid/Small Cap (World Stock)	U	U	U		Y	5,000
Hartford Global Impact Fund Class R3	HGXRX	NAS CM	Open End	Global Equity Mid/Small Cap (World Stock)	U	U	U		Y	0
Hartford Global Impact Fund Class R4	HGXSX	NAS CM	Open End	Global Equity Mid/Small Cap (World Stock)	U	U	U		Y	0
Hartford Global Impact Fund Class R5	HGXTX	NAS CM	Open End	Global Equity Mid/Small Cap (World Stock)	U	U	U		Y	0
Hartford Global Impact Fund Class R6	HGXVX	NAS CM	Open End	Global Equity Mid/Small Cap (World Stock)	U	U	U		Y	0
Hartford Global Impact Fund Class Y	HGXYX	NAS CM	Open End	Global Equity Mid/Small Cap (World Stock)	U	U	U		Y	250,000
Hartford Global Real Asset Fund Class A	HRLAX	NAS CM	Open End	Alloc (Asset Alloc)	C	C	C	Up	Y	5,000
Hartford Global Real Asset Fund Class F	HRLFX	NAS CM	Open End	Alloc (Asset Alloc)	C	C	C	Up	Y	1,000,000
Hartford Global Real Asset Fund Class I	HRLIX	NAS CM	Open End	Alloc (Asset Alloc)	C	C	C	Up	Y	5,000
Hartford Global Real Asset Fund Class R3	HRLRX	NAS CM	Open End	Alloc (Asset Alloc)	C	C	C	Up	Y	0
Hartford Global Real Asset Fund Class R4	HRLSX	NAS CM	Open End	Alloc (Asset Alloc)	C	C	C	Up	Y	0
Hartford Global Real Asset Fund Class R5	HRLTX	NAS CM	Open End	Alloc (Asset Alloc)	C	C	C	Up	Y	0
Hartford Global Real Asset Fund Class Y	HRLYX	NAS CM	Open End	Alloc (Asset Alloc)	C	C	C	Up	Y	250,000
Hartford Growth Allocation Fund Class A	HRAAX	NAS CM	Open End	Alloc (Asset Alloc)	C+	C+	C+	Down	Y	2,000
Hartford Growth Allocation Fund Class C	HRACX	NAS CM	Open End	Alloc (Asset Alloc)	C+	C+	C+	Down	Y	2,000
Hartford Growth Allocation Fund Class F	HRAFX	NAS CM	Open End	Alloc (Asset Alloc)	C+	C+	C+	Down	Y	1,000,000
Hartford Growth Allocation Fund Class I	HRAIX	NAS CM	Open End	Alloc (Asset Alloc)	C+	C+	B-	Down	Y	2,000
Hartford Growth Allocation Fund Class R3	HRARX	NAS CM	Open End	Alloc (Asset Alloc)	C+	C+	C+	Down	Y	0
Hartford Growth Allocation Fund Class R4	HRASX	NAS CM	Open End	Alloc (Asset Alloc)	C+	C+	C+	Down	Y	0
Hartford Growth Allocation Fund Class R5	HRATX	NAS CM	Open End	Alloc (Asset Alloc)	C+	C+	B-	Down	Y	0

★ Expanded analysis of this fund is included in Section II.

Min Additional Investment	3-Month Total Return	6-Month Total Return	1-Year Total Return	3-Year Total Return	5-Year Total Return	Dividend Yield (TTM)	Expense Ratio	3-Yr Std Deviation	3-Year Beta	NAV	Total Assets (MIL)	%Cash	%Stocks	%Bonds	%Other	Turnover Ratio	Last Bull Market Total Return	Last Bear Market Total Return	Front End Fee (%)	Back End Fee (%)	Inception Date
TOTAL RETURNS						PERFORMANCE				ASSETS		ASSET ALLOCATION & TURNOVER					BULL & BEAR		FEES		
	2.41	7.49	21.69			0.62	1.61			12.49	39.1	3	97	0	0						Feb-16
	2.41	7.49	21.78			0.82	1.31			12.49	39.1	3	97	0	0						Feb-16
	2.43	7.50	21.78			1.02	1.01			12.49	39.1	3	97	0	0						Feb-16
	2.44	7.51	21.89			1.08	0.91			12.49	39.1	3	97	0	0						Feb-16
	2.41	7.49	21.86			1.08	0.91			12.48	39.1	3	97	0	0						Feb-16
50	2.91	6.28	16.06	20.22	34.55	0.7	1.99	6.88		10.61	311.1	18	43	33	4	95	11.12	-15.9		1.00	May-10
	3.15	6.82	17.33	24.23	42.14		0.89	6.91		10.77	311.1	18	43	33	4	95	11.72	-15.51			Feb-17
50	3.17	6.75	17.26	23.92	41.39	1.68	0.99	6.87		10.77	311.1	18	43	33	4	95	11.72	-15.52			May-10
	2.97	6.48	16.57	22.00	37.82	1.22	1.54	6.89		10.74	311.1	18	43	33	4	95	11.49	-15.8			May-10
	3.08	6.63	16.92	23.12	39.97	1.46	1.24	6.89		10.88	311.1	18	43	33	4	95	11.61	-15.69			May-10
	3.14	6.84	17.43	23.45	40.98	1.87	0.94	6.98		10.69	311.1	18	43	33	4	95	11.65	-15.51			May-10
50	3.41	6.70	20.57	22.04	76.14	0.63	1.26	11.08	1.02	18.8	1,081	1	97	0	1	100	24.34	-25.47	5.50		Apr-05
50	3.26	6.29	19.73	19.40	69.92	0.03	2	11.06	1.02	17.24	1,081	1	97	0	1	100	23.75	-25.66		1.00	Apr-05
	3.52	6.89	21.09	23.34	79.33		0.86	11.08	1.02	19.36	1,081	1	97	0	1	100	24.68	-25.31			Feb-17
50	3.46	6.83	20.91	23.08	78.70	0.86	0.97	11.1	1.02	19.36	1,081	1	97	0	1	100	24.61	-25.38			Aug-06
	3.39	6.62	20.48	21.68	75.21	0.56	1.36	11.09	1.02	18.52	1,081	1	97	0	1	100	24.2	-25.59			Dec-06
	3.50	6.80	20.83	22.78	77.95	0.81	1.06	11.09	1.02	19.07	1,081	1	97	0	1	100	24.39	-25.4			Dec-06
	3.50	6.90	20.98	23.20	78.79	0.84	0.96	11.09	1.02	19.49	1,081	1	97	0	1	100	24.59	-25.35			Dec-06
	3.50	6.87	21.01	23.25	79.20	0.92	0.91	11.09	1.02	19.65	1,081	1	97	0	1	100	24.67	-25.31			Apr-05
50	3.02	8.55	19.80	24.33	67.02	1.84	1.25	10.51	0.96	12.82	168.1	2	97	0	1	28	20.59	-22.91	5.50		Feb-08
50	2.82	8.10	18.92	21.59	60.80	1.19	2	10.47	0.96	12.51	168.1	2	97	0	1	28	20.18	-23.14		1.00	Feb-08
	3.04	8.76	20.31	25.71	70.35		0.8	10.51	0.96	12.83	168.1	2	97	0	1	28	21.12	-22.82			Feb-17
50	3.08	8.72	20.12	25.46	69.28	2.02	1	10.46	0.95	12.85	168.1	2	97	0	1	28	20.88	-22.87			Feb-08
	2.97	8.43	19.56	23.62	65.38	1.65	1.45	10.49	0.96	12.81	168.1	2	97	0	1	28	20.62	-23.06			Feb-08
	2.95	8.56	19.82	24.60	67.78	1.91	1.15	10.45	0.95	12.86	168.1	2	97	0	1	28	20.82	-22.91			Feb-08
	3.03	8.74	20.21	25.77	70.22	2.18	0.85	10.52	0.96	12.84	168.1	2	97	0	1	28	21.02	-22.87			Feb-08
	3.08	8.78	20.33	25.73	70.38	2.27	0.8	10.51	0.96	12.69	168.1	2	97	0	1	28	21.11	-22.82			Feb-08
	5.80	12.32	32.72	44.97	116.10	0.47	0.82	11.09	0.98	27.89	520.7	1	96	0	3	65	24.64	-24.78			Oct-98
	5.74	12.17	32.36	43.92	113.42	0.25	1.07	11.1	0.98	27.63	520.7	1	96	0	3	65	24.46	-24.86			Sep-98
50	7.85	14.70					1.25			11.9	28.7	1	99	0	1				5.50		Feb-17
50	7.72	14.28					2			11.77	28.7	1	99	0	1					1.00	Feb-17
	8.00	14.96					0.85			11.92	28.7	1	99	0	1						Feb-17
50	7.99	14.95					1			11.81	28.7	1	99	0	1						Feb-17
	7.91	14.77					1.55			11.76	28.7	1	99	0	1						Feb-17
	7.99	14.85					1.25			11.87	28.7	1	99	0	1						Feb-17
	8.05	14.91					0.95			11.76	28.7	1	99	0	1						Feb-17
	8.04	15.00					0.85			11.76	28.7	1	99	0	1						Feb-17
	8.06	14.92					0.9			11.75	28.7	1	99	0	1						Feb-17
50	4.87	11.84	9.21	7.94	-6.17	0.4	1.26	11.8		9.45	288.6	2	67	10	21	115	8.02	-20.22	5.50		May-10
	5.00	12.11	9.59	9.07	-4.38		0.91	11.82		9.43	288.6	2	67	10	21	115	8.28	-20.09			Feb-17
50	4.95	12.06	9.55	8.80	-4.93	0.65	1.01	11.82		9.43	288.6	2	67	10	21	115	8.15	-20.11			May-10
	4.87	11.71	8.97	7.11	-7.33	0.23	1.51	11.83		9.52	288.6	2	67	10	21	115	7.86	-20.3			May-10
	4.91	11.88	9.25	7.97	-6.00	0.35	1.21	11.81		9.46	288.6	2	67	10	21	115	7.96	-20.19			May-10
	4.95	12.05	9.54	8.94	-4.76	0.71	0.96	11.79		9.44	288.6	2	67	10	21	115	8.22	-20.09			May-10
	4.96	12.07	9.55	9.03	-4.42	0.72	0.91	11.82		9.43	288.6	2	67	10	21	115	8.28	-20.09			May-10
50	2.31	6.19	15.74	16.77	45.24	0.37	1.29	8.77		12.35	688.2	2	81	15	2	98	18.84	-17.59	5.50		May-04
50	2.87	6.56	15.68	15.10	40.97	0	2.02	8.78		12.17	688.2	2	81	15	2	98	18.29	-17.88		1.00	May-04
	2.07	6.05	15.72	16.75	45.21		0.9	8.79		12.27	688.2	2	81	15	2	98	18.85	-17.59			Feb-17
50	1.99	5.96	15.66	17.46	47.13	0.64	0.98	8.78		12.26	688.2	2	81	15	2	98	19.04	-17.49			Aug-06
	2.54	6.34	15.61	16.03	43.50	0.09	1.6	8.77		12.07	688.2	2	81	15	2	98	18.61	-17.67			Dec-06
	2.33	6.22	15.73	16.83	45.26	0.37	1.3	8.8		12.28	688.2	2	81	15	2	98	18.77	-17.59			Dec-06
	2.15	6.09	15.74	17.56	47.15	0.63	1	8.8		12.35	688.2	2	81	15	2	98	19.03	-17.5			Dec-06

	MARKET			FUND TYPE, CATEGORY & OBJECTIVE	RATINGS				MINIMUMS	
Fund Name	Ticker Symbol	Traded On	Fund Type	Category and (Prospectus Objective)	Overall Rating	Reward Rating	Risk Rating	Recent Up/ Downgrade	Open to New Investors	Min Initial Investment
Hartford Growth Opportunities HLS Fund Class IA	HAGOX	NAS CM	Open End	US Equity Large Cap Growth (Growth)	A-	A-	B+	Up	Y	0
Hartford Growth Opportunities HLS Fund Class IB	HBGOX	NAS CM	Open End	US Equity Large Cap Growth (Growth)	A-	A-	B+	Up	Y	0
Hartford Growth Opportunities HLS Fund Class IC	HCGOX	NAS CM	Open End	US Equity Large Cap Growth (Growth)	A-	A-	B+	Up	Y	0
Hartford Healthcare HLS Fund Class IA	HIAHX	NAS CM	Open End	Healthcare Sector Equity (Health)	B-	C+	B	Down	Y	0
Hartford Healthcare HLS Fund Class IB	HBGHX	NAS CM	Open End	Healthcare Sector Equity (Health)	B-	C+	B	Down	Y	0
Hartford International Equity Fund Class A	HDVAX	NAS CM	Open End	Global Equity Large Cap (Growth)	B	B	B	Up	Y	2,000
Hartford International Equity Fund Class C	HDVCX	NAS CM	Open End	Global Equity Large Cap (Growth)	B-	B-	B	Up	Y	2,000
Hartford International Equity Fund Class F	HDVFX	NAS CM	Open End	Global Equity Large Cap (Growth)	B	B	B	Up	Y	1,000,000
Hartford International Equity Fund Class I	HDVIX	NAS CM	Open End	Global Equity Large Cap (Growth)	B	B	B	Up	Y	2,000
Hartford International Equity Fund Class R3	HDVRX	NAS CM	Open End	Global Equity Large Cap (Growth)	B	B	B	Up	Y	0
Hartford International Equity Fund Class R4	HDVSX	NAS CM	Open End	Global Equity Large Cap (Growth)	B	B	B	Up	Y	0
Hartford International Equity Fund Class R5	HDVTX	NAS CM	Open End	Global Equity Large Cap (Growth)	B	B	B	Up	Y	0
Hartford International Equity Fund Class Y	HDVYX	NAS CM	Open End	Global Equity Large Cap (Growth)	B	B	B	Up	Y	250,000
Hartford International Growth Fund Class A	HNCAX	NAS CM	Open End	Global Equity Large Cap (Foreign Stock)	B	B	B	Up	Y	2,000
Hartford International Growth Fund Class C	HNCCX	NAS CM	Open End	Global Equity Large Cap (Foreign Stock)	B-	B-	B	Up	Y	2,000
Hartford International Growth Fund Class F	HNCFX	NAS CM	Open End	Global Equity Large Cap (Foreign Stock)	B	B	B	Up	Y	1,000,000
Hartford International Growth Fund Class I	HNCJX	NAS CM	Open End	Global Equity Large Cap (Foreign Stock)	B	B	B	Up	Y	2,000
Hartford International Growth Fund Class R3	HNCRX	NAS CM	Open End	Global Equity Large Cap (Foreign Stock)	B	B-	B	Up	Y	0
Hartford International Growth Fund Class R4	HNCSX	NAS CM	Open End	Global Equity Large Cap (Foreign Stock)	B	B	B	Up	Y	0
Hartford International Growth Fund Class R5	HNCTX	NAS CM	Open End	Global Equity Large Cap (Foreign Stock)	B	B	B	Up	Y	0
Hartford International Growth Fund Class Y	HNCYX	NAS CM	Open End	Global Equity Large Cap (Foreign Stock)	B	B	B	Up	Y	250,000
Hartford International Opportunities HLS Fund Class IA	HIAOX	NAS CM	Open End	Global Equity Large Cap (Foreign Stock)	B	B	B	Up	Y	0
Hartford International Opportunities HLS Fund Class IB	HBIOX	NAS CM	Open End	Global Equity Large Cap (Foreign Stock)	B	B-	B	Up	Y	0
Hartford International Small Company Fund Class A	HNSAX	NAS CM	Open End	Global Equity Mid/Small Cap (Foreign Stock)	B	B	B	Up	Y	2,000
Hartford International Small Company Fund Class C	HNSCX	NAS CM	Open End	Global Equity Mid/Small Cap (Foreign Stock)	B	B	B	Up	Y	2,000
Hartford International Small Company Fund Class F	HNSFX	NAS CM	Open End	Global Equity Mid/Small Cap (Foreign Stock)	B	B+	B	Up	Y	1,000,000
Hartford International Small Company Fund Class I	HNSJX	NAS CM	Open End	Global Equity Mid/Small Cap (Foreign Stock)	B	B+	B	Up	Y	2,000
Hartford International Small Company Fund Class R3	HNSRX	NAS CM	Open End	Global Equity Mid/Small Cap (Foreign Stock)	B	B	B	Up	Y	0
Hartford International Small Company Fund Class R4	HNSSX	NAS CM	Open End	Global Equity Mid/Small Cap (Foreign Stock)	B	B+	B	Up	Y	0
Hartford International Small Company Fund Class R5	HNSTX	NAS CM	Open End	Global Equity Mid/Small Cap (Foreign Stock)	B	B+	B	Up	Y	0
Hartford International Small Company Fund Class Y	HNSYX	NAS CM	Open End	Global Equity Mid/Small Cap (Foreign Stock)	B	B+	B	Up	Y	250,000
Hartford International Value Fund Class A	HILAX	NAS CM	Open End	Global Equity Large Cap (Foreign Stock)	B	B	C+	Up		2,000
Hartford International Value Fund Class C	HILCX	NAS CM	Open End	Global Equity Large Cap (Foreign Stock)	B	B	C+	Up		2,000
Hartford International Value Fund Class F	HILDX	NAS CM	Open End	Global Equity Large Cap (Foreign Stock)	B	B	C+	Up	Y	1,000,000
Hartford International Value Fund Class I	HILIX	NAS CM	Open End	Global Equity Large Cap (Foreign Stock)	B	B	C+	Up		2,000
Hartford International Value Fund Class R3	HILRX	NAS CM	Open End	Global Equity Large Cap (Foreign Stock)	B	B	C+	Up		0
Hartford International Value Fund Class R4	HILSX	NAS CM	Open End	Global Equity Large Cap (Foreign Stock)	B	B	C+	Up		0
Hartford International Value Fund Class R5	HILTX	NAS CM	Open End	Global Equity Large Cap (Foreign Stock)	B	B	C+	Up		0
Hartford Long/Short Global Equity Fund Class A	HLOAX	NAS CM	Open End	Long/Short Equity (Growth)	B	B-	B+	Up	Y	5,000
Hartford Long/Short Global Equity Fund Class C	HLOCX	NAS CM	Open End	Long/Short Equity (Growth)	B-	C+	B	Up	Y	5,000
Hartford Long/Short Global Equity Fund Class F	HLOFX	NAS CM	Open End	Long/Short Equity (Growth)	B	B-	B+	Up	Y	1,000,000
Hartford Long/Short Global Equity Fund Class I	HLOIX	NAS CM	Open End	Long/Short Equity (Growth)	B	B-	B+	Up	Y	5,000
Hartford Long/Short Global Equity Fund Class Y	HLOYX	NAS CM	Open End	Long/Short Equity (Growth)	B	B-	B+	Up	Y	250,000
Hartford MidCap HLS Fund Class IA	HIMCX	NAS CM	Open End	US Equity Mid Cap (Growth)	B	B+	B	Up	Y	0
Hartford MidCap HLS Fund Class IB	HBMCX	NAS CM	Open End	US Equity Mid Cap (Growth)	B	B+	B-	Up	Y	0
Hartford MidCap Value Fund Class A	HMVAX	NAS CM	Open End	US Equity Mid Cap (Growth)	B	B-	B	Up	Y	2,000
Hartford MidCap Value Fund Class C	HMVCX	NAS CM	Open End	US Equity Mid Cap (Growth)	B-	C+	B	Up	Y	2,000
Hartford MidCap Value Fund Class F	HMVFX	NAS CM	Open End	US Equity Mid Cap (Growth)	B	B-	B	Up	Y	1,000,000
Hartford MidCap Value Fund Class I	HMVJX	NAS CM	Open End	US Equity Mid Cap (Growth)	B	B-	B	Up	Y	2,000
Hartford MidCap Value Fund Class R3	HMVRX	NAS CM	Open End	US Equity Mid Cap (Growth)	B-	B-	B	Up	Y	0
Hartford MidCap Value Fund Class R4	HMVSX	NAS CM	Open End	US Equity Mid Cap (Growth)	B	B-	B	Up	Y	0
Hartford MidCap Value Fund Class R5	HMVTX	NAS CM	Open End	US Equity Mid Cap (Growth)	B	B-	B	Up	Y	0

★ Expanded analysis of this fund is included in Section II.

	TOTAL RETURNS					PERFORMANCE				ASSETS		ASSET ALLOCATION & TURNOVER					BULL & BEAR		FEES		
Min Additional Investment	3-Month Total Return	6-Month Total Return	1-Year Total Return	3-Year Total Return	5-Year Total Return	Dividend Yield (TTM)	Expense Ratio	3-Yr Std Deviation	3-Year Beta	NAV	Total Assets (MIL)	%Cash	%Stocks	%Bonds	%Other	Turnover Ratio	Last Bull Market Total Return	Last Bear Market Total Return	Front End Fee (%)	Back End Fee (%)	Inception Date
	5.28	11.21	30.44	44.26	128.22	0	0.65	11.91	1.01	38.42	1,526	0	95	0	1	138	27.19	-22.88			Mar-87
	5.18	11.05	30.13	43.14	125.31	0	0.9	11.9	1.01	36.91	1,526	0	95	0	1	138	27	-22.96			May-02
	5.12	10.92	29.80	42.09	123.37	0	1.15	11.91	1.01	37.71	1,526	0	95	0	1	138	27	-22.96			Apr-14
	-1.44	0.10	22.26	26.21	148.15	0	0.89	15.77	1.22	22.46	339.4	2	98	0	0	36	23.17	-12.53			May-00
	-1.52	0.01	21.96	25.28	145.03	0	1.14	15.76	1.21	21.35	339.4	2	98	0	0	36	22.99	-12.63			May-00
50	3.81	10.89	28.54	32.36	50.16	1.48	1.12	10.97	0.88	11.35	56.1	4	93	0	3	95	15.19	-23.47	5.50		Jun-08
50	3.59	10.42	27.49	29.49	44.57	0.87	1.87	10.98	0.88	11.25	56.1	4	93	0	3	95	14.86	-23.72		1.00	Jun-08
	3.95	11.07	29.00	33.64	52.86		0.67	10.96	0.88	11.46	56.1	4	93	0	3	95	15.49	-23.37			Feb-17
50	3.87	11.00	28.80	33.43	52.62	1.58	0.87	10.95	0.88	11.43	56.1	4	93	0	3	95	15.49	-23.37			Jun-08
	3.74	10.74	28.16	31.18	48.15	1.57	1.42	10.96	0.88	11.32	56.1	4	93	0	3	95	15.03	-23.55			Jun-08
	3.78	10.84	28.47	32.33	50.31	1.64	1.17	10.94	0.88	11.36	56.1	4	93	0	3	95	15.4	-23.52			Jun-08
	3.92	11.05	28.89	32.80	51.88	12.34	0.87	10.92	0.88	9.97	56.1	4	93	0	3	95	15.61	-23.4			Jun-08
	3.92	11.06	29.02	33.91	53.29	1.76	0.77	10.93	0.88	11.41	56.1	4	93	0	3	95	15.52	-23.37			Jun-08
50	3.76	11.64	33.01	28.14	56.76	0.92	1.3	11.12	0.89	15.35	267.3	4	94	0	2	89	17.23	-24.21	5.50		Apr-01
50	3.57	11.21	31.90	25.24	51.14	0.32	2.05	11.11	0.89	14.18	267.3	4	94	0	2	89	16.74	-24.49		1.00	Apr-01
	3.91	11.94	33.56	29.69	60.48		0.9	11.17	0.9	15.22	267.3	4	94	0	2	89	17.49	-23.98			Feb-17
50	3.86	11.82	33.31	29.26	59.38	1.18	1	11.1	0.89	15.21	267.3	4	94	0	2	89	17.37	-24.09			Aug-06
	3.74	11.54	32.61	27.10	55.34	0.54	1.6	11.12	0.89	15.57	267.3	4	94	0	2	89	17.01	-24.24			Dec-06
	3.77	11.68	32.98	28.29	57.66	0.92	1.3	11.08	0.89	15.75	267.3	4	94	0	2	89	17.44	-24.16			Dec-06
	3.85	11.84	33.41	29.47	60.04	1.14	1	11.14	0.89	15.86	267.3	4	94	0	2	89	17.47	-24.04			Dec-06
	3.88	11.92	33.54	29.68	60.46	1.18	0.95	11.16	0.89	15.91	267.3	4	94	0	2	89	17.49	-23.98			Apr-01
	3.62	9.18	25.25	28.65	52.89	1.36	0.76	10.79	0.85	17.46	1,578	2	95	0	3	95	18.43	-23.52			Jul-90
	3.57	9.06	24.99	27.71	51.00	1.11	1.01	10.82	0.85	17.68	1,578	2	95	0	3	95	18.26	-23.6			Apr-98
50	6.03	12.38	34.25	37.04	68.15	0.32	1.48	11.77	0.95	16.71	393.5	4	94	0	2	43	17.2	-21.44	5.50		Apr-01
50	5.78	11.99	33.23	34.10	62.18	0	2.22	11.73	0.95	15.04	393.5	4	94	0	2	43	16.71	-21.72		1.00	Apr-01
	6.14	12.67	34.98	39.12	72.42		1	11.75	0.95	16.56	393.5	4	94	0	2	43	17.53	-21.28			Feb-17
50	6.08	12.55	34.74	38.66	71.26	0.64	1.12	11.78	0.96	16.55	393.5	4	94	0	2	43	17.5	-21.26			May-07
	5.95	12.26	33.93	36.27	66.67	0.19	1.67	11.72	0.95	16.84	393.5	4	94	0	2	43	17.07	-21.41			May-10
	6.01	12.42	34.33	37.48	69.20	0.48	1.37	11.76	0.95	16.9	393.5	4	94	0	2	43	17.36	-21.36			May-10
	6.11	12.56	34.72	38.68	71.68	0.7	1.07	11.74	0.95	16.98	393.5	4	94	0	2	43	17.47	-21.22			May-10
	6.08	12.59	34.84	38.97	72.23	0.75	1.02	11.74	0.95	16.99	393.5	4	94	0	2	43	17.53	-21.28			Apr-01
50	3.79	10.23	24.33	41.77	73.40	1.48	1.35	12.27	0.91	17.11	2,769	5	94	0	0	32	14.29	-22.76	5.50		May-10
50	3.58	9.90	23.57	39.03	67.81	0.96	2	12.31	0.91	16.93	2,769	5	94	0	0	32	13.81	-22.94		1.00	May-10
	3.85	10.55	24.86	43.52	76.91		0.89	12.27	0.91	17.27	2,769	5	94	0	0	32	14.56	-22.58			Feb-17
50	3.88	10.45	24.76	43.40	76.76	1.81	0.98	12.26	0.91	17.27	2,769	5	94	0	0	32	14.56	-22.58			May-10
	3.70	10.09	23.97	40.70	71.30	1.41	1.61	12.32	0.91	17.24	2,769	5	94	0	0	32	14.07	-22.78			May-10
	3.73	10.26	24.35	41.97	73.97	1.59	1.3	12.28	0.91	17.22	2,769	5	94	0	0	32	14.42	-22.74			May-10
	3.90	10.52	24.71	43.31	76.68	1.8	1	12.26	0.91	17.32	2,769	5	94	0	0	32	14.47	-22.58			May-10
50	3.17	8.52	17.08	27.19		0	1.96	7.25	0.54	11.85	44.4	37	64	0	-1	399			5.50		Aug-14
50	3.15	8.42	16.91	25.24		0	2.71	7.22	0.54	11.64	44.4	37	64	0	-1	399				1.00	Aug-14
	3.27	8.60	17.21	28.06			1.56	7.2	0.54	11.92	44.4	37	64	0	-1	399					Feb-17
50	3.20	8.52	17.13	27.97		0	1.71	7.19	0.54	11.93	44.4	37	64	0	-1	399					Aug-14
	3.26	8.67	17.29	28.13		0	1.56	7.23	0.54	11.93	44.4	37	64	0	-1	399					Aug-14
	7.42	11.07	24.46	40.50	123.83	0.12	0.7	11.79	1	40.1	2,185	0	100	0	0	32	29.46	-25.59			Jul-97
	7.37	10.92	24.16	39.47	121.01	0	0.95	11.8	1	39.18	2,185	0	100	0	0	32	29.27	-25.67			Nov-99
50	4.58	9.19	13.03	23.79	82.99	0.01	1.28	12.38	1	15.71	694.1	2	98	0	0	56	31.58	-25.59	5.50		Apr-01
50	4.41	8.81	12.18	21.12	76.42	0	2	12.33	0.99	13.02	694.1	2	98	0	0	56	30.99	-25.78		1.00	Apr-01
	4.71	9.43	13.49	25.47	87.15		0.83	12.42	1	15.82	694.1	2	98	0	0	56	31.96	-25.43			Feb-17
50	4.62	9.27	13.16	24.60	85.61	0.28	1.04	12.42	1	15.82	694.1	2	98	0	0	56	31.84	-25.45			May-10
	4.49	9.08	12.64	22.70	80.57	0	1.54	12.39	1	16.5	694.1	2	98	0	0	56	31.4	-25.6			May-10
	4.60	9.25	13.06	23.88	83.37	0.02	1.24	12.38	0.99	16.8	694.1	2	98	0	0	56	31.59	-25.52			May-10
	4.70	9.37	13.35	24.98	86.14	0.27	0.94	12.42	1	16.99	694.1	2	98	0	0	56	31.89	-25.43			May-10

	MARKET			FUND TYPE, CATEGORY & OBJECTIVE	RATINGS					MINIMUMS
Fund Name	Ticker Symbol	Traded On	Fund Type	Category and (Prospectus Objective)	Overall Rating	Reward Rating	Risk Rating	Recent Up/ Downgrade	Open to New Investors	Min Initial Investment
Hartford MidCap Value Fund Class Y	HMVYX	NAS CM	Open End	US Equity Mid Cap (Growth)	B	B-	B	Up	Y	250,000
Hartford MidCap Value HLS Fund Class IA	HMVIX	NAS CM	Open End	US Equity Mid Cap (Growth)	B	B-	B	Up	Y	0
Hartford MidCap Value HLS Fund Class IB	HBMVX	NAS CM	Open End	US Equity Mid Cap (Growth)	B	B-	B	Up	Y	0
Hartford Moderate Allocation Fund Class A	HBAAX	NAS CM	Open End	Alloc (Balanced)	C+	C+	B-	Down	Y	2,000
Hartford Moderate Allocation Fund Class C	HBACX	NAS CM	Open End	Alloc (Balanced)	C+	C+	B-	Down	Y	2,000
Hartford Moderate Allocation Fund Class F	HBADX	NAS CM	Open End	Alloc (Balanced)	C+	C+	B-	Down	Y	1,000,000
Hartford Moderate Allocation Fund Class I	HBAIX	NAS CM	Open End	Alloc (Balanced)	B-	C+	B-	Down	Y	2,000
Hartford Moderate Allocation Fund Class R3	HBARX	NAS CM	Open End	Alloc (Balanced)	C+	C+	B-	Down	Y	0
Hartford Moderate Allocation Fund Class R4	HBASX	NAS CM	Open End	Alloc (Balanced)	C+	C+	B-	Down	Y	0
Hartford Moderate Allocation Fund Class R5	HBATX	NAS CM	Open End	Alloc (Balanced)	B-	C+	B-	Down	Y	0
Hartford Multi-Asset Income Fund Class A	HAFAX	NAS CM	Open End	Alloc (Income)	C+	C+	B-	Down	Y	2,000
Hartford Multi-Asset Income Fund Class C	HAICX	NAS CM	Open End	Alloc (Income)	C+	C	B-	Down	Y	2,000
Hartford Multi-Asset Income Fund Class F	HAFDX	NAS CM	Open End	Alloc (Income)	C+	C+	B-	Down	Y	1,000,000
Hartford Multi-Asset Income Fund Class I	HAFIX	NAS CM	Open End	Alloc (Income)	C+	C+	B-	Down	Y	2,000
Hartford Multi-Asset Income Fund Class R3	HAFRX	NAS CM	Open End	Alloc (Income)	C+	C+	B-	Down	Y	0
Hartford Multi-Asset Income Fund Class R4	HAFSX	NAS CM	Open End	Alloc (Income)	C+	C+	B-	Down	Y	0
Hartford Multi-Asset Income Fund Class R5	HAFTX	NAS CM	Open End	Alloc (Income)	C+	C+	B-	Down	Y	0
Hartford Multi-Asset Income Fund Class Y	HAFYX	NAS CM	Open End	Alloc (Income)	C+	C+	B-	Down	Y	250,000
Hartford Quality Value Fund Class A	HVOAX	NAS CM	Open End	US Equity Large Cap Value (Growth)	B-	C+	B	Up	Y	2,000
Hartford Quality Value Fund Class C	HVOCX	NAS CM	Open End	US Equity Large Cap Value (Growth)	B-	C+	B	Up	Y	2,000
Hartford Quality Value Fund Class F	HVOFX	NAS CM	Open End	US Equity Large Cap Value (Growth)	B-	C+	B	Up	Y	1,000,000
Hartford Quality Value Fund Class I	HVOIX	NAS CM	Open End	US Equity Large Cap Value (Growth)	B-	C+	B	Up	Y	2,000
Hartford Quality Value Fund Class R3	HVORX	NAS CM	Open End	US Equity Large Cap Value (Growth)	B-	C+	B	Up	Y	0
Hartford Quality Value Fund Class R4	HVOSX	NAS CM	Open End	US Equity Large Cap Value (Growth)	B-	C+	B	Up	Y	0
Hartford Quality Value Fund Class R5	HVOTX	NAS CM	Open End	US Equity Large Cap Value (Growth)	B-	C+	B	Up	Y	0
Hartford Quality Value Fund Class Y	HVOYX	NAS CM	Open End	US Equity Large Cap Value (Growth)	B-	C+	B	Up	Y	250,000
Hartford Real Total Return Fund Class A	HABMX	NAS CM	Open End	Multialternative (Growth)	C-	D+	C	Up	Y	5,000
Hartford Real Total Return Fund Class C	HABNX	NAS CM	Open End	Multialternative (Growth)	C-	D+	C	Up	Y	5,000
Hartford Real Total Return Fund Class F	HABAX	NAS CM	Open End	Multialternative (Growth)	C-	D+	C	Up	Y	1,000,000
Hartford Real Total Return Fund Class I	HABOX	NAS CM	Open End	Multialternative (Growth)	C-	D+	C	Up	Y	5,000
Hartford Real Total Return Fund Class R3	HABFX	NAS CM	Open End	Multialternative (Growth)	C-	D+	C	Up	Y	0
Hartford Real Total Return Fund Class R4	HABQX	NAS CM	Open End	Multialternative (Growth)	C-	D+	C	Up	Y	0
Hartford Real Total Return Fund Class R5	HABRX	NAS CM	Open End	Multialternative (Growth)	C-	D+	C	Up	Y	0
Hartford Real Total Return Fund Class Y	HABPX	NAS CM	Open End	Multialternative (Growth)	C-	D+	C	Up	Y	250,000
Hartford Schroders Emerging Markets Equity Fund Class A	SEMVX	NAS CM	Open End	Emerging Markets Equity (Div Emerging Mkts)	B	B	C	Up	Y	2,000
Hartford Schroders Emerging Markets Equity Fund Class C	HHHCX	NAS CM	Open End	Emerging Markets Equity (Div Emerging Mkts)	B-	B	C	Up	Y	2,000
Hartford Schroders Emerging Markets Equity Fund Class F	HHHFX	NAS CM	Open End	Emerging Markets Equity (Div Emerging Mkts)	B	B+	C	Up	Y	1,000,000
Hartford Schroders Emerging Markets Equity Fund Class I	SEMNX	NAS CM	Open End	Emerging Markets Equity (Div Emerging Mkts)	B	B+	C	Up	Y	2,000
Hartford Schroders Emerging Markets Equity Fund Class R3	HHHRX	NAS CM	Open End	Emerging Markets Equity (Div Emerging Mkts)	B	B	C	Up	Y	0
Hartford Schroders Emerging Markets Equity Fund Class R4	HHHSX	NAS CM	Open End	Emerging Markets Equity (Div Emerging Mkts)	B	B	C	Up	Y	0
Hartford Schroders Emerging Markets Equity Fund Class R5	HHHTX	NAS CM	Open End	Emerging Markets Equity (Div Emerging Mkts)	B	B+	C	Up	Y	0
Hartford Schroders Emerging Markets Equity Fund Class SDR	SEMTX	NAS CM	Open End	Emerging Markets Equity (Div Emerging Mkts)	B	B+	C	Up	Y	5,000,000
Hartford Schroders Emerging Markets Equity Fund Class Y	HHHYX	NAS CM	Open End	Emerging Markets Equity (Div Emerging Mkts)	B	B+	C	Up	Y	250,000
Hartford Schroders Intl Multi-Cap Value Fund Cls A	SIDVX	NAS CM	Open End	Global Equity Large Cap (Foreign Stock)	B-	B-	B-	Up	Y	2,000
Hartford Schroders Intl Multi-Cap Value Fund Cls C	HFYCX	NAS CM	Open End	Global Equity Large Cap (Foreign Stock)	B-	C+	B-	Up	Y	2,000
Hartford Schroders Intl Multi-Cap Value Fund Cls F	HFYFX	NAS CM	Open End	Global Equity Large Cap (Foreign Stock)	B-	C+	B-	Up	Y	1,000,000
Hartford Schroders Intl Multi-Cap Value Fund Cls I	SIDNX	NAS CM	Open End	Global Equity Large Cap (Foreign Stock)	B-	B-	B-	Up	Y	2,000
Hartford Schroders Intl Multi-Cap Value Fund Cls R3	HFYRX	NAS CM	Open End	Global Equity Large Cap (Foreign Stock)	B-	C+	B-	Up	Y	0
Hartford Schroders Intl Multi-Cap Value Fund Cls R4	HFYSX	NAS CM	Open End	Global Equity Large Cap (Foreign Stock)	B-	B-	B-	Up	Y	0
Hartford Schroders Intl Multi-Cap Value Fund Cls R5	HFYTX	NAS CM	Open End	Global Equity Large Cap (Foreign Stock)	B-	B-	B-	Up	Y	0
Hartford Schroders Intl Multi-Cap Value Fund Cls SDR	SIDRX	NAS CM	Open End	Global Equity Large Cap (Foreign Stock)	B-	B-	B-	Up	Y	5,000,000
Hartford Schroders Intl Multi-Cap Value Fund Cls Y	HFYYX	NAS CM	Open End	Global Equity Large Cap (Foreign Stock)	B-	B-	B-	Up	Y	250,000

★ Expanded analysis of this fund is included in Section II.

	TOTAL RETURNS					PERFORMANCE				ASSETS		ASSET ALLOCATION & TURNOVER					BULL & BEAR		FEES		
Min Additional Investment	3-Month Total Return	6-Month Total Return	1-Year Total Return	3-Year Total Return	5-Year Total Return	Dividend Yield (TTM)	Expense Ratio	3-Yr Std Deviation	3-Year Beta	NAV	Total Assets (MIL)	%Cash	%Stocks	%Bonds	%Other	Turnover Ratio	Last Bull Market Total Return	Last Bear Market Total Return	Front End Fee (%)	Back End Fee (%)	Inception Date
	4.65	9.37	13.35	25.31	86.91	0.34	0.88	12.42	1	17.02	694.1	2	98	0	0	56	31.96	-25.43			Apr-01
	4.73	9.54	13.46	25.43	87.65	0.53	0.86	12.41	1	12.6	377.7	0	99	0	1	38	31.65	-25.24			Apr-01
	4.69	9.32	13.18	24.43	85.29	0.29	1.11	12.4	1	12.5	377.7	0	99	0	1	38	31.46	-25.31			Apr-01
50	0.92	4.07	11.60	13.34	26.09	0.83	1.25	6.65		12.08	476.8	2	63	33	2	81	15.36	-13.01	5.50		May-04
50	1.54	4.51	11.71	11.67	22.50	0.14	1.99	6.64		11.9	476.8	2	63	33	2	81	14.93	-13.3		1.00	May-04
	0.75	3.88	11.57	13.31	26.06		0.88	6.65		12.11	476.8	2	63	33	2	81	15.36	-13.01			Feb-17
50	0.75	3.97	11.66	14.05	27.79	1.1	0.95	6.63		12.11	476.8	2	63	33	2	81	15.55	-12.88			Aug-06
	1.20	4.23	11.68	12.59	24.39	0.56	1.58	6.62		11.92	476.8	2	63	33	2	81	15.19	-13.14			Dec-06
	1.01	4.16	11.70	13.27	26.00	0.8	1.28	6.64		12.08	476.8	2	63	33	2	81	15.36	-13.03			Dec-06
	0.83	3.97	11.76	13.97	27.48	1.08	0.98	6.61		12.12	476.8	2	63	33	2	81	15.51	-12.89			Dec-06
50	1.82	4.12	9.68	12.35		4.07	1.13	5.52		9.34	65.4	7	16	56	6	80			4.50		Apr-14
50	1.74	3.76	9.07	10.01		3.41	1.88	5.52		9.35	65.4	7	16	56	6	80				1.00	Apr-14
	1.89	4.26	9.92	13.19			0.73	5.54		9.34	65.4	7	16	56	6	80					Feb-17
50	1.85	4.19	9.84	12.96		4.22	0.83	5.61		9.34	65.4	7	16	56	6	80					Apr-14
	1.89	4.06	9.62	11.47		3.89	1.43	5.57		9.35	65.4	7	16	56	6	80					Apr-14
	1.92	4.22	9.74	12.28		4.02	1.13	5.58		9.35	65.4	7	16	56	6	80					Apr-14
	1.85	4.18	9.80	12.78		4.18	0.83	5.59		9.34	65.4	7	16	56	6	80					Apr-14
	1.97	4.22	9.90	13.16		4.27	0.78	5.54		9.34	65.4	7	16	56	6	80					Apr-14
50	4.14	6.58	11.37	23.52	80.43	0.65	1.05	12.44	1.16	20.38	274.2	2	98	0	0	41	24.5	-22.13	5.50		Feb-02
50	3.96	6.18	10.52	20.83	73.98	0.17	1.78	12.42	1.15	17.55	274.2	2	98	0	0	41	24.02	-22.39		1.00	Feb-02
	4.16	6.74	11.65	23.84	80.89		0.64	12.45	1.16	20.06	274.2	2	98	0	0	41	24.5	-22.13			Feb-17
50	4.21	6.74	11.65	24.66	83.29	0.98	0.78	12.44	1.16	20.09	274.2	2	98	0	0	41	24.72	-22.01			Aug-06
	4.04	6.40	10.94	22.35	77.88	0.37	1.35	12.43	1.15	20.71	274.2	2	98	0	0	41	24.4	-22.21			Dec-06
	4.13	6.57	11.36	23.51	80.77	0.63	1.05	12.41	1.15	20.87	274.2	2	98	0	0	41	24.62	-22.09			Dec-06
	4.21	6.73	11.66	24.65	83.39	0.9	0.75	12.41	1.15	21	274.2	2	98	0	0	41	24.86	-22.04			Dec-06
	4.18	6.75	11.72	25.01	84.06	1	0.69	12.42	1.15	21.04	274.2	2	98	0	0	41	24.87	-22			Feb-02
50	0.70	1.84	2.42	-6.33		0	1.47	6.19	-22.44	8.02	92.0	13	47	36	5	239			5.50		Nov-13
50	0.59	1.41	1.77	-8.39		0	2.22	6.18	-21.9	7.8	92.0	13	47	36	5	239				1.00	Nov-13
	0.89	2.02	2.94	-5.18			1.07	6.26	-22.66	8.1	92.0	13	47	36	5	239					Feb-17
50	0.82	1.95	2.64	-5.56		0	1.22	6.22	-22.9	8.1	92.0	13	47	36	5	239					Nov-13
	0.64	1.79	2.84	-6.51		0	1.77	6.19	-27.47	7.98	92.0	13	47	36	5	239					Nov-13
	0.78	1.80	2.62	-6.16		0	1.47	6.22	-23.32	8.04	92.0	13	47	36	5	239					Nov-13
	0.73	1.98	2.78	-5.44		0	1.17	6.23	-22.36	8.09	92.0	13	47	36	5	239					Nov-13
	0.45	0.79	1.81	-6.22		0	1.12	6.21	-23.28	8.04	92.0	13	47	36	5	239					Nov-13
50	6.87	16.85	40.53	34.75	26.88	0.52	1.45	14.44	0.9	16.68	2,799	2	98	0	0	47	21.91	-27.29	5.50		Mar-06
50	6.68	16.41	39.50	31.90	22.30	0.67	2.2	14.42	0.89	16.53	2,799	2	98	0	0	47	21.19	-27.5		1.00	Oct-16
	7.00	16.99	40.96	35.78	28.44		1.1	14.44	0.9	16.63	2,799	2	98	0	0	47	21.89	-27.19			Feb-17
50	6.93	16.91	40.86	35.69	28.35	0.69	1.27	14.45	0.9	16.64	2,799	2	98	0	0	47	21.89	-27.19			Mar-06
	6.87	16.86	40.61	34.17	25.66	0.61	1.81	14.44	0.9	16.61	2,799	2	98	0	0	47	21.54	-27.35			Oct-16
	6.84	16.75	40.48	34.74	26.82	0.66	1.51	14.43	0.89	16.62	2,799	2	98	0	0	47	21.72	-27.27			Oct-16
	6.96	16.95	40.91	35.85	28.51	0.69	1.21	14.43	0.89	16.64	2,799	2	98	0	0	47	21.89	-27.19			Oct-16
	6.98	17.03	41.09	36.27	28.90	0.71	1.1	14.44	0.9	16.66	2,799	2	98	0	0	47	21.89	-27.19			Dec-14
	6.97	16.94	41.10	36.07	28.71	0.71	1.15	14.43	0.89	16.65	2,799	2	98	0	0	47	21.89	-27.19			Oct-16
50	3.57	8.39	22.95	26.05	44.71	1.56	1.15	10.89	0.88	10.26	1,441	8	88	0	3	94	12.82	-22.26	5.50		Aug-06
50	3.34	8.01	22.04	23.34	39.61	1.25	1.9	10.89	0.87	10.2	1,441	8	88	0	3	94	12.12	-22.49		1.00	Oct-16
	3.57	7.95	21.95	25.72	45.16		0.75	10.91	0.88	10.25	1,441	8	88	0	3	94	12.77	-22.16			Feb-17
50	3.54	8.43	23.28	27.09	46.75	1.81	0.89	10.92	0.88	10.25	1,441	8	88	0	3	94	12.77	-22.16			Aug-06
	3.44	8.19	22.50	25.12	43.04	1.38	1.52	10.9	0.87	10.23	1,441	8	88	0	3	94	12.44	-22.32			Oct-16
	3.57	8.38	22.88	26.16	44.94	1.61	1.22	10.89	0.87	10.24	1,441	8	88	0	3	94	12.6	-22.24			Oct-16
	3.54	8.43	23.14	27.07	46.73	1.78	0.92	10.89	0.87	10.24	1,441	8	88	0	3	94	12.77	-22.16			Oct-16
	3.57	8.49	23.26	27.43	47.31	1.88	0.75	10.92	0.88	10.24	1,441	8	88	0	3	94	12.77	-22.16			Dec-14
	3.66	8.55	23.48	27.45	47.17	1.96	0.87	10.9	0.88	10.25	1,441	8	88	0	3	94	12.77	-22.16			Oct-16

	MARKET		FUND TYPE, CATEGORY & OBJECTIVE		RATINGS				MINIMUMS	
Fund Name	Ticker Symbol	Traded On	Fund Type	Category and (Prospectus Objective)	Overall Rating	Reward Rating	Risk Rating	Recent Up/ Downgrade	Open to New Investors	Min Initial Investment
Hartford Schroders International Stock Fund Class A	SCVEX	NAS CM	Open End	Global Equity Large Cap (Foreign Stock)	B-	B-	B	Up	Y	2,000
Hartford Schroders International Stock Fund Class C	HSWCX	NAS CM	Open End	Global Equity Large Cap (Foreign Stock)	B-	B-	B	Up	Y	2,000
Hartford Schroders International Stock Fund Class F	HSWFX	NAS CM	Open End	Global Equity Large Cap (Foreign Stock)	B	B-	B	Up	Y	1,000,000
Hartford Schroders International Stock Fund Class I	SCIEX	NAS CM	Open End	Global Equity Large Cap (Foreign Stock)	B	B-	B	Up	Y	2,000
Hartford Schroders International Stock Fund Class R3	HSWRX	NAS CM	Open End	Global Equity Large Cap (Foreign Stock)	B-	B-	B	Up	Y	0
Hartford Schroders International Stock Fund Class R4	HSWSX	NAS CM	Open End	Global Equity Large Cap (Foreign Stock)	B-	B-	B	Up	Y	0
Hartford Schroders International Stock Fund Class R5	HSWTX	NAS CM	Open End	Global Equity Large Cap (Foreign Stock)	B	B-	B	Up	Y	0
Hartford Schroders International Stock Fund Class SDR	SCIJX	NAS CM	Open End	Global Equity Large Cap (Foreign Stock)	B	B-	B	Up	Y	5,000,000
Hartford Schroders International Stock Fund Class Y	HSWYX	NAS CM	Open End	Global Equity Large Cap (Foreign Stock)	B	B-	B	Up	Y	250,000
Hartford Schroders US Small Cap Opportunities Fund Class A	SCUVX	NAS CM	Open End	US Equity Small Cap (Growth)	B	B	B+	Up	Y	2,000
Hartford Schroders US Small Cap Opportunities Fund Class C	HOOCX	NAS CM	Open End	US Equity Small Cap (Growth)	B	B	B	Up	Y	2,000
Hartford Schroders US Small Cap Opportunities Fund Class F	HOOFX	NAS CM	Open End	US Equity Small Cap (Growth)	B	B	B+		Y	1,000,000
Hartford Schroders US Small Cap Opportunities Fund Class I	SCUIX	NAS CM	Open End	US Equity Small Cap (Growth)	B	B	B+	Up	Y	2,000
Hartford Schroders US Small Cap Opportunities Fund Cls R3	HOORX	NAS CM	Open End	US Equity Small Cap (Growth)	B	B	B+	Up	Y	0
Hartford Schroders US Small Cap Opportunities Fund Cls R4	HOOSX	NAS CM	Open End	US Equity Small Cap (Growth)	B	B	B+	Up	Y	0
Hartford Schroders US Small Cap Opportunities Fund Cls R5	HOOTX	NAS CM	Open End	US Equity Small Cap (Growth)	B	B	B+	Up	Y	0
Hartford Schroders US Small Cap Opportunities Fund Cls SDR	SCURX	NAS CM	Open End	US Equity Small Cap (Growth)	B	B	B+	Up	Y	5,000,000
Hartford Schroders US Small Cap Opportunities Fund Class Y	HOOYX	NAS CM	Open End	US Equity Small Cap (Growth)	B	B	B+	Up	Y	250,000
Hartford Schroders US Small/Mid Cap Opp Fund Cls F	HFDFX	NAS CM	Open End	US Equity Mid Cap (Growth)	B	B	B+		Y	1,000,000
Hartford Schroders US Small/Mid-Cap Opp Fund Cls A	SMDVX	NAS CM	Open End	US Equity Mid Cap (Growth)	B	B	B+		Y	2,000
Hartford Schroders US Small/Mid-Cap Opp Fund Cls C	HFDCX	NAS CM	Open End	US Equity Mid Cap (Growth)	B	B-	B+		Y	2,000
Hartford Schroders US Small/Mid-Cap Opp Fund Cls I	SMDIX	NAS CM	Open End	US Equity Mid Cap (Growth)	B	B	B+		Y	2,000
Hartford Schroders US Small/Mid-Cap Opp Fund Cls R3	HFDRX	NAS CM	Open End	US Equity Mid Cap (Growth)	B	B	B+		Y	0
Hartford Schroders US Small/Mid-Cap Opp Fund Cls R4	HFDSX	NAS CM	Open End	US Equity Mid Cap (Growth)	B	B	B+		Y	0
Hartford Schroders US Small/Mid-Cap Opp Fund Cls R5	HFDTX	NAS CM	Open End	US Equity Mid Cap (Growth)	B	B	B+		Y	0
Hartford Schroders US Small/Mid-Cap Opp Fund Cls SDR	SMDRX	NAS CM	Open End	US Equity Mid Cap (Growth)	B	B	A-		Y	5,000,000
Hartford Schroders US Small/Mid-Cap Opp Fund Cls Y	HFDYX	NAS CM	Open End	US Equity Mid Cap (Growth)	B	B	B+		Y	250,000
Hartford Small Cap Core Fund Class A	HSMAX	NAS CM	Open End	US Equity Small Cap (Small Company)	B-	B-	B	Up	Y	2,000
Hartford Small Cap Core Fund Class C	HTSCX	NAS CM	Open End	US Equity Small Cap (Small Company)	B-	C+	B	Up	Y	2,000
Hartford Small Cap Core Fund Class F	HSMFX	NAS CM	Open End	US Equity Small Cap (Small Company)	B	B	B	Up	Y	1,000,000
Hartford Small Cap Core Fund Class I	HSEIX	NAS CM	Open End	US Equity Small Cap (Small Company)	B	B-	B	Up	Y	2,000
Hartford Small Cap Core Fund Class R3	HSMRX	NAS CM	Open End	US Equity Small Cap (Small Company)	B-	B-	B	Up	Y	0
Hartford Small Cap Core Fund Class R4	HSMSX	NAS CM	Open End	US Equity Small Cap (Small Company)	B-	B-	B	Up	Y	0
Hartford Small Cap Core Fund Class R5	HSMTX	NAS CM	Open End	US Equity Small Cap (Small Company)	B	B-	B	Up	Y	0
Hartford Small Cap Core Fund Class Y	HSMYX	NAS CM	Open End	US Equity Small Cap (Small Company)	B	B	B	Up	Y	250,000
Hartford Small Cap Growth Fund Class A	HSLAX	NAS CM	Open End	US Equity Small Cap (Small Company)	B	B+	B	Up		2,000
Hartford Small Cap Growth Fund Class C	HSLCX	NAS CM	Open End	US Equity Small Cap (Small Company)	B	B	B	Up		2,000
Hartford Small Cap Growth Fund Class F	HSLFX	NAS CM	Open End	US Equity Small Cap (Small Company)	B	B+	B	Up	Y	1,000,000
Hartford Small Cap Growth Fund Class I	HSLIX	NAS CM	Open End	US Equity Small Cap (Small Company)	B	B+	B	Up		2,000
Hartford Small Cap Growth Fund Class R3	HSLRX	NAS CM	Open End	US Equity Small Cap (Small Company)	B	B+	B	Up		0
Hartford Small Cap Growth Fund Class R4	HSLSX	NAS CM	Open End	US Equity Small Cap (Small Company)	B	B+	B	Up		0
Hartford Small Cap Growth Fund Class R5	HSLTX	NAS CM	Open End	US Equity Small Cap (Small Company)	B	B+	B	Up		0
Hartford Small Cap Growth Fund Class R6	HSLVX	NAS CM	Open End	US Equity Small Cap (Small Company)	B	B+	B	Up		0
Hartford Small Cap Growth Fund Class Y	HSLYX	NAS CM	Open End	US Equity Small Cap (Small Company)	B	B+	B	Up		250,000
Hartford Small Cap Growth HLS Fund Class IA	HISCX	NAS CM	Open End	US Equity Small Cap (Small Company)	B	B+	B	Up		0
Hartford Small Cap Growth HLS Fund Class IB	HBSGX	NAS CM	Open End	US Equity Small Cap (Small Company)	B	B+	B	Up		0
Hartford Small Company HLS Fund Class IA	HIASX	NAS CM	Open End	US Equity Small Cap (Small Company)	C+	B-	C	Up		0
Hartford Small Company HLS Fund Class IB	HDMBX	NAS CM	Open End	US Equity Small Cap (Small Company)	C+	C+	C	Up		0
Hartford Small/Mid Cap Equity HLS Fund Class IA	HMCSX	NAS CM	Open End	US Equity Small Cap (Growth & Income)	B	B	B	Up	Y	0
Hartford Small/Mid Cap Equity HLS Fund Class IB	HMCVX	NAS CM	Open End	US Equity Small Cap (Growth & Income)	B	B	B	Up	Y	0
Hartford Stock HLS Fund Class IA	HSTAX	NAS CM	Open End	US Equity Large Cap Blend (Growth)	B	B-	B+		Y	0
Hartford Stock HLS Fund Class IB	HIBSX	NAS CM	Open End	US Equity Large Cap Blend (Growth)	B	B-	B+		Y	0

★ Expanded analysis of this fund is included in Section II.

Min Additional Investment	TOTAL RETURNS: 3-Month Total Return	6-Month Total Return	1-Year Total Return	3-Year Total Return	5-Year Total Return	PERFORMANCE: Dividend Yield (TTM)	Expense Ratio	3-Yr Std Deviation	3-Year Beta	ASSETS: NAV	Total Assets (MIL)	ASSET ALLOCATION & TURNOVER: %Cash	%Stocks	%Bonds	%Other	Turnover Ratio	BULL & BEAR: Last Bull Market Total Return	Last Bear Market Total Return	FEES: Front End Fee (%)	Back End Fee (%)	Inception Date
50	3.39	11.47	29.43	26.05	45.49	1.14	1.2	11.61	0.91	13.69	204.1	3	96	0	1	53	17.29	-27.17	5.50		May-06
50	3.19	11.04	28.56	23.28	40.19	1.25	1.95	11.59	0.91	13.15	204.1	3	96	0	1	53	16.71	-27.34		1.00	Oct-16
	3.44	11.71	29.87	27.07	47.40		0.8	11.62	0.91	13.25	204.1	3	96	0	1	53	17.39	-27.04			Feb-17
50	3.45	11.54	29.69	26.88	47.19	1.38	0.95	11.6	0.91	13.24	204.1	3	96	0	1	53	17.39	-27.04			Dec-85
	3.35	11.53	29.56	25.46	44.09	1.3	1.5	11.62	0.91	13.25	204.1	3	96	0	1	53	17.05	-27.19			Oct-16
	3.41	11.51	29.65	26.19	45.66	1.34	1.2	11.59	0.91	13.25	204.1	3	96	0	1	53	17.22	-27.12			Oct-16
	3.39	11.56	29.82	27.02	47.34	1.39	0.9	11.59	0.91	13.25	204.1	3	96	0	1	53	17.39	-27.04			Oct-16
	3.43	11.69	29.84	27.39	47.77	1.4	0.8	11.59	0.91	13.25	204.1	3	96	0	1	53	17.39	-27.04			Dec-14
	3.43	11.69	29.97	27.17	47.53	1.39	0.85	11.62	0.91	13.26	204.1	3	96	0	1	53	17.39	-27.04			Oct-16
50	3.80	7.33	14.31	32.82	97.62	0.22	1.3	11.16	0.77	26.1	210.9	7	93	0	0	51	23.93	-23.02	5.50		May-06
50	3.62	6.94	13.53	29.90	90.72	0.29	2.05	11.15	0.77	26.94	210.9	7	93	0	0	51	23.38	-23.25		1.00	Oct-16
	3.90	7.55	14.79	34.00	100.70		0.96	11.17	0.77	27.23	210.9	7	93	0	0	51	24.09	-22.92			Feb-17
50	3.89	7.50	14.73	33.94	100.60	0.32	1.03	11.17	0.77	27.22	210.9	7	93	0	0	51	24.09	-22.92			Aug-93
	3.74	7.28	14.33	32.10	95.88	0.21	1.66	11.14	0.77	27.16	210.9	7	93	0	0	51	23.73	-23.09			Oct-16
	3.84	7.41	14.51	32.99	98.18	0.26	1.36	11.15	0.77	27.21	210.9	7	93	0	0	51	23.91	-23.01			Oct-16
	3.88	7.50	14.65	33.84	100.44	0.31	1.06	11.15	0.77	27.21	210.9	7	93	0	0	51	24.09	-22.92			Oct-16
	3.93	7.54	14.80	34.23	101.03	0.33	0.96	11.16	0.77	27.27	210.9	7	93	0	0	51	24.09	-22.92			Sep-15
	3.93	7.55	14.78	34.01	100.70	0.32	1.01	11.15	0.77	27.23	210.9	7	93	0	0	51	24.09	-22.92			Oct-16
	5.13	7.69	15.56	37.92	113.40		0.92	9.37	0.73	14.8	882.8	9	91	0	0	72	24.11	-20.99			Feb-17
50	5.05	7.55	15.27	36.87	110.58	0.13	1.26	9.4	0.73	14.25	882.8	9	91	0	0	72	23.92	-21.04	5.50		Mar-06
50	4.91	7.11	14.37	33.80	102.94	0.18	2.01	9.35	0.73	14.64	882.8	9	91	0	0	72	23.39	-21.32		1.00	Oct-16
50	5.21	7.69	15.56	37.92	113.40	0.21	1	9.36	0.73	14.81	882.8	9	91	0	0	72	24.11	-20.99			Mar-06
	4.96	7.37	14.81	35.70	107.88	0.15	1.62	9.37	0.73	14.72	882.8	9	91	0	0	72	23.75	-21.16			Oct-16
	5.05	7.54	15.24	36.73	110.50	0.16	1.32	9.36	0.73	14.77	882.8	9	91	0	0	72	23.93	-21.07			Oct-16
	5.08	7.64	15.42	37.75	113.14	0.2	1.02	9.36	0.73	14.79	882.8	9	91	0	0	72	24.11	-20.99			Oct-16
	5.13	7.68	15.62	38.32	113.84	0.22	0.92	9.39	0.73	14.83	882.8	9	91	0	0	72	24.11	-20.99			Dec-14
	5.12	7.68	15.54	37.91	113.39	0.21	0.97	9.37	0.73	14.8	882.8	9	91	0	0	72	24.11	-20.99			Oct-16
50	2.53	7.61	9.42	19.75	75.19	0.72	1.4	13.73	0.95	13.7	157.5	1	99	0	0	94	24.57	-22.38	5.50		Dec-04
50	2.35	7.22	8.65	17.06	68.79	0.16	2.15	13.68	0.95	12.47	157.5	1	99	0	0	94	24.17	-22.69		1.00	Dec-04
	2.65	7.89	9.99	21.37	78.97		0.95	13.69	0.95	13.69	157.5	1	99	0	0	94	24.97	-22.23			Feb-17
50	2.63	7.87	9.85	20.94	78.34	1	1.1	13.69	0.95	13.7	157.5	1	99	0	0	94	24.97	-22.23			Mar-15
	2.52	7.54	9.22	18.98	73.43	0.47	1.6	13.67	0.94	14.1	157.5	1	99	0	0	94	24.53	-22.39			Sep-11
	2.55	7.69	9.52	20.04	75.95	0.56	1.3	13.7	0.95	14.21	157.5	1	99	0	0	94	24.76	-22.31			Sep-11
	2.65	7.87	9.87	21.17	78.63	0.97	1	13.7	0.95	14.17	157.5	1	99	0	0	94	24.95	-22.23			Sep-11
	2.68	7.89	9.97	21.34	78.93	1.05	0.95	13.68	0.95	14.16	157.5	1	99	0	0	94	24.97	-22.23			Dec-04
50	3.55	9.26	19.61	31.24	106.98	0	1.24	13.78	0.92	55.85	1,338	4	96	0	0	45	28.77	-24.07	5.50		Feb-02
50	3.35	8.87	18.74	28.49	99.90	0	1.93	13.77	0.92	42.53	1,338	4	96	0	0	45	28.22	-24.31		1.00	Feb-02
	3.66	9.50	20.11	32.97	111.79		0.78	13.78	0.92	57.75	1,338	4	96	0	0	45	29.11	-23.89			Feb-17
50	3.62	9.40	19.88	32.24	109.97	0	0.98	13.78	0.92	57.65	1,338	4	96	0	0	45	28.99	-23.95			Aug-06
	3.46	9.08	19.23	30.11	104.30	0	1.5	13.79	0.92	55.46	1,338	4	96	0	0	45	28.6	-24.11			Dec-06
	3.55	9.26	19.61	31.37	107.60	0	1.18	13.79	0.92	57.63	1,338	4	96	0	0	45	28.85	-24.04			Dec-06
	3.63	9.43	19.98	32.59	110.75	0	0.88	13.79	0.92	60	1,338	4	96	0	0	45	29.04	-23.92			Dec-06
	3.66	9.50	20.10	32.80	111.52	0	0.78	13.77	0.92	60.63	1,338	4	96	0	0	45	29.11	-23.89			Nov-14
	3.64	9.47	20.05	32.92	111.70	0	0.83	13.78	0.92	60.69	1,338	4	96	0	0	45	29.11	-23.89			Feb-02
	3.67	9.33	20.07	33.57	110.34	0.04	0.66	13.78	0.92	32.13	1,350	3	97	0	0	51	29.3	-23.51			May-94
	3.61	9.17	19.75	32.57	107.65	0	0.91	13.79	0.92	31.28	1,350	3	97	0	0	51	29.11	-23.59			May-02
	6.29	12.07	26.36	17.85	86.64	0	0.75	14.97	0.96	20.42	640.2	5	93	0	0	94	27.07	-24.54			Aug-96
	6.21	11.91	26.04	16.95	84.35	0	1	14.97	0.96	18.97	640.2	5	93	0	0	94	26.88	-24.62			Apr-98
	5.63	10.97	14.42	25.91	87.31	0.8	0.94	12.28	0.98	8.81	100.3	1	99	0	0	96	24.88	-22.28			May-98
	5.42	10.75	13.93	24.90	84.85	0.56	1.19	12.27	0.98	8.75	100.3	1	99	0	0	96	24.69	-22.36			Mar-08
	5.75	9.71	19.84	30.98	96.97	1.51	0.52	9.13	0.84	79.57	1,527	0	98	0	2	29	26.88	-19.42			Aug-77
	5.68	9.56	19.54	30.00	94.51	1.29	0.77	9.12	0.84	79.54	1,527	0	98	0	2	29	26.69	-19.51			Apr-98

	MARKET			FUND TYPE, CATEGORY & OBJECTIVE	RATINGS					MINIMUMS
Fund Name	Ticker Symbol	Traded On	Fund Type	Category and (Prospectus Objective)	Overall Rating	Reward Rating	Risk Rating	Recent Up/ Downgrade	Open to New Investors	Min Initial Investment
Hartford Value HLS Fund Class IA	HIAVX	NAS CM	Open End	US Equity Large Cap Value (Growth)	B	B-	B	Up	Y	0
Hartford Value HLS Fund Class IB	HBVLX	NAS CM	Open End	US Equity Large Cap Value (Growth)	B	B-	B	Up	Y	0
Hatteras Alpha Hedged Strategies Fund Class A	APHAX	NAS CM	Open End	Multialternative (Income)	C-	D+	C		Y	1,000
Hatteras Alpha Hedged Strategies Fund Class C	APHCX	NAS CM	Open End	Multialternative (Income)	C-	D+	C		Y	1,000
Hatteras Alpha Hedged Strategies Fund Institutional Class	ALPIX	NAS CM	Open End	Multialternative (Income)	C	C-	C	Up	Y	1,000,000
Haverford Quality Growth Stock Fund	HAVGX	NAS CM	Open End	US Equity Large Cap Blend (Growth)	B-	C+	B-	Down	Y	2,500
HC The ESG Growth Portfolio HC Advisors Shares	HCSGX	NAS CM	Open End	Alloc (Growth & Income)	U	U	U		Y	0
HC The ESG Growth Portfolio HC Strategic Shares	HCESX	NAS CM	Open End	Alloc (Growth & Income)	U	U	U		Y	0
HCM Dividend Sector Plus Fund Class A	HCMNX	NAS CM	Open End	US Equity Large Cap Value (Equity-Income)	B-	B-	B-	Up	Y	2,500
HCM Dividend Sector Plus Fund Class A1	HCMWX	NAS CM	Open End	US Equity Large Cap Value (Equity-Income)	B-	B-	B-	Up	Y	2,500
HCM Dividend Sector Plus Fund Class I	HCMQX	NAS CM	Open End	US Equity Large Cap Value (Equity-Income)	B-	B-	B-	Up	Y	500,000
HCM Dividend Sector Plus Fund Class R	HCMZX	NAS CM	Open End	US Equity Large Cap Value (Equity-Income)	B-	B-	B-	Up	Y	0
HCM Dividend Sector Plus Fund Investor Class	HCMPX	NAS CM	Open End	US Equity Large Cap Value (Equity-Income)	B-	C+	B-	Up	Y	2,500
HCM Income Plus Fund Class A Shares	HCMEX	NAS CM	Open End	Alloc (Income)	D	D+	A		Y	2,500
HCM Income Plus Fund Investor Class Shares	HCMKX	NAS CM	Open End	Alloc (Income)	D	D+	A		Y	2,500
HCM Tactical Growth Fund Class A	HCMGX	NAS CM	Open End	US Equity Large Cap Blend (Growth)	B	A	C+	Up	Y	2,500
HCM Tactical Growth Fund Class I	HCMIX	NAS CM	Open End	US Equity Large Cap Blend (Growth)	B	A	C+	Up	Y	100,000
HCM Tactical Growth Fund Class R	HCMSX	NAS CM	Open End	US Equity Large Cap Blend (Growth)	B	A	C+	Up	Y	2,500
HCM Tactical Growth Fund Investor Class	HCMDX	NAS CM	Open End	US Equity Large Cap Blend (Growth)	B	B+	C	Up	Y	2,500
Heartland International Value Fund	HINVX	NAS CM	Open End	Global Equity Mid/Small Cap (Foreign Stock)	C	C+	C		Y	1,000
Heartland International Value Fund Institutional Class	HNNVX	NAS CM	Open End	Global Equity Mid/Small Cap (Foreign Stock)	C+	C+	C+	Up	Y	500,000
Heartland Mid Cap Value Fund Institutional Class	HNMDX	NAS CM	Open End	US Equity Mid Cap (Growth & Income)	C+	C+	C+	Up	Y	500,000
Heartland Mid Cap Value Fund Investor Class	HRMDX	NAS CM	Open End	US Equity Mid Cap (Growth & Income)	C+	C+	C+	Up	Y	1,000
Heartland Select Value Fund Institutional Class	HNSVX	NAS CM	Open End	US Equity Mid Cap (Growth)	B	B	B	Up	Y	500,000
Heartland Select Value Fund Investor Class	HRSVX	NAS CM	Open End	US Equity Mid Cap (Growth)	B	B	B	Up	Y	1,000
Heartland Value Fund Institutional Class	HNTVX	NAS CM	Open End	US Equity Small Cap (Small Company)	C+	C+	C+	Up	Y	500,000
Heartland Value Fund Investor Class	HRTVX	NAS CM	Open End	US Equity Small Cap (Small Company)	C+	C+	C+	Up	Y	1,000
Heartland Value Plus Fund Institutional Class	HNVIX	NAS CM	Open End	US Equity Small Cap (Equity-Income)	C+	C+	C	Up		500,000
Heartland Value Plus Fund Investor Class	HRVIX	NAS CM	Open End	US Equity Small Cap (Equity-Income)	C+	C+	C	Up		1,000
Hedeker Strategic Appreciation Fund Institutional Shares	SAFFX	NAS CM	Open End	Convertibles (Convertible Bond)	D-	D+	B-		Y	1,000
HedgeRow Income and Opportunity Fund Class A	HROAX	NAS CM	Open End	Long/Short Equity (Growth & Income)	C-	C-	B+	Up	Y	1,000
HedgeRow Income and Opportunity Fund Institutional Class	HIOIX	NAS CM	Open End	Long/Short Equity (Growth & Income)	C-	C-	B+	Up	Y	2,000
Hennessy Balanced Fund Investor Class	HBFBX	NAS CM	Open End	Moderate Alloc (Balanced)	B-	C+	B	Down	Y	2,500
Hennessy Cornerstone Growth Fund Class Institutional	HICGX	NAS CM	Open End	US Equity Mid Cap (Growth)	B+	B+	B+	Up	Y	250,000
Hennessy Cornerstone Growth Fund Investor Class	HFCGX	NAS CM	Open End	US Equity Mid Cap (Growth)	B	B	B+	Up	Y	2,500
Hennessy Cornerstone Large Growth Fund Institutional Class	HILGX	NAS CM	Open End	US Equity Large Cap Value (Growth)	B-	B-	B		Y	250,000
Hennessy Cornerstone Large Growth Fund Investor Class	HFLGX	NAS CM	Open End	US Equity Large Cap Value (Growth)	B-	C+	B		Y	2,500
Hennessy Cornerstone Mid Cap 30 Fund Institutional Class	HIMDX	NAS CM	Open End	US Equity Mid Cap (Growth)	B	B	B+	Up	Y	250,000
Hennessy Cornerstone Mid Cap 30 Fund Investor Class	HFMDX	NAS CM	Open End	US Equity Mid Cap (Growth)	B	B	B+	Up	Y	2,500
Hennessy Cornerstone Value Fund Class Institutional	HICVX	NAS CM	Open End	US Equity Large Cap Value (Equity-Income)	B-	B-	B-	Down	Y	250,000
Hennessy Cornerstone Value Fund Investor Class	HFCVX	NAS CM	Open End	US Equity Large Cap Value (Equity-Income)	B-	B-	B-	Down	Y	2,500
Hennessy Equity and Income Fund Institutional Class	HEIIX	NAS CM	Open End	Moderate Alloc (Balanced)	B-	C+	B	Down	Y	250,000
Hennessy Equity and Income Fund Investor Class	HEIFX	NAS CM	Open End	Moderate Alloc (Balanced)	B-	C+	B	Down	Y	2,500
Hennessy Focus Fund Institutional Class	HFCIX	NAS CM	Open End	US Equity Mid Cap (Growth)	B	B	B		Y	250,000
Hennessy Focus Fund Investor Class	HFCSX	NAS CM	Open End	US Equity Mid Cap (Growth)	B	B	B		Y	2,500
Hennessy Gas Utility Fund Institutional Class	HGASX	NAS CM	Open End	Utilities Sector Equity (Utility)	C	C	C+	Down	Y	250,000
Hennessy Gas Utility Fund Investor Class	GASFX	NAS CM	Open End	Utilities Sector Equity (Utility)	C	C	C+	Down	Y	2,500
Hennessy Japan Fund Institutional Class	HJPIX	NAS CM	Open End	Japan Equity (Pacific Stock)	A	A	A-	Up	Y	250,000
Hennessy Japan Fund Investor Class	HJPNX	NAS CM	Open End	Japan Equity (Pacific Stock)	A	A	A-	Up	Y	2,500
Hennessy Japan Small Cap Fund Institutional Class	HJSIX	NAS CM	Open End	Japan Equity (Pacific Stock)	A	A+	A-	Up	Y	250,000
Hennessy Japan Small Cap Fund Investor Class	HJPSX	NAS CM	Open End	Japan Equity (Pacific Stock)	A	A+	A-	Up	Y	2,500
Hennessy Large Cap Financial Fund Institutional Class	HILFX	NAS CM	Open End	Financials Sector Equity (Financial)	B	A-	B-		Y	250,000

★ Expanded analysis of this fund is included in Section II.

Min Additional Investment	TOTAL RETURNS: 3-Month Total Return	6-Month Total Return	1-Year Total Return	3-Year Total Return	5-Year Total Return	PERFORMANCE: Dividend Yield (TTM)	Expense Ratio	3-Yr Std Deviation	3-Year Beta	ASSETS: NAV	Total Assets (MIL)	ASSET ALLOCATION & TURNOVER: %Cash	%Stocks	%Bonds	%Other	Turnover Ratio	BULL & BEAR: Last Bull Market Total Return	Last Bear Market Total Return	FEES: Front End Fee (%)	Back End Fee (%)	Inception Date
	5.72	8.87	15.43	26.00	89.76	1.53	0.8	11.25	1.08	16.05	527.2	0	99	0	1	15	27.44	-20.51			Apr-01
	5.60	8.69	15.03	24.95	87.29	1.32	1.05	11.24	1.08	16.02	527.2	0	99	0	1	15	27.25	-20.6			Apr-01
250	0.74	1.69	3.36	-4.23	3.65	1.42	3.49	4.81	19.14	9.95	31.7	11	53	26	9	60	4.27	-5.16	4.75		May-11
250	0.59	1.38	2.60	-6.21	0.00	0	4.24	4.82	17.89	9.46	31.7	11	53	26	9	60	3.76	-5.35		1.00	Aug-06
	0.81	1.83	3.55	-3.19	6.46	1.02	3.24	4.81	20.32	10.3	31.7	11	53	26	9	60	4.85	-5.35			Sep-11
	7.17	9.34	18.46	20.90	84.63	1.11	0.83	10.16	0.97	16.86	193.9	1	99	0	0	15	22.09	-17.11			Jun-04
	-4.97						0.56				117.7										Jul-15
	-4.97						0.31				117.7										Jul-15
500	8.62	12.77	19.09			1.38	1.76			13.11	318.1	4	121	-25	0	100			5.75		Mar-15
500	8.55	12.71	18.83			1.38	1.91			13.11	318.1	4	121	-25	0	100			5.75		Mar-15
500	8.62	12.77	19.09			1.38	2.01			13.11	318.1	4	121	-25	0	100					Mar-15
	8.62	12.77	19.09			1.38	1.86			13.11	318.1	4	121	-25	0	100					Mar-15
500	8.45	12.39	18.27			1.22	2.51			12.98	318.1	4	121	-25	0	100					Mar-15
500	2.02	4.48	8.57			0.54	2.03			10.6	96.3	3	45	30	0	26			5.75		Nov-16
500	1.83	4.10	7.76			0.54	2.78			10.55	96.3	3	45	30	0	26					Nov-16
500	9.09	16.40	33.23	42.06		0	2.5	15.82	1.5	13.55	99.9	-46	146	0	0	67			5.75		Jul-14
500	9.09	16.39	33.20	42.01		0	2.15	15.81	1.5	13.56	99.9	-46	146	0	0	67					Jul-14
500	9.09	16.39	33.20	42.01		0	2.25	15.81	1.5	13.56	99.9	-46	146	0	0	67					Jul-14
500	9.00	16.02	32.40	39.51		0	3.25	15.85	1.5	13.32	99.9	-46	146	0	0	67					Jul-14
100	3.98	6.74	19.03	15.10	24.95	1.26	1.25	13.58	1.07	10.76	29.0	5	94	0	1	55	4.09	-20			Oct-10
100	4.00	6.86	19.05	15.11	24.97		0.99	13.59	1.07	10.75	29.0	5	94	0	1	55	4.09	-20			May-17
100	6.74	6.12	8.36	28.86		0.67	0.99	12.23	1.08	11.99	7.5	0	100	0	0	76					Oct-14
100	6.75	6.04	8.10	27.98		0.65	1.25	12.24	1.08	11.99	7.5	0	100	0	0	76					Oct-14
100	5.85	10.27	12.69	28.40	86.42	1.15	1	11.68	1.03	28	237.9	4	96	0	0	49	21.26	-21.85			May-08
100	5.79	10.13	12.41	27.46	83.88	0.94	1.23	11.67	1.03	28.09	237.9	4	96	0	0	49	20.99	-21.96			Oct-96
100	0.93	5.73	8.58	12.67	55.48	0	0.92	14.44	0.92	41.98	820.1	8	92	0	0	47	20.29	-24.05			May-08
100	0.93	5.67	8.42	12.13	54.22	0	1.09	14.45	0.92	41.18	820.1	8	92	0	0	47	20.16	-24.11			Dec-84
100	5.29	12.76	10.07	14.84	54.81	0.69	0.97	17.08	1.12	33.11	421.6	-1	101	0	0	77	24.91	-25.02			May-08
100	5.22	12.59	9.80	14.16	53.05	0.6	1.19	17.08	1.12	33.26	421.6	-1	101	0	0	77	24.7	-25.1			Oct-93
100	-1.07	-0.84	1.83				1.47			24.7	51.1	-6	1	0	1	113					Dec-16
100	2.21	4.59	8.42			0	2.34			10.9	6.0	17	83	0	0				5.50		Jan-16
100	2.38	4.76	8.68			0	2.09			10.96	6.0	17	83	0	0						Jan-16
	2.56	6.59	8.34	17.18	36.04	0.36	1.69	5.79		12.28	12.4	4	51	44	0	51	8.97	-3.66			Mar-96
	3.75	17.20	16.98	25.11	100.02	0	0.99	12.36	0.75	24.86	224.6	2	98	0	0	97	42.73	-32.63			Mar-08
	3.64	16.99	16.60	24.02	97.26	0	1.33	12.37	0.75	24.16	224.6	2	98	0	0	97	42.4	-32.73			Nov-96
	8.36	10.31	17.33	25.01	100.43	1.18	1.02	11.82	0.97	12.37	109.7	4	96	0	0	53	21.92	-16.46			Mar-09
	8.24	10.20	17.07	24.24	98.46	0.99	1.26	11.85	0.97	12.26	109.7	4	96	0	0	53	21.68	-16.54			Mar-09
	7.78	13.99	20.96	27.48	100.38	0	0.97	11.59	0.91	20.26	982.0	2	98	0	0	108	25.36	-20.23			Mar-08
	7.69	13.79	20.50	26.20	97.37	0	1.35	11.57	0.9	19.73	982.0	2	98	0	0	108	25.06	-20.33			Sep-03
	6.61	12.40	19.47	30.22	84.26	2.21	0.95	11.04	0.98	19.69	294.2	3	96	0	0	36	17.42	-11.16			Mar-08
	6.58	12.32	19.15	29.47	82.45	1.95	1.22	11.02	0.97	19.69	294.2	3	96	0	0	36	17.14	-11.23			Nov-96
	4.75	7.96	13.87	17.50	53.09	1.08	1.08	6.32	0.6	15.11	267.0	1	63	34	0	24	15.14	-5.08			Jun-97
	4.67	7.79	13.50	16.18	50.59	0.67	1.48	6.31	0.6	16.01	267.0	1	63	34	0	24	15.02	-5.2			Sep-01
	5.80	10.87	19.71	32.02	102.79	0	1.13	10.36	0.95	90.69	2,778	6	94	0	0	2	31.28	-15.39			May-08
	5.71	10.67	19.26	30.58	99.33	0	1.5	10.37	0.95	88.37	2,778	6	94	0	0	2	31.07	-15.47			Jan-97
	-1.00	1.10	7.28	7.39	67.98		0.64	10.41		29.42	1,397	1	99	0	0	38	17.82	-3.79			Mar-17
	-1.09	0.93	7.03	7.13	67.57	2.3	1.01	10.4		29.45	1,397	1	99	0	0	38	17.82	-3.79			May-89
	11.65	16.10	32.60	67.03	128.40	0	1.11	12.4	0.86	35.8	308.7	4	96	0	0	5	4.24	-2.6			Oct-03
	11.50	15.84	32.04	65.30	125.09	0	1.49	12.39	0.86	34.84	308.7	4	96	0	0	5	4.08	-2.69			Oct-03
	11.83	21.12	50.26	81.34	165.16	0.6	1.51	10.09	0.79	15.68	127.5	9	91	0	0	22	7.59	-0.37			Jun-15
	11.64	20.86	49.57	79.98	163.17	0.76	1.84	10.1	0.8	15.9	127.5	9	91	0	0	22	7.59	-0.37			Aug-07
	7.96	14.43	19.73	28.74	102.63	1.36	1.23	16	1.17	21.74	33.6	4	96	0	0	141	31.81	-25.05			Jun-15

	MARKET		FUND TYPE, CATEGORY & OBJECTIVE		RATINGS				MINIMUMS	
Fund Name	Ticker Symbol	Traded On	Fund Type	Category and (Prospectus Objective)	Overall Rating	Reward Rating	Risk Rating	Recent Up/ Downgrade	Open to New Investors	Min Initial Investment
Hennessy Large Cap Financial Fund Investor Class	HLFNX	NAS CM	Open End	Financials Sector Equity (Financial)	B	B+	B-		Y	2,500
Hennessy Small Cap Financial Fund Institutional Class	HISFX	NAS CM	Open End	Financials Sector Equity (Financial)	B+	A-	B	Up	Y	250,000
Hennessy Small Cap Financial Fund Investor Class	HSFNX	NAS CM	Open End	Financials Sector Equity (Financial)	B+	A-	B	Up	Y	2,500
Hennessy Technology Fund Institutional Class	HTCIX	NAS CM	Open End	Technology Sector Equity (Technology)	B	B	B	Up	Y	250,000
Hennessy Technology Fund Investor Class	HTECX	NAS CM	Open End	Technology Sector Equity (Technology)	B	B-	B	Up	Y	2,500
Hennessy Total Return Fund Investor Class	HDOGX	NAS CM	Open End	Aggressive Alloc (Balanced)	B	C+	B+		Y	2,500
Henssler Equity Fund Institutional Class	HEQCX	NAS CM	Open End	US Equity Large Cap Blend (Growth)	B	C+	B+		Y	1,000,000
Henssler Equity Fund Investor Class	HEQFX	NAS CM	Open End	US Equity Large Cap Blend (Growth)	B	C+	B		Y	2,000
Herzfeld Caribbean Basin Fund	CUBA	NAS CM	Closed End	US Equity Mid Cap (World Stock)	C	C	C	Down	Y	
Highland Energy MLP Fund Class A	HEFAX	NAS CM	Open End	Energy Sector Equity (Natl Res)	D-	D-	D	Down	Y	1,000
Highland Energy MLP Fund Class C	HEFCX	NAS CM	Open End	Energy Sector Equity (Natl Res)	D-	D-	D	Down	Y	1,000
Highland Energy MLP Fund Class Y	HEFYX	NAS CM	Open End	Energy Sector Equity (Natl Res)	D-	D-	D	Down	Y	0
Highland Global Allocation Fund Class A	HCOAX	NAS CM	Open End	Alloc (Growth & Income)	C	C	C-	Up	Y	1,000
Highland Global Allocation Fund Class C	HCOCX	NAS CM	Open End	Alloc (Growth & Income)	C-	C	D+		Y	1,000
Highland Global Allocation Fund Class Y	HCOYX	NAS CM	Open End	Alloc (Growth & Income)	C	C	C-	Up	Y	0
Highland Long/Short Equity Fund Class A	HEOAX	NAS CM	Open End	Long/Short Equity (Equity-Income)	B-	C+	B	Up	Y	2,500
Highland Long/Short Equity Fund Class C	HEOCX	NAS CM	Open End	Long/Short Equity (Equity-Income)	B-	C	B	Up	Y	2,500
Highland Long/Short Equity Fund Class Z	HEOZX	NAS CM	Open End	Long/Short Equity (Equity-Income)	C+	C+	B-		Y	2,500
Highland Long/Short Healthcare Fund Class A	HHCAX	NAS CM	Open End	Long/Short Equity (Health)	D	D	C-	Down	Y	2,500
Highland Long/Short Healthcare Fund Class C	HHCCX	NAS CM	Open End	Long/Short Equity (Health)	D	D	D+	Down	Y	2,500
Highland Long/Short Healthcare Fund Class Z	HHCZX	NAS CM	Open End	Long/Short Equity (Health)	D+	D	C-	Down	Y	2,500
Highland Merger Arbitrage Fund Class A	HMEAX	NAS CM	Open End	Market Neutral (Growth & Income)	B-	C	A-	Up	Y	2,500
Highland Merger Arbitrage Fund Class C	HMECX	NAS CM	Open End	Market Neutral (Growth & Income)	B-	C	A-	Up	Y	2,500
Highland Merger Arbitrage Fund Class Z	HMEZX	NAS CM	Open End	Market Neutral (Growth & Income)	B-	C	A-	Up	Y	2,500
Highland Premier Growth Equity Fund Class A	HPEAX	NAS CM	Open End	US Equity Large Cap Growth (Growth)	B	B	B+	Up	Y	1,000
Highland Premier Growth Equity Fund Class C	HPECX	NAS CM	Open End	US Equity Large Cap Growth (Growth)	B	B-	B+	Up	Y	1,000
Highland Premier Growth Equity Fund Class Y	HPEYX	NAS CM	Open End	US Equity Large Cap Growth (Growth)	B	B	A-	Up	Y	0
Highland Resolute Fund Class I	RMRGX	NAS CM	Open End	Multialternative (Growth)	B	C	A-	Up	Y	1,000,000
Highland Small-Cap Equity Fund Class A	HSZAX	NAS CM	Open End	US Equity Small Cap (Small Company)	C	C	C+	Down	Y	1,000
Highland Small-Cap Equity Fund Class C	HSZCX	NAS CM	Open End	US Equity Small Cap (Small Company)	C	C	C+	Down	Y	1,000
Highland Small-Cap Equity Fund Class Y	HSZYX	NAS CM	Open End	US Equity Small Cap (Small Company)	C	C	C+	Down	Y	0
Highland Total Return Fund Class A	HTAAX	NAS CM	Open End	Moderate Alloc (Asset Alloc)	B-	C+	B	Down	Y	1,000
Highland Total Return Fund Class C	HTACX	NAS CM	Open End	Moderate Alloc (Asset Alloc)	B-	C	B	Up	Y	1,000
Highland Total Return Fund Class Y	HTAYX	NAS CM	Open End	Moderate Alloc (Asset Alloc)	B-	C+	B	Down	Y	0
Highmore Managed Volatility Fund Institutional Class	HMVZX	NAS CM	Open End	Multialternative (Growth & Income)	D-	D+	D+		Y	25,000
Hillman Fund No Load Shares	HCMAX	NAS CM	Open End	US Equity Large Cap Value (Aggr Growth)	B	B	B		Y	5,000
Hodges Blue Chip Equity Income Fund Retail Class	HDPBX	NAS CM	Open End	US Equity Large Cap Growth (Growth & Income)	B	B-	B		Y	1,000
Hodges Fund Institutional Class	HDPIX	NAS CM	Open End	US Equity Mid Cap (Growth)	B	B+	C+	Up	Y	1,000,000
Hodges Fund Retail Class	HDPMX	NAS CM	Open End	US Equity Mid Cap (Growth)	B	B+	C+	Up	Y	250
Hodges Pure Contrarian Fund Retail Class	HDPCX	NAS CM	Open End	US Equity Small Cap (Growth)	C-	C-	C-		Y	1,000
Hodges Small Cap Fund Institutional Class	HDSIX	NAS CM	Open End	US Equity Small Cap (Small Company)	C	C+	C		Y	1,000,000
Hodges Small Cap Fund Retail Class	HDPSX	NAS CM	Open End	US Equity Small Cap (Small Company)	C	C+	C		Y	1,000
Hodges Small Intrinsic Value Fund Retail Class	HDSVX	NAS CM	Open End	US Equity Small Cap (Growth)	B	B+	B-	Up	Y	1,000
Hodges Small-Mid Cap Fund Retail Class	HDSMX	NAS CM	Open End	US Equity Mid Cap (Growth)	B-	B	C+	Up	Y	1,000
Holland Balanced Fund	HOLBX	NAS CM	Open End	Moderate Alloc (Balanced)	B	C+	A+		Y	1,000
Homestead Funds Value Fund	HOVLX	NAS CM	Open End	US Equity Large Cap Value (Growth & Income)	B	B	B		Y	500
Homestead Growth Fund	HNASX	NAS CM	Open End	US Equity Large Cap Growth (Growth)	A-	A	B	Up	Y	500
Homestead International Equity Fund	HISIX	NAS CM	Open End	Global Equity Large Cap (Growth)	B-	B-	B-	Up	Y	500
Homestead Small Company Stock Fund	HSCSX	NAS CM	Open End	US Equity Small Cap (Small Company)	B	B+	B	Up	Y	500
Homestead Stock Index Fund	HSTIX	NAS CM	Open End	US Equity Large Cap Blend (Growth)	B	B	B		Y	500
Hood River Small-Cap Growth Fund Class Institutional	HRSMX	NAS CM	Open End	US Equity Small Cap (Growth)	B	B	B	Down	Y	25,000
Hood River Small-Cap Growth Fund Investor Shares	HRSRX	NAS CM	Open End	US Equity Small Cap (Growth)	B	B	B	Down	Y	1,000

★ Expanded analysis of this fund is included in Section II.

Min Additional Investment	TOTAL RETURNS 3-Month Total Return	6-Month Total Return	1-Year Total Return	3-Year Total Return	5-Year Total Return	PERFORMANCE Dividend Yield (TTM)	Expense Ratio	3-Yr Std Deviation	3-Year Beta	ASSETS NAV	Total Assets (MIL)	ASSET ALLOCATION & TURNOVER %Cash	%Stocks	%Bonds	%Other	Turnover Ratio	BULL & BEAR Last Bull Market Total Return	Last Bear Market Total Return	FEES Front End Fee (%)	Back End Fee (%)	Inception Date
	7.98	14.30	19.37	27.42	100.55	0.46	1.68	16.01	1.17	21.84	33.6	4	96	0	0	141	31.81	-25.05			Jan-97
	0.58	5.15	0.13	49.40	102.71	0.92	1.18	16.43	1.09	14.53	210.0	3	97	0	0	46	25.46	-27.54			May-08
	0.52	4.98	-0.20	47.79	99.11	0.22	1.55	16.44	1.09	24.12	210.0	3	97	0	0	46	25.43	-27.65			Jan-97
	3.62	8.13	20.56	27.14	73.45	0	0.99	13.22	1	17.4	4.5	7	93	0	0	80	25.23	-23.1			Mar-10
	3.54	7.97	20.19	25.77	70.68	0	1.24	13.2	1	17.03	4.5	7	93	0	0	80	24.89	-23.16			Feb-02
	3.66	9.17	11.16	25.65	60.29	1.26	1.18	7.88		13.54	78.2	51	49	0	0	44	14.88	-5.72			Jul-98
	3.82	8.06	10.85	22.30	88.31	0.8	0.98	9.42	0.83	6.22	42.1	2	98	0	0	146	21.4	-15.77			Jun-11
200	3.84	7.81	10.37	20.47	83.67	0.53	1.48	9.37	0.83	5.86	42.1	2	98	0	0	146	21	-15.9			Jun-98
	0.45	1.65	13.37	14.53	26.14	0	3.35	14.56	0.82	8.3388	51.6	3	97	0	0	16	21.9	-20.43			May-94
1,000	-1.34	-3.87	-17.63	-54.16	-42.07	11.9	7.61	31.55	1.24	3.86	24.5	0	100	0	0	8			5.75		Dec-11
1,000	-1.52	-4.48	-18.30	-55.26	-44.16	11.07	8.36	31.55	1.24	3.84	24.5	0	100	0	0	8				1.00	Dec-11
	-1.28	-3.98	-17.31	-54.16	-41.62	12.31	7.36	31.66	1.24	3.84	24.5	0	100	0	0	8					Dec-11
1,000	2.31	2.00	-0.59	-2.43	48.57	7.81	1.16	16.43	0.99	8.4	606.6	0	65	26	10	66	24.24	-19.3	5.75		Sep-93
1,000	2.16	1.73	-1.32	-4.54	43.22	8.13	1.91	16.37	0.99	7.33	606.6	0	65	26	10	66	23.71	-19.53		1.00	Sep-99
	2.50	2.19	-0.27	-1.75	50.40	6.74	0.91	16.36	0.98	10.08	606.6	0	65	26	10	66	24.54	-19.28			Jan-98
50	4.16	6.63	13.34	11.41	35.48	0	1.94	6.51	0.51	12.27	390.9	0	62	0	38	404	8.21	-6.78	5.50		Dec-06
50	4.04	6.31	12.66	9.28	31.15	0	2.59	6.5	0.51	11.36	390.9	0	62	0	38	404	8.05	-7.12		1.00	Dec-06
50	4.32	6.87	13.81	12.60	37.92	0	1.59	6.53	0.51	12.8	390.9	0	62	0	38	404	8.26	-6.52			Dec-06
50	1.12	4.96	8.32	-14.64	34.26	0	2.09	14.23	0.23	12.1	84.4	24	71	0	1	964	-1.15	0	5.50		May-08
50	0.97	4.57	7.63	-16.08	30.24	0	2.74	14.24	0.23	11.42	84.4	24	71	0	1	964	-1.51	-0.23		1.00	May-08
50	1.23	5.11	8.73	-13.60	36.90	0	1.74	14.26	0.24	12.5	84.4	24	71	0	1	964	-1.05	0.23			May-08
50	-0.35	-0.70	5.14			2.03	1.86			20.17	37.3	0	18	0	82	233			5.50		Aug-16
50	-0.54	-1.07	4.43			2.05	2.48			20.12	37.3	0	18	0	82	233				1.00	Aug-16
50	-0.27	-0.52	5.45			2.03	1.53			20.32	37.3	0	18	0	82	233					Aug-16
1,000	8.78	14.66	25.39	33.92	110.89	0	1.22	12.98	1.14	27.02	161.0	0	96	0	4	83	28.21	-17.17	5.75		Dec-96
1,000	8.58	14.25	24.51	31.00	103.23	0	1.97	12.97	1.14	18.49	161.0	0	96	0	4	83	27.64	-17.42		1.00	Sep-99
	8.84	14.82	25.75	34.93	113.55	0	0.97	12.98	1.14	28.65	161.0	0	96	0	4	83	28.38	-17.08			Dec-96
	2.61	5.45	8.14	10.29	24.09	1.13	0.98	4.28	1.05		393.7	-30	41	72	9	94					Dec-11
1,000	2.46	-1.60	13.33	33.68	92.15	0.56	1.42	17.2	0.96	13.12	55.9	-1	101	0	0	84	26.31	-20.64	5.75		Sep-98
1,000	2.25	-1.93	12.46	30.76	84.99	0.28	2.17	17.17	0.96	8.8	55.9	-1	101	0	0	84	25.72	-20.9		1.00	Sep-99
	2.54	-1.37	13.64	34.74	94.56	0.69	1.17	17.2	0.96	14.49	55.9	-1	101	0	0	84	26.45	-20.55			Sep-98
1,000	0.37	0.41	7.87	17.62	43.47	1.04	1.37	8.3	0.7	22.85	105.6	22	54	21	0	99	14.93	-14.46	5.75		Feb-93
1,000	0.14	0.01	7.00	14.98	38.15	0.29	2.12	8.28	0.7	20.46	105.6	22	54	21	0	99	14.41	-14.71		1.00	Sep-99
	0.41	0.53	8.11	18.43	45.19	1.26	1.12	8.3	0.7	23.2	105.6	22	54	21	0	99	15.13	-14.36			Nov-93
250	-0.98	-1.84	-9.50				2.25			9.04	65.2	34	7	56	4						Dec-16
500	4.41	8.37	16.36	30.52	102.50	0.51	1.52	10.87	0.97	23.06	38.0	10	92	1	-2	90	27.22	-21.84			Dec-00
50	8.05	14.48	24.57	36.87	105.35	0.91	1.3	10.3	0.93	16.36	22.3	0	100	0	0	59	21.23	-14.63			Sep-09
50	11.85	17.90	14.11	41.44	146.14	0	0.93	19.06	1.41	50.48	271.7	0	100	0	0	145	21.46	-24.68			Dec-08
50	11.80	17.77	13.83	40.08	142.23	0	1.18	19.06	1.41	49.56	271.7	0	100	0	0	145	21.27	-24.81			Oct-92
50	7.08	9.13	-2.82	4.23	49.05	0	1.41	23.78	0.84	12.44	7.6	0	100	0	0	185	19.56	-28.31			Sep-09
50	10.93	16.51	9.51	16.13	86.20	0.26	0.98	15.5	1.03	20.07	652.1	0	100	0	0	44	31.62	-18.94			Dec-08
50	10.80	16.31	9.19	15.04	83.27	0.02	1.28	15.5	1.03	19.38	652.1	0	100	0	0	44	31.4	-19.05			Dec-07
50	3.26	10.78	8.75	28.59		0	1.3	15.48	1.02	13.89	105.6	0	100	0	0	11					Dec-13
50	9.51	14.43	9.16	31.99		0	1.41	16.42	1.23	13.3	16.5	0	100	0	0	115					Dec-13
500	4.85	6.24	9.24	16.58	57.80	0	2	6.54	0.6	20.03	31.6	9	63	27	0	30	17.36	-10.06			Oct-95
	8.00	14.53	22.16	34.19	112.76	1.78	0.62	12.09	1.11	55.26	1,107	3	96	0	1	9	26.16	-20.64			Nov-90
	7.25	15.10	37.67	53.53	145.34	0	0.95	12.55	1.09	10.36	177.3	2	98	0	0	39	29.43	-16.9			Jan-01
	4.24	9.85	28.11	29.08	47.47	0.76	0.99	11.78	0.91	8.49	73.1	4	91	0	5	112	9.38	-24.31			Jan-01
	4.54	10.62	11.99	25.20	89.39	0.29	0.89	14.73	0.96	44.11	1,303	0	99	0	1	14	28.82	-24.35			Mar-98
	6.47	11.09	21.16	34.63	106.01	1.26	0.58	10.1	1	20.02	144.5	1	99	0	0	3	24.79	-16.46			Oct-99
	2.21	5.80	20.69	37.67	120.20	0	1.1	13.97	0.86	37.76	283.2	2	98	0	0	134	33.14	-25.33			Jan-03
	2.14	5.74	20.50	36.94	117.94	0	1.35	13.98	0.86	37.59	283.2	2	98	0	0	134	32.94	-25.41			Jul-15

	MARKET			FUND TYPE, CATEGORY & OBJECTIVE	RATINGS				MINIMUMS	
Fund Name	Ticker Symbol	Traded On	Fund Type	Category and (Prospectus Objective)	Overall Rating	Reward Rating	Risk Rating	Recent Up/ Downgrade	Open to New Investors	Min Initial Investment
Hood River Small-Cap Growth Fund Retirement Shares	HRSIX	NAS CM	Open End	US Equity Small Cap (Growth)	B	B	B	Down	Y	0
Horizon Active Asset Allocation Fund Class A	HASAX	NAS CM	Open End	Moderate Alloc (Asset Alloc)	C+	B-	C+	Down	Y	2,500
Horizon Active Asset Allocation Fund Class I	HASIX	NAS CM	Open End	Moderate Alloc (Asset Alloc)	B-	B-	C+	Up	Y	10,000,000
Horizon Active Asset Allocation Fund Investor Class	AAANX	NAS CM	Open End	Moderate Alloc (Asset Alloc)	C+	B-	C+	Down	Y	2,500
Horizon Active Dividend Fund Advisor Class	HADUX	NAS CM	Open End	US Equity Large Cap Value (Equity-Income)	D-	D+	A-		Y	2,500
Horizon Active Dividend Fund Investor Class	HNDDX	NAS CM	Open End	US Equity Large Cap Value (Equity-Income)	D-	D+	A-		Y	2,500
Horizon Active Risk Assist® Fund Class A	ARAAX	NAS CM	Open End	Aggressive Alloc (Asset Alloc)	C+	C+	C+	Down	Y	2,500
Horizon Active Risk Assist® Fund Class I	ACRIX	NAS CM	Open End	Aggressive Alloc (Asset Alloc)	C+	C+	C+	Down	Y	10,000,000
Horizon Active Risk Assist® Fund Investor Class	ARANX	NAS CM	Open End	Aggressive Alloc (Asset Alloc)	C+	C+	C+	Down	Y	2,500
Hotchkis & Wiley Capital Income Fund Class A	HWIAX	NAS CM	Open End	Moderate Alloc (Income)	B-	C+	B-	Up	Y	2,500
Hotchkis & Wiley Capital Income Fund Class I	HWIIX	NAS CM	Open End	Moderate Alloc (Income)	B-	C+	B-		Y	250,000
Hotchkis & Wiley Diversified Value Fund Class A	HWCAX	NAS CM	Open End	US Equity Large Cap Value (Growth)	B	B	B-	Up	Y	2,500
Hotchkis & Wiley Diversified Value Fund Class C	HWCCX	NAS CM	Open End	US Equity Large Cap Value (Growth)	B	B	B-	Up	Y	2,500
Hotchkis & Wiley Diversified Value Fund Cls Institutional	HWCIX	NAS CM	Open End	US Equity Large Cap Value (Growth)	B	B	B-	Up	Y	250,000
Hotchkis & Wiley Global Value Fund Class A	HWGAX	NAS CM	Open End	Global Equity (World Stock)	B-	B-	B-	Up	Y	2,500
Hotchkis & Wiley Global Value Fund Class I	HWGIX	NAS CM	Open End	Global Equity (World Stock)	B-	B	B-	Up	Y	250,000
Hotchkis & Wiley International Value Fund Class I	HWNIX	NAS CM	Open End	Global Equity Large Cap (World Stock)	C-	C	B+	Up	Y	250,000
Hotchkis & Wiley Large Cap Value Fund Class A	HWLAX	NAS CM	Open End	US Equity Large Cap Value (Equity-Income)	B	B	B-	Up	Y	2,500
Hotchkis & Wiley Large Cap Value Fund Class C	HWLCX	NAS CM	Open End	US Equity Large Cap Value (Equity-Income)	B	B	B-	Up	Y	2,500
Hotchkis & Wiley Large Cap Value Fund Class I	HWLIX	NAS CM	Open End	US Equity Large Cap Value (Equity-Income)	B	B	B	Up	Y	250,000
Hotchkis & Wiley Large Cap Value Fund Class R	HWLRX	NAS CM	Open End	US Equity Large Cap Value (Equity-Income)	B	B	B-	Up	Y	2,500
Hotchkis & Wiley Mid-Cap Value Fund Class A	HWMAX	NAS CM	Open End	US Equity Mid Cap (Growth)	C+	C+	C+	Up		2,500
Hotchkis & Wiley Mid-Cap Value Fund Class C	HWMCX	NAS CM	Open End	US Equity Mid Cap (Growth)	C+	C+	C+	Up		2,500
Hotchkis & Wiley Mid-Cap Value Fund Class I	HWMIX	NAS CM	Open End	US Equity Mid Cap (Growth)	C+	C+	C+	Up		250,000
Hotchkis & Wiley Mid-Cap Value Fund Class R	HWMRX	NAS CM	Open End	US Equity Mid Cap (Growth)	C+	C+	C+	Up		2,500
Hotchkis & Wiley Small Cap Diversified Value Fund Class A	HWVAX	NAS CM	Open End	US Equity Small Cap (Small Company)	B+	A	B-	Up	Y	2,500
Hotchkis & Wiley Small Cap Diversified Value Fund Class I	HWVIX	NAS CM	Open End	US Equity Small Cap (Small Company)	B+	A	B-	Up	Y	250,000
Hotchkis & Wiley Small Cap Value Fund Class A	HWSAX	NAS CM	Open End	US Equity Small Cap (Small Company)	B-	B-	B-	Up		2,500
Hotchkis & Wiley Small Cap Value Fund Class C	HWSCX	NAS CM	Open End	US Equity Small Cap (Small Company)	B-	B-	C+	Up		2,500
Hotchkis & Wiley Small Cap Value Fund Class I	HWSIX	NAS CM	Open End	US Equity Small Cap (Small Company)	B-	B	B-	Up		250,000
Hotchkis & Wiley Value Opportunities Fund Class A	HWAAX	NAS CM	Open End	US Equity Large Cap Value (Growth)	B	B-	B	Up	Y	2,500
Hotchkis & Wiley Value Opportunities Fund Class C	HWACX	NAS CM	Open End	US Equity Large Cap Value (Growth)	B	B-	B	Up	Y	2,500
Hotchkis & Wiley Value Opp Fund Cls Inst	HWAIX	NAS CM	Open End	US Equity Large Cap Value (Growth)	B	B	B	Up	Y	250,000
HSBC Asia ex-Japan Smaller Companies Equity Fund Class A	HAJAX	NAS CM	Open End	Asia ex-Japan Equity (Growth)	C+	B-	C	Down	Y	1,000
HSBC Asia ex-Japan Smaller Companies Equity Fund Class I	HAJIX	NAS CM	Open End	Asia ex-Japan Equity (Growth)	C+	B-	C	Down	Y	1,000,000
HSBC Asia ex-Japan Smaller Companies Equity Fund Class S	HAJSX	NAS CM	Open End	Asia ex-Japan Equity (Growth)	U	U	U		Y	25,000,000
HSBC Frontier Markets Fund Class A	HSFAX	NAS CM	Open End	Emerging Markets Equity (Growth)	C+	C+	C+	Up		1,000
HSBC Frontier Markets Fund Class I	HSFIX	NAS CM	Open End	Emerging Markets Equity (Growth)	C+	C+	C+	Up		1,000,000
HSBC Funds - HSBC Global Equity Volatility Focused Fund A	HGEAX	NAS CM	Open End	Global Equity (World Stock)	C	C-	B+	Up	Y	1,000
HSBC Funds - HSBC Global Equity Volatility Focused Fund I	HGEIX	NAS CM	Open End	Global Equity (World Stock)	C	C-	B+	Up	Y	1,000,000
HSBC Opportunity Fund Class A	HSOAX	NAS CM	Open End	US Equity Mid Cap (Growth)	C+	B-	C	Up	Y	1,000
HSBC Opportunity Fund Class B	HOPBX	NAS CM	Open End	US Equity Mid Cap (Growth)	C+	B-	C	Up		1,000
HSBC Opportunity Fund Class C	HOPCX	NAS CM	Open End	US Equity Mid Cap (Growth)	C+	B-	C	Up	Y	1,000
HSBC Opportunity Fund Class I	RESCX	NAS CM	Open End	US Equity Mid Cap (Growth)	B-	B	C	Up	Y	5,000,000
Huber Capital Diversified Large Cap Value Fund Inst Cls	HUDEX	NAS CM	Open End	US Equity Large Cap Value (Growth & Income)	B	B-	B	Up	Y	1,000,000
Huber Capital Diversified Large Cap Value Fund Inv Cls	HUDIX	NAS CM	Open End	US Equity Large Cap Value (Growth & Income)	B-	B-	B	Up	Y	5,000
Huber Capital Equity Income Fund Institutional Class	HULEX	NAS CM	Open End	US Equity Large Cap Value (Equity-Income)	B-	B-	B		Y	1,000,000
Huber Capital Equity Income Fund Investor Class	HULIX	NAS CM	Open End	US Equity Large Cap Value (Equity-Income)	B-	B-	B		Y	5,000
Huber Capital Mid Cap Value Fund Institutional Class	HUMEX	NAS CM	Open End	US Equity Small Cap (Growth & Income)	C-	C-	B+	Up	Y	1,000,000
Huber Capital Mid Cap Value Fund Investor Class	HUMDX	NAS CM	Open End	US Equity Small Cap (Growth & Income)	C-	C-	B	Up	Y	5,000
Huber Capital Small Cap Value Fund Institutional Class	HUSEX	NAS CM	Open End	US Equity Small Cap (Small Company)	C+	C+	C	Up	Y	1,000,000
Huber Capital Small Cap Value Fund Investor Class	HUSIX	NAS CM	Open End	US Equity Small Cap (Small Company)	C	C+	C		Y	5,000

★ Expanded analysis of this fund is included in Section II.

	TOTAL RETURNS					PERFORMANCE				ASSETS		ASSET ALLOCATION & TURNOVER					BULL & BEAR		FEES		
Min Additional Investment	3-Month Total Return	6-Month Total Return	1-Year Total Return	3-Year Total Return	5-Year Total Return	Dividend Yield (TTM)	Expense Ratio	3-Yr Std Deviation	3-Year Beta	NAV	Total Assets (MIL)	%Cash	%Stocks	%Bonds	%Other	Turnover Ratio	Last Bull Market Total Return	Last Bear Market Total Return	Front End Fee (%)	Back End Fee (%)	Inception Date
	2.24	5.85	20.78	37.77	120.37		1	13.97	0.86	37.79	283.2	2	98	0	0	134	33.14	-25.33			Mar-17
250	5.76	11.02	22.11	20.64	65.87	0.9	1.64	10.45	1.01		427.4	2	92	0	5				5.75		Sep-15
	4.92	10.11	21.90	21.01	66.11	0.94	1.39	10.45	1.01	12.74	427.4	2	92	0	5						Sep-16
250	4.85	10.05	21.63	20.74	65.75	0.74	1.49	10.44	1	12.72	427.4	2	92	0	5						Jan-12
250	6.83	11.72	22.56				1.24			60.33	27.9	7	93	0	0						Jun-17
250	6.87	11.58	22.50				1.09			60.33	27.9	7	93	0	0						Dec-16
250	-0.21	3.93	13.26	9.11		0.75	1.64	8.74	0.83	21.88	424.5	4	90	0	5	563			5.75		Sep-15
	3.36	7.70	17.58	13.58		0.9	1.4	8.74	0.83	21.9	424.5	4	90	0	5	563					Sep-16
250	-0.10	4.00	13.37	9.46		0.73	1.49	8.71	0.82	21.89	424.5	4	90	0	5	563					Aug-14
100	1.32	3.50	9.98	21.71	63.55	3.56	1.07	9.63	0.79	13.21	39.2	1	58	40	0	71	18.59	-10.09	4.75		Feb-11
100	1.36	3.69	10.22	22.49	65.32	3.96	0.82	9.67	0.8	12.7	39.2	1	58	40	0	71	18.01	-9.99			Dec-10
100	6.03	9.91	18.09	28.62	102.05	4.37	1.2	14.09	1.23	18.91	115.0	2	98	0	0	25	27.8	-21.53	5.25		Aug-04
100	5.85	9.52	17.26	25.74	94.72	3.94	1.95	14.07	1.23	18.77	115.0	2	98	0	0	25	27.37	-21.84		1.00	Aug-04
100	6.08	10.04	18.39	29.61	104.60	4.49	0.95	14.08	1.23	18.84	115.0	2	98	0	0	25	28.09	-21.5			Aug-04
100	2.89	7.87	16.52	25.96	75.80	0.59	1.35	12.95	1.1	13.1	8.6	1	99	0	0	38			5.25		Aug-13
100	2.88	7.94	16.78	26.81	77.81	0.7	1.1	12.96	1.1	13.1	8.6	1	99	0	0	38					Dec-12
100	1.16	6.71	18.18			1.37	1.15			11.93	2.6	1	97	0	0	34					Dec-15
100	6.29	9.98	18.59	28.99	109.12	1.46	1.24	13.92	1.22	33.44	381.8	2	98	0	0	27	26.98	-20.48	5.25		Oct-01
100	6.10	9.58	17.70	26.13	101.30	0.54	1.99	13.92	1.22	32.88	381.8	2	98	0	0	27	26.41	-20.71		1.00	Feb-02
100	6.36	10.13	18.86	29.99	111.67	1.68	0.99	13.93	1.22	33.61	381.8	2	98	0	0	27	27.21	-20.39			Jun-87
100	6.25	9.89	18.29	28.07	106.58	1.32	1.49	13.95	1.22	33.69	381.8	2	98	0	0	27	26.88	-20.57			Aug-03
100	4.54	8.17	7.52	12.41	83.36	0.18	1.28	17.25	1.4	37.02	1,920	3	97	0	0	37	44.3	-31.12	5.25		Jan-01
100	4.33	7.75	6.73	9.90	76.64	0	2.03	17.23	1.4	32.3	1,920	3	97	0	0	37	43.68	-31.36		1.00	Jan-01
100	4.58	8.27	7.77	13.24	85.66	0.29	1.03	17.25	1.4	37.58	1,920	3	97	0	0	37	44.57	-31.09			Jan-97
100	4.45	7.99	7.23	11.55	81.07	0.09	1.53	17.24	1.4	37.05	1,920	3	97	0	0	37	44.1	-31.23			Aug-03
100	3.99	10.22	13.53	37.04		0.49	1.32	15.14	1	11.42	24.7	0	100	0	0	58			5.25		Jun-14
100	3.96	10.26	13.75	38.12		0.68	1.07	15.17	1	11.46	24.7	0	100	0	0	58					Jun-14
100	1.82	6.97	7.46	16.14	93.39	0	1.29	16.79	1.12	60.08	804.3	2	98	0	0	29	30.39	-29.19	5.25		Oct-00
100	1.64	6.58	6.66	13.56	86.23	0	2.04	16.77	1.12	50.01	804.3	2	98	0	0	29	29.83	-29.42		1.00	Feb-02
100	1.89	7.12	7.74	17.03	95.82	0.38	1.04	16.8	1.12	60.39	804.3	2	98	0	0	29	30.54	-29.11			Sep-85
100	5.11	8.45	13.56	29.71	99.82	1.76	1.24	13.36	1.1	29.48	586.1	0	94	2	3	83	31.09	-23.67	5.25		Dec-02
100	4.93	8.03	12.75	26.83	92.49	1.19	1.99	13.35	1.1	27.47	586.1	0	94	2	3	83	30.47	-23.92		1.00	Aug-03
100	5.18	8.56	13.85	30.67	102.40	2.02	0.99	13.35	1.1	29.42	586.1	0	94	2	3	83	31.21	-23.59			Dec-02
100	4.98	12.51	34.52	51.59		0.92	1.27	16.26	1.05	12.25	15.1	3	91	0	7	93			5.00		Nov-14
0	5.10	12.73	34.92	53.18		1.16	0.92	16.21	1.05	12.24	15.1	3	91	0	7	93					Nov-14
0	10.02	5.34	34.25			1.56	1.33				12.0	2	96	0	2	93					Nov-14
100	1.60	5.68	21.20	17.28	55.77	1.62	2.2	12.23	0.94	14.11	44.9	4	93	0	0	8	14.1		5.00		Sep-11
0	1.78	5.92	21.60	18.45	58.49	1.96	1.85	12.22	0.94	14.16	44.9	4	93	0	0	8	14.32				Sep-11
100	6.30	8.22	17.32			1.41	1.3			11.63	12.2	3	94	0	2				5.00		Nov-15
0	6.36	8.46	17.77			1.47	0.95			11.7	12.2	3	94	0	2						Nov-15
100	9.26	13.75	29.57	25.11	86.19	0	1.65	15.11	1.1	10.66	143.6	3	97	0	0	96	29.48	-24.85	5.00		Sep-96
100	9.10	13.25	28.50	22.24	79.23	0	2.4	15.01	1.09	6.18	143.6	3	97	0	0	96	28.75	-25.04		4.00	Jan-98
100	9.09	13.36	28.46	22.29	79.39	0	2.4	14.99	1.09	6.55	143.6	3	97	0	0	96	28.82	-25.11		1.00	Nov-98
0	9.41	14.06	30.14	27.04	91.10	0	1.1	15.07	1.09	14.27	143.6	3	97	0	0	96	29.79	-24.67			Sep-96
5,000	6.96	13.43	21.41	28.77	75.26	1.52	0.76	10.71	0.94	14.95	5.1	6	94	0	0	26					Dec-12
100	7.05	13.40	21.23	27.87	72.34	1.32	1.16	10.74	0.94	14.89	5.1	6	94	0	0	26					Dec-12
5,000	6.92	12.82	19.93	24.61	75.93	1.41	0.99	11.74	1.01	16.34	89.8	1	99	0	0	16	24.56	-16.1			Oct-11
100	6.83	12.67	19.53	23.21	72.58	1.08	1.39	11.73	1.01	16.39	89.8	1	99	0	0	16	24.39	-16.1			Jun-07
5,000	6.88	10.55	15.39			0.99	1.11			12.79	1.7	1	99	0	0						Dec-15
100	6.81	10.39	15.03			0.8	1.41			12.77	1.7	1	99	0	0						Dec-15
5,000	4.90	9.03	12.01	11.10	40.28	1.27	1.35	15.94	1.03	17.83	94.3	2	98	0	0	15	37.54	-24.08			Oct-11
100	4.87	8.99	11.73	10.15	37.77	1.05	1.75	15.92	1.03	17.64	94.3	2	98	0	0	15	37.2	-24.08			Jun-07

Fund Name	MARKET Ticker Symbol	Traded On	FUND TYPE, CATEGORY & OBJECTIVE Fund Type	Category and (Prospectus Objective)	RATINGS Overall Rating	Reward Rating	Risk Rating	Recent Up/ Downgrade	Open to New Investors	MINIMUMS Min Initial Investment
Hundredfold Select Alternative Fund Investor Class	HFSAX	NAS CM	Open End	Moderate Alloc (Growth & Income)	B	C+	A		Y	1,000,000
Hundredfold Select Alternative Fund Service Class	SFHYX	NAS CM	Open End	Moderate Alloc (Growth & Income)	B	C+	A-	Up	Y	5,000
Hussman Strategic Growth Fund	HSGFX	NAS CM	Open End	Market Neutral (Growth)	D-	D-	D	Down	Y	1,000
Hussman Strategic International Fund	HSIEX	NAS CM	Open End	Market Neutral (Foreign Stock)	C	D+	C+	Up	Y	1,000
Hussman Strategic Total Return Fund	HSTRX	NAS CM	Open End	Moderate Alloc (Growth & Income)	C	C	C	Down	Y	1,000
Hussman Strategic Value Fund	HSVLX	NAS CM	Open End	US Equity Large Cap Value (Growth & Income)	D+	D	C-		Y	1,000
HVIA Equity Fund Institutional Class	HVEIX	NAS CM	Open End	US Equity Large Cap Growth (Growth)	D	C	B		Y	25,000
ICM Small Company Portfolio	ICSCX	NAS CM	Open End	US Equity Small Cap (Small Company)	A-	A	B	Up	Y	2,500,000
ICON Consumer Discretionary Fund Class A	ICCAX	NAS CM	Open End	Consumer Goods Sec Equity ()	B-	C	B+		Y	1,000
ICON Consumer Discretionary Fund Class S	ICCCX	NAS CM	Open End	Consumer Goods Sec Equity ()	B-	C	B+	Down	Y	1,000
ICON Consumer Staples Fund Class A	ICRAX	NAS CM	Open End	Consumer Goods Sec Equity ()	B	C+	A		Y	1,000
ICON Consumer Staples Fund Class S	ICLEX	NAS CM	Open End	Consumer Goods Sec Equity ()	B	C+	A		Y	1,000
ICON Emerging Markets Fund Class A	IPCAX	NAS CM	Open End	Emerging Markets Equity (Div Emerging Mkts)	B-	C+	B	Up	Y	1,000
ICON Emerging Markets Fund Class S	ICARX	NAS CM	Open End	Emerging Markets Equity (Div Emerging Mkts)	B-	C+	B	Up	Y	1,000
ICON Energy Fund Class A	ICEAX	NAS CM	Open End	Energy Sector Equity ()	D+	D+	D+	Down	Y	1,000
ICON Energy Fund Class S	ICENX	NAS CM	Open End	Energy Sector Equity ()	D+	D+	D+	Down	Y	1,000
ICON Equity Income Fund Class A	IEQAX	NAS CM	Open End	Aggressive Alloc (Equity-Income)	B	B-	B+		Y	1,000
ICON Equity Income Fund Class C	IOECX	NAS CM	Open End	Aggressive Alloc (Equity-Income)	B	B-	B		Y	1,000
ICON Equity Income Fund Class S	IOEZX	NAS CM	Open End	Aggressive Alloc (Equity-Income)	B	B-	B+		Y	1,000
ICON Financial Fund Class A	ICFAX	NAS CM	Open End	Financials Sector Equity (Financial)	B	B	B	Up	Y	1,000
ICON Financial Fund Class S	ICFSX	NAS CM	Open End	Financials Sector Equity (Financial)	B	B+	B	Up	Y	1,000
ICON Fund Class A	ICNAX	NAS CM	Open End	US Equity Mid Cap (Growth & Income)	B-	B	C	Up	Y	1,000
ICON Fund Class C	ICNCX	NAS CM	Open End	US Equity Mid Cap (Growth & Income)	B-	B	C+	Up	Y	1,000
ICON Fund Class S	ICNZX	NAS CM	Open End	US Equity Mid Cap (Growth & Income)	B-	B	C	Up	Y	1,000
ICON Healthcare Fund Class A	ICHAX	NAS CM	Open End	Healthcare Sector Equity (Health)	C	C	B-	Down	Y	1,000
ICON Healthcare Fund Class S	ICHCX	NAS CM	Open End	Healthcare Sector Equity (Health)	C	C	B-	Down	Y	1,000
ICON Industrials Fund Class A	ICIAX	NAS CM	Open End	Industrials Sector Equity ()	B-	B-	B-	Down	Y	1,000
ICON Industrials Fund Class S	ICTRX	NAS CM	Open End	Industrials Sector Equity ()	B-	B-	B-	Down	Y	1,000
ICON Information Technology Fund Class A	ICTTX	NAS CM	Open End	Technology Sector Equity (Technology)	A-	A	B	Up	Y	1,000
ICON Information Technology Fund Class S	ICTEX	NAS CM	Open End	Technology Sector Equity (Technology)	A-	A	B	Up	Y	1,000
ICON International Equity Fund Class A	IIQAX	NAS CM	Open End	Global Equity Large Cap (Foreign Stock)	B-	C+	B	Up	Y	1,000
ICON International Equity Fund Class C	IIQCX	NAS CM	Open End	Global Equity Large Cap (Foreign Stock)	B-	C+	B	Up	Y	1,000
ICON International Equity Fund Class S	ICNEX	NAS CM	Open End	Global Equity Large Cap (Foreign Stock)	B-	C+	B	Up	Y	1,000
ICON Long/Short Fund Class A	ISTAX	NAS CM	Open End	US Equity Mid Cap (Growth)	B	A-	C		Y	1,000
ICON Long/Short Fund Class C	IOLCX	NAS CM	Open End	US Equity Mid Cap (Growth)	B	B+	B-	Up	Y	1,000
ICON Long/Short Fund Class S	IOLZX	NAS CM	Open End	US Equity Mid Cap (Growth)	B	A-	C		Y	1,000
ICON Natural Resources Fund Class A	ICBAX	NAS CM	Open End	Natl Resources Sec Equity (Natl Res)	C+	B-	C	Up	Y	1,000
ICON Natural Resources Fund Class C	ICBCX	NAS CM	Open End	Natl Resources Sec Equity (Natl Res)	C+	C+	C	Up	Y	1,000
ICON Natural Resources Fund Class S	ICBMX	NAS CM	Open End	Natl Resources Sec Equity (Natl Res)	C+	B-	C	Up	Y	1,000
ICON Opportunities Fund	ICONX	NAS CM	Open End	US Equity Small Cap (Small Company)	A-	A	B	Up	Y	1,000
ICON Risk-Managed Balanced Fund Class A	IOCAX	NAS CM	Open End	Moderate Alloc (Growth & Income)	B-	C+	B	Up	Y	1,000
ICON Risk-Managed Balanced Fund Class C	IOCCX	NAS CM	Open End	Moderate Alloc (Growth & Income)	B-	C+	B	Up	Y	1,000
ICON Risk-Managed Balanced Fund Class S	IOCZX	NAS CM	Open End	Moderate Alloc (Growth & Income)	B-	C+	B	Up	Y	1,000
ICON Utilities Fund Class A	ICTVX	NAS CM	Open End	Utilities Sector Equity (Utility)	B-	C+	B	Down	Y	1,000
ICON Utilities Fund Class S	ICTUX	NAS CM	Open End	Utilities Sector Equity (Utility)	B-	B-	B	Down	Y	1,000
Iman Fund Class K	IMANX	NAS CM	Open End	US Equity Large Cap Growth (Growth)	A-	A	B	Up	Y	250
IMS Capital Value Fund	IMSCX	NAS CM	Open End	US Equity Mid Cap (Growth)	B-	C+	B	Up	Y	5,000
IMS Dividend Growth Fund	IMSAX	NAS CM	Open End	US Equity Large Cap Value (Growth)	C+	B-	C+	Down	Y	5,000
IMS Strategic Income Fund	IMSIX	NAS CM	Open End	Moderate Alloc (Equity-Income)	D	D	D		Y	5,000
Independent Franchise Partners US Equity Fund	IFPUX	NAS CM	Open End	US Equity Large Cap Blend (Income)	B	B-	A		Y	3,000,000
Index Funds S&P 500 Equal Weight No Load Shares	INDEX	NAS CM	Open End	US Equity Large Cap Blend (Growth & Income)	B-	C+	B	Up	Y	1,000
Infinity Q Diversified Alpha Fund Institutional Class	IQDNX	NAS CM	Open End	Multialternative (Growth & Income)	C+	C	B	Down	Y	1,000,000

★ Expanded analysis of this fund is included in Section II.

Min Additional Investment	TOTAL RETURNS 3-Month Total Return	6-Month Total Return	1-Year Total Return	3-Year Total Return	5-Year Total Return	PERFORMANCE Dividend Yield (TTM)	Expense Ratio	3-Yr Std Deviation	3-Year Beta	ASSETS NAV	Total Assets (ML)	ASSET ALLOCATION & TURNOVER %Cash	%Stocks	%Bonds	%Other	Turnover Ratio	BULL & BEAR Last Bull Market Total Return	Last Bear Market Total Return	FEES Front End Fee (%)	Back End Fee (%)	Inception Date
0	2.21	4.30	9.92	21.13	34.59	1.54	2	3.95	0.11	22.62	52.4	50	10	39	1	419	8.85	-3.05			Oct-12
1,000	1.98	3.79	8.95	17.90	28.64	0.64	2.9	3.92	0.11	21.65	52.4	50	10	39	1	419	8.85	-3.05			Sep-04
100	-1.69	-5.66	-12.72	-28.84	-40.08	0.31	1.31	8.3	-0.75	6.27	341.7	55	41	0	5	209	-12.24	9.02			Jul-00
100	-0.13	1.68	1.33	-0.34	-4.78	0	2.01	5.42	-0.05	8.9	28.6	2	91	0	7	102	-2.45	-1.99			Dec-09
100	-0.15	0.70	1.21	8.04	3.35	0.2	0.84	5.87	1.29	12.03	339.6	24	11	65	0	341	1.26	2.34			Sep-02
100	1.95	0.54	-2.80	-9.03	-2.31	0.79	1.38	6.05	-0.09	8.38	6.5	34	65	0	2	118					Feb-12
	5.51	10.42	22.69			0.12	0.99			12.97	14.1	6	94	0	0						Oct-16
1,000	3.51	10.39	13.13	42.55	105.63	0.07	0.95	14.11	0.98	33.08	794.1	1	99	0	0	32	31.19	-24.97			Apr-89
100	4.49	1.97	8.30	13.53	68.19	0	1.99	11.01	0.89	13.46	27.0	6	94	0	0	152	30.17	-9.13	5.75		Sep-10
100	4.65	2.31	8.94	15.47	72.20	0	1.42	11	0.89	14.12	27.0	6	94	0	0	152	30.14	-8.72			Jul-97
100	5.32	5.60	11.34	22.67	74.16	0.15	1.76	7.5	0.72	6.95	14.8	8	92	0	0	118	14.45	-6.66	5.75		Sep-10
100	5.48	5.76	11.64	23.67	76.34	0.25	1.51	7.5	0.72	6.99	14.8	8	92	0	0	118	14.68	-7.51			May-97
100	2.98	5.52	24.25	22.01	28.63	0	1.8	11.31	0.63	16.24	63.5	0	97	0	2	169	20.62	-26.49	5.75		May-06
100	3.03	5.62	24.48	22.98	29.89	0	1.55	11.3	0.63	16.35	63.5	0	97	0	2	169	20.76	-26.45			Feb-97
100	3.97	12.47	-4.06	-7.94	-7.30	0.53	1.73	20.48	1.06	12.74	226.4	-1	101	0	0	74	15.49	-28.18	5.75		Sep-10
100	3.94	12.56	-3.83	-7.20	-6.01	0.62	1.44	20.54	1.06	12.82	226.4	-1	101	0	0	74	15.71	-27.99			Nov-97
100	2.56	5.90	12.35	26.19	75.76	2.86	1.44	9.38	0.86	18.01	88.1	3	85	9	0	206	20.01	-16.72	5.75		May-06
100	2.59	5.70	11.81	23.64	69.57	2.18	2.19	9.4	0.86	18.22	88.1	3	85	9	0	206	19.61	-17.03		1.00	Nov-02
100	2.55	6.01	12.65	27.05	77.85	3.1	1.19	9.38	0.86	18.06	88.1	3	85	9	0	206	20.23	-16.6			May-04
100	8.44	13.33	19.59	28.52	81.39	0.74	1.91	17.03	1.1	10.81	44.7	2	98	0	0	68	28.83	-25.47	5.75		Sep-10
100	8.57	13.47	20.03	29.84	84.38	0.82	1.56	17.07	1.1	10.78	44.7	2	98	0	0	68	29.32	-25.43			Jul-97
100	6.13	11.45	28.12	22.41	75.89	0	1.51	14.16	1.2	18.68	52.6	0	100	0	0	15	27.06	-21.37	5.75		May-06
100	5.99	11.02	27.16	19.69	69.47	0	2.26	14.14	1.19	17.32	52.6	0	100	0	0	15	26.8	-21.29		1.00	Nov-00
100	6.26	11.64	28.64	23.83	79.15	0	1.12	14.17	1.2	19.85	52.6	0	100	0	0	15	27.09	-20.82			May-04
100	-1.43	-0.39	12.05	14.25	108.77	0	1.75	13.82	1.05	15.64	82.4	7	93	0	0	174	19.42	-11.74	5.75		Sep-10
100	-1.31	-0.25	12.47	15.38	112.47	0	1.44	13.82	1.05	16.33	82.4	7	93	0	0	174	19.66	-11.54			Feb-97
100	4.19	6.56	15.95	25.18	84.77	0	1.75	12.54	0.98	15.41	17.1	9	91	0	0	75	26.29	-26.2	5.75		Sep-10
100	4.34	6.69	16.22	25.95	86.98	0	1.5	12.58	0.99	15.62	17.1	9	91	0	0	75	27.9	-25.92			May-97
100	2.74	11.38	32.07	60.73	135.32	0	1.75	12.65	0.82	15.26	70.7	2	98	0	0	116	29.39	-13.59	5.75		Sep-10
100	2.90	11.65	32.54	62.32	139.98	0	1.49	12.67	0.83	15.82	70.7	2	98	0	0	116	29.8	-13.47			Feb-97
100	3.78	7.69	22.64	17.19	19.27	0	1.8	10.8	0.8	13.43	51.4	7	90	0	2	209	17.75	-33.18	5.75		May-06
100	3.69	7.38	21.91	14.62	15.06	0	2.55	10.77	0.8	12.07	51.4	7	90	0	2	209	17.29	-33.43		1.00	Feb-04
100	3.87	7.88	23.02	18.23	21.28	0	1.45	10.79	0.8	13.68	51.4	7	90	0	2	209	18.01	-33.09			Feb-97
100	5.05	11.32	26.40	28.24	84.28	0	1.58	14.3	1.19	25.56	24.3	0	100	0	0	24	24.82	-16.25	5.75		May-06
100	4.88	10.89	25.45	25.39	77.44	0	2.33	14.31	1.19	23.21	24.3	0	100	0	0	24	24.24	-16.48		1.00	Oct-02
100	5.13	11.47	26.77	29.38	87.11	0	1.28	14.3	1.19	26.42	24.3	0	100	0	0	24	24.97	-16.05			May-04
100	5.62	13.56	16.62	18.15	59.50	0.48	1.78	17.08	1.36	15.83	83.6	3	97	0	0	68	26.23	-27.13	5.75		Sep-10
100	5.41	13.14	15.76	15.51	53.48	0.33	2.54	17.05	1.36	15.25	83.6	3	97	0	0	68	25.61	-27.3		1.00	Sep-10
100	5.63	13.71	16.92	19.06	61.75	0.47	1.53	17.08	1.36	16	83.6	3	97	0	0	68	26.53	-27			May-97
100	5.14	12.60	24.85	46.27	108.60	0	1.51	15.46	1.01	19.56	20.9	0	100	0	0	26					Sep-12
100	2.95	5.16	11.45	15.35	42.57	1.25	1.54	6.1	0.57	15.57	36.1	3	51	42	0	83	10.72	-10.65	5.75		May-06
100	1.31	3.31	9.05	11.24	35.38	0.67	2.29	6.08	0.57	14.61	36.1	3	51	42	0	83	10.33	-10.98		1.00	Nov-02
100	1.39	3.58	9.98	14.40	41.92	1.46	1.29	6.14	0.58	15.96	36.1	3	51	42	0	83	11.01	-10.59			May-04
100	-1.44	0.52	6.86	19.66	73.14	2.37	1.75	11.02	0.83	8.53	42.9	1	99	0	0	160	6.95	-0.16	5.75		Sep-10
100	-1.41	0.68	7.07	20.52	75.26	2.56	1.5	11.04	0.83	8.68	42.9	1	99	0	0	160	7.1	0.02			Jul-97
50	7.91	13.39	28.48	46.37	111.72	0.02	1.35	11.5		13.15	95.8	0	100	0	0	75	22.44	-20.28			Jun-00
100	4.09	5.22	11.87	17.04	65.07	0	1.69	11.39	1	24.79	38.3	0	100	0	0	84	27.24	-29.29			Aug-96
100	7.63	10.34	17.51	24.11	72.49	0.69	1.95	11.01	1.04	16.17	11.9	1	99	0	0	33	19.06	-14.67			Nov-02
100	-3.15	-3.16	-5.37	-28.84	-30.81	7.04	1.95	10	-0.4	2.75	5.3	4	31	65	0	506	9.43	-10.47			Nov-02
250,000	5.46	5.22	19.92	39.71	99.59	1.17	0.79	10.61	0.8	17.73	1,999	0	95	0	5	31					Dec-11
1,000	6.25	10.02	18.78			0.96	0.25			30.36	24.3	0	100	0	0	32					Apr-15
10,000	0.85	1.14	7.29	15.36		2.29	2.04	3.62	-0.17	10.59	169.7	24	63	2	11	62					Sep-14

	MARKET			FUND TYPE, CATEGORY & OBJECTIVE	RATINGS					MINIMUMS
Fund Name	Ticker Symbol	Traded On	Fund Type	Category and (Prospectus Objective)	Overall Rating	Reward Rating	Risk Rating	Recent Up/ Downgrade	Open to New Investors	Min Initial Investment
Infinity Q Diversified Alpha Fund Investor Class	IQDAX	NAS CM	Open End	Multialternative (Growth & Income)	C+	C	B	Down	Y	100,000
Innovator McKinley Income Fund Investor Class	IMIFX	NAS CM	Open End	US Equity Mid Cap (Growth & Income)	C+	C	B-		Y	2,000
Insignia Macro Fund Class A	IGMFX	NAS CM	Open End	Other Alternative (Growth & Income)	D+	D	C-	Down	Y	2,500
Insignia Macro Fund Class I	IGMLX	NAS CM	Open End	Other Alternative (Growth & Income)	D+	D	C-	Down	Y	250,000
Integrity Dividend Harvest Fund Class A Shares	IDIVX	NAS CM	Open End	US Equity Large Cap Value (Equity-Income)	B	B-	A		Y	1,000
Integrity Dividend Harvest Fund Class C	IDHCX	NAS CM	Open End	US Equity Large Cap Value (Equity-Income)	B	B-	A-		Y	1,000
Integrity Dividend Harvest Fund Class I	IDHIX	NAS CM	Open End	US Equity Large Cap Value (Equity-Income)	B	B-	A		Y	1,000
Integrity Energized Dividend Fund Class A	NRGDX	NAS CM	Open End	Energy Sector Equity (Equity-Income)	D+	C	B+	Up	Y	1,000
Integrity Energized Dividend Fund Class C	NRGUX	NAS CM	Open End	Energy Sector Equity (Equity-Income)	D+	C-	B	Up	Y	1,000
Integrity Energized Dividend Fund Class I	NRIGX	NAS CM	Open End	Energy Sector Equity (Equity-Income)	D+	C	B+	Up	Y	1,000
Integrity Growth & Income Fund Class A	IGIAX	NAS CM	Open End	US Equity Large Cap Blend (Growth & Income)	B-	B-	B-	Down	Y	1,000
Integrity Growth & Income Fund Class C	IGIUX	NAS CM	Open End	US Equity Large Cap Blend (Growth & Income)	B-	C+	B-	Down	Y	1,000
Integrity Growth & Income Fund Class I	IGIVX	NAS CM	Open End	US Equity Large Cap Blend (Growth & Income)	B-	B-	B-	Down	Y	1,000
Intrepid Capital Fund Institutional Class	ICMVX	NAS CM	Open End	Moderate Alloc (Growth & Income)	C+	C+	B-	Down	Y	250,000
Intrepid Capital Fund Investor Class	ICMBX	NAS CM	Open End	Moderate Alloc (Growth & Income)	C+	C+	B-	Down	Y	2,500
Intrepid Disciplined Value Fund Investor Class	ICMCX	NAS CM	Open End	US Equity Mid Cap (Growth)	B-	C+	B	Down	Y	2,500
Intrepid Endurance Fund Institutional Class	ICMZX	NAS CM	Open End	US Equity Small Cap (Small Company)	C+	C	B		Y	250,000
Intrepid Endurance Fund Investor Class	ICMAX	NAS CM	Open End	US Equity Small Cap (Small Company)	C+	C	B	Up	Y	2,500
Intrepid International Fund Investor Class	ICMIX	NAS CM	Open End	Global Equity Mid/Small Cap (Foreign Stock)	B-	C	B+	Up	Y	2,500
Intrepid Select Fund Investor Class	ICMTX	NAS CM	Open End	US Equity Small Cap (Growth & Income)	C	C+	B	Up	Y	2,500
Invesco All Cap Market Neutral Fund Class A	CPNAX	NAS CM	Open End	Market Neutral (Growth & Income)	D+	D	C	Down	Y	1,000
Invesco All Cap Market Neutral Fund Class C	CPNCX	NAS CM	Open End	Market Neutral (Growth & Income)	D+	D	C-	Down	Y	1,000
Invesco All Cap Market Neutral Fund Class R	CPNRX	NAS CM	Open End	Market Neutral (Growth & Income)	D+	D	C	Down	Y	0
Invesco All Cap Market Neutral Fund Class R5	CPNFX	NAS CM	Open End	Market Neutral (Growth & Income)	C-	D	C	Down	Y	10,000,000
Invesco All Cap Market Neutral Fund Class R6	CPNSX	NAS CM	Open End	Market Neutral (Growth & Income)	C-	D	C	Down	Y	10,000,000
Invesco All Cap Market Neutral Fund Class Y	CPNYX	NAS CM	Open End	Market Neutral (Growth & Income)	C-	D	C	Down	Y	1,000
Invesco Alternative Strategies Fund Class A	LQLAX	NAS CM	Open End	Multialternative (Growth)	C+	C	B		Y	1,000
Invesco Alternative Strategies Fund Class C	LQLCX	NAS CM	Open End	Multialternative (Growth)	C+	C	B		Y	1,000
Invesco Alternative Strategies Fund Class R	LQLRX	NAS CM	Open End	Multialternative (Growth)	C+	C	B		Y	0
Invesco Alternative Strategies Fund Class R5	LQLFX	NAS CM	Open End	Multialternative (Growth)	C+	C	B		Y	10,000,000
Invesco Alternative Strategies Fund Class R6	LQLSX	NAS CM	Open End	Multialternative (Growth)	C+	C	B		Y	10,000,000
Invesco Alternative Strategies Fund Class Y	LQLYX	NAS CM	Open End	Multialternative (Growth)	C+	C	B		Y	1,000
Invesco American Franchise Fund Class A	VAFAX	NAS CM	Open End	US Equity Large Cap Growth (Growth)	B	B	B+	Down	Y	1,000
Invesco American Franchise Fund Class B	VAFBX	NAS CM	Open End	US Equity Large Cap Growth (Growth)	B	B	B+	Down		1,000
Invesco American Franchise Fund Class C	VAFCX	NAS CM	Open End	US Equity Large Cap Growth (Growth)	B	B	B+	Down	Y	1,000
Invesco American Franchise Fund Class R	VAFRX	NAS CM	Open End	US Equity Large Cap Growth (Growth)	B	B	B+	Down	Y	0
Invesco American Franchise Fund Class R6	VAFFX	NAS CM	Open End	US Equity Large Cap Growth (Growth)	B	B	B+	Down	Y	10,000,000
Invesco American Franchise Fund Class Y	VAFIX	NAS CM	Open End	US Equity Large Cap Growth (Growth)	B	B	B+	Down	Y	1,000
Invesco American Franchise Fund R5 Class	VAFNX	NAS CM	Open End	US Equity Large Cap Growth (Growth)	B	B	B+	Down	Y	10,000,000
Invesco American Value Fund Class A	MSAVX	NAS CM	Open End	US Equity Mid Cap (Growth & Income)	C+	C+	B-	Up	Y	1,000
Invesco American Value Fund Class B	MGAVX	NAS CM	Open End	US Equity Mid Cap (Growth & Income)	C+	C+	B-	Up		1,000
Invesco American Value Fund Class C	MSVCX	NAS CM	Open End	US Equity Mid Cap (Growth & Income)	C+	C+	C+	Up	Y	1,000
Invesco American Value Fund Class R	MSARX	NAS CM	Open End	US Equity Mid Cap (Growth & Income)	C+	C+	C+	Up	Y	0
Invesco American Value Fund Class R6	MSAFX	NAS CM	Open End	US Equity Mid Cap (Growth & Income)	C+	C+	B-	Up	Y	10,000,000
Invesco American Value Fund Class Y	MSAIX	NAS CM	Open End	US Equity Mid Cap (Growth & Income)	C+	C+	B-	Up	Y	1,000
Invesco American Value Fund R5 Class	MSAJX	NAS CM	Open End	US Equity Mid Cap (Growth & Income)	C+	C+	B-	Up	Y	10,000,000
Invesco Asia Pacific Growth Fund Class A	ASIAX	NAS CM	Open End	Asia ex-Japan Equity (Pacific Stock)	B-	B-	C+	Up	Y	1,000
Invesco Asia Pacific Growth Fund Class B	ASIBX	NAS CM	Open End	Asia ex-Japan Equity (Pacific Stock)	C+	B-	C+	Down		1,000
Invesco Asia Pacific Growth Fund Class C	ASICX	NAS CM	Open End	Asia ex-Japan Equity (Pacific Stock)	C+	B-	C+	Down	Y	1,000
Invesco Asia Pacific Growth Fund Class R6	ASISX	NAS CM	Open End	Asia ex-Japan Equity (Pacific Stock)	B-	B-	C+	Up	Y	10,000,000
Invesco Asia Pacific Growth Fund Class Y	ASIYX	NAS CM	Open End	Asia ex-Japan Equity (Pacific Stock)	B-	B-	C+	Up	Y	1,000
Invesco Balanced-Risk Allocation Fund Class A	ABRZX	NAS CM	Open End	Flexible Alloc (Growth & Income)	B-	C+	B	Up	Y	1,000

★ Expanded analysis of this fund is included in Section II.

	TOTAL RETURNS					PERFORMANCE				ASSETS		ASSET ALLOCATION & TURNOVER					BULL & BEAR		FEES		
Min Additional Investment	3-Month Total Return	6-Month Total Return	1-Year Total Return	3-Year Total Return	5-Year Total Return	Dividend Yield (TTM)	Expense Ratio	3-Yr Std Deviation	3-Year Beta	NAV	Total Assets (MIL)	%Cash	%Stocks	%Bonds	%Other	Turnover Ratio	Last Bull Market Total Return	Last Bear Market Total Return	Front End Fee (%)	Back End Fee (%)	Inception Date
100	0.66	0.95	7.01	14.46		2.08	2.29	3.63	-0.19	10.53	169.7	24	63	2	11	62			5.00		Sep-14
1,000	1.04	3.07	9.13	11.55		10.18	2.73	10.09	0.83	15.85	28.8	3	95	2	0	64					Mar-13
	-0.49	-2.12	-3.51	-4.79		0.09	2.01	4.6	0.8	9.48	36.1	38	0	73	-11	129			5.50		Dec-13
	-0.41	-2.05	-3.44	-4.59		0.16	1.76	4.61	0.8	9.48	36.1	38	0	73	-11	129					Dec-13
50	5.16	8.38	11.09	34.45	89.67	2.65	0.95	8.24	0.67	14.68	149.3	0	100	0	0	38			5.00		May-12
50	4.94	7.98	10.25	31.45	82.68	2.05	1.7	8.2	0.67	14.59	149.3	0	100	0	0	38				1.00	Aug-15
50	5.29	8.51	11.36	34.91	90.32	2.88	0.7	8.24	0.67	14.69	149.3	0	100	0	0	38					Aug-16
50	9.87	22.88	17.46			4.05	1.05			12.43	4.5	0	100	0	0				5.00		May-16
50	9.69	22.42	16.63			3.48	1.8			12.4	4.5	0	100	0	0					1.00	May-16
50	9.92	23.02	17.74			4.28	0.8			12.43	4.5	0	100	0	0						Aug-16
50	7.43	11.65	18.67	26.51	76.19	1.24	1.25	9.89	0.95	53.51	35.1	0	100	0	0	50	24.44	-20.89	5.00		Jan-95
50	7.23	11.23	17.78	23.93	70.03	0.65	2	9.86	0.95	53.49	35.1	0	100	0	0	50	23.9	-21.13		1.00	Aug-15
50	7.49	11.77	18.96	26.99	76.85	1.41	1	9.89	0.95	53.49	35.1	0	100	0	0	50	24.44	-20.89			Aug-16
100	3.61	4.90	8.30	16.63	43.07	2.13	1.15	7.23	0.59	12.08	412.3	24	45	28	0	47	13.23	-9.52			Apr-10
100	3.52	4.74	8.09	15.70	41.32	1.89	1.4	7.22	0.59	12.07	412.3	24	45	28	0	47	13	-9.56			Jan-05
100	1.82	2.29	6.72	14.57	48.88	0.51	1.3	6.24	0.49	10.71	45.8	36	64	0	0	13	18.29	-14.69			Oct-07
100	1.40	2.16	2.44	4.53	20.16	0.02	1.15	3.88	0.14	14.5	174.9	59	15	20	2	43	13.63	-10.55			Nov-09
100	1.37	2.00	2.14	3.67	18.69	0	1.4	3.89	0.14	14.15	174.9	59	15	20	2	43	13.5	-10.6			Oct-05
100	6.67	13.65	14.46	28.38		3.44	1.4			10.6	23.1	3	76	10	0	51					Dec-14
100	5.39	8.12	15.10			0.83	1.4			11.8	19.8	11	77	0	7	29					Jul-15
50	-3.18	-1.78	-9.27	-0.71		0	1.45	9.55	46.14	8.36	126.2	98	2	0	0	168			5.50		Dec-13
50	-3.36	-2.13	-9.95	-2.92		0	2.2	9.53	45.31	8.09	126.2	98	2	0	0	168				1.00	Dec-13
	-3.20	-1.78	-9.43	-1.41		0	1.7	9.59	46.97	8.27	126.2	98	2	0	0	168					Dec-13
	-3.03	-1.55	-8.82	0.16		0	1.05	9.52	45.82	8.46	126.2	98	2	0	0	168					Dec-13
	-3.04	-1.55	-8.83	0.06		0	1.04	9.51	46.44	8.45	126.2	98	2	0	0	168					Dec-13
50	-3.15	-1.66	-9.03	-0.05		0	1.2	9.52	44.33	8.44	126.2	98	2	0	0	168					Dec-13
50	1.74	3.87	3.76	7.06		3.39	1.44	3.72	25.86	9.79	2.6	15	53	23	8	45			5.50		Oct-14
50	1.58	3.52	3.08	4.77		2.78	2.19	3.7	26.12	9.72	2.6	15	53	23	8	45				1.00	Oct-14
	1.64	3.68	3.57	6.27		3.18	1.69	3.73	26.66	9.77	2.6	15	53	23	8	45					Oct-14
	1.86	3.99	4.10	7.89		3.57	1.19	3.76	26.34	9.81	2.6	15	53	23	8	45					Oct-14
	1.86	3.99	4.10	7.89		3.57	1.19	3.76	26.34	9.81	2.6	15	53	23	8	45					Oct-14
50	1.75	3.99	4.10	7.88		3.57	1.19	3.75	25.49	9.82	2.6	15	53	23	8	45					Oct-14
50	3.17	7.83	27.10	35.00	110.40	0	1.06	12.82	1.11	19.71	10,350	0	100	0	0	48	23.17	-19.31	5.50		Jun-05
50	3.10	7.84	27.03	34.98	110.19	0	1.06	12.81	1.11	19.14	10,350	0	100	0	0	48	23.2	-19.47		5.00	Jun-05
50	2.93	7.41	26.13	32.02	102.58	0	1.81	12.78	1.11	18.19	10,350	0	100	0	0	48	22.65	-19.61		1.00	Jun-05
	3.07	7.69	26.69	33.94	107.71	0	1.31	12.8	1.11	19.34	10,350	0	100	0	0	48	23	-19.48			May-11
	3.24	8.05	27.59	36.75	114.91	0	0.64	12.81	1.11	20.25	10,350	0	100	0	0	48	23.32	-19.28			Sep-12
50	3.21	7.94	27.36	35.97	112.85	0	0.81	12.81	1.11	20.11	10,350	0	100	0	0	48	23.32	-19.28			Jun-05
	3.20	7.98	27.45	36.38	114.05	0	0.72	12.77	1.11	20.15	10,350	0	100	0	0	48	23.39	-19.2			Dec-10
50	5.45	7.55	9.44	14.27	71.75	0.19	1.23	13.26	1.19	37.09	1,568	3	97	0	0	42	32.64	-21.77	5.50		Oct-93
50	5.47	7.56	9.44	14.24	71.71	0.22	1.23	13.27	1.19	32.33	1,568	3	97	0	0	42	32.72	-21.76		5.00	Aug-95
50	5.27	7.17	8.68	11.83	65.58	0	1.96	13.26	1.19	30.6	1,568	3	97	0	0	42	32.03	-21.97		1.00	Oct-93
	5.38	7.41	9.17	13.40	69.56	0	1.48	13.26	1.19	36.9	1,568	3	97	0	0	42	32.4	-21.85			Mar-07
	5.58	7.80	9.93	15.84	75.58	0.57	0.78	13.26	1.19	37.38	1,568	3	97	0	0	42	32.64	-21.77			Sep-12
50	5.51	7.70	9.73	15.11	73.87	0.39	0.98	13.26	1.19	37.34	1,568	3	97	0	0	42	32.82	-21.69			Feb-06
	5.55	7.73	9.82	15.52	74.83	0.49	0.87	13.28	1.19	37.36	1,568	3	97	0	0	42	33	-21.58			Jun-10
50	5.81	10.10	29.05	28.40	44.79	0.78	1.47	11.7	0.77	35.39	970.8	15	85	0	0	9	24.53	-19.8	5.50		Nov-97
50	5.62	9.70	28.09	25.56	39.48	0.18	2.22	11.69	0.77	32.87	970.8	15	85	0	0	9	24	-20.05		5.00	Nov-97
50	5.63	9.67	28.10	25.54	39.50	0.18	2.22	11.69	0.77	32.64	970.8	15	85	0	0	9	24.04	-20.08		1.00	Nov-97
	5.90	10.34	29.43	28.78	45.21		1.07	11.71	0.77	35.41	970.8	15	85	0	0	9	24.53	-19.8			Apr-17
50	5.90	10.25	29.35	29.37	46.62	0.98	1.22	11.68	0.77	35.44	970.8	15	85	0	0	9	24.75	-19.72			Oct-08
50	4.98	7.63	9.77	15.91	25.43	3.47	1.28	5.55	0.3	10.84	4,978	28	22	39	12	96	11.89	1.39	5.50		Jun-09

	MARKET			FUND TYPE, CATEGORY & OBJECTIVE	RATINGS				MINIMUMS	
Fund Name	Ticker Symbol	Traded On	Fund Type	Category and (Prospectus Objective)	Overall Rating	Reward Rating	Risk Rating	Recent Up/ Downgrade	Open to New Investors	Min Initial Investment
Invesco Balanced-Risk Allocation Fund Class B	ABRBX	NAS CM	Open End	Flexible Alloc (Growth & Income)	B-	C+	B	Up		1,000
Invesco Balanced-Risk Allocation Fund Class C	ABRCX	NAS CM	Open End	Flexible Alloc (Growth & Income)	B-	C+	B	Up	Y	1,000
Invesco Balanced-Risk Allocation Fund Class R	ABRRX	NAS CM	Open End	Flexible Alloc (Growth & Income)	B-	C+	B	Up	Y	0
Invesco Balanced-Risk Allocation Fund Class R6	ALLFX	NAS CM	Open End	Flexible Alloc (Growth & Income)	B-	C+	B		Y	10,000,000
Invesco Balanced-Risk Allocation Fund Class Y	ABRYX	NAS CM	Open End	Flexible Alloc (Growth & Income)	B-	C+	B		Y	1,000
Invesco Balanced-Risk Allocation Fund R5 Class	ABRIX	NAS CM	Open End	Flexible Alloc (Growth & Income)	B-	C+	B		Y	10,000,000
Invesco Balanced-Risk Commodity Strategy Fund Class A	BRCAX	NAS CM	Open End	Commodities Broad Basket (Growth & Income)	C-	C-	C-	Up	Y	1,000
Invesco Balanced-Risk Commodity Strategy Fund Class B	BRCBX	NAS CM	Open End	Commodities Broad Basket (Growth & Income)	D+	D+	D+	Up		1,000
Invesco Balanced-Risk Commodity Strategy Fund Class C	BRCCX	NAS CM	Open End	Commodities Broad Basket (Growth & Income)	D+	D+	D+	Up	Y	1,000
Invesco Balanced-Risk Commodity Strategy Fund Class R	BRCRX	NAS CM	Open End	Commodities Broad Basket (Growth & Income)	C-	C-	C-	Up	Y	0
Invesco Balanced-Risk Commodity Strategy Fund Class R6	IBRFX	NAS CM	Open End	Commodities Broad Basket (Growth & Income)	C-	C	C-	Up	Y	10,000,000
Invesco Balanced-Risk Commodity Strategy Fund Class Y	BRCYX	NAS CM	Open End	Commodities Broad Basket (Growth & Income)	C-	C	C-	Up	Y	1,000
Invesco Balanced-Risk Commodity Strategy Fund R5 Class	BRCNX	NAS CM	Open End	Commodities Broad Basket (Growth & Income)	C-	C	C-	Up	Y	10,000,000
Invesco Balanced-Risk Retirement 2020 Fund Class A	AFTAX	NAS CM	Open End	Target Date 2000-2020 (Asset Alloc)	B-	C	B	Up	Y	1,000
Invesco Balanced-Risk Retirement 2020 Fund Class AX	VRCAX	NAS CM	Open End	Target Date 2000-2020 (Asset Alloc)	B-	C	B	Up		1,000
Invesco Balanced-Risk Retirement 2020 Fund Class B	AFTBX	NAS CM	Open End	Target Date 2000-2020 (Asset Alloc)	B-	C	B	Up		1,000
Invesco Balanced-Risk Retirement 2020 Fund Class C	AFTCX	NAS CM	Open End	Target Date 2000-2020 (Asset Alloc)	B-	C	B	Up	Y	1,000
Invesco Balanced-Risk Retirement 2020 Fund Class CX	VRCCX	NAS CM	Open End	Target Date 2000-2020 (Asset Alloc)	B-	C	B	Up		1,000
Invesco Balanced-Risk Retirement 2020 Fund Class R	ATFRX	NAS CM	Open End	Target Date 2000-2020 (Asset Alloc)	B-	C	B	Up	Y	0
Invesco Balanced-Risk Retirement 2020 Fund Class R6	VRCFX	NAS CM	Open End	Target Date 2000-2020 (Asset Alloc)	C+	C+	B-	Down	Y	10,000,000
Invesco Balanced-Risk Retirement 2020 Fund Class RX	VRCRX	NAS CM	Open End	Target Date 2000-2020 (Asset Alloc)	B-	C	B	Up		0
Invesco Balanced-Risk Retirement 2020 Fund Class Y	AFTYX	NAS CM	Open End	Target Date 2000-2020 (Asset Alloc)	B-	C+	B	Up	Y	1,000
Invesco Balanced-Risk Retirement 2020 Fund R5 Class	AFTSX	NAS CM	Open End	Target Date 2000-2020 (Asset Alloc)	B-	C+	B	Up	Y	10,000,000
Invesco Balanced-Risk Retirement 2030 Fund Class A	TNAAX	NAS CM	Open End	Target Date 2021-2045 (Asset Alloc)	B-	C+	B	Up	Y	1,000
Invesco Balanced-Risk Retirement 2030 Fund Class AX	VREAX	NAS CM	Open End	Target Date 2021-2045 (Asset Alloc)	B-	C+	B	Up		1,000
Invesco Balanced-Risk Retirement 2030 Fund Class B	TNABX	NAS CM	Open End	Target Date 2021-2045 (Asset Alloc)	B-	C+	B	Up		1,000
Invesco Balanced-Risk Retirement 2030 Fund Class C	TNACX	NAS CM	Open End	Target Date 2021-2045 (Asset Alloc)	B-	C+	B	Up	Y	1,000
Invesco Balanced-Risk Retirement 2030 Fund Class CX	VRECX	NAS CM	Open End	Target Date 2021-2045 (Asset Alloc)	B-	C+	B	Up		1,000
Invesco Balanced-Risk Retirement 2030 Fund Class R	TNARX	NAS CM	Open End	Target Date 2021-2045 (Asset Alloc)	B-	C+	B	Up	Y	0
Invesco Balanced-Risk Retirement 2030 Fund Class R6	TNAFX	NAS CM	Open End	Target Date 2021-2045 (Asset Alloc)	B-	C+	B	Up	Y	10,000,000
Invesco Balanced-Risk Retirement 2030 Fund Class RX	VRERX	NAS CM	Open End	Target Date 2021-2045 (Asset Alloc)	B-	C+	B	Up		0
Invesco Balanced-Risk Retirement 2030 Fund Class Y	TNAYX	NAS CM	Open End	Target Date 2021-2045 (Asset Alloc)	B-	C+	B		Y	1,000
Invesco Balanced-Risk Retirement 2030 Fund R5 Class	TNAIX	NAS CM	Open End	Target Date 2021-2045 (Asset Alloc)	B-	C+	B	Up	Y	10,000,000
Invesco Balanced-Risk Retirement 2040 Fund Class A	TNDAX	NAS CM	Open End	Target Date 2021-2045 (Asset Alloc)	B-	B-	B		Y	1,000
Invesco Balanced-Risk Retirement 2040 Fund Class AX	VRGAX	NAS CM	Open End	Target Date 2021-2045 (Asset Alloc)	B-	B-	B			1,000
Invesco Balanced-Risk Retirement 2040 Fund Class B	TNDBX	NAS CM	Open End	Target Date 2021-2045 (Asset Alloc)	B-	C+	B	Up		1,000
Invesco Balanced-Risk Retirement 2040 Fund Class C	TNDCX	NAS CM	Open End	Target Date 2021-2045 (Asset Alloc)	B-	C+	B-	Up	Y	1,000
Invesco Balanced-Risk Retirement 2040 Fund Class CX	VRGCX	NAS CM	Open End	Target Date 2021-2045 (Asset Alloc)	B-	C+	B	Up		1,000
Invesco Balanced-Risk Retirement 2040 Fund Class R	TNDRX	NAS CM	Open End	Target Date 2021-2045 (Asset Alloc)	B-	B-	B		Y	0
Invesco Balanced-Risk Retirement 2040 Fund Class R6	TNDFX	NAS CM	Open End	Target Date 2021-2045 (Asset Alloc)	B-	B-	B		Y	10,000,000
Invesco Balanced-Risk Retirement 2040 Fund Class RX	VRGRX	NAS CM	Open End	Target Date 2021-2045 (Asset Alloc)	B-	B-	B			0
Invesco Balanced-Risk Retirement 2040 Fund Class Y	TNDYX	NAS CM	Open End	Target Date 2021-2045 (Asset Alloc)	B-	B-	B		Y	1,000
Invesco Balanced-Risk Retirement 2040 Fund R5 Class	TNDIX	NAS CM	Open End	Target Date 2021-2045 (Asset Alloc)	B-	B-	B		Y	10,000,000
Invesco Balanced-Risk Retirement 2050 Fund Class A	TNEAX	NAS CM	Open End	Target Date 2046+ (Asset Alloc)	B	B	B-	Up	Y	1,000
Invesco Balanced-Risk Retirement 2050 Fund Class AX	VRIAX	NAS CM	Open End	Target Date 2046+ (Asset Alloc)	B	B	B-	Up		1,000
Invesco Balanced-Risk Retirement 2050 Fund Class B	TNEBX	NAS CM	Open End	Target Date 2046+ (Asset Alloc)	B-	B-	B-			1,000
Invesco Balanced-Risk Retirement 2050 Fund Class C	TNECX	NAS CM	Open End	Target Date 2046+ (Asset Alloc)	B-	B-	B-		Y	1,000
Invesco Balanced-Risk Retirement 2050 Fund Class CX	VRICX	NAS CM	Open End	Target Date 2046+ (Asset Alloc)	B-	B-	B-			1,000
Invesco Balanced-Risk Retirement 2050 Fund Class R	TNERX	NAS CM	Open End	Target Date 2046+ (Asset Alloc)	B	B	B-	Up	Y	0
Invesco Balanced-Risk Retirement 2050 Fund Class R5	TNEIX	NAS CM	Open End	Target Date 2046+ (Asset Alloc)	B	B	B	Up	Y	10,000,000
Invesco Balanced-Risk Retirement 2050 Fund Class R6	TNEFX	NAS CM	Open End	Target Date 2046+ (Asset Alloc)	B	B	B	Up	Y	10,000,000
Invesco Balanced-Risk Retirement 2050 Fund Class RX	VRIRX	NAS CM	Open End	Target Date 2046+ (Asset Alloc)	B	B	B-	Up		0

★ Expanded analysis of this fund is included in Section II.

Min Additional Investment	TOTAL RETURNS: 3-Month Total Return	6-Month Total Return	1-Year Total Return	3-Year Total Return	5-Year Total Return	PERFORMANCE: Dividend Yield (TTM)	Expense Ratio	3-Yr Std Deviation	3-Year Beta	ASSETS: NAV	Total Assets (MIL)	ASSET ALLOCATION & TURNOVER: %Cash	%Stocks	%Bonds	%Other	Turnover Ratio	BULL & BEAR: Last Bull Market Total Return	Last Bear Market Total Return	FEES: Front End Fee (%)	Back End Fee (%)	Inception Date
50	4.71	7.24	8.93	13.35	20.80	2.83	2.03	5.58	0.31	10.36	4,978	28	22	39	12	96	11.44	1.05		5.00	Jun-09
50	4.71	7.24	8.82	13.35	20.80	2.83	2.03	5.58	0.31	10.36	4,978	28	22	39	12	96	11.45	1.05		1.00	Jun-09
	4.87	7.45	9.41	15.06	23.87	3.27	1.53	5.59	0.31	10.66	4,978	28	22	39	12	96	11.78	1.31			Jun-09
	5.00	7.80	10.13	17.26	27.82	3.81	0.9	5.57	0.31	11.01	4,978	28	22	39	12	96	12.01	1.56			Sep-12
50	4.92	7.72	9.94	16.80	26.96	3.68	1.03	5.56	0.3	10.99	4,978	28	22	39	12	96	12.01	1.56			Jun-09
	5.00	7.81	10.04	16.92	27.32	3.74	0.97	5.53	0.3	11	4,978	28	22	39	12	96	12.01	1.56			Jun-09
50	7.21	11.50	4.49	-4.16	-29.62	2.57	1.56	11.31	0.79	6.98	871.0	47	0	31	22	98	14.37	-17.17	5.50		Nov-10
50	7.05	11.14	3.72	-6.13	-32.15	2.31	2.31	11.25	0.78	6.68	871.0	47	0	31	22	98	13.94	-17.47		5.00	Nov-10
50	7.06	11.35	3.89	-6.14	-32.19	2.32	2.31	11.28	0.78	6.67	871.0	47	0	31	22	98	13.94	-17.47		1.00	Nov-10
	7.14	11.65	4.38	-4.70	-30.42	2.47	1.81	11.28	0.78	6.9	871.0	47	0	31	22	98	14.38	-17.26			Nov-10
	7.40	11.94	5.04	-2.71	-28.20	2.8	1.12	11.24	0.78	7.15	871.0	47	0	31	22	98	14.73	-17.06			Sep-12
50	7.25	11.80	4.88	-3.37	-28.75	2.72	1.31	11.28	0.79	7.11	871.0	47	0	31	22	98	14.73	-17.06			Nov-10
	7.25	11.79	4.88	-3.06	-28.45	2.73	1.22	11.21	0.78	7.13	871.0	47	0	31	22	98	14.85	-17.14			Nov-10
50	3.66	5.66	7.24	12.21	20.48	2.55	0.91	4.33		9.05	64.8	48	16	28	8	11	11.09	1.47	5.50		Jan-07
50	3.66	5.66	7.24	12.21	20.48	2.55	0.91	4.34		9.05	64.8	48	16	28	8	11	11.09	1.47	5.50		Jun-10
50	3.33	5.11	6.46	9.71	15.98	1.83	1.66	4.3		8.96	64.8	48	16	28	8	11	10.58	1.14		5.00	Jan-07
50	3.34	5.12	6.35	9.73	16.02	1.83	1.66	4.36		8.94	64.8	48	16	28	8	11	10.72	1.03		1.00	Jan-07
50	3.34	5.24	6.47	9.72	16.01	1.83	1.66	4.27		8.94	64.8	48	16	28	8	11	10.6	1.15		1.00	Jun-10
	3.52	5.40	6.99	11.35	18.94	2.32	1.16	4.31		9.01	64.8	48	16	28	8	11	11.01	1.25			Jan-07
	3.67	5.77	7.47	12.91	21.95	2.77	0.66	4.36		9.1	64.8	48	16	28	8	11	11.29	1.58			Sep-12
	3.52	5.40	6.86	11.35	18.94	2.32	1.16	4.31		9.01	64.8	48	16	28	8	11	11.01	1.25			Jun-10
50	3.58	5.69	7.52	13.00	21.96	2.79	0.66	4.29		9.04	64.8	48	16	28	8	11	11.34	1.47			Oct-08
	3.56	5.66	7.47	12.92	21.85	2.77	0.66	4.34		9.09	64.8	48	16	28	8	11	11.29	1.58			Jan-07
50	5.04	7.94	10.20	17.18	28.05	4.46	1.08	5.92		8.71	72.7	27	22	39	12	11	11.79	1.43	5.50		Jan-07
50	5.15	7.93	10.32	17.16	28.16	4.45	1.08	5.95		8.72	72.7	27	22	39	12	11	11.78	1.43	5.50		Jun-10
50	4.79	7.47	9.34	14.56	23.26	3.76	1.83	5.89		8.62	72.7	27	22	39	12	11	11.28	1.08		5.00	Jan-07
50	4.79	7.47	9.34	14.70	23.41	3.76	1.83	5.9		8.62	72.7	27	22	39	12	11	11.29	1.08		1.00	Jan-07
50	4.91	7.60	9.47	14.83	23.55	3.76	1.83	5.91		8.63	72.7	27	22	39	12	11	11.29	1.08		1.00	Jun-10
	5.04	7.84	9.97	16.46	26.67	4.23	1.33	5.91		8.67	72.7	27	22	39	12	11	11.6	1.31			Jan-07
	5.16	8.05	10.43	18.02	29.56	4.67	0.83	5.96		8.75	72.7	27	22	39	12	11	11.98	1.54			Sep-12
	5.05	7.72	9.98	16.48	26.55	4.23	1.33	5.89		8.66	72.7	27	22	39	12	11	11.48	1.44			Jun-10
50	5.17	8.07	10.45	18.07	29.64	4.68	0.83	5.92		8.73	72.7	27	22	39	12	11	12.01	1.42			Oct-08
	5.15	8.17	10.55	18.15	29.70	4.67	0.83	5.92		8.76	72.7	27	22	39	12	11	11.98	1.54			Jan-07
50	5.76	9.11	11.77	20.04	32.49	4.52	1.12	6.79		7.94	53.2	25	23	41	11	13	11.84	1.37	5.50		Jan-07
50	5.77	9.13	11.79	20.05	32.36	4.52	1.12	6.86		7.93	53.2	25	23	41	11	13	11.86	1.37	5.50		Jun-10
50	5.59	8.70	10.93	17.58	27.92	3.87	1.87	6.89		7.86	53.2	25	23	41	11	13	11.35	1.13		5.00	Jan-07
50	5.60	8.71	10.94	17.76	27.96	3.87	1.87	6.84		7.85	53.2	25	23	41	11	13	11.37	1.13		1.00	Jan-07
50	5.60	8.72	10.96	17.64	27.85	3.88	1.87	6.85		7.84	53.2	25	23	41	11	13	11.24	1.13		1.00	Jun-10
	5.67	9.04	11.41	19.33	30.96	4.3	1.37	6.85		7.9	53.2	25	23	41	11	13	11.64	1.25			Jan-07
	5.86	9.20	12.00	20.89	34.07	4.72	0.87	6.86		7.97	53.2	25	23	41	11	13	11.92	1.49			Sep-12
	5.67	9.04	11.57	19.18	30.78	4.3	1.37	6.86		7.9	53.2	25	23	41	11	13	11.77	1.25			Jun-10
50	5.87	9.36	12.01	20.92	34.13	4.72	0.87	6.87		7.96	53.2	25	23	41	11	13	11.8	1.61			Oct-08
	5.99	9.34	12.14	21.04	34.23	4.72	0.87	6.88		7.98	53.2	25	23	41	11	13	11.92	1.49			Jan-07
50	6.49	10.24	13.15	22.64	36.83	6.89	1.16	7.74		7.79	38.1	22	25	44	10	34	11.63	1.52	5.50		Jan-07
50	6.48	10.22	13.29	22.61	36.80	6.88	1.16	7.73		7.8	38.1	22	25	44	10	34	11.75	1.4	5.50		Jun-10
50	6.37	9.89	12.53	20.32	32.17	6.35	1.91	7.71		7.68	38.1	22	25	44	10	34	11.17	1.16		5.00	Jan-07
50	6.36	9.87	12.35	20.11	32.08	6.34	1.91	7.76		7.69	38.1	22	25	44	10	34	11.28	1.15		1.00	Jan-07
50	6.36	9.87	12.51	20.29	32.12	6.34	1.91	7.7		7.69	38.1	22	25	44	10	34	11.15	1.15		1.00	Jun-10
	6.41	10.18	12.96	21.82	35.20	6.71	1.41	7.76		7.75	38.1	22	25	44	10	34	11.46	1.4			Jan-07
	6.69	10.58	13.65	23.61	38.56	7.06	0.91	7.76		7.83	38.1	22	25	44	10	34	11.93	1.52			Jan-07
	6.68	10.57	13.63	23.57	38.66	7.06	0.91	7.77		7.84	38.1	22	25	44	10	34	11.93	1.52			Sep-12
	6.54	10.17	13.10	21.96	35.33	6.7	1.41	7.73		7.76	38.1	22	25	44	10	34	11.59	1.27			Jun-10

	MARKET			FUND TYPE, CATEGORY & OBJECTIVE	RATINGS				MINIMUMS	
Fund Name	Ticker Symbol	Traded On	Fund Type	Category and (Prospectus Objective)	Overall Rating	Reward Rating	Risk Rating	Recent Up/ Downgrade	Open to New Investors	Min Initial Investment
Invesco Balanced-Risk Retirement 2050 Fund Class Y	TNEYX	NAS CM	Open End	Target Date 2046+ (Asset Alloc)	B	B	B	Up	Y	1,000
Invesco Balanced-Risk Retirement Now Fund Class A	IANAX	NAS CM	Open End	Target Date 2000-2020 (Asset Alloc)	B-	C	B	Up	Y	1,000
Invesco Balanced-Risk Retirement Now Fund Class AX	VIRAX	NAS CM	Open End	Target Date 2000-2020 (Asset Alloc)	B-	C	B	Up		1,000
Invesco Balanced-Risk Retirement Now Fund Class B	IANBX	NAS CM	Open End	Target Date 2000-2020 (Asset Alloc)	C+	C	B			1,000
Invesco Balanced-Risk Retirement Now Fund Class C	IANCX	NAS CM	Open End	Target Date 2000-2020 (Asset Alloc)	C+	C	B		Y	1,000
Invesco Balanced-Risk Retirement Now Fund Class CX	VIRCX	NAS CM	Open End	Target Date 2000-2020 (Asset Alloc)	C+	C	B			1,000
Invesco Balanced-Risk Retirement Now Fund Class R	IANRX	NAS CM	Open End	Target Date 2000-2020 (Asset Alloc)	B-	C	B	Up	Y	0
Invesco Balanced-Risk Retirement Now Fund Class R6	IANFX	NAS CM	Open End	Target Date 2000-2020 (Asset Alloc)	C+	C	B	Down	Y	10,000,000
Invesco Balanced-Risk Retirement Now Fund Class RX	VIRRX	NAS CM	Open End	Target Date 2000-2020 (Asset Alloc)	B-	C	B	Up		0
Invesco Balanced-Risk Retirement Now Fund Class Y	IANYX	NAS CM	Open End	Target Date 2000-2020 (Asset Alloc)	B-	C	B	Up	Y	1,000
Invesco Balanced-Risk Retirement Now Fund R5 Class	IANIX	NAS CM	Open End	Target Date 2000-2020 (Asset Alloc)	B-	C	B	Up	Y	10,000,000
Invesco Charter Fund Class A	CHTRX	NAS CM	Open End	US Equity Large Cap Blend (Growth)	B-	C+	B-	Down	Y	1,000
Invesco Charter Fund Class B	BCHTX	NAS CM	Open End	US Equity Large Cap Blend (Growth)	C+	C+	B-	Down		1,000
Invesco Charter Fund Class C	CHTCX	NAS CM	Open End	US Equity Large Cap Blend (Growth)	C+	C+	B-	Down	Y	1,000
Invesco Charter Fund Class R	CHRRX	NAS CM	Open End	US Equity Large Cap Blend (Growth)	C+	C+	B-	Down	Y	0
Invesco Charter Fund Class R6	CHFTX	NAS CM	Open End	US Equity Large Cap Blend (Growth)	C+	C+	C+	Down	Y	10,000,000
Invesco Charter Fund Class S	CHRSX	NAS CM	Open End	US Equity Large Cap Blend (Growth)	C+	C+	C+	Down	Y	0
Invesco Charter Fund Class Y	CHTYX	NAS CM	Open End	US Equity Large Cap Blend (Growth)	C+	C+	C+	Down	Y	1,000
Invesco Charter Fund R5 Class	CHTVX	NAS CM	Open End	US Equity Large Cap Blend (Growth)	C+	C+	C+	Down	Y	10,000,000
Invesco Comstock Fund Class A	ACSTX	NAS CM	Open End	US Equity Large Cap Value (Growth & Income)	B	B	B-	Up	Y	1,000
Invesco Comstock Fund Class B	ACSWX	NAS CM	Open End	US Equity Large Cap Value (Growth & Income)	B	B	B-	Up		1,000
Invesco Comstock Fund Class C	ACSYX	NAS CM	Open End	US Equity Large Cap Value (Growth & Income)	B-	B-	B-	Up	Y	1,000
Invesco Comstock Fund Class R	ACSRX	NAS CM	Open End	US Equity Large Cap Value (Growth & Income)	B	B	B-	Up	Y	0
Invesco Comstock Fund Class R6	ICSFX	NAS CM	Open End	US Equity Large Cap Value (Growth & Income)	B	B	B	Up	Y	10,000,000
Invesco Comstock Fund Class Y	ACSDX	NAS CM	Open End	US Equity Large Cap Value (Growth & Income)	B	B	B-	Up	Y	1,000
Invesco Comstock Fund R5 Class	ACSHX	NAS CM	Open End	US Equity Large Cap Value (Growth & Income)	B	B	B	Up	Y	10,000,000
Invesco Conservative Allocation Fund Class A	CAAMX	NAS CM	Open End	Cautious Alloc (Asset Alloc)	C+	C	B		Y	1,000
Invesco Conservative Allocation Fund Class B	CMBAX	NAS CM	Open End	Cautious Alloc (Asset Alloc)	C+	C	B	Up		1,000
Invesco Conservative Allocation Fund Class C	CACMX	NAS CM	Open End	Cautious Alloc (Asset Alloc)	C+	C	B	Up	Y	1,000
Invesco Conservative Allocation Fund Class R	CMARX	NAS CM	Open End	Cautious Alloc (Asset Alloc)	C+	C	B	Up	Y	0
Invesco Conservative Allocation Fund Class R6	CNSSX	NAS CM	Open End	Cautious Alloc (Asset Alloc)	B-	C+	B	Up	Y	10,000,000
Invesco Conservative Allocation Fund Class S	CMASX	NAS CM	Open End	Cautious Alloc (Asset Alloc)	B-	C+	B	Up	Y	0
Invesco Conservative Allocation Fund Class Y	CAAYX	NAS CM	Open End	Cautious Alloc (Asset Alloc)	B-	C+	B	Up	Y	1,000
Invesco Conservative Allocation Fund R5 Class	CMAIX	NAS CM	Open End	Cautious Alloc (Asset Alloc)	B-	C+	B	Up	Y	10,000,000
Invesco Convertible Securities Fund Class A	CNSAX	NAS CM	Open End	Convertibles (Convertible Bond)	C+	C+	B-	Down	Y	1,000
Invesco Convertible Securities Fund Class B	CNSBX	NAS CM	Open End	Convertibles (Convertible Bond)	C+	C+	B-	Down		1,000
Invesco Convertible Securities Fund Class C	CNSCX	NAS CM	Open End	Convertibles (Convertible Bond)	C+	C+	B-	Down	Y	1,000
Invesco Convertible Securities Fund Class R6	CNSFX	NAS CM	Open End	Convertibles (Convertible Bond)	C+	C+	B-	Down	Y	10,000,000
Invesco Convertible Securities Fund Class Y	CNSDX	NAS CM	Open End	Convertibles (Convertible Bond)	C+	C+	B-	Down	Y	1,000
Invesco Convertible Securities Fund R5 Shares	CNSIX	NAS CM	Open End	Convertibles (Convertible Bond)	C+	C+	B-	Down	Y	10,000,000
Invesco Developing Markets Fund Class A	GTDDX	NAS CM	Open End	Emerging Markets Equity (Div Emerging Mkts)	C+	B-	C	Up		1,000
Invesco Developing Markets Fund Class B	GTDBX	NAS CM	Open End	Emerging Markets Equity (Div Emerging Mkts)	C+	B-	C	Up		1,000
Invesco Developing Markets Fund Class C	GTDCX	NAS CM	Open End	Emerging Markets Equity (Div Emerging Mkts)	C+	B-	C	Up		1,000
Invesco Developing Markets Fund Class R6	GTDFX	NAS CM	Open End	Emerging Markets Equity (Div Emerging Mkts)	C+	B-	C	Up		10,000,000
Invesco Developing Markets Fund Class Y	GTDYX	NAS CM	Open End	Emerging Markets Equity (Div Emerging Mkts)	C+	B-	C	Up		1,000
Invesco Developing Markets Fund R5 Class	GTDIX	NAS CM	Open End	Emerging Markets Equity (Div Emerging Mkts)	C+	B-	C	Up		10,000,000
Invesco Diversified Dividend Fund Class A	LCEAX	NAS CM	Open End	US Equity Large Cap Value (Equity-Income)	B	C+	A+		Y	1,000
Invesco Diversified Dividend Fund Class B	LCEDX	NAS CM	Open End	US Equity Large Cap Value (Equity-Income)	B	C+	A			1,000
Invesco Diversified Dividend Fund Class C	LCEVX	NAS CM	Open End	US Equity Large Cap Value (Equity-Income)	B	C+	A		Y	1,000
Invesco Diversified Dividend Fund Class R	DDFRX	NAS CM	Open End	US Equity Large Cap Value (Equity-Income)	B	C+	A+		Y	0
Invesco Diversified Dividend Fund Class R6	LCEFX	NAS CM	Open End	US Equity Large Cap Value (Equity-Income)	B	C+	A+		Y	10,000,000
Invesco Diversified Dividend Fund Class Y	LCEYX	NAS CM	Open End	US Equity Large Cap Value (Equity-Income)	B	C+	A+		Y	1,000

★Expanded analysis of this fund is included in Section II.

	TOTAL RETURNS					PERFORMANCE				ASSETS		ASSET ALLOCATION & TURNOVER					BULL & BEAR		FEES		
Min Additional Investment	3-Month Total Return	6-Month Total Return	1-Year Total Return	3-Year Total Return	5-Year Total Return	Dividend Yield (TTM)	Expense Ratio	3-Yr Std Deviation	3-Year Beta	NAV	Total Assets (MIL)	%Cash	%Stocks	%Bonds	%Other	Turnover Ratio	Last Bull Market Total Return	Last Bear Market Total Return	Front End Fee (%)	Back End Fee (%)	Inception Date
50	6.70	10.45	13.67	23.63	38.60	7.07	0.91	7.73		7.82	38.1	22	25	44	10	34	11.81	1.52			Oct-08
50	3.03	4.75	6.10	9.94	15.49	3.23	0.81	3.36		8.47	24.7	57	13	23	7	10	7.07	0.92	5.50		Jan-07
50	3.03	4.63	5.98	9.82	15.37	3.23	0.81	3.38		8.45	24.7	57	13	23	7	10	7.08	0.8	5.50		Jun-10
50	2.82	4.35	5.27	7.53	11.27	2.88	1.56	3.37		8.16	24.7	57	13	23	7	10	6.47	0.57		5.00	Jan-07
50	2.82	4.34	5.26	7.65	11.39	2.87	1.56	3.43		8.17	24.7	57	13	23	7	10	6.58	0.57		1.00	Jan-07
50	2.82	4.22	5.27	7.53	11.26	2.88	1.56	3.36		8.16	24.7	57	13	23	7	10	6.47	0.57		1.00	Jun-10
	3.04	4.66	5.83	8.98	13.93	3.11	1.06	3.34		8.37	24.7	57	13	23	7	10	6.83	0.8			Jan-07
	3.13	4.85	6.38	10.66	16.78	3.35	0.56	3.35		8.56	24.7	57	13	23	7	10	7.19	1.03			Sep-12
	2.92	4.54	5.83	9.10	13.94	3.11	1.06	3.37		8.36	24.7	57	13	23	7	10	6.84	0.69			Jun-10
50	3.13	4.84	6.50	10.79	16.92	3.34	0.56	3.34		8.57	24.7	57	13	23	7	10	7.19	1.03			Oct-08
	3.13	4.85	6.38	10.67	16.79	3.35	0.56	3.33		8.56	24.7	57	13	23	7	10	7.19	1.03			Jan-07
50	2.43	4.82	13.25	16.11	63.89	0.79	1.12	9.54	0.9	18.05	3,780	11	89	0	0	28	18.22	-15.11	5.50		Nov-68
50	2.26	4.39	12.37	13.52	57.81	0.08	1.87	9.51	0.9	16.92	3,780	11	89	0	0	28	17.68	-15.37		5.00	Jun-95
50	2.25	4.43	12.45	13.60	57.95	0.08	1.87	9.56	0.9	17	3,780	11	89	0	0	28	17.78	-15.44		1.00	Aug-97
	2.37	4.67	12.97	15.25	61.85	0.56	1.37	9.53	0.9	17.9	3,780	11	89	0	0	28	18.07	-15.26			Jun-02
	2.54	5.00	13.69	17.61	67.36	1.15	0.69	9.51	0.9	18.84	3,780	11	89	0	0	28	18.22	-15.11			Sep-12
	2.49	4.88	13.37	16.50	64.75	0.88	1.02	9.54	0.9	18.05	3,780	11	89	0	0	28	18.31	-15.1			Sep-09
50	2.53	4.97	13.56	17.06	66.00	1.02	0.87	9.55	0.9	18.11	3,780	11	89	0	0	28	18.41	-15.07			Oct-08
	2.51	4.96	13.59	17.30	66.67	1.08	0.76	9.52	0.9	18.85	3,780	11	89	0	0	28	18.52	-14.98			Jul-91
50	7.44	13.87	17.76	29.31	95.82	1.75	0.84	13.22	1.23	26.86	12,696	3	97	0	0	18	25.08	-20.2	5.50		Oct-68
50	7.49	13.92	17.81	29.37	95.20	1.75	0.84	13.2	1.23	26.86	12,696	3	97	0	0	18	25.08	-20.2		5.00	Oct-92
50	7.25	13.50	16.95	26.53	88.76	1.11	1.59	13.18	1.22	26.87	12,696	3	97	0	0	18	24.52	-20.44		1.00	Oct-93
	7.42	13.77	17.52	28.39	93.45	1.53	1.09	13.19	1.22	26.87	12,696	3	97	0	0	18	24.92	-20.25			Oct-02
	7.56	14.17	18.33	31.04	100.10	2.12	0.41	13.19	1.23	26.84	12,696	3	97	0	0	18	25.08	-20.2			Sep-12
50	7.55	14.05	18.10	30.29	98.28	1.97	0.59	13.18	1.22	26.86	12,696	3	97	0	0	18	25.23	-20.1			Oct-04
	7.58	14.11	18.21	30.66	99.22	2.04	0.51	13.22	1.23	26.85	12,696	3	97	0	0	18	25.45	-20.03			Jun-10
50	1.65	3.56	7.87	11.19	24.06	1.89	1.05	4.2	0.35	11.63	323.5	9	31	57	1	45	11.07	-4.92	5.50		Apr-05
50	1.45	3.19	7.02	8.74	19.49	1.16	1.8	4.22	0.35	11.49	323.5	9	31	57	1	45	10.62	-5.16		5.00	Apr-05
50	1.45	3.19	7.01	8.73	19.48	1.17	1.8	4.21	0.35	11.51	323.5	9	31	57	1	45	10.6	-5.24		1.00	Apr-05
	1.49	3.34	7.52	10.27	22.37	1.65	1.3	4.22	0.35	11.58	323.5	9	31	57	1	45	10.91	-4.93			Apr-05
	1.63	3.60	8.16	12.18	25.82		0.7	4.24	0.35	11.67	323.5	9	31	57	1	45	11.19	-4.71			Apr-17
	1.58	3.61	7.97	11.52	24.61	1.99	0.95	4.26	0.36	11.64	323.5	9	31	57	1	45	11.1	-4.74			Jun-11
50	1.71	3.69	8.14	12.03	25.60	2.13	0.8	4.25	0.35	11.62	323.5	9	31	57	1	45	11.15	-4.82			Oct-08
	1.71	3.69	8.16	12.18	25.82	2.18	0.75	4.24	0.35	11.68	323.5	9	31	57	1	45	11.19	-4.71			Apr-05
50	1.87	4.68	10.41	12.78	44.12	4.21	0.89	6.7	0.82	24.41	1,407	2	0	0	0	42	12.57	-14.81	5.50		Jul-97
50	1.71	4.32	9.60	10.27	38.77	3.48	1.65	6.68	0.82	24.49	1,407	2	0	0	0	42	11.99	-15.01		5.00	Oct-85
50	1.68	4.34	9.57	10.39	39.10	3.52	1.62	6.67	0.82	24.3	1,407	2	0	0	0	42	12.03	-15.04		1.00	Jul-97
	2.00	4.91	10.81	14.03	46.75	4.56	0.53	6.69	0.82	24.43	1,407	2	0	0	0	42	11.99	-15.01			Sep-12
50	1.93	4.85	10.67	13.61	45.90	4.44	0.65	6.68	0.82	24.44	1,407	2	0	0	0	42	12.75	-14.73			Jul-97
	1.94	4.83	10.73	13.73	46.28	4.48	0.63	6.7	0.82	24.42	1,407	2	0	0	0	42	12.78	-14.65			May-11
50	3.61	12.84	30.34	26.66	19.82	0.68	1.42	15.69	0.92	37.63	3,439	12	85	0	0	3	19.91	-20.27	5.50		Jan-94
50	3.43	12.40	29.35	23.84	15.39	0.09	2.17	15.69	0.92	36.8	3,439	12	85	0	0	3	19.4	-20.55		5.00	Nov-97
50	3.40	12.39	29.36	23.84	15.38	0.09	2.17	15.68	0.92	36.75	3,439	12	85	0	0	3	19.38	-20.55		1.00	Mar-99
	3.70	13.04	30.86	28.26	22.35	1.01	1	15.7	0.92	37.51	3,439	12	85	0	0	3	19.91	-20.27			Sep-12
50	3.66	12.96	30.64	27.57	21.29	0.88	1.17	15.68	0.92	37.62	3,439	12	85	0	0	3	20.09	-20.18			Oct-08
	3.72	13.02	30.79	28.08	22.14	0.97	1.05	15.69	0.92	37.53	3,439	12	85	0	0	3	20.21	-20.13			Oct-05
50	2.92	4.87	8.20	24.69	84.27	1.59	0.82	7.12	0.63	20.36	24,220	13	87	0	0	11	21.17	-15.87	5.50		Dec-01
50	2.70	4.42	7.36	21.89	77.42	0.89	1.57	7.12	0.63	20.13	24,220	13	87	0	0	11	20.64	-16.2		5.00	Dec-01
50	2.76	4.48	7.36	21.92	77.40	0.89	1.57	7.1	0.63	20.11	24,220	13	87	0	0	11	20.66	-16.15		1.00	Dec-01
	2.85	4.73	7.96	23.76	81.87	1.36	1.07	7.1	0.63	20.43	24,220	13	87	0	0	11	20.96	-16			Oct-05
	3.03	5.08	8.63	26.18	87.90	1.96	0.42	7.13	0.63	20.36	24,220	13	87	0	0	11	21.17	-15.87			Sep-12
50	2.94	4.95	8.41	25.55	86.39	1.83	0.57	7.11	0.63	20.37	24,220	13	87	0	0	11	21.3	-15.81			Oct-08

Fund Name	MARKET Ticker Symbol	Traded On	FUND TYPE, CATEGORY & OBJECTIVE Fund Type	Category and (Prospectus Objective)	RATINGS Overall Rating	Reward Rating	Risk Rating	Recent Up/ Downgrade	MINIMUMS Open to New Investors	Min Initial Investment
Invesco Diversified Dividend Fund Investor Class	LCEIX	NAS CM	Open End	US Equity Large Cap Value (Equity-Income)	B	C+	A+		Y	1,000
Invesco Diversified Dividend Fund R5 Class	DDFIX	NAS CM	Open End	US Equity Large Cap Value (Equity-Income)	B	C+	A+		Y	10,000,000
Invesco Dividend Income Fund Class A	IAUTX	NAS CM	Open End	US Equity Large Cap Value (Equity-Income)	B	B-	A+		Y	1,000
Invesco Dividend Income Fund Class B	IBUTX	NAS CM	Open End	US Equity Large Cap Value (Equity-Income)	B	C+	A+			1,000
Invesco Dividend Income Fund Class C	IUTCX	NAS CM	Open End	US Equity Large Cap Value (Equity-Income)	B	C+	A+		Y	1,000
Invesco Dividend Income Fund Class R6	IFUTX	NAS CM	Open End	US Equity Large Cap Value (Equity-Income)	B	B-	A+		Y	10,000,000
Invesco Dividend Income Fund Class Y	IAUYX	NAS CM	Open End	US Equity Large Cap Value (Equity-Income)	B	B-	A+		Y	1,000
Invesco Dividend Income Fund Investor Class	FSTUX	NAS CM	Open End	US Equity Large Cap Value (Equity-Income)	B	B-	A+			1,000
Invesco Dividend Income Fund R5 Class	FSIUX	NAS CM	Open End	US Equity Large Cap Value (Equity-Income)	B	B-	A+		Y	10,000,000
Invesco Emerging Markets Equity Fund Class A	IEMAX	NAS CM	Open End	Emerging Markets Equity (Div Emerging Mkts)	B	B+	C+	Up	Y	1,000
Invesco Emerging Markets Equity Fund Class C	IEMCX	NAS CM	Open End	Emerging Markets Equity (Div Emerging Mkts)	B	B	C+	Up	Y	1,000
Invesco Emerging Markets Equity Fund Class R	IEMRX	NAS CM	Open End	Emerging Markets Equity (Div Emerging Mkts)	B	B	C+	Up	Y	0
Invesco Emerging Markets Equity Fund Class R6	EMEFX	NAS CM	Open End	Emerging Markets Equity (Div Emerging Mkts)	B	B+	C+	Up	Y	10,000,000
Invesco Emerging Markets Equity Fund Class Y	IEMYX	NAS CM	Open End	Emerging Markets Equity (Div Emerging Mkts)	B	B+	C+	Up	Y	1,000
Invesco Emerging Markets Equity Fund R5 Class	IEMIX	NAS CM	Open End	Emerging Markets Equity (Div Emerging Mkts)	B	B+	C+	Up	Y	10,000,000
Invesco Endeavor Fund Class A	ATDAX	NAS CM	Open End	US Equity Mid Cap (Growth)	B-	B-	C+	Up	Y	1,000
Invesco Endeavor Fund Class B	ATDBX	NAS CM	Open End	US Equity Mid Cap (Growth)	C+	B-	C+	Down		1,000
Invesco Endeavor Fund Class C	ATDCX	NAS CM	Open End	US Equity Mid Cap (Growth)	C+	B-	C+	Down	Y	1,000
Invesco Endeavor Fund Class R	ATDRX	NAS CM	Open End	US Equity Mid Cap (Growth)	B-	B-	C+	Up	Y	0
Invesco Endeavor Fund Class R6	ATDFX	NAS CM	Open End	US Equity Mid Cap (Growth)	B-	B	C+	Up	Y	10,000,000
Invesco Endeavor Fund Class Y	ATDYX	NAS CM	Open End	US Equity Mid Cap (Growth)	B-	B-	C+	Up	Y	1,000
Invesco Endeavor Fund R5 Class	ATDIX	NAS CM	Open End	US Equity Mid Cap (Growth)	B-	B	C+	Up	Y	10,000,000
Invesco Energy Fund Class A	IENAX	NAS CM	Open End	Energy Sector Equity (Natl Res)	D	D	D	Down	Y	1,000
Invesco Energy Fund Class B	IENBX	NAS CM	Open End	Energy Sector Equity (Natl Res)	D	D	D	Down		1,000
Invesco Energy Fund Class C	IEFCX	NAS CM	Open End	Energy Sector Equity (Natl Res)	D	D	D	Down	Y	1,000
Invesco Energy Fund Class Y	IENYX	NAS CM	Open End	Energy Sector Equity (Natl Res)	D	D	D	Down	Y	1,000
Invesco Energy Fund Investor Class	FSTEX	NAS CM	Open End	Energy Sector Equity (Natl Res)	D	D	D	Down		1,000
Invesco Energy Fund R5 Class	IENIX	NAS CM	Open End	Energy Sector Equity (Natl Res)	D	D	D	Down	Y	10,000,000
Invesco Equally-Weighted S&P 500 Fund Class A	VADAX	NAS CM	Open End	US Equity Large Cap Blend (Growth & Income)	B-	B-	B-	Down	Y	1,000
Invesco Equally-Weighted S&P 500 Fund Class B	VADBX	NAS CM	Open End	US Equity Large Cap Blend (Growth & Income)	B-	B-	B-	Down		1,000
Invesco Equally-Weighted S&P 500 Fund Class C	VADCX	NAS CM	Open End	US Equity Large Cap Blend (Growth & Income)	B-	B-	B-	Down	Y	1,000
Invesco Equally-Weighted S&P 500 Fund Class R	VADRX	NAS CM	Open End	US Equity Large Cap Blend (Growth & Income)	B-	B-	B-	Down	Y	0
Invesco Equally-Weighted S&P 500 Fund Class R6	VADFX	NAS CM	Open End	US Equity Large Cap Blend (Growth & Income)	B-	B	B-	Down	Y	10,000,000
Invesco Equally-Weighted S&P 500 Fund Class Y	VADDX	NAS CM	Open End	US Equity Large Cap Blend (Growth & Income)	B-	B-	B-	Down	Y	1,000
Invesco Equity and Income Fund Class A	ACEIX	NAS CM	Open End	Moderate Alloc (Equity-Income)	B	C+	B+	Up	Y	1,000
Invesco Equity and Income Fund Class B	ACEQX	NAS CM	Open End	Moderate Alloc (Equity-Income)	B-	C+	B	Down		1,000
Invesco Equity and Income Fund Class C	ACERX	NAS CM	Open End	Moderate Alloc (Equity-Income)	B-	C+	B	Down	Y	1,000
Invesco Equity and Income Fund Class R	ACESX	NAS CM	Open End	Moderate Alloc (Equity-Income)	B	C+	B	Up	Y	0
Invesco Equity and Income Fund Class R6	IEIFX	NAS CM	Open End	Moderate Alloc (Equity-Income)	B	B-	B+	Up	Y	10,000,000
Invesco Equity and Income Fund Class Y	ACETX	NAS CM	Open End	Moderate Alloc (Equity-Income)	B	C+	B+	Up	Y	1,000
Invesco Equity and Income Fund R5 Class	ACEKX	NAS CM	Open End	Moderate Alloc (Equity-Income)	B	B-	B+	Up	Y	10,000,000
Invesco European Growth Fund Class A	AEDAX	NAS CM	Open End	Europe Equity Large Cap (Europe Stock)	B	B	B	Up	Y	1,000
Invesco European Growth Fund Class B	AEDBX	NAS CM	Open End	Europe Equity Large Cap (Europe Stock)	B	B-	B	Up		1,000
Invesco European Growth Fund Class C	AEDCX	NAS CM	Open End	Europe Equity Large Cap (Europe Stock)	B	B-	B	Up	Y	1,000
Invesco European Growth Fund Class R	AEDRX	NAS CM	Open End	Europe Equity Large Cap (Europe Stock)	B	B	B	Up	Y	0
Invesco European Growth Fund Class R6	AEGSX	NAS CM	Open End	Europe Equity Large Cap (Europe Stock)	B	B	B	Up	Y	10,000,000
Invesco European Growth Fund Class Y	AEDYX	NAS CM	Open End	Europe Equity Large Cap (Europe Stock)	B	B	B	Up	Y	1,000
Invesco European Growth Fund Investor Class	EGINX	NAS CM	Open End	Europe Equity Large Cap (Europe Stock)	B	B	B	Up		1,000
Invesco European Small Company Fund Class A	ESMAX	NAS CM	Open End	Europe Equity Large Cap (Europe Stock)	B+	B	A	Up		1,000
Invesco European Small Company Fund Class B	ESMBX	NAS CM	Open End	Europe Equity Large Cap (Europe Stock)	B+	B	A	Up		1,000
Invesco European Small Company Fund Class C	ESMCX	NAS CM	Open End	Europe Equity Large Cap (Europe Stock)	B+	B	A	Up		1,000
Invesco European Small Company Fund Class R6	ESMSX	NAS CM	Open End	Europe Equity Large Cap (Europe Stock)	B	B	B+	Down	Y	10,000,000

★Expanded analysis of this fund is included in Section II.

	TOTAL RETURNS					PERFORMANCE				ASSETS		ASSET ALLOCATION & TURNOVER					BULL & BEAR		FEES		
Min Additional Investment	3-Month Total Return	6-Month Total Return	1-Year Total Return	3-Year Total Return	5-Year Total Return	Dividend Yield (TTM)	Expense Ratio	3-Yr Std Deviation	3-Year Beta	NAV	Total Assets (MIL)	%Cash	%Stocks	%Bonds	%Other	Turnover Ratio	Last Bull Market Total Return	Last Bear Market Total Return	Front End Fee (%)	Back End Fee (%)	Inception Date
50	2.94	4.84	8.24	24.76	84.44	1.62	0.78	7.11	0.63	20.34	24,220	13	87	0	0	11	21.21	-15.91			Jul-05
	3.00	5.03	8.53	25.81	87.02	1.87	0.52	7.12	0.63	20.36	24,220	13	87	0	0	11	21.5	-15.8			Oct-05
50	3.38	5.83	9.07	29.16	85.70	1.73	1.06	6.43	0.48	24.48	2,391	8	92	0	0	6	7.02	0.21	5.50		Mar-02
50	3.18	5.42	8.24	26.28	78.80	1.02	1.81	6.42	0.48	24.55	2,391	8	92	0	0	6	6.53	-0.03		5.00	Mar-02
50	3.19	5.42	8.26	26.26	78.84	1.02	1.81	6.43	0.48	24.79	2,391	8	92	0	0	6	6.55	-0.08		1.00	Feb-00
	3.48	6.03	9.45	30.62	88.93	2.11	0.67	6.44	0.48	24.5	2,391	8	92	0	0	6	6.97	0.28			Sep-12
50	3.46	5.96	9.37	30.17	88.07	1.97	0.81	6.41	0.48	24.72	2,391	8	92	0	0	6	7.17	0.34			Oct-08
50	3.40	5.83	9.05	29.15	85.67	1.73	1.06	6.42	0.48	24.71	2,391	8	92	0	0	6	6.97	0.28			Jun-86
	3.42	5.94	9.36	30.18	88.32	2.03	0.75	6.43	0.48	24.48	2,391	8	92	0	0	6	7.26	0.46			Oct-05
50	10.43	22.22	47.52	41.71	25.98	0.07	1.34	13.74	0.82	9.83	46.4	2	98	0	0	47	15.71		5.50		May-11
50	10.15	21.81	46.24	38.60	21.20	0	2.09	13.7	0.82	9.55	46.4	2	98	0	0	47	15.28			1.00	May-11
	10.30	22.05	47.12	40.54	24.12	0	1.59	13.73	0.82	9.74	46.4	2	98	0	0	47	15.46				May-11
	10.45	22.37	47.44	42.62	27.22	0.25	1.09	13.71	0.83	9.84	46.4	2	98	0	0	47	15.79				Sep-12
50	10.43	22.34	47.80	42.96	27.51	0.25	1.09	13.76	0.83	9.85	46.4	2	98	0	0	47	15.79				May-11
	10.44	22.35	47.81	42.77	27.35	0.25	1.09	13.75	0.82	9.85	46.4	2	98	0	0	47	15.79				May-11
50	7.25	9.24	17.42	26.11	76.10	0	1.36	12.76	0.91	20.1	249.8	17	83	0	0	28	18.86	-18.15	5.50		Nov-03
50	7.03	8.85	16.57	23.34	69.61	0	2.11	12.78	0.91	17.37	249.8	17	83	0	0	28	18.31	-18.38		5.00	Nov-03
50	7.02	8.78	16.56	23.33	69.55	0	2.11	12.79	0.91	17.38	249.8	17	83	0	0	28	18.31	-18.38		1.00	Nov-03
	7.17	9.11	17.15	25.17	73.89	0	1.61	12.77	0.91	19.29	249.8	17	83	0	0	28	18.69	-18.21			Apr-04
	7.34	9.48	17.96	27.91	80.16	0	0.87	12.76	0.91	21.47	249.8	17	83	0	0	28	18.86	-18.15			Sep-12
50	7.30	9.34	17.73	27.05	78.21	0	1.11	12.79	0.91	20.72	249.8	17	83	0	0	28	19.06	-18.04			Oct-08
	7.33	9.42	17.87	27.61	79.41	0	0.96	12.77	0.91	21.36	249.8	17	83	0	0	28	19.23	-18			Apr-04
50	5.29	14.31	-8.28	-19.71	-16.25	1.26	1.27	26.19	1.4	25.16	637.2	0	99	0	0	22	20.14	-31.31	5.50		Mar-02
50	5.13	13.93	-8.93	-21.48	-19.32	0.58	2.02	26.15	1.4	22.23	637.2	0	99	0	0	22	19.59	-31.53		5.00	Mar-02
50	5.14	13.93	-8.95	-21.50	-19.31	0.59	2.02	26.15	1.4	21.58	637.2	0	99	0	0	22	19.64	-31.56		1.00	Feb-00
50	5.42	14.46	-8.05	-19.11	-15.18	1.53	1.02	26.16	1.4	25.16	637.2	0	99	0	0	22	20.28	-31.24			Oct-08
50	5.35	14.37	-8.24	-19.69	-16.22	1.27	1.27	26.16	1.4	25.06	637.2	0	99	0	0	22	20.12	-31.31			Jan-84
	5.44	14.59	-7.87	-18.67	-14.55	1.67	0.86	26.18	1.4	25.73	637.2	0	99	0	0	22	20.41	-31.22			Jan-06
50	6.07	9.76	18.26	30.00	105.75	0.88	0.53	10.42	1	59.97	8,015	1	99	0	0	24	25.31	-19.88	5.50		Jul-97
50	5.87	9.33	17.36	27.08	98.12	0.31	1.28	10.41	1	59.65	8,015	1	99	0	0	24	24.75	-20.13		5.00	Dec-87
50	5.91	9.38	17.41	27.25	98.40	0.41	1.28	10.41	1	57.56	8,015	1	99	0	0	24	24.76	-20.14		1.00	Jul-97
	6.00	9.60	17.96	29.03	103.17	0.7	0.78	10.42	1	59.69	8,015	1	99	0	0	24	25.06	-19.97			Mar-08
	6.17	9.94	18.70	31.48	109.33	1.15	0.16	10.43	1	60.56	8,015	1	99	0	0	24	24.75	-20.12			Sep-12
50	6.13	9.88	18.55	30.97	108.32	1.06	0.28	10.43	1	60.5	8,015	1	99	0	0	24	25.49	-19.79			Jul-97
50	3.25	6.46	10.88	23.50	71.14	1.49	0.8	8.5	0.79	10.96	14,928	6	66	21	0	94	17.71	-15.36	5.50		Aug-60
50	3.11	6.09	10.06	20.71	64.86	0.8	1.55	8.45	0.79	10.7	14,928	6	66	21	0	94	17.56	-15.36		5.00	May-92
50	3.10	6.06	10.02	20.76	64.88	0.82	1.55	8.49	0.79	10.76	14,928	6	66	21	0	94	17.11	-15.57		1.00	Jul-93
	3.17	6.30	10.55	22.60	68.99	1.26	1.05	8.5	0.8	11.02	14,928	6	66	21	0	94	17.36	-15.39			Oct-02
	3.45	6.68	11.33	25.06	74.74	1.87	0.39	8.48	0.79	10.96	14,928	6	66	21	0	94	17.71	-15.36			Sep-12
50	3.32	6.60	11.16	24.44	73.30	1.73	0.55	8.5	0.79	10.96	14,928	6	66	21	0	94	17.87	-15.25			Dec-04
	3.33	6.63	11.23	24.58	73.91	1.78	0.49	8.5	0.8	10.96	14,928	6	66	21	0	94	17.79	-15.16			Jun-10
50	3.59	10.14	26.89	28.68	50.57	1.27	1.36	11.17	0.82	41.26	1,732	13	82	0	0	16	18.22	-20.63	5.50		Nov-97
50	3.41	9.74	25.93	25.80	45.07	0.62	2.11	11.19	0.82	38.41	1,732	13	82	0	0	16	17.73	-20.9		5.00	Nov-97
50	3.41	9.73	25.93	25.81	45.05	0.62	2.11	11.19	0.82	38.45	1,732	13	82	0	0	16	17.71	-20.88		1.00	Nov-97
	3.54	9.99	26.57	27.71	48.72	1.04	1.61	11.19	0.82	41.13	1,732	13	82	0	0	16	18.06	-20.73			Jun-02
	3.69	10.33	27.22	29.01	50.96		1.01	11.18	0.82	41.27	1,732	13	82	0	0	16	18.22	-20.63			Apr-17
50	3.67	10.26	27.19	29.63	52.46	1.5	1.11	11.17	0.82	41.29	1,732	13	82	0	0	16	18.39	-20.54			Oct-08
50	3.61	10.17	26.94	28.80	50.86	1.3	1.33	11.19	0.82	41.14	1,732	13	82	0	0	16	18.23	-20.64			Sep-03
50	2.73	5.71	28.28	48.85	82.95	1.65	1.43	10.23	0.67	16.58	811.8	28	72	0	0	11	14.54	-19.14	5.50		Aug-00
50	2.48	5.26	27.22	45.45	76.11	1.12	2.18	10.26	0.68	15.49	811.8	28	72	0	0	11	14.14	-19.45		5.00	Aug-00
50	2.55	5.32	27.26	45.47	76.24	1.11	2.18	10.22	0.67	15.52	811.8	28	72	0	0	11	14.12	-19.5		1.00	Aug-00
	2.77	5.86	28.43	49.02	83.16		1.09	10.22	0.67	16.64	811.8	28	72	0	0	11	14.54	-19.14			Apr-17

	MARKET			FUND TYPE, CATEGORY & OBJECTIVE	RATINGS					MINIMUMS
Fund Name	Ticker Symbol	Traded On	Fund Type	Category and (Prospectus Objective)	Overall Rating	Reward Rating	Risk Rating	Recent Up/ Downgrade	Open to New Investors	Min Initial Investment
Invesco European Small Company Fund Class Y	ESMYX	NAS CM	Open End	Europe Equity Large Cap (Europe Stock)	B+	B	A	Up		1,000
Invesco Exchange Fund	ACEHX	NAS CM	Open End	US Equity Large Cap Value (Growth)	C+	C+	B-	Down		0
Invesco Funds - Invesco Energy Fund Class R6	IENSX	NAS CM	Open End	Energy Sector Equity (Natl Res)	D	D	D	Down	Y	10,000,000
Invesco Global Core Equity Fund Class A	AWSAX	NAS CM	Open End	Global Equity (World Stock)	B-	B-	B	Up	Y	1,000
Invesco Global Core Equity Fund Class B	AWSBX	NAS CM	Open End	Global Equity (World Stock)	C+	C+	C+	Down		1,000
Invesco Global Core Equity Fund Class C	AWSCX	NAS CM	Open End	Global Equity (World Stock)	B-	B-	B	Up	Y	1,000
Invesco Global Core Equity Fund Class R6	AWSSX	NAS CM	Open End	Global Equity (World Stock)	B-	B-	C+	Up	Y	10,000,000
Invesco Global Core Equity Fund Class Y	AWSYX	NAS CM	Open End	Global Equity (World Stock)	B	B-	B	Up	Y	1,000
Invesco Global Core Equity Fund ClassR	AWSRX	NAS CM	Open End	Global Equity (World Stock)	B-	B-	B	Up	Y	0
Invesco Global Core Equity Fund R5 Class	AWSIX	NAS CM	Open End	Global Equity (World Stock)	B-	B-	C+	Up	Y	10,000,000
Invesco Global Growth Fund Class A	AGGAX	NAS CM	Open End	Global Equity (World Stock)	B-	C+	B	Up	Y	1,000
Invesco Global Growth Fund Class B	AGGBX	NAS CM	Open End	Global Equity (World Stock)	B-	C+	B	Up		1,000
Invesco Global Growth Fund Class C	AGGCX	NAS CM	Open End	Global Equity (World Stock)	B-	C+	B	Up	Y	1,000
Invesco Global Growth Fund Class R5	GGAIX	NAS CM	Open End	Global Equity (World Stock)	B-	C+	B	Up	Y	10,000,000
Invesco Global Growth Fund Class R6	AGGFX	NAS CM	Open End	Global Equity (World Stock)	B-	C+	B	Up	Y	10,000,000
Invesco Global Growth Fund Class Y	AGGYX	NAS CM	Open End	Global Equity (World Stock)	B-	C+	B	Up	Y	1,000
Invesco Global Health Care Fund Class A	GGHCX	NAS CM	Open End	Healthcare Sector Equity (Health)	C	C	C+		Y	1,000
Invesco Global Health Care Fund Class B	GTHBX	NAS CM	Open End	Healthcare Sector Equity (Health)	C	C	C+			1,000
Invesco Global Health Care Fund Class C	GTHCX	NAS CM	Open End	Healthcare Sector Equity (Health)	C	C	C+		Y	1,000
Invesco Global Health Care Fund Class R6	GGHSX	NAS CM	Open End	Healthcare Sector Equity (Health)	C	C	C+		Y	10,000,000
Invesco Global Health Care Fund Class Y	GGHYX	NAS CM	Open End	Healthcare Sector Equity (Health)	C	C	B-		Y	1,000
Invesco Global Health Care Fund Investor Class	GTHIX	NAS CM	Open End	Healthcare Sector Equity (Health)	C	C	C+		Y	1,000
Invesco Global Infrastructure Fund Class A	GIZAX	NAS CM	Open End	Other Sector Equity (World Stock)	C+	C+	C+	Up	Y	1,000
Invesco Global Infrastructure Fund Class C	GIZCX	NAS CM	Open End	Other Sector Equity (World Stock)	C+	C+	C	Up	Y	1,000
Invesco Global Infrastructure Fund Class R	GIZRX	NAS CM	Open End	Other Sector Equity (World Stock)	C+	C+	C+	Up	Y	0
Invesco Global Infrastructure Fund Class R5	GIZFX	NAS CM	Open End	Other Sector Equity (World Stock)	C+	C+	C+	Up	Y	10,000,000
Invesco Global Infrastructure Fund Class R6	GIZSX	NAS CM	Open End	Other Sector Equity (World Stock)	C+	C+	C+	Up	Y	10,000,000
Invesco Global Infrastructure Fund Class Y	GIZYX	NAS CM	Open End	Other Sector Equity (World Stock)	C+	C+	C+	Up	Y	1,000
Invesco Global Low Volatility Equity Yield Fund Class A	GTNDX	NAS CM	Open End	Global Equity (World Stock)	C+	C+	C+	Up	Y	1,000
Invesco Global Low Volatility Equity Yield Fund Class B	GNDBX	NAS CM	Open End	Global Equity (World Stock)	C+	C	C+	Up		1,000
Invesco Global Low Volatility Equity Yield Fund Class C	GNDCX	NAS CM	Open End	Global Equity (World Stock)	C+	C	C+	Up	Y	1,000
Invesco Global Low Volatility Equity Yield Fund Class R	GTNRX	NAS CM	Open End	Global Equity (World Stock)	C+	C+	C+	Up	Y	0
Invesco Global Low Volatility Equity Yield Fund Class R6	GNDSX	NAS CM	Open End	Global Equity (World Stock)	C+	C+	C+	Up	Y	10,000,000
Invesco Global Low Volatility Equity Yield Fund Class Y	GTNYX	NAS CM	Open End	Global Equity (World Stock)	C+	C+	C+	Up	Y	1,000
Invesco Global Low Volatility Equity Yield Fund R5 Class	GNDIX	NAS CM	Open End	Global Equity (World Stock)	C+	C+	C+	Up	Y	10,000,000
Invesco Global Market Neutral Fund Class A	MKNAX	NAS CM	Open End	Market Neutral (Growth & Income)	C-	D+	C	Up	Y	1,000
Invesco Global Market Neutral Fund Class C	MKNCX	NAS CM	Open End	Market Neutral (Growth & Income)	D+	D	C		Y	1,000
Invesco Global Market Neutral Fund Class R	MKNRX	NAS CM	Open End	Market Neutral (Growth & Income)	C-	D+	C	Up	Y	0
Invesco Global Market Neutral Fund Class R5	MKNFX	NAS CM	Open End	Market Neutral (Growth & Income)	C	D+	C+	Up	Y	10,000,000
Invesco Global Market Neutral Fund Class R6	MKNSX	NAS CM	Open End	Market Neutral (Growth & Income)	C-	D+	C	Up	Y	10,000,000
Invesco Global Market Neutral Fund Class Y	MKNYX	NAS CM	Open End	Market Neutral (Growth & Income)	C-	D+	C	Up	Y	1,000
Invesco Global Opportunities Fund Class A	IAOPX	NAS CM	Open End	Global Equity (World Stock)	B	B	C+	Up	Y	1,000
Invesco Global Opportunities Fund Class C	ICOPX	NAS CM	Open End	Global Equity (World Stock)	B	B	C+	Up	Y	1,000
Invesco Global Opportunities Fund Class R	IROPX	NAS CM	Open End	Global Equity (World Stock)	B	B	C+	Up	Y	0
Invesco Global Opportunities Fund Class R6	IFOPX	NAS CM	Open End	Global Equity (World Stock)	B	B	C+	Up	Y	10,000,000
Invesco Global Opportunities Fund Class Y	IYOPX	NAS CM	Open End	Global Equity (World Stock)	B	B	C+	Up	Y	1,000
Invesco Global Opportunities Fund R5 Class	IIOPX	NAS CM	Open End	Global Equity (World Stock)	B	B	C+	Up	Y	10,000,000
Invesco Global Real Estate Fund Class A	AGREX	NAS CM	Open End	Real Estate Sector Equity (Real Estate)	B-	C+	B	Up	Y	1,000
Invesco Global Real Estate Fund Class B	BGREX	NAS CM	Open End	Real Estate Sector Equity (Real Estate)	B-	C	B	Up		1,000
Invesco Global Real Estate Fund Class C	CGREX	NAS CM	Open End	Real Estate Sector Equity (Real Estate)	B-	C	B	Up	Y	1,000
Invesco Global Real Estate Fund Class R	RGREX	NAS CM	Open End	Real Estate Sector Equity (Real Estate)	B-	C+	B	Up	Y	0
Invesco Global Real Estate Fund Class R6	FGREX	NAS CM	Open End	Real Estate Sector Equity (Real Estate)	B-	C+	B	Up	Y	10,000,000

★ Expanded analysis of this fund is included in Section II.

Min Additional Investment	TOTAL RETURNS 3-Month Total Return	6-Month Total Return	1-Year Total Return	3-Year Total Return	5-Year Total Return	PERFORMANCE Dividend Yield (TTM)	Expense Ratio	3-Yr Std Deviation	3-Year Beta	ASSETS NAV	Total Assets (MIL)	ASSET ALLOCATION & TURNOVER %Cash	%Stocks	%Bonds	%Other	Turnover Ratio	BULL & BEAR Last Bull Market Total Return	Last Bear Market Total Return	FEES Front End Fee (%)	Back End Fee (%)	Inception Date
50	2.73	5.82	28.47	49.86	85.13	1.85	1.18	10.24	0.68	16.64	811.8	28	72	0	0	11	14.77	-19.14			Oct-08
	6.01	11.52	10.36	21.06	65.31	1.73	0.54	11.52		572.5	61.2	1	99	0	0	1	17.71	-18.62			Dec-76
	5.44	14.58	-7.97	-19.46	-15.97		0.79	26.17	1.4	25.72	637.2	0	99	0	0	22	20.12	-31.31			Apr-17
50	4.92	10.50	22.83	27.38	59.26	0.82	1.22	10.65	0.99	16.2	933.5	-1	101	0	0	39	16.23	-24.01	5.50		Dec-00
50	4.69	10.05	21.94	24.54	53.78	0.2	1.97	10.66	0.99	15.4	933.5	-1	101	0	0	39	16	-24.11		5.00	Dec-00
50	4.68	10.09	21.97	24.56	53.42	0.2	1.97	10.68	0.99	15.44	933.5	-1	101	0	0	39	15.72	-24.19		1.00	Dec-00
	4.92	10.55	23.00	27.56	59.48		0.89	10.66	0.99	16.41	933.5	-1	101	0	0	39	16.23	-24.01			Apr-17
50	4.92	10.63	23.14	28.33	61.19	1.04	0.97	10.67	0.99	16.19	933.5	-1	101	0	0	39	16.32	-23.92			Oct-08
	4.79	10.37	22.53	26.43	57.24	0.62	1.47	10.69	0.99	16.19	933.5	-1	101	0	0	39	16.03	-24.09			May-11
	4.92	10.62	23.13	28.62	61.80	1.11	0.94	10.66	0.99	16.41	933.5	-1	101	0	0	39	16.53	-23.86			Oct-05
50	2.01	5.22	18.63	19.95	60.30	0.29	1.22	10.82	0.99	31.98	684.3	6	93	0	0	19	20.01	-19.5	5.50		Sep-94
50	1.85	4.81	17.75	17.31	54.40	0	1.97	10.82	0.99	29.38	684.3	6	93	0	0	19	19.5	-19.74		5.00	Sep-94
50	1.82	4.81	17.71	17.31	54.40	0	1.97	10.8	0.99	29.38	684.3	6	93	0	0	19	19.55	-19.74		1.00	Aug-97
	2.12	5.38	19.01	21.29	63.60	0.64	0.9	10.82	0.99	31.77	684.3	6	93	0	0	19	20.32	-19.29			Sep-07
	2.12	5.38	19.02	21.30	63.63	0.64	0.9	10.81	0.99	31.76	684.3	6	93	0	0	19	20.01	-19.5			Sep-12
50	2.07	5.34	18.89	20.87	62.27	0.51	0.97	10.8	0.99	32.02	684.3	6	93	0	0	19	20.18	-19.38			Oct-08
50	-3.38	1.11	15.46	4.34	82.37	0.19	1.09	15.62	1.06	35.56	1,419	2	95	0	0	21	19.89	-13.83	5.50		Aug-89
50	-3.55	0.77	14.60	2.04	75.66	0	1.84	15.62	1.06	24.7	1,419	2	95	0	0	21	19.35	-14.11		5.00	Apr-93
50	-3.58	0.73	14.57	2.03	75.65	0	1.84	15.62	1.06	24.74	1,419	2	95	0	0	21	19.38	-14.1		1.00	Mar-99
	-3.32	1.25	15.65	4.52	82.68		0.72	15.62	1.06	36.23	1,419	2	95	0	0	21	19.89	-13.83			Apr-17
50	-3.32	1.22	15.74	5.11	84.64	0.43	0.84	15.64	1.06	36.21	1,419	2	95	0	0	21	20.06	-13.74			Oct-08
50	-3.38	1.11	15.45	4.34	82.34	0.19	1.09	15.62	1.06	35.57	1,419	2	95	0	0	21	19.89	-13.85			Jul-05
50	1.40	5.05	18.02	8.77		1.73	1.28	10.68	0.66	10.53	22.5	1	99	0	0	85			5.50		May-14
50	1.11	4.67	17.17	6.25		1.04	2.03	10.71	0.66	10.51	22.5	1	99	0	0	85				1.00	May-14
	1.24	4.93	17.74	7.86		1.5	1.53	10.68	0.66	10.52	22.5	1	99	0	0	85					May-14
	1.46	5.18	18.31	9.49		1.96	1.03	10.73	0.66	10.53	22.5	1	99	0	0	85					May-14
	1.46	5.18	18.31	9.49		1.96	1.03	10.69	0.66	10.53	22.5	1	99	0	0	85					May-14
50	1.46	5.18	18.31	9.49		1.96	1.03	10.7	0.66	10.53	22.5	1	99	0	0	85					May-14
50	2.51	5.45	15.84	10.68	45.15	3.04	1.52	10.28	0.88	13.9	105.2	3	96	0	1	83	18	-18.31	5.50		Sep-97
50	2.34	5.03	14.99	8.25	39.95	2.33	2.27	10.26	0.88	13.16	105.2	3	96	0	1	83	17.5	-18.6		5.00	Sep-97
50	2.34	5.04	15.01	8.17	39.84	2.33	2.27	10.25	0.88	13.14	105.2	3	96	0	1	83	17.41	-18.54		1.00	Jan-98
	2.44	5.31	15.63	9.85	43.34	2.8	1.77	10.27	0.88	13.92	105.2	3	96	0	1	83	17.81	-18.39			Oct-05
	2.59	5.62	16.08	10.91	45.44		1.05	10.28	0.88	14.06	105.2	3	96	0	1	83	18	-18.31			Apr-17
50	2.57	5.57	16.20	11.53	47.03	3.28	1.27	10.28	0.88	13.93	105.2	3	96	0	1	83	18.2	-18.25			Oct-08
	2.59	5.62	16.27	11.87	48.24	3.45	1.1	10.26	0.88	14.06	105.2	3	96	0	1	83	18.44	-18.12			Apr-04
50	-0.75	0.96	-0.85	-3.03		0	1.5	4.37	9.97	9.21	16.7	-83	174	2	7	79			5.50		Dec-13
50	-0.97	0.57	-1.58	-5.11		0	2.25	4.42	9.79	8.95	16.7	-83	174	2	7	79				1.00	Dec-13
	-0.75	0.88	-1.05	-3.71		0	1.75	4.4	10.3	9.13	16.7	-83	174	2	7	79					Dec-13
	-0.63	1.17	-0.53	-2.23		0	1.25	4.42	8.81	9.3	16.7	-83	174	2	7	79					Dec-13
	-0.74	1.06	-0.64	-2.34		0	1.25	4.38	10.43	9.29	16.7	-83	174	2	7	79					Dec-13
50	-0.64	1.17	-0.54	-2.33		0	1.25	4.45	10.9	9.29	16.7	-83	174	2	7	79					Dec-13
50	3.13	10.40	27.16	36.88	85.28	1.03	1.02	12.85	1.14	16.79	29.8	2	98	0	0	22			5.50		Aug-12
50	2.92	9.97	26.14	33.87	78.36	0.45	1.77	12.84	1.13	16.49	29.8	2	98	0	0	22				1.00	Aug-12
	3.06	10.30	26.87	35.84	82.88	0.84	1.27	12.84	1.14	16.7	29.8	2	98	0	0	22					Aug-12
	3.23	10.55	27.45	37.97	87.60	1.23	0.77	12.83	1.13	16.84	29.8	2	98	0	0	22					Sep-12
50	3.23	10.62	27.55	37.97	87.59	1.23	0.77	12.82	1.13	16.84	29.8	2	98	0	0	22					Aug-12
	3.17	10.55	27.45	37.97	87.59	1.23	0.77	12.87	1.14	16.84	29.8	2	98	0	0	22					Aug-12
50	3.67	6.26	12.65	11.47	32.81	3.24	1.36	10.65	0.67	13.5	1,390	1	97	0	2	57	23.9	-20.05	5.50		Apr-05
50	3.48	5.86	11.80	8.99	27.95	2.53	2.11	10.58	0.67	13.52	1,390	1	97	0	2	57	23.2	-20.29		5.00	Apr-05
50	3.55	5.94	11.89	8.99	28.04	2.53	2.11	10.63	0.67	13.53	1,390	1	97	0	2	57	23.31	-20.29		1.00	Apr-05
	3.60	6.13	12.37	10.64	31.28	3.01	1.61	10.63	0.67	13.51	1,390	1	97	0	2	57	23.62	-20.16			Apr-05
	3.69	6.42	13.03	13.20	36.56	3.73	0.81	10.66	0.67	13.46	1,390	1	97	0	2	57	24.17	-19.77			Sep-12

	MARKET			FUND TYPE, CATEGORY & OBJECTIVE	RATINGS				MINIMUMS	
Fund Name	Ticker Symbol	Traded On	Fund Type	Category and (Prospectus Objective)	Overall Rating	Reward Rating	Risk Rating	Recent Up/ Downgrade	Open to New Investors	Min Initial Investment
Invesco Global Real Estate Fund Class Y	ARGYX	NAS CM	Open End	Real Estate Sector Equity (Real Estate)	B-	C+	B	Up	Y	1,000
Invesco Global Real Estate Fund R5 Class	IGREX	NAS CM	Open End	Real Estate Sector Equity (Real Estate)	B-	C+	B	Up	Y	10,000,000
Invesco Global Real Estate Income Fund Class A	ASRAX	NAS CM	Open End	Real Estate Sector Equity (Real Estate)	B-	C+	B+		Y	1,000
Invesco Global Real Estate Income Fund Class B	SARBX	NAS CM	Open End	Real Estate Sector Equity (Real Estate)	B-	C	B	Up		1,000
Invesco Global Real Estate Income Fund Class C	ASRCX	NAS CM	Open End	Real Estate Sector Equity (Real Estate)	B-	C	B	Up	Y	1,000
Invesco Global Real Estate Income Fund Class R5	ASRIX	NAS CM	Open End	Real Estate Sector Equity (Real Estate)	B-	C+	B+	Down	Y	10,000,000
Invesco Global Real Estate Income Fund Class R6	ASRFX	NAS CM	Open End	Real Estate Sector Equity (Real Estate)	B-	C+	B+	Down	Y	10,000,000
Invesco Global Real Estate Income Fund Class Y	ASRYX	NAS CM	Open End	Real Estate Sector Equity (Real Estate)	B-	C+	B+		Y	1,000
Invesco Global Responsibility Equity Fund Class A	VSQAX	NAS CM	Open End	Global Equity (Growth)	D	C	B		Y	1,000
Invesco Global Responsibility Equity Fund Class C	VSQCX	NAS CM	Open End	Global Equity (Growth)	D	C	B		Y	1,000
Invesco Global Responsibility Equity Fund Class R	VSQRX	NAS CM	Open End	Global Equity (Growth)	D	C	B		Y	0
Invesco Global Responsibility Equity Fund Class R5	VSQFX	NAS CM	Open End	Global Equity (Growth)	D	C	B		Y	10,000,000
Invesco Global Responsibility Equity Fund Class R6	VSQSX	NAS CM	Open End	Global Equity (Growth)	D	C	B		Y	10,000,000
Invesco Global Responsibility Equity Fund Class Y	VSQYX	NAS CM	Open End	Global Equity (Growth)	D	C	B		Y	1,000
Invesco Global Small & Mid Cap Growth Fund Class A	AGAAX	NAS CM	Open End	Global Equity Mid/Small Cap (World Stock)	B-	C+	B	Up	Y	1,000
Invesco Global Small & Mid Cap Growth Fund Class B	AGABX	NAS CM	Open End	Global Equity Mid/Small Cap (World Stock)	B-	C+	B	Up		1,000
Invesco Global Small & Mid Cap Growth Fund Class C	AGACX	NAS CM	Open End	Global Equity Mid/Small Cap (World Stock)	B-	C+	B	Up	Y	1,000
Invesco Global Small & Mid Cap Growth Fund Class R5	GAIIX	NAS CM	Open End	Global Equity Mid/Small Cap (World Stock)	B-	B-	B	Up	Y	10,000,000
Invesco Global Small & Mid Cap Growth Fund Class R6	AGSSX	NAS CM	Open End	Global Equity Mid/Small Cap (World Stock)	B-	C+	B	Up	Y	10,000,000
Invesco Global Small & Mid Cap Growth Fund Class Y	AGAYX	NAS CM	Open End	Global Equity Mid/Small Cap (World Stock)	B-	C+	B	Up	Y	1,000
Invesco Global Targeted Returns Fund Class A	GLTAX	NAS CM	Open End	Multialternative (Growth & Income)	C	C	C		Y	1,000
Invesco Global Targeted Returns Fund Class C	GLTCX	NAS CM	Open End	Multialternative (Growth & Income)	C	C	C	Down	Y	1,000
Invesco Global Targeted Returns Fund Class R	GLTRX	NAS CM	Open End	Multialternative (Growth & Income)	C	C	C		Y	0
Invesco Global Targeted Returns Fund Class R5	GLTFX	NAS CM	Open End	Multialternative (Growth & Income)	C	C	C		Y	10,000,000
Invesco Global Targeted Returns Fund Class R6	GLTSX	NAS CM	Open End	Multialternative (Growth & Income)	C	C	C		Y	10,000,000
Invesco Global Targeted Returns Fund Class Y	GLTYX	NAS CM	Open End	Multialternative (Growth & Income)	C	C	C		Y	1,000
Invesco Gold & Precious Metals Fund Class R6	IGDSX	NAS CM	Open End	Precious Metals Sector Equity (Precious Metals)	D+	C-	D	Down	Y	10,000,000
Invesco Gold and Precious Metals Fund Class A	IGDAX	NAS CM	Open End	Precious Metals Sector Equity (Precious Metals)	D+	C-	D	Down	Y	1,000
Invesco Gold and Precious Metals Fund Class B	IGDBX	NAS CM	Open End	Precious Metals Sector Equity (Precious Metals)	D+	C-	D	Down		1,000
Invesco Gold and Precious Metals Fund Class C	IGDCX	NAS CM	Open End	Precious Metals Sector Equity (Precious Metals)	D+	C-	D	Down	Y	1,000
Invesco Gold and Precious Metals Fund Class Investor	FGLDX	NAS CM	Open End	Precious Metals Sector Equity (Precious Metals)	D+	C-	D	Down		1,000
Invesco Gold and Precious Metals Fund Class Y	IGDYX	NAS CM	Open End	Precious Metals Sector Equity (Precious Metals)	D+	C-	D	Down	Y	1,000
Invesco Greater China Fund Class A	AACFX	NAS CM	Open End	Greater China Equity (Pacific Stock)	B+	A	B-	Up	Y	1,000
Invesco Greater China Fund Class B	ABCFX	NAS CM	Open End	Greater China Equity (Pacific Stock)	B+	A	B-	Up		1,000
Invesco Greater China Fund Class C	CACFX	NAS CM	Open End	Greater China Equity (Pacific Stock)	B+	A	B-	Up	Y	1,000
Invesco Greater China Fund Class R5	IACFX	NAS CM	Open End	Greater China Equity (Pacific Stock)	B+	A	B-	Up	Y	10,000,000
Invesco Greater China Fund Class R6	CACSX	NAS CM	Open End	Greater China Equity (Pacific Stock)	B+	A	B-	Up	Y	10,000,000
Invesco Greater China Fund Class Y	AMCYX	NAS CM	Open End	Greater China Equity (Pacific Stock)	B+	A	B-	Up	Y	1,000
Invesco Growth Allocation Fund Class A	AADAX	NAS CM	Open End	Aggressive Alloc (Asset Alloc)	B-	C+	B-	Down	Y	1,000
Invesco Growth Allocation Fund Class B	AAEBX	NAS CM	Open End	Aggressive Alloc (Asset Alloc)	C+	C+	B-	Down		1,000
Invesco Growth Allocation Fund Class C	AADCX	NAS CM	Open End	Aggressive Alloc (Asset Alloc)	C+	C+	B-	Down	Y	1,000
Invesco Growth Allocation Fund Class R	AADRX	NAS CM	Open End	Aggressive Alloc (Asset Alloc)	B-	C+	B-	Down	Y	0
Invesco Growth Allocation Fund Class R6	AAESX	NAS CM	Open End	Aggressive Alloc (Asset Alloc)	B-	C+	B-	Down	Y	10,000,000
Invesco Growth Allocation Fund Class S	AADSX	NAS CM	Open End	Aggressive Alloc (Asset Alloc)	B-	C+	B-	Down	Y	0
Invesco Growth Allocation Fund Class Y	AADYX	NAS CM	Open End	Aggressive Alloc (Asset Alloc)	B-	C+	B-	Down	Y	1,000
Invesco Growth Allocation Fund R5 Class	AADIX	NAS CM	Open End	Aggressive Alloc (Asset Alloc)	B-	C+	B-	Down	Y	10,000,000
Invesco Growth and Income Fund Class A	ACGIX	NAS CM	Open End	US Equity Large Cap Value (Growth & Income)	B	B	B	Up	Y	1,000
Invesco Growth and Income Fund Class B	ACGJX	NAS CM	Open End	US Equity Large Cap Value (Growth & Income)	B	B	B	Up		1,000
Invesco Growth and Income Fund Class C	ACGKX	NAS CM	Open End	US Equity Large Cap Value (Growth & Income)	B	B	B	Up	Y	1,000
Invesco Growth and Income Fund Class R	ACGLX	NAS CM	Open End	US Equity Large Cap Value (Growth & Income)	B	B	B	Up	Y	0
Invesco Growth and Income Fund Class R6	GIFFX	NAS CM	Open End	US Equity Large Cap Value (Growth & Income)	B	B	B	Up	Y	10,000,000
Invesco Growth and Income Fund Class Y	ACGMX	NAS CM	Open End	US Equity Large Cap Value (Growth & Income)	B	B	B	Up	Y	1,000

★ Expanded analysis of this fund is included in Section II.

Min Additional Investment	TOTAL RETURNS 3-Month Total Return	6-Month Total Return	1-Year Total Return	3-Year Total Return	5-Year Total Return	PERFORMANCE Dividend Yield (TTM)	Expense Ratio	3-Yr Std Deviation	3-Year Beta	ASSETS NAV	Total Assets (MIL)	ASSET ALLOCATION & TURNOVER %Cash	%Stocks	%Bonds	%Other	Turnover Ratio	BULL & BEAR Last Bull Market Total Return	Last Bear Market Total Return	FEES Front End Fee (%)	Back End Fee (%)	Inception Date
50	3.81	6.47	13.02	12.39	34.68	3.48	1.11	10.64	0.67	13.51	1,390	1	97	0	2	57	24.03	-19.93			Oct-08
	3.75	6.45	13.12	13.05	36.25	3.66	0.88	10.65	0.67	13.47	1,390	1	97	0	2	57	24.16	-19.77			Apr-05
50	2.35	4.06	8.76	11.73	29.07	3.38	1.26	6.81	0.37	9.11	1,123	11	57	19	1	43	14.45	-8.21	5.50		May-02
50	2.04	3.67	7.95	9.24	24.29	2.65	2.01	6.8	0.38	9.1	1,123	11	57	19	1	43	13.9	-8.46		5.00	Mar-07
50	2.15	3.78	8.07	9.36	24.42	2.65	2.01	6.8	0.38	9.11	1,123	11	57	19	1	43	13.9	-8.46		1.00	Mar-07
	2.43	4.24	9.13	12.95	31.36	3.7	0.94	6.76	0.37	9.1	1,123	11	57	19	1	43	14.84	-8.16			Mar-07
	2.45	4.28	9.23	13.12	31.91	3.78	0.85	6.77	0.37	9.1	1,123	11	57	19	1	43	14.45	-8.21			Sep-12
50	2.41	4.19	9.05	12.58	30.74	3.62	1.01	6.72	0.37	9.08	1,123	11	57	19	1	43	14.64	-8.12			Oct-08
50	5.92	12.11	23.73			0.45	0.85			12.78	6.3	5	95	0	0				5.50		Jul-16
50	5.73	11.74	22.92			0.14	1.6			12.72	6.3	5	95	0	0					1.00	Jul-16
	5.91	12.01	23.53			0.35	1.1			12.76	6.3	5	95	0	0						Jul-16
	6.07	12.35	24.09			0.54	0.6			12.81	6.3	5	95	0	0						Jul-16
	6.07	12.35	24.09			0.54	0.6			12.81	6.3	5	95	0	0						Jul-16
50	6.07	12.34	24.09			0.54	0.6			12.81	6.3	5	95	0	0						Jul-16
50	2.52	8.42	24.21	22.56	61.14	0.58	1.36	10.49	0.92	19.8	549.1	8	92	0	0	22	18.6	-21.94	5.50		Sep-94
50	2.27	7.97	23.22	19.85	55.17	0	2.11	10.5	0.92	16.08	549.1	8	92	0	0	22	18.13	-22.2		5.00	Sep-94
50	2.28	7.97	23.28	19.82	55.22	0	2.11	10.52	0.92	16.1	549.1	8	92	0	0	22	18.12	-22.19		1.00	Aug-97
	2.52	8.50	24.54	23.87	64.15	0.92	0.98	10.51	0.92	19.63	549.1	8	92	0	0	22	18.97	-21.78			Sep-07
	2.59	8.62	24.53	22.87	61.55		0.93	10.49	0.92	19.63	549.1	8	92	0	0	22	18.6	-21.94			Apr-17
50	2.57	8.50	24.48	23.48	63.12	0.8	1.11	10.49	0.92	19.82	549.1	8	92	0	0	22	18.83	-21.89			Oct-08
50	0.00	-0.99	1.32	0.94		1.26	1.44	3.2	-5.94	9.92	152.2	25	30	33	10	23			5.50		Dec-13
50	-0.20	-1.42	0.51	-1.36		0.61	2.19	3.19	-6.68	9.71	152.2	25	30	33	10	23				1.00	Dec-13
	-0.20	-1.20	0.92	0.06		1.05	1.69	3.25	-5.9	9.85	152.2	25	30	33	10	23					Dec-13
	0.00	-0.89	1.52	1.66		1.51	1.19	3.23	-5.68	9.97	152.2	25	30	33	10	23					Dec-13
	0.00	-0.89	1.52	1.66		1.51	1.19	3.21	-6.66	9.96	152.2	25	30	33	10	23					Dec-13
50	0.00	-0.89	1.42	1.65		1.51	1.19	3.26	-5.76	9.96	152.2	25	30	33	10	23					Dec-13
	0.25	0.01	5.16	22.49	-36.84		0.97	36.54	0.78	4.25	277.6	4	90	0	6	28	-9.75	-17.11			Apr-17
50	0.30	-0.17	4.77	22.15	-36.92	9.61	1.44	36.46	0.78	4.16	277.6	4	90	0	6	28	-9.8	-17.11	5.50		Mar-02
50	-0.05	-0.55	3.89	19.43	-39.43	8.89	2.19	36.47	0.78	3.89	277.6	4	90	0	6	28	-10.24	-17.35		5.00	Mar-02
50	-0.04	-0.51	4.11	19.48	-39.31	8.27	2.19	36.52	0.78	4.19	277.6	4	90	0	6	28	-10.16	-17.36		1.00	Feb-00
50	0.06	-0.17	4.74	22.00	-37.09	9.56	1.44	36.55	0.78	4.18	277.6	4	90	0	6	28	-9.75	-17.1			Jan-84
50	0.16	-0.06	4.78	22.91	-36.39	9.85	1.19	36.58	0.78	4.24	277.6	4	90	0	6	28	-9.75	-17.04			Oct-08
50	4.98	16.47	42.40	53.33	60.90	0.52	1.93	17.15	0.94	29.64	96.6	2	98	0	0	52	16.68	-29.92	5.50		Mar-06
50	4.79	16.04	41.33	49.94	55.01	0	2.68	17.14	0.94	28.86	96.6	2	98	0	0	52	16.15	-30.13		5.00	Mar-06
50	4.76	16.07	41.36	49.92	54.99	0	2.68	17.12	0.94	28.81	96.6	2	98	0	0	52	16.18	-30.14		1.00	Mar-06
	5.06	16.71	42.96	55.40	64.56	0.87	1.45	17.16	0.94	29.61	96.6	2	98	0	0	52	17.07	-29.8			Mar-06
	5.04	16.70	42.94	55.38	64.55		1.4	17.15	0.94	29.6	96.6	2	98	0	0	52	17.07	-29.8			Apr-17
50	5.01	16.62	42.71	54.44	62.88	0.7	1.68	17.13	0.94	29.63	96.6	2	98	0	0	52	16.91	-29.86			Oct-08
50	3.71	7.89	15.76	19.76	46.38	0.98	1.15	7.59	0.71	16.05	1,062	9	74	14	1	52	17.34	-13.55	5.50		Apr-04
50	3.54	7.49	14.95	17.10	40.75	0.29	1.9	7.6	0.72	15.9	1,062	9	74	14	1	52	16.92	-13.86		5.00	Apr-04
50	3.54	7.49	14.94	17.09	40.84	0.29	1.9	7.6	0.72	15.91	1,062	9	74	14	1	52	16.92	-13.86		1.00	Apr-04
	3.65	7.70	15.42	18.87	44.42	0.75	1.4	7.62	0.72	16.01	1,062	9	74	14	1	52	17.26	-13.67			Apr-04
	3.80	8.09	16.18	21.02	49.01		0.72	7.6	0.72	16.11	1,062	9	74	14	1	52	17.5	-13.4			Apr-17
	3.75	7.93	15.89	20.07	47.05	1.07	1.05	7.59	0.71	16.03	1,062	9	74	14	1	52	17.44	-13.47			Sep-09
50	3.84	8.10	16.08	20.73	48.19	1.2	0.9	7.62	0.72	16.02	1,062	9	74	14	1	52	17.49	-13.47			Oct-08
	3.86	8.16	16.25	21.10	49.11	1.3	0.77	7.6	0.72	16.12	1,062	9	74	14	1	52	17.5	-13.4			Apr-04
50	4.69	9.19	14.20	31.24	98.22	1.38	0.82	12.22	1.13	26.97	8,263	2	98	0	0	16	23.21	-19.71	5.50		Aug-46
50	4.69	9.22	14.20	31.25	98.29	1.38	0.82	12.23	1.13	26.71	8,263	2	98	0	0	16	23.26	-19.72		5.00	Aug-93
50	4.49	8.79	13.33	28.31	91.00	0.72	1.57	12.23	1.13	26.65	8,263	2	98	0	0	16	22.73	-20		1.00	Aug-93
	4.62	9.08	13.91	30.23	95.81	1.16	1.07	12.23	1.13	27	8,263	2	98	0	0	16	23.05	-19.8			Oct-02
	4.80	9.41	14.66	32.94	102.53	1.76	0.39	12.23	1.13	27.01	8,263	2	98	0	0	16	23.21	-19.71			Sep-12
50	4.71	9.32	14.48	32.17	100.66	1.6	0.57	12.24	1.13	26.98	8,263	2	98	0	0	16	23.43	-19.65			Oct-04

	MARKET		FUND TYPE, CATEGORY & OBJECTIVE		RATINGS				MINIMUMS	
Fund Name	Ticker Symbol	Traded On	Fund Type	Category and (Prospectus Objective)	Overall Rating	Reward Rating	Risk Rating	Recent Up/ Downgrade	Open to New Investors	Min Initial Investment
Invesco Growth and Income Fund R5 Class	ACGQX	NAS CM	Open End	US Equity Large Cap Value (Growth & Income)	B	B	B	Up	Y	10,000,000
Invesco Income Allocation Fund Class A	ALAAX	NAS CM	Open End	Cautious Alloc (Asset Alloc)	B-	C+	B	Up	Y	1,000
Invesco Income Allocation Fund Class B	BLIAX	NAS CM	Open End	Cautious Alloc (Asset Alloc)	B	C+	A-	Up		1,000
Invesco Income Allocation Fund Class C	CLIAX	NAS CM	Open End	Cautious Alloc (Asset Alloc)	B-	C+	B	Up	Y	1,000
Invesco Income Allocation Fund Class R	RLIAX	NAS CM	Open End	Cautious Alloc (Asset Alloc)	B	C+	A-	Up	Y	0
Invesco Income Allocation Fund Class R6	IIASX	NAS CM	Open End	Cautious Alloc (Asset Alloc)	B-	C+	B	Up	Y	10,000,000
Invesco Income Allocation Fund Class Y	ALAYX	NAS CM	Open End	Cautious Alloc (Asset Alloc)	B-	C+	B	Up	Y	1,000
Invesco Income Allocation Fund R5 Class	ILAAX	NAS CM	Open End	Cautious Alloc (Asset Alloc)	B	C+	A-	Up	Y	10,000,000
Invesco International Allocation Fund Class A	AINAX	NAS CM	Open End	Global Equity Large Cap (Growth)	C+	C+	C+	Up	Y	1,000
Invesco International Allocation Fund Class B	INABX	NAS CM	Open End	Global Equity Large Cap (Growth)	C+	C+	C+	Up		1,000
Invesco International Allocation Fund Class C	INACX	NAS CM	Open End	Global Equity Large Cap (Growth)	C+	C+	C+	Up	Y	1,000
Invesco International Allocation Fund Class R	RINAX	NAS CM	Open End	Global Equity Large Cap (Growth)	C+	C+	C+	Up	Y	0
Invesco International Allocation Fund Class R6	INASX	NAS CM	Open End	Global Equity Large Cap (Growth)	C+	C+	C+	Up	Y	10,000,000
Invesco International Allocation Fund Class Y	AINYX	NAS CM	Open End	Global Equity Large Cap (Growth)	C+	C+	C+	Up	Y	1,000
Invesco International Allocation Fund R5 Class	INAIX	NAS CM	Open End	Global Equity Large Cap (Growth)	C+	C+	C+	Up	Y	10,000,000
Invesco International Companies Fund Class A	IZIAX	NAS CM	Open End	Global Equity Large Cap (Growth)	C-	C	B+	Up	Y	1,000
Invesco International Companies Fund Class C	IZICX	NAS CM	Open End	Global Equity Large Cap (Growth)	C-	C	B+	Up	Y	1,000
Invesco International Companies Fund Class R	IZIRX	NAS CM	Open End	Global Equity Large Cap (Growth)	C-	C	B+	Up	Y	0
Invesco International Companies Fund Class R5	IZIFX	NAS CM	Open End	Global Equity Large Cap (Growth)	C-	C	B+	Up	Y	10,000,000
Invesco International Companies Fund Class R6	IZISX	NAS CM	Open End	Global Equity Large Cap (Growth)	C-	C	B+	Up	Y	10,000,000
Invesco International Companies Fund Class Y	IZIYX	NAS CM	Open End	Global Equity Large Cap (Growth)	C-	C	B+	Up	Y	1,000
Invesco International Core Equity Fund Class A	IBVAX	NAS CM	Open End	Global Equity Large Cap (Foreign Stock)	B-	C+	B	Up	Y	1,000
Invesco International Core Equity Fund Class B	IBVBX	NAS CM	Open End	Global Equity Large Cap (Foreign Stock)	B-	C+	B	Up		1,000
Invesco International Core Equity Fund Class C	IBVCX	NAS CM	Open End	Global Equity Large Cap (Foreign Stock)	B-	C+	B	Up	Y	1,000
Invesco International Core Equity Fund Class R	IIBRX	NAS CM	Open End	Global Equity Large Cap (Foreign Stock)	B-	C+	B	Up	Y	0
Invesco International Core Equity Fund Class R5	IBVIX	NAS CM	Open End	Global Equity Large Cap (Foreign Stock)	B-	B-	B	Up	Y	10,000,000
Invesco International Core Equity Fund Class R6	IBVFX	NAS CM	Open End	Global Equity Large Cap (Foreign Stock)	B-	B-	B	Up	Y	10,000,000
Invesco International Core Equity Fund Class Y	IBVYX	NAS CM	Open End	Global Equity Large Cap (Foreign Stock)	B-	C+	B	Up	Y	1,000
Invesco International Core Equity Fund Investor Class	IIBCX	NAS CM	Open End	Global Equity Large Cap (Foreign Stock)	B-	C+	B	Up		1,000
Invesco International Growth Fund Class A	AIIEX	NAS CM	Open End	Global Equity Large Cap (Foreign Stock)	B-	C+	B	Up		1,000
Invesco International Growth Fund Class B	AIEBX	NAS CM	Open End	Global Equity Large Cap (Foreign Stock)	B-	C+	B	Up		1,000
Invesco International Growth Fund Class C	AIECX	NAS CM	Open End	Global Equity Large Cap (Foreign Stock)	B-	C+	B	Up		1,000
Invesco International Growth Fund Class R	AIERX	NAS CM	Open End	Global Equity Large Cap (Foreign Stock)	B-	C+	B	Up		0
Invesco International Growth Fund Class R6	IGFRX	NAS CM	Open End	Global Equity Large Cap (Foreign Stock)	B-	C+	B	Up		10,000,000
Invesco International Growth Fund Class Y	AIIYX	NAS CM	Open End	Global Equity Large Cap (Foreign Stock)	B-	C+	B	Up		1,000
Invesco International Growth Fund R5 Class	AIEVX	NAS CM	Open End	Global Equity Large Cap (Foreign Stock)	B-	C+	B	Up		10,000,000
Invesco International Small Company Fund Class A	IEGAX	NAS CM	Open End	Global Equity Mid/Small Cap (Foreign Stock)	B-	B	C+	Up	Y	1,000
Invesco International Small Company Fund Class B	IEGBX	NAS CM	Open End	Global Equity Mid/Small Cap (Foreign Stock)	B-	B	C+	Up		1,000
Invesco International Small Company Fund Class C	IEGCX	NAS CM	Open End	Global Equity Mid/Small Cap (Foreign Stock)	B-	B	C+	Up	Y	1,000
Invesco International Small Company Fund Class R6	IEGFX	NAS CM	Open End	Global Equity Mid/Small Cap (Foreign Stock)	B	B	C+	Up	Y	10,000,000
Invesco International Small Company Fund Class Y	IEGYX	NAS CM	Open End	Global Equity Mid/Small Cap (Foreign Stock)	B	B	C+	Up	Y	1,000
Invesco International Small Company Fund R5 Class	IEGIX	NAS CM	Open End	Global Equity Mid/Small Cap (Foreign Stock)	B	B	C+	Up	Y	10,000,000
Invesco Long/Short Equity Fund Class A	LSQAX	NAS CM	Open End	Long/Short Equity (Growth)	B	B	B+	Up	Y	1,000
Invesco Long/Short Equity Fund Class C	LSQCX	NAS CM	Open End	Long/Short Equity (Growth)	B	B-	B+	Up	Y	1,000
Invesco Long/Short Equity Fund Class R	LSQRX	NAS CM	Open End	Long/Short Equity (Growth)	B	B	B+	Up	Y	0
Invesco Long/Short Equity Fund Class R5	LSQFX	NAS CM	Open End	Long/Short Equity (Growth)	B	B	B+	Up	Y	10,000,000
Invesco Long/Short Equity Fund Class R6	LSQSX	NAS CM	Open End	Long/Short Equity (Growth)	B	B	B+	Up	Y	10,000,000
Invesco Long/Short Equity Fund Class Y	LSQYX	NAS CM	Open End	Long/Short Equity (Growth)	B	B	B+	Up	Y	1,000
Invesco Low Volatility Emerging Markets Fund Class A	LVLAX	NAS CM	Open End	Emerging Markets Equity (Growth)	C+	C+	C	Up	Y	1,000
Invesco Low Volatility Emerging Markets Fund Class C	LVLCX	NAS CM	Open End	Emerging Markets Equity (Growth)	C+	C+	C	Up	Y	1,000
Invesco Low Volatility Emerging Markets Fund Class R	LVLRX	NAS CM	Open End	Emerging Markets Equity (Growth)	C+	C+	C	Up	Y	0
Invesco Low Volatility Emerging Markets Fund Class R5	LVLFX	NAS CM	Open End	Emerging Markets Equity (Growth)	C+	C+	C	Up	Y	10,000,000

★Expanded analysis of this fund is included in Section II.

	TOTAL RETURNS					PERFORMANCE				ASSETS		ASSET ALLOCATION & TURNOVER					BULL & BEAR		FEES		
Min Additional Investment	3-Month Total Return	6-Month Total Return	1-Year Total Return	3-Year Total Return	5-Year Total Return	Dividend Yield (TTM)	Expense Ratio	3-Yr Std Deviation	3-Year Beta	NAV	Total Assets (MIL)	%Cash	%Stocks	%Bonds	%Other	Turnover Ratio	Last Bull Market Total Return	Last Bear Market Total Return	Front End Fee (%)	Back End Fee (%)	Inception Date
	4.77	9.36	14.56	32.57	101.68	1.67	0.49	12.23	1.13	27.01	8,263	2	98	0	0	16	23.49	-19.61			Jun-10
50	1.42	3.23	7.99	16.28	35.08	3.34	0.83	4.24	0.32	11.7	618.5	6	29	57	1	38	9.37	-5.05	5.50		Oct-05
50	1.14	2.84	7.17	13.79	30.21	2.6	1.58	4.23	0.32	11.72	618.5	6	29	57	1	38	8.84	-5.3		5.00	Oct-05
50	1.14	2.84	7.18	13.69	30.10	2.6	1.58	4.25	0.32	11.71	618.5	6	29	57	1	38	8.84	-5.3		1.00	Oct-05
	1.27	3.10	7.62	15.41	33.40	3.09	1.08	4.2	0.32	11.7	618.5	6	29	57	1	38	9.23	-5.17			Oct-05
	1.39	3.36	8.26	17.16	36.78		0.58	4.24	0.32	11.7	618.5	6	29	57	1	38	9.51	-4.93			Apr-17
50	1.48	3.36	8.26	17.16	36.92	3.58	0.58	4.23	0.32	11.7	618.5	6	29	57	1	38	9.51	-4.92			Oct-08
	1.39	3.36	8.26	17.16	36.78	3.58	0.58	4.24	0.32	11.7	618.5	6	29	57	1	38	9.51	-4.92			Oct-05
50	3.97	9.84	24.94	19.58	34.46	1.19	1.47	11.66	0.94	12.21	157.8	5	90	0	2	47	13.69	-20.18	5.50		Oct-05
50	3.73	9.41	23.98	16.82	29.42	0.54	2.22	11.67	0.94	12.23	157.8	5	90	0	2	47	13.13	-20.4		5.00	Oct-05
50	3.73	9.41	23.98	16.93	29.42	0.54	2.22	11.71	0.94	12.23	157.8	5	90	0	2	47	13.13	-20.4		1.00	Oct-05
	3.89	9.76	24.61	18.61	32.67	0.97	1.72	11.7	0.94	12.22	157.8	5	90	0	2	47	13.5	-20.27			Oct-05
	4.07	10.12	25.49	21.14	37.55		0.98	11.7	0.94	12.19	157.8	5	90	0	2	47	13.86	-20.16			Apr-17
50	4.07	10.06	25.25	20.52	36.13	1.4	1.22	11.73	0.94	12.16	157.8	5	90	0	2	47	13.77	-20.07			Oct-08
	4.06	10.12	25.38	21.03	37.43	1.55	1.03	11.69	0.94	12.19	157.8	5	90	0	2	47	13.86	-20.16			Oct-05
50	3.49	10.45	31.15			0.74	1.12			12.21	106.9	7	92	0	0	35			5.50		Dec-15
50	3.26	10.02	30.08			0.57	1.87			12.08	106.9	7	92	0	0	35				1.00	Dec-15
	3.39	10.29	30.77			0.67	1.37			12.16	106.9	7	92	0	0	35					Dec-15
	3.56	10.60	31.41			0.87	0.87			12.23	106.9	7	92	0	0	35					Dec-15
	3.56	10.60	31.41			0.87	0.87			12.23	106.9	7	92	0	0	35					Dec-15
50	3.56	10.51	31.41			0.87	0.87			12.23	106.9	7	92	0	0	35					Dec-15
50	5.49	12.01	24.46	23.81	38.02	1.36	1.12	11.48	0.91	12.68	92.2	1	99	0	0	37	10.06	-22.46	5.50		Mar-02
50	5.27	11.57	23.56	21.05	32.75	0.7	1.87	11.46	0.9	12.78	92.2	1	99	0	0	37	9.5	-22.67		5.00	Mar-02
50	5.35	11.64	23.55	21.08	32.86	0.72	1.87	11.43	0.9	12.42	92.2	1	99	0	0	37	9.53	-22.74		1.00	Feb-00
	5.47	11.89	24.19	22.88	36.27	1.15	1.37	11.4	0.9	12.72	92.2	1	99	0	0	37	9.83	-22.52			Nov-03
	5.60	12.17	24.74	25.24	40.94	1.71	0.87	11.46	0.9	12.58	92.2	1	99	0	0	37	10.53	-22.31			Apr-04
	5.60	12.17	24.87	25.27	41.14	1.72	0.87	11.45	0.9	12.58	92.2	1	99	0	0	37	10.02	-22.54			Sep-12
50	5.55	12.15	24.75	24.76	39.65	1.56	0.87	11.46	0.9	12.88	92.2	1	99	0	0	37	10.33	-22.46			Oct-08
50	5.48	12.08	24.45	23.80	37.92	1.34	1.12	11.48	0.91	12.89	92.2	1	99	0	0	37	10.02	-22.54			Oct-98
50	3.07	7.50	22.63	18.14	41.66	1.01	1.32	10.79	0.85	36.28	9,060	9	90	0	0	12	16.89	-20.29	5.50		Apr-92
50	2.87	7.08	21.71	15.52	36.47	0.37	2.07	10.78	0.85	33.36	9,060	9	90	0	0	12	16.43	-20.56		5.00	Sep-94
50	2.86	7.07	21.68	15.50	36.42	0.36	2.07	10.8	0.85	33.39	9,060	9	90	0	0	12	16.36	-20.51		1.00	Aug-97
	2.99	7.33	22.32	17.24	39.90	0.8	1.57	10.79	0.85	35.86	9,060	9	90	0	0	12	16.72	-20.36			Jun-02
	3.17	7.72	23.16	19.64	44.65	1.38	0.89	10.79	0.85	36.79	9,060	9	90	0	0	12	16.89	-20.29			Sep-12
50	3.12	7.64	22.94	19.04	43.45	1.24	1.07	10.78	0.85	36.34	9,060	9	90	0	0	12	17.1	-20.21			Oct-08
	3.15	7.67	23.02	19.30	44.08	1.3	0.98	10.79	0.85	36.81	9,060	9	90	0	0	12	17.18	-20.14			Mar-02
50	3.93	10.33	33.41	31.92	37.99	1.75	1.58	12.66	1.02	19.33	322.3	12	88	0	0	15	15.61	-17.59	5.50		Aug-00
50	3.72	9.91	32.45	29.08	32.98	1.19	2.33	12.59	1.02	18.38	322.3	12	88	0	0	15	15.07	-17.82		5.00	Aug-00
50	3.72	9.98	32.45	29.01	32.92	1.19	2.33	12.66	1.02	18.38	322.3	12	88	0	0	15	15.07	-17.86		1.00	Aug-00
	4.01	10.63	34.04	33.71	40.93	2.08	1.14	12.69	1.02	19.17	322.3	12	88	0	0	15	15.61	-17.59			Sep-12
50	4.00	10.50	33.73	32.91	39.75	1.94	1.33	12.61	1.02	19.36	322.3	12	88	0	0	15	15.76	-17.53			Oct-08
	4.02	10.57	33.96	33.47	40.49	2.02	1.2	12.65	1.02	19.19	322.3	12	88	0	0	15	15.85	-17.44			Oct-05
50	9.62	21.95	18.62	28.48		0	1.59	11.69	0.68	11.92	75.2	1	99	0	0	102			5.50		Dec-13
50	9.56	21.65	17.85	25.89		0	2.34	11.66	0.68	11.68	75.2	1	99	0	0	102				1.00	Dec-13
	8.72	20.83	17.41	26.59		0	1.84	11.66	0.68	11.84	75.2	1	99	0	0	102					Dec-13
	9.31	21.71	18.60	29.10		0	1.26	11.66	0.68	12	75.2	1	99	0	0	102					Dec-13
	9.40	21.81	18.71	29.22		0	1.26	11.66	0.68	12	75.2	1	99	0	0	102					Dec-13
50	9.12	21.41	18.21	28.79		0	1.34	11.66	0.68	12	75.2	1	99	0	0	102					Dec-13
50	7.02	13.12	31.76	18.42		1.05	1.34	15.47	1.06	8.8	46.3	5	95	0	1	63			5.50		Dec-13
50	6.88	12.77	30.77	15.85		0.14	2.09	15.48	1.07	8.77	46.3	5	95	0	1	63				1.00	Dec-13
	6.15	12.21	30.38	16.71		0.77	1.59	15.52	1.08	8.79	46.3	5	95	0	1	63					Dec-13
	6.80	13.00	31.59	18.99		1.23	1.09	15.48	1.08	8.8	46.3	5	95	0	1	63					Dec-13

	MARKET		FUND TYPE, CATEGORY & OBJECTIVE		RATINGS				MINIMUMS	
Fund Name	Ticker Symbol	Traded On	Fund Type	Category and (Prospectus Objective)	Overall Rating	Reward Rating	Risk Rating	Recent Up/ Downgrade	Open to New Investors	Min Initial Investment
Invesco Low Volatility Emerging Markets Fund Class R6	LVLSX	NAS CM	Open End	Emerging Markets Equity (Growth)	C+	C+	C	Up	Y	10,000,000
Invesco Low Volatility Emerging Markets Fund Class Y	LVLYX	NAS CM	Open End	Emerging Markets Equity (Growth)	C+	C+	C	Up	Y	1,000
Invesco Low Volatility Equity Yield Fund Class A	SCAUX	NAS CM	Open End	US Equity Large Cap Value (Growth & Income)	C+	C+	C+	Down	Y	1,000
Invesco Low Volatility Equity Yield Fund Class B	SBCUX	NAS CM	Open End	US Equity Large Cap Value (Growth & Income)	C+	C+	C+	Down		1,000
Invesco Low Volatility Equity Yield Fund Class C	SCCUX	NAS CM	Open End	US Equity Large Cap Value (Growth & Income)	C+	C+	C+	Down	Y	1,000
Invesco Low Volatility Equity Yield Fund Class R	SCRUX	NAS CM	Open End	US Equity Large Cap Value (Growth & Income)	C+	C+	C+	Down	Y	0
Invesco Low Volatility Equity Yield Fund Class R6	SLESX	NAS CM	Open End	US Equity Large Cap Value (Growth & Income)	C+	C+	C+	Down	Y	10,000,000
Invesco Low Volatility Equity Yield Fund Class Y	SCAYX	NAS CM	Open End	US Equity Large Cap Value (Growth & Income)	C+	C+	C+	Down	Y	1,000
Invesco Low Volatility Equity Yield Fund Investor Class	SCNUX	NAS CM	Open End	US Equity Large Cap Value (Growth & Income)	C+	C+	C+	Down	Y	1,000
Invesco Low Volatility Equity Yield Fund R5 Class	SCIUX	NAS CM	Open End	US Equity Large Cap Value (Growth & Income)	C+	C+	B-	Down	Y	10,000,000
Invesco Macro Allocation Strategy Fund Class A	GMSDX	NAS CM	Open End	Moderate Alloc (Multi-Asset Global)	B-	C+	B	Down	Y	1,000
Invesco Macro Allocation Strategy Fund Class C	GMSEX	NAS CM	Open End	Moderate Alloc (Multi-Asset Global)	B-	C+	B		Y	1,000
Invesco Macro Allocation Strategy Fund Class R	GMSJX	NAS CM	Open End	Moderate Alloc (Multi-Asset Global)	B-	C+	B	Down	Y	0
Invesco Macro Allocation Strategy Fund Class R5	GMSKX	NAS CM	Open End	Moderate Alloc (Multi-Asset Global)	B-	C+	B+	Down	Y	10,000,000
Invesco Macro Allocation Strategy Fund Class R6	GMSLX	NAS CM	Open End	Moderate Alloc (Multi-Asset Global)	B-	C+	B+	Down	Y	10,000,000
Invesco Macro Allocation Strategy Fund Class Y	GMSHX	NAS CM	Open End	Moderate Alloc (Multi-Asset Global)	B-	C+	B+	Down	Y	1,000
Invesco Mid Cap Core Equity Fund Class A	GTAGX	NAS CM	Open End	US Equity Mid Cap (Growth)	B-	C+	B	Up	Y	1,000
Invesco Mid Cap Core Equity Fund Class B	GTABX	NAS CM	Open End	US Equity Mid Cap (Growth)	B-	C+	B	Up		1,000
Invesco Mid Cap Core Equity Fund Class C	GTACX	NAS CM	Open End	US Equity Mid Cap (Growth)	B-	C+	B	Up	Y	1,000
Invesco Mid Cap Core Equity Fund Class R	GTARX	NAS CM	Open End	US Equity Mid Cap (Growth)	B-	C+	B	Up	Y	0
Invesco Mid Cap Core Equity Fund Class R6	GTAFX	NAS CM	Open End	US Equity Mid Cap (Growth)	B-	C+	B	Down	Y	10,000,000
Invesco Mid Cap Core Equity Fund Class Y	GTAYX	NAS CM	Open End	US Equity Mid Cap (Growth)	B-	C+	B		Y	1,000
Invesco Mid Cap Core Equity Fund R5 Class	GTAVX	NAS CM	Open End	US Equity Mid Cap (Growth)	B-	C+	B		Y	10,000,000
Invesco Mid Cap Growth Fund Class A	VGRAX	NAS CM	Open End	US Equity Mid Cap (Growth)	B	B-	B	Up	Y	1,000
Invesco Mid Cap Growth Fund Class B	VGRBX	NAS CM	Open End	US Equity Mid Cap (Growth)	B	B-	B	Up		1,000
Invesco Mid Cap Growth Fund Class C	VGRCX	NAS CM	Open End	US Equity Mid Cap (Growth)	B-	B-	B	Up	Y	1,000
Invesco Mid Cap Growth Fund Class R	VGRRX	NAS CM	Open End	US Equity Mid Cap (Growth)	B-	B-	B	Up	Y	0
Invesco Mid Cap Growth Fund Class R5	VGRJX	NAS CM	Open End	US Equity Mid Cap (Growth)	B	B-	B	Up	Y	10,000,000
Invesco Mid Cap Growth Fund Class R6	VGRFX	NAS CM	Open End	US Equity Mid Cap (Growth)	B	B-	B	Up	Y	10,000,000
Invesco Mid Cap Growth Fund Class Y	VGRDX	NAS CM	Open End	US Equity Mid Cap (Growth)	B	B-	B	Up	Y	1,000
Invesco MLP Fund Class A	ILPAX	NAS CM	Open End	Energy Sector Equity (Growth & Income)	D	D	D	Down	Y	1,000
Invesco MLP Fund Class C	ILPCX	NAS CM	Open End	Energy Sector Equity (Growth & Income)	D	D	D	Down	Y	1,000
Invesco MLP Fund Class R	ILPRX	NAS CM	Open End	Energy Sector Equity (Growth & Income)	D	D	D	Down	Y	0
Invesco MLP Fund Class R5	ILPFX	NAS CM	Open End	Energy Sector Equity (Growth & Income)	D	D	D	Down	Y	10,000,000
Invesco MLP Fund Class R6	ILPQX	NAS CM	Open End	Energy Sector Equity (Growth & Income)	D	D	D	Down	Y	10,000,000
Invesco MLP Fund Class Y	ILPYX	NAS CM	Open End	Energy Sector Equity (Growth & Income)	D	D	D	Down	Y	1,000
Invesco Moderate Allocation Fund Class A	AMKAX	NAS CM	Open End	Moderate Alloc (Asset Alloc)	B-	C+	B-	Up	Y	1,000
Invesco Moderate Allocation Fund Class B	AMKBX	NAS CM	Open End	Moderate Alloc (Asset Alloc)	C+	C+	B-	Down		1,000
Invesco Moderate Allocation Fund Class C	AMKCX	NAS CM	Open End	Moderate Alloc (Asset Alloc)	C+	C+	B-	Down	Y	1,000
Invesco Moderate Allocation Fund Class R	AMKRX	NAS CM	Open End	Moderate Alloc (Asset Alloc)	C+	C+	B-		Y	0
Invesco Moderate Allocation Fund Class R6	AMLSX	NAS CM	Open End	Moderate Alloc (Asset Alloc)	B-	C+	B-	Up	Y	10,000,000
Invesco Moderate Allocation Fund Class S	AMKSX	NAS CM	Open End	Moderate Alloc (Asset Alloc)	B-	C+	B-	Up	Y	0
Invesco Moderate Allocation Fund Class Y	ABKYX	NAS CM	Open End	Moderate Alloc (Asset Alloc)	B-	C+	B-	Up	Y	1,000
Invesco Moderate Allocation Fund R5 Class	AMLIX	NAS CM	Open End	Moderate Alloc (Asset Alloc)	B-	C+	B-	Up	Y	10,000,000
Invesco Multi-Asset Income Fund Class A	PIAFX	NAS CM	Open End	Flexible Alloc (Income)	B	C+	A-		Y	1,000
Invesco Multi-Asset Income Fund Class C	PICFX	NAS CM	Open End	Flexible Alloc (Income)	B	C+	B+		Y	1,000
Invesco Multi-Asset Income Fund Class R	PIRFX	NAS CM	Open End	Flexible Alloc (Income)	B	C+	A-		Y	0
Invesco Multi-Asset Income Fund Class R5	IPNFX	NAS CM	Open End	Flexible Alloc (Income)	B	C+	A-		Y	10,000,000
Invesco Multi-Asset Income Fund Class R6	PIFFX	NAS CM	Open End	Flexible Alloc (Income)	B	C+	A-		Y	10,000,000
Invesco Multi-Asset Income Fund Class Y	PIYFX	NAS CM	Open End	Flexible Alloc (Income)	B	C+	A-		Y	1,000
Invesco Multi-Asset Inflation Fund Class A	MIZAX	NAS CM	Open End	Cautious Alloc (Growth & Income)	C	C	C+	Up	Y	1,000
Invesco Multi-Asset Inflation Fund Class C	MIZCX	NAS CM	Open End	Cautious Alloc (Growth & Income)	C	C	C	Up	Y	1,000

★ Expanded analysis of this fund is included in Section II.

	TOTAL RETURNS					PERFORMANCE				ASSETS		ASSET ALLOCATION & TURNOVER					BULL & BEAR		FEES		
Min Additional Investment	3-Month Total Return	6-Month Total Return	1-Year Total Return	3-Year Total Return	5-Year Total Return	Dividend Yield (TTM)	Expense Ratio	3-Yr Std Deviation	3-Year Beta	NAV	Total Assets (MIL)	%Cash	%Stocks	%Bonds	%Other	Turnover Ratio	Last Bull Market Total Return	Last Bear Market Total Return	Front End Fee (%)	Back End Fee (%)	Inception Date
	6.81	13.02	31.64	18.88		1.23	1.09	15.58	1.08	8.79	46.3	5	95	0	1	63					Dec-13
50	6.53	12.71	31.26	18.68		1.23	1.09	15.48	1.08	8.8	46.3	5	95	0	1	63					Dec-13
50	3.31	7.23	15.84	13.94	65.43	2.26	1.21	9.01	0.71	11.26	273.2	2	97	0	0	108	25.44	-17.64	5.50		Mar-06
50	3.16	6.92	14.95	11.48	59.33	1.55	1.96	8.99	0.7	11.11	273.2	2	97	0	0	108	24.78	-17.79		5.00	Mar-06
50	3.07	6.84	14.99	11.39	59.30	1.55	1.96	9.06	0.71	11.08	273.2	2	97	0	0	108	25	-17.84		1.00	Mar-06
	3.26	7.13	15.62	13.22	63.70	2.02	1.46	9.02	0.71	11.21	273.2	2	97	0	0	108	25.29	-17.71			Mar-06
	3.42	7.55	16.41	15.51	68.98		0.74	9.07	0.71	11.32	273.2	2	97	0	0	108	25.64	-17.48			Apr-17
50	3.36	7.44	16.18	14.88	67.59	2.49	0.96	9	0.71	11.31	273.2	2	97	0	0	108	25.63	-17.48			Oct-08
50	3.30	7.31	15.91	14.02	65.58	2.26	1.21	9.08	0.71	11.3	273.2	2	97	0	0	108	25.51	-17.7			Apr-08
	3.41	7.53	16.39	15.49	68.95	2.67	0.77	9.07	0.71	11.32	273.2	2	97	0	0	108	25.64	-17.48			Mar-06
50	5.13	7.41	7.30	13.53	26.50	13.23	1.45	6.26	-8.94	9.45	43.5	32	35	19	14	75			5.50		Aug-13
50	4.82	6.99	6.41	11.09	21.97	12.38	2.2	6.25	-8.58	9.4	43.5	32	35	19	14	75				1.00	Aug-13
	5.02	7.18	6.95	12.69	25.14	12.92	1.7	6.18	-8.73	9.45	43.5	32	35	19	14	75					Aug-13
	5.11	7.61	7.49	14.48	28.33	13.45	1.2	6.24	-9.44	9.5	43.5	32	35	19	14	75					Aug-13
	5.11	7.50	7.50	14.38	27.97	13.47	1.2	6.22	-8.83	9.48	43.5	32	35	19	14	75					Aug-13
50	5.11	7.50	7.50	14.48	28.08	13.45	1.2	6.26	-8.7	9.49	43.5	32	35	19	14	75					Sep-12
50	3.91	7.11	15.04	22.43	69.03	0.25	1.24	9.32	0.83	21.53	1,218	20	80	0	0	20	18.54	-20.83	5.50		Jun-87
50	3.75	6.73	14.20	19.74	62.86	0	1.99	9.32	0.83	12.83	1,218	20	80	0	0	20	18.03	-21.07		5.00	Apr-93
50	3.76	6.75	14.18	19.75	62.92	0	1.99	9.32	0.83	12.77	1,218	20	80	0	0	20	18.07	-21.11		1.00	May-99
	3.88	7.01	14.74	21.50	66.95	0.02	1.49	9.34	0.83	20.63	1,218	20	80	0	0	20	18.37	-20.9			Jun-02
	4.03	7.35	15.52	24.13	72.90	0.95	0.78	9.35	0.83	23.69	1,218	20	80	0	0	20	18.54	-20.83			Sep-12
50	4.02	7.25	15.32	23.35	71.22	0.46	0.99	9.34	0.83	21.96	1,218	20	80	0	0	20	18.75	-20.75			Oct-08
	4.07	7.36	15.48	23.87	72.22	0.68	0.86	9.34	0.83	23.68	1,218	20	80	0	0	20	18.84	-20.71			Mar-02
50	4.12	7.35	22.21	23.60	87.45	0	1.21	12.07	1.04	37.76	2,848	2	98	0	0	53	23.62	-25.9	5.50		Dec-95
50	4.10	7.36	22.21	23.61	87.49	0	1.21	12.06	1.04	31.04	2,848	2	98	0	0	53	23.76	-25.92		5.00	Dec-95
50	3.92	6.98	21.32	20.95	80.79	0	1.93	12.05	1.03	28.28	2,848	2	98	0	0	53	23.11	-26.15		1.00	Dec-95
	4.05	7.23	21.90	22.68	85.14	0	1.46	12.05	1.04	36.62	2,848	2	98	0	0	53	23.41	-25.95			Jul-08
	4.18	7.53	22.62	24.98	90.91	0	0.83	12.06	1.04	39.85	2,848	2	98	0	0	53	23.93	-25.74			Jun-10
	4.22	7.58	22.75	25.31	91.18	0	0.75	12.07	1.04	40.03	2,848	2	98	0	0	53	23.62	-25.9			Jul-13
50	4.15	7.47	22.50	24.53	89.81	0	0.96	12.07	1.04	39.44	2,848	2	98	0	0	53	23.8	-25.8			Aug-05
50	0.34	-2.34	-6.64	-24.96		6.04	1.98	19.07	1.17	5.64	10.2	1	99	0	0	57			5.50		Aug-14
50	-0.01	-2.88	-7.37	-26.73		5.18	2.73	19.1	1.17	5.63	10.2	1	99	0	0	57				1.00	Aug-14
	0.28	-2.46	-6.87	-25.53		5.75	2.23	19.06	1.17	5.64	10.2	1	99	0	0	57					Aug-14
	0.40	-2.22	-6.40	-24.37		6.33	1.73	19.08	1.18	5.64	10.2	1	99	0	0	57					Aug-14
	0.40	-2.22	-6.40	-24.37		6.33	1.73	19.08	1.18	5.64	10.2	1	99	0	0	57					Aug-14
50	0.40	-2.39	-6.40	-24.37		6.33	1.73	19.05	1.17	5.64	10.2	1	99	0	0	57					Aug-14
50	2.99	6.31	12.66	16.37	35.75	2.12	1.06	6.07	0.56	13.62	774.1	10	55	34	1	47	14.42	-9.6	5.50		Apr-04
50	2.81	5.87	11.81	13.76	30.74	1.41	1.81	6.12	0.56	13.52	774.1	10	55	34	1	47	13.91	-9.85		5.00	Apr-04
50	2.81	5.87	11.82	13.77	30.76	1.41	1.81	6.08	0.56	13.51	774.1	10	55	34	1	47	13.81	-9.85		1.00	Apr-04
	2.93	6.19	12.40	15.52	34.05	1.89	1.31	6.1	0.56	13.59	774.1	10	55	34	1	47	14.28	-9.71			Apr-04
	3.07	6.46	12.97	17.20	37.42		0.69	6.17	0.56	13.67	774.1	10	55	34	1	47	14.53	-9.48			Apr-17
	3.02	6.37	12.69	16.64	36.39	2.22	0.96	6.11	0.56	13.61	774.1	10	55	34	1	47	14.43	-9.52			Sep-09
50	3.06	6.36	12.85	17.15	37.40	2.36	0.81	6.1	0.56	13.63	774.1	10	55	34	1	47	14.55	-9.42			Oct-08
	3.06	6.45	12.96	17.19	37.41	2.41	0.75	6.17	0.56	13.68	774.1	10	55	34	1	47	14.53	-9.48			Apr-04
50	0.91	3.32	10.71	24.14	31.74	4.47	0.85	5.43	0.98	10.93	683.5	5	31	42	4	101			5.50		Dec-11
50	0.72	2.93	9.88	21.37	26.88	3.73	1.6	5.4	0.98	10.92	683.5	5	31	42	4	101				1.00	Dec-11
	0.85	3.19	10.43	23.21	30.10	4.22	1.1	5.35	0.96	10.93	683.5	5	31	42	4	101					Dec-11
	0.98	3.45	11.08	25.06	33.39	4.71	0.6	5.35	0.96	10.94	683.5	5	31	42	4	101					Dec-11
	0.98	3.36	10.98	24.95	33.39	4.71	0.6	5.35	0.96	10.93	683.5	5	31	42	4	101					Sep-12
50	0.98	3.36	10.98	25.07	33.26	4.71	0.6	5.34	0.95	10.93	683.5	5	31	42	4	101					Dec-11
50	3.49	6.51	6.27	3.06		1.94	1.02	8.18	56.86	9.26	1.4	13	44	36	6	72			5.50		Oct-14
50	3.27	6.07	5.48	0.80		1.68	1.77	8.16	57.13	9.2	1.4	13	44	36	6	72				1.00	Oct-14

	MARKET			FUND TYPE, CATEGORY & OBJECTIVE	RATINGS				MINIMUMS	
Fund Name	Ticker Symbol	Traded On	Fund Type	Category and (Prospectus Objective)	Overall Rating	Reward Rating	Risk Rating	Recent Up/ Downgrade	Open to New Investors	Min Initial Investment
Invesco Multi-Asset Inflation Fund Class R	MIZRX	NAS CM	Open End	Cautious Alloc (Growth & Income)	C	C	C+	Up	Y	0
Invesco Multi-Asset Inflation Fund Class R5	MIZFX	NAS CM	Open End	Cautious Alloc (Growth & Income)	C	C	C+	Up	Y	10,000,000
Invesco Multi-Asset Inflation Fund Class R6	MIZSX	NAS CM	Open End	Cautious Alloc (Growth & Income)	C	C	C+	Up	Y	10,000,000
Invesco Multi-Asset Inflation Fund Class Y	MIZYX	NAS CM	Open End	Cautious Alloc (Growth & Income)	C	C	C+	Up	Y	1,000
Invesco Pacific Growth Fund Class A	TGRAX	NAS CM	Open End	Asia Equity (Pacific Stock)	A-	A	B	Up	Y	1,000
Invesco Pacific Growth Fund Class B	TGRBX	NAS CM	Open End	Asia Equity (Pacific Stock)	B+	A	B	Up		1,000
Invesco Pacific Growth Fund Class C	TGRCX	NAS CM	Open End	Asia Equity (Pacific Stock)	B+	A	B	Up	Y	1,000
Invesco Pacific Growth Fund Class R	TGRRX	NAS CM	Open End	Asia Equity (Pacific Stock)	A-	A	B	Up	Y	0
Invesco Pacific Growth Fund Class R6	TGRUX	NAS CM	Open End	Asia Equity (Pacific Stock)	A-	A	B	Up	Y	10,000,000
Invesco Pacific Growth Fund Class Y	TGRDX	NAS CM	Open End	Asia Equity (Pacific Stock)	A-	A	B	Up	Y	1,000
Invesco Pacific Growth Fund R5 Shares	TGRSX	NAS CM	Open End	Asia Equity (Pacific Stock)	A-	A	B	Up	Y	10,000,000
Invesco Real Estate Fund Class A	IARAX	NAS CM	Open End	Real Estate Sector Equity (Real Estate)	B	B-	B+	Up	Y	1,000
Invesco Real Estate Fund Class B	AARBX	NAS CM	Open End	Real Estate Sector Equity (Real Estate)	B	C+	B	Up		1,000
Invesco Real Estate Fund Class C	IARCX	NAS CM	Open End	Real Estate Sector Equity (Real Estate)	B	C+	B	Up	Y	1,000
Invesco Real Estate Fund Class R	IARRX	NAS CM	Open End	Real Estate Sector Equity (Real Estate)	B	B-	B+	Up	Y	0
Invesco Real Estate Fund Class R6	IARFX	NAS CM	Open End	Real Estate Sector Equity (Real Estate)	B	B-	B+	Up	Y	10,000,000
Invesco Real Estate Fund Class Y	IARYX	NAS CM	Open End	Real Estate Sector Equity (Real Estate)	B	B-	B+	Up	Y	1,000
Invesco Real Estate Fund Investor Class	REINX	NAS CM	Open End	Real Estate Sector Equity (Real Estate)	B	B-	B+	Up		1,000
Invesco Real Estate Fund R5 Class	IARIX	NAS CM	Open End	Real Estate Sector Equity (Real Estate)	B	B-	B+	Up	Y	10,000,000
Invesco S&P 500 Index Class R6	SPISX	NAS CM	Open End	US Equity Large Cap Blend (Growth & Income)	B	B	B		Y	10,000,000
Invesco S&P 500 Index Fund Class A	SPIAX	NAS CM	Open End	US Equity Large Cap Blend (Growth & Income)	B	B	B		Y	1,000
Invesco S&P 500 Index Fund Class B	SPIBX	NAS CM	Open End	US Equity Large Cap Blend (Growth & Income)	B-	B-	B	Down		1,000
Invesco S&P 500 Index Fund Class C	SPICX	NAS CM	Open End	US Equity Large Cap Blend (Growth & Income)	B-	B-	B	Down	Y	1,000
Invesco S&P 500 Index Fund Class Y	SPIDX	NAS CM	Open End	US Equity Large Cap Blend (Growth & Income)	B	B	B		Y	1,000
Invesco Select Companies Fund Class A	ATIAX	NAS CM	Open End	US Equity Small Cap (Small Company)	B-	B-	C	Up		1,000
Invesco Select Companies Fund Class B	ATIBX	NAS CM	Open End	US Equity Small Cap (Small Company)	C+	B-	C			1,000
Invesco Select Companies Fund Class C	ATICX	NAS CM	Open End	US Equity Small Cap (Small Company)	C+	B-	C			1,000
Invesco Select Companies Fund Class R	ATIRX	NAS CM	Open End	US Equity Small Cap (Small Company)	C+	B-	C			0
Invesco Select Companies Fund Class R6	ATISX	NAS CM	Open End	US Equity Small Cap (Small Company)	B-	B-	C	Up	Y	10,000,000
Invesco Select Companies Fund Class Y	ATIYX	NAS CM	Open End	US Equity Small Cap (Small Company)	B-	B	C	Up		1,000
Invesco Select Companies Fund R5 Class	ATIIX	NAS CM	Open End	US Equity Small Cap (Small Company)	B-	B	C	Up		10,000,000
Invesco Select Opportunities Fund Class A	IZSAX	NAS CM	Open End	Global Equity Mid/Small Cap (Small Company)	C+	C+	C+	Up	Y	1,000
Invesco Select Opportunities Fund Class C	IZSCX	NAS CM	Open End	Global Equity Mid/Small Cap (Small Company)	C+	C+	C+	Up	Y	1,000
Invesco Select Opportunities Fund Class R	IZSRX	NAS CM	Open End	Global Equity Mid/Small Cap (Small Company)	C+	C+	C+	Up	Y	0
Invesco Select Opportunities Fund Class R6	IZFSX	NAS CM	Open End	Global Equity Mid/Small Cap (Small Company)	C+	C+	C+	Up	Y	10,000,000
Invesco Select Opportunities Fund Class Y	IZSYX	NAS CM	Open End	Global Equity Mid/Small Cap (Small Company)	C+	C+	C+	Up	Y	1,000
Invesco Select Opportunities Fund R5 Class	IZSIX	NAS CM	Open End	Global Equity Mid/Small Cap (Small Company)	C+	C+	C+	Up	Y	10,000,000
Invesco Small Cap Discovery Fund Class A	VASCX	NAS CM	Open End	US Equity Small Cap (Small Company)	B	B	B	Up	Y	1,000
Invesco Small Cap Discovery Fund Class B	VBSCX	NAS CM	Open End	US Equity Small Cap (Small Company)	B	B	B	Up		1,000
Invesco Small Cap Discovery Fund Class C	VCSCX	NAS CM	Open End	US Equity Small Cap (Small Company)	B	B	B-	Up	Y	1,000
Invesco Small Cap Discovery Fund Class R5	VESCX	NAS CM	Open End	US Equity Small Cap (Small Company)	B	B	B	Up	Y	10,000,000
Invesco Small Cap Discovery Fund Class R6	VFSCX	NAS CM	Open End	US Equity Small Cap (Small Company)	B	B	B	Up	Y	10,000,000
Invesco Small Cap Discovery Fund Class Y	VISCX	NAS CM	Open End	US Equity Small Cap (Small Company)	B	B	B	Up	Y	1,000
Invesco Small Cap Equity Fund Class A	SMEAX	NAS CM	Open End	US Equity Small Cap (Small Company)	B-	B-	B	Up	Y	1,000
Invesco Small Cap Equity Fund Class B	SMEBX	NAS CM	Open End	US Equity Small Cap (Small Company)	B-	C+	B	Up		1,000
Invesco Small Cap Equity Fund Class C	SMECX	NAS CM	Open End	US Equity Small Cap (Small Company)	B-	C+	B	Up	Y	1,000
Invesco Small Cap Equity Fund Class R	SMERX	NAS CM	Open End	US Equity Small Cap (Small Company)	B-	C+	B	Up	Y	0
Invesco Small Cap Equity Fund Class R6	SMEFX	NAS CM	Open End	US Equity Small Cap (Small Company)	B	B-	B	Up	Y	10,000,000
Invesco Small Cap Equity Fund Class Y	SMEYX	NAS CM	Open End	US Equity Small Cap (Small Company)	B-	B-	B	Up	Y	1,000
Invesco Small Cap Equity Fund R5 Class	SMEIX	NAS CM	Open End	US Equity Small Cap (Small Company)	B	B-	B	Up	Y	10,000,000
Invesco Small Cap Growth Fund Class A	GTSAX	NAS CM	Open End	US Equity Small Cap (Small Company)	B+	A-	B	Up		1,000
Invesco Small Cap Growth Fund Class B	GTSBX	NAS CM	Open End	US Equity Small Cap (Small Company)	B+	B+	B	Up		1,000

★Expanded analysis of this fund is included in Section II.

	TOTAL RETURNS					PERFORMANCE				ASSETS		ASSET ALLOCATION & TURNOVER					BULL & BEAR		FEES		
Min Additional Investment	3-Month Total Return	6-Month Total Return	1-Year Total Return	3-Year Total Return	5-Year Total Return	Dividend Yield (TTM)	Expense Ratio	3-Yr Std Deviation	3-Year Beta	NAV	Total Assets (MIL)	%Cash	%Stocks	%Bonds	%Other	Turnover Ratio	Last Bull Market Total Return	Last Bear Market Total Return	Front End Fee (%)	Back End Fee (%)	Inception Date
	3.39	6.40	6.05	2.39		1.85	1.27	8.13	55.1	9.25	1.4	13	44	36	6	72					Oct-14
	3.62	6.74	6.62	3.97		2.06	0.77	8.14	55.84	9.29	1.4	13	44	36	6	72					Oct-14
	3.62	6.74	6.62	3.97		2.06	0.77	8.14	55.84	9.29	1.4	13	44	36	6	72					Oct-14
50	3.61	6.74	6.62	3.97		2.06	0.77	8.14	55.48	9.29	1.4	13	44	36	6	72					Oct-14
50	12.02	21.38	46.88	53.53	70.89	0.15	1.64	12.13	0.7	35.59	111.1	4	96	0	0	31	11.31	-22.21	5.50		Jul-97
50	11.83	20.98	45.77	50.18	64.61	0	2.39	12.12	0.7	32.8	111.1	4	96	0	0	31	10.8	-22.49		5.00	Nov-90
50	11.80	20.93	45.82	50.22	64.63	0	2.37	12.14	0.7	32.87	111.1	4	96	0	0	31	10.86	-22.47		1.00	Jul-97
	11.93	21.23	46.48	52.38	68.61	0	1.89	12.12	0.7	35.17	111.1	4	96	0	0	31	11.18	-22.33			Mar-08
	12.10	21.60	46.82	51.25	65.79		1.22	12.17	0.7	36.31	111.1	4	96	0	0	31	10.8	-22.49			Apr-17
50	12.09	21.56	47.23	54.74	72.95	0.34	1.39	12.13	0.7	36.25	111.1	4	96	0	0	31	11.54	-22.17			Jul-97
	12.10	21.60	47.36	55.24	74.04	0.43	1.28	12.14	0.7	36.31	111.1	4	96	0	0	31	11.58	-22.12			May-11
50	3.31	3.92	8.43	14.87	54.01	1.56	1.24	12.36	0.59	21.28	1,657	1	98	0	0	52	29.78	-16.21	5.50		Dec-96
50	3.12	3.53	7.62	12.31	48.32	0.9	1.99	12.35	0.59	21.28	1,657	1	98	0	0	52	29.22	-16.5		5.00	Mar-98
50	3.13	3.50	7.60	12.32	48.35	0.9	1.99	12.34	0.59	21.17	1,657	1	98	0	0	52	29.21	-16.51		1.00	May-95
	3.24	3.78	8.15	14.00	52.06	1.34	1.49	12.36	0.59	21.31	1,657	1	98	0	0	52	29.61	-16.31			Apr-04
	3.42	4.16	8.95	16.44	57.55	1.98	0.8	12.35	0.59	21.25	1,657	1	98	0	0	52	29.21	-16.51			Sep-12
50	3.33	4.00	8.65	15.69	55.88	1.78	0.99	12.37	0.59	21.26	1,657	1	98	0	0	52	29.96	-16.14			Oct-08
50	3.32	3.93	8.51	14.92	54.13	1.57	1.23	12.34	0.58	21.23	1,657	1	98	0	0	52	29.73	-16.23			Sep-03
	3.40	4.11	8.85	16.13	56.92	1.9	0.89	12.36	0.59	21.26	1,657	1	98	0	0	52	30.09	-16.07			Apr-04
	6.56	11.28	21.49	35.56	108.30		0.25	10.1	1	29.21	1,167	2	98	0	0	4	24.88	-16.44			Apr-17
50	6.48	11.09	21.12	34.53	105.65	1.07	0.58	10.04	1	28.88	1,167	2	98	0	0	4	24.64	-16.48	5.50		Sep-97
50	6.29	10.67	20.26	31.57	98.11	0.54	1.33	10.08	1	28.27	1,167	2	98	0	0	4	24.15	-16.79		5.00	Sep-97
50	6.32	10.75	20.27	31.61	98.25	0.56	1.31	10.07	1	27.93	1,167	2	98	0	0	4	24.15	-16.74		1.00	Sep-97
50	6.56	11.24	21.45	35.52	108.23	1.24	0.33	10.09	1	29.21	1,167	2	98	0	0	4	24.88	-16.44			Sep-97
50	8.60	9.37	20.11	25.03	72.81	0	1.25	12.77	0.96	18.79	482.7	10	90	0	0	20	18.75	-14.77	5.50		Nov-03
50	8.35	8.92	19.17	22.21	66.33	0	2	12.78	0.96	15.87	482.7	10	90	0	0	20	18.25	-15.07		5.00	Nov-03
50	8.36	8.93	19.21	22.27	66.39	0	2	12.78	0.96	15.84	482.7	10	90	0	0	20	18.19	-15.03		1.00	Nov-03
	8.51	9.20	19.80	24.12	70.61	0	1.5	12.8	0.96	17.86	482.7	10	90	0	0	20	18.58	-14.89			Apr-04
	8.64	9.57	20.44	25.37	73.28		0.85	12.77	0.96	20.21	482.7	10	90	0	0	20	18.75	-14.77			Apr-17
50	8.66	9.47	20.36	25.93	74.90	0	1	12.79	0.96	19.28	482.7	10	90	0	0	20	18.93	-14.69			Oct-08
	8.65	9.53	20.52	26.32	75.64	0	0.9	12.81	0.96	20.2	482.7	10	90	0	0	20	18.99	-14.63			Apr-04
50	5.70	8.55	18.71	21.15	58.21	0	1.02	12.04	0.94	16.49	54.1	8	92	0	0	26			5.50		Aug-12
50	5.58	8.17	17.89	18.52	52.36	0	1.77	12.05	0.95	15.88	54.1	8	92	0	0	26				1.00	Aug-12
	5.64	8.45	18.47	20.30	56.38	0	1.27	12.06	0.94	16.29	54.1	8	92	0	0	26					Aug-12
	5.76	8.72	19.03	22.14	60.21	0	0.77	12.04	0.94	16.7	54.1	8	92	0	0	26					Sep-12
50	5.82	8.78	19.10	22.22	60.31	0	0.77	12.04	0.94	16.71	54.1	8	92	0	0	26					Aug-12
	5.75	8.71	19.01	22.13	60.30	0	0.77	12.04	0.94	16.71	54.1	8	92	0	0	26					Aug-12
50	4.77	8.10	24.14	26.52	84.44	0	1.4	13.99	1.14	9.66	603.1	3	97	0	0	39	28.36	-25.01	5.50		Nov-00
50	4.71	8.07	24.11	26.52	84.33	0	1.4	14	1.14	8.23	603.1	3	97	0	0	39	28.38	-24.95		5.00	Nov-00
50	4.61	7.68	23.37	23.77	77.79	0	2.14	14	1.14	7.26	603.1	3	97	0	0	39	27.67	-25.14		1.00	Nov-00
	4.83	8.35	24.77	28.27	88.62	0	0.95	13.97	1.14	10.39	603.1	3	97	0	0	39	28.37	-25.01			Sep-12
	4.91	8.42	24.82	28.33	88.80	0	0.91	14.01	1.15	10.42	603.1	3	97	0	0	39	28.37	-25.01			Sep-12
50	4.79	8.25	24.58	27.47	86.92	0	1.15	14	1.15	10.26	603.1	3	97	0	0	39	28.45	-24.9			Feb-06
50	3.88	8.33	13.57	18.74	70.33	0	1.31	13.47	1.12	15.35	1,291	1	99	0	0	35	28.99	-24.87	5.50		Aug-00
50	3.73	7.98	12.78	16.22	64.21	0	2.06	13.42	1.12	12.36	1,291	1	99	0	0	35	28.43	-25.09		5.00	Aug-00
50	3.73	7.98	12.78	16.13	64.12	0	2.06	13.44	1.12	12.35	1,291	1	99	0	0	35	28.33	-25.03		1.00	Aug-00
	3.84	8.25	13.31	17.91	68.20	0	1.56	13.49	1.12	14.44	1,291	1	99	0	0	35	28.68	-24.87			Jun-02
	4.06	8.69	14.19	20.59	74.75	0	0.79	13.48	1.12	16.99	1,291	1	99	0	0	35	28.99	-24.87			Sep-12
50	3.95	8.48	13.88	19.63	72.46	0	1.06	13.48	1.12	15.86	1,291	1	99	0	0	35	29.12	-24.76			Oct-08
	3.96	8.54	13.99	20.26	73.94	0	0.87	13.48	1.12	16.88	1,291	1	99	0	0	35	29.38	-24.68			Apr-05
50	6.62	13.10	24.91	35.56	109.55	0	1.23	12.66	1.07	37.31	2,866	1	99	0	0	26	28.88	-23.65	5.50		Oct-95
50	6.42	12.69	24.02	32.57	101.90	0	1.98	12.64	1.07	25.4	2,866	1	99	0	0	26	28.28	-23.86		5.00	Oct-95

	MARKET			FUND TYPE, CATEGORY & OBJECTIVE	RATINGS				MINIMUMS	
Fund Name	Ticker Symbol	Traded On	Fund Type	Category and (Prospectus Objective)	Overall Rating	Reward Rating	Risk Rating	Recent Up/ Downgrade	Open to New Investors	Min Initial Investment
Invesco Small Cap Growth Fund Class C	GTSDX	NAS CM	Open End	US Equity Small Cap (Small Company)	B	B+	C+	Up		1,000
Invesco Small Cap Growth Fund Class R	GTSRX	NAS CM	Open End	US Equity Small Cap (Small Company)	B+	A-	B	Up		0
Invesco Small Cap Growth Fund Class R6	GTSFX	NAS CM	Open End	US Equity Small Cap (Small Company)	B+	A-	B	Up		10,000,000
Invesco Small Cap Growth Fund Class Y	GTSYX	NAS CM	Open End	US Equity Small Cap (Small Company)	B+	A-	B	Up		1,000
Invesco Small Cap Growth Fund Investor Class	GTSIX	NAS CM	Open End	US Equity Small Cap (Small Company)	B	A-	C+	Up		1,000
Invesco Small Cap Growth Fund R5 Class	GTSVX	NAS CM	Open End	US Equity Small Cap (Small Company)	B+	A-	B	Up		10,000,000
Invesco Small Cap Value Class R6	SMVSX	NAS CM	Open End	US Equity Small Cap (Small Company)	B	A-	B-	Up	Y	10,000,000
Invesco Small Cap Value Fund Class A	VSCAX	NAS CM	Open End	US Equity Small Cap (Small Company)	B	A-	B-	Up		1,000
Invesco Small Cap Value Fund Class B	VSMBX	NAS CM	Open End	US Equity Small Cap (Small Company)	B	B	B-	Up		1,000
Invesco Small Cap Value Fund Class C	VSMCX	NAS CM	Open End	US Equity Small Cap (Small Company)	B	B	B-	Up		1,000
Invesco Small Cap Value Fund Class Y	VSMIX	NAS CM	Open End	US Equity Small Cap (Small Company)	B	A-	B-	Up		1,000
Invesco Summit Fund Class A	ASMMX	NAS CM	Open End	US Equity Large Cap Growth (Growth)	B	B	B	Down	Y	1,000
Invesco Summit Fund Class B	BSMMX	NAS CM	Open End	US Equity Large Cap Growth (Growth)	B	B	B	Down		1,000
Invesco Summit Fund Class C	CSMMX	NAS CM	Open End	US Equity Large Cap Growth (Growth)	B	B	B	Down	Y	1,000
Invesco Summit Fund Class P	SMMIX	NAS CM	Open End	US Equity Large Cap Growth (Growth)	B+	B	B+	Up		0
Invesco Summit Fund Class R6	SMISX	NAS CM	Open End	US Equity Large Cap Growth (Growth)	B+	B+	B+	Up	Y	10,000,000
Invesco Summit Fund Class S	SMMSX	NAS CM	Open End	US Equity Large Cap Growth (Growth)	B	B	B	Down	Y	0
Invesco Summit Fund Class Y	ASMYX	NAS CM	Open End	US Equity Large Cap Growth (Growth)	B	B+	B	Down	Y	1,000
Invesco Summit Fund R5 Class	SMITX	NAS CM	Open End	US Equity Large Cap Growth (Growth)	B+	B+	B+	Up	Y	10,000,000
Invesco Technology Fund Class A	ITYAX	NAS CM	Open End	Technology Sector Equity (Technology)	B+	B+	B	Up	Y	1,000
Invesco Technology Fund Class B	ITYBX	NAS CM	Open End	Technology Sector Equity (Technology)	B+	B+	B	Up		1,000
Invesco Technology Fund Class C	ITHCX	NAS CM	Open End	Technology Sector Equity (Technology)	B+	B+	B	Up	Y	1,000
Invesco Technology Fund Class R6	FTPSX	NAS CM	Open End	Technology Sector Equity (Technology)	B+	A-	B	Up	Y	10,000,000
Invesco Technology Fund Class Y	ITYYX	NAS CM	Open End	Technology Sector Equity (Technology)	B+	A-	B	Up	Y	1,000
Invesco Technology Fund Investor Class	FTCHX	NAS CM	Open End	Technology Sector Equity (Technology)	B+	A-	B	Up		1,000
Invesco Technology Fund R5 Class	FTPIX	NAS CM	Open End	Technology Sector Equity (Technology)	B+	A-	B	Up	Y	10,000,000
Invesco Technology Sector Fund Class A	IFOAX	NAS CM	Open End	Technology Sector Equity (Technology)	B+	B+	B	Up		1,000
Invesco Technology Sector Fund Class B	IFOBX	NAS CM	Open End	Technology Sector Equity (Technology)	B+	B+	B	Up		1,000
Invesco Technology Sector Fund Class C	IFOCX	NAS CM	Open End	Technology Sector Equity (Technology)	B+	B+	B	Up		1,000
Invesco Technology Sector Fund Class Y	IFODX	NAS CM	Open End	Technology Sector Equity (Technology)	B+	A-	B	Up		1,000
Invesco Value Opportunities Fund Class A	VVOAX	NAS CM	Open End	US Equity Large Cap Value (Growth & Income)	B-	B	C	Up	Y	1,000
Invesco Value Opportunities Fund Class B	VVOBX	NAS CM	Open End	US Equity Large Cap Value (Growth & Income)	B-	B	C	Up		1,000
Invesco Value Opportunities Fund Class C	VVOCX	NAS CM	Open End	US Equity Large Cap Value (Growth & Income)	C+	B-	C		Y	1,000
Invesco Value Opportunities Fund Class R	VVORX	NAS CM	Open End	US Equity Large Cap Value (Growth & Income)	B-	B	C	Up	Y	0
Invesco Value Opportunities Fund Class R5	VVONX	NAS CM	Open End	US Equity Large Cap Value (Growth & Income)	B-	B	C+	Up	Y	10,000,000
Invesco Value Opportunities Fund Class R6	VVOSX	NAS CM	Open End	US Equity Large Cap Value (Growth & Income)	B-	B	C	Up	Y	10,000,000
Invesco Value Opportunities Fund Class Y	VVOIX	NAS CM	Open End	US Equity Large Cap Value (Growth & Income)	B-	B	C+	Up	Y	1,000
InvestEd Aggressive Portfolio	WAGPX	NAS CM	Open End	Aggressive Alloc (Growth)	U	U	U		Y	250
InvestEd Balanced Portfolio	WBLAX	NAS CM	Open End	Moderate Alloc (Growth & Income)	B-	C+	B	Down	Y	250
InvestEd Conservative Portfolio	WICAX	NAS CM	Open End	Moderate Alloc (Income)	B-	C	B	Up	Y	250
InvestEd Growth Portfolio	WAGRX	NAS CM	Open End	Aggressive Alloc (Growth)	B	B-	B+	Up	Y	250
InvestEd Income Portfolio	WICPX	NAS CM	Open End	Cautious Alloc (Income)	U	U	U		Y	250
IPS Strategic Absolute Return Fund Inst Cls Shares	IPSAX	NAS CM	Open End	Long/Short Equity (Growth)	D+	C-	B	Up	Y	5,000
IQ Hedge Multi-Strategy Plus Fund Class A	IQHOX	NAS CM	Open End	Multialternative (Growth)	C	C	C+	Up	Y	25,000
IQ Hedge Multi-Strategy Plus Fund Class I	IQHIX	NAS CM	Open End	Multialternative (Growth)	C+	C	B	Up	Y	5,000,000
Iron Equity Premium Income Fund Institutional Class	CALLX	NAS CM	Open End	Long/Short Equity (Growth & Income)	C	C-	B+	Up	Y	10,000
Iron Equity Premium Income Fund Investor Class	CALIX	NAS CM	Open End	Long/Short Equity (Growth & Income)	C	C-	B+	Up	Y	10,000
IronBridge Large Cap Fund	IBLCX	NAS CM	Open End	US Equity Large Cap Growth (Growth)	B	B-	B+		Y	100,000
IronBridge Small Cap Fund	IBSCX	NAS CM	Open End	US Equity Small Cap (Growth)	B	B-	B	Up	Y	100,000
IronBridge SMID Cap Fund	IBSMX	NAS CM	Open End	US Equity Mid Cap (Growth)	B	B-	B+	Up	Y	100,000
Ironclad Managed Risk Fund	IRONX	NAS CM	Open End	Long/Short Equity (Growth)	C+	C	B	Up	Y	2,500
iShares Developed Real Estate Index Fund Class K	BKRDX	NAS CM	Open End	Real Estate Sector Equity (Real Estate)	C	C	B	Up	Y	5,000,000

★ Expanded analysis of this fund is included in Section II.

Min Additional Investment	TOTAL RETURNS 3-Month Total Return	6-Month Total Return	1-Year Total Return	3-Year Total Return	5-Year Total Return	PERFORMANCE Dividend Yield (TTM)	Expense Ratio	3-Yr Std Deviation	3-Year Beta	ASSETS NAV	Total Assets (MIL)	ASSET ALLOCATION & TURNOVER %Cash	%Stocks	%Bonds	%Other	Turnover Ratio	BULL & BEAR Last Bull Market Total Return	Last Bear Market Total Return	FEES Front End Fee (%)	Back End Fee (%)	Inception Date
50	6.44	12.69	23.98	32.55	101.86	0	1.98	12.65	1.07	25.33	2,866	1	99	0	0	26	28.32	-23.88		1.00	May-99
	6.56	12.95	24.59	34.54	106.94	0	1.48	12.66	1.07	34.58	2,866	1	99	0	0	26	28.66	-23.72			Jun-02
	6.75	13.37	25.48	37.51	114.60	0.33	0.74	12.66	1.07	42.2	2,866	1	99	0	0	26	28.88	-23.65			Sep-12
50	6.69	13.26	25.24	36.57	112.23	0.18	0.98	12.67	1.07	38.44	2,866	1	99	0	0	26	29.07	-23.56			Oct-08
50	6.65	13.12	24.94	35.60	109.65	0	1.23	12.65	1.07	39.22	2,866	1	99	0	0	26	28.84	-23.63			Apr-06
	6.73	13.32	25.40	37.12	113.72	0.27	0.84	12.67	1.07	42.02	2,866	1	99	0	0	26	29.18	-23.49			Mar-02
	6.39	13.13	18.67	27.32	103.26		0.72	18.82	1.23	19.84	2,700	3	97	0	0	32	36.31	-29			Feb-17
50	6.25	12.85	18.28	26.90	102.59	0.15	1.11	18.82	1.23	18.96	2,700	3	97	0	0	32	36.31	-29	5.50		Jun-99
50	6.01	12.43	17.41	24.08	95.03	0	1.86	18.84	1.24	14.29	2,700	3	97	0	0	32	36.05	-29.07		5.00	Jun-99
50	6.13	12.52	17.47	24.15	95.23	0	1.85	18.8	1.23	13.64	2,700	3	97	0	0	32	35.76	-29.21		1.00	Jun-99
50	6.35	13.04	18.58	27.87	105.08	0.36	0.86	18.81	1.23	19.81	2,700	3	97	0	0	32	36.49	-28.88			Aug-05
50	4.12	10.62	29.69	40.05	115.97	0	1.05	12.81	1.12	19.64	2,170	0	100	0	0	47	23.96	-18.36	5.50		Oct-05
50	3.88	10.19	28.63	36.88	107.83	0	1.8	12.78	1.12	17.93	2,170	0	100	0	0	47	23.61	-18.64		5.00	Oct-05
50	3.89	10.22	28.66	36.93	107.86	0	1.8	12.78	1.12	17.87	2,170	0	100	0	0	47	23.33	-18.65		1.00	Oct-05
	4.13	10.72	29.87	40.66	117.56	0.05	0.9	12.78	1.12	19.9	2,170	0	100	0	0	47	24.09	-18.33			Nov-82
	4.14	10.78	30.01	40.80	117.78		0.73	12.78	1.12	19.91	2,170	0	100	0	0	47	24.09	-18.33			Apr-17
	4.10	10.68	29.73	40.42	116.97	0.01	0.95	12.79	1.12	19.75	2,170	0	100	0	0	47	24.06	-18.33			Sep-09
50	4.19	10.80	30.02	41.07	118.59	0.13	0.8	12.78	1.12	19.84	2,170	0	100	0	0	47	24.22	-18.33			Oct-08
	4.20	10.79	30.01	41.37	119.54	0.17	0.74	12.78	1.12	19.91	2,170	0	100	0	0	47	24.29	-18.31			Oct-08
50	2.91	10.14	34.66	40.94	100.14	0	1.43	15.43	1.17	44.23	861.6	0	100	0	0	49	26.02	-17.4	5.50		Mar-02
50	2.71	9.73	33.64	37.81	92.78	0	2.18	15.44	1.17	37.64	861.6	0	100	0	0	49	25.48	-17.59		5.00	Mar-02
50	2.71	9.72	33.64	37.80	92.81	0	2.18	15.43	1.17	36.01	861.6	0	100	0	0	49	25.48	-17.61		1.00	Feb-00
	3.02	10.36	35.09	41.62	101.50		0.92	15.44	1.17	51.75	861.6	0	100	0	0	49	26.05	-17.39			Apr-17
50	2.98	10.27	34.99	41.97	102.67	0	1.18	15.43	1.17	44.8	861.6	0	100	0	0	49	26.21	-17.29			Oct-08
50	2.92	10.18	34.77	41.29	101.02	0	1.35	15.43	1.17	43.97	861.6	0	100	0	0	49	26.05	-17.39			Jan-84
	3.00	10.37	35.26	42.96	105.45	0	0.92	15.44	1.17	51.74	861.6	0	100	0	0	49	26.52	-17.15			Dec-98
50	2.90	10.07	34.53	40.35	100.50	0	1.67	15.41	1.17	22.09	97.8	0	100	0	0	49	27.94	-18.13	5.50		Jul-97
50	2.67	9.61	33.48	37.23	93.07	0	2.42	15.38	1.17	18.63	97.8	0	100	0	0	49	27.62	-18.51		5.00	Nov-95
50	2.67	9.67	33.46	37.21	93.17	0	2.39	15.4	1.17	18.64	97.8	0	100	0	0	49	27.62	-18.51		1.00	Jul-97
50	2.93	10.18	34.79	41.32	102.91	0	1.42	15.39	1.17	23.28	97.8	0	100	0	0	49	28.29	-18.1			Jul-97
50	5.39	10.22	17.10	22.68	77.36	0.13	1.27	17.04	1.41	14.65	861.4	3	97	0	0	33	27.06	-20.82	5.50		Jun-01
50	5.42	10.26	17.17	22.76	77.43	0.14	1.27	17.04	1.41	14.39	861.4	3	97	0	0	33	27.07	-20.91		5.00	Jun-01
50	5.20	9.92	16.35	20.16	71.14	0	1.98	17.04	1.41	13.97	861.4	3	97	0	0	33	26.45	-21		1.00	Jun-01
	5.36	10.14	16.87	21.81	75.19	0	1.52	17.09	1.42	14.55	861.4	3	97	0	0	33	26.87	-20.9			May-12
	5.45	10.43	17.58	24.25	81.08	0.49	0.86	17.05	1.41	14.69	861.4	3	97	0	0	33	27.63	-20.7			May-11
	5.52	10.50	17.48	23.08	77.93		0.78	17.03	1.41	14.7	861.4	3	97	0	0	33	27.06	-20.82			Apr-17
50	5.48	10.40	17.39	23.63	79.61	0.36	1.02	17.08	1.41	14.63	861.4	3	97	0	0	33	27.29	-20.8			Mar-05
	4.98						1.02			10.54	16.6	2	85	11	1				2.50		Sep-17
	3.43	8.25	16.60	19.49	51.27	0.74	0.96	7.75		11.65	81.5	1	58	37	2	25	15.15	-13.71	2.50		Oct-01
	2.37	5.29	8.82	10.50	30.34	1.17	0.91	5.09		10.68	87.7	2	39	55	2	64	5.66	-0.27	2.50		Oct-01
	4.27	9.56	21.84	25.07	71.54	0.2	1.02	9.55		12.61	135.6	1	72	23	2	24	17.89	-18.08	2.50		Oct-01
	1.49						0.86			10.16	96.2	4	25	69	1				2.50		Sep-17
200	5.46	8.78	13.55			0	1.6			10.44	84.1	85	15	0	0	0					Apr-16
	1.90	3.77	6.38	0.59	10.93	0	2.12	4.06	1.02	10.17	47.1	-6	50	49	2	280	5.26	-6.95	5.50		Jun-08
	1.88	3.84	6.54	1.82	13.19	0	1.68	4.04	1.01	10.26	47.1	-6	50	49	2	280	5.28	-6.65			Jun-08
1,000	4.62	8.29	16.70			4.05	1.11			11.6	8.5	2	98	0	0	6					Oct-15
1,000	4.54	8.13	16.33			3.74	1.46			11.6	8.5	2	98	0	0	6					Oct-15
1,000	5.72	9.93	18.53	32.50	93.20	1.08	0.8	9.63	0.93	14.53	34.4	2	98	0	0	26					Mar-12
1,000	2.23	7.57	10.43	22.01	77.20	0.26	1.11	11.74	0.79	17.12	269.2	5	95	0	0	32	26.25	-23.22			Aug-02
1,000	3.98	7.84	13.66	25.45	75.25	0.26	0.96	10.76	0.83	11.36	266.4	3	97	0	0	34	24.49	-22.95			Dec-04
500	0.00	0.27	3.32	6.53	23.82	0	1.25	4.93		10.19	92.6	60	0	40	0	47	10.28	-3.66			Oct-10
	3.53	5.37	10.99			2.34	0.26			10.48	1,524	1	98	0	1	11					Aug-15

	MARKET			FUND TYPE, CATEGORY & OBJECTIVE	RATINGS				MINIMUMS	
Fund Name	Ticker Symbol	Traded On	Fund Type	Category and (Prospectus Objective)	Overall Rating	Reward Rating	Risk Rating	Recent Up/ Downgrade	Open to New Investors	Min Initial Investment
iShares Developed Real Estate Index Fund Inst Shares	BIRDX	NAS CM	Open End	Real Estate Sector Equity (Real Estate)	C	C	B	Up	Y	2,000,000
iShares Developed Real Estate Index Fund Investor A Shares	BARDX	NAS CM	Open End	Real Estate Sector Equity (Real Estate)	C	C	B	Up	Y	1,000
iShares Edge MSCI Min Vol EAFE Index Fund Class K	BKEVX	NAS CM	Open End	Global Equity Large Cap (Growth & Income)	D	C-	B-		Y	5,000,000
iShares Edge MSCI Min Vol EAFE Index Fund Inst Shares	BIEVX	NAS CM	Open End	Global Equity Large Cap (Growth & Income)	D	C-	B-		Y	2,000,000
iShares Edge MSCI Min Vol USA Index Fund Class K	BKMVX	NAS CM	Open End	US Equity Large Cap Blend (Growth & Income)	D	C	B		Y	5,000,000
iShares Edge MSCI Min Vol USA Index Fund Inst Shares	BIMVX	NAS CM	Open End	US Equity Large Cap Blend (Growth & Income)	D	C	B		Y	2,000,000
iShares Edge MSCI Multifactor Intl Index Fund Class K	BKIMX	NAS CM	Open End	Global Equity Large Cap (Growth & Income)	D	C	B		Y	5,000,000
iShares Edge MSCI Multifactor Intl Index Fund Inst Shares	BIIMX	NAS CM	Open End	Global Equity Large Cap (Growth & Income)	D	C	B		Y	2,000,000
iShares Edge MSCI Multifactor USA Index Fund Class K	BKMFX	NAS CM	Open End	US Equity Large Cap Blend (Growth & Income)	D	C	B+		Y	5,000,000
iShares Edge MSCI Multifactor USA Index Fund Inst Shares	BIMFX	NAS CM	Open End	US Equity Large Cap Blend (Growth & Income)	D	C	B+		Y	2,000,000
iShares Edge MSCI USA Momentum Factor Index Fund Class K	BKMTX	NAS CM	Open End	US Equity Large Cap Growth (Growth & Income)	D-	D+	A		Y	5,000,000
iShares Edge MSCI USA Momentum Factor Ind Fund Inst Shares	BIMTX	NAS CM	Open End	US Equity Large Cap Growth (Growth & Income)	D-	D+	A		Y	2,000,000
iShares Edge MSCI USA Quality Factor Index Fund Class K	BQFKX	NAS CM	Open End	US Equity Large Cap Blend (Growth & Income)	D-	D+	A-		Y	5,000,000
iShares Edge MSCI USA Quality Factor Ind Fund Inst Shares	BQFIX	NAS CM	Open End	US Equity Large Cap Blend (Growth & Income)	D-	D+	A-		Y	2,000,000
iShares Edge MSCI USA Size Factor Index Fund Class K	BKSFX	NAS CM	Open End	US Equity Large Cap Blend (Growth & Income)	D-	D+	A		Y	5,000,000
iShares Edge MSCI USA Size Factor Index Fund Inst Shares	BISFX	NAS CM	Open End	US Equity Large Cap Blend (Growth & Income)	D-	D+	A		Y	2,000,000
iShares Edge MSCI USA Value Factor Index Fund Class K	BKVFX	NAS CM	Open End	US Equity Large Cap Value (Growth & Income)	D-	D+	B+		Y	5,000,000
iShares Edge MSCI USA Value Factor Index Fund Inst Shares	BIVFX	NAS CM	Open End	US Equity Large Cap Value (Growth & Income)	D-	D+	B+		Y	2,000,000
iShares MSCI Asia ex Japan Index Fund Class K	BAJKX	NAS CM	Open End	Asia ex-Japan Equity (Growth & Income)	C	B-	B-	Up	Y	5,000,000
iShares MSCI Asia ex Japan Index Fund Institutional Shares	BAJIX	NAS CM	Open End	Asia ex-Japan Equity (Growth & Income)	C	B-	B-	Up	Y	2,000,000
iShares MSCI Developed World Index Fund Class K	BWIKX	NAS CM	Open End	Global Equity (World Stock)	C	C+	B	Up	Y	5,000,000
iShares MSCI Developed World Index Fund Inst Shares	BWIIX	NAS CM	Open End	Global Equity (World Stock)	C	C+	B	Up	Y	2,000,000
iShares MSCI EAFE International Index Fund Class K	BTMKX	NAS CM	Open End	Global Equity Large Cap (Foreign Stock)	B-	C+	B	Up	Y	5,000,000
iShares MSCI EAFE Intl Index Fund Inst Shares	MAIIX	NAS CM	Open End	Global Equity Large Cap (Foreign Stock)	B-	C+	B	Up	Y	2,000,000
iShares MSCI EAFE Intl Index Fund Inv A Shares	MDIIX	NAS CM	Open End	Global Equity Large Cap (Foreign Stock)	B-	C+	B	Up	Y	1,000
iShares MSCI Total International Index Fund Class K	BDOKX	NAS CM	Open End	Global Equity Large Cap (Foreign Stock)	B-	B-	B-	Up	Y	5,000,000
iShares MSCI Total Intl Index Fund Inst Shares	BDOIX	NAS CM	Open End	Global Equity Large Cap (Foreign Stock)	B-	B-	B-	Up	Y	2,000,000
iShares MSCI Total Intl Index Fund Inv A Shares	BDOAX	NAS CM	Open End	Global Equity Large Cap (Foreign Stock)	B-	B-	B-	Up	Y	1,000
iShares Russell 1000 Large-Cap Index Fund Class K	BRGKX	NAS CM	Open End	US Equity Large Cap Blend (Growth)	B	B	B		Y	5,000,000
iShares Russell 1000 Large-Cap Index Fund Inst Shares	BRGNX	NAS CM	Open End	US Equity Large Cap Blend (Growth)	B	B	B		Y	2,000,000
iShares Russell 1000 Large-Cap Index Fund Inv A Shares	BRGAX	NAS CM	Open End	US Equity Large Cap Blend (Growth)	B	B	B		Y	1,000
iShares Russell 2000 Small-Cap Index Fund Class K	BDBKX	NAS CM	Open End	US Equity Small Cap (Small Company)	B+	A-	B	Up	Y	5,000,000
iShares Russell 2000 Small-Cap Index Fund Inst Shares	MASKX	NAS CM	Open End	US Equity Small Cap (Small Company)	B+	A-	B	Up	Y	2,000,000
iShares Russell 2000 Small-Cap Index Fund Inv A Shares	MDSKX	NAS CM	Open End	US Equity Small Cap (Small Company)	B+	A-	B	Up	Y	1,000
iShares Russell Mid-Cap Index Fund Class K	BRMKX	NAS CM	Open End	US Equity Mid Cap (Growth)	C+	C+	B-	Up	Y	5,000,000
iShares Russell Mid-Cap Index Fund Institutional Shares	BRMIX	NAS CM	Open End	US Equity Mid Cap (Growth)	C+	C+	B-	Up	Y	2,000,000
iShares Russell Mid-Cap Index Fund Investor A Shares	BRMAX	NAS CM	Open End	US Equity Mid Cap (Growth)	C+	C+	B-	Up	Y	1,000
iShares Russell Small/Mid-Cap Index Fund Class K	BSMKX	NAS CM	Open End	US Equity Small Cap (Growth & Income)	C	C+	B	Up	Y	5,000,000
iShares Russell Small/Mid-Cap Index Fund Inst Shares	BSMIX	NAS CM	Open End	US Equity Small Cap (Growth & Income)	C	C+	B	Up	Y	2,000,000
iShares Russell Small/Mid-Cap Index Fund Investor A Shares	BSMAX	NAS CM	Open End	US Equity Small Cap (Growth & Income)	C	C+	B	Up	Y	1,000
iShares S&P 500 Index Fund Class K	WFSPX	NAS CM	Open End	US Equity Large Cap Blend (Growth & Income)	B	B	B		Y	5,000,000
iShares S&P 500 Index Fund Institutional Shares	BSPIX	NAS CM	Open End	US Equity Large Cap Blend (Growth & Income)	B	B	B		Y	2,000,000
iShares S&P 500 Index Fund Investor A Shares	BSPAX	NAS CM	Open End	US Equity Large Cap Blend (Growth & Income)	B	B	B		Y	1,000
iShares S&P 500 Index Fund Investor C1 Shares	BSPZX	NAS CM	Open End	US Equity Large Cap Blend (Growth & Income)	B-	B-	B	Down	Y	1,000
iShares S&P 500 Index Fund Service Shares	BSPSX	NAS CM	Open End	US Equity Large Cap Blend (Growth & Income)	B	B	B		Y	5,000
iShares Total U.S. Stock Market Index Fund Class K	BKTSX	NAS CM	Open End	US Equity Large Cap Blend (Growth)	C	C+	B+	Up	Y	5,000,000
iShares Total U.S. Stock Mkt Index Fund Inst Shares	BITSX	NAS CM	Open End	US Equity Large Cap Blend (Growth)	C	C+	B+	Up	Y	2,000,000
iShares Total U.S. Stock Mkt Index Fund Inv A Shares	BASMX	NAS CM	Open End	US Equity Large Cap Blend (Growth)	C	C+	B+	Up	Y	1,000
Issachar Fund Class N	LIONX	NAS CM	Open End	Moderate Alloc (Growth)	C+	C	B		Y	1,000
IVA International Fund Class A	IVIOX	NAS CM	Open End	Global Equity Mid/Small Cap (Growth)	B	C+	B+	Up		5,000
IVA International Fund Class C	IVICX	NAS CM	Open End	Global Equity Mid/Small Cap (Growth)	B	C+	B+	Up		5,000
IVA International Fund Class I	IVIQX	NAS CM	Open End	Global Equity Mid/Small Cap (Growth)	B	C+	B+	Up		1,000,000

★ Expanded analysis of this fund is included in Section II.

	TOTAL RETURNS					PERFORMANCE				ASSETS		ASSET ALLOCATION & TURNOVER					BULL & BEAR		FEES		
Min Additional Investment	3-Month Total Return	6-Month Total Return	1-Year Total Return	3-Year Total Return	5-Year Total Return	Dividend Yield (TTM)	Expense Ratio	3-Yr Std Deviation	3-Year Beta	NAV	Total Assets (MIL)	%Cash	%Stocks	%Bonds	%Other	Turnover Ratio	Last Bull Market Total Return	Last Bear Market Total Return	Front End Fee (%)	Back End Fee (%)	Inception Date
	3.51	5.33	10.82			2.3	0.31			10.5	1,524	1	98	0	1	11					Aug-15
50	3.47	5.23	10.69			2.08	0.51			10.48	1,524	1	98	0	1	11					Aug-15
	3.27	6.11	21.15			2.9	0.19			10.88	140.0	1	99	0	0	48					Jul-16
	3.26	6.09	21.12			2.87	0.24			10.88	140.0	1	99	0	0	48					Jul-16
	5.22	8.80	19.02			1.94	0.13			11.24	12.0	0	100	0	0	25					Jul-16
	5.21	8.78	18.98			1.92	0.18			11.24	12.0	0	100	0	0	25					Jul-16
	4.82	11.95	28.52			2.45	0.3			12.43	12.6	1	98	0	1	44					Jul-16
	4.81	12.02	28.48			2.42	0.35			12.43	12.6	1	98	0	1	44					Jul-16
	6.65	11.76	21.08			1.86	0.2			12.29	12.9	0	100	0	0	43					Jul-16
	6.63	11.73	21.04			1.83	0.25			12.29	12.9	0	100	0	0	43					Jul-16
	7.95	16.48	37.30				0.15			12.62	13.5	0	100	0	0	68					Dec-16
	7.93	16.44	37.24				0.2			12.62	13.5	0	100	0	0	68					Dec-16
	7.85	13.45	25.15				0.15			11.67	12.0	0	100	0	0	18					Dec-16
	7.82	13.41	25.09				0.2			11.67	12.0	0	100	0	0	18					Dec-16
	5.86	8.90	18.90				0.15			11.44	11.5	0	100	0	0	9					Dec-16
	5.84	8.86	18.84				0.2			11.44	11.5	0	100	0	0	9					Dec-16
	8.66	14.87	21.95				0.15			11.64	11.6	0	100	0	0	10					Dec-16
	8.54	14.73	21.79				0.2			11.63	11.6	0	100	0	0	10					Dec-16
	7.07	14.58	40.26			1.74	0.46			11.93	37.5	1	99	0	0	1					Nov-15
	7.16	14.58	40.26			1.73	0.51			11.93	37.5	1	99	0	0	1					Jun-15
	5.34	10.42	22.71			1.82	0.15			11.85	841.3	1	99	0	0	6					Nov-15
	5.42	10.49	22.67			1.79	0.2			11.84	841.3	1	99	0	0	6					Jun-15
	3.80	9.18	25.17	24.72	44.73	2.29	0.06	11.52	0.93	14.18	10,415	1	96	0	3	42	13.19	-23.36			Mar-11
	3.77	9.15	25.24	24.72	44.54	2.26	0.12	11.55	0.93	14.18	10,415	1	96	0	3	42	13.33	-23.44			Apr-97
50	3.72	9.05	24.84	23.66	42.58	2.09	0.37	11.52	0.93	14.09	10,415	1	96	0	3	42	13.13	-23.51			Apr-97
	4.50	11.02	27.61	24.98	37.57	2.34	0.11	11.7	0.95	9.82	607.4	1	99	0	0	15	13.13				Jun-11
	4.51	10.97	27.56	24.75	37.28	2.37	0.16	11.79	0.95	9.54	607.4	1	99	0	0	15	13.12				Jun-11
50	4.45	10.85	27.32	23.83	35.56	2.15	0.41	11.76	0.95	9.52	607.4	1	99	0	0	15	12.92				Jun-11
	6.54	11.31	21.59	35.96	109.65	1.64	0.08	10.19	1	17.76	205.4	1	100	0	0	13	25.45	-17.15			Mar-11
	6.50	11.25	21.45	35.65	109.78	1.6	0.13	10.14	1	17.82	205.4	1	100	0	0	13	25.42	-17.17			Mar-11
50	6.46	11.10	21.15	34.60	106.56	1.41	0.38	10.14	1	17.72	205.4	1	100	0	0	13	25.26	-17.27			Mar-11
	3.29	9.22	14.68	32.13	98.28	0.94	0.08	14.1	1	19.77	873.8	1	99	0	0	39	27.79	-25.26			Mar-11
	3.31	9.14	14.55	31.87	97.80	0.92	0.13	14.13	1	19.72	873.8	1	99	0	0	39	27.66	-25.28			Apr-97
50	3.24	9.06	14.34	31.00	95.40	0.73	0.38	14.14	1	19.74	873.8	1	99	0	0	39	27.44	-25.3			Apr-97
	6.05	9.75	18.39			2.34	0.07			10.27	832.4	1	99	0	0	41					May-15
	6.04	9.67	18.29			2.33	0.12			10.25	832.4	1	99	0	0	41					May-15
50	5.95	9.54	18.05			2.21	0.34			10.22	832.4	1	99	0	0	41					Nov-15
	5.29	10.29	16.74			1.32	0.08			12.34	93.9	0	100	0	0	48					Aug-15
	5.26	10.26	16.69			1.29	0.13			12.34	93.9	0	100	0	0	48					Aug-15
50	5.15	10.09	16.37			1.1	0.38			12.32	93.9	0	100	0	0	48					Aug-15
	6.64	11.40	21.77	36.70	111.02	1.72	0.04	10.09	1	318.38	12,674	1	99	0	0	4	25	-16.31			Jul-93
	6.61	11.36	21.68	36.41	110.32	1.65	0.11	10.09	1	318.31	12,674	1	99	0	0	4	25	-16.31			Apr-13
50	6.55	11.22	21.38	35.39	107.71	1.44	0.36	10.09	1	318.24	12,674	1	99	0	0	4	24.82	-16.39			Apr-13
50	6.36	10.83	20.51	32.49	100.39	0.67	1.08	10.08	1	318.76	12,674	1	99	0	0	4	24.35	-16.62		1.00	Apr-13
	6.59	11.30	21.54	35.93	109.04	1.55	0.23	10.09	1	318.3	12,674	1	99	0	0	4	24.89	-16.36			Apr-13
	6.33	11.15	21.01			1.71	0.03			12.79	707.1	1	99	0	0	1					Aug-15
	6.31	11.12	20.98			1.69	0.08			12.79	707.1	1	99	0	0	1					Aug-15
50	6.19	10.95	20.64			1.5	0.33			12.77	707.1	1	99	0	0	1					Aug-15
100	-1.72	-2.63	0.62	5.50		1.72	2.58	3.84	-0.05	9.98	12.2	101	0	0	-1	779					Feb-14
100	2.37	6.08	16.98	20.96	42.34	0.17	1.24	6.28	0.49	17.83	4,237	28	62	3	7	23	5.89	-9.69	5.00		Oct-08
100	2.20	5.67	16.16	18.31	37.18	0	1.99	6.26	0.48	17.54	4,237	28	62	3	7	23	5.37	-9.97		1.00	Oct-08
100	2.44	6.14	17.24	21.84	44.18	0.38	0.99	6.25	0.48	17.84	4,237	28	62	3	7	23	5.96	-9.56			Oct-08

	MARKET			FUND TYPE, CATEGORY & OBJECTIVE	RATINGS					MINIMUMS
Fund Name	Ticker Symbol	Traded On	Fund Type	Category and (Prospectus Objective)	Overall Rating	Reward Rating	Risk Rating	Recent Up/ Downgrade	Open to New Investors	Min Initial Investment
IVA Worldwide Fund Class A	IVWAX	NAS CM	Open End	Alloc (Growth)	B-	C+	B	Up		5,000
IVA Worldwide Fund Class C	IVWCX	NAS CM	Open End	Alloc (Growth)	B-	C+	B	Up		5,000
IVA Worldwide Fund Class I	IVWIX	NAS CM	Open End	Alloc (Growth)	B-	C+	B	Up		1,000,000
Ivy Advantus Real Estate Securities Fund Class A	IRSAX	NAS CM	Open End	Real Estate Sector Equity (Real Estate)	B-	C+	B		Y	750
Ivy Advantus Real Estate Securities Fund Class B	IRSBX	NAS CM	Open End	Real Estate Sector Equity (Real Estate)	B-	C+	B	Up		750
Ivy Advantus Real Estate Securities Fund Class C	IRSCX	NAS CM	Open End	Real Estate Sector Equity (Real Estate)	B-	C+	B	Up	Y	750
Ivy Advantus Real Estate Securities Fund Class E	IREEX	NAS CM	Open End	Real Estate Sector Equity (Real Estate)	B-	C+	B		Y	250
Ivy Advantus Real Estate Securities Fund Class I	IREIX	NAS CM	Open End	Real Estate Sector Equity (Real Estate)	B-	C+	B+		Y	0
Ivy Advantus Real Estate Securities Fund Class N	IRSEX	NAS CM	Open End	Real Estate Sector Equity (Real Estate)	B-	C+	B+		Y	1,000,000
Ivy Advantus Real Estate Securities Fund Class R	IRSRX	NAS CM	Open End	Real Estate Sector Equity (Real Estate)	B-	C+	B	Up	Y	0
Ivy Advantus Real Estate Securities Fund Class Y	IRSYX	NAS CM	Open End	Real Estate Sector Equity (Real Estate)	B-	C+	B		Y	0
Ivy Apollo Multi-Asset Income Fund Class A	IMAAX	NAS CM	Open End	Cautious Alloc (Income)	C	C	B	Up	Y	750
Ivy Apollo Multi-Asset Income Fund Class C	IMACX	NAS CM	Open End	Cautious Alloc (Income)	C	C	B	Up	Y	750
Ivy Apollo Multi-Asset Income Fund Class I	IMAIX	NAS CM	Open End	Cautious Alloc (Income)	C	C	B	Up	Y	0
Ivy Apollo Multi-Asset Income Fund Class N	IMURX	NAS CM	Open End	Cautious Alloc (Income)	C	C	B	Up	Y	1,000,000
Ivy Apollo Multi-Asset Income Fund Class Y	IMAYX	NAS CM	Open End	Cautious Alloc (Income)	C	C	B	Up	Y	0
Ivy Asset Strategy Fund Class A	WASAX	NAS CM	Open End	Alloc (Asset Alloc)	C	C	C+	Up	Y	750
Ivy Asset Strategy Fund Class B	WASBX	NAS CM	Open End	Alloc (Asset Alloc)	C	C	C+	Up		750
Ivy Asset Strategy Fund Class C	WASCX	NAS CM	Open End	Alloc (Asset Alloc)	C	C	C+	Up	Y	750
Ivy Asset Strategy Fund Class E	IASEX	NAS CM	Open End	Alloc (Asset Alloc)	C	C	C+	Up	Y	250
Ivy Asset Strategy Fund Class I	IVAEX	NAS CM	Open End	Alloc (Asset Alloc)	C	C	C+	Up	Y	0
Ivy Asset Strategy Fund Class N	IASTX	NAS CM	Open End	Alloc (Asset Alloc)	C+	C	C+	Up	Y	1,000,000
Ivy Asset Strategy Fund Class R	IASRX	NAS CM	Open End	Alloc (Asset Alloc)	C	C	C+	Up	Y	0
Ivy Asset Strategy Fund Class Y	WASYX	NAS CM	Open End	Alloc (Asset Alloc)	C	C	C+	Up	Y	0
Ivy Balanced Fund Class A	IBNAX	NAS CM	Open End	Moderate Alloc (Balanced)	B-	C+	B+	Down	Y	750
Ivy Balanced Fund Class B	IBNBX	NAS CM	Open End	Moderate Alloc (Balanced)	B-	C	B+	Up		750
Ivy Balanced Fund Class C	IBNCX	NAS CM	Open End	Moderate Alloc (Balanced)	B-	C	B+	Up	Y	750
Ivy Balanced Fund Class I	IYBIX	NAS CM	Open End	Moderate Alloc (Balanced)	B	C+	B+	Up	Y	0
Ivy Balanced Fund Class N	IBARX	NAS CM	Open End	Moderate Alloc (Balanced)	B	C+	A-	Up	Y	1,000,000
Ivy Balanced Fund Class R	IYBFX	NAS CM	Open End	Moderate Alloc (Balanced)	B-	C	B+	Up	Y	0
Ivy Balanced Fund Class Y	IBNYX	NAS CM	Open End	Moderate Alloc (Balanced)	B-	C+	B+	Down	Y	0
Ivy Core Equity Fund Class A	WCEAX	NAS CM	Open End	US Equity Large Cap Growth (Growth)	B	C+	B	Up	Y	750
Ivy Core Equity Fund Class B	WCEBX	NAS CM	Open End	US Equity Large Cap Growth (Growth)	B-	C+	B	Down		750
Ivy Core Equity Fund Class C	WTRCX	NAS CM	Open End	US Equity Large Cap Growth (Growth)	C+	C+	B-	Down	Y	750
Ivy Core Equity Fund Class E	ICFEX	NAS CM	Open End	US Equity Large Cap Growth (Growth)	B-	C+	B-	Down	Y	250
Ivy Core Equity Fund Class I	ICIEX	NAS CM	Open End	US Equity Large Cap Growth (Growth)	B-	B-	B-	Down	Y	0
Ivy Core Equity Fund Class N	ICEQX	NAS CM	Open End	US Equity Large Cap Growth (Growth)	B-	B-	B-	Down	Y	1,000,000
Ivy Core Equity Fund Class R	IYCEX	NAS CM	Open End	US Equity Large Cap Growth (Growth)	B-	C+	B-	Down	Y	0
Ivy Core Equity Fund Class Y	WCEYX	NAS CM	Open End	US Equity Large Cap Growth (Growth)	B-	B-	B-	Down	Y	0
Ivy Cundill Global Value Fund Class A	ICDAX	NAS CM	Open End	Global Equity (World Stock)	C+	C+	C	Up	Y	750
Ivy Cundill Global Value Fund Class B	ICDBX	NAS CM	Open End	Global Equity (World Stock)	C+	C+	C	Up		750
Ivy Cundill Global Value Fund Class C	ICDCX	NAS CM	Open End	Global Equity (World Stock)	C+	C+	C	Up	Y	750
Ivy Cundill Global Value Fund Class I	ICVIX	NAS CM	Open End	Global Equity (World Stock)	C+	C+	C+	Up	Y	0
Ivy Cundill Global Value Fund Class N	ICNGX	NAS CM	Open End	Global Equity (World Stock)	C+	C+	C+	Up	Y	1,000,000
Ivy Cundill Global Value Fund Class R	IYCUX	NAS CM	Open End	Global Equity (World Stock)	C+	C+	C	Up	Y	0
Ivy Cundill Global Value Fund Class Y	ICDYX	NAS CM	Open End	Global Equity (World Stock)	C+	C+	C	Up	Y	0
Ivy Dividend Opportunities Fund Class A	IVDAX	NAS CM	Open End	US Equity Large Cap Blend (Growth & Income)	B-	C+	B-	Down	Y	750
Ivy Dividend Opportunities Fund Class B	IVDBX	NAS CM	Open End	US Equity Large Cap Blend (Growth & Income)	C+	C+	B-	Down		750
Ivy Dividend Opportunities Fund Class C	IVDCX	NAS CM	Open End	US Equity Large Cap Blend (Growth & Income)	C+	C+	B-	Down	Y	750
Ivy Dividend Opportunities Fund Class E	IDIEX	NAS CM	Open End	US Equity Large Cap Blend (Growth & Income)	B-	C+	B-	Down	Y	250
Ivy Dividend Opportunities Fund Class I	IVDIX	NAS CM	Open End	US Equity Large Cap Blend (Growth & Income)	B-	C+	B-	Down	Y	0
Ivy Dividend Opportunities Fund Class N	IDOTX	NAS CM	Open End	US Equity Large Cap Blend (Growth & Income)	B-	C+	B-	Down	Y	1,000,000

★Expanded analysis of this fund is included in Section II.

	TOTAL RETURNS					PERFORMANCE				ASSETS		ASSET ALLOCATION & TURNOVER					BULL & BEAR		FEES		
Min Additional Investment	3-Month Total Return	6-Month Total Return	1-Year Total Return	3-Year Total Return	5-Year Total Return	Dividend Yield (TTM)	Expense Ratio	3-Yr Std Deviation	3-Year Beta	NAV	Total Assets (MIL)	%Cash	%Stocks	%Bonds	%Other	Turnover Ratio	Last Bull Market Total Return	Last Bear Market Total Return	Front End Fee (%)	Back End Fee (%)	Inception Date
100	2.70	5.77	13.54	17.11	42.86	0	1.25	5.18	0.46	18.87	8,328	40	51	2	6	14	8.8	-11.74	5.00		Oct-08
100	2.52	5.35	12.71	14.50	37.62	0	2	5.13	0.46	18.49	8,328	40	51	2	6	14	8.39	-12.05		1.00	Oct-08
100	2.77	5.94	13.83	17.98	44.73	0	1	5.15	0.46	18.92	8,328	40	51	2	6	14	9.02	-11.67			Oct-08
	2.00	2.15	5.26	12.57	51.27	0.82	1.43	13.59	1.02	24.19	554.4	0	98	0	2	77	31.54	-18.22	5.75		Feb-99
	1.75	1.68	4.27	9.52	44.18	0.22	2.34	13.59	1.02	23.29	554.4	0	98	0	2	77	30.69	-18.6		5.00	Dec-03
	1.78	1.74	4.42	10.09	45.79	0.35	2.16	13.6	1.02	23.66	554.4	0	98	0	2	77	30.95	-18.48		1.00	Dec-03
	2.00	2.15	5.26	12.41	50.60	0.79	1.43	13.6	1.02	24.19	554.4	0	98	0	2	77	31.64	-18.22	2.50		Apr-07
	2.08	2.32	5.63	13.92	54.67	1.11	1.05	13.62	1.02	24.35	554.4	0	98	0	2	77	32.01	-18.03			Apr-07
	2.12	2.41	5.81	14.47	54.20	1.28	0.87	13.64	1.02	24.38	554.4	0	98	0	2	77	31.54	-18.22			Jul-14
	1.93	2.03	4.98	11.86	49.93	0.67	1.64	13.61	1.02	24.16	554.4	0	98	0	2	77	31.56	-18.22			Dec-05
	2.04	2.23	5.43	13.16	52.93	0.92	1.26	13.61	1.02	24.22	554.4	0	98	0	2	77	31.8	-18.06			Dec-03
	2.16	5.39	10.49			2.72	1.3			11.04	566.5	5	49	44	2	84			5.75		Oct-15
	1.94	4.98	9.68			2.1	2.01			11.04	566.5	5	49	44	2	84				1.00	Oct-15
	2.23	5.55	10.81			3.02	0.93			11.04	566.5	5	49	44	2	84					Oct-15
	2.24	5.51	10.98			3.2	0.89			11.04	566.5	5	49	44	2	84					Oct-15
	2.17	5.42	10.56			2.78	1.25			11.04	566.5	5	49	44	2	84					Oct-15
	4.51	9.74	18.36	1.69	23.31	0	1.12	8.85	0.74	23.86	3,572	9	76	9	6	51	23.32	-22.07	5.75		Jul-00
	4.26	9.27	17.48	-0.59	18.74	0	1.83	8.87	0.74	22.43	3,572	9	76	9	6	51	22.77	-22.34		5.00	Jul-00
	4.29	9.32	17.53	-0.48	18.97	0	1.83	8.86	0.74	22.6	3,572	9	76	9	6	51	22.81	-22.31		1.00	Apr-95
	4.54	9.79	18.54	1.83	23.47	0	1.03	8.87	0.74	23.93	3,572	9	76	9	6	51	23.31	-22.09	2.50		Apr-07
	4.57	9.91	18.75	2.51	24.89	0	0.85	8.86	0.74	24.15	3,572	9	76	9	6	51	23.52	-22.02			Apr-07
	4.58	9.95	18.86	2.89	23.61	0	0.69	8.89	0.74	24.2	3,572	9	76	9	6	51	22.81	-22.31			Jul-14
	4.39	9.54	18.03	0.65	21.21	0	1.43	8.87	0.74	23.59	3,572	9	76	9	6	51	23.1	-22.2			Jul-08
	4.53	9.74	18.45	1.75	23.43	0	1.08	8.87	0.74	23.92	3,572	9	76	9	6	51	23.33	-22.1			Dec-95
	3.80	5.15	11.38	12.59	51.64	1.73	1.11	7.46	0.69	24.89	1,897	2	62	24	0	47	18.74	-11.74	5.75		Nov-87
	3.64	4.81	10.60	10.22	46.20	1.07	1.84	7.44	0.69	24.64	1,897	2	62	24	0	47	18.25	-12.04		5.00	Dec-03
	3.64	4.77	10.59	10.32	46.47	1.09	1.8	7.46	0.69	24.72	1,897	2	62	24	0	47	18.22	-11.96		1.00	Dec-03
	3.91	5.29	11.65	13.51	53.64	1.97	0.85	7.48	0.7	24.89	1,897	2	62	24	0	47	18.93	-11.62			Apr-07
	3.94	5.35	11.85	14.00	53.77	2.11	0.7	7.46	0.69	24.93	1,897	2	62	24	0	47	18.74	-11.74			Jul-14
	3.76	5.00	11.02	11.51	49.14	1.42	1.44	7.44	0.69	24.86	1,897	2	62	24	0	47	18.57	-11.83			Dec-12
	3.85	5.16	11.38	12.66	51.76	1.73	1.1	7.47	0.69	24.9	1,897	2	62	24	0	47	18.77	-11.72			Dec-03
	6.27	13.46	20.38	22.79	82.08	0.37	1.15	11.31	1.06	14.62	4,815	0	98	1	1	90	26.64	-17.25	5.75		Jul-00
	5.91	12.88	19.18	19.29	73.45	0	2.13	11.25	1.05	12.11	4,815	0	98	1	1	90	25.75	-17.57		5.00	Jul-00
	6.03	12.95	19.44	20.04	75.14	0	1.92	11.27	1.06	12.58	4,815	0	98	1	1	90	25.94	-17.44		1.00	Sep-92
	6.29	13.43	20.38	22.55	81.01	0.33	1.13	11.25	1.06	14.56	4,815	0	98	1	1	90	26.62	-17.27	2.50		Apr-07
	6.34	13.59	20.81	23.90	84.92	0.77	0.84	11.26	1.06	16.3	4,815	0	98	1	1	90	26.83	-17.12			Apr-07
	6.35	13.67	20.88	24.28	82.26	0.9	0.76	11.26	1.06	16.32	4,815	0	98	1	1	90	25.94	-17.44			Jul-14
	6.13	13.21	19.98	21.52	78.91	0.08	1.51	11.27	1.06	14.52	4,815	0	98	1	1	90	25.94	-17.44			Dec-12
	6.21	13.51	20.67	23.83	84.73	0.78	0.84	11.3	1.06	15.83	4,815	0	98	1	1	90	26.65	-17.13			Dec-95
	5.17	10.53	16.27	14.60	43.92	0.31	1.65	13.97	1.2	18.9	197.2	0	96	0	0	51	15.16	-23.54	5.75		Sep-01
	4.76	9.80	14.72	10.29	35.49	0	2.94	13.98	1.2	17.14	197.2	0	96	0	0	51	14.55	-23.84		5.00	Sep-01
	4.95	10.21	15.56	12.62	39.72	0	2.21	14	1.2	17.79	197.2	0	96	0	0	51	14.85	-23.73		1.00	Oct-01
	5.21	10.76	16.72	16.18	47.36	0.71	1.17	13.98	1.2	19.3	197.2	0	96	0	0	51	15.6	-23.36			Apr-07
	5.26	10.85	16.94	16.76	46.88	0.82	1	14.01	1.2	19.34	197.2	0	96	0	0	51	15.16	-23.54			Jul-14
	5.06	10.43	16.03	14.19	43.08	0.25	1.75	14.01	1.2	18.87	197.2	0	96	0	0	51	14.99	-23.62			Dec-12
	5.19	10.61	16.47	15.29	45.44	0.51	1.41	13.99	1.2	19.15	197.2	0	96	0	0	51	15.71	-23.4			Jul-03
	4.24	8.64	15.28	19.31	73.51	1.39	1.26	10.09	0.96	18.86	901.1	3	97	0	0	54	26.91	-23.49	5.75		Jul-03
	4.06	8.25	14.46	16.61	66.78	0.67	2.04	10.12	0.96	18.5	901.1	3	97	0	0	54	26.27	-23.8		5.00	Jul-03
	4.13	8.32	14.53	16.96	67.83	0.76	1.93	10.12	0.96	18.61	901.1	3	97	0	0	54	26.39	-23.72		1.00	Jul-03
	4.29	8.76	15.41	19.45	73.25	1.51	1.13	10.14	0.96	18.79	901.1	3	97	0	0	54	26.8	-23.53	2.50		Apr-07
	4.36	8.88	15.69	20.48	76.26	1.67	0.95	10.13	0.96	18.94	901.1	3	97	0	0	54	27.1	-23.32			Apr-07
	4.40	8.92	15.84	20.99	76.28	1.83	0.8	10.1	0.96	18.97	901.1	3	97	0	0	54	26.91	-23.49			Jul-14

	MARKET			FUND TYPE, CATEGORY & OBJECTIVE	RATINGS				MINIMUMS	
Fund Name	Ticker Symbol	Traded On	Fund Type	Category and (Prospectus Objective)	Overall Rating	Reward Rating	Risk Rating	Recent Up/ Downgrade	Open to New Investors	Min Initial Investment
Ivy Dividend Opportunities Fund Class R	IYDVX	NAS CM	Open End	US Equity Large Cap Blend (Growth & Income)	C+	C+	B-	Down	Y	0
Ivy Dividend Opportunities Fund Class Y	IVDYX	NAS CM	Open End	US Equity Large Cap Blend (Growth & Income)	B-	C+	B-	Down	Y	0
Ivy Emerging Markets Equity Fund Class A	IPOAX	NAS CM	Open End	Emerging Markets Equity (Div Emerging Mkts)	B+	A	C+	Up	Y	750
Ivy Emerging Markets Equity Fund Class B	IPOBX	NAS CM	Open End	Emerging Markets Equity (Div Emerging Mkts)	B	A	C+	Up		750
Ivy Emerging Markets Equity Fund Class C	IPOCX	NAS CM	Open End	Emerging Markets Equity (Div Emerging Mkts)	B	A	C+	Up	Y	750
Ivy Emerging Markets Equity Fund Class I	IPOIX	NAS CM	Open End	Emerging Markets Equity (Div Emerging Mkts)	B+	A	C+	Up	Y	0
Ivy Emerging Markets Equity Fund Class N	IMEGX	NAS CM	Open End	Emerging Markets Equity (Div Emerging Mkts)	B+	A	C+	Up	Y	1,000,000
Ivy Emerging Markets Equity Fund Class R	IYPCX	NAS CM	Open End	Emerging Markets Equity (Div Emerging Mkts)	B	A	C+	Up	Y	0
Ivy Emerging Markets Equity Fund Class T	IPOTX	NAS CM	Open End	Emerging Markets Equity (Div Emerging Mkts)	B+	A	C+	Up	Y	0
Ivy Emerging Markets Equity Fund Class Y	IPOYX	NAS CM	Open End	Emerging Markets Equity (Div Emerging Mkts)	B+	A	C+	Up	Y	0
Ivy Energy Fund Class A	IEYAX	NAS CM	Open End	Energy Sector Equity (Natl Res)	D	D	D	Down	Y	750
Ivy Energy Fund Class B	IEYBX	NAS CM	Open End	Energy Sector Equity (Natl Res)	D	D	D	Down		750
Ivy Energy Fund Class C	IEYCX	NAS CM	Open End	Energy Sector Equity (Natl Res)	D	D	D	Down	Y	750
Ivy Energy Fund Class I	IVEIX	NAS CM	Open End	Energy Sector Equity (Natl Res)	D	D	D	Down	Y	0
Ivy Energy Fund Class N	IENRX	NAS CM	Open End	Energy Sector Equity (Natl Res)	D	D	D	Down	Y	1,000,000
Ivy Energy Fund Class R	IYEFX	NAS CM	Open End	Energy Sector Equity (Natl Res)	D	D	D	Down	Y	0
Ivy Energy Fund Class Y	IEYYX	NAS CM	Open End	Energy Sector Equity (Natl Res)	D	D	D	Down	Y	0
Ivy European Opportunities Fund Class A	IEOAX	NAS CM	Open End	Europe Equity Large Cap (Europe Stock)	B-	B-	C+	Up	Y	750
Ivy European Opportunities Fund Class B	IEOBX	NAS CM	Open End	Europe Equity Large Cap (Europe Stock)	C+	C+	C+	Up		750
Ivy European Opportunities Fund Class C	IEOCX	NAS CM	Open End	Europe Equity Large Cap (Europe Stock)	B-	B-	C+	Up	Y	750
Ivy European Opportunities Fund Class I	IEOIX	NAS CM	Open End	Europe Equity Large Cap (Europe Stock)	B-	B	C+	Up	Y	0
Ivy European Opportunities Fund Class N	IEURX	NAS CM	Open End	Europe Equity Large Cap (Europe Stock)	B-	B	C+	Up	Y	1,000,000
Ivy European Opportunities Fund Class R	IYEUX	NAS CM	Open End	Europe Equity Large Cap (Europe Stock)	B-	B-	C+	Up	Y	0
Ivy European Opportunities Fund Class Y	IEOYX	NAS CM	Open End	Europe Equity Large Cap (Europe Stock)	B-	B	C+	Up	Y	0
Ivy Global Equity Income Fund Class A	IBIAX	NAS CM	Open End	Global Equity (Growth & Income)	B-	C+	B-	Up	Y	750
Ivy Global Equity Income Fund Class B	IBIBX	NAS CM	Open End	Global Equity (Growth & Income)	C+	C+	B-	Down		750
Ivy Global Equity Income Fund Class C	IBICX	NAS CM	Open End	Global Equity (Growth & Income)	C+	C+	B-	Down	Y	750
Ivy Global Equity Income Fund Class I	IBIIX	NAS CM	Open End	Global Equity (Growth & Income)	B-	C+	B-	Up	Y	0
Ivy Global Equity Income Fund Class N	IICNX	NAS CM	Open End	Global Equity (Growth & Income)	B-	B-	B-	Up	Y	1,000,000
Ivy Global Equity Income Fund Class R	IYGEX	NAS CM	Open End	Global Equity (Growth & Income)	B-	C+	B-	Up	Y	0
Ivy Global Equity Income Fund Class Y	IBIYX	NAS CM	Open End	Global Equity (Growth & Income)	B-	C+	B-	Up	Y	0
Ivy Global Growth Fund Class A	IVINX	NAS CM	Open End	Global Equity (Growth)	B-	C+	B	Up	Y	750
Ivy Global Growth Fund Class B	IVIBX	NAS CM	Open End	Global Equity (Growth)	B-	C+	B	Up		750
Ivy Global Growth Fund Class C	IVNCX	NAS CM	Open End	Global Equity (Growth)	B-	C+	B	Up	Y	750
Ivy Global Growth Fund Class I	IGIIX	NAS CM	Open End	Global Equity (Growth)	B-	C+	B	Up	Y	0
Ivy Global Growth Fund Class N	ITGRX	NAS CM	Open End	Global Equity (Growth)	B-	B-	B	Up	Y	1,000,000
Ivy Global Growth Fund Class R	IYIGX	NAS CM	Open End	Global Equity (Growth)	B-	C+	B	Up	Y	0
Ivy Global Growth Fund Class Y	IVIYX	NAS CM	Open End	Global Equity (Growth)	B-	C+	B	Up	Y	0
Ivy Global Income Allocation Fund Class A	IVBAX	NAS CM	Open End	Alloc (Growth & Income)	B-	C+	B	Up	Y	750
Ivy Global Income Allocation Fund Class B	IVBBX	NAS CM	Open End	Alloc (Growth & Income)	C+	C+	B-	Down		750
Ivy Global Income Allocation Fund Class C	IVBCX	NAS CM	Open End	Alloc (Growth & Income)	C+	C+	B-	Down	Y	750
Ivy Global Income Allocation Fund Class E	IIBEX	NAS CM	Open End	Alloc (Growth & Income)	C+	C+	B-	Down	Y	250
Ivy Global Income Allocation Fund Class I	IIBIX	NAS CM	Open End	Alloc (Growth & Income)	C+	C+	B-	Down	Y	0
Ivy Global Income Allocation Fund Class N	ILIAX	NAS CM	Open End	Alloc (Growth & Income)	C+	C+	B-	Down	Y	1,000,000
Ivy Global Income Allocation Fund Class R	IYGBX	NAS CM	Open End	Alloc (Growth & Income)	C+	C+	B-	Down	Y	0
Ivy Global Income Allocation Fund Class Y	IVBYX	NAS CM	Open End	Alloc (Growth & Income)	C+	C+	B-	Down	Y	0
Ivy IG International Small Cap Fund Class A	IVJAX	NAS CM	Open End	Global Equity Mid/Small Cap (Small Company)	D-	D+	B+		Y	750
Ivy IG International Small Cap Fund Class C	IVJCX	NAS CM	Open End	Global Equity Mid/Small Cap (Small Company)	D-	D+	B+		Y	750
Ivy IG International Small Cap Fund Class I	IVJIX	NAS CM	Open End	Global Equity Mid/Small Cap (Small Company)	D-	D+	B+		Y	0
Ivy IG International Small Cap Fund Class N	IVJRX	NAS CM	Open End	Global Equity Mid/Small Cap (Small Company)	D-	D+	B+		Y	1,000,000
Ivy IG International Small Cap Fund Class Y	IVJYX	NAS CM	Open End	Global Equity Mid/Small Cap (Small Company)	D-	D+	B+		Y	0
Ivy International Core Equity Fund Class A	IVIAX	NAS CM	Open End	Global Equity Large Cap (Foreign Stock)	B-	C+	B	Up	Y	750

★ Expanded analysis of this fund is included in Section II.

	TOTAL RETURNS					PERFORMANCE				ASSETS		ASSET ALLOCATION & TURNOVER					BULL & BEAR		FEES		
Min Additional Investment	3-Month Total Return	6-Month Total Return	1-Year Total Return	3-Year Total Return	5-Year Total Return	Dividend Yield (TTM)	Expense Ratio	3-Yr Std Deviation	3-Year Beta	NAV	Total Assets (MIL)	%Cash	%Stocks	%Bonds	%Other	Turnover Ratio	Last Bull Market Total Return	Last Bear Market Total Return	Front End Fee (%)	Back End Fee (%)	Inception Date
	4.17	8.50	14.97	18.34	71.14	1.12	1.53	10.13	0.96	18.84	901.1	3	97	0	0	54	26.73	-23.57			Dec-12
	4.29	8.71	15.37	19.57	74.09	1.45	1.19	10.11	0.96	18.9	901.1	3	97	0	0	54	26.95	-23.43			Jul-03
	5.40	17.51	42.46	37.64	53.69	0	1.58	17.04	1.02	21.07	2,135	0	91	0	2	59	17.25	-30.01	5.75		Oct-93
	5.17	16.98	41.14	33.67	45.77	0	2.5	17.05	1.02	17.29	2,135	0	91	0	2	59	16.44	-30.31		5.00	Oct-93
	5.22	17.06	41.48	34.29	47.53	0	2.36	17.04	1.02	18.11	2,135	0	91	0	2	59	16.74	-30.21		1.00	Apr-96
	5.54	17.74	43.10	39.04	56.62	0	0.99	17.06	1.02	21.73	2,135	0	91	0	2	59	17.57	-29.82			Apr-07
	5.57	17.83	43.24	39.54	56.07	0	0.99	17.07	1.02	21.85	2,135	0	91	0	2	59	17.25	-30.01			Jul-14
	5.34	17.35	42.10	36.46	51.80	0	1.82	17.04	1.02	20.89	2,135	0	91	0	2	59	17.08	-30.08			Dec-12
	5.43	17.54	42.50	37.68	53.74		1.58	17.04	1.02	21.08	2,135	0	91	0	2	59	17.25	-30.01	2.50		Jul-17
	5.40	17.51	42.55	37.81	54.37	0	1.5	17.02	1.02	21.47	2,135	0	91	0	2	59	17.37	-29.9			Jul-03
	7.98	14.24	-13.09	-10.65	4.35	0	1.41	24.22	1.23	12.38	643.8	0	98	0	2	39	23.31	-31.66	5.75		Apr-06
	7.74	13.72	-13.83	-12.97	0.08	0	2.29	24.19	1.23	11.27	643.8	0	98	0	2	39	22.62	-31.87		5.00	Apr-06
	7.87	13.84	-13.65	-12.40	1.14	0	2.11	24.18	1.23	11.51	643.8	0	98	0	2	39	22.75	-31.84		1.00	Apr-06
	8.13	14.45	-12.74	-9.63	6.52	0	1.08	24.24	1.23	12.85	643.8	0	98	0	2	39	23.53	-31.51			Apr-07
	8.12	14.51	-12.66	-9.25	6.62	0	0.93	24.21	1.23	12.9	643.8	0	98	0	2	39	23.35	-31.61			Jul-14
	7.89	14.10	-13.31	-11.25	3.36	0	1.67	24.2	1.23	12.28	643.8	0	98	0	2	39	23.17	-31.68			Dec-12
	8.04	14.31	-12.97	-10.31	5.16	0	1.34	24.2	1.23	12.56	643.8	0	98	0	2	39	23.35	-31.61			Apr-06
	0.83	10.05	21.17	21.75	44.32	1.11	1.71	11.59	0.85	32.66	253.3	1	98	0	0	79	20.68	-26.73	5.75		May-99
	0.63	9.47	19.93	17.82	36.47	0.59	2.81	11.58	0.85	30.05	253.3	1	98	0	0	79	19.94	-26.99		5.00	May-99
	0.71	9.73	20.42	19.45	39.81	0.83	2.34	11.58	0.85	30.84	253.3	1	98	0	0	79	20.19	-26.92		1.00	Oct-99
	0.99	10.33	21.74	23.46	47.98	1.46	1.22	11.6	0.85	32.93	253.3	1	98	0	0	79	21.11	-26.5			Apr-07
	1.03	10.39	21.92	24.02	47.41	1.56	1.06	11.61	0.85	33.07	253.3	1	98	0	0	79	20.68	-26.73			Jul-14
	0.82	9.98	21.02	21.29	43.64	1.06	1.81	11.59	0.85	32.63	253.3	1	98	0	0	79	20.51	-26.81			Dec-12
	0.95	10.20	21.54	22.49	46.07	1.2	1.5	11.58	0.85	32.9	253.3	1	98	0	0	79	20.96	-26.61			Jul-03
	3.95	10.15	18.65	23.21	56.50	2.76	1.3	8.44	0.78	13.97	297.4	0	100	0	0	103			5.75		Jun-12
	3.71	9.81	17.82	20.77	51.20	2.18	1.95	8.43	0.78	13.96	297.4	0	100	0	0	103				5.00	Jun-12
	3.79	9.90	17.90	20.87	51.52	2.18	1.95	8.37	0.77	13.97	297.4	0	100	0	0	103				1.00	Jun-12
	4.03	10.40	19.01	24.48	59.36	3.06	0.96	8.45	0.78	13.98	297.4	0	100	0	0	103					Jun-12
	4.07	10.50	19.19	24.99	60.11	3.2	0.81	8.44	0.78	13.99	297.4	0	100	0	0	103					Jul-14
	3.88	10.09	18.32	22.24	54.35	2.53	1.56	8.42	0.78	13.98	297.4	0	100	0	0	103					Dec-12
	3.98	10.21	18.77	23.57	57.41	2.85	1.19	8.44	0.78	13.97	297.4	0	100	0	0	103					Jun-12
	4.23	10.57	24.36	23.19	49.82	0	1.48	10.94	0.96	45.51	439.8	0	96	1	2	66	20.21	-21.94	5.75		Apr-86
	4.01	10.10	23.06	19.28	42.29	0	2.67	10.95	0.96	38.53	439.8	0	96	1	2	66	19.53	-22.27		5.00	Oct-93
	4.04	10.15	23.47	20.48	44.26	0	2.21	10.94	0.96	38.95	439.8	0	96	1	2	66	19.6	-22.27		1.00	Apr-96
	4.30	10.73	24.75	24.50	52.57	0	1.11	10.95	0.96	46.41	439.8	0	96	1	2	66	20.48	-21.84			Apr-07
	4.35	10.82	24.96	25.11	52.47	0	0.95	10.95	0.96	46.64	439.8	0	96	1	2	66	20.21	-21.94			Jul-14
	4.17	10.43	24.06	22.33	48.13	0	1.69	10.95	0.96	45.2	439.8	0	96	1	2	66	20.02	-22.03			Dec-12
	4.26	10.61	24.44	23.56	50.64	0	1.36	10.95	0.96	45.73	439.8	0	96	1	2	66	20.32	-21.91			Jul-03
	3.35	5.68	13.73	17.13	33.17	3.6	1.46	8.08		15.6	686.5	1	60	26	1	70	10.63	-14.09	5.75		Sep-94
	3.11	5.26	12.74	14.05	27.42	2.86	2.33	8.08		15.3	686.5	1	60	26	1	70	10	-14.46		5.00	Dec-03
	3.15	5.34	13.05	14.89	29.05	3.08	2.08	8.07		15.4	686.5	1	60	26	1	70	10.24	-14.38		1.00	Dec-03
	3.32	5.64	13.67	16.87	32.96	3.56	1.49	8.06		15.6	686.5	1	60	26	1	70	10.72	-14.09	2.50		Apr-07
	3.46	5.86	14.12	18.34	35.70	3.89	1.12	8.09		15.74	686.5	1	60	26	1	70	10.91	-13.95			Apr-07
	3.50	5.94	14.29	18.87	35.44	4.04	0.96	8.1		15.75	686.5	1	60	26	1	70	10.63	-14.09			Jul-14
	3.27	5.53	13.45	16.20	31.59	3.37	1.7	8.07		15.59	686.5	1	60	26	1	70	10.47	-14.18			Dec-12
	3.41	5.82	13.92	17.56	34.12	3.69	1.35	8.08		15.68	686.5	1	60	26	1	70	10.79	-14.11			Dec-03
	5.96	14.10	28.17				1.45			12.76	143.0	0	94	4	0	38			5.75		Jan-17
	5.66	13.51	27.30				2.21			12.68	143.0	0	94	4	0	38				1.00	Jan-17
	5.98	14.20	28.52				1.15			12.77	143.0	0	94	4	0	38					Jan-17
	5.93	14.14	28.45				1.15			12.76	143.0	0	94	4	0	38					Jan-17
	5.88	14.01	28.07				1.45			12.75	143.0	0	94	4	0	38					Jan-17
	4.22	7.68	22.74	22.34	56.57	1.32	1.29	11.78	0.93	20.23	6,950	1	97	0	2	80	14.41	-24.58	5.75		May-97

Fund Name	Ticker Symbol	Traded On	Fund Type	Category and (Prospectus Objective)	Overall Rating	Reward Rating	Risk Rating	Recent Up/ Downgrade	Open to New Investors	Min Initial Investment
	MARKET		FUND TYPE, CATEGORY & OBJECTIVE		RATINGS				MINIMUMS	
Ivy International Core Equity Fund Class B	IIFBX	NAS CM	Open End	Global Equity Large Cap (Foreign Stock)	B-	C+	B-	Up		750
Ivy International Core Equity Fund Class C	IVIFX	NAS CM	Open End	Global Equity Large Cap (Foreign Stock)	B-	C+	B-	Up	Y	750
Ivy International Core Equity Fund Class E	IICEX	NAS CM	Open End	Global Equity Large Cap (Foreign Stock)	B-	C+	B	Up	Y	250
Ivy International Core Equity Fund Class I	ICEIX	NAS CM	Open End	Global Equity Large Cap (Foreign Stock)	B-	B-	B	Up	Y	0
Ivy International Core Equity Fund Class N	IINCX	NAS CM	Open End	Global Equity Large Cap (Foreign Stock)	B-	B-	B	Up	Y	1,000,000
Ivy International Core Equity Fund Class R	IYITX	NAS CM	Open End	Global Equity Large Cap (Foreign Stock)	B-	C+	B	Up	Y	0
Ivy International Core Equity Fund Class T	IICTX	NAS CM	Open End	Global Equity Large Cap (Foreign Stock)	B-	B-	B	Up	Y	0
Ivy International Core Equity Fund Class Y	IVVYX	NAS CM	Open End	Global Equity Large Cap (Foreign Stock)	B-	B-	B	Up	Y	0
Ivy Large Cap Growth Fund Class A	WLGAX	NAS CM	Open End	US Equity Large Cap Growth (Growth)	B+	A-	B	Up	Y	750
Ivy Large Cap Growth Fund Class B	WLGBX	NAS CM	Open End	US Equity Large Cap Growth (Growth)	B+	B+	B	Up		750
Ivy Large Cap Growth Fund Class C	WLGCX	NAS CM	Open End	US Equity Large Cap Growth (Growth)	A-	B+	A-	Up	Y	750
Ivy Large Cap Growth Fund Class E	ILCEX	NAS CM	Open End	US Equity Large Cap Growth (Growth)	A-	A-	A-	Up	Y	250
Ivy Large Cap Growth Fund Class I	IYGIX	NAS CM	Open End	US Equity Large Cap Growth (Growth)	B+	A-	B	Up	Y	0
Ivy Large Cap Growth Fund Class N	ILGRX	NAS CM	Open End	US Equity Large Cap Growth (Growth)	A-	A-	A-	Up	Y	1,000,000
Ivy Large Cap Growth Fund Class R	WLGRX	NAS CM	Open End	US Equity Large Cap Growth (Growth)	A-	A-	A-	Up	Y	0
Ivy Large Cap Growth Fund Class Y	WLGYX	NAS CM	Open End	US Equity Large Cap Growth (Growth)	A-	A-	A-	Up	Y	0
Ivy LaSalle Global Real Estate Fund Class A	IREAX	NAS CM	Open End	Real Estate Sector Equity (Real Estate)	B-	C	B	Up	Y	750
Ivy LaSalle Global Real Estate Fund Class B	IREBX	NAS CM	Open End	Real Estate Sector Equity (Real Estate)	C+	C	B-	Up		750
Ivy LaSalle Global Real Estate Fund Class C	IRECX	NAS CM	Open End	Real Estate Sector Equity (Real Estate)	C	C	C+		Y	750
Ivy LaSalle Global Real Estate Fund Class I	IRESX	NAS CM	Open End	Real Estate Sector Equity (Real Estate)	B-	C	B	Up	Y	0
Ivy LaSalle Global Real Estate Fund Class N	IRENX	NAS CM	Open End	Real Estate Sector Equity (Real Estate)	B-	C	B	Up	Y	1,000,000
Ivy LaSalle Global Real Estate Fund Class R	IRERX	NAS CM	Open End	Real Estate Sector Equity (Real Estate)	C+	C	B	Up	Y	0
Ivy LaSalle Global Real Estate Fund Class Y	IREYX	NAS CM	Open End	Real Estate Sector Equity (Real Estate)	B-	C	B	Up	Y	0
Ivy LaSalle Global Risk-Managed Real Estate Fund Class A	IVRAX	NAS CM	Open End	Real Estate Sector Equity (Real Estate)	C+	C	B-	Up	Y	750
Ivy LaSalle Global Risk-Managed Real Estate Fund Class B	IVRBX	NAS CM	Open End	Real Estate Sector Equity (Real Estate)	C	C	C	Down		750
Ivy LaSalle Global Risk-Managed Real Estate Fund Class C	IVRCX	NAS CM	Open End	Real Estate Sector Equity (Real Estate)	C	C	C	Down	Y	750
Ivy LaSalle Global Risk-Managed Real Estate Fund Class I	IVIRX	NAS CM	Open End	Real Estate Sector Equity (Real Estate)	C+	C	B	Up	Y	0
Ivy LaSalle Global Risk-Managed Real Estate Fund Class N	IVRNX	NAS CM	Open End	Real Estate Sector Equity (Real Estate)	C+	C	B-	Up	Y	1,000,000
Ivy LaSalle Global Risk-Managed Real Estate Fund Class R	IVRRX	NAS CM	Open End	Real Estate Sector Equity (Real Estate)	C+	C	C+	Up	Y	0
Ivy LaSalle Global Risk-Managed Real Estate Fund Class Y	IVRYX	NAS CM	Open End	Real Estate Sector Equity (Real Estate)	C+	C	B-	Up	Y	0
Ivy Managed International Opportunities Fund Class A	IVTAX	NAS CM	Open End	Global Equity Large Cap (Growth)	B-	B-	B	Up	Y	750
Ivy Managed International Opportunities Fund Class B	IVTBX	NAS CM	Open End	Global Equity Large Cap (Growth)	B-	C+	B-	Up		750
Ivy Managed International Opportunities Fund Class C	IVTCX	NAS CM	Open End	Global Equity Large Cap (Growth)	B-	C+	B-	Up	Y	750
Ivy Managed International Opportunities Fund Class I	IVTIX	NAS CM	Open End	Global Equity Large Cap (Growth)	B-	B-	B	Up	Y	0
Ivy Managed International Opportunities Fund Class N	IVTNX	NAS CM	Open End	Global Equity Large Cap (Growth)	C+	B-	C+		Y	1,000,000
Ivy Managed International Opportunities Fund Class R	IYMGX	NAS CM	Open End	Global Equity Large Cap (Growth)	B-	C+	B	Up	Y	0
Ivy Managed International Opportunities Fund Class Y	IVTYX	NAS CM	Open End	Global Equity Large Cap (Growth)	B-	B-	B	Up	Y	0
Ivy Micro Cap Growth Fund Class A	IGWAX	NAS CM	Open End	US Equity Small Cap (Growth)	C+	C+	C+	Up	Y	750
Ivy Micro Cap Growth Fund Class B	IGWBX	NAS CM	Open End	US Equity Small Cap (Growth)	C+	C+	C+	Up		750
Ivy Micro Cap Growth Fund Class C	IGWCX	NAS CM	Open End	US Equity Small Cap (Growth)	C+	C+	C+	Up	Y	750
Ivy Micro Cap Growth Fund Class I	IGWIX	NAS CM	Open End	US Equity Small Cap (Growth)	C+	C+	C+	Up	Y	0
Ivy Micro Cap Growth Fund Class N	IMIGX	NAS CM	Open End	US Equity Small Cap (Growth)	C+	C+	C+	Up	Y	1,000,000
Ivy Micro Cap Growth Fund Class R	IYMRX	NAS CM	Open End	US Equity Small Cap (Growth)	C+	C+	C+	Up	Y	0
Ivy Micro Cap Growth Fund Class Y	IGWYX	NAS CM	Open End	US Equity Small Cap (Growth)	C+	C+	C+	Up	Y	0
Ivy Mid Cap Growth Fund Class A	WMGAX	NAS CM	Open End	US Equity Mid Cap (Growth)	B-	B	C	Up	Y	750
Ivy Mid Cap Growth Fund Class B	WMGBX	NAS CM	Open End	US Equity Mid Cap (Growth)	C+	B-	C	Down		750
Ivy Mid Cap Growth Fund Class C	WMGCX	NAS CM	Open End	US Equity Mid Cap (Growth)	C+	B-	C	Down	Y	750
Ivy Mid Cap Growth Fund Class E	IMCEX	NAS CM	Open End	US Equity Mid Cap (Growth)	B-	B-	C	Up	Y	250
Ivy Mid Cap Growth Fund Class I	IYMIX	NAS CM	Open End	US Equity Mid Cap (Growth)	B-	B	C	Up	Y	0
Ivy Mid Cap Growth Fund Class N	IGRFX	NAS CM	Open End	US Equity Mid Cap (Growth)	B-	B	C	Up	Y	1,000,000
Ivy Mid Cap Growth Fund Class R	WMGRX	NAS CM	Open End	US Equity Mid Cap (Growth)	C+	B-	C	Down	Y	0
Ivy Mid Cap Growth Fund Class Y	WMGYX	NAS CM	Open End	US Equity Mid Cap (Growth)	B-	B	C	Up	Y	0

★Expanded analysis of this fund is included in Section II.

	TOTAL RETURNS					PERFORMANCE				ASSETS		ASSET ALLOCATION & TURNOVER					BULL & BEAR		FEES		
Min Additional Investment	3-Month Total Return	6-Month Total Return	1-Year Total Return	3-Year Total Return	5-Year Total Return	Dividend Yield (TTM)	Expense Ratio	3-Yr Std Deviation	3-Year Beta	NAV	Total Assets (MIL)	%Cash	%Stocks	%Bonds	%Other	Turnover Ratio	Last Bull Market Total Return	Last Bear Market Total Return	Front End Fee (%)	Back End Fee (%)	Inception Date
	3.97	7.12	21.63	19.02	49.80	0.73	2.22	11.74	0.93	17.97	6,950	1	97	0	2	80	13.75	-24.87		5.00	May-97
	4.04	7.24	21.88	19.82	51.36	0.93	1.97	11.75	0.93	18.02	6,950	1	97	0	2	80	13.93	-24.8		1.00	May-97
	4.20	7.58	22.67	21.96	55.73	1.26	1.28	11.78	0.93	20.36	6,950	1	97	0	2	80	14.35	-24.59	2.50		Apr-07
	4.29	7.78	23.11	23.52	59.19	1.58	0.97	11.79	0.93	20.33	6,950	1	97	0	2	80	14.66	-24.44			Apr-07
	4.32	7.85	23.28	24.05	59.09	1.69	0.82	11.76	0.93	20.39	6,950	1	97	0	2	80	14.41	-24.58			Jul-14
	4.16	7.51	22.43	21.37	54.61	1.11	1.56	11.76	0.93	20.23	6,950	1	97	0	2	80	14.24	-24.66			Dec-12
	4.32	7.84	22.93	22.53	56.81		1.29	11.78	0.93	20.25	6,950	1	97	0	2	80	14.41	-24.58	2.50		Jul-17
	4.25	7.68	22.78	22.52	57.18	1.36	1.24	11.77	0.93	20.36	6,950	1	97	0	2	80	14.49	-24.5			Jul-03
	6.09	14.25	29.03	38.30	114.73	0	1.15	11.28	1	21.76	1,889	0	97	0	3	43	27.14	-14.81	5.75		Jun-00
	5.86	13.79	27.95	34.59	105.15	0	2.08	11.33	1	16.81	1,889	0	97	0	3	43	26.36	-15.2		5.00	Jul-00
	5.89	13.83	28.17	35.33	107.03	0	1.87	11.3	1	18.16	1,889	0	97	0	3	43	26.58	-15.14		1.00	Jul-00
	6.05	14.21	29.01	38.21	114.67	0	1.15	11.29	1	21.73	1,889	0	97	0	3	43	27.16	-14.82	2.50		Apr-07
	6.16	14.36	29.37	39.37	117.61	0	0.88	11.3	1	22.84	1,889	0	97	0	3	43	27.29	-14.74			Apr-07
	6.18	14.48	29.63	40.07	117.92	0	0.72	11.31	1	22.94	1,889	0	97	0	3	43	27.14	-14.81			Jul-14
	6.02	14.07	28.67	36.95	111.23	0	1.47	11.29	1	20.95	1,889	0	97	0	3	43	27	-14.98			Dec-05
	6.08	14.25	29.15	38.60	115.69	0	1.06	11.29	1	22.31	1,889	0	97	0	3	43	27.17	-14.81			Jul-00
	3.91	5.10	8.32	7.91		0.88	1.51	10.79	0.97	10.8	65.9	0	100	0	0	49			5.75		Apr-13
	3.65	4.74	7.64	4.90		0.13	2.54	10.79	0.97	10.76	65.9	0	100	0	0	49				5.00	Apr-13
	3.67	4.67	7.56	4.61		0.05	2.66	10.8	0.97	10.76	65.9	0	100	0	0	49				1.00	Apr-13
	4.02	5.31	8.95	8.28		0.75	1.05	10.73	0.96	10.82	65.9	0	100	0	0	49					Apr-13
	4.00	5.29	8.51	8.11			1.05	10.78	0.97	10.83	65.9	0	100	0	0	49					Jul-17
	3.81	4.90	8.11	6.17		0.4	2.13	10.84	0.97	10.79	65.9	0	100	0	0	49					Apr-13
	3.87	5.05	8.43	8.44		0.87	1.51	10.81	0.97	10.92	65.9	0	100	0	0	49					Apr-13
	3.40	4.36	5.94	11.32		1.1	1.51	11	0.97	11.11	99.5	0	100	0	0	54			5.75		Apr-13
	3.27	4.04	5.23	8.62		0.54	2.31	11.01	0.97	11.08	99.5	0	100	0	0	54				5.00	Apr-13
	3.27	3.95	5.13	8.58		0.55	2.29	10.99	0.97	11.08	99.5	0	100	0	0	54				1.00	Apr-13
	3.50	4.56	6.35	12.04		1.24	1.16	11.03	0.97	11.12	99.5	0	100	0	0	54					Apr-13
	3.50	4.57	6.15	11.42			1.16	11.01	0.97	11.13	99.5	0	100	0	0	54					Jul-17
	3.41	4.19	5.57	9.85		0.81	1.9	11.01	0.97	11.1	99.5	0	100	0	0	54					Apr-13
	3.49	4.46	6.04	11.30		1.1	1.51	11.01	0.97	11.12	99.5	0	100	0	0	54					Apr-13
	3.76	9.74	24.43	23.01	44.61	0.86	1.55	10.84	0.85	11.89	214.7	1	92	4	2	24	15.95	-24.5	5.75		Apr-07
	3.74	9.58	23.99	20.32	39.31	0.37	2.46	11.05	0.87	11.66	214.7	1	92	4	2	24	15.57	-25.12		5.00	Apr-07
	3.73	9.54	24.02	20.70	39.88	0.43	2.33	11.03	0.87	11.69	214.7	1	92	4	2	24	15.74	-25.07		1.00	Apr-07
	3.89	9.85	24.71	24.10	46.51	1.04	1.22	10.81	0.85	11.94	214.7	1	92	4	2	24	16.06	-24.32			Apr-07
	3.90	9.86	24.72	24.12	46.53		1.22	10.81	0.85	11.95	214.7	1	92	4	2	24	16.06	-24.32			Jul-17
	3.74	9.65	24.24	22.49	43.44	0.75	1.72	10.82	0.85	11.86	214.7	1	92	4	2	24	15.73	-24.48			Dec-12
	3.84	9.82	24.52	23.39	45.29	0.92	1.44	10.87	0.85	11.89	214.7	1	92	4	2	24	15.99	-24.52			Apr-07
	1.36	1.36	8.31	11.48	71.19	0	1.68	16.04	0.93	25.28	161.2	4	93	3	0	32	38.21	-28.59	5.75		Feb-09
	1.11	0.85	7.33	8.45	63.38	0	2.6	16.02	0.93	23.56	161.2	4	93	3	0	32	37.27	-28.96		5.00	Feb-09
	1.13	0.92	7.48	8.93	64.82	0	2.45	16.02	0.93	23.97	161.2	4	93	3	0	32	37.58	-28.83		1.00	Feb-09
	1.44	1.52	8.69	12.83	74.79	0	1.27	16.04	0.93	26	161.2	4	93	3	0	32	38.64	-28.48			Feb-09
	1.47	1.58	8.89	13.44	75.85	0	1.09	16.04	0.93	26.2	161.2	4	93	3	0	32	38.64	-28.48			Jul-14
	1.29	1.24	8.09	10.88	69.68	0	1.85	16.04	0.93	25.11	161.2	4	93	3	0	32	38.23	-28.63			Dec-12
	1.39	1.43	8.45	12.03	76.22	0	1.51	16.04	0.93	26.17	161.2	4	93	3	0	32	38.4	-28.56			Feb-09
	7.16	12.56	26.99	25.91	79.72	0	1.31	12.24	1.06	22.92	2,406	1	99	0	0	14	25.39	-20.68	5.75		Jun-00
	6.97	12.16	25.97	23.08	72.85	0	2.1	12.21	1.06	18.3	2,406	1	99	0	0	14	24.71	-20.98		5.00	Jul-00
	6.90	12.17	26.04	23.19	73.30	0	2.04	12.22	1.06	19.56	2,406	1	99	0	0	14	24.75	-20.88		1.00	Jul-00
	7.14	12.57	26.99	25.69	78.30	0	1.3	12.24	1.06	22.36	2,406	1	99	0	0	14	25.2	-20.7	2.50		Apr-07
	7.22	12.73	27.30	26.97	82.40	0	1.04	12.23	1.06	24.66	2,406	1	99	0	0	14	25.62	-20.53			Apr-07
	7.21	12.78	27.50	27.57	82.49	0	0.87	12.25	1.07	24.83	2,406	1	99	0	0	14	25.39	-20.68			Jul-14
	7.04	12.41	26.57	24.75	77.00	0	1.62	12.22	1.06	22.37	2,406	1	99	0	0	14	25.18	-20.73			Dec-05
	7.16	12.59	27.01	26.13	80.26	0	1.26	12.24	1.06	23.94	2,406	1	99	0	0	14	25.47	-20.6			Jul-00

	MARKET		FUND TYPE, CATEGORY & OBJECTIVE		RATINGS					MINIMUMS
Fund Name	Ticker Symbol	Traded On	Fund Type	Category and (Prospectus Objective)	Overall Rating	Reward Rating	Risk Rating	Recent Up/ Downgrade	Open to New Investors	Min Initial Investment
Ivy Mid Cap Income Opportunities Fund Class A	IVOAX	NAS CM	Open End	US Equity Mid Cap (Income)	C+	C+	B-	Down	Y	750
Ivy Mid Cap Income Opportunities Fund Class C	IVOCX	NAS CM	Open End	US Equity Mid Cap (Income)	C+	C+	B-	Down	Y	750
Ivy Mid Cap Income Opportunities Fund Class E	IVOEX	NAS CM	Open End	US Equity Mid Cap (Income)	C+	C+	B-	Down	Y	250
Ivy Mid Cap Income Opportunities Fund Class I	IVOIX	NAS CM	Open End	US Equity Mid Cap (Income)	C+	C+	B-	Down	Y	0
Ivy Mid Cap Income Opportunities Fund Class N	IVOSX	NAS CM	Open End	US Equity Mid Cap (Income)	C+	C+	B-	Down	Y	1,000,000
Ivy Mid Cap Income Opportunities Fund Class R	IVORX	NAS CM	Open End	US Equity Mid Cap (Income)	C+	C+	B-	Down	Y	0
Ivy Mid Cap Income Opportunities Fund Class Y	IVOYX	NAS CM	Open End	US Equity Mid Cap (Income)	C+	C+	B-	Down	Y	0
Ivy Natural Resources Fund Class A	IGNAX	NAS CM	Open End	Natl Resources Sec Equity (Natl Res)	C	C	C	Up	Y	750
Ivy Natural Resources Fund Class B	IGNBX	NAS CM	Open End	Natl Resources Sec Equity (Natl Res)	C-	C-	D+			750
Ivy Natural Resources Fund Class C	IGNCX	NAS CM	Open End	Natl Resources Sec Equity (Natl Res)	C-	C	C-		Y	750
Ivy Natural Resources Fund Class E	IGNEX	NAS CM	Open End	Natl Resources Sec Equity (Natl Res)	C	C	C	Up	Y	750
Ivy Natural Resources Fund Class I	IGNIX	NAS CM	Open End	Natl Resources Sec Equity (Natl Res)	C	C	C	Up	Y	0
Ivy Natural Resources Fund Class N	INRSX	NAS CM	Open End	Natl Resources Sec Equity (Natl Res)	C	C	C	Up	Y	1,000,000
Ivy Natural Resources Fund Class R	IGNRX	NAS CM	Open End	Natl Resources Sec Equity (Natl Res)	C	C	C	Up	Y	0
Ivy Natural Resources Fund Class Y	IGNYX	NAS CM	Open End	Natl Resources Sec Equity (Natl Res)	C	C	C	Up	Y	0
Ivy ProShares MSCI ACWI Index Fund Class A	IMWAX	NAS CM	Open End	Global Equity (World Stock)	U	U	U		Y	750
Ivy ProShares MSCI ACWI Index Fund Class E	IMWEX	NAS CM	Open End	Global Equity (World Stock)	U	U	U		Y	250
Ivy ProShares MSCI ACWI Index Fund Class I	IMWIX	NAS CM	Open End	Global Equity (World Stock)	U	U	U		Y	0
Ivy ProShares MSCI ACWI Index Fund Class N	IMCNX	NAS CM	Open End	Global Equity (World Stock)	U	U	U		Y	1,000,000
Ivy ProShares MSCI ACWI Index Fund Class R	IMCRX	NAS CM	Open End	Global Equity (World Stock)	U	U	U		Y	0
Ivy ProShares Russell 2000 Div Growers Index Fund Cls A	IRUAX	NAS CM	Open End	US Equity Small Cap (Equity-Income)	U	U	U		Y	750
Ivy ProShares Russell 2000 Div Growers Index Fund Cls E	IRUEX	NAS CM	Open End	US Equity Small Cap (Equity-Income)	U	U	U		Y	250
Ivy ProShares Russell 2000 Div Growers Index Fund Cls I	IRUIX	NAS CM	Open End	US Equity Small Cap (Equity-Income)	U	U	U		Y	0
Ivy ProShares Russell 2000 Div Growers Index Fund Cls N	IRUNX	NAS CM	Open End	US Equity Small Cap (Equity-Income)	U	U	U		Y	1,000,000
Ivy ProShares Russell 2000 Div Growers Index Fund Cls R	IRURX	NAS CM	Open End	US Equity Small Cap (Equity-Income)	U	U	U		Y	0
Ivy ProShares S&P 500 Div Aristocrats Index Fund Cls A	IDAAX	NAS CM	Open End	US Equity Large Cap Value (Equity-Income)	U	U	U		Y	750
Ivy ProShares S&P 500 Div Aristocrats Index Fund Cls E	IDAEX	NAS CM	Open End	US Equity Large Cap Value (Equity-Income)	U	U	U		Y	250
Ivy ProShares S&P 500 Div Aristocrats Index Fund Cls I	IDAIX	NAS CM	Open End	US Equity Large Cap Value (Equity-Income)	U	U	U		Y	0
Ivy ProShares S&P 500 Div Aristocrats Index Fund Cls N	IDANX	NAS CM	Open End	US Equity Large Cap Value (Equity-Income)	U	U	U		Y	1,000,000
Ivy ProShares S&P 500 Div Aristocrats Index Fund Cls R	IDARX	NAS CM	Open End	US Equity Large Cap Value (Equity-Income)	U	U	U		Y	0
Ivy Science And Technology Fund Class A	WSTAX	NAS CM	Open End	Technology Sector Equity (Technology)	B	A	C	Up	Y	750
Ivy Science And Technology Fund Class B	WSTBX	NAS CM	Open End	Technology Sector Equity (Technology)	B	A-	C	Up		750
Ivy Science And Technology Fund Class C	WSTCX	NAS CM	Open End	Technology Sector Equity (Technology)	B	A-	C	Up	Y	750
Ivy Science and Technology Fund Class E	ISTEX	NAS CM	Open End	Technology Sector Equity (Technology)	B	A-	C	Up	Y	250
Ivy Science and Technology Fund Class I	ISTIX	NAS CM	Open End	Technology Sector Equity (Technology)	B	A	C	Up	Y	0
Ivy Science and Technology Fund Class N	ISTNX	NAS CM	Open End	Technology Sector Equity (Technology)	B	A	C	Up	Y	1,000,000
Ivy Science and Technology Fund Class R	WSTRX	NAS CM	Open End	Technology Sector Equity (Technology)	B	A-	C	Up	Y	0
Ivy Science And Technology Fund Class Y	WSTYX	NAS CM	Open End	Technology Sector Equity (Technology)	B	A	C	Up	Y	0
Ivy Small Cap Core Fund Class A	IYSAX	NAS CM	Open End	US Equity Small Cap (Small Company)	B+	A-	B	Up	Y	750
Ivy Small Cap Core Fund Class B	IYSBX	NAS CM	Open End	US Equity Small Cap (Small Company)	B	B+	B	Up		750
Ivy Small Cap Core Fund Class C	IYSCX	NAS CM	Open End	US Equity Small Cap (Small Company)	B	B+	B	Up	Y	750
Ivy Small Cap Core Fund Class I	IVVIX	NAS CM	Open End	US Equity Small Cap (Small Company)	B+	A-	B	Up	Y	0
Ivy Small Cap Core Fund Class N	ISPVX	NAS CM	Open End	US Equity Small Cap (Small Company)	B+	A-	B	Up	Y	1,000,000
Ivy Small Cap Core Fund Class R	IYSMX	NAS CM	Open End	US Equity Small Cap (Small Company)	B+	B+	B	Up	Y	0
Ivy Small Cap Core Fund Class T	IYCTX	NAS CM	Open End	US Equity Small Cap (Small Company)	B+	A-	B	Up	Y	0
Ivy Small Cap Core Fund Class Y	IYSYX	NAS CM	Open End	US Equity Small Cap (Small Company)	B+	A-	B	Up	Y	0
Ivy Small Cap Growth Fund Class A	WSGAX	NAS CM	Open End	US Equity Small Cap (Small Company)	B+	B+	B	Up	Y	750
Ivy Small Cap Growth Fund Class B	WSGBX	NAS CM	Open End	US Equity Small Cap (Small Company)	B	B+	B	Up		750
Ivy Small Cap Growth Fund Class C	WRGCX	NAS CM	Open End	US Equity Small Cap (Small Company)	B	B+	B	Up	Y	750
Ivy Small Cap Growth Fund Class E	ISGEX	NAS CM	Open End	US Equity Small Cap (Small Company)	B+	B+	B	Up	Y	250
Ivy Small Cap Growth Fund Class Institutional	IYSIX	NAS CM	Open End	US Equity Small Cap (Small Company)	B+	B+	B	Up	Y	0
Ivy Small Cap Growth Fund Class N	IRGFX	NAS CM	Open End	US Equity Small Cap (Small Company)	B+	B+	B	Up	Y	1,000,000

★Expanded analysis of this fund is included in Section II.

	TOTAL RETURNS					PERFORMANCE				ASSETS		ASSET ALLOCATION & TURNOVER					BULL & BEAR		FEES		
Min Additional Investment	3-Month Total Return	6-Month Total Return	1-Year Total Return	3-Year Total Return	5-Year Total Return	Dividend Yield (TTM)	Expense Ratio	3-Yr Std Deviation	3-Year Beta	NAV	Total Assets (MIL)	%Cash	%Stocks	%Bonds	%Other	Turnover Ratio	Last Bull Market Total Return	Last Bear Market Total Return	Front End Fee (%)	Back End Fee (%)	Inception Date
	6.23	9.30	11.96	31.19		0.82	1.35	10.12	0.88	13.7	343.2	0	99	0	1	28			5.75		Oct-14
	5.96	8.90	11.11	28.34		0.34	2.07	10.05	0.87	13.64	343.2	0	99	0	1	28				1.00	Oct-14
	6.19	9.33	12.09	31.45		0.99	1.23	10.07	0.87	13.7	343.2	0	99	0	1	28			2.50		Oct-14
	6.30	9.51	12.29	32.32		1.1	1.05	10.1	0.87	13.72	343.2	0	99	0	1	28					Oct-14
	6.25	9.50	12.42	32.49		1.2	0.98	10.11	0.87	13.72	343.2	0	99	0	1	28					Oct-14
	6.08	9.16	11.55	29.61		0.53	1.73	10.11	0.87	13.68	343.2	0	99	0	1	28					Oct-14
	6.15	9.30	11.97	31.08		0.84	1.35	10.09	0.87	13.7	343.2	0	99	0	1	28					Oct-14
	7.91	14.28	2.88	-1.87	-4.91	0.06	1.72	18.57		15.68	587.0	3	97	0	0	64	18.81	-40.1	5.75		Jan-97
	7.49	13.51	1.69	-4.97	-9.53	0	2.77	18.55		13.19	587.0	3	97	0	0	64	18.31	-40.3		5.00	Jan-97
	7.66	13.86	2.19	-3.75	-7.89	0	2.34	18.56		13.06	587.0	3	97	0	0	64	18.4	-40.28		1.00	Jan-97
	8.04	14.57	3.40	-0.50	-3.06	0.44	1.27	18.6		16.11	587.0	3	97	0	0	64	19.02	-40.08	2.50		Apr-07
	7.98	14.55	3.41	-0.34	-2.52	0.53	1.19	18.56		16.37	587.0	3	97	0	0	64	19.06	-39.98			Apr-07
	8.08	14.71	3.65	0.23	-2.67	0.69	1.02	18.59		16.45	587.0	3	97	0	0	64	18.81	-40.1			Jul-14
	7.87	14.32	2.85	-2.02	-5.32	0	1.77	18.6		15.48	587.0	3	97	0	0	64	18.72	-40.13			Dec-05
	7.92	14.45	3.21	-1.00	-3.66	0.31	1.43	18.55		16.07	587.0	3	97	0	0	64	18.96	-40.02			Jul-03
	5.35	10.60					0.9			11.46	75.3	0	99	1	0	51			2.50		Apr-17
	5.39	10.60					0.75			11.46	75.3	0	99	1	0	51			2.50		Apr-17
	5.51	10.76					0.65			11.47	75.3	0	99	1	0	51					Apr-17
	5.51	10.76					0.65			11.47	75.3	0	99	1	0	51					Apr-17
	5.32	10.37					1.4			11.46	75.3	0	99	1	0	51					Apr-17
	-1.00	2.17					0.9			10.28	77.3	0	99	1	0	12			2.50		Apr-17
	-0.98	2.23					0.8			10.28	77.3	0	99	1	0	12			2.50		Apr-17
	-0.94	2.33					0.65			10.28	77.3	0	99	1	0	12					Apr-17
	-0.94	2.33					0.65			10.28	77.3	0	99	1	0	12					Apr-17
	-1.17	1.85					1.44			10.27	77.3	0	99	1	0	12					Apr-17
	8.05	11.72					0.75			11.43	239.9	0	99	1	0	4			2.50		Apr-17
	8.05	11.72					0.75			11.43	239.9	0	99	1	0	4			2.50		Apr-17
	8.11	11.78					0.5			11.43	239.9	0	99	1	0	4					Apr-17
	8.11	11.78					0.5			11.43	239.9	0	99	1	0	4					Apr-17
	7.80	11.36					1.26			11.42	239.9	0	99	1	0	4					Apr-17
	3.46	13.82	32.82	29.73	111.41	0	1.3	15.06	0.91	63.57	4,284	2	98	1	0	16	22.03	-19.83	5.75		Jul-00
	3.25	13.38	31.80	26.83	103.47	0	2.06	15.05	0.91	52.73	4,284	2	98	1	0	16	21.41	-20.11		5.00	Jul-00
	3.26	13.40	31.84	27.00	104.10	0	2	15.05	0.9	54.79	4,284	2	98	1	0	16	21.47	-20.06		1.00	Jul-97
	3.44	13.78	32.75	29.40	110.23	0	1.3	15.06	0.91	63.14	4,284	2	98	1	0	16	21.96	-19.85	2.50		Apr-07
	3.52	13.94	33.13	30.85	114.47	0	1	15.06	0.91	69.87	4,284	2	98	1	0	16	22.24	-19.72			Apr-07
	3.56	14.03	33.35	31.44	112.21	0	0.85	15.06	0.91	70.19	4,284	2	98	1	0	16	21.47	-20.06			Jul-14
	3.37	13.61	32.35	28.54	108.11	0	1.59	15.05	0.91	62.02	4,284	2	98	1	0	16	21.82	-19.92			Dec-05
	3.46	13.81	32.80	29.88	111.80	0	1.24	15.06	0.91	67.04	4,284	2	98	1	0	16	22.06	-19.8			Jun-98
	4.01	8.25	13.30	35.27	97.78	0	1.5	11.94	0.8	18.99	642.4	0	97	1	2	133	22.94	-27.1	5.75		Jan-97
	3.78	7.68	12.20	31.43	88.40	0	2.44	11.91	0.79	15.38	642.4	0	97	1	2	133	22.08	-27.4		5.00	Dec-03
	3.86	7.85	12.54	32.59	91.33	0	2.17	11.89	0.79	16.44	642.4	0	97	1	2	133	22.4	-27.3		1.00	Dec-03
	4.13	8.43	13.72	37.00	102.12	0	1.1	11.94	0.8	20.53	642.4	0	97	1	2	133	23.42	-26.93			Apr-07
	4.14	8.53	13.90	37.57	101.61	0	0.95	11.93	0.8	20.69	642.4	0	97	1	2	133	22.94	-27.1			Jul-14
	3.91	8.10	13.04	34.58	96.15	0	1.69	11.95	0.8	18.88	642.4	0	97	1	2	133	22.76	-27.17			Dec-12
	4.12	8.41	13.47	35.47	98.08		1.5	11.95	0.8	19.02	642.4	0	97	1	2	133	22.94	-27.1	2.50		Jul-17
	4.07	8.33	13.46	35.96	99.57	0	1.35	11.93	0.8	19.93	642.4	0	97	1	2	133	23.15	-27.02			Dec-03
	5.40	9.34	23.69	36.59	103.20	0	1.41	13.44	0.87	17.82	1,163	2	95	0	3	53	24.18	-24.73	5.75		Jul-00
	5.17	8.90	22.57	33.12	94.38	0	2.24	13.43	0.87	12.99	1,163	2	95	0	3	53	23.43	-25.12		5.00	Jul-00
	5.20	8.97	22.77	33.92	96.63	0	2.07	13.42	0.87	14.34	1,163	2	95	0	3	53	23.73	-24.96		1.00	Sep-92
	5.45	9.37	23.62	36.46	102.56	0	1.35	13.41	0.87	17.66	1,163	2	95	0	3	53	24.07	-24.78	2.50		Apr-07
	5.48	9.53	24.02	37.99	106.84	0	1.07	13.44	0.87	23.28	1,163	2	95	0	3	53	24.48	-24.62			Apr-07
	5.56	9.64	24.24	38.63	104.69	0	0.91	13.46	0.87	23.41	1,163	2	95	0	3	53	23.73	-24.96			Jul-14

	MARKET			FUND TYPE, CATEGORY & OBJECTIVE	RATINGS					MINIMUMS
Fund Name	Ticker Symbol	Traded On	Fund Type	Category and (Prospectus Objective)	Overall Rating	Reward Rating	Risk Rating	Recent Up/ Downgrade	Open to New Investors	Min Initial Investment
Ivy Small Cap Growth Fund Class R	WSGRX	NAS CM	Open End	US Equity Small Cap (Small Company)	B+	B+	B	Up	Y	0
Ivy Small Cap Growth Fund Class T	IYSTX	NAS CM	Open End	US Equity Small Cap (Small Company)	B+	B+	B	Up	Y	0
Ivy Small Cap Growth Fund Class Y	WSCYX	NAS CM	Open End	US Equity Small Cap (Small Company)	B+	B+	B	Up	Y	0
Ivy Tax-Managed Equity Class A	IYEAX	NAS CM	Open End	US Equity Large Cap Growth (Growth)	B+	B	A-	Up	Y	750
Ivy Tax-Managed Equity Class B	IYEBX	NAS CM	Open End	US Equity Large Cap Growth (Growth)	B	B	B+			750
Ivy Tax-Managed Equity Class C	IYECX	NAS CM	Open End	US Equity Large Cap Growth (Growth)	B	B	B+		Y	750
Ivy Tax-Managed Equity Class I	WYTMX	NAS CM	Open End	US Equity Large Cap Growth (Growth)	B+	B+	A-	Up	Y	0
Ivy Tax-Managed Equity Class Y	IYEYX	NAS CM	Open End	US Equity Large Cap Growth (Growth)	B+	B	A-	Up	Y	0
Ivy Tax-Managed Equity Fund Class N	IYENX	NAS CM	Open End	US Equity Large Cap Growth (Growth)	B+	B+	A-	Up	Y	1,000,000
Ivy Value Fund Class A	IYVAX	NAS CM	Open End	US Equity Large Cap Value (Growth)	B-	C+	B	Up	Y	750
Ivy Value Fund Class B	IYVBX	NAS CM	Open End	US Equity Large Cap Value (Growth)	B-	C+	B	Up		750
Ivy Value Fund Class C	IYVCX	NAS CM	Open End	US Equity Large Cap Value (Growth)	B-	C+	B	Up	Y	750
Ivy Value Fund Class I	IYAIX	NAS CM	Open End	US Equity Large Cap Value (Growth)	B-	C+	B	Up	Y	0
Ivy Value Fund Class N	IVALX	NAS CM	Open End	US Equity Large Cap Value (Growth)	B-	C+	B		Y	1,000,000
Ivy Value Fund Class R	IYVLX	NAS CM	Open End	US Equity Large Cap Value (Growth)	B-	C+	B	Up	Y	0
Ivy Value Fund Class Y	IYVYX	NAS CM	Open End	US Equity Large Cap Value (Growth)	B-	C+	B	Up	Y	0
Jackson Square All Cap Growth Fund IS Class	JSSSX	NAS CM	Open End	US Equity Large Cap Growth (Growth)	D	C	B		Y	1,000,000
Jackson Square Global Growth Fund Institutional Class	JSPTX	NAS CM	Open End	Global Equity (Growth)	D	C	B		Y	100,000
Jackson Square Global Growth Fund IS Class	JSPUX	NAS CM	Open End	Global Equity (Growth)	D	C	B		Y	1,000,000
Jackson Square Large-Cap Growth Fund Institutional Class	JSPIX	NAS CM	Open End	US Equity Large Cap Growth (Growth)	B	B	A-	Up	Y	100,000
Jackson Square Large-Cap Growth Fund Investor Class	JSPJX	NAS CM	Open End	US Equity Large Cap Growth (Growth)	B	B	A-	Up	Y	2,500
Jackson Square Large-Cap Growth Fund IS Class	DPLGX	NAS CM	Open End	US Equity Large Cap Growth (Growth)	B	B	A-	Up	Y	1,000,000
Jackson Square Select 20 Growth Fund IS Class	DPCEX	NAS CM	Open End	US Equity Large Cap Growth (Growth)	B	C+	B+	Up	Y	1,000,000
Jackson Square SMID-Cap Growth Fund Institutional Class	JSMTX	NAS CM	Open End	US Equity Mid Cap (Growth)	B+	A-	B	Up	Y	100,000
Jackson Square SMID-Cap Growth Fund Investor Class	JSMVX	NAS CM	Open End	US Equity Mid Cap (Growth)	B+	A-	B	Up	Y	2,500
Jackson Square SMID-Cap Growth Fund IS Class	DCGTX	NAS CM	Open End	US Equity Mid Cap (Growth)	B+	A-	B	Up	Y	1,000,000
Jacob Internet Investor Class	JAMFX	NAS CM	Open End	Technology Sector Equity (Technology)	B+	A	B	Up	Y	2,500
Jacob Micro Cap Growth Fund Institutional Class shares	JMIGX	NAS CM	Open End	US Equity Small Cap (Growth)	C	C	C	Up	Y	1,000,000
Jacob Micro Cap Growth Fund Investor Class shares	JMCGX	NAS CM	Open End	US Equity Small Cap (Growth)	C	C	C	Up	Y	2,500
Jacob Small Cap Growth Fund Institutional Class shares	JSIGX	NAS CM	Open End	US Equity Small Cap (Small Company)	C+	C+	C	Up	Y	1,000,000
Jacob Small Cap Growth Fund Investor Class shares	JSCGX	NAS CM	Open End	US Equity Small Cap (Small Company)	C	C+	C	Up	Y	2,500
JAG Large Cap Growth Fund Class A	JLGAX	NAS CM	Open End	US Equity Large Cap Growth (Growth)	A-	A	B+	Up	Y	2,500
JAG Large Cap Growth Fund Class I	JLGIX	NAS CM	Open End	US Equity Large Cap Growth (Growth)	A-	A	B+	Up	Y	250,000
James Aggressive Allocation Fund	JAVAX	NAS CM	Open End	Aggressive Alloc (Growth & Income)	C	C	B	Up	Y	10,000
James Alpha Equity Hedge Portfolio Class C Shares	JAHCX	NAS CM	Open End	Long/Short Equity (Growth)	U	U	U		Y	2,500
James Alpha Equity Hedge Portfolio Class I Shares	JEHIX	NAS CM	Open End	Long/Short Equity (Growth)	U	U	U		Y	1,000,000
James Alpha Equity Hedge Portfolio Class S Shares	JAHSX	NAS CM	Open End	Long/Short Equity (Growth)	U	U	U		Y	0
James Alpha Event Driven Portfolio Class A Shares	JAEAX	NAS CM	Open End	Multialternative (Growth)	U	U	U		Y	2,500
James Alpha Event Driven Portfolio Class C Shares	JAECX	NAS CM	Open End	Multialternative (Growth)	U	U	U		Y	2,500
James Alpha Event Driven Portfolio Class I Shares	JAEIX	NAS CM	Open End	Multialternative (Growth)	U	U	U		Y	1,000,000
James Alpha Event Driven Portfolio Class S Shares	JAESX	NAS CM	Open End	Multialternative (Growth)	U	U	U		Y	0
James Alpha Family Office Portfolio Class A	JFOAX	NAS CM	Open End	Miscellaneous (Growth & Income)	U	U	U		Y	2,500
James Alpha Family Office Portfolio Class C	JFOCX	NAS CM	Open End	Miscellaneous (Growth & Income)	U	U	U		Y	2,500
James Alpha Family Office Portfolio Class I	JFOIX	NAS CM	Open End	Miscellaneous (Growth & Income)	U	U	U		Y	1,000,000
James Alpha Family Office Portfolio Class S Shares	JFOSX	NAS CM	Open End	Miscellaneous (Growth & Income)	U	U	U		Y	0
James Alpha Global Real Estate Inv Port Cls A Shares	JAREX	NAS CM	Open End	Real Estate Sector Equity (Real Estate)	B	B-	B+	Up	Y	2,500
James Alpha Global Real Estate Inv Port Cls C Shares	JACRX	NAS CM	Open End	Real Estate Sector Equity (Real Estate)	B	B-	B	Up	Y	2,500
James Alpha Global Real Estate Inv Port Cls I Shares	JARIX	NAS CM	Open End	Real Estate Sector Equity (Real Estate)	B	B-	B+	Up	Y	1,000,000
James Alpha Global Real Estate Inv Port Cls S Shares	JARSX	NAS CM	Open End	Real Estate Sector Equity (Real Estate)	B	B-	B+		Y	0
James Alpha Macro Portfolio Class A	GRRAX	NAS CM	Open End	Moderate Alloc (Income)	D+	D	C	Up	Y	2,500
James Alpha Macro Portfolio Class C	GRRCX	NAS CM	Open End	Moderate Alloc (Income)	D	D	C-		Y	2,500
James Alpha Macro Portfolio Class I	GRRIX	NAS CM	Open End	Moderate Alloc (Income)	D+	D	C	Up	Y	1,000,000

★ Expanded analysis of this fund is included in Section II.

	TOTAL RETURNS					PERFORMANCE				ASSETS		ASSET ALLOCATION & TURNOVER					BULL & BEAR		FEES		
Min Additional Investment	3-Month Total Return	6-Month Total Return	1-Year Total Return	3-Year Total Return	5-Year Total Return	Dividend Yield (TTM)	Expense Ratio	3-Yr Std Deviation	3-Year Beta	NAV	Total Assets (MIL)	%Cash	%Stocks	%Bonds	%Other	Turnover Ratio	Last Bull Market Total Return	Last Bear Market Total Return	Front End Fee (%)	Back End Fee (%)	Inception Date
	5.34	9.23	23.28	35.50	100.84	0	1.66	13.42	0.87	17.49	1,163	2	95	0	3	53	24.06	-24.81			Dec-05
	5.49	9.44	23.30	34.50	97.48		1.41	13.44	0.87	17.82	1,163	2	95	0	3	53	23.73	-24.96	2.50		Jul-17
	5.43	9.40	23.74	37.00	104.43	0	1.31	13.42	0.87	22	1,163	2	95	0	3	53	24.33	-24.71			Dec-95
	7.62	14.67	30.03	36.09	108.70	0	1.2	11.71	1.04	24.69	571.7	0	99	1	0	46	23.7	-14.93	5.75		May-09
	7.43	14.27	29.16	33.13	101.64	0	1.91	11.74	1.05	23.53	571.7	0	99	1	0	46	23.27	-15.19		5.00	May-09
	7.37	14.17	28.97	32.87	100.97	0	1.96	11.72	1.04	23.43	571.7	0	99	1	0	46	23.29	-15.2		1.00	May-09
	7.66	14.74	30.32	36.87	111.09	0	0.96	11.72	1.04	24.98	571.7	0	99	1	0	46	23.89	-14.84			Apr-00
	7.65	14.63	30.15	36.07	108.83	0	1.33	11.77	1.05	24.74	571.7	0	99	1	0	46	23.79	-15			May-09
	7.70	14.83	30.42	36.98	111.26		0.81	11.72	1.04	25	571.7	0	99	1	0	46	23.89	-14.84			Jul-17
	5.03	5.80	12.16	18.05	79.98	1.06	1.33	12.05	1.1	23.77	1,216	8	92	1	0	53	23.9	-22.08	5.75		Sep-94
	4.78	5.31	11.13	14.64	71.78	0.4	2.36	12.07	1.1	22.05	1,216	8	92	1	0	53	23.03	-22.51		5.00	Dec-03
	4.84	5.40	11.41	15.71	74.00	0.64	1.97	12.04	1.1	22.92	1,216	8	92	1	0	53	23.32	-22.3		1.00	Dec-03
	5.09	5.95	12.53	19.23	83.04	1.4	0.97	12.04	1.1	23.86	1,216	8	92	1	0	53	24.12	-21.9			Apr-07
	5.16	6.07	12.72	19.85	83.09	1.56	0.82	12.07	1.1	23.93	1,216	8	92	1	0	53	23.9	-22.08			Jul-14
	4.95	5.65	11.87	17.16	77.71	0.89	1.57	12.03	1.1	23.74	1,216	8	92	1	0	53	23.72	-22.16			Dec-12
	5.02	5.78	12.15	18.26	80.57	1.1	1.21	12.04	1.1	23.81	1,216	8	92	1	0	53	24.01	-22.01			Dec-03
	3.13	11.23	21.80			0.03	0.9			21.5	5.1	3	97	0	0						Sep-16
	3.25	14.42	33.79			0	1.15			22.7	9.3	5	95	0	0						Sep-16
	3.25	14.46	33.83			0	1.05			22.72	9.3	5	95	0	0						Sep-16
	3.24	12.40	28.39	27.27	98.51	0.22	0.74	11.65	0.95	13.48	154.3	1	99	0	0	27	28.4	-12.39			Sep-16
100	3.18	12.27	28.05	26.28	95.99	0.17	0.99	11.66	0.95	13.47	154.3	1	99	0	0	27	28.21	-12.48			Sep-16
	3.18	12.42	28.41	27.34	98.61	0.24	0.64	11.66	0.95	13.47	154.3	1	99	0	0	27	28.4	-12.38			Nov-05
	0.66	6.50	17.08	13.83	67.51	0	0.87	12.26	0.95	5.14	6.2	1	99	0	0	22	27.06	-8.7			Mar-00
	5.37	11.99	20.34	38.56	103.69	0.1	0.97	9.84	0.67	21.65	386.8	3	97	0	0	20	26.17	-16			Sep-16
100	5.24	11.80	19.97	37.47	101.09	0.07	1.22	9.82	0.67	21.57	386.8	3	97	0	0	20	25.99	-16.08			Sep-16
	5.37	12.04	20.40	38.71	103.92	0.11	0.87	9.84	0.67	21.66	386.8	3	97	0	0	20	26.17	-15.99			Dec-03
100	2.52	11.17	24.14	53.96	123.19	0	2.51	14.78	0.89	4.43	45.3	5	95	0	0	46	17.73	-21.82			Dec-99
1,000	6.86	17.00	28.90	5.99	41.73	0	2.61	21.18	0.89	13.69	8.9	9	91	0	0	48	40.24	-30.71			Dec-97
100	6.88	16.82	28.65	5.14	39.71	0	2.86	21.14	0.89	12.57	8.9	9	91	0	0	48	40.09	-30.82			May-01
1,000	7.86	14.16	20.96	12.80	61.20	0	2.04	21.03	1.16	21.12	15.4	1	99	0	0	60	18.58	-31.91			Nov-12
100	7.75	14.01	20.61	11.87	58.86	0	2.26	21	1.16	20.83	15.4	1	99	0	0	60	18.58	-31.91			Feb-10
50	4.29	14.32	34.68	46.01	114.77	0	1.5	12.29	1.03	17.31	64.3	1	99	0	0	125			5.75		Dec-11
50	4.38	14.51	35.01	47.01	117.43	0	1.25	12.32	1.03	17.63	64.3	1	99	0	0	125					Dec-11
	5.55	9.77	11.44			0.82	1.01			10.9	10.7	1	76	23	0	198					Jul-15
	3.26						2.91			10.61	2.8	17	65	15	1					1.00	Aug-17
	3.33						1.91			10.61	2.8	17	65	15	1						Aug-17
	3.42						0.91			10.62	2.8	17	65	15	1						Aug-17
100	0.76						2.56			10.23	5.9	15	41	42	0				5.75		Aug-17
100	0.76						3.31			10.23	5.9	15	41	42	0					1.00	Aug-17
	0.76						2.31			10.23	5.9	15	41	42	0						Aug-17
	0.86						1.31			10.23	5.9	15	41	42	0						Aug-17
	3.48	6.17					2.54			10.57	5.0	-3	81	20	2				5.75		Jun-17
	3.26	5.94					3.29			10.57	5.0	-3	81	20	2					1.00	Jun-17
	3.55	6.24					2.29			10.57	5.0	-3	81	20	2						Jun-17
	3.64	6.44					1.09			10.59	5.0	-3	81	20	2						Jun-17
	4.77	7.23	16.78	27.03	43.02	1.2	1.69	11.19	0.91	18.71	533.2	-1	97	0	4	141	27.39	-21.27	5.75		Oct-09
	4.64	6.93	16.00	24.46	39.24	0.53	2.37	11.17	0.9	18.9	533.2	-1	97	0	4	141	26.97	-21.52		1.00	Jan-12
	4.93	7.51	17.32	28.94	47.65	1.4	1.19	11.19	0.9	19.22	533.2	-1	97	0	4	141	27.53	-20.45			Aug-11
	5.03	7.57	17.15	27.44	43.48		0.98	11.2	0.91	19.25	533.2	-1	97	0	4	141	27.38	-21.27			Aug-17
	1.86	2.77	0.65	-7.68	-8.38	0	1.71	4.27	-0.06	9.26	10.8	56	14	25	4	83	3.5	-0.49	5.75		Feb-11
	1.71	2.42	-0.11	-9.71	-11.68	0	2.46	4.25	-0.06	8.88	10.8	56	14	25	4	83	3.01	-0.91		1.00	Jan-12
	1.98	2.88	0.98	-6.95	-7.19	0	1.46	4.24	-0.06	9.27	10.8	56	14	25	4	83	3.65	-0.49			Feb-11

	MARKET		FUND TYPE, CATEGORY & OBJECTIVE		RATINGS				MINIMUMS	
Fund Name	Ticker Symbol	Traded On	Fund Type	Category and (Prospectus Objective)	Overall Rating	Reward Rating	Risk Rating	Recent Up/ Downgrade	Open to New Investors	Min Initial Investment
James Alpha Macro Portfolio Class S Shares	GRRSX	NAS CM	Open End	Moderate Alloc (Income)	D+	D	C		Y	0
James Alpha Managed Risk Domestic Equity Portfolio Class A	JDAEX	NAS CM	Open End	Long/Short Equity (Growth)	C	C	B+	Up	Y	2,500
James Alpha Managed Risk Domestic Equity Portfolio Class C	JDCEX	NAS CM	Open End	Long/Short Equity (Growth)	C	C	B+	Up	Y	2,500
James Alpha Managed Risk Domestic Equity Portfolio Class I	JDIEX	NAS CM	Open End	Long/Short Equity (Growth)	C	C	B+	Up	Y	1,000,000
James Alpha Managed Risk Domestic Eq Port Cls S Shares	JDSEX	NAS CM	Open End	Long/Short Equity (Growth)	C	C	B+		Y	0
James Alpha Managed Risk Emerging Mkts Eq Port Cls A	JEAMX	NAS CM	Open End	Long/Short Equity (Growth)	C	C	B	Up	Y	2,500
James Alpha Managed Risk Emerging Mkts Eq Port Cls C	JECMX	NAS CM	Open End	Long/Short Equity (Growth)	C	C	B	Up	Y	2,500
James Alpha Managed Risk Emerging Mkts Eq Port Cls I	JEIMX	NAS CM	Open End	Long/Short Equity (Growth)	C	C	B	Up	Y	1,000,000
James Alpha Managed Risk Emerg Mkts Eq Cls S Shares	JESMX	NAS CM	Open End	Long/Short Equity (Growth)	C	C	B		Y	0
James Alpha Multi Strat Alternative Income Cls A Shares	JAAMX	NAS CM	Open End	Long/Short Equity (Growth & Income)	C	C	C		Y	2,500
James Alpha Multi Strat Alternative Income Cls C Shares	JACMX	NAS CM	Open End	Long/Short Equity (Growth & Income)	C	C	C-	Up	Y	2,500
James Alpha Multi Strat Alternative Income Cls I Shares	JAIMX	NAS CM	Open End	Long/Short Equity (Growth & Income)	C	C	C		Y	1,000,000
James Alpha Multi Strat Alternative Income Cls S Shares	JASMX	NAS CM	Open End	Long/Short Equity (Growth & Income)	C	C	C		Y	0
James Alpha Relative Value Portfolio A Shares	JRVAX	NAS CM	Open End	Market Neutral (Growth)	U	U	U		Y	2,500
James Alpha Relative Value Portfolio C Shares	JRVCX	NAS CM	Open End	Market Neutral (Growth)	U	U	U		Y	2,500
James Alpha Relative Value Portfolio Class S Shares	JRSVX	NAS CM	Open End	Market Neutral (Growth)	U	U	U		Y	0
James Alpha Relative Value Portfolio I Shares	JRVIX	NAS CM	Open End	Market Neutral (Growth)	U	U	U		Y	1,000,000
James Alpha Total Hedge Portfolio A Shares	JTHAX	NAS CM	Open End	Multialternative (Growth)	U	U	U		Y	2,500
James Alpha Total Hedge Portfolio C Shares	JTHCX	NAS CM	Open End	Multialternative (Growth)	U	U	U		Y	2,500
James Alpha Total Hedge Portfolio Class S Shares	JTHSX	NAS CM	Open End	Multialternative (Growth)	U	U	U		Y	0
James Alpha Total Hedge Portfolio I Shares	JTHIX	NAS CM	Open End	Multialternative (Growth)	U	U	U		Y	1,000,000
James Alpha Yorkville MLP Portfolio Class A	JAMLX	NAS CM	Open End	Energy Sector Equity (Growth & Income)	D+	D+	D	Down	Y	2,500
James Alpha Yorkville MLP Portfolio Class C	MLPCX	NAS CM	Open End	Energy Sector Equity (Growth & Income)	D	D	D	Down	Y	2,500
James Alpha Yorkville MLP Portfolio Class I	JMLPX	NAS CM	Open End	Energy Sector Equity (Growth & Income)	D+	D+	D	Down	Y	1,000,000
James Balanced Golden Rainbow Fund Retail Class	GLRBX	NAS CM	Open End	Cautious Alloc (Balanced)	B-	C	A-	Up	Y	2,000
James Balanced: Golden Rainbow Fund Institutional Class	GLRIX	NAS CM	Open End	Cautious Alloc (Balanced)	B-	C	A-	Up	Y	50,000
James Long-Short Fund	JAZZX	NAS CM	Open End	Long/Short Equity (Growth)	C+	C+	B	Down	Y	2,000
James Micro Cap Fund	JMCRX	NAS CM	Open End	US Equity Small Cap (Small Company)	B	B+	B	Up	Y	10,000
James Mid Cap Fund	JAMDX	NAS CM	Open End	US Equity Mid Cap (Growth & Income)	B	C+	A-	Up	Y	2,000
James Small Cap Fund	JASCX	NAS CM	Open End	US Equity Small Cap (Small Company)	B-	C+	B	Up	Y	2,000
Jamestown Equity Fund	JAMEX	NAS CM	Open End	US Equity Large Cap Blend (Growth)	B-	C+	B	Down	Y	5,000
Janus Henderson Adaptive Global Allocation Fund Class A	JAGAX	NAS CM	Open End	Alloc (Growth & Income)	C	C+	B	Up	Y	2,500
Janus Henderson Adaptive Global Allocation Fund Class C	JAVCX	NAS CM	Open End	Alloc (Growth & Income)	C	C	B	Up	Y	2,500
Janus Henderson Adaptive Global Allocation Fund Class D	JAGDX	NAS CM	Open End	Alloc (Growth & Income)	C	C+	B	Up	Y	2,500
Janus Henderson Adaptive Global Allocation Fund Class I	JVGIX	NAS CM	Open End	Alloc (Growth & Income)	C	C+	B	Up	Y	1,000,000
Janus Henderson Adaptive Global Allocation Fund Class N	JAGNX	NAS CM	Open End	Alloc (Growth & Income)	C	C+	B	Up	Y	1,000,000
Janus Henderson Adaptive Global Allocation Fund Class S	JAGSX	NAS CM	Open End	Alloc (Growth & Income)	C	C+	B	Up	Y	2,500
Janus Henderson Adaptive Global Allocation Fund Class T	JVGTX	NAS CM	Open End	Alloc (Growth & Income)	C	C+	B	Up	Y	2,500
Janus Henderson All Asset Fund Class A	HGAAX	NAS CM	Open End	Alloc (Asset Alloc)	B-	C+	B+	Up	Y	2,500
Janus Henderson All Asset Fund Class C	HGACX	NAS CM	Open End	Alloc (Asset Alloc)	C+	C	B	Up	Y	2,500
Janus Henderson All Asset Fund Class D	HGADX	NAS CM	Open End	Alloc (Asset Alloc)	B-	C+	B	Up	Y	2,500
Janus Henderson All Asset Fund Class I	HGAIX	NAS CM	Open End	Alloc (Asset Alloc)	B-	C+	B	Up	Y	1,000,000
Janus Henderson All Asset Fund Class N	HGARX	NAS CM	Open End	Alloc (Asset Alloc)	B-	C+	B	Up	Y	1,000,000
Janus Henderson All Asset Fund Class S	HGAQX	NAS CM	Open End	Alloc (Asset Alloc)	C+	C+	B	Up	Y	2,500
Janus Henderson All Asset Fund Class T	HGATX	NAS CM	Open End	Alloc (Asset Alloc)	B-	C+	B	Up	Y	2,500
Janus Henderson Asia Equity Fund Class A	JAQAX	NAS CM	Open End	Asia ex-Japan Equity (Pacific Stock)	B+	A	C+	Up	Y	2,500
Janus Henderson Asia Equity Fund Class C	JAQCX	NAS CM	Open End	Asia ex-Japan Equity (Pacific Stock)	B	A	C+	Up	Y	2,500
Janus Henderson Asia Equity Fund Class D	JAQDX	NAS CM	Open End	Asia ex-Japan Equity (Pacific Stock)	B+	A	C+	Up		2,500
Janus Henderson Asia Equity Fund Class I	JAQIX	NAS CM	Open End	Asia ex-Japan Equity (Pacific Stock)	B+	A	C+	Up	Y	1,000,000
Janus Henderson Asia Equity Fund Class S	JAQSX	NAS CM	Open End	Asia ex-Japan Equity (Pacific Stock)	B+	A	C+	Up	Y	2,500
Janus Henderson Asia Equity Fund Class T	JAQTX	NAS CM	Open End	Asia ex-Japan Equity (Pacific Stock)	B+	A	C+	Up	Y	2,500
Janus Henderson Balanced Fund Class A	JDBAX	NAS CM	Open End	Moderate Alloc (Balanced)	B-	C+	B	Down	Y	2,500

★ Expanded analysis of this fund is included in Section II.

	TOTAL RETURNS					PERFORMANCE				ASSETS		ASSET ALLOCATION & TURNOVER					BULL & BEAR		FEES		
Min Additional Investment	3-Month Total Return	6-Month Total Return	1-Year Total Return	3-Year Total Return	5-Year Total Return	Dividend Yield (TTM)	Expense Ratio	3-Yr Std Deviation	3-Year Beta	NAV	Total Assets (MIL)	%Cash	%Stocks	%Bonds	%Other	Turnover Ratio	Last Bull Market Total Return	Last Bear Market Total Return	Front End Fee (%)	Back End Fee (%)	Inception Date
	2.09	2.88	0.97	-6.95	-7.20		0.74	4.26	-0.05	9.28	10.8	56	14	25	4	83	3.65	-0.49			Aug-17
	2.05	3.25	6.25			0	2.48			10.35	11.1	12	88	0	0	11			5.75		Jul-15
	1.92	2.93	5.42			0	3.23			10.27	11.1	12	88	0	0	11				1.00	Jul-15
	2.18	3.57	6.67			0.1	2.02			10.41	11.1	12	88	0	0	11					Jul-15
	2.18	3.87	6.98				1.02			10.41	11.1	12	88	0	0	11					Aug-17
	2.71	5.20	11.14			0	2.59			9.7	9.4	13	87	0	0	152			5.75		Jul-15
	2.58	4.77	10.28			0	3.22			9.62	9.4	13	87	0	0	152				1.00	Jul-15
	2.80	5.49	11.54			0.17	2.19			9.74	9.4	13	87	0	0	152					Jul-15
	2.91	5.80	11.88				1.37			9.75	9.4	13	87	0	0	152					Aug-17
	1.50	2.23	4.79	-1.39		1.62	2.86	8.84	0.48	8.98	14.6	21	72	4	1	118			5.75		Sep-14
	1.33	1.76	3.81	-3.63		1.29	3.61	8.81	0.48	8.82	14.6	21	72	4	1	118				1.00	Sep-14
	1.56	2.24	5.00	-0.73		1.76	2.61	8.85	0.48	9	14.6	21	72	4	1	118					Sep-14
	1.78	2.58	5.35	-0.40			1.5	8.86	0.48	9.02	14.6	21	72	4	1	118					Aug-17
	0.35						2.45			10.13	4.2	11	15	71	1				5.75		Aug-17
	0.35						3.2			10.13	4.2	11	15	71	1					1.00	Aug-17
	0.35						1.2			10.13	4.2	11	15	71	1						Aug-17
	0.35						2.2			10.13	4.2	11	15	71	1						Aug-17
	2.09	4.64					2.37			10.38	2.2	19	36	39	3				5.75		Jun-17
	1.90	4.45					3.12			10.39	2.2	19	36	39	3					1.00	Jun-17
	2.17	4.82					1.12			10.39	2.2	19	36	39	3						Jun-17
	2.17	4.82					2.12			10.39	2.2	19	36	39	3						Jun-17
	3.20	0.54	-9.27			6.78	2.27			6.23	5.3	1	99	0	0	101			5.75		Mar-15
	3.01	0.15	-9.98			5.91	3.02			6.22	5.3	1	99	0	0	101				1.00	Mar-15
	3.27	0.51	-9.16			7.1	2.02			6.22	5.3	1	99	0	0	101					Mar-15
	2.46	4.61	6.04	9.27	33.99	1.05	0.97	4.59	0.39	24.08	3,035	5	44	51	0	46	10.82	-5.43			Jul-91
	2.51	4.71	6.29	10.07	35.64	1.31	0.72	4.61	0.4	23.81	3,035	5	44	51	0	46	10.98	-5.33			Mar-09
	5.02	7.30	13.48	8.89	51.38	0	1.57	8.93	0.71	15.32	22.2	19	81	0	0	38	19.13				May-11
	2.68	7.56	2.91	26.14	102.04	0	1.52	14.56	0.77	17.23	30.9	4	96	0	0	97	32.44	-24.27			Jul-10
	4.25	10.57	14.66	20.64	73.55	0.11	1.52	9.3	0.6	11.38	16.2	8	92	0	0	150	21.83	-21.58			Jun-06
	4.11	11.77	6.56	17.14	69.40	0.45	1.52	13.6	0.84	30.23	67.2	0	100	0	0	129	24.21	-16.37			Oct-98
	7.83	11.63	19.74	22.66	87.01	0.9	1.03	11.52	1.11	22.3	38.8	4	96	0	0	27	23.61	-16.48			Dec-92
	4.15	8.10	16.97			0.78	1.06			10.61	65.4	2	84	13	0	302			5.75		Jun-15
	3.95	7.72	16.02			0.15	1.81			10.56	65.4	2	84	13	0	302				1.00	Jun-15
100	4.19	8.24	17.01			0.83	0.96			10.6	65.4	2	84	13	0	302					Jun-15
	4.15	8.19	17.17			1	0.81			10.62	65.4	2	84	13	0	302					Jun-15
	4.20	8.24	17.23			1	0.81			10.62	65.4	2	84	13	0	302					Jun-15
	4.12	8.07	16.72			0.68	1.06			10.6	65.4	2	84	13	0	302					Jun-15
	4.17	8.12	17.00			0.88	1.06			10.6	65.4	2	84	13	0	302					Jun-15
	2.39	5.35	10.95	13.43	25.28	0.39	1.29	4.79	14.82	10.51	50.1	37	33	22	7	55			5.75		Mar-12
	2.19	5.02	10.19	10.93	20.47	0	2.05	4.77	15.27	10.34	50.1	37	33	22	7	55				1.00	Mar-12
100	2.42	5.49	11.22	14.32	26.78		1.11	4.73	14.75	10.44	50.1	37	33	22	7	55					Jun-17
	2.42	5.49	11.23	14.32	26.79	0.63	1.03	4.73	14.29	10.44	50.1	37	33	22	7	55					Mar-12
	2.45	5.53	11.28	14.31	26.78	0.75	0.97	4.75	15.09	10.42	50.1	37	33	22	7	55					Nov-15
	2.30	5.27	10.85	13.37	25.10		1.46	4.73	14.55	10.45	50.1	37	33	22	7	55					Jun-17
	2.44	5.51	11.25	14.34	26.81		1.21	4.73	14.66	10.46	50.1	37	33	22	7	55					Jun-17
	7.14	11.83	39.25	36.80	47.14	0.93	1.66	15.52	1.01	11.94	42.3	0	94	0	3	120	23.68		5.75		Jul-11
	6.93	11.34	38.36	33.96	41.98	0.33	2.34	15.56	1.01	11.87	42.3	0	94	0	3	120	23.55			1.00	Jul-11
100	7.10	11.84	39.42	37.62	48.37	0.89	1.46	15.55	1.01	12.05	42.3	0	94	0	3	120	24.25				Jul-11
	7.14	11.89	39.64	38.13	49.43	1.1	1.32	15.53	1.01	12.04	42.3	0	94	0	3	120	23.82				Jul-11
	7.10	11.78	39.25	37.01	47.29	0.8	1.79	15.45	1	11.98	42.3	0	94	0	3	120	23.68				Jul-11
	7.12	11.82	39.49	37.53	48.31	0.7	1.55	15.55	1.01	11.91	42.3	0	94	0	3	120	23.68				Jul-11
	5.19	9.20	18.24	23.18	61.61	1.72	0.94	6.71	0.64	32.86	13,878	1	65	32	2	60	17.76	-12.35	5.75		Jul-09

	MARKET			FUND TYPE, CATEGORY & OBJECTIVE	RATINGS				MINIMUMS	
Fund Name	Ticker Symbol	Traded On	Fund Type	Category and (Prospectus Objective)	Overall Rating	Reward Rating	Risk Rating	Recent Up/ Downgrade	Open to New Investors	Min Initial Investment
Janus Henderson Balanced Fund Class C	JABCX	NAS CM	Open End	Moderate Alloc (Balanced)	B-	C+	B	Down	Y	2,500
Janus Henderson Balanced Fund Class D	JANBX	NAS CM	Open End	Moderate Alloc (Balanced)	B-	C+	B	Down		2,500
Janus Henderson Balanced Fund Class I	JBALX	NAS CM	Open End	Moderate Alloc (Balanced)	B-	C+	B	Down	Y	1,000,000
Janus Henderson Balanced Fund Class N	JABNX	NAS CM	Open End	Moderate Alloc (Balanced)	B-	B-	B	Down	Y	0
Janus Henderson Balanced Fund Class R	JDBRX	NAS CM	Open End	Moderate Alloc (Balanced)	B-	C+	B	Down	Y	2,500
Janus Henderson Balanced Fund Class S	JABRX	NAS CM	Open End	Moderate Alloc (Balanced)	B-	C+	B	Down	Y	2,500
Janus Henderson Balanced Fund Class T	JABAX	NAS CM	Open End	Moderate Alloc (Balanced)	B-	C+	B	Down	Y	2,500
Janus Henderson Contrarian Fund Class A	JCNAX	NAS CM	Open End	US Equity Mid Cap (Growth)	C	C	C+		Y	2,500
Janus Henderson Contrarian Fund Class C	JCNCX	NAS CM	Open End	US Equity Mid Cap (Growth)	C	C	C		Y	2,500
Janus Henderson Contrarian Fund Class D	JACNX	NAS CM	Open End	US Equity Mid Cap (Growth)	C	C	C+			2,500
Janus Henderson Contrarian Fund Class I	JCONX	NAS CM	Open End	US Equity Mid Cap (Growth)	C	C	C+		Y	1,000,000
Janus Henderson Contrarian Fund Class N	JCNNX	NAS CM	Open End	US Equity Mid Cap (Growth)	C	C	C+		Y	0
Janus Henderson Contrarian Fund Class R	JCNRX	NAS CM	Open End	US Equity Mid Cap (Growth)	C	C	C		Y	2,500
Janus Henderson Contrarian Fund Class S	JCNIX	NAS CM	Open End	US Equity Mid Cap (Growth)	C	C	C+		Y	2,500
Janus Henderson Contrarian Fund Class T	JSVAX	NAS CM	Open End	US Equity Mid Cap (Growth)	C	C	C+		Y	2,500
Janus Henderson Diversified Alternatives Fund Class A	JDDAX	NAS CM	Open End	Multialternative (Growth & Income)	B-	C	B	Up	Y	2,500
Janus Henderson Diversified Alternatives Fund Class C	JDDCX	NAS CM	Open End	Multialternative (Growth & Income)	C+	C	B	Down	Y	2,500
Janus Henderson Diversified Alternatives Fund Class D	JDADX	NAS CM	Open End	Multialternative (Growth & Income)	B-	C	B	Up	Y	2,500
Janus Henderson Diversified Alternatives Fund Class I	JDAIX	NAS CM	Open End	Multialternative (Growth & Income)	B-	C	B	Down	Y	1,000,000
Janus Henderson Diversified Alternatives Fund Class N	JDANX	NAS CM	Open End	Multialternative (Growth & Income)	B-	C	B	Down	Y	1,000,000
Janus Henderson Diversified Alternatives Fund Class S	JDASX	NAS CM	Open End	Multialternative (Growth & Income)	B-	C	B	Up	Y	2,500
Janus Henderson Diversified Alternatives Fund Class T	JDATX	NAS CM	Open End	Multialternative (Growth & Income)	B-	C	B		Y	2,500
Janus Henderson Dividend & Income Builder Fund Class A	HDAVX	NAS CM	Open End	Alloc (Equity-Income)	B-	C+	B	Down	Y	2,500
Janus Henderson Dividend & Income Builder Fund Class C	HDCVX	NAS CM	Open End	Alloc (Equity-Income)	B	C+	B+	Up	Y	2,500
Janus Henderson Dividend & Income Builder Fund Class D	HDDVX	NAS CM	Open End	Alloc (Equity-Income)	B-	C+	B	Down	Y	2,500
Janus Henderson Dividend & Income Builder Fund Class I	HDIVX	NAS CM	Open End	Alloc (Equity-Income)	B-	C+	B	Down	Y	1,000,000
Janus Henderson Dividend & Income Builder Fund Class N	HDRVX	NAS CM	Open End	Alloc (Equity-Income)	B-	C+	B	Down	Y	1,000,000
Janus Henderson Dividend & Income Builder Fund Class S	HDQVX	NAS CM	Open End	Alloc (Equity-Income)	B-	C+	B	Down	Y	2,500
Janus Henderson Dividend & Income Builder Fund Class T	HDTVX	NAS CM	Open End	Alloc (Equity-Income)	B-	C+	B	Down	Y	2,500
Janus Henderson Emerging Markets Fund Class A	HEMAX	NAS CM	Open End	Emerging Markets Equity (Div Emerging Mkts)	C+	C+	C+		Y	2,500
Janus Henderson Emerging Markets Fund Class C	HEMCX	NAS CM	Open End	Emerging Markets Equity (Div Emerging Mkts)	C+	C+	C+	Up	Y	2,500
Janus Henderson Emerging Markets Fund Class D	HEMDX	NAS CM	Open End	Emerging Markets Equity (Div Emerging Mkts)	C+	B-	C+		Y	2,500
Janus Henderson Emerging Markets Fund Class I	HEMIX	NAS CM	Open End	Emerging Markets Equity (Div Emerging Mkts)	C+	B-	C+		Y	1,000,000
Janus Henderson Emerging Markets Fund Class N	HEMRX	NAS CM	Open End	Emerging Markets Equity (Div Emerging Mkts)	C+	B-	C+		Y	1,000,000
Janus Henderson Emerging Markets Fund Class S	HEMSX	NAS CM	Open End	Emerging Markets Equity (Div Emerging Mkts)	C+	C+	C+		Y	2,500
Janus Henderson Emerging Markets Fund Class T	HEMTX	NAS CM	Open End	Emerging Markets Equity (Div Emerging Mkts)	C+	B-	C+		Y	2,500
Janus Henderson Emerging Mkts Managed Vol Fund Cls A	JOLAX	NAS CM	Open End	Emerging Markets Equity (Growth)	C+	C+	C	Up	Y	2,500
Janus Henderson Emerging Mkts Managed Vol Fund Cls C	JOLCX	NAS CM	Open End	Emerging Markets Equity (Growth)	C+	C+	C	Up	Y	2,500
Janus Henderson Emerging Mkts Managed Vol Fund Cls D	JOLDX	NAS CM	Open End	Emerging Markets Equity (Growth)	C+	C+	C	Up	Y	2,500
Janus Henderson Emerging Mkts Managed Vol Fund Cls I	JOLIX	NAS CM	Open End	Emerging Markets Equity (Growth)	C+	C+	C	Up	Y	1,000,000
Janus Henderson Emerging Mkts Managed Vol Fund Cls N	JOLNX	NAS CM	Open End	Emerging Markets Equity (Growth)	C+	C+	C		Y	1,000,000
Janus Henderson Emerging Mkts Managed Vol Fund Cls S	JOLSX	NAS CM	Open End	Emerging Markets Equity (Growth)	C+	C+	C	Up	Y	2,500
Janus Henderson Emerging Mkts Managed Vol Fund Cls T	JOLTX	NAS CM	Open End	Emerging Markets Equity (Growth)	C+	C+	C	Up	Y	2,500
Janus Henderson Enterprise Fund Class A	JDMAX	NAS CM	Open End	US Equity Mid Cap (Growth)	B	B+	B-	Down	Y	2,500
Janus Henderson Enterprise Fund Class C	JGRCX	NAS CM	Open End	US Equity Mid Cap (Growth)	B	B+	B-	Down	Y	2,500
Janus Henderson Enterprise Fund Class D	JANEX	NAS CM	Open End	US Equity Mid Cap (Growth)	B	B+	B	Down		2,500
Janus Henderson Enterprise Fund Class I	JMGRX	NAS CM	Open End	US Equity Mid Cap (Growth)	B	B+	B	Down	Y	1,000,000
Janus Henderson Enterprise Fund Class N	JDMNX	NAS CM	Open End	US Equity Mid Cap (Growth)	B	B+	B	Down	Y	0
Janus Henderson Enterprise Fund Class R	JDMRX	NAS CM	Open End	US Equity Mid Cap (Growth)	B	B+	B-	Down	Y	2,500
Janus Henderson Enterprise Fund Class S	JGRTX	NAS CM	Open End	US Equity Mid Cap (Growth)	B	B+	B-	Down	Y	2,500
Janus Henderson Enterprise Fund Class T	JAENX	NAS CM	Open End	US Equity Mid Cap (Growth)	B	B+	B	Down	Y	2,500
Janus Henderson European Focus Fund Class A	HFEAX	NAS CM	Open End	Europe Equity Large Cap (Europe Stock)	C+	C	C+	Up	Y	2,500

★ Expanded analysis of this fund is included in Section II.

	TOTAL RETURNS					PERFORMANCE				ASSETS		ASSET ALLOCATION & TURNOVER					BULL & BEAR		FEES		
Min Additional Investment	3-Month Total Return	6-Month Total Return	1-Year Total Return	3-Year Total Return	5-Year Total Return	Dividend Yield (TTM)	Expense Ratio	3-Yr Std Deviation	3-Year Beta	NAV	Total Assets (MIL)	%Cash	%Stocks	%Bonds	%Other	Turnover Ratio	Last Bull Market Total Return	Last Bear Market Total Return	Front End Fee (%)	Back End Fee (%)	Inception Date
	5.02	8.84	17.42	20.69	55.98	1.18	1.67	6.7	0.64	32.58	13,878	1	65	32	2	60	17.3	-12.67		1.00	Jul-09
100	5.27	9.34	18.51	23.95	63.29	1.93	0.73	6.73	0.64	32.93	13,878	1	65	32	2	60	17.88	-12.28			Sep-92
	5.29	9.38	18.58	24.24	63.90	1.99	0.67	6.71	0.64	32.94	13,878	1	65	32	2	60	17.94	-12.25			Jul-09
	5.32	9.42	18.68	24.52	64.48	2.05	0.59	6.72	0.64	32.91	13,878	1	65	32	2	60	17.88	-12.28			May-12
	5.08	8.99	17.79	21.74	58.48	1.46	1.34	6.7	0.64	32.68	13,878	1	65	32	2	60	17.51	-12.53			Jul-09
	5.16	9.11	18.05	22.64	60.49	1.63	1.09	6.74	0.64	32.84	13,878	1	65	32	2	60	17.68	-12.43			Jul-09
	5.22	9.26	18.38	23.61	62.55	1.85	0.84	6.72	0.64	32.89	13,878	1	65	32	2	60	17.84	-12.33			Sep-92
	2.28	2.33	5.13	-2.08	62.67	0.02	0.9	11.82	0.87	18.89	2,612	4	96	0	0	116	24.69	-26.04	5.75		Jul-09
	2.09	1.99	4.43	-4.13	56.69	0	1.66	11.8	0.87	17.72	2,612	4	96	0	0	116	24.28	-26.3		1.00	Jul-09
100	2.36	2.47	5.37	-1.46	64.31	0.31	0.7	11.82	0.87	18.9	2,612	4	96	0	0	116	25	-26.06			Feb-00
	2.35	2.45	5.41	-1.22	64.98	0.37	0.63	11.82	0.87	18.91	2,612	4	96	0	0	116	24.91	-26.06			Jul-09
	2.33	2.49	5.39	-1.44	64.34		0.55	11.82	0.87	18.86	2,612	4	96	0	0	116	25	-26.06			Aug-17
	2.17	2.12	4.70	-3.18	59.63	0	1.3	11.82	0.87	18.42	2,612	4	96	0	0	116	24.53	-26.25			Jul-09
	2.23	2.23	4.97	-2.49	61.65	0	1.04	11.82	0.87	18.86	2,612	4	96	0	0	116	24.75	-26.19			Jul-09
	2.27	2.37	5.27	-1.69	63.67	0.24	0.79	11.83	0.87	18.89	2,612	4	96	0	0	116	24.93	-26.12			Feb-00
	1.17	1.96	3.59	6.84	8.44	2.71	1.36	4.87	0.47	10.1	106.6	59	0	41	0	16			5.75		Dec-12
	1.01	1.52	2.87	4.39	5.01	2.11	2.1	4.88	0.46	9.94	106.6	59	0	41	0	16				1.00	Dec-12
100	1.26	2.05	3.78	7.25	9.07	2.8	1.24	4.85	0.48	10.14	106.6	59	0	41	0	16					Dec-12
	1.24	2.04	3.86	7.58	9.62	2.93	1.13	4.88	0.46	10.15	106.6	59	0	41	0	16					Dec-12
	1.34	2.13	3.95	7.74	9.89	2.9	1.09	4.89	0.46	10.18	106.6	59	0	41	0	16					Dec-12
	1.29	1.89	3.64	6.76	7.93	2.89	1.34	4.83	0.46	10.06	106.6	59	0	41	0	16					Dec-12
	1.19	1.99	3.72	7.30	8.90	3.01	1.34	4.88	0.45	10.09	106.6	59	0	41	0	16					Dec-12
	2.62	7.30	17.47	23.47	52.39	2.58	1.15	8.51	0.76	13.7	153.8	6	76	14	2	55			5.75		Aug-12
	2.44	6.93	16.60	20.71	46.69	2.03	1.92	8.52	0.76	13.55	153.8	6	76	14	2	55				1.00	Aug-12
100	2.58	7.39	17.79	24.37	54.11		1	8.5	0.76	13.69	153.8	6	76	14	2	55					Jun-17
	2.65	7.38	17.77	24.35	54.09	2.77	0.94	8.49	0.76	13.7	153.8	6	76	14	2	55					Aug-12
	2.67	7.44	17.66	24.15	53.84	2.9	1	8.5	0.76	13.67	153.8	6	76	14	2	55					Nov-15
	2.60	7.23	17.46	23.41	52.16		1.35	8.49	0.76	13.69	153.8	6	76	14	2	55					Jun-17
	2.58	7.30	17.69	24.26	53.97		1.1	8.49	0.76	13.68	153.8	6	76	14	2	55					Jun-17
	7.11	12.66	29.49	26.76	26.48	0.59	1.42	12.56	0.74	10.78	194.2	6	94	0	0	2	29.31	-28.76	5.75		Dec-10
	6.93	12.21	28.58	24.02	21.90	0.14	2.18	12.55	0.74	10.44	194.2	6	94	0	0	2	28.71	-29.02		1.00	Dec-10
100	7.22	12.75	29.66	27.56	28.05		1.21	12.59	0.74	10.83	194.2	6	94	0	0	2	29.57	-28.74			Jun-17
	7.15	12.89	29.82	27.72	28.21	0.71	1.12	12.58	0.74	10.82	194.2	6	94	0	0	2	29.57	-28.74			Dec-10
	7.14	12.88	29.96	27.72	28.20	0.73	1.21	12.6	0.74	10.82	194.2	6	94	0	0	2	29.57	-28.74			Nov-15
	7.07	12.58	29.31	26.58	26.43		1.54	12.57	0.74	10.83	194.2	6	94	0	0	2	29.38	-28.81			Jun-17
	7.09	12.71	29.62	27.52	28.01		1.29	12.57	0.74	10.83	194.2	6	94	0	0	2	29.57	-28.74			Jun-17
	6.19	15.32	34.16	21.61		0.83	1.3			11.86	8.8	1	99	0	0	116			5.75		Dec-14
	5.93	14.86	33.24	18.90		0.18	2.04			11.84	8.8	1	99	0	0	116				1.00	Dec-14
100	6.17	15.40	34.40	21.99		0.95	5.76			11.85	8.8	1	99	0	0	116					Dec-14
	6.21	15.43	34.57	22.49		1.04	1.12			11.91	8.8	1	99	0	0	116					Dec-14
	6.18	15.50	34.64	22.55			0.97			11.86	8.8	1	99	0	0	116					Aug-17
	6.16	15.29	34.12	21.35		0.75	1.31			11.87	8.8	1	99	0	0	116					Dec-14
	6.14	15.36	34.33	22.04		0.94	1.31			11.86	8.8	1	99	0	0	116					Dec-14
	5.40	10.74	26.07	44.03	114.80	0	1.18	10.05	0.88	115.08	16,122	7	92	0	0	10	24.26	-19.05	5.75		Jul-09
	5.25	10.44	25.34	41.34	107.84	0	1.81	10.04	0.88	107.66	16,122	7	92	0	0	10	23.74	-19.31		1.00	Jul-09
100	5.47	10.92	26.46	45.32	117.91	0.07	0.84	10.06	0.88	117.68	16,122	7	92	0	0	10	24.41	-19.03			Sep-92
	5.50	10.95	26.53	45.64	118.67	0.13	0.78	10.05	0.88	118.24	16,122	7	92	0	0	10	24.47	-18.97			Jul-09
	5.52	11.00	26.64	46.03	119.73	0.17	0.68	10.05	0.88	118.59	16,122	7	92	0	0	10	24.41	-19.03			Jul-12
	5.32	10.58	25.71	42.79	111.67	0	1.43	10.04	0.88	111.88	16,122	7	92	0	0	10	23.99	-19.22			Jul-09
	5.38	10.72	26.02	43.86	114.38	0	1.18	10.05	0.88	114.58	16,122	7	92	0	0	10	24.18	-19.15			Jul-09
	5.45	10.87	26.34	44.96	117.07	0.05	0.93	10.06	0.88	116.99	16,122	7	92	0	0	10	24.35	-19.05			Sep-92
	0.76	6.99	16.11	10.16	44.31	2.23	1.27	12.93	0.93	34.69	1,663	0	97	0	3	6	25.05	-33.19	5.75		Aug-01

	MARKET			FUND TYPE, CATEGORY & OBJECTIVE	RATINGS					MINIMUMS
Fund Name	Ticker Symbol	Traded On	Fund Type	Category and (Prospectus Objective)	Overall Rating	Reward Rating	Risk Rating	Recent Up/ Downgrade	Open to New Investors	Min Initial Investment
Janus Henderson European Focus Fund Class C	HFECX	NAS CM	Open End	Europe Equity Large Cap (Europe Stock)	C	C	C+	Up	Y	2,500
Janus Henderson European Focus Fund Class D	HFEDX	NAS CM	Open End	Europe Equity Large Cap (Europe Stock)	C+	C	C+	Up	Y	2,500
Janus Henderson European Focus Fund Class I	HFEIX	NAS CM	Open End	Europe Equity Large Cap (Europe Stock)	C+	C	C+	Up	Y	1,000,000
Janus Henderson European Focus Fund Class N	HFERX	NAS CM	Open End	Europe Equity Large Cap (Europe Stock)	C+	C	C+	Up	Y	1,000,000
Janus Henderson European Focus Fund Class S	HFESX	NAS CM	Open End	Europe Equity Large Cap (Europe Stock)	C+	C	C+	Up	Y	2,500
Janus Henderson European Focus Fund Class T	HFETX	NAS CM	Open End	Europe Equity Large Cap (Europe Stock)	C+	C	C+	Up	Y	2,500
Janus Henderson Forty Fund Class A	JDCAX	NAS CM	Open End	US Equity Large Cap Growth (Growth)	B+	B+	A-	Up	Y	2,500
Janus Henderson Forty Fund Class C	JACCX	NAS CM	Open End	US Equity Large Cap Growth (Growth)	B+	B+	A-	Up	Y	2,500
Janus Henderson Forty Fund Class D	JFRDX	NAS CM	Open End	US Equity Large Cap Growth (Growth)	B+	B+	A-	Up	Y	2,500
Janus Henderson Forty Fund Class I	JCAPX	NAS CM	Open End	US Equity Large Cap Growth (Growth)	B+	B+	A-	Up	Y	1,000,000
Janus Henderson Forty Fund Class N	JFRNX	NAS CM	Open End	US Equity Large Cap Growth (Growth)	B+	B+	A-	Up	Y	0
Janus Henderson Forty Fund Class R	JDCRX	NAS CM	Open End	US Equity Large Cap Growth (Growth)	B+	B+	A-	Up	Y	2,500
Janus Henderson Forty Fund Class S	JARTX	NAS CM	Open End	US Equity Large Cap Growth (Growth)	B+	B+	A-	Up	Y	2,500
Janus Henderson Forty Fund Class T	JACTX	NAS CM	Open End	US Equity Large Cap Growth (Growth)	B+	B+	A-	Up	Y	2,500
Janus Henderson Global Alloc Fund - Conservative Cls A	JCAAX	NAS CM	Open End	Alloc (Growth & Income)	B-	C+	B+	Up	Y	2,500
Janus Henderson Global Alloc Fund - Conservative Cls C	JCACX	NAS CM	Open End	Alloc (Growth & Income)	B-	C	B+	Up	Y	2,500
Janus Henderson Global Alloc Fund - Conservative Cls D	JMSCX	NAS CM	Open End	Alloc (Growth & Income)	B-	C+	B+	Up		2,500
Janus Henderson Global Alloc Fund - Conservative Cls I	JCAIX	NAS CM	Open End	Alloc (Growth & Income)	B-	C+	B+	Up	Y	1,000,000
Janus Henderson Global Alloc Fund - Conservative Cls S	JCASX	NAS CM	Open End	Alloc (Growth & Income)	B-	C+	B+	Up	Y	2,500
Janus Henderson Global Alloc Fund - Conservative Cls T	JSPCX	NAS CM	Open End	Alloc (Growth & Income)	B-	C+	B+	Up	Y	2,500
Janus Henderson Global Allocation Fund - Growth Class A	JGCAX	NAS CM	Open End	Alloc (Growth & Income)	B-	C+	B	Up	Y	2,500
Janus Henderson Global Allocation Fund - Growth Class C	JGCCX	NAS CM	Open End	Alloc (Growth & Income)	B-	C+	B	Up	Y	2,500
Janus Henderson Global Allocation Fund - Growth Class D	JNSGX	NAS CM	Open End	Alloc (Growth & Income)	B-	C+	B	Down		2,500
Janus Henderson Global Allocation Fund - Growth Class I	JGCIX	NAS CM	Open End	Alloc (Growth & Income)	B-	C+	B	Down	Y	1,000,000
Janus Henderson Global Allocation Fund - Growth Class S	JGCSX	NAS CM	Open End	Alloc (Growth & Income)	B-	C+	B	Up	Y	2,500
Janus Henderson Global Allocation Fund - Growth Class T	JSPGX	NAS CM	Open End	Alloc (Growth & Income)	B-	C+	B	Down	Y	2,500
Janus Henderson Global Allocation Fund - Moderate Class A	JMOAX	NAS CM	Open End	Alloc (Growth & Income)	B-	C+	B	Down	Y	2,500
Janus Henderson Global Allocation Fund - Moderate Class C	JMOCX	NAS CM	Open End	Alloc (Growth & Income)	B-	C+	B	Up	Y	2,500
Janus Henderson Global Allocation Fund - Moderate Class D	JNSMX	NAS CM	Open End	Alloc (Growth & Income)	B-	C+	B+	Down		2,500
Janus Henderson Global Allocation Fund - Moderate Class I	JMOIX	NAS CM	Open End	Alloc (Growth & Income)	B-	C+	B+	Down	Y	1,000,000
Janus Henderson Global Allocation Fund - Moderate Class S	JMOSX	NAS CM	Open End	Alloc (Growth & Income)	B-	C+	B	Down	Y	2,500
Janus Henderson Global Allocation Fund - Moderate Class T	JSPMX	NAS CM	Open End	Alloc (Growth & Income)	B-	C+	B+	Down	Y	2,500
Janus Henderson Global Equity Income Fund Class A	HFQAX	NAS CM	Open End	Global Equity Large Cap (Equity-Income)	B-	C+	B-	Up	Y	2,500
Janus Henderson Global Equity Income Fund Class C	HFQCX	NAS CM	Open End	Global Equity Large Cap (Equity-Income)	B-	C+	B	Up	Y	2,500
Janus Henderson Global Equity Income Fund Class D	HFQDX	NAS CM	Open End	Global Equity Large Cap (Equity-Income)	B-	C+	B-		Y	2,500
Janus Henderson Global Equity Income Fund Class I	HFQIX	NAS CM	Open End	Global Equity Large Cap (Equity-Income)	B-	C+	B-	Up	Y	1,000,000
Janus Henderson Global Equity Income Fund Class N	HFQRX	NAS CM	Open End	Global Equity Large Cap (Equity-Income)	B-	C+	B-	Up	Y	1,000,000
Janus Henderson Global Equity Income Fund Class S	HFQSX	NAS CM	Open End	Global Equity Large Cap (Equity-Income)	B-	C+	B		Y	2,500
Janus Henderson Global Equity Income Fund Class T	HFQTX	NAS CM	Open End	Global Equity Large Cap (Equity-Income)	B-	C+	B-		Y	2,500
Janus Henderson Global Income Managed Vol Fund Cls A	JGDAX	NAS CM	Open End	Global Equity (Income)	B	C+	A		Y	2,500
Janus Henderson Global Income Managed Vol Fund Cls C	JGDCX	NAS CM	Open End	Global Equity (Income)	B	C+	A		Y	2,500
Janus Henderson Global Income Managed Vol Fund Cls D	JGDDX	NAS CM	Open End	Global Equity (Income)	B	B-	A		Y	2,500
Janus Henderson Global Income Managed Vol Fund Cls I	JGDIX	NAS CM	Open End	Global Equity (Income)	B	B-	A		Y	1,000,000
Janus Henderson Global Income Managed Vol Fund Cls N	JGGNX	NAS CM	Open End	Global Equity (Income)	B	B-	A		Y	1,000,000
Janus Henderson Global Income Managed Vol Fund Cls S	JGDSX	NAS CM	Open End	Global Equity (Income)	B	C+	A		Y	2,500
Janus Henderson Global Income Managed Vol Fund Cls T	JDGTX	NAS CM	Open End	Global Equity (Income)	B	B-	A		Y	2,500
Janus Henderson Global Life Sciences Fund Class A	JFNAX	NAS CM	Open End	Healthcare Sector Equity (Health)	C+	C	B-	Down	Y	2,500
Janus Henderson Global Life Sciences Fund Class C	JFNCX	NAS CM	Open End	Healthcare Sector Equity (Health)	C+	C	B-	Down	Y	2,500
Janus Henderson Global Life Sciences Fund Class D	JNGLX	NAS CM	Open End	Healthcare Sector Equity (Health)	C+	C	B-	Down		2,500
Janus Henderson Global Life Sciences Fund Class I	JFNIX	NAS CM	Open End	Healthcare Sector Equity (Health)	C+	C	B-	Down	Y	1,000,000
Janus Henderson Global Life Sciences Fund Class S	JFNSX	NAS CM	Open End	Healthcare Sector Equity (Health)	C+	C	B-	Down	Y	2,500
Janus Henderson Global Life Sciences Fund Class T	JAGLX	NAS CM	Open End	Healthcare Sector Equity (Health)	C+	C	B-	Down	Y	2,500

★ Expanded analysis of this fund is included in Section II.

	TOTAL RETURNS					PERFORMANCE				ASSETS		ASSET ALLOCATION & TURNOVER					BULL & BEAR		FEES		
Min Additional Investment	3-Month Total Return	6-Month Total Return	1-Year Total Return	3-Year Total Return	5-Year Total Return	Dividend Yield (TTM)	Expense Ratio	3-Yr Std Deviation	3-Year Beta	NAV	Total Assets (MIL)	%Cash	%Stocks	%Bonds	%Other	Turnover Ratio	Last Bull Market Total Return	Last Bear Market Total Return	Front End Fee (%)	Back End Fee (%)	Inception Date
	0.58	6.59	15.26	7.61	38.86	1.57	2.06	12.92	0.93	32.61	1,663	0	97	0	3	6	24.46	-33.41		1.00	Aug-01
100	0.80	7.06	16.19	10.23	44.41		1.1	12.93	0.93	34.51	1,663	0	97	0	3	6	25.05	-33.19			Jun-17
	0.82	7.10	16.41	10.96	46.20	2.72	1.03	12.94	0.93	34.47	1,663	0	97	0	3	6	25.32	-33.14			Mar-09
	0.84	7.11	16.31	10.65	44.95	2.77	1.04	12.93	0.93	34.51	1,663	0	97	0	3	6	25.05	-33.19			Nov-15
	0.73	6.96	16.08	10.13	44.27		1.45	12.93	0.93	34.51	1,663	0	97	0	3	6	25.05	-33.19			Jun-17
	0.76	7.03	16.15	10.20	44.36		1.2	12.93	0.93	34.5	1,663	0	97	0	3	6	25.05	-33.19			Jun-17
	4.38	10.15	29.19	46.52	115.55	0	1.1	11.99	1.06	31.56	11,753	5	95	0	0	56	28.16	-18.49	5.75		Sep-04
	4.26	9.86	28.39	44.25	108.92	0	1.83	11.91	1.05	26.36	11,753	5	95	0	0	56	27.59	-18.84		1.00	Sep-02
100	4.45	10.31	29.50	46.51	115.61		0.85	11.97	1.06	30.52	11,753	5	95	0	0	56	28.1	-18.64			Jan-17
	4.47	10.34	29.60	47.89	118.99	0	0.78	11.96	1.06	32.59	11,753	5	95	0	0	56	28.36	-18.49			Nov-05
	4.50	10.40	29.71	48.14	119.92	0	0.71	11.98	1.06	32.68	11,753	5	95	0	0	56	28.1	-18.64			May-12
	4.31	9.98	28.73	44.92	111.83	0	1.47	11.96	1.06	28.46	11,753	5	95	0	0	56	27.88	-18.71			Sep-04
	4.37	10.13	29.09	46.05	114.94	0	1.21	11.96	1.06	30.41	11,753	5	95	0	0	56	28.1	-18.64			May-97
	4.43	10.25	29.36	47.06	117.29	0	0.96	11.97	1.06	30.92	11,753	5	95	0	0	56	28.25	-18.53			Jul-09
	2.56	5.30	12.74	12.00	29.82	0.37	0.78	4.99	0.5	12.67	237.1	7	43	48	1	25	10.69	-7.18	5.75		Jul-09
	2.36	4.90	11.90	10.47	26.24	0.13	1.51	4.93	0.5	12.43	237.1	7	43	48	1	25	10.28	-7.55		1.00	Jul-09
100	2.63	5.44	12.87	12.74	31.19	0.83	0.58	5.01	0.5	12.71	237.1	7	43	48	1	25	10.81	-7.15			Dec-05
	2.61	5.43	12.94	12.86	31.40	0.91	0.53	5.02	0.5	12.7	237.1	7	43	48	1	25	10.9	-7.15			Jul-09
	2.50	5.18	12.46	11.51	28.83	0.49	0.71	5	0.5	12.61	237.1	7	43	48	1	25	10.55	-7.26			Jul-09
	2.63	5.37	12.80	12.48	30.91	0.76	0.68	4.97	0.49	12.69	237.1	7	43	48	1	25	10.79	-7.15			Dec-05
	4.17	8.35	19.55	20.17	50.25	1.02	1.01	7.98	0.74	14.25	262.7	6	81	12	1	35	16.9	-17.47	5.75		Jul-09
	3.98	7.99	18.70	18.15	45.53	0.43	1.79	7.92	0.73	14.02	262.7	6	81	12	1	35	16.4	-17.77		1.00	Jul-09
100	4.19	8.40	19.71	20.67	51.35	1.12	0.85	7.99	0.74	14.34	262.7	6	81	12	1	35	17.12	-17.41			Dec-05
	4.22	8.52	19.84	20.98	51.97	1.18	0.77	7.99	0.74	14.34	262.7	6	81	12	1	35	17.22	-17.48			Jul-09
	4.11	8.22	19.29	19.54	48.99	0.79	0.96	8	0.74	14.18	262.7	6	81	12	1	35	16.81	-17.53			Jul-09
	4.21	8.43	19.67	20.59	51.09	1.07	0.93	8.02	0.74	14.33	262.7	6	81	12	1	35	17.08	-17.48			Dec-05
	3.39	6.85	16.03	16.04	39.77	0.81	1.26	6.45	0.58	13.11	264.5	8	61	29	1	32	13.8	-12.5	5.75		Jul-09
	3.20	6.39	15.29	14.10	35.27	0.22	2.02	6.36	0.57	12.94	264.5	8	61	29	1	32	13.36	-12.76		1.00	Jul-09
100	3.41	6.93	16.25	16.73	40.96	1.01	1.08	6.42	0.58	13.18	264.5	8	61	29	1	32	14	-12.46			Dec-05
	3.48	6.92	16.34	16.86	41.27	1.06	1.03	6.44	0.58	13.17	264.5	8	61	29	1	32	14.09	-12.47			Jul-09
	3.30	6.63	15.77	15.41	38.45	0.7	1.19	6.4	0.58	13.01	264.5	8	61	29	1	32	13.7	-12.55			Jul-09
	3.43	6.88	16.22	16.56	40.55	0.94	1.18	6.41	0.58	13.15	264.5	8	61	29	1	32	13.95	-12.48			Dec-05
	3.42	8.16	19.13	23.61	47.82	6.06	1.08	9.31	0.81	7.97	5,369	3	96	0	0	21	13.99	-16.12	5.75		Nov-06
	3.28	7.86	18.46	21.07	42.45	5.43	1.84	9.35	0.81	7.92	5,369	3	96	0	0	21	13.55	-16.45		1.00	Nov-06
100	3.50	8.31	19.30	23.79	48.03		0.91	9.33	0.81	7.96	5,369	3	96	0	0	21	13.99	-16.12			Jun-17
	3.63	8.46	19.59	24.69	49.84	6.3	0.83	9.32	0.81	7.99	5,369	3	96	0	0	21	14.15	-16			Mar-09
	3.65	8.49	19.67	24.57	48.97	6.36	0.78	9.32	0.81	7.99	5,369	3	96	0	0	21	13.99	-16.12			Nov-15
	3.42	8.12	19.09	23.57	47.77		1.25	9.31	0.81	7.96	5,369	3	96	0	0	21	13.99	-16.12			Jun-17
	3.61	8.44	19.43	23.93	48.20		1	9.32	0.81	7.96	5,369	3	96	0	0	21	13.99	-16.12			Jun-17
	2.22	3.81	15.90	30.24	58.15	3.14	0.85	8.15	0.44	13.62	246.3	1	99	0	0	58			5.75		Dec-11
	2.00	3.50	15.10	27.36	52.30	2.53	1.59	8.13	0.44	13.52	246.3	1	99	0	0	58				1.00	Dec-11
100	2.21	3.95	16.16	31.03	59.60	3.4	0.22	8.16	0.44	13.58	246.3	1	99	0	0	58					Dec-11
	2.22	3.97	16.24	31.38	60.42	3.44	0.58	8.14	0.44	13.65	246.3	1	99	0	0	58					Dec-11
	2.23	3.99	16.27	31.41	60.46		0.5	8.14	0.44	13.65	246.3	1	99	0	0	58					Aug-17
	2.22	3.81	15.85	30.14	58.42	3.14	0.75	8.13	0.44	13.59	246.3	1	99	0	0	58					Dec-11
	2.26	3.90	16.03	30.66	59.00	3.3	0.75	8.17	0.44	13.6	246.3	1	99	0	0	58					Dec-11
	-2.00	2.11	22.34	15.44	145.82	0.05	1.04	16.52	1.26	54.08	3,595	2	95	0	2	38	26.76	-13.08	5.75		Jul-09
	-2.19	1.73	21.46	12.87	136.64	0	1.84	16.52	1.26	50.37	3,595	2	95	0	2	38	26.19	-13.34		1.00	Jul-09
100	-1.97	2.19	22.59	16.10	148.12	0.24	0.84	16.54	1.26	54.78	3,595	2	95	0	2	38	26.92	-13.06			Dec-98
	-1.95	2.25	22.66	16.34	148.77	0.3	0.78	16.53	1.26	54.82	3,595	2	95	0	2	38	26.97	-13.03			Jul-09
	-2.05	2.01	22.15	14.97	144.08	0.01	1.19	16.51	1.26	53.41	3,595	2	95	0	2	38	26.65	-13.14			Jul-09
	-1.98	2.16	22.46	15.78	147.01	0.14	0.94	16.52	1.26	54.63	3,595	2	95	0	2	38	26.82	-13.03			Dec-98

	MARKET		FUND TYPE, CATEGORY & OBJECTIVE		RATINGS				MINIMUMS	
Fund Name	Ticker Symbol	Traded On	Fund Type	Category and (Prospectus Objective)	Overall Rating	Reward Rating	Risk Rating	Recent Up/ Downgrade	Open to New Investors	Min Initial Investment
Janus Henderson Global Real Estate Fund Class A	JERAX	NAS CM	Open End	Real Estate Sector Equity (Real Estate)	B-	C+	B	Up	Y	2,500
Janus Henderson Global Real Estate Fund Class C	JERCX	NAS CM	Open End	Real Estate Sector Equity (Real Estate)	B-	C+	B	Up	Y	2,500
Janus Henderson Global Real Estate Fund Class D	JNGSX	NAS CM	Open End	Real Estate Sector Equity (Real Estate)	B-	C+	B	Up		2,500
Janus Henderson Global Real Estate Fund Class I	JERIX	NAS CM	Open End	Real Estate Sector Equity (Real Estate)	B-	C+	B	Up	Y	1,000,000
Janus Henderson Global Real Estate Fund Class S	JERSX	NAS CM	Open End	Real Estate Sector Equity (Real Estate)	B-	C+	B	Up	Y	2,500
Janus Henderson Global Real Estate Fund Class T	JERTX	NAS CM	Open End	Real Estate Sector Equity (Real Estate)	B-	C+	B	Up	Y	2,500
Janus Henderson Global Research Fund Class A	JDWAX	NAS CM	Open End	Global Equity (World Stock)	B-	B-	B	Up	Y	2,500
Janus Henderson Global Research Fund Class C	JWWCX	NAS CM	Open End	Global Equity (World Stock)	B-	B-	B	Up	Y	2,500
Janus Henderson Global Research Fund Class D	JANWX	NAS CM	Open End	Global Equity (World Stock)	B-	B-	B	Up		2,500
Janus Henderson Global Research Fund Class I	JWWFX	NAS CM	Open End	Global Equity (World Stock)	B-	B-	B	Up	Y	1,000,000
Janus Henderson Global Research Fund Class N	JDWNX	NAS CM	Open End	Global Equity (World Stock)	B-	B-	B		Y	0
Janus Henderson Global Research Fund Class R	JDWRX	NAS CM	Open End	Global Equity (World Stock)	B-	B-	B	Up	Y	2,500
Janus Henderson Global Research Fund Class S	JWGRX	NAS CM	Open End	Global Equity (World Stock)	B-	B-	B	Up	Y	2,500
Janus Henderson Global Research Fund Class T	JAWWX	NAS CM	Open End	Global Equity (World Stock)	B-	B-	B	Up	Y	2,500
Janus Henderson Global Select Fund Class A	JORAX	NAS CM	Open End	Global Equity (Aggr Growth)	B-	B	C	Up	Y	2,500
Janus Henderson Global Select Fund Class C	JORCX	NAS CM	Open End	Global Equity (Aggr Growth)	C+	B-	C		Y	2,500
Janus Henderson Global Select Fund Class D	JANRX	NAS CM	Open End	Global Equity (Aggr Growth)	B-	B	C	Up		2,500
Janus Henderson Global Select Fund Class I	JORFX	NAS CM	Open End	Global Equity (Aggr Growth)	B-	B	C	Up	Y	1,000,000
Janus Henderson Global Select Fund Class N	JSLNX	NAS CM	Open End	Global Equity (Aggr Growth)	B-	B	C		Y	0
Janus Henderson Global Select Fund Class R	JORRX	NAS CM	Open End	Global Equity (Aggr Growth)	B-	B-	C	Up	Y	2,500
Janus Henderson Global Select Fund Class S	JORIX	NAS CM	Open End	Global Equity (Aggr Growth)	B-	B	C	Up	Y	2,500
Janus Henderson Global Select Fund Class T	JORNX	NAS CM	Open End	Global Equity (Aggr Growth)	B-	B	C	Up	Y	2,500
Janus Henderson Global Technology Fund Class A	JATAX	NAS CM	Open End	Technology Sector Equity (Technology)	A	A+	B+	Up	Y	2,500
Janus Henderson Global Technology Fund Class C	JAGCX	NAS CM	Open End	Technology Sector Equity (Technology)	A	A+	B+	Up	Y	2,500
Janus Henderson Global Technology Fund Class D	JNGTX	NAS CM	Open End	Technology Sector Equity (Technology)	A	A+	B+	Up		2,500
Janus Henderson Global Technology Fund Class I	JATIX	NAS CM	Open End	Technology Sector Equity (Technology)	A	A+	B+	Up	Y	1,000,000
Janus Henderson Global Technology Fund Class N	JATNX	NAS CM	Open End	Technology Sector Equity (Technology)	A	A+	B+	Up	Y	0
Janus Henderson Global Technology Fund Class S	JATSX	NAS CM	Open End	Technology Sector Equity (Technology)	A	A+	B+	Up	Y	2,500
Janus Henderson Global Technology Fund Class T	JAGTX	NAS CM	Open End	Technology Sector Equity (Technology)	A	A+	B+	Up	Y	2,500
Janus Henderson Global Value Fund Class A	JPPAX	NAS CM	Open End	Global Equity (World Stock)	B-	C+	B	Down	Y	2,500
Janus Henderson Global Value Fund Class C	JPPCX	NAS CM	Open End	Global Equity (World Stock)	B-	C+	B-	Up	Y	2,500
Janus Henderson Global Value Fund Class D	JNGOX	NAS CM	Open End	Global Equity (World Stock)	B-	C+	B	Down		2,500
Janus Henderson Global Value Fund Class I	JPPIX	NAS CM	Open End	Global Equity (World Stock)	B-	C+	B	Down	Y	1,000,000
Janus Henderson Global Value Fund Class N	JPPNX	NAS CM	Open End	Global Equity (World Stock)	B-	C+	B	Down	Y	0
Janus Henderson Global Value Fund Class S	JPPSX	NAS CM	Open End	Global Equity (World Stock)	B-	C+	B	Down	Y	2,500
Janus Henderson Global Value Fund Class T	JGVAX	NAS CM	Open End	Global Equity (World Stock)	B-	C+	B	Down	Y	2,500
Janus Henderson Growth And Income Fund Class A	JDNAX	NAS CM	Open End	US Equity Large Cap Blend (Growth & Income)	B	B	B		Y	2,500
Janus Henderson Growth And Income Fund Class C	JGICX	NAS CM	Open End	US Equity Large Cap Blend (Growth & Income)	B	B	B		Y	2,500
Janus Henderson Growth And Income Fund Class D	JNGIX	NAS CM	Open End	US Equity Large Cap Blend (Growth & Income)	B	B	B			2,500
Janus Henderson Growth And Income Fund Class I	JGINX	NAS CM	Open End	US Equity Large Cap Blend (Growth & Income)	B	B	B		Y	1,000,000
Janus Henderson Growth And Income Fund Class N	JDNNX	NAS CM	Open End	US Equity Large Cap Blend (Growth & Income)	B	B	B		Y	0
Janus Henderson Growth And Income Fund Class R	JDNRX	NAS CM	Open End	US Equity Large Cap Blend (Growth & Income)	B	B	B		Y	2,500
Janus Henderson Growth And Income Fund Class S	JADGX	NAS CM	Open End	US Equity Large Cap Blend (Growth & Income)	B	B	B		Y	2,500
Janus Henderson Growth And Income Fund Class T	JAGIX	NAS CM	Open End	US Equity Large Cap Blend (Growth & Income)	B	B	B		Y	2,500
Janus Henderson International Long/Short Equity Fund Cls A	HLNAX	NAS CM	Open End	Long/Short Equity (Growth)	C-	C-	C	Down	Y	2,500
Janus Henderson International Long/Short Equity Fund Cls C	HLNCX	NAS CM	Open End	Long/Short Equity (Growth)	C-	C-	C	Down	Y	2,500
Janus Henderson International Long/Short Equity Fund Cls D	HLNDX	NAS CM	Open End	Long/Short Equity (Growth)	C	C	C		Y	2,500
Janus Henderson International Long/Short Equity Fund Cls I	HLNIX	NAS CM	Open End	Long/Short Equity (Growth)	C	C	C		Y	1,000,000
Janus Henderson International Long/Short Equity Fund Cls N	HLNRX	NAS CM	Open End	Long/Short Equity (Growth)	C	C	C		Y	1,000,000
Janus Henderson International Long/Short Equity Fund Cls S	HLNSX	NAS CM	Open End	Long/Short Equity (Growth)	C	C	C		Y	2,500
Janus Henderson International Long/Short Equity Fund Cls T	HLNTX	NAS CM	Open End	Long/Short Equity (Growth)	C	C	C		Y	2,500
Janus Henderson Intl Managed Volatility Fund Cls A	JMIAX	NAS CM	Open End	Global Equity Large Cap (Growth)	B	B-	B	Up	Y	2,500

★ Expanded analysis of this fund is included in Section II.

Min Additional Investment	3-Month Total Return	6-Month Total Return	1-Year Total Return	3-Year Total Return	5-Year Total Return	Dividend Yield (TTM)	Expense Ratio	3-Yr Std Deviation	3-Year Beta	NAV	Total Assets (MIL)	%Cash	%Stocks	%Bonds	%Other	Turnover Ratio	Last Bull Market Total Return	Last Bear Market Total Return	Front End Fee (%)	Back End Fee (%)	Inception Date
TOTAL RETURNS						PERFORMANCE				ASSETS		ASSET ALLOCATION & TURNOVER					BULL & BEAR		FEES		
	4.65	8.24	17.43	18.02	45.06	2.85	1.26	10.59	0.87	11.44	222.9	0	98	0	2	72	25.31	-23.84	5.75		Nov-07
	4.41	7.86	16.56	15.34	39.71	2.35	2.03	10.59	0.87	11.29	222.9	0	98	0	2	72	24.88	-24.12		1.00	Nov-07
100	4.67	8.29	17.63	18.42	46.24	3.13	1.08	10.57	0.86	11.51	222.9	0	98	0	2	72	25.48	-23.78			Feb-10
	4.70	8.27	17.71	18.83	46.98	3.24	0.98	10.58	0.86	11.49	222.9	0	98	0	2	72	25.54	-23.72			Nov-07
	4.52	8.07	17.18	17.30	43.80	2.83	1.4	10.56	0.86	11.41	222.9	0	98	0	2	72	25.37	-23.89			Nov-07
	4.65	8.27	17.55	18.28	45.84	3.07	1.14	10.6	0.87	11.5	222.9	0	98	0	2	72	25.51	-23.77			Jul-09
	4.96	9.86	26.47	24.61	69.51	0.41	1.02	11.39	1.05	79.77	2,816	1	98	0	1	48	23.52	-20.92	5.75		Jul-09
	4.78	9.50	25.66	22.03	63.47	0	1.74	11.38	1.05	78.14	2,816	1	98	0	1	48	22.87	-21.16		1.00	Jul-09
100	5.03	10.02	26.86	25.53	71.40	0.66	0.78	11.39	1.05	78.77	2,816	1	98	0	1	48	23.57	-20.85			Feb-05
	5.06	10.06	26.98	25.90	72.18	0.73	0.69	11.4	1.05	79.85	2,816	1	98	0	1	48	23.63	-20.82			Jul-09
	5.06	10.07	26.93	25.59	71.49		0.67	11.4	1.05	78.6	2,816	1	98	0	1	48	23.57	-20.85			Aug-17
	4.87	9.69	26.12	23.36	66.54	0.2	1.37	11.39	1.05	79.16	2,816	1	98	0	1	48	23.22	-21.02			Mar-13
	4.94	9.83	26.44	24.29	68.67	0.36	1.11	11.38	1.05	79.93	2,816	1	98	0	1	48	23.34	-20.99			Jul-09
	5.01	9.97	26.75	25.26	70.82	0.6	0.86	11.39	1.05	78.72	2,816	1	98	0	1	48	23.53	-20.87			Feb-05
	5.68	12.65	30.87	27.91	77.24	0.71	1.06	12.25	1.09	16.95	2,221	2	97	0	0	42	17.88	-26.11	5.75		Jul-09
	5.45	12.17	29.87	24.91	70.05	0.08	1.86	12.23	1.09	16.52	2,221	2	97	0	0	42	17.36	-26.32		1.00	Jul-09
100	5.69	12.71	31.08	28.55	78.51	0.88	0.88	12.26	1.09	16.83	2,221	2	97	0	0	42	18.09	-26.04			Jun-00
	5.64	12.78	31.20	28.97	79.80	0.96	0.75	12.24	1.09	16.88	2,221	2	97	0	0	42	18.07	-26.04			Jul-09
	5.76	12.77	31.15	28.62	78.61		0.69	12.26	1.09	16.85	2,221	2	97	0	0	42	18.09	-26.04			Aug-17
	5.48	12.36	30.34	26.32	73.63	0.45	1.46	12.26	1.09	16.78	2,221	2	97	0	0	42	17.66	-26.21			Jul-09
	5.61	12.54	30.72	27.38	75.94	0.61	1.2	12.28	1.1	17.08	2,221	2	97	0	0	42	18.21	-26.1			Jul-09
	5.71	12.72	31.06	28.39	78.14	0.83	0.94	12.24	1.09	16.86	2,221	2	97	0	0	42	18.05	-26.06			Jun-00
	7.76	16.87	44.49	69.79	156.48	0	1.08	14.53	1.22	30.2	2,353	0	99	0	0	30	23.98	-19.08	5.75		Jul-09
	7.55	16.40	43.43	66.34	147.99	0	1.82	14.49	1.21	27.83	2,353	0	99	0	0	30	23.52	-19.35		1.00	Jul-09
100	7.77	16.95	44.72	70.73	158.94	0	0.88	14.51	1.22	30.83	2,353	0	99	0	0	30	24.23	-19.03			Dec-98
	7.82	17.02	44.88	71.27	160.15	0	0.8	14.53	1.22	31.07	2,353	0	99	0	0	30	24.22	-18.98			Jul-09
	7.85	17.07	44.93	70.80	158.84		0.71	14.51	1.22	30.73	2,353	0	99	0	0	30	24.12	-19			Jan-17
	7.71	16.81	44.31	69.21	155.04	0	1.21	14.52	1.22	29.8	2,353	0	99	0	0	30	23.94	-19.1			Jul-09
	7.77	16.91	44.65	70.47	158.34	0	0.95	14.5	1.22	30.67	2,353	0	99	0	0	30	24.12	-19			Dec-98
	4.46	7.95	18.72	18.85	53.43	1.64	0.96	7.72	0.71	15.14	256.3	12	86	0	0	29	12.56	-10.47	5.75		Jul-09
	4.22	7.49	17.82	16.25	47.81	0.95	1.72	7.68	0.71	14.82	256.3	12	86	0	0	29	12.66	-10.71		1.00	Jul-09
100	4.50	8.04	18.87	19.40	54.48	1.79	0.82	7.72	0.71	15.23	256.3	12	86	0	0	29	12.54	-10.43			Jun-01
	4.53	8.05	19.00	19.73	55.46	1.94	0.69	7.74	0.71	14.97	256.3	12	86	0	0	29	12.7	-10.42			Jul-09
	4.51	8.04	19.13	20.03	56.04	2.01	0.62	7.74	0.71	14.89	256.3	12	86	0	0	29	12.54	-10.43			May-12
	4.39	7.81	18.50	18.33	52.09	1.08	1.13	7.73	0.71	15.4	256.3	12	86	0	0	29	12.35	-10.56			Jul-09
	4.43	7.97	18.83	19.24	54.08	1.73	0.87	7.73	0.71	15.2	256.3	12	86	0	0	29	12.49	-10.44			Jun-01
	8.99	14.18	24.70	41.02	112.08	1.79	0.95	10.23	0.98	55.07	5,178	0	100	0	0	16	29.41	-21.55	5.75		Jul-09
	8.76	13.74	23.77	37.94	104.08	1.25	1.74	10.22	0.98	54.41	5,178	0	100	0	0	16	28.84	-21.81		1.00	Jul-09
100	9.03	14.26	24.90	41.67	113.81	1.93	0.79	10.23	0.98	55.12	5,178	0	100	0	0	16	29.5	-21.48			May-91
	9.04	14.29	24.97	41.99	114.58	1.98	0.72	10.24	0.99	55.15	5,178	0	100	0	0	16	29.58	-21.46			Jul-09
	9.05	14.31	24.96	41.72	113.89		0.64	10.23	0.98	55.07	5,178	0	100	0	0	16	29.5	-21.48			Aug-17
	8.86	13.90	24.13	39.13	107.51	1.47	1.39	10.22	0.98	54.78	5,178	0	100	0	0	16	29.04	-21.69			Jul-09
	8.92	14.05	24.45	40.23	110.20	1.66	1.14	10.22	0.98	55.03	5,178	0	100	0	0	16	29.27	-21.63			Jul-09
	8.99	14.20	24.77	41.33	112.94	1.86	0.88	10.23	0.98	55.08	5,178	0	100	0	0	16	29.43	-21.53			May-91
	-0.32	-0.42	2.75	0.54		0	3.06			9.16	13.3	82	17	0	2	186			5.75		Dec-14
	-0.26	-0.47	2.24	-1.19		1.87	3.77			9.04	13.3	82	17	0	2	186				1.00	Dec-14
100	0.03	0.13	3.28	1.86			1.67			9.02	13.3	82	17	0	2	186					Jun-17
	-0.18	0.02	3.16	1.74		2.3	2.8			9.04	13.3	82	17	0	2	186					Dec-14
	0.00	0.10	3.35	1.87		2.32	2.75			9.01	13.3	82	17	0	2	186					Nov-15
	-0.03	-0.03	2.97	1.05			3.24			9.02	13.3	82	17	0	2	186					Jun-17
	-0.01	0.09	3.23	1.81			2.99			9.02	13.3	82	17	0	2	186					Jun-17
	4.67	10.82	28.17	26.70	52.55	1.45	1.14	9.86	0.69	9.39	109.4	1	99	0	0	134	12.52	-24.79	5.75		May-07

	MARKET			FUND TYPE, CATEGORY & OBJECTIVE	RATINGS				MINIMUMS	
Fund Name	Ticker Symbol	Traded On	Fund Type	Category and (Prospectus Objective)	Overall Rating	Reward Rating	Risk Rating	Recent Up/ Downgrade	Open to New Investors	Min Initial Investment
Janus Henderson Intl Managed Volatility Fund Cls C	JMICX	NAS CM	Open End	Global Equity Large Cap (Growth)	B-	C+	B	Up	Y	2,500
Janus Henderson Intl Managed Volatility Fund Cls D	JIIDX	NAS CM	Open End	Global Equity Large Cap (Growth)	B	B-	B	Up	Y	2,500
Janus Henderson Intl Managed Volatility Fund Cls I	JMIIX	NAS CM	Open End	Global Equity Large Cap (Growth)	B	B-	B	Up	Y	1,000,000
Janus Henderson Intl Managed Volatility Fund Cls N	JMRNX	NAS CM	Open End	Global Equity Large Cap (Growth)	B	B-	B	Up	Y	1,000,000
Janus Henderson Intl Managed Volatility Fund Cls S	JMISX	NAS CM	Open End	Global Equity Large Cap (Growth)	B	B-	B	Up	Y	2,500
Janus Henderson Intl Managed Volatility Fund Cls T	JRMTX	NAS CM	Open End	Global Equity Large Cap (Growth)	B	B-	B	Up	Y	2,500
Janus Henderson International Opportunities Fund Class A	HFOAX	NAS CM	Open End	Global Equity Large Cap (Foreign Stock)	B-	C+	B	Up	Y	2,500
Janus Henderson International Opportunities Fund Class C	HFOCX	NAS CM	Open End	Global Equity Large Cap (Foreign Stock)	B-	C+	B	Up	Y	2,500
Janus Henderson International Opportunities Fund Class D	HFODX	NAS CM	Open End	Global Equity Large Cap (Foreign Stock)	B-	C+	B	Up	Y	2,500
Janus Henderson International Opportunities Fund Class I	HFOIX	NAS CM	Open End	Global Equity Large Cap (Foreign Stock)	B-	C+	B	Up	Y	1,000,000
Janus Henderson International Opportunities Fund Class N	HFOQX	NAS CM	Open End	Global Equity Large Cap (Foreign Stock)	B-	C+	B	Up	Y	1,000,000
Janus Henderson International Opportunities Fund Class R	HFORX	NAS CM	Open End	Global Equity Large Cap (Foreign Stock)	B-	C+	B	Up	Y	2,500
Janus Henderson International Opportunities Fund Class S	HFOSX	NAS CM	Open End	Global Equity Large Cap (Foreign Stock)	B-	C+	B	Up	Y	2,500
Janus Henderson International Opportunities Fund Class T	HFOTX	NAS CM	Open End	Global Equity Large Cap (Foreign Stock)	B-	C+	B	Up	Y	2,500
Janus Henderson International Small Cap Fund Class A	HIZAX	NAS CM	Open End	Global Equity Mid/Small Cap (Foreign Stock)	D-	D+	A-		Y	2,500
Janus Henderson International Small Cap Fund Class C	HIZCX	NAS CM	Open End	Global Equity Mid/Small Cap (Foreign Stock)	D-	D+	A-		Y	2,500
Janus Henderson International Small Cap Fund Class D	HIZDX	NAS CM	Open End	Global Equity Mid/Small Cap (Foreign Stock)	D-	D+	A-		Y	2,500
Janus Henderson International Small Cap Fund Class I	HIZIX	NAS CM	Open End	Global Equity Mid/Small Cap (Foreign Stock)	D-	D+	A-		Y	1,000,000
Janus Henderson International Small Cap Fund Class N	HIZRX	NAS CM	Open End	Global Equity Mid/Small Cap (Foreign Stock)	D	D+	A-			1,000,000
Janus Henderson International Small Cap Fund Class S	HIZSX	NAS CM	Open End	Global Equity Mid/Small Cap (Foreign Stock)	D-	D+	A-		Y	2,500
Janus Henderson International Small Cap Fund Class T	HIZTX	NAS CM	Open End	Global Equity Mid/Small Cap (Foreign Stock)	D-	D+	A-		Y	2,500
Janus Henderson International Value Fund Class A	JIFAX	NAS CM	Open End	Global Equity Large Cap (Growth & Income)	B-	C+	B	Up	Y	2,500
Janus Henderson International Value Fund Class C	JIFCX	NAS CM	Open End	Global Equity Large Cap (Growth & Income)	B-	C+	B	Up	Y	2,500
Janus Henderson International Value Fund Class D	JIFDX	NAS CM	Open End	Global Equity Large Cap (Growth & Income)	B-	C+	B	Up		2,500
Janus Henderson International Value Fund Class I	JIFIX	NAS CM	Open End	Global Equity Large Cap (Growth & Income)	B-	C+	B	Up	Y	1,000,000
Janus Henderson International Value Fund Class N	JIFNX	NAS CM	Open End	Global Equity Large Cap (Growth & Income)	B-	C+	B	Up	Y	0
Janus Henderson International Value Fund Class S	JIFSX	NAS CM	Open End	Global Equity Large Cap (Growth & Income)	B-	C+	B	Up	Y	2,500
Janus Henderson International Value Fund Class T	JIFTX	NAS CM	Open End	Global Equity Large Cap (Growth & Income)	B-	C+	B	Up	Y	2,500
Janus Henderson Large Cap Value Fund Class A	JAPAX	NAS CM	Open End	US Equity Large Cap Value (Growth)	B-	C+	B	Down	Y	2,500
Janus Henderson Large Cap Value Fund Class C	JAPCX	NAS CM	Open End	US Equity Large Cap Value (Growth)	B-	C+	B	Down	Y	2,500
Janus Henderson Large Cap Value Fund Class D	JNPLX	NAS CM	Open End	US Equity Large Cap Value (Growth)	B-	B-	B-	Down		2,500
Janus Henderson Large Cap Value Fund Class I	JAPIX	NAS CM	Open End	US Equity Large Cap Value (Growth)	B	B-	B	Up	Y	1,000,000
Janus Henderson Large Cap Value Fund Class N	JPLNX	NAS CM	Open End	US Equity Large Cap Value (Growth)	B	B-	B	Up	Y	1,000,000
Janus Henderson Large Cap Value Fund Class S	JAPSX	NAS CM	Open End	US Equity Large Cap Value (Growth)	B-	C+	B-	Down	Y	2,500
Janus Henderson Large Cap Value Fund Class T	JPLTX	NAS CM	Open End	US Equity Large Cap Value (Growth)	B-	B-	B	Down	Y	2,500
Janus Henderson Mid Cap Value Fund Class A	JDPAX	NAS CM	Open End	US Equity Mid Cap (Growth)	B	B-	B		Y	2,500
Janus Henderson Mid Cap Value Fund Class C	JMVCX	NAS CM	Open End	US Equity Mid Cap (Growth)	B	B-	B		Y	2,500
Janus Henderson Mid Cap Value Fund Class D	JNMCX	NAS CM	Open End	US Equity Mid Cap (Growth)	B	B-	B			2,500
Janus Henderson Mid Cap Value Fund Class I	JMVAX	NAS CM	Open End	US Equity Mid Cap (Growth)	B	B-	B		Y	1,000,000
Janus Henderson Mid Cap Value Fund Class L	JMIVX	NAS CM	Open End	US Equity Mid Cap (Growth)	B	B-	B			250,000
Janus Henderson Mid Cap Value Fund Class N	JDPNX	NAS CM	Open End	US Equity Mid Cap (Growth)	B	B-	B		Y	1,000,000
Janus Henderson Mid Cap Value Fund Class R	JDPRX	NAS CM	Open End	US Equity Mid Cap (Growth)	B	B-	B		Y	2,500
Janus Henderson Mid Cap Value Fund Class S	JMVIX	NAS CM	Open End	US Equity Mid Cap (Growth)	B	B-	B		Y	2,500
Janus Henderson Mid Cap Value Fund Class T	JMCVX	NAS CM	Open End	US Equity Mid Cap (Growth)	B	B-	B		Y	2,500
Janus Henderson Overseas Fund Class A	JDIAX	NAS CM	Open End	Global Equity Large Cap (Foreign Stock)	C+	C+	C+	Up	Y	2,500
Janus Henderson Overseas Fund Class C	JIGCX	NAS CM	Open End	Global Equity Large Cap (Foreign Stock)	C	C	C+	Up	Y	2,500
Janus Henderson Overseas Fund Class D	JNOSX	NAS CM	Open End	Global Equity Large Cap (Foreign Stock)	C+	C+	C+	Up		2,500
Janus Henderson Overseas Fund Class I	JIGFX	NAS CM	Open End	Global Equity Large Cap (Foreign Stock)	C+	C+	C+	Up	Y	1,000,000
Janus Henderson Overseas Fund Class N	JDINX	NAS CM	Open End	Global Equity Large Cap (Foreign Stock)	C+	C+	C+	Up	Y	0
Janus Henderson Overseas Fund Class R	JDIRX	NAS CM	Open End	Global Equity Large Cap (Foreign Stock)	C+	C+	C+	Up	Y	2,500
Janus Henderson Overseas Fund Class S	JIGRX	NAS CM	Open End	Global Equity Large Cap (Foreign Stock)	C+	C+	C+	Up	Y	2,500
Janus Henderson Overseas Fund Class T	JAOSX	NAS CM	Open End	Global Equity Large Cap (Foreign Stock)	C+	C+	C+	Up	Y	2,500

★ Expanded analysis of this fund is included in Section II.

Min Additional Investment	TOTAL RETURNS: 3-Month Total Return	6-Month Total Return	1-Year Total Return	3-Year Total Return	5-Year Total Return	PERFORMANCE: Dividend Yield (TTM)	Expense Ratio	3-Yr Std Deviation	3-Year Beta	ASSETS: NAV	Total Assets (MIL)	ASSET ALLOCATION & TURNOVER: %Cash	%Stocks	%Bonds	%Other	Turnover Ratio	BULL & BEAR: Last Bull Market Total Return	Last Bear Market Total Return	FEES: Front End Fee (%)	Back End Fee (%)	Inception Date
	4.50	10.52	27.51	24.31	50.25	1.02	1.89	9.85	0.69	9.17	109.4	1	99	0	0	134	12.7	-24.91		1.00	May-07
100	4.70	11.04	28.76	27.98	54.96	1.43	0.99	9.84	0.69	9.23	109.4	1	99	0	0	134	12.54	-24.67			Apr-15
	4.67	11.10	28.76	28.15	55.17	1.3	0.8	9.9	0.7	9.26	109.4	1	99	0	0	134	12.53	-24.67			May-07
	4.83	11.15	29.02	28.59	55.71	1.63	0.8	9.89	0.69	9.25	109.4	1	99	0	0	134	12.53	-24.67			Oct-16
	4.69	10.96	28.45	27.00	53.41	1.43	1.2	9.83	0.69	9.37	109.4	1	99	0	0	134	12.35	-24.67			May-07
	4.71	11.05	28.62	27.54	53.42	1.46	1	9.9	0.7	9.24	109.4	1	99	0	0	134	12.39	-24.82			Jul-09
	3.15	8.21	21.18	18.38	49.77	1.28	1.33	11.56	0.91	30.14	4,890	1	95	0	4	5	15.23	-24.69	5.75		Aug-01
	2.98	7.81	20.29	15.67	44.09	0.74	2.09	11.55	0.91	28.25	4,890	1	95	0	4	5	14.75	-24.96		1.00	Aug-01
100	3.21	8.36	21.35	18.54	49.97		1.1	11.56	0.91	30.04	4,890	1	95	0	4	5	15.23	-24.69			Jun-17
	3.26	8.41	21.53	19.37	51.91	1.64	1.03	11.56	0.91	30.03	4,890	1	95	0	4	5	15.47	-24.63			Mar-09
	3.14	8.21	21.18	18.38	49.76		1.06	11.56	0.91	30.02	4,890	1	95	0	4	5	15.23	-24.69			Jun-17
	3.06	8.05	20.75	17.20	47.46	1.27	1.68	11.56	0.91	29.5	4,890	1	95	0	4	5	15.07	-24.81			Sep-05
	3.27	8.42	21.54	19.07	50.63	1.62	1.45	11.58	0.91	30.01	4,890	1	95	0	4	5	15.23	-24.69			Nov-15
	3.20	8.31	21.29	18.49	49.90		1.2	11.56	0.91	30.03	4,890	1	95	0	4	5	15.23	-24.69			Jun-17
	5.56	16.36	36.80				1.45			13.19	10.4	4	92	0	4	18			5.75		Jun-17
	5.41	15.84	35.67				2.13			13.16	10.4	4	92	0	4	18				1.00	Jun-17
100	5.56	16.44	37.06				1.25			13.24	10.4	4	92	0	4	18					Jun-17
	5.56	16.35	36.95				1.11			13.19	10.4	4	92	0	4	18					Jun-17
	5.64	16.53	37.17				1.08			13.08	10.4	4	92	0	4	18					Dec-16
	5.51	16.21	36.63				1.58			13.18	10.4	4	92	0	4	18					Jun-17
	5.54	16.33	36.93				1.34			13.22	10.4	4	92	0	4	18					Jun-17
	3.77	8.57	22.59	21.50		1.83	1.18	9.27	0.72	11.63	52.6	7	90	0	0	24			5.75		Apr-13
	3.50	8.22	21.76	18.87		1.22	1.9	9.27	0.72	11.61	52.6	7	90	0	0	24				1.00	Apr-13
100	3.68	8.58	22.76	22.07		1.98	1.02	9.28	0.72	11.59	52.6	7	90	0	0	24					Apr-13
	3.74	8.65	22.85	22.29		2.03	0.95	9.31	0.72	11.58	52.6	7	90	0	0	24					Apr-13
	3.76	8.75	23.06	22.65		2.09	0.87	9.28	0.72	11.61	52.6	7	90	0	0	24					Apr-13
	3.70	8.49	22.59	21.35		1.78	1.37	9.25	0.72	11.65	52.6	7	90	0	0	24					Apr-13
	3.80	8.61	22.68	21.67		1.92	1.12	9.26	0.72	11.59	52.6	7	90	0	0	24					Apr-13
	4.96	7.64	14.24	22.08	75.47	1.31	0.95	9.6	0.91	15.6	138.3	3	97	0	0	43	20.78	-17.46	5.75		Dec-08
	4.84	7.30	13.46	20.02	70.19	0.58	1.7	9.48	0.9	15.34	138.3	3	97	0	0	43	20.23	-17.7		1.00	Dec-08
100	5.05	7.74	14.45	22.87	77.17	1.45	0.74	9.59	0.9	15.42	138.3	3	97	0	0	43	20.92	-17.34			Feb-10
	5.06	7.81	14.57	23.00	78.00	1.45	0.69	9.59	0.9	15.5	138.3	3	97	0	0	43	21.01	-17.31			Dec-08
	5.08	7.83	14.68	23.35	78.49	1.54	0.6	9.55	0.9	15.47	138.3	3	97	0	0	43	21.01	-17.31			May-12
	5.04	7.70	14.24	22.13	75.37	1.22	0.85	9.54	0.9	15.68	138.3	3	97	0	0	43	20.68	-17.46			Dec-08
	5.03	7.73	14.38	22.55	76.38	1.37	0.85	9.58	0.9	15.4	138.3	3	97	0	0	43	20.82	-17.36			Jul-09
	5.12	8.04	13.66	28.04	79.42	0.41	0.94	9.74	0.9	17.11	4,087	5	95	0	0	53	19.52	-19.24	5.75		Jul-09
	4.95	7.69	12.99	26.00	74.04	0	1.6	9.67	0.89	16.69	4,087	5	95	0	0	53	18.97	-19.44		1.00	Jul-09
100	5.19	8.22	14.06	29.17	82.02	0.72	0.62	9.7	0.89	16.82	4,087	5	95	0	0	53	19.74	-19.09			Aug-98
	5.19	8.16	13.99	29.15	82.16	0.71	0.61	9.73	0.9	16.84	4,087	5	95	0	0	53	19.73	-19.13			Jul-09
	5.20	8.22	14.11	29.72	82.65	0.73	0.62	9.71	0.89	17.3	4,087	5	95	0	0	53	19.61	-19.07			Aug-98
	5.23	8.27	14.20	29.76	83.39	0.85	0.48	9.7	0.89	16.77	4,087	5	95	0	0	53	19.61	-19.07			May-12
	5.03	7.87	13.34	26.85	76.65	0.2	1.22	9.7	0.89	16.85	4,087	5	95	0	0	53	19.34	-19.34			Jul-09
	5.09	8.02	13.65	27.83	78.87	0.44	0.87	9.71	0.89	17.05	4,087	5	95	0	0	53	19.48	-19.26			Jul-09
	5.12	8.13	13.87	28.80	81.25	0.63	0.72	9.73	0.9	16.91	4,087	5	95	0	0	53	19.64	-19.18			Aug-98
	3.97	9.70	30.92	11.31	9.05	0.64	0.91	17.22	1.31	32.99	1,717	1	98	0	0	39	12.64	-33.39	5.75		Jul-09
	3.75	9.26	29.92	8.76	4.92	0	1.71	17.19	1.3	32.49	1,717	1	98	0	0	39	12.2	-33.6		1.00	Jul-09
100	4.04	9.86	31.32	12.30	10.61	1.02	0.58	17.2	1.3	32.6	1,717	1	98	0	0	39	12.88	-33.33			May-94
	4.06	9.89	31.36	12.40	10.89	0.99	0.52	17.2	1.3	32.73	1,717	1	98	0	0	39	12.89	-33.32			Jul-09
	4.08	9.95	31.51	12.73	11.38	1.15	0.41	17.21	1.3	32.53	1,717	1	98	0	0	39	12.88	-33.33			May-12
	3.89	9.54	30.54	10.37	7.44	0.48	1.16	17.21	1.3	32.41	1,717	1	98	0	0	39	12.49	-33.49			Jul-09
	3.97	9.68	30.90	11.18	8.79	0.68	0.91	17.22	1.31	32.65	1,717	1	98	0	0	39	12.67	-33.43			Jul-09
	3.99	9.79	31.16	12.02	10.19	0.94	0.66	17.21	1.3	32.64	1,717	1	98	0	0	39	12.8	-33.35			May-94

	MARKET		FUND TYPE, CATEGORY & OBJECTIVE		RATINGS				MINIMUMS	
Fund Name	Ticker Symbol	Traded On	Fund Type	Category and (Prospectus Objective)	Overall Rating	Reward Rating	Risk Rating	Recent Up/ Downgrade	Open to New Investors	Min Initial Investment
Janus Henderson Research Fund Class A	JRAAX	NAS CM	Open End	US Equity Large Cap Growth (Growth)	B	B	A-	Up	Y	2,500
Janus Henderson Research Fund Class C	JRACX	NAS CM	Open End	US Equity Large Cap Growth (Growth)	B	B	A-	Up	Y	2,500
Janus Henderson Research Fund Class D	JNRFX	NAS CM	Open End	US Equity Large Cap Growth (Growth)	B	B	A-			2,500
Janus Henderson Research Fund Class I	JRAIX	NAS CM	Open End	US Equity Large Cap Growth (Growth)	B	B	A-	Down	Y	1,000,000
Janus Henderson Research Fund Class N	JRANX	NAS CM	Open End	US Equity Large Cap Growth (Growth)	B	B	A-	Down	Y	0
Janus Henderson Research Fund Class R	JRARX	NAS CM	Open End	US Equity Large Cap Growth (Growth)	B	B	A-	Up	Y	2,500
Janus Henderson Research Fund Class S	JRASX	NAS CM	Open End	US Equity Large Cap Growth (Growth)	B	B	A-	Up	Y	2,500
Janus Henderson Research Fund Class T	JAMRX	NAS CM	Open End	US Equity Large Cap Growth (Growth)	B	B	A-		Y	2,500
Janus Henderson Select Value Fund Class A	JVSAX	NAS CM	Open End	US Equity Mid Cap (Growth)	B	B	B+		Y	2,500
Janus Henderson Select Value Fund Class C	JVSCX	NAS CM	Open End	US Equity Mid Cap (Growth)	B	B-	B+		Y	2,500
Janus Henderson Select Value Fund Class D	JSVDX	NAS CM	Open End	US Equity Mid Cap (Growth)	B	B	B+		Y	2,500
Janus Henderson Select Value Fund Class I	JVSIX	NAS CM	Open End	US Equity Mid Cap (Growth)	B	B	B+		Y	1,000,000
Janus Henderson Select Value Fund Class N	JVSNX	NAS CM	Open End	US Equity Mid Cap (Growth)	B	B	B+		Y	1,000,000
Janus Henderson Select Value Fund Class S	JSVSX	NAS CM	Open End	US Equity Mid Cap (Growth)	B	B	B+		Y	2,500
Janus Henderson Select Value Fund Class T	JSVTX	NAS CM	Open End	US Equity Mid Cap (Growth)	B	B	B+		Y	2,500
Janus Henderson Small Cap Value Fund Class A	JDSAX	NAS CM	Open End	US Equity Small Cap (Small Company)	B+	B+	B+	Up	Y	2,500
Janus Henderson Small Cap Value Fund Class C	JCSCX	NAS CM	Open End	US Equity Small Cap (Small Company)	B	B	B		Y	2,500
Janus Henderson Small Cap Value Fund Class D	JNPSX	NAS CM	Open End	US Equity Small Cap (Small Company)	B+	B+	B+	Up		2,500
Janus Henderson Small Cap Value Fund Class I	JSCOX	NAS CM	Open End	US Equity Small Cap (Small Company)	B+	B+	B+	Up	Y	1,000,000
Janus Henderson Small Cap Value Fund Class L	JSIVX	NAS CM	Open End	US Equity Small Cap (Small Company)	B+	B+	B+	Up		250,000
Janus Henderson Small Cap Value Fund Class N	JDSNX	NAS CM	Open End	US Equity Small Cap (Small Company)	B+	B+	B+	Up	Y	1,000,000
Janus Henderson Small Cap Value Fund Class R	JDSRX	NAS CM	Open End	US Equity Small Cap (Small Company)	B+	B+	B	Up	Y	2,500
Janus Henderson Small Cap Value Fund Class S	JISCX	NAS CM	Open End	US Equity Small Cap (Small Company)	B+	B+	B+	Up	Y	2,500
Janus Henderson Small Cap Value Fund Class T	JSCVX	NAS CM	Open End	US Equity Small Cap (Small Company)	B+	B+	B+	Up	Y	2,500
Janus Henderson Triton Fund Class A	JGMAX	NAS CM	Open End	US Equity Small Cap (Growth)	B	A-	C+	Down		2,500
Janus Henderson Triton Fund Class C	JGMCX	NAS CM	Open End	US Equity Small Cap (Growth)	B	A-	C+			2,500
Janus Henderson Triton Fund Class D	JANIX	NAS CM	Open End	US Equity Small Cap (Growth)	B	A-	B-	Down		2,500
Janus Henderson Triton Fund Class I	JSMGX	NAS CM	Open End	US Equity Small Cap (Growth)	B	A-	B-	Down		1,000,000
Janus Henderson Triton Fund Class N	JGMNX	NAS CM	Open End	US Equity Small Cap (Growth)	B	A-	B-	Down		0
Janus Henderson Triton Fund Class R	JGMRX	NAS CM	Open End	US Equity Small Cap (Growth)	B	A-	C+			2,500
Janus Henderson Triton Fund Class S	JGMIX	NAS CM	Open End	US Equity Small Cap (Growth)	B	A-	C+	Down		2,500
Janus Henderson Triton Fund Class T	JATTX	NAS CM	Open End	US Equity Small Cap (Growth)	B	A-	B-	Down		2,500
Janus Henderson U.S. Growth Opportunities Fund Class A	HGRAX	NAS CM	Open End	US Equity Large Cap Growth (Growth)	B-	C+	B+	Up	Y	2,500
Janus Henderson U.S. Growth Opportunities Fund Class C	HGRCX	NAS CM	Open End	US Equity Large Cap Growth (Growth)	B-	C	B	Up	Y	2,500
Janus Henderson U.S. Growth Opportunities Fund Class D	HGRDX	NAS CM	Open End	US Equity Large Cap Growth (Growth)	B-	C+	B+		Y	2,500
Janus Henderson U.S. Growth Opportunities Fund Class I	HGRIX	NAS CM	Open End	US Equity Large Cap Growth (Growth)	B-	C+	B	Up	Y	1,000,000
Janus Henderson U.S. Growth Opportunities Fund Class N	HGRRX	NAS CM	Open End	US Equity Large Cap Growth (Growth)	B-	C+	B	Up	Y	1,000,000
Janus Henderson U.S. Growth Opportunities Fund Class S	HGRSX	NAS CM	Open End	US Equity Large Cap Growth (Growth)	B-	C	B		Y	2,500
Janus Henderson U.S. Growth Opportunities Fund Class T	HGRTX	NAS CM	Open End	US Equity Large Cap Growth (Growth)	B-	C+	B		Y	2,500
Janus Henderson U.S. Managed Volatility Fund Class A	JRSAX	NAS CM	Open End	US Equity Large Cap Blend (Growth)	B	B	B		Y	2,500
Janus Henderson U.S. Managed Volatility Fund Class C	JRSCX	NAS CM	Open End	US Equity Large Cap Blend (Growth)	B	B	B		Y	2,500
Janus Henderson U.S. Managed Volatility Fund Class S	JRSSX	NAS CM	Open End	US Equity Large Cap Blend (Growth)	B	B	B		Y	2,500
Janus Henderson Value Plus Income Fund Class A	JPVAX	NAS CM	Open End	Moderate Alloc (Income)	B-	C+	B	Up	Y	2,500
Janus Henderson Value Plus Income Fund Class C	JPVCX	NAS CM	Open End	Moderate Alloc (Income)	B-	C+	B	Up	Y	2,500
Janus Henderson Value Plus Income Fund Class D	JPVDX	NAS CM	Open End	Moderate Alloc (Income)	B-	C+	B	Up	Y	2,500
Janus Henderson Value Plus Income Fund Class I	JPVIX	NAS CM	Open End	Moderate Alloc (Income)	B-	C+	B	Up	Y	1,000,000
Janus Henderson Value Plus Income Fund Class N	JPVNX	NAS CM	Open End	Moderate Alloc (Income)	B-	C+	B		Y	1,000,000
Janus Henderson Value Plus Income Fund Class S	JPVSX	NAS CM	Open End	Moderate Alloc (Income)	B-	C+	B	Up	Y	2,500
Janus Henderson Value Plus Income Fund Class T	JPVTX	NAS CM	Open End	Moderate Alloc (Income)	B-	C+	B	Up	Y	2,500
Janus Henderson Venture Fund Class A	JVTAX	NAS CM	Open End	US Equity Small Cap (Growth)	B+	B+	B	Up		2,500
Janus Henderson Venture Fund Class C	JVTCX	NAS CM	Open End	US Equity Small Cap (Growth)	B	B+	B	Up		2,500
Janus Henderson Venture Fund Class D	JANVX	NAS CM	Open End	US Equity Small Cap (Growth)	B+	B+	B	Up		2,500

★ Expanded analysis of this fund is included in Section II.

Min Additional Investment	3-Month Total Return	6-Month Total Return	1-Year Total Return	3-Year Total Return	5-Year Total Return	Dividend Yield (TTM)	Expense Ratio	3-Yr Std Deviation	3-Year Beta	NAV	Total Assets (MIL)	%Cash	%Stocks	%Bonds	%Other	Turnover Ratio	Last Bull Market Total Return	Last Bear Market Total Return	Front End Fee (%)	Back End Fee (%)	Inception Date
	TOTAL RETURNS					PERFORMANCE				ASSETS		ASSET ALLOCATION & TURNOVER					BULL & BEAR		FEES		
	6.83	9.99	25.98	33.18	110.03	0.02	1.04	10.9	0.99	46.11	13,532	1	99	0	0	46	24.04	-18.55	5.75		Jul-09
	6.66	9.62	25.11	30.42	102.68	0	1.81	10.87	0.99	43.61	13,532	1	99	0	0	46	23.44	-18.82		1.00	Jul-09
100	6.90	10.09	26.22	33.90	112.21	0.38	0.85	10.92	0.99	46.39	13,532	1	99	0	0	46	24.18	-18.51			May-93
	6.92	10.14	26.29	34.26	113.02	0.48	0.77	10.9	0.99	46.3	13,532	1	99	0	0	46	24.24	-18.46			Jul-09
	6.92	10.16	26.38	34.54	113.90	0.58	0.68	10.91	0.99	46.29	13,532	1	99	0	0	46	24.18	-18.51			May-12
	6.73	9.75	25.47	31.78	106.77		1.44	10.91	0.99	46.29	13,532	1	99	0	0	46	23.82	-18.68			Jan-17
	6.79	9.92	25.79	32.57	108.69	0.15	1.18	10.89	0.99	45.46	13,532	1	99	0	0	46	23.9	-18.6			Jul-09
	6.88	10.04	26.13	33.61	111.42	0.26	0.94	10.89	0.99	46.42	13,532	1	99	0	0	46	24.08	-18.53			May-93
	4.73	7.64	13.78	34.68	79.88	0.78	1.13	9.18	0.83	14.02	128.9	6	94	0	0	49			5.75		Dec-11
	4.55	7.27	12.90	31.37	72.98	0.55	1.91	9.14	0.83	13.67	128.9	6	94	0	0	49				1.00	Dec-11
100	4.84	7.81	14.02	35.52	82.14	0.81	0.92	9.15	0.83	14.06	128.9	6	94	0	0	49					Dec-11
	4.80	7.84	14.05	35.67	82.94	0.8	0.87	9.17	0.83	14.08	128.9	6	94	0	0	49					Dec-11
	4.82	7.86	14.07	35.69	82.98		0.77	9.17	0.83	14.06	128.9	6	94	0	0	49					Aug-17
	4.72	7.62	13.77	34.66	79.58	0.75	1.02	9.13	0.82	14.01	128.9	6	94	0	0	49					Dec-11
	4.83	7.73	13.94	35.24	81.38	0.79	1.02	9.17	0.83	14.04	128.9	6	94	0	0	49					Dec-11
	5.03	8.20	12.42	36.45	93.15	0.18	1.36	11.17	0.76	23.13	2,999	5	96	0	0	83	20.38	-20.74	5.75		Jul-09
	4.84	7.88	11.67	34.16	87.17	0.01	1.99	11.15	0.76	21.88	2,999	5	96	0	0	83	19.92	-21.03		1.00	Jul-09
100	5.07	8.36	12.72	37.69	95.97	0.44	1.04	11.18	0.76	22.9	2,999	5	96	0	0	83	20.64	-20.63			Oct-87
	5.15	8.42	12.81	37.85	96.45	0.47	1.03	11.2	0.76	23.03	2,999	5	96	0	0	83	20.71	-20.66			Jul-09
	5.12	8.44	12.87	38.25	97.31	0.47	1.02	11.18	0.76	23.63	2,999	5	96	0	0	83	20.75	-20.59			Feb-85
	5.12	8.45	12.90	38.33	97.61	0.51	0.88	11.2	0.76	22.97	2,999	5	96	0	0	83	20.75	-20.59			May-12
	4.94	8.04	12.10	35.28	90.34	0.1	1.64	11.16	0.76	22.51	2,999	5	96	0	0	83	20.24	-20.85			Jul-09
	5.01	8.17	12.35	36.29	92.77	0.19	1.27	11.17	0.76	22.81	2,999	5	96	0	0	83	20.4	-20.78			Jul-09
	5.07	8.31	12.61	37.32	95.14	0.37	1.13	11.17	0.76	22.95	2,999	5	96	0	0	83	20.6	-20.68			Oct-87
	5.50	11.46	26.64	39.88	112.61	0	1.17	12.43	0.93	28.12	9,515	6	93	0	0	30	27.45	-20.01	5.75		Jul-09
	5.29	11.09	25.81	37.28	105.70	0	1.82	12.41	0.93	26.19	9,515	6	93	0	0	30	26.84	-20.3		1.00	Jul-09
100	5.57	11.63	27.00	41.20	115.90	0.11	0.83	12.44	0.93	28.7	9,515	6	93	0	0	30	27.56	-19.91			Feb-05
	5.61	11.67	27.07	41.41	116.42	0.13	0.78	12.44	0.93	28.88	9,515	6	93	0	0	30	27.61	-19.9			Jul-09
	5.63	11.72	27.23	41.83	117.58	0.19	0.68	12.45	0.93	28.97	9,515	6	93	0	0	30	27.56	-19.91			May-12
	5.41	11.32	26.24	38.68	109.56	0	1.44	12.44	0.93	27.37	9,515	6	93	0	0	30	27.2	-20.15			Jul-09
	5.47	11.44	26.59	39.68	112.18	0	1.18	12.45	0.93	27.88	9,515	6	93	0	0	30	27.32	-20.05			Jul-09
	5.53	11.59	26.90	40.79	114.99	0.06	0.93	12.43	0.93	28.51	9,515	6	93	0	0	30	27.55	-19.98			Feb-05
	4.74	8.12	19.18	28.71		0	1.17			12.95	8.9	2	98	0	0	2			5.75		Dec-14
	4.60	7.78	18.37	25.85		0	1.92			12.66	8.9	2	98	0	0	2				1.00	Dec-14
100	4.79	8.24	19.44	29.69			0.96			13.05	8.9	2	98	0	0	2					Jun-17
	4.87	8.15	19.35	29.59		0	0.82			13.04	8.9	2	98	0	0	2					Dec-14
	4.88	8.26	19.17	29.40		0	0.83			13.02	8.9	2	98	0	0	2					Nov-15
	4.79	8.07	19.11	28.69			1.31			13.03	8.9	2	98	0	0	2					Jun-17
	4.87	8.24	19.44	29.69			1.06			13.05	8.9	2	98	0	0	2					Jun-17
	5.20	11.06	20.18	32.06	100.26	1.54	0.92	8.23	0.63	11	1,285	1	99	0	0	108	23.53	-18.08	5.75		Dec-05
	5.07	10.65	19.32	29.44	93.65	0.78	1.69	8.18	0.62	10.71	1,285	1	99	0	0	108	23.15	-18.4		1.00	Dec-05
	5.22	10.99	20.05	31.69	100.33	1.29	1.04	8.21	0.63	10.98	1,285	1	99	0	0	108	23.41	-18.1			Dec-05
	2.84	4.63	9.28	17.52	47.00	2.14	0.93	5.85	0.54	11.65	59.6	1	52	44	2	86	13.24	-9.32	5.75		Jul-10
	2.64	4.31	8.53	14.87	41.67	1.41	1.7	5.84	0.54	11.68	59.6	1	52	44	2	86	13.06	-9.6		1.00	Jul-10
100	2.96	4.78	9.50	17.94	48.07	2.26	0.82	5.88	0.54	11.66	59.6	1	52	44	2	86	13.31	-9.27			Jul-10
	2.98	4.81	9.57	18.15	48.69	2.32	0.75	5.87	0.54	11.67	59.6	1	52	44	2	86	13.26	-9.15			Jul-10
	2.90	4.82	9.59	18.17	48.71		0.68	5.87	0.54	11.66	59.6	1	52	44	2	86	13.26	-9.15			Aug-17
	2.82	4.56	9.15	17.32	46.59	2.03	0.93	5.76	0.53	11.66	59.6	1	52	44	2	86	13.07	-9.41			Jul-10
	2.85	4.72	9.30	17.75	47.75	2.17	0.93	5.84	0.54	11.66	59.6	1	52	44	2	86	13.23	-9.32			Jul-10
	3.95	9.52	24.01	30.64	107.51	0	1.04	13.72	0.89	75.41	3,217	3	97	0	0	25	28.98	-20.37	5.75		May-11
	3.76	9.12	23.08	27.85	100.44	0	1.8	13.68	0.89	70.68	3,217	3	97	0	0	25	28.58	-20.89		1.00	May-11
100	4.01	9.66	24.28	31.54	110.22	0	0.82	13.72	0.89	77.3	3,217	3	97	0	0	25	29.21	-20.31			Apr-85

	MARKET		FUND TYPE, CATEGORY & OBJECTIVE		RATINGS				MINIMUMS	
Fund Name	Ticker Symbol	Traded On	Fund Type	Category and (Prospectus Objective)	Overall Rating	Reward Rating	Risk Rating	Recent Up/ Downgrade	Open to New Investors	Min Initial Investment
Janus Henderson Venture Fund Class I	JVTIX	NAS CM	Open End	US Equity Small Cap (Growth)	B+	B+	B	Up		1,000,000
Janus Henderson Venture Fund Class N	JVTNX	NAS CM	Open End	US Equity Small Cap (Growth)	B+	B+	B	Up		0
Janus Henderson Venture Fund Class S	JVTSX	NAS CM	Open End	US Equity Small Cap (Growth)	B+	B+	B	Up		2,500
Janus Henderson Venture Fund Class T	JAVTX	NAS CM	Open End	US Equity Small Cap (Growth)	B+	B+	B	Up		2,500
Janus Henderson VIT Balanced Portfolio Institutional Class	JABLX	NAS CM	Open End	Moderate Alloc (Balanced)	B-	C+	B	Down	Y	0
Janus Henderson VIT Balanced Portfolio Service Class	US4710216916		Open End	Moderate Alloc (Balanced)	B-	C+	B	Down	Y	0
Janus Henderson VIT Enterprise Portfolio Institutional Cls	JAAGX	NAS CM	Open End	US Equity Mid Cap (Growth)	B+	A-	B	Up	Y	0
Janus Henderson VIT Enterprise Portfolio Service Class	US4710217179		Open End	US Equity Mid Cap (Growth)	B	A-	B	Down	Y	0
Janus Henderson VIT Forty Portfolio Institutional Class	JACAX	NAS CM	Open End	US Equity Large Cap Growth (Growth)	B+	B+	A-	Up	Y	0
Janus Henderson VIT Forty Portfolio Service Class	US4710216189		Open End	US Equity Large Cap Growth (Growth)	B+	B+	A-	Up	Y	0
Janus Henderson VIT Global Alloc Port - Moderate Inst Cls	JMAPX	NAS CM	Open End	Alloc (Asset Alloc)	B-	C+	B+	Down	Y	0
Janus Henderson VIT Global Alloc Port - Moderate Serv Cls	US4710214283		Open End	Alloc (Asset Alloc)	B-	C+	B	Down	Y	0
Janus Henderson VIT Global Research Portfolio Inst Cls	JAWGX	NAS CM	Open End	Global Equity (World Stock)	B-	B-	B	Up	Y	0
Janus Henderson VIT Global Research Portfolio Service Cls	US4710216429		Open End	Global Equity (World Stock)	B-	B-	B	Up	Y	0
Janus Henderson VIT Global Technology Portfolio Inst Cls	JGLTX	NAS CM	Open End	Technology Sector Equity (Technology)	A-	A+	B	Up	Y	0
Janus Henderson VIT Global Technology Port Serv Cls	US4710215504		Open End	Technology Sector Equity (Technology)	A	A+	B+	Up	Y	0
Janus Henderson VIT Mid Cap Value Portfolio Inst Cls	JAMVX	NAS CM	Open End	US Equity Mid Cap (Growth)	B	B-	B		Y	0
Janus Henderson VIT Mid Cap Value Portfolio Service Class	US4710214515		Open End	US Equity Mid Cap (Growth)	B	B-	B		Y	0
Janus Henderson VIT Overseas Portfolio Institutional Class	JAIGX	NAS CM	Open End	Global Equity Large Cap (Foreign Stock)	C+	C+	C+	Up	Y	0
Janus Henderson VIT Overseas Portfolio Service Class	US4710216676		Open End	Global Equity Large Cap (Foreign Stock)	C+	C+	C+	Up		0
Janus Henderson VIT Research Portfolio Institutional Class	JAGRX	NAS CM	Open End	US Equity Large Cap Growth (Growth)	B	B	A-	Down	Y	0
Janus Henderson VIT Research Portfolio Service Class	US4710216759		Open End	US Equity Large Cap Growth (Growth)	B	B	A-	Up	Y	0
Janus Henderson VIT U.S. Low Vol Port Serv Shares	US4710213780		Open End	US Equity Large Cap Blend (Growth)	B	B-	A+		Y	0
Japan Smaller Capitalization Fund	JOF	NYSE	Closed End	Japan Equity (Pacific Stock)	A	A	A-	Up	Y	
Jensen Quality Growth Fund Class I	JENIX	NAS CM	Open End	US Equity Large Cap Growth (Growth)	B	B	B+	Down	Y	250,000
Jensen Quality Growth Fund Class J	JENSX	NAS CM	Open End	US Equity Large Cap Growth (Growth)	B	B	B+	Down	Y	2,500
Jensen Quality Growth Fund Class Y	JENYX	NAS CM	Open End	US Equity Large Cap Growth (Growth)	B	B	B+	Down	Y	1,000,000
Jensen Quality Growth FundClass R	JENRX	NAS CM	Open End	US Equity Large Cap Growth (Growth)	B	B	B+	Down	Y	2,500
Jensen Quality Value Fund Class I	JNVIX	NAS CM	Open End	US Equity Mid Cap (Growth)	B-	C+	B-		Y	250,000
Jensen Quality Value Fund Class J	JNVSX	NAS CM	Open End	US Equity Mid Cap (Growth)	B-	C+	B-		Y	2,500
JHancock Intl Strategic Equity Allocation Fund Cls NAV	US47805T7735		Open End	Global Equity Large Cap (Growth)	D	D+	A-		Y	0
JHancock U.S. Strategic Equity Allocation Fund Class NAV	US47805T7651		Open End	US Equity Large Cap Blend (Growth)	D	C	B		Y	0
JNL Aggressive Growth Allocation Fund Class A	US46648L5912		Open End	Aggressive Alloc (Growth)	B-	B-	B-	Down	Y	0
JNL Aggressive Growth Allocation Fund Class I	US46648L5839		Open End	Aggressive Alloc (Growth)	B-	B-	B-		Y	0
JNL Growth Allocation Fund Class A	US46648L5599		Open End	Aggressive Alloc (Growth & Income)	B-	B-	B-	Down	Y	0
JNL Growth Allocation Fund Class I	US46648L5425		Open End	Aggressive Alloc (Growth & Income)	B-	B-	B-		Y	0
JNL Institutional Alt 25 Fund Class A	US46644W5913		Open End	Moderate Alloc (Growth & Income)	B-	C+	B	Up	Y	0
JNL Institutional Alt 25 Fund Class I	US46644W5830		Open End	Moderate Alloc (Growth & Income)	B-	C+	B		Y	0
JNL Institutional Alt 50 Fund Class A	US46644W5590		Open End	Cautious Alloc (Growth & Income)	C+	C+	B	Up	Y	0
JNL Institutional Alt 50 Fund Class I	US46644W5426		Open End	Cautious Alloc (Growth & Income)	B-	C+	B		Y	0
JNL Moderate Growth Allocation Fund Class A	US46648L5755		Open End	Moderate Alloc (Growth)	B-	C+	B	Up	Y	0
JNL Moderate Growth Allocation Fund Class I	US46648L5672		Open End	Moderate Alloc (Growth)	B-	C+	B		Y	0
JNL Multi-Manager Alternative Fund Class A	US46644W5186		Open End	Multialternative (Growth)	C+	C	B	Up	Y	0
JNL Multi-Manager Alternative Fund Class I	US46644W4924		Open End	Multialternative (Growth)	C+	C	B		Y	0
JNL Multi-Manager Mid Cap Fund Class A	US46644W8727		Open End	US Equity Mid Cap (Growth & Income)	D	C-	B		Y	0
JNL Multi-Manager Mid Cap Fund Class I	US46644W4841		Open End	US Equity Mid Cap (Growth & Income)	D	C-	B		Y	0
JNL Multi-Manager Small Cap Growth Fund Class A	US46644W4767		Open End	US Equity Small Cap (Small Company)	B	B+	B-	Up	Y	0
JNL Multi-Manager Small Cap Growth Fund Class I	US46644W4684		Open End	US Equity Small Cap (Small Company)	B	B+	C	Up	Y	0
JNL Multi-Manager Small Cap Value Fund Class A	US46644W4502		Open End	US Equity Small Cap (Small Company)	B-	B	B-	Up	Y	0
JNL Multi-Manager Small Cap Value Fund Class I	US46644W4437		Open End	US Equity Small Cap (Small Company)	B-	B	B-	Up	Y	0
JNL S&P 500 Index Fund Class I	US46648L3289		Open End	US Equity Large Cap Blend (Growth)	U	U	U		Y	0
JNL/AB Dynamic Asset Allocation Fund Class A	US46644W2522		Open End	Moderate Alloc (Growth & Income)	B-	C+	B-	Down	Y	0

★ Expanded analysis of this fund is included in Section II.

	TOTAL RETURNS					PERFORMANCE				ASSETS		ASSET ALLOCATION & TURNOVER					BULL & BEAR		FEES		
Min Additional Investment	3-Month Total Return	6-Month Total Return	1-Year Total Return	3-Year Total Return	5-Year Total Return	Dividend Yield (TTM)	Expense Ratio	3-Yr Std Deviation	3-Year Beta	NAV	Total Assets (MIL)	%Cash	%Stocks	%Bonds	%Other	Turnover Ratio	Last Bull Market Total Return	Last Bear Market Total Return	Front End Fee (%)	Back End Fee (%)	Inception Date
	4.03	9.68	24.35	31.77	110.89	0	0.77	13.72	0.89	77.58	3,217	3	97	0	0	25	29.26	-20.28			May-11
	4.04	9.72	24.44	32.08	111.68	0	0.68	13.72	0.89	77.98	3,217	3	97	0	0	25	29.21	-20.31			May-12
	3.91	9.45	23.83	30.12	106.44	0	1.19	13.72	0.89	74.8	3,217	3	97	0	0	25	29.04	-20.43			May-11
	3.98	9.60	24.16	31.15	109.21	0	0.93	13.7	0.89	76.4	3,217	3	97	0	0	25	29.1	-20.33			Apr-85
	5.17	9.15	18.42	24.01	64.08	1.77	0.64	6.68	0.64	35.27	3,268	2	63	34	1	80	18.02	-12.25			Sep-93
	5.09	9.02	18.13	23.11	62.00	1.53	0.89	6.69	0.64	37.09	3,268	2	63	34	1	80	17.82	-12.32			Dec-99
	5.71	11.45	27.41	47.79	125.63	0.29	0.74	10.14	0.89	70.65	1,155	4	96	0	0	20	24.98	-19.18			Sep-93
	5.64	11.32	27.08	46.67	122.80	0.15	0.98	10.13	0.89	66.67	1,155	4	96	0	0	20	24.83	-19.27			Dec-99
	4.08	9.47	30.31	48.49	117.92	0	0.74	12.04	1.06	39.76	790.2	3	97	0	0	53	28.82	-18.42			May-97
	4.01	9.33	29.99	47.39	115.24	0	0.99	12.04	1.06	37.84	790.2	3	97	0	0	53	28.62	-18.51			Dec-99
	3.35	6.93	16.54	17.17	40.79	0.7	0.94	6.4	0.58	12.87	7.5	8	62	28	1	14	17.77				Aug-11
	3.33	6.83	16.25	16.36	39.59	0.64	1.19	6.41	0.58	12.84	7.5	8	62	28	1	14	17.88				Aug-11
	5.06	10.09	27.02	25.77	77.75	0.76	0.67	11.43	1.05	51.2	747.0	0	98	0	1	45	18.42	-23.69			Sep-93
	4.98	9.94	26.68	24.83	75.53	0.65	0.92	11.42	1.05	50.17	747.0	0	98	0	1	45	18.25	-23.76			Dec-99
	7.75	16.68	45.08	72.30	162.97	0	0.78	14.56	1.22	11.4	391.8	1	99	0	0	62	24.37	-19.19			Jan-00
	7.73	16.65	44.91	71.24	160.24	0	1.04	14.52	1.21	11.56	391.8	1	99	0	0	62	24.23	-19.37			Jan-00
	5.23	8.19	13.93	29.67	82.08	0.82	0.6	9.74	0.9	18.02	121.3	5	95	0	0	69	20.26	-19.71			May-03
	5.15	8.07	13.63	28.71	79.85	0.69	0.86	9.7	0.89	17.49	121.3	5	95	0	0	69	19.95	-19.79			Dec-02
	3.97	9.92	31.11	12.46	15.41	1.6	0.52	16.91	1.29	31.98	819.7	0	100	0	0	103	13.01	-31.85			May-94
	3.91	9.76	30.80	11.64	13.97	1.53	0.77	16.89	1.29	30.74	819.7	0	100	0	0	103	12.85	-31.91			Dec-99
	6.93	10.15	27.87	34.41	103.15	0.36	0.64	11.07	1	36.51	540.9	1	99	0	0	58	25.43	-18.51			Sep-93
	6.88	10.04	27.55	33.40	100.70	0.23	0.89	11.05	0.99	35.68	540.9	1	99	0	0	58	25.24	-18.58			Dec-99
	6.69	8.27	15.44	30.28	96.07	1.24	0.83	7.51	0.53	17.43	1,151	1	99	0	0	29					Sep-12
	8.43	18.02	37.23	74.01	126.81	2.22	1.32	10.83	0.95	13.44	425.3	1	99	0	1	20	4.76	2.06			Mar-90
100	7.80	9.95	23.55	39.91	112.41	1.1	0.61	9.63	0.89	46.66	6,644	4	96	0	0	7	19.96	-16.1			Jul-03
100	7.72	9.81	23.21	38.87	109.80	0.87	0.88	9.63	0.89	46.65	6,644	4	96	0	0	7	19.74	-16.22			Aug-92
100	7.82	9.99	23.61	39.44	110.66	1.15	0.57	9.64	0.89	46.65	6,644	4	96	0	0	7	19.74	-16.22			Sep-16
100	7.63	9.60	22.77	37.37	106.04	0.56	1.25	9.63	0.89	46.44	6,644	4	96	0	0	7	19.6	-16.27			Jul-03
100	7.64	8.80	15.27	20.34	94.88	1.15	0.9	10.75	0.76	12.71	36.3	4	96	0	0	71	16.9	-14.47			Mar-10
100	7.53	8.71	15.07	19.85	93.44	0.98	1.05	10.73	0.76	12.78	36.3	4	96	0	0	71	16.89	-14.53			Mar-10
	4.13	10.28	25.83			0.23	0.69			11.68	2,076	3	96	0	1	112					Oct-16
	6.30	10.97	19.72			0.28	0.66			11.88	2,006	3	97	0	0	119					Sep-16
	4.50	9.06	21.40	27.05	68.63	0	0.97	9.07	1.07	12.99	1,509	4	76	18	1	38	18.37	-18.06			Jan-07
	4.58	9.15	21.49	27.15	68.76		0.67	9.07	1.07	13	1,509	4	76	18	1	38	18.37	-18.06			Sep-17
	3.98	7.87	18.63	24.25	63.13	0	0.99	7.83	0.92	13.56	2,481	5	67	25	1	41	17.33	-15.46			Jan-07
	4.06	7.95	18.71	24.34	63.25		0.69	7.83	0.92	13.58	2,481	5	67	25	1	41	17.33	-15.47			Sep-17
	3.39	6.62	14.33	18.01	39.09	0	1.2	6.38	1	17.07	3,311	7	57	32	1	26	13.33	-13.9			Apr-09
	3.45	6.68	14.40	18.08	39.17		0.9	6.38	1	17.08	3,311	7	57	32	1	26	13.33	-13.9			Sep-17
	2.82	5.09	10.52	12.28	27.74	0	1.43	5.16	0.8	17.12	2,911	8	50	36	1	22	12.09	-15.44			Apr-09
	3.00	5.27	10.71	12.48	27.96		1.13	5.17	0.81	17.15	2,911	8	50	36	1	22	12.09	-15.44			Sep-17
	3.08	6.11	14.53	20.12	50.09	0	0.98	6.35	1	13.71	2,467	7	54	37	1	44	15.14	-11.75			Jan-07
	3.15	6.19	14.61	20.21	50.20		0.68	6.35	1	13.72	2,467	7	54	37	1	44	15.14	-11.75			Sep-17
	1.09	3.48	6.38			0.54	2.09			10.19	1,032	28	23	33	0	278					Apr-15
	1.19	3.59	6.49				1.79			10.2	1,032	28	23	33	0	278					Sep-17
	5.11	7.94	16.03			0.08	1.1			12.34	960.3	4	96	0	0	13					Sep-16
	5.28	8.12	16.22				0.8			12.36	960.3	4	96	0	0	13					Sep-17
	4.98	11.84	27.23	27.83	75.88	0	0.98	15.07	0.99	25.88	1,713	3	97	0	0	119	24.74	-22.01			Sep-96
	5.08	11.99	27.50	28.63	77.74	0	0.68	15.07	0.99	27.07	1,713	3	97	0	0	119	24.9	-21.97			Mar-04
	3.09	8.16	11.06	23.52	70.68	0.57	1.08	13.96	0.96	15.33	1,236	2	98	0	0	84	31.42	-24.85			May-05
	3.15	8.21	11.25	24.23	72.41	0.74	0.78	13.97	0.96	15.35	1,236	2	98	0	0	84	31.63	-24.76			May-05
	6.54						0.19			10.74	5.4	0	100	0	0						Sep-17
	3.65	7.12	15.88	17.84		2.19	1.21	7.15	1.13	11.64	37.9	7	85	7	0	83					Apr-14

	MARKET		FUND TYPE, CATEGORY & OBJECTIVE		RATINGS				MINIMUMS	
Fund Name	Ticker Symbol	Traded On	Fund Type	Category and (Prospectus Objective)	Overall Rating	Reward Rating	Risk Rating	Recent Up/ Downgrade	Open to New Investors	Min Initial Investment
JNL/AB Dynamic Asset Allocation Fund Class I	US46644W2456		Open End	Moderate Alloc (Growth & Income)	B-	C+	B-		Y	0
JNL/American Funds Balanced Fund Class A	US46644W7992		Open End	Alloc (Asset Alloc)	B	C+	B+	Up	Y	0
JNL/American Funds Balanced Fund Class I	US46644W7810		Open End	Alloc (Asset Alloc)	B	C+	B+	Up	Y	0
JNL/American Funds Blue Chip Income & Growth Fund Cls A	US46644W4197		Open End	US Equity Large Cap Value (Income)	B	B-	B		Y	0
JNL/American Funds Blue Chip Income & Growth Fund Cls I	US46644W3934		Open End	US Equity Large Cap Value (Income)	B	B-	B		Y	0
JNL/American Funds Global Small Capitalization Fund Cls A	US46644W3694		Open End	Global Equity Mid/Small Cap (Small Company)	B	B-	B	Up	Y	0
JNL/American Funds Global Small Capitalization Fund Cls I	US46644W3512		Open End	Global Equity Mid/Small Cap (Small Company)	B	B	B	Up	Y	0
JNL/American Funds Growth Allocation Fund Class A	US46644W3447		Open End	Aggressive Alloc (Growth)	B-	B-	B	Down	Y	0
JNL/American Funds Growth Allocation Fund Class I	US46644W3363		Open End	Aggressive Alloc (Growth)	B-	B-	B		Y	0
JNL/American Funds Growth-Income Fund Class A	US46644W3280		Open End	US Equity Large Cap Blend (Growth & Income)	B	B	B		Y	0
JNL/American Funds Growth-Income Fund Class I	US46644W3108		Open End	US Equity Large Cap Blend (Growth & Income)	B	B	B		Y	0
JNL/American Funds International Fund Class A	US46644W2944		Open End	Global Equity Large Cap (Foreign Stock)	B-	B-	B-	Up	Y	0
JNL/American Funds International Fund Class I	US46644W2860		Open End	Global Equity Large Cap (Foreign Stock)	B-	B	B-	Up	Y	0
JNL/American Funds Moderate Growth Allocation Class A	US46644W4353		Open End	Moderate Alloc (Balanced)	B	C+	A-	Up	Y	0
JNL/American Funds Moderate Growth Allocation Class I	US46644W4270		Open End	Moderate Alloc (Balanced)	B	C+	A-		Y	0
JNL/American Funds New World Fund Class A	US46644W2787		Open End	Emerging Markets Equity (Growth)	B-	B-	B-	Up	Y	0
JNL/American Funds New World Fund Class I	US46644W2605		Open End	Emerging Markets Equity (Growth)	B-	B-	B-	Up	Y	0
JNL/AQR Large Cap Relaxed Constraint Equity Fund Class A	US46644W7166		Open End	US Equity Large Cap Blend (Growth)	B-	B	B-	Down	Y	0
JNL/AQR Large Cap Relaxed Constraint Equity Fund Class I	US46644W6903		Open End	US Equity Large Cap Blend (Growth)	B	B	B-	Up	Y	0
JNL/AQR Managed Futures Strategy Fund Class A	US46648M8055		Open End	Other Alternative (Growth)	D	D	D+	Down	Y	0
JNL/AQR Managed Futures Strategy Fund Class I	US46648M8881		Open End	Other Alternative (Growth)	D	D	D+	Down	Y	0
JNL/BlackRock Global Allocation Fund Class A	US46648M8543		Open End	Alloc (Asset Alloc)	B-	C+	B+	Down	Y	0
JNL/BlackRock Global Allocation Fund Class I	US46648M8477		Open End	Alloc (Asset Alloc)	B-	C+	B	Down	Y	0
JNL/BlackRock Global Natural Resources Fund Class A	US46648M8709		Open End	Natl Resources Sec Equity (Natl Res)	D+	D+	D+	Up	Y	0
JNL/BlackRock Global Natural Resources Fund Class I	US46648M8626		Open End	Natl Resources Sec Equity (Natl Res)	D+	D+	D+	Up	Y	0
JNL/BlackRock Large Cap Select Growth Fund Class A	US46644W4015		Open End	US Equity Large Cap Growth (Growth)	B+	A-	B+	Up	Y	0
JNL/BlackRock Large Cap Select Growth Fund Class I	US46644W5004		Open End	US Equity Large Cap Growth (Growth)	A-	A-	B+	Up	Y	0
JNL/Boston Partners Global Long Short Equity Fund Class A	US46648M8394		Open End	Long/Short Equity (Equity-Income)	B	C	A+	Up	Y	0
JNL/Boston Partners Global Long Short Equity Fund Class I	US46648M8212		Open End	Long/Short Equity (Equity-Income)	B	C	A+		Y	0
JNL/Brookfield Global Infrastructure and MLP Fund Class A	US46648M8139		Open End	Other Sector Equity (Growth & Income)	C	C	C-		Y	0
JNL/Brookfield Global Infrastructure and MLP Fund Class I	US46648M7974		Open End	Other Sector Equity (Growth & Income)	C	C	C-		Y	0
JNL/Causeway International Value Select Fund Class A	US46648M1449		Open End	Global Equity Large Cap (Foreign Stock)	C+	C+	C	Up	Y	0
JNL/Causeway International Value Select Fund Class I	US46648M1365		Open End	Global Equity Large Cap (Foreign Stock)	B-	B-	B-	Up	Y	0
JNL/ClearBridge Large Cap Growth Fund Class A	US46649B7901		Open End	US Equity Large Cap Growth (Growth)	U	U	U		Y	0
JNL/ClearBridge Large Cap Growth Fund Class I	US46649B7828		Open End	US Equity Large Cap Growth (Growth)	U	U	U		Y	0
JNL/DFA Growth Allocation Fund (A)	US46644W8644		Open End	Aggressive Alloc (Growth & Income)	U	U	U		Y	0
JNL/DFA Growth Allocation Fund Class I	US46644W6663		Open End	Aggressive Alloc (Growth & Income)	U	U	U		Y	0
JNL/DFA Moderate Growth Allocation Fund Class A	US46644W8560		Open End	Moderate Alloc (Growth & Income)	U	U	U		Y	0
JNL/DFA Moderate Growth Allocation Fund Class I	US46644W2373		Open End	Moderate Alloc (Growth & Income)	U	U	U		Y	0
JNL/DFA U.S. Core Equity Fund Class A	US46649B7588		Open End	US Equity Large Cap Blend (Growth)	B	B	B-	Up	Y	0
JNL/DFA U.S. Core Equity Fund Class I	US46649B7414		Open End	US Equity Large Cap Blend (Growth)	B	B	B-	Up	Y	0
JNL/DoubleLine® Shiller Enhanced CAPE® Fund Class A	US46644W1045		Open End	US Equity Large Cap Value (Growth & Income)	C	C+	B	Up	Y	0
JNL/DoubleLine® Shiller Enhanced CAPE® Fund Class I	US46644W6333		Open End	US Equity Large Cap Value (Growth & Income)	C	C	B		Y	0
JNL/FPA + DoubleLine Flexible Allocation Fund Class A	US46644W8073		Open End	Moderate Alloc (Growth & Income)	C+	C	C+	Up	Y	0
JNL/FPA + DoubleLine Flexible Allocation Fund Class I	US46644W8800		Open End	Moderate Alloc (Growth & Income)	C+	C	C+	Up	Y	0
JNL/Franklin Templeton Founding Strategy Fund Class A	US46648M7891		Open End	Aggressive Alloc (Growth)	C+	C+	C+	Down	Y	0
JNL/Franklin Templeton Founding Strategy Fund Class I	US46648M7719		Open End	Aggressive Alloc (Growth)	C+	C+	C+		Y	0
JNL/Franklin Templeton Global Fund Class A	US46644W7737		Open End	Global Equity (Growth)	B-	C+	B-	Up	Y	0
JNL/Franklin Templeton Global Fund Class I	US46644W7653		Open End	Global Equity (Growth)	C+	C+	C	Up	Y	0
JNL/Franklin Templeton Income Fund Class A	US46648M4336		Open End	Cautious Alloc (Income)	C+	C+	B-	Down	Y	0
JNL/Franklin Templeton Income Fund Class I	US46648M4252		Open End	Cautious Alloc (Income)	C+	C+	B-		Y	0
JNL/Franklin Templeton Intl Small Cap Growth Fund Cls A	US46648M4179		Open End	Global Equity Mid/Small Cap (Foreign Stock)	B	B	B	Up	Y	0

★Expanded analysis of this fund is included in Section II.

	TOTAL RETURNS					PERFORMANCE				ASSETS		ASSET ALLOCATION & TURNOVER					BULL & BEAR		FEES		
Min Additional Investment	3-Month Total Return	6-Month Total Return	1-Year Total Return	3-Year Total Return	5-Year Total Return	Dividend Yield (TTM)	Expense Ratio	3-Yr Std Deviation	3-Year Beta	NAV	Total Assets (MIL)	%Cash	%Stocks	%Bonds	%Other	Turnover Ratio	Last Bull Market Total Return	Last Bear Market Total Return	Front End Fee (%)	Back End Fee (%)	Inception Date
	3.73	7.22	15.98	17.94			0.91	7.16	1.13	11.65	37.9	7	85	7	0	83					Sep-17
	2.93	7.23	16.70	20.98	42.47	1.32	0.89	7.78	0.69	11.56	730.3	5	61	30	5	57	13.92	-14.96			May-00
	3.02	7.38	17.03	21.79	43.86	1.46	0.59	7.8	0.69	11.92	730.3	5	61	30	5	57	14.11	-14.99			Mar-04
	7.06	10.48	16.60	32.09	106.22	0	1	10.27	0.94	22.12	3,371	1	95	0	4	1	22.6	-16.26			May-10
	7.19	10.63	16.88	32.98	108.39	0	0.7	10.27	0.94	22.36	3,371	1	95	0	4	1	22.64	-16.12			May-10
	5.06	11.59	25.52	27.38	68.83	0.17	1.29	12.14	0.97	14.31	676.5	9	89	2	0	11	18.74	-26.11			May-10
	5.15	11.71	25.77	28.20	70.47	0.31	0.99	12.12	0.96	14.48	676.5	9	89	2	0	11	18.71	-25.96			May-10
	4.21	9.08	20.60	29.48	65.36	0	1.09	8.52	1	16.33	2,025	2	75	19	4	19					Apr-12
	4.33	9.21	20.75	29.63	65.56		0.79	8.52	1	16.35	2,025	2	75	19	4	19					Sep-17
	5.55	11.26	21.87	35.71	103.24	0	0.96	10.19	0.99	22.23	5,732	2	92	1	4	1	22.39	-17.24			May-10
	5.64	11.40	22.18	36.57	105.30	0	0.66	10.19	0.99	22.47	5,732	2	92	1	4	1	22.45	-17.2			May-10
	4.77	11.28	31.63	28.41	52.92	0.61	1.19	11.78	0.92	14.92	1,953	3	89	1	6	4	16.62	-25.5			May-10
	4.79	11.37	31.93	29.15	54.35	0.71	0.89	11.78	0.92	15.07	1,953	3	89	1	6	4	16.57	-25.27			May-10
	3.18	6.81	15.69	23.60	50.17	0	1.07	6.65	1.05	14.89	2,198	3	55	38	4	15					Apr-12
	3.18	6.81	15.69	23.60	50.17		0.77	6.65	1.05	14.89	2,198	3	55	38	4	15					Sep-17
	4.94	12.90	28.89	29.93	34.03	0.29	1.43	11.5	0.95	13.16	1,368	4	93	3	0	3	17.05	-21.9			May-10
	4.98	13.01	29.22	30.69	35.35	0.41	1.13	11.54	0.96	13.28	1,368	4	93	3	0	3	17.01	-21.76			May-10
	6.16	12.41	22.98	29.37	102.93	0.57	1.85	11.52	1.09	12.75	646.6	2	98	0	0	119	24.32	-23.02			Jan-07
	6.24	12.49	23.23	30.17	105.12	0.7	1.55	11.54	1.09	12.93	646.6	2	98	0	0	119	24.21	-22.86			Jan-07
	4.88	4.75	-1.29	-7.32	8.60	0	1.38	9.09	33.71	8.37	417.9	39	32	25	3	0	-5.68				Aug-11
	4.98	4.85	-1.05	-6.79	9.64	0	1.08	9.11	36.33	8.42	417.9	39	32	25	3	0	-5.58				Aug-11
	2.68	5.75	13.83	16.37	37.20	1.54	1.08	6.35	0.59	12.62	4,014	7	54	32	6	133	11.08	-13.58			Oct-10
	2.74	5.82	14.12	17.08	38.42	1.71	0.78	6.31	0.58	12.72	4,014	7	54	32	6	133	11.04	-13.45			Oct-10
	8.80	13.67	-2.90	-6.99	-10.54	0.95	1	19.47	0.82	8.77	821.4	3	97	0	0	4	13.82	-24.25			Jan-07
	8.85	13.91	-2.67	-6.31	-9.51	1.14	0.7	19.43	0.82	8.85	821.4	3	97	0	0	4	13.9	-24.22			Jan-07
	7.67	13.65	33.62	41.47	120.39	0	0.89	12.31	1.08	36.46	3,082	2	97	0	0	92	25.46	-17.5			May-95
	7.72	13.75	33.91	42.33	122.71	0	0.59	12.29	1.08	37.8	3,082	2	97	0	0	92	26.78	-17.43			Mar-04
	3.36	5.32	7.68	15.77		0	2.35	5.12	0.41	11.07	623.9	3	98	0	0	157					Sep-14
	3.54	5.51	7.87	15.98			2.05	5.14	0.41	11.09	623.9	3	98	0	0	157					Sep-17
	-0.49	1.28	9.90	0.19	35.30	1.81	1.15	11.58	1.03	13.95	1,027	2	98	0	0	100					Dec-11
	-0.42	1.36	10.19	0.78	36.72	1.97	0.85	11.58	1.02	14.02	1,027	2	98	0	0	100					Dec-11
	5.07	12.32	28.46	23.23	36.58	0.97	1.01	12.2	0.89	17.17	1,827	3	97	0	0	33	13.26	-25.14			Mar-98
	5.19	12.48	28.74	24.05	38.04	1.03	0.71	12.24	0.9	17.63	1,827	3	97	0	0	33	13.49	-25.2			Mar-04
	7.00						0.95			10.85	448.9	3	97	0	0						Sep-17
	7.00						0.65			10.85	448.9	3	97	0	0						Sep-17
	4.40	8.85					0.89			10.88	72.1	0	76	22	2						Apr-17
	4.47	8.93					0.54			10.88	72.1	0	76	22	2						Sep-17
	3.47	7.11					0.86			10.71	54.0	0	59	40	2						Apr-17
	3.63	7.27					0.51			10.72	54.0	0	59	40	2						Sep-17
	6.77	11.74	20.22	33.03	102.70	0.83	0.8	10.55	1.02	13.72	1,189	0	100	0	0	16	20.69	-16.6			Sep-96
	6.92	11.94	20.54	33.90	104.70	0.91	0.45	10.58	1.02	14.52	1,189	0	100	0	0	16	20.79	-16.48			Mar-04
	5.72	8.58	21.50			0	1.11			14.96	1,369	12	0	78	10	106					Sep-15
	5.79	8.66	21.58				0.81			14.97	1,369	12	0	78	10	106					Sep-17
	3.41	5.45	11.05	3.83	26.57	0.93	1.21	8.04	0.68	12.71	2,190	3	52	42	3	230	21.4	-21.43			Sep-09
	3.48	5.71	11.40	4.58	27.85	1.11	0.91	8.06	0.68	12.77	2,190	3	52	42	3	230	21.4	-21.3			Sep-09
	2.11	4.72	11.75	18.23	53.09	0	1.05	9.69	1.09	13.97	1,470	6	78	13	2	8	16.71	-16.9			Jan-07
	2.19	4.79	11.84	18.31	53.20		0.75	9.69	1.09	13.98	1,470	6	78	13	2	8	16.71	-16.9			Sep-17
	2.98	6.35	17.56	21.00	57.07	1.62	1.02	12.53	1.14	11.74	1,032	6	93	1	0	23	17.37	-22.27			Jan-07
	3.05	6.51	17.92	21.70	58.71	1.79	0.72	12.52	1.14	11.79	1,032	6	93	1	0	23	17.5	-22.22			Jan-07
	1.52	5.19	9.93	15.52	37.70	3.83	0.95	7.73	0.66	11.98	2,537	7	51	35	1	43	13.04	-11.15			May-06
	1.59	5.35	10.20	16.25	39.11	4.19	0.65	7.72	0.66	11.47	2,537	7	51	35	1	43	13.1	-11.05			May-06
	3.32	10.36	32.28	35.71	64.47	0.97	1.29	11.48	0.91	11.51	734.0	6	90	0	3	18	13.09	-20.52			Dec-07

	MARKET		FUND TYPE, CATEGORY & OBJECTIVE		RATINGS				MINIMUMS	
Fund Name	Ticker Symbol	Traded On	Fund Type	Category and (Prospectus Objective)	Overall Rating	Reward Rating	Risk Rating	Recent Up/ Downgrade	Open to New Investors	Min Initial Investment
JNL/Franklin Templeton Intl Small Cap Growth Fund Cls I	US46648M3916		Open End	Global Equity Mid/Small Cap (Foreign Stock)	B	B	B	Up	Y	0
JNL/Franklin Templeton Mutual Shares Fund Class A	US46648M3833		Open End	Aggressive Alloc (Growth)	B-	C+	B	Down	Y	0
JNL/Franklin Templeton Mutual Shares Fund Class I	US46648M3759		Open End	Aggressive Alloc (Growth)	B-	C+	B	Up	Y	0
JNL/GQG Emerging Markets Equity Fund Class A	US46648M3593		Open End	Emerging Markets Equity (Div Emerging Mkts)	U	U	U		Y	0
JNL/GQG Emerging Markets Equity Fund Class I	US46648M3676		Open End	Emerging Markets Equity (Div Emerging Mkts)	U	U	U		Y	0
JNL/Harris Oakmark Global Equity Fund Class A	US46648M2926		Open End	Global Equity (World Stock)	C+	C+	C+	Up	Y	0
JNL/Harris Oakmark Global Equity Fund Class I	US46648M2843		Open End	Global Equity (World Stock)	C+	C+	C+		Y	0
JNL/Invesco China-India Fund Class A	US46648M2769		Open End	Other Equity (Foreign Stock)	B+	A	B-	Up	Y	0
JNL/Invesco China-India Fund Class I	US46648M2686		Open End	Other Equity (Foreign Stock)	B+	A	B-	Up	Y	0
JNL/Invesco Diversified Dividend Fund Class A	US46648M2504		Open End	US Equity Large Cap Value (Equity-Income)	U	U	U		Y	0
JNL/Invesco Diversified Dividend Fund Class I	US46648M2439		Open End	US Equity Large Cap Value (Equity-Income)	U	U	U		Y	0
JNL/Invesco Global Real Estate Fund Class A	US46648M1852		Open End	Real Estate Sector Equity (Real Estate)	B-	C	B	Up	Y	0
JNL/Invesco Global Real Estate Fund Class I	US46648M1779		Open End	Real Estate Sector Equity (Real Estate)	B-	C+	B	Up	Y	0
JNL/Invesco International Growth Fund Class A	US46648M2355		Open End	Global Equity Large Cap (Foreign Stock)	B-	C+	B	Up	Y	0
JNL/Invesco International Growth Fund Class I	US46648M2272		Open End	Global Equity Large Cap (Foreign Stock)	B-	C+	B	Up	Y	0
JNL/Invesco Mid Cap Value Fund Class A	US46648M1696		Open End	US Equity Mid Cap (Growth & Income)	C+	C+	B-	Up	Y	0
JNL/Invesco Mid Cap Value Fund Class I	US46648M1514		Open End	US Equity Mid Cap (Growth & Income)	C+	C+	B-	Up	Y	0
JNL/Invesco Small Cap Growth Fund Class A	US46648M2199		Open End	US Equity Small Cap (Small Company)	B	A-	C+	Up	Y	0
JNL/Invesco Small Cap Growth Fund Class I	US46648M1936		Open End	US Equity Small Cap (Small Company)	B	A-	C+	Up	Y	0
JNL/JPMorgan MidCap Growth Fund Class A	US46648M1282		Open End	US Equity Mid Cap (Growth)	B	B+	C+	Up	Y	0
JNL/JPMorgan MidCap Growth Fund Class I	US46648M1100		Open End	US Equity Mid Cap (Growth)	B	B+	C+	Up	Y	0
JNL/Lazard Emerging Markets Fund Class A	US46644W1953		Open End	Emerging Markets Equity (Div Emerging Mkts)	C+	B-	C	Up		0
JNL/Lazard Emerging Markets Fund Class I	US46644W1870		Open End	Emerging Markets Equity (Div Emerging Mkts)	C+	B-	C	Up		0
JNL/Mellon Capital 10 x 10 Fund Class A	US46648M5739		Open End	Aggressive Alloc (Balanced)	B-	B-	B-	Down	Y	0
JNL/Mellon Capital 10 x 10 Fund Class I	US46648M4419		Open End	Aggressive Alloc (Balanced)	B-	B-	B-		Y	0
JNL/Mellon Capital Consumer Discretionary Sector Cls A	US47760W3088		Open End	Consumer Goods Sec Equity (Growth & Income)	B	B	A-		Y	0
JNL/Mellon Capital Consumer Discretionary Sector Cls I	US47760W4078		Open End	Consumer Goods Sec Equity (Growth & Income)	B	B	A-		Y	0
JNL/Mellon Capital Consumers Staples Sector Fund Class A	US46648M5242		Open End	Consumer Goods Sec Equity ()	U	U	U		Y	0
JNL/Mellon Capital Consumers Staples Sector Fund Class I	US46648M5168		Open End	Consumer Goods Sec Equity ()	U	U	U		Y	0
JNL/Mellon Capital Dow Index Fund Class A	US47760W7048		Open End	US Equity Large Cap Value (Growth & Income)	B	B+	B-			0
JNL/Mellon Capital Dow Index Fund Class I	US47760W8038		Open End	US Equity Large Cap Value (Growth & Income)	B	B+	B-		Y	0
JNL/Mellon Capital Emerging Markets Index Fund Class A	US46648M7487		Open End	Emerging Markets Equity (Div Emerging Mkts)	C+	B-	C	Up	Y	0
JNL/Mellon Capital Emerging Markets Index Fund Class I	US46648M7305		Open End	Emerging Markets Equity (Div Emerging Mkts)	C+	B-	C	Up	Y	0
JNL/Mellon Capital Energy Sector Fund Class A	US47760W7386		Open End	Energy Sector Equity (Natl Res)	C-	D+	C		Y	0
JNL/Mellon Capital Energy Sector Fund Class I	US47760W7204		Open End	Energy Sector Equity (Natl Res)	C-	D+	C		Y	0
JNL/Mellon Capital European 30 Fund Class A	US46648M7222		Open End	Europe Equity Large Cap (Growth)	B-	C+	B-	Up	Y	0
JNL/Mellon Capital European 30 Fund Class I	US46648M7149		Open End	Europe Equity Large Cap (Growth)	B-	C+	B-	Up	Y	0
JNL/Mellon Capital Financial Sector Fund Class A	US47760W7535		Open End	Financials Sector Equity (Financial)	A-	A	B	Up	Y	0
JNL/Mellon Capital Financial Sector Fund Class I	US47760W7469		Open End	Financials Sector Equity (Financial)	A-	A	B	Up	Y	0
JNL/Mellon Capital Healthcare Sector Fund Class A	US47760W7790		Open End	Healthcare Sector Equity (Health)	B	B-	B	Up	Y	0
JNL/Mellon Capital Healthcare Sector Fund Class I	US47760W7618		Open End	Healthcare Sector Equity (Health)	B	B-	B	Up	Y	0
JNL/Mellon Capital Index 5 Fund Class A	US46648M5812		Open End	Aggressive Alloc (Growth)	B-	B-	B-	Down	Y	0
JNL/Mellon Capital Index 5 Fund Class I	US46648M4583		Open End	Aggressive Alloc (Growth)	B-	B-	B-		Y	0
JNL/Mellon Capital Industrials Sector Fund Class A	US46648M4906		Open End	Industrials Sector Equity ()	U	U	U		Y	0
JNL/Mellon Capital Industrials Sector Fund Class I	US46648M4823		Open End	Industrials Sector Equity ()	U	U	U		Y	0
JNL/Mellon Capital Information Technology Sector Cls A	US47760W7956		Open End	Technology Sector Equity (Technology)	A-	A	B	Up	Y	0
JNL/Mellon Capital Information Technology Sector Cls I	US47760W7873		Open End	Technology Sector Equity (Technology)	A-	A+	B	Up	Y	0
JNL/Mellon Capital International Index Fund Class A	US46648M5408		Open End	Global Equity Large Cap (Foreign Stock)	B-	C+	B	Up	Y	0
JNL/Mellon Capital International Index Fund Class I	US46648M5325		Open End	Global Equity Large Cap (Foreign Stock)	B-	C+	B	Up	Y	0
JNL/Mellon Capital JNL 5 Fund Class A	US47760W8459		Open End	US Equity Large Cap Value (Growth & Income)	B	B-	B+	Up	Y	0
JNL/Mellon Capital JNL 5 Fund Class I	US47760W8376		Open End	US Equity Large Cap Value (Growth & Income)	B	B-	B+	Up	Y	0
JNL/Mellon Capital Materials Sector Fund Class A	US46648M4740		Open End	Natl Resources Sec Equity ()	U	U	U		Y	0

★ Expanded analysis of this fund is included in Section II.

Min Additional Investment	TOTAL RETURNS					PERFORMANCE				ASSETS		ASSET ALLOCATION & TURNOVER					BULL & BEAR		FEES		Inception Date
	3-Month Total Return	6-Month Total Return	1-Year Total Return	3-Year Total Return	5-Year Total Return	Dividend Yield (TTM)	Expense Ratio	3-Yr Std Deviation	3-Year Beta	NAV	Total Assets (MIL)	%Cash	%Stocks	%Bonds	%Other	Turnover Ratio	Last Bull Market Total Return	Last Bear Market Total Return	Front End Fee (%)	Back End Fee (%)	
	3.37	10.51	32.49	36.53	66.04	1.11	0.99	11.48	0.9	11.63	734.0	6	90	0	3	18	13.18	-20.41			Dec-07
	2.01	2.74	8.10	18.25	66.10	3.03	1.01	9.75	0.89	11.66	1,210	6	89	2	2	20	19.65	-17.24			Jan-07
	2.07	2.91	8.41	18.99	67.83	3.19	0.71	9.74	0.89	11.78	1,210	6	89	2	2	20	19.82	-17.24			Jan-07
	5.31						1.35			10.51	404.6	10	90	0	0						Sep-17
	5.30						1.05			10.52	404.6	10	90	0	0						Sep-17
	2.10	9.83	22.85			0.21	1.19			12.1	1,098	2	96	0	3	42					Apr-15
	2.19	9.92	22.95				0.89			12.11	1,098	2	96	0	3	42					Sep-17
	7.58	18.66	52.32	40.80	54.53	0.24	1.22	15.68	0.64	10.5	714.3	2	98	0	0	118	9.26	-29.2			Dec-07
	7.72	18.84	52.83	41.86	56.18	0.35	0.92	15.72	0.64	10.6	714.3	2	98	0	0	118	9.38	-29.12			Dec-07
	3.09						0.98			10.33	551.4	8	92	0	0						Sep-17
	3.19						0.68			10.34	551.4	8	92	0	0						Sep-17
	4.07	5.22	10.19	10.55	33.61	3.11	1.05	10.6	0.95	9.97	1,967	1	97	0	2	65	24.17	-19.73			May-05
	4.21	5.44	10.46	11.26	35.06	3.24	0.75	10.65	0.96	10.13	1,967	1	97	0	2	65	24.37	-19.67			May-05
	3.44	7.83	23.19	19.07	43.81	1.38	0.98	10.78	0.87	14.1	1,475	9	91	0	0	21	17.1	-20.01			May-95
	3.47	8.04	23.55	19.85	45.21	1.47	0.68	10.77	0.87	14.87	1,475	9	91	0	0	21	17.12	-19.89			Mar-04
	5.53	7.78	9.73	14.12	67.49	1.17	0.98	13.31	1.19	17.34	547.4	3	97	0	0	45	22.05	-21.4			Mar-98
	5.59	7.81	9.88	14.71	69.04	1.33	0.68	13.27	1.19	17.54	547.4	3	97	0	0	45	22.25	-21.37			Mar-04
	6.63	13.14	24.96	35.97	110.40	0	1.1	12.6	0.82	24.91	1,913	2	98	0	0	33	28.82	-23.79			Oct-01
	6.73	13.26	25.25	36.79	112.51	0	0.8	12.58	0.82	25.82	1,913	2	98	0	0	33	28.91	-23.76			Mar-04
	5.69	11.99	29.40	33.35	115.24	0	0.93	12.77	1.1	34.51	2,102	4	96	0	0	44	30.6	-23.81			May-95
	5.80	12.17	29.73	34.24	117.45	0	0.63	12.78	1.1	35.34	2,102	4	96	0	0	44	29.67	-23.77			Mar-04
	6.40	13.72	28.59	24.72	17.90	1.22	1.22	16.18	0.98	11.46	980.5	2	97	0	0	32	18.85	-23.04			May-06
	6.47	13.84	28.93	25.55	19.17	1.38	0.92	16.19	0.98	11.51	980.5	2	97	0	0	32	19.04	-23.01			May-06
	5.01	10.46	16.21	26.38	78.56	0	0.66	8.97	0.81	13.83	493.3	1	90	9	0	12	21.81	-18.65			Apr-07
	5.08	10.54	16.30	26.48	78.69		0.36	8.98	0.81	13.84	493.3	1	90	9	0	12	21.81	-18.65			Sep-17
	8.89	10.22	22.10	36.73	118.62	1.07	0.65	11.34	1	20.81	1,109	0	100	0	0	13	28.81	-12.56			Jul-99
	8.99	10.38	22.43	37.66	120.86	1.22	0.3	11.31	1	21.21	1,109	0	100	0	0	13	28.98	-12.54			Mar-04
	6.20						0.69			10.61	10.7	1	99	0	0						Sep-17
	6.30						0.34			10.62	10.7	1	99	0	0						Sep-17
	10.81	16.80	27.64	45.12	112.93	0	0.66	11.15	0.97	27.66	797.4	3	97	0	0	6	18.19	-5.38			Jul-99
	10.93	16.93	27.78	45.27	113.16		0.31	11.16	0.97	27.69	797.4	3	97	0	0	6	18.19	-5.38			Sep-17
	6.89	14.91	36.11	26.79	18.61	0.86	0.75	15.45	0.98	11.78	1,339	5	95	0	0	11	17.81				Aug-11
	7.04	15.04	36.58	27.60	19.87	0.96	0.45	15.51	0.98	11.85	1,339	5	95	0	0	11	17.92				Aug-11
	6.26	13.28	-2.93	-5.93	8.74	2.17	0.64	19.18	1	26.11	1,464	0	100	0	0	7	21.73	-25.88			Jul-99
	6.33	13.43	-2.72	-5.34	9.87	2.34	0.29	19.2	1	26.52	1,464	0	100	0	0	7	21.89	-25.82			Mar-04
	0.59	7.34	23.73	18.44	51.60	2.83	0.65	13.14	0.97	13.55	477.8	0	100	0	0	81	8.51	-23.62			Oct-08
	0.73	7.53	24.00	19.12	53.20	2.98	0.35	13.18	0.98	13.68	477.8	0	100	0	0	81	8.63	-23.53			Oct-08
	7.47	12.69	19.32	44.60	123.62	0.86	0.65	14.72	1	13.94	1,439	0	100	0	0	37	31.65	-25.23			Jul-99
	7.62	12.87	19.60	45.55	125.88	0.96	0.3	14.74	1	13.97	1,439	0	100	0	0	37	31.73	-25.13			Mar-04
	1.38	5.00	22.63	24.56	124.38	0.82	0.64	13.08	1	25.63	3,038	0	100	0	0	7	20.39	-10.61			Jul-99
	1.49	5.17	22.95	25.37	126.79	1	0.29	13.08	1	25.76	3,038	0	100	0	0	7	20.54	-10.54			Mar-04
	4.13	8.05	15.29	26.41	67.98	0	0.63	8.26	0.94	14.62	1,025	2	79	18	0	6	18.33	-17.03			Apr-07
	4.20	8.13	15.37	26.50	68.10		0.33	8.26	0.94	14.63	1,025	2	79	18	0	6	18.33	-17.03			Sep-17
	6.06						0.69			10.67	18.8	2	98	0	0						Sep-17
	6.06						0.34			10.67	18.8	2	98	0	0						Sep-17
	8.42	17.20	36.31	59.61	150.48	0.54	0.64	14.28	1	15.31	2,369	0	100	0	0	13	28.72	-13.31			Jul-99
	8.48	17.40	36.62	60.58	153.40	0.64	0.29	14.26	1	15.6	2,369	0	100	0	0	13	28.72	-13.28			Mar-04
	4.00	9.19	25.03	24.00	43.70	2.76	0.63	11.56	0.94	15.59	2,054	1	99	0	0	7	13.11	-23.39			Jan-02
	4.11	9.40	25.45	24.72	45.20	2.86	0.33	11.53	0.93	16.21	2,054	1	99	0	0	7	13.2	-23.25			Mar-04
	5.83	12.79	16.93	26.16	89.51	2.01	0.64	9.92	0.92	15.61	3,782	0	100	0	0	74	25.66	-20.34			Oct-04
	5.95	12.94	17.24	27.02	91.49	2.16	0.34	9.88	0.91	15.66	3,782	0	100	0	0	74	25.84	-20.27			Oct-04
	6.05						0.69			10.68	44.2	2	98	0	0						Sep-17

	MARKET		FUND TYPE, CATEGORY & OBJECTIVE		RATINGS				MINIMUMS	
Fund Name	Ticker Symbol	Traded On	Fund Type	Category and (Prospectus Objective)	Overall Rating	Reward Rating	Risk Rating	Recent Up/ Downgrade	Open to New Investors	Min Initial Investment
JNL/Mellon Capital Materials Sector Fund Class I	US46648M4666		Open End	Natl Resources Sec Equity ()	U	U	U		Y	0
JNL/Mellon Capital MSCI KLD 400 Social Index Fund (A)	US46644W8313		Open End	US Equity Large Cap Blend (Growth & Income)	U	U	U		Y	0
JNL/Mellon Capital MSCI KLD 400 Social Index Fund Class I	US46644W6259		Open End	US Equity Large Cap Blend (Growth & Income)	U	U	U		Y	0
JNL/Mellon Capital MSCI World Index Fund Class A	US47760W8863		Open End	Global Equity (World Stock)	B-	B-	B	Up	Y	0
JNL/Mellon Capital MSCI World Index Fund Class I	US47760W8780		Open End	Global Equity (World Stock)	B-	B-	B		Y	0
JNL/Mellon Capital Nasdaq® 100 Index Fund Class A	US47760W8608		Open End	US Equity Large Cap Growth (Growth)	B+	A-	B	Down	Y	0
JNL/Mellon Capital Nasdaq® 100 Index Fund Class I	US47760W8525		Open End	US Equity Large Cap Growth (Growth)	B+	A-	B	Down	Y	0
JNL/Mellon Capital Pacific RIM 30 Fund Class A	US46648M6984		Open End	Asia Equity (Growth)	B	B	B-	Up	Y	0
JNL/Mellon Capital Pacific Rim 30 Fund Class I	US46648M6802		Open End	Asia Equity (Growth)	B	B	B-		Y	0
JNL/Mellon Capital Real Estate Sector Fund Class A	US46648L3776		Open End	Real Estate Sector Equity (Real Estate)	U	U	U		Y	0
JNL/Mellon Capital Real Estate Sector Fund Class I	US46648L3693		Open End	Real Estate Sector Equity (Real Estate)	U	U	U		Y	0
JNL/Mellon Capital S&P 1500 Growth Index Fund Class A	US46648M6729		Open End	US Equity Large Cap Growth (Growth)	U	U	U		Y	0
JNL/Mellon Capital S&P 1500 Growth Index Fund Class I	US46648M6646		Open End	US Equity Large Cap Growth (Growth)	U	U	U		Y	0
JNL/Mellon Capital S&P 1500 Value Index Fund Class A	US46649B7745		Open End	US Equity Large Cap Value (Growth)	U	U	U		Y	0
JNL/Mellon Capital S&P 1500 Value Index Fund Class I	US46649B7661		Open End	US Equity Large Cap Value (Growth)	U	U	U		Y	0
JNL/Mellon Capital S&P 400 MidCap Index Fund Class A	US46648M6315		Open End	US Equity Mid Cap (Growth)	B	B	B		Y	0
JNL/Mellon Capital S&P 400 MidCap Index Fund Class I	US46648M6232		Open End	US Equity Mid Cap (Growth)	B	B	B		Y	0
JNL/Mellon Capital S&P 500 Index Fund Class A	US46648M6562		Open End	US Equity Large Cap Blend (Growth)	B	B	B		Y	0
JNL/Mellon Capital S&P 500 Index Fund Class I	US46648M6497		Open End	US Equity Large Cap Blend (Growth)	B	B	B		Y	0
JNL/Mellon Capital S&P® SMid 60 Fund Class A	US47760W8293		Open End	US Equity Small Cap (Growth)	C+	C+	C+	Up	Y	0
JNL/Mellon Capital S&P® SMid 60 Fund Class I	US47760W8111		Open End	US Equity Small Cap (Growth)	C+	C+	C+	Up	Y	0
JNL/Mellon Capital Small Cap Index Fund Class A	US46648M6158		Open End	US Equity Small Cap (Small Company)	B+	A-	B	Up	Y	0
JNL/Mellon Capital Small Cap Index Fund Class I	US46648M5994		Open End	US Equity Small Cap (Small Company)	B+	A-	B	Up	Y	0
JNL/Mellon Capital Telecommunications Sector Fund Class A	US47760W5067		Open End	Communications Sector Equity (Comm)	B-	C	B	Up	Y	0
JNL/Mellon Capital Telecommunications Sector Fund Class I	US47760W6057		Open End	Communications Sector Equity (Comm)	B-	C+	B	Up	Y	0
JNL/Mellon Capital Utilities Sector Fund Class A	US46648L3511		Open End	Utilities Sector Equity (Utility)	B	B	B		Y	0
JNL/Mellon Capital Utilities Sector Fund Class I	US46648L3446		Open End	Utilities Sector Equity (Utility)	B	B	B		Y	0
JNL/MFS Mid Cap Value Fund Class A	US46644W7323		Open End	US Equity Mid Cap (Growth)	B-	C+	B-	Up	Y	0
JNL/MFS Mid Cap Value Fund Class I	US46644W7240		Open End	US Equity Mid Cap (Growth)	B-	C+	B-	Up	Y	0
JNL/MMRS Conservative Fund Class A	US46648L3107		Open End	Cautious Alloc (Growth)	B-	C+	B+	Up	Y	0
JNL/MMRS Conservative Fund Class I	US46648L2943		Open End	Cautious Alloc (Growth)	B	C+	B+		Y	0
JNL/MMRS Growth Fund Class A	US46648L2869		Open End	Aggressive Alloc (Growth)	C+	C+	B-	Up	Y	0
JNL/MMRS Growth Fund Class I	US46648L2786		Open End	Aggressive Alloc (Growth)	C+	C+	B-		Y	0
JNL/MMRS Moderate Fund Class A	US46648L2604		Open End	Moderate Alloc (Growth)	C+	C+	B-	Down	Y	0
JNL/MMRS Moderate Fund Class I	US46648L2521		Open End	Moderate Alloc (Growth)	C+	C+	B-		Y	0
JNL/Oppenheimer Emerging Markets Innovator Fund Class A	US46648L2299		Open End	Emerging Markets Equity (Div Emerging Mkts)	C+	C+	C+	Up	Y	0
JNL/Oppenheimer Emerging Markets Innovator Fund Class I	US46648L2117		Open End	Emerging Markets Equity (Div Emerging Mkts)	C+	C+	C+		Y	0
JNL/Oppenheimer Global Growth Fund Class A	US46644W2035		Open End	Global Equity (World Stock)	B+	B+	B	Up	Y	0
JNL/Oppenheimer Global Growth Fund Class I	US46644W3025		Open End	Global Equity (World Stock)	B+	B+	B	Up	Y	0
JNL/PPM America Mid Cap Value Fund Class A	US46648M3007		Open End	US Equity Mid Cap (Growth)	B	B	B-	Up	Y	0
JNL/PPM America Mid Cap Value Fund Class I	US46648M4096		Open End	US Equity Mid Cap (Growth)	B	B+	B-	Up	Y	0
JNL/PPM America Small Cap Value Fund Class A	US46648M5085		Open End	US Equity Small Cap (Small Company)	A-	A	B	Up	Y	0
JNL/PPM America Small Cap Value Fund Class I	US46648M6075		Open End	US Equity Small Cap (Small Company)	A-	A	B	Up	Y	0
JNL/PPM America Value Equity Fund Class A	US46648L1044		Open End	US Equity Large Cap Value (Growth)	B-	B-	B-	Up	Y	0
JNL/PPM America Value Equity Fund Class I	US46648L2034		Open End	US Equity Large Cap Value (Growth)	B-	B	B-	Up	Y	0
JNL/S&P 4 Fund Class A	US46648L7322		Open End	US Equity Large Cap Value (Growth)	B-	C+	B	Down	Y	0
JNL/S&P 4 Fund Class I	US46648L7249		Open End	US Equity Large Cap Value (Growth)	B-	C+	B		Y	0
JNL/S&P Competitive Advantage Fund Class A	US46648L8494		Open End	US Equity Large Cap Growth (Growth)	B	C+	A-	Up	Y	0
JNL/S&P Competitive Advantage Fund Class I	US46648L8312		Open End	US Equity Large Cap Growth (Growth)	B	B-	A-	Up	Y	0
JNL/S&P Dividend Income & Growth Fund Class A	US46648L8239		Open End	US Equity Large Cap Value (Growth)	B	B-	A		Y	0
JNL/S&P Dividend Income & Growth Fund Class I	US46648L8155		Open End	US Equity Large Cap Value (Growth)	B	B-	A		Y	0
JNL/S&P International 5 Fund Class A	US46648L7165		Open End	Global Equity Large Cap (World Stock)	B	B	C+	Up	Y	0

★ Expanded analysis of this fund is included in Section II.

	TOTAL RETURNS					PERFORMANCE				ASSETS		ASSET ALLOCATION & TURNOVER					BULL & BEAR		FEES		
Min Additional Investment	3-Month Total Return	6-Month Total Return	1-Year Total Return	3-Year Total Return	5-Year Total Return	Dividend Yield (TTM)	Expense Ratio	3-Yr Std Deviation	3-Year Beta	NAV	Total Assets (MIL)	%Cash	%Stocks	%Bonds	%Other	Turnover Ratio	Last Bull Market Total Return	Last Bear Market Total Return	Front End Fee (%)	Back End Fee (%)	Inception Date
	6.05						0.34			10.68	44.2	2	98	0	0						Sep-17
	5.89	10.55					0.76			11.06	14.2	0	100	0	0						Apr-17
	5.89	10.55					0.41			11.05	14.2	0	100	0	0						Sep-17
	5.43	11.70	21.24	18.96	51.97	0	0.66	12.53	1.01	28.54	366.5	1	99	0	0	5	19.32	-21.96			Jul-99
	5.57	11.85	21.40	19.13	52.18		0.31	12.53	1.01	28.59	366.5	1	99	0	0	5	19.32	-21.96			Sep-17
	7.06	13.46	32.09	43.20	146.48	0.28	0.68	13.28	0.96	22.87	2,155	1	99	0	0	148	22.31	-10.98			Oct-04
	7.17	13.65	32.42	44.17	149.12	0.56	0.33	13.32	0.96	15.08	2,155	1	99	0	0	148	22.35	-10.84			Dec-07
	3.91	7.43	23.23	40.96	66.16	3.05	0.66	12.32	0.87	16.73	315.5	0	100	0	0	96	10.02	-6.21			Oct-08
	3.99	7.57	23.48	41.88	67.78	3.17	0.36	12.31	0.87	16.9	315.5	0	100	0	0	96	10.15	-6.11			Oct-08
	2.19						0.69			10.23	166.4	0	100	0	0						Sep-17
	2.40						0.34			10.24	166.4	0	100	0	0						Sep-17
	6.44						0.67			10.74	18.5	0	100	0	0						Sep-17
	6.44						0.32			10.74	18.5	0	100	0	0						Sep-17
	5.94						0.67			10.7	8.6	1	99	0	0						Sep-17
	5.84						0.32			10.69	8.6	1	99	0	0						Sep-17
	6.17	9.41	15.66	33.80	99.60	0.9	0.57	11.04	1	21.66	3,143	1	99	0	0	33	27.55	-22.7			Jan-02
	6.21	9.56	15.88	34.20	100.91	1.03	0.27	11.07	1	22.06	3,143	1	99	0	0	33	27.65	-22.58			Mar-04
	6.50	11.09	21.16	34.69	106.08	1.26	0.54	10.1	1	21.94	7,748	2	98	0	0	5	24.57	-16.4			Jan-02
	6.60	11.26	21.48	35.30	107.71	1.38	0.24	10.12	1	22.45	7,748	2	98	0	0	5	24.79	-16.35			Mar-04
	3.27	7.92	-2.21	23.23	79.89	0.66	0.66	16.29	1.24	9.15	586.7	0	100	0	0	56	34.42	-30.42			Apr-07
	3.34	8.02	-1.87	23.96	81.90	0.83	0.31	16.22	1.23	8.97	586.7	0	100	0	0	56	34.46	-30.34			Apr-07
	3.84	9.90	12.83	34.62	100.43	0.78	0.57	14.16	1.02	19.71	2,375	1	99	0	0	22	27.51	-25.14			Jan-02
	3.93	10.07	13.08	35.36	102.22	0.92	0.27	14.15	1.02	20.06	2,375	1	99	0	0	22	27.7	-25.07			Mar-04
	0.06	2.38	3.53	30.29	70.03	3.45	0.68	12.66	1	14.55	120.7	0	100	0	0	24	12.03	-12.53			Jul-99
	0.14	2.47	3.76	30.91	71.80	3.89	0.33	12.71	1	13.69	120.7	0	100	0	0	24	11.75	-12.5			Mar-04
	0.38	3.29	11.61	21.08		2.27	0.69	12.31	1	13.18	86.9	0	100	0	0	25					Apr-13
	0.53	3.44	11.78	21.26			0.34	12.31	1	13.2	86.9	0	100	0	0	25					Sep-17
	4.56	7.10	13.02	15.88	78.41	1.22	0.97	11	1.02	12.13	940.6	1	99	0	0	135	23.65	-22.1			May-05
	4.72	7.24	13.32	16.66	80.31	1.45	0.67	10.96	1.02	12.2	940.6	1	99	0	0	135	23.84	-22.06			May-05
	2.69	4.97	10.78	12.36		0	1.15	4.69	1.03	11.81	380.6	6	43	51	0	27					Apr-14
	2.86	5.15	10.97	12.55			0.85	4.69	1.04	11.83	380.6	6	43	51	0	27					Sep-17
	6.05	10.74	21.36	16.96		0	1.14	6.88	0.75	12.27	48.7	3	97	0	0	224					Apr-14
	6.13	10.83	21.46	17.06			0.84	6.9	0.75	12.28	48.7	3	97	0	0	224					Sep-17
	4.29	7.69	15.54	13.23		0	1.15	6.59	0.98	11.89	190.7	4	69	26	0	159					Apr-14
	4.38	7.78	15.64	13.33			0.85	6.6	0.98	11.9	190.7	4	69	26	0	159					Sep-17
	7.96	17.03	41.27			0.07	1.49			11.93	478.0	3	96	0	0	23					Apr-15
	8.14	17.23	41.51				1.19			11.95	478.0	3	96	0	0	23					Sep-17
	7.27	13.72	36.15	40.47	84.25	0.7	0.96	12.82	1.12	18.57	2,577	3	97	0	0	19	17.44	-22.68			May-01
	7.39	13.89	36.39	41.29	86.12	0.82	0.66	12.84	1.12	18.89	2,577	3	97	0	0	19	17.59	-22.6			Mar-04
	5.20	10.47	12.36	29.95	109.63	0.62	0.98	14.63	1.28	15.76	695.7	0	100	0	0	37	32.61	-30.13			Mar-08
	5.30	10.63	12.66	30.79	111.77	0.75	0.68	14.66	1.28	15.88	695.7	0	100	0	0	37	32.73	-29.99			Mar-08
	3.54	12.03	17.16	46.06	119.58	0.34	0.99	15.82	1.03	15.18	898.9	0	100	0	0	44	32.57	-31.95			Mar-08
	3.58	12.14	17.40	49.86	126.02	0.45	0.69	15.52	1.01	15.59	898.9	0	100	0	0	44	32.7	-31.86			Mar-08
	6.71	12.61	14.97	26.22	105.35	1.3	0.85	13.38	1.23	23.85	226.7	0	100	0	0	30	30.64	-24.19			May-95
	6.75	12.74	15.19	27.06	107.54	1.44	0.55	13.4	1.24	24.01	226.7	0	100	0	0	30	30.85	-24.1			Mar-04
	8.50	11.95	15.37	19.78	102.07	0	0.71	10.92	0.91	20.41	7,028	0	100	0	0	7	22.83	-13.64			Dec-07
	8.55	12.01	15.43	19.84	102.17		0.41	10.92	0.91	20.42	7,028	0	100	0	0	7	22.83	-13.64			Sep-17
	12.25	17.38	19.66	27.30	105.26	1.26	0.66	11.92	0.88	16.86	2,858	0	100	0	0	57	28.7	-9.97			Dec-07
	12.30	17.49	19.92	28.00	107.21	1.44	0.36	11.91	0.88	16.97	2,858	0	100	0	0	57	28.83	-9.96			Dec-07
	6.10	9.85	11.96	31.35	99.99	2.69	0.64	8.39	0.68	15.99	5,437	0	100	0	0	51	22.32	-7.94			Dec-07
	6.22	9.99	12.21	32.11	102.14	2.83	0.34	8.4	0.68	16.21	5,437	0	100	0	0	51	22.5	-7.82			Dec-07
	4.91	10.64	33.09	40.27		10.08	0.8	11.8	0.9	11.53	45.4	0	100	0	0	73					Sep-14

Fund Name	MARKET Ticker Symbol	Traded On	FUND TYPE, CATEGORY & OBJECTIVE Fund Type	Category and (Prospectus Objective)	RATINGS Overall Rating	Reward Rating	Risk Rating	Recent Up/ Downgrade	MINIMUMS Open to New Investors	Min Initial Investment
JNL/S&P International 5 Fund Class I	US46648L6902		Open End	Global Equity Large Cap (World Stock)	B	B	C+		Y	0
JNL/S&P Intrinsic Value Fund Class A	US46648L7991		Open End	US Equity Large Cap Value (Growth)	C+	C	B-	Up	Y	0
JNL/S&P Intrinsic Value Fund Class I	US46648L7819		Open End	US Equity Large Cap Value (Growth)	C+	C	B-	Up	Y	0
JNL/S&P Managed Aggressive Growth Fund Class A	US46648L6662		Open End	Aggressive Alloc (Aggr Growth)	B-	B-	B-	Down	Y	0
JNL/S&P Managed Aggressive Growth Fund Class I	US46648L6589		Open End	Aggressive Alloc (Aggr Growth)	B-	B-	B-		Y	0
JNL/S&P Managed Conservative Fund Class A	US46648L6415		Open End	Cautious Alloc (Income)	B-	C	B	Up	Y	0
JNL/S&P Managed Conservative Fund Class I	US46648L6332		Open End	Cautious Alloc (Income)	B-	C	B		Y	0
JNL/S&P Managed Growth Fund Class A	US46648L3933		Open End	Aggressive Alloc (Growth)	B-	B-	B	Down	Y	0
JNL/S&P Managed Growth Fund Class I	US46648L3859		Open End	Aggressive Alloc (Growth)	B-	B-	B		Y	0
JNL/S&P Managed Moderate Fund Class A	US46648L6258		Open End	Cautious Alloc (Growth & Income)	B-	C+	B	Up	Y	0
JNL/S&P Managed Moderate Fund Class I	US46648L6175		Open End	Cautious Alloc (Growth & Income)	B-	C+	B		Y	0
JNL/S&P Managed Moderate Growth Fund Class A	US46648L6829		Open End	Moderate Alloc (Growth & Income)	B-	C+	B	Down	Y	0
JNL/S&P Managed Moderate Growth Fund Class I	US46648L6746		Open End	Moderate Alloc (Growth & Income)	B-	C+	B		Y	0
JNL/S&P Mid 3 Fund Class A	US46648L7579		Open End	US Equity Mid Cap (Growth)	C+	C+	C+	Up	Y	0
JNL/S&P MID 3 Fund Class I	US46648L7405		Open End	US Equity Mid Cap (Growth)	C+	C+	C+	Up	Y	0
JNL/S&P Total Yield Fund Class A	US46648L7736		Open End	US Equity Large Cap Value (Growth)	B-	C+	B		Y	0
JNL/S&P Total Yield Fund Class I	US46648L7652		Open End	US Equity Large Cap Value (Growth)	B-	C+	B		Y	0
JNL/T. Rowe Price Established Growth Fund Class A	US46648L5003		Open End	US Equity Large Cap Growth (Growth)	B+	B+	B	Down	Y	0
JNL/T. Rowe Price Established Growth Fund Class I	US46648L6092		Open End	US Equity Large Cap Growth (Growth)	B+	B+	B	Down	Y	0
JNL/T. Rowe Price Mid-Cap Growth Fund Class A	US46648L7082		Open End	US Equity Mid Cap (Growth)	B	B	B	Down	Y	0
JNL/T. Rowe Price Mid-Cap Growth Fund Class I	US46648L8072		Open End	US Equity Mid Cap (Growth)	B	B	B	Down	Y	0
JNL/T. Rowe Price Value Fund Class A	US46648L8643		Open End	US Equity Large Cap Value (Growth)	B-	B-	B-	Down	Y	0
JNL/T. Rowe Price Value Fund Class I	US46648L8569		Open End	US Equity Large Cap Value (Growth)	B-	B	B-	Down	Y	0
JNL/Vanguard Capital Growth Fund Class A	US46648L5342		Open End	US Equity Large Cap Growth (Growth)	B	B+	B-		Y	0
JNL/Vanguard Capital Growth Fund Class I	US46648L5268		Open End	US Equity Large Cap Growth (Growth)	B	A-	B-		Y	0
JNL/Vanguard Equity Income Fund Class A	US46648L5185		Open End	US Equity Large Cap Value (Equity-Income)	B-	B-	B		Y	0
JNL/Vanguard Equity Income Fund Class I	US46648L4923		Open End	US Equity Large Cap Value (Equity-Income)	B-	B-	B		Y	0
JNL/Vanguard Growth Allocation Fund Class A	US46649B7091		Open End	Aggressive Alloc (Multi-Asset Global)	U	U	U		Y	0
JNL/Vanguard Growth Allocation Fund Class I	US46649B8081		Open End	Aggressive Alloc (Multi-Asset Global)	U	U	U		Y	0
JNL/Vanguard International Fund Class A	US46648L4840		Open End	Global Equity Large Cap (Foreign Stock)	B+	A	B-		Y	0
JNL/Vanguard International Fund Class I	US46648L4766		Open End	Global Equity Large Cap (Foreign Stock)	B+	A	B-		Y	0
JNL/Vanguard International Stock Market Index Fund Class A	US46648L4279		Open End	Global Equity Large Cap (Foreign Stock)	U	U	U		Y	0
JNL/Vanguard International Stock Market Index Fund Class I	US46648L4196		Open End	Global Equity Large Cap (Foreign Stock)	U	U	U		Y	0
JNL/Vanguard Moderate Allocation Fund Class A	US46649B3033		Open End	Cautious Alloc (Growth)	U	U	U		Y	0
JNL/Vanguard Moderate Allocation Fund Class I	US46649B4023		Open End	Cautious Alloc (Growth)	U	U	U		Y	0
JNL/Vanguard Moderate Growth Allocation Fund Class A	US46649B5012		Open End	Moderate Alloc (Growth)	U	U	U		Y	0
JNL/Vanguard Moderate Growth Allocation Fund Class I	US46649B6002		Open End	Moderate Alloc (Growth)	U	U	U		Y	0
JNL/Vanguard Small Company Growth Fund Class A	US46648L4683		Open End	US Equity Small Cap (Small Company)	B	A-	C		Y	0
JNL/Vanguard Small Company Growth Fund Class I	US46648L4501		Open End	US Equity Small Cap (Small Company)	B	A-	C		Y	0
JNL/Vanguard U.S. Stock Market Index Fund Class A	US46648L4436		Open End	US Equity Large Cap Blend (Growth)	U	U	U		Y	0
JNL/Vanguard U.S. Stock Market Index Fund Class I	US46648L4352		Open End	US Equity Large Cap Blend (Growth)	U	U	U		Y	0
JNL/Westchester Capital Event Driven Fund Class A	US46649B8248		Open End	Multialternative (Growth)	C+	C	B	Up	Y	0
JNL/Westchester Capital Event Driven Fund Class I	US46649B8164		Open End	Multialternative (Growth)	C+	C	B		Y	0
JNL/WMC Balanced Fund Class A	US46649B8818		Open End	Moderate Alloc (Balanced)	B-	C+	B	Down	Y	0
JNL/WMC Balanced Fund Class I	US46649B8735		Open End	Moderate Alloc (Balanced)	B-	C+	B	Down	Y	0
JNL/WMC Value Fund Class A	US46649B8404		Open End	US Equity Large Cap Value (Growth)	B	B-	B	Up	Y	0
JNL/WMC Value Fund Class I	US46649B8321		Open End	US Equity Large Cap Value (Growth)	B	B-	B	Up	Y	0
JOHCM Asia Ex-Japan Equity Fund Class I	JOAIX	NAS CM	Open End	Asia ex-Japan Equity (Pacific Stock)	B	B	B-	Up	Y	0
JOHCM Asia Ex-Japan Equity Fund Class II	JOAAX	NAS CM	Open End	Asia ex-Japan Equity (Pacific Stock)	B	B	B-	Up	Y	0
JOHCM Asia Ex-Japan Equity Fund Institutional Shares	JOAMX	NAS CM	Open End	Asia ex-Japan Equity (Pacific Stock)	B	B	B-	Up	Y	1,000,000
JOHCM Emerging Markets Opportunities Fund Class I	JOEIX	NAS CM	Open End	Emerging Markets Equity (Div Emerging Mkts)	B	B	C+	Up	Y	0
JOHCM Emerging Markets Opportunities Fund Class II Shares	JOEAX	NAS CM	Open End	Emerging Markets Equity (Div Emerging Mkts)	B	B	C+	Up	Y	0

★ Expanded analysis of this fund is included in Section II.

Min Additional Investment	3-Month Total Return	6-Month Total Return	1-Year Total Return	3-Year Total Return	5-Year Total Return	Dividend Yield (TTM)	Expense Ratio	3-Yr Std Deviation	3-Year Beta	NAV	Total Assets (MIL)	%Cash	%Stocks	%Bonds	%Other	Turnover Ratio	Last Bull Market Total Return	Last Bear Market Total Return	Front End Fee (%)	Back End Fee (%)	Inception Date
	TOTAL RETURNS					PERFORMANCE				ASSETS		ASSET ALLOCATION & TURNOVER					BULL & BEAR		FEES		
	4.81	10.54	32.97	40.14			0.45	11.8	0.9	11.53	45.4	0	100	0	0	73					Sep-17
	8.92	12.93	18.91	6.82	94.64	2.53	0.66	14.25	1.12	14.65	2,600	0	100	0	0	53	15.69	-12.58			Dec-07
	9.05	13.06	19.11	7.50	96.53	2.68	0.36	14.25	1.12	14.93	2,600	0	100	0	0	53	15.75	-12.47			Dec-07
	5.26	9.89	23.25	29.50	77.39	0	1.13	9.76	0.91	22.21	2,220	4	87	8	0	16	21.57	-19.51			Apr-98
	5.35	9.99	23.36	29.62	77.55		0.83	9.76	0.91	22.23	2,220	4	87	8	0	16	21.57	-19.51			Sep-17
	1.13	2.75	6.84	10.27	19.35	0	1.06	3.27	1.02	13.42	1,498	7	20	72	1	16	8	-3.67			Oct-04
	1.20	2.83	6.92	10.35	19.44		0.76	3.28	1.02	13.43	1,498	7	20	72	1	16	8	-3.67			Sep-17
	4.83	9.08	21.05	27.17	67.94	0	1.1	8.78	1.03	18.86	5,685	4	79	16	0	15	19.78	-17.18			Apr-98
	4.89	9.13	21.11	27.24	68.03		0.8	8.78	1.03	18.87	5,685	4	79	16	0	15	19.79	-17.19			Sep-17
	2.25	4.68	11.16	15.66	33.99	0	1.07	5.08	1.05	15.43	3,335	6	40	52	1	9	11.69	-8.18			Oct-04
	2.31	4.74	11.23	15.74	34.08		0.77	5.08	1.05	15.44	3,335	6	40	52	1	9	11.69	-8.18			Sep-17
	3.48	6.82	16.00	21.04	48.61	0	1.09	6.91	1.07	17.54	6,400	5	59	34	1	13	15.7	-12.71			Apr-98
	3.59	6.94	16.13	21.18	48.78		0.79	6.91	1.07	17.56	6,400	5	59	34	1	13	15.7	-12.71			Sep-17
	10.04	8.83	12.00	16.91		1.78	0.75	12.78	1.07	12.82	306.3	0	100	0	0	159					Apr-14
	10.21	9.08	12.25	17.72		2	0.4	12.75	1.06	12.84	306.3	0	100	0	0	159					Apr-14
	6.66	7.70	11.02	14.31	106.40	2.08	0.67	11.76	0.96	14.08	2,278	0	100	0	0	65	25.11	-23.57			Dec-07
	6.83	7.83	11.37	15.08	108.58	2.26	0.37	11.71	0.96	14.23	2,278	0	100	0	0	65	25.31	-23.5			Dec-07
	6.05	11.77	33.62	49.13	130.69	0.05	0.83	12.14	1.07	43.98	8,763	2	97	1	1	42	30.88	-16.54			May-95
	6.14	11.90	33.89	50.03	133.09	0.19	0.53	12.13	1.06	45.26	8,763	2	97	1	1	42	30.98	-16.46			Mar-04
	4.34	8.79	24.46	39.52	120.27	0	1	10.72	0.95	47.27	5,304	6	93	0	0	30	25	-20.25			May-95
	4.42	8.93	24.75	40.40	122.48	0	0.7	10.7	0.95	49.29	5,304	6	93	0	0	30	25.1	-20.15			Mar-04
	5.94	9.44	18.70	27.73	103.86	1.49	0.89	10.4	0.97	17.46	4,963	0	99	0	0	105	24.79	-20.6			May-00
	6.06	9.59	18.99	28.50	105.93	1.58	0.59	10.41	0.97	18.2	4,963	0	99	0	0	105	24.92	-20.49			Mar-04
	6.82	12.42	27.77	41.96	133.78		0.94	10.78	1	10.8	53.7	8	92	0	0		19.48	-17.8			Sep-17
	7.02	12.72	28.29	43.40	137.56		0.64	10.79	1	10.82	53.7	8	92	0	0		19.69	-17.7			Sep-17
	6.16	10.88	17.26	32.47	93.38		0.88	9.4	1	10.67	17.1	4	96	0	0		22.8	-12.52			Sep-17
	6.36	11.17	17.75	33.81	96.51		0.58	9.4	1	10.69	17.1	4	96	0	0		23.01	-12.41			Sep-17
	4.27						0.69			10.49	25.1	15	68	16	0						Sep-17
	4.47						0.27			10.51	25.1	15	68	16	0						Sep-17
	3.81	14.48	41.44	39.55	60.90		0.97	14.37	1.12	10.34	57.1	5	92	0	3		19.1	-25.78			Sep-17
	3.91	14.68	41.90	40.83	63.35		0.67	14.37	1.12	10.34	57.1	5	92	0	3		19.31	-25.69			Sep-17
	4.70						0.69			10.45	98.4	2	97	0	1						Sep-17
	4.70						0.39			10.45	98.4	2	97	0	1						Sep-17
	2.09						0.69			10.23	20.8	17	33	49	0						Sep-17
	2.19						0.27			10.24	20.8	17	33	49	0						Sep-17
	3.28						0.69			10.37	31.8	17	50	33	0						Sep-17
	3.38						0.27			10.38	31.8	17	50	33	0						Sep-17
	5.08	10.61	22.46	33.92	103.89		0.95	14.16	1.06	10.74	45.6	8	92	0	0		27.66	-22.07			Sep-17
	5.18	10.79	22.84	35.15	106.98		0.65	14.16	1.06	10.75	45.6	8	92	0	0		27.88	-21.97			Sep-17
	6.25						0.59			10.71	30.7	1	99	0	0						Sep-17
	6.24						0.29			10.72	30.7	1	99	0	0						Sep-17
	0.60	0.99	5.57			2.4	2.18			10	244.9	4	55	35	-1	251					Apr-15
	0.50	0.88	5.46				1.88			10	244.9	4	55	35	-1	251					Sep-17
	3.98	6.98	12.48	22.62	63.35	1.34	0.73	6.71	0.65	24.02	7,674	7	63	30	0	58	15.5	-10.61			May-95
	4.07	7.14	12.74	23.43	65.07	1.45	0.43	6.73	0.65	24.75	7,674	7	63	30	0	58	15.69	-10.62			Mar-04
	5.65	8.75	15.20	25.40	87.41	1.62	0.78	11.26	1.08	24.48	1,580	1	99	0	0	15	26.7	-20.35			Sep-02
	5.76	8.94	15.53	26.28	89.50	1.76	0.48	11.25	1.08	25.14	1,580	1	99	0	0	15	26.8	-20.21			Mar-04
	4.87	10.75	31.23	28.12		0.43	1.39	11.58	0.61	12.66	373.1	2	98	0	0	49					Jun-14
	4.75	10.63	30.91	27.31		0.3	1.54	11.53	0.61	12.62	373.1	2	98	0	0	49					Jun-14
	4.80	10.77	31.25	28.39		0.49	1.29	11.54	0.61	12.65	373.1	2	98	0	0	49					Mar-14
	6.76	14.21	38.64	31.78	37.69	0.59	1.39	15.85	0.95	12.31	380.0	3	97	0	0	23					Nov-12
	6.77	14.22	38.53	31.43	36.82	0.46	1.54	15.89	0.95	12.31	380.0	3	97	0	0	23					Dec-13

	MARKET			FUND TYPE, CATEGORY & OBJECTIVE	RATINGS					MINIMUMS
Fund Name	Ticker Symbol	Traded On	Fund Type	Category and (Prospectus Objective)	Overall Rating	Reward Rating	Risk Rating	Recent Up/ Downgrade	Open to New Investors	Min Initial Investment
JOHCM Emerging Mkts Opp Fund Inst Shares	JOEMX	NAS CM	Open End	Emerging Markets Equity (Div Emerging Mkts)	B	B+	C+	Up	Y	1,000,000
JOHCM Emerging Markets Small Mid Cap Equity Fund Class I	JOMEX	NAS CM	Open End	Emerging Markets Equity (Div Emerging Mkts)	C+	B-	C	Up	Y	0
JOHCM Emerging Mkts Small Mid Cap Eq Fund Cls Inst Shares	JOMMX	NAS CM	Open End	Emerging Markets Equity (Div Emerging Mkts)	C+	B-	C	Up	Y	1,000,000
JOHCM Global Equity Fund Class I	JOGEX	NAS CM	Open End	Global Equity (World Stock)	C+	C+	B-	Up	Y	0
JOHCM Global Equity Fund Institutional Shares	JOGIX	NAS CM	Open End	Global Equity (World Stock)	B-	C+	B-	Up	Y	1,000,000
JOHCM Intl Opp Fund Inst Shares	JOPSX	NAS CM	Open End	Global Equity Large Cap (Foreign Stock)	D	C-	B		Y	1,000,000
JOHCM International Select Fund Class I Shares	JOHIX	NAS CM	Open End	Global Equity Large Cap (Foreign Stock)	B-	B-	B	Up		0
JOHCM International Select Fund Class II Shares	JOHAX	NAS CM	Open End	Global Equity Large Cap (Foreign Stock)	B-	B-	B	Up		0
JOHCM International Small Cap Equity Fund Class I	JOISX	NAS CM	Open End	Global Equity Mid/Small Cap (Small Company)	B	B	B	Up	Y	0
JOHCM International Small Cap Equity Fund Class II	JOSAX	NAS CM	Open End	Global Equity Mid/Small Cap (Small Company)	B	B	B	Up	Y	0
JOHCM Intl Small Cap Equity Fund Inst Shares	JOSMX	NAS CM	Open End	Global Equity Mid/Small Cap (Small Company)	B	B	B	Up	Y	1,000,000
JOHCM US Small Mid Cap Equity Fund Class I	JODIX	NAS CM	Open End	US Equity Mid Cap (Growth)	C+	C+	C+	Down	Y	0
JOHCM US Small Mid Cap Equity Fund Institutional Shares	JODMX	NAS CM	Open End	US Equity Mid Cap (Growth)	C+	C+	C+	Down	Y	1,000,000
John Hancock Balanced Fund Class A	SVBAX	NAS CM	Open End	Moderate Alloc (Balanced)	B-	C+	B	Down	Y	1,000
John Hancock Balanced Fund Class B	SVBBX	NAS CM	Open End	Moderate Alloc (Balanced)	B-	C+	B	Down		1,000
John Hancock Balanced Fund Class C	SVBCX	NAS CM	Open End	Moderate Alloc (Balanced)	B-	C+	B	Down	Y	1,000
John Hancock Balanced Fund Class I	SVBIX	NAS CM	Open End	Moderate Alloc (Balanced)	B-	C+	B	Down	Y	250,000
John Hancock Balanced Fund Class R1	JBAOX	NAS CM	Open End	Moderate Alloc (Balanced)	B-	C+	B	Down	Y	0
John Hancock Balanced Fund Class R2	JBATX	NAS CM	Open End	Moderate Alloc (Balanced)	B-	C+	B	Down	Y	0
John Hancock Balanced Fund Class R3	JBAHX	NAS CM	Open End	Moderate Alloc (Balanced)	B-	C+	B	Down	Y	0
John Hancock Balanced Fund Class R4	JBAFX	NAS CM	Open End	Moderate Alloc (Balanced)	B-	C+	B	Down	Y	0
John Hancock Balanced Fund Class R5	JBAVX	NAS CM	Open End	Moderate Alloc (Balanced)	B-	C+	B	Down	Y	0
John Hancock Balanced Fund Class R6	JBAWX	NAS CM	Open End	Moderate Alloc (Balanced)	B-	C+	B	Down	Y	1,000,000
John Hancock Capital Series Classic Value Fund Class R3	JCVHX	NAS CM	Open End	US Equity Large Cap Value (Growth)	B	B	B-	Up	Y	0
John Hancock Capital Series Classic Value Fund Class R4	JCVFX	NAS CM	Open End	US Equity Large Cap Value (Growth)	B	B+	B-	Up	Y	0
John Hancock Capital Series Classic Value Fund Class R5	JCVVX	NAS CM	Open End	US Equity Large Cap Value (Growth)	B	B+	B-	Up	Y	0
John Hancock Classic Value Fund Class A	PZFVX	NAS CM	Open End	US Equity Large Cap Value (Growth)	B	B+	B-	Up	Y	1,000
John Hancock Classic Value Fund Class B	JCVBX	NAS CM	Open End	US Equity Large Cap Value (Growth)	B	B	B-	Up		1,000
John Hancock Classic Value Fund Class C	JCVCX	NAS CM	Open End	US Equity Large Cap Value (Growth)	B	B	B-	Up	Y	1,000
John Hancock Classic Value Fund Class I	JCVIX	NAS CM	Open End	US Equity Large Cap Value (Growth)	B	B+	B-	Up	Y	250,000
John Hancock Classic Value Fund Class R1	JCVRX	NAS CM	Open End	US Equity Large Cap Value (Growth)	B	B	B-	Up	Y	0
John Hancock Classic Value Fund Class R2	JCVSX	NAS CM	Open End	US Equity Large Cap Value (Growth)	B	B	B-	Up	Y	0
John Hancock Classic Value Fund Class R6	JCVWX	NAS CM	Open End	US Equity Large Cap Value (Growth)	B	B+	B	Up	Y	1,000,000
John Hancock Disciplined Value International Fund Class A	JDIBX	NAS CM	Open End	Global Equity Large Cap (Foreign Stock)	B-	C+	B	Up	Y	1,000
John Hancock Disciplined Value International Fund Class C	JDICX	NAS CM	Open End	Global Equity Large Cap (Foreign Stock)	B-	C+	B	Up	Y	1,000
John Hancock Disciplined Value International Fund Class I	JDVIX	NAS CM	Open End	Global Equity Large Cap (Foreign Stock)	B-	B-	B	Up	Y	250,000
John Hancock Disciplined Value International Fund Cls NAV	JDIVX	NAS CM	Open End	Global Equity Large Cap (Foreign Stock)	B-	B-	B	Up	Y	0
John Hancock Disciplined Value International Fund Class R2	JDISX	NAS CM	Open End	Global Equity Large Cap (Foreign Stock)	B-	C+	B	Up	Y	0
John Hancock Disciplined Value International Fund Class R4	JDITX	NAS CM	Open End	Global Equity Large Cap (Foreign Stock)	B-	B-	B	Up	Y	0
John Hancock Disciplined Value International Fund Class R6	JDIUX	NAS CM	Open End	Global Equity Large Cap (Foreign Stock)	B-	B-	B	Up	Y	1,000,000
John Hancock Emerging Markets Equity Fund Class A	JEMQX	NAS CM	Open End	Emerging Markets Equity (Div Emerging Mkts)	C	C+	B-	Up	Y	1,000
John Hancock Emerging Markets Equity Fund Class C	JEMZX	NAS CM	Open End	Emerging Markets Equity (Div Emerging Mkts)	C	C+	B-	Up	Y	1,000
John Hancock Emerging Markets Equity Fund Class I	JEMMX	NAS CM	Open End	Emerging Markets Equity (Div Emerging Mkts)	C	C+	B-	Up	Y	250,000
John Hancock Emerging Markets Equity Fund Class NAV	US47803P1791		Open End	Emerging Markets Equity (Div Emerging Mkts)	C	C+	B-	Up	Y	0
John Hancock Emerging Markets Equity Fund Class R2	JEMKX	NAS CM	Open End	Emerging Markets Equity (Div Emerging Mkts)	C	C+	B-	Up	Y	0
John Hancock Emerging Markets Equity Fund Class R4	JEMNX	NAS CM	Open End	Emerging Markets Equity (Div Emerging Mkts)	C	C+	B-	Up	Y	0
John Hancock Emerging Markets Equity Fund Class R6	JEMGX	NAS CM	Open End	Emerging Markets Equity (Div Emerging Mkts)	C	C+	B-	Up	Y	1,000,000
John Hancock Enduring Assets Fund Class A	JEEBX	NAS CM	Open End	Other Sector Equity (Growth & Income)	C+	C	B	Down	Y	1,000
John Hancock Enduring Assets Fund Class C	JEEFX	NAS CM	Open End	Other Sector Equity (Growth & Income)	C+	C	B	Down	Y	1,000
John Hancock Enduring Assets Fund Class I	JEEIX	NAS CM	Open End	Other Sector Equity (Growth & Income)	B-	C	B		Y	250,000
John Hancock Enduring Assets Fund Class NAV	US47803P4191		Open End	Other Sector Equity (Growth & Income)	B-	C	B		Y	0
John Hancock Enduring Assets Fund Class R6	JEEDX	NAS CM	Open End	Other Sector Equity (Growth & Income)	B-	C	B		Y	1,000,000

★ Expanded analysis of this fund is included in Section II.

Min Additional Investment	TOTAL RETURNS 3-Month Total Return	6-Month Total Return	1-Year Total Return	3-Year Total Return	5-Year Total Return	PERFORMANCE Dividend Yield (TTM)	Expense Ratio	3-Yr Std Deviation	3-Year Beta	ASSETS NAV	Total Assets (MIL)	ASSET ALLOCATION & TURNOVER %Cash	%Stocks	%Bonds	%Other	Turnover Ratio	BULL & BEAR Last Bull Market Total Return	Last Bear Market Total Return	FEES Front End Fee (%)	Back End Fee (%)	Inception Date
	6.81	14.35	38.90	32.11	38.22	0.63	1.29	15.91	0.96	12.34	380.0	3	97	0	0	23					Nov-12
	9.35	19.81	43.57	60.32		1.51	1.64			13.54	7.9	2	98	0	0	174					Jan-16
	9.41	19.87	43.62	60.76		1.53	1.54			13.55	7.9	2	98	0	0	174					Dec-14
	6.40	14.30	25.20	17.43		0.18	1.18	11.72	0.83	15.95	518.2	7	93	0	0	51					Mar-13
	6.42	14.31	25.38	17.73		0.26	1.08	11.76	0.83	15.97	518.2	7	93	0	0	51					Mar-13
	0.33	5.22	18.18			0.75	0.89			10.56	2.3	19	79	0	0	69					Sep-16
	4.04	10.02	22.88	23.69	82.24	0.59	1.01	11.33	0.74	22.54	6,797	11	87	0	0	35	17.41	-23.54			Jul-09
	3.95	9.86	22.56	22.74	79.82	0.43	1.28	11.3	0.74	22.59	6,797	11	87	0	0	35	17.25	-23.62			Mar-10
	3.27	6.53	27.35	38.03		0.96	1.34	11.9	0.95	13.08	242.7	1	98	0	0	16					Dec-13
	3.97	7.23	28.15	38.52		0.85	1.49	11.88	0.94	13.16	242.7	1	98	0	0	16					Nov-13
	4.04	7.33	28.32	39.41		1.07	1.24	11.89	0.94	13.06	242.7	1	98	0	0	16					Oct-13
	6.50	10.50	19.15	37.75		0	1.09	13.26	1.04	12.54	6.9	2	98	0	0	40					Oct-14
	6.53	10.51	19.24	37.98		0.01	0.99	13.32	1.05	12.57	6.9	2	98	0	0	40					Oct-14
	4.58	7.40	13.91	20.01	57.62	1.56	1.14	6.74	-0.19	20.46	1,957	3	63	32	1	52	19.28	-14.53	5.00		Oct-92
	4.46	7.04	13.09	17.55	52.22	0.92	1.84	6.73	-0.19	20.43	1,957	3	63	32	1	52	18.84	-14.82		5.00	Oct-92
	4.41	7.04	13.09	17.54	52.18	0.92	1.84	6.72	-0.19	20.44	1,957	3	63	32	1	52	18.83	-14.81		1.00	May-99
	4.66	7.58	14.22	21.15	60.08	1.85	0.83	6.73	-0.19	20.44	1,957	3	63	32	1	52	19.56	-14.39			Mar-02
	4.47	7.19	13.46	18.76	54.96	1.23	1.49	6.73	-0.19	20.54	1,957	3	63	32	1	52	19.15	-14.69			Sep-08
	4.56	7.36	13.77	19.67	57.40	1.48	1.24	6.72	-0.19	20.43	1,957	3	63	32	1	52	19.28	-14.53			Mar-12
	4.56	7.25	13.60	19.17	55.78	1.33	1.39	6.7	-0.2	20.51	1,957	3	63	32	1	52	19.23	-14.65			Sep-08
	4.65	7.51	14.08	20.60	58.94	1.69	0.99	6.74	-0.2	20.55	1,957	3	63	32	1	52	19.46	-14.55			Sep-08
	4.71	7.62	14.32	21.36	60.54	1.88	0.79	6.72	-0.19	20.52	1,957	3	63	32	1	52	19.64	-14.38			Sep-08
	4.68	7.62	14.31	21.52	61.05	1.94	0.74	6.71	-0.19	20.46	1,957	3	63	32	1	52	19.64	-14.53			Sep-11
	7.15	11.15	16.17	29.61	105.43	1.36	1.48	15.02	1.36	33.71	2,262	4	96	0	0	45	27.22	-23.64			May-09
	7.26	11.43	16.72	31.57	110.46	1.73	1.08	15.02	1.36	33.78	2,262	4	96	0	0	45	27.5	-23.57			May-09
	7.31	11.47	16.83	32.01	111.75	1.81	0.88	15.02	1.36	33.81	2,262	4	96	0	0	45	27.57	-23.45			May-09
	7.22	11.28	16.45	30.75	108.07	1.57	1.19	15	1.36	33.75	2,262	4	96	0	0	45	27.32	-23.57	5.00		Jun-96
	7.02	10.90	15.62	27.80	100.51	1.04	1.94	15.01	1.36	33.3	2,262	4	96	0	0	45	26.81	-23.84		5.00	Nov-02
	7.02	10.90	15.63	27.80	100.44	1.03	1.94	15	1.36	33.29	2,262	4	96	0	0	45	26.73	-23.8		1.00	Nov-02
	7.26	11.42	16.75	31.75	110.96	1.77	0.93	15.02	1.36	33.79	2,262	4	96	0	0	45	27.58	-23.46			Nov-02
	7.09	11.07	15.99	29.21	104.28	1.29	1.58	15.01	1.36	33.84	2,262	4	96	0	0	45	27.07	-23.68			Aug-03
	7.19	11.23	16.29	30.25	107.51	1.48	1.33	15	1.36	33.71	2,262	4	96	0	0	45	27.32	-23.57			Mar-12
	7.32	11.52	16.88	32.19	112.06	1.85	0.83	15.04	1.36	33.81	2,262	4	96	0	0	45	27.59	-23.54			Aug-11
	4.37	10.36	24.87	25.45	54.31	0.95	1.31	11.1	0.85	14.27	1,009	7	92	0	1	63			5.00		Sep-14
	4.14	9.89	23.95	22.79	49.05	0.4	2.01	11.1	0.85	14.27	1,009	7	92	0	1	63				1.00	Sep-14
	4.37	10.51	25.23	26.61	56.68	1.21	0.98	11.1	0.85	14.27	1,009	7	92	0	1	63					Sep-14
	4.40	10.53	25.37	26.94	57.19	1.29	0.88	11.06	0.84	14.26	1,009	7	92	0	1	63					Apr-15
	4.35	10.33	24.81	25.38	54.33	0.89	1.4	11.1	0.85	14.3	1,009	7	92	0	1	63					Sep-14
	4.40	10.46	25.18	26.33	55.61	1.15	1.15	11.08	0.84	14.28	1,009	7	92	0	1	63					Sep-14
	4.47	10.61	25.45	27.02	57.30	1.29	0.88	11.08	0.84	14.27	1,009	7	92	0	1	63					Dec-11
	6.65	15.67	40.04			0.12	1.51			12.13	1,051	0	100	0	0	54			5.00		Jun-15
	7.57	16.48	40.56			0	2.21			11.97	1,051	0	100	0	0	54				1.00	Jun-15
	7.82	17.14	41.94			0.31	1.26			12.13	1,051	0	100	0	0	54					Jun-15
	7.92	17.14	42.24			0.42	1.16			12.13	1,051	0	100	0	0	54					Jun-15
	6.71	15.74	40.27			0.23	1.61			12.12	1,051	0	100	0	0	54					Jun-15
	6.70	15.82	40.34			0.3	1.36			12.13	1,051	0	100	0	0	54					Jun-15
	7.91	17.24	42.23			0.42	1.18			12.13	1,051	0	100	0	0	54					Jun-15
	-0.36	4.00	17.08	16.82		1.96	1.48	10.26	0.64	11.98	114.0	8	89	1	2	14			5.00		Dec-13
	-0.46	3.66	16.29	14.24		1.32	2.18	10.25	0.64	11.9	114.0	8	89	1	2	14				1.00	May-14
	-0.20	4.16	17.44	17.86		2.26	1.17	10.24	0.64	11.99	114.0	8	89	1	2	14					Dec-13
	-0.25	4.21	17.62	18.32		2.33	1.06	10.2	0.64	12.01	114.0	8	89	1	2	14					Dec-13
	-0.17	4.29	17.70	18.40		2.32	1.08	10.23	0.64	12.02	114.0	8	89	1	2	14					Dec-13

	MARKET			FUND TYPE, CATEGORY & OBJECTIVE	RATINGS				MINIMUMS	
Fund Name	Ticker Symbol	Traded On	Fund Type	Category and (Prospectus Objective)	Overall Rating	Reward Rating	Risk Rating	Recent Up/ Downgrade	Open to New Investors	Min Initial Investment
John Hancock ESG All Cap Core Fund Class A	JHKAX	NAS CM	Open End	US Equity Large Cap Growth (Growth)	D+	C-	B+	Up	Y	1,000
John Hancock ESG All Cap Core Fund Class C	JHKCX	NAS CM	Open End	US Equity Large Cap Growth (Growth)	D+	C-	B+	Up	Y	1,000
John Hancock ESG All Cap Core Fund Class I	JHKIX	NAS CM	Open End	US Equity Large Cap Growth (Growth)	D+	C-	B+	Up	Y	250,000
John Hancock ESG All Cap Core Fund Class R6	JHKRX	NAS CM	Open End	US Equity Large Cap Growth (Growth)	D+	C-	B+	Up	Y	1,000,000
John Hancock ESG International Equity Fund Class A	JTQAX	NAS CM	Open End	Global Equity Large Cap (Foreign Stock)	D	D+	A-		Y	1,000
John Hancock ESG International Equity Fund Class I	JTQIX	NAS CM	Open End	Global Equity Large Cap (Foreign Stock)	D	D+	A-		Y	250,000
John Hancock ESG International Equity Fund Class R6	JTQRX	NAS CM	Open End	Global Equity Large Cap (Foreign Stock)	D	D+	A-		Y	1,000,000
John Hancock ESG Large Cap Core Fund Class A	JHJAX	NAS CM	Open End	US Equity Large Cap Blend (Growth)	D+	C-	B+	Up	Y	1,000
John Hancock ESG Large Cap Core Fund Class C	JHJCX	NAS CM	Open End	US Equity Large Cap Blend (Growth)	D+	C-	B+	Up	Y	1,000
John Hancock ESG Large Cap Core Fund Class I	JHJIX	NAS CM	Open End	US Equity Large Cap Blend (Growth)	D+	C-	B+	Up	Y	250,000
John Hancock ESG Large Cap Core Fund Class R6	JHJRX	NAS CM	Open End	US Equity Large Cap Blend (Growth)	D+	C-	B+	Up	Y	1,000,000
John Hancock Financial Industries Fund Class A	FIDAX	NAS CM	Open End	Financials Sector Equity (Financial)	B	B+	B	Up	Y	1,000
John Hancock Financial Industries Fund Class B	FIDBX	NAS CM	Open End	Financials Sector Equity (Financial)	B	B+	B	Up		1,000
John Hancock Financial Industries Fund Class C	FIDCX	NAS CM	Open End	Financials Sector Equity (Financial)	B	B+	B	Up	Y	1,000
John Hancock Financial Industries Fund Class I	JFIFX	NAS CM	Open End	Financials Sector Equity (Financial)	B	B+	B	Up	Y	250,000
John Hancock Financial Industries Fund Class NAV	US4099058178		Open End	Financials Sector Equity (Financial)	B	B+	B	Up	Y	0
John Hancock Financial Industries Fund Class R6	JFDRX	NAS CM	Open End	Financials Sector Equity (Financial)	B	B+	B		Y	1,000,000
John Hancock Financial Opportunities Fund	BTO	NYSE	Closed End	Financials Sector Equity (Financial)	A-	A	B	Up	Y	
John Hancock Fundamental Large Cap Core Fund Class A	TAGRX	NAS CM	Open End	US Equity Large Cap Blend (Growth)	B	B	B		Y	1,000
John Hancock Fundamental Large Cap Core Fund Class B	TSGWX	NAS CM	Open End	US Equity Large Cap Blend (Growth)	B	B	B	Up		1,000
John Hancock Fundamental Large Cap Core Fund Class C	JHLVX	NAS CM	Open End	US Equity Large Cap Blend (Growth)	B	B	B	Up	Y	1,000
John Hancock Fundamental Large Cap Core Fund Class I	JLVIX	NAS CM	Open End	US Equity Large Cap Blend (Growth)	B	B	B		Y	250,000
John Hancock Fundamental Large Cap Core Fund Class NAV	US47803N5547		Open End	US Equity Large Cap Blend (Growth)	B	B	B		Y	0
John Hancock Fundamental Large Cap Core Fund Class R1	JLCRX	NAS CM	Open End	US Equity Large Cap Blend (Growth)	B	B	B		Y	0
John Hancock Fundamental Large Cap Core Fund Class R2	JLCYX	NAS CM	Open End	US Equity Large Cap Blend (Growth)	B	B	B		Y	0
John Hancock Fundamental Large Cap Core Fund Class R3	JLCHX	NAS CM	Open End	US Equity Large Cap Blend (Growth)	B	B	B		Y	0
John Hancock Fundamental Large Cap Core Fund Class R4	JLCFX	NAS CM	Open End	US Equity Large Cap Blend (Growth)	B	B	B		Y	0
John Hancock Fundamental Large Cap Core Fund Class R5	JLCVX	NAS CM	Open End	US Equity Large Cap Blend (Growth)	B	B	B		Y	0
John Hancock Fundamental Large Cap Core Fund Class R6	JLCWX	NAS CM	Open End	US Equity Large Cap Blend (Growth)	B	B	B		Y	1,000,000
John Hancock Funds Alternative Asset Allocation Fund Cls A	JAAAX	NAS CM	Open End	Multialternative (Asset Alloc)	C+	C	B	Up	Y	1,000
John Hancock Funds Alternative Asset Allocation Fund Cls C	JAACX	NAS CM	Open End	Multialternative (Asset Alloc)	C+	C	B	Up	Y	1,000
John Hancock Funds Alternative Asset Allocation Fund Cls I	JAAIX	NAS CM	Open End	Multialternative (Asset Alloc)	C+	C	B	Up	Y	250,000
John Hancock Funds Alternative Asset Alloc Fund Cls R2	JAAPX	NAS CM	Open End	Multialternative (Asset Alloc)	C+	C	B	Down	Y	0
John Hancock Funds Alternative Asset Alloc Fund Cls R4	JAASX	NAS CM	Open End	Multialternative (Asset Alloc)	C+	C	B	Up	Y	0
John Hancock Funds Alternative Asset Alloc Fund Cls R6	JAARX	NAS CM	Open End	Multialternative (Asset Alloc)	C+	C	B	Up	Y	1,000,000
John Hancock Funds Disciplined Value Fund Class A	JVLAX	NAS CM	Open End	US Equity Large Cap Value (Growth & Income)	B	B-	B	Up	Y	1,000
John Hancock Funds Disciplined Value Fund Class B	JVLBX	NAS CM	Open End	US Equity Large Cap Value (Growth & Income)	B-	B-	B	Down		1,000
John Hancock Funds Disciplined Value Fund Class C	JVLCX	NAS CM	Open End	US Equity Large Cap Value (Growth & Income)	B-	B-	B	Down	Y	1,000
John Hancock Funds Disciplined Value Fund Class I	JVLIX	NAS CM	Open End	US Equity Large Cap Value (Growth & Income)	B	B-	B	Up	Y	250,000
John Hancock Funds Disciplined Value Fund Class I2	JVLTX	NAS CM	Open End	US Equity Large Cap Value (Growth & Income)	B	B-	B	Up	Y	250,000
John Hancock Funds Disciplined Value Fund Class NAV	JDVNX	NAS CM	Open End	US Equity Large Cap Value (Growth & Income)	B-	B-	C+	Down	Y	0
John Hancock Funds Disciplined Value Fund Class R1	JDVOX	NAS CM	Open End	US Equity Large Cap Value (Growth & Income)	B-	B-	B	Down	Y	0
John Hancock Funds Disciplined Value Fund Class R2	JDVPX	NAS CM	Open End	US Equity Large Cap Value (Growth & Income)	B	B-	B	Up	Y	0
John Hancock Funds Disciplined Value Fund Class R3	JDVHX	NAS CM	Open End	US Equity Large Cap Value (Growth & Income)	B-	B-	B	Down	Y	0
John Hancock Funds Disciplined Value Fund Class R4	JDVFX	NAS CM	Open End	US Equity Large Cap Value (Growth & Income)	B	B-	B	Up	Y	0
John Hancock Funds Disciplined Value Fund Class R5	JDVVX	NAS CM	Open End	US Equity Large Cap Value (Growth & Income)	B	B-	B	Up	Y	0
John Hancock Funds Disciplined Value Fund Class R6	JDVWX	NAS CM	Open End	US Equity Large Cap Value (Growth & Income)	B	B-	B	Up	Y	1,000,000
John Hancock Funds Disciplined Value Mid Cap Fund Class A	JVMAX	NAS CM	Open End	US Equity Mid Cap (Growth)	B	B	B+	Up		1,000
John Hancock Funds Disciplined Value Mid Cap Fund Cls ADV	JVMVX	NAS CM	Open End	US Equity Mid Cap (Growth)	B	B	B+	Up		0
John Hancock Funds Disciplined Value Mid Cap Fund Class C	JVMCX	NAS CM	Open End	US Equity Mid Cap (Growth)	B	B	B+	Up		1,000
John Hancock Funds Disciplined Value Mid Cap Fund Class I	JVMIX	NAS CM	Open End	US Equity Mid Cap (Growth)	B	B	A-			250,000
John Hancock Funds Disciplined Value Mid Cap Fund Class R2	JVMSX	NAS CM	Open End	US Equity Mid Cap (Growth)	B	B	B+	Up		0

★ Expanded analysis of this fund is included in Section II.

Min Additional Investment	3-Month Total Return	6-Month Total Return	1-Year Total Return	3-Year Total Return	5-Year Total Return	Dividend Yield (TTM)	Expense Ratio	3-Yr Std Deviation	3-Year Beta	NAV	Total Assets (MIL)	%Cash	%Stocks	%Bonds	%Other	Turnover Ratio	Last Bull Market Total Return	Last Bear Market Total Return	Front End Fee (%)	Back End Fee (%)	Inception Date
	TOTAL RETURNS					PERFORMANCE				ASSETS		ASSET ALLOCATION & TURNOVER					BULL & BEAR		FEES		
	5.61	8.66	18.16			0.56	1.19			12.15	21.2	2	98	0	0	21			5.00		Jun-16
	5.39	8.26	17.21			0.2	1.94			12.09	21.2	2	98	0	0	21				1.00	Jun-16
	5.57	8.80	18.42			0.67	0.94			12.15	21.2	2	98	0	0	21					Jun-16
	5.69	8.83	18.55			0.73	0.81			12.15	21.2	2	98	0	0	21					Jun-16
	2.84	9.60	29.71				1.28			12.97	56.4	0	100	0	0	10			5.00		Dec-16
	3.43	10.30	30.63				1.02			12.98	56.4	0	100	0	0	10					Dec-16
	3.44	10.31	30.74				0.93			12.98	56.4	0	100	0	0	10					Dec-16
	5.03	8.10	16.24			0.64	1.19			12.07	39.3	1	99	0	0	17			5.00		Jun-16
	4.89	7.78	15.39			0.29	1.94			12.01	39.3	1	99	0	0	17				1.00	Jun-16
	4.26	7.50	15.58			0.76	0.94			12.08	39.3	1	99	0	0	17					Jun-16
	5.20	8.37	16.62			0.82	0.81			12.08	39.3	1	99	0	0	17					Jun-16
	3.62	8.40	13.29	31.56	95.86	0.66	1.58	16.41	1.02	19.97	976.3	2	93	1	4	24	36.02	-28.88	5.00		Mar-96
	3.46	8.06	12.52	28.78	88.73	0.18	2.28	16.39	1.02	18.15	976.3	2	93	1	4	24	35.53	-29.15		5.00	Jan-97
	3.45	8.04	12.49	28.80	88.99	0.18	2.28	16.38	1.02	18.18	976.3	2	93	1	4	24	35.53	-29.15		1.00	Mar-99
	3.73	8.57	13.65	32.05	96.59	0.89	1.26	16.41	1.02	19.93	976.3	2	93	1	4	24	36.02	-28.88			Sep-16
	3.74	8.63	13.71	33.17	99.65	0.96	1.15	16.43	1.02	19.92	976.3	2	93	1	4	24	36.02	-28.88			Jul-13
	3.73	8.57	13.46	31.77	96.16		1.17	16.42	1.02	19.92	976.3	2	93	1	4	24	36.02	-28.88			Aug-17
	3.34	8.85	10.20	66.07	155.06	1.28		18.29	1.12	36.94	703.9	1	88	6	0	11	37.87	-24.89			Aug-94
	4.29	9.32	20.19	38.73	102.88	0.35	1.06	12.64	1.18	48.82	5,199	1	99	0	0	54	25.48	-23.38	5.00		Oct-84
	4.10	8.91	19.28	35.62	95.37	0	1.81	12.63	1.18	43.61	5,199	1	99	0	0	54	24.96	-23.64		5.00	Aug-91
	4.08	8.89	19.28	35.63	95.41	0	1.81	12.63	1.18	43.6	5,199	1	99	0	0	54	24.91	-23.64		1.00	May-98
	4.34	9.43	20.49	39.80	105.63	0.53	0.78	12.64	1.18	50.94	5,199	1	99	0	0	54	25.72	-23.28			Mar-01
	4.38	9.50	20.54	39.13	103.47		0.68	12.64	1.18	51.01	5,199	1	99	0	0	54	25.48	-23.38			Feb-17
	4.17	9.08	19.73	37.09	99.05	0.06	1.45	12.62	1.18	50.29	5,199	1	99	0	0	54	25.28	-23.51			May-09
	4.26	9.23	20.03	38.14	101.83	0.24	1.2	12.63	1.18	50.82	5,199	1	99	0	0	54	25.47	-23.38			Mar-12
	4.21	9.16	19.86	37.55	100.08	0.13	1.35	12.63	1.18	50.41	5,199	1	99	0	0	54	25.28	-23.46			May-09
	4.30	9.36	20.31	39.16	104.05	0.42	0.95	12.64	1.18	50.71	5,199	1	99	0	0	54	25.49	-23.36			May-09
	4.36	9.47	20.54	39.98	106.03	0.56	0.75	12.63	1.18	51.02	5,199	1	99	0	0	54	25.76	-23.29			May-09
	4.38	9.52	20.64	40.28	106.69	0.6	0.7	12.64	1.18	51.03	5,199	1	99	0	0	54	25.82	-23.38			Sep-11
	1.23	2.35	6.10	7.25	12.82	0.72	1.87	3.08	0.78	14.59	732.2	19	37	38	4	10	7.21	-9.05	5.00		Jan-09
	1.08	1.99	5.27	5.01	8.90	0.07	2.57	3.09	0.79	14.66	732.2	19	37	38	4	10	6.84	-9.35		1.00	Jun-11
	1.31	2.50	6.40	8.23	14.69	1.01	1.56	3.06	0.78	14.59	732.2	19	37	38	4	10	7.42	-8.9			Dec-10
	1.20	2.25	5.92	6.89	12.02	0.65	1.96	3.07	0.78	14.58	732.2	19	37	38	4	10	7.28	-9.05			Mar-12
	1.30	2.42	6.24	7.83	13.50	0.87	1.71	3.07	0.79	14.61	732.2	19	37	38	4	10	7.21	-9.05			Jun-13
	1.41	2.60	6.51	8.66	15.13	1.12	1.46	3.08	0.78	14.59	732.2	19	37	38	4	10	7.5	-9.05			Sep-11
	6.86	11.80	18.92	26.88	95.01	0.81	1.07	11.68	1.1	22.53	15,171	2	98	0	0	65	28.48	-19.91	5.00		Dec-08
	6.65	11.36	17.98	23.95	87.37	0.26	1.82	11.67	1.1	21.19	15,171	2	98	0	0	65	27.82	-20.14		5.00	Dec-08
	6.63	11.32	17.98	24.00	87.69	0.26	1.82	11.67	1.09	21.25	15,171	2	98	0	0	65	27.91	-20.14		1.00	Dec-08
	6.94	11.91	19.19	27.86	97.70	1.04	0.81	11.68	1.1	21.84	15,171	2	98	0	0	65	28.79	-19.74			Jan-97
	6.94	11.91	19.19	27.79	97.57	1.04	0.81	11.68	1.1	21.84	15,171	2	98	0	0	65	28.73	-19.78			Dec-08
	6.93	12.01	19.34	28.23	98.76	1.13	0.7	11.68	1.1	21.87	15,171	2	98	0	0	65	28.78	-19.71			May-09
	6.74	11.52	18.43	25.25	91.00	0.53	1.47	11.67	1.1	21.83	15,171	2	98	0	0	65	28.12	-19.97			Jul-09
	6.84	11.72	18.75	26.27	93.57	0.73	1.22	11.69	1.1	21.84	15,171	2	98	0	0	65	28.54	-19.82			Mar-12
	6.75	11.63	18.55	25.69	91.95	0.61	1.37	11.7	1.1	21.82	15,171	2	98	0	0	65	28.05	-19.95			May-09
	6.88	11.80	19.01	27.22	96.03	0.92	0.97	11.7	1.1	21.85	15,171	2	98	0	0	65	28.53	-19.88			May-09
	6.92	11.94	19.27	27.97	98.34	1.07	0.77	11.66	1.09	21.87	15,171	2	98	0	0	65	28.68	-19.78			May-09
	6.97	11.99	19.33	28.28	98.74	1.13	0.72	11.69	1.1	21.87	15,171	2	98	0	0	65	28.69	-19.74			Sep-11
	5.00	8.58	15.28	33.52	115.96	0.59	1.12	11.72	1.07	22.45	14,869	2	98	0	0	50	28.35	-21.39	5.00		Jun-97
	5.01	8.60	15.31	33.46	115.35	0.59	1.12	11.71	1.07	22.4	14,869	2	98	0	0	50	28.51	-21.41			Jul-10
	4.79	8.19	14.45	30.54	107.87	0	1.87	11.71	1.07	22.56	14,869	2	98	0	0	50	27.83	-21.6		1.00	Aug-11
	5.11	8.75	15.64	34.59	118.88	0.78	0.86	11.7	1.07	23.31	14,869	2	98	0	0	50	28.58	-21.26			Jun-97
	5.00	8.51	15.14	32.99	114.55	0.46	1.27	11.73	1.07	23.25	14,869	2	98	0	0	50	28.42	-21.34			Mar-12

	MARKET			FUND TYPE, CATEGORY & OBJECTIVE	RATINGS				MINIMUMS	
Fund Name	Ticker Symbol	Traded On	Fund Type	Category and (Prospectus Objective)	Overall Rating	Reward Rating	Risk Rating	Recent Up/ Downgrade	Open to New Investors	Min Initial Investment
John Hancock Funds Disciplined Value Mid Cap Fund Class R4	JVMTX	NAS CM	Open End	US Equity Mid Cap (Growth)	B	B	B+			0
John Hancock Funds Disciplined Value Mid Cap Fund Class R6	JVMRX	NAS CM	Open End	US Equity Mid Cap (Growth)	B	B	A-			1,000,000
John Hancock Funds Diversified Strategies Fund Class A	JDSTX	NAS CM	Open End	Moderate Alloc (Growth & Income)	C+	C	B	Up	Y	1,000
John Hancock Funds Diversified Strategies Fund Class I	JDSIX	NAS CM	Open End	Moderate Alloc (Growth & Income)	B-	C	B+	Up	Y	250,000
John Hancock Funds Fundamental All Cap Core Fund Class A	JFCAX	NAS CM	Open End	US Equity Large Cap Growth (Growth)	B+	A	B	Up	Y	1,000
John Hancock Funds Fundamental All Cap Core Fund Class C	JFCCX	NAS CM	Open End	US Equity Large Cap Growth (Growth)	B+	A-	B	Up	Y	1,000
John Hancock Funds Fundamental All Cap Core Fund Class I	JFCIX	NAS CM	Open End	US Equity Large Cap Growth (Growth)	B+	A	B	Up	Y	250,000
John Hancock Funds Fundamental All Cap Core Fund Class R2	JFACX	NAS CM	Open End	US Equity Large Cap Growth (Growth)	B+	A	B	Up	Y	0
John Hancock Funds Fundamental All Cap Core Fund Class R4	JFARX	NAS CM	Open End	US Equity Large Cap Growth (Growth)	B+	A	B	Up	Y	0
John Hancock Funds Fundamental All Cap Core Fund Class R6	JFAIX	NAS CM	Open End	US Equity Large Cap Growth (Growth)	B+	A	B	Up	Y	1,000,000
John Hancock Funds Fundamental Global Franchise Fund Cls A	JFGAX	NAS CM	Open End	Global Equity (Growth)	B	B	A	Up	Y	1,000
John Hancock Funds Fundamental Global Franchise Fund Cls I	JFGIX	NAS CM	Open End	Global Equity (Growth)	B	B	A	Up	Y	250,000
John Hancock Funds Fundament Global Franchise Fund Cls NAV	US47804M2585		Open End	Global Equity (Growth)	B	B	A	Up	Y	0
John Hancock Funds Fundament Global Franchise Fund Cls R6	JFGFX	NAS CM	Open End	Global Equity (Growth)	B	B	A	Up	Y	1,000,000
John Hancock Funds Fundamental Large Cap Value Fund Cls A	JFVAX	NAS CM	Open End	US Equity Large Cap Value (Growth)	B-	C+	B	Up	Y	1,000
John Hancock Funds Fundamental Large Cap Value Fund Cls C	JFVCX	NAS CM	Open End	US Equity Large Cap Value (Growth)	B-	C+	B	Up	Y	1,000
John Hancock Funds Fundamental Large Cap Value Fund Cls I	JFVIX	NAS CM	Open End	US Equity Large Cap Value (Growth)	B	B-	B	Up	Y	250,000
John Hancock Funds Fundament Large Cap Value Fund Cls NAV	US47804M1009		Open End	US Equity Large Cap Value (Growth)	B	B-	B	Up	Y	0
John Hancock Funds Fundamental Large Cap Value Fund Cls R2	JFLCX	NAS CM	Open End	US Equity Large Cap Value (Growth)	B-	C+	B	Up	Y	0
John Hancock Funds Fundamental Large Cap Value Fund Cls R4	JFLRX	NAS CM	Open End	US Equity Large Cap Value (Growth)	B	C+	B	Up	Y	0
John Hancock Funds Fundamental Large Cap Value Fund Cls R6	JFLVX	NAS CM	Open End	US Equity Large Cap Value (Growth)	B	B-	B	Up	Y	1,000,000
John Hancock Funds Global Absolute Return Strategies Cls C	JHACX	NAS CM	Open End	Multialternative (Multi-Asset Global)	C-	D+	C	Down	Y	1,000
John Hancock Funds Global Absolute Return Strat Cls R6	JHASX	NAS CM	Open End	Multialternative (Multi-Asset Global)	C	C	B		Y	1,000,000
John Hancock Funds Global Absolute Return Strat Fund Cls A	JHAAX	NAS CM	Open End	Multialternative (Multi-Asset Global)	C	C-	C+		Y	1,000
John Hancock Funds Global Absolute Return Strat Fund Cls I	JHAIX	NAS CM	Open End	Multialternative (Multi-Asset Global)	C	C	B-		Y	250,000
John Hancock Funds Global Absolute Return Strat Cls NAV	US47804M8608		Open End	Multialternative (Multi-Asset Global)	C	C	B		Y	0
John Hancock Funds Global Absolute Return Strat Cls R2	JHARX	NAS CM	Open End	Multialternative (Multi-Asset Global)	C	C-	C+		Y	0
John Hancock Funds Global Equity Fund Class A	JHGEX	NAS CM	Open End	Global Equity (World Stock)	B-	C+	B	Down	Y	1,000
John Hancock Funds Global Equity Fund Class C	JGECX	NAS CM	Open End	Global Equity (World Stock)	C+	C+	B-	Down	Y	1,000
John Hancock Funds Global Equity Fund Class I	JGEFX	NAS CM	Open End	Global Equity (World Stock)	B-	C+	B-	Down	Y	250,000
John Hancock Funds Global Equity Fund Class NAV	US47804M1181		Open End	Global Equity (World Stock)	B-	B-	B-	Down	Y	0
John Hancock Funds Global Equity Fund Class R2	JGERX	NAS CM	Open End	Global Equity (World Stock)	B-	C+	B	Down	Y	0
John Hancock Funds Global Equity Fund Class R4	JGETX	NAS CM	Open End	Global Equity (World Stock)	B-	C+	B-	Down	Y	0
John Hancock Funds Global Equity Fund Class R6	JGEMX	NAS CM	Open End	Global Equity (World Stock)	B-	B-	B-	Down	Y	1,000,000
John Hancock Funds II Blue Chip Growth Fund Class 1	JIBCX	NAS CM	Open End	US Equity Large Cap Growth (Growth & Income)	A-	A	B	Up	Y	0
John Hancock Funds II Blue Chip Growth Fund Class A	JBGAX	NAS CM	Open End	US Equity Large Cap Growth (Growth & Income)	A-	A	B	Up	Y	1,000
John Hancock Funds II Blue Chip Growth Fund Class C	JBGCX	NAS CM	Open End	US Equity Large Cap Growth (Growth & Income)	A-	A	B	Up	Y	1,000
John Hancock Funds II Blue Chip Growth Fund Class NAV	JHBCX	NAS CM	Open End	US Equity Large Cap Growth (Growth & Income)	A-	A	B	Up	Y	0
John Hancock Funds II Capital Appreciation Fund Class 1	JICPX	NAS CM	Open End	US Equity Large Cap Growth (Growth)	A-	A	B+	Up	Y	0
John Hancock Funds II Capital Appreciation Fund Class NAV	JHCPX	NAS CM	Open End	US Equity Large Cap Growth (Growth)	A-	A	B+	Up	Y	0
John Hancock Funds II Emerging Markets Fund Class A	JEVAX	NAS CM	Open End	Emerging Markets Equity (Div Emerging Mkts)	C+	B-	C	Up	Y	1,000
John Hancock Funds II Emerging Markets Fund Class C	JEVCX	NAS CM	Open End	Emerging Markets Equity (Div Emerging Mkts)	C+	B-	C	Up	Y	1,000
John Hancock Funds II Emerging Markets Fund Class I	JEVIX	NAS CM	Open End	Emerging Markets Equity (Div Emerging Mkts)	C+	B-	C	Up	Y	250,000
John Hancock Funds II Emerging Markets Fund Class NAV	JEVNX	NAS CM	Open End	Emerging Markets Equity (Div Emerging Mkts)	C+	B-	C	Up	Y	0
John Hancock Funds II Emerging Markets Fund Class R6	JEVRX	NAS CM	Open End	Emerging Markets Equity (Div Emerging Mkts)	C+	B-	C	Up	Y	1,000,000
John Hancock Funds II Equity Income Fund Class 1	JIEMX	NAS CM	Open End	US Equity Large Cap Value (Equity-Income)	B-	B-	C+	Down	Y	0
John Hancock Funds II Equity Income Fund Class A	JHEIX	NAS CM	Open End	US Equity Large Cap Value (Equity-Income)	B-	B-	C+	Down	Y	1,000
John Hancock Funds II Equity Income Fund Class C	JHERX	NAS CM	Open End	US Equity Large Cap Value (Equity-Income)	B-	B-	C+	Down	Y	1,000
John Hancock Funds II Equity Income Fund Class NAV	US47803V7964		Open End	US Equity Large Cap Value (Equity-Income)	B-	B-	C+	Down	Y	0
John Hancock Funds II Global Real Estate Fund Class NAV	JHAMX	NAS CM	Open End	Real Estate Sector Equity (Real Estate)	B-	C+	B		Y	0
John Hancock Funds II International Small Cap Fund Class 1	JIIMX	NAS CM	Open End	Global Equity Mid/Small Cap (Small Company)	B	B	B	Up	Y	0
John Hancock Funds II International Small Cap Fund Cls NAV	JHISX	NAS CM	Open End	Global Equity Mid/Small Cap (Small Company)	B	B	B	Up	Y	0

★Expanded analysis of this fund is included in Section II.

	TOTAL RETURNS					PERFORMANCE				ASSETS		ASSET ALLOCATION & TURNOVER					BULL & BEAR		FEES		
Min Additional Investment	3-Month Total Return	6-Month Total Return	1-Year Total Return	3-Year Total Return	5-Year Total Return	Dividend Yield (TTM)	Expense Ratio	3-Yr Std Deviation	3-Year Beta	NAV	Total Assets (MIL)	%Cash	%Stocks	%Bonds	%Other	Turnover Ratio	Last Bull Market Total Return	Last Bear Market Total Return	Front End Fee (%)	Back End Fee (%)	Inception Date
	5.05	8.69	15.42	33.96	116.99	0.65	1.02	11.73	1.07	23.3	14,869	2	98	0	0	50	28.39	-21.34			Jul-13
	5.06	8.75	15.69	34.97	119.78	0.85	0.77	11.71	1.07	23.29	14,869	2	98	0	0	50	28.61	-21.26			Sep-11
	0.84	2.68	7.00	8.69	17.39	1.5	1.77	4.58	-0.1	10.32	43.0	19	34	43	2	73	8.94		5.00		Sep-11
	0.84	2.77	7.30	9.68	19.28	1.78	1.46	4.64	-0.11	10.33	43.0	19	34	43	2	73	9.25				Sep-11
	7.00	14.47	27.14	41.19	111.75	0.11	1.35	14.12	1.28	18.87	86.7	4	95	0	0	52	26.48		5.00		Jun-11
	6.79	14.06	26.24	38.27	104.66	0	2.05	14.12	1.28	18.49	86.7	4	95	0	0	52	26.18			1.00	Jun-14
	7.09	14.68	27.56	42.60	115.36	0.33	1.04	14.13	1.28	19.07	86.7	4	95	0	0	52	26.91				Jun-11
	7.07	14.62	27.37	41.79	113.06	0.25	1.45	14.14	1.28	19.02	86.7	4	95	0	0	52	26.72				Mar-15
	7.07	14.67	27.48	42.19	113.66	0.32	1.2	14.13	1.28	19.04	86.7	4	95	0	0	52	26.72				Mar-15
	7.10	14.75	27.63	42.89	115.78	0.41	0.95	14.14	1.28	19.07	86.7	4	95	0	0	52	26.91				Mar-15
	3.21	8.26	24.29	44.66	84.48	0.25	1.3	11.33	0.91	12.54	481.4	7	93	0	0	54			5.00		Jun-12
	3.28	8.46	24.67	46.03	87.83	0.5	0.99	11.3	0.9	12.58	481.4	7	93	0	0	54					Jun-12
	3.31	8.49	24.80	46.50	88.53	0.59	0.88	11.33	0.91	12.58	481.4	7	93	0	0	54					Jun-14
	3.37	8.56	24.77	46.15	87.98		0.9	11.3	0.91	12.59	481.4	7	93	0	0	54					Feb-17
	4.98	9.32	15.56	23.82	82.99	1.87	1.11	13.15	1.2	14.41	814.9	2	98	0	0	49	29.96		5.00		Jun-11
	4.80	8.92	14.72	21.07	76.52	1.33	1.81	13.14	1.2	14.43	814.9	2	98	0	0	49	29.46			1.00	Jun-14
	5.06	9.45	15.92	24.93	85.76	2.11	0.8	13.17	1.21	14.47	814.9	2	98	0	0	49	30.21				Jun-11
	5.10	9.50	16.06	25.35	87.44	2.2	0.69	13.18	1.21	14.45	814.9	2	98	0	0	49	30.39				Aug-11
	5.04	9.38	15.61	24.07	83.56	1.92	1.21	13.15	1.2	14.45	814.9	2	98	0	0	49	30.02				Mar-15
	5.07	9.48	15.95	24.78	84.61	2.08	0.96	13.14	1.2	14.46	814.9	2	98	0	0	49	30.02				Mar-15
	5.17	9.57	16.05	25.43	86.51	2.19	0.71	13.17	1.2	14.46	814.9	2	98	0	0	49	30.21				Mar-15
	1.57	1.57	2.79	-0.07	6.84	0	2.35	3.66	-5.6	10.31	4,956	6	32	54	8	59				1.00	Aug-12
	1.83	2.13	3.94	3.31	12.95	0	1.24	3.7	-5.59	10.54	4,956	6	32	54	8	59					Mar-12
	1.65	1.85	3.36	1.89	10.57	0	1.65	3.71	-5.58	10.44	4,956	6	32	54	8	59			5.00		Dec-11
	1.74	2.03	3.74	2.90	12.37	0	1.33	3.7	-5.52	10.52	4,956	6	32	54	8	59					Dec-11
	1.83	2.13	3.94	3.22	13.00	0	1.22	3.7	-5.59	10.53	4,956	6	32	54	8	59					Dec-11
	1.75	1.95	3.37	1.54	9.48	0	1.74	3.71	-5.65	10.41	4,956	6	32	54	8	59					Mar-12
	3.69	5.68	16.45	23.93		1.32	1.31	9.04	0.82	11.69	859.4	1	99	0	0	46			5.00		May-13
	3.60	5.33	15.66	21.53		0.74	2.02	9.06	0.82	11.71	859.4	1	99	0	0	46				1.00	Mar-15
	3.82	5.80	16.78	25.06		1.57	1.01	9.07	0.82	11.69	859.4	1	99	0	0	46					May-13
	3.85	5.92	16.92	25.63		1.67	0.89	9.07	0.82	11.68	859.4	1	99	0	0	46					May-13
	3.73	5.71	16.56	24.39		1.37	1.41	9.07	0.82	11.72	859.4	1	99	0	0	46					Mar-15
	3.85	5.84	16.72	25.00		1.53	1.16	9.08	0.82	11.69	859.4	1	99	0	0	46					Mar-15
	3.82	5.90	16.90	25.60		1.67	0.91	9.07	0.82	11.68	859.4	1	99	0	0	46					Mar-15
	6.94	14.33	36.24	51.55	139.77	0.03	0.84	12.3	1.06	36.21	2,733	1	99	0	0	26	30.88	-14.86			Oct-05
	6.87	14.12	35.80	50.28	136.58	0	1.14	12.3	1.06	35.87	2,733	1	99	0	0	26	30.75	-14.98	5.00		Mar-15
	6.69	13.71	34.80	46.97	128.17	0	1.89	12.28	1.06	34.96	2,733	1	99	0	0	26	30.22	-15.22		1.00	Mar-15
	6.96	14.35	36.32	51.82	140.44	0.05	0.79	12.29	1.06	36.25	2,733	1	99	0	0	26	30.98	-14.87			Oct-05
	6.95	16.14	36.63	48.77	130.70	0.05	0.79	12.82	1.12	15.98	1,796	2	99	0	0	45	26.87	-13.78			Oct-05
	6.98	16.16	36.68	49.05	131.28	0.09	0.74	12.79	1.12	16.02	1,796	2	99	0	0	45	26.91	-13.77			Oct-05
	7.19	13.57	34.88	26.91	21.32	1.18	1.47	14.87	0.93	12.1	1,144	3	97	0	0	14	16.69	-31.03	5.00		Mar-11
	6.95	13.11	33.84	23.99	17.33	0.65	2.17	14.82	0.93	12.15	1,144	3	97	0	0	14	16.52	-31.14		1.00	Jun-14
	7.32	13.71	35.37	28.06	23.25	1.41	1.16	14.81	0.93	12.07	1,144	3	97	0	0	14	17.02	-30.87			Mar-11
	7.33	13.71	35.50	28.50	24.10	1.49	1.02	14.81	0.93	12.07	1,144	3	97	0	0	14	17.2	-30.85			May-07
	7.33	13.72	35.41	28.52	23.80	1.48	1.06	14.84	0.93	12.05	1,144	3	97	0	0	14	17.08	-30.85			Sep-11
	5.55	10.08	16.19	27.52	82.27	1.99	0.82	11.04	1.05	20.44	1,733	1	95	0	2	21	23.72	-18.22			Oct-05
	5.47	9.96	15.83	26.30	79.56	1.71	1.14	11.03	1.05	20.43	1,733	1	95	0	2	21	23.51	-18.34	5.00		Mar-15
	5.22	9.49	14.95	23.56	73.25	1.05	1.89	11.05	1.05	20.48	1,733	1	95	0	2	21	23.01	-18.58		1.00	Mar-15
	5.57	10.18	16.27	27.75	82.71	2.03	0.77	11.06	1.05	20.42	1,733	1	95	0	2	21	23.72	-18.24			Oct-05
	4.31	5.85	11.60	14.85	40.77	4.59	1	10.72	0.94	9.9	239.9	2	95	0	4	124	24.14	-20.44			Apr-06
	5.39	11.47	34.95	32.19	54.61	1.23	1.08	11.92	0.97	22.55	627.6	8	90	0	2	20	15.88	-24.61			Oct-05
	5.39	11.47	35.03	32.33	55.02	1.27	1.03	11.88	0.96	22.54	627.6	8	90	0	2	20	15.87	-24.61			Oct-05

	MARKET		FUND TYPE, CATEGORY & OBJECTIVE		RATINGS				MINIMUMS	
Fund Name	Ticker Symbol	Traded On	Fund Type	Category and (Prospectus Objective)	Overall Rating	Reward Rating	Risk Rating	Recent Up/ Downgrade	Open to New Investors	Min Initial Investment
John Hancock Funds II Intl Small Company Fund Cls A	JISAX	NAS CM	Open End	Global Equity Mid/Small Cap (Small Company)	B	B	B+	Up	Y	1,000
John Hancock Funds II Intl Small Company Fund Cls C	JISDX	NAS CM	Open End	Global Equity Mid/Small Cap (Small Company)	B	B	B	Up	Y	1,000
John Hancock Funds II Intl Small Company Fund Cls I	JSCIX	NAS CM	Open End	Global Equity Mid/Small Cap (Small Company)	B	B	B+	Up	Y	250,000
John Hancock Funds II Intl Small Company Fund Cls NAV	JHATX	NAS CM	Open End	Global Equity Mid/Small Cap (Small Company)	B+	B	B+	Up	Y	0
John Hancock Funds II Intl Small Company Fund Cls R6	JHSMX	NAS CM	Open End	Global Equity Mid/Small Cap (Small Company)	B+	B	B+		Y	1,000,000
John Hancock Funds II International Value Fund Class 1	JIVIX	NAS CM	Open End	Global Equity Large Cap (Growth)	C+	C+	B-	Up	Y	0
John Hancock Funds II International Value Fund Class NAV	JHVIX	NAS CM	Open End	Global Equity Large Cap (Growth)	C+	C+	B-	Up	Y	0
John Hancock Funds II Mid Cap Stock Fund Class 1	JIMSX	NAS CM	Open End	US Equity Mid Cap (Growth)	B	B	B	Up	Y	0
John Hancock Funds II Mid Cap Stock Fund Class NAV	JHMSX	NAS CM	Open End	US Equity Mid Cap (Growth)	B	B	B	Up	Y	0
John Hancock Funds II MultiMgr 2010 Lifetime Port Cls 1	JLAOX	NAS CM	Open End	Target Date 2000-2020 (Asset Alloc)	B-	C+	B	Up	Y	0
John Hancock Funds II MultiMgr 2010 Lifetime Port Cls A	JLAAX	NAS CM	Open End	Target Date 2000-2020 (Asset Alloc)	B-	C+	B	Up	Y	1,000
John Hancock Funds II MultiMgr 2010 Lifetime Port Cls I	JHRLX	NAS CM	Open End	Target Date 2000-2020 (Asset Alloc)	B-	C+	B	Up	Y	250,000
John Hancock Funds II MultiMgr 2010 Lifetime Port Cls R1	JLADX	NAS CM	Open End	Target Date 2000-2020 (Asset Alloc)	B-	C+	B	Up	Y	0
John Hancock Funds II MultiMgr 2010 Lifetime Port Cls R2	JLAEX	NAS CM	Open End	Target Date 2000-2020 (Asset Alloc)	B-	C+	B	Up	Y	0
John Hancock Funds II MultiMgr 2010 Lifetime Port Cls R3	JLAFX	NAS CM	Open End	Target Date 2000-2020 (Asset Alloc)	B-	C+	B	Up	Y	0
John Hancock Funds II MultiMgr 2010 Lifetime Port Cls R4	JLAGX	NAS CM	Open End	Target Date 2000-2020 (Asset Alloc)	B-	C+	B	Up	Y	0
John Hancock Funds II MultiMgr 2010 Lifetime Port Cls R5	JLAHX	NAS CM	Open End	Target Date 2000-2020 (Asset Alloc)	B-	C+	B	Up	Y	0
John Hancock Funds II MultiMgr 2010 Lifetime Port Cls R6	JLAIX	NAS CM	Open End	Target Date 2000-2020 (Asset Alloc)	B-	C+	B	Up	Y	1,000,000
John Hancock Funds II MultiMgr 2015 Lifetime Port Cls 1	JLBOX	NAS CM	Open End	Target Date 2000-2020 (Asset Alloc)	B-	C+	B	Up	Y	0
John Hancock Funds II MultiMgr 2015 Lifetime Port Cls A	JLBAX	NAS CM	Open End	Target Date 2000-2020 (Asset Alloc)	B-	C+	B	Up	Y	1,000
John Hancock Funds II MultiMgr 2015 Lifetime Port Cls I	JHREX	NAS CM	Open End	Target Date 2000-2020 (Asset Alloc)	B-	C+	B	Up	Y	250,000
John Hancock Funds II MultiMgr 2015 Lifetime Port Cls R1	JLBDX	NAS CM	Open End	Target Date 2000-2020 (Asset Alloc)	B-	C+	B	Up	Y	0
John Hancock Funds II MultiMgr 2015 Lifetime Port Cls R2	JLBKX	NAS CM	Open End	Target Date 2000-2020 (Asset Alloc)	B-	C+	B	Up	Y	0
John Hancock Funds II MultiMgr 2015 Lifetime Port Cls R3	JLBFX	NAS CM	Open End	Target Date 2000-2020 (Asset Alloc)	B-	C+	B	Up	Y	0
John Hancock Funds II MultiMgr 2015 Lifetime Port Cls R4	JLBGX	NAS CM	Open End	Target Date 2000-2020 (Asset Alloc)	B-	C+	B	Up	Y	0
John Hancock Funds II MultiMgr 2015 Lifetime Port Cls R5	JLBHX	NAS CM	Open End	Target Date 2000-2020 (Asset Alloc)	B-	C+	B	Up	Y	0
John Hancock Funds II MultiMgr 2015 Lifetime Port Cls R6	JLBJX	NAS CM	Open End	Target Date 2000-2020 (Asset Alloc)	B-	C+	B	Up	Y	1,000,000
John Hancock Funds II MultiMgr 2020 Lifetime Port Cls 1	JLDOX	NAS CM	Open End	Target Date 2000-2020 (Asset Alloc)	B-	C+	B	Up	Y	0
John Hancock Funds II MultiMgr 2020 Lifetime Port Cls A	JLDAX	NAS CM	Open End	Target Date 2000-2020 (Asset Alloc)	B-	C+	B	Up	Y	1,000
John Hancock Funds II MultiMgr 2020 Lifetime Port Cls I	JHRVX	NAS CM	Open End	Target Date 2000-2020 (Asset Alloc)	B-	C+	B	Up	Y	250,000
John Hancock Funds II MultiMgr 2020 Lifetime Port Cls R1	JLDDX	NAS CM	Open End	Target Date 2000-2020 (Asset Alloc)	B-	C+	B	Down	Y	0
John Hancock Funds II MultiMgr 2020 Lifetime Port Cls R2	JLDEX	NAS CM	Open End	Target Date 2000-2020 (Asset Alloc)	B-	C+	B	Up	Y	0
John Hancock Funds II MultiMgr 2020 Lifetime Port Cls R3	JLDFX	NAS CM	Open End	Target Date 2000-2020 (Asset Alloc)	B-	C+	B	Down	Y	0
John Hancock Funds II MultiMgr 2020 Lifetime Port Cls R4	JLDGX	NAS CM	Open End	Target Date 2000-2020 (Asset Alloc)	B-	C+	B	Down	Y	0
John Hancock Funds II MultiMgr 2020 Lifetime Port Cls R5	JLDHX	NAS CM	Open End	Target Date 2000-2020 (Asset Alloc)	B-	C+	B	Up	Y	0
John Hancock Funds II MultiMgr 2020 Lifetime Port Cls R6	JLDIX	NAS CM	Open End	Target Date 2000-2020 (Asset Alloc)	B-	C+	B	Up	Y	1,000,000
John Hancock Funds II MultiMgr 2025 Lifetime Port Cls 1	JLEOX	NAS CM	Open End	Target Date 2021-2045 (Asset Alloc)	B-	C+	B	Down	Y	0
John Hancock Funds II MultiMgr 2025 Lifetime Port Cls A	JLEAX	NAS CM	Open End	Target Date 2021-2045 (Asset Alloc)	B-	C+	B	Down	Y	1,000
John Hancock Funds II MultiMgr 2025 Lifetime Port Cls I	JHRNX	NAS CM	Open End	Target Date 2021-2045 (Asset Alloc)	B-	C+	B	Down	Y	250,000
John Hancock Funds II MultiMgr 2025 Lifetime Port Cls R1	JLEDX	NAS CM	Open End	Target Date 2021-2045 (Asset Alloc)	B-	C+	B	Down	Y	0
John Hancock Funds II MultiMgr 2025 Lifetime Port Cls R2	JLEEX	NAS CM	Open End	Target Date 2021-2045 (Asset Alloc)	B-	C+	B	Down	Y	0
John Hancock Funds II MultiMgr 2025 Lifetime Port Cls R3	JLEFX	NAS CM	Open End	Target Date 2021-2045 (Asset Alloc)	B-	C+	B	Down	Y	0
John Hancock Funds II MultiMgr 2025 Lifetime Port Cls R4	JLEGX	NAS CM	Open End	Target Date 2021-2045 (Asset Alloc)	B-	C+	B	Down	Y	0
John Hancock Funds II MultiMgr 2025 Lifetime Port Cls R5	JLEHX	NAS CM	Open End	Target Date 2021-2045 (Asset Alloc)	B-	C+	B	Down	Y	0
John Hancock Funds II MultiMgr 2025 Lifetime Port Cls R6	JLEIX	NAS CM	Open End	Target Date 2021-2045 (Asset Alloc)	B-	C+	B	Down	Y	1,000,000
John Hancock Funds II MultiMgr 2030 Lifetime Port Cls 1	JLFOX	NAS CM	Open End	Target Date 2021-2045 (Asset Alloc)	B-	B-	B-	Down	Y	0
John Hancock Funds II MultiMgr 2030 Lifetime Port Cls A	JLFAX	NAS CM	Open End	Target Date 2021-2045 (Asset Alloc)	B-	B-	B-	Down	Y	1,000
John Hancock Funds II MultiMgr 2030 Lifetime Port Cls I	JHRGX	NAS CM	Open End	Target Date 2021-2045 (Asset Alloc)	B-	B-	B-	Down	Y	250,000
John Hancock Funds II MultiMgr 2030 Lifetime Port Cls R1	JLFDX	NAS CM	Open End	Target Date 2021-2045 (Asset Alloc)	B-	C+	B-	Down	Y	0
John Hancock Funds II MultiMgr 2030 Lifetime Port Cls R2	JLFEX	NAS CM	Open End	Target Date 2021-2045 (Asset Alloc)	B-	B-	B-	Down	Y	0
John Hancock Funds II MultiMgr 2030 Lifetime Port Cls R3	JLFFX	NAS CM	Open End	Target Date 2021-2045 (Asset Alloc)	B-	C+	B-	Down	Y	0
John Hancock Funds II MultiMgr 2030 Lifetime Port Cls R4	JLFGX	NAS CM	Open End	Target Date 2021-2045 (Asset Alloc)	B-	B-	B-	Down	Y	0

★ Expanded analysis of this fund is included in Section II.

	TOTAL RETURNS					PERFORMANCE				ASSETS		ASSET ALLOCATION & TURNOVER					BULL & BEAR		FEES		
Min Additional Investment	3-Month Total Return	6-Month Total Return	1-Year Total Return	3-Year Total Return	5-Year Total Return	Dividend Yield (TTM)	Expense Ratio	3-Yr Std Deviation	3-Year Beta	NAV	Total Assets (MIL)	%Cash	%Stocks	%Bonds	%Other	Turnover Ratio	Last Bull Market Total Return	Last Bear Market Total Return	Front End Fee (%)	Back End Fee (%)	Inception Date
	4.35	11.66	29.98	42.32	69.35	1.59	1.39	11.26	0.95	13.02	640.7	4	94	0	2	13	13.89	-23.71	5.00		Jun-13
	4.18	11.21	28.95	39.09	63.66	0.98	2.18	11.23	0.95	13.06	640.7	4	94	0	2	13	13.43	-23.93		1.00	Jun-14
	4.48	11.81	30.17	43.48	72.01	1.76	1.17	11.25	0.95	13	640.7	4	94	0	2	13	14.09	-23.61			Jun-13
	4.42	11.74	30.32	43.97	72.90	1.85	1.05	11.29	0.96	12.99	640.7	4	94	0	2	13	14.09	-23.61			Apr-06
	4.49	11.81	30.41	44.06	73.02		1.07	11.29	0.96	13	640.7	4	94	0	2	13	14.09	-23.61			Aug-17
	2.25	5.31	17.25	21.75	35.47	2.06	0.9	13.54	1.01	17.19	1,213	7	93	0	0	31	10.41	-24.05			Oct-05
	2.31	5.38	17.36	21.92	35.81	2.11	0.85	13.56	1.01	17.14	1,213	7	93	0	0	31	10.42	-24.05			Oct-05
	5.16	9.07	28.37	32.57	98.23	0	0.92	12.66	1.06	21.37	1,635	9	83	0	1	89	24.82	-24.41			Oct-05
	5.16	9.08	28.40	32.72	98.79	0	0.87	12.65	1.06	21.57	1,635	9	83	0	1	89	24.89	-24.44			Oct-05
	2.24	4.64	10.89	17.39	37.44	2.89	0.55	5.11		9.17	239.3	6	35	55	2	39	14.02	-11.15			Oct-06
	2.11	4.50	10.50	16.20	34.71	2.55	0.93	5.16		9.18	239.3	6	35	55	2	39	13.74	-11.35	5.00		Oct-06
	2.19	4.69	10.83	17.16	37.17	2.83	0.61	5.16		9.17	239.3	6	35	55	2	39	14.02	-11.15			Mar-15
	2.04	4.33	10.10	15.09	32.82	2.28	1.25	5.17		9.15	239.3	6	35	55	2	39	13.61	-11.38			Oct-06
	2.12	4.41	10.29	15.82	34.27	2.48	1	5.12		9.17	239.3	6	35	55	2	39	14.02	-11.22			Mar-12
	1.98	4.27	10.15	15.21	33.20	2.35	1.15	5.16		9.15	239.3	6	35	55	2	39	13.66	-11.37			Oct-06
	2.15	4.55	10.56	16.70	35.98	2.71	0.75	5.13		9.16	239.3	6	35	55	2	39	13.85	-11.25			Oct-06
	2.13	4.64	10.77	17.39	37.31	2.9	0.55	5.22		9.16	239.3	6	35	55	2	39	14.08	-11.15			Oct-06
	2.19	4.69	10.94	17.57	37.79	2.94	0.5	5.11		9.17	239.3	6	35	55	2	39	14.07	-11.15			Sep-11
	2.50	5.28	12.15	18.97	42.87	2.69	0.58	5.78		9.62	415.0	6	41	50	2	38	15.65	-13.11			Oct-06
	2.34	5.01	11.63	17.62	40.01	2.35	0.96	5.84		9.63	415.0	6	41	50	2	38	15.37	-13.21	5.00		Oct-06
	2.43	5.21	12.08	18.72	42.57	2.63	0.65	5.84		9.62	415.0	6	41	50	2	38	15.65	-13.11			Mar-15
	2.32	4.90	11.29	16.41	37.92	2.06	1.28	5.82		9.61	415.0	6	41	50	2	38	15.22	-13.32			Oct-06
	2.37	4.95	11.47	17.27	39.50	2.29	1.03	5.77		9.59	415.0	6	41	50	2	38	15.54	-13.18			Mar-12
	2.31	4.89	11.40	16.86	38.60	2.15	1.18	5.81		9.61	415.0	6	41	50	2	38	15.28	-13.32			Oct-06
	2.41	5.20	11.84	18.30	41.42	2.52	0.78	5.78		9.6	415.0	6	41	50	2	38	15.5	-13.22			Oct-06
	2.50	5.28	12.15	18.97	42.87	2.69	0.58	5.81		9.62	415.0	6	41	50	2	38	15.7	-13.1			Oct-06
	2.54	5.32	12.19	19.12	43.34	2.74	0.53	5.85		9.62	415.0	6	41	50	2	38	15.72	-13.11			Sep-11
	2.87	6.13	13.89	21.13	50.22	2.37	0.6	6.69		10.44	1,004	6	50	41	2	35	17.48	-15.42			Oct-06
	2.90	5.97	13.59	19.89	47.35	2.04	0.97	6.68		10.47	1,004	6	50	41	2	35	17.32	-15.61	5.00		Oct-06
	3.00	6.17	13.92	21.11	50.19	2.31	0.66	6.72		10.46	1,004	6	50	41	2	35	17.48	-15.42			Mar-15
	2.76	5.83	13.14	18.66	45.20	1.75	1.3	6.7		10.44	1,004	6	50	41	2	35	17.05	-15.64			Oct-06
	2.81	5.89	13.42	19.67	47.02	1.98	1.05	6.72		10.43	1,004	6	50	41	2	35	17.24	-15.49			Mar-12
	2.76	5.83	13.25	19.01	45.75	1.84	1.2	6.68		10.44	1,004	6	50	41	2	35	17.1	-15.63			Oct-06
	2.87	6.05	13.71	20.47	48.88	2.2	0.8	6.72		10.42	1,004	6	50	41	2	35	17.35	-15.63			Oct-06
	2.87	6.13	13.89	21.13	50.22	2.37	0.6	6.73		10.44	1,004	6	50	41	2	35	17.52	-15.4			Oct-06
	2.93	6.20	14.08	21.35	50.67	2.42	0.55	6.71		10.43	1,004	6	50	41	2	35	17.56	-15.42			Sep-11
	3.45	7.19	16.20	23.81	58.72	2.05	0.62	7.72		11.13	1,376	5	61	30	2	37	19.12	-17.47			Oct-06
	3.44	7.08	15.94	22.47	55.66	1.72	1	7.7		11.19	1,376	5	61	30	2	37	18.91	-17.63	5.00		Oct-06
	3.57	7.31	16.34	23.67	58.55	1.99	0.68	7.72		11.14	1,376	5	61	30	2	37	19.12	-17.47			Mar-15
	3.32	6.88	15.45	21.29	53.29	1.44	1.32	7.72		11.13	1,376	5	61	30	2	37	18.67	-17.68			Oct-06
	3.37	6.93	15.72	22.20	55.19	1.66	1.07	7.7		11.12	1,376	5	61	30	2	37	19	-17.54			Mar-12
	3.31	6.96	15.64	21.62	53.97	1.53	1.22	7.73		11.14	1,376	5	61	30	2	37	18.71	-17.58			Oct-06
	3.40	7.14	16.03	23.12	57.21	1.87	0.82	7.69		11.15	1,376	5	61	30	2	37	18.92	-17.47			Oct-06
	3.45	7.19	16.20	23.81	58.73	2.05	0.62	7.72		11.13	1,376	5	61	30	2	37	19.18	-17.47			Oct-06
	3.50	7.24	16.38	24.01	59.01	2.09	0.57	7.68		11.12	1,376	5	61	30	2	37	19.18	-17.47			Sep-11
	4.01	8.22	18.41	26.09	65.46	1.78	0.62	8.72		11.48	1,307	5	71	21	2	36	20.36	-18.95			Oct-06
	3.92	8.02	17.95	24.65	62.04	1.46	1	8.7		11.52	1,307	5	71	21	2	36	19.88	-19.01	5.00		Oct-06
	3.95	8.15	18.22	25.83	65.12	1.73	0.69	8.7		11.48	1,307	5	71	21	2	36	20.36	-18.95			Mar-15
	3.86	7.81	17.55	23.43	59.69	1.19	1.32	8.68		11.47	1,307	5	71	21	2	36	19.91	-19.16			Oct-06
	3.85	7.89	17.75	24.39	61.59	1.41	1.07	8.67		11.45	1,307	5	71	21	2	36	20.24	-19.02			Mar-12
	3.87	7.90	17.65	23.89	60.59	1.28	1.22	8.66		11.48	1,307	5	71	21	2	36	19.95	-19.07			Oct-06
	3.99	8.11	18.20	25.36	63.76	1.62	0.82	8.68		11.47	1,307	5	71	21	2	36	20.18	-18.97			Oct-06

Fund Name	MARKET Ticker Symbol	Traded On	FUND TYPE, CATEGORY & OBJECTIVE Fund Type	Category and (Prospectus Objective)	RATINGS Overall Rating	Reward Rating	Risk Rating	Recent Up/ Downgrade	Open to New Investors	MINIMUMS Min Initial Investment
John Hancock Funds II MultiMgr 2030 Lifetime Port Cls R5	JLFHX	NAS CM	Open End	Target Date 2021-2045 (Asset Alloc)	B-	B-	B-	Down	Y	0
John Hancock Funds II MultiMgr 2030 Lifetime Port Cls R6	JLFIX	NAS CM	Open End	Target Date 2021-2045 (Asset Alloc)	B-	B-	B-	Down	Y	1,000,000
John Hancock Funds II MultiMgr 2035 Lifetime Port Cls 1	JLHOX	NAS CM	Open End	Target Date 2021-2045 (Asset Alloc)	B-	B-	B-	Down	Y	0
John Hancock Funds II MultiMgr 2035 Lifetime Port Cls A	JLHAX	NAS CM	Open End	Target Date 2021-2045 (Asset Alloc)	B-	B-	B-	Down	Y	1,000
John Hancock Funds II MultiMgr 2035 Lifetime Port Cls I	JHRMX	NAS CM	Open End	Target Date 2021-2045 (Asset Alloc)	B-	B-	B-	Down	Y	250,000
John Hancock Funds II MultiMgr 2035 Lifetime Port Cls R1	JLHDX	NAS CM	Open End	Target Date 2021-2045 (Asset Alloc)	B-	B-	B-	Down	Y	0
John Hancock Funds II MultiMgr 2035 Lifetime Port Cls R2	JLHEX	NAS CM	Open End	Target Date 2021-2045 (Asset Alloc)	B-	B-	B-	Down	Y	0
John Hancock Funds II MultiMgr 2035 Lifetime Port Cls R3	JLHFX	NAS CM	Open End	Target Date 2021-2045 (Asset Alloc)	B-	B-	B-	Down	Y	0
John Hancock Funds II MultiMgr 2035 Lifetime Port Cls R4	JLHGX	NAS CM	Open End	Target Date 2021-2045 (Asset Alloc)	B-	B-	B-	Down	Y	0
John Hancock Funds II MultiMgr 2035 Lifetime Port Cls R5	JLHHX	NAS CM	Open End	Target Date 2021-2045 (Asset Alloc)	B-	B-	B-	Down	Y	0
John Hancock Funds II MultiMgr 2035 Lifetime Port Cls R6	JLHIX	NAS CM	Open End	Target Date 2021-2045 (Asset Alloc)	B-	B-	B-	Down	Y	1,000,000
John Hancock Funds II MultiMgr 2040 Lifetime Port Cls 1	JLIOX	NAS CM	Open End	Target Date 2021-2045 (Asset Alloc)	B-	B-	B-	Down	Y	0
John Hancock Funds II MultiMgr 2040 Lifetime Port Cls A	JLIAX	NAS CM	Open End	Target Date 2021-2045 (Asset Alloc)	B-	B-	B-	Down	Y	1,000
John Hancock Funds II MultiMgr 2040 Lifetime Port Cls I	JHRDX	NAS CM	Open End	Target Date 2021-2045 (Asset Alloc)	B-	B-	B-	Down	Y	250,000
John Hancock Funds II MultiMgr 2040 Lifetime Port Cls R1	JLIDX	NAS CM	Open End	Target Date 2021-2045 (Asset Alloc)	B-	B-	B-	Down	Y	0
John Hancock Funds II MultiMgr 2040 Lifetime Port Cls R2	JLIEX	NAS CM	Open End	Target Date 2021-2045 (Asset Alloc)	B-	B-	B-	Down	Y	0
John Hancock Funds II MultiMgr 2040 Lifetime Port Cls R3	JLIFX	NAS CM	Open End	Target Date 2021-2045 (Asset Alloc)	B-	B-	B-	Down	Y	0
John Hancock Funds II MultiMgr 2040 Lifetime Port Cls R4	JLIGX	NAS CM	Open End	Target Date 2021-2045 (Asset Alloc)	B-	B-	B-	Down	Y	0
John Hancock Funds II MultiMgr 2040 Lifetime Port Cls R5	JLIHX	NAS CM	Open End	Target Date 2021-2045 (Asset Alloc)	B-	B-	B-	Down	Y	0
John Hancock Funds II MultiMgr 2040 Lifetime Port Cls R6	JLIIX	NAS CM	Open End	Target Date 2021-2045 (Asset Alloc)	B-	B-	B-	Down	Y	1,000,000
John Hancock Funds II MultiMgr 2045 Lifetime Port Cls 1	JLJOX	NAS CM	Open End	Target Date 2021-2045 (Asset Alloc)	B-	B-	B-	Down	Y	0
John Hancock Funds II MultiMgr 2045 Lifetime Port Cls A	JLJAX	NAS CM	Open End	Target Date 2021-2045 (Asset Alloc)	B-	B-	B-	Down	Y	1,000
John Hancock Funds II MultiMgr 2045 Lifetime Port Cls I	JHROX	NAS CM	Open End	Target Date 2021-2045 (Asset Alloc)	B-	B-	B-	Down	Y	250,000
John Hancock Funds II MultiMgr 2045 Lifetime Port Cls R1	JLJDX	NAS CM	Open End	Target Date 2021-2045 (Asset Alloc)	B-	B-	B-	Down	Y	0
John Hancock Funds II MultiMgr 2045 Lifetime Port Cls R2	JLJEX	NAS CM	Open End	Target Date 2021-2045 (Asset Alloc)	B-	B-	B-	Down	Y	0
John Hancock Funds II MultiMgr 2045 Lifetime Port Cls R3	JLJFX	NAS CM	Open End	Target Date 2021-2045 (Asset Alloc)	B-	B-	B-	Down	Y	0
John Hancock Funds II MultiMgr 2045 Lifetime Port Cls R4	JLJGX	NAS CM	Open End	Target Date 2021-2045 (Asset Alloc)	B-	B-	B-	Down	Y	0
John Hancock Funds II MultiMgr 2045 Lifetime Port Cls R5	JLJHX	NAS CM	Open End	Target Date 2021-2045 (Asset Alloc)	B-	B-	B-	Down	Y	0
John Hancock Funds II MultiMgr 2045 Lifetime Port Cls R6	JLJIX	NAS CM	Open End	Target Date 2021-2045 (Asset Alloc)	B-	B-	B-	Down	Y	1,000,000
John Hancock Funds II Multimgr Lifest Aggress Port Cls 1	JILAX	NAS CM	Open End	Aggressive Alloc (Aggr Growth)	B-	B-	B-	Down	Y	0
John Hancock Funds II Multimgr Lifest Aggress Port Cls A	JALAX	NAS CM	Open End	Aggressive Alloc (Aggr Growth)	B-	B-	B-	Down	Y	1,000
John Hancock Funds II Multimgr Lifest Aggress Port Cls B	JBLAX	NAS CM	Open End	Aggressive Alloc (Aggr Growth)	B-	B-	C+	Up		1,000
John Hancock Funds II Multimgr Lifest Aggress Port Cls C	JCLAX	NAS CM	Open End	Aggressive Alloc (Aggr Growth)	B-	B-	C+	Up	Y	1,000
John Hancock Funds II Multimgr Lifest Aggress Port Cls I	JTAIX	NAS CM	Open End	Aggressive Alloc (Aggr Growth)	B-	B-	B-	Down	Y	250,000
John Hancock Funds II Multimgr Lifest Aggress Port Cls R1	JPLAX	NAS CM	Open End	Aggressive Alloc (Aggr Growth)	B-	B-	C+	Down	Y	0
John Hancock Funds II Multimgr Lifest Aggress Port Cls R2	JQLAX	NAS CM	Open End	Aggressive Alloc (Aggr Growth)	B-	B-	B-	Down	Y	0
John Hancock Funds II Multimgr Lifest Aggress Port Cls R3	JRLAX	NAS CM	Open End	Aggressive Alloc (Aggr Growth)	B-	B-	C+	Down	Y	0
John Hancock Funds II Multimgr Lifest Aggress Port Cls R4	JSLAX	NAS CM	Open End	Aggressive Alloc (Aggr Growth)	B-	B-	B-	Down	Y	0
John Hancock Funds II Multimgr Lifest Aggress Port Cls R5	JTLAX	NAS CM	Open End	Aggressive Alloc (Aggr Growth)	B-	B-	B-	Down	Y	0
John Hancock Funds II Multimgr Lifest Aggress Port Cls R6	JULAX	NAS CM	Open End	Aggressive Alloc (Aggr Growth)	B-	B-	B-	Down	Y	1,000,000
John Hancock Funds II Multimgr Lifest Balanced Port Cls 1	JILBX	NAS CM	Open End	Moderate Alloc (Balanced)	B-	C+	B	Down	Y	0
John Hancock Funds II Multimgr Lifest Balanced Port Cls 5	JHLAX	NAS CM	Open End	Moderate Alloc (Balanced)	B-	C+	B	Down	Y	0
John Hancock Funds II Multimgr Lifest Balanced Port Cls A	JALBX	NAS CM	Open End	Moderate Alloc (Balanced)	B-	C+	B	Down	Y	1,000
John Hancock Funds II Multimgr Lifest Balanced Port Cls B	JBLBX	NAS CM	Open End	Moderate Alloc (Balanced)	B-	C+	B	Down		1,000
John Hancock Funds II Multimgr Lifest Balanced Port Cls C	JCLBX	NAS CM	Open End	Moderate Alloc (Balanced)	B-	C+	B	Down	Y	1,000
John Hancock Funds II Multimgr Lifest Balanced Port Cls I	JTBIX	NAS CM	Open End	Moderate Alloc (Balanced)	B-	C+	B	Down	Y	250,000
John Hancock Funds II Multimgr Lifest Balanced Port Cls R1	JPLBX	NAS CM	Open End	Moderate Alloc (Balanced)	B-	C+	B	Down	Y	0
John Hancock Funds II Multimgr Lifest Balanced Port Cls R2	JQLBX	NAS CM	Open End	Moderate Alloc (Balanced)	B-	C+	B	Down	Y	0
John Hancock Funds II Multimgr Lifest Balanced Port Cls R3	JRLBX	NAS CM	Open End	Moderate Alloc (Balanced)	B-	C+	B	Down	Y	0
John Hancock Funds II Multimgr Lifest Balanced Port Cls R4	JSLBX	NAS CM	Open End	Moderate Alloc (Balanced)	B-	C+	B	Down	Y	0
John Hancock Funds II Multimgr Lifest Balanced Port Cls R5	JTSBX	NAS CM	Open End	Moderate Alloc (Balanced)	B-	C+	B	Down	Y	0
John Hancock Funds II Multimgr Lifest Balanced Port Cls R6	JULBX	NAS CM	Open End	Moderate Alloc (Balanced)	B-	C+	B	Down	Y	1,000,000

★ Expanded analysis of this fund is included in Section II.

Min Additional Investment	TOTAL RETURNS 3-Month Total Return	6-Month Total Return	1-Year Total Return	3-Year Total Return	5-Year Total Return	PERFORMANCE Dividend Yield (TTM)	Expense Ratio	3-Yr Std Deviation	3-Year Beta	ASSETS NAV	Total Assets (MIL)	ASSET ALLOCATION & TURNOVER %Cash	%Stocks	%Bonds	%Other	Turnover Ratio	BULL & BEAR Last Bull Market Total Return	Last Bear Market Total Return	FEES Front End Fee (%)	Back End Fee (%)	Inception Date
	3.93	8.14	18.32	26.00	65.35	1.79	0.62	8.69		11.47	1,307	5	71	21	2	36	20.39	-18.93			Oct-06
	4.07	8.19	18.37	26.30	65.94	1.83	0.57	8.69		11.47	1,307	5	71	21	2	36	20.42	-18.95			Sep-11
	4.51	9.10	20.17	28.01	70.30	1.59	0.64	9.3		12.01	1,100	5	79	14	2	35	21.12	-19.67			Oct-06
	4.35	8.88	19.67	26.54	66.94	1.28	1.01	9.29		11.95	1,100	5	79	14	2	35	20.78	-19.84	5.00		Oct-06
	4.45	9.04	20.00	27.76	69.98	1.53	0.7	9.32		12.01	1,100	5	79	14	2	35	21.12	-19.67			Mar-15
	4.28	8.64	19.33	25.37	64.51	1.01	1.34	9.31		11.93	1,100	5	79	14	2	35	20.62	-19.86			Oct-06
	4.33	8.84	19.59	26.35	66.55	1.22	1.09	9.31		12	1,100	5	79	14	2	35	20.99	-19.74			Mar-12
	4.28	8.73	19.30	25.71	65.22	1.09	1.24	9.26		11.94	1,100	5	79	14	2	35	20.66	-19.77			Oct-06
	4.40	8.91	19.86	27.28	68.56	1.42	0.84	9.27		12	1,100	5	79	14	2	35	20.82	-19.77			Oct-06
	4.51	9.10	20.18	28.01	70.31	1.59	0.64	9.3		12.01	1,100	5	79	14	2	35	21.04	-19.58			Oct-06
	4.48	9.16	20.25	28.22	70.78	1.63	0.59	9.29		12	1,100	5	79	14	2	35	21.18	-19.67			Sep-11
	4.71	9.67	21.37	29.51	72.79	1.53	0.64	9.47		12.13	879.0	5	85	8	2	32	21.05	-19.65			Oct-06
	4.71	9.43	20.94	28.11	69.26	1.22	1.02	9.5		12.09	879.0	5	85	8	2	32	20.7	-19.73	5.00		Oct-06
	4.73	9.60	21.29	29.35	72.57	1.47	0.71	9.48		12.14	879.0	5	85	8	2	32	21.05	-19.65			Mar-15
	4.56	9.20	20.50	26.71	66.68	0.95	1.34	9.47		12.06	879.0	5	85	8	2	32	20.55	-19.84			Oct-06
	4.62	9.41	20.79	27.73	69.00	1.16	1.09	9.52		12.12	879.0	5	85	8	2	32	20.93	-19.72			Mar-12
	4.66	9.31	20.64	27.23	67.76	1.04	1.24	9.44		12.05	879.0	5	85	8	2	32	20.56	-19.76			Oct-06
	4.68	9.40	21.01	28.63	70.93	1.37	0.84	9.45		12.08	879.0	5	85	8	2	32	20.81	-19.71			Oct-06
	4.70	9.56	21.35	29.36	72.69	1.53	0.64	9.49		12.14	879.0	5	85	8	2	32	21.09	-19.63			Oct-06
	4.76	9.64	21.45	29.61	73.09	1.57	0.59	9.46		12.12	879.0	5	85	8	2	32	20.99	-19.65			Sep-11
	4.81	9.73	21.44	29.61	72.90	1.52	0.64	9.46		11.97	811.4	5	86	7	2	30	21.05	-19.65			Oct-06
	4.75	9.61	21.04	28.24	69.46	1.22	1.02	9.44		11.92	811.4	5	86	7	2	30	20.72	-19.82	5.00		Oct-06
	4.76	9.68	21.38	29.48	72.72	1.47	0.71	9.46		11.97	811.4	5	86	7	2	30	21.06	-19.65			Mar-15
	4.68	9.46	20.70	27.06	67.02	0.95	1.34	9.46		11.9	811.4	5	86	7	2	30	20.56	-19.76			Oct-06
	4.73	9.58	20.97	27.96	69.14	1.15	1.09	9.45		11.96	811.4	5	86	7	2	30	20.93	-19.72			Mar-12
	4.70	9.38	20.70	27.32	67.81	1.03	1.24	9.43		11.9	811.4	5	86	7	2	30	20.69	-19.84			Oct-06
	4.78	9.63	21.25	28.92	71.29	1.36	0.84	9.49		11.94	811.4	5	86	7	2	30	20.93	-19.78			Oct-06
	4.81	9.82	21.52	29.69	72.97	1.52	0.64	9.45		11.99	811.4	5	86	7	2	30	21.1	-19.63			Oct-06
	4.78	9.79	21.52	29.83	73.22	1.57	0.59	9.47		11.96	811.4	5	86	7	2	30	21	-19.65			Sep-11
	5.57	10.35	23.30	29.97	75.29	1.02	1.06	10.12	0.95	16.45	4,334	5	91	1	2	31	21.46	-20.88			Oct-05
	4.90	10.07	22.79	28.55	72.00	0.72	1.41	10.08	0.95	16.52	4,334	5	91	1	2	31	21.11	-21.04	5.00		Oct-05
	4.71	9.69	21.97	25.78	65.70	0.13	2.13	10.15	0.95	16.55	4,334	5	91	1	2	31	20.67	-21.34		5.00	Oct-05
	4.77	9.69	22.02	25.83	66.04	0.13	2.13	10.15	0.95	16.57	4,334	5	91	1	2	31	20.65	-21.26		1.00	Oct-05
	5.57	10.27	23.20	29.69	74.92	0.97	1.12	10.16	0.95	16.47	4,334	5	91	1	2	31	21.45	-20.88			May-15
	4.87	9.91	22.44	27.12	68.56	0.45	1.77	10.08	0.95	16.55	4,334	5	91	1	2	31	20.84	-21.2			Sep-06
	4.90	10.04	22.67	28.12	71.06	0.65	1.52	10.09	0.95	16.42	4,334	5	91	1	2	31	21.33	-20.94			Mar-12
	4.86	9.92	22.58	27.51	69.33	0.51	1.67	10.1	0.95	16.48	4,334	5	91	1	2	31	20.97	-21.15			Oct-05
	4.94	10.13	22.98	28.99	72.56	0.85	1.27	10.12	0.95	16.45	4,334	5	91	1	2	31	21.13	-21.07			Oct-05
	5.00	10.25	23.24	29.86	74.56	1.01	1.07	10.14	0.95	16.48	4,334	5	91	1	2	31	21.47	-20.98			Oct-05
	5.05	10.31	23.31	30.19	75.78	1.06	1.02	10.12	0.95	16.47	4,334	5	91	1	2	31	21.46	-20.88			Sep-11
	3.15	6.64	15.14	21.52	49.18	1.82	0.97	6.86	0.64	15.19	12,976	6	55	36	2	23	15.81	-13.92			Oct-05
	3.22	6.66	15.27	21.69	49.53	1.87	0.92	6.9	0.64	15.2	12,976	6	55	36	2	23	15.83	-13.83			Jul-06
	3.10	6.40	14.79	20.16	46.41	1.49	1.33	6.85	0.64	15.29	12,976	6	55	36	2	23	15.46	-14.07	5.00		Oct-05
	2.92	6.03	13.93	17.64	41.13	0.87	2.05	6.85	0.64	15.28	12,976	6	55	36	2	23	14.98	-14.31		5.00	Oct-05
	2.92	6.09	13.99	17.71	41.27	0.87	2.05	6.87	0.64	15.3	12,976	6	55	36	2	23	14.97	-14.29		1.00	Oct-05
	3.13	6.60	15.14	21.37	49.01	1.77	1.04	6.9	0.64	15.2	12,976	6	55	36	2	23	15.81	-13.92			May-15
	3.02	6.24	14.38	18.90	43.64	1.19	1.69	6.84	0.63	15.22	12,976	6	55	36	2	23	15.24	-14.17			Sep-06
	3.03	6.32	14.60	19.74	45.50	1.41	1.44	6.86	0.64	15.2	12,976	6	55	36	2	23	15.61	-14			Mar-12
	3.04	6.29	14.46	19.29	44.54	1.27	1.59	6.85	0.64	15.25	12,976	6	55	36	2	23	15.29	-14.11			Oct-05
	3.14	6.49	14.98	20.71	47.53	1.62	1.19	6.86	0.64	15.26	12,976	6	55	36	2	23	15.48	-14.04			Oct-05
	3.19	6.59	15.19	21.46	48.90	1.8	0.99	6.84	0.63	15.28	12,976	6	55	36	2	23	15.71	-13.96			Oct-05
	3.23	6.66	15.27	21.69	49.45	1.86	0.94	6.87	0.64	15.2	12,976	6	55	36	2	23	15.71	-13.92			Sep-11

	MARKET			FUND TYPE, CATEGORY & OBJECTIVE	RATINGS					MINIMUMS
Fund Name	Ticker Symbol	Traded On	Fund Type	Category and (Prospectus Objective)	Overall Rating	Reward Rating	Risk Rating	Recent Up/ Downgrade	Open to New Investors	Min Initial Investment
John Hancock Funds II Multimgr Lifest Cons Cls 1	JILCX	NAS CM	Open End	Cautious Alloc (Income)	B	C	A-	Up	Y	0
John Hancock Funds II Multimgr Lifest Cons Cls A	JALRX	NAS CM	Open End	Cautious Alloc (Income)	B-	C	B+	Up	Y	1,000
John Hancock Funds II Multimgr Lifest Cons Cls B	JBLCX	NAS CM	Open End	Cautious Alloc (Income)	B-	C	B+	Up		1,000
John Hancock Funds II Multimgr Lifest Cons Cls C	JCLCX	NAS CM	Open End	Cautious Alloc (Income)	B-	C	B+	Up	Y	1,000
John Hancock Funds II Multimgr Lifest Cons Cls I	JTOIX	NAS CM	Open End	Cautious Alloc (Income)	B-	C	A-	Up	Y	250,000
John Hancock Funds II Multimgr Lifest Cons Cls R1	JPLCX	NAS CM	Open End	Cautious Alloc (Income)	B-	C	B+	Up	Y	0
John Hancock Funds II Multimgr Lifest Cons Cls R2	JQLCX	NAS CM	Open End	Cautious Alloc (Income)	B-	C	B+	Up	Y	0
John Hancock Funds II Multimgr Lifest Cons Cls R3	JRLCX	NAS CM	Open End	Cautious Alloc (Income)	B-	C	B+	Up	Y	0
John Hancock Funds II Multimgr Lifest Cons Cls R4	JSLCX	NAS CM	Open End	Cautious Alloc (Income)	B-	C	B+	Up	Y	0
John Hancock Funds II Multimgr Lifest Cons Cls R5	JTLRX	NAS CM	Open End	Cautious Alloc (Income)	B-	C	A-	Up	Y	0
John Hancock Funds II Multimgr Lifest Cons Cls R6	JULCX	NAS CM	Open End	Cautious Alloc (Income)	B	C	A-	Up	Y	1,000,000
John Hancock Funds II Multimgr Lifest Growth Port Cls 1	JILGX	NAS CM	Open End	Aggressive Alloc (Growth)	B-	B-	B-	Down	Y	0
John Hancock Funds II Multimgr Lifest Growth Port Cls 5	JHLGX	NAS CM	Open End	Aggressive Alloc (Growth)	B-	B-	B-	Down	Y	0
John Hancock Funds II Multimgr Lifest Growth Port Cls A	JALGX	NAS CM	Open End	Aggressive Alloc (Growth)	B-	C+	B-	Down	Y	1,000
John Hancock Funds II Multimgr Lifest Growth Port Cls B	JBLGX	NAS CM	Open End	Aggressive Alloc (Growth)	B-	C+	B-	Down		1,000
John Hancock Funds II Multimgr Lifest Growth Port Cls C	JCLGX	NAS CM	Open End	Aggressive Alloc (Growth)	B-	C+	B-	Down	Y	1,000
John Hancock Funds II Multimgr Lifest Growth Port Cls I	JTGIX	NAS CM	Open End	Aggressive Alloc (Growth)	B-	B-	B-	Down	Y	250,000
John Hancock Funds II Multimgr Lifest Growth Port Cls R1	JPLGX	NAS CM	Open End	Aggressive Alloc (Growth)	B-	C+	B-	Down	Y	0
John Hancock Funds II Multimgr Lifest Growth Port Cls R2	JQLGX	NAS CM	Open End	Aggressive Alloc (Growth)	B-	C+	B-	Down	Y	0
John Hancock Funds II Multimgr Lifest Growth Port Cls R3	JRLGX	NAS CM	Open End	Aggressive Alloc (Growth)	B-	C+	B-	Down	Y	0
John Hancock Funds II Multimgr Lifest Growth Port Cls R4	JSLGX	NAS CM	Open End	Aggressive Alloc (Growth)	B-	B-	B-	Down	Y	0
John Hancock Funds II Multimgr Lifest Growth Port Cls R5	JTLGX	NAS CM	Open End	Aggressive Alloc (Growth)	B-	B-	B-	Down	Y	0
John Hancock Funds II Multimgr Lifest Growth Port Cls R6	JULGX	NAS CM	Open End	Aggressive Alloc (Growth)	B-	B-	B-	Down	Y	1,000,000
John Hancock Funds II Multimgr Lifest Mod Port Cls 1	JILMX	NAS CM	Open End	Cautious Alloc (Growth & Income)	B-	C+	B	Up	Y	0
John Hancock Funds II Multimgr Lifest Mod Port Cls 5	JHLMX	NAS CM	Open End	Cautious Alloc (Growth & Income)	B	C+	B+	Up	Y	0
John Hancock Funds II Multimgr Lifest Mod Port Cls A	JALMX	NAS CM	Open End	Cautious Alloc (Growth & Income)	B-	C+	B	Up	Y	1,000
John Hancock Funds II Multimgr Lifest Mod Port Cls B	JBLMX	NAS CM	Open End	Cautious Alloc (Growth & Income)	B-	C+	B+	Up		1,000
John Hancock Funds II Multimgr Lifest Mod Port Cls C	JCLMX	NAS CM	Open End	Cautious Alloc (Growth & Income)	B-	C+	B	Up	Y	1,000
John Hancock Funds II Multimgr Lifest Mod Port Cls I	JTMIX	NAS CM	Open End	Cautious Alloc (Growth & Income)	B-	C+	B	Up	Y	250,000
John Hancock Funds II Multimgr Lifest Mod Port Cls R1	JPLMX	NAS CM	Open End	Cautious Alloc (Growth & Income)	B-	C+	B+	Up	Y	0
John Hancock Funds II Multimgr Lifest Mod Port Cls R2	JQLMX	NAS CM	Open End	Cautious Alloc (Growth & Income)	B-	C+	B	Up	Y	0
John Hancock Funds II Multimgr Lifest Mod Port Cls R3	JRLMX	NAS CM	Open End	Cautious Alloc (Growth & Income)	B-	C+	B	Up	Y	0
John Hancock Funds II Multimgr Lifest Mod Port Cls R4	JSLMX	NAS CM	Open End	Cautious Alloc (Growth & Income)	B	C+	B+	Up	Y	0
John Hancock Funds II Multimgr Lifest Mod Port Cls R5	JTLMX	NAS CM	Open End	Cautious Alloc (Growth & Income)	B-	C+	B	Up	Y	0
John Hancock Funds II Multimgr Lifest Mod Port Cls R6	JULMX	NAS CM	Open End	Cautious Alloc (Growth & Income)	B-	C+	B	Up	Y	1,000,000
John Hancock Funds II Natural Resources Fund Class 1	JINRX	NAS CM	Open End	Natl Resources Sec Equity (Natl Res)	C	C	C-	Up	Y	0
John Hancock Funds II Natural Resources Fund Class A	JNRAX	NAS CM	Open End	Natl Resources Sec Equity (Natl Res)	C	C	C-	Up	Y	1,000
John Hancock Funds II Natural Resources Fund Class I	JNRIX	NAS CM	Open End	Natl Resources Sec Equity (Natl Res)	C	C	C-	Up	Y	250,000
John Hancock Funds II Natural Resources Fund Class NAV	JHNRX	NAS CM	Open End	Natl Resources Sec Equity (Natl Res)	C	C	C-	Up	Y	0
John Hancock Funds II New Opportunities Fund Class 1	JISOX	NAS CM	Open End	US Equity Small Cap (Small Company)	B	B	B	Up	Y	0
John Hancock Funds II New Opportunities Fund Class A	JASOX	NAS CM	Open End	US Equity Small Cap (Small Company)	B	B	B	Up	Y	1,000
John Hancock Funds II New Opportunities Fund Class C	JBSOX	NAS CM	Open End	US Equity Small Cap (Small Company)	B	B	B	Up	Y	1,000
John Hancock Funds II New Opportunities Fund Class I	JHSOX	NAS CM	Open End	US Equity Small Cap (Small Company)	B	B	B	Up	Y	250,000
John Hancock Funds II New Opportunities Fund Class NAV	US47803X8838		Open End	US Equity Small Cap (Small Company)	B	B	B	Up	Y	0
John Hancock Funds II New Opportunities Fund Class R1	JRSOX	NAS CM	Open End	US Equity Small Cap (Small Company)	B	B	B	Up	Y	0
John Hancock Funds II New Opportunities Fund Class R2	JSSOX	NAS CM	Open End	US Equity Small Cap (Small Company)	B	B	B	Up	Y	0
John Hancock Funds II New Opportunities Fund Class R3	JTSOX	NAS CM	Open End	US Equity Small Cap (Small Company)	B	B	B	Up	Y	0
John Hancock Funds II New Opportunities Fund Class R4	JUSOX	NAS CM	Open End	US Equity Small Cap (Small Company)	B	B	B	Up	Y	0
John Hancock Funds II New Opportunities Fund Class R5	JVSOX	NAS CM	Open End	US Equity Small Cap (Small Company)	B	B	B	Up	Y	0
John Hancock Funds II New Opportunities Fund Class R6	JWSOX	NAS CM	Open End	US Equity Small Cap (Small Company)	B	B	B	Up	Y	1,000,000
John Hancock Funds II Real Estate Equity Fund Class NAV	JHAZX	NAS CM	Open End	Real Estate Sector Equity (Real Estate)	B	C+	B+	Up	Y	0
John Hancock Funds II Real Estate Securities Fund Class 1	JIREX	NAS CM	Open End	Real Estate Sector Equity (Real Estate)	B-	C+	B		Y	0

★ Expanded analysis of this fund is included in Section II.

	TOTAL RETURNS					PERFORMANCE				ASSETS		ASSET ALLOCATION & TURNOVER					BULL & BEAR		FEES		
Min Additional Investment	3-Month Total Return	6-Month Total Return	1-Year Total Return	3-Year Total Return	5-Year Total Return	Dividend Yield (TTM)	Expense Ratio	3-Yr Std Deviation	3-Year Beta	NAV	Total Assets (MIL)	%Cash	%Stocks	%Bonds	%Other	Turnover Ratio	Last Bull Market Total Return	Last Bear Market Total Return	Front End Fee (%)	Back End Fee (%)	Inception Date
	1.21	2.92	7.42	12.07	22.58	2.49	0.89	3.5	0.44	13.03	2,945	6	20	70	2	23	9.18	-4.85			Oct-05
	1.19	2.73	7.11	10.84	20.35	2.14	1.25	3.45	0.43	13.06	2,945	6	20	70	2	23	8.82	-5	5.00		Oct-05
	1.01	2.36	6.35	8.55	16.08	1.46	1.97	3.48	0.43	13.07	2,945	6	20	70	2	23	8.35	-5.34		5.00	Oct-05
	0.93	2.36	6.27	8.47	16.05	1.46	1.97	3.45	0.42	13.06	2,945	6	20	70	2	23	8.36	-5.26		1.00	Oct-05
	1.27	2.89	7.44	11.96	22.46	2.44	0.96	3.49	0.44	13.04	2,945	6	20	70	2	23	9.18	-4.85			May-15
	1.10	2.55	6.74	9.67	17.93	1.82	1.61	3.48	0.44	13.05	2,945	6	20	70	2	23	8.44	-5.18			Sep-06
	1.09	2.68	6.91	10.49	19.72	2.04	1.36	3.5	0.43	13.04	2,945	6	20	70	2	23	8.98	-4.93			Mar-12
	1.14	2.63	6.91	10.19	18.85	1.96	1.51	3.48	0.43	13.03	2,945	6	20	70	2	23	8.67	-5.2			Oct-05
	1.15	2.81	7.19	11.22	20.83	2.29	1.11	3.49	0.42	13.03	2,945	6	20	70	2	23	8.75	-4.99			Oct-05
	1.28	2.91	7.48	11.92	22.28	2.48	0.91	3.47	0.43	13.04	2,945	6	20	70	2	23	9.08	-4.9			Oct-05
	1.29	2.94	7.56	12.24	22.83	2.54	0.86	3.48	0.42	13.03	2,945	6	20	70	2	23	9.18	-4.85			Sep-11
	4.10	8.48	19.25	25.71	63.76	1.44	1.01	8.61	0.81	16.08	13,119	4	74	18	2	28	19.32	-18.12			Oct-05
	4.15	8.47	19.33	25.85	64.26	1.49	0.96	8.64	0.81	16.06	13,119	4	74	18	2	28	19.31	-18.07			Jul-06
	4.04	8.28	18.83	24.34	60.81	1.13	1.36	8.6	0.81	16.16	13,119	4	74	18	2	28	18.96	-18.22	5.00		Oct-05
	3.79	7.89	17.94	21.72	55.13	0.52	2.08	8.61	0.81	16.2	13,119	4	74	18	2	28	18.39	-18.44		5.00	Oct-05
	3.79	7.90	17.96	21.67	55.12	0.52	2.08	8.61	0.81	16.18	13,119	4	74	18	2	28	18.43	-18.45		1.00	Oct-05
	4.10	8.42	19.20	25.57	63.59	1.39	1.07	8.61	0.81	16.07	13,119	4	74	18	2	28	19.32	-18.12			May-15
	3.94	8.10	18.45	23.05	57.87	0.85	1.72	8.62	0.81	16.23	13,119	4	74	18	2	28	18.7	-18.36			Sep-06
	3.97	8.24	18.71	23.92	59.92	1.06	1.47	8.62	0.81	16.05	13,119	4	74	18	2	28	19.11	-18.19			Mar-12
	3.94	8.12	18.53	23.42	58.66	0.92	1.62	8.62	0.81	16.13	13,119	4	74	18	2	28	18.85	-18.32			Oct-05
	4.07	8.37	19.03	24.85	61.81	1.26	1.22	8.63	0.81	16.14	13,119	4	74	18	2	28	18.94	-18.22			Oct-05
	4.06	8.42	19.21	25.61	63.44	1.42	1.02	8.62	0.81	16.16	13,119	4	74	18	2	28	19.24	-18.14			Oct-05
	4.13	8.51	19.29	25.88	64.18	1.48	0.97	8.61	0.81	16.08	13,119	4	74	18	2	28	19.34	-18.12			Sep-11
	2.18	4.68	11.06	16.94	35.36	2.23	0.93	5.03	0.17	13.79	3,876	6	37	54	2	25	12.24	-8.7			Oct-05
	2.12	4.71	11.13	17.04	35.64	2.28	0.88	5.05	0.16	13.77	3,876	6	37	54	2	25	12.19	-8.68			Jul-06
	2.01	4.48	10.64	15.63	32.84	1.89	1.28	5.04	0.18	13.83	3,876	6	37	54	2	25	11.96	-8.9	5.00		Oct-05
	1.91	4.12	9.96	13.19	28.09	1.23	2	5.07	0.18	13.82	3,876	6	37	54	2	25	11.39	-9.16		5.00	Oct-05
	1.83	4.11	9.86	13.17	28.04	1.23	2	5.05	0.16	13.83	3,876	6	37	54	2	25	11.39	-9.15		1.00	Oct-05
	2.17	4.66	11.01	16.75	35.14	2.17	0.99	5.01	0.17	13.78	3,876	6	37	54	2	25	12.24	-8.7			May-15
	2.00	4.31	10.37	14.37	30.19	1.58	1.64	5.06	0.17	13.81	3,876	6	37	54	2	25	11.64	-9.09			Sep-06
	2.00	4.45	10.57	15.24	32.05	1.8	1.39	5.06	0.18	13.78	3,876	6	37	54	2	25	12.13	-8.77			Mar-12
	1.95	4.36	10.39	14.75	30.83	1.66	1.54	5.06	0.16	13.8	3,876	6	37	54	2	25	11.75	-9.02			Oct-05
	2.13	4.58	10.93	16.16	33.56	2.04	1.14	5.07	0.18	13.78	3,876	6	37	54	2	25	11.92	-8.91			Oct-05
	2.18	4.68	11.05	16.84	34.85	2.21	0.94	5.04	0.16	13.79	3,876	6	37	54	2	25	12.09	-8.74			Oct-05
	2.20	4.71	11.13	17.05	35.58	2.28	0.89	5.07	0.17	13.77	3,876	6	37	54	2	25	12.26	-8.7			Sep-11
	9.06	19.18	5.85	0.13	-18.69	0.95	1.02	22.42	1.18	12.77	509.2	9	90	0	1	28	12.8	-32.47			Oct-05
	8.95	19.06	5.46	-0.91	-20.41	0.63	1.39	22.42	1.19	12.68	509.2	9	90	0	1	28	12.43	-32.59	5.00		Jan-10
	9.02	19.15	5.79	-0.27	-19.54	0.9	1.08	22.44	1.19	12.64	509.2	9	90	0	1	28	12.64	-32.51			Jan-10
	9.09	19.20	5.86	0.28	-18.51	1	0.97	22.34	1.18	12.67	509.2	9	90	0	1	28	12.83	-32.45			Oct-05
	5.30	10.07	14.23	28.13	89.24	0.32	0.84	13.97	0.96	28.7	601.6	7	93	0	0	41	29.47	-25.75			Oct-05
	5.20	9.89	13.82	26.78	86.30	0.06	1.21	13.93	0.96	28.5	601.6	7	93	0	0	41	29.26	-25.82	5.00		May-15
	5.02	9.51	13.06	24.21	80.00	0	1.91	13.94	0.96	28	601.6	7	93	0	0	41	28.73	-26.04		1.00	May-15
	5.28	10.09	14.19	28.00	89.22	0.28	0.9	13.96	0.96	28.52	601.6	7	93	0	0	41	29.48	-25.73			May-15
	5.31	10.11	14.30	28.37	89.76	0.35	0.79	13.96	0.96	28.51	601.6	7	93	0	0	41	29.48	-25.73			Oct-05
	5.18	9.84	13.74	26.45	85.08	0	1.56	13.97	0.96	28.48	601.6	7	93	0	0	41	29.11	-25.88			May-15
	5.24	10.05	13.86	27.20	87.10	0.17	1.31	13.96	0.96	28.51	601.6	7	93	0	0	41	29.29	-25.81			May-15
	5.17	9.83	13.68	26.40	85.00	0	1.46	13.96	0.96	28.47	601.6	7	93	0	0	41	29.11	-25.88			May-15
	5.31	10.03	14.13	27.69	87.82	0.24	1.06	13.97	0.96	28.53	601.6	7	93	0	0	41	29.29	-25.81			May-15
	5.32	10.13	14.31	28.33	89.71	0.34	0.86	13.95	0.96	28.54	601.6	7	93	0	0	41	29.48	-25.73			May-15
	5.29	10.10	14.29	28.23	89.57	0.34	0.81	13.96	0.96	28.5	601.6	7	93	0	0	41	29.48	-25.73			May-15
	3.28	4.08	4.29	13.66	56.39	1.88	0.93	12.75	0.94	10.19	222.5	0	96	0	3	16	32.22	-16.41			Apr-06
	2.38	3.01	6.22	14.81	54.96	3.48	0.79	13.39	0.99	12.39	474.9	0	100	0	0	159	32.02	-17.1			Oct-05

	MARKET		FUND TYPE, CATEGORY & OBJECTIVE		RATINGS				MINIMUMS	
Fund Name	Ticker Symbol	Traded On	Fund Type	Category and (Prospectus Objective)	Overall Rating	Reward Rating	Risk Rating	Recent Up/ Downgrade	Open to New Investors	Min Initial Investment
John Hancock Funds II Science & Technology Cls NAV Shares	US47803M1430		Open End	Technology Sector Equity (Technology)	A	A+	B+	Up	Y	0
John Hancock Funds II Small Company Growth Fund Class NAV	US47803X5453		Open End	US Equity Small Cap (Small Company)	B	A-	C+	Up	Y	0
John Hancock Funds II Small Company Value Fund Class 1	JISVX	NAS CM	Open End	US Equity Small Cap (Small Company)	A-	A	B	Up	Y	0
John Hancock Funds II Small Company Value Fund Class NAV	JHSVX	NAS CM	Open End	US Equity Small Cap (Small Company)	A-	A	B	Up	Y	0
John Hancock Funds II Strategic Equity Allocation Fund NAV	US47804M7204		Open End	Aggressive Alloc (Equity-Income)	B-	B	B-	Down	Y	0
John Hancock Funds II U.S. Growth Fund Class 1	JHUPX	NAS CM	Open End	US Equity Large Cap Blend (Growth)	B	B	B+		Y	0
John Hancock Funds II U.S. Growth Fund Class A	JHUAX	NAS CM	Open End	US Equity Large Cap Blend (Growth)	B	B	B+		Y	1,000
John Hancock Funds II U.S. Growth Fund Class C	JHUCX	NAS CM	Open End	US Equity Large Cap Blend (Growth)	B	B	B		Y	1,000
John Hancock Funds II U.S. Growth Fund Class I	JHUIX	NAS CM	Open End	US Equity Large Cap Blend (Growth)	B	B	B+		Y	250,000
John Hancock Funds II U.S. Growth Fund Class NAV	JHUMX	NAS CM	Open End	US Equity Large Cap Blend (Growth)	B+	B	B+	Up	Y	0
John Hancock Funds II U.S. Growth Fund Class R6	JUSEX	NAS CM	Open End	US Equity Large Cap Blend (Growth)	B+	B	B+	Up	Y	1,000,000
John Hancock Funds Income Allocation Fund Class A	JIAFX	NAS CM	Open End	Cautious Alloc (Growth & Income)	C+	C	B	Up	Y	1,000
John Hancock Funds Income Allocation Fund Class C	JIAGX	NAS CM	Open End	Cautious Alloc (Growth & Income)	C+	C	B	Up	Y	1,000
John Hancock Funds Income Allocation Fund Class I	JIAIX	NAS CM	Open End	Cautious Alloc (Growth & Income)	B-	C	B	Up	Y	250,000
John Hancock Funds Income Allocation Fund Class R6	JIASX	NAS CM	Open End	Cautious Alloc (Growth & Income)	C+	C	B	Up	Y	1,000,000
John Hancock Funds International Growth Fund Class 1	GOIOX	NAS CM	Open End	Global Equity Large Cap (Foreign Stock)	A-	A-	B+	Up	Y	0
John Hancock Funds International Growth Fund Class A	GOIGX	NAS CM	Open End	Global Equity Large Cap (Foreign Stock)	B+	A-	B+	Up	Y	1,000
John Hancock Funds International Growth Fund Class B	GONBX	NAS CM	Open End	Global Equity Large Cap (Foreign Stock)	B+	B+	B	Up		1,000
John Hancock Funds International Growth Fund Class C	GONCX	NAS CM	Open End	Global Equity Large Cap (Foreign Stock)	B+	B+	B	Up	Y	1,000
John Hancock Funds International Growth Fund Class I	GOGIX	NAS CM	Open End	Global Equity Large Cap (Foreign Stock)	A-	A-	B+	Up	Y	250,000
John Hancock Funds International Growth Fund Class NAV	JIGHX	NAS CM	Open End	Global Equity Large Cap (Foreign Stock)	A-	A-	B+	Up	Y	0
John Hancock Funds International Growth Fund Class R2	JHIGX	NAS CM	Open End	Global Equity Large Cap (Foreign Stock)	B+	A-	B+	Up	Y	0
John Hancock Funds International Growth Fund Class R4	JIGIX	NAS CM	Open End	Global Equity Large Cap (Foreign Stock)	B+	A-	B+	Up	Y	0
John Hancock Funds International Growth Fund Class R6	JIGTX	NAS CM	Open End	Global Equity Large Cap (Foreign Stock)	A-	A-	B+	Up	Y	1,000,000
John Hancock Funds Multi-Index 2010 Lifetime Port Cls 1	JRLDX	NAS CM	Open End	Target Date 2000-2020 (Asset Alloc)	B-	C+	B	Up	Y	0
John Hancock Funds Multi-Index 2010 Lifetime Port Cls R6	JRLHX	NAS CM	Open End	Target Date 2000-2020 (Asset Alloc)	B-	C+	B	Up	Y	1,000,000
John Hancock Funds Multi-Index 2015 Lifetime Port Cls 1	JRLIX	NAS CM	Open End	Target Date 2000-2020 (Asset Alloc)	B-	C+	B	Up	Y	0
John Hancock Funds Multi-Index 2015 Lifetime Port Cls R6	JRLLX	NAS CM	Open End	Target Date 2000-2020 (Asset Alloc)	B-	C+	B	Up	Y	1,000,000
John Hancock Funds Multi-Index 2020 Lifetime Port Cls 1	JRLOX	NAS CM	Open End	Target Date 2000-2020 (Asset Alloc)	B-	C+	B	Up	Y	0
John Hancock Funds Multi-Index 2020 Lifetime Port Cls R6	JRTAX	NAS CM	Open End	Target Date 2000-2020 (Asset Alloc)	B-	C+	B	Up	Y	1,000,000
John Hancock Funds Multi-Ind 2020 Preserv Port Cls 1	JRWOX	NAS CM	Open End	Target Date 2000-2020 (Asset Alloc)	B	C	A-	Up	Y	0
John Hancock Funds Multi-Ind 2020 Preserv Port Cls R1	JRWQX	NAS CM	Open End	Target Date 2000-2020 (Asset Alloc)	B-	C	A-	Up	Y	0
John Hancock Funds Multi-Ind 2020 Preserv Port Cls R2	JRWRX	NAS CM	Open End	Target Date 2000-2020 (Asset Alloc)	B-	C	A-	Up	Y	0
John Hancock Funds Multi-Ind 2020 Preserv Port Cls R4	JRWPX	NAS CM	Open End	Target Date 2000-2020 (Asset Alloc)	B	C	A-	Up	Y	0
John Hancock Funds Multi-Ind 2020 Preserv Port Cls R6	JRWSX	NAS CM	Open End	Target Date 2000-2020 (Asset Alloc)	B	C	A-	Up	Y	1,000,000
John Hancock Funds Multi-Index 2025 Lifetime Port Cls 1	JRTBX	NAS CM	Open End	Target Date 2021-2045 (Asset Alloc)	B-	C+	B	Down	Y	0
John Hancock Funds Multi-Index 2025 Lifetime Port Cls R6	JRTFX	NAS CM	Open End	Target Date 2021-2045 (Asset Alloc)	B-	C+	B	Down	Y	1,000,000
John Hancock Funds Multi-Ind 2025 Preserv Port Cls 1	JREOX	NAS CM	Open End	Target Date 2021-2045 (Asset Alloc)	B-	C+	B	Up	Y	0
John Hancock Funds Multi-Ind 2025 Preserv Port Cls R1	JREQX	NAS CM	Open End	Target Date 2021-2045 (Asset Alloc)	B-	C+	B	Up	Y	0
John Hancock Funds Multi-Ind 2025 Preserv Port Cls R2	JRERX	NAS CM	Open End	Target Date 2021-2045 (Asset Alloc)	B-	C+	B	Up	Y	0
John Hancock Funds Multi-Ind 2025 Preserv Port Cls R4	JREPX	NAS CM	Open End	Target Date 2021-2045 (Asset Alloc)	B-	C+	B	Up	Y	0
John Hancock Funds Multi-Ind 2025 Preserv Port Cls R6	JRESX	NAS CM	Open End	Target Date 2021-2045 (Asset Alloc)	B-	C+	B	Up	Y	1,000,000
John Hancock Funds Multi-Index 2030 Lifetime Port Cls 1	JRTGX	NAS CM	Open End	Target Date 2021-2045 (Asset Alloc)	B-	B-	B-	Down	Y	0
John Hancock Funds Multi-Index 2030 Lifetime Port Cls R6	JRTJX	NAS CM	Open End	Target Date 2021-2045 (Asset Alloc)	B-	B-	B	Down	Y	1,000,000
John Hancock Funds Multi-Ind 2030 Preserv Port Cls 1	JRHOX	NAS CM	Open End	Target Date 2021-2045 (Asset Alloc)	B-	C+	B	Up	Y	0
John Hancock Funds Multi-Ind 2030 Preserv Port Cls R1	JRHQX	NAS CM	Open End	Target Date 2021-2045 (Asset Alloc)	B-	C+	B	Up	Y	0
John Hancock Funds Multi-Ind 2030 Preserv Port Cls R2	JRHRX	NAS CM	Open End	Target Date 2021-2045 (Asset Alloc)	B-	C+	B	Up	Y	0
John Hancock Funds Multi-Ind 2030 Preserv Port Cls R4	JRHPX	NAS CM	Open End	Target Date 2021-2045 (Asset Alloc)	B-	C+	B	Up	Y	0
John Hancock Funds Multi-Ind 2030 Preserv Port Cls R6	JRHSX	NAS CM	Open End	Target Date 2021-2045 (Asset Alloc)	B-	C+	B	Up	Y	1,000,000
John Hancock Funds Multi-Index 2035 Lifetime Port Cls 1	JRTKX	NAS CM	Open End	Target Date 2021-2045 (Asset Alloc)	B-	B-	B-	Down	Y	0
John Hancock Funds Multi-Index 2035 Lifetime Port Cls R6	JRTNX	NAS CM	Open End	Target Date 2021-2045 (Asset Alloc)	B-	B-	B-	Down	Y	1,000,000
John Hancock Funds Multi-Ind 2035 Preserv Port Cls 1	JRYOX	NAS CM	Open End	Target Date 2021-2045 (Asset Alloc)	B-	C+	B	Down	Y	0

★ Expanded analysis of this fund is included in Section II.

	TOTAL RETURNS					PERFORMANCE				ASSETS		ASSET ALLOCATION & TURNOVER					BULL & BEAR		FEES		
Min Additional Investment	3-Month Total Return	6-Month Total Return	1-Year Total Return	3-Year Total Return	5-Year Total Return	Dividend Yield (TTM)	Expense Ratio	3-Yr Std Deviation	3-Year Beta	NAV	Total Assets (MIL)	%Cash	%Stocks	%Bonds	%Other	Turnover Ratio	Last Bull Market Total Return	Last Bear Market Total Return	Front End Fee (%)	Back End Fee (%)	Inception Date
	7.17	16.02	40.92	62.51		0.14	1.07	14.19	1.22	4.98	289.5	3	92	0	4	93					Feb-13
	6.54	13.12	25.13	35.86	110.93	0	0.95	12.66	0.83	20.86	233.0	7	93	0	0	39	28.71	-23.57			Oct-05
	3.47	9.85	11.50	38.30	86.55	0.65	1.27	12.93	0.89	28.46	296.3	2	96	0	2	22	28.41	-23.36			Oct-05
	3.49	9.87	11.56	38.54	87.03	0.69	1.22	12.92	0.89	28.42	296.3	2	96	0	2	22	28.48	-23.35			Oct-05
	5.37	10.72	22.11	30.96	82.73	1.51	0.67	10.13	0.98	12.89	7,694	3	97	0	0	67					Apr-12
	6.76	13.19	29.80	34.45	95.49	0.79	0.8	10.75	0.96	10.1	122.4	0	100	0	0	112	20.36	-9.52			May-12
	6.66	13.06	29.27	32.94	91.51	0.71	1.17	10.74	0.96	10.14	122.4	0	100	0	0	112	19.96	-9.62	5.00		Oct-11
	6.45	12.60	28.39	30.14	85.39	0.55	1.87	10.68	0.96	10.12	122.4	0	100	0	0	112	19.7	-9.88		1.00	Aug-14
	6.72	13.15	29.59	34.13	94.77	0.78	0.85	10.7	0.96	10.1	122.4	0	100	0	0	112	20.39	-9.51			Oct-11
	6.77	13.18	30.20	35.00	96.46	0.8	0.75	10.71	0.96	10.13	122.4	0	100	0	0	112	20.4	-9.51			Oct-05
	6.79	13.22	29.83	34.77	96.13	0.8	0.75	10.71	0.96	10.1	122.4	0	100	0	0	112	20.4	-9.51			Nov-16
	1.30	3.20	8.00	12.76		2.98	1.24	4.07	0.63	9.97	12.4	6	25	62	1	17			4.00		Nov-14
	1.13	2.85	7.28	10.29		2.31	1.93	4.11	0.64	9.94	12.4	6	25	62	1	17				1.00	Nov-14
	1.38	3.36	8.33	13.85		3.29	0.93	4.04	0.6	9.98	12.4	6	25	62	1	17					Nov-14
	1.40	3.41	8.44	14.20		3.38	0.83	4.07	0.63	9.98	12.4	6	25	62	1	17					Nov-14
	4.63	12.68	36.72	39.47	75.46	0.75	0.96	10.85	0.83	27.67	7,998	2	96	0	2	94	16.15	-20.42			Jun-06
	4.54	12.52	36.25	37.90	72.02	0.46	1.33	10.85	0.83	27.65	7,998	2	96	0	2	94	15.83	-20.55	5.00		Jun-06
	4.32	12.09	35.30	34.90	65.76	0	2.03	10.86	0.83	27.25	7,998	2	96	0	2	94	15.36	-20.81		5.00	Jun-06
	4.33	12.12	35.34	35.00	65.84	0	2.03	10.86	0.83	27.19	7,998	2	96	0	2	94	15.33	-20.8		1.00	Jun-06
	4.61	12.70	36.67	39.17	74.81	0.7	1.02	10.86	0.83	27.69	7,998	2	96	0	2	94	16.02	-20.4			Jun-06
	4.63	12.73	36.84	39.61	75.64	0.78	0.91	10.86	0.83	27.67	7,998	2	96	0	2	94	16.15	-20.42			Jun-15
	4.52	12.45	36.14	37.45	72.23	0.38	1.43	10.85	0.83	27.68	7,998	2	96	0	2	94	16.01	-20.48			Mar-15
	4.59	12.60	36.49	38.41	73.43	0.59	1.18	10.86	0.83	27.69	7,998	2	96	0	2	94	16.01	-20.48			Mar-15
	4.61	12.74	36.83	39.63	75.66	0.78	0.93	10.85	0.83	27.7	7,998	2	96	0	2	94	16.15	-20.42			Mar-15
	2.16	4.44	9.85	16.26		2.57	0.42	5.09		10.68	30.9	2	36	62	0	52					Nov-13
	2.11	4.49	9.90	16.43		2.61	0.37	5.05		10.68	30.9	2	36	62	0	52					Nov-13
	2.40	5.00	10.96	17.75		2.3	0.43	5.67		10.87	46.3	3	41	55	0	47					Nov-13
	2.44	5.05	11.01	17.81		2.35	0.38	5.72		10.87	46.3	3	41	55	0	47					Nov-13
	2.89	6.00	12.72	20.18		2.14	0.44	6.58		11.23	146.7	2	51	46	0	37					Nov-13
	3.02	6.04	12.86	20.35		2.18	0.39	6.54		11.24	146.7	2	51	46	0	37					Nov-13
	1.07	2.73	6.67	11.14	25.55	2.02	0.38	3.42		11.66	851.2	2	19	79	0	13	10.59	-6.25			Apr-10
	0.87	2.35	5.91	9.32	21.86	1.55	1.08	3.43		11.72	851.2	2	19	79	0	13	10.3	-6.43			Sep-12
	0.93	2.41	6.06	9.68	22.77	1.59	0.83	3.39		11.71	851.2	2	19	79	0	13	10.46	-6.33			Sep-12
	1.01	2.58	6.50	10.68	24.61	1.9	0.58	3.42		11.7	851.2	2	19	79	0	13	10.46	-6.33			May-12
	1.03	2.69	6.62	11.30	25.85	2.06	0.33	3.39		11.66	851.2	2	19	79	0	13	10.59	-6.25			Sep-12
	3.50	7.11	15.02	22.89		1.99	0.44	7.53		11.54	210.3	3	63	34	0	28					Nov-13
	3.63	7.24	15.17	23.18		2.03	0.39	7.54		11.55	210.3	3	63	34	0	28					Nov-13
	2.16	4.78	10.54	16.19	38.81	1.96	0.4	5.04		12.99	1,463	2	40	58	0	14	14.53	-10.58			Apr-10
	1.99	4.37	9.75	13.79	34.01	1.32	1.1	5.05		13.04	1,463	2	40	58	0	14	14.23	-10.75			Sep-12
	2.11	4.64	10.30	15.24	36.41	1.7	0.85	5.09		13.04	1,463	2	40	58	0	14	14.4	-10.66			Sep-12
	2.18	4.72	10.45	15.81	37.85	1.85	0.6	5.08		13.05	1,463	2	40	58	0	14	14.4	-10.66			May-12
	2.21	4.83	10.68	16.37	39.16	2	0.35	5.04		12.99	1,463	2	40	58	0	14	14.53	-10.58			Sep-12
	4.10	8.20	17.13	25.46		1.78	0.43	8.43		11.82	218.7	3	73	24	0	25					Nov-13
	4.15	8.25	17.29	25.65		1.83	0.38	8.43		11.82	218.7	3	73	24	0	25					Nov-13
	3.17	6.70	14.28	20.98	50.46	1.88	0.41	6.74		13.93	1,501	3	58	39	0	15	16.76	-13.07			Apr-10
	3.09	6.40	13.61	18.72	45.57	1.28	1.11	6.72		13.99	1,501	3	58	39	0	15	16.46	-13.23			Sep-12
	3.07	6.45	13.84	19.33	47.17	1.49	0.86	6.72		13.96	1,501	3	58	39	0	15	16.63	-13.14			Sep-12
	3.25	6.70	14.25	20.62	49.42	1.78	0.61	6.71		14.01	1,501	3	58	39	0	15	16.63	-13.14			May-12
	3.22	6.75	14.42	21.25	50.97	1.93	0.36	6.71		13.93	1,501	3	58	39	0	15	16.77	-13.07			Sep-12
	4.59	9.10	18.85	27.34		1.65	0.41	9.09		12.07	195.5	3	81	15	0	22					Nov-13
	4.63	9.15	19.02	27.65		1.69	0.36	9.17		12.07	195.5	3	81	15	0	22					Nov-13
	3.87	7.97	16.76	24.08	57.89	1.88	0.41	7.69		14.48	1,275	3	69	27	0	15	18.2	-14.5			Apr-10

	MARKET			FUND TYPE, CATEGORY & OBJECTIVE	RATINGS				MINIMUMS	
Fund Name	Ticker Symbol	Traded On	Fund Type	Category and (Prospectus Objective)	Overall Rating	Reward Rating	Risk Rating	Recent Up/ Downgrade	Open to New Investors	Min Initial Investment
John Hancock Funds Multi-Ind 2035 Preserv Port Cls R1	JRYQX	NAS CM	Open End	Target Date 2021-2045 (Asset Alloc)	B-	C+	B-	Down	Y	0
John Hancock Funds Multi-Ind 2035 Preserv Port Cls R2	JRYRX	NAS CM	Open End	Target Date 2021-2045 (Asset Alloc)	B-	C+	B	Down	Y	0
John Hancock Funds Multi-Ind 2035 Preserv Port Cls R4	JRYPX	NAS CM	Open End	Target Date 2021-2045 (Asset Alloc)	B-	C+	B	Down	Y	0
John Hancock Funds Multi-Ind 2035 Preserv Port Cls R6	JRYSX	NAS CM	Open End	Target Date 2021-2045 (Asset Alloc)	B-	B-	B	Down	Y	1,000,000
John Hancock Funds Multi-Index 2040 Lifetime Port Cls 1	JRTTX	NAS CM	Open End	Target Date 2021-2045 (Asset Alloc)	B-	B-	B-	Down	Y	0
John Hancock Funds Multi-Index 2040 Lifetime Port Cls R6	JRTWX	NAS CM	Open End	Target Date 2021-2045 (Asset Alloc)	B-	B-	B-	Down	Y	1,000,000
John Hancock Funds Multi-Ind 2040 Preserv Port Cls 1	JRROX	NAS CM	Open End	Target Date 2021-2045 (Asset Alloc)	B-	B-	B-	Down	Y	0
John Hancock Funds Multi-Ind 2040 Preserv Port Cls R1	JRRQX	NAS CM	Open End	Target Date 2021-2045 (Asset Alloc)	B-	B-	B-	Down	Y	0
John Hancock Funds Multi-Ind 2040 Preserv Port Cls R2	JRRRX	NAS CM	Open End	Target Date 2021-2045 (Asset Alloc)	B-	B-	B-	Down	Y	0
John Hancock Funds Multi-Ind 2040 Preserv Port Cls R4	JRRPX	NAS CM	Open End	Target Date 2021-2045 (Asset Alloc)	B-	B-	B-	Down	Y	0
John Hancock Funds Multi-Ind 2040 Preserv Port Cls R6	JRRSX	NAS CM	Open End	Target Date 2021-2045 (Asset Alloc)	B-	B-	B-	Down	Y	1,000,000
John Hancock Funds Multi-Index 2045 Lifetime Port Cls 1	JRLQX	NAS CM	Open End	Target Date 2021-2045 (Asset Alloc)	B-	B-	B-	Down	Y	0
John Hancock Funds Multi-Index 2045 Lifetime Port Cls R6	JRLVX	NAS CM	Open End	Target Date 2021-2045 (Asset Alloc)	B-	B-	B-	Down	Y	1,000,000
John Hancock Funds Multi-Ind 2045 Preserv Port Cls 1	JRVOX	NAS CM	Open End	Target Date 2021-2045 (Asset Alloc)	B-	B-	B-	Down	Y	0
John Hancock Funds Multi-Ind 2045 Preserv Port Cls R1	JRVQX	NAS CM	Open End	Target Date 2021-2045 (Asset Alloc)	B-	B-	B-	Down	Y	0
John Hancock Funds Multi-Ind 2045 Preserv Port Cls R2	JRVRX	NAS CM	Open End	Target Date 2021-2045 (Asset Alloc)	B-	B-	B-	Down	Y	0
John Hancock Funds Multi-Ind 2045 Preserv Port Cls R4	JRVPX	NAS CM	Open End	Target Date 2021-2045 (Asset Alloc)	B-	B-	B-	Down	Y	0
John Hancock Funds Multi-Ind 2045 Preserv Port Cls R6	JRVSX	NAS CM	Open End	Target Date 2021-2045 (Asset Alloc)	B-	B-	B-	Down	Y	1,000,000
John Hancock Funds Multi-Index 2050 Lifetime Port Cls 1	JRLWX	NAS CM	Open End	Target Date 2046+ (Asset Alloc)	B-	B-	B-	Down	Y	0
John Hancock Funds Multi-Index 2050 Lifetime Port Cls R6	JRLZX	NAS CM	Open End	Target Date 2046+ (Asset Alloc)	B-	B-	B-	Down	Y	1,000,000
John Hancock Funds Multi-Ind 2050 Preserv Port Cls 1	JRIOX	NAS CM	Open End	Target Date 2046+ (Asset Alloc)	B-	B-	B-	Down	Y	0
John Hancock Funds Multi-Ind 2050 Preserv Port Cls R1	JRIQX	NAS CM	Open End	Target Date 2046+ (Asset Alloc)	B-	B-	B-	Down	Y	0
John Hancock Funds Multi-Ind 2050 Preserv Port Cls R2	JRINX	NAS CM	Open End	Target Date 2046+ (Asset Alloc)	B-	B-	B-	Down	Y	0
John Hancock Funds Multi-Ind 2050 Preserv Port Cls R4	JRIPX	NAS CM	Open End	Target Date 2046+ (Asset Alloc)	B-	B-	B-	Down	Y	0
John Hancock Funds Multi-Ind 2050 Preserv Port Cls R6	JRISX	NAS CM	Open End	Target Date 2046+ (Asset Alloc)	B-	B-	B-	Down	Y	1,000,000
John Hancock Funds Multi-Index 2055 Lifetime Port Cls 1	JLKZX	NAS CM	Open End	Target Date 2046+ (Asset Alloc)	B-	B-	B-	Down	Y	0
John Hancock Funds Multi-Index 2055 Lifetime Port Cls R6	JLKYX	NAS CM	Open End	Target Date 2046+ (Asset Alloc)	B-	B-	B-	Down	Y	1,000,000
John Hancock Funds Multi-Ind 2055 Preserv Port Cls 1	JRIYX	NAS CM	Open End	Target Date 2046+ (Asset Alloc)	B-	B-	B-	Down	Y	0
John Hancock Funds Multi-Ind 2055 Preserv Port Cls R1	JRITX	NAS CM	Open End	Target Date 2046+ (Asset Alloc)	B-	B-	B-	Down	Y	0
John Hancock Funds Multi-Ind 2055 Preserv Port Cls R2	JRIUX	NAS CM	Open End	Target Date 2046+ (Asset Alloc)	B-	B-	B-	Down	Y	0
John Hancock Funds Multi-Ind 2055 Preserv Port Cls R4	JRIVX	NAS CM	Open End	Target Date 2046+ (Asset Alloc)	B-	B-	B-	Down	Y	0
John Hancock Funds Multi-Ind 2055 Preserv Port Cls R6	JRIWX	NAS CM	Open End	Target Date 2046+ (Asset Alloc)	B-	B-	B-	Down	Y	1,000,000
John Hancock Funds Multi-Index 2060 Lifetime Port Cls 1	JRODX	NAS CM	Open End	Target Date 2046+ (Asset Alloc)	D+	C	B+	Up	Y	0
John Hancock Funds Multi-Index 2060 Lifetime Port Cls R4	JHIKX	NAS CM	Open End	Target Date 2046+ (Asset Alloc)	D+	C	B+	Up	Y	0
John Hancock Funds Multi-Index 2060 Lifetime Port Cls R6	JIEHX	NAS CM	Open End	Target Date 2046+ (Asset Alloc)	D+	C	B+	Up	Y	1,000,000
John Hancock Funds Multi-Ind 2060 Preserv Port Cls 1	JCHOX	NAS CM	Open End	Target Date 2046+ (Asset Alloc)	D+	C	A-	Up	Y	0
John Hancock Funds Multi-Ind 2060 Preserv Port Cls R1	JKIMX	NAS CM	Open End	Target Date 2046+ (Asset Alloc)	D+	C	A-	Up	Y	0
John Hancock Funds Multi-Ind 2060 Preserv Port Cls R2	JSATX	NAS CM	Open End	Target Date 2046+ (Asset Alloc)	D+	C	A-	Up	Y	0
John Hancock Funds Multi-Ind 2060 Preserv Port Cls R4	JPORX	NAS CM	Open End	Target Date 2046+ (Asset Alloc)	D+	C	A-	Up	Y	0
John Hancock Funds Multi-Ind 2060 Preserv Port Cls R6	JTFOX	NAS CM	Open End	Target Date 2046+ (Asset Alloc)	D+	C	A-	Up	Y	1,000,000
John Hancock Funds Multi-Ind Income Preserv Port Cls 1	JRFOX	NAS CM	Open End	Target Date 2000-2020 (Asset Alloc)	B	C	A	Up	Y	0
John Hancock Funds Multi-Ind Income Preserv Port Cls R1	JRFQX	NAS CM	Open End	Target Date 2000-2020 (Asset Alloc)	B-	C	A	Up	Y	0
John Hancock Funds Multi-Ind Income Preserv Port Cls R2	JRFNX	NAS CM	Open End	Target Date 2000-2020 (Asset Alloc)	B-	C	A	Up	Y	0
John Hancock Funds Multi-Ind Income Preserv Port Cls R4	JRFPX	NAS CM	Open End	Target Date 2000-2020 (Asset Alloc)	B	C	A	Up	Y	0
John Hancock Funds Multi-Ind Income Preserv Port Cls R6	JRFSX	NAS CM	Open End	Target Date 2000-2020 (Asset Alloc)	B	C	A	Up	Y	1,000,000
John Hancock Funds Multi-Ind Lifestyle Aggress Port Cls 1	JIIOX	NAS CM	Open End	Aggressive Alloc (Aggr Growth)	B-	B-	B-	Down	Y	0
John Hancock Funds Multi-Ind Lifestyle Aggress Port Cls R6	JIIRX	NAS CM	Open End	Aggressive Alloc (Aggr Growth)	B-	B-	B-	Down	Y	1,000,000
John Hancock Funds Multi-Ind Lifestyle Balanced Port Cls 1	JIBOX	NAS CM	Open End	Moderate Alloc (Balanced)	B-	C+	B	Up	Y	0
John Hancock Funds Multi-Ind Lifest Bal Cls R6	JIBRX	NAS CM	Open End	Moderate Alloc (Balanced)	B-	C+	B	Up	Y	1,000,000
John Hancock Funds Multi-Ind Lifest Cons Cls 1	JLCGX	NAS CM	Open End	Cautious Alloc (Asset Alloc)	B	C	A-	Up	Y	0
John Hancock Funds Multi-Ind Lifest Cons Cls R6	JLCSX	NAS CM	Open End	Cautious Alloc (Asset Alloc)	B	C	A-	Up	Y	1,000,000
John Hancock Funds Multi-Index Lifestyle Growth Port Cls 1	JLGOX	NAS CM	Open End	Aggressive Alloc (Growth)	B-	B-	B	Down	Y	0

★ Expanded analysis of this fund is included in Section II.

	TOTAL RETURNS					PERFORMANCE				ASSETS		ASSET ALLOCATION & TURNOVER					BULL & BEAR		FEES		
Min Additional Investment	3-Month Total Return	6-Month Total Return	1-Year Total Return	3-Year Total Return	5-Year Total Return	Dividend Yield (TTM)	Expense Ratio	3-Yr Std Deviation	3-Year Beta	NAV	Total Assets (MIL)	%Cash	%Stocks	%Bonds	%Other	Turnover Ratio	Last Bull Market Total Return	Last Bear Market Total Return	Front End Fee (%)	Back End Fee (%)	Inception Date
	3.76	7.63	15.95	21.70	52.78	1.29	1.11	7.71		14.55	1,275	3	69	27	0	15	17.89	-14.66			Sep-12
	3.77	7.78	16.22	22.48	54.54	1.5	0.86	7.69		14.52	1,275	3	69	27	0	15	18.07	-14.57			Sep-12
	3.88	7.96	16.63	23.69	56.76	1.78	0.61	7.72		14.56	1,275	3	69	27	0	15	18.07	-14.57			May-12
	3.92	8.01	16.80	24.34	58.36	1.92	0.36	7.7		14.49	1,275	3	69	27	0	15	18.2	-14.5			Sep-12
	4.99	9.74	20.20	29.22		1.63	0.41	9.46		12.3	160.3	3	87	9	0	19					Nov-13
	5.04	9.79	20.14	29.29		1.68	0.36	9.44		12.3	160.3	3	87	9	0	19					Nov-13
	4.31	8.71	18.17	25.87	62.05	1.86	0.41	8.26		14.81	1,005	3	76	21	0	13	18.82	-15.17			Apr-10
	4.15	8.39	17.47	23.82	57.31	1.42	1.11	8.28		14.86	1,005	3	76	21	0	13	18.5	-15.33			Sep-12
	4.24	8.55	17.75	24.49	58.83	1.63	0.86	8.28		14.84	1,005	3	76	21	0	13	18.68	-15.24			Sep-12
	4.33	8.70	18.04	25.48	60.89	1.76	0.61	8.26		14.89	1,005	3	76	21	0	13	18.68	-15.24			May-12
	4.30	8.77	18.17	26.00	62.40	1.91	0.36	8.26		14.79	1,005	3	76	21	0	13	18.81	-15.17			Sep-12
	5.04	9.89	20.29	29.08		1.62	0.41	9.48		12.26	130.4	3	88	8	0	21					Nov-13
	5.08	9.85	20.35	29.27		1.66	0.36	9.47		12.26	130.4	3	88	8	0	21					Nov-13
	4.53	9.04	18.72	26.79	63.63	1.86	0.42	8.49		14.96	778.3	3	78	18	0	12	18.88	-15.24			Apr-10
	4.29	8.58	17.87	24.19	57.97	1.29	1.12	8.5		15	778.3	3	78	18	0	12	18.57	-15.4			Sep-12
	4.40	8.84	18.25	25.21	60.09	1.49	0.87	8.53		15	778.3	3	78	18	0	12	18.75	-15.31			Sep-12
	4.47	8.96	18.59	26.32	62.35	1.75	0.62	8.53		15.03	778.3	3	78	18	0	12	18.75	-15.31			May-12
	4.51	9.09	18.87	26.98	64.02	1.9	0.37	8.5		14.96	778.3	3	78	18	0	12	18.88	-15.24			Sep-12
	4.98	9.81	20.27	29.14		1.61	0.41	9.4		12.34	89.2	3	88	8	0	16					Nov-13
	5.03	9.86	20.33	29.46		1.65	0.36	9.39		12.34	89.2	3	88	8	0	16					Nov-13
	4.58	9.09	18.91	26.89	63.62	1.87	0.43	8.52		13.3	600.0	3	79	17	0	12	18.84	-15.16			Apr-11
	4.44	8.78	18.17	24.72	58.53	1.39	1.13	8.5		13.35	600.0	3	79	17	0	12	18.53	-15.32			Sep-12
	4.39	8.89	18.39	25.65	60.54	1.6	0.88	8.51		13.33	600.0	3	79	17	0	12	18.7	-15.24			Sep-12
	4.46	9.03	18.61	26.34	62.10	1.76	0.63	8.49		13.35	600.0	3	79	17	0	12	18.7	-15.24			May-12
	4.55	9.14	18.96	27.08	64.01	1.91	0.38	8.54		13.3	600.0	3	79	17	0	12	18.84	-15.16			Sep-12
	5.06	9.93	20.36	29.24		1.6	0.41	9.44		12.22	60.0	3	88	8	0	15					Mar-14
	5.12	9.89	20.33	29.34		1.64	0.36	9.44		12.21	60.0	3	88	8	0	15					Mar-14
	4.50	9.11	18.78	26.79		1.75	0.43	8.56		11.75	226.6	3	79	17	0	11					Mar-14
	4.42	8.86	18.29	25.11		1.37	1.13	8.49		11.75	226.6	3	79	17	0	11					Mar-14
	4.47	9.00	18.56	26.01		1.57	0.88	8.56		11.75	226.6	3	79	17	0	11					Mar-14
	4.57	9.10	18.77	26.48		1.65	0.63	8.5		11.76	226.6	3	79	17	0	11					Mar-14
	4.55	9.16	18.94	27.08		1.79	0.38	8.49		11.76	226.6	3	79	17	0	11					Mar-14
	5.05	9.79	20.14			1.39	0.42			12.38	7.9	4	88	8	0	46					Mar-16
	5.02	9.77	20.12				0.64			12.39	7.9	4	88	8	0	46					Apr-17
	5.01	9.84	20.30			1.42	0.37			12.38	7.9	4	88	8	0	46					Mar-16
	4.55	9.14	18.87			1.35	0.42			12.2	35.0	4	78	17	0	14					Mar-16
	4.36	8.87	18.26			1.05	1.12			12.19	35.0	4	78	17	0	14					Mar-16
	4.43	8.93	18.54			1.21	0.87			12.19	35.0	4	78	17	0	14					Mar-16
	4.52	9.02	18.74			1.27	0.62			12.2	35.0	4	78	17	0	14					Mar-16
	4.60	9.10	18.93			1.38	0.37			12.2	35.0	4	78	17	0	14					Mar-16
	0.53	1.59	4.27	7.88	14.56	1.78	0.39	2.19		11.06	482.7	1	11	88	0	5	6.02	-0.93			Apr-10
	0.51	1.40	3.78	6.31	11.32	1.3	1.09	2.2		11.12	482.7	1	11	88	0	5	5.75	-1.12			Sep-12
	0.53	1.51	3.99	6.95	12.55	1.47	0.84	2.2		11.1	482.7	1	11	88	0	5	5.9	-1.02			Sep-12
	0.59	1.56	4.14	7.56	13.66	1.66	0.59	2.2		11.08	482.7	1	11	88	0	5	5.9	-1.02			May-12
	0.67	1.74	4.42	8.05	14.85	1.83	0.34	2.17		11.06	482.7	1	11	88	0	5	6.02	-0.93			Sep-12
	5.47	10.58	21.52	30.33		1.37	0.68	9.96	0.97	12.54	280.2	3	97	0	0	13					Dec-13
	5.51	10.62	21.57	30.59		1.39	0.65	9.94	0.96	12.54	280.2	3	97	0	0	13					Dec-13
	3.21	6.42	13.55	20.66		1.84	0.74	6.58	0.09	11.53	796.3	2	57	40	0	22					Dec-13
	3.31	6.53	13.70	20.90		1.87	0.7	6.53	0.09	11.54	796.3	2	57	40	0	22					Dec-13
	1.13	2.74	6.56	11.79		2.13	0.76	3.67	0.7	10.63	144.3	2	19	78	0	36					Dec-13
	1.14	2.76	6.59	11.90		2.16	0.73	3.71	0.73	10.63	144.3	2	19	78	0	36					Dec-13
	4.33	8.50	17.51	25.40		1.54	0.71	8.25	0.79	12.12	686.1	3	76	20	0	15					Dec-13

Fund Name	MARKET Ticker Symbol	Traded On	FUND TYPE, CATEGORY & OBJECTIVE Fund Type	Category and (Prospectus Objective)	RATINGS Overall Rating	Reward Rating	Risk Rating	Recent Up/ Downgrade	MINIMUMS Open to New Investors	Min Initial Investment
John Hancock Funds Multi-Ind Lifestyle Growth Port Cls R6	JLGSX	NAS CM	Open End	Aggressive Alloc (Growth)	B-	B-	B	Down	Y	1,000,000
John Hancock Funds Multi-Ind Lifestyle Mod Port Cls 1	JLMOX	NAS CM	Open End	Cautious Alloc (Growth)	B	C+	A-	Up	Y	0
John Hancock Funds Multi-Ind Lifestyle Mod Port Cls R6	JLMRX	NAS CM	Open End	Cautious Alloc (Growth)	B-	C+	B	Up	Y	1,000,000
John Hancock Funds Multimanager 2050 Lifetime Port Cls 1	JLKOX	NAS CM	Open End	Target Date 2046+ (Asset Alloc)	B-	B-	B-	Down	Y	0
John Hancock Funds Multimanager 2050 Lifetime Port Cls A	JLKAX	NAS CM	Open End	Target Date 2046+ (Asset Alloc)	B-	B-	B-	Down	Y	1,000
John Hancock Funds Multimanager 2050 Lifetime Port Cls I	JHRPX	NAS CM	Open End	Target Date 2046+ (Asset Alloc)	B-	B-	B-	Down	Y	250,000
John Hancock Funds Multimanager 2050 Lifetime Port Cls R1	JLKDX	NAS CM	Open End	Target Date 2046+ (Asset Alloc)	B-	B-	B-	Down	Y	0
John Hancock Funds Multimanager 2050 Lifetime Port Cls R2	JLKEX	NAS CM	Open End	Target Date 2046+ (Asset Alloc)	B-	B-	B-	Down	Y	0
John Hancock Funds Multimanager 2050 Lifetime Port Cls R3	JLKFX	NAS CM	Open End	Target Date 2046+ (Asset Alloc)	B-	B-	B-	Down	Y	0
John Hancock Funds Multimanager 2050 Lifetime Port Cls R4	JLKGX	NAS CM	Open End	Target Date 2046+ (Asset Alloc)	B-	B-	B-	Down	Y	0
John Hancock Funds Multimanager 2050 Lifetime Port Cls R5	JLKHX	NAS CM	Open End	Target Date 2046+ (Asset Alloc)	B-	B-	B-	Down	Y	0
John Hancock Funds Multimanager 2050 Lifetime Port Cls R6	JLKRX	NAS CM	Open End	Target Date 2046+ (Asset Alloc)	B-	B-	B-	Down	Y	1,000,000
John Hancock Funds Multimanager 2055 Lifetime Port Cls 1	JLKUX	NAS CM	Open End	Target Date 2046+ (Asset Alloc)	B-	B-	B-	Down	Y	0
John Hancock Funds Multimanager 2055 Lifetime Port Cls A	JLKLX	NAS CM	Open End	Target Date 2046+ (Asset Alloc)	B-	B-	B-	Down	Y	1,000
John Hancock Funds Multimanager 2055 Lifetime Port Cls I	JHRTX	NAS CM	Open End	Target Date 2046+ (Asset Alloc)	B-	B-	B-	Down	Y	250,000
John Hancock Funds Multimanager 2055 Lifetime Port Cls R1	JLKMX	NAS CM	Open End	Target Date 2046+ (Asset Alloc)	B-	B-	B-	Down	Y	0
John Hancock Funds Multimanager 2055 Lifetime Port Cls R2	JLKNX	NAS CM	Open End	Target Date 2046+ (Asset Alloc)	B-	B-	B-	Down	Y	0
John Hancock Funds Multimanager 2055 Lifetime Port Cls R3	JLKPX	NAS CM	Open End	Target Date 2046+ (Asset Alloc)	B-	B-	B-	Down	Y	0
John Hancock Funds Multimanager 2055 Lifetime Port Cls R4	JLKQX	NAS CM	Open End	Target Date 2046+ (Asset Alloc)	B-	B-	B-	Down	Y	0
John Hancock Funds Multimanager 2055 Lifetime Port Cls R5	JLKSX	NAS CM	Open End	Target Date 2046+ (Asset Alloc)	B-	B-	B-	Down	Y	0
John Hancock Funds Multimanager 2055 Lifetime Port Cls R6	JLKTX	NAS CM	Open End	Target Date 2046+ (Asset Alloc)	B-	B-	B-	Down	Y	1,000,000
John Hancock Funds Multimanager 2060 Lifetime Port Cls 1	JRETX	NAS CM	Open End	Target Date 2046+ (Asset Alloc)	D+	C	B+	Up	Y	0
John Hancock Funds Multimanager 2060 Lifetime Port Cls A	JJERX	NAS CM	Open End	Target Date 2046+ (Asset Alloc)	D+	C	B+	Up	Y	1,000
John Hancock Funds Multimanager 2060 Lifetime Port Cls I	JMENX	NAS CM	Open End	Target Date 2046+ (Asset Alloc)	D+	C	B+	Up	Y	250,000
John Hancock Funds Multimanager 2060 Lifetime Port Cls R1	JTLOX	NAS CM	Open End	Target Date 2046+ (Asset Alloc)	D+	C	B+	Up	Y	0
John Hancock Funds Multimanager 2060 Lifetime Port Cls R2	JVIMX	NAS CM	Open End	Target Date 2046+ (Asset Alloc)	D+	C	B+	Up	Y	0
John Hancock Funds Multimanager 2060 Lifetime Port Cls R3	JGTHX	NAS CM	Open End	Target Date 2046+ (Asset Alloc)	D+	C	B+	Up	Y	0
John Hancock Funds Multimanager 2060 Lifetime Port Cls R4	JROUX	NAS CM	Open End	Target Date 2046+ (Asset Alloc)	D+	C	B+	Up	Y	0
John Hancock Funds Multimanager 2060 Lifetime Port Cls R5	JGHTX	NAS CM	Open End	Target Date 2046+ (Asset Alloc)	D+	C	B+	Up	Y	0
John Hancock Funds Multimanager 2060 Lifetime Port Cls R6	JESRX	NAS CM	Open End	Target Date 2046+ (Asset Alloc)	D+	C	B+	Up	Y	1,000,000
John Hancock Funds Redwood Fund Class A	JTRAX	NAS CM	Open End	Long/Short Equity (Growth)	C+	C	B	Down	Y	1,000
John Hancock Funds Redwood Fund Class C	JTRCX	NAS CM	Open End	Long/Short Equity (Growth)	C+	C	B	Up	Y	1,000
John Hancock Funds Redwood Fund Class I	JTRIX	NAS CM	Open End	Long/Short Equity (Growth)	C+	C	B	Down	Y	250,000
John Hancock Funds Redwood Fund Class NAV	US47804M8038		Open End	Long/Short Equity (Growth)	C+	C	B	Down	Y	0
John Hancock Funds Redwood Fund Class R6	JTRRX	NAS CM	Open End	Long/Short Equity (Growth)	C+	C	B	Down	Y	1,000,000
John Hancock Funds Strategic Growth Fund Class A	JSGAX	NAS CM	Open End	US Equity Large Cap Growth (Growth)	B+	B+	B	Up	Y	1,000
John Hancock Funds Strategic Growth Fund Class C	JSGCX	NAS CM	Open End	US Equity Large Cap Growth (Growth)	B	B	B		Y	1,000
John Hancock Funds Strategic Growth Fund Class I	JSGIX	NAS CM	Open End	US Equity Large Cap Growth (Growth)	B+	B+	B	Up	Y	250,000
John Hancock Funds Strategic Growth Fund Class NAV	US47803W8441		Open End	US Equity Large Cap Growth (Growth)	B+	B+	B	Up	Y	0
John Hancock Funds Strategic Growth Fund Class R2	JSGRX	NAS CM	Open End	US Equity Large Cap Growth (Growth)	B	B+	B	Down	Y	0
John Hancock Funds Strategic Growth Fund Class R4	JHSGX	NAS CM	Open End	US Equity Large Cap Growth (Growth)	B+	B+	B	Up	Y	0
John Hancock Funds Strategic Growth Fund Class R6	JSGTX	NAS CM	Open End	US Equity Large Cap Growth (Growth)	B+	B+	B	Up	Y	1,000,000
John Hancock Funds Technical Opportunities Fund Class A	JTCAX	NAS CM	Open End	US Equity Large Cap Growth (Growth)	B-	B-	C+	Up	Y	1,000
John Hancock Funds Technical Opportunities Fund Class C	JTCDX	NAS CM	Open End	US Equity Large Cap Growth (Growth)	C+	B-	C+	Up	Y	1,000
John Hancock Funds Technical Opportunities Fund Class I	JTCIX	NAS CM	Open End	US Equity Large Cap Growth (Growth)	B-	B	C+	Up	Y	250,000
John Hancock Funds Technical Opportunities Fund Class NAV	JTCNX	NAS CM	Open End	US Equity Large Cap Growth (Growth)	B-	B	C+	Up	Y	0
John Hancock Funds Technical Opportunities Fund Cls R6 New	JTOPX	NAS CM	Open End	US Equity Large Cap Growth (Growth)	B-	B	C+	Up	Y	1,000,000
John Hancock Global Cons Absolute Return Cls A	JHRAX	NAS CM	Open End	Multialternative (Income)	C-	C-	C		Y	1,000
John Hancock Global Cons Absolute Return Cls C	JHRCX	NAS CM	Open End	Multialternative (Income)	D+	D	C		Y	1,000
John Hancock Global Cons Absolute Return Cls I	JHRIX	NAS CM	Open End	Multialternative (Income)	C	C	C		Y	250,000
John Hancock Global Cons Absolute Return Cls NAV	US41014P7143		Open End	Multialternative (Income)	C	C	C		Y	0
John Hancock Global Cons Absolute Return Cls R6	JHRRX	NAS CM	Open End	Multialternative (Income)	C	C	C		Y	1,000,000

★ Expanded analysis of this fund is included in Section II.

Min Additional Investment	TOTAL RETURNS 3-Month Total Return	6-Month Total Return	1-Year Total Return	3-Year Total Return	5-Year Total Return	PERFORMANCE Dividend Yield (TTM)	Expense Ratio	3-Yr Std Deviation	3-Year Beta	ASSETS NAV	Total Assets (MIL)	ASSET ALLOCATION & TURNOVER %Cash	%Stocks	%Bonds	%Other	Turnover Ratio	BULL & BEAR Last Bull Market Total Return	Last Bear Market Total Return	FEES Front End Fee (%)	Back End Fee (%)	Inception Date
	4.35	8.53	17.53	25.61		1.57	0.67	8.24	0.79	12.13	686.1	3	76	20	0	15					Dec-13
	2.18	4.52	9.96	16.13		1.95	0.75	4.89	0.42	11.06	222.8	2	38	59	0	24					Dec-13
	2.18	4.54	9.90	16.25		1.99	0.71	4.92	0.43	11.06	222.8	2	38	59	0	24					Dec-13
	4.86	9.76	21.50	29.55	72.96	1.5	0.65	9.49		12.78	389.5	5	86	7	2	38	21.12	-19.64			Apr-11
	4.76	9.58	21.10	28.15	69.48	1.2	1.02	9.47		12.78	389.5	5	86	7	2	38	20.84	-19.72	5.00		Mar-12
	4.80	9.70	21.32	29.29	72.62	1.45	0.71	9.44		12.78	389.5	5	86	7	2	38	21.12	-19.64			Mar-15
	4.60	9.33	20.63	26.85	67.11	0.96	1.35	9.43		12.77	389.5	5	86	7	2	38	20.72	-19.79			Mar-12
	4.76	9.58	21.00	27.97	69.24	1.14	1.1	9.47		12.79	389.5	5	86	7	2	38	20.88	-19.7			Mar-12
	4.69	9.43	20.74	27.33	68.06	1.08	1.25	9.46		12.77	389.5	5	86	7	2	38	20.72	-19.79			Mar-12
	4.76	9.66	21.29	28.90	71.45	1.35	0.85	9.45		12.78	389.5	5	86	7	2	38	20.88	-19.7			Mar-12
	4.87	9.85	21.59	29.78	73.27	1.53	0.65	9.46		12.8	389.5	5	86	7	2	38	21	-19.64			Mar-12
	4.83	9.80	21.54	29.71	73.49	1.54	0.6	9.47		12.79	389.5	5	86	7	2	38	21	-19.64			Mar-12
	4.88	9.79	21.49	29.42		1.45	0.64	9.46		11.73	159.6	5	86	7	2	33					Mar-14
	4.72	9.54	21.11	27.94		1.14	1.02	9.46		11.72	159.6	5	86	7	2	33			5.00		Mar-14
	4.83	9.74	21.43	29.19		1.4	0.7	9.38		11.73	159.6	5	86	7	2	33					Mar-15
	4.71	9.53	20.88	27.60		1.07	1.34	9.43		11.72	159.6	5	86	7	2	33					Mar-14
	4.71	9.53	21.09	28.39		1.23	1.09	9.42		11.72	159.6	5	86	7	2	33					Mar-14
	4.76	9.49	20.84	27.53		1.05	1.24	9.42		11.72	159.6	5	86	7	2	33					Mar-14
	4.87	9.78	21.37	29.02		1.35	0.84	9.44		11.73	159.6	5	86	7	2	33					Mar-14
	4.81	9.72	21.51	29.48		1.47	0.64	9.42		11.73	159.6	5	86	7	2	33					Mar-14
	4.84	9.84	21.55	29.61		1.49	0.59	9.4		11.73	159.6	5	86	7	2	33					Mar-14
	4.79	9.66	21.34			1.23	0.63			12.41	29.9	5	85	7	2	24					Mar-16
	4.78	9.57	20.94			1	1.01			12.41	29.9	5	85	7	2	24			5.00		Mar-16
	4.90	9.78	21.37			1.19	0.7			12.42	29.9	5	85	7	2	24					Mar-16
	4.68	9.47	20.82			0.94	1.33			12.41	29.9	5	85	7	2	24					Mar-16
	4.75	9.63	21.10			1.1	1.08			12.41	29.9	5	85	7	2	24					Mar-16
	4.68	9.47	20.82			0.94	1.23			12.41	29.9	5	85	7	2	24					Mar-16
	4.78	9.65	21.23			1.16	0.83			12.41	29.9	5	85	7	2	24					Mar-16
	4.82	9.69	21.38			1.25	0.63			12.41	29.9	5	85	7	2	24					Mar-16
	4.92	9.79	21.49			1.26	0.58			12.42	29.9	5	85	7	2	24					Mar-16
	0.94	3.08	5.01	5.49	15.08	0	1.65	4.39	-0.77	10.69	99.7	14	87	0	-2	124	10.72		5.00		Dec-13
	0.86	2.75	4.29	3.28	11.14	0	2.35	4.35	-0.49	10.45	99.7	14	87	0	-2	124	10.27			1.00	Jun-14
	1.12	3.24	5.35	6.43	16.87	0	1.33	4.34	-0.88	10.83	99.7	14	87	0	-2	124	10.91				Dec-13
	1.11	3.22	5.41	6.88	17.46	0	1.22	4.41	-0.56	10.9	99.7	14	87	0	-2	124	10.91				Sep-11
	1.11	3.21	5.41	6.79	17.57	0	1.24	4.37	-0.55	10.9	99.7	14	87	0	-2	124	10.91				Dec-13
	5.66	12.32	28.83	37.74	114.00	0.2	1.11	10.89	0.99	17.42	1,922	3	97	0	0	94			5.00		Dec-11
	5.48	11.87	27.79	34.59	107.06	0	1.86	10.88	0.99	17.23	1,922	3	97	0	0	94				1.00	Aug-14
	5.76	12.44	29.10	38.90	117.31	0.41	0.85	10.89	0.99	17.52	1,922	3	97	0	0	94					Dec-11
	5.81	12.54	29.28	39.43	119.03	0.49	0.73	10.88	0.99	17.54	1,922	3	97	0	0	94					Dec-11
	5.63	12.24	28.68	37.43	114.82	0.16	1.25	10.92	1	17.57	1,922	3	97	0	0	94					Mar-15
	5.72	12.39	29.02	38.28	116.15	0.35	1	10.9	0.99	17.55	1,922	3	97	0	0	94					Mar-15
	5.79	12.52	29.32	39.47	119.10	0.49	0.75	10.89	0.99	17.55	1,922	3	97	0	0	94					Mar-15
	5.82	12.39	33.58	22.18	94.21	0	1.29	13.18	0.85	11.51	568.1	13	87	0	0	375	7.06	-21.09	5.00		Aug-09
	5.66	11.94	32.75	19.56	88.79	0	1.99	13.21	0.85	11.69	568.1	13	87	0	0	375	6.9	-21.16		1.00	Aug-14
	5.90	12.50	34.09	23.26	97.22	0	0.96	13.18	0.86	11.99	568.1	13	87	0	0	375	7.31	-21.01			Aug-09
	5.89	12.63	34.20	23.72	98.76	0	0.86	13.15	0.86	12.23	568.1	13	87	0	0	375	7.39	-20.9			Aug-09
	5.95	12.62	34.18	23.70	98.73		0.88	13.16	0.86	12.23	568.1	13	87	0	0	375	7.39	-20.9			Feb-17
	-0.43	-0.64	-0.75	1.15		4.91	1.14	2.23	10.34	9.24	68.3	35	0	51	7	196			3.00		Jul-13
	-0.64	-1.07	-1.49	-1.22		4.14	1.89	2.24	11.26	9.2	68.3	35	0	51	7	196				1.00	Jun-14
	-0.42	-0.53	-0.64	1.73		5.15	0.89	2.27	10.95	9.27	68.3	35	0	51	7	196					Jul-13
	-0.42	-0.53	-0.53	2.13		5.26	0.78	2.24	10.73	9.28	68.3	35	0	51	7	196					Jul-13
	-0.42	-0.53	-0.53	2.13		5.26	0.8	2.22	11.43	9.28	68.3	35	0	51	7	196					Jul-13

	MARKET		FUND TYPE, CATEGORY & OBJECTIVE		RATINGS				MINIMUMS	
Fund Name	Ticker Symbol	Traded On	Fund Type	Category and (Prospectus Objective)	Overall Rating	Reward Rating	Risk Rating	Recent Up/ Downgrade	Open to New Investors	Min Initial Investment
John Hancock Global Focused Strategies Fund Class A	JGFOX	NAS CM	Open End	Multialternative (Growth & Income)	D+	D+	B-	Up	Y	1,000
John Hancock Global Focused Strategies Fund Class C	JGFEX	NAS CM	Open End	Multialternative (Growth & Income)	D+	D+	C	Up	Y	1,000
John Hancock Global Focused Strategies Fund Class I	JGFGX	NAS CM	Open End	Multialternative (Growth & Income)	D+	D+	B-	Up	Y	250,000
John Hancock Global Focused Strategies Fund Class NAV	US47803N8285		Open End	Multialternative (Growth & Income)	D+	D+	B-	Up	Y	0
John Hancock Global Focused Strategies Fund Class R6	JGFDX	NAS CM	Open End	Multialternative (Growth & Income)	D+	D+	B-	Up	Y	1,000,000
John Hancock Global Shareholder Yield Fund Class A	JGYAX	NAS CM	Open End	Global Equity (Growth & Income)	B-	C+	B		Y	1,000
John Hancock Global Shareholder Yield Fund Class B	JGYBX	NAS CM	Open End	Global Equity (Growth & Income)	C+	C+	B-	Down		1,000
John Hancock Global Shareholder Yield Fund Class C	JGYCX	NAS CM	Open End	Global Equity (Growth & Income)	B-	C+	B-		Y	1,000
John Hancock Global Shareholder Yield Fund Class I	JGYIX	NAS CM	Open End	Global Equity (Growth & Income)	B-	C+	B		Y	250,000
John Hancock Global Shareholder Yield Fund Class NAV	US47803U4004		Open End	Global Equity (Growth & Income)	B-	C+	B		Y	0
John Hancock Global Shareholder Yield Fund Class R2	JGSRX	NAS CM	Open End	Global Equity (Growth & Income)	B-	C+	B		Y	0
John Hancock Global Shareholder Yield Fund Class R6	JGRSX	NAS CM	Open End	Global Equity (Growth & Income)	B-	C+	B		Y	1,000,000
John Hancock Greater China Opportunities Fund Class A	JCOAX	NAS CM	Open End	Greater China Equity (Growth)	B+	A	C+	Up	Y	1,000
John Hancock Greater China Opportunities Fund Class B	JCOBX	NAS CM	Open End	Greater China Equity (Growth)	B	A	C+	Up		1,000
John Hancock Greater China Opportunities Fund Class C	JCOCX	NAS CM	Open End	Greater China Equity (Growth)	B	A	C+	Up	Y	1,000
John Hancock Greater China Opportunities Fund Class I	JCOIX	NAS CM	Open End	Greater China Equity (Growth)	B+	A	C+	Up	Y	250,000
John Hancock Greater China Opportunities Fund Class NAV	JGCNX	NAS CM	Open End	Greater China Equity (Growth)	B+	A	C+	Up	Y	0
John Hancock Hedged Equity & Income Fund	HEQ	NYSE	Closed End	Global Equity (Corporate Bond)	B-	C+	B	Up	Y	
John Hancock II Capital Appreciation Value Fund Class NAV	JCAVX	NAS CM	Open End	Moderate Alloc (Growth)	B	B-	A-	Down	Y	0
John Hancock II Health Sciences Fund Class NAV	US47804M7048		Open End	Healthcare Sector Equity (Health)	B	B	B	Up	Y	0
John Hancock II International Growth Stock Fund Class NAV	JGSNX	NAS CM	Open End	Global Equity Large Cap (Growth)	B-	C+	B	Up	Y	0
John Hancock II Mid Value Fund Class NAV	JMVNX	NAS CM	Open End	US Equity Mid Cap (Growth)	B	B-	B	Up	Y	0
John Hancock II Small Cap Growth Fund Class NAV	US47804A3124		Open End	US Equity Small Cap (Small Company)	C+	C+	C	Up	Y	0
John Hancock II Small Cap Value Fund Class A	JSCAX	NAS CM	Open End	US Equity Small Cap (Small Company)	B	B	B	Up	Y	1,000
John Hancock II Small Cap Value Fund Class I	JSCBX	NAS CM	Open End	US Equity Small Cap (Small Company)	B	B	B	Up	Y	250,000
John Hancock II Small Cap Value Fund Class NAV	JSCNX	NAS CM	Open End	US Equity Small Cap (Small Company)	B	B	B	Up	Y	0
John Hancock II Small Cap Value Fund Class R6	JSCCX	NAS CM	Open End	US Equity Small Cap (Small Company)	B	B	B	Up	Y	1,000,000
John Hancock International Value Equity Fund Class A	JIEAX	NAS CM	Open End	Global Equity Large Cap (Foreign Stock)	C+	C+	C+	Up	Y	1,000
John Hancock International Value Equity Fund Class C	JIEVX	NAS CM	Open End	Global Equity Large Cap (Foreign Stock)	C+	C+	C	Up	Y	1,000
John Hancock International Value Equity Fund Class I	JIEEX	NAS CM	Open End	Global Equity Large Cap (Foreign Stock)	C+	C+	C+	Up	Y	250,000
John Hancock International Value Equity Fund Class NAV	US47803U4269		Open End	Global Equity Large Cap (Foreign Stock)	C+	C+	C+	Up	Y	0
John Hancock International Value Equity Fund Class R2	JIVSX	NAS CM	Open End	Global Equity Large Cap (Foreign Stock)	C+	C+	C+	Up	Y	0
John Hancock International Value Equity Fund Class R4	JIVTX	NAS CM	Open End	Global Equity Large Cap (Foreign Stock)	C+	C+	C+	Up	Y	0
John Hancock International Value Equity Fund Class R6	JIVUX	NAS CM	Open End	Global Equity Large Cap (Foreign Stock)	C+	C+	C+	Up	Y	1,000,000
John Hancock Preferred Income Fund	HPI	NYSE	Closed End	US Fixed Income (Income)	B	C+	A	Up	Y	
John Hancock Preferred Income Fund II	HPF	NYSE	Closed End	US Fixed Income (Income)	B	C+	A	Up	Y	
John Hancock Preferred Income Fund III	HPS	NYSE	Closed End	US Fixed Income (Income)	B	C+	A	Up	Y	
John Hancock Premium Dividend Fund	PDT	NYSE	Closed End	US Fixed Income (Income)	B	B-	A	Up	Y	
John Hancock Regional Bank Fund Class A	FRBAX	NAS CM	Open End	Financials Sector Equity (Financial)	A-	A	B	Up	Y	1,000
John Hancock Regional Bank Fund Class B	FRBFX	NAS CM	Open End	Financials Sector Equity (Financial)	A-	A	B	Up		1,000
John Hancock Regional Bank Fund Class C	FRBCX	NAS CM	Open End	Financials Sector Equity (Financial)	A-	A	B	Up	Y	1,000
John Hancock Regional Bank Fund Class I	JRBFX	NAS CM	Open End	Financials Sector Equity (Financial)	A-	A	B	Up	Y	250,000
John Hancock Regional Bank Fund Class R6	JRGRX	NAS CM	Open End	Financials Sector Equity (Financial)	A-	A	B		Y	1,000,000
John Hancock Seaport Fund Class A	JSFBX	NAS CM	Open End	Long/Short Equity (Growth)	B	C+	A-	Up	Y	1,000
John Hancock Seaport Fund Class C	JSFTX	NAS CM	Open End	Long/Short Equity (Growth)	B-	C+	B+	Up	Y	1,000
John Hancock Seaport Fund Class I	JSFDX	NAS CM	Open End	Long/Short Equity (Growth)	B	C+	A-	Up	Y	250,000
John Hancock Seaport Fund Class NAV	US47803P4506		Open End	Long/Short Equity (Growth)	B	C+	A-	Up	Y	0
John Hancock Seaport Fund Class R6	JSFRX	NAS CM	Open End	Long/Short Equity (Growth)	B	C+	A-	Up	Y	1,000,000
John Hancock Small Cap Core Fund Class I	JCCIX	NAS CM	Open End	US Equity Small Cap (Small Company)	B+	B+	B	Up	Y	250,000
John Hancock Small Cap Core Fund Class NAV	US47803P5420		Open End	US Equity Small Cap (Small Company)	B+	B+	B	Up	Y	0
John Hancock Small Cap Core Fund Class R6	JORSX	NAS CM	Open End	US Equity Small Cap (Small Company)	B+	B+	B		Y	1,000,000
John Hancock Small Company Fund Class A	JCSAX	NAS CM	Open End	US Equity Small Cap (Small Company)	B	B	B	Up	Y	1,000

★Expanded analysis of this fund is included in Section II.

Min Additional Investment	3-Month Total Return	6-Month Total Return	1-Year Total Return	3-Year Total Return	5-Year Total Return	Dividend Yield (TTM)	Expense Ratio	3-Yr Std Deviation	3-Year Beta	NAV	Total Assets (MIL)	%Cash	%Stocks	%Bonds	%Other	Turnover Ratio	Last Bull Market Total Return	Last Bear Market Total Return	Front End Fee (%)	Back End Fee (%)	Inception Date
	TOTAL RETURNS					PERFORMANCE				ASSETS		ASSET ALLOCATION & TURNOVER					BULL & BEAR		FEES		
	-0.51	0.39	2.69			0.62	2			9.78	46.9	39	44	6	7	91			5.00		Apr-16
	-0.72	-0.01	1.96			0.08	2.75			9.71	46.9	39	44	6	7	91				1.00	Apr-16
	-0.51	0.39	2.90			0.8	1.73			9.8	46.9	39	44	6	7	91					Apr-16
	-0.51	0.49	3.00			0.89	1.62			9.81	46.9	39	44	6	7	91					Apr-16
	-0.51	0.49	3.00			0.89	1.62			9.81	46.9	39	44	6	7	91					Apr-16
	3.18	6.69	16.49	17.03	55.51	2.59	1.09	9.08	0.73	11.75	2,491	5	95	0	0	25	13.45	-12.26	5.00		Mar-07
	2.89	6.20	15.62	14.54	49.74	1.91	1.84	9.12	0.73	11.76	2,491	5	95	0	0	25	13.05	-12.58		5.00	Mar-07
	2.98	6.29	15.61	14.61	50.08	1.91	1.84	9.07	0.72	11.77	2,491	5	95	0	0	25	12.92	-12.48		1.00	Mar-07
	3.23	6.80	16.71	18.10	57.81	2.83	0.84	9.1	0.73	11.79	2,491	5	95	0	0	25	13.67	-12.03			Mar-07
	3.17	6.86	16.84	18.40	58.84	2.92	0.86	9.11	0.73	11.78	2,491	5	95	0	0	25	13.7	-12			Apr-08
	3.12	6.58	16.35	16.66	54.54	2.46	1.24	9.06	0.72	11.8	2,491	5	95	0	0	25	13.41	-12.12			Mar-12
	3.17	6.77	16.85	18.42	58.62	2.93	0.74	9.03	0.72	11.77	2,491	5	95	0	0	25	13.67	-12.02			Sep-11
	9.62	25.12	53.77	46.48	71.58	0.86	1.72	17.97	1.02	25.59	67.0	0	100	0	0	55	14.15	-29.87	5.00		Jun-05
	9.42	24.57	52.52	43.29	64.87	0.42	2.42	17.92	1.02	24.52	67.0	0	100	0	0	55	13.65	-30.1		5.00	Jun-05
	9.42	24.62	52.58	43.27	64.94	0.41	2.42	17.96	1.02	24.53	67.0	0	100	0	0	55	13.67	-30.11		1.00	Jun-05
	9.73	25.24	54.20	48.02	74.85	1.12	1.34	17.94	1.02	25.46	67.0	0	100	0	0	55	14.32	-29.84			Jun-05
	9.75	25.30	54.30	48.23	75.34	1.13	1.3	17.97	1.02	25.84	67.0	0	100	0	0	55	14.56	-29.73			Dec-06
	2.42	6.29	15.14	26.09	54.35	3.06	1.2	7.27		17.64	218.8	1	79	14	6	43	19.36				May-11
	2.87	5.60	15.25	30.41	81.42	1.56	0.85	6.44	0.6	11.42	1,907	1	62	21	12	61	19.92	-12.88			Jan-11
	1.47	6.07	26.66	26.74	157.53	0	1.1	15.73	0.98	4.3	325.2	0	99	1	0	131	27.6				Sep-11
	2.64	7.11	22.03	17.65	42.24	1.23	0.86	10.87	0.88	14.17	831.7	8	91	0	1	37	17.01	-20.05			Sep-10
	5.11	7.94	11.21	32.14	96.22	0.78	0.99	10.59	0.98	16.29	1,419	3	89	0	8	55	20.45	-19.57			Jan-09
	5.19	11.72	26.48	16.67	84.16	0	1.06	15.33	0.99	9.99	241.2	7	92	0	1	101	25.5	-25.7			Sep-08
	2.81	6.11	3.39	22.94	77.98	0.27	1.58	14.07	0.95	21.03	536.2	7	93	0	0	26	27.36	-21.49	5.00		Dec-13
	2.92	6.31	3.73	24.12	80.74	0.53	1.26	14.09	0.96	21.05	536.2	7	93	0	0	26	27.58	-21.39			Dec-13
	2.93	6.33	3.84	24.54	81.75	0.62	1.15	14.06	0.95	21.03	536.2	7	93	0	0	26	27.58	-21.39			Dec-08
	2.92	6.36	3.83	24.49	81.68	0.61	1.17	14.08	0.95	21.05	536.2	7	93	0	0	26	27.58	-21.39			Dec-13
	3.57	8.26	21.25	20.16	33.18	1.38	1.33	10.85	0.88	8.7	666.9	3	96	0	1	27	13.27	-23.52	5.00		Apr-98
	3.40	7.91	20.43	17.46	28.19	0.77	2.08	10.79	0.88	8.81	666.9	3	96	0	1	27	12.78	-23.76		1.00	Aug-14
	3.69	8.50	21.67	21.10	35.15	1.6	1.07	10.8	0.88	8.71	666.9	3	96	0	1	27	13.51	-23.39			Feb-11
	3.69	8.49	21.66	21.50	36.27	1.68	0.95	10.82	0.88	8.7	666.9	3	96	0	1	27	13.41	-23.52			Dec-11
	3.53	8.20	21.13	19.67	32.57	1.31	1.47	10.83	0.88	8.74	666.9	3	96	0	1	27	13.27	-23.52			Jul-13
	3.64	8.44	21.58	20.87	34.31	1.55	1.22	10.9	0.89	8.72	666.9	3	96	0	1	27	13.27	-23.52			Jul-13
	3.68	8.49	21.67	21.51	35.62	1.69	0.97	10.85	0.88	8.69	666.9	3	96	0	1	27	13.27	-23.52			Jul-13
	1.27	1.80	11.04	24.83	45.90	6.12	0	5.39	1.19	21.52	558.0	0	15	-8	0	20	13.75	-3.72			Aug-02
	1.19	1.87	11.23	23.83	45.40	5.93	0	5.35	1	21.27	451.1	0	14	-8	0	21	12.98	-3.15			Nov-02
	1.05	1.74	11.25	24.51	47.86	6.6	0	5.34	0.97	18.95	597.4	0	14	-8	0	21	14.55	-4.61			Jun-03
	1.12	2.41	11.94	28.06	66.59	5.57		7.43	1.8	15.23	779.0	0	44	-9	0	14	16	-0.66			Dec-89
	4.07	8.91	10.49	61.27	150.29	0.5	1.28	17.76	0.83	27.63	1,946	3	96	1	0	4	38.35	-25.7	5.00		Jan-92
	3.91	8.55	9.76	57.92	141.76	0.01	1.98	17.75	0.83	26.21	1,946	3	96	1	0	4	37.8	-25.91		5.00	Oct-85
	3.90	8.53	9.74	57.93	141.78	0.01	1.98	17.74	0.83	26.26	1,946	3	96	1	0	4	37.73	-25.87		1.00	Mar-99
	4.18	9.07	10.85	59.89	144.77	0.75	0.96	17.79	0.83	27.63	1,946	3	96	1	0	4	37.8	-25.91			Sep-16
	4.21	8.95	10.17	58.51	142.66		0.87	17.76	0.83	27.63	1,946	3	96	1	0	4	37.8	-25.91			Aug-17
	2.04	3.81	15.43	17.65		0	2.01	7.52	0.6	11.05	655.8	39	57	0	3	485			5.00		Dec-13
	1.91	3.44	14.69	15.33		0	2.71	7.52	0.6	10.79	655.8	39	57	0	3	485				1.00	May-14
	2.10	3.94	15.85	18.87		0	1.69	7.53	0.6	11.21	655.8	39	57	0	3	485					Dec-13
	2.09	4.00	15.97	19.20		0	1.58	7.52	0.6	11.28	655.8	39	57	0	3	485					Dec-13
	2.09	4.00	15.86	19.20		0	1.6	7.52	0.6	11.28	655.8	39	57	0	3	485					Dec-13
	2.76	7.29	16.12	44.56		0.63	1.1	13.8	0.94	12.6	181.3	3	97	0	0	68					Dec-13
	2.80	7.41	16.24	45.03		0.71	0.99	13.77	0.94	12.6	181.3	3	97	0	0	68					Dec-13
	2.86	7.47	16.31	45.10			1.01	13.77	0.94	12.61	181.3	3	97	0	0	68					Aug-17
	3.60	8.07	12.94	26.21	83.64	0	1.44	12.75	0.87	28.23	363.4	3	97	0	0	123	27.8	-25.81	5.00		Dec-09

	MARKET			FUND TYPE, CATEGORY & OBJECTIVE	RATINGS				MINIMUMS	
Fund Name	Ticker Symbol	Traded On	Fund Type	Category and (Prospectus Objective)	Overall Rating	Reward Rating	Risk Rating	Recent Up/ Downgrade	Open to New Investors	Min Initial Investment
John Hancock Small Company Fund Class ADV	JCSDX	NAS CM	Open End	US Equity Small Cap (Small Company)	B	B	B	Up	Y	0
John Hancock Small Company Fund Class I	JCSIX	NAS CM	Open End	US Equity Small Cap (Small Company)	B	B	B	Up	Y	250,000
John Hancock Small Company Fund Class R1	JCSOX	NAS CM	Open End	US Equity Small Cap (Small Company)	B	B	B	Up	Y	0
John Hancock Small Company Fund Class R2	JCSPX	NAS CM	Open End	US Equity Small Cap (Small Company)	B	B	B	Up	Y	0
John Hancock Small Company Fund Class R3	JCSHX	NAS CM	Open End	US Equity Small Cap (Small Company)	B	B	B	Up	Y	0
John Hancock Small Company Fund Class R4	JCSFX	NAS CM	Open End	US Equity Small Cap (Small Company)	B	B	B	Up	Y	0
John Hancock Small Company Fund Class R5	JCSVX	NAS CM	Open End	US Equity Small Cap (Small Company)	B	B	B	Up	Y	0
John Hancock Small Company Fund Class R6	JCSWX	NAS CM	Open End	US Equity Small Cap (Small Company)	B	B	B	Up	Y	1,000,000
John Hancock Tax Advantage Global Shareholder Yield Fund	XHTYX	NYSE	Closed End	Global Equity (World Stock)	B-	C+	B	Up	Y	
John Hancock Tax-Advantaged Dividend Income Fund	HTD	NYSE	Closed End	Moderate Alloc (Equity-Income)	B	B-	A	Up	Y	
John Hancock U.S. Global Leaders Growth Fund Class A	USGLX	NAS CM	Open End	US Equity Large Cap Growth (Growth)	B	B-	A-		Y	1,000
John Hancock U.S. Global Leaders Growth Fund Class B	USLBX	NAS CM	Open End	US Equity Large Cap Growth (Growth)	B	B-	A-	Up		1,000
John Hancock U.S. Global Leaders Growth Fund Class C	USLCX	NAS CM	Open End	US Equity Large Cap Growth (Growth)	B	B-	A-	Up	Y	1,000
John Hancock U.S. Global Leaders Growth Fund Class I	USLIX	NAS CM	Open End	US Equity Large Cap Growth (Growth)	B	B-	A-		Y	250,000
John Hancock U.S. Global Leaders Growth Fund Class R2	USLYX	NAS CM	Open End	US Equity Large Cap Growth (Growth)	B	B-	A-	Up	Y	0
John Hancock U.S. Global Leaders Growth Fund Class R6	UGLSX	NAS CM	Open End	US Equity Large Cap Growth (Growth)	B	B-	A-		Y	1,000,000
John Hancock Value Equity Fund Class A	JVEAX	NAS CM	Open End	US Equity Large Cap Value (Equity-Income)	B	B	B	Up	Y	1,000
John Hancock Value Equity Fund Class C	JVECX	NAS CM	Open End	US Equity Large Cap Value (Equity-Income)	B-	B-	B-	Up	Y	1,000
John Hancock Value Equity Fund Class I	JVEIX	NAS CM	Open End	US Equity Large Cap Value (Equity-Income)	B-	B	B-	Up	Y	250,000
John Hancock Value Equity Fund Class NAV	US47803P3441		Open End	US Equity Large Cap Value (Equity-Income)	B-	B	B-	Up	Y	0
John Hancock Value Equity Fund Class R6	JVERX	NAS CM	Open End	US Equity Large Cap Value (Equity-Income)	B-	B	B-	Up	Y	1,000,000
John Hancock Var Ins Trust 500 Index Trust B Series I	JFIVX	NAS CM	Open End	US Equity Large Cap Blend (Growth & Income)	U	U	U		Y	0
John Hancock Var Ins Trust All Cap Core Trust Series I	JEACX	NAS CM	Open End	US Equity Large Cap Blend (Growth)	U	U	U		Y	0
John Hancock Var Ins Trust Financial Ind Trust Series I	JEFSX	NAS CM	Open End	Financials Sector Equity (Financial)	U	U	U		Y	0
John Hancock Var Ins Trust Fundament All Cap Core Trust Se	JEQAX	NAS CM	Open End	US Equity Large Cap Growth (Growth)	U	U	U		Y	0
John Hancock Var Ins Trust Intl Eq Index Trust B Series I	JIEQX	NAS CM	Open End	Global Equity Large Cap (Foreign Stock)	U	U	U		Y	0
John Hancock Var Ins Trust Mid Cap Index Trust Series I	JECIX	NAS CM	Open End	US Equity Mid Cap (Growth)	U	U	U		Y	0
John Hancock Var Ins Trust Mid Value Trust Series I	JEMUX	NAS CM	Open End	US Equity Mid Cap (Growth)	U	U	U		Y	0
John Hancock Var Ins Trust Science & Technology Trust Ser	JESTX	NAS CM	Open End	Technology Sector Equity (Technology)	U	U	U		Y	0
John Hancock Var Ins Trust Small Cap Growth Trust Series I	JESGX	NAS CM	Open End	US Equity Small Cap (Growth)	U	U	U		Y	0
John Hancock Var Ins Trust Small Cap Index Trust Series I	JESIX	NAS CM	Open End	US Equity Small Cap (Growth)	U	U	U		Y	0
John Hancock Var Ins Trust Small Cap Value Trust Series I	JESVX	NAS CM	Open End	US Equity Small Cap (Growth)	U	U	U		Y	0
John Hancock Var Ins Trust Total Stock Mkt Ind Trust Ser I	JETSX	NAS CM	Open End	US Equity Large Cap Blend (Growth & Income)	U	U	U		Y	0
John Hancock Var Ins Trust Utilities Trust Series I	JEUTX	NAS CM	Open End	Utilities Sector Equity (Utility)	U	U	U		Y	0
John Hancock Variable Insurance Trust Value Trust Series I	JEVLX	NAS CM	Open End	US Equity Mid Cap (Growth)	U	U	U		Y	0
John HancockRetirement Income 2040 Fund Class R6	JRIFX	NAS CM	Open End	Cautious Alloc (Asset Alloc)	U	U	U		Y	1,000,000
Johnson Enhanced Return Fund	JENHX	NAS CM	Open End	US Equity Large Cap Blend (Growth)	B	B	B		Y	1,000,000
Johnson Equity Income Fund	JEQIX	NAS CM	Open End	US Equity Large Cap Blend (Growth & Income)	B-	B-	B-	Down	Y	2,000
Johnson Growth Fund	JGRWX	NAS CM	Open End	US Equity Large Cap Growth (Growth)	B-	B-	B-	Down	Y	2,000
Johnson International Fund	JINTX	NAS CM	Open End	Global Equity Large Cap (Foreign Stock)	C+	C+	B-	Up	Y	2,000
Johnson Opportunity Fund	JOPPX	NAS CM	Open End	US Equity Mid Cap (Growth)	B	B	B+	Up	Y	2,000
Johnson Realty Fund	JRLTX	NAS CM	Open End	Real Estate Sector Equity (Real Estate)	B	C+	B+	Up	Y	2,000
JPMorgan Commodities Strategy Fund Class A Shares	CSAFX	NAS CM	Open End	Commodities Broad Basket (Growth & Income)	D+	D+	D	Up	Y	1,000
JPMorgan Commodities Strategy Fund Class C Shares	CCSFX	NAS CM	Open End	Commodities Broad Basket (Growth & Income)	D+	D+	D	Up	Y	1,000
JPMorgan Commodities Strategy Fund Class I Shares	CSFSX	NAS CM	Open End	Commodities Broad Basket (Growth & Income)	D+	C-	D	Up	Y	1,000,000
JPMorgan Commodities Strategy Fund Class R6 Shares	CSFVX	NAS CM	Open End	Commodities Broad Basket (Growth & Income)	D+	C-	D+	Up	Y	15,000,000
JPMorgan Diversified Fund Class A	JDVAX	NAS CM	Open End	Moderate Alloc (Balanced)	B-	C+	B	Down	Y	1,000
JPMorgan Diversified Fund Class C	JDVCX	NAS CM	Open End	Moderate Alloc (Balanced)	B-	C+	B	Down	Y	1,000
JPMorgan Diversified Fund Class I	JDVSX	NAS CM	Open End	Moderate Alloc (Balanced)	B-	C+	B	Down	Y	1,000,000
JPMorgan Diversified Fund Class L	JPDVX	NAS CM	Open End	Moderate Alloc (Balanced)	B-	C+	B	Down	Y	3,000,000
JPMorgan Diversified Fund Class R6	JDVZX	NAS CM	Open End	Moderate Alloc (Balanced)	B-	C+	B		Y	15,000,000
JPMorgan Dynamic Small Cap Growth Fund Class A	VSCOX	NAS CM	Open End	US Equity Small Cap (Small Company)	B	A	C	Up		1,000

★ Expanded analysis of this fund is included in Section II.

	TOTAL RETURNS					PERFORMANCE				ASSETS		ASSET ALLOCATION & TURNOVER					BULL & BEAR		FEES		
Min Additional Investment	3-Month Total Return	6-Month Total Return	1-Year Total Return	3-Year Total Return	5-Year Total Return	Dividend Yield (TTM)	Expense Ratio	3-Yr Std Deviation	3-Year Beta	NAV	Total Assets (MIL)	%Cash	%Stocks	%Bonds	%Other	Turnover Ratio	Last Bull Market Total Return	Last Bear Market Total Return	Front End Fee (%)	Back End Fee (%)	Inception Date
	3.64	8.15	13.07	26.54	84.53	0	1.35	12.73	0.87	28.49	363.4	3	97	0	0	123	27.99	-25.81			Dec-09
	3.67	8.24	13.31	27.34	86.47	0	1.14	12.75	0.87	29.08	363.4	3	97	0	0	123	28.13	-25.68			Dec-09
	3.47	7.88	12.52	24.79	80.30	0	1.81	12.76	0.87	27.28	363.4	3	97	0	0	123	27.59	-25.94			Apr-10
	3.54	8.00	12.82	25.82	82.67	0	1.56	12.77	0.88	28.23	363.4	3	97	0	0	123	27.8	-25.81			Mar-12
	3.55	7.96	12.69	25.22	81.27	0	1.71	12.76	0.88	27.55	363.4	3	97	0	0	123	27.66	-25.88			Apr-10
	3.66	8.16	13.18	26.83	85.08	0	1.31	12.77	0.88	28.59	363.4	3	97	0	0	123	27.92	-25.81			Apr-10
	3.67	8.26	13.33	27.44	86.73	0	1.11	12.76	0.87	29.13	363.4	3	97	0	0	123	28.15	-25.72			Apr-10
	3.71	8.25	13.37	27.74	87.57	0	1.07	12.76	0.88	29.31	363.4	3	97	0	0	123	28.19	-25.81			Sep-11
	2.26	5.29	14.14	14.95	37.72	7.04	1.3	7.96	0.59	8.85	99.6	1	98	0	1	220	11.97	-9.67			Sep-07
	0.20	1.83	11.38	28.96	80.86	4.68	0	9.02	0.6	25.23	943.0	1	58	-9	0	11	18.58	-3.64			Feb-04
	5.22	7.16	25.32	35.38	90.09	0	1.18	11.66	1.01	45.43	1,493	8	92	0	0	41	31.15	-14.43	5.00		Sep-95
	5.03	6.77	24.40	32.38	83.08	0	1.93	11.65	1.01	38.58	1,493	8	92	0	0	41	30.58	-14.72		5.00	May-02
	5.03	6.77	24.39	32.40	83.08	0	1.93	11.64	1.01	38.6	1,493	8	92	0	0	41	30.57	-14.71		1.00	May-02
	5.28	7.30	25.64	36.47	92.67	0	0.92	11.65	1.01	48.66	1,493	8	92	0	0	41	31.48	-14.3			May-02
	5.20	7.09	25.14	34.84	88.94	0	1.32	11.64	1.01	47.84	1,493	8	92	0	0	41	31.14	-14.43			Mar-12
	5.30	7.34	25.74	36.89	93.68	0	0.82	11.66	1.01	48.89	1,493	8	92	0	0	41	31.52	-14.43			Sep-11
	4.73	8.57	17.07	29.44		0.89	1.12	11.06	1.03	12.34	638.4	2	98	0	0	30			5.00		Jun-14
	4.64	8.24	16.33	26.80		0.34	1.82	11.06	1.03	12.33	638.4	2	98	0	0	30				1.00	Jun-14
	4.86	8.70	17.52	30.58		1.14	0.81	11.05	1.02	12.34	638.4	2	98	0	0	30					Jun-14
	4.87	8.80	17.62	31.26		1.21	0.7	11.07	1.03	12.35	638.4	2	98	0	0	30					Jun-14
	4.86	8.79	17.60	31.24		1.21	0.72	11.01	1.02	12.35	638.4	2	98	0	0	30					Jun-14
	2.79	10.79	12.28	36.25	99.50	1.59	0.3	11.1	1		3,913	3	97	0	0	4	24.92	-16.35			Nov-12
	4.87	11.26	8.35	31.07	95.80	0.95	0.87	11.77	1		247.9	8	91	0	1	238	24.64	-19.51			Jul-96
	0.26	12.81	-0.28	17.72	61.44	0.83	1.07	14.68	1.13		143.0	4	92	2	1	27	20.01	-19.65			Apr-01
	5.62	19.09	10.89	34.95	115.56	0	0.76	15	1.24		1,580	4	96	0	0	49	26.97	-20.63			May-03
	4.69	14.50	5.24	4.32	22.48	2.51	0.39	13.03	0.97		598.0	1	98	0	1	4	14.51	-24.49			Nov-12
	5.69	17.62	16.83	32.54	102.80	0.92	0.46	12.19	1		933.0	7	93	0	0	23	27.56	-22.71			May-00
	4.37	19.34	20.87	37.44	106.17	0.95	1.06	11.46	0.97		788.2	10	89	0	0	93	20.66	-19.45			Apr-05
	10.02	19.39	23.94	52.30	111.82	0	1.13	14.81	1.18		511.5	12	86	0	1	118	21.42	-20.58			Dec-96
	8.58	18.45	-3.33	10.90	70.87	0	1.14	16.78	0.99		407.4	13	84	0	3	87	24.97	-25.48			Apr-05
	8.80	20.79	13.53	23.37	94.77	0.96	0.53	15.09	1		442.4	12	88	0	0	19	27.71	-25.26			May-00
	3.75	15.89	17.69	29.59	103.02	0.4	1.17	14.24	0.96		677.5	7	93	0	0	22	28.22	-21.24			Apr-05
	3.21	11.86	10.67	31.87	94.09	1.25	0.58	11.26	1.01		606.5	4	96	0	0	4	25.11	-17.75			May-00
	1.19	13.85	4.16	16.65	55.29	2.98	0.92	11.95	0.82		376.4	8	88	0	1	37	14.73	-12.24			Apr-01
	3.98	18.94	7.49	20.57	96.19	0.5	0.89	13.73	1.12		538.2	4	96	0	0	26	32.8	-21.58			Dec-96
	2.13	3.24					0.51			51.19	24.4	1	24	75	0						Jul-17
100	6.21	10.94	21.38	37.23	114.06	1.37	0.36	10.15	1	16.27	135.6	10	0	90	0	65	26.05	-15.81			Dec-05
100	7.60	12.16	25.02	29.79	87.72	1.07	1.01	10.15	0.96	25.12	196.0	4	96	0	0	42	22.68	-14.93			Dec-05
100	5.89	10.29	23.60	23.69	85.98	0.44	1.01	10.05	0.95	31.79	51.5	0	100	0	0	40	22.79	-17.92			Jan-93
100	4.28	9.00	20.49	15.72	33.41	1.78	1.01	11.49	0.92	26.37	17.5	2	98	0	0	8	17.4	-25.04			Dec-08
100	6.33	10.94	16.90	33.35	104.50	0.54	1	11.31	0.88	42.89	58.4	6	94	0	0	35	28.8	-30.13			May-94
100	1.97	2.49	5.93	14.18	52.95	2.38	1	12.96	0.95	15.93	11.0	2	98	0	0	4	28.69	-15.12			Jan-98
50	4.35	6.92	0.66	-17.70	-38.65	0	0.95	13.08	1	9.11	168.1	82	0	18	0	0			5.25		Dec-12
50	4.10	6.60	0.11	-18.97	-40.16	0	1.45	13.13	1.01	8.88	168.1	82	0	18	0	0				1.00	Dec-12
	4.42	7.09	0.99	-17.05	-37.83	0	0.7	13.1	1	9.22	168.1	82	0	18	0	0					Dec-12
	4.35	7.12	1.17	-16.68	-37.37	0	0.55	13.09	1	9.28	168.1	82	0	18	0	0					Dec-12
50	3.98	8.29	17.35	21.86	54.76	1.6	1.22	7		17.69	1,574	5	64	31	0	72	18.02	-14.18	4.50		Mar-03
50	3.82	8.00	16.72	19.94	50.85	1.13	1.72	7.01		17.56	1,574	5	64	31	0	72	17.63	-14.37		1.00	Mar-03
	4.02	8.37	17.60	22.71	56.65	1.82	0.97	6.99		17.78	1,574	5	64	31	0	72	18.09	-14.04			Sep-01
	4.05	8.48	17.88	23.60	58.50	2.05	0.79	7.03		17.75	1,574	5	64	31	0	72	18.34	-13.95			Sep-93
	4.09	8.52	17.92	23.65	58.56		0.72	7.03		17.75	1,574	5	64	31	0	72	18.34	-13.95			Nov-17
50	7.94	17.69	41.45	48.81	122.90	0	1.31	17.19	1.12	23.14	199.5	2	98	0	0	41	30.62	-27.99	5.25		May-97

	MARKET		FUND TYPE, CATEGORY & OBJECTIVE		RATINGS				MINIMUMS	
Fund Name	Ticker Symbol	Traded On	Fund Type	Category and (Prospectus Objective)	Overall Rating	Reward Rating	Risk Rating	Recent Up/ Downgrade	Open to New Investors	Min Initial Investment
JPMorgan Dynamic Small Cap Growth Fund Class C	VSCCX	NAS CM	Open End	US Equity Small Cap (Small Company)	B+	A	B-	Up		1,000
JPMorgan Dynamic Small Cap Growth Fund Class I	JDSCX	NAS CM	Open End	US Equity Small Cap (Small Company)	B+	A	B-	Up		1,000,000
JPMorgan Emerging Economies Fund Class A Shares	JEEAX	NAS CM	Open End	Emerging Markets Equity (Div Emerging Mkts)	B-	B	C	Up	Y	1,000
JPMorgan Emerging Economies Fund Class C Shares	JEECX	NAS CM	Open End	Emerging Markets Equity (Div Emerging Mkts)	C+	B-	C	Up	Y	1,000
JPMorgan Emerging Economies Fund Class I Shares	JEESX	NAS CM	Open End	Emerging Markets Equity (Div Emerging Mkts)	B-	B	C	Up	Y	1,000,000
JPMorgan Emerging Economies Fund Class R5 Shares	JEERX	NAS CM	Open End	Emerging Markets Equity (Div Emerging Mkts)	B-	B	C	Up	Y	0
JPMorgan Emerging Economies Fund Class R6	JEEEX	NAS CM	Open End	Emerging Markets Equity (Div Emerging Mkts)	B-	B	C	Up	Y	15,000,000
JPMorgan Emerging Markets Equity Fund Class A	JFAMX	NAS CM	Open End	Emerging Markets Equity (Div Emerging Mkts)	B	B	C	Up	Y	1,000
JPMorgan Emerging Markets Equity Fund Class C	JEMCX	NAS CM	Open End	Emerging Markets Equity (Div Emerging Mkts)	B-	B	C	Up	Y	1,000
JPMorgan Emerging Markets Equity Fund Class I	JEMSX	NAS CM	Open End	Emerging Markets Equity (Div Emerging Mkts)	B	B+	C	Up	Y	1,000,000
JPMorgan Emerging Markets Equity Fund Class L	JMIEX	NAS CM	Open End	Emerging Markets Equity (Div Emerging Mkts)	B	B+	C	Up	Y	3,000,000
JPMorgan Emerging Markets Equity Fund Class R2	JHUJX	NAS CM	Open End	Emerging Markets Equity (Div Emerging Mkts)	B-	B	C		Y	0
JPMorgan Emerging Markets Equity Fund Class R3	JHURX	NAS CM	Open End	Emerging Markets Equity (Div Emerging Mkts)	B	B	C		Y	0
JPMorgan Emerging Markets Equity Fund Class R4	JHUKX	NAS CM	Open End	Emerging Markets Equity (Div Emerging Mkts)	B	B+	C		Y	0
JPMorgan Emerging Markets Equity Fund Class R5	JEMOX	NAS CM	Open End	Emerging Markets Equity (Div Emerging Mkts)	B	B+	C	Up	Y	0
JPMorgan Emerging Markets Equity Fund Class R6	JEMWX	NAS CM	Open End	Emerging Markets Equity (Div Emerging Mkts)	B	B+	C	Up	Y	15,000,000
JPMorgan Equity Focus Fund Class A	JPFAX	NAS CM	Open End	US Equity Large Cap Growth (Growth)	B	B	B		Y	1,000
JPMorgan Equity Focus Fund Class C	JPFCX	NAS CM	Open End	US Equity Large Cap Growth (Growth)	B	B	B		Y	1,000
JPMorgan Equity Focus Fund Class I	JPFSX	NAS CM	Open End	US Equity Large Cap Growth (Growth)	B	B	B		Y	1,000,000
JPMorgan Equity Income Fund Class A	OIEIX	NAS CM	Open End	US Equity Large Cap Value (Equity-Income)	B	B-	B+		Y	1,000
JPMorgan Equity Income Fund Class C	OINCX	NAS CM	Open End	US Equity Large Cap Value (Equity-Income)	B	B-	B		Y	1,000
JPMorgan Equity Income Fund Class I	HLIEX	NAS CM	Open End	US Equity Large Cap Value (Equity-Income)	B	B-	B+		Y	1,000,000
JPMorgan Equity Income Fund Class R2	OIEFX	NAS CM	Open End	US Equity Large Cap Value (Equity-Income)	B-	B-	B-	Down	Y	0
JPMorgan Equity Income Fund Class R3	OIEPX	NAS CM	Open End	US Equity Large Cap Value (Equity-Income)	B-	B-	B-	Down	Y	0
JPMorgan Equity Income Fund Class R4	OIEQX	NAS CM	Open End	US Equity Large Cap Value (Equity-Income)	B-	B-	B-	Down	Y	0
JPMorgan Equity Income Fund Class R5	OIERX	NAS CM	Open End	US Equity Large Cap Value (Equity-Income)	B	B	B		Y	0
JPMorgan Equity Income Fund Class R6	OIEJX	NAS CM	Open End	US Equity Large Cap Value (Equity-Income)	B	B	B+		Y	15,000,000
JPMorgan Equity Index Fund Class A	OGEAX	NAS CM	Open End	US Equity Large Cap Blend (Growth)	B	B	B		Y	1,000
JPMorgan Equity Index Fund Class C	OEICX	NAS CM	Open End	US Equity Large Cap Blend (Growth)	B	B-	B		Y	1,000
JPMorgan Equity Index Fund Class I	HLEIX	NAS CM	Open End	US Equity Large Cap Blend (Growth)	B	B	B		Y	1,000,000
JPMorgan Equity Index Fund Class R6	OGFAX	NAS CM	Open End	US Equity Large Cap Blend (Growth)	B	B	B		Y	15,000,000
JPMorgan Global Allocation Fund Class A	GAOAX	NAS CM	Open End	Alloc (Growth & Income)	B	C+	B+	Up	Y	1,000
JPMorgan Global Allocation Fund Class C	GAOCX	NAS CM	Open End	Alloc (Growth & Income)	B-	C+	B	Down	Y	1,000
JPMorgan Global Allocation Fund Class I	GAOSX	NAS CM	Open End	Alloc (Growth & Income)	B-	C+	B	Down	Y	1,000,000
JPMorgan Global Allocation Fund Class R2	GAONX	NAS CM	Open End	Alloc (Growth & Income)	B	C+	B+	Up	Y	0
JPMorgan Global Allocation Fund Class R6	GAOZX	NAS CM	Open End	Alloc (Growth & Income)	B-	C+	B		Y	15,000,000
JPMorgan Global Allocation Fund Class T	JGCTX	NAS CM	Open End	Alloc (Growth & Income)	B-	C+	B	Down	Y	1,000
JPMorgan Global Research Enhanced Index Fund Class I	JEITX	NAS CM	Open End	Global Equity (Growth)	B-	B-	B-	Down	Y	1,000,000
JPMorgan Global Research Enhanced Index Fund Class R6	JEIYX	NAS CM	Open End	Global Equity (Growth)	B-	B-	B-		Y	15,000,000
JPMorgan Global Unconstrained Equity Fund Class A	JFUAX	NAS CM	Open End	Global Equity (Foreign Stock)	B-	B-	B-	Up	Y	1,000
JPMorgan Global Unconstrained Equity Fund Class C	JFECX	NAS CM	Open End	Global Equity (Foreign Stock)	B-	B-	C+	Up	Y	1,000
JPMorgan Global Unconstrained Equity Fund Class I	JMESX	NAS CM	Open End	Global Equity (Foreign Stock)	B-	B-	B-	Up	Y	1,000,000
JPMorgan Global Unconstrained Equity Fund Class R5	JFETX	NAS CM	Open End	Global Equity (Foreign Stock)	B-	B	B-	Up	Y	0
JPMorgan Global Unconstrained Equity Fund Class R6	JFEUX	NAS CM	Open End	Global Equity (Foreign Stock)	B-	B	B-	Up	Y	15,000,000
JPMorgan Growth Advantage Fund Class A	VHIAX	NAS CM	Open End	US Equity Large Cap Growth (Aggr Growth)	A-	A	B	Up	Y	1,000
JPMorgan Growth Advantage Fund Class C	JGACX	NAS CM	Open End	US Equity Large Cap Growth (Aggr Growth)	A-	A	B	Up	Y	1,000
JPMorgan Growth Advantage Fund Class I	JGASX	NAS CM	Open End	US Equity Large Cap Growth (Aggr Growth)	A-	A	B	Up	Y	1,000,000
JPMorgan Growth Advantage Fund Class R2	JGRJX	NAS CM	Open End	US Equity Large Cap Growth (Aggr Growth)	A-	A	B		Y	0
JPMorgan Growth Advantage Fund Class R3	JGTTX	NAS CM	Open End	US Equity Large Cap Growth (Aggr Growth)	A-	A	B	Up	Y	0
JPMorgan Growth Advantage Fund Class R4	JGTUX	NAS CM	Open End	US Equity Large Cap Growth (Aggr Growth)	A-	A	B	Up	Y	0
JPMorgan Growth Advantage Fund Class R5	JGVRX	NAS CM	Open End	US Equity Large Cap Growth (Aggr Growth)	A-	A	B	Up	Y	0
JPMorgan Growth Advantage Fund Class R6	JGVVX	NAS CM	Open End	US Equity Large Cap Growth (Aggr Growth)	A-	A	B	Up	Y	15,000,000

★Expanded analysis of this fund is included in Section II.

Min Additional Investment	TOTAL RETURNS: 3-Month Total Return	6-Month Total Return	1-Year Total Return	3-Year Total Return	5-Year Total Return	PERFORMANCE: Dividend Yield (TTM)	Expense Ratio	3-Yr Std Deviation	3-Year Beta	ASSETS: NAV	Total Assets (MIL)	ASSET ALLOCATION & TURNOVER: %Cash	%Stocks	%Bonds	%Other	Turnover Ratio	BULL & BEAR: Last Bull Market Total Return	Last Bear Market Total Return	FEES: Front End Fee (%)	Back End Fee (%)	Inception Date
50	7.81	17.38	40.73	46.53	117.22	0	1.81	17.18	1.11	17.31	199.5	2	98	0	0	41	30.23	-28.13		1.00	Jan-98
	8.00	17.83	41.82	49.92	125.74	0	1.06	17.21	1.12	26.47	199.5	2	98	0	0	41	30.94	-27.92			Apr-99
50	4.83	15.31	36.68	27.01	16.21	1.02	1.14	15.34	0.95	14.85	2,032	4	96	0	0	72	23.42	-29.24	5.25		Feb-08
50	4.76	15.07	35.98	25.23	13.39	0.44	1.64	15.28	0.94	14.78	2,032	4	96	0	0	72	23.14	-29.46		1.00	Feb-08
	4.94	15.45	37.01	28.02	17.72	1.04	0.89	15.3	0.94	15.03	2,032	4	96	0	0	72	23.61	-29.16			Feb-08
	4.97	15.55	37.17	28.76	18.78	1.14	0.79	15.29	0.94	15.17	2,032	4	96	0	0	72	23.72	-29.12			Feb-08
	5.03	15.60	37.43	29.16	19.14	1.23	0.69	15.29	0.94	14.95	2,032	4	96	0	0	72	23.72	-29.12			Sep-15
50	7.29	16.42	42.13	34.17	28.26	0.37	1.24	15	0.88	29.11	4,585	3	97	0	1	23	18.56	-24.37	5.25		Sep-01
50	7.16	16.18	41.43	32.23	25.09	0.03	1.74	15	0.88	28.3	4,585	3	97	0	1	23	18.19	-24.53		1.00	Feb-06
	7.35	16.60	42.49	35.20	29.85	0.48	0.99	15.04	0.89	29.79	4,585	3	97	0	1	23	18.72	-24.29			Sep-01
	7.39	16.66	42.70	35.82	30.81	0.59	0.95	15.02	0.88	29.99	4,585	3	97	0	1	23	18.8	-24.24			Nov-93
	7.21	16.27	41.86	33.68	27.47		1.54	15.01	0.88	29.04	4,585	3	97	0	1	23	18.45	-24.4			Jul-17
	7.28	16.41	42.21	34.69	29.07		1.29	15.02	0.88	29.04	4,585	3	97	0	1	23	18.62	-24.32			Jul-17
	7.35	16.56	42.56	35.70	30.69		1.04	15.02	0.89	29.76	4,585	3	97	0	1	23	18.8	-24.24			Jul-17
	7.37	16.65	42.68	35.84	30.83	0.64	0.89	15.02	0.88	29.95	4,585	3	97	0	1	23	18.8	-24.24			Sep-16
	7.41	16.74	42.84	36.26	31.33	0.65	0.79	15	0.88	29.93	4,585	3	97	0	1	23	18.8	-24.24			Dec-13
50	7.02	11.84	24.03	38.51	113.47	0.03	1.1	11.49	1.05	30.95	217.2	4	96	0	0	84	30.31		5.25		Jul-11
50	6.86	11.54	23.42	36.43	108.27	0	1.6	11.47	1.05	29.96	217.2	4	96	0	0	84	29.9			1.00	Jul-11
	7.07	11.96	24.34	39.59	116.22	0.22	0.85	11.48	1.05	31.2	217.2	4	96	0	0	84	30.42				Jul-11
50	6.87	11.12	17.20	29.49	97.71	1.38	1.01	9.43	0.89	17.12	16,369	3	97	0	0	14	23.88	-13.2	5.25		Feb-92
50	6.71	10.80	16.58	27.59	92.76	1.07	1.5	9.45	0.89	16.81	16,369	3	97	0	0	14	23.42	-13.24		1.00	Nov-97
	6.95	11.27	17.54	30.50	100.18	1.57	0.75	9.46	0.9	17.4	16,369	3	97	0	0	14	24	-13.05			Jul-87
	6.85	11.00	16.91	28.54	95.23	1.21	1.26	9.5	0.9	17.05	16,369	3	97	0	0	14	23.64	-13.16			Feb-11
	6.89	11.07	17.21	29.54	97.72	1.42	1.04	9.45	0.9	17.1	16,369	3	97	0	0	14	23.82	-13.14			Sep-16
	6.96	11.22	17.51	30.46	100.13	1.59	0.79	9.46	0.9	17.39	16,369	3	97	0	0	14	24	-13.05			Sep-16
	6.99	11.36	17.72	31.30	102.20	1.72	0.59	9.48	0.9	17.41	16,369	3	97	0	0	14	24.12	-12.97			Feb-11
	7.02	11.42	17.84	31.58	102.84	1.8	0.5	9.43	0.89	17.4	16,369	3	97	0	0	14	23.95	-13.05			Jan-12
50	7.15	11.85	21.99	35.81	108.02	1.33	0.45	10.07	1	40.92	1,892	0	100	0	0	21	24.78	-16.4	5.25		Feb-92
50	7.01	11.50	21.29	33.03	100.70	0.83	1.15	10.07	1	40.56	1,892	0	100	0	0	21	24.27	-16.68		1.00	Nov-97
	7.23	12.00	22.33	36.85	110.67	1.54	0.2	10.09	1	40.97	1,892	0	100	0	0	21	24.97	-16.32			Jul-91
	7.27	12.09	22.52	37.16	111.14	1.67	0.05	10.09	1	40.97	1,892	0	100	0	0	21	24.97	-16.32			Sep-16
50	3.83	7.28	16.81	21.48	48.50	1.68	1.03	6.83	0.61	18.62	2,478	10	55	33	1	64	13.94		4.50		May-11
50	3.68	6.99	16.21	19.65	44.79	1.39	1.53	6.82	0.61	18.4	2,478	10	55	33	1	64	13.57			1.00	May-11
	3.87	7.36	17.11	22.34	50.35	1.86	0.78	6.79	0.61	18.69	2,478	10	55	33	1	64	14.13				May-11
	3.75	7.08	16.53	20.58	46.57	1.57	1.4	6.82	0.61	18.56	2,478	10	55	33	1	64	13.84				May-11
	3.96	7.46	17.21	22.45	50.49		0.65	6.79	0.61	18.68	2,478	10	55	33	1	64	14.13				Nov-17
50	3.78	7.18	16.76	21.37	48.41		1.03	6.8	0.61	18.6	2,478	10	55	33	1	64	13.96		2.50		Jun-17
	5.41	10.49	22.30	29.31		1.84	0.34	10.31	0.98	22.69	8,890	1	99	0	0	35					Feb-13
	5.43	10.51	22.32	29.33			0.25	10.31	0.98	22.45	8,890	1	99	0	0	35					Nov-17
50	8.48	12.40	23.21	29.96	71.92	0	1	12.73	1.1	17.02	3.8	0	100	0	0	1,256			5.25		Nov-11
50	8.43	12.19	22.68	28.04	67.74	0	1.5	12.72	1.1	16.83	3.8	0	100	0	0	1,256				1.00	Nov-11
	5.58	9.44	20.18	27.58	69.75	0.22	0.75	12.75	1.1	17.15	3.8	0	100	0	0	1,256					Nov-11
	8.64	12.68	23.78	31.73	75.81	0.55	0.65	12.74	1.1	17.1	3.8	0	100	0	0	1,256					Nov-11
	8.63	12.67	23.87	31.86	76.23	0.59	0.55	12.74	1.1	17.08	3.8	0	100	0	0	1,256					Nov-11
50	7.14	14.25	35.18	47.46	139.08	0	1.14	12.22	1.06	19.67	8,056	5	95	0	0	34	32.2	-19.09	5.25		Oct-99
50	7.03	13.99	34.52	45.41	133.16	0	1.64	12.19	1.06	17.39	8,056	5	95	0	0	34	31.92	-19.29		1.00	May-06
	7.22	14.44	35.51	48.42	141.44	0	0.89	12.2	1.06	20.22	8,056	5	95	0	0	34	32.43	-19.06			May-06
	7.24	14.27	35.04	46.57	136.44		1.39	12.21	1.06	19.65	8,056	5	95	0	0	34	32.01	-19.17			Jul-17
	7.19	14.30	35.25	47.53	139.19		1.14	12.22	1.06	19.68	8,056	5	95	0	0	34	32.2	-19.09			May-17
	7.22	14.39	35.40	47.70	139.47		0.89	12.22	1.06	20.21	8,056	5	95	0	0	34	32.2	-19.09			May-17
	7.25	14.49	35.68	49.23	143.56	0	0.74	12.18	1.06	20.56	8,056	5	95	0	0	34	32.65	-18.98			Jan-09
	7.28	14.54	35.82	49.74	143.63	0	0.64	12.23	1.06	20.65	8,056	5	95	0	0	34	32.2	-19.09			Dec-13

	MARKET			FUND TYPE, CATEGORY & OBJECTIVE	RATINGS				MINIMUMS	
Fund Name	Ticker Symbol	Traded On	Fund Type	Category and (Prospectus Objective)	Overall Rating	Reward Rating	Risk Rating	Recent Up/ Downgrade	Open to New Investors	Min Initial Investment
JPMorgan Growth And Income Fund Class A	VGRIX	NAS CM	Open End	US Equity Large Cap Value (Growth & Income)	B	B	B	Up	Y	1,000
JPMorgan Growth And Income Fund Class C	VGICX	NAS CM	Open End	US Equity Large Cap Value (Growth & Income)	B	B-	B	Up	Y	1,000
JPMorgan Growth And Income Fund Class I	VGIIX	NAS CM	Open End	US Equity Large Cap Value (Growth & Income)	B	B	B+		Y	1,000,000
JPMorgan Growth and Income Fund Class R2	VGRTX	NAS CM	Open End	US Equity Large Cap Value (Growth & Income)	B	B-	B	Up	Y	0
JPMorgan Growth and Income Fund Class R3	JGAVX	NAS CM	Open End	US Equity Large Cap Value (Growth & Income)	B	B	B		Y	0
JPMorgan Growth and Income Fund Class R4	JGRUX	NAS CM	Open End	US Equity Large Cap Value (Growth & Income)	B	B	B		Y	0
JPMorgan Growth and Income Fund Class R5	VGIFX	NAS CM	Open End	US Equity Large Cap Value (Growth & Income)	B	B	B		Y	0
JPMorgan Growth and Income Fund Class R6	VGINX	NAS CM	Open End	US Equity Large Cap Value (Growth & Income)	B	B	B		Y	15,000,000
JPMorgan Hedged Equity Fund Class A	JHQAX	NAS CM	Open End	Long/Short Equity (Growth)	B-	C+	B	Down	Y	1,000
JPMorgan Hedged Equity Fund Class C	JHQCX	NAS CM	Open End	Long/Short Equity (Growth)	B-	C+	B	Down	Y	1,000
JPMorgan Hedged Equity Fund Class I	JHEQX	NAS CM	Open End	Long/Short Equity (Growth)	B-	C+	B	Down	Y	1,000,000
JPMorgan Hedged Equity Fund Class R5	JHQPX	NAS CM	Open End	Long/Short Equity (Growth)	B-	C+	B	Down	Y	0
JPMorgan Hedged Equity Fund Class R6	JHQRX	NAS CM	Open End	Long/Short Equity (Growth)	B-	C+	B	Down	Y	15,000,000
JPMorgan Income Builder Fund Class A Shares	JNBAX	NAS CM	Open End	Cautious Alloc (Income)	B-	C+	B	Up	Y	1,000
JPMorgan Income Builder Fund Class C Shares	JNBCX	NAS CM	Open End	Cautious Alloc (Income)	B-	C+	B	Up	Y	1,000
JPMorgan Income Builder Fund Class I Shares	JNBSX	NAS CM	Open End	Cautious Alloc (Income)	B-	C+	B	Up	Y	1,000,000
JPMorgan Income Builder Fund Class R6	JNBZX	NAS CM	Open End	Cautious Alloc (Income)	B-	C+	B		Y	15,000,000
JPMorgan Income Builder Fund Class T	JIBTX	NAS CM	Open End	Cautious Alloc (Income)	B-	C+	B	Up	Y	1,000
JPMorgan Insurance Trust Global Allocation Portfolio Cls 1	US4809067428		Open End	Alloc (Growth & Income)	C+	C+	B	Down	Y	0
JPMorgan Insurance Trust Global Allocation Portfolio Cls 2	US4809067675		Open End	Alloc (Growth & Income)	C+	C+	B	Down	Y	0
JPMorgan Insurance Trust Income Builder Portfolio Class 1	US4809067345		Open End	Cautious Alloc (Growth & Income)	B-	C	B	Up	Y	0
JPMorgan Insurance Trust Income Builder Portfolio Class 2	US4809067592		Open End	Cautious Alloc (Growth & Income)	B-	C	B	Up	Y	0
JPMorgan International Equity Fund Class A	JSEAX	NAS CM	Open End	Global Equity Large Cap (Foreign Stock)	B-	B-	B-	Up	Y	1,000
JPMorgan International Equity Fund Class C	JIECX	NAS CM	Open End	Global Equity Large Cap (Foreign Stock)	B-	B-	B-	Up	Y	1,000
JPMorgan International Equity Fund Class I	VSIEX	NAS CM	Open End	Global Equity Large Cap (Foreign Stock)	B-	B-	B-	Up	Y	1,000,000
JPMorgan International Equity Fund Class R2	JIEZX	NAS CM	Open End	Global Equity Large Cap (Foreign Stock)	B-	B-	B-	Up	Y	0
JPMorgan International Equity Fund Class R5	JIERX	NAS CM	Open End	Global Equity Large Cap (Foreign Stock)	B-	B-	B-	Up	Y	0
JPMorgan International Equity Fund Class R6	JNEMX	NAS CM	Open End	Global Equity Large Cap (Foreign Stock)	B-	B	B-	Up	Y	15,000,000
JPMorgan International Equity Income Fund Class A	JEIAX	NAS CM	Open End	Global Equity Large Cap (Equity-Income)	B-	C+	B	Up	Y	1,000
JPMorgan International Equity Income Fund Class C	JEICX	NAS CM	Open End	Global Equity Large Cap (Equity-Income)	B-	C+	B	Up	Y	1,000
JPMorgan International Equity Income Fund Class I	JEISX	NAS CM	Open End	Global Equity Large Cap (Equity-Income)	B-	C+	B	Up	Y	1,000,000
JPMorgan International Equity Income Fund Class R2	JGEZX	NAS CM	Open End	Global Equity Large Cap (Equity-Income)	B-	C+	B	Up	Y	0
JPMorgan International Equity Income Fund Class R5	JEIRX	NAS CM	Open End	Global Equity Large Cap (Equity-Income)	B-	C+	B	Up	Y	0
JPMorgan International Equity Income Fund Class R6	JIEFX	NAS CM	Open End	Global Equity Large Cap (Equity-Income)	B-	C+	B	Up	Y	15,000,000
JPMorgan International Research Enhanced Equity Fund Cls A	OEIAX	NAS CM	Open End	Global Equity Large Cap (Foreign Stock)	B-	B-	B	Up	Y	1,000
JPMorgan International Research Enhanced Equity Fund Cls I	OIEAX	NAS CM	Open End	Global Equity Large Cap (Foreign Stock)	B-	B-	B	Up	Y	1,000,000
JPMorgan Intl Research Enhanced Equity Fund Cls R6	JEIQX	NAS CM	Open End	Global Equity Large Cap (Foreign Stock)	B-	B-	C+		Y	15,000,000
JPMorgan International Unconstrained Equity Fund Class A	IUAEX	NAS CM	Open End	Global Equity Large Cap (Foreign Stock)	B	B	B	Up	Y	1,000
JPMorgan International Unconstrained Equity Fund Class C	IUCEX	NAS CM	Open End	Global Equity Large Cap (Foreign Stock)	B	B	B	Up	Y	1,000
JPMorgan International Unconstrained Equity Fund Class I	IUESX	NAS CM	Open End	Global Equity Large Cap (Foreign Stock)	B	B	B	Up	Y	1,000,000
JPMorgan International Unconstrained Equity Fund Class R2	IUERX	NAS CM	Open End	Global Equity Large Cap (Foreign Stock)	B	B	B	Up	Y	0
JPMorgan International Unconstrained Equity Fund Class R5	IUEFX	NAS CM	Open End	Global Equity Large Cap (Foreign Stock)	B	B	B	Up	Y	0
JPMorgan International Unconstrained Equity Fund Class R6	IUENX	NAS CM	Open End	Global Equity Large Cap (Foreign Stock)	B	B	B	Up	Y	15,000,000
JPMorgan International Value Fund Class A	JFEAX	NAS CM	Open End	Global Equity Large Cap (Foreign Stock)	C+	C+	C	Up	Y	1,000
JPMorgan International Value Fund Class C	JIUCX	NAS CM	Open End	Global Equity Large Cap (Foreign Stock)	C+	C+	C	Up	Y	1,000
JPMorgan International Value Fund Class I	JIESX	NAS CM	Open End	Global Equity Large Cap (Foreign Stock)	C+	C+	C	Up	Y	1,000,000
JPMorgan International Value Fund Class L	JNUSX	NAS CM	Open End	Global Equity Large Cap (Foreign Stock)	C+	C+	C	Up	Y	3,000,000
JPMorgan International Value Fund Class R2	JPVZX	NAS CM	Open End	Global Equity Large Cap (Foreign Stock)	C+	C+	C	Up	Y	0
JPMorgan International Value Fund Class R5	JPVRX	NAS CM	Open End	Global Equity Large Cap (Foreign Stock)	C+	C+	C	Up	Y	0
JPMorgan International Value Fund Class R6	JNVMX	NAS CM	Open End	Global Equity Large Cap (Foreign Stock)	C+	C+	C	Up	Y	15,000,000
JPMorgan Intrepid America Fund Class A	JIAAX	NAS CM	Open End	US Equity Large Cap Blend (Growth)	B	B	B-	Up	Y	1,000
JPMorgan Intrepid America Fund Class C	JIACX	NAS CM	Open End	US Equity Large Cap Blend (Growth)	B-	B-	B-	Down	Y	1,000

★Expanded analysis of this fund is included in Section II.

	TOTAL RETURNS					PERFORMANCE				ASSETS		ASSET ALLOCATION & TURNOVER					BULL & BEAR		FEES		
Min Additional Investment	3-Month Total Return	6-Month Total Return	1-Year Total Return	3-Year Total Return	5-Year Total Return	Dividend Yield (TTM)	Expense Ratio	3-Yr Std Deviation	3-Year Beta	NAV	Total Assets (MIL)	%Cash	%Stocks	%Bonds	%Other	Turnover Ratio	Last Bull Market Total Return	Last Bear Market Total Return	Front End Fee (%)	Back End Fee (%)	Inception Date
50	7.16	12.47	17.14	29.67	103.34	1.04	0.94	10.67	1.01	50.26	586.8	3	97	0	0	28	26.95	-17.93	5.25		Sep-87
50	7.00	12.18	16.54	27.72	98.21	0.76	1.44	10.66	1.01	45.39	586.8	3	97	0	0	28	26.64	-18.11		1.00	Jan-98
	7.21	12.61	17.42	30.63	105.77	1.2	0.69	10.68	1.01	52.91	586.8	3	97	0	0	28	27.22	-17.84			Jan-96
	7.09	12.32	16.85	28.69	100.81	0.83	1.19	10.67	1.01	50.49	586.8	3	97	0	0	28	26.77	-18.02			Nov-15
	7.68	13.05	17.75	30.34	104.39		0.94	10.67	1.01	52.9	586.8	3	97	0	0	28	26.95	-17.93			Jul-17
	7.73	13.13	17.83	30.44	104.55		0.69	10.67	1.01	52.9	586.8	3	97	0	0	28	26.95	-17.93			Jul-17
	7.26	12.71	17.66	30.86	105.21	1.35	0.54	10.68	1.01	53.24	586.8	3	97	0	0	28	26.95	-17.93			Nov-15
	7.26	12.73	17.70	31.01	105.45	1.4	0.44	10.69	1.01	53.24	586.8	3	97	0	0	28	26.95	-17.93			Nov-15
50	2.90	6.16	12.44	21.01		0.79	0.85	5.98	0.53	19.29	1,443	3	97	0	0	31			5.25		Dec-13
50	2.76	5.92	11.89	19.21		0.42	1.35	5.98	0.53	19.2	1,443	3	97	0	0	31				1.00	Dec-13
	2.96	6.28	12.69	21.87		1.02	0.6	5.96	0.53	19.33	1,443	3	97	0	0	31					Dec-13
	3.00	6.36	12.92	22.61		1.17	0.4	5.97	0.53	19.36	1,443	3	97	0	0	31					Dec-13
	2.96	6.39	12.91	22.74		1.21	0.35	5.96	0.53	19.35	1,443	3	97	0	0	31					Dec-13
50	2.86	5.57	11.84	18.70	35.56	3.81	0.75	5.51	0.49	10.75	12,883	2	44	45	1	52	14.56	-11.85	4.50		May-07
50	2.64	5.32	11.20	16.95	32.16	3.33	1.25	5.5	0.49	10.72	12,883	2	44	45	1	52	14.13	-11.96		1.00	May-07
	2.80	5.64	11.88	19.18	36.50	3.96	0.6	5.54	0.49	10.76	12,883	2	44	45	1	52	14.64	-11.8			May-07
	2.81	5.65	11.89	19.19	36.51		0.52	5.54	0.49	10.76	12,883	2	44	45	1	52	14.64	-11.8			Nov-17
50	2.76	5.55	11.65	18.33	34.85		0.75	5.54	0.49	10.75	12,883	2	44	45	1	52	14.48	-11.9	2.50		Jun-17
	3.73	7.30	17.10	22.34		2.64	1.03			16.57	61.5	9	50	30	10	61					Dec-14
	3.66	7.18	16.84	21.49		2.46	1.28			16.55	61.5	9	50	30	10	61					Dec-14
	2.68	5.61	11.88	18.38		2.99	0.68			10.62	49.6	4	40	48	7	46					Dec-14
	2.69	5.53	11.70	17.58		2.8	0.93			10.62	49.6	4	40	48	7	46					Dec-14
50	5.41	12.07	29.36	27.02	38.72	0.23	0.95	12.63	1	18.04	4,061	1	99	0	0	11	18.25	-23.66	5.25		Feb-02
50	5.32	11.80	28.81	25.21	35.32	0.08	1.45	12.64	1	17.1	4,061	1	99	0	0	11	17.91	-23.83		1.00	Jan-03
	5.51	12.20	29.72	28.04	40.48	0.32	0.7	12.61	1	18.31	4,061	1	99	0	0	11	18.42	-23.6			Dec-96
	5.41	11.91	29.08	26.10	36.97	0.13	1.25	12.65	1	17.95	4,061	1	99	0	0	11	18.07	-23.73			Nov-08
	5.53	12.27	29.91	28.69	41.74	0.38	0.6	12.66	1	18.33	4,061	1	99	0	0	11	18.62	-23.58			May-06
	5.55	12.35	30.04	28.96	42.27	0.42	0.5	12.63	1	18.33	4,061	1	99	0	0	11	18.64	-23.51			Nov-10
50	3.50	7.94	19.41	16.47	44.89	2.77	0.95	9.23	0.72	16.84	202.0	1	98	0	1	162	14.85	-19.42	5.25		Feb-11
50	3.34	7.69	18.86	14.69	41.20	2.46	1.45	9.18	0.72	16.72	202.0	1	98	0	1	162	14.53	-19.62		1.00	Feb-11
	3.56	8.16	19.84	17.68	47.04	3	0.7	9.21	0.72	16.89	202.0	1	98	0	1	162	15.06	-19.41			Feb-11
	3.44	7.81	19.19	15.56	43.00	2.61	1.25	9.22	0.72	16.81	202.0	1	98	0	1	162	14.72	-19.56			Feb-11
	3.58	8.20	20.02	17.96	48.06	3.09	0.6	9.22	0.72	16.9	202.0	1	98	0	1	162	15.16	-19.3			Feb-11
	3.67	8.25	20.11	18.09	48.22	3.13	0.5	9.21	0.72	16.89	202.0	1	98	0	1	162	15.16	-19.3			Jan-15
50	3.64	8.44	23.34	25.66	45.12	1.83	0.6	11.98	0.97	18.75	5,126	5	95	0	1	24	11.16	-25.72	5.25		Apr-93
	3.71	8.59	23.69	26.70	47.04	2.07	0.35	12	0.97	18.96	5,126	5	95	0	1	24	11.3	-25.6			Oct-92
	3.69	8.57	23.68	26.68	47.03		0.25	12	0.97	18.89	5,126	5	95	0	1	24	11.3	-25.6			Nov-17
50	4.00	10.29	28.01	30.29	45.18	1.65	1	12.23	0.96	21.39	388.2	4	96	0	0	51			5.25		Nov-11
50	3.86	9.99	27.32	28.27	41.43	1.21	1.5	12.2	0.96	21.16	388.2	4	96	0	0	51				1.00	Nov-11
	4.05	10.49	28.46	31.58	47.31	1.88	0.75	12.24	0.96	21.63	388.2	4	96	0	0	51					Nov-11
	3.92	10.10	27.64	29.23	43.25	1.42	1.3	12.22	0.96	21.32	388.2	4	96	0	0	51					Nov-11
	4.10	10.49	28.54	31.97	48.34	1.95	0.65	12.23	0.96	21.61	388.2	4	96	0	0	51					Nov-11
	4.13	10.57	28.64	32.26	48.79	1.99	0.55	12.24	0.96	21.62	388.2	4	96	0	0	51					Nov-11
50	4.12	9.34	21.62	19.24	31.34	4.8	1	12.41	0.92	14.31	798.0	1	99	0	0	61	14.11	-25.37	5.25		Sep-01
50	4.00	9.15	21.03	17.47	28.01	4.83	1.5	12.42	0.93	13.89	798.0	1	99	0	0	61	13.72	-25.49		1.00	Jul-06
	4.19	9.51	21.99	20.35	33.12	5.26	0.75	12.4	0.92	14.64	798.0	1	99	0	0	61	14.27	-25.27			Sep-01
	4.32	9.68	22.26	20.84	34.09	5.34	0.83	12.43	0.93	14.57	798.0	1	99	0	0	61	14.25	-25.2			Nov-93
	4.05	9.29	21.40	18.33	29.62	4.79	1.3	12.4	0.92	14.07	798.0	1	99	0	0	61	13.86	-25.41			Nov-08
	4.28	9.66	22.18	20.73	33.97	5.6	0.65	12.44	0.93	14.51	798.0	1	99	0	0	61	14.26	-25.2			Sep-16
	4.23	9.67	22.37	21.34	34.98	5.61	0.55	12.41	0.92	14.52	798.0	1	99	0	0	61	14.38	-25.2			Nov-10
50	8.47	14.55	22.99	30.22	108.19	0.59	0.84	10.94	1.06	39.91	4,398	3	97	0	0	95	24.57	-18.46	5.25		Feb-05
50	8.32	14.24	22.35	28.28	103.10	0.24	1.34	10.94	1.06	39.74	4,398	3	97	0	0	95	24.18	-18.6		1.00	Feb-05

	MARKET			FUND TYPE, CATEGORY & OBJECTIVE	RATINGS				MINIMUMS	
Fund Name	Ticker Symbol	Traded On	Fund Type	Category and (Prospectus Objective)	Overall Rating	Reward Rating	Risk Rating	Recent Up/ Downgrade	Open to New Investors	Min Initial Investment
JPMorgan Intrepid America Fund Class I	JPIAX	NAS CM	Open End	US Equity Large Cap Blend (Growth)	B	B	B-	Up	Y	1,000,000
JPMorgan Intrepid America Fund Class R2	JIAZX	NAS CM	Open End	US Equity Large Cap Blend (Growth)	B-	B-	B-	Down	Y	0
JPMorgan Intrepid America Fund Class R5	JIARX	NAS CM	Open End	US Equity Large Cap Blend (Growth)	B	B	B-	Up	Y	0
JPMorgan Intrepid America Fund Class R6	JIAPX	NAS CM	Open End	US Equity Large Cap Blend (Growth)	B	B	B-	Up	Y	15,000,000
JPMorgan Intrepid European Fund Class A	VEUAX	NAS CM	Open End	Europe Equity Large Cap (Europe Stock)	B-	C+	B-	Up	Y	1,000
JPMorgan Intrepid European Fund Class C	VEUCX	NAS CM	Open End	Europe Equity Large Cap (Europe Stock)	C+	C+	B-	Up	Y	1,000
JPMorgan Intrepid European Fund Class I	JFESX	NAS CM	Open End	Europe Equity Large Cap (Europe Stock)	B-	B-	B-	Up	Y	1,000,000
JPMorgan Intrepid European Fund Class L	JFEIX	NAS CM	Open End	Europe Equity Large Cap (Europe Stock)	B-	B-	C+	Up	Y	3,000,000
JPMorgan Intrepid Growth Fund Class A	JIGAX	NAS CM	Open End	US Equity Large Cap Growth (Growth)	B+	A-	B	Up	Y	1,000
JPMorgan Intrepid Growth Fund Class C	JCICX	NAS CM	Open End	US Equity Large Cap Growth (Growth)	B	A-	B	Down	Y	1,000
JPMorgan Intrepid Growth Fund Class I	JPGSX	NAS CM	Open End	US Equity Large Cap Growth (Growth)	A-	A	B	Up	Y	1,000,000
JPMorgan Intrepid Growth Fund Class R2	JIGZX	NAS CM	Open End	US Equity Large Cap Growth (Growth)	B+	A-	B	Up	Y	0
JPMorgan Intrepid Growth Fund Class R5	JGIRX	NAS CM	Open End	US Equity Large Cap Growth (Growth)	A-	A	B	Up	Y	0
JPMorgan Intrepid Growth Fund Class R6	JGISX	NAS CM	Open End	US Equity Large Cap Growth (Growth)	A-	A	B	Up	Y	15,000,000
JPMorgan Intrepid International Fund Class A	JFTAX	NAS CM	Open End	Global Equity Large Cap (Foreign Stock)	B-	C+	B	Up	Y	1,000
JPMorgan Intrepid International Fund Class C	JIICX	NAS CM	Open End	Global Equity Large Cap (Foreign Stock)	B-	C+	B	Up	Y	1,000
JPMorgan Intrepid International Fund Class I	JISIX	NAS CM	Open End	Global Equity Large Cap (Foreign Stock)	B-	B-	B	Up	Y	1,000,000
JPMorgan Intrepid International Fund Class R2	JIIZX	NAS CM	Open End	Global Equity Large Cap (Foreign Stock)	B-	C+	B	Up	Y	0
JPMorgan Intrepid International Fund Class R6	JIFFX	NAS CM	Open End	Global Equity Large Cap (Foreign Stock)	B-	B-	B	Up	Y	15,000,000
JPMorgan Intrepid Mid Cap Fund Class A	PECAX	NAS CM	Open End	US Equity Mid Cap (Growth)	B-	B-	B	Up	Y	1,000
JPMorgan Intrepid Mid Cap Fund Class C	ODMCX	NAS CM	Open End	US Equity Mid Cap (Growth)	B-	C+	B	Up	Y	1,000
JPMorgan Intrepid Mid Cap Fund Class I	WOOPX	NAS CM	Open End	US Equity Mid Cap (Growth)	B-	B-	B	Up	Y	1,000,000
JPMorgan Intrepid Mid Cap Fund Class R3	WOOOX	NAS CM	Open End	US Equity Mid Cap (Growth)	B-	B-	B	Up	Y	0
JPMorgan Intrepid Mid Cap Fund Class R4	WOOQX	NAS CM	Open End	US Equity Mid Cap (Growth)	B-	B-	B	Up	Y	0
JPMorgan Intrepid Mid Cap Fund Class R6	WOOSX	NAS CM	Open End	US Equity Mid Cap (Growth)	B-	B-	B	Up	Y	15,000,000
JPMorgan Intrepid Sustainable Equity Fund Class A Shares	JICAX	NAS CM	Open End	US Equity Large Cap Blend (Growth)	B-	B-	B-	Down	Y	1,000
JPMorgan Intrepid Sustainable Equity Fund Class C Shares	JICCX	NAS CM	Open End	US Equity Large Cap Blend (Growth)	B-	B-	B-	Down	Y	1,000
JPMorgan Intrepid Sustainable Equity Fund I Class	JIISX	NAS CM	Open End	US Equity Large Cap Blend (Growth)	B-	B-	B	Down	Y	1,000,000
JPMorgan Intrepid Value Fund Class A Shares	JIVAX	NAS CM	Open End	US Equity Large Cap Value (Growth)	B-	C+	B	Up	Y	1,000
JPMorgan Intrepid Value Fund Class C Shares	JIVCX	NAS CM	Open End	US Equity Large Cap Value (Growth)	B-	C+	B	Up	Y	1,000
JPMorgan Intrepid Value Fund Class I Shares	JPIVX	NAS CM	Open End	US Equity Large Cap Value (Growth)	B-	B-	B	Up	Y	1,000,000
JPMorgan Intrepid Value Fund Class R2 Shares	JIVZX	NAS CM	Open End	US Equity Large Cap Value (Growth)	B-	C+	B	Up	Y	0
JPMorgan Intrepid Value Fund Class R5 Shares	JIVRX	NAS CM	Open End	US Equity Large Cap Value (Growth)	B-	B-	B	Up	Y	0
JPMorgan Intrepid Value Fund Class R6 Shares	JIVMX	NAS CM	Open End	US Equity Large Cap Value (Growth)	B-	B-	B	Up	Y	15,000,000
JPMorgan Investor Balanced Fund Class A	OGIAX	NAS CM	Open End	Moderate Alloc (Balanced)	B-	C+	B	Up	Y	500
JPMorgan Investor Balanced Fund Class C	OGBCX	NAS CM	Open End	Moderate Alloc (Balanced)	B-	C+	B	Up	Y	500
JPMorgan Investor Balanced Fund Class I	OIBFX	NAS CM	Open End	Moderate Alloc (Balanced)	B-	C+	B	Up	Y	1,000,000
JPMorgan Investor Balanced Fund Class R6	JFQUX	NAS CM	Open End	Moderate Alloc (Balanced)	B-	C+	B		Y	15,000,000
JPMorgan Investor Balanced Fund Class T	JPBTX	NAS CM	Open End	Moderate Alloc (Balanced)	B-	C+	B	Up	Y	1,000
JPMorgan Investor Conservative Growth Fund Class A	OICAX	NAS CM	Open End	Cautious Alloc (Growth & Income)	B-	C+	B	Up	Y	500
JPMorgan Investor Conservative Growth Fund Class C	OCGCX	NAS CM	Open End	Cautious Alloc (Growth & Income)	B-	C	B	Up	Y	500
JPMorgan Investor Conservative Growth Fund Class I	ONCFX	NAS CM	Open End	Cautious Alloc (Growth & Income)	B-	C+	B	Up	Y	1,000,000
JPMorgan Investor Conservative Growth Fund Class R6	JFLJX	NAS CM	Open End	Cautious Alloc (Growth & Income)	B-	C+	B		Y	15,000,000
JPMorgan Investor Conservative Growth Fund Class T	JICTX	NAS CM	Open End	Cautious Alloc (Growth & Income)	B-	C+	B	Up	Y	1,000
JPMorgan Investor Growth & Income Fund Class A	ONGIX	NAS CM	Open End	Aggressive Alloc (Growth & Income)	B-	C+	B	Down	Y	500
JPMorgan Investor Growth & Income Fund Class C	ONECX	NAS CM	Open End	Aggressive Alloc (Growth & Income)	B-	C+	B	Down	Y	500
JPMorgan Investor Growth & Income Fund Class I	ONGFX	NAS CM	Open End	Aggressive Alloc (Growth & Income)	B-	C+	B	Down	Y	1,000,000
JPMorgan Investor Growth & Income Fund Class R6	JFBUX	NAS CM	Open End	Aggressive Alloc (Growth & Income)	B-	C+	B		Y	15,000,000
JPMorgan Investor Growth & Income Fund Class T	JGITX	NAS CM	Open End	Aggressive Alloc (Growth & Income)	B-	C+	B	Down	Y	1,000
JPMorgan Investor Growth Fund Class A	ONGAX	NAS CM	Open End	Aggressive Alloc (Growth)	B-	B-	B-	Down	Y	500
JPMorgan Investor Growth Fund Class C	OGGCX	NAS CM	Open End	Aggressive Alloc (Growth)	B-	B-	B-	Down	Y	500
JPMorgan Investor Growth Fund Class I	ONIFX	NAS CM	Open End	Aggressive Alloc (Growth)	B-	B-	B-	Down	Y	1,000,000

★ Expanded analysis of this fund is included in Section II.

	TOTAL RETURNS					PERFORMANCE				ASSETS		ASSET ALLOCATION & TURNOVER					BULL & BEAR		FEES		
Min Additional Investment	3-Month Total Return	6-Month Total Return	1-Year Total Return	3-Year Total Return	5-Year Total Return	Dividend Yield (TTM)	Expense Ratio	3-Yr Std Deviation	3-Year Beta	NAV	Total Assets (MIL)	%Cash	%Stocks	%Bonds	%Other	Turnover Ratio	Last Bull Market Total Return	Last Bear Market Total Return	Front End Fee (%)	Back End Fee (%)	Inception Date
	8.52	14.67	23.30	31.32	111.03	0.88	0.59	10.95	1.06	41.01	4,398	3	97	0	0	95	24.79	-18.37			Feb-03
	8.40	14.42	22.68	29.28	105.66	0.44	1.09	10.93	1.06	39.09	4,398	3	97	0	0	95	24.4	-18.54			Nov-08
	8.59	14.80	23.52	32.02	113.00	1.04	0.44	10.94	1.06	40.88	4,398	3	97	0	0	95	24.88	-18.28			May-06
	8.59	14.83	23.63	32.05	112.20	1.13	0.34	10.94	1.06	40.2	4,398	3	97	0	0	95	24.79	-18.37			Nov-15
50	0.97	6.39	22.26	18.28	52.45	1.59	1.24	11.15	0.82	26.59	963.5	3	97	0	0	142	19.25	-27.52	5.25		Nov-95
50	0.84	6.12	21.68	16.56	48.71	1.38	1.74	11.12	0.82	23.67	963.5	3	97	0	0	142	18.96	-27.66		1.00	Oct-98
	1.01	6.52	22.61	19.40	54.67	1.77	0.99	11.14	0.82	27.08	963.5	3	97	0	0	142	19.43	-27.42			Sep-01
	1.05	6.59	22.80	20.04	56.05	2.01	0.89	11.15	0.82	27.31	963.5	3	97	0	0	142	19.59	-27.39			Sep-01
50	8.09	15.44	31.54	39.96	123.86	0.47	0.84	11.02	1.01	55.84	1,148	3	97	0	0	68	24.49	-16.89	5.25		Feb-05
50	7.97	15.15	30.93	37.90	118.38	0.07	1.34	11.03	1.01	54.94	1,148	3	97	0	0	68	24.12	-17.05		1.00	Feb-05
	8.16	15.57	31.88	41.00	126.65	0.68	0.59	11.02	1.01	56.66	1,148	3	97	0	0	68	24.63	-16.79			Feb-03
	8.03	15.28	31.25	38.95	121.12	0.42	1.09	11.02	1.01	54.83	1,148	3	97	0	0	68	24.31	-16.94			Nov-08
	8.21	15.67	32.14	41.84	128.96	0.83	0.44	11.02	1.01	55.94	1,148	3	97	0	0	68	24.82	-16.73			May-06
	8.23	15.71	32.20	41.71	127.80	0.87	0.34	11.03	1.01	55.91	1,148	3	97	0	0	68	24.63	-16.79			Nov-15
50	3.03	8.88	22.82	23.90	44.28	1.69	1	11.27	0.9	22.05	3,154	2	98	0	1	38	15.71	-25.91	5.25		Apr-01
50	2.85	8.57	22.12	22.01	40.61	1.14	1.5	11.27	0.9	22.37	3,154	2	98	0	1	38	15.4	-26.05		1.00	Feb-06
	3.08	9.05	23.19	25.10	46.47	2.02	0.75	11.28	0.9	22.91	3,154	2	98	0	1	38	15.88	-25.8			Feb-06
	2.94	8.74	22.46	22.94	42.40	1.62	1.3	11.29	0.9	21.78	3,154	2	98	0	1	38	15.57	-25.97			Nov-08
	3.12	9.13	23.40	25.56	46.21	2.12	0.55	11.3	0.9	22.54	3,154	2	98	0	1	38	15.71	-25.91			May-15
50	6.07	10.15	16.70	21.39	101.41	0.15	1.14	10.34	0.97	22.55	964.4	3	97	0	0	70	26.75	-23.07	5.25		May-92
50	5.90	9.88	16.02	19.21	95.19	0.06	1.64	10.32	0.97	19.09	964.4	3	97	0	0	70	26.33	-23.3		1.00	Mar-99
	6.14	10.30	16.95	22.32	103.90	0.19	0.89	10.31	0.96	23.76	964.4	3	97	0	0	70	26.85	-23.02			May-91
	6.10	10.18	16.69	21.38	101.32	0.15	1.14	10.32	0.97	22.49	964.4	3	97	0	0	70	26.67	-23.1			Sep-16
	6.13	10.29	16.94	22.26	103.80	0.19	0.89	10.32	0.97	23.7	964.4	3	97	0	0	70	26.85	-23.02			Sep-16
	6.22	10.42	17.28	22.93	104.91	0.24	0.64	10.32	0.97	23.76	964.4	3	97	0	0	70	26.85	-23.02			Nov-15
50	4.97	10.47	20.98	31.59	106.65	0.79	0.84	10.62	1.03	40.76	20.4	4	96	0	0	53	27.98	-19.67	5.25		Feb-05
50	4.82	10.19	20.38	29.60	101.55	0.33	1.34	10.62	1.03	40.02	20.4	4	96	0	0	53	27.54	-19.8		1.00	Feb-05
	5.02	10.59	21.28	32.56	109.25	1.01	0.59	10.61	1.03	40.98	20.4	4	96	0	0	53	28.16	-19.58			Feb-03
50	7.11	12.37	16.44	20.68	90.88	1.54	0.83	11.8	1.11	34.32	1,105	2	98	0	0	81	23.7	-19.26	5.25		Feb-05
50	6.94	12.08	15.85	18.88	86.16	1.11	1.33	11.8	1.11	33.88	1,105	2	98	0	0	81	23.31	-19.38		1.00	Feb-05
	7.15	12.48	16.65	21.26	92.38	1.67	0.59	11.81	1.11	34.5	1,105	2	98	0	0	81	23.82	-19.2			Feb-03
	6.99	12.19	16.06	19.66	88.41	1.3	1.09	11.8	1.11	34.07	1,105	2	98	0	0	81	23.5	-19.31			Nov-08
	7.20	12.59	16.86	21.96	94.25	1.85	0.44	11.81	1.11	34.59	1,105	2	98	0	0	81	23.9	-19.1			May-06
	7.22	12.59	16.93	22.15	94.74	1.9	0.34	11.81	1.11	34.59	1,105	2	98	0	0	81	23.92	-19.08			Nov-10
50	3.25	6.36	13.01	18.63	46.30	1.44	1.04	5.64	-0.47	15.39	5,001	8	51	41	0	4	13.57	-10.44	4.50		Dec-96
50	2.09	5.05	11.25	15.50	41.03	0.93	1.62	5.63	-0.45	15.15	5,001	8	51	41	0	4	13.25	-10.63		1.00	Jul-97
	3.31	6.47	13.27	19.44	48.03	1.67	0.79	5.66	-0.47	15.41	5,001	8	51	41	0	4	13.68	-10.31			Dec-96
	3.35	6.55	13.36	19.53	48.14		0.64	5.66	-0.47	15.41	5,001	8	51	41	0	4	13.68	-10.31			Jul-17
50	3.24	6.34	12.99	18.55	46.19		1.04	5.66	-0.46	15.37	5,001	8	51	41	0	4	13.52	-10.4	2.50		Jun-17
50	2.04	4.27	8.93	13.14	30.25	1.76	1.01	3.69	0.06	12.77	3,733	8	31	59	0	6	9.41	-6.09	4.50		Dec-96
50	1.30	3.29	7.71	10.57	26.06	1.2	1.59	3.69	0.04	12.71	3,733	8	31	59	0	6	9.02	-6.3		1.00	Jul-97
	2.17	4.45	9.32	14.11	31.98	1.98	0.76	3.71	0.04	12.85	3,733	8	31	59	0	6	9.52	-5.97			Dec-96
	2.13	4.44	9.30	14.09	31.96		0.63	3.71	0.04	12.84	3,733	8	31	59	0	6	9.52	-5.97			Jul-17
50	2.02	4.24	8.96	13.17	30.24		1.01	3.71	0.04	12.77	3,733	8	31	59	0	6	9.36	-6.07	2.50		Jun-17
50	2.90	6.76	15.06	21.53	58.67	1.17	1.04	7.4	0.7	17.4	3,020	7	67	26	0	7	17.87	-14.08	4.50		Dec-96
50	2.88	6.56	14.46	19.65	54.61	0.68	1.62	7.4	0.71	16.9	3,020	7	67	26	0	7	17.5	-14.3		1.00	Jul-97
	2.89	6.81	15.18	22.35	60.62	1.42	0.79	7.44	0.71	17.12	3,020	7	67	26	0	7	17.97	-13.98			Dec-96
	4.45	8.46	16.97	24.24	63.11		0.65	7.45	0.71	17.12	3,020	7	67	26	0	7	17.97	-13.98			Jul-17
50	4.63	8.62	16.66	23.12	61.40		1.04	7.44	0.71		3,020	7	67	26	0	7	17.8	-14.07	2.50		Jun-17
50	3.77	8.55	19.07	26.68	80.01	0.78	1.02	9.44	0.9	20.69	2,718	4	86	9	0	8	22.31	-18.15	4.50		Dec-96
50	5.35	10.07	20.35	26.65	78.14	0.62	1.6	9.42	0.9	19.37	2,718	4	86	9	0	8	22.03	-18.4		1.00	Jul-97
	3.79	8.64	19.30	27.60	82.25	0.98	0.77	9.41	0.9	21.12	2,718	4	86	9	0	8	22.53	-18.1			Dec-96

	MARKET			FUND TYPE, CATEGORY & OBJECTIVE	RATINGS				MINIMUMS	
Fund Name	Ticker Symbol	Traded On	Fund Type	Category and (Prospectus Objective)	Overall Rating	Reward Rating	Risk Rating	Recent Up/ Downgrade	Open to New Investors	Min Initial Investment
JPMorgan Investor Growth Fund Class R6	JFTUX	NAS CM	Open End	Aggressive Alloc (Growth)	B-	B-	B-		Y	15,000,000
JPMorgan Investor Growth Fund Class T	JPITX	NAS CM	Open End	Aggressive Alloc (Growth)	B-	B-	B-	Down	Y	1,000
JPMorgan Large Cap Growth Fund Class A	OLGAX	NAS CM	Open End	US Equity Large Cap Growth (Growth)	A-	A	B	Up	Y	1,000
JPMorgan Large Cap Growth Fund Class C	OLGCX	NAS CM	Open End	US Equity Large Cap Growth (Growth)	B+	A	B	Up	Y	1,000
JPMorgan Large Cap Growth Fund Class I	SEEGX	NAS CM	Open End	US Equity Large Cap Growth (Growth)	A-	A	B	Up	Y	1,000,000
JPMorgan Large Cap Growth Fund Class R2	JLGZX	NAS CM	Open End	US Equity Large Cap Growth (Growth)	A-	A	B	Up	Y	0
JPMorgan Large Cap Growth Fund Class R3	JLGPX	NAS CM	Open End	US Equity Large Cap Growth (Growth)	A-	A	B	Up	Y	0
JPMorgan Large Cap Growth Fund Class R4	JLGQX	NAS CM	Open End	US Equity Large Cap Growth (Growth)	A-	A	B	Up	Y	0
JPMorgan Large Cap Growth Fund Class R5	JLGRX	NAS CM	Open End	US Equity Large Cap Growth (Growth)	A-	A	B	Up	Y	0
JPMorgan Large Cap Growth Fund Class R6	JLGMX	NAS CM	Open End	US Equity Large Cap Growth (Growth)	A-	A	B	Up	Y	15,000,000
JPMorgan Large Cap Value Fund Class A	OLVAX	NAS CM	Open End	US Equity Large Cap Value (Growth)	B	B	B		Y	1,000
JPMorgan Large Cap Value Fund Class C	OLVCX	NAS CM	Open End	US Equity Large Cap Value (Growth)	B	B	B		Y	1,000
JPMorgan Large Cap Value Fund Class I	HLQVX	NAS CM	Open End	US Equity Large Cap Value (Growth)	B+	B+	B	Up	Y	1,000,000
JPMorgan Large Cap Value Fund Class R2	JLVZX	NAS CM	Open End	US Equity Large Cap Value (Growth)	B	B	B		Y	0
JPMorgan Large Cap Value Fund Class R5	JLVRX	NAS CM	Open End	US Equity Large Cap Value (Growth)	B+	B+	B+	Up	Y	0
JPMorgan Large Cap Value Fund Class R6	JLVMX	NAS CM	Open End	US Equity Large Cap Value (Growth)	B+	B+	B+	Up	Y	15,000,000
JPMorgan Market Expansion Enhanced Index Fund Class A	OMEAX	NAS CM	Open End	US Equity Mid Cap (Growth)	B+	B+	B	Up	Y	1,000
JPMorgan Market Expansion Enhanced Index Fund Class C	OMECX	NAS CM	Open End	US Equity Mid Cap (Growth)	B	B+	B	Up	Y	1,000
JPMorgan Market Expansion Enhanced Index Fund Class I	PGMIX	NAS CM	Open End	US Equity Mid Cap (Growth)	B+	B+	B	Up	Y	1,000,000
JPMorgan Market Expansion Enhanced Index Fund Class R2	JMEZX	NAS CM	Open End	US Equity Mid Cap (Growth)	B+	B+	B	Up	Y	0
JPMorgan Mid Cap Equity Fund Class A	JCMAX	NAS CM	Open End	US Equity Mid Cap (Growth)	B-	B	B-	Down		1,000
JPMorgan Mid Cap Equity Fund Class C	JMCCX	NAS CM	Open End	US Equity Mid Cap (Growth)	B-	B-	C+	Down		1,000
JPMorgan Mid Cap Equity Fund Class I	VSNGX	NAS CM	Open End	US Equity Mid Cap (Growth)	B-	B	B-	Down		1,000,000
JPMorgan Mid Cap Equity Fund Class R2	JMCEX	NAS CM	Open End	US Equity Mid Cap (Growth)	B-	B	B-	Down		0
JPMorgan Mid Cap Equity Fund Class R5	JMEEX	NAS CM	Open End	US Equity Mid Cap (Growth)	B-	B	B-	Down		0
JPMorgan Mid Cap Equity Fund Class R6	JPPEX	NAS CM	Open End	US Equity Mid Cap (Growth)	B-	B	B-	Down		15,000,000
JPMorgan Mid Cap Growth Fund Class A	OSGIX	NAS CM	Open End	US Equity Mid Cap (Growth)	B	B	B	Up	Y	1,000
JPMorgan Mid Cap Growth Fund Class C	OMGCX	NAS CM	Open End	US Equity Mid Cap (Growth)	B	B	B	Up	Y	1,000
JPMorgan Mid Cap Growth Fund Class I	HLGEX	NAS CM	Open End	US Equity Mid Cap (Growth)	B	B+	B	Up	Y	1,000,000
JPMorgan Mid Cap Growth Fund Class R2	JMGZX	NAS CM	Open End	US Equity Mid Cap (Growth)	B	B	C+	Up	Y	0
JPMorgan Mid Cap Growth Fund Class R3	JMGPX	NAS CM	Open End	US Equity Mid Cap (Growth)	B	B	C+	Up	Y	0
JPMorgan Mid Cap Growth Fund Class R4	JMGQX	NAS CM	Open End	US Equity Mid Cap (Growth)	B	B+	C+	Up	Y	0
JPMorgan Mid Cap Growth Fund Class R5	JMGFX	NAS CM	Open End	US Equity Mid Cap (Growth)	B	B+	B	Up	Y	0
JPMorgan Mid Cap Growth Fund Class R6	JMGMX	NAS CM	Open End	US Equity Mid Cap (Growth)	B	B+	C+	Up	Y	15,000,000
JPMorgan Mid Cap Value Fund Class A	JAMCX	NAS CM	Open End	US Equity Mid Cap (Growth)	B	B-	B+			1,000
JPMorgan Mid Cap Value Fund Class C	JCMVX	NAS CM	Open End	US Equity Mid Cap (Growth)	B	C+	B	Up		1,000
JPMorgan Mid Cap Value Fund Class I	JMVSX	NAS CM	Open End	US Equity Mid Cap (Growth)	B	B-	B+			1,000,000
JPMorgan Mid Cap Value Fund Class L	FLMVX	NAS CM	Open End	US Equity Mid Cap (Growth)	B	B-	B+			3,000,000
JPMorgan Mid Cap Value Fund Class R2	JMVZX	NAS CM	Open End	US Equity Mid Cap (Growth)	B	B-	B			0
JPMorgan Mid Cap Value Fund Class R3	JMVPX	NAS CM	Open End	US Equity Mid Cap (Growth)	B	B-	B+		Y	0
JPMorgan Mid Cap Value Fund Class R4	JMVQX	NAS CM	Open End	US Equity Mid Cap (Growth)	B	B-	B+		Y	0
JPMorgan Mid Cap Value Fund Class R5	JMVRX	NAS CM	Open End	US Equity Mid Cap (Growth)	B	B-	B+		Y	0
JPMorgan Mid Cap Value Fund Class R6	JMVYX	NAS CM	Open End	US Equity Mid Cap (Growth)	B	B-	B+		Y	15,000,000
JPMorgan Multi-Cap Market Neutral Fund Class A	OGNAX	NAS CM	Open End	Market Neutral (Growth & Income)	C+	C	B	Up	Y	1,000
JPMorgan Multi-Cap Market Neutral Fund Class C	OGNCX	NAS CM	Open End	Market Neutral (Growth & Income)	C	C	B	Up	Y	1,000
JPMorgan Multi-Cap Market Neutral Fund Class I	OGNIX	NAS CM	Open End	Market Neutral (Growth & Income)	C+	C	B	Up	Y	1,000,000
JPMorgan Multi-Manager Alternatives Fund Class A	JMMAX	NAS CM	Open End	Multialternative (Growth)	C	C	B	Down	Y	1,000
JPMorgan Multi-Manager Alternatives Fund Class C	JMCMX	NAS CM	Open End	Multialternative (Growth)	C	C	C+	Up	Y	1,000
JPMorgan Multi-Manager Alternatives Fund Class I	JMMSX	NAS CM	Open End	Multialternative (Growth)	C+	C	B	Up	Y	1,000,000
JPMorgan Multi-Manager Alternatives Fund Class R5	JMMRX	NAS CM	Open End	Multialternative (Growth)	C+	C	B	Up	Y	0
JPMorgan Multi-Manager Alternatives Fund Class R6	JMMYX	NAS CM	Open End	Multialternative (Growth)	C+	C	B	Up	Y	15,000,000
JPMorgan Opportunistic Equity Long/Short Fund Class A	JOELX	NAS CM	Open End	Long/Short Equity (Growth)	B	C+	A+	Up	Y	1,000

★Expanded analysis of this fund is included in Section II.

	TOTAL RETURNS					PERFORMANCE				ASSETS		ASSET ALLOCATION & TURNOVER					BULL & BEAR		FEES		
Min Additional Investment	3-Month Total Return	6-Month Total Return	1-Year Total Return	3-Year Total Return	5-Year Total Return	Dividend Yield (TTM)	Expense Ratio	3-Yr Std Deviation	3-Year Beta	NAV	Total Assets (MIL)	%Cash	%Stocks	%Bonds	%Other	Turnover Ratio	Last Bull Market Total Return	Last Bear Market Total Return	Front End Fee (%)	Back End Fee (%)	Inception Date
	3.84	8.68	19.34	27.64	82.31		0.63	9.41	0.9	21.12	2,718	4	86	9	0	8	22.53	-18.1			Jul-17
50	3.77	8.54	19.04	26.69	80.05		1.02	9.41	0.9	20.67	2,718	4	86	9	0	8	22.36	-18.18	2.50		Jun-17
50	7.95	13.85	37.71	43.77	116.57	0	0.94	12.38	1.07	37.61	13,040	1	99	0	0	22	27.95	-13.05	5.25		Feb-94
50	7.81	13.55	37.01	41.60	111.23	0	1.44	12.37	1.07	30.38	13,040	1	99	0	0	22	27.6	-13.22		1.00	Nov-97
	8.00	13.95	37.98	44.45	118.30	0	0.69	12.38	1.07	37.93	13,040	1	99	0	0	22	28.05	-12.97			Feb-92
	7.86	13.67	37.32	42.63	113.82	0	1.19	12.38	1.07	36.53	13,040	1	99	0	0	22	27.74	-13.13			Nov-08
	7.94	13.82	37.62	43.40	115.64	0	0.94	12.37	1.07	37.79	13,040	1	99	0	0	22	27.86	-13.06			Sep-16
	8.03	13.96	37.99	44.45	118.31	0	0.69	12.38	1.07	37.93	13,040	1	99	0	0	22	28.05	-12.97			Sep-16
	8.06	14.06	38.22	45.29	120.47	0	0.54	12.39	1.07	38.61	13,040	1	99	0	0	22	28.25	-12.88			Apr-09
	8.09	14.13	38.37	45.71	121.41	0	0.44	12.39	1.07	38.85	13,040	1	99	0	0	22	28.29	-12.88			Nov-10
50	7.09	10.75	17.49	38.88	120.94	0.79	0.93	12.54	1.11	15.78	1,364	2	98	0	0	145	25.48	-21.45	5.25		Feb-92
50	6.98	10.51	16.92	36.77	115.26	0.44	1.44	12.52	1.1	15.17	1,364	2	98	0	0	145	25.03	-21.58		1.00	Mar-99
	7.20	10.90	17.71	39.58	122.73	0.96	0.69	12.5	1.1	15.52	1,364	2	98	0	0	145	25.44	-21.31			Mar-91
	7.09	10.63	17.15	37.73	117.98	0.53	1.19	12.53	1.11	15.67	1,364	2	98	0	0	145	25.17	-21.51			Nov-08
	7.17	10.96	17.87	40.28	124.73	1.07	0.54	12.55	1.11	15.66	1,364	2	98	0	0	145	25.69	-21.32			May-06
	7.24	11.00	17.91	40.60	125.29	1.14	0.44	12.52	1.11	15.56	1,364	2	98	0	0	145	25.61	-21.3			Nov-10
50	5.19	9.94	14.30	35.61	107.35	0.31	0.6	11.87	1.01	11.33	1,072	2	98	0	0	30	28.24	-23.33	5.25		Jul-98
50	5.06	9.64	13.68	33.16	100.68	0.2	1.1	11.9	1.01	9.5	1,072	2	98	0	0	30	27.66	-23.49		1.00	Mar-99
	5.21	9.99	14.55	36.68	109.90	0.39	0.35	11.86	1.01	11.47	1,072	2	98	0	0	30	28.49	-23.22			Jul-98
	5.13	9.85	14.04	34.78	105.02	0.25	0.83	11.88	1.01	11.16	1,072	2	98	0	0	30	28.09	-23.43			Nov-08
50	5.11	9.31	20.96	28.23	101.34	0.01	1.14	10.92	1.01	50.16	3,047	4	96	0	0	38	28.82	-20.62	5.25		Nov-09
50	4.97	9.03	20.33	26.31	96.18	0	1.64	10.91	1.01	48.42	3,047	4	96	0	0	38	28.42	-20.79		1.00	Nov-09
	5.18	9.49	21.35	29.56	104.50	0.12	0.89	10.91	1.01	50.83	3,047	4	96	0	0	38	29.05	-20.5			Dec-96
	5.03	9.17	20.63	27.25	98.75	0	1.39	10.91	1.01	49.74	3,047	4	96	0	0	38	28.67	-20.67			Mar-14
	5.20	9.55	21.46	29.94	105.29	0.16	0.74	10.92	1.01	50.82	3,047	4	96	0	0	38	29.05	-20.5			Mar-14
	5.24	9.56	21.54	30.15	105.69	0.19	0.64	10.91	1.01	50.83	3,047	4	96	0	0	38	29.05	-20.5			Mar-14
50	5.59	11.82	29.06	31.53	111.10	0	1.24	12.82	1.1	29.13	3,490	5	95	0	0	41	30.46	-23.79	5.25		Feb-92
50	5.46	11.57	28.42	29.62	105.87	0	1.74	12.78	1.1	23.08	3,490	5	95	0	0	41	30.05	-23.95		1.00	Nov-97
	5.69	12.01	29.50	32.78	114.32	0	0.93	12.81	1.1	33.43	3,490	5	95	0	0	41	30.67	-23.67			Mar-89
	5.54	11.71	28.80	30.87	109.29	0	1.49	12.8	1.1	31.68	3,490	5	95	0	0	41	30.3	-23.83			Jun-09
	5.59	11.82	29.04	31.69	111.50	0	1.24	12.79	1.1	33.28	3,490	5	95	0	0	41	30.48	-23.75			Sep-16
	5.67	11.95	29.39	32.67	114.14	0	0.99	12.8	1.1	33.4	3,490	5	95	0	0	41	30.67	-23.67			Sep-16
	5.70	12.05	29.67	33.32	115.82	0	0.79	12.82	1.1	33.79	3,490	5	95	0	0	41	30.72	-23.67			Nov-11
	5.70	12.07	29.72	33.50	116.40	0	0.74	12.81	1.1	33.92	3,490	5	95	0	0	41	30.72	-23.67			Nov-11
50	4.67	6.78	13.25	24.34	91.59	0.33	1.24	9.82	0.91	39.41	19,353	4	96	0	0	23	27.15	-17.71	5.25		Apr-01
50	4.51	6.50	12.67	22.46	86.72	0	1.75	9.83	0.91	37.93	19,353	4	96	0	0	23	26.8	-17.91		1.00	Apr-01
	4.71	6.90	13.53	25.29	93.90	0.56	0.99	9.83	0.91	39.82	19,353	4	96	0	0	23	27.35	-17.64			Oct-01
	4.67	6.91	13.67	26.04	96.03	0.73	0.75	9.83	0.91	40.28	19,353	4	96	0	0	23	27.57	-17.57			Nov-97
	4.60	6.64	12.98	23.39	89.11	0.17	1.5	9.82	0.91	37.85	19,353	4	96	0	0	23	27	-17.81			Nov-08
	4.54	6.65	13.14	24.75	93.06	0.66	1.25	9.82	0.91	39.14	19,353	4	96	0	0	23	27.39	-17.66			Sep-16
	4.58	6.77	13.37	25.61	95.36	0.72	1	9.83	0.91	39.67	19,353	4	96	0	0	23	27.57	-17.57			Sep-16
	4.66	6.85	13.57	25.91	95.82	0.76	0.85	9.82	0.91	40.24	19,353	4	96	0	0	23	27.57	-17.57			Sep-16
	4.67	6.89	13.68	26.04	96.03	0.77	0.75	9.83	0.91	40.26	19,353	4	96	0	0	23	27.57	-17.57			Sep-16
50	1.36	3.91	3.08	2.67	8.70	0	1.25	3.02	-7.78	10.36	123.7	100	0	0	0	229	1.03	-1.02	5.25		May-03
50	1.25	3.65	2.55	1.04	5.92	0	1.75	2.99	-7.27	9.65	123.7	100	0	0	0	229	0.64	-1.37		1.00	May-03
	1.43	4.00	3.30	3.40	10.03	0	0.99	2.99	-7.41	10.64	123.7	100	0	0	0	229	1.22	-0.91			May-03
50	0.52	0.98	3.01	2.56		0	2.23	2.35	-4.43	14.91	196.7	13	34	39	3	453			5.25		Nov-14
50	0.37	0.70	2.40	1.01		0	2.73	2.34	-4.04	14.71	196.7	13	34	39	3	453				1.00	Nov-14
	0.63	1.16	3.24	3.34		0	1.98	2.37	-4.37	15.02	196.7	13	34	39	3	453					Nov-14
	0.62	1.21	3.42	3.99		0	1.78	2.37	-4.7	15.07	196.7	13	34	39	3	453					Nov-14
	0.66	1.25	3.52	4.17		0	1.73	2.39	-4.63	15.09	196.7	13	34	39	3	453					Nov-14
50	4.88	4.89	16.27	25.57		0	1.86	7.77	0.48	18.03	162.9	9	91	0	0	749			5.25		Aug-14

	MARKET			FUND TYPE, CATEGORY & OBJECTIVE	RATINGS				MINIMUMS	
Fund Name	Ticker Symbol	Traded On	Fund Type	Category and (Prospectus Objective)	Overall Rating	Reward Rating	Risk Rating	Recent Up/ Downgrade	Open to New Investors	Min Initial Investment
JPMorgan Opportunistic Equity Long/Short Fund Class C	JOECX	NAS CM	Open End	Long/Short Equity (Growth)	B	C+	B+	Up	Y	1,000
JPMorgan Opportunistic Equity Long/Short Fund Class I	JOEQX	NAS CM	Open End	Long/Short Equity (Growth)	B	C+	A+	Up	Y	1,000,000
JPMorgan Opportunistic Equity Long/Short Fund Class R2	JOEZX	NAS CM	Open End	Long/Short Equity (Growth)	B	C+	A+	Up	Y	0
JPMorgan Opportunistic Equity Long/Short Fund Class R5	JOEPX	NAS CM	Open End	Long/Short Equity (Growth)	B	C+	B+	Up	Y	0
JPMorgan Opportunistic Equity Long/Short Fund Class R6	JOERX	NAS CM	Open End	Long/Short Equity (Growth)	B	C+	A+	Up	Y	15,000,000
JPMorgan Realty Income Fund Class A	URTAX	NAS CM	Open End	Real Estate Sector Equity (Real Estate)	B-	C+	B		Y	1,000
JPMorgan Realty Income Fund Class C	URTCX	NAS CM	Open End	Real Estate Sector Equity (Real Estate)	B-	C	B		Y	1,000
JPMorgan Realty Income Fund Class I	URTDX	NAS CM	Open End	Real Estate Sector Equity (Real Estate)	B-	C+	B+		Y	1,000,000
JPMorgan Realty Income Fund Class L	URTLX	NAS CM	Open End	Real Estate Sector Equity (Real Estate)	B-	C+	B+		Y	3,000,000
JPMorgan Realty Income Fund Class R5	JRIRX	NAS CM	Open End	Real Estate Sector Equity (Real Estate)	B-	C+	B+		Y	0
JPMorgan Realty Income Fund Class R6	JPINX	NAS CM	Open End	Real Estate Sector Equity (Real Estate)	B-	C+	B+		Y	15,000,000
JPMorgan Research Market Neutral Fund Class A	JMNAX	NAS CM	Open End	Market Neutral (Growth)	C	C-	B-		Y	1,000
JPMorgan Research Market Neutral Fund Class C	JMNCX	NAS CM	Open End	Market Neutral (Growth)	C	C-	C	Up	Y	1,000
JPMorgan Research Market Neutral Fund Class I	JMNSX	NAS CM	Open End	Market Neutral (Growth)	C	C	B-		Y	1,000,000
JPMorgan Research Market Neutral Fund Class L	JPMNX	NAS CM	Open End	Market Neutral (Growth)	C+	C	B	Up	Y	3,000,000
JPMorgan Small Cap Core Fund Class A	VSSBX	NAS CM	Open End	US Equity Small Cap (Small Company)	B+	A-	B	Up	Y	1,000
JPMorgan Small Cap Core Fund Class C	VSSRX	NAS CM	Open End	US Equity Small Cap (Small Company)	B+	A-	B	Up	Y	1,000
JPMorgan Small Cap Core Fund Class I	VSSWX	NAS CM	Open End	US Equity Small Cap (Small Company)	B+	A-	B	Up	Y	1,000,000
JPMorgan Small Cap Core Fund Class R2	JRJUX	NAS CM	Open End	US Equity Small Cap (Small Company)	B+	A-	B		Y	0
JPMorgan Small Cap Core Fund Class R3	JGAUX	NAS CM	Open End	US Equity Small Cap (Small Company)	B+	A-	B		Y	0
JPMorgan Small Cap Core Fund Class R4	JGREX	NAS CM	Open End	US Equity Small Cap (Small Company)	B+	A-	B		Y	0
JPMorgan Small Cap Core Fund Class R5	VSSCX	NAS CM	Open End	US Equity Small Cap (Small Company)	B+	A-	B	Up	Y	0
JPMorgan Small Cap Core Fund Class R6	VSSLX	NAS CM	Open End	US Equity Small Cap (Small Company)	B+	A-	B	Up	Y	15,000,000
JPMorgan Small Cap Equity Fund Class A	VSEAX	NAS CM	Open End	US Equity Small Cap (Small Company)	B	B	B			1,000
JPMorgan Small Cap Equity Fund Class C	JSECX	NAS CM	Open End	US Equity Small Cap (Small Company)	B	B	B			1,000
JPMorgan Small Cap Equity Fund Class I	VSEIX	NAS CM	Open End	US Equity Small Cap (Small Company)	B	B+	B			1,000,000
JPMorgan Small Cap Equity Fund Class R2	JSEZX	NAS CM	Open End	US Equity Small Cap (Small Company)	B	B	B			0
JPMorgan Small Cap Equity Fund Class R3	JSEPX	NAS CM	Open End	US Equity Small Cap (Small Company)	B	B	B		Y	0
JPMorgan Small Cap Equity Fund Class R4	JSEQX	NAS CM	Open End	US Equity Small Cap (Small Company)	B	B+	B		Y	0
JPMorgan Small Cap Equity Fund Class R5	JSERX	NAS CM	Open End	US Equity Small Cap (Small Company)	B+	B+	B	Up		0
JPMorgan Small Cap Equity Fund Class R6	VSENX	NAS CM	Open End	US Equity Small Cap (Small Company)	B	B+	B		Y	15,000,000
JPMorgan Small Cap Growth Fund Class A	PGSGX	NAS CM	Open End	US Equity Small Cap (Small Company)	B+	A	B-	Up		1,000
JPMorgan Small Cap Growth Fund Class C	OSGCX	NAS CM	Open End	US Equity Small Cap (Small Company)	B	A	C	Up		1,000
JPMorgan Small Cap Growth Fund Class I	OGGFX	NAS CM	Open End	US Equity Small Cap (Small Company)	B	A	C	Up		1,000,000
JPMorgan Small Cap Growth Fund Class L	JISGX	NAS CM	Open End	US Equity Small Cap (Small Company)	B	A	C	Up		3,000,000
JPMorgan Small Cap Growth Fund Class R2	JSGZX	NAS CM	Open End	US Equity Small Cap (Small Company)	B+	A	B-	Up		0
JPMorgan Small Cap Growth Fund Class R3	JGRQX	NAS CM	Open End	US Equity Small Cap (Small Company)	B	A	C		Y	0
JPMorgan Small Cap Growth Fund Class R4	JGLYX	NAS CM	Open End	US Equity Small Cap (Small Company)	B	A	C		Y	0
JPMorgan Small Cap Growth Fund Class R5	JGSVX	NAS CM	Open End	US Equity Small Cap (Small Company)	B	A	C	Up	Y	0
JPMorgan Small Cap Growth Fund Class R6	JGSMX	NAS CM	Open End	US Equity Small Cap (Small Company)	B	A	C	Up		15,000,000
JPMorgan Small Cap Value Fund Class A	PSOAX	NAS CM	Open End	US Equity Small Cap (Small Company)	B	B	B-	Up	Y	1,000
JPMorgan Small Cap Value Fund Class C	OSVCX	NAS CM	Open End	US Equity Small Cap (Small Company)	B	B	B-	Up	Y	1,000
JPMorgan Small Cap Value Fund Class I	PSOPX	NAS CM	Open End	US Equity Small Cap (Small Company)	B	B	B-	Up	Y	1,000,000
JPMorgan Small Cap Value Fund Class R2	JSVZX	NAS CM	Open End	US Equity Small Cap (Small Company)	B	B	B-	Up	Y	0
JPMorgan Small Cap Value Fund Class R3	JSVPX	NAS CM	Open End	US Equity Small Cap (Small Company)	B	B	B-	Up	Y	0
JPMorgan Small Cap Value Fund Class R4	JSVQX	NAS CM	Open End	US Equity Small Cap (Small Company)	B	B	B-	Up	Y	0
JPMorgan Small Cap Value Fund Class R5	JSVRX	NAS CM	Open End	US Equity Small Cap (Small Company)	B	B	B-	Up	Y	0
JPMorgan Small Cap Value Fund Class R6	JSVUX	NAS CM	Open End	US Equity Small Cap (Small Company)	B	B	B-	Up	Y	15,000,000
JPMorgan SmartRetirement® 2020 Fund Class A	JTTAX	NAS CM	Open End	Target Date 2000-2020 (Asset Alloc)	B-	C+	B	Up	Y	500
JPMorgan SmartRetirement® 2020 Fund Class C	JTTCX	NAS CM	Open End	Target Date 2000-2020 (Asset Alloc)	B-	C+	B	Up	Y	500
JPMorgan SmartRetirement® 2020 Fund Class I	JTTSX	NAS CM	Open End	Target Date 2000-2020 (Asset Alloc)	B-	C+	B	Up	Y	1,000,000
JPMorgan SmartRetirement® 2020 Fund Class R2	JTTZX	NAS CM	Open End	Target Date 2000-2020 (Asset Alloc)	B	C+	A-	Up	Y	0

★Expanded analysis of this fund is included in Section II.

	TOTAL RETURNS					PERFORMANCE				ASSETS		ASSET ALLOCATION & TURNOVER					BULL & BEAR		FEES		
Min Additional Investment	3-Month Total Return	6-Month Total Return	1-Year Total Return	3-Year Total Return	5-Year Total Return	Dividend Yield (TTM)	Expense Ratio	3-Yr Std Deviation	3-Year Beta	NAV	Total Assets (MIL)	%Cash	%Stocks	%Bonds	%Other	Turnover Ratio	Last Bull Market Total Return	Last Bear Market Total Return	Front End Fee (%)	Back End Fee (%)	Inception Date
50	4.79	4.62	15.66	23.68		0	2.36	7.72	0.48	17.71	162.9	9	91	0	0	749				1.00	Aug-14
	4.26	4.26	15.75	25.59		0	1.61	7.73	0.48	18.19	162.9	9	91	0	0	749					Aug-14
	4.81	4.75	15.93	24.62		0	2.11	7.75	0.48	17.87	162.9	9	91	0	0	749					Aug-14
	4.98	5.10	16.74	27.24		0	1.41	7.76	0.48	18.33	162.9	9	91	0	0	749					Aug-14
	5.03	5.15	16.85	27.44		0	1.36	7.76	0.48	18.36	162.9	9	91	0	0	749					Aug-14
50	1.97	2.70	3.67	8.82	46.76	1.56	1.18	13.36	0.99	13.14	2,588	4	96	0	0	116	32.15	-16.48	5.25		Jun-04
50	1.81	2.38	3.13	7.20	43.14	1.52	1.68	13.35	0.99	12.71	2,588	4	96	0	0	116	31.62	-16.59		1.00	Jun-04
	2.05	2.82	4.01	10.03	49.59		0.93	13.38	0.99	13.28	2,588	4	96	0	0	116	32.37	-16.25			Feb-17
	2.05	2.87	4.06	10.08	49.66	1.78	0.78	13.37	0.99	13.3	2,588	4	96	0	0	116	32.37	-16.25			Dec-97
	2.05	2.85	4.11	10.20	50.03	1.83	0.73	13.35	0.99	13.36	2,588	4	96	0	0	116	32.41	-16.23			May-06
	2.07	2.94	4.22	10.34	50.01	1.9	0.68	13.33	0.99	13.31	2,588	4	96	0	0	116	32.37	-16.25			Nov-15
50	0.87	1.57	5.38	-1.23	3.46	0	1.25	3.49	-7.6	14.22	214.5	98	2	0	0	298	-0.69	-3.27	5.25		Feb-02
50	0.71	1.30	4.87	-2.71	0.83	0	1.75	3.49	-8.12	13.31	214.5	98	2	0	0	298	-0.92	-3.44		1.00	Nov-09
	0.97	1.71	5.67	-0.41	4.80	0	0.99	3.54	-7.76	14.83	214.5	98	2	0	0	298	-0.54	-3.13			Nov-09
	0.95	1.75	5.85	0.04	5.84	0	0.85	3.53	-7.8	15.11	214.5	98	2	0	0	298	-0.33	-3.12			Dec-98
50	3.07	9.69	14.78	28.91	106.30	0.31	1.24	15.11	1.06	52.97	255.2	3	97	0	0	61	30.08	-27.27	5.25		May-16
50	2.95	9.41	14.21	27.00	101.23	0.14	1.74	15.1	1.06	52.64	255.2	3	97	0	0	61	29.71	-27.43		1.00	May-16
	3.15	9.84	15.09	30.07	109.21		0.99	15.11	1.06	53.17	255.2	3	97	0	0	61	30.27	-27.2			Jan-17
	4.08	10.71	15.80	29.57	106.34		1.49	15.11	1.06	53.18	255.2	3	97	0	0	61	29.9	-27.35			Jul-17
	4.16	10.85	16.10	30.55	108.93		1.24	15.11	1.06	53.19	255.2	3	97	0	0	61	30.08	-27.27			Jul-17
	4.20	10.98	16.37	31.52	111.53		0.99	15.12	1.06	53.19	255.2	3	97	0	0	61	30.27	-27.2			Jul-17
	3.20	9.95	15.29	30.30	109.57	0.25	0.8	15.12	1.06	53.29	255.2	3	97	0	0	61	30.27	-27.2			Dec-96
	3.20	9.96	15.33	30.40	109.74	0.4	0.74	15.12	1.06	53.2	255.2	3	97	0	0	61	30.27	-27.2			May-16
50	4.17	8.24	15.28	36.51	103.50	0.22	1.24	11.07	0.76	49.64	6,513	4	96	0	0	21	30.37	-20.53	5.25		Dec-94
50	4.04	7.96	14.71	34.51	98.50	0.26	1.74	11.08	0.76	37.13	6,513	4	96	0	0	21	29.97	-20.67		1.00	Feb-05
	4.22	8.38	15.58	37.70	106.51	0.35	0.99	11.07	0.76	57.22	6,513	4	96	0	0	21	30.6	-20.42			May-96
	4.09	8.10	14.98	35.50	100.97	0.19	1.49	11.06	0.76	48.76	6,513	4	96	0	0	21	30.14	-20.59			Nov-08
	4.17	8.25	15.30	36.56	103.58	0.42	1.24	11.07	0.76	49.35	6,513	4	96	0	0	21	30.37	-20.53			Sep-16
	4.23	8.37	15.57	36.98	104.20	0.42	0.99	11.09	0.76	57.13	6,513	4	96	0	0	21	30.37	-20.53			Sep-16
	4.29	8.47	15.81	38.53	108.61	0.42	0.8	11.07	0.76	57.33	6,513	4	96	0	0	21	30.72	-20.35			May-06
	4.30	8.51	15.88	37.68	105.25	0.48	0.74	11.09	0.76	57.31	6,513	4	96	0	0	21	30.37	-20.53			May-16
50	7.94	17.78	41.12	48.52	123.96	0	1.31	17.06	1.11	16.08	1,542	2	98	0	0	42	30.81	-27.92	5.25		Jul-91
50	7.78	17.47	40.34	46.32	118.14	0	1.81	17.03	1.11	11.83	1,542	2	98	0	0	42	30.51	-28.11		1.00	Nov-97
	8.00	17.95	41.49	49.60	126.71	0	1.06	17.04	1.11	17.71	1,542	2	98	0	0	42	31.07	-27.86			Mar-96
	8.01	17.97	41.70	50.27	128.26	0	0.92	17.03	1.1	18.22	1,542	2	98	0	0	42	31.16	-27.81			Feb-05
	7.85	17.59	40.78	47.41	121.11	0	1.56	17.03	1.11	15.56	1,542	2	98	0	0	42	30.71	-28.01			Nov-08
	7.98	17.82	41.18	48.57	124.04		1.31	17.06	1.11	16.08	1,542	2	98	0	0	42	30.81	-27.92			Jul-17
	8.04	17.96	41.34	48.75	124.30		1.06	17.06	1.11	16.1	1,542	2	98	0	0	42	30.81	-27.92			Jul-17
	8.07	18.03	41.77	49.32	125.17	0	0.91	17.07	1.11	18.23	1,542	2	98	0	0	42	30.81	-27.92			Sep-16
	8.06	18.07	41.80	50.74	129.53	0	0.81	17.08	1.11	18.39	1,542	2	98	0	0	42	31.13	-27.79			Nov-10
50	1.71	5.64	2.89	22.05	77.83	0.38	1.24	14.47	1.01	28.9	2,073	1	99	0	0	41	30.52	-25.42	5.25		Jan-95
50	1.56	5.38	2.29	19.87	72.53	0.2	1.74	14.46	1.01	24	2,073	1	99	0	0	41	30	-25.59		1.00	Mar-99
	1.74	5.77	3.15	22.93	80.06	0.47	0.99	14.47	1.01	30.61	2,073	1	99	0	0	41	30.68	-25.36			Jan-95
	1.63	5.48	2.57	21.05	75.53	0.26	1.49	14.46	1.01	28.64	2,073	1	99	0	0	41	30.35	-25.52			Nov-08
	1.69	5.63	2.87	21.96	77.75	0.41	1.24	14.47	1.01	28.86	2,073	1	99	0	0	41	30.49	-25.44			Sep-16
	1.74	5.75	3.08	22.85	79.94	0.47	0.99	14.48	1.01	30.58	2,073	1	99	0	0	41	30.68	-25.36			Sep-16
	1.81	5.87	3.29	23.37	81.03	0.59	0.84	14.46	1.01	30.62	2,073	1	99	0	0	41	30.74	-25.29			May-06
	1.83	5.92	3.39	23.81	81.94	0.69	0.74	14.46	1.01	30.65	2,073	1	99	0	0	41	30.75	-25.29			Feb-05
50	3.18	6.51	13.72	18.35	45.18	1.91	0.81	5.81	1	19.73	7,320	5	48	47	0	19	16.64	-12.87	4.50		May-06
50	3.03	6.20	13.04	16.10	40.49	1.28	1.41	5.82	1	19.65	7,320	5	48	47	0	19	16.25	-13.12		1.00	May-06
	3.20	6.60	13.85	18.79	45.89	1.99	0.66	5.82	1	19.8	7,320	5	48	47	0	19	16.73	-12.81			May-06
	3.04	6.25	13.27	17.33	43.10	1.58	1.2	5.8	1	19.67	7,320	5	48	47	0	19	16.48	-12.92			Nov-08

Fund Name	Ticker Symbol	Traded On	Fund Type	Category and (Prospectus Objective)	Overall Rating	Reward Rating	Risk Rating	Recent Up/ Downgrade	Open to New Investors	Min Initial Investment
	MARKET		**FUND TYPE, CATEGORY & OBJECTIVE**		**RATINGS**				**MINIMUMS**	
JPMorgan SmartRetirement® 2020 Fund Class R3	JTTPX	NAS CM	Open End	Target Date 2000-2020 (Asset Alloc)	B-	C+	B	Up	Y	0
JPMorgan SmartRetirement® 2020 Fund Class R4	JTTQX	NAS CM	Open End	Target Date 2000-2020 (Asset Alloc)	B	C+	A-	Up	Y	0
JPMorgan SmartRetirement® 2020 Fund Class R5	JTTIX	NAS CM	Open End	Target Date 2000-2020 (Asset Alloc)	B-	C+	B	Up	Y	0
JPMorgan SmartRetirement® 2020 Fund Class R6	JTTYX	NAS CM	Open End	Target Date 2000-2020 (Asset Alloc)	B-	C+	B	Up	Y	15,000,000
JPMorgan SmartRetirement® 2025 Fund Class A	JNSAX	NAS CM	Open End	Target Date 2021-2045 (Asset Alloc)	B-	C+	B	Down	Y	500
JPMorgan SmartRetirement® 2025 Fund Class C	JNSCX	NAS CM	Open End	Target Date 2021-2045 (Asset Alloc)	B	C+	B+	Up	Y	500
JPMorgan SmartRetirement® 2025 Fund Class I	JNSSX	NAS CM	Open End	Target Date 2021-2045 (Asset Alloc)	B-	C+	B	Down	Y	1,000,000
JPMorgan SmartRetirement® 2025 Fund Class R2	JNSZX	NAS CM	Open End	Target Date 2021-2045 (Asset Alloc)	B-	C+	B	Down	Y	0
JPMorgan SmartRetirement® 2025 Fund Class R3	JNSPX	NAS CM	Open End	Target Date 2021-2045 (Asset Alloc)	B-	C+	B	Down	Y	0
JPMorgan SmartRetirement® 2025 Fund Class R4	JNSQX	NAS CM	Open End	Target Date 2021-2045 (Asset Alloc)	B	C+	B+	Up	Y	0
JPMorgan SmartRetirement® 2025 Fund Class R5	JNSIX	NAS CM	Open End	Target Date 2021-2045 (Asset Alloc)	B-	C+	B	Down	Y	0
JPMorgan SmartRetirement® 2025 Fund Class R6	JNSYX	NAS CM	Open End	Target Date 2021-2045 (Asset Alloc)	B-	C+	B	Down	Y	15,000,000
JPMorgan SmartRetirement® 2030 Fund Class A	JSMAX	NAS CM	Open End	Target Date 2021-2045 (Asset Alloc)	B-	C+	B	Down	Y	500
JPMorgan SmartRetirement® 2030 Fund Class C	JSMCX	NAS CM	Open End	Target Date 2021-2045 (Asset Alloc)	B-	C+	B-	Down	Y	500
JPMorgan SmartRetirement® 2030 Fund Class I	JSMSX	NAS CM	Open End	Target Date 2021-2045 (Asset Alloc)	B-	C+	B	Down	Y	1,000,000
JPMorgan SmartRetirement® 2030 Fund Class R2	JSMZX	NAS CM	Open End	Target Date 2021-2045 (Asset Alloc)	B-	C+	B-	Down	Y	0
JPMorgan SmartRetirement® 2030 Fund Class R3	JSMNX	NAS CM	Open End	Target Date 2021-2045 (Asset Alloc)	B-	C+	B	Down	Y	0
JPMorgan SmartRetirement® 2030 Fund Class R4	JSMQX	NAS CM	Open End	Target Date 2021-2045 (Asset Alloc)	B-	C+	B	Down	Y	0
JPMorgan SmartRetirement® 2030 Fund Class R5	JSMIX	NAS CM	Open End	Target Date 2021-2045 (Asset Alloc)	B-	B-	B	Down	Y	0
JPMorgan SmartRetirement® 2030 Fund Class R6	JSMYX	NAS CM	Open End	Target Date 2021-2045 (Asset Alloc)	B-	B-	B	Down	Y	15,000,000
JPMorgan SmartRetirement® 2035 Fund Class A	SRJAX	NAS CM	Open End	Target Date 2021-2045 (Asset Alloc)	B-	B-	B-	Down	Y	500
JPMorgan SmartRetirement® 2035 Fund Class C	SRJCX	NAS CM	Open End	Target Date 2021-2045 (Asset Alloc)	B-	C+	B-	Down	Y	500
JPMorgan SmartRetirement® 2035 Fund Class I	SRJSX	NAS CM	Open End	Target Date 2021-2045 (Asset Alloc)	B-	B-	B-	Down	Y	1,000,000
JPMorgan SmartRetirement® 2035 Fund Class R2	SRJZX	NAS CM	Open End	Target Date 2021-2045 (Asset Alloc)	B-	B-	B-	Down	Y	0
JPMorgan SmartRetirement® 2035 Fund Class R3	SRJPX	NAS CM	Open End	Target Date 2021-2045 (Asset Alloc)	B-	B-	B-	Down	Y	0
JPMorgan SmartRetirement® 2035 Fund Class R4	SRJQX	NAS CM	Open End	Target Date 2021-2045 (Asset Alloc)	B-	B-	B-	Down	Y	0
JPMorgan SmartRetirement® 2035 Fund Class R5	SRJIX	NAS CM	Open End	Target Date 2021-2045 (Asset Alloc)	B-	B-	B-	Down	Y	0
JPMorgan SmartRetirement® 2035 Fund Class R6	SRJYX	NAS CM	Open End	Target Date 2021-2045 (Asset Alloc)	B-	B-	B-	Down	Y	15,000,000
JPMorgan SmartRetirement® 2040 Fund Class A	SMTAX	NAS CM	Open End	Target Date 2021-2045 (Asset Alloc)	B-	B-	B-	Down	Y	500
JPMorgan SmartRetirement® 2040 Fund Class C	SMTCX	NAS CM	Open End	Target Date 2021-2045 (Asset Alloc)	B-	B-	B-	Down	Y	500
JPMorgan SmartRetirement® 2040 Fund Class I	SMTSX	NAS CM	Open End	Target Date 2021-2045 (Asset Alloc)	B-	B-	B-	Down	Y	1,000,000
JPMorgan SmartRetirement® 2040 Fund Class R2	SMTZX	NAS CM	Open End	Target Date 2021-2045 (Asset Alloc)	B-	B-	B-	Down	Y	0
JPMorgan SmartRetirement® 2040 Fund Class R3	SMTPX	NAS CM	Open End	Target Date 2021-2045 (Asset Alloc)	B-	B-	B-	Down	Y	0
JPMorgan SmartRetirement® 2040 Fund Class R4	SMTQX	NAS CM	Open End	Target Date 2021-2045 (Asset Alloc)	B-	B-	B-	Down	Y	0
JPMorgan SmartRetirement® 2040 Fund Class R5	SMTIX	NAS CM	Open End	Target Date 2021-2045 (Asset Alloc)	B-	B-	B-	Down	Y	0
JPMorgan SmartRetirement® 2040 Fund Class R6	SMTYX	NAS CM	Open End	Target Date 2021-2045 (Asset Alloc)	B-	B-	B-	Down	Y	15,000,000
JPMorgan SmartRetirement® 2045 Fund Class A	JSAAX	NAS CM	Open End	Target Date 2021-2045 (Asset Alloc)	B-	B-	B-	Down	Y	500
JPMorgan SmartRetirement® 2045 Fund Class C	JSACX	NAS CM	Open End	Target Date 2021-2045 (Asset Alloc)	B-	B-	B-	Down	Y	500
JPMorgan SmartRetirement® 2045 Fund Class I	JSASX	NAS CM	Open End	Target Date 2021-2045 (Asset Alloc)	B-	B-	B-	Down	Y	1,000,000
JPMorgan SmartRetirement® 2045 Fund Class R2	JSAZX	NAS CM	Open End	Target Date 2021-2045 (Asset Alloc)	B-	B-	B-	Down	Y	0
JPMorgan SmartRetirement® 2045 Fund Class R3	JSAPX	NAS CM	Open End	Target Date 2021-2045 (Asset Alloc)	B-	B-	B-	Down	Y	0
JPMorgan SmartRetirement® 2045 Fund Class R4	JSAQX	NAS CM	Open End	Target Date 2021-2045 (Asset Alloc)	B-	B-	B-	Down	Y	0
JPMorgan SmartRetirement® 2045 Fund Class R5	JSAIX	NAS CM	Open End	Target Date 2021-2045 (Asset Alloc)	B-	B-	B-	Down	Y	0
JPMorgan SmartRetirement® 2045 Fund Class R6	JSAYX	NAS CM	Open End	Target Date 2021-2045 (Asset Alloc)	B-	B-	B-	Down	Y	15,000,000
JPMorgan SmartRetirement® 2050 Fund Class A	JTSAX	NAS CM	Open End	Target Date 2046+ (Asset Alloc)	B-	B-	B-	Down	Y	500
JPMorgan SmartRetirement® 2050 Fund Class C	JTSCX	NAS CM	Open End	Target Date 2046+ (Asset Alloc)	B-	B-	B-	Down	Y	500
JPMorgan SmartRetirement® 2050 Fund Class I	JTSSX	NAS CM	Open End	Target Date 2046+ (Asset Alloc)	B-	B-	B-	Down	Y	1,000,000
JPMorgan SmartRetirement® 2050 Fund Class R2	JTSZX	NAS CM	Open End	Target Date 2046+ (Asset Alloc)	B-	B-	B-	Down	Y	0
JPMorgan SmartRetirement® 2050 Fund Class R3	JTSPX	NAS CM	Open End	Target Date 2046+ (Asset Alloc)	B-	B-	B-	Down	Y	0
JPMorgan SmartRetirement® 2050 Fund Class R4	JTSQX	NAS CM	Open End	Target Date 2046+ (Asset Alloc)	B-	B-	B-	Down	Y	0
JPMorgan SmartRetirement® 2050 Fund Class R5	JTSIX	NAS CM	Open End	Target Date 2046+ (Asset Alloc)	B-	B-	B-	Down	Y	0
JPMorgan SmartRetirement® 2050 Fund Class R6	JTSYX	NAS CM	Open End	Target Date 2046+ (Asset Alloc)	B-	B-	B-	Down	Y	15,000,000

★ Expanded analysis of this fund is included in Section II.

	TOTAL RETURNS					PERFORMANCE				ASSETS		ASSET ALLOCATION & TURNOVER					BULL & BEAR		FEES		
Min Additional Investment	3-Month Total Return	6-Month Total Return	1-Year Total Return	3-Year Total Return	5-Year Total Return	Dividend Yield (TTM)	Expense Ratio	3-Yr Std Deviation	3-Year Beta	NAV	Total Assets (MIL)	%Cash	%Stocks	%Bonds	%Other	Turnover Ratio	Last Bull Market Total Return	Last Bear Market Total Return	Front End Fee (%)	Back End Fee (%)	Inception Date
	3.15	6.43	13.50	18.05	44.71	2.4	0.95	5.8	1	19.68	7,320	5	48	47	0	19	16.71	-12.88			Sep-16
	3.20	6.54	13.77	18.93	46.52	2.52	0.7	5.8	1	19.77	7,320	5	48	47	0	19	16.88	-12.79			Sep-16
	3.23	6.65	13.96	19.18	46.84	2.09	0.55	5.81	1	19.82	7,320	5	48	47	0	19	16.88	-12.79			May-06
	3.30	6.71	14.13	19.53	47.26	2.18	0.45	5.79	0.99	19.83	7,320	5	48	47	0	19	16.88	-12.79			Nov-14
50	3.75	7.59	15.98	20.71	53.54	1.72	0.84	6.71	1.02	19.53	7,833	5	57	38	0	17	19.03	-15.58	4.50		Jul-07
50	2.67	6.26	14.27	17.37	47.32	1.11	1.43	6.74	1.03	19.46	7,833	5	57	38	0	17	18.51	-15.79		1.00	Jul-07
	3.77	7.64	16.14	21.12	54.27	1.8	0.68	6.71	1.02	19.57	7,833	5	57	38	0	17	19.05	-15.52			Jul-07
	3.61	7.34	15.55	19.69	51.41	1.41	1.21	6.7	1.02	19.46	7,833	5	57	38	0	17	18.79	-15.64			Nov-08
	3.71	7.44	15.78	20.38	53.14	2.5	0.96	6.71	1.02	19.47	7,833	5	57	38	0	17	18.94	-15.54			Sep-16
	3.77	7.63	16.07	21.30	55.07	2.61	0.71	6.71	1.02	19.55	7,833	5	57	38	0	17	19.12	-15.45			Sep-16
	3.85	7.74	16.31	21.60	55.46	1.91	0.56	6.72	1.02	19.6	7,833	5	57	38	0	17	19.12	-15.45			Jul-07
	3.82	7.74	16.43	21.90	55.84	2	0.46	6.68	1.02	19.6	7,833	5	57	38	0	17	19.12	-15.45			Nov-14
50	4.49	8.93	18.65	22.96	60.95	1.63	0.86	7.73	1.07	21.37	8,612	4	66	29	0	22	20.68	-17.78	4.50		May-06
50	3.28	7.53	16.71	19.38	54.25	1.04	1.45	7.74	1.07	21.17	8,612	4	66	29	0	22	20.19	-17.95		1.00	May-06
	4.47	8.97	18.73	23.30	61.65	1.71	0.7	7.76	1.07	21.42	8,612	4	66	29	0	22	20.69	-17.71			May-06
	3.31	7.60	16.97	20.59	57.11	1.32	1.23	7.74	1.07	21.29	8,612	4	66	29	0	22	20.53	-17.88			Nov-08
	4.43	8.81	18.44	22.63	60.53	2.29	0.98	7.74	1.07	21.32	8,612	4	66	29	0	22	20.64	-17.71			Sep-16
	4.47	8.98	18.74	23.49	62.46	2.43	0.73	7.75	1.07	21.39	8,612	4	66	29	0	22	20.82	-17.62			Sep-16
	4.53	9.01	18.88	23.76	62.82	1.81	0.58	7.75	1.07	21.47	8,612	4	66	29	0	22	20.82	-17.62			May-06
	4.56	9.12	19.00	24.06	63.21	1.9	0.48	7.74	1.07	21.47	8,612	4	66	29	0	22	20.82	-17.62			Nov-14
50	4.83	9.66	20.15	24.51	66.54	1.51	0.88	8.39	1.07	20.79	6,440	4	74	22	0	17	22.35	-19.26	4.50		Jul-07
50	3.63	8.20	18.19	20.89	59.59	0.92	1.46	8.4	1.07	20.62	6,440	4	74	22	0	17	21.9	-19.46		1.00	Jul-07
	4.84	9.73	20.23	24.92	67.37	1.58	0.71	8.4	1.07	20.89	6,440	4	74	22	0	17	22.41	-19.22			Jul-07
	3.66	8.33	18.46	22.19	62.56	1.2	1.24	8.42	1.07	20.73	6,440	4	74	22	0	17	22.1	-19.35			Nov-08
	4.81	9.57	19.88	24.19	66.09	2.26	0.99	8.41	1.07	20.72	6,440	4	74	22	0	17	22.4	-19.3			Sep-16
	4.90	9.73	20.24	25.18	68.26	2.37	0.74	8.41	1.07	20.87	6,440	4	74	22	0	17	22.57	-19.22			Sep-16
	4.92	9.78	20.41	25.42	68.58	1.69	0.59	8.41	1.07	20.91	6,440	4	74	22	0	17	22.57	-19.22			Jul-07
	4.95	9.84	20.53	25.65	68.89	1.78	0.49	8.42	1.07	20.91	6,440	4	74	22	0	17	22.57	-19.22			Nov-14
50	3.93	9.02	20.14	24.71	68.22	1.4	0.89	9.02	1.09	22.52	6,524	4	80	15	0	16	22.45	-19.39	4.50		May-06
50	5.07	10.00	20.80	23.78	64.76	0.84	1.47	9.02	1.09	22.23	6,524	4	80	15	0	16	22	-19.62		1.00	May-06
	3.97	9.07	20.28	25.04	69.01	1.48	0.72	9.03	1.09	22.59	6,524	4	80	15	0	16	22.52	-19.31			May-06
	3.96	8.96	19.81	23.73	66.06	1.1	1.25	9.01	1.09	22.41	6,524	4	80	15	0	16	22.22	-19.45			Nov-08
	3.94	8.96	19.96	24.41	67.87	2.21	1	9.03	1.09	22.47	6,524	4	80	15	0	16	22.4	-19.36			Sep-16
	5.24	10.41	21.71	26.79	71.94	2.35	0.75	9.04	1.09	22.56	6,524	4	80	15	0	16	22.57	-19.28			Sep-16
	5.25	10.43	21.82	27.03	72.26	1.58	0.6	9.04	1.09	22.64	6,524	4	80	15	0	16	22.57	-19.28			May-06
	5.27	10.48	21.94	27.34	72.68	1.67	0.5	9.04	1.09	22.64	6,524	4	80	15	0	16	22.57	-19.27			Nov-14
50	4.02	9.16	20.32	24.98	68.52	1.36	0.89	9.03	1.04	21.42	4,298	4	82	14	0	13	22.44	-19.3	4.50		Jul-07
50	5.08	10.09	20.95	24.02	65.02	0.82	1.47	9.03	1.04	21.25	4,298	4	82	14	0	13	21.96	-19.53		1.00	Jul-07
	4.00	9.15	20.40	25.31	69.31	1.44	0.72	9.01	1.04	21.49	4,298	4	82	14	0	13	22.52	-19.28			Jul-07
	4.03	9.02	20.02	24.00	66.30	1.06	1.25	9	1.04	21.34	4,298	4	82	14	0	13	22.28	-19.41			Nov-08
	3.98	9.06	20.16	24.69	68.04	2.22	1	9.02	1.04	21.36	4,298	4	82	14	0	13	22.41	-19.29			Sep-16
	5.27	10.49	21.88	27.11	72.16	2.35	0.75	9.03	1.04	21.46	4,298	4	82	14	0	13	22.58	-19.21			Sep-16
	4.00	9.17	20.55	25.77	70.35	1.55	0.6	9.02	1.04	21.51	4,298	4	82	14	0	13	22.58	-19.21			Jul-07
	5.37	10.64	22.17	27.65	72.89	1.63	0.5	9.03	1.04	21.51	4,298	4	82	14	0	13	22.58	-19.21			Nov-14
50	4.07	9.18	20.38	24.98	68.47	1.37	0.89	9.04	1	21.39	3,605	5	81	14	0	16	22.52	-19.37	4.50		Jul-07
50	5.14	10.11	21.01	24.03	65.00	0.82	1.47	9.01	1	21.2	3,605	5	81	14	0	16	21.97	-19.55		1.00	Jul-07
	4.06	9.22	20.45	25.31	69.26	1.45	0.72	9.04	1	21.46	3,605	5	81	14	0	16	22.6	-19.29			Jul-07
	4.04	9.04	19.95	24.01	66.18	1.07	1.25	9.01	1	21.3	3,605	5	81	14	0	16	22.29	-19.43			Nov-08
	4.03	9.13	20.13	24.67	68.05	2.26	1	9	1	21.33	3,605	5	81	14	0	16	22.49	-19.36			Sep-16
	5.27	10.49	21.85	27.08	72.15	2.39	0.75	9	1	21.44	3,605	5	81	14	0	16	22.66	-19.27			Sep-16
	4.10	9.29	20.58	25.81	70.44	1.55	0.6	9.01	1	21.5	3,605	5	81	14	0	16	22.66	-19.27			Jul-07
	5.36	10.64	22.12	27.67	72.95	1.64	0.5	9.02	1	21.5	3,605	5	81	14	0	16	22.66	-19.27			Nov-14

	MARKET			FUND TYPE, CATEGORY & OBJECTIVE	RATINGS				MINIMUMS	
Fund Name	Ticker Symbol	Traded On	Fund Type	Category and (Prospectus Objective)	Overall Rating	Reward Rating	Risk Rating	Recent Up/ Downgrade	Open to New Investors	Min Initial Investment
JPMorgan SmartRetirement® 2055 Fund Class A	JFFAX	NAS CM	Open End	Target Date 2046+ (Asset Alloc)	B-	B-	B-	Down	Y	500
JPMorgan SmartRetirement® 2055 Fund Class C	JFFCX	NAS CM	Open End	Target Date 2046+ (Asset Alloc)	B-	B-	B-	Down	Y	500
JPMorgan SmartRetirement® 2055 Fund Class I	JFFSX	NAS CM	Open End	Target Date 2046+ (Asset Alloc)	B-	B-	B-	Down	Y	1,000,000
JPMorgan SmartRetirement® 2055 Fund Class R2	JFFRX	NAS CM	Open End	Target Date 2046+ (Asset Alloc)	B-	B-	B-	Down	Y	0
JPMorgan SmartRetirement® 2055 Fund Class R3	JFFPX	NAS CM	Open End	Target Date 2046+ (Asset Alloc)	B-	B-	B-	Down	Y	0
JPMorgan SmartRetirement® 2055 Fund Class R4	JFFQX	NAS CM	Open End	Target Date 2046+ (Asset Alloc)	B-	B-	B-	Down	Y	0
JPMorgan SmartRetirement® 2055 Fund Class R5	JFFIX	NAS CM	Open End	Target Date 2046+ (Asset Alloc)	B-	B-	B-	Down	Y	0
JPMorgan SmartRetirement® 2055 Fund Class R6	JFFYX	NAS CM	Open End	Target Date 2046+ (Asset Alloc)	B-	B-	B-	Down	Y	15,000,000
JPMorgan SmartRetirement® 2060 Fund Class A	JAKAX	NAS CM	Open End	Target Date 2046+ (Asset Alloc)	D	C	B	Up	Y	500
JPMorgan SmartRetirement® 2060 Fund Class C	JAKCX	NAS CM	Open End	Target Date 2046+ (Asset Alloc)	D	C	B	Up	Y	500
JPMorgan SmartRetirement® 2060 Fund Class I	JAKSX	NAS CM	Open End	Target Date 2046+ (Asset Alloc)	D	C	B+	Up	Y	1,000,000
JPMorgan SmartRetirement® 2060 Fund Class R2	JAKZX	NAS CM	Open End	Target Date 2046+ (Asset Alloc)	D	C	B	Up	Y	0
JPMorgan SmartRetirement® 2060 Fund Class R3	JAKPX	NAS CM	Open End	Target Date 2046+ (Asset Alloc)	D	C	B	Up	Y	0
JPMorgan SmartRetirement® 2060 Fund Class R4	JAKQX	NAS CM	Open End	Target Date 2046+ (Asset Alloc)	D	C	B	Up	Y	0
JPMorgan SmartRetirement® 2060 Fund Class R5	JAKIX	NAS CM	Open End	Target Date 2046+ (Asset Alloc)	D	C	B+	Up	Y	0
JPMorgan SmartRetirement® 2060 Fund Class R6	JAKYX	NAS CM	Open End	Target Date 2046+ (Asset Alloc)	D	C	B	Up	Y	15,000,000
JPMorgan SmartRetirement® Blend 2020 Fund Class I	JSSRX	NAS CM	Open End	Target Date 2000-2020 (Asset Alloc)	B	C+	A-	Up	Y	1,000,000
JPMorgan SmartRetirement® Blend 2020 Fund Class R2	JIORX	NAS CM	Open End	Target Date 2000-2020 (Asset Alloc)	B-	C+	B	Up	Y	0
JPMorgan SmartRetirement® Blend 2020 Fund Class R3	JSTKX	NAS CM	Open End	Target Date 2000-2020 (Asset Alloc)	B	C+	A-	Up	Y	0
JPMorgan SmartRetirement® Blend 2020 Fund Class R4	JSTLX	NAS CM	Open End	Target Date 2000-2020 (Asset Alloc)	B-	C+	B	Up	Y	0
JPMorgan SmartRetirement® Blend 2020 Fund Class R5	JBSRX	NAS CM	Open End	Target Date 2000-2020 (Asset Alloc)	B	C+	A-	Up	Y	0
JPMorgan SmartRetirement® Blend 2020 Fund Class R6	JSYRX	NAS CM	Open End	Target Date 2000-2020 (Asset Alloc)	B-	C+	B	Up	Y	15,000,000
JPMorgan SmartRetirement® Blend 2025 Fund Class I	JBSSX	NAS CM	Open End	Target Date 2021-2045 (Asset Alloc)	B-	C+	B	Up	Y	1,000,000
JPMorgan SmartRetirement® Blend 2025 Fund Class R2	JBRSX	NAS CM	Open End	Target Date 2021-2045 (Asset Alloc)	B-	C+	B	Up	Y	0
JPMorgan SmartRetirement® Blend 2025 Fund Class R3	JBTUX	NAS CM	Open End	Target Date 2021-2045 (Asset Alloc)	B-	C+	B	Up	Y	0
JPMorgan SmartRetirement® Blend 2025 Fund Class R4	JBTBX	NAS CM	Open End	Target Date 2021-2045 (Asset Alloc)	B-	C+	B	Up	Y	0
JPMorgan SmartRetirement® Blend 2025 Fund Class R5	JBBSX	NAS CM	Open End	Target Date 2021-2045 (Asset Alloc)	B-	C+	B	Up	Y	0
JPMorgan SmartRetirement® Blend 2025 Fund Class R6	JBYSX	NAS CM	Open End	Target Date 2021-2045 (Asset Alloc)	B-	C+	B	Up	Y	15,000,000
JPMorgan SmartRetirement® Blend 2030 Fund Class I	JRBEX	NAS CM	Open End	Target Date 2021-2045 (Asset Alloc)	B-	C+	B	Down	Y	1,000,000
JPMorgan SmartRetirement® Blend 2030 Fund Class R2	JRBRX	NAS CM	Open End	Target Date 2021-2045 (Asset Alloc)	B-	C+	B	Down	Y	0
JPMorgan SmartRetirement® Blend 2030 Fund Class R3	JUTPX	NAS CM	Open End	Target Date 2021-2045 (Asset Alloc)	B-	C+	B	Down	Y	0
JPMorgan SmartRetirement® Blend 2030 Fund Class R4	JUTUX	NAS CM	Open End	Target Date 2021-2045 (Asset Alloc)	B-	C+	B	Down	Y	0
JPMorgan SmartRetirement® Blend 2030 Fund Class R5	JRBBX	NAS CM	Open End	Target Date 2021-2045 (Asset Alloc)	B-	C+	B	Down	Y	0
JPMorgan SmartRetirement® Blend 2030 Fund Class R6	JRBYX	NAS CM	Open End	Target Date 2021-2045 (Asset Alloc)	B-	B-	B	Down	Y	15,000,000
JPMorgan SmartRetirement® Blend 2035 Fund Class I	JPSRX	NAS CM	Open End	Target Date 2021-2045 (Asset Alloc)	B-	B-	B	Down	Y	1,000,000
JPMorgan SmartRetirement® Blend 2035 Fund Class R2	JPRRX	NAS CM	Open End	Target Date 2021-2045 (Asset Alloc)	B-	C+	B	Down	Y	0
JPMorgan SmartRetirement® Blend 2035 Fund Class R3	JPTLX	NAS CM	Open End	Target Date 2021-2045 (Asset Alloc)	B-	B-	B	Down	Y	0
JPMorgan SmartRetirement® Blend 2035 Fund Class R4	JPTKX	NAS CM	Open End	Target Date 2021-2045 (Asset Alloc)	B-	B-	B	Down	Y	0
JPMorgan SmartRetirement® Blend 2035 Fund Class R5	JPBRX	NAS CM	Open End	Target Date 2021-2045 (Asset Alloc)	B-	B-	B	Down	Y	0
JPMorgan SmartRetirement® Blend 2035 Fund Class R6	JPYRX	NAS CM	Open End	Target Date 2021-2045 (Asset Alloc)	B-	B-	B	Down	Y	15,000,000
JPMorgan SmartRetirement® Blend 2040 Fund Class I	JOBEX	NAS CM	Open End	Target Date 2021-2045 (Asset Alloc)	B-	B-	B-	Down	Y	1,000,000
JPMorgan SmartRetirement® Blend 2040 Fund Class R2	JOBRX	NAS CM	Open End	Target Date 2021-2045 (Asset Alloc)	B-	B-	B-	Down	Y	0
JPMorgan SmartRetirement® Blend 2040 Fund Class R3	JNTEX	NAS CM	Open End	Target Date 2021-2045 (Asset Alloc)	B-	B-	B-	Down	Y	0
JPMorgan SmartRetirement® Blend 2040 Fund Class R4	JNTNX	NAS CM	Open End	Target Date 2021-2045 (Asset Alloc)	B-	B-	B-	Down	Y	0
JPMorgan SmartRetirement® Blend 2040 Fund Class R5	JOBBX	NAS CM	Open End	Target Date 2021-2045 (Asset Alloc)	B-	B-	B-	Down	Y	0
JPMorgan SmartRetirement® Blend 2040 Fund Class R6	JOBYX	NAS CM	Open End	Target Date 2021-2045 (Asset Alloc)	B-	B-	B-	Down	Y	15,000,000
JPMorgan SmartRetirement® Blend 2045 Fund Class I	JMSSX	NAS CM	Open End	Target Date 2021-2045 (Asset Alloc)	B-	B-	B-	Down	Y	1,000,000
JPMorgan SmartRetirement® Blend 2045 Fund Class R2	JNARX	NAS CM	Open End	Target Date 2021-2045 (Asset Alloc)	B-	B-	B-	Down	Y	0
JPMorgan SmartRetirement® Blend 2045 Fund Class R3	JNTOX	NAS CM	Open End	Target Date 2021-2045 (Asset Alloc)	B-	B-	B-	Down	Y	0
JPMorgan SmartRetirement® Blend 2045 Fund Class R4	JNTLX	NAS CM	Open End	Target Date 2021-2045 (Asset Alloc)	B-	B-	B-	Down	Y	0
JPMorgan SmartRetirement® Blend 2045 Fund Class R5	JMBRX	NAS CM	Open End	Target Date 2021-2045 (Asset Alloc)	B-	B-	B-	Down	Y	0
JPMorgan SmartRetirement® Blend 2045 Fund Class R6	JMYAX	NAS CM	Open End	Target Date 2021-2045 (Asset Alloc)	B-	B-	B-	Down	Y	15,000,000

★Expanded analysis of this fund is included in Section II.

Min Additional Investment	3-Month Total Return	6-Month Total Return	1-Year Total Return	3-Year Total Return	5-Year Total Return	Dividend Yield (TTM)	Expense Ratio	3-Yr Std Deviation	3-Year Beta	NAV	Total Assets (MIL)	%Cash	%Stocks	%Bonds	%Other	Turnover Ratio	Last Bull Market Total Return	Last Bear Market Total Return	Front End Fee (%)	Back End Fee (%)	Inception Date
	TOTAL RETURNS					PERFORMANCE				ASSETS		ASSET ALLOCATION & TURNOVER					BULL & BEAR		FEES		
50	4.04	9.11	20.27	24.94	68.62	1.35	0.89	9.01	0.98	23.88	1,262	5	81	14	0	10			4.50		Jan-12
50	5.13	10.11	20.95	23.97	65.22	0.8	1.47	8.99	0.97	23.78	1,262	5	81	14	0	10				1.00	Jan-12
	4.04	9.17	20.37	25.30	69.48	1.43	0.72	8.99	0.98	23.92	1,262	5	81	14	0	10					Jan-12
	4.05	9.01	19.99	23.96	66.55	1.06	1.25	8.99	0.97	23.84	1,262	5	81	14	0	10					Jan-12
	4.01	9.06	20.10	24.64	68.21	2.09	1	9	0.98	23.83	1,262	5	81	14	0	10					Sep-16
	4.04	9.15	20.39	25.55	70.30	2.19	0.75	8.99	0.98	23.91	1,262	5	81	14	0	10					Sep-16
	4.03	9.19	20.51	25.74	70.56	1.53	0.6	9	0.98	23.94	1,262	5	81	14	0	10					Jan-12
	5.34	10.59	22.11	27.65	73.06	1.62	0.5	9	0.98	23.95	1,262	5	81	14	0	10					Nov-14
50	3.94	9.12	20.16			1.23	0.9			17.99	25.9	3	91	5	0				4.50		Aug-16
50	5.03	10.04	20.83			0.71	1.48			17.97	25.9	3	91	5	0					1.00	Aug-16
	4.06	9.19	20.39			1.23	0.73			18.02	25.9	3	91	5	0						Aug-16
	3.94	8.98	19.90			0.95	1.26			17.99	25.9	3	91	5	0						Aug-16
	4.00	9.08	20.04			1.05	1.01			18	25.9	3	91	5	0						Sep-16
	4.06	9.16	20.32			1.21	0.76			18.02	25.9	3	91	5	0						Sep-16
	4.00	9.23	20.44			1.35	0.61			18.01	25.9	3	91	5	0						Aug-16
	5.29	10.61	22.06			1.4	0.51			18.03	25.9	3	91	5	0						Aug-16
	3.10	6.20	13.07	18.76	43.99	2	0.54	5.67	0.98	20.02	475.9	5	49	46	0	33					Jul-12
	3.02	5.93	12.57	17.21	40.97	1.53	1.04	5.68	0.98	20.03	475.9	5	49	46	0	33					Jul-12
	3.04	6.07	12.90	18.55	43.72		0.79	5.68	0.98	20.01	475.9	5	49	46	0	33					May-17
	3.10	6.20	13.18	19.44	45.53		0.54	5.68	0.98	20.01	475.9	5	49	46	0	33					May-17
	3.14	6.28	13.24	19.42	45.31	2.14	0.39	5.68	0.98	20.03	475.9	5	49	46	0	33					Jul-12
	3.21	6.38	13.40	19.67	45.80	2.22	0.29	5.68	0.98	20.04	475.9	5	49	46	0	33					Jul-12
	3.65	7.23	15.28	21.44	51.42	1.96	0.54	6.54	1	21.19	515.3	5	58	37	0	21					Jul-12
	3.49	6.93	14.68	19.77	48.17	1.5	1.04	6.51	1	21.18	515.3	5	58	37	0	21					Jul-12
	3.54	7.05	15.11	21.24	51.16		0.79	6.55	1	21.18	515.3	5	58	37	0	21					May-17
	3.60	7.18	15.40	22.15	53.06		0.54	6.55	1	21.18	515.3	5	58	37	0	21					May-17
	3.64	7.31	15.45	22.05	52.92	2.1	0.39	6.56	1.01	21.2	515.3	5	58	37	0	21					Jul-12
	3.66	7.36	15.56	22.32	53.27	2.18	0.29	6.56	1.01	21.2	515.3	5	58	37	0	21					Jul-12
	4.14	8.15	17.22	23.86	58.27	1.89	0.54	7.47	1.04	22.29	547.2	4	68	28	0	22					Jul-12
	3.96	7.83	16.58	22.19	54.89	1.44	1.04	7.45	1.04	22.29	547.2	4	68	28	0	22					Jul-12
	4.03	7.97	16.97	23.49	57.67		0.79	7.46	1.04	22.27	547.2	4	68	28	0	22					May-17
	4.09	8.10	17.26	24.42	59.65		0.54	7.46	1.04	22.27	547.2	4	68	28	0	22					May-17
	4.13	8.18	17.34	24.51	59.76	2.04	0.39	7.46	1.04	22.29	547.2	4	68	28	0	22					Jul-12
	4.15	8.22	17.43	24.76	60.17	2.12	0.29	7.45	1.04	22.3	547.2	4	68	28	0	22					Jul-12
	4.53	8.85	18.63	25.67	63.71	1.84	0.54	8.09	1.04	23.17	415.5	3	75	21	0	24					Jul-12
	4.35	8.53	17.99	23.96	60.25	1.39	1.04	8.1	1.04	23.17	415.5	3	75	21	0	24					Jul-12
	4.42	8.67	18.39	25.45	63.43		0.79	8.11	1.04	23.16	415.5	3	75	21	0	24					May-17
	4.49	8.80	18.69	26.40	65.49		0.54	8.11	1.04	23.16	415.5	3	75	21	0	24					May-17
	4.57	8.92	18.79	26.40	65.29	1.98	0.39	8.1	1.04	23.19	415.5	3	75	21	0	24					Jul-12
	4.59	8.98	18.90	26.62	65.78	2.06	0.29	8.12	1.04	23.19	415.5	3	75	21	0	24					Jul-12
	4.86	9.44	19.96	27.36	67.70	1.79	0.54	8.73	1.06	23.78	418.9	2	83	14	0	19					Jul-12
	4.73	9.21	19.42	25.69	64.10	1.34	1.04	8.69	1.06	23.79	418.9	2	83	14	0	19					Jul-12
	4.75	9.30	19.75	26.96	67.01		0.79	8.7	1.06	23.77	418.9	2	83	14	0	19					May-17
	4.82	9.44	20.05	27.92	69.11		0.54	8.7	1.06	23.77	418.9	2	83	14	0	19					May-17
	4.90	9.55	20.18	28.05	69.29	1.92	0.39	8.7	1.06	23.8	418.9	2	83	14	0	19					Jul-12
	4.92	9.61	20.29	28.34	69.80	2.01	0.29	8.7	1.06	23.8	418.9	2	83	14	0	19					Jul-12
	4.92	9.64	20.16	27.74	67.84	1.77	0.54	8.7	1.01	23.75	285.2	3	84	13	0	17					Jul-12
	4.79	9.37	19.57	25.98	64.30	1.32	1.04	8.7	1.01	23.75	285.2	3	84	13	0	17					Jul-12
	4.82	9.47	19.98	27.50	67.65		0.79	8.72	1.02	23.73	285.2	3	84	13	0	17					May-17
	4.92	9.65	20.33	28.52	69.82		0.54	8.72	1.02	23.74	285.2	3	84	13	0	17					May-17
	4.96	9.72	20.39	28.41	69.39	1.9	0.39	8.71	1.01	23.76	285.2	3	84	13	0	17					Jul-12
	4.98	9.76	20.48	28.68	70.03	1.99	0.29	8.72	1.02	23.78	285.2	3	84	13	0	17					Jul-12

	MARKET		FUND TYPE, CATEGORY & OBJECTIVE		RATINGS				MINIMUMS	
Fund Name	Ticker Symbol	Traded On	Fund Type	Category and (Prospectus Objective)	Overall Rating	Reward Rating	Risk Rating	Recent Up/ Downgrade	Open to New Investors	Min Initial Investment
JPMorgan SmartRetirement® Blend 2050 Fund Class I	JNEAX	NAS CM	Open End	Target Date 2046+ (Asset Alloc)	B-	B-	B-	Down	Y	1,000,000
JPMorgan SmartRetirement® Blend 2050 Fund Class R2	JNNRX	NAS CM	Open End	Target Date 2046+ (Asset Alloc)	B-	B-	B-	Down	Y	0
JPMorgan SmartRetirement® Blend 2050 Fund Class R3	JNTKX	NAS CM	Open End	Target Date 2046+ (Asset Alloc)	B-	B-	B-	Down	Y	0
JPMorgan SmartRetirement® Blend 2050 Fund Class R4	JNTPX	NAS CM	Open End	Target Date 2046+ (Asset Alloc)	B-	B-	B-	Down	Y	0
JPMorgan SmartRetirement® Blend 2050 Fund Class R5	JNABX	NAS CM	Open End	Target Date 2046+ (Asset Alloc)	B-	B-	B-	Down	Y	0
JPMorgan SmartRetirement® Blend 2050 Fund Class R6	JNYAX	NAS CM	Open End	Target Date 2046+ (Asset Alloc)	B-	B-	B-	Down	Y	15,000,000
JPMorgan SmartRetirement® Blend 2055 Fund Class I	JPTBX	NAS CM	Open End	Target Date 2046+ (Asset Alloc)	B-	B-	B-	Down	Y	1,000,000
JPMorgan SmartRetirement® Blend 2055 Fund Class R2	JTRBX	NAS CM	Open End	Target Date 2046+ (Asset Alloc)	B-	B-	B-	Down	Y	0
JPMorgan SmartRetirement® Blend 2055 Fund Class R3	JTTUX	NAS CM	Open End	Target Date 2046+ (Asset Alloc)	B-	B-	B-	Down	Y	0
JPMorgan SmartRetirement® Blend 2055 Fund Class R4	JTTLX	NAS CM	Open End	Target Date 2046+ (Asset Alloc)	B-	B-	B	Down	Y	0
JPMorgan SmartRetirement® Blend 2055 Fund Class R5	JTBBX	NAS CM	Open End	Target Date 2046+ (Asset Alloc)	B-	B-	B-	Down	Y	0
JPMorgan SmartRetirement® Blend 2055 Fund Class R6	JTYBX	NAS CM	Open End	Target Date 2046+ (Asset Alloc)	B-	B-	B	Down	Y	15,000,000
JPMorgan SmartRetirement® Blend 2060 Fund Class I	JACSX	NAS CM	Open End	Target Date 2046+ (Asset Alloc)	D	C	B	Up	Y	1,000,000
JPMorgan SmartRetirement® Blend 2060 Fund Class R2	JATPX	NAS CM	Open End	Target Date 2046+ (Asset Alloc)	D	C	B	Up	Y	0
JPMorgan SmartRetirement® Blend 2060 Fund Class R3	JATQX	NAS CM	Open End	Target Date 2046+ (Asset Alloc)	D	C	B	Up	Y	0
JPMorgan SmartRetirement® Blend 2060 Fund Class R4	JATUX	NAS CM	Open End	Target Date 2046+ (Asset Alloc)	D	C	B	Up	Y	0
JPMorgan SmartRetirement® Blend 2060 Fund Class R5	JAABX	NAS CM	Open End	Target Date 2046+ (Asset Alloc)	D	C	B	Up	Y	0
JPMorgan SmartRetirement® Blend 2060 Fund Class R6	JAAYX	NAS CM	Open End	Target Date 2046+ (Asset Alloc)	D	C	B	Up	Y	15,000,000
JPMorgan SmartRetirement® Blend Inc Fund Class R3	JITLX	NAS CM	Open End	Target Date 2000-2020 (Asset Alloc)	B	C+	A-	Up	Y	0
JPMorgan SmartRetirement® Blend Inc Fund Class R4	JITKX	NAS CM	Open End	Target Date 2000-2020 (Asset Alloc)	B-	C+	B	Up	Y	0
JPMorgan SmartRetirement® Blend Income Fund Class I	JIJSX	NAS CM	Open End	Target Date 2000-2020 (Asset Alloc)	B	C+	A-	Up	Y	1,000,000
JPMorgan SmartRetirement® Blend Income Fund Class R2	JIRBX	NAS CM	Open End	Target Date 2000-2020 (Asset Alloc)	B	C+	A-	Up	Y	0
JPMorgan SmartRetirement® Blend Income Fund Class R5	JIBBX	NAS CM	Open End	Target Date 2000-2020 (Asset Alloc)	B	C+	A-	Up	Y	0
JPMorgan SmartRetirement® Blend Income Fund Class R6	JIYBX	NAS CM	Open End	Target Date 2000-2020 (Asset Alloc)	B-	C+	B	Up	Y	15,000,000
JPMorgan SmartRetirement® Income Fund Class A	JSRAX	NAS CM	Open End	Target Date 2000-2020 (Income)	B	C+	A-	Up	Y	500
JPMorgan SmartRetirement® Income Fund Class C	JSRCX	NAS CM	Open End	Target Date 2000-2020 (Income)	B	C+	B+	Up	Y	500
JPMorgan SmartRetirement® Income Fund Class I	JSRSX	NAS CM	Open End	Target Date 2000-2020 (Income)	B	C+	A-	Up	Y	1,000,000
JPMorgan SmartRetirement® Income Fund Class R2	JSIZX	NAS CM	Open End	Target Date 2000-2020 (Income)	B-	C+	B	Up	Y	0
JPMorgan SmartRetirement® Income Fund Class R3	JSIPX	NAS CM	Open End	Target Date 2000-2020 (Income)	B	C+	A-	Up	Y	0
JPMorgan SmartRetirement® Income Fund Class R4	JSIQX	NAS CM	Open End	Target Date 2000-2020 (Income)	B-	C+	B	Up	Y	0
JPMorgan SmartRetirement® Income Fund Class R5	JSIIX	NAS CM	Open End	Target Date 2000-2020 (Income)	B-	C+	B	Up	Y	0
JPMorgan SmartRetirement® Income Fund Class R6	JSIYX	NAS CM	Open End	Target Date 2000-2020 (Income)	B	C+	A-	Up	Y	15,000,000
JPMorgan Systematic Alpha Fund Class A	JSALX	NAS CM	Open End	Multialternative (Growth & Income)	C	C	C		Y	1,000
JPMorgan Systematic Alpha Fund Class C	JSYAX	NAS CM	Open End	Multialternative (Growth & Income)	C-	D+	C	Down	Y	1,000
JPMorgan Systematic Alpha Fund Class I	SSALX	NAS CM	Open End	Multialternative (Growth & Income)	C	C	C+		Y	1,000,000
JPMorgan Systematic Alpha Fund Class R6	JALPX	NAS CM	Open End	Multialternative (Growth & Income)	C	C	B-	Down	Y	15,000,000
JPMorgan Tax Aware Equity Fund Class A	JPEAX	NAS CM	Open End	US Equity Large Cap Blend (Growth & Income)	B	B	B-		Y	1,000
JPMorgan Tax Aware Equity Fund Class C	JPECX	NAS CM	Open End	US Equity Large Cap Blend (Growth & Income)	B	B	B-		Y	1,000
JPMorgan U.S. Dynamic Plus Fund Class A	JPSAX	NAS CM	Open End	US Equity Large Cap Blend (Growth)	B	B	B-	Up	Y	1,000
JPMorgan U.S. Dynamic Plus Fund Class C	JPSCX	NAS CM	Open End	US Equity Large Cap Blend (Growth)	B-	B-	B-	Down	Y	1,000
JPMorgan U.S. Dynamic Plus Fund Class I	JILSX	NAS CM	Open End	US Equity Large Cap Blend (Growth)	B	B	B-		Y	1,000,000
JPMorgan U.S. Equity Fund Class A	JUEAX	NAS CM	Open End	US Equity Large Cap Blend (Growth)	B	B	B-		Y	1,000
JPMorgan U.S. Equity Fund Class C	JUECX	NAS CM	Open End	US Equity Large Cap Blend (Growth)	B-	B	B-	Down	Y	1,000
JPMorgan U.S. Equity Fund Class I	JUESX	NAS CM	Open End	US Equity Large Cap Blend (Growth)	B	B	B-		Y	1,000,000
JPMorgan U.S. Equity Fund Class L	JMUEX	NAS CM	Open End	US Equity Large Cap Blend (Growth)	B	B	B-		Y	3,000,000
JPMorgan U.S. Equity Fund Class R2	JUEZX	NAS CM	Open End	US Equity Large Cap Blend (Growth)	B-	B	B-	Down	Y	0
JPMorgan U.S. Equity Fund Class R3	JUEPX	NAS CM	Open End	US Equity Large Cap Blend (Growth)	B	B	B-		Y	0
JPMorgan U.S. Equity Fund Class R4	JUEQX	NAS CM	Open End	US Equity Large Cap Blend (Growth)	B	B	B-		Y	0
JPMorgan U.S. Equity Fund Class R5	JUSRX	NAS CM	Open End	US Equity Large Cap Blend (Growth)	B	B	B-		Y	0
JPMorgan U.S. Equity Fund Class R6	JUEMX	NAS CM	Open End	US Equity Large Cap Blend (Growth)	B	B	B-		Y	15,000,000
JPMorgan U.S. Large Cap Core Plus Fund Class A Shares	JLCAX	NAS CM	Open End	US Equity Large Cap Blend (Growth)	B-	B	B-	Down		1,000
JPMorgan U.S. Large Cap Core Plus Fund Class C Shares	JLPCX	NAS CM	Open End	US Equity Large Cap Blend (Growth)	B-	B	B-	Down		1,000

★ Expanded analysis of this fund is included in Section II.

	TOTAL RETURNS					PERFORMANCE				ASSETS		ASSET ALLOCATION & TURNOVER					BULL & BEAR		FEES		
Min Additional Investment	3-Month Total Return	6-Month Total Return	1-Year Total Return	3-Year Total Return	5-Year Total Return	Dividend Yield (TTM)	Expense Ratio	3-Yr Std Deviation	3-Year Beta	NAV	Total Assets (MIL)	%Cash	%Stocks	%Bonds	%Other	Turnover Ratio	Last Bull Market Total Return	Last Bear Market Total Return	Front End Fee (%)	Back End Fee (%)	Inception Date
	4.91	9.59	20.20	27.68	67.95	1.77	0.54	8.73	0.98	23.75	218.7	3	84	13	0	17					Jul-12
	4.78	9.31	19.61	25.94	64.36	1.31	1.04	8.7	0.97	23.75	218.7	3	84	13	0	17					Jul-12
	4.85	9.45	20.02	27.47	67.63		0.79	8.7	0.97	23.74	218.7	3	84	13	0	17					May-17
	4.92	9.59	20.32	28.43	69.74		0.54	8.7	0.97	23.74	218.7	3	84	13	0	17					May-17
	4.95	9.67	20.43	28.37	69.46	1.9	0.39	8.69	0.97	23.76	218.7	3	84	13	0	17					Jul-12
	4.97	9.71	20.53	28.65	70.03	1.98	0.29	8.7	0.97	23.77	218.7	3	84	13	0	17					Jul-12
	4.93	9.58	20.14	27.83	67.37	1.79	0.54	8.66	0.94	23.37	86.0	3	84	13	0	16					Jul-12
	4.80	9.31	19.55	26.08	63.83	1.34	1.04	8.67	0.95	23.37	86.0	3	84	13	0	16					Jul-12
	4.82	9.45	19.90	27.60	67.08		0.79	8.67	0.95	23.35	86.0	3	84	13	0	16					May-17
	4.93	9.64	20.25	28.62	69.26		0.54	8.67	0.95	23.36	86.0	3	84	13	0	16					May-17
	4.97	9.66	20.31	28.51	69.00	1.92	0.39	8.7	0.95	23.38	86.0	3	84	13	0	16					Jul-12
	4.99	9.75	20.41	28.78	69.47	2.01	0.29	8.68	0.95	23.39	86.0	3	84	13	0	16					Jul-12
	4.93	9.48	20.14			1.86	0.54			17.69	5.6	1	89	9	0						Aug-16
	4.74	9.15	19.48			1.42	1.04			17.68	5.6	1	89	9	0						Aug-16
	4.81	9.28	19.97				0.79			17.68	5.6	1	89	9	0						May-17
	4.88	9.42	20.27				0.54			17.68	5.6	1	89	9	0						May-17
	4.97	9.57	20.36			2.03	0.39			17.69	5.6	1	89	9	0						Aug-16
	5.00	9.61	20.51			2.09	0.29			17.69	5.6	1	89	9	0						Aug-16
	2.43	4.94	10.27	14.95	29.74		0.79	4.23	1.28	17.89	259.0	14	36	50	0	35					May-17
	2.50	5.07	10.54	15.82	31.37		0.54	4.24	1.28	17.89	259.0	14	36	50	0	35					May-17
	2.49	5.06	10.43	15.07	29.86	1.89	0.54	4.23	1.28	17.9	259.0	14	36	50	0	35					Jul-12
	2.37	4.80	9.88	13.53	27.10	1.42	1.04	4.21	1.27	17.9	259.0	14	36	50	0	35					Jul-12
	2.54	5.09	10.54	15.66	31.11	2.05	0.39	4.22	1.27	17.9	259.0	14	36	50	0	35					Jul-12
	2.56	5.19	10.70	15.98	31.56	2.13	0.29	4.24	1.28	17.91	259.0	14	36	50	0	35					Jul-12
50	2.53	5.26	10.88	14.61	30.44	1.96	0.72	4.35	1.29	18.58	4,457	13	36	51	0	29	11.05	-7.51	4.50		May-06
50	2.36	4.92	10.17	12.42	26.26	1.3	1.35	4.37	1.3	18.51	4,457	13	36	51	0	29	10.6	-7.7		1.00	May-06
	2.61	5.36	11.03	15.01	31.18	2.04	0.6	4.36	1.29	18.62	4,457	13	36	51	0	29	11.09	-7.46			May-06
	2.42	5.03	10.45	13.60	28.60	1.61	1.16	4.33	1.29	18.54	4,457	13	36	51	0	29	10.91	-7.63			Nov-08
	2.52	5.19	10.68	14.27	30.02	1.93	0.91	4.33	1.29	18.53	4,457	13	36	51	0	29	11	-7.48			Sep-16
	2.55	5.29	10.97	15.15	31.68	2.02	0.66	4.33	1.29	18.6	4,457	13	36	51	0	29	11.16	-7.38			Sep-16
	2.62	5.40	11.11	15.42	31.98	2.12	0.51	4.33	1.29	18.65	4,457	13	36	51	0	29	11.16	-7.38			May-06
	2.65	5.45	11.22	15.67	32.28	2.22	0.41	4.37	1.3	18.65	4,457	13	36	51	0	29	11.16	-7.38			Nov-14
50	-0.60	-1.46	-1.98	1.03		0	1.25	2.98	-5.67	14.84	469.2	34	55	0	0	151			4.50		Feb-13
50	-0.68	-1.69	-2.35	-0.39		0	1.75	2.92	-6.07	14.54	469.2	34	55	0	0	151				1.00	Feb-13
	-0.52	-1.35	-1.73	1.79		0.08	1	2.99	-5.88	15.28	469.2	34	55	0	0	151					Feb-13
	-0.45	-1.23	-1.42	2.60		0.23	0.75	2.96	-7.17	15.17	469.2	34	55	0	0	151					Feb-13
50	7.08	11.31	22.83	35.56	112.65	0.52	0.98	11.32	1.09	33.29	1,313	1	99	0	0	41	26.32	-18.64	5.25		Mar-11
50	6.91	11.04	22.21	33.56	107.36	0.18	1.47	11.31	1.09	33.01	1,313	1	99	0	0	41	25.92	-18.82		1.00	Mar-11
50	7.29	13.62	20.10	28.51	103.81	1.3	1.2	11.83	1.13	18.81	340.2	2	98	0	0	122	23.55	-16.21	5.25		Jan-06
50	7.15	13.39	19.52	26.58	98.81	0.87	1.7	11.84	1.14	18.14	340.2	2	98	0	0	122	23.13	-16.34		1.00	Jan-06
	7.33	13.79	20.38	29.50	106.38	0.43	0.95	11.86	1.14	19.34	340.2	2	98	0	0	122	23.74	-16.14			Jan-06
50	6.73	11.26	21.12	33.15	110.32	0.6	0.94	10.91	1.06	16.24	15,686	1	99	0	0	86	25.81	-17.78	5.25		Sep-01
50	6.67	11.05	20.49	31.25	105.31	0.21	1.44	10.93	1.06	15.77	15,686	1	99	0	0	86	25.54	-18.02		1.00	Sep-01
	6.84	11.41	21.40	34.01	112.38	0.77	0.69	10.89	1.06	16.28	15,686	1	99	0	0	86	25.9	-17.71			Sep-01
	6.87	11.53	21.52	34.51	113.91	0.88	0.61	10.91	1.06	16.3	15,686	1	99	0	0	86	26.07	-17.72			Sep-93
	6.72	11.13	20.76	32.21	107.71	0.39	1.19	10.92	1.06	16.11	15,686	1	99	0	0	86	25.57	-17.93			Nov-08
	6.76	11.23	21.02	33.18	110.74	0.7	0.94	10.92	1.06	16.19	15,686	1	99	0	0	86	25.89	-17.8			Sep-16
	6.85	11.44	21.37	34.21	113.43	0.79	0.69	10.91	1.06	16.27	15,686	1	99	0	0	86	26.07	-17.72			Sep-16
	6.87	11.49	21.58	34.71	114.36	0.93	0.54	10.92	1.06	16.3	15,686	1	99	0	0	86	26.1	-17.7			May-06
	6.88	11.58	21.70	35.00	115.09	0.98	0.44	10.9	1.06	16.33	15,686	1	99	0	0	86	26.1	-17.66			Nov-10
50	6.74	11.28	21.23	30.87	109.69	0.04	1.1	11.83	1.12	29.6	9,648	2	98	0	0	131	24.55	-18.52	5.25		Nov-05
50	6.62	11.00	20.58	28.92	104.48	0	1.6	11.82	1.12	28.24	9,648	2	98	0	0	131	24.26	-18.7		1.00	Nov-05

	MARKET			FUND TYPE, CATEGORY & OBJECTIVE	RATINGS					MINIMUMS
Fund Name	Ticker Symbol	Traded On	Fund Type	Category and (Prospectus Objective)	Overall Rating	Reward Rating	Risk Rating	Recent Up/ Downgrade	Open to New Investors	Min Initial Investment
JPMorgan U.S. Large Cap Core Plus Fund Class I Shares	JLPSX	NAS CM	Open End	US Equity Large Cap Blend (Growth)	B-	B	B-	Down		1,000,000
JPMorgan U.S. Large Cap Core Plus Fund Class R2 Shares	JLPZX	NAS CM	Open End	US Equity Large Cap Blend (Growth)	B	B	B			0
JPMorgan U.S. Large Cap Core Plus Fund Class R5 Shares	JCPRX	NAS CM	Open End	US Equity Large Cap Blend (Growth)	B	B	B-			0
JPMorgan U.S. Large Cap Core Plus Fund Class R6	JLPYX	NAS CM	Open End	US Equity Large Cap Blend (Growth)	B-	B	B-		Y	15,000,000
JPMorgan U.S. Research Enhanced Equity Fund Class A	JDEAX	NAS CM	Open End	US Equity Large Cap Blend (Growth)	B-	B-	B-	Down	Y	1,000
JPMorgan U.S. Research Enhanced Equity Fund Class I	JDESX	NAS CM	Open End	US Equity Large Cap Blend (Growth)	B-	B-	B-	Down	Y	1,000,000
JPMorgan U.S. Research Enhanced Equity Fund Class L	JPIEX	NAS CM	Open End	US Equity Large Cap Blend (Growth)	B-	B-	B-	Down	Y	3,000,000
JPMorgan U.S. Research Enhanced Equity Fund Class R6	JDEUX	NAS CM	Open End	US Equity Large Cap Blend (Growth)	B-	B-	B-	Down	Y	15,000,000
JPMorgan U.S. Small Company Fund Class A	JTUAX	NAS CM	Open End	US Equity Small Cap (Small Company)	B	B	B	Up	Y	1,000
JPMorgan U.S. Small Company Fund Class C	JTUCX	NAS CM	Open End	US Equity Small Cap (Small Company)	B	B	B	Up	Y	1,000
JPMorgan U.S. Small Company Fund Class I	JSCSX	NAS CM	Open End	US Equity Small Cap (Small Company)	B	B	B	Up	Y	1,000,000
JPMorgan U.S. Small Company Fund Class L	JUSSX	NAS CM	Open End	US Equity Small Cap (Small Company)	B	B	B	Up	Y	3,000,000
JPMorgan U.S. Small Company Fund Class R2	JSCZX	NAS CM	Open End	US Equity Small Cap (Small Company)	B	B	B	Up	Y	0
JPMorgan U.S. Small Company Fund Class R3	JUSPX	NAS CM	Open End	US Equity Small Cap (Small Company)	B	B	B	Up	Y	0
JPMorgan U.S. Small Company Fund Class R4	JUSQX	NAS CM	Open End	US Equity Small Cap (Small Company)	B	B	B	Up	Y	0
JPMorgan U.S. Small Company Fund Class R5	JUSYX	NAS CM	Open End	US Equity Small Cap (Small Company)	B	B	B	Up	Y	0
JPMorgan U.S. Small Company Fund Class R6	JUSMX	NAS CM	Open End	US Equity Small Cap (Small Company)	B	B	B	Up	Y	15,000,000
JPMorgan Value Advantage Fund Class A	JVAAX	NAS CM	Open End	US Equity Large Cap Value (Growth & Income)	B	B-	B	Up	Y	1,000
JPMorgan Value Advantage Fund Class C	JVACX	NAS CM	Open End	US Equity Large Cap Value (Growth & Income)	B-	B-	B	Down	Y	1,000
JPMorgan Value Advantage Fund Class I	JVASX	NAS CM	Open End	US Equity Large Cap Value (Growth & Income)	B	B-	B	Up	Y	1,000,000
JPMorgan Value Advantage Fund Class L	JVAIX	NAS CM	Open End	US Equity Large Cap Value (Growth & Income)	B	B-	B	Up	Y	3,000,000
JPMorgan Value Advantage Fund Class R2	JGAQX	NAS CM	Open End	US Equity Large Cap Value (Growth & Income)	B-	B-	B		Y	0
JPMorgan Value Advantage Fund Class R3	JVAPX	NAS CM	Open End	US Equity Large Cap Value (Growth & Income)	B	B-	B	Up	Y	0
JPMorgan Value Advantage Fund Class R4	JVAQX	NAS CM	Open End	US Equity Large Cap Value (Growth & Income)	B	B-	B	Up	Y	0
JPMorgan Value Advantage Fund Class R5	JVARX	NAS CM	Open End	US Equity Large Cap Value (Growth & Income)	B	B-	B	Up	Y	0
JPMorgan Value Advantage Fund Class R6	JVAYX	NAS CM	Open End	US Equity Large Cap Value (Growth & Income)	B	B-	B	Up	Y	15,000,000
Kayne Anderson Energy Development Company	KED	NYSE	Closed End	Energy Sector Equity (Growth & Income)	D	D	D	Down	Y	
Kayne Anderson Energy Total Return Fund	KYE	NYSE	Closed End	Energy Sector Equity (Natl Res)	D	D	D	Down	Y	
Kayne Anderson Midstream/Energy Fund, Inc.	KMF	NYSE	Closed End	Energy Sector Equity (Natl Res)	D	D	D	Down	Y	
Kayne Anderson MLP Investment Company	KYN	NYSE	Closed End	Energy Sector Equity (Natl Res)	D	D	D	Down	Y	
KCM Macro Trends Fund Class R-1	KCMTX	NAS CM	Open End	Multialternative (Growth)	B-	B-	B	Up	Y	5,000
KCM Macro Trends Fund Institutional Class	KCMIX	NAS CM	Open End	Multialternative (Growth)	B-	B-	B	Up	Y	250,000
Keeley All Cap Value Fund Class A	KACVX	NAS CM	Open End	US Equity Mid Cap (Growth)	C+	C+	C+	Up	Y	2,500
Keeley All Cap Value Fund Class I	KACIX	NAS CM	Open End	US Equity Mid Cap (Growth)	C+	C+	C+	Up	Y	1,000,000
Keeley Mid Cap Dividend Value Fund Class A	KMDVX	NAS CM	Open End	US Equity Mid Cap (Growth)	B	B	B	Up	Y	2,500
Keeley Mid Cap Dividend Value Fund Class I	KMDIX	NAS CM	Open End	US Equity Mid Cap (Growth)	B	B+	B	Up	Y	1,000,000
Keeley Small Cap Dividend Value Fund Class A	KSDVX	NAS CM	Open End	US Equity Small Cap (Small Company)	B	B	B-	Up	Y	2,500
Keeley Small Cap Dividend Value Fund Class I	KSDIX	NAS CM	Open End	US Equity Small Cap (Small Company)	B	B	B-	Up	Y	1,000,000
Keeley Small Cap Value Fund Class A	KSCVX	NAS CM	Open End	US Equity Small Cap (Small Company)	C+	C+	B-	Up	Y	2,500
Keeley Small Cap Value Fund Class I	KSCIX	NAS CM	Open End	US Equity Small Cap (Small Company)	C+	C+	B-	Up	Y	1,000,000
Keeley Small-Mid Cap Value Fund Class A	KSMVX	NAS CM	Open End	US Equity Small Cap (Growth)	B-	B-	B-	Up	Y	2,500
Keeley Small-Mid Cap Value Fund Class I	KSMIX	NAS CM	Open End	US Equity Small Cap (Growth)	B-	B	B-	Up	Y	1,000,000
Kellner Merger Fund Institutional Class	GAKIX	NAS CM	Open End	Market Neutral (World Stock)	C+	C	B		Y	100,000
Kellner Merger Fund Investor Class	GAKAX	NAS CM	Open End	Market Neutral (World Stock)	C+	C	B		Y	2,000
Kempner Multi-Cap Deep Value Fund Institutional Class	FIKDX	NAS CM	Open End	US Equity Large Cap Value (Growth & Income)	C+	C+	C+		Y	500,000
Kempner Multi-Cap Deep Value Fund Investor Class	FAKDX	NAS CM	Open End	US Equity Large Cap Value (Growth & Income)	C+	C+	C+		Y	500
Kinetics Global Fund Class Advisor Class A	KGLAX	NAS CM	Open End	Global Equity (World Stock)	B	B+	C	Up	Y	2,500
Kinetics Global Fund Class Advisor Class C	KGLCX	NAS CM	Open End	Global Equity (World Stock)	B-	B	C	Up	Y	2,500
Kinetics Global No Load Class	WWWEX	NAS CM	Open End	Global Equity (World Stock)	B	B+	C	Up	Y	2,500
Kinetics Internet Advisor Fund Class A	KINAX	NAS CM	Open End	US Equity Large Cap Growth (Technology)	B	A	C	Up	Y	2,500
Kinetics Internet Advisor Fund Class C	KINCX	NAS CM	Open End	US Equity Large Cap Growth (Technology)	B	A	C	Up	Y	2,500
Kinetics Internet Fund No Load Class	WWWFX	NAS CM	Open End	US Equity Large Cap Growth (Technology)	B	A	C	Up	Y	2,500

★ Expanded analysis of this fund is included in Section II.

Min Additional Investment	TOTAL RETURNS 3-Month Total Return	6-Month Total Return	1-Year Total Return	3-Year Total Return	5-Year Total Return	PERFORMANCE Dividend Yield (TTM)	Expense Ratio	3-Yr Std Deviation	3-Year Beta	ASSETS NAV	Total Assets (MIL)	ASSET ALLOCATION & TURNOVER %Cash	%Stocks	%Bonds	%Other	Turnover Ratio	BULL & BEAR Last Bull Market Total Return	Last Bear Market Total Return	FEES Front End Fee (%)	Back End Fee (%)	Inception Date
	6.81	11.41	21.48	31.86	112.29	0.27	0.85	11.82	1.12	29.96	9,648	2	98	0	0	131	24.77	-18.45			Nov-05
	6.66	11.11	20.86	29.87	107.01	0	1.45	11.82	1.12	28.87	9,648	2	98	0	0	131	24.36	-18.58			Nov-08
	6.84	11.52	21.72	32.64	114.37	0.41	0.8	11.83	1.12	30.09	9,648	2	98	0	0	131	24.93	-18.39			May-06
	6.81	11.41	21.47	31.85	112.28		0.7	11.82	1.12	30.06	9,648	2	98	0	0	131	24.77	-18.45			Nov-17
50	6.46	11.22	21.23	27.84	102.09	1.14	0.6	10.65	1.03	28.09	7,921	1	99	0	0	40	24.78	-16.25	5.25		Sep-01
	6.52	11.30	21.48	28.74	104.55	1.36	0.35	10.66	1.04	28.32	7,921	1	99	0	0	40	25.02	-16.18			Sep-01
	6.53	11.32	21.49	29.05	105.78	1.35	0.45	10.68	1.04	28.28	7,921	1	99	0	0	40	25.07	-16.09			Jan-97
	6.55	11.37	21.63	29.52	106.90	1.46	0.25	10.65	1.03	28.29	7,921	1	99	0	0	40	25.13	-16.04			Mar-03
50	3.35	7.86	8.52	24.95	94.37	0.07	1.22	14.21	0.99	18.31	1,857	4	96	0	0	53	30.04	-26.64	5.25		Nov-07
50	3.21	7.54	7.97	23.11	89.59	0	1.74	14.22	0.99	17.51	1,857	4	96	0	0	53	29.67	-26.69		1.00	Nov-07
	3.40	7.93	8.75	25.88	96.86	0.27	0.97	14.18	0.99	18.7	1,857	4	96	0	0	53	30.22	-26.49			Sep-01
	3.43	8.02	8.97	26.57	98.69	0.43	0.81	14.21	0.99	18.68	1,857	4	96	0	0	53	30.29	-26.45			Nov-93
	3.29	7.70	8.25	23.99	91.97	0	1.49	14.2	0.99	17.98	1,857	4	96	0	0	53	29.82	-26.6			Nov-11
	3.38	7.85	8.51	25.43	95.91	0.38	1.23	14.22	0.99	18.21	1,857	4	96	0	0	53	30.1	-26.52			Sep-16
	3.42	7.97	8.79	26.30	98.26	0.43	1.01	14.22	1	18.64	1,857	4	96	0	0	53	30.29	-26.45			Sep-16
	3.42	8.02	8.90	26.50	98.58	0.49	0.86	14.21	0.99	18.65	1,857	4	96	0	0	53	30.29	-26.45			Sep-16
	3.48	8.07	9.07	26.97	99.47	0.49	0.72	14.24	1	18.69	1,857	4	96	0	0	53	30.37	-26.45			Nov-11
50	6.03	9.20	13.66	24.96	90.75	0.82	1.14	10.09	0.94	35.84	12,225	4	96	0	0	24	26.63	-17.35	5.25		Feb-05
50	5.88	8.94	13.10	23.06	86.01	0.48	1.64	10.1	0.94	35.74	12,225	4	96	0	0	24	26.24	-17.54		1.00	Feb-05
	6.09	9.34	13.95	25.91	93.16	1.09	0.89	10.1	0.94	36.02	12,225	4	96	0	0	24	26.82	-17.26			Feb-05
	6.15	9.47	14.22	26.81	95.47	1.27	0.75	10.11	0.94	36.01	12,225	4	96	0	0	24	27.01	-17.22			Feb-05
	5.97	9.09	13.54	24.81	90.47		1.39	10.1	0.94	35.72	12,225	4	96	0	0	24	26.64	-17.39			Jul-17
	6.01	9.20	13.64	25.51	92.51	1.23	1.14	10.1	0.94	35.56	12,225	4	96	0	0	24	26.82	-17.31			Sep-16
	6.09	9.31	13.93	26.43	94.88	1.28	0.89	10.1	0.94	35.88	12,225	4	96	0	0	24	27.01	-17.22			Sep-16
	6.14	9.43	14.12	26.70	95.29	1.33	0.74	10.11	0.94	35.96	12,225	4	96	0	0	24	27.01	-17.22			Sep-16
	6.18	9.50	14.22	26.84	95.51	1.34	0.64	10.1	0.94	35.98	12,225	4	96	0	0	24	27.01	-17.22			Sep-16
	4.80	2.64	-1.48	-22.37	16.27	1.04	11.11	21.01		18.01	174.1	-49	149	0	0	38	34.24	-15.98			Sep-06
	-1.60	0.81	-11.39	-45.94	-30.82	8.33	0	35.72	1.65	10.94	385.4	-24	117	5	1	44	34.11	-23.95			Jun-05
	-1.26	0.60	-10.65	-44.47	-18.52	7.94	2.03	35.9		14.83	312.2	-41	124	16	1	48	39.19	-16.9			Nov-10
	10.16	7.21	2.87	-25.45	9.33	0	5.18	25.05	1.28	18.67	1,822	-79	175	0	0	15	23.34	-13.34			Sep-04
100	9.37	18.08	22.53	24.41	77.70	0	1.65	9.4	1.42	13.25	94.6	0	100	0	0		12.32	-21.7			Aug-08
	9.61	18.34	22.80	24.68	78.09		1.4	9.4	1.42	13.25	94.6	0	100	0	0		12.32	-21.7			Mar-17
50	6.03	12.15	12.29	17.72	69.27	0.37	1.42	11.69	1.03	17.19	58.2	1	99	0	0	84	28.61	-21.99	4.50		Jun-06
10,000	6.09	12.30	12.58	18.59	71.46	0.59	1.17	11.65	1.03	17.36	58.2	1	99	0	0	84	28.95	-22.01			Dec-07
50	6.45	13.17	15.68	35.33	107.20	0.65	1.3	11.83	1.08	23.21	124.3	3	97	0	0	43			4.50		Oct-11
10,000	6.51	13.31	15.97	36.32	109.79	0.87	1.05	11.84	1.09	23.21	124.3	3	97	0	0	43					Oct-11
50	2.84	7.30	7.27	25.95	76.08	1.19	1.45	13.66	0.95	18.63	100.2	3	97	0	0	22	26.63	-19.53	4.50		Dec-09
10,000	2.90	7.48	7.52	26.95	78.23	1.42	1.2	13.67	0.95	18.66	100.2	3	97	0	0	22	26.83	-19.42			Dec-09
50	1.19	5.41	4.65	9.28	51.27	0.42	1.4	13.29	0.91	31.6	818.4	2	98	0	0	28	26.9	-26.93	4.50		Oct-93
10,000	1.25	5.54	4.88	10.10	53.16	0.6	1.15	13.29	0.91	32.01	818.4	2	98	0	0	28	27.1	-26.86			Dec-07
50	5.60	11.66	17.75	25.25	77.99	0.1	1.4	12.93	1.04	14.14	134.9	2	98	0	0	20	34.89	-28.05	4.50		Aug-07
10,000	5.70	11.80	18.13	26.30	80.36	0.3	1.15	12.99	1.05	14.44	134.9	2	98	0	0	20	35.03	-27.98			Aug-07
100	-0.83	-0.37	3.26	5.71	15.58	0	1.55	3.81	-11.36	10.74	151.5	52	48	0	0	224					Jun-12
100	-0.94	-0.47	3.03	4.99	13.52	0	1.8	3.77	-11.62	10.53	151.5	52	48	0	0	224					Jun-12
100	4.57	8.71	12.84	15.99	61.86	1.91	0.86	11.3	1.03	10.5	84.9	13	87	0	0	18	19.24	-18.18			Apr-08
100	4.51	8.58	12.48	15.22	59.94	1.74	1.11	11.24	1.02	10.49	84.9	13	87	0	0	18	19.07	-18.26			Jun-08
	21.68	38.30	50.29	47.29	67.99	0	1.66	15.34	0.81	7.15	13.2	39	48	0	12	11	18.85	-20.37	5.75		May-08
	21.48	36.52	48.02	43.55	61.88	0	2.16	15.44	0.81	6.76	13.2	39	48	0	12	11	18.56	-20.76		1.00	May-08
	21.73	36.89	49.19	47.07	68.05	0	1.41	15.59	0.82	7.15	13.2	39	48	0	12	11	18.85	-20.37			Dec-99
	27.30	38.70	57.05	50.55	121.12	0	2.12	15.1	0.98	49.27	149.1	38	49	0	12	2	21.45	-22.15	5.75		Apr-01
	27.18	38.43	56.36	48.38	115.86	0	2.62	15.1	0.99	44.24	149.1	38	49	0	12	2	21.18	-22.34		1.00	Feb-07
	27.37	38.85	57.42	51.68	123.88	0	1.87	15.11	0.99	52.18	149.1	38	49	0	12	2	21.67	-22.11			Oct-96

	MARKET			FUND TYPE, CATEGORY & OBJECTIVE	RATINGS					MINIMUMS
Fund Name	Ticker Symbol	Traded On	Fund Type	Category and (Prospectus Objective)	Overall Rating	Reward Rating	Risk Rating	Recent Up/ Downgrade	Open to New Investors	Min Initial Investment
Kinetics Market Opportunities Fund Advisor Class A	KMKAX	NAS CM	Open End	Financials Sector Equity (Growth)	B+	A	C+	Up	Y	2,500
Kinetics Market Opportunities Fund Advisor Class C	KMKCX	NAS CM	Open End	Financials Sector Equity (Growth)	B+	A	C+	Up	Y	2,500
Kinetics Market Opportunities Fund Class Institutional	KMKYX	NAS CM	Open End	Financials Sector Equity (Growth)	B+	A	C+	Up	Y	1,000,000
Kinetics Market Opportunities Fund No Load Class	KMKNX	NAS CM	Open End	Financials Sector Equity (Growth)	B+	A	C+	Up	Y	2,500
Kinetics Medical Advisor Fund Class C	KRXCX	NAS CM	Open End	Healthcare Sector Equity (Health)	C+	C	B-	Up	Y	2,500
Kinetics Medical Fund Class A	KRXAX	NAS CM	Open End	Healthcare Sector Equity (Health)	C+	C	B-	Up	Y	2,500
Kinetics Medical Fund No Load Class	MEDRX	NAS CM	Open End	Healthcare Sector Equity (Health)	C+	C	B	Up	Y	2,500
Kinetics Paradigm Fund Advisor Class A	KNPAX	NAS CM	Open End	US Equity Mid Cap (Growth)	B	B	B-	Up	Y	2,500
Kinetics Paradigm Fund Advisor Class C	KNPCX	NAS CM	Open End	US Equity Mid Cap (Growth)	B	B	C+	Up	Y	2,500
Kinetics Paradigm Fund Class Institutional	KNPYX	NAS CM	Open End	US Equity Mid Cap (Growth)	B	B+	B-	Up	Y	1,000,000
Kinetics Paradigm Fund No Load Class	WWNPX	NAS CM	Open End	US Equity Mid Cap (Growth)	B	B+	B-	Up	Y	2,500
Kinetics Small Capital Opportunities Advisor Fund Class A	KSOAX	NAS CM	Open End	US Equity Small Cap (Small Company)	B-	B	C	Up	Y	2,500
Kinetics Small Capital Opportunities Fund Advisor Class C	KSOCX	NAS CM	Open End	US Equity Small Cap (Small Company)	B-	B	C	Up	Y	2,500
Kinetics Small Capital Opp Fund Cls Inst	KSCYX	NAS CM	Open End	US Equity Small Cap (Small Company)	B-	B	C	Up	Y	1,000,000
Kinetics Small Capital Opportunities Fund No Load Class	KSCOX	NAS CM	Open End	US Equity Small Cap (Small Company)	B-	B	C	Up	Y	2,500
Kinetics Spin-Off & Corporate Restructuring Fund Adv Cls A	LSHAX	NAS CM	Open End	US Equity Mid Cap (World Stock)	C+	C+	C	Up	Y	2,500
Kinetics Spin-Off & Corporate Restructuring Fund Adv Cls C	LSHCX	NAS CM	Open End	US Equity Mid Cap (World Stock)	C+	C+	C	Up	Y	2,500
Kinetics Spin-Off & Corporate Restructuring Fund Inst Cls	LSHUX	NAS CM	Open End	US Equity Mid Cap (World Stock)	C+	C+	C	Up	Y	1,000,000
Kirr Marbach Partners Value Fund	KMVAX	NAS CM	Open End	US Equity Mid Cap (Growth)	B-	C+	B	Up	Y	1,000
KL Allocation Fund Advisor Class	GAVAX	NAS CM	Open End	Aggressive Alloc (Asset Alloc)	B	C+	A		Y	2,500
KL Allocation Fund Institutional Class	GAVIX	NAS CM	Open End	Aggressive Alloc (Asset Alloc)	B	C+	A		Y	500,000
Knights of Columbus International Equity Fund Class S	KCISX	NAS CM	Open End	Global Equity Large Cap (World Stock)	C+	C+	C+	Up	Y	0
Knights of Columbus Intl Equity Fund Inst Cls	KCIIX	NAS CM	Open End	Global Equity Large Cap (World Stock)	C+	C+	C+	Up	Y	25,000
Knights of Columbus Intl Equity Fund Inv Shares	KCIVX	NAS CM	Open End	Global Equity Large Cap (World Stock)	C+	C+	C+	Up	Y	1,000
Knights of Columbus Large Cap Growth Fund Class S	KCGSX	NAS CM	Open End	US Equity Large Cap Growth (Growth)	B-	C+	B-	Up	Y	0
Knights of Columbus Large Cap Growth Fund Inst Cls	KCGIX	NAS CM	Open End	US Equity Large Cap Growth (Growth)	B-	C+	B-	Up	Y	25,000
Knights of Columbus Large Cap Growth Fund Investor Shares	KCGVX	NAS CM	Open End	US Equity Large Cap Growth (Growth)	C+	C+	B-	Up	Y	1,000
Knights of Columbus Large Cap Value Fund Class S	KCVSX	NAS CM	Open End	US Equity Large Cap Value (Growth)	B-	C+	B	Up	Y	0
Knights of Columbus Large Cap Value Fund Institutional Cls	KCVIX	NAS CM	Open End	US Equity Large Cap Value (Growth)	B-	C+	B	Up	Y	25,000
Knights of Columbus Large Cap Value Fund Investor Shares	KCVVX	NAS CM	Open End	US Equity Large Cap Value (Growth)	B-	C+	B-	Up	Y	1,000
Knights of Columbus Small Cap Equity Fund Class S	KCSSX	NAS CM	Open End	US Equity Small Cap (Small Company)	C+	C+	B-	Up	Y	0
Knights of Columbus Small Cap Equity Fund Inst Cls	KCSIX	NAS CM	Open End	US Equity Small Cap (Small Company)	C+	C+	B-	Up	Y	25,000
Knights of Columbus Small Cap Equity Fund Investor Shares	KCSVX	NAS CM	Open End	US Equity Small Cap (Small Company)	C+	C+	B-	Up	Y	1,000
Kopernik Global All-Cap Fund Class A	KGGAX	NAS CM	Open End	Global Equity Mid/Small Cap (World Stock)	B	B+	C	Up	Y	3,000
Kopernik Global All-Cap Fund Class I	KGGIX	NAS CM	Open End	Global Equity Mid/Small Cap (World Stock)	B	B+	C	Up	Y	1,000,000
Kopernik International Fund Class I	KGIIX	NAS CM	Open End	Global Equity Large Cap (Foreign Stock)	C	C+	B	Up	Y	1,000,000
Korea Fund Inc	KF	NYSE	Closed End	Other Equity (Pacific Stock)	B	A-	B-	Up	Y	
KP International Equity Fund Institutional Shares	KPIEX	NAS CM	Open End	Global Equity Large Cap (Foreign Stock)	B-	B-	B-	Up	Y	0
KP Large Cap Equity Fund Institutional Shares	KPLCX	NAS CM	Open End	US Equity Large Cap Blend (Growth)	B	B	B		Y	0
KP Retirement Path 2015 Fund Institutional Shares	KPRAX	NAS CM	Open End	Target Date 2000-2020 (Asset Alloc)	B-	C+	B	Up	Y	0
KP Retirement Path 2020 Fund Institutional Shares	KPRBX	NAS CM	Open End	Target Date 2000-2020 (Asset Alloc)	B-	C+	B	Up	Y	0
KP Retirement Path 2025 Fund Institutional Shares	KPRCX	NAS CM	Open End	Target Date 2021-2045 (Asset Alloc)	B-	C+	B	Up	Y	0
KP Retirement Path 2030 Fund Institutional Shares	KPRDX	NAS CM	Open End	Target Date 2021-2045 (Asset Alloc)	B-	C+	B	Down	Y	0
KP Retirement Path 2035 Fund Institutional Shares	KPREX	NAS CM	Open End	Target Date 2021-2045 (Asset Alloc)	B-	B-	B	Down	Y	0
KP Retirement Path 2040 Fund Institutional Shares	KPRFX	NAS CM	Open End	Target Date 2021-2045 (Asset Alloc)	B-	B-	B-	Down	Y	0
KP Retirement Path 2045 Fund Institutional Shares	KPRGX	NAS CM	Open End	Target Date 2021-2045 (Asset Alloc)	B-	B-	B-	Down	Y	0
KP Retirement Path 2050 Fund Institutional Shares	KPRHX	NAS CM	Open End	Target Date 2046+ (Asset Alloc)	B-	B-	B-	Down	Y	0
KP Retirement Path 2055 Fund Institutional Shares	KPRIX	NAS CM	Open End	Target Date 2046+ (Asset Alloc)	B-	B-	B-	Down	Y	0
KP Retirement Path 2060 Fund Institutional Shares	KPRJX	NAS CM	Open End	Target Date 2046+ (Asset Alloc)	B-	B-	B-	Down	Y	0
KP Small Cap Equity Fund Institutional Shares	KPSCX	NAS CM	Open End	US Equity Small Cap (Small Company)	B+	A-	B	Up	Y	0
Ladenburg Aggressive Growth Fund Class A	LAWAX	NAS CM	Open End	Aggressive Alloc (Aggr Growth)	C	C+	B	Up	Y	1,000
Ladenburg Aggressive Growth Fund Class C	LAWCX	NAS CM	Open End	Aggressive Alloc (Aggr Growth)	C	C+	B	Up	Y	1,000

★ Expanded analysis of this fund is included in Section II.

Min Additional Investment	TOTAL RETURNS 3-Month Total Return	6-Month Total Return	1-Year Total Return	3-Year Total Return	5-Year Total Return	PERFORMANCE Dividend Yield (TTM)	Expense Ratio	3-Yr Std Deviation	3-Year Beta	ASSETS NAV	Total Assets (ML)	ASSET ALLOCATION & TURNOVER %Cash	%Stocks	%Bonds	%Other	Turnover Ratio	BULL & BEAR Last Bull Market Total Return	Last Bear Market Total Return	FEES Front End Fee (%)	Back End Fee (%)	Inception Date
	19.41	36.27	46.90	59.82	123.72	0	1.89	13.22	0.68	26.41	65.1	29	60	0	11	5	20.76	-18.66	5.75		Jan-06
	19.22	35.95	46.12	57.45	118.01	0	2.39	13.22	0.68	25.53	65.1	29	60	0	11	5	20.51	-18.9		1.00	Feb-07
	19.59	36.68	47.64	62.13	129.11	0	1.44	13.24	0.68	27.04	65.1	29	60	0	11	5	21.18	-18.55			May-08
	19.47	36.51	47.27	61.03	126.44	0	1.64	13.21	0.68	26.72	65.1	29	60	0	11	5	20.96	-18.6			Jan-06
	-3.02	1.07	9.85	5.95	84.16	0	2.14	14.73	0.97	23.57	19.7	6	94	0	0	0	12.64	-15.62		1.00	Feb-07
	-2.90	1.36	10.43	7.57	88.97	0.33	1.64	14.74	0.97	24.33	19.7	6	94	0	0	0	12.96	-15.46	5.75		Apr-01
	-2.86	1.44	10.70	8.36	91.31	0.71	1.39	14.74	0.97	25.33	19.7	6	94	0	0	0	13.1	-15.34			Sep-99
	7.75	19.96	28.07	39.80	103.58	0	1.89	12.86	0.92	46.99	744.6	7	91	0	2	2	23.4	-24.98	5.75		Apr-01
	7.61	19.68	27.47	37.72	98.49	0	2.39	12.87	0.93	44.21	744.6	7	91	0	2	2	23.05	-25.14		1.00	Jun-02
	7.85	20.22	28.65	41.70	108.22	0	1.44	12.87	0.92	48.62	744.6	7	91	0	2	2	23.72	-24.84			May-05
	7.80	20.10	28.40	40.87	106.09	0	1.64	12.87	0.92	48.32	744.6	7	91	0	2	2	23.58	-24.9			Dec-99
	6.77	21.13	25.94	36.61	104.97	0	1.91	13.86	0.69	49.81	178.2	7	87	0	6	4	26.46	-22.13	5.75		Dec-01
	6.62	20.81	25.31	34.56	99.95	0	2.41	13.86	0.69	47.77	178.2	7	87	0	6	4	26.15	-22.33		1.00	Feb-07
	6.87	21.40	26.50	38.48	109.62	0	1.46	13.87	0.69	52.07	178.2	7	87	0	6	4	26.82	-21.99			Aug-05
	6.81	21.27	26.23	37.62	107.57	0	1.66	13.87	0.69	51.25	178.2	7	87	0	6	4	26.7	-22.08			Mar-00
	2.32	12.49	15.66	13.84	57.95	0	1.5	13.44	1.07	10.67	24.2	1	99	0	0	11	23.52	-23.85	5.75		May-07
	2.03	11.95	14.74	11.24	52.41	0	2.25	13.38	1.06	10.17	24.2	1	99	0	0	11	23.12	-24.01		1.00	May-07
	2.36	12.61	15.89	14.66	59.94	0	1.25	13.42	1.07	10.68	24.2	1	99	0	0	11	23.77	-23.84			Jul-07
100	6.49	9.82	16.09	22.11	70.15	0	1.46	13.72	1.21	24.95	78.8	10	90	0	0	16	35.82	-25.77			Dec-98
250	5.09	9.64	15.88	22.88	56.32	0.24	1.47	7.02	0.51	15	481.1	11	67	20	2	117	14.51	-2.31			Sep-10
25,000	5.16	9.80	16.13	23.71	58.23	0.43	1.22	7.03	0.51	15.18	481.1	11	67	20	2	117	14.83	-2.21			Sep-10
	7.17	13.99	31.07			1.39	1.3			12.13	64.9	2	97	0	1	55					Jul-15
250	7.11	13.90	30.97			1.4	1.1			12.13	64.9	2	97	0	1	55					Feb-15
	7.13	13.88	30.77			1.15	1.55			12.13	64.9	2	97	0	1	55					Jun-16
	8.03	13.40	26.61			0.2	1.1			12.67	50.7	1	99	0	0	75					Jul-15
250	8.03	13.36	26.70			0.2	0.9			12.68	50.7	1	99	0	0	75					Feb-15
	7.98	13.16	26.16			0.02	1.35			12.65	50.7	1	99	0	0	75					Jun-16
	6.27	10.01	15.74			1.25	1.1			12.06	50.4	3	97	0	0	57					Jul-15
250	6.30	9.92	15.78			1.26	0.9			12.06	50.4	3	97	0	0	57					Feb-15
	6.33	9.79	15.37			1	1.35			12.06	50.4	3	97	0	0	57					Jun-16
	3.69	9.79	15.37			0.09	1.25			11.96	79.9	2	98	0	0	83					Jul-15
250	3.69	9.79	15.37			0.11	1.05			11.97	79.9	2	98	0	0	83					Feb-15
	3.70	9.79	15.17			0.02	1.5			11.94	79.9	2	98	0	0	83					Jun-16
250	1.99	11.60	8.74	43.06		2.89	1.35	21.58	1.18	10.58	1,160	6	90	1	3	39			5.75		Nov-13
	2.07	11.71	8.95	44.06		3.11	1.1	21.52	1.18	10.53	1,160	6	90	1	3	39					Nov-13
	2.88	10.29	10.49			0.3	0.45			12.09	87.9	35	64	0	1	50					Jun-15
	11.38	13.77	40.87	38.49	28.30	0.56	0	15.51	0.92	46.65	286.7	1	99	0	0	67	18.08	-26.46			Aug-84
	4.96	11.68	28.94	28.58		1.57	0.49	11.46	0.93	11.2	1,419	3	95	0	2						Jan-14
	6.43	11.66	23.84	39.08		1.22	0.34	10.28	1.01	12.98	2,215	2	98	0	0						Jan-14
	2.32	4.86	10.02	15.72		2	0.33	3.46	0.67	10.51	442.7	5	36	58	1						Jan-14
	2.77	5.85	12.03	18.18		1.91	0.37	4.39	0.75	10.9	870.4	5	45	49	1						Jan-14
	3.38	6.99	14.58	21.28		1.81	0.4	5.75	0.88	11.22	1,047	5	56	39	1						Jan-14
	3.83	7.98	16.92	24.20		1.72	0.44	7.2	1	11.44	994.8	5	65	29	1						Jan-14
	4.38	8.98	18.92	26.79		1.62	0.47	8.11	1.04	11.68	1,112	5	73	22	1	9					Jan-14
	4.60	9.55	20.28	28.47		1.53	0.48	8.75	1.06	11.83	1,024	4	78	17	1	8					Jan-14
	4.68	9.80	21.00	29.22		1.47	0.48	9.08	1.05	11.9	748.3	4	80	14	1	9					Jan-14
	4.83	10.12	21.52	29.85		1.45	0.48	9.08	1.01	12.01	401.7	4	82	12	1	10					Jan-14
	4.95	10.16	21.59	30.01		1.45	0.48	9.07	0.99	12.03	106.6	4	83	12	1	16					Jan-14
	4.90	10.17	21.65	30.05		1.45	0.48	9.11	0.99	12	21.5	4	83	12	1	51					Jan-14
	4.61	10.93	17.95	32.11		0.64	0.53	13.7	0.96	12.08	1,071	3	97	0	0						Jan-14
1,000	5.35	9.16	18.95			0	1.19			12.78	9.8	4	92	3	1	6			5.00		Aug-15
1,000	5.18	8.80	17.95			0	1.94			12.52	9.8	4	92	3	1	6				1.00	Aug-15

Fund Name	Ticker Symbol	Traded On	Fund Type	Category and (Prospectus Objective)	Overall Rating	Reward Rating	Risk Rating	Recent Up/ Downgrade	Open to New Investors	Min Initial Investment
	MARKET		FUND TYPE, CATEGORY & OBJECTIVE		RATINGS				MINIMUMS	
Ladenburg Aggressive Growth Fund Class I	LAGIX	NAS CM	Open End	Aggressive Alloc (Aggr Growth)	C	C+	B	Up	Y	1,000,000
Ladenburg Growth & Income Fund Class A	LOWAX	NAS CM	Open End	Moderate Alloc (Growth & Income)	C	C	B	Up	Y	1,000
Ladenburg Growth & Income Fund Class C	LOWCX	NAS CM	Open End	Moderate Alloc (Growth & Income)	C	C	B	Up	Y	1,000
Ladenburg Growth & Income Fund Class I	LOWIX	NAS CM	Open End	Moderate Alloc (Growth & Income)	C	C	B	Up	Y	1,000,000
Ladenburg Growth Fund Class A	LGWAX	NAS CM	Open End	Aggressive Alloc (Growth)	C	C+	B	Up	Y	1,000
Ladenburg Growth Fund Class C	LGWCX	NAS CM	Open End	Aggressive Alloc (Growth)	C	C	B	Up	Y	1,000
Ladenburg Growth Fund Class I	LGWIX	NAS CM	Open End	Aggressive Alloc (Growth)	C	C+	B	Up	Y	1,000,000
Ladenburg Income & Growth Fund Class A	LNOAX	NAS CM	Open End	Cautious Alloc (Growth & Income)	C	C	B	Up	Y	1,000
Ladenburg Income & Growth Fund Class C	LNOCX	NAS CM	Open End	Cautious Alloc (Growth & Income)	C	C	B	Up	Y	1,000
Ladenburg Income & Growth Fund Class I	LNOIX	NAS CM	Open End	Cautious Alloc (Growth & Income)	C	C	B	Up	Y	1,000,000
Ladenburg Income Fund Class A	LNCAX	NAS CM	Open End	Cautious Alloc (Income)	C	C	B	Up	Y	1,000
Ladenburg Income Fund Class C	LNCCX	NAS CM	Open End	Cautious Alloc (Income)	C	C	B	Up	Y	1,000
Ladenburg Income Fund Class I	LNCIX	NAS CM	Open End	Cautious Alloc (Income)	C	C	B	Up	Y	1,000,000
Lateef Fund Class A	LIMAX	NAS CM	Open End	US Equity Large Cap Growth (Growth)	B	B-	B	Up	Y	5,000
Lateef Fund Class C	LIMCX	NAS CM	Open End	US Equity Large Cap Growth (Growth)	B-	C+	B-	Down	Y	5,000
Lateef Fund Class I	LIMIX	NAS CM	Open End	US Equity Large Cap Growth (Growth)	B-	B-	B-	Down	Y	1,000,000
Latin American Discovery Fund	LDF	NYSE	Closed End	Latin America Equity (Foreign Stock)	C	C	C		Y	
Laudus International MarketMasters Fund™ - Investor Shares	SWOIX	NAS CM	Open End	Global Equity Large Cap (Foreign Stock)	B	B	B	Up	Y	100
Laudus International MarketMasters Fund™ - Select Shares®	SWMIX	NAS CM	Open End	Global Equity Large Cap (Foreign Stock)	B	B	B	Up	Y	50,000
Laudus Mondrian Emerging Markets Fund	LEMNX	NAS CM	Open End	Emerging Markets Equity (Div Emerging Mkts)	C	C+	C		Y	0
Laudus Mondrian International Equity Fund	LIEIX	NAS CM	Open End	Global Equity Large Cap (Foreign Stock)	B-	C+	B	Up	Y	0
Laudus Small-Cap MarketMasters Fund™ - Investor Shares	SWOSX	NAS CM	Open End	US Equity Small Cap (Small Company)	B	B	B	Up	Y	100
Laudus Small-Cap MarketMasters Fund™ - Select Shares®	SWMSX	NAS CM	Open End	US Equity Small Cap (Small Company)	B	B	B	Up	Y	50,000
Laudus U.S. Large Cap Growth Fund	LGILX	NAS CM	Open End	US Equity Large Cap Growth (Growth)	A-	A-	B+	Up	Y	100
Lazard Capital Allocator Opportunistic Strat Inst Shares	LCAIX	NAS CM	Open End	Moderate Alloc (Growth)	B-	C+	B-	Down	Y	100,000
Lazard Capital Allocator Opportunistic Strat Open Shares	LCAOX	NAS CM	Open End	Moderate Alloc (Growth)	B-	C+	B-	Down	Y	2,500
Lazard Developing Mkts Eq Port Institutiona Shares	LDMIX	NAS CM	Open End	Emerging Markets Equity (Div Emerging Mkts)	B	A	C	Up	Y	100,000
Lazard Developing Markets Equity Portfolio Open Shares	LDMOX	NAS CM	Open End	Emerging Markets Equity (Div Emerging Mkts)	B	A-	C	Up	Y	2,500
Lazard Emerging Mkts Core Equity Portfolio Inst Shares	ECEIX	NAS CM	Open End	Emerging Markets Equity (Div Emerging Mkts)	B-	B	C+	Up	Y	100,000
Lazard Emerging Markets Core Equity Portfolio Open Shares	ECEOX	NAS CM	Open End	Emerging Markets Equity (Div Emerging Mkts)	B-	B	C+	Up	Y	2,500
Lazard Emerging Mkts Eq Advantage Port Inst Shares	LEAIX	NAS CM	Open End	Emerging Markets Equity (Div Emerging Mkts)	B-	B-	B-	Up	Y	100,000
Lazard Emerging Mkts Eq Advantage Port Open Shares	LEAOX	NAS CM	Open End	Emerging Markets Equity (Div Emerging Mkts)	B-	B-	B-	Up	Y	2,500
Lazard Emerging Mkts Equity Blend Portfolio Inst Shares	EMBIX	NAS CM	Open End	Emerging Markets Equity (Div Emerging Mkts)	B-	B	C	Up	Y	100,000
Lazard Emerging Markets Equity Blend Portfolio Open Shares	EMBOX	NAS CM	Open End	Emerging Markets Equity (Div Emerging Mkts)	B-	B	C	Up	Y	2,500
Lazard Emerging Mkts Equity Portfolio Inst Shares	LZEMX	NAS CM	Open End	Emerging Markets Equity (Div Emerging Mkts)	C+	B-	C	Up		100,000
Lazard Emerging Markets Equity Portfolio Open Shares	LZOEX	NAS CM	Open End	Emerging Markets Equity (Div Emerging Mkts)	C+	B-	C	Up		2,500
Lazard Emerging Markets Equity Portfolio R6 Shares	RLEMX	NAS CM	Open End	Emerging Markets Equity (Div Emerging Mkts)	C+	B-	C	Up		1,000,000
Lazard Emerging Mkts Multi Asset Portfolio Inst Shares	EMMIX	NAS CM	Open End	Emerging Markets Equity (Asset Alloc)	C+	C+	C+	Up	Y	100,000
Lazard Emerging Markets Multi Asset Portfolio Open Shares	EMMOX	NAS CM	Open End	Emerging Markets Equity (Asset Alloc)	C+	C+	C+	Up	Y	2,500
Lazard Equity Franchise Portfolio Institutional Shares	LZFIX	NAS CM	Open End	Global Equity Large Cap (World Stock)	U	U	U		Y	100,000
Lazard Equity Franchise Portfolio Open Shares	LZFOX	NAS CM	Open End	Global Equity Large Cap (World Stock)	U	U	U		Y	2,500
Lazard Fundamental Long/Short Portfolio Inst Shares	LLSIX	NAS CM	Open End	Long/Short Equity (Equity-Income)	C	C-	C+	Down	Y	100,000
Lazard Fundamental Long/Short Portfolio Open Shares	LLSOX	NAS CM	Open End	Long/Short Equity (Equity-Income)	C	C-	C+	Down	Y	2,500
Lazard Global Dynamic Multi Asset Portfolio Inst Shares	GDMIX	NAS CM	Open End	Alloc (Asset Alloc)	D+	C-	B	Up	Y	100,000
Lazard Global Dynamic Multi Asset Portfolio Open Shares	GDMOX	NAS CM	Open End	Alloc (Asset Alloc)	D+	C-	B	Up	Y	2,500
Lazard Global Equity Select Portfolio Institutional Shares	GESIX	NAS CM	Open End	Global Equity (Growth)	B	B-	B+	Up	Y	100,000
Lazard Global Equity Select Portfolio Open Shares	GESOX	NAS CM	Open End	Global Equity (Growth)	B	B-	B+	Up	Y	2,500
Lazard Global Listed Infrastructure Portfolio Inst Shares	GLIFX	NAS CM	Open End	Other Sector Equity (Equity-Income)	B+	B	A	Down	Y	100,000
Lazard Global Listed Infrastructure Portfolio Open Shares	GLFOX	NAS CM	Open End	Other Sector Equity (Equity-Income)	B+	B	A	Down	Y	2,500
Lazard Global Realty Equity Portfolio Institutional Shares	LITIX	NAS CM	Open End	Real Estate Sector Equity (Real Estate)	B-	C+	B		Y	100,000
Lazard Global Realty Equity Portfolio Open Shares	LITOX	NAS CM	Open End	Real Estate Sector Equity (Real Estate)	B-	C+	B	Up	Y	2,500
Lazard Global Strategic Equity Portfolio Inst Shares	LSTIX	NAS CM	Open End	Global Equity (Growth)	B-	C+	B	Up	Y	100,000

★Expanded analysis of this fund is included in Section II.

	TOTAL RETURNS					PERFORMANCE				ASSETS		ASSET ALLOCATION & TURNOVER					BULL & BEAR		FEES		
Min Additional Investment	3-Month Total Return	6-Month Total Return	1-Year Total Return	3-Year Total Return	5-Year Total Return	Dividend Yield (TTM)	Expense Ratio	3-Yr Std Deviation	3-Year Beta	NAV	Total Assets (MIL)	%Cash	%Stocks	%Bonds	%Other	Turnover Ratio	Last Bull Market Total Return	Last Bear Market Total Return	Front End Fee (%)	Back End Fee (%)	Inception Date
1,000	5.41	9.37	19.23			0	0.94			12.6	9.8	4	92	3	1	6				1.00	Aug-15
1,000	3.88	6.84	14.00			1.06	1.23			11.6	56.0	5	69	25	1	3			5.00		Aug-15
1,000	3.71	6.45	13.15			0.44	1.98			11.51	56.0	5	69	25	1	3				1.00	Aug-15
1,000	3.94	7.00	14.27			1.04	0.98			11.61	56.0	5	69	25	1	3				1.00	Aug-15
1,000	4.68	8.11	16.44			0.43	1.23			12.03	21.7	4	82	12	1	2			5.00		Aug-15
1,000	4.55	7.73	15.58			0	1.98			11.92	21.7	4	82	12	1	2				1.00	Aug-15
1,000	4.79	8.33	16.77			0.57	0.98			12.01	21.7	4	82	12	1	2				1.00	Aug-15
1,000	2.45	4.66	9.90			1.14	1.26			11.06	17.5	5	46	44	1	4			5.00		Aug-15
1,000	2.21	4.20	9.02			0.57	2.01			11.01	17.5	5	46	44	1	4				1.00	Aug-15
1,000	2.51	4.77	10.33			1.43	1.01			11.11	17.5	5	46	44	1	4				1.00	Aug-15
1,000	1.37	2.90	6.69			0.96	1.3			10.73	6.6	6	29	61	1	3			5.00		Aug-15
1,000	1.18	2.54	5.93			0.29	2.05			10.67	6.6	6	29	61	1	3				1.00	Aug-15
1,000	1.44	3.04	6.99			1.21	1.05			10.71	6.6	6	29	61	1	3				1.00	Aug-15
250	5.55	8.77	20.52	22.52	72.71	0	1.1	13.09	1.2	8.38	100.3	1	99	0	0	42	29.32	-15.7	5.00		Sep-07
250	5.42	8.34	19.64	19.83	66.45	0	1.85	13.1	1.2	7.07	100.3	1	99	0	0	42	28.7	-15.98			Sep-07
	5.58	8.81	20.86	23.39	74.73	0	0.85	13.08	1.2	8.69	100.3	1	99	0	0	42	29.44	-15.63			Sep-07
	-4.78	9.31	22.80	7.47	-18.61	0.73	0	23.39	0.92	13.04	85.1	2	96	0	1	13	15.91	-26.79			Jun-92
	4.76	13.42	33.39	34.34	56.88	0.54	1.4	11.19	0.87	26.51	1,754	3	94	0	3	69	18.42	-23.72			Oct-96
	4.83	13.55	33.65	34.99	58.19	0.66	1.25	11.22	0.87	26.47	1,754	3	94	0	3	69	18.51	-23.67			Apr-04
	5.65	9.74	26.84	10.88	-0.74	2.19	1.2	13.57	0.81	8.55	304.9	0	97	2	0	32	20.25	-20.86			Nov-07
	3.44	8.49	21.05	22.13	47.78	2.33	0.9	10.81	0.84	6.66	120.9	0	99	0	0	34	6.79	-16.76			Jun-08
	4.18	8.34	11.88	24.62	72.98	0.12	1.35	14.41	1	18.42	192.9	4	96	0	0	85	25.19	-25.88			Sep-97
	4.19	8.43	12.07	25.22	74.35	0.23	1.2	14.4	1	18.86	192.9	4	96	0	0	85	25.47	-25.92			Jun-04
	7.64	13.82	33.90	42.30	119.20	0	0.76	12.35	1.09	19.35	1,858	0	98	2	0	73	29.41	-15.39			Oct-97
50	3.44	8.45	17.73	18.61	40.91	1.27	1.71	7.4	0.67	10.6	156.0	18	71	17	-6	238	12.39	-12.74			Mar-08
50	3.43	8.37	17.47	17.05	38.27	1.06	2.01	7.4	0.67	10.55	156.0	18	71	17	-6	238	12.18	-12.97			Mar-08
50	6.53	18.25	41.14	41.92	23.09	0.68	1.23	17.08	1.03	14.48	270.2	1	92	0	7	56	23.21	-32.3			Sep-08
50	6.40	18.05	40.56	40.28	20.91	0.45	1.6	17.11	1.03	14.45	270.2	1	92	0	7	56	23.11	-32.42			Sep-08
50	5.81	16.91	40.34	30.44		0.57	1.3	13.81	0.83	12.3	208.4	2	96	0	2	62					Oct-13
50	5.70	16.63	39.80	28.90		0.36	1.6	13.78	0.83	12.27	208.4	2	96	0	2	62					Oct-13
50	6.46	16.55	42.51			1.1	1.1			12.27	4.4	1	91	0	6	57					May-15
50	6.32	16.42	42.09			0.89	1.4			12.27	4.4	1	91	0	6	57					May-15
50	5.27	14.40	35.97	33.94	22.36	0.38	1.26	15.51	0.95	12.93	382.1	4	93	0	3	47	21.63	-27.02			May-10
50	5.19	14.13	35.37	32.86	20.69	0.15	1.6	15.55	0.95	12.95	382.1	4	93	0	3	47	21.4	-27.16			May-10
50	6.26	13.50	28.01	22.75	17.95	1.22	1.09	16.33	0.98	20.02	12,896	1	99	0	0	12	18.86	-23.09			Jul-94
50	6.20	13.42	27.73	21.87	16.39	0.99	1.35	16.36	0.99	20.6	12,896	1	99	0	0	12	18.65	-23.21			Jan-97
	6.26	13.50	28.01	22.72	17.93	1.22	1.09	16.39	0.99	20.02	12,896	1	99	0	0	12	18.86	-23.09			Jan-15
50	3.83	10.11	22.08	17.41	8.99	0.85	1.31	11.42	0.69	9.72	244.9	18	61	14	6	1	13.69	-17.07			Mar-11
50	3.58	9.73	21.64	16.14	7.20	0.6	1.61	11.47	0.7	9.73	244.9	18	61	14	6	1	13.57	-17.17			Mar-11
50	4.24						0.95			10.38	5.5	0	100	0	0						Sep-17
50	4.18						1.2			10.38	5.5	0	100	0	0						Sep-17
50	1.31	2.30	5.66	2.84		0	1.65	4.77	0.25	11.56	78.2	69	32	0	0	257					Apr-14
50	1.14	2.04	5.43	1.95		0	1.93	4.78	0.25	11.45	78.2	69	32	0	0	257					Apr-14
50	5.11	9.92	20.69			0.42	0.91			11.49	68.4	1	81	13	4	67					May-16
50	5.07	9.78	20.32			0.27	1.21			11.49	68.4	1	81	13	4	67					May-16
50	6.47	12.30	28.51	31.38		0.56	1.06	10.64	0.95	13.04	54.2	4	95	0	1	40					Dec-13
50	6.40	12.06	28.01	30.20		0.33	1.36	10.66	0.95	13.04	54.2	4	95	0	1	40					Dec-13
50	0.16	4.11	20.80	43.48	116.43	2.65	0.97	8.83	0.77	16	5,458	9	91	0	0	35	6.99	-9.84			Dec-09
50	0.04	3.97	20.47	42.28	113.61	2.49	1.23	8.86	0.77	16.01	5,458	9	91	0	0	35	6.81	-10.09			Dec-09
50	4.55	5.79	14.68	17.07	32.98	2.61	1	10.86	0.95	15.52	5.1	2	94	0	3	38	22.22	-24.51			Sep-11
50	4.51	5.62	14.36	15.95	30.96	2.34	1.3	10.86	0.95	15.5	5.1	2	94	0	3	38	22.12	-24.51			Dec-08
50	6.24	10.99	24.19	20.97		0.55	1.1	9.73	0.86	2.31	5.7	0	97	0	3	67					Aug-14

Fund Name	MARKET Ticker Symbol	Traded On	FUND TYPE, CATEGORY & OBJECTIVE Fund Type	Category and (Prospectus Objective)	RATINGS Overall Rating	Reward Rating	Risk Rating	Recent Up/ Downgrade	Open to New Investors	MINIMUMS Min Initial Investment
Lazard Global Strategic Equity Portfolio Open Shares	LSTOX	NAS CM	Open End	Global Equity (Growth)	B-	C+	B	Up	Y	2,500
Lazard Global Total Return and Income Fund Inc	LGI	NYSE	Closed End	Global Equity (World Stock)	B-	B	C	Up	Y	
Lazard Intl Equity Advantage Portfolio Inst Shares	IEAIX	NAS CM	Open End	Global Equity Large Cap (Foreign Stock)	C+	C+	B-	Up	Y	100,000
Lazard Intl Equity Advantage Portfolio Open Shares	IEAOX	NAS CM	Open End	Global Equity Large Cap (Foreign Stock)	C+	C+	B-	Up	Y	2,500
Lazard Intl Equity Concentrated Portfolio Inst Shares	LCNIX	NAS CM	Open End	Global Equity Large Cap (World Stock)	C+	C+	C+	Up	Y	100,000
Lazard Intl Equity Concentrated Portfolio Open Shares	LCNOX	NAS CM	Open End	Global Equity Large Cap (World Stock)	C+	C+	C+	Up	Y	2,500
Lazard International Equity Portfolio Institutional Shares	LZIEX	NAS CM	Open End	Global Equity Large Cap (Foreign Stock)	B-	C+	B	Up	Y	100,000
Lazard International Equity Portfolio Open Shares	LZIOX	NAS CM	Open End	Global Equity Large Cap (Foreign Stock)	B-	C+	B	Up	Y	2,500
Lazard International Equity Portfolio R6 Shares	RLIEX	NAS CM	Open End	Global Equity Large Cap (Foreign Stock)	B-	C+	B	Up	Y	1,000,000
Lazard Intl Equity Select Portfolio Inst Shares	LZSIX	NAS CM	Open End	Global Equity Large Cap (Foreign Stock)	B-	C+	B-	Up	Y	100,000
Lazard International Equity Select Portfolio Open Shares	LZESX	NAS CM	Open End	Global Equity Large Cap (Foreign Stock)	B-	C+	B-	Up	Y	2,500
Lazard Intl Small Cap Equity Portfolio Inst Shares	LZISX	NAS CM	Open End	Global Equity Mid/Small Cap (Foreign Stock)	B+	A-	B	Up	Y	100,000
Lazard Intl Small Cap Equity Portfolio Open Shares	LZSMX	NAS CM	Open End	Global Equity Mid/Small Cap (Foreign Stock)	B+	A-	B	Up	Y	2,500
Lazard Intl Strategic Equity Portfolio Inst Shares	LISIX	NAS CM	Open End	Global Equity Large Cap (Growth)	B-	C+	B	Up	Y	100,000
Lazard Intl Strategic Equity Portfolio Open Shares	LISOX	NAS CM	Open End	Global Equity Large Cap (Growth)	B-	C+	B	Up	Y	2,500
Lazard International Strategic Equity Portfolio R6 Shares	RLITX	NAS CM	Open End	Global Equity Large Cap (Growth)	B-	C+	B	Up	Y	1,000,000
Lazard Managed Equity Volatility Portfolio Inst Shares	MEVIX	NAS CM	Open End	Global Equity (Growth & Income)	B-	C+	B+	Up	Y	100,000
Lazard Managed Equity Volatility Portfolio Open Shares	MEVOX	NAS CM	Open End	Global Equity (Growth & Income)	B-	C+	B+	Up	Y	2,500
Lazard Real Assets & Pricing Opp Portfolio Inst Shares	RALIX	NAS CM	Open End	Alloc (Growth)	D-	D+	A		Y	100,000
Lazard Real Assets & Pricing Opp Portfolio Open Shares	RALOX	NAS CM	Open End	Alloc (Growth)	D-	D+	A		Y	2,500
Lazard US Equity Concentrated Portfolio Inst Shares	LEVIX	NAS CM	Open End	US Equity Large Cap Blend (Growth)	B	B-	A		Y	100,000
Lazard US Equity Concentrated Portfolio Open Shares	LEVOX	NAS CM	Open End	US Equity Large Cap Blend (Growth)	B	B-	A		Y	2,500
Lazard US Equity Concentrated Portfolio R6 Shares	RLUEX	NAS CM	Open End	US Equity Large Cap Blend (Growth)	B	B-	A		Y	1,000,000
Lazard US Realty Equity Portfolio Institutional Shares	LREIX	NAS CM	Open End	Real Estate Sector Equity (Real Estate)	B	C+	A-	Up	Y	100,000
Lazard US Realty Equity Portfolio Open Shares	LREOX	NAS CM	Open End	Real Estate Sector Equity (Real Estate)	B	C+	A-	Up	Y	2,500
Lazard US Realty Income Portfolio Institutional Shares	LRIIX	NAS CM	Open End	Real Estate Sector Equity (Real Estate)	C	C	C		Y	100,000
Lazard US Realty Income Portfolio Open Shares	LRIOX	NAS CM	Open End	Real Estate Sector Equity (Real Estate)	C	C	C		Y	2,500
Lazard US Small-Mid Cap Equity Portfolio Inst Shares	LZSCX	NAS CM	Open End	US Equity Small Cap (Growth)	B	B	B	Up	Y	100,000
Lazard US Small-Mid Cap Equity Portfolio Open Shares	LZCOX	NAS CM	Open End	US Equity Small Cap (Growth)	B	B	B	Up	Y	2,500
Lazard US Strategic Equity Portfolio Institutional Shares	LZUSX	NAS CM	Open End	US Equity Large Cap Blend (Growth)	B-	B-	B-	Down	Y	100,000
Lazard US Strategic Equity Portfolio Open Shares	LZUOX	NAS CM	Open End	US Equity Large Cap Blend (Growth)	B-	B-	B-	Down	Y	2,500
Lazard US Strategic Equity Portfolio R6 Shares	RLUSX	NAS CM	Open End	US Equity Large Cap Blend (Growth)	B-	B-	B-	Down	Y	1,000,000
Lazard World Dividend & Income Fund Inc	LOR	NYSE	Closed End	Global Equity (World Stock)	C	C+	C		Y	
Legg Mason BW Alternative Credit Fund Class A	LMAPX	NAS CM	Open End	Other Alternative (Growth & Income)	C+	C	B-		Y	1,000
Legg Mason BW Alternative Credit Fund Class C	LMAQX	NAS CM	Open End	Other Alternative (Growth & Income)	C+	C	B-	Up	Y	1,000
Legg Mason BW Alternative Credit Fund Class FI	LMAOX	NAS CM	Open End	Other Alternative (Growth & Income)	C+	C	B-		Y	0
Legg Mason BW Alternative Credit Fund Class I	LMANX	NAS CM	Open End	Other Alternative (Growth & Income)	C+	C	B-		Y	1,000,000
Legg Mason BW Alternative Credit Fund Class IS	LMAMX	NAS CM	Open End	Other Alternative (Growth & Income)	C+	C	B-	Down	Y	1,000,000
Legg Mason BW Diversified Large Cap Value Fund Class A	LBWAX	NAS CM	Open End	US Equity Large Cap Value (Growth)	B	B	B	Up	Y	1,000
Legg Mason BW Diversified Large Cap Value Fund Class A2	LLVAX	NAS CM	Open End	US Equity Large Cap Value (Growth)	B	B	B	Up	Y	1,000
Legg Mason BW Diversified Large Cap Value Fund Class C	LBWCX	NAS CM	Open End	US Equity Large Cap Value (Growth)	B	B-	B	Up	Y	1,000
Legg Mason BW Diversified Large Cap Value Fund Class I	LBWIX	NAS CM	Open End	US Equity Large Cap Value (Growth)	B	B	B	Up	Y	1,000,000
Legg Mason BW Diversified Large Cap Value Fund Class IS	LBISX	NAS CM	Open End	US Equity Large Cap Value (Growth)	B	B	B	Up	Y	1,000,000
Legg Mason BW Diversified Large Cap Value Fund Class R	LBDRX	NAS CM	Open End	US Equity Large Cap Value (Growth)	B	B	B	Up	Y	0
Legg Mason BW Dynamic Large Cap Value Fund Class A	LMBJX	NAS CM	Open End	US Equity Large Cap Value (Growth)	B	B-	B	Up	Y	1,000
Legg Mason BW Dynamic Large Cap Value Fund Class C	LMBBX	NAS CM	Open End	US Equity Large Cap Value (Growth)	B-	B-	B	Up	Y	1,000
Legg Mason BW Dynamic Large Cap Value Fund Class I	LMBEX	NAS CM	Open End	US Equity Large Cap Value (Growth)	B	B-	B	Up	Y	1,000,000
Legg Mason BW Dynamic Large Cap Value Fund Class IS	LMBGX	NAS CM	Open End	US Equity Large Cap Value (Growth)	B-	B-	B-	Down	Y	1,000,000
Legg Mason BW Dynamic Large Cap Value Fund Class R	LMBHX	NAS CM	Open End	US Equity Large Cap Value (Growth)	B-	B-	B	Down	Y	0
Leigh Baldwin Total Return Fund	LEBOX	NAS CM	Open End	Long/Short Equity (Growth & Income)	D+	D	C	Down	Y	1,000
Leland Real Asset Opportunities Fund Class A	GHTAX	NAS CM	Open End	Global Equity Mid/Small Cap (Income)	C	C+	C		Y	2,500
Leland Real Asset Opportunities Fund Class C	GHTCX	NAS CM	Open End	Global Equity Mid/Small Cap (Income)	C	C+	C		Y	2,500

★ Expanded analysis of this fund is included in Section II.

Min Additional Investment	TOTAL RETURNS 3-Month Total Return	6-Month Total Return	1-Year Total Return	3-Year Total Return	5-Year Total Return	PERFORMANCE Dividend Yield (TTM)	Expense Ratio	3-Yr Std Deviation	3-Year Beta	ASSETS NAV	Total Assets (MIL)	ASSET ALLOCATION & TURNOVER %Cash	%Stocks	%Bonds	%Other	Turnover Ratio	BULL & BEAR Last Bull Market Total Return	Last Bear Market Total Return	FEES Front End Fee (%)	Back End Fee (%)	Inception Date
50	6.12	10.78	23.71	19.77		0.31	1.4	9.74	0.86	2.3	5.7	0	97	0	3	67					Aug-14
	7.07	13.61	33.26	32.81	56.60	3.31	0	12.92	1.18	19.81	187.5	5	86	8	1	103	19.05	-16.93			Apr-04
50	3.20	9.06	24.97			1.45	0.9			10.92	2.6	1	96	0	3	92					May-15
50	3.17	8.84	24.60			1.22	1.2			10.92	2.6	1	96	0	3	92					May-15
50	5.22	9.22	23.28	12.85		1.11	1.05	13.27	0.96	10.43	68.8	4	94	0	2	92					Aug-14
50	5.11	9.10	22.86	11.95		0.86	1.35	13.32	0.96	10.45	68.8	4	94	0	2	92					Aug-14
50	4.49	9.49	22.80	18.74	39.34	0.71	0.84	10.92	0.85	19.61	3,855	4	94	0	1	25	18.72	-19.62			Oct-91
50	4.46	9.34	22.50	17.73	37.39	0.49	1.1	10.88	0.85	19.83	3,855	4	94	0	1	25	18.47	-19.69			Jan-97
	4.51	9.51	22.84	18.84	39.46	0.73	0.8	10.91	0.85	19.59	3,855	4	94	0	1	25	18.72	-19.62			Apr-15
50	5.05	11.54	28.30	21.94	36.12	0.67	1.06	11.31	0.88	11.02	55.0	4	95	0	1	42	18.7	-19.83			May-01
50	4.94	11.42	27.88	20.79	33.78	0.38	1.36	11.33	0.88	11.03	55.0	4	95	0	1	42	18.64	-20.04			May-01
50	7.31	16.96	36.66	42.27	81.95	1.04	1.06	11.52	0.92	13.79	80.9	2	96	0	2	63	16.34	-19.95			Dec-93
50	7.21	16.72	36.29	41.04	79.49	0.84	1.3	11.51	0.92	13.82	80.9	2	96	0	2	63	16.15	-20.08			Feb-97
50	6.10	12.16	27.85	18.31	47.79	1.28	0.82	10.99	0.85	15.7	7,119	5	92	0	3	47	19.14	-21.78			Oct-05
50	6.06	12.00	27.44	17.38	45.93	1.07	1.07	10.99	0.85	15.83	7,119	5	92	0	3	47	19	-21.92			Feb-06
	6.08	12.14	27.81	17.99	47.40	1.28	0.82	10.99	0.85	15.71	7,119	5	92	0	3	47	19.14	-21.78			Jan-15
50	5.75	9.20	20.57			1.59	0.75			11.57	4.3	9	87	0	4	91					May-15
50	5.62	8.98	20.11			1.34	1.05			11.56	4.3	9	87	0	4	91					May-15
50	3.46	5.16	9.89				0.9			10.72	16.8	8	57	26	9	0					Dec-16
50	3.40	4.99	9.68				1.15			10.71	16.8	8	57	26	9	0					Jan-17
50	5.57	7.23	15.49	31.61	107.52	0.28	0.78	9.93	0.87	15.31	1,624	9	91	0	0	84	25.44	-20.23			Sep-05
50	5.51	7.09	15.21	30.61	103.93	0.06	1.04	9.91	0.87	15.42	1,624	9	91	0	0	84	25.08	-20.32			Sep-05
	5.54	7.20	15.52	31.56	107.45	0.17	0.78	9.92	0.87	15.34	1,624	9	91	0	0	84	25.44	-20.23			Nov-16
50	3.43	2.58	7.92	17.19	53.89	1.3	1	12.18	0.94	18.85	67.5	5	95	0	0	41	40.97	-19.31			Sep-11
50	3.42	2.47	7.68	16.25	51.90	1.03	1.29	12.2	0.94	18.94	67.5	5	95	0	0	41	40.73	-19.31			Dec-08
50	3.07	0.84	3.19	-0.18	26.39	2.9	1	11	0.78	7.33	28.1	4	64	0	0	75	21.52	-12.28			Sep-11
50	3.00	0.69	2.89	-1.03	24.67	2.62	1.3	11.08	0.78	7.31	28.1	4	64	0	0	75	21.35	-12.28			Jul-08
50	4.87	9.37	14.20	28.86	99.91	0.61	0.9	12.23	0.96	14.65	205.4	2	98	0	0	91	28.77	-29.13			Oct-91
50	4.79	9.19	13.82	27.73	96.88	0.41	1.2	12.2	0.95	13.72	205.4	2	98	0	0	91	28.52	-29.21			Jan-97
50	5.17	9.50	18.17	22.29	85.10	1.18	0.75	10.5	1.01	12.43	85.9	3	97	0	0	68	22.41	-17			Dec-04
50	5.08	9.32	17.74	21.23	82.24	0.93	1.05	10.46	1.01	12.48	85.9	3	97	0	0	68	22.26	-17.18			Dec-04
	5.16	9.50	18.16	22.47	85.32	1.19	0.75	10.45	1.01	12.43	85.9	3	97	0	0	68	22.41	-17			May-14
	3.76	8.09	20.91	9.05	22.93	5.09	0	12.92	1.12	12.7	85.6	4	85	9	2	82	19.96	-21.36			Jun-05
50	0.83	2.52	8.81	8.02	27.03	2.64	1.66	4.14	-32.12	10.36	467.2	42	0	55	2	156	9.98	4.66	4.25		Dec-13
50	0.64	2.14	8.11	5.73	22.58	2.16	2.41	4.16	-30.78	10.3	467.2	42	0	55	2	156	9.5	4.33		1.00	Dec-13
	0.84	2.54	8.94	7.92	26.95	2.75	1.55	4.14	-31.18	10.35	467.2	42	0	55	2	156	9.98	4.66			Dec-13
	0.89	2.65	9.19	9.10	28.82	2.93	1.37	4.15	-31.81	10.38	467.2	42	0	55	2	156	10.14	4.77			Dec-13
	0.90	2.77	9.35	9.50	29.30	2.98	1.27	4.17	-30.83	10.4	467.2	42	0	55	2	156	10.14	4.77			Dec-13
50	6.98	11.98	19.65	30.08	96.51	1.13	1.09	11.48	1.09	20.85	870.3	0	99	0	1	38	24.3	-15.61	5.75		Sep-10
50	7.00	11.94	19.48	29.53	95.02	1.11	1.18	11.48	1.09	20.65	870.3	0	99	0	1	38	24.57	-15.58	5.75		Oct-12
50	6.82	11.60	18.82	27.22	89.31	0.35	1.82	11.5	1.09	20.64	870.3	0	99	0	1	38	23.84	-15.93		1.00	Sep-10
	7.13	12.18	19.98	31.19	99.22	1.39	0.81	11.48	1.09	20.84	870.3	0	99	0	1	38	24.62	-15.49			Sep-10
	7.15	12.25	20.12	31.56	99.87	1.45	0.71	11.5	1.09	20.85	870.3	0	99	0	1	38	24.75	-15.49			Sep-10
	7.01	11.91	19.40	29.09	94.18	0.94	1.36	11.5	1.09	20.85	870.3	0	99	0	1	38	24.39	-15.67			Jan-14
50	8.50	14.48	21.50	27.11	114.06	1	1.1	11.92	1.07	12.35	157.1	1	99	0	0	83	27.82	-17.18	5.75		Nov-14
50	8.33	14.06	20.66	24.26	105.93	0.24	1.85	11.95	1.08	12.26	157.1	1	99	0	0	83	27.27	-17.44		1.00	Nov-14
	8.58	14.65	21.90	28.18	116.79	1.09	0.75	11.93	1.07	12.37	157.1	1	99	0	0	83	28.01	-17.1			Nov-14
	8.62	14.69	21.94	28.47	117.14	1.15	0.65	11.99	1.08	12.37	157.1	1	99	0	0	83	28.01	-17.1			Oct-14
	8.49	14.37	21.15	25.92	110.89	0.59	1.35	11.99	1.08	12.36	157.1	1	99	0	0	83	27.64	-17.27			Nov-14
100	0.29	0.73	-1.26	-3.99	-4.61	0	1.82	2.57	0.16	6.92	2.5	6	86	0	8	373	2.76	-6.26			Aug-08
250	0.67	2.66	1.75	9.86		4.02	1.43	12.22	0.9	9.02	40.0	18	82	0	0	37			5.75		Sep-13
250	0.41	2.23	0.94	7.44		3.35	2.18	12.19	0.9	8.94	40.0	18	82	0	0	37				1.00	Sep-13

Fund Name	Ticker Symbol	Traded On	Fund Type	Category and (Prospectus Objective)	Overall Rating	Reward Rating	Risk Rating	Recent Up/ Downgrade	Open to New Investors	Min Initial Investment
	MARKET		FUND TYPE, CATEGORY & OBJECTIVE		RATINGS				MINIMUMS	
Leland Real Asset Opportunities Fund Class I	GHTIX	NAS CM	Open End	Global Equity Mid/Small Cap (Income)	C	C+	C		Y	5,000,000
Leland Thomson Reuters Private Equity Index Fund Class A	LDPAX	NAS CM	Open End	US Equity Large Cap Blend (Growth)	C	C+	B-	Up	Y	2,500
Leland Thomson Reuters Private Equity Index Fund Class C	LDPCX	NAS CM	Open End	US Equity Large Cap Blend (Growth)	C	C+	B-	Up	Y	2,500
Leland Thomson Reuters Private Equity Index Fund Class I	LDPIX	NAS CM	Open End	US Equity Large Cap Blend (Growth)	C	C+	B-	Up	Y	5,000,000
Leland Thomson Reuters Venture Capital Index Fund Class A	LDVAX	NAS CM	Open End	US Equity Large Cap Growth (Growth)	B	B-	B	Up	Y	2,500
Leland Thomson Reuters Venture Capital Index Fund Class C	LDVCX	NAS CM	Open End	US Equity Large Cap Growth (Growth)	B	B-	B	Up	Y	2,500
Leland Thomson Reuters Venture Capital Index Fund Class I	LDVIX	NAS CM	Open End	US Equity Large Cap Growth (Growth)	B	B-	B	Up	Y	5,000,000
Leuthold Core Investment Fund Class Institutional	LCRIX	NAS CM	Open End	Moderate Alloc (Growth & Income)	B-	C+	B	Up	Y	1,000,000
Leuthold Core Investment Fund Retail Class	LCORX	NAS CM	Open End	Moderate Alloc (Growth & Income)	B-	C+	B	Up	Y	10,000
Leuthold Global Fund Class Institutional	GLBIX	NAS CM	Open End	Alloc (Growth & Income)	B-	C+	B	Up	Y	1,000,000
Leuthold Global Fund Class Retail	GLBLX	NAS CM	Open End	Alloc (Growth & Income)	B-	C+	B+	Up	Y	10,000
Leuthold Global Industries Fund Institutional Class	LGIIX	NAS CM	Open End	Global Equity (World Stock)	B-	B-	C+	Up	Y	1,000,000
Leuthold Global Industries Fund Retail Class	LGINX	NAS CM	Open End	Global Equity (World Stock)	B-	B-	C+	Up	Y	10,000
Leuthold Select Industries Fund	LSLTX	NAS CM	Open End	US Equity Mid Cap (Growth)	B	B	B-	Up	Y	10,000
Liberty All-Star Equity	USA	NYSE	Closed End	US Equity Large Cap Blend (Growth & Income)	B-	B-	B-		Y	
Liberty All-Star Growth	ASG	NYSE	Closed End	US Equity Mid Cap (Growth)	B	B	C+	Up	Y	
Linde Hansen Contrarian Value Fund Class A Shares	LHVAX	NAS CM	Open End	US Equity Mid Cap (Growth & Income)	C+	C	B	Up	Y	2,500
Linde Hansen Contrarian Value Fund Class I Shares	LHVIX	NAS CM	Open End	US Equity Mid Cap (Growth & Income)	C+	C	B	Up	Y	1,000,000
Litman Gregory Masters Alternative Strat Fund Inst Cls	MASFX	NAS CM	Open End	Multialternative (Growth & Income)	B-	C	B	Up	Y	100,000
Litman Gregory Masters Alternative Strategies Fund Inv Cls	MASNX	NAS CM	Open End	Multialternative (Growth & Income)	B-	C	B	Up	Y	1,000
Litman Gregory Masters Equity Fund Institutional Class	MSEFX	NAS CM	Open End	US Equity Large Cap Growth (Growth)	B	B	B-	Up	Y	100,000
Litman Gregory Masters Equity Fund Investor Class	MSENX	NAS CM	Open End	US Equity Large Cap Growth (Growth)	B	B	B-	Up	Y	1,000
Litman Gregory Masters Intl Fund Inst Cls	MSILX	NAS CM	Open End	Global Equity Large Cap (Foreign Stock)	C+	C+	C	Up	Y	100,000
Litman Gregory Masters International Fund Investor Class	MNILX	NAS CM	Open End	Global Equity Large Cap (Foreign Stock)	C+	C+	C	Up	Y	1,000
Litman Gregory Masters Smaller Companies Fund Inst Cls	MSSFX	NAS CM	Open End	US Equity Small Cap (Small Company)	C+	C+	C+	Up	Y	10,000
Live Oak Health Sciences Fund	LOGSX	NAS CM	Open End	Healthcare Sector Equity (Health)	B-	C	B+		Y	2,000
LJM Preservation and Growth Fund Class A	LJMAX	NAS CM	Open End	Long/Short Equity (Growth & Income)	B	B-	B+		Y	2,500
LJM Preservation and Growth Fund Class C	LJMCX	NAS CM	Open End	Long/Short Equity (Growth & Income)	B	C+	B+		Y	2,500
LJM Preservation and Growth Fund Class I	LJMIX	NAS CM	Open End	Long/Short Equity (Growth & Income)	B	B-	B+		Y	100,000
LK Balanced Fund Institutional Class Shares	LKBLX	NAS CM	Open End	Moderate Alloc (Balanced)	B-	C+	B	Up	Y	50,000
LKCM Aquinas Catholic Equity Fund	AQEIX	NAS CM	Open End	US Equity Large Cap Blend (Growth)	B-	B-	B	Down	Y	2,000
LKCM Balanced Fund	LKBAX	NAS CM	Open End	Moderate Alloc (Balanced)	B-	C+	B	Down	Y	2,000
LKCM Equity Fund Institutional Class	LKEQX	NAS CM	Open End	US Equity Large Cap Growth (Growth)	B-	B	B-	Down	Y	2,000
LKCM Small Capital Equity Fund Advisor Class	LKSAX	NAS CM	Open End	US Equity Small Cap (Small Company)	B-	B-	B	Up	Y	2,000
LKCM Small Capital Equity Fund Class Institutional	LKSCX	NAS CM	Open End	US Equity Small Cap (Small Company)	B-	B-	B	Up	Y	2,000
LKCM Small-Mid Cap Equity Fund Institutional Class	LKSMX	NAS CM	Open End	US Equity Mid Cap (Growth)	C+	C+	C+	Up	Y	2,000
LMCG Global Market Neutral Fund Institutional Shares	GMNIX	NAS CM	Open End	Market Neutral (Growth)	C	C-	B-	Up	Y	100,000
LMCG Global Market Neutral Fund Investor Shares	GMNRX	NAS CM	Open End	Market Neutral (Growth)	C	C-	B-	Up	Y	2,500
LMCG Global MultiCap Fund Institutional Shares	GMCIX	NAS CM	Open End	Global Equity (Growth)	B-	B	B-	Down	Y	100,000
LMCG Global MultiCap Fund Investor Shares	GMCRX	NAS CM	Open End	Global Equity (Growth)	B-	B	C+	Down	Y	2,500
LMCG International Small Cap Fund Institutional Shares	ISMIX	NAS CM	Open End	Global Equity Mid/Small Cap (Growth)	A-	A-	A-	Up	Y	100,000
LMCG International Small Cap Fund Investor shares	ISMRX	NAS CM	Open End	Global Equity Mid/Small Cap (Growth)	A-	A-	A-	Up	Y	2,500
LMP Capital and Income Fund Inc	SCD	NYSE	Closed End	Aggressive Alloc (Growth & Income)	C	C	C		Y	
LoCorr Dynamic Equity Fund Class A	LEQAX	NAS CM	Open End	Long/Short Equity (Growth)	B-	C+	B	Up	Y	2,500
LoCorr Dynamic Equity Fund Class C	LEQCX	NAS CM	Open End	Long/Short Equity (Growth)	C+	C+	B	Up	Y	2,500
LoCorr Dynamic Equity Fund Class I	LEQIX	NAS CM	Open End	Long/Short Equity (Growth)	B-	C+	B	Up	Y	100,000
LoCorr Long/Short Commodity Strategies Fund Class A	LCSAX	NAS CM	Open End	Other Alternative (Growth)	C+	C	B	Up	Y	2,500
LoCorr Long/Short Commodity Strategies Fund Class I	LCSIX	NAS CM	Open End	Other Alternative (Growth)	C+	C	B	Up	Y	100,000
LoCorr Long/Short Commodity Strategies Fund ClassC	LCSCX	NAS CM	Open End	Other Alternative (Growth)	C	C	B-	Up	Y	2,500
LoCorr Macro Strategies Fund Class A	LFMAX	NAS CM	Open End	Other Alternative (Growth)	B-	C	B	Up	Y	2,500
LoCorr Macro Strategies Fund Class C	LFMCX	NAS CM	Open End	Other Alternative (Growth)	C+	C	B	Up	Y	2,500
LoCorr Macro Strategies Fund Class I	LFMIX	NAS CM	Open End	Other Alternative (Growth)	B-	C	B+	Up	Y	100,000

★ Expanded analysis of this fund is included in Section II.

Min Additional Investment	TOTAL RETURNS 3-Month Total Return	6-Month Total Return	1-Year Total Return	3-Year Total Return	5-Year Total Return	PERFORMANCE Dividend Yield (TTM)	Expense Ratio	3-Yr Std Deviation	3-Year Beta	ASSETS NAV	Total Assets (MIL)	ASSET ALLOCATION & TURNOVER %Cash	%Stocks	%Bonds	%Other	Turnover Ratio	BULL & BEAR Last Bull Market Total Return	Last Bear Market Total Return	FEES Front End Fee (%)	Back End Fee (%)	Inception Date
10,000	0.64	2.73	2.00	10.69		4.3	1.18	12.2	0.9	8.88	40.0	18	82	0	0	37					Sep-13
250	12.09	17.56	28.25			0	1.76			12.69	12.6	4	95	0	1	48			5.75		Sep-15
250	11.87	17.07	27.19			0	2.51			12.63	12.6	4	95	0	1	48				1.00	Sep-15
10,000	12.17	17.72	28.50			0	1.51			12.74	12.6	4	95	0	1	48					Sep-15
100	9.07	19.98	51.24	70.30		0	1.77	21.65	0.96	14.5	19.1	4	91	0	5	88			5.75		Oct-14
250	9.04	19.76	50.18	66.67		0	2.52	21.63	0.96	14.29	19.1	4	91	0	5	88				1.00	Sep-15
10,000	9.19	20.15	51.49	71.07		0	1.52	21.66	0.96	14.56	19.1	4	91	0	5	88					Oct-14
100	3.14	7.88	15.88	19.59	57.06	0.16	1.12	5.21	0.39	20.55	865.9	18	63	18	1	52	10.31	-15.34			Jan-06
100	3.14	7.83	15.76	19.21	56.33	0.05	1.24	5.23	0.39	20.53	865.9	18	63	18	1	52	10.24	-15.39			Nov-95
100	3.89	8.78	16.71	16.20	43.43	0.13	1.22	5.14	0.37	9.65	96.0	17	63	20	0	63	9.92	-14.31			Apr-08
100	3.88	8.64	16.52	15.47	41.89	0	1.47	5.14	0.37	9.54	96.0	17	63	20	0	63	9.81	-14.32			Jul-08
100	6.09	13.51	25.02	25.12	83.09	0.52	1.25	10.28	0.88	17.85	11.8	1	99	0	0	87	17.63	-24.65			May-10
100	6.02	13.34	24.66	24.20	80.78	0.35	1.5	10.28	0.88	17.75	11.8	1	99	0	0	87	17.42	-24.71			May-10
100	4.71	11.57	21.83	26.30	113.77	0	1.5	11.22	0.96	26.27	20.0	3	97	0	0	63	21.41	-25.31			Jun-00
	5.96	10.22	22.06	27.27	87.68	0.53	1.01	11.73	1.13	6.87	1,291	2	98	0	0	46	25.67	-21.97			Oct-86
	5.55	9.69	27.89	37.45	99.39	0	0	12.46	1.14	5.67	149.5	2	98	0	0	100	24.13	-18.83			Mar-86
250	-0.28	-0.43	0.00	7.02	44.07	0	1.4	8.9	0.74	13.76	39.9	17	83	0	0	9			5.25		Feb-12
1,000	-0.21	-0.28	0.29	7.77	45.87	0.06	1.15	8.89	0.74	13.91	39.9	17	83	0	0	9					Feb-12
250	0.67	2.02	4.50	10.63	22.38	2.28	1.47	3.1	0.02	11.69	2,007	23	27	46	3	142	7.91				Sep-11
100	0.51	1.88	4.14	9.83	20.92	2.03	1.72	3.04	0	11.7	2,007	23	27	46	3	142	7.84				Sep-11
250	5.74	12.30	21.15	32.10	103.19	0.67	1.2	11.59	1.08	19.1	347.5	9	91	0	0	27	20.12	-19.88			Dec-96
100	5.72	12.19	20.86	31.11	101.50	0.46	1.45	11.54	1.07	18.81	347.5	9	91	0	0	27	19.84	-19.88			Apr-09
250	2.68	7.65	23.61	10.89	33.14	3.46	1.06	12.62	0.94	17.73	678.4	3	95	0	1	44	13.36	-26.29			Dec-97
100	2.65	7.53	23.35	10.02	31.46	3.12	1.31	12.62	0.94	17.83	678.4	3	95	0	1	44	13.15	-26.36			Apr-09
250	6.94	10.59	14.43	17.26	57.89	0	1.26	13.86	0.79	23.7	33.3	11	89	0	0	51	33.39	-24.67			Jun-03
25	1.94	-0.17	13.40	20.85	105.49	0.48	1.11	11.43	0.88	19.42	65.3	4	96	0	0	14	14.44	-10.35			Jun-01
500	1.41	3.65	9.17	35.98		0	2.49	6.23	0.05	10.6	781.9	101	-1	0	0	0			5.75		Jan-13
500	1.24	3.21	8.42	33.30		0	3.24	6.17	0.06	10.48	781.9	101	-1	0	0	0				1.00	Feb-16
1,000	1.57	3.79	9.45	37.01		0	2.24	6.19	0.05	10.76	781.9	101	-1	0	0	0					Jan-13
500	4.46	10.47	14.03	20.06	45.01	0.65	1.01	7.27	0.64	48.5	28.0	8	68	22	0	11	14.66	-16.84			Jun-12
500	8.39	11.11	20.78	26.89	78.62	0.19	1	12.13	1.13	17.19	67.6	1	99	0	0	18	24.27	-19.71			Jul-05
1,000	3.80	6.38	12.87	24.08	65.08	0.82	0.81	7.45	0.72	22.18	81.3	2	69	29	0	16	18.98	-10.62			Dec-97
1,000	6.07	10.31	21.68	29.81	84.83	0.69	0.8	11.22	1.06	26.02	341.9	3	97	0	0	16	25.81	-16.35			Jan-96
1,000	3.93	9.07	16.69	18.57	59.55	0	1.25	13.73	0.93	17.13	214.2	1	99	0	0	50	25.61	-20.49			Jun-03
1,000	4.04	9.31	17.03	19.50	61.63	0	1	13.74	0.93	18.44	214.2	1	99	0	0	50	25.79	-20.4			Jul-94
1,000	8.17	15.10	24.13	22.50	61.96	0	1.02	11.98	0.89	10.6	19.6	1	99	0	0	80	23.02				May-11
	-0.54	2.34	-0.81	0.83		0	1.61	5.37	2.18	10.91	51.9	98	3	0	-1						May-13
100	-0.73	2.17	-1.09	0.00		0	1.86	5.35	2.07	10.82	51.9	98	3	0	-1						May-13
	5.54	11.26	22.47	32.09		0.88	0.91	10.84	1	12.98	2.3	3	97	0	0						Sep-13
100	5.41	11.06	22.27	31.18		0.84	1.16	10.85	1	13	2.3	3	97	0	0						Sep-13
	5.56	13.85	32.73	47.27	100.66	2.32	0.86			12.81	35.0	2	97	0	1		12.74	-21			Apr-16
100	5.50	13.61	32.22	46.05	98.01	2.24	1.11			12.79	35.0	2	97	0	1		12.57	-21.08			Apr-16
	2.17	2.32	7.99	1.54	56.40	3.8	0	12.42		15.33	275.9	2	89	0	1	29	20.34	-13.32			Feb-04
500	1.20	2.97	2.37	25.22		0	3.21	12.64	0.86	11.82	64.7	35	65	0	0	343			5.75		May-13
500	0.98	2.64	1.67	22.47		0	3.96	12.58	0.86	11.39	64.7	35	65	0	0	343				1.00	May-13
500	1.18	3.11	2.60	26.12		0	2.96	12.58	0.86	11.96	64.7	35	65	0	0	343					May-13
500	2.55	9.24	5.91	25.85	40.95	2.87	2.71	9.14	-0.25	9.71	83.1	3	0	73	24	105			5.75		Dec-11
500	2.74	9.38	6.18	26.86	42.63	3.14	2.46	9.11	-0.26	9.81	83.1	3	0	73	24	105					Dec-11
500	2.42	8.81	5.04	23.06	35.61	2.35	3.46	9.09	-0.25	9.41	83.1	3	0	73	24	105				1.00	Dec-11
500	4.53	5.61	2.65	13.30	22.85	0	2.3	9.08	-0.07	8.64	809.2	5	0	92	4	62	-6.79	-7.17	5.75		Mar-11
500	4.34	5.22	1.92	10.85	18.30	0	3.05	9.02	-0.07	8.27	809.2	5	0	92	4	62	-7.23	-7.46		1.00	Mar-11
500	4.58	5.77	2.95	14.19	24.44	0.01	2.05	9.11	-0.07	8.77	809.2	5	0	92	4	62	-6.57	-7.08			Mar-11

	MARKET			FUND TYPE, CATEGORY & OBJECTIVE	RATINGS				MINIMUMS	
Fund Name	Ticker Symbol	Traded On	Fund Type	Category and (Prospectus Objective)	Overall Rating	Reward Rating	Risk Rating	Recent Up/ Downgrade	Open to New Investors	Min Initial Investment
LoCorr Market Trend Fund Class A	LOTAX	NAS CM	Open End	Other Alternative (Growth)	D+	D	D+	Up	Y	2,500
LoCorr Market Trend Fund Class C	LOTCX	NAS CM	Open End	Other Alternative (Growth)	D+	D	D+	Up	Y	2,500
LoCorr Market Trend Fund Class I	LOTIX	NAS CM	Open End	Other Alternative (Growth)	D+	D	C-	Up	Y	100,000
LoCorr Multi-Strategy Fund Class A	LMUAX	NAS CM	Open End	Multialternative (Growth)	C-	D+	C-	Up	Y	2,500
LoCorr Multi-Strategy Fund Class C	LMUCX	NAS CM	Open End	Multialternative (Growth)	D+	D	C-		Y	2,500
LoCorr Multi-Strategy Fund Class I	LMUIX	NAS CM	Open End	Multialternative (Growth)	C-	C-	C	Up	Y	100,000
LoCorr Spectrum Income Fund Class A	LSPAX	NAS CM	Open End	Aggressive Alloc (Income)	C-	C-	C-	Down	Y	2,500
LoCorr Spectrum Income Fund Class C	LSPCX	NAS CM	Open End	Aggressive Alloc (Income)	C-	C-	C-		Y	2,500
LoCorr Spectrum Income Fund Class I	LSPIX	NAS CM	Open End	Aggressive Alloc (Income)	C	C	C	Up	Y	100,000
Logan Capital Large Cap Growth Fund Institutional Class	LGNGX	NAS CM	Open End	US Equity Large Cap Growth (Growth)	B+	A-	B	Up	Y	100,000
Logan Capital Large Cap Growth Fund Investor Class	LGNHX	NAS CM	Open End	US Equity Large Cap Growth (Growth)	B+	A-	B	Up	Y	5,000
Longboard Alternative Growth Fund Class A	LONAX	NAS CM	Open End	Long/Short Equity (Growth)	C+	C+	C+	Up	Y	2,500
Longboard Alternative Growth Fund Class I	LONGX	NAS CM	Open End	Long/Short Equity (Growth)	C+	C+	B-	Up	Y	100,000
Longboard Managed Futures Strategy Fund Class A Shares	WAVEX	NAS CM	Open End	Other Alternative (Growth & Income)	C+	C	B-	Up	Y	2,500
Longboard Managed Futures Strategy Fund Class I Shares	WAVIX	NAS CM	Open End	Other Alternative (Growth & Income)	C+	C	B-	Up	Y	10,000
Longleaf Partners Fund	LLPFX	NAS CM	Open End	US Equity Large Cap Blend (Growth)	C+	C+	C	Up	Y	10,000
Longleaf Partners Global Fund	LLGLX	NAS CM	Open End	Global Equity (World Stock)	B-	B	C	Up	Y	10,000
Longleaf Partners International Fund	LLINX	NAS CM	Open End	Global Equity Large Cap (Foreign Stock)	C+	B-	C+	Up	Y	10,000
Longleaf Partners Small-Cap Fund	LLSCX	NAS CM	Open End	US Equity Mid Cap (Small Company)	B-	B-	B-	Up		10,000
Loomis Sayles Dividend Income Fund Class A	LSCAX	NAS CM	Open End	US Equity Large Cap Value (Equity-Income)	B-	C+	B	Down	Y	2,500
Loomis Sayles Dividend Income Fund Class C	LSCCX	NAS CM	Open End	US Equity Large Cap Value (Equity-Income)	B-	C+	B	Down	Y	2,500
Loomis Sayles Dividend Income Fund Class N	LDINX	NAS CM	Open End	US Equity Large Cap Value (Equity-Income)	B-	C+	B	Down	Y	1,000,000
Loomis Sayles Dividend Income Fund Class Y	LSCYX	NAS CM	Open End	US Equity Large Cap Value (Equity-Income)	B-	C+	B	Down	Y	100,000
Loomis Sayles Global Allocation Fund Class A	LGMAX	NAS CM	Open End	Alloc (Multi-Asset Global)	B	B-	A-	Up	Y	2,500
Loomis Sayles Global Allocation Fund Class C	LGMCX	NAS CM	Open End	Alloc (Multi-Asset Global)	B	C+	B+	Up	Y	2,500
Loomis Sayles Global Allocation Fund Class N	LGMNX	NAS CM	Open End	Alloc (Multi-Asset Global)	B	B-	A-	Up	Y	1,000,000
Loomis Sayles Global Allocation Fund Class Y	LSWWX	NAS CM	Open End	Alloc (Multi-Asset Global)	B	B-	A-	Up	Y	100,000
Loomis Sayles Global Growth Fund Class A	LSAGX	NAS CM	Open End	Global Equity (Growth)	D+	C	B+	Up	Y	2,500
Loomis Sayles Global Growth Fund Class C	LSCGX	NAS CM	Open End	Global Equity (Growth)	D+	C	B+	Up	Y	2,500
Loomis Sayles Global Growth Fund Class N	LSNGX	NAS CM	Open End	Global Equity (Growth)	D+	C	B+	Up	Y	1,000,000
Loomis Sayles Global Growth Fund Class Y	LSGGX	NAS CM	Open End	Global Equity (Growth)	D+	C	B+	Up	Y	100,000
Loomis Sayles Growth Fund Class A	LGRRX	NAS CM	Open End	US Equity Large Cap Growth (Growth)	A-	A-	A	Up	Y	2,500
Loomis Sayles Growth Fund Class C	LGRCX	NAS CM	Open End	US Equity Large Cap Growth (Growth)	A-	B+	A	Up	Y	2,500
Loomis Sayles Growth Fund Class N	LGRNX	NAS CM	Open End	US Equity Large Cap Growth (Growth)	A-	A-	A	Up	Y	1,000,000
Loomis Sayles Growth Fund Class Y	LSGRX	NAS CM	Open End	US Equity Large Cap Growth (Growth)	A-	A-	A	Up	Y	100,000
Loomis Sayles Multi-Asset Income Fund Class A	IIDPX	NAS CM	Open End	Moderate Alloc (Growth & Income)	B-	C+	B	Up	Y	2,500
Loomis Sayles Multi-Asset Income Fund Class C	CIDPX	NAS CM	Open End	Moderate Alloc (Growth & Income)	B-	C+	B	Down	Y	2,500
Loomis Sayles Multi-Asset Income Fund Class N	LMINX	NAS CM	Open End	Moderate Alloc (Growth & Income)	B-	C+	B	Up	Y	1,000,000
Loomis Sayles Multi-Asset Income Fund Class Y	YIDPX	NAS CM	Open End	Moderate Alloc (Growth & Income)	B-	C+	B	Up	Y	100,000
Loomis Sayles Small Cap Growth Fund Class N	LSSNX	NAS CM	Open End	US Equity Small Cap (Small Company)	B	A-	C+	Up		1,000,000
Loomis Sayles Small Cap Growth Fund Institutional Class	LSSIX	NAS CM	Open End	US Equity Small Cap (Small Company)	B	A-	C+	Up		100,000
Loomis Sayles Small Cap Growth Fund Retail Class	LCGRX	NAS CM	Open End	US Equity Small Cap (Small Company)	B	A-	C+	Up		2,500
Loomis Sayles Small Cap Value Fund Class N	LSCNX	NAS CM	Open End	US Equity Small Cap (Small Company)	B+	A-	B	Up		1,000,000
Loomis Sayles Small Capital Value Fund Admin Class	LSVAX	NAS CM	Open End	US Equity Small Cap (Small Company)	B+	A-	B	Up		0
Loomis Sayles Small Capital Value Fund Institutional Class	LSSCX	NAS CM	Open End	US Equity Small Cap (Small Company)	B+	A-	B	Up		100,000
Loomis Sayles Small Capital Value Fund Retail Class	LSCRX	NAS CM	Open End	US Equity Small Cap (Small Company)	B+	A-	B	Up		2,500
Loomis Sayles Small/Mid Cap Growth Fund Institutional Cls	LSMIX	NAS CM	Open End	US Equity Mid Cap (Growth)	C	C+	B-	Up	Y	1,000,000
Loomis Sayles Value Fund Admin Class	LSAVX	NAS CM	Open End	US Equity Large Cap Value (Growth & Income)	B-	C+	B	Down	Y	0
Loomis Sayles Value Fund Class A	LSVRX	NAS CM	Open End	US Equity Large Cap Value (Growth & Income)	B-	C+	B	Down	Y	2,500
Loomis Sayles Value Fund Class C	LSCVX	NAS CM	Open End	US Equity Large Cap Value (Growth & Income)	B-	C+	B	Up	Y	2,500
Loomis Sayles Value Fund Class N	LSVNX	NAS CM	Open End	US Equity Large Cap Value (Growth & Income)	B-	C+	B	Down	Y	1,000,000
Loomis Sayles Value Fund Class Y	LSGIX	NAS CM	Open End	US Equity Large Cap Value (Growth & Income)	B-	C+	B	Down	Y	100,000

★ Expanded analysis of this fund is included in Section II.

Min Additional Investment	3-Month Total Return	6-Month Total Return	1-Year Total Return	3-Year Total Return	5-Year Total Return	Dividend Yield (TTM)	Expense Ratio	3-Yr Std Deviation	3-Year Beta	NAV	Total Assets (MIL)	%Cash	%Stocks	%Bonds	%Other	Turnover Ratio	Last Bull Market Total Return	Last Bear Market Total Return	Front End Fee (%)	Back End Fee (%)	Inception Date
TOTAL RETURNS						PERFORMANCE				ASSETS		ASSET ALLOCATION & TURNOVER					BULL & BEAR		FEES		
500	8.99	7.19	3.56	-1.06		1.74	2.03	10.67	-0.23	11.03	697.4	7	3	86	5	83			5.75		Jul-14
500	8.84	6.80	2.84	-3.31		1.39	2.78	10.65	-0.23	10.83	697.4	7	3	86	5	83				1.00	Jul-14
500	9.15	7.25	3.83	-0.35		1.87	1.78	10.73	-0.23	11.09	697.4	7	3	86	5	83					Jul-14
500	9.17	7.20	5.17			3.48	3.42			8.28	26.6	0	67	10	19	95			5.75		Apr-15
500	9.02	6.80	4.55			2.52	4.17			8.31	26.6	0	67	10	19	95				1.00	Apr-15
500	9.26	7.37	5.50			3.8	3.17			8.27	26.6	0	67	10	19	95					Apr-15
500	0.47	0.79	3.50	1.77		7.95	3.09	10.04	0.69	7.39	94.4	-1	76	18	1	92			5.75		Dec-13
500	0.22	0.42	2.62	-0.61		6.89	3.84	10.03	0.7	7.42	94.4	-1	76	18	1	92				1.00	Dec-13
500	0.43	0.96	3.84	2.51		8.31	2.84	10.05	0.69	7.38	94.4	-1	76	18	1	92					Dec-13
50	7.57	12.61	31.31	42.90	110.96	0	1.24	12.67	1.12	21.43	28.4	1	99	0	0	9					Jun-12
50	7.58	12.56	31.14	42.01	108.54	0	1.49	12.68	1.12	21.14	28.4	1	99	0	0	9					Jun-12
250	5.11	10.40	18.91			18.5	2.24			2.75	13.9	164	0	0	-64	0			5.75		Dec-15
2,500	5.17	10.47	19.29			18.73	1.99			2.72	13.9	164	0	0	-64	0					Mar-15
250	7.13	11.04	13.22	14.24	35.29	0	3.12	11.85	0.93	11.56	460.5	84	19	0	-4	0			5.75		Mar-13
2,500	7.22	11.19	13.45	15.17	37.19	0	2.87	11.87	0.94	11.72	460.5	84	19	0	-4	0					Jun-12
0	3.62	6.98	15.51	12.29	58.87	0.01	0.95	15.18	1.24	26.84	3,292	29	71	0	0	17	22.63	-20.66			Apr-87
0	2.64	5.73	26.33	30.75	58.39	0.4	1.52	17.24	1.42	14.94	231.3	16	84	0	0	33					Dec-12
0	-0.30	5.31	24.22	28.07	41.60	1.96	1.33	17.01	1.25	16.63	1,168	26	74	0	0	21	7.14	-24.47			Oct-98
0	1.73	3.85	8.98	22.87	83.17	0.32	0.91	11.79	0.62	27.6	3,836	28	61	4	3	31	18.84	-16.72			Feb-89
50	2.37	4.31	10.19	21.61	73.13	2.23	1.1	10.06	0.94	11.32	45.6	0	97	0	0	35			5.75		Mar-12
50	2.18	3.92	9.34	18.77	66.64	1.59	1.85	10.09	0.95	11.26	45.6	0	97	0	0	35				1.00	Mar-12
	2.45	4.46	10.51	22.45	75.28		0.8	10.09	0.95	11.32	45.6	0	97	0	0	35					Mar-17
50	2.44	4.43	10.47	22.41	75.21	2.47	0.85	10.09	0.95	11.32	45.6	0	97	0	0	35					Mar-12
50	4.53	8.65	21.78	28.54	55.90	1.05	1.17	7.92	0.7	22.1	1,877	4	68	26	2	35	19.89	-16.57	5.75		Feb-06
50	4.32	8.23	20.90	25.63	50.09	0.39	1.92	7.93	0.7	21.91	1,877	4	68	26	2	35	19.33	-16.81		1.00	Feb-06
	4.59	8.80	22.06	29.45	57.85		0.84	7.95	0.71	22.19	1,877	4	68	26	2	35	20.04	-16.46			Feb-17
50	4.58	8.79	22.11	29.50	57.91	1.26	0.92	7.95	0.71	22.21	1,877	4	68	26	2	35	20.04	-16.46			May-96
50	5.44	11.75	31.75			0.23	1.3			13.19	17.7	0	100	0	0	12			5.75		Mar-16
50	5.20	11.29	30.74			0.02	2.05			13.06	17.7	0	100	0	0	12				1.00	Mar-16
	5.45	11.93	32.04				1			13.21	17.7	0	100	0	0	12					Mar-17
50	5.50	11.89	32.00			0.34	1.05			13.21	17.7	0	100	0	0	12					Mar-16
50	6.19	12.69	32.29	51.91	133.14	0.31	0.92	11.89	1.04	14.57	7,788	1	99	0	0	8	20.4	-12.95	5.75		Dec-96
50	5.97	12.22	31.39	48.58	124.20	0	1.66	11.94	1.05	13.4	7,788	1	99	0	0	8	19.83	-13.18		1.00	Sep-03
	6.24	12.79	32.75	53.55	135.53	0.47	0.58	11.93	1.05	15.52	7,788	1	99	0	0	8	20.6	-12.85			Feb-13
50	6.23	12.78	32.63	53.03	135.70	0.42	0.66	11.89	1.04	15.53	7,788	1	99	0	0	8	20.6	-12.85			May-91
50	3.54	6.68	12.41	20.47	46.13	3.09	1.08	6.09	0.68	13.87	142.3	3	64	27	2	341	15.83	-7.45	4.25		Nov-05
50	3.42	6.30	11.70	17.84	40.77	2.4	1.83	6.09	0.67	13.82	142.3	3	64	27	2	341	15.41	-7.76		1.00	Nov-05
	3.64	6.81	12.82	21.31	47.14	3.38	0.78	6.12	0.69	13.79	142.3	3	64	27	2	341	15.83	-7.45			Aug-15
50	3.71	6.86	12.76	21.42	47.38	3.34	0.83	6.09	0.67	13.8	142.3	3	64	27	2	341	15.83	-7.45			Dec-12
	4.48	11.15	27.02	35.52	107.17	0	0.83	14.34	0.92	25.54	1,270	5	95	0	0	45	26.16	-22.45			Feb-13
50	4.47	11.08	26.85	35.13	106.24	0	0.95	14.33	0.92	25.4	1,270	5	95	0	0	45	26.16	-22.45			Dec-96
50	4.39	10.91	26.55	34.09	103.49	0	1.2	14.32	0.92	23.46	1,270	5	95	0	0	45	25.89	-22.47			Dec-96
	3.06	9.75	10.12	33.58	96.59	0.39	0.89	13.91	0.96	34.24	1,105	1	99	0	0	25	29.96	-23.86			Feb-13
	2.91	9.43	9.50	31.32	91.10	0	1.45	13.91	0.96	32.38	1,105	1	99	0	0	25	29.55	-24			Jan-98
50	3.04	9.71	10.02	33.30	95.92	0.33	0.96	13.92	0.96	34.22	1,105	1	99	0	0	25	29.96	-23.86			May-91
50	3.01	9.58	9.77	32.31	93.49	0.12	1.21	13.92	0.96	33.7	1,105	1	99	0	0	25	29.72	-23.91			Dec-96
50,000	7.06	15.10	31.79			0.14	0.85			13.18	15.7	3	96	0	0	49					Jun-15
	4.84	7.36	14.16	19.33	82.11	0	1.19	11.55	1.1	21.19	1,184	1	99	0	0	27	24.98	-21.52			Feb-10
50	4.92	7.48	14.43	20.52	84.73	1.57	0.94	11.52	1.1	21.22	1,184	1	99	0	0	27	25.14	-21.44	5.75		Jun-06
50	4.72	7.07	13.55	17.83	77.86	0.85	1.69	11.52	1.1	21.02	1,184	1	99	0	0	27	24.63	-21.72		1.00	Jun-07
	5.07	7.77	14.94	21.98	88.24	1.83	0.57	11.52	1.1	21.25	1,184	1	99	0	0	27	25.35	-21.36			Feb-13
50	4.97	7.61	14.70	21.37	86.99	1.72	0.69	11.54	1.1	21.29	1,184	1	99	0	0	27	25.35	-21.36			May-91

	MARKET		FUND TYPE, CATEGORY & OBJECTIVE		RATINGS					MINIMUMS
Fund Name	Ticker Symbol	Traded On	Fund Type	Category and (Prospectus Objective)	Overall Rating	Reward Rating	Risk Rating	Recent Up/ Downgrade	Open to New Investors	Min Initial Investment
Lord Abbett Affiliated Fund Class A	LAFFX	NAS CM	Open End	US Equity Large Cap Value (Growth & Income)	B	B-	B		Y	1,000
Lord Abbett Affiliated Fund Class B	LAFBX	NAS CM	Open End	US Equity Large Cap Value (Growth & Income)	B-	B-	B	Down		1,000
Lord Abbett Affiliated Fund Class C	LAFCX	NAS CM	Open End	US Equity Large Cap Value (Growth & Income)	B-	B-	B	Down	Y	1,000
Lord Abbett Affiliated Fund Class F	LAAFX	NAS CM	Open End	US Equity Large Cap Value (Growth & Income)	B	B-	B		Y	0
Lord Abbett Affiliated Fund Class F3	LTFOX	NAS CM	Open End	US Equity Large Cap Value (Growth & Income)	B	B-	B		Y	0
Lord Abbett Affiliated Fund Class I	LAFYX	NAS CM	Open End	US Equity Large Cap Value (Growth & Income)	B	B-	B		Y	1,000,000
Lord Abbett Affiliated Fund Class P	LAFPX	NAS CM	Open End	US Equity Large Cap Value (Growth & Income)	B-	B-	B-	Down		0
Lord Abbett Affiliated Fund Class R2	LAFQX	NAS CM	Open End	US Equity Large Cap Value (Growth & Income)	B-	B-	B-	Down	Y	0
Lord Abbett Affiliated Fund Class R3	LAFRX	NAS CM	Open End	US Equity Large Cap Value (Growth & Income)	B	B-	B		Y	0
Lord Abbett Affiliated Fund Class R4	LAFSX	NAS CM	Open End	US Equity Large Cap Value (Growth & Income)	B-	B-	B-	Down	Y	0
Lord Abbett Affiliated Fund Class R5	LAFTX	NAS CM	Open End	US Equity Large Cap Value (Growth & Income)	B-	B-	B-	Down	Y	0
Lord Abbett Affiliated Fund Class R6	LAFVX	NAS CM	Open End	US Equity Large Cap Value (Growth & Income)	B-	B-	B-	Down	Y	0
Lord Abbett Affiliated Fund Class T	LAETX	NAS CM	Open End	US Equity Large Cap Value (Growth & Income)	B-	B-	B-		Y	1,000
Lord Abbett Alpha Strategy Fund Class A	ALFAX	NAS CM	Open End	US Equity Small Cap (Growth)	B	B	C+	Up	Y	1,500
Lord Abbett Alpha Strategy Fund Class B	ALFBX	NAS CM	Open End	US Equity Small Cap (Growth)	B	B	B	Up		1,500
Lord Abbett Alpha Strategy Fund Class C	ALFCX	NAS CM	Open End	US Equity Small Cap (Growth)	B	B	B	Up	Y	1,500
Lord Abbett Alpha Strategy Fund Class F	ALFFX	NAS CM	Open End	US Equity Small Cap (Growth)	B	B	C+	Up	Y	0
Lord Abbett Alpha Strategy Fund Class F3	ALFOX	NAS CM	Open End	US Equity Small Cap (Growth)	B	B	C+	Up	Y	0
Lord Abbett Alpha Strategy Fund Class I	ALFYX	NAS CM	Open End	US Equity Small Cap (Growth)	B	B	C+	Up	Y	1,000,000
Lord Abbett Alpha Strategy Fund Class R2	ALFQX	NAS CM	Open End	US Equity Small Cap (Growth)	B-	B	C+	Up	Y	0
Lord Abbett Alpha Strategy Fund Class R3	ALFRX	NAS CM	Open End	US Equity Small Cap (Growth)	B-	B	C+	Up	Y	0
Lord Abbett Alpha Strategy Fund Class R4	ALFKX	NAS CM	Open End	US Equity Small Cap (Growth)	B	B	C+	Up	Y	0
Lord Abbett Alpha Strategy Fund Class R5	ALFTX	NAS CM	Open End	US Equity Small Cap (Growth)	B	B	C+	Up	Y	0
Lord Abbett Alpha Strategy Fund Class R6	ALFVX	NAS CM	Open End	US Equity Small Cap (Growth)	B	B	C+	Up	Y	0
Lord Abbett Calibrated Dividend Growth Fund Class A	LAMAX	NAS CM	Open End	US Equity Large Cap Blend (Growth & Income)	B-	B-	B-	Down	Y	1,000
Lord Abbett Calibrated Dividend Growth Fund Class B	LAMBX	NAS CM	Open End	US Equity Large Cap Blend (Growth & Income)	B-	B-	B-	Down		1,000
Lord Abbett Calibrated Dividend Growth Fund Class C	LAMCX	NAS CM	Open End	US Equity Large Cap Blend (Growth & Income)	B	B-	B		Y	1,000
Lord Abbett Calibrated Dividend Growth Fund Class F	LAMFX	NAS CM	Open End	US Equity Large Cap Blend (Growth & Income)	B-	B-	B-	Down	Y	0
Lord Abbett Calibrated Dividend Growth Fund Class F3	LRMAX	NAS CM	Open End	US Equity Large Cap Blend (Growth & Income)	B-	B-	B-	Down	Y	0
Lord Abbett Calibrated Dividend Growth Fund Class I	LAMYX	NAS CM	Open End	US Equity Large Cap Blend (Growth & Income)	B-	B-	B-	Down	Y	1,000,000
Lord Abbett Calibrated Dividend Growth Fund Class P	LAMPX	NAS CM	Open End	US Equity Large Cap Blend (Growth & Income)	B-	B-	B-	Down		0
Lord Abbett Calibrated Dividend Growth Fund Class R2	LAMQX	NAS CM	Open End	US Equity Large Cap Blend (Growth & Income)	B-	B-	B-	Down	Y	0
Lord Abbett Calibrated Dividend Growth Fund Class R3	LAMRX	NAS CM	Open End	US Equity Large Cap Blend (Growth & Income)	B-	B-	B-	Down	Y	0
Lord Abbett Calibrated Dividend Growth Fund Class R4	LAMSX	NAS CM	Open End	US Equity Large Cap Blend (Growth & Income)	B-	B-	B-	Down	Y	0
Lord Abbett Calibrated Dividend Growth Fund Class R5	LAMTX	NAS CM	Open End	US Equity Large Cap Blend (Growth & Income)	B-	B-	B-	Down	Y	0
Lord Abbett Calibrated Dividend Growth Fund Class R6	LAMHX	NAS CM	Open End	US Equity Large Cap Blend (Growth & Income)	B-	B-	B-	Down	Y	0
Lord Abbett Calibrated Dividend Growth Fund Class T	LBDTX	NAS CM	Open End	US Equity Large Cap Blend (Growth & Income)	B-	B-	B-		Y	1,000
Lord Abbett Calibrated Large Cap Value Class R4	LCASX	NAS CM	Open End	US Equity Large Cap Value (Growth & Income)	B-	C+	B	Down	Y	0
Lord Abbett Calibrated Large Cap Value Class R5	LCAUX	NAS CM	Open End	US Equity Large Cap Value (Growth & Income)	B-	C+	B	Down	Y	0
Lord Abbett Calibrated Large Cap Value Class R6	LCAVX	NAS CM	Open End	US Equity Large Cap Value (Growth & Income)	B-	C+	B	Down	Y	0
Lord Abbett Calibrated Large Cap Value Fund Class A	LCAAX	NAS CM	Open End	US Equity Large Cap Value (Growth & Income)	B-	C+	B	Down	Y	1,500
Lord Abbett Calibrated Large Cap Value Fund Class C	LCACX	NAS CM	Open End	US Equity Large Cap Value (Growth & Income)	B-	C+	B	Up	Y	1,500
Lord Abbett Calibrated Large Cap Value Fund Class F	LCAFX	NAS CM	Open End	US Equity Large Cap Value (Growth & Income)	B-	C+	B	Down	Y	0
Lord Abbett Calibrated Large Cap Value Fund Class F3	LCAYX	NAS CM	Open End	US Equity Large Cap Value (Growth & Income)	B-	C+	B	Down	Y	0
Lord Abbett Calibrated Large Cap Value Fund Class I	LVCIX	NAS CM	Open End	US Equity Large Cap Value (Growth & Income)	B-	C+	B	Down	Y	1,000,000
Lord Abbett Calibrated Large Cap Value Fund Class R2	LCAQX	NAS CM	Open End	US Equity Large Cap Value (Growth & Income)	B-	C+	B	Down	Y	0
Lord Abbett Calibrated Large Cap Value Fund Class R3	LCARX	NAS CM	Open End	US Equity Large Cap Value (Growth & Income)	B-	C+	B	Down	Y	0
Lord Abbett Calibrated Mid Cap Value Fund Class A	LVMAX	NAS CM	Open End	US Equity Mid Cap (Growth & Income)	B-	C+	B		Y	1,500
Lord Abbett Calibrated Mid Cap Value Fund Class C	LVMCX	NAS CM	Open End	US Equity Mid Cap (Growth & Income)	B-	C+	B	Up	Y	1,500
Lord Abbett Calibrated Mid Cap Value Fund Class F	LVMFX	NAS CM	Open End	US Equity Mid Cap (Growth & Income)	B-	C+	B	Down	Y	0
Lord Abbett Calibrated Mid Cap Value Fund Class F3	LVMOX	NAS CM	Open End	US Equity Mid Cap (Growth & Income)	B-	B-	B	Down	Y	0
Lord Abbett Calibrated Mid Cap Value Fund Class I	LVMIX	NAS CM	Open End	US Equity Mid Cap (Growth & Income)	B-	B-	B	Down	Y	1,000,000

★ Expanded analysis of this fund is included in Section II.

Min Additional Investment	TOTAL RETURNS 3-Month Total Return	6-Month Total Return	1-Year Total Return	3-Year Total Return	5-Year Total Return	PERFORMANCE Dividend Yield (TTM)	Expense Ratio	3-Yr Std Deviation	3-Year Beta	ASSETS NAV	Total Assets (MIL)	ASSET ALLOCATION & TURNOVER %Cash	%Stocks	%Bonds	%Other	Turnover Ratio	BULL & BEAR Last Bull Market Total Return	Last Bear Market Total Return	FEES Front End Fee (%)	Back End Fee (%)	Inception Date
	5.50	8.71	15.50	28.45	95.38	2.17	0.74	10.26	0.98	15.81	6,828	0	100	0	0	73	25.6	-24.11	5.75		Jan-50
	5.70	8.65	14.99	26.03	88.98	1.2	1.49	10.27	0.98	16.03	6,828	0	100	0	0	73	25.19	-24.34		5.00	Aug-96
	5.50	8.52	14.81	25.86	88.76	1.44	1.49	10.26	0.98	15.82	6,828	0	100	0	0	73	25.09	-24.38		1.00	Aug-96
	6.16	9.37	16.29	29.70	98.05	2.31	0.59	10.27	0.98	15.81	6,828	0	100	0	0	73	25.75	-24.07			Sep-07
	6.15	9.44	16.34	29.39	96.80		0.39	10.28	0.98	15.9	6,828	0	100	0	0	73	25.6	-24.11			Apr-17
	6.09	9.38	16.32	30.04	98.96	2.38	0.49	10.23	0.97	15.87	6,828	0	100	0	0	73	25.98	-24.11			Mar-98
	6.07	9.30	16.06	29.15	96.49	2.16	0.94	10.27	0.98	15.78	6,828	0	100	0	0	73	25.54	-24.16			Nov-97
	5.97	9.08	15.63	27.78	93.10	1.89	1.09	10.28	0.98	15.81	6,828	0	100	0	0	73	25.38	-24.23			Sep-07
	6.01	9.18	15.79	28.19	94.26	1.95	0.99	10.26	0.98	15.79	6,828	0	100	0	0	73	25.56	-24.24			Sep-07
	5.50	8.73	15.45	28.46	95.39	2.28	0.74	10.3	0.98	15.79	6,828	0	100	0	0	73	25.6	-24.11			Jun-15
	5.53	8.80	15.71	29.20	96.51	2.38	0.49	10.27	0.98	15.88	6,828	0	100	0	0	73	25.6	-24.11			Jun-15
	5.59	8.86	15.78	29.49	96.96	2.41	0.39	10.28	0.98	15.91	6,828	0	100	0	0	73	25.6	-24.11			Jun-15
	5.56	8.80	15.59	28.56	95.54		0.74	10.27	0.98	15.82	6,828	0	100	0	0	73	25.6	-24.11	2.50		Jul-17
	4.81	10.81	20.59	29.50	94.15	0	1.63	11.57		26.6	1,144	0	100	0	0	13	26.38	-25.35	5.75		Mar-98
	4.58	10.36	19.69	26.63	87.01	0	2.38	11.56		22.98	1,144	0	100	0	0	13	25.82	-25.57		5.00	Mar-98
	4.62	10.40	19.69	26.68	87.09	0	2.38	11.58		22.56	1,144	0	100	0	0	13	25.84	-25.55		1.00	Mar-98
	4.85	10.87	20.75	30.11	95.60	0	1.48	11.57		26.75	1,144	0	100	0	0	13	26.52	-25.31			Sep-07
	4.89	10.97	20.88	29.81	94.62		1.25	11.58		27.23	1,144	0	100	0	0	13	26.38	-25.35			Apr-17
	4.85	10.93	20.86	30.48	96.55	0	1.38	11.59		27.21	1,144	0	100	0	0	13	26.56	-25.24			Oct-04
	4.70	10.63	20.15	28.19	90.82	0	1.98	11.57		25.71	1,144	0	100	0	0	13	26.17	-25.45			Sep-07
	4.74	10.68	20.29	28.58	91.81	0	1.88	11.56		25.9	1,144	0	100	0	0	13	26.18	-25.42			Sep-07
	4.81	10.83	20.62	29.55	94.23	0	1.63	11.56		26.56	1,144	0	100	0	0	13	26.38	-25.35			Jun-15
	4.89	10.97	20.94	30.42	95.53	0	1.38	11.58		27.23	1,144	0	100	0	0	13	26.38	-25.35			Jun-15
	4.92	11.00	21.02	30.49	95.64	0	1.25	11.56		27.24	1,144	0	100	0	0	13	26.38	-25.35			Jun-15
	7.65	11.28	19.08	32.55	93.71	1.54	0.95	9.28	0.86	15.39	2,475	0	100	0	0	70	20.94	-16.02	5.75		Dec-01
	7.45	10.85	18.16	29.61	86.57	0.68	1.7	9.3	0.86	15.31	2,475	0	100	0	0	70	20.51	-16.22		5.00	Dec-01
	7.49	10.88	18.21	29.66	86.58	0.92	1.7	9.23	0.86	15.2	2,475	0	100	0	0	70	20.49	-16.24		1.00	Dec-01
	7.68	11.37	19.27	33.24	95.26	1.68	0.7	9.28	0.86	15.38	2,475	0	100	0	0	70	21.11	-15.92			Sep-07
	7.76	11.51	19.48	33.71	96.31		0.6	9.28	0.86	15.57	2,475	0	100	0	0	70	21.12	-15.86			Apr-17
	7.71	11.46	19.35	33.56	96.09	1.73	0.7	9.28	0.86	15.53	2,475	0	100	0	0	70	21.12	-15.86			Dec-01
	7.63	11.19	18.83	31.75	91.77	1.35	1.15	9.28	0.86	15.47	2,475	0	100	0	0	70	20.91	-16.03			Dec-01
	7.56	11.13	18.65	31.16	90.26	1.24	1.3	9.31	0.87	15.54	2,475	0	100	0	0	70	20.79	-16.12			Sep-07
	7.56	11.14	18.75	31.55	91.38	1.35	1.2	9.3	0.86	15.31	2,475	0	100	0	0	70	20.92	-16.11			Sep-07
	7.67	11.31	19.10	32.58	93.68	1.59	0.95	9.27	0.86	15.38	2,475	0	100	0	0	70	20.94	-15.95			Jun-15
	7.71	11.39	19.36	33.50	96.00	1.74	0.7	9.28	0.86	15.52	2,475	0	100	0	0	70	21.12	-15.86			Jun-15
	7.76	11.51	19.48	33.93	96.62	1.75	0.6	9.29	0.86	15.57	2,475	0	100	0	0	70	21.12	-15.86			Jun-15
	7.72	11.36	19.09	32.61	93.73		0.95	9.28	0.86	15.39	2,475	0	100	0	0	70	20.94	-15.95	2.50		Jul-17
	5.04	8.29	10.88	21.17	82.06	1.68	0.85	11.14	1.07	20.8	507.2	0	100	0	0	76					Jun-15
	5.09	8.38	11.12	22.05	84.30	1.92	0.6	11.14	1.07	20.86	507.2	0	100	0	0	76					Jun-15
	5.09	8.43	11.17	22.16	84.48	1.92	0.58	11.14	1.07	20.88	507.2	0	100	0	0	76					Jun-15
	5.02	8.27	10.85	21.15	82.07	1.67	0.85	11.11	1.06	20.84	507.2	0	100	0	0	76			5.75		Dec-11
	4.84	7.88	10.07	18.50	75.50	0.9	1.6	11.1	1.06	20.52	507.2	0	100	0	0	76				1.00	Dec-11
	5.12	8.42	11.16	21.87	83.71	1.77	0.6	11.13	1.07	20.89	507.2	0	100	0	0	76					Dec-11
	5.08	8.42	11.17	22.13	84.43		0.58	11.13	1.07	20.88	507.2	0	100	0	0	76					Apr-17
	5.08	8.43	11.12	22.08	84.34	1.92	0.6	11.14	1.07	20.87	507.2	0	100	0	0	76					Dec-11
	4.95	8.13	10.48	19.94	79.75	1.35	1.2	11.13	1.07	20.98	507.2	0	100	0	0	76					Dec-11
	4.99	8.16	10.59	20.30	79.94	1.49	1.1	11.1	1.06	20.72	507.2	0	100	0	0	76					Dec-11
	4.76	6.18	10.85	19.88	90.73	1.13	0.95	11.65	1.1	21.66	1,035	0	100	0	0	93			5.75		Dec-11
	4.53	5.78	10.01	17.22	83.85	0.41	1.7	11.63	1.1	21.26	1,035	0	100	0	0	93				1.00	Dec-11
	4.81	6.32	11.09	20.53	92.38	1.27	0.7	11.64	1.1	21.69	1,035	0	100	0	0	93					Dec-11
	4.80	6.31	11.12	20.82	93.20		0.65	11.63	1.1	21.71	1,035	0	100	0	0	93					Apr-17
	4.80	6.31	11.07	20.76	93.11	1.4	0.7	11.63	1.1	21.71	1,035	0	100	0	0	93					Dec-11

	MARKET			FUND TYPE, CATEGORY & OBJECTIVE	RATINGS				MINIMUMS	
Fund Name	Ticker Symbol	Traded On	Fund Type	Category and (Prospectus Objective)	Overall Rating	Reward Rating	Risk Rating	Recent Up/ Downgrade	Open to New Investors	Min Initial Investment
Lord Abbett Calibrated Mid Cap Value Fund Class R2	LVMQX	NAS CM	Open End	US Equity Mid Cap (Growth & Income)	B-	C+	B		Y	0
Lord Abbett Calibrated Mid Cap Value Fund Class R3	LVMRX	NAS CM	Open End	US Equity Mid Cap (Growth & Income)	B-	C+	B		Y	0
Lord Abbett Calibrated Mid Cap Value Fund Class R4	LVMSX	NAS CM	Open End	US Equity Mid Cap (Growth & Income)	B-	C+	B		Y	0
Lord Abbett Calibrated Mid Cap Value Fund Class R5	LVMTX	NAS CM	Open End	US Equity Mid Cap (Growth & Income)	B-	B-	B	Down	Y	0
Lord Abbett Calibrated Mid Cap Value Fund Class R6	LVMHX	NAS CM	Open End	US Equity Mid Cap (Growth & Income)	B-	B-	B	Down	Y	0
Lord Abbett Convertible Fund Class A	LACFX	NAS CM	Open End	Convertibles (Convertible Bond)	C+	B-	C+	Down	Y	1,500
Lord Abbett Convertible Fund Class B	LBCFX	NAS CM	Open End	Convertibles (Convertible Bond)	C+	C+	C+	Down		1,500
Lord Abbett Convertible Fund Class C	LACCX	NAS CM	Open End	Convertibles (Convertible Bond)	C+	C+	C+	Down	Y	1,500
Lord Abbett Convertible Fund Class F	LBFFX	NAS CM	Open End	Convertibles (Convertible Bond)	C+	B-	C+	Down	Y	0
Lord Abbett Convertible Fund Class F3	LOCFX	NAS CM	Open End	Convertibles (Convertible Bond)	C+	B-	C+	Down	Y	0
Lord Abbett Convertible Fund Class I	LCFYX	NAS CM	Open End	Convertibles (Convertible Bond)	C+	B-	C+	Down	Y	1,000,000
Lord Abbett Convertible Fund Class P	LCFPX	NAS CM	Open End	Convertibles (Convertible Bond)	C+	C+	C+	Down		0
Lord Abbett Convertible Fund Class R2	LBCQX	NAS CM	Open End	Convertibles (Convertible Bond)	C+	C+	C+	Down	Y	0
Lord Abbett Convertible Fund Class R3	LCFRX	NAS CM	Open End	Convertibles (Convertible Bond)	C+	C+	C+	Down	Y	0
Lord Abbett Convertible Fund Class R4	LCFSX	NAS CM	Open End	Convertibles (Convertible Bond)	C+	B-	C+	Down	Y	0
Lord Abbett Convertible Fund Class R5	LCFTX	NAS CM	Open End	Convertibles (Convertible Bond)	C+	B-	C+	Down	Y	0
Lord Abbett Convertible Fund Class R6	LCFVX	NAS CM	Open End	Convertibles (Convertible Bond)	C+	B-	C+	Down	Y	0
Lord Abbett Developing Growth Fund Class A	LAGWX	NAS CM	Open End	US Equity Small Cap (Growth)	C+	C+	C+	Up		1,000
Lord Abbett Developing Growth Fund Class B	LADBX	NAS CM	Open End	US Equity Small Cap (Growth)	C+	C+	C+	Up		1,000
Lord Abbett Developing Growth Fund Class C	LADCX	NAS CM	Open End	US Equity Small Cap (Growth)	C+	C+	C+	Up		1,000
Lord Abbett Developing Growth Fund Class F	LADFX	NAS CM	Open End	US Equity Small Cap (Growth)	C+	C+	C+	Up		0
Lord Abbett Developing Growth Fund Class F3	LOGWX	NAS CM	Open End	US Equity Small Cap (Growth)	C+	C+	C+	Up	Y	0
Lord Abbett Developing Growth Fund Class I	LADYX	NAS CM	Open End	US Equity Small Cap (Growth)	C+	C+	C+	Up		1,000,000
Lord Abbett Developing Growth Fund Class P	LADPX	NAS CM	Open End	US Equity Small Cap (Growth)	C+	C+	C+	Up		0
Lord Abbett Developing Growth Fund Class R2	LADQX	NAS CM	Open End	US Equity Small Cap (Growth)	C+	C+	C+	Up		0
Lord Abbett Developing Growth Fund Class R3	LADRX	NAS CM	Open End	US Equity Small Cap (Growth)	C+	C+	C+	Up		0
Lord Abbett Developing Growth Fund Class R4	LADSX	NAS CM	Open End	US Equity Small Cap (Growth)	C+	C+	C+	Up		0
Lord Abbett Developing Growth Fund Class R5	LADTX	NAS CM	Open End	US Equity Small Cap (Growth)	C+	C+	C+	Up		0
Lord Abbett Developing Growth Fund Class R6	LADVX	NAS CM	Open End	US Equity Small Cap (Growth)	C+	C+	C+	Up		0
Lord Abbett Fundamental Equity Class R4	LAVSX	NAS CM	Open End	US Equity Large Cap Value (Growth)	B-	B-	B	Down	Y	0
Lord Abbett Fundamental Equity Class R5	LAVTX	NAS CM	Open End	US Equity Large Cap Value (Growth)	B-	B-	B	Down	Y	0
Lord Abbett Fundamental Equity Class R6	LAVVX	NAS CM	Open End	US Equity Large Cap Value (Growth)	B-	B-	B	Down	Y	0
Lord Abbett Fundamental Equity Fund Class A	LDFVX	NAS CM	Open End	US Equity Large Cap Value (Growth)	B-	B-	B	Down	Y	1,500
Lord Abbett Fundamental Equity Fund Class B	GILBX	NAS CM	Open End	US Equity Large Cap Value (Growth)	B-	C+	B	Down		1,500
Lord Abbett Fundamental Equity Fund Class C	GILAX	NAS CM	Open End	US Equity Large Cap Value (Growth)	B-	C+	B	Down	Y	1,500
Lord Abbett Fundamental Equity Fund Class F	LAVFX	NAS CM	Open End	US Equity Large Cap Value (Growth)	B	B-	B	Up	Y	0
Lord Abbett Fundamental Equity Fund Class F3	LDFOX	NAS CM	Open End	US Equity Large Cap Value (Growth)	B-	B-	B	Down	Y	0
Lord Abbett Fundamental Equity Fund Class I	LAVYX	NAS CM	Open End	US Equity Large Cap Value (Growth)	B	B-	B	Up	Y	1,000,000
Lord Abbett Fundamental Equity Fund Class P	LAVPX	NAS CM	Open End	US Equity Large Cap Value (Growth)	B-	B-	B	Down		0
Lord Abbett Fundamental Equity Fund Class R2	LAVQX	NAS CM	Open End	US Equity Large Cap Value (Growth)	B-	B-	B	Down	Y	0
Lord Abbett Fundamental Equity Fund Class R3	LAVRX	NAS CM	Open End	US Equity Large Cap Value (Growth)	B-	B-	B	Down	Y	0
Lord Abbett Global Core Equity Fund Class A	LGCAX	NAS CM	Open End	Global Equity (World Stock)	U	U	U		Y	1,500
Lord Abbett Global Core Equity Fund Class C	LGCCX	NAS CM	Open End	Global Equity (World Stock)	U	U	U		Y	1,500
Lord Abbett Global Core Equity Fund Class F	LGCFX	NAS CM	Open End	Global Equity (World Stock)	U	U	U		Y	0
Lord Abbett Global Core Equity Fund Class F3	LGCOX	NAS CM	Open End	Global Equity (World Stock)	U	U	U		Y	0
Lord Abbett Global Core Equity Fund Class I	LGCYX	NAS CM	Open End	Global Equity (World Stock)	U	U	U		Y	1,000,000
Lord Abbett Global Core Equity Fund Class R2	LGCQX	NAS CM	Open End	Global Equity (World Stock)	U	U	U		Y	0
Lord Abbett Global Core Equity Fund Class R3	LGCRX	NAS CM	Open End	Global Equity (World Stock)	U	U	U		Y	0
Lord Abbett Global Core Equity Fund Class R4	LGCSX	NAS CM	Open End	Global Equity (World Stock)	U	U	U		Y	0
Lord Abbett Global Core Equity Fund Class R5	LGCVX	NAS CM	Open End	Global Equity (World Stock)	U	U	U		Y	0
Lord Abbett Global Core Equity Fund Class R6	LGCWX	NAS CM	Open End	Global Equity (World Stock)	U	U	U		Y	0
Lord Abbett Growth Leaders Fund Class A	LGLAX	NAS CM	Open End	US Equity Large Cap Growth (Growth)	A-	A-	A-	Up	Y	1,500

★Expanded analysis of this fund is included in Section II.

Min Additional Investment	TOTAL RETURNS: 3-Month Total Return	6-Month Total Return	1-Year Total Return	3-Year Total Return	5-Year Total Return	PERFORMANCE: Dividend Yield (TTM)	Expense Ratio	3-Yr Std Deviation	3-Year Beta	ASSETS: NAV	Total Assets (MIL)	ASSET ALLOCATION & TURNOVER: %Cash	%Stocks	%Bonds	%Other	Turnover Ratio	BULL & BEAR: Last Bull Market Total Return	Last Bear Market Total Return	FEES: Front End Fee (%)	Back End Fee (%)	Inception Date
	4.67	6.00	10.45	18.64	88.38	0.8	1.3	11.62	1.1	21.71	1,035	0	100	0	0	93					Dec-11
	4.70	6.03	10.52	18.97	89.13	0.96	1.2	11.62	1.1	21.7	1,035	0	100	0	0	93					Dec-11
	4.74	6.17	10.79	19.88	90.75	1.2	0.95	11.64	1.1	21.59	1,035	0	100	0	0	93					Jun-15
	4.80	6.31	11.07	20.78	93.14	1.4	0.7	11.64	1.1	21.71	1,035	0	100	0	0	93					Jun-15
	4.80	6.31	11.13	20.80	93.18	1.4	0.65	11.63	1.1	21.71	1,035	0	100	0	0	93					Jun-15
	2.13	6.29	16.18	19.64	61.96	2.81	1.05	8.98	1.12	13.14	874.4	0	18	0	0	241	11.4	-17.34	2.25		Jun-03
	2.28	6.20	15.66	17.16	56.10	1.82	1.85	8.93	1.12	13.2	874.4	0	18	0	0	241	10.83	-17.61		5.00	Jun-03
	2.14	6.17	15.64	17.57	57.15	2.25	1.68	9	1.12	13.07	874.4	0	18	0	0	241	10.98	-17.54		1.00	Jun-03
	2.13	6.32	16.26	19.93	62.75	2.89	0.95	8.96	1.12	13.14	874.4	0	18	0	0	241	11.46	-17.29			Sep-07
	2.19	6.39	16.34	20.26	63.52		0.82	8.97	1.12	13.22	874.4	0	18	0	0	241	11.58	-17.34			Apr-17
	2.20	6.39	16.34	20.27	63.53	2.96	0.85	8.98	1.12	13.21	874.4	0	18	0	0	241	11.58	-17.34			Jun-03
	2.17	6.21	15.98	19.16	60.58	2.53	1.3	8.95	1.12	13.34	874.4	0	18	0	0	241	11.25	-17.44			Jun-03
	2.18	6.26	15.93	18.34	58.96	2.38	1.45	8.97	1.12	13.33	874.4	0	18	0	0	241	11.08	-17.45			Sep-07
	2.14	6.24	15.92	18.64	59.71	2.57	1.35	8.98	1.12	13.09	874.4	0	18	0	0	241	11.17	-17.43			Sep-07
	2.21	6.28	16.23	19.41	61.55	2.76	1.1	8.98	1.12	13.14	874.4	0	18	0	0	241	11.42	-17.42			Jun-15
	2.27	6.47	16.53	20.38	63.68	2.97	0.85	8.94	1.12	13.21	874.4	0	18	0	0	241	11.58	-17.34			Jun-15
	2.12	6.30	16.35	20.29	63.55	2.97	0.82	8.97	1.12	13.22	874.4	0	18	0	0	241	11.58	-17.34			Jun-15
	7.61	15.21	29.91	14.68	90.79	0	0.96	15.76	0.99	23.32	1,933	0	100	0	0	134	23.66	-23.64	5.75		Oct-73
	7.40	14.76	28.90	12.07	83.95	0	1.71	15.73	0.99	17.26	1,933	0	100	0	0	134	23.17	-23.87		5.00	Aug-96
	7.44	14.78	28.92	12.19	84.04	0	1.71	15.76	0.99	17.47	1,933	0	100	0	0	134	23.16	-23.87		1.00	Aug-96
	7.66	15.32	30.11	15.23	92.59	0	0.81	15.78	0.99	24.15	1,933	0	100	0	0	134	23.85	-23.59			Sep-07
	7.72	15.43	30.26	14.99	91.30		0.6	15.77	0.99	26.77	1,933	0	100	0	0	134	23.66	-23.64			Apr-17
	7.66	15.39	30.27	15.60	93.49	0	0.71	15.76	0.99	26.68	1,933	0	100	0	0	134	23.84	-23.53			Dec-97
	7.61	15.23	29.92	14.74	91.05	0	1.16	15.75	0.99	22.62	1,933	0	100	0	0	134	23.62	-23.64			Jan-98
	7.50	15.03	29.43	13.52	87.75	0	1.31	15.77	0.99	22.34	1,933	0	100	0	0	134	23.45	-23.73			Sep-07
	7.58	15.11	29.64	13.84	88.79	0	1.21	15.76	0.99	22.7	1,933	0	100	0	0	134	23.52	-23.69			Sep-07
	7.61	15.27	29.91	14.68	90.79	0	0.96	15.76	0.99	23.32	1,933	0	100	0	0	134	23.66	-23.64			Jun-15
	7.71	15.39	30.27	15.43	92.04	0	0.71	15.77	0.99	26.68	1,933	0	100	0	0	134	23.66	-23.64			Jun-15
	7.72	15.43	30.39	15.82	92.68	0	0.6	15.75	0.99	26.77	1,933	0	100	0	0	134	23.66	-23.64			Jun-15
	5.57	8.89	13.03	25.00	84.74	1.32	0.98	10.41	0.99	12.89	2,680	0	100	0	0	135	24.43	-22.18			Jun-15
	5.57	9.01	13.28	25.74	85.83	1.49	0.73	10.43	1	13.02	2,680	0	100	0	0	135	24.43	-22.18			Jun-15
	5.63	9.07	13.42	26.10	86.37	1.49	0.61	10.39	0.99	13.06	2,680	0	100	0	0	135	24.43	-22.18			Jun-15
	5.54	8.84	12.96	25.42	87.87	1.23	0.98	10.37	0.99	12.95	2,680	0	100	0	0	135	24.85	-21.99	5.75		Jul-96
	5.34	8.44	12.10	22.65	81.22	0	1.73	10.39	0.99	11.8	2,680	0	100	0	0	135	24.32	-22.16		5.00	Jun-97
	5.27	8.41	12.11	22.55	81.11	0.56	1.73	10.4	0.99	11.56	2,680	0	100	0	0	135	24.44	-22.18		1.00	Jan-94
	5.60	8.93	13.18	25.99	89.60	1.39	0.83	10.4	0.99	12.81	2,680	0	100	0	0	135	24.97	-21.87			Sep-07
	5.56	8.99	13.03	23.55	82.59		0.61	10.42	1	13.05	2,680	0	100	0	0	135	24.43	-22.18			Apr-17
	5.56	8.92	13.19	26.29	90.46	1.49	0.73	10.4	0.99	13.01	2,680	0	100	0	0	135	25.07	-21.89			Mar-03
	5.46	8.74	12.76	24.68	86.32	0.95	1.18	10.41	1	12.72	2,680	0	100	0	0	135	24.79	-22.03			Aug-01
	5.44	8.65	12.59	24.17	84.85	0.92	1.33	10.4	0.99	12.67	2,680	0	100	0	0	135	24.55	-22			Sep-07
	5.44	8.71	12.63	24.46	85.82	1	1.23	10.4	0.99	12.73	2,680	0	100	0	0	135	24.64	-21.96			Sep-07
	5.11	10.47	17.20				1.05			11.28	4.5	0	100	0	0				5.75		Jan-17
	4.92	9.99	16.48				1.8			11.23	4.5	0	100	0	0					1.00	Jan-17
	5.23	10.59	17.44				0.9			11.29	4.5	0	100	0	0						Jan-17
	5.24	10.60					0.75			11.29	4.5	0	100	0	0						Apr-17
	5.23	10.58	17.54				0.8			11.29	4.5	0	100	0	0						Jan-17
	5.04	10.20	16.81				1.4			11.28	4.5	0	100	0	0						Jan-17
	5.04	10.30	16.92				1.3			11.28	4.5	0	100	0	0						Jan-17
	5.18	10.44	17.18				1.05			11.28	4.5	0	100	0	0						Jan-17
	5.23	10.58	17.54				0.8			11.29	4.5	0	100	0	0						Jan-17
	5.24	10.60	17.56				0.75			11.29	4.5	0	100	0	0						Jan-17
	7.48	14.48	31.19	39.75	131.66	0	0.95	11.68	1.03	27.85	3,095	0	100	0	0	246	23.04		5.75		Jun-11

	MARKET			FUND TYPE, CATEGORY & OBJECTIVE	RATINGS					MINIMUMS
Fund Name	Ticker Symbol	Traded On	Fund Type	Category and (Prospectus Objective)	Overall Rating	Reward Rating	Risk Rating	Recent Up/ Downgrade	Open to New Investors	Min Initial Investment
Lord Abbett Growth Leaders Fund Class B	GLABX	NAS CM	Open End	US Equity Large Cap Growth (Growth)	A-	A-	B+	Up	Y	1,500
Lord Abbett Growth Leaders Fund Class C	LGLCX	NAS CM	Open End	US Equity Large Cap Growth (Growth)	A-	A-	B+	Up	Y	1,500
Lord Abbett Growth Leaders Fund Class F	LGLFX	NAS CM	Open End	US Equity Large Cap Growth (Growth)	A-	A-	A-	Up	Y	0
Lord Abbett Growth Leaders Fund Class F3	LGLOX	NAS CM	Open End	US Equity Large Cap Growth (Growth)	A-	A-	A-	Up	Y	0
Lord Abbett Growth Leaders Fund Class I	LGLIX	NAS CM	Open End	US Equity Large Cap Growth (Growth)	A-	A-	A-	Up	Y	1,000,000
Lord Abbett Growth Leaders Fund Class R2	LGLQX	NAS CM	Open End	US Equity Large Cap Growth (Growth)	A-	A-	B+	Up	Y	0
Lord Abbett Growth Leaders Fund Class R3	LGLRX	NAS CM	Open End	US Equity Large Cap Growth (Growth)	A-	A-	A-	Up	Y	0
Lord Abbett Growth Leaders Fund Class R4	LGLSX	NAS CM	Open End	US Equity Large Cap Growth (Growth)	A-	A-	A-	Up	Y	0
Lord Abbett Growth Leaders Fund Class R5	LGLUX	NAS CM	Open End	US Equity Large Cap Growth (Growth)	A-	A-	A-	Up	Y	0
Lord Abbett Growth Leaders Fund Class R6	LGLVX	NAS CM	Open End	US Equity Large Cap Growth (Growth)	A-	A-	A-	Up	Y	0
Lord Abbett Growth Leaders Fund Class T	LGWTX	NAS CM	Open End	US Equity Large Cap Growth (Growth)	A-	A-	A-		Y	1,500
Lord Abbett Growth Opportunities Fund Class A	LMGAX	NAS CM	Open End	US Equity Mid Cap (Growth)	B	B	B	Up	Y	1,000
Lord Abbett Growth Opportunities Fund Class B	LMGBX	NAS CM	Open End	US Equity Mid Cap (Growth)	B	B-	B	Up		1,000
Lord Abbett Growth Opportunities Fund Class C	LMGCX	NAS CM	Open End	US Equity Mid Cap (Growth)	B	B-	B	Up	Y	1,000
Lord Abbett Growth Opportunities Fund Class F	LGOFX	NAS CM	Open End	US Equity Mid Cap (Growth)	B	B	B	Up	Y	0
Lord Abbett Growth Opportunities Fund Class F3	LOMGX	NAS CM	Open End	US Equity Mid Cap (Growth)	B	B	B	Up	Y	0
Lord Abbett Growth Opportunities Fund Class I	LMGYX	NAS CM	Open End	US Equity Mid Cap (Growth)	B	B	B	Up	Y	1,000,000
Lord Abbett Growth Opportunities Fund Class P	LGOPX	NAS CM	Open End	US Equity Mid Cap (Growth)	B	B-	B	Up		0
Lord Abbett Growth Opportunities Fund Class R2	LGOQX	NAS CM	Open End	US Equity Mid Cap (Growth)	B	B-	B	Up	Y	0
Lord Abbett Growth Opportunities Fund Class R3	LGORX	NAS CM	Open End	US Equity Mid Cap (Growth)	B	B-	B	Up	Y	0
Lord Abbett Growth Opportunities Fund Class R4	LGOSX	NAS CM	Open End	US Equity Mid Cap (Growth)	B	B	B	Up	Y	0
Lord Abbett Growth Opportunities Fund Class R5	LGOTX	NAS CM	Open End	US Equity Mid Cap (Growth)	B	B	B	Up	Y	0
Lord Abbett Growth Opportunities Fund Class R6	LGOVX	NAS CM	Open End	US Equity Mid Cap (Growth)	B	B	B	Up	Y	0
Lord Abbett International Dividend Income Fund Class A	LIDAX	NAS CM	Open End	Global Equity Large Cap (Equity-Income)	C+	C+	C+	Up	Y	1,500
Lord Abbett International Dividend Income Fund Class C	LIDCX	NAS CM	Open End	Global Equity Large Cap (Equity-Income)	C+	C+	C+	Up	Y	1,500
Lord Abbett International Dividend Income Fund Class F	LIDFX	NAS CM	Open End	Global Equity Large Cap (Equity-Income)	C+	C+	C+	Up	Y	0
Lord Abbett International Dividend Income Fund Class F3	LIDOX	NAS CM	Open End	Global Equity Large Cap (Equity-Income)	C+	C+	C+	Up	Y	0
Lord Abbett International Dividend Income Fund Class I	LAIDX	NAS CM	Open End	Global Equity Large Cap (Equity-Income)	C+	C+	C+	Up	Y	1,000,000
Lord Abbett International Dividend Income Fund Class R2	LIDRX	NAS CM	Open End	Global Equity Large Cap (Equity-Income)	C+	C+	C+	Up	Y	0
Lord Abbett International Dividend Income Fund Class R3	LIRRX	NAS CM	Open End	Global Equity Large Cap (Equity-Income)	C+	C+	C+	Up	Y	0
Lord Abbett International Dividend Income Fund Class R4	LIRSX	NAS CM	Open End	Global Equity Large Cap (Equity-Income)	C+	C+	C+	Up	Y	0
Lord Abbett International Dividend Income Fund Class R5	LIRTX	NAS CM	Open End	Global Equity Large Cap (Equity-Income)	C+	C+	C+	Up	Y	0
Lord Abbett International Dividend Income Fund Class R6	LIRVX	NAS CM	Open End	Global Equity Large Cap (Equity-Income)	C+	C+	C+	Up	Y	0
Lord Abbett International Equity Fund Class A	LICAX	NAS CM	Open End	Global Equity Large Cap (Foreign Stock)	B-	C+	B-	Up	Y	1,500
Lord Abbett International Equity Fund Class B	LICBX	NAS CM	Open End	Global Equity Large Cap (Foreign Stock)	C+	C+	B-	Up		1,500
Lord Abbett International Equity Fund Class C	LICCX	NAS CM	Open End	Global Equity Large Cap (Foreign Stock)	C+	C+	B-	Up	Y	1,500
Lord Abbett International Equity Fund Class F	LICFX	NAS CM	Open End	Global Equity Large Cap (Foreign Stock)	B-	C+	B-	Up	Y	0
Lord Abbett International Equity Fund Class F3	LICOX	NAS CM	Open End	Global Equity Large Cap (Foreign Stock)	B-	C+	B-	Up	Y	0
Lord Abbett International Equity Fund Class I	LICYX	NAS CM	Open End	Global Equity Large Cap (Foreign Stock)	B-	C+	B-	Up	Y	1,000,000
Lord Abbett International Equity Fund Class P	LICPX	NAS CM	Open End	Global Equity Large Cap (Foreign Stock)	B-	C+	B-	Up		0
Lord Abbett International Equity Fund Class R2	LICQX	NAS CM	Open End	Global Equity Large Cap (Foreign Stock)	C+	C+	B-	Up	Y	0
Lord Abbett International Equity Fund Class R3	LICRX	NAS CM	Open End	Global Equity Large Cap (Foreign Stock)	C+	C+	B-	Up	Y	0
Lord Abbett International Equity Fund Class R4	LICSX	NAS CM	Open End	Global Equity Large Cap (Foreign Stock)	B-	C+	B-	Up	Y	0
Lord Abbett International Equity Fund Class R5	LICTX	NAS CM	Open End	Global Equity Large Cap (Foreign Stock)	B-	C+	B-	Up	Y	0
Lord Abbett International Equity Fund Class R6	LICVX	NAS CM	Open End	Global Equity Large Cap (Foreign Stock)	B-	C+	B-	Up	Y	0
Lord Abbett International Opportunities Fund Clas R4	LINSX	NAS CM	Open End	Global Equity Mid/Small Cap (Foreign Stock)	A-	A-	A-	Up	Y	0
Lord Abbett International Opportunities Fund Clas R5	LINTX	NAS CM	Open End	Global Equity Mid/Small Cap (Foreign Stock)	A-	A	A-	Up	Y	0
Lord Abbett International Opportunities Fund Clas R6	LINVX	NAS CM	Open End	Global Equity Mid/Small Cap (Foreign Stock)	A-	A	A-	Up	Y	0
Lord Abbett International Opportunities Fund Class A	LAIEX	NAS CM	Open End	Global Equity Mid/Small Cap (Foreign Stock)	A-	A-	A-	Up	Y	1,500
Lord Abbett International Opportunities Fund Class B	LINBX	NAS CM	Open End	Global Equity Mid/Small Cap (Foreign Stock)	A-	A-	A-	Up		1,500
Lord Abbett International Opportunities Fund Class C	LINCX	NAS CM	Open End	Global Equity Mid/Small Cap (Foreign Stock)	A-	A-	A-	Up	Y	1,500
Lord Abbett International Opportunities Fund Class F	LINFX	NAS CM	Open End	Global Equity Mid/Small Cap (Foreign Stock)	A-	A	A-	Up	Y	0

★ Expanded analysis of this fund is included in Section II.

Min Additional Investment	TOTAL RETURNS: 3-Month Total Return	6-Month Total Return	1-Year Total Return	3-Year Total Return	5-Year Total Return	PERFORMANCE: Dividend Yield (TTM)	Expense Ratio	3-Yr Std Deviation	3-Year Beta	ASSETS: NAV	Total Assets (MIL)	ASSET ALLOCATION & TURNOVER: %Cash	%Stocks	%Bonds	%Other	Turnover Ratio	BULL & BEAR: Last Bull Market Total Return	Last Bear Market Total Return	FEES: Front End Fee (%)	Back End Fee (%)	Inception Date
	7.25	14.02	30.23	36.67	123.29	0	1.7	11.69	1.03	26.75	3,095	0	100	0	0	246	22.7			5.00	Feb-13
	7.30	14.05	30.23	36.67	123.49	0	1.7	11.68	1.03	26.45	3,095	0	100	0	0	246	22.62			1.00	Jun-11
	7.55	14.62	31.51	40.54	133.76	0	0.7	11.71	1.03	28.16	3,095	0	100	0	0	246	23.29				Jun-11
	7.57	14.68	31.59	40.90	134.94		0.6	11.68	1.03	28.37	3,095	0	100	0	0	246	23.41				Apr-17
	7.55	14.62	31.54	40.84	134.85	0	0.7	11.67	1.03	28.31	3,095	0	100	0	0	246	23.41				Jun-11
	7.41	14.28	30.76	38.31	128.89	0	1.3	11.71	1.04	27.65	3,095	0	100	0	0	246	23.29				Jun-11
	7.44	14.34	30.90	38.68	128.94	0	1.2	11.7	1.03	27.55	3,095	0	100	0	0	246	23.29				Jun-11
	7.47	14.48	31.23	39.75	131.86	0	0.95	11.69	1.03	27.86	3,095	0	100	0	0	246	23.23				Jun-15
	7.54	14.62	31.58	40.89	134.93	0	0.7	11.69	1.03	28.32	3,095	0	100	0	0	246	23.41				Jun-15
	7.57	14.68	31.63	41.12	135.31	0	0.6	11.69	1.03	28.37	3,095	0	100	0	0	246	23.41				Jun-15
	7.51	14.53	31.26	39.84	132.02		0.95	11.67	1.03	27.87	3,095	0	100	0	0	246	23.23		2.50		Jul-17
	4.81	9.25	22.83	26.57	89.04	0	1.27	11.24	0.98	20.37	515.9	0	100	0	0		30.68	-27.57	5.75		Aug-95
	4.59	8.79	21.91	23.77	82.31	0	2.02	11.21	0.98	15.23	515.9	0	100	0	0		30.11	-27.74		5.00	Oct-98
	4.66	8.86	21.92	23.86	82.49	0	2.02	11.24	0.98	15.23	515.9	0	100	0	0		30.14	-27.76		1.00	Oct-98
	4.83	9.31	23.04	27.18	90.70	0	1.12	11.24	0.98	21.17	515.9	0	100	0	0		30.81	-27.48			Sep-07
	4.90	9.43	23.11	26.85	89.46		0.86	11.24	0.98	23.22	515.9	0	100	0	0		30.68	-27.57			Apr-17
	4.87	9.38	23.19	27.56	91.69	0	1.02	11.23	0.98	23.12	515.9	0	100	0	0		30.89	-27.46			Dec-98
	4.78	9.15	22.64	25.84	87.43	0	1.47	11.22	0.98	19.88	515.9	0	100	0	0		30.6	-27.58			Aug-00
	4.73	9.08	22.46	25.32	86.05	0	1.62	11.23	0.98	19.42	515.9	0	100	0	0		30.45	-27.61			Sep-07
	4.74	9.12	22.52	25.67	86.98	0	1.52	11.23	0.98	19.8	515.9	0	100	0	0		30.53	-27.61			Sep-07
	4.81	9.25	22.83	26.57	89.04	0	1.27	11.22	0.98	20.37	515.9	0	100	0	0		30.68	-27.57			Jun-15
	4.87	9.37	23.17	27.44	90.34	0	1.02	11.24	0.98	23.14	515.9	0	100	0	0		30.68	-27.57			Jun-15
	4.90	9.43	23.32	27.83	90.92	0	0.86	11.24	0.98	23.22	515.9	0	100	0	0		30.68	-27.57			Jun-15
	3.67	9.47	21.23	9.06	23.11	3.18	1.12	11.39	0.87	7.87	1,052	0	100	0	0	58	12.66	-22.9	5.75		Jun-08
	3.50	9.13	20.51	6.73	18.87	2.49	1.87	11.39	0.87	7.81	1,052	0	100	0	0	58	12.15	-22.98		1.00	Jun-08
	3.82	9.66	21.68	9.92	24.58	3.32	0.91	11.41	0.87	7.9	1,052	0	100	0	0	58	12.77	-22.7			Jun-08
	3.71	9.70	21.76	9.99	24.66		0.81	11.43	0.87	7.91	1,052	0	100	0	0	58	12.77	-22.7			Apr-17
	3.84	9.69	21.74	10.27	25.16	3.4	0.81	11.46	0.88	7.92	1,052	0	100	0	0	58	12.79	-22.72			Jun-08
	3.60	9.31	20.93	8.02	21.16	2.78	1.47	11.44	0.88	8.05	1,052	0	100	0	0	58	12.44	-22.87			Jun-08
	3.56	9.38	21.04	8.32	21.80	2.92	1.37	11.45	0.88	7.95	1,052	0	100	0	0	58	12.46	-22.87			Jun-08
	3.67	9.50	21.33	9.13	23.32	3.24	1.12	11.38	0.87	7.86	1,052	0	100	0	0	58	12.67	-22.75			Jun-15
	3.85	9.70	21.78	10.07	24.75	3.41	0.87	11.44	0.88	7.91	1,052	0	100	0	0	58	12.77	-22.7			Jun-15
	3.84	9.84	21.75	10.21	24.91	3.41	0.81	11.43	0.88	7.92	1,052	0	100	0	0	58	12.77	-22.7			Jun-15
	4.54	12.27	25.10	18.69	34.07	1.8	1.12	11.14	0.85	14.28	654.5	0	100	0	0	164	13.31	-23.48	5.75		Dec-03
	4.40	11.91	24.12	15.98	29.49	0.92	1.87	11.13	0.85	14.46	654.5	0	100	0	0	164	12.93	-23.67		5.00	Dec-03
	4.38	11.87	24.16	16.06	29.59	1.15	1.87	11.08	0.85	14.18	654.5	0	100	0	0	164	12.89	-23.69		1.00	Dec-03
	4.57	12.36	25.28	19.46	35.65	1.98	0.87	11.08	0.85	14.18	654.5	0	100	0	0	164	13.5	-23.4			Sep-07
	4.69	12.53	25.59	19.90	36.53		0.7	11.07	0.85	14.41	654.5	0	100	0	0	164	13.51	-23.29			Apr-17
	4.61	12.46	25.52	19.83	36.45	2.04	0.77	11.07	0.85	14.38	654.5	0	100	0	0	164	13.51	-23.29			Dec-03
	4.49	12.22	24.83	18.01	33.12	1.66	1.32	11.1	0.85	14.3	654.5	0	100	0	0	164	13.18	-23.43			Dec-03
	4.45	12.12	24.66	17.43	32.08	1.54	1.47	11.12	0.85	14.27	654.5	0	100	0	0	164	13.19	-23.5			Sep-07
	4.42	12.11	24.71	17.77	32.78	1.67	1.37	11.13	0.85	14.07	654.5	0	100	0	0	164	13.29	-23.54			Sep-07
	4.54	12.22	25.07	18.63	34.42	1.85	1.12	11.1	0.85	14.22	654.5	0	100	0	0	164	13.35	-23.37			Jun-15
	4.62	12.41	25.28	19.48	36.06	2.03	0.87	11.07	0.85	14.34	654.5	0	100	0	0	164	13.51	-23.29			Jun-15
	4.69	12.54	25.59	20.04	36.69	2.05	0.7	11.09	0.85	14.4	654.5	0	100	0	0	164	13.51	-23.29			Jun-15
	5.80	14.75	37.88	45.61	81.99	0.67	1.27	12.34	1.01	20.62	834.3	0	99	0	0	82	19.37	-24.25			Jun-15
	5.91	14.90	38.31	46.52	83.13	0.72	1.02	12.35	1.01	21.23	834.3	0	99	0	0	82	19.37	-24.25			Jun-15
	5.85	14.92	38.35	46.99	83.72	0.75	0.91	12.35	1.01	21.29	834.3	0	99	0	0	82	19.37	-24.25			Jun-15
	5.82	14.75	37.97	45.65	82.05	0.53	1.27	12.35	1.01	20.69	834.3	0	99	0	0	82	19.37	-24.25	5.75		Dec-96
	5.61	14.32	36.89	42.41	75.61	0	2.02	12.38	1.02	19.63	834.3	0	99	0	0	82	18.92	-24.45		5.00	Jun-97
	5.60	14.30	36.95	42.43	75.58	0	2.02	12.34	1.01	19.29	834.3	0	99	0	0	82	18.92	-24.45		1.00	Jun-97
	5.82	14.83	38.14	46.27	83.63	0.65	1.12	12.34	1.01	20.48	834.3	0	99	0	0	82	19.49	-24.2			Sep-07

Fund Name	MARKET Ticker Symbol	MARKET Traded On	FUND TYPE, CATEGORY & OBJECTIVE Fund Type	FUND TYPE, CATEGORY & OBJECTIVE Category and (Prospectus Objective)	RATINGS Overall Rating	RATINGS Reward Rating	RATINGS Risk Rating	RATINGS Recent Up/ Downgrade	MINIMUMS Open to New Investors	MINIMUMS Min Initial Investment
Lord Abbett International Opportunities Fund Class F3	LOIEX	NAS CM	Open End	Global Equity Mid/Small Cap (Foreign Stock)	A-	A-	A-	Up	Y	0
Lord Abbett International Opportunities Fund Class I	LINYX	NAS CM	Open End	Global Equity Mid/Small Cap (Foreign Stock)	A-	A	A-	Up	Y	1,000,000
Lord Abbett International Opportunities Fund Class P	LINPX	NAS CM	Open End	Global Equity Mid/Small Cap (Foreign Stock)	A-	A-	A-	Up		0
Lord Abbett International Opportunities Fund Class R2	LINQX	NAS CM	Open End	Global Equity Mid/Small Cap (Foreign Stock)	A-	A-	A-	Up	Y	0
Lord Abbett International Opportunities Fund Class R3	LINRX	NAS CM	Open End	Global Equity Mid/Small Cap (Foreign Stock)	A-	A-	A-	Up	Y	0
Lord Abbett Micro Cap Growth Fund Class I	LMIYX	NAS CM	Open End	US Equity Small Cap (Growth)	B	A	C+	Up	Y	1,000,000
Lord Abbett Micro Cap Value Fund Class I	LMVYX	NAS CM	Open End	US Equity Small Cap (Growth)	A-	A-	B+	Up	Y	1,000,000
Lord Abbett Mid Cap Stock Fund Class A	LAVLX	NAS CM	Open End	US Equity Mid Cap (Growth)	B-	C+	B		Y	1,000
Lord Abbett Mid Cap Stock Fund Class B	LMCBX	NAS CM	Open End	US Equity Mid Cap (Growth)	B-	C+	B			1,000
Lord Abbett Mid Cap Stock Fund Class C	LMCCX	NAS CM	Open End	US Equity Mid Cap (Growth)	B-	C+	B		Y	1,000
Lord Abbett Mid Cap Stock Fund Class F	LMCFX	NAS CM	Open End	US Equity Mid Cap (Growth)	B-	C+	B		Y	0
Lord Abbett Mid Cap Stock Fund Class F3	LOVLX	NAS CM	Open End	US Equity Mid Cap (Growth)	B-	C+	B		Y	0
Lord Abbett Mid Cap Stock Fund Class I	LMCYX	NAS CM	Open End	US Equity Mid Cap (Growth)	B-	C+	B		Y	1,000,000
Lord Abbett Mid Cap Stock Fund Class P	LMCPX	NAS CM	Open End	US Equity Mid Cap (Growth)	B-	C+	B			0
Lord Abbett Mid Cap Stock Fund Class R2	LMCQX	NAS CM	Open End	US Equity Mid Cap (Growth)	B-	C+	B		Y	0
Lord Abbett Mid Cap Stock Fund Class R3	LMCRX	NAS CM	Open End	US Equity Mid Cap (Growth)	B-	C+	B		Y	0
Lord Abbett Mid Cap Stock Fund Class R4	LMCSX	NAS CM	Open End	US Equity Mid Cap (Growth)	B-	C+	B		Y	0
Lord Abbett Mid Cap Stock Fund Class R5	LMCTX	NAS CM	Open End	US Equity Mid Cap (Growth)	B-	C+	B		Y	0
Lord Abbett Mid Cap Stock Fund Class R6	LMCHX	NAS CM	Open End	US Equity Mid Cap (Growth)	B-	C+	B		Y	0
Lord Abbett Multi-Asset Balanced Opportunity Fund Class A	LABFX	NAS CM	Open End	Moderate Alloc (Growth & Income)	C+	C+	B-	Down	Y	1,500
Lord Abbett Multi-Asset Balanced Opportunity Fund Class B	LABBX	NAS CM	Open End	Moderate Alloc (Growth & Income)	B-	C+	B	Up		1,500
Lord Abbett Multi-Asset Balanced Opportunity Fund Class C	BFLAX	NAS CM	Open End	Moderate Alloc (Growth & Income)	B-	C+	B	Up	Y	1,500
Lord Abbett Multi-Asset Balanced Opportunity Fund Class F	BLAFX	NAS CM	Open End	Moderate Alloc (Growth & Income)	B-	C+	B	Down	Y	0
Lord Abbett Multi-Asset Balanced Opportunity Fund Class F3	LOBFX	NAS CM	Open End	Moderate Alloc (Growth & Income)	C+	C+	B-	Down	Y	0
Lord Abbett Multi-Asset Balanced Opportunity Fund Class I	LABYX	NAS CM	Open End	Moderate Alloc (Growth & Income)	C+	C+	B-	Down	Y	1,000,000
Lord Abbett Multi-Asset Balanced Opportunity Fund Class P	LABPX	NAS CM	Open End	Moderate Alloc (Growth & Income)	C+	C+	B-	Down		0
Lord Abbett Multi-Asset Balanced Opportunity Fund Class R2	BLAQX	NAS CM	Open End	Moderate Alloc (Growth & Income)	C+	C+	B-	Down	Y	0
Lord Abbett Multi-Asset Balanced Opportunity Fund Class R3	BLARX	NAS CM	Open End	Moderate Alloc (Growth & Income)	C+	C+	B-	Down	Y	0
Lord Abbett Multi-Asset Balanced Opportunity Fund Class R4	BLASX	NAS CM	Open End	Moderate Alloc (Growth & Income)	C+	C+	B-	Down	Y	0
Lord Abbett Multi-Asset Balanced Opportunity Fund Class R5	BLATX	NAS CM	Open End	Moderate Alloc (Growth & Income)	C+	C+	B-	Down	Y	0
Lord Abbett Multi-Asset Balanced Opportunity Fund Class R6	BLAVX	NAS CM	Open End	Moderate Alloc (Growth & Income)	C+	C+	B-	Down	Y	0
Lord Abbett Multi-Asset Balanced Opportunity Fund Class T	LABTX	NAS CM	Open End	Moderate Alloc (Growth & Income)	C+	C+	B-		Y	1,500
Lord Abbett Multi-Asset Focused Growth Fund Class A	LDSAX	NAS CM	Open End	Aggressive Alloc (Growth)	B-	C+	B-	Down	Y	1,500
Lord Abbett Multi-Asset Focused Growth Fund Class B	LDSBX	NAS CM	Open End	Aggressive Alloc (Growth)	B-	C+	B	Up		1,500
Lord Abbett Multi-Asset Focused Growth Fund Class C	LDSCX	NAS CM	Open End	Aggressive Alloc (Growth)	C+	C+	B-	Down	Y	1,500
Lord Abbett Multi-Asset Focused Growth Fund Class F	LDSFX	NAS CM	Open End	Aggressive Alloc (Growth)	B-	C+	B-	Down	Y	0
Lord Abbett Multi-Asset Focused Growth Fund Class F3	LDSOX	NAS CM	Open End	Aggressive Alloc (Growth)	B-	C+	B-	Down	Y	0
Lord Abbett Multi-Asset Focused Growth Fund Class I	LDSYX	NAS CM	Open End	Aggressive Alloc (Growth)	B	C+	B+	Up	Y	1,000,000
Lord Abbett Multi-Asset Focused Growth Fund Class R2	LDSQX	NAS CM	Open End	Aggressive Alloc (Growth)	B-	C+	B	Up	Y	0
Lord Abbett Multi-Asset Focused Growth Fund Class R3	LDSRX	NAS CM	Open End	Aggressive Alloc (Growth)	B	C+	B	Up	Y	0
Lord Abbett Multi-Asset Focused Growth Fund Class R4	LDSSX	NAS CM	Open End	Aggressive Alloc (Growth)	B-	C+	B-	Down	Y	0
Lord Abbett Multi-Asset Focused Growth Fund Class R5	LDSTX	NAS CM	Open End	Aggressive Alloc (Growth)	B-	C+	B-	Down	Y	0
Lord Abbett Multi-Asset Focused Growth Fund Class R6	LDSVX	NAS CM	Open End	Aggressive Alloc (Growth)	B-	C+	B-	Down	Y	0
Lord Abbett Multi-Asset Global Opportunity Fund Class A	LAGEX	NAS CM	Open End	Alloc (Growth & Income)	C+	C+	C+	Down	Y	1,000
Lord Abbett Multi-Asset Global Opportunity Fund Class B	LAGBX	NAS CM	Open End	Alloc (Growth & Income)	C+	C+	C+	Up		1,000
Lord Abbett Multi-Asset Global Opportunity Fund Class C	LAGCX	NAS CM	Open End	Alloc (Growth & Income)	C+	C+	C+	Up	Y	1,000
Lord Abbett Multi-Asset Global Opportunity Fund Class F	LAGFX	NAS CM	Open End	Alloc (Growth & Income)	C+	C+	C+	Down	Y	0
Lord Abbett Multi-Asset Global Opportunity Fund Class F3	LOGEX	NAS CM	Open End	Alloc (Growth & Income)	C+	C+	C+	Down	Y	0
Lord Abbett Multi-Asset Global Opportunity Fund Class I	LGEYX	NAS CM	Open End	Alloc (Growth & Income)	C+	C+	C+	Down	Y	1,000,000
Lord Abbett Multi-Asset Global Opportunity Fund Class R2	LAGQX	NAS CM	Open End	Alloc (Growth & Income)	C+	C+	C+	Down	Y	0
Lord Abbett Multi-Asset Global Opportunity Fund Class R3	LARRX	NAS CM	Open End	Alloc (Growth & Income)	C+	C+	C+	Down	Y	0
Lord Abbett Multi-Asset Global Opportunity Fund Class R4	LARSX	NAS CM	Open End	Alloc (Growth & Income)	C+	C+	C+	Down	Y	0

★ Expanded analysis of this fund is included in Section II.

	TOTAL RETURNS					PERFORMANCE				ASSETS		ASSET ALLOCATION & TURNOVER					BULL & BEAR		FEES		
Min Additional Investment	3-Month Total Return	6-Month Total Return	1-Year Total Return	3-Year Total Return	5-Year Total Return	Dividend Yield (TTM)	Expense Ratio	3-Yr Std Deviation	3-Year Beta	NAV	Total Assets (MIL)	%Cash	%Stocks	%Bonds	%Other	Turnover Ratio	Last Bull Market Total Return	Last Bear Market Total Return	Front End Fee (%)	Back End Fee (%)	Inception Date
	5.90	14.92	38.17	45.86	82.31		0.91	12.36	1.01	21.29	834.3	0	99	0	0	82	19.37	-24.25			Apr-17
	5.88	14.92	38.25	46.74	84.48	0.72	1.02	12.37	1.02	21.23	834.3	0	99	0	0	82	19.59	-24.17			Dec-97
	5.76	14.63	37.64	44.71	80.45	0.29	1.47	12.36	1.02	21.13	834.3	0	99	0	0	82	19.24	-24.3			Mar-99
	5.76	14.60	37.52	44.11	79.19	0.43	1.62	12.34	1.01	20.38	834.3	0	99	0	0	82	19.18	-24.35			Sep-07
	5.79	14.66	37.65	44.71	80.24	0.45	1.52	12.34	1.01	20.34	834.3	0	99	0	0	82	19.26	-24.28			Sep-07
	3.31	17.39	38.37	32.33	166.28	0	1.67	19.26	1	17.81	137.7	0	98	0	0	161	30.59	-26.03			Jul-99
	2.13	6.54	7.50	42.57	102.16	0	1.65	13.48	0.79	30.96	138.2	0	100	0	0	52	30.46	-27.14			Jul-99
	2.67	2.80	7.03	19.18	77.85	0.58	0.97	10.77	1	29.9	2,081	0	100	0	0	69	26.39	-24.17	5.75		Jun-83
	2.45	2.38	6.23	16.52	71.62	0.03	1.72	10.81	1	27.94	2,081	0	100	0	0	69	25.96	-24.35		5.00	May-97
	2.45	2.37	6.24	16.52	71.64	0.03	1.72	10.76	1	27.8	2,081	0	100	0	0	69	25.9	-24.34		1.00	May-97
	2.72	2.86	7.19	19.68	79.57	0.74	0.82	10.78	1	29.65	2,081	0	100	0	0	69	26.61	-24.1			Sep-07
	2.76	2.97	7.28	19.45	78.26		0.63	10.78	1	29.74	2,081	0	100	0	0	69	26.39	-24.17			Apr-17
	2.71	2.91	7.29	20.06	80.39	0.82	0.72	10.79	1	29.66	2,081	0	100	0	0	69	26.64	-24.03			May-99
	2.63	2.70	6.83	18.50	76.96	0.42	1.17	10.78	1	28.99	2,081	0	100	0	0	69	26.43	-24.14			Nov-97
	2.58	2.61	6.67	17.90	75.13	0.35	1.32	10.8	1	29.4	2,081	0	100	0	0	69	26.19	-24.23			Mar-08
	2.57	2.64	6.76	18.28	76.06	0.4	1.22	10.78	1	29.58	2,081	0	100	0	0	69	26.32	-24.21			Mar-08
	2.67	2.77	7.05	19.22	77.92	0.8	0.97	10.77	1	29.79	2,081	0	100	0	0	69	26.39	-24.17			Jun-15
	2.72	2.93	7.30	19.93	78.98	0.83	0.72	10.78	1	29.66	2,081	0	100	0	0	69	26.39	-24.17			Jun-15
	2.76	2.97	7.41	20.29	79.51	0.83	0.63	10.78	1	29.74	2,081	0	100	0	0	69	26.39	-24.17			Jun-15
	2.73	5.05	10.10	15.72	46.88	2.78	1.23	7.22		11.8	1,838	1	57	31	2	25	17.65	-16.61	2.25		Dec-94
	2.57	4.75	9.42	13.27	41.46	1.95	1.98	7.24		11.81	1,838	1	57	31	2	25	17.14	-16.97		5.00	May-98
	2.62	4.75	9.41	13.28	41.61	2.07	1.98	7.2		11.73	1,838	1	57	31	2	25	17.1	-16.84		1.00	Jul-96
	2.85	5.21	10.35	16.35	47.99	2.93	1.08	7.19		11.8	1,838	1	57	31	2	25	17.76	-16.64			Sep-07
	2.78	5.17	10.27	15.91	47.12		0.88	7.22		11.8	1,838	1	57	31	2	25	17.64	-16.61			Apr-17
	2.78	5.25	10.45	16.69	48.68	3.02	0.98	7.24		11.8	1,838	1	57	31	2	25	17.7	-16.52			Oct-04
	2.71	4.99	9.95	15.11	45.41	2.6	1.43	7.26		11.75	1,838	1	57	31	2	25	17.56	-16.66			Dec-02
	2.70	4.96	9.80	14.70	44.33	2.37	1.58	7.2		12.05	1,838	1	57	31	2	25	17.38	-16.76			Sep-07
	2.70	4.96	9.88	14.94	45.03	2.55	1.48	7.25		11.77	1,838	1	57	31	2	25	17.39	-16.71			Sep-07
	2.74	5.06	10.14	15.78	46.96	2.82	1.23	7.18		11.8	1,838	1	57	31	2	25	17.65	-16.61			Jun-15
	2.78	5.16	10.34	16.45	47.81	3.01	0.98	7.2		11.81	1,838	1	57	31	2	25	17.65	-16.61			Jun-15
	2.78	5.26	10.47	16.48	47.85	3.04	0.88	7.19		11.8	1,838	1	57	31	2	25	17.65	-16.61			Jun-15
	2.82	5.15	10.20	15.83	47.02		1.23	7.22		11.81	1,838	1	57	31	2	25	17.65	-16.61	2.50		Jul-17
	4.28	7.51	16.12	22.93	79.01	1.28	1.42	9.88	0.95	17.21	239.7	0	92	4	0	7	24.29	-23.26	2.25		Jun-06
	4.09	7.14	15.34	20.26	72.43	0.27	2.17	9.87	0.95	17.24	239.7	0	92	4	0	7	23.81	-23.53		5.00	Jun-06
	4.12	7.09	15.33	20.28	72.60	0.64	2.17	9.84	0.95	16.67	239.7	0	92	4	0	7	23.77	-23.52		1.00	Jun-06
	4.33	7.62	16.30	23.45	80.26	1.37	1.27	9.88	0.95	17.2	239.7	0	92	4	0	7	24.39	-23.27			Sep-07
	4.33	7.59	16.45	23.87	81.25		1.01	9.85	0.95	17.36	239.7	0	92	4	0	7	24.5	-23.23			Apr-17
	4.33	7.65	16.45	23.87	81.25	1.5	1.17	9.85	0.95	17.37	239.7	0	92	4	0	7	24.5	-23.23			Jun-06
	4.22	7.37	15.80	20.33	74.04	0.76	1.77	9.99	0.96	17.74	239.7	0	92	4	0	7	24	-23.38			Sep-07
	4.25	7.40	15.90	22.07	76.88	1.08	1.67	9.86	0.95	17.01	239.7	0	92	4	0	7	24.18	-23.38			Sep-07
	4.29	7.53	16.16	22.95	79.01	1.31	1.42	9.86	0.95	17.14	239.7	0	92	4	0	7	24.32	-23.31			Jun-15
	4.38	7.70	16.51	23.93	81.34	1.5	1.17	9.86	0.95	17.38	239.7	0	92	4	0	7	24.5	-23.23			Jun-15
	4.36	7.67	16.55	23.97	81.40	1.53	1.01	9.86	0.95	17.37	239.7	0	92	4	0	7	24.5	-23.23			Jun-15
	2.30	5.38	11.69	11.90	32.96	2.57	1.36	7.96		11.63	241.8	1	67	24	2	24	15.75	-19.75	2.25		Sep-88
	2.26	5.13	10.99	9.58	28.34	2.05	2.11	8.01		10.47	241.8	1	67	24	2	24	15.4	-20.08		5.00	Aug-96
	2.27	5.10	10.92	9.54	28.19	2.18	2.11	8.01		10.44	241.8	1	67	24	2	24	15.28	-20.02		1.00	Aug-96
	2.30	5.42	11.72	12.30	33.90	2.72	1.21	8.02		11.63	241.8	1	67	24	2	24	15.83	-19.75			Sep-07
	2.28	5.50	11.90	12.11	33.21		0.98	7.96		11.72	241.8	1	67	24	2	24	15.75	-19.75			Apr-17
	2.28	5.40	11.81	12.66	34.52	2.79	1.11	8.01		11.71	241.8	1	67	24	2	24	15.91	-19.69			Oct-04
	2.34	5.29	11.37	10.86	30.81	2.22	1.71	8.02		11.88	241.8	1	67	24	2	24	15.73	-19.92			Jun-08
	2.29	5.37	11.50	11.22	31.66	2.32	1.61	7.98		11.71	241.8	1	67	24	2	24	15.56	-19.82			Jun-08
	2.30	5.39	11.69	11.92	32.99	2.66	1.36	7.99		11.62	241.8	1	67	24	2	24	15.75	-19.75			Jun-15

	MARKET		FUND TYPE, CATEGORY & OBJECTIVE		RATINGS				MINIMUMS	
Fund Name	Ticker Symbol	Traded On	Fund Type	Category and (Prospectus Objective)	Overall Rating	Reward Rating	Risk Rating	Recent Up/ Downgrade	Open to New Investors	Min Initial Investment
Lord Abbett Multi-Asset Global Opportunity Fund Class R5	LARTX	NAS CM	Open End	Alloc (Growth & Income)	C+	C+	C+	Down	Y	0
Lord Abbett Multi-Asset Global Opportunity Fund Class R6	LARVX	NAS CM	Open End	Alloc (Growth & Income)	C+	C+	C+	Down	Y	0
Lord Abbett Multi-Asset Growth Fund Class A	LWSAX	NAS CM	Open End	Aggressive Alloc (Growth & Income)	C+	C+	B-	Down	Y	1,500
Lord Abbett Multi-Asset Growth Fund Class B	LWSBX	NAS CM	Open End	Aggressive Alloc (Growth & Income)	C+	C+	B-	Down		1,500
Lord Abbett Multi-Asset Growth Fund Class C	LWSCX	NAS CM	Open End	Aggressive Alloc (Growth & Income)	B-	C+	B	Up	Y	1,500
Lord Abbett Multi-Asset Growth Fund Class F	LGXFX	NAS CM	Open End	Aggressive Alloc (Growth & Income)	C+	C+	B-	Down	Y	0
Lord Abbett Multi-Asset Growth Fund Class F3	LOWSX	NAS CM	Open End	Aggressive Alloc (Growth & Income)	C+	C+	B-	Down	Y	0
Lord Abbett Multi-Asset Growth Fund Class I	LWSYX	NAS CM	Open End	Aggressive Alloc (Growth & Income)	C+	C+	B-	Down	Y	1,000,000
Lord Abbett Multi-Asset Growth Fund Class R2	LGIQX	NAS CM	Open End	Aggressive Alloc (Growth & Income)	C+	C+	B-	Down	Y	0
Lord Abbett Multi-Asset Growth Fund Class R3	LGIRX	NAS CM	Open End	Aggressive Alloc (Growth & Income)	B-	C+	B	Down	Y	0
Lord Abbett Multi-Asset Growth Fund Class R4	LGIKX	NAS CM	Open End	Aggressive Alloc (Growth & Income)	C+	C+	B-	Down	Y	0
Lord Abbett Multi-Asset Growth Fund Class R5	LGITX	NAS CM	Open End	Aggressive Alloc (Growth & Income)	C+	C+	B-	Down	Y	0
Lord Abbett Multi-Asset Growth Fund Class R6	LGIVX	NAS CM	Open End	Aggressive Alloc (Growth & Income)	C+	C+	B-	Down	Y	0
Lord Abbett Multi-Asset Income Fund Class A	ISFAX	NAS CM	Open End	Cautious Alloc (Equity-Income)	B-	C+	B	Up	Y	1,500
Lord Abbett Multi-Asset Income Fund Class B	ISFBX	NAS CM	Open End	Cautious Alloc (Equity-Income)	C+	C+	B	Down		1,500
Lord Abbett Multi-Asset Income Fund Class C	ISFCX	NAS CM	Open End	Cautious Alloc (Equity-Income)	C+	C+	B	Down	Y	1,500
Lord Abbett Multi-Asset Income Fund Class F	LIGFX	NAS CM	Open End	Cautious Alloc (Equity-Income)	B-	C+	B	Up	Y	0
Lord Abbett Multi-Asset Income Fund Class F3	ISFOX	NAS CM	Open End	Cautious Alloc (Equity-Income)	B-	C+	B	Up	Y	0
Lord Abbett Multi-Asset Income Fund Class I	ISFYX	NAS CM	Open End	Cautious Alloc (Equity-Income)	B-	C+	B	Up	Y	1,000,000
Lord Abbett Multi-Asset Income Fund Class R2	LIGQX	NAS CM	Open End	Cautious Alloc (Equity-Income)	C+	C+	B	Down	Y	0
Lord Abbett Multi-Asset Income Fund Class R3	LIXRX	NAS CM	Open End	Cautious Alloc (Equity-Income)	C+	C+	B	Down	Y	0
Lord Abbett Multi-Asset Income Fund Class R4	LIXSX	NAS CM	Open End	Cautious Alloc (Equity-Income)	C+	C+	B	Down	Y	0
Lord Abbett Multi-Asset Income Fund Class R5	LIXTX	NAS CM	Open End	Cautious Alloc (Equity-Income)	B-	C+	B	Up	Y	0
Lord Abbett Multi-Asset Income Fund Class R6	LIXVX	NAS CM	Open End	Cautious Alloc (Equity-Income)	B-	C+	B	Up	Y	0
Lord Abbett Multi-Asset Income Fund Class T	ISFTX	NAS CM	Open End	Cautious Alloc (Equity-Income)	B-	C+	B		Y	1,500
Lord Abbett Small Cap Value Fund Class A	LRSCX	NAS CM	Open End	US Equity Small Cap (Small Company)	B	B-	B	Up	Y	1,000
Lord Abbett Small Cap Value Fund Class B	LRSBX	NAS CM	Open End	US Equity Small Cap (Small Company)	B-	B-	B	Up		1,000
Lord Abbett Small Cap Value Fund Class C	LSRCX	NAS CM	Open End	US Equity Small Cap (Small Company)	B	B-	B	Up	Y	1,000
Lord Abbett Small Cap Value Fund Class F	LRSFX	NAS CM	Open End	US Equity Small Cap (Small Company)	B	B	B	Up	Y	0
Lord Abbett Small Cap Value Fund Class F3	LRSOX	NAS CM	Open End	US Equity Small Cap (Small Company)	B	B	B	Up	Y	0
Lord Abbett Small Cap Value Fund Class I	LRSYX	NAS CM	Open End	US Equity Small Cap (Small Company)	B	B	B	Up	Y	1,000,000
Lord Abbett Small Cap Value Fund Class P	LRSPX	NAS CM	Open End	US Equity Small Cap (Small Company)	B	B-	B	Up		0
Lord Abbett Small Cap Value Fund Class R2	LRSQX	NAS CM	Open End	US Equity Small Cap (Small Company)	B	B-	B	Up	Y	0
Lord Abbett Small Cap Value Fund Class R3	LRSRX	NAS CM	Open End	US Equity Small Cap (Small Company)	B	B-	B	Up	Y	0
Lord Abbett Small Cap Value Fund Class R4	LRSSX	NAS CM	Open End	US Equity Small Cap (Small Company)	B	B-	B	Up	Y	0
Lord Abbett Small Cap Value Fund Class R5	LRSTX	NAS CM	Open End	US Equity Small Cap (Small Company)	B	B	B	Up	Y	0
Lord Abbett Small Cap Value Fund Class R6	LRSVX	NAS CM	Open End	US Equity Small Cap (Small Company)	B	B	B	Up	Y	0
Lord Abbett Value Opportunities Fund Class A	LVOAX	NAS CM	Open End	US Equity Mid Cap (Growth)	B	B-	B	Up	Y	1,500
Lord Abbett Value Opportunities Fund Class B	LVOBX	NAS CM	Open End	US Equity Mid Cap (Growth)	B-	C+	B	Up		1,500
Lord Abbett Value Opportunities Fund Class C	LVOCX	NAS CM	Open End	US Equity Mid Cap (Growth)	B-	C+	B	Up	Y	1,500
Lord Abbett Value Opportunities Fund Class F	LVOFX	NAS CM	Open End	US Equity Mid Cap (Growth)	B	B-	B	Up	Y	0
Lord Abbett Value Opportunities Fund Class F3	LVOOX	NAS CM	Open End	US Equity Mid Cap (Growth)	B	B-	B	Up	Y	0
Lord Abbett Value Opportunities Fund Class I	LVOYX	NAS CM	Open End	US Equity Mid Cap (Growth)	B	B-	B	Up	Y	1,000,000
Lord Abbett Value Opportunities Fund Class P	LVOPX	NAS CM	Open End	US Equity Mid Cap (Growth)	B-	C+	B	Up		0
Lord Abbett Value Opportunities Fund Class R2	LVOQX	NAS CM	Open End	US Equity Mid Cap (Growth)	B-	C+	B	Up	Y	0
Lord Abbett Value Opportunities Fund Class R3	LVORX	NAS CM	Open End	US Equity Mid Cap (Growth)	B-	C+	B	Up	Y	0
Lord Abbett Value Opportunities Fund Class R4	LVOSX	NAS CM	Open End	US Equity Mid Cap (Growth)	B	B-	B	Up	Y	0
Lord Abbett Value Opportunities Fund Class R5	LVOTX	NAS CM	Open End	US Equity Mid Cap (Growth)	B	B-	B	Up	Y	0
Lord Abbett Value Opportunities Fund Class R6	LVOVX	NAS CM	Open End	US Equity Mid Cap (Growth)	B	B-	B	Up	Y	0
Lord Abbett Value Opportunities Fund Class T	LVATX	NAS CM	Open End	US Equity Mid Cap (Growth)	B-	C+	B		Y	1,500
Low Beta Tactical 500 Fund Institutional Class	LBETX	NAS CM	Open End	US Equity Large Cap Blend (Growth & Income)	U	U	U		Y	100,000
Low Beta Tactical 500 Fund Investor Class	LBTTX	NAS CM	Open End	US Equity Large Cap Blend (Growth & Income)	U	U	U		Y	2,500

★Expanded analysis of this fund is included in Section II.

Min Additional Investment	TOTAL RETURNS 3-Month Total Return	6-Month Total Return	1-Year Total Return	3-Year Total Return	5-Year Total Return	PERFORMANCE Dividend Yield (TTM)	Expense Ratio	3-Yr Std Deviation	3-Year Beta	ASSETS NAV	Total Assets (MIL)	ASSET ALLOCATION & TURNOVER %Cash	%Stocks	%Bonds	%Other	Turnover Ratio	BULL & BEAR Last Bull Market Total Return	Last Bear Market Total Return	FEES Front End Fee (%)	Back End Fee (%)	Inception Date
	2.28	5.40	11.80	12.55	33.73	2.79	1.11	7.99		11.72	241.8	1	67	24	2	24	15.75	-19.75			Jun-15
	2.28	5.50	11.94	12.65	33.85	2.83	0.98	7.99		11.72	241.8	1	67	24	2	24	15.75	-19.75			Jun-15
	2.49	5.16	10.43	17.21	54.62	2.45	1.25	8.07		17.47	1,023	0	72	20	1	21	19.68	-18.69	2.25		Jun-05
	2.68	5.10	9.94	15.01	49.42	1.57	2	8.03		17.42	1,023	0	72	20	1	21	19.1	-18.95		5.00	Jun-05
	2.52	4.96	9.85	14.86	49.38	1.76	2	8.03		17.31	1,023	0	72	20	1	21	19.13	-18.93		1.00	Jun-05
	2.54	5.20	10.56	17.75	55.78	2.6	1.1	8.06		17.46	1,023	0	72	20	1	21	19.77	-18.64			Sep-07
	2.51	5.24	10.69	18.12	56.58		0.88	8.04		17.58	1,023	0	72	20	1	21	19.83	-18.64			Apr-17
	2.53	5.19	10.64	18.06	56.51	2.67	1	8.04		17.56	1,023	0	72	20	1	21	19.83	-18.64			Jun-05
	2.55	5.08	10.18	16.18	52.14	1.86	1.6	8.07		17.88	1,023	0	72	20	1	21	19.44	-18.83			Sep-07
	2.56	5.12	10.28	16.53	52.95	2.24	1.5	8.04		17.42	1,023	0	72	20	1	21	19.48	-18.76			Sep-07
	2.47	5.09	10.36	17.28	54.70	2.52	1.25	8.03		17.45	1,023	0	72	20	1	21	19.66	-18.72			Jun-15
	2.57	5.23	10.68	18.16	56.64	2.67	1	8.06		17.58	1,023	0	72	20	1	21	19.83	-18.64			Jun-15
	2.57	5.30	10.83	18.30	56.83	2.7	0.88	8.07		17.59	1,023	0	72	20	1	21	19.83	-18.64			Jun-15
	1.82	3.97	8.73	14.56	32.41	3.13	1.15	4.88		14.94	1,659	1	38	45	2	26	12.54	-9.82	2.25		Jun-05
	1.70	3.66	7.96	12.09	27.54	2.24	1.9	4.89		15.18	1,659	1	38	45	2	26	11.99	-10.02		5.00	Jun-05
	1.66	3.59	7.93	12.03	27.50	2.35	1.9	4.89		15.15	1,659	1	38	45	2	26	12	-10.06		1.00	Jun-05
	1.84	4.04	8.88	15.07	33.38	3.28	1	4.88		14.94	1,659	1	38	45	2	26	12.56	-9.7			Sep-07
	1.87	4.11	8.96	15.43	34.03		0.82	4.92		14.86	1,659	1	38	45	2	26	12.67	-9.7			Apr-17
	1.80	4.04	8.89	15.35	33.94	3.39	0.9	4.92		14.85	1,659	1	38	45	2	26	12.67	-9.7			Jun-05
	1.71	3.77	8.28	13.39	30.04	2.69	1.5	4.88		15.33	1,659	1	38	45	2	26	12.24	-9.88			Sep-07
	1.77	3.87	8.42	13.74	30.76	2.89	1.4	4.88		14.94	1,659	1	38	45	2	26	12.3	-9.84			Sep-07
	1.81	3.98	8.69	14.56	32.36	3.16	1.15	4.89		14.94	1,659	1	38	45	2	26	12.51	-9.79			Jun-15
	1.87	4.11	8.96	15.42	34.02	3.39	0.9	4.89		14.86	1,659	1	38	45	2	26	12.67	-9.7			Jun-15
	1.87	4.11	9.05	15.47	34.08	3.41	0.82	4.88		14.86	1,659	1	38	45	2	26	12.67	-9.7			Jun-15
	1.82	3.98	8.69	14.57	32.37		1.15	4.92		14.94	1,659	1	38	45	2	26	12.51	-9.79	2.50		Jul-17
	3.94	6.01	6.30	25.38	75.72	0	1.17	12.12	0.83	20.42	1,162	0	100	0	0	44	33.42	-28.31	5.75		Dec-95
	3.77	5.59	5.51	22.59	69.37	0	1.92	12.1	0.83	11.52	1,162	0	100	0	0	44	32.83	-28.5		5.00	Nov-96
	3.76	5.65	5.58	22.71	69.50	0	1.92	12.11	0.83	11.56	1,162	0	100	0	0	44	32.87	-28.51		1.00	Apr-97
	3.97	6.08	6.47	25.98	77.15	0	1.02	12.12	0.83	20.54	1,162	0	100	0	0	44	33.56	-28.24			Sep-07
	4.04	6.19	6.56	25.68	76.14		0.83	12.13	0.83	24.26	1,162	0	100	0	0	44	33.42	-28.31			Apr-17
	3.98	6.14	6.60	26.33	78.05	0	0.92	12.12	0.83	24.17	1,162	0	100	0	0	44	33.6	-28.21			Dec-97
	3.88	5.90	6.10	24.63	74.13	0	1.37	12.12	0.83	19.41	1,162	0	100	0	0	44	33.26	-28.35			Jun-99
	3.87	5.85	5.95	24.10	72.76	0	1.52	12.12	0.83	19.23	1,162	0	100	0	0	44	33.14	-28.38			Mar-08
	3.87	5.88	6.08	24.53	73.85	0	1.42	12.12	0.83	19.5	1,162	0	100	0	0	44	33.22	-28.34			Mar-08
	3.94	6.02	6.36	25.43	75.79	0	1.17	12.12	0.83	20.43	1,162	0	100	0	0	44	33.42	-28.31			Jun-15
	3.99	6.14	6.60	26.23	76.91	0	0.92	12.13	0.83	24.19	1,162	0	100	0	0	44	33.42	-28.31			Jun-15
	4.02	6.21	6.67	26.52	77.32	0	0.83	12.13	0.83	24.26	1,162	0	100	0	0	44	33.42	-28.31			Jun-15
	4.18	6.63	10.15	23.38	87.71	0	1.15	10.3	0.81	20.09	3,227	0	100	0	0	37	24.33	-23	5.75		Dec-05
	4.04	6.29	9.37	20.65	81.10	0	1.9	10.3	0.81	17.96	3,227	0	100	0	0	37	23.87	-23.22		5.00	Dec-05
	3.99	6.29	9.31	20.65	81.10	0	1.9	10.28	0.81	17.96	3,227	0	100	0	0	37	23.87	-23.22		1.00	Dec-05
	4.20	6.70	10.27	23.92	89.43	0.04	1	10.3	0.81	20.48	3,227	0	100	0	0	37	24.48	-22.91			Sep-07
	4.32	6.88	10.54	24.45	90.56		0.79	10.28	0.81	20.93	3,227	0	100	0	0	37	24.58	-22.9			Apr-17
	4.23	6.79	10.41	24.30	90.33	0.23	0.9	10.28	0.81	20.86	3,227	0	100	0	0	37	24.58	-22.89			Dec-05
	4.15	6.58	9.93	22.68	86.17	0	1.35	10.32	0.81	19.74	3,227	0	100	0	0	37	24.29	-23.04			Dec-05
	4.13	6.50	9.79	22.11	84.81	0	1.5	10.3	0.81	19.33	3,227	0	100	0	0	37	24.19	-23.09			Sep-07
	4.15	6.55	9.87	22.48	85.64	0	1.4	10.29	0.81	19.52	3,227	0	100	0	0	37	24.23	-23.02			Sep-07
	4.17	6.67	10.13	23.39	87.99	0.08	1.15	10.29	0.81	20.06	3,227	0	100	0	0	37	24.4	-22.98			Jun-15
	4.29	6.85	10.41	24.36	90.41	0.19	0.9	10.31	0.81	20.88	3,227	0	100	0	0	37	24.58	-22.9			Jun-15
	4.28	6.83	10.54	24.69	90.92	0.24	0.79	10.29	0.81	20.93	3,227	0	100	0	0	37	24.58	-22.9			Jun-15
	4.25	6.72	10.19	23.44	88.07		1.15	10.28	0.81	20.07	3,227	0	100	0	0	37	24.4	-22.98	2.50		Jul-17
1,000	4.55	6.56					1.7			10.4	18.6	100	0	0	0						Jun-17
1,000	4.46	6.35					1.95			10.38	18.6	100	0	0	0						Jun-17

Fund Name	MARKET Ticker Symbol	Traded On	FUND TYPE, CATEGORY & OBJECTIVE Fund Type	Category and (Prospectus Objective)	RATINGS Overall Rating	Reward Rating	Risk Rating	Recent Up/ Downgrade	Open to New Investors	MINIMUMS Min Initial Investment
LS Opportunity Fund	LSOFX	NAS CM	Open End	Long/Short Equity (Growth)	B-	C+	B	Down	Y	5,000
LS Theta Fund Institutional Class	LQTIX	NAS CM	Open End	Long/Short Equity (Income)	B	C	A-	Up	Y	100,000
LS Theta Fund Investor Class	LQTVX	NAS CM	Open End	Long/Short Equity (Income)	B	C	A-	Up	Y	1,000
LSV Conservative Value Equity Fund	LSVVX	NAS CM	Open End	US Equity Large Cap Value (Growth)	B	B-	B	Up	Y	100,000
LSV Conservative Value Equity Fund Investor Class	LVAVX	NAS CM	Open End	US Equity Large Cap Value (Growth)	B	B-	B	Up	Y	1,000
LSV Global Managed Volatility Fund Institutional Class	LSVFX	NAS CM	Open End	Global Equity (Income)	B-	B-	B-		Y	100,000
LSV Global Managed Volatility Fund Investor Class	LVAFX	NAS CM	Open End	Global Equity (Income)	B-	C+	B		Y	1,000
LSV Global Value Fund Institutional Class	LSVGX	NAS CM	Open End	Global Equity (Growth)	B-	B-	C+	Up	Y	100,000
LSV Global Value Fund Investor Class	LVAGX	NAS CM	Open End	Global Equity (Growth)	C+	B-	C+	Down	Y	1,000
LSV Small Cap Value Fund Institutional Class	LSVQX	NAS CM	Open End	US Equity Small Cap (Small Company)	B	B+	B	Up	Y	100,000
LSV Small Cap Value Fund Investor Class	LVAQX	NAS CM	Open End	US Equity Small Cap (Small Company)	B	B+	B	Up	Y	1,000
LSV U.S. Managed Volatility Fund Institutional Class	LSVMX	NAS CM	Open End	US Equity Large Cap Value (Growth)	B-	B-	B	Down	Y	100,000
LSV U.S. Managed Volatility Fund Investor Class	LVAMX	NAS CM	Open End	US Equity Large Cap Value (Growth)	B-	B-	B	Down	Y	1,000
LSV Value Equity Fund	LSVEX	NAS CM	Open End	US Equity Large Cap Value (Growth)	B	B	B	Up	Y	100,000
LSV Value Equity Fund Investor Class	LVAEX	NAS CM	Open End	US Equity Large Cap Value (Growth)	B	B	B	Up	Y	1,000
LWAS/DFA International High Book To Market Portfolio	DFHBX	NAS CM	Open End	Global Equity Large Cap (Foreign Stock)	B-	B-	B-	Up		0
LWAS/DFA U.S. High Book To Market Portfolio	DFBMX	NAS CM	Open End	US Equity Large Cap Value (Growth)	B	B	B	Up		0
Lyrical U.S. Hedged Value Fund Institutional Class	LYRHX	NAS CM	Open End	Long/Short Equity (Growth)	B-	C+	B	Up	Y	100,000
Lyrical U.S. Hedged Value Fund Investor Class	LYRDX	NAS CM	Open End	Long/Short Equity (Growth)	B-	C+	B	Up	Y	2,500
Lyrical U.S. Value Equity Fund Institutional Class	LYRIX	NAS CM	Open End	US Equity Large Cap Value (Growth)	B	B	B	Up	Y	100,000
Lyrical U.S. Value Equity Fund Investor Class	LYRBX	NAS CM	Open End	US Equity Large Cap Value (Growth)	B	B	B	Up	Y	2,500
M.D. Sass Equity Income Plus Fund Institutional Class	MDEIX	NAS CM	Open End	Long/Short Equity (Growth & Income)	B-	C	B	Up	Y	1,000,000
M.D. Sass Equity Income Plus Fund Investor Class	MDEPX	NAS CM	Open End	Long/Short Equity (Growth & Income)	B-	C	B	Up	Y	2,500
Macquarie Global Infrastructure Total Return Fund Inc.	MGU	NYSE	Closed End	Other Sector Equity (World Stock)	C+	C+	C+	Up	Y	
Macquarie Pooled Trust Emerging Markets Portfolio	DPEMX	NAS CM	Open End	Emerging Markets Equity (Div Emerging Mkts)	C+	C+	C	Up		1,000,000
Macquarie Pooled Trust Emerging Markets Portfolio II	DPEGX	NAS CM	Open End	Emerging Markets Equity (Div Emerging Mkts)	B-	B	C	Up	Y	1,000,000
Macquarie Pooled Trust Labor Select Intl Equity Portfolio	DELPX	NAS CM	Open End	Global Equity Large Cap (Foreign Stock)	B-	C+	B	Up	Y	1,000,000
Macquarie Pooled Trust Large Cap Value Portfolio	DPDEX	NAS CM	Open End	US Equity Large Cap Value (Growth)	B	B-	B+		Y	1,000,000
Macquarie/First Trust Global Infrastr/Util Div & Income	MFD	NYSE	Closed End	Utilities Sector Equity (Utility)	C	C	C	Up	Y	
Madison Aggressive Allocation Fund Class A	MAGSX	NAS CM	Open End	Aggressive Alloc (Asset Alloc)	B-	B-	B	Down	Y	1,000
Madison Aggressive Allocation Fund Class B	MAGBX	NAS CM	Open End	Aggressive Alloc (Asset Alloc)	B-	C+	B	Down	Y	1,000
Madison Aggressive Allocation Fund Class C	MAACX	NAS CM	Open End	Aggressive Alloc (Asset Alloc)	B-	C+	B	Down	Y	1,000
Madison Conservative Allocation Fund Class A	MCNAX	NAS CM	Open End	Cautious Alloc (Asset Alloc)	B	C+	A-	Up	Y	1,000
Madison Conservative Allocation Fund Class B	MCNBX	NAS CM	Open End	Cautious Alloc (Asset Alloc)	B	C	A-	Up	Y	1,000
Madison Conservative Allocation Fund Class C	MCOCX	NAS CM	Open End	Cautious Alloc (Asset Alloc)	B	C	A-	Up	Y	1,000
Madison Covered Call & Equity Income Fund Class A	MENAX	NAS CM	Open End	Long/Short Equity (Equity-Income)	B-	C	B+	Down	Y	1,000
Madison Covered Call & Equity Income Fund Class C	MENCX	NAS CM	Open End	Long/Short Equity (Equity-Income)	B-	C	B+		Y	1,000
Madison Covered Call & Equity Income Fund Class R6	MENRX	NAS CM	Open End	Long/Short Equity (Equity-Income)	B-	C+	B+	Down	Y	500,000
Madison Covered Call & Equity Income Fund Class Y	MENYX	NAS CM	Open End	Long/Short Equity (Equity-Income)	B-	C+	B+	Down	Y	0
Madison Covered Call and Equity Strategy Fund	MCN	NYSE	Closed End	US Equity Large Cap Growth (Equity-Income)	B-	C+	B+	Up	Y	
Madison Diversified Income Fund Class A	MBLAX	NAS CM	Open End	Moderate Alloc (Growth & Income)	B-	C+	B	Up	Y	1,000
Madison Diversified Income Fund Class B	MBLNX	NAS CM	Open End	Moderate Alloc (Growth & Income)	B-	C+	B	Down	Y	1,000
Madison Diversified Income Fund Class C	MBLCX	NAS CM	Open End	Moderate Alloc (Growth & Income)	B-	C+	B	Down	Y	1,000
Madison Dividend Income Fund Class Y	BHBFX	NAS CM	Open End	US Equity Large Cap Value (Equity-Income)	B	B-	B		Y	0
Madison International Stock Fund Class A	MINAX	NAS CM	Open End	Global Equity Large Cap (Foreign Stock)	B-	C+	B	Up	Y	1,000
Madison International Stock Fund Class B	MINBX	NAS CM	Open End	Global Equity Large Cap (Foreign Stock)	C+	C+	B	Up	Y	1,000
Madison International Stock Fund Class Y	MINYX	NAS CM	Open End	Global Equity Large Cap (Foreign Stock)	B-	C+	B	Up	Y	0
Madison Investors Fund Class A	MNVAX	NAS CM	Open End	US Equity Large Cap Growth (Growth)	B	B	B+		Y	1,000
Madison Investors Fund Class R6	MNVRX	NAS CM	Open End	US Equity Large Cap Growth (Growth)	B	B	B+		Y	500,000
Madison Investors Fund Class Y	MINVX	NAS CM	Open End	US Equity Large Cap Growth (Growth)	B	B	B+		Y	0
Madison Large Cap Value Fund Class A	MGWAX	NAS CM	Open End	US Equity Large Cap Value (Growth & Income)	B-	B-	B	Down	Y	1,000
Madison Large Cap Value Fund Class B	MGWBX	NAS CM	Open End	US Equity Large Cap Value (Growth & Income)	B-	C+	B	Down	Y	1,000

★ Expanded analysis of this fund is included in Section II.

Min Additional Investment	TOTAL RETURNS: 3-Month Total Return	6-Month Total Return	1-Year Total Return	3-Year Total Return	5-Year Total Return	PERFORMANCE: Dividend Yield (TTM)	Expense Ratio	3-Yr Std Deviation	3-Year Beta	ASSETS: NAV	Total Assets (MIL)	ASSET ALLOCATION & TURNOVER: %Cash	%Stocks	%Bonds	%Other	Turnover Ratio	BULL & BEAR: Last Bull Market Total Return	Last Bear Market Total Return	FEES: Front End Fee (%)	Back End Fee (%)	Inception Date
100	3.70	6.55	9.57	18.17	49.96	0	1.95	6.46	0.51	13.78	37.1	38	63	0	-1	75	3.65	-11.34			Sep-10
1,000	1.19	2.54	5.75	14.33		0	1.25	3.17		53.4	304.8	37	0	61	2						Mar-14
100	1.12	2.40	5.50	13.51		0	1.5	3.15		52.89	304.8	37	0	61	2						Mar-14
	6.57	10.98	16.17	27.92	105.51	2.07	0.35	10.92	1.04	13.41	120.4	1	99	0	0		25.76	-21.09			Mar-07
	6.49	10.83	15.83	27.04	102.89	1.95	0.6	10.89	1.04	13.36	120.4	1	99	0	0		25.58	-21.17			Jun-14
	6.36	9.97	19.03	25.30		1.78	0.75	8.57	0.75	11.16	8.2	2	97	0	0						Jun-14
	6.17	9.76	18.66	24.32		1.42	1	8.58	0.75	11.2	8.2	2	97	0	0						Jun-14
	5.95	11.97	21.85	28.00		1.66	0.9	10.86	0.98	11.77	4.6	0	97	0	1						Jun-14
	5.90	11.92	21.69	27.06		1.48	1.15	10.91	0.98	11.78	4.6	0	97	0	1						Jun-14
	2.18	7.02	6.11	29.82		1.1	0.85	14.15	0.98	15.55	359.9	2	98	0	0						Feb-13
	2.14	6.93	5.81	28.83		1.04	1.1	14.13	0.98	15.49	359.9	2	98	0	0						Jun-14
	5.36	8.42	13.69	26.37		1.52	0.55	7.94	0.69	12.58	92.9	0	97	0	2						Jun-14
	5.28	8.33	13.51	25.85		1.36	0.8	7.93	0.69	12.6	92.9	0	97	0	2						Jun-14
	7.30	13.15	18.30	34.01	120.92	1.76	0.66	11.68	1.1	28.95	2,181	0	100	0	0		27.46	-23.28			Mar-99
	7.21	12.96	17.99	32.98	118.09	1.61	0.91	11.68	1.1	28.82	2,181	0	100	0	0		27.28	-23.36			Jun-14
	5.57	14.29	26.26	27.31	48.40	3.03	0.29	13.68	1.08	8.9	58.0	1	96	0	3	15	10.58	-26.9			Jun-93
	7.50	12.44	19.00	34.99	114.56	1.76	0.18	12.08	1.15	19.05	58.5	1	99	0	0	15	25.84	-23.95			Jun-96
	1.64	2.93	9.13	8.53		0	1.76	8.5	0.62	10.41	1.5	46	54	0	0	17					Jul-14
	1.65	2.86	8.87	7.72		0	2.01	8.5	0.62	10.32	1.5	46	54	0	0	17					Jul-14
	5.15	9.48	21.29	28.79		1.19	1.38	13.38	1.16	18.62	1,163	2	98	0	0	36					Feb-13
	5.06	9.29	20.88	27.67		0.87	1.7	13.39	1.17	18.54	1,163	2	98	0	0	36					Feb-14
25,000	0.99	3.38	7.27	8.27		1.85	0.75	6.12	0.77	11.13	61.2	9	91	0	0	77					Jun-13
100	0.90	3.19	6.99	7.20		1.57	1.1	6.16	0.78	11.1	61.2	9	91	0	0	77			5.75		Jun-13
	0.79	4.16	24.59	16.68	70.59	1.19	0	13.83	0.85	27.7	354.6	0	138	0	-39	65	22.05	-20.05			Aug-05
	5.52	9.31	26.57	15.20	6.87	3.01	1.19	13.32	0.8	8.79	136.2	2	98	0	0	28	19.98	-20.61			Apr-97
	3.18	16.70	44.46	33.72	39.90	0.87	1.2	17.93	1.09	10.42	44.8	0	100	0	0	20	15.73	-28.79			Jun-10
	2.37	8.04	21.70	19.85	43.68	2.49	0.86	11.54	0.88	14.97	493.6	0	99	0	1	22	7.26	-16.2			Dec-95
	5.41	10.56	13.69	28.00	99.37	1.67	0.65	10.13	0.93	26.18	173.7	6	99	0	-5	13	24.35	-13.57			Feb-92
	-1.51	1.33	10.40	-0.37	27.41	7.86	0	11.14	0.71	13.26	113.9	0	73	27	0	199	16.52	-14.73			Mar-04
50	4.44	8.61	18.04	24.76	65.79	0.96	1.15	7.44	0.72	12.33	66.5	7	77	13	3	98	14.58	-13.31	5.75		Jun-06
150	4.27	8.18	17.19	21.93	59.63	0.5	1.9	7.42	0.72	12.04	66.5	7	77	13	3	98	14.05	-13.59		4.50	Jun-06
50	4.26	8.18	17.18	22.01	59.73	0.5	1.9	7.45	0.72	12.05	66.5	7	77	13	3	98	14.03	-13.58		1.00	Feb-08
50	2.21	4.49	9.67	13.25	29.12	1.63	1.13	3.69	0.48	10.79	73.6	7	34	57	3	82	8.37	-5.15	5.75		Jun-06
150	2.06	4.03	8.74	10.66	24.32	0.8	1.88	3.64	0.47	10.88	73.6	7	34	57	3	82	7.91	-5.41		4.50	Jun-06
50	2.06	4.02	8.84	10.66	24.43	0.8	1.88	3.65	0.47	10.89	73.6	7	34	57	3	82	7.91	-5.5		1.00	Feb-08
50	2.31	4.25	7.17	13.83	38.99	4.23	1.28	5.66	0.48	8.89	129.7	25	74	0	1	135	22.06	-11.21	5.75		Oct-09
50	2.23	3.90	6.43	11.43	34.07	4.4	2.03	5.7	0.48	8.47	129.7	25	74	0	1	135	21.55	-11.53		1.00	Jul-12
50,000	2.41	4.42	7.62	15.16	41.67	4.17	0.9	5.68	0.48	9.15	129.7	25	74	0	1	135	22.26	-11.16			Jul-12
	2.43	4.46	7.56	14.77	40.89	4.21	1.03	5.69	0.48	9.08	129.7	25	74	0	1	135	22.25	-11.16			Oct-09
	2.45	4.47	7.20	14.40	45.83	1.26	0	5.78	0.48	8.27	160.7	12	87	0	1	134	19.7	-14.79			Jul-04
50	4.49	7.59	12.83	21.86	51.69	1.58	1.1	5.35	0.48	16.13	168.2	2	63	35	0	35	11.51	-5.03	5.75		Dec-97
150	4.27	7.14	11.99	19.13	46.13	0.88	1.85	5.32	0.48	16.23	168.2	2	63	35	0	35	11.03	-5.3		4.50	Dec-97
50	4.27	7.15	12.00	19.14	46.16	0.88	1.85	5.31	0.48	16.22	168.2	2	63	35	0	35	11.02	-5.33		1.00	Jul-12
	7.05	11.77	19.92	34.00	94.35	1.6	0.95	9.32	0.88	26.7	111.2	2	98	0	0	33	15.32	-9.67			Dec-86
50	4.41	9.32	21.98	16.72	35.44	1	1.6	10.92	0.85	14.31	31.6	3	97	0	0	34	16.46	-20.39	5.75		Dec-97
150	4.16	8.84	21.05	14.09	30.43	0.49	2.35	10.88	0.84	14	31.6	3	97	0	0	34	15.91	-20.63		4.50	Dec-97
	4.47	9.45	22.31	17.62	37.13	1.17	1.35	10.92	0.84	14.32	31.6	3	97	0	0	34	16.63	-20.24			Jun-06
50	0.70	4.58	15.71	29.29	88.74	0	1.2	8.89	0.83	22.83	314.6	5	95	0	0	27	21.1	-15.07	5.75		Sep-13
50,000	0.43	4.36	15.72	30.50	92.02	0.33	0.77	8.89	0.83	22.96	314.6	5	95	0	0	27	21.28	-14.98			Sep-13
	0.52	4.48	15.69	29.93	90.69	0.19	0.95	8.87	0.83	22.85	314.6	5	95	0	0	27	21.28	-14.98			Nov-78
50	6.97	10.83	14.83	23.78	83.57	1.01	1.16	8.73	0.78		92.5	1	99	0	0	74	22.51	-14.48	5.75		Dec-97
150	6.75	10.41	13.99	21.04	76.87	0.32	1.91	8.74	0.78		92.5	1	99	0	0	74	21.95	-14.75		4.50	Dec-97

	MARKET		FUND TYPE, CATEGORY & OBJECTIVE		RATINGS				MINIMUMS	
Fund Name	Ticker Symbol	Traded On	Fund Type	Category and (Prospectus Objective)	Overall Rating	Reward Rating	Risk Rating	Recent Up/ Downgrade	Open to New Investors	Min Initial Investment
Madison Large Cap Value Fund Class Y	MYLVX	NAS CM	Open End	US Equity Large Cap Value (Growth & Income)	B-	B-	B	Down	Y	0
Madison Mid Cap Fund Class A	MERAX	NAS CM	Open End	US Equity Mid Cap (Growth)	B	B-	B+		Y	1,000
Madison Mid Cap Fund Class B	MERBX	NAS CM	Open End	US Equity Mid Cap (Growth)	B	B-	B+		Y	1,000
Madison Mid Cap Fund Class R6	MMCRX	NAS CM	Open End	US Equity Mid Cap (Growth)	B	B	A-		Y	500,000
Madison Mid Cap Fund Class Y	GTSGX	NAS CM	Open End	US Equity Mid Cap (Growth)	B	B-	B+		Y	0
Madison Moderate Allocation Fund Class A	MMDAX	NAS CM	Open End	Moderate Alloc (Asset Alloc)	B-	C+	B	Up	Y	1,000
Madison Moderate Allocation Fund Class B	MMDRX	NAS CM	Open End	Moderate Alloc (Asset Alloc)	B-	C+	B	Up	Y	1,000
Madison Moderate Allocation Fund Class C	MMDCX	NAS CM	Open End	Moderate Alloc (Asset Alloc)	B-	C+	B	Up	Y	1,000
Madison Small Cap Fund Class A	MASVX	NAS CM	Open End	US Equity Small Cap (Small Company)	B	B	B	Up	Y	1,000
Madison Small Cap Fund Class B	MBSVX	NAS CM	Open End	US Equity Small Cap (Small Company)	B	B	B	Up	Y	1,000
Madison Small Cap Fund Class Y	MYSVX	NAS CM	Open End	US Equity Small Cap (Small Company)	B	B	B	Up	Y	0
Madison Strategic Sector Premium Fund	MSP	NYSE	Closed End	US Equity Large Cap Growth (Equity-Income)	B-	C+	B+	Up	Y	
MAI Managed Volatility Fund Institutional Class	MAIPX	NAS CM	Open End	Long/Short Equity (Growth)	B-	C+	B	Up	Y	50,000
MAI Managed Volatility Fund Investor Class	DIVPX	NAS CM	Open End	Long/Short Equity (Growth)	B-	C+	B	Up	Y	2,500
Main BuyWrite Fund Class I Shares	BUYWX	NAS CM	Open End	Long/Short Equity (Growth & Income)	C-	D+	A-	Up	Y	100,000
MainGate MLP Fund Class A	AMLPX	NAS CM	Open End	Energy Sector Equity (Growth & Income)	D	D	D	Down	Y	2,500
MainGate MLP Fund Class C	MLCPX	NAS CM	Open End	Energy Sector Equity (Growth & Income)	D	D	D	Down	Y	2,500
MainGate MLP Fund Class I	IMLPX	NAS CM	Open End	Energy Sector Equity (Growth & Income)	D	D	D	Down	Y	1,000,000
MainStay Absolute Return Multi-Strategy Fund Class A	MSAKX	NAS CM	Open End	Multialternative (Growth)	C	C	B	Up	Y	15,000
MainStay Absolute Return Multi-Strategy Fund Class C	MSHEX	NAS CM	Open End	Multialternative (Growth)	C	C-	C	Up	Y	2,500
MainStay Absolute Return Multi-Strategy Fund Class I	MSNIX	NAS CM	Open End	Multialternative (Growth)	C	C	B	Up	Y	5,000,000
MainStay Absolute Return Multi-Strategy Fund Investor Cls	MSANX	NAS CM	Open End	Multialternative (Growth)	C	C	B-	Up	Y	2,500
MainStay Balanced Fund Class A	MBNAX	NAS CM	Open End	Moderate Alloc (Balanced)	B-	C+	B	Up	Y	25,000
MainStay Balanced Fund Class B	MBNBX	NAS CM	Open End	Moderate Alloc (Balanced)	B-	C+	B+	Up		1,000
MainStay Balanced Fund Class C	MBACX	NAS CM	Open End	Moderate Alloc (Balanced)	B-	C+	B+	Up	Y	1,000
MainStay Balanced Fund Class I	MBAIX	NAS CM	Open End	Moderate Alloc (Balanced)	B	C+	B+	Up	Y	5,000,000
MainStay Balanced Fund Class R1	MBNRX	NAS CM	Open End	Moderate Alloc (Balanced)	B-	C+	B	Up	Y	0
MainStay Balanced Fund Class R2	MBCRX	NAS CM	Open End	Moderate Alloc (Balanced)	B	C+	B+	Up	Y	0
MainStay Balanced Fund Class R3	MBDRX	NAS CM	Open End	Moderate Alloc (Balanced)	B-	C+	B	Up	Y	0
MainStay Balanced Fund Class R6	MBERX	NAS CM	Open End	Moderate Alloc (Balanced)	U	U	U		Y	0
MainStay Balanced Fund Investor Class	MBINX	NAS CM	Open End	Moderate Alloc (Balanced)	B-	C+	B	Up	Y	1,000
MainStay Common Stock Fund Class A	MSOAX	NAS CM	Open End	US Equity Large Cap Blend (Growth)	B	B	B	Up	Y	25,000
MainStay Common Stock Fund Class B	MOPBX	NAS CM	Open End	US Equity Large Cap Blend (Growth)	B-	B-	B-	Down		1,000
MainStay Common Stock Fund Class C	MGOCX	NAS CM	Open End	US Equity Large Cap Blend (Growth)	B-	B-	B-	Down	Y	1,000
MainStay Common Stock Fund Class I	MSOIX	NAS CM	Open End	US Equity Large Cap Blend (Growth)	B	B	B		Y	5,000,000
MainStay Common Stock Fund Class R3	MSOSX	NAS CM	Open End	US Equity Large Cap Blend (Growth)	B	B	B	Up	Y	0
MainStay Common Stock Fund Investor Class	MCSSX	NAS CM	Open End	US Equity Large Cap Blend (Growth)	B	B	B	Up	Y	1,000
MainStay Conservative Allocation Fund Class A	MCKAX	NAS CM	Open End	Cautious Alloc (Asset Alloc)	B-	C+	B	Up	Y	25,000
MainStay Conservative Allocation Fund Class B	MCKBX	NAS CM	Open End	Cautious Alloc (Asset Alloc)	C+	C	B	Up		1,000
MainStay Conservative Allocation Fund Class C	MCKCX	NAS CM	Open End	Cautious Alloc (Asset Alloc)	C+	C	B	Up	Y	1,000
MainStay Conservative Allocation Fund Class I	MCKIX	NAS CM	Open End	Cautious Alloc (Asset Alloc)	B-	C+	B	Up	Y	5,000,000
MainStay Conservative Allocation Fund Class R3	MCKRX	NAS CM	Open End	Cautious Alloc (Asset Alloc)	B-	C+	B	Up	Y	0
MainStay Conservative Allocation Fund Investor Class	MCKNX	NAS CM	Open End	Cautious Alloc (Asset Alloc)	B-	C+	B	Up	Y	1,000
MainStay Convertible Fund Class A	MCOAX	NAS CM	Open End	Convertibles (Convertible Bond)	B	C+	B	Up	Y	25,000
MainStay Convertible Fund Class B	MCSVX	NAS CM	Open End	Convertibles (Convertible Bond)	B-	C+	B	Down		1,000
MainStay Convertible Fund Class C	MCCVX	NAS CM	Open End	Convertibles (Convertible Bond)	B-	C+	B	Down	Y	1,000
MainStay Convertible Fund Class I	MCNVX	NAS CM	Open End	Convertibles (Convertible Bond)	B	C+	B+	Up	Y	5,000,000
MainStay Convertible Fund Investor Class	MCINX	NAS CM	Open End	Convertibles (Convertible Bond)	B	C+	B	Up	Y	1,000
MainStay Cornerstone Growth Fund Class A	KLGAX	NAS CM	Open End	US Equity Large Cap Growth (Growth)	B	B	B	Up	Y	25,000
MainStay Cornerstone Growth Fund Class B	KLGBX	NAS CM	Open End	US Equity Large Cap Growth (Growth)	B-	B	B-	Down	Y	1,000
MainStay Cornerstone Growth Fund Class C	KLGCX	NAS CM	Open End	US Equity Large Cap Growth (Growth)	B-	B	B-	Down	Y	2,500
MainStay Cornerstone Growth Fund Class I	KLGIX	NAS CM	Open End	US Equity Large Cap Growth (Growth)	B	B	B	Up	Y	5,000,000

★ Expanded analysis of this fund is included in Section II.

	TOTAL RETURNS					PERFORMANCE				ASSETS		ASSET ALLOCATION & TURNOVER					BULL & BEAR		FEES		
Min Additional Investment	3-Month Total Return	6-Month Total Return	1-Year Total Return	3-Year Total Return	5-Year Total Return	Dividend Yield (TTM)	Expense Ratio	3-Yr Std Deviation	3-Year Beta	NAV	Total Assets (MIL)	%Cash	%Stocks	%Bonds	%Other	Turnover Ratio	Last Bull Market Total Return	Last Bear Market Total Return	Front End Fee (%)	Back End Fee (%)	Inception Date
	6.96	10.90	15.06	24.66	85.75	1.24	0.91	8.71	0.78		92.5	1	99	0	0	74	22.71	-14.4			Jun-06
50	1.39	5.34	11.03	23.81	77.47	0	1.4	9.9	0.89	9.46	351.8	7	93	0	0	27	26.24	-18.52	5.75		Apr-13
150	0.38	4.15	9.27	20.20	69.64	0	2.15	9.89	0.89	7.78	351.8	7	93	0	0	27	25.69	-18.78		4.50	Apr-13
50,000	1.71	5.89	11.90	26.55	83.64	0	0.77	9.86	0.89	10.06	351.8	7	93	0	0	27	26.62	-18.44			Feb-12
	1.54	5.67	11.65	25.34	80.48	0	0.98	9.84	0.89	9.87	351.8	7	93	0	0	27	26.42	-18.44			Jul-83
50	3.47	6.75	14.28	19.59	48.37	1.22	1.15	5.58	0.52	11.86	149.1	8	58	32	3	97	12.26	-9.53	5.75		Jun-06
150	3.23	6.26	13.41	16.87	42.90	0.55	1.9	5.59	0.52	11.79	149.1	8	58	32	3	97	11.68	-9.66		4.50	Jun-06
50	3.23	6.35	13.40	16.85	42.86	0.55	1.9	5.56	0.52	11.8	149.1	8	58	32	3	97	11.68	-9.75		1.00	Feb-08
50	2.84	6.50	3.33	23.86	76.85	0.13	1.55	14.38	0.95		98.2	3	97	0	0	19	28.06	-21.94	5.75		Dec-06
150	2.65	6.07	2.59	21.15	70.37	0	2.3	14.4	0.96		98.2	3	97	0	0	19	27.57	-22.25		4.50	Dec-06
	3.55	7.36	3.79	24.51	79.68	0.37	1.3	14.44	0.96		98.2	3	97	0	0	19	28.34	-21.91			Jan-07
	2.55	4.50	6.99	14.82	44.77	0.98	0	5.75	0.48	12.35	72.1	13	86	0	1	138	18.53	-13.38			Apr-05
5,000	2.54	4.70	8.65	14.16	33.30	0.42	1.06	4.92	0.47	11.33	123.3	30	46	24	0	60	13.15	-7.29			Sep-10
100	2.51	4.61	8.39	13.36	32.01	0	1.31	4.92	0.47	11.53	123.3	30	46	24	0	60	12.91	-7.35			Dec-10
	1.83	4.66	8.62			0.51	1.37			10.88	26.9	6	94	0	0	73					Dec-15
100	-0.36	-2.97	-8.20	-19.16	15.88	7.64	1.67	20.9	1.19	8.83	1,618	0	100	0	0	25	15.49	-6.86	5.75		Feb-11
100	-0.48	-3.24	-8.81	-20.90	11.78	7.79	2.42	20.87	1.19	8.66	1,618	0	100	0	0	25	15	-7.05		1.00	Mar-14
10,000	-0.24	-2.80	-7.95	-18.52	17.46	7.47	1.42	20.84	1.19	9.03	1,618	0	100	0	0	25	15.67	-6.67			Feb-11
	-1.00	0.68	-1.40			1.58	1.8			9.82	110.3	63	14	6	18	168			5.50		Jun-15
50	-1.10	0.31	-2.29			1	2.82			9.74	110.3	63	14	6	18	168				1.00	Jun-15
	-0.85	0.94	-1.05			1.8	1.57			9.83	110.3	63	14	6	18	168					Jun-15
50	-0.93	0.66	-1.52			1.44	2.07			9.81	110.3	63	14	6	18	168			5.50		Jun-15
	3.59	5.84	9.61	16.09	58.54	1.12	1.15	6.35	0.59	32.67	770.9	1	58	41	0	271	15.19	-11.18	5.50		Jan-04
50	3.33	5.35	8.58	12.98	51.46	0.3	2.05	6.35	0.59	32.54	770.9	1	58	41	0	271	14.55	-11.54		5.00	Jan-04
50	3.33	5.35	8.59	12.99	51.45	0.3	2.05	6.35	0.59	32.52	770.9	1	58	41	0	271	14.52	-11.54		1.00	Dec-02
	3.65	5.96	9.86	16.96	60.53	1.35	0.9	6.34	0.59	32.74	770.9	1	58	41	0	271	15.35	-11.09			May-89
	3.63	5.95	9.75	16.62	59.75	1.25	1	6.34	0.59	32.7	770.9	1	58	41	0	271	15.27	-11.14			Jan-04
	3.53	5.78	9.64	15.90	57.96	1.01	1.25	6.35	0.59	32.71	770.9	1	58	41	0	271	15.09	-11.23			Jan-04
	3.47	5.65	9.20	14.86	55.72	0.79	1.5	6.34	0.59	32.64	770.9	1	58	41	0	271	14.95	-11.31			Apr-06
	3.65	5.96	9.86	17.71	58.76		0.78			32.74	770.9	1	58	41	0	271	15.35	-11.08			Dec-17
50	3.51	5.76	9.40	15.53	57.19	0.95	1.3	6.33	0.59	32.69	770.9	1	58	41	0	271	15.08	-11.27	5.50		Feb-08
	8.56	13.88	23.82	32.64	111.88	1	0.98	10.33	1.01	25.58	193.1	0	100	0	0	164	24.36	-17.27	5.50		Jun-98
50	8.27	13.26	22.58	28.74	101.26	0.17	1.98	10.3	1	23.56	193.1	0	100	0	0	164	23.44	-17.69		5.00	Jun-98
50	8.32	13.27	22.59	28.75	101.17	0.17	1.98	10.3	1	23.55	193.1	0	100	0	0	164	23.44	-17.69		1.00	Sep-98
	8.64	13.99	24.14	33.61	114.41	1.2	0.73	10.33	1.01	25.65	193.1	0	100	0	0	164	24.52	-17.16			Dec-04
	8.48	13.61	23.38	31.37	108.79	0.78	1.34	10.34	1.01	25.52	193.1	0	100	0	0	164	24.18	-17.35			Feb-16
50	8.53	13.70	23.51	31.69	108.88	0.79	1.23	10.33	1.01	25.61	193.1	0	100	0	0	164	24.03	-17.48	5.50		Feb-08
	2.55	5.38	10.30	14.38	36.00	1.85	1.33	5.16	0.48	12.32	473.0	10	40	46	2	44	12.89	-8.44	5.50		Apr-05
50	2.40	4.98	9.32	11.39	30.09	0.98	2.22	5.11	0.47	12.28	473.0	10	40	46	2	44	12.34	-8.87		5.00	Apr-05
50	2.32	4.90	9.24	11.31	29.99	0.98	2.22	5.16	0.48	12.27	473.0	10	40	46	2	44	12.34	-8.79		1.00	Apr-05
	2.67	5.55	10.49	15.28	37.69	2.07	1.08	5.13	0.47	12.42	473.0	10	40	46	2	44	13.15	-8.36			Apr-05
	2.50	5.25	9.88	13.40	34.11	1.52	1.68	5.13	0.47	12.31	473.0	10	40	46	2	44	12.82	-8.55			Feb-16
50	2.59	5.36	10.20	13.92	35.04	1.7	1.47	5.16	0.47	12.33	473.0	10	40	46	2	44	12.8	-8.49	5.50		Feb-08
	2.38	4.50	10.80	21.27	65.94	1.32	1.01	8.84	1.08	16.81	1,199	10	5	0	0	24	16.65	-19.56	5.50		Jan-95
50	2.15	3.96	9.79	18.00	58.36	0.48	1.93	8.84	1.08	16.74	1,199	10	5	0	0	24	15.94	-19.86		5.00	May-86
50	2.15	3.97	9.80	17.96	58.34	0.48	1.93	8.83	1.08	16.72	1,199	10	5	0	0	24	15.95	-19.87		1.00	Sep-98
	2.48	4.69	11.23	22.33	68.16	1.6	0.61	8.87	1.08	16.84	1,199	10	5	0	0	24	16.78	-19.48			Nov-08
50	2.34	4.41	10.68	20.73	64.44	1.16	1.18	8.86	1.08	16.81	1,199	10	5	0	0	24	16.45	-19.59	5.50		Feb-08
	9.17	15.83	30.04	31.98	82.59	0	1.16	12.23	1.06	34.35	661.6	0	100	0	0	137	28.62	-18.62	5.50		Aug-06
50	8.90	15.24	28.76	28.29	74.14	0	2.1	12.24	1.06	32.47	661.6	0	100	0	0	137	28.06	-18.87		5.00	Jan-13
50	8.90	15.25	28.77	28.25	74.10	0	2.1	12.24	1.06	32.46	661.6	0	100	0	0	137	28.06	-18.87		1.00	Jan-13
	9.25	15.97	30.37	32.92	84.82	0	0.98	12.24	1.06	35.1	661.6	0	100	0	0	137	28.88	-18.52			Nov-09

Fund Name	MARKET Ticker Symbol	Traded On	FUND TYPE, CATEGORY & OBJECTIVE Fund Type	Category and (Prospectus Objective)	RATINGS Overall Rating	Reward Rating	Risk Rating	Recent Up/ Downgrade	Open to New Investors	MINIMUMS Min Initial Investment
MainStay Cornerstone Growth Fund Class R2	KLGRX	NAS CM	Open End	US Equity Large Cap Growth (Growth)	B	B	B	Up	Y	0
MainStay Cornerstone Growth Fund Investor Class	KLGNX	NAS CM	Open End	US Equity Large Cap Growth (Growth)	B	B	B	Up	Y	2,500
MainStay Cushing® Energy Income Fund Class A	CURAX	NAS CM	Open End	Energy Sector Equity (Natl Res)	D	D	D	Down	Y	25,000
MainStay Cushing® Energy Income Fund Class C	CURCX	NAS CM	Open End	Energy Sector Equity (Natl Res)	D	D	D	Down	Y	2,500
MainStay Cushing® Energy Income Fund Class I	CURZX	NAS CM	Open End	Energy Sector Equity (Natl Res)	D	D+	D	Down	Y	5,000,000
MainStay Cushing® Energy Income Fund Investor Class	CURNX	NAS CM	Open End	Energy Sector Equity (Natl Res)	D	D	D	Down	Y	2,500
MainStay Cushing® MLP Premier Fund Class A	CSHAX	NAS CM	Open End	Energy Sector Equity (Equity-Income)	D	D	D	Down	Y	25,000
MainStay Cushing® MLP Premier Fund Class C	CSHCX	NAS CM	Open End	Energy Sector Equity (Equity-Income)	D	D	D	Down	Y	2,500
MainStay Cushing® MLP Premier Fund Class I	CSHZX	NAS CM	Open End	Energy Sector Equity (Equity-Income)	D	D	D	Down	Y	5,000,000
MainStay Cushing® MLP Premier Fund Investor Class	CSHNX	NAS CM	Open End	Energy Sector Equity (Equity-Income)	D	D	D	Down	Y	2,500
MainStay Cushing® Renaissance Advantage Fund Class A	CRZAX	NAS CM	Open End	Natl Resources Sec Equity (Natl Res)	C	C	C-	Up	Y	25,000
MainStay Cushing® Renaissance Advantage Fund Class C	CRZCX	NAS CM	Open End	Natl Resources Sec Equity (Natl Res)	C	C	C-	Up	Y	2,500
MainStay Cushing® Renaissance Advantage Fund Class I	CRZZX	NAS CM	Open End	Natl Resources Sec Equity (Natl Res)	C	C	C	Up	Y	5,000,000
MainStay Cushing® Renaissance Advantage Fund Investor Cls	CRZNX	NAS CM	Open End	Natl Resources Sec Equity (Natl Res)	C	C	C-	Up	Y	2,500
MainStay Emerging Markets Equity Fund Class A	MEOAX	NAS CM	Open End	Emerging Markets Equity (Div Emerging Mkts)	B-	B	C	Up	Y	25,000
MainStay Emerging Markets Equity Fund Class C	MEOCX	NAS CM	Open End	Emerging Markets Equity (Div Emerging Mkts)	C+	B-	C	Up	Y	2,500
MainStay Emerging Markets Equity Fund Class I	MEOIX	NAS CM	Open End	Emerging Markets Equity (Div Emerging Mkts)	B-	B	C	Up	Y	5,000,000
MainStay Emerging Markets Equity Fund Investor Class	MEOVX	NAS CM	Open End	Emerging Markets Equity (Div Emerging Mkts)	C+	B	C	Up	Y	2,500
MainStay Epoch Capital Growth Fund Class A	MECDX	NAS CM	Open End	Global Equity (Growth)	D	C	B		Y	25,000
MainStay Epoch Capital Growth Fund Class C	MECEX	NAS CM	Open End	Global Equity (Growth)	D	C	B		Y	2,500
MainStay Epoch Capital Growth Fund Class I	MECFX	NAS CM	Open End	Global Equity (Growth)	D	C	B		Y	5,000,000
MainStay Epoch Capital Growth Fund Investor Class	MECVX	NAS CM	Open End	Global Equity (Growth)	D	C	B		Y	2,500
Mainstay Epoch Global Choice Fund Class A	EPAPX	NAS CM	Open End	Global Equity (World Stock)	B-	B-	B	Up	Y	25,000
Mainstay Epoch Global Choice Fund Class C	EPAKX	NAS CM	Open End	Global Equity (World Stock)	B-	B-	B	Up	Y	2,500
Mainstay Epoch Global Choice Fund Class I	EPACX	NAS CM	Open End	Global Equity (World Stock)	B-	B-	B	Up	Y	5,000,000
Mainstay Epoch Global Choice Fund Investor Class	EPAIX	NAS CM	Open End	Global Equity (World Stock)	B-	B-	B	Up	Y	2,500
MainStay Epoch Global Equity Yield Fund Class A	EPSPX	NAS CM	Open End	Global Equity (Equity-Income)	B-	C+	B		Y	25,000
MainStay Epoch Global Equity Yield Fund Class C	EPSKX	NAS CM	Open End	Global Equity (Equity-Income)	B-	C+	B-		Y	2,500
Mainstay Epoch Global Equity Yield Fund Class I	EPSYX	NAS CM	Open End	Global Equity (Equity-Income)	B-	C+	B		Y	5,000,000
MainStay Epoch Global Equity Yield Fund Class R2	EPSZX	NAS CM	Open End	Global Equity (Equity-Income)	B-	C+	B		Y	0
MainStay Epoch Global Equity Yield Fund Class R3	EPSHX	NAS CM	Open End	Global Equity (Equity-Income)	B-	C+	B		Y	0
MainStay Epoch Global Equity Yield Fund Class R6	EPSRX	NAS CM	Open End	Global Equity (Equity-Income)	B-	C+	B		Y	0
MainStay Epoch Global Equity Yield Fund Investor Class	EPSIX	NAS CM	Open End	Global Equity (Equity-Income)	B-	C+	B		Y	2,500
MainStay Epoch International Choice Fund Class A	ICEVX	NAS CM	Open End	Global Equity Large Cap (Foreign Stock)	C+	C+	B-	Up	Y	25,000
MainStay Epoch International Choice Fund Class C	ICEWX	NAS CM	Open End	Global Equity Large Cap (Foreign Stock)	C+	C+	B-	Up	Y	1,000
MainStay Epoch International Choice Fund Class I	ICEUX	NAS CM	Open End	Global Equity Large Cap (Foreign Stock)	C+	C+	B-	Up	Y	5,000,000
MainStay Epoch International Choice Fund Class R1	ICETX	NAS CM	Open End	Global Equity Large Cap (Foreign Stock)	C+	C+	B-	Up	Y	0
MainStay Epoch International Choice Fund Class R2	ICEYX	NAS CM	Open End	Global Equity Large Cap (Foreign Stock)	C+	C+	B-	Up	Y	0
MainStay Epoch International Choice Fund Class R3	ICEZX	NAS CM	Open End	Global Equity Large Cap (Foreign Stock)	C+	C+	B-	Up	Y	0
MainStay Epoch International Choice Fund Investor Class	ICELX	NAS CM	Open End	Global Equity Large Cap (Foreign Stock)	C+	C+	B-	Up	Y	1,000
MainStay Epoch International Small Cap Fund Class A	EPIPX	NAS CM	Open End	Global Equity Mid/Small Cap (Small Company)	B+	B+	B	Up	Y	25,000
MainStay Epoch International Small Cap Fund Class C	EPIKX	NAS CM	Open End	Global Equity Mid/Small Cap (Small Company)	B	B	B	Up	Y	2,500
MainStay Epoch International Small Cap Fund Class I	EPIEX	NAS CM	Open End	Global Equity Mid/Small Cap (Small Company)	B+	B+	B+	Up	Y	5,000,000
MainStay Epoch International Small Cap Fund Investor Class	EPIIX	NAS CM	Open End	Global Equity Mid/Small Cap (Small Company)	B	B	B	Up	Y	2,500
MainStay Epoch U.S. All Cap Fund Class A	MAAAX	NAS CM	Open End	US Equity Large Cap Blend (Growth)	B	B	B	Up	Y	25,000
MainStay Epoch U.S. All Cap Fund Class B	MAWBX	NAS CM	Open End	US Equity Large Cap Blend (Growth)	B	B-	B	Up		1,000
MainStay Epoch U.S. All Cap Fund Class C	MAWCX	NAS CM	Open End	US Equity Large Cap Blend (Growth)	B	B-	B	Up	Y	1,000
MainStay Epoch U.S. All Cap Fund Class I	MATIX	NAS CM	Open End	US Equity Large Cap Blend (Growth)	B	B	B		Y	5,000,000
MainStay Epoch U.S. All Cap Fund Investor Class	MAWNX	NAS CM	Open End	US Equity Large Cap Blend (Growth)	B	B	B	Up	Y	1,000
MainStay Epoch U.S. Equity Yield Fund Class A	EPLPX	NAS CM	Open End	US Equity Large Cap Value (Growth & Income)	B-	B-	B	Down	Y	25,000
MainStay Epoch U.S. Equity Yield Fund Class B	EPLBX	NAS CM	Open End	US Equity Large Cap Value (Growth & Income)	B-	B-	B	Down	Y	1,000
MainStay Epoch U.S. Equity Yield Fund Class C	EPLKX	NAS CM	Open End	US Equity Large Cap Value (Growth & Income)	B-	B-	B	Down	Y	2,500

★ Expanded analysis of this fund is included in Section II.

	TOTAL RETURNS					PERFORMANCE				ASSETS		ASSET ALLOCATION & TURNOVER					BULL & BEAR		FEES		
Min Additional Investment	3-Month Total Return	6-Month Total Return	1-Year Total Return	3-Year Total Return	5-Year Total Return	Dividend Yield (TTM)	Expense Ratio	3-Yr Std Deviation	3-Year Beta	NAV	Total Assets (MIL)	%Cash	%Stocks	%Bonds	%Other	Turnover Ratio	Last Bull Market Total Return	Last Bear Market Total Return	Front End Fee (%)	Back End Fee (%)	Inception Date
	9.11	15.77	29.93	31.57	81.47	0	1.24	12.23	1.06	34.14	661.6	0	100	0	0	137	28.62	-18.62			Jan-13
50	9.06	15.63	29.68	31.11	80.71	0	1.35	12.24	1.06	33.97	661.6	0	100	0	0	137	28.62	-18.62	5.50		Jan-13
	5.65	12.39	-0.96	-42.74	-63.58	4.77	1.45	28.96	1.49	4.52	56.9	1	88	7	0	64			5.50		Jul-12
50	5.66	11.85	-1.86	-44.18	-65.05	4.07	2.33	28.92	1.48	4.34	56.9	1	88	7	0	64				1.00	Jul-12
	5.88	12.63	-0.69	-42.27	-63.09	4.99	1.21	28.99	1.49	4.58	56.9	1	88	7	0	64					Jul-12
50	5.86	12.33	-1.05	-42.89	-63.68	4.7	1.55	28.92	1.48	4.51	56.9	1	88	7	0	64			5.50		Jul-14
	-0.03	-1.37	-8.42	-24.31	-2.79	11.45	1.53	21.59	1.26	12.2	1,242	1	98	0	0	52	9.87	-8.16	5.50		Oct-10
50	-0.12	-1.73	-9.06	-26.01	-6.38	12.34	2.3	21.56	1.26	11.3	1,242	1	98	0	0	52	9.36	-8.43		1.00	Oct-10
	0.12	-1.27	-8.18	-23.73	-1.52	11.18	1.28	21.59	1.26	12.5	1,242	1	98	0	0	52	10.02	-8.06			Oct-10
50	-0.03	-1.45	-8.42	-24.31	-2.81	11.45	1.55	21.57	1.26	12.2	1,242	1	98	0	0	52	9.86	-8.16	5.50		Jul-14
	11.85	19.79	8.34	7.21		2.7	1.61	19.56	1.39	22.29	163.6	0	100	0	0	314			5.50		Apr-13
50	11.59	19.25	7.32	4.41		2.81	2.51	19.54	1.4	21.39	163.6	0	100	0	0	314				1.00	Apr-13
	11.92	19.90	8.60	8.06		2.67	1.36	19.55	1.4	22.55	163.6	0	100	0	0	314					Apr-13
50	11.79	19.63	8.11	6.74		2.71	1.76	19.54	1.4	22.2	163.6	0	100	0	0	314			5.50		Jul-14
	5.94	14.72	40.13	25.57		2.62	1.63	16.41	1.02	10.98	173.8	0	97	0	2	149			5.50		Nov-13
50	5.57	14.09	38.66	21.80		2.02	2.62	16.4	1.01	10.87	173.8	0	97	0	2	149				1.00	Nov-13
	5.94	14.70	40.19	26.25		2.8	1.38	16.35	1.01	11	173.8	0	97	0	2	149					Nov-13
50	5.85	14.54	39.66	24.48		2.48	1.87	16.35	1.01	10.95	173.8	0	97	0	2	149			5.50		Nov-13
	6.28	11.61	26.82			0.17	1.2			12.69	111.0	3	96	1	1	26			5.50		Jun-16
50	6.03	11.01	25.62			0	1.95			12.62	111.0	3	96	1	1	26				1.00	Jun-16
	6.35	11.77	27.11			0.26	0.95			12.7	111.0	3	96	1	1	26					Jun-16
50	6.21	11.45	26.64			0.17	1.2			12.68	111.0	3	96	1	1	26			5.50		Jun-16
	4.52	10.18	27.86	22.22	62.45	0.64	1.3	10.97	0.98	21	206.9	3	97	0	0	70	18.41	-17.22	5.50		Aug-06
50	4.25	9.60	26.58	18.64	54.56	0	2.29	10.94	0.98	19.83	206.9	3	97	0	0	70	17.77	-17.56		1.00	Nov-09
	4.54	10.29	28.17	23.16	64.45	0.82	1.05	10.96	0.98	21.64	206.9	3	97	0	0	70	18.5	-17.08			Jul-05
50	4.43	10.01	27.54	21.31	60.38	0.44	1.54	10.93	0.97	20.9	206.9	3	97	0	0	70	18.21	-17.31	5.50		Nov-09
	3.22	6.80	16.52	17.69	57.02	2.46	1.11	9.18	0.73	20.07	3,967	3	96	0	1	21	13.4	-12.23	5.50		Aug-06
50	3.06	6.42	15.68	15.13	51.22	1.79	1.86	9.16	0.73	19.94	3,967	3	96	0	1	21	12.87	-12.49		1.00	Nov-09
	3.34	6.95	16.84	18.61	59.09	2.7	0.86	9.18	0.73	20.04	3,967	3	96	0	1	21	13.54	-12.15			Dec-05
	3.25	6.75	16.46	17.42	56.59	2.37	1.21	9.16	0.73	20.08	3,967	3	96	0	1	21	13.38	-12.24			Feb-14
	3.19	6.58	16.15	16.63	54.87	2.18	1.45	9.16	0.73	20.06	3,967	3	96	0	1	21	13.21	-12.33			Feb-16
	3.33	7.04	17.02	19.07	59.89	2.83	0.74	9.2	0.74	20.04	3,967	3	96	0	1	21	13.54	-12.15			Jun-13
50	3.29	6.85	16.66	17.75	56.97	2.49	1.11	9.17	0.73	20.04	3,967	3	96	0	1	21	13.42	-12.17	5.50		Nov-09
	2.09	6.91	25.26	15.56	32.62	2.58	1.24	13.61	1.08	36.1	634.1	5	95	0	0	46	12.7	-22.92	5.50		Sep-06
50	1.84	6.41	24.12	12.47	26.83	1.87	2.14	13.61	1.08	35.58	634.1	5	95	0	0	46	12.13	-23.19		1.00	Sep-06
	2.11	6.98	25.59	16.49	34.48	2.88	0.95	13.62	1.08	36.06	634.1	5	95	0	0	46	12.92	-22.79			Dec-97
	2.11	6.96	25.47	16.16	33.81	2.77	1.09	13.62	1.08	35.99	634.1	5	95	0	0	46	12.89	-22.86			Sep-06
	2.05	6.80	25.14	15.29	32.06	2.55	1.34	13.62	1.08	36.09	634.1	5	95	0	0	46	12.62	-22.95			Sep-06
	1.98	6.73	24.82	14.34	30.31	2.29	1.59	13.62	1.08	35.91	634.1	5	95	0	0	46	12.48	-23.03			Sep-06
50	2.03	6.79	25.01	15.01	31.64	2.53	1.39	13.61	1.08	36.08	634.1	5	95	0	0	46	12.58	-22.95	5.50		Apr-08
	5.53	14.07	30.65	35.89	55.20	0.38	1.65	12.52	1.04	25.61	38.2	2	95	0	3	43	15.09	-28.2	5.50		Aug-06
50	5.29	13.57	29.44	32.12	47.92	0	2.62	12.52	1.04	25.05	38.2	2	95	0	3	43	14.53	-28.43		1.00	Nov-09
	5.64	14.25	30.98	36.92	57.14	0.59	1.4	12.53	1.04	26.4	38.2	2	95	0	3	43	15.27	-28.1			Jan-05
50	5.51	13.98	30.41	35.11	53.50	0.21	1.87	12.53	1.04	25.56	38.2	2	95	0	3	43	14.98	-28.19	5.50		Nov-09
	6.39	11.22	22.38	28.50	102.74	1.5	1.15	11.61	1.11	25.41	783.1	2	98	0	0	45	25.64	-20.89	5.50		Jan-04
50	6.07	10.60	21.15	24.53	92.06	0.82	2.23	11.6	1.11	21.4	783.1	2	98	0	0	45	24.82	-21.31		5.00	Jan-04
50	6.07	10.59	21.08	24.46	91.87	0.82	2.23	11.62	1.11	21.41	783.1	2	98	0	0	45	24.8	-21.29		1.00	Jan-04
	6.44	11.37	22.72	29.48	105.29	1.54	0.9	11.6	1.11	28.46	783.1	2	98	0	0	45	25.85	-20.8			Jan-91
50	6.32	11.06	22.15	27.41	99.45	1.28	1.48	11.62	1.11	24.89	783.1	2	98	0	0	45	25.31	-21.01	5.50		Feb-08
	5.36	8.86	16.65	28.21	95.32	1.76	1.03	8.27	0.65	16.23	1,254	2	98	0	0	14	23.53	-19.01	5.50		Feb-09
50	5.15	8.40	15.62	25.24	87.99		2.01	8.25	0.64	15.71	1,254	2	98	0	0	14	22.97	-19.26		5.00	May-17
50	5.09	8.40	15.56	24.86	86.74	1.01	2.01	8.24	0.64	15.71	1,254	2	98	0	0	14	23.01	-19.3		1.00	Nov-09

	MARKET		FUND TYPE, CATEGORY & OBJECTIVE		RATINGS				MINIMUMS	
Fund Name	Ticker Symbol	Traded On	Fund Type	Category and (Prospectus Objective)	Overall Rating	Reward Rating	Risk Rating	Recent Up/ Downgrade	Open to New Investors	Min Initial Investment
MainStay Epoch U.S. Equity Yield Fund Class I	EPLCX	NAS CM	Open End	US Equity Large Cap Value (Growth & Income)	B-	B-	B	Down	Y	5,000,000
MainStay Epoch U.S. Equity Yield Fund Class R1	EPLRX	NAS CM	Open End	US Equity Large Cap Value (Growth & Income)	B-	B-	B	Down	Y	0
MainStay Epoch U.S. Equity Yield Fund Class R2	EPLSX	NAS CM	Open End	US Equity Large Cap Value (Growth & Income)	B-	B-	B	Down	Y	0
MainStay Epoch U.S. Equity Yield Fund Class R3	EPLTX	NAS CM	Open End	US Equity Large Cap Value (Growth & Income)	B-	B-	B	Down	Y	0
MainStay Epoch U.S. Equity Yield Fund Class R6	EPLDX	NAS CM	Open End	US Equity Large Cap Value (Growth & Income)	B-	B-	B	Down	Y	0
MainStay Epoch U.S. Equity Yield Fund Investor Class	EPLIX	NAS CM	Open End	US Equity Large Cap Value (Growth & Income)	B-	B-	B	Down	Y	2,500
MainStay Epoch U.S. Small Cap Fund Class A	MOPAX	NAS CM	Open End	US Equity Small Cap (Small Company)	B	B	B	Up	Y	25,000
MainStay Epoch U.S. Small Cap Fund Class B	MOTBX	NAS CM	Open End	US Equity Small Cap (Small Company)	B	B-	B	Up	Y	1,000
MainStay Epoch U.S. Small Cap Fund Class C	MOPCX	NAS CM	Open End	US Equity Small Cap (Small Company)	B	B-	B	Up	Y	1,000
MainStay Epoch U.S. Small Cap Fund Class I	MOPIX	NAS CM	Open End	US Equity Small Cap (Small Company)	B	B	B	Up	Y	5,000,000
MainStay Epoch U.S. Small Cap Fund Class R1	MOPRX	NAS CM	Open End	US Equity Small Cap (Small Company)	B	B	B	Up	Y	0
MainStay Epoch U.S. Small Cap Fund Class R2	MOTRX	NAS CM	Open End	US Equity Small Cap (Small Company)	B	B	B	Up	Y	0
MainStay Epoch U.S. Small Cap Fund Class R3	MOVRX	NAS CM	Open End	US Equity Small Cap (Small Company)	B	B	B	Up	Y	0
MainStay Epoch U.S. Small Cap Fund Investor Class	MOINX	NAS CM	Open End	US Equity Small Cap (Small Company)	B	B	B	Up	Y	1,000
MainStay Growth Allocation Class R3	MGXRX	NAS CM	Open End	Aggressive Alloc (Asset Alloc)	C+	B-	C+	Down	Y	0
MainStay Growth Allocation Fund Class A	MGXAX	NAS CM	Open End	Aggressive Alloc (Asset Alloc)	C+	B-	C+	Down	Y	25,000
MainStay Growth Allocation Fund Class B	MGXBX	NAS CM	Open End	Aggressive Alloc (Asset Alloc)	C+	C+	C+	Down		1,000
MainStay Growth Allocation Fund Class C	MGXCX	NAS CM	Open End	Aggressive Alloc (Asset Alloc)	C+	C+	C+	Down	Y	1,000
MainStay Growth Allocation Fund Class I	MGXIX	NAS CM	Open End	Aggressive Alloc (Asset Alloc)	B-	B-	C+	Up	Y	5,000,000
MainStay Growth Allocation Fund Investor Class	MGXNX	NAS CM	Open End	Aggressive Alloc (Asset Alloc)	C+	B-	C+	Down	Y	1,000
MainStay Income Builder Fund Class A	MTRAX	NAS CM	Open End	Alloc (Income)	B-	C+	B	Down	Y	25,000
MainStay Income Builder Fund Class B	MKTRX	NAS CM	Open End	Alloc (Income)	C+	C+	B-	Down		1,000
MainStay Income Builder Fund Class C	MCTRX	NAS CM	Open End	Alloc (Income)	C+	C+	B-	Down	Y	1,000
MainStay Income Builder Fund Class I	MTOIX	NAS CM	Open End	Alloc (Income)	B-	C+	B	Down	Y	5,000,000
MainStay Income Builder Fund Class R2	MTXRX	NAS CM	Open End	Alloc (Income)	B-	C+	B	Down	Y	0
MainStay Income Builder Fund Class R3	MTXVX	NAS CM	Open End	Alloc (Income)	C+	C+	B-	Down	Y	0
MainStay Income Builder Fund Investor Class	MTINX	NAS CM	Open End	Alloc (Income)	B-	C+	B-	Down	Y	1,000
MainStay International Equity Fund Class A	MSEAX	NAS CM	Open End	Global Equity Large Cap (Foreign Stock)	B	B	B	Up	Y	25,000
MainStay International Equity Fund Class B	MINEX	NAS CM	Open End	Global Equity Large Cap (Foreign Stock)	B	B-	B	Up		1,000
MainStay International Equity Fund Class C	MIECX	NAS CM	Open End	Global Equity Large Cap (Foreign Stock)	B	B-	B	Up	Y	1,000
MainStay International Equity Fund Class I	MSIIX	NAS CM	Open End	Global Equity Large Cap (Foreign Stock)	B	B	B	Up	Y	5,000,000
MainStay International Equity Fund Class R1	MIERX	NAS CM	Open End	Global Equity Large Cap (Foreign Stock)	B	B	B	Up	Y	0
MainStay International Equity Fund Class R2	MIRRX	NAS CM	Open End	Global Equity Large Cap (Foreign Stock)	B	B	B	Up	Y	0
MainStay International Equity Fund Class R3	MIFRX	NAS CM	Open End	Global Equity Large Cap (Foreign Stock)	B	B-	B	Up	Y	0
MainStay International Equity Fund Investor Class	MINNX	NAS CM	Open End	Global Equity Large Cap (Foreign Stock)	B	B-	B	Up	Y	1,000
Mainstay International Opportunities Fund Class A	MYITX	NAS CM	Open End	Global Equity Large Cap (Foreign Stock)	C+	B-	C+	Up	Y	25,000
Mainstay International Opportunities Fund Class C	MYICX	NAS CM	Open End	Global Equity Large Cap (Foreign Stock)	C+	C+	C	Up	Y	1,000
Mainstay International Opportunities Fund Class I	MYIIX	NAS CM	Open End	Global Equity Large Cap (Foreign Stock)	B-	B-	C+	Up	Y	5,000,000
Mainstay International Opportunities Fund Investor Class	MYINX	NAS CM	Open End	Global Equity Large Cap (Foreign Stock)	C+	B-	C+	Up	Y	1,000
MainStay Large Cap Growth Fund Class A	MLAAX	NAS CM	Open End	US Equity Large Cap Growth (Growth)	B+	B+	B+	Up	Y	25,000
MainStay Large Cap Growth Fund Class B	MLABX	NAS CM	Open End	US Equity Large Cap Growth (Growth)	B	B	B+	Up		1,000
MainStay Large Cap Growth Fund Class C	MLACX	NAS CM	Open End	US Equity Large Cap Growth (Growth)	B	B	B+	Up	Y	1,000
MainStay Large Cap Growth Fund Class I	MLAIX	NAS CM	Open End	US Equity Large Cap Growth (Growth)	B+	B+	B+	Up	Y	5,000,000
MainStay Large Cap Growth Fund Class R1	MLRRX	NAS CM	Open End	US Equity Large Cap Growth (Growth)	B+	B+	B+	Up	Y	0
MainStay Large Cap Growth Fund Class R2	MLRTX	NAS CM	Open End	US Equity Large Cap Growth (Growth)	B+	B	B+	Up	Y	0
MainStay Large Cap Growth Fund Class R3	MLGRX	NAS CM	Open End	US Equity Large Cap Growth (Growth)	B+	B	B+	Up	Y	0
MainStay Large Cap Growth Fund Class R6	MLRSX	NAS CM	Open End	US Equity Large Cap Growth (Growth)	B+	B+	B+	Up	Y	0
MainStay Large Cap Growth Fund Investor Class	MLINX	NAS CM	Open End	US Equity Large Cap Growth (Growth)	B+	B	B+	Up	Y	1,000
MainStay MAP Equity Fund Class A	MAPAX	NAS CM	Open End	US Equity Large Cap Blend (Growth)	B-	B-	C+	Down	Y	25,000
MainStay MAP Equity Fund Class B	MAPBX	NAS CM	Open End	US Equity Large Cap Blend (Growth)	B-	B-	C+	Down		1,000
MainStay MAP Equity Fund Class C	MMPCX	NAS CM	Open End	US Equity Large Cap Blend (Growth)	B-	B-	C+	Down	Y	1,000
MainStay MAP Equity Fund Class I	MUBFX	NAS CM	Open End	US Equity Large Cap Blend (Growth)	B-	B-	C+	Down	Y	5,000,000

★ Expanded analysis of this fund is included in Section II.

Min Additional Investment	TOTAL RETURNS 3-Month Total Return	6-Month Total Return	1-Year Total Return	3-Year Total Return	5-Year Total Return	PERFORMANCE Dividend Yield (TTM)	Expense Ratio	3-Yr Std Deviation	3-Year Beta	ASSETS NAV	Total Assets (MIL)	ASSET ALLOCATION & TURNOVER %Cash	%Stocks	%Bonds	%Other	Turnover Ratio	BULL & BEAR Last Bull Market Total Return	Last Bear Market Total Return	FEES Front End Fee (%)	Back End Fee (%)	Inception Date
	5.37	9.05	16.91	29.18	97.81	1.95	0.78	8.26	0.65	16.38	1,254	2	98	0	0	14	23.69	-18.93			Dec-08
	5.41	9.00	16.83	29.10	97.67		0.88	8.26	0.65	16.38	1,254	2	98	0	0	14	23.69	-18.93			May-17
	5.33	8.81	16.53	28.12	95.20		1.13	8.26	0.65	16.23	1,254	2	98	0	0	14	23.51	-19.01			May-17
	5.26	8.67	16.29	27.22	92.87		1.38	8.25	0.65	16.23	1,254	2	98	0	0	14	23.33	-19.1			May-17
	5.46	9.10	16.98	29.27	97.93		0.71	8.26	0.65	16.38	1,254	2	98	0	0	14	23.69	-18.93			May-17
50	5.27	8.77	16.42	27.58	93.63	1.6	1.26	8.27	0.65	16.16	1,254	2	98	0	0	14	23.53	-19.09	5.50		Nov-09
	6.34	8.71	15.32	26.95	89.90	0.32	1.25	12.4	0.96	31.04	615.0	0	100	0	0	65	26.57	-21.78	5.50		Jan-04
50	6.06	8.12	14.14	23.15	80.41	0	2.28	12.41	0.96	27.42	615.0	0	100	0	0	65	25.86	-22.17		5.00	Jan-04
50	6.06	8.12	14.15	23.11	80.35	0	2.28	12.41	0.96	27.41	615.0	0	100	0	0	65	25.88	-22.22		1.00	Dec-02
	6.44	8.85	15.61	27.92	92.30	0.51	1	12.41	0.96	31.91	615.0	0	100	0	0	65	26.84	-21.76			Jan-87
	6.42	8.80	15.54	27.57	91.39	0.45	1.1	12.42	0.97	31.83	615.0	0	100	0	0	65	26.84	-21.76			Jul-12
	6.33	8.63	15.22	26.57	88.98	0.27	1.35	12.4	0.96	30.93	615.0	0	100	0	0	65	26.65	-21.84			Jul-12
	6.27	8.50	14.93	25.76	87.18	0.19	1.61	12.41	0.96	30.88	615.0	0	100	0	0	65	26.47	-21.92			Feb-16
50	6.27	8.56	15.01	25.97	87.33	0.12	1.53	12.41	0.96	30.57	615.0	0	100	0	0	65	26.34	-21.9	5.50		Feb-08
	5.82	11.25	20.80	23.57	75.08	0.49	2.07	10.82	1.04	16.67	401.5	2	97	0	1	25	22.83	-20.25			Feb-16
	5.98	11.47	21.27	24.80	77.60	0.73	1.72	10.82	1.04	16.72	401.5	2	97	0	1	25	22.92	-20.2	5.50		Apr-05
50	5.69	10.90	20.18	21.49	69.84	0.02	2.61	10.81	1.04	16.34	401.5	2	97	0	1	25	22.25	-20.46		5.00	Apr-05
50	5.68	10.88	20.14	21.44	69.68	0.01	2.61	10.84	1.04	16.36	401.5	2	97	0	1	25	22.34	-20.44		1.00	Apr-05
	5.95	11.55	21.52	25.69	79.86	0.91	1.47	10.84	1.04	16.96	401.5	2	97	0	1	25	23.19	-20.08			Apr-05
50	5.91	11.33	21.05	24.18	76.26	0.62	1.86	10.85	1.04	16.72	401.5	2	97	0	1	25	22.87	-20.28	5.50		Feb-08
	2.62	5.21	12.14	17.13	51.34	2.98	1.02	7.22		19.66	1,837	6	50	41	2	27	15.3	-10.94	5.50		Jan-95
50	2.37	4.70	11.13	14.01	44.45	1.98	1.91	7.23		19.79	1,837	6	50	41	2	27	14.6	-11.34		5.00	Dec-87
50	2.32	4.71	11.09	14.04	44.46	1.98	1.91	7.24		19.75	1,837	6	50	41	2	27	14.62	-11.31		1.00	Sep-98
	2.61	5.29	12.36	17.97	53.22	3.23	0.77	7.24		19.83	1,837	6	50	41	2	27	15.49	-10.87			Jan-04
	2.54	5.10	11.98	16.62	47.75	2.88	1.12	7.23		19.64	1,837	6	50	41	2	27	14.6	-11.34			Feb-15
	2.48	4.97	11.70	15.08	45.81	2.6	1.36	7.26		19.65	1,837	6	50	41	2	27	14.6	-11.34			Feb-16
50	2.53	5.07	11.98	16.62	49.94	2.83	1.16	7.24		19.67	1,837	6	50	41	2	27	15.1	-11.03	5.50		Feb-08
	5.58	11.59	32.08	31.09	47.28	0.22	1.33	11.43	0.79	16.96	307.6	2	94	0	3	33	20.73	-25.58	5.50		Jan-95
50	5.29	11.01	30.68	26.84	39.48	0	2.45	11.4	0.79	15.12	307.6	2	94	0	3	33	20.03	-25.93		5.00	Sep-94
50	5.29	11.01	30.68	26.84	39.35	0	2.45	11.44	0.79	15.12	307.6	2	94	0	3	33	20.03	-25.93		1.00	Sep-98
	5.60	11.73	32.33	32.03	49.07	0.43	1.08	11.43	0.79	17.02	307.6	2	94	0	3	33	20.87	-25.5			Jan-04
	5.60	11.68	32.30	31.70	48.43	0.34	1.18	11.44	0.8	16.94	307.6	2	94	0	3	33	20.88	-25.58			Jan-04
	5.53	11.52	31.93	30.64	46.60	0.13	1.42	11.41	0.79	17.01	307.6	2	94	0	3	33	20.66	-25.6			Jan-04
	5.45	11.42	31.59	29.67	44.68	0	1.68	11.44	0.8	16.9	307.6	2	94	0	3	33	20.46	-25.67			Apr-06
50	5.47	11.38	31.56	29.64	44.75	0	1.7	11.42	0.79	16.89	307.6	2	94	0	3	33	20.44	-25.64	5.50		Feb-08
	2.72	9.78	22.93	22.59	56.22	2.38	1.57	11.66	0.91	9.6	765.2	4	92	0	3	137	15	-24.31	5.50		Sep-07
50	2.41	9.22	21.86	19.39	49.37	1.62	2.51	11.6	0.9	9.29	765.2	4	92	0	3	137	14.44	-24.5		1.00	Sep-07
	2.73	9.84	23.19	23.52	58.14	2.6	1.31	11.74	0.92	9.66	765.2	4	92	0	3	137	15.26	-24.25			Sep-07
50	2.65	9.62	22.80	22.05	55.23	2.27	1.78	11.68	0.91	9.56	765.2	4	92	0	3	137	14.88	-24.21	5.50		Feb-08
	5.74	11.74	32.15	35.11	109.10	0	0.99	12.3	1.09	9.05	12,363	0	100	0	0	84	26.84	-17.71	5.50		Jul-95
50	5.51	11.27	31.01	31.81	101.01	0	1.8	12.38	1.1	7.57	12,363	0	100	0	0	84	26.14	-18.05		5.00	Apr-05
50	5.63	11.29	31.06	31.88	100.92	0	1.8	12.39	1.1	7.56	12,363	0	100	0	0	84	26.36	-18.08		1.00	Apr-05
	5.86	11.93	32.38	36.04	111.89	0	0.74	12.38	1.1	9.71	12,363	0	100	0	0	84	26.98	-17.7			Apr-05
	5.83	11.82	32.41	35.69	110.89	0	0.84	12.4	1.1	9.48	12,363	0	100	0	0	84	26.96	-17.75			Apr-05
	5.76	11.66	31.94	34.63	108.30	0	1.09	12.35	1.1	9.02	12,363	0	100	0	0	84	26.75	-17.77			Apr-05
	5.71	11.62	31.69	33.73	105.79	0	1.34	12.37	1.1	8.59	12,363	0	100	0	0	84	26.66	-17.87			Apr-06
	5.85	11.90	32.50	36.56	112.64	0	0.62	12.31	1.09	9.76	12,363	0	100	0	0	84	26.84	-17.71			Jun-13
50	5.71	11.66	31.97	34.80	108.48	0	1.05	12.31	1.09	8.93	12,363	0	100	0	0	84	26.81	-17.78	5.50		Feb-08
	5.92	10.82	22.48	27.31	85.41	1.05	1.09	11.53	1.11	40.86	1,249	1	98	0	0	42	23.27	-19.76	5.50		Jun-99
50	5.67	10.28	21.32	23.80	77.01	0.33	2.04	11.51	1.11	36.51	1,249	1	98	0	0	42	22.6	-20.06		5.00	Jun-99
50	5.67	10.28	21.32	23.80	76.95	0.33	2.04	11.51	1.11	36.51	1,249	1	98	0	0	42	22.6	-20.08		1.00	Jun-99
	5.98	10.93	22.77	28.26	87.70	1.22	0.84	11.53	1.11	42.06	1,249	1	98	0	0	42	23.45	-19.65			Jan-71

	MARKET		FUND TYPE, CATEGORY & OBJECTIVE		RATINGS					MINIMUMS
Fund Name	Ticker Symbol	Traded On	Fund Type	Category and (Prospectus Objective)	Overall Rating	Reward Rating	Risk Rating	Recent Up/ Downgrade	Open to New Investors	Min Initial Investment
MainStay MAP Equity Fund Class R1	MAPRX	NAS CM	Open End	US Equity Large Cap Blend (Growth)	B-	B-	C+	Down	Y	0
MainStay MAP Equity Fund Class R2	MPRRX	NAS CM	Open End	US Equity Large Cap Blend (Growth)	B-	B-	C+	Down	Y	0
MainStay MAP Equity Fund Class R3	MMAPX	NAS CM	Open End	US Equity Large Cap Blend (Growth)	B-	B-	C+	Down	Y	0
MainStay MAP Equity Fund Investor Class	MSMIX	NAS CM	Open End	US Equity Large Cap Blend (Growth)	B-	B-	C+	Down	Y	1,000
MainStay Moderate Allocation Class R3	MMRHX	NAS CM	Open End	Moderate Alloc (Asset Alloc)	B-	C+	B	Down	Y	0
MainStay Moderate Allocation Fund Class A	MMRAX	NAS CM	Open End	Moderate Alloc (Asset Alloc)	B-	C+	B	Down	Y	25,000
MainStay Moderate Allocation Fund Class B	MMRBX	NAS CM	Open End	Moderate Alloc (Asset Alloc)	B-	C+	B	Down		1,000
MainStay Moderate Allocation Fund Class C	MMRCX	NAS CM	Open End	Moderate Alloc (Asset Alloc)	B-	C+	B	Down	Y	1,000
MainStay Moderate Allocation Fund Class I	MMRIX	NAS CM	Open End	Moderate Alloc (Asset Alloc)	B-	C+	B	Down	Y	5,000,000
MainStay Moderate Allocation Fund Investor Class	MMRDX	NAS CM	Open End	Moderate Alloc (Asset Alloc)	B-	C+	B	Down	Y	1,000
MainStay Moderate Growth Allocation Class R3	MGDRX	NAS CM	Open End	Aggressive Alloc (Asset Alloc)	B-	C+	B-	Down	Y	0
MainStay Moderate Growth Allocation Fund Class A	MGDAX	NAS CM	Open End	Aggressive Alloc (Asset Alloc)	B-	C+	B-	Down	Y	25,000
MainStay Moderate Growth Allocation Fund Class B	MGDBX	NAS CM	Open End	Aggressive Alloc (Asset Alloc)	C+	C+	B-	Down		1,000
MainStay Moderate Growth Allocation Fund Class C	MGDCX	NAS CM	Open End	Aggressive Alloc (Asset Alloc)	C+	C+	B-	Down	Y	1,000
MainStay Moderate Growth Allocation Fund Class I	MGDIX	NAS CM	Open End	Aggressive Alloc (Asset Alloc)	B-	C+	B-	Down	Y	5,000,000
MainStay Moderate Growth Allocation Fund Investor Class	MGDNX	NAS CM	Open End	Aggressive Alloc (Asset Alloc)	B-	C+	B-	Down	Y	1,000
MainStay Retirement 2010 Fund Class A	MYRAX	NAS CM	Open End	Target Date 2000-2020 (Asset Alloc)	B-	C+	B	Up	Y	25,000
MainStay Retirement 2010 Fund Class I	MYRIX	NAS CM	Open End	Target Date 2000-2020 (Asset Alloc)	B-	C+	B	Up	Y	5,000,000
MainStay Retirement 2010 Fund Class R1	MYRRX	NAS CM	Open End	Target Date 2000-2020 (Asset Alloc)	B	C+	A-	Up	Y	0
MainStay Retirement 2010 Fund Class R2	MYRWX	NAS CM	Open End	Target Date 2000-2020 (Asset Alloc)	B-	C+	B	Up	Y	0
MainStay Retirement 2010 Fund Class R3	MYREX	NAS CM	Open End	Target Date 2000-2020 (Asset Alloc)	B-	C+	B	Up	Y	0
MainStay Retirement 2010 Fund Investor Class	MYRDX	NAS CM	Open End	Target Date 2000-2020 (Asset Alloc)	B-	C+	B	Up	Y	1,000
MainStay Retirement 2020 Fund Class A	MYROX	NAS CM	Open End	Target Date 2000-2020 (Asset Alloc)	B-	C+	B	Up	Y	25,000
MainStay Retirement 2020 Fund Class I	MYRTX	NAS CM	Open End	Target Date 2000-2020 (Asset Alloc)	B-	C+	B	Up	Y	5,000,000
MainStay Retirement 2020 Fund Class R1	MYRUX	NAS CM	Open End	Target Date 2000-2020 (Asset Alloc)	B-	C+	B	Up	Y	0
MainStay Retirement 2020 Fund Class R2	MYRVX	NAS CM	Open End	Target Date 2000-2020 (Asset Alloc)	B-	C+	B	Up	Y	0
MainStay Retirement 2020 Fund Class R3	MYRZX	NAS CM	Open End	Target Date 2000-2020 (Asset Alloc)	B-	C+	B	Up	Y	0
MainStay Retirement 2020 Fund Investor Class	MYRYX	NAS CM	Open End	Target Date 2000-2020 (Asset Alloc)	B-	C+	B	Up	Y	1,000
MainStay Retirement 2030 Fund Class A	MRTTX	NAS CM	Open End	Target Date 2021-2045 (Asset Alloc)	B-	C+	B	Down	Y	25,000
MainStay Retirement 2030 Fund Class I	MRTIX	NAS CM	Open End	Target Date 2021-2045 (Asset Alloc)	B-	C+	B	Down	Y	5,000,000
MainStay Retirement 2030 Fund Class R1	MRTOX	NAS CM	Open End	Target Date 2021-2045 (Asset Alloc)	B-	C+	B	Down	Y	0
MainStay Retirement 2030 Fund Class R2	MRTUX	NAS CM	Open End	Target Date 2021-2045 (Asset Alloc)	B-	C+	B	Down	Y	0
MainStay Retirement 2030 Fund Class R3	MRTVX	NAS CM	Open End	Target Date 2021-2045 (Asset Alloc)	B-	C+	B	Down	Y	0
MainStay Retirement 2030 Fund Investor Class	MRTFX	NAS CM	Open End	Target Date 2021-2045 (Asset Alloc)	B-	C+	B	Down	Y	1,000
MainStay Retirement 2040 Fund Class A	MSRTX	NAS CM	Open End	Target Date 2021-2045 (Asset Alloc)	B-	B-	B-	Down	Y	25,000
MainStay Retirement 2040 Fund Class I	MSRYX	NAS CM	Open End	Target Date 2021-2045 (Asset Alloc)	B-	B-	B-	Down	Y	5,000,000
MainStay Retirement 2040 Fund Class R1	MSREX	NAS CM	Open End	Target Date 2021-2045 (Asset Alloc)	B-	B-	B-	Down	Y	0
MainStay Retirement 2040 Fund Class R2	MSRQX	NAS CM	Open End	Target Date 2021-2045 (Asset Alloc)	B-	B-	B-	Down	Y	0
MainStay Retirement 2040 Fund Class R3	MSRZX	NAS CM	Open End	Target Date 2021-2045 (Asset Alloc)	B-	B-	B-	Down	Y	0
MainStay Retirement 2040 Fund Investor Class	MSRUX	NAS CM	Open End	Target Date 2021-2045 (Asset Alloc)	B-	B-	B-	Down	Y	1,000
MainStay Retirement 2050 Fund Class A	MSRLX	NAS CM	Open End	Target Date 2046+ (Asset Alloc)	B-	B-	B-	Down	Y	25,000
MainStay Retirement 2050 Fund Class I	MSRMX	NAS CM	Open End	Target Date 2046+ (Asset Alloc)	B-	B-	B-	Down	Y	5,000,000
MainStay Retirement 2050 Fund Class R1	MSROX	NAS CM	Open End	Target Date 2046+ (Asset Alloc)	B-	B-	B-	Down	Y	0
MainStay Retirement 2050 Fund Class R2	MSRPX	NAS CM	Open End	Target Date 2046+ (Asset Alloc)	B-	B-	B-	Down	Y	0
MainStay Retirement 2050 Fund Class R3	MSRWX	NAS CM	Open End	Target Date 2046+ (Asset Alloc)	B-	B-	B-	Down	Y	0
MainStay Retirement 2050 Fund Investor Class	MSRVX	NAS CM	Open End	Target Date 2046+ (Asset Alloc)	B-	B-	B-	Down	Y	1,000
MainStay Retirement 2060 Fund Class A	MYSQX	NAS CM	Open End	Target Date 2046+ (Asset Alloc)	C-	C	B+	Up	Y	25,000
MainStay Retirement 2060 Fund Class I	MYSSX	NAS CM	Open End	Target Date 2046+ (Asset Alloc)	C-	C	B+	Up	Y	5,000,000
MainStay Retirement 2060 Fund Class R1	MYSTX	NAS CM	Open End	Target Date 2046+ (Asset Alloc)	C-	C	B+	Up	Y	0
MainStay Retirement 2060 Fund Class R2	MYSWX	NAS CM	Open End	Target Date 2046+ (Asset Alloc)	C-	C	B+	Up	Y	0
MainStay Retirement 2060 Fund Class R3	MYSZX	NAS CM	Open End	Target Date 2046+ (Asset Alloc)	C-	C	B+	Up	Y	0
MainStay Retirement 2060 Fund Investor Class	MYSRX	NAS CM	Open End	Target Date 2046+ (Asset Alloc)	C-	C	B+	Up	Y	1,000

★ Expanded analysis of this fund is included in Section II.

	TOTAL RETURNS					PERFORMANCE				ASSETS		ASSET ALLOCATION & TURNOVER					BULL & BEAR		FEES		
Min Additional Investment	3-Month Total Return	6-Month Total Return	1-Year Total Return	3-Year Total Return	5-Year Total Return	Dividend Yield (TTM)	Expense Ratio	3-Yr Std Deviation	3-Year Beta	NAV	Total Assets (MIL)	%Cash	%Stocks	%Bonds	%Other	Turnover Ratio	Last Bull Market Total Return	Last Bear Market Total Return	Front End Fee (%)	Back End Fee (%)	Inception Date
	5.96	10.90	22.65	27.88	86.81	1.15	0.94	11.54	1.11	41.13	1,249	1	98	0	0	42	23.4	-19.71			Jan-04
	5.91	10.76	22.36	26.92	84.44	0.95	1.2	11.52	1.11	41.08	1,249	1	98	0	0	42	23.2	-19.78			Jan-04
	5.83	10.62	22.07	26.01	82.18	0.75	1.44	11.52	1.11	40.93	1,249	1	98	0	0	42	23.01	-19.85			Apr-06
50	5.87	10.69	22.25	26.59	83.76	0.89	1.29	11.52	1.11	40.87	1,249	1	98	0	0	42	23.14	-19.83	5.50		Feb-08
	3.66	7.34	14.19	17.70	49.01	1.39	1.8	7.09	0.67	13.78	744.2	8	60	29	1	37	16.42	-12.8			Feb-16
	3.77	7.53	14.64	18.86	51.16	1.68	1.45	7.12	0.68	13.8	744.2	8	60	29	1	37	16.54	-12.68	5.50		Apr-05
50	3.47	7.03	13.58	15.64	44.43	0.87	2.38	7.13	0.68	13.69	744.2	8	60	29	1	37	16.01	-13.05		5.00	Apr-05
50	3.47	6.96	13.50	15.57	44.33	0.87	2.38	7.13	0.68	13.68	744.2	8	60	29	1	37	15.9	-12.97		1.00	Apr-05
	3.85	7.66	14.91	19.75	53.13	1.88	1.2	7.1	0.67	13.88	744.2	8	60	29	1	37	16.76	-12.62			Apr-05
50	3.71	7.46	14.40	18.28	49.94	1.53	1.63	7.13	0.68	13.82	744.2	8	60	29	1	37	16.5	-12.84	5.50		Feb-08
	4.75	9.29	17.28	21.27	63.62	0.99	1.93	9.08	0.87	15.59	768.2	7	79	12	1	32	19.99	-17.24			Feb-16
	4.89	9.50	17.73	22.35	65.95	1.19	1.58	9.13	0.87	15.64	768.2	7	79	12	1	32	20.2	-17.11	5.50		Apr-05
50	4.64	8.96	16.61	19.01	58.55	0.41	2.52	9.12	0.87	15.48	768.2	7	79	12	1	32	19.63	-17.49		5.00	Apr-05
50	4.65	8.96	16.61	19.01	58.55	0.41	2.52	9.11	0.87	15.48	768.2	7	79	12	1	32	19.62	-17.49		1.00	Apr-05
	5.02	9.65	18.05	23.39	68.14	1.39	1.33	9.08	0.87	15.8	768.2	7	79	12	1	32	20.34	-17.07			Apr-05
50	4.83	9.37	17.51	21.74	64.53	1.05	1.77	9.11	0.87	15.66	768.2	7	79	12	1	32	20.06	-17.2	5.50		Feb-08
	2.28	4.66	10.01	14.23	36.28	2.4	0.93	4.49	0.41	9.77	38.4	7	33	58	0	45	14.43	-10.59	5.50		Jun-07
	2.33	4.70	10.22	14.96	37.93	2.59	0.68	4.47	0.4	9.83	38.4	7	33	58	0	45	14.62	-10.43			Jun-07
	2.26	4.75	10.13	14.71	37.49	0	0.78	4.49	0.41	10.14	38.4	7	33	58	0	45	14.62	-10.43			Aug-14
	2.26	4.53	9.83	13.86	35.61	1.96	1.03	4.5	0.41	9.83	38.4	7	33	58	0	45	14.36	-10.58			Jan-09
	2.22	4.45	9.65	13.07	34.08	1.8	1.28	4.49	0.41	10.03	38.4	7	33	58	0	45	14.18	-10.67			May-08
50	2.22	4.60	9.91	13.94	35.61	2.31	1.03	4.49	0.41	9.84	38.4	7	33	58	0	45	14.37	-10.56	5.50		Feb-08
	3.27	6.57	13.96	18.46	47.96	1.85	1	6.46	0.61	10.67	125.3	6	53	39	0	48	16.93	-13.86	5.50		Jun-07
	3.36	6.74	14.21	19.32	49.89	2.03	0.75	6.4	0.61	10.72	125.3	6	53	39	0	48	17.16	-13.8			Jun-07
	3.28	6.68	14.07	18.95	49.30	0	0.85	6.41	0.61	10.99	125.3	6	53	39	0	48	17.16	-13.8			Aug-14
	3.11	6.38	13.71	17.88	46.97	1.15	1.1	6.43	0.61	10.74	125.3	6	53	39	0	48	16.92	-13.94			Jan-09
	3.22	6.37	13.62	17.14	45.36	0.95	1.35	6.43	0.61	10.88	125.3	6	53	39	0	48	16.76	-13.97			May-08
50	3.18	6.47	13.74	17.95	47.09	1.76	1.1	6.43	0.61	10.7	125.3	6	53	39	0	48	16.9	-13.93	5.50		Feb-08
	4.28	8.28	17.51	22.42	60.76	1.57	1.07	8.31	0.8	11.44	253.1	6	70	23	0	43	19.67	-17.32	5.50		Jun-07
	4.34	8.40	17.77	23.20	62.56	1.72	0.82	8.33	0.8	11.53	253.1	6	70	23	0	43	20.01	-17.3			Jun-07
	4.29	8.36	17.75	22.92	62.05	0	0.92	8.3	0.8	11.77	253.1	6	70	23	0	43	20.01	-17.29			Aug-14
	4.08	8.07	17.27	21.87	59.62	1.25	1.17	8.25	0.79	11.46	253.1	6	70	23	0	43	19.66	-17.42			Jan-09
	4.15	8.10	17.07	20.99	57.72	1.04	1.42	8.28	0.8	11.61	253.1	6	70	23	0	43	19.42	-17.4			May-08
50	4.26	8.25	17.46	22.11	60.00	1.48	1.17	8.32	0.8	11.48	253.1	6	70	23	0	43	19.65	-17.38	5.50		Feb-08
	4.81	9.37	19.91	24.69	68.52	1.35	1.08	9.48	0.91	11.95	213.2	5	82	11	0	38	21.07	-18.85	5.50		Jun-07
	4.85	9.54	20.30	25.75	70.66	1.49	0.83	9.52	0.92	12.09	213.2	5	82	11	0	38	21.28	-18.8			Jun-07
	4.87	9.48	20.13	25.38	70.16	0	0.93	9.49	0.91	12.32	213.2	5	82	11	0	38	21.28	-18.8			Aug-14
	4.54	9.17	19.64	24.18	67.43	1.13	1.18	9.48	0.91	12.03	213.2	5	82	11	0	38	20.98	-18.91			Jan-09
	4.68	9.17	19.55	23.40	65.73	0.95	1.43	9.48	0.91	12.13	213.2	5	82	11	0	38	20.84	-19.03			May-08
50	4.73	9.36	19.85	24.41	67.80	1.26	1.18	9.52	0.92	12.03	213.2	5	82	11	0	38	21.01	-18.87	5.50		Feb-08
	5.01	9.95	21.60	26.19	72.11	1.16	1.1	9.89	0.95	11.99	115.8	5	87	6	0	38	21.66	-19.7	5.50		Jun-07
	5.10	10.10	21.91	27.10	74.23	1.33	0.85	9.88	0.95	12.06	115.8	5	87	6	0	38	21.97	-19.62			Jun-07
	5.06	10.04	21.79	26.73	73.57	0.97	0.95	9.93	0.95	12.12	115.8	5	87	6	0	38	21.97	-19.62			Aug-14
	5.16	10.02	21.66	25.89	71.49	1.04	1.2	9.88	0.95	12.02	115.8	5	87	6	0	38	21.64	-19.79			Jan-09
	5.00	9.83	21.17	24.84	69.20	0.86	1.45	9.91	0.95	12.08	115.8	5	87	6	0	38	21.49	-19.77			May-08
50	5.06	9.93	21.49	25.71	71.18	1.09	1.21	9.89	0.95	11.97	115.8	5	87	6	0	38	21.73	-19.81	5.50		Feb-08
	5.30	10.41	22.93			1.08	1.1			13.1	8.7	4	92	2	0	26			5.50		Feb-16
	5.33	10.60	23.23			1.19	0.85			13.06	8.7	4	92	2	0	26					Feb-16
	5.28	10.46	23.08			1.13	0.95			13.06	8.7	4	92	2	0	26					Feb-16
	5.07	10.17	22.57			1.01	1.2			13.07	8.7	4	92	2	0	26					Feb-16
	5.15	10.18	22.50			0.97	1.45			13.06	8.7	4	92	2	0	26					Feb-16
50	5.23	10.34	22.77			1.11	1.2			13.08	8.7	4	92	2	0	26			5.50		Feb-16

	MARKET			FUND TYPE, CATEGORY & OBJECTIVE	RATINGS				MINIMUMS	
Fund Name	Ticker Symbol	Traded On	Fund Type	Category and (Prospectus Objective)	Overall Rating	Reward Rating	Risk Rating	Recent Up/ Downgrade	Open to New Investors	Min Initial Investment
MainStay S&P 500 Index Fund Class A	MSXAX	NAS CM	Open End	US Equity Large Cap Blend (Growth & Income)	B	B	B		Y	25,000
MainStay S&P 500 Index Fund Class I	MSPIX	NAS CM	Open End	US Equity Large Cap Blend (Growth & Income)	B	B	B		Y	5,000,000
MainStay S&P 500 Index Fund Investor Class	MYSPX	NAS CM	Open End	US Equity Large Cap Blend (Growth & Income)	B	B-	B		Y	1,000
Mainstay U.S. Equity Opportunities Fund Class A	MYCTX	NAS CM	Open End	US Equity Large Cap Blend (Growth)	A-	A-	A-	Up	Y	25,000
Mainstay U.S. Equity Opportunities Fund Class C	MYCCX	NAS CM	Open End	US Equity Large Cap Blend (Growth)	B+	B+	A-	Up	Y	1,000
Mainstay U.S. Equity Opportunities Fund Class I	MYCIX	NAS CM	Open End	US Equity Large Cap Blend (Growth)	A-	A-	B	Up	Y	5,000,000
Mainstay U.S. Equity Opportunities Fund Investor Class	MYCNX	NAS CM	Open End	US Equity Large Cap Blend (Growth)	A-	A-	A-	Up	Y	1,000
Mairs & Power Balanced Fund Investor Class	MAPOX	NAS CM	Open End	Moderate Alloc (Balanced)	B-	C+	B	Down	Y	2,500
Mairs & Power Growth Fund Investor Class	MPGFX	NAS CM	Open End	US Equity Large Cap Blend (Growth)	B	B-	B		Y	2,500
Mairs & Power Small Cap Fund	MSCFX	NAS CM	Open End	US Equity Small Cap (Small Company)	B	B	B	Up	Y	2,500
Managed Account Series Advantage Global SmallCap Fund	MGCSX	NAS CM	Open End	Global Equity Mid/Small Cap (Small Company)	C+	B-	C	Up	Y	0
Managed Account Series Mid Cap Dividend Fund	MMCVX	NAS CM	Open End	US Equity Mid Cap (Growth)	B	B-	B	Up	Y	0
Manning & Napier Disciplined Value Series Class I	MNDFX	NAS CM	Open End	US Equity Large Cap Value (Equity-Income)	B	B	B-		Y	1,000,000
Manning & Napier Disciplined Value Series Class S	MDFSX	NAS CM	Open End	US Equity Large Cap Value (Equity-Income)	B	B	B-		Y	2,000
Manning & Napier Equity Income Series Class I	MNEIX	NAS CM	Open End	US Equity Large Cap Value (Equity-Income)	B-	B-	B-	Down	Y	1,000,000
Manning & Napier Equity Income Series Class S	MNESX	NAS CM	Open End	US Equity Large Cap Value (Equity-Income)	B	B-	B		Y	2,000
Manning & Napier Equity Series Class S	EXEYX	NAS CM	Open End	US Equity Large Cap Growth (Growth)	B	B	B	Up	Y	2,000
Manning & Napier International Series Class I	MNIIX	NAS CM	Open End	Global Equity Large Cap (Foreign Stock)	B-	B-	B-	Up	Y	1,000,000
Manning & Napier International Series Class S Shares	EXITX	NAS CM	Open End	Global Equity Large Cap (Foreign Stock)	B-	C+	B-	Up	Y	2,000
Manning & Napier Overseas Series Class I	EXOSX	NAS CM	Open End	Global Equity Large Cap (Foreign Stock)	B-	C+	B-	Up	Y	1,000,000
Manning & Napier Pro-Blend Conservative Term Series Cls I	MNCIX	NAS CM	Open End	Cautious Alloc (Asset Alloc)	B-	C	B+	Up	Y	1,000,000
Manning & Napier Pro-Blend Conservative Term Series Cls R	MNCRX	NAS CM	Open End	Cautious Alloc (Asset Alloc)	B-	C	B	Up	Y	2,000
Manning & Napier Pro-Blend Conservative Term Series Cls R2	MNCCX	NAS CM	Open End	Cautious Alloc (Asset Alloc)	C+	C	B	Down	Y	2,000
Manning & Napier Pro-Blend Conservative Term Series Cls S	EXDAX	NAS CM	Open End	Cautious Alloc (Asset Alloc)	B-	C	B	Up	Y	2,000
Manning & Napier Pro-Blend Extended Term Series Class I	MNBIX	NAS CM	Open End	Moderate Alloc (Asset Alloc)	B-	C+	B	Up	Y	1,000,000
Manning & Napier Pro-Blend Extended Term Series Class R	MNBRX	NAS CM	Open End	Moderate Alloc (Asset Alloc)	B-	C+	B	Up	Y	2,000
Manning & Napier Pro-Blend Extended Term Series Class R2	MNECX	NAS CM	Open End	Moderate Alloc (Asset Alloc)	B-	C+	B	Up	Y	2,000
Manning & Napier Pro-Blend Extended Term Series Class S	MNBAX	NAS CM	Open End	Moderate Alloc (Asset Alloc)	B-	C+	B	Up	Y	2,000
Manning & Napier Pro-Blend Maximum Term Series Class I	MNHIX	NAS CM	Open End	Aggressive Alloc (Growth)	B-	B-	B	Up	Y	1,000,000
Manning & Napier Pro-Blend Maximum Term Series Class R	MNHRX	NAS CM	Open End	Aggressive Alloc (Growth)	B-	C+	B	Up	Y	2,000
Manning & Napier Pro-Blend Maximum Term Series Class R2	MNHCX	NAS CM	Open End	Aggressive Alloc (Growth)	B-	C+	B-	Up	Y	2,000
Manning & Napier Pro-Blend Maximum Term Series Class S	EXHAX	NAS CM	Open End	Aggressive Alloc (Growth)	B-	B-	B	Up	Y	2,000
Manning & Napier Pro-Blend Moderate Term Series Class I	MNMIX	NAS CM	Open End	Cautious Alloc (Asset Alloc)	B-	C+	B	Up	Y	1,000,000
Manning & Napier Pro-Blend Moderate Term Series Class R	MNMRX	NAS CM	Open End	Cautious Alloc (Asset Alloc)	B-	C	B	Up	Y	2,000
Manning & Napier Pro-Blend Moderate Term Series Class R2	MNMCX	NAS CM	Open End	Cautious Alloc (Asset Alloc)	C+	C	B		Y	2,000
Manning & Napier Pro-Blend Moderate Term Series Class S	EXBAX	NAS CM	Open End	Cautious Alloc (Asset Alloc)	B-	C	B	Up	Y	2,000
Manning & Napier Quality Equity Series Class I	MNQIX	NAS CM	Open End	Global Equity (Growth)	C	C	B	Up	Y	1,000,000
Manning & Napier Quality Equity Series Class S	MNQSX	NAS CM	Open End	Global Equity (Growth)	C	C	B	Up	Y	2,000
Manning & Napier Rainier Intl Discovery Series Cls I	RAIIX	NAS CM	Open End	Global Equity Mid/Small Cap (World Stock)	A-	A	B	Up	Y	1,000,000
Manning & Napier Rainier Intl Discovery Series Cls K	RISAX	NAS CM	Open End	Global Equity Mid/Small Cap (World Stock)	A-	A	B	Up	Y	2,000
Manning & Napier Rainier Intl Discovery Series Cls R6	RAIRX	NAS CM	Open End	Global Equity Mid/Small Cap (World Stock)	A-	A	B		Y	0
Manning & Napier Real Estate Series Class I	MNRIX	NAS CM	Open End	Real Estate Sector Equity (Real Estate)	B	B-	B+		Y	1,000,000
Manning & Napier Real Estate Series Class S	MNREX	NAS CM	Open End	Real Estate Sector Equity (Real Estate)	B	B-	B+	Up	Y	2,000
Manning & Napier Strat Income Conservative Series Cls I	MSCIX	NAS CM	Open End	Cautious Alloc (Income)	B-	C+	B	Up	Y	1,000,000
Manning & Napier Strat Income Conservative Series Cls S	MSCBX	NAS CM	Open End	Cautious Alloc (Income)	B-	C+	B	Up	Y	2,000
Manning & Napier Strategic Income Moderate Series Class I	MSMAX	NAS CM	Open End	Moderate Alloc (Income)	B-	C+	B	Up	Y	1,000,000
Manning & Napier Strategic Income Moderate Series Class S	MSMSX	NAS CM	Open End	Moderate Alloc (Income)	B-	C+	B	Up	Y	2,000
Manning & Napier Target 2015 Series Class I	MTJIX	NAS CM	Open End	Target Date 2000-2020 (Asset Alloc)	B-	C	B	Up	Y	1,000,000
Manning & Napier Target 2015 Series Class K	MTJKX	NAS CM	Open End	Target Date 2000-2020 (Asset Alloc)	B-	C	B	Up	Y	2,000
Manning & Napier Target 2015 Series Class R	MTJRX	NAS CM	Open End	Target Date 2000-2020 (Asset Alloc)	B-	C	B	Up	Y	2,000
Manning & Napier Target 2015 Series R6	MTJZX	NAS CM	Open End	Target Date 2000-2020 (Asset Alloc)	B-	C	B		Y	0
Manning & Napier Target 2020 Series Class I	MTNIX	NAS CM	Open End	Target Date 2000-2020 (Asset Alloc)	B-	C+	B	Up	Y	1,000,000

★Expanded analysis of this fund is included in Section II.

	TOTAL RETURNS					PERFORMANCE				ASSETS		ASSET ALLOCATION & TURNOVER					BULL & BEAR		FEES		
Min Additional Investment	3-Month Total Return	6-Month Total Return	1-Year Total Return	3-Year Total Return	5-Year Total Return	Dividend Yield (TTM)	Expense Ratio	3-Yr Std Deviation	3-Year Beta	NAV	Total Assets (MIL)	%Cash	%Stocks	%Bonds	%Other	Turnover Ratio	Last Bull Market Total Return	Last Bear Market Total Return	Front End Fee (%)	Back End Fee (%)	Inception Date
	6.48	11.09	21.13	34.52	105.63	1.83	0.53	10.07	1	48.04	1,321	2	98	0	0	4	24.7	-16.45	3.00		Jan-04
	6.54	11.25	21.45	35.53	108.22	2.01	0.27	10.07	1	48.62	1,321	2	98	0	0	4	24.86	-16.34			Jan-91
50	6.46	11.06	21.01	34.11	104.56	1.79	0.76	10.08	1	48.03	1,321	2	98	0	0	4	24.63	-16.48	3.00		Feb-08
	8.99	16.81	22.98	40.80	134.80	0	1.38	10.79	0.99	9.85	979.0	3	94	0	3	159	23.94	-16.5	5.50		Jun-07
50	8.69	16.38	21.89	37.17	124.24	0	2.22	10.87	1	8.56	979.0	3	94	0	3	159	23.32	-16.88		1.00	Jun-07
	8.94	16.89	23.14	41.74	137.38	0.1	1.13	10.78	0.99	9.95	979.0	3	94	0	3	159	24.16	-16.47			Jun-07
50	8.96	16.78	22.78	40.31	132.89	0	1.47	10.75	0.99	9.69	979.0	3	94	0	3	159	23.88	-16.56	5.50		Feb-08
100	4.00	6.07	11.89	20.80	57.53	2.09	0.72	6.56		94.01	985.2	2	65	31	0	14	19.85	-11.45			Nov-61
100	6.26	7.98	16.52	28.93	93.97	1.19	0.66	10.1	0.92	121.12	4,812	2	98	0	0	11	29.13	-18.05			Nov-58
100	1.46	2.78	7.63	29.77	97.06	0.29	1.05	12.65	0.88	25.32	446.5	1	99	0	0	21	42.81				Aug-11
	5.17	11.98	22.45	26.78	81.52	2.21	0	12.28	1.09	13.36	104.0	3	97	0	0	143	21.05	-23.19			Aug-05
	5.07	8.05	9.51	26.54	89.63	1.42	0	12.34	1.13	12.14	93.2	1	99	0	0	144	27.11	-21.41			Aug-05
	8.93	14.26	23.10	40.01	98.24	2.01	0.57	9.71	0.88	14.54	152.6	1	99	0	0	39	17.81	-10.61			Nov-08
	8.85	14.05	22.82	38.90	95.72	2.68	0.82	9.71	0.88	8.82	152.6	1	99	0	0	39	17.67	-10.61			Mar-12
	5.89	10.02	15.30	27.47		3.31	0.99	10.27	0.96	12.12	87.1	0	100	0	0	45					Dec-13
	5.83	9.90	15.18	26.84		3.02	1.19	10.27	0.96	12.12	87.1	0	100	0	0	45					Dec-13
	6.81	11.97	28.77	31.29	93.82	0	1.05	12	1.05	13.8	83.7	2	98	0	0	40	20.06	-19.94			May-98
	3.83	10.60	25.50	26.58	43.17	0.62	0.86	11.88	0.89	11.93	541.3	2	98	0	0	47	7.35	-22.61			Mar-12
	3.73	10.38	25.13	25.49	41.29	0.59	1.11	11.85	0.88	9.39	541.3	2	98	0	0	47	7.24	-22.61			Aug-92
	2.71	7.95	23.91	21.57	33.53	1.4	0.75	11.95	0.92	24.95	658.7	12	88	0	0	37	16.5	-27.02			Jul-02
	1.39	3.60	9.09	10.44	25.05	1.76	0.7	4.31	0.38	10.38	933.6	1	29	69	0	65	7.8	-4.04			Mar-08
	1.26	3.26	8.59	8.84	22.03	1.28	1.2	4.35	0.38	9.96	933.6	1	29	69	0	65	7.39	-4.15			Jun-10
	1.16	3.05	8.03	7.20	19.06	0.84	1.7	4.33	0.37	9.97	933.6	1	29	69	0	65	7.2	-4.48			Jan-10
	1.38	3.53	8.92	9.82	23.89	1.15	0.9	4.31	0.37	13.67	933.6	1	29	69	0	65	7.66	-4.13			Nov-95
	1.85	5.25	15.09	13.83	41.67	1.26	0.83	7.3	0.27	9.29	681.2	2	49	49	0	63	14.56	-13.15			Mar-08
	1.79	5.02	14.64	12.12	38.23	0.59	1.33	7.36	0.27	10.85	681.2	2	49	49	0	63	14.21	-13.23			Jun-10
	1.68	4.74	13.98	10.43	34.77	0.22	1.83	7.29	0.27	10.09	681.2	2	49	49	0	63	13.87	-13.4			Jan-10
	1.84	5.16	14.86	12.98	39.98	0.47	1.08	7.34	0.27	17.3	681.2	2	49	49	0	63	14.27	-13.17			Oct-93
	5.17	9.71	24.49	23.25	67.87	0.63	0.84	10.37	0.88	10.34	486.6	1	87	11	0	49	18.62	-20.01			Mar-08
	5.02	9.39	23.93	21.44	63.83	0.22	1.34	10.31	0.88	13.15	486.6	1	87	11	0	49	18.27	-20.21			Jun-10
	4.90	9.11	23.23	19.58	59.74	0.09	1.84	10.37	0.89	10.93	486.6	1	87	11	0	49	17.96	-20.35			Jan-10
	5.10	9.52	24.19	22.35	65.96	0.17	1.09	10.34	0.88	20.8	486.6	1	87	11	0	49	18.5	-20.14			Nov-95
	1.32	3.95	11.75	10.77	30.68	1.28	0.83	5.75	0.36	9.99	697.9	2	37	61	0	67	12.32	-9.85			Mar-08
	1.30	3.80	11.28	9.14	27.52	0.72	1.33	5.73	0.35	10.56	697.9	2	37	61	0	67	12.01	-10.05			Jun-10
	1.09	3.49	10.65	7.45	24.25	0.3	1.83	5.74	0.36	10.15	697.9	2	37	61	0	67	11.7	-10.28			Jan-10
	1.35	3.93	11.57	9.98	29.11	0.73	1.08	5.76	0.35	13.49	697.9	2	37	61	0	67	12.24	-10.02			Sep-93
	6.02	7.40	18.53			0.91	0.71			11.38	2.4	1	99	0	0	43					Jun-15
	5.88	7.27	18.28			0.75	0.96			11.37	2.4	1	99	0	0	43					Jun-15
	6.26	18.26	42.04	53.03	105.76	0	1.16	10.36	0.71	21.66	316.3	6	94	0	0	123					Mar-12
	6.23	18.16	41.71	51.91	103.44	0	1.41	10.34	0.71	21.47	316.3	6	94	0	0	123			5.75		Nov-12
	6.30	18.30	42.09	53.09	105.83		1.01	10.36	0.71	21.66	316.3	6	94	0	0	123					Aug-17
	2.13	3.96	8.85	21.31	64.47	3.82	0.85	11.95	0.88	6.81	323.3	0	100	0	0	46	33.17	-17.18			Aug-12
	2.08	3.91	8.65	20.46	62.53	1.7	1.1	11.93	0.88	14.93	323.3	0	100	0	0	46	33.17	-17.18			Nov-09
	2.13	3.90	7.32	14.34	29.15	2.8	0.59	3.67	0.41	10.46	28.5	2	33	65	0	41					Aug-12
	2.05	3.76	7.17	13.49	27.49	2.57	0.84	3.64	0.39	10.46	28.5	2	33	65	0	41					Aug-12
	3.57	6.18	10.66	19.55	44.45	2.99	0.64	5.43	0.11	11.27	32.9	2	53	45	0	28					Aug-12
	3.49	6.03	10.39	18.78	42.75	2.76	0.89	5.39	0.11	11.27	32.9	2	53	45	0	28					Aug-12
	1.23	3.75	10.69	9.70	29.73	1.54	0.67	5.58	1.02	11.2	4.1	1	34	65	0	49					Jun-12
	1.18	3.52	10.34	8.78	27.99	1.31	0.92	5.6	1.03	11.16	4.1	1	34	65	0	49					Jun-12
	1.13	3.44	10.06	7.94	26.59	0.05	1.17	5.53	1.01	11.32	4.1	1	34	65	0	49					Jun-12
	1.17	3.69	10.63	9.64	29.66		0.52	5.58	1.02	11.19	4.1	1	34	65	0	49					Oct-17
	1.26	4.03	12.14	10.80	34.08	1.51	0.71	6.12	0.95	9.46	114.9	2	39	60	0	16	13.53	-11.94			Mar-08

Fund Name	MARKET Ticker Symbol	Traded On	FUND TYPE, CATEGORY & OBJECTIVE Fund Type	Category and (Prospectus Objective)	RATINGS Overall Rating	Reward Rating	Risk Rating	Recent Up/ Downgrade	MINIMUMS Open to New Investors	Min Initial Investment
Manning & Napier Target 2020 Series Class K	MTNKX	NAS CM	Open End	Target Date 2000-2020 (Asset Alloc)	B-	C	B	Up	Y	2,000
Manning & Napier Target 2020 Series Class R	MTNRX	NAS CM	Open End	Target Date 2000-2020 (Asset Alloc)	B-	C	B	Up	Y	2,000
Manning & Napier Target 2020 Series Fund R6	MTNZX	NAS CM	Open End	Target Date 2000-2020 (Asset Alloc)	B-	C+	B		Y	0
Manning & Napier Target 2025 Series Class I	MTOAX	NAS CM	Open End	Target Date 2021-2045 (Asset Alloc)	B-	C+	B	Up	Y	1,000,000
Manning & Napier Target 2025 Series Class K	MTOKX	NAS CM	Open End	Target Date 2021-2045 (Asset Alloc)	B-	C+	B	Up	Y	2,000
Manning & Napier Target 2025 Series Class R	MTORX	NAS CM	Open End	Target Date 2021-2045 (Asset Alloc)	B-	C+	B	Up	Y	2,000
Manning & Napier Target 2025 Series R6	MTOZX	NAS CM	Open End	Target Date 2021-2045 (Asset Alloc)	B-	C+	B		Y	0
Manning & Napier Target 2030 Series Class I	MTPIX	NAS CM	Open End	Target Date 2021-2045 (Asset Alloc)	B-	C+	B	Up	Y	1,000,000
Manning & Napier Target 2030 Series Class K	MTPKX	NAS CM	Open End	Target Date 2021-2045 (Asset Alloc)	B-	C+	B	Up	Y	2,000
Manning & Napier Target 2030 Series Class R	MTPRX	NAS CM	Open End	Target Date 2021-2045 (Asset Alloc)	B-	C+	B	Up	Y	2,000
Manning & Napier Target 2030 Series Fund R6	MTPZX	NAS CM	Open End	Target Date 2021-2045 (Asset Alloc)	B-	C+	B		Y	0
Manning & Napier Target 2035 Series Class I	MTQIX	NAS CM	Open End	Target Date 2021-2045 (Asset Alloc)	B-	C+	B	Up	Y	1,000,000
Manning & Napier Target 2035 Series Class K	MTQKX	NAS CM	Open End	Target Date 2021-2045 (Asset Alloc)	B-	C+	B	Up	Y	2,000
Manning & Napier Target 2035 Series Class R	MTQRX	NAS CM	Open End	Target Date 2021-2045 (Asset Alloc)	B-	C+	B	Up	Y	2,000
Manning & Napier Target 2035 Series R6	MTQZX	NAS CM	Open End	Target Date 2021-2045 (Asset Alloc)	B-	C+	B		Y	0
Manning & Napier Target 2040 Series Class I	MTTIX	NAS CM	Open End	Target Date 2021-2045 (Asset Alloc)	B-	C+	B	Up	Y	1,000,000
Manning & Napier Target 2040 Series Class K	MTTKX	NAS CM	Open End	Target Date 2021-2045 (Asset Alloc)	B-	C+	B	Up	Y	2,000
Manning & Napier Target 2040 Series Class R	MTTRX	NAS CM	Open End	Target Date 2021-2045 (Asset Alloc)	B-	C+	B	Up	Y	2,000
Manning & Napier Target 2040 Series Fund R6	MTTZX	NAS CM	Open End	Target Date 2021-2045 (Asset Alloc)	B-	C+	B		Y	0
Manning & Napier Target 2045 Series Class I	MTUIX	NAS CM	Open End	Target Date 2021-2045 (Asset Alloc)	B-	C+	B	Up	Y	1,000,000
Manning & Napier Target 2045 Series Class K	MTUKX	NAS CM	Open End	Target Date 2021-2045 (Asset Alloc)	B-	C+	B	Up	Y	2,000
Manning & Napier Target 2045 Series Class R	MTURX	NAS CM	Open End	Target Date 2021-2045 (Asset Alloc)	B-	C+	B	Up	Y	2,000
Manning & Napier Target 2045 Series R6	MTUZX	NAS CM	Open End	Target Date 2021-2045 (Asset Alloc)	B-	C+	B		Y	0
Manning & Napier Target 2050 Series Class I	MTYIX	NAS CM	Open End	Target Date 2046+ (Asset Alloc)	B-	B-	B	Up	Y	1,000,000
Manning & Napier Target 2050 Series Class K	MTYKX	NAS CM	Open End	Target Date 2046+ (Asset Alloc)	B-	B-	B	Up	Y	2,000
Manning & Napier Target 2050 Series Class R	MTYRX	NAS CM	Open End	Target Date 2046+ (Asset Alloc)	B-	C+	B	Up	Y	2,000
Manning & Napier Target 2050 Series Fund R6	MTYZX	NAS CM	Open End	Target Date 2046+ (Asset Alloc)	B-	B-	B		Y	0
Manning & Napier Target 2055 Series Class I	MTZIX	NAS CM	Open End	Target Date 2046+ (Asset Alloc)	B-	B-	B	Up	Y	1,000,000
Manning & Napier Target 2055 Series Class K	MTZKX	NAS CM	Open End	Target Date 2046+ (Asset Alloc)	B-	B-	B	Up	Y	2,000
Manning & Napier Target 2055 Series Class R	MTZRX	NAS CM	Open End	Target Date 2046+ (Asset Alloc)	B-	C+	B	Up	Y	2,000
Manning & Napier Target 2055 Series R6	MTZZX	NAS CM	Open End	Target Date 2046+ (Asset Alloc)	B-	B-	B		Y	0
Manning & Napier Target 2060 Series Class I	MTKIX	NAS CM	Open End	Target Date 2046+ (Asset Alloc)	C	C+	B	Up	Y	1,000,000
Manning & Napier Target 2060 Series Class K	MTKKX	NAS CM	Open End	Target Date 2046+ (Asset Alloc)	C	C+	B	Up	Y	2,000
Manning & Napier Target 2060 Series Class R	MTKRX	NAS CM	Open End	Target Date 2046+ (Asset Alloc)	C	C+	B	Up	Y	2,000
Manning & Napier Target 2060 Series R6	MTKZX	NAS CM	Open End	Target Date 2046+ (Asset Alloc)	C	C	B		Y	0
Manning & Napier Target Income Series Class I	MTDIX	NAS CM	Open End	Target Date 2000-2020 (Asset Alloc)	B-	C	B+	Up	Y	1,000,000
Manning & Napier Target Income Series Class K	MTDKX	NAS CM	Open End	Target Date 2000-2020 (Asset Alloc)	B-	C	B	Up	Y	2,000
Manning & Napier Target Income Series Class R	MTDRX	NAS CM	Open End	Target Date 2000-2020 (Asset Alloc)	B-	C	B	Up	Y	2,000
Manning & Napier Target Income Series Fund R6	MTDZX	NAS CM	Open End	Target Date 2000-2020 (Asset Alloc)	B-	C	B+		Y	0
Manning & Napier World Opportunities Series Class S	EXWAX	NAS CM	Open End	Global Equity Large Cap (Foreign Stock)	B-	C+	B-	Up	Y	2,000
Manor Investment Funds Growth Fund	MNRGX	NAS CM	Open End	US Equity Large Cap Growth (Growth)	B	B	B-		Y	1,000
Manor Investment Funds Manor Fund	MNRMX	NAS CM	Open End	US Equity Large Cap Blend (Growth & Income)	B-	B-	C+	Down	Y	1,000
Marathon Value Portfolio	MVPFX	NAS CM	Open End	US Equity Large Cap Blend (Growth)	B	B-	B+		Y	2,500
Marketfield Fund Class A	MFADX	NAS CM	Open End	Long/Short Equity (Growth)	C	C	C+	Up	Y	2,500
Marketfield Fund Class C	MFCDX	NAS CM	Open End	Long/Short Equity (Growth)	C	C	C+	Up	Y	2,500
Marketfield Fund Class I	MFLDX	NAS CM	Open End	Long/Short Equity (Growth)	C+	C	C+	Up	Y	25,000
Marketfield Fund Class R6	MFRIX	NAS CM	Open End	Long/Short Equity (Growth)	C+	C	C+	Up	Y	250,000
MarketGrader 100 Enhanced Index Fund Class I	KHMIX	NAS CM	Open End	US Equity Mid Cap (Growth & Income)	C-	C	B+	Up	Y	10,000
Marshfield Concentrated Opportunity Fund	MRFOX	NAS CM	Open End	US Equity Large Cap Blend (Growth)	C-	C	B+	Up	Y	10,000
Marsico 21st Century Fund	MXXIX	NAS CM	Open End	US Equity Mid Cap (Growth)	B	B	B	Up	Y	2,500
Marsico Flexible Capital Fund	MFCFX	NAS CM	Open End	Aggressive Alloc (Growth)	B	C+	B+	Up	Y	2,500
Marsico Focus Fund	MFOCX	NAS CM	Open End	US Equity Large Cap Growth (Growth)	B	B	B	Up	Y	2,500

★ Expanded analysis of this fund is included in Section II.

Min Additional Investment	TOTAL RETURNS 3-Month Total Return	6-Month Total Return	1-Year Total Return	3-Year Total Return	5-Year Total Return	PERFORMANCE Dividend Yield (TTM)	Expense Ratio	3-Yr Std Deviation	3-Year Beta	ASSETS NAV	Total Assets (MIL)	ASSET ALLOCATION & TURNOVER %Cash	%Stocks	%Bonds	%Other	Turnover Ratio	BULL & BEAR Last Bull Market Total Return	Last Bear Market Total Return	FEES Front End Fee (%)	Back End Fee (%)	Inception Date
	1.24	3.91	11.89	10.10	32.40	1.26	0.96	6.08	0.94	9.43	114.9	2	39	60	0	16	13.49	-12.08			Mar-08
	1.29	3.88	11.69	9.26	30.91	1.1	1.21	6.1	0.95	9.31	114.9	2	39	60	0	16	13.27	-12.19			Mar-08
	1.40	4.18	12.29	10.96	34.27		0.56	6.12	0.95	9.47	114.9	2	39	60	0	16	13.53	-11.94			Oct-17
	1.50	4.59	13.66	11.83	40.12	1.56	0.73	7.18	1	11.97	41.6	2	44	54	0	51					Jun-12
	1.47	4.46	13.38	11.01	38.63	1.34	0.98	7.14	0.99	12.01	41.6	2	44	54	0	51					Jun-12
	1.40	4.38	13.16	10.21	36.82	1.13	1.23	7.18	1	12.05	41.6	2	44	54	0	51					Jun-12
	1.53	4.62	13.69	11.86	40.16		0.58	7.18	1	11.97	41.6	2	44	54	0	51					Oct-17
	2.25	5.80	16.32	14.75	47.31	1.55	0.75	7.98	1.02	9.7	143.8	2	55	43	0	22	14.95	-14.65			Mar-08
	2.14	5.62	15.96	13.87	45.46	1.34	1	7.92	1.01	9.6	143.8	2	55	43	0	22	14.73	-14.74			Mar-08
	2.08	5.47	15.81	13.02	43.62	1.12	1.25	7.95	1.01	9.52	143.8	2	55	43	0	22	14.46	-14.82			Mar-08
	2.28	5.84	16.36	14.79	47.35		0.6	7.98	1.02	9.69	143.8	2	55	43	0	22	14.95	-14.65			Oct-17
	3.02	6.85	18.62	17.04	53.73	1.4	0.75	8.72	1.03	12.72	27.5	2	65	33	0	22					Jun-12
	3.08	6.75	18.43	16.29	51.94	1.19	1	8.71	1.03	12.68	27.5	2	65	33	0	22					Jun-12
	3.01	6.67	18.14	15.36	50.21	0.87	1.25	8.72	1.03	12.73	27.5	2	65	33	0	22					Jun-12
	3.13	6.96	18.75	17.17	53.90		0.6	8.72	1.03	12.73	27.5	2	65	33	0	22					Oct-17
	3.95	8.08	21.02	19.49	60.34	1.3	0.75	9.49	1.07	10.11	86.8	1	75	24	0	26	18.63	-20.16			Mar-08
	3.85	7.90	20.75	18.56	58.29	1.07	1	9.51	1.08	10.03	86.8	1	75	24	0	26	18.41	-20.18			Mar-08
	3.80	7.77	20.48	17.60	56.33	0.88	1.25	9.49	1.07	9.95	86.8	1	75	24	0	26	18.28	-20.29			Mar-08
	3.98	8.12	21.05	19.53	60.39		0.6	9.49	1.07	10.11	86.8	1	75	24	0	26	18.63	-20.16			Oct-17
	4.78	9.15	23.35	21.84	65.01	1.17	0.75	10.26	1.12	13.1	16.5	1	84	15	0	26					Jun-12
	4.74	9.03	23.11	20.95	63.00	0.97	1	10.3	1.12	13.08	16.5	1	84	15	0	26					Jun-12
	4.62	8.85	22.73	20.01	60.91	0.71	1.25	10.33	1.12	13	16.5	1	84	15	0	26					Jun-12
	4.89	9.27	23.48	21.97	65.19		0.6	10.26	1.12	13.11	16.5	1	84	15	0	26					Oct-17
	5.09	9.61	24.27	22.98	67.42	1.17	0.75	10.38	1.08	10.64	37.5	1	87	11	0	31	18.52	-20.12			Mar-08
	5.00	9.44	24.06	22.13	65.37	0.97	1	10.35	1.08	10.56	37.5	1	87	11	0	31	18.34	-20.16			Mar-08
	4.97	9.36	23.71	21.19	63.18	0.74	1.25	10.36	1.08	10.44	37.5	1	87	11	0	31	18.27	-20.28			Mar-08
	5.12	9.64	24.31	23.02	67.47		0.6	10.38	1.08	10.64	37.5	1	87	11	0	31	18.52	-20.12			Oct-17
	5.06	9.55	24.21	22.94	66.88	1.12	0.75	10.4	1.06	12.95	7.5	1	87	12	0	30					Jun-12
	4.99	9.42	23.98	22.07	64.59	0.94	1	10.44	1.06	12.83	7.5	1	87	12	0	30					Jun-12
	4.92	9.23	23.65	21.13	62.44	0.77	1.25	10.43	1.06	12.68	7.5	1	87	12	0	30					Jun-12
	5.17	9.66	24.34	23.07	67.06		0.6	10.4	1.06	12.96	7.5	1	87	12	0	30					Oct-17
	5.11	9.68	24.26			1.11	0.75			11.53	5.2	1	87	11	0	14					Sep-15
	4.97	9.45	23.88			0.92	1			11.52	5.2	1	87	11	0	14					Sep-15
	4.94	9.33	23.74			0.71	1.25			11.5	5.2	1	87	11	0	14					Sep-15
	5.12	9.69	24.27				0.6			11.53	5.2	1	87	11	0	14					Oct-17
	1.17	3.37	8.91	10.09	24.51	1.68	0.65	4.3	1.24	9.94	102.6	1	29	69	0	6	7.8	-4.03			Mar-08
	1.16	3.26	8.58	9.33	22.96	1.45	0.9	4.35	1.25	9.91	102.6	1	29	69	0	6	7.57	-4.14			Mar-08
	1.14	3.16	8.32	8.43	21.41	1.35	1.15	4.35	1.25	9.79	102.6	1	29	69	0	6	7.45	-4.28			Mar-08
	1.21	3.41	8.94	10.13	24.55		0.5	4.3	1.24	9.94	102.6	1	29	69	0	6	7.8	-4.03			Oct-17
	2.61	7.67	23.32	18.33	28.68	1.41	1.07	12.04	0.93	8.32	756.9	5	95	0	0	27	15.81	-27.08			Sep-96
25	5.12	12.62	25.17	29.63	103.06	0.05	0.99	10.7	0.96	25.24	10.6	2	98	0	0	13	21.35	-15.68			Jun-99
25	6.80	10.58	21.67	25.97	93.94	0.44	1.25	12.11	1.09	26.53	7.6	2	98	0	0	20	19.34	-15.4			Sep-95
100	5.70	8.02	16.44	28.76	79.17	0.43	1.1	9.7	0.92	27.24	73.2	7	88	4	0	15	21.46	-14.27			Mar-00
0	6.03	13.28	20.82	6.62	9.96	0	1.9	6.68	0.33	17.23	489.0	35	64	0	1	86	15.49	-7.12	5.50		Oct-12
50	5.88	12.88	20.00	4.21	5.89	0	2.67	6.69	0.33	16.56	489.0	35	64	0	1	86	14.99	-7.41		1.00	Oct-12
0	6.08	13.46	21.19	7.38	11.30	0	1.66	6.72	0.33	17.44	489.0	35	64	0	1	86	15.66	-7.03			Jul-07
0	6.17	13.51	21.36	7.86	12.01	0	1.53	6.7	0.33	17.55	489.0	35	64	0	1	86	15.66	-7.03			Jun-13
1,000	7.05	14.07	24.52			0	1.5			13.05	112.7	1	99	0	0	105					Dec-15
	7.81	14.52	25.92			0.13	1.1			13.88	15.2	12	88	0	0	11					Dec-15
100	5.26	8.92	30.04	26.99	100.94	0	1.41	11.52	0.96	27.57	242.9	10	88	0	2	28	28.52	-25.45			Feb-00
100	5.00	8.79	18.80	17.17	71.09	1.4	1.37	9.05	0.82	14.37	246.0	5	83	7	0	20	25.12	-18.02			Dec-06
100	3.06	11.04	33.98	25.33	98.17	0	1.27	11.87	0.96	17.07	567.4	0	99	1	0	67	27.67	-17.72			Dec-97

	MARKET			FUND TYPE, CATEGORY & OBJECTIVE	RATINGS				MINIMUMS	
Fund Name	Ticker Symbol	Traded On	Fund Type	Category and (Prospectus Objective)	Overall Rating	Reward Rating	Risk Rating	Recent Up/ Downgrade	Open to New Investors	Min Initial Investment
Marsico Global Fund	MGLBX	NAS CM	Open End	Global Equity (World Stock)	B+	A-	B	Up	Y	2,500
Marsico Growth Fund	MGRIX	NAS CM	Open End	US Equity Large Cap Growth (Growth)	B	B-	B	Up	Y	2,500
Marsico International Opportunities Fund	MIOFX	NAS CM	Open End	Global Equity Large Cap (Foreign Stock)	B	B+	B	Up	Y	2,500
Martin Currie Emerging Markets Fund Class FI	MEFIX	NAS CM	Open End	Emerging Markets Equity (Div Emerging Mkts)	B-	B-	B-	Up	Y	0
Martin Currie Emerging Markets Fund Class I	MCEIX	NAS CM	Open End	Emerging Markets Equity (Div Emerging Mkts)	B-	B-	B-	Up	Y	1,000,000
Martin Currie Emerging Markets Fund Class IS	MCEMX	NAS CM	Open End	Emerging Markets Equity (Div Emerging Mkts)	B-	B-	B-	Up	Y	1,000,000
Martin Currie Intl Unconstrained Equity Fund Cls A	LUFIX	NAS CM	Open End	Global Equity Large Cap (Foreign Stock)	C	C	B-	Up	Y	1,000
Martin Currie Intl Unconstrained Equity Fund Cls I	LUEIX	NAS CM	Open End	Global Equity Large Cap (Foreign Stock)	C	C	B-	Up	Y	1,000,000
Martin Currie Intl Unconstrained Equity Fund Cls IS	LUISX	NAS CM	Open End	Global Equity Large Cap (Foreign Stock)	C	C	B-	Up	Y	1,000,000
MassMutual Premier Balanced Fund Administrative Class	MMBLX	NAS CM	Open End	Moderate Alloc (Balanced)	B-	C+	B	Up	Y	0
MassMutual Premier Balanced Fund Class A	MMBDX	NAS CM	Open End	Moderate Alloc (Balanced)	B-	C+	B	Up	Y	0
MassMutual Premier Balanced Fund Class I	MBBIX	NAS CM	Open End	Moderate Alloc (Balanced)	B-	C+	B	Up	Y	0
MassMutual Premier Balanced Fund Class R3	MMBRX	NAS CM	Open End	Moderate Alloc (Balanced)	B-	C+	B	Up	Y	0
MassMutual Premier Balanced Fund Class R4	MBBRX	NAS CM	Open End	Moderate Alloc (Balanced)	B-	C+	B	Up	Y	0
MassMutual Premier Balanced Fund Class R5	MBLDX	NAS CM	Open End	Moderate Alloc (Balanced)	B-	C+	B	Up	Y	0
MassMutual Premier Balanced Fund Service Class	MBAYX	NAS CM	Open End	Moderate Alloc (Balanced)	B-	C+	B	Up	Y	0
MassMutual Premier Disciplined Growth Fund Admin Cls	MPGLX	NAS CM	Open End	US Equity Large Cap Growth (Growth)	B+	A-	B	Up	Y	0
MassMutual Premier Disciplined Growth Fund Class A	MPGAX	NAS CM	Open End	US Equity Large Cap Growth (Growth)	B+	A-	B	Up	Y	0
MassMutual Premier Disciplined Growth Fund Class I	MPDIX	NAS CM	Open End	US Equity Large Cap Growth (Growth)	A-	A-	B	Up	Y	0
MassMutual Premier Disciplined Growth Fund Class R3	MPDRX	NAS CM	Open End	US Equity Large Cap Growth (Growth)	B+	B+	B	Up	Y	0
MassMutual Premier Disciplined Growth Fund Class R4	MPDGX	NAS CM	Open End	US Equity Large Cap Growth (Growth)	B+	A-	B	Up	Y	0
MassMutual Premier Disciplined Growth Fund Class R5	MPGSX	NAS CM	Open End	US Equity Large Cap Growth (Growth)	A-	A-	B	Up	Y	0
MassMutual Premier Disciplined Growth Fund Service Class	DEIGX	NAS CM	Open End	US Equity Large Cap Growth (Growth)	B+	A-	B	Up	Y	0
MassMutual Premier Disciplined Value Fund Admin Cls	MPILX	NAS CM	Open End	US Equity Large Cap Value (Growth)	B-	B-	B	Down	Y	0
MassMutual Premier Disciplined Value Fund Class A	MEPAX	NAS CM	Open End	US Equity Large Cap Value (Growth)	B-	B-	B	Down	Y	0
MassMutual Premier Disciplined Value Fund Class I	MPIVX	NAS CM	Open End	US Equity Large Cap Value (Growth)	B	B-	B	Up	Y	0
MassMutual Premier Disciplined Value Fund Class R3	MPINX	NAS CM	Open End	US Equity Large Cap Value (Growth)	B-	B-	B	Down	Y	0
MassMutual Premier Disciplined Value Fund Class R4	MPIRX	NAS CM	Open End	US Equity Large Cap Value (Growth)	B-	B-	B	Down	Y	0
MassMutual Premier Disciplined Value Fund Class R5	MEPSX	NAS CM	Open End	US Equity Large Cap Value (Growth)	B-	B-	B	Down	Y	0
MassMutual Premier Disciplined Value Fund Service Class	DENVX	NAS CM	Open End	US Equity Large Cap Value (Growth)	B-	B-	B	Down	Y	0
MassMutual Premier Global Fund Administrative Class	MGFLX	NAS CM	Open End	Global Equity (Foreign Stock)	B	B+	C+	Up	Y	0
MassMutual Premier Global Fund Class A	MGFAX	NAS CM	Open End	Global Equity (Foreign Stock)	B	B+	C+	Up	Y	0
MassMutual Premier Global Fund Class I	MGFZX	NAS CM	Open End	Global Equity (Foreign Stock)	B	B+	C+	Up	Y	0
MassMutual Premier Global Fund Class R3	MGFNX	NAS CM	Open End	Global Equity (Foreign Stock)	B	B+	C+	Up	Y	0
MassMutual Premier Global Fund Class R4	MGFRX	NAS CM	Open End	Global Equity (Foreign Stock)	B	B+	C+	Up	Y	0
MassMutual Premier Global Fund Class R5	MGFSX	NAS CM	Open End	Global Equity (Foreign Stock)	B+	B+	B	Up	Y	0
MassMutual Premier Global Fund Service Class	MGFYX	NAS CM	Open End	Global Equity (Foreign Stock)	B+	B+	B	Up	Y	0
MassMutual Premier Intl Equity Fund Admin Cls	MIELX	NAS CM	Open End	Global Equity Large Cap (Foreign Stock)	B	B	B	Up	Y	0
MassMutual Premier International Equity Fund Class A	MMIAX	NAS CM	Open End	Global Equity Large Cap (Foreign Stock)	B	B-	B	Up	Y	0
MassMutual Premier International Equity Fund Class I	MIZIX	NAS CM	Open End	Global Equity Large Cap (Foreign Stock)	B	B	B	Up	Y	0
MassMutual Premier International Equity Fund Class R3	MEERX	NAS CM	Open End	Global Equity Large Cap (Foreign Stock)	B	B-	B	Up	Y	0
MassMutual Premier International Equity Fund Class R4	MEIRX	NAS CM	Open End	Global Equity Large Cap (Foreign Stock)	B	B-	B	Up	Y	0
MassMutual Premier International Equity Fund Class R5	MIEDX	NAS CM	Open End	Global Equity Large Cap (Foreign Stock)	B	B	B	Up	Y	0
MassMutual Premier International Equity Fund Service Class	MYIEX	NAS CM	Open End	Global Equity Large Cap (Foreign Stock)	B	B	B	Up	Y	0
MassMutual Premier Main Street Fund Administrative Class	MMSLX	NAS CM	Open End	US Equity Large Cap Blend (Growth)	B	B-	B+		Y	0
MassMutual Premier Main Street Fund Class A	MSSAX	NAS CM	Open End	US Equity Large Cap Blend (Growth)	B	B-	B+		Y	0
MassMutual Premier Main Street Fund Class I	MSZIX	NAS CM	Open End	US Equity Large Cap Blend (Growth)	B	B-	B+		Y	0
MassMutual Premier Main Street Fund Class R3	MMSNX	NAS CM	Open End	US Equity Large Cap Blend (Growth)	B	B-	B+		Y	0
MassMutual Premier Main Street Fund Class R4	MSSRX	NAS CM	Open End	US Equity Large Cap Blend (Growth)	B	B-	B+		Y	0
MassMutual Premier Main Street Fund Class R5	MMSSX	NAS CM	Open End	US Equity Large Cap Blend (Growth)	B	B-	B+		Y	0
MassMutual Premier Main Street Fund Service Class	MMSYX	NAS CM	Open End	US Equity Large Cap Blend (Growth)	B	B-	B+		Y	0
MassMutual Premier Small Cap Opp Fund Admin Cls	MSCLX	NAS CM	Open End	US Equity Small Cap (Growth)	B	B	B	Up	Y	0

★ Expanded analysis of this fund is included in Section II.

	TOTAL RETURNS					PERFORMANCE				ASSETS		ASSET ALLOCATION & TURNOVER					BULL & BEAR		FEES		
Min Additional Investment	3-Month Total Return	6-Month Total Return	1-Year Total Return	3-Year Total Return	5-Year Total Return	Dividend Yield (TTM)	Expense Ratio	3-Yr Std Deviation	3-Year Beta	NAV	Total Assets (MIL)	%Cash	%Stocks	%Bonds	%Other	Turnover Ratio	Last Bull Market Total Return	Last Bear Market Total Return	Front End Fee (%)	Back End Fee (%)	Inception Date
100	4.36	14.67	40.23	34.43	100.70	0	1.6	12.7	1.03	14.45	48.5	5	95	0	0	79	29.69	-24.24			Jun-07
100	4.77	11.40	31.10	24.31	88.18	0	1.36	11.34	0.98	17.61	281.4	0	100	0	0	50	27.99	-17.43			Dec-97
100	4.81	15.33	44.08	32.48	55.41	0	1.6	14.15	1.01	20.23	65.3	0	98	0	1	108	21.2	-25.17			Jun-00
	7.08	18.87	46.34			1.09	1.39			13.17	107.1	2	97	0	1	7					May-15
	7.15	19.03	46.80			1.23	1.04			13.21	107.1	2	97	0	1	7					May-15
	7.14	19.29	47.09			1.41	0.94			13.23	107.1	2	97	0	1	7					May-15
50	3.32	5.50	28.21			0.77	1.2			11.68	4.9	1	96	0	0	22			5.75		Nov-15
	3.41	5.58	28.48			0.86	0.85			11.71	4.9	1	96	0	0	22					Nov-15
	3.40	5.67	28.47			0.88	0.75			11.7	4.9	1	96	0	0	22					Nov-15
	4.68	8.66	15.85	22.81	57.98	1.49	0.93	7.05	0.69	12.28	119.7	3	68	28	1	108	15.47	-10.25			Apr-99
	4.49	8.39	15.55	21.74	55.93	1.28	1.18	7.01	0.68	11.94	119.7	3	68	28	1	108	15.27	-10.35	5.75		Dec-97
	4.72	8.80	16.23	23.88	60.49	1.69	0.63	7.02	0.68	12.22	119.7	3	68	28	1	108	15.64	-10.12			Apr-14
	4.45	8.31	15.33	21.26	55.30	1.27	1.33	7.01	0.68	11.81	119.7	3	68	28	1	108	15.3	-10.3			Apr-14
	4.54	8.47	15.68	22.14	57.11	1.38	1.08	7.05	0.69	11.85	119.7	3	68	28	1	108	15.47	-10.21			Apr-14
	4.70	8.69	16.10	23.47	59.86	1.6	0.73	7	0.68	12.23	119.7	3	68	28	1	108	15.64	-10.12			Sep-94
	4.65	8.62	15.97	23.02	58.76	1.39	0.83	7.03	0.69	12.85	119.7	3	68	28	1	108	15.65	-10.23			Dec-97
	7.72	14.99	28.29	40.69	119.34	0.9	0.81	10.87	1	12.69	400.1	0	100	0	0	105	27.02	-15.84			Nov-04
	7.63	14.81	27.99	39.51	116.43	0.72	1.06	10.88	1	12.36	400.1	0	100	0	0	105	26.94	-15.99	5.75		Nov-04
	7.82	15.19	28.70	41.88	122.30	1.16	0.51	10.89	1	12.5	400.1	0	100	0	0	105	27.09	-15.79			Apr-14
	7.65	14.80	27.83	38.90	115.11	0.54	1.21	10.84	1	12.27	400.1	0	100	0	0	105	26.72	-15.97			Apr-14
	7.64	14.86	28.12	39.92	117.81	0.9	0.96	10.88	1	12.27	400.1	0	100	0	0	105	26.9	-15.88			Apr-14
	7.70	15.06	28.54	41.38	121.47	1.07	0.61	10.84	1	12.51	400.1	0	100	0	0	105	27.25	-15.82			Nov-04
	7.66	15.00	28.44	40.94	120.36	0.96	0.71	10.82	1	12.55	400.1	0	100	0	0	105	27.09	-15.79			Dec-00
	5.36	9.14	14.24	25.36	91.54	2.48	0.83	10.39	1	16.7	206.6	0	100	0	0	102	22.96	-18.37			Nov-04
	5.30	9.00	13.95	24.44	89.14	2.41	1.08	10.36	1	16.25	206.6	0	100	0	0	102	22.65	-18.45	5.75		Nov-04
	5.43	9.33	14.57	26.42	93.87	2.78	0.53	10.38	1	16.46	206.6	0	100	0	0	102	22.87	-18.32			Apr-14
	5.25	8.90	13.80	23.91	87.37	2.03	1.23	10.36	1	16.39	206.6	0	100	0	0	102	22.38	-18.61			Nov-04
	5.31	9.02	14.07	24.75	90.14	2.63	0.98	10.39	1	16.13	206.6	0	100	0	0	102	22.69	-18.4			Apr-14
	5.36	9.19	14.41	26.13	93.63	2.71	0.63	10.37	1	16.49	206.6	0	100	0	0	102	23	-18.31			Nov-04
	5.42	9.22	14.41	25.75	92.60	2.58	0.73	10.35	0.99	16.38	206.6	0	100	0	0	102	22.87	-18.32			Dec-00
	7.12	13.61	35.98	39.60	83.21	0.79	1.15	12.94	1.13	15.63	333.8	2	96	0	2	30	17.68	-23.12			Dec-04
	7.04	13.46	35.74	38.50	80.83	0.56	1.4	12.92	1.13	15.48	333.8	2	96	0	2	30	17.44	-23.25	5.75		Dec-04
	7.23	13.80	36.40	40.83	85.81	1.03	0.85	12.92	1.13	15.62	333.8	2	96	0	2	30	17.79	-23.08			Apr-14
	7.00	13.36	35.50	37.99	79.60	0.57	1.55	12.94	1.13	15.42	333.8	2	96	0	2	30	17.46	-23.3			Dec-04
	7.03	13.50	35.83	38.91	82.08	0.77	1.3	12.96	1.13	15.3	333.8	2	96	0	2	30	17.61	-23.17			Apr-14
	7.12	13.67	36.34	40.35	85.14	0.95	0.95	12.92	1.12	15.63	333.8	2	96	0	2	30	17.79	-23.08			Dec-04
	7.13	13.67	36.14	40.01	84.10	0.85	1.05	12.95	1.13	15.5	333.8	2	96	0	2	30	17.8	-23.15			Dec-04
	3.57	9.40	26.22	26.14	49.21	0.83	1.25	11.76	0.88	13.67	552.7	3	97	0	0	44	18.15	-20.78			May-99
	3.52	9.27	25.92	25.21	47.38	0.61	1.5	11.72	0.88	13.29	552.7	3	97	0	0	44	17.97	-20.86	5.75		Jan-98
	3.65	9.61	26.65	27.36	51.29	1.07	0.95	11.75	0.88	13.76	552.7	3	97	0	0	44	18.2	-20.67			Apr-14
	3.41	9.12	25.72	24.64	46.49	0.72	1.65	11.81	0.89	13.14	552.7	3	97	0	0	44	17.86	-20.84			Apr-14
	3.50	9.29	26.09	25.55	48.36	0.92	1.4	11.77	0.89	13.16	552.7	3	97	0	0	44	18.03	-20.75			Apr-14
	3.55	9.41	26.40	26.83	50.67	0.98	1.05	11.74	0.88	13.76	552.7	3	97	0	0	44	18.2	-20.67			Jan-95
	3.63	9.43	26.38	26.57	50.04	0.91	1.15	11.76	0.89	13.73	552.7	3	97	0	0	44	18.28	-20.73			Jan-98
	1.99	6.65	16.58	32.12	97.11	0.95	1.02	10.02	0.97	11.26	140.0	1	99	0	0	35	26.43	-15.24			Dec-04
	1.88	6.41	16.22	31.05	94.68	0.78	1.27	10.01	0.97	11.11	140.0	1	99	0	0	35	26.41	-15.45	5.75		Dec-04
	2.03	6.77	16.92	33.22	99.80	1.21	0.72	10.03	0.97	11.26	140.0	1	99	0	0	35	26.81	-15.22			Apr-14
	1.85	6.37	16.06	30.53	92.87	0.91	1.42	10.06	0.97	11.14	140.0	1	99	0	0	35	26.15	-15.49			Dec-04
	1.97	6.53	16.43	31.62	95.98	1.12	1.17	10.01	0.96	11.03	140.0	1	99	0	0	35	26.63	-15.31			Apr-14
	2.02	6.66	16.80	32.91	99.06	1.13	0.82	10.03	0.97	11.26	140.0	1	99	0	0	35	26.81	-15.22			Dec-04
	2.01	6.61	16.61	32.51	98.30	0.88	0.92	10.04	0.97	11.65	140.0	1	99	0	0	35	26.75	-15.25			Dec-04
	1.80	6.59	14.01	25.56	103.45	0.84	1.01	12.75	0.88	14.6	213.6	5	95	0	0	62	30.05	-23.37			Nov-04

Fund Name	Ticker Symbol	Traded On	Fund Type	Category and (Prospectus Objective)	Overall Rating	Reward Rating	Risk Rating	Recent Up/ Downgrade	Open to New Investors	Min Initial Investment
	MARKET		FUND TYPE, CATEGORY & OBJECTIVE		RATINGS				MINIMUMS	
MassMutual Premier Small Cap Opportunities Fund Class A	DLBMX	NAS CM	Open End	US Equity Small Cap (Growth)	B	B	B	Up	Y	0
MassMutual Premier Small Cap Opportunities Fund Class I	MSOOX	NAS CM	Open End	US Equity Small Cap (Growth)	B	B	B	Up	Y	0
MassMutual Premier Small Cap Opportunities Fund Class R3	MCCRX	NAS CM	Open End	US Equity Small Cap (Growth)	B	B	B	Up	Y	0
MassMutual Premier Small Cap Opportunities Fund Class R4	MOORX	NAS CM	Open End	US Equity Small Cap (Growth)	B	B	B	Up	Y	0
MassMutual Premier Small Cap Opportunities Fund Class R5	MSCDX	NAS CM	Open End	US Equity Small Cap (Growth)	B	B	B	Up	Y	0
MassMutual Premier Small Cap Opp Fund Service Cls	MSVYX	NAS CM	Open End	US Equity Small Cap (Growth)	B	B	B	Up	Y	0
MassMutual Premier Strategic Emerging Mkts Fund Admin Cls	MPLSX	NAS CM	Open End	Emerging Markets Equity (Div Emerging Mkts)	C+	B-	C	Up	Y	0
MassMutual Premier Strategic Emerging Markets Fund Class A	MPASX	NAS CM	Open End	Emerging Markets Equity (Div Emerging Mkts)	C+	B-	C	Up	Y	0
MassMutual Premier Strategic Emerging Markets Fund Class I	MPZSX	NAS CM	Open End	Emerging Markets Equity (Div Emerging Mkts)	C+	B-	C	Up	Y	0
MassMutual Premier Strategic Emerging Markets Fund Cls R3	MPZRX	NAS CM	Open End	Emerging Markets Equity (Div Emerging Mkts)	C+	B-	C	Up	Y	0
MassMutual Premier Strategic Emerging Markets Fund Cls R4	MPRSX	NAS CM	Open End	Emerging Markets Equity (Div Emerging Mkts)	C+	B-	C	Up	Y	0
MassMutual Premier Strategic Emerging Markets Fund Cls R5	MPSMX	NAS CM	Open End	Emerging Markets Equity (Div Emerging Mkts)	C+	B-	C	Up	Y	0
MassMutual Premier Strategic Emerging Mkts Fund Serv Cls	MPEYX	NAS CM	Open End	Emerging Markets Equity (Div Emerging Mkts)	C+	B-	C	Up	Y	0
MassMutual Premier Value Fund Administrative Class Share	DLBVX	NAS CM	Open End	US Equity Large Cap Value (Growth)	B-	B-	B-	Down	Y	0
MassMutual Premier Value Fund Class A	MCEAX	NAS CM	Open End	US Equity Large Cap Value (Growth)	B-	B-	B-	Down	Y	0
MassMutual Premier Value Fund Class I	MCZIX	NAS CM	Open End	US Equity Large Cap Value (Growth)	B-	B-	B-	Down	Y	0
MassMutual Premier Value Fund Class R3	MCENX	NAS CM	Open End	US Equity Large Cap Value (Growth)	B	B-	B	Up	Y	0
MassMutual Premier Value Fund Class R4	MCERX	NAS CM	Open End	US Equity Large Cap Value (Growth)	B-	B-	B-	Down	Y	0
MassMutual Premier Value Fund Class R5	MVEDX	NAS CM	Open End	US Equity Large Cap Value (Growth)	B-	B-	B-	Down	Y	0
MassMutual Premier Value Fund Service Class	MCEYX	NAS CM	Open End	US Equity Large Cap Value (Growth)	B	B-	B	Up	Y	0
MassMutual RetireSMART 2010 Fund Administrative Class	MRXYX	NAS CM	Open End	Target Date 2000-2020 (Growth & Income)	B-	C+	B	Up	Y	0
MassMutual RetireSMART 2010 Fund Class A	MRXAX	NAS CM	Open End	Target Date 2000-2020 (Growth & Income)	B-	C+	B	Up	Y	0
MassMutual RetireSMART 2010 Fund Class I	MRXUX	NAS CM	Open End	Target Date 2000-2020 (Growth & Income)	B-	C+	B	Up	Y	0
MassMutual RetireSMART 2010 Fund Class R3	MRXNX	NAS CM	Open End	Target Date 2000-2020 (Growth & Income)	B-	C+	B+	Up	Y	0
MassMutual RetireSMART 2010 Fund Class R4	MRXZX	NAS CM	Open End	Target Date 2000-2020 (Growth & Income)	B-	C+	B	Up	Y	0
MassMutual RetireSMART 2010 Fund Class R5	MRXTX	NAS CM	Open End	Target Date 2000-2020 (Growth & Income)	B-	C+	B	Up	Y	0
MassMutual RetireSMART 2010 Fund Service Class	MRXSX	NAS CM	Open End	Target Date 2000-2020 (Growth & Income)	B-	C+	B+	Up	Y	0
MassMutual RetireSMART 2015 Fund Administrative Class	MMJYX	NAS CM	Open End	Target Date 2000-2020 (Growth & Income)	B-	C+	B+	Up	Y	0
MassMutual RetireSMART 2015 Fund Class A	MMJAX	NAS CM	Open End	Target Date 2000-2020 (Growth & Income)	B-	C+	B+	Up	Y	0
MassMutual RetireSMART 2015 Fund Class I	MMJUX	NAS CM	Open End	Target Date 2000-2020 (Growth & Income)	B-	C+	B	Up	Y	0
MassMutual RetireSMART 2015 Fund Class R3	MMJNX	NAS CM	Open End	Target Date 2000-2020 (Growth & Income)	B-	C+	B	Up	Y	0
MassMutual RetireSMART 2015 Fund Class R4	MMJZX	NAS CM	Open End	Target Date 2000-2020 (Growth & Income)	B-	C+	B	Up	Y	0
MassMutual RetireSMART 2015 Fund Class R5	MMJTX	NAS CM	Open End	Target Date 2000-2020 (Growth & Income)	B-	C+	B	Up	Y	0
MassMutual RetireSMART 2015 Fund Service Class	MMJSX	NAS CM	Open End	Target Date 2000-2020 (Growth & Income)	B-	C+	B	Up	Y	0
MassMutual RetireSMART 2020 Fund Administrative Class	MRTYX	NAS CM	Open End	Target Date 2000-2020 (Growth & Income)	B-	C+	B	Down	Y	0
MassMutual RetireSMART 2020 Fund Class A	MRTAX	NAS CM	Open End	Target Date 2000-2020 (Growth & Income)	B-	C+	B	Down	Y	0
MassMutual RetireSMART 2020 Fund Class I	MRTDX	NAS CM	Open End	Target Date 2000-2020 (Growth & Income)	B-	C+	B	Down	Y	0
MassMutual RetireSMART 2020 Fund Class R3	MRTNX	NAS CM	Open End	Target Date 2000-2020 (Growth & Income)	B-	C+	B	Down	Y	0
MassMutual RetireSMART 2020 Fund Class R4	MRTHX	NAS CM	Open End	Target Date 2000-2020 (Growth & Income)	B-	C+	B	Down	Y	0
MassMutual RetireSMART 2020 Fund Class R5	MRTBX	NAS CM	Open End	Target Date 2000-2020 (Growth & Income)	B-	C+	B	Down	Y	0
MassMutual RetireSMART 2020 Fund Service Class	MRTSX	NAS CM	Open End	Target Date 2000-2020 (Growth & Income)	B-	C+	B	Down	Y	0
MassMutual RetireSMART 2025 Fund Administrative Class	MMIYX	NAS CM	Open End	Target Date 2021-2045 (Growth & Income)	B-	C+	B-	Down	Y	0
MassMutual RetireSMART 2025 Fund Class A	MMSDX	NAS CM	Open End	Target Date 2021-2045 (Growth & Income)	C+	C+	B-	Down	Y	0
MassMutual RetireSMART 2025 Fund Class I	MMNUX	NAS CM	Open End	Target Date 2021-2045 (Growth & Income)	B-	C+	B-	Down	Y	0
MassMutual RetireSMART 2025 Fund Class R3	MMNRX	NAS CM	Open End	Target Date 2021-2045 (Growth & Income)	C+	C+	B-	Down	Y	0
MassMutual RetireSMART 2025 Fund Class R4	MMNZX	NAS CM	Open End	Target Date 2021-2045 (Growth & Income)	B-	C+	B-	Down	Y	0
MassMutual RetireSMART 2025 Fund Class R5	MMNTX	NAS CM	Open End	Target Date 2021-2045 (Growth & Income)	B-	C+	B-	Down	Y	0
MassMutual RetireSMART 2025 Fund Service Class	MMISX	NAS CM	Open End	Target Date 2021-2045 (Growth & Income)	B-	C+	B-	Down	Y	0
MassMutual RetireSMART 2030 Fund Administrative Class	MRYYX	NAS CM	Open End	Target Date 2021-2045 (Growth & Income)	B-	C+	B-	Down	Y	0
MassMutual RetireSMART 2030 Fund Class A	MRYAX	NAS CM	Open End	Target Date 2021-2045 (Growth & Income)	C+	C+	B-	Down	Y	0
MassMutual RetireSMART 2030 Fund Class I	MRYUX	NAS CM	Open End	Target Date 2021-2045 (Growth & Income)	B-	C+	B-	Down	Y	0
MassMutual RetireSMART 2030 Fund Class R3	MRYNX	NAS CM	Open End	Target Date 2021-2045 (Growth & Income)	C+	C+	B-	Down	Y	0

★ Expanded analysis of this fund is included in Section II.

Min Additional Investment	3-Month Total Return	6-Month Total Return	1-Year Total Return	3-Year Total Return	5-Year Total Return	Dividend Yield (TTM)	Expense Ratio	3-Yr Std Deviation	3-Year Beta	NAV	Total Assets (MIL)	%Cash	%Stocks	%Bonds	%Other	Turnover Ratio	Last Bull Market Total Return	Last Bear Market Total Return	Front End Fee (%)	Back End Fee (%)	Inception Date
	TOTAL RETURNS					PERFORMANCE				ASSETS		ASSET ALLOCATION & TURNOVER					BULL & BEAR		FEES		
	1.73	6.47	13.72	24.60	100.71	0.63	1.26	12.71	0.88	14.29	213.6	5	95	0	0	62	29.89	-23.46	5.75		Jul-98
	1.89	6.77	14.36	26.82	105.09	1.04	0.71	12.73	0.88	14.73	213.6	5	95	0	0	62	29.89	-23.46			Apr-14
	1.68	6.33	13.48	24.10	99.00	0.67	1.41	12.75	0.88	14.12	213.6	5	95	0	0	62	29.7	-23.54			Apr-14
	1.72	6.50	13.80	24.95	101.52	0.83	1.16	12.76	0.88	14.18	213.6	5	95	0	0	62	29.89	-23.46			Apr-14
	1.84	6.73	14.18	26.29	105.46	0.96	0.81	12.75	0.88	14.71	213.6	5	95	0	0	62	30.19	-23.36			Nov-04
	1.81	6.64	14.10	25.93	104.38	0.9	0.91	12.72	0.88	14.68	213.6	5	95	0	0	62	30.18	-23.38			Nov-04
	4.95	13.28	33.62	21.98	10.43	0.8	1.35	14.4	0.86	13.41	255.7	4	94	0	1	51	14.51	-27.65			Nov-08
	4.86	13.21	33.33	21.11	9.14	0.16	1.6	14.38	0.86	13.38	255.7	4	94	0	1	51	14.35	-27.81	5.75		Nov-08
	5.03	13.58	34.07	23.16	12.33	0.94	1.05	14.39	0.86	13.35	255.7	4	94	0	1	51	14.8	-27.62			Mar-11
	4.83	13.09	33.18	20.62	8.55	0.58	1.75	14.37	0.86	13.26	255.7	4	94	0	1	51	14.3	-27.78			Apr-14
	4.95	13.30	33.52	21.60	10.03	0.77	1.5	14.38	0.86	13.27	255.7	4	94	0	1	51	14.46	-27.71			Apr-14
	5.02	13.45	33.97	22.67	11.60	0.83	1.15	14.36	0.86	13.54	255.7	4	94	0	1	51	14.63	-27.63			Nov-08
	4.97	13.44	33.68	22.39	11.03	0.77	1.25	14.34	0.86	13.35	255.7	4	94	0	1	51	14.61	-27.65			Nov-08
	5.21	9.02	16.46	25.67	85.56	1.26	0.9	11.3	1.06	26.13	50.7	3	97	0	0	58	19.7	-21.04			Jul-95
	5.12	8.89	16.17	24.70	83.14	1.05	1.15	11.29	1.06	26.12	50.7	3	97	0	0	58	19.47	-21.1	5.75		Nov-04
	5.30	9.21	16.78	26.77	87.63	1.51	0.6	11.31	1.07	25.98	50.7	3	97	0	0	58	19.7	-21.04			Apr-14
	5.09	8.80	15.97	24.16	81.44	0.97	1.3	11.3	1.07	25.93	50.7	3	97	0	0	58	19.23	-21.19			Nov-04
	5.17	8.95	16.25	25.07	83.94	1.15	1.05	11.3	1.06	25.98	50.7	3	97	0	0	58	19.53	-21.12			Apr-14
	5.26	9.13	16.70	26.41	87.51	1.43	0.7	11.28	1.06	25.99	50.7	3	97	0	0	58	19.88	-20.95			Nov-04
	5.22	9.07	16.56	26.01	86.49	1.35	0.8	11.29	1.06	26.08	50.7	3	97	0	0	58	19.74	-21			Nov-04
	2.30	4.85	10.35	13.44	31.12	2.61	0.83	4.87	1.17	12.41	64.7	3	39	55	3	46	12.83	-9.86			Dec-03
	2.28	4.77	10.21	12.71	29.52	2.37	1.08	4.83	1.16	12.34	64.7	3	39	55	3	46	12.57	-9.96	5.75		Dec-03
	2.43	5.08	10.83	14.60	32.84	2.92	0.53	4.87	1.17	12.31	64.7	3	39	55	3	46	12.69	-9.72			Apr-14
	2.20	4.64	9.98	12.09	28.24	2.33	1.23	4.86	1.17	12.1	64.7	3	39	55	3	46	12.31	-10.03			Dec-03
	2.25	4.84	10.23	13.03	30.28	2.51	0.98	4.85	1.17	12.23	64.7	3	39	55	3	46	12.53	-9.81			Apr-14
	2.34	4.97	10.57	14.21	32.27	2.78	0.63	4.84	1.16	12.4	64.7	3	39	55	3	46	12.69	-9.72			Apr-14
	2.32	4.94	10.53	13.84	31.99	2.68	0.73	4.82	1.16	12.45	64.7	3	39	55	3	46	12.69	-9.72			Dec-03
	2.53	5.31	11.25	14.54	36.96	1.78	0.86	5.36	1.07	11.9	81.0	3	44	50	3	42	16.02	-13.21			Apr-10
	2.41	5.12	10.89	13.68	35.15	1.59	1.11	5.32	1.06	11.83	81.0	3	44	50	3	42	15.82	-13.33	5.75		Apr-10
	2.60	5.46	11.49	15.59	38.58	2.04	0.56	5.33	1.06	11.92	81.0	3	44	50	3	42	15.95	-13.2			Apr-14
	2.45	5.18	10.79	13.25	34.28	1.4	1.26	5.34	1.06	11.78	81.0	3	44	50	3	42	15.61	-13.38			Apr-14
	2.56	5.28	11.09	14.07	35.88	1.65	1.01	5.37	1.07	11.78	81.0	3	44	50	3	42	15.78	-13.29			Apr-14
	2.59	5.44	11.47	15.29	38.21	1.92	0.66	5.33	1.06	11.93	81.0	3	44	50	3	42	15.95	-13.2			Apr-14
	2.64	5.41	11.43	15.03	37.71	1.81	0.76	5.35	1.06	11.95	81.0	3	44	50	3	42	15.95	-13.2			Apr-10
	2.96	6.23	13.44	16.93	44.75	1.76	0.86	6.64	1.15	13	474.6	2	53	42	3	33	17.84	-15.56			Dec-03
	3.00	6.21	13.27	16.19	42.84	1.53	1.11	6.66	1.15	12.95	474.6	2	53	42	3	33	17.62	-15.73	5.75		Dec-03
	3.14	6.50	13.81	18.10	46.69	2.05	0.56	6.65	1.15	12.99	474.6	2	53	42	3	33	17.94	-15.58			Apr-14
	2.93	6.05	13.01	15.55	41.40	1.5	1.26	6.66	1.15	12.59	474.6	2	53	42	3	33	17.42	-15.82			Dec-03
	3.00	6.25	13.40	16.54	43.73	1.71	1.01	6.64	1.14	12.77	474.6	2	53	42	3	33	17.77	-15.67			Apr-14
	3.14	6.42	13.74	17.78	46.17	1.97	0.66	6.68	1.15	12.98	474.6	2	53	42	3	33	17.94	-15.58			Apr-14
	3.05	6.31	13.60	17.34	45.50	1.84	0.76	6.67	1.15	13.03	474.6	2	53	42	3	33	17.94	-15.58			Dec-03
	3.61	7.42	15.85	19.89	51.98	1.64	0.85	7.66	1.17	13.04	279.0	2	65	30	3	42	19.76	-17.56			Apr-10
	3.53	7.29	15.50	19.00	49.90	1.44	1.1	7.67	1.17	12.95	279.0	2	65	30	3	42	19.54	-17.67	5.75		Apr-10
	3.73	7.62	16.14	21.03	53.76	1.87	0.55	7.68	1.18	13.06	279.0	2	65	30	3	42	19.8	-17.54			Apr-14
	3.57	7.27	15.33	18.49	48.97	1.36	1.25	7.64	1.17	12.87	279.0	2	65	30	3	42	19.46	-17.71			Apr-14
	3.60	7.38	15.61	19.34	50.71	1.53	1	7.68	1.18	12.89	279.0	2	65	30	3	42	19.63	-17.63			Apr-14
	3.75	7.55	16.16	20.67	53.31	1.67	0.65	7.68	1.18	13.08	279.0	2	65	30	3	42	19.8	-17.54			Apr-14
	3.69	7.57	16.00	20.29	52.73	1.66	0.75	7.66	1.17	13.08	279.0	2	65	30	3	42	19.8	-17.54			Apr-10
	4.05	8.26	17.42	21.61	55.98	1.59	0.89	8.4	1.17	13.4	551.4	2	72	23	2	35	20.39	-18.22			Dec-03
	4.00	8.08	17.18	20.68	53.96	1.4	1.14	8.38	1.17	13.33	551.4	2	72	23	2	35	20.18	-18.41	5.75		Dec-03
	4.14	8.44	17.78	22.75	58.07	1.86	0.59	8.34	1.16	13.4	551.4	2	72	23	2	35	20.48	-18.25			Apr-14
	3.95	8.03	17.00	20.19	52.47	1.36	1.29	8.35	1.16	13.07	551.4	2	72	23	2	35	19.95	-18.44			Dec-03

Fund Name	MARKET Ticker Symbol	Traded On	FUND TYPE, CATEGORY & OBJECTIVE Fund Type	Category and (Prospectus Objective)	RATINGS Overall Rating	Reward Rating	Risk Rating	Recent Up/ Downgrade	Open to New Investors	MINIMUMS Min Initial Investment
MassMutual RetireSMART 2030 Fund Class R4	MRYZX	NAS CM	Open End	Target Date 2021-2045 (Growth & Income)	B-	C+	B-	Down	Y	0
MassMutual RetireSMART 2030 Fund Class R5	MRYTX	NAS CM	Open End	Target Date 2021-2045 (Growth & Income)	B-	C+	B-	Down	Y	0
MassMutual RetireSMART 2030 Fund Service Class	MRYSX	NAS CM	Open End	Target Date 2021-2045 (Growth & Income)	B-	C+	B-	Down	Y	0
MassMutual RetireSMART 2035 Fund Administrative Class	MMXYX	NAS CM	Open End	Target Date 2021-2045 (Growth & Income)	B-	C+	B-	Down	Y	0
MassMutual RetireSMART 2035 Fund Class A	MMXAX	NAS CM	Open End	Target Date 2021-2045 (Growth & Income)	B-	C+	B-	Down	Y	0
MassMutual RetireSMART 2035 Fund Class I	MMXUX	NAS CM	Open End	Target Date 2021-2045 (Growth & Income)	B-	B-	B-	Down	Y	0
MassMutual RetireSMART 2035 Fund Class R3	MMXNX	NAS CM	Open End	Target Date 2021-2045 (Growth & Income)	C+	C+	B-	Down	Y	0
MassMutual RetireSMART 2035 Fund Class R4	MMXZX	NAS CM	Open End	Target Date 2021-2045 (Growth & Income)	B-	C+	B-	Down	Y	0
MassMutual RetireSMART 2035 Fund Class R5	MMXTX	NAS CM	Open End	Target Date 2021-2045 (Growth & Income)	B-	C+	B-	Down	Y	0
MassMutual RetireSMART 2035 Fund Service Class	MMXSX	NAS CM	Open End	Target Date 2021-2045 (Growth & Income)	B-	C+	B-	Down	Y	0
MassMutual RetireSMART 2040 Fund Administrative Class	MRFYX	NAS CM	Open End	Target Date 2021-2045 (Growth & Income)	B-	C+	B-	Down	Y	0
MassMutual RetireSMART 2040 Fund Class A	MRFAX	NAS CM	Open End	Target Date 2021-2045 (Growth & Income)	C+	C+	B-	Down	Y	0
MassMutual RetireSMART 2040 Fund Class I	MRFUX	NAS CM	Open End	Target Date 2021-2045 (Growth & Income)	B-	B-	B-	Down	Y	0
MassMutual RetireSMART 2040 Fund Class R3	MFRNX	NAS CM	Open End	Target Date 2021-2045 (Growth & Income)	B-	C+	B-	Down	Y	0
MassMutual RetireSMART 2040 Fund Class R4	MRFZX	NAS CM	Open End	Target Date 2021-2045 (Growth & Income)	B-	C+	B-	Down	Y	0
MassMutual RetireSMART 2040 Fund Class R5	MRFTX	NAS CM	Open End	Target Date 2021-2045 (Growth & Income)	B-	B-	B-	Down	Y	0
MassMutual RetireSMART 2040 Fund Service Class	MFRSX	NAS CM	Open End	Target Date 2021-2045 (Growth & Income)	B-	C+	B-	Down	Y	0
MassMutual RetireSMART 2045 Fund Administrative Class	MMKYX	NAS CM	Open End	Target Date 2021-2045 (Growth & Income)	B-	B-	B-	Down	Y	0
MassMutual RetireSMART 2045 Fund Class A	MMKAX	NAS CM	Open End	Target Date 2021-2045 (Growth & Income)	B-	C+	B-	Down	Y	0
MassMutual RetireSMART 2045 Fund Class I	MMKUX	NAS CM	Open End	Target Date 2021-2045 (Growth & Income)	B-	B-	B-	Down	Y	0
MassMutual RetireSMART 2045 Fund Class R3	MMKNX	NAS CM	Open End	Target Date 2021-2045 (Growth & Income)	B-	C+	B-	Up	Y	0
MassMutual RetireSMART 2045 Fund Class R4	MMKZX	NAS CM	Open End	Target Date 2021-2045 (Growth & Income)	B-	C+	B-	Down	Y	0
MassMutual RetireSMART 2045 Fund Class R5	MMKTX	NAS CM	Open End	Target Date 2021-2045 (Growth & Income)	B-	B-	B-	Down	Y	0
MassMutual RetireSMART 2045 Fund Service Class	MMKSX	NAS CM	Open End	Target Date 2021-2045 (Growth & Income)	B-	B-	B-	Down	Y	0
MassMutual RetireSMART 2050 Fund Administrative Class	MMRYX	NAS CM	Open End	Target Date 2046+ (Growth & Income)	B-	B-	B-	Down	Y	0
MassMutual RetireSMART 2050 Fund Class A	MMARX	NAS CM	Open End	Target Date 2046+ (Growth & Income)	B-	B-	B-	Up	Y	0
MassMutual RetireSMART 2050 Fund Class I	MMRUX	NAS CM	Open End	Target Date 2046+ (Growth & Income)	B-	B-	B-	Down	Y	0
MassMutual RetireSMART 2050 Fund Class R3	MMRNX	NAS CM	Open End	Target Date 2046+ (Growth & Income)	C+	B-	C+	Down	Y	0
MassMutual RetireSMART 2050 Fund Class R4	MMRZX	NAS CM	Open End	Target Date 2046+ (Growth & Income)	B-	B-	B-	Down	Y	0
MassMutual RetireSMART 2050 Fund Class R5	MMRTX	NAS CM	Open End	Target Date 2046+ (Growth & Income)	B-	B-	B-	Down	Y	0
MassMutual RetireSMART 2050 Fund Service Class	MMTSX	NAS CM	Open End	Target Date 2046+ (Growth & Income)	B-	B-	B-	Down	Y	0
MassMutual RetireSMART 2055 Fund Administrative Class	MMWYX	NAS CM	Open End	Target Date 2046+ (Growth & Income)	B-	B-	C+	Down	Y	0
MassMutual RetireSMART 2055 Fund Class A	MMWAX	NAS CM	Open End	Target Date 2046+ (Growth & Income)	C+	B-	C+	Down	Y	0
MassMutual RetireSMART 2055 Fund Class I	MMWZX	NAS CM	Open End	Target Date 2046+ (Growth & Income)	B-	B-	C+	Down	Y	0
MassMutual RetireSMART 2055 Fund Class R3	MMWTX	NAS CM	Open End	Target Date 2046+ (Growth & Income)	C+	B-	C+	Down	Y	0
MassMutual RetireSMART 2055 Fund Class R4	MMWEX	NAS CM	Open End	Target Date 2046+ (Growth & Income)	B-	B-	C+	Down	Y	0
MassMutual RetireSMART 2055 Fund Class R5	MMWUX	NAS CM	Open End	Target Date 2046+ (Growth & Income)	B-	B-	C+	Down	Y	0
MassMutual RetireSMART 2055 Fund Service Class	MMWSX	NAS CM	Open End	Target Date 2046+ (Growth & Income)	B-	B-	C+	Down	Y	0
MassMutual RetireSMART 2060 Fund Administrative Class	MMWFX	NAS CM	Open End	Target Date 2046+ (Growth & Income)	C	C	B+	Up	Y	0
MassMutual RetireSMART 2060 Fund Class A	MMWDX	NAS CM	Open End	Target Date 2046+ (Growth & Income)	C	C	B+	Up	Y	0
MassMutual RetireSMART 2060 Fund Class I	MMWIX	NAS CM	Open End	Target Date 2046+ (Growth & Income)	C	C	B+	Up	Y	0
MassMutual RetireSMART 2060 Fund Class R3	MMWBX	NAS CM	Open End	Target Date 2046+ (Growth & Income)	C	C	B+	Up	Y	0
MassMutual RetireSMART 2060 Fund Class R4	MMWCX	NAS CM	Open End	Target Date 2046+ (Growth & Income)	C	C	B+	Up	Y	0
MassMutual RetireSMART 2060 Fund Class R5	MMWHX	NAS CM	Open End	Target Date 2046+ (Growth & Income)	C	C	B+	Up	Y	0
MassMutual RetireSMART 2060 Fund Service Class	MMWGX	NAS CM	Open End	Target Date 2046+ (Growth & Income)	C	C	B+	Up	Y	0
MassMutual RetireSMART Conservative Fund Admin Cls	MRCLX	NAS CM	Open End	Cautious Alloc (Asset Alloc)	B-	C	B+	Up	Y	0
MassMutual RetireSMART Conservative Fund Class A	MCTAX	NAS CM	Open End	Cautious Alloc (Asset Alloc)	B-	C	B+	Up	Y	0
MassMutual RetireSMART Conservative Fund Class I	MRCUX	NAS CM	Open End	Cautious Alloc (Asset Alloc)	B	C	A-	Up	Y	0
MassMutual RetireSMART Conservative Fund Class R3	MRCVX	NAS CM	Open End	Cautious Alloc (Asset Alloc)	B-	C	B+	Up	Y	0
MassMutual RetireSMART Conservative Fund Class R4	MRCZX	NAS CM	Open End	Cautious Alloc (Asset Alloc)	B-	C	B+	Up	Y	0
MassMutual RetireSMART Conservative Fund Class R5	MRCSX	NAS CM	Open End	Cautious Alloc (Asset Alloc)	B	C	A-	Up	Y	0
MassMutual RetireSMART Conservative Fund Service Class	MRCYX	NAS CM	Open End	Cautious Alloc (Asset Alloc)	B-	C	A-	Up	Y	0

★ Expanded analysis of this fund is included in Section II.

	TOTAL RETURNS					PERFORMANCE				ASSETS		ASSET ALLOCATION & TURNOVER					BULL & BEAR		FEES		
Min Additional Investment	3-Month Total Return	6-Month Total Return	1-Year Total Return	3-Year Total Return	5-Year Total Return	Dividend Yield (TTM)	Expense Ratio	3-Yr Std Deviation	3-Year Beta	NAV	Total Assets (MIL)	%Cash	%Stocks	%Bonds	%Other	Turnover Ratio	Last Bull Market Total Return	Last Bear Market Total Return	Front End Fee (%)	Back End Fee (%)	Inception Date
	4.00	8.18	17.25	21.04	54.76	1.54	1.04	8.36	1.16	13.23	551.4	2	72	23	2	35	20.31	-18.33			Apr-14
	4.06	8.36	17.63	22.39	57.34	1.8	0.69	8.34	1.16	13.37	551.4	2	72	23	2	35	20.48	-18.25			Apr-14
	4.07	8.29	17.52	21.96	56.84	1.68	0.79	8.32	1.16	13.41	551.4	2	72	23	2	35	20.48	-18.25			Dec-03
	4.41	8.82	18.46	22.66	58.90	1.44	0.91	8.76	1.12	13.71	211.9	2	79	16	2	41	20.94	-18.77			Apr-10
	4.39	8.76	18.20	21.81	56.72	1.24	1.16	8.76	1.12	13.62	211.9	2	79	16	2	41	20.74	-18.89	5.75		Apr-10
	4.43	9.02	18.94	23.89	60.66	1.68	0.61	8.74	1.12	13.61	211.9	2	79	16	2	41	20.94	-18.77			Apr-14
	4.30	8.61	17.99	21.28	55.45	1.18	1.31	8.78	1.12	13.53	211.9	2	79	16	2	41	20.59	-18.94			Apr-14
	4.34	8.80	18.37	22.16	57.55	1.36	1.06	8.75	1.12	13.55	211.9	2	79	16	2	41	20.76	-18.86			Apr-14
	4.38	8.97	18.71	23.37	59.98	1.57	0.71	8.76	1.12	13.6	211.9	2	79	16	2	41	20.94	-18.77			Apr-14
	4.41	8.88	18.60	23.03	59.65	1.49	0.81	8.77	1.12	13.75	211.9	2	79	16	2	41	21	-18.84			Apr-10
	4.58	9.13	19.02	23.16	59.89	1.4	0.9	8.88	1.08	13.23	333.5	2	82	14	2	37	21.26	-19.02			Dec-03
	4.48	8.98	18.72	22.26	57.68	1.22	1.15	8.9	1.08	13.15	333.5	2	82	14	2	37	20.94	-19.06	5.75		Dec-03
	4.60	9.30	19.29	24.18	61.63	1.66	0.6	8.95	1.08	13.23	333.5	2	82	14	2	37	21.21	-18.95			Apr-14
	4.45	8.96	18.51	21.69	56.17	1.2	1.3	8.91	1.08	12.87	333.5	2	82	14	2	37	20.71	-19.16			Dec-03
	4.46	8.99	18.80	22.50	58.58	1.35	1.05	8.92	1.08	13.04	333.5	2	82	14	2	37	21.03	-19.04			Apr-14
	4.59	9.21	19.19	23.97	61.21	1.59	0.7	8.92	1.08	13.23	333.5	2	82	14	2	37	21.21	-18.95			Apr-14
	4.61	9.23	19.11	23.56	60.71	1.48	0.8	8.92	1.08	13.26	333.5	2	82	14	2	37	21.21	-18.95			Dec-03
	4.63	9.21	19.31	23.45	63.66	1.34	0.88	9.25	1.08	13.76	127.4	2	83	13	2	39	22.62	-20.35			Apr-10
	4.48	9.10	18.99	22.53	61.30	1.15	1.13	9.22	1.07	13.66	127.4	2	83	13	2	39	22.33	-20.47	5.75		Apr-10
	4.67	9.40	19.68	24.59	65.42	1.56	0.58	9.26	1.08	13.79	127.4	2	83	13	2	39	22.62	-20.35			Apr-14
	4.46	9.03	18.77	21.93	60.23	1.09	1.28	9.22	1.07	13.57	127.4	2	83	13	2	39	22.26	-20.52			Apr-14
	4.55	9.11	19.13	22.88	62.19	1.25	1.03	9.25	1.08	13.59	127.4	2	83	13	2	39	22.44	-20.44			Apr-14
	4.69	9.41	19.59	24.32	64.94	1.39	0.68	9.22	1.07	13.81	127.4	2	83	13	2	39	22.62	-20.35			Apr-14
	4.64	9.29	19.46	23.80	64.34	1.39	0.78	9.26	1.08	13.79	127.4	2	83	13	2	39	22.55	-20.27			Apr-10
	4.97	9.81	20.55	24.62	65.16	1.26	0.89	9.74	1.09	9.72	176.6	2	89	7	2	43	22.35	-20.12			Dec-07
	4.78	9.65	20.18	23.57	62.82	1.09	1.14	9.62	1.07	9.66	176.6	2	89	7	2	43	22	-20.18	5.75		Dec-07
	5.04	10.00	20.88	25.68	67.04	1.49	0.59	9.68	1.08	9.72	176.6	2	89	7	2	43	22.24	-20.01			Apr-14
	4.89	9.70	20.07	23.11	61.40	1.04	1.29	9.7	1.08	9.56	176.6	2	89	7	2	43	21.82	-20.35			Dec-07
	4.86	9.75	20.32	23.99	63.88	1.17	1.04	9.65	1.08	9.62	176.6	2	89	7	2	43	22.06	-20.09			Apr-14
	4.96	9.91	20.66	25.38	66.44	1.42	0.69	9.62	1.07	9.71	176.6	2	89	7	2	43	22.24	-20.01			Apr-14
	4.95	9.90	20.65	24.94	65.83	1.33	0.79	9.65	1.08	9.72	176.6	2	89	7	2	43	22.24	-20.01			Dec-07
	4.88	9.77	20.59	24.81		1.25	0.87	9.67	1.06	11.47	43.8	2	89	7	2	47					Sep-13
	4.84	9.74	20.34	23.86		1.04	1.12	9.64	1.05	11.47	43.8	2	89	7	2	47			5.75		Sep-13
	4.94	10.02	20.96	25.87		1.41	0.57	9.64	1.05	11.49	43.8	2	89	7	2	47					Apr-14
	4.80	9.64	20.06	23.29		1.01	1.27	9.66	1.06	11.4	43.8	2	89	7	2	47					Apr-14
	4.82	9.73	20.35	24.24		1.16	1.02	9.67	1.06	11.43	43.8	2	89	7	2	47					Apr-14
	4.91	9.89	20.80	25.48		1.27	0.67	9.65	1.05	11.5	43.8	2	89	7	2	47					Apr-14
	4.94	9.91	20.70	25.19		1.28	0.77	9.6	1.05	11.52	43.8	2	89	7	2	47					Sep-13
	4.90	9.83	20.49			1.4	0.87			11.35	13.2	2	89	7	2	29					Nov-15
	4.76	9.68	20.10			1.12	1.12			11.35	13.2	2	89	7	2	29			5.75		Nov-15
	4.95	9.96	20.73			1.53	0.57			11.37	13.2	2	89	7	2	29					Nov-15
	4.75	9.59	19.90			1.15	1.27			11.32	13.2	2	89	7	2	29					Nov-15
	4.87	9.80	20.21			1.18	1.02			11.36	13.2	2	89	7	2	29					Nov-15
	4.95	9.87	20.63			1.45	0.67			11.37	13.2	2	89	7	2	29					Nov-15
	4.89	9.81	20.57			1.4	0.77			11.36	13.2	2	89	7	2	29					Nov-15
	1.67	3.74	8.50	11.33	23.57	1.99	0.77	3.73	0.39	9.93	219.0	4	28	64	3	39	9.25				Jun-11
	1.68	3.64	8.26	10.43	22.01	1.31	1.02	3.72	0.38	9.99	219.0	4	28	64	3	39	9.23		5.75		Jun-11
	1.78	3.96	8.83	12.27	25.17	2.29	0.47	3.71	0.4	9.93	219.0	4	28	64	3	39	9.33				Apr-14
	1.58	3.57	8.01	9.96	21.15	1.8	1.17	3.76	0.4	9.84	219.0	4	28	64	3	39	9.01				Apr-14
	1.68	3.77	8.33	10.89	22.81	2.06	0.92	3.7	0.4	9.86	219.0	4	28	64	3	39	9.17				Apr-14
	1.79	3.86	8.74	12.01	24.74	2.2	0.57	3.7	0.41	9.92	219.0	4	28	64	3	39	9.33				Jun-11
	1.68	3.75	8.50	11.60	24.10	2.06	0.67	3.67	0.39	9.92	219.0	4	28	64	3	39	9.34				Jun-11

Fund Name	Ticker Symbol	Traded On	Fund Type	Category and (Prospectus Objective)	Overall Rating	Reward Rating	Risk Rating	Recent Up/ Downgrade	Open to New Investors	Min Initial Investment
	MARKET			FUND TYPE, CATEGORY & OBJECTIVE	RATINGS				MINIMUMS	
MassMutual RetireSMART Growth Fund Administrative Class	MRGLX	NAS CM	Open End	Aggressive Alloc (Asset Alloc)	B-	B-	C+	Up	Y	0
MassMutual RetireSMART Growth Fund Class A	MRRAX	NAS CM	Open End	Aggressive Alloc (Asset Alloc)	C+	B-	C+	Down	Y	0
MassMutual RetireSMART Growth Fund Class I	MRGUX	NAS CM	Open End	Aggressive Alloc (Asset Alloc)	B-	B-	B-	Down	Y	0
MassMutual RetireSMART Growth Fund Class R3	MRGVX	NAS CM	Open End	Aggressive Alloc (Asset Alloc)	C+	B-	C+	Down	Y	0
MassMutual RetireSMART Growth Fund Class R4	MRGZX	NAS CM	Open End	Aggressive Alloc (Asset Alloc)	C+	B-	C+	Down	Y	0
MassMutual RetireSMART Growth Fund Class R5	MRRSX	NAS CM	Open End	Aggressive Alloc (Asset Alloc)	B-	B-	B-	Down	Y	0
MassMutual RetireSMART Growth Fund Service Class	MRGYX	NAS CM	Open End	Aggressive Alloc (Asset Alloc)	B-	B-	C+	Down	Y	0
MassMutual RetireSMART In Retmnt Fund Admin Cls	MDRYX	NAS CM	Open End	Target Date 2000-2020 (Growth & Income)	B-	C	B+	Up	Y	0
MassMutual RetireSMART In Retirement Fund Class A	MRDAX	NAS CM	Open End	Target Date 2000-2020 (Growth & Income)	B-	C	B+	Up	Y	0
MassMutual RetireSMART In Retirement Fund Class I	MDRVX	NAS CM	Open End	Target Date 2000-2020 (Growth & Income)	B-	C+	B	Up	Y	0
MassMutual RetireSMART In Retirement Fund Class R3	MDRNX	NAS CM	Open End	Target Date 2000-2020 (Growth & Income)	B-	C	B+	Up	Y	0
MassMutual RetireSMART In Retirement Fund Class R4	MDRZX	NAS CM	Open End	Target Date 2000-2020 (Growth & Income)	B-	C	B+	Up	Y	0
MassMutual RetireSMART In Retirement Fund Class R5	MDRTX	NAS CM	Open End	Target Date 2000-2020 (Growth & Income)	B-	C+	B+	Up	Y	0
MassMutual RetireSMART In Retirement Fund Service Class	MDRSX	NAS CM	Open End	Target Date 2000-2020 (Growth & Income)	B-	C+	B+	Up	Y	0
MassMutual RetireSMART Moderate Fund Administrative Class	MRMLX	NAS CM	Open End	Moderate Alloc (Asset Alloc)	B-	C+	B	Up	Y	0
MassMutual RetireSMART Moderate Fund Class A	MRMAX	NAS CM	Open End	Moderate Alloc (Asset Alloc)	B-	C+	B	Up	Y	0
MassMutual RetireSMART Moderate Fund Class I	MRMUX	NAS CM	Open End	Moderate Alloc (Asset Alloc)	B-	C+	B	Up	Y	0
MassMutual RetireSMART Moderate Fund Class R3	MRMTX	NAS CM	Open End	Moderate Alloc (Asset Alloc)	B-	C+	B	Up	Y	0
MassMutual RetireSMART Moderate Fund Class R4	MRMZX	NAS CM	Open End	Moderate Alloc (Asset Alloc)	B-	C+	B	Up	Y	0
MassMutual RetireSMART Moderate Fund Class R5	MROSX	NAS CM	Open End	Moderate Alloc (Asset Alloc)	B-	C+	B	Up	Y	0
MassMutual RetireSMART Moderate Fund Service Class	MRMYX	NAS CM	Open End	Moderate Alloc (Asset Alloc)	B-	C+	B	Up	Y	0
MassMutual RetireSMART Moderate Growth Fund Admin Cls	MRSLX	NAS CM	Open End	Aggressive Alloc (Asset Alloc)	B-	C+	B-	Down	Y	0
MassMutual RetireSMART Moderate Growth Fund Class A	MOGAX	NAS CM	Open End	Aggressive Alloc (Asset Alloc)	B-	C+	B-	Down	Y	0
MassMutual RetireSMART Moderate Growth Fund Class I	MROUX	NAS CM	Open End	Aggressive Alloc (Asset Alloc)	B-	C+	B-	Down	Y	0
MassMutual RetireSMART Moderate Growth Fund Class R3	MROTX	NAS CM	Open End	Aggressive Alloc (Asset Alloc)	B-	C+	B-	Down	Y	0
MassMutual RetireSMART Moderate Growth Fund Class R4	MROZX	NAS CM	Open End	Aggressive Alloc (Asset Alloc)	B-	C+	B-	Down	Y	0
MassMutual RetireSMART Moderate Growth Fund Class R5	MRSSX	NAS CM	Open End	Aggressive Alloc (Asset Alloc)	B-	C+	B-	Down	Y	0
MassMutual RetireSMART Moderate Growth Fund Service Class	MROYX	NAS CM	Open End	Aggressive Alloc (Asset Alloc)	B-	C+	B-	Down	Y	0
MassMutual Select BlackRock Global Alloc Fund Admin Cls	MGSLX	NAS CM	Open End	Alloc (Growth & Income)	B-	C+	B+	Down	Y	0
MassMutual Select BlackRock Global Allocation Fund Class A	MGJAX	NAS CM	Open End	Alloc (Growth & Income)	B-	C+	B+	Down	Y	0
MassMutual Select BlackRock Global Allocation Fund Class I	MGJIX	NAS CM	Open End	Alloc (Growth & Income)	B	C+	B+	Up	Y	0
MassMutual Select BlackRock Global Allocation Fund Cls R3	MGJRX	NAS CM	Open End	Alloc (Growth & Income)	C+	C+	B	Down	Y	0
MassMutual Select BlackRock Global Allocation Fund Cls R4	MGJFX	NAS CM	Open End	Alloc (Growth & Income)	B-	C+	B	Down	Y	0
MassMutual Select BlackRock Global Allocation Fund Cls R5	MGSSX	NAS CM	Open End	Alloc (Growth & Income)	B-	C+	B	Down	Y	0
MassMutual Select BlackRock Global Alloc Fund Serv Cls	MGSYX	NAS CM	Open End	Alloc (Growth & Income)	B-	C+	B	Down	Y	0
MassMutual Select Blue Chip Growth Fund Administrative Cls	MBCLX	NAS CM	Open End	US Equity Large Cap Growth (Growth)	A-	A-	A-	Up	Y	0
MassMutual Select Blue Chip Growth Fund Class A	MBCGX	NAS CM	Open End	US Equity Large Cap Growth (Growth)	A-	A-	A-	Up	Y	0
MassMutual Select Blue Chip Growth Fund Class I	MBCZX	NAS CM	Open End	US Equity Large Cap Growth (Growth)	A-	A	A-	Up	Y	0
MassMutual Select Blue Chip Growth Fund Class R3	MBCNX	NAS CM	Open End	US Equity Large Cap Growth (Growth)	A-	A-	A-	Up	Y	0
MassMutual Select Blue Chip Growth Fund Class R4	MBGFX	NAS CM	Open End	US Equity Large Cap Growth (Growth)	A-	A-	A-	Up	Y	0
MassMutual Select Blue Chip Growth Fund Class R5	MBCSX	NAS CM	Open End	US Equity Large Cap Growth (Growth)	A-	A	A-	Up	Y	0
MassMutual Select Blue Chip Growth Fund Service Class	MBCYX	NAS CM	Open End	US Equity Large Cap Growth (Growth)	A-	A	A-	Up	Y	0
MassMutual Select Diversified Value Fund Admin Cls	MDDLX	NAS CM	Open End	US Equity Large Cap Value (Growth & Income)	B	B-	B	Up	Y	0
MassMutual Select Diversified Value Fund Class A	MDDAX	NAS CM	Open End	US Equity Large Cap Value (Growth & Income)	B	B-	B	Up	Y	0
MassMutual Select Diversified Value Fund Class I	MDDIX	NAS CM	Open End	US Equity Large Cap Value (Growth & Income)	B	B	B	Up	Y	0
MassMutual Select Diversified Value Fund Class R3	MDVNX	NAS CM	Open End	US Equity Large Cap Value (Growth & Income)	B	B-	B	Up	Y	0
MassMutual Select Diversified Value Fund Class R4	MDDRX	NAS CM	Open End	US Equity Large Cap Value (Growth & Income)	B	B-	B	Up	Y	0
MassMutual Select Diversified Value Fund Class R5	MDVSX	NAS CM	Open End	US Equity Large Cap Value (Growth & Income)	B	B-	B	Up	Y	0
MassMutual Select Diversified Value Fund Service Class	MDVYX	NAS CM	Open End	US Equity Large Cap Value (Growth & Income)	B	B-	B	Up	Y	0
MassMutual Select Equity Opp Fund Admin Cls	MMFVX	NAS CM	Open End	US Equity Large Cap Blend (Growth)	B-	B	C	Down	Y	0
MassMutual Select Equity Opportunities Fund Class A	MFVAX	NAS CM	Open End	US Equity Large Cap Blend (Growth)	B-	B	C	Down	Y	0
MassMutual Select Equity Opportunities Fund Class I	MFVZX	NAS CM	Open End	US Equity Large Cap Blend (Growth)	B-	B	C	Down	Y	0

★ Expanded analysis of this fund is included in Section II.

Min Additional Investment	3-Month Total Return	6-Month Total Return	1-Year Total Return	3-Year Total Return	5-Year Total Return	Dividend Yield (TTM)	Expense Ratio	3-Yr Std Deviation	3-Year Beta	NAV	Total Assets (MIL)	%Cash	%Stocks	%Bonds	%Other	Turnover Ratio	Last Bull Market Total Return	Last Bear Market Total Return	Front End Fee (%)	Back End Fee (%)	Inception Date
	TOTAL RETURNS					PERFORMANCE				ASSETS		ASSET ALLOCATION & TURNOVER					BULL & BEAR		FEES		
	4.92	9.94	20.83	24.66	65.91	1.23	0.94	9.81	0.94	11.68	118.7	2	90	5	2	39	22.8				Jun-11
	4.91	9.84	20.51	23.81	63.88	1	1.19	9.85	0.94	11.68	118.7	2	90	5	2	39	22.52		5.75		Jun-11
	5.04	10.16	21.21	25.89	67.97	1.5	0.64	9.81	0.93	11.66	118.7	2	90	5	2	39	22.86				Apr-14
	4.90	9.79	20.33	23.28	62.72	1.08	1.34	9.79	0.93	11.56	118.7	2	90	5	2	39	22.5				Apr-14
	4.87	9.84	20.59	24.12	64.67	1.3	1.09	9.82	0.94	11.57	118.7	2	90	5	2	39	22.68				Apr-14
	5.03	10.05	20.96	25.50	67.40	1.41	0.74	9.87	0.94	11.67	118.7	2	90	5	2	39	22.74				Jun-11
	5.00	10.02	20.91	25.10	66.78	1.33	0.84	9.83	0.94	11.69	118.7	2	90	5	2	39	22.86				Jun-11
	1.99	4.25	9.07	11.84	24.82	2.04	0.85	4.12	1.22	11.6	83.7	3	33	61	3	47	10.05	-6.34			Dec-03
	1.87	4.04	8.79	11.01	23.00	1.84	1.1	4.12	1.23	11.52	83.7	3	33	61	3	47	9.92	-6.49	5.75		Dec-03
	1.97	4.32	9.36	12.74	26.15	2.34	0.55	4.15	1.24	11.55	83.7	3	33	61	3	47	10.18	-6.34			Apr-14
	1.82	4.03	8.65	10.56	22.02	1.83	1.25	4.09	1.22	11.36	83.7	3	33	61	3	47	9.7	-6.59			Dec-03
	1.94	4.14	9.03	11.45	23.74	1.99	1	4.07	1.21	11.44	83.7	3	33	61	3	47	10.02	-6.44			Apr-14
	1.96	4.31	9.24	12.49	25.64	2.25	0.65	4.16	1.24	11.57	83.7	3	33	61	3	47	10.18	-6.34			Apr-14
	2.02	4.28	9.30	12.18	25.35	2.14	0.75	4.13	1.23	11.6	83.7	3	33	61	3	47	10.18	-6.34			Dec-03
	3.16	6.46	13.62	17.17	41.12	1.78	0.84	6.18	0.57	10.32	307.5	3	55	39	3	30	15.1				Jun-11
	3.07	6.36	13.37	16.32	39.44	1.5	1.09	6.19	0.57	10.36	307.5	3	55	39	3	30	14.96		5.75		Jun-11
	3.19	6.61	13.91	18.24	42.84	2.07	0.54	6.22	0.57	10.28	307.5	3	55	39	3	30	15.18				Apr-14
	3.05	6.27	13.22	15.95	38.41	1.57	1.24	6.16	0.57	10.26	307.5	3	55	39	3	30	14.84				Apr-14
	3.18	6.40	13.47	16.74	40.08	1.84	0.99	6.19	0.57	10.27	307.5	3	55	39	3	30	15.01				Apr-14
	3.20	6.61	13.91	18.05	42.49	1.99	0.64	6.16	0.57	10.29	307.5	3	55	39	3	30	15.18				Jun-11
	3.17	6.57	13.72	17.55	41.84	1.75	0.74	6.17	0.57	10.34	307.5	3	55	39	3	30	15.31				Jun-11
	4.35	8.89	18.40	22.66	57.53	1.58	0.89	8.62	0.82	10.78	263.2	2	79	16	2	33	20.13				Jun-11
	4.36	8.79	18.14	21.78	55.64	1.33	1.14	8.6	0.81	10.82	263.2	2	79	16	2	33	19.98		5.75		Jun-11
	4.49	9.04	18.71	23.67	59.22	1.87	0.59	8.57	0.81	10.74	263.2	2	79	16	2	33	20.21				Apr-14
	4.30	8.78	17.99	21.31	54.47	1.44	1.29	8.57	0.81	10.7	263.2	2	79	16	2	33	19.86				Apr-14
	4.38	8.84	18.28	22.21	56.42	1.65	1.04	8.65	0.82	10.72	263.2	2	79	16	2	33	20.03				Apr-14
	4.48	9.04	18.70	23.48	58.83	1.8	0.69	8.62	0.82	10.75	263.2	2	79	16	2	33	20.21				Jun-11
	4.45	8.99	18.62	23.12	58.29	1.53	0.79	8.6	0.82	10.79	263.2	2	79	16	2	33	20.11				Jun-11
	2.40	5.43	13.46	15.83	36.45	0.51	1.09	6.34	0.59	11.52	610.3	7	53	32	6	153	11.26	-13.63			Dec-09
	2.36	5.31	13.08	14.96	34.70	0.32	1.34	6.33	0.58	11.14	610.3	7	53	32	6	153	11.22	-14.11	5.75		Dec-09
	2.51	5.63	13.82	16.90	38.50	0.85	0.79	6.3	0.58	11.17	610.3	7	53	32	6	153	11.68	-13.96			Apr-14
	2.34	5.23	12.97	14.51	34.08	0.41	1.49	6.33	0.58	11	610.3	7	53	32	6	153	11.36	-14.14			Apr-14
	2.37	5.34	13.17	15.28	35.68	0.52	1.24	6.31	0.58	11.03	610.3	7	53	32	6	153	11.52	-14.05			Apr-14
	2.47	5.55	13.62	16.42	37.65	0.74	0.89	6.35	0.59	11.32	610.3	7	53	32	6	153	11.68	-13.96			Dec-09
	2.40	5.52	13.50	16.17	37.05	0.64	0.99	6.37	0.59	11.16	610.3	7	53	32	6	153	11.5	-13.97			Dec-09
	6.65	13.66	34.69	51.03	138.54	0.24	0.96	12.02	1.07	19.74	2,372	0	99	0	1	27	30.72	-14.79			May-01
	6.55	13.47	34.31	49.93	135.85	0.05	1.21	12.02	1.07	18.94	2,372	0	99	0	1	27	30.53	-14.91	5.75		Jun-01
	6.74	13.81	35.08	52.40	142.09	0.46	0.66	12.06	1.07	20.2	2,372	0	99	0	1	27	30.85	-14.75			Apr-14
	6.53	13.44	34.11	49.32	133.62	0.15	1.36	12.03	1.07	17.74	2,372	0	99	0	1	27	30.31	-15.03			Dec-02
	6.60	13.54	34.42	50.39	137.44	0.23	1.11	12.04	1.07	18.89	2,372	0	99	0	1	27	30.66	-14.84			Apr-14
	6.70	13.79	35.00	52.00	141.19	0.37	0.76	12.03	1.07	20.18	2,372	0	99	0	1	27	30.85	-14.75			May-01
	6.67	13.70	34.85	51.52	140.04	0.29	0.86	12.05	1.07	20	2,372	0	99	0	1	27	30.87	-14.8			May-01
	7.24	11.15	18.71	28.16	96.77	1.69	0.87	11.46	1.09	12.88	247.3	1	99	0	0	71	25.24	-18.87			Oct-04
	7.19	11.07	18.44	27.28	94.36	1.45	1.12	11.45	1.09	12.78	247.3	1	99	0	0	71	24.93	-18.93	5.75		Oct-04
	7.36	11.37	19.06	29.35	99.62	1.92	0.57	11.45	1.09	12.76	247.3	1	99	0	0	71	25.21	-18.75			Apr-14
	7.23	10.98	18.29	26.71	92.54	1.45	1.27	11.43	1.09	12.73	247.3	1	99	0	0	71	24.75	-19.05			Oct-04
	7.24	11.13	18.55	27.65	95.73	1.69	1.02	11.43	1.09	12.65	247.3	1	99	0	0	71	25.02	-18.83			Apr-14
	7.31	11.31	18.99	28.96	98.82	1.75	0.67	11.46	1.09	12.79	247.3	1	99	0	0	71	25.21	-18.75			Oct-04
	7.33	11.26	18.86	28.56	97.79	1.73	0.77	11.47	1.09	12.79	247.3	1	99	0	0	71	25.23	-18.77			Oct-04
	6.36	10.23	21.29	28.72	104.45	0.88	1.03	15	1.37	16.37	707.2	2	98	0	0	131	33.26	-20.79			Apr-00
	6.28	10.08	20.97	27.74	101.84	0.64	1.28	14.97	1.37	15.61	707.2	2	98	0	0	131	33.09	-20.88	5.75		May-00
	6.44	10.43	21.67	29.92	107.73	1.12	0.73	14.98	1.37	16.86	707.2	2	98	0	0	131	33.58	-20.65			Nov-10

	MARKET		FUND TYPE, CATEGORY & OBJECTIVE		RATINGS					MINIMUMS
Fund Name	Ticker Symbol	Traded On	Fund Type	Category and (Prospectus Objective)	Overall Rating	Reward Rating	Risk Rating	Recent Up/ Downgrade	Open to New Investors	Min Initial Investment
MassMutual Select Equity Opportunities Fund Class R3	MFVNX	NAS CM	Open End	US Equity Large Cap Blend (Growth)	B-	B	C	Down	Y	0
MassMutual Select Equity Opportunities Fund Class R4	MFVFX	NAS CM	Open End	US Equity Large Cap Blend (Growth)	B-	B	C	Down	Y	0
MassMutual Select Equity Opportunities Fund Class R5	MFVSX	NAS CM	Open End	US Equity Large Cap Blend (Growth)	B-	B	C	Down	Y	0
MassMutual Select Equity Opportunities Fund Service Class	MMFYX	NAS CM	Open End	US Equity Large Cap Blend (Growth)	B-	B	C	Down	Y	0
MassMutual Select Fundamental Growth Fund Admin Cls	MOTLX	NAS CM	Open End	US Equity Large Cap Growth (Growth)	B+	B+	B+	Up	Y	0
MassMutual Select Fundamental Growth Fund Class A	MOTAX	NAS CM	Open End	US Equity Large Cap Growth (Growth)	B+	B+	B+	Up	Y	0
MassMutual Select Fundamental Growth Fund Class I	MOTZX	NAS CM	Open End	US Equity Large Cap Growth (Growth)	B+	B+	B+	Up	Y	0
MassMutual Select Fundamental Growth Fund Class R3	MOTNX	NAS CM	Open End	US Equity Large Cap Growth (Growth)	B+	B+	B+	Up	Y	0
MassMutual Select Fundamental Growth Fund Class R4	MFGFX	NAS CM	Open End	US Equity Large Cap Growth (Growth)	B+	B+	B+	Up	Y	0
MassMutual Select Fundamental Growth Fund Class R5	MOTCX	NAS CM	Open End	US Equity Large Cap Growth (Growth)	B+	B+	B+	Up	Y	0
MassMutual Select Fundamental Growth Fund Service Class	MOTYX	NAS CM	Open End	US Equity Large Cap Growth (Growth)	B+	B+	B+	Up	Y	0
MassMutual Select Fundamental Value Fund Admin Cls	MFULX	NAS CM	Open End	US Equity Large Cap Value (Growth & Income)	B-	B-	B	Down	Y	0
MassMutual Select Fundamental Value Fund Class A	MFUAX	NAS CM	Open End	US Equity Large Cap Value (Growth & Income)	B-	B-	B	Down	Y	0
MassMutual Select Fundamental Value Fund Class I	MFUZX	NAS CM	Open End	US Equity Large Cap Value (Growth & Income)	B	B-	B	Up	Y	0
MassMutual Select Fundamental Value Fund Class R3	MFUNX	NAS CM	Open End	US Equity Large Cap Value (Growth & Income)	B-	B-	B	Down	Y	0
MassMutual Select Fundamental Value Fund Class R4	MFUFX	NAS CM	Open End	US Equity Large Cap Value (Growth & Income)	B-	B-	B	Down	Y	0
MassMutual Select Fundamental Value Fund Class R5	MVUSX	NAS CM	Open End	US Equity Large Cap Value (Growth & Income)	B	B-	B	Up	Y	0
MassMutual Select Fundamental Value Fund Service Class	MFUYX	NAS CM	Open End	US Equity Large Cap Value (Growth & Income)	B	B-	B	Up	Y	0
MassMutual Select Growth Opp Fund Admin Cls	MAGLX	NAS CM	Open End	US Equity Large Cap Growth (Growth)	B	B	B+	Up	Y	0
MassMutual Select Growth Opportunities Fund Class A	MMAAX	NAS CM	Open End	US Equity Large Cap Growth (Growth)	B	B	B	Up	Y	0
MassMutual Select Growth Opportunities Fund Class I	MMAZX	NAS CM	Open End	US Equity Large Cap Growth (Growth)	B	B	B+	Up	Y	0
MassMutual Select Growth Opportunities Fund Class R3	MMANX	NAS CM	Open End	US Equity Large Cap Growth (Growth)	B	B	B	Up	Y	0
MassMutual Select Growth Opportunities Fund Class R4	MMGFX	NAS CM	Open End	US Equity Large Cap Growth (Growth)	B	B	B+	Up	Y	0
MassMutual Select Growth Opportunities Fund Class R5	MGRSX	NAS CM	Open End	US Equity Large Cap Growth (Growth)	B	B	B+	Up	Y	0
MassMutual Select Growth Opportunities Fund Service Class	MAGYX	NAS CM	Open End	US Equity Large Cap Growth (Growth)	B	B	B+	Up	Y	0
MassMutual Select Large Cap Value Fund Administrative Cls	MLVLX	NAS CM	Open End	US Equity Large Cap Value (Growth & Income)	B	B-	B	Up	Y	0
MassMutual Select Large Cap Value Fund Class A	MMLAX	NAS CM	Open End	US Equity Large Cap Value (Growth & Income)	B-	B-	B-	Down	Y	0
MassMutual Select Large Cap Value Fund Class I	MLVZX	NAS CM	Open End	US Equity Large Cap Value (Growth & Income)	B-	B	B-	Down	Y	0
MassMutual Select Large Cap Value Fund Class R3	MLVNX	NAS CM	Open End	US Equity Large Cap Value (Growth & Income)	B-	B-	B-	Down	Y	0
MassMutual Select Large Cap Value Fund Class R4	MLVFX	NAS CM	Open End	US Equity Large Cap Value (Growth & Income)	B-	B-	B-	Down	Y	0
MassMutual Select Large Cap Value Fund Class R5	MLVSX	NAS CM	Open End	US Equity Large Cap Value (Growth & Income)	B-	B-	B-	Down	Y	0
MassMutual Select Large Cap Value Fund Service Class	MMLYX	NAS CM	Open End	US Equity Large Cap Value (Growth & Income)	B	B-	B	Up	Y	0
MassMutual Select Mid Cap Growth Fund Administrative Class	MMELX	NAS CM	Open End	US Equity Mid Cap (Growth)	B	B	B		Y	0
MassMutual Select Mid Cap Growth Fund Class A	MEFAX	NAS CM	Open End	US Equity Mid Cap (Growth)	B	B	B		Y	0
MassMutual Select Mid Cap Growth Fund Class I	MEFZX	NAS CM	Open End	US Equity Mid Cap (Growth)	B	B	B	Down	Y	0
MassMutual Select Mid Cap Growth Fund Class R3	MEFNX	NAS CM	Open End	US Equity Mid Cap (Growth)	B	B	B		Y	0
MassMutual Select Mid Cap Growth Fund Class R4	MEFFX	NAS CM	Open End	US Equity Mid Cap (Growth)	B	B	B		Y	0
MassMutual Select Mid Cap Growth Fund Class R5	MGRFX	NAS CM	Open End	US Equity Mid Cap (Growth)	B	B	B	Down	Y	0
MassMutual Select Mid Cap Growth Fund Service Class	MEFYX	NAS CM	Open End	US Equity Mid Cap (Growth)	B	B	B	Down	Y	0
MassMutual Select Mid Cap Value Fund Administrative Class	MLULX	NAS CM	Open End	US Equity Mid Cap (Growth)	B	B-	B	Up	Y	0
MassMutual Select Mid Cap Value Fund Class A	MLUAX	NAS CM	Open End	US Equity Mid Cap (Growth)	B	B-	B	Up	Y	0
MassMutual Select Mid Cap Value Fund Class R3	MLUNX	NAS CM	Open End	US Equity Mid Cap (Growth)	B-	B-	B	Down	Y	0
MassMutual Select Mid Cap Value Fund Class R4	MLUFX	NAS CM	Open End	US Equity Mid Cap (Growth)	B	B-	B	Up	Y	0
MassMutual Select Mid Cap Value Fund Class R5	MLUSX	NAS CM	Open End	US Equity Mid Cap (Growth)	B	B	B	Up	Y	0
MassMutual Select Mid Cap Value Fund Service Class	MLUYX	NAS CM	Open End	US Equity Mid Cap (Growth)	B	B-	B	Up	Y	0
MassMutual Select Mid-Cap Value Fund Class I	MLUZX	NAS CM	Open End	US Equity Mid Cap (Growth)	B	B	B	Up	Y	0
MassMutual Select Overseas Fund Administrative Class	MOSLX	NAS CM	Open End	Global Equity Large Cap (Foreign Stock)	B-	B-	C	Up	Y	0
MassMutual Select Overseas Fund Class A	MOSAX	NAS CM	Open End	Global Equity Large Cap (Foreign Stock)	B-	B-	B-	Up	Y	0
MassMutual Select Overseas Fund Class I	MOSZX	NAS CM	Open End	Global Equity Large Cap (Foreign Stock)	B-	B	C	Up	Y	0
MassMutual Select Overseas Fund Class R3	MOSNX	NAS CM	Open End	Global Equity Large Cap (Foreign Stock)	C+	B-	C	Up	Y	0
MassMutual Select Overseas Fund Class R4	MOSFX	NAS CM	Open End	Global Equity Large Cap (Foreign Stock)	C+	B-	C	Up	Y	0
MassMutual Select Overseas Fund Class R5	MOSSX	NAS CM	Open End	Global Equity Large Cap (Foreign Stock)	B-	B	C	Up	Y	0

★Expanded analysis of this fund is included in Section II.

Min Additional Investment	3-Month Total Return	6-Month Total Return	1-Year Total Return	3-Year Total Return	5-Year Total Return	Dividend Yield (TTM)	Expense Ratio	3-Yr Std Deviation	3-Year Beta	NAV	Total Assets (MIL)	%Cash	%Stocks	%Bonds	%Other	Turnover Ratio	Last Bull Market Total Return	Last Bear Market Total Return	Front End Fee (%)	Back End Fee (%)	Inception Date
	TOTAL RETURNS					PERFORMANCE				ASSETS		ASSET ALLOCATION & TURNOVER					BULL & BEAR		FEES		
	6.20	9.98	20.74	27.10	99.95	0.76	1.43	14.99	1.37	14.51	707.2	2	98	0	0	131	32.93	-21.01			Dec-02
	6.30	10.13	21.12	28.14	103.29	0.97	1.18	15	1.37	15.38	707.2	2	98	0	0	131	33.29	-20.79			Apr-14
	6.41	10.33	21.53	29.47	106.67	1.03	0.83	14.97	1.37	16.93	707.2	2	98	0	0	131	33.49	-20.7			Apr-00
	6.38	10.26	21.39	29.09	105.60	0.97	0.93	15	1.38	16.6	707.2	2	98	0	0	131	33.45	-20.79			Apr-00
	5.96	12.05	27.18	38.29	108.08	0.64	1	10.5	0.96	7.97	149.5	2	98	0	0	52	23.93	-10.76			Apr-00
	5.84	11.90	26.97	37.24	105.20	0.42	1.25	10.57	0.96	7.62	149.5	2	98	0	0	52	23.85	-11.03	5.75		Apr-00
	5.86	12.11	27.46	39.36	110.64	0.86	0.7	10.56	0.96	8.31	149.5	2	98	0	0	52	24.24	-10.8			Apr-14
	5.78	11.77	26.69	36.64	103.42	0.59	1.4	10.59	0.97	7.11	149.5	2	98	0	0	52	23.62	-11.03			Dec-02
	5.93	11.91	27.12	37.61	106.66	0.76	1.15	10.5	0.96	7.54	149.5	2	98	0	0	52	24.05	-10.89			Apr-14
	5.88	12.11	27.42	39.01	109.93	0.77	0.8	10.54	0.96	8.34	149.5	2	98	0	0	52	24.24	-10.8			Apr-00
	5.78	12.00	27.28	38.59	108.87	0.71	0.9	10.53	0.96	8.16	149.5	2	98	0	0	52	24.02	-10.76			Apr-00
	5.50	8.58	14.91	24.66	86.44	1.42	0.93	11.32	1.08	11.7	1,266	1	99	0	0	13	26.62	-20.51			Dec-01
	5.47	8.50	14.72	23.83	84.30	1.16	1.18	11.26	1.08	11.56	1,266	1	99	0	0	13	26.48	-20.68	5.75		Dec-01
	5.64	8.82	15.30	25.82	89.62	1.69	0.63	11.25	1.08	11.61	1,266	1	99	0	0	13	26.98	-20.41			Nov-10
	5.43	8.41	14.52	23.22	82.54	1.17	1.33	11.22	1.07	11.37	1,266	1	99	0	0	13	26.31	-20.73			Dec-02
	5.46	8.52	14.81	24.19	85.53	1.56	1.08	11.25	1.08	11.39	1,266	1	99	0	0	13	26.53	-20.53			Apr-14
	5.58	8.75	15.20	25.51	88.42	1.6	0.73	11.26	1.08	11.67	1,266	1	99	0	0	13	26.71	-20.45			Dec-01
	5.54	8.63	15.10	25.07	87.45	1.5	0.83	11.3	1.08	11.62	1,266	1	99	0	0	13	26.78	-20.49			Dec-01
	3.45	11.30	31.34	26.19	97.57	0	1.04	13.15	1.1	10.06	797.1	1	99	0	0	19	31.49	-12.21			Apr-00
	3.38	11.09	30.88	25.25	95.11	0	1.29	13.18	1.1	9.34	797.1	1	99	0	0	19	31.38	-12.43	5.75		Apr-00
	3.48	11.38	31.74	27.40	100.75	0	0.74	13.2	1.1	10.86	797.1	1	99	0	0	19	31.64	-12.14			Dec-11
	3.32	11.01	30.75	24.66	93.24	0	1.44	13.2	1.1	8.61	797.1	1	99	0	0	19	30.99	-12.42			Dec-02
	3.37	11.15	31.01	25.63	96.63	0	1.19	13.2	1.1	9.39	797.1	1	99	0	0	19	31.45	-12.23			Apr-14
	3.42	11.30	31.44	26.87	99.52	0	0.84	13.19	1.1	10.74	797.1	1	99	0	0	19	31.65	-12.14			Apr-00
	3.42	11.20	31.32	26.55	98.66	0	0.94	13.13	1.1	10.44	797.1	1	99	0	0	19	31.57	-12.15			Apr-00
	6.49	10.76	19.90	28.64	80.62	1.94	0.93	10.53	0.98	8.08	195.1	4	96	0	0	22	23.18	-20.08			Apr-00
	6.36	10.63	19.61	27.66	78.30	1.72	1.18	10.6	0.99	8.07	195.1	4	96	0	0	22	23.13	-20.24	5.75		May-00
	6.53	11.07	20.24	29.81	83.22	2.21	0.63	10.58	0.98	8.08	195.1	4	96	0	0	22	23.36	-20.01			Apr-14
	6.26	10.63	19.34	27.15	76.88	1.56	1.33	10.55	0.98	7.88	195.1	4	96	0	0	22	22.87	-20.28			Dec-02
	6.45	10.76	19.68	28.13	79.67	2.09	1.08	10.54	0.98	7.99	195.1	4	96	0	0	22	23.18	-20.1			Apr-14
	6.54	10.93	20.23	29.45	82.44	2.11	0.73	10.55	0.98	8.1	195.1	4	96	0	0	22	23.36	-20.01			Apr-00
	6.50	10.87	20.11	29.15	81.80	1.85	0.83	10.62	0.99	8.15	195.1	4	96	0	0	22	23.39	-20.12			Apr-00
	4.34	8.69	24.26	37.99	116.19	0	1.03	10.76	0.96	19.93	5,628	4	94	0	3	36	25.46	-20.28			May-00
	4.28	8.60	24.02	37.04	113.64	0	1.28	10.75	0.95	18.5	5,628	4	94	0	3	36	25.29	-20.37	5.75		May-00
	4.41	8.88	24.66	39.28	119.70	0.13	0.73	10.75	0.96	21.47	5,628	4	94	0	3	36	25.76	-20.14			Nov-10
	4.25	8.52	23.87	36.43	111.68	0	1.43	10.74	0.95	17.15	5,628	4	94	0	3	36	25.01	-20.45			Dec-02
	4.31	8.67	24.18	37.50	115.29	0	1.18	10.74	0.95	18.6	5,628	4	94	0	3	36	25.47	-20.29			Apr-14
	4.40	8.86	24.56	38.92	118.58	0.05	0.83	10.72	0.95	21.29	5,628	4	94	0	3	36	25.65	-20.21			May-00
	4.35	8.80	24.46	38.46	117.56	0	0.93	10.76	0.96	20.81	5,628	4	94	0	3	36	25.51	-20.17			May-00
	5.66	9.34	11.90	27.42	86.27	1.14	1.1	11.77	1.09	14	93.1	3	97	0	0	88	27.16	-22.07			Aug-06
	5.58	9.25	11.60	26.45	84.00	0.84	1.35	11.75	1.09	13.79	93.1	3	97	0	0	88	27.01	-22.02	5.75		Aug-06
	5.56	9.11	11.48	25.90	82.33	0.75	1.5	11.75	1.09	13.63	93.1	3	97	0	0	88	26.76	-22.08			Aug-06
	5.57	9.19	11.63	26.76	85.11	1.02	1.25	11.75	1.09	13.67	93.1	3	97	0	0	88	27.08	-21.88			Apr-14
	5.73	9.46	12.11	28.21	88.20	1.22	0.9	11.8	1.09	13.82	93.1	3	97	0	0	88	27.27	-21.8			Aug-06
	5.65	9.46	12.05	27.79	87.40	1.09	1	11.74	1.09	13.78	93.1	3	97	0	0	88	27.2	-21.83			Aug-06
	5.67	9.49	12.17	28.53	89.23	1.3	0.8	11.75	1.09	13.71	93.1	3	97	0	0	88	27.52	-21.8			Dec-11
	3.25	9.01	26.76	25.92	45.73	1.56	1.22	12.26	0.98	9.8	645.3	1	98	0	1	29	16.52	-24.04			Apr-01
	3.27	8.92	26.44	24.95	44.15	1.37	1.47	12.26	0.98	9.61	645.3	1	98	0	1	29	16.52	-24.14	5.75		Apr-01
	3.37	9.29	27.20	27.11	48.22	1.8	0.92	12.32	0.98	9.74	645.3	1	98	0	1	29	16.75	-23.94			Nov-10
	3.14	8.83	26.16	24.24	42.52	1.34	1.62	12.31	0.98	9.53	645.3	1	98	0	1	29	16.29	-24.29			Dec-02
	3.23	8.97	26.66	25.32	44.46	1.52	1.37	12.29	0.98	9.44	645.3	1	98	0	1	29	16.35	-24.12			Apr-14
	3.26	9.15	26.97	26.57	47.04	1.71	1.02	12.31	0.98	9.77	645.3	1	98	0	1	29	16.58	-23.95			Apr-01

	MARKET		FUND TYPE, CATEGORY & OBJECTIVE		RATINGS				MINIMUMS	
Fund Name	Ticker Symbol	Traded On	Fund Type	Category and (Prospectus Objective)	Overall Rating	Reward Rating	Risk Rating	Recent Up/ Downgrade	Open to New Investors	Min Initial Investment
MassMutual Select Overseas Fund Service Class	MOSYX	NAS CM	Open End	Global Equity Large Cap (Foreign Stock)	B-	B-	C	Up	Y	0
MassMutual Select Small Cap Growth Equity Fund Admin Cls	MSGLX	NAS CM	Open End	US Equity Small Cap (Small Company)	B	B	B	Up	Y	0
MassMutual Select Small Cap Growth Equity Fund Class A	MMGEX	NAS CM	Open End	US Equity Small Cap (Small Company)	B	B	B-	Up	Y	0
MassMutual Select Small Cap Growth Equity Fund Class I	MSGZX	NAS CM	Open End	US Equity Small Cap (Small Company)	B	B+	B	Up	Y	0
MassMutual Select Small Cap Growth Equity Fund Class R3	MSGNX	NAS CM	Open End	US Equity Small Cap (Small Company)	B	B	B-	Up	Y	0
MassMutual Select Small Cap Growth Equity Fund Class R4	MSERX	NAS CM	Open End	US Equity Small Cap (Small Company)	B-	B	C	Up	Y	0
MassMutual Select Small Cap Growth Equity Fund Class R5	MSGSX	NAS CM	Open End	US Equity Small Cap (Small Company)	B	B+	B	Up	Y	0
MassMutual Select Small Cap Growth Equity Fund Service Cls	MSCYX	NAS CM	Open End	US Equity Small Cap (Small Company)	B	B	B	Up	Y	0
MassMutual Select Small Cap Val Equity Fund Class I	MMQIX	NAS CM	Open End	US Equity Small Cap (Small Company)	B+	A-	B	Up	Y	0
MassMutual Select Small Cap Val Equity Fund Class R3	MMQTX	NAS CM	Open End	US Equity Small Cap (Small Company)	B	B+	B	Up	Y	0
MassMutual Select Small Cap Val Equity Fund Class R4	MMQFX	NAS CM	Open End	US Equity Small Cap (Small Company)	B+	B+	B	Up	Y	0
MassMutual Select Small Cap Value Equity Fund Admin Cls	MMQLX	NAS CM	Open End	US Equity Small Cap (Small Company)	B+	A-	B	Up	Y	0
MassMutual Select Small Cap Value Equity Fund Class A	MMQAX	NAS CM	Open End	US Equity Small Cap (Small Company)	B	B+	B	Up	Y	0
MassMutual Select Small Cap Value Equity Fund Class R5	MMQSX	NAS CM	Open End	US Equity Small Cap (Small Company)	B+	A-	B	Up	Y	0
MassMutual Select Small Cap Value Equity Fund Service Cls	MMQYX	NAS CM	Open End	US Equity Small Cap (Small Company)	B+	A-	B	Up	Y	0
MassMutual Select Small Company Value Fund Admin Cls	MMYLX	NAS CM	Open End	US Equity Small Cap (Small Company)	B	B	B	Up	Y	0
MassMutual Select Small Company Value Fund Class A	MMYAX	NAS CM	Open End	US Equity Small Cap (Small Company)	B	B	B	Up	Y	0
MassMutual Select Small Company Value Fund Class I	MSVZX	NAS CM	Open End	US Equity Small Cap (Small Company)	B	B+	B	Up	Y	0
MassMutual Select Small Company Value Fund Class R3	MSVNX	NAS CM	Open End	US Equity Small Cap (Small Company)	B	B	B	Up	Y	0
MassMutual Select Small Company Value Fund Class R4	MMVFX	NAS CM	Open End	US Equity Small Cap (Small Company)	B	B	B	Up	Y	0
MassMutual Select Small Company Value Fund Class R5	MSVSX	NAS CM	Open End	US Equity Small Cap (Small Company)	B	B	B	Up	Y	0
MassMutual Select Small Company Value Fund Service Class	MMVYX	NAS CM	Open End	US Equity Small Cap (Small Company)	B	B	B	Up	Y	0
Matisse Discounted Closed-End Fund Strategy Class A Shares	MDCAX	NAS CM	Open End	Moderate Alloc (Growth & Income)	B-	B-	C+	Down	Y	1,000
Matisse Discounted Closed-End Fund Strat Inst Cls Shares	MDCEX	NAS CM	Open End	Moderate Alloc (Growth & Income)	B-	B-	C+	Down	Y	1,000
Matrix Advisors Dividend Fund	MADFX	NAS CM	Open End	US Equity Large Cap Value (Equity-Income)	D	D+	B		Y	1,000
Matrix Advisors Value Fund	MAVFX	NAS CM	Open End	US Equity Large Cap Value (Growth & Income)	C+	C+	C+	Down	Y	1,000
Matthew 25 Fund	MXXVX	NAS CM	Open End	US Equity Large Cap Blend (Growth)	B	A-	C+	Up	Y	10,000
Matthews Asia Dividend Fund Institutional Class	MIPIX	NAS CM	Open End	Asia Equity (Pacific Stock)	B+	A-	B	Up	Y	100,000
Matthews Asia Dividend Fund Investor Class	MAPIX	NAS CM	Open End	Asia Equity (Pacific Stock)	B+	A-	B	Up	Y	2,500
Matthews Asia ESG Fund Institutional Class	MISFX	NAS CM	Open End	Asia ex-Japan Equity (Pacific Stock)	C+	C+	B-	Up	Y	100,000
Matthews Asia ESG Fund Investor Class	MASGX	NAS CM	Open End	Asia ex-Japan Equity (Pacific Stock)	C+	C+	B-	Up	Y	2,500
Matthews Asia Focus Fund Institutional Class	MIFSX	NAS CM	Open End	Asia ex-Japan Equity (Pacific Stock)	C+	B-	C+	Up	Y	100,000
Matthews Asia Focus Fund Investor Class	MAFSX	NAS CM	Open End	Asia ex-Japan Equity (Pacific Stock)	C+	B-	C+	Up	Y	2,500
Matthews Asia Growth Fund Institutional Class	MIAPX	NAS CM	Open End	Asia Equity (Pacific Stock)	B	B+	B-	Up	Y	100,000
Matthews Asia Growth Fund Investor Class	MPACX	NAS CM	Open End	Asia Equity (Pacific Stock)	B	B+	B-	Up	Y	2,500
Matthews Asia Innovators Fund Institutional Class Shares	MITEX	NAS CM	Open End	Asia ex-Japan Equity (Pacific Stock)	B+	A	B-	Up	Y	100,000
Matthews Asia Innovators Fund Investor Class Shares	MATFX	NAS CM	Open End	Asia ex-Japan Equity (Pacific Stock)	B+	A	B-	Up	Y	2,500
Matthews Asia Small Companies Fund Institutional Class	MISMX	NAS CM	Open End	Asia ex-Japan Equity (Pacific Stock)	C+	C+	C+	Up	Y	100,000
Matthews Asia Small Companies Fund Investor Class Shares	MSMLX	NAS CM	Open End	Asia ex-Japan Equity (Pacific Stock)	C+	C+	C+	Up	Y	2,500
Matthews Asia Value Fund Institutional Class	MAVAX	NAS CM	Open End	Asia Equity (Growth)	C	C	B+	Up	Y	100,000
Matthews Asia Value Fund Investor Class	MAVRX	NAS CM	Open End	Asia Equity (Growth)	C	C	B+	Up	Y	2,500
Matthews Asian Growth and Income Fund Institutional Class	MICSX	NAS CM	Open End	Asia ex-Japan Equity (Pacific Stock)	C+	C+	B-	Up	Y	100,000
Matthews Asian Growth and Income Fund Investor Class	MACSX	NAS CM	Open End	Asia ex-Japan Equity (Pacific Stock)	C+	C+	B-	Up	Y	2,500
Matthews China Dividend Fund Institutional Class	MICDX	NAS CM	Open End	Greater China Equity (Pacific Stock)	B+	A	B-	Up	Y	100,000
Matthews China Dividend Fund Investor Class	MCDFX	NAS CM	Open End	Greater China Equity (Pacific Stock)	B+	A	B-	Up	Y	2,500
Matthews China Fund Institutional Class	MICFX	NAS CM	Open End	Greater China Equity (Pacific Stock)	B+	A+	C+	Up	Y	100,000
Matthews China Fund Investor Class	MCHFX	NAS CM	Open End	Greater China Equity (Pacific Stock)	B+	A+	C+	Up	Y	2,500
Matthews China Small Companies Fund	MCSMX	NAS CM	Open End	Greater China Equity (Pacific Stock)	B+	A	C+	Up	Y	2,500
Matthews Emerging Asia Fund Institutional Class	MIASX	NAS CM	Open End	Asia ex-Japan Equity (Pacific Stock)	B	B	B-	Down	Y	100,000
Matthews Emerging Asia Fund Investor Class	MEASX	NAS CM	Open End	Asia ex-Japan Equity (Pacific Stock)	B	B	B-	Down	Y	2,500
Matthews India Fund Institutional Class	MIDNX	NAS CM	Open End	India Equity (Pacific Stock)	B	B	B	Up	Y	100,000
Matthews India Fund Investor Class	MINDX	NAS CM	Open End	India Equity (Pacific Stock)	B	B	B	Up	Y	2,500

★ Expanded analysis of this fund is included in Section II.

Min Additional Investment	3-Month Total Return	6-Month Total Return	1-Year Total Return	3-Year Total Return	5-Year Total Return	Dividend Yield (TTM)	Expense Ratio	3-Yr Std Deviation	3-Year Beta	NAV	Total Assets (MIL)	%Cash	%Stocks	%Bonds	%Other	Turnover Ratio	Last Bull Market Total Return	Last Bear Market Total Return	Front End Fee (%)	Back End Fee (%)	Inception Date
TOTAL RETURNS						PERFORMANCE				ASSETS		ASSET ALLOCATION & TURNOVER					BULL & BEAR		FEES		
	3.28	9.09	26.85	26.26	46.57	1.64	1.12	12.27	0.98	9.72	645.3	1	98	0	1	29	16.66	-24.06			Apr-01
	5.89	11.28	24.50	28.22	104.79	0	1.18	13.48	0.89	14	561.7	1	98	0	1	86	27.59	-27.24			May-99
	5.80	11.13	24.15	27.25	102.09	0	1.43	13.47	0.89	12.58	561.7	1	98	0	1	86	27.49	-27.36	5.75		May-99
	5.89	11.41	24.85	29.28	108.01	0	0.88	13.49	0.89	15.79	561.7	1	98	0	1	86	27.91	-27.14			Nov-10
	5.74	11.07	23.90	26.73	100.17	0	1.58	13.53	0.89	11.24	561.7	1	98	0	1	86	27.18	-27.42			Dec-02
	5.85	11.24	24.33	27.73	103.75	0	1.33	13.44	0.89	12.65	561.7	1	98	0	1	86	27.59	-27.23			Apr-14
	5.96	11.40	24.70	28.99	107.06	0	0.98	13.5	0.89	15.62	561.7	1	98	0	1	86	27.78	-27.15			May-99
	5.91	11.39	24.64	28.64	105.95	0	1.08	13.5	0.89	14.84	561.7	1	98	0	1	86	27.65	-27.21			May-99
	3.69	9.70	9.44	29.51	98.63	0.39	0.82	13.8	0.94	16.63	195.7	2	98	0	0	21	36.22	-27.2			Apr-14
	3.49	9.26	8.68	26.84	92.44	0	1.52	13.77	0.94	16.42	195.7	2	98	0	0	21	35.82	-27.35			Apr-14
	3.54	9.43	8.98	27.79	94.75	0.07	1.27	13.76	0.93	16.43	195.7	2	98	0	0	21	36.02	-27.27			Apr-14
	3.59	9.56	9.11	28.40	95.99	0.25	1.12	13.79	0.94	16.63	195.7	2	98	0	0	21	35.91	-27.42			Mar-06
	3.55	9.35	8.84	27.39	93.54	0.01	1.37	13.78	0.94	16.54	195.7	2	98	0	0	21	35.82	-27.37	5.75		Mar-06
	3.70	9.65	9.39	29.16	98.12	0.29	0.92	13.79	0.94	16.66	195.7	2	98	0	0	21	36.22	-27.2			Mar-06
	3.59	9.58	9.20	28.78	97.12	0.23	1.02	13.81	0.94	16.69	195.7	2	98	0	0	21	36.23	-27.22			Mar-06
	2.91	9.10	10.25	27.50	79.61	0.69	1.24	13.21	0.92	11.23	251.7	3	97	0	0	57	26.93	-24.26			Dec-01
	2.82	9.01	9.92	26.58	77.28	0.44	1.49	13.2	0.92	10.87	251.7	3	97	0	0	57	26.7	-24.34	5.75		Dec-01
	2.95	9.29	10.51	28.66	82.41	0.92	0.94	13.21	0.92	11.43	251.7	3	97	0	0	57	27.16	-24.12			Nov-10
	2.76	8.88	9.75	26.01	75.70	0.53	1.64	13.21	0.92	10.08	251.7	3	97	0	0	57	26.5	-24.47			Dec-02
	2.87	9.03	10.04	26.95	78.36	0.8	1.39	13.23	0.92	10.73	251.7	3	97	0	0	57	26.77	-24.28			Apr-14
	2.97	9.20	10.42	28.27	81.32	0.84	1.04	13.23	0.92	11.5	251.7	3	97	0	0	57	27.02	-24.24			Dec-01
	2.94	9.11	10.33	27.90	80.52	0.73	1.14	13.25	0.92	11.44	251.7	3	97	0	0	57	26.96	-24.2			Dec-01
100	2.05	6.00	19.33	29.04	48.07	1.81	2.92	10.81	0.91		117.3	5	72	19	3	100			5.75		May-13
100	3.23	7.18	20.69	30.66	52.42	2.01	2.67	10.85	0.91	11.32	117.3	5	72	19	3	100					Oct-12
100	5.89	10.80	12.74			1.95	0.9			23.32	7.9	2	98	0	0						Oct-16
100	6.37	9.92	14.03	19.26	93.57	2.15	0.99	13.07	1.18	71.61	60.7	0	100	0	0	22	25.64	-25.98			Jul-96
100	10.01	18.17	24.68	38.03	107.80	0.74	1.09	15.19	1.22	34.05	408.0	1	90	0	0	11	42.81	-15.96			Oct-95
100	8.85	13.22	34.77	45.85	63.78	1.58	0.93	11.2	0.8	19.73	6,888	1	99	0	0	40	13.79	-13.43			Oct-10
100	8.88	13.16	34.69	45.38	62.91	1.48	1.06	11.22	0.8	19.74	6,888	1	99	0	0	40	13.75	-13.54			Oct-06
100	4.48	9.58	30.72			1.24	1.25			11.5	17.3	4	96	0	0	16					Apr-15
100	4.64	9.63	30.66			1.12	1.48			11.56	17.3	4	96	0	0	16					Apr-15
100	9.95	13.80	37.35	26.65		1.18	1.25	13.13	0.8	12.24	13.3	4	96	0	0	21					Apr-13
100	9.92	13.68	36.98	25.75		1.1	1.5	13.18	0.8	12.18	13.3	4	96	0	0	21					Apr-13
100	9.71	17.23	39.64	40.85	73.90	0.97	0.96	11.97	0.78	27.45	801.5	3	97	0	0	14	12.61	-17.27			Oct-10
100	9.64	17.12	39.38	40.06	72.20	0.83	1.14	11.94	0.77	27.25	801.5	3	97	0	0	14	12.5	-17.34			Oct-03
100	9.69	17.58	53.18	45.75	120.14	0	1.01	15.78	0.89	14.26	200.9	1	99	0	0	92	13.17	-23.49			Apr-13
100	9.66	17.51	52.88	44.88	118.14	0	1.24	15.75	0.89	14.19	200.9	1	99	0	0	92	13.17	-23.49			Dec-99
100	7.65	14.11	30.85	18.13	42.02	0.55	1.25	12.34	0.79	22.86	429.2	5	95	0	0	44	12.6	-21.73			Apr-13
100	7.65	14.06	30.59	17.38	40.57	0.34	1.47	12.33	0.79	22.89	429.2	5	95	0	0	44	12.6	-21.73			Sep-08
100	3.79	12.01	36.35			5.27	1.25			12.73	27.9	12	87	0	1	20					Nov-15
100	3.73	11.95	36.12			4.36	1.5			12.83	27.9	12	87	0	1	20					Nov-15
100	5.53	6.08	21.99	18.07	24.70	2.44	0.94	10.79	0.65	17.43	2,921	4	85	0	0	16	13.45	-14.59			Oct-10
100	5.57	6.07	21.85	17.60	23.82	2.3	1.09	10.77	0.64	17.46	2,921	4	85	0	0	16	13.32	-14.63			Sep-94
100	8.46	17.65	37.87	60.42	86.30	1.55	1.06	17.58	0.76	17.61	309.0	2	96	0	1	73	19.59	-19.03			Oct-10
100	8.45	17.57	37.69	59.67	84.49	1.43	1.22	17.57	0.76	17.61	309.0	2	96	0	1	73	19.57	-19.17			Nov-09
100	9.64	22.68	59.71	56.82	62.64	1.11	1.03	21.06	0.96	22.17	877.1	2	98	0	0	84	17.16	-26.28			Oct-10
100	9.57	22.53	59.37	56.15	61.40	1	1.18	21.06	0.96	22.2	877.1	2	98	0	0	84	17.02	-26.33			Feb-98
100	8.90	24.96	53.87	57.57	98.36	0.23	1.5	19.98	0.69	11.89	31.8	2	97	0	1	63	14.68				May-11
100	7.25	6.67	18.69	39.14		0.96	1.25	9.28	0.37	15.57	457.1	4	95	0	0	35					Apr-13
100	7.12	6.46	18.42	38.08		0.82	1.47	9.29	0.37	15.51	457.1	4	95	0	0	35					Apr-13
100	10.10	11.22	36.04	37.39	112.87	0	0.91	14.22	0.74	34.51	2,300	2	98	0	0	16	-1.68	-19.22			Oct-10
100	10.04	11.13	35.78	36.56	110.88	0	1.12	14.22	0.74	34.31	2,300	2	98	0	0	16	-1.74	-19.27			Oct-05

	MARKET			FUND TYPE, CATEGORY & OBJECTIVE	RATINGS					MINIMUMS
Fund Name	Ticker Symbol	Traded On	Fund Type	Category and (Prospectus Objective)	Overall Rating	Reward Rating	Risk Rating	Recent Up/ Downgrade	Open to New Investors	Min Initial Investment
Matthews Japan Fund Institutional Class	MIJFX	NAS CM	Open End	Japan Equity (Pacific Stock)	A-	A	B+	Up		100,000
Matthews Japan Fund Investor Class	MJFOX	NAS CM	Open End	Japan Equity (Pacific Stock)	A-	A	B+	Up	Y	2,500
Matthews Korea Fund Institutional Class	MIKOX	NAS CM	Open End	Other Equity (Pacific Stock)	B+	A-	B	Up	Y	100,000
Matthews Korea Fund Investor Class	MAKOX	NAS CM	Open End	Other Equity (Pacific Stock)	B+	A-	B	Up	Y	2,500
Matthews Pacific Tiger Fund Institutional Class	MIPTX	NAS CM	Open End	Asia ex-Japan Equity (Pacific Stock)	B	B	B-	Up	Y	100,000
Matthews Pacific Tiger Fund Investor Class	MAPTX	NAS CM	Open End	Asia ex-Japan Equity (Pacific Stock)	B	B	B-	Up	Y	2,500
McKee International Equity Fund Class Institutional	MKIEX	NAS CM	Open End	Global Equity Large Cap (Foreign Stock)	B-	B-	B-	Up	Y	2,500
Measured Risk Strategy Fund Class A	MRPAX	NAS CM	Open End	Long/Short Equity (Growth & Income)	D-	D	B		Y	2,500
Measured Risk Strategy Fund Class I	MRPIX	NAS CM	Open End	Long/Short Equity (Growth & Income)	D-	D	B		Y	100,000
Meeder Aggressive Allocation Fund Adviser Class	AGHAX	NAS CM	Open End	Aggressive Alloc (Aggr Growth)	B-	C+	B	Up	Y	2,500
Meeder Aggressive Allocation Fund Institutional Class	AGHIX	NAS CM	Open End	Aggressive Alloc (Aggr Growth)	B-	C+	B	Up	Y	1,000,000
Meeder Aggressive Allocation Fund Retail Class	FLAGX	NAS CM	Open End	Aggressive Alloc (Aggr Growth)	B-	C+	B	Up	Y	2,500
Meeder Balanced Fund Adviser Class	BLNAX	NAS CM	Open End	Moderate Alloc (Balanced)	B-	C+	B-	Down	Y	2,500
Meeder Balanced Fund Institutional Class	BLNIX	NAS CM	Open End	Moderate Alloc (Balanced)	B-	C+	B-	Down	Y	1,000,000
Meeder Balanced Fund Retail Class	FLDFX	NAS CM	Open End	Moderate Alloc (Balanced)	B-	C+	B	Down	Y	2,500
Meeder Conservative Allocation Fund Adviser Class	IFAAX	NAS CM	Open End	Other Sector Equity (Utility)	C+	C+	C+	Up	Y	2,500
Meeder Conservative Allocation Fund Institutional Class	IFAIX	NAS CM	Open End	Other Sector Equity (Utility)	C+	C+	C+	Up	Y	1,000,000
Meeder Conservative Allocation Fund Retail Class	FLRUX	NAS CM	Open End	Other Sector Equity (Utility)	C+	C+	C+	Up	Y	2,500
Meeder Dynamic Allocation Fund Adviser Class	DYGAX	NAS CM	Open End	Aggressive Alloc (Growth)	B-	B-	C+	Down	Y	2,500
Meeder Dynamic Allocation Fund Institutional Class	DYGIX	NAS CM	Open End	Aggressive Alloc (Growth)	B-	B-	C+	Down	Y	1,000,000
Meeder Dynamic Allocation Fund Retail Class	FLDGX	NAS CM	Open End	Aggressive Alloc (Growth)	B-	B-	C+	Down	Y	2,500
Meeder Global Allocation Fund Adviser Class	GBPAX	NAS CM	Open End	Global Equity (Growth)	B-	C+	B-	Up	Y	2,500
Meeder Global Allocation Fund Institutional Class	GBPIX	NAS CM	Open End	Global Equity (Growth)	B-	C+	B-	Up	Y	1,000,000
Meeder Global Allocation Fund Retail Class	FLFGX	NAS CM	Open End	Global Equity (Growth)	C+	C+	C+	Up	Y	2,500
Meeder Moderate Allocation Fund Adviser Class	DVOAX	NAS CM	Open End	US Equity Large Cap Value (Growth & Income)	C	C+	B	Up	Y	2,500
Meeder Moderate Allocation Fund Institutional Class	DVOIX	NAS CM	Open End	US Equity Large Cap Value (Growth & Income)	C	C+	B	Up	Y	1,000,000
Meeder Moderate Allocation Fund Retail Class	FLDOX	NAS CM	Open End	US Equity Large Cap Value (Growth & Income)	C	C+	B	Up	Y	2,500
Meeder Muirfield Fund Adviser Class	FLMAX	NAS CM	Open End	Moderate Alloc (Growth)	C+	C+	C+	Down	Y	2,500
Meeder Muirfield Fund Institutional Class	FLMIX	NAS CM	Open End	Moderate Alloc (Growth)	C+	C+	C+	Down	Y	1,000,000
Meeder Muirfield Fund Retail Class	FLMFX	NAS CM	Open End	Moderate Alloc (Growth)	C+	C+	C+	Down	Y	2,500
Meeder Quantex Fund Adviser Class	QNTAX	NAS CM	Open End	US Equity Mid Cap (Growth)	B	B	B	Up	Y	2,500
Meeder Quantex Fund Institutional Class	QNTIX	NAS CM	Open End	US Equity Mid Cap (Growth)	B	B	B	Up	Y	1,000,000
Meeder Quantex Fund Retail Class	FLCGX	NAS CM	Open End	US Equity Mid Cap (Growth)	B	B	B	Up	Y	2,500
Meeder Spectrum Fund Adviser Class	SRUAX	NAS CM	Open End	Long/Short Equity (Growth)	C+	C+	B	Down	Y	2,500
Meeder Spectrum Fund Institutional Class	SRUIX	NAS CM	Open End	Long/Short Equity (Growth)	C+	C+	B	Down	Y	1,000,000
Meeder Spectrum Fund Retail Class	FLSPX	NAS CM	Open End	Long/Short Equity (Growth)	C+	C+	B	Down	Y	2,500
Meehan Focus Fund	MEFOX	NAS CM	Open End	US Equity Large Cap Blend (Growth)	B-	C+	B	Down	Y	5,000
Meridian Contrarian Fund A Class	MFCAX	NAS CM	Open End	US Equity Mid Cap (Growth)	B+	A-	B	Up	Y	2,500
Meridian Contrarian Fund Class C	MFCCX	NAS CM	Open End	US Equity Mid Cap (Growth)	B	B+	B	Up	Y	2,500
Meridian Contrarian Fund Investor Class	MFCIX	NAS CM	Open End	US Equity Mid Cap (Growth)	B+	A-	B	Up	Y	99,999
Meridian Contrarian Fund Legacy Class	MVALX	NAS CM	Open End	US Equity Mid Cap (Growth)	B+	A	B	Up		1,000
Meridian Equity Income Fund® A Class	MRAEX	NAS CM	Open End	US Equity Large Cap Growth (Equity-Income)	B	B	B	Up	Y	2,500
Meridian Equity Income Fund® Class C	MRCEX	NAS CM	Open End	US Equity Large Cap Growth (Equity-Income)	B	B	B	Up	Y	2,500
Meridian Equity Income Fund® Investor Class	MRIEX	NAS CM	Open End	US Equity Large Cap Growth (Equity-Income)	B	B	B	Up	Y	99,999
Meridian Equity Income Fund® Legacy Class	MEIFX	NAS CM	Open End	US Equity Large Cap Growth (Equity-Income)	B	B	B	Up		1,000
Meridian Growth Fund® A Class	MRAGX	NAS CM	Open End	US Equity Small Cap (Growth)	B	B+	C+	Up	Y	2,500
Meridian Growth Fund® Class C	MRCGX	NAS CM	Open End	US Equity Small Cap (Growth)	B	B+	C+	Up	Y	2,500
Meridian Growth Fund® Institutional Class	MRRGX	NAS CM	Open End	US Equity Small Cap (Growth)	B	B+	C+	Up	Y	1,000,000
Meridian Growth Fund® Investor Class	MRIGX	NAS CM	Open End	US Equity Small Cap (Growth)	B	B+	C+	Up	Y	99,999
Meridian Growth Fund® Legacy Class	MERDX	NAS CM	Open End	US Equity Small Cap (Growth)	B+	B+	B	Up		1,000
Meridian Small Cap Growth Fund A Class	MSGAX	NAS CM	Open End	US Equity Small Cap (Small Company)	B	A-	C	Up	Y	2,500
Meridian Small Cap Growth Fund Class C	MSGCX	NAS CM	Open End	US Equity Small Cap (Small Company)	B	B+	C	Up	Y	2,500

★ Expanded analysis of this fund is included in Section II.

	TOTAL RETURNS					PERFORMANCE				ASSETS		ASSET ALLOCATION & TURNOVER					BULL & BEAR		FEES		
Min Additional Investment	3-Month Total Return	6-Month Total Return	1-Year Total Return	3-Year Total Return	5-Year Total Return	Dividend Yield (TTM)	Expense Ratio	3-Yr Std Deviation	3-Year Beta	NAV	Total Assets (MIL)	%Cash	%Stocks	%Bonds	%Other	Turnover Ratio	Last Bull Market Total Return	Last Bear Market Total Return	Front End Fee (%)	Back End Fee (%)	Inception Date
100	8.21	16.22	33.22	59.72	113.48	0.75	0.88	12.65	0.66	24.16	4,191	3	97	0	0	55	4.09	-5.46			Oct-10
100	8.24	16.16	33.13	59.27	112.41	0.66	0.98	12.65	0.66	24.12	4,191	3	97	0	0	55	4.01	-5.46			Dec-98
100	9.88	10.20	40.11	51.85	67.69	1.16	0.97	14.54	0.85	6.95	225.9	1	94	0	0	35	18.2	-21.83			Oct-10
100	9.94	10.27	39.88	51.19	66.74	1.05	1.15	14.53	0.85	6.91	225.9	1	94	0	0	35	18	-21.86			Jan-95
100	11.26	16.51	40.17	38.74	63.12	0.55	0.9	13.56	0.84	31.63	9,228	3	96	0	1	6	14.78	-17.44			Oct-10
100	11.23	16.43	39.96	38.01	61.69	0.41	1.08	13.56	0.84	31.66	9,228	3	96	0	1	6	14.68	-17.49			Sep-94
100	5.04	11.27	26.23	26.96	43.52	1.35	1.02	12.39	1	13.87	196.3	2	97	0	1	7	15.75	-25.86			May-94
100	1.63	-2.90	21.85				2.4			10.81	14.4	23	-4	81	0				4.75		Dec-16
5,000	1.72	-2.73	22.17				2.15			10.84	14.4	23	-4	81	0						Dec-16
100	4.80	9.51	13.22	16.06	77.30	0.3	1.46	10.3	0.8	10.45	42.0	0	95	5	0	361	22.55	-21.71			Oct-16
100	4.98	9.80	13.52	16.34	77.72	0.27	1.3	10.31	0.8	10.46	42.0	0	95	5	0	361	22.55	-21.71			Oct-16
100	4.70	9.41	12.91	15.60	76.59	0.18	1.65	10.27	0.8	10.45	42.0	0	95	5	0	361	22.55	-21.71			Feb-00
100	4.05	7.78	15.21	14.55	51.73	0.66	1.47	6.12	0.58	11.68	230.4	6	65	28	0	322	14.1	-14.04			Oct-16
100	4.09	7.92	15.25	14.66	51.88	0.8	1.31	6.12	0.58	11.68	230.4	6	65	28	0	322	14.1	-14.04			Oct-16
100	3.92	7.66	14.73	14.06	51.09	0.78	1.67	6.1	0.58	11.61	230.4	6	65	28	0	322	14.1	-14.04			Jan-06
100	0.75	3.35	6.93	5.50	52.84	0.04	1.56	10.77	0.36	22.82	19.1	-2	35	65	0	44	15.59	-15.75			Oct-16
100	0.83	3.44	7.07	5.62	53.02	0.03	1.36	10.76	0.36	22.85	19.1	-2	35	65	0	44	15.59	-15.75			Oct-16
100	-0.17	2.36	5.72	4.22	50.99	0.05	1.76	10.76	0.36	22.54	19.1	-2	35	65	0	44	15.59	-15.75			Jun-95
100	6.03	11.66	21.42	22.48	87.19	0.44	1.24	10.04	0.98	10.88	129.4	1	95	5	0	369	23.09	-20.34			Oct-16
100	5.98	11.71	21.60	22.56	87.30	0.54	1.06	10.04	0.98	10.86	129.4	1	95	5	0	369	23.09	-20.34			Oct-16
100	5.97	11.50	21.20	22.12	86.64	0.39	1.48	10.02	0.98	10.85	129.4	1	95	5	0	369	23.09	-20.34			Feb-00
100	5.23	11.96	22.84	17.15	57.55	0.69	1.47	10.14	0.93	11.54	74.4	1	89	10	0	169	22.36	-23.33			Oct-16
100	5.44	12.17	23.06	17.36	57.83	0.6	1.31	10.15	0.93	11.55	74.4	1	89	10	0	169	22.36	-23.33			Oct-16
100	5.12	11.75	22.33	16.52	56.71	0.55	1.64	10.13	0.93	11.53	74.4	1	89	10	0	169	22.36	-23.33			Jan-06
100	6.36	10.95	16.39			0.69	1.54			11.66	60.6	1	89	10	0	250					Oct-16
100	6.40	11.09	16.54			0.61	1.34			11.68	60.6	1	89	10	0	250					Oct-16
100	6.24	10.74	15.98			0.48	1.74			11.66	60.6	1	89	10	0	250					Jun-15
100	5.85	10.87	20.49	19.36	79.41	0.31	1.25	8.46	0.8	7.57	452.5	8	92	0	0	414	19.05	-19.8			Oct-16
100	5.94	11.11	20.60	19.51	79.63	0.34	1.07	8.48	0.8	7.57	452.5	8	92	0	0	414	19.05	-19.8			Oct-16
100	5.92	10.96	20.28	19.00	78.87	0.32	1.41	8.45	0.8	7.54	452.5	8	92	0	0	414	19.04	-19.8			Aug-88
100	5.78	10.05	13.68	27.05	103.15	0.19	1.37	13.95	1.18	36.78	94.5	0	100	0	0	91	23.63	-23.07			Oct-16
100	5.44	9.73	13.38	26.72	102.62	0.24	1.2	13.95	1.18	36.77	94.5	0	100	0	0	91	23.63	-23.07			Oct-16
100	5.74	9.98	13.41	26.66	102.53	0.07	1.54	13.95	1.18	36.76	94.5	0	100	0	0	91	23.63	-23.08			Mar-85
100	6.41	11.62	19.65	26.55		0.15	1.78			11.53	142.7	8	92	0	0	235					Oct-16
100	6.40	11.71	19.74	26.70		0.18	1.61			11.54	142.7	8	92	0	0	235					Oct-16
100	6.34	11.37	19.28	26.05		0.16	2.03			11.48	142.7	8	92	0	0	235					Jan-15
100	7.79	12.93	21.88	21.63	77.39	0.25	1.02	12.07	1.14	25.21	65.3	2	98	0	0	44	20.71	-15.12			Dec-99
50	7.46	16.37	24.20	37.55	100.45	0	1.6	12.41	0.95	41.15	659.9	6	94	0	0	54	28.24	-20.63	5.75		Nov-13
50	7.31	16.06	23.57	35.38	94.69	0	2.21	12.4	0.95	40.81	659.9	6	94	0	0	54	27.68	-20.88	1.00	1.00	Jul-15
	7.54	16.52	24.51	38.65	103.09	0	1.34	12.39	0.95	41.7	659.9	6	94	0	0	54	28.43	-20.55			Nov-13
50	7.60	16.66	24.82	39.57	104.74	0.02	1.15	12.41	0.95	41.96	659.9	6	94	0	0	54	28.43	-20.55			Feb-94
50	9.94	18.64	27.40	38.36	93.64	0.36	1.6	11.79	1.05	15.86	55.4	7	79	6	8	44	21.08	-15.08	5.75		Nov-13
50	9.79	18.35	26.82	36.36	88.08	0.09	2	11.81	1.06	15.86	55.4	7	79	6	8	44	20.55	-15.35		1.00	Jul-15
	10.05	18.79	27.71	39.35	96.02	0.51	1.34	11.83	1.06	15.98	55.4	7	79	6	8	44	21.25	-15			Nov-13
50	10.07	18.90	27.94	39.80	96.71	0.62	1.25	11.86	1.06	15.97	55.4	7	79	6	8	44	21.25	-14.99			Jan-05
50	5.55	10.87	25.25	35.77	92.99	0	1.17	12.67	0.9	40.61	1,605	7	92	0	0	34	29.51	-19.22	5.75		Nov-13
50	5.37	10.46	24.32	33.35	87.62	0	1.92	12.63	0.9	40.46	1,605	7	92	0	0	34	28.95	-19.47		1.00	Jul-15
	5.65	11.05	25.63	37.49	97.28	0	0.87	12.64	0.9	41.61	1,605	7	92	0	0	34	29.7	-19.14			Dec-14
	5.61	10.99	25.55	37.11	96.11	0	0.95	12.65	0.9	41.29	1,605	7	92	0	0	34	29.7	-19.14			Nov-13
50	5.65	11.04	25.62	37.54	97.41	0	0.89	12.64	0.9	41.63	1,605	7	92	0	0	34	29.7	-19.14			Aug-84
50	3.52	10.41	22.59	36.40		0	1.49	12.94	0.83	15.77	1,290	10	89	0	1	39			5.75		Dec-13
50	3.30	10.02	21.64	33.73		0	2.29	12.92	0.83	15.57	1,290	10	89	0	1	39				1.00	Jul-15

	MARKET			FUND TYPE, CATEGORY & OBJECTIVE	RATINGS					MINIMUMS
Fund Name	Ticker Symbol	Traded On	Fund Type	Category and (Prospectus Objective)	Overall Rating	Reward Rating	Risk Rating	Recent Up/ Downgrade	Open to New Investors	Min Initial Investment
Meridian Small Cap Growth Fund Institutional Class	MSGRX	NAS CM	Open End	US Equity Small Cap (Small Company)	B	A-	C	Up	Y	1,000,000
Meridian Small Cap Growth Fund Investor Shares	MISGX	NAS CM	Open End	US Equity Small Cap (Small Company)	B	A-	C	Up	Y	99,999
Meridian Small Cap Growth Fund Legacy Class	MSGGX	NAS CM	Open End	US Equity Small Cap (Small Company)	B	A-	C	Up		1,000
Meritage Growth Equity Fund Institutional Shares	MPGIX	NAS CM	Open End	US Equity Large Cap Growth (Growth)	B	B+	B	Down	Y	100,000
Meritage Growth Equity Fund Investor Shares	MPGEX	NAS CM	Open End	US Equity Large Cap Growth (Growth)	B	B+	B	Down	Y	2,500
Meritage Value Equity Fund Institutional Shares	MVEBX	NAS CM	Open End	US Equity Large Cap Value (Growth & Income)	B	C+	B+	Up	Y	100,000
Meritage Yield-Focus Equity Fund Institutional Shares	MPYIX	NAS CM	Open End	US Equity Large Cap Value (Growth & Income)	C+	C+	C+		Y	100,000
Meritage Yield-Focus Equity Fund Investor Shares	MPYEX	NAS CM	Open End	US Equity Large Cap Value (Growth & Income)	C+	C+	C+		Y	2,500
Metropolitan West AlphaTrak 500 Fund	MWATX	NAS CM	Open End	US Equity Large Cap Blend (Growth)	B	B	B	Down	Y	5,000
Mexico Equity & Income Fund	MXE	NYSE	Closed End	Other Equity (Foreign Stock)	D	D	D+	Down	Y	
Mexico Fund, Inc	MXF	NYSE	Closed End	Other Equity (Foreign Stock)	D+	D+	D+	Down	Y	
MFG Infrastructure Fund Service Class Shares	MGKSX	NAS CM	Open End	Other Sector Equity (Utility)	U	U	U		Y	10,000
MFS Special Value Trust	MFV	NYSE	Closed End	Cautious Alloc (Income)	B-	C+	B	Up	Y	
MFS® Aggressive Growth Allocation Fund Class 529A	EAGTX	NAS CM	Open End	Aggressive Alloc (Aggr Growth)	B	B-	B+	Up	Y	250
MFS® Aggressive Growth Allocation Fund Class 529B	EBAAX	NAS CM	Open End	Aggressive Alloc (Aggr Growth)	B	B-	B+	Up	Y	250
MFS® Aggressive Growth Allocation Fund Class 529C	ECAAX	NAS CM	Open End	Aggressive Alloc (Aggr Growth)	B	B-	B+	Up	Y	250
MFS® Aggressive Growth Allocation Fund Class A	MAAGX	NAS CM	Open End	Aggressive Alloc (Aggr Growth)	B	B-	B+	Up	Y	1,000
MFS® Aggressive Growth Allocation Fund Class B	MBAGX	NAS CM	Open End	Aggressive Alloc (Aggr Growth)	B	B-	B+	Up	Y	1,000
MFS® Aggressive Growth Allocation Fund Class C	MCAGX	NAS CM	Open End	Aggressive Alloc (Aggr Growth)	B	B-	B+	Up	Y	1,000
MFS® Aggressive Growth Allocation Fund Class I	MIAGX	NAS CM	Open End	Aggressive Alloc (Aggr Growth)	B-	B-	B-	Down	Y	0
MFS® Aggressive Growth Allocation Fund Class R1	MAAFX	NAS CM	Open End	Aggressive Alloc (Aggr Growth)	B	B-	B+	Up	Y	0
MFS® Aggressive Growth Allocation Fund Class R2	MAWAX	NAS CM	Open End	Aggressive Alloc (Aggr Growth)	B	B-	B+	Up	Y	0
MFS® Aggressive Growth Allocation Fund Class R3	MAAHX	NAS CM	Open End	Aggressive Alloc (Aggr Growth)	B	B-	B+	Up	Y	0
MFS® Aggressive Growth Allocation Fund Class R4	MAALX	NAS CM	Open End	Aggressive Alloc (Aggr Growth)	B	B-	B+	Up	Y	0
MFS® Blended Research Core Equity Fund Class A	MUEAX	NAS CM	Open End	US Equity Large Cap Blend (Growth)	B-	B-	B-	Down	Y	1,000
MFS® Blended Research Core Equity Fund Class B	MUSBX	NAS CM	Open End	US Equity Large Cap Blend (Growth)	B-	B-	B-	Down	Y	1,000
MFS® Blended Research Core Equity Fund Class C	MUECX	NAS CM	Open End	US Equity Large Cap Blend (Growth)	B-	B-	B-	Down	Y	1,000
MFS® Blended Research Core Equity Fund Class I	MUSEX	NAS CM	Open End	US Equity Large Cap Blend (Growth)	B-	B-	B-	Down	Y	0
MFS® Blended Research Core Equity Fund Class R1	MUERX	NAS CM	Open End	US Equity Large Cap Blend (Growth)	B-	B-	B-	Down	Y	0
MFS® Blended Research Core Equity Fund Class R2	MUESX	NAS CM	Open End	US Equity Large Cap Blend (Growth)	B-	B-	B-	Down	Y	0
MFS® Blended Research Core Equity Fund Class R3	MUETX	NAS CM	Open End	US Equity Large Cap Blend (Growth)	B-	B-	B-	Down	Y	0
MFS® Blended Research Core Equity Fund Class R4	MUEUX	NAS CM	Open End	US Equity Large Cap Blend (Growth)	B-	B-	B-	Down	Y	0
MFS® Blended Research Core Equity Fund Class R6	MUEVX	NAS CM	Open End	US Equity Large Cap Blend (Growth)	B-	B-	B	Down	Y	0
MFS® Blended Research Emerging Markets Equity Fund Class A	BRKAX	NAS CM	Open End	Emerging Markets Equity (Div Emerging Mkts)	C	B-	B	Up	Y	1,000
MFS® Blended Research Emerging Markets Equity Fund Class B	BRKBX	NAS CM	Open End	Emerging Markets Equity (Div Emerging Mkts)	C	B-	B	Up	Y	1,000
MFS® Blended Research Emerging Markets Equity Fund Class C	BRKCX	NAS CM	Open End	Emerging Markets Equity (Div Emerging Mkts)	C	B-	B	Up	Y	1,000
MFS® Blended Research Emerging Markets Equity Fund Class I	BRKIX	NAS CM	Open End	Emerging Markets Equity (Div Emerging Mkts)	C	B-	B	Up	Y	0
MFS® Blended Research Emerging Markets Equity Fund Cls R1	BRKRX	NAS CM	Open End	Emerging Markets Equity (Div Emerging Mkts)	C	B-	B	Up	Y	0
MFS® Blended Research Emerging Markets Equity Fund Cls R2	BRKSX	NAS CM	Open End	Emerging Markets Equity (Div Emerging Mkts)	C	B-	B	Up	Y	0
MFS® Blended Research Emerging Markets Equity Fund Cls R3	BRKTX	NAS CM	Open End	Emerging Markets Equity (Div Emerging Mkts)	C	B-	B	Up	Y	0
MFS® Blended Research Emerging Markets Equity Fund Cls R4	BRKUX	NAS CM	Open End	Emerging Markets Equity (Div Emerging Mkts)	C	B-	B	Up	Y	0
MFS® Blended Research Emerging Markets Equity Fund Cls R6	BRKVX	NAS CM	Open End	Emerging Markets Equity (Div Emerging Mkts)	C	B-	B	Up	Y	0
MFS® Blended Research Global Equity Fund Class A	BRLAX	NAS CM	Open End	Global Equity (World Stock)	C	C+	B	Up	Y	1,000
MFS® Blended Research Global Equity Fund Class B	BRLBX	NAS CM	Open End	Global Equity (World Stock)	C	C+	B	Up	Y	1,000
MFS® Blended Research Global Equity Fund Class C	BRLCX	NAS CM	Open End	Global Equity (World Stock)	C	C+	B	Up	Y	1,000
MFS® Blended Research Global Equity Fund Class I	BRLJX	NAS CM	Open End	Global Equity (World Stock)	C	C+	B	Up	Y	0
MFS® Blended Research Global Equity Fund Class R1	BRLRX	NAS CM	Open End	Global Equity (World Stock)	C	C+	B	Up	Y	0
MFS® Blended Research Global Equity Fund Class R2	BRLSX	NAS CM	Open End	Global Equity (World Stock)	C	C+	B	Up	Y	0
MFS® Blended Research Global Equity Fund Class R3	BRLTX	NAS CM	Open End	Global Equity (World Stock)	C	C+	B	Up	Y	0
MFS® Blended Research Global Equity Fund Class R4	BRLUX	NAS CM	Open End	Global Equity (World Stock)	C	C+	B	Up	Y	0
MFS® Blended Research Global Equity Fund Class R6	BRLYX	NAS CM	Open End	Global Equity (World Stock)	C	C+	B	Up	Y	0
MFS® Blended Research Growth Equity Fund Class A	BRWAX	NAS CM	Open End	US Equity Large Cap Growth (Growth)	C	C+	B	Up	Y	1,000

★Expanded analysis of this fund is included in Section II.

	TOTAL RETURNS					PERFORMANCE				ASSETS		ASSET ALLOCATION & TURNOVER					BULL & BEAR		FEES		
Min Additional Investment	3-Month Total Return	6-Month Total Return	1-Year Total Return	3-Year Total Return	5-Year Total Return	Dividend Yield (TTM)	Expense Ratio	3-Yr Std Deviation	3-Year Beta	NAV	Total Assets (MIL)	%Cash	%Stocks	%Bonds	%Other	Turnover Ratio	Last Bull Market Total Return	Last Bear Market Total Return	Front End Fee (%)	Back End Fee (%)	Inception Date
	3.59	10.59	22.96	38.18		0	1.15	12.96	0.83	16.04	1,290	10	89	0	1	39					Dec-14
	3.55	10.50	22.82	37.52		0	1.32	12.96	0.83	15.96	1,290	10	89	0	1	39					Dec-13
50	3.54	10.55	22.86	37.76		0	1.25	12.93	0.83	15.99	1,290	10	89	0	1	39					Dec-13
1,000	5.90	11.12	25.98	41.81		0.2	1.03	10.21	0.92	14.52	26.0	5	95	0	0	82					Dec-13
100	5.83	11.00	25.65	40.72		0	1.28	10.16	0.91	14.41	26.0	5	95	0	0	82					Dec-13
1,000	4.93	10.37	15.70	21.32		0.73	1.04	8.86	0.78	13.34	17.6	1	99	0	0	81					Dec-13
1,000	3.74	8.10	12.61	14.30		3.35	1.15	9.22	0.76	10.95	27.7	3	91	0	0	60					Dec-13
100	3.63	7.99	12.78	13.82		2.35	1.4	9.23	0.76	11.06	27.7	3	91	0	0	60					Dec-13
0	6.49	10.92	20.83	44.71	127.20	0.98	0.9	10.66	1.01	10.14	18.3	5	45	50	0	505	26.72	-18.56			Jun-98
	-9.60	-9.12	11.82	-12.17	-1.73	0	1.51	17.8	0.72	11.84	89.6	2	92	4	2	316	24.92	-20.85			Aug-90
	-6.20	-5.16	16.01	-6.63	-13.57	0.72	1.03	17.72	0.98	18.1243	272.6	6	95	0	-1	31	26.06	-23.97			Jun-81
1,000	4.48	7.31					0.95			10.52	1.1	10	90	0	0						May-17
	1.85	4.09	10.70	21.14	43.73	3.23		6.67	1.06	5.98	42.6	6	39	54	0	26	14.48	-11.49			Nov-89
	5.50	9.76	22.86	30.54	73.99	0.79	1.15	9.25	0.87	22.95	1,775	4	93	4	0	2	20.94	-19.02	5.75		Jul-02
	5.26	9.31	21.89	27.57	67.49	0.05	1.9	9.28	0.88	22.54	1,775	4	93	4	0	2	20.43	-19.25		4.00	Jul-02
	5.31	9.31	21.93	27.60	67.59	0.15	1.9	9.26	0.87	22.25	1,775	4	93	4	0	2	20.52	-19.29		1.00	Jul-02
	5.49	9.73	22.91	30.64	74.23	0.81	1.1	9.25	0.87	23.1	1,775	4	93	4	0	2	20.98	-18.97	5.75		Jun-02
	5.28	9.34	21.96	27.69	67.79	0.17	1.85	9.26	0.87	22.8	1,775	4	93	4	0	2	20.48	-19.25		4.00	Jun-02
	5.27	9.32	21.94	27.70	67.87	0.21	1.85	9.25	0.87	22.57	1,775	4	93	4	0	2	20.43	-19.23		1.00	Jun-02
	5.56	9.87	23.22	31.63	76.49	1.01	0.85	9.26	0.87	23.46	1,775	4	93	4	0	2	21.15	-18.91			Jun-02
	5.30	9.30	21.98	27.73	67.79	0.23	1.85	9.26	0.87	22.25	1,775	4	93	4	0	2	20.46	-19.23			Apr-05
	5.42	9.65	22.63	29.66	72.07	0.61	1.35	9.25	0.87	22.64	1,775	4	93	4	0	2	20.74	-19.07			Oct-03
	5.49	9.76	22.88	30.63	74.21	0.81	1.1	9.26	0.87	22.91	1,775	4	93	4	0	2	20.98	-18.97			Apr-05
	5.59	9.91	23.26	31.65	76.49	1.02	0.85	9.26	0.87	23.16	1,775	4	93	4	0	2	21.16	-18.89			Apr-05
	6.67	10.92	20.33	29.60	102.24	0.83	0.74	10.04	0.98	27.46	1,587	1	99	0	0	62	25.11	-16.9	5.75		Aug-97
	6.47	10.53	19.43	26.71	94.78	0.28	1.49	10.06	0.99	26.59	1,587	1	99	0	0	62	24.59	-17.12		4.00	Aug-97
	6.45	10.47	19.40	26.68	94.64	0.28	1.49	10.05	0.98	26.2	1,587	1	99	0	0	62	24.56	-17.08		1.00	Aug-97
	6.71	11.03	20.63	30.53	104.75	1.01	0.49	10.05	0.98	27.81	1,587	1	99	0	0	62	25.33	-16.78			Jan-94
	6.46	10.51	19.45	26.75	94.83	0.27	1.49	10.02	0.98	26.32	1,587	1	99	0	0	62	24.6	-17.12			Sep-08
	6.62	10.77	20.04	28.60	99.67	0.68	0.99	10.01	0.98	26.39	1,587	1	99	0	0	62	24.94	-16.96			Sep-08
	6.64	10.92	20.32	29.54	102.05	0.83	0.74	10.07	0.99	27.36	1,587	1	99	0	0	62	25.09	-16.83			Sep-08
	6.72	11.04	20.62	30.54	104.74	1.02	0.49	10.04	0.98	27.56	1,587	1	99	0	0	62	25.29	-16.78			Sep-08
	6.77	11.13	20.81	31.02	105.84	1.09	0.42	10.04	0.98	27.85	1,587	1	99	0	0	62	25.33	-16.78			Jun-12
	6.63	15.89	38.73			0.42	1.24			14.7	21.2	2	98	0	0	92			5.75		Sep-15
	6.46	15.52	37.70			0.01	1.99			14.64	21.2	2	98	0	0	92				4.00	Sep-15
	6.47	15.56	37.83			0.2	1.99			14.6	21.2	2	98	0	0	92				1.00	Sep-15
	6.77	16.10	39.17			0.53	0.99			14.74	21.2	2	98	0	0	92					Sep-15
	6.49	15.55	37.74			0	1.99			14.68	21.2	2	98	0	0	92					Sep-15
	6.57	15.83	38.43			0.16	1.49			14.73	21.2	2	98	0	0	92					Sep-15
	6.66	15.92	38.74			0.34	1.24			14.73	21.2	2	98	0	0	92					Sep-15
	6.74	16.08	39.15			0.52	0.99			14.74	21.2	2	98	0	0	92					Sep-15
	6.76	16.17	39.26			0.55	0.95			14.74	21.2	2	98	0	0	92					Sep-15
	4.68	11.04	24.60			1.39	0.89			12.76	6.5	1	99	0	0	55			5.75		Sep-15
	4.45	10.64	23.62			0.74	1.64			12.76	6.5	1	99	0	0	55				4.00	Sep-15
	4.52	10.63	23.62			0.82	1.64			12.75	6.5	1	99	0	0	55				1.00	Sep-15
	4.73	11.16	24.94			1.51	0.64			12.79	6.5	1	99	0	0	55					Sep-15
	4.46	10.65	23.63			0.74	1.64			12.77	6.5	1	99	0	0	55					Sep-15
	4.59	10.95	24.29			1.13	1.14			12.78	6.5	1	99	0	0	55					Sep-15
	4.67	11.02	24.57			1.32	0.89			12.78	6.5	1	99	0	0	55					Sep-15
	4.73	11.17	24.95			1.51	0.64			12.79	6.5	1	99	0	0	55					Sep-15
	4.71	11.23	25.02			1.52	0.6			12.79	6.5	1	99	0	0	55					Sep-15
	7.22	13.19	26.55			0.2	0.74			13.44	191.6	2	98	0	0	57			5.75		Sep-15

	MARKET			FUND TYPE, CATEGORY & OBJECTIVE	RATINGS					MINIMUMS
Fund Name	Ticker Symbol	Traded On	Fund Type	Category and (Prospectus Objective)	Overall Rating	Reward Rating	Risk Rating	Recent Up/ Downgrade	Open to New Investors	Min Initial Investment
MFS® Blended Research Growth Equity Fund Class B	BRWBX	NAS CM	Open End	US Equity Large Cap Growth (Growth)	C	C+	B	Up	Y	1,000
MFS® Blended Research Growth Equity Fund Class C	BRWCX	NAS CM	Open End	US Equity Large Cap Growth (Growth)	C	C+	B	Up	Y	1,000
MFS® Blended Research Growth Equity Fund Class I	BRWJX	NAS CM	Open End	US Equity Large Cap Growth (Growth)	C	C+	B	Up	Y	0
MFS® Blended Research Growth Equity Fund Class R1	BRWRX	NAS CM	Open End	US Equity Large Cap Growth (Growth)	C	C+	B	Up	Y	0
MFS® Blended Research Growth Equity Fund Class R2	BRWSX	NAS CM	Open End	US Equity Large Cap Growth (Growth)	C	C+	B	Up	Y	0
MFS® Blended Research Growth Equity Fund Class R3	BRWTX	NAS CM	Open End	US Equity Large Cap Growth (Growth)	C	C+	B	Up	Y	0
MFS® Blended Research Growth Equity Fund Class R4	BRWUX	NAS CM	Open End	US Equity Large Cap Growth (Growth)	C	C+	B	Up	Y	0
MFS® Blended Research Growth Equity Fund Class R6	BRWVX	NAS CM	Open End	US Equity Large Cap Growth (Growth)	C	C+	B	Up	Y	0
MFS® Blended Research International Equity Fund Class A	BRXAX	NAS CM	Open End	Global Equity Large Cap (Foreign Stock)	C	C+	B	Up	Y	1,000
MFS® Blended Research International Equity Fund Class B	BRXBX	NAS CM	Open End	Global Equity Large Cap (Foreign Stock)	C	C+	B-	Up	Y	1,000
MFS® Blended Research International Equity Fund Class C	BRXCX	NAS CM	Open End	Global Equity Large Cap (Foreign Stock)	C	C+	B-	Up	Y	1,000
MFS® Blended Research International Equity Fund Class I	BRXIX	NAS CM	Open End	Global Equity Large Cap (Foreign Stock)	C	C+	B	Up	Y	0
MFS® Blended Research International Equity Fund Class R1	BRXRX	NAS CM	Open End	Global Equity Large Cap (Foreign Stock)	C	C+	B-	Up	Y	0
MFS® Blended Research International Equity Fund Class R2	BRXSX	NAS CM	Open End	Global Equity Large Cap (Foreign Stock)	C	C+	B-	Up	Y	0
MFS® Blended Research International Equity Fund Class R3	BRXTX	NAS CM	Open End	Global Equity Large Cap (Foreign Stock)	C	C+	B-	Up	Y	0
MFS® Blended Research International Equity Fund Class R4	BRXUX	NAS CM	Open End	Global Equity Large Cap (Foreign Stock)	C	C+	B	Up	Y	0
MFS® Blended Research International Equity Fund Class R6	BRXVX	NAS CM	Open End	Global Equity Large Cap (Foreign Stock)	C	C+	B	Up	Y	0
MFS® Blended Research Mid Cap Equity Fund A	BMSFX	NAS CM	Open End	US Equity Mid Cap (Growth)	D	C	B+	Up	Y	1,000
MFS® Blended Research Mid Cap Equity Fund B	BMSBX	NAS CM	Open End	US Equity Mid Cap (Growth)	D	C-	B+	Up	Y	1,000
MFS® Blended Research Mid Cap Equity Fund C	BMSDX	NAS CM	Open End	US Equity Mid Cap (Growth)	D	C-	B+	Up	Y	1,000
MFS® Blended Research Mid Cap Equity Fund I	BMSLX	NAS CM	Open End	US Equity Mid Cap (Growth)	D	C	A-	Up	Y	0
MFS® Blended Research Mid Cap Equity Fund R1	BMSRX	NAS CM	Open End	US Equity Mid Cap (Growth)	D	C-	B+	Up	Y	0
MFS® Blended Research Mid Cap Equity Fund R2	BMSSX	NAS CM	Open End	US Equity Mid Cap (Growth)	D	C	B+	Up	Y	0
MFS® Blended Research Mid Cap Equity Fund R3	BMSTX	NAS CM	Open End	US Equity Mid Cap (Growth)	D	C	B+	Up	Y	0
MFS® Blended Research Mid Cap Equity Fund R4	BMSVX	NAS CM	Open End	US Equity Mid Cap (Growth)	D	C	A-	Up	Y	0
MFS® Blended Research Mid Cap Equity Fund R6	BMSYX	NAS CM	Open End	US Equity Mid Cap (Growth)	D	C	A-	Up	Y	0
MFS® Blended Research Small Cap Equity Fund 529A	BRSNX	NAS CM	Open End	US Equity Small Cap (Small Company)	C	C+	B	Up	Y	250
MFS® Blended Research Small Cap Equity Fund 529B	BRSQX	NAS CM	Open End	US Equity Small Cap (Small Company)	C	C+	B	Up	Y	250
MFS® Blended Research Small Cap Equity Fund 529C	BRSWX	NAS CM	Open End	US Equity Small Cap (Small Company)	C	C+	B	Up	Y	250
MFS® Blended Research Small Cap Equity Fund Class A	BRSDX	NAS CM	Open End	US Equity Small Cap (Small Company)	C	C+	B	Up	Y	1,000
MFS® Blended Research Small Cap Equity Fund Class B	BRSBX	NAS CM	Open End	US Equity Small Cap (Small Company)	C	C+	B	Up	Y	1,000
MFS® Blended Research Small Cap Equity Fund Class C	BRSHX	NAS CM	Open End	US Equity Small Cap (Small Company)	C	C+	B	Up	Y	1,000
MFS® Blended Research Small Cap Equity Fund Class I	BRSJX	NAS CM	Open End	US Equity Small Cap (Small Company)	C	C+	B	Up	Y	0
MFS® Blended Research Small Cap Equity Fund Class R1	BRSPX	NAS CM	Open End	US Equity Small Cap (Small Company)	C	C+	B	Up	Y	0
MFS® Blended Research Small Cap Equity Fund Class R2	BRSSX	NAS CM	Open End	US Equity Small Cap (Small Company)	C	C+	B	Up	Y	0
MFS® Blended Research Small Cap Equity Fund Class R3	BRSTX	NAS CM	Open End	US Equity Small Cap (Small Company)	C	C+	B	Up	Y	0
MFS® Blended Research Small Cap Equity Fund Class R4	BRSUX	NAS CM	Open End	US Equity Small Cap (Small Company)	C	C+	B	Up	Y	0
MFS® Blended Research Small Cap Equity Fund Class R6	BRSYX	NAS CM	Open End	US Equity Small Cap (Small Company)	C	C+	B	Up	Y	0
MFS® Blended Research Value Equity Fund Class A	BRUDX	NAS CM	Open End	US Equity Large Cap Value (Growth)	C	C+	B	Up	Y	1,000
MFS® Blended Research Value Equity Fund Class B	BRUEX	NAS CM	Open End	US Equity Large Cap Value (Growth)	C	C+	B	Up	Y	1,000
MFS® Blended Research Value Equity Fund Class C	BRUGX	NAS CM	Open End	US Equity Large Cap Value (Growth)	C	C+	B	Up	Y	1,000
MFS® Blended Research Value Equity Fund Class I	BRUHX	NAS CM	Open End	US Equity Large Cap Value (Growth)	C	C+	B	Up	Y	0
MFS® Blended Research Value Equity Fund Class R1	BRUJX	NAS CM	Open End	US Equity Large Cap Value (Growth)	C	C+	B	Up	Y	0
MFS® Blended Research Value Equity Fund Class R2	BRUKX	NAS CM	Open End	US Equity Large Cap Value (Growth)	C	C+	B	Up	Y	0
MFS® Blended Research Value Equity Fund Class R3	BRULX	NAS CM	Open End	US Equity Large Cap Value (Growth)	C	C+	B	Up	Y	0
MFS® Blended Research Value Equity Fund Class R4	BRUMX	NAS CM	Open End	US Equity Large Cap Value (Growth)	C	C+	B	Up	Y	0
MFS® Blended Research Value Equity Fund Class R6	BRUNX	NAS CM	Open End	US Equity Large Cap Value (Growth)	C	C+	B	Up	Y	0
MFS® Commodity Strategy Fund Class A	MCSAX	NAS CM	Open End	Commodities Broad Basket (Growth)	C-	C-	D+	Up	Y	1,000
MFS® Commodity Strategy Fund Class I	MCSIX	NAS CM	Open End	Commodities Broad Basket (Growth)	C-	C-	D+	Up	Y	0
MFS® Commodity Strategy Fund Class R6	MCSRX	NAS CM	Open End	Commodities Broad Basket (Growth)	C-	C-	D+	Up	Y	0
MFS® Conservative Allocation Fund Class 529A	ECLAX	NAS CM	Open End	Cautious Alloc (Balanced)	B	C+	A-	Up	Y	250
MFS® Conservative Allocation Fund Class 529B	EBCAX	NAS CM	Open End	Cautious Alloc (Balanced)	B	C+	A-	Up	Y	250

★Expanded analysis of this fund is included in Section II.

	TOTAL RETURNS					PERFORMANCE				ASSETS		ASSET ALLOCATION & TURNOVER					BULL & BEAR		FEES		
Min Additional Investment	3-Month Total Return	6-Month Total Return	1-Year Total Return	3-Year Total Return	5-Year Total Return	Dividend Yield (TTM)	Expense Ratio	3-Yr Std Deviation	3-Year Beta	NAV	Total Assets (MIL)	%Cash	%Stocks	%Bonds	%Other	Turnover Ratio	Last Bull Market Total Return	Last Bear Market Total Return	Front End Fee (%)	Back End Fee (%)	Inception Date
	7.07	12.82	25.67			0	1.49			13.35	191.6	2	98	0	0	57				4.00	Sep-15
	7.16	12.82	25.67			0	1.49			13.35	191.6	2	98	0	0	57				1.00	Sep-15
	7.37	13.33	26.91			0.31	0.49			13.5	191.6	2	98	0	0	57					Sep-15
	7.16	12.82	25.67			0	1.49			13.35	191.6	2	98	0	0	57					Sep-15
	7.26	13.06	26.30			0	0.99			13.46	191.6	2	98	0	0	57					Sep-15
	7.37	13.25	26.71			0.11	0.74			13.5	191.6	2	98	0	0	57					Sep-15
	7.36	13.41	26.99			0.3	0.49			13.5	191.6	2	98	0	0	57					Sep-15
	7.50	13.47	27.17			0.33	0.45			13.51	191.6	2	98	0	0	57					Sep-15
	3.96	10.77	26.84			0.32	0.89			12.18	293.8	2	98	0	0	63			5.75		Sep-15
	3.72	10.39	25.88			0	1.64			12.17	293.8	2	98	0	0	63				4.00	Sep-15
	3.76	10.33	25.82			0	1.64			12.11	293.8	2	98	0	0	63				1.00	Sep-15
	3.96	10.85	27.14			0.43	0.64			12.22	293.8	2	98	0	0	63					Sep-15
	3.71	10.38	25.87			0	1.64			12.16	293.8	2	98	0	0	63					Sep-15
	3.83	10.63	26.42			0.03	1.14			12.22	293.8	2	98	0	0	63					Sep-15
	3.88	10.74	26.70			0	0.89			12.27	293.8	2	98	0	0	63					Sep-15
	4.04	10.94	27.11			0.42	0.64			12.23	293.8	2	98	0	0	63					Sep-15
	4.00	10.89	27.05			0.45	0.6			12.22	293.8	2	98	0	0	63					Sep-15
	6.03	9.91	18.81			0.33	0.84			11.91	290.5	1	99	0	0				5.75		Aug-16
	5.84	9.44	17.88			0.09	1.59			11.91	290.5	1	99	0	0					4.00	Aug-16
	5.79	9.38	17.82			0.09	1.59			11.9	290.5	1	99	0	0					1.00	Aug-16
	6.05	10.02	19.04			0.39	0.59			11.93	290.5	1	99	0	0						Aug-16
	5.84	9.44	17.88			0.09	1.59			11.91	290.5	1	99	0	0						Aug-16
	6.03	9.72	18.50			0.24	1.09			11.93	290.5	1	99	0	0						Aug-16
	6.08	9.87	18.77			0.32	0.84			11.93	290.5	1	99	0	0						Aug-16
	6.05	10.02	19.04			0.39	0.59			11.93	290.5	1	99	0	0						Aug-16
	6.15	10.03	19.05			0.4	0.55			11.93	290.5	1	99	0	0						Aug-16
	3.05	8.69	13.41			0.22	1.04			12.9	99.7	2	98	0	0	90			5.75		Jul-16
	2.89	8.22	12.58			0	1.79			12.76	99.7	2	98	0	0	90				4.00	Jul-16
	2.89	8.32	12.59			0	1.79			12.75	99.7	2	98	0	0	90				1.00	Jul-16
	3.07	8.70	13.51			0.21	0.99			12.88	99.7	2	98	0	0	90			5.75		Sep-15
	2.88	8.30	12.66			0	1.74			12.77	99.7	2	98	0	0	90				4.00	Sep-15
	2.89	8.31	12.67			0	1.74			12.76	99.7	2	98	0	0	90				1.00	Sep-15
	3.10	8.80	13.80			0.26	0.74			12.93	99.7	2	98	0	0	90					Sep-15
	2.88	8.30	12.66			0	1.74			12.77	99.7	2	98	0	0	90					Sep-15
	3.01	8.57	13.19			0	1.24			12.9	99.7	2	98	0	0	90					Sep-15
	3.07	8.69	13.50			0.06	0.99			12.93	99.7	2	98	0	0	90					Sep-15
	3.15	8.85	13.85			0.25	0.74			12.94	99.7	2	98	0	0	90					Sep-15
	3.21	8.92	13.92			0.28	0.7			12.94	99.7	2	98	0	0	90					Sep-15
	5.81	10.88	16.36			0.47	0.74			12.97	185.6	3	97	0	0	51			5.75		Sep-15
	5.66	10.48	15.56			0.04	1.49			12.99	185.6	3	97	0	0	51				4.00	Sep-15
	5.69	10.45	15.55			0.26	1.49			12.94	185.6	3	97	0	0	51				1.00	Sep-15
	5.87	11.01	16.68			0.62	0.49			13.03	185.6	3	97	0	0	51					Sep-15
	5.68	10.50	15.48			0	1.49			12.98	185.6	3	97	0	0	51					Sep-15
	5.82	10.80	16.07			0.22	0.99			13.02	185.6	3	97	0	0	51					Sep-15
	5.87	10.94	16.41			0.42	0.74			13.03	185.6	3	97	0	0	51					Sep-15
	5.87	11.01	16.67			0.61	0.49			13.03	185.6	3	97	0	0	51					Sep-15
	5.93	11.07	16.74			0.64	0.45			13.04	185.6	3	97	0	0	51					Sep-15
	5.32	9.24	3.37	-13.33	-34.17	0.37	1.08	12.22	0.93	5.98	585.4	27	0	73	0	32	1.29	-20.98	5.75		Jun-10
	5.41	9.33	3.64	-12.56	-33.28	0.61	0.83	12.14	0.93	5.97	585.4	27	0	73	0	32	1.41	-20.89			Jun-10
	5.58	9.51	3.81	-12.54	-33.25	0.61	0.83	12.16	0.93	5.98	585.4	27	0	73	0	32	1.41	-20.89			Sep-12
	2.34	4.50	10.81	15.44	31.35	1.59	0.98	4.36	0.37	15.42	2,981	4	36	59	0	3	10.71	-6.4	5.75		Jul-02
	2.09	4.02	9.92	12.82	26.42	0.9	1.73	4.38	0.37	15.18	2,981	4	36	59	0	3	10.18	-6.66		4.00	Jul-02

	MARKET		FUND TYPE, CATEGORY & OBJECTIVE		RATINGS				MINIMUMS	
Fund Name	Ticker Symbol	Traded On	Fund Type	Category and (Prospectus Objective)	Overall Rating	Reward Rating	Risk Rating	Recent Up/ Downgrade	Open to New Investors	Min Initial Investment
MFS® Conservative Allocation Fund Class 529C	ECACX	NAS CM	Open End	Cautious Alloc (Balanced)	B	C+	A-	Up	Y	250
MFS® Conservative Allocation Fund Class A	MACFX	NAS CM	Open End	Cautious Alloc (Balanced)	B	C+	A-	Up	Y	1,000
MFS® Conservative Allocation Fund Class B	MACBX	NAS CM	Open End	Cautious Alloc (Balanced)	B	C+	A-	Up	Y	1,000
MFS® Conservative Allocation Fund Class C	MACVX	NAS CM	Open End	Cautious Alloc (Balanced)	B	C+	A-	Up	Y	1,000
MFS® Conservative Allocation Fund Class I	MACIX	NAS CM	Open End	Cautious Alloc (Balanced)	B	C+	A-	Up	Y	0
MFS® Conservative Allocation Fund Class R1	MACKX	NAS CM	Open End	Cautious Alloc (Balanced)	B	C+	A-	Up	Y	0
MFS® Conservative Allocation Fund Class R2	MCARX	NAS CM	Open End	Cautious Alloc (Balanced)	B	C+	A-	Up	Y	0
MFS® Conservative Allocation Fund Class R3	MACNX	NAS CM	Open End	Cautious Alloc (Balanced)	B	C+	A-	Up	Y	0
MFS® Conservative Allocation Fund Class R4	MACJX	NAS CM	Open End	Cautious Alloc (Balanced)	B	C+	A-	Up	Y	0
MFS® Core Equity Fund Class A	MRGAX	NAS CM	Open End	US Equity Large Cap Blend (Growth)	B	B	B-		Y	1,000
MFS® Core Equity Fund Class B	MRGBX	NAS CM	Open End	US Equity Large Cap Blend (Growth)	B	B	B-	Up	Y	1,000
MFS® Core Equity Fund Class C	MRGCX	NAS CM	Open End	US Equity Large Cap Blend (Growth)	B	B	B-	Up	Y	1,000
MFS® Core Equity Fund Class I	MRGRX	NAS CM	Open End	US Equity Large Cap Blend (Growth)	B	B	B-		Y	0
MFS® Core Equity Fund Class R1	MRGGX	NAS CM	Open End	US Equity Large Cap Blend (Growth)	B	B	B-	Up	Y	0
MFS® Core Equity Fund Class R2	MRERX	NAS CM	Open End	US Equity Large Cap Blend (Growth)	B	B	B-		Y	0
MFS® Core Equity Fund Class R3	MRGHX	NAS CM	Open End	US Equity Large Cap Blend (Growth)	B	B	B-		Y	0
MFS® Core Equity Fund Class R4	MRGJX	NAS CM	Open End	US Equity Large Cap Blend (Growth)	B	B	B-		Y	0
MFS® Core Equity Fund Class R6	MRGKX	NAS CM	Open End	US Equity Large Cap Blend (Growth)	B	B	B-		Y	0
MFS® Diversified Income Fund Class A	DIFAX	NAS CM	Open End	Cautious Alloc (Growth & Income)	B	C+	A-	Up	Y	1,000
MFS® Diversified Income Fund Class C	DIFCX	NAS CM	Open End	Cautious Alloc (Growth & Income)	B-	C+	B+	Up	Y	1,000
MFS® Diversified Income Fund Class I	DIFIX	NAS CM	Open End	Cautious Alloc (Growth & Income)	B	C+	A-	Up	Y	0
MFS® Diversified Income Fund Class R1	DIFDX	NAS CM	Open End	Cautious Alloc (Growth & Income)	B-	C+	B+	Up	Y	0
MFS® Diversified Income Fund Class R2	DIFEX	NAS CM	Open End	Cautious Alloc (Growth & Income)	B	C+	B+	Up	Y	0
MFS® Diversified Income Fund Class R3	DIFFX	NAS CM	Open End	Cautious Alloc (Growth & Income)	B	C+	A-	Up	Y	0
MFS® Diversified Income Fund Class R4	DIFGX	NAS CM	Open End	Cautious Alloc (Growth & Income)	B	C+	A-	Up	Y	0
MFS® Diversified Income Fund Class R6	DIFHX	NAS CM	Open End	Cautious Alloc (Growth & Income)	B	C+	A-	Up	Y	0
MFS® Emerging Markets Equity Fund Class A	MEMAX	NAS CM	Open End	Emerging Markets Equity (Div Emerging Mkts)	B-	B-	C	Up	Y	1,000
MFS® Emerging Markets Equity Fund Class B	MEMBX	NAS CM	Open End	Emerging Markets Equity (Div Emerging Mkts)	C+	B-	C	Up	Y	1,000
MFS® Emerging Markets Equity Fund Class C	MEMCX	NAS CM	Open End	Emerging Markets Equity (Div Emerging Mkts)	C+	B-	C	Up	Y	1,000
MFS® Emerging Markets Equity Fund Class I	MEMIX	NAS CM	Open End	Emerging Markets Equity (Div Emerging Mkts)	B-	B	C	Up	Y	0
MFS® Emerging Markets Equity Fund Class R1	MEMRX	NAS CM	Open End	Emerging Markets Equity (Div Emerging Mkts)	C+	B-	C	Up	Y	0
MFS® Emerging Markets Equity Fund Class R2	MEMFX	NAS CM	Open End	Emerging Markets Equity (Div Emerging Mkts)	C+	B-	C	Up	Y	0
MFS® Emerging Markets Equity Fund Class R3	MEMGX	NAS CM	Open End	Emerging Markets Equity (Div Emerging Mkts)	B-	B-	C	Up	Y	0
MFS® Emerging Markets Equity Fund Class R4	MEMHX	NAS CM	Open End	Emerging Markets Equity (Div Emerging Mkts)	B-	B	C	Up	Y	0
MFS® Emerging Markets Equity Fund Class R6	MEMJX	NAS CM	Open End	Emerging Markets Equity (Div Emerging Mkts)	B-	B	C	Up	Y	0
MFS® Equity Income Fund Class A	EQNAX	NAS CM	Open End	US Equity Large Cap Value (Equity-Income)	B-	B-	B-	Down	Y	1,000
MFS® Equity Income Fund Class B	EQNBX	NAS CM	Open End	US Equity Large Cap Value (Equity-Income)	B-	B-	B-	Down	Y	1,000
MFS® Equity Income Fund Class C	EQNCX	NAS CM	Open End	US Equity Large Cap Value (Equity-Income)	B-	B-	B-	Down	Y	1,000
MFS® Equity Income Fund Class I	EQNIX	NAS CM	Open End	US Equity Large Cap Value (Equity-Income)	B-	B-	B-	Down	Y	0
MFS® Equity Income Fund Class R1	EQNRX	NAS CM	Open End	US Equity Large Cap Value (Equity-Income)	B-	B-	B-	Down	Y	0
MFS® Equity Income Fund Class R2	EQNSX	NAS CM	Open End	US Equity Large Cap Value (Equity-Income)	B-	B-	B-	Down	Y	0
MFS® Equity Income Fund Class R3	EQNTX	NAS CM	Open End	US Equity Large Cap Value (Equity-Income)	B-	B-	B-	Down	Y	0
MFS® Equity Income Fund Class R4	EQNUX	NAS CM	Open End	US Equity Large Cap Value (Equity-Income)	B-	B-	B-	Down	Y	0
MFS® Equity Income Fund Class R6	EQNVX	NAS CM	Open End	US Equity Large Cap Value (Equity-Income)	B-	B-	B-	Down	Y	0
MFS® Equity Opportunities Fund Class A	SRFAX	NAS CM	Open End	US Equity Large Cap Blend (Growth)	B	B-	B+		Y	1,000
MFS® Equity Opportunities Fund Class B	SRFBX	NAS CM	Open End	US Equity Large Cap Blend (Growth)	B	B-	B+	Up	Y	1,000
MFS® Equity Opportunities Fund Class C	SRFCX	NAS CM	Open End	US Equity Large Cap Blend (Growth)	B	B-	B+	Up	Y	1,000
MFS® Equity Opportunities Fund Class I	SRFIX	NAS CM	Open End	US Equity Large Cap Blend (Growth)	B	B	B+		Y	0
MFS® Equity Opportunities Fund Class R1	SRFDX	NAS CM	Open End	US Equity Large Cap Blend (Growth)	B	B-	B+	Up	Y	0
MFS® Equity Opportunities Fund Class R2	SRFEX	NAS CM	Open End	US Equity Large Cap Blend (Growth)	B	B-	B+		Y	0
MFS® Equity Opportunities Fund Class R3	SRFFX	NAS CM	Open End	US Equity Large Cap Blend (Growth)	B	B-	B+		Y	0
MFS® Equity Opportunities Fund Class R4	SRFGX	NAS CM	Open End	US Equity Large Cap Blend (Growth)	B	B	B+		Y	0

★ Expanded analysis of this fund is included in Section II.

	TOTAL RETURNS					PERFORMANCE				ASSETS		ASSET ALLOCATION & TURNOVER					BULL & BEAR		FEES		
Min Additional Investment	3-Month Total Return	6-Month Total Return	1-Year Total Return	3-Year Total Return	5-Year Total Return	Dividend Yield (TTM)	Expense Ratio	3-Yr Std Deviation	3-Year Beta	NAV	Total Assets (MIL)	%Cash	%Stocks	%Bonds	%Other	Turnover Ratio	Last Bull Market Total Return	Last Bear Market Total Return	Front End Fee (%)	Back End Fee (%)	Inception Date
	2.10	4.11	9.97	12.78	26.44	0.92	1.73	4.4	0.36	15.13	2,981	4	36	59	0	3	10.23	-6.71		1.00	Jul-02
	2.33	4.50	10.78	15.56	31.61	1.61	0.93	4.36	0.37	15.5	2,981	4	36	59	0	3	10.69	-6.33	5.75		Jun-02
	2.13	4.10	10.00	13.03	26.80	0.9	1.68	4.36	0.37	15.42	2,981	4	36	59	0	3	10.26	-6.66		4.00	Jun-02
	2.15	4.15	10.03	13.05	26.77	0.92	1.68	4.38	0.38	15.28	2,981	4	36	59	0	3	10.26	-6.68		1.00	Jun-02
	2.32	4.59	11.03	16.44	33.23	1.84	0.68	4.38	0.37	15.63	2,981	4	36	59	0	3	10.91	-6.25			Jun-02
	2.07	4.10	9.96	12.95	26.76	0.94	1.68	4.37	0.37	14.98	2,981	4	36	59	0	3	10.29	-6.66			Apr-05
	2.26	4.35	10.52	14.68	29.92	1.42	1.18	4.36	0.36	15.07	2,981	4	36	59	0	3	10.65	-6.45			Oct-03
	2.28	4.46	10.80	15.53	31.62	1.63	0.93	4.37	0.37	15.37	2,981	4	36	59	0	3	10.77	-6.38			Apr-05
	2.34	4.63	11.05	16.42	33.25	1.85	0.68	4.33	0.36	15.5	2,981	4	36	59	0	3	10.9	-6.29			Apr-05
	6.15	11.41	24.45	36.55	108.83	0.47	1.02	10.16	0.97	30.95	1,853	2	98	0	0	46	24.33	-17.61	5.75		Jan-96
	5.94	11.01	23.55	33.53	101.18	0	1.77	10.15	0.97	27.48	1,853	2	98	0	0	46	23.83	-17.92		4.00	Jan-97
	5.93	10.98	23.50	33.54	101.20	0	1.77	10.15	0.97	27.16	1,853	2	98	0	0	46	23.78	-17.88		1.00	Jan-97
	6.21	11.54	24.76	37.58	111.48	0.69	0.77	10.16	0.97	32.65	1,853	2	98	0	0	46	24.53	-17.53			Jan-97
	5.93	10.99	23.52	33.51	101.10	0	1.77	10.14	0.97	27.14	1,853	2	98	0	0	46	23.83	-17.91			Apr-05
	6.09	11.29	24.18	35.55	106.30	0.27	1.27	10.16	0.97	30.23	1,853	2	98	0	0	46	24.17	-17.69			Oct-03
	6.14	11.38	24.43	36.49	108.77	0.47	1.02	10.17	0.97	30.88	1,853	2	98	0	0	46	24.37	-17.65			Apr-05
	6.19	11.55	24.77	37.56	111.46	0.66	0.77	10.16	0.97	31.17	1,853	2	98	0	0	46	24.55	-17.55			Apr-05
	6.23	11.60	24.85	37.95	112.37	0.72	0.68	10.16	0.97	32.69	1,853	2	98	0	0	46	24.33	-17.61			Jan-13
	1.26	3.57	8.60	14.73	36.64	2.97	1.02	5.3	0.41	12.57	4,106	3	40	56	0	46	15.56	-8.2	4.25		May-06
	1.08	3.19	7.72	12.20	31.54	2.24	1.77	5.26	0.41	12.56	4,106	3	40	56	0	46	15.08	-8.59		1.00	May-06
	1.40	3.69	8.87	15.58	38.35	3.21	0.77	5.31	0.42	12.57	4,106	3	40	56	0	46	15.72	-8.11			May-06
	1.08	3.19	7.82	12.20	31.56	2.24	1.77	5.28	0.41	12.55	4,106	3	40	56	0	46	15.2	-8.59			Jul-08
	1.20	3.44	8.25	13.88	34.85	2.72	1.27	5.24	0.41	12.56	4,106	3	40	56	0	46	15.41	-8.31			Jul-08
	1.26	3.57	8.51	14.73	36.52	2.97	1.02	5.3	0.41	12.57	4,106	3	40	56	0	46	15.68	-8.3			Jul-08
	1.32	3.69	8.78	15.58	38.34	3.21	0.77	5.27	0.41	12.57	4,106	3	40	56	0	46	15.84	-8.2			Jul-08
	1.34	3.74	8.97	15.93	39.01	3.3	0.67	5.28	0.41	12.57	4,106	3	40	56	0	46	15.72	-8.11			Jul-12
	5.84	14.68	37.37	29.69	15.66	0.4	1.5	13.87	0.84	35.11	1,318	3	96	0	0	43	19.54	-25.58	5.75		Oct-95
	5.64	14.24	36.36	26.76	11.38	0	2.25	13.86	0.84	32.4	1,318	3	96	0	0	43	19.06	-25.85		4.00	Oct-95
	5.64	14.26	36.37	26.76	11.37	0	2.25	13.86	0.84	31.64	1,318	3	96	0	0	43	19.04	-25.85		1.00	Jun-96
	5.95	14.85	37.74	30.64	17.11	0.58	1.25	13.87	0.84	36.95	1,318	3	96	0	0	43	19.73	-25.53			Jan-97
	5.65	14.27	36.37	26.78	11.36	0	2.25	13.86	0.84	31.38	1,318	3	96	0	0	43	19.03	-25.82			Oct-08
	5.79	14.59	37.04	28.69	14.21	0.36	1.75	13.88	0.84	32.11	1,318	3	96	0	0	43	19.36	-25.67			Oct-08
	5.86	14.71	37.41	29.68	15.69	0.37	1.5	13.88	0.84	34.97	1,318	3	96	0	0	43	19.59	-25.61			Oct-08
	5.94	14.86	37.75	30.63	17.09	0.61	1.25	13.88	0.84	34.94	1,318	3	96	0	0	43	19.74	-25.53			Oct-08
	5.94	14.91	37.86	31.07	17.71	0.65	1.15	13.87	0.84	36.94	1,318	3	96	0	0	43	19.54	-25.58			Jun-12
	5.29	9.62	19.64	29.39	89.25	1.78	0.89	9.53	0.91	15.77	199.4	1	98	0	0	47			5.75		Sep-12
	5.07	9.12	18.71	26.52	82.23	1.11	1.64	9.5	0.91	15.76	199.4	1	98	0	0	47				4.00	Sep-12
	5.07	9.13	18.70	26.49	82.29	1.1	1.64	9.49	0.91	15.76	199.4	1	98	0	0	47				1.00	Sep-12
	5.36	9.83	20.02	30.52	91.69	2.01	0.64	9.52	0.91	15.78	199.4	1	98	0	0	47					Sep-12
	5.09	9.14	18.76	26.53	82.20	1.1	1.64	9.48	0.91	15.84	199.4	1	98	0	0	47					Sep-12
	5.15	9.40	19.29	28.38	86.71	1.54	1.14	9.5	0.91	15.8	199.4	1	98	0	0	47					Sep-12
	5.28	9.53	19.60	29.34	89.14	1.78	0.89	9.51	0.91	15.79	199.4	1	98	0	0	47					Sep-12
	5.36	9.68	19.93	30.32	91.50	2	0.64	9.47	0.91	15.78	199.4	1	98	0	0	47					Sep-12
	5.43	9.84	20.11	30.88	93.56	2.09	0.55	9.5	0.91	15.87	199.4	1	98	0	0	47					Sep-12
	5.02	7.65	18.08	31.31	101.43	0.48	1.2	9.72	0.9	33.85	468.8	1	99	0	0	109	26.82	-18.71	5.75		Aug-00
	4.80	7.23	17.18	28.37	93.88	0	1.95	9.72	0.9	32.12	468.8	1	99	0	0	109	26.32	-18.99		4.00	Jan-07
	4.80	7.23	17.16	28.33	93.94	0	1.95	9.7	0.9	32.15	468.8	1	99	0	0	109	26.23	-18.97		1.00	Mar-04
	5.07	7.76	18.31	32.27	103.86	0.7	0.95	9.7	0.9	33.89	468.8	1	99	0	0	109	27.05	-18.66			Feb-11
	4.78	7.22	17.15	28.32	93.92	0	1.95	9.7	0.9	32.03	468.8	1	99	0	0	109	26.28	-18.94			May-08
	4.94	7.55	17.77	30.31	98.84	0.32	1.45	9.72	0.9	32.91	468.8	1	99	0	0	109	26.66	-18.77			May-08
	5.01	7.65	18.04	31.31	101.35	0.5	1.2	9.7	0.9	33.73	468.8	1	99	0	0	109	26.77	-18.68			May-08
	5.08	7.79	18.34	32.26	103.88	0.7	0.95	9.72	0.9	33.97	468.8	1	99	0	0	109	26.96	-18.61			May-08

Fund Name	MARKET Ticker Symbol	Traded On	FUND TYPE, CATEGORY & OBJECTIVE Fund Type	Category and (Prospectus Objective)	RATINGS Overall Rating	Reward Rating	Risk Rating	Recent Up/ Downgrade	MINIMUMS Open to New Investors	Min Initial Investment
MFS® Equity Opportunities Fund Class R6	SRFHX	NAS CM	Open End	US Equity Large Cap Blend (Growth)	B	B	B+		Y	0
MFS® Global Alternative Strategy Fund Class A	DVRAX	NAS CM	Open End	Multialternative (Growth & Income)	C	C	C		Y	1,000
MFS® Global Alternative Strategy Fund Class B	DVRBX	NAS CM	Open End	Multialternative (Growth & Income)	C	C-	C		Y	1,000
MFS® Global Alternative Strategy Fund Class C	DVRCX	NAS CM	Open End	Multialternative (Growth & Income)	C	C-	C		Y	1,000
MFS® Global Alternative Strategy Fund Class I	DVRIX	NAS CM	Open End	Multialternative (Growth & Income)	C	C	C		Y	0
MFS® Global Alternative Strategy Fund Class R1	DVRFX	NAS CM	Open End	Multialternative (Growth & Income)	C	C-	C		Y	0
MFS® Global Alternative Strategy Fund Class R2	DVRHX	NAS CM	Open End	Multialternative (Growth & Income)	C	C	C		Y	0
MFS® Global Alternative Strategy Fund Class R3	DVRJX	NAS CM	Open End	Multialternative (Growth & Income)	C	C	C		Y	0
MFS® Global Alternative Strategy Fund Class R4	DVRKX	NAS CM	Open End	Multialternative (Growth & Income)	C	C	C		Y	0
MFS® Global Alternative Strategy Fund Class R6	DVRLX	NAS CM	Open End	Multialternative (Growth & Income)	C	C	C		Y	0
MFS® Global Equity Fund Class A	MWEFX	NAS CM	Open End	Global Equity (World Stock)	B	B-	B	Up	Y	1,000
MFS® Global Equity Fund Class B	MWEBX	NAS CM	Open End	Global Equity (World Stock)	B	B-	B	Up	Y	1,000
MFS® Global Equity Fund Class C	MWECX	NAS CM	Open End	Global Equity (World Stock)	B	B-	B	Up	Y	1,000
MFS® Global Equity Fund Class I	MWEIX	NAS CM	Open End	Global Equity (World Stock)	B	B-	B+	Up	Y	0
MFS® Global Equity Fund Class R1	MWEGX	NAS CM	Open End	Global Equity (World Stock)	B	B-	B	Up	Y	0
MFS® Global Equity Fund Class R2	MEQRX	NAS CM	Open End	Global Equity (World Stock)	B	B-	B	Up	Y	0
MFS® Global Equity Fund Class R3	MWEHX	NAS CM	Open End	Global Equity (World Stock)	B	B-	B	Up	Y	0
MFS® Global Equity Fund Class R4	MWELX	NAS CM	Open End	Global Equity (World Stock)	B	B-	B+	Up	Y	0
MFS® Global Equity Fund Class R6	MWEMX	NAS CM	Open End	Global Equity (World Stock)	B	B-	B+	Up	Y	0
MFS® Global Growth Fund Class A	MWOFX	NAS CM	Open End	Global Equity (World Stock)	B	B	B	Up	Y	1,000
MFS® Global Growth Fund Class B	MWOBX	NAS CM	Open End	Global Equity (World Stock)	B	B	B	Up	Y	1,000
MFS® Global Growth Fund Class C	MWOCX	NAS CM	Open End	Global Equity (World Stock)	B	B	B	Up	Y	1,000
MFS® Global Growth Fund Class I	MWOIX	NAS CM	Open End	Global Equity (World Stock)	B	B	B	Up	Y	0
MFS® Global Growth Fund Class R1	MWOGX	NAS CM	Open End	Global Equity (World Stock)	B	B	B	Up	Y	0
MFS® Global Growth Fund Class R2	MGWRX	NAS CM	Open End	Global Equity (World Stock)	B	B	B	Up	Y	0
MFS® Global Growth Fund Class R3	MWOHX	NAS CM	Open End	Global Equity (World Stock)	B	B	B	Up	Y	0
MFS® Global Growth Fund Class R4	MWOJX	NAS CM	Open End	Global Equity (World Stock)	B	B	B	Up	Y	0
MFS® Global Growth Fund Class R6	MWOKX	NAS CM	Open End	Global Equity (World Stock)	B	B	B	Up	Y	0
MFS® Global Multi-Asset Fund Class A	GLMAX	NAS CM	Open End	Alloc (Growth)	C+	C	B-	Up	Y	1,000
MFS® Global Multi-Asset Fund Class B	GLMBX	NAS CM	Open End	Alloc (Growth)	C+	C	B-	Up	Y	1,000
MFS® Global Multi-Asset Fund Class C	GLMCX	NAS CM	Open End	Alloc (Growth)	C+	C	B-	Up	Y	1,000
MFS® Global Multi-Asset Fund Class I	GLMIX	NAS CM	Open End	Alloc (Growth)	C+	C	B-		Y	0
MFS® Global Multi-Asset Fund Class R1	GLMRX	NAS CM	Open End	Alloc (Growth)	C+	C	B-	Up	Y	0
MFS® Global Multi-Asset Fund Class R2	GLMSX	NAS CM	Open End	Alloc (Growth)	C+	C	B-	Up	Y	0
MFS® Global Multi-Asset Fund Class R3	GLMTX	NAS CM	Open End	Alloc (Growth)	C+	C	B-	Up	Y	0
MFS® Global Multi-Asset Fund Class R4	GLMUX	NAS CM	Open End	Alloc (Growth)	C+	C	B-		Y	0
MFS® Global Multi-Asset Fund Class R6	GLMVX	NAS CM	Open End	Alloc (Growth)	C+	C	B-		Y	0
MFS® Global New Discovery Fund Class A	GLNAX	NAS CM	Open End	Global Equity Mid/Small Cap (World Stock)	B+	B	B+	Up	Y	1,000
MFS® Global New Discovery Fund Class B	GLNBX	NAS CM	Open End	Global Equity Mid/Small Cap (World Stock)	B	B	B+	Up	Y	1,000
MFS® Global New Discovery Fund Class C	GLNCX	NAS CM	Open End	Global Equity Mid/Small Cap (World Stock)	B	B	B+	Up	Y	1,000
MFS® Global New Discovery Fund Class I	GLNIX	NAS CM	Open End	Global Equity Mid/Small Cap (World Stock)	B+	B	B+	Up	Y	0
MFS® Global New Discovery Fund Class R1	GLNJX	NAS CM	Open End	Global Equity Mid/Small Cap (World Stock)	B	B	B+	Up	Y	0
MFS® Global New Discovery Fund Class R2	GLNKX	NAS CM	Open End	Global Equity Mid/Small Cap (World Stock)	B+	B	B+	Up	Y	0
MFS® Global New Discovery Fund Class R3	GLNLX	NAS CM	Open End	Global Equity Mid/Small Cap (World Stock)	B+	B	B+	Up	Y	0
MFS® Global New Discovery Fund Class R4	GLNMX	NAS CM	Open End	Global Equity Mid/Small Cap (World Stock)	B+	B	B+	Up	Y	0
MFS® Global New Discovery Fund Class R6	GLNNX	NAS CM	Open End	Global Equity Mid/Small Cap (World Stock)	B+	B+	B+	Up	Y	0
MFS® Global Real Estate Fund Class A	MGLAX	NAS CM	Open End	Real Estate Sector Equity (Real Estate)	B-	C+	B		Y	1,000
MFS® Global Real Estate Fund Class B	MGLDX	NAS CM	Open End	Real Estate Sector Equity (Real Estate)	B-	C+	B		Y	1,000
MFS® Global Real Estate Fund Class C	MGLCX	NAS CM	Open End	Real Estate Sector Equity (Real Estate)	B-	C+	B		Y	1,000
MFS® Global Real Estate Fund Class I	MGLIX	NAS CM	Open End	Real Estate Sector Equity (Real Estate)	B-	C+	B		Y	0
MFS® Global Real Estate Fund Class R1	MGLJX	NAS CM	Open End	Real Estate Sector Equity (Real Estate)	B-	C+	B		Y	0
MFS® Global Real Estate Fund Class R2	MGLKX	NAS CM	Open End	Real Estate Sector Equity (Real Estate)	B-	C+	B		Y	0

★Expanded analysis of this fund is included in Section II.

Min Additional Investment	3-Month Total Return	6-Month Total Return	1-Year Total Return	3-Year Total Return	5-Year Total Return	Dividend Yield (TTM)	Expense Ratio	3-Yr Std Deviation	3-Year Beta	NAV	Total Assets (MIL)	%Cash	%Stocks	%Bonds	%Other	Turnover Ratio	Last Bull Market Total Return	Last Bear Market Total Return	Front End Fee (%)	Back End Fee (%)	Inception Date
	TOTAL RETURNS					PERFORMANCE				ASSETS		ASSET ALLOCATION & TURNOVER					BULL & BEAR		FEES		
	5.11	7.85	18.45	32.67	104.85	0.77	0.85	9.7	0.9	34.49	468.8	1	99	0	0	109	26.95	-18.64			Mar-08
	-0.66	-0.08	6.18	0.32	10.19	2.35	1.47	4.36	0.43	9.98	298.1	12	70	18	0	51	5.18	1.2	5.75		Dec-07
	-0.81	-0.41	5.40	-1.86	6.10	1.64	2.22	4.33	0.37	9.8	298.1	12	70	18	0	51	4.68	1		4.00	Dec-07
	-0.92	-0.42	5.40	-1.91	6.12	1.54	2.22	4.33	0.44	9.82	298.1	12	70	18	0	51	4.68	0.89		1.00	Dec-07
	-0.61	0.06	6.40	1.06	11.48	2.68	1.22	4.37	0.46	10.04	298.1	12	70	18	0	51	5.27	1.41			Dec-07
	-0.83	-0.43	5.44	-1.89	6.15	2.04	2.22	4.35	0.41	9.7	298.1	12	70	18	0	51	4.69	1			Dec-07
	-0.72	-0.13	5.88	-0.43	8.76	2.37	1.72	4.36	0.4	9.84	298.1	12	70	18	0	51	4.99	1.1			Dec-07
	-0.69	-0.01	6.23	0.32	10.06	2.63	1.47	4.29	0.34	10	298.1	12	70	18	0	51	5.16	1.2			Dec-07
	-0.64	0.12	6.44	0.64	11.04	2.76	1.22	4.46	0.38	10.07	298.1	12	70	18	0	51	5.27	1.41			Dec-07
	-0.55	0.12	6.64	1.44	12.06	2.83	1.12	4.33	0.37	10.09	298.1	12	70	18	0	51	5.27	1.3			Dec-07
	4.33	7.11	23.62	29.19	73.98	0.47	1.22	10.28	0.95	43.57	3,386	1	99	0	0	8	22.95	-19.73	5.75		Sep-93
	4.13	6.69	22.67	26.32	67.54	0	1.97	10.28	0.95	40.3	3,386	1	99	0	0	8	22.43	-19.99		4.00	Dec-86
	4.13	6.69	22.68	26.32	67.56	0	1.97	10.28	0.95	38.55	3,386	1	99	0	0	8	22.47	-20		1.00	Jan-94
	4.39	7.22	23.90	30.12	76.15	0.67	0.97	10.29	0.95	44.66	3,386	1	99	0	0	8	23.13	-19.63			Jan-97
	4.13	6.69	22.70	26.31	67.52	0	1.97	10.28	0.95	39.41	3,386	1	99	0	0	8	22.52	-19.97			Apr-05
	4.25	6.94	23.28	28.21	71.77	0.27	1.47	10.27	0.95	42.36	3,386	1	99	0	0	8	22.81	-19.81			Oct-03
	4.32	7.11	23.62	29.20	73.99	0.47	1.22	10.3	0.95	43.28	3,386	1	99	0	0	8	22.94	-19.72			Apr-05
	4.37	7.21	23.91	30.15	76.07	0.67	0.97	10.28	0.95	43.67	3,386	1	99	0	0	8	23.12	-19.64			Apr-05
	4.40	7.28	24.03	30.49	76.85	0.73	0.88	10.29	0.95	44.67	3,386	1	99	0	0	8	22.43	-19.99			Jun-12
	6.75	11.60	31.38	34.35	72.18	0.05	1.4	11.1	0.98	40.71	303.8	1	99	0	0	28	21.18	-19.25	5.75		Nov-93
	6.54	11.14	30.38	31.33	65.77	0	2.15	11.1	0.98	35.64	303.8	1	99	0	0	28	20.66	-19.55		4.00	Nov-93
	6.53	11.15	30.39	31.34	65.78	0	2.15	11.1	0.98	35.21	303.8	1	99	0	0	28	20.68	-19.55		1.00	Jan-94
	6.79	11.70	31.68	35.30	74.23	0.27	1.15	11.11	0.98	41.66	303.8	1	99	0	0	28	21.37	-19.19			Jan-97
	6.55	11.15	30.38	31.29	65.78	0	2.15	11.09	0.98	35.13	303.8	1	99	0	0	28	20.66	-19.54			Apr-05
	6.69	11.46	31.03	33.32	69.98	0	1.65	11.11	0.98	39.48	303.8	1	99	0	0	28	21.04	-19.37			Oct-03
	6.73	11.55	31.35	34.28	72.10	0.05	1.4	11.09	0.98	40.49	303.8	1	99	0	0	28	21.21	-19.32			Apr-05
	6.81	11.71	31.67	35.30	74.25	0.23	1.15	11.11	0.98	40.74	303.8	1	99	0	0	28	21.36	-19.18			Apr-05
	6.83	11.74	31.77	35.65	74.76	0.29	1.08	11.1	0.98	41.64	303.8	1	99	0	0	28	21.18	-19.25			Mar-13
	2.35	3.76	9.99	8.88	12.84	0.09	1.5	6.36	0.4	9.59	22.5	12	36	52	0	30	5.81	-14.4	5.75		Mar-11
	2.17	3.41	9.22	6.43	8.71	0	2.25	6.32	0.41	9.26	22.5	12	36	52	0	30	5.34	-14.61		4.00	Mar-11
	2.22	3.35	9.15	6.49	8.64	0	2.25	6.37	0.41	9.25	22.5	12	36	52	0	30	5.25	-14.6		1.00	Mar-11
	2.51	3.86	10.28	9.76	14.25	0.15	1.25	6.38	0.41	9.69	22.5	12	36	52	0	30	5.92	-14.25			Mar-11
	2.22	3.35	9.13	6.48	8.61	0	2.25	6.37	0.41	9.28	22.5	12	36	52	0	30	5.29	-14.61			Mar-11
	2.31	3.56	9.71	8.01	11.36	0.03	1.75	6.36	0.41	9.5	22.5	12	36	52	0	30	5.55	-14.47			Mar-11
	2.47	3.77	10.02	8.91	12.83	0.09	1.5	6.32	0.41	9.58	22.5	12	36	52	0	30	5.79	-14.36			Mar-11
	2.40	3.75	10.17	9.65	14.14	0.15	1.25	6.33	0.41	9.68	22.5	12	36	52	0	30	5.92	-14.25			Mar-11
	2.41	3.88	10.29	9.89	14.46	0.16	1.24	6.36	0.42	9.7	22.5	12	36	52	0	30	5.92	-14.25			Nov-12
	6.60	12.83	29.42	40.78	74.73	0.11	1.5	10.5	0.89	19.48	41.2	1	98	0	0	37			5.75		Dec-11
	6.44	12.49	28.45	37.65	68.27	0	2.25	10.49	0.89	18.61	41.2	1	98	0	0	37				4.00	Dec-11
	6.44	12.49	28.45	37.65	68.41	0	2.25	10.51	0.89	18.61	41.2	1	98	0	0	37				1.00	Dec-11
	6.69	13.05	29.75	41.90	76.94	0.42	1.25	10.54	0.89	19.7	41.2	1	98	0	0	37					Dec-11
	6.39	12.43	28.46	37.68	68.32	0	2.25	10.5	0.89	18.6	41.2	1	98	0	0	37					Dec-11
	6.58	12.78	29.11	39.75	72.51	0.04	1.75	10.52	0.89	19.2	41.2	1	98	0	0	37					Dec-11
	6.66	12.90	29.42	40.84	74.81	0.21	1.5	10.51	0.89	19.48	41.2	1	98	0	0	37					Dec-11
	6.69	13.04	29.80	41.76	76.77	0.37	1.25	10.52	0.89	19.72	41.2	1	98	0	0	37					Dec-11
	6.74	13.09	29.86	42.29	77.66	0.46	1.22	10.51	0.89	19.73	41.2	1	98	0	0	37					Jan-13
	4.41	5.77	12.64	20.05	47.32	3.49	1.35	10.12	0.9	15.65	735.3	4	96	0	0	29	22.57	-19.66	5.75		Mar-09
	4.24	5.32	11.73	17.37	41.76	5.36	2.1	10.13	0.9	8.59	735.3	4	96	0	0	29	22.01	-19.81		4.00	Dec-14
	4.27	5.35	11.79	17.33	41.70	5.63	2.1	10.2	0.91	8.53	735.3	4	96	0	0	29	22.01	-19.81		1.00	Dec-14
	4.49	5.91	12.93	20.87	48.95	3.65	1.1	10.16	0.9	15.69	735.3	4	96	0	0	29	22.72	-19.48			Mar-09
	4.18	5.36	11.85	17.44	41.84	5.27	2.1	10.16	0.9	8.67	735.3	4	96	0	0	29	22.01	-19.81			Dec-14
	4.37	5.68	12.34	19.25	45.47	6.04	1.6	10.15	0.9	8.62	735.3	4	96	0	0	29	22.36	-19.64			Dec-14

	MARKET			FUND TYPE, CATEGORY & OBJECTIVE	RATINGS				MINIMUMS	
Fund Name	Ticker Symbol	Traded On	Fund Type	Category and (Prospectus Objective)	Overall Rating	Reward Rating	Risk Rating	Recent Up/ Downgrade	Open to New Investors	Min Initial Investment
MFS® Global Real Estate Fund Class R3	MGLLX	NAS CM	Open End	Real Estate Sector Equity (Real Estate)	B-	C+	B		Y	0
MFS® Global Real Estate Fund Class R4	MGLMX	NAS CM	Open End	Real Estate Sector Equity (Real Estate)	B-	C+	B		Y	0
MFS® Global Real Estate Fund Class R6	MGLRX	NAS CM	Open End	Real Estate Sector Equity (Real Estate)	B	C+	B	Up	Y	0
MFS® Global Total Return Fund Class A	MFWTX	NAS CM	Open End	Alloc (Balanced)	B	C+	B+		Y	1,000
MFS® Global Total Return Fund Class B	MFWBX	NAS CM	Open End	Alloc (Balanced)	B-	C+	B+	Up	Y	1,000
MFS® Global Total Return Fund Class C	MFWCX	NAS CM	Open End	Alloc (Balanced)	B-	C+	B+	Up	Y	1,000
MFS® Global Total Return Fund Class I	MFWIX	NAS CM	Open End	Alloc (Balanced)	B	C+	B+		Y	0
MFS® Global Total Return Fund Class R1	MFWGX	NAS CM	Open End	Alloc (Balanced)	B-	C+	B+	Up	Y	0
MFS® Global Total Return Fund Class R2	MGBRX	NAS CM	Open End	Alloc (Balanced)	B	C+	B+		Y	0
MFS® Global Total Return Fund Class R3	MFWHX	NAS CM	Open End	Alloc (Balanced)	B	C+	B+		Y	0
MFS® Global Total Return Fund Class R4	MFWJX	NAS CM	Open End	Alloc (Balanced)	B	C+	B+		Y	0
MFS® Global Total Return Fund Class R6	MFWLX	NAS CM	Open End	Alloc (Balanced)	B	C+	B+		Y	0
MFS® Growth Allocation Fund Class 529A	EAGWX	NAS CM	Open End	Aggressive Alloc (Balanced)	B-	B-	B	Down	Y	250
MFS® Growth Allocation Fund Class 529B	EBGWX	NAS CM	Open End	Aggressive Alloc (Balanced)	B	C+	B+	Up	Y	250
MFS® Growth Allocation Fund Class 529C	ECGWX	NAS CM	Open End	Aggressive Alloc (Balanced)	B	C+	B+	Up	Y	250
MFS® Growth Allocation Fund Class A	MAGWX	NAS CM	Open End	Aggressive Alloc (Balanced)	B	B-	B+	Up	Y	1,000
MFS® Growth Allocation Fund Class B	MBGWX	NAS CM	Open End	Aggressive Alloc (Balanced)	B	C+	B+	Up	Y	1,000
MFS® Growth Allocation Fund Class C	MCGWX	NAS CM	Open End	Aggressive Alloc (Balanced)	B	C+	B+	Up	Y	1,000
MFS® Growth Allocation Fund Class I	MGWIX	NAS CM	Open End	Aggressive Alloc (Balanced)	B	B-	B+	Up	Y	0
MFS® Growth Allocation Fund Class R1	MAGMX	NAS CM	Open End	Aggressive Alloc (Balanced)	B	C+	B+	Up	Y	0
MFS® Growth Allocation Fund Class R2	MGALX	NAS CM	Open End	Aggressive Alloc (Balanced)	B	B-	B+	Up	Y	0
MFS® Growth Allocation Fund Class R3	MAGEX	NAS CM	Open End	Aggressive Alloc (Balanced)	B	B-	B+	Up	Y	0
MFS® Growth Allocation Fund Class R4	MAGJX	NAS CM	Open End	Aggressive Alloc (Balanced)	B	B-	B+	Up	Y	0
MFS® Growth Fund Class A	MFEGX	NAS CM	Open End	US Equity Large Cap Growth (Growth)	A-	B+	A	Up	Y	1,000
MFS® Growth Fund Class B	MEGBX	NAS CM	Open End	US Equity Large Cap Growth (Growth)	B+	B+	A	Up	Y	1,000
MFS® Growth Fund Class C	MFECX	NAS CM	Open End	US Equity Large Cap Growth (Growth)	B+	B+	A	Up	Y	1,000
MFS® Growth Fund Class I	MFEIX	NAS CM	Open End	US Equity Large Cap Growth (Growth)	A-	B+	A	Up	Y	0
MFS® Growth Fund Class R1	MFELX	NAS CM	Open End	US Equity Large Cap Growth (Growth)	B+	B+	A	Up	Y	0
MFS® Growth Fund Class R2	MEGRX	NAS CM	Open End	US Equity Large Cap Growth (Growth)	A-	B+	A	Up	Y	0
MFS® Growth Fund Class R3	MFEHX	NAS CM	Open End	US Equity Large Cap Growth (Growth)	A-	B+	A	Up	Y	0
MFS® Growth Fund Class R4	MFEJX	NAS CM	Open End	US Equity Large Cap Growth (Growth)	A-	B+	A	Up	Y	0
MFS® Growth Fund Class R6	MFEKX	NAS CM	Open End	US Equity Large Cap Growth (Growth)	A-	B+	A	Up	Y	0
MFS® Institutional International Equity Fund	MIEIX	NAS CM	Open End	Global Equity Large Cap (Foreign Stock)	B	B-	B	Up	Y	3,000,000
MFS® International Diversification Fund Class A	MDIDX	NAS CM	Open End	Global Equity Large Cap (Growth)	B	B	B	Up	Y	1,000
MFS® International Diversification Fund Class B	MDIFX	NAS CM	Open End	Global Equity Large Cap (Growth)	B-	B-	B	Up	Y	1,000
MFS® International Diversification Fund Class C	MDIGX	NAS CM	Open End	Global Equity Large Cap (Growth)	B-	B-	B	Up	Y	1,000
MFS® International Diversification Fund Class I	MDIJX	NAS CM	Open End	Global Equity Large Cap (Growth)	B	B	B	Up	Y	0
MFS® International Diversification Fund Class R1	MDIOX	NAS CM	Open End	Global Equity Large Cap (Growth)	B-	B-	B	Up	Y	0
MFS® International Diversification Fund Class R2	MDIKX	NAS CM	Open End	Global Equity Large Cap (Growth)	B	B-	B	Up	Y	0
MFS® International Diversification Fund Class R3	MDIHX	NAS CM	Open End	Global Equity Large Cap (Growth)	B	B	B	Up	Y	0
MFS® International Diversification Fund Class R4	MDITX	NAS CM	Open End	Global Equity Large Cap (Growth)	B	B	B	Up	Y	0
MFS® International Diversification Fund Class R6	MDIZX	NAS CM	Open End	Global Equity Large Cap (Growth)	B	B	B		Y	0
MFS® International Growth Fund Class A	MGRAX	NAS CM	Open End	Global Equity Large Cap (Foreign Stock)	B	B	B	Up	Y	1,000
MFS® International Growth Fund Class B	MGRBX	NAS CM	Open End	Global Equity Large Cap (Foreign Stock)	B	B	B	Up	Y	1,000
MFS® International Growth Fund Class C	MGRCX	NAS CM	Open End	Global Equity Large Cap (Foreign Stock)	B	B	B	Up	Y	1,000
MFS® International Growth Fund Class I	MQGIX	NAS CM	Open End	Global Equity Large Cap (Foreign Stock)	B	B	B	Up	Y	0
MFS® International Growth Fund Class R1	MGRRX	NAS CM	Open End	Global Equity Large Cap (Foreign Stock)	B	B	B	Up	Y	0
MFS® International Growth Fund Class R2	MGRQX	NAS CM	Open End	Global Equity Large Cap (Foreign Stock)	B	B	B	Up	Y	0
MFS® International Growth Fund Class R3	MGRTX	NAS CM	Open End	Global Equity Large Cap (Foreign Stock)	B	B	B	Up	Y	0
MFS® International Growth Fund Class R4	MGRVX	NAS CM	Open End	Global Equity Large Cap (Foreign Stock)	B	B	B	Up	Y	0
MFS® International Growth Fund Class R6	MGRDX	NAS CM	Open End	Global Equity Large Cap (Foreign Stock)	B	B	B	Up	Y	0
MFS® International New Discovery Fund Class 529A	EAIDX	NAS CM	Open End	Global Equity Mid/Small Cap (Foreign Stock)	B	B	B+	Up	Y	250

★ Expanded analysis of this fund is included in Section II.

	TOTAL RETURNS					PERFORMANCE				ASSETS		ASSET ALLOCATION & TURNOVER					BULL & BEAR		FEES		
Min Additional Investment	3-Month Total Return	6-Month Total Return	1-Year Total Return	3-Year Total Return	5-Year Total Return	Dividend Yield (TTM)	Expense Ratio	3-Yr Std Deviation	3-Year Beta	NAV	Total Assets (MIL)	%Cash	%Stocks	%Bonds	%Other	Turnover Ratio	Last Bull Market Total Return	Last Bear Market Total Return	Front End Fee (%)	Back End Fee (%)	Inception Date
	4.39	5.82	12.61	20.15	47.29	6.04	1.35	10.19	0.91	8.63	735.3	4	96	0	0	29	22.54	-19.56			Dec-14
	4.57	5.88	12.94	21.04	49.13	6.21	1.1	10.12	0.9	8.64	735.3	4	96	0	0	29	22.72	-19.48			Dec-14
	4.47	5.89	12.97	21.12	49.25	3.68	1.05	10.17	0.91	15.71	735.3	4	96	0	0	29	22.72	-19.48			Jul-12
	2.88	5.91	15.13	18.76	43.95	1.49	1.09	6.27	0.54	18.18	2,194	10	60	30	0	36	11.88	-9.25	5.75		Sep-90
	2.71	5.53	14.26	16.16	38.74	0.9	1.84	6.3	0.54	18.53	2,194	10	60	30	0	36	11.43	-9.49		4.00	Sep-93
	2.70	5.52	14.30	16.12	38.74	0.93	1.84	6.3	0.54	18.27	2,194	10	60	30	0	36	11.41	-9.52		1.00	Jan-94
	2.98	6.05	15.45	19.74	45.82	1.75	0.84	6.3	0.54	18	2,194	10	60	30	0	36	12.04	-9.14			Jan-97
	2.70	5.53	14.30	16.12	38.69	0.94	1.84	6.29	0.54	18.2	2,194	10	60	30	0	36	11.46	-9.54			Apr-05
	2.88	5.81	14.91	17.95	42.20	1.32	1.34	6.28	0.53	18	2,194	10	60	30	0	36	11.84	-9.37			Oct-03
	2.88	5.92	15.18	18.84	44.12	1.51	1.09	6.29	0.54	18.13	2,194	10	60	30	0	36	11.92	-9.27			Apr-05
	3.00	6.09	15.46	19.75	45.84	1.72	0.84	6.3	0.54	18.21	2,194	10	60	30	0	36	12.1	-9.14			Apr-05
	3.01	6.10	15.56	20.08	46.48	1.84	0.78	6.27	0.53	18	2,194	10	60	30	0	36	11.88	-9.25			Jun-12
	4.43	8.07	18.83	25.84	59.45	1.01	1.09	7.85	0.73	20.38	5,109	4	74	22	0	1	18.03	-15.24	5.75		Jul-02
	4.21	7.62	17.95	22.99	53.54	0.31	1.84	7.82	0.73	20.19	5,109	4	74	22	0	1	17.53	-15.43		4.00	Jul-02
	4.21	7.67	17.95	23.04	53.57	0.39	1.84	7.83	0.73	19.91	5,109	4	74	22	0	1	17.61	-15.54		1.00	Jul-02
	4.42	8.09	18.89	26.01	59.76	1.03	1.04	7.83	0.73	20.54	5,109	4	74	22	0	1	18.07	-15.2	5.75		Jun-02
	4.22	7.71	18.01	23.20	53.87	0.36	1.79	7.83	0.73	20.39	5,109	4	74	22	0	1	17.52	-15.4		4.00	Jun-02
	4.23	7.70	18.06	23.17	53.92	0.4	1.79	7.82	0.73	20.17	5,109	4	74	22	0	1	17.57	-15.44		1.00	Jun-02
	4.49	8.23	19.20	26.99	61.85	1.24	0.79	7.84	0.73	20.71	5,109	4	74	22	0	1	18.22	-15.1			Jun-02
	4.26	7.69	18.06	23.21	53.87	0.38	1.79	7.83	0.73	19.77	5,109	4	74	22	0	1	17.62	-15.48			Apr-05
	4.34	7.93	18.58	25.01	57.75	0.83	1.29	7.82	0.73	20.09	5,109	4	74	22	0	1	17.96	-15.31			Oct-03
	4.40	8.10	18.94	25.97	59.80	1.04	1.04	7.83	0.73	20.36	5,109	4	74	22	0	1	18.07	-15.18			Apr-05
	4.48	8.20	19.21	26.93	61.80	1.25	0.79	7.85	0.73	20.51	5,109	4	74	22	0	1	18.27	-15.08			Apr-05
	6.40	11.69	30.54	41.79	115.60	0	0.97	10.93	0.98	89.95	16,680	2	98	0	0	24	24.12	-14.39	5.75		Sep-93
	6.19	11.26	29.56	38.63	107.63	0	1.72	10.92	0.98	73.18	16,680	2	98	0	0	24	23.6	-14.66		4.00	Dec-86
	6.19	11.25	29.55	38.60	107.62	0	1.72	10.93	0.98	72.62	16,680	2	98	0	0	24	23.57	-14.65		1.00	Apr-96
	6.47	11.83	30.86	42.84	118.25	0	0.72	10.93	0.98	95.4	16,680	2	98	0	0	24	24.31	-14.29			Jan-97
	6.19	11.26	29.55	38.59	107.60	0	1.72	10.92	0.98	72.88	16,680	2	98	0	0	24	23.59	-14.66			Apr-05
	6.33	11.54	30.20	40.71	112.86	0	1.22	10.93	0.98	85.22	16,680	2	98	0	0	24	23.93	-14.47			Oct-03
	6.40	11.69	30.52	41.77	115.58	0	0.97	10.93	0.98	89.51	16,680	2	98	0	0	24	24.11	-14.38			Apr-05
	6.47	11.83	30.87	42.85	118.25	0	0.72	10.93	0.98	92.87	16,680	2	98	0	0	24	24.29	-14.31			Apr-05
	6.50	11.89	30.98	43.25	119.30	0	0.62	10.93	0.98	95.65	16,680	2	98	0	0	24	24.23	-14.58			Aug-11
	3.99	8.52	28.02	27.94	47.39	1.41	0.71	11.65	0.93	25.46	9,538	1	99	0	0	17	19.23	-23.06			Jan-96
	5.72	10.70	29.93	32.07	49.96	1.53	1.16	10.8	0.84	19.69	9,950	3	97	0	0	3	16.32	-20.01	5.75		Sep-04
	5.55	10.29	28.90	29.16	44.46	0.86	1.91	10.82	0.84	19.49	9,950	3	97	0	0	3	15.73	-20.25		4.00	Sep-04
	5.52	10.31	28.99	29.13	44.53	0.94	1.91	10.77	0.84	19.27	9,950	3	97	0	0	3	15.77	-20.23		1.00	Sep-04
	5.84	10.90	30.28	33.12	51.92	1.71	0.91	10.81	0.84	19.88	9,950	3	97	0	0	3	16.4	-19.93			Sep-04
	5.55	10.29	28.95	29.16	44.44	0.97	1.91	10.81	0.84	18.99	9,950	3	97	0	0	3	15.74	-20.21			Apr-05
	5.67	10.55	29.55	31.12	48.14	1.38	1.41	10.82	0.84	19.37	9,950	3	97	0	0	3	16.01	-20.05			Sep-04
	5.72	10.74	29.89	32.06	49.97	1.55	1.16	10.79	0.84	19.55	9,950	3	97	0	0	3	16.22	-19.95			Apr-05
	5.81	10.88	30.24	33.10	51.85	1.72	0.91	10.78	0.84	19.81	9,950	3	97	0	0	3	16.36	-19.86			Apr-05
	5.82	10.87	30.24	33.09	51.88		0.81	10.81	0.84	19.87	9,950	3	97	0	0	3	16.4	-19.93			Oct-17
	5.80	10.87	32.17	34.78	46.76	0.78	1.18	11.41	0.93	33.76	5,450	1	99	0	0	21	19.97	-21.81	5.75		Oct-95
	5.57	10.41	31.12	31.70	41.32	0.22	1.93	11.4	0.93	31.69	5,450	1	99	0	0	21	19.44	-22.06		4.00	Oct-95
	5.58	10.44	31.13	31.73	41.34	0.28	1.93	11.42	0.93	30.84	5,450	1	99	0	0	21	19.45	-22.06		1.00	Jul-96
	5.84	10.98	32.45	35.74	48.60	0.91	0.93	11.41	0.93	37.54	5,450	1	99	0	0	21	20.13	-21.73			Jan-97
	5.60	10.44	31.16	31.78	41.33	0.5	1.93	11.42	0.93	30.27	5,450	1	99	0	0	21	19.48	-22.06			Oct-08
	5.71	10.71	31.82	33.73	44.92	0.68	1.43	11.41	0.93	30.93	5,450	1	99	0	0	21	19.82	-21.91			Oct-08
	5.79	10.85	32.10	34.72	46.73	0.77	1.18	11.42	0.93	33.52	5,450	1	99	0	0	21	20.02	-21.8			Oct-08
	5.86	11.01	32.48	35.76	48.58	0.94	0.93	11.42	0.93	33.8	5,450	1	99	0	0	21	20.15	-21.75			Oct-08
	5.89	11.04	32.57	36.24	49.41	1.11	0.82	11.4	0.93	33.77	5,450	1	99	0	0	21	20.08	-21.77			May-06
	6.56	12.01	31.70	35.15	58.03	1.07	1.38	10.14	0.82	34.16	6,233	4	96	0	0	17	20.12	-20.17	5.75		Jul-02

	MARKET			FUND TYPE, CATEGORY & OBJECTIVE	RATINGS					MINIMUMS
Fund Name	Ticker Symbol	Traded On	Fund Type	Category and (Prospectus Objective)	Overall Rating	Reward Rating	Risk Rating	Recent Up/ Downgrade	Open to New Investors	Min Initial Investment
MFS® International New Discovery Fund Class 529B	EBIDX	NAS CM	Open End	Global Equity Mid/Small Cap (Foreign Stock)	B	B	B	Up	Y	250
MFS® International New Discovery Fund Class 529C	ECIDX	NAS CM	Open End	Global Equity Mid/Small Cap (Foreign Stock)	B	B	B	Up	Y	250
MFS® International New Discovery Fund Class A	MIDAX	NAS CM	Open End	Global Equity Mid/Small Cap (Foreign Stock)	B	B	B+	Up	Y	1,000
MFS® International New Discovery Fund Class B	MIDBX	NAS CM	Open End	Global Equity Mid/Small Cap (Foreign Stock)	B	B	B	Up	Y	1,000
MFS® International New Discovery Fund Class C	MIDCX	NAS CM	Open End	Global Equity Mid/Small Cap (Foreign Stock)	B	B	B	Up	Y	1,000
MFS® International New Discovery Fund Class I	MWNIX	NAS CM	Open End	Global Equity Mid/Small Cap (Foreign Stock)	B	B	B+	Up	Y	0
MFS® International New Discovery Fund Class R1	MIDGX	NAS CM	Open End	Global Equity Mid/Small Cap (Foreign Stock)	B	B	B	Up	Y	0
MFS® International New Discovery Fund Class R2	MIDRX	NAS CM	Open End	Global Equity Mid/Small Cap (Foreign Stock)	B	B	B+	Up	Y	0
MFS® International New Discovery Fund Class R3	MIDHX	NAS CM	Open End	Global Equity Mid/Small Cap (Foreign Stock)	B	B	B+	Up	Y	0
MFS® International New Discovery Fund Class R4	MIDJX	NAS CM	Open End	Global Equity Mid/Small Cap (Foreign Stock)	B	B	B+	Up	Y	0
MFS® International New Discovery Fund Class R6	MIDLX	NAS CM	Open End	Global Equity Mid/Small Cap (Foreign Stock)	B	B	B+	Up	Y	0
MFS® International Value Fund Class A	MGIAX	NAS CM	Open End	Global Equity Large Cap (Foreign Stock)	B	B	A-			1,000
MFS® International Value Fund Class B	MGIBX	NAS CM	Open End	Global Equity Large Cap (Foreign Stock)	B	B	B+			1,000
MFS® International Value Fund Class C	MGICX	NAS CM	Open End	Global Equity Large Cap (Foreign Stock)	B	B	B+			1,000
MFS® International Value Fund Class I	MINIX	NAS CM	Open End	Global Equity Large Cap (Foreign Stock)	B+	B	A	Up		0
MFS® International Value Fund Class R1	MINRX	NAS CM	Open End	Global Equity Large Cap (Foreign Stock)	B	B	B+			0
MFS® International Value Fund Class R2	MINFX	NAS CM	Open End	Global Equity Large Cap (Foreign Stock)	B	B	B+			0
MFS® International Value Fund Class R3	MINGX	NAS CM	Open End	Global Equity Large Cap (Foreign Stock)	B	B	A-			0
MFS® International Value Fund Class R4	MINHX	NAS CM	Open End	Global Equity Large Cap (Foreign Stock)	B+	B	A	Up		0
MFS® International Value Fund Class R6	MINJX	NAS CM	Open End	Global Equity Large Cap (Foreign Stock)	B+	B	A	Up		0
MFS® Lifetime 2020 Fund Class A	MFLAX	NAS CM	Open End	Target Date 2000-2020 (Asset Alloc)	B	C+	A-	Up	Y	1,000
MFS® Lifetime 2020 Fund Class B	MFLBX	NAS CM	Open End	Target Date 2000-2020 (Asset Alloc)	B	C+	A-	Up	Y	1,000
MFS® Lifetime 2020 Fund Class C	MFLCX	NAS CM	Open End	Target Date 2000-2020 (Asset Alloc)	B	C+	A-	Up	Y	1,000
MFS® Lifetime 2020 Fund Class I	MFLIX	NAS CM	Open End	Target Date 2000-2020 (Asset Alloc)	B	C+	A-	Up	Y	0
MFS® Lifetime 2020 Fund Class R1	MFLEX	NAS CM	Open End	Target Date 2000-2020 (Asset Alloc)	B	C+	A-	Up	Y	0
MFS® Lifetime 2020 Fund Class R2	MFLGX	NAS CM	Open End	Target Date 2000-2020 (Asset Alloc)	B	C+	A-	Up	Y	0
MFS® Lifetime 2020 Fund Class R3	MFLHX	NAS CM	Open End	Target Date 2000-2020 (Asset Alloc)	B	C+	A-	Up	Y	0
MFS® Lifetime 2020 Fund Class R4	MFLJX	NAS CM	Open End	Target Date 2000-2020 (Asset Alloc)	B	C+	A-	Up	Y	0
MFS® Lifetime 2020 Fund Class R6	MFLKX	NAS CM	Open End	Target Date 2000-2020 (Asset Alloc)	B	C+	A-	Up	Y	0
MFS® Lifetime 2025 Fund Class A	LTTAX	NAS CM	Open End	Target Date 2021-2045 (Asset Alloc)	B	C+	A-	Up	Y	1,000
MFS® Lifetime 2025 Fund Class B	LTTBX	NAS CM	Open End	Target Date 2021-2045 (Asset Alloc)	B-	C+	B	Up	Y	1,000
MFS® Lifetime 2025 Fund Class C	LTTCX	NAS CM	Open End	Target Date 2021-2045 (Asset Alloc)	B	C+	B+	Up	Y	1,000
MFS® Lifetime 2025 Fund Class I	LTTIX	NAS CM	Open End	Target Date 2021-2045 (Asset Alloc)	B-	C+	B	Up	Y	0
MFS® Lifetime 2025 Fund Class R1	LTTRX	NAS CM	Open End	Target Date 2021-2045 (Asset Alloc)	B	C+	B+	Up	Y	0
MFS® Lifetime 2025 Fund Class R2	LTTSX	NAS CM	Open End	Target Date 2021-2045 (Asset Alloc)	B	C+	A-	Up	Y	0
MFS® Lifetime 2025 Fund Class R3	LTTTX	NAS CM	Open End	Target Date 2021-2045 (Asset Alloc)	B-	C+	B	Up	Y	0
MFS® Lifetime 2025 Fund Class R4	LTTUX	NAS CM	Open End	Target Date 2021-2045 (Asset Alloc)	B-	C+	B	Up	Y	0
MFS® Lifetime 2025 Fund Class R6	LTTKX	NAS CM	Open End	Target Date 2021-2045 (Asset Alloc)	B-	C+	B	Up	Y	0
MFS® Lifetime 2030 Fund Class A	MLTAX	NAS CM	Open End	Target Date 2021-2045 (Asset Alloc)	B-	C+	B	Down	Y	1,000
MFS® Lifetime 2030 Fund Class B	MLTBX	NAS CM	Open End	Target Date 2021-2045 (Asset Alloc)	B-	C+	B	Down	Y	1,000
MFS® Lifetime 2030 Fund Class C	MLTCX	NAS CM	Open End	Target Date 2021-2045 (Asset Alloc)	B	C+	B+	Up	Y	1,000
MFS® Lifetime 2030 Fund Class I	MLTIX	NAS CM	Open End	Target Date 2021-2045 (Asset Alloc)	B-	B-	B	Down	Y	0
MFS® Lifetime 2030 Fund Class R1	MLTEX	NAS CM	Open End	Target Date 2021-2045 (Asset Alloc)	B-	C+	B	Down	Y	0
MFS® Lifetime 2030 Fund Class R2	MLTGX	NAS CM	Open End	Target Date 2021-2045 (Asset Alloc)	B-	C+	B	Down	Y	0
MFS® Lifetime 2030 Fund Class R3	MLTHX	NAS CM	Open End	Target Date 2021-2045 (Asset Alloc)	B-	C+	B	Down	Y	0
MFS® Lifetime 2030 Fund Class R4	MLTJX	NAS CM	Open End	Target Date 2021-2045 (Asset Alloc)	B-	B-	B	Down	Y	0
MFS® Lifetime 2030 Fund Class R6	MLTKX	NAS CM	Open End	Target Date 2021-2045 (Asset Alloc)	B	B-	B+	Up	Y	0
MFS® Lifetime 2035 Fund Class A	LFEAX	NAS CM	Open End	Target Date 2021-2045 (Asset Alloc)	B-	B-	B	Down	Y	1,000
MFS® Lifetime 2035 Fund Class B	LFEBX	NAS CM	Open End	Target Date 2021-2045 (Asset Alloc)	B-	B-	B	Down	Y	1,000
MFS® Lifetime 2035 Fund Class C	LFECX	NAS CM	Open End	Target Date 2021-2045 (Asset Alloc)	B-	B-	B	Down	Y	1,000
MFS® Lifetime 2035 Fund Class I	LFEDX	NAS CM	Open End	Target Date 2021-2045 (Asset Alloc)	B-	B-	B	Down	Y	0
MFS® Lifetime 2035 Fund Class R1	LFERX	NAS CM	Open End	Target Date 2021-2045 (Asset Alloc)	B-	B-	B	Down	Y	0

★ Expanded analysis of this fund is included in Section II.

	TOTAL RETURNS					PERFORMANCE				ASSETS		ASSET ALLOCATION & TURNOVER					BULL & BEAR		FEES		
Min Additional Investment	3-Month Total Return	6-Month Total Return	1-Year Total Return	3-Year Total Return	5-Year Total Return	Dividend Yield (TTM)	Expense Ratio	3-Yr Std Deviation	3-Year Beta	NAV	Total Assets (MIL)	%Cash	%Stocks	%Bonds	%Other	Turnover Ratio	Last Bull Market Total Return	Last Bear Market Total Return	Front End Fee (%)	Back End Fee (%)	Inception Date
	6.58	11.97	31.17	33.64	53.79	1.11	2.13	10.12	0.82	32.44	6,233	4	96	0	0	17	19.63	-20.43		4.00	Jul-02
	6.39	11.58	30.68	32.02	51.96	0.5	2.13	10.14	0.82	32.1	6,233	4	96	0	0	17	19.58	-20.4		1.00	Jul-02
	6.59	12.02	31.75	35.22	58.10	1.03	1.33	10.14	0.82	34.74	6,233	4	96	0	0	17	20.17	-20.15	5.75		Oct-97
	6.39	11.60	30.71	32.17	52.25	0.39	2.08	10.12	0.81	33.8	6,233	4	96	0	0	17	19.62	-20.39		4.00	Oct-00
	6.39	11.62	30.74	32.21	52.24	0.48	2.08	10.12	0.81	33.18	6,233	4	96	0	0	17	19.66	-20.4		1.00	Oct-00
	6.63	12.14	32.04	36.21	60.01	1.23	1.08	10.15	0.82	35.72	6,233	4	96	0	0	17	20.33	-20.06			Oct-97
	6.39	11.60	30.74	32.19	52.21	0.59	2.08	10.15	0.82	32.38	6,233	4	96	0	0	17	19.66	-20.42			Apr-05
	6.50	11.87	31.39	34.19	56.08	0.85	1.58	10.14	0.82	33.83	6,233	4	96	0	0	17	19.99	-20.25			Oct-03
	6.58	12.02	31.70	35.17	58.07	1.07	1.33	10.12	0.81	34.43	6,233	4	96	0	0	17	20.17	-20.16			Apr-05
	6.63	12.13	32.02	36.21	59.99	1.26	1.08	10.15	0.82	34.67	6,233	4	96	0	0	17	20.29	-20.05			Apr-05
	6.68	12.22	32.15	36.71	60.97	1.32	0.96	10.14	0.82	35.74	6,233	4	96	0	0	17	20.33	-20.06			Jun-12
	5.84	9.21	26.82	39.80	82.03	1.21	1.01	9.78	0.58	43.18	29,692	7	93	0	0	7	12.93	-13.24	5.75		Oct-95
	5.64	8.79	25.85	36.68	75.37	0.64	1.76	9.78	0.58	41.18	29,692	7	93	0	0	7	12.45	-13.52		4.00	Oct-95
	5.65	8.78	25.86	36.69	75.36	0.7	1.76	9.77	0.58	39.28	29,692	7	93	0	0	7	12.48	-13.51		1.00	Jul-96
	5.93	9.34	27.15	40.85	84.34	1.37	0.76	9.78	0.58	45.26	29,692	7	93	0	0	7	13.1	-13.16			Jan-97
	5.66	8.80	25.89	36.67	75.33	0.75	1.76	9.8	0.58	39.76	29,692	7	93	0	0	7	12.42	-13.48			Oct-08
	5.77	9.05	26.50	38.74	79.76	1.12	1.26	9.78	0.58	40.42	29,692	7	93	0	0	7	12.77	-13.33			Oct-08
	5.84	9.20	26.80	39.78	82.07	1.26	1.01	9.78	0.58	42.88	29,692	7	93	0	0	7	12.94	-13.24			Oct-08
	5.92	9.33	27.15	40.85	84.35	1.44	0.76	9.79	0.58	43.26	29,692	7	93	0	0	7	13.08	-13.14			Oct-08
	5.94	9.37	27.25	41.27	85.20	1.53	0.66	9.8	0.58	43.29	29,692	7	93	0	0	7	13.03	-13.18			May-06
	2.11	4.29	9.65	15.17	34.84	1.46	0.83	4.29		13.09	416.5	2	32	66	0	35	13.59	-10.07	5.75		Sep-05
	1.92	3.88	8.82	12.69	29.90	0.7	1.58	4.28		13.03	416.5	2	32	66	0	35	13.03	-10.32		4.00	Sep-05
	1.96	3.87	8.88	12.68	29.88	0.78	1.58	4.28		12.85	416.5	2	32	66	0	35	12.99	-10.32		1.00	Sep-05
	2.14	4.39	9.97	16.13	36.61	1.67	0.58	4.3		13.17	416.5	2	32	66	0	35	13.69	-9.94			Sep-05
	1.91	3.86	8.88	12.60	29.87	0.55	1.58	4.27		13.05	416.5	2	32	66	0	35	13.01	-10.34			Sep-05
	2.03	4.15	9.37	14.36	33.23	1.28	1.08	4.29		13	416.5	2	32	66	0	35	13.31	-10.13			Sep-05
	2.15	4.33	9.69	15.28	34.95	1.45	0.83	4.27		13.1	416.5	2	32	66	0	35	13.48	-10.06			Sep-05
	2.18	4.43	10.02	16.10	36.59	1.67	0.58	4.26		13.17	416.5	2	32	66	0	35	13.7	-9.95			Sep-05
	2.20	4.44	10.03	16.34	36.86	1.71	0.44	4.29		13.15	416.5	2	32	66	0	35	13.69	-9.94			Aug-16
	3.07	5.95	13.06	19.83	48.36	1.28	0.84	5.91		12.88	270.2	0	49	52	0	33			5.75		Nov-12
	2.87	5.51	12.18	17.08	42.85	0.65	1.59	5.92		12.81	270.2	0	49	52	0	33				4.00	Nov-12
	2.88	5.53	12.13	17.13	42.90	0.63	1.59	5.92		12.75	270.2	0	49	52	0	33				1.00	Nov-12
	3.03	5.97	13.15	20.61	50.13	1.47	0.59	5.91		12.91	270.2	0	49	52	0	33					Nov-12
	2.79	5.50	12.13	17.02	42.81	1	1.59	5.91		12.84	270.2	0	49	52	0	33					Nov-12
	3.01	5.73	12.67	18.83	46.52	1.25	1.09	5.9		12.81	270.2	0	49	52	0	33					Nov-12
	3.01	5.88	12.90	19.71	48.22	1.31	0.84	5.93		12.86	270.2	0	49	52	0	33					Nov-12
	3.02	5.96	13.24	20.60	49.95	1.47	0.59	5.91		12.92	270.2	0	49	52	0	33					Nov-12
	3.08	6.02	13.38	20.82	50.38	1.51	0.45	5.92		12.92	270.2	0	49	52	0	33					Aug-16
	4.09	7.79	16.91	25.33	60.44	1.13	0.87	7.64		15.48	594.8	3	66	31	0	50	18.93	-16.33	5.75		Sep-05
	3.85	7.32	16.02	22.51	54.52	0.47	1.62	7.62		15.3	594.8	3	66	31	0	50	18.37	-16.5		4.00	Sep-05
	3.89	7.38	16.06	22.55	54.53	0.49	1.62	7.62		15.21	594.8	3	66	31	0	50	18.43	-16.63		1.00	Sep-05
	4.11	7.87	17.19	25.98	62.02	1.31	0.62	7.63		15.54	594.8	3	66	31	0	50	19.1	-16.18			Sep-05
	3.86	7.31	15.97	22.49	54.53	0.37	1.62	7.65		15.36	594.8	3	66	31	0	50	18.36	-16.57			Sep-05
	4.02	7.62	16.56	24.36	58.43	0.96	1.12	7.66		15.34	594.8	3	66	31	0	50	18.8	-16.46			Sep-05
	4.12	7.83	16.97	25.31	60.49	1.12	0.87	7.61		15.45	594.8	3	66	31	0	50	18.95	-16.35			Sep-05
	4.11	7.94	17.18	26.26	62.45	1.31	0.62	7.66		15.56	594.8	3	66	31	0	50	19.12	-16.19			Sep-05
	4.17	7.99	17.32	26.54	62.74	1.35	0.48	7.64		15.55	594.8	3	66	31	0	50	19.1	-16.18			Aug-16
	4.78	8.95	19.13	28.33	67.16	0.99	0.89	8.13		14.59	249.1	2	79	19	0	43			5.75		Nov-12
	4.55	8.52	18.18	25.38	60.99	0.34	1.64	8.16		14.5	249.1	2	79	19	0	43				4.00	Nov-12
	4.57	8.55	18.25	25.44	61.09	0.27	1.64	8.16		14.46	249.1	2	79	19	0	43				1.00	Nov-12
	4.80	9.04	19.48	28.94	68.84	1.16	0.64	8.18		14.6	249.1	2	79	19	0	43					Nov-12
	4.54	8.49	18.20	25.45	60.98	0.85	1.64	8.17		14.51	249.1	2	79	19	0	43					Nov-12

	MARKET			FUND TYPE, CATEGORY & OBJECTIVE	RATINGS				MINIMUMS	
Fund Name	Ticker Symbol	Traded On	Fund Type	Category and (Prospectus Objective)	Overall Rating	Reward Rating	Risk Rating	Recent Up/ Downgrade	Open to New Investors	Min Initial Investment
MFS® Lifetime 2035 Fund Class R2	LFESX	NAS CM	Open End	Target Date 2021-2045 (Asset Alloc)	B-	B-	B	Down	Y	0
MFS® Lifetime 2035 Fund Class R3	LFETX	NAS CM	Open End	Target Date 2021-2045 (Asset Alloc)	B-	B-	B	Down	Y	0
MFS® Lifetime 2035 Fund Class R4	LFEUX	NAS CM	Open End	Target Date 2021-2045 (Asset Alloc)	B-	B-	B	Down	Y	0
MFS® Lifetime 2035 Fund Class R6	LFEKX	NAS CM	Open End	Target Date 2021-2045 (Asset Alloc)	B-	B-	B	Down	Y	0
MFS® Lifetime 2040 Fund Class A	MLFAX	NAS CM	Open End	Target Date 2021-2045 (Asset Alloc)	B-	B-	B	Down	Y	1,000
MFS® Lifetime 2040 Fund Class B	MLFBX	NAS CM	Open End	Target Date 2021-2045 (Asset Alloc)	B-	B-	B	Down	Y	1,000
MFS® Lifetime 2040 Fund Class C	MLFCX	NAS CM	Open End	Target Date 2021-2045 (Asset Alloc)	B-	B-	B	Down	Y	1,000
MFS® Lifetime 2040 Fund Class I	MLFIX	NAS CM	Open End	Target Date 2021-2045 (Asset Alloc)	B-	B-	B	Down	Y	0
MFS® Lifetime 2040 Fund Class R1	MLFEX	NAS CM	Open End	Target Date 2021-2045 (Asset Alloc)	B-	B-	B	Down	Y	0
MFS® Lifetime 2040 Fund Class R2	MLFGX	NAS CM	Open End	Target Date 2021-2045 (Asset Alloc)	B-	B-	B	Down	Y	0
MFS® Lifetime 2040 Fund Class R3	MLFHX	NAS CM	Open End	Target Date 2021-2045 (Asset Alloc)	B-	B-	B	Down	Y	0
MFS® Lifetime 2040 Fund Class R4	MLFJX	NAS CM	Open End	Target Date 2021-2045 (Asset Alloc)	B-	B-	B	Down	Y	0
MFS® Lifetime 2040 Fund Class R6	MLFKX	NAS CM	Open End	Target Date 2021-2045 (Asset Alloc)	B-	B-	B	Down	Y	0
MFS® Lifetime 2045 Fund Class A	LTMAX	NAS CM	Open End	Target Date 2021-2045 (Asset Alloc)	B-	B-	B	Down	Y	1,000
MFS® Lifetime 2045 Fund Class B	LTMBX	NAS CM	Open End	Target Date 2021-2045 (Asset Alloc)	B-	B-	B-	Down	Y	1,000
MFS® Lifetime 2045 Fund Class C	LTMDX	NAS CM	Open End	Target Date 2021-2045 (Asset Alloc)	B-	B-	B-	Down	Y	1,000
MFS® Lifetime 2045 Fund Class I	LTMKX	NAS CM	Open End	Target Date 2021-2045 (Asset Alloc)	B-	B-	B	Down	Y	0
MFS® Lifetime 2045 Fund Class R1	LTMRX	NAS CM	Open End	Target Date 2021-2045 (Asset Alloc)	B-	B-	B-	Down	Y	0
MFS® Lifetime 2045 Fund Class R2	LTMSX	NAS CM	Open End	Target Date 2021-2045 (Asset Alloc)	B-	B-	B	Down	Y	0
MFS® Lifetime 2045 Fund Class R3	LTMTX	NAS CM	Open End	Target Date 2021-2045 (Asset Alloc)	B-	B-	B	Down	Y	0
MFS® Lifetime 2045 Fund Class R4	LTMUX	NAS CM	Open End	Target Date 2021-2045 (Asset Alloc)	B-	B-	B	Down	Y	0
MFS® Lifetime 2045 Fund Class R6	LTMLX	NAS CM	Open End	Target Date 2021-2045 (Asset Alloc)	B-	B-	B	Down	Y	0
MFS® Lifetime 2050 Fund Class A	MFFSX	NAS CM	Open End	Target Date 2046+ (Asset Alloc)	B-	B-	B	Down	Y	1,000
MFS® Lifetime 2050 Fund Class B	MFFRX	NAS CM	Open End	Target Date 2046+ (Asset Alloc)	B-	B-	B-	Down	Y	1,000
MFS® Lifetime 2050 Fund Class C	MFFDX	NAS CM	Open End	Target Date 2046+ (Asset Alloc)	B-	B-	B-	Down	Y	1,000
MFS® Lifetime 2050 Fund Class I	MFFIX	NAS CM	Open End	Target Date 2046+ (Asset Alloc)	B-	B-	B	Down	Y	0
MFS® Lifetime 2050 Fund Class R1	MFFMX	NAS CM	Open End	Target Date 2046+ (Asset Alloc)	B-	B-	B-	Down	Y	0
MFS® Lifetime 2050 Fund Class R2	MFFNX	NAS CM	Open End	Target Date 2046+ (Asset Alloc)	B-	B-	B	Down	Y	0
MFS® Lifetime 2050 Fund Class R3	MFFOX	NAS CM	Open End	Target Date 2046+ (Asset Alloc)	B-	B-	B	Down	Y	0
MFS® Lifetime 2050 Fund Class R4	MFFPX	NAS CM	Open End	Target Date 2046+ (Asset Alloc)	B-	B-	B	Down	Y	0
MFS® Lifetime 2050 Fund Class R6	MFFKX	NAS CM	Open End	Target Date 2046+ (Asset Alloc)	B-	B-	B	Down	Y	0
MFS® Lifetime 2055 Fund Class A	LFIAX	NAS CM	Open End	Target Date 2046+ (Asset Alloc)	B-	B-	B	Down	Y	1,000
MFS® Lifetime 2055 Fund Class B	LFIBX	NAS CM	Open End	Target Date 2046+ (Asset Alloc)	B-	B-	B	Down	Y	1,000
MFS® Lifetime 2055 Fund Class C	LFICX	NAS CM	Open End	Target Date 2046+ (Asset Alloc)	B-	B-	B	Down	Y	1,000
MFS® Lifetime 2055 Fund Class I	LFIIX	NAS CM	Open End	Target Date 2046+ (Asset Alloc)	B-	B-	B	Down	Y	0
MFS® Lifetime 2055 Fund Class R1	LFIRX	NAS CM	Open End	Target Date 2046+ (Asset Alloc)	B-	B-	B	Down	Y	0
MFS® Lifetime 2055 Fund Class R2	LFISX	NAS CM	Open End	Target Date 2046+ (Asset Alloc)	B-	B-	B	Down	Y	0
MFS® Lifetime 2055 Fund Class R3	LFITX	NAS CM	Open End	Target Date 2046+ (Asset Alloc)	B-	B-	B	Down	Y	0
MFS® Lifetime 2055 Fund Class R4	LFIUX	NAS CM	Open End	Target Date 2046+ (Asset Alloc)	B-	B-	B	Down	Y	0
MFS® Lifetime 2055 Fund Class R6	LFIKX	NAS CM	Open End	Target Date 2046+ (Asset Alloc)	B-	B-	B	Down	Y	0
MFS® Lifetime 2060 Fund Class A	MFJAX	NAS CM	Open End	Target Date 2046+ (Asset Alloc)	D	D+	A		Y	1,000
MFS® Lifetime 2060 Fund Class B	MFJBX	NAS CM	Open End	Target Date 2046+ (Asset Alloc)	D	D+	A		Y	1,000
MFS® Lifetime 2060 Fund Class C	MFJCX	NAS CM	Open End	Target Date 2046+ (Asset Alloc)	D	D+	A		Y	1,000
MFS® Lifetime 2060 Fund Class I	MFJIX	NAS CM	Open End	Target Date 2046+ (Asset Alloc)	D	D+	A		Y	0
MFS® Lifetime 2060 Fund Class R1	MFJEX	NAS CM	Open End	Target Date 2046+ (Asset Alloc)	D	D+	A		Y	0
MFS® Lifetime 2060 Fund Class R2	MFJGX	NAS CM	Open End	Target Date 2046+ (Asset Alloc)	D	D+	A		Y	0
MFS® Lifetime 2060 Fund Class R3	MFJTX	NAS CM	Open End	Target Date 2046+ (Asset Alloc)	D	D+	A		Y	0
MFS® Lifetime 2060 Fund Class R4	MFJUX	NAS CM	Open End	Target Date 2046+ (Asset Alloc)	D	D+	A		Y	0
MFS® Lifetime 2060 Fund Class R6	MFJKX	NAS CM	Open End	Target Date 2046+ (Asset Alloc)	D	D+	A		Y	0
MFS® Lifetime Income Fund Class 529A	MLLQX	NAS CM	Open End	Target Date 2000-2020 (Asset Alloc)	B	C	A-	Up	Y	250
MFS® Lifetime Income Fund Class 529B	MLLRX	NAS CM	Open End	Target Date 2000-2020 (Asset Alloc)	B-	C	A-	Up	Y	250
MFS® Lifetime Income Fund Class 529C	MLLSX	NAS CM	Open End	Target Date 2000-2020 (Asset Alloc)	B-	C	A-	Up	Y	250

★ Expanded analysis of this fund is included in Section II.

	TOTAL RETURNS					PERFORMANCE				ASSETS		ASSET ALLOCATION & TURNOVER					BULL & BEAR		FEES		
Min Additional Investment	3-Month Total Return	6-Month Total Return	1-Year Total Return	3-Year Total Return	5-Year Total Return	Dividend Yield (TTM)	Expense Ratio	3-Yr Std Deviation	3-Year Beta	NAV	Total Assets (MIL)	%Cash	%Stocks	%Bonds	%Other	Turnover Ratio	Last Bull Market Total Return	Last Bear Market Total Return	Front End Fee (%)	Back End Fee (%)	Inception Date
	4.70	8.81	18.83	27.34	65.16	0.93	1.14	8.18		14.53	249.1	2	79	19	0	43					Nov-12
	4.71	8.88	19.12	28.25	67.23	1	0.89	8.15		14.6	249.1	2	79	19	0	43					Nov-12
	4.83	9.06	19.47	29.24	69.24	1.16	0.64	8.14		14.65	249.1	2	79	19	0	43					Nov-12
	4.87	9.18	19.60	29.53	69.62	1.2	0.5	8.19		14.65	249.1	2	79	19	0	43					Aug-16
	5.09	9.52	20.46	29.90	70.66	0.88	0.9	8.63		16.33	465.2	4	85	12	0	54	20.21	-17.94	5.75		Sep-05
	4.94	9.14	19.57	26.98	64.47	0.25	1.65	8.64		16.22	465.2	4	85	12	0	54	19.72	-18.22		4.00	Sep-05
	4.92	9.16	19.56	27.01	64.48	0.26	1.65	8.63		16.02	465.2	4	85	12	0	54	19.61	-18.18		1.00	Sep-05
	5.16	9.71	20.78	30.51	72.46	1.07	0.65	8.65		16.41	465.2	4	85	12	0	54	20.36	-17.85			Sep-05
	4.96	9.18	19.57	26.99	64.41	0.04	1.65	8.64		16.16	465.2	4	85	12	0	54	19.59	-18.15			Sep-05
	5.07	9.40	20.17	28.88	68.64	0.7	1.15	8.64		16.21	465.2	4	85	12	0	54	20.06	-18.06			Sep-05
	5.10	9.54	20.49	29.84	70.73	0.88	0.9	8.64		16.32	465.2	4	85	12	0	54	20.2	-17.94			Sep-05
	5.22	9.70	20.83	30.85	72.95	1.07	0.65	8.65		16.45	465.2	4	85	12	0	54	20.38	-17.86			Sep-05
	5.21	9.75	20.88	31.05	73.18	1.1	0.51	8.66		16.44	465.2	4	85	12	0	54	20.36	-17.85			Aug-16
	5.25	9.78	20.87	30.35	71.69	0.87	0.9	8.64		15.1	169.4	2	89	9	0	45			5.75		Nov-12
	5.13	9.40	20.07	27.58	65.19	0.29	1.65	8.63		15.03	169.4	2	89	9	0	45				4.00	Nov-12
	5.15	9.43	20.06	27.53	65.26	0.35	1.65	8.66		14.97	169.4	2	89	9	0	45				1.00	Nov-12
	5.36	9.95	21.19	31.52	73.83	1.05	0.65	8.66		15.16	169.4	2	89	9	0	45					Nov-12
	5.16	9.40	20.04	27.53	65.20	0.43	1.65	8.67		15.06	169.4	2	89	9	0	45					Nov-12
	5.20	9.69	20.57	29.36	69.32	0.84	1.15	8.7		15	169.4	2	89	9	0	45					Nov-12
	5.26	9.79	20.89	30.40	71.48	0.9	0.9	8.7		15.09	169.4	2	89	9	0	45					Nov-12
	5.32	9.91	21.17	31.39	73.53	1.05	0.65	8.66		15.14	169.4	2	89	9	0	45					Nov-12
	5.35	9.94	21.29	31.48	73.78	1.09	0.51	8.66		15.13	169.4	2	89	9	0	45					Aug-16
	5.26	9.75	20.86	30.37	71.37	0.87	0.9	8.67		18.24	201.3	2	89	9	0	52	20.15	-17.63	5.75		Sep-10
	5.13	9.43	20.03	27.56	65.16	0.25	1.65	8.65		18.06	201.3	2	89	9	0	52	19.57	-17.91		4.00	Sep-10
	5.09	9.42	20.01	27.50	65.18	0.35	1.65	8.7		17.95	201.3	2	89	9	0	52	19.63	-17.91		1.00	Sep-10
	5.36	9.99	21.20	31.49	73.76	1.04	0.65	8.67		18.22	201.3	2	89	9	0	52	20.43	-17.6			Sep-10
	5.10	9.35	19.99	27.44	65.11	0.38	1.65	8.68		17.95	201.3	2	89	9	0	52	19.61	-17.91			Sep-10
	5.21	9.64	20.57	29.36	69.30	0.74	1.15	8.68		18.02	201.3	2	89	9	0	52	20.09	-17.79			Sep-10
	5.30	9.82	20.93	30.36	71.29	0.88	0.9	8.65		18.12	201.3	2	89	9	0	52	20.11	-17.61			Sep-10
	5.37	10.00	21.23	31.44	73.58	1.04	0.65	8.7		18.21	201.3	2	89	9	0	52	20.43	-17.6			Sep-10
	5.41	9.98	21.36	31.55	73.84	1.08	0.51	8.68		18.19	201.3	2	89	9	0	52	20.43	-17.6			Aug-16
	5.28	9.82	20.92	30.41	71.60	0.82	0.91	8.58		15.41	68.3	1	90	9	0	45			5.75		Nov-12
	5.12	9.38	20.02	27.53	65.31	0.29	1.66	8.59		15.38	68.3	1	90	9	0	45				4.00	Nov-12
	5.09	9.37	20.01	27.51	65.27	0.25	1.66	8.59		15.27	68.3	1	90	9	0	45				1.00	Nov-12
	5.35	9.89	21.18	30.88	73.00	0.99	0.66	8.59		15.4	68.3	1	90	9	0	45					Nov-12
	5.06	9.40	19.89	27.39	65.15	0.79	1.66	8.56		15.31	68.3	1	90	9	0	45					Nov-12
	5.20	9.69	20.56	29.43	69.41	0.76	1.16	8.54		15.33	68.3	1	90	9	0	45					Nov-12
	5.25	9.79	20.80	30.29	71.54	0.85	0.91	8.56		15.4	68.3	1	90	9	0	45					Nov-12
	5.33	9.93	21.08	31.37	73.65	0.98	0.66	8.59		15.46	68.3	1	90	9	0	45					Nov-12
	5.39	10.06	21.31	31.68	74.05	1.02	0.52	8.61		15.47	68.3	1	90	9	0	45					Aug-16
	5.25	9.83	20.91				0.9			11.81	2.0	6	85	8	0				5.75		Dec-16
	5.11	9.42	20.03				1.65			11.81	2.0	6	85	8	0					4.00	Dec-16
	5.11	9.42	20.02				1.65			11.8	2.0	6	85	8	0					1.00	Dec-16
	5.36	9.95	21.26				0.65			11.83	2.0	6	85	8	0						Dec-16
	5.14	9.45	20.06				1.65			11.82	2.0	6	85	8	0						Dec-16
	5.17	9.66	20.61				1.15			11.81	2.0	6	85	8	0						Dec-16
	5.27	9.86	20.94				0.9			11.81	2.0	6	85	8	0						Dec-16
	5.37	9.95	21.27				0.65			11.83	2.0	6	85	8	0						Dec-16
	5.47	10.05	21.38				0.51			11.84	2.0	6	85	8	0						Dec-16
	0.90	2.71	7.06	11.36	22.37	1.81	0.86	3.27		10.19	628.2	3	26	71	0	25	8.29	-4.04	5.75		Jan-15
	0.78	2.39	6.33	8.96	17.95	1.09	1.61	3.24		10.19	628.2	3	26	71	0	25	7.83	-4.34		4.00	Jan-15
	0.68	2.29	6.23	8.86	17.84	1.09	1.61	3.26		10.18	628.2	3	26	71	0	25	7.83	-4.34		1.00	Jan-15

	MARKET		FUND TYPE, CATEGORY & OBJECTIVE		RATINGS				MINIMUMS	
Fund Name	Ticker Symbol	Traded On	Fund Type	Category and (Prospectus Objective)	Overall Rating	Reward Rating	Risk Rating	Recent Up/ Downgrade	Open to New Investors	Min Initial Investment
MFS® Lifetime Income Fund Class A	MLLAX	NAS CM	Open End	Target Date 2000-2020 (Asset Alloc)	B	C	A-	Up	Y	1,000
MFS® Lifetime Income Fund Class B	MLLBX	NAS CM	Open End	Target Date 2000-2020 (Asset Alloc)	B-	C	A-	Up	Y	1,000
MFS® Lifetime Income Fund Class C	MLLCX	NAS CM	Open End	Target Date 2000-2020 (Asset Alloc)	B-	C	A-	Up	Y	1,000
MFS® Lifetime Income Fund Class I	MLLIX	NAS CM	Open End	Target Date 2000-2020 (Asset Alloc)	B	C+	A-	Up	Y	0
MFS® Lifetime Income Fund Class R1	MLLEX	NAS CM	Open End	Target Date 2000-2020 (Asset Alloc)	B-	C	A-	Up	Y	0
MFS® Lifetime Income Fund Class R2	MLLGX	NAS CM	Open End	Target Date 2000-2020 (Asset Alloc)	B	C	A-	Up	Y	0
MFS® Lifetime Income Fund Class R3	MLLHX	NAS CM	Open End	Target Date 2000-2020 (Asset Alloc)	B	C	A-	Up	Y	0
MFS® Lifetime Income Fund Class R4	MLLJX	NAS CM	Open End	Target Date 2000-2020 (Asset Alloc)	B	C+	A-	Up	Y	0
MFS® Lifetime Income Fund Class R6	MLLKX	NAS CM	Open End	Target Date 2000-2020 (Asset Alloc)	B	C+	A-	Up	Y	0
MFS® Low Volatility Equity Fund Class A	MLVAX	NAS CM	Open End	US Equity Large Cap Blend (Equity-Income)	B	B-	B+		Y	1,000
MFS® Low Volatility Equity Fund Class B	MLVBX	NAS CM	Open End	US Equity Large Cap Blend (Equity-Income)	B	B-	B+		Y	1,000
MFS® Low Volatility Equity Fund Class C	MLVGX	NAS CM	Open End	US Equity Large Cap Blend (Equity-Income)	B	B-	B+		Y	1,000
MFS® Low Volatility Equity Fund Class I	MLVHX	NAS CM	Open End	US Equity Large Cap Blend (Equity-Income)	B	B-	B+		Y	0
MFS® Low Volatility Equity Fund Class R1	MLVMX	NAS CM	Open End	US Equity Large Cap Blend (Equity-Income)	B	B-	A+		Y	0
MFS® Low Volatility Equity Fund Class R2	MLVOX	NAS CM	Open End	US Equity Large Cap Blend (Equity-Income)	B	B-	A+		Y	0
MFS® Low Volatility Equity Fund Class R3	MLVPX	NAS CM	Open End	US Equity Large Cap Blend (Equity-Income)	B	B-	B+		Y	0
MFS® Low Volatility Equity Fund Class R4	MLVRX	NAS CM	Open End	US Equity Large Cap Blend (Equity-Income)	B	B-	A+		Y	0
MFS® Low Volatility Equity Fund Class R6	MLVTX	NAS CM	Open End	US Equity Large Cap Blend (Equity-Income)	B	B-	B+		Y	0
MFS® Low Volatility Global Equity Fund Class A	MVGAX	NAS CM	Open End	Global Equity (World Stock)	B	B-	B+		Y	1,000
MFS® Low Volatility Global Equity Fund Class B	MVGBX	NAS CM	Open End	Global Equity (World Stock)	B	C+	B+		Y	1,000
MFS® Low Volatility Global Equity Fund Class C	MVGCX	NAS CM	Open End	Global Equity (World Stock)	B	C+	B+		Y	1,000
MFS® Low Volatility Global Equity Fund Class I	MVGIX	NAS CM	Open End	Global Equity (World Stock)	B	B-	B+		Y	0
MFS® Low Volatility Global Equity Fund Class R1	MVGJX	NAS CM	Open End	Global Equity (World Stock)	B	C+	B+		Y	0
MFS® Low Volatility Global Equity Fund Class R2	MVGKX	NAS CM	Open End	Global Equity (World Stock)	B	C+	B+		Y	0
MFS® Low Volatility Global Equity Fund Class R3	MVGLX	NAS CM	Open End	Global Equity (World Stock)	B	C+	B+		Y	0
MFS® Low Volatility Global Equity Fund Class R4	MVGMX	NAS CM	Open End	Global Equity (World Stock)	B	B-	B+		Y	0
MFS® Low Volatility Global Equity Fund Class R6	MVGNX	NAS CM	Open End	Global Equity (World Stock)	B	B-	B+		Y	0
MFS® Managed Wealth Fund Class A	MNWAX	NAS CM	Open End	Long/Short Equity (Growth & Income)	B-	C	A-	Up	Y	1,000
MFS® Managed Wealth Fund Class B	MNWBX	NAS CM	Open End	Long/Short Equity (Growth & Income)	B-	C	A-	Up	Y	1,000
MFS® Managed Wealth Fund Class C	MNWCX	NAS CM	Open End	Long/Short Equity (Growth & Income)	B-	C	A-	Up	Y	1,000
MFS® Managed Wealth Fund Class I	MNWIX	NAS CM	Open End	Long/Short Equity (Growth & Income)	B-	C	A-	Up	Y	0
MFS® Managed Wealth Fund Class R1	MNWRX	NAS CM	Open End	Long/Short Equity (Growth & Income)	B-	C	A-	Up	Y	0
MFS® Managed Wealth Fund Class R2	MNWSX	NAS CM	Open End	Long/Short Equity (Growth & Income)	B-	C	A-	Up	Y	0
MFS® Managed Wealth Fund Class R3	MNWTX	NAS CM	Open End	Long/Short Equity (Growth & Income)	B-	C	A-	Up	Y	0
MFS® Managed Wealth Fund Class R4	MNWUX	NAS CM	Open End	Long/Short Equity (Growth & Income)	B-	C	A-	Up	Y	0
MFS® Managed Wealth Fund Class R6	MNWZX	NAS CM	Open End	Long/Short Equity (Growth & Income)	B-	C	A-		Y	0
MFS® Massachusetts Investors Growth Stock Fund Class 529A	EISTX	NAS CM	Open End	US Equity Large Cap Growth (Growth)	B	B	A-		Y	250
MFS® Massachusetts Investors Growth Stock Fund Class 529B	EMIVX	NAS CM	Open End	US Equity Large Cap Growth (Growth)	B	B	B+		Y	250
MFS® Massachusetts Investors Growth Stock Fund Class 529C	EMICX	NAS CM	Open End	US Equity Large Cap Growth (Growth)	B	B	B+		Y	250
MFS® Massachusetts Investors Growth Stock Fund Class A	MIGFX	NAS CM	Open End	US Equity Large Cap Growth (Growth)	B	B	A-		Y	1,000
MFS® Massachusetts Investors Growth Stock Fund Class B	MIGBX	NAS CM	Open End	US Equity Large Cap Growth (Growth)	B	B	B+		Y	1,000
MFS® Massachusetts Investors Growth Stock Fund Class C	MIGDX	NAS CM	Open End	US Equity Large Cap Growth (Growth)	B	B	B+		Y	1,000
MFS® Massachusetts Investors Growth Stock Fund Class I	MGTIX	NAS CM	Open End	US Equity Large Cap Growth (Growth)	B	B	A-		Y	0
MFS® Massachusetts Investors Growth Stock Fund Class R1	MIGMX	NAS CM	Open End	US Equity Large Cap Growth (Growth)	B	B	B+		Y	0
MFS® Massachusetts Investors Growth Stock Fund Class R2	MIRGX	NAS CM	Open End	US Equity Large Cap Growth (Growth)	B	B	A-		Y	0
MFS® Massachusetts Investors Growth Stock Fund Class R3	MIGHX	NAS CM	Open End	US Equity Large Cap Growth (Growth)	B	B	A-		Y	0
MFS® Massachusetts Investors Growth Stock Fund Class R4	MIGKX	NAS CM	Open End	US Equity Large Cap Growth (Growth)	B	B	A-		Y	0
MFS® Massachusetts Investors Growth Stock Fund Class R6	MIGNX	NAS CM	Open End	US Equity Large Cap Growth (Growth)	B	B	A-		Y	0
MFS® Massachusetts Investors Trust Class 529A	EAMTX	NAS CM	Open End	US Equity Large Cap Blend (Growth)	B	B-	B		Y	250
MFS® Massachusetts Investors Trust Class 529B	EBMTX	NAS CM	Open End	US Equity Large Cap Blend (Growth)	B-	B-	B-	Down	Y	250
MFS® Massachusetts Investors Trust Class 529C	ECITX	NAS CM	Open End	US Equity Large Cap Blend (Growth)	B-	B-	B-	Down	Y	250
MFS® Massachusetts Investors Trust Class A	MITTX	NAS CM	Open End	US Equity Large Cap Blend (Growth)	B	B	B		Y	1,000

★Expanded analysis of this fund is included in Section II.

Min Additional Investment	TOTAL RETURNS 3-Month Total Return	6-Month Total Return	1-Year Total Return	3-Year Total Return	5-Year Total Return	PERFORMANCE Dividend Yield (TTM)	Expense Ratio	3-Yr Std Deviation	3-Year Beta	ASSETS NAV	Total Assets (MIL)	ASSET ALLOCATION & TURNOVER %Cash	%Stocks	%Bonds	%Other	Turnover Ratio	BULL & BEAR Last Bull Market Total Return	Last Bear Market Total Return	FEES Front End Fee (%)	Back End Fee (%)	Inception Date
	1.17	2.97	7.40	11.83	22.88	1.86	0.81	3.25		12.41	628.2	3	26	71	0	25	8.3	-4.05	5.75		Sep-05
	0.99	2.59	6.52	9.35	18.38	1.14	1.56	3.24		12.41	628.2	3	26	71	0	25	7.93	-4.43		4.00	Sep-05
	0.91	2.51	6.53	9.27	18.29	1.14	1.56	3.25		12.4	628.2	3	26	71	0	25	7.93	-4.35		1.00	Sep-05
	1.15	3.01	7.58	12.66	24.41	2.1	0.56	3.25		12.41	628.2	3	26	71	0	25	8.45	-3.94			Sep-05
	0.90	2.59	6.52	9.35	18.37	1.14	1.56	3.25		12.42	628.2	3	26	71	0	25	7.83	-4.34			Sep-05
	1.03	2.76	7.05	10.99	21.25	1.62	1.06	3.25		12.41	628.2	3	26	71	0	25	8.14	-4.14			Sep-05
	1.17	2.97	7.31	11.82	22.88	1.86	0.81	3.25		12.41	628.2	3	26	71	0	25	8.4	-4.05			Sep-05
	1.15	3.09	7.58	12.66	24.41	2.1	0.56	3.25		12.41	628.2	3	26	71	0	25	8.55	-3.94			Sep-05
	1.25	3.14	7.75	13.16	24.97	2.19	0.46	3.26		12.45	628.2	3	26	71	0	25	8.45	-3.94			Aug-16
	5.31	7.47	16.53	32.20		1.09	0.89	7.88	0.71	14.3	91.0	1	99	0	0	36			5.75		Dec-13
	5.09	7.06	15.57	29.18		0.39	1.64	7.84	0.71	14.29	91.0	1	99	0	0	36				4.00	Dec-13
	5.11	7.09	15.65	29.20		0.43	1.64	7.82	0.71	14.25	91.0	1	99	0	0	36				1.00	Dec-13
	5.38	7.61	16.80	33.00		1.3	0.64	7.85	0.71	14.31	91.0	1	99	0	0	36					Dec-13
	5.08	7.04	15.61	29.19		0.46	1.64	7.86	0.71	14.32	91.0	1	99	0	0	36					Dec-13
	5.28	7.30	16.23	31.13		0.85	1.14	7.87	0.71	14.37	91.0	1	99	0	0	36					Dec-13
	5.29	7.37	16.46	32.01		1.07	0.89	7.88	0.71	14.34	91.0	1	99	0	0	36					Dec-13
	5.37	7.60	16.77	33.01		1.3	0.64	7.86	0.71	14.32	91.0	1	99	0	0	36					Dec-13
	5.40	7.65	16.88	33.36		1.39	0.57	7.83	0.71	14.32	91.0	1	99	0	0	36					Dec-13
	4.79	6.90	18.14	25.60		1.35	0.99	8.36	0.69	13.33	187.1	1	99	0	0	24			5.75		Dec-13
	4.60	6.51	17.26	22.62		0.65	1.74	8.34	0.68	13.26	187.1	1	99	0	0	24				4.00	Dec-13
	4.59	6.49	17.26	22.58		0.64	1.74	8.35	0.69	13.24	187.1	1	99	0	0	24				1.00	Dec-13
	4.85	7.02	18.48	26.37		1.54	0.74	8.37	0.69	13.33	187.1	1	99	0	0	24					Dec-13
	4.65	6.55	17.26	22.67		0.65	1.74	8.34	0.68	13.32	187.1	1	99	0	0	24					Dec-13
	4.70	6.82	17.87	24.50		1.07	1.24	8.37	0.69	13.34	187.1	1	99	0	0	24					Dec-13
	4.73	6.84	18.06	25.38		1.33	0.99	8.34	0.68	13.34	187.1	1	99	0	0	24					Dec-13
	4.85	7.02	18.48	26.33		1.53	0.74	8.33	0.68	13.33	187.1	1	99	0	0	24					Dec-13
	4.80	6.98	18.46	26.52		1.57	0.68	8.38	0.69	13.31	187.1	1	99	0	0	24					Dec-13
	0.69	0.99	6.67	6.49		0	1.45	3.4	-2.38	10.17	23.0	8	92	0	0	5			5.75		Jun-14
	0.50	0.50	5.68	3.71		0	2.2	3.44	-1.3	10.03	23.0	8	92	0	0	5				4.00	Jun-14
	0.40	0.50	5.72	3.72		0	2.2	3.41	-1.18	9.98	23.0	8	92	0	0	5				1.00	Jun-14
	0.64	1.03	6.70	6.82		0	1.2	3.4	-2.72	10.18	23.0	8	92	0	0	5					Jun-14
	0.40	0.50	5.68	3.71		0	2.2	3.43	-1.33	10.03	23.0	8	92	0	0	5					Jun-14
	0.57	0.77	6.23	5.32		0	1.7	3.44	-2.72	10.14	23.0	8	92	0	0	5					Jun-14
	0.62	0.81	6.47	6.03		0	1.45	3.43	-1.28	10.17	23.0	8	92	0	0	5					Jun-14
	0.67	1.06	6.73	6.85		0	1.2	3.4	-2.39	10.18	23.0	8	92	0	0	5					Jun-14
	0.62	1.01	6.68	6.80			1.17	3.4	-2.23	10.18	23.0	8	92	0	0	5					Oct-17
	7.53	11.54	28.63	35.16	100.72	0.62	0.79	10.8	0.98	27.4	7,262	1	99	0	0	24	22.32	-13.19	5.75		Jul-02
	7.32	11.15	27.67	32.09	93.19	0.1	1.54	10.81	0.98	23.54	7,262	1	99	0	0	24	21.84	-13.41		4.00	Jul-02
	7.30	11.11	27.64	32.10	93.16	0.17	1.54	10.79	0.98	23.32	7,262	1	99	0	0	24	21.85	-13.45		1.00	Jul-02
	7.54	11.62	28.69	35.40	101.15	0.6	0.74	10.84	0.98	27.81	7,262	1	99	0	0	24	22.36	-13.13	5.75		Jan-35
	7.31	11.13	27.66	32.29	93.65	0.03	1.49	10.81	0.98	24.21	7,262	1	99	0	0	24	21.87	-13.45		4.00	Sep-93
	7.31	11.16	27.67	32.26	93.59	0.1	1.49	10.8	0.98	24	7,262	1	99	0	0	24	21.88	-13.44		1.00	Nov-97
	7.60	11.73	28.98	36.33	103.55	0.79	0.49	10.81	0.98	28.56	7,262	1	99	0	0	24	22.55	-13.04			Jan-97
	7.33	11.17	27.66	32.27	93.63	0.11	1.49	10.82	0.98	23.76	7,262	1	99	0	0	24	21.87	-13.47			Apr-05
	7.42	11.40	28.29	34.26	98.45	0.41	0.99	10.83	0.98	27.04	7,262	1	99	0	0	24	22.22	-13.26			Oct-03
	7.53	11.57	28.65	35.33	101.05	0.6	0.74	10.82	0.98	27.51	7,262	1	99	0	0	24	22.46	-13.21			Apr-05
	7.61	11.71	28.98	36.31	103.51	0.78	0.49	10.81	0.98	27.98	7,262	1	99	0	0	24	22.56	-13.06			Apr-05
	7.63	11.80	29.13	36.77	104.59	0.87	0.38	10.83	0.98	28.58	7,262	1	99	0	0	24	22.36	-13.13			Jun-12
	6.60	10.26	23.47	33.37	99.88	0.75	0.78	9.97	0.96	31.38	6,571	1	99	0	0	12	25.03	-17.95	5.75		Jul-02
	6.45	9.87	22.56	30.83	93.10	0.31	1.53	9.95	0.96	29.68	6,571	1	99	0	0	12	24.48	-18.22		4.00	Jul-02
	6.40	9.83	22.53	30.34	92.34	0.15	1.53	9.96	0.96	29.28	6,571	1	99	0	0	12	24.49	-18.19		1.00	Jul-02
	6.63	10.32	23.56	33.57	100.30	0.74	0.73	9.97	0.96	32.15	6,571	1	99	0	0	12	25.02	-17.89	5.75		Jul-24

	MARKET			FUND TYPE, CATEGORY & OBJECTIVE	RATINGS				MINIMUMS	
Fund Name	Ticker Symbol	Traded On	Fund Type	Category and (Prospectus Objective)	Overall Rating	Reward Rating	Risk Rating	Recent Up/ Downgrade	Open to New Investors	Min Initial Investment
MFS® Massachusetts Investors Trust Class B	MITBX	NAS CM	Open End	US Equity Large Cap Blend (Growth)	B-	B-	B-	Down	Y	1,000
MFS® Massachusetts Investors Trust Class C	MITCX	NAS CM	Open End	US Equity Large Cap Blend (Growth)	B-	B-	B-	Down	Y	1,000
MFS® Massachusetts Investors Trust Class I	MITIX	NAS CM	Open End	US Equity Large Cap Blend (Growth)	B	B	B		Y	0
MFS® Massachusetts Investors Trust Class R1	MITGX	NAS CM	Open End	US Equity Large Cap Blend (Growth)	B-	B-	B-	Down	Y	0
MFS® Massachusetts Investors Trust Class R2	MIRTX	NAS CM	Open End	US Equity Large Cap Blend (Growth)	B-	B-	B	Down	Y	0
MFS® Massachusetts Investors Trust Class R3	MITHX	NAS CM	Open End	US Equity Large Cap Blend (Growth)	B	B	B		Y	0
MFS® Massachusetts Investors Trust Class R4	MITDX	NAS CM	Open End	US Equity Large Cap Blend (Growth)	B	B	B		Y	0
MFS® Massachusetts Investors Trust Class R6	MITJX	NAS CM	Open End	US Equity Large Cap Blend (Growth)	B	B	B		Y	0
MFS® Mid Cap Growth Fund Class 529A	EAMCX	NAS CM	Open End	US Equity Mid Cap (Growth)	B+	B	A-	Up	Y	250
MFS® Mid Cap Growth Fund Class 529B	EBCGX	NAS CM	Open End	US Equity Mid Cap (Growth)	B+	B	A-	Up	Y	250
MFS® Mid Cap Growth Fund Class 529C	ECGRX	NAS CM	Open End	US Equity Mid Cap (Growth)	B+	B	A-	Up	Y	250
MFS® Mid Cap Growth Fund Class A	OTCAX	NAS CM	Open End	US Equity Mid Cap (Growth)	B+	B	A-	Up	Y	1,000
MFS® Mid Cap Growth Fund Class B	OTCBX	NAS CM	Open End	US Equity Mid Cap (Growth)	B+	B	A-	Up	Y	1,000
MFS® Mid Cap Growth Fund Class C	OTCCX	NAS CM	Open End	US Equity Mid Cap (Growth)	B+	B	A-	Up	Y	1,000
MFS® Mid Cap Growth Fund Class I	OTCIX	NAS CM	Open End	US Equity Mid Cap (Growth)	B+	B	A-	Up	Y	0
MFS® Mid Cap Growth Fund Class R1	OTCGX	NAS CM	Open End	US Equity Mid Cap (Growth)	B+	B	A-	Up	Y	0
MFS® Mid Cap Growth Fund Class R2	MCPRX	NAS CM	Open End	US Equity Mid Cap (Growth)	B	B	B	Up	Y	0
MFS® Mid Cap Growth Fund Class R3	OTCHX	NAS CM	Open End	US Equity Mid Cap (Growth)	B+	B	A-	Up	Y	0
MFS® Mid Cap Growth Fund Class R4	OTCJX	NAS CM	Open End	US Equity Mid Cap (Growth)	B+	B+	A-	Up	Y	0
MFS® Mid Cap Growth Fund Class R6	OTCKX	NAS CM	Open End	US Equity Mid Cap (Growth)	B+	B+	A-	Up	Y	0
MFS® Mid Cap Value Fund Class 529A	EACVX	NAS CM	Open End	US Equity Mid Cap (Growth)	B	B-	B+	Up		250
MFS® Mid Cap Value Fund Class 529B	EBCVX	NAS CM	Open End	US Equity Mid Cap (Growth)	B	C+	B	Up		250
MFS® Mid Cap Value Fund Class 529C	ECCVX	NAS CM	Open End	US Equity Mid Cap (Growth)	B	C+	B	Up		250
MFS® Mid Cap Value Fund Class A	MVCAX	NAS CM	Open End	US Equity Mid Cap (Growth)	B	B-	B+	Up	Y	1,000
MFS® Mid Cap Value Fund Class B	MCBVX	NAS CM	Open End	US Equity Mid Cap (Growth)	B	C+	B	Up	Y	1,000
MFS® Mid Cap Value Fund Class C	MVCCX	NAS CM	Open End	US Equity Mid Cap (Growth)	B	C+	B	Up	Y	1,000
MFS® Mid Cap Value Fund Class I	MCVIX	NAS CM	Open End	US Equity Mid Cap (Growth)	B	B-	B+	Up	Y	0
MFS® Mid Cap Value Fund Class R1	MVCGX	NAS CM	Open End	US Equity Mid Cap (Growth)	B	C+	B	Up	Y	0
MFS® Mid Cap Value Fund Class R2	MCVRX	NAS CM	Open End	US Equity Mid Cap (Growth)	B	B-	B	Up	Y	0
MFS® Mid Cap Value Fund Class R3	MVCHX	NAS CM	Open End	US Equity Mid Cap (Growth)	B	B-	B+	Up	Y	0
MFS® Mid Cap Value Fund Class R4	MVCJX	NAS CM	Open End	US Equity Mid Cap (Growth)	B	B-	B+	Up	Y	0
MFS® Mid Cap Value Fund Class R6	MVCKX	NAS CM	Open End	US Equity Mid Cap (Growth)	B	B-	B+	Up	Y	0
MFS® Moderate Allocation Fund Class 529A	EAMDX	NAS CM	Open End	Moderate Alloc (Asset Alloc)	B	C+	A-	Up	Y	250
MFS® Moderate Allocation Fund Class 529B	EBMDX	NAS CM	Open End	Moderate Alloc (Asset Alloc)	B	C+	B+	Up	Y	250
MFS® Moderate Allocation Fund Class 529C	ECMAX	NAS CM	Open End	Moderate Alloc (Asset Alloc)	B	C+	B+	Up	Y	250
MFS® Moderate Allocation Fund Class A	MAMAX	NAS CM	Open End	Moderate Alloc (Asset Alloc)	B	C+	A-	Up	Y	1,000
MFS® Moderate Allocation Fund Class B	MMABX	NAS CM	Open End	Moderate Alloc (Asset Alloc)	B	C+	B+	Up	Y	1,000
MFS® Moderate Allocation Fund Class C	MMACX	NAS CM	Open End	Moderate Alloc (Asset Alloc)	B	C+	B+	Up	Y	1,000
MFS® Moderate Allocation Fund Class I	MMAIX	NAS CM	Open End	Moderate Alloc (Asset Alloc)	B	C+	A-	Up	Y	0
MFS® Moderate Allocation Fund Class R1	MAMFX	NAS CM	Open End	Moderate Alloc (Asset Alloc)	B	C+	B+	Up	Y	0
MFS® Moderate Allocation Fund Class R2	MARRX	NAS CM	Open End	Moderate Alloc (Asset Alloc)	B	C+	A-	Up	Y	0
MFS® Moderate Allocation Fund Class R3	MAMHX	NAS CM	Open End	Moderate Alloc (Asset Alloc)	B	C+	A-	Up	Y	0
MFS® Moderate Allocation Fund Class R4	MAMJX	NAS CM	Open End	Moderate Alloc (Asset Alloc)	B	C+	A-	Up	Y	0
MFS® New Discovery Fund Class 529A	EANDX	NAS CM	Open End	US Equity Small Cap (Growth)	B	B+	C	Up	Y	250
MFS® New Discovery Fund Class 529B	EBNDX	NAS CM	Open End	US Equity Small Cap (Growth)	B-	B	C	Up	Y	250
MFS® New Discovery Fund Class 529C	ECNDX	NAS CM	Open End	US Equity Small Cap (Growth)	B-	B	C	Up	Y	250
MFS® New Discovery Fund Class A	MNDAX	NAS CM	Open End	US Equity Small Cap (Growth)	B	B+	C	Up	Y	1,000
MFS® New Discovery Fund Class B	MNDBX	NAS CM	Open End	US Equity Small Cap (Growth)	B-	B	C	Up	Y	1,000
MFS® New Discovery Fund Class C	MNDCX	NAS CM	Open End	US Equity Small Cap (Growth)	B-	B	C	Up	Y	1,000
MFS® New Discovery Fund Class I	MNDIX	NAS CM	Open End	US Equity Small Cap (Growth)	B	B+	C	Up	Y	0
MFS® New Discovery Fund Class R1	MNDGX	NAS CM	Open End	US Equity Small Cap (Growth)	B-	B	C	Up	Y	0
MFS® New Discovery Fund Class R2	MNDRX	NAS CM	Open End	US Equity Small Cap (Growth)	B	B	C	Up	Y	0

★ Expanded analysis of this fund is included in Section II.

	TOTAL RETURNS					PERFORMANCE				ASSETS		ASSET ALLOCATION & TURNOVER					BULL & BEAR		FEES		
Min Additional Investment	3-Month Total Return	6-Month Total Return	1-Year Total Return	3-Year Total Return	5-Year Total Return	Dividend Yield (TTM)	Expense Ratio	3-Yr Std Deviation	3-Year Beta	NAV	Total Assets (MIL)	%Cash	%Stocks	%Bonds	%Other	Turnover Ratio	Last Bull Market Total Return	Last Bear Market Total Return	Front End Fee (%)	Back End Fee (%)	Inception Date
	6.43	9.87	22.60	30.54	92.80	0.1	1.48	9.96	0.96	31.24	6,571	1	99	0	0	12	24.51	-18.14		4.00	Sep-93
	6.43	9.89	22.62	30.55	92.78	0.13	1.48	9.97	0.96	30.65	6,571	1	99	0	0	12	24.48	-18.16		1.00	Jul-96
	6.69	10.40	23.79	34.46	102.58	0.95	0.48	9.97	0.96	31.26	6,571	1	99	0	0	12	25.25	-17.82			Jan-97
	6.41	9.89	22.58	30.50	92.81	0.1	1.48	9.96	0.96	30.47	6,571	1	99	0	0	12	24.46	-18.15			Apr-05
	6.56	10.13	23.18	32.47	97.60	0.54	0.98	9.96	0.96	30.69	6,571	1	99	0	0	12	24.85	-17.99			Oct-03
	6.63	10.28	23.50	33.48	100.09	0.73	0.73	9.98	0.96	31.87	6,571	1	99	0	0	12	25.09	-17.93			Apr-05
	6.69	10.42	23.83	34.49	102.67	0.92	0.48	9.96	0.96	32.42	6,571	1	99	0	0	12	25.26	-17.84			Apr-05
	6.72	10.47	23.92	34.86	103.51	1.03	0.39	9.97	0.96	31.28	6,571	1	99	0	0	12	25.02	-17.89			Jun-12
	4.96	10.22	25.96	36.12	107.41	0	1.26	10.6	0.91	15.52	2,561	3	97	0	0	30	23.3	-19.73	5.75		Jul-02
	4.72	9.74	24.94	32.99	99.43	0	2.01	10.54	0.9	13.01	2,561	3	97	0	0	30	22.65	-19.84		4.00	Jul-02
	4.70	9.70	24.94	32.86	99.17	0	2.01	10.62	0.91	12.61	2,561	3	97	0	0	30	22.77	-19.95		1.00	Jul-02
	4.95	10.20	25.99	36.19	107.37	0	1.21	10.61	0.91	15.99	2,561	3	97	0	0	30	23.27	-19.69	5.75		Dec-93
	4.76	9.75	25.01	33.11	99.91	0	1.96	10.6	0.91	13.33	2,561	3	97	0	0	30	22.58	-19.95		4.00	Dec-93
	4.75	9.71	25.00	33.09	99.66	0	1.96	10.6	0.91	12.93	2,561	3	97	0	0	30	22.67	-19.86		1.00	Aug-94
	4.99	10.31	26.28	37.07	109.84	0	0.96	10.59	0.91	16.89	2,561	3	97	0	0	30	23.32	-19.55			Jan-97
	4.78	9.80	25.03	33.16	99.70	0	1.96	10.59	0.91	13.27	2,561	3	97	0	0	30	22.82	-20.02			Apr-05
	4.89	10.06	25.61	35.05	104.90	0	1.46	10.6	0.91	15.11	2,561	3	97	0	0	30	23.06	-19.75			Oct-03
	4.98	10.19	25.99	36.14	107.39	0	1.21	10.59	0.91	15.89	2,561	3	97	0	0	30	23.27	-19.69			Apr-05
	4.98	10.28	26.28	37.10	110.03	0	0.96	10.59	0.91	16.51	2,561	3	97	0	0	30	23.39	-19.6			Apr-05
	5.03	10.39	26.38	37.52	110.91	0	0.85	10.62	0.91	16.98	2,561	3	97	0	0	30	23.27	-19.69			Jan-13
	4.53	7.03	13.34	26.19	93.59	0.99	1.21	10.64	0.98	22.87	7,150	2	98	0	0	29	25.08	-20.98	5.75		Jul-02
	4.30	6.58	12.46	23.33	86.27	0.28	1.96	10.66	0.99	21.31	7,150	2	98	0	0	29	24.48	-21.14		4.00	Jul-02
	4.34	6.60	12.53	23.43	86.59	0.43	1.96	10.64	0.98	21.39	7,150	2	98	0	0	29	24.37	-21.12		1.00	Jul-02
	4.50	7.01	13.38	26.32	93.86	1	1.16	10.65	0.99	23.24	7,150	2	98	0	0	29	24.96	-20.85	5.75		Aug-01
	4.36	6.62	12.55	23.57	86.87	0.4	1.91	10.67	0.99	21.99	7,150	2	98	0	0	29	24.54	-21.14		4.00	Nov-01
	4.33	6.65	12.55	23.52	86.84	0.52	1.91	10.65	0.98	21.9	7,150	2	98	0	0	29	24.47	-21.16		1.00	Nov-01
	4.61	7.16	13.68	27.27	96.43	1.19	0.91	10.65	0.99	23.8	7,150	2	98	0	0	29	25.26	-20.81			Nov-01
	4.35	6.60	12.54	23.55	86.79	0.52	1.91	10.65	0.99	21.55	7,150	2	98	0	0	29	24.49	-21.13			Apr-05
	4.46	6.90	13.09	25.35	91.55	0.86	1.41	10.66	0.99	22.7	7,150	2	98	0	0	29	24.93	-21.01			Oct-03
	4.53	7.05	13.39	26.36	93.98	1.01	1.16	10.66	0.99	23.16	7,150	2	98	0	0	29	25.01	-20.85			Apr-05
	4.60	7.15	13.65	27.25	96.32	1.2	0.91	10.65	0.99	23.33	7,150	2	98	0	0	29	25.22	-20.8			Apr-05
	4.62	7.21	13.84	27.87	97.52	1.29	0.75	10.65	0.99	23.81	7,150	2	98	0	0	29	24.96	-20.85			Feb-13
	3.38	6.34	14.78	20.38	45.21	1.33	1.03	6.05	0.55	17.66	5,882	4	55	40	0	1	14.3	-10.77	5.75		Jul-02
	3.18	5.91	13.84	17.67	39.74	0.64	1.78	6.06	0.55	17.37	5,882	4	55	40	0	1	13.88	-11.06		4.00	Jul-02
	3.15	5.91	13.84	17.68	39.73	0.7	1.78	6.07	0.55	17.25	5,882	4	55	40	0	1	13.86	-11.07		1.00	Jul-02
	3.43	6.39	14.81	20.55	45.52	1.35	0.98	6.07	0.55	17.75	5,882	4	55	40	0	1	14.35	-10.76	5.75		Jun-02
	3.21	5.93	13.94	17.79	40.10	0.67	1.73	6.05	0.55	17.55	5,882	4	55	40	0	1	13.85	-11.01		4.00	Jun-02
	3.18	5.92	13.90	17.80	40.08	0.67	1.73	6.06	0.55	17.43	5,882	4	55	40	0	1	13.84	-11.02		1.00	Jun-02
	3.45	6.43	15.08	21.37	47.27	1.57	0.73	6.05	0.55	17.98	5,882	4	55	40	0	1	14.57	-10.68			Jun-02
	3.20	5.93	13.89	17.80	40.09	0.7	1.73	6.07	0.55	17.07	5,882	4	55	40	0	1	13.86	-11.08			Apr-05
	3.32	6.21	14.52	19.61	43.58	1.15	1.23	6.06	0.55	17.37	5,882	4	55	40	0	1	14.15	-10.79			Oct-03
	3.40	6.38	14.80	20.50	45.46	1.37	0.98	6.06	0.55	17.61	5,882	4	55	40	0	1	14.37	-10.76			Apr-05
	3.50	6.46	15.10	21.48	47.28	1.59	0.73	6.09	0.55	17.73	5,882	4	55	40	0	1	14.58	-10.66			Apr-05
	6.57	13.79	25.96	33.53	78.49	0	1.4	13.31	0.84	26.34	1,213	3	97	0	0	53	26.86	-27.4	5.75		Jul-02
	6.38	13.37	25.04	30.52	71.91	0	2.15	13.3	0.84	21.3	1,213	3	97	0	0	53	26.23	-27.58		4.00	Jul-02
	6.39	13.37	25.05	30.47	71.73	0	2.15	13.31	0.84	21.29	1,213	3	97	0	0	53	26.21	-27.57		1.00	Jul-02
	6.59	13.83	26.08	33.65	78.85	0	1.35	13.3	0.84	27.26	1,213	3	97	0	0	53	26.8	-27.35	5.75		Jan-97
	6.35	13.35	25.05	30.63	72.23	0	2.1	13.31	0.84	22.09	1,213	3	97	0	0	53	26.31	-27.56		4.00	Nov-97
	6.38	13.37	25.11	30.68	72.22	0	2.1	13.32	0.84	22.14	1,213	3	97	0	0	53	26.28	-27.6		1.00	Nov-97
	6.64	13.94	26.34	34.65	80.99	0	1.1	13.32	0.84	30.09	1,213	3	97	0	0	53	27.04	-27.29			Jan-97
	6.40	13.35	25.07	30.68	72.21	0	2.1	13.31	0.84	21.93	1,213	3	97	0	0	53	26.24	-27.55			Apr-05
	6.54	13.67	25.73	32.67	76.59	0	1.6	13.3	0.84	25.67	1,213	3	97	0	0	53	26.66	-27.42			Oct-03

	MARKET			FUND TYPE, CATEGORY & OBJECTIVE	RATINGS				MINIMUMS	
Fund Name	Ticker Symbol	Traded On	Fund Type	Category and (Prospectus Objective)	Overall Rating	Reward Rating	Risk Rating	Recent Up/ Downgrade	Open to New Investors	Min Initial Investment
MFS® New Discovery Fund Class R3	MNDHX	NAS CM	Open End	US Equity Small Cap (Growth)	B	B+	C	Up	Y	0
MFS® New Discovery Fund Class R4	MNDJX	NAS CM	Open End	US Equity Small Cap (Growth)	B	B+	C	Up	Y	0
MFS® New Discovery Fund Class R6	MNDKX	NAS CM	Open End	US Equity Small Cap (Growth)	B	B+	C	Up	Y	0
MFS® New Discovery Value Fund Class A	NDVAX	NAS CM	Open End	US Equity Small Cap (Growth)	B+	A-	B	Up	Y	1,000
MFS® New Discovery Value Fund Class B	NDVBX	NAS CM	Open End	US Equity Small Cap (Growth)	B+	A-	B	Up	Y	1,000
MFS® New Discovery Value Fund Class C	NDVCX	NAS CM	Open End	US Equity Small Cap (Growth)	B+	A-	B	Up	Y	1,000
MFS® New Discovery Value Fund Class I	NDVIX	NAS CM	Open End	US Equity Small Cap (Growth)	A-	A-	B	Up	Y	0
MFS® New Discovery Value Fund Class R1	NDVRX	NAS CM	Open End	US Equity Small Cap (Growth)	B+	A-	B	Up	Y	0
MFS® New Discovery Value Fund Class R2	NDVSX	NAS CM	Open End	US Equity Small Cap (Growth)	B+	A-	B	Up	Y	0
MFS® New Discovery Value Fund Class R3	NDVTX	NAS CM	Open End	US Equity Small Cap (Growth)	B+	A-	B	Up	Y	0
MFS® New Discovery Value Fund Class R4	NDVUX	NAS CM	Open End	US Equity Small Cap (Growth)	B+	A-	B	Up	Y	0
MFS® New Discovery Value Fund Class R6	NDVVX	NAS CM	Open End	US Equity Small Cap (Growth)	A-	A	B	Up	Y	0
MFS® Research Fund Class A	MFRFX	NAS CM	Open End	US Equity Large Cap Blend (Growth & Income)	B	B	B		Y	1,000
MFS® Research Fund Class B	MFRBX	NAS CM	Open End	US Equity Large Cap Blend (Growth & Income)	B-	B-	B-	Down	Y	1,000
MFS® Research Fund Class C	MFRCX	NAS CM	Open End	US Equity Large Cap Blend (Growth & Income)	B-	B-	B-	Down	Y	1,000
MFS® Research Fund Class I	MRFIX	NAS CM	Open End	US Equity Large Cap Blend (Growth & Income)	B	B	B		Y	0
MFS® Research Fund Class R1	MFRLX	NAS CM	Open End	US Equity Large Cap Blend (Growth & Income)	B-	B-	B-	Down	Y	0
MFS® Research Fund Class R2	MSRRX	NAS CM	Open End	US Equity Large Cap Blend (Growth & Income)	B	B	B		Y	0
MFS® Research Fund Class R3	MFRHX	NAS CM	Open End	US Equity Large Cap Blend (Growth & Income)	B	B	B		Y	0
MFS® Research Fund Class R4	MFRJX	NAS CM	Open End	US Equity Large Cap Blend (Growth & Income)	B	B	B		Y	0
MFS® Research Fund Class R6	MFRKX	NAS CM	Open End	US Equity Large Cap Blend (Growth & Income)	B	B	B		Y	0
MFS® Research International Fund Class 529A	EARSX	NAS CM	Open End	Global Equity Large Cap (Foreign Stock)	B-	C+	B-	Up	Y	250
MFS® Research International Fund Class 529B	EBRIX	NAS CM	Open End	Global Equity Large Cap (Foreign Stock)	B-	C+	B-	Up	Y	250
MFS® Research International Fund Class 529C	ECRIX	NAS CM	Open End	Global Equity Large Cap (Foreign Stock)	B-	C+	B-	Up	Y	250
MFS® Research International Fund Class A	MRSAX	NAS CM	Open End	Global Equity Large Cap (Foreign Stock)	B-	C+	B-	Up	Y	1,000
MFS® Research International Fund Class B	MRIBX	NAS CM	Open End	Global Equity Large Cap (Foreign Stock)	B-	C+	B-	Up	Y	1,000
MFS® Research International Fund Class C	MRICX	NAS CM	Open End	Global Equity Large Cap (Foreign Stock)	B-	C+	B-	Up	Y	1,000
MFS® Research International Fund Class I	MRSIX	NAS CM	Open End	Global Equity Large Cap (Foreign Stock)	B-	C+	B-	Up	Y	0
MFS® Research International Fund Class R1	MRSGX	NAS CM	Open End	Global Equity Large Cap (Foreign Stock)	B-	C+	B-	Up	Y	0
MFS® Research International Fund Class R2	MRSRX	NAS CM	Open End	Global Equity Large Cap (Foreign Stock)	B-	C+	B-	Up	Y	0
MFS® Research International Fund Class R3	MRSHX	NAS CM	Open End	Global Equity Large Cap (Foreign Stock)	B-	C+	B-	Up	Y	0
MFS® Research International Fund Class R4	MRSJX	NAS CM	Open End	Global Equity Large Cap (Foreign Stock)	B-	C+	B-	Up	Y	0
MFS® Research International Fund Class R6	MRSKX	NAS CM	Open End	Global Equity Large Cap (Foreign Stock)	B-	C+	B-	Up	Y	0
MFS® Technology Fund Class A	MTCAX	NAS CM	Open End	Technology Sector Equity (Technology)	A	A	A-	Up	Y	1,000
MFS® Technology Fund Class B	MTCBX	NAS CM	Open End	Technology Sector Equity (Technology)	A	A	A-	Up	Y	1,000
MFS® Technology Fund Class C	MTCCX	NAS CM	Open End	Technology Sector Equity (Technology)	A	A	A-	Up	Y	1,000
MFS® Technology Fund Class I	MTCIX	NAS CM	Open End	Technology Sector Equity (Technology)	A	A	A-	Up	Y	0
MFS® Technology Fund Class R1	MTCKX	NAS CM	Open End	Technology Sector Equity (Technology)	A	A	A-	Up	Y	0
MFS® Technology Fund Class R2	MTERX	NAS CM	Open End	Technology Sector Equity (Technology)	A	A	A-	Up	Y	0
MFS® Technology Fund Class R3	MTCHX	NAS CM	Open End	Technology Sector Equity (Technology)	A	A	A-	Up	Y	0
MFS® Technology Fund Class R4	MTCJX	NAS CM	Open End	Technology Sector Equity (Technology)	A	A	A-	Up	Y	0
MFS® Technology Fund Class R6	MTCLX	NAS CM	Open End	Technology Sector Equity (Technology)	A	A	A-	Up	Y	0
MFS® Total Return Fund Class 529A	EATRX	NAS CM	Open End	Moderate Alloc (Balanced)	B-	C+	B	Up	Y	250
MFS® Total Return Fund Class 529B	EBTRX	NAS CM	Open End	Moderate Alloc (Balanced)	B-	C+	B	Up	Y	250
MFS® Total Return Fund Class 529C	ECTRX	NAS CM	Open End	Moderate Alloc (Balanced)	B-	C+	B	Up	Y	250
MFS® Total Return Fund Class A	MSFRX	NAS CM	Open End	Moderate Alloc (Balanced)	B-	C+	B	Up	Y	1,000
MFS® Total Return Fund Class B	MTRBX	NAS CM	Open End	Moderate Alloc (Balanced)	B-	C+	B	Up	Y	1,000
MFS® Total Return Fund Class C	MTRCX	NAS CM	Open End	Moderate Alloc (Balanced)	B-	C+	B	Up	Y	1,000
MFS® Total Return Fund Class I	MTRIX	NAS CM	Open End	Moderate Alloc (Balanced)	B-	C+	B	Down	Y	0
MFS® Total Return Fund Class R1	MSFFX	NAS CM	Open End	Moderate Alloc (Balanced)	B-	C+	B	Up	Y	0
MFS® Total Return Fund Class R2	MTRRX	NAS CM	Open End	Moderate Alloc (Balanced)	B-	C+	B	Up	Y	0
MFS® Total Return Fund Class R3	MSFHX	NAS CM	Open End	Moderate Alloc (Balanced)	B-	C+	B	Up	Y	0

★Expanded analysis of this fund is included in Section II.

Min Additional Investment	TOTAL RETURNS: 3-Month Total Return	6-Month Total Return	1-Year Total Return	3-Year Total Return	5-Year Total Return	PERFORMANCE: Dividend Yield (TTM)	Expense Ratio	3-Yr Std Deviation	3-Year Beta	ASSETS: NAV	Total Assets (MIL)	ASSET ALLOCATION & TURNOVER: %Cash	%Stocks	%Bonds	%Other	Turnover Ratio	BULL & BEAR: Last Bull Market Total Return	Last Bear Market Total Return	FEES: Front End Fee (%)	Back End Fee (%)	Inception Date
	6.55	13.81	26.01	33.64	78.72	0	1.35	13.31	0.84	27.22	1,213	3	97	0	0	53	26.81	-27.33			Apr-05
	6.75	14.06	26.46	34.74	81.19	0	1.1	13.34	0.84	28.64	1,213	3	97	0	0	53	26.99	-27.28			Apr-05
	6.65	13.98	26.49	35.14	82.08	0	0.97	13.33	0.84	30.32	1,213	3	97	0	0	53	27.04	-27.29			Jun-12
	5.50	10.60	14.65	38.89	104.77	0.36	1.37	12.12	0.82	15.74	1,208	2	98	0	0	60	35.56		5.75		May-11
	5.27	10.14	13.81	35.81	97.34	0.05	2.12	12.15	0.82	15.21	1,208	2	98	0	0	60	34.92			4.00	May-11
	5.29	10.19	13.79	35.80	97.32	0	2.12	12.12	0.82	15.14	1,208	2	98	0	0	60	34.99			1.00	May-11
	5.50	10.64	14.83	39.90	107.24	0.47	1.12	12.14	0.82	15.81	1,208	2	98	0	0	60	35.91				May-11
	5.26	10.21	13.80	35.81	97.35	0	2.12	12.1	0.82	15.22	1,208	2	98	0	0	60	35.05				May-11
	5.38	10.48	14.38	37.94	102.37	0.21	1.62	12.15	0.82	15.69	1,208	2	98	0	0	60	35.41				May-11
	5.49	10.57	14.60	38.95	104.94	0.3	1.37	12.15	0.82	15.78	1,208	2	98	0	0	60	35.57				May-11
	5.45	10.66	14.83	39.89	107.42	0.47	1.12	12.11	0.82	15.83	1,208	2	98	0	0	60	35.74				May-11
	5.53	10.74	15.00	40.38	108.22	0.51	0.99	12.16	0.82	15.83	1,208	2	98	0	0	60	35.91				Jul-12
	5.87	10.41	23.34	33.96	100.33	0.8	0.82	9.81	0.95	42.1	5,567	1	99	0	0	38	25.12	-16.87	5.75		Oct-71
	5.64	9.97	22.38	30.94	92.88	0.22	1.57	9.81	0.95	38.4	5,567	1	99	0	0	38	24.63	-17.16		4.00	Sep-93
	5.66	10.00	22.43	30.99	92.92	0.29	1.57	9.79	0.95	38.1	5,567	1	99	0	0	38	24.58	-17.14		1.00	Jan-94
	5.93	10.54	23.63	34.97	102.78	0.97	0.57	9.81	0.95	43.18	5,567	1	99	0	0	38	25.28	-16.81			Jan-97
	5.67	9.99	22.41	31.00	92.93	0.29	1.57	9.81	0.95	37.48	5,567	1	99	0	0	38	24.63	-17.16			Apr-05
	5.80	10.26	23.04	32.97	97.82	0.61	1.07	9.82	0.95	40.83	5,567	1	99	0	0	38	24.99	-17.01			Oct-03
	5.86	10.40	23.32	33.95	100.26	0.79	0.82	9.82	0.95	41.86	5,567	1	99	0	0	38	25.11	-16.89			Apr-05
	5.94	10.56	23.64	34.98	102.82	0.99	0.57	9.81	0.95	42.15	5,567	1	99	0	0	38	25.32	-16.84			Apr-05
	5.95	10.57	23.71	35.29	103.67	1.07	0.48	9.82	0.95	42.06	5,567	1	99	0	0	38	25.26	-16.85			May-06
	5.33	10.18	27.99	23.17	37.99	1.63	1.16	11.73	0.93	18.94	7,938	1	99	0	0	33	13.65	-22.03	5.75		Jul-02
	5.18	9.80	27.01	20.41	32.85	1.49	1.92	11.73	0.93	17.93	7,938	1	99	0	0	33	13.12	-22.29		4.00	Jul-02
	5.17	9.81	27.09	20.42	32.83	1.53	1.91	11.73	0.93	17.58	7,938	1	99	0	0	33	13.15	-22.25		1.00	Jul-02
	5.36	10.25	28.04	23.32	38.20	1.36	1.11	11.72	0.93	19.31	7,938	1	99	0	0	33	13.6	-21.96	5.75		Jan-97
	5.17	9.86	27.07	20.55	33.13	0.6	1.87	11.72	0.93	18.68	7,938	1	99	0	0	33	13.12	-22.24		4.00	Jan-98
	5.10	9.78	27.06	20.54	33.14	0.75	1.87	11.73	0.93	18.19	7,938	1	99	0	0	33	13.2	-22.28		1.00	Jan-98
	5.40	10.41	28.37	24.27	39.97	1.56	0.87	11.73	0.93	19.96	7,938	1	99	0	0	33	13.83	-21.91			Jan-97
	5.17	9.86	27.07	20.59	33.14	0.67	1.86	11.71	0.93	17.92	7,938	1	99	0	0	33	13.17	-22.24			Apr-05
	5.25	10.12	27.66	22.36	36.45	1.22	1.36	11.72	0.93	18.67	7,938	1	99	0	0	33	13.46	-22.06			Oct-03
	5.37	10.24	28.08	23.33	38.20	1.35	1.12	11.72	0.93	19.11	7,938	1	99	0	0	33	13.71	-22.02			Apr-05
	5.42	10.36	28.38	24.20	39.90	1.47	0.86	11.74	0.93	19.33	7,938	1	99	0	0	33	13.87	-21.92			Apr-05
	5.41	10.44	28.45	24.59	40.67	1.71	0.77	11.73	0.93	19.18	7,938	1	99	0	0	33	13.76	-21.95			May-06
	6.69	14.86	38.46	63.75	152.18	0	1.27	14.07	0.96	36.7	940.7	2	98	0	0	43	24.04	-12.5	5.75		Jan-97
	6.47	14.41	37.37	60.07	142.91	0	1.99	14.08	0.96	31.95	940.7	2	98	0	0	43	23.42	-12.7		4.00	Apr-00
	6.49	14.44	37.41	60.09	142.84	0	1.99	14.06	0.96	31.89	940.7	2	98	0	0	43	23.46	-12.72		1.00	Apr-00
	6.74	15.02	38.80	64.94	155.29	0	0.99	14.07	0.96	39.11	940.7	2	98	0	0	43	24.16	-12.37			Jan-97
	6.47	14.43	37.40	60.06	142.86	0	1.99	14.1	0.96	31.82	940.7	2	98	0	0	43	23.51	-12.74			Apr-05
	6.60	14.72	38.07	62.53	149.06	0	1.49	14.07	0.96	35.06	940.7	2	98	0	0	43	23.81	-12.54			Oct-03
	6.66	14.87	38.44	63.73	152.20	0	1.24	14.08	0.96	36.68	940.7	2	98	0	0	43	24.04	-12.45			Apr-05
	6.75	15.03	38.81	64.99	155.36	0	1.02	14.08	0.96	38.1	940.7	2	98	0	0	43	24.16	-12.36			Apr-05
	6.76	15.06	38.90	65.44	156.51	0	0.9	14.07	0.96	39.32	940.7	2	98	0	0	43	24.04	-12.5			Jan-13
	3.34	5.52	12.09	20.74	57.41	1.93	0.79	5.71	0.55	19.07	8,026	1	60	39	0	38	15.12	-10.36	5.75		Jul-02
	3.18	5.14	11.24	18.05	51.55	1.2	1.54	5.7	0.55	19.15	8,026	1	60	39	0	38	14.57	-10.57		4.00	Jul-02
	3.16	5.12	11.26	18.02	51.57	1.2	1.54	5.74	0.55	19.23	8,026	1	60	39	0	38	14.6	-10.64		1.00	Jul-02
	3.40	5.58	12.16	20.96	57.84	1.97	0.74	5.74	0.55	19.13	8,026	1	60	39	0	38	15.2	-10.38	5.75		Oct-70
	3.19	5.16	11.29	18.24	51.94	1.24	1.49	5.72	0.55	19.15	8,026	1	60	39	0	38	14.69	-10.61		4.00	Aug-93
	3.17	5.14	11.23	18.16	51.88	1.23	1.49	5.72	0.55	19.24	8,026	1	60	39	0	38	14.63	-10.62		1.00	Aug-94
	3.46	5.65	12.37	21.82	59.74	2.2	0.49	5.7	0.55	19.12	8,026	1	60	39	0	38	15.37	-10.23			Jan-97
	3.20	5.13	11.27	18.18	51.97	1.25	1.49	5.74	0.55	19.1	8,026	1	60	39	0	38	14.65	-10.61			Apr-05
	3.32	5.37	11.84	20.01	55.81	1.72	0.99	5.74	0.55	19.18	8,026	1	60	39	0	38	14.91	-10.39			Oct-03
	3.39	5.57	12.14	20.92	57.75	1.96	0.74	5.74	0.55	19.14	8,026	1	60	39	0	38	15.19	-10.31			Apr-05

	MARKET			FUND TYPE, CATEGORY & OBJECTIVE	RATINGS				MINIMUMS	
Fund Name	Ticker Symbol	Traded On	Fund Type	Category and (Prospectus Objective)	Overall Rating	Reward Rating	Risk Rating	Recent Up/ Downgrade	Open to New Investors	Min Initial Investment
MFS® Total Return Fund Class R4	MSFJX	NAS CM	Open End	Moderate Alloc (Balanced)	B-	C+	B	Up	Y	0
MFS® Total Return Fund Class R6	MSFKX	NAS CM	Open End	Moderate Alloc (Balanced)	B-	C+	B	Down	Y	0
MFS® Utilities Fund Class A	MMUFX	NAS CM	Open End	Utilities Sector Equity (Utility)	C	C	C+	Down	Y	1,000
MFS® Utilities Fund Class B	MMUBX	NAS CM	Open End	Utilities Sector Equity (Utility)	C	C	C	Down	Y	1,000
MFS® Utilities Fund Class C	MMUCX	NAS CM	Open End	Utilities Sector Equity (Utility)	C	C	C	Down	Y	1,000
MFS® Utilities Fund Class I	MMUIX	NAS CM	Open End	Utilities Sector Equity (Utility)	C+	C	C+		Y	0
MFS® Utilities Fund Class R1	MMUGX	NAS CM	Open End	Utilities Sector Equity (Utility)	C	C	C	Down	Y	0
MFS® Utilities Fund Class R2	MURRX	NAS CM	Open End	Utilities Sector Equity (Utility)	C	C	C+	Down	Y	0
MFS® Utilities Fund Class R3	MMUHX	NAS CM	Open End	Utilities Sector Equity (Utility)	C	C	C+	Down	Y	0
MFS® Utilities Fund Class R4	MMUJX	NAS CM	Open End	Utilities Sector Equity (Utility)	C+	C	C+		Y	0
MFS® Utilities Fund Class R6	MMUKX	NAS CM	Open End	Utilities Sector Equity (Utility)	C+	C	C+		Y	0
MFS® Value Fund Class 529A	EAVLX	NAS CM	Open End	US Equity Large Cap Value (Growth)	B	B-	B		Y	250
MFS® Value Fund Class 529B	EBVLX	NAS CM	Open End	US Equity Large Cap Value (Growth)	B-	B-	B-	Down	Y	250
MFS® Value Fund Class 529C	ECVLX	NAS CM	Open End	US Equity Large Cap Value (Growth)	B-	B-	B-	Down	Y	250
MFS® Value Fund Class A	MEIAX	NAS CM	Open End	US Equity Large Cap Value (Growth)	B	B-	B		Y	1,000
MFS® Value Fund Class B	MFEBX	NAS CM	Open End	US Equity Large Cap Value (Growth)	B-	B-	B-	Down	Y	1,000
MFS® Value Fund Class C	MEICX	NAS CM	Open End	US Equity Large Cap Value (Growth)	B-	B-	B-	Down	Y	1,000
MFS® Value Fund Class I	MEIIX	NAS CM	Open End	US Equity Large Cap Value (Growth)	B	B	B		Y	0
MFS® Value Fund Class R1	MEIGX	NAS CM	Open End	US Equity Large Cap Value (Growth)	B-	B-	B-	Down	Y	0
MFS® Value Fund Class R2	MVRRX	NAS CM	Open End	US Equity Large Cap Value (Growth)	B-	B-	B	Down	Y	0
MFS® Value Fund Class R3	MEIHX	NAS CM	Open End	US Equity Large Cap Value (Growth)	B-	B-	B	Down	Y	0
MFS® Value Fund Class R4	MEIJX	NAS CM	Open End	US Equity Large Cap Value (Growth)	B	B	B		Y	0
MFS® Value Fund Class R6	MEIKX	NAS CM	Open End	US Equity Large Cap Value (Growth)	B	B	B		Y	0
MH Elite Fund of Funds Fund	MHEFX	NAS CM	Open End	Aggressive Alloc (Growth)	B-	B-	B-	Down	Y	10,000
MH Elite Select Portfolio of Funds Fund	MHESX	NAS CM	Open End	Global Equity (Growth)	B-	C+	B-	Up	Y	10,000
MH Elite Small Capital Fund of Funds	MHELX	NAS CM	Open End	Aggressive Alloc (Small Company)	B-	B-	B	Up	Y	10,000
Midas Fund	MIDSX	NAS CM	Open End	Precious Metals Sector Equity (Precious Metals)	D+	C-	D	Down	Y	1,000
Miles Capital Alternatives Advantage Fund Class I	MILIX	NAS CM	Open End	Multialternative (Growth)	C-	D+	B	Up	Y	50,000
Miles Capital Alternatives Advantage Fund Class N	MILNX	NAS CM	Open End	Multialternative (Growth)	C-	D+	B	Up	Y	2,500
Miller Convertible Bond Fund Class A	MCFAX	NAS CM	Open End	Convertibles (Convertible Bond)	B	C+	A-	Up	Y	2,500
Miller Convertible Bond Fund Class C	MCFCX	NAS CM	Open End	Convertibles (Convertible Bond)	B	C+	A-	Up	Y	2,500
Miller Convertible Bond Fund Class I	MCIFX	NAS CM	Open End	Convertibles (Convertible Bond)	B	C+	A-	Up	Y	1,000,000
Miller Convertible Plus Fund Class A	MCPAX	NAS CM	Open End	Convertibles (Convertible Bond)	C+	C	B-	Down	Y	2,500
Miller Convertible Plus Fund Class C	MCCCX	NAS CM	Open End	Convertibles (Convertible Bond)	C+	C	B-	Down	Y	2,500
Miller Convertible Plus Fund Class I	MCPIX	NAS CM	Open End	Convertibles (Convertible Bond)	C+	C	B-	Down	Y	1,000,000
Miller Income Fund Class A	LMCJX	NAS CM	Open End	Aggressive Alloc (Income)	C+	C+	C	Up	Y	1,000
Miller Income Fund Class C	LCMNX	NAS CM	Open End	Aggressive Alloc (Income)	C+	C+	C	Up	Y	1,000
Miller Income Fund Class FI	LMCKX	NAS CM	Open End	Aggressive Alloc (Income)	C+	C+	C	Up	Y	0
Miller Income Fund Class I	LMCLX	NAS CM	Open End	Aggressive Alloc (Income)	C+	C+	C	Up	Y	1,000,000
Miller Income Fund Class IS	LMCMX	NAS CM	Open End	Aggressive Alloc (Income)	C+	C+	C	Up	Y	1,000,000
Miller Opportunity Trust Class A	LGOAX	NAS CM	Open End	US Equity Mid Cap (Growth)	B-	B-	C+	Up	Y	1,000
Miller Opportunity Trust Class C	LMOPX	NAS CM	Open End	US Equity Mid Cap (Growth)	B-	B-	C+	Up	Y	1,000
Miller Opportunity Trust Class FI	LMOFX	NAS CM	Open End	US Equity Mid Cap (Growth)	B-	B-	C+	Up	Y	0
Miller Opportunity Trust Class I	LMNOX	NAS CM	Open End	US Equity Mid Cap (Growth)	B-	B-	C+	Up	Y	1,000,000
Miller Opportunity Trust Class R	LMORX	NAS CM	Open End	US Equity Mid Cap (Growth)	B-	B-	C+	Up	Y	0
Miller/Howard Drill Bit to Burner Tip® Adviser Cls Shares	DBBDX	NAS CM	Open End	Energy Sector Equity (Growth & Income)	C-	D	C	Up	Y	2,500
Miller/Howard Drill Bit to Burner Tip® Fund Class I Shares	DBBEX	NAS CM	Open End	Energy Sector Equity (Growth & Income)	C-	D	C	Up	Y	100,000
Miller/Howard High Income Equity	HIE	NYSE	Closed End	US Equity Mid Cap (Growth & Income)	C	C	C-		Y	
Miller/Howard Income-Equity Fund Adviser Class Shares	MHIDX	NAS CM	Open End	US Equity Large Cap Value (Equity-Income)	C-	C-	B+	Up	Y	2,500
Miller/Howard Income-Equity Fund Class I Shares	MHIEX	NAS CM	Open End	US Equity Large Cap Value (Equity-Income)	C-	C-	B+	Up	Y	100,000
MIP International Tilts Master Portfolio	US5763536019		Open End	Global Equity Large Cap (Foreign Stock)	U	U	U		Y	0
Mirae Asset Asia Fund Class A	MALAX	NAS CM	Open End	Asia ex-Japan Equity (Pacific Stock)	B	B	C+	Up	Y	2,000

★ Expanded analysis of this fund is included in Section II.

	TOTAL RETURNS					PERFORMANCE				ASSETS		ASSET ALLOCATION & TURNOVER					BULL & BEAR		FEES		
Min Additional Investment	3-Month Total Return	6-Month Total Return	1-Year Total Return	3-Year Total Return	5-Year Total Return	Dividend Yield (TTM)	Expense Ratio	3-Yr Std Deviation	3-Year Beta	NAV	Total Assets (MIL)	%Cash	%Stocks	%Bonds	%Other	Turnover Ratio	Last Bull Market Total Return	Last Bear Market Total Return	Front End Fee (%)	Back End Fee (%)	Inception Date
	3.40	5.65	12.36	21.79	59.75	2.19	0.49	5.72	0.55	19.14	8,026	1	60	39	0	38	15.36	-10.22			Apr-05
	3.48	5.75	12.52	22.19	60.47	2.28	0.41	5.74	0.55	19.13	8,026	1	60	39	0	38	15.2	-10.38			Jun-12
	0.19	4.28	14.68	7.68	48.90	3.35	0.99	11.1	0.73	20.17	3,789	3	92	0	0	27	14.64	-12.3	5.75		Feb-92
	0.05	3.95	13.89	5.32	43.48	2.63	1.74	11.07	0.72	20.08	3,789	3	92	0	0	27	14.15	-12.56		4.00	Sep-93
	0.05	3.91	13.84	5.28	43.45	2.64	1.74	11.07	0.73	20.07	3,789	3	92	0	0	27	14.22	-12.61		1.00	Jan-94
	0.26	4.45	15.03	8.49	50.82	3.57	0.74	11.12	0.73	20.25	3,789	3	92	0	0	27	14.83	-12.18			Jan-97
	0.00	3.91	13.87	5.30	43.46	2.64	1.74	11.1	0.73	20.03	3,789	3	92	0	0	27	14.17	-12.58			Apr-05
	0.18	4.21	14.43	6.92	47.07	3.12	1.24	11.09	0.73	20.12	3,789	3	92	0	0	27	14.45	-12.36			Oct-03
	0.19	4.28	14.68	7.68	48.93	3.35	0.99	11.09	0.73	20.16	3,789	3	92	0	0	27	14.66	-12.31			Apr-05
	0.26	4.46	15.01	8.51	50.82	3.58	0.74	11.1	0.73	20.19	3,789	3	92	0	0	27	14.8	-12.2			Apr-05
	0.33	4.49	15.13	8.83	51.63	3.66	0.64	11.08	0.73	20.26	3,789	3	92	0	0	27	14.64	-12.3			Jun-12
	4.91	7.74	17.43	31.40	100.72	1.53	0.89	10.21	0.96	40.24	47,021	2	98	0	0	14	25.08	-18.02	5.75		Jul-02
	4.71	7.33	16.65	29.32	94.55	1.13	1.64	10.22	0.96	39.81	47,021	2	98	0	0	14	24.51	-18.21		4.00	Jul-02
	4.71	7.34	16.51	28.33	92.88	0.86	1.64	10.21	0.96	39.63	47,021	2	98	0	0	14	24.51	-18.25		1.00	Jul-02
	4.90	7.76	17.44	31.42	100.68	1.5	0.84	10.22	0.96	40.57	47,021	2	98	0	0	14	25.11	-17.97	5.75		Jan-96
	4.72	7.34	16.57	28.48	93.34	0.84	1.59	10.21	0.96	40.38	47,021	2	98	0	0	14	24.5	-18.22		4.00	Nov-97
	4.71	7.35	16.55	28.48	93.33	0.85	1.59	10.21	0.96	40.11	47,021	2	98	0	0	14	24.57	-18.23		1.00	Nov-97
	4.99	7.88	17.76	32.43	103.24	1.74	0.59	10.22	0.96	40.79	47,021	2	98	0	0	14	25.24	-17.86			Jan-97
	4.72	7.35	16.58	28.49	93.36	0.87	1.59	10.21	0.96	39.82	47,021	2	98	0	0	14	24.53	-18.22			Apr-05
	4.85	7.62	17.15	30.43	98.20	1.32	1.09	10.22	0.96	40.16	47,021	2	98	0	0	14	24.9	-18.06			Oct-03
	4.92	7.77	17.46	31.42	100.74	1.53	0.84	10.23	0.97	40.42	47,021	2	98	0	0	14	25.08	-17.97			Apr-05
	4.97	7.90	17.74	32.41	103.28	1.75	0.59	10.22	0.96	40.56	47,021	2	98	0	0	14	25.26	-17.89			Apr-05
	5.03	7.96	17.86	32.83	104.34	1.84	0.49	10.23	0.96	40.56	47,021	2	98	0	0	14	25.17	-17.89			May-06
1,000	5.64	10.19	20.43	24.30	76.61	0	1.85	10.45	1.01	6.92	12.6	5	85	4	6	42	21.87	-20.14			Jan-04
1,000	4.50	9.23	21.70	18.52	31.40	0	2.12	9.36	0.75	6.27	5.8	3	91	4	2	34	11.95	-20.76			Apr-06
1,000	3.54	7.64	12.39	20.79	68.86	0	2.03	12.19	0.85	7.6	7.0	6	91	2	1	45	26.74	-25.68			Sep-98
100	2.48	4.20	5.98	24.00	-50.79	0	3.39	37.7	0.25	1.24	17.5	0	90	1	9	2	-20.98	-26.05			Jan-86
1,000	1.31	2.80	5.17			0	2.97			10.48	18.6	37	37	19	2						Mar-16
1,000	1.22	2.61	4.88			0	3.22			10.43	18.6	37	37	19	2						Mar-16
100	2.01	3.92	6.83	15.98	47.14	3.13	1.49	6.95	-0.57	12.95	974.2	1	-7	8	7	46	12.42	-15.19	5.75		Dec-07
100	1.88	3.59	6.18	14.20	43.46	2.66	1.99	6.95	-0.56	12.86	974.2	1	-7	8	7	46	12.14	-15.33			Dec-09
100	2.16	4.13	7.29	17.70	50.88	3.62	0.99	6.93	-0.56	12.93	974.2	1	-7	8	7	46	12.83	-15.01			Dec-07
100	2.18	4.51	6.84	29.75		2.11	4			23.66	137.5	-45	0	11	0	81			5.75		Dec-14
100	1.86	4.03	5.96	26.70		1.56	3.62			23.44	137.5	-45	0	11	0	81					Dec-14
100	2.18	4.57	7.09	30.59		2.57	2.62			23.63	137.5	-45	0	11	0	81					Dec-14
50	0.60	4.47	16.41	12.59		7.56	2.34	12.76	1.48	8.47	126.8	0	68	17	1	52			5.75		Feb-14
50	0.54	4.10	15.58	10.10		6.86	3.09	12.68	1.48	8.46	126.8	0	68	17	1	52				1.00	Feb-14
	0.61	4.49	16.39	12.42		7.68	2.34	12.79	1.48	8.44	126.8	0	68	17	1	52					Feb-14
	0.80	4.63	16.94	13.59		7.86	2.04	12.73	1.47	8.46	126.8	0	68	17	1	52					Feb-14
	0.82	4.81	17.05	13.91		7.95	1.94	12.78	1.48	8.46	126.8	0	68	17	1	52					Feb-14
50	5.43	4.96	25.94	25.68	140.73	0	1.36	21.47	1.67	23.88	1,458	0	100	0	0	85	32.04	-38.54	5.75		Feb-09
50	5.22	4.54	24.99	22.88	131.56	0	2.13	21.48	1.67	22.55	1,458	0	100	0	0	85	31.37	-38.78		1.00	Dec-99
	5.43	4.94	25.90	25.58	140.08	0	1.42	21.47	1.67	24.64	1,458	0	100	0	0	85	32.13	-38.65			Feb-04
	5.45	5.06	26.20	26.76	143.97	0	1.09	21.51	1.67	25.91	1,458	0	100	0	0	85	32.22	-38.44			Jun-00
	5.36	4.80	25.54	24.50	136.20	0	1.71	21.45	1.67	23.98	1,458	0	100	0	0	85	31.35	-38.63			Dec-06
	2.57	5.96	-1.02			0	1.56			11.55	7.0	1	99	0	0						Dec-15
	2.74	6.12	-0.77			0.23	1.31			11.52	7.0	1	99	0	0						Dec-15
	0.44	2.19	7.58	-7.08		11.27	1.7	14.36	1.15	12.57	167.9	1	99	0	0	85					Nov-14
	3.54	6.39	13.40			3.01	1.21			11.62	109.1	1	99	0	0						Dec-15
	3.69	6.52	13.59			3.3	0.96			11.63	109.1	1	99	0	0						Dec-15
	-9.70	-14.64	-9.17			0	0.45				--	3	96	0	1	120					Oct-13
100	10.94	19.29	48.28	34.62	66.59	0	1.5	14.27	0.88	13.79	17.9	3	97	0	0	113	25.05	-30.52	5.75		Sep-10

Fund Name	Ticker Symbol	Traded On	Fund Type	Category and (Prospectus Objective)	Overall Rating	Reward Rating	Risk Rating	Recent Up/ Downgrade	Open to New Investors	Min Initial Investment
	MARKET		FUND TYPE, CATEGORY & OBJECTIVE		RATINGS				MINIMUMS	
Mirae Asset Asia Fund Class C	MCLAX	NAS CM	Open End	Asia ex-Japan Equity (Pacific Stock)	B-	B	C+	Up	Y	2,000
Mirae Asset Asia Fund Class I	MILAX	NAS CM	Open End	Asia ex-Japan Equity (Pacific Stock)	B	B	C+	Up	Y	250,000
Mirae Asset Emerging Markets Fund Class A	MALGX	NAS CM	Open End	Emerging Markets Equity (Div Emerging Mkts)	B	A-	C	Up	Y	2,000
Mirae Asset Emerging Markets Fund Class C	MCLGX	NAS CM	Open End	Emerging Markets Equity (Div Emerging Mkts)	B	B+	C	Up	Y	2,000
Mirae Asset Emerging Markets Fund Class I	MILGX	NAS CM	Open End	Emerging Markets Equity (Div Emerging Mkts)	B	A-	C	Up	Y	250,000
Mirae Asset Emerging Markets Great Consumer Fund Class A	MECGX	NAS CM	Open End	Emerging Markets Equity (Div Emerging Mkts)	C+	B-	C	Up	Y	2,000
Mirae Asset Emerging Markets Great Consumer Fund Class C	MCCGX	NAS CM	Open End	Emerging Markets Equity (Div Emerging Mkts)	C+	B-	C	Up	Y	2,000
Mirae Asset Emerging Markets Great Consumer Fund Class I	MICGX	NAS CM	Open End	Emerging Markets Equity (Div Emerging Mkts)	C+	B-	C	Up	Y	250,000
Mirova Global Sustainable Equity Fund Class A	ESGMX	NAS CM	Open End	Global Equity (Growth)	D+	C	B	Up	Y	2,500
Mirova Global Sustainable Equity Fund Class C	ESGCX	NAS CM	Open End	Global Equity (Growth)	D+	C	B	Up	Y	2,500
Mirova Global Sustainable Equity Fund Class N	ESGNX	NAS CM	Open End	Global Equity (Growth)	D+	C	B	Up	Y	1,000,000
Mirova Global Sustainable Equity Fund Class Y	ESGYX	NAS CM	Open End	Global Equity (Growth)	D+	C	B	Up	Y	100,000
MM MSCI EAFE® International Index Fund Administrative Cls	MKRYX	NAS CM	Open End	Global Equity Large Cap (Growth)	B-	C+	B	Up	Y	0
MM MSCI EAFE® International Index Fund Class A	MKRAX	NAS CM	Open End	Global Equity Large Cap (Growth)	B-	C+	B	Up	Y	0
MM MSCI EAFE® International Index Fund Class I	MKRZX	NAS CM	Open End	Global Equity Large Cap (Growth)	B-	B-	B	Up	Y	0
MM MSCI EAFE® International Index Fund Class R3	MKRTX	NAS CM	Open End	Global Equity Large Cap (Growth)	B-	C+	B	Up	Y	0
MM MSCI EAFE® International Index Fund Class R4	MKRFX	NAS CM	Open End	Global Equity Large Cap (Growth)	B-	C+	B	Up	Y	0
MM MSCI EAFE® International Index Fund Class R5	MKRIX	NAS CM	Open End	Global Equity Large Cap (Growth)	B-	C+	B	Up	Y	0
MM MSCI EAFE® International Index Fund Service Cls shares	MKRSX	NAS CM	Open End	Global Equity Large Cap (Growth)	B-	C+	B	Up	Y	0
MM Russell 2000® Small Cap Index Fund Administrative Class	MCJYX	NAS CM	Open End	US Equity Small Cap (Small Company)	B+	A-	B	Up	Y	0
MM Russell 2000® Small Cap Index Fund Class A	MCJAX	NAS CM	Open End	US Equity Small Cap (Small Company)	B+	A-	B	Up	Y	0
MM Russell 2000® Small Cap Index Fund Class I	MCJZX	NAS CM	Open End	US Equity Small Cap (Small Company)	B+	A-	B	Up	Y	0
MM Russell 2000® Small Cap Index Fund Class R3	MCJTX	NAS CM	Open End	US Equity Small Cap (Small Company)	B+	B+	B	Up	Y	0
MM Russell 2000® Small Cap Index Fund Class R4	MCJFX	NAS CM	Open End	US Equity Small Cap (Small Company)	B+	A-	B	Up	Y	0
MM Russell 2000® Small Cap Index Fund Class R5	MCJIX	NAS CM	Open End	US Equity Small Cap (Small Company)	B+	A-	B	Up	Y	0
MM Russell 2000® Small Cap Index Fund Service Class shares	MCJSX	NAS CM	Open End	US Equity Small Cap (Small Company)	B+	A-	B	Up	Y	0
MM S&P 500® Index Fund Class A	MMFFX	NAS CM	Open End	US Equity Large Cap Blend (Growth & Income)	B	B-	B		Y	0
MM S&P 500® Index Fund Class Administrative Class	MIEYX	NAS CM	Open End	US Equity Large Cap Blend (Growth & Income)	B	B	B		Y	0
MM S&P 500® Index Fund Class I	MMIZX	NAS CM	Open End	US Equity Large Cap Blend (Growth & Income)	B	B	B		Y	0
MM S&P 500® Index Fund Class R3	MMINX	NAS CM	Open End	US Equity Large Cap Blend (Growth & Income)	B	B-	B		Y	0
MM S&P 500® Index Fund Class R4	MIEAX	NAS CM	Open End	US Equity Large Cap Blend (Growth & Income)	B	B	B		Y	0
MM S&P 500® Index Fund Class R5	MIEZX	NAS CM	Open End	US Equity Large Cap Blend (Growth & Income)	B	B	B		Y	0
MM S&P 500® Index Fund Class Service Class	MMIEX	NAS CM	Open End	US Equity Large Cap Blend (Growth & Income)	B	B	B		Y	0
MM S&P® Mid Cap Index Fund Class A	MDKAX	NAS CM	Open End	US Equity Mid Cap (Growth)	B	B	B	Up	Y	0
MM S&P® Mid Cap Index Fund Class I	MDKZX	NAS CM	Open End	US Equity Mid Cap (Growth)	B	B	B		Y	0
MM S&P® Mid Cap Index Fund Class R3	MDKTX	NAS CM	Open End	US Equity Mid Cap (Growth)	B	B	B	Up	Y	0
MM S&P® Mid Cap Index Fund Class R4	MDKFX	NAS CM	Open End	US Equity Mid Cap (Growth)	B	B	B		Y	0
MM S&P® Mid Cap Index Fund Class R5	MDKIX	NAS CM	Open End	US Equity Mid Cap (Growth)	B	B	B		Y	0
MM S&P® Mid Cap Index Fund Service Class shares	MDKSX	NAS CM	Open End	US Equity Mid Cap (Growth)	B	B	B		Y	0
MM S&P® Mid Cap R5ndex Fund Administrative Class	MDKYX	NAS CM	Open End	US Equity Mid Cap (Growth)	B	B	B		Y	0
MM Select Equity Asset Fund Class I	MSEJX	NAS CM	Open End	Global Equity (World Stock)	D	C	B		Y	0
Moerus Worldwide Value Fund Class N	MOWNX	NAS CM	Open End	Global Equity Mid/Small Cap (World Stock)	D+	C	B+	Up	Y	2,500
Moerus Worldwide Value Fund Institutional Class	MOWIX	NAS CM	Open End	Global Equity Mid/Small Cap (World Stock)	D+	C	B+	Up	Y	100,000
Mondrian International Equity Fund	DPIEX	NAS CM	Open End	Global Equity Large Cap (Foreign Stock)	B-	C+	B-	Up		1,000,000
Monetta Fund	MONTX	NAS CM	Open End	US Equity Large Cap Growth (Growth)	B	B	B	Up	Y	1,000
Monetta Young Investor Fund	MYIFX	NAS CM	Open End	US Equity Large Cap Growth (Growth)	B	B	B		Y	1,000
Monongahela All Cap Value Fund	MCMVX	NAS CM	Open End	US Equity Mid Cap (Growth)	B	B+	B		Y	5,000
Monteagle Informed Investor Growth Fund Class I	MIIFX	NAS CM	Open End	US Equity Large Cap Growth (Growth)	B	B	A-	Up	Y	50,000
Monteagle Quality Growth Fund Class I	MFGIX	NAS CM	Open End	US Equity Large Cap Growth (Growth)	B	B	B-		Y	50,000
Monteagle Select Value Fund Class I	MVEIX	NAS CM	Open End	US Equity Large Cap Value (Growth)	C+	C+	C+	Up	Y	50,000
Monteagle Value Fund Class I	MVRGX	NAS CM	Open End	US Equity Large Cap Value (Growth)	C+	B-	C+		Y	50,000
Morgan Dempsey Small/Micro Cap Value Fund	MITYX	NAS CM	Open End	US Equity Small Cap (Growth)	B	B	C+	Up	Y	2,500

★ Expanded analysis of this fund is included in Section II.

	TOTAL RETURNS					PERFORMANCE				ASSETS		ASSET ALLOCATION & TURNOVER					BULL & BEAR		FEES		
Min Additional Investment	3-Month Total Return	6-Month Total Return	1-Year Total Return	3-Year Total Return	5-Year Total Return	Dividend Yield (TTM)	Expense Ratio	3-Yr Std Deviation	3-Year Beta	NAV	Total Assets (MIL)	%Cash	%Stocks	%Bonds	%Other	Turnover Ratio	Last Bull Market Total Return	Last Bear Market Total Return	Front End Fee (%)	Back End Fee (%)	Inception Date
100	10.75	18.86	47.16	31.65	60.50	0	2.25	14.24	0.87	12.98	17.9	3	97	0	0	113	24.55	-30.72		1.00	Sep-10
25,000	11.03	19.40	48.62	35.55	68.61	0	1.25	14.31	0.88	14.09	17.9	3	97	0	0	113	25.21	-30.44			Sep-10
100	8.73	19.99	45.29	39.70	42.97	0	1.5	14.65	0.87	13.44	36.4	2	95	0	0		20.6	-28.69	5.75		Sep-10
100	8.54	19.58	44.15	36.41	37.44	0	2.25	14.67	0.87	12.7	36.4	2	95	0	0		19.84	-28.82		1.00	Sep-10
25,000	8.75	20.14	45.62	40.68	44.53	0	1.25	14.7	0.87	13.66	36.4	2	95	0	0		20.69	-28.62			Sep-10
100	9.87	21.22	47.39	26.75	34.53	0	1.5	14.49	0.84	15.02	218.3	3	94	0	0	55	23.86	-24.6	5.75		Nov-10
100	9.72	20.81	46.29	23.97	29.58	0	2.25	14.44	0.83	14.22	218.3	3	94	0	0	55	23.22	-24.85		1.00	Nov-10
25,000	9.85	21.28	47.67	27.67	36.04	0	1.25	14.46	0.84	15.27	218.3	3	94	0	0	55	24.03	-24.49			Sep-10
50	5.33	10.94	30.44			0.03	1.3			12.77	68.8	3	97	0	0	20			5.75		Mar-16
50	5.16	10.45	29.40			0	2.05			12.63	68.8	3	97	0	0	20				1.00	Mar-16
	5.37	11.06	30.79				1			12.81	68.8	3	97	0	0	20					May-17
50	5.34	11.02	30.74			0.07	1.05			12.81	68.8	3	97	0	0	20					Mar-16
	3.79	9.03	24.79	23.59	43.57	4.12	0.6	11.46	0.93	13.24	232.5	2	97	0	0	35					Jul-12
	3.67	8.84	24.39	22.63	41.68	3.94	0.85	11.45	0.92	13.21	232.5	2	97	0	0	35			5.75		Jul-12
	3.81	9.19	25.10	24.92	46.09	4.38	0.25	11.46	0.92	13.29	232.5	2	97	0	0	35					Jul-12
	3.58	8.78	24.24	22.18	41.22	4	1	11.51	0.93	13.11	232.5	2	97	0	0	35					Apr-14
	3.68	8.88	24.52	23.03	42.94	4.14	0.75	11.51	0.93	13.14	232.5	2	97	0	0	35					Apr-14
	3.78	9.08	25.08	24.50	45.39	4.31	0.35	11.49	0.93	13.29	232.5	2	97	0	0	35					Jul-12
	3.75	8.98	24.82	23.95	44.16	4.21	0.5	11.46	0.92	13.24	232.5	2	97	0	0	35					Jul-12
	3.24	8.98	14.12	30.56	93.77	0.96	0.55	14.11	1	13.14	298.3	1	98	0	0	38					Jul-12
	3.23	8.92	13.91	29.70	91.18	0.79	0.8	14.16	1	13.08	298.3	1	98	0	0	38			5.75		Jul-12
	3.35	9.21	14.60	32.06	97.29	1.2	0.2	14.17	1	13.21	298.3	1	98	0	0	38					Jul-12
	3.16	8.81	13.65	29.13	90.51	0.81	0.95	14.08	1	12.97	298.3	1	98	0	0	38					Apr-14
	3.19	8.89	13.98	30.03	92.89	0.91	0.7	14.14	1	13.02	298.3	1	98	0	0	38					Apr-14
	3.25	9.11	14.41	31.52	96.25	1.14	0.3	14.15	1	13.2	298.3	1	98	0	0	38					Jul-12
	3.20	9.02	14.18	30.91	94.51	1.06	0.45	14.14	1	13.1	298.3	1	98	0	0	38					Jul-12
	6.42	11.02	20.98	33.94	104.34	1.45	0.72	10.11	1	18.02	3,367	0	99	0	1	5	24.57	-16.47	5.75		Apr-14
	6.52	11.21	21.30	34.96	106.88	1.62	0.47	10.11	1	18.33	3,367	0	99	0	1	5	24.77	-16.47			Feb-98
	6.67	11.41	21.72	36.40	110.68	1.87	0.12	10.1	1	18.55	3,367	0	99	0	1	5	25	-16.38			Dec-11
	6.44	10.94	20.78	33.42	102.53	1.49	0.87	10.1	1	17.71	3,367	0	99	0	1	5	24.38	-16.65			Dec-02
	6.46	11.08	21.07	34.36	105.16	1.52	0.62	10.1	1	18.13	3,367	0	99	0	1	5	24.56	-16.5			Feb-98
	6.58	11.32	21.59	36.00	109.42	1.78	0.22	10.1	1	18.6	3,367	0	99	0	1	5	24.96	-16.38			Apr-01
	6.56	11.24	21.37	35.35	107.68	1.63	0.37	10.1	1	18.64	3,367	0	99	0	1	5	24.76	-16.38			Feb-98
	6.13	9.30	15.26	32.61	96.15	0.86	0.8	11.04	1	14.12	493.0	1	99	0	0	33			5.75		Jul-12
	6.21	9.58	15.85	34.90	102.05	1.32	0.2	11.08	1	14.22	493.0	1	99	0	0	33					Jul-12
	6.00	9.19	15.01	31.93	95.31	0.89	0.95	11.02	1	13.99	493.0	1	99	0	0	33					Apr-14
	6.09	9.35	15.34	32.86	97.71	1.02	0.7	11.09	1	14.04	493.0	1	99	0	0	33					Apr-14
	6.20	9.58	15.78	34.45	100.90	1.26	0.3	11.05	1	14.18	493.0	1	99	0	0	33					Jul-12
	6.22	9.46	15.59	33.99	99.72	1.16	0.45	11.04	1	14.13	493.0	1	99	0	0	33					Jul-12
	6.12	9.44	15.48	33.50	98.72	1.06	0.55	11.06	1	14.13	493.0	1	99	0	0	33					Jul-12
	5.44	10.57	22.14			0.47	0.22			11.77	1,121	1	97	0	2	31					Sep-16
1,000	0.38	6.78	19.05			0.35	1.71			12.97	46.5	12	88	0	0						May-16
200	0.41	6.89	19.35			0.4	1.46			12.99	46.5	12	88	0	0						May-16
100	2.98	8.42	21.42	20.57	45.48	1.91	0.79	11.53	0.89	15.73	576.0	1	99	0	0	20	7.83	-17.12			Feb-92
	5.31	10.20	19.18	30.46	93.67	0.01	1.46	11.08	1.02	18.89	58.1	6	94	0	0	120	18.92	-24.04			May-86
	7.50	12.59	23.10	36.19	103.51	0.47	1.26	10.36	1.01	24	144.9	5	95	0	0	42	23.52	-13.44			Dec-06
250	6.40	11.11	20.75	38.09		1.04	0.85	10.67	0.94	14.09	9.4	8	92	0	0	51					Jul-13
	5.63	10.34	16.52	30.21	71.59	0	1.44	11.14	0.71	11.06	12.6	46	54	0	0	610	26.11	-17.51			Apr-08
	6.07	11.21	24.59	31.13	87.93	0.22	1.33	9.94	0.95	14.31	29.0	10	90	0	0	31	24.3	-15.91			Mar-98
	7.33	10.66	11.08	18.88	104.94	1.47	1.4	13.67	1.02	13.37	12.9	6	94	0	0	127	18.01	-22.94			Mar-98
	8.04	11.35	10.20	25.38	75.97	1.42	1.34	12.98	1.05	16.12	22.6	12	88	0	0	30	17.95	-18.87			Dec-99
50	3.74	10.64	11.73	29.05	67.38	0.27	1.3	13.08	0.85	15.94	24.1	2	98	0	0	24	22.27	-21.71			Dec-10

	MARKET			FUND TYPE, CATEGORY & OBJECTIVE	RATINGS				MINIMUMS	
Fund Name	Ticker Symbol	Traded On	Fund Type	Category and (Prospectus Objective)	Overall Rating	Reward Rating	Risk Rating	Recent Up/ Downgrade	Open to New Investors	Min Initial Investment
Morgan Stanley China A Share Fund	CAF	NYSE	Closed End	Greater China Equity (Pacific Stock)	B	A	C+	Up	Y	
Morgan Stanley Emerging Mkts Breakout Nations Port Cls A	EMAPX	NAS CM	Open End	Emerging Markets Equity (Div Emerging Mkts)	D	D+	A-		Y	1,000
Morgan Stanley Emerging Mkts Breakout Nations Port Cls C	EMCPX	NAS CM	Open End	Emerging Markets Equity (Div Emerging Mkts)	D	D+	A-		Y	1,000
Morgan Stanley Emerging Mkts Breakout Nations Port Cls I	EMIPX	NAS CM	Open End	Emerging Markets Equity (Div Emerging Mkts)	D	D+	A-		Y	5,000,000
Morgan Stanley Emerging Mkts Breakout Nations Port Cls IS	EMSPX	NAS CM	Open End	Emerging Markets Equity (Div Emerging Mkts)	D	D+	A-		Y	10,000,000
Morgan Stanley European Equity Fund Inc. Class A	EUGAX	NAS CM	Open End	Europe Equity Large Cap (Europe Stock)	C+	C+	B-	Up	Y	1,000
Morgan Stanley European Equity Fund Inc. Class B	EUGBX	NAS CM	Open End	Europe Equity Large Cap (Europe Stock)	C+	C+	B-	Up		1,000
Morgan Stanley European Equity Fund Inc. Class C	MSEEX	NAS CM	Open End	Europe Equity Large Cap (Europe Stock)	C+	C+	C+	Up	Y	1,000
Morgan Stanley European Equity Fund Inc. Class I	EUGDX	NAS CM	Open End	Europe Equity Large Cap (Europe Stock)	C+	C+	B-	Up	Y	5,000,000
Morgan Stanley European Equity Fund Inc. Class L	EUGCX	NAS CM	Open End	Europe Equity Large Cap (Europe Stock)	C+	C+	C+	Up		1,000
Morgan Stanley Inst Trust Global Strategist Cls A	MBAAX	NAS CM	Open End	Alloc (Growth & Income)	B-	C+	B-	Up	Y	1,000
Morgan Stanley Inst Trust Global Strategist Cls C	MSSOX	NAS CM	Open End	Alloc (Growth & Income)	C+	C+	B-	Down	Y	1,000
Morgan Stanley Inst Trust Global Strategist Cls Inst	MPBAX	NAS CM	Open End	Alloc (Growth & Income)	B-	C+	B	Up	Y	5,000,000
Morgan Stanley Inst Trust Global Strategist Cls IS	MGPOX	NAS CM	Open End	Alloc (Growth & Income)	C+	C+	B-	Down	Y	10,000,000
Morgan Stanley Inst Trust Global Strategist Cls L	MSDLX	NAS CM	Open End	Alloc (Growth & Income)	C+	C+	B-	Down		1,000
Morgan Stanley Inst Fund Trust Mid Cap Growth Port Cls A	MACGX	NAS CM	Open End	US Equity Mid Cap (Growth)	C+	C+	C+	Up		1,000
Morgan Stanley Inst Fund Trust Mid Cap Growth Port Cls C	MSMFX	NAS CM	Open End	US Equity Mid Cap (Growth)	C+	C+	C+		Y	1,000
Morgan Stanley Inst Fund Trust Mid Cap Growth Port Cls I	MPEGX	NAS CM	Open End	US Equity Mid Cap (Growth)	C+	C+	C+	Up		5,000,000
Morgan Stanley Inst Fund Trust Mid Cap Growth Port Cls IS	MMCGX	NAS CM	Open End	US Equity Mid Cap (Growth)	C+	C+	C+	Up		10,000,000
Morgan Stanley Inst Fund Trust Mid Cap Growth Port Cls L	MSKLX	NAS CM	Open End	US Equity Mid Cap (Growth)	C+	C+	C+	Up		1,000
Morgan Stanley Inst Fund, Inc. Active Intl Alloc Cls A	MSIBX	NAS CM	Open End	Global Equity Large Cap (Foreign Stock)	B-	C+	B-	Up	Y	1,000
Morgan Stanley Inst Fund, Inc. Active Intl Alloc Cls C	MSAAX	NAS CM	Open End	Global Equity Large Cap (Foreign Stock)	C+	C+	B-	Up	Y	1,000
Morgan Stanley Inst Fund, Inc. Active Intl Alloc Cls I	MSACX	NAS CM	Open End	Global Equity Large Cap (Foreign Stock)	B-	C+	B-	Up	Y	5,000,000
Morgan Stanley Inst Fund, Inc. Active Intl Alloc Cls L	MSLLX	NAS CM	Open End	Global Equity Large Cap (Foreign Stock)	B-	C+	B-	Up		1,000
Morgan Stanley Inst Fund, Inc. Advantage Portfolio Cls A	MAPPX	NAS CM	Open End	US Equity Large Cap Growth (Growth)	B+	B+	A-	Up	Y	1,000
Morgan Stanley Inst Fund, Inc. Advantage Portfolio Cls C	MSPRX	NAS CM	Open End	US Equity Large Cap Growth (Growth)	B+	B	A-	Up	Y	1,000
Morgan Stanley Inst Fund, Inc. Advantage Portfolio Cls I	MPAIX	NAS CM	Open End	US Equity Large Cap Growth (Growth)	B+	B+	A-	Up		5,000,000
Morgan Stanley Inst Fund, Inc. Advantage Portfolio Cls IS	MADSX	NAS CM	Open End	US Equity Large Cap Growth (Growth)	B+	B+	A-	Up	Y	10,000,000
Morgan Stanley Inst Fund, Inc. Advantage Portfolio Cls L	MAPLX	NAS CM	Open End	US Equity Large Cap Growth (Growth)	B+	B+	A-	Up		1,000
Morgan Stanley Inst Fund, Inc. Asia Opp Portfolio Cls A	MSAUX	NAS CM	Open End	Asia ex-Japan Equity (Growth)	C-	C	B	Up	Y	1,000
Morgan Stanley Inst Fund, Inc. Asia Opp Portfolio Cls C	MSAWX	NAS CM	Open End	Asia ex-Japan Equity (Growth)	C-	C	B	Up	Y	1,000
Morgan Stanley Inst Fund, Inc. Asia Opp Portfolio Cls I	MSAQX	NAS CM	Open End	Asia ex-Japan Equity (Growth)	C-	C	B	Up	Y	5,000,000
Morgan Stanley Inst Fund, Inc. Asia Opp Portfolio Cls IS	MSAYX	NAS CM	Open End	Asia ex-Japan Equity (Growth)	C-	C	B	Up	Y	10,000,000
Morgan Stanley Inst Fund, Inc. Emerg Mkts Leaders Cls A	MELAX	NAS CM	Open End	Emerging Markets Equity (Div Emerging Mkts)	C+	C+	C+	Up	Y	1,000
Morgan Stanley Inst Fund, Inc. Emerg Mkts Leaders Cls C	MEMLX	NAS CM	Open End	Emerging Markets Equity (Div Emerging Mkts)	C+	C+	C+	Up	Y	1,000
Morgan Stanley Inst Fund, Inc. Emerg Mkts Leaders Cls I	MELIX	NAS CM	Open End	Emerging Markets Equity (Div Emerging Mkts)	C+	C+	C+		Y	5,000,000
Morgan Stanley Inst Fund, Inc. Emerg Mkts Leaders Cls IS	MELSX	NAS CM	Open End	Emerging Markets Equity (Div Emerging Mkts)	C+	C+	C+		Y	10,000,000
Morgan Stanley Inst Fund, Inc. Emerging Mkts Port Cls A	MMKBX	NAS CM	Open End	Emerging Markets Equity (Div Emerging Mkts)	C+	B-	C	Up	Y	1,000
Morgan Stanley Inst Fund, Inc. Emerging Mkts Port Cls C	MSEPX	NAS CM	Open End	Emerging Markets Equity (Div Emerging Mkts)	C+	B-	C	Up	Y	1,000
Morgan Stanley Inst Fund, Inc. Emerging Mkts Port Cls I	MGEMX	NAS CM	Open End	Emerging Markets Equity (Div Emerging Mkts)	C+	B-	C	Up	Y	5,000,000
Morgan Stanley Inst Fund, Inc. Emerging Mkts Port Cls IS	MMMPX	NAS CM	Open End	Emerging Markets Equity (Div Emerging Mkts)	B-	B-	C	Up	Y	10,000,000
Morgan Stanley Inst Fund, Inc. Emerging Mkts Port Cls L	MSELX	NAS CM	Open End	Emerging Markets Equity (Div Emerging Mkts)	C+	B-	C	Up		1,000
Morgan Stanley Inst Fund, Inc. Emerg Mkts Small Cap Cls A	MSEOX	NAS CM	Open End	Emerging Markets Equity (Div Emerging Mkts)	C	C	B	Up	Y	1,000
Morgan Stanley Inst Fund, Inc. Emerg Mkts Small Cap Cls C	MSESX	NAS CM	Open End	Emerging Markets Equity (Div Emerging Mkts)	C	C	B	Up	Y	1,000
Morgan Stanley Inst Fund, Inc. Emerg Mkts Small Cap Cls I	MSEMX	NAS CM	Open End	Emerging Markets Equity (Div Emerging Mkts)	C	C	B	Up	Y	5,000,000
Morgan Stanley Inst Fund, Inc. Emerg Mkts Small Cap Cls IS	MSETX	NAS CM	Open End	Emerging Markets Equity (Div Emerging Mkts)	C	C	B	Up	Y	10,000,000
Morgan Stanley Inst Fund, Inc. Frontier Mkts Port Cls A	MFMPX	NAS CM	Open End	Emerging Markets Equity (Div Emerging Mkts)	C+	C+	C+	Up	Y	1,000
Morgan Stanley Inst Fund, Inc. Frontier Mkts Port Cls C	MSFEX	NAS CM	Open End	Emerging Markets Equity (Div Emerging Mkts)	C	C	C+		Y	1,000
Morgan Stanley Inst Fund, Inc. Frontier Mkts Port Cls I	MFMIX	NAS CM	Open End	Emerging Markets Equity (Div Emerging Mkts)	C+	C+	C+	Up	Y	5,000,000
Morgan Stanley Inst Fund, Inc. Frontier Mkts Port Cls IS	MSRFX	NAS CM	Open End	Emerging Markets Equity (Div Emerging Mkts)	C+	C+	C+	Up	Y	10,000,000
Morgan Stanley Inst Fund, Inc. Frontier Mkts Port Cls L	MFMLX	NAS CM	Open End	Emerging Markets Equity (Div Emerging Mkts)	C	C	C+			1,000
Morgan Stanley Inst Fund, Inc. Global Advantage Port Cls A	MIGPX	NAS CM	Open End	Global Equity (World Stock)	B+	B+	B	Up	Y	1,000

★Expanded analysis of this fund is included in Section II.

Min Additional Investment	TOTAL RETURNS 3-Month Total Return	6-Month Total Return	1-Year Total Return	3-Year Total Return	5-Year Total Return	PERFORMANCE Dividend Yield (TTM)	Expense Ratio	3-Yr Std Deviation	3-Year Beta	ASSETS NAV	Total Assets (MIL)	ASSET ALLOCATION & TURNOVER %Cash	%Stocks	%Bonds	%Other	Turnover Ratio	BULL & BEAR Last Bull Market Total Return	Last Bear Market Total Return	FEES Front End Fee (%)	Back End Fee (%)	Inception Date
	8.35	13.82	41.39	42.62	127.74	0.12	1.75	23.86	0.74	28.14	612.7	1	97	1	0	69	3.45	-15.03			Sep-06
	4.88	8.61	21.29				1.56			11.9	6.0	10	88	0	0	16			5.25		Dec-16
	4.74	8.17	20.37				2.31			11.81	6.0	10	88	0	0	16				1.00	Dec-16
	4.98	8.82	21.83				1.14			11.91	6.0	10	88	0	0	16					Dec-16
	5.01	8.85	21.87				1.11			11.91	6.0	10	88	0	0	16					Dec-16
100	2.51	5.37	22.70	11.63	30.18	1.94	1.4	12.52	0.94	18.83	119.4	0	99	1	0	23	16.03	-25.09	5.25		Jul-97
100	2.50	5.39	22.68	11.66	30.19	2.18	1.39	12.52	0.94	17.83	119.4	0	99	1	0	23	16.06	-25.1		5.00	Jun-90
100	2.27	4.96	21.76	9.13	25.32	1.05	2.15	12.47	0.94	17.96	119.4	0	99	1	0	23	15.55	-25.33		1.00	Apr-15
	2.58	5.54	23.11	12.80	32.39	2.28	1.05	12.52	0.94	19.57	119.4	0	99	1	0	23	16.15	-25			Jul-97
100	2.37	5.11	22.11	9.95	26.81	1.67	1.9	12.5	0.94	18.02	119.4	0	99	1	0	23	15.46	-25.33			Jul-97
	3.37	6.89	16.26	13.72	36.60	0.71	1.07	7.36	0.67	16.85	338.6	9	60	29	2	176	16.49	-9.43	5.25		Nov-96
	3.13	6.44	15.28	11.16	31.62	0	1.84	7.34	0.66	16.7	338.6	9	60	29	2	176	16.08	-9.79		1.00	Apr-15
	3.45	7.13	16.67	14.88	38.76	0.99	0.74	7.41	0.67	16.97	338.6	9	60	29	2	176	16.75	-9.42			Dec-92
	3.42	7.10	16.63	14.95	38.85	1.02	0.71	7.4	0.67	16.97	338.6	9	60	29	2	176	16.75	-9.42			May-15
	3.18	6.60	15.59	11.92	33.11	0.17	1.59	7.4	0.67	16.74	338.6	9	60	29	2	176	16.24	-9.7			Apr-12
	6.68	9.20	38.90	11.97	59.47	0	1	14.41	0.99	14.27	613.8	3	97	0	0	59	17.97	-21.22	5.25		Jan-97
	6.43	8.68	37.75	9.47	53.58		1.86	14.41	0.99	14.15	613.8	3	97	0	0	59	17.44	-21.46		1.00	May-17
	6.79	9.39	39.34	12.97	61.67	0	0.74	14.42	0.99	16.83	613.8	3	97	0	0	59	18.13	-21.13			Mar-90
	6.79	9.38	39.35	13.26	62.37	0	0.62	14.39	0.99	16.97	613.8	3	97	0	0	59	18.13	-21.13			Sep-13
	6.53	8.84	37.95	9.93	54.92	0	1.61	14.41	0.99	13.04	613.8	3	97	0	0	59	17.61	-21.38			Jun-12
	3.19	9.21	24.29	19.84	37.35	1.76	1.25	11.68	0.92	14.79	226.4	1	86	12	1	40	10.91	-23.61	5.25		Jan-96
	3.02	8.81	23.42	17.03	32.35	0.15	2	11.66	0.92	14.77	226.4	1	86	12	1	40	10.43	-23.89		1.00	Apr-15
	3.33	9.49	24.76	21.13	39.74	2.12	0.9	11.66	0.92	14.46	226.4	1	86	12	1	40	11.07	-23.57			Jan-92
	3.12	9.03	23.79	17.91	33.79	1.25	1.75	11.64	0.91	14.73	226.4	1	86	12	1	40	10.59	-23.81			Jun-12
	9.32	13.32	31.63	50.00	125.59	0	1.2	11.63	0.99	21.1	111.5	0	95	5	0	79	25.37	-10.66	5.25		May-10
	9.13	12.93	30.76	46.66	117.70	0	1.95	11.65	1	20.82	111.5	0	95	5	0	79	24.79	-11.01		1.00	Apr-15
	9.38	13.48	32.06	51.48	129.38	0.2	0.85	11.62	0.99	21.45	111.5	0	95	5	0	79	25.52	-10.63			Jun-08
	9.47	13.57	32.21	51.74	129.75	0.22	0.81	11.65	1	21.49	111.5	0	95	5	0	79	25.52	-10.63			Sep-13
	9.34	13.44	31.96	51.10	128.23	0.12	0.92	11.62	0.99	21.42	111.5	0	95	5	0	79	25.54	-10.63			Jun-08
	11.49	29.55	76.17			1.14	1.45			16.84	17.8	0	92	8	0	44			5.25		Dec-15
	11.28	29.10	74.85			0.59	2.2			16.73	17.8	0	92	8	0	44				1.00	Dec-15
	11.57	29.86	76.81			1.28	1.09			16.92	17.8	0	92	8	0	44					Dec-15
	11.57	29.86	76.81			1.31	1.05			16.92	17.8	0	92	8	0	44					Dec-15
	3.95	6.79	25.45	14.15	23.89	0	1.58			12.06	88.1	4	95	0	0	45	22.66		5.25		Jan-15
	3.75	6.34	24.52	11.52	19.26	0	2.33			11.9	88.1	4	95	0	0	45	22.12			1.00	Apr-15
	4.07	6.98	26.00	15.62	26.11	0.03	1.15			12.14	88.1	4	95	0	0	45	22.83				Jan-15
	4.09	6.99	26.02	15.66	26.15	0.03	1.13			12.14	88.1	4	95	0	0	45	22.83				Jan-15
	5.23	12.44	34.53	27.54	21.60	0.46	1.36	13.84	0.85	27.23	1,354	2	92	0	4	33	16.01	-22.83	5.25		Jan-96
	5.04	11.99	33.45	24.57	17.17	0.15	2.15	13.84	0.85	26.65	1,354	2	92	0	4	33	15.52	-23.07		1.00	Apr-15
	5.31	12.59	34.97	28.76	23.54	0.71	1.03	13.87	0.85	27.94	1,354	2	92	0	4	33	16.19	-22.75			Sep-92
	5.32	12.64	35.09	29.07	23.96	0.75	0.95	13.86	0.85	27.94	1,354	2	92	0	4	33	16.19	-22.75			Sep-13
	5.08	12.13	33.79	25.47	18.42	0.09	1.9	13.86	0.85	26.84	1,354	2	92	0	4	33	15.69	-22.99			Apr-12
	8.72	13.99	33.78			0.48	2.06			12.72	25.5	1	96	0	2	69			5.25		Dec-15
	8.45	13.54	32.70			0	2.81			12.6	25.5	1	96	0	2	69				1.00	Dec-15
	8.78	14.13	34.29			0.79	1.67			12.77	25.5	1	96	0	2	69					Dec-15
	8.78	14.23	34.29			0.8	1.66			12.77	25.5	1	96	0	2	69					Dec-15
	2.65	5.33	18.54	8.74	49.28	0.88	2.03	10.18	0.84	20.52	706.7	3	93	0	4	30	8.94	-21.62	5.25		Sep-12
	2.49	4.96	17.69	6.24	43.81	0.29	2.89	10.16	0.84	20.09	706.7	3	93	0	4	30	8.47	-21.86		1.00	Apr-15
	2.78	5.50	18.97	9.88	51.72	1.15	1.69	10.17	0.84	20.69	706.7	3	93	0	4	30	9.1	-21.54			Aug-08
	2.78	5.51	18.98	9.94	51.81	1.2	1.64	10.18	0.84	20.68	706.7	3	93	0	4	30	9.1	-21.54			Feb-15
	2.57	5.01	17.79	6.58	44.74	0.07	2.7	10.16	0.84	20.32	706.7	3	93	0	4	30	8.63	-21.78			Sep-12
	8.70	14.98	41.02	44.40	91.65	0	1.45	12.35	1.02	15.21	11.9	3	95	0	1	90	27.91	-15.84	5.25		Dec-10

Fund Name	MARKET: Ticker Symbol	MARKET: Traded On	FUND TYPE, CATEGORY & OBJECTIVE: Fund Type	Category and (Prospectus Objective)	RATINGS: Overall Rating	Reward Rating	Risk Rating	Recent Up/ Downgrade	MINIMUMS: Open to New Investors	Min Initial Investment
Morgan Stanley Inst Fund, Inc. Global Advantage Port Cls C	MSPTX	NAS CM	Open End	Global Equity (World Stock)	B	B	B	Up	Y	1,000
Morgan Stanley Inst Fund, Inc. Global Advantage Port Cls I	MIGIX	NAS CM	Open End	Global Equity (World Stock)	B+	B+	B+	Up	Y	5,000,000
Morgan Stanley Inst Fund, Inc. Global Advantage Port Cls L	MIGLX	NAS CM	Open End	Global Equity (World Stock)	B	B+	B	Up		1,000
Morgan Stanley Inst Fund, Inc. Global Conc Port Cls A	MLNAX	NAS CM	Open End	Global Equity (Growth)	D+	C	B	Up	Y	1,000
Morgan Stanley Inst Fund, Inc. Global Conc Port Cls C	MLNCX	NAS CM	Open End	Global Equity (Growth)	D+	C	B	Up	Y	1,000
Morgan Stanley Inst Fund, Inc. Global Conc Port Cls I	MLNIX	NAS CM	Open End	Global Equity (Growth)	D+	C	B	Up	Y	5,000,000
Morgan Stanley Inst Fund, Inc. Global Conc Port Cls IS	MLNSX	NAS CM	Open End	Global Equity (Growth)	D+	C	B	Up	Y	10,000,000
Morgan Stanley Inst Fund, Inc. Global Core Portfolio Cls A	MLMAX	NAS CM	Open End	US Equity Large Cap Blend (Growth)	D+	C	B	Up	Y	1,000
Morgan Stanley Inst Fund, Inc. Global Core Portfolio Cls C	MLMCX	NAS CM	Open End	US Equity Large Cap Blend (Growth)	D+	C	B	Up	Y	1,000
Morgan Stanley Inst Fund, Inc. Global Core Portfolio Cls I	MLMIX	NAS CM	Open End	US Equity Large Cap Blend (Growth)	D+	C	B	Up	Y	5,000,000
Morgan Stanley Inst Fund, Inc. Global Core Port Cls IS	MLMSX	NAS CM	Open End	US Equity Large Cap Blend (Growth)	D+	C	B	Up	Y	10,000,000
Morgan Stanley Inst Fund, Inc. Global Discovery Port Cls A	MGDPX	NAS CM	Open End	Global Equity Mid/Small Cap (World Stock)	B	B+	C+	Down	Y	1,000
Morgan Stanley Inst Fund, Inc. Global Discovery Port Cls C	MSPCX	NAS CM	Open End	Global Equity Mid/Small Cap (World Stock)	B	B+	C+	Down	Y	1,000
Morgan Stanley Inst Fund, Inc. Global Discovery Port Cls I	MLDIX	NAS CM	Open End	Global Equity Mid/Small Cap (World Stock)	B	B+	C+	Down	Y	5,000,000
Morgan Stanley Inst Fund, Inc. Global Discovery Port Cls L	MGDLX	NAS CM	Open End	Global Equity Mid/Small Cap (World Stock)	B	B+	C+	Down		1,000
Morgan Stanley Inst Fund, Inc. Global Franchise Port Cls A	MSFBX	NAS CM	Open End	Global Equity (World Stock)	B	B	A	Down		1,000
Morgan Stanley Inst Fund, Inc. Global Franchise Port Cls C	MSGFX	NAS CM	Open End	Global Equity (World Stock)	B	B-	A		Y	1,000
Morgan Stanley Inst Fund, Inc. Global Franchise Port Cls I	MSFAX	NAS CM	Open End	Global Equity (World Stock)	B+	B	A	Up		5,000,000
Morgan Stanley Inst Fund, Inc. Global Franch Port Cls IS	MGISX	NAS CM	Open End	Global Equity (World Stock)	B+	B	A	Up	Y	10,000,000
Morgan Stanley Inst Fund, Inc. Global Franchise Port Cls L	MSFLX	NAS CM	Open End	Global Equity (World Stock)	B	B-	A			1,000
Morgan Stanley Inst Fund, Inc. Global Infrastr Port Cls A	MTIPX	NAS CM	Open End	Other Sector Equity (World Stock)	C+	C+	C+		Y	1,000
Morgan Stanley Inst Fund, Inc. Global Infrastr Port Cls C	MSGTX	NAS CM	Open End	Other Sector Equity (World Stock)	C	C	C+	Down	Y	1,000
Morgan Stanley Inst Fund, Inc. Global Infrastr Port Cls I	MTIIX	NAS CM	Open End	Other Sector Equity (World Stock)	C+	C+	C+		Y	5,000,000
Morgan Stanley Inst Fund, Inc. Global Infrastr Port Cls IS	MSGPX	NAS CM	Open End	Other Sector Equity (World Stock)	C+	C+	C+		Y	10,000,000
Morgan Stanley Inst Fund, Inc. Global Infrastr Port Cls L	MTILX	NAS CM	Open End	Other Sector Equity (World Stock)	C	C	C+	Down		1,000
Morgan Stanley Inst Fund, Inc. Global Insight Port Cls A	MBPHX	NAS CM	Open End	Global Equity Mid/Small Cap (World Stock)	B	B+	C+	Down	Y	1,000
Morgan Stanley Inst Fund, Inc. Global Insight Port Cls C	MSIZX	NAS CM	Open End	Global Equity Mid/Small Cap (World Stock)	B	B+	C+	Down	Y	1,000
Morgan Stanley Inst Fund, Inc. Global Insight Port Cls I	MBPIX	NAS CM	Open End	Global Equity Mid/Small Cap (World Stock)	B	B+	C+	Down	Y	5,000,000
Morgan Stanley Inst Fund, Inc. Global Insight Port Cls L	MBPLX	NAS CM	Open End	Global Equity Mid/Small Cap (World Stock)	B	B+	C+	Down		1,000
Morgan Stanley Inst Fund, Inc. Global Opp Portfolio Cls A	MGGPX	NAS CM	Open End	Global Equity (World Stock)	A	A+	A-	Up	Y	1,000
Morgan Stanley Inst Fund, Inc. Global Opp Portfolio Cls C	MSOPX	NAS CM	Open End	Global Equity (World Stock)	A	A	B+	Up	Y	1,000
Morgan Stanley Inst Fund, Inc. Global Opp Portfolio Cls I	MGGIX	NAS CM	Open End	Global Equity (World Stock)	A	A+	A-	Up	Y	5,000,000
Morgan Stanley Inst Fund, Inc. Global Opp Portfolio Cls IS	MGTSX	NAS CM	Open End	Global Equity (World Stock)	A	A+	A-	Up	Y	10,000,000
Morgan Stanley Inst Fund, Inc. Global Opp Portfolio Cls L	MGGLX	NAS CM	Open End	Global Equity (World Stock)	A	A+	B+	Up		1,000
Morgan Stanley Inst Fund, Inc. Global Quality Port Cls A	MGQAX	NAS CM	Open End	Global Equity (World Stock)	B	B-	A		Y	1,000
Morgan Stanley Inst Fund, Inc. Global Quality Port Cls C	MSGQX	NAS CM	Open End	Global Equity (World Stock)	B	B-	A		Y	1,000
Morgan Stanley Inst Fund, Inc. Global Quality Port Cls I	MGQIX	NAS CM	Open End	Global Equity (World Stock)	B	B-	A		Y	5,000,000
Morgan Stanley Inst Fund, Inc. Global Quality Port Cls IS	MGQSX	NAS CM	Open End	Global Equity (World Stock)	B	B-	A		Y	10,000,000
Morgan Stanley Inst Fund, Inc. Global Quality Port Cls L	MGQLX	NAS CM	Open End	Global Equity (World Stock)	B	B-	A			1,000
Morgan Stanley Inst Fund, Inc. Global Real Est Cls A	MRLBX	NAS CM	Open End	Real Estate Sector Equity (Real Estate)	B-	C	B	Up	Y	1,000
Morgan Stanley Inst Fund, Inc. Global Real Est Cls C	MSRDX	NAS CM	Open End	Real Estate Sector Equity (Real Estate)	C+	C	B	Up	Y	1,000
Morgan Stanley Inst Fund, Inc. Global Real Est Cls I	MRLAX	NAS CM	Open End	Real Estate Sector Equity (Real Estate)	B-	C	B	Up	Y	5,000,000
Morgan Stanley Inst Fund, Inc. Global Real Est Cls IS	MGREX	NAS CM	Open End	Real Estate Sector Equity (Real Estate)	B-	C	B	Up	Y	10,000,000
Morgan Stanley Inst Fund, Inc. Global Real Est Cls L	MGRLX	NAS CM	Open End	Real Estate Sector Equity (Real Estate)	C+	C	B			1,000
Morgan Stanley Inst Fund, Inc. Growth Portfolio Cls A	MSEGX	NAS CM	Open End	US Equity Large Cap Growth (Growth)	B+	A-	B+	Up	Y	1,000
Morgan Stanley Inst Fund, Inc. Growth Portfolio Cls C	MSGUX	NAS CM	Open End	US Equity Large Cap Growth (Growth)	B+	A-	B+	Up	Y	1,000
Morgan Stanley Inst Fund, Inc. Growth Portfolio Cls I	MSEQX	NAS CM	Open End	US Equity Large Cap Growth (Growth)	A-	A-	B+	Up	Y	5,000,000
Morgan Stanley Inst Fund, Inc. Growth Portfolio Cls IS	MGRPX	NAS CM	Open End	US Equity Large Cap Growth (Growth)	A-	A-	B+	Up	Y	10,000,000
Morgan Stanley Inst Fund, Inc. Growth Portfolio Cls L	MSHLX	NAS CM	Open End	US Equity Large Cap Growth (Growth)	B+	A-	B+	Up		1,000
Morgan Stanley Inst Fund, Inc. Insight Portfolio Cls A	MFPHX	NAS CM	Open End	US Equity Mid Cap (Growth)	B	B	C+		Y	1,000
Morgan Stanley Inst Fund, Inc. Insight Portfolio Cls C	MSSPX	NAS CM	Open End	US Equity Mid Cap (Growth)	B	B	C+		Y	1,000
Morgan Stanley Inst Fund, Inc. Insight Portfolio Cls I	MFPIX	NAS CM	Open End	US Equity Mid Cap (Growth)	B	B	C+		Y	5,000,000

★ Expanded analysis of this fund is included in Section II.

Min Additional Investment	TOTAL RETURNS 3-Month Total Return	6-Month Total Return	1-Year Total Return	3-Year Total Return	5-Year Total Return	PERFORMANCE Dividend Yield (TTM)	Expense Ratio	3-Yr Std Deviation	3-Year Beta	ASSETS NAV	Total Assets (MIL)	ASSET ALLOCATION & TURNOVER %Cash	%Stocks	%Bonds	%Other	Turnover Ratio	BULL & BEAR Last Bull Market Total Return	Last Bear Market Total Return	FEES Front End Fee (%)	Back End Fee (%)	Inception Date
	8.48	14.49	40.02	41.27	84.96	0	2.2	12.37	1.02	14.6	11.9	3	95	0	1	90	27.44	-16.09		1.00	Apr-15
	8.79	15.14	41.55	46.06	95.09	0	1.1	12.38	1.02	15.43	11.9	3	95	0	1	90	28.19	-15.74			Dec-10
	8.53	14.57	40.33	42.23	86.96	0	1.95	12.35	1.02	14.75	11.9	3	95	0	1	90	27.47	-15.97			Dec-10
	2.48	9.93	22.17			0.64	1.35			12.37	14.1	0	98	2	0				5.25		May-16
	2.33	9.53	21.18			0.38	2.1			12.27	14.1	0	98	2	0					1.00	May-16
	2.63	10.16	22.63			0.74	0.97			12.42	14.1	0	98	2	0						May-16
	2.57	10.09	22.66			0.75	0.95			12.42	14.1	0	98	2	0						May-16
	5.39	10.06	21.81			0.61	1.35			12.18	13.3	0	98	2	0	22			5.25		May-16
	5.13	9.72	20.92			0.43	2.1			12.08	13.3	0	98	2	0	22				1.00	May-16
	5.43	10.28	22.26			0.73	0.99			12.2	13.3	0	98	2	0	22					May-16
	5.45	10.30	22.29			0.74	0.95			12.2	13.3	0	98	2	0	22					May-16
	2.85	8.84	24.88	61.49	125.61	0.11	1.7	11.89	0.9	15.8	113.9	0	92	8	0	64	29.22	-27.72	5.25		Dec-10
	2.63	8.39	23.89	57.78	117.51	0.1	2.45	11.88	0.89	15.41	113.9	0	92	8	0	64	28.53	-27.91		1.00	Apr-15
	2.94	9.04	25.39	63.26	129.58	0.23	1.35	11.91	0.89	15.87	113.9	0	92	8	0	64	29.28	-27.61			Dec-10
	2.72	8.56	24.26	59.11	120.00	0.09	2.2	11.93	0.9	15.62	113.9	0	92	8	0	64	28.83	-27.86			Dec-10
	7.86	7.96	25.58	39.67	76.55	0.88	1.23	11.38	0.85	24.21	1,034	2	98	0	0	30	17.79	-6.53	5.25		Nov-01
	7.62	7.53	24.62	36.51	70.14	0.53	2	11.38	0.85	23.82	1,034	2	98	0	0	30	17.37	-6.83		1.00	Sep-15
	7.89	8.08	25.84	40.68	78.85	1.05	0.98	11.4	0.85	24.72	1,034	2	98	0	0	30	18.05	-6.44			Nov-01
	7.92	8.15	25.99	40.93	79.17	1.09	0.94	11.38	0.85	24.72	1,034	2	98	0	0	30	18.05	-6.44			May-15
	7.69	7.69	24.97	37.67	72.26	0.38	1.72	11.39	0.86	24.18	1,034	2	98	0	0	30	17.54	-6.73			Apr-12
	0.97	3.35	12.37	10.52	52.10	2.09	1.21	11.11	1.01	14.6	402.4	6	91	0	3	48	18.14	-6.79	5.25		Sep-10
	0.76	2.92	11.41	7.76	46.34	1.87	2.07	11.11	1.01	14.36	402.4	6	91	0	3	48	17.62	-7.09		1.00	Apr-15
	1.09	3.54	12.69	11.32	54.21	2.31	0.96	11.11	1.01	14.64	402.4	6	91	0	3	48	18.3	-6.7			Sep-10
	1.05	3.50	12.65	11.30	54.18	2.33	0.94	11.1	1.01	14.63	402.4	6	91	0	3	48	18.3	-6.7			Sep-13
	0.87	3.13	11.79	8.55	47.86	1.57	1.78	11.12	1.01	14.55	402.4	6	91	0	3	48	17.81	-6.98			Sep-10
	3.67	8.92	26.98	54.56	98.92	0.03	1.7	12.98	1.08	14.78	13.6	0	94	6	0	54			5.25		Dec-11
	3.57	8.60	26.08	51.31	92.07	0.03	2.45	12.96	1.08	14.46	13.6	0	94	6	0	54				1.00	Apr-15
	3.76	9.17	27.38	56.12	102.16	0.22	1.35	12.96	1.08	14.77	13.6	0	94	6	0	54					Dec-11
	3.61	8.67	26.34	52.00	93.83	0.03	2.2	12.97	1.08	14.56	13.6	0	94	6	0	54					Dec-11
	6.56	17.79	49.02	76.04	173.72	0	1.18	12.77	0.99	22.28	1,720	8	91	0	0	37	20.92	-21.44	5.25		May-10
	6.35	17.39	47.91	72.51	164.76	0	1.85	12.78	1	21.64	1,720	8	91	0	0	37	20.44	-21.76		1.00	Apr-15
	6.61	17.97	49.44	77.92	178.54	0	0.81	12.75	0.99	22.94	1,720	8	91	0	0	37	21.14	-21.43			May-08
	6.64	18.04	49.54	78.24	179.22	0	0.72	12.79	1	23	1,720	8	91	0	0	37	21.14	-21.43			Sep-13
	6.55	17.73	48.91	75.72	172.83	0	1.26	12.77	1	22.01	1,720	8	91	0	0	37	21.05	-21.54			May-08
	5.77	6.29	22.44	32.55		1.12	1.33	10.69	0.86	12.44	10.6	2	98	0	0	35			5.25		Aug-13
	5.52	5.88	21.45	29.40		0.62	2.1	10.63	0.85	12.26	10.6	2	98	0	0	35				1.00	Apr-15
	5.81	6.41	22.85	33.81		1.43	0.99	10.68	0.86	12.47	10.6	2	98	0	0	35					Aug-13
	5.86	6.46	22.91	33.98		1.48	0.95	10.69	0.86	12.47	10.6	2	98	0	0	35					Sep-13
	5.59	6.02	21.79	30.54		0.69	1.81	10.6	0.85	12.41	10.6	2	98	0	0	35					Aug-13
	4.65	5.97	9.43	10.14	32.16	3.13	1.36	11.04	0.99	11.1	1,545	0	98	1	2	26	25.33	-21.94	5.25		Aug-06
	4.36	5.42	8.53	7.52	27.25	2.77	2.15	10.97	0.98	10.83	1,545	0	98	1	2	26	24.71	-22.14		1.00	Apr-15
	4.67	5.99	9.73	11.02	34.03	3.48	1.04	10.99	0.98	11.13	1,545	0	98	1	2	26	25.43	-21.82			Aug-06
	4.64	6.05	9.80	11.32	34.52	3.6	0.97	10.99	0.98	11.13	1,545	0	98	1	2	26	25.43	-21.82			Sep-13
	4.47	5.61	8.89	8.57	29.10	2.18	1.82	10.98	0.98	11.01	1,545	0	98	1	2	26	24.89	-22.05			Jun-08
	7.32	12.48	43.44	55.27	151.22	0	0.92	14.79	1.15	39.77	4,194	0	93	3	1	39	22.19	-16	5.25		Jan-96
	7.13	12.07	42.37	51.87	141.91	0	1.7	14.77	1.15	37.76	4,194	0	93	3	1	39	21.71	-16.26		1.00	Apr-15
	7.40	12.64	43.82	56.67	154.57	0	0.63	14.78	1.15	41.65	4,194	0	93	3	1	39	22.42	-15.91			Apr-91
	7.43	12.71	43.98	57.05	155.66	0	0.54	14.79	1.15	41.89	4,194	0	93	3	1	39	22.42	-15.91			Sep-13
	7.19	12.20	42.69	52.68	144.46	0	1.45	14.78	1.15	37.99	4,194	0	93	3	1	39	21.88	-16.17			Apr-12
	5.56	9.24	17.81	44.09	118.66	0	1.4	11.19	0.93	16.45	100.9	0	84	16	0	42			5.25		Dec-11
	5.35	8.85	16.92	41.02	111.13	0	2.15	11.15	0.92	15.89	100.9	0	84	16	0	42				1.00	Apr-15
	5.67	9.48	18.27	45.60	122.38	0.03	1.05	11.14	0.92	16.54	100.9	0	84	16	0	42					Dec-11

Fund Name	MARKET Ticker Symbol	MARKET Traded On	FUND TYPE, CATEGORY & OBJECTIVE Fund Type	FUND TYPE, CATEGORY & OBJECTIVE Category and (Prospectus Objective)	RATINGS Overall Rating	RATINGS Reward Rating	RATINGS Risk Rating	RATINGS Recent Up/ Downgrade	MINIMUMS Open to New Investors	MINIMUMS Min Initial Investment
Morgan Stanley Inst Fund, Inc. Insight Portfolio Cls L	MFPLX	NAS CM	Open End	US Equity Mid Cap (Growth)	B	B	C+			1,000
Morgan Stanley Inst Fund, Inc. Intl Advantage Port Cls A	MFAPX	NAS CM	Open End	Global Equity Large Cap (Foreign Stock)	A-	A-	A-	Up	Y	1,000
Morgan Stanley Inst Fund, Inc. Intl Advantage Port Cls C	MSIAX	NAS CM	Open End	Global Equity Large Cap (Foreign Stock)	A-	A-	A-	Up	Y	1,000
Morgan Stanley Inst Fund, Inc. Intl Advantage Port Cls I	MFAIX	NAS CM	Open End	Global Equity Large Cap (Foreign Stock)	A-	A-	A-	Up	Y	5,000,000
Morgan Stanley Inst Fund, Inc. Intl Advantage Port Cls L	MSALX	NAS CM	Open End	Global Equity Large Cap (Foreign Stock)	A-	A-	A-	Up		1,000
Morgan Stanley Inst Fund, Inc. Intl Equity Portfolio Cls A	MIQBX	NAS CM	Open End	Global Equity Large Cap (Foreign Stock)	B-	C+	B	Up	Y	1,000
Morgan Stanley Inst Fund, Inc. Intl Equity Portfolio Cls C	MSECX	NAS CM	Open End	Global Equity Large Cap (Foreign Stock)	B-	C+	B	Up	Y	1,000
Morgan Stanley Inst Fund, Inc. Intl Equity Portfolio Cls I	MSIQX	NAS CM	Open End	Global Equity Large Cap (Foreign Stock)	B-	C+	B	Up	Y	5,000,000
Morgan Stanley Inst Fund, Inc. Intl Eq Port Cls IS	MIQPX	NAS CM	Open End	Global Equity Large Cap (Foreign Stock)	B-	C+	B	Up	Y	10,000,000
Morgan Stanley Inst Fund, Inc. Intl Equity Portfolio Cls L	MSQLX	NAS CM	Open End	Global Equity Large Cap (Foreign Stock)	B-	C+	B	Up		1,000
Morgan Stanley Inst Fund, Inc. Intl Opp Portfolio Cls A	MIOPX	NAS CM	Open End	Global Equity Large Cap (Foreign Stock)	A-	A	B+	Up	Y	1,000
Morgan Stanley Inst Fund, Inc. Intl Opp Portfolio Cls C	MSOCX	NAS CM	Open End	Global Equity Large Cap (Foreign Stock)	A-	A	B+	Up	Y	1,000
Morgan Stanley Inst Fund, Inc. Intl Opp Portfolio Cls I	MIOIX	NAS CM	Open End	Global Equity Large Cap (Foreign Stock)	A	A+	B+	Up	Y	5,000,000
Morgan Stanley Inst Fund, Inc. Intl Opp Portfolio Cls IS	MNOPX	NAS CM	Open End	Global Equity Large Cap (Foreign Stock)	A	A+	B+	Up	Y	10,000,000
Morgan Stanley Inst Fund, Inc. Intl Opp Portfolio Cls L	MIOLX	NAS CM	Open End	Global Equity Large Cap (Foreign Stock)	A-	A	B+	Up		1,000
Morgan Stanley Inst Fund, Inc. Intl Real Estate Port Cls A	IERBX	NAS CM	Open End	Real Estate Sector Equity (Real Estate)	C+	C	B	Up	Y	1,000
Morgan Stanley Inst Fund, Inc. Intl Real Estate Port Cls C	MSIJX	NAS CM	Open End	Real Estate Sector Equity (Real Estate)	C+	C	B	Up	Y	1,000
Morgan Stanley Inst Fund, Inc. Intl Real Estate Port Cls I	MSUAX	NAS CM	Open End	Real Estate Sector Equity (Real Estate)	C+	C	B	Up	Y	5,000,000
Morgan Stanley Inst Fund, Inc. Intl Real Est Cls IS	MIREX	NAS CM	Open End	Real Estate Sector Equity (Real Estate)	C+	C	B	Up	Y	10,000,000
Morgan Stanley Inst Fund, Inc. Intl Real Estate Port Cls L	MSOLX	NAS CM	Open End	Real Estate Sector Equity (Real Estate)	C+	C	B	Up		1,000
Morgan Stanley Inst Fund, Inc. Multi-Asset Portfolio Cls A	MMPPX	NAS CM	Open End	Multialternative (Multi-Asset Global)	D+	D+	C-	Up	Y	1,000
Morgan Stanley Inst Fund, Inc. Multi-Asset Portfolio Cls C	MSMEX	NAS CM	Open End	Multialternative (Multi-Asset Global)	D+	D+	D+	Up	Y	1,000
Morgan Stanley Inst Fund, Inc. Multi-Asset Portfolio Cls I	MMPIX	NAS CM	Open End	Multialternative (Multi-Asset Global)	D+	D+	C-		Y	5,000,000
Morgan Stanley Inst Fund, Inc. Multi-Asset Port Cls IS	MSPMX	NAS CM	Open End	Multialternative (Multi-Asset Global)	D+	D+	C-	Up	Y	10,000,000
Morgan Stanley Inst Fund, Inc. Multi-Asset Portfolio Cls L	MMPLX	NAS CM	Open End	Multialternative (Multi-Asset Global)	D+	D+	D+	Up		1,000
Morgan Stanley Inst Fund, Inc. Small Company Growth Cls A	MSSMX	NAS CM	Open End	US Equity Small Cap (Small Company)	C+	C+	C+	Up		1,000
Morgan Stanley Inst Fund, Inc. Small Company Growth Cls C	MSCOX	NAS CM	Open End	US Equity Small Cap (Small Company)	C+	C	C+	Up	Y	1,000
Morgan Stanley Inst Fund, Inc. Small Company Growth Cls I	MSSGX	NAS CM	Open End	US Equity Small Cap (Small Company)	C+	C+	C+	Up	Y	5,000,000
Morgan Stanley Inst Fund, Inc. Small Company Growth Cls IS	MFLLX	NAS CM	Open End	US Equity Small Cap (Small Company)	C+	C+	C+	Up	Y	10,000,000
Morgan Stanley Inst Fund, Inc. Small Company Growth Cls L	MSSLX	NAS CM	Open End	US Equity Small Cap (Small Company)	C+	C+	C+	Up		1,000
Morgan Stanley Inst Fund, Inc. U.S. Real Estate Port Cls A	MUSDX	NAS CM	Open End	Real Estate Sector Equity (Real Estate)	B-	C	B	Up	Y	1,000
Morgan Stanley Inst Fund, Inc. U.S. Real Estate Port Cls C	MSURX	NAS CM	Open End	Real Estate Sector Equity (Real Estate)	C+	C	B		Y	1,000
Morgan Stanley Inst Fund, Inc. U.S. Real Estate Port Cls I	MSUSX	NAS CM	Open End	Real Estate Sector Equity (Real Estate)	B-	C+	B	Up	Y	5,000,000
Morgan Stanley Inst Fund, Inc. U.S. Real Est Cls IS	MURSX	NAS CM	Open End	Real Estate Sector Equity (Real Estate)	B-	C+	B	Up	Y	10,000,000
Morgan Stanley Inst Fund, Inc. U.S. Real Estate Port Cls L	MSULX	NAS CM	Open End	Real Estate Sector Equity (Real Estate)	C+	C	B			1,000
Morgan Stanley Inst Fund, Inc. US Core Portfolio Cls A	MUOAX	NAS CM	Open End	US Equity Large Cap Blend (Growth)	D+	C-	B+	Up	Y	1,000
Morgan Stanley Inst Fund, Inc. US Core Portfolio Cls C	MUOCX	NAS CM	Open End	US Equity Large Cap Blend (Growth)	D+	C-	B+	Up	Y	1,000
Morgan Stanley Inst Fund, Inc. US Core Portfolio Cls I	MUOIX	NAS CM	Open End	US Equity Large Cap Blend (Growth)	D+	C	B+	Up	Y	5,000,000
Morgan Stanley Inst Fund, Inc. US Core Portfolio Cls IS	MUOSX	NAS CM	Open End	US Equity Large Cap Blend (Growth)	D+	C	B+	Up	Y	10,000,000
Morgan Stanley Inst Global Multi-Asset Income Port Cls A	MSGOX	NAS CM	Open End	Alloc (Growth & Income)	C+	C	B	Up	Y	1,000
Morgan Stanley Inst Global Multi-Asset Income Port Cls C	MSGYX	NAS CM	Open End	Alloc (Growth & Income)	C+	C	B	Up	Y	1,000
Morgan Stanley Inst Global Multi-Asset Income Port Cls I	MSGMX	NAS CM	Open End	Alloc (Growth & Income)	C+	C	B	Up	Y	5,000,000
Morgan Stanley Inst Global Multi-Asset Income Port Cls IS	MSMUX	NAS CM	Open End	Alloc (Growth & Income)	C+	C	B	Up	Y	10,000,000
Morgan Stanley Multi Cap Growth Trust Class A	CPOAX	NAS CM	Open End	US Equity Large Cap Growth (Growth)	A-	A	B	Up	Y	1,000
Morgan Stanley Multi Cap Growth Trust Class B	CPOBX	NAS CM	Open End	US Equity Large Cap Growth (Growth)	A-	A	B	Up		1,000
Morgan Stanley Multi Cap Growth Trust Class C	MSCMX	NAS CM	Open End	US Equity Large Cap Growth (Growth)	A-	A	B	Up	Y	1,000
Morgan Stanley Multi Cap Growth Trust Class I	CPODX	NAS CM	Open End	US Equity Large Cap Growth (Growth)	A-	A	B	Up	Y	5,000,000
Morgan Stanley Multi Cap Growth Trust Class IS	MCRTX	NAS CM	Open End	US Equity Large Cap Growth (Growth)	A-	A	B	Up	Y	10,000,000
Morgan Stanley Multi Cap Growth Trust Class L	CPOCX	NAS CM	Open End	US Equity Large Cap Growth (Growth)	A-	A	B	Up		1,000
Morningstar Aggressive Growth ETF Asset Alloc Port Cls I	US00162T8606		Open End	Aggressive Alloc (Aggr Growth)	B-	B-	B-	Down	Y	0
Morningstar Balanced ETF Asset Allocation Portfolio Cls I	US00162T7046		Open End	Moderate Alloc (Balanced)	B-	C+	B	Up	Y	0
Morningstar Conservative ETF Asset Alloc Port Cls I	US00162T3086		Open End	Cautious Alloc (Income)	B	C	A-	Up	Y	0

★ Expanded analysis of this fund is included in Section II.

	TOTAL RETURNS					PERFORMANCE				ASSETS		ASSET ALLOCATION & TURNOVER					BULL & BEAR		FEES		
Min Additional Investment	3-Month Total Return	6-Month Total Return	1-Year Total Return	3-Year Total Return	5-Year Total Return	Dividend Yield (TTM)	Expense Ratio	3-Yr Std Deviation	3-Year Beta	NAV	Total Assets (MIL)	%Cash	%Stocks	%Bonds	%Other	Turnover Ratio	Last Bull Market Total Return	Last Bear Market Total Return	Front End Fee (%)	Back End Fee (%)	Inception Date
	5.38	9.01	17.21	42.04	113.31	0	1.9	11.15	0.92	16	100.9	0	84	16	0	42					Dec-11
	4.27	13.46	44.17	61.07	87.78	0	1.35	11.49	0.82	16.75	281.3	9	91	0	0	23	23.49	-15.88	5.25		Dec-10
	4.13	13.10	43.16	57.63	81.26	0	2.1	11.5	0.83	16.3	281.3	9	91	0	0	23	22.93	-16.04		1.00	Apr-15
	4.42	13.71	44.75	62.70	90.85	0	1	11.52	0.83	16.89	281.3	9	91	0	0	23	23.65	-15.69			Dec-10
	4.16	13.22	43.41	58.59	83.04	0	1.85	11.5	0.82	16.43	281.3	9	91	0	0	23	23.27	-16.1			Dec-10
	3.72	7.13	24.77	21.12	37.92	1.1	1.3	11.57	0.89	17.75	4,155	2	98	0	0	33	16.74	-20.13	5.25		Jan-96
	3.49	6.70	23.77	18.49	33.03	0.63	2.05	11.6	0.89	17.51	4,155	2	98	0	0	33	16.16	-20.36		1.00	Apr-15
	3.79	7.28	25.16	22.38	40.16	1.39	0.95	11.58	0.89	17.97	4,155	2	98	0	0	33	16.84	-20.03			Aug-89
	3.77	7.32	25.21	22.47	40.29	1.43	0.91	11.57	0.89	17.97	4,155	2	98	0	0	33	16.83	-20.03			Sep-13
	3.56	6.80	24.05	19.27	34.40	0.65	1.8	11.58	0.89	17.7	4,155	2	98	0	0	33	16.33	-20.28			Jun-12
	5.52	17.80	53.01	67.15	120.72	0	1.35	13.13	0.93	22.25	528.6	0	85	15	0	42	20.32	-26.17	5.25		Mar-10
	5.32	17.35	51.77	63.45	113.07	0	2.1	13.13	0.93	21.46	528.6	0	85	15	0	42	19.81	-26.37		1.00	Apr-15
	5.60	17.92	53.38	68.78	124.44	0	1	13.14	0.93	22.52	528.6	0	85	15	0	42	20.5	-26.06			Mar-10
	5.59	17.96	53.41	68.84	124.69	0	0.94	13.13	0.93	22.54	528.6	0	85	15	0	42	20.5	-26.06			Sep-13
	5.38	17.44	52.10	64.42	114.90	0	1.85	13.15	0.94	21.63	528.6	0	85	15	0	42	20	-26.28			Mar-10
	5.45	8.17	18.78	11.44	20.85	7.51	1.35	11.37	0.98	19.37	31.5	0	97	1	1	21	20.99	-24.99	5.25		Oct-97
	5.22	7.76	17.77	8.93	16.56	7.01	2.1	11.37	0.98	19	31.5	0	97	1	1	21	20.42	-25.2		1.00	Apr-15
	5.53	8.37	19.12	12.59	22.91	7.86	1	11.36	0.98	19.36	31.5	0	97	1	1	21	21.12	-24.89			Oct-97
	5.52	8.41	19.18	12.75	23.07	7.92	0.97	11.36	0.98	19.35	31.5	0	97	1	1	21	21.12	-24.89			Sep-13
	5.28	7.85	18.13	9.74	17.85	7.18	1.85	11.37	0.98	19.29	31.5	0	97	1	1	21	20.6	-25.12			Apr-12
	-1.23	-2.64	-1.23	-14.83	0.70	0	1.46	5.39	-64.01	9.56	75.1	111	88	-102	3	353			5.25		Jun-12
	-1.27	-2.92	-1.90	-16.60	-2.89	0	2.21	5.34	-63.03	9.29	75.1	111	88	-102	3	353				1.00	Apr-15
	-1.02	-2.32	-0.72	-13.83	2.34	0	1.11	5.31	-62.8	9.65	75.1	111	88	-102	3	353					Jun-12
	-1.02	-2.32	-0.82	-13.84	2.33	0	1.08	5.31	-61.27	9.64	75.1	111	88	-102	3	353					May-15
	-1.25	-2.78	-1.66	-15.97	-1.68	0	1.92	5.33	-61.29	9.44	75.1	111	88	-102	3	353					Jun-12
	7.01	5.62	21.57	8.61	61.06	0	1.35	15.35	0.88	8.99	360.4	0	92	3	0	51	20.83	-24.69	5.25		Jan-96
	6.86	5.21	20.62	6.40	55.58		2.1	15.34	0.87	8.93	360.4	0	92	3	0	51	20.32	-24.91		1.00	May-17
	7.04	5.75	21.86	9.66	63.57	0	1	15.34	0.88	10.9	360.4	0	92	3	0	51	21.02	-24.59			Nov-89
	7.12	5.83	22.07	10.01	64.18	0	0.93	15.35	0.88	10.96	360.4	0	92	3	0	51	21.02	-24.59			Sep-13
	6.88	5.42	20.94	7.00	57.01	0	1.85	15.3	0.87	8.46	360.4	0	92	3	0	51	20.5	-24.83			Nov-11
	3.87	4.09	2.97	10.19	50.56	3.07	1.3	13.34	0.98	14.76	606.3	1	99	0	0	24	30.35	-17.48	5.25		Jan-96
	3.66	3.73	2.13	7.65	45.14	2.38	2.1	13.36	0.98	14.68	606.3	1	99	0	0	24	29.89	-17.77		1.00	Apr-15
	3.94	4.24	3.30	11.19	52.93	3.3	1	13.36	0.98	15.24	606.3	1	99	0	0	24	30.65	-17.43			Feb-95
	3.96	4.29	3.31	11.47	53.35	3.39	0.9	13.36	0.98	15.24	606.3	1	99	0	0	24	30.65	-17.43			Sep-13
	3.67	3.81	2.37	8.36	46.61	2.58	1.84	13.35	0.98	14.74	606.3	1	99	0	0	24	30.01	-17.69			Nov-11
	5.64	10.83	18.79			0.73	1.15			12.38	12.7	0	98	2	0				5.25		May-16
	5.40	10.33	17.96			0.56	1.9			12.28	12.7	0	98	2	0					1.00	May-16
	5.77	11.04	19.33			0.81	0.77			12.41	12.7	0	98	2	0						May-16
	5.80	11.08	19.37			0.83	0.75			12.41	12.7	0	98	2	0						May-16
	2.00	4.24	11.21			1.06	1.35			10.42	15.7	11	42	46	1	218			5.25		Apr-15
	1.66	3.72	10.33			0.48	2.1			10.36	15.7	11	42	46	1	218				1.00	May-15
	1.97	4.30	11.46			1.39	1			10.42	15.7	11	42	46	1	218					Apr-15
	2.00	4.34	11.63			1.44	0.95			10.43	15.7	11	42	46	1	218					Apr-15
100	10.20	15.46	47.81	52.20	145.24	0	1.24	15.32	1.18	31.98	426.4	0	91	3	0	46	20.53	-16.8	5.25		Jul-97
100	9.97	14.97	46.61	48.68	135.86	0	2.02	15.31	1.18	23.44	426.4	0	91	3	0	46	20.03	-17.07		5.00	Feb-96
100	9.98	15.02	46.66	48.74	135.96	0	2.02	15.31	1.17	23.51	426.4	0	91	3	0	46	20.03	-17.07		1.00	Apr-15
	10.28	15.63	48.23	53.72	149.15	0	0.92	15.33	1.18	35.15	426.4	0	91	3	0	46	20.75	-16.73			Jul-97
	10.29	15.66	48.33	53.99	148.00	0	0.84	15.31	1.18	35.3	426.4	0	91	3	0	46	20.03	-17.07			Sep-13
100	10.06	15.14	46.97	49.80	138.89	0	1.77	15.32	1.18	23.74	426.4	0	91	3	0	46	20.01	-17.06			Jul-97
	5.02	9.97	20.17	29.39	63.84	1.28	0.66	8.71		13.03	99.7	1	91	8	0	46	18.33	-19.1			Apr-07
	3.21	6.53	13.65	20.45	43.48	1.81	0.68	6.02		11.29	194.6	3	57	40	0	34	13.62	-12.21			Apr-07
	1.09	2.72	6.45	10.38	17.38	1.72	0.71	2.95		11.16	35.3	2	17	80	0	55	5.93	-2.62			Apr-07

	MARKET		FUND TYPE, CATEGORY & OBJECTIVE		RATINGS				MINIMUMS	
Fund Name	Ticker Symbol	Traded On	Fund Type	Category and (Prospectus Objective)	Overall Rating	Reward Rating	Risk Rating	Recent Up/ Downgrade	Open to New Investors	Min Initial Investment
Morningstar Growth ETF Asset Allocation Portfolio Class I	US00162T8861		Open End	Aggressive Alloc (Growth)	B-	B-	B-	Down	Y	0
Morningstar Income & Growth ETF Asset Alloc Port Cls I	US00162T5065		Open End	Cautious Alloc (Growth & Income)	B-	C+	B	Up	Y	0
Motley Fool Emerging Markets Fund Investor Shares	TMFEX	NAS CM	Open End	Global Equity Mid/Small Cap (Growth)	C+	B-	C+	Up	Y	500
Motley Fool Great America Fund Institutional Shares	FOGIX	NAS CM	Open End	US Equity Mid Cap (Growth)	B	B+	B	Up	Y	100,000
Motley Fool Great America Fund Investor Shares	TMFGX	NAS CM	Open End	US Equity Mid Cap (Growth)	B	B	B	Up	Y	500
Motley Fool Independence Fund Institutional Shares	FOIIX	NAS CM	Open End	Global Equity (Growth & Income)	B	B	B	Up	Y	100,000
Motley Fool Independence Fund Investor Shares	FOOLX	NAS CM	Open End	Global Equity (Growth & Income)	B	B-	B	Up	Y	500
Mount Lucas U.S. Focused Equity Fund Class I	BMLEX	NAS CM	Open End	US Equity Large Cap Value (Growth)	B-	B-	B	Down	Y	10,000
MS Asia-Pacific Fund, Inc.	APF	NYSE	Closed End	Asia Equity (Pacific Stock)	B	B	B-	Up	Y	
MS Emerging Markets Fund	MSF	NYSE	Closed End	Emerging Markets Equity (World Stock)	C+	B-	C	Up	Y	
MS India Investment Fund	IIF	NYSE	Closed End	India Equity (Pacific Stock)	B	B+	B	Up	Y	
Muhlenkamp Fund	MUHLX	NAS CM	Open End	US Equity Large Cap Blend (Growth & Income)	C+	C+	C+	Up	Y	1,500
Multimanager Aggressive Equity Portfolio Class IA	US4049924719		Open End	US Equity Large Cap Growth (Growth)	B+	A-	B	Up	Y	0
Multimanager Aggressive Equity Portfolio Class IB	US4049924891		Open End	US Equity Large Cap Growth (Growth)	B+	A-	B	Up	Y	0
Multimanager Aggressive Equity Portfolio Class K	US00247C5360		Open End	US Equity Large Cap Growth (Growth)	B+	A-	B	Up	Y	0
Multi-Manager Alternative Strategies Fund Class A	CPASX	NAS CM	Open End	Multialternative (Growth & Income)	D+	D	C-		Y	100
Multi-Manager Alternative Strategies Fund Inst Cls	CZAMX	NAS CM	Open End	Multialternative (Growth & Income)	D+	D	C-		Y	100
Multi-Mgr Directional Alternative Strat Fund Cls A	CDAAX	NAS CM	Open End	Long/Short Equity (Growth)	D	D+	A		Y	100
Multi-Mgr Directional Alternative Strat Fund Inst Cls	CDAZX	NAS CM	Open End	Long/Short Equity (Growth)	D	D+	A		Y	100
Multi-Manager Growth Strategies Fund Class A	CSLGX	NAS CM	Open End	US Equity Large Cap Growth (Growth)	B	B	B	Down	Y	100
Multi-Manager Growth Strategies Fund Institutional Class	CZMGX	NAS CM	Open End	US Equity Large Cap Growth (Growth)	B	B	B	Down	Y	100
Multimanager Mid Cap Growth Portfolio Class IA	US00247C7002		Open End	US Equity Mid Cap (Growth)	B	B+	C	Up	Y	0
Multimanager Mid Cap Growth Portfolio Class IB	US00247C8091		Open End	US Equity Mid Cap (Growth)	B	B+	C	Up	Y	0
Multimanager Mid Cap Growth Portfolio Class K	US00247C4785		Open End	US Equity Mid Cap (Growth)	B	A-	C+	Up	Y	0
Multimanager Mid Cap Value Portfolio Class IA	US00247C8828		Open End	US Equity Mid Cap (Growth)	B-	C+	B	Up	Y	0
Multimanager Mid Cap Value Portfolio Class IB	US00247C8745		Open End	US Equity Mid Cap (Growth)	B-	C+	B	Up	Y	0
Multimanager Mid Cap Value Portfolio Class K	US00247C4603		Open End	US Equity Mid Cap (Growth)	B-	B-	B	Up	Y	0
Multi-Manager Small Cap Equity Strategies Fund Class A	CSCEX	NAS CM	Open End	US Equity Small Cap (Small Company)	B+	A-	B	Up	Y	100
Multi-Manager Small Cap Equity Strategies Fund Inst Cls	CZMSX	NAS CM	Open End	US Equity Small Cap (Small Company)	B+	A-	B	Up	Y	100
Multimanager Technology Portfolio Class IA	US00247C8414		Open End	Technology Sector Equity (Technology)	A-	A	B		Y	0
Multimanager Technology Portfolio Class IB	US00247C8331		Open End	Technology Sector Equity (Technology)	A	A	B+	Up	Y	0
Multimanager Technology Portfolio Class K	US00247C4298		Open End	Technology Sector Equity (Technology)	A-	A+	B		Y	0
Multi-Manager Value Strategies Fund Class A	CDEIX	NAS CM	Open End	US Equity Large Cap Value (Growth)	B-	B	B-	Down	Y	100
Multi-Manager Value Strategies Fund Institutional Class	CZMVX	NAS CM	Open End	US Equity Large Cap Value (Growth)	B-	B	B-	Down	Y	100
Multi-Strategy Growth & Income Fund Class A Shares	MSFDX	NAS CM	Closed End	Multialternative (Growth & Income)	B-	C	B+	Up	Y	2,500
Multi-Strategy Growth & Income Fund Class C Shares	US62546J4067		Closed End	Multialternative (Growth & Income)	B-	C	B	Up	Y	2,500
Multi-Strategy Growth & Income Fund Class I Shares	US62546J2087		Closed End	Multialternative (Growth & Income)	B-	C	B+	Up	Y	1,000,000
Multi-Strategy Growth & Income Fund Class L Shares	US62546J3077		Closed End	Multialternative (Growth & Income)	B-	C	B+	Up	Y	2,500
Mundoval Fund	MUNDX	NAS CM	Open End	Global Equity (Growth)	C+	C+	C		Y	10,000
Mutual of America 2010 Retirement Fund			Open End	Target Date 2000-2020 (Growth & Income)	U	U	U		Y	0
Mutual of America 2015 Retirement Fund			Open End	Target Date 2000-2020 (Growth & Income)	U	U	U		Y	0
Mutual of America 2020 Retirement Fund			Open End	Target Date 2000-2020 (Growth & Income)	U	U	U		Y	0
Mutual of America 2025 Retirement Fund			Open End	Target Date 2021-2045 (Growth & Income)	U	U	U		Y	0
Mutual of America 2030 Retirement Fund			Open End	Target Date 2021-2045 (Growth & Income)	U	U	U		Y	0
Mutual of America 2035 Retirement Fund			Open End	Target Date 2021-2045 (Growth & Income)	U	U	U		Y	0
Mutual of America 2040 Retirement Fund			Open End	Target Date 2021-2045 (Growth & Income)	U	U	U		Y	0
Mutual of America 2045 Retirement Fund			Open End	Target Date 2021-2045 (Growth & Income)	U	U	U		Y	0
Mutual of America 2050 Retirement Fund			Open End	Target Date 2046+ (Growth & Income)	U	U	U		Y	0
Mutual of America Institutional Funds Inc All America Fund	MALLX	NAS CM	Open End	US Equity Large Cap Blend (Growth)	B+	B+	B+	Up	Y	25,000
Mutual of America Inst Funds Inc Equity Index Fund	MAEQX	NAS CM	Open End	US Equity Large Cap Blend (Growth)	B	B	B		Y	25,000
Mutual of America Inst Funds Inc Mid-Cap Equity Index Fund	MAMQX	NAS CM	Open End	US Equity Mid Cap (Growth)	B	B	B		Y	25,000
Mutual of America Inst Funds Inc Small Cap Growth Fund	MASSX	NAS CM	Open End	US Equity Small Cap (Small Company)	B	A-	C+	Up	Y	25,000

★Expanded analysis of this fund is included in Section II.

Min Additional Investment	TOTAL RETURNS 3-Month Total Return	6-Month Total Return	1-Year Total Return	3-Year Total Return	5-Year Total Return	PERFORMANCE Dividend Yield (TTM)	Expense Ratio	3-Yr Std Deviation	3-Year Beta	ASSETS NAV	Total Assets (MIL)	ASSET ALLOCATION & TURNOVER %Cash	%Stocks	%Bonds	%Other	Turnover Ratio	BULL & BEAR Last Bull Market Total Return	Last Bear Market Total Return	FEES Front End Fee (%)	Back End Fee (%)	Inception Date
	4.26	8.53	17.67	25.54	56.46	1.49	0.66	7.8		12.15	227.0	1	76	22	0	37	16.68	-16.76			Apr-07
	2.15	4.67	10.11	15.42	29.66	1.96	0.7	4.41		10.26	80.7	3	37	60	0	40	9.49	-7.44			Apr-07
50	1.62	6.35	26.09	24.72	37.56	0.46	1.15	11.89	0.64	14.27	34.2	0	96	0	4	21					Nov-11
	11.76	18.04	29.38	34.77	106.07	0	0.95	12.73	0.9	24.48	267.5	0	96	0	4	24	25.74	-17.34			Jun-14
50	11.73	17.93	29.19	33.89	104.68	0	1.15	12.73	0.9	24.35	267.5	0	96	0	4	24	25.74	-17.34			Nov-10
	6.85	10.27	30.60	31.66	78.75	0.34	0.95	10.98	0.98	22.76	429.2	0	94	2	4	38	18.04	-16.13			Jun-14
50	6.82	10.19	30.37	31.02	77.77	0.15	1.14	10.97	0.98	22.72	429.2	0	94	2	4	38	18.04	-16.13			Jun-09
	8.97	14.68	23.90	24.26	104.37	3.74	0.95	12.72	1.1	10.73	10.9	0	99	0	0	92	26.09	-23.92			Oct-07
	7.70	12.09	35.23	30.67	37.98	0.71	0	13.48		21.01	277.1	2	93	0	5	41	10.52	-18.23			Aug-94
	5.27	12.64	35.25	28.22	22.63	0.46	0	13.87	0.85	20.39	279.8	1	94	0	4	35	16.08	-22.49			Nov-91
	7.46	14.39	44.78	52.18	115.35	0	1.29	17.41	0.73	37.32	578.9	1	97	0	1	16	-1.36	-23.64			Feb-94
50	4.72	10.39	18.77	6.62	47.79	0	1.25	10.69	0.95	55.21	262.2	8	88	0	3	40	19.31	-18.96			Nov-88
	7.81	14.66	30.20	39.06	118.52	0.41	1	11.29	1.03		1,184	1	99	0	0	63	22.56	-19.21			Jan-86
	7.81	14.66	30.20	39.05	118.46	0.41	1	11.29	1.03		1,184	1	99	0	0	63	22.47	-19.32			Oct-96
	7.88	14.80	30.54	39.71	120.65	0.61	0.75	11.28	1.03		1,184	1	99	0	0	63	22.64	-19.21			Aug-11
	1.44	1.89	0.54	-6.22	5.42	0	1.48	3.95	26.82	9.15	583.4	34	13	49	1	444					Apr-12
	1.55	2.11	1.10	-5.70	6.00		1.23	3.96	25.34	9.17	583.4	34	13	49	1	444					Jan-17
	3.02	7.42	12.87			0.06	2.2			11.01	1,108	33	67	0	0	100					Oct-16
	3.04	7.54	13.00				1.95			10.96	1,108	33	67	0	0	100					Jan-17
	5.77	10.88	31.44	36.44	116.76	0	1.13	13.78	1.18	14.73	2,657	1	99	0	0	48					Apr-12
	5.74	10.92	31.90	36.92	117.52		0.88	13.78	1.18	14.54	2,657	1	99	0	0	48					Jan-17
	7.43	14.16	27.09	32.76	101.15	0.07	1.1	13.58	1.02		189.2	2	98	0	0	49	23.41	-24.76			Dec-01
	7.43	14.18	27.14	32.80	101.21	0.08	1.1	13.59	1.02		189.2	2	98	0	0	49	23.49	-24.9			Dec-01
	7.49	14.33	27.47	33.84	103.66	0.28	0.85	13.64	1.02		189.2	2	98	0	0	49	23.54	-24.76			Aug-11
	4.23	7.49	9.61	22.36	79.97	0.88	1.1	11.25	0.93		194.7	2	98	0	0	42	16.81	-25.63			Dec-01
	4.19	7.52	9.62	22.26	79.98	0.89	1.1	11.25	0.93		194.7	2	98	0	0	42	16.64	-25.71			Dec-01
	4.29	7.67	9.87	23.27	82.23	1.12	0.85	11.24	0.93		194.7	2	98	0	0	42	16.81	-25.63			Aug-11
	3.36	11.03	14.83	34.34	96.71	0.06	1.34	13.41	0.94	15.54	1,260	2	98	0	0	85					Apr-12
	3.43	11.20	15.18	34.74	97.31		1.09	13.42	0.94	15.5	1,260	2	98	0	0	85					Jan-17
	8.34	17.30	38.77	59.52	154.24	0.01	1.3	14.15	1.18		1,085	1	99	0	0	64	24	-17.2			Dec-01
	8.34	17.25	38.69	59.45	154.22	0.01	1.3	14.16	1.18		1,085	1	99	0	0	64	23.89	-17.25			Dec-01
	8.39	17.43	39.07	60.59	158.29	0.19	1.05	14.15	1.18		1,085	1	99	0	0	64	24	-17.2			Aug-12
	6.54	11.02	19.60	33.64	93.48	1.01	1.06	10.3	0.97	14.11	2,633	1	99	0	0	97					Apr-12
	6.52	11.11	19.64	33.69	93.54		0.81	10.3	0.97	13.96	2,633	1	99	0	0	97					Jan-17
100	0.19	1.84	2.73	8.51	30.77	6.13	3.27	4.08		15.11	--	1	47	8	41	49			5.75		Mar-12
100	0.02	1.40	1.99	6.10	27.43	6.15	4.02	4.11		14.77	--	1	47	8	41	49					Jul-14
	0.27	1.98	3.04	9.92	32.04	6.12	3.02	4.2		15.31	--	1	47	8	41	49					Jul-14
100	0.10	1.62	2.28	6.92	28.60	6.14	3.77	4.07		14.89	--	1	47	8	41	49			2.00		Jul-14
100	3.59	10.25	18.86	18.66	53.44	0.42	1.53	12.37	1.05	17.63	23.5	8	92	0	0	31	15.36	-17.33			Sep-04
	2.28	5.71	7.18	19.72	43.99	2.04	0.38	4.53	0.39		25.2	7	35	58	0	23	11.8	-7.1			Nov-07
	2.72	6.28	7.71	21.18	50.49	2	0.4	5.56	0.48		146.6	4	44	51	0	18	13.38	-9.4			Nov-07
	3.20	6.76	8.24	22.31	57.15	1.64	0.38	6.63	0.59		400.1	4	55	41	0	8	15.45	-11.5			Nov-07
	3.69	7.39	8.95	23.95	65.63	1.48	0.36	7.88	0.7		461.7	3	67	30	0	4	17.96	-13.92			Nov-07
	4.03	7.86	9.37	25.50	71.87	1.44	0.35	8.67	0.77		377.6	3	74	23	0	5	19.52	-15.54			Nov-07
	4.36	8.18	9.51	25.76	76.09	1.36	0.35	9.43	0.84		317.4	3	82	15	0	5	20.97	-17.26			Nov-07
	4.54	8.41	9.20	25.03	76.77	1.3	0.36	9.92	0.88		258.4	3	85	12	0	5	21.36	-18.15			Nov-07
	4.68	8.48	9.07	24.57	76.51	1.32	0.37	10.14	0.9		303.2	3	87	10	0	4	21.3	-18.38			Nov-07
	4.78	8.60	9.02	24.32		0.72	0.39	10.34	0.91		133.8	3	89	8	0	3					Oct-12
5,000	5.62	10.68	19.57	32.56	100.05	1.14	0.5	10.19	1	11.6824	13.1	2	98	0	0	47	24.35	-18.27			May-96
5,000	6.61	11.36	21.66	36.47	110.41	1.7	0.13	10.1	1	11.8034	42.9	1	100	0	0	11	25.01	-16.31			Apr-99
5,000	6.20	9.58	15.99	35.16	103.06	1.23	0.13	11.04	1	11.7826	25.1	5	95	0	0	35	27.91	-22.63			Sep-00
5,000	4.62	11.49	24.19	30.75	100.62	0.02	0.85	13.61	0.9	13.1427	8.5	0	100	0	0	54	23.13	-23.85			May-07

	MARKET			FUND TYPE, CATEGORY & OBJECTIVE	RATINGS					MINIMUMS
Fund Name	Ticker Symbol	Traded On	Fund Type	Category and (Prospectus Objective)	Overall Rating	Reward Rating	Risk Rating	Recent Up/ Downgrade	Open to New Investors	Min Initial Investment
Mutual of America Inst Funds Inc Small Cap Value Fund	MAVSX	NAS CM	Open End	US Equity Small Cap (Small Company)	B	B	B	Up	Y	25,000
Nationwide Bailard Cognitive Value Fund Class A	NWHDX	NAS CM	Open End	US Equity Small Cap (Small Company)	B	B	B	Up	Y	2,000
Nationwide Bailard Cognitive Value Fund Class C	NWHEX	NAS CM	Open End	US Equity Small Cap (Small Company)	B	B	B	Up	Y	2,000
Nationwide Bailard Cognitive Value Fund Class M	NWHFX	NAS CM	Open End	US Equity Small Cap (Small Company)	B	B	B	Up	Y	5,000
Nationwide Bailard Cognitive Value Fund Class R6	NWHGX	NAS CM	Open End	US Equity Small Cap (Small Company)	B	B	B	Up	Y	1,000,000
Nationwide Bailard Cognitive Value Fund Inst Service Cls	NWHHX	NAS CM	Open End	US Equity Small Cap (Small Company)	B	B	B	Up	Y	50,000
Nationwide Bailard Emerging Markets Equity Fund Class A	NWWAX	NAS CM	Open End	Emerging Markets Equity (Div Emerging Mkts)	C	C	C		Y	2,000
Nationwide Bailard Emerging Markets Equity Fund Class C	NWWBX	NAS CM	Open End	Emerging Markets Equity (Div Emerging Mkts)	C	C	C		Y	2,000
Nationwide Bailard Emerging Markets Equity Fund Class M	NWWEX	NAS CM	Open End	Emerging Markets Equity (Div Emerging Mkts)	C	C	C		Y	5,000
Nationwide Bailard Emerging Markets Equity Fund Class R6	NWWCX	NAS CM	Open End	Emerging Markets Equity (Div Emerging Mkts)	C	C	C		Y	1,000,000
Nationwide Bailard Emerging Mkts Eq Fund Inst Serv Cls	NWWDX	NAS CM	Open End	Emerging Markets Equity (Div Emerging Mkts)	C	C	C		Y	50,000
Nationwide Bailard International Equities Fund Class A	NWHJX	NAS CM	Open End	Global Equity Large Cap (Foreign Stock)	B-	C+	B	Up	Y	2,000
Nationwide Bailard International Equities Fund Class C	NWHKX	NAS CM	Open End	Global Equity Large Cap (Foreign Stock)	B-	C+	B	Up	Y	2,000
Nationwide Bailard International Equities Fund Class M	NWHLX	NAS CM	Open End	Global Equity Large Cap (Foreign Stock)	B-	C+	B	Up	Y	5,000
Nationwide Bailard International Equities Fund Class R6	NWHMX	NAS CM	Open End	Global Equity Large Cap (Foreign Stock)	B-	C+	B	Up	Y	1,000,000
Nationwide Bailard Intl Equities Fund Inst Service Cls	NWHNX	NAS CM	Open End	Global Equity Large Cap (Foreign Stock)	B-	C+	B	Up	Y	50,000
Nationwide Bailard Technology and Science Fund Class A	NWHOX	NAS CM	Open End	Technology Sector Equity (Technology)	A-	A	B	Up	Y	2,000
Nationwide Bailard Technology and Science Fund Class C	NWHPX	NAS CM	Open End	Technology Sector Equity (Technology)	A-	A	B	Up	Y	2,000
Nationwide Bailard Technology and Science Fund Class M	NWHQX	NAS CM	Open End	Technology Sector Equity (Technology)	A-	A+	B	Up	Y	5,000
Nationwide Bailard Technology and Science Fund Class R6	NWHTX	NAS CM	Open End	Technology Sector Equity (Technology)	A-	A+	B	Up	Y	1,000,000
Nationwide Bailard Technology & Science Fund Inst Serv Cls	NWHUX	NAS CM	Open End	Technology Sector Equity (Technology)	A-	A+	B	Up	Y	50,000
Nationwide Destination 2010 Fund Class A	NWDAX	NAS CM	Open End	Target Date 2000-2020 (Asset Alloc)	B-	C+	B	Up	Y	2,000
Nationwide Destination 2010 Fund Class C	NWDCX	NAS CM	Open End	Target Date 2000-2020 (Asset Alloc)	B-	C	B	Up	Y	2,000
Nationwide Destination 2010 Fund Class R	NWDBX	NAS CM	Open End	Target Date 2000-2020 (Asset Alloc)	B-	C+	B	Up	Y	0
Nationwide Destination 2010 Fund Class R6	NWDIX	NAS CM	Open End	Target Date 2000-2020 (Asset Alloc)	B-	C+	B	Up	Y	1,000,000
Nationwide Destination 2010 Fund Institutional Service Cls	NWDSX	NAS CM	Open End	Target Date 2000-2020 (Asset Alloc)	B-	C+	B	Up	Y	50,000
Nationwide Destination 2015 Fund Class A	NWEAX	NAS CM	Open End	Target Date 2000-2020 (Asset Alloc)	B-	C+	B	Up	Y	2,000
Nationwide Destination 2015 Fund Class C	NWECX	NAS CM	Open End	Target Date 2000-2020 (Asset Alloc)	B-	C+	B	Up	Y	2,000
Nationwide Destination 2015 Fund Class R	NWEBX	NAS CM	Open End	Target Date 2000-2020 (Asset Alloc)	B-	C+	B	Up	Y	0
Nationwide Destination 2015 Fund Class R6	NWEIX	NAS CM	Open End	Target Date 2000-2020 (Asset Alloc)	B-	C+	B	Up	Y	1,000,000
Nationwide Destination 2015 Fund Institutional Service Cls	NWESX	NAS CM	Open End	Target Date 2000-2020 (Asset Alloc)	B-	C+	B	Up	Y	50,000
Nationwide Destination 2020 Fund Class A	NWAFX	NAS CM	Open End	Target Date 2000-2020 (Asset Alloc)	B-	C+	B	Up	Y	2,000
Nationwide Destination 2020 Fund Class C	NWFCX	NAS CM	Open End	Target Date 2000-2020 (Asset Alloc)	B-	C+	B	Up	Y	2,000
Nationwide Destination 2020 Fund Class R	NWFTX	NAS CM	Open End	Target Date 2000-2020 (Asset Alloc)	B-	C+	B	Up	Y	0
Nationwide Destination 2020 Fund Class R6	NWFIX	NAS CM	Open End	Target Date 2000-2020 (Asset Alloc)	B-	C+	B	Up	Y	1,000,000
Nationwide Destination 2020 Fund Institutional Service Cls	NWFSX	NAS CM	Open End	Target Date 2000-2020 (Asset Alloc)	B-	C+	B	Up	Y	50,000
Nationwide Destination 2025 Fund Class A	NWHAX	NAS CM	Open End	Target Date 2021-2045 (Asset Alloc)	B-	C+	B	Down	Y	2,000
Nationwide Destination 2025 Fund Class C	NWHCX	NAS CM	Open End	Target Date 2021-2045 (Asset Alloc)	B-	C+	B	Down	Y	2,000
Nationwide Destination 2025 Fund Class R	NWHBX	NAS CM	Open End	Target Date 2021-2045 (Asset Alloc)	B-	C+	B	Down	Y	0
Nationwide Destination 2025 Fund Class R6	NWHIX	NAS CM	Open End	Target Date 2021-2045 (Asset Alloc)	B-	C+	B	Down	Y	1,000,000
Nationwide Destination 2025 Fund Institutional Service Cls	NWHSX	NAS CM	Open End	Target Date 2021-2045 (Asset Alloc)	B-	C+	B	Down	Y	50,000
Nationwide Destination 2030 Fund Class A	NWIAX	NAS CM	Open End	Target Date 2021-2045 (Asset Alloc)	B-	C+	B-	Down	Y	2,000
Nationwide Destination 2030 Fund Class C	NWICX	NAS CM	Open End	Target Date 2021-2045 (Asset Alloc)	B-	C+	B-	Down	Y	2,000
Nationwide Destination 2030 Fund Class R	NWBIX	NAS CM	Open End	Target Date 2021-2045 (Asset Alloc)	B-	C+	B-	Down	Y	0
Nationwide Destination 2030 Fund Class R6	NWIIX	NAS CM	Open End	Target Date 2021-2045 (Asset Alloc)	B-	C+	B	Down	Y	1,000,000
Nationwide Destination 2030 Fund Institutional Service Cls	NWISX	NAS CM	Open End	Target Date 2021-2045 (Asset Alloc)	B-	C+	B	Down	Y	50,000
Nationwide Destination 2035 Fund Class A	NWLAX	NAS CM	Open End	Target Date 2021-2045 (Asset Alloc)	B-	C+	B-	Down	Y	2,000
Nationwide Destination 2035 Fund Class C	NWLCX	NAS CM	Open End	Target Date 2021-2045 (Asset Alloc)	B-	C+	B-	Down	Y	2,000
Nationwide Destination 2035 Fund Class R	NWLBX	NAS CM	Open End	Target Date 2021-2045 (Asset Alloc)	B-	C+	B-	Down	Y	0
Nationwide Destination 2035 Fund Class R6	NWLIX	NAS CM	Open End	Target Date 2021-2045 (Asset Alloc)	B-	B-	B-	Down	Y	1,000,000
Nationwide Destination 2035 Fund Institutional Service Cls	NWLSX	NAS CM	Open End	Target Date 2021-2045 (Asset Alloc)	B-	B-	B-	Down	Y	50,000
Nationwide Destination 2040 Fund Class A	NWMAX	NAS CM	Open End	Target Date 2021-2045 (Asset Alloc)	B-	B-	B-	Down	Y	2,000

★ Expanded analysis of this fund is included in Section II.

Min Additional Investment	TOTAL RETURNS 3-Month Total Return	6-Month Total Return	1-Year Total Return	3-Year Total Return	5-Year Total Return	PERFORMANCE Dividend Yield (TTM)	Expense Ratio	3-Yr Std Deviation	3-Year Beta	ASSETS NAV	Total Assets (MIL)	ASSET ALLOCATION & TURNOVER %Cash	%Stocks	%Bonds	%Other	Turnover Ratio	BULL & BEAR Last Bull Market Total Return	Last Bear Market Total Return	FEES Front End Fee (%)	Back End Fee (%)	Inception Date
5,000	1.35	6.30	8.21	24.46	73.85	0.99	0.85	12.03	0.83	13.2387	11.1	0	100	0	0	35	22.83	-21.71			May-07
100	0.86	5.76	3.57	24.17	74.69	0.41	1.44	13.29	0.88	13.49	100.5	2	98	0	0	115	27.95	-23.27	5.75		Apr-06
100	0.68	5.29	2.74	21.50	68.62	0.24	2.21	13.31	0.88	12.54	100.5	2	98	0	0	115	27.44	-23.44		1.00	Apr-06
100	0.95	5.95	3.90	25.50	77.93	0.63	1.12	13.29	0.88	13.49	100.5	2	98	0	0	115	28.23	-23.13			May-01
	0.88	5.88	3.84	25.52	77.81	0.63	1.12	13.29	0.88	13.48	100.5	2	98	0	0	115	28.23	-23.13			Sep-13
	0.91	5.90	3.78	25.32	77.31	0.54	1.22	13.26	0.88	13.51	100.5	2	98	0	0	115	28.23	-23.21			Apr-06
100	4.07	11.81	31.16	17.74		1.44	1.53	14.67	0.89	11.13	160.4	2	98	0	0	89			5.75		Mar-14
100	3.82	11.40	30.14	15.25		1.05	2.28	14.63	0.88	11.03	160.4	2	98	0	0	89				1.00	Mar-14
100	4.18	12.03	31.55	18.84		1.64	1.13	14.64	0.88	11.06	160.4	2	98	0	0	89					Mar-14
	4.14	12.03	31.53	18.81		1.63	1.13	14.64	0.88	11.15	160.4	2	98	0	0	89					Mar-14
	4.06	11.95	31.24	18.56		1.55	1.24	14.6	0.88	11.02	160.4	2	98	0	0	89					Mar-14
100	3.63	9.53	24.22	21.51	46.08	2	1.24	10.34	0.81	8.95	506.1	1	97	0	1	96	15.73	-26.14	5.75		Apr-06
100	3.41	9.09	23.21	18.58	40.65	1.46	1.99	10.4	0.82	8.84	506.1	1	97	0	1	96	15.47	-26.41		1.00	Apr-06
100	3.77	9.65	24.70	22.70	48.52	2.29	0.87	10.42	0.82	8.94	506.1	1	97	0	1	96	16.09	-26.1			Sep-79
	3.76	9.77	24.67	22.84	48.70	2.29	0.87	10.39	0.82	8.95	506.1	1	97	0	1	96	16.09	-26.1			Sep-13
	3.63	9.61	24.44	22.20	47.67	2.2	0.99	10.35	0.81	8.93	506.1	1	97	0	1	96	16.02	-26.14			Apr-06
100	6.25	16.96	37.61	59.79	150.67	0.1	1.3	13.88	0.94	20.39	143.8	0	100	0	0	26	28.49	-17.62	5.75		Apr-06
100	6.05	16.53	36.60	56.22	142.00	0	2.09	13.89	0.94	18.49	143.8	0	100	0	0	26	27.98	-17.86		1.00	Apr-06
100	6.34	17.22	38.10	61.36	155.10	0.15	0.98	13.91	0.95	21.33	143.8	0	100	0	0	26	28.83	-17.53			May-01
	6.31	17.20	38.05	61.36	155.26	0.15	0.98	13.91	0.95	21.28	143.8	0	100	0	0	26	28.83	-17.53			Sep-13
	6.30	17.14	37.95	60.97	153.77	0.13	1.09	13.87	0.94	21.3	143.8	0	100	0	0	26	28.73	-17.46			Apr-06
100	2.10	4.17	9.08	14.20	29.50	1.82	0.86	4.47	1	8.38	21.8	22	36	42	0	57	8.56	-10.12	5.75		Aug-07
100	1.97	3.89	8.36	12.00	25.62	1.25	1.51	4.46	0.99	8.31	21.8	22	36	42	0	57	8.3	-10.37		1.00	Aug-07
	2.16	4.04	8.83	13.26	27.79	1.58	1.12	4.44	0.99	8.36	21.8	22	36	42	0	57	8.36	-10.15			Aug-07
	2.35	4.56	9.75	15.97	32.78	2.28	0.37	4.46	1	8.4	21.8	22	36	42	0	57	8.81	-9.98			Aug-07
	2.35	4.43	9.72	15.55	32.32	2.22	0.62	4.43	0.98	8.39	21.8	22	36	42	0	57	8.96	-10			Aug-07
100	2.66	5.04	10.77	16.27	35.10	1.78	0.87	5.24	1.05	8.59	90.1	17	46	37	0	35	10.16	-11.4	5.75		Aug-07
100	2.57	4.82	10.26	14.31	31.38	1.29	1.44	5.24	1.05	8.54	90.1	17	46	37	0	35	9.77	-11.63		1.00	Aug-07
	2.51	4.95	10.41	15.20	33.05	1.53	1.14	5.3	1.06	8.55	90.1	17	46	37	0	35	9.97	-11.44			Aug-07
	2.82	5.45	11.44	17.93	38.28	2.22	0.39	5.25	1.05	8.62	90.1	17	46	37	0	35	10.4	-11.23			Aug-07
	2.75	5.20	11.05	17.05	36.61	1.99	0.64	5.29	1.06	8.6	90.1	17	46	37	0	35	10.27	-11.27			Aug-07
100	3.18	6.02	12.38	18.09	41.27	1.81	0.87	6.12	1.08	9.46	255.8	13	57	31	0	34	11.49	-12.74	5.75		Aug-07
100	3.05	5.77	11.75	15.80	37.00	1.27	1.49	6.09	1.08	9.33	255.8	13	57	31	0	34	11.29	-13.03		1.00	Aug-07
	3.11	5.88	12.09	16.93	39.08	1.55	1.14	6.11	1.08	9.43	255.8	13	57	31	0	34	11.43	-12.87			Aug-07
	3.28	6.34	12.95	19.72	44.44	2.22	0.39	6.09	1.08	9.52	255.8	13	57	31	0	34	11.96	-12.66			Aug-07
	3.23	6.23	12.72	18.77	42.68	2	0.64	6.06	1.08	9.48	255.8	13	57	31	0	34	11.74	-12.71			Aug-07
100	3.61	6.77	13.97	20.23	48.89	1.76	0.87	7.06	1.08	9.84	321.4	10	65	26	0	41	13.67	-14.8	5.75		Aug-07
100	3.39	6.42	13.17	18.00	44.55	1.3	1.46	7.09	1.09	9.73	321.4	10	65	26	0	41	13.3	-14.97		1.00	Aug-07
	3.55	6.64	13.57	19.19	46.83	1.51	1.14	7.09	1.09	9.81	321.4	10	65	26	0	41	13.49	-14.83			Aug-07
	3.62	6.98	14.42	21.86	52.25	2.17	0.39	7.1	1.09	9.9	321.4	10	65	26	0	41	13.99	-14.61			Aug-07
	3.57	6.88	14.21	20.94	50.50	1.95	0.64	7.1	1.09	9.85	321.4	10	65	26	0	41	13.85	-14.76			Aug-07
100	3.97	7.54	15.10	22.20	56.03	1.7	0.88	7.85	1.03	9.56	320.4	6	73	21	0	42	16.16	-16.8	5.75		Aug-07
100	3.76	7.10	14.48	20.05	51.87	1.29	1.44	7.83	1.03	9.45	320.4	6	73	21	0	42	15.8	-16.95		1.00	Aug-07
	3.81	7.33	14.76	21.12	53.91	1.47	1.15	7.84	1.03	9.5	320.4	6	73	21	0	42	15.86	-16.74			Aug-07
	4.07	7.75	15.67	23.92	59.80	2.11	0.4	7.83	1.03	9.62	320.4	6	73	21	0	42	16.48	-16.6			Aug-07
	4.03	7.67	15.36	23.02	57.84	1.9	0.65	7.87	1.03	9.57	320.4	6	73	21	0	42	16.2	-16.65			Aug-07
100	4.18	7.93	16.07	23.51	61.21	1.66	0.88	8.44	0.98	10.26	268.9	1	79	20	0	43	17.81	-17.8	5.75		Aug-07
100	4.00	7.65	15.35	21.20	56.53	1.27	1.49	8.38	0.98	10.07	268.9	1	79	20	0	43	17.52	-18.1		1.00	Aug-07
	4.13	7.83	15.79	22.58	59.09	1.47	1.15	8.39	0.98	10.2	268.9	1	79	20	0	43	17.66	-17.89			Aug-07
	4.28	8.24	16.61	25.20	65.17	2.06	0.4	8.4	0.98	10.33	268.9	1	79	20	0	43	18.28	-17.69			Aug-07
	4.23	8.05	16.30	24.30	63.06	1.85	0.65	8.41	0.98	10.27	268.9	1	79	20	0	43	18	-17.7			Aug-07
100	4.64	8.55	16.99	25.01	65.13	1.54	0.87	8.69	0.94	10.05	221.2	1	85	14	0	36	18.56	-18.94	5.75		Aug-07

Fund Name	Ticker Symbol	Traded On	Fund Type	Category and (Prospectus Objective)	Overall Rating	Reward Rating	Risk Rating	Recent Up/ Downgrade	Open to New Investors	Min Initial Investment
	MARKET		FUND TYPE, CATEGORY & OBJECTIVE		RATINGS				MINIMUMS	
Nationwide Destination 2040 Fund Class C	NWMCX	NAS CM	Open End	Target Date 2021-2045 (Asset Alloc)	B-	C+	B-	Down	Y	2,000
Nationwide Destination 2040 Fund Class R	NWMDX	NAS CM	Open End	Target Date 2021-2045 (Asset Alloc)	B-	B-	B-	Down	Y	0
Nationwide Destination 2040 Fund Class R6	NWMHX	NAS CM	Open End	Target Date 2021-2045 (Asset Alloc)	B-	B-	B-	Down	Y	1,000,000
Nationwide Destination 2040 Fund Institutional Service Cls	NWMSX	NAS CM	Open End	Target Date 2021-2045 (Asset Alloc)	B-	B-	B-	Down	Y	50,000
Nationwide Destination 2045 Fund Class A	NWNAX	NAS CM	Open End	Target Date 2021-2045 (Asset Alloc)	B-	B-	B-	Down	Y	2,000
Nationwide Destination 2045 Fund Class C	NWNCX	NAS CM	Open End	Target Date 2021-2045 (Asset Alloc)	B-	B-	B-	Down	Y	2,000
Nationwide Destination 2045 Fund Class R	NWNBX	NAS CM	Open End	Target Date 2021-2045 (Asset Alloc)	B-	B-	B-	Down	Y	0
Nationwide Destination 2045 Fund Class R6	NWNIX	NAS CM	Open End	Target Date 2021-2045 (Asset Alloc)	B-	B-	B-	Down	Y	1,000,000
Nationwide Destination 2045 Fund Institutional Service Cls	NWNSX	NAS CM	Open End	Target Date 2021-2045 (Asset Alloc)	B-	B-	B-	Down	Y	50,000
Nationwide Destination 2050 Fund Class A	NWOAX	NAS CM	Open End	Target Date 2046+ (Asset Alloc)	B-	B-	B-	Down	Y	2,000
Nationwide Destination 2050 Fund Class C	NWOCX	NAS CM	Open End	Target Date 2046+ (Asset Alloc)	B-	B-	B-	Down	Y	2,000
Nationwide Destination 2050 Fund Class R	NWOBX	NAS CM	Open End	Target Date 2046+ (Asset Alloc)	B-	B-	B-	Down	Y	0
Nationwide Destination 2050 Fund Class R6	NWOIX	NAS CM	Open End	Target Date 2046+ (Asset Alloc)	B-	B-	B-	Down	Y	1,000,000
Nationwide Destination 2050 Fund Institutional Service Cls	NWOSX	NAS CM	Open End	Target Date 2046+ (Asset Alloc)	B-	B-	B-	Down	Y	50,000
Nationwide Destination 2055 Fund Class A	NTDAX	NAS CM	Open End	Target Date 2046+ (Asset Alloc)	B-	B-	B-	Down	Y	2,000
Nationwide Destination 2055 Fund Class C	NTDCX	NAS CM	Open End	Target Date 2046+ (Asset Alloc)	B-	B-	B-	Down	Y	2,000
Nationwide Destination 2055 Fund Class R	NTDTX	NAS CM	Open End	Target Date 2046+ (Asset Alloc)	B-	B-	B-	Down	Y	0
Nationwide Destination 2055 Fund Class R6	NTDIX	NAS CM	Open End	Target Date 2046+ (Asset Alloc)	B-	B-	B-	Down	Y	1,000,000
Nationwide Destination 2055 Fund Institutional Service Cls	NTDSX	NAS CM	Open End	Target Date 2046+ (Asset Alloc)	B-	B-	B-	Down	Y	50,000
Nationwide Destination 2060 Fund Class A	NWWRX	NAS CM	Open End	Target Date 2046+ (Asset Alloc)	C+	C+	B-	Down	Y	2,000
Nationwide Destination 2060 Fund Class C	NWWSX	NAS CM	Open End	Target Date 2046+ (Asset Alloc)	C+	C+	B-	Down	Y	2,000
Nationwide Destination 2060 Fund Class R	NWWTX	NAS CM	Open End	Target Date 2046+ (Asset Alloc)	C+	C+	B-	Down	Y	0
Nationwide Destination 2060 Fund Class R6	NWWUX	NAS CM	Open End	Target Date 2046+ (Asset Alloc)	C+	C+	B-	Down	Y	1,000,000
Nationwide Destination 2060 Fund Institutional Service Cls	NWWVX	NAS CM	Open End	Target Date 2046+ (Asset Alloc)	C+	C+	B-	Down	Y	50,000
Nationwide Fund Class A	NWFAX	NAS CM	Open End	US Equity Large Cap Blend (Growth & Income)	B	B	B-		Y	2,000
Nationwide Fund Class C	GTRCX	NAS CM	Open End	US Equity Large Cap Blend (Growth & Income)	B-	B	B-	Down	Y	2,000
Nationwide Fund Class R	GNWRX	NAS CM	Open End	US Equity Large Cap Blend (Growth & Income)	B	B	B-		Y	0
Nationwide Fund Institutional Service Class	MUIFX	NAS CM	Open End	US Equity Large Cap Blend (Growth & Income)	B	B	B-		Y	50,000
Nationwide Geneva Mid Cap Growth Fund Class A	NWHVX	NAS CM	Open End	US Equity Mid Cap (Growth)	B	B	A-	Up	Y	2,000
Nationwide Geneva Mid Cap Growth Fund Class C	NWHWX	NAS CM	Open End	US Equity Mid Cap (Growth)	B	B-	A-	Up	Y	2,000
Nationwide Geneva Mid Cap Growth Fund Class R6	NWKAX	NAS CM	Open End	US Equity Mid Cap (Growth)	B	B	A-	Up	Y	1,000,000
Nationwide Geneva Mid Cap Growth Fund Inst Service Cls	NWHYX	NAS CM	Open End	US Equity Mid Cap (Growth)	B	B	A-	Up	Y	50,000
Nationwide Geneva Small Cap Growth Fund Class A	NWHZX	NAS CM	Open End	US Equity Small Cap (Small Company)	A-	A	A-	Up	Y	2,000
Nationwide Geneva Small Cap Growth Fund Class C	NWKBX	NAS CM	Open End	US Equity Small Cap (Small Company)	A-	A-	A-	Up	Y	2,000
Nationwide Geneva Small Cap Growth Fund Class R6	NWKCX	NAS CM	Open End	US Equity Small Cap (Small Company)	A-	A	B	Up	Y	1,000,000
Nationwide Geneva Small Cap Growth Fund Inst Service Cls	NWKDX	NAS CM	Open End	US Equity Small Cap (Small Company)	A-	A	A-	Up	Y	50,000
Nationwide Global Sustainable Equity Fund Class A	GGEAX	NAS CM	Open End	Global Equity (World Stock)	C+	B-	C	Down	Y	2,000
Nationwide Global Sustainable Equity Fund Class C	GGECX	NAS CM	Open End	Global Equity (World Stock)	C+	B-	C	Up	Y	2,000
Nationwide Global Sustainable Equity Fund Class R6	GGEIX	NAS CM	Open End	Global Equity (World Stock)	C+	B-	C	Down	Y	1,000,000
Nationwide Global Sustainable Equity Fund Inst Service Cls	GGESX	NAS CM	Open End	Global Equity (World Stock)	C+	B-	C		Y	50,000
Nationwide Growth Fund Class A	NMFAX	NAS CM	Open End	US Equity Large Cap Growth (Growth)	B	B	B	Up	Y	2,000
Nationwide Growth Fund Class C	GCGRX	NAS CM	Open End	US Equity Large Cap Growth (Growth)	B	B	B	Up	Y	2,000
Nationwide Growth Fund Class R	GGFRX	NAS CM	Open End	US Equity Large Cap Growth (Growth)	B	B	B	Up	Y	0
Nationwide Growth Fund Class R6	MUIGX	NAS CM	Open End	US Equity Large Cap Growth (Growth)	B	B	B	Up	Y	1,000,000
Nationwide Growth Fund Institutional Service Class	NGISX	NAS CM	Open End	US Equity Large Cap Growth (Growth)	B	B	B	Up	Y	50,000
Nationwide International Index Fund Class A	GIIAX	NAS CM	Open End	Global Equity Large Cap (Foreign Stock)	B-	C+	B	Up	Y	2,000
Nationwide International Index Fund Class C	GIICX	NAS CM	Open End	Global Equity Large Cap (Foreign Stock)	B-	C+	B	Up	Y	2,000
Nationwide International Index Fund Class R	GIIRX	NAS CM	Open End	Global Equity Large Cap (Foreign Stock)	B-	C+	B	Up	Y	0
Nationwide International Index Fund Class R6	GIXIX	NAS CM	Open End	Global Equity Large Cap (Foreign Stock)	B-	C+	B	Up	Y	1,000,000
Nationwide International Index Fund Institutional Service	NWXPX	NAS CM	Open End	Global Equity Large Cap (Foreign Stock)	C+	C+	C+	Up	Y	50,000
Nationwide International Small Cap Fund Class A	NWXSX	NAS CM	Open End	Global Equity Mid/Small Cap (Foreign Stock)	D-	D+	A-		Y	2,000
Nationwide International Small Cap Fund Class R6	NWXUX	NAS CM	Open End	Global Equity Mid/Small Cap (Foreign Stock)	D-	D+	A-		Y	1,000,000

★ Expanded analysis of this fund is included in Section II.

Min Additional Investment	3-Month Total Return	6-Month Total Return	1-Year Total Return	3-Year Total Return	5-Year Total Return	Dividend Yield (TTM)	Expense Ratio	3-Yr Std Deviation	3-Year Beta	NAV	Total Assets (MIL)	%Cash	%Stocks	%Bonds	%Other	Turnover Ratio	Last Bull Market Total Return	Last Bear Market Total Return	Front End Fee (%)	Back End Fee (%)	Inception Date
TOTAL RETURNS						PERFORMANCE				ASSETS		ASSET ALLOCATION & TURNOVER					BULL & BEAR		FEES		
100	4.41	8.19	16.36	22.74	60.43	1.23	1.43	8.69	0.94	9.99	221.2	1	85	14	0	36	18.15	-19.03		1.00	Aug-07
	4.48	8.33	16.72	23.88	62.82	1.36	1.14	8.65	0.94	9.99	221.2	1	85	14	0	36	18.27	-18.95			Aug-07
	4.72	8.74	17.63	26.77	68.97	1.93	0.39	8.69	0.94	10.13	221.2	1	85	14	0	36	18.74	-18.65			Aug-07
	4.57	8.52	17.28	25.67	66.79	1.72	0.64	8.75	0.95	10.09	221.2	1	85	14	0	36	18.56	-18.72			Aug-07
100	4.74	8.86	17.85	26.35	68.32	1.44	0.87	9.3	0.98	10.51	172.2	1	89	10	0	34	18.58	-19.08	5.75		Aug-07
100	4.64	8.52	17.05	24.04	63.24	1.05	1.49	9.26	0.97	10.39	172.2	1	89	10	0	34	18.24	-19.2		1.00	Aug-07
	4.70	8.67	17.40	25.30	65.90	1.27	1.14	9.29	0.98	10.42	172.2	1	89	10	0	34	18.32	-19.11			Aug-07
	4.94	9.06	18.37	28.14	72.40	1.8	0.39	9.32	0.98	10.57	172.2	1	89	10	0	34	18.95	-18.92			Aug-07
	4.81	9.00	18.11	27.17	70.20	1.61	0.64	9.32	0.98	10.49	172.2	1	89	10	0	34	18.82	-18.95			Aug-07
100	4.94	9.00	18.16	26.95	68.92	1.42	0.87	9.38	0.97	9.11	133.1	0	91	8	0	33	18.55	-19.21	5.75		Aug-07
100	4.78	8.64	17.34	24.64	64.37	1.09	1.44	9.38	0.97	8.94	133.1	0	91	8	0	33	18.27	-19.45		1.00	Aug-07
	4.82	8.85	17.75	25.87	66.77	1.26	1.14	9.35	0.97	8.99	133.1	0	91	8	0	33	18.45	-19.35			Aug-07
	5.06	9.37	18.63	28.78	73.01	1.79	0.39	9.35	0.97	9.13	133.1	0	91	8	0	33	18.94	-19.15			Aug-07
	5.01	9.14	18.39	27.77	70.96	1.58	0.64	9.37	0.97	9.1	133.1	0	91	8	0	33	18.62	-19.14			Aug-07
100	4.97	9.22	18.45	27.30	69.36	1.38	0.88	9.46	0.98	13.89	69.9	0	93	6	0	26	18.8	-19.24	5.75		Dec-10
100	4.90	8.93	17.88	25.20	64.82	1.01	1.43	9.47	0.98	13.88	69.9	0	93	6	0	26	18.35	-19.41		1.00	Dec-10
	4.91	9.02	18.18	26.25	67.08	1.21	1.14	9.5	0.98	13.86	69.9	0	93	6	0	26	18.48	-19.35			Dec-10
	5.14	9.43	19.06	29.15	73.56	1.76	0.39	9.47	0.98	13.96	69.9	0	93	6	0	26	19	-19.14			Dec-10
	5.08	9.31	18.80	28.24	71.44	1.55	0.64	9.48	0.98	13.95	69.9	0	93	6	0	26	18.97	-19.14			Dec-10
100	4.99	9.22	18.56	27.57		1.4	0.89	9.48	0.97	11.2	12.0	0	93	6	0	45			5.75		Nov-14
100	4.86	8.95	17.87	25.36		1.02	1.64	9.45	0.97	11.18	12.0	0	93	6	0	45				1.00	Nov-14
	4.93	9.00	18.26	26.72		1.27	1.14	9.46	0.97	11.19	12.0	0	93	6	0	45					Nov-14
	5.10	9.46	19.04	29.18		1.78	0.39	9.49	0.97	11.22	12.0	0	93	6	0	45					Nov-14
	4.95	9.23	18.78	28.42		1.57	0.64	9.48	0.97	11.21	12.0	0	93	6	0	45					Nov-14
100	5.80	10.51	19.90	33.23	98.66	0.93	1	10.27	1.01	25.03	1,043	0	100	0	0	79	23.58	-18.43	5.75		May-98
100	5.61	10.06	19.04	30.17	91.17	0.35	1.75	10.3	1.01	23.21	1,043	0	100	0	0	79	23.09	-18.66		1.00	Mar-01
	5.70	10.25	19.40	31.43	94.52	0.53	1.42	10.3	1.01	24.47	1,043	0	100	0	0	79	23.39	-18.57			Oct-03
	5.89	10.65	20.20	34.19	100.94	1.15	0.74	10.31	1.01	24.61	1,043	0	100	0	0	79	23.81	-18.39			May-33
100	6.20	8.21	23.00	28.84	79.58	0	1.14	10.74	0.89	25.08	1,060	3	97	0	0	25	29.06	-17.05	5.75		Jan-99
100	5.99	7.82	22.09	26.01	73.48	0	1.89	10.7	0.89	20.32	1,060	3	97	0	0	25	28.65	-17.24		1.00	May-00
	6.30	8.41	23.45	30.30	82.61	0	0.78	10.7	0.89	26.17	1,060	3	97	0	0	25	29.06	-17.05			Sep-13
	6.28	8.35	23.30	29.76	81.84	0	0.93	10.71	0.89	25.96	1,060	3	97	0	0	25	29.27	-16.96			Jun-09
100	2.83	9.19	21.84	46.97	106.57	0	1.3	11.87	0.73	54.12	734.2	5	95	0	0	22	22.97	-18.3	5.75		Jun-09
100	2.64	8.80	20.96	43.78	99.62	0	2.02	11.87	0.73	50.7	734.2	5	95	0	0	22	22.51	-18.5		1.00	Jun-09
	2.92	9.41	22.30	48.64	110.34	0	0.93	11.88	0.73	55.89	734.2	5	95	0	0	22	23.12	-18.18			Sep-13
	2.90	9.34	22.15	48.16	109.38	0	1.03	11.86	0.73	55.61	734.2	5	95	0	0	22	23.12	-18.18			Jun-09
100	4.77	10.54	24.06	22.82	59.98	1.11	1.37	12.28	1.13	18.63	57.8	2	98	0	0	38	24.45	-25.53	5.75		Jun-97
100	4.62	10.10	23.16	19.98	54.05	0.59	2.12	12.29	1.13	17.65	57.8	2	98	0	0	38	23.85	-25.81		1.00	Nov-01
	4.89	10.75	24.62	24.29	62.91	1.37	0.95	12.26	1.13	19.16	57.8	2	98	0	0	38	24.6	-25.41			Jan-94
	4.84	10.70	24.48	23.86	62.19	1.29	1.06	12.29	1.13	19.17	57.8	2	98	0	0	38	24.59	-25.41			Nov-12
100	7.29	13.44	26.85	35.57	107.76	0.17	0.98	10.52	0.96	11.65	216.8	2	98	0	0	82	26.79	-17.02	5.75		May-98
100	7.00	12.93	25.62	32.24	99.74	0.05	1.77	10.52	0.96	8.97	216.8	2	98	0	0	82	26.37	-17.36		1.00	Mar-01
	7.07	13.14	26.17	34.70	105.24	0.1	1.41	10.61	0.97	11.38	216.8	2	98	0	0	82	26.54	-17.18			Oct-03
	7.35	13.59	27.15	36.75	110.94	0.37	0.66	10.5	0.96	12.27	216.8	2	98	0	0	82	27.02	-17.04			Feb-61
	7.25	13.48	26.85	35.83	108.67	0.22	0.87	10.51	0.96	12.33	216.8	2	98	0	0	82	27.14	-17.04			Nov-11
100	3.68	9.01	24.73	23.34	42.78	1.93	0.71	11.53	0.93	8.47	1,553	0	100	0	0	6	12.9	-23.58	5.75		Dec-99
100	3.60	8.57	24.00	20.95	38.08	1.5	1.39	11.48	0.93	7.96	1,553	0	100	0	0	6	12.45	-23.67		1.00	Feb-05
	3.60	8.85	24.30	22.29	41.11	1.74	1	11.49	0.93	8.47	1,553	0	100	0	0	6	12.84	-23.53			Mar-07
	3.86	9.15	25.19	24.82	45.52	2.27	0.31	11.58	0.94	8.52	1,553	0	100	0	0	6	13.12	-23.34			Dec-99
	3.73	9.12	24.99	24.62	45.29		0.56	11.6	0.94	8.51	1,553	0	100	0	0	6	13.13	-23.34			Dec-16
100	5.51	13.42	30.36				1.49			11.78	567.2	1	99	0	0	90			5.75		Dec-16
	5.54	13.63	30.82				0.99			11.8	567.2	1	99	0	0	90					Dec-16

	MARKET		FUND TYPE, CATEGORY & OBJECTIVE		RATINGS				MINIMUMS	
Fund Name	Ticker Symbol	Traded On	Fund Type	Category and (Prospectus Objective)	Overall Rating	Reward Rating	Risk Rating	Recent Up/ Downgrade	Open to New Investors	Min Initial Investment
Nationwide Intl Small Cap Fund Inst Service Cls	NWXVX	NAS CM	Open End	Global Equity Mid/Small Cap (Foreign Stock)	D-	D+	A-		Y	50,000
Nationwide Investor Destinations Aggressive Fund Class A	NDAAX	NAS CM	Open End	Aggressive Alloc (Growth & Income)	B-	B-	B-	Down	Y	2,000
Nationwide Investor Destinations Aggressive Fund Class C	NDACX	NAS CM	Open End	Aggressive Alloc (Growth & Income)	B-	B-	B-	Down	Y	2,000
Nationwide Investor Destinations Aggressive Fund Class R	GAFRX	NAS CM	Open End	Aggressive Alloc (Growth & Income)	B-	B-	B-	Down	Y	0
Nationwide Investor Destinations Aggressive Fund Class R6	GAIDX	NAS CM	Open End	Aggressive Alloc (Growth & Income)	B-	B-	B-	Down	Y	1,000,000
Nationwide Inv Destinations Aggressive Fund Inst Serv Cls	NWWHX	NAS CM	Open End	Aggressive Alloc (Growth & Income)	B-	B-	B-	Down	Y	50,000
Nationwide Inv Destinations Aggressive Fund Service Cls	NDASX	NAS CM	Open End	Aggressive Alloc (Growth & Income)	B-	B-	B-	Down	Y	50,000
Nationwide Investor Destinations Conservative Fund Class A	NDCAX	NAS CM	Open End	Cautious Alloc (Growth & Income)	B-	C	B	Up	Y	2,000
Nationwide Investor Destinations Conservative Fund Class C	NDCCX	NAS CM	Open End	Cautious Alloc (Growth & Income)	B-	C	A-	Up	Y	2,000
Nationwide Investor Destinations Conservative Fund Class R	GCFRX	NAS CM	Open End	Cautious Alloc (Growth & Income)	B	C	A	Up	Y	0
Nationwide Investor Destinations Conservative Fund Cls R6	GIMCX	NAS CM	Open End	Cautious Alloc (Growth & Income)	B-	C	B+	Up	Y	1,000,000
Nationwide Inv Destinations Cons Inst Serv Cls	NWWLX	NAS CM	Open End	Cautious Alloc (Growth & Income)	B-	C	B+	Up	Y	50,000
Nationwide Inv Destinations Conservative Fund Service Cls	NDCSX	NAS CM	Open End	Cautious Alloc (Growth & Income)	B-	C	B	Up	Y	50,000
Nationwide Investor Destinations Moderate Fund Class A	NADMX	NAS CM	Open End	Moderate Alloc (Growth & Income)	B-	C+	B	Up	Y	2,000
Nationwide Investor Destinations Moderate Fund Class C	NCDMX	NAS CM	Open End	Moderate Alloc (Growth & Income)	B-	C+	B	Up	Y	2,000
Nationwide Investor Destinations Moderate Fund Class R	GMDRX	NAS CM	Open End	Moderate Alloc (Growth & Income)	B-	C+	B	Up	Y	0
Nationwide Investor Destinations Moderate Fund Class R6	GMDIX	NAS CM	Open End	Moderate Alloc (Growth & Income)	B-	C+	B	Up	Y	1,000,000
Nationwide Investor Destinations Moderate Fund Cls Service	NSDMX	NAS CM	Open End	Moderate Alloc (Growth & Income)	B-	C+	B	Up	Y	50,000
Nationwide Inv Destinations Moderate Fund Inst Service Cls	NWWJX	NAS CM	Open End	Moderate Alloc (Growth & Income)	B-	C+	B	Up	Y	50,000
Nationwide Inv Destinations Mod Aggress Fund Cls A	NDMAX	NAS CM	Open End	Aggressive Alloc (Growth & Income)	B-	B-	B-	Down	Y	2,000
Nationwide Inv Destinations Mod Aggress Fund Cls C	NDMCX	NAS CM	Open End	Aggressive Alloc (Growth & Income)	B-	C+	B-	Down	Y	2,000
Nationwide Inv Destinations Mod Aggress Fund Cls R	GMARX	NAS CM	Open End	Aggressive Alloc (Growth & Income)	B-	C+	B-	Down	Y	0
Nationwide Inv Destinations Mod Aggress Fund Cls R6	GMIAX	NAS CM	Open End	Aggressive Alloc (Growth & Income)	B-	B-	B-	Down	Y	1,000,000
Nationwide Inv Destinations Mod Aggress Fund Inst Serv Cls	NWWIX	NAS CM	Open End	Aggressive Alloc (Growth & Income)	B-	B-	B-	Down	Y	50,000
Nationwide Inv Destinations Mod Aggress Fund Serv Cls	NDMSX	NAS CM	Open End	Aggressive Alloc (Growth & Income)	B-	B-	B-	Down	Y	50,000
Nationwide Inv Destinations Mod Conservative Fund Cls A	NADCX	NAS CM	Open End	Cautious Alloc (Growth & Income)	B-	C+	B	Up	Y	2,000
Nationwide Inv Destinations Mod Conservative Fund Cls C	NCDCX	NAS CM	Open End	Cautious Alloc (Growth & Income)	B-	C+	B	Up	Y	2,000
Nationwide Inv Destinations Mod Conservative Fund Cls R	GMMRX	NAS CM	Open End	Cautious Alloc (Growth & Income)	B-	C+	B	Up	Y	0
Nationwide Inv Destinations Mod Conservative Fund Cls R6	GMIMX	NAS CM	Open End	Cautious Alloc (Growth & Income)	B-	C+	B	Up	Y	1,000,000
Nationwide Inv Destinations Mod Cons Inst Serv Cls	NWWKX	NAS CM	Open End	Cautious Alloc (Growth & Income)	B-	C+	B	Up	Y	50,000
Nationwide Inv Destinations Mod Conservative Fund Serv Cls	NSDCX	NAS CM	Open End	Cautious Alloc (Growth & Income)	B-	C+	B	Up	Y	50,000
Nationwide Large Cap Equity Fund Class A	NWGHX	NAS CM	Open End	US Equity Large Cap Blend (Growth)	B-	B	B-	Down	Y	2,000
Nationwide Large Cap Equity Fund Class C	NWGIX	NAS CM	Open End	US Equity Large Cap Blend (Growth)	B-	B-	B-	Down	Y	2,000
Nationwide Large Cap Equity Fund Class R6	NWGJX	NAS CM	Open End	US Equity Large Cap Blend (Growth)	B	B	B-		Y	1,000,000
Nationwide Large Cap Equity Fund Institutional Service Cls	NWGKX	NAS CM	Open End	US Equity Large Cap Blend (Growth)	B	B	B-		Y	50,000
Nationwide Long/Short Equity Fund Class R6	NWLFX	NAS CM	Open End	Long/Short Equity (Growth)	B-	C+	B-	Down	Y	1,000,000
Nationwide Long/Short Equity Fund Inst Service Cls	NWLGX	NAS CM	Open End	Long/Short Equity (Growth)	B-	C+	B	Down	Y	50,000
Nationwide Loomis All Cap Growth Fund Class A	NWZLX	NAS CM	Open End	US Equity Large Cap Growth (Growth)	U	U	U		Y	2,000
Nationwide Loomis All Cap Growth Fund Class R6	NWZMX	NAS CM	Open End	US Equity Large Cap Growth (Growth)	U	U	U		Y	1,000,000
Nationwide Loomis All Cap Growth Fund Inst Service Cls	NWZNX	NAS CM	Open End	US Equity Large Cap Growth (Growth)	U	U	U		Y	50,000
Nationwide Mid Cap Market Index Fund Class A	GMXAX	NAS CM	Open End	US Equity Mid Cap (Growth)	B	B	B		Y	2,000
Nationwide Mid Cap Market Index Fund Class C	GMCCX	NAS CM	Open End	US Equity Mid Cap (Growth)	B	B	B	Up	Y	2,000
Nationwide Mid Cap Market Index Fund Class R	GMXRX	NAS CM	Open End	US Equity Mid Cap (Growth)	B	B	B	Up	Y	0
Nationwide Mid Cap Market Index Fund Class R6	GMXIX	NAS CM	Open End	US Equity Mid Cap (Growth)	B	B	B		Y	1,000,000
Nationwide Mid Cap Mkt Index Fund Inst Service Cls	NWXQX	NAS CM	Open End	US Equity Mid Cap (Growth)	B	B	B		Y	50,000
Nationwide S&P 500 Index Fund Class A	GRMAX	NAS CM	Open End	US Equity Large Cap Blend (Growth & Income)	B	B	B		Y	2,000
Nationwide S&P 500 Index Fund Class C	GRMCX	NAS CM	Open End	US Equity Large Cap Blend (Growth & Income)	B-	B-	B	Down	Y	2,000
Nationwide S&P 500 Index Fund Class R	GRMRX	NAS CM	Open End	US Equity Large Cap Blend (Growth & Income)	B	B-	B		Y	0
Nationwide S&P 500 Index Fund Class R6	GRMIX	NAS CM	Open End	US Equity Large Cap Blend (Growth & Income)	B	B	B		Y	1,000,000
Nationwide S&P 500 Index Fund Institutional Service Class	GRISX	NAS CM	Open End	US Equity Large Cap Blend (Growth & Income)	B	B	B		Y	50,000
Nationwide S&P 500 Index Fund Service Class	GRMSX	NAS CM	Open End	US Equity Large Cap Blend (Growth & Income)	B	B-	B		Y	25,000
Nationwide Small Cap Index Fund Class A	GMRAX	NAS CM	Open End	US Equity Small Cap (Small Company)	B+	A-	B	Up	Y	2,000

★Expanded analysis of this fund is included in Section II.

Min Additional Investment	3-Month Total Return	6-Month Total Return	1-Year Total Return	3-Year Total Return	5-Year Total Return	Dividend Yield (TTM)	Expense Ratio	3-Yr Std Deviation	3-Year Beta	NAV	Total Assets (MIL)	%Cash	%Stocks	%Bonds	%Other	Turnover Ratio	Last Bull Market Total Return	Last Bear Market Total Return	Front End Fee (%)	Back End Fee (%)	Inception Date
TOTAL RETURNS						PERFORMANCE				ASSETS		ASSET ALLOCATION & TURNOVER					BULL & BEAR		FEES		
	5.58	13.57	30.76				1.24			11.8	567.2	1	99	0	0	90					Dec-16
100	4.99	9.76	19.88	27.71	72.30	1.56	0.88	9.12	0.86	10.2	1,098	0	92	7	0	29	20.59	-19.58	5.75		Mar-00
100	4.66	9.27	18.94	24.87	66.20	1.01	1.62	9.12	0.86	9.83	1,098	0	92	7	0	29	19.97	-19.79		1.00	Mar-01
	4.82	9.50	19.38	26.59	69.71	1.33	1.18	9.18	0.87	9.96	1,098	0	92	7	0	29	20.22	-19.6			Oct-03
	5.02	9.93	20.24	29.07	75.30	1.83	0.53	9.19	0.87	10.34	1,098	0	92	7	0	29	20.75	-19.41			Dec-04
	5.05	9.89	20.14	28.76	73.87	1.76	0.64	9.17	0.87	10.21	1,098	0	92	7	0	29	20.53	-19.62			Mar-14
	4.86	9.71	19.76	27.58	71.82	1.51	0.92	9.19	0.87	10.22	1,098	0	92	7	0	29	20.53	-19.62			Mar-00
100	1.48	3.00	5.84	10.33	19.29	2.04	0.81	2.28	0.34	10.29	742.6	30	21	49	0	31	5.45	-2.3	5.75		Mar-00
100	1.30	2.53	4.99	7.90	15.02	1.34	1.56	2.25	0.33	10.24	742.6	30	21	49	0	31	5	-2.59		1.00	Mar-01
	1.40	2.84	5.51	9.37	17.39	1.73	1.12	2.26	0.33	10.27	742.6	30	21	49	0	31	5.17	-2.41			Oct-03
	1.66	3.26	6.26	11.59	21.42	2.35	0.48	2.24	0.33	10.35	742.6	30	21	49	0	31	5.57	-2.18			Dec-04
	1.54	3.12	6.08	11.21	20.25	2.27	0.56	2.25	0.32	10.32	742.6	30	21	49	0	31	5.37	-2.38			Mar-14
	1.56	2.96	5.75	10.28	18.92	1.97	0.87	2.24	0.33	10.33	742.6	30	21	49	0	31	5.37	-2.38			Mar-00
100	3.65	7.01	13.74	20.04	46.43	1.93	0.87	6.04	0.56	10.15	1,403	14	62	24	0	24	13.58	-11.58	5.75		Mar-00
100	3.43	6.54	12.80	17.45	41.23	1.27	1.59	6.06	0.56	9.94	1,403	14	62	24	0	24	13.18	-11.84		1.00	Mar-01
	3.58	6.84	13.45	19.10	44.26	1.71	1.15	6.02	0.56	9.87	1,403	14	62	24	0	24	13.38	-11.73			Oct-03
	3.67	7.14	14.11	21.36	48.85	2.25	0.51	6.02	0.56	10.09	1,403	14	62	24	0	24	13.89	-11.47			Dec-04
	3.66	7.02	13.63	20.00	46.15	1.89	0.91	6.07	0.57	10.1	1,403	14	62	24	0	24	13.55	-11.65			Mar-00
	3.65	7.10	14.05	20.93	47.79	2.2	0.59	6.05	0.56	10.08	1,403	14	62	23	0	24	13.55	-11.65			Mar-14
100	4.43	8.79	17.67	24.87	61.68	1.73	0.9	8.07	0.76	10.52	1,733	1	82	17	0	27	17.43	-16.16	5.75		Mar-00
100	4.27	8.34	16.74	22.25	55.84	1.11	1.63	8.03	0.76	10.21	1,733	1	82	17	0	27	17.04	-16.41		1.00	Mar-01
	4.38	8.58	17.26	23.89	59.24	1.51	1.19	8.06	0.76	10.22	1,733	1	82	17	0	27	17.28	-16.32			Oct-03
	4.63	9.00	18.09	26.38	64.62	2.03	0.54	8.08	0.76	10.51	1,733	1	82	17	0	27	17.66	-16.06			Dec-04
	4.62	8.97	18.04	25.91	63.43	1.97	0.64	8.09	0.76	10.49	1,733	1	82	17	0	27	17.43	-16.16			Mar-14
	4.53	8.79	17.64	24.88	61.24	1.68	0.94	8.05	0.76	10.5	1,733	1	82	17	0	27	17.44	-16.25			Mar-00
100	2.49	4.77	9.46	15.22	32.45	2.04	0.83	4.05	0.11	10.2	488.6	23	41	37	0	23	9.8	-6.72	5.75		Mar-00
100	2.41	4.51	8.78	12.89	27.84	1.33	1.57	3.96	0.12	10.16	488.6	23	41	37	0	23	9.35	-7		1.00	Mar-01
	2.51	4.71	9.20	14.23	30.46	1.73	1.13	3.98	0.11	10.23	488.6	23	41	37	0	23	9.6	-6.98			Oct-03
	2.55	5.00	9.82	16.47	34.75	2.32	0.49	4.04	0.12	10.32	488.6	23	41	37	0	23	9.99	-6.63			Dec-04
	2.64	4.98	9.77	16.19	33.61	2.25	0.59	4.02	0.12	10.28	488.6	23	41	37	0	23	9.81	-6.85			Mar-14
	2.55	4.91	9.53	15.14	32.21	1.96	0.88	4.02	0.11	10.28	488.6	23	41	37	0	23	9.81	-6.86			Mar-00
100	7.94	11.76	21.93	32.18	96.84	0.47	1.19	10.55	0.95	13.71	75.6	2	98	0	0	82	25.89	-15.05	5.75		Jun-00
100	7.72	11.38	21.10	29.73	90.95	0.17	1.88	10.53	0.95	13.06	75.6	2	98	0	0	82	25.64	-15.39		1.00	Nov-03
	8.01	11.93	22.41	33.73	100.76	0.78	0.82	10.57	0.95	13.75	75.6	2	98	0	0	82	26.33	-15.05			Sep-13
	7.97	11.85	22.14	33.23	99.49	0.65	0.89	10.52	0.95	13.76	75.6	2	98	0	0	82	26.33	-15.05			May-00
	4.72	8.32	16.50	21.85	53.71	0	1.77	8.81	0.78	14.19	11.2	34	66	0	0	35					Aug-15
	4.58	8.19	16.20	21.34	53.06	0	1.87	8.82	0.78	14.13	11.2	34	66	0	0	35					Sep-12
100	5.62	12.47					1.35			11.27	205.9	1	99	0	0	12			5.75		May-17
	6.13	13.22					0.85			11.3	205.9	1	99	0	0	12					May-17
	5.71	12.56					1.1			11.29	205.9	1	99	0	0	12					May-17
100	6.08	9.33	15.43	33.11	97.88	0.72	0.68	11.08	1	17.74	1,283	0	100	0	0	18	27.3	-23.02	5.75		Dec-99
100	5.90	8.93	14.62	30.42	91.41	0.47	1.37	11.05	1	16.38	1,283	0	100	0	0	18	26.96	-23.2		1.00	Oct-03
	5.97	9.12	15.08	32.00	95.51	0.57	0.97	11.06	1	17.51	1,283	0	100	0	0	18	27.39	-23.09			Mar-07
	6.15	9.52	15.85	34.74	101.84	1.05	0.27	11.07	1	18.03	1,283	0	100	0	0	18	27.71	-22.89			Dec-99
	6.17	9.46	15.76	33.48	98.44		0.52	11.09	1	18.03	1,283	0	100	0	0	18	27.3	-23.02			Dec-16
100	6.49	11.10	21.09	34.45	105.65	1.28	0.6	10.12	1	16.01	2,942	0	100	0	0	12	24.79	-16.54	5.75		Dec-99
100	6.34	10.74	20.36	31.89	99.29	0.8	1.24	10.08	1	15.67	2,942	0	100	0	0	12	24.22	-16.71		1.00	Oct-03
	6.40	10.94	20.74	33.37	102.63	1.18	0.87	10.05	1	15.96	2,942	0	100	0	0	12	24.39	-16.6			Jan-07
	6.61	11.38	21.63	36.22	110.09	1.62	0.17	10.09	1	16.15	2,942	0	100	0	0	12	25	-16.35			Dec-99
	6.57	11.20	21.31	35.21	107.39	1.41	0.42	10.11	1	16.11	2,942	0	100	0	0	12	24.84	-16.47			Nov-98
	6.49	11.10	21.16	34.60	105.81	1.29	0.57	10.1	1	16.03	2,942	0	100	0	0	12	24.68	-16.45			Nov-98
100	3.17	8.90	13.97	30.20	93.38	0.74	0.66	14.13	1	13.76	595.6	0	100	0	0	15	27.29	-25.17	5.75		Dec-99

	MARKET			FUND TYPE, CATEGORY & OBJECTIVE	RATINGS				MINIMUMS	
Fund Name	Ticker Symbol	Traded On	Fund Type	Category and (Prospectus Objective)	Overall Rating	Reward Rating	Risk Rating	Recent Up/ Downgrade	Open to New Investors	Min Initial Investment
Nationwide Small Cap Index Fund Class C	GMRCX	NAS CM	Open End	US Equity Small Cap (Small Company)	B	B+	B	Up	Y	2,000
Nationwide Small Cap Index Fund Class R	GMSRX	NAS CM	Open End	US Equity Small Cap (Small Company)	B+	A-	B	Up	Y	0
Nationwide Small Cap Index Fund Class R6	GMRIX	NAS CM	Open End	US Equity Small Cap (Small Company)	B+	A-	B	Up	Y	1,000,000
Nationwide Small Cap Index Fund Institutional Service Cls	NWXRX	NAS CM	Open End	US Equity Small Cap (Small Company)	B+	A-	B	Up	Y	50,000
Nationwide Small Company Growth Fund Class A	NWSAX	NAS CM	Open End	US Equity Small Cap (Small Company)	A-	A	B	Up	Y	2,000
Nationwide Small Company Growth Fund Inst Service Cls	NWSIX	NAS CM	Open End	US Equity Small Cap (Small Company)	A-	A	B	Up	Y	50,000
Nationwide U.S. Small Cap Value Fund Class A	NWUAX	NAS CM	Open End	US Equity Small Cap (Small Company)	B	B	B-	Up	Y	2,000
Nationwide U.S. Small Cap Value Fund Class C	NWUCX	NAS CM	Open End	US Equity Small Cap (Small Company)	B-	B	B-	Up	Y	2,000
Nationwide U.S. Small Cap Value Fund Class R6	NWUIX	NAS CM	Open End	US Equity Small Cap (Small Company)	B	B	B	Up	Y	1,000,000
Nationwide U.S. Small Cap Value Fund Inst Service Cls	NWUSX	NAS CM	Open End	US Equity Small Cap (Small Company)	B	B	B-	Up	Y	50,000
Nationwide WCM Focused Small Cap Fund Class A	NWGPX	NAS CM	Open End	US Equity Small Cap (Small Company)	B+	A-	B	Up	Y	2,000
Nationwide WCM Focused Small Cap Fund Class C	NWGQX	NAS CM	Open End	US Equity Small Cap (Small Company)	B+	A-	B	Up	Y	2,000
Nationwide WCM Focused Small Cap Fund Class R6	NWKEX	NAS CM	Open End	US Equity Small Cap (Small Company)	B+	A-	B	Up	Y	1,000,000
Nationwide WCM Focused Small Cap Fund Inst Service Cls	NWGSX	NAS CM	Open End	US Equity Small Cap (Small Company)	B+	A-	B	Up	Y	50,000
Nationwide Ziegler Equity Income Fund Class A	NWGYX	NAS CM	Open End	US Equity Large Cap Value (Equity-Income)	B-	B-	B-	Down	Y	2,000
Nationwide Ziegler Equity Income Fund Class C	NWGZX	NAS CM	Open End	US Equity Large Cap Value (Equity-Income)	B-	B-	B-	Down	Y	2,000
Nationwide Ziegler Equity Income Fund Class R6	NWJAX	NAS CM	Open End	US Equity Large Cap Value (Equity-Income)	B	B-	B		Y	1,000,000
Nationwide Ziegler Equity Income Fund Inst Service Cls	NWJBX	NAS CM	Open End	US Equity Large Cap Value (Equity-Income)	B-	B-	B-	Down	Y	50,000
Nationwide Ziegler NYSE Arca Tech 100 Index Fund Class A	NWJCX	NAS CM	Open End	US Equity Large Cap Growth (Technology)	B+	A	C+	Up	Y	2,000
Nationwide Ziegler NYSE Arca Tech 100 Index Fund Class C	NWJDX	NAS CM	Open End	US Equity Large Cap Growth (Technology)	B+	A	C+	Up	Y	2,000
Nationwide Ziegler NYSE Arca Tech 100 Index Fund Class R6	NWJEX	NAS CM	Open End	US Equity Large Cap Growth (Technology)	B+	A	C+	Down	Y	1,000,000
Nationwide Ziegler NYSE Arca Tech 100 Ind Inst Serv Cls	NWJFX	NAS CM	Open End	US Equity Large Cap Growth (Technology)	B+	A	C+	Up	Y	50,000
Natixis ASG Dynamic Allocation Fund Class A	DAAFX	NAS CM	Open End	Alloc (Asset Alloc)	C	C	B+	Up	Y	2,500
Natixis ASG Dynamic Allocation Fund Class C	DACFX	NAS CM	Open End	Alloc (Asset Alloc)	C	C	B+	Up	Y	2,500
Natixis ASG Dynamic Allocation Fund Class Y	DAYFX	NAS CM	Open End	Alloc (Asset Alloc)	C	C	B+	Up	Y	100,000
Natixis ASG Managed Futures Strategy Fund Class A	AMFAX	NAS CM	Open End	Other Alternative (Growth)	C-	C-	C-	Up	Y	2,500
Natixis ASG Managed Futures Strategy Fund Class C	ASFCX	NAS CM	Open End	Other Alternative (Growth)	C-	C-	C-	Up	Y	2,500
Natixis ASG Managed Futures Strategy Fund Class N	AMFNX	NAS CM	Open End	Other Alternative (Growth)	C-	C-	C	Up	Y	1,000,000
Natixis ASG Managed Futures Strategy Fund Class Y	ASFYX	NAS CM	Open End	Other Alternative (Growth)	C-	C-	C	Up	Y	100,000
Natixis ASG Tactical U.S. Market Fund Class A	USMAX	NAS CM	Open End	Long/Short Equity (Growth)	B-	B-	B-	Down	Y	2,500
Natixis ASG Tactical U.S. Market Fund Class C	USMCX	NAS CM	Open End	Long/Short Equity (Growth)	B-	B-	B-	Down	Y	2,500
Natixis ASG Tactical U.S. Market Fund Class Y	USMYX	NAS CM	Open End	Long/Short Equity (Growth)	B-	B-	B-	Down	Y	100,000
Natixis Funds Trust I Oakmark International Fund Class A	NOIAX	NAS CM	Open End	Global Equity Large Cap (Foreign Stock)	B	B+	C	Up	Y	2,500
Natixis Funds Trust I Oakmark International Fund Class C	NOICX	NAS CM	Open End	Global Equity Large Cap (Foreign Stock)	B-	B	C	Up	Y	2,500
Natixis Funds Trust I Oakmark International Fund Class N	NIONX	NAS CM	Open End	Global Equity Large Cap (Foreign Stock)	B	B+	C	Up	Y	1,000,000
Natixis Funds Trust I Oakmark International Fund Class Y	NOIYX	NAS CM	Open End	Global Equity Large Cap (Foreign Stock)	B	B+	C	Up	Y	100,000
Natixis Funds Trust I U.S. Equity Opportunities Fund Cls A	NEFSX	NAS CM	Open End	US Equity Large Cap Growth (Growth)	B	B	B	Down	Y	2,500
Natixis Funds Trust I U.S. Equity Opportunities Fund Cls C	NECCX	NAS CM	Open End	US Equity Large Cap Growth (Growth)	B	B	B	Down	Y	2,500
Natixis Funds Trust I U.S. Equity Opportunities Fund Cls N	NESNX	NAS CM	Open End	US Equity Large Cap Growth (Growth)	B	B	B	Down	Y	1,000,000
Natixis Funds Trust I U.S. Equity Opportunities Fund Cls Y	NESYX	NAS CM	Open End	US Equity Large Cap Growth (Growth)	B	B	B	Down	Y	100,000
Natixis Funds Trust I Vaughan Nelson Small Cap Value Cls A	NEFJX	NAS CM	Open End	US Equity Small Cap (Small Company)	B	B	B	Up		2,500
Natixis Funds Trust I Vaughan Nelson Small Cap Value Cls C	NEJCX	NAS CM	Open End	US Equity Small Cap (Small Company)	B-	B-	B	Up		2,500
Natixis Funds Trust I Vaughan Nelson Small Cap Value Cls N	VSCNX	NAS CM	Open End	US Equity Small Cap (Small Company)	B	B	B	Up	Y	1,000,000
Natixis Funds Trust I Vaughan Nelson Small Cap Value Cls Y	NEJYX	NAS CM	Open End	US Equity Small Cap (Small Company)	B	B	B	Up		100,000
Natixis Funds Trust II ASG Global Alternatives Fund Cls A	GAFAX	NAS CM	Open End	Multialternative (Growth)	C	C	C+	Up	Y	2,500
Natixis Funds Trust II ASG Global Alternatives Fund Cls C	GAFCX	NAS CM	Open End	Multialternative (Growth)	C	C	C+	Up	Y	2,500
Natixis Funds Trust II ASG Global Alternatives Fund Cls N	GAFNX	NAS CM	Open End	Multialternative (Growth)	C	C	C+		Y	1,000,000
Natixis Funds Trust II ASG Global Alternatives Fund Cls Y	GAFYX	NAS CM	Open End	Multialternative (Growth)	C	C	C+		Y	100,000
Natixis Funds Trust II Oakmark Fund Class A	NEFOX	NAS CM	Open End	US Equity Large Cap Blend (Growth)	B	B	B	Up	Y	2,500
Natixis Funds Trust II Oakmark Fund Class C	NECOX	NAS CM	Open End	US Equity Large Cap Blend (Growth)	B	B	B	Up	Y	2,500
Natixis Funds Trust II Oakmark Fund Class N	NOANX	NAS CM	Open End	US Equity Large Cap Blend (Growth)	B	B	C+		Y	1,000,000
Natixis Funds Trust II Oakmark Fund Class Y	NEOYX	NAS CM	Open End	US Equity Large Cap Blend (Growth)	B	B	B	Up	Y	100,000

★ Expanded analysis of this fund is included in Section II.

	TOTAL RETURNS					PERFORMANCE				ASSETS		ASSET ALLOCATION & TURNOVER					BULL & BEAR		FEES		
Min Additional Investment	3-Month Total Return	6-Month Total Return	1-Year Total Return	3-Year Total Return	5-Year Total Return	Dividend Yield (TTM)	Expense Ratio	3-Yr Std Deviation	3-Year Beta	NAV	Total Assets (MIL)	%Cash	%Stocks	%Bonds	%Other	Turnover Ratio	Last Bull Market Total Return	Last Bear Market Total Return	Front End Fee (%)	Back End Fee (%)	Inception Date
100	2.99	8.49	13.18	27.47	86.84	0.48	1.36	14.11	1	13.06	595.6	0	100	0	0	15	26.89	-25.36		1.00	Oct-03
	3.13	8.81	13.80	29.64	92.19	0.68	0.91	14.15	1	13.61	595.6	0	100	0	0	15	27.21	-25.23			Mar-07
	3.33	9.16	14.53	31.87	97.42	1.06	0.26	14.18	1	14.04	595.6	0	100	0	0	15	27.56	-25.01			Dec-99
	3.24	9.09	14.33	31.63	97.06		0.51	14.18	1	14.03	595.6	0	100	0	0	15	27.56	-25.01			Dec-16
100	5.21	9.43	27.98	50.20	127.00	0	1.31	14.49	0.87	17.18	248.6	5	95	0	0	16			5.75		Jan-12
	5.28	9.60	28.20	50.86	128.97	0	1.19	14.5	0.87	17.35	248.6	5	95	0	0	16					Jan-12
100	3.23	8.66	7.56	25.92	86.31	0.12	1.36	14.53	1.01	13.49	186.7	0	100	0	0	39	29.55	-26.62	5.75		Dec-07
100	2.99	8.20	6.70	23.05	79.56	0	2.12	14.54	1.01	12.54	186.7	0	100	0	0	39	29.08	-26.88		1.00	Dec-07
	3.25	8.77	7.92	27.21	89.48	0.36	1.01	14.55	1.01	13.83	186.7	0	100	0	0	39	29.77	-26.53			Dec-07
	3.28	8.75	7.74	26.38	87.24	0.17	1.26	14.57	1.01	13.6	186.7	0	100	0	0	39	29.56	-26.55			Dec-07
100	2.19	8.70	13.56	32.10	106.48	0	1.39	14.57	1.01	36.98	201.4	11	89	0	0	96	29.31	-25.94	5.75		Mar-07
100	1.98	8.28	12.70	29.11	99.32	0	2.15	14.58	1.01	34.39	201.4	11	89	0	0	96	28.87	-26.12		1.00	Mar-07
	2.28	8.90	13.97	33.54	110.11	0.09	1.03	14.58	1.01	37.97	201.4	11	89	0	0	96	29.6	-25.86			Sep-13
	2.28	8.86	13.88	33.26	109.55	0.03	1.11	14.58	1.01	37.89	201.4	11	89	0	0	96	29.61	-25.86			Mar-07
100	7.73	12.37	17.97	28.90	90.16	2.49	0.91	9.48	0.88	15.24	489.1	0	100	0	0	60	23.22	-14.12	5.75		Apr-05
100	7.47	11.92	17.12	26.02	83.54	1.85	1.65	9.44	0.88	15.1	489.1	0	100	0	0	60	22.85	-14.35		1.00	Apr-05
	7.80	12.51	18.37	30.18	93.00	2.78	0.57	9.48	0.88	15.3	489.1	0	100	0	0	60	23.22	-14.12			Sep-13
	7.77	12.52	18.24	29.84	92.27	2.68	0.68	9.45	0.88	15.3	489.1	0	100	0	0	60	23.46	-14.07			Jul-09
100	4.86	14.55	31.27	43.15	126.00	0.65	0.84	11.45	0.99	76.46	477.9	1	99	0	0	24	27.12	-16.45	5.75		Jun-96
100	4.66	14.13	30.32	40.00	118.22	0.34	1.58	11.44	0.99	68.25	477.9	1	99	0	0	24	26.66	-16.66		1.00	May-00
	4.95	14.75	31.75	44.72	129.47	0.94	0.48	11.45	1	77.16	477.9	1	99	0	0	24	27.12	-16.45			Sep-13
	4.93	14.67	31.57	44.12	128.64	0.83	0.61	11.44	0.99	77.19	477.9	1	99	0	0	24	27.34	-16.34			Jul-09
50	5.59	10.40	20.78			0.15	1.23			11.1	38.9	25	52	21	2	9			5.75		Nov-15
50	5.39	10.05	19.91			0	1.97			10.99	38.9	25	52	21	2	9				1.00	Nov-15
50	5.67	10.57	21.18			0.27	0.97			11.12	38.9	25	52	21	2	9					Nov-15
50	4.95	9.03	6.13	-0.74	35.53	0	1.74	10.52	0.87	10.38	3,356	58	59	-26	9		-5	-6.32	5.75		Jul-10
50	4.74	8.64	5.41	-2.95	30.59	0	2.49	10.54	0.87	9.93	3,356	58	59	-26	9		-5.34	-6.62		1.00	Jul-10
	5.44	8.72	6.51	0.13	37.90		1.39	10.54	0.87	10.46	3,356	58	59	-26	9		-4.78	-6.23			May-17
50	5.08	9.25	6.47	0.05	37.29	0.01	1.49	10.53	0.87	10.46	3,356	58	59	-26	9		-4.78	-6.23			Jul-10
50	8.31	13.97	25.36	24.79		0.33	1.24	8.83	0.78	14.11	97.9	22	77	1	0	42			5.75		Sep-13
50	8.11	13.47	24.36	21.83		0.02	1.99	8.78	0.78	13.75	97.9	22	77	1	0	42				1.00	Sep-13
50	8.39	14.11	25.67	25.82		0.6	0.99	8.82	0.78	14.17	97.9	22	77	1	0	42					Sep-13
50	1.75	11.01	29.56	32.04	61.47	1.34	1.34	15.28	1.17	15.58	1,112	6	93	0	1	41	15.22	-22.81	5.75		Dec-10
50	1.55	10.53	28.55	29.09	55.37	0.72	2.09	15.28	1.17	15.3	1,112	6	93	0	1	41	14.81	-23.06		1.00	Dec-10
	1.88	11.29	29.88	32.36	61.88		0.97	15.29	1.17	15.58	1,112	6	93	0	1	41	15.22	-22.81			May-17
50	1.79	11.11	29.77	32.25	61.74		1.09	15.29	1.17	15.56	1,112	6	93	0	1	41	15.22	-22.81			May-17
50	5.70	11.62	26.28	48.23	133.24	0.25	1.18	11.93	1.13	36.9	999.0	3	96	0	1	17	25.61	-20.08	5.75		Jul-94
50	5.50	11.22	25.35	44.91	124.67	0.01	1.93	11.95	1.13	25.73	999.0	3	96	0	1	17	25.02	-20.34		1.00	Jul-94
	5.81	11.87	26.57	48.57	133.77		0.84	11.94	1.13	42.63	999.0	3	96	0	1	17	25.61	-20.08			May-17
50	5.76	11.76	26.60	49.33	136.13	0.38	0.93	11.93	1.13	42.61	999.0	3	96	0	1	17	25.76	-19.99			Nov-94
100	3.42	7.77	6.27	26.44	96.53	0.07	1.53	13.04	0.86	18.71	305.8	0	100	0	0	74	24.87	-23.31	5.75		Dec-96
100	3.21	7.31	5.49	23.62	89.33	0.01	2.28	13.07	0.86	11.67	305.8	0	100	0	0	74	24.24	-23.56		1.00	Dec-96
	3.51	8.00	6.53	26.75	97.00		1.19	13.04	0.86	19.37	305.8	0	100	0	0	74	24.87	-23.31			May-17
100	3.51	7.89	6.59	27.45	99.05	0.28	1.28	13.04	0.86	19.37	305.8	0	100	0	0	74	24.98	-23.22			Aug-06
50	4.90	7.54	10.66	2.86	24.01	0	1.56	6.58		11.04	1,634	93	66	-63	4		3.93	-9.76	5.75		Sep-08
50	4.76	7.15	9.89	0.59	19.51	0	2.31	6.6		10.33	1,634	93	66	-63	4		3.41	-10.01		1.00	Sep-08
	5.18	7.78	10.95	3.38	25.98	0	1.24	6.6		11.22	1,634	93	66	-63	4		4	-9.62			May-13
50	4.95	7.65	10.92	3.60	25.58	0	1.31	6.59		11.22	1,634	93	66	-63	4		4	-9.62			Sep-08
50	5.84	11.84	20.74	35.50	111.36	0.62	1.18	12.61	1.18	24.72	311.4	5	95	0	0	16	27.84	-19.1	5.75		May-31
50	5.61	11.38	19.84	32.45	103.54	0.06	1.93	12.6	1.18	21.58	311.4	5	95	0	0	16	27.24	-19.34		1.00	May-95
	5.93	12.07	21.03	35.82	111.87		0.81	12.61	1.18	25.91	311.4	5	95	0	0	16	27.84	-19.1			May-17
50	5.88	11.97	21.04	36.51	113.99	0.78	0.92	12.6	1.18	25.9	311.4	5	95	0	0	16	28	-19.03			Nov-98

Fund Name	MARKET Ticker Symbol	Traded On	FUND TYPE, CATEGORY & OBJECTIVE Fund Type	Category and (Prospectus Objective)	RATINGS Overall Rating	Reward Rating	Risk Rating	Recent Up/ Downgrade	MINIMUMS Open to New Investors	Min Initial Investment
Natixis Funds Trust II Vaughan Nelson Value Opp Fund Cls A	VNVAX	NAS CM	Open End	US Equity Mid Cap (Growth)	B-	C+	B	Up	Y	2,500
Natixis Funds Trust II Vaughan Nelson Value Opp Fund Cls C	VNVCX	NAS CM	Open End	US Equity Mid Cap (Growth)	C+	C+	B	Up	Y	2,500
Natixis Funds Trust II Vaughan Nelson Value Opp Fund Cls N	VNVNX	NAS CM	Open End	US Equity Mid Cap (Growth)	B-	C+	B	Up	Y	1,000,000
Natixis Funds Trust II Vaughan Nelson Value Opp Fund Cls Y	VNVYX	NAS CM	Open End	US Equity Mid Cap (Growth)	B-	C+	B	Up	Y	100,000
Natixis Funds Trust IV AEW Real Estate Fund Class A	NRFAX	NAS CM	Open End	Real Estate Sector Equity (Real Estate)	B-	C+	B+		Y	2,500
Natixis Funds Trust IV AEW Real Estate Fund Class C	NRCFX	NAS CM	Open End	Real Estate Sector Equity (Real Estate)	B-	C+	B		Y	2,500
Natixis Funds Trust IV AEW Real Estate Fund Class N	NRFNX	NAS CM	Open End	Real Estate Sector Equity (Real Estate)	B	C+	B+	Up	Y	1,000,000
Natixis Funds Trust IV AEW Real Estate Fund Class Y	NRFYX	NAS CM	Open End	Real Estate Sector Equity (Real Estate)	B	C+	B+	Up	Y	100,000
Natixis Sustainable Future 2015 Fund Class N	NSFBX	NAS CM	Open End	Target Date 2000-2020 (Asset Alloc)	U	U	U		Y	1,000,000
Natixis Sustainable Future 2020 Fund Class N	NSFDX	NAS CM	Open End	Target Date 2000-2020 (Asset Alloc)	U	U	U		Y	1,000,000
Natixis Sustainable Future 2025 Fund Class N	NSFEX	NAS CM	Open End	Target Date 2021-2045 (Asset Alloc)	U	U	U		Y	1,000,000
Natixis Sustainable Future 2030 Fund Class N	NSFFX	NAS CM	Open End	Target Date 2021-2045 (Asset Alloc)	U	U	U		Y	1,000,000
Natixis Sustainable Future 2035 Fund Class N	NSFGX	NAS CM	Open End	Target Date 2021-2045 (Asset Alloc)	U	U	U		Y	1,000,000
Natixis Sustainable Future 2040 Fund Class N	NSFHX	NAS CM	Open End	Target Date 2021-2045 (Asset Alloc)	U	U	U		Y	1,000,000
Natixis Sustainable Future 2045 Fund Class N	NSFJX	NAS CM	Open End	Target Date 2021-2045 (Asset Alloc)	U	U	U		Y	1,000,000
Natixis Sustainable Future 2050 Fund Class N	NSFKX	NAS CM	Open End	Target Date 2046+ (Asset Alloc)	U	U	U		Y	1,000,000
Natixis Sustainable Future 2055 Fund Class N	NSFLX	NAS CM	Open End	Target Date 2046+ (Asset Alloc)	U	U	U		Y	1,000,000
Natixis Sustainable Future 2060 Fund Class N	NSFMX	NAS CM	Open End	Target Date 2046+ (Asset Alloc)	U	U	U		Y	1,000,000
Natixis Vaughan Nelson Select Fund Class A	VNSAX	NAS CM	Open End	US Equity Large Cap Growth (Growth)	B	B	B		Y	2,500
Natixis Vaughan Nelson Select Fund Class C	VNSCX	NAS CM	Open End	US Equity Large Cap Growth (Growth)	B	B	B-		Y	2,500
Natixis Vaughan Nelson Select Fund Class N	VNSNX	NAS CM	Open End	US Equity Large Cap Growth (Growth)	B	B	B		Y	1,000,000
Natixis Vaughan Nelson Select Fund Class Y	VNSYX	NAS CM	Open End	US Equity Large Cap Growth (Growth)	B	B	B		Y	100,000
Navian Waycross Long/Short Equity Fund	WAYEX	NAS CM	Open End	Long/Short Equity (Growth)	C+	C	B	Up	Y	5,000
Navigator Equity Hedged Fund Class A	NAVAX	NAS CM	Open End	Long/Short Equity (Growth)	B-	C+	B	Up	Y	5,000
Navigator Equity Hedged Fund Class C	NAVCX	NAS CM	Open End	Long/Short Equity (Growth)	C+	C+	B	Up	Y	5,000
Navigator Equity Hedged Fund Class I	NAVIX	NAS CM	Open End	Long/Short Equity (Growth)	B-	C+	B	Up	Y	25,000
Navigator Sentry Managed Volatility Fund Class A	NVXAX	NAS CM	Open End	Other Alternative (Equity-Income)	E+	E+	E+	Down	Y	5,000
Navigator Sentry Managed Volatility Fund Class C	NVXCX	NAS CM	Open End	Other Alternative (Equity-Income)	E+	E+	E+	Down	Y	5,000
Navigator Sentry Managed Volatility Fund Class I	NVXIX	NAS CM	Open End	Other Alternative (Equity-Income)	E+	E+	E+	Down	Y	25,000
Nebraska Fund Class C Shares	NEBCX	NAS CM	Open End	Alloc (Equity-Income)	C+	C+	B-	Up	Y	1,000
Nebraska Fund Institutional Class Shares	NEBIX	NAS CM	Open End	Alloc (Equity-Income)	C+	C+	B-	Up	Y	1,000
Needham Aggressive Growth Fund Institutional Class	NEAIX	NAS CM	Open End	US Equity Small Cap (Aggr Growth)	B+	A-	B-	Up	Y	100,000
Needham Aggressive Growth Fund Retail Class	NEAGX	NAS CM	Open End	US Equity Small Cap (Aggr Growth)	B+	A-	B-	Up	Y	2,000
Needham Growth Fund Institutional Class	NEEIX	NAS CM	Open End	US Equity Mid Cap (Growth)	B-	B-	B	Up	Y	100,000
Needham Growth Fund Retail Class	NEEGX	NAS CM	Open End	US Equity Mid Cap (Growth)	B-	C+	B	Up	Y	2,000
Needham Small Cap Growth Fund Institutional Class	NESIX	NAS CM	Open End	US Equity Small Cap (Small Company)	B+	A	B-	Up	Y	100,000
Needham Small Cap Growth Fund Retail Class	NESGX	NAS CM	Open End	US Equity Small Cap (Small Company)	B+	A	B-	Up	Y	2,000
Neiman Balanced Allocation Fund Class A	NBAFX	NAS CM	Open End	Moderate Alloc (Balanced)	B-	C+	B	Up	Y	2,500
Neiman Balanced Allocation Fund Class C	NBCFX	NAS CM	Open End	Moderate Alloc (Balanced)	C+	C+	B	Up	Y	2,500
Neiman Large Cap Value Fund A Shares	NEAMX	NAS CM	Open End	US Equity Large Cap Value (Growth)	B-	B-	B	Down	Y	2,500
Neiman Large Cap Value Fund No-Load Shares	NEIMX	NAS CM	Open End	US Equity Large Cap Value (Growth)	B-	B-	B	Down	Y	2,500
Neiman Opportunities Fund Class A	NEOMX	NAS CM	Open End	US Equity Mid Cap (Growth)	D+	C	B+	Up	Y	2,500
Neuberger Berman Absolute Return Multi-Manager Fund Cls A	NABAX	NAS CM	Open End	Multialternative (Growth)	C	C	C+	Up	Y	1,000
Neuberger Berman Absolute Return Multi-Manager Fund Cls C	NABCX	NAS CM	Open End	Multialternative (Growth)	C	C-	C	Up	Y	1,000
Neuberger Berman Absolute Return Multi-Manager Fund Cls R6	NRABX	NAS CM	Open End	Multialternative (Growth)	C	C	B-	Up	Y	0
Neuberger Berman Absolute Return Multi-Mgr Fund Inst Cls	NABIX	NAS CM	Open End	Multialternative (Growth)	C	C	B-	Up	Y	1,000,000
Neuberger Berman Advisers Mgmt Trust Guardian Port Cls I	US6412224015		Open End	US Equity Large Cap Growth (Growth)	B-	B-	C+	Down	Y	0
Neuberger Berman Advisers Mgmt Trust Guardian Port Cls S	US6412228727		Open End	US Equity Large Cap Growth (Growth)	B-	B-	C+	Down	Y	0
Neuberger Berman Advisers Mgmt Trust Intl Portfolio Cls S	US6412223025		Open End	Global Equity Large Cap (Foreign Stock)	B	B	B	Up	Y	0
Neuberger Berman Advisers Mgmt Trust Large Cap Value Cls I	US6412221045		Open End	US Equity Large Cap Value (Growth)	B-	B-	B-		Y	0
Neuberger Berman Advisers Mgmt Trust Mid-Cap Growth Cls I	US6412225004		Open End	US Equity Mid Cap (Growth)	B	B	C+	Up	Y	0
Neuberger Berman Advisers Mgmt Trust Mid-Cap Growth Cls S	US6412228560		Open End	US Equity Mid Cap (Growth)	B	B	C+	Up	Y	0

★ Expanded analysis of this fund is included in Section II.

Min Additional Investment	3-Month Total Return	6-Month Total Return	1-Year Total Return	3-Year Total Return	5-Year Total Return	Dividend Yield (TTM)	Expense Ratio	3-Yr Std Deviation	3-Year Beta	NAV	Total Assets (MIL)	%Cash	%Stocks	%Bonds	%Other	Turnover Ratio	Last Bull Market Total Return	Last Bear Market Total Return	Front End Fee (%)	Back End Fee (%)	Inception Date
	TOTAL RETURNS					PERFORMANCE				ASSETS		ASSET ALLOCATION & TURNOVER					BULL & BEAR		FEES		
50	4.95	8.74	12.92	14.40	83.70	0.2	1.48	12.42	1.08	22.65	1,008	1	99	0	0	57	24.48	-23.92	5.75		Oct-08
50	4.75	8.33	12.11	11.86	76.98	0	2.23	12.44	1.08	21.5	1,008	1	99	0	0	57	23.96	-24.18		1.00	Oct-08
	5.01	8.90	13.31	15.61	86.36	0.66	1.13	12.42	1.08	22.87	1,008	1	99	0	0	57	24.73	-23.88			May-13
50	5.00	8.84	13.19	15.28	85.92	0.56	1.23	12.43	1.08	22.89	1,008	1	99	0	0	57	24.73	-23.88			Oct-08
50	1.15	2.08	3.59	12.76	51.82	1.86	1.25	13.37	0.99	15.08	156.8	2	98	0	0	13	30.57	-14.95	5.75		Dec-00
50	0.93	1.67	2.80	10.20	46.18	1.1	2	13.36	0.99	15.13	156.8	2	98	0	0	13	30	-15.19		1.00	Dec-00
	1.24	2.26	3.93	14.08	54.56	2.32	0.95	13.38	0.99	14.06	156.8	2	98	0	0	13	30.77	-14.83			May-13
50	1.23	2.24	3.85	13.62	53.79	2.24	1	13.4	0.99	14.03	156.8	2	98	0	0	13	30.77	-14.83			Aug-00
	3.42	6.41					0.65			10.85	4.4	30	26	44	1						Feb-17
	3.81	7.29					0.65			11	4.5	31	29	39	1						Feb-17
	4.17	7.94					0.65			11.13	3.4	34	33	32	0						Feb-17
	4.74	9.01					0.65			11.31	2.9	38	37	24	0						Feb-17
	5.20	9.75					0.65			11.47	2.9	42	41	16	0						Feb-17
	5.56	10.51					0.65			11.59	2.9	45	45	10	0						Feb-17
	5.72	10.97					0.65			11.66	2.3	46	47	7	0						Feb-17
	5.90	11.24					0.65			11.71	2.4	47	48	5	0						Feb-17
	5.90	11.24					0.65			11.71	2.4	47	48	5	0						Feb-17
	5.86	11.20					0.65			11.71	2.4	47	48	5	0						Feb-17
50	5.48	10.66	23.51	34.05	117.36	0.04	1.25	10.53	0.99	17.28	153.5	1	99	0	0	64			5.75		Jun-12
50	5.23	10.21	22.57	31.06	109.44	0	2	10.52	0.99	16.6	153.5	1	99	0	0	64				1.00	Jun-12
	5.58	10.92	23.97	35.26	120.50		0.95	10.59	1	17.37	153.5	1	99	0	0	64					Mar-17
50	5.48	10.82	23.79	35.06	120.17	0.23	1	10.59	1	17.35	153.5	1	99	0	0	64					Jun-12
	1.69	6.72	11.92			0	2.02			10.79	17.1	46	54	0	0	192					Apr-15
500	2.84	7.23	11.76	11.92	28.10	0.75	1.65	7.35	0.59	8.82	44.5	13	87	0	1	371	7.11	-15.43	5.50		Dec-10
500	2.59	6.79	10.96	9.47	23.48	0	2.4	7.37	0.6	8.37	44.5	13	87	0	1	371	6.66	-15.76			Dec-10
	2.92	7.39	12.02	12.72	29.80	0.91	1.4	7.32	0.59	8.74	44.5	13	87	0	1	371	7.24	-15.4			Dec-10
500	-18.78	-37.00	-55.30	-78.55		0	1.78	20.31		1.6	8.2	94	6	0	0	0			3.75		Mar-14
500	-18.68	-37.10	-55.27	-78.41		0	2.53	20.27		1.61	8.2	94	6	0	0	0					Mar-14
	-18.68	-37.10	-55.27	-78.41		0	1.53	20.27		1.61	8.2	94	6	0	0	0					Mar-14
50	6.80	12.76	15.12	14.89	32.83	0.2	2.23	8.62	0.65	12.31	4.9	10	90	0	0	84				1.00	Sep-12
50	6.89	13.20	16.41	18.53	39.61	0.32	1.23	8.63	0.65	12.27	4.9	10	90	0	0	84					Sep-12
	-2.84	7.76	9.36	23.78	84.86		1.4	12.26	0.9	23.21	64.9	0	100	0	0	14	29.89	-30.25			Dec-16
100	-2.97	7.47	8.72	23.06	83.79	0	1.95	12.26	0.9	23.07	64.9	0	100	0	0	14	29.89	-30.25			Sep-01
	-2.40	4.41	8.88	13.74	70.80		1.41	11.31	0.9	43.15	121.0	1	99	0	0	12	30.11	-28.5			Dec-16
100	-2.54	4.12	8.32	13.15	69.92	0	1.85	11.3	0.9	42.91	121.0	1	99	0	0	12	30.11	-28.5			Jan-96
	-1.13	4.84	12.48	34.88	77.34		1.46	14.18	0.82	15.77	30.6	2	97	0	0	99	22.44	-29.04			Dec-16
100	-1.26	4.54	11.87	34.16	76.39	0	2.01	14.16	0.82	15.68	30.6	2	97	0	0	99	22.44	-29.04			May-02
100	3.73	6.80	12.89	16.13	40.23	1.02	2.23	6.18	0.59	13.14	9.3	3	64	32	0	42	14.43	-13.18	5.75		Jul-10
100	3.46	6.31	11.96	13.45	34.88	0.26	2.98	6.19	0.59	13.01	9.3	3	64	32	0	42	13.81	-13.49			Jul-10
100	8.06	12.60	18.99	27.76	80.94	1.06	1.46	8.32	0.78	27.98	26.6	7	93	0	0	32	18.12	-14.65	5.75		Aug-12
100	8.06	12.60	18.98	27.76	80.81	1.06	1.46	8.31	0.77	27.98	26.6	7	93	0	0	32	18.29	-14.56			Apr-03
100	4.12	11.72	19.90			0.06	1.53			12.86	4.3	17	83	0	0	98			5.75		Apr-16
100	1.13	1.91	3.89	0.24	10.54	0	2.38	3.92	0.98	10.66	343.4	26	40	33	0	485			5.75		May-12
100	0.88	1.48	3.12	-2.03	6.47	0	3.13	3.94	0.98	10.23	343.4	26	40	33	0	485				1.00	May-12
	1.31	2.08	4.35	1.31	12.80	0	1.95	3.91	0.98	10.79	343.4	26	40	33	0	485					Dec-13
	1.21	2.08	4.25	1.33	12.65	0	2.02	3.9	0.97	10.79	343.4	26	40	33	0	485					May-12
	6.89	11.29	25.41	28.31	99.16	0.31	1.22	10	0.96	16.15	61.0	2	97	0	1	72	20.08	-20.09			Nov-97
	6.90	11.21	24.73	27.47	97.25	0.26	1.26	9.94	0.96	15.95	61.0	2	97	0	1	72	20	-20.16			Aug-02
	3.58	10.25	26.75	25.79	45.63	0.62	1.51	11.29	0.86	13.63	86.4	3	97	0	1	28	13.86	-23.21			Apr-05
	5.08	8.45	13.36	26.41	86.65	0.56	1.19	13.25	1.17	16.71	73.3	13	87	0	0	93	19.64	-26.32			Mar-94
	7.05	11.79	25.28	31.65	92.26	0	1	11.69	1	27.79	423.9	5	95	0	0	54	25.43	-16.51			Nov-97
	6.98	11.66	24.56	30.25	89.21	0	1.11	11.68	1	25.77	423.9	5	95	0	0	54	25.31	-16.62			Feb-03

	MARKET		FUND TYPE, CATEGORY & OBJECTIVE		RATINGS				MINIMUMS	
Fund Name	Ticker Symbol	Traded On	Fund Type	Category and (Prospectus Objective)	Overall Rating	Reward Rating	Risk Rating	Recent Up/ Downgrade	Open to New Investors	Min Initial Investment
Neuberger Berman Advisers Mgmt Trust Social Resp Cls S	US6412228230		Open End	US Equity Large Cap Growth (Growth)	B	B-	B+		Y	0
Neuberger Berman Advisers Mgmt Trust Socially Resp Cls I	US6412226093		Open End	US Equity Large Cap Growth (Growth)	B	B-	B+		Y	0
Neuberger Berman Advisers Mgmt Trust U.S. Eq Ind PutWrite	US6412227810		Open End	Multialternative (Multi-Asset Global)	C+	C	B	Up	Y	0
Neuberger Berman AMT Mid-Cap Intrinsic Value Port Cls I	US6412227083		Open End	US Equity Mid Cap (Growth)	B-	B-	B	Up	Y	0
Neuberger Berman AMT Mid-Cap Intrinsic Value Port Cls S	US6412228313		Open End	US Equity Mid Cap (Growth)	B-	B-	B	Up	Y	0
Neuberger Berman Dividend Growth Fund Class A	NDGAX	NAS CM	Open End	US Equity Large Cap Value (Equity-Income)	C	C	B+	Up	Y	1,000
Neuberger Berman Dividend Growth Fund Class C	NDGCX	NAS CM	Open End	US Equity Large Cap Value (Equity-Income)	C	C	B+	Up	Y	1,000
Neuberger Berman Dividend Growth Fund Class Institutional	NDGIX	NAS CM	Open End	US Equity Large Cap Value (Equity-Income)	C	C	B+	Up	Y	1,000,000
Neuberger Berman Dividend Growth Fund Class R6	NRDGX	NAS CM	Open End	US Equity Large Cap Value (Equity-Income)	C	C	B+	Up	Y	0
Neuberger Berman Emerging Markets Equity Fund Class A	NEMAX	NAS CM	Open End	Emerging Markets Equity (Div Emerging Mkts)	B	B	C	Up	Y	1,000
Neuberger Berman Emerging Markets Equity Fund Class C	NEMCX	NAS CM	Open End	Emerging Markets Equity (Div Emerging Mkts)	B-	B	C	Up	Y	1,000
Neuberger Berman Emerging Markets Equity Fund Class R3	NEMRX	NAS CM	Open End	Emerging Markets Equity (Div Emerging Mkts)	B-	B	C	Up	Y	0
Neuberger Berman Emerging Markets Equity Fund Class R6	NREMX	NAS CM	Open End	Emerging Markets Equity (Div Emerging Mkts)	B	B+	C	Up	Y	0
Neuberger Berman Emerging Mkts Equity Fund Inst Cls	NEMIX	NAS CM	Open End	Emerging Markets Equity (Div Emerging Mkts)	B	B+	C	Up	Y	1,000,000
Neuberger Berman Equity Income Fund Class A	NBHAX	NAS CM	Open End	US Equity Large Cap Value (Equity-Income)	B-	B-	B-	Down	Y	1,000
Neuberger Berman Equity Income Fund Class C	NBHCX	NAS CM	Open End	US Equity Large Cap Value (Equity-Income)	C+	C+	B-	Down	Y	1,000
Neuberger Berman Equity Income Fund Class R3	NBHRX	NAS CM	Open End	US Equity Large Cap Value (Equity-Income)	B-	B-	B-	Down	Y	0
Neuberger Berman Equity Income Fund Institutional Class	NBHIX	NAS CM	Open End	US Equity Large Cap Value (Equity-Income)	B-	B-	B-	Down	Y	1,000,000
Neuberger Berman Focus Fund Advisor Class	NBFAX	NAS CM	Open End	US Equity Large Cap Blend (Growth)	B-	B-	B-	Down		0
Neuberger Berman Focus Fund Class A	NFAAX	NAS CM	Open End	US Equity Large Cap Blend (Growth)	B-	B-	B-	Down	Y	1,000
Neuberger Berman Focus Fund Class C	NFACX	NAS CM	Open End	US Equity Large Cap Blend (Growth)	B-	B-	B-	Down	Y	1,000
Neuberger Berman Focus Fund Institutional Class	NFALX	NAS CM	Open End	US Equity Large Cap Blend (Growth)	B-	B-	B-	Down	Y	1,000,000
Neuberger Berman Focus Fund Investor Class	NBSSX	NAS CM	Open End	US Equity Large Cap Blend (Growth)	B-	B-	B-	Down		1,000
Neuberger Berman Focus Fund Trust Class	NBFCX	NAS CM	Open End	US Equity Large Cap Blend (Growth)	B-	B-	B-	Down		0
Neuberger Berman Genesis Fund Advisor Class	NBGAX	NAS CM	Open End	US Equity Small Cap (Small Company)	B	B	B+	Up	Y	0
Neuberger Berman Genesis Fund Class R6	NRGSX	NAS CM	Open End	US Equity Small Cap (Small Company)	B+	B+	A-	Up	Y	0
Neuberger Berman Genesis Fund Investor Class	NBGNX	NAS CM	Open End	US Equity Small Cap (Small Company)	B+	B+	B+	Up	Y	1,000
Neuberger Berman Genesis Fund Trust Class	NBGEX	NAS CM	Open End	US Equity Small Cap (Small Company)	B+	B+	B+	Up	Y	0
Neuberger Berman Global Allocation Fund Class A	NGLAX	NAS CM	Open End	Alloc (Multi-Asset Global)	B-	C+	B	Up	Y	1,000
Neuberger Berman Global Allocation Fund Class C	NGLCX	NAS CM	Open End	Alloc (Multi-Asset Global)	B-	C+	B	Up	Y	1,000
Neuberger Berman Global Allocation Fund Institutional Cls	NGLIX	NAS CM	Open End	Alloc (Multi-Asset Global)	B-	C+	B	Up	Y	1,000,000
Neuberger Berman Global Equity Fund Class A	NGQAX	NAS CM	Open End	Global Equity (World Stock)	B	B-	B	Up	Y	1,000
Neuberger Berman Global Equity Fund Class C	NGQCX	NAS CM	Open End	Global Equity (World Stock)	B-	B-	B	Up	Y	1,000
Neuberger Berman Global Equity Fund Institutional Class	NGQIX	NAS CM	Open End	Global Equity (World Stock)	B	B-	B	Up	Y	1,000,000
Neuberger Berman Global Real Estate Fund Class A	NGRAX	NAS CM	Open End	Real Estate Sector Equity (Real Estate)	C+	C	B-	Up	Y	1,000
Neuberger Berman Global Real Estate Fund Class C	NGRCX	NAS CM	Open End	Real Estate Sector Equity (Real Estate)	C+	C	B-	Up	Y	1,000
Neuberger Berman Global Real Estate Fund Institutional Cls	NGRIX	NAS CM	Open End	Real Estate Sector Equity (Real Estate)	C+	C	B-	Up	Y	1,000,000
Neuberger Berman Greater China Equity Fund Class A	NCEAX	NAS CM	Open End	Greater China Equity (Pacific Stock)	B+	A+	C+	Up	Y	1,000
Neuberger Berman Greater China Equity Fund Class C	NCECX	NAS CM	Open End	Greater China Equity (Pacific Stock)	B+	A+	C+	Up	Y	1,000
Neuberger Berman Greater China Equity Fund Inst Cls	NCEIX	NAS CM	Open End	Greater China Equity (Pacific Stock)	B+	A+	C+	Up	Y	1,000,000
Neuberger Berman Guardian Fund Class A	NGDAX	NAS CM	Open End	US Equity Large Cap Growth (Growth)	B-	B-	C+	Down	Y	1,000
Neuberger Berman Guardian Fund Class Advisor	NBGUX	NAS CM	Open End	US Equity Large Cap Growth (Growth)	B-	B-	C+	Down		0
Neuberger Berman Guardian Fund Class C	NGDCX	NAS CM	Open End	US Equity Large Cap Growth (Growth)	B-	B-	C+	Down	Y	1,000
Neuberger Berman Guardian Fund Class Institutional	NGDLX	NAS CM	Open End	US Equity Large Cap Growth (Growth)	B-	B-	B-	Down	Y	1,000,000
Neuberger Berman Guardian Fund Class Investor	NGUAX	NAS CM	Open End	US Equity Large Cap Growth (Growth)	B-	B-	C+	Down		1,000
Neuberger Berman Guardian Fund Class R3	NGDRX	NAS CM	Open End	US Equity Large Cap Growth (Growth)	B-	B-	C+	Down	Y	0
Neuberger Berman Guardian Fund Class Trust	NBGTX	NAS CM	Open End	US Equity Large Cap Growth (Growth)	B-	B-	C+	Down		0
Neuberger Berman Hedged Option Premium Fund Class A	NHOAX	NAS CM	Open End	Long/Short Equity (Growth & Income)	U	U	U		Y	1,000
Neuberger Berman Hedged Option Premium Fund Class C	NHOCX	NAS CM	Open End	Long/Short Equity (Growth & Income)	U	U	U		Y	1,000
Neuberger Berman Hedged Option Premium Fund Class R6	NHORX	NAS CM	Open End	Long/Short Equity (Growth & Income)	U	U	U		Y	0
Neuberger Berman Hedged Option Premium Fund Inst Cls	NHOIX	NAS CM	Open End	Long/Short Equity (Growth & Income)	U	U	U		Y	1,000,000
Neuberger Berman International Equity Fund Class A	NIQAX	NAS CM	Open End	Global Equity Large Cap (Foreign Stock)	B	B	B	Up	Y	1,000

★ Expanded analysis of this fund is included in Section II.

Min Additional Investment	3-Month Total Return	6-Month Total Return	1-Year Total Return	3-Year Total Return	5-Year Total Return	Dividend Yield (TTM)	Expense Ratio	3-Yr Std Deviation	3-Year Beta	NAV	Total Assets (MIL)	%Cash	%Stocks	%Bonds	%Other	Turnover Ratio	Last Bull Market Total Return	Last Bear Market Total Return	Front End Fee (%)	Back End Fee (%)	Inception Date
TOTAL RETURNS						PERFORMANCE				ASSETS		ASSET ALLOCATION & TURNOVER					BULL & BEAR		FEES		
	5.32	8.13	18.10	27.55	97.75	0.33	1.18	9.94	0.95	25.69	461.2	3	97	0	0	31	20.13	-20.79			May-06
	5.44	8.30	18.42	28.37	99.71	0.5	1	9.93	0.94	25.61	461.2	3	97	0	0	31	20.19	-20.76			Feb-99
	1.95	4.31	6.68	0.42		0	1.05	4.32	0.32	9.9	12.0	0	0	100	0	547					May-14
	3.24	6.70	16.73	23.26	97.35	0.82	1.06	11.66	1.03	19.58	177.7	10	90	0	0	36	27.39	-25.53			Aug-01
	3.17	6.52	16.34	22.34	94.97	0.48	1.26	11.66	1.03	22.22	177.7	10	90	0	0	36	27.25	-25.57			Apr-05
100	4.25	8.54	17.16			1.06	1.06			13.43	47.5	10	88	0	0	44			5.75		Dec-15
100	4.16	8.22	16.36			0.35	1.81			13.42	47.5	10	88	0	0	44				1.00	Dec-15
	4.45	8.84	17.70			1.61	0.7			13.4	47.5	10	88	0	0	44					Dec-15
	4.45	8.83	17.69			1.65	0.64			13.39	47.5	10	88	0	0	44					Dec-15
100	7.29	17.63	41.29	36.10	34.21	0.26	1.51	14.33	0.88	21.39	1,033	6	94	0	0	25	16.42	-27.95	5.75		Oct-08
100	7.06	17.17	40.22	32.98	29.19	0	2.26	14.33	0.88	20.55	1,033	6	94	0	0	25	15.96	-28.22		1.00	Oct-08
	7.13	17.32	40.60	34.32	31.37	0.05	1.92	14.34	0.88	20.91	1,033	6	94	0	0	25	16.2	-28.08			Jun-10
	7.35	17.80	41.69	37.35	36.35	0.43	1.19	14.33	0.88	21.52	1,033	6	94	0	0	25	16.63	-27.92			Mar-13
	7.28	17.73	41.61	37.07	35.82	0.38	1.26	14.36	0.89	21.5	1,033	6	94	0	0	25	16.63	-27.92			Oct-08
100	4.42	7.95	12.83	23.87	54.90	2.08	1.06	8.37	0.77	13.11	1,728	1	90	0	0	53	12.43	-9.84	5.75		Jun-08
100	4.18	7.50	12.08	21.18	49.28	1.41	1.8	8.37	0.77	13.03	1,728	1	90	0	0	53	12.01	-10.11		1.00	Jun-08
	4.33	7.79	12.60	22.89	52.81	1.82	1.34	8.35	0.76	13.09	1,728	1	90	0	0	53	12.31	-9.95			Jun-10
	4.51	8.12	13.22	25.22	57.74	2.42	0.69	8.4	0.77	13.15	1,728	1	90	0	0	53	12.72	-9.66			Nov-06
	3.04	5.97	18.96	25.45	91.18	1.27	1.27	11.5	1.07	4.56	757.8	5	95	0	0	72	24.85	-20.48			Sep-96
100	3.12	6.11	19.12	26.08	92.72	0.49	1.12	11.48	1.07	14.34	757.8	5	95	0	0	72	25	-20.47	5.75		Jun-10
100	2.95	5.75	18.19	23.16	85.83	0.73	1.87	11.38	1.06	4.09	757.8	5	95	0	0	72	24.33	-20.64		1.00	Jun-10
	3.18	6.26	19.53	27.38	96.23	0.45	0.76	11.47	1.07	26.56	757.8	5	95	0	0	72	25.27	-20.34			Jun-10
100	3.15	6.20	19.34	26.73	94.55	0.3	0.93	11.47	1.07	26.53	757.8	5	95	0	0	72	25.09	-20.38			Oct-55
	3.16	6.11	19.19	26.08	92.82	0.44	1.11	11.5	1.07	14.55	757.8	5	95	0	0	72	24.92	-20.43			Aug-93
	5.60	9.75	15.21	34.19	86.51	0.25	1.36	11.43	0.76	57.69	11,160	2	98	0	0	20	19.91	-17.72			Apr-97
	5.75	10.07	15.87	36.60	92.02	0.33	0.75	11.43	0.76	57.46	11,160	2	98	0	0	20	20.17	-17.62			Mar-13
100	5.67	9.94	15.59	35.64	89.86	0.37	1.02	11.42	0.76	57.6	11,160	2	98	0	0	20	20.17	-17.62			Sep-88
	5.66	9.88	15.50	35.28	89.05	0.04	1.09	11.42	0.76	57.65	11,160	2	98	0	0	20	20.08	-17.64			Aug-93
100	3.39	8.21	17.62	14.89	31.83	0	1.22	7.51		11.7	20.3	8	23	66	3	176	10.21	-5.91	5.75		Dec-10
100	3.16	7.74	16.62	12.23	26.97	0	1.97	7.51		11.4	20.3	8	23	66	3	176	9.85	-6.21		1.00	Dec-10
	3.52	8.41	17.99	16.10	34.13	0.38	0.86	7.52		11.77	20.3	8	23	66	3	176	10.46	-5.72			Dec-10
100	4.13	10.29	25.12	24.85	60.03	0.12	1.11	11.05	0.99	7.98	4.9	3	95	0	0	16	15.47		5.75		Jun-11
100	3.96	9.82	24.18	22.12	54.30	0	1.86	11.06	0.99	7.6	4.9	3	95	0	0	16	14.92			1.00	Jun-11
	4.05	10.43	25.47	25.95	62.79	0.45	0.75	11.12	0.99	8.06	4.9	3	95	0	0	16	15.66				Jun-11
100	3.61	6.13	13.71	15.82		2.33	1.37			10.75	2.8	1	99	0	0	61			5.75		Dec-14
100	3.54	5.83	12.94	13.38		1.71	2.12			10.74	2.8	1	99	0	0	61				1.00	Dec-14
	3.77	6.36	14.12	17.14		2.75	1.01			10.75	2.8	1	99	0	0	61					Dec-14
100	12.53	24.98	65.41	62.88		0.01	1.87	21.71	0.98	15.98	140.0	4	97	0	0	116			5.75		Jul-13
100	12.28	24.46	64.06	58.74		0	2.62	21.58	0.98	15.56	140.0	4	97	0	0	116				1.00	Jul-13
	12.62	25.17	66.00	64.05		0.28	1.51	21.61	0.98	15.98	140.0	4	97	0	0	116					Jul-13
100	6.92	11.39	24.89	28.25	98.75	0.75	1.1	9.95	0.96	10.27	1,255	3	96	0	1	37	19.81	-20.09	5.75		May-09
	6.91	11.31	24.85	27.36	96.06	0.3	1.39	9.99	0.96	13.75	1,255	3	96	0	1	37	19.57	-20.22			Sep-96
100	6.72	10.97	23.93	25.36	91.27	0.2	1.84	9.91	0.96	13.11	1,255	3	96	0	1	37	19.3	-20.32		1.00	May-09
	7.09	11.61	25.41	29.69	102.50	0.69	0.72	9.93	0.96	17.53	1,255	3	96	0	1	37	20.11	-19.96			May-09
100	7.00	11.46	25.20	28.93	100.62	0.53	0.9	9.94	0.96	17.49	1,255	3	96	0	1	37	19.92	-20			Jun-50
	6.89	11.23	24.64	27.20	96.21	0.32	1.37	9.93	0.96	13.65	1,255	3	96	0	1	37	19.65	-20.16			May-09
	7.03	11.44	25.10	28.43	99.09	0.75	1.07	9.94	0.96	10.46	1,255	3	96	0	1	37	19.85	-20.1			Aug-93
100	-0.13	0.68					1.01			25.2	13.0	7	0	94	0				5.75		Apr-17
100	-0.35	0.31					1.76			25.1	13.0	7	0	94	0					1.00	Apr-17
	-0.02	0.90					0.58			25.2	13.0	7	0	94	0						Apr-17
	-0.04	0.87					0.65			25.2	13.0	7	0	94	0						Apr-17
100	3.58	10.19	26.65	26.46	47.74	0.16	1.22	11.08	0.84	28.13	1,949	4	95	0	1	27	13.75	-23.06	5.75		Jan-13

	MARKET		FUND TYPE, CATEGORY & OBJECTIVE		RATINGS				MINIMUMS	
Fund Name	Ticker Symbol	Traded On	Fund Type	Category and (Prospectus Objective)	Overall Rating	Reward Rating	Risk Rating	Recent Up/ Downgrade	Open to New Investors	Min Initial Investment
Neuberger Berman International Equity Fund Class C	NIQCX	NAS CM	Open End	Global Equity Large Cap (Foreign Stock)	B	B-	B	Up	Y	1,000
Neuberger Berman International Equity Fund Class R6	NRIQX	NAS CM	Open End	Global Equity Large Cap (Foreign Stock)	B	B	B	Up	Y	0
Neuberger Berman Intl Equity Fund Inst Cls	NBIIX	NAS CM	Open End	Global Equity Large Cap (Foreign Stock)	B	B	B	Up	Y	1,000,000
Neuberger Berman International Equity Fund Investor Class	NIQVX	NAS CM	Open End	Global Equity Large Cap (Foreign Stock)	B	B	B	Up	Y	1,000
Neuberger Berman International Equity Fund Trust Class	NIQTX	NAS CM	Open End	Global Equity Large Cap (Foreign Stock)	B	B	B	Up		0
Neuberger Berman International Select Fund Class A	NBNAX	NAS CM	Open End	Global Equity Large Cap (Foreign Stock)	B	B-	B	Up	Y	1,000
Neuberger Berman International Select Fund Class C	NBNCX	NAS CM	Open End	Global Equity Large Cap (Foreign Stock)	B-	B-	B	Up	Y	1,000
Neuberger Berman Intl Select Fund Cls Inst	NILIX	NAS CM	Open End	Global Equity Large Cap (Foreign Stock)	B	B	B	Up	Y	1,000,000
Neuberger Berman International Select Fund Class R3	NBNRX	NAS CM	Open End	Global Equity Large Cap (Foreign Stock)	B	B-	B	Up	Y	0
Neuberger Berman International Select Fund Class R6	NRILX	NAS CM	Open End	Global Equity Large Cap (Foreign Stock)	B	B-	B	Up	Y	0
Neuberger Berman International Select Fund Class Trust	NILTX	NAS CM	Open End	Global Equity Large Cap (Foreign Stock)	B	B-	B	Up		1,000
Neuberger Berman International Small Cap Fund Class A	NIOAX	NAS CM	Open End	Global Equity Mid/Small Cap (Small Company)	D	D+	A-		Y	1,000
Neuberger Berman International Small Cap Fund Class C	NIOCX	NAS CM	Open End	Global Equity Mid/Small Cap (Small Company)	D	D+	A-		Y	1,000
Neuberger Berman International Small Cap Fund Class R6	NIORX	NAS CM	Open End	Global Equity Mid/Small Cap (Small Company)	D	D+	A-		Y	0
Neuberger Berman Intl Small Cap Fund Inst Cls	NIOIX	NAS CM	Open End	Global Equity Mid/Small Cap (Small Company)	D	D+	A-		Y	1,000,000
Neuberger Berman Intrinsic Value Fund Class A	NINAX	NAS CM	Open End	US Equity Small Cap (Growth)	B	B	B	Up	Y	1,000
Neuberger Berman Intrinsic Value Fund Class C	NINCX	NAS CM	Open End	US Equity Small Cap (Growth)	B	B	B	Up	Y	1,000
Neuberger Berman Intrinsic Value Fund Institutional Class	NINLX	NAS CM	Open End	US Equity Small Cap (Growth)	B	B	B	Up	Y	1,000,000
Neuberger Berman Large Cap Value Fund Advisor Class	NBPBX	NAS CM	Open End	US Equity Large Cap Value (Growth)	B-	B-	B-			0
Neuberger Berman Large Cap Value Fund Class A	NPNAX	NAS CM	Open End	US Equity Large Cap Value (Growth)	B-	B-	B-		Y	1,000
Neuberger Berman Large Cap Value Fund Class C	NPNCX	NAS CM	Open End	US Equity Large Cap Value (Growth)	B-	B-	C+		Y	1,000
Neuberger Berman Large Cap Value Fund Class R3	NPNRX	NAS CM	Open End	US Equity Large Cap Value (Growth)	B-	B-	C+		Y	0
Neuberger Berman Large Cap Value Fund Institutional Class	NBPIX	NAS CM	Open End	US Equity Large Cap Value (Growth)	B-	B-	B-		Y	1,000,000
Neuberger Berman Large Cap Value Fund Investor Class	NPRTX	NAS CM	Open End	US Equity Large Cap Value (Growth)	B-	B-	B-			1,000
Neuberger Berman Large Cap Value Fund Trust Class	NBPTX	NAS CM	Open End	US Equity Large Cap Value (Growth)	B-	B-	B-			0
Neuberger Berman Long Short Credit Fund Class A	NLNAX	NAS CM	Open End	Other Alternative (Growth & Income)	C	C	B	Up	Y	1,000
Neuberger Berman Long Short Credit Fund Class C	NLNCX	NAS CM	Open End	Other Alternative (Growth & Income)	C	C	B	Up	Y	1,000
Neuberger Berman Long Short Credit Fund Class R6	NRLNX	NAS CM	Open End	Other Alternative (Growth & Income)	C	C	B	Up	Y	0
Neuberger Berman Long Short Credit Fund Institutional Cls	NLNIX	NAS CM	Open End	Other Alternative (Growth & Income)	C	C	B	Up	Y	1,000,000
Neuberger Berman Long Short Fund Class A	NLSAX	NAS CM	Open End	Long/Short Equity (Growth)	C+	C+	B	Down	Y	1,000
Neuberger Berman Long Short Fund Class C	NLSCX	NAS CM	Open End	Long/Short Equity (Growth)	C+	C	B-	Down	Y	1,000
Neuberger Berman Long Short Fund Institutional Class	NLSIX	NAS CM	Open End	Long/Short Equity (Growth)	C+	C+	B	Down	Y	1,000,000
Neuberger Berman Mid Cap Growth Fund Advisor Class	NBMBX	NAS CM	Open End	US Equity Mid Cap (Growth)	B	B	C+	Up		0
Neuberger Berman Mid Cap Growth Fund Class A	NMGAX	NAS CM	Open End	US Equity Mid Cap (Growth)	B	B+	B	Up	Y	1,000
Neuberger Berman Mid Cap Growth Fund Class C	NMGCX	NAS CM	Open End	US Equity Mid Cap (Growth)	B	B	C+	Up	Y	1,000
Neuberger Berman Mid Cap Growth Fund Class R3	NMGRX	NAS CM	Open End	US Equity Mid Cap (Growth)	B	B	C+	Up	Y	0
Neuberger Berman Mid Cap Growth Fund Class R6	NRMGX	NAS CM	Open End	US Equity Mid Cap (Growth)	B	B+	C+	Up	Y	0
Neuberger Berman Mid Cap Growth Fund Institutional Class	NBMLX	NAS CM	Open End	US Equity Mid Cap (Growth)	B	B+	C+	Up	Y	1,000,000
Neuberger Berman Mid Cap Growth Fund Investor Class	NMANX	NAS CM	Open End	US Equity Mid Cap (Growth)	B	B+	B	Up		1,000
Neuberger Berman Mid Cap Growth Fund Trust Class	NBMTX	NAS CM	Open End	US Equity Mid Cap (Growth)	B	B+	B	Up		0
Neuberger Berman Mid Cap Intrinsic Value Fund Class A	NBRAX	NAS CM	Open End	US Equity Mid Cap (Growth)	B-	B-	B		Y	1,000
Neuberger Berman Mid Cap Intrinsic Value Fund Class C	NBRCX	NAS CM	Open End	US Equity Mid Cap (Growth)	B-	B-	B	Up	Y	1,000
Neuberger Berman Mid Cap Intrinsic Value Fund Class R3	NBRRX	NAS CM	Open End	US Equity Mid Cap (Growth)	B-	B-	B		Y	0
Neuberger Berman Mid Cap Intrinsic Value Fund Class Trust	NBREX	NAS CM	Open End	US Equity Mid Cap (Growth)	B-	B-	B			0
Neuberger Berman Mid Cap Intrinsic Value Fund Inst Cls	NBRTX	NAS CM	Open End	US Equity Mid Cap (Growth)	B-	B-	B	Down	Y	1,000,000
Neuberger Berman Mid Cap Intrinsic Value Fund Investor Cls	NBRVX	NAS CM	Open End	US Equity Mid Cap (Growth)	B-	B-	B	Down		1,000
Neuberger Berman MLP Income Fund Inc.	NML	AMEX	Closed End	Energy Sector Equity (Natl Res)	D	D	D	Down	Y	
Neuberger Berman Multi-Asset Income Fund Class A	NANAX	NAS CM	Open End	Cautious Alloc (Growth & Income)	B-	C	B	Up	Y	1,000
Neuberger Berman Multi-Asset Income Fund Class C	NANCX	NAS CM	Open End	Cautious Alloc (Growth & Income)	C+	C	B	Up	Y	1,000
Neuberger Berman Multi-Asset Income Fund Class R6	NRANX	NAS CM	Open End	Cautious Alloc (Growth & Income)	B-	C	B	Up	Y	0
Neuberger Berman Multi-Asset Income Fund Institutional Cls	NANIX	NAS CM	Open End	Cautious Alloc (Growth & Income)	B-	C	B	Up	Y	1,000,000
Neuberger Berman Multi-Cap Opportunities Fund Class A	NMUAX	NAS CM	Open End	US Equity Large Cap Blend (Growth & Income)	B	B	B-		Y	1,000

★ Expanded analysis of this fund is included in Section II.

	TOTAL RETURNS					PERFORMANCE				ASSETS		ASSET ALLOCATION & TURNOVER					BULL & BEAR		FEES		
Min Additional Investment	3-Month Total Return	6-Month Total Return	1-Year Total Return	3-Year Total Return	5-Year Total Return	Dividend Yield (TTM)	Expense Ratio	3-Yr Std Deviation	3-Year Beta	NAV	Total Assets (MIL)	%Cash	%Stocks	%Bonds	%Other	Turnover Ratio	Last Bull Market Total Return	Last Bear Market Total Return	Front End Fee (%)	Back End Fee (%)	Inception Date
100	3.43	9.78	25.78	23.67	42.27	0	1.97	11.08	0.84	27.37	1,949	4	95	0	1	27	13.26	-23.3		1.00	Jan-13
	3.66	10.45	27.23	28.18	50.91	1.2	0.78	11.14	0.85	13.51	1,949	4	95	0	1	27	13.99	-22.94			Sep-13
	3.75	10.45	27.16	27.91	50.47	1.15	0.86	11.1	0.85	13.4	1,949	4	95	0	1	27	13.99	-22.94			Jun-05
100	3.65	10.26	27.35	27.54	49.49	0.36	1.23	11.09	0.85	25.33	1,949	4	95	0	1	27	13.92	-22.98			Jan-13
	3.63	10.23	27.34	27.35	48.97	0.28	1.27	11.11	0.85	28.34	1,949	4	95	0	1	27	13.83	-23.02			Jan-13
100	3.24	10.45	27.25	24.60	43.31	0.92	1.16	11.18	0.86	13.03	245.5	2	94	0	1	27	13.6	-24.56	5.75		Dec-07
100	3.04	9.98	26.21	21.89	38.10	0.28	1.91	11.1	0.86	12.9	245.5	2	94	0	1	27	13.02	-24.74		1.00	Dec-07
	3.25	10.59	27.54	25.93	45.85	1.21	0.8	11.14	0.86	13.08	245.5	2	94	0	1	27	13.85	-24.42			Oct-06
	3.03	10.20	26.75	23.66	41.41	0.8	1.41	11.1	0.85	12.92	245.5	2	94	0	1	27	13.32	-24.6			May-09
	3.23	10.56	27.59	25.04	43.64		0.73	11.16	0.86	13.08	245.5	2	94	0	1	27	13.54	-24.51			Apr-17
100	3.23	10.47	27.25	24.71	43.26	0.91	1.15	11.16	0.86	13.13	245.5	2	94	0	1	27	13.54	-24.51			Aug-06
100	5.61	12.14	36.48				1.44			13.09	1.8	3	96	0	1	43			5.75		Dec-16
100	5.40	11.69	35.38				2.19			13.04	1.8	3	96	0	1	43				1.00	Dec-16
	5.73	12.33	37.01				1.01			13.1	1.8	3	96	0	1	43					Dec-16
	5.75	12.36	36.94				1.08			13.1	1.8	3	96	0	1	43					Dec-16
100	1.41	7.69	16.25	25.91	88.85	0	1.37	13.4	0.84	15.83	914.8	4	95	0	0	26	24.09	-29.4	5.75		May-10
100	1.24	7.26	15.40	23.19	82.01	0	2.12	13.36	0.83	14.82	914.8	4	95	0	0	26	23.47	-29.61		1.00	May-10
	1.55	7.92	16.71	27.41	92.57	0	1.01	13.41	0.84	16.34	914.8	4	95	0	0	26	24.31	-29.29			May-10
	4.97	8.36	13.01	25.28	86.25	1.16	1.21	13.32	1.18	31.31	1,514	14	86	0	0	74	19.79	-26.46			Aug-96
100	5.00	8.38	13.16	25.72	87.26	0.87	1.08	13.37	1.18	31.28	1,514	14	86	0	0	74	19.9	-26.42	5.75		Jun-10
100	4.81	8.01	12.35	22.99	80.45	0.83	1.83	13.38	1.18	31.43	1,514	14	86	0	0	74	19.31	-26.65		1.00	Jun-10
	4.95	8.21	12.78	24.64	84.67	1.03	1.37	13.37	1.18	31.35	1,514	14	86	0	0	74	19.73	-26.49			Jun-10
	5.11	8.62	13.56	27.21	90.95	0.73	0.71	13.37	1.18	31.2	1,514	14	86	0	0	74	20.11	-26.29			Jun-06
100	5.07	8.49	13.39	26.51	89.36	0.57	0.88	13.36	1.18	31.23	1,514	14	86	0	0	74	20.02	-26.36			Jan-75
	5.01	8.44	13.21	25.89	87.70	0.85	1.06	13.37	1.18	31.28	1,514	14	86	0	0	74	19.87	-26.39			Aug-93
100	-0.05	1.57	3.96			3.62	1.58			9.58	25.3	15	0	72	3	190			4.25		Jun-15
100	-0.29	1.14	3.14			2.87	2.33			9.57	25.3	15	0	72	3	190				1.00	Jun-15
	0.05	1.79	4.41			4.05	1.14			9.58	25.3	15	0	72	3	190					Jun-15
	0.03	1.76	4.34			3.98	1.22			9.58	25.3	15	0	72	3	190					Jun-15
100	3.30	4.80	13.03	11.46	31.37	0	1.72	5.38	0.88	14.39	3,172	43	51	5	1	86			5.75		Dec-11
100	3.06	4.39	12.21	8.93	26.50	0	2.46	5.36	0.88	13.78	3,172	43	51	5	1	86				1.00	Dec-11
	3.31	4.94	13.39	12.62	33.61	0	1.35	5.39	0.89	14.65	3,172	43	51	5	1	86					Dec-11
	6.91	11.65	24.84	31.02	89.30	0	1.24	11.8	1.01	14.71	1,274	4	96	0	0	47	24.32	-15.2			Sep-96
100	6.91	11.70	25.00	31.48	90.53	0	1.12	11.81	1.01	14.71	1,274	4	96	0	0	47	24.58	-15.07	5.75		May-09
100	6.76	11.34	24.10	28.62	83.69	0	1.87	11.81	1.01	14.7	1,274	4	96	0	0	47	23.99	-15.3		1.00	May-09
	6.89	11.61	24.71	30.54	88.33	0	1.37	11.81	1.01	14.71	1,274	4	96	0	0	47	24.43	-15.16			May-09
	7.05	11.96	25.57	33.28	94.86	0	0.65	11.81	1.01	14.72	1,274	4	96	0	0	47	24.64	-15.03			Mar-13
	7.05	11.98	25.46	32.98	94.23	0	0.73	11.79	1.01	14.72	1,274	4	96	0	0	47	24.91	-14.99			Apr-07
100	7.02	11.86	25.33	32.31	92.39	0	0.93	11.8	1.01	14.72	1,274	4	96	0	0	47	24.64	-15.03			Mar-79
	7.02	11.84	25.25	32.08	91.88	0	0.98	11.81	1.01	14.72	1,274	4	96	0	0	47	24.63	-15.03			Aug-93
100	3.07	6.52	16.50	25.19	98.01	0.54	1.21	12.14	1.08	18.47	102.8	10	90	0	0	31	27.06	-25.68	5.75		Jun-10
100	2.86	6.12	15.57	22.42	90.68	0.31	1.96	12.15	1.08	18	102.8	10	90	0	0	31	26.55	-25.99		1.00	Jun-10
	2.97	6.37	16.17	24.26	95.56	0.46	1.46	12.14	1.08	18.42	102.8	10	90	0	0	31	27.03	-25.89			Jun-10
	3.02	6.53	16.43	25.07	97.58	0.54	1.25	12.14	1.08	18.49	102.8	10	90	0	0	31	27.09	-25.73			Jun-99
	3.16	6.72	16.92	26.55	101.65	0.71	0.85	12.13	1.08	22.83	102.8	10	90	0	0	31	27.42	-25.64			Mar-10
100	3.05	6.61	16.70	25.67	99.56	0.44	1.25	12.14	1.08	22.84	102.8	10	90	0	0	31	27.37	-25.76			Jun-99
	-2.77	-2.43	-2.99	-35.64		0	1.98	31.9		9.74	520.7	3	121	0	-28	49					Mar-13
100	1.92	4.99	11.13			3.19	1.15			10.26	23.1	5	40	52	1	94			4.25		Mar-15
100	1.73	4.60	10.31			2.46	1.9			10.26	23.1	5	40	52	1	94				1.00	Mar-15
	2.02	5.22	11.61			3.62	0.71			10.26	23.1	5	40	52	1	94					Mar-15
	2.01	5.18	11.53			3.55	0.78			10.26	23.1	5	40	52	1	94					Mar-15
100	6.96	11.53	24.42	37.54	113.96	0.36	1.1	11.08	1.05	18.46	2,064	1	99	0	0	23	27.04	-17.64	5.75		Dec-09

Fund Name	MARKET: Ticker Symbol	MARKET: Traded On	FUND TYPE, CATEGORY & OBJECTIVE: Fund Type	FUND TYPE, CATEGORY & OBJECTIVE: Category and (Prospectus Objective)	RATINGS: Overall Rating	RATINGS: Reward Rating	RATINGS: Risk Rating	RATINGS: Recent Up/ Downgrade	MINIMUMS: Open to New Investors	MINIMUMS: Min Initial Investment
Neuberger Berman Multi-Cap Opportunities Fund Class C	NMUCX	NAS CM	Open End	US Equity Large Cap Blend (Growth & Income)	B	B	B-		Y	1,000
Neuberger Berman Multi-Cap Opp Fund Inst Cls	NMULX	NAS CM	Open End	US Equity Large Cap Blend (Growth & Income)	B	B	B-		Y	1,000,000
Neuberger Berman Real Estate Fund Class A	NREAX	NAS CM	Open End	Real Estate Sector Equity (Real Estate)	B	B-	B+	Up	Y	1,000
Neuberger Berman Real Estate Fund Class C	NRECX	NAS CM	Open End	Real Estate Sector Equity (Real Estate)	B	B-	B	Up	Y	1,000
Neuberger Berman Real Estate Fund Class R3	NRERX	NAS CM	Open End	Real Estate Sector Equity (Real Estate)	B	B-	B+	Up	Y	0
Neuberger Berman Real Estate Fund Class R6	NRREX	NAS CM	Open End	Real Estate Sector Equity (Real Estate)	B	B-	B+	Up	Y	0
Neuberger Berman Real Estate Fund Institutional Class	NBRIX	NAS CM	Open End	Real Estate Sector Equity (Real Estate)	B	B-	B+	Up	Y	1,000,000
Neuberger Berman Real Estate Fund Trust Class	NBRFX	NAS CM	Open End	Real Estate Sector Equity (Real Estate)	B	B-	B+	Up		1,000
Neuberger Berman Real Estate Securities Income Fund Inc	NRO	AMEX	Closed End	Real Estate Sector Equity (Real Estate)	C+	C	B	Down	Y	
Neuberger Berman Risk Balanced Commodity Strat Fund Cls A	NRBAX	NAS CM	Open End	Commodities Broad Basket (Balanced)	C-	C-	D+	Up	Y	1,000
Neuberger Berman Risk Balanced Commodity Strat Fund Cls C	NRBCX	NAS CM	Open End	Commodities Broad Basket (Balanced)	C-	C-	D+	Up	Y	1,000
Neuberger Berman Risk Bal Commod Strat Inst Cls	NRBIX	NAS CM	Open End	Commodities Broad Basket (Balanced)	C-	C-	D+	Up	Y	1,000,000
Neuberger Berman Small Cap Growth Fund Advisor Class	NBMVX	NAS CM	Open End	US Equity Small Cap (Small Company)	B	B+	C	Up		0
Neuberger Berman Small Cap Growth Fund Class A	NSNAX	NAS CM	Open End	US Equity Small Cap (Small Company)	B	B+	B-	Up	Y	1,000
Neuberger Berman Small Cap Growth Fund Class C	NSNCX	NAS CM	Open End	US Equity Small Cap (Small Company)	B	B+	B-	Up	Y	1,000
Neuberger Berman Small Cap Growth Fund Class R3	NSNRX	NAS CM	Open End	US Equity Small Cap (Small Company)	B	B+	B-	Up	Y	0
Neuberger Berman Small Cap Growth Fund Institutional Class	NBSMX	NAS CM	Open End	US Equity Small Cap (Small Company)	B	B+	C	Up	Y	1,000,000
Neuberger Berman Small Cap Growth Fund Investor Class	NBMIX	NAS CM	Open End	US Equity Small Cap (Small Company)	B	B+	C	Up		1,000
Neuberger Berman Small Cap Growth Fund Trust Class	NBMOX	NAS CM	Open End	US Equity Small Cap (Small Company)	B	B+	C	Up		0
Neuberger Berman Socially Responsive Fund Class A	NRAAX	NAS CM	Open End	US Equity Large Cap Growth (Growth)	B	B-	B+		Y	1,000
Neuberger Berman Socially Responsive Fund Class C	NRACX	NAS CM	Open End	US Equity Large Cap Growth (Growth)	B	B-	B+	Up	Y	1,000
Neuberger Berman Socially Responsive Fund Class R3	NRARX	NAS CM	Open End	US Equity Large Cap Growth (Growth)	B	B-	B+		Y	0
Neuberger Berman Socially Responsive Fund Class R6	NRSRX	NAS CM	Open End	US Equity Large Cap Growth (Growth)	B	B-	B+		Y	0
Neuberger Berman Socially Responsive Fund Inst Cls	NBSLX	NAS CM	Open End	US Equity Large Cap Growth (Growth)	B	B-	B+		Y	1,000,000
Neuberger Berman Socially Responsive Fund Investor Class	NBSRX	NAS CM	Open End	US Equity Large Cap Growth (Growth)	B	B-	B+			1,000
Neuberger Berman Socially Responsive Fund Trust Class	NBSTX	NAS CM	Open End	US Equity Large Cap Growth (Growth)	A	A+	B+	Up		0
Neuberger Berman U.S. Eq Ind PutWrite Strat Fund Cls A	NUPAX	NAS CM	Open End	Long/Short Equity (Growth & Income)	D	C-	A-		Y	1,000
Neuberger Berman U.S. Eq Ind PutWrite Strat Fund Cls C	NUPCX	NAS CM	Open End	Long/Short Equity (Growth & Income)	D	C-	A-		Y	1,000
Neuberger Berman U.S. Eq Ind PutWrite Strat Fund Cls R6	NUPRX	NAS CM	Open End	Long/Short Equity (Growth & Income)	D	C-	A-		Y	0
Neuberger Berman U.S. Eq Ind PutWrite Strat Fund Inst Cls	NUPIX	NAS CM	Open End	Long/Short Equity (Growth & Income)	D	C-	A-		Y	1,000,000
Neuberger Berman Value Fund Class A	NVAAX	NAS CM	Open End	US Equity Large Cap Value (Growth)	B-	B-	C+		Y	1,000
Neuberger Berman Value Fund Class C	NVACX	NAS CM	Open End	US Equity Large Cap Value (Growth)	B-	B-	C+		Y	1,000
Neuberger Berman Value Fund Institutional Class	NLRLX	NAS CM	Open End	US Equity Large Cap Value (Growth)	B-	B-	C+		Y	1,000,000
New Alternatives Fund Class A	NALFX	NAS CM	Open End	Global Equity Mid/Small Cap (Growth & Income)	C	C	C+	Down	Y	2,500
New Alternatives Fund Investor Shares	NAEFX	NAS CM	Open End	Global Equity Mid/Small Cap (Growth & Income)	C	C	C+	Down	Y	3,500
New Covenant Balanced Growth Fund	NCBGX	NAS CM	Open End	Moderate Alloc (Balanced)	B-	C+	B	Up	Y	500
New Covenant Balanced Income Fund	NCBIX	NAS CM	Open End	Cautious Alloc (Balanced)	B-	C+	B	Up	Y	500
New Covenant Growth Fund	NCGFX	NAS CM	Open End	US Equity Large Cap Growth (Growth)	B-	B-	B-	Down	Y	500
New Covenant Growth Fund	GF	NYSE	Closed End	Other Equity (Europe Stock)	A	A	A-	Up	Y	
New Ireland Fund	IRL	NYSE	Closed End	Other Equity (Europe Stock)	C+	C+	C+	Up	Y	
Newfound Multi-Asset Income Fund Class A	NFMAX	NAS CM	Open End	Moderate Alloc (Growth & Income)	B-	C	B	Up	Y	2,500
Newfound Multi-Asset Income Fund Class C	NFMCX	NAS CM	Open End	Moderate Alloc (Growth & Income)	C+	C	B		Y	2,500
Newfound Multi-Asset Income Fund Class I	NFMIX	NAS CM	Open End	Moderate Alloc (Growth & Income)	B-	C	B	Up	Y	1,000,000
Newfound Risk Managed Global Sectors Fund Class A	NFGAX	NAS CM	Open End	Moderate Alloc (Growth)	C+	C+	C+	Down	Y	2,500
Newfound Risk Managed Global Sectors Fund Class C	NFGCX	NAS CM	Open End	Moderate Alloc (Growth)	C+	C+	C+	Up	Y	2,500
Newfound Risk Managed Global Sectors Fund Class I	NFGIX	NAS CM	Open End	Moderate Alloc (Growth)	C+	C+	C+	Down	Y	1,000,000
Newfound Risk Managed U.S. Sectors Fund Class A	NFDAX	NAS CM	Open End	Moderate Alloc (Growth & Income)	C	C+	B-	Up	Y	2,500
Newfound Risk Managed U.S. Sectors Fund Class C	NFDCX	NAS CM	Open End	Moderate Alloc (Growth & Income)	C	C+	B-	Up	Y	2,500
Newfound Risk Managed U.S. Sectors Fund Class I	NFDIX	NAS CM	Open End	Moderate Alloc (Growth & Income)	C	C+	B-	Up	Y	1,000,000
NexPoint Credit Strategies Fund	NHF	NYSE	Closed End	Moderate Alloc (Multisector Bond)	C+	B-	C+	Up	Y	
NexPoint Real Estate Strategies Fund Class A	US65342M1018		Closed End	Real Estate Sector Equity (Real Estate)	D	D+	B		Y	500
NexPoint Real Estate Strategies Fund Class C	US65342M2008		Closed End	Real Estate Sector Equity (Real Estate)	D	D+	B		Y	500

★ Expanded analysis of this fund is included in Section II.

Min Additional Investment	TOTAL RETURNS: 3-Month Total Return	6-Month Total Return	1-Year Total Return	3-Year Total Return	5-Year Total Return	PERFORMANCE: Dividend Yield (TTM)	Expense Ratio	3-Yr Std Deviation	3-Year Beta	ASSETS: NAV	Total Assets (MIL)	ASSET ALLOCATION & TURNOVER: %Cash	%Stocks	%Bonds	%Other	Turnover Ratio	BULL & BEAR: Last Bull Market Total Return	Last Bear Market Total Return	FEES: Front End Fee (%)	Back End Fee (%)	Inception Date
100	6.72	11.09	23.52	34.52	105.79	0	1.84	11.05	1.04	17.69	2,064	1	99	0	0	23	26.54	-17.97		1.00	Dec-09
	6.98	11.64	24.81	39.01	117.56	0.7	0.75	11.04	1.04	18.56	2,064	1	99	0	0	23	27.38	-17.61			Nov-06
100	3.75	5.19	11.54	17.52	50.04	1.82	1.22	12.28	0.96	13.16	507.2	0	99	1	0	45	31.02	-16.78	5.75		Jun-10
100	3.62	4.76	10.65	14.92	44.48	1.13	1.97	12.29	0.96	13.19	507.2	0	99	1	0	45	30.45	-17.12		1.00	Jun-10
	3.69	5.06	11.19	16.68	48.20	1.6	1.47	12.29	0.96	13.14	507.2	0	99	1	0	45	30.87	-16.93			Jun-10
	3.85	5.40	11.92	19.04	53.27	2.2	0.79	12.28	0.96	13.19	507.2	0	99	1	0	45	31.12	-16.7			Mar-13
	3.83	5.37	11.92	18.77	52.76	2.14	0.86	12.31	0.96	13.2	507.2	0	99	1	0	45	31.27	-16.67			Jun-08
100	3.79	5.20	11.57	18.06	51.23	1.98	1.41	12.34	0.96	13.15	507.2	0	99	1	0	45	31.13	-16.7			May-02
	-0.09	1.02	7.48	13.57	49.20	7.71		12.55	0.96	5.75	273.6	1	57	0	0	14	30.85	-16.4			Oct-03
100	5.16	9.47	6.03	-13.21	-34.50	0	1.1	12.78	0.96	6.18	126.3	17	0	68	16	58			5.75		Aug-12
100	5.02	9.16	5.20	-15.83	-37.47	0	1.85	12.74	0.96	5.97	126.3	17	0	68	16	58				1.00	Aug-12
	5.47	9.72	6.50	-12.22	-33.19	0	0.74	12.75	0.96	6.29	126.3	17	0	68	16	58					Aug-12
	4.75	11.59	27.69	26.79	96.77	0	1.61	15.74	0.98	24.09	76.6	2	98	0	0	215	21.79	-21.19			May-02
100	4.83	11.72	28.02	27.73	99.28	0	1.27	15.75	0.99	38.43	76.6	2	98	0	0	215	22.08	-21.08	5.75		May-09
100	4.69	11.31	27.09	24.94	92.00	0	2.02	15.73	0.98	23.06	76.6	2	98	0	0	215	21.59	-21.32		1.00	May-09
	4.78	11.55	27.72	26.82	96.85	0	1.52	15.71	0.98	24.16	76.6	2	98	0	0	215	21.84	-21.11			May-09
	4.94	11.92	28.48	29.13	102.92	0	0.91	15.73	0.98	36.14	76.6	2	98	0	0	215	22.36	-20.95			Apr-08
100	4.84	11.75	28.12	27.97	99.76	0	1.31	15.75	0.99	35.09	76.6	2	98	0	0	215	22.11	-21.05			Oct-98
	4.83	11.67	27.90	27.32	97.99	0	1.41	15.72	0.98	38.01	76.6	2	98	0	0	215	22.03	-21.13			Nov-98
100	5.44	8.24	18.36	28.09	99.61	0.95	1.04	10.04	0.96	38.19	2,466	3	97	0	0	26	20	-20.64	5.75		May-09
100	5.25	7.83	17.43	25.24	92.26	0.37	1.78	10.03	0.96	38.32	2,466	3	97	0	0	26	19.49	-20.9		1.00	May-09
	5.39	8.08	18.07	27.16	97.30	0.8	1.28	10.02	0.95	38.28	2,466	3	97	0	0	26	19.86	-20.73			May-09
	5.56	8.44	18.84	29.80	104.00	0.77	0.59	10.04	0.96	38.04	2,466	3	97	0	0	26	20.15	-20.58			Mar-13
	5.54	8.42	18.76	29.49	103.41	0.71	0.67	10.03	0.95	38.06	2,466	3	97	0	0	26	20.29	-20.53			Nov-07
100	5.50	8.33	18.56	28.81	101.58	0.54	0.85	10.04	0.96	38.13	2,466	3	97	0	0	26	20.15	-20.58			Mar-94
	85.01	89.87	107.70	124.85	250.62	0.94	1.02	10.02	0.95	38.19	2,466	3	97	0	0	26	20.05	-20.65			Mar-97
100	2.13	4.58	10.97			0.09	1.01			10.89	188.6	9	0	91	0				5.75		Sep-16
100	1.92	4.16	10.10			0	1.76			10.79	188.6	9	0	91	0					1.00	Sep-16
	2.13	4.79	11.48			0.42	0.58			10.9	188.6	9	0	91	0						Sep-16
	2.11	4.75	11.32			0.38	0.65			10.89	188.6	9	0	91	0						Sep-16
100	5.24	8.73	13.51	26.21	84.30	0.36	1.13	13.35	1.18	17.72	16.9	10	90	0	0	115	20.51	-15.81	5.75		Mar-11
100	5.02	8.29	12.64	23.42	77.59	0.49	1.88	13.36	1.18	17.23	16.9	10	90	0	0	115	19.99	-16.1		1.00	Mar-11
	5.32	8.96	13.99	27.64	88.07	0.61	0.77	13.38	1.18	17.74	16.9	10	90	0	0	115	20.9	-15.79			Nov-06
250	0.33	1.60	21.22	29.97	76.79	1.15	1.12	16.45	0.84	55.56	211.3	5	95	0	0	30	2.53	-24.72	3.50		Sep-82
250	-1.97	-0.81	18.20	26.12	70.70	0.96	1.37	16.44	0.84	55.43	211.3	5	95	0	0	30	2.38	-24.8			Jan-15
100	3.85	6.91	13.47	18.61	49.18	1	1.1	6.23	0.6	101.83	295.4	0	59	41	0	4	16.11	-11.39			Jun-99
100	2.16	4.24	8.69	13.00	29.99	1.25	1.05	3.68	0.34	21.25	80.7	-2	34	68	0	5	10.67	-6.14			Jun-99
100	6.50	11.29	21.59	27.78	84.56	0.73	1.13	10.6	1.03	41.98	442.9	4	96	0	0	50	24.68	-18.95			Jun-99
	8.36	20.72	48.54	67.62	128.19	1.98		13.97	0.96	21.49	442.9	0	96	6	-4	65	25	-32.53			Jan-90
	-5.95	-1.99	16.46	30.36	96.20	0	0	14.28	0.7	14.36	58.4	0	99	0	1	22	20.17	-19.77			Mar-90
250	0.56	2.42	7.48	8.52		2.91	2.06	3.82	0.14	9.97	85.2	3	30	50	1	120			5.75		Sep-14
250	0.37	2.06	6.79	6.20		2.15	2.81	3.86	0.14	9.94	85.2	3	30	50	1	120					Sep-14
10,000	0.72	2.65	7.84	9.40		3.23	1.81	3.82	0.14	9.98	85.2	3	30	50	1	120					Sep-14
250	4.58	8.85	17.92	14.34		0.26	2.22	7.46	0.58	11.41	56.0	1	99	0	0	106			5.75		May-14
250	4.36	8.39	17.10	11.85		0	2.97	7.43	0.58	11.23	56.0	1	99	0	0	106					May-14
10,000	4.58	8.95	18.25	15.25		0.54	1.97	7.51	0.59	11.42	56.0	1	99	0	0	106					May-14
250	5.55	9.49	16.91			0.36	1.64			11.02	42.0	0	100	0	0	190			5.75		Jun-15
250	5.37	9.15	16.08			0	2.39			10.97	42.0	0	100	0	0	190					Jun-15
10,000	5.68	9.89	17.47			0.53	1.39			11.08	42.0	0	100	0	0	190					Jun-15
	8.96	11.40	17.49	12.49	126.22	9.24	1.94	14.55	-1.03	26.35	590.5	1	61	18	2	41	7.73	-8.19			Jun-06
50	10.86	5.13	10.09			6.18	2.67			20.79	--								5.75		Jul-16
50	11.26	5.35	9.82			5.38	3.67			20.87	--									1.00	Jul-16

	MARKET		FUND TYPE, CATEGORY & OBJECTIVE		RATINGS				MINIMUMS	
Fund Name	Ticker Symbol	Traded On	Fund Type	Category and (Prospectus Objective)	Overall Rating	Reward Rating	Risk Rating	Recent Up/ Downgrade	Open to New Investors	Min Initial Investment
NexPoint Real Estate Strategies Fund Class Z	US65342M3097		Closed End	Real Estate Sector Equity (Real Estate)	D	D+	B		Y	0
Nicholas Equity Income Fund Class I	NSEIX	NAS CM	Open End	US Equity Mid Cap (Equity-Income)	B-	C+	B		Y	500
Nicholas Fund	NICSX	NAS CM	Open End	US Equity Large Cap Growth (Growth)	B-	C+	B	Up	Y	500
Nicholas II Fund Class I	NCTWX	NAS CM	Open End	US Equity Mid Cap (Growth)	B	B	B-	Up	Y	100,000
Nicholas II Fund Class N	NNTWX	NAS CM	Open End	US Equity Mid Cap (Growth)	B	B	B-	Up	Y	500
Nicholas Limited Edition Fund Class Institutional	NCLEX	NAS CM	Open End	US Equity Small Cap (Growth)	B	B	B	Up	Y	100,000
Nicholas Limited Edition Fund Class N	NNLEX	NAS CM	Open End	US Equity Small Cap (Growth)	B	B	B	Up	Y	500
Nile Africa, Frontier and Emerging Fund Class A	NAFAX	NAS CM	Open End	Other Equity (Div Emerging Mkts)	C	C-	C	Up	Y	1,000
Nile Africa, Frontier and Emerging Fund Class C	NAFCX	NAS CM	Open End	Other Equity (Div Emerging Mkts)	C-	C-	C-	Up	Y	1,000
Nile Africa, Frontier & Emerging Fund Institutional Cls	NAFIX	NAS CM	Open End	Other Equity (Div Emerging Mkts)	C	C-	C	Up	Y	250,000
North Country Equity Growth Fund	NCEGX	NAS CM	Open End	US Equity Large Cap Growth (Growth)	B	B	B		Y	1,000
North Star Dividend Fund Class I	NSDVX	NAS CM	Open End	US Equity Small Cap (Equity-Income)	B+	B+	B+	Up	Y	5,000
North Star Micro Cap Fund Class I	NSMVX	NAS CM	Open End	US Equity Small Cap (Growth)	B-	B	C+	Up	Y	5,000
North Star Opportunity Fund Class A Shares	NSOPX	NAS CM	Open End	Aggressive Alloc (Growth)	C+	C+	C+		Y	2,500
North Star Opportunity Fund Class I Shares	NSOIX	NAS CM	Open End	Aggressive Alloc (Growth)	C+	C+	C+		Y	5,000
Northern Active M Emerging Market Equity Fund	NMMEX	NAS CM	Open End	Emerging Markets Equity (Div Emerging Mkts)	C+	B-	C	Up	Y	2,500
Northern Active M International Equity Fund	NMIEX	NAS CM	Open End	Global Equity Large Cap (Foreign Stock)	B-	C+	B-	Up	Y	2,500
Northern Active M U.S. Equity Fund	NMUSX	NAS CM	Open End	US Equity Large Cap Blend (Growth)	D+	C-	B+	Up	Y	2,500
Northern Emerging Markets Equity Index Fund	NOEMX	NAS CM	Open End	Emerging Markets Equity (Div Emerging Mkts)	B-	B	C	Up	Y	2,500
Northern Global Real Estate Index Fund	NGREX	NAS CM	Open End	Real Estate Sector Equity (Real Estate)	B-	C+	B		Y	2,500
Northern Global Sustainability Index Fund	NSRIX	NAS CM	Open End	Global Equity (World Stock)	B-	B-	B-	Down	Y	2,500
Northern Global Tactical Asset Allocation Fund	BBALX	NAS CM	Open End	Alloc (Asset Alloc)	B-	C+	B	Up	Y	2,500
Northern Income Equity Fund	NOIEX	NAS CM	Open End	US Equity Large Cap Value (Equity-Income)	B	B-	B		Y	2,500
Northern International Equity Fund	NOIGX	NAS CM	Open End	Global Equity Large Cap (Foreign Stock)	C+	C+	B-	Up	Y	2,500
Northern International Equity Index Fund	NOINX	NAS CM	Open End	Global Equity Large Cap (Foreign Stock)	B-	C+	B	Up	Y	2,500
Northern Large Cap Core Fund	NOLCX	NAS CM	Open End	US Equity Large Cap Value (Growth & Income)	B-	B-	B-	Down	Y	2,500
Northern Large Cap Value Fund	NOLVX	NAS CM	Open End	US Equity Large Cap Value (Growth)	B-	B-	B	Up	Y	2,500
Northern Mid Cap Index Fund	NOMIX	NAS CM	Open End	US Equity Mid Cap (Growth)	B	B	B		Y	2,500
Northern Multi-Manager Global Listed Infrastructure Fund	NMFIX	NAS CM	Open End	Other Sector Equity (Utility)	C+	C+	C+	Down	Y	2,500
Northern Multi-Manager Global Real Estate Fund	NMMGX	NAS CM	Open End	Real Estate Sector Equity (Real Estate)	B-	C+	B	Up	Y	2,500
Northern Small Cap Core Fund	NSGRX	NAS CM	Open End	US Equity Small Cap (Small Company)	B	B+	B	Up	Y	2,500
Northern Small Cap Index Fund	NSIDX	NAS CM	Open End	US Equity Small Cap (Small Company)	B+	A-	B	Up	Y	2,500
Northern Small Cap Value Fund	NOSGX	NAS CM	Open End	US Equity Small Cap (Small Company)	B+	B+	B	Up	Y	2,500
Northern Stock Index Fund	NOSIX	NAS CM	Open End	US Equity Large Cap Blend (Growth)	B	B	B		Y	2,500
Northern U.S. Quality ESG Fund	NUESX	NAS CM	Open End	US Equity Large Cap Blend (Growth)	U	U	U		Y	2,500
NorthPointe Large Cap Value Fund Institutional Shares	NPILX	NAS CM	Open End	US Equity Large Cap Value (Growth)	B	B-	B	Up	Y	100,000
NorthPointe Large Cap Value Fund Investor Shares	NPLVX	NAS CM	Open End	US Equity Large Cap Value (Growth)	B	B-	B	Up	Y	1,000
NorthPointe Small Cap Value Fund Institutional Shares	NPIVX	NAS CM	Open End	US Equity Small Cap (Small Company)	C+	C+	C+	Up	Y	100,000
NorthPointe Small Cap Value Fund Investor Shares	NPSVX	NAS CM	Open End	US Equity Small Cap (Small Company)	C+	C	C+	Up	Y	1,000
NorthQuest Capital Fund	NQCFX	NAS CM	Open End	US Equity Large Cap Growth (Growth & Income)	B-	B-	B-	Down	Y	1,000
Nuance Concentrated Value Fund Institutional Class	NCVLX	NAS CM	Open End	US Equity Mid Cap (Growth)	B	B-	B	Up	Y	10,000
Nuance Concentrated Value Fund Investor Class	NCAVX	NAS CM	Open End	US Equity Mid Cap (Growth)	B	B-	B	Up	Y	2,500
Nuance Concentrated Value Long-Short Fund Inst Cls Shares	NCLSX	NAS CM	Open End	Long/Short Equity (Growth)	C-	D+	B-	Up	Y	10,000
Nuance Concentrated Value Long-Short Fund Inv Cls Shares	NCLIX	NAS CM	Open End	Long/Short Equity (Growth)	C-	D+	B-	Up	Y	2,500
Nuance Mid Cap Value Fund Institutional Class	NMVLX	NAS CM	Open End	US Equity Mid Cap (Growth)	B	B	B+		Y	10,000
Nuance Mid Cap Value Fund Investor Class	NMAVX	NAS CM	Open End	US Equity Mid Cap (Growth)	B+	B	A	Up	Y	2,500
Nuance Mid Cap Value Fund Z Class Shares	NMVZX	NAS CM	Open End	US Equity Mid Cap (Growth)	B	B	B+		Y	2,500
Nuveen All Cap Energy MLP Opportunities Fund	JMLP	NYSE	Closed End	Energy Sector Equity (Income)	D+	C-	D	Up	Y	
Nuveen Concentrated Core Fund Class A	NCADX	NAS CM	Open End	US Equity Large Cap Value (Growth)	B-	C+	B	Up	Y	3,000
Nuveen Concentrated Core Fund Class C	NCAEX	NAS CM	Open End	US Equity Large Cap Value (Growth)	B-	C+	B	Up	Y	3,000
Nuveen Concentrated Core Fund Class I	NCAFX	NAS CM	Open End	US Equity Large Cap Value (Growth)	B-	C+	B	Up	Y	100,000
Nuveen Concentrated Core Fund Class R6	NCARX	NAS CM	Open End	US Equity Large Cap Value (Growth)	B-	C+	B	Up	Y	5,000,000

★ Expanded analysis of this fund is included in Section II.

Min Additional Investment	3-Month Total Return	6-Month Total Return	1-Year Total Return	3-Year Total Return	5-Year Total Return	Dividend Yield (TTM)	Expense Ratio	3-Yr Std Deviation	3-Year Beta	NAV	Total Assets (MIL)	%Cash	%Stocks	%Bonds	%Other	Turnover Ratio	Last Bull Market Total Return	Last Bear Market Total Return	Front End Fee (%)	Back End Fee (%)	Inception Date
TOTAL RETURNS						PERFORMANCE				ASSETS		ASSET ALLOCATION & TURNOVER					BULL & BEAR		FEES		
	11.68	5.96	11.11			6.38	2.33			20.88	--										Jul-16
100	4.82	6.71	12.40	20.94	78.62	2.71	0.72	10.39	0.98	20.66	507.1	9	89	0	0	36	19.28	-15.06			Nov-93
100	4.64	7.20	17.54	14.23	89.05	0.69	0.72	9.55	0.84	61.81	2,811	5	95	0	0	41	25.44	-15.66			Jul-69
100	6.69	10.69	25.63	32.04	99.73	0.24	0.61	11.06	0.97	27.67	842.2	3	97	0	0	29	27.62	-19.58			Oct-83
100	6.60	10.51	25.19	30.71	96.27	0	0.96	11.05	0.96	27.14	842.2	3	97	0	0	29	27.35	-19.67			Feb-05
100	3.08	7.32	19.92	31.41	91.44	0	0.86	11.96	0.77	26.32	398.3	6	94	0	0	42	24.19	-19.03			May-87
100	3.03	7.15	19.56	30.08	88.26	0	1.21	11.96	0.77	24.74	398.3	6	94	0	0	42	23.92	-19.13			Feb-05
100	13.32	15.13	12.63	-3.14	3.67	0	2.5	17.85	0.9	12.93	13.7	5	95	0	0	72	32.17	-23.81	5.75		Apr-10
100	13.11	14.68	11.89	-5.25	-0.10	0	3.25	17.82	0.9	12.42	13.7	5	95	0	0	72	31.53	-24.02			Apr-10
25,000	13.43	15.33	12.94	-2.38	4.98	0	2.25	17.83	0.9	13.09	13.7	5	95	0	0	72	32.33	-23.73			Nov-10
100	7.07	11.25	23.79	35.96	102.56	0.36	1.04	10.45	1	17.89	127.7	4	96	0	0	21	23.14	-16.26			Mar-01
500	2.66	6.22	8.27	29.28	83.40	2.04	1.49	8.71	0.46	21.64	80.8	2	96	0	0	23	16.36	-12.22			May-13
500	-0.58	4.19	4.83	18.04	85.69	0	1.47	12.95	0.75	28.3	83.0	8	92	0	0	33	22.73	-14.47			May-13
500	5.95	7.12	12.03	15.45	63.54	0.72	1.75	12.34	1.05	13.73	81.1	11	73	10	0	61			5.75		Dec-11
500	5.98	7.22	12.29	15.83	64.39	0.97	1.5	12.42	1.05	13.68	81.1	11	73	10	0	61					Dec-11
50	6.31	14.67	35.41	28.11	24.35	1.45	1.11	15.39	0.96	21.72	1,178	0	100	0	0	60	20.28	-25.52			Nov-08
50	4.73	11.40	29.04	20.51	33.19	1.36	0.85	11.72	0.96	11.74	1,419	0	98	0	0	115	14.15	-23.3			Jun-06
50	4.93	9.40	17.43			1.03	0.68			12.54	577.7	0	100	0	0	15					May-16
50	7.01	15.62	37.33	28.67	21.86	1.44	0.31	15.48	0.98	12.86	2,979	0	100	0	0	30	18.51	-27.2			Apr-06
50	3.48	6.80	14.36	16.77	37.41	2.86	0.5	10.93	0.98	10.76	1,882	0	98	0	2	6	23.8	-20.74			Jul-06
50	4.86	9.99	21.20	28.11	73.97	1.88	0.31	9.97	0.97	13.96	371.0	0	99	0	0	19	18.14	-19.3			Mar-08
50	3.70	7.52	14.17	21.30	40.19	2.43	0.64	6.13	0.56	13.19	91.3	1	63	35	1	28	14.45	-11.19			Jul-93
50	7.20	12.29	20.20	33.08	85.44	1.88	1.01	8.82	0.81	14.38	238.2	0	100	0	0	32	17.27	-15.26			Mar-94
50	2.41	7.83	22.89	19.41	39.84	1.3	0.51	13.26	1.03	10.26	234.3	0	97	0	1	101	16.72	-26.14			Mar-94
50	3.82	9.14	25.26	24.81	45.32	2.59	0.25	11.49	0.93	12.91	6,046	0	100	0	0	28	13.41	-23.59			Mar-05
50	7.43	12.45	20.31	30.38	107.94	1.63	0.46	10.3	1.01	19.06	246.7	0	100	0	0	67	25.04	-15.51			Dec-05
50	5.63	8.80	12.54	22.34	88.30	1.36	0.57	11.2	1.06	16.31	94.2	0	100	0	0	71	26.97	-25.5			Aug-00
50	6.18	9.60	16.03	35.14	102.71	1.11	0.16	11.08	1	19.32	2,409	0	100	0	0	20	27.72	-22.71			Mar-05
50	-0.16	3.83	22.20	21.93	65.80	2.57	1.01	10.41	0.94	13.39	1,236	0	100	0	0	81					Sep-12
50	3.33	4.07	9.67	12.01	30.20	3.73	0.93	10.46	0.92	10.84	153.7	0	98	0	2	167	23.66	-20.01			Nov-08
50	2.95	8.25	13.02	29.63	97.07	0.51	0.65	13.17	0.93	25.57	498.0	0	100	0	0	16	27.13	-23.81			Sep-99
50	3.32	9.15	14.58	31.54	96.36	0.9	0.15	14.14	1	13.62	1,275	0	100	0	0	19	27.48	-25.1			Sep-99
50	1.29	6.46	6.42	28.45	93.39	0.83	1.01	13.16	0.92	23.4	3,959	0	100	0	0	11	26.9	-21.39			Mar-94
50	6.61	11.38	21.70	36.46	110.66	1.73	0.1	10.09	1	31.75	8,114	0	100	0	0	4	24.99	-16.33			Oct-96
50	4.78						0.43			10.55	12.3										Oct-17
10,000	6.56	12.07	15.10	24.91		0.99	0.8	10.55	1	13.09	49.3	1	99	0	0						Mar-14
500	6.42	11.85	14.78	24.14		0.85	1.05	10.54	1	13.06	49.3	1	99	0	0						Mar-14
10,000	-1.55	-0.84	-2.86	13.76		0	1	15.47	1.02	10.54	28.7	1	99	0	0						Mar-14
500	-1.66	-1.03	-3.05	13.05		0	1.25	15.43	1.01	10.46	28.7	1	99	0	0						Mar-14
100	5.51	9.04	22.73	26.46	75.12	0	1.79	8.44	0.72	16.38	3.8	1	99	0	0	31	21.01	-16.93			Jan-02
100	3.71	6.41	11.06	27.99	87.95	0.53	1.18	10.18	0.86	14.67	619.8	27	73	0	0	96	19.45				May-11
100	3.70	6.28	10.72	26.87	85.44	0.31	1.43	10.16	0.85	14.63	619.8	27	73	0	0	96	19.27		5.00		Jul-12
100	-1.70	-0.57	-2.05			0	1.34			10.74	56.8	101	-1	0	0	93					Dec-15
100	-1.81	-0.76	-2.49			0	1.59			10.66	56.8	101	-1	0	0	93					Dec-15
100	4.83	7.96	15.00	39.89		0.62	0.95	10.53	0.88	12.48	474.0	17	77	0	0						Dec-13
100	4.86	7.84	14.80	38.85		0.38	1.2	10.49	0.88	12.46	474.0	17	77	0	0				5.00		Dec-13
100	4.92	8.08	14.90	39.77			0.8	10.52	0.88	12.49	474.0	17	77	0	0						May-17
	-0.21	0.63	-8.30	-29.51		0	1.99	36.55	1.76	8.64	108.1	1	99	0	0	37					Mar-14
100	2.07	8.37	16.72	16.23		1.76	1.07	12.72	1.13	30.33	98.8	0	100	0	0	137			5.75		Jun-13
100	1.85	7.96	15.82	13.61		1.14	1.82	12.72	1.13	29.9	98.8	0	100	0	0	137				1.00	Jun-13
	2.10	8.51	16.99	17.07		1.96	0.82	12.75	1.13	30.34	98.8	0	100	0	0	137					Jun-13
	2.13	8.54	17.11	17.22		2.02	0.71	12.75	1.13	30.36	98.8	0	100	0	0	137					Jun-16

		MARKET	FUND TYPE, CATEGORY & OBJECTIVE		RATINGS				MINIMUMS	
Fund Name	Ticker Symbol	Traded On	Fund Type	Category and (Prospectus Objective)	Overall Rating	Reward Rating	Risk Rating	Recent Up/ Downgrade	Open to New Investors	Min Initial Investment
Nuveen Core Equity Alpha Fund	JCE	NYSE	Closed End	US Equity Large Cap Growth (Growth & Income)	B-	B-	B	Up	Y	
Nuveen Diversified Dividend and Income Fund	JDD	NYSE	Closed End	Alloc (Multi-Asset Global)	B	C+	B+	Up	Y	
Nuveen Dividend Value Fund Class A	FFEIX	NAS CM	Open End	US Equity Large Cap Value (Equity-Income)	B	B-	B	Up	Y	3,000
Nuveen Dividend Value Fund Class C	FFECX	NAS CM	Open End	US Equity Large Cap Value (Equity-Income)	B-	B-	B	Down	Y	3,000
Nuveen Dividend Value Fund Class I	FAQIX	NAS CM	Open End	US Equity Large Cap Value (Equity-Income)	B	B	B	Up	Y	100,000
Nuveen Dividend Value Fund Class R3	FEISX	NAS CM	Open End	US Equity Large Cap Value (Equity-Income)	B	B-	B	Up	Y	0
Nuveen Dividend Value Fund Class R6	FFEFX	NAS CM	Open End	US Equity Large Cap Value (Equity-Income)	B	B	B	Up	Y	1,000,000
Nuveen Dow 30 Dynamic Overwrite Fund	DIAX	NYSE	Closed End	Long/Short Equity (Equity-Income)	B	B	B		Y	
Nuveen Energy MLP Total Return Fund	JMF	NYSE	Closed End	Energy Sector Equity (Growth & Income)	D	D	D	Down	Y	
Nuveen Equity Long/Short Fund Class A	NELAX	NAS CM	Open End	Long/Short Equity (Growth)	B	B-	B+	Up	Y	3,000
Nuveen Equity Long/Short Fund Class C	NELCX	NAS CM	Open End	Long/Short Equity (Growth)	B	C+	B+	Up	Y	3,000
Nuveen Equity Long/Short Fund Class I	NELIX	NAS CM	Open End	Long/Short Equity (Growth)	B	B-	B+	Up	Y	100,000
Nuveen Equity Market Neutral Fund Class A	NMAEX	NAS CM	Open End	Market Neutral (Growth)	B	C+	A-	Up	Y	3,000
Nuveen Equity Market Neutral Fund Class C	NMECX	NAS CM	Open End	Market Neutral (Growth)	B-	C	A-	Up	Y	3,000
Nuveen Equity Market Neutral Fund Class I	NIMEX	NAS CM	Open End	Market Neutral (Growth)	B	C+	A-	Up	Y	100,000
Nuveen Global Infrastructure Fund Class A	FGIAX	NAS CM	Open End	Other Sector Equity (Utility)	B-	C+	B-		Y	3,000
Nuveen Global Infrastructure Fund Class C	FGNCX	NAS CM	Open End	Other Sector Equity (Utility)	C+	C+	B-	Down	Y	3,000
Nuveen Global Infrastructure Fund Class I	FGIYX	NAS CM	Open End	Other Sector Equity (Utility)	B-	C+	B-		Y	100,000
Nuveen Global Infrastructure Fund Class R3	FGNRX	NAS CM	Open End	Other Sector Equity (Utility)	B-	C+	B-		Y	0
Nuveen Global Infrastructure Fund Class R6	FGIWX	NAS CM	Open End	Other Sector Equity (Utility)	B-	C+	B-		Y	5,000,000
Nuveen Gresham Diversified Commodity Strategy Fund Class A	NGVAX	NAS CM	Open End	Commodities Broad Basket (Growth & Income)	C-	C-	D+	Up	Y	3,000
Nuveen Gresham Diversified Commodity Strategy Fund Class C	NGVCX	NAS CM	Open End	Commodities Broad Basket (Growth & Income)	D+	C-	D+	Up	Y	3,000
Nuveen Gresham Diversified Commodity Strategy Fund Class I	NGVIX	NAS CM	Open End	Commodities Broad Basket (Growth & Income)	C-	C-	D+	Up	Y	100,000
Nuveen Growth Fund Class A	NSAGX	NAS CM	Open End	US Equity Large Cap Growth (Growth)	B	B	B		Y	3,000
Nuveen Growth Fund Class C	NSRCX	NAS CM	Open End	US Equity Large Cap Growth (Growth)	B	B	B		Y	3,000
Nuveen Growth Fund Class I	NSRGX	NAS CM	Open End	US Equity Large Cap Growth (Growth)	B	B	B		Y	100,000
Nuveen Growth Fund Class R3	NBGRX	NAS CM	Open End	US Equity Large Cap Growth (Growth)	B	B	B		Y	0
Nuveen International Growth Fund Class A	NBQAX	NAS CM	Open End	Global Equity Large Cap (Foreign Stock)	B	B	B-	Up	Y	3,000
Nuveen International Growth Fund Class C	NBQCX	NAS CM	Open End	Global Equity Large Cap (Foreign Stock)	B-	B-	B-	Up	Y	3,000
Nuveen International Growth Fund Class I	NBQIX	NAS CM	Open End	Global Equity Large Cap (Foreign Stock)	B	B	B-	Up	Y	100,000
Nuveen International Growth Fund Class R3	NBQBX	NAS CM	Open End	Global Equity Large Cap (Foreign Stock)	B	B	B-	Up	Y	0
Nuveen International Growth Fund Class R6	NBQFX	NAS CM	Open End	Global Equity Large Cap (Foreign Stock)	B	B	B-	Up	Y	1,000,000
Nuveen Large Cap Core Fund Class A	NLACX	NAS CM	Open End	US Equity Large Cap Blend (Growth)	B	B	B	Up	Y	3,000
Nuveen Large Cap Core Fund Class C	NLCDX	NAS CM	Open End	US Equity Large Cap Blend (Growth)	B	B-	B	Up	Y	3,000
Nuveen Large Cap Core Fund Class I	NLCIX	NAS CM	Open End	US Equity Large Cap Blend (Growth)	B	B	B	Up	Y	100,000
Nuveen Large Cap Core Fund Class R6	NLCFX	NAS CM	Open End	US Equity Large Cap Blend (Growth)	B	B	B	Up	Y	5,000,000
Nuveen Large Cap Growth Fund Class A	NLAGX	NAS CM	Open End	US Equity Large Cap Growth (Growth)	B	B	B-	Up	Y	3,000
Nuveen Large Cap Growth Fund Class C	NLCGX	NAS CM	Open End	US Equity Large Cap Growth (Growth)	B-	B	B-	Down	Y	3,000
Nuveen Large Cap Growth Fund Class I	NLIGX	NAS CM	Open End	US Equity Large Cap Growth (Growth)	B	B	B-	Up	Y	100,000
Nuveen Large Cap Growth Fund Class R6	NLAFX	NAS CM	Open End	US Equity Large Cap Growth (Growth)	B	B	B-	Up	Y	5,000,000
Nuveen Large Cap Select Fund Class A	FLRAX	NAS CM	Open End	US Equity Large Cap Blend (Growth & Income)	B	B	C+		Y	3,000
Nuveen Large Cap Select Fund Class C	FLYCX	NAS CM	Open End	US Equity Large Cap Blend (Growth & Income)	B	B	C+		Y	3,000
Nuveen Large Cap Select Fund Class I	FLRYX	NAS CM	Open End	US Equity Large Cap Blend (Growth & Income)	B	B+	B-		Y	100,000
Nuveen Large-Cap Value Fund Class A	NNGAX	NAS CM	Open End	US Equity Large Cap Value (Growth)	B-	B-	B-	Up	Y	3,000
Nuveen Large-Cap Value Fund Class C	NNGCX	NAS CM	Open End	US Equity Large Cap Value (Growth)	B-	B-	C+	Up	Y	3,000
Nuveen Large-Cap Value Fund Class I	NNGRX	NAS CM	Open End	US Equity Large Cap Value (Growth)	B-	B-	B-	Up	Y	100,000
Nuveen Large-Cap Value Fund Class R3	NMMTX	NAS CM	Open End	US Equity Large Cap Value (Growth)	B-	B-	B-	Up	Y	0
Nuveen Large-Cap Value Fund Class R6	NNGFX	NAS CM	Open End	US Equity Large Cap Value (Growth)	B-	B-	B-	Up	Y	5,000,000
Nuveen Mid Cap Growth Opportunities Fund Class A	FRSLX	NAS CM	Open End	US Equity Mid Cap (Growth)	B	B-	B	Up	Y	3,000
Nuveen Mid Cap Growth Opportunities Fund Class C	FMECX	NAS CM	Open End	US Equity Mid Cap (Growth)	B-	B-	B	Up	Y	3,000
Nuveen Mid Cap Growth Opportunities Fund Class I	FISGX	NAS CM	Open End	US Equity Mid Cap (Growth)	B	B	B	Up	Y	100,000
Nuveen Mid Cap Growth Opportunities Fund Class R3	FMEYX	NAS CM	Open End	US Equity Mid Cap (Growth)	B	B-	B	Up	Y	0

★ Expanded analysis of this fund is included in Section II.

Min Additional Investment	TOTAL RETURNS 3-Month Total Return	6-Month Total Return	1-Year Total Return	3-Year Total Return	5-Year Total Return	PERFORMANCE Dividend Yield (TTM)	Expense Ratio	3-Yr Std Deviation	3-Year Beta	ASSETS NAV	Total Assets (MIL)	ASSET ALLOCATION & TURNOVER %Cash	%Stocks	%Bonds	%Other	Turnover Ratio	BULL & BEAR Last Bull Market Total Return	Last Bear Market Total Return	FEES Front End Fee (%)	Back End Fee (%)	Inception Date
	4.90	9.26	21.70	26.25	92.23	0.87	1.07	8.97		14.76	265.5	1	97	1	1	110	25.11	-14.46			Mar-07
	2.95	5.93	12.36	21.98	58.44	4.17	0	8.82	0.6	12.71	260.0	3	51	40	5	74	23.6	-15.56			Sep-03
100	6.62	11.18	17.05	29.94	88.43	1.19	1.07	10.66	1.02	14.81	1,154	1	99	0	0	67	24.99	-16.96	5.75		Dec-92
100	6.47	10.82	16.18	27.11	81.62	0.6	1.82	10.69	1.02	14.55	1,154	1	99	0	0	67	24.42	-17.19		1.00	Feb-99
	6.67	11.33	17.29	30.87	90.93	1.39	0.82	10.66	1.02	15	1,154	1	99	0	0	67	25.13	-16.85			Aug-94
	6.58	11.09	16.75	28.99	86.25	1.09	1.33	10.69	1.02	14.75	1,154	1	99	0	0	67	24.88	-17.09			Sep-01
	6.71	11.42	17.44	31.34	91.67	1.39	0.72	10.67	1.02	15.09	1,154	1	99	0	0	67	24.99	-16.96			Feb-13
	8.63	13.32	22.15	36.09	85.72	1.55	0	8.68	0.77	19.05	686.3	1	99	0	0	6	20.92	-12.8			Apr-05
	1.36	-1.50	-7.88	-26.88	4.22	0	13.16	26.57		11.64	446.3	0	103	0	-3	28	22.08	-16.58			Feb-11
100	6.12	12.49	18.99	23.02	80.99	0	1.62	10.8	0.88	41.14	130.3	0	65	0	35	186	27.07	-17.53	5.75		Dec-08
100	5.90	12.05	18.09	20.28	74.37	0	2.37	10.78	0.88	38.13	130.3	0	65	0	35	186	26.48	-17.77		1.00	Dec-08
	6.18	12.64	19.30	23.96	83.27	0	1.36	10.79	0.88	42.13	130.3	0	65	0	35	186	27.27	-17.46			Dec-08
100	2.59	6.93	5.07	12.07		0	1.61	5.91	-10.66	23.76	86.2	0	-2	0	102	159			5.75		Jun-13
100	2.41	6.55	4.32	9.61		0	2.37	5.9	-10.88	22.95	86.2	0	-2	0	102	159				1.00	Jun-13
	2.60	7.03	5.33	12.95		0	1.37	5.92	-10.82	24.04	86.2	0	-2	0	102	159					Jun-13
100	2.36	4.78	19.37	18.73	58.40	2.49	1.23	10.04	0.93	10.93	621.7	0	95	0	5	149	16.38	-15.51	5.75		Dec-07
100	2.18	4.43	18.54	16.14	52.58	1.84	1.98	10.05	0.93	10.85	621.7	0	95	0	5	149	15.79	-15.68		1.00	Nov-08
	2.43	4.94	19.61	19.57	60.45	2.71	0.98	10.02	0.93	10.89	621.7	0	95	0	5	149	16.61	-15.45			Dec-07
	2.30	4.68	19.02	17.87	56.42	2.27	1.48	10	0.92	11.11	621.7	0	95	0	5	149	16.2	-16			Nov-08
	2.52	5.13	19.94	19.89	60.89	2.88	0.87	10.01	0.92	10.91	621.7	0	95	0	5	149	16.61	-15.45			Jun-16
100	5.92	10.04	4.15	-15.78	-35.17	0	1.31	13.35	1.01	12.22	97.3	33	0	67	0	0			5.75		Jul-12
100	5.75	9.62	3.39	-17.72	-37.48	0	2.06	13.36	1.01	11.87	97.3	33	0	67	0	0				1.00	Jul-12
	6.03	10.20	4.46	-15.12	-34.22	0	1.06	13.36	1.02	12.37	97.3	33	0	67	0	0					Jul-12
100	8.94	15.27	25.66	35.12	109.39	0.57	1.02	10.61	0.95	30.46	49.9	0	100	0	0	55	24.5	-16.45	5.75		Mar-06
100	8.72	14.86	24.70	32.11	101.77	0	1.77	10.59	0.95	27.68	49.9	0	100	0	0	55	24.04	-16.73		1.00	Mar-06
	8.98	15.44	25.97	36.13	112.12	0.77	0.77	10.6	0.95	31.03	49.9	0	100	0	0	55	24.71	-16.36			Mar-06
	8.88	15.16	25.39	34.14	106.86	0.38	1.27	10.62	0.95	30.2	49.9	0	100	0	0	55	24.39	-16.57			Mar-09
100	7.12	17.53	37.52	30.49	69.29	0	1.14	11.66	0.85	48.31	425.8	0	94	0	6	318	15.83	-25.37	5.75		Apr-09
100	6.92	17.09	36.49	27.57	63.06	0	1.89	11.66	0.85	46.04	425.8	0	94	0	6	318	15.37	-25.61		1.00	Apr-09
	7.20	17.68	37.85	31.47	71.37	0	0.89	11.65	0.85	48.69	425.8	0	94	0	6	318	15.99	-25.27			Apr-09
	7.06	17.38	37.19	29.52	67.09	0	1.39	11.64	0.85	47.73	425.8	0	94	0	6	318	15.68	-25.45			Apr-09
	7.21	17.71	37.99	31.69	71.65	0	0.77	11.65	0.85	48.77	425.8	0	94	0	6	318	15.99	-25.27			Jun-16
100	6.44	11.84	19.49	29.20		1.02	1	12.22	1.12	32.62	571.1	0	100	0	0	121			5.75		Jun-13
100	6.26	11.40	18.64	26.35		0.01	1.75	12.2	1.12	32.18	571.1	0	100	0	0	121				1.00	Jun-13
	6.50	11.96	19.78	30.18		1.41	0.75	12.18	1.12	32.57	571.1	0	100	0	0	121					Jun-13
	6.56	12.02	19.89	30.35		1.44	0.69	12.19	1.12	32.6	571.1	0	100	0	0	121					Jun-16
100	6.94	12.99	23.60	31.92		0.81	0.98	11.38	0.97	30.7	345.2	0	100	0	0	136			5.75		Jun-13
100	6.73	12.54	22.65	28.99		0.02	1.73	11.36	0.97	30.11	345.2	0	100	0	0	136				1.00	Jun-13
	7.04	13.16	23.91	32.94		1.19	0.73	11.39	0.97	30.73	345.2	0	100	0	0	136					Jun-13
	7.00	13.16	23.91	33.00		1.22	0.64	11.38	0.97	30.73	345.2	0	100	0	0	136					Jun-16
100	8.12	13.90	24.64	39.31	116.97	0.33	1.14	11.53	1.07	28.66	64.3	0	100	0	0	116	29.93	-23.26	5.75		Jan-03
100	7.90	13.44	23.68	36.22	108.90	0	1.89	11.49	1.07	26.74	64.3	0	100	0	0	116	29.27	-23.47		1.00	Jan-03
	8.15	14.00	24.94	40.34	119.62	0.51	0.89	11.52	1.07	28.85	64.3	0	100	0	0	116	30.09	-23.21			Jan-03
100	6.67	12.56	16.48	24.40	97.19	2.23	1.04	13.17	1.2	25.96	457.6	0	100	0	0	152	24.16	-19.55	5.75		Aug-96
100	6.48	12.11	15.56	21.63	89.90	1.02	1.79	13.16	1.2	24.85	457.6	0	100	0	0	152	23.63	-19.78		1.00	Aug-96
	6.73	12.66	16.75	25.32	99.62	2.63	0.79	13.14	1.2	26.05	457.6	0	100	0	0	152	24.37	-19.48			Aug-96
	6.62	12.38	16.13	23.48	94.72	1.82	1.29	13.15	1.2	26.23	457.6	0	100	0	0	152	23.99	-19.64			Aug-08
	6.77	12.71	16.79	25.48	99.87	2.71	0.73	13.15	1.2	26.06	457.6	0	100	0	0	152	24.37	-19.48			Jun-16
100	4.44	9.67	24.47	23.98	87.92	0	1.17	11.82	1.02	36.78	814.9	0	100	0	0	89	26.24	-20.49	5.75		Jan-95
100	4.23	9.25	23.53	21.19	81.00	0	1.92	11.81	1.02	27.01	814.9	0	100	0	0	89	25.66	-20.73		1.00	Sep-01
	4.50	9.81	24.78	24.91	90.29	0	0.92	11.83	1.02	44.38	814.9	0	100	0	0	89	26.42	-20.4			Dec-89
	4.39	9.53	24.19	23.05	85.63	0	1.42	11.84	1.02	34.16	814.9	0	100	0	0	89	26.07	-20.57			Dec-00

	MARKET			FUND TYPE, CATEGORY & OBJECTIVE	RATINGS				MINIMUMS	
Fund Name	Ticker Symbol	Traded On	Fund Type	Category and (Prospectus Objective)	Overall Rating	Reward Rating	Risk Rating	Recent Up/ Downgrade	Open to New Investors	Min Initial Investment
Nuveen Mid Cap Growth Opportunities Fund Class R6	FMEFX	NAS CM	Open End	US Equity Mid Cap (Growth)	B	B	B	Up	Y	1,000,000
Nuveen Mid Cap Value Fund Class A	FASEX	NAS CM	Open End	US Equity Mid Cap (Growth)	B	B	B	Up	Y	3,000
Nuveen Mid Cap Value Fund Class C	FACSX	NAS CM	Open End	US Equity Mid Cap (Growth)	B	B	B	Up	Y	3,000
Nuveen Mid Cap Value Fund Class I	FSEIX	NAS CM	Open End	US Equity Mid Cap (Growth)	B	B	B	Up	Y	100,000
Nuveen Mid Cap Value Fund Class R3	FMVSX	NAS CM	Open End	US Equity Mid Cap (Growth)	B	B	B	Up	Y	0
Nuveen Multi-Asset Income Fund Class A	NMKAX	NAS CM	Open End	Cautious Alloc (Multi-Asset Global)	D	C-	B+		Y	3,000
Nuveen Multi-Asset Income Fund Class C	NMKCX	NAS CM	Open End	Cautious Alloc (Multi-Asset Global)	D	C-	B+		Y	3,000
Nuveen Multi-Asset Income Fund Class I	NMKIX	NAS CM	Open End	Cautious Alloc (Multi-Asset Global)	D	C-	B+		Y	100,000
Nuveen Multi-Asset Income Fund Class R6	NMKRX	NAS CM	Open End	Cautious Alloc (Multi-Asset Global)	D	C-	B+		Y	1,000,000
Nuveen Multi-Asset Income Tax-Aware Fund Class A	NMXAX	NAS CM	Open End	Cautious Alloc (Multi-Asset Global)	D	C-	B+		Y	3,000
Nuveen Multi-Asset Income Tax-Aware Fund Class C	NMXCX	NAS CM	Open End	Cautious Alloc (Multi-Asset Global)	D	D+	B+		Y	3,000
Nuveen Multi-Asset Income Tax-Aware Fund Class I	NMXIX	NAS CM	Open End	Cautious Alloc (Multi-Asset Global)	D	C-	B+		Y	100,000
Nuveen Multi-Asset Income Tax-Aware Fund Class R6	NMXRX	NAS CM	Open End	Cautious Alloc (Multi-Asset Global)	D	C-	B+		Y	1,000,000
Nuveen NASDAQ 100 Dynamic Overwrite Fund	QQQX	NAS CM	Closed End	Long/Short Equity (Equity-Income)	B+	B+	B	Up	Y	
Nuveen NWQ Flexible Income Fund Class A	NWQAX	NAS CM	Open End	Cautious Alloc (Growth & Income)	B	C+	A-	Up	Y	3,000
Nuveen NWQ Flexible Income Fund Class C	NWQCX	NAS CM	Open End	Cautious Alloc (Growth & Income)	B	C+	A-	Up	Y	3,000
Nuveen NWQ Flexible Income Fund Class I	NWQIX	NAS CM	Open End	Cautious Alloc (Growth & Income)	B	C+	A-	Up	Y	100,000
Nuveen NWQ Flexible Income Fund Class R6	NQWFX	NAS CM	Open End	Cautious Alloc (Growth & Income)	B	C+	A-	Up	Y	5,000,000
Nuveen NWQ Global All-Cap Fund Class A	NGEAX	NAS CM	Open End	Global Equity (Growth)	B	B-	B	Up	Y	3,000
Nuveen NWQ Global All-Cap Fund Class C	NGECX	NAS CM	Open End	Global Equity (Growth)	B-	C+	B	Up	Y	3,000
Nuveen NWQ Global All-Cap Fund Class I	NGEIX	NAS CM	Open End	Global Equity (Growth)	B	B-	B	Up		100,000
Nuveen NWQ Global Equity Income Fund Class A	NQGAX	NAS CM	Open End	Global Equity (Equity-Income)	B-	C+	B-	Up	Y	3,000
Nuveen NWQ Global Equity Income Fund Class C	NQGCX	NAS CM	Open End	Global Equity (Equity-Income)	C+	C+	B-	Up	Y	3,000
Nuveen NWQ Global Equity Income Fund Class I	NQGIX	NAS CM	Open End	Global Equity (Equity-Income)	B-	C+	B-	Up	Y	100,000
Nuveen NWQ Global Equity Income Fund Class R3	NQGRX	NAS CM	Open End	Global Equity (Equity-Income)	B-	C+	B-	Up	Y	0
Nuveen NWQ International Value Fund Class A	NAIGX	NAS CM	Open End	Global Equity Large Cap (Foreign Stock)	B-	C+	B	Up	Y	3,000
Nuveen NWQ International Value Fund Class C	NCIGX	NAS CM	Open End	Global Equity Large Cap (Foreign Stock)	B-	C+	B	Up	Y	3,000
Nuveen NWQ International Value Fund Class I	NGRRX	NAS CM	Open End	Global Equity Large Cap (Foreign Stock)	B-	C+	B	Up	Y	100,000
Nuveen NWQ International Value Fund Class R3	NTITX	NAS CM	Open End	Global Equity Large Cap (Foreign Stock)	B-	C+	B	Up	Y	0
Nuveen NWQ Large Cap Value Fund Class A	NQCAX	NAS CM	Open End	US Equity Large Cap Value (Growth)	B-	B-	B	Up	Y	3,000
Nuveen NWQ Large Cap Value Fund Class C	NQCCX	NAS CM	Open End	US Equity Large Cap Value (Growth)	B-	C+	B	Up	Y	3,000
Nuveen NWQ Large Cap Value Fund Class I	NQCRX	NAS CM	Open End	US Equity Large Cap Value (Growth)	B-	B-	B	Up	Y	100,000
Nuveen NWQ Large Cap Value Fund Class R3	NQCQX	NAS CM	Open End	US Equity Large Cap Value (Growth)	B-	B-	B	Up	Y	0
Nuveen NWQ Multi Cap Value Fund Class A	NQVAX	NAS CM	Open End	US Equity Large Cap Value (Growth)	B-	B-	B-	Up	Y	3,000
Nuveen NWQ Multi Cap Value Fund Class C	NQVCX	NAS CM	Open End	US Equity Large Cap Value (Growth)	B-	B-	B-	Up	Y	3,000
Nuveen NWQ Multi Cap Value Fund Class I	NQVRX	NAS CM	Open End	US Equity Large Cap Value (Growth)	B-	B-	B-	Up	Y	100,000
Nuveen NWQ Multi-Cap Value Fund Class R3	NMCTX	NAS CM	Open End	US Equity Large Cap Value (Growth)	B-	B-	B-	Up	Y	0
Nuveen NWQ Small Mid/Cap Value Fund Class R3	NWQRX	NAS CM	Open End	US Equity Small Cap (Growth)	B-	B-	B-	Up	Y	0
Nuveen NWQ Small/Mid Cap Value Fund Class A	NSMAX	NAS CM	Open End	US Equity Small Cap (Growth)	B-	B	B-	Up	Y	3,000
Nuveen NWQ Small/Mid Cap Value Fund Class C	NSMCX	NAS CM	Open End	US Equity Small Cap (Growth)	B-	B-	B-	Up	Y	3,000
Nuveen NWQ Small/Mid Cap Value Fund Class I	NSMRX	NAS CM	Open End	US Equity Small Cap (Growth)	B	B	B-	Up	Y	100,000
Nuveen NWQ Small/Mid Cap Value Fund Class R6	NWQFX	NAS CM	Open End	US Equity Small Cap (Growth)	B	B	B-	Up	Y	5,000,000
Nuveen NWQ Small-Cap Value Fund Class A	NSCAX	NAS CM	Open End	US Equity Small Cap (Small Company)	B	A-	B	Up	Y	3,000
Nuveen NWQ Small-Cap Value Fund Class C	NSCCX	NAS CM	Open End	US Equity Small Cap (Small Company)	B	B	B	Up	Y	3,000
Nuveen NWQ Small-Cap Value Fund Class I	NSCRX	NAS CM	Open End	US Equity Small Cap (Small Company)	B+	A-	B	Up	Y	100,000
Nuveen NWQ Small-Cap Value Fund Class R3	NSCQX	NAS CM	Open End	US Equity Small Cap (Small Company)	B	B+	B	Up	Y	0
Nuveen NWQ Small-Cap Value Fund Class R6	NSCFX	NAS CM	Open End	US Equity Small Cap (Small Company)	B+	A-	B	Up	Y	5,000,000
Nuveen Preferred & Income Opportunities Fund	JPC	NYSE	Closed End	US Fixed Income (Income)	B	C+	A+	Up	Y	
Nuveen Preferred & Income Securities Fund	JPS	NYSE	Closed End	US Fixed Income (Income)	B	B-	A+	Up	Y	
Nuveen Preferred & Income Term Fund	JPI	NYSE	Closed End	US Fixed Income (Growth & Income)	B	B-	A+	Up	Y	
Nuveen Preferred Securities & Income Fund Class A	NPSAX	NAS CM	Open End	US Fixed Income (Growth & Income)	B	C+	A+	Up	Y	3,000
Nuveen Preferred Securities & Income Fund Class C	NPSCX	NAS CM	Open End	US Fixed Income (Growth & Income)	B	C+	A+	Up	Y	3,000

★ Expanded analysis of this fund is included in Section II.

Min Additional Investment	TOTAL RETURNS 3-Month Total Return	6-Month Total Return	1-Year Total Return	3-Year Total Return	5-Year Total Return	PERFORMANCE Dividend Yield (TTM)	Expense Ratio	3-Yr Std Deviation	3-Year Beta	ASSETS NAV	Total Assets (MIL)	ASSET ALLOCATION & TURNOVER %Cash	%Stocks	%Bonds	%Other	Turnover Ratio	BULL & BEAR Last Bull Market Total Return	Last Bear Market Total Return	FEES Front End Fee (%)	Back End Fee (%)	Inception Date
	4.52	9.89	24.99	25.45	91.56	0	0.78	11.83	1.02	44.79	814.9	0	100	0	0	89	26.42	-20.4			Feb-13
100	6.11	11.21	19.16	31.72	106.23	0.71	1.17	11.96	1.09	40.89	115.9	1	99	0	0	44	24.18	-24.2	5.75		Dec-87
100	5.91	10.78	18.26	28.75	98.58	0.13	1.92	11.97	1.09	38.84	115.9	1	99	0	0	44	23.64	-24.44		1.00	Feb-99
	6.16	11.35	19.45	32.70	108.78	0.91	0.92	11.96	1.09	40.98	115.9	1	99	0	0	44	24.28	-24.1			Feb-94
	6.04	11.07	18.88	30.74	103.71	0.52	1.42	11.95	1.09	40.59	115.9	1	99	0	0	44	23.94	-24.25			Sep-01
100	2.04	4.57	10.24			3.98	0.96			21.09	10.7	6	42	47	0	46			5.75		Sep-16
100	1.92	4.20	9.50			3.25	1.7			21.07	10.7	6	42	47	0	46				1.00	Sep-16
	2.13	4.67	10.53			4.2	0.71			21.1	10.7	6	42	47	0	46					Sep-16
	2.13	4.67	10.53			4.2	0.71			21.1	10.7	6	42	47	0	46					Sep-16
100	2.21	5.08	11.21			3.14	0.93			21.07	10.5	6	48	51	-5	48			5.75		Sep-16
100	2.09	4.75	10.41			2.41	1.68			21.05	10.5	6	48	51	-5	48				1.00	Sep-16
	2.25	5.18	11.40			3.37	0.68			21.07	10.5	6	48	51	-5	48					Sep-16
	2.25	5.18	11.40			3.37	0.67			21.07	10.5	6	48	51	-5	48					Sep-16
	5.45	11.86	24.63	40.31	118.34	0.41	1.07	10.81	0.78	22.84	843.9	0	101	0	-1	17	26.89	-9.14			Jan-07
100	0.49	1.59	8.38	20.12	32.47	5.09	0.96	5.44	0.49	21.99	716.4	3	17	56	1	24	11.65	-3.39	4.75		Dec-09
100	0.32	1.27	7.66	17.41	27.49	4.35	1.71	5.43	0.49	21.94	716.4	3	17	56	1	24	11.13	-3.66		1.00	Dec-09
	0.49	1.65	8.64	21.03	34.16	5.36	0.71	5.46	0.49	22.01	716.4	3	17	56	1	24	11.81	-3.28			Dec-09
	0.53	1.74	8.52	20.95	34.06	5.35	0.63	5.46	0.49	22.05	716.4	3	17	56	1	24	11.81	-3.28			Jun-16
100	3.85	7.83	22.40	25.86		0.64	1.11	11.58	1.04	24.62	1.7	0	100	0	0	46			5.75		Apr-14
100	3.66	7.43	21.48	23.02		0.06	1.86	11.6	1.04	24.51	1.7	0	100	0	0	46				1.00	Apr-14
	3.88	7.94	22.69	26.78		0.83	0.86	11.62	1.04	24.61	1.7	0	100	0	0	46					Apr-14
100	2.88	7.39	18.43	21.41	69.79	3.64	1.11	10.1	0.93	28.99	320.9	1	97	1	1	86	20.23	-20.32	5.75		Sep-09
100	2.67	6.97	17.56	18.71	63.54	2.95	1.86	10.09	0.93	28.92	320.9	1	97	1	1	86	19.68	-20.61		1.00	Sep-09
	2.95	7.52	18.72	22.32	71.96	3.86	0.86	10.1	0.93	29	320.9	1	97	1	1	86	20.37	-20.25			Sep-09
	2.83	7.23	18.17	20.55	67.80	3.52	1.36	10.09	0.93	28.94	320.9	1	97	1	1	86	20.02	-20.41			Jul-16
100	4.97	8.00	20.43	25.11	41.94	1.61	1.15	10.97	0.86	26.15	289.6	1	99	0	0	23	-1.65	-18.44	5.75		Dec-99
100	4.76	7.64	19.54	22.36	36.70	0.99	1.9	10.99	0.86	24.97	289.6	1	99	0	0	23	-2.07	-18.71		1.00	Dec-99
	5.00	8.15	20.74	26.00	43.71	1.82	0.9	10.99	0.86	26.25	289.6	1	99	0	0	23	-1.52	-18.34			Dec-99
	4.87	7.88	20.14	24.13	40.12	1.41	1.4	10.99	0.86	26.36	289.6	1	99	0	0	23	-1.77	-18.52			Aug-08
100	3.77	8.38	15.10	21.71	71.58	1.1	1	13.01	1.2	6.7	82.0	1	99	0	0	46	21.02	-22.77	5.75		Dec-06
100	3.38	7.86	14.07	18.76	65.05	0.49	1.75	12.96	1.19	5.95	82.0	1	99	0	0	46	20.47	-23		1.00	Dec-06
	3.75	8.47	15.32	22.54	73.67	1.3	0.75	13	1.2	6.72	82.0	1	99	0	0	46	21.16	-22.64			Dec-06
	3.68	8.33	14.81	20.71	69.39	0.89	1.25	13.03	1.2	6.63	82.0	1	99	0	0	46	20.83	-22.8			Sep-09
100	5.23	8.41	18.36	24.99	71.50	0.67	1.15	13.18	1.18	31.06	97.6	1	99	0	0	46	25.19	-23.79	5.75		Dec-02
100	5.06	8.00	17.50	22.22	65.21	0.09	1.9	13.17	1.18	29.35	97.6	1	99	0	0	46	24.61	-24		1.00	Dec-02
	5.28	8.51	18.67	25.91	73.66	0.86	0.9	13.19	1.18	31.21	97.6	1	99	0	0	46	25.29	-23.68			Nov-97
	5.17	8.27	18.10	24.05	69.45	0.48	1.4	13.18	1.18	30.76	97.6	1	99	0	0	46	25.01	-23.86			Aug-08
	5.10	8.38	9.74	23.07	73.57	0	1.56	14.55	1.14	33.31	61.3	2	98	0	0	88	26.34	-23.11			Sep-09
100	5.14	8.50	9.99	24.02	75.79	0	1.31	14.54	1.14	34.29	61.3	2	98	0	0	88	26.51	-23.04	5.75		Dec-06
100	4.97	8.09	9.19	21.29	69.36	0	2.06	14.56	1.15	31.41	61.3	2	98	0	0	88	25.98	-23.25		1.00	Dec-06
	5.23	8.61	10.28	24.95	78.03	0	1.06	14.56	1.14	34.7	61.3	2	98	0	0	88	26.7	-22.97			Dec-06
	5.28	8.72	10.46	25.26	78.47	0	0.9	14.56	1.15	34.79	61.3	2	98	0	0	88	26.7	-22.97			Jun-16
100	5.66	11.07	11.75	29.53	99.63	0	1.3	15.09	1	52.47	768.5	6	94	0	0	57	27.22	-21.3	5.75		Dec-04
100	5.45	10.65	10.93	26.62	92.26	0	2.05	15.08	1	47.64	768.5	6	94	0	0	57	26.66	-21.58		1.00	Dec-04
	5.73	11.21	12.03	30.49	102.11	0	1.05	15.09	1	53.85	768.5	6	94	0	0	57	27.42	-21.22			Dec-04
	5.60	10.93	11.48	28.56	97.23	0	1.55	15.08	1	51.68	768.5	6	94	0	0	57	27.05	-21.41			Sep-09
	5.76	11.32	12.22	31.13	103.53	0	0.86	15.11	1	54.27	768.5	6	94	0	0	57	27.42	-21.22			Feb-13
	1.35	3.02	13.35	29.04	52.18	7.19	0	4.95	0.84	10.75	1,112	-6	0	24	9	32	16.17	-13.07			Mar-03
	1.91	4.17	17.26	31.23	56.22	7.17	0	5.42	0.42	10.36	2,114	-6	0	26	10	13	14.02	-7.01			Sep-02
	1.81	3.90	15.48	31.77	57.78	6.76		4.74	0.89	25.95	590.1	0	2	18	2	19					Jul-12
100	1.06	2.69	10.89	21.49	38.21	5.27	1.07	3.44	0.88	17.68	3,997	1	1	23	3	9	13.94	-8.2	4.75		Dec-06
100	0.93	2.31	10.07	18.85	33.25	4.55	1.82	3.46	0.88	17.7	3,997	1	1	23	3	9	13.43	-8.48		1.00	Dec-06

	MARKET		FUND TYPE, CATEGORY & OBJECTIVE		RATINGS					MINIMUMS
Fund Name	Ticker Symbol	Traded On	Fund Type	Category and (Prospectus Objective)	Overall Rating	Reward Rating	Risk Rating	Recent Up/ Downgrade	Open to New Investors	Min Initial Investment
Nuveen Preferred Securities & Income Fund Class I	NPSRX	NAS CM	Open End	US Fixed Income (Growth & Income)	B	C+	A+	Up	Y	100,000
Nuveen Preferred Securities & Income Fund Class R3	NPSTX	NAS CM	Open End	US Fixed Income (Growth & Income)	B	C+	A+	Up	Y	0
Nuveen Preferred Securities & Income Fund Class R6	NPSFX	NAS CM	Open End	US Fixed Income (Growth & Income)	B	C+	A-	Up	Y	1,000,000
Nuveen Real Asset Income and Growth Fund	JRI	NYSE	Closed End	Moderate Alloc (Growth & Income)	B-	B-	B	Up	Y	
Nuveen Real Asset Income Fund Class A	NRIAX	NAS CM	Open End	Alloc (Income)	B-	C+	B	Down	Y	3,000
Nuveen Real Asset Income Fund Class C	NRICX	NAS CM	Open End	Alloc (Income)	B-	C+	B	Down	Y	3,000
Nuveen Real Asset Income Fund Class I	NRIIX	NAS CM	Open End	Alloc (Income)	B-	C+	B	Down	Y	100,000
Nuveen Real Asset Income Fund Class R6	NRIFX	NAS CM	Open End	Alloc (Income)	B-	C+	B	Down	Y	5,000,000
Nuveen Real Estate Income Fund	JRS	NYSE	Closed End	Real Estate Sector Equity (Real Estate)	B	B-	B+	Up	Y	
Nuveen Real Estate Securities Fund Class A	FREAX	NAS CM	Open End	Real Estate Sector Equity (Real Estate)	B	C+	B+	Up		3,000
Nuveen Real Estate Securities Fund Class C	FRLCX	NAS CM	Open End	Real Estate Sector Equity (Real Estate)	B-	C+	B+	Up		3,000
Nuveen Real Estate Securities Fund Class I	FARCX	NAS CM	Open End	Real Estate Sector Equity (Real Estate)	B	C+	B+	Up		100,000
Nuveen Real Estate Securities Fund Class R3	FRSSX	NAS CM	Open End	Real Estate Sector Equity (Real Estate)	B-	C+	B+			0
Nuveen Real Estate Securities Fund Class R6	FREGX	NAS CM	Open End	Real Estate Sector Equity (Real Estate)	B	C+	B+	Up		5,000,000
Nuveen S&P 500 Buy-Write Income Fund	BXMX	NYSE	Closed End	Long/Short Equity (Equity-Income)	B	B-	B+	Up	Y	
Nuveen S&P 500 Dynamic Overwrite Fund	SPXX	NYSE	Closed End	Long/Short Equity (Equity-Income)	B-	B-	B	Up	Y	
Nuveen Santa Barbara Dividend Growth Fund Class A	NSBAX	NAS CM	Open End	US Equity Large Cap Blend (Equity-Income)	B-	B-	B-	Down	Y	3,000
Nuveen Santa Barbara Dividend Growth Fund Class C	NSBCX	NAS CM	Open End	US Equity Large Cap Blend (Equity-Income)	B-	B-	B-	Down	Y	3,000
Nuveen Santa Barbara Dividend Growth Fund Class I	NSBRX	NAS CM	Open End	US Equity Large Cap Blend (Equity-Income)	B-	B-	B-	Down	Y	100,000
Nuveen Santa Barbara Dividend Growth Fund Class R3	NBDRX	NAS CM	Open End	US Equity Large Cap Blend (Equity-Income)	B-	B-	B-	Down	Y	0
Nuveen Santa Barbara Dividend Growth Fund Class R6	NSBFX	NAS CM	Open End	US Equity Large Cap Blend (Equity-Income)	B-	B-	B-	Down	Y	1,000,000
Nuveen Santa Barbara Global Dividend Growth Fund Class A	NUGAX	NAS CM	Open End	Global Equity (Equity-Income)	B-	B-	B-	Down	Y	3,000
Nuveen Santa Barbara Global Dividend Growth Fund Class C	NUGCX	NAS CM	Open End	Global Equity (Equity-Income)	B-	C+	B-	Down	Y	3,000
Nuveen Santa Barbara Global Dividend Growth Fund Class I	NUGIX	NAS CM	Open End	Global Equity (Equity-Income)	B-	B-	B-	Down	Y	100,000
Nuveen Santa Barbara Global Dividend Growth Fund Class R3	NUGRX	NAS CM	Open End	Global Equity (Equity-Income)	B-	B-	B-	Down	Y	0
Nuveen Santa Barbara Intl Dividend Growth Fund Cls A	NUIAX	NAS CM	Open End	Global Equity Large Cap (Equity-Income)	B-	C+	B	Up	Y	3,000
Nuveen Santa Barbara Intl Dividend Growth Fund Cls C	NUICX	NAS CM	Open End	Global Equity Large Cap (Equity-Income)	B-	C+	B	Up	Y	3,000
Nuveen Santa Barbara Intl Dividend Growth Fund Cls I	NUIIX	NAS CM	Open End	Global Equity Large Cap (Equity-Income)	B-	C+	B	Up	Y	100,000
Nuveen Santa Barbara Intl Dividend Growth Fund Cls R3	NUIRX	NAS CM	Open End	Global Equity Large Cap (Equity-Income)	B-	C+	B	Up	Y	0
Nuveen Small Cap Growth Opportunities Fund Class A	FRMPX	NAS CM	Open End	US Equity Small Cap (Small Company)	B	B+	B	Up	Y	3,000
Nuveen Small Cap Growth Opportunities Fund Class C	FMPCX	NAS CM	Open End	US Equity Small Cap (Small Company)	B	B	B-	Up	Y	3,000
Nuveen Small Cap Growth Opportunities Fund Class I	FIMPX	NAS CM	Open End	US Equity Small Cap (Small Company)	B	B+	B	Up	Y	100,000
Nuveen Small Cap Growth Opportunities Fund Class R3	FMPYX	NAS CM	Open End	US Equity Small Cap (Small Company)	B	B+	B	Up	Y	0
Nuveen Small Cap Growth Opportunities Fund Class R6	FMPFX	NAS CM	Open End	US Equity Small Cap (Small Company)	B+	A-	B	Up	Y	1,000,000
Nuveen Small Cap Select Fund Class A	EMGRX	NAS CM	Open End	US Equity Small Cap (Small Company)	B	B	B	Up	Y	3,000
Nuveen Small Cap Select Fund Class C	FHMCX	NAS CM	Open End	US Equity Small Cap (Small Company)	B	B	B	Up	Y	3,000
Nuveen Small Cap Select Fund Class I	ARSTX	NAS CM	Open End	US Equity Small Cap (Small Company)	B	B	B	Up	Y	100,000
Nuveen Small Cap Select Fund Class R3	ASEIX	NAS CM	Open End	US Equity Small Cap (Small Company)	B	B	B	Up	Y	0
Nuveen Small Cap Value Fund Class A	FSCAX	NAS CM	Open End	US Equity Small Cap (Small Company)	B+	A-	B	Up	Y	3,000
Nuveen Small Cap Value Fund Class C	FSCVX	NAS CM	Open End	US Equity Small Cap (Small Company)	B+	B+	B	Up	Y	3,000
Nuveen Small Cap Value Fund Class I	FSCCX	NAS CM	Open End	US Equity Small Cap (Small Company)	B+	A-	B	Up	Y	100,000
Nuveen Small Cap Value Fund Class R3	FSVSX	NAS CM	Open End	US Equity Small Cap (Small Company)	B+	B+	B	Up	Y	0
Nuveen Small Cap Value Fund Class R6	FSCWX	NAS CM	Open End	US Equity Small Cap (Small Company)	B+	A-	B	Up	Y	1,000,000
Nuveen Strategy Aggressive Growth Allocation Fund Class A	FAAGX	NAS CM	Open End	Aggressive Alloc (Aggr Growth)	B-	B-	B-	Down	Y	3,000
Nuveen Strategy Aggressive Growth Allocation Fund Class C	FSACX	NAS CM	Open End	Aggressive Alloc (Aggr Growth)	C+	C+	B-	Down	Y	3,000
Nuveen Strategy Aggressive Growth Allocation Fund Class I	FSAYX	NAS CM	Open End	Aggressive Alloc (Aggr Growth)	B-	B-	B-	Down	Y	100,000
Nuveen Strategy Aggressive Growth Allocation Fund Class R3	FSASX	NAS CM	Open End	Aggressive Alloc (Aggr Growth)	B-	C+	B-	Down	Y	0
Nuveen Strategy Balanced Allocation Fund Class A	FSGNX	NAS CM	Open End	Moderate Alloc (Balanced)	B	C+	B+	Up	Y	3,000
Nuveen Strategy Balanced Allocation Fund Class C	FSKCX	NAS CM	Open End	Moderate Alloc (Balanced)	B-	C+	B+	Up	Y	3,000
Nuveen Strategy Balanced Allocation Fund Class I	FSKYX	NAS CM	Open End	Moderate Alloc (Balanced)	B-	C+	B	Up	Y	100,000
Nuveen Strategy Balanced Allocation Fund Class R3	FSKSX	NAS CM	Open End	Moderate Alloc (Balanced)	B-	C+	B	Up	Y	0
Nuveen Strategy Conservative Allocation Fund Class A	FSFIX	NAS CM	Open End	Cautious Alloc (Asset Alloc)	B-	C	B+	Up	Y	3,000

★Expanded analysis of this fund is included in Section II.

	TOTAL RETURNS					PERFORMANCE				ASSETS		ASSET ALLOCATION & TURNOVER					BULL & BEAR		FEES		
Min Additional Investment	3-Month Total Return	6-Month Total Return	1-Year Total Return	3-Year Total Return	5-Year Total Return	Dividend Yield (TTM)	Expense Ratio	3-Yr Std Deviation	3-Year Beta	NAV	Total Assets (MIL)	%Cash	%Stocks	%Bonds	%Other	Turnover Ratio	Last Bull Market Total Return	Last Bear Market Total Return	Front End Fee (%)	Back End Fee (%)	Inception Date
	1.17	2.87	11.21	22.50	40.04	5.51	0.82	3.46	0.88	17.7	3,997	1	1	23	3	9	14.04	-8.09			Dec-06
	1.06	2.57	10.64	20.63	36.56	5.03	1.32	3.48	0.89	17.81	3,997	1	1	23	3	9	13.7	-8.28			Sep-09
	0.73	2.41	10.71	22.03	39.49	5.5	0.75	3.48	0.89	17.71	3,997	1	1	23	3	9	14.04	-8.09			Jun-16
	1.37	3.93	15.96	22.96	64.62	5.49	0	10.04		19.62	539.4	1	37	23	7	107					Apr-12
100	0.63	3.30	11.65	18.31	45.61	4.89	1.17	7.03	0.92	24.14	2,058	0	40	24	6	89	12.96		5.75		Sep-11
100	0.49	2.98	10.90	15.67	40.33	4.17	1.92	7.01	0.92	24.15	2,058	0	40	24	6	89	12.43			1.00	Sep-11
	0.67	3.41	11.91	19.20	47.34	5.14	0.92	7.03	0.92	24.14	2,058	0	40	24	6	89	13.09				Sep-11
	0.71	3.45	11.99	19.33	47.50	5.17	0.83	7.03	0.92	24.24	2,058	0	40	24	6	89	13.09				Jun-16
	3.29	4.82	8.80	19.84	67.60	5.18	0	12.43	0.94	11.35	333.1	1	60	0	0	101	29.89	-14.56			Nov-01
100	2.40	2.78	5.34	14.07	54.96	2.31	1.3	13.05	0.97	20.23	3,943	2	98	0	0	139	30.87	-16.39	5.75		Sep-95
100	2.20	2.38	4.58	11.55	49.27	1.61	2.05	13.02	0.96	19.64	3,943	2	98	0	0	139	30.39	-16.67		1.00	Feb-00
	2.39	2.83	5.60	14.89	56.84	2.54	1.05	13.05	0.97	20.55	3,943	2	98	0	0	139	31.13	-16.29			Jun-95
	2.31	2.62	5.08	13.23	52.99	2.2	1.55	13.05	0.96	20.56	3,943	2	98	0	0	139	30.73	-16.49			Sep-01
	2.47	2.96	5.77	15.49	58.08	2.54	0.87	13.04	0.96	20.75	3,943	2	98	0	0	139	31.13	-16.29			Apr-13
	2.58	6.04	12.90	28.51	57.62	1.58	0	5.5	0.5	14.3077	1,501	2	99	0	-1	5	16.72	-8.67			Oct-04
	4.51	8.00	16.77	27.27	62.05	2.16	0	7.91	0.76	16.447	267.0	0	100	0	0	13	17.38	-9.51			Nov-05
100	6.32	10.54	19.71	27.94	85.80	1.37	0.97	10.04	0.96	41.08	3,116	2	98	0	0	22	23.37	-13.94	5.75		Mar-06
100	6.13	10.12	18.82	25.11	78.99	0.7	1.72	10.04	0.96	41.03	3,116	2	98	0	0	22	22.85	-14.25		1.00	Mar-06
	6.38	10.67	20.02	28.88	88.11	1.59	0.72	10.04	0.96	41.1	3,116	2	98	0	0	22	23.56	-13.9			Mar-06
	6.24	10.39	19.41	27.00	83.49	1.25	1.22	10.05	0.96	41.35	3,116	2	98	0	0	22	23.2	-14.06			Mar-09
	6.40	10.72	20.07	29.18	88.78	1.59	0.65	10.04	0.96	41.46	3,116	2	98	0	0	22	23.56	-13.9			Mar-13
100	4.37	8.27	19.50	25.37	60.67	3.18	1.15	9.83	0.92	27.27	20.4	4	94	0	2	33			5.75		Jun-12
100	4.23	7.90	18.66	22.62	54.83	2.5	1.9	9.83	0.92	27.21	20.4	4	94	0	2	33				1.00	Jun-12
	4.47	8.45	19.84	26.32	62.68	3.4	0.9	9.86	0.92	27.27	20.4	4	94	0	2	33					Jun-12
	4.31	8.16	19.25	24.46	58.66	3.06	1.4	9.86	0.92	27.21	20.4	4	94	0	2	33					Jun-12
100	1.99	5.55	19.96	21.00	37.96	2.76	1.15	10.47	0.82	27.92	6.0	3	95	0	0	25			5.75		Jun-12
100	1.84	5.18	19.10	18.33	32.91	2.07	1.9	10.47	0.82	27.66	6.0	3	95	0	0	25				1.00	Jun-12
	2.05	5.68	20.23	21.91	39.66	2.99	0.9	10.47	0.82	27.95	6.0	3	95	0	0	25					Jun-12
	1.94	5.40	19.63	20.13	36.20	2.64	1.4	10.47	0.82	27.82	6.0	3	95	0	0	25					Jun-12
100	1.97	7.78	16.52	24.14	91.74	0	1.24	15.72	1.03	22.15	104.2	1	99	0	0	106	30.67	-25.27	5.75		Aug-95
100	1.75	7.36	15.66	21.35	84.64	0	1.99	15.7	1.03	17.05	104.2	1	99	0	0	106	30.07	-25.53		1.00	Sep-01
	2.06	7.92	16.80	25.09	94.08	0	0.99	15.71	1.03	26.1	104.2	1	99	0	0	106	30.82	-25.19			Aug-95
	1.90	7.64	16.17	23.19	89.23	0	1.49	15.68	1.03	20.89	104.2	1	99	0	0	106	30.49	-25.36			Dec-00
	2.09	7.99	16.95	25.34	94.48	0	0.86	15.72	1.03	26.16	104.2	1	99	0	0	106	30.82	-25.19			Jun-16
100	2.10	7.14	9.74	29.43	85.23	0.04	1.24	15.27	1.07	9.2	130.3	2	98	0	0	66	32.24	-27.06	5.75		May-92
100	1.90	6.73	8.98	26.53	78.52	0	1.99	15.22	1.06	6	130.3	2	98	0	0	66	31.67	-27.26		1.00	Sep-01
	2.16	7.23	9.96	30.29	87.61	0.24	0.99	15.25	1.06	11.75	130.3	2	98	0	0	66	32.48	-27.02			May-92
	1.96	6.99	9.44	28.43	82.90	0	1.49	15.24	1.06	8.33	130.3	2	98	0	0	66	32.21	-27.22			Jan-94
100	4.45	7.30	6.08	41.30	111.34	0.35	1.22	14.9	1.02	25.71	2,066	1	99	0	0	40	32.39	-24.17	5.75		Aug-94
100	4.23	6.92	5.28	38.21	103.56	0	1.97	14.89	1.02	21.85	2,066	1	99	0	0	40	31.91	-24.46		1.00	Feb-99
	4.48	7.44	6.34	42.35	114.06	0.54	0.97	14.9	1.02	26.58	2,066	1	99	0	0	40	32.66	-24.15			Aug-94
	4.34	7.17	5.78	40.22	108.63	0.16	1.47	14.9	1.02	25.16	2,066	1	99	0	0	40	32.2	-24.24			Sep-01
	4.52	7.53	6.30	42.41	114.15	0.59	0.85	14.9	1.02	26.58	2,066	1	99	0	0	40	32.66	-24.15			Jun-16
100	4.79	9.52	19.53	24.39	63.80	1.14	1.38	8.94	0.91	16	76.1	5	76	18	1	14	20.15	-19.38	5.75		Sep-01
100	4.68	9.18	18.68	21.67	57.85	0.53	2.13	8.96	0.91	15.36	76.1	5	76	18	1	14	19.67	-19.62		1.00	Sep-01
	4.90	9.68	19.84	25.33	65.88	1.34	1.13	8.94	0.91	16.04	76.1	5	76	18	1	14	20.41	-19.34			Sep-01
	4.79	9.44	19.26	23.52	61.79	0.94	1.63	8.94	0.91	15.8	76.1	5	76	18	1	14	19.99	-19.52			Oct-96
100	3.00	5.86	12.39	15.87	41.95	1.29	1.29	5.81	0.94	10.64	254.1	4	56	39	1	18	15.47	-13.29	5.75		Sep-01
100	2.83	5.43	11.56	13.29	36.61	0.64	2.04	5.81	0.94	10.46	254.1	4	56	39	1	18	15.02	-13.62		1.00	Sep-01
	3.07	6.01	12.60	16.67	43.72	1.52	1.04	5.76	0.93	10.6	254.1	4	56	39	1	18	15.66	-13.29			Sep-01
	2.86	5.68	12.04	14.95	40.06	1.17	1.54	5.83	0.94	10.49	254.1	4	56	39	1	18	15.49	-13.53			Oct-96
100	2.01	4.09	9.28	10.62	23.98	3.43	1.18	4.08	0.94	11.73	89.9	4	36	58	1	18	10.23	-6.44	5.75		Sep-01

	MARKET		FUND TYPE, CATEGORY & OBJECTIVE		RATINGS				MINIMUMS	
Fund Name	Ticker Symbol	Traded On	Fund Type	Category and (Prospectus Objective)	Overall Rating	Reward Rating	Risk Rating	Recent Up/ Downgrade	Open to New Investors	Min Initial Investment
Nuveen Strategy Conservative Allocation Fund Class C	FSJCX	NAS CM	Open End	Cautious Alloc (Asset Alloc)	B-	C	B+	Up	Y	3,000
Nuveen Strategy Conservative Allocation Fund Class I	FSFYX	NAS CM	Open End	Cautious Alloc (Asset Alloc)	B-	C	B+	Up	Y	100,000
Nuveen Strategy Conservative Allocation Fund Class R3	FSJSX	NAS CM	Open End	Cautious Alloc (Asset Alloc)	B-	C	B+	Up	Y	0
Nuveen Strategy Growth Allocation Fund Class A	FSNAX	NAS CM	Open End	Moderate Alloc (Growth)	B-	C+	B	Down	Y	3,000
Nuveen Strategy Growth Allocation Fund Class C	FSNCX	NAS CM	Open End	Moderate Alloc (Growth)	B-	C+	B-	Down	Y	3,000
Nuveen Strategy Growth Allocation Fund Class I	FSGYX	NAS CM	Open End	Moderate Alloc (Growth)	B-	C+	B	Down	Y	100,000
Nuveen Strategy Growth Allocation Fund Class R3	FSNSX	NAS CM	Open End	Moderate Alloc (Growth)	B-	C+	B	Down	Y	0
Nuveen Symphony International Equity Fund Class A	NSIAX	NAS CM	Open End	Global Equity Large Cap (Foreign Stock)	B-	B-	B	Up	Y	3,000
Nuveen Symphony International Equity Fund Class C	NSECX	NAS CM	Open End	Global Equity Large Cap (Foreign Stock)	B-	B-	B-	Up	Y	3,000
Nuveen Symphony International Equity Fund Class I	NSIEX	NAS CM	Open End	Global Equity Large Cap (Foreign Stock)	B	B	B	Up	Y	100,000
Nuveen Symphony International Equity Fund Class R3	NSREX	NAS CM	Open End	Global Equity Large Cap (Foreign Stock)	B-	B-	B	Up	Y	0
Nuveen Symphony Large Cap Growth Fund Class A	NCGAX	NAS CM	Open End	US Equity Large Cap Growth (Growth)	B+	B+	B	Up	Y	3,000
Nuveen Symphony Large Cap Growth Fund Class C	NCGCX	NAS CM	Open End	US Equity Large Cap Growth (Growth)	B	B	B		Y	3,000
Nuveen Symphony Large Cap Growth Fund Class I	NSGIX	NAS CM	Open End	US Equity Large Cap Growth (Growth)	B+	A-	B	Up	Y	100,000
Nuveen Symphony Large-Cap Growth Fund Class R3	NSGQX	NAS CM	Open End	US Equity Large Cap Growth (Growth)	B+	B+	B	Up	Y	0
Nuveen Symphony Low Volatility Equity Fund A	NOPAX	NAS CM	Open End	US Equity Large Cap Blend (Growth)	B	B-	B+		Y	3,000
Nuveen Symphony Low Volatility Equity Fund C	NOPCX	NAS CM	Open End	US Equity Large Cap Blend (Growth)	B	B-	B+	Up	Y	3,000
Nuveen Symphony Low Volatility Equity Fund Class R6	NOPFX	NAS CM	Open End	US Equity Large Cap Blend (Growth)	B	B-	B+		Y	5,000,000
Nuveen Symphony Low Volatility Equity Fund I	NOPRX	NAS CM	Open End	US Equity Large Cap Blend (Growth)	B	B-	B+		Y	100,000
Nuveen Symphony Mid Cap Core Fund Class A	NCCAX	NAS CM	Open End	US Equity Mid Cap (Growth)	B	C+	B	Up	Y	3,000
Nuveen Symphony Mid Cap Core Fund Class C	NCCCX	NAS CM	Open End	US Equity Mid Cap (Growth)	B-	C+	B	Up	Y	3,000
Nuveen Symphony Mid-Cap Core Fund Class I	NCCIX	NAS CM	Open End	US Equity Mid Cap (Growth)	B	C+	B	Up	Y	100,000
Nuveen Symphony Mid-Cap Core Fund Class R3	NMCRX	NAS CM	Open End	US Equity Mid Cap (Growth)	B-	C+	B	Up	Y	0
Nuveen Symphony Small Cap Core Fund Class A	NSSAX	NAS CM	Open End	US Equity Small Cap (Small Company)	B+	A-	B	Up	Y	3,000
Nuveen Symphony Small Cap Core Fund Class C	NSSCX	NAS CM	Open End	US Equity Small Cap (Small Company)	B	B	B	Up	Y	3,000
Nuveen Symphony Small Cap Core Fund Class I	NSSIX	NAS CM	Open End	US Equity Small Cap (Small Company)	B+	A-	B	Up	Y	100,000
Nuveen Tax-Advantaged Dividend Growth Fund	JTD	NYSE	Closed End	Aggressive Alloc (Equity-Income)	B	B-	B	Up	Y	
Nuveen Tax-Advantaged Total Return Strategy Fund	JTA	NYSE	Closed End	Alloc (Equity-Income)	B-	B-	C+	Up	Y	
Nuveen Winslow Large-Cap Growth Fund Class A	NWCAX	NAS CM	Open End	US Equity Large Cap Growth (Growth)	B+	B+	B+	Up	Y	3,000
Nuveen Winslow Large-Cap Growth Fund Class C	NWCCX	NAS CM	Open End	US Equity Large Cap Growth (Growth)	B+	B	B+	Up	Y	3,000
Nuveen Winslow Large-Cap Growth Fund Class I	NVLIX	NAS CM	Open End	US Equity Large Cap Growth (Growth)	B+	B+	B+	Up	Y	100,000
Nuveen Winslow Large-Cap Growth Fund Class R3	NWCRX	NAS CM	Open End	US Equity Large Cap Growth (Growth)	B+	B+	B+	Up	Y	0
Nuveen Winslow Large-Cap Growth Fund Class R6	NWCFX	NAS CM	Open End	US Equity Large Cap Growth (Growth)	B+	B+	B+	Up	Y	0
NWM Momentum Fund	MOMOX	NAS CM	Open End	Moderate Alloc (Growth)	B	B-	A+		Y	5,000
NWS Global Property Fund Institutional Shares	NWSGX	NAS CM	Open End	Real Estate Sector Equity (Real Estate)	D-	D+	B+		Y	1,000,000
NWS International Property Fund Institutional Shares	NWSOX	NAS CM	Open End	Real Estate Sector Equity (Real Estate)	C+	C+	C+	Up	Y	1,000,000
Nysa Fund	NYSAX	NAS CM	Open End	US Equity Small Cap (Growth)	C	C	C+	Up	Y	1,000
Oak Ridge Disciplined Growth Fund Class I	ODGIX	NAS CM	Open End	US Equity Large Cap Growth (Growth)	D	C	B		Y	1,000,000
Oak Ridge Dividend Growth Fund Class A	ORDAX	NAS CM	Open End	US Equity Large Cap Blend (Equity-Income)	B-	B-	B-	Down	Y	1,000
Oak Ridge Dividend Growth Fund Class I	ORDNX	NAS CM	Open End	US Equity Large Cap Blend (Equity-Income)	B-	B-	B-	Down	Y	1,000,000
Oak Ridge Dynamic Small Cap Fund Class A	ORSAX	NAS CM	Open End	US Equity Small Cap (Small Company)	A-	A-	B+	Up	Y	1,000
Oak Ridge Dynamic Small Cap Fund Class I	ORSIX	NAS CM	Open End	US Equity Small Cap (Small Company)	A-	A-	B+	Up	Y	1,000,000
Oak Ridge Global Res & Infrastr Fund Cls A Shares	INNAX	NAS CM	Open End	Natl Resources Sec Equity (Natl Res)	C	C+	C		Y	1,000
Oak Ridge Global Res & Infrastr Fund Cls I Shares	INNNX	NAS CM	Open End	Natl Resources Sec Equity (Natl Res)	C	C+	C		Y	1,000,000
Oak Ridge International Small Cap Fund Class A	ORIAX	NAS CM	Open End	Global Equity Mid/Small Cap (Small Company)	C	C	B	Up	Y	1,000
Oak Ridge International Small Cap Fund Class I	ORIIX	NAS CM	Open End	Global Equity Mid/Small Cap (Small Company)	C	C+	B	Up	Y	1,000,000
Oak Ridge Multi Strategy Fund Class A	ORILX	NAS CM	Open End	US Equity Large Cap Growth (Growth)	B	B	A-	Up	Y	1,000
Oak Ridge Multi Strategy Fund Class C	ORLCX	NAS CM	Open End	US Equity Large Cap Growth (Growth)	B	B-	A-	Up	Y	1,000
Oak Ridge Multi Strategy Fund Class I	PORYX	NAS CM	Open End	US Equity Large Cap Growth (Growth)	B	B	A-	Up	Y	1,000,000
Oak Ridge Small Cap Growth Fund Class A	ORIGX	NAS CM	Open End	US Equity Small Cap (Small Company)	C+	C+	B-	Up	Y	1,000
Oak Ridge Small Cap Growth Fund Class C	ORICX	NAS CM	Open End	US Equity Small Cap (Small Company)	C+	C+	B-	Up	Y	1,000
Oak Ridge Small Cap Growth Fund Class I	ORIYX	NAS CM	Open End	US Equity Small Cap (Small Company)	C+	C+	B-	Up	Y	1,000,000

★ Expanded analysis of this fund is included in Section II.

Min Additional Investment	3-Month Total Return	6-Month Total Return	1-Year Total Return	3-Year Total Return	5-Year Total Return	Dividend Yield (TTM)	Expense Ratio	3-Yr Std Deviation	3-Year Beta	NAV	Total Assets (MIL)	%Cash	%Stocks	%Bonds	%Other	Turnover Ratio	Last Bull Market Total Return	Last Bear Market Total Return	Front End Fee (%)	Back End Fee (%)	Inception Date
	TOTAL RETURNS					PERFORMANCE				ASSETS		ASSET ALLOCATION & TURNOVER					BULL & BEAR		FEES		
100	1.84	3.65	8.35	8.09	19.34	2.72	1.93	4.06	0.94	11.65	89.9	4	36	58	1	18	9.7	-6.68		1.00	Sep-01
	2.08	4.14	9.45	11.40	25.51	3.66	0.93	4.08	0.95	11.72	89.9	4	36	58	1	18	10.3	-6.33			Sep-01
	1.95	3.97	8.92	9.78	22.44	3.18	1.43	4.08	0.94	11.7	89.9	4	36	58	1	18	10.01	-6.53			Oct-96
100	4.04	8.10	16.56	21.51	55.52	1.06	1.35	7.67	0.94	12.9	138.4	4	75	20	1	13	17.74	-16.08	5.75		Sep-01
100	3.92	7.76	15.85	18.90	49.86	0.43	2.1	7.66	0.93	12.57	138.4	4	75	20	1	13	17.25	-16.36		1.00	Sep-01
	4.12	8.25	16.96	22.43	57.48	1.27	1.1	7.66	0.93	12.96	138.4	4	75	20	1	13	17.86	-16.01			Sep-01
	4.06	8.02	16.40	20.65	53.62	0.85	1.6	7.61	0.93	12.73	138.4	4	75	20	1	13	17.54	-16.18			Oct-96
100	4.17	11.02	27.67	27.58	49.20	0.98	1.2	11.82	0.93	21.25	17.4	2	96	0	2	96	18.23	-22.27	5.75		May-08
100	3.93	10.58	26.66	24.65	43.64	0.39	1.95	11.8	0.92	21.05	17.4	2	96	0	2	96	17.74	-22.54		1.00	May-08
	4.26	11.23	28.00	28.54	51.08	1.17	0.95	11.83	0.93	21.23	17.4	2	96	0	2	96	18.39	-22.21			May-08
	4.12	10.90	27.37	26.64	47.32	0.78	1.45	11.8	0.93	21.31	17.4	2	96	0	2	96	18.05	-22.35			Oct-10
100	7.93	14.21	29.45	40.13	106.12	0.22	1.13	10.78	0.99	38.78	156.5	0	100	0	0	54	32.01	-16.54	5.75		Dec-06
100	7.69	13.75	28.46	37.02	98.46	0	1.88	10.77	0.99	35.64	156.5	0	100	0	0	54	31.4	-16.79		1.00	Dec-06
	7.97	14.34	29.72	41.18	108.69	0.41	0.88	10.78	0.99	39.33	156.5	0	100	0	0	54	32.16	-16.45			Dec-06
	7.84	14.05	29.09	39.07	103.53	0.03	1.38	10.77	0.99	38.69	156.5	0	100	0	0	54	31.74	-16.61			Sep-09
100	6.68	11.67	19.43	29.66	98.58	0.95	1.01	8.97	0.85	31.61	140.9	0	100	0	0	67	22.51	-13.33	5.75		Sep-07
100	6.47	11.25	18.50	26.75	91.24	0.34	1.76	8.96	0.85	30.63	140.9	0	100	0	0	67	21.99	-13.61		1.00	Sep-07
	6.73	11.86	19.82	30.86	101.38	1.18	0.64	8.98	0.86	31.68	140.9	0	100	0	0	67	22.72	-13.27			Jun-16
	6.74	11.80	19.72	30.65	101.06	1.15	0.76	8.98	0.85	31.64	140.9	0	100	0	0	67	22.72	-13.27			Sep-07
100	4.76	8.57	16.51	20.58	81.37	0	1.17	9.67	0.89	41.16	32.0	1	99	0	0	66	28.32	-22.76	5.75		May-06
100	4.56	8.17	15.68	17.92	74.71	0	1.92	9.69	0.89	38.04	32.0	1	99	0	0	66	27.78	-23.03		1.00	May-06
	4.81	8.69	16.81	21.49	83.59	0	0.92	9.68	0.89	42.09	32.0	1	99	0	0	66	28.53	-22.7			May-06
	4.68	8.42	16.25	19.78	79.25	0	1.42	9.68	0.89	40.78	32.0	1	99	0	0	66	28.12	-22.82			May-09
100	6.79	13.07	19.22	33.90		0	1.3	12.87	0.88	27.53	34.6	1	99	0	0	65			5.75		Dec-13
100	6.60	12.64	18.34	30.95		0	2.05	12.85	0.88	26.68	34.6	1	99	0	0	65				1.00	Dec-13
	6.84	13.23	19.49	34.90		0	1.05	12.89	0.88	27.81	34.6	1	99	0	0	65					Dec-13
	5.66	10.22	25.32	30.28	74.42	2.84	0	10.23		18.07	261.7	3	75	5	0	19	26.66	-15.4			Jun-07
	3.13	7.75	20.15	23.27	79.00	4.02	0	11.71	0.94	14.22	199.3	3	72	17	0	42	24.04	-21.27			Jan-04
100	5.74	11.88	32.56	36.39	110.30	0	0.98	12.26	1.09	37.1	600.9	1	99	0	0	65	26.31	-17.69	5.75		May-09
100	5.54	11.48	31.56	33.38	102.53	0	1.73	12.24	1.08	33.23	600.9	1	99	0	0	65	25.79	-17.99		1.00	May-09
	5.79	12.00	32.84	37.38	112.88	0.06	0.73	12.25	1.09	38.17	600.9	1	99	0	0	65	26.52	-17.61			May-09
	5.65	11.72	32.16	35.32	107.61	0	1.23	12.24	1.08	35.82	600.9	1	99	0	0	65	26.14	-17.78			May-09
	5.84	12.10	33.10	38.09	114.47	0.06	0.57	12.25	1.09	38.59	600.9	1	99	0	0	65	26.52	-17.61			Mar-13
100	0.38	5.80	12.17	39.46		1.39	1.81	6.79	-0.24	10.18	77.8	12	46	33	0	396					Apr-14
	4.77	6.92	13.93				1			10.85	1.3	2	98	0	0						Dec-16
	6.04	11.68	27.91			5.78	1			9.11	5.7	7	93	0	0	30					Mar-15
250	0.21	5.58	11.54	1.33	-23.18	0	5.38	15.81	1.04	4.54	1.8	4	93	3	0	42	5.25	-21.4	2.50		May-97
	8.55	10.82	25.18			0.2	0.97			12.18	14.7	4	72	0	25						Jul-16
100	7.42	12.39	20.15	29.73		0.95	1.26	10.33	1	15.24	9.8	8	215	0	-123	22			5.75		Jun-13
	7.51	12.59	20.56	30.71		1.16	1.01	10.32	1	15.35	9.8	8	215	0	-123	22					Jun-13
100	5.31	14.28	15.42	40.78	124.29	0	1.41			13.91	28.2	3	97	0	0	181	26.75	-21.43	5.75		Dec-15
	5.37	14.40	15.63	41.77	126.99	0	1.16			13.97	28.2	3	97	0	0	181	26.94	-21.35			Sep-15
100	9.49	18.74	11.49	13.86	33.78	0.28	1.41	17.09	1.14	12.71	19.4	1	100	0	0	52			5.75		Sep-12
	9.52	18.94	11.81	14.75	35.47	0.28	1.16	17.07	1.14	12.76	19.4	1	100	0	0	52					Sep-12
100	3.94	13.00	31.25			0.78	1.51			13.1	83.6	4	94	0	0	124			5.75		Dec-15
	4.03	13.26	31.65			0.91	1.26			13.12	83.6	4	94	0	0	124					Sep-15
100	6.48	12.92	26.35	30.87	95.12	0	2.18	10.62	0.94	25.6	67.7	9	93	2	-4	23	28.3	-16.39	5.75		Mar-99
100	6.19	12.43	25.21	27.38	86.49	0	2.75	10.67	0.94	22.79	67.7	9	93	2	-4	23	27.6	-16.69		1.00	Feb-04
	6.40	12.90	26.35	30.98	95.50	0	1.81	10.64	0.94	26.08	67.7	9	93	2	-4	23	28.41	-16.37			Aug-04
100	7.08	11.04	18.96	15.23	70.31	0	1.42	14.26	0.91	15.55	681.9	0	98	0	2	30	19.95	-21.49	5.75		Jan-94
100	6.79	10.55	18.02	12.52	63.95	0	2.15	14.25	0.91	6.75	681.9	0	98	0	2	30	19.47	-21.76		1.00	Mar-97
	7.15	11.22	19.35	16.35	73.27	0	1.15	14.25	0.91	16.86	681.9	0	98	0	2	30	20.25	-21.43			Dec-09

	MARKET			FUND TYPE, CATEGORY & OBJECTIVE	RATINGS					MINIMUMS
Fund Name	Ticker Symbol	Traded On	Fund Type	Category and (Prospectus Objective)	Overall Rating	Reward Rating	Risk Rating	Recent Up/ Downgrade	Open to New Investors	Min Initial Investment
Oak Ridge Small Cap Growth Fund Class K	ORIKX	NAS CM	Open End	US Equity Small Cap (Small Company)	C+	C+	B-	Up	Y	1,000,000
Oakhurst Strategic Defined Risk Fund Insitutional Class	OASDX	NAS CM	Open End	Multialternative (Growth)	U	U	U		Y	25,000
Oakmark Equity and Income Fund Class Advisor	OAYBX	NAS CM	Open End	Moderate Alloc (Balanced)	B-	C+	B	Down	Y	100,000
Oakmark Equity and Income Fund Class Institutional	OANBX	NAS CM	Open End	Moderate Alloc (Balanced)	B	C+	B	Up	Y	1,000,000
Oakmark Equity And Income Fund Investor Class	OAKBX	NAS CM	Open End	Moderate Alloc (Balanced)	B-	C+	B	Down	Y	1,000
Oakmark Equity And Income Fund Service Class	OARBX	NAS CM	Open End	Moderate Alloc (Balanced)	B-	C+	B	Down	Y	0
Oakmark Fund Advisor Class	OAYMX	NAS CM	Open End	US Equity Large Cap Blend (Growth)	B	B	B-	Up	Y	100,000
Oakmark Fund Institutional Class	OANMX	NAS CM	Open End	US Equity Large Cap Blend (Growth)	B	B	B	Up	Y	1,000,000
Oakmark Fund Investor Class	OAKMX	NAS CM	Open End	US Equity Large Cap Blend (Growth)	B	B	B	Up	Y	1,000
Oakmark Fund Service Class	OARMX	NAS CM	Open End	US Equity Large Cap Blend (Growth)	B	B	B	Up	Y	0
Oakmark Global Fund Class Advisor	OAYGX	NAS CM	Open End	Global Equity (World Stock)	B-	B	C	Up	Y	100,000
Oakmark Global Fund Class Institutional	OANGX	NAS CM	Open End	Global Equity (World Stock)	B-	B	C	Up	Y	1,000,000
Oakmark Global Fund Investor Class	OAKGX	NAS CM	Open End	Global Equity (World Stock)	B-	B	C	Up		1,000
Oakmark Global Fund Service Class	OARGX	NAS CM	Open End	Global Equity (World Stock)	B-	B	C	Up	Y	0
Oakmark Global Select Fund Class Advisor	OAYWX	NAS CM	Open End	Global Equity (World Stock)	B	B	B-	Up	Y	100,000
Oakmark Global Select Fund Class Institutional	OANWX	NAS CM	Open End	Global Equity (World Stock)	B	B	B-	Up	Y	1,000,000
Oakmark Global Select Fund Investor Class	OAKWX	NAS CM	Open End	Global Equity (World Stock)	B	B	B-	Up	Y	1,000
Oakmark International Fund Class Advisor	OAYIX	NAS CM	Open End	Global Equity Large Cap (Foreign Stock)	B	A-	C	Up	Y	100,000
Oakmark International Fund Class Institutional	OANIX	NAS CM	Open End	Global Equity Large Cap (Foreign Stock)	B	A-	C	Up	Y	1,000,000
Oakmark International Fund Investor Class	OAKIX	NAS CM	Open End	Global Equity Large Cap (Foreign Stock)	B	A-	C	Up		1,000
Oakmark International Fund Service Class	OARIX	NAS CM	Open End	Global Equity Large Cap (Foreign Stock)	B	B+	C	Up		0
Oakmark International Small Cap Fund Class Advisor	OAYEX	NAS CM	Open End	Global Equity Mid/Small Cap (Small Company)	B	B-	B	Up	Y	100,000
Oakmark International Small Cap Fund Class Institutional	OANEX	NAS CM	Open End	Global Equity Mid/Small Cap (Small Company)	B	B-	B	Up	Y	1,000,000
Oakmark International Small Cap Fund Investor Class	OAKEX	NAS CM	Open End	Global Equity Mid/Small Cap (Small Company)	B	B-	B	Up		1,000
Oakmark International Small Cap Service Class	OAREX	NAS CM	Open End	Global Equity Mid/Small Cap (Small Company)	B-	B-	B	Up	Y	0
Oakmark Select Fund Class Advisor	OAYLX	NAS CM	Open End	US Equity Large Cap Blend (Growth)	B	B	B	Up	Y	100,000
Oakmark Select Fund Class Institutional	OANLX	NAS CM	Open End	US Equity Large Cap Blend (Growth)	B	B	B	Up	Y	1,000,000
Oakmark Select Fund Investor Class	OAKLX	NAS CM	Open End	US Equity Large Cap Blend (Growth)	B	B	B	Up	Y	1,000
Oakmark Select Fund Service Class	OARLX	NAS CM	Open End	US Equity Large Cap Blend (Growth)	B	B	B	Up	Y	0
Oberweis China Opportunities Fund	OBCHX	NAS CM	Open End	Greater China Equity (Foreign Stock)	B	A	C	Up	Y	1,000
Oberweis China Opportunities Fund Institutional Class	OCHIX	NAS CM	Open End	Greater China Equity (Foreign Stock)	B	A	C	Up	Y	1,000,000
Oberweis Emerging Growth Fund	OBEGX	NAS CM	Open End	Global Equity Mid/Small Cap (Small Company)	B+	A-	B	Up	Y	1,000
Oberweis Emerging Growth Fund Institutional Class	OBGIX	NAS CM	Open End	Global Equity Mid/Small Cap (Small Company)	B+	A-	B	Up	Y	1,000,000
Oberweis International Opportunities Fund	OBIOX	NAS CM	Open End	Global Equity Mid/Small Cap (Foreign Stock)	A-	A	B+	Up	Y	1,000
Oberweis International Opportunities Institutional Fund	OBIIX	NAS CM	Open End	Global Equity Mid/Small Cap (Foreign Stock)	A-	A	B+	Up	Y	1,000,000
Oberweis Micro Cap Fund Institutional Class	OMCIX	NAS CM	Open End	US Equity Small Cap (Small Company)	A-	A+	B	Up	Y	1,000,000
Oberweis Micro-Cap Fund	OBMCX	NAS CM	Open End	US Equity Small Cap (Small Company)	A-	A+	B	Up	Y	1,000
Oberweis Small-Cap Opportunities Fund	OBSOX	NAS CM	Open End	US Equity Small Cap (Small Company)	B+	A-	B	Up	Y	1,000
Oberweis Small-Cap Opportunities Fund Institutional Class	OBSIX	NAS CM	Open End	US Equity Small Cap (Small Company)	B+	A-	B	Up	Y	1,000,000
Oberweis Small-Cap Value Fund Institutional Class	OBVLX	NAS CM	Open End	US Equity Small Cap (Small Company)	B-	B	C+	Up	Y	1,000,000
OCM Gold Fund Advisors Class	OCMAX	NAS CM	Open End	Precious Metals Sector Equity (Precious Metals)	C-	C	D	Down	Y	5,000
OCM Gold Fund Investor Class	OCMGX	NAS CM	Open End	Precious Metals Sector Equity (Precious Metals)	C-	C	D	Down	Y	1,000
Old Westbury All Cap Core Fund	OWACX	NAS CM	Open End	Global Equity (Growth)	C+	B-	C+	Down	Y	1,000
Old Westbury Large Cap Strategies Fund	OWLSX	NAS CM	Open End	Global Equity (World Stock)	B	C+	B	Up	Y	1,000
Old Westbury Small & Mid Cap Strategies Fund	OWSMX	NAS CM	Open End	Global Equity Mid/Small Cap (World Stock)	B-	B-	B-	Down	Y	1,000
Old Westbury Strategic Opportunities Fund	OWSOX	NAS CM	Open End	Alloc (World Stock)	B-	C+	B	Down	Y	1,000
Olstein All Cap Value Fund Class Advisor	OFAFX	NAS CM	Open End	US Equity Large Cap Blend (Growth)	B-	C+	B	Up	Y	1,000
Olstein All Cap Value Fund Class C	OFALX	NAS CM	Open End	US Equity Large Cap Blend (Growth)	B-	C+	B-	Up	Y	1,000
Olstein Strategic Opportunities Fund Adviser Class	OFSFX	NAS CM	Open End	US Equity Small Cap (Growth)	C+	C+	C+	Up	Y	1,000
Olstein Strategic Opportunities Fund Class A	OFSAX	NAS CM	Open End	US Equity Small Cap (Growth)	C+	C+	C+	Up	Y	1,000
Olstein Strategic Opportunities Fund Class C	OFSCX	NAS CM	Open End	US Equity Small Cap (Growth)	C+	C+	C+	Up	Y	1,000
OnTrack Core Fund Advisor Class	OTRGX	NAS CM	Open End	Multialternative (Growth & Income)	C+	C+	B	Down	Y	1,000

★ Expanded analysis of this fund is included in Section II.

	TOTAL RETURNS					PERFORMANCE				ASSETS		ASSET ALLOCATION & TURNOVER					BULL & BEAR		FEES		
Min Additional Investment	3-Month Total Return	6-Month Total Return	1-Year Total Return	3-Year Total Return	5-Year Total Return	Dividend Yield (TTM)	Expense Ratio	3-Yr Std Deviation	3-Year Beta	NAV	Total Assets (MIL)	%Cash	%Stocks	%Bonds	%Other	Turnover Ratio	Last Bull Market Total Return	Last Bear Market Total Return	Front End Fee (%)	Back End Fee (%)	Inception Date
	7.18	11.28	19.47	16.82	74.43	0	1	14.26	0.91	16.63	681.9	0	98	0	2	30	19.95	-21.5			Dec-12
250	1.67	3.79					2.58			10.41	21.1	18	57	15	10						May-17
	4.25	8.16	14.63	20.61	63.17	0	0.69	7.78	0.7	32.19	16,501	11	62	23	4	18	17.1	-13.65			Nov-16
	4.27	8.14	14.65	20.62	63.20	0	0.59	7.78	0.7	32.19	16,501	11	62	23	4	18	17.1	-13.65			Nov-16
100	4.21	8.06	14.46	20.38	62.87	0	0.79	7.77	0.7	32.19	16,501	11	62	23	4	18	17.1	-13.65			Nov-95
	4.14	7.94	14.15	19.30	60.37	0	1.1	7.77	0.7	32.03	16,501	11	62	23	4	18	16.85	-13.75			Jul-00
	6.01	12.16	21.30	36.73	114.36	0	0.81	12.28	1.14	84.34	19,380	7	93	0	0	19	26.73	-16.29			Nov-16
	6.02	12.17	21.33	36.75	114.39	0	0.71	12.28	1.14	84.33	19,380	7	93	0	0	19	26.73	-16.29			Nov-16
100	5.98	12.08	21.14	36.50	113.99	0	0.89	12.28	1.14	84.33	19,380	7	93	0	0	19	26.73	-16.29			Aug-91
	5.89	11.93	20.82	35.19	110.75	0	1.21	12.28	1.14	84.08	19,380	7	93	0	0	19	26.54	-16.5			Apr-01
	3.95	13.28	27.24	26.25	79.36	0	1.08	14.44	1.26	33.13	2,732	0	99	0	1	32	19.13	-21.09			Nov-16
	3.96	13.32	27.33	26.34	79.50	0	0.98	14.44	1.26	33.14	2,732	0	99	0	1	32	19.13	-21.09			Nov-16
100	3.90	13.23	27.08	26.04	79.07	0	1.17	14.44	1.26	33.13	2,732	0	99	0	1	32	19.13	-21.09			Aug-99
	3.85	13.09	26.78	24.81	76.14	0	1.5	14.43	1.26	32.24	2,732	0	99	0	1	32	18.89	-21.24			Oct-01
	2.98	7.88	21.36	34.96	88.57	0	1.09	13.45	1.19	19.3	2,866	3	97	0	0	39	20.88	-18.36			Nov-16
	3.02	7.92	21.40	35.01	88.64	0	0.98	13.44	1.19	19.3	2,866	3	97	0	0	39	20.88	-18.36			Nov-16
100	2.98	7.83	21.18	34.75	88.29	0	1.15	13.44	1.19	19.3	2,866	3	97	0	0	39	20.88	-18.36			Oct-06
	2.38	11.76	29.92	34.04	66.24	0	0.92	15.34	1.18	28.58	41,961	3	92	0	5	41	15.09	-22.78			Nov-16
	2.43	11.82	29.99	34.11	66.33	0	0.81	15.34	1.18	28.59	41,961	3	92	0	5	41	15.09	-22.78			Nov-16
100	2.37	11.69	29.75	33.80	65.94	0	1	15.34	1.18	28.57	41,961	3	92	0	5	41	15.08	-22.78			Sep-92
	2.30	11.56	29.44	32.55	63.22	0	1.34	15.36	1.18	28.76	41,961	3	92	0	5	41	14.88	-22.91			Nov-99
	1.63	5.53	26.19	34.78	60.49	0	1.29	13.63	1.09	17.73	3,029	5	92	0	1	34	21.02	-23.79			Nov-16
	1.67	5.63	26.31	34.90	60.64	0	1.17	13.63	1.09	17.74	3,029	5	92	0	1	34	21.02	-23.79			Nov-16
100	1.58	5.48	26.07	34.56	60.23	0	1.38	13.62	1.09	17.74	3,029	5	92	0	1	34	21.02	-23.79			Nov-95
	1.55	5.41	25.71	33.45	58.00	0	1.69	13.61	1.09	17.65	3,029	5	92	0	1	34	20.89	-23.94			Jan-01
	4.14	10.36	15.87	27.67	106.87	0	0.91	13.64	1.2	47.76	6,336	6	94	0	0	22	27.64	-16.88			Nov-16
	4.15	10.39	15.91	27.71	106.94	0	0.82	13.65	1.2	47.77	6,336	6	94	0	0	22	27.64	-16.88			Nov-16
100	4.10	10.28	15.72	27.47	106.55	0	0.98	13.64	1.2	47.76	6,336	6	94	0	0	22	27.64	-16.88			Nov-96
	4.02	10.15	15.38	26.26	103.38	0	1.32	13.65	1.2	47.2	6,336	6	94	0	0	22	27.4	-16.97			Dec-99
100	5.22	24.17	55.04	38.75	112.94	0	1.99	20.64	0.7	15.95	121.9	0	100	0	0	125	24.85	-41.64			Oct-05
	5.27	24.31	55.21	38.91	113.17		1.74	20.65	0.7	15.93	121.9	0	100	0	0	125	24.85	-41.64			May-17
100	3.29	14.62	33.29	44.45	111.41	0	1.59	13.66	1.02	28.36	56.0	0	96	0	4	126	25.59	-32.93			Jan-87
	3.35	14.77	33.51	44.68	111.75		1.34	13.67	1.02	28.41	56.0	0	96	0	4	126	25.59	-32.93			May-17
100	7.45	17.24	40.76	52.45	129.98	0.05	1.6	11.11	0.81	25.49	927.9	0	94	0	6	139	24.61	-25.39			Feb-07
	7.48	17.22	40.98	53.20		0.29	1.1	11.06	0.81	12.77	1,039	3	93	0	5	123					Mar-14
	3.53	13.96	28.07	70.56	163.97		1.4	13.62	0.84	25.17	99.3	0	95	0	5	102	29.46	-28.95			May-17
100	3.46	13.80	27.89	70.33	163.60	0	1.65	13.61	0.83	25.12	99.3	0	95	0	5	102	29.46	-28.95			Dec-95
100	4.98	14.64	25.53	41.36	103.92	0	1.55	14.89	0.94	16.4	11.2	0	98	0	2	150	24.28	-23.38			Sep-96
	5.03	14.83	25.74	41.60	104.26		1.3	14.9	0.94	16.44	11.2	0	98	0	2	150	24.28	-23.38			May-17
	3.80	9.48	9.63	21.88	90.33	1.25	1.3	13.83	0.94	21.63	41.6	0	99	0	1	76	25.12	-20.74			Jul-14
50	2.91	4.14	10.51	28.06	-33.47	0	1.78	39.94	-0.23	9.8	37.6	0	94	0	5	11	-13.67	-11.56			Mar-10
50	2.78	3.65	9.66	25.17	-35.88	0	2.66	39.94	-0.24	9.16	37.6	0	94	0	5	11	-13.91	-11.77	4.50		Feb-88
100	5.35	9.77	20.93	23.08	65.62	0.9	1.05	9.58	0.87	16.68	1,809	3	97	0	0	34	6.4	-18.31			Mar-98
100	4.84	8.18	19.39	22.63	68.24	0.64	1.15	9.72	0.89	14.46	17,483	3	96	0	0	50	15.04	-25.49			Oct-93
100	3.81	6.89	18.18	29.77	67.55	0.48	1.12	9.22	0.83	16.76	6,654	4	95	0	0	48	20.83	-21.96			Apr-05
100	2.63	5.72	13.26	16.83	35.86	1.69	1.36	6.75	0.62	7.82	5,572	22	28	40	2	114	9.18	-15.41			Nov-07
100	6.48	7.01	15.38	17.82	93.20	0	1.27	11.76	1.05	24.72	698.2	6	94	0	0	56	28.73	-19.1			Sep-99
100	6.21	6.48	14.29	14.33	84.17	0	2.27	11.79	1.05	19.96	698.2	6	94	0	0	56	28.18	-19.35		1.00	Sep-95
100	5.32	3.59	6.21	9.20	80.12	0	1.36	14.98	1.15	17.6	141.8	7	93	0	0	65	32.25	-23.95			May-15
100	5.23	3.43	5.87	8.46	78.91	0	1.61	14.97	1.15	17.48	141.8	7	93	0	0	65	32.25	-23.95	5.50		Nov-06
100	5.03	3.05	5.10	6.05	72.29	0	2.36	14.97	1.15	15.86	141.8	7	93	0	0	65	31.66	-24.17		1.00	Nov-06
500	0.64	2.00	6.26	11.67		6.4	3.18	4.99	24.9	49.21	35.8	65	0	29	1	435					Jun-13

	MARKET		FUND TYPE, CATEGORY & OBJECTIVE		RATINGS				MINIMUMS	
Fund Name	Ticker Symbol	Traded On	Fund Type	Category and (Prospectus Objective)	Overall Rating	Reward Rating	Risk Rating	Recent Up/ Downgrade	Open to New Investors	Min Initial Investment
OnTrack Core Fund Investor Class	OTRFX	NAS CM	Open End	Multialternative (Growth & Income)	C+	C+	B	Down	Y	1,000
Oppenheimer Capital Appreciation Fund Class A	OPTFX	NAS CM	Open End	US Equity Large Cap Growth (Growth)	B	B	B	Up	Y	1,000
Oppenheimer Capital Appreciation Fund Class B	OTGBX	NAS CM	Open End	US Equity Large Cap Growth (Growth)	B	B-	B	Up		1,000
Oppenheimer Capital Appreciation Fund Class C	OTFCX	NAS CM	Open End	US Equity Large Cap Growth (Growth)	B	B-	B	Up	Y	1,000
Oppenheimer Capital Appreciation Fund Class I	OPTIX	NAS CM	Open End	US Equity Large Cap Growth (Growth)	B	B	B		Y	1,000,000
Oppenheimer Capital Appreciation Fund Class R	OTCNX	NAS CM	Open End	US Equity Large Cap Growth (Growth)	B	B-	B	Up	Y	1,000
Oppenheimer Capital Appreciation Fund Class Y	OTCYX	NAS CM	Open End	US Equity Large Cap Growth (Growth)	B	B	B		Y	0
Oppenheimer Capital Income Fund Class A	OPPEX	NAS CM	Open End	Cautious Alloc (Equity-Income)	B-	C+	B	Up	Y	1,000
Oppenheimer Capital Income Fund Class B	OPEBX	NAS CM	Open End	Cautious Alloc (Equity-Income)	B-	C	B	Up		1,000
Oppenheimer Capital Income Fund Class C	OPECX	NAS CM	Open End	Cautious Alloc (Equity-Income)	B-	C	B	Up	Y	1,000
Oppenheimer Capital Income Fund Class I	OCIIX	NAS CM	Open End	Cautious Alloc (Equity-Income)	B-	C+	B	Down	Y	1,000,000
Oppenheimer Capital Income Fund Class R	OCINX	NAS CM	Open End	Cautious Alloc (Equity-Income)	B-	C	B	Up	Y	0
Oppenheimer Capital Income Fund Class Y	OCIYX	NAS CM	Open End	Cautious Alloc (Equity-Income)	B-	C+	B	Down	Y	0
Oppenheimer Developing Markets Fund Class A	ODMAX	NAS CM	Open End	Emerging Markets Equity (Div Emerging Mkts)	C+	B-	C	Up		1,000
Oppenheimer Developing Markets Fund Class B	ODVBX	NAS CM	Open End	Emerging Markets Equity (Div Emerging Mkts)	C+	B-	C	Up		1,000
Oppenheimer Developing Markets Fund Class C	ODVCX	NAS CM	Open End	Emerging Markets Equity (Div Emerging Mkts)	C+	B-	C	Up		1,000
Oppenheimer Developing Markets Fund Class I	ODVIX	NAS CM	Open End	Emerging Markets Equity (Div Emerging Mkts)	C+	B-	C	Up		1,000,000
Oppenheimer Developing Markets Fund Class R	ODVNX	NAS CM	Open End	Emerging Markets Equity (Div Emerging Mkts)	C+	B-	C	Up		1,000
Oppenheimer Developing Markets Fund Class Y	ODVYX	NAS CM	Open End	Emerging Markets Equity (Div Emerging Mkts)	C+	B-	C	Up		0
Oppenheimer Discovery Fund Class A	OPOCX	NAS CM	Open End	US Equity Small Cap (Small Company)	B+	A-	B	Up		1,000
Oppenheimer Discovery Fund Class B	ODIBX	NAS CM	Open End	US Equity Small Cap (Small Company)	B+	A-	B	Up		1,000
Oppenheimer Discovery Fund Class C	ODICX	NAS CM	Open End	US Equity Small Cap (Small Company)	B+	A-	B	Up		1,000
Oppenheimer Discovery Fund Class I	ODIIX	NAS CM	Open End	US Equity Small Cap (Small Company)	B+	A-	B	Up		1,000,000
Oppenheimer Discovery Fund Class R	ODINX	NAS CM	Open End	US Equity Small Cap (Small Company)	B+	A-	B	Up		1,000
Oppenheimer Discovery Fund Class Y	ODIYX	NAS CM	Open End	US Equity Small Cap (Small Company)	B+	A-	B	Up		0
Oppenheimer Discovery Mid Cap Growth Fund A	OEGAX	NAS CM	Open End	US Equity Mid Cap (Growth)	A-	A-	B+	Up	Y	1,000
Oppenheimer Discovery Mid Cap Growth Fund B	OEGBX	NAS CM	Open End	US Equity Mid Cap (Growth)	B+	B+	B+	Up		1,000
Oppenheimer Discovery Mid Cap Growth Fund C	OEGCX	NAS CM	Open End	US Equity Mid Cap (Growth)	B+	B+	B+	Up	Y	1,000
Oppenheimer Discovery Mid Cap Growth Fund I	OEGIX	NAS CM	Open End	US Equity Mid Cap (Growth)	A-	A-	B+	Up	Y	1,000,000
Oppenheimer Discovery Mid Cap Growth Fund R	OEGNX	NAS CM	Open End	US Equity Mid Cap (Growth)	A-	A-	B+	Up	Y	0
Oppenheimer Discovery Mid Cap Growth Fund Y	OEGYX	NAS CM	Open End	US Equity Mid Cap (Growth)	A-	A-	B+	Up	Y	0
Oppenheimer Dividend Opportunity Fund Class A	OSVAX	NAS CM	Open End	US Equity Large Cap Value (Growth & Income)	B-	B-	B-	Down	Y	1,000
Oppenheimer Dividend Opportunity Fund Class B	OSVBX	NAS CM	Open End	US Equity Large Cap Value (Growth & Income)	B-	C+	B-	Down		1,000
Oppenheimer Dividend Opportunity Fund Class C	OSCVX	NAS CM	Open End	US Equity Large Cap Value (Growth & Income)	B	C+	B+	Up	Y	1,000
Oppenheimer Dividend Opportunity Fund Class I	OSVIX	NAS CM	Open End	US Equity Large Cap Value (Growth & Income)	B-	B-	B	Down	Y	1,000,000
Oppenheimer Dividend Opportunity Fund Class R	OSVNX	NAS CM	Open End	US Equity Large Cap Value (Growth & Income)	B	B-	B+	Up	Y	0
Oppenheimer Dividend Opportunity Fund Class Y	OSVYX	NAS CM	Open End	US Equity Large Cap Value (Growth & Income)	B-	B-	B-	Down	Y	0
Oppenheimer Emerging Markets Innovators Fund Class A	EMIAX	NAS CM	Open End	Emerging Markets Equity (Div Emerging Mkts)	B-	B-	B-	Up	Y	1,000
Oppenheimer Emerging Markets Innovators Fund Class C	EMVCX	NAS CM	Open End	Emerging Markets Equity (Div Emerging Mkts)	B-	B-	C+	Up	Y	1,000
Oppenheimer Emerging Markets Innovators Fund Class I	EMVIX	NAS CM	Open End	Emerging Markets Equity (Div Emerging Mkts)	B-	B-	B-	Up	Y	1,000,000
Oppenheimer Emerging Markets Innovators Fund Class R	EMIRX	NAS CM	Open End	Emerging Markets Equity (Div Emerging Mkts)	B-	B-	C+	Up	Y	0
Oppenheimer Emerging Markets Innovators Fund Class Y	EMIYX	NAS CM	Open End	Emerging Markets Equity (Div Emerging Mkts)	B-	B-	B-	Up	Y	0
Oppenheimer Equity Income Fund Class A	OAEIX	NAS CM	Open End	US Equity Large Cap Value (Equity-Income)	C+	C+	B-	Down	Y	1,000
Oppenheimer Equity Income Fund Class B	OBEIX	NAS CM	Open End	US Equity Large Cap Value (Equity-Income)	C+	C+	B-	Down		1,000
Oppenheimer Equity Income Fund Class C	OCEIX	NAS CM	Open End	US Equity Large Cap Value (Equity-Income)	C+	C+	B-	Down	Y	1,000
Oppenheimer Equity Income Fund Class I	OEIIX	NAS CM	Open End	US Equity Large Cap Value (Equity-Income)	B-	C+	B-	Up	Y	1,000,000
Oppenheimer Equity Income Fund Class R	ONEIX	NAS CM	Open End	US Equity Large Cap Value (Equity-Income)	C+	C+	B-	Down	Y	0
Oppenheimer Equity Income Fund Class Y	OYEIX	NAS CM	Open End	US Equity Large Cap Value (Equity-Income)	C+	C+	B-	Down	Y	0
Oppenheimer Fundamental Alternatives Fund A	QVOPX	NAS CM	Open End	Multialternative (Asset Alloc)	B-	C	A-	Up	Y	1,000
Oppenheimer Fundamental Alternatives Fund B	QOPBX	NAS CM	Open End	Multialternative (Asset Alloc)	C	C	C+	Down		1,000
Oppenheimer Fundamental Alternatives Fund C	QOPCX	NAS CM	Open End	Multialternative (Asset Alloc)	C	C	C+	Down	Y	1,000
Oppenheimer Fundamental Alternatives Fund I	QOPIX	NAS CM	Open End	Multialternative (Asset Alloc)	B-	C	A	Up	Y	1,000,000

★ Expanded analysis of this fund is included in Section II.

Min Additional Investment	3-Month Total Return	6-Month Total Return	1-Year Total Return	3-Year Total Return	5-Year Total Return	Dividend Yield (TTM)	Expense Ratio	3-Yr Std Deviation	3-Year Beta	NAV	Total Assets (MIL)	%Cash	%Stocks	%Bonds	%Other	Turnover Ratio	Last Bull Market Total Return	Last Bear Market Total Return	Front End Fee (%)	Back End Fee (%)	Inception Date
	TOTAL RETURNS					PERFORMANCE				ASSETS		ASSET ALLOCATION & TURNOVER					BULL & BEAR		FEES		
500	0.69	2.12	6.49	12.40		6.61	3.06	4.99	25	48.96	35.8	65	0	29	1	435					Jan-13
	5.86	9.90	26.52	26.38	93.45	0.06	1.07	11.55	1.03	58.38	5,215	1	99	0	0	63	24.5	-16.56	5.75		Jan-81
	5.65	9.46	25.55	23.49	86.10	0	1.83	11.55	1.03	44.54	5,215	1	99	0	0	63	23.89	-16.86		5.00	Nov-95
	5.65	9.48	25.56	23.51	86.20	0	1.82	11.55	1.03	44.13	5,215	1	99	0	0	63	23.93	-16.85		1.00	Dec-93
	5.97	10.13	27.03	27.97	97.58	0.38	0.63	11.56	1.03	63.31	5,215	1	99	0	0	63	24.7	-16.56			Dec-11
	5.79	9.76	26.19	25.39	90.95	0	1.32	11.56	1.03	55.08	5,215	1	99	0	0	63	24.32	-16.65			Mar-01
	5.92	10.03	26.81	27.25	95.93	0.21	0.82	11.55	1.03	63.08	5,215	1	99	0	0	63	24.79	-16.41			Nov-97
	1.72	3.36	6.97	13.49	30.63	2.57	1.03	3.34	0.28	10.25	2,779	7	31	54	2	92	8.43	-4.87	5.75		Dec-70
	1.56	2.90	6.11	10.97	25.42	1.76	1.79	3.34	0.28	10.05	2,779	7	31	54	2	92	7.84	-5.26		5.00	Aug-93
	1.57	2.96	6.17	10.96	25.64	1.93	1.79	3.32	0.28	9.92	2,779	7	31	54	2	92	7.95	-5.18		1.00	Nov-95
	1.85	3.59	7.43	14.97	32.91	2.98	0.6	3.36	0.28	10.24	2,779	7	31	54	2	92	8.43	-4.87			Dec-13
	1.69	3.20	6.73	12.68	28.90	2.39	1.29	3.36	0.28	10.11	2,779	7	31	54	2	92	8.23	-5.09			Mar-01
	1.79	3.39	7.24	14.33	32.17	2.81	0.79	3.34	0.28	10.24	2,779	7	31	54	2	92	8.59	-4.68			Jan-11
	5.03	13.63	34.77	23.55	28.75	0.17	1.32	14.56	0.87	43.56	38,199	4	93	0	4	33	18.46	-23.19	5.75		Nov-96
	4.82	13.20	33.73	20.81	23.89	0	2.08	14.52	0.87	41.74	38,199	4	93	0	4	33	17.86	-23.47		5.00	Nov-96
	4.83	13.22	33.78	20.81	24.11	0	2.07	14.53	0.87	40.75	38,199	4	93	0	4	33	17.97	-23.41		1.00	Nov-96
	5.13	13.87	35.32	25.20	31.66	0.55	0.88	14.54	0.87	42.93	38,199	4	93	0	4	33	18.59	-23.19			Dec-11
	4.97	13.49	34.46	22.65	27.10	0.01	1.57	14.54	0.87	41.88	38,199	4	93	0	4	33	18.2	-23.3			Mar-01
	5.09	13.78	35.10	24.49	30.52	0.4	1.07	14.55	0.87	42.94	38,199	4	93	0	4	33	18.69	-23.1			Sep-05
	6.97	12.94	29.11	36.43	100.03	0	1.12	13.31	0.83	77.54	2,197	1	99	0	0	107	27.59	-22.32	5.75		Sep-86
	6.75	12.48	28.11	33.32	92.40	0	1.88	13.3	0.83	53.42	2,197	1	99	0	0	107	26.95	-22.55		5.00	Apr-94
	6.76	12.50	28.12	33.35	92.57	0	1.87	13.3	0.83	55.86	2,197	1	99	0	0	107	27.02	-22.56		1.00	Oct-95
	7.09	13.18	29.64	38.17	104.54	0	0.68	13.31	0.83	88.63	2,197	1	99	0	0	107	27.75	-22.32			Jan-12
	6.91	12.80	28.78	35.37	97.40	0	1.37	13.3	0.83	71.89	2,197	1	99	0	0	107	27.36	-22.4			Mar-01
	7.04	13.06	29.40	37.39	102.55	0	0.87	13.31	0.83	87.31	2,197	1	99	0	0	107	27.92	-22.19			Jun-94
	6.66	12.13	27.98	37.43	100.43	0	1.15	10.88	0.91	19.94	1,053	2	98	0	0	128	27.32	-19.66	5.75		Nov-00
	6.50	11.79	27.06	34.37	92.68	0	1.91	10.88	0.91	16.34	1,053	2	98	0	0	128	26.75	-19.95		5.00	Nov-00
	6.45	11.69	27.07	34.33	92.96	0	1.9	10.89	0.91	16.47	1,053	2	98	0	0	128	26.84	-19.95		1.00	Nov-00
	6.74	12.39	28.53	39.22	105.20	0	0.71	10.86	0.91	22.54	1,053	2	98	0	0	128	27.73	-19.48			Feb-13
	6.54	11.99	27.64	36.41	97.73	0	1.4	10.88	0.91	18.67	1,053	2	98	0	0	128	27.21	-19.77			Mar-01
	6.73	12.33	28.37	38.53	103.27	0	0.9	10.88	0.91	22.29	1,053	2	98	0	0	128	27.73	-19.48			Nov-00
	5.74	8.66	14.40	29.06	71.43	2.66	1.15	9.09	0.82	24.09	268.9	1	99	0	0	64	16.19	-24.66	5.75		Nov-02
	5.52	8.19	13.46	25.97	64.77	1.91	1.93	9.06	0.82	23.36	268.9	1	99	0	0	64	15.65	-24.94		5.00	Feb-04
	5.55	8.27	13.59	26.18	65.15	2.08	1.9	9.08	0.82	23.26	268.9	1	99	0	0	64	15.7	-24.95		1.00	Feb-04
	5.88	8.92	14.92	30.81	74.09	3.07	0.7	9.07	0.82	24.06	268.9	1	99	0	0	64	16.19	-24.66			Aug-14
	5.69	8.52	14.14	28.11	69.38	2.48	1.39	9.09	0.82	23.85	268.9	1	99	0	0	64	16.11	-24.75			Feb-04
	5.82	8.82	14.72	30.04	73.80	2.91	0.9	9.09	0.82	24.06	268.9	1	99	0	0	64	16.49	-24.54			Feb-04
	7.76	16.68	40.50	30.36		0	1.71	12.46	0.72	11.54	382.1	7	93	0	0	23			5.75		Jun-14
	7.44	16.20	39.35	27.23		0	2.5	12.45	0.72	11.26	382.1	7	93	0	0	23				1.00	Jun-14
	7.83	16.96	41.14	32.24		0	1.25	12.41	0.72	11.68	382.1	7	93	0	0	23					Jun-14
	7.58	16.44	39.90	29.17		0	2.01	12.4	0.72	11.45	382.1	7	93	0	0	23					Jun-14
	7.71	16.77	40.75	31.39		0	1.46	12.45	0.73	11.61	382.1	7	93	0	0	23					Jun-14
	4.78	8.05	12.59	15.49	71.20	2.15	1.05	11.93	1.09	32.35	3,798	0	93	0	0	46	24.24	-22.15	5.75		Feb-87
	4.56	7.64	11.71	12.88	64.44	1.93	1.8	11.92	1.09	25.74	3,798	0	93	0	0	46	23.59	-22.46		5.00	Mar-97
	4.61	7.66	11.77	12.90	64.82	2.09	1.8	11.94	1.09	25.71	3,798	0	93	0	0	46	23.65	-22.36		1.00	Mar-97
	4.91	8.31	13.06	17.00	74.80	2.55	0.61	11.94	1.09	32.29	3,798	0	93	0	0	46	24.35	-22.15			Feb-12
	4.73	7.90	12.31	14.59	68.77	2.02	1.29	11.92	1.09	30.93	3,798	0	93	0	0	46	23.9	-22.3			Mar-01
	4.86	8.19	12.85	16.32	73.36	2.38	0.8	11.93	1.09	32.31	3,798	0	93	0	0	46	24.37	-22.05			Feb-11
	-0.66	-0.59	1.28	4.33	19.52	0.25	1.34	2.97	0.32	26.82	1,239	35	28	26	4	131	0.87	-10.17	5.75		Jan-89
	-0.86	-1.03	0.50	1.88	14.86	0.2	2.08	2.97	0.32	24.02	1,239	35	28	26	4	131	0.39	-10.52		5.00	Sep-93
	-0.87	-0.99	0.53	1.97	15.03	0.2	2.1	2.97	0.32	23.79	1,239	35	28	26	4	131	0.43	-10.45		1.00	Sep-93
	-0.55	-0.38	1.74	5.71	22.06	0.7	0.95	2.96	0.32	27.5	1,239	35	28	26	4	131	0.87	-10.17			Feb-13

	MARKET			FUND TYPE, CATEGORY & OBJECTIVE	RATINGS					MINIMUMS
Fund Name	Ticker Symbol	Traded On	Fund Type	Category and (Prospectus Objective)	Overall Rating	Reward Rating	Risk Rating	Recent Up/ Downgrade	Open to New Investors	Min Initial Investment
Oppenheimer Fundamental Alternatives Fund R	QOPNX	NAS CM	Open End	Multialternative (Asset Alloc)	C+	C	B	Up	Y	0
Oppenheimer Fundamental Alternatives Fund Y	QOPYX	NAS CM	Open End	Multialternative (Asset Alloc)	B-	C	A	Up	Y	0
Oppenheimer Global Allocation Fund Class A	QVGIX	NAS CM	Open End	Alloc (Asset Alloc)	B	C+	A-	Up	Y	1,000
Oppenheimer Global Allocation Fund Class B	QGRBX	NAS CM	Open End	Alloc (Asset Alloc)	B	C+	B+	Up		1,000
Oppenheimer Global Allocation Fund Class C	QGRCX	NAS CM	Open End	Alloc (Asset Alloc)	B	C+	B+	Up	Y	1,000
Oppenheimer Global Allocation Fund Class I	QGRIX	NAS CM	Open End	Alloc (Asset Alloc)	B	C+	A-	Up	Y	1,000,000
Oppenheimer Global Allocation Fund Class R	QGRNX	NAS CM	Open End	Alloc (Asset Alloc)	B	C+	A-	Up	Y	0
Oppenheimer Global Allocation Fund Class Y	QGRYX	NAS CM	Open End	Alloc (Asset Alloc)	B	C+	A-	Up	Y	0
Oppenheimer Global Fund Class A	OPPAX	NAS CM	Open End	Global Equity (World Stock)	B+	B+	B	Up	Y	1,000
Oppenheimer Global Fund Class B	OGLBX	NAS CM	Open End	Global Equity (World Stock)	B	B+	B	Up		1,000
Oppenheimer Global Fund Class C	OGLCX	NAS CM	Open End	Global Equity (World Stock)	B	B+	B	Up	Y	1,000
Oppenheimer Global Fund Class Fund Class Y	OGLYX	NAS CM	Open End	Global Equity (World Stock)	B+	B+	B	Up	Y	0
Oppenheimer Global Fund Class I	OGLIX	NAS CM	Open End	Global Equity (World Stock)	B+	A-	B	Up	Y	1,000,000
Oppenheimer Global Fund Class R	OGLNX	NAS CM	Open End	Global Equity (World Stock)	B+	B+	B	Up	Y	1,000
Oppenheimer Global Multi Strategies Fund Class A	OARAX	NAS CM	Open End	Multialternative (Growth & Income)	C	C	C	Up	Y	1,000
Oppenheimer Global Multi Strategies Fund Class C	OARCX	NAS CM	Open End	Multialternative (Growth & Income)	C	C-	C	Up	Y	1,000
Oppenheimer Global Multi Strategies Fund Class I	OAIIX	NAS CM	Open End	Multialternative (Growth & Income)	C	C	C	Up	Y	1,000,000
Oppenheimer Global Multi Strategies Fund Class Y	OARYX	NAS CM	Open End	Multialternative (Growth & Income)	C	C	C	Up	Y	0
Oppenheimer Global Multi-Alternatives Fund A	ODAAX	NAS CM	Open End	Multialternative (Growth)	C	C	C	Down	Y	1,000
Oppenheimer Global Multi-Alternatives Fund C	ODACX	NAS CM	Open End	Multialternative (Growth)	C-	C-	C	Down	Y	1,000
Oppenheimer Global Multi-Alternatives Fund I	ODAIX	NAS CM	Open End	Multialternative (Growth)	C	C	C	Down	Y	1,000,000
Oppenheimer Global Multi-Alternatives Fund R	ODANX	NAS CM	Open End	Multialternative (Growth)	C	C-	C		Y	0
Oppenheimer Global Multi-Alternatives Fund Y	ODAYX	NAS CM	Open End	Multialternative (Growth)	C	C	C	Down	Y	0
Oppenheimer Global Multi-Asset Growth Fund Class A	QMGAX	NAS CM	Open End	Alloc (Multi-Asset Global)	C	C+	B	Up	Y	1,000
Oppenheimer Global Multi-Asset Growth Fund Class C	QMGCX	NAS CM	Open End	Alloc (Multi-Asset Global)	C	C+	B	Up	Y	1,000
Oppenheimer Global Multi-Asset Growth Fund Class I	QMGIX	NAS CM	Open End	Alloc (Multi-Asset Global)	C	C+	B	Up	Y	1,000,000
Oppenheimer Global Multi-Asset Growth Fund Class R	QMGRX	NAS CM	Open End	Alloc (Multi-Asset Global)	C	C+	B	Up	Y	0
Oppenheimer Global Multi-Asset Growth Fund Class Y	QMGYX	NAS CM	Open End	Alloc (Multi-Asset Global)	C	C+	B	Up	Y	0
Oppenheimer Global Multi-Asset Income Fund Class A	QMAAX	NAS CM	Open End	Cautious Alloc (Growth & Income)	C+	C	B	Up	Y	1,000
Oppenheimer Global Multi-Asset Income Fund Class C	QMACX	NAS CM	Open End	Cautious Alloc (Growth & Income)	C+	C	B	Up	Y	1,000
Oppenheimer Global Multi-Asset Income Fund Class I	QMAIX	NAS CM	Open End	Cautious Alloc (Growth & Income)	C+	C	B	Up	Y	1,000,000
Oppenheimer Global Multi-Asset Income Fund Class R	QMARX	NAS CM	Open End	Cautious Alloc (Growth & Income)	C+	C	B	Up	Y	0
Oppenheimer Global Multi-Asset Income Fund Class Y	QMAYX	NAS CM	Open End	Cautious Alloc (Growth & Income)	C+	C	B	Up	Y	0
Oppenheimer Global Opportunities Fund Class A	OPGIX	NAS CM	Open End	Global Equity Mid/Small Cap (World Stock)	A	A+	B+	Up	Y	1,000
Oppenheimer Global Opportunities Fund Class B	OGGIX	NAS CM	Open End	Global Equity Mid/Small Cap (World Stock)	A	A+	B+	Up		1,000
Oppenheimer Global Opportunities Fund Class C	OGICX	NAS CM	Open End	Global Equity Mid/Small Cap (World Stock)	A	A+	B+	Up	Y	1,000
Oppenheimer Global Opportunities Fund Class I	OGIIX	NAS CM	Open End	Global Equity Mid/Small Cap (World Stock)	A	A+	B+	Up	Y	1,000,000
Oppenheimer Global Opportunities Fund Class R	OGINX	NAS CM	Open End	Global Equity Mid/Small Cap (World Stock)	A	A+	B+	Up	Y	1,000
Oppenheimer Global Opportunities Fund Class Y	OGIYX	NAS CM	Open End	Global Equity Mid/Small Cap (World Stock)	A	A+	B+	Up	Y	0
Oppenheimer Global Real Estate Fund Class A	OGRAX	NAS CM	Open End	Real Estate Sector Equity (Real Estate)	C+	C	B	Up	Y	1,000
Oppenheimer Global Real Estate Fund Class C	OGRCX	NAS CM	Open End	Real Estate Sector Equity (Real Estate)	C+	C	B	Up	Y	1,000
Oppenheimer Global Real Estate Fund Class I	OIRGX	NAS CM	Open End	Real Estate Sector Equity (Real Estate)	B-	C+	B	Up	Y	1,000,000
Oppenheimer Global Real Estate Fund Class R	OGRNX	NAS CM	Open End	Real Estate Sector Equity (Real Estate)	C+	C	B	Up	Y	0
Oppenheimer Global Real Estate Fund Class Y	OGRYX	NAS CM	Open End	Real Estate Sector Equity (Real Estate)	B-	C+	B	Up	Y	0
Oppenheimer Global Value Fund Class A	GLVAX	NAS CM	Open End	Global Equity (World Stock)	B	B-	B	Up	Y	1,000
Oppenheimer Global Value Fund Class C	GLVCX	NAS CM	Open End	Global Equity (World Stock)	B-	B-	B	Up	Y	1,000
Oppenheimer Global Value Fund Class I	GLVIX	NAS CM	Open End	Global Equity (World Stock)	B	B	B	Up	Y	1,000,000
Oppenheimer Global Value Fund Class R	GLVNX	NAS CM	Open End	Global Equity (World Stock)	B	B-	B	Up	Y	0
Oppenheimer Global Value Fund Class Y	GLVYX	NAS CM	Open End	Global Equity (World Stock)	B	B	B	Up	Y	0
Oppenheimer Gold & Special Minerals Fund Class A	OPGSX	NAS CM	Open End	Precious Metals Sector Equity (Precious Metals)	C-	C	D		Y	1,000
Oppenheimer Gold & Special Minerals Fund Class C	OGMCX	NAS CM	Open End	Precious Metals Sector Equity (Precious Metals)	C-	C	D		Y	1,000
Oppenheimer Gold & Special Minerals Fund Class I	OGMIX	NAS CM	Open End	Precious Metals Sector Equity (Precious Metals)	C-	C	D+		Y	1,000,000

★ Expanded analysis of this fund is included in Section II.

Min Additional Investment	TOTAL RETURNS 3-Month Total Return	6-Month Total Return	1-Year Total Return	3-Year Total Return	5-Year Total Return	PERFORMANCE Dividend Yield (TTM)	Expense Ratio	3-Yr Std Deviation	3-Year Beta	ASSETS NAV	Total Assets (MIL)	ASSET ALLOCATION & TURNOVER %Cash	%Stocks	%Bonds	%Other	Turnover Ratio	BULL & BEAR Last Bull Market Total Return	Last Bear Market Total Return	FEES Front End Fee (%)	Back End Fee (%)	Inception Date
	-0.72	-0.72	1.04	3.53	17.89	0.21	1.61	2.98	0.32	25.67	1,239	35	28	26	4	131	0.72	-10.28			Mar-01
	-0.60	-0.50	1.52	5.04	20.88	0.54	1.15	2.97	0.32	27.4	1,239	35	28	26	4	131	1.06	-10.06			Dec-96
	2.29	4.67	14.83	20.49	42.87	2.58	1.3	6.74	0.59	19.76	1,640	11	63	25	0	84	9.03	-14.95	5.75		Nov-91
	2.05	4.24	13.91	17.73	37.36	2.35	2.07	6.74	0.59	18.91	1,640	11	63	25	0	84	8.54	-15.29		5.00	Sep-93
	2.04	4.24	13.97	17.78	37.60	2.39	2.04	6.74	0.59	18.92	1,640	11	63	25	0	84	8.55	-15.23		1.00	Sep-93
	2.36	4.86	15.28	22.06	46.01	2.88	0.8	6.76	0.59	19.72	1,640	11	63	25	0	84	9.08	-14.95			Feb-12
	2.16	4.47	14.53	19.62	41.03	2.51	1.54	6.73	0.59	19.38	1,640	11	63	25	0	84	8.82	-15.03			Mar-01
	2.28	4.78	15.10	21.40	44.83	2.77	1.04	6.74	0.59	19.72	1,640	11	63	25	0	84	9.25	-14.82			May-00
	7.12	13.61	36.24	40.82	85.20	0.51	1.15	12.88	1.12	95.98	11,177	1	98	0	1	7	17.76	-23.19	5.75		Dec-69
	6.90	13.17	35.20	37.60	78.02	0	1.9	12.87	1.12	87.17	11,177	1	98	0	1	7	17.17	-23.48		5.00	Aug-93
	6.91	13.18	35.19	37.61	78.38	0	1.89	12.87	1.12	88.5	11,177	1	98	0	1	7	17.25	-23.41		1.00	Oct-95
	7.18	13.76	36.56	41.81	87.47	0.7	0.89	12.88	1.12	96.05	11,177	1	98	0	1	7	17.95	-23.11			Nov-98
	7.21	13.84	36.78	42.59	89.23	0.84	0.7	12.88	1.12	96.02	11,177	1	98	0	1	7	17.91	-23.19			Jan-12
	7.04	13.47	35.88	39.70	82.79	0.32	1.39	12.88	1.12	95.56	11,177	1	98	0	1	7	17.52	-23.29			Mar-01
	0.67	0.80	2.51	-0.48	8.65	8.64	1.37	3.69	16.22	22.68	106.8	7	52	40	0	111	-2.88	-7.19	5.75		Mar-07
	0.45	0.36	1.65	-2.90	4.28	7.83	2.2	3.69	16.12	22.33	106.8	7	52	40	0	111	-3.32	-7.48		1.00	Jan-12
	0.73	0.90	2.74	0.31	10.05	8.94	1.12	3.69	16.49	22.76	106.8	7	52	40	0	111	-2.8	-7.19			Jan-12
	0.74	0.87	2.64	-0.18	8.86	8.36	1.27	3.7	16.38	22.59	106.8	7	52	40	0	111	-2.84	-7.19			Jan-12
	0.36	-0.27	0.47	1.39	1.88	3.72	1.37	3.38	13.54	9.05	28.7	16	37	44	1	21			5.75		Dec-12
	0.07	-0.78	-0.35	-1.18	-2.84	2.81	2.12	3.31	13.98	8.97	28.7	16	37	44	1	21				1.00	Dec-12
	0.48	-0.04	1.03	2.68	3.84	4.15	0.93	3.38	13.8	9.07	28.7	16	37	44	1	21					Dec-12
	0.25	-0.49	0.14	0.38	-0.26	3.5	1.62	3.36	13.02	8.98	28.7	16	37	44	1	21					Dec-12
	0.32	-0.21	0.64	1.86	2.39	4	1.12	3.43	14.82	9.06	28.7	16	37	44	1	21					Dec-12
	3.23	6.77	18.99			4.22	1.21			11.59	70.1	6	72	20	1	61			5.75		Aug-15
	2.91	6.27	18.06			3.84	1.96			11.5	70.1	6	72	20	1	61				1.00	Aug-15
	3.19	6.81	19.13			4.41	0.96			11.59	70.1	6	72	20	1	61					Aug-15
	3.03	6.57	18.56			4.18	1.46			11.56	70.1	6	72	20	1	61					Aug-15
	3.25	6.78	19.20			4.26	1.06			11.61	70.1	6	72	20	1	61					Aug-15
	1.74	2.24	6.29	12.06		5.03	0.95			9.7	108.1	9	22	45	14	71			4.75		Dec-14
	1.65	1.82	5.50	9.45		4.29	1.75			9.69	108.1	9	22	45	14	71				1.00	Dec-14
	1.90	2.36	6.64	12.93		5.26	0.7			9.71	108.1	9	22	45	14	71					Dec-14
	1.76	2.06	6.07	11.12		4.73	1.25			9.7	108.1	9	22	45	14	71					Dec-14
	1.79	2.32	6.59	12.59		5.22	0.75			9.7	108.1	9	22	45	14	71					Dec-14
	14.29	22.25	52.52	91.92	166.36	0.18	1.17	17.19	1.12	68.54	6,911	0	99	0	1	18	16.64	-19.52	5.75		Oct-90
	14.08	21.79	51.36	87.54	155.93	0	1.93	17.19	1.12	60.53	6,911	0	99	0	1	18	16.09	-19.85		5.00	Oct-95
	14.08	21.80	51.39	87.59	156.47	0	1.92	17.19	1.12	60.62	6,911	0	99	0	1	18	16.16	-19.78		1.00	Dec-93
	14.43	22.52	53.18	94.38	172.19	0.45	0.73	17.2	1.12	69.61	6,911	0	99	0	1	18	16.77	-19.52			Jan-12
	14.23	22.11	52.16	90.44	162.74	0.08	1.42	17.19	1.12	65.97	6,911	0	99	0	1	18	16.44	-19.65			Mar-01
	14.38	22.43	52.93	93.33	169.70	0.36	0.92	17.19	1.12	69.34	6,911	0	99	0	1	18	16.85	-19.44			Feb-01
	4.41	6.33	11.81	10.23		4.62	1.45	10.87	0.94	10.53	50.9	2	98	0	1	124			5.75		Mar-13
	4.25	5.86	11.03	7.63		3.89	2.25	10.86	0.94	10.47	50.9	2	98	0	1	124				1.00	Mar-13
	4.52	6.55	12.35	11.62		4.99	1.05	10.9	0.94	10.55	50.9	2	98	0	1	124					Mar-13
	4.34	6.09	11.44	9.24		4.37	1.75	10.86	0.94	10.5	50.9	2	98	0	1	124					Mar-13
	4.51	6.53	12.18	11.34		4.92	1.1	10.84	0.94	10.54	50.9	2	98	0	1	124					Mar-13
	0.87	7.22	25.08	22.10	69.61	0	1.31	14.58	1.27	50.36	561.6	1	99	0	0	59	19.11	-22.05	5.75		Oct-07
	0.69	6.83	24.15	19.35	63.25	0	2.06	14.59	1.28	47.31	561.6	1	99	0	0	59	18.6	-22.29		1.00	Oct-07
	0.98	7.46	25.61	23.72	73.34	0	0.86	14.6	1.28	51.71	561.6	1	99	0	0	59	19.36	-21.94			Aug-12
	0.81	7.09	24.80	21.18	67.38	0	1.56	14.59	1.28	49.26	561.6	1	99	0	0	59	18.99	-22.14			Oct-07
	0.93	7.35	25.41	23.01	71.79	0	1.05	14.59	1.28	51.26	561.6	1	99	0	0	59	19.36	-21.94			Oct-07
	1.20	4.37	17.19	34.27	-38.97	6.58	1.17	37.07	0.35	16.5	1,012	3	97	0	0	65	-13.91	-21.07	5.75		Jul-83
	0.99	3.97	16.29	31.29	-41.28	6.44	1.92	37.03	0.35	15.13	1,012	3	97	0	0	65	-14.25	-21.29		1.00	Nov-95
	1.26	4.54	17.62	35.97	-37.57	7.03	0.73	37.11	0.35	16.54	1,012	3	97	0	0	65	-13.91	-21.07			Oct-12

Fund Name	MARKET Ticker Symbol	Traded On	FUND TYPE, CATEGORY & OBJECTIVE Fund Type	Category and (Prospectus Objective)	RATINGS Overall Rating	Reward Rating	Risk Rating	Recent Up/ Downgrade	Open to New Investors	MINIMUMS Min Initial Investment
Oppenheimer Gold & Special Minerals Fund Class Y	OGMYX	NAS CM	Open End	Precious Metals Sector Equity (Precious Metals)	C-	C	D		Y	0
Oppenheimer Gold and Special Minerals Fund Class B	OGMBX	NAS CM	Open End	Precious Metals Sector Equity (Precious Metals)	C-	C	D			1,000
Oppenheimer Gold and Special Minerals Fund Class R	OGMNX	NAS CM	Open End	Precious Metals Sector Equity (Precious Metals)	C-	C	D		Y	0
Oppenheimer International Diversified Fund Class A	OIDAX	NAS CM	Open End	Global Equity Large Cap (Growth)	B	B	B	Up	Y	1,000
Oppenheimer International Diversified Fund Class B	OIDBX	NAS CM	Open End	Global Equity Large Cap (Growth)	B	B	B	Up		1,000
Oppenheimer International Diversified Fund Class C	OIDCX	NAS CM	Open End	Global Equity Large Cap (Growth)	B	B	B	Up	Y	1,000
Oppenheimer International Diversified Fund Class I	OIDIX	NAS CM	Open End	Global Equity Large Cap (Growth)	B	B	B	Up	Y	1,000,000
Oppenheimer International Diversified Fund Class R	OIDNX	NAS CM	Open End	Global Equity Large Cap (Growth)	B	B	B	Up	Y	0
Oppenheimer International Diversified Fund Class Y	OIDYX	NAS CM	Open End	Global Equity Large Cap (Growth)	B	B	B	Up	Y	0
Oppenheimer International Equity Fund Class A	QIVAX	NAS CM	Open End	Global Equity Large Cap (Foreign Stock)	B	B	B	Up	Y	1,000
Oppenheimer International Equity Fund Class B	QIVBX	NAS CM	Open End	Global Equity Large Cap (Foreign Stock)	B	B	B	Up		1,000
Oppenheimer International Equity Fund Class C	QIVCX	NAS CM	Open End	Global Equity Large Cap (Foreign Stock)	B	B	B	Up	Y	1,000
Oppenheimer International Equity Fund Class I	QIVIX	NAS CM	Open End	Global Equity Large Cap (Foreign Stock)	B	B	B	Up	Y	1,000,000
Oppenheimer International Equity Fund Class R	QIVNX	NAS CM	Open End	Global Equity Large Cap (Foreign Stock)	B	B	B	Up	Y	0
Oppenheimer International Equity Fund Class Y	QIVYX	NAS CM	Open End	Global Equity Large Cap (Foreign Stock)	B	B	B	Up	Y	0
Oppenheimer International Growth & Income Fund A	OIMAX	NAS CM	Open End	Global Equity Large Cap (Growth & Income)	D	D+	B+		Y	1,000
Oppenheimer International Growth & Income Fund C	OCIMX	NAS CM	Open End	Global Equity Large Cap (Growth & Income)	D	D+	B+		Y	1,000
Oppenheimer International Growth & Income Fund I	OIMIX	NAS CM	Open End	Global Equity Large Cap (Growth & Income)	D	D+	B+		Y	1,000,000
Oppenheimer International Growth & Income Fund R	OIMRX	NAS CM	Open End	Global Equity Large Cap (Growth & Income)	D	D+	B+		Y	0
Oppenheimer International Growth & Income Fund Y	OIMYX	NAS CM	Open End	Global Equity Large Cap (Growth & Income)	D	D+	B+		Y	0
Oppenheimer International Growth Fund Class A	OIGAX	NAS CM	Open End	Global Equity Large Cap (Foreign Stock)	B	B	B	Up	Y	1,000
Oppenheimer International Growth Fund Class B	IGRWX	NAS CM	Open End	Global Equity Large Cap (Foreign Stock)	B	B-	B	Up	Y	1,000
Oppenheimer International Growth Fund Class C	OIGCX	NAS CM	Open End	Global Equity Large Cap (Foreign Stock)	B	B-	B	Up	Y	1,000
Oppenheimer International Growth Fund Class I	OIGIX	NAS CM	Open End	Global Equity Large Cap (Foreign Stock)	B	B	B	Up	Y	1,000,000
Oppenheimer International Growth Fund Class R	OIGNX	NAS CM	Open End	Global Equity Large Cap (Foreign Stock)	B	B	B	Up	Y	0
Oppenheimer International Growth Fund Class Y	OIGYX	NAS CM	Open End	Global Equity Large Cap (Foreign Stock)	B	B	B	Up	Y	0
Oppenheimer International Small-Mid Company Fund Class A	OSMAX	NAS CM	Open End	Global Equity Mid/Small Cap (Growth)	A-	B+	A	Up	Y	1,000
Oppenheimer International Small-Mid Company Fund Class B	OSMBX	NAS CM	Open End	Global Equity Mid/Small Cap (Growth)	B+	B+	A	Up		1,000
Oppenheimer International Small-Mid Company Fund Class C	OSMCX	NAS CM	Open End	Global Equity Mid/Small Cap (Growth)	B+	B+	A	Up	Y	1,000
Oppenheimer International Small-Mid Company Fund Class I	OSCIX	NAS CM	Open End	Global Equity Mid/Small Cap (Growth)	A-	B+	A	Up		1,000,000
Oppenheimer International Small-Mid Company Fund Class R	OSMNX	NAS CM	Open End	Global Equity Mid/Small Cap (Growth)	A-	B+	A	Up		1,000
Oppenheimer International Small-Mid Company Fund Class Y	OSMYX	NAS CM	Open End	Global Equity Mid/Small Cap (Growth)	A-	B+	A	Up		0
Oppenheimer Macquarie Global Infrastructure Fund Class A	OQGAX	NAS CM	Open End	Other Sector Equity (Growth & Income)	D+	C-	B-	Up	Y	1,000
Oppenheimer Macquarie Global Infrastructure Fund Class C	OQGCX	NAS CM	Open End	Other Sector Equity (Growth & Income)	D+	C-	B-	Up	Y	1,000
Oppenheimer Macquarie Global Infrastructure Fund Class I	OQGIX	NAS CM	Open End	Other Sector Equity (Growth & Income)	D+	C	B-	Up	Y	1,000,000
Oppenheimer Macquarie Global Infrastructure Fund Class R	OQGRX	NAS CM	Open End	Other Sector Equity (Growth & Income)	D+	C-	B-	Up	Y	0
Oppenheimer Macquarie Global Infrastructure Fund Class Y	OQGYX	NAS CM	Open End	Other Sector Equity (Growth & Income)	D+	C	B-	Up	Y	0
Oppenheimer Main Street All Cap Fund Class A	OMSOX	NAS CM	Open End	US Equity Large Cap Blend (Growth)	B	B	B-		Y	1,000
Oppenheimer Main Street All Cap Fund Class B	OMOBX	NAS CM	Open End	US Equity Large Cap Blend (Growth)	B-	C+	B-	Down		1,000
Oppenheimer Main Street All Cap Fund Class C	OMSCX	NAS CM	Open End	US Equity Large Cap Blend (Growth)	B-	C+	B-	Down	Y	1,000
Oppenheimer Main Street All Cap Fund Class R	OMSNX	NAS CM	Open End	US Equity Large Cap Blend (Growth)	B-	B-	B-	Down	Y	1,000
Oppenheimer Main Street All Cap Fund Class Y	OMSYX	NAS CM	Open End	US Equity Large Cap Blend (Growth)	B-	B-	B-	Down	Y	0
Oppenheimer Main Street Fund Class A	MSIGX	NAS CM	Open End	US Equity Large Cap Blend (Growth & Income)	B	B-	B+		Y	1,000
Oppenheimer Main Street Fund Class B	OMSBX	NAS CM	Open End	US Equity Large Cap Blend (Growth & Income)	B	B-	B+			1,000
Oppenheimer Main Street Fund Class C	MIGCX	NAS CM	Open End	US Equity Large Cap Blend (Growth & Income)	B	B-	B+		Y	1,000
Oppenheimer Main Street Fund Class I	OMSIX	NAS CM	Open End	US Equity Large Cap Blend (Growth & Income)	B	B-	B+		Y	1,000,000
Oppenheimer Main Street Fund Class R	OMGNX	NAS CM	Open End	US Equity Large Cap Blend (Growth & Income)	B	B-	B+		Y	1,000
Oppenheimer Main Street Fund Class Y	MIGYX	NAS CM	Open End	US Equity Large Cap Blend (Growth & Income)	B	B-	B+		Y	0
Oppenheimer Main Street Mid Cap Fund Class A	OPMSX	NAS CM	Open End	US Equity Mid Cap (Growth)	B	B	B	Up	Y	1,000
Oppenheimer Main Street Mid Cap Fund Class B	OPMBX	NAS CM	Open End	US Equity Mid Cap (Growth)	B	B	B-	Up		1,000
Oppenheimer Main Street Mid Cap Fund Class C	OPMCX	NAS CM	Open End	US Equity Mid Cap (Growth)	B	B	B-	Up	Y	1,000
Oppenheimer Main Street Mid Cap Fund Class I	OPMIX	NAS CM	Open End	US Equity Mid Cap (Growth)	B	B	B	Up	Y	1,000,000

★ Expanded analysis of this fund is included in Section II.

Min Additional Investment	TOTAL RETURNS 3-Month Total Return	6-Month Total Return	1-Year Total Return	3-Year Total Return	5-Year Total Return	PERFORMANCE Dividend Yield (TTM)	Expense Ratio	3-Yr Std Deviation	3-Year Beta	ASSETS NAV	Total Assets (MIL)	ASSET ALLOCATION & TURNOVER %Cash	%Stocks	%Bonds	%Other	Turnover Ratio	BULL & BEAR Last Bull Market Total Return	Last Bear Market Total Return	FEES Front End Fee (%)	Back End Fee (%)	Inception Date
	1.21	4.44	17.36	35.21	-38.31	6.87	0.92	37.09	0.35	16.44	1,012	3	97	0	0	65	-13.86	-20.92			Sep-10
	0.96	3.88	16.19	31.08	-41.40	5.69	1.94	37.04	0.35	15.64	1,012	3	97	0	0	65	-14.32	-21.32		5.00	Nov-95
	1.13	4.19	16.91	33.24	-39.71	6.66	1.42	37.11	0.35	15.74	1,012	3	97	0	0	65	-14.08	-21.17			Mar-01
	4.68	11.42	32.40	33.73	57.75	0.31	1.33	11.06	0.86	18.28	3,860	5	94	0	0	16	12.91	-21.25	5.75		Sep-05
	4.45	10.95	31.31	30.64	51.65	0	2.08	11.04	0.86	17.82	3,860	5	94	0	0	16	12.41	-21.6		5.00	Sep-05
	4.46	10.98	31.31	30.69	51.93	0	2.08	11.02	0.86	17.78	3,860	5	94	0	0	16	12.47	-21.49		1.00	Sep-05
	4.80	11.64	32.96	35.46	61.91	0.67	0.89	11.04	0.86	18.51	3,860	5	94	0	0	16	13.13	-21.2			Aug-12
	4.58	11.20	31.97	32.63	55.67	0.14	1.58	11.05	0.86	18.06	3,860	5	94	0	0	16	12.78	-21.33			Sep-05
	4.75	11.54	32.75	34.75	59.75	0.54	1.08	11.08	0.86	18.45	3,860	5	94	0	0	16	13.13	-21.2			Sep-05
	3.86	9.67	31.09	31.83	55.79	1.56	1.25	11.09	0.85	22.35	1,838	4	96	0	0	79	6.95	-26.82	5.75		Jul-90
	3.61	9.16	30.01	28.64	49.80	0.66	2.1	11.09	0.85	20.36	1,838	4	96	0	0	79	6.37	-27.12		5.00	Sep-93
	3.63	9.26	30.15	28.93	49.99	1.13	2	11.07	0.85	19.94	1,838	4	96	0	0	79	6.44	-27.04		1.00	Sep-93
	3.94	9.88	31.61	33.54	59.08	1.93	0.8	11.09	0.85	22.21	1,838	4	96	0	0	79	6.95	-26.82			Mar-13
	3.75	9.51	30.71	30.82	53.76	1.38	1.5	11.09	0.85	22.09	1,838	4	96	0	0	79	6.72	-26.91			Mar-01
	3.89	9.80	31.39	32.82	57.45	1.78	0.85	11.09	0.85	22.52	1,838	4	96	0	0	79	7.25	-26.59			Nov-08
	0.92	2.82	16.97			1.94	1.25			11.49	11.3	2	98	0	0	4			5.75		Oct-16
	0.63	2.38	16.03			1.42	2			11.47	11.3	2	98	0	0	4				1.00	Oct-16
	0.93	3.01	17.40			2.16	0.9			11.5	11.3	2	98	0	0	4					Oct-16
	0.75	2.58	16.56			1.72	1.5			11.48	11.3	2	98	0	0	4					Oct-16
	0.91	2.86	17.22			2.11	1			11.49	11.3	2	98	0	0	4					Oct-16
	3.61	9.52	26.60	27.10	49.76	0.82	1.14	11.75	0.88	43.91	27,302	3	97	0	0	9	18.05	-20.36	5.75		Mar-96
	3.40	9.10	25.64	24.24	44.20	0	1.89	11.75	0.88	42.18	27,302	3	97	0	0	9	17.48	-20.6		5.00	Mar-96
	3.42	9.10	25.67	24.26	44.26	0.22	1.89	11.76	0.88	41.7	27,302	3	97	0	0	9	17.54	-20.56		1.00	Mar-96
	3.73	9.74	27.15	28.77	53.12	1.23	0.7	11.75	0.88	43.63	27,302	3	97	0	0	9	18.16	-20.36			Mar-12
	3.54	9.35	26.25	26.12	47.87	0.7	1.38	11.77	0.89	43.1	27,302	3	97	0	0	9	17.87	-20.41			Mar-01
	3.66	9.63	26.89	28.04	51.69	1.07	0.89	11.77	0.89	43.62	27,302	3	97	0	0	9	18.34	-20.19			Sep-05
	6.17	12.93	37.92	57.36	130.64	0.11	1.41	10.09	0.73	49.55	10,129	11	88	0	1	22	14.05	-18.89	5.75		Nov-97
	5.95	12.48	36.87	53.82	121.96	0	2.17	10.08	0.73	46.34	10,129	11	88	0	1	22	13.44	-19.23		5.00	Nov-97
	5.99	12.50	36.92	53.87	122.18	0	2.16	10.08	0.73	45.67	10,129	11	88	0	1	22	13.58	-19.19		1.00	Nov-97
	6.28	13.17	38.53	59.41	135.62	0.45	0.97	10.09	0.73	49.22	10,129	11	88	0	1	22	14.22	-18.89			Dec-11
	6.11	12.78	37.62	56.20	127.71	0	1.66	10.08	0.73	47.37	10,129	11	88	0	1	22	13.78	-19			Mar-01
	6.24	13.08	38.30	58.52	133.63	0.32	1.16	10.09	0.73	49.12	10,129	11	88	0	1	22	14.36	-18.79			Sep-05
	0.65	3.59	18.82			1.95	1.36			11.1	23.4	4	96	0	0	125			5.75		May-16
	0.51	3.17	17.90			1.35	2.16			11.08	23.4	4	96	0	0	125				1.00	May-16
	0.84	3.78	19.32			2.26	1.01			11.11	23.4	4	96	0	0	125					May-16
	0.66	3.44	18.54			1.74	1.66			11.1	23.4	4	96	0	0	125					May-16
	0.81	3.78	19.12			2.12	1.11			11.12	23.4	4	96	0	0	125					May-16
	3.32	6.99	16.07	42.16	102.97	1.59	1.16	13.16	0.95	17.95	1,261	1	99	0	0	89	25.97	-14.5	5.75		Sep-00
	3.16	6.63	15.23	21.63	70.94	0	1.91	9.59	0.9	16.32	1,261	1	99	0	0	89	25.3	-14.78		5.00	Sep-00
	3.18	6.62	15.23	21.65	71.16	0.38	1.9	9.57	0.9	16.43	1,261	1	99	0	0	89	25.51	-14.76		1.00	Sep-00
	3.25	6.90	15.78	23.46	75.35	0.75	1.41	9.62	0.91	17.44	1,261	1	99	0	0	89	25.66	-14.58			Mar-01
	3.43	7.18	16.40	25.30	80.02	1.09	0.91	9.6	0.9	18.36	1,261	1	99	0	0	89	26.2	-14.41			Sep-00
	2.05	6.67	16.73	32.72	98.19	0.92	0.94	9.97	0.96	51.01	10,187	2	98	0	0	40	26.45	-15.14	5.75		Feb-88
	1.85	6.25	15.82	29.71	90.48	0	1.7	9.96	0.96	49.07	10,187	2	98	0	0	40	25.85	-15.49		5.00	Oct-94
	1.82	6.25	15.82	29.73	90.83	0.38	1.69	9.97	0.96	48.38	10,187	2	98	0	0	40	25.93	-15.39		1.00	Dec-93
	2.13	6.88	17.18	34.40	102.35	1.29	0.5	9.97	0.96	50.46	10,187	2	98	0	0	40	26.61	-15.14			Dec-11
	1.96	6.52	16.40	31.69	95.67	0.76	1.19	9.96	0.96	50.1	10,187	2	98	0	0	40	26.26	-15.22			Mar-01
	2.10	6.80	16.98	33.66	100.63	1.13	0.69	9.98	0.96	50.55	10,187	2	98	0	0	40	26.77	-14.99			Nov-96
	-8.74	-6.76	0.32	19.62	83.70	0.76	1.11	9.41	0.85	26.57	2,935	2	98	0	0	68	29.9	-23.58	5.75		Aug-99
	-10.59	-8.81	-2.23	16.90	76.71	0	1.86	9.39	0.85	21.78	2,935	2	98	0	0	68	29.27	-23.82		5.00	Aug-99
	-10.50	-8.73	-2.14	16.91	76.84	0.3	1.86	9.4	0.85	21.93	2,935	2	98	0	0	68	29.36	-23.83		1.00	Aug-99
	-8.32	-6.22	1.15	21.17	87.81	1.07	0.67	9.44	0.85	28.61	2,935	2	98	0	0	68	30.2	-23.45			Oct-12

	MARKET			FUND TYPE, CATEGORY & OBJECTIVE	RATINGS				MINIMUMS	
Fund Name	Ticker Symbol	Traded On	Fund Type	Category and (Prospectus Objective)	Overall Rating	Reward Rating	Risk Rating	Recent Up/ Downgrade	Open to New Investors	Min Initial Investment
Oppenheimer Main Street Mid Cap Fund Class R	OPMNX	NAS CM	Open End	US Equity Mid Cap (Growth)	B	B	B	Up	Y	0
Oppenheimer Main Street Mid Cap Fund Class Y	OPMYX	NAS CM	Open End	US Equity Mid Cap (Growth)	B	B	B	Up	Y	0
Oppenheimer Main Street Small Cap Fund Class A	OSCAX	NAS CM	Open End	US Equity Small Cap (Small Company)	B	B	B	Up	Y	1,000
Oppenheimer Main Street Small Cap Fund Class C	OSCCX	NAS CM	Open End	US Equity Small Cap (Small Company)	B	B	B	Up	Y	1,000
Oppenheimer Main Street Small Cap Fund Class I	OSSIX	NAS CM	Open End	US Equity Small Cap (Small Company)	B	B	B	Up	Y	1,000,000
Oppenheimer Main Street Small Cap Fund Class R	OSCNX	NAS CM	Open End	US Equity Small Cap (Small Company)	B	B	B	Up	Y	0
Oppenheimer Main Street Small Cap Fund Class Y	OSCYX	NAS CM	Open End	US Equity Small Cap (Small Company)	B	B	B	Up	Y	0
Oppenheimer Mid Cap Value Fund Class A	QVSCX	NAS CM	Open End	US Equity Mid Cap (Growth)	B	B	B	Up	Y	1,000
Oppenheimer Mid Cap Value Fund Class B	QSCBX	NAS CM	Open End	US Equity Mid Cap (Growth)	B-	B-	B	Up		1,000
Oppenheimer Mid Cap Value Fund Class C	QSCCX	NAS CM	Open End	US Equity Mid Cap (Growth)	B-	B-	B	Up	Y	1,000
Oppenheimer Mid Cap Value Fund Class I	QSCIX	NAS CM	Open End	US Equity Mid Cap (Growth)	B	B	B	Up	Y	1,000,000
Oppenheimer Mid Cap Value Fund Class R	QSCNX	NAS CM	Open End	US Equity Mid Cap (Growth)	B	B	B	Up	Y	0
Oppenheimer Mid Cap Value Fund Class Y	QSCYX	NAS CM	Open End	US Equity Mid Cap (Growth)	B	B	B	Up	Y	0
Oppenheimer Portfolio Series Active Allocation Fund Cls A	OAAAX	NAS CM	Open End	Aggressive Alloc (Asset Alloc)	B-	C+	B	Down	Y	1,000
Oppenheimer Portfolio Series Active Allocation Fund Cls B	OAABX	NAS CM	Open End	Aggressive Alloc (Asset Alloc)	B-	C+	B-	Down		1,000
Oppenheimer Portfolio Series Active Allocation Fund Cls C	OAACX	NAS CM	Open End	Aggressive Alloc (Asset Alloc)	B	C+	B+	Up	Y	1,000
Oppenheimer Portfolio Series Active Allocation Fund Cls R	OAANX	NAS CM	Open End	Aggressive Alloc (Asset Alloc)	B	C+	B+	Up	Y	0
Oppenheimer Portfolio Series Active Allocation Fund Cls Y	OAAYX	NAS CM	Open End	Aggressive Alloc (Asset Alloc)	B	C+	B+	Up	Y	0
Oppenheimer Portfolio Series Conservative Inv Fund Cls A	OACIX	NAS CM	Open End	Cautious Alloc (Asset Alloc)	B	C	A-	Up	Y	1,000
Oppenheimer Portfolio Series Conservative Inv Fund Cls B	OBCIX	NAS CM	Open End	Cautious Alloc (Asset Alloc)	B-	C	B+	Up		1,000
Oppenheimer Portfolio Series Conservative Inv Fund Cls C	OCCIX	NAS CM	Open End	Cautious Alloc (Asset Alloc)	B-	C	B+	Up	Y	1,000
Oppenheimer Portfolio Series Conservative Inv Fund Cls R	ONCIX	NAS CM	Open End	Cautious Alloc (Asset Alloc)	B-	C	B+	Up	Y	0
Oppenheimer Portfolio Series Conservative Inv Fund Cls Y	OYCIX	NAS CM	Open End	Cautious Alloc (Asset Alloc)	B	C+	A-	Up	Y	0
Oppenheimer Portfolio Series Equity Investor Fund Class A	OAAIX	NAS CM	Open End	Global Equity (Growth)	B	B-	B	Up	Y	1,000
Oppenheimer Portfolio Series Equity Investor Fund Class B	OBAIX	NAS CM	Open End	Global Equity (Growth)	B	B-	B	Up		1,000
Oppenheimer Portfolio Series Equity Investor Fund Class C	OCAIX	NAS CM	Open End	Global Equity (Growth)	B	B-	B	Up	Y	1,000
Oppenheimer Portfolio Series Equity Investor Fund Class R	ONAIX	NAS CM	Open End	Global Equity (Growth)	B	B-	B	Up	Y	0
Oppenheimer Portfolio Series Equity Investor Fund Class Y	OYAIX	NAS CM	Open End	Global Equity (Growth)	B	B-	B	Up	Y	0
Oppenheimer Portfolio Series Moderate Investor Fund Cls A	OAMIX	NAS CM	Open End	Moderate Alloc (Asset Alloc)	B-	C+	B	Down	Y	1,000
Oppenheimer Portfolio Series Moderate Investor Fund Cls B	OBMIX	NAS CM	Open End	Moderate Alloc (Asset Alloc)	B	C+	B+	Up		1,000
Oppenheimer Portfolio Series Moderate Investor Fund Cls C	OCMIX	NAS CM	Open End	Moderate Alloc (Asset Alloc)	B	C+	B+	Up	Y	1,000
Oppenheimer Portfolio Series Moderate Investor Fund Cls R	ONMIX	NAS CM	Open End	Moderate Alloc (Asset Alloc)	B-	C+	B	Down	Y	0
Oppenheimer Portfolio Series Moderate Investor Fund Cls Y	OYMIX	NAS CM	Open End	Moderate Alloc (Asset Alloc)	B-	C+	B	Down	Y	0
Oppenheimer Real Estate Fund Class A	OREAX	NAS CM	Open End	Real Estate Sector Equity (Real Estate)	B-	C+	B		Y	1,000
Oppenheimer Real Estate Fund Class B	OREBX	NAS CM	Open End	Real Estate Sector Equity (Real Estate)	B-	C+	B			1,000
Oppenheimer Real Estate Fund Class C	ORECX	NAS CM	Open End	Real Estate Sector Equity (Real Estate)	B-	C+	B		Y	1,000
Oppenheimer Real Estate Fund Class I	OREIX	NAS CM	Open End	Real Estate Sector Equity (Real Estate)	B-	C+	B+		Y	1,000,000
Oppenheimer Real Estate Fund Class R	ORENX	NAS CM	Open End	Real Estate Sector Equity (Real Estate)	B-	C+	B		Y	0
Oppenheimer Real Estate Fund Class Y	OREYX	NAS CM	Open End	Real Estate Sector Equity (Real Estate)	B-	C+	B		Y	0
Oppenheimer Rising Dividends Fund Class A	OARDX	NAS CM	Open End	US Equity Large Cap Blend (Growth)	B-	C+	B-	Down	Y	1,000
Oppenheimer Rising Dividends Fund Class B	OBRDX	NAS CM	Open End	US Equity Large Cap Blend (Growth)	B-	C+	B-	Down		1,000
Oppenheimer Rising Dividends Fund Class C	OCRDX	NAS CM	Open End	US Equity Large Cap Blend (Growth)	B-	C+	B-	Down	Y	1,000
Oppenheimer Rising Dividends Fund Class I	OIRDX	NAS CM	Open End	US Equity Large Cap Blend (Growth)	B-	B-	B-	Down	Y	1,000,000
Oppenheimer Rising Dividends Fund Class R	ONRDX	NAS CM	Open End	US Equity Large Cap Blend (Growth)	B-	C+	B-	Down	Y	0
Oppenheimer Rising Dividends Fund Class Y	OYRDX	NAS CM	Open End	US Equity Large Cap Blend (Growth)	B-	C+	B-	Down	Y	0
Oppenheimer Small Cap Value Fund A	OVSAX	NAS CM	Open End	US Equity Small Cap (Small Company)	C	C-	B	Up	Y	1,000
Oppenheimer Small Cap Value Fund C	OVSCX	NAS CM	Open End	US Equity Small Cap (Small Company)	C	C-	B	Up	Y	1,000
Oppenheimer Small Cap Value Fund I	OVSIX	NAS CM	Open End	US Equity Small Cap (Small Company)	C	C-	B	Up	Y	1,000,000
Oppenheimer Small Cap Value Fund R	OVSRX	NAS CM	Open End	US Equity Small Cap (Small Company)	C	C-	B	Up	Y	0
Oppenheimer Small Cap Value Fund Y	OVSYX	NAS CM	Open End	US Equity Small Cap (Small Company)	C	C-	B	Up	Y	0
Oppenheimer SteelPath MLP Alpha Fund Class A	MLPAX	NAS CM	Open End	Energy Sector Equity (Natl Res)	D	D	D	Down	Y	1,000
Oppenheimer SteelPath MLP Alpha Fund Class C Shares	MLPGX	NAS CM	Open End	Energy Sector Equity (Natl Res)	D	D	D	Down	Y	1,000

★Expanded analysis of this fund is included in Section II.

Min Additional Investment	TOTAL RETURNS 3-Month Total Return	6-Month Total Return	1-Year Total Return	3-Year Total Return	5-Year Total Return	PERFORMANCE Dividend Yield (TTM)	Expense Ratio	3-Yr Std Deviation	3-Year Beta	ASSETS NAV	Total Assets (MIL)	ASSET ALLOCATION & TURNOVER %Cash	%Stocks	%Bonds	%Other	Turnover Ratio	BULL & BEAR Last Bull Market Total Return	Last Bear Market Total Return	FEES Front End Fee (%)	Back End Fee (%)	Inception Date
	-9.16	-7.22	-0.28	18.72	81.28	0.6	1.36	9.41	0.85	25.2	2,935	2	98	0	0	68	29.71	-23.68			Mar-01
	-8.16	-6.09	1.17	20.52	86.12	0.91	0.86	9.41	0.85	28.7	2,935	2	98	0	0	68	30.2	-23.45			Aug-99
	1.61	6.29	13.47	24.25		0.22	1.24	12.71	0.88	15.11	568.6	2	98	0	0	67			5.75		May-13
	1.50	5.94	12.72	21.57		0	1.98	12.63	0.88	14.68	568.6	2	98	0	0	67				1.00	May-13
	1.79	6.57	14.05	26.00		0.51	0.78	12.66	0.88	15.19	568.6	2	98	0	0	67					May-13
	1.56	6.21	13.21	23.34		0.06	1.49	12.68	0.88	14.98	568.6	2	98	0	0	67					May-13
	1.70	6.49	13.89	25.49		0.42	0.9	12.66	0.88	15.17	568.6	2	98	0	0	67					May-13
	5.42	9.49	13.28	25.43	96.06	0.37	1.2	12.4	1.14	57.39	1,402	0	100	0	0	34	18.01	-24.25	5.75		Jan-89
	5.22	9.04	12.42	22.58	88.54	0	1.95	12.39	1.13	47.2	1,402	0	100	0	0	34	17.44	-24.54		5.00	Sep-93
	5.23	9.08	12.46	22.62	88.81	0.02	1.95	12.39	1.13	47.27	1,402	0	100	0	0	34	17.46	-24.51		1.00	Sep-93
	5.54	9.72	13.77	27.05	100.46	0.74	0.76	12.4	1.14	58.38	1,402	0	100	0	0	34	18.11	-24.25			Feb-12
	5.38	9.35	13.01	24.49	93.61	0.17	1.45	12.4	1.14	54.95	1,402	0	100	0	0	34	17.8	-24.35			Mar-01
	5.49	9.62	13.57	26.35	98.75	0.58	0.95	12.39	1.13	58.91	1,402	0	100	0	0	34	18.24	-24.17			Oct-05
	4.04	7.93	19.37	22.46	57.63	0.82	1.19	8.28	0.77	14.59	2,562	4	78	17	0	5	13.89	-15.74	5.75		Apr-05
	3.78	7.47	18.43	19.57	51.67	0	1.94	8.24	0.77	14.52	2,562	4	78	17	0	5	13.34	-15.97		5.00	Apr-05
	3.82	7.48	18.49	19.71	51.91	0.2	1.94	8.26	0.77	14.28	2,562	4	78	17	0	5	13.4	-16.07		1.00	Apr-05
	3.97	7.79	19.01	21.48	55.76	0.62	1.44	8.25	0.77	14.51	2,562	4	78	17	0	5	13.7	-15.83			Apr-05
	4.08	7.99	19.58	23.37	59.64	1.06	0.94	8.26	0.77	14.74	2,562	4	78	17	0	5	14.14	-15.65			Apr-05
	1.95	3.91	9.17	12.22	24.88	2	0.98	4.01	0.45	9.51	633.7	8	33	58	0	9	8.93	-7.3	5.75		Apr-05
	1.81	3.44	8.30	9.62	20.18	0.9	1.74	3.98	0.44	9.67	633.7	8	33	58	0	9	8.32	-7.49		5.00	Apr-05
	1.84	3.61	8.44	9.75	20.27	1.29	1.73	4.02	0.45	9.41	633.7	8	33	58	0	9	8.4	-7.5		1.00	Apr-05
	1.94	3.80	8.82	11.27	23.26	1.82	1.23	4.06	0.45	9.49	633.7	8	33	58	0	9	8.7	-7.33			Apr-05
	2.11	4.06	9.42	13.00	26.41	2.21	0.73	4.01	0.47	9.55	633.7	8	33	58	0	9	9.08	-7.15			Apr-05
	4.61	9.66	24.90	28.00	70.38	0.87	1.18	10.23	0.94	18.43	918.4	3	97	0	0	6	19.24	-20.98	5.75		Apr-05
	4.42	9.26	23.90	25.16	64.04	0	1.94	10.19	0.93	18.23	918.4	3	97	0	0	6	18.63	-21.17		5.00	Apr-05
	4.47	9.27	24.02	25.24	64.15	0.27	1.93	10.23	0.94	17.98	918.4	3	97	0	0	6	18.72	-21.16		1.00	Apr-05
	4.58	9.57	24.58	27.12	68.24	0.66	1.43	10.23	0.94	18.42	918.4	3	97	0	0	6	19.02	-20.98			Apr-05
	4.72	9.80	25.21	29.02	72.58	1.06	0.93	10.21	0.94	18.52	918.4	3	97	0	0	6	19.48	-20.81			Apr-05
	3.29	6.37	15.01	18.42	45.54	1.42	1.04	6.46	-0.02	12.24	1,669	5	60	34	0	7	12.38	-11.86	5.75		Apr-05
	3.09	6.02	14.19	15.83	40.16	0.36	1.79	6.37	-0.02	12.31	1,669	5	60	34	0	7	11.93	-12.26		5.00	Apr-05
	3.12	5.99	14.27	15.85	40.10	0.78	1.78	6.42	-0.02	12.01	1,669	5	60	34	0	7	12.01	-12.18		1.00	Apr-05
	3.16	6.26	14.74	17.54	43.78	1.22	1.28	6.46	-0.01	12.17	1,669	5	60	34	0	7	12.38	-11.95			Apr-05
	3.37	6.53	15.43	19.33	47.43	1.63	0.78	6.38	-0.01	12.31	1,669	5	60	34	0	7	12.49	-11.7			Apr-05
	1.94	2.69	4.06	11.22	54.40	1.61	1.33	13.15	0.98	24.71	1,174	1	99	0	0	114	30.53	-17.05	5.75		Mar-02
	1.72	2.25	3.25	8.66	48.63	0.84	2.09	13.15	0.98	24.16	1,174	1	99	0	0	114	29.97	-17.3		5.00	Oct-03
	1.76	2.29	3.28	8.75	48.71	0.96	2.08	13.15	0.98	24.05	1,174	1	99	0	0	114	29.94	-17.31		1.00	Oct-03
	2.03	2.88	4.50	12.66	57.89	1.99	0.89	13.19	0.98	24.95	1,174	1	99	0	0	114	30.53	-17.05			Aug-12
	1.90	2.55	3.80	10.38	52.48	1.4	1.58	13.16	0.98	24.59	1,174	1	99	0	0	114	30.33	-17.16			Oct-03
	2.05	2.81	4.34	12.07	56.31	1.83	1.08	13.17	0.98	24.99	1,174	1	99	0	0	114	30.75	-16.9			Oct-03
	3.95	7.42	16.76	19.97	74.08	1.33	1.07	10.02	0.97	19.35	3,318	0	100	0	0	78	23.82	-15.84	5.75		Apr-80
	3.77	7.06	15.89	17.28	67.32	0.81	1.83	9.98	0.97	16.57	3,318	0	100	0	0	78	23.1	-16.17		5.00	Sep-93
	3.77	7.07	15.93	17.31	67.71	0.93	1.82	10	0.97	16.37	3,318	0	100	0	0	78	23.22	-16.14		1.00	Sep-93
	4.05	7.63	17.22	21.50	77.74	1.66	0.63	10	0.97	20	3,318	0	100	0	0	78	23.86	-15.84			Feb-12
	3.90	7.27	16.45	19.06	71.69	1.12	1.32	10.01	0.97	19.22	3,318	0	100	0	0	78	23.51	-15.96			Mar-01
	4.03	7.56	17.02	20.86	76.05	1.5	0.82	10.01	0.97	20.05	3,318	0	100	0	0	78	23.98	-15.81			Dec-96
	2.09	4.56	5.33			0.42	1.25			12.52	31.8	3	97	0	0	52			5.75		Dec-15
	1.95	4.22	4.57			0.04	2			12.47	31.8	3	97	0	0	52				1.00	Dec-15
	2.18	4.64	5.64			0.7	0.93			12.51	31.8	3	97	0	0	52					Dec-15
	2.02	4.43	5.10			0.22	1.5			12.53	31.8	3	97	0	0	52					Dec-15
	2.16	4.73	5.62			0.67	1			12.53	31.8	3	97	0	0	52					Dec-15
	-2.53	-4.06	-7.21	-19.16	8.17	8.57	4.07	17.35	0.99	8.08	2,759	0	96	0	4	35	10.44	-5.84	5.75		Mar-10
	-2.78	-4.39	-7.88	-20.94	4.17	9.03	4.82	17.34	0.99	7.66	2,759	0	96	0	4	35	9.89	-6.14		1.00	Aug-11

	MARKET		FUND TYPE, CATEGORY & OBJECTIVE		RATINGS					MINIMUMS
Fund Name	Ticker Symbol	Traded On	Fund Type	Category and (Prospectus Objective)	Overall Rating	Reward Rating	Risk Rating	Recent Up/ Downgrade	Open to New Investors	Min Initial Investment
Oppenheimer SteelPath MLP Alpha Fund Class I	OSPAX	NAS CM	Open End	Energy Sector Equity (Natl Res)	D	D	D	Down	Y	1,000,000
Oppenheimer SteelPath MLP Alpha Fund Class Y	MLPOX	NAS CM	Open End	Energy Sector Equity (Natl Res)	D	D	D	Down	Y	0
Oppenheimer SteelPath MLP Alpha Plus Fund Class A	MLPLX	NAS CM	Open End	Energy Sector Equity (Growth & Income)	D	D	D	Down	Y	1,000
Oppenheimer SteelPath MLP Alpha Plus Fund Class C	MLPMX	NAS CM	Open End	Energy Sector Equity (Growth & Income)	D	D	D	Down	Y	1,000
Oppenheimer SteelPath MLP Alpha Plus Fund Class I	OSPPX	NAS CM	Open End	Energy Sector Equity (Growth & Income)	D	D	D	Down	Y	1,000,000
Oppenheimer SteelPath MLP Alpha Plus Fund Class Y	MLPNX	NAS CM	Open End	Energy Sector Equity (Growth & Income)	D	D	D	Down	Y	0
Oppenheimer SteelPath MLP Income Fund Class A	MLPDX	NAS CM	Open End	Energy Sector Equity (Natl Res)	D	D	D	Down		1,000
Oppenheimer SteelPath MLP Income Fund Class C Shares	MLPRX	NAS CM	Open End	Energy Sector Equity (Natl Res)	D	D	D	Down		1,000
Oppenheimer SteelPath MLP Income Fund Class I	OSPMX	NAS CM	Open End	Energy Sector Equity (Natl Res)	D	D	D	Down		1,000,000
Oppenheimer SteelPath MLP Income Fund Class Y	MLPZX	NAS CM	Open End	Energy Sector Equity (Natl Res)	D	D	D	Down		0
Oppenheimer SteelPath MLP Select 40 Fund Class A	MLPFX	NAS CM	Open End	Energy Sector Equity (Natl Res)	D	D	D	Down	Y	1,000
Oppenheimer SteelPath MLP Select 40 Fund Class C	MLPEX	NAS CM	Open End	Energy Sector Equity (Natl Res)	D	D	D	Down	Y	1,000
Oppenheimer SteelPath MLP Select 40 Fund Class I	OSPSX	NAS CM	Open End	Energy Sector Equity (Natl Res)	D	D+	D	Down	Y	1,000,000
Oppenheimer SteelPath MLP Select 40 Fund Class W	MLPYX	NAS CM	Open End	Energy Sector Equity (Natl Res)	D	D+	D	Down	Y	0
Oppenheimer SteelPath MLP Select 40 Fund Class Y	MLPTX	NAS CM	Open End	Energy Sector Equity (Natl Res)	D	D+	D	Down	Y	0
Oppenheimer SteelPath Panoramic Fund Class A	EESAX	NAS CM	Open End	Energy Sector Equity (Growth & Income)	D+	D	C-	Up	Y	1,000
Oppenheimer SteelPath Panoramic Fund Class C	EESCX	NAS CM	Open End	Energy Sector Equity (Growth & Income)	D	D	C-		Y	1,000
Oppenheimer SteelPath Panoramic Fund Class I	EESIX	NAS CM	Open End	Energy Sector Equity (Growth & Income)	D+	D	C-	Up	Y	1,000,000
Oppenheimer SteelPath Panoramic Fund Class R	EESRX	NAS CM	Open End	Energy Sector Equity (Growth & Income)	D	D	C-		Y	0
Oppenheimer SteelPath Panoramic Fund Class Y	EESYX	NAS CM	Open End	Energy Sector Equity (Growth & Income)	D+	D	C-	Up	Y	0
Oppenheimer Value Fund Class A	CGRWX	NAS CM	Open End	US Equity Large Cap Value (Growth)	B	B-	B	Up	Y	1,000
Oppenheimer Value Fund Class B	CGRBX	NAS CM	Open End	US Equity Large Cap Value (Growth)	B-	C+	B	Down		1,000
Oppenheimer Value Fund Class C	CGRCX	NAS CM	Open End	US Equity Large Cap Value (Growth)	B-	C+	B	Down	Y	1,000
Oppenheimer Value Fund Class I	OGRIX	NAS CM	Open End	US Equity Large Cap Value (Growth)	B	B-	B	Up	Y	1,000,000
Oppenheimer Value Fund Class R	CGRNX	NAS CM	Open End	US Equity Large Cap Value (Growth)	B-	B-	B	Down	Y	0
Oppenheimer Value Fund Class Y	CGRYX	NAS CM	Open End	US Equity Large Cap Value (Growth)	B	B-	B	Up	Y	0
Optimum International Fund Class A	OAIEX	NAS CM	Open End	Global Equity Large Cap (Foreign Stock)	B-	B-	B-	Up	Y	1,000
Optimum International Fund Class C	OCIEX	NAS CM	Open End	Global Equity Large Cap (Foreign Stock)	B-	B-	B-	Up	Y	1,000
Optimum International Fund Institutional Class	OIIEX	NAS CM	Open End	Global Equity Large Cap (Foreign Stock)	B	B	B	Up	Y	0
Optimum Large Cap Growth Fund Class A	OALGX	NAS CM	Open End	US Equity Large Cap Growth (Growth)	B	B	B	Down	Y	1,000
Optimum Large Cap Growth Fund Class C	OCLGX	NAS CM	Open End	US Equity Large Cap Growth (Growth)	B	B	B	Down	Y	1,000
Optimum Large Cap Growth Fund Institutional Class	OILGX	NAS CM	Open End	US Equity Large Cap Growth (Growth)	B	B	B	Down	Y	0
Optimum Large Cap Value Fund Class A	OALVX	NAS CM	Open End	US Equity Large Cap Blend (Growth)	B-	C+	B	Down	Y	1,000
Optimum Large Cap Value Fund Class C	OCLVX	NAS CM	Open End	US Equity Large Cap Blend (Growth)	B-	C+	B	Down	Y	1,000
Optimum Large Cap Value Fund Institutional Class	OILVX	NAS CM	Open End	US Equity Large Cap Blend (Growth)	B-	C+	B	Down	Y	0
Optimum Small-Mid Cap Growth Fund Class A	OASGX	NAS CM	Open End	US Equity Small Cap (Growth)	B-	B-	B-	Up	Y	1,000
Optimum Small-Mid Cap Growth Fund Class C	OCSGX	NAS CM	Open End	US Equity Small Cap (Growth)	B-	B-	B-	Up	Y	1,000
Optimum Small-Mid Cap Growth Fund Institutional Class	OISGX	NAS CM	Open End	US Equity Small Cap (Growth)	B-	B	B-	Up	Y	0
Optimum Small-Mid Cap Value Fund Class A	OASVX	NAS CM	Open End	US Equity Small Cap (Growth)	C+	C+	B-	Up	Y	1,000
Optimum Small-Mid Cap Value Fund Class C	OCSVX	NAS CM	Open End	US Equity Small Cap (Growth)	C+	C+	C+	Up	Y	1,000
Optimum Small-Mid Cap Value Fund Institutional Class	OISVX	NAS CM	Open End	US Equity Small Cap (Growth)	C+	C+	B-	Up	Y	0
Orchard Small Cap Value Fund Class I	OCSIX	NAS CM	Open End	US Equity Small Cap (Small Company)	C-	C-	B	Up	Y	1,000,000
Orchard Small Cap Value Fund Class N	OCSNX	NAS CM	Open End	US Equity Small Cap (Small Company)	C-	C-	B	Up	Y	1,000
Orinda Income Opportunities Fund Class A	OIOAX	NAS CM	Open End	US Fixed Income (Income)	C+	C+	B	Down	Y	5,000
Orinda Income Opportunities Fund Class D	OIODX	NAS CM	Open End	US Fixed Income (Income)	C+	C	B-	Down	Y	5,000
Orinda Income Opportunities Fund Class I	OIOIX	NAS CM	Open End	US Fixed Income (Income)	C+	C+	B	Down	Y	100,000
O'Shaughnessy All Cap Core Fund Class A	OFAAX	NAS CM	Open End	US Equity Large Cap Blend (Growth)	B	B	B-		Y	2,500
O'Shaughnessy All Cap Core Fund Class C	OFACX	NAS CM	Open End	US Equity Large Cap Blend (Growth)	B	B	B-	Up	Y	2,500
O'Shaughnessy All Cap Core Fund Class I	OFAIX	NAS CM	Open End	US Equity Large Cap Blend (Growth)	B	B	B-		Y	10,000
O'Shaughnessy Enhanced Dividend Fund Class I	OFDIX	NAS CM	Open End	Global Equity (Equity-Income)	C+	C+	C+	Up	Y	10,000
O'Shaughnessy Market Leaders Value Fund Class I	OFVIX	NAS CM	Open End	US Equity Large Cap Value (Growth & Income)	C-	C	B+	Up	Y	10,000
O'Shaughnessy Small Cap Value Fund Class I	OFSIX	NAS CM	Open End	US Equity Small Cap (Small Company)	C-	C	B+	Up	Y	10,000

★ Expanded analysis of this fund is included in Section II.

	TOTAL RETURNS					PERFORMANCE				ASSETS		ASSET ALLOCATION & TURNOVER					BULL & BEAR		FEES		
Min Additional Investment	3-Month Total Return	6-Month Total Return	1-Year Total Return	3-Year Total Return	5-Year Total Return	Dividend Yield (TTM)	Expense Ratio	3-Yr Std Deviation	3-Year Beta	NAV	Total Assets (MIL)	%Cash	%Stocks	%Bonds	%Other	Turnover Ratio	Last Bull Market Total Return	Last Bear Market Total Return	Front End Fee (%)	Back End Fee (%)	Inception Date
	-2.57	-3.95	-6.93	-18.34	9.87	8.32	3.72	17.37	0.99	8.32	2,759	0	96	0	4	35	10.59	-5.73			Jun-13
	-2.46	-3.96	-6.95	-18.59	9.53	8.35	3.82	17.35	1	8.29	2,759	0	96	0	4	35	10.59	-5.73			Mar-10
	-1.25	-4.02	-11.16	-30.27	0.83	10.47	2.99	26.67	1.55	6.79	208.7	0	127	0	-27	45			5.75		Feb-12
	-1.47	-4.50	-11.89	-31.92	-2.86	11.02	3.74	26.64	1.56	6.45	208.7	0	127	0	-27	45				1.00	May-12
	-1.22	-3.93	-10.81	-29.41	2.67	10.21	2.56	26.64	1.55	6.97	208.7	0	127	0	-27	45					Jun-13
	-1.23	-3.82	-10.97	-29.76	2.16	10.28	2.75	26.7	1.56	6.93	208.7	0	127	0	-27	45					Dec-11
	-4.37	-5.04	-8.59	-19.56	3.76	11.07	3.44	20.38	1.19	6.42	3,495	0	93	0	7	22	10.19	-9.61	5.75		Mar-10
	-4.48	-5.33	-9.19	-21.28	-0.03	11.78	4.19	20.44	1.2	6.04	3,495	0	93	0	7	22	9.77	-9.91		1.00	Jun-11
	-4.24	-4.90	-8.24	-18.73	5.37	10.74	3.08	20.42	1.19	6.62	3,495	0	93	0	7	22	10.47	-9.58			Jun-13
	-4.26	-4.92	-8.39	-18.96	4.99	10.79	3.19	20.38	1.19	6.59	3,495	0	93	0	7	22	10.47	-9.58			Mar-10
	-1.03	-1.63	-4.01	-13.80	13.99	8.66	4.91	13.88	0.89	8.45	3,117	0	101	0	-3	10	10.78	-7.41	5.75		Mar-10
	-1.09	-1.95	-4.64	-15.68	9.88	9.09	5.66	13.9	0.9	8.04	3,117	0	101	0	-3	10	10.55	-7.7		1.00	Jul-11
	-0.78	-1.47	-3.58	-12.84	15.98	8.39	4.59	13.88	0.9	8.73	3,117	0	101	0	-3	10	11.02	-7.29			Jun-13
	-0.78	-1.47	-3.70	-13.03	15.63	8.41	4.66	13.88	0.9	8.7	3,117	0	101	0	-3	10	11.02	-7.28			Mar-10
	-0.78	-1.47	-3.70	-13.03	15.63	8.41	4.66	13.88	0.9	8.7	3,117	0	101	0	-3	10	11.02	-7.28			Mar-10
	5.19	10.48	-8.74			0	1.56			10.33	19.5	0	100	0	0	35			5.75		Nov-15
	4.94	10.05	-9.43			0	2.31			10.18	19.5	0	100	0	0	35				1.00	Nov-15
	5.35	10.72	-8.26			0	1.11			10.43	19.5	0	100	0	0	35					Nov-15
	5.10	10.39	-8.93			0	1.81			10.3	19.5	0	100	0	0	35					Nov-15
	5.26	10.65	-8.45			0	1.31			10.39	19.5	0	100	0	0	35					Nov-15
	5.02	8.80	15.94	24.21	83.14	1.22	0.97	11.23	1.06	37.32	2,140	2	98	0	0	64	19.25	-20.87	5.75		Sep-85
	4.82	8.39	15.06	21.37	76.18	0.53	1.72	11.22	1.06	36.84	2,140	2	98	0	0	64	18.62	-21.18		5.00	Oct-95
	4.84	8.41	15.07	21.42	76.42	0.69	1.71	11.22	1.06	35.62	2,140	2	98	0	0	64	18.73	-21.16		1.00	May-96
	5.15	9.04	16.44	25.85	87.19	1.57	0.52	11.24	1.06	38.08	2,140	2	98	0	0	64	19.34	-20.87			Feb-12
	4.96	8.67	15.64	23.28	80.89	1.03	1.21	11.24	1.06	36.59	2,140	2	98	0	0	64	19.04	-20.98			Mar-01
	5.09	8.92	16.21	25.11	85.53	1.41	0.71	11.23	1.06	38.14	2,140	2	98	0	0	64	19.52	-20.71			Dec-96
100	3.67	10.78	30.07	30.24	45.54	0.72	1.37	11.1	0.85	14.44	641.6	1	98	0	0	68	10.56	-20.98	5.75		Aug-03
100	3.51	10.39	29.15	27.37	40.47	0.18	2.12	11.08	0.85	14.11	641.6	1	98	0	0	68	10.2	-21.18		1.00	Aug-03
	3.74	10.95	30.45	31.28	47.63	0.91	1.12	11.06	0.85	14.54	641.6	1	98	0	0	68	10.81	-20.86			Aug-03
100	6.41	12.06	32.15	42.46	121.48	0	1.27	11.85	1.06	16.78	1,704	1	98	0	0	52	28.12	-18.17	5.75		Aug-03
100	6.28	11.69	31.24	39.32	113.57	0	2.02	11.85	1.06	14.28	1,704	1	98	0	0	52	27.69	-18.47		1.00	Aug-03
	6.51	12.25	32.47	43.58	124.55	0	1.02	11.82	1.06	17.98	1,704	1	98	0	0	52	28.38	-18.08			Aug-03
100	5.58	9.27	16.05	22.75	75.22	0.94	1.23	10.66	1.01	16.32	1,482	2	98	0	0	82	24.78	-17	5.75		Aug-03
100	5.45	8.91	15.21	20.01	68.97	0.35	1.98	10.64	1.01	16.15	1,482	2	98	0	0	82	24.38	-17.18		1.00	Aug-03
	5.68	9.43	16.36	23.66	77.61	1.15	0.98	10.66	1.01	16.35	1,482	2	98	0	0	82	25.16	-16.86			Aug-03
100	7.04	12.70	27.29	22.60	79.15	0	1.54	13.53	1	14.86	501.5	3	96	0	0	180	26.05	-24.5	5.75		Aug-03
100	6.83	12.27	26.40	19.86	72.85	0	2.29	13.55	1	12.78	501.5	3	96	0	0	180	25.68	-24.68		1.00	Aug-03
	7.11	12.78	27.61	23.51	81.68	0	1.29	13.54	1	15.92	501.5	3	96	0	0	180	26.41	-24.4			Aug-03
100	3.65	7.03	9.49	14.10	53.73	0.32	1.47	12.47	0.99	14.02	463.0	1	99	0	0	30	30.75	-25.7	5.75		Aug-03
100	3.48	6.70	8.66	11.58	48.13	0	2.22	12.44	0.99	12.35	463.0	1	99	0	0	30	30.26	-25.92		1.00	Aug-03
	3.69	7.18	9.74	14.93	55.69	0.49	1.22	12.43	0.99	14.82	463.0	1	99	0	0	30	31	-25.6			Aug-03
1,000	5.26	9.63	9.79			0	1.6			14.03	5.9	9	91	0	0						Dec-15
100	5.22	9.53	9.53			0	1.85			13.95	5.9	9	91	0	0						Dec-15
0	-0.25	0.75	6.46	12.34		6.97	1.64	6.26	0.42	22.75	345.6	16	9	2	0				5.00		Jun-13
0	-0.44	0.39	5.71	10.23		6.54	2.32	6.24	0.42	22.63	345.6	16	9	2	0						Sep-13
	-0.21	0.89	6.79	13.36		7.19	1.34	6.26	0.41	22.83	345.6	16	9	2	0						Jun-13
100	6.33	10.90	19.31	35.07	111.30	1.7	0.85	10.95	0.99	12.32	14.5	0	100	0	0	61	26.11	-19.73	5.25		Aug-10
100	6.13	10.48	18.44	31.78	103.21	1.22	1.6	10.91	0.99	11.68	14.5	0	100	0	0	61	25.63	-20.03		1.00	Aug-10
	6.34	10.93	19.57	35.75	113.46	1.94	0.6	10.9	0.99	12.14	14.5	0	100	0	0	61	26.23	-19.65			Aug-10
	6.50	13.62	18.28	24.71	35.74	2.46	0.99	12.89	1.05	12.04	11.1	0	100	0	0	37	13.24	-16.65			Aug-10
	8.49	15.19	24.64			0.87	0.65			14.22	67.7	0	100	0	0	63					Feb-16
	4.39	8.53	11.24			1.03	0.99			13.52	8.9	0	100	0	0	78					Feb-16

	MARKET			FUND TYPE, CATEGORY & OBJECTIVE	RATINGS				MINIMUMS	
Fund Name	Ticker Symbol	Traded On	Fund Type	Category and (Prospectus Objective)	Overall Rating	Reward Rating	Risk Rating	Recent Up/ Downgrade	Open to New Investors	Min Initial Investment
O'Shaughnessy Small/Mid Cap Growth Fund Class I	OFMIX	NAS CM	Open End	US Equity Small Cap (Growth)	B	B	B+	Up	Y	10,000
Osterweis Emerging Opportunity Fund	OSTGX	NAS CM	Open End	US Equity Small Cap (Growth)	B+	A-	B	Up	Y	5,000
Osterweis Fund	OSTFX	NAS CM	Open End	US Equity Large Cap Blend (Growth)	C+	C+	B-	Down	Y	5,000
Osterweis Strategic Investment Investment	OSTVX	NAS CM	Open End	Moderate Alloc (Growth & Income)	C+	C+	C+	Down	Y	5,000
Otter Creek Long/Short Opportunity Fund Institutional Cls	OTTRX	NAS CM	Open End	Long/Short Equity (Growth)	C	D	B-		Y	100,000
Otter Creek Long/Short Opportunity Fund Investor Class	OTCRX	NAS CM	Open End	Long/Short Equity (Growth)	C-	D	B-	Down	Y	2,500
PACE Alternative Strategies Investments Class A	PASIX	NAS CM	Open End	Multialternative (Growth)	C+	C	B	Up	Y	1,000
PACE Alternative Strategies Investments Class C	PASOX	NAS CM	Open End	Multialternative (Growth)	C	C	B-		Y	1,000
PACE Alternative Strategies Investments Class P	PASPX	NAS CM	Open End	Multialternative (Growth)	C+	C	B		Y	10,000
PACE Alternative Strategies Investments Class Y	PASYX	NAS CM	Open End	Multialternative (Growth)	C+	C	B	Up	Y	5,000,000
PACE Global Real Estate Securities Investments Class A	PREAX	NAS CM	Open End	Real Estate Sector Equity (Real Estate)	B-	C+	B	Up	Y	1,000
PACE Global Real Estate Securities Investments Class C	PREEX	NAS CM	Open End	Real Estate Sector Equity (Real Estate)	C+	C	B		Y	1,000
PACE Global Real Estate Securities Investments Class P	PREQX	NAS CM	Open End	Real Estate Sector Equity (Real Estate)	B-	C+	B	Up	Y	10,000
PACE Global Real Estate Securities Investments Class Y	PREYX	NAS CM	Open End	Real Estate Sector Equity (Real Estate)	B-	C+	B	Up	Y	5,000,000
PACE Intl Emerging Mkts Equity Investments Cls A	PWEAX	NAS CM	Open End	Emerging Markets Equity (Div Emerging Mkts)	C+	C+	C	Up	Y	1,000
PACE Intl Emerging Mkts Equity Investments Cls C	PWECX	NAS CM	Open End	Emerging Markets Equity (Div Emerging Mkts)	C+	C+	C	Up	Y	1,000
PACE Intl Emerging Mkts Equity Investments Cls P	PCEMX	NAS CM	Open End	Emerging Markets Equity (Div Emerging Mkts)	C+	B-	C	Up	Y	10,000
PACE Intl Emerging Mkts Equity Investments Cls Y	PWEYX	NAS CM	Open End	Emerging Markets Equity (Div Emerging Mkts)	C+	B-	C	Up	Y	5,000,000
PACE International Equity Investments Class A	PWGAX	NAS CM	Open End	Global Equity Large Cap (Growth)	B-	B-	B	Up	Y	1,000
PACE International Equity Investments Class C	PWGCX	NAS CM	Open End	Global Equity Large Cap (Growth)	B-	C+	B	Up	Y	1,000
PACE International Equity Investments Class P	PCIEX	NAS CM	Open End	Global Equity Large Cap (Growth)	B-	B-	B	Up	Y	10,000
PACE International Equity Investments Class Y	PWIYX	NAS CM	Open End	Global Equity Large Cap (Growth)	B-	B-	B	Up	Y	5,000,000
PACE Large Co Growth Equity Investments Class A	PLAAX	NAS CM	Open End	US Equity Large Cap Growth (Growth)	B+	B	A-	Up	Y	1,000
PACE Large Co Growth Equity Investments Class C	PLACX	NAS CM	Open End	US Equity Large Cap Growth (Growth)	B+	B	A-	Up	Y	1,000
PACE Large Co Growth Equity Investments Class P	PCLCX	NAS CM	Open End	US Equity Large Cap Growth (Growth)	B+	B	A-	Up	Y	10,000
PACE Large Co Growth Equity Investments Class Y	PLAYX	NAS CM	Open End	US Equity Large Cap Growth (Growth)	B+	B	A-	Up	Y	5,000,000
PACE Large Co Value Equity Investments Class A	PCPAX	NAS CM	Open End	US Equity Large Cap Value (Growth & Income)	B	B-	B		Y	1,000
PACE Large Co Value Equity Investments Class C	PLVCX	NAS CM	Open End	US Equity Large Cap Value (Growth & Income)	B-	B-	B	Down	Y	1,000
PACE Large Co Value Equity Investments Class P	PCLVX	NAS CM	Open End	US Equity Large Cap Value (Growth & Income)	B	B-	B		Y	10,000
PACE Large Co Value Equity Investments Class Y	PLVYX	NAS CM	Open End	US Equity Large Cap Value (Growth & Income)	B	B-	B		Y	5,000,000
PACE Small/Medium Co Growth Equity Investments Class A	PQUAX	NAS CM	Open End	US Equity Small Cap (Growth)	B	B	B	Up	Y	1,000
PACE Small/Medium Co Growth Equity Investments Class C	PUMCX	NAS CM	Open End	US Equity Small Cap (Growth)	B-	B-	B-	Up	Y	1,000
PACE Small/Medium Co Growth Equity Investments Class P	PCSGX	NAS CM	Open End	US Equity Small Cap (Growth)	B	B	B	Up	Y	10,000
PACE Small/Medium Co Growth Equity Investments Class Y	PUMYX	NAS CM	Open End	US Equity Small Cap (Growth)	B	B	B	Up	Y	5,000,000
PACE Small/Medium Co Value Equity Investments Class A	PEVAX	NAS CM	Open End	US Equity Small Cap (Growth)	B	B	B	Up	Y	1,000
PACE Small/Medium Co Value Equity Investments Class C	PEVCX	NAS CM	Open End	US Equity Small Cap (Growth)	B	B-	B	Up	Y	1,000
PACE Small/Medium Co Value Equity Investments Class P	PCSVX	NAS CM	Open End	US Equity Small Cap (Growth)	B	B	B	Up	Y	10,000
PACE Small/Medium Co Value Equity Investments Class Y	PVEYX	NAS CM	Open End	US Equity Small Cap (Growth)	B	B	B	Up	Y	5,000,000
Pacific Advisors Balanced Fund Class A	PAABX	NAS CM	Open End	Aggressive Alloc (Balanced)	C-	C-	C		Y	1,000
Pacific Advisors Balanced Fund Class C	PGBCX	NAS CM	Open End	Aggressive Alloc (Balanced)	C-	D+	C-		Y	10,000
Pacific Advisors Income and Equity Fund Class A	PADIX	NAS CM	Open End	Cautious Alloc (Equity-Income)	B-	C	B	Up	Y	1,000
Pacific Advisors Income and Equity Fund Class C	PIECX	NAS CM	Open End	Cautious Alloc (Equity-Income)	B-	C	B	Up	Y	10,000
Pacific Advisors Large Cap Value Fund Class A	PAGTX	NAS CM	Open End	US Equity Large Cap Blend (Growth)	B-	B-	B-	Down	Y	1,000
Pacific Advisors Large Cap Value Fund Class C	PGCCX	NAS CM	Open End	US Equity Large Cap Blend (Growth)	B-	C+	B-	Down	Y	10,000
Pacific Advisors Mid Cap Value Fund Class A	PAMVX	NAS CM	Open End	US Equity Mid Cap (Growth)	C	C	C		Y	1,000
Pacific Advisors Mid Cap Value Fund Class C	PMVCX	NAS CM	Open End	US Equity Mid Cap (Growth)	C	C	C		Y	10,000
Pacific Advisors Small Cap Value Fund Class A	PASMX	NAS CM	Open End	US Equity Small Cap (Small Company)	C	C	C-		Y	1,000
Pacific Advisors Small Cap Value Fund Class C	PGSCX	NAS CM	Open End	US Equity Small Cap (Small Company)	C	C	C-		Y	10,000
Pacific Advisors Small Cap Value Fund Class I	PGISX	NAS CM	Open End	US Equity Small Cap (Small Company)	C	C	C-		Y	250,000
Pacific Financial Core Equity Fund Class Institutional	PFGQX	NAS CM	Open End	US Equity Large Cap Blend (Growth)	B-	B-	B-	Down	Y	5,000
Pacific Financial Core Equity Fund Class Investor	PFLQX	NAS CM	Open End	US Equity Large Cap Blend (Growth)	B-	B-	B-	Down	Y	5,000
Pacific Financial Dynamic Allocation Fund Inst Cls	PFGDX	NAS CM	Open End	Moderate Alloc (Growth & Income)	C	C	B	Up	Y	5,000

★ Expanded analysis of this fund is included in Section II.

Min Additional Investment	3-Month Total Return	6-Month Total Return	1-Year Total Return	3-Year Total Return	5-Year Total Return	Dividend Yield (TTM)	Expense Ratio	3-Yr Std Deviation	3-Year Beta	NAV	Total Assets (MIL)	%Cash	%Stocks	%Bonds	%Other	Turnover Ratio	Last Bull Market Total Return	Last Bear Market Total Return	Front End Fee (%)	Back End Fee (%)	Inception Date
TOTAL RETURNS						PERFORMANCE				ASSETS		ASSET ALLOCATION & TURNOVER					BULL & BEAR		FEES		
	2.39	9.26	13.85	29.17	88.12	0.26	1.19	10.54	0.74	15.62	15.8	0	100	0	0	99	25.92	-28.36			Aug-10
100	4.59	12.51	26.44	39.35	122.21	0	1.28			10.74	55.9	20	80	0	0						Nov-16
100	4.28	6.78	14.42	11.43	61.00	0.98	1.14	9.44	0.84	19.74	206.4	4	95	1	0	50	19.97	-20.58			Oct-93
100	3.25	5.63	12.85	16.21	53.96	3.25	1.15	7.39	-0.18	15.24	189.5	0	56	38	0	53	16.75	-13.93			Aug-10
	-0.59	0.60	-3.49	5.25		0	1.7	7.08	-0.08	11.61	269.2	62	38	0	0	80					Dec-13
	-0.60	0.52	-3.76	4.54		0	1.95	7.11	-0.09	11.51	269.2	62	38	0	0	80					Dec-13
100	1.39	2.15	3.70	3.17	17.91	0	1.94	2.88	9.67	10.91	674.0	42	51	3	4	292	7.57	-8.38	5.50		Apr-06
100	1.18	1.79	2.92	0.99	13.64	0	2.71	2.87	9.58	10.21	674.0	42	51	3	4	292	7.16	-8.75		1.00	Apr-06
500	1.49	2.36	4.03	4.07	19.53	0	1.72	2.91	9.4	10.83	674.0	42	51	3	4	292	7.77	-8.35			Apr-06
0	1.49	2.26	3.92	4.10	19.49	0	1.77	2.88	9.68	10.86	674.0	42	51	3	4	292	7.74	-8.33			Jul-08
100	3.77	4.73	10.40	11.89	37.73	3.9	1.45	11.56	1.02	7.64	140.6	1	98	0	1	98	24.88	-20.13	5.50		Dec-06
100	3.68	4.40	9.69	9.60	32.87	3.34	2.2	11.6	1.02	7.35	140.6	1	98	0	1	98	24.38	-20.36		1.00	Dec-06
500	3.96	4.81	10.70	12.85	39.51	4.23	1.2	11.56	1.02	7.35	140.6	1	98	0	1	98	25.05	-19.96			Jan-07
0	3.94	4.79	10.66	12.53	39.20	4.01	1.2	11.54	1.02	7.38	140.6	1	98	0	1	98	25.21	-20.06			Dec-08
100	6.38	13.38	33.78	17.35	12.51	0.66	1.7	14.02	0.88	14.51	477.2	1	98	0	1	65	18.47	-25.37	5.50		Dec-00
100	6.18	12.95	32.77	14.79	8.52	0.08	2.45	13.99	0.88	13.42	477.2	1	98	0	1	65	18.06	-25.62		1.00	Dec-00
500	6.46	13.53	34.12	18.12	13.69	0.85	1.45	13.99	0.88	14.54	477.2	1	98	0	1	65	18.47	-25.3			Aug-95
0	6.43	13.54	34.02	18.17	13.93	0.87	1.45	13.97	0.88	14.61	477.2	1	98	0	1	65	18.6	-25.26			Feb-01
100	4.42	10.80	25.15	25.65	47.77	1.65	1.35	11.28	0.9	17.08	1,207	1	97	0	2	81	13.97	-22.31	5.50		Nov-00
100	4.25	10.35	24.14	22.76	42.03	0.92	2.1	11.22	0.9	16.79	1,207	1	97	0	2	81	13.48	-22.66		1.00	Nov-00
500	4.48	10.90	25.45	26.71	49.81	1.89	1.1	11.26	0.9	16.95	1,207	1	97	0	2	81	14.17	-22.23			Aug-95
0	4.46	10.87	25.46	26.70	49.79	1.89	1.1	11.24	0.9	16.99	1,207	1	97	0	2	81	14.15	-22.26			Jan-01
100	5.72	12.19	29.53	35.31	108.75	0.1	1.18	10.7	0.96	24.73	1,383	1	99	0	0	40	26.62	-17.43	5.50		Nov-00
100	5.47	11.71	28.50	32.07	100.28	0	1.93	10.69	0.96	19.9	1,383	1	99	0	0	40	25.95	-17.7		1.00	Nov-00
500	5.76	12.30	29.84	36.37	111.34	0.29	0.93	10.71	0.96	25.56	1,383	1	99	0	0	40	26.81	-17.32			Aug-95
0	5.77	12.35	29.88	36.39	111.45	0.3	0.92	10.7	0.96	25.76	1,383	1	99	0	0	40	26.78	-17.3			Feb-01
100	5.76	9.33	13.81	26.66	94.23	1.36	1.12	11.04	1.05	23.56	1,383	2	98	0	0	71	25.3	-20.63	5.50		Nov-00
100	5.59	8.92	12.93	23.72	86.76	0.64	1.89	11.07	1.05	23.68	1,383	2	98	0	0	71	24.75	-20.91		1.00	Nov-00
500	5.80	9.43	14.02	27.50	96.56	1.56	0.89	11.05	1.05	23.47	1,383	2	98	0	0	71	25.43	-20.53			Aug-95
0	5.83	9.44	14.07	27.56	96.66	1.57	0.87	11.06	1.05	23.59	1,383	2	98	0	0	71	25.49	-20.58			Jan-01
100	5.32	7.72	23.02	23.28	77.41	0	1.23	14.43	1.04	17.01	516.3	1	99	0	0	93	27.94	-22.94	5.50		Nov-00
100	5.10	7.28	22.06	20.46	70.79	0	2	14.43	1.04	13	516.3	1	99	0	0	93	27.3	-23.16		1.00	Nov-00
500	5.34	7.78	23.18	23.71	78.46	0	1.08	14.41	1.04	18.13	516.3	1	99	0	0	93	28.05	-22.89			Aug-95
0	5.37	7.77	23.16	23.60	78.26	0	1.08	14.43	1.04	18.41	516.3	1	99	0	0	93	28.07	-22.89			Feb-01
100	4.38	8.14	9.19	28.61	88.59	1.21	1.23	13.32	1.09	20.1	544.4	6	94	0	0	102	31.19	-27.71	5.50		Nov-00
100	4.20	7.70	8.32	25.65	81.56	0.78	1.99	13.31	1.09	16.48	544.4	6	94	0	0	102	30.63	-27.96		1.00	Nov-00
500	4.45	8.21	9.33	29.16	89.88	1.28	1.04	13.32	1.09	20.7	544.4	6	94	0	0	102	31.29	-27.68			Aug-95
0	4.49	8.25	9.31	29.12	89.81	1.18	1.04	13.32	1.09	20.96	544.4	6	94	0	0	102	31.34	-27.68			Dec-00
25	5.43	7.88	10.54	-8.37	10.55	0	4.5	11.91	0.93	12.45	5.5	4	71	24	0	55	16.93	-14.57	5.75		Feb-93
500	5.23	7.50	9.64	-10.48	6.44	0	5.25	11.89	0.93	10.89	5.5	4	71	24	0	55	16.46	-14.88		1.00	Apr-98
25	2.95	5.13	5.25	9.35	33.29	0.35	3.63	4.89	0.23	13.01	17.2	1	48	46	0	14	8.32	-5.03	4.75		Feb-93
500	2.73	4.64	4.38	6.81	28.27	0	4.39	4.91	0.26	12.38	17.2	1	48	46	0	14	7.84	-5.37		1.00	Apr-98
25	7.67	10.20	17.55	24.75	81.21	0	4.6	10.62	1.01	17.32	7.8	0	100	0	0	0	21.57	-10.93	5.75		May-99
500	7.41	9.74	16.66	21.95	74.31	0	5.34	10.62	1.01	14.7	7.8	0	100	0	0	0	21.08	-11.18		1.00	May-99
25	5.68	15.80	11.97	-2.80	17.97	0	4.74	18.3	1.32	13.19	5.8	0	100	0	0	13	30.81	-33.48	5.75		Apr-02
500	5.46	15.33	11.13	-5.00	13.52	0	5.54	18.28	1.31	11.58	5.8	0	100	0	0	13	30.08	-33.73		1.00	Apr-02
25	6.48	18.70	12.47	-0.98	27.86	0	4.19	27.42	1.59	29.29	23.4	0	100	0	0	11	47.32	-29.97	5.75		Feb-93
500	6.28	18.22	11.59	-3.22	23.08	0	4.95	27.4	1.59	20.75	23.4	0	100	0	0	11	46.61	-30.19		1.00	Apr-98
500	6.54	18.84	12.71	-0.23	29.38	0	3.93	27.31	1.58	38.17	23.4	0	100	0	0	11	47.49	-29.9			Oct-06
250	5.77	10.08	17.42	25.44	80.21	0.48	1.64	10.19	0.98	9.66	595.2	1	94	4	1	105	22.12	-22.32			Jul-07
250	5.31	9.31	16.15	22.36	73.20	0.11	2.39	10.17	0.98	9.03	595.2	1	94	4	1	105	21.63	-22.53			Jan-09
500	3.76	6.58	12.70			0.55	1.84			10.44	484.5	4	60	34	1	41					Sep-15

	MARKET		FUND TYPE, CATEGORY & OBJECTIVE		RATINGS				MINIMUMS	
Fund Name	Ticker Symbol	Traded On	Fund Type	Category and (Prospectus Objective)	Overall Rating	Reward Rating	Risk Rating	Recent Up/ Downgrade	Open to New Investors	Min Initial Investment
Pacific Financial Dynamic Allocation Fund Investor Class	PFLDX	NAS CM	Open End	Moderate Alloc (Growth & Income)	C	C	B	Up	Y	5,000
Pacific Financial Explorer Fund Class Institutional	PFGPX	NAS CM	Open End	US Equity Large Cap Blend (Growth)	B-	B-	B-	Down	Y	5,000
Pacific Financial Explorer Fund Class Investor	PFLPX	NAS CM	Open End	US Equity Large Cap Blend (Growth)	B-	B-	B-	Down	Y	5,000
Pacific Financial Faith & Values Based Mod Inv Cls Shares	FVMLX	NAS CM	Open End	Moderate Alloc (Growth & Income)	C+	C+	B	Up	Y	5,000
Pacific Financial Flexible Growth & Income Fund Inst Cls	PFGFX	NAS CM	Open End	Multialternative (Growth & Income)	C	C-	A-	Up	Y	5,000
Pacific Financial Flexible Growth & Income Fund Inv Cls	PFLFX	NAS CM	Open End	Multialternative (Growth & Income)	C	C-	A-	Up	Y	5,000
Pacific Financial International Fund Class Institutional	PFGIX	NAS CM	Open End	Global Equity Large Cap (Foreign Stock)	B-	C+	B	Up	Y	5,000
Pacific Financial International Fund Class Investor	PFLIX	NAS CM	Open End	Global Equity Large Cap (Foreign Stock)	B-	C+	B-	Up	Y	5,000
Pacific Financial Tactical Fund Class Institutional	PFGTX	NAS CM	Open End	Moderate Alloc (Growth)	C+	C	B	Up	Y	5,000
Pacific Financial Tactical Fund Class Investor	PFTLX	NAS CM	Open End	Moderate Alloc (Growth)	C+	C	B	Up	Y	5,000
Pacific Funds Diversified Alternatives Fund Advisor Class	PLDLX	NAS CM	Open End	Multialternative (Growth & Income)	B-	C+	B	Down	Y	0
Pacific Funds Diversified Alternatives Fund Class A	PLALX	NAS CM	Open End	Multialternative (Growth & Income)	B	C+	A-	Up	Y	1,000
Pacific Funds Diversified Alternatives Fund Class C	PLCLX	NAS CM	Open End	Multialternative (Growth & Income)	B-	C	B+	Up	Y	1,000
Pacific Funds Large-Cap Advisor Class	PFCDX	NAS CM	Open End	US Equity Large Cap Blend (Growth)	C+	C+	B-	Down	Y	0
Pacific Funds Large-Cap Class A	PFLAX	NAS CM	Open End	US Equity Large Cap Blend (Growth)	C+	C+	B-	Down	Y	1,000
Pacific Funds Large-Cap Class C	PFCCX	NAS CM	Open End	US Equity Large Cap Blend (Growth)	C+	C+	B-	Down	Y	1,000
Pacific Funds Large-Cap Investor Class	PFCRX	NAS CM	Open End	US Equity Large Cap Blend (Growth)	C+	C+	B-	Down	Y	0
Pacific Funds Large-Cap S Class	PFKIX	NAS CM	Open End	US Equity Large Cap Blend (Growth)	C+	C+	B-	Down	Y	0
Pacific Funds Large-Cap Value Advisor Class	PFVDX	NAS CM	Open End	US Equity Large Cap Value (Growth)	C+	C+	B	Down	Y	0
Pacific Funds Large-Cap Value Class A	PFAAX	NAS CM	Open End	US Equity Large Cap Value (Growth)	C+	C+	B	Down	Y	1,000
Pacific Funds Large-Cap Value Class C	PFVCX	NAS CM	Open End	US Equity Large Cap Value (Growth)	C+	C+	B	Down	Y	1,000
Pacific Funds Large-Cap Value Investor Class	PFVRX	NAS CM	Open End	US Equity Large Cap Value (Growth)	C+	C+	B	Down	Y	0
Pacific Funds Large-Cap Value S Class	PFVIX	NAS CM	Open End	US Equity Large Cap Value (Growth)	C+	C+	B	Down	Y	0
Pacific Funds Optimization Aggress-Growth Adv Cls	POEDX	NAS CM	Open End	Aggressive Alloc (Asset Alloc)	B-	B-	B-	Down	Y	0
Pacific Funds Port Optimization Aggress-Growth Fund Cls A	POEAX	NAS CM	Open End	Aggressive Alloc (Asset Alloc)	B-	B-	B-	Down	Y	1,000
Pacific Funds Port Optimization Aggress-Growth Fund Cls B	POEBX	NAS CM	Open End	Aggressive Alloc (Asset Alloc)	B-	B-	B-	Down	Y	1,000
Pacific Funds Port Optimization Aggress-Growth Fund Cls C	POCEX	NAS CM	Open End	Aggressive Alloc (Asset Alloc)	B-	B-	B-	Down	Y	1,000
Pacific Funds Optimization Aggress-Growth Retmnt Cls	POERX	NAS CM	Open End	Aggressive Alloc (Asset Alloc)	B-	B-	B-	Down	Y	0
Pacific Funds Port Optimization Conservative Fund Adv Cls	PLCDX	NAS CM	Open End	Cautious Alloc (Asset Alloc)	B-	C+	B	Up	Y	0
Pacific Funds Port Optimization Conservative Fund Cls A	POAAX	NAS CM	Open End	Cautious Alloc (Asset Alloc)	B-	C	B	Up	Y	1,000
Pacific Funds Port Optimization Conservative Fund Cls B	POABX	NAS CM	Open End	Cautious Alloc (Asset Alloc)	C+	C	B	Up	Y	1,000
Pacific Funds Port Optimization Conservative Fund Cls C	POACX	NAS CM	Open End	Cautious Alloc (Asset Alloc)	C+	C	B	Up	Y	1,000
Pacific Funds Optimization Cons Cls Retmnt	POARX	NAS CM	Open End	Cautious Alloc (Asset Alloc)	B-	C	B+	Up	Y	0
Pacific Funds Portfolio Optimization Growth Fund Adv Cls	PMADX	NAS CM	Open End	Aggressive Alloc (Asset Alloc)	B-	B-	B	Down	Y	0
Pacific Funds Portfolio Optimization Growth Fund Class A	PODAX	NAS CM	Open End	Aggressive Alloc (Asset Alloc)	B-	C+	B	Down	Y	1,000
Pacific Funds Portfolio Optimization Growth Fund Class B	PODBX	NAS CM	Open End	Aggressive Alloc (Asset Alloc)	B-	C+	B-	Down	Y	1,000
Pacific Funds Portfolio Optimization Growth Fund Class C	PODCX	NAS CM	Open End	Aggressive Alloc (Asset Alloc)	B-	C+	B-	Down	Y	1,000
Pacific Funds Port Optimization Growth Fund Cls Retmnt	PODRX	NAS CM	Open End	Aggressive Alloc (Asset Alloc)	B-	C+	B	Down	Y	0
Pacific Funds Portfolio Optimization Moderate Fund Adv Cls	POMDX	NAS CM	Open End	Moderate Alloc (Asset Alloc)	B-	C+	B	Up	Y	0
Pacific Funds Portfolio Optimization Moderate Fund Class A	POCAX	NAS CM	Open End	Moderate Alloc (Asset Alloc)	B-	C+	B	Up	Y	1,000
Pacific Funds Portfolio Optimization Moderate Fund Class B	POMBX	NAS CM	Open End	Moderate Alloc (Asset Alloc)	B-	C+	B	Down	Y	1,000
Pacific Funds Portfolio Optimization Moderate Fund Class C	POMCX	NAS CM	Open End	Moderate Alloc (Asset Alloc)	B-	C+	B	Up	Y	1,000
Pacific Funds Port Optimization Moderate Fund Cls Retmnt	POCRX	NAS CM	Open End	Moderate Alloc (Asset Alloc)	B-	C+	B	Up	Y	0
Pacific Funds Optimization Mod-Cons Adv Cls	PMCDX	NAS CM	Open End	Cautious Alloc (Asset Alloc)	B-	C+	B	Up	Y	0
Pacific Funds Optimization Mod-Cons Cls A	POBAX	NAS CM	Open End	Cautious Alloc (Asset Alloc)	B-	C+	B	Up	Y	1,000
Pacific Funds Optimization Mod-Cons Cls B	POBBX	NAS CM	Open End	Cautious Alloc (Asset Alloc)	B-	C+	B	Up	Y	1,000
Pacific Funds Optimization Mod-Cons Cls C	POBCX	NAS CM	Open End	Cautious Alloc (Asset Alloc)	B-	C+	B	Up	Y	1,000
Pacific Funds Optimization Mod-Cons Cls Retmnt	POBRX	NAS CM	Open End	Cautious Alloc (Asset Alloc)	B-	C+	B	Up	Y	0
Pacific Funds Small/Mid-Cap Advisor Class	PFMDX	NAS CM	Open End	US Equity Small Cap (Growth)	C+	C+	B-	Down	Y	0
Pacific Funds Small/Mid-Cap Class A	PFDAX	NAS CM	Open End	US Equity Small Cap (Growth)	C+	C+	B-	Down	Y	1,000
Pacific Funds Small/Mid-Cap Class C	PFPCX	NAS CM	Open End	US Equity Small Cap (Growth)	C+	C+	B-	Down	Y	1,000
Pacific Funds Small/Mid-Cap Investor Class	PFIRX	NAS CM	Open End	US Equity Small Cap (Growth)	C+	C+	B-	Down	Y	0

★Expanded analysis of this fund is included in Section II.

Min Additional Investment	3-Month Total Return	6-Month Total Return	1-Year Total Return	3-Year Total Return	5-Year Total Return	Dividend Yield (TTM)	Expense Ratio	3-Yr Std Deviation	3-Year Beta	NAV	Total Assets (MIL)	%Cash	%Stocks	%Bonds	%Other	Turnover Ratio	Last Bull Market Total Return	Last Bear Market Total Return	Front End Fee (%)	Back End Fee (%)	Inception Date
TOTAL RETURNS						PERFORMANCE				ASSETS		ASSET ALLOCATION & TURNOVER					BULL & BEAR		FEES		
500	3.71	6.36	11.87			0.15	2.6			10.32	484.5	4	60	34	1	41					Sep-15
250	5.82	9.82	19.28	25.75	85.62	0	1.79	10.12	0.98	10.33	180.3	0	100	0	0		20.64	-25.25			Jul-07
250	5.64	9.54	18.51	23.16	79.13	0	2.54	10.1	0.98	9.72	180.3	0	100	0	0		20.06	-25.34			Jan-09
500	3.36	5.59	10.35	12.78		0	3.23			9.84	12.1	1	65	28	0	57					May-13
500	1.86	4.63	8.85			1.15	2.73			10.02	232.6	10	47	23	13						Nov-15
500	1.88	4.47	8.16			0.72	3.48			9.93	232.6	10	47	23	13						Nov-15
250	2.95	8.50	24.35	16.29	41.52	0	2.56	9.96	0.75	5.87	94.9	6	92	0	2	41	8.42	-30.04			Jul-07
250	3.13	8.29	23.64	13.99	36.82	0	3.31	10.04	0.76	5.51	94.9	6	92	0	2	41	7.88	-30.22			Jan-09
250	0.28	1.41	3.77	3.79	6.48	2.65	2.42	1.32	4.45	9.73	101.3	16	10	60	4	15	0.5	-2.24			Jul-07
250	0.40	1.36	3.33	1.85	2.89	1.08	3.17	1.31	4.87	9.54	101.3	16	10	60	4	15	0.1	-2.59			Jan-09
	0.89	3.37	7.08	14.01		6.35	1.58	3.41	1.87	9.87	24.3	24	20	56	0	37					Dec-13
50	0.85	3.33	6.83	13.27		6.16	1.83	3.42	3.45	9.84	24.3	24	20	56	0	37			5.50		Dec-13
50	0.62	2.92	6.01	10.73		5.98	2.58	3.46	4.62	9.69	24.3	24	20	56	0	37				1.00	Dec-13
	6.13	11.99	21.34	30.61		0.72	0.75			12.61	15.2	1	99	0	0	108					Jan-16
50	6.10	11.79	21.05	30.06		0.72	1			12.53	15.2	1	99	0	0	108			4.25		Jan-16
50	5.90	11.34	20.05	27.10		0.33	1.75			12.49	15.2	1	99	0	0	108				1.00	Jan-16
	6.05	11.72	20.99	29.99		1.77	1			12.38	15.2	1	99	0	0	108					Dec-14
	6.12	11.93	21.36	31.12		1.38	0.65			12.38	15.2	1	99	0	0	108					Mar-15
	6.68	11.42	15.48	24.93		0.79	0.85			11.61	33.0	2	98	0	0	65					Jan-16
50	6.48	11.23	15.08	24.41		0.8	1.1			11.58	33.0	2	98	0	0	65			4.25		Jan-16
50	6.38	10.76	14.29	21.58		0.52	1.85			11.51	33.0	2	98	0	0	65				1.00	Jan-16
	6.57	11.27	15.28	24.51		1.76	1.1			11.46	33.0	2	98	0	0	65					Dec-14
	6.70	11.46	15.65	25.25		1.23	0.75			11.58	33.0	2	98	0	0	65					Jan-16
	4.30	9.00	19.40	27.59	63.13	1.17	1.19	9.35	0.9	17.17	340.1	4	91	5	0	41	21.83	-19.37			Dec-12
50	4.25	8.90	19.15	26.61	61.18	1.02	1.44	9.38	0.9	17.14	340.1	4	91	5	0	41	21.83	-19.37	5.50		Dec-03
50	4.07	8.50	18.25	23.80	56.01	0.58	2.19	9.57	0.92	16.76	340.1	4	91	5	0	41	21.94	-20.03		5.00	Dec-03
50	4.10	8.46	18.23	23.74	56.12	0.58	2.19	9.55	0.92	16.73	340.1	4	91	5	0	41	21.94	-20.03		1.00	Dec-03
	4.22	8.76	18.84	25.67	59.43	0.87	1.69	9.43	0.9	17.03	340.1	4	91	5	0	41	21.84	-19.57			Sep-05
	1.38	3.55	8.08	12.98	20.09	2.03	1.02	4.3	0.34	11.35	320.1	10	24	66	0	57	8.55	-4.6			Dec-12
50	1.28	3.36	7.79	12.24	18.87	1.85	1.27	4.33	0.34	11.33	320.1	10	24	66	0	57	8.55	-4.6	5.50		Dec-03
50	1.06	2.99	7.00	9.69	14.66	1.34	2.02	4.42	0.35	11.11	320.1	10	24	66	0	57	8.2	-4.92		5.00	Dec-03
50	1.07	3.00	6.91	9.69	14.64	1.33	2.02	4.36	0.34	11.1	320.1	10	24	66	0	57	8.25	-4.92		1.00	Dec-03
	1.22	3.31	7.57	11.41	17.52	1.71	1.52	4.34	0.34	11.26	320.1	10	24	66	0	57	8.34	-4.62			Sep-05
	3.62	7.73	16.59	24.80	56.24	1.53	1.16	8.43	0.81	15.64	1,038	5	77	18	0	43	19.47	-15.98			Dec-12
50	3.58	7.63	16.34	23.91	54.35	1.38	1.41	8.45	0.81	15.61	1,038	5	77	18	0	43	19.47	-15.98	5.50		Dec-03
50	3.38	7.20	15.43	21.16	48.96	0.92	2.16	8.49	0.81	15.4	1,038	5	77	18	0	43	19.19	-16.46		5.00	Dec-03
50	3.32	7.23	15.41	21.17	49.06	0.91	2.16	8.49	0.81	15.35	1,038	5	77	18	0	43	19.2	-16.42		1.00	Dec-03
	3.47	7.53	16.01	23.01	52.50	1.19	1.66	8.43	0.81	15.57	1,038	5	77	18	0	43	19.33	-16.08			Sep-05
	2.91	6.42	13.77	20.96	43.84	1.75	1.11	6.9	0.65	14.4	1,386	7	60	33	0	48	16.16	-12.2			Dec-12
50	2.87	6.31	13.50	20.05	42.12	1.58	1.36	6.92	0.66	14.38	1,386	7	60	33	0	48	16.16	-12.2	5.50		Dec-03
50	2.67	5.86	12.60	17.39	37.13	1.1	2.11	6.97	0.66	14.21	1,386	7	60	33	0	48	15.72	-12.54		5.00	Dec-03
50	2.61	5.87	12.54	17.34	37.08	1.09	2.11	6.97	0.66	14.18	1,386	7	60	33	0	48	15.8	-12.56		1.00	Dec-03
	2.85	6.15	13.18	19.16	40.43	1.41	1.61	6.93	0.66	14.34	1,386	7	60	33	0	48	16.05	-12.32			Sep-05
	1.96	4.81	10.72	16.69	31.42	1.96	1.06	5.22	0.08	12.71	475.5	8	40	52	0	53	12.11	-8.34			Dec-12
50	1.94	4.62	10.45	15.78	30.07	1.78	1.31	5.25	0.1	12.68	475.5	8	40	52	0	53	12.11	-8.34	5.50		Dec-03
50	1.77	4.26	9.71	13.32	25.51	1.3	2.06	5.3	0.09	12.47	475.5	8	40	52	0	53	11.75	-8.83		5.00	Dec-03
50	1.70	4.27	9.63	13.32	25.47	1.29	2.06	5.28	0.1	12.46	475.5	8	40	52	0	53	11.79	-8.75		1.00	Dec-03
	1.92	4.54	10.22	14.94	28.59	1.64	1.56	5.23	0.1	12.61	475.5	8	40	52	0	53	11.89	-8.53			Sep-05
	5.31	9.36	17.12	35.16		0.05	1.05			13.35	192.7	2	98	0	0	45					Jan-16
50	5.24	9.30	16.77	34.32		0	1.3			13.31	192.7	2	98	0	0	45			4.25		Jan-16
50	5.07	8.82	15.93	31.24		0	2.05			13.11	192.7	2	98	0	0	45				1.00	Jan-16
	5.25	9.23	16.71	34.02		0	1.35			13.28	192.7	2	98	0	0	45					Jan-16

	MARKET		FUND TYPE, CATEGORY & OBJECTIVE		RATINGS				MINIMUMS	
Fund Name	Ticker Symbol	Traded On	Fund Type	Category and (Prospectus Objective)	Overall Rating	Reward Rating	Risk Rating	Recent Up/ Downgrade	Open to New Investors	Min Initial Investment
Pacific Funds Small/Mid-Cap S Class	PFOIX	NAS CM	Open End	US Equity Small Cap (Growth)	C+	C+	B-	Down	Y	0
Pacific Funds Small-Cap Advisor Class	PFQDX	NAS CM	Open End	US Equity Small Cap (Small Company)	C+	C+	B-	Down	Y	0
Pacific Funds Small-Cap Class A	PFKAX	NAS CM	Open End	US Equity Small Cap (Small Company)	C+	C+	B-	Down	Y	1,000
Pacific Funds Small-Cap Class C	PFACX	NAS CM	Open End	US Equity Small Cap (Small Company)	C+	C+	C+	Down	Y	1,000
Pacific Funds Small-Cap Growth Advisor Class	PFWDX	NAS CM	Open End	US Equity Small Cap (Small Company)	C+	C+	C+	Up	Y	0
Pacific Funds Small-Cap Growth Class A	PFMAX	NAS CM	Open End	US Equity Small Cap (Small Company)	C+	C+	C+	Up	Y	1,000
Pacific Funds Small-Cap Growth Class C	PFMCX	NAS CM	Open End	US Equity Small Cap (Small Company)	C+	C+	C+	Up	Y	1,000
Pacific Funds Small-Cap Growth Class P	US69448A3187		Open End	US Equity Small Cap (Small Company)	C+	C+	C+	Up	Y	0
Pacific Funds Small-Cap Growth Investor Class	PFWRX	NAS CM	Open End	US Equity Small Cap (Small Company)	C+	C+	C+	Up	Y	0
Pacific Funds Small-Cap Growth S Class	PFYIX	NAS CM	Open End	US Equity Small Cap (Small Company)	C+	C+	C+	Up	Y	0
Pacific Funds Small-Cap Investor Class	PFBRX	NAS CM	Open End	US Equity Small Cap (Small Company)	C+	C+	B-	Down	Y	0
Pacific Funds Small-Cap S Class	PFJIX	NAS CM	Open End	US Equity Small Cap (Small Company)	C+	C+	B-	Down	Y	0
Pacific Funds Small-Cap Value Advisor Class	PFFDX	NAS CM	Open End	US Equity Small Cap (Small Company)	C+	C+	B-	Up	Y	0
Pacific Funds Small-Cap Value Class A	PFEAX	NAS CM	Open End	US Equity Small Cap (Small Company)	C+	C+	B-	Up	Y	1,000
Pacific Funds Small-Cap Value Class C	PFHCX	NAS CM	Open End	US Equity Small Cap (Small Company)	C+	C+	B-	Up	Y	1,000
Pacific Funds Small-Cap Value Investor Class	PFQRX	NAS CM	Open End	US Equity Small Cap (Small Company)	C+	C+	B-	Up	Y	0
Pacific Funds Small-Cap Value S Class	PFEIX	NAS CM	Open End	US Equity Small Cap (Small Company)	C+	C+	B-	Up	Y	0
Palmer Square SSI Alternative Income Fund Class A	PSCAX	NAS CM	Open End	Market Neutral (Convertible Bond)	C+	C	B		Y	2,500
Palmer Square SSI Alternative Income Fund Class I	PSCIX	NAS CM	Open End	Market Neutral (Convertible Bond)	C+	C	B		Y	1,000,000
Palmer Square Strategic Credit Fund Class A	PSQAX	NAS CM	Open End	Multialternative (Growth)	C	C	C+		Y	2,500
Palmer Square Strategic Credit Fund Class I	PSQIX	NAS CM	Open End	Multialternative (Growth)	C	C	C+		Y	1,000,000
Papp Small & Mid-Cap Growth Fund	PAPPX	NAS CM	Open End	US Equity Mid Cap (Growth)	B	B	B-		Y	5,000
Paradigm Micro-Cap Fund	PVIVX	NAS CM	Open End	US Equity Small Cap (Growth)	B	B+	B-	Up	Y	2,500
Paradigm Opportunity Fund	PFOPX	NAS CM	Open End	US Equity Small Cap (Growth)	B	B	B	Up	Y	2,500
Paradigm Select Fund	PFSLX	NAS CM	Open End	US Equity Small Cap (Growth)	B	B+	B	Up	Y	2,500
Paradigm Value Fund	PVFAX	NAS CM	Open End	US Equity Small Cap (Growth)	A-	A-	B+	Up	Y	2,500
Parametric Commodity Strategy Fund Institutional Class	EIPCX	NAS CM	Open End	Commodities Broad Basket (Growth)	C-	C-	D+	Up	Y	50,000
Parametric Commodity Strategy Fund Investor Class	EAPCX	NAS CM	Open End	Commodities Broad Basket (Growth)	C-	C-	D+	Up	Y	1,000
Parametric Dividend Income Fund Institutional Class	EIPDX	NAS CM	Open End	US Equity Large Cap Value (Equity-Income)	B	B-	B		Y	50,000
Parametric Dividend Income Fund Investor Class	EAPDX	NAS CM	Open End	US Equity Large Cap Value (Equity-Income)	B-	B-	B	Down	Y	1,000
Parametric Emerging Markets Fund Class C	ECEMX	NAS CM	Open End	Emerging Markets Equity (Div Emerging Mkts)	C+	C+	C	Up		1,000
Parametric Emerging Markets Fund Class R6	EREMX	NAS CM	Open End	Emerging Markets Equity (Div Emerging Mkts)	C+	C+	C	Up	Y	1,000,000
Parametric Emerging Markets Fund Institutional Class	EIEMX	NAS CM	Open End	Emerging Markets Equity (Div Emerging Mkts)	C+	C+	C	Up	Y	50,000
Parametric Emerging Markets Fund Investor Class	EAEMX	NAS CM	Open End	Emerging Markets Equity (Div Emerging Mkts)	C+	C+	C	Up	Y	1,000
Parametric International Equity Fund Class R	ERISX	NAS CM	Open End	Global Equity Large Cap (Foreign Stock)	B	B-	B	Up	Y	1,000
Parametric International Equity Fund Class R6	ESISX	NAS CM	Open End	Global Equity Large Cap (Foreign Stock)	B	B	B	Up	Y	1,000,000
Parametric International Equity Fund Institutional Class	EIISX	NAS CM	Open End	Global Equity Large Cap (Foreign Stock)	B	B	B	Up	Y	50,000
Parametric International Equity Fund Investor Class	EAISX	NAS CM	Open End	Global Equity Large Cap (Foreign Stock)	B	B-	B	Up	Y	1,000
Parametric Tax-Managed Emerging Mkts Fund Inst Cls	EITEX	NAS CM	Open End	Emerging Markets Equity (Div Emerging Mkts)	C+	C+	C	Up	Y	50,000
Parametric Tax-Managed International Equity Fund Class C	ECIGX	NAS CM	Open End	Global Equity Large Cap (Foreign Stock)	B-	C+	B	Up		1,000
Parametric Tax-Managed Intl Equity Fund Inst Cls	EITIX	NAS CM	Open End	Global Equity Large Cap (Foreign Stock)	B	B-	B	Up	Y	50,000
Parametric Tax-Managed Intl Equity Fund Inv Cls	ETIGX	NAS CM	Open End	Global Equity Large Cap (Foreign Stock)	B	B-	B	Up	Y	1,000
Parametric Vol Risk Premium - Defensive Fund Inst Cls	EIVPX	NAS CM	Open End	Long/Short Equity (Growth & Income)	U	U	U		Y	50,000
Parnassus Asia Fund	PAFSX	NAS CM	Open End	Asia Equity (Growth)	C+	B-	C	Up	Y	2,000
Parnassus Asia Fund Institutional Shares	PFPSX	NAS CM	Open End	Asia Equity (Growth)	C+	B-	C	Down	Y	100,000
Parnassus Core Equity Fund - Institutional Shares	PRILX	NAS CM	Open End	US Equity Large Cap Blend (Equity-Income)	B	B-	B+	Up	Y	100,000
Parnassus Core Equity Fund - Investor Shares	PRBLX	NAS CM	Open End	US Equity Large Cap Blend (Equity-Income)	B	B-	B+	Up	Y	2,000
Parnassus Endeavor Fund Institutional Shares	PFPWX	NAS CM	Open End	US Equity Large Cap Growth (Growth)	B+	A-	B	Up	Y	100,000
Parnassus Endeavor Fund Investor Shares	PARWX	NAS CM	Open End	US Equity Large Cap Growth (Growth)	B+	A-	B	Up	Y	2,000
Parnassus Fund	PARNX	NAS CM	Open End	US Equity Large Cap Growth (Growth)	B	B-	B+	Up	Y	2,000
Parnassus Fund Institutional Shares	PFPRX	NAS CM	Open End	US Equity Large Cap Growth (Growth)	B	B-	B+	Up	Y	100,000
Parnassus Mid Cap Fund	PARMX	NAS CM	Open End	US Equity Mid Cap (Growth)	B	B-	B		Y	2,000

★Expanded analysis of this fund is included in Section II.

	TOTAL RETURNS					PERFORMANCE				ASSETS		ASSET ALLOCATION & TURNOVER					BULL & BEAR		FEES		
Min Additional Investment	3-Month Total Return	6-Month Total Return	1-Year Total Return	3-Year Total Return	5-Year Total Return	Dividend Yield (TTM)	Expense Ratio	3-Yr Std Deviation	3-Year Beta	NAV	Total Assets (MIL)	%Cash	%Stocks	%Bonds	%Other	Turnover Ratio	Last Bull Market Total Return	Last Bear Market Total Return	Front End Fee (%)	Back End Fee (%)	Inception Date
	5.39	9.44	17.21	35.33		0.09	1			13.36	192.7	2	98	0	0	45					Dec-14
	4.90	9.92	15.44	34.19		0.07	1.05			13.11	15.6	1	99	0	0	62					Jan-16
50	4.82	9.81	15.09	33.25		0.79	1.3			12.94	15.6	1	99	0	0	62			4.25		Jan-16
50	4.60	9.32	14.29	30.22		0	2.05			12.86	15.6	1	99	0	0	62				1.00	Jan-16
	6.45	9.66	18.43	29.67		0	1.05			12.24	39.5	2	98	0	0	49					Jan-16
50	6.32	9.45	18.14	28.76		0	1.3			12.15	39.5	2	98	0	0	49			4.25		Jan-16
50	6.14	9.02	17.22	26.05		0	2.05			11.97	39.5	2	98	0	0	49				1.00	Jan-16
	6.45	9.66	18.44	29.30		0	1.05			12.23	39.5	2	98	0	0	49					Jun-16
	6.32	9.55	18.16	28.95		0.19	1.25			12.14	39.5	2	98	0	0	49					Dec-14
	6.53	9.74	18.62	29.89		0.01	0.9			12.26	39.5	2	98	0	0	49					Jan-16
	4.79	9.74	15.08	32.96		0.15	1.35			13.02	15.6	1	99	0	0	62					Jan-16
	4.91	9.99	15.47	34.11		7.5	1			12.06	15.6	1	99	0	0	62					Dec-14
	2.41	8.98	7.58	29.33		0.29	1.05			11.53	36.4	1	99	0	0	76					Jan-16
50	2.36	8.80	7.30	28.23		0.47	1.3			11.47	36.4	1	99	0	0	76			4.25		Jan-16
50	2.21	8.41	6.45	25.53		0.12	2.05			11.37	36.4	1	99	0	0	76				1.00	Jan-16
	2.35	8.70	7.20	28.06		0.51	1.35			11.45	36.4	1	99	0	0	76					Jan-16
	2.40	8.98	7.58	29.45		0.51	1			11.5	36.4	1	99	0	0	76					Dec-14
100	0.40	1.51	4.05	6.87	7.66	1.2	1.82	2.64	25.49	10	296.5	12	-37	0	37	54			5.75		May-12
5,000	0.46	1.67	4.35	7.64	9.08	1.48	1.57	2.63	25.05	9.99	296.5	12	-37	0	37	54					May-12
100	0.34	0.11	1.98	0.40	7.51	1.17	1.65	7.46	31.97	8.61	21.2	18	1	41	37	255	2		5.75		May-11
5,000	0.34	0.11	2.06	1.25	8.93	1.47	1.4	7.45	32.15	8.64	21.2	18	1	41	37	255	2.21				May-11
1,000	5.98	9.06	25.82	31.34	80.51	0	1.25	9.6	0.8	20.78	30.9	2	98	0	0	14	25.43	-19.21			Mar-10
100	-0.48	0.55	15.79	32.00	94.97	0	1.26	17.1	0.94	32.4	51.1	4	96	0	0	89	22.4	-21.21			Dec-07
100	4.78	13.58	14.48	24.05	74.73	0	1.26	11.55	0.67	40.48	7.9	2	98	0	0	11	20.11	-19.05			Jan-05
100	5.58	9.63	16.11	31.87	87.77	0.01	1.18	11.25	0.84	37.44	25.3	5	95	0	0	31	24.25	-18.82			Jan-05
100	3.45	8.79	14.06	34.60	71.88	0	1.5	13.06	0.85	48.96	62.9	4	96	0	0	13	21.04	-21.56			Dec-02
	4.34	9.49	7.06	-6.34	-27.35	6.32	0.65	11.72	0.85	5.48	253.3	22	0	76	3	0	1.77				May-11
	4.16	9.15	6.70	-7.03	-28.24	6.24	0.9	11.71	0.85	5.42	253.3	22	0	76	3	0	1.68				Jan-12
	6.33	10.68	15.79	36.48		2.34	0.4	9.08	0.91	13.12	26.4	1	99	0	0	26					Mar-14
	6.28	10.58	15.46	35.45		2.18	0.65	9.08	0.91	13.1	26.4	1	99	0	0	26					Mar-14
	4.79	11.29	26.11	15.86	11.37	1.03	2.13	13.87	0.85	15.45	2,902	0	94	0	4	6	15.55	-24.93		1.00	Jun-06
	5.05	11.84	27.39	19.55	17.26	1.52	1.08	13.9	0.85	15.79	2,902	0	94	0	4	6	16.15	-24.57			Jul-14
	5.01	11.87	27.34	19.43	17.10	1.48	1.13	13.85	0.85	15.79	2,902	0	94	0	4	6	16.15	-24.57			Jun-06
	4.94	11.68	27.01	18.51	15.62	1.28	1.38	13.85	0.85	15.73	2,902	0	94	0	4	6	16.01	-24.69			Jun-06
	3.44	8.57	25.17	28.32	46.78	1.28	1	10.78	0.86	13.68	255.4	0	95	0	4	22	12.05	-21.32			Aug-15
	3.53	8.86	25.77	30.24	50.46	1.37	0.47	10.82	0.86	13.78	255.4	0	95	0	4	22	12.37	-21.16			Aug-15
	3.56	8.81	25.70	30.12	50.32	1.35	0.5	10.84	0.86	13.78	255.4	0	95	0	4	22	12.37	-21.16			Apr-10
	3.46	8.73	25.48	29.23	48.52	1.26	0.75	10.85	0.87	13.73	255.4	0	95	0	4	22	12.11	-21.28			Apr-10
	4.63	11.51	27.09	19.89	19.27	1.37	0.95	13.71	0.84	52.29	3,551	0	95	0	4	8	16.56	-24.15			Jun-98
	3.25	8.08	23.86	23.86	40.06	0.88	1.8	10.6	0.84	10.67	41.0	0	96	0	4	14	17.86	-28.11		1.00	Apr-98
	3.50	8.67	25.21	27.70	47.25	1.66	0.8	10.56	0.84	11.22	41.0	0	96	0	4	14	18.66	-27.75			Sep-08
	3.52	8.59	24.81	26.72	45.46	1.44	1.05	10.6	0.84	11.26	41.0	0	96	0	4	14	18.37	-27.82			Apr-98
	2.60	5.47					0.55			10.9	180.5	9	51	41	0						Feb-17
50	5.01	6.00	20.38	20.82		0	1.25	13.93	0.98	19.02	16.3	6	94	0	0	46					Apr-13
50	5.04	6.08	20.60	21.61		0	0.96	13.88	0.98	19.1	16.3	6	94	0	0	46					Apr-15
50	5.54	9.12	16.81	27.42	100.78	1.16	0.66	8.73	0.83	42.73	16,256	3	97	0	0	23	20.6	-14.65			Apr-06
50	5.51	9.04	16.57	26.65	98.97	0.95	0.87	8.74	0.83	42.67	16,256	3	97	0	0	23	20.51	-14.79			Aug-92
50	5.23	8.99	20.02	49.98	137.83	0.92	0.74	11.68	1.01	37.21	5,204	7	93	0	0	34	29.6	-19.94			Apr-15
50	5.17	8.88	19.80	49.19	136.59	0.81	0.95	11.68	1.01	37.18	5,204	7	93	0	0	34	29.6	-19.94			Apr-05
50	4.71	6.03	16.07	31.27	106.79	0.7	0.86	12.34	1.06	48.27	1,081	1	99	0	0	42	35.21	-25.88			Dec-84
50	4.75	6.09	16.24	31.76	107.56	0.82	0.71	12.33	1.06	48.25	1,081	1	99	0	0	42	35.21	-25.88			Apr-15
50	4.07	6.52	15.78	31.98	92.81	0.33	0.99	9.12	0.82	32.07	2,805	7	93	0	0	19	26.64	-20.42			Apr-05

Fund Name	Ticker Symbol	Traded On	Fund Type	Category and (Prospectus Objective)	Overall Rating	Reward Rating	Risk Rating	Recent Up/ Downgrade	Open to New Investors	Min Initial Investment
		MARKET		FUND TYPE, CATEGORY & OBJECTIVE	RATINGS				MINIMUMS	
Parnassus Mid Cap Fund Institutional Shares	PFPMX	NAS CM	Open End	US Equity Mid Cap (Growth)	B	B	B		Y	100,000
Parnassus Mid Cap Fund Institutional Shares	ATBAX	NAS CM	Open End	Aggressive Alloc (Balanced)	B-	C+	B	Up	Y	1,000
Parnassus Mid Cap Fund Institutional Shares	ATBTX	NAS CM	Open End	Aggressive Alloc (Balanced)	B-	C+	B	Up	Y	1,000
Parnassus Mid Cap Fund Institutional Shares	ATBIX	NAS CM	Open End	Aggressive Alloc (Balanced)	B-	C+	B	Up	Y	1,000,000
Parnassus Mid Cap Fund Institutional Shares	TRFAX	NAS CM	Open End	US Equity Large Cap Blend (Growth)	B	B-	B+		Y	1,000
Parnassus Mid Cap Fund Institutional Shares	TRFCX	NAS CM	Open End	US Equity Large Cap Blend (Growth)	B	B-	B+		Y	1,000
Parnassus Mid Cap Fund Institutional Shares	TRFTX	NAS CM	Open End	US Equity Large Cap Blend (Growth)	B	B-	B+		Y	1,000,000
Pax Balanced Fund Class Institutional	PAXIX	NAS CM	Open End	Moderate Alloc (Balanced)	B-	C+	B	Up	Y	250,000
Pax Balanced Fund Individual Investor Class	PAXWX	NAS CM	Open End	Moderate Alloc (Balanced)	B-	C+	B	Up	Y	1,000
Pax Ellevate Global Women's Index Fund Individual Inv Cls	PXWEX	NAS CM	Open End	Global Equity (Growth)	B-	B-	B-	Down	Y	1,000
Pax Ellevate Global Women's Index Fund Institutional Class	PXWIX	NAS CM	Open End	Global Equity (Growth)	B-	B-	B-	Down	Y	250,000
Pax ESG Beta Dividend Fund Individual Investor Class	PAXDX	NAS CM	Open End	US Equity Large Cap Blend (Equity-Income)	D-	D+	A		Y	1,000
Pax ESG Beta Dividend Fund Institutional Class	PXDIX	NAS CM	Open End	US Equity Large Cap Blend (Equity-Income)	D-	D+	A		Y	250,000
Pax ESG Beta Quality Fund Class A	PXGAX	NAS CM	Open End	US Equity Large Cap Growth (Growth)	B	B-	B	Up	Y	1,000
Pax ESG Beta Quality Fund Individual Investor Class	PXWGX	NAS CM	Open End	US Equity Large Cap Growth (Growth)	B	B-	B	Up	Y	1,000
Pax ESG Beta Quality Fund Institutional Class	PWGIX	NAS CM	Open End	US Equity Large Cap Growth (Growth)	B	B	B	Up	Y	250,000
Pax Global Environmental Markets Fund Class A	PXEAX	NAS CM	Open End	Global Equity Mid/Small Cap (Growth)	B	B	B	Up	Y	1,000
Pax Global Environmental Mkts Fund Individual Inv Cls	PGRNX	NAS CM	Open End	Global Equity Mid/Small Cap (Growth)	B	B	B	Up	Y	1,000
Pax Global Environmental Markets Fund Institutional Class	PGINX	NAS CM	Open End	Global Equity Mid/Small Cap (Growth)	B	B	B	Up	Y	250,000
Pax Large Cap Fund Individual Investor Class	PAXLX	NAS CM	Open End	US Equity Large Cap Blend (Growth)	D-	D+	A-		Y	1,000
Pax Large Cap Fund Institutional Class	PXLIX	NAS CM	Open End	US Equity Large Cap Blend (Growth)	D-	D+	A-		Y	250,000
Pax Mid Cap Fund Individual Investor Class	PWMDX	NAS CM	Open End	US Equity Mid Cap (Growth)	D+	C-	B+	Up	Y	1,000
Pax Mid Cap Fund Institutional Class	PMIDX	NAS CM	Open End	US Equity Mid Cap (Growth)	D+	C-	B+	Up	Y	250,000
Pax MSCI EAFE ESG Leaders Index Fund Individual Inv Cls	PXINX	NAS CM	Open End	Global Equity Large Cap (Pacific Stock)	B-	C+	B	Up	Y	1,000
Pax MSCI EAFE ESG Leaders Index Fund Institutional Class	PXNIX	NAS CM	Open End	Global Equity Large Cap (Pacific Stock)	B-	C+	B	Up	Y	250,000
Pax Small Cap Fund Class A	PXSAX	NAS CM	Open End	US Equity Small Cap (Small Company)	B-	C+	B	Up	Y	1,000
Pax Small Cap Fund Individual Investor Class	PXSCX	NAS CM	Open End	US Equity Small Cap (Small Company)	B-	C+	B	Up	Y	1,000
Pax Small Cap Fund Institutional Class	PXSIX	NAS CM	Open End	US Equity Small Cap (Small Company)	B-	B-	B	Up	Y	250,000
Payden Equity Income Fund	PYVLX	NAS CM	Open End	US Equity Large Cap Value (Growth & Income)	B	B-	B		Y	100,000
Payden Equity Income Fund Adviser Class	PYVAX	NAS CM	Open End	US Equity Large Cap Value (Growth & Income)	B-	B-	B	Down	Y	5,000
Payden Equity Income Fund SI Class	PYVSX	NAS CM	Open End	US Equity Large Cap Value (Growth & Income)	B	B-	B		Y	50,000,000
Payson Total Return Fund	PBFDX	NAS CM	Open End	US Equity Large Cap Blend (Growth & Income)	B-	B-	C+	Down	Y	2,000
PCS Commodity Strategy Fund Class A	PCYAX	NAS CM	Open End	Commodities Broad Basket (Growth)	C-	C	D+	Up	Y	5,000
PCS Commodity Strategy Fund Class C	PCYCX	NAS CM	Open End	Commodities Broad Basket (Growth)	C-	C-	D+	Up	Y	5,000
PCS Commodity Strategy Fund Class I	PCYIX	NAS CM	Open End	Commodities Broad Basket (Growth)	C-	C	D+	Up	Y	5,000,000
Pear Tree PanAgora Emerging Markets Fund Institutional Cls	QEMAX	NAS CM	Open End	Emerging Markets Equity (Div Emerging Mkts)	C+	C+	C	Up	Y	1,000,000
Pear Tree PanAgora Emerging Markets Fund Ordinary Class	QFFOX	NAS CM	Open End	Emerging Markets Equity (Div Emerging Mkts)	C	C+	C	Up	Y	2,500
Pear Tree PanAgora Risk Parity Emerg Mkts Inst Shares	EMRPX	NAS CM	Open End	Emerging Markets Equity (Growth)	C	C	C	Up	Y	1,000,000
Pear Tree PanAgora Risk Parity Emerg Mkts Ordinary Shares	RPEMX	NAS CM	Open End	Emerging Markets Equity (Growth)	C	C	C	Up	Y	2,500
Pear Tree Polaris Foreign Value Fund Class Institutional	QFVIX	NAS CM	Open End	Global Equity Large Cap (Foreign Stock)	B-	B	C+	Up	Y	1,000,000
Pear Tree Polaris Foreign Value Fund Class Ordinary	QFVOX	NAS CM	Open End	Global Equity Large Cap (Foreign Stock)	B-	B	C+	Up	Y	2,500
Pear Tree Polaris Foreign Value Fund Class R6	QFVRX	NAS CM	Open End	Global Equity Large Cap (Foreign Stock)	B-	B	C+	Up	Y	100,000
Pear Tree Polaris Foreign Value Small Cap Fund Class R6	QUSRX	NAS CM	Open End	Global Equity Mid/Small Cap (Foreign Stock)	B+	A-	B	Up	Y	100,000
Pear Tree Polaris Foreign Value Small Cap Fund Inst Cls	QUSIX	NAS CM	Open End	Global Equity Mid/Small Cap (Foreign Stock)	B+	A-	B	Up	Y	1,000,000
Pear Tree Polaris Foreign Value Small Cap Ordinary Cls	QUSOX	NAS CM	Open End	Global Equity Mid/Small Cap (Foreign Stock)	B+	A-	B	Up	Y	2,500
Pear Tree Polaris Small Cap Fund Institutional Class	QBNAX	NAS CM	Open End	US Equity Small Cap (Small Company)	B	B	B	Up	Y	1,000,000
Pear Tree Polaris Small Cap Fund Ordinary Class	USBNX	NAS CM	Open End	US Equity Small Cap (Small Company)	B	B	B	Up	Y	2,500
Pear Tree Quality Fund Institutional Shares	QGIAX	NAS CM	Open End	US Equity Large Cap Blend (Growth)	A-	B	A+	Up	Y	1,000,000
Pear Tree Quality Fund Ordinary Shares	USBOX	NAS CM	Open End	US Equity Large Cap Blend (Growth)	B+	B	A+	Up	Y	2,500
Penn Capital Managed Alpha SMID Cap Equity Fund Inst Cls	PSMPX	NAS CM	Open End	US Equity Small Cap (Growth & Income)	C	C	B	Up	Y	100,000
Penn Capital Special Situations Small Cap Eq Fund Inst Cls	PSCNX	NAS CM	Open End	US Equity Small Cap (Small Company)	C-	C-	B	Up	Y	100,000
Perkins Discovery Fund	PDFDX	NAS CM	Open End	US Equity Small Cap (Aggr Growth)	C+	C+	C+	Up	Y	2,500

★ Expanded analysis of this fund is included in Section II.

Min Additional Investment	TOTAL RETURNS 3-Month Total Return	6-Month Total Return	1-Year Total Return	3-Year Total Return	5-Year Total Return	PERFORMANCE Dividend Yield (TTM)	Expense Ratio	3-Yr Std Deviation	3-Year Beta	ASSETS NAV	Total Assets (MIL)	ASSET ALLOCATION & TURNOVER %Cash	%Stocks	%Bonds	%Other	Turnover Ratio	BULL & BEAR Last Bull Market Total Return	Last Bear Market Total Return	FEES Front End Fee (%)	Back End Fee (%)	Inception Date
50	4.15	6.63	16.04	32.79	94.00	0.43	0.8	9.1	0.82	32.11	2,805	7	93	0	0	19	26.64	-20.42			Apr-15
100	3.93	6.45	10.93	14.19	43.05	0.48	2.3	6.87	0.64	13.92	2,805	7	66	13	0	25			5.75		Oct-11
100	3.72	6.07	10.16	11.68	37.63	0	3.1	6.89	0.64	13.58	2,805	7	66	13	0	25					Oct-11
25,000	3.95	6.54	11.26	15.02	44.88	0.74	2.1	6.89	0.64	13.95	2,805	7	66	13	0	25					Oct-11
100	5.63	9.66	17.79	32.55	98.47	0	2.41	8.69	0.82	17.76	2,805	2	98	0	0	41			5.75		Mar-12
100	5.44	9.23	16.98	29.66	91.37	0	3.16	8.7	0.82	16.98	2,805	2	98	0	0	41					Mar-12
25,000	5.71	9.75	18.13	33.55	101.17	0	2.16	8.65	0.82	18.06	2,805	2	98	0	0	41					Mar-12
	3.88	6.62	13.42	19.24	53.39	1.2	0.68	6.29	0.6	23.01	1,989	1	63	34	1		17.64	-15.77			Apr-07
50	3.80	6.48	13.16	18.33	51.41	0.96	0.93	6.27	0.6	22.66	1,989	1	63	34	1		17.51	-15.86			Aug-71
50	6.02	11.17	24.86	29.73	74.97	1.49	0.9	9.32		25.02	173.0	0	100	0	0		19.47	-22.24			Oct-93
	6.09	11.26	25.14	30.67	77.11	1.7	0.65	9.34		25.13	173.0	0	100	0	0		19.64	-22.18			Apr-06
50	7.55	11.68	19.23				0.9			11.5	152.5	0	99	0	1						Dec-16
	7.56	11.69	19.44				0.65			11.5	152.5	0	99	0	1						Dec-16
50	7.39	12.43	21.96	31.24	95.04	1.16	0.9	10.82	0.98	19.65	212.3	0	98	0	0		24.02	-20.08	5.50		May-13
50	7.33	12.35	21.89	31.15	94.89	1.12	0.9	10.85	0.98	19.69	212.3	0	98	0	0		24.02	-20.08			Jun-97
	7.37	12.49	22.21	32.13	97.27	1.31	0.65	10.84	0.98	20.23	212.3	0	98	0	0		24.22	-20.02			Apr-07
50	5.27	9.81	26.45	37.19	79.61	0.45	1.23	11.62	1.01	16.09	582.6	2	98	0	0		22.48	-23.73	5.50		May-13
50	5.21	9.81	26.42	37.15	79.43	0.46	1.23	11.6	1.01	16.11	582.6	2	98	0	0		22.46	-23.7			Mar-08
	5.31	9.95	26.78	38.24	81.80	0.66	0.98	11.62	1.01	16.22	582.6	2	98	0	0		22.66	-23.65			Mar-08
50	7.07	11.09	20.65				0.96			10.56	733.4	0	99	0	1						Dec-16
	7.18	11.30	20.96				0.71			10.57	733.4	0	99	0	1						Dec-16
50	3.85	5.95	13.57			0.94	1.15			11.14	143.9	6	94	0	0						Mar-16
	3.88	6.07	13.91			1.13	0.9			11.14	143.9	6	94	0	0						Mar-16
50	3.01	7.96	23.00	21.09	43.03	2.06	0.81	11.22	0.94	9.36	671.0	0	97	0	0		12.41	-21.2			Mar-14
	3.09	8.14	23.34	22.13	44.80	2.32	0.56	11.23	0.94	9.19	671.0	0	97	0	0		12.58	-21.12			Jan-11
50	5.52	8.16	8.79	22.55	92.16	0.76	1.19	9.88	0.66	16.38	845.3	4	96	0	0		23.74	-23.91	5.50		May-13
50	5.51	8.14	8.77	22.50	92.16	0.75	1.19	9.87	0.66	16.41	845.3	4	96	0	0		23.74	-23.91			Mar-08
	5.59	8.34	9.10	23.46	94.65	0.98	0.94	9.88	0.66	16.53	845.3	4	96	0	0		23.92	-23.83			Mar-08
250	6.28	10.87	15.70	33.94	92.48	2.13	0.8	8.73	0.76	16.56	997.8	0	95	0	0	25	19.63	-5.55			Nov-96
250	6.24	10.76	15.50	33.06	90.24	1.93	1.05	8.73	0.76	16.56	997.8	0	95	0	0	25	19.47	-5.65			Dec-11
250	6.29	10.92	15.92	34.54	93.46	2.25	0.65	8.73	0.76	16.57	997.8	0	95	0	0	25	19.63	-5.55			Aug-14
250	5.04	11.28	21.71	26.85	74.13	1.06	0.98	10.78	1.02	17.5	93.6	2	98	0	0	30	24.54	-14.51			Nov-91
500	6.02	10.28	3.00	-17.17		0	1.35			7.94	30.1	53	0	47	0	0			5.50		Dec-14
500	5.69	9.85	2.22	-18.75		0	2.1			7.8	30.1	53	0	47	0	0				1.00	Dec-14
10,000	5.90	10.43	3.17	-16.60		0	1.1			7.98	30.1	53	0	47	0	0					Dec-14
50	7.28	11.95	26.67	13.18	7.47	1.64	1.27	14.16	0.88	23.52	111.5	1	96	0	3	47	17.42	-24.95			Apr-96
50	7.19	11.67	26.25	12.21	5.97	1.42	1.65	14.16	0.88	23.2	111.5	1	96	0	3	47	17.27	-25.03			Sep-94
50	4.35	8.92	21.93	6.81		1.13	0.95	13.91	0.84	10.03	62.9	0	95	0	4	42					Jun-13
50	4.24	8.71	21.49	5.85		0.9	1.34	13.98	0.85	9.99	62.9	0	95	0	4	42					Jun-13
50	4.84	10.12	25.68	30.91	59.66	1.06	1.05	12.84	0.97	22.11	2,193	5	95	0	0	15	15.88	-23.58			Dec-98
50	4.71	9.87	25.24	29.82	57.43	0.83	1.43	12.82	0.97	22.17	2,193	5	95	0	0	15	15.72	-23.65			May-98
	4.89	10.15	25.64	30.24	57.94		1.04	12.83	0.97	11.86	2,193	5	95	0	0	15	15.72	-23.65			Feb-17
	3.88	12.66	33.44	35.69	81.65		1.04	11.55	0.92	12.31	899.7	4	94	0	3	46	13.73	-22.06			Feb-17
50	3.84	12.54	33.43	35.68	81.64	1.06	1.08	11.55	0.92	16.04	899.7	4	94	0	3	46	13.72	-22.06			May-08
50	3.79	12.43	33.05	34.50	79.13	0.85	1.45	11.63	0.93	16.03	899.7	4	94	0	3	46	13.63	-22.18			May-08
50	3.38	4.51	6.77	27.15	70.75	0.61	1.17	13.89	0.95	30.78	120.3	2	98	0	0	37	30.77	-21.6			Jan-93
50	3.29	4.30	6.42	26.10	68.50	0.52	1.54	13.9	0.95	26.1	120.3	2	98	0	0	37	30.63	-21.69			Aug-92
50	7.90	10.95	28.90	41.73	101.49	1.01	0.93	9.96	0.89	20.6	134.0	1	99	0	0	31	20.5	-7.76			Mar-91
50	7.75	10.70	28.45	40.55	98.68	0.89	1.3	9.98	0.89	19.26	134.0	1	99	0	0	31	20.12	-7.85			May-85
100	8.79	13.42	19.97			0	1.06			13.09	13.2	4	96	0	0	91					Nov-15
100	7.50	12.18	15.84			0	1.09			11.74	20.8	2	98	0	0	101					Dec-15
100	-2.92	3.29	11.57	8.71	46.68	0	2.5	19.51	1.06	38.55	7.1	6	94	0	0	18	11.63	-26.71			Apr-98

	MARKET		FUND TYPE, CATEGORY & OBJECTIVE		RATINGS					MINIMUMS
Fund Name	Ticker Symbol	Traded On	Fund Type	Category and (Prospectus Objective)	Overall Rating	Reward Rating	Risk Rating	Recent Up/ Downgrade	Open to New Investors	Min Initial Investment
Permanent Portfolio Aggressive Growth Portfolio Class A	PAGDX	NAS CM	Open End	US Equity Large Cap Growth (Aggr Growth)	C+	C+	C+	Down	Y	1,000
Permanent Portfolio Aggressive Growth Portfolio Class C	PAGHX	NAS CM	Open End	US Equity Large Cap Growth (Aggr Growth)	C+	C+	C+	Down	Y	1,000
Permanent Portfolio Aggressive Growth Portfolio Class I	PAGRX	NAS CM	Open End	US Equity Large Cap Growth (Aggr Growth)	C+	B-	C+	Down	Y	1,000
Permanent Portfolio Permanent Portfolio Class A	PRPDX	NAS CM	Open End	Cautious Alloc (Multi-Asset Global)	C+	C+	B-		Y	1,000
Permanent Portfolio Permanent Portfolio Class C	PRPHX	NAS CM	Open End	Cautious Alloc (Multi-Asset Global)	C+	C	B-	Up	Y	1,000
Permanent Portfolio Permanent Portfolio Class I	PRPFX	NAS CM	Open End	Cautious Alloc (Multi-Asset Global)	C+	C+	B-		Y	1,000
Perritt Low Priced Stock Fund Investor Class	PLOWX	NAS CM	Open End	US Equity Small Cap (Small Company)	B+	A-	B	Up	Y	1,000
Perritt MicroCap Opportunities Fund Investor Class	PRCGX	NAS CM	Open End	US Equity Small Cap (Growth)	B	B	B-	Up	Y	1,000
Perritt Ultra MicroCap Fund	PREOX	NAS CM	Open End	US Equity Small Cap (Growth)	B+	A-	B	Up	Y	1,000
Persimmon Long/Short Fund Class A Shares	LSEAX	NAS CM	Open End	Long/Short Equity (Growth)	U	U	U		Y	2,500
Persimmon Long/Short Fund Class I Shares	LSEIX	NAS CM	Open End	Long/Short Equity (Growth)	C+	C	B		Y	100,000
PF Comstock Fund Class P	US69447T6073		Open End	US Equity Large Cap Value (Growth)	B	B	B-	Up	Y	0
PF Developing Growth Fund Class P	US69447T8541		Open End	US Equity Small Cap (Small Company)	C+	C+	C+	Up	Y	0
PF Emerging Markets Fund Class P	US69447T1108		Open End	Emerging Markets Equity (Div Emerging Mkts)	C+	B-	C	Up	Y	0
PF Equity Long/Short Fund Class P	US69448A6800		Open End	Long/Short Equity (Growth)	B-	C+	B+	Up	Y	0
PF Growth Fund Class P	US69447T7063		Open End	US Equity Large Cap Growth (Growth)	A-	B+	A	Up	Y	0
PF International Large-Cap Fund Class P	US69447T1280		Open End	Global Equity Large Cap (World Stock)	B-	B-	B	Up	Y	0
PF International Small-Cap Fund Class P	US69448A7147		Open End	Global Equity Mid/Small Cap (Small Company)	B-	C+	B-	Up	Y	0
PF International Value Fund Class P	US69447T1363		Open End	Global Equity Large Cap (Foreign Stock)	C+	C+	C	Up	Y	0
PF Large-Cap Growth Fund Class P	US69447T8053		Open End	US Equity Large Cap Growth (Growth)	A-	A-	B+	Up	Y	0
PF Large-Cap Value Fund Class P	US69447T8210		Open End	US Equity Large Cap Value (Growth)	B	C+	B	Up	Y	0
PF Main Street® Core Fund Class P	US69447T8889		Open End	US Equity Large Cap Blend (Growth)	B	B-	B+		Y	0
PF Mid-Cap Equity Fund Class P	US69447T8707		Open End	US Equity Mid Cap (Growth)	B+	A	B-	Up	Y	0
PF Mid-Cap Growth Fund Class P	US69447T8624		Open End	US Equity Mid Cap (Growth)	B-	B	C	Up	Y	0
PF Mid-Cap Value Fund Class P	US69448A6644		Open End	US Equity Mid Cap (Growth)	C	C+	B+	Up	Y	0
PF Real Estate Fund Class P	US69447T8392		Open End	Real Estate Sector Equity (Growth)	B-	C+	B	Up	Y	0
PF Small-Cap Value Fund Class P	US69447T8475		Open End	US Equity Small Cap (Small Company)	B+	A-	B	Up	Y	0
PhaseCapital Dynamic Multi-Asset Growth Inst Cls Shares	PHDIX	NAS CM	Open End	Alloc (Multi-Asset Global)	U	U	U		Y	100,000
Phocas Real Estate Fund	PHREX	NAS CM	Open End	Real Estate Sector Equity (Real Estate)	B	B-	B	Up	Y	5,000
Piedmont Select Equity Fund	PSVFX	NAS CM	Open End	US Equity Large Cap Growth (Growth)	B	C+	A-	Up	Y	5,000
PIMCO All Asset All Authority Fund Class A	PAUAX	NAS CM	Open End	Moderate Alloc (Asset Alloc)	C+	C+	C+	Up	Y	1,000
PIMCO All Asset All Authority Fund Class C	PAUCX	NAS CM	Open End	Moderate Alloc (Asset Alloc)	C	C	C+		Y	1,000
PIMCO All Asset All Authority Fund Class D	PAUDX	NAS CM	Open End	Moderate Alloc (Asset Alloc)	C+	C+	C+	Up	Y	1,000
PIMCO All Asset All Authority Fund Class P	PAUPX	NAS CM	Open End	Moderate Alloc (Asset Alloc)	C+	C+	C+	Up	Y	1,000,000
PIMCO All Asset All Authority Fund Institutional Class	PAUIX	NAS CM	Open End	Moderate Alloc (Asset Alloc)	C+	C+	C+	Up	Y	1,000,000
PIMCO All Asset Fund Administrative Class	PAALX	NAS CM	Open End	Moderate Alloc (Asset Alloc)	C+	C+	C+		Y	1,000,000
PIMCO All Asset Fund Class A	PASAX	NAS CM	Open End	Moderate Alloc (Asset Alloc)	C+	C+	C+		Y	1,000
PIMCO All Asset Fund Class C	PASCX	NAS CM	Open End	Moderate Alloc (Asset Alloc)	C+	C+	C+		Y	1,000
PIMCO All Asset Fund Class D	PASDX	NAS CM	Open End	Moderate Alloc (Asset Alloc)	C+	C+	C+		Y	1,000
PIMCO All Asset Fund Class P	PALPX	NAS CM	Open End	Moderate Alloc (Asset Alloc)	C+	C+	C+		Y	1,000,000
PIMCO All Asset Fund Class R	PATRX	NAS CM	Open End	Moderate Alloc (Asset Alloc)	C+	C+	C+		Y	0
PIMCO All Asset Fund Institutional Class	PAAIX	NAS CM	Open End	Moderate Alloc (Asset Alloc)	C+	C+	C+		Y	1,000,000
PIMCO Capital Securities and Financials Fund Class A	PFANX	NAS CM	Open End	US Fixed Income (Growth & Income)	B-	C+	B+	Up	Y	1,000
PIMCO Capital Securities and Financials Fund Class C	PFCNX	NAS CM	Open End	US Fixed Income (Growth & Income)	B-	C	B	Up	Y	1,000
PIMCO Capital Securities and Financials Fund Class D	PFDNX	NAS CM	Open End	US Fixed Income (Growth & Income)	B-	C+	B+	Up	Y	1,000
PIMCO Capital Securities and Financials Fund Class P	PFPNX	NAS CM	Open End	US Fixed Income (Growth & Income)	B-	C+	A-	Up	Y	1,000,000
PIMCO Capital Securities & Financials Fund Inst Cls	PFINX	NAS CM	Open End	US Fixed Income (Growth & Income)	B-	C+	B+	Up	Y	1,000,000
PIMCO CommoditiesPLUS® Strategy Fund Administrative Class	PCPSX	NAS CM	Open End	Commodities Broad Basket (Growth & Income)	C	C	C-	Up	Y	1,000,000
PIMCO CommoditiesPLUS® Strategy Fund Class A	PCLAX	NAS CM	Open End	Commodities Broad Basket (Growth & Income)	C	C	C-	Up	Y	1,000
PIMCO CommoditiesPLUS® Strategy Fund Class C	PCPCX	NAS CM	Open End	Commodities Broad Basket (Growth & Income)	C	C	C-	Up	Y	1,000
PIMCO CommoditiesPLUS® Strategy Fund Class D	PCLDX	NAS CM	Open End	Commodities Broad Basket (Growth & Income)	C	C	C-	Up	Y	1,000
PIMCO CommoditiesPLUS® Strategy Fund Class P	PCLPX	NAS CM	Open End	Commodities Broad Basket (Growth & Income)	C	C	C-	Up	Y	1,000,000

★Expanded analysis of this fund is included in Section II.

Min Additional Investment	3-Month Total Return	6-Month Total Return	1-Year Total Return	3-Year Total Return	5-Year Total Return	Dividend Yield (TTM)	Expense Ratio	3-Yr Std Deviation	3-Year Beta	NAV	Total Assets (MIL)	%Cash	%Stocks	%Bonds	%Other	Turnover Ratio	Last Bull Market Total Return	Last Bear Market Total Return	Front End Fee (%)	Back End Fee (%)	Inception Date
TOTAL RETURNS						PERFORMANCE				ASSETS		ASSET ALLOCATION & TURNOVER					BULL & BEAR		FEES		
100	5.63	13.13	20.88	19.57	86.97	0.39	1.46	14.31	1.11	63.27	29.0	2	98	0	0		25.72	-25.33	5.00		May-16
100	5.43	12.72	19.98	16.94	80.14	0.03	2.21	14.3	1.11	62.83	29.0	2	98	0	0		25.17	-25.56		1.00	May-16
100	5.71	13.31	21.20	20.50	89.37	0.5	1.21	14.31	1.11	63.33	29.0	2	98	0	0		25.9	-25.25			Jan-90
100	2.70	6.64	11.13	12.95	11.18	0.69	1.07	7.09	29.61	41.12	2,525	1	38	34	27		8.05	-8.4	5.00		May-16
100	2.52	6.25	10.31	10.45	7.10	0.55	1.82	7.08	29.45	40.9	2,525	1	38	34	27		7.58	-8.68		1.00	May-16
100	2.77	6.76	11.42	13.79	12.56	0.76	0.82	7.09	29.48	41.18	2,525	1	38	34	27		8.21	-8.3			Dec-82
50	2.25	7.80	13.73	35.29	109.83	0	1.4	13.65	0.9	19.19	8.0	4	96	0	0	75					Feb-14
50	0.67	6.41	5.33	24.80	86.39	0.23	1.23	13.11	0.83	30	199.8	3	97	0	0	18	30.85	-28.97			May-88
50	3.94	10.49	17.93	39.73	110.22	0	1.78	10.71	0.65	17.27	69.5	7	93	0	0	43	16.44	-22.66			Aug-04
100	1.88	-4.53	-2.28	8.41		0	3.27	5.63	0.41		28.3	81	19	0	0	214			5.00		Dec-12
100	2.48	5.39	13.39	10.35	24.59	0	2.76	5.76	0.43	10.82	23.8	32	66	0	2	207					Dec-12
	7.36	13.78	17.65	28.56	94.75	1.97	0.89	13.08	1.22	15.96	191.0	4	96	0	0	22	25.07	-19.98			Sep-01
	7.71	15.44	30.34	15.05	59.40	0	0.75	15.79	1	13.83	9.3	1	99	0	0	123	28.97	-26.08			Sep-01
	4.96	13.91	35.34	24.04	29.78	0.4	0.95	14.45	0.86	16.74	208.1	3	97	0	0	69	18.34	-23.22			Sep-05
	3.60	11.14	18.21			16.29	1.31			9.71	74.9	39	16	45	0	0					Apr-15
	6.54	12.03	31.37	43.29	113.73	0.08	0.7	11.05	0.99	24.1	142.3	1	99	0	0	43	24.39	-18.38			Sep-01
	3.73	8.07	27.55	25.87	43.40	1.57	1	11.57	0.92	21.1	179.6	0	99	0	1	16	19.09	-23.45			Sep-01
	4.39	13.18	31.83			3.17	1.1			11.36	44.3	1	99	0	0	53					Jan-15
	3.45	9.63	22.07	21.96	35.53	2.72	0.8	12.26	0.96	10.21	173.4	1	99	0	0	67	14.64	-24.75			Sep-01
	7.60	13.88	34.00	41.94	117.54	0	0.86	12.41	1.09	10.02	95.3	0	100	0	0	80	29.66	-15.37			Sep-01
	4.61	7.02	13.99	23.63	86.58	1.08	0.8	10.53	0.99	17.71	432.3	3	97	0	0	21	25.81	-16.37			Sep-01
	2.13	6.84	17.17	34.27	101.14	1.06	0.6	9.99	0.96	14.37	303.4	2	98	0	0	51	26.59	-14.88			Sep-05
	7.50	13.80	24.37	48.29	116.27	1.12	0.8	10.21	0.92	10.9	70.6	0	100	0	0	101	22.5	-21.46			Dec-04
	7.23	13.19	27.93	27.16	87.62	1	0.83	12.11	1.05	7.8	15.3	1	99	0	0	19	16.81	-21.52			Sep-01
	5.06	8.72	15.58			1.05	0.92			12.7	200.5	2	98	0	0	56					Jul-15
	3.87	4.21	3.31	10.49	49.89	2.4	1.05	13.56	0.66	12.87	36.9	1	99	0	0	27	31.67	-18			Dec-04
	3.86	9.01	8.83	37.02	99.27	0.51	0.9	14.98	1.03	11.49	119.6	1	99	0	0	49	21.9	-18.45			Jun-07
10,000	1.57						1.39			10.15	10.1										Oct-17
200	2.66	3.74	7.35	15.14	66.30	0.97	1.5	13.03	0.99	32.39	12.8	2	98	0	0	26	31.95	-18.01			Sep-06
250	4.42	6.99	15.76	20.89	67.29	0	1.36	9.71	0.9	15.5	25.6	8	92	0	0	45	26.06	-14.41			Apr-05
50	1.96	5.06	11.57	11.08	1.15	4.47	1.65	8.54	0.42	8.93	8,125	-7	17	78	11	51	13.04	-7.39	5.50		Jul-05
50	1.75	4.63	10.75	8.44	-2.67	3.83	2.4	8.6	0.42	8.92	8,125	-7	17	78	11	51	12.47	-7.66		1.00	Jul-05
50	1.97	5.10	11.65	11.13	1.37	4.54	1.65	8.55	0.42	8.89	8,125	-7	17	78	11	51	13	-7.36			Jul-05
	2.17	5.26	12.06	12.25	2.92	4.8	1.3	8.59	0.43	8.93	8,125	-7	17	78	11	51	13.15	-7.2			Jul-08
	2.09	5.32	12.04	12.59	3.46	4.89	1.2	8.61	0.43	8.92	8,125	-7	17	78	11	51	13.3	-7.24			Oct-03
	3.05	6.41	13.68	16.90	18.38	4.12	1.12	7.72	1.5	12.18	19,572	3	33	59	4	54	11.38	-7.4			Dec-02
50	3.00	6.30	13.49	16.14	16.94	3.95	1.32	7.73	1.51	12.17	19,572	3	33	59	4	54	11.21	-7.47	3.75		Apr-03
50	2.80	5.90	12.65	13.55	12.60	3.26	2.07	7.76	1.51	12.12	19,572	3	33	59	4	54	10.77	-7.79		1.00	Apr-03
50	2.92	6.24	13.45	16.30	17.37	4	1.32	7.75	1.51	12.15	19,572	3	33	59	4	54	11.25	-7.41			Apr-03
	3.10	6.50	13.84	17.42	19.27	4.27	0.97	7.75	1.52	12.18	19,572	3	33	59	4	54	11.43	-7.32			Apr-08
	2.86	6.11	13.12	15.13	15.46	3.74	1.57	7.74	1.51	12.09	19,572	3	33	59	4	54	11.07	-7.62			Jan-06
	3.13	6.48	13.98	17.71	19.75	4.37	0.87	7.74	1.52	12.15	19,572	3	33	59	4	54	11.58	-7.36			Jul-02
50	1.81	4.81	12.93			6.19	1.15			10.51	160.0	18	0	23	8	123			3.75		Apr-15
50	1.57	4.40	12.04			5.66	1.9			10.45	160.0	18	0	23	8	123				1.00	Apr-15
50	1.81	4.82	12.96			6.02	1.15			10.49	160.0	18	0	23	8	123					Apr-15
	1.75	4.88	13.19			6.33	0.9			10.51	160.0	18	0	23	8	123					Apr-15
	1.86	4.98	13.27			6.33	0.8			10.52	160.0	18	0	23	8	123					Apr-15
	10.21	20.02	10.56	-6.84	-30.50	8.62	0.99	18.69	1.01	6.24	3,046	29	0	25	46	211	10.35	-21.63			Jul-14
50	10.11	19.75	10.27	-7.50	-31.36	8.56	1.19	18.79	1.02	6.16	3,046	29	0	25	46	211	10.21	-21.75	5.50		May-10
50	9.94	19.34	9.32	-9.57	-33.85	8.54	1.94	18.69	1.01	5.93	3,046	29	0	25	46	211	9.76	-22.04		1.00	May-10
50	10.11	19.88	10.14	-7.60	-31.40	8.59	1.19	18.75	1.01	6.16	3,046	29	0	25	46	211	10.27	-21.78			May-10
	10.11	19.97	10.52	-6.48	-30.04	8.85	0.84	18.66	1.01	6.22	3,046	29	0	25	46	211	10.45	-21.57			May-10

	MARKET		FUND TYPE, CATEGORY & OBJECTIVE		RATINGS					MINIMUMS
Fund Name	Ticker Symbol	Traded On	Fund Type	Category and (Prospectus Objective)	Overall Rating	Reward Rating	Risk Rating	Recent Up/ Downgrade	Open to New Investors	Min Initial Investment
PIMCO CommoditiesPLUS® Strategy Fund Institutional Class	PCLIX	NAS CM	Open End	Commodities Broad Basket (Growth & Income)	C	C	C-	Up	Y	1,000,000
PIMCO CommodityRealReturn Strategy Fund Administrative Cls	PCRRX	NAS CM	Open End	Commodities Broad Basket (Growth & Income)	D+	C-	D+	Up	Y	1,000,000
PIMCO CommodityRealReturn Strategy Fund Class A	PCRAX	NAS CM	Open End	Commodities Broad Basket (Growth & Income)	D+	C-	D+	Up	Y	1,000
PIMCO CommodityRealReturn Strategy Fund Class C	PCRCX	NAS CM	Open End	Commodities Broad Basket (Growth & Income)	D+	C-	D	Up	Y	1,000
PIMCO CommodityRealReturn Strategy Fund Class D	PCRDX	NAS CM	Open End	Commodities Broad Basket (Growth & Income)	D+	C-	D	Up	Y	1,000
PIMCO CommodityRealReturn Strategy Fund Class P	PCRPX	NAS CM	Open End	Commodities Broad Basket (Growth & Income)	C-	C-	D+	Up	Y	1,000,000
PIMCO CommodityRealReturn Strategy Fund Class R	PCSRX	NAS CM	Open End	Commodities Broad Basket (Growth & Income)	D+	C-	D	Up	Y	0
PIMCO CommodityRealReturn Strategy Fund Institutional Cls	PCRIX	NAS CM	Open End	Commodities Broad Basket (Growth & Income)	C-	C-	D+	Up	Y	1,000,000
PIMCO Credit Absolute Return Fund Class A	PZCRX	NAS CM	Open End	Other Alternative (Income)	B-	C	B	Up	Y	1,000
PIMCO Credit Absolute Return Fund Class C	PCCRX	NAS CM	Open End	Other Alternative (Income)	C+	C	B	Down	Y	1,000
PIMCO Credit Absolute Return Fund Class D	PDCRX	NAS CM	Open End	Other Alternative (Income)	B-	C	B	Up	Y	1,000
PIMCO Credit Absolute Return Fund Class P	PPCRX	NAS CM	Open End	Other Alternative (Income)	B-	C+	B	Up	Y	1,000,000
PIMCO Credit Absolute Return Fund Institutional	PCARX	NAS CM	Open End	Other Alternative (Income)	B-	C+	B	Up	Y	1,000,000
PIMCO Dividend and Income Fund Class A	PQIZX	NAS CM	Open End	Alloc (Growth & Income)	C+	C+	C	Up	Y	1,000
PIMCO Dividend and Income Fund Class C	PQICX	NAS CM	Open End	Alloc (Growth & Income)	C+	C+	C	Up	Y	1,000
PIMCO Dividend and Income Fund Class D	PQIDX	NAS CM	Open End	Alloc (Growth & Income)	C+	C+	C	Up	Y	1,000
PIMCO Dividend and Income Fund Class P	PQIPX	NAS CM	Open End	Alloc (Growth & Income)	C+	C+	C	Up	Y	1,000,000
PIMCO Dividend and Income Fund Institutional Class	PQIIX	NAS CM	Open End	Alloc (Growth & Income)	C+	C+	C	Up	Y	1,000,000
PIMCO EqS® Long/Short Fund Class A	PMHAX	NAS CM	Open End	Long/Short Equity (Growth)	B	C	A-	Up	Y	1,000
PIMCO EqS® Long/Short Fund Class C	PMHCX	NAS CM	Open End	Long/Short Equity (Growth)	B	C	A-	Up	Y	1,000
PIMCO EqS® Long/Short Fund Class D	PMHDX	NAS CM	Open End	Long/Short Equity (Growth)	B	C	A-	Up	Y	1,000
PIMCO EqS® Long/Short Fund Class P	PMHBX	NAS CM	Open End	Long/Short Equity (Growth)	B	C+	A-	Up	Y	1,000,000
PIMCO EqS® Long/Short Fund Institutional Class	PMHIX	NAS CM	Open End	Long/Short Equity (Growth)	B-	C+	B	Up	Y	1,000,000
PIMCO Global Multi-Asset Fund Class A	PGMAX	NAS CM	Open End	Alloc (Growth & Income)	C+	C+	B-	Down	Y	1,000
PIMCO Global Multi-Asset Fund Class C	PGMCX	NAS CM	Open End	Alloc (Growth & Income)	B-	C+	B	Up	Y	1,000
PIMCO Global Multi-Asset Fund Class D	PGMDX	NAS CM	Open End	Alloc (Growth & Income)	C+	C+	B-	Down	Y	1,000
PIMCO Global Multi-Asset Fund Class P	PGAPX	NAS CM	Open End	Alloc (Growth & Income)	B-	C+	B-	Down	Y	1,000,000
PIMCO Global Multi-Asset Fund Class R	PGMRX	NAS CM	Open End	Alloc (Growth & Income)	C+	C+	B-	Down	Y	0
PIMCO Global Multi-Asset Fund Institutional Class	PGAIX	NAS CM	Open End	Alloc (Growth & Income)	B-	C+	B-	Down	Y	1,000,000
PIMCO Global StocksPLUS and Income Fund	PGP	NYSE	Closed End	Global Equity (Multi-Asset Global)	B	B+	B-	Up	Y	
PIMCO Inflation Response Multi-Asset Fund Class A	PZRMX	NAS CM	Open End	Cautious Alloc (Growth & Income)	C+	C	B-	Up	Y	1,000
PIMCO Inflation Response Multi-Asset Fund Class P	PPRMX	NAS CM	Open End	Cautious Alloc (Growth & Income)	C+	C	B-	Up	Y	1,000,000
PIMCO Inflation Response Multi-Asset Fund Institutional	PIRMX	NAS CM	Open End	Cautious Alloc (Growth & Income)	C+	C	B-	Up	Y	1,000,000
PIMCO Multi-Strategy Alternative Fund Class A	PXAAX	NAS CM	Open End	Multialternative (Growth & Income)	C+	C	B	Up	Y	1,000
PIMCO Multi-Strategy Alternative Fund Class D	PXADX	NAS CM	Open End	Multialternative (Growth & Income)	C+	C	B	Up	Y	1,000
PIMCO Multi-Strategy Alternative Fund Class P	PXAPX	NAS CM	Open End	Multialternative (Growth & Income)	C+	C	B	Up	Y	1,000,000
PIMCO Multi-Strategy Alternative Fund Institutional Class	PXAIX	NAS CM	Open End	Multialternative (Growth & Income)	C+	C	B	Up	Y	1,000,000
PIMCO RAE Fundamental Advantage PLUS Fund Class A	PTFAX	NAS CM	Open End	Market Neutral (Growth & Income)	C-	D+	C	Up	Y	1,000
PIMCO RAE Fundamental Advantage PLUS Fund Class C	PTRCX	NAS CM	Open End	Market Neutral (Growth & Income)	C-	D+	C	Up	Y	1,000
PIMCO RAE Fundamental Advantage PLUS Fund Class D	PFSDX	NAS CM	Open End	Market Neutral (Growth & Income)	C-	D+	C	Up	Y	1,000
PIMCO RAE Fundamental Advantage PLUS Fund Class P	PFAPX	NAS CM	Open End	Market Neutral (Growth & Income)	C	C-	C	Up	Y	1,000,000
PIMCO RAE Fundamental Advantage PLUS Fund Inst Cls	PFATX	NAS CM	Open End	Market Neutral (Growth & Income)	C	C-	C	Up	Y	1,000,000
PIMCO RAE Fundamental Emerging Markets Fund Class A	PEAFX	NAS CM	Open End	Emerging Markets Equity (Div Emerging Mkts)	B-	B	C	Up	Y	1,000
PIMCO RAE Fundamental Emerging Markets Fund Class C	PECFX	NAS CM	Open End	Emerging Markets Equity (Div Emerging Mkts)	C+	B-	C	Up	Y	1,000
PIMCO RAE Fundamental Emerging Markets Fund Class P	PEPFX	NAS CM	Open End	Emerging Markets Equity (Div Emerging Mkts)	B-	B	C	Up	Y	1,000,000
PIMCO RAE Fundamental Emerging Mkts Fund Inst Cls	PEIFX	NAS CM	Open End	Emerging Markets Equity (Div Emerging Mkts)	B-	B	C	Up	Y	1,000,000
PIMCO RAE Fundamental Global ex-US Fund Class A	PZRAX	NAS CM	Open End	Global Equity Large Cap (Growth & Income)	C	C+	B-	Up	Y	1,000
PIMCO RAE Fundamental Global ex-US Fund Class C	PZRCX	NAS CM	Open End	Global Equity Large Cap (Growth & Income)	C	C+	B-	Up	Y	1,000
PIMCO RAE Fundamental Global ex-US Fund Class P	PZRPX	NAS CM	Open End	Global Equity Large Cap (Growth & Income)	C	C+	B-	Up	Y	1,000,000
PIMCO RAE Fundamental Global ex-US Fund Institutional Cls	PZRIX	NAS CM	Open End	Global Equity Large Cap (Growth & Income)	C	C+	B-	Up	Y	1,000,000
PIMCO RAE Fundamental Global Fund Class A	PFQAX	NAS CM	Open End	Global Equity (Growth & Income)	C	C+	B-	Up	Y	1,000
PIMCO RAE Fundamental Global Fund Class C	PFQCX	NAS CM	Open End	Global Equity (Growth & Income)	C	C+	B-	Up	Y	1,000

★ Expanded analysis of this fund is included in Section II.

	TOTAL RETURNS					PERFORMANCE				ASSETS		ASSET ALLOCATION & TURNOVER					BULL & BEAR		FEES		
Min Additional Investment	3-Month Total Return	6-Month Total Return	1-Year Total Return	3-Year Total Return	5-Year Total Return	Dividend Yield (TTM)	Expense Ratio	3-Yr Std Deviation	3-Year Beta	NAV	Total Assets (MIL)	%Cash	%Stocks	%Bonds	%Other	Turnover Ratio	Last Bull Market Total Return	Last Bear Market Total Return	Front End Fee (%)	Back End Fee (%)	Inception Date
	10.27	20.14	10.83	-6.13	-29.59	8.95	0.74	18.7	1.01	6.25	3,046	29	0	25	46	211	10.51	-21.55			May-10
	5.37	8.61	2.51	-14.47	-39.72	6.04	0.99	14.44	1.1	6.65	6,168	-8	0	85	23	176	6.04	-20.06			Feb-03
50	5.33	8.53	2.33	-14.82	-40.37	5.89	1.19	14.3	1.09	6.62	6,168	-8	0	85	23	176	5.83	-20.03	5.50		Nov-02
50	5.05	8.19	1.56	-16.82	-42.54	5.62	1.94	14.34	1.09	6.3	6,168	-8	0	85	23	176	5.58	-20.32		1.00	Nov-02
50	5.16	8.49	2.15	-14.93	-40.40	5.86	1.19	14.3	1.09	6.63	6,168	-8	0	85	23	176	5.98	-20.08			Nov-02
	5.32	8.71	2.60	-14.00	-39.37	6.11	0.84	14.38	1.09	6.75	6,168	-8	0	85	23	176	6.07	-19.9			Apr-08
	5.06	8.25	2.00	-15.63	-41.19	5.82	1.44	14.4	1.1	6.47	6,168	-8	0	85	23	176	5.66	-20.11			Mar-10
	5.33	8.75	2.69	-13.76	-39.08	6.18	0.74	14.42	1.1	6.77	6,168	-8	0	85	23	176	6.13	-19.84			Jun-02
50	0.50	2.51	6.55	11.61	14.13	3.49	1.3	3.43	14.08	10.16	461.3	62	0	38	0	146	5.17		3.75		Aug-11
50	0.31	2.13	5.73	9.08	10.00	3.07	2.05	3.4	13.88	10.03	461.3	62	0	38	0	146	4.8			1.00	Aug-11
50	0.51	2.56	6.51	11.57	14.21	3.61	1.3	3.43	14.04	10.13	461.3	62	0	38	0	146	5.24				Aug-11
	0.60	2.69	6.82	12.57	15.90	3.84	1	3.48	13.32	10.11	461.3	62	0	38	0	146	5.43				Aug-11
	0.51	2.71	6.94	12.84	16.45	3.82	0.9	3.46	14.49	10.14	461.3	62	0	38	0	146	5.49				Aug-11
50	4.06	9.11	15.73	13.55	39.16	2.23	1.14	9.53	0.86	11.87	338.3	-12	74	37	0	93			5.50		Dec-11
50	3.86	8.65	14.84	10.96	33.96	1.39	1.89	9.56	0.86	11.84	338.3	-12	74	37	0	93				1.00	Dec-11
50	4.14	9.10	15.81	13.60	39.21	2.19	1.14	9.51	0.86	11.88	338.3	-12	74	37	0	93					Dec-11
	4.12	9.22	16.07	14.55	41.03	2.47	0.89	9.53	0.86	11.9	338.3	-12	74	37	0	93					Dec-11
	4.16	9.28	16.20	14.81	41.58	2.59	0.79	9.56	0.86	11.88	338.3	-12	74	37	0	93					Dec-11
50	1.70	1.19	9.66	11.25	48.46	2.73	1.84	5.18	2.06	11.55	534.3	58	46	-4	0	251	2.89	-7.7	5.50		Apr-12
50	1.50	0.80	8.74	8.66	43.00	2.44	2.59	5.15	3.32	11.1	534.3	58	46	-4	0	251	2.45	-7.98		1.00	Apr-12
50	1.70	1.19	9.54	11.21	48.49	2.63	1.84	5.16	2.31	11.57	534.3	58	46	-4	0	251	2.89	-7.7			Apr-12
	1.76	1.26	9.82	12.02	50.30	2.81	1.59	5.22	2.04	11.7	534.3	58	46	-4	0	251	3.04	-7.6			Apr-12
	1.75	1.34	9.95	12.39	51.20	2.85	1.49	5.17	1.42	11.78	534.3	58	46	-4	0	251	3.1	-7.56			Apr-12
50	3.17	6.56	14.25	17.70	15.96	1.14	1.41	7.99		12.65	503.2	-29	56	54	16	327	7.42	-10.13	5.50		Oct-08
50	2.97	6.15	13.37	15.14	11.78	0.49	2.16	7.97		12.32	503.2	-29	56	54	16	327	6.9	-10.44		1.00	Oct-08
50	3.26	6.64	14.24	17.79	16.05	1.14	1.41	7.98		12.66	503.2	-29	56	54	16	327	7.41	-10.13			Oct-08
	3.33	6.77	14.70	19.31	18.72	1.46	1.06	7.98		12.74	503.2	-29	56	54	16	327	7.73	-9.96			Oct-08
	3.14	6.42	13.93	16.87	14.60	0.92	1.66	7.98		12.52	503.2	-29	56	54	16	327	7.3	-10.26			Oct-08
	3.35	6.83	14.78	19.69	19.32	1.54	0.96	8.02		12.76	503.2	-29	56	54	16	327	7.85	-9.99			Oct-08
	2.69	8.31	30.07	49.89	97.45	15.58	0	11.62	0.82	11.2	121.1	-296	101	280	0	25	25.4	-24.33			May-05
50	2.85	5.76	7.95	10.06	0.83	3.1	1.14	6.42		8.68	1,017	-3	10	60	32	184	6.82		5.50		Aug-11
	2.93	5.92	8.37	11.25	2.69	3.59	0.79	6.41		8.75	1,017	-3	10	60	32	184	6.95				Aug-11
	2.95	6.09	8.58	11.63	3.19	3.68	0.69	6.39		8.75	1,017	-3	10	60	32	184	6.97				Aug-11
50	2.46	3.61	3.82	6.90		3.62	1.56			10	111.7	-23	38	57	28	110			3.75		Dec-14
50	2.41	3.57	3.78	6.66		3.69	1.56			9.87	111.7	-23	38	57	28	110					Dec-14
	2.52	3.78	4.10	7.73		3.7	1.26			9.94	111.7	-23	38	57	28	110					Dec-14
	2.59	3.85	4.28	8.05		3.75	1.16			9.95	111.7	-23	38	57	28	110					Dec-14
50	1.09	1.89	-1.09	-1.72	-0.05	0.62	1.29	3.47	5.26	9.93	596.4	84	-13	5	21	398	4.37	-5.31	3.75		Jul-08
50	0.91	1.43	-1.78	-4.07	-3.74	0.39	2.04	3.49	4.66	9.88	596.4	84	-13	5	21	398	4.08	-5.6		1.00	Jul-08
50	1.01	1.81	-1.09	-1.88	-0.15	0.6	1.29	3.49	5.87	9.88	596.4	84	-13	5	21	398	4.62	-5.33			Jul-08
	1.16	2.03	-0.74	-0.78	1.57	0.74	0.99	3.48	5.43	10.12	596.4	84	-13	5	21	398	4.42	-5.09			Jun-10
	1.20	2.00	-0.74	-0.68	1.91	0.79	0.89	3.44	5.05	10.14	596.4	84	-13	5	21	398	4.7	-5.11			Feb-08
50	6.81	15.40	28.87	22.85	28.27	2.11	1.1			11.51	1,842	0	99	0	0	43	17.38	-26.83	3.75		Jun-15
50	6.54	14.94	27.90	19.95	23.40	2.1	1.85			11.33	1,842	0	99	0	0	43	16.87	-27.06		1.00	Jun-15
	6.78	15.39	29.03	23.50	29.59	2.23	0.85			11.49	1,842	0	99	0	0	43	17.55	-26.75			Jun-15
	6.91	15.60	29.33	24.17	30.55	2.25	0.75			11.55	1,842	0	99	0	0	43	17.61	-26.72			Jun-15
50	4.27	11.96	25.55			2.09	0.9			11.24	86.4	0	100	0	0	8			3.75		Jun-15
50	4.10	11.55	24.70			1.76	1.65			11.12	86.4	0	100	0	0	8				1.00	Jun-15
	4.28	12.04	25.73			2.09	0.65			11.27	86.4	0	100	0	0	8					Jun-15
	4.30	12.16	25.97			2.1	0.55			11.3	86.4	0	100	0	0	8					Jun-15
50	5.32	11.91	21.91			1.95	0.85			11.28	428.9	0	100	0	0	13			3.75		Jun-15
50	5.18	11.54	21.02			1.72	1.6			11.13	428.9	0	100	0	0	13				1.00	Jun-15

Fund Name	MARKET Ticker Symbol	Traded On	FUND TYPE, CATEGORY & OBJECTIVE Fund Type	Category and (Prospectus Objective)	RATINGS Overall Rating	Reward Rating	Risk Rating	Recent Up/ Downgrade	MINIMUMS Open to New Investors	Min Initial Investment
PIMCO RAE Fundamental Global Fund Class P	PFQPX	NAS CM	Open End	Global Equity (Growth & Income)	C	C+	B-	Up	Y	1,000,000
PIMCO RAE Fundamental Global Fund Institutional Class	PFQIX	NAS CM	Open End	Global Equity (Growth & Income)	C	C+	B-	Up	Y	1,000,000
PIMCO RAE Fundamental International Fund Class A	PPYAX	NAS CM	Open End	Global Equity Large Cap (Growth & Income)	C	C+	B-	Up	Y	1,000
PIMCO RAE Fundamental International Fund Class C	PPYCX	NAS CM	Open End	Global Equity Large Cap (Growth & Income)	C	C+	B-	Up	Y	1,000
PIMCO RAE Fundamental International Fund Class P	PPYPX	NAS CM	Open End	Global Equity Large Cap (Growth & Income)	C	C+	B-	Up	Y	1,000,000
PIMCO RAE Fundamental International Fund Institutional Cls	PPYIX	NAS CM	Open End	Global Equity Large Cap (Growth & Income)	C	C+	B-	Up	Y	1,000,000
PIMCO RAE Fundamental PLUS EMG Fund Administrative Class	PEFAX	NAS CM	Open End	Emerging Markets Equity (Growth & Income)	B	B+	C	Up	Y	1,000,000
PIMCO RAE Fundamental PLUS EMG Fund Class A	PEFFX	NAS CM	Open End	Emerging Markets Equity (Growth & Income)	B-	B+	C	Up	Y	1,000
PIMCO RAE Fundamental PLUS EMG Fund Class C	PEFCX	NAS CM	Open End	Emerging Markets Equity (Growth & Income)	B-	B	C	Up	Y	1,000
PIMCO RAE Fundamental PLUS EMG Fund Class D	PEFDX	NAS CM	Open End	Emerging Markets Equity (Growth & Income)	B-	B+	C	Up	Y	1,000
PIMCO RAE Fundamental PLUS EMG Fund Class P	PEFPX	NAS CM	Open End	Emerging Markets Equity (Growth & Income)	B	B+	C	Up	Y	1,000,000
PIMCO RAE Fundamental PLUS EMG Fund Institutional Class	PEFIX	NAS CM	Open End	Emerging Markets Equity (Growth & Income)	B	B+	C	Up	Y	1,000,000
PIMCO RAE Fundamental PLUS Fund Administrative Class	PXTAX	NAS CM	Open End	US Equity Large Cap Value (Growth & Income)	B	B	B-	Up	Y	1,000,000
PIMCO RAE Fundamental PLUS Fund Class A	PIXAX	NAS CM	Open End	US Equity Large Cap Value (Growth & Income)	B	B	B-	Up	Y	1,000
PIMCO RAE Fundamental PLUS Fund Class C	PIXCX	NAS CM	Open End	US Equity Large Cap Value (Growth & Income)	B-	B-	C+	Down	Y	1,000
PIMCO RAE Fundamental PLUS Fund Class D	PIXDX	NAS CM	Open End	US Equity Large Cap Value (Growth & Income)	B	B	B-	Up	Y	1,000
PIMCO RAE Fundamental PLUS Fund Class P	PIXPX	NAS CM	Open End	US Equity Large Cap Value (Growth & Income)	B	B	B-	Up	Y	1,000,000
PIMCO RAE Fundamental PLUS Fund Institutional Class	PXTIX	NAS CM	Open End	US Equity Large Cap Value (Growth & Income)	B	B	B-	Up	Y	1,000,000
PIMCO RAE Fundamental PLUS International Fund Class A	PTSOX	NAS CM	Open End	Global Equity Large Cap (Growth & Income)	B-	B	C	Up	Y	1,000
PIMCO RAE Fundamental PLUS International Fund Class C	PTSKX	NAS CM	Open End	Global Equity Large Cap (Growth & Income)	B-	B	C	Up	Y	1,000
PIMCO RAE Fundamental PLUS International Fund Class D	PTSLX	NAS CM	Open End	Global Equity Large Cap (Growth & Income)	B-	B	C	Up	Y	1,000
PIMCO RAE Fundamental PLUS International Fund Class P	PTIPX	NAS CM	Open End	Global Equity Large Cap (Growth & Income)	B-	B	C	Up	Y	1,000,000
PIMCO RAE Fundamental PLUS Intl Fund Inst Cls	PTSIX	NAS CM	Open End	Global Equity Large Cap (Growth & Income)	B-	B	C	Up	Y	1,000,000
PIMCO RAE Fundamental PLUS Small Fund Class A	PCFAX	NAS CM	Open End	US Equity Small Cap (Small Company)	B+	A-	B-	Up	Y	1,000
PIMCO RAE Fundamental PLUS Small Fund Class C	PCFEX	NAS CM	Open End	US Equity Small Cap (Small Company)	B+	A-	B-	Up	Y	1,000
PIMCO RAE Fundamental PLUS Small Fund Class D	PCFDX	NAS CM	Open End	US Equity Small Cap (Small Company)	B+	A-	B-	Up	Y	1,000
PIMCO RAE Fundamental PLUS Small Fund Class P	PCCPX	NAS CM	Open End	US Equity Small Cap (Small Company)	B+	A	B-	Up	Y	1,000,000
PIMCO RAE Fundamental PLUS Small Fund Institutional Class	PCFIX	NAS CM	Open End	US Equity Small Cap (Small Company)	B+	A	B-	Up	Y	1,000,000
PIMCO RAE Fundamental US Fund Class A	PKAAX	NAS CM	Open End	US Equity Large Cap Value (Growth & Income)	B	B-	B		Y	1,000
PIMCO RAE Fundamental US Fund Class C	PKACX	NAS CM	Open End	US Equity Large Cap Value (Growth & Income)	B-	B-	B	Down	Y	1,000
PIMCO RAE Fundamental US Fund Class P	PKAPX	NAS CM	Open End	US Equity Large Cap Value (Growth & Income)	B	B-	B		Y	1,000,000
PIMCO RAE Fundamental US Fund Institutional Class	PKAIX	NAS CM	Open End	US Equity Large Cap Value (Growth & Income)	B	B-	B		Y	1,000,000
PIMCO RAE Fundamental US Small Fund Class A	PMJAX	NAS CM	Open End	US Equity Small Cap (Small Company)	B	B+	B	Up	Y	1,000
PIMCO RAE Fundamental US Small Fund Class C	PMJCX	NAS CM	Open End	US Equity Small Cap (Small Company)	B	B	B-	Up	Y	1,000
PIMCO RAE Fundamental US Small Fund Class P	PMJPX	NAS CM	Open End	US Equity Small Cap (Small Company)	B	A-	B	Up	Y	1,000,000
PIMCO RAE Fundamental US Small Fund Institutional Class	PMJIX	NAS CM	Open End	US Equity Small Cap (Small Company)	B+	A-	B	Up	Y	1,000,000
PIMCO RAE Low Volatility PLUS EMG Fund Class A	PLVVX	NAS CM	Open End	Emerging Markets Equity (Div Emerging Mkts)	C+	C+	C	Up	Y	1,000
PIMCO RAE Low Volatility PLUS EMG Fund Class P	PLVWX	NAS CM	Open End	Emerging Markets Equity (Div Emerging Mkts)	C+	C+	C	Up	Y	1,000,000
PIMCO RAE Low Volatility PLUS EMG Fund Institutional Class	PLVLX	NAS CM	Open End	Emerging Markets Equity (Div Emerging Mkts)	C+	C+	C	Up	Y	1,000,000
PIMCO RAE Low Volatility PLUS Fund Class A	PXLVX	NAS CM	Open End	US Equity Large Cap Value (Growth & Income)	B-	B-	B-	Down	Y	1,000
PIMCO RAE Low Volatility PLUS Fund Class C	POLVX	NAS CM	Open End	US Equity Large Cap Value (Growth & Income)	B-	B-	B-	Down	Y	1,000
PIMCO RAE Low Volatility PLUS Fund Class P	PPLVX	NAS CM	Open End	US Equity Large Cap Value (Growth & Income)	B	B	B-		Y	1,000,000
PIMCO RAE Low Volatility PLUS Fund Institutional Class	PILVX	NAS CM	Open End	US Equity Large Cap Value (Growth & Income)	B	B	B-		Y	1,000,000
PIMCO RAE Low Volatility PLUS International Fund Class A	PLVBX	NAS CM	Open End	Global Equity Large Cap (Growth & Income)	B-	B	C	Up	Y	1,000
PIMCO RAE Low Volatility PLUS International Fund Class P	PLVZX	NAS CM	Open End	Global Equity Large Cap (Growth & Income)	B	B	B	Up	Y	1,000,000
PIMCO RAE Low Volatility PLUS Intl Fund Inst Cls	PLVTX	NAS CM	Open End	Global Equity Large Cap (Growth & Income)	B	B	B	Up	Y	1,000,000
PIMCO RAE Worldwide Long/Short PLUS Fund Class A	PWLAX	NAS CM	Open End	Long/Short Equity (Growth)	C+	C+	B-	Up	Y	1,000
PIMCO RAE Worldwide Long/Short PLUS Fund Class P	PWLPX	NAS CM	Open End	Long/Short Equity (Growth)	C+	C+	B-	Up	Y	1,000,000
PIMCO RAE Worldwide Long/Short PLUS Fund Institutional Cls	PWLIX	NAS CM	Open End	Long/Short Equity (Growth)	C+	C+	B-	Up	Y	1,000,000
PIMCO RealEstateRealReturn Strategy Fund Class A	PETAX	NAS CM	Open End	Real Estate Sector Equity (Real Estate)	B-	C+	B		Y	1,000
PIMCO RealEstateRealReturn Strategy Fund Class C	PETCX	NAS CM	Open End	Real Estate Sector Equity (Real Estate)	B-	C+	B	Up	Y	1,000
PIMCO RealEstateRealReturn Strategy Fund Class D	PETDX	NAS CM	Open End	Real Estate Sector Equity (Real Estate)	B-	C+	B		Y	1,000

★ Expanded analysis of this fund is included in Section II.

	TOTAL RETURNS					PERFORMANCE				ASSETS		ASSET ALLOCATION & TURNOVER					BULL & BEAR		FEES		
Min Additional Investment	3-Month Total Return	6-Month Total Return	1-Year Total Return	3-Year Total Return	5-Year Total Return	Dividend Yield (TTM)	Expense Ratio	3-Yr Std Deviation	3-Year Beta	NAV	Total Assets (MIL)	%Cash	%Stocks	%Bonds	%Other	Turnover Ratio	Last Bull Market Total Return	Last Bear Market Total Return	Front End Fee (%)	Back End Fee (%)	Inception Date
	5.42	12.09	22.32			2.04	0.6			11.33	428.9	0	100	0	0	13					Jun-15
	5.36	12.11	22.32			2.05	0.5			11.35	428.9	0	100	0	0	13					Jun-15
50	3.64	11.14	24.51			1.75	0.85			11.09	519.9	0	100	0	0	39			3.75		Jun-15
50	3.45	10.75	23.64			1.56	1.6			10.91	519.9	0	100	0	0	39				1.00	Jun-15
	3.74	11.34	24.88			1.97	0.6			11.12	519.9	0	100	0	0	39					Jun-15
	3.69	11.27	24.89			1.88	0.5			11.14	519.9	0	100	0	0	39					Jun-15
	6.73	16.25	31.51	32.49	20.92	8.06	1.4	21.18	1.26	11.13	2,030	-35	100	24	11	368	24.48	-29.08			May-12
50	6.82	16.20	31.30	31.98	20.33	8.04	1.55	21.26	1.27	11.12	2,030	-35	100	24	11	368	24.37	-29.13	3.75		May-13
50	6.60	15.68	30.37	29.02	15.65	7.72	2.3	21.26	1.27	10.81	2,030	-35	100	24	11	368	23.83	-29.35		1.00	May-13
50	6.79	16.19	31.46	32.02	19.97	7.99	1.55	21.27	1.27	11.08	2,030	-35	100	24	11	368	24.37	-29.13			May-13
	6.80	16.27	31.65	33.08	21.93	8.13	1.25	21.27	1.27	11.24	2,030	-35	100	24	11	368	24.69	-29.14			Jan-11
	6.81	16.40	31.83	33.53	22.54	8.16	1.15	21.23	1.26	11.25	2,030	-35	100	24	11	368	24.66	-29.01			Nov-08
	7.40	12.93	19.07	30.97	102.24	2.73	1.04	12.06	1.15	7.51	1,841	-37	100	26	11	552	31.56	-18.59			Jun-05
50	7.40	12.71	18.77	30.19	100.55	2.74	1.19	12.01	1.15	7.32	1,841	-37	100	26	11	552	31.13	-18.41	3.75		Jun-05
50	7.17	12.33	17.93	27.25	93.05	2.65	1.94	12.05	1.15	6.77	1,841	-37	100	26	11	552	30.98	-18.79		1.00	Jun-05
50	7.42	12.90	18.81	30.42	100.81	2.74	1.19	12.03	1.15	7.31	1,841	-37	100	26	11	552	31.32	-18.47			Jun-05
	7.46	12.96	19.21	31.58	103.86	2.75	0.89	12.02	1.15	7.63	1,841	-37	100	26	11	552	31.5	-18.37			Apr-08
	7.58	13.08	19.32	31.78	104.63	2.77	0.79	12.01	1.15	7.68	1,841	-37	100	26	11	552	31.67	-18.33			Jun-05
50	4.24	12.80	28.05	27.35	49.11	2.77	1.17	15.59	1.23	9.99	1,228	-33	100	23	9	250	13.43		3.75		Feb-14
50	3.91	12.26	26.97	24.33	43.53	2.3	1.92	15.63	1.23	9.85	1,228	-33	100	23	9	250	12.93			1.00	Feb-14
50	4.21	12.73	27.99	27.27	49.01	2.81	1.17	15.6	1.22	9.98	1,228	-33	100	23	9	250	13.43				Feb-14
	4.18	12.92	28.31	28.10	50.99	2.98	0.92	15.59	1.22	9.99	1,228	-33	100	23	9	250	13.59				May-14
	4.20	12.96	28.38	28.49	51.68	3.05	0.82	15.57	1.22	10	1,228	-33	100	23	9	250	13.66				Sep-11
50	3.89	10.32	12.51	33.22	101.81	2.32	1.19	15.42	1.06	11.79	97.8	-26	97	20	9	352	31.54		3.75		Feb-14
50	3.77	9.88	11.70	30.43	94.57	1.76	1.94	15.39	1.06	11.6	97.8	-26	97	20	9	352	30.97			1.00	Feb-14
50	3.97	10.29	12.49	33.32	101.99	2.24	1.19	15.4	1.06	11.82	97.8	-26	97	20	9	352	31.54				Feb-14
	4.02	10.47	12.85	34.28	104.63	2.58	0.94	15.39	1.06	11.86	97.8	-26	97	20	9	352	31.73				May-14
	4.03	10.52	12.88	34.71	105.63	2.61	0.84	15.4	1.06	11.89	97.8	-26	97	20	9	352	31.81				Sep-11
50	7.22	11.72	16.14	28.95	98.46	1.8	0.8			11.09	641.7	1	99	0	0	42	23.38	-17.48	3.75		Jun-15
50	7.02	11.36	15.26	26.00	91.06	1.71	1.55			10.92	641.7	1	99	0	0	42	22.84	-17.73		1.00	Jun-15
	7.21	11.89	16.42	30.27	101.69	1.89	0.5			11.14	641.7	1	99	0	0	42	23.59	-17.37			Jun-15
	7.24	11.91	16.54	30.66	102.70	1.88	0.4			11.17	641.7	1	99	0	0	42	23.67	-17.34			Jun-15
50	3.76	9.39	8.80	31.96	97.66	1.06	0.9			11.56	116.6	1	99	0	0	85	27.69	-25.63	3.75		Jun-15
50	3.55	8.98	7.99	29.08	90.49	0.86	1.65			11.35	116.6	1	99	0	0	85	27.13	-25.86		1.00	Jun-15
	3.83	9.55	9.06	33.13	100.61	1.11	0.6			11.58	116.6	1	99	0	0	85	27.91	-25.53			Jun-15
	3.86	9.66	9.27	33.61	101.74	1.13	0.5			11.62	116.6	1	99	0	0	85	27.98	-25.5			Jun-15
50	5.33	10.45	25.69	13.87		3.56	1.41	16.78	1.02	10.19	1,781	-28	101	16	11	278			3.75		Dec-13
	5.41	10.65	25.99	14.92		3.73	1.11	16.82	1.02	10.22	1,781	-28	101	16	11	278					Dec-13
	5.33	10.54	26.01	15.10		3.86	1.01	16.8	1.02	10.22	1,781	-28	101	16	11	278					Dec-13
50	7.26	11.54	17.59	32.00		1.69	1.19	9.94	0.88	11.81	190.3	-56	95	45	15	342			3.75		Dec-13
50	7.06	11.14	16.81	29.20		1.16	1.94	9.89	0.87	11.61	190.3	-56	95	45	15	342				1.00	Dec-13
	7.34	11.77	17.98	33.25		1.88	0.89	9.91	0.87	11.9	190.3	-56	95	45	15	342					Dec-13
	7.44	11.87	18.16	33.72		1.94	0.79	9.93	0.88	11.94	190.3	-56	95	45	15	342					Dec-13
50	5.65	11.09	23.54	29.54		2.07	1.17	11.96	0.91	11.11	672.3	-45	101	39	5	350			3.75		Dec-13
	5.71	11.10	23.88	30.40		2.31	0.92	12.01	0.91	11.13	672.3	-45	101	39	5	350					Dec-13
	5.82	11.22	24.02	30.94		2.41	0.82	11.97	0.91	11.16	672.3	-45	101	39	5	350					Dec-13
50	4.84	7.32	11.28	19.06		6.04	1.59			9.74	894.0	-25	69	20	36	231			5.50		Dec-14
	4.91	7.46	11.60	20.27		6.24	1.29			9.78	894.0	-25	69	20	36	231					Dec-14
	5.02	7.57	11.80	20.65		6.22	1.19			9.8	894.0	-25	69	20	36	231					Dec-14
50	1.78	2.32	3.94	16.15	41.36	0.61	1.14	15.01	1.09	7.61	2,001	-94	68	93	33	186	39.86	-10.33	5.50		Oct-03
50	1.70	2.01	3.16	13.57	36.05	0.21	1.89	14.99	1.09	6.64	2,001	-94	68	93	33	186	39.11	-10.55		1.00	Oct-03
50	1.77	2.31	3.91	16.04	41.31	0.61	1.14	14.98	1.09	7.65	2,001	-94	68	93	33	186	39.78	-10.28			Oct-03

Fund Name	MARKET Ticker Symbol	Traded On	Fund Type	FUND TYPE, CATEGORY & OBJECTIVE Category and (Prospectus Objective)	RATINGS Overall Rating	Reward Rating	Risk Rating	Recent Up/ Downgrade	Open to New Investors	MINIMUMS Min Initial Investment
PIMCO RealEstateRealReturn Strategy Fund Class P	PETPX	NAS CM	Open End	Real Estate Sector Equity (Real Estate)	B-	C+	B		Y	1,000,000
PIMCO RealEstateRealReturn Strategy Fund Institutional Cls	PRRSX	NAS CM	Open End	Real Estate Sector Equity (Real Estate)	B-	C+	B		Y	1,000,000
PIMCO RealPath Blend 2020 Fund Administrative Class	PBZDX	NAS CM	Open End	Target Date 2000-2020 (Asset Alloc)	B-	C	B	Up	Y	1,000,000
PIMCO RealPath Blend 2020 Fund Class A	PBZAX	NAS CM	Open End	Target Date 2000-2020 (Asset Alloc)	B-	C	B	Up	Y	1,000
PIMCO RealPath Blend 2020 Fund Institutional Class	PBZNX	NAS CM	Open End	Target Date 2000-2020 (Asset Alloc)	B-	C	B	Up	Y	1,000,000
PIMCO RealPath Blend 2025 Fund Administrative Class	PPZDX	NAS CM	Open End	Target Date 2021-2045 (Asset Alloc)	B-	C+	B	Up	Y	1,000,000
PIMCO RealPath Blend 2025 Fund Class A	PPZAX	NAS CM	Open End	Target Date 2021-2045 (Asset Alloc)	C+	C	B	Up	Y	1,000
PIMCO RealPath Blend 2025 Fund Institutional Class	PPZRX	NAS CM	Open End	Target Date 2021-2045 (Asset Alloc)	B-	C+	B	Up	Y	1,000,000
PIMCO RealPath Blend 2030 Fund Administrative Class	PBPRX	NAS CM	Open End	Target Date 2021-2045 (Asset Alloc)	C+	C+	B-	Down	Y	1,000,000
PIMCO RealPath Blend 2030 Fund Class A	PBPAX	NAS CM	Open End	Target Date 2021-2045 (Asset Alloc)	C+	C+	B-	Down	Y	1,000
PIMCO RealPath Blend 2030 Fund Institutional Class	PBPNX	NAS CM	Open End	Target Date 2021-2045 (Asset Alloc)	C+	C+	B	Down	Y	1,000,000
PIMCO RealPath Blend 2035 Fund Administrative Class	PDGDX	NAS CM	Open End	Target Date 2021-2045 (Asset Alloc)	C+	C+	B-	Down	Y	1,000,000
PIMCO RealPath Blend 2035 Fund Class A	PDGAX	NAS CM	Open End	Target Date 2021-2045 (Asset Alloc)	C+	C+	B-	Up	Y	1,000
PIMCO RealPath Blend 2035 Fund Institutional Class	PDGZX	NAS CM	Open End	Target Date 2021-2045 (Asset Alloc)	C+	C+	B-	Down	Y	1,000,000
PIMCO RealPath Blend 2040 Fund Administrative Class	PVPRX	NAS CM	Open End	Target Date 2021-2045 (Asset Alloc)	C+	C+	B-	Down	Y	1,000,000
PIMCO RealPath Blend 2040 Fund Class A	PVPAX	NAS CM	Open End	Target Date 2021-2045 (Asset Alloc)	C+	C+	B-	Up	Y	1,000
PIMCO RealPath Blend 2040 Fund Institutional Class	PVPNX	NAS CM	Open End	Target Date 2021-2045 (Asset Alloc)	C+	C+	B-	Down	Y	1,000,000
PIMCO RealPath Blend 2045 Fund Administrative Class	PVQDX	NAS CM	Open End	Target Date 2021-2045 (Asset Alloc)	C+	C+	B-	Up	Y	1,000,000
PIMCO RealPath Blend 2045 Fund Class A	PVQAX	NAS CM	Open End	Target Date 2021-2045 (Asset Alloc)	C+	C+	B-	Up	Y	1,000
PIMCO RealPath Blend 2045 Fund Institutional Class	PVQNX	NAS CM	Open End	Target Date 2021-2045 (Asset Alloc)	C+	C+	B-	Down	Y	1,000,000
PIMCO RealPath Blend 2050 Fund Administrative Class	PPQDX	NAS CM	Open End	Target Date 2046+ (Asset Alloc)	C+	C+	B-	Up	Y	1,000,000
PIMCO RealPath Blend 2050 Fund Class A	PPQAX	NAS CM	Open End	Target Date 2046+ (Asset Alloc)	C+	C+	B-	Up	Y	1,000
PIMCO RealPath Blend 2050 Fund Institutional Class	PPQZX	NAS CM	Open End	Target Date 2046+ (Asset Alloc)	C+	C+	B-	Up	Y	1,000,000
PIMCO RealPath Blend 2055 Fund Administrative Class	PRQDX	NAS CM	Open End	Target Date 2046+ (Asset Alloc)	C+	C+	B-	Up	Y	1,000,000
PIMCO RealPath Blend 2055 Fund Class A	PRQAX	NAS CM	Open End	Target Date 2046+ (Asset Alloc)	C+	C+	B-	Up	Y	1,000
PIMCO RealPath Blend 2055 Fund Institutional Class	PRQZX	NAS CM	Open End	Target Date 2046+ (Asset Alloc)	C+	C+	B-	Up	Y	1,000,000
PIMCO RealPath Blend Income Fund Administrative Class	PBRDX	NAS CM	Open End	Target Date 2000-2020 (Asset Alloc)	B-	C	B	Up	Y	1,000,000
PIMCO RealPath Blend Income Fund Class A	PBRAX	NAS CM	Open End	Target Date 2000-2020 (Asset Alloc)	B-	C	B	Up	Y	1,000
PIMCO RealPath Blend Income Fund Institutional Class	PBRNX	NAS CM	Open End	Target Date 2000-2020 (Asset Alloc)	B-	C	B	Up	Y	1,000,000
PIMCO RealPath™ 2020 Fund Administrative Class	PFNAX	NAS CM	Open End	Target Date 2000-2020 (Asset Alloc)	B-	C+	B	Up	Y	1,000,000
PIMCO RealPath™ 2020 Fund Class A	PTYAX	NAS CM	Open End	Target Date 2000-2020 (Asset Alloc)	B-	C+	B	Down	Y	1,000
PIMCO RealPath™ 2020 Fund Institutional Class	PRWIX	NAS CM	Open End	Target Date 2000-2020 (Asset Alloc)	B-	C+	B	Up	Y	1,000,000
PIMCO RealPath™ 2025 Fund Administrative Class	PENMX	NAS CM	Open End	Target Date 2021-2045 (Asset Alloc)	C+	C+	B-	Down	Y	1,000,000
PIMCO RealPath™ 2025 Fund Class A	PENZX	NAS CM	Open End	Target Date 2021-2045 (Asset Alloc)	B-	C+	B	Down	Y	1,000
PIMCO RealPath™ 2025 Fund Institutional Class	PENTX	NAS CM	Open End	Target Date 2021-2045 (Asset Alloc)	B-	C+	B	Down	Y	1,000,000
PIMCO RealPath™ 2030 Fund Administrative Class	PNLAX	NAS CM	Open End	Target Date 2021-2045 (Asset Alloc)	B-	C+	B-	Down	Y	1,000,000
PIMCO RealPath™ 2030 Fund Class A	PEHAX	NAS CM	Open End	Target Date 2021-2045 (Asset Alloc)	C+	C+	C+	Down	Y	1,000
PIMCO RealPath™ 2030 Fund Institutional Class	PRLIX	NAS CM	Open End	Target Date 2021-2045 (Asset Alloc)	C+	C+	B-	Down	Y	1,000,000
PIMCO RealPath™ 2035 Fund Administrative Class	PIVNX	NAS CM	Open End	Target Date 2021-2045 (Asset Alloc)	C+	C+	C+	Down	Y	1,000,000
PIMCO RealPath™ 2035 Fund Class A	PIVAX	NAS CM	Open End	Target Date 2021-2045 (Asset Alloc)	C+	C+	C+	Down	Y	1,000
PIMCO RealPath™ 2035 Fund Institutional Class	PIVIX	NAS CM	Open End	Target Date 2021-2045 (Asset Alloc)	C+	C+	C+	Down	Y	1,000,000
PIMCO RealPath™ 2040 Fund Administrative Class	PEOAX	NAS CM	Open End	Target Date 2021-2045 (Asset Alloc)	C+	C+	C+	Down	Y	1,000,000
PIMCO RealPath™ 2040 Fund Class A	POFAX	NAS CM	Open End	Target Date 2021-2045 (Asset Alloc)	C+	C+	C+	Down	Y	1,000
PIMCO RealPath™ 2040 Fund Institutional Class	PROIX	NAS CM	Open End	Target Date 2021-2045 (Asset Alloc)	C+	C+	C+	Down	Y	1,000,000
PIMCO RealPath™ 2045 Fund Administrative Class	PFZMX	NAS CM	Open End	Target Date 2021-2045 (Asset Alloc)	C+	C+	C+	Down	Y	1,000,000
PIMCO RealPath™ 2045 Fund Class A	PFZAX	NAS CM	Open End	Target Date 2021-2045 (Asset Alloc)	C+	C+	C+	Down	Y	1,000
PIMCO RealPath™ 2045 Fund Institutional Class	PFZIX	NAS CM	Open End	Target Date 2021-2045 (Asset Alloc)	C+	C+	C+	Down	Y	1,000,000
PIMCO RealPath™ 2050 Fund Administrative Class	POTAX	NAS CM	Open End	Target Date 2046+ (Asset Alloc)	C+	C+	C+	Down	Y	1,000,000
PIMCO RealPath™ 2050 Fund Class A	PFYAX	NAS CM	Open End	Target Date 2046+ (Asset Alloc)	C+	C+	C+	Down	Y	1,000
PIMCO RealPath™ 2050 Fund Institutional Class	PRMIX	NAS CM	Open End	Target Date 2046+ (Asset Alloc)	C+	C+	C+	Down	Y	1,000,000
PIMCO RealPath™ 2055 Fund Administrative Class	PQRZX	NAS CM	Open End	Target Date 2046+ (Asset Alloc)	C+	C+	C+	Up	Y	1,000,000
PIMCO RealPath™ 2055 Fund Class A	PQRAX	NAS CM	Open End	Target Date 2046+ (Asset Alloc)	C+	C+	C+	Up	Y	1,000

★Expanded analysis of this fund is included in Section II.

	TOTAL RETURNS					PERFORMANCE				ASSETS		ASSET ALLOCATION & TURNOVER					BULL & BEAR		FEES		
Min Additional Investment	3-Month Total Return	6-Month Total Return	1-Year Total Return	3-Year Total Return	5-Year Total Return	Dividend Yield (TTM)	Expense Ratio	3-Yr Std Deviation	3-Year Beta	NAV	Total Assets (MIL)	%Cash	%Stocks	%Bonds	%Other	Turnover Ratio	Last Bull Market Total Return	Last Bear Market Total Return	Front End Fee (%)	Back End Fee (%)	Inception Date
	1.97	2.53	4.22	17.12	43.53	0.8	0.84	14.96	1.08	8.25	2,001	-94	68	93	33	186	40.08	-10.11			Apr-08
	1.96	2.55	4.31	17.57	43.97	0.92	0.74	15.02	1.09	8.4	2,001	-94	68	93	33	186	40.24	-10.23			Oct-03
	3.43	6.64	13.49	19.24		1.93	0.59			11.1	11.7	-3	47	54	0	36					Dec-14
50	3.41	6.58	13.21	18.50		1.83	0.84			11.1	11.7	-3	47	54	0	36			5.50		Dec-14
	3.53	6.80	13.79	20.23		2.16	0.34			11.11	11.7	-3	47	54	0	36					Dec-14
	3.90	7.47	15.09	20.69		1.93	0.55			11.25	11.6	-2	56	44	0	27					Dec-14
50	3.87	7.39	14.87	19.94		1.82	0.8			11.26	11.6	-2	56	44	0	27			5.50		Dec-14
	3.99	7.61	15.46	21.69		2.14	0.3			11.27	11.6	-2	56	44	0	27					Dec-14
	4.24	8.23	16.66	23.25		2.24	0.52			11.47	17.4	0	64	35	0	23					Dec-14
50	4.21	8.16	16.60	22.46		2.18	0.77			11.46	17.4	0	64	35	0	23			5.50		Dec-14
	4.42	8.38	17.05	24.24		2.43	0.27			11.49	17.4	0	64	35	0	23					Dec-14
	4.63	8.75	17.92	24.26		1.81	0.49			11.64	21.9	0	71	28	0	20					Dec-14
50	4.50	8.64	17.56	23.46		1.72	0.74			11.68	21.9	0	71	28	0	20			5.50		Dec-14
	4.64	8.90	18.12	25.27		2.04	0.24			11.65	21.9	0	71	28	0	20					Dec-14
	4.83	9.17	18.64	25.40		1.49	0.47			11.74	30.6	1	76	22	0	15					Dec-14
50	4.62	8.90	18.25	24.40		1.38	0.72			11.72	30.6	1	76	22	0	15			5.50		Dec-14
	4.74	9.22	18.94	26.30		1.7	0.22			11.75	30.6	1	76	22	0	15					Dec-14
	4.87	9.37	19.25	25.30		1.34	0.45			11.79	42.3	2	80	17	0	10					Dec-14
50	4.84	9.19	18.93	24.36		1.21	0.7			11.79	42.3	2	80	17	0	10			5.50		Dec-14
	5.05	9.61	19.63	26.37		1.53	0.2			11.82	42.3	2	80	17	0	10					Dec-14
	4.88	9.45	19.40	25.82		1.43	0.44			11.85	51.4	2	82	15	0	10					Dec-14
50	4.95	9.48	19.23	25.02		1.32	0.69			11.83	51.4	2	82	15	0	10			5.50		Dec-14
	5.06	9.68	19.87	26.96		1.62	0.19			11.88	51.4	2	82	15	0	10					Dec-14
	4.89	9.41	19.36	25.71		1.39	0.44			11.77	9.9	2	82	16	0	14					Dec-14
50	4.84	9.32	19.08	24.62		1.37	0.69			11.72	9.9	2	82	16	0	14			5.50		Dec-14
	4.96	9.53	19.64	26.63		1.69	0.19			11.76	9.9	2	82	16	0	14					Dec-14
	2.96	6.02	12.38	18.55		2.11	0.6			11.04	8.0	-3	42	60	0	30					Dec-14
50	2.89	5.87	12.01	17.64		2.05	0.85			11	8.0	-3	42	60	0	30			5.50		Dec-14
	3.16	6.25	12.74	19.48		2.39	0.35			11.04	8.0	-3	42	60	0	30					Dec-14
	3.22	6.21	12.91	15.73	23.52	3.9	0.83	6.1	1	8.37	30.4	-24	20	75	27	33	6.76	-4.7			Jun-08
50	3.11	6.04	12.70	14.85	22.06	3.77	1.03	6.07	1	8.13	30.4	-24	20	75	27	33	6.62	-4.79	5.50		Mar-08
	3.23	6.36	13.06	16.44	24.92	4.23	0.58	6.13	1	8.15	30.4	-24	20	75	27	33	6.81	-4.54			Mar-08
	3.63	7.04	14.40	17.42	27.46	4.26	0.85	7.02	1.03	9.47	35.5	-26	25	68	32	35	8.62				Jun-11
50	3.67	6.97	14.27	16.64	26.09	4.07	1.05	6.96	1.02	9.48	35.5	-26	25	68	32	35	8.59		5.50		Jun-11
	3.69	7.16	14.69	18.33	29.08	4.43	0.6	6.99	1.02	9.46	35.5	-26	25	68	32	35	8.89				Jun-11
	4.05	7.76	16.05	19.56	32.50	4.88	0.88	7.9	1.06	7.84	46.1	-28	28	62	37	21	7.71	-7.7			Jun-08
50	4.09	7.57	15.88	18.73	30.88	4.72	1.08	7.89	1.06	7.78	46.1	-28	28	62	37	21	7.45	-7.71	5.50		Mar-08
	4.07	7.85	16.35	20.35	34.16	5.06	0.63	7.96	1.07	7.83	46.1	-28	28	62	37	21	7.77	-7.59			Mar-08
	4.25	8.04	16.93	19.83	35.25	5.29	0.9	8.82	1.1	9.94	28.9	-31	32	57	41	22	10.18				Jun-11
50	4.09	8.02	16.73	18.95	33.63	4.99	1.1	8.82	1.1	9.91	28.9	-31	32	57	41	22	10.14		5.50		Jun-11
	4.31	8.28	17.29	20.72	37.04	5.5	0.65	8.84	1.1	9.94	28.9	-31	32	57	41	22	10.34				Jun-11
	4.48	8.52	17.96	20.09	36.60	6.83	0.9	9.12	1.08	7.54	29.5	-32	35	53	44	16	10.1	-10.58			Jun-08
50	4.41	8.38	17.51	19.19	34.88	6.7	1.1	9.09	1.08	7.48	29.5	-32	35	53	44	16	9.99	-10.63	5.50		Mar-08
	4.50	8.61	17.95	20.91	38.19	7.01	0.65	9.09	1.08	7.53	29.5	-32	35	53	44	16	10.14	-10.44			Mar-08
	4.47	8.75	18.27	19.77	37.29	8.96	0.92	9.55	1.08	9.78	19.6	-34	37	50	46	22					Feb-12
50	4.45	8.61	18.07	18.93	35.64	8.72	1.12	9.56	1.08	9.77	19.6	-34	37	50	46	22			5.50		Feb-12
	4.63	8.86	18.59	20.66	39.00	8.75	0.67	9.58	1.08	9.84	19.6	-34	37	50	46	22					Feb-12
	4.64	8.83	18.37	20.53	37.82	8.5	0.92	9.64	1.05	7.46	30.8	-33	37	49	47	23	10.27	-11.89			Jun-08
50	4.49	8.74	18.14	19.59	36.21	8.37	1.12	9.66	1.06	7.4	30.8	-33	37	49	47	23	10.33	-12.03	5.50		Mar-08
	4.57	8.94	18.49	21.32	39.44	8.62	0.67	9.65	1.05	7.48	30.8	-33	37	49	47	23	10.57	-11.75			Mar-08
	4.65	8.85	18.69	22.34		5.62	0.93			9.89	4.9	-32	37	48	47	36					Dec-14
50	4.59	8.81	18.45	21.55		5.23	1.13			9.89	4.9	-32	37	48	47	36			5.50		Dec-14

Fund Name	Ticker Symbol	Traded On	Fund Type	Category and (Prospectus Objective)	Overall Rating	Reward Rating	Risk Rating	Recent Up/ Downgrade	Open to New Investors	Min Initial Investment
	MARKET		FUND TYPE, CATEGORY & OBJECTIVE		RATINGS				MINIMUMS	
PIMCO RealPath™ 2055 Fund Institutional Class	PRQIX	NAS CM	Open End	Target Date 2046+ (Asset Alloc)	C+	C+	C+	Up	Y	1,000,000
PIMCO RealPath™ Income Fund Administrative Class	PRNAX	NAS CM	Open End	Target Date 2000-2020 (Asset Alloc)	B-	C+	B	Down	Y	1,000,000
PIMCO RealPath™ Income Fund Class A	PTNAX	NAS CM	Open End	Target Date 2000-2020 (Asset Alloc)	C+	C+	B-	Down	Y	1,000
PIMCO RealPath™ Income Fund Institutional Class	PRIEX	NAS CM	Open End	Target Date 2000-2020 (Asset Alloc)	B-	C+	B	Down	Y	1,000,000
PIMCO StocksPLUS® Absolute Return Fund Class A	PTOAX	NAS CM	Open End	US Equity Large Cap Blend (Growth & Income)	B-	B	C+	Down	Y	1,000
PIMCO StocksPLUS® Absolute Return Fund Class C	PSOCX	NAS CM	Open End	US Equity Large Cap Blend (Growth & Income)	B-	B	C+	Down	Y	1,000
PIMCO StocksPLUS® Absolute Return Fund Class D	PSTDX	NAS CM	Open End	US Equity Large Cap Blend (Growth & Income)	B-	B	C+	Down	Y	1,000
PIMCO StocksPLUS® Absolute Return Fund Class P	PTOPX	NAS CM	Open End	US Equity Large Cap Blend (Growth & Income)	B	B	C+		Y	1,000,000
PIMCO StocksPLUS® Absolute Return Fund Class R	PTORX	NAS CM	Open End	US Equity Large Cap Blend (Growth & Income)	B-	B	C+	Down	Y	0
PIMCO StocksPLUS® Absolute Return Fund Institutional Class	PSPTX	NAS CM	Open End	US Equity Large Cap Blend (Growth & Income)	B	B	C+		Y	1,000,000
PIMCO StocksPLUS® Fund Administrative Class	PPLAX	NAS CM	Open End	US Equity Large Cap Blend (Growth & Income)	B	B	B-		Y	1,000,000
PIMCO StocksPLUS® Fund Class A	PSPAX	NAS CM	Open End	US Equity Large Cap Blend (Growth & Income)	B-	B	B-	Down	Y	1,000
PIMCO StocksPLUS® Fund Class C	PSPCX	NAS CM	Open End	US Equity Large Cap Blend (Growth & Income)	B-	B-	B-	Down	Y	1,000
PIMCO StocksPLUS® Fund Class D	PSPDX	NAS CM	Open End	US Equity Large Cap Blend (Growth & Income)	B	B	B-		Y	1,000
PIMCO StocksPLUS® Fund Class P	PSKPX	NAS CM	Open End	US Equity Large Cap Blend (Growth & Income)	B	B	B-		Y	1,000,000
PIMCO StocksPLUS® Fund Class R	PSPRX	NAS CM	Open End	US Equity Large Cap Blend (Growth & Income)	B-	B	B-	Down	Y	0
PIMCO StocksPLUS® Fund Institutional Class	PSTKX	NAS CM	Open End	US Equity Large Cap Blend (Growth & Income)	B	B	B-		Y	1,000,000
PIMCO StocksPLUS® Intl Fund (U.S. Dollar-Hedged) Cls A	PIPAX	NAS CM	Open End	Global Equity Large Cap (Growth & Income)	B	B	B-	Up	Y	1,000
PIMCO StocksPLUS® Intl Fund (U.S. Dollar-Hedged) Cls C	PIPCX	NAS CM	Open End	Global Equity Large Cap (Growth & Income)	B	B	B-	Up	Y	1,000
PIMCO StocksPLUS® Intl Fund (U.S. Dollar-Hedged) Cls D	PIPDX	NAS CM	Open End	Global Equity Large Cap (Growth & Income)	B	B	B-	Up	Y	1,000
PIMCO StocksPLUS® Intl Fund (U.S. Dollar-Hedged) Cls P	PIUHX	NAS CM	Open End	Global Equity Large Cap (Growth & Income)	B-	B	C		Y	1,000,000
PIMCO StocksPLUS® Intl Fund (U.S. Dollar-Hedged) Cls R	PIRHX	NAS CM	Open End	Global Equity Large Cap (Growth & Income)	B-	B	C		Y	0
PIMCO StocksPLUS® Intl Fund (U.S. Dollar-Hedged) Inst Cls	PISIX	NAS CM	Open End	Global Equity Large Cap (Growth & Income)	B	B	B	Up	Y	1,000,000
PIMCO StocksPLUS® Intl Fund (Unhedged) Admin Cls	PSKAX	NAS CM	Open End	Global Equity Large Cap (Growth & Income)	B-	B	C	Up	Y	1,000,000
PIMCO StocksPLUS® International Fund (Unhedged) Class A	PPUAX	NAS CM	Open End	Global Equity Large Cap (Growth & Income)	B-	B	C	Up	Y	1,000
PIMCO StocksPLUS® International Fund (Unhedged) Class C	PPUCX	NAS CM	Open End	Global Equity Large Cap (Growth & Income)	C+	B-	C	Up	Y	1,000
PIMCO StocksPLUS® International Fund (Unhedged) Class D	PPUDX	NAS CM	Open End	Global Equity Large Cap (Growth & Income)	B-	B	C	Up	Y	1,000
PIMCO StocksPLUS® International Fund (Unhedged) Class P	PPLPX	NAS CM	Open End	Global Equity Large Cap (Growth & Income)	B-	B	C	Up	Y	1,000,000
PIMCO StocksPLUS® Intl Fund (Unhedged) Inst Cls	PSKIX	NAS CM	Open End	Global Equity Large Cap (Growth & Income)	B-	B	C	Up	Y	1,000,000
PIMCO StocksPLUS® Long Duration Fund Institutional Class	PSLDX	NAS CM	Open End	Aggressive Alloc (Growth & Income)	A-	A	B		Y	1,000,000
PIMCO StocksPLUS® Short Fund Class A	PSSAX	NAS CM	Open End	Other Alternative (Growth & Income)	D	D-	D		Y	1,000
PIMCO StocksPLUS® Short Fund Class C	PSSCX	NAS CM	Open End	Other Alternative (Growth & Income)	D	D-	D		Y	1,000
PIMCO StocksPLUS® Short Fund Class D	PSSDX	NAS CM	Open End	Other Alternative (Growth & Income)	D	D-	D		Y	1,000
PIMCO StocksPLUS® Short Fund Class P	PSPLX	NAS CM	Open End	Other Alternative (Growth & Income)	D	D-	D		Y	1,000,000
PIMCO StocksPLUS® Short Fund Institutional Class	PSTIX	NAS CM	Open End	Other Alternative (Growth & Income)	D	D-	D		Y	1,000,000
PIMCO StocksPLUS® Small Fund Administrative Class	PCKTX	NAS CM	Open End	US Equity Small Cap (Growth & Income)	B+	A	B-	Up	Y	1,000,000
PIMCO StocksPLUS® Small Fund Class A	PCKAX	NAS CM	Open End	US Equity Small Cap (Growth & Income)	B+	A	B-	Up	Y	1,000
PIMCO StocksPLUS® Small Fund Class C	PCKCX	NAS CM	Open End	US Equity Small Cap (Growth & Income)	B+	A-	B-	Up	Y	1,000
PIMCO StocksPLUS® Small Fund Class D	PCKDX	NAS CM	Open End	US Equity Small Cap (Growth & Income)	B+	A	B-	Up	Y	1,000
PIMCO StocksPLUS® Small Fund Class P	PCKPX	NAS CM	Open End	US Equity Small Cap (Growth & Income)	B+	A	B-	Up	Y	1,000,000
PIMCO StocksPLUS® Small Fund Class R	PCKRX	NAS CM	Open End	US Equity Small Cap (Growth & Income)	B+	A-	B-	Up	Y	0
PIMCO StocksPLUS® Small Fund Institutional Class	PSCSX	NAS CM	Open End	US Equity Small Cap (Growth & Income)	B+	A	B-	Up	Y	1,000,000
PIMCO TRENDS Managed Futures Strategy Fund Class A	PQTAX	NAS CM	Open End	Other Alternative (Income)	C-	C-	C	Up	Y	1,000
PIMCO TRENDS Managed Futures Strategy Fund Class C	PQTCX	NAS CM	Open End	Other Alternative (Income)	C-	D+	C-	Up	Y	1,000
PIMCO TRENDS Managed Futures Strategy Fund Class D	PQTDX	NAS CM	Open End	Other Alternative (Income)	C-	C-	C	Up	Y	1,000
PIMCO TRENDS Managed Futures Strategy Fund Class P	PQTPX	NAS CM	Open End	Other Alternative (Income)	C-	C-	C	Up	Y	1,000,000
PIMCO TRENDS Managed Futures Strategy Fund Inst Cls	PQTIX	NAS CM	Open End	Other Alternative (Income)	C	C-	C	Up	Y	1,000,000
Pin Oak Equity Fund	POGSX	NAS CM	Open End	US Equity Large Cap Blend (Aggr Growth)	B	B	A-		Y	2,000
PineBridge Dynamic Asset Allocation Fund Inst Shares	PDAIX	NAS CM	Open End	Alloc (Asset Alloc)	C-	C-	A-	Up	Y	1,000,000
PineBridge Dynamic Asset Alloc Fund Inv Servicing Shares	PDAVX	NAS CM	Open End	Alloc (Asset Alloc)	C-	C-	B+	Up	Y	100,000
Pinnacle Sherman Multi-Strategy Core Fund Class A	APSHX	NAS CM	Open End	Moderate Alloc (Growth & Income)	C	C	B	Up	Y	2,000
Pinnacle Sherman Multi-Strategy Core Fund Class C	CPSHX	NAS CM	Open End	Moderate Alloc (Growth & Income)	C	C	B	Up	Y	2,000

★ Expanded analysis of this fund is included in Section II.

Min Additional Investment	3-Month Total Return	6-Month Total Return	1-Year Total Return	3-Year Total Return	5-Year Total Return	Dividend Yield (TTM)	Expense Ratio	3-Yr Std Deviation	3-Year Beta	NAV	Total Assets (MIL)	%Cash	%Stocks	%Bonds	%Other	Turnover Ratio	Last Bull Market Total Return	Last Bear Market Total Return	Front End Fee (%)	Back End Fee (%)	Inception Date
	TOTAL RETURNS					PERFORMANCE				ASSETS		ASSET ALLOCATION & TURNOVER					BULL & BEAR		FEES		
	4.70	9.04	19.00	23.24		5.84	0.68			9.92	4.9	-32	37	48	47	36					Dec-14
	2.92	5.89	12.22	16.15	22.50	4.28	0.8	5.42	1.6	8.24	31.5	-24	19	80	24	35	5.42	-1.84			Jun-08
50	2.81	5.70	11.95	15.38	21.06	4.1	1	5.37	1.58	8.21	31.5	-24	19	80	24	35	5.26	-1.94	5.50		Mar-08
	3.08	6.00	12.43	17.11	24.14	4.51	0.55	5.41	1.59	8.23	31.5	-24	19	80	24	35	5.59	-1.73			Mar-08
50	6.39	11.59	23.41	36.16	108.48	0.87	1.04	12.13	1.19	10.53	1,626	-31	100	21	10	339	32.47	-19.02	3.75		Jul-03
50	6.17	11.16	22.32	32.97	100.55	0.52	1.79	12.15	1.19	9.61	1,626	-31	100	21	10	339	31.94	-19.32		1.00	Jul-03
50	6.50	11.68	23.36	36.14	108.51	0.89	1.04	12.22	1.2	10.35	1,626	-31	100	21	10	339	32.3	-19.1			Jul-03
	6.45	11.71	23.74	37.27	111.49	1.16	0.74	12.19	1.2	10.58	1,626	-31	100	21	10	339	32.64	-18.86			Apr-08
	6.27	11.43	23.08	35.17	105.83	0.83	1.29	12.17	1.19	10.46	1,626	-31	100	21	10	339	32.29	-19.09			Nov-15
	6.58	11.82	23.89	37.84	112.63	1.2	0.64	12.14	1.19	10.71	1,626	-31	100	21	10	339	32.79	-18.87			Jun-02
	6.73	11.57	22.13	35.51	112.27	1.08	0.75	10.64	1.05	10.73	876.0	-75	101	63	11	132	28.63	-18.71			Jan-97
50	6.65	11.38	21.96	34.92	110.27	1	0.9	10.68	1.06	10.63	876.0	-75	101	63	11	132	28.19	-18.81	3.75		Jan-97
50	6.55	11.14	21.34	32.92	105.24	0.65	1.4	10.67	1.06	10.11	876.0	-75	101	63	11	132	27.78	-18.93		1.00	Jan-97
50	6.69	11.46	21.98	34.92	110.47	1.03	0.9	10.67	1.06	10.57	876.0	-75	101	63	11	132	28.15	-18.72			Apr-98
	6.64	11.54	22.28	36.04	113.62	1.16	0.6	10.69	1.06	11.4	876.0	-75	101	63	11	132	28.51	-18.86			Apr-08
	6.59	11.34	21.75	33.94	107.94	0.77	1.15	10.68	1.06	10.94	876.0	-75	101	63	11	132	28.1	-18.89			Dec-02
	6.75	11.67	22.42	36.48	114.60	1.23	0.5	10.66	1.05	11.43	876.0	-75	101	63	11	132	28.4	-18.6			May-93
50	3.78	8.37	18.32	30.12	69.17	5.37	1.15	13.7	1.19	8.07	3,170	-42	99	32	11	256	16.99	-19.47	3.75		Oct-03
50	3.63	7.80	17.33	27.15	62.88	5.19	1.9	13.68	1.18	7.45	3,170	-42	99	32	11	256	16.51	-19.75		1.00	Oct-03
50	3.77	8.34	18.27	30.03	68.95	5.36	1.15	13.71	1.19	8.08	3,170	-42	99	32	11	256	16.97	-19.47			Oct-03
	3.84	8.47	18.61	31.17	71.70	5.42	0.85	13.75	1.19	8.4	3,170	-42	99	32	11	256	17.42	-19.49			Mar-12
	3.75	8.19	18.00	29.24	66.97	5.43	1.4	13.74	1.19	8.02	3,170	-42	99	32	11	256	16.87	-19.67			Nov-15
	3.96	8.58	18.84	31.69	72.36	5.44	0.75	13.72	1.19	8.47	3,170	-42	99	32	11	256	17.31	-19.46			Oct-03
	4.02	10.16	26.55	25.47	45.30	1.89	0.89	14.24	1.16	6.83	1,848	-40	97	30	13	278	20.17	-24.44			Nov-06
50	3.73	9.88	26.38	24.60	43.81	1.86	1.04	14.31	1.16	6.75	1,848	-40	97	30	13	278	19.27	-24.64	3.75		Nov-06
50	3.57	9.45	25.40	21.90	38.52	1.66	1.79	14.3	1.16	6.45	1,848	-40	97	30	13	278	18.88	-24.73		1.00	Nov-06
50	3.86	10.03	26.46	24.62	43.89	1.88	1.04	14.23	1.16	6.79	1,848	-40	97	30	13	278	19.29	-24.48			Nov-06
	3.86	10.06	26.55	25.82	46.03	1.91	0.74	14.31	1.16	6.96	1,848	-40	97	30	13	278	19.65	-24.45			Apr-08
	4.03	10.30	27.11	26.25	47.01	1.96	0.64	14.24	1.16	6.95	1,848	-40	97	30	13	278	19.76	-24.47			Nov-06
	8.43	14.65	32.86	53.41	151.15	3.99	0.59	13	1.02	7.21	727.9	-113	101	111	0	141	30.79	-5.9			Aug-07
50	-5.60	-8.57	-14.34	-24.62	-52.00	1.31	1.04	7.97	-0.77	8.16	2,218	155	-100	34	10	237	-17.01	12.88	3.75		Jul-06
50	-5.79	-8.93	-15.03	-26.34	-53.85	1.05	1.79	7.98	-0.77	7.8	2,218	155	-100	34	10	237	-17.27	12.5		1.00	Jul-06
50	-5.51	-8.47	-14.25	-24.48	-52.05	1.36	1.04	7.88	-0.76	8.14	2,218	155	-100	34	10	237	-17.03	12.91			Jul-06
	-5.46	-8.38	-14.03	-23.97	-51.33	1.41	0.74	8.06	-0.78	8.42	2,218	155	-100	34	10	237	-16.8	12.91			Jan-10
	-5.55	-8.41	-14.04	-23.83	-51.07	1.49	0.64	8.08	-0.78	8.42	2,218	155	-100	34	10	237	-16.73	13.12			Jul-03
	3.10	9.83	17.30	35.36	102.66	4.21	0.94	15.67	1.1	10.53	1,361	-38	100	29	9	383	34.96	-27.89			Jun-14
50	3.13	9.85	17.21	34.85	101.29	4.43	1.09	15.66	1.1	10.32	1,361	-38	100	29	9	383	35.14	-28.07	3.75		Jul-06
50	2.98	9.45	16.42	31.82	93.80	4.02	1.84	15.62	1.09	9.54	1,361	-38	100	29	9	383	34.34	-28.22		1.00	Jul-06
50	3.05	9.82	17.10	34.67	101.19	4.46	1.09	15.67	1.1	10.24	1,361	-38	100	29	9	383	34.95	-27.91			Jul-06
	3.17	10.00	17.58	35.92	104.34	4.69	0.79	15.67	1.1	10.46	1,361	-38	100	29	9	383	35.25	-27.96			Apr-08
	3.02	9.59	16.94	33.72	98.55	4.4	1.34	15.64	1.1	10.25	1,361	-38	100	29	9	383	34.64	-28.01			Nov-15
	3.16	10.07	17.62	36.35	105.10	4.74	0.69	15.64	1.09	10.54	1,361	-38	100	29	9	383	35.16	-27.82			Mar-06
50	3.44	5.43	1.85	-4.67		0.06	1.55	7.86	12.58	9.61	383.4	-129	48	157	23	69			5.50		Dec-13
50	3.18	5.02	1.07	-6.80		0	2.3	7.9	14.32	9.4	383.4	-129	48	157	23	69				1.00	Dec-13
50	3.34	5.38	1.80	-4.69		0	1.55	7.86	13.47	9.59	383.4	-129	48	157	23	69					Dec-13
	3.52	5.66	2.21	-3.91		0.2	1.25	7.96	13.69	9.68	383.4	-129	48	157	23	69					Dec-13
	3.52	5.71	2.37	-3.49		0.25	1.15	7.89	13.82	9.69	383.4	-129	48	157	23	69					Dec-13
25	6.75	8.94	15.15	42.23	117.12	0.54	1.08	12.93	1.15	65.86	219.2	6	94	0	0	10	30.87	-20.79			Aug-92
	4.87	8.30	16.11			1.08	0.54			11.26	165.3	19	61	20	0						Mar-16
	4.82	8.25	16.05			1.08	0.54			11.27	165.3	19	61	20	0						Mar-16
500	3.58	7.18	10.84			0.2	1.86			11.34	120.7	4	96	0	0	337			5.75	1.00	Oct-15
500	3.46	6.81	9.98			0	2.61			11.17	120.7	4	96	0	0	337				1.00	Oct-15

Fund Name	Ticker Symbol	Traded On	Fund Type	Category and (Prospectus Objective)	Overall Rating	Reward Rating	Risk Rating	Recent Up/ Downgrade	Open to New Investors	Min Initial Investment
	MARKET		FUND TYPE, CATEGORY & OBJECTIVE		RATINGS				MINIMUMS	
Pinnacle Sherman Multi-Strategy Core Fund Class I	IPSHX	NAS CM	Open End	Moderate Alloc (Growth & Income)	C	C	B	Up	Y	1,000,000
Pinnacle Sherman Tactical Allocation Fund Class A Shares	PTAFX	NAS CM	Open End	Moderate Alloc (Growth & Income)	C	C	C	Down	Y	2,000
Pinnacle Sherman Tactical Allocation Fund Class C Shares	PTCFX	NAS CM	Open End	Moderate Alloc (Growth & Income)	C	C	C	Up	Y	2,000
Pinnacle Sherman Tactical Allocation Fund Class I Shares	PTIFX	NAS CM	Open End	Moderate Alloc (Growth & Income)	C	C	C	Down	Y	1,000,000
Pinnacle Value Fund	PVFIX	NAS CM	Open End	US Equity Small Cap (Small Company)	C+	C	B-	Up	Y	2,500
Pioneer Classic Balanced Fund Class A	AOBLX	NAS CM	Open End	Moderate Alloc (Balanced)	B-	C+	B	Down	Y	1,000
Pioneer Classic Balanced Fund Class C	PCBCX	NAS CM	Open End	Moderate Alloc (Balanced)	B-	C+	B	Down	Y	1,000
Pioneer Classic Balanced Fund Class K	PCBKX	NAS CM	Open End	Moderate Alloc (Balanced)	B-	C+	B	Down	Y	5,000,000
Pioneer Classic Balanced Fund Class R	CBPRX	NAS CM	Open End	Moderate Alloc (Balanced)	B-	C+	B	Down	Y	0
Pioneer Classic Balanced Fund Class Y	AYBLX	NAS CM	Open End	Moderate Alloc (Balanced)	B-	C+	B	Down	Y	5,000,000
Pioneer Core Equity Fund Class A	PIOTX	NAS CM	Open End	US Equity Large Cap Blend (Growth)	B	B	B-	Up	Y	1,000
Pioneer Core Equity Fund Class C	PCOTX	NAS CM	Open End	US Equity Large Cap Blend (Growth)	B-	B-	B-	Down	Y	1,000
Pioneer Core Equity Fund Class Y	PVFYX	NAS CM	Open End	US Equity Large Cap Blend (Growth)	B	B	B-	Up	Y	5,000,000
Pioneer Disciplined Growth Fund Class A	PINDX	NAS CM	Open End	US Equity Large Cap Growth (Growth)	B	B	B		Y	1,000
Pioneer Disciplined Growth Fund Class C	INDCX	NAS CM	Open End	US Equity Large Cap Growth (Growth)	B	B	B		Y	1,000
Pioneer Disciplined Growth Fund Class Y	INYDX	NAS CM	Open End	US Equity Large Cap Growth (Growth)	B	B	B		Y	5,000,000
Pioneer Disciplined Value Fund Class A	CVFCX	NAS CM	Open End	US Equity Large Cap Value (Growth)	B	B	C+		Y	1,000
Pioneer Disciplined Value Fund Class C	CVCFX	NAS CM	Open End	US Equity Large Cap Value (Growth)	B-	B	C+	Down	Y	1,000
Pioneer Disciplined Value Fund Class R	CVRFX	NAS CM	Open End	US Equity Large Cap Value (Growth)	B-	B	C+	Down	Y	0
Pioneer Disciplined Value Fund Class Y	CVFYX	NAS CM	Open End	US Equity Large Cap Value (Growth)	B	B	C+		Y	5,000,000
Pioneer Equity Income Fund Class A	PEQIX	NAS CM	Open End	US Equity Large Cap Value (Equity-Income)	B	B	A-		Y	1,000
Pioneer Equity Income Fund Class C	PCEQX	NAS CM	Open End	US Equity Large Cap Value (Equity-Income)	B	B-	A-		Y	1,000
Pioneer Equity Income Fund Class K	PEQKX	NAS CM	Open End	US Equity Large Cap Value (Equity-Income)	B+	B	A	Up	Y	5,000,000
Pioneer Equity Income Fund Class R	PQIRX	NAS CM	Open End	US Equity Large Cap Value (Equity-Income)	B	B	A-		Y	0
Pioneer Equity Income Fund Class Y	PYEQX	NAS CM	Open End	US Equity Large Cap Value (Equity-Income)	B+	B	A	Up	Y	5,000,000
Pioneer Flexible Opportunities Fund Class A	PMARX	NAS CM	Open End	Moderate Alloc (Growth & Income)	B	B-	B	Up	Y	1,000
Pioneer Flexible Opportunities Fund Class C	PRRCX	NAS CM	Open End	Moderate Alloc (Growth & Income)	B-	C+	B	Up	Y	1,000
Pioneer Flexible Opportunities Fund Class R	MUARX	NAS CM	Open End	Moderate Alloc (Growth & Income)	B-	C+	B	Up	Y	0
Pioneer Flexible Opportunities Fund Class Y	PMYRX	NAS CM	Open End	Moderate Alloc (Growth & Income)	B	B-	B	Up	Y	5,000,000
Pioneer Fund Class A	PIODX	NAS CM	Open End	US Equity Large Cap Blend (Growth & Income)	B-	B	B-	Down	Y	1,000
Pioneer Fund Class C	PCODX	NAS CM	Open End	US Equity Large Cap Blend (Growth & Income)	B-	B-	B-	Down	Y	1,000
Pioneer Fund Class R	PIORX	NAS CM	Open End	US Equity Large Cap Blend (Growth & Income)	B-	B-	B-	Down	Y	0
Pioneer Fund Class Y	PYODX	NAS CM	Open End	US Equity Large Cap Blend (Growth & Income)	B	B	B-		Y	5,000,000
Pioneer Fundamental Growth Fund Class A	PIGFX	NAS CM	Open End	US Equity Large Cap Growth (Growth)	B	B-	A+		Y	1,000
Pioneer Fundamental Growth Fund Class C	FUNCX	NAS CM	Open End	US Equity Large Cap Growth (Growth)	B	B-	A		Y	1,000
Pioneer Fundamental Growth Fund Class K Shares	PFGKX	NAS CM	Open End	US Equity Large Cap Growth (Growth)	B+	B	A+	Up	Y	5,000,000
Pioneer Fundamental Growth Fund Class R	PFGRX	NAS CM	Open End	US Equity Large Cap Growth (Growth)	B	B-	B+		Y	0
Pioneer Fundamental Growth Fund Class Y	FUNYX	NAS CM	Open End	US Equity Large Cap Growth (Growth)	B	B-	B+		Y	5,000,000
Pioneer Global Equity Fund Class A	GLOSX	NAS CM	Open End	Global Equity (World Stock)	B-	B-	C+	Up	Y	1,000
Pioneer Global Equity Fund Class C	GCSLX	NAS CM	Open End	Global Equity (World Stock)	C+	B-	C+	Down	Y	1,000
Pioneer Global Equity Fund Class K	PGEKX	NAS CM	Open End	Global Equity (World Stock)	B-	B	C+	Down	Y	5,000,000
Pioneer Global Equity Fund Class R	PRGEX	NAS CM	Open End	Global Equity (World Stock)	B-	B-	C+	Up	Y	0
Pioneer Global Equity Fund Class Y	PGSYX	NAS CM	Open End	Global Equity (World Stock)	B-	B	C+	Down	Y	5,000,000
Pioneer International Equity Fund Class A	PIIFX	NAS CM	Open End	Global Equity Large Cap (Foreign Stock)	B-	B-	B	Up	Y	1,000
Pioneer International Equity Fund Class C	PCITX	NAS CM	Open End	Global Equity Large Cap (Foreign Stock)	B-	C+	B	Up	Y	1,000
Pioneer International Equity Fund Class Y	INVYX	NAS CM	Open End	Global Equity Large Cap (Foreign Stock)	B-	B-	B	Up	Y	5,000,000
Pioneer Mid Cap Value Fund Class A	PCGRX	NAS CM	Open End	US Equity Mid Cap (Growth)	B-	B-	B	Up	Y	1,000
Pioneer Mid Cap Value Fund Class C	PCCGX	NAS CM	Open End	US Equity Mid Cap (Growth)	B-	C+	B	Up	Y	1,000
Pioneer Mid Cap Value Fund Class K	PMCKX	NAS CM	Open End	US Equity Mid Cap (Growth)	B-	B-	B	Up	Y	5,000,000
Pioneer Mid Cap Value Fund Class R	PCMRX	NAS CM	Open End	US Equity Mid Cap (Growth)	B-	C+	B	Up	Y	0
Pioneer Mid Cap Value Fund Class Y	PYCGX	NAS CM	Open End	US Equity Mid Cap (Growth)	B-	B-	B	Up	Y	5,000,000
Pioneer Multi-Asset Income Fund A	PMAIX	NAS CM	Open End	Cautious Alloc (Multi-Asset Global)	B-	B-	B-	Down	Y	1,000

★ Expanded analysis of this fund is included in Section II.

Min Additional Investment	TOTAL RETURNS 3-Month Total Return	6-Month Total Return	1-Year Total Return	3-Year Total Return	5-Year Total Return	PERFORMANCE Dividend Yield (TTM)	Expense Ratio	3-Yr Std Deviation	3-Year Beta	ASSETS NAV	Total Assets (MIL)	ASSET ALLOCATION & TURNOVER %Cash	%Stocks	%Bonds	%Other	Turnover Ratio	BULL & BEAR Last Bull Market Total Return	Last Bear Market Total Return	FEES Front End Fee (%)	Back End Fee (%)	Inception Date
5,000	3.70	7.38	11.13			0.3	1.61			11.39	120.7	4	96	0	0	337					Oct-15
500	1.64	3.00	5.94	1.14		0.07	1.87	5.2	0.56	10.63	41.9	2	59	8	20	422			5.75		Jun-13
500	1.52	2.71	5.19	-1.13		0.01	2.62	5.15	0.56	10.34	41.9	2	59	8	20	422				1.00	Jun-13
5,000	1.70	3.15	6.29	1.89		0.14	1.62	5.16	0.56	10.68	41.9	2	59	8	20	422					Jun-13
100	3.07	4.00	-0.12	9.71	34.70	0	1.67	8.94	0.44	15.62	61.7	50	50	0	0	43	11.79	-7.64			Apr-03
100	4.46	8.07	15.00	20.07	60.38	1.82	1.29	6.36	0.61	9.52	275.8	0	64	35	0	51	16.41	-12.04	4.50		Dec-91
500	4.30	7.71	14.17	17.51	54.31	1.06	2.04	6.36	0.61	9.46	275.8	0	64	35	0	51	15.84	-12.36		1.00	Sep-05
	4.55	8.39	15.46	21.14	62.63	2.17	0.98	6.33	0.61	9.52	275.8	0	64	35	0	51	16.59	-11.94			Dec-15
	4.41	8.02	14.84	19.50	58.82	1.57	1.43	6.35	0.61	9.53	275.8	0	64	35	0	51	16.25	-12.12			Jul-15
	4.48	8.18	15.19	20.90	62.30	2.02	1.08	6.36	0.61	9.58	275.8	0	64	35	0	51	16.59	-11.94			Dec-91
100	5.89	12.46	24.77	31.84	96.02	0.91	0.94	10.77	1.04	20.58	1,696	2	98	0	0	80	25.31	-16.3	5.75		Nov-99
500	5.70	12.03	23.74	28.75	88.01	0.44	1.76	10.77	1.04	18.26	1,696	2	98	0	0	80	24.81	-16.66		1.00	Nov-99
	5.98	12.64	25.10	33.07	99.15	1.13	0.63	10.77	1.04	20.8	1,696	2	98	0	0	80	25.58	-16.24			Aug-04
100	6.13	11.42	26.25	33.70	108.95	0.21	1.13	10.96	0.99	18.2	1,245	4	96	0	0	76	27.16	-17.54	5.75		Dec-05
500	5.86	10.91	25.20	30.34	100.22	0	1.98	10.9	0.98	16.22	1,245	4	96	0	0	76	26.61	-17.94		1.00	Jul-08
	6.14	11.55	26.54	34.78	112.22	0.41	0.86	10.93	0.99	18.59	1,245	4	96	0	0	76	27.43	-17.45			Jul-08
100	4.88	10.22	21.43	29.16	88.00	0.79	1.18	11.01	1.04	15.92	590.2	0	100	0	0	115	24.23	-18.51	5.75		Dec-05
500	4.71	9.76	20.49	26.24	81.13	0.15	1.9	11.02	1.04	15.65	590.2	0	100	0	0	115	23.68	-18.89		1.00	Jul-08
	4.82	10.00	21.07	28.15	85.93	0.67	1.4	11.05	1.04	15.39	590.2	0	100	0	0	115	24.24	-18.51			Dec-05
	5.02	10.41	21.82	30.39	91.18	1.1	0.84	11.02	1.04	15.99	590.2	0	100	0	0	115	24.53	-18.47			Jul-08
100	5.79	10.37	14.95	35.94	102.36	1.39	1.04	9.53	0.89	35.79	2,312	1	99	0	0	35	19.42	-14.37	5.75		Jul-90
100	5.57	9.97	14.09	32.99	95.10	0.7	1.77	9.53	0.89	35.17	2,312	1	99	0	0	35	18.91	-14.65		1.00	Jan-96
	5.86	10.54	15.35	37.44	106.33	1.7	0.67	9.54	0.89	35.85	2,312	1	99	0	0	35	19.42	-14.37			Dec-12
	5.60	10.14	14.50	34.43	98.77	1.03	1.4	9.54	0.89	36.42	2,312	1	99	0	0	35	19.29	-14.55			Apr-03
	5.79	10.48	15.21	37.01	105.22	1.58	0.77	9.53	0.89	36.22	2,312	1	99	0	0	35	19.69	-14.24			Jul-98
100	4.51	11.82	23.24	29.77	44.39	0.87	1.22	9.14	0.95	13.48	660.5	13	77	5	4	230	11.37	-5.73	4.50		May-10
500	4.34	11.45	22.44	26.84	39.02	0.43	1.97	9.13	0.95	13.27	660.5	13	77	5	4	230	10.88	-6.03		1.00	May-10
	4.54	11.67	22.78	27.32	41.09	0.55	1.74	9.19	0.95	13.42	660.5	13	77	5	4	230	11.18	-5.74			Sep-13
	4.62	12.00	23.66	30.97	46.55	1.13	0.93	9.17	0.95	13.54	660.5	13	77	5	4	230	11.51	-5.55			May-10
100	6.37	11.49	21.53	31.30	98.77	0.87	0.98	9.84	0.96	28.81	5,008	1	99	0	0	62	21.1	-20.2	5.75		Feb-28
500	6.14	11.01	20.57	28.21	91.09	0.27	1.77	9.85	0.96	25.17	5,008	1	99	0	0	62	20.51	-20.43		1.00	Jul-96
	6.24	11.20	20.98	29.73	94.98	0.48	1.41	9.85	0.96	28.93	5,008	1	99	0	0	62	20.93	-20.31			Apr-03
	6.41	11.63	21.85	32.34	101.59	1.06	0.73	9.83	0.96	29.17	5,008	1	99	0	0	62	21.37	-20.07			May-99
100	4.36	8.29	22.61	33.94	107.75	0.24	1.09	10.08	0.9	22.5	6,346	2	98	0	0	23	24.31	-11.31	5.75		Aug-02
500	4.16	7.96	21.76	31.23	100.65	0	1.77	10.08	0.9	20.61	6,346	2	98	0	0	23	23.72	-11.58		1.00	Dec-05
	4.47	8.54	23.19	35.69	112.15	0.54	0.67	10.08	0.9	22.5	6,346	2	98	0	0	23	24.31	-11.31			Dec-12
	4.29	8.14	22.28	32.76	104.71	0.05	1.4	10.08	0.9	22.17	6,346	2	98	0	0	23	24.13	-11.41			Apr-12
	4.46	8.50	23.02	35.25	110.96	0.48	0.77	10.07	0.9	22.69	6,346	2	98	0	0	23	24.52	-11.11			Apr-09
100	5.85	13.74	28.44	30.23	84.12	2.15	1.25	11.4	1.03	16.3	317.1	5	95	0	0	85	17.93	-21.3	5.75		Dec-05
500	5.78	13.34	27.57	27.42	76.92	0.86	2.15	11.4	1.03	16.01	317.1	5	95	0	0	85	17.23	-21.63		1.00	Dec-05
	5.97	13.93	29.00	32.03	86.66	2.99	0.8	11.39	1.03	16.27	317.1	5	95	0	0	85	17.93	-21.3			Dec-14
	5.76	13.48	27.98	29.26	81.83	1.73	1.55	11.38	1.03	16.22	317.1	5	95	0	0	85	17.76	-21.38			Jul-15
	5.94	13.95	29.01	31.98	88.48	2.95	0.8	11.4	1.03	16.32	317.1	5	95	0	0	85	18.12	-21.11			Dec-08
100	3.76	10.19	27.10	25.07	46.74	0.71	1.25	11.55	0.91	24.64	185.4	3	97	0	0	29	10.33	-22.05	5.75		Mar-93
500	3.48	9.67	25.88	21.67	40.22	0.08	2.15	11.55	0.91	21.53	185.4	3	97	0	0	29	9.83	-22.38		1.00	Jan-96
	3.83	10.39	27.57	26.52	49.50	1.01	0.9	11.56	0.91	24.62	185.4	3	97	0	0	29	10.62	-21.91			Apr-09
100	5.71	9.82	12.85	21.36	89.99	0.39	1.08	11.62	1.06	25.26	979.3	0	100	0	0	70	23.83	-22.94	5.75		Jul-90
500	5.50	9.33	11.89	18.31	82.15	0	1.92	11.58	1.06	17.54	979.3	0	100	0	0	70	23.2	-23.23		1.00	Jan-96
	5.81	10.00	13.22	22.59	91.92	0.71	0.71	11.6	1.06	25.25	979.3	0	100	0	0	70	23.83	-22.94			Mar-15
	5.57	9.59	12.34	19.89	86.32	0.05	1.47	11.61	1.06	24.72	979.3	0	100	0	0	70	23.56	-23.06			Apr-03
	5.79	9.98	13.12	22.30	92.94	0.57	0.82	11.61	1.06	27.18	979.3	0	100	0	0	70	24.16	-22.82			Jul-98
100	2.42	5.94	16.17	25.76	48.52	4.61	1.16	7.04	-0.07	11.88	988.4	10	47	37	2	131			4.50		Dec-11

	MARKET			FUND TYPE, CATEGORY & OBJECTIVE	RATINGS				MINIMUMS	
Fund Name	Ticker Symbol	Traded On	Fund Type	Category and (Prospectus Objective)	Overall Rating	Reward Rating	Risk Rating	Recent Up/ Downgrade	Open to New Investors	Min Initial Investment
Pioneer Multi-Asset Income Fund C	PMACX	NAS CM	Open End	Cautious Alloc (Multi-Asset Global)	B-	C+	B-	Down	Y	1,000
Pioneer Multi-Asset Income Fund Class K	PMFKX	NAS CM	Open End	Cautious Alloc (Multi-Asset Global)	B-	B-	B-	Down	Y	5,000,000
Pioneer Multi-Asset Income Fund Class R	PMFRX	NAS CM	Open End	Cautious Alloc (Multi-Asset Global)	B-	C+	B-	Down	Y	0
Pioneer Multi-Asset Income Fund Y	PMFYX	NAS CM	Open End	Cautious Alloc (Multi-Asset Global)	B-	B-	B-	Down	Y	5,000,000
Pioneer Real Estate Fund Class A	PWREX	NAS CM	Open End	Real Estate Sector Equity (Real Estate)	B-	C+	B+		Y	1,000
Pioneer Real Estate Fund Class C	PCREX	NAS CM	Open End	Real Estate Sector Equity (Real Estate)	B-	C+	B		Y	1,000
Pioneer Real Estate Fund Class Y	PYREX	NAS CM	Open End	Real Estate Sector Equity (Real Estate)	B	C+	B+	Up	Y	5,000,000
Pioneer Select Mid Cap Growth Fund Class A	PGOFX	NAS CM	Open End	US Equity Mid Cap (Growth)	B	B+	B-	Up	Y	1,000
Pioneer Select Mid Cap Growth Fund Class C	GOFCX	NAS CM	Open End	US Equity Mid Cap (Growth)	B	B	C+	Up	Y	1,000
Pioneer Select Mid Cap Growth Fund Class K	PSMKX	NAS CM	Open End	US Equity Mid Cap (Growth)	B	B+	B-	Up	Y	5,000,000
Pioneer Select Mid Cap Growth Fund Class R	PGRRX	NAS CM	Open End	US Equity Mid Cap (Growth)	B	B	B-	Up	Y	0
Pioneer Select Mid Cap Growth Fund Class Y	GROYX	NAS CM	Open End	US Equity Mid Cap (Growth)	B	B+	B-	Up	Y	5,000,000
Pioneer Solutions - Balanced Fund Class A	PIALX	NAS CM	Open End	Moderate Alloc (Asset Alloc)	B-	C+	B+	Up	Y	1,000
Pioneer Solutions - Balanced Fund Class C	PIDCX	NAS CM	Open End	Moderate Alloc (Asset Alloc)	B-	C	B+	Up	Y	1,000
Pioneer Solutions - Balanced Fund Class R	BALRX	NAS CM	Open End	Moderate Alloc (Asset Alloc)	C+	C+	B	Up	Y	0
Pioneer Solutions - Balanced Fund Class Y	IMOYX	NAS CM	Open End	Moderate Alloc (Asset Alloc)	B-	C+	B+	Up	Y	5,000,000
Pioneer Solutions - Conservative Fund Class A	PIAVX	NAS CM	Open End	Cautious Alloc (Asset Alloc)	B-	C	A-	Up	Y	1,000
Pioneer Solutions - Conservative Fund Class C	PICVX	NAS CM	Open End	Cautious Alloc (Asset Alloc)	B-	C	B+	Up	Y	1,000
Pioneer Solutions - Conservative Fund Class R	PSMRX	NAS CM	Open End	Cautious Alloc (Asset Alloc)	B-	C	A-	Up	Y	0
Pioneer Solutions - Conservative Fund Class Y	IBBCX	NAS CM	Open End	Cautious Alloc (Asset Alloc)	B-	C	A-	Up	Y	5,000,000
Pioneer Solutions - Growth Fund Class A	GRAAX	NAS CM	Open End	Aggressive Alloc (Asset Alloc)	B-	C+	B-	Up	Y	1,000
Pioneer Solutions - Growth Fund Class C	GRACX	NAS CM	Open End	Aggressive Alloc (Asset Alloc)	B-	C+	B	Up	Y	1,000
Pioneer Solutions - Growth Fund Class R	SOGRX	NAS CM	Open End	Aggressive Alloc (Asset Alloc)	B-	C+	B-	Up	Y	0
Pioneer Solutions - Growth Fund Class Y	IBGYX	NAS CM	Open End	Aggressive Alloc (Asset Alloc)	B-	C+	B-	Down	Y	5,000,000
Plumb Balanced Fund	PLBBX	NAS CM	Open End	Moderate Alloc (Balanced)	B-	B-	B	Down	Y	2,500
Plumb Equity Fund	PLBEX	NAS CM	Open End	US Equity Large Cap Growth (Growth)	B+	A	B-	Up	Y	2,500
PMC Diversified Equity Fund	PMDEX	NAS CM	Open End	US Equity Large Cap Blend (Growth)	C+	B-	C+	Down	Y	1,000
PNC Balanced Allocation Class T	PBTTX	NAS CM	Open End	Moderate Alloc (Balanced)	B	C+	A-	Up	Y	1,000
PNC Balanced Allocation Fund Class A	PBAAX	NAS CM	Open End	Moderate Alloc (Balanced)	B-	C+	B	Up	Y	1,000
PNC Balanced Allocation Fund Class C	PBCCX	NAS CM	Open End	Moderate Alloc (Balanced)	B	C+	A-	Up	Y	1,000
PNC Balanced Allocation Fund Class I	PBLIX	NAS CM	Open End	Moderate Alloc (Balanced)	B	C+	A-	Up	Y	0
PNC Emerging Markets Equity Fund Class I	PIEFX	NAS CM	Open End	Emerging Markets Equity (Div Emerging Mkts)	U	U	U		Y	1,000
PNC International Equity Fund Class A	PMIEX	NAS CM	Open End	Global Equity Large Cap (Foreign Stock)	B	B	B	Up	Y	1,000
PNC International Equity Fund Class C	PIUCX	NAS CM	Open End	Global Equity Large Cap (Foreign Stock)	B	B	B	Up	Y	1,000
PNC International Equity Fund Class Institutional	PIUIX	NAS CM	Open End	Global Equity Large Cap (Foreign Stock)	B	B	B	Up	Y	0
PNC International Growth Fund Class A	PIGAX	NAS CM	Open End	Global Equity Large Cap (Growth)	C-	C	B-	Up	Y	1,000
PNC International Growth Fund Class I	PIGDX	NAS CM	Open End	Global Equity Large Cap (Growth)	C-	C	B-	Up	Y	0
PNC Multi Factor Small Cap Growth Fund Class A	PLWAX	NAS CM	Open End	US Equity Small Cap (Small Company)	B+	B+	B+	Up	Y	1,000
PNC Multi Factor Small Cap Growth Fund Class C	PLWCX	NAS CM	Open End	US Equity Small Cap (Small Company)	B+	B+	B+	Up	Y	1,000
PNC Multi Factor Small Cap Growth Fund Class I	PLTIX	NAS CM	Open End	US Equity Small Cap (Small Company)	B+	B+	B+	Up	Y	0
PNC Multi-Factor All Cap Fund Class A	PLEAX	NAS CM	Open End	US Equity Large Cap Blend (Growth)	B	B	A		Y	1,000
PNC Multi-Factor All Cap Fund Class C	PLECX	NAS CM	Open End	US Equity Large Cap Blend (Growth)	B	B-	A-	Up	Y	1,000
PNC Multi-Factor All Cap Fund Class I	PLEIX	NAS CM	Open End	US Equity Large Cap Blend (Growth)	B+	B	A	Up	Y	0
PNC Multi-Factor Large Cap Growth Fund Class A	PEWAX	NAS CM	Open End	US Equity Large Cap Growth (Growth)	A-	B+	A-	Up	Y	1,000
PNC Multi-Factor Large Cap Growth Fund Class C	PEWCX	NAS CM	Open End	US Equity Large Cap Growth (Growth)	B+	B	A-	Up	Y	1,000
PNC Multi-Factor Large Cap Growth Fund Class I	PEWIX	NAS CM	Open End	US Equity Large Cap Growth (Growth)	A-	A-	A	Up	Y	0
PNC Multi-Factor Large Cap Value Fund Class A	PLVAX	NAS CM	Open End	US Equity Large Cap Value (Growth)	B	C+	A-	Up	Y	1,000
PNC Multi-Factor Large Cap Value Fund Class C	PALVX	NAS CM	Open End	US Equity Large Cap Value (Growth)	B	C+	A-	Up	Y	1,000
PNC Multi-Factor Large Cap Value Fund Class I	PLIVX	NAS CM	Open End	US Equity Large Cap Value (Growth)	B	C+	A-	Up	Y	0
PNC Multiple Factor Small Cap Core Fund Class A	PLOAX	NAS CM	Open End	US Equity Small Cap (Small Company)	B+	B+	B+	Up	Y	1,000
PNC Multiple Factor Small Cap Core Fund Class C	PLOCX	NAS CM	Open End	US Equity Small Cap (Small Company)	B+	B+	B+	Up	Y	1,000
PNC Multiple Factor Small Cap Core Fund Class I	PLOIX	NAS CM	Open End	US Equity Small Cap (Small Company)	B+	B+	B+	Up	Y	0

★Expanded analysis of this fund is included in Section II.

	TOTAL RETURNS					PERFORMANCE				ASSETS		ASSET ALLOCATION & TURNOVER					BULL & BEAR		FEES		
Min Additional Investment	3-Month Total Return	6-Month Total Return	1-Year Total Return	3-Year Total Return	5-Year Total Return	Dividend Yield (TTM)	Expense Ratio	3-Yr Std Deviation	3-Year Beta	NAV	Total Assets (MIL)	%Cash	%Stocks	%Bonds	%Other	Turnover Ratio	Last Bull Market Total Return	Last Bear Market Total Return	Front End Fee (%)	Back End Fee (%)	Inception Date
500	2.28	5.51	15.26	22.73	42.58	3.85	2	7.06	-0.07	11.84	988.4	10	47	37	2	131				1.00	Dec-11
	2.44	5.98	16.46	28.22	52.07	4.83	0.94	7	-0.03	12.04	988.4	10	47	37	2	131					Dec-14
	2.34	5.64	15.63	24.48	46.17	4.17	1.68	7.01	-0.06	11.92	988.4	10	47	37	2	131					Dec-14
	2.46	6.03	16.41	26.39	49.90	4.8	0.96	7.04	-0.07	11.86	988.4	10	47	37	2	131					Dec-11
100	0.95	1.96	3.19	12.45	51.37	2.6	1.41	13.44	0.99	24.59	118.9	2	98	0	0	15	30.47	-15.64	5.75		Oct-93
500	0.81	1.61	2.45	9.80	45.27	1.88	2.22	13.42	0.99	24.09	118.9	2	98	0	0	15	29.84	-15.96		1.00	Jan-96
	1.12	2.18	3.58	13.67	54.44	2.89	1.07	13.45	0.99	24.56	118.9	2	98	0	0	15	30.85	-15.4			Apr-98
100	8.55	15.55	29.78	35.37	113.50	0	1.06	11.34	1	41.99	1,577	1	99	0	0	99	28.59	-21.01	5.75		Jun-93
500	8.31	15.08	28.75	32.16	104.83	0	1.86	11.36	1	30.92	1,577	1	99	0	0	99	27.84	-21.26		1.00	Jan-02
	8.65	15.75	30.24	36.92	115.93	0	0.68	11.35	1	42.53	1,577	1	99	0	0	99	28.59	-21.01			Dec-14
	8.42	15.29	29.24	33.82	109.79	0	1.43	11.34	1	40.46	1,577	1	99	0	0	99	28.59	-21.01			Jun-93
	8.59	15.68	30.09	36.44	116.55	0	0.82	11.36	1	45.34	1,577	1	99	0	0	99	28.93	-20.86			Jun-04
100	2.57	5.79	12.89	12.63	37.46	1.95	1.36	6.04	-0.09	12.23	166.2	5	64	28	1	27	13.58	-13.34	5.75		Aug-04
500	2.32	5.45	11.97	10.23	32.69	1.43	2.06	6.06	-0.11	11.26	166.2	5	64	28	1	27	13.06	-13.54		1.00	Aug-04
	2.53	5.77	12.60	11.92	35.92	1.88	1.58	6.04	-0.1	12.17	166.2	5	64	28	1	27	13.41	-13.43			Jul-15
	2.65	5.92	13.13	13.44	39.28	2.17	1.15	6.06	-0.09	12.39	166.2	5	64	28	1	27	13.93	-13.27			Sep-05
100	1.56	3.40	7.93	9.26	23.47	2.18	1.26	3.45	0.34	10.61	56.1	3	28	65	2	31	8.75	-7.44	5.75		May-05
500	1.34	3.03	7.15	6.80	19.00	1.47	2.01	3.49	0.33	10.3	56.1	3	28	65	2	31	8.31	-7.82		1.00	May-05
	1.46	3.30	7.72	8.53	22.04	1.99	1.46	3.49	0.32	10.59	56.1	3	28	65	2	31	8.59	-7.54			Jul-15
	1.46	3.40	7.88	9.30	22.59	2.4	1.21	3.5	0.35	9.97	56.1	3	28	65	2	31	8.82	-8.04			Oct-05
100	2.72	7.20	16.77	17.84	49.22	1.1	1.36	8.09	-0.42	13.88	312.6	4	95	0	1	26	16.11	-16.11	5.75		Aug-04
500	3.20	7.57	16.71	16.17	45.02	0.53	2.07	8.08	-0.41	13.08	312.6	4	95	0	1	26	15.51	-16.25		1.00	Aug-04
	4.13	8.71	18.08	18.27	49.52	1.07	1.62	8.1	-0.42		312.6	4	95	0	1	26	15.94	-16.2			Jul-15
	2.59	7.19	16.83	18.57	50.83	1.34	1.13	8.04	-0.41	14.18	312.6	4	95	0	1	26	16.13	-16.89			Sep-05
100	5.82	8.80	23.22	27.89	75.49	0.42	1.19	7.56	0.67	28.37	39.6	6	61	26	0	29	15.18	-13.12			May-07
100	9.97	15.55	39.70	45.59	119.62	0	1.19	11.51	0.99	27.45	26.0	2	98	0	0	18	19.43	-18.8			May-07
50	5.61	10.75	21.05	23.15	71.05	0.49	1.39	10.24	0.95	27.34	722.8	2	98	0	0	139	22.24	-20.82			Aug-09
50	3.72	7.49	15.34	20.05	47.98	0.33	1.53	5.64	0.52	13.45	22.2	3	59	38	0	88	17.43	-12.46	3.50		Apr-15
50	3.78	7.55	15.36	19.13	47.60	0.51	1.29	5.9	0.54	13.33	22.2	3	59	38	0	88	17.8	-12.41	4.75		Jul-98
50	3.55	7.13	14.61	16.65	42.51	0	2.03	5.88	0.54	13.11	22.2	3	59	38	0	88	17.1	-12.62		1.00	Apr-00
	3.87	7.73	15.75	20.19	49.63	0.79	1.03	5.91	0.54	13.27	22.2	3	59	38	0	88	17.77	-12.27			Jul-98
	8.75	20.43					1.27			13.62	13.3	4	96	0	0	7					Mar-17
50	5.33	12.75	32.86	33.43	66.21	0.57	1.29	11.53	0.9	24.23	1,227	9	91	0	0	32	17.51	-25.41	5.50		Aug-97
50	5.17	12.38	31.95	30.93	60.94	0.01	1.99	11.55	0.9	23.26	1,227	9	91	0	0	32	16.83	-25.63		1.00	Jan-00
	5.43	12.92	33.27	34.75	68.73	0.74	0.99	11.54	0.9	24.44	1,227	9	91	0	0	32	17.54	-25.31			Aug-97
50	6.09	16.12	42.19			0	1.12			14.35	7.4	4	96	0	0	49			5.50		Feb-16
	6.15	16.18	42.37			0	0.86			14.34	7.4	4	96	0	0	49					Feb-16
50	2.46	7.93	14.76	31.80	110.18	0	1.15	13.14	0.84	23.75	158.6	1	99	0	0	94	21.39	-19.95	5.50		Sep-05
50	2.26	7.58	13.97	29.15	102.97	0	1.85	13.11	0.84	22.9	158.6	1	99	0	0	94	20.77	-20.23		1.00	Sep-05
	2.52	8.10	15.09	32.95	112.92	0	0.85	13.14	0.84	24.25	158.6	1	99	0	0	94	21.51	-19.87			Sep-05
50	5.56	11.43	19.58	30.32	94.49	0.85	0.95	10.21	0.94	20.89	9.9	2	98	0	0	134	24.49	-15.28	5.50		Aug-97
50	5.38	11.02	18.74	27.66	87.90	0.61	1.65	10.15	0.93	19.18	9.9	2	98	0	0	134	23.95	-15.56		1.00	Jan-00
	5.61	11.57	19.93	31.45	97.12	1.12	0.65	10.17	0.93	21.35	9.9	2	98	0	0	134	24.56	-15.17			Aug-97
50	8.60	15.98	31.21	36.30	116.12	0.42	0.96	10.32	0.91	37.36	95.6	2	98	0	0	131	27.78	-15.37	5.50		Apr-91
50	8.44	15.60	30.42	33.83	109.94	0	1.66	10.32	0.91	33.78	95.6	2	98	0	0	131	27.1	-15.58		1.00	Jan-00
	8.67	16.14	31.63	37.54	118.97	0.59	0.66	10.33	0.91	38.01	95.6	2	98	0	0	131	27.86	-15.27			Dec-89
50	6.00	9.81	14.62	22.62	88.48	0.99	0.96	9.75	0.9	25.69	107.1	1	99	0	0	141	23.11	-17.52	5.50		Aug-94
50	5.81	9.50	13.93	20.59	83.05	0.52	1.66	9.74	0.9	25.19	107.1	1	99	0	0	141	22.45	-17.77		1.00	Jan-00
	6.06	9.96	14.90	23.65	90.86	1.3	0.66	9.72	0.9	25.75	107.1	1	99	0	0	141	23.21	-17.45			Jul-94
50	3.05	9.15	12.19	28.78	113.87	0.27	1.16	11.79	0.8	26.25	416.9	2	98	0	0	82	23.33	-19.88	5.50		Sep-05
	2.84	8.77	11.41	27.23	109.26	0.48	1.86	11.77	0.8	26.3	416.9	2	98	0	0	82	22.97	-20.08		1.00	Sep-16
	3.13	9.31	12.52	29.92	116.91	0.48	0.86	11.8	0.8	26.45	416.9	2	98	0	0	82	23.5	-19.83			Sep-05

	MARKET		FUND TYPE, CATEGORY & OBJECTIVE		RATINGS				MINIMUMS	
Fund Name	Ticker Symbol	Traded On	Fund Type	Category and (Prospectus Objective)	Overall Rating	Reward Rating	Risk Rating	Recent Up/ Downgrade	Open to New Investors	Min Initial Investment
PNC Multiple Factor Small Cap Value Fund Class A	PMRRX	NAS CM	Open End	US Equity Small Cap (Small Company)	B-	B	B-	Up	Y	1,000
PNC Multiple Factor Small Cap Value Fund Class C	PSVCX	NAS CM	Open End	US Equity Small Cap (Small Company)	B-	B-	B-	Up	Y	1,000
PNC Multiple Factor Small Cap Value Fund Class I	PMUIX	NAS CM	Open End	US Equity Small Cap (Small Company)	B	B	B-	Up	Y	0
PNC Small Cap Fund Class A	PPCAX	NAS CM	Open End	US Equity Small Cap (Small Company)	B	B	B	Up	Y	1,000
PNC Small Cap Fund Class C	PPCCX	NAS CM	Open End	US Equity Small Cap (Small Company)	B	B	B	Up	Y	1,000
PNC Small Cap Fund Class I	PPCIX	NAS CM	Open End	US Equity Small Cap (Small Company)	B	B	B	Up	Y	0
Polaris Global Value Fund	PGVFX	NAS CM	Open End	Global Equity Mid/Small Cap (Growth)	B	B	B-	Up	Y	2,500
Polen Global Growth Fund Institutional Class	PGIIX	NAS CM	Open End	Global Equity (Growth)	B	C+	B+	Up	Y	100,000
Polen Global Growth Fund Investor Class	PGIRX	NAS CM	Open End	Global Equity (Growth)	B	C+	B+	Up	Y	3,000
Polen Growth Fund Institutional Class	POLIX	NAS CM	Open End	US Equity Large Cap Growth (Growth)	B+	B	A	Up	Y	100,000
Polen Growth Fund Investor Class	POLRX	NAS CM	Open End	US Equity Large Cap Growth (Growth)	B+	B	A	Up	Y	3,000
Polen International Growth Fund Institutional Class	POIIX	NAS CM	Open End	Global Equity Large Cap (Foreign Stock)	D-	D+	A-		Y	100,000
Polen International Growth Fund Investor Class	POIRX	NAS CM	Open End	Global Equity Large Cap (Foreign Stock)	D-	D+	A-		Y	3,000
Polen U.S. Small Company Growth Fund Institutional Class	PBSIX	NAS CM	Open End	US Equity Small Cap (Small Company)	U	U	U		Y	100,000
Poplar Forest Cornerstone Fund Class A	PFCFX	NAS CM	Open End	Moderate Alloc (Balanced)	C+	C	B-	Up	Y	25,000
Poplar Forest Cornerstone Fund Institutional Class	IPFCX	NAS CM	Open End	Moderate Alloc (Balanced)	C+	C	B-	Up	Y	100,000
Poplar Forest Outliers Fund Institutional Class	IPFOX	NAS CM	Open End	US Equity Mid Cap (Growth)	C	C	C		Y	100,000
Poplar Forest Partners Fund Class A	PFPFX	NAS CM	Open End	US Equity Large Cap Value (Growth)	C+	C+	C+		Y	25,000
Poplar Forest Partners Fund Institutional Class	IPFPX	NAS CM	Open End	US Equity Large Cap Value (Growth)	C+	C+	C+		Y	100,000
Port Street Inst Opp Fund Inst Cls	PSOFX	NAS CM	Open End	Moderate Alloc (Growth)	C-	C-	A	Up	Y	1,000
Port Street Quality Growth Fund Institutional Class	PSQGX	NAS CM	Open End	US Equity Large Cap Blend (Growth)	B	C+	A-		Y	2,000
Portfolio 21 Global Equity Fund Class Institutional	PORIX	NAS CM	Open End	Global Equity (World Stock)	B	B	B+	Up	Y	100,000
Portfolio 21 Global Equity Fund Class R	PORTX	NAS CM	Open End	Global Equity (World Stock)	B	B	B+	Up	Y	5,000
Power Dividend Index Fund Class A	PWDAX	NAS CM	Open End	US Equity Large Cap Value (Equity-Income)	B-	C+	B-		Y	1,000
Power Dividend Index Fund Class C	PWDCX	NAS CM	Open End	US Equity Large Cap Value (Equity-Income)	C+	C+	B-	Down	Y	2,500
Power Dividend Index Fund Class I	PWDIX	NAS CM	Open End	US Equity Large Cap Value (Equity-Income)	B-	C+	B		Y	100,000
Power Dividend Index VIT Fund Class 1 shares	US66537U5020		Open End	US Equity Large Cap Value (Growth & Income)	C+	C	B	Up	Y	0
Power Momentum Index Fund Classs A Shares	MOJAX	NAS CM	Open End	Moderate Alloc (Growth & Income)	D-	D+	A-		Y	1,000
Power Momentum Index Fund Classs C Shares	MOJCX	NAS CM	Open End	Moderate Alloc (Growth & Income)	D-	D+	A-		Y	1,000
Power Momentum Index Fund Classs I Shares	MOJOX	NAS CM	Open End	Moderate Alloc (Growth & Income)	D-	D+	A-		Y	100,000
Power Momentum Index VIT Fund Class 1 shares	US66537U4031		Open End	Flexible Alloc (Growth & Income)	B-	B-	B-	Down	Y	0
Praxis Genesis Balanced Portfolio Class A	MBAPX	NAS CM	Open End	Moderate Alloc (Balanced)	B-	C+	B	Up	Y	1,000
Praxis Genesis Conservative Portfolio Class A	MCONX	NAS CM	Open End	Cautious Alloc (Growth & Income)	B	C	A-	Up	Y	1,000
Praxis Genesis Growth Portfolio Class A	MGAFX	NAS CM	Open End	Aggressive Alloc (Growth)	B-	C+	B	Down	Y	1,000
Praxis Growth Index Fund Class A	MGNDX	NAS CM	Open End	US Equity Large Cap Growth (Growth)	B	B	B+	Down	Y	2,500
Praxis Growth Index Fund Class I	MMDEX	NAS CM	Open End	US Equity Large Cap Growth (Growth)	B	B	B+	Down	Y	100,000
Praxis International Index Fund Class A	MPLAX	NAS CM	Open End	Global Equity Large Cap (Foreign Stock)	B-	C+	B-	Up	Y	2,500
Praxis International Index Fund Class I	MPLIX	NAS CM	Open End	Global Equity Large Cap (Foreign Stock)	B-	B-	B-	Up	Y	100,000
Praxis Small Cap Index Fund Class A	MMSCX	NAS CM	Open End	US Equity Small Cap (Small Company)	B-	C+	B	Up	Y	2,500
Praxis Small Cap Index Fund Class I	MMSIX	NAS CM	Open End	US Equity Small Cap (Small Company)	B-	C+	B	Up	Y	100,000
Praxis Value Index Fund Class A	MVIAX	NAS CM	Open End	US Equity Large Cap Value (Growth)	B-	B-	B	Down	Y	2,500
Praxis Value Index Fund Class I	MVIIX	NAS CM	Open End	US Equity Large Cap Value (Growth)	B-	B-	B	Down	Y	100,000
PREDEX Fund	US74036J1016		Closed End	Real Estate Sector Equity (Growth)	D	D+	A-		Y	1,000,000
Preserver Alternative Opp Fund Inst Shares	PAOIX	NAS CM	Open End	Flexible Alloc (Growth & Income)	C-	C-	A	Up	Y	100,000
Preserver Alternative Opportunities Fund Retail Shares	PAORX	NAS CM	Open End	Flexible Alloc (Growth & Income)	C-	C-	A-	Up	Y	2,000
PRIMECAP Odyssey Aggressive Growth Fund	POAGX	NAS CM	Open End	US Equity Mid Cap (Aggr Growth)	A-	A	B	Up		2,000
PRIMECAP Odyssey Growth Fund	POGRX	NAS CM	Open End	US Equity Large Cap Growth (Growth)	A-	A	B+	Up	Y	2,000
PRIMECAP Odyssey Stock Fund	POSKX	NAS CM	Open End	US Equity Large Cap Blend (Growth)	B	B+	B		Y	2,000
Princeton Long/Short Treasury Fund Class A shares	PTAAX	NAS CM	Open End	Other Alternative (Growth & Income)	U	U	U		Y	2,500
Princeton Long/Short Treasury Fund Class I shares	PTAIX	NAS CM	Open End	Other Alternative (Growth & Income)	U	U	U		Y	100,000
Princeton Premium Fund Class A	PPFAX	NAS CM	Open End	Long/Short Equity (Growth & Income)	D	D+	A		Y	2,500
Princeton Premium Fund Class I	PPFIX	NAS CM	Open End	Long/Short Equity (Growth & Income)	D	D+	A		Y	100,000

★ Expanded analysis of this fund is included in Section II.

Min Additional Investment	TOTAL RETURNS 3-Month Total Return	6-Month Total Return	1-Year Total Return	3-Year Total Return	5-Year Total Return	PERFORMANCE Dividend Yield (TTM)	Expense Ratio	3-Yr Std Deviation	3-Year Beta	ASSETS NAV	Total Assets (MIL)	ASSET ALLOCATION & TURNOVER %Cash	%Stocks	%Bonds	%Other	Turnover Ratio	BULL & BEAR Last Bull Market Total Return	Last Bear Market Total Return	FEES Front End Fee (%)	Back End Fee (%)	Inception Date
50	0.27	4.26	0.96	20.18	92.15	2.23	1.37	12.49	0.83	21.62	29.6	0	100	0	0	106	20.14	-19.61	5.50		Aug-94
50	0.11	3.89	0.32	18.06	86.11	1.92	2.07	12.48	0.83	19.24	29.6	0	100	0	0	106	19.54	-19.89		1.00	Jan-00
	0.36	4.41	1.25	21.24	94.32	2.27	1.07	12.48	0.83	23.54	29.6	0	100	0	0	106	20.19	-19.47			Jul-94
50	4.39	11.31	9.64	25.12	87.26	0	1.25	14.46	0.95	23.06	806.8	2	98	0	0	42	33.56	-20.97	5.50		Apr-04
50	4.21	10.88	8.84	22.55	80.94	0	2	14.42	0.95	20.61	806.8	2	98	0	0	42	32.77	-21.21		1.00	Apr-04
	4.49	11.46	9.97	26.19	89.93	0	1	14.45	0.95	23.96	806.8	2	98	0	0	42	33.62	-20.9			Apr-04
250	5.49	9.43	20.60	36.18	95.70	1.11	0.99	10.32	0.92	27.71	543.8	4	96	0	0	33	22.03	-22.51			Jun-98
0	6.11	10.91	31.51	42.49		0	1.1			14.23	23.6	5	95	0	0	12					Dec-14
100	6.08	10.73	31.19	41.33		0	1.35			14.13	23.6	5	95	0	0	12					Jul-15
0	4.90	8.84	26.45	44.79	111.24	0.01	1	10.56	0.91	24.23	1,752	4	96	0	0	14	25.02	-8.84			Sep-10
100	4.85	8.70	26.11	43.74	108.71	0	1.25	10.52	0.91	23.85	1,752	4	96	0	0	14	24.8	-8.93			Dec-10
0	3.13	9.74	33.66				1.1			13.28	4.4	6	94	0	0						Dec-16
100	3.04	9.57	33.27				1.35			13.25	4.4	6	94	0	0						Mar-17
0	2.04						1.25			10	0.50										Nov-17
1,000	3.90	5.69	5.73	19.76		0.56	1.16			27.07	30.0	10	66	24	0	25			5.00		Dec-14
1,000	3.97	5.83	5.99	20.68		0.78	0.91			27.11	30.0	10	66	24	0	25					Dec-14
1,000	5.89	7.83	6.73	3.67		0.02	1.13			25.13	6.1	9	91	0	0	50					Dec-14
1,000	5.50	8.33	6.53	23.43	103.42	0.35	1.25	14.94	1.17	51.22	777.6	1	98	1	0	31	24.1	-21.73	5.00		Dec-09
1,000	5.56	8.47	6.79	24.35	105.97	0.75	1	14.95	1.17	51.26	777.6	1	98	1	0	31	24.28	-21.63			Dec-09
100	3.04	5.71	11.80			0.44	1.8			11.64	60.8	13	61	23	2	49					Dec-15
100	5.24	7.27	14.99	21.09		0.02	1.23	5.64	0.48	12.72	91.3	45	55	0	0	12					Mar-14
1,000	5.60	11.85	28.22	35.28	68.69	0.8	1.08	10.01	0.91	42.77	502.3	1	99	0	0	19	14.05	-19.46			Mar-07
100	5.53	11.68	27.86	34.19	66.37	0.61	1.33	10	0.91	42.98	502.3	1	99	0	0	19	13.82	-19.52			Sep-99
100	4.18	8.16	11.25	19.03		2.23	1.45	8.31	0.46	12.48	831.6	1	99	0	0	56			5.00		Nov-13
500	4.03	7.75	10.37	16.36		1.59	2.2	8.24	0.45	12.39	831.6	1	99	0	0	56					Nov-14
	4.16	8.20	11.41	19.82		2.45	1.2	8.29	0.46	12.48	831.6	1	99	0	0	56					Nov-13
	4.22	8.17	10.89	6.40	38.97	1.38	1.27	7.51	0.52	17.29	21.3	1	99	0	0	166	18.21	-9.22			May-07
100	5.25	11.24	14.99				2.27			10.85	45.0	1	89	10	0				5.00		Dec-16
100	5.00	10.78	14.19				3.02			10.77	45.0	1	89	10	0						Dec-16
	5.24	11.33	15.25				2.02			10.87	45.0	1	89	10	0						Dec-16
	5.39	11.50	20.92	24.91	89.09	0	1.23	9.5	1.01	33.82	81.8	2	88	10	0	141	27.95	-21			May-07
50	1.69	4.79	11.51	16.13	43.05	1.22	1.08	5.94	0.94	13.71	72.7	0	61	39	0	10	13.29	-10.9	5.25		Dec-09
50	1.15	2.93	7.53	10.94	25.26	1.57	1.12	3.18	0.85	11.75	23.0	1	31	68	0	11	7.77	-3.75	5.25		Dec-09
50	4.31	8.34	16.70	21.82	58.48	0.89	1.13	8.07	0.97	15.09	64.5	0	80	19	0	9	17.08	-15.36	5.25		Dec-09
100	6.67	11.94	26.28	38.95	114.69	0.52	0.86	10.74	1	23.05	261.8	0	99	1	0	43	26.17	-13.82	5.25		May-07
	6.75	12.14	26.78	40.65	119.17	0.86	0.44	10.75	1	23.21	261.8	0	99	1	0	43	26.46	-13.51			May-07
100	3.99	9.78	24.97	22.99	34.58	1.16	1.27	11.66	0.94	11.69	283.3	0	99	1	0	10	14.43	-25.32	5.25		Dec-10
	4.19	10.04	25.67	24.92	38.30	1.56	0.72	11.61	0.94	11.75	283.3	0	99	1	0	10	15.02	-25.25			Dec-10
100	3.62	9.00	10.69	13.05	50.80	0	1.12	13.46	0.92	8.63	54.0	0	99	1	0	60	25.37	-19.61	5.25		May-07
	2.84	8.31	10.29	14.12	54.07	0	0.45	13.47	0.92	9.36	54.0	0	99	1	0	60	25.87	-19.53			May-07
100	5.59	9.23	15.19	23.81	87.88	1.6	0.94	10.55	1	13.82	194.4	0	99	0	0	48	22.5	-19.46	5.25		May-01
	6.79	10.57	16.91	26.98	94.73	1.99	0.44	10.61	1.01	13.74	194.4	0	99	0	0	48	22.92	-19.15			May-06
	1.80	3.41	4.40			1.22	1			25.77	--	10	25	0	65						Jun-16
5,000	1.34	5.05	12.41			2.23	2.05			11.5	19.2	9	63	20	2						Mar-16
500	1.27	4.93	12.09			1.99	2.3			11.48	19.2	9	63	20	2						Mar-16
100	11.08	15.47	33.58	55.69	186.29	0	0.64	14.36	1.19	44.33	9,529	3	96	0	0	15	24.35	-20.48			Nov-04
100	9.17	15.44	32.05	51.26	145.05	0.36	0.66	13.23	1.14	37.25	10,362	3	96	0	0	9	21.42	-20.12			Nov-04
100	7.19	12.64	25.96	43.43	126.04	0.94	0.69	11.39	1.07	31.91	9,094	5	94	0	0	8	20.21	-16.02			Nov-04
100	1.78	1.08					1.76			10.25	142.6	76	24	0	0				5.75		Feb-17
100	1.78	1.17					1.51			10.29	142.6	76	24	0	0						Feb-17
100	1.46	3.57	9.81			0	2.21			10.65	59.7	100	0	0	0	0			5.75		Nov-16
100	1.55	3.66	10.11			0	1.96			10.68	59.7	100	0	0	0	0					Nov-16

	MARKET		FUND TYPE, CATEGORY & OBJECTIVE		RATINGS					MINIMUMS
Fund Name	Ticker Symbol	Traded On	Fund Type	Category and (Prospectus Objective)	Overall Rating	Reward Rating	Risk Rating	Recent Up/ Downgrade	Open to New Investors	Min Initial Investment
Principal Blue Chip Fund Class A	PBLAX	NAS CM	Open End	US Equity Large Cap Growth (Growth)	B+	B+	B	Up	Y	1,000
Principal Blue Chip Fund Class C	PBLCX	NAS CM	Open End	US Equity Large Cap Growth (Growth)	B+	B+	B	Up	Y	1,000
Principal Blue Chip Fund Class J	PBCJX	NAS CM	Open End	US Equity Large Cap Growth (Growth)	B+	A-	B		Y	1,000
Principal Blue Chip Fund Class R-3	PGBEX	NAS CM	Open End	US Equity Large Cap Growth (Growth)	B+	B+	B	Up	Y	0
Principal Blue Chip Fund Class R-4	PGBFX	NAS CM	Open End	US Equity Large Cap Growth (Growth)	B+	A-	B	Up	Y	0
Principal Blue Chip Fund Class R-5	PGBGX	NAS CM	Open End	US Equity Large Cap Growth (Growth)	B+	A-	B	Up	Y	0
Principal Blue Chip Fund Class R-6	PGBHX	NAS CM	Open End	US Equity Large Cap Growth (Growth)	B+	A-	B	Up	Y	0
Principal Blue Chip Fund Class T	PBLTX	NAS CM	Open End	US Equity Large Cap Growth (Growth)	B+	B+	B	Up	Y	1,000
Principal Blue Chip Fund Institutional Class	PBCKX	NAS CM	Open End	US Equity Large Cap Growth (Growth)	B+	A-	B	Up	Y	0
Principal Capital Appreciation Fund Class A	CMNWX	NAS CM	Open End	US Equity Large Cap Blend (Growth)	B	B	B		Y	1,000
Principal Capital Appreciation Fund Class C	CMNCX	NAS CM	Open End	US Equity Large Cap Blend (Growth)	B-	B-	B	Down	Y	1,000
Principal Capital Appreciation Fund Institutional Class	PWCIX	NAS CM	Open End	US Equity Large Cap Blend (Growth)	B	B	B+		Y	0
Principal Capital Appreciation Fund R-1 Class	PCAMX	NAS CM	Open End	US Equity Large Cap Blend (Growth)	B	B-	B		Y	0
Principal Capital Appreciation Fund R-2 Class	PCANX	NAS CM	Open End	US Equity Large Cap Blend (Growth)	B	B-	B		Y	0
Principal Capital Appreciation Fund R-3 Class	PCAOX	NAS CM	Open End	US Equity Large Cap Blend (Growth)	B	B	B		Y	0
Principal Capital Appreciation Fund R-4 Class	PCAPX	NAS CM	Open End	US Equity Large Cap Blend (Growth)	B	B	B		Y	0
Principal Capital Appreciation Fund R-5 Class	PCAQX	NAS CM	Open End	US Equity Large Cap Blend (Growth)	B	B	B		Y	0
Principal Capital Securities Fund Class S	PCSFX	NAS CM	Open End	US Fixed Income (Income)	B	C+	A-	Up	Y	0
Principal Diversified International Fund Class A	PRWLX	NAS CM	Open End	Global Equity Large Cap (Foreign Stock)	B-	B-	B	Up	Y	1,000
Principal Diversified International Fund Class C	PDNCX	NAS CM	Open End	Global Equity Large Cap (Foreign Stock)	B-	C+	B	Up	Y	1,000
Principal Diversified International Fund Class J	PIIJX	NAS CM	Open End	Global Equity Large Cap (Foreign Stock)	B-	B-	B	Up	Y	1,000
Principal Diversified International Fund Institutional Cls	PIIIX	NAS CM	Open End	Global Equity Large Cap (Foreign Stock)	B	B-	B	Up	Y	0
Principal Diversified International Fund R-1 Class	PDVIX	NAS CM	Open End	Global Equity Large Cap (Foreign Stock)	B-	B-	B	Up	Y	0
Principal Diversified International Fund R-2 Class	PINNX	NAS CM	Open End	Global Equity Large Cap (Foreign Stock)	B-	B-	B	Up	Y	0
Principal Diversified International Fund R-3 Class	PINRX	NAS CM	Open End	Global Equity Large Cap (Foreign Stock)	B-	B-	B	Up	Y	0
Principal Diversified International Fund R-4 Class	PINLX	NAS CM	Open End	Global Equity Large Cap (Foreign Stock)	B-	B-	B	Up	Y	0
Principal Diversified International Fund R-5 Class	PINPX	NAS CM	Open End	Global Equity Large Cap (Foreign Stock)	B	B-	B	Up	Y	0
Principal Diversified Real Asset Fund Class A	PRDAX	NAS CM	Open End	Cautious Alloc (Growth)	C	C	C	Up	Y	1,000
Principal Diversified Real Asset Fund Class C	PRDCX	NAS CM	Open End	Cautious Alloc (Growth)	C	C	C	Up	Y	1,000
Principal Diversified Real Asset Fund Class R-3	PGDRX	NAS CM	Open End	Cautious Alloc (Growth)	C	C	C	Up	Y	0
Principal Diversified Real Asset Fund Class R-4	PGDSX	NAS CM	Open End	Cautious Alloc (Growth)	C	C	C	Up	Y	0
Principal Diversified Real Asset Fund Class R-5	PGDTX	NAS CM	Open End	Cautious Alloc (Growth)	C	C	C	Up	Y	0
Principal Diversified Real Asset Fund Class R-6	PDARX	NAS CM	Open End	Cautious Alloc (Growth)	C	C	C	Up	Y	0
Principal Diversified Real Asset Fund Institutional Class	PDRDX	NAS CM	Open End	Cautious Alloc (Growth)	C	C	C	Up	Y	0
Principal EDGE MidCap Fund Class Institutional	PEDGX	NAS CM	Open End	US Equity Mid Cap (Growth)	C	C+	B	Up	Y	0
Principal EDGE MidCap Fund R-6	PEDMX	NAS CM	Open End	US Equity Mid Cap (Growth)	C	C	B	Up	Y	0
Principal Equity Income Fund Class A	PQIAX	NAS CM	Open End	US Equity Large Cap Value (Equity-Income)	B-	B	B-	Down	Y	1,000
Principal Equity Income Fund Class C	PEUCX	NAS CM	Open End	US Equity Large Cap Value (Equity-Income)	B-	B-	B-	Down	Y	1,000
Principal Equity Income Fund Institutional Class	PEIIX	NAS CM	Open End	US Equity Large Cap Value (Equity-Income)	B	B	B-		Y	0
Principal Equity Income Fund R-1 Class	PIEMX	NAS CM	Open End	US Equity Large Cap Value (Equity-Income)	B-	B-	B-	Down	Y	0
Principal Equity Income Fund R-2 Class	PEINX	NAS CM	Open End	US Equity Large Cap Value (Equity-Income)	B-	B-	B-	Down	Y	0
Principal Equity Income Fund R-3 Class	PEIOX	NAS CM	Open End	US Equity Large Cap Value (Equity-Income)	B-	B-	B-	Down	Y	0
Principal Equity Income Fund R-4 Class	PEIPX	NAS CM	Open End	US Equity Large Cap Value (Equity-Income)	B-	B	B-	Down	Y	0
Principal Equity Income Fund R-5 Class	PEIQX	NAS CM	Open End	US Equity Large Cap Value (Equity-Income)	B-	B	B-	Down	Y	0
Principal Global Diversified Income Fund Class A	PGBAX	NAS CM	Open End	Cautious Alloc (Income)	B-	C+	B	Up	Y	1,000
Principal Global Diversified Income Fund Class C	PGDCX	NAS CM	Open End	Cautious Alloc (Income)	B-	C+	B	Up	Y	1,000
Principal Global Diversified Income Fund Class R-6	PGBLX	NAS CM	Open End	Cautious Alloc (Income)	B	C+	B+	Up	Y	0
Principal Global Diversified Income Fund Class T	PGKTX	NAS CM	Open End	Cautious Alloc (Income)	B-	C+	B	Up	Y	1,000
Principal Global Diversified Income Fund Institutional Cls	PGDIX	NAS CM	Open End	Cautious Alloc (Income)	B-	C+	B	Up	Y	0
Principal Global Invs Funds Preferred Sec Fund Cls T	PPBTX	NAS CM	Open End	US Fixed Income (Income)	B	C+	A+	Up	Y	1,000
Principal Global Invs Funds Preferred Securities Fund R-6	PPREX	NAS CM	Open End	US Fixed Income (Income)	B	C+	A+	Up	Y	0
Principal Global Multi-Strategy Fund Class A Shares	PMSAX	NAS CM	Open End	Multialternative (Growth)	C+	C	B	Up	Y	1,000

★ Expanded analysis of this fund is included in Section II.

	TOTAL RETURNS					PERFORMANCE				ASSETS		ASSET ALLOCATION & TURNOVER					BULL & BEAR		FEES		
Min Additional Investment	3-Month Total Return	6-Month Total Return	1-Year Total Return	3-Year Total Return	5-Year Total Return	Dividend Yield (TTM)	Expense Ratio	3-Yr Std Deviation	3-Year Beta	NAV	Total Assets (MIL)	%Cash	%Stocks	%Bonds	%Other	Turnover Ratio	Last Bull Market Total Return	Last Bear Market Total Return	Front End Fee (%)	Back End Fee (%)	Inception Date
100	6.73	13.06	28.30	44.36	109.26	0	1.28	10.83	0.97	20.93	2,340	0	100	0	0	27			5.50		Sep-13
100	6.51	12.60	27.29	41.08	101.50	0	2.08	10.83	0.97	20.29	2,340	0	100	0	0	27				1.00	Sep-13
100	6.76	13.17	28.63	45.96	113.02		1.04	10.89	0.97	21.14	2,340	0	100	0	0	27				1.00	Sep-17
	6.64	12.95	28.09	44.75	110.83	0.14	1.25	10.86	0.97	21.01	2,340	0	100	0	0	27					Mar-16
	6.73	13.08	28.43	45.61	112.71	0.2	1.06	10.86	0.97	21.08	2,340	0	100	0	0	27					Mar-16
	6.77	13.12	28.53	46.04	113.78	0.23	0.94	10.87	0.97	21.11	2,340	0	100	0	0	27					Mar-16
	6.83	13.28	28.78	46.58	114.56		0.69	10.88	0.97	21.16	2,340	0	100	0	0	27					Jan-17
100	6.67	13.01	28.38	45.39	111.76		1.22	10.88	0.97	21.1	2,340	0	100	0	0	27			2.50		Jun-17
	6.83	13.28	28.85	46.66	114.68	0.36	0.69	10.89	0.97	21.16	2,340	0	100	0	0	27					Jun-12
100	6.44	11.08	20.64	32.73	102.31	0.83	0.84	9.96	0.96	61.57	2,412	3	97	0	0	35	23.92	-17.59	5.50		Nov-86
100	6.24	10.64	19.68	29.54	94.12	0.47	1.67	9.96	0.96	47.99	2,412	3	97	0	0	35	23.34	-17.9		1.00	Mar-02
	6.54	11.29	21.06	34.18	106.09	1.09	0.47	9.97	0.96	62.64	2,412	3	97	0	0	35	24.27	-17.45			Jun-99
	6.31	10.80	20.03	30.76	97.31	0.31	1.33	9.96	0.96	61.68	2,412	3	97	0	0	35	23.62	-17.74			Mar-10
	6.34	10.88	20.18	31.26	98.62	0.54	1.2	9.96	0.96	61.71	2,412	3	97	0	0	35	23.69	-17.7			Mar-10
	6.41	10.99	20.42	32.01	100.45	0.68	1.02	9.95	0.96	61.67	2,412	3	97	0	0	35	23.82	-17.64			Mar-10
	6.46	11.09	20.64	32.74	102.36	0.81	0.83	9.96	0.96	62.12	2,412	3	97	0	0	35	23.95	-17.57			Mar-10
	6.47	11.15	20.78	33.19	103.54	0.91	0.71	9.96	0.96	62.3	2,412	3	97	0	0	35	24.08	-17.54			Mar-10
	1.23	2.81	11.56	22.37		4.97	0.01	3.62	0.89	10.38	496.7	2	0	37	0	8					Mar-14
100	2.96	11.02	28.08	26.13	46.03	0.91	1.36	10.67	0.84	13.99	12,112	2	98	0	1	48	16.58	-22.36	5.50		Jun-05
100	2.74	10.63	27.06	23.47	40.81	0.27	2.08	10.65	0.83	14.02	12,112	2	98	0	1	48	16.09	-22.52		1.00	Jan-07
100	2.94	11.09	28.25	26.71	46.91	1.08	1.16	10.68	0.84	13.82	12,112	2	98	0	1	48	16.54	-22.38		1.00	Mar-01
	3.08	11.26	28.66	28.08	49.75	1.35	0.85	10.64	0.83	13.9	12,112	2	98	0	1	48	16.93	-22.24			Mar-01
	2.85	10.86	27.61	24.74	43.39	0.58	1.72	10.62	0.83	13.97	12,112	2	98	0	1	48	16.17	-22.48			Nov-04
	2.88	10.83	27.75	25.19	44.27	0.69	1.59	10.64	0.83	13.9	12,112	2	98	0	1	48	16.33	-22.4			Dec-00
	2.94	10.95	27.95	25.97	45.52	0.83	1.41	10.66	0.83	13.94	12,112	2	98	0	1	48	16.5	-22.37			Dec-00
	3.04	11.11	28.22	26.64	47.02	1.02	1.22	10.63	0.83	14.12	12,112	2	98	0	1	48	16.61	-22.34			Dec-00
	2.98	11.15	28.31	27.05	47.79	1.13	1.1	10.68	0.83	14.08	12,112	2	98	0	1	48	16.66	-22.22			Dec-00
100	2.39	5.49	9.69	0.39	8.91	2.19	1.27	7.35		11.63	4,004	6	62	31	0	65	12	-12.8	3.75		Mar-10
100	2.24	5.12	8.98	-1.76	4.97	1.24	2.02	7.38		11.44	4,004	6	62	31	0	65	11.57	-13.12		1.00	Mar-10
	2.35	5.35	9.55	0.32	9.12	2.08	1.41	7.34		11.63	4,004	6	62	31	0	65	12.15	-12.77			Mar-16
	2.43	5.44	9.83	0.90	10.08	2.2	1.22	7.31		11.64	4,004	6	62	31	0	65	12.25	-12.71			Mar-16
	2.47	5.57	9.97	1.26	10.69	2.29	1.1	7.32		11.64	4,004	6	62	31	0	65	12.31	-12.68			Mar-16
	2.54	5.73	10.23	1.68	11.15	2.41	0.85	7.35		11.64	4,004	6	62	31	0	65	12.31	-12.68			Dec-14
	2.48	5.67	10.17	1.57	11.04	2.41	0.89	7.34		11.64	4,004	6	62	31	0	65	12.31	-12.68			Mar-10
	4.71	7.58	14.00			0.73	0.8			13.62	463.4	2	98	0	0	12					Sep-15
	4.78	8.31	14.77				0.78			13.65	463.4	2	98	0	0	12					Jan-17
100	7.10	11.87	20.54	31.70	91.41	1.38	0.91	9.53	0.88	31.43	6,859	2	98	0	0	16	21.74	-14.18	5.50		May-39
100	6.93	11.47	19.68	28.82	84.42	0.8	1.65	9.54	0.88	30.65	6,859	2	98	0	0	16	21.24	-14.45		1.00	Mar-02
	7.23	12.10	21.03	33.26	95.10	1.69	0.52	9.55	0.88	31.47	6,859	2	98	0	0	16	22.06	-14.08			Aug-00
	6.99	11.60	19.96	29.80	86.72	0.98	1.39	9.55	0.88	31.32	6,859	2	98	0	0	16	21.5	-14.39			Mar-10
	7.03	11.70	20.12	30.33	88.01	1.06	1.26	9.53	0.88	31.44	6,859	2	98	0	0	16	21.53	-14.3			Mar-10
	7.10	11.79	20.37	31.01	89.75	1.22	1.08	9.53	0.88	31.34	6,859	2	98	0	0	16	21.68	-14.26			Mar-10
	7.10	11.84	20.54	31.71	91.49	1.37	0.89	9.53	0.88	31.39	6,859	2	98	0	0	16	21.76	-14.15			Mar-10
	7.16	11.97	20.71	32.24	92.63	1.48	0.77	9.56	0.88	31.44	6,859	2	98	0	0	16	21.86	-14.13			Mar-10
100	1.57	4.24	9.85	16.78	31.86	4.96	1.1	4.62	0.72	14.2	12,450	7	34	56	1	101	13.82	-8.86	3.75		Dec-08
100	1.32	3.79	9.00	14.09	26.92	4.25	1.86	4.64	0.72	14.11	12,450	7	34	56	1	101	13.42	-9.15		1.00	Dec-08
	1.66	4.42	10.25	17.90	34.02		0.74	4.63	0.72	14.14	12,450	7	34	56	1	101	14.1	-8.72			Jun-17
100	2.53	5.24	10.97	18.08	33.55		1.1	4.65	0.72	14.28	12,450	7	34	56	1	101	13.93	-8.82	2.50		Jun-17
	1.65	4.40	10.23	17.88	33.99	5.28	0.77	4.63	0.72	14.14	12,450	7	34	56	1	101	14.1	-8.73			Dec-08
100	0.88	2.22	10.23	19.38	35.03		1.08	3.16	0.86	10.39	6,014	1	0	28	0	16	10.37	-5.87	2.50		Jun-17
	0.98	2.39	10.52	20.30	36.74		0.73	3.16	0.86	10.39	6,014	1	0	28	0	16	10.53	-5.77			Jan-17
100	1.44	3.08	6.22	8.03	17.42	0	1.94	2.49	0.62	11.2	2,814	39	30	26	1	318			3.75		Oct-11

	MARKET		FUND TYPE, CATEGORY & OBJECTIVE		RATINGS					MINIMUMS
Fund Name	Ticker Symbol	Traded On	Fund Type	Category and (Prospectus Objective)	Overall Rating	Reward Rating	Risk Rating	Recent Up/ Downgrade	Open to New Investors	Min Initial Investment
Principal Global Multi-Strategy Fund Class C	PMSCX	NAS CM	Open End	Multialternative (Growth)	C+	C	B	Up	Y	1,000
Principal Global Multi-Strategy Fund Inst Cls Shares	PSMIX	NAS CM	Open End	Multialternative (Growth)	B-	C	B	Up	Y	0
Principal Global Multi-Strategy Fund R-6	PGLSX	NAS CM	Open End	Multialternative (Growth)	B-	C	B	Up	Y	0
Principal Global Opportunities Fund Class A	PGLAX	NAS CM	Open End	Global Equity (Growth)	B-	C+	B	Up	Y	1,000
Principal Global Opportunities Fund Class C	PGOCX	NAS CM	Open End	Global Equity (Growth)	B-	C+	B	Up	Y	1,000
Principal Global Opportunities Fund Institutional Class	PGOIX	NAS CM	Open End	Global Equity (Growth)	B	C+	B	Up	Y	0
Principal Global Real Estate Securities Fund Class A	POSAX	NAS CM	Open End	Real Estate Sector Equity (Real Estate)	B-	C+	B	Up	Y	1,000
Principal Global Real Estate Securities Fund Class C	POSCX	NAS CM	Open End	Real Estate Sector Equity (Real Estate)	B-	C+	B	Up	Y	1,000
Principal Global Real Estate Securities Fund Class R-6	PGRSX	NAS CM	Open End	Real Estate Sector Equity (Real Estate)	B-	C+	B	Up	Y	0
Principal Global Real Estate Securities Fund Inst Cls	POSIX	NAS CM	Open End	Real Estate Sector Equity (Real Estate)	B-	C+	B		Y	0
Principal Global Real Estate Securities Fund R-3	PGRKX	NAS CM	Open End	Real Estate Sector Equity (Real Estate)	B-	C+	B	Up	Y	0
Principal Global Real Estate Securities Fund R-4	PGRVX	NAS CM	Open End	Real Estate Sector Equity (Real Estate)	B-	C+	B	Up	Y	0
Principal Global Real Estate Securities Fund R-5	PGRUX	NAS CM	Open End	Real Estate Sector Equity (Real Estate)	B-	C+	B	Up	Y	0
Principal International Emerging Markets Fund Class A	PRIAX	NAS CM	Open End	Emerging Markets Equity (Div Emerging Mkts)	B-	B	C	Up	Y	1,000
Principal International Emerging Markets Fund Class C	PMKCX	NAS CM	Open End	Emerging Markets Equity (Div Emerging Mkts)	B-	B-	C	Up	Y	1,000
Principal International Emerging Markets Fund Class J	PIEJX	NAS CM	Open End	Emerging Markets Equity (Div Emerging Mkts)	B-	B	C	Up	Y	1,000
Principal International Emerging Markets Fund Class R-6	PIIMX	NAS CM	Open End	Emerging Markets Equity (Div Emerging Mkts)	B-	B	C	Up	Y	0
Principal Intl Emerging Mkts Fund Inst Cls	PIEIX	NAS CM	Open End	Emerging Markets Equity (Div Emerging Mkts)	B-	B	C	Up	Y	0
Principal International Emerging Markets Fund R-1 Class	PIXEX	NAS CM	Open End	Emerging Markets Equity (Div Emerging Mkts)	B-	B	C	Up	Y	0
Principal International Emerging Markets Fund R-2 Class	PEASX	NAS CM	Open End	Emerging Markets Equity (Div Emerging Mkts)	B-	B	C	Up	Y	0
Principal International Emerging Markets Fund R-3 Class	PEAPX	NAS CM	Open End	Emerging Markets Equity (Div Emerging Mkts)	B-	B	C	Up	Y	0
Principal International Emerging Markets Fund R-4 Class	PESSX	NAS CM	Open End	Emerging Markets Equity (Div Emerging Mkts)	B-	B	C	Up	Y	0
Principal International Emerging Markets Fund R-5 Class	PEPSX	NAS CM	Open End	Emerging Markets Equity (Div Emerging Mkts)	B-	B	C	Up	Y	0
Principal Intl Equity Index Fund Inst Cls	PIDIX	NAS CM	Open End	Global Equity Large Cap (Foreign Stock)	B-	C+	B	Up	Y	0
Principal International Equity Index Fund R-1 Class	PILIX	NAS CM	Open End	Global Equity Large Cap (Foreign Stock)	B-	C+	B	Up	Y	0
Principal International Equity Index Fund R-2 Class	PINEX	NAS CM	Open End	Global Equity Large Cap (Foreign Stock)	B-	C+	B	Up	Y	0
Principal International Equity Index Fund R-3 Class	PIIOX	NAS CM	Open End	Global Equity Large Cap (Foreign Stock)	B-	C+	B	Up	Y	0
Principal International Equity Index Fund R-4 Class	PIIPX	NAS CM	Open End	Global Equity Large Cap (Foreign Stock)	B-	C+	B	Up	Y	0
Principal International Equity Index Fund R-5 Class	PIIQX	NAS CM	Open End	Global Equity Large Cap (Foreign Stock)	B-	C+	B	Up	Y	0
Principal International Equity Index Fund R-6	PFIEX	NAS CM	Open End	Global Equity Large Cap (Foreign Stock)	B-	C+	B	Up	Y	0
Principal International Fund I Class A	PFAFX	NAS CM	Open End	Global Equity Large Cap (Foreign Stock)	B	B	B	Up	Y	1,000
Principal International Fund I Class R-6	PIIDX	NAS CM	Open End	Global Equity Large Cap (Foreign Stock)	B	B	B	Up	Y	0
Principal International Fund I Institutional Class	PINIX	NAS CM	Open End	Global Equity Large Cap (Foreign Stock)	B	B	B	Up	Y	0
Principal International Fund I R-1 Class	PPISX	NAS CM	Open End	Global Equity Large Cap (Foreign Stock)	B	B	B	Up	Y	0
Principal International Fund I R-2 Class	PSPPX	NAS CM	Open End	Global Equity Large Cap (Foreign Stock)	B	B	B	Up	Y	0
Principal International Fund I R-3 Class	PRPPX	NAS CM	Open End	Global Equity Large Cap (Foreign Stock)	B	B	B	Up	Y	0
Principal International Fund I R-4 Class	PUPPX	NAS CM	Open End	Global Equity Large Cap (Foreign Stock)	B	B	B	Up	Y	0
Principal International Fund I R-5 Class	PTPPX	NAS CM	Open End	Global Equity Large Cap (Foreign Stock)	B	B	B	Up	Y	0
Principal International Small Company Fund Class A	PICAX	NAS CM	Open End	Global Equity Mid/Small Cap (Small Company)	A-	A	A-	Up	Y	1,000
Principal Intl Small Company Fund Inst Cls	PISMX	NAS CM	Open End	Global Equity Mid/Small Cap (Small Company)	A-	A	A-	Up	Y	0
Principal International Small Company Fund R-6	PFISX	NAS CM	Open End	Global Equity Mid/Small Cap (Small Company)	A-	A	A-	Up	Y	0
Principal LargeCap Growth Fund Class A	PRGWX	NAS CM	Open End	US Equity Large Cap Growth (Growth)	B	B	B+	Up	Y	1,000
Principal LargeCap Growth Fund Class C	PLGCX	NAS CM	Open End	US Equity Large Cap Growth (Growth)	B	B	B	Up	Y	1,000
Principal LargeCap Growth Fund Class J	PGLJX	NAS CM	Open End	US Equity Large Cap Growth (Growth)	B	B	B+	Up	Y	1,000
Principal LargeCap Growth Fund I Class A	PLGAX	NAS CM	Open End	US Equity Large Cap Growth (Growth)	A-	A	A-	Up	Y	1,000
Principal LargeCap Growth Fund I Class J	PLGJX	NAS CM	Open End	US Equity Large Cap Growth (Growth)	A-	A	B	Up	Y	1,000
Principal LargeCap Growth Fund I Class R-6	PLCGX	NAS CM	Open End	US Equity Large Cap Growth (Growth)	A-	A	B	Up	Y	0
Principal LargeCap Growth Fund I Institutional Class	PLGIX	NAS CM	Open End	US Equity Large Cap Growth (Growth)	A-	A	B	Up	Y	0
Principal LargeCap Growth Fund I R-1 Class	PCRSX	NAS CM	Open End	US Equity Large Cap Growth (Growth)	A-	A-	A-	Up	Y	0
Principal LargeCap Growth Fund I R-2 Class	PPUNX	NAS CM	Open End	US Equity Large Cap Growth (Growth)	A-	A	B	Up	Y	0
Principal LargeCap Growth Fund I R-3 Class	PPUMX	NAS CM	Open End	US Equity Large Cap Growth (Growth)	A-	A	B	Up	Y	0
Principal LargeCap Growth Fund I R-4 Class	PPUSX	NAS CM	Open End	US Equity Large Cap Growth (Growth)	A-	A	B	Up	Y	0

★Expanded analysis of this fund is included in Section II.

Min Additional Investment	3-Month Total Return	6-Month Total Return	1-Year Total Return	3-Year Total Return	5-Year Total Return	Dividend Yield (TTM)	Expense Ratio	3-Yr Std Deviation	3-Year Beta	NAV	Total Assets (MIL)	%Cash	%Stocks	%Bonds	%Other	Turnover Ratio	Last Bull Market Total Return	Last Bear Market Total Return	Front End Fee (%)	Back End Fee (%)	Inception Date
		TOTAL RETURNS				PERFORMANCE				ASSETS		ASSET ALLOCATION & TURNOVER					BULL & BEAR		FEES		
100	1.27	2.67	5.39	5.44	12.92	0	2.77	2.53	0.64	10.91	2,814	39	30	26	1	318				1.00	Jun-12
	1.56	3.36	6.59	9.17	19.46	0.14	1.61	2.51	0.63	11.3	2,814	39	30	26	1	318					Oct-11
	1.53	3.24	6.46	9.04	19.31		1.57	2.5	0.63	11.29	2,814	39	30	26	1	318					Jun-17
100	4.76	9.42	21.60	21.26	57.76	0.91	1.5	9.08	0.82	12.52	947.6	2	98	0	0	117			5.50		Sep-13
100	4.47	8.99	20.69	18.44	51.90	0.16	2.25	9.04	0.82	12.43	947.6	2	98	0	0	117				1.00	Sep-13
	4.81	9.77	22.31	23.55	62.47	1.46	0.85	9.07	0.82	12.6	947.6	2	98	0	0	117					Dec-12
100	4.56	7.25	14.30	14.42	42.50	2.45	1.32	11.2	1	8.88	2,447	1	99	0	0	55	25.51	-20.96	5.50		Oct-07
100	4.40	6.91	13.45	11.78	37.03	1.98	2.11	11.17	1	8.59	2,447	1	99	0	0	55	24.95	-21.23		1.00	Oct-07
	4.59	7.44	14.77	15.69	45.54	2.66	0.88	11.18	1	9.52	2,447	1	99	0	0	55	25.8	-20.73			Nov-14
	4.58	7.41	14.72	15.73	45.58	2.65	0.9	11.15	1	9.52	2,447	1	99	0	0	55	25.81	-20.73			Oct-07
	4.55	7.25	14.22	14.48	43.30	2.25	1.44	11.16	1	9.52	2,447	1	99	0	0	55	25.62	-20.81			Mar-16
	4.49	7.24	14.26	14.87	44.22	2.37	1.25	11.17	1	9.51	2,447	1	99	0	0	55	25.73	-20.76			Mar-16
	4.63	7.41	14.63	15.45	45.23	2.48	1.13	11.15	1	9.53	2,447	1	99	0	0	55	25.81	-20.73			Mar-16
100	5.88	17.48	40.73	31.27	20.58	0.69	1.61	14.84	0.92	29.96	976.8	2	98	0	0	120	20.44	-26.19	5.50		Jun-05
100	5.63	16.88	39.33	27.21	14.60	0	2.66	14.84	0.92	28.64	976.8	2	98	0	0	120	19.8	-26.48		1.00	Jan-07
100	5.90	17.52	40.88	31.63	21.23	0.81	1.52	14.85	0.92	28.84	976.8	2	98	0	0	120	20.49	-26.16		1.00	Mar-01
	5.99	17.72	41.22	32.37	22.34	1.05	1.21	14.85	0.92	29.63	976.8	2	98	0	0	120	20.67	-26.11			Nov-16
	5.95	17.63	41.17	32.90	23.46	1.04	1.27	14.83	0.92	29.63	976.8	2	98	0	0	120	20.83	-26.03			Mar-01
	5.74	17.15	40.03	29.63	18.29	0.36	2.13	14.83	0.92	29.62	976.8	2	98	0	0	120	20.21	-26.31			Nov-04
	5.82	17.27	40.27	30.15	19.09	0.51	2	14.83	0.92	29.44	976.8	2	98	0	0	120	20.33	-26.27			Dec-00
	5.84	17.34	40.51	30.82	20.17	0.61	1.82	14.85	0.92	29.6	976.8	2	98	0	0	120	20.43	-26.23			Dec-00
	5.92	17.50	40.78	31.58	21.35	0.78	1.63	14.83	0.92	29.72	976.8	2	98	0	0	120	20.58	-26.17			Dec-00
	5.91	17.56	40.89	32.04	22.03	0.83	1.51	14.84	0.92	29.74	976.8	2	98	0	0	120	20.67	-26.11			Dec-00
	3.68	8.93	24.86	23.98	43.77	2.29	0.35	11.42	0.92	10.81	1,084	0	100	0	0	25	13.07	-23.38			Dec-09
	3.37	8.46	23.78	20.79	37.62	1.57	1.22	11.54	0.93	10.49	1,084	0	100	0	0	25	12.34	-23.51			Dec-09
	3.47	8.53	23.91	21.28	38.57	1.62	1.09	11.5	0.93	10.8	1,084	0	100	0	0	25	12.35	-23.57			Dec-09
	3.51	8.64	24.17	21.91	39.75	1.89	0.91	11.56	0.94	10.63	1,084	0	100	0	0	25	12.7	-23.48			Dec-09
	3.55	8.73	24.35	22.58	41.11	2.03	0.72	11.51	0.93	10.74	1,084	0	100	0	0	25	12.74	-23.37			Dec-09
	3.56	8.84	24.58	23.04	42.01	2.09	0.6	11.5	0.93	10.76	1,084	0	100	0	0	25	12.75	-23.35			Dec-09
	3.60	8.95	24.76	23.88	43.65		0.28	11.43	0.92	10.8	1,084	0	100	0	0	25	13.07	-23.38			Jan-17
100	6.32	17.21	38.28	31.51	61.72	0.35	1.46	12.07	0.87	17.05	466.9	0	99	0	0	70	16.34	-26.02	5.50		Jun-14
	6.38	17.51	38.85	33.29	64.86	0.79	0.93	12.11	0.87	17.1	466.9	0	99	0	0	70	16.51	-25.95			Nov-16
	6.38	17.51	38.83	33.34	64.92	0.77	1.01	12.11	0.87	17.12	466.9	0	99	0	0	70	16.51	-25.95			Dec-03
	6.22	17.01	37.77	30.05	58.27	0	1.86	12.08	0.87	17.11	466.9	0	99	0	0	70	15.93	-26.19			Nov-04
	6.25	17.09	37.90	30.51	59.26	0.24	1.73	12.1	0.87	17.15	466.9	0	99	0	0	70	16	-26.17			Jun-04
	6.31	17.23	38.22	31.31	60.76	0.36	1.55	12.07	0.87	17.12	466.9	0	99	0	0	70	16.08	-26.09			Jun-04
	6.34	17.33	38.41	32.05	62.20	0.45	1.36	12.1	0.87	17.13	466.9	0	99	0	0	70	16.16	-26.03			Jun-04
	6.34	17.34	38.57	32.36	63.10	0.61	1.24	12.1	0.87	17.09	466.9	0	99	0	0	70	16.37	-26.07			Jun-04
100	5.44	15.31	35.60	46.95		0.07	1.6	11.26	0.92	12.61	1,044	3	97	0	0	59			5.50		Jun-14
	5.57	15.48	35.76	48.48		0.22	1.2	11.25	0.91	12.66	1,044	3	97	0	0	59					Dec-14
	5.56	15.53	36.23	47.63			1.07	11.26	0.92	12.7	1,044	3	97	0	0	59					Jan-17
100	7.52	15.72	34.16	31.21	98.88	0.08	1.11	11.59	1	9.02	1,083	1	99	0	0	63	26.52	-16.66	5.50		Jun-05
100	7.28	15.24	33.04	27.98	90.71	0	1.98	11.65	1	7.72	1,083	1	99	0	0	63	26.06	-17.09		1.00	Jan-07
100	7.62	15.80	34.35	31.77	99.97	0.23	0.94	11.68	1.01	8.31	1,083	1	99	0	0	63	26.7	-16.68		1.00	Mar-01
100	7.58	14.02	33.09	42.55	115.08	0	1.15	11.71	1.05	14.05	8,131	0	99	0	0	33	29.8	-17.49	5.50		Mar-13
100	7.61	14.14	33.49	43.74	117.64	0	0.88	11.71	1.05	12	8,131	0	99	0	0	33	29.58	-17.61		1.00	Mar-01
	7.72	14.34	33.77	44.86	121.37	0.06	0.6	11.73	1.06	14.42	8,131	0	99	0	0	33	29.99	-17.4			Nov-14
	7.68	14.29	33.69	44.87	121.36	0.06	0.62	11.74	1.06	14.43	8,131	0	99	0	0	33	29.99	-17.4			Dec-00
	7.47	13.81	32.70	41.38	112.09	0	1.47	11.75	1.06	12.52	8,131	0	99	0	0	33	29.29	-17.69			Nov-04
	7.56	13.87	32.75	41.90	113.45	0	1.34	11.73	1.05	12.22	8,131	0	99	0	0	33	29.42	-17.66			Dec-00
	7.64	14.04	33.04	42.64	115.36	0	1.16	11.72	1.05	13.22	8,131	0	99	0	0	33	29.53	-17.52			Dec-00
	7.60	14.06	33.23	43.47	117.31	0	0.97	11.71	1.05	13.44	8,131	0	99	0	0	33	29.58	-17.48			Dec-00

	MARKET			FUND TYPE, CATEGORY & OBJECTIVE	RATINGS				MINIMUMS	
Fund Name	Ticker Symbol	Traded On	Fund Type	Category and (Prospectus Objective)	Overall Rating	Reward Rating	Risk Rating	Recent Up/ Downgrade	Open to New Investors	Min Initial Investment
Principal LargeCap Growth Fund I R-5 Class	PPUPX	NAS CM	Open End	US Equity Large Cap Growth (Growth)	A-	A	B	Up	Y	0
Principal LargeCap Growth Fund Institutional Class	PGLIX	NAS CM	Open End	US Equity Large Cap Growth (Growth)	B+	B	B+	Up	Y	0
Principal LargeCap Growth Fund R-1 Class	PLSGX	NAS CM	Open End	US Equity Large Cap Growth (Growth)	B	B	B+	Up	Y	0
Principal LargeCap Growth Fund R-2 Class	PCPPX	NAS CM	Open End	US Equity Large Cap Growth (Growth)	B	B	B+	Up	Y	0
Principal LargeCap Growth Fund R-3 Class	PLGPX	NAS CM	Open End	US Equity Large Cap Growth (Growth)	B	B	B+	Up	Y	0
Principal LargeCap Growth Fund R-4 Class	PEPPX	NAS CM	Open End	US Equity Large Cap Growth (Growth)	B	B	B+	Up	Y	0
Principal LargeCap Growth Fund R-5 Class	PDPPX	NAS CM	Open End	US Equity Large Cap Growth (Growth)	B	B	B+	Up	Y	0
Principal LargeCap S&P 500 Index Fund Class A	PLSAX	NAS CM	Open End	US Equity Large Cap Blend (Growth)	B	B-	B		Y	1,000
Principal LargeCap S&P 500 Index Fund Class C	PLICX	NAS CM	Open End	US Equity Large Cap Blend (Growth)	B-	B-	B	Down	Y	1,000
Principal LargeCap S&P 500 Index Fund Class J	PSPJX	NAS CM	Open End	US Equity Large Cap Blend (Growth)	B	B	B		Y	1,000
Principal LargeCap S&P 500 Index Fund Institutional Class	PLFIX	NAS CM	Open End	US Equity Large Cap Blend (Growth)	B	B	B		Y	0
Principal LargeCap S&P 500 Index Fund R-1 Class	PLPIX	NAS CM	Open End	US Equity Large Cap Blend (Growth)	B	B-	B		Y	0
Principal LargeCap S&P 500 Index Fund R-2 Class	PLFNX	NAS CM	Open End	US Equity Large Cap Blend (Growth)	B	B-	B		Y	0
Principal LargeCap S&P 500 Index Fund R-3 Class	PLFMX	NAS CM	Open End	US Equity Large Cap Blend (Growth)	B	B-	B		Y	0
Principal LargeCap S&P 500 Index Fund R-4 Class	PLFSX	NAS CM	Open End	US Equity Large Cap Blend (Growth)	B	B	B		Y	0
Principal LargeCap S&P 500 Index Fund R-5 Class	PLFPX	NAS CM	Open End	US Equity Large Cap Blend (Growth)	B	B	B		Y	0
Principal LargeCap Value Fund Class A	PCACX	NAS CM	Open End	US Equity Large Cap Value (Growth)	B	C+	B+	Up	Y	1,000
Principal LargeCap Value Fund Class C	PLUCX	NAS CM	Open End	US Equity Large Cap Value (Growth)	B-	C+	B	Down	Y	1,000
Principal LargeCap Value Fund Class J	PVLJX	NAS CM	Open End	US Equity Large Cap Value (Growth)	B	C+	B+	Up	Y	1,000
Principal LargeCap Value Fund III Class J	PLVJX	NAS CM	Open End	US Equity Large Cap Value (Growth)	B-	B-	B-	Down	Y	1,000
Principal LargeCap Value Fund III Institutional Class	PLVIX	NAS CM	Open End	US Equity Large Cap Value (Growth)	B-	B-	B-	Down	Y	0
Principal LargeCap Value Fund III R-1 Class	PESAX	NAS CM	Open End	US Equity Large Cap Value (Growth)	B-	B-	B-	Down	Y	0
Principal LargeCap Value Fund III R-2 Class	PPSNX	NAS CM	Open End	US Equity Large Cap Value (Growth)	B-	B-	B-	Down	Y	0
Principal LargeCap Value Fund III R-3 Class	PPSFX	NAS CM	Open End	US Equity Large Cap Value (Growth)	B-	B-	B-	Down	Y	0
Principal LargeCap Value Fund III R-4 Class	PPSSX	NAS CM	Open End	US Equity Large Cap Value (Growth)	B	B-	B	Up	Y	0
Principal LargeCap Value Fund III R-5 Class	PPSRX	NAS CM	Open End	US Equity Large Cap Value (Growth)	B-	B-	B-	Down	Y	0
Principal LargeCap Value Fund Institutional Class	PVLIX	NAS CM	Open End	US Equity Large Cap Value (Growth)	B	B-	B+	Up	Y	0
Principal LargeCap Value Fund R-1 Class	PLSVX	NAS CM	Open End	US Equity Large Cap Value (Growth)	B	C+	B	Up	Y	0
Principal LargeCap Value Fund R-2 Class	PLVNX	NAS CM	Open End	US Equity Large Cap Value (Growth)	B	C+	B	Up	Y	0
Principal LargeCap Value Fund R-3 Class	PLVMX	NAS CM	Open End	US Equity Large Cap Value (Growth)	B	C+	B+	Up	Y	0
Principal LargeCap Value Fund R-4 Class	PLVSX	NAS CM	Open End	US Equity Large Cap Value (Growth)	B	C+	B+	Up	Y	0
Principal LargeCap Value Fund R-5 Class	PLVPX	NAS CM	Open End	US Equity Large Cap Value (Growth)	B	C+	B+	Up	Y	0
Principal LifeTime 2010 Fund Class A	PENAX	NAS CM	Open End	Target Date 2000-2020 (Asset Alloc)	B	C+	A-	Up	Y	1,000
Principal LifeTime 2010 Fund Class J	PTAJX	NAS CM	Open End	Target Date 2000-2020 (Asset Alloc)	B-	C+	B	Up	Y	1,000
Principal LifeTime 2010 Fund Institutional Class	PTTIX	NAS CM	Open End	Target Date 2000-2020 (Asset Alloc)	B-	C+	B	Up	Y	0
Principal LifeTime 2010 Fund R-1 Class	PVASX	NAS CM	Open End	Target Date 2000-2020 (Asset Alloc)	B-	C+	B+	Up	Y	0
Principal LifeTime 2010 Fund R-2 Class	PTANX	NAS CM	Open End	Target Date 2000-2020 (Asset Alloc)	B-	C+	B	Up	Y	0
Principal LifeTime 2010 Fund R-3 Class	PTAMX	NAS CM	Open End	Target Date 2000-2020 (Asset Alloc)	B	C+	A-	Up	Y	0
Principal LifeTime 2010 Fund R-4 Class	PTASX	NAS CM	Open End	Target Date 2000-2020 (Asset Alloc)	B	C+	A-	Up	Y	0
Principal LifeTime 2010 Fund R-5 Class	PTAPX	NAS CM	Open End	Target Date 2000-2020 (Asset Alloc)	B-	C+	B	Up	Y	0
Principal LifeTime 2015 Fund Institutional Class	LTINX	NAS CM	Open End	Target Date 2000-2020 (Asset Alloc)	B-	C+	B	Up	Y	0
Principal LifeTime 2015 Fund R-1 Class	LTSGX	NAS CM	Open End	Target Date 2000-2020 (Asset Alloc)	B-	C+	B	Up	Y	0
Principal LifeTime 2015 Fund R-2 Class	LTASX	NAS CM	Open End	Target Date 2000-2020 (Asset Alloc)	B	C+	B+	Up	Y	0
Principal LifeTime 2015 Fund R-3 Class	LTAPX	NAS CM	Open End	Target Date 2000-2020 (Asset Alloc)	B-	C+	B	Up	Y	0
Principal LifeTime 2015 Fund R-4 Class	LTSLX	NAS CM	Open End	Target Date 2000-2020 (Asset Alloc)	B-	C+	B	Up	Y	0
Principal LifeTime 2015 Fund R-5 Class	LTPFX	NAS CM	Open End	Target Date 2000-2020 (Asset Alloc)	B-	C+	B	Up	Y	0
Principal LifeTime 2020 Fund Class A	PTBAX	NAS CM	Open End	Target Date 2000-2020 (Asset Alloc)	B	C+	B+	Up	Y	1,000
Principal LifeTime 2020 Fund Class J	PLFJX	NAS CM	Open End	Target Date 2000-2020 (Asset Alloc)	B	C+	B+	Up	Y	1,000
Principal LifeTime 2020 Fund Institutional Class	PLWIX	NAS CM	Open End	Target Date 2000-2020 (Asset Alloc)	B-	C+	B	Up	Y	0
Principal LifeTime 2020 Fund R-1 Class	PWASX	NAS CM	Open End	Target Date 2000-2020 (Asset Alloc)	B-	C+	B	Up	Y	0
Principal LifeTime 2020 Fund R-2 Class	PTBNX	NAS CM	Open End	Target Date 2000-2020 (Asset Alloc)	B-	C+	B	Up	Y	0
Principal LifeTime 2020 Fund R-3 Class	PTBMX	NAS CM	Open End	Target Date 2000-2020 (Asset Alloc)	B	C+	B+	Up	Y	0

★ Expanded analysis of this fund is included in Section II.

	TOTAL RETURNS					PERFORMANCE				ASSETS		ASSET ALLOCATION & TURNOVER					BULL & BEAR		FEES		
Min Additional Investment	3-Month Total Return	6-Month Total Return	1-Year Total Return	3-Year Total Return	5-Year Total Return	Dividend Yield (TTM)	Expense Ratio	3-Yr Std Deviation	3-Year Beta	NAV	Total Assets (MIL)	%Cash	%Stocks	%Bonds	%Other	Turnover Ratio	Last Bull Market Total Return	Last Bear Market Total Return	Front End Fee (%)	Back End Fee (%)	Inception Date
	7.72	14.24	33.45	44.02	118.72	0	0.85	11.78	1.06	13.93	8,131	0	99	0	0	33	29.85	-17.5			Dec-00
	7.63	15.87	34.57	32.98	103.46	0.39	0.65	11.69	1.01	9.58	1,083	1	99	0	0	63	27.14	-16.62			Mar-01
	7.44	15.37	33.59	29.60	95.07	0	1.52	11.7	1.01	8.4	1,083	1	99	0	0	63	26.48	-16.84			Nov-04
	7.46	15.46	33.73	30.05	96.25	0	1.39	11.65	1	8.64	1,083	1	99	0	0	63	26.58	-16.84			Dec-00
	7.52	15.55	33.97	30.85	98.04	0	1.21	11.66	1.01	9.85	1,083	1	99	0	0	63	26.62	-16.66			Dec-00
	7.54	15.72	34.24	31.62	99.99	0.09	1.02	11.67	1.01	9.82	1,083	1	99	0	0	63	26.87	-16.7			Dec-00
	7.55	15.82	34.47	32.14	101.06	0.22	0.9	11.65	1	9.69	1,083	1	99	0	0	63	27.04	-16.64			Dec-00
100	6.52	11.14	21.23	34.89	106.32	1.37	0.48	10.09	1	17.53	5,749	0	100	0	0	4	24.55	-16.38	1.50		Jun-05
100	6.34	10.73	20.30	31.60	98.21	0.81	1.3	10.06	1	17.19	5,749	0	100	0	0	4	24.14	-16.71		1.00	Jan-07
100	6.55	11.21	21.33	35.20	106.76	1.45	0.4	10.06	1	17.35	5,749	0	100	0	0	4	24.73	-16.5		1.00	Mar-01
	6.62	11.31	21.64	36.19	109.84	1.61	0.16	10.07	1	17.51	5,749	0	100	0	0	4	24.89	-16.28			Mar-01
	6.32	10.83	20.55	32.67	100.79	0.89	1.04	10.06	1	17.5	5,749	0	100	0	0	4	24.25	-16.54			Nov-04
	6.38	10.85	20.64	33.10	102.16	0.99	0.91	10.06	1	17.63	5,749	0	100	0	0	4	24.49	-16.56			Dec-00
	6.42	11.04	20.96	33.92	104.06	1.15	0.73	10.08	1	17.56	5,749	0	100	0	0	4	24.47	-16.45			Dec-00
	6.46	11.12	21.17	34.67	105.88	1.3	0.54	10.08	1	17.6	5,749	0	100	0	0	4	24.76	-16.51			Dec-00
	6.51	11.14	21.25	35.14	107.24	1.4	0.42	10.07	1	17.75	5,749	0	100	0	0	4	24.81	-16.4			Dec-00
100	6.84	11.41	16.18	21.94	81.91	1.66	0.87	9.96	0.93	10.91	1,401	0	100	0	0	99	25.78	-19.92	5.50		Jun-05
100	6.60	11.02	15.22	18.95	74.38	1.03	1.7	9.96	0.93	10.57	1,401	0	100	0	0	99	25.09	-20.03		1.00	Jan-07
100	6.87	11.53	16.41	22.46	82.68	1.83	0.73	9.96	0.93	10.64	1,401	0	100	0	0	99	25.62	-19.8		1.00	Mar-01
100	6.51	9.31	16.53	27.23	91.46	1.35	1.08	10.12	0.97	16.72	2,177	0	100	0	0	35	23.78	-21.32		1.00	Mar-01
	6.60	9.50	16.86	28.48	94.75	1.58	0.78	10.16	0.97	16.93	2,177	0	100	0	0	35	24.12	-21.16			Dec-00
	6.33	8.98	15.80	25.16	86.48	0.82	1.66	10.14	0.97	16.92	2,177	0	100	0	0	35	23.49	-21.49			Nov-04
	6.42	9.06	16.01	25.67	87.74	0.89	1.53	10.16	0.97	16.98	2,177	0	100	0	0	35	23.64	-21.4			Dec-00
	6.48	9.21	16.25	26.37	89.51	1.05	1.35	10.15	0.97	17.69	2,177	0	100	0	0	35	23.67	-21.34			Dec-00
	6.52	9.29	16.41	27.11	91.23	1.24	1.16	10.15	0.97	16.95	2,177	0	100	0	0	35	23.91	-21.31			Dec-00
	6.55	9.36	16.59	27.50	92.38	1.36	1.04	10.16	0.97	17.07	2,177	0	100	0	0	35	23.93	-21.28			Dec-00
	6.97	11.72	16.72	23.67	86.03	2.04	0.43	9.98	0.93	10.88	1,401	0	100	0	0	99	26.11	-19.67			Mar-01
	6.67	11.10	15.62	20.36	77.97	1.26	1.3	10.01	0.93	10.79	1,401	0	100	0	0	99	25.53	-19.98			Nov-04
	6.68	11.18	15.79	20.76	79.04	1.46	1.17	9.96	0.93	10.84	1,401	0	100	0	0	99	25.43	-19.84			Dec-00
	6.76	11.37	16.01	21.55	80.69	1.62	0.99	9.96	0.93	10.78	1,401	0	100	0	0	99	25.65	-19.92			Dec-00
	6.81	11.42	16.25	22.13	82.37	1.69	0.8	9.95	0.93	10.77	1,401	0	100	0	0	99	25.8	-19.8			Dec-00
	6.87	11.52	16.40	22.65	83.47	1.83	0.68	9.95	0.93	10.91	1,401	0	100	0	0	99	25.95	-19.74			Dec-00
100	2.36	5.07	10.87	14.37	33.36	1.52	1.03	4.51	1.08	13.64	1,039	4	42	53	0	15	12.82	-10.1	3.75		Jun-05
100	2.41	5.15	11.09	14.91	34.20	1.7	0.87	4.47	1.07	13.49	1,039	4	42	53	0	15	12.88	-10.17		1.00	Jun-01
	2.42	5.30	11.23	15.55	35.88	1.86	0.67	4.48	1.08	13.53	1,039	4	42	53	0	15	13.05	-9.98			Mar-01
	2.16	4.74	10.31	12.60	29.98	0.92	1.55	4.49	1.08	13.54	1,039	4	42	53	0	15	12.46	-10.3			Nov-04
	2.23	4.89	10.48	13.03	30.88	1.06	1.42	4.52	1.08	13.54	1,039	4	42	53	0	15	12.63	-10.32			Mar-01
	2.28	5.03	10.65	13.70	32.12	1.31	1.24	4.54	1.09	13.46	1,039	4	42	53	0	15	12.61	-10.15			Mar-01
	2.31	5.06	10.83	14.33	33.35	1.5	1.05	4.48	1.08	13.48	1,039	4	42	53	0	15	12.89	-10.13			Mar-01
	2.38	5.12	10.98	14.75	34.15	1.6	0.93	4.48	1.08	13.49	1,039	4	42	53	0	15	12.87	-10.02			Mar-01
	2.80	6.11	13.19	17.68	41.92	1.76	0.68	5.21	1.04	10.41	641.5	3	50	45	0	14	15.63	-12.58			Feb-08
	2.59	5.68	12.21	14.53	35.89	1	1.56	5.21	1.04	10.19	641.5	3	50	45	0	14	14.99	-12.82			Feb-08
	2.68	5.75	12.25	15.01	36.70	0.92	1.43	5.25	1.04	10.25	641.5	3	50	45	0	14	15.17	-12.79			Feb-08
	2.67	5.85	12.50	15.62	37.95	1.26	1.25	5.17	1.03	10.2	641.5	3	50	45	0	14	15.17	-12.75			Feb-08
	2.76	6.02	12.74	16.33	39.39	1.43	1.06	5.2	1.04	10.28	641.5	3	50	45	0	14	15.29	-12.62			Feb-08
	2.84	6.10	12.93	16.77	40.23	1.55	0.94	5.17	1.03	10.29	641.5	3	50	45	0	14	15.49	-12.59			Feb-08
100	3.24	6.90	14.61	18.39	46.02	1.37	1.08	6.09	1.05	14.33	5,497	3	59	37	0	12	17.71	-14.65	5.50		Jun-05
100	3.21	6.98	14.79	18.92	46.88	1.56	0.91	6.09	1.05	14.15	5,497	3	59	37	0	12	17.61	-14.62		1.00	Jun-01
	3.28	7.10	14.96	19.68	48.75	1.7	0.71	6.07	1.05	14.22	5,497	3	59	37	0	12	17.95	-14.56			Mar-01
	3.07	6.55	13.99	16.61	42.36	0.94	1.59	6.1	1.05	14.17	5,497	3	59	37	0	12	17.23	-14.82			Nov-04
	3.13	6.69	14.15	17.09	43.31	1.01	1.46	6.11	1.06	14.15	5,497	3	59	37	0	12	17.39	-14.79			Mar-01
	3.14	6.78	14.35	17.67	44.60	1.19	1.28	6.08	1.05	14.11	5,497	3	59	37	0	12	17.51	-14.75			Mar-01

Fund Name	MARKET Ticker Symbol	Traded On	FUND TYPE, CATEGORY & OBJECTIVE Fund Type	Category and (Prospectus Objective)	RATINGS Overall Rating	Reward Rating	Risk Rating	Recent Up/ Downgrade	Open to New Investors	MINIMUMS Min Initial Investment
Principal LifeTime 2020 Fund R-4 Class	PTBSX	NAS CM	Open End	Target Date 2000-2020 (Asset Alloc)	B-	C+	B	Up	Y	0
Principal LifeTime 2020 Fund R-5 Class	PTBPX	NAS CM	Open End	Target Date 2000-2020 (Asset Alloc)	B-	C+	B	Up	Y	0
Principal LifeTime 2025 Fund Institutional Class	LTSTX	NAS CM	Open End	Target Date 2021-2045 (Asset Alloc)	B-	C+	B	Down	Y	0
Principal LifeTime 2025 Fund R-1 Class	LTSNX	NAS CM	Open End	Target Date 2021-2045 (Asset Alloc)	B-	C+	B	Down	Y	0
Principal LifeTime 2025 Fund R-2 Class	LTADX	NAS CM	Open End	Target Date 2021-2045 (Asset Alloc)	B-	C+	B	Down	Y	0
Principal LifeTime 2025 Fund R-3 Class	LTVPX	NAS CM	Open End	Target Date 2021-2045 (Asset Alloc)	B-	C+	B	Down	Y	0
Principal LifeTime 2025 Fund R-4 Class	LTEEX	NAS CM	Open End	Target Date 2021-2045 (Asset Alloc)	B-	C+	B	Down	Y	0
Principal LifeTime 2025 Fund R-5 Class	LTPDX	NAS CM	Open End	Target Date 2021-2045 (Asset Alloc)	B-	C+	B	Down	Y	0
Principal LifeTime 2030 Fund Class A	PTCAX	NAS CM	Open End	Target Date 2021-2045 (Asset Alloc)	B-	C+	B	Down	Y	1,000
Principal LifeTime 2030 Fund Class J	PLTJX	NAS CM	Open End	Target Date 2021-2045 (Asset Alloc)	B-	C+	B	Down	Y	1,000
Principal LifeTime 2030 Fund Institutional Class	PMTIX	NAS CM	Open End	Target Date 2021-2045 (Asset Alloc)	B-	C+	B	Down	Y	0
Principal LifeTime 2030 Fund R-1 Class	PXASX	NAS CM	Open End	Target Date 2021-2045 (Asset Alloc)	B-	C+	B	Down	Y	0
Principal LifeTime 2030 Fund R-2 Class	PTCNX	NAS CM	Open End	Target Date 2021-2045 (Asset Alloc)	B-	C+	B	Down	Y	0
Principal LifeTime 2030 Fund R-3 Class	PTCMX	NAS CM	Open End	Target Date 2021-2045 (Asset Alloc)	B-	C+	B	Down	Y	0
Principal LifeTime 2030 Fund R-4 Class	PTCSX	NAS CM	Open End	Target Date 2021-2045 (Asset Alloc)	B-	C+	B	Down	Y	0
Principal LifeTime 2030 Fund R-5 Class	PTCPX	NAS CM	Open End	Target Date 2021-2045 (Asset Alloc)	B-	C+	B	Down	Y	0
Principal LifeTime 2035 Fund Institutional Class	LTIUX	NAS CM	Open End	Target Date 2021-2045 (Asset Alloc)	B-	B-	B	Down	Y	0
Principal LifeTime 2035 Fund R-1 Class	LTANX	NAS CM	Open End	Target Date 2021-2045 (Asset Alloc)	B-	C+	B	Down	Y	0
Principal LifeTime 2035 Fund R-2 Class	LTVIX	NAS CM	Open End	Target Date 2021-2045 (Asset Alloc)	B	C+	B+	Up	Y	0
Principal LifeTime 2035 Fund R-3 Class	LTAOX	NAS CM	Open End	Target Date 2021-2045 (Asset Alloc)	B-	C+	B	Down	Y	0
Principal LifeTime 2035 Fund R-4 Class	LTSEX	NAS CM	Open End	Target Date 2021-2045 (Asset Alloc)	B-	C+	B	Down	Y	0
Principal LifeTime 2035 Fund R-5 Class	LTPEX	NAS CM	Open End	Target Date 2021-2045 (Asset Alloc)	B-	C+	B	Down	Y	0
Principal LifeTime 2040 Fund Class A	PTDAX	NAS CM	Open End	Target Date 2021-2045 (Asset Alloc)	B-	B-	B	Down	Y	1,000
Principal LifeTime 2040 Fund Class J	PTDJX	NAS CM	Open End	Target Date 2021-2045 (Asset Alloc)	B-	B-	B	Down	Y	1,000
Principal LifeTime 2040 Fund Institutional Class	PTDIX	NAS CM	Open End	Target Date 2021-2045 (Asset Alloc)	B-	B-	B	Down	Y	0
Principal LifeTime 2040 Fund R-1 Class	PYASX	NAS CM	Open End	Target Date 2021-2045 (Asset Alloc)	B-	C+	B-	Down	Y	0
Principal LifeTime 2040 Fund R-2 Class	PTDNX	NAS CM	Open End	Target Date 2021-2045 (Asset Alloc)	B-	C+	B-	Down	Y	0
Principal LifeTime 2040 Fund R-3 Class	PTDMX	NAS CM	Open End	Target Date 2021-2045 (Asset Alloc)	B-	C+	B-	Down	Y	0
Principal LifeTime 2040 Fund R-4 Class	PTDSX	NAS CM	Open End	Target Date 2021-2045 (Asset Alloc)	B-	B-	B	Down	Y	0
Principal LifeTime 2040 Fund R-5 Class	PTDPX	NAS CM	Open End	Target Date 2021-2045 (Asset Alloc)	B-	B-	B	Down	Y	0
Principal LifeTime 2045 Fund Institutional Class	LTRIX	NAS CM	Open End	Target Date 2021-2045 (Asset Alloc)	B-	B-	B-	Down	Y	0
Principal LifeTime 2045 Fund R-1 Class	LTRGX	NAS CM	Open End	Target Date 2021-2045 (Asset Alloc)	B-	C+	B-	Down	Y	0
Principal LifeTime 2045 Fund R-2 Class	LTRSX	NAS CM	Open End	Target Date 2021-2045 (Asset Alloc)	B-	B-	B-	Down	Y	0
Principal LifeTime 2045 Fund R-3 Class	LTRVX	NAS CM	Open End	Target Date 2021-2045 (Asset Alloc)	B-	B-	B-	Down	Y	0
Principal LifeTime 2045 Fund R-4 Class	LTRLX	NAS CM	Open End	Target Date 2021-2045 (Asset Alloc)	B-	B-	B-	Down	Y	0
Principal LifeTime 2045 Fund R-5 Class	LTRDX	NAS CM	Open End	Target Date 2021-2045 (Asset Alloc)	B-	B-	B-	Down	Y	0
Principal LifeTime 2050 Fund Class A	PPEAX	NAS CM	Open End	Target Date 2046+ (Asset Alloc)	B-	B-	B-	Down	Y	1,000
Principal LifeTime 2050 Fund Class J	PFLJX	NAS CM	Open End	Target Date 2046+ (Asset Alloc)	B-	B-	B-	Down	Y	1,000
Principal LifeTime 2050 Fund Institutional Class	PPLIX	NAS CM	Open End	Target Date 2046+ (Asset Alloc)	B-	B-	B-	Down	Y	0
Principal LifeTime 2050 Fund R-1 Class	PZASX	NAS CM	Open End	Target Date 2046+ (Asset Alloc)	B-	B-	B-	Down	Y	0
Principal LifeTime 2050 Fund R-2 Class	PTENX	NAS CM	Open End	Target Date 2046+ (Asset Alloc)	B-	B-	B-	Down	Y	0
Principal LifeTime 2050 Fund R-3 Class	PTERX	NAS CM	Open End	Target Date 2046+ (Asset Alloc)	B-	B-	B-	Down	Y	0
Principal LifeTime 2050 Fund R-4 Class	PTESX	NAS CM	Open End	Target Date 2046+ (Asset Alloc)	B-	B-	B-	Down	Y	0
Principal LifeTime 2050 Fund R-5 Class	PTEFX	NAS CM	Open End	Target Date 2046+ (Asset Alloc)	B-	B-	B-	Down	Y	0
Principal LifeTime 2055 Fund Institutional Class	LTFIX	NAS CM	Open End	Target Date 2046+ (Asset Alloc)	B-	B-	B-	Down	Y	0
Principal LifeTime 2055 Fund R-1 Class	LTFGX	NAS CM	Open End	Target Date 2046+ (Asset Alloc)	B-	B-	B-	Down	Y	0
Principal LifeTime 2055 Fund R-2 Class	LTFSX	NAS CM	Open End	Target Date 2046+ (Asset Alloc)	B-	B-	B-	Down	Y	0
Principal LifeTime 2055 Fund R-3 Class	LTFDX	NAS CM	Open End	Target Date 2046+ (Asset Alloc)	B-	B-	B-	Down	Y	0
Principal LifeTime 2055 Fund R-4 Class	LTFLX	NAS CM	Open End	Target Date 2046+ (Asset Alloc)	B-	B-	B-	Down	Y	0
Principal LifeTime 2055 Fund R-5 Class	LTFPX	NAS CM	Open End	Target Date 2046+ (Asset Alloc)	B-	B-	B-	Down	Y	0
Principal LifeTime 2060 Fund Class J	PLTAX	NAS CM	Open End	Target Date 2046+ (Asset Alloc)	B-	B-	B-	Down	Y	1,000
Principal LifeTime 2060 Fund Class R-1	PLTRX	NAS CM	Open End	Target Date 2046+ (Asset Alloc)	B-	B-	B-	Down	Y	0

★ Expanded analysis of this fund is included in Section II.

	TOTAL RETURNS					PERFORMANCE				ASSETS		ASSET ALLOCATION & TURNOVER					BULL & BEAR		FEES		
Min Additional Investment	3-Month Total Return	6-Month Total Return	1-Year Total Return	3-Year Total Return	5-Year Total Return	Dividend Yield (TTM)	Expense Ratio	3-Yr Std Deviation	3-Year Beta	NAV	Total Assets (MIL)	%Cash	%Stocks	%Bonds	%Other	Turnover Ratio	Last Bull Market Total Return	Last Bear Market Total Return	Front End Fee (%)	Back End Fee (%)	Inception Date
	3.23	6.86	14.50	18.33	45.93	1.4	1.09	6.08	1.05	14.13	5,497	3	59	37	0	12	17.62	-14.66			Mar-01
	3.23	6.93	14.64	18.74	46.71	1.46	0.97	6.07	1.05	14.16	5,497	3	59	37	0	12	17.71	-14.62			Mar-01
	3.67	7.85	16.75	21.66	53.86	1.57	0.73	6.73	1.03	11.48	1,781	3	67	29	0	14	19.01	-15.74			Feb-08
	3.47	7.36	15.74	18.55	47.22	0.87	1.6	6.71	1.03	11.26	1,781	3	67	29	0	14	18.43	-16.05			Feb-08
	3.48	7.46	15.83	19.00	48.18	0.9	1.47	6.72	1.03	11.29	1,781	3	67	29	0	14	18.4	-15.94			Feb-08
	3.55	7.52	16.12	19.59	49.64	1.12	1.29	6.76	1.04	11.28	1,781	3	67	29	0	14	18.54	-15.91			Feb-08
	3.55	7.68	16.33	20.26	51.00	1.29	1.1	6.74	1.03	11.38	1,781	3	67	29	0	14	18.61	-15.75			Feb-08
	3.71	7.74	16.46	20.80	51.91	1.38	0.98	6.73	1.03	11.42	1,781	3	67	29	0	14	18.81	-15.8			Feb-08
100	4.09	8.58	18.01	22.10	55.82	1.19	1.1	7.31	1.02	14.8	6,679	3	74	22	0	15	19.39	-16.62	5.50		Jun-05
100	4.04	8.62	18.21	22.65	56.70	1.34	0.95	7.31	1.02	14.7	6,679	3	74	22	0	15	19.39	-16.62		1.00	Jun-01
	4.12	8.76	18.42	23.51	58.74	1.5	0.73	7.3	1.02	14.74	6,679	3	74	22	0	15	19.69	-16.52			Mar-01
	3.93	8.24	17.40	20.27	51.87	0.77	1.61	7.29	1.01	14.67	6,679	3	74	22	0	15	19.07	-16.86			Nov-04
	3.93	8.37	17.61	20.78	52.93	0.84	1.48	7.31	1.02	14.71	6,679	3	74	22	0	15	19.13	-16.78			Mar-01
	3.96	8.48	17.81	21.40	54.26	1.02	1.3	7.31	1.02	14.7	6,679	3	74	22	0	15	19.26	-16.73			Mar-01
	3.99	8.51	17.95	22.08	55.75	1.15	1.11	7.3	1.02	15.19	6,679	3	74	22	0	15	19.41	-16.71			Mar-01
	4.06	8.63	18.20	22.57	56.75	1.26	0.99	7.29	1.01	14.74	6,679	3	74	22	0	15	19.49	-16.61			Mar-01
	4.45	9.39	19.70	24.28	62.81	1.3	0.69	7.78	1	12.28	1,361	1	79	20	0	15	20.58	-17.52			Feb-08
	4.27	8.94	18.64	21.19	55.80	0.64	1.56	7.79	1	12.09	1,361	1	79	20	0	15	19.98	-17.75			Feb-08
	4.29	8.96	18.78	21.56	56.81	0.69	1.43	7.79	1	12.07	1,361	1	79	20	0	15	20.07	-17.75			Feb-08
	4.39	9.14	19.04	22.31	58.37	0.86	1.25	7.81	1	12.12	1,361	1	79	20	0	15	20.18	-17.68			Feb-08
	4.39	9.20	19.25	23.06	59.79	1.02	1.06	7.8	1	12.2	1,361	1	79	20	0	15	20.27	-17.61			Feb-08
	4.40	9.27	19.41	23.40	60.75	1.1	0.94	7.79	1	12.23	1,361	1	79	20	0	15	20.49	-17.57			Feb-08
100	4.60	9.66	20.24	24.09	63.03	1	1.08	8.34	1.01	15.43	4,553	1	84	15	0	18	20.93	-18.34	5.50		Jun-05
100	4.69	9.77	20.43	24.53	63.75	1.11	0.94	8.29	1	15.57	4,553	1	84	15	0	18	20.95	-18.38		1.00	Jun-01
	4.75	9.87	20.69	25.46	66.18	1.27	0.71	8.29	1	15.7	4,553	1	84	15	0	18	21.1	-18.13			Mar-01
	4.47	9.42	19.64	22.16	58.91	0.55	1.59	8.31	1	15.59	4,553	1	84	15	0	18	20.53	-18.51			Nov-04
	4.52	9.47	19.77	22.64	59.94	0.66	1.46	8.33	1.01	15.58	4,553	1	84	15	0	18	20.6	-18.43			Mar-01
	4.56	9.53	19.95	23.33	61.36	0.82	1.28	8.32	1.01	15.52	4,553	1	84	15	0	18	20.81	-18.37			Mar-01
	4.59	9.61	20.20	24.06	62.98	0.98	1.09	8.3	1	15.54	4,553	1	84	15	0	18	20.83	-18.28			Mar-01
	4.71	9.78	20.39	24.52	64.04	1.03	0.97	8.33	1.01	15.64	4,553	1	84	15	0	18	20.97	-18.27			Mar-01
	4.90	10.23	21.39	26.28	68.55	1.22	0.73	8.66	1	12.85	946.8	1	88	11	0	15	21.53	-18.51			Feb-08
	4.69	9.82	20.39	23.11	61.39	0.57	1.6	8.65	1	12.52	946.8	1	88	11	0	15	20.9	-18.86			Feb-08
	4.76	9.80	20.48	23.49	62.45	0.63	1.47	8.65	1	12.51	946.8	1	88	11	0	15	21.03	-18.75			Feb-08
	4.75	9.93	20.68	24.14	63.90	0.83	1.29	8.68	1.01	12.57	946.8	1	88	11	0	15	21.3	-18.77			Feb-08
	4.82	10.06	20.95	24.91	65.49	0.95	1.1	8.65	1	12.67	946.8	1	88	11	0	15	21.37	-18.7			Feb-08
	4.89	10.13	21.10	25.36	66.53	0.99	0.98	8.69	1.01	12.69	946.8	1	88	11	0	15	21.48	-18.66			Feb-08
100	5.02	10.35	21.66	25.74	67.68	0.91	1.1	8.91	0.99	15.76	2,598	1	90	9	0	17	21.8	-19.32	5.50		Jun-05
100	5.00	10.43	21.85	25.92	67.66	0.98	1.05	8.91	0.99	15.25	2,598	1	90	9	0	17	21.76	-19.43		1.00	Jun-01
	5.06	10.56	22.12	27.11	70.89	1.19	0.74	8.91	0.99	15.67	2,598	1	90	9	0	17	22.15	-19.25			Mar-01
	4.85	10.05	20.98	23.76	63.43	0.53	1.61	8.9	0.99	15.54	2,598	1	90	9	0	17	21.49	-19.49			Nov-04
	4.88	10.15	21.18	24.24	64.50	0.62	1.48	8.94	1	15.52	2,598	1	90	9	0	17	21.55	-19.47			Mar-01
	4.91	10.18	21.39	24.98	66.08	0.78	1.3	8.92	0.99	15.51	2,598	1	90	9	0	17	21.75	-19.45			Mar-01
	4.97	10.36	21.61	25.71	67.69	0.91	1.11	8.9	0.99	15.59	2,598	1	90	9	0	17	21.8	-19.33			Mar-01
	4.96	10.34	21.73	26.13	68.54	0.93	0.99	8.9	0.99	15.62	2,598	1	90	9	0	17	21.99	-19.29			Mar-01
	5.13	10.76	22.52	27.74	71.63	1.16	0.75	9.15	1	13.6	399.5	1	93	7	0	12	22.14	-19.43			Feb-08
	4.93	10.22	21.48	24.48	64.41	0.6	1.61	9.11	0.99	13.19	399.5	1	93	7	0	12	21.6	-19.78			Feb-08
	5.00	10.36	21.70	25.00	65.50	0.62	1.48	9.13	0.99	13.23	399.5	1	93	7	0	12	21.54	-19.68			Feb-08
	5.02	10.44	21.83	25.61	66.95	0.82	1.3	9.16	1	13.29	399.5	1	93	7	0	12	21.77	-19.66			Feb-08
	5.11	10.57	22.08	26.38	68.63	0.92	1.11	9.1	0.99	13.4	399.5	1	93	7	0	12	21.81	-19.58			Feb-08
	5.14	10.58	22.25	26.81	69.57	0.94	0.99	9.15	1	13.45	399.5	1	93	7	0	12	21.93	-19.47			Feb-08
100	5.13	10.68	22.27	26.53		0.91	1.11	9.11	0.98	14.13	264.4	0	94	6	0	15				1.00	Mar-13
	4.93	10.31	21.65	24.52		0.66	1.63	9.14	0.98	13.92	264.4	0	94	6	0	15					Mar-13

	MARKET		FUND TYPE, CATEGORY & OBJECTIVE		RATINGS				MINIMUMS	
Fund Name	Ticker Symbol	Traded On	Fund Type	Category and (Prospectus Objective)	Overall Rating	Reward Rating	Risk Rating	Recent Up/ Downgrade	Open to New Investors	Min Initial Investment
Principal LifeTime 2060 Fund Class R-2	PLTBX	NAS CM	Open End	Target Date 2046+ (Asset Alloc)	B-	B-	B-	Down	Y	0
Principal LifeTime 2060 Fund Class R-3	PLTCX	NAS CM	Open End	Target Date 2046+ (Asset Alloc)	B-	B-	B-	Down	Y	0
Principal LifeTime 2060 Fund Class R-4	PLTMX	NAS CM	Open End	Target Date 2046+ (Asset Alloc)	B-	B-	B-	Down	Y	0
Principal LifeTime 2060 Fund Class R-5	PLTOX	NAS CM	Open End	Target Date 2046+ (Asset Alloc)	B-	B-	B-	Down	Y	0
Principal LifeTime 2060 Fund Institutional Class	PLTZX	NAS CM	Open End	Target Date 2046+ (Asset Alloc)	B-	B-	B-	Down	Y	0
Principal LifeTime 2065 Class R-1 Shares	PLJAX	NAS CM	Open End	Target Date 2046+ (Asset Alloc)	U	U	U		Y	0
Principal LifeTime 2065 Class R-2 Shares	PLJBX	NAS CM	Open End	Target Date 2046+ (Asset Alloc)	U	U	U		Y	0
Principal LifeTime 2065 Class R-3 Shares	PLJCX	NAS CM	Open End	Target Date 2046+ (Asset Alloc)	U	U	U		Y	0
Principal LifeTime 2065 Class R-4 Shares	PLJDX	NAS CM	Open End	Target Date 2046+ (Asset Alloc)	U	U	U		Y	0
Principal LifeTime 2065 Class R-5 Shares	PLJEX	NAS CM	Open End	Target Date 2046+ (Asset Alloc)	U	U	U		Y	0
Principal LifeTime 2065 Institutional Class Shares	PLJIX	NAS CM	Open End	Target Date 2046+ (Asset Alloc)	U	U	U		Y	0
Principal LifeTime Hybrid 2015 Fund Institutional Class	PHTMX	NAS CM	Open End	Target Date 2000-2020 (Asset Alloc)	B-	C	B	Up	Y	0
Principal LifeTime Hybrid 2015 Fund R-6	PLRRX	NAS CM	Open End	Target Date 2000-2020 (Asset Alloc)	B-	C	B	Up	Y	0
Principal LifeTime Hybrid 2020 Fund Institutional Class	PHTTX	NAS CM	Open End	Target Date 2000-2020 (Asset Alloc)	B-	C	B	Up	Y	0
Principal LifeTime Hybrid 2020 Fund R-6	PLTTX	NAS CM	Open End	Target Date 2000-2020 (Asset Alloc)	B-	C	B	Up	Y	0
Principal LifeTime Hybrid 2025 Fund Institutional Class	PHTQX	NAS CM	Open End	Target Date 2021-2045 (Asset Alloc)	B-	C+	B	Up	Y	0
Principal LifeTime Hybrid 2025 Fund R-6	PLFTX	NAS CM	Open End	Target Date 2021-2045 (Asset Alloc)	B-	C+	B	Up	Y	0
Principal LifeTime Hybrid 2030 Fund Institutional Class	PHTNX	NAS CM	Open End	Target Date 2021-2045 (Asset Alloc)	B-	C+	B	Up	Y	0
Principal LifeTime Hybrid 2030 Fund R-6	PLZTX	NAS CM	Open End	Target Date 2021-2045 (Asset Alloc)	B-	C+	B	Up	Y	0
Principal LifeTime Hybrid 2035 Fund Institutional Class	PHTJX	NAS CM	Open End	Target Date 2021-2045 (Asset Alloc)	B-	C+	B	Up	Y	0
Principal LifeTime Hybrid 2035 Fund R-6	PLRTX	NAS CM	Open End	Target Date 2021-2045 (Asset Alloc)	B-	C+	B	Up	Y	0
Principal LifeTime Hybrid 2040 Fund Institutional Class	PLTQX	NAS CM	Open End	Target Date 2021-2045 (Asset Alloc)	B-	C+	B	Up	Y	0
Principal LifeTime Hybrid 2040 Fund R-6	PLMTX	NAS CM	Open End	Target Date 2021-2045 (Asset Alloc)	B-	C+	B	Up	Y	0
Principal LifeTime Hybrid 2045 Fund Institutional Class	PHTYX	NAS CM	Open End	Target Date 2021-2045 (Asset Alloc)	B-	C+	B	Up	Y	0
Principal LifeTime Hybrid 2045 Fund R-6	PLNTX	NAS CM	Open End	Target Date 2021-2045 (Asset Alloc)	B-	C+	B	Up	Y	0
Principal LifeTime Hybrid 2050 Fund Institutional Class	PHTUX	NAS CM	Open End	Target Date 2046+ (Asset Alloc)	C+	C+	B-	Down	Y	0
Principal LifeTime Hybrid 2050 Fund R-6	PLJTX	NAS CM	Open End	Target Date 2046+ (Asset Alloc)	C+	C+	B-	Down	Y	0
Principal LifeTime Hybrid 2055 Fund Institutional Class	PLTNX	NAS CM	Open End	Target Date 2046+ (Asset Alloc)	C+	C+	B-	Down	Y	0
Principal LifeTime Hybrid 2055 Fund R-6	PLHTX	NAS CM	Open End	Target Date 2046+ (Asset Alloc)	C+	C+	B-	Down	Y	0
Principal LifeTime Hybrid 2060 Fund Institutional Class	PLTHX	NAS CM	Open End	Target Date 2046+ (Asset Alloc)	C+	C+	B-	Down	Y	0
Principal LifeTime Hybrid 2060 Fund R-6	PLKTX	NAS CM	Open End	Target Date 2046+ (Asset Alloc)	C+	C+	B-	Down	Y	0
Principal LifeTime Hybrid 2065 Class R-6 Shares	PLHRX	NAS CM	Open End	Target Date 2046+ (Asset Alloc)	U	U	U		Y	0
Principal LifeTime Hybrid 2065 Institutional Class Shares	PLHHX	NAS CM	Open End	Target Date 2046+ (Asset Alloc)	U	U	U		Y	0
Principal LifeTime Hybrid Income Fund Institutional Class	PHTFX	NAS CM	Open End	Target Date 2000-2020 (Asset Alloc)	C+	C	B	Up	Y	0
Principal LifeTime Hybrid Income Fund R-6	PLTYX	NAS CM	Open End	Target Date 2000-2020 (Asset Alloc)	C+	C	B	Up	Y	0
Principal LifeTime Strategic Income Fund Class A	PALTX	NAS CM	Open End	Target Date 2000-2020 (Asset Alloc)	B	C	A-	Up	Y	1,000
Principal LifeTime Strategic Income Fund Class J	PLSJX	NAS CM	Open End	Target Date 2000-2020 (Asset Alloc)	B	C	A-	Up	Y	1,000
Principal LifeTime Strategic Income Fund Institutional Cls	PLSIX	NAS CM	Open End	Target Date 2000-2020 (Asset Alloc)	B	C+	A-	Up	Y	0
Principal LifeTime Strategic Income Fund R-1 Class	PLAIX	NAS CM	Open End	Target Date 2000-2020 (Asset Alloc)	B-	C	A-	Up	Y	0
Principal LifeTime Strategic Income Fund R-2 Class	PLSNX	NAS CM	Open End	Target Date 2000-2020 (Asset Alloc)	B-	C	A-	Up	Y	0
Principal LifeTime Strategic Income Fund R-3 Class	PLSMX	NAS CM	Open End	Target Date 2000-2020 (Asset Alloc)	B	C	A-	Up	Y	0
Principal LifeTime Strategic Income Fund R-4 Class	PLSSX	NAS CM	Open End	Target Date 2000-2020 (Asset Alloc)	B	C	A-	Up	Y	0
Principal LifeTime Strategic Income Fund R-5 Class	PLSPX	NAS CM	Open End	Target Date 2000-2020 (Asset Alloc)	B	C	A-	Up	Y	0
Principal MidCap Fund Class A	PEMGX	NAS CM	Open End	US Equity Mid Cap (Growth)	B	B	B-			1,000
Principal MidCap Fund Class C	PMBCX	NAS CM	Open End	US Equity Mid Cap (Growth)	B	B	B-			1,000
Principal MidCap Fund Class J	PMBJX	NAS CM	Open End	US Equity Mid Cap (Growth)	B	B	B-			1,000
PRINCIPAL MIDCAP FUND Class R-6	PMAQX	NAS CM	Open End	US Equity Mid Cap (Growth)	B	B	B-		Y	0
Principal MidCap Fund Institutional Class	PCBIX	NAS CM	Open End	US Equity Mid Cap (Growth)	B	B	B-			0
Principal MidCap Fund R-1 Class	PMSBX	NAS CM	Open End	US Equity Mid Cap (Growth)	B	B	B-			0
Principal MidCap Fund R-2 Class	PMBNX	NAS CM	Open End	US Equity Mid Cap (Growth)	B	B	B-			0
Principal MidCap Fund R-3 Class	PMBMX	NAS CM	Open End	US Equity Mid Cap (Growth)	B	B	B-			0
Principal MidCap Fund R-4 Class	PMBSX	NAS CM	Open End	US Equity Mid Cap (Growth)	B	B	B-			0

★Expanded analysis of this fund is included in Section II.

	TOTAL RETURNS					PERFORMANCE				ASSETS		ASSET ALLOCATION & TURNOVER					BULL & BEAR		FEES		
Min Additional Investment	3-Month Total Return	6-Month Total Return	1-Year Total Return	3-Year Total Return	5-Year Total Return	Dividend Yield (TTM)	Expense Ratio	3-Yr Std Deviation	3-Year Beta	NAV	Total Assets (MIL)	%Cash	%Stocks	%Bonds	%Other	Turnover Ratio	Last Bull Market Total Return	Last Bear Market Total Return	Front End Fee (%)	Back End Fee (%)	Inception Date
	4.95	10.40	21.80	24.97		0.71	1.5	9.12	0.98	13.96	264.4	0	94	6	0	15					Mar-13
	5.08	10.57	22.09	25.69		0.81	1.32	9.08	0.98	14.08	264.4	0	94	6	0	15					Mar-13
	5.14	10.61	22.33	26.40		0.93	1.13	9.09	0.98	14.09	264.4	0	94	6	0	15					Mar-13
	5.08	10.62	22.40	26.74		0.98	1.01	9.12	0.98	14.12	264.4	0	94	6	0	15					Mar-13
	5.25	10.85	22.69	27.74		1.15	0.77	9.15	0.98	14.2	264.4	0	94	6	0	15					Mar-13
	5.06						1.65			10.55	0.06	1	92	7	0						Sep-17
	5.06						1.52			10.55	0.06	1	92	7	0						Sep-17
	5.16						1.34			10.56	0.06	1	92	7	0						Sep-17
	5.15						1.15			10.57	0.06	1	92	7	0						Sep-17
	5.15						1.03			10.57	0.06	1	92	7	0						Sep-17
	5.25						0.82			10.58	0.06	1	92	7	0						Sep-17
	2.61	5.63	11.77	17.26		1.52	0.46	4.88	0.97	10.89	34.2	2	47	51	0	28					Sep-14
	2.61	5.72	11.86	17.35		1.51	0.43	4.9	0.98	10.91	34.2	2	47	51	0	28					Aug-15
	3.07	6.62	13.51	19.73		1.63	0.46	5.8	1	11.15	125.4	1	56	43	0	15					Sep-14
	2.99	6.55	13.53	19.76		1.63	0.43	5.78	1	11.15	125.4	1	56	43	0	15					Aug-15
	3.50	7.50	15.23	21.97		1.52	0.47	6.48	0.99	11.43	92.3	1	64	35	0	26					Sep-14
	3.41	7.40	15.12	21.84		1.52	0.44	6.51	1	11.43	92.3	1	64	35	0	26					Aug-15
	3.86	8.21	16.81	23.94		1.59	0.47	7.03	0.98	11.61	125.3	1	72	27	0	12					Sep-14
	3.88	8.32	16.71	23.96		1.59	0.44	7.05	0.98	11.61	125.3	1	72	27	0	12					Aug-15
	4.24	8.92	18.14	25.67		1.49	0.47	7.6	0.97	11.87	74.0	0	78	22	0	25					Sep-14
	4.15	8.82	18.02	25.67		1.49	0.44	7.56	0.97	11.87	74.0	0	78	22	0	25					Aug-15
	4.45	9.39	19.16	27.04		1.51	0.48	8.05	0.98	11.99	90.6	0	83	17	0	13					Sep-14
	4.45	9.38	19.14	27.14		1.51	0.45	8.09	0.98	12	90.6	0	83	17	0	13					Aug-15
	4.65	9.84	19.82	27.80		1.47	0.49	8.5	0.99	12.13	46.1	0	87	12	0	11					Sep-14
	4.65	9.83	19.91	28.03		1.47	0.46	8.47	0.98	12.14	46.1	0	87	12	0	11					Aug-15
	4.81	10.17	20.49	29.02		1.51	0.49	8.76	0.98	12.19	41.4	0	90	9	0	12					Sep-14
	4.81	10.17	20.60	29.02		1.51	0.46	8.81	0.98	12.19	41.4	0	90	9	0	12					Aug-15
	4.92	10.44	21.04	29.76		1.47	0.49	8.98	0.98	12.34	12.2	0	93	7	0	20					Sep-14
	4.92	10.43	21.02	29.86		1.47	0.46	8.95	0.98	12.35	12.2	0	93	7	0	20					Aug-15
	5.00	10.51	21.32	30.36		1.47	0.49	9.01	0.97	12.35	2.4	0	94	6	0	22					Sep-14
	4.99	10.58	21.40	30.56		1.47	0.46	8.99	0.97	12.37	2.4	0	94	6	0	22					Aug-15
	5.14						0.44			10.58	0.02	0	93	7	0						Sep-17
	5.14						0.47			10.58	0.02	0	93	7	0						Sep-17
	1.54	3.52	7.62	12.18		1.26	0.44	3.09	0.89	10.37	24.6	1	27	71	0	26					Sep-14
	1.64	3.62	7.61	12.28		1.26	0.41	3.06	0.88	10.38	24.6	1	27	71	0	26					Aug-15
100	1.67	3.86	8.27	11.55	22.56	1.54	0.99	3.15	0.94	12.47	570.2	5	31	63	0	18	8.65	-4.66	3.75		Jun-05
100	1.76	3.99	8.55	11.99	23.19	1.75	0.89	3.19	0.95	12.3	570.2	5	31	63	0	18	8.63	-4.71		1.00	Jun-01
	1.79	4.09	8.72	12.73	24.89	1.95	0.64	3.18	0.95	12.35	570.2	5	31	63	0	18	8.9	-4.59			Mar-01
	1.63	3.67	7.83	9.91	19.61	1	1.51	3.17	0.94	12.42	570.2	5	31	63	0	18	8.32	-4.88			Nov-04
	1.58	3.70	7.96	10.28	20.34	1.19	1.38	3.18	0.95	12.41	570.2	5	31	63	0	18	8.4	-4.79			Mar-01
	1.61	3.76	8.15	10.88	21.38	1.43	1.2	3.19	0.95	12.27	570.2	5	31	63	0	18	8.65	-4.82			Mar-01
	1.79	3.93	8.32	11.57	22.61	1.62	1.01	3.21	0.96	12.29	570.2	5	31	63	0	18	8.69	-4.72			Mar-01
	1.74	3.95	8.49	11.96	23.34	1.69	0.89	3.2	0.95	12.36	570.2	5	31	63	0	18	8.74	-4.69			Mar-01
100	4.82	10.88	24.92	37.79	110.96	0.11	0.99	11.43	1.03	26.73	15,667	0	100	0	0	22	26.67	-15.86	5.50		Jun-05
100	4.64	10.50	24.07	34.89	103.39	0	1.73	11.42	1.03	24.37	15,667	0	100	0	0	22	26.05	-16.05		1.00	Jan-07
100	4.88	11.00	25.19	38.48	112.29	0.23	0.82	11.42	1.03	25.75	15,667	0	100	0	0	22	26.65	-15.82		1.00	Mar-01
	4.94	11.11	25.40	38.76	112.99	0.37	0.61	11.43	1.03	27.25	15,667	0	100	0	0	22	26.84	-15.8			Nov-16
	4.89	11.05	25.32	39.11	114.35	0.32	0.68	11.43	1.03	27.28	15,667	0	100	0	0	22	26.97	-15.69			Mar-01
	4.70	10.61	24.40	35.83	105.93	0	1.47	11.43	1.03	24.96	15,667	0	100	0	0	22	26.34	-15.99			Nov-04
	4.71	10.68	24.50	36.39	107.27	0	1.34	11.42	1.03	25.33	15,667	0	100	0	0	22	26.51	-15.94			Dec-00
	4.76	10.75	24.73	37.10	109.17	0	1.16	11.42	1.03	26.2	15,667	0	100	0	0	22	26.53	-15.87			Dec-00
	4.78	10.87	24.95	37.89	111.08	0.08	0.97	11.41	1.03	27.16	15,667	0	100	0	0	22	26.7	-15.8			Dec-00

Fund Name	MARKET Ticker Symbol	MARKET Traded On	FUND TYPE, CATEGORY & OBJECTIVE Fund Type	Category and (Prospectus Objective)	RATINGS Overall Rating	Reward Rating	Risk Rating	Recent Up/ Downgrade	Open to New Investors	MINIMUMS Min Initial Investment
Principal MidCap Fund R-5 Class	PMBPX	NAS CM	Open End	US Equity Mid Cap (Growth)	B	B	B-			0
Principal MidCap Growth Fund Class J	PMGJX	NAS CM	Open End	US Equity Mid Cap (Growth)	B+	A-	B	Up	Y	1,000
Principal MidCap Growth Fund III Class J	PPQJX	NAS CM	Open End	US Equity Mid Cap (Growth)	B-	B-	C+	Up	Y	1,000
Principal MidCap Growth Fund III Institutional Class	PPIMX	NAS CM	Open End	US Equity Mid Cap (Growth)	B-	B	C+	Down	Y	0
Principal MidCap Growth Fund III R-1 Class	PHASX	NAS CM	Open End	US Equity Mid Cap (Growth)	C+	B-	C+	Down	Y	0
Principal MidCap Growth Fund III R-2 Class	PPQNX	NAS CM	Open End	US Equity Mid Cap (Growth)	B-	B-	C+	Up	Y	0
Principal MidCap Growth Fund III R-3 Class	PPQMX	NAS CM	Open End	US Equity Mid Cap (Growth)	B-	B-	C+	Up	Y	0
Principal MidCap Growth Fund III R-4 Class	PPQSX	NAS CM	Open End	US Equity Mid Cap (Growth)	B-	B-	C+	Up	Y	0
Principal MidCap Growth Fund III R-5 Class	PPQPX	NAS CM	Open End	US Equity Mid Cap (Growth)	B-	B-	C+	Up	Y	0
Principal MidCap Growth Fund Institutional Class	PGWIX	NAS CM	Open End	US Equity Mid Cap (Growth)	B+	A-	B	Up	Y	0
Principal MidCap Growth Fund R-1 Class	PMSGX	NAS CM	Open End	US Equity Mid Cap (Growth)	B+	B+	B	Up	Y	0
Principal MidCap Growth Fund R-2 Class	PGPPX	NAS CM	Open End	US Equity Mid Cap (Growth)	B+	A-	B	Up	Y	0
Principal MidCap Growth Fund R-3 Class	PFPPX	NAS CM	Open End	US Equity Mid Cap (Growth)	B+	A-	B	Up	Y	0
Principal MidCap Growth Fund R-4 Class	PIPPX	NAS CM	Open End	US Equity Mid Cap (Growth)	B+	A-	B	Up	Y	0
Principal MidCap Growth Fund R-5 Class	PHPPX	NAS CM	Open End	US Equity Mid Cap (Growth)	B+	A-	B	Up	Y	0
Principal MidCap S&P 400 Index Fund Class J	PMFJX	NAS CM	Open End	US Equity Mid Cap (Growth)	B	B	B		Y	1,000
Principal MidCap S&P 400 Index Fund Class R-6	PMAPX	NAS CM	Open End	US Equity Mid Cap (Growth)	B	B	B		Y	0
Principal MidCap S&P 400 Index Fund Institutional Class	MPSIX	NAS CM	Open End	US Equity Mid Cap (Growth)	B	B	B		Y	0
Principal MidCap S&P 400 Index Fund R-1 Class	PMSSX	NAS CM	Open End	US Equity Mid Cap (Growth)	B	B	B	Up	Y	0
Principal MidCap S&P 400 Index Fund R-2 Class	PMFNX	NAS CM	Open End	US Equity Mid Cap (Growth)	B	B	B	Up	Y	0
Principal MidCap S&P 400 Index Fund R-3 Class	PMFMX	NAS CM	Open End	US Equity Mid Cap (Growth)	B	B	B	Up	Y	0
Principal MidCap S&P 400 Index Fund R-4 Class	PMFSX	NAS CM	Open End	US Equity Mid Cap (Growth)	B	B	B		Y	0
Principal MidCap S&P 400 Index Fund R-5 Class	PMFPX	NAS CM	Open End	US Equity Mid Cap (Growth)	B	B	B		Y	0
Principal MidCap Value Fund I Class J	PVEJX	NAS CM	Open End	US Equity Mid Cap (Growth)	B-	C+	B	Up	Y	1,000
Principal MidCap Value Fund I Institutional Class	PVMIX	NAS CM	Open End	US Equity Mid Cap (Growth)	B-	B-	B	Up	Y	0
Principal MidCap Value Fund I R-1 Class	PLASX	NAS CM	Open End	US Equity Mid Cap (Growth)	B-	C+	B	Up	Y	0
Principal MidCap Value Fund I R-2 Class	PABUX	NAS CM	Open End	US Equity Mid Cap (Growth)	B-	C+	B	Up	Y	0
Principal MidCap Value Fund I R-3 Class	PMPRX	NAS CM	Open End	US Equity Mid Cap (Growth)	B-	C+	B	Up	Y	0
Principal MidCap Value Fund I R-4 Class	PABWX	NAS CM	Open End	US Equity Mid Cap (Growth)	B-	C+	B	Up	Y	0
Principal MidCap Value Fund I R-5 Class	PABVX	NAS CM	Open End	US Equity Mid Cap (Growth)	B-	B-	B	Up	Y	0
Principal MidCap Value Fund III Class A	PVCAX	NAS CM	Open End	US Equity Mid Cap (Growth)	B-	B-	B	Up	Y	1,000
Principal MidCap Value Fund III Class J	PMCJX	NAS CM	Open End	US Equity Mid Cap (Growth)	B-	B-	B	Down	Y	1,000
Principal MidCap Value Fund III Class R-6	PCMIX	NAS CM	Open End	US Equity Mid Cap (Growth)	B-	B-	C+	Down	Y	0
Principal MidCap Value Fund III Institutional Class	PVUIX	NAS CM	Open End	US Equity Mid Cap (Growth)	B	B-	B	Up	Y	0
Principal MidCap Value Fund III R-1 Class	PMSVX	NAS CM	Open End	US Equity Mid Cap (Growth)	B-	C+	B	Up	Y	0
Principal MidCap Value Fund III R-2 Class	PKPPX	NAS CM	Open End	US Equity Mid Cap (Growth)	B-	C+	B	Up	Y	0
Principal MidCap Value Fund III R-3 Class	PJPPX	NAS CM	Open End	US Equity Mid Cap (Growth)	B-	B-	B	Down	Y	0
Principal MidCap Value Fund III R-4 Class	PMPPX	NAS CM	Open End	US Equity Mid Cap (Growth)	B-	B-	B	Down	Y	0
Principal MidCap Value Fund III R-5 Class	PLPPX	NAS CM	Open End	US Equity Mid Cap (Growth)	B-	B-	B	Down	Y	0
Principal Multi-Manager Equity Long/Short Fund Class A	PGMMX	NAS CM	Open End	Long/Short Equity (Growth)	D+	C-	A-	Up	Y	1,000
Principal Multi-Manager Equity Long/Short Fund Class R-6	PGPMX	NAS CM	Open End	Long/Short Equity (Growth)	D+	C-	A-	Up	Y	0
Principal Multi-Manager Equity Long/Short Fund Inst Cls	PGPIX	NAS CM	Open End	Long/Short Equity (Growth)	D+	C-	A-	Up	Y	0
Principal Origin Emerging Markets Fund Class A	POEYX	NAS CM	Open End	Emerging Markets Equity (Div Emerging Mkts)	C+	B-	C	Up	Y	1,000
Principal Origin Emerging Markets Fund Class R-6	POEFX	NAS CM	Open End	Emerging Markets Equity (Div Emerging Mkts)	C+	B-	C	Up	Y	0
Principal Origin Emerging Markets Fund Institutional Class	POEIX	NAS CM	Open End	Emerging Markets Equity (Div Emerging Mkts)	C+	B-	C	Up	Y	0
Principal Overseas Fund Institutional Class	PINZX	NAS CM	Open End	Global Equity Large Cap (World Stock)	C+	C+	C	Up	Y	0
Principal Overseas Fund R-1 Class	PINQX	NAS CM	Open End	Global Equity Large Cap (World Stock)	C+	C+	C	Up	Y	0
Principal Overseas Fund R-2 Class	PINSX	NAS CM	Open End	Global Equity Large Cap (World Stock)	C+	C+	C	Up	Y	0
Principal Overseas Fund R-3 Class	PINTX	NAS CM	Open End	Global Equity Large Cap (World Stock)	C+	C+	C	Up	Y	0
Principal Overseas Fund R-4 Class	PINUX	NAS CM	Open End	Global Equity Large Cap (World Stock)	B-	C+	B-	Up	Y	0
Principal Overseas Fund R-5 Class	PINGX	NAS CM	Open End	Global Equity Large Cap (World Stock)	C+	C+	C	Up	Y	0
Principal Preferred Securities Fund Class A	PPSAX	NAS CM	Open End	US Fixed Income (Income)	B	C+	A+	Up	Y	1,000

★ Expanded analysis of this fund is included in Section II.

Min Additional Investment	TOTAL RETURNS 3-Month Total Return	6-Month Total Return	1-Year Total Return	3-Year Total Return	5-Year Total Return	PERFORMANCE Dividend Yield (TTM)	Expense Ratio	3-Yr Std Deviation	3-Year Beta	ASSETS NAV	Total Assets (MIL)	ASSET ALLOCATION & TURNOVER %Cash	%Stocks	%Bonds	%Other	Turnover Ratio	BULL & BEAR Last Bull Market Total Return	Last Bear Market Total Return	FEES Front End Fee (%)	Back End Fee (%)	Inception Date
	4.86	10.95	25.16	38.42	112.47	0.19	0.85	11.42	1.03	26.97	15,667	0	100	0	0	22	26.84	-15.8			Dec-00
100	6.57	13.20	28.83	34.28	106.91	0.12	1.02	11.99	1.01	6.97	171.1	2	98	0	0	110	22.92	-22.44		1.00	Mar-01
100	6.33	10.91	24.22	25.67	86.05	0	1.25	10.65	0.95	9.07	1,127	-1	101	0	0	65	23.65	-22.43		1.00	Mar-01
	6.30	10.98	24.58	27.04	89.76	0	0.91	10.62	0.94	11.12	1,127	-1	101	0	0	65	24.16	-22.35			Mar-01
	6.18	10.59	23.56	23.86	81.68	0	1.78	10.65	0.94	9.15	1,127	-1	101	0	0	65	23.54	-22.63			Nov-04
	6.23	10.70	23.70	24.39	82.95	0	1.65	10.63	0.94	9.57	1,127	-1	101	0	0	65	23.48	-22.54			Dec-00
	6.22	10.77	23.91	24.93	84.43	0	1.47	10.66	0.95	10.42	1,127	-1	101	0	0	65	23.64	-22.52			Dec-00
	6.24	10.87	24.16	25.55	86.24	0	1.28	10.59	0.94	10.73	1,127	-1	101	0	0	65	23.81	-22.4			Dec-00
	6.35	10.90	24.37	26.07	87.36	0	1.16	10.63	0.94	11.21	1,127	-1	101	0	0	65	23.94	-22.43			Dec-00
	6.66	13.30	29.02	35.41	110.56	0.27	0.75	12	1.01	8.8	171.1	2	98	0	0	110	23.16	-22.24			Mar-01
	6.46	12.99	28.12	32.41	102.49	0	1.55	11.99	1	7.25	171.1	2	98	0	0	110	22.6	-22.52			Nov-04
	6.55	13.08	28.26	32.90	103.69	0	1.42	12.01	1.01	7.81	171.1	2	98	0	0	110	22.68	-22.45			Dec-00
	6.54	13.12	28.49	33.49	105.68	0	1.24	12.03	1.01	8.3	171.1	2	98	0	0	110	22.78	-22.42			Dec-00
	6.57	13.22	28.64	34.25	107.62	0.05	1.05	12.02	1.01	8.76	171.1	2	98	0	0	110	22.94	-22.35			Dec-00
	6.68	13.38	28.93	34.85	108.89	0.11	0.93	11.95	1	9.09	171.1	2	98	0	0	110	23.04	-22.36			Dec-00
100	6.18	9.45	15.74	33.78	98.69	1	0.49	11.06	1	20.85	1,463	0	100	0	0	18	27.34	-22.72		1.00	Mar-01
	6.25	9.60	15.96	34.30	100.24	1.19	0.17	11.06	1	21.4	1,463	0	100	0	0	18	27.57	-22.66			Nov-16
	6.25	9.59	15.96	34.86	102.04	1.17	0.2	11.06	1	21.42	1,463	0	100	0	0	18	27.68	-22.58			Mar-01
	6.00	9.11	14.99	31.53	93.67	0.4	1.04	11.04	1	21.25	1,463	0	100	0	0	18	27.07	-22.83			Nov-04
	6.06	9.19	15.18	32.08	94.97	0.61	0.91	11.04	1	21.91	1,463	0	100	0	0	18	27.25	-22.82			Dec-00
	6.07	9.26	15.33	32.76	96.71	0.74	0.73	11.06	1	21.81	1,463	0	100	0	0	18	27.33	-22.79			Dec-00
	6.14	9.37	15.60	33.48	98.62	0.8	0.54	11.07	1	21.87	1,463	0	100	0	0	18	27.46	-22.7			Dec-00
	6.16	9.47	15.71	33.96	99.74	0.98	0.42	11.05	1	22.04	1,463	0	100	0	0	18	27.57	-22.66			Dec-00
100	5.59	9.37	14.31	20.19	85.78	1.16	1.2	10.96	1.03	14.92	1,083	0	100	0	0	131	25	-22.2		1.00	Mar-09
	5.67	9.55	14.61	21.34	89.16	1.39	0.91	10.97	1.03	15.07	1,083	0	100	0	0	131	25.44	-22.02			Dec-03
	5.43	9.08	13.67	18.27	81.24	0.6	1.76	10.96	1.03	14.49	1,083	0	100	0	0	131	24.77	-22.3			Nov-04
	5.52	9.15	13.86	18.71	82.37	0.75	1.63	10.94	1.03	14.63	1,083	0	100	0	0	131	24.93	-22.28			Jun-04
	5.53	9.25	13.97	19.37	84.05	0.88	1.45	10.93	1.03	14.88	1,083	0	100	0	0	131	25.05	-22.21			Jun-04
	5.57	9.35	14.23	20.06	85.78	1.09	1.26	10.94	1.03	14.91	1,083	0	100	0	0	131	25.22	-22.16			Jun-04
	5.64	9.40	14.41	20.46	86.95	1.19	1.14	10.92	1.02	14.98	1,083	0	100	0	0	131	25.23	-22.09			Jun-04
100	4.97	8.63	15.54	21.52	88.30	0.74	1.31	10.36	0.96	21.22	1,385	0	100	0	0	74	25.42	-20.18	5.50		Jun-14
100	5.09	8.90	15.95	22.83	90.89	1.06	0.92	10.34	0.96	20.08	1,385	0	100	0	0	74	25.51	-20.15		1.00	Mar-01
	5.10	8.97	16.73	24.31	93.78	1.16	0.66	10.34	0.96	21.49	1,385	0	100	0	0	74	25.6	-20.1			Nov-14
	5.06	8.94	16.15	23.76	93.74	1.21	0.66	10.37	0.96	21.38	1,385	0	100	0	0	74	25.93	-19.94			Mar-01
	4.87	8.49	15.24	20.67	85.77	0.43	1.52	10.36	0.96	20.24	1,385	0	100	0	0	74	25.27	-20.31			Nov-04
	4.96	8.61	15.43	21.17	86.95	0.62	1.39	10.34	0.96	20.39	1,385	0	100	0	0	74	25.32	-20.26			Dec-00
	4.98	8.71	15.66	21.85	88.62	0.81	1.21	10.34	0.96	20.2	1,385	0	100	0	0	74	25.5	-20.19			Dec-00
	5.07	8.84	15.87	22.57	90.50	1.02	1.02	10.36	0.96	19.98	1,385	0	100	0	0	74	25.6	-20.15			Dec-00
	5.03	8.86	15.94	22.94	91.65	1.08	0.9	10.35	0.96	20.18	1,385	0	100	0	0	74	25.6	-20.1			Dec-00
100	3.49	8.38	11.84			0.42	2.05			10.72	339.7	47	49	4	0	301			5.50		Mar-16
	3.58	8.65	12.20			0.41	1.62			10.76	339.7	47	49	4	0	301					Mar-16
	3.54	8.61	12.05			0.41	1.7			10.75	339.7	47	49	4	0	301					Mar-16
100	6.50	20.65	50.48			0.24	1.76			12.48	741.5	0	100	0	0	66			5.50		Jan-15
	6.57	20.89	51.03			0.57	1.22			12.3	741.5	0	100	0	0	66					Jan-15
	6.56	20.88	51.03			0.59	1.25			12.3	741.5	0	100	0	0	66					Jan-15
	3.71	10.31	25.58	20.91	41.50	1.64	1.07	11.74	0.88	11.43	3,659	0	100	0	0	32	15.2	-24.87			Sep-08
	3.52	9.78	24.36	17.70	35.33	1.19	1.94	11.72	0.88	11.38	3,659	0	100	0	0	32	14.99	-24.98			Mar-12
	3.58	9.81	24.57	18.21	36.36	0.99	1.81	11.75	0.88	11.4	3,659	0	100	0	0	32	14.91	-24.96			Mar-12
	3.57	9.91	24.86	18.87	37.59	1.18	1.63	11.71	0.88	11.35	3,659	0	100	0	0	32	14.93	-24.95			Mar-12
	3.67	10.11	25.03	19.60	38.99	1.36	1.44	11.73	0.88	11.4	3,659	0	100	0	0	32	15.14	-24.9			Mar-12
	3.66	10.09	25.13	19.97	39.65	1.45	1.32	11.74	0.88	11.39	3,659	0	100	0	0	32	15.2	-24.87			Mar-12
100	0.78	2.20	10.22	19.18	34.65	4.4	1.08	3.16	0.86	10.46	6,014	1	0	28	0	16	10.28	-5.91	3.75		Jun-05

	MARKET			FUND TYPE, CATEGORY & OBJECTIVE	RATINGS					MINIMUMS
Fund Name	Ticker Symbol	Traded On	Fund Type	Category and (Prospectus Objective)	Overall Rating	Reward Rating	Risk Rating	Recent Up/ Downgrade	Open to New Investors	Min Initial Investment
Principal Preferred Securities Fund Class C	PRFCX	NAS CM	Open End	US Fixed Income (Income)	B	C+	A+	Up	Y	1,000
Principal Preferred Securities Fund Class J	PPSJX	NAS CM	Open End	US Fixed Income (Income)	B	C+	A+	Up	Y	1,000
Principal Preferred Securities Fund Institutional Class	PPSIX	NAS CM	Open End	US Fixed Income (Income)	B	C+	A+	Up	Y	0
Principal Preferred Securities Fund R-1 Class	PUSAX	NAS CM	Open End	US Fixed Income (Income)	B	C+	A+	Up	Y	0
Principal Preferred Securities Fund R-2 Class	PPRSX	NAS CM	Open End	US Fixed Income (Income)	B	C+	A+	Up	Y	0
Principal Preferred Securities Fund R-3 Class	PNARX	NAS CM	Open End	US Fixed Income (Income)	B	C+	A+	Up	Y	0
Principal Preferred Securities Fund R-4 Class	PQARX	NAS CM	Open End	US Fixed Income (Income)	B	C+	A+	Up	Y	0
Principal Preferred Securities Fund R-5 Class	PPARX	NAS CM	Open End	US Fixed Income (Income)	B	C+	A+	Up	Y	0
Principal Real Estate Allocation Fund Class A	PAEDX	NAS CM	Open End	Real Estate Sector Equity (Real Estate)	C+	C	B	Up	Y	1,000
Principal Real Estate Allocation Fund Institutional Class	PADDX	NAS CM	Open End	Real Estate Sector Equity (Real Estate)	C+	C	B	Up	Y	0
Principal Real Estate Income Fund	PGZ	NYSE	Closed End	Real Estate Sector Equity (Real Estate)	B	C+	B+	Up	Y	
Principal Real Estate Securities Fund Class A	PRRAX	NAS CM	Open End	Real Estate Sector Equity (Real Estate)	B	B-	B+	Up	Y	1,000
Principal Real Estate Securities Fund Class C	PRCEX	NAS CM	Open End	Real Estate Sector Equity (Real Estate)	B	C+	B+	Up	Y	1,000
Principal Real Estate Securities Fund Class J	PREJX	NAS CM	Open End	Real Estate Sector Equity (Real Estate)	B	B-	B+	Up	Y	1,000
Principal Real Estate Securities Fund Class R-6	PFRSX	NAS CM	Open End	Real Estate Sector Equity (Real Estate)	B	B-	B+	Up	Y	0
Principal Real Estate Securities Fund Institutional Class	PIREX	NAS CM	Open End	Real Estate Sector Equity (Real Estate)	B	B-	B+	Up	Y	0
Principal Real Estate Securities Fund R-1 Class	PRAEX	NAS CM	Open End	Real Estate Sector Equity (Real Estate)	B	B-	B+	Up	Y	0
Principal Real Estate Securities Fund R-2 Class	PRENX	NAS CM	Open End	Real Estate Sector Equity (Real Estate)	B	B-	B+	Up	Y	0
Principal Real Estate Securities Fund R-3 Class	PRERX	NAS CM	Open End	Real Estate Sector Equity (Real Estate)	B	B-	B+	Up	Y	0
Principal Real Estate Securities Fund R-4 Class	PRETX	NAS CM	Open End	Real Estate Sector Equity (Real Estate)	B	B-	B+	Up	Y	0
Principal Real Estate Securities Fund R-5 Class	PREPX	NAS CM	Open End	Real Estate Sector Equity (Real Estate)	B	B-	B+	Up	Y	0
Principal SmallCap Fund Class A	PLLAX	NAS CM	Open End	US Equity Small Cap (Small Company)	B	B+	B	Up	Y	1,000
Principal SmallCap Fund Class C	PSMCX	NAS CM	Open End	US Equity Small Cap (Small Company)	B	B	B	Up	Y	1,000
Principal SmallCap Fund Class J	PSBJX	NAS CM	Open End	US Equity Small Cap (Small Company)	B+	B+	B	Up	Y	1,000
Principal SmallCap Fund Class R-6	PSMLX	NAS CM	Open End	US Equity Small Cap (Small Company)	B+	B+	B	Up	Y	0
Principal SmallCap Fund Institutional Class	PSLIX	NAS CM	Open End	US Equity Small Cap (Small Company)	B+	B+	B	Up	Y	0
Principal SmallCap Fund R-1 Class	PSABX	NAS CM	Open End	US Equity Small Cap (Small Company)	B	B	B	Up	Y	0
Principal SmallCap Fund R-2 Class	PSBNX	NAS CM	Open End	US Equity Small Cap (Small Company)	B	B	B	Up	Y	0
Principal SmallCap Fund R-3 Class	PSBMX	NAS CM	Open End	US Equity Small Cap (Small Company)	B	B+	B	Up	Y	0
Principal SmallCap Fund R-4 Class	PSBSX	NAS CM	Open End	US Equity Small Cap (Small Company)	B	B+	B	Up	Y	0
Principal SmallCap Fund R-5 Class	PSBPX	NAS CM	Open End	US Equity Small Cap (Small Company)	B+	B+	B	Up	Y	0
Principal SmallCap Growth Fund I Class J	PSIJX	NAS CM	Open End	US Equity Small Cap (Growth)	B	A-	C+	Up	Y	1,000
Principal SmallCap Growth Fund I Class R-6	PCSMX	NAS CM	Open End	US Equity Small Cap (Growth)	B	A-	C+	Up	Y	0
Principal SmallCap Growth Fund I Institutional Class	PGRTX	NAS CM	Open End	US Equity Small Cap (Growth)	B	A-	C+	Up	Y	0
Principal SmallCap Growth Fund I R-1 Class	PNASX	NAS CM	Open End	US Equity Small Cap (Growth)	B	A-	C+	Up	Y	0
Principal SmallCap Growth Fund I R-2 Class	PPNNX	NAS CM	Open End	US Equity Small Cap (Growth)	B	A-	C+	Up	Y	0
Principal SmallCap Growth Fund I R-3 Class	PPNMX	NAS CM	Open End	US Equity Small Cap (Growth)	B	A-	C+	Up	Y	0
Principal SmallCap Growth Fund I R-4 Class	PPNSX	NAS CM	Open End	US Equity Small Cap (Growth)	B	A-	C+	Up	Y	0
Principal SmallCap Growth Fund I R-5 Class	PPNPX	NAS CM	Open End	US Equity Small Cap (Growth)	B	A-	C+	Up	Y	0
Principal SmallCap S&P 600 Index Fund Class J	PSSJX	NAS CM	Open End	US Equity Small Cap (Small Company)	B+	A-	B	Up	Y	1,000
Principal SmallCap S&P 600 Index Fund Class R-6	PSPIX	NAS CM	Open End	US Equity Small Cap (Small Company)	B+	A-	B	Up	Y	0
Principal SmallCap S&P 600 Index Fund Institutional Class	PSSIX	NAS CM	Open End	US Equity Small Cap (Small Company)	A-	A-	B	Up	Y	0
Principal SmallCap S&P 600 Index Fund R-1 Class	PSAPX	NAS CM	Open End	US Equity Small Cap (Small Company)	B+	A-	B	Up	Y	0
Principal SmallCap S&P 600 Index Fund R-2 Class	PSSNX	NAS CM	Open End	US Equity Small Cap (Small Company)	B+	A-	B	Up	Y	0
Principal SmallCap S&P 600 Index Fund R-3 Class	PSSMX	NAS CM	Open End	US Equity Small Cap (Small Company)	B+	A-	B	Up	Y	0
Principal SmallCap S&P 600 Index Fund R-4 Class	PSSSX	NAS CM	Open End	US Equity Small Cap (Small Company)	B+	A-	B	Up	Y	0
Principal SmallCap S&P 600 Index Fund R-5 Class	PSSPX	NAS CM	Open End	US Equity Small Cap (Small Company)	B+	A-	B	Up	Y	0
Principal SmallCap Value Fund II Class A	PSVAX	NAS CM	Open End	US Equity Small Cap (Small Company)	B	B	B	Up	Y	1,000
Principal SmallCap Value Fund II Class J	PSMJX	NAS CM	Open End	US Equity Small Cap (Small Company)	B	B	B	Up	Y	1,000
Principal SmallCap Value Fund II Class R-6	PSMVX	NAS CM	Open End	US Equity Small Cap (Small Company)	B	B	B	Up	Y	0
Principal SmallCap Value Fund II Institutional Class	PPVIX	NAS CM	Open End	US Equity Small Cap (Small Company)	B	B	B	Up	Y	0
Principal SmallCap Value Fund II R-1 Class	PCPTX	NAS CM	Open End	US Equity Small Cap (Small Company)	B	B	B	Up	Y	0

★ Expanded analysis of this fund is included in Section II.

Min Additional Investment	TOTAL RETURNS 3-Month Total Return	6-Month Total Return	1-Year Total Return	3-Year Total Return	5-Year Total Return	PERFORMANCE Dividend Yield (TTM)	Expense Ratio	3-Yr Std Deviation	3-Year Beta	ASSETS NAV	Total Assets (MIL)	ASSET ALLOCATION & TURNOVER %Cash	%Stocks	%Bonds	%Other	Turnover Ratio	BULL & BEAR Last Bull Market Total Return	Last Bear Market Total Return	FEES Front End Fee (%)	Back End Fee (%)	Inception Date
100	0.69	1.81	9.40	16.56	29.77	3.67	1.82	3.17	0.86	10.45	6,014	1	0	28	0	16	9.71	-6.19		1.00	Jan-07
100	0.83	2.20	10.26	19.32	34.36	4.6	1.06	3.15	0.85	10.19	6,014	1	0	28	0	16	10.1	-5.98		1.00	Dec-03
	0.86	2.34	10.50	20.27	36.71	4.71	0.77	3.16	0.86	10.39	6,014	1	0	28	0	16	10.53	-5.77			May-02
	0.66	1.94	9.66	17.36	31.26	3.95	1.59	3.16	0.86	10.34	6,014	1	0	28	0	16	9.93	-6.13			Nov-04
	0.70	2.03	9.77	17.82	32.11	4.11	1.46	3.14	0.86	10.28	6,014	1	0	28	0	16	10.04	-6			Jun-04
	0.74	2.11	9.91	18.48	33.37	4.25	1.28	3.16	0.86	10.32	6,014	1	0	28	0	16	10.13	-5.91			Jun-04
	0.79	2.20	10.14	19.08	34.58	4.44	1.09	3.17	0.86	10.3	6,014	1	0	28	0	16	10.25	-5.94			Jun-04
	0.92	2.27	10.34	19.66	35.50	4.55	0.97	3.16	0.86	10.35	6,014	1	0	28	0	16	10.31	-5.88			Jun-04
100	2.28	4.00	8.74	10.18		2.66	1.27			10.13	1.6	2	50	48	0	44			5.50		Dec-14
	2.36	4.26	9.20	11.42		2.63	0.92			10.25	1.6	2	50	48	0	44					Dec-14
	2.41	5.46	15.23	21.59		6.56	2.62	6.84		19.73	135.0	-40	50	89	2	41					Jun-13
100	3.49	4.73	8.64	17.04	64.42	0.96	1.25	13.1	0.96	23.75	3,654	1	99	0	0	25	31.59	-16.32	5.50		Jun-05
100	3.29	4.36	7.79	14.35	58.03	0.3	2.07	13.12	0.96	23.34	3,654	1	99	0	0	25	30.99	-16.6		1.00	Jan-07
100	3.56	4.84	8.87	17.59	65.25	1.16	1.12	13.14	0.96	23.07	3,654	1	99	0	0	25	31.65	-16.29		1.00	Mar-01
	3.62	4.99	9.08	17.99	66.45	1.32	0.83	13.14	0.96	23.76	3,654	1	99	0	0	25	31.86	-16.28			Nov-16
	3.56	4.94	9.02	18.46	67.77	1.33	0.88	13.11	0.96	23.76	3,654	1	99	0	0	25	32.06	-16.19			Mar-01
	3.35	4.51	8.18	15.55	60.97	0.58	1.7	13.1	0.96	23.46	3,654	1	99	0	0	25	31.3	-16.44			Nov-04
	3.41	4.61	8.33	16.04	62.07	0.79	1.57	13.11	0.96	22.61	3,654	1	99	0	0	25	31.38	-16.39			Dec-00
	3.46	4.67	8.51	16.69	63.52	0.91	1.39	13.12	0.96	23.17	3,654	1	99	0	0	25	31.58	-16.33			Dec-00
	3.51	4.83	8.73	17.38	65.16	1.09	1.2	13.14	0.96	22.92	3,654	1	99	0	0	25	31.76	-16.3			Dec-00
	3.54	4.84	8.85	17.75	66.10	1.2	1.08	13.14	0.96	22.96	3,654	1	99	0	0	25	31.85	-16.28			Dec-00
100	4.89	9.86	12.40	29.61	105.67	0.35	1.26	13.12	0.91	22.82	640.4	2	98	0	0	59	31.89	-24.8	5.50		Jun-05
100	4.69	9.46	11.56	26.47	97.35	0	2.1	13.11	0.91	20.66	640.4	2	98	0	0	59	31.38	-25.08		1.00	Jan-07
100	4.95	9.99	12.64	30.31	107.30	0.58	1.04	13.11	0.91	21.85	640.4	2	98	0	0	59	32.1	-24.8		1.00	Mar-01
	5.03	10.19	12.97	30.76	108.47	0.7	0.79	13.12	0.91	24.41	640.4	2	98	0	0	59	32.27	-24.72			Nov-16
	5.04	10.15	12.93	31.29	110.33	0.66	0.82	13.12	0.91	24.43	640.4	2	98	0	0	59	32.38	-24.64			Mar-01
	4.75	9.64	11.97	28.04	101.58	0.07	1.66	13.11	0.91	21.75	640.4	2	98	0	0	59	31.72	-24.87			Nov-04
	4.84	9.74	12.16	28.55	102.94	0.32	1.53	13.12	0.91	21.98	640.4	2	98	0	0	59	31.84	-24.83			Dec-00
	4.85	9.82	12.31	29.24	104.79	0.3	1.35	13.12	0.91	22.8	640.4	2	98	0	0	59	31.98	-24.76			Dec-00
	4.89	9.92	12.53	29.98	106.76	0.45	1.16	13.1	0.91	23.68	640.4	2	98	0	0	59	32.23	-24.75			Dec-00
	4.95	10.02	12.67	30.44	107.96	0.51	1.04	13.12	0.91	24.2	640.4	2	98	0	0	59	32.27	-24.72			Dec-00
100	5.38	12.33	25.91	37.58	102.75	0	1.35	14.47	0.96	10.41	1,634	0	100	0	0	57	32.45	-25.33		1.00	Mar-01
	5.39	12.55	26.36	39.01	106.68	0	1.03	14.48	0.96	13.9	1,634	0	100	0	0	57	32.9	-25.12			Nov-14
	5.38	12.54	26.31	39.07	106.91	0	1.03	14.46	0.96	13.92	1,634	0	100	0	0	57	32.9	-25.11			Dec-00
	5.16	12.06	25.29	35.57	98.22	0	1.89	14.48	0.96	11.47	1,634	0	100	0	0	57	32.16	-25.38			Nov-04
	5.21	12.11	25.37	36.08	99.57	0	1.76	14.5	0.96	11.14	1,634	0	100	0	0	57	32.26	-25.32			Dec-00
	5.27	12.17	25.65	36.78	101.41	0	1.58	14.47	0.96	11.82	1,634	0	100	0	0	57	32.47	-25.29			Dec-00
	5.39	12.38	25.93	37.68	103.39	0	1.39	14.48	0.96	12.54	1,634	0	100	0	0	57	32.53	-25.18			Dec-00
	5.32	12.38	26.00	38.06	104.60	0	1.27	14.45	0.96	13.09	1,634	0	100	0	0	57	32.63	-25.16			Dec-00
100	3.85	9.92	12.76	37.38	108.22	0.75	0.46	13.76	1	25.71	1,360	0	100	0	0	21	28.91	-22.22		1.00	Mar-01
	3.92	10.06	13.03	37.86	109.70	0.91	0.17	13.78	1	27.07	1,360	0	100	0	0	21	29.09	-22.09			Nov-16
	3.90	10.00	13.01	38.40	111.40	0.88	0.21	13.79	1	27.09	1,360	0	100	0	0	21	29.31	-22.06			Mar-01
	3.69	9.59	12.11	35.04	102.77	0.3	1.04	13.78	1	26.72	1,360	0	100	0	0	21	28.71	-22.35			Nov-04
	3.69	9.60	12.19	35.53	104.11	0.38	0.91	13.78	1	27.43	1,360	0	100	0	0	21	28.72	-22.27			Dec-00
	3.76	9.74	12.44	36.28	105.98	0.48	0.73	13.78	1	27.64	1,360	0	100	0	0	21	28.9	-22.27			Dec-00
	3.79	9.83	12.64	37.06	107.92	0.61	0.54	13.78	1	27.89	1,360	0	100	0	0	21	29.03	-22.19			Dec-00
	3.85	9.90	12.78	37.55	109.22	0.71	0.42	13.78	1	28.03	1,360	0	100	0	0	21	29.09	-22.09			Dec-00
100	2.82	7.87	6.38	25.72	90.01	0.25	1.51	13.82	0.96	13.06	1,257	0	100	0	0	53	27.18	-25.94	5.50		Jun-14
100	2.83	7.87	6.44	25.84	89.32	0.17	1.46	13.86	0.96	12.86	1,257	0	100	0	0	53	26.73	-26.04		1.00	Mar-09
	3.01	8.18	6.94	27.54	93.99	0.43	1.04	13.86	0.96	13.17	1,257	0	100	0	0	53	27.37	-25.87			Nov-14
	2.98	8.15	6.91	27.49	93.89	0.43	1.05	13.8	0.96	13.18	1,257	0	100	0	0	53	27.37	-25.87			Jun-04
	2.73	7.66	5.97	24.25	85.63	0	1.91	13.85	0.96	12.02	1,257	0	100	0	0	53	26.69	-26.1			Nov-04

	MARKET		FUND TYPE, CATEGORY & OBJECTIVE		RATINGS					MINIMUMS
Fund Name	Ticker Symbol	Traded On	Fund Type	Category and (Prospectus Objective)	Overall Rating	Reward Rating	Risk Rating	Recent Up/ Downgrade	Open to New Investors	Min Initial Investment
Principal SmallCap Value Fund II R-2 Class	PKARX	NAS CM	Open End	US Equity Small Cap (Small Company)	B	B	B	Up	Y	0
Principal SmallCap Value Fund II R-3 Class	PJARX	NAS CM	Open End	US Equity Small Cap (Small Company)	B	B	B	Up	Y	0
Principal SmallCap Value Fund II R-4 Class	PSTWX	NAS CM	Open End	US Equity Small Cap (Small Company)	B	B	B	Up	Y	0
Principal SmallCap Value Fund II R-5 Class	PLARX	NAS CM	Open End	US Equity Small Cap (Small Company)	B	B	B	Up	Y	0
Principal Small-MidCap Dividend Income Fund Class A	PMDAX	NAS CM	Open End	US Equity Small Cap (Equity-Income)	B	B	B			1,000
Principal Small-MidCap Dividend Income Fund Class C	PMDDX	NAS CM	Open End	US Equity Small Cap (Equity-Income)	B	B	B			1,000
Principal Small-MidCap Dividend Income Fund Inst Cls	PMDIX	NAS CM	Open End	US Equity Small Cap (Equity-Income)	B	B	B			0
Principal Small-MidCap Dividend Income Fund R-6	PMDHX	NAS CM	Open End	US Equity Small Cap (Equity-Income)	B	B	B		Y	0
Principal Strategic Asset Mgmt Balanced Portfolio Cls A	SABPX	NAS CM	Open End	Moderate Alloc (Balanced)	B-	C+	B	Up	Y	1,000
Principal Strategic Asset Mgmt Balanced Portfolio Cls C	SCBPX	NAS CM	Open End	Moderate Alloc (Balanced)	B-	C+	B	Up	Y	1,000
Principal Strategic Asset Mgmt Balanced Portfolio Cls J	PSAJX	NAS CM	Open End	Moderate Alloc (Balanced)	B-	C+	B	Up	Y	1,000
Principal Strategic Asset Mgmt Balanced Portfolio Inst Cls	PSBIX	NAS CM	Open End	Moderate Alloc (Balanced)	B-	C+	B	Up	Y	0
Principal Strategic Asset Mgmt Balanced Portfolio R-1 Cls	PSBGX	NAS CM	Open End	Moderate Alloc (Balanced)	B-	C+	B	Up	Y	0
Principal Strategic Asset Mgmt Balanced Portfolio R-2 Cls	PSBVX	NAS CM	Open End	Moderate Alloc (Balanced)	B-	C+	B	Up	Y	0
Principal Strategic Asset Mgmt Balanced Portfolio R-3 Cls	PBAPX	NAS CM	Open End	Moderate Alloc (Balanced)	B-	C+	B	Up	Y	0
Principal Strategic Asset Mgmt Balanced Portfolio R-4 Cls	PSBLX	NAS CM	Open End	Moderate Alloc (Balanced)	B-	C+	B	Up	Y	0
Principal Strategic Asset Mgmt Balanced Portfolio R-5 Cls	PSBFX	NAS CM	Open End	Moderate Alloc (Balanced)	B-	C+	B	Up	Y	0
Principal Strat Asset Mgmt Cons Bal Cls A	SAIPX	NAS CM	Open End	Cautious Alloc (Corporate Bond)	B-	C+	B	Up	Y	1,000
Principal Strat Asset Mgmt Cons Bal Cls C	SCIPX	NAS CM	Open End	Cautious Alloc (Corporate Bond)	B	C+	B+	Up	Y	1,000
Principal Strat Asset Mgmt Cons Bal Cls J	PCBJX	NAS CM	Open End	Cautious Alloc (Corporate Bond)	B-	C+	B	Up	Y	1,000
Principal Strat Asset Mgmt Cons Bal Inst Cls	PCCIX	NAS CM	Open End	Cautious Alloc (Corporate Bond)	B-	C+	B	Up	Y	0
Principal Strat Asset Mgmt Cons Bal R-1 Cls	PCSSX	NAS CM	Open End	Cautious Alloc (Corporate Bond)	B-	C+	B	Up	Y	0
Principal Strat Asset Mgmt Cons Bal R-2 Cls	PCNSX	NAS CM	Open End	Cautious Alloc (Corporate Bond)	B-	C+	B	Up	Y	0
Principal Strat Asset Mgmt Cons Bal R-3 Cls	PCBPX	NAS CM	Open End	Cautious Alloc (Corporate Bond)	B-	C+	B	Up	Y	0
Principal Strat Asset Mgmt Cons Bal R-4 Cls	PCBLX	NAS CM	Open End	Cautious Alloc (Corporate Bond)	B-	C+	B	Up	Y	0
Principal Strat Asset Mgmt Cons Bal R-5 Cls	PCBFX	NAS CM	Open End	Cautious Alloc (Corporate Bond)	B-	C+	B	Up	Y	0
Principal Strat Asset Mgmt Conservative Growth Fund Cls A	SAGPX	NAS CM	Open End	Aggressive Alloc (Growth)	B-	B-	B	Down	Y	1,000
Principal Strat Asset Mgmt Conservative Growth Fund Cls C	SCGPX	NAS CM	Open End	Aggressive Alloc (Growth)	B	C+	B+	Up	Y	1,000
Principal Strat Asset Mgmt Conservative Growth Fund Cls J	PCGJX	NAS CM	Open End	Aggressive Alloc (Growth)	B-	B-	B	Down	Y	1,000
Principal Strat Asset Mgmt Cons Growth Inst Cls	PCWIX	NAS CM	Open End	Aggressive Alloc (Growth)	B-	B-	B	Down	Y	0
Principal Strat Asset Mgmt Cons Growth R-1 Cls	PCGGX	NAS CM	Open End	Aggressive Alloc (Growth)	B-	C+	B	Down	Y	0
Principal Strat Asset Mgmt Cons Growth R-2 Cls	PCGVX	NAS CM	Open End	Aggressive Alloc (Growth)	B-	C+	B	Down	Y	0
Principal Strat Asset Mgmt Cons Growth R-3 Cls	PCGPX	NAS CM	Open End	Aggressive Alloc (Growth)	B-	B-	B	Down	Y	0
Principal Strat Asset Mgmt Cons Growth R-4 Cls	PCWSX	NAS CM	Open End	Aggressive Alloc (Growth)	B-	B-	B	Down	Y	0
Principal Strat Asset Mgmt Cons Growth R-5 Cls	PCWPX	NAS CM	Open End	Aggressive Alloc (Growth)	B-	B-	B	Down	Y	0
Principal Strategic Asset Mgmt Flexible Income Fund Cls A	SAUPX	NAS CM	Open End	Cautious Alloc (Corporate Bond)	B-	C+	B	Up	Y	1,000
Principal Strategic Asset Mgmt Flexible Income Fund Cls C	SCUPX	NAS CM	Open End	Cautious Alloc (Corporate Bond)	B-	C	B+	Up	Y	1,000
Principal Strategic Asset Mgmt Flexible Income Fund Cls J	PFIJX	NAS CM	Open End	Cautious Alloc (Corporate Bond)	B-	C+	B	Up	Y	1,000
Principal Strat Asset Mgmt Flexible Income Fund Inst Cls	PIFIX	NAS CM	Open End	Cautious Alloc (Corporate Bond)	B-	C+	B	Up	Y	0
Principal Strat Asset Mgmt Flexible Income Fund R-1 Cls	PFIGX	NAS CM	Open End	Cautious Alloc (Corporate Bond)	B-	C	B	Up	Y	0
Principal Strat Asset Mgmt Flexible Income Fund R-2 Cls	PFIVX	NAS CM	Open End	Cautious Alloc (Corporate Bond)	B-	C	B	Up	Y	0
Principal Strat Asset Mgmt Flexible Income Fund R-3 Cls	PFIPX	NAS CM	Open End	Cautious Alloc (Corporate Bond)	B	C	A-	Up	Y	0
Principal Strat Asset Mgmt Flexible Income Fund R-4 Cls	PFILX	NAS CM	Open End	Cautious Alloc (Corporate Bond)	B	C	A-	Up	Y	0
Principal Strat Asset Mgmt Flexible Income Fund R-5 Cls	PFIFX	NAS CM	Open End	Cautious Alloc (Corporate Bond)	B-	C+	B	Up	Y	0
Principal Strategic Asset Mgmt Strategic Growth Fund Cls A	SACAX	NAS CM	Open End	Aggressive Alloc (Growth)	B	B-	B	Up	Y	1,000
Principal Strategic Asset Mgmt Strategic Growth Fund Cls C	SWHCX	NAS CM	Open End	Aggressive Alloc (Growth)	B	B-	B	Up	Y	1,000
Principal Strategic Asset Mgmt Strategic Growth Fund Cls J	PSWJX	NAS CM	Open End	Aggressive Alloc (Growth)	B-	B-	B-	Down	Y	1,000
Principal Strat Asset Mgmt Strat Growth Fund Inst Cls	PSWIX	NAS CM	Open End	Aggressive Alloc (Growth)	B-	B-	B-	Down	Y	0
Principal Strat Asset Mgmt Strat Growth Fund R-1 Cls	PSGGX	NAS CM	Open End	Aggressive Alloc (Growth)	B-	B-	B-	Down	Y	0
Principal Strat Asset Mgmt Strat Growth Fund R-2 Cls	PSGVX	NAS CM	Open End	Aggressive Alloc (Growth)	B-	B-	B-	Down	Y	0
Principal Strat Asset Mgmt Strat Growth Fund R-3 Cls	PSGPX	NAS CM	Open End	Aggressive Alloc (Growth)	B-	B-	B-	Down	Y	0
Principal Strat Asset Mgmt Strat Growth Fund R-4 Cls	PSGLX	NAS CM	Open End	Aggressive Alloc (Growth)	B-	B-	B-	Down	Y	0

★Expanded analysis of this fund is included in Section II.

	TOTAL RETURNS					PERFORMANCE				ASSETS		ASSET ALLOCATION & TURNOVER					BULL & BEAR		FEES		
Min Additional Investment	3-Month Total Return	6-Month Total Return	1-Year Total Return	3-Year Total Return	5-Year Total Return	Dividend Yield (TTM)	Expense Ratio	3-Yr Std Deviation	3-Year Beta	NAV	Total Assets (MIL)	%Cash	%Stocks	%Bonds	%Other	Turnover Ratio	Last Bull Market Total Return	Last Bear Market Total Return	Front End Fee (%)	Back End Fee (%)	Inception Date
	2.77	7.71	6.13	24.72	86.79	0	1.78	13.82	0.96	12.21	1,257	0	100	0	0	53	26.85	-26.09			Jun-04
	2.83	7.86	6.32	25.50	88.58	0.03	1.6	13.78	0.96	12.68	1,257	0	100	0	0	53	26.75	-25.96			Jun-04
	2.87	7.92	6.49	26.09	90.27	0.13	1.41	13.84	0.96	12.85	1,257	0	100	0	0	53	26.93	-25.97			Jun-04
	2.88	8.04	6.62	26.58	91.65	0.27	1.29	13.82	0.96	12.98	1,257	0	100	0	0	53	27.14	-25.92			Jun-04
100	3.58	7.68	12.94	39.77	98.92	1.92	1.5	11.3	0.9	17.11	3,378	3	97	0	0	26	26.46		5.50		Jun-11
100	3.40	7.35	12.14	36.60	91.19	1.39	2.27	11.29	0.9	16.98	3,378	3	97	0	0	26	26.07			1.00	Jun-12
	3.64	7.89	13.29	41.10	102.35	2.17	1.15	11.28	0.9	17.18	3,378	3	97	0	0	26	26.8				Jun-11
	3.66	7.87	13.35	41.16	102.44		1.13	11.28	0.9	17.18	3,378	3	97	0	0	26	26.8				Jan-17
100	2.01	5.80	13.12	18.19	49.30	1.31	1.37	6.17	0.57	15.95	4,917	4	62	31	0	17	16.19	-12.18	5.50		Jul-96
100	3.19	6.89	13.87	17.19	45.82	0.69	2.11	6.18	0.57	15.72	4,917	4	62	31	0	17	15.67	-12.42		1.00	Mar-02
100	2.01	5.83	13.27	18.59	49.85	1.51	1.22	6.18	0.57	15.43	4,917	4	62	31	0	17	16.27	-12.25		1.00	Jan-07
	3.46	7.45	15.03	21.03	53.85	1.63	1.02	6.15	0.57	15.7	4,917	4	62	31	0	17	16.42	-12.08			Jan-07
	1.99	5.64	12.63	16.47	45.42	0.86	1.9	6.18	0.57	15.67	4,917	4	62	31	0	17	15.87	-12.42			Jan-07
	1.99	5.67	12.75	16.84	46.36	0.96	1.77	6.15	0.57	15.62	4,917	4	62	31	0	17	16.01	-12.35			Jan-07
	1.99	5.71	12.95	17.44	47.66	1.04	1.59	6.15	0.57	15.66	4,917	4	62	31	0	17	16.06	-12.26			Jan-07
	1.98	5.75	13.08	18.03	48.91	1.29	1.4	6.16	0.57	15.68	4,917	4	62	31	0	17	16.24	-12.24			Jan-07
	1.98	5.78	13.19	18.43	49.83	1.41	1.28	6.19	0.58	15.68	4,917	4	62	31	0	17	16.3	-12.2			Jan-07
100	2.35	5.24	10.88	15.76	36.87	1.85	1.31	4.54	0.19	12.24	1,814	4	43	50	0	17	12.29	-8.41	5.50		Jul-96
100	1.00	3.68	8.89	11.85	30.41	1.17	2.06	4.56	0.2	12.11	1,814	4	43	50	0	17	11.86	-8.64		1.00	Mar-02
100	2.34	5.40	11.13	16.13	37.48	2.04	1.16	4.6	0.19	12.08	1,814	4	43	50	0	17	12.42	-8.4		1.00	Jan-07
	2.46	5.46	11.26	16.82	39.03	2.18	0.97	4.56	0.18	12.12	1,814	4	43	50	0	17	12.57	-8.31			Jan-07
	2.15	5.01	10.25	13.81	33.06	1.39	1.84	4.56	0.19	12.08	1,814	4	43	50	0	17	12.04	-8.64			Jan-07
	0.99	3.79	9.16	12.96	32.46	1.43	1.71	4.56	0.19	12.17	1,814	4	43	50	0	17	12.12	-8.59			Jan-07
	2.32	5.18	10.66	14.92	35.20	1.65	1.53	4.59	0.19	12.1	1,814	4	43	50	0	17	12.29	-8.55			Jan-07
	2.28	5.27	10.86	15.52	36.52	1.84	1.34	4.55	0.18	12.11	1,814	4	43	50	0	17	12.4	-8.39			Jan-07
	2.31	5.32	10.99	15.88	37.26	1.95	1.22	4.56	0.18	12.11	1,814	4	43	50	0	17	12.45	-8.33			Jan-07
100	4.39	9.60	19.33	24.20	66.10	0.99	1.42	7.9	0.75	18.22	3,267	4	80	14	0	22	20.1	-16.17	5.50		Jul-96
100	4.17	9.18	18.38	21.41	60.02	0.44	2.18	7.89	0.75	16.98	3,267	4	80	14	0	22	19.46	-16.36		1.00	Mar-02
100	4.38	9.70	19.49	24.69	66.84	1.16	1.28	7.91	0.75	17.57	3,267	4	80	14	0	22	20.06	-16.09		1.00	Jan-07
	4.46	9.78	19.67	25.51	68.97	1.3	1.08	7.91	0.75	17.8	3,267	4	80	14	0	22	20.28	-16.01			Jan-07
	4.22	9.31	18.72	22.29	61.73	0.54	1.95	7.91	0.75	17.62	3,267	4	80	14	0	22	19.78	-16.35			Jan-07
	4.28	9.36	18.77	22.70	62.72	0.63	1.82	7.92	0.75	17.64	3,267	4	80	14	0	22	19.84	-16.28			Jan-07
	4.25	9.46	19.02	23.32	64.19	0.75	1.64	7.89	0.74	17.58	3,267	4	80	14	0	22	19.95	-16.21			Jan-07
	4.31	9.52	19.21	24.02	65.80	0.97	1.45	7.91	0.75	17.75	3,267	4	80	14	0	22	20.02	-16.12			Jan-07
	4.41	9.65	19.37	24.57	66.82	1.12	1.33	7.91	0.75	17.71	3,267	4	80	14	0	22	20.2	-16.09			Jan-07
100	1.76	3.75	7.80	12.54	27.88	2.35	1.18	3.69	0.4	12.5	2,772	2	27	66	0	10	10.18	-5.55	3.75		Jul-96
100	0.92	2.72	6.37	9.34	22.33	1.63	1.95	3.69	0.39	12.38	2,772	2	27	66	0	10	9.69	-5.81		1.00	Mar-02
100	1.81	3.86	8.04	12.96	28.43	2.53	1.06	3.71	0.38	12.4	2,772	2	27	66	0	10	10.14	-5.51		1.00	Jan-07
	1.83	3.91	8.14	13.55	29.89	2.65	0.86	3.65	0.36	12.46	2,772	2	27	66	0	10	10.4	-5.44			Jan-07
	1.62	3.49	7.26	10.63	24.44	1.83	1.73	3.67	0.39	12.41	2,772	2	27	66	0	10	9.8	-5.7			Jan-07
	1.57	3.45	7.37	11.09	25.24	1.94	1.6	3.7	0.37	12.44	2,772	2	27	66	0	10	9.86	-5.64			Jan-07
	1.70	3.63	7.55	11.72	26.43	2.1	1.42	3.66	0.38	12.44	2,772	2	27	66	0	10	10.09	-5.65			Jan-07
	1.74	3.73	7.76	12.37	27.63	2.3	1.23	3.67	0.37	12.45	2,772	2	27	66	0	10	10.11	-5.5			Jan-07
	1.78	3.79	7.89	12.72	28.34	2.42	1.11	3.66	0.37	12.44	2,772	2	27	66	0	10	10.18	-5.45			Jan-07
100	4.71	10.61	21.69	24.79	75.36	0.86	1.44	8.91	0.84	20.58	2,007	4	89	7	0	23	23.25	-18.91	5.50		Jul-96
100	4.51	10.19	20.80	22.03	68.88	0.34	2.19	8.91	0.84	18.8	2,007	4	89	7	0	23	22.73	-19.15		1.00	Mar-02
100	4.78	10.76	21.97	25.38	76.31	1.03	1.28	8.94	0.84	19.89	2,007	4	89	7	0	23	23.24	-18.91		1.00	Jan-07
	4.84	10.82	22.11	26.14	78.55	1.18	1.07	8.92	0.84	20.09	2,007	4	89	7	0	23	23.59	-18.79			Jan-07
	4.58	10.31	21.05	22.88	70.91	0.35	1.94	8.92	0.84	19.95	2,007	4	89	7	0	23	22.86	-19.05			Jan-07
	4.61	10.37	21.20	23.34	71.99	0.47	1.81	8.92	0.84	19.9	2,007	4	89	7	0	23	22.99	-19.02			Jan-07
	4.67	10.55	21.49	24.08	73.59	0.64	1.63	8.94	0.84	19.88	2,007	4	89	7	0	23	23.16	-18.98			Jan-07
	4.70	10.60	21.66	24.73	75.22	0.87	1.44	8.94	0.84	19.99	2,007	4	89	7	0	23	23.26	-18.9			Jan-07

	MARKET			FUND TYPE, CATEGORY & OBJECTIVE	RATINGS				MINIMUMS	
Fund Name	Ticker Symbol	Traded On	Fund Type	Category and (Prospectus Objective)	Overall Rating	Reward Rating	Risk Rating	Recent Up/ Downgrade	Open to New Investors	Min Initial Investment
Principal Strat Asset Mgmt Strat Growth Fund R-5 Cls	PSGFX	NAS CM	Open End	Aggressive Alloc (Growth)	B-	B-	B-	Down	Y	0
Principal SystematEx International Fund Class R-6	PSTMX	NAS CM	Open End	Global Equity Large Cap (Growth)	C	C+	B	Up	Y	0
Principal SystematEx International Fund Institutional Cls	PSOMX	NAS CM	Open End	Global Equity Large Cap (Growth)	C	C+	B	Up	Y	0
Principal SystematEx Large Value Fund Class R-6	PSLVX	NAS CM	Open End	US Equity Large Cap Value (Growth)	C	C+	B	Up	Y	0
Private Capital Management Value Fund Class A	VFPAX	NAS CM	Open End	US Equity Small Cap (Growth)	B-	C+	B-	Up	Y	5,000
Private Capital Management Value Fund Class I	VFPIX	NAS CM	Open End	US Equity Small Cap (Growth)	B-	B-	B-	Up	Y	750,000
Private Capital Management Value Fund Class I	PROAX	NAS CM	Open End	Long/Short Equity (Growth)	B-	C+	B	Up	Y	2,500
Private Capital Management Value Fund Class I	PROCX	NAS CM	Open End	Long/Short Equity (Growth)	B-	C+	B	Up	Y	2,500
Private Capital Management Value Fund Class I	PROTX	NAS CM	Open End	Long/Short Equity (Growth)	C+	C+	B-	Down	Y	2,500
ProFunds Banks UltraSector Fund Investor Class	BKPIX	NAS CM	Open End	Trading Tools (Financial)	B+	A+	C	Up	Y	15,000
ProFunds Banks UltraSector Fund Service Class	BKPSX	NAS CM	Open End	Trading Tools (Financial)	B+	A+	C	Up	Y	15,000
ProFunds Basic Materials UltraSector Fund Investor Class	BMPIX	NAS CM	Open End	Trading Tools ()	B	A	C	Up	Y	15,000
ProFunds Basic Materials UltraSector Fund Service Class	BMPSX	NAS CM	Open End	Trading Tools ()	B	B+	C	Up	Y	15,000
ProFunds Bear Fund Investor Class	BRPIX	NAS CM	Open End	Other Alternative (Growth)	D-	D-	D-	Down	Y	15,000
ProFunds Bear Fund Service Class	BRPSX	NAS CM	Open End	Other Alternative (Growth)	D-	D-	D-	Down	Y	15,000
ProFunds Biotechnology UltraSector Fund Investor Class	BIPIX	NAS CM	Open End	Trading Tools (Health)	C	C	C	Up	Y	15,000
ProFunds Biotechnology UltraSector Fund Service Class	BIPSX	NAS CM	Open End	Trading Tools (Health)	C	C	C	Down	Y	15,000
ProFunds Bull Fund Investor Class	BLPIX	NAS CM	Open End	Trading Tools (Growth & Income)	B-	B-	B	Down	Y	15,000
ProFunds Bull Fund Service Class	BLPSX	NAS CM	Open End	Trading Tools (Growth & Income)	B-	B-	B-	Down	Y	15,000
ProFunds Consumer Goods Ultra Sector Fund Investor Class	CNPIX	NAS CM	Open End	Trading Tools ()	B	B-	A-	Down	Y	15,000
ProFunds Consumer Goods Ultra Sector Fund Service Class	CNPSX	NAS CM	Open End	Trading Tools ()	B	B-	A-		Y	15,000
ProFunds Consumer Services UltraSector Fund Investor Class	CYPIX	NAS CM	Open End	Trading Tools ()	B	B	B		Y	15,000
ProFunds Consumer Services UltraSector Fund Service Class	CYPSX	NAS CM	Open End	Trading Tools ()	B	B	B		Y	15,000
ProFunds Europe 30 Fund Investor Class	UEPIX	NAS CM	Open End	Europe Equity Large Cap (Europe Stock)	C+	C+	C+	Up	Y	15,000
ProFunds Europe 30 Fund Service Class	UEPSX	NAS CM	Open End	Europe Equity Large Cap (Europe Stock)	C+	C+	C+	Up	Y	15,000
ProFunds Financials UltraSector Fund Investor Class	FNPIX	NAS CM	Open End	Trading Tools (Financial)	B+	A	B-	Up	Y	15,000
ProFunds Financials UltraSector Fund Service Class	FNPSX	NAS CM	Open End	Trading Tools (Financial)	B+	A	B-	Up	Y	15,000
ProFunds Industrial Ultra Sector Fund Investor Class	IDPIX	NAS CM	Open End	Trading Tools (Growth)	B+	A+	C	Up	Y	15,000
ProFunds Industrial Ultra Sector Fund Service Class	IDPSX	NAS CM	Open End	Trading Tools (Growth)	B+	A+	C	Up	Y	15,000
ProFunds Internet UltraSector Fund Investor Class	INPIX	NAS CM	Open End	Trading Tools (Technology)	A-	A+	B-	Up	Y	15,000
ProFunds Internet UltraSector Fund Service Class	INPSX	NAS CM	Open End	Trading Tools (Technology)	A-	A+	B-	Up	Y	15,000
ProFunds Large Cap Growth Fund Investor Class	LGPIX	NAS CM	Open End	US Equity Large Cap Growth (Growth)	B	B	B	Down	Y	15,000
ProFunds Large Cap Growth Fund Service Class	LGPSX	NAS CM	Open End	US Equity Large Cap Growth (Growth)	B	B	B	Up	Y	15,000
ProFunds Large Cap Value Fund Investor Class	LVPIX	NAS CM	Open End	US Equity Large Cap Value (Growth & Income)	B-	B-	B	Down	Y	15,000
ProFunds Large Cap Value Fund Service Class	LVPSX	NAS CM	Open End	US Equity Large Cap Value (Growth & Income)	B-	C+	B-	Down	Y	15,000
ProFunds Mid Cap Fund Investor Class	MDPIX	NAS CM	Open End	US Equity Mid Cap (Growth)	B	B	B	Up	Y	15,000
ProFunds Mid Cap Fund Service Class	MDPSX	NAS CM	Open End	US Equity Mid Cap (Growth)	B	B-	B	Up	Y	15,000
ProFunds Mid Cap Growth Fund Investor Class	MGPIX	NAS CM	Open End	US Equity Mid Cap (Growth)	B	B	B	Up	Y	15,000
ProFunds Mid Cap Growth Fund Service Class	MGPSX	NAS CM	Open End	US Equity Mid Cap (Growth)	B	B	B	Up	Y	15,000
ProFunds Mid Cap Value Fund Investor Class	MLPIX	NAS CM	Open End	US Equity Mid Cap (Growth)	B	B	B	Up	Y	15,000
ProFunds Mid Cap Value Fund Service Class	MLPSX	NAS CM	Open End	US Equity Mid Cap (Growth)	B-	B-	B-	Up	Y	15,000
ProFunds NASDAQ-100 Fund Investor Class	OTPIX	NAS CM	Open End	US Equity Large Cap Growth (Growth)	B+	A-	B	Down	Y	15,000
ProFunds NASDAQ-100 Fund Service Class	OTPSX	NAS CM	Open End	US Equity Large Cap Growth (Growth)	B+	B+	B+	Down	Y	15,000
ProFunds Oil Equipment Service & Distribution Fund Inv Cls	OEPIX	NAS CM	Open End	Energy Sector Equity (Utility)	D	D	D		Y	15,000
ProFunds Oil Equipment Serv & Distribution Fund Serv Cls	OEPSX	NAS CM	Open End	Energy Sector Equity (Utility)	D	D	D		Y	15,000
ProFunds Pharmaceuticals UltraSector Fund Investor Class	PHPIX	NAS CM	Open End	Trading Tools (Health)	B-	C+	B-	Up	Y	15,000
ProFunds Pharmaceuticals UltraSector Fund Service Class	PHPSX	NAS CM	Open End	Trading Tools (Health)	C+	C+	C+		Y	15,000
ProFunds Precious Metals UltraSector Fund Investor Class	PMPIX	NAS CM	Open End	Trading Tools (Precious Metals)	D	C-	D	Down	Y	15,000
ProFunds Precious Metals UltraSector Fund Service Class	PMPSX	NAS CM	Open End	Trading Tools (Precious Metals)	D	C-	D	Down	Y	15,000
ProFunds Real Estate UltraSector Fund Investor Class	REPIX	NAS CM	Open End	Trading Tools (Real Estate)	B-	B-	B-	Up	Y	15,000
ProFunds Real Estate UltraSector Fund Service Class	REPSX	NAS CM	Open End	Trading Tools (Real Estate)	B-	B-	B-	Up	Y	15,000
ProFunds Rising Rates Opportunity 10 Fund Investor Class	RTPIX	NAS CM	Open End	Trading Tools (Govt Bond - Treasury)	D+	D	C	Down	Y	15,000

★Expanded analysis of this fund is included in Section II.

Min Additional Investment	TOTAL RETURNS: 3-Month Total Return	6-Month Total Return	1-Year Total Return	3-Year Total Return	5-Year Total Return	PERFORMANCE: Dividend Yield (TTM)	Expense Ratio	3-Yr Std Deviation	3-Year Beta	ASSETS: NAV	Total Assets (MIL)	ASSET ALLOCATION & TURNOVER: %Cash	%Stocks	%Bonds	%Other	Turnover Ratio	BULL & BEAR: Last Bull Market Total Return	Last Bear Market Total Return	FEES: Front End Fee (%)	Back End Fee (%)	Inception Date
	4.75	10.72	21.84	25.24	76.40	1	1.32	8.93	0.84	19.94	2,007	4	89	7	0	23	23.36	-18.88			Jan-07
	3.61	9.44	25.02			1.76	0.62			12.33	79.9	0	99	0	1	44					Sep-15
	3.54	9.33	24.27			1.77	0.75			12.23	79.9	0	99	0	1	44					Sep-15
	6.04	10.55	15.17			1.82	0.43			13.2	10.2	0	100	0	0	47					Sep-15
50	2.44	6.78	15.19	13.74	80.84	0.97	1.35	13.23	0.92	17.17	77.6	11	89	0	0	11	24.02	-20.3	5.00		Oct-10
	2.53	6.94	15.49	14.57	83.16	1.2	1.1	13.22	0.92	17.4	77.6	11	89	0	0	11	24.21	-20.22			May-10
100	6.15	6.52	15.76	11.14	39.93	0	2.43	11.13	0.93	10.79	77.6	40	56	0	4	2,011	32.73	-17.53	5.75		Jan-14
100	6.07	6.16	14.95	8.73	34.74	0	3.18	11.12	0.93	10.44	77.6	40	56	0	4	2,011	32.16	-17.79			Jan-14
100	6.27	6.74	16.02	11.94	41.72	0	2.18	11.19	0.93	10.91	77.6	40	56	0	4	2,011	32.93	-17.45			Dec-13
	12.84	19.50	26.77	63.91	200.11	0	1.55	31.17		53.6	53.4	26	74	0	0	252	56.57	-46.07			Sep-01
	12.56	18.91	25.53	58.95	185.33	0	2.55	31.16		49.99	53.4	26	74	0	0	252	55.17	-46.21			Sep-01
	9.71	21.52	34.95	33.97	83.17	0.12	1.67	26.27		74.86	56.9	29	71	0	0	179	36.28	-45.73			Sep-01
	9.46	20.94	33.67	30.08	74.38	0	2.67	26.25		67.8	56.9	29	71	0	0	179	35.5	-45.98			Sep-01
	-6.17	-10.17	-18.03	-31.72	-58.27	0	1.63	9.56		32.5	17.9	100	0	0	0	1,297	-22.61	14.81			Dec-97
	-6.40	-10.59	-18.79	-33.73	-60.32	0	2.63	9.52		30.55	17.9	100	0	0	0	1,297	-23.03	14.37			Dec-97
	-7.50	9.45	34.66	4.54	238.65	0	1.45	30.76		62.47	303.1	27	73	0	0	14	45.79	-16.7			Jun-00
	-7.72	8.91	33.35	1.46	222.15	0	2.45	30.75		50.02	303.1	27	73	0	0	14	44.93	-17.04			Jun-00
	6.21	10.40	19.50	29.31	92.22	0	1.58	10.08	1	122.41	77.3	47	52	0	0	4	23.65	-17.06			Dec-97
	5.95	9.86	18.33	25.52	82.83	0	2.58	10.08	1	102.99	77.3	47	52	0	0	4	22.91	-17.37			Dec-97
	7.54	6.22	22.79	34.03	132.64	0	1.75	13.22		110.89	11.3	28	72	0	0	199	27.87	-13.61			Jan-04
	7.27	5.71	21.60	30.10	121.37	0	2.75	13.21		101.17	11.3	28	72	0	0	199	27.12	-14			Jan-04
	13.77	13.58	28.24	44.17	193.64	0	1.58	16.57		112.29	35.4	25	74	0	1	123	44.32	-19.69			Jan-04
	13.48	13.01	26.96	39.91	179.31	0	2.58	16.56		98.78	35.4	25	74	0	1	123	43.46	-20.02			Jan-04
	1.03	6.08	19.91	14.02	28.43	0.97	1.78	12.86		14.3	19.6	0	100	0	0	1,157	14.34	-27.69			Mar-99
	0.66	5.36	18.50	10.55	21.96	0	2.78	12.8		15.11	19.6	0	100	0	0	1,157	13.76	-28.02			Mar-99
	9.87	16.77	27.18	48.39	178.74	0	1.61	19.56		22.69	30.3	23	77	0	0	211	47.67	-37.37			Jun-00
	9.61	16.24	26.02	44.08	165.35	0	2.61	19.58		19.61	30.3	23	77	0	0	211	47.25	-37.79			Jun-00
	9.42	18.23	34.58	58.02	189.00	0	1.69	17.78		107.28	27.6	29	71	0	0	294	45.36	-35.63			Jan-04
	9.13	17.64	33.26	53.38	174.95	0	2.69	17.76		95.15	27.6	29	71	0	0	294	44.55	-35.91			Jan-04
	10.52	23.31	57.91	119.55	326.56	0	1.46	23.06		69.01	148.9	30	70	0	0	27	37.54	-32.94			Jun-00
	10.26	22.72	56.40	113.14	305.78	0	2.46	23.07		54.29	148.9	30	70	0	0	27	36.75	-33.23			Jun-00
	6.30	11.32	25.08	34.39	102.41	0	1.66	10.73	1	82.67	22.8	0	100	0	0	592	22.78	-13.7			Oct-02
	6.03	10.77	23.84	30.43	92.51	0	2.66	10.73	1	70.68	22.8	0	100	0	0	592	22.08	-14.08			Oct-02
	5.86	9.01	13.24	23.09	80.58	0.19	1.78	10.36	0.99	65.56	10.2	0	99	0	1	498	24.44	-20.07			Oct-02
	5.59	8.48	12.13	19.43	71.69	0	2.78	10.36	0.99	59.75	10.2	0	99	0	1	498	23.69	-20.38			Oct-02
	5.79	8.57	14.16	28.86	87.11	0	1.57	11.05	1	87.55	51.1	47	53	0	0	603	26.27	-23.26			Sep-01
	5.53	8.03	13.02	25.02	77.93	0	2.57	11.04	1	74	51.1	47	53	0	0	603	25.58	-23.62			Sep-01
	6.65	9.63	18.07	31.89	86.19	0	1.73	10.46	1	89.56	14.1	0	100	0	0	242	24.25	-21.6			Sep-01
	6.38	9.07	16.89	27.94	77.01	0	2.73	10.46	0.99	75.69	14.1	0	100	0	0	242	23.57	-21.92			Sep-01
	4.89	7.85	10.41	24.49	84.70	0.22	1.78	12.33	0.99	75.35	8.2	0	100	0	0	281	28.72	-24.71			Sep-01
	4.64	7.32	9.32	20.67	75.60	0	2.78	12.32	0.99	62.99	8.2	0	100	0	0	281	27.95	-25.01			Sep-01
	6.79	12.74	30.40	45.71	135.34	0	1.49	13.62	1	63.47	77.0	50	50	0	0	4	26.44	-11.43			Aug-00
	6.52	12.18	29.11	41.34	123.67	0	2.49	13.6	1	52.74	77.0	50	50	0	0	4	25.69	-11.79			Aug-00
	-1.31	5.18	-22.68	-39.98	-28.80	0.08	1.61	32.41		12.31	8.6	29	69	0	1	201	38.36	-47.08			Jun-06
	-1.56	4.75	-23.39	-41.74	-32.28	0	2.61	32.38		11.13	8.6	29	69	0	1	201	37.6	-47.32			Jun-06
	-0.55	0.53	15.04	12.62	126.36	0	1.74	18.09		24.66	11.0	31	69	0	0	159	26.72	-8.43			Jun-00
	-0.79	0.06	13.87	9.26	115.26	0	2.74	18.08		21.86	11.0	31	69	0	0	159	25.91	-8.84			Jun-00
	-1.22	4.18	6.54	-1.98	-68.84	0	1.52	66.19		38.57	22.7	20	77	0	3	309	-16.97	-26.62			Jun-02
	-1.45	3.75	5.49	-4.81	-70.34	0	2.52	66.1		33.98	22.7	20	77	0	3	309	-17.45	-26.94			Jun-02
	2.99	3.90	11.31	17.31	69.45	2.92	1.68	18.72		44.66	7.9	28	72	0	1	195	44	-26.39			Jun-00
	2.75	3.40	10.22	13.83	61.18	2.8	2.68	18.7		42.57	7.9	28	72	0	1	195	43.19	-26.71			Jun-00
	0.00	-0.46	-3.05	-8.13	-13.57	0	1.73	6		14.9	8.9	100	0	0	0	1,297	-3.03	-13.83			Jan-05

	MARKET			FUND TYPE, CATEGORY & OBJECTIVE	RATINGS					MINIMUMS
Fund Name	Ticker Symbol	Traded On	Fund Type	Category and (Prospectus Objective)	Overall Rating	Reward Rating	Risk Rating	Recent Up/ Downgrade	Open to New Investors	Min Initial Investment
ProFunds Rising Rates Opportunity 10 Fund Service Class	RTPSX	NAS CM	Open End	Trading Tools (Govt Bond - Treasury)	D+	D	C-	Down	Y	15,000
ProFunds Rising Rates Opportunity Fund Investor Class	RRPIX	NAS CM	Open End	Trading Tools (Govt Bond - Treasury)	D	D	D+	Down	Y	15,000
ProFunds Rising Rates Opportunity Fund Service Class	RRPSX	NAS CM	Open End	Trading Tools (Govt Bond - Treasury)	D	D	D	Down	Y	15,000
ProFunds Semiconductor UltraSector Fund Investor Class	SMPIX	NAS CM	Open End	Trading Tools (Technology)	B+	A+	C+	Up	Y	15,000
ProFunds Semiconductor UltraSector Fund Service Class	SMPSX	NAS CM	Open End	Trading Tools (Technology)	B+	A+	C+	Up	Y	15,000
ProFunds Short NASDAQ-100 Fund Investor Class	SOPIX	NAS CM	Open End	Other Alternative (Growth)	D-	D-	D-	Down	Y	15,000
ProFunds Short NASDAQ-100 Fund Service Class	SOPSX	NAS CM	Open End	Other Alternative (Growth)	D-	D-	D-	Down	Y	15,000
ProFunds Short Oil & Gas Fund Investor Class	SNPIX	NAS CM	Open End	Trading Tools (Natl Res)	D	D	D	Down	Y	15,000
ProFunds Short Oil & Gas Fund Service Class	SNPSX	NAS CM	Open End	Trading Tools (Natl Res)	D	D	D	Down	Y	15,000
ProFunds Short Precious Metals Fund Investor Class	SPPIX	NAS CM	Open End	Trading Tools (Precious Metals)	D	D	D		Y	15,000
ProFunds Short Precious Metals Fund Service Class	SPPSX	NAS CM	Open End	Trading Tools (Precious Metals)	D	D	D		Y	15,000
ProFunds Short Real Estate Fund Investor Class	SRPIX	NAS CM	Open End	Trading Tools (Real Estate)	D	D	D		Y	15,000
ProFunds Short Real Estate Fund Service Class	SRPSX	NAS CM	Open End	Trading Tools (Real Estate)	D	D-	D		Y	15,000
ProFunds Short Small Cap Fund Investor Class	SHPIX	NAS CM	Open End	Other Alternative (Small Company)	D-	D-	D-	Down	Y	15,000
ProFunds Short Small Cap Fund Service Class	SHPSX	NAS CM	Open End	Other Alternative (Small Company)	D-	D-	D-	Down	Y	15,000
ProFunds Small Cap Fund Investor Class	SLPIX	NAS CM	Open End	US Equity Small Cap (Small Company)	B	B	B	Up	Y	15,000
ProFunds Small Cap Fund Service Class	SLPSX	NAS CM	Open End	US Equity Small Cap (Small Company)	B	B	B	Up	Y	15,000
ProFunds Small Cap Growth Fund Investor Class	SGPIX	NAS CM	Open End	US Equity Small Cap (Small Company)	B+	A-	B+	Up	Y	15,000
ProFunds Small Cap Growth Fund Service Class	SGPSX	NAS CM	Open End	US Equity Small Cap (Small Company)	B+	B+	B	Up	Y	15,000
ProFunds Small Cap Value Fund Investor Class	SVPIX	NAS CM	Open End	US Equity Small Cap (Small Company)	B	B+	B-	Up	Y	15,000
ProFunds Small Cap Value Fund Services Class	SVPSX	NAS CM	Open End	US Equity Small Cap (Small Company)	B	B	B-	Up	Y	15,000
ProFunds Technology UltraSector Fund Investor Class	TEPIX	NAS CM	Open End	Trading Tools (Technology)	A-	A+	B	Up	Y	15,000
ProFunds Technology UltraSector Fund Service Class	TEPSX	NAS CM	Open End	Trading Tools (Technology)	A-	A+	B	Up	Y	15,000
ProFunds Telecommunications UltraSector Fund Investor Cls	TCPIX	NAS CM	Open End	Trading Tools (Comm)	C	C	C-	Down	Y	15,000
ProFunds Telecommunications UltraSector Fund Service Class	TCPSX	NAS CM	Open End	Trading Tools (Comm)	C-	C	C-	Down	Y	15,000
ProFunds U.S. Government Plus Fund Investor Class	GVPIX	NAS CM	Open End	Trading Tools (Govt Bond - Treasury)	C	C	C-	Up	Y	15,000
ProFunds U.S. Government Plus Fund Service Class	GVPSX	NAS CM	Open End	Trading Tools (Govt Bond - Treasury)	C-	C-	C-	Down	Y	15,000
ProFunds Ultra Dow 30 Fund Investor Class	UDPIX	NAS CM	Open End	Trading Tools (Growth)	B+	A+	C	Down	Y	15,000
ProFunds Ultra Dow 30 Fund Service Class	UDPSX	NAS CM	Open End	Trading Tools (Growth)	B+	A+	C	Down	Y	15,000
ProFunds Ultra International Fund Investor Class	UNPIX	NAS CM	Open End	Trading Tools (Growth)	B-	B	C	Up	Y	15,000
ProFunds Ultra International Fund Service Class	UNPSX	NAS CM	Open End	Trading Tools (Growth)	B-	B	C	Up	Y	15,000
ProFunds UltraBear Fund Investor Class	URPIX	NAS CM	Open End	Other Alternative (Growth)	E+	E+	D-	Down	Y	15,000
ProFunds UltraBear Fund Service Class	URPSX	NAS CM	Open End	Other Alternative (Growth)	E+	E+	D-	Down	Y	15,000
ProFunds UltraBull Fund Investor Class	ULPIX	NAS CM	Open End	Trading Tools (Growth & Income)	B+	A+	C+	Down	Y	15,000
ProFunds UltraBull Fund Service Class	ULPSX	NAS CM	Open End	Trading Tools (Growth & Income)	B+	A+	C+	Up	Y	15,000
ProFunds UltraChina Fund Investor Class	UGPIX	NAS CM	Open End	Trading Tools (Foreign Stock)	B	A+	D+	Up	Y	15,000
ProFunds UltraChina Fund Service Class	UGPSX	NAS CM	Open End	Trading Tools (Foreign Stock)	B	A+	D+	Up	Y	15,000
ProFunds UltraEmerging Markets Fund Investor Class	UUPIX	NAS CM	Open End	Trading Tools (Growth)	C	B-	C-		Y	15,000
ProFunds UltraEmerging Markets Fund Service Class	UUPSX	NAS CM	Open End	Trading Tools (Growth)	C	C+	C-		Y	15,000
ProFunds UltraJapan Fund Investor Class	UJPIX	NAS CM	Open End	Trading Tools (Pacific Stock)	B	A	C-	Up	Y	15,000
ProFunds UltraJapan Fund Service Class	UJPSX	NAS CM	Open End	Trading Tools (Pacific Stock)	B	A	C-	Up	Y	15,000
ProFunds UltraLatin America Fund Investor Class	UBPIX	NAS CM	Open End	Trading Tools (Growth)	C-	C	D+	Down	Y	15,000
ProFunds UltraLatin America Fund Service Class	UBPSX	NAS CM	Open End	Trading Tools (Growth)	C-	C	D+	Down	Y	15,000
ProFunds UltraMid Cap Fund Investor Class	UMPIX	NAS CM	Open End	Trading Tools (Growth)	B+	A+	C+	Up	Y	15,000
ProFunds UltraMid Cap Fund Service Class	UMPSX	NAS CM	Open End	Trading Tools (Growth)	B+	A+	C+	Up	Y	15,000
ProFunds UltraNASDAQ-100 Fund Investor Class	UOPIX	NAS CM	Open End	Trading Tools (Growth)	A-	A+	B-	Up	Y	15,000
ProFunds UltraNASDAQ-100 Fund Service Class	UOPSX	NAS CM	Open End	Trading Tools (Growth)	A-	A+	B-	Up	Y	15,000
ProFunds UltraSector Health Care Fund Investor Class	HCPIX	NAS CM	Open End	Trading Tools (Health)	B	B	B-	Up	Y	15,000
ProFunds UltraSector Health Care Fund Service Class	HCPSX	NAS CM	Open End	Trading Tools (Health)	B	B	B-	Up	Y	15,000
ProFunds UltraSector Mobile Telecommunications Inv Cls	WCPIX	NAS CM	Open End	Trading Tools (Comm)	C	C	C-	Down	Y	15,000
ProFunds UltraSector Mobile Telecommunications Serv Cls	WCPSX	NAS CM	Open End	Trading Tools (Comm)	C	C	C-	Down	Y	15,000
ProFunds UltraSector Oil & Gas Fund Investor Class	ENPIX	NAS CM	Open End	Trading Tools (Natl Res)	D+	D+	D+	Up	Y	15,000

★ Expanded analysis of this fund is included in Section II.

Min Additional Investment	3-Month Total Return	6-Month Total Return	1-Year Total Return	3-Year Total Return	5-Year Total Return	Dividend Yield (TTM)	Expense Ratio	3-Yr Std Deviation	3-Year Beta	NAV	Total Assets (MIL)	%Cash	%Stocks	%Bonds	%Other	Turnover Ratio	Last Bull Market Total Return	Last Bear Market Total Return	Front End Fee (%)	Back End Fee (%)	Inception Date
	TOTAL RETURNS					PERFORMANCE				ASSETS		ASSET ALLOCATION & TURNOVER					BULL & BEAR		FEES		
	-0.28	-0.98	-4.00	-10.85	-17.84	0	2.73	6.01		14.13	8.9	100	0	0	0	1,297	-3.64	-14.14			Jan-05
	-4.01	-4.50	-11.94	-17.79	-31.14	0	1.54	16.25		39	30.0	100	0	0	0	1,297	-2.32	-33.22			May-02
	-4.23	-4.95	-12.77	-20.24	-34.63	0	2.54	16.16		35.09	30.0	100	0	0	0	1,297	-2.67	-33.5			May-02
	15.13	37.74	56.74	108.04	415.23	0.09	1.46	28.06		56.48	307.9	27	73	0	0	27	34.05	-29.9			Jun-00
	14.85	37.09	55.19	101.91	390.20	0	2.46	28.02		47.5	307.9	27	73	0	0	27	33.48	-30.17			Jun-00
	-6.84	-12.31	-25.24	-41.89	-68.65	0	1.78	12.74		10.75	2.9	100	0	0	0	1,297	-24.75	7.15			May-02
	-6.99	-12.68	-25.95	-43.44	-70.04	0	2.78	12.75		9.84	2.9	100	0	0	0	1,297	-25.3	6.59			May-02
	-6.33	-12.59	-0.43	-13.11	-32.12	0	1.78	18.14		43.44	2.0	100	0	0	0	166	-22.43	26.76			Sep-05
	-6.59	-13.04	-1.41	-15.71	-35.45	0	2.78	18.12		41.67	2.0	100	0	0	0	166	-22.79	26.19			Sep-05
	-0.52	-5.98	-13.42	-50.33	-26.85	0	1.78	41.77		39.73	4.1	100	0	0	0		3.2	15.31			Jan-06
	-0.74	-6.38	-14.24	-51.87	-30.54	0	2.78	41.74		39.73	4.1	100	0	0	0		2.72	14.85			Jan-06
	-2.66	-4.03	-10.07	-23.85	-46.90	0	1.78	11.87		15	1.5	100	0	0	0	1,298	-26.19	13.86			Sep-05
	-2.84	-4.48	-10.90	-25.95	-49.38	0	2.78	11.88		13.64	1.5	100	0	0	0	1,298	-26.62	13.43			Sep-05
	-3.63	-8.88	-14.48	-33.09	-59.62	0	1.78	13.73		14.05	2.8	100	0	0	0		-26.94	24.17			May-02
	-3.78	-9.30	-15.23	-35.03	-61.51	0	2.78	13.72		13.74	2.8	100	0	0	0		-27.32	23.85			May-02
	2.77	7.91	12.05	24.77	80.30	0	1.67	14.1	1	83.95	41.3	81	19	0	0	401	26.62	-25.23			Sep-01
	2.56	7.44	11.01	21.20	71.69	0	2.67	14.08	1	71.27	41.3	81	19	0	0	401	25.94	-25.56			Sep-01
	3.46	8.79	12.73	35.31	98.53	0	1.59	13.31	1	86.94	20.6	0	100	0	0	511	26.57	-21.98			Sep-01
	3.20	8.26	11.60	31.29	88.77	0	2.59	13.3	1	72.69	20.6	0	100	0	0	511	25.8	-22.31			Sep-01
	3.59	9.56	9.52	27.50	88.64	0	1.74	14.68	1	90.53	14.8	0	100	0	0	393	30.03	-23.22			Sep-01
	3.33	9.03	8.45	23.79	79.38	0	2.74	14.65	1	77.46	14.8	0	100	0	0	393	29.22	-23.53			Sep-01
	12.52	24.83	55.87	85.35	244.57	0	1.52	22.82		108.98	104.4	24	76	0	0	107	42.92	-20.66			Jun-00
	12.24	24.21	54.32	79.94	227.78	0	2.52	22.8		92.68	104.4	24	76	0	0	107	42.12	-20.99			Jun-00
	5.24	14.18	-4.31	27.82	57.36	0	1.78	23.36		24.48	3.3	26	66	0	8	562	23.04	-15.32			Jun-00
	4.96	13.67	-5.22	24.00	49.68	0	2.78	23.36		23.38	3.3	26	66	0	8	562	22.32	-15.69			Jun-00
	3.43	3.13	9.92	3.95	12.13	0	1.28	16.46		56.27	28.5	77	0	22	0	397	-3.15	41.98			May-02
	3.18	2.63	8.74	0.98	6.48	0	2.28	16.49		52.11	28.5	77	0	22	0	397	-3.68	41.44			May-02
	21.99	34.61	57.64	92.24	276.72	0	1.57	22.41		126.55	57.3	23	76	0	0	0	46.18	-28.5			Jun-02
	21.69	33.96	56.11	86.66	258.38	0	2.57	22.4		111.41	57.3	23	76	0	0	0	45.27	-28.82			Jun-02
	6.36	16.11	48.19	27.30	55.39	0	1.78	23.16		18.88	15.3	99	0	0	1	1,297	22.83	-46.54			Apr-06
	6.06	15.49	46.74	23.57	47.88	0	2.78	23.18		17.14	15.3	99	0	0	1	1,297	22	-46.74			Apr-06
	-11.84	-19.20	-32.58	-53.48	-82.53	0	1.66	18.68		26.42	10.3	100	0	0	0	1,297	-41.15	28.05			Dec-97
	-12.05	-19.58	-33.25	-54.75	-83.38	0	2.66	18.54		24.43	10.3	100	0	0	0	1,297	-41.51	27.68			Dec-97
	12.71	21.74	42.76	64.59	263.65	0	1.42	20.61		172.92	117.5	19	81	0	0	9	50.57	-33.14			Nov-97
	12.42	21.12	41.37	59.77	245.91	0	2.42	20.59		145.7	117.5	19	81	0	0	9	49.75	-33.41			Nov-97
	6.42	37.05	105.73	61.05	149.50	0	1.78	42.65		18.62	42.7	11	87	0	2	513	27.07	-54.07			Feb-08
	6.14	36.28	103.77	56.43	137.26	0	2.78	42.64		16.96	42.7	11	87	0	2	513	26.33	-54.23			Feb-08
	3.70	25.17	75.02	35.62	9.58	0	1.62	37.21		66.21	41.5	15	82	0	1	225	26.53	-45.74			Apr-06
	3.46	24.52	73.27	31.60	4.11	0	2.62	37.14		61.79	41.5	15	82	0	1	225	25.87	-45.99			Apr-06
	23.63	27.25	39.71	44.67	218.61	0	1.7	34.02		25.68	33.4	31	69	0	0	1,297	17.8	-27.36			Feb-00
	23.40	26.63	38.42	40.69	203.81	0	2.7	33.96		22.3	33.4	31	69	0	0	1,297	16.88	-27.65			Feb-00
	-3.68	26.92	46.58	-7.16	-57.93	0.25	1.66	56.01		38.89	28.5	12	81	0	2	228	41.19	-47.46			Oct-07
	-3.91	26.30	45.18	-9.85	-59.93	0	2.66	55.87		37.5	28.5	12	81	0	2	228	40.3	-47.66			Oct-07
	11.64	17.73	29.53	60.63	234.45	0	1.46	22.41		132	108.2	27	73	0	0	35	55.63	-43.32			Feb-00
	11.44	17.22	28.43	56.10	218.55	0	2.46	22.4		110.02	108.2	27	73	0	0	35	54.7	-43.57			Feb-00
	13.73	26.38	68.58	104.77	434.52	0	1.43	27.95		182.86	436.3	37	63	0	0	4	58.29	-23.31			Dec-97
	13.45	25.74	66.91	98.73	408.62	0	2.43	27.94		152.13	436.3	37	63	0	0	4	57.45	-23.63			Dec-97
	1.75	6.92	32.17	29.65	201.53	0	1.58	19.07		53.98	28.7	27	72	0	0	215	30.76	-16.67			Jun-00
	1.49	6.37	30.85	25.81	186.86	0	2.58	19.07		45.61	28.7	27	72	0	0	215	30.06	-17.02			Jun-00
	-5.47	-6.29	-1.69	48.95	82.54	0	1.78	26.73		67.12	3.7	45	55	0	0	562	18.54	-29.81			Jun-00
	-5.70	-6.75	-2.68	44.65	73.61	0	2.78	26.71		56.2	3.7	45	55	0	0	562	17.9	-30.08			Jun-00
	8.99	19.24	-5.58	-16.50	0.19	0.64	1.6	28.15		38.22	22.5	22	76	0	2	110	31.39	-37.72			Jun-00

	MARKET			FUND TYPE, CATEGORY & OBJECTIVE	RATINGS				MINIMUMS	
Fund Name	Ticker Symbol	Traded On	Fund Type	Category and (Prospectus Objective)	Overall Rating	Reward Rating	Risk Rating	Recent Up/ Downgrade	Open to New Investors	Min Initial Investment
ProFunds UltraSector Oil & Gas Fund Service Class	ENPSX	NAS CM	Open End	Trading Tools (Natl Res)	D+	D+	D	Up	Y	15,000
ProFunds UltraShort China Fund Investor Class	UHPIX	NAS CM	Open End	Other Alternative (Foreign Stock)	E+	E+	D-	Down	Y	15,000
ProFunds UltraShort China Fund Service Class	UHPSX	NAS CM	Open End	Other Alternative (Foreign Stock)	E+	E+	D-	Down	Y	15,000
ProFunds UltraShort Dow 30 Fund Investor Class	UWPIX	NAS CM	Open End	Other Alternative (Aggr Growth)	E+	E+	E+	Down	Y	15,000
ProFunds UltraShort Dow 30 Fund Service Class	UWPSX	NAS CM	Open End	Other Alternative (Aggr Growth)	E+	E+	E+	Down	Y	15,000
ProFunds UltraShort Emerging Market Fund Investor Class	UVPIX	NAS CM	Open End	Other Alternative (Growth)	D-	E+	D-	Down	Y	15,000
ProFunds UltraShort Emerging Market Fund Service Class	UVPSX	NAS CM	Open End	Other Alternative (Growth)	D-	E+	D-	Down	Y	15,000
ProFunds UltraShort International Fund Investor Class	UXPIX	NAS CM	Open End	Other Alternative (Growth)	D-	D-	D-	Down	Y	15,000
ProFunds UltraShort International Fund Service Class	UXPSX	NAS CM	Open End	Other Alternative (Growth)	D-	D-	D-	Down	Y	15,000
ProFunds UltraShort Japan Fund Investor Class	UKPIX	NAS CM	Open End	Other Alternative (Growth)	E+	E+	E+	Down	Y	15,000
ProFunds UltraShort Japan Fund Service Class	UKPSX	NAS CM	Open End	Other Alternative (Growth)	E+	E+	E+	Down	Y	15,000
ProFunds UltraShort Latin America Fund Investor Class	UFPIX	NAS CM	Open End	Other Alternative (Growth)	D-	E+	D-	Down	Y	15,000
ProFunds UltraShort Latin America Fund Service Class	UFPSX	NAS CM	Open End	Other Alternative (Growth)	D-	E+	D-	Down	Y	15,000
ProFunds UltraShort Mid-Cap Fund Investor Class	UIPIX	NAS CM	Open End	Other Alternative (Growth)	E+	D-	E+	Down	Y	15,000
ProFunds UltraShort Mid-Cap Fund Service Class	UIPSX	NAS CM	Open End	Other Alternative (Growth)	E+	E+	E+	Down	Y	15,000
ProFunds UltraShort NASDAQ-100 Fund Investor Class	USPIX	NAS CM	Open End	Other Alternative (Growth)	E+	E+	E+	Down	Y	15,000
ProFunds UltraShort NASDAQ-100 Fund Service Class	USPSX	NAS CM	Open End	Other Alternative (Growth)	E+	E+	E+	Down	Y	15,000
ProFunds UltraShort Small-Cap Fund Investor Class	UCPIX	NAS CM	Open End	Other Alternative (Small Company)	E+	E+	E+	Down	Y	15,000
ProFunds UltraShort Small-Cap Fund Service Class	UCPSX	NAS CM	Open End	Other Alternative (Small Company)	E+	E+	E+	Down	Y	15,000
ProFunds UltraSmall Cap Fund Investor Class	UAPIX	NAS CM	Open End	Trading Tools (Small Company)	B+	A+	C	Up	Y	15,000
ProFunds UltraSmall Cap Fund Service Class	UAPSX	NAS CM	Open End	Trading Tools (Small Company)	B+	A+	C	Up	Y	15,000
ProFunds Utilities UltraSector Fund Investor Class	UTPIX	NAS CM	Open End	Trading Tools (Utility)	B	B+	B-	Down	Y	15,000
ProFunds Utilities UltraSector Fund Service Class	UTPSX	NAS CM	Open End	Trading Tools (Utility)	B	B	B-	Down	Y	15,000
Prospector Capital Appreciation Fund	PCAFX	NAS CM	Open End	Aggressive Alloc (Growth)	B	C+	B	Up	Y	10,000
Prospector Opportunity Fund	POPFX	NAS CM	Open End	US Equity Mid Cap (Growth)	B+	B	A	Up	Y	10,000
Provident Trust Strategy Fund	PROVX	NAS CM	Open End	US Equity Large Cap Growth (Growth)	A-	A-	B+	Up	Y	1,000
Prudential 60/40 Allocation Fund R6	PALDX	NAS CM	Open End	Moderate Alloc (Balanced)	U	U	U		Y	0
Prudential Balanced Fund Class A	PIBAX	NAS CM	Open End	Moderate Alloc (Balanced)	B-	C+	B	Up	Y	2,500
Prudential Balanced Fund Class B	PBFBX	NAS CM	Open End	Moderate Alloc (Balanced)	B-	C+	B	Up		2,500
Prudential Balanced Fund Class C	PABCX	NAS CM	Open End	Moderate Alloc (Balanced)	B-	C+	B	Up	Y	2,500
Prudential Balanced Fund Class Q	PIBQX	NAS CM	Open End	Moderate Alloc (Balanced)	B-	C+	B		Y	5,000,000
Prudential Balanced Fund Class R	PALRX	NAS CM	Open End	Moderate Alloc (Balanced)	B-	C+	B	Up	Y	0
Prudential Balanced Fund Class Z	PABFX	NAS CM	Open End	Moderate Alloc (Balanced)	B-	C+	B	Down	Y	5,000,000
Prudential Commodity Strategies Fund Class Q	PQCMX	NAS CM	Open End	Commodities Broad Basket (Growth & Income)	D	D+	B-		Y	0
Prudential Conservative Allocation Fund Class A	JDUAX	NAS CM	Open End	Cautious Alloc (Balanced)	B-	C+	B	Up	Y	2,500
Prudential Conservative Allocation Fund Class B	JDABX	NAS CM	Open End	Cautious Alloc (Balanced)	B-	C+	B	Up		2,500
Prudential Conservative Allocation Fund Class C	JDACX	NAS CM	Open End	Cautious Alloc (Balanced)	B-	C+	B	Up	Y	2,500
Prudential Conservative Allocation Fund Class Q	JDAQX	NAS CM	Open End	Cautious Alloc (Balanced)	B-	C+	B		Y	5,000,000
Prudential Conservative Allocation Fund Class R	JDARX	NAS CM	Open End	Cautious Alloc (Balanced)	B-	C+	B	Up	Y	0
Prudential Conservative Allocation Fund Class Z	JDAZX	NAS CM	Open End	Cautious Alloc (Balanced)	B-	C+	B	Up	Y	5,000,000
Prudential Day One 2010 Fund Class R1	PDBDX	NAS CM	Open End	Target Date 2000-2020 (Asset Alloc)	D+	D+	A+		Y	0
Prudential Day One 2010 Fund Class R2	PDBEX	NAS CM	Open End	Target Date 2000-2020 (Asset Alloc)	D+	D+	A+		Y	2,500
Prudential Day One 2010 Fund Class R3	PDBFX	NAS CM	Open End	Target Date 2000-2020 (Asset Alloc)	D+	D+	A+		Y	0
Prudential Day One 2010 Fund Class R4	PDBGX	NAS CM	Open End	Target Date 2000-2020 (Asset Alloc)	D+	D+	A+		Y	0
Prudential Day One 2010 Fund Class R5	PDBHX	NAS CM	Open End	Target Date 2000-2020 (Asset Alloc)	D+	D+	A+		Y	2,500
Prudential Day One 2010 Fund Class R6	PDBJX	NAS CM	Open End	Target Date 2000-2020 (Asset Alloc)	D+	D+	A+		Y	0
Prudential Day One 2015 Fund Class R1	PDCDX	NAS CM	Open End	Target Date 2000-2020 (Asset Alloc)	D+	D+	A+		Y	0
Prudential Day One 2015 Fund Class R2	PDCEX	NAS CM	Open End	Target Date 2000-2020 (Asset Alloc)	D+	D+	A+		Y	2,500
Prudential Day One 2015 Fund Class R3	PDCFX	NAS CM	Open End	Target Date 2000-2020 (Asset Alloc)	D+	D+	A+		Y	0
Prudential Day One 2015 Fund Class R4	PDCGX	NAS CM	Open End	Target Date 2000-2020 (Asset Alloc)	D+	D+	A+		Y	0
Prudential Day One 2015 Fund Class R5	PDCHX	NAS CM	Open End	Target Date 2000-2020 (Asset Alloc)	D+	D+	A+		Y	2,500
Prudential Day One 2015 Fund Class R6	PDCJX	NAS CM	Open End	Target Date 2000-2020 (Asset Alloc)	D+	D+	A+		Y	0

★Expanded analysis of this fund is included in Section II.

	TOTAL RETURNS					PERFORMANCE				ASSETS		ASSET ALLOCATION & TURNOVER					BULL & BEAR		FEES		
Min Additional Investment	3-Month Total Return	6-Month Total Return	1-Year Total Return	3-Year Total Return	5-Year Total Return	Dividend Yield (TTM)	Expense Ratio	3-Yr Std Deviation	3-Year Beta	NAV	Total Assets (MIL)	%Cash	%Stocks	%Bonds	%Other	Turnover Ratio	Last Bull Market Total Return	Last Bear Market Total Return	Front End Fee (%)	Back End Fee (%)	Inception Date
	8.75	18.66	-6.49	-18.93	-4.62	0	2.6	28.13		32.8	22.5	22	76	0	2	110	30.64	-37.99			Jun-00
	-9.13	-32.07	-57.67	-70.24	-87.75	0	1.78	38.65		5.57	2.0	100	0	0	0		-38.28	72.51			Feb-08
	-9.31	-32.26	-58.04	-71.10	-88.36	0	2.78	38.59		5.06	2.0	100	0	0	0		-38.81	71.97			Feb-08
	-18.66	-26.91	-39.01	-60.42	-83.30	0	1.78	20.37		20.04	3.5	100	0	0	0	181	-37.85	23.52			Jul-04
	-18.87	-27.26	-39.59	-61.60	-84.15	0	2.78	20.31		18.09	3.5	100	0	0	0	181	-38.27	23.1			Jul-04
	-5.48	-23.58	-48.36	-57.39	-62.19	0	1.78	34.51		19.47	2.5	100	0	0	0	1,298	-35.05	51.78			Apr-06
	-5.67	-23.97	-48.87	-58.60	-64.03	0	2.78	34.47		18.11	2.5	100	0	0	0	1,298	-35.41	51.35			Apr-06
	-7.27	-16.42	-37.29	-50.20	-68.79	0	1.78	21.89		13.13	2.3	100	0	0	0		-33.46	47.18			Apr-06
	-7.50	-16.86	-37.92	-51.69	-70.39	0	2.78	21.84		12.08	2.3	100	0	0	0		-33.81	46.53			Apr-06
	-20.96	-24.37	-34.24	-62.81	-90.67	0	1.78	31.48		7.01	1.8	100	0	0	0		-24.42	21.65			Mar-06
	-21.19	-24.76	-34.90	-63.89	-91.11	0	2.78	31.45		6.47	1.8	100	0	0	0		-24.83	21.2			Mar-06
	-0.14	-26.11	-45.62	-61.71	-46.74	0	1.78	52.21		6.96	17.6	100	0	0	0		-42.23	55.55			Oct-07
	-0.31	-26.54	-46.16	-62.79	-49.23	0	2.78	52.2		6.31	17.6	100	0	0	0		-42.59	55.39			Oct-07
	-11.45	-17.17	-27.32	-55.62	-83.10	0	1.78	20.66		23.43	1.4	99	0	0	1		-45.83	43.66			Jan-04
	-11.66	-17.55	-28.02	-57.03	-83.95	0	2.78	20.74		21.27	1.4	99	0	0	1		-46.07	43.63			Jan-04
	-13.36	-23.49	-44.56	-66.30	-89.66	0	1.69	24.9		22.17	13.9	99	0	0	1	1,297	-43.86	12.96			Jun-98
	-13.55	-23.81	-45.05	-67.26	-90.17	0	2.69	24.82		21.62	13.9	99	0	0	1	1,297	-44.17	12.45			Jun-98
	-6.87	-17.39	-27.19	-56.71	-84.35	0	1.78	27.17		9.21	5.9	99	0	0	1	1,297	-49.27	47.55			Jan-04
	-7.20	-17.90	-28.07	-58.12	-85.20	0	2.78	27.11		8.76	5.9	99	0	0	1	1,297	-49.43	46.52			Jan-04
	5.41	16.44	25.25	49.30	207.93	0	1.5	28.64		59.68	77.4	55	45	0	0	71	53.14	-47.47			Feb-00
	5.11	15.82	23.94	44.80	192.80	0	2.5	28.64		50.08	77.4	55	45	0	0	71	52.34	-47.71			Feb-00
	-0.01	3.82	15.82	24.42	120.23	0.65	1.65	18.84		44.78	19.7	23	77	0	1	97	12.43	0.1			Jul-00
	-0.25	3.29	14.66	20.65	109.42	0	2.65	18.84		42.42	19.7	23	77	0	1	97	11.83	-0.31			Jul-00
1,000	4.64	7.04	11.37	23.56	56.45	1.18	1.3	7.89	0.72	17.63	26.6	3	76	2	0	32	9.41	-16.13			Sep-07
1,000	4.52	7.86	10.32	34.32	87.62	0.97	1.3	9.82	0.63	20.85	117.7	8	92	0	0	42	18.32	-15.58			Sep-07
100	9.08	15.93	29.37	48.23	101.74	0.07	1.01	10.6	0.9	14.73	148.8	10	90	0	0	4	19.29	-15.63			Dec-86
	5.00						0.4			10.44	0.01	14	52	33	1						Sep-17
100	4.09	7.84	14.04	23.04	62.27	1.05	1.17	6.23		15.82	589.8	-1	55	46	0	180	16.09	-10.51	5.50		Nov-96
100	3.89	7.42	13.17	20.42	56.58	0.41	2.12	6.27		15.93	589.8	-1	55	46	0	180	15.63	-10.79		5.00	Nov-96
100	3.96	7.56	13.24	20.50	56.81	0.41	1.86	6.25		15.93	589.8	-1	55	46	0	180	15.63	-10.79		1.00	Nov-96
	4.16	8.03	14.35	24.13	64.75		0.88	6.27		15.93	589.8	-1	55	46	0	180	16.24	-10.45			Nov-17
	4.02	7.70	13.73	22.28	60.64	0.87	1.63	6.28		15.84	589.8	-1	55	46	0	180	15.96	-10.59			Dec-04
	4.16	8.03	14.35	24.13	64.75	1.31	0.88	6.27		15.93	589.8	-1	55	46	0	180	16.24	-10.45			Jan-93
	4.97	7.93	1.19			0	1			10.54	15.1	80	0	0	20						Nov-16
100	2.71	5.61	11.17	14.88	31.79	1.57	1.3	4.48		12.99	130.2	2	39	20	39	17	10.42	-8.11	5.50		Mar-04
100	2.52	5.15	10.31	12.31	26.85	0.85	2.05	4.48		12.94	130.2	2	39	20	39	17	10.03	-8.46		5.00	Mar-04
100	2.52	5.23	10.31	12.31	26.94	0.85	2.05	4.44		12.95	130.2	2	39	20	39	17	10.03	-8.46		1.00	Mar-04
	2.82	5.78	11.39	15.75	33.46		1.05	4.48		13.04	130.2	2	39	20	39	17	10.68	-8.1			Nov-17
	2.58	5.40	10.85	13.96	30.04	1.32	1.55	4.45		13.04	130.2	2	39	20	39	17	10.27	-8.3			Jan-07
	2.82	5.77	11.39	15.75	33.46	1.8	1.05	4.48		13.05	130.2	2	39	20	39	17	10.68	-8.1			Mar-04
	2.59	4.67	8.45				1.15			10.7	4.7	15	32	52	1						Dec-16
100	2.65	4.73	8.73				0.9			10.7	4.7	15	32	52	1						Dec-16
	2.61	4.78	8.88				0.75			10.7	4.7	15	32	52	1						Dec-16
	2.71	4.90	9.00				0.65			10.7	4.7	15	32	52	1						Dec-16
100	2.72	4.90	9.11				0.55			10.7	4.7	15	32	52	1						Dec-16
	2.68	5.06	9.06				0.4			10.7	4.7	15	32	52	1						Dec-16
	2.74	5.02	9.44				1.15			10.8	5.9	15	37	47	1						Dec-16
100	2.80	5.18	9.72				0.9			10.8	5.9	15	37	47	1						Dec-16
	2.86	5.24	9.88				0.75			10.8	5.9	15	37	47	1						Dec-16
	2.87	5.24	9.89				0.65			10.79	5.9	15	37	47	1						Dec-16
100	2.87	5.35	10.11				0.55			10.8	5.9	15	37	47	1						Dec-16
	2.94	5.40	10.05				0.4			10.8	5.9	15	37	47	1						Dec-16

	MARKET		FUND TYPE, CATEGORY & OBJECTIVE		RATINGS					MINIMUMS
Fund Name	Ticker Symbol	Traded On	Fund Type	Category and (Prospectus Objective)	Overall Rating	Reward Rating	Risk Rating	Recent Up/ Downgrade	Open to New Investors	Min Initial Investment
Prudential Day One 2020 Fund Class R1	PDDDX	NAS CM	Open End	Target Date 2000-2020 (Asset Alloc)	D+	D+	A+		Y	0
Prudential Day One 2020 Fund Class R2	PDDEX	NAS CM	Open End	Target Date 2000-2020 (Asset Alloc)	D+	D+	A+		Y	2,500
Prudential Day One 2020 Fund Class R3	PDDFX	NAS CM	Open End	Target Date 2000-2020 (Asset Alloc)	D+	D+	A+		Y	0
Prudential Day One 2020 Fund Class R4	PDDGX	NAS CM	Open End	Target Date 2000-2020 (Asset Alloc)	D+	D+	A+		Y	0
Prudential Day One 2020 Fund Class R5	PDDHX	NAS CM	Open End	Target Date 2000-2020 (Asset Alloc)	D+	D+	A+		Y	2,500
Prudential Day One 2020 Fund Class R6	PDDJX	NAS CM	Open End	Target Date 2000-2020 (Asset Alloc)	D+	D+	A+		Y	0
Prudential Day One 2025 Fund Class R1	PDEDX	NAS CM	Open End	Target Date 2021-2045 (Asset Alloc)	D+	D+	A+		Y	0
Prudential Day One 2025 Fund Class R2	PDEEX	NAS CM	Open End	Target Date 2021-2045 (Asset Alloc)	D+	D+	A+		Y	2,500
Prudential Day One 2025 Fund Class R3	PDEFX	NAS CM	Open End	Target Date 2021-2045 (Asset Alloc)	D+	D+	A+		Y	0
Prudential Day One 2025 Fund Class R4	PDEGX	NAS CM	Open End	Target Date 2021-2045 (Asset Alloc)	D+	D+	A+		Y	0
Prudential Day One 2025 Fund Class R5	PDEHX	NAS CM	Open End	Target Date 2021-2045 (Asset Alloc)	D+	D+	A+		Y	2,500
Prudential Day One 2025 Fund Class R6	PDEJX	NAS CM	Open End	Target Date 2021-2045 (Asset Alloc)	D+	D+	A+		Y	0
Prudential Day One 2030 Fund Class R1	PDFCX	NAS CM	Open End	Target Date 2021-2045 (Asset Alloc)	D+	D+	A+		Y	0
Prudential Day One 2030 Fund Class R2	PDFEX	NAS CM	Open End	Target Date 2021-2045 (Asset Alloc)	D+	D+	A+		Y	2,500
Prudential Day One 2030 Fund Class R3	PDFFX	NAS CM	Open End	Target Date 2021-2045 (Asset Alloc)	D+	D+	A+		Y	0
Prudential Day One 2030 Fund Class R4	PDFGX	NAS CM	Open End	Target Date 2021-2045 (Asset Alloc)	D+	D+	A+		Y	0
Prudential Day One 2030 Fund Class R5	PDFHX	NAS CM	Open End	Target Date 2021-2045 (Asset Alloc)	D+	D+	A+		Y	2,500
Prudential Day One 2030 Fund Class R6	PDFJX	NAS CM	Open End	Target Date 2021-2045 (Asset Alloc)	D+	D+	A+		Y	0
Prudential Day One 2035 Fund Class R1	PDGCX	NAS CM	Open End	Target Date 2021-2045 (Asset Alloc)	D	D+	A		Y	0
Prudential Day One 2035 Fund Class R2	PDGEX	NAS CM	Open End	Target Date 2021-2045 (Asset Alloc)	D	D+	A		Y	2,500
Prudential Day One 2035 Fund Class R3	PDGFX	NAS CM	Open End	Target Date 2021-2045 (Asset Alloc)	D	D+	A		Y	0
Prudential Day One 2035 Fund Class R4	PDGGX	NAS CM	Open End	Target Date 2021-2045 (Asset Alloc)	D	D+	A		Y	0
Prudential Day One 2035 Fund Class R5	PDGHX	NAS CM	Open End	Target Date 2021-2045 (Asset Alloc)	D	D+	A		Y	2,500
Prudential Day One 2035 Fund Class R6	PDGJX	NAS CM	Open End	Target Date 2021-2045 (Asset Alloc)	D	D+	A		Y	0
Prudential Day One 2040 Fund Class R1	PDHDX	NAS CM	Open End	Target Date 2021-2045 (Asset Alloc)	D	D+	A		Y	0
Prudential Day One 2040 Fund Class R2	PDHEX	NAS CM	Open End	Target Date 2021-2045 (Asset Alloc)	D	D+	A		Y	2,500
Prudential Day One 2040 Fund Class R3	PDHFX	NAS CM	Open End	Target Date 2021-2045 (Asset Alloc)	D	D+	A		Y	0
Prudential Day One 2040 Fund Class R4	PDHGX	NAS CM	Open End	Target Date 2021-2045 (Asset Alloc)	D	D+	A		Y	0
Prudential Day One 2040 Fund Class R5	PDHHX	NAS CM	Open End	Target Date 2021-2045 (Asset Alloc)	D	D+	A		Y	2,500
Prudential Day One 2040 Fund Class R6	PDHJX	NAS CM	Open End	Target Date 2021-2045 (Asset Alloc)	D	D+	A		Y	0
Prudential Day One 2045 Fund Class R1	PDIDX	NAS CM	Open End	Target Date 2021-2045 (Asset Alloc)	D	D+	A		Y	0
Prudential Day One 2045 Fund Class R2	PDIEX	NAS CM	Open End	Target Date 2021-2045 (Asset Alloc)	D	D+	A		Y	2,500
Prudential Day One 2045 Fund Class R3	PDIKX	NAS CM	Open End	Target Date 2021-2045 (Asset Alloc)	D	D+	A		Y	0
Prudential Day One 2045 Fund Class R4	PDIGX	NAS CM	Open End	Target Date 2021-2045 (Asset Alloc)	D	D+	A		Y	0
Prudential Day One 2045 Fund Class R5	PDIHX	NAS CM	Open End	Target Date 2021-2045 (Asset Alloc)	D	D+	A		Y	2,500
Prudential Day One 2045 Fund Class R6	PDIJX	NAS CM	Open End	Target Date 2021-2045 (Asset Alloc)	D	D+	A		Y	0
Prudential Day One 2050 Fund Class R1	PDJDX	NAS CM	Open End	Target Date 2046+ (Asset Alloc)	D	D+	A		Y	0
Prudential Day One 2050 Fund Class R2	PDJEX	NAS CM	Open End	Target Date 2046+ (Asset Alloc)	D	D+	A		Y	2,500
Prudential Day One 2050 Fund Class R3	PDJFX	NAS CM	Open End	Target Date 2046+ (Asset Alloc)	D	D+	A		Y	0
Prudential Day One 2050 Fund Class R4	PDJGX	NAS CM	Open End	Target Date 2046+ (Asset Alloc)	D	D+	A		Y	0
Prudential Day One 2050 Fund Class R5	PDJHX	NAS CM	Open End	Target Date 2046+ (Asset Alloc)	D	D+	A		Y	2,500
Prudential Day One 2050 Fund Class R6	PDJJX	NAS CM	Open End	Target Date 2046+ (Asset Alloc)	D	D+	A		Y	0
Prudential Day One 2055 Fund Class R1	PDKDX	NAS CM	Open End	Target Date 2046+ (Asset Alloc)	D	D+	A		Y	0
Prudential Day One 2055 Fund Class R2	PDKEX	NAS CM	Open End	Target Date 2046+ (Asset Alloc)	D	D+	A		Y	2,500
Prudential Day One 2055 Fund Class R3	PDKFX	NAS CM	Open End	Target Date 2046+ (Asset Alloc)	D	D+	A		Y	0
Prudential Day One 2055 Fund Class R4	PDKGX	NAS CM	Open End	Target Date 2046+ (Asset Alloc)	D	D+	A		Y	0
Prudential Day One 2055 Fund Class R5	PDKHX	NAS CM	Open End	Target Date 2046+ (Asset Alloc)	D	D+	A		Y	2,500
Prudential Day One 2055 Fund Class R6	PDKJX	NAS CM	Open End	Target Date 2046+ (Asset Alloc)	D	D+	A		Y	0
Prudential Day One 2060 Fund Class R1	PDLDX	NAS CM	Open End	Target Date 2046+ (Asset Alloc)	D	D+	A		Y	0
Prudential Day One 2060 Fund Class R2	PDLEX	NAS CM	Open End	Target Date 2046+ (Asset Alloc)	D	D+	A		Y	2,500
Prudential Day One 2060 Fund Class R3	PDLFX	NAS CM	Open End	Target Date 2046+ (Asset Alloc)	D	D+	A		Y	0
Prudential Day One 2060 Fund Class R4	PDLGX	NAS CM	Open End	Target Date 2046+ (Asset Alloc)	D	D+	A		Y	0

★Expanded analysis of this fund is included in Section II.

	TOTAL RETURNS					PERFORMANCE				ASSETS		ASSET ALLOCATION & TURNOVER					BULL & BEAR		FEES		
Min Additional Investment	3-Month Total Return	6-Month Total Return	1-Year Total Return	3-Year Total Return	5-Year Total Return	Dividend Yield (TTM)	Expense Ratio	3-Yr Std Deviation	3-Year Beta	NAV	Total Assets (MIL)	%Cash	%Stocks	%Bonds	%Other	Turnover Ratio	Last Bull Market Total Return	Last Bear Market Total Return	Front End Fee (%)	Back End Fee (%)	Inception Date
	3.04	5.61	10.39				1.15			10.89	15.3	14	42	43	1						Dec-16
100	3.10	5.77	10.66				0.9			10.89	15.3	14	42	43	1						Dec-16
	3.24	5.91	10.92				0.75			10.9	15.3	14	42	43	1						Dec-16
	3.16	5.83	10.93				0.65			10.89	15.3	14	42	43	1						Dec-16
100	3.17	5.84	11.05				0.55			10.89	15.3	14	42	43	1						Dec-16
	3.24	6.02	10.70				0.4			10.86	15.3	14	42	43	1						Dec-16
	3.54	6.51	12.09				1.15			11.02	23.2	13	50	35	1						Dec-16
100	3.62	6.69	12.39				0.9			11.02	23.2	13	50	35	1						Dec-16
	3.66	6.84	12.65				0.75			11.03	23.2	13	50	35	1						Dec-16
	3.68	6.75	12.56				0.65			11.02	23.2	13	50	35	1						Dec-16
100	3.69	6.76	12.67				0.55			11.02	23.2	13	50	35	1						Dec-16
	3.84	7.01	12.93				0.4			11.04	23.2	13	50	35	1						Dec-16
	4.27	7.92	15.22				1.15			11.29	14.0	10	64	25	1						Dec-16
100	4.41	8.16	15.59				0.9			11.3	14.0	10	64	25	1						Dec-16
	4.37	8.12	15.65				0.75			11.29	14.0	10	64	25	1						Dec-16
	4.39	8.14	15.78				0.65			11.29	14.0	10	64	25	1						Dec-16
100	4.40	8.14	15.89				0.55			11.29	14.0	10	64	25	1						Dec-16
	4.46	8.29	15.94				0.4			11.3	14.0	10	64	25	1						Dec-16
	4.79	8.93	17.09				1.15			11.42	15.3	7	73	19	1						Dec-16
100	4.85	9.10	17.26				0.9			11.42	15.3	7	73	19	1						Dec-16
	4.89	9.23	17.51				0.75			11.43	15.3	7	73	19	1						Dec-16
	5.01	9.25	17.64				0.65			11.43	15.3	7	73	19	1						Dec-16
100	4.92	9.26	17.66				0.55			11.42	15.3	7	73	19	1						Dec-16
	4.89	9.21	17.71				0.4			11.42	15.3	7	73	19	1						Dec-16
	5.09	9.52	18.62				1.15			11.54	8.9	6	78	14	1						Dec-16
100	5.06	9.57	18.90				0.9			11.54	8.9	6	78	14	1						Dec-16
	5.10	9.61	18.93				0.75			11.54	8.9	6	78	14	1						Dec-16
	5.12	9.73	19.06				0.65			11.54	8.9	6	78	14	1						Dec-16
100	5.13	9.74	19.18				0.55			11.54	8.9	6	78	14	1						Dec-16
	5.19	9.89	19.34				0.4			11.55	8.9	6	78	14	1						Dec-16
	5.13	9.73	19.51				1.15			11.61	9.6	5	82	11	1						Dec-16
100	5.28	9.98	19.90				0.9			11.62	9.6	5	82	11	1						Dec-16
	5.32	10.02	20.05				0.75			11.62	9.6	5	82	11	1						Dec-16
	5.34	10.14	20.18				0.65			11.62	9.6	5	82	11	1						Dec-16
100	5.36	10.14	20.30				0.55			11.62	9.6	5	82	11	1						Dec-16
	5.32	10.19	20.33				0.4			11.63	9.6	5	82	11	1						Dec-16
	5.39	10.11	19.71				1.15			11.61	3.1	5	85	9	1						Dec-16
100	5.38	10.29	19.90				0.9			11.61	3.1	5	85	9	1						Dec-16
	5.43	10.34	20.06				0.75			11.61	3.1	5	85	9	1						Dec-16
	5.45	10.35	20.19				0.65			11.61	3.1	5	85	9	1						Dec-16
100	5.46	10.46	20.31				0.55			11.61	3.1	5	85	9	1						Dec-16
	5.60	10.60	20.56				0.4			11.63	3.1	5	85	9	1						Dec-16
	5.58	10.45	21.43				1.15			11.78	4.4	5	89	5	1						Dec-16
100	5.55	10.61	21.71				0.9			11.78	4.4	5	89	5	1						Dec-16
	5.69	10.65	21.87				0.75			11.78	4.4	5	89	5	1						Dec-16
	5.70	10.76	22.11				0.65			11.79	4.4	5	89	5	1						Dec-16
100	5.72	10.87	22.23				0.55			11.79	4.4	5	89	5	1						Dec-16
	5.78	10.93	22.16				0.4			11.79	4.4	5	89	5	1						Dec-16
	5.63	10.73	21.07				1.15			11.73	0.35	5	91	3	1						Dec-16
100	5.69	10.78	21.23				0.9			11.73	0.35	5	91	3	1						Dec-16
	5.82	10.92	21.49				0.75			11.74	0.35	5	91	3	1						Dec-16
	5.84	11.04	21.63				0.65			11.74	0.35	5	91	3	1						Dec-16

	MARKET			FUND TYPE, CATEGORY & OBJECTIVE	RATINGS				MINIMUMS	
Fund Name	Ticker Symbol	Traded On	Fund Type	Category and (Prospectus Objective)	Overall Rating	Reward Rating	Risk Rating	Recent Up/ Downgrade	Open to New Investors	Min Initial Investment
Prudential Day One 2060 Fund Class R5	PDLHX	NAS CM	Open End	Target Date 2046+ (Asset Alloc)	D	D+	A		Y	2,500
Prudential Day One 2060 Fund Class R6	PDLJX	NAS CM	Open End	Target Date 2046+ (Asset Alloc)	D	D+	A		Y	0
Prudential Day One Income Fund Class R1	PDADX	NAS CM	Open End	Target Date 2000-2020 (Asset Alloc)	D+	D+	A+		Y	0
Prudential Day One Income Fund Class R2	PDAEX	NAS CM	Open End	Target Date 2000-2020 (Asset Alloc)	D+	D+	A+		Y	2,500
Prudential Day One Income Fund Class R3	PDAFX	NAS CM	Open End	Target Date 2000-2020 (Asset Alloc)	D+	D+	A+		Y	0
Prudential Day One Income Fund Class R4	PDAGX	NAS CM	Open End	Target Date 2000-2020 (Asset Alloc)	D+	D+	A+		Y	0
Prudential Day One Income Fund Class R5	PDAHX	NAS CM	Open End	Target Date 2000-2020 (Asset Alloc)	D+	D+	A+		Y	2,500
Prudential Day One Income Fund Class R6	PDAJX	NAS CM	Open End	Target Date 2000-2020 (Asset Alloc)	D	D+	A		Y	0
Prudential Global Real Estate Fund Class A	PURAX	NAS CM	Open End	Real Estate Sector Equity (Real Estate)	B-	C	B	Up	Y	2,500
Prudential Global Real Estate Fund Class B	PURBX	NAS CM	Open End	Real Estate Sector Equity (Real Estate)	C+	C	B	Up		2,500
Prudential Global Real Estate Fund Class C	PURCX	NAS CM	Open End	Real Estate Sector Equity (Real Estate)	C+	C	B	Up	Y	2,500
Prudential Global Real Estate Fund Class Q	PGRQX	NAS CM	Open End	Real Estate Sector Equity (Real Estate)	B-	C+	B	Up	Y	5,000,000
Prudential Global Real Estate Fund Class R	PURRX	NAS CM	Open End	Real Estate Sector Equity (Real Estate)	B-	C	B	Up	Y	0
Prudential Global Real Estate Fund Class Z	PURZX	NAS CM	Open End	Real Estate Sector Equity (Real Estate)	B-	C+	B	Up	Y	5,000,000
Prudential Growth Allocation Fund Class A	JDAAX	NAS CM	Open End	Aggressive Alloc (Growth)	B-	B-	C+	Down	Y	2,500
Prudential Growth Allocation Fund Class B	JDGBX	NAS CM	Open End	Aggressive Alloc (Growth)	C+	B-	C+	Down		2,500
Prudential Growth Allocation Fund Class C	JDGCX	NAS CM	Open End	Aggressive Alloc (Growth)	C+	B-	C+	Down	Y	2,500
Prudential Growth Allocation Fund Class Q	JDGQX	NAS CM	Open End	Aggressive Alloc (Growth)	B-	B-	C+		Y	5,000,000
Prudential Growth Allocation Fund Class R	JGARX	NAS CM	Open End	Aggressive Alloc (Growth)	B-	B-	C+	Down	Y	0
Prudential Growth Allocation Fund Class Z	JDGZX	NAS CM	Open End	Aggressive Alloc (Growth)	B-	B-	C+	Down	Y	5,000,000
Prudential Income Builder Fund Class A	PCGAX	NAS CM	Open End	Moderate Alloc (Growth & Income)	C+	C+	B-	Down	Y	2,500
Prudential Income Builder Fund Class B	PBCFX	NAS CM	Open End	Moderate Alloc (Growth & Income)	C+	C	B	Up		2,500
Prudential Income Builder Fund Class C	PCCFX	NAS CM	Open End	Moderate Alloc (Growth & Income)	C+	C	B	Up	Y	2,500
Prudential Income Builder Fund Class Q	PCGQX	NAS CM	Open End	Moderate Alloc (Growth & Income)	C+	C+	B-	Down	Y	5,000,000
Prudential Income Builder Fund Class Retirement	PCLRX	NAS CM	Open End	Moderate Alloc (Growth & Income)	C+	C+	B-	Down	Y	0
Prudential Income Builder Fund Class Z	PDCZX	NAS CM	Open End	Moderate Alloc (Growth & Income)	C+	C+	B-	Down	Y	5,000,000
Prudential Jennison 20/20 Focus Fund Class A	PTWAX	NAS CM	Open End	US Equity Large Cap Growth (Growth)	B	B	B	Up	Y	2,500
Prudential Jennison 20/20 Focus Fund Class B	PTWBX	NAS CM	Open End	US Equity Large Cap Growth (Growth)	B	B	B	Up		2,500
Prudential Jennison 20/20 Focus Fund Class C	PTWCX	NAS CM	Open End	US Equity Large Cap Growth (Growth)	B	B	B	Up	Y	2,500
Prudential Jennison 20/20 Focus Fund Class R	JTWRX	NAS CM	Open End	US Equity Large Cap Growth (Growth)	B	B	B	Up	Y	0
Prudential Jennison 20/20 Focus Fund Class Z	PTWZX	NAS CM	Open End	US Equity Large Cap Growth (Growth)	B	B	B	Up	Y	5,000,000
Prudential Jennison 20-20 Focus Fund Class Q	PJTQX	NAS CM	Open End	US Equity Large Cap Growth (Growth)	B	B	B	Up	Y	5,000,000
Prudential Jennison Blend Fund Class A	PBQAX	NAS CM	Open End	US Equity Large Cap Growth (Growth)	B-	B-	B-	Down	Y	2,500
Prudential Jennison Blend Fund Class B	PBQFX	NAS CM	Open End	US Equity Large Cap Growth (Growth)	B-	B-	B-	Up		2,500
Prudential Jennison Blend Fund Class C	PRECX	NAS CM	Open End	US Equity Large Cap Growth (Growth)	B-	B-	B-	Up	Y	2,500
Prudential Jennison Blend Fund Class Q	PBQQX	NAS CM	Open End	US Equity Large Cap Growth (Growth)	B-	B-	B-		Y	5,000,000
Prudential Jennison Blend Fund Class Z	PEQZX	NAS CM	Open End	US Equity Large Cap Growth (Growth)	B-	B	B-	Down	Y	5,000,000
Prudential Jennison Diversified Growth Fund Class A	TBDAX	NAS CM	Open End	US Equity Large Cap Growth (Growth)	B	B	B-		Y	2,500
Prudential Jennison Diversified Growth Fund Class B	TBDBX	NAS CM	Open End	US Equity Large Cap Growth (Growth)	B	B	B-	Up		2,500
Prudential Jennison Diversified Growth Fund Class C	TBDCX	NAS CM	Open End	US Equity Large Cap Growth (Growth)	B	B	B-	Up	Y	2,500
Prudential Jennison Diversified Growth Fund Class Q	TBDQX	NAS CM	Open End	US Equity Large Cap Growth (Growth)	B	B	B-		Y	5,000,000
Prudential Jennison Diversified Growth Fund Class Z	TBDZX	NAS CM	Open End	US Equity Large Cap Growth (Growth)	B	B	B-		Y	5,000,000
Prudential Jennison Emerging Markets Equity Fund Class A	PDEAX	NAS CM	Open End	Emerging Markets Equity (Growth)	C+	B-	C	Up	Y	2,500
Prudential Jennison Emerging Markets Equity Fund Class C	PDECX	NAS CM	Open End	Emerging Markets Equity (Growth)	C+	B-	C	Up	Y	2,500
Prudential Jennison Emerging Markets Equity Fund Class Q	PDEQX	NAS CM	Open End	Emerging Markets Equity (Growth)	C+	B-	C	Up	Y	5,000,000
Prudential Jennison Emerging Markets Equity Fund Class Z	PDEZX	NAS CM	Open End	Emerging Markets Equity (Growth)	C+	B-	C	Up	Y	5,000,000
Prudential Jennison Equity Income Fund Class A	SPQAX	NAS CM	Open End	US Equity Large Cap Blend (Equity-Income)	C+	C+	C+	Down	Y	2,500
Prudential Jennison Equity Income Fund Class B	JEIBX	NAS CM	Open End	US Equity Large Cap Blend (Equity-Income)	C+	C+	C+	Down		2,500
Prudential Jennison Equity Income Fund Class C	AGOCX	NAS CM	Open End	US Equity Large Cap Blend (Equity-Income)	B-	C+	B-	Up	Y	2,500
Prudential Jennison Equity Income Fund Class Q	PJIQX	NAS CM	Open End	US Equity Large Cap Blend (Equity-Income)	C+	C+	C+	Down	Y	5,000,000
Prudential Jennison Equity Income Fund Class R	PJERX	NAS CM	Open End	US Equity Large Cap Blend (Equity-Income)	B-	C+	B	Up	Y	0
Prudential Jennison Equity Income Fund Class Z	JDEZX	NAS CM	Open End	US Equity Large Cap Blend (Equity-Income)	B-	C+	B	Up	Y	5,000,000

★ Expanded analysis of this fund is included in Section II.

	TOTAL RETURNS					PERFORMANCE				ASSETS		ASSET ALLOCATION & TURNOVER					BULL & BEAR		FEES		
Min Additional Investment	3-Month Total Return	6-Month Total Return	1-Year Total Return	3-Year Total Return	5-Year Total Return	Dividend Yield (TTM)	Expense Ratio	3-Yr Std Deviation	3-Year Beta	NAV	Total Assets (MIL)	%Cash	%Stocks	%Bonds	%Other	Turnover Ratio	Last Bull Market Total Return	Last Bear Market Total Return	Front End Fee (%)	Back End Fee (%)	Inception Date
100	5.85	11.04	21.74				0.55			11.74	0.35	5	91	3	1						Dec-16
	5.82	11.01	21.57				0.4			11.73	0.35	5	91	3	1						Dec-16
	2.41	4.47	7.81				1.15			10.61	3.5	16	30	53	1						Dec-16
100	2.48	4.50	8.06				0.9			10.61	3.5	16	30	53	1						Dec-16
	2.53	4.57	8.21				0.75			10.61	3.5	16	30	53	1						Dec-16
	2.56	4.64	8.34				0.65			10.61	3.5	16	30	53	1						Dec-16
100	2.49	4.70	8.46				0.55			10.61	3.5	16	30	53	1						Dec-16
	2.63	4.86	8.49				0.4			10.62	3.5	16	30	53	1						Dec-16
100	3.81	5.86	11.05	10.27	33.04	2.31	1.24	10.22	0.92	24.14	2,691	0	98	0	2	66	24.51	-18.99	5.50		May-98
100	3.59	5.46	10.28	7.97	28.42	1.87	1.94	10.21	0.92	23.63	2,691	0	98	0	2	66	23.97	-19.22		5.00	May-98
100	3.63	5.50	10.28	7.97	28.42	1.87	1.94	10.21	0.92	23.62	2,691	0	98	0	2	66	23.91	-19.22		1.00	May-98
	3.92	6.09	11.59	11.79	35.96	2.73	0.79	10.22	0.92	24.23	2,691	0	98	0	2	66	24.75	-18.91			Aug-13
	3.73	5.73	10.81	9.59	31.66	2.16	1.44	10.21	0.92	24.07	2,691	0	98	0	2	66	24.35	-19.04			Jun-08
	3.88	6.00	11.40	11.27	35.03	2.57	0.94	10.19	0.91	24.24	2,691	0	98	0	2	66	24.75	-18.91			May-98
100	5.31	10.96	21.06	25.60	66.44	0.91	1.4	9.16		18.36	109.7	2	80	4	14	23	19.05	-18.79	5.50		Mar-04
100	5.14	10.58	20.25	22.81	60.25	0.36	2.15	9.14		17.62	109.7	2	80	4	14	23	18.6	-19.06		5.00	Mar-04
100	5.13	10.57	20.22	22.86	60.28	0.36	2.15	9.15		17.64	109.7	2	80	4	14	23	18.58	-19.05		1.00	Mar-04
	5.37	11.14	21.43	26.48	68.48		1.15	9.17		18.58	109.7	2	80	4	14	23	19.15	-18.66			Nov-17
	5.27	10.91	20.80	24.74	64.36	0.72	1.65	9.18		18.23	109.7	2	80	4	14	23	18.97	-18.88			Jan-07
	5.37	11.14	21.43	26.47	68.47	1.1	1.15	9.17		18.58	109.7	2	80	4	14	23	19.15	-18.66			Mar-04
100	1.57	3.63	7.84	11.98	30.70	4.35	0.95	6.15	0.5	9.68	452.5	2	44	42	1	102	11.73	-6.63	4.50		Nov-98
100	1.42	3.32	7.08	9.55	26.00	3.69	1.7	6.12	0.49	9.5	452.5	2	44	42	1	102	11.22	-7		5.00	Nov-98
100	1.42	3.32	7.08	9.55	26.01	3.69	1.7	6.12	0.5	9.5	452.5	2	44	42	1	102	11.22	-7		1.00	Nov-98
	1.73	3.84	8.20	12.92	32.54		0.7	6.13	0.5	9.75	452.5	2	44	42	1	102	11.82	-6.5			Dec-16
	1.51	3.62	7.58	11.26	29.15	4.11	1.2	6.13	0.49	9.67	452.5	2	44	42	1	102	11.48	-6.73			Oct-04
	1.63	3.84	8.16	12.87	32.48	4.57	0.7	6.14	0.5	9.75	452.5	2	44	42	1	102	11.82	-6.5			Nov-98
100	5.22	12.39	26.58	35.13	90.41	0	1.2	11.61	1.05	14.6	1,182	1	99	0	0	73	20.7	-18.56	5.50		Jul-98
100	5.00	11.96	25.56	32.21	83.76	0	1.9	11.64	1.05	10.29	1,182	1	99	0	0	73	20.2	-18.83		5.00	Jul-98
100	5.07	12.03	25.63	32.28	83.83	0	1.9	11.65	1.06	10.31	1,182	1	99	0	0	73	20.19	-18.76		1.00	Jul-98
	5.13	12.25	26.25	34.28	88.44	0	1.4	11.61	1.05	13.86	1,182	1	99	0	0	73	20.55	-18.63			Jun-04
	5.29	12.56	26.90	36.32	93.23	0.07	0.9	11.62	1.05	16.18	1,182	1	99	0	0	73	20.86	-18.43			Jul-98
	5.37	12.67	27.08	36.87	94.58	0.17	0.77	11.62	1.05	16.32	1,182	1	99	0	0	73	21	-18.44			Mar-11
100	5.34	10.71	21.58	27.85	87.40	0.71	0.95	11.33	1.06	20.84	1,017	2	98	0	0	53	23.13	-20.98	5.50		Jan-90
100	5.05	10.17	20.64	25.04	80.75	0.26	1.91	11.33	1.06	18.64	1,017	2	98	0	0	53	22.62	-21.21		5.00	Mar-82
100	5.10	10.28	20.69	25.15	80.90	0.26	1.73	11.34	1.06	18.66	1,017	2	98	0	0	53	22.69	-21.21		1.00	Aug-94
	5.30	10.43	20.92	25.33	81.17		0.68	11.33	1.06	20.86	1,017	2	98	0	0	53	22.62	-21.21			Oct-17
	5.38	10.85	21.90	28.94	90.17	0.95	0.68	11.35	1.06	20.86	1,017	2	98	0	0	53	23.29	-20.81			Mar-96
100	6.46	10.84	22.93	33.90	104.30	0.42	1.26	10.8	0.96	12.36	240.9	1	99	0	0	181	21.64	-15.44	5.50		Nov-99
100	6.16	10.37	21.88	30.83	96.53	0	2.26	10.82	0.97	10.33	240.9	1	99	0	0	181	21.33	-15.81		5.00	Nov-99
100	6.24	10.45	22.08	30.93	96.87	0	1.97	10.82	0.97	10.35	240.9	1	99	0	0	181	21.17	-15.81		1.00	Nov-99
	6.46	10.84	22.94	33.90	104.30		1	10.81	0.97	12.36	240.9	1	99	0	0	181	21.64	-15.45			Sep-17
	6.46	10.84	22.94	33.90	104.30		1	10.8	0.96	12.36	240.9	1	99	0	0	181	21.64	-15.45			Sep-17
100	6.94	16.63	40.40	25.52		0	1.45	15.51	0.85	11.85	16.5	3	97	0	0	45			5.50		Sep-14
100	6.74	16.18	39.27	22.58		0	2.2	15.52	0.86	11.56	16.5	3	97	0	0	45				1.00	Sep-14
	6.98	16.82	40.63	26.48		0	1.2	15.52	0.86	11.94	16.5	3	97	0	0	45					Sep-14
	6.98	16.82	40.80	26.34		0	1.2	15.52	0.86	11.94	16.5	3	97	0	0	45					Sep-14
100	5.54	9.94	15.58	15.56	68.69	2.22	1.16	9.73	0.9	16.62	2,034	1	95	0	1	75	20.01	-17.15	5.50		Apr-04
100	5.38	9.49	14.62	12.96	62.41	1.75	1.91	9.73	0.9	15.33	2,034	1	95	0	1	75	19.49	-17.44		5.00	Apr-04
100	5.41	9.53	14.68	13.02	62.52	1.75	1.91	9.73	0.9	15.29	2,034	1	95	0	1	75	19.63	-17.48		1.00	Dec-97
	5.64	10.06	15.96	16.78	71.74	2.52	0.79	9.72	0.9	16.63	2,034	1	95	0	1	75	20.31	-17.02			Jan-11
	5.46	9.78	15.20	14.62	66.61	1.99	1.41	9.71	0.9	16.62	2,034	1	95	0	1	75	19.86	-17.25			Jan-11
	5.63	10.03	15.81	16.37	70.75	2.44	0.91	9.74	0.9	16.6	2,034	1	95	0	1	75	20.26	-17.11			Aug-08

	MARKET			FUND TYPE, CATEGORY & OBJECTIVE	RATINGS				MINIMUMS	
Fund Name	Ticker Symbol	Traded On	Fund Type	Category and (Prospectus Objective)	Overall Rating	Reward Rating	Risk Rating	Recent Up/ Downgrade	Open to New Investors	Min Initial Investment
Prudential Jennison Equity Opportunity Fund Class A	PJIAX	NAS CM	Open End	US Equity Large Cap Blend (Growth)	B	B-	B	Up	Y	2,500
Prudential Jennison Equity Opportunity Fund Class B	PJIBX	NAS CM	Open End	US Equity Large Cap Blend (Growth)	B-	B-	B	Up		2,500
Prudential Jennison Equity Opportunity Fund Class C	PJGCX	NAS CM	Open End	US Equity Large Cap Blend (Growth)	B-	B-	B	Up	Y	2,500
Prudential Jennison Equity Opportunity Fund Class Q	PJOQX	NAS CM	Open End	US Equity Large Cap Blend (Growth)	B	B	B	Up	Y	5,000,000
Prudential Jennison Equity Opportunity Fund Class R	PJORX	NAS CM	Open End	US Equity Large Cap Blend (Growth)	B	B-	B	Up	Y	0
Prudential Jennison Equity Opportunity Fund Class Z	PJGZX	NAS CM	Open End	US Equity Large Cap Blend (Growth)	B	B	B	Up	Y	5,000,000
Prudential Jennison Financial Services Fund Class A	PFSAX	NAS CM	Open End	Financials Sector Equity (Financial)	C	C+	C		Y	2,500
Prudential Jennison Financial Services Fund Class B	PUFBX	NAS CM	Open End	Financials Sector Equity (Financial)	C	C+	C			2,500
Prudential Jennison Financial Services Fund Class C	PUFCX	NAS CM	Open End	Financials Sector Equity (Financial)	C+	C+	C+	Up	Y	2,500
Prudential Jennison Financial Services Fund Class R	PSSRX	NAS CM	Open End	Financials Sector Equity (Financial)	C	C+	C		Y	0
Prudential Jennison Financial Services Fund Class Z	PFSZX	NAS CM	Open End	Financials Sector Equity (Financial)	C	C+	C		Y	5,000,000
Prudential Jennison Focused Growth Fund Class A	SPFAX	NAS CM	Open End	US Equity Large Cap Growth (Aggr Growth)	A-	A	B+	Up	Y	2,500
Prudential Jennison Focused Growth Fund Class B	SPFBX	NAS CM	Open End	US Equity Large Cap Growth (Aggr Growth)	A-	A-	B+	Up		2,500
Prudential Jennison Focused Growth Fund Class C	SPFCX	NAS CM	Open End	US Equity Large Cap Growth (Aggr Growth)	A-	A-	B+	Up	Y	2,500
Prudential Jennison Focused Growth Fund Class Q	PSGQX	NAS CM	Open End	US Equity Large Cap Growth (Aggr Growth)	A-	A	B+	Up	Y	5,000,000
Prudential Jennison Focused Growth Fund Class Z	SPFZX	NAS CM	Open End	US Equity Large Cap Growth (Aggr Growth)	A-	A	B+	Up	Y	5,000,000
Prudential Jennison Global Infrastructure Fund Class A	PGJAX	NAS CM	Open End	Other Sector Equity (Growth & Income)	C+	C+	C+	Up	Y	2,500
Prudential Jennison Global Infrastructure Fund Class C	PGJCX	NAS CM	Open End	Other Sector Equity (Growth & Income)	C+	C+	C+	Up	Y	2,500
Prudential Jennison Global Infrastructure Fund Class Q	PGJQX	NAS CM	Open End	Other Sector Equity (Growth & Income)	C+	C+	B-		Y	5,000,000
Prudential Jennison Global Infrastructure Fund Class Z	PGJZX	NAS CM	Open End	Other Sector Equity (Growth & Income)	C+	C+	B-	Up	Y	5,000,000
Prudential Jennison Global Opportunities Fund Class A	PRJAX	NAS CM	Open End	Global Equity (World Stock)	A-	A	B	Up	Y	2,500
Prudential Jennison Global Opportunities Fund Class C	PRJCX	NAS CM	Open End	Global Equity (World Stock)	A-	A	B	Up	Y	2,500
Prudential Jennison Global Opportunities Fund Class Q	PRJQX	NAS CM	Open End	Global Equity (World Stock)	A-	A	B	Up	Y	5,000,000
Prudential Jennison Global Opportunities Fund Class Z	PRJZX	NAS CM	Open End	Global Equity (World Stock)	A-	A	B	Up	Y	5,000,000
Prudential Jennison Growth Fund Class A	PJFAX	NAS CM	Open End	US Equity Large Cap Growth (Growth)	A-	A	B+	Up	Y	2,500
Prudential Jennison Growth Fund Class B	PJFBX	NAS CM	Open End	US Equity Large Cap Growth (Growth)	A-	A	B+	Up		2,500
Prudential Jennison Growth Fund Class C	PJFCX	NAS CM	Open End	US Equity Large Cap Growth (Growth)	A-	A	B+	Up	Y	2,500
Prudential Jennison Growth Fund Class Q	PJFQX	NAS CM	Open End	US Equity Large Cap Growth (Growth)	A-	A	B+		Y	5,000,000
Prudential Jennison Growth Fund Class R	PJGRX	NAS CM	Open End	US Equity Large Cap Growth (Growth)	A-	A	B+	Up	Y	0
Prudential Jennison Growth Fund Class R2	PJFOX	NAS CM	Open End	US Equity Large Cap Growth (Growth)	A-	A	B+		Y	0
Prudential Jennison Growth Fund Class R4	PJFPX	NAS CM	Open End	US Equity Large Cap Growth (Growth)	A-	A	B+		Y	0
Prudential Jennison Growth Fund Class Z	PJFZX	NAS CM	Open End	US Equity Large Cap Growth (Growth)	A-	A	B+	Up	Y	5,000,000
Prudential Jennison Health Sciences Class R	PJHRX	NAS CM	Open End	Healthcare Sector Equity (Health)	C+	B-	C	Up		0
Prudential Jennison Health Sciences Fund Class A	PHLAX	NAS CM	Open End	Healthcare Sector Equity (Health)	C+	B-	C	Up		2,500
Prudential Jennison Health Sciences Fund Class B	PHLBX	NAS CM	Open End	Healthcare Sector Equity (Health)	C+	C+	C	Up		2,500
Prudential Jennison Health Sciences Fund Class C	PHLCX	NAS CM	Open End	Healthcare Sector Equity (Health)	C+	C+	C	Up		2,500
Prudential Jennison Health Sciences Fund Class Q	PHLQX	NAS CM	Open End	Healthcare Sector Equity (Health)	C+	B-	C	Up	Y	5,000,000
Prudential Jennison Health Sciences Fund Class Z	PHSZX	NAS CM	Open End	Healthcare Sector Equity (Health)	C+	B-	C	Up		5,000,000
Prudential Jennison International Opportunities Fund Cls A	PWJAX	NAS CM	Open End	Global Equity Large Cap (Foreign Stock)	B+	A-	B-	Up	Y	2,500
Prudential Jennison International Opportunities Fund Cls C	PWJCX	NAS CM	Open End	Global Equity Large Cap (Foreign Stock)	B	B+	B-	Up	Y	2,500
Prudential Jennison International Opportunities Fund Cls Q	PWJQX	NAS CM	Open End	Global Equity Large Cap (Foreign Stock)	B+	A	B	Up	Y	5,000,000
Prudential Jennison International Opportunities Fund Cls R	PWJRX	NAS CM	Open End	Global Equity Large Cap (Foreign Stock)	B	A-	B-		Y	0
Prudential Jennison International Opportunities Fund Cls Z	PWJZX	NAS CM	Open End	Global Equity Large Cap (Foreign Stock)	B+	A	B	Up	Y	5,000,000
Prudential Jennison Mid-Cap Growth Fund, Inc Class A	PEEAX	NAS CM	Open End	US Equity Mid Cap (Growth)	C+	B-	C+	Down		2,500
Prudential Jennison Mid-Cap Growth Fund, Inc Class B	PEEBX	NAS CM	Open End	US Equity Mid Cap (Growth)	B-	C+	B	Up		2,500
Prudential Jennison Mid-Cap Growth Fund, Inc Class C	PEGCX	NAS CM	Open End	US Equity Mid Cap (Growth)	C+	C+	C+	Down		2,500
Prudential Jennison Mid-Cap Growth Fund, Inc Class Q	PJGQX	NAS CM	Open End	US Equity Mid Cap (Growth)	B-	B-	C+	Up		5,000,000
Prudential Jennison Mid-Cap Growth Fund, Inc Class R	JDERX	NAS CM	Open End	US Equity Mid Cap (Growth)	C+	B-	C+	Down		0
Prudential Jennison Mid-Cap Growth Fund, Inc Class Z	PEGZX	NAS CM	Open End	US Equity Mid Cap (Growth)	B-	B-	C+	Up		5,000,000
Prudential Jennison MLP Fund Class A	PRPAX	NAS CM	Open End	Energy Sector Equity (Income)	D	D+	D	Down	Y	2,500
Prudential Jennison MLP Fund Class C	PRPCX	NAS CM	Open End	Energy Sector Equity (Income)	D	D	D	Down	Y	2,500
Prudential Jennison MLP Fund Class Z	PRPZX	NAS CM	Open End	Energy Sector Equity (Income)	D	D+	D	Down	Y	5,000,000

★Expanded analysis of this fund is included in Section II.

Min Additional Investment	TOTAL RETURNS: 3-Month Total Return	6-Month Total Return	1-Year Total Return	3-Year Total Return	5-Year Total Return	PERFORMANCE: Dividend Yield (TTM)	Expense Ratio	3-Yr Std Deviation	3-Year Beta	ASSETS: NAV	Total Assets (MIL)	ASSET ALLOCATION & TURNOVER: %Cash	%Stocks	%Bonds	%Other	Turnover Ratio	BULL & BEAR: Last Bull Market Total Return	Last Bear Market Total Return	FEES: Front End Fee (%)	Back End Fee (%)	Inception Date
100	6.95	10.17	15.95	29.24	91.24	0.67	1.07	12.02	1.1	19.44	430.7	3	96	0	1	49	24.91	-19.94	5.50		Nov-96
100	6.70	9.72	15.06	26.49	84.61	0.29	2.03	12	1.1	15.88	430.7	3	96	0	1	49	24.44	-20.17		5.00	Nov-96
100	6.76	9.77	15.12	26.55	84.70	0.29	1.8	12	1.1	15.88	430.7	3	96	0	1	49	24.44	-20.17		1.00	Nov-96
	6.98	10.39	16.36	30.95	94.94	0.95	0.72	12.01	1.1	20.25	430.7	3	96	0	1	49	25.2	-19.83			Nov-14
	6.77	9.96	15.58	28.37	89.23	0.62	1.53	12.01	1.1	17.04	430.7	3	96	0	1	49	24.79	-19.98			Dec-04
	6.97	10.33	16.25	30.36	94.14	0.87	0.77	12.02	1.1	20.24	430.7	3	96	0	1	49	25.2	-19.83			Nov-96
100	4.69	9.67	23.16	11.78	38.12	1.38	1.42	17.21	0.89	14.35	184.2	3	97	0	0	68	27.52	-30.1	5.50		Jun-99
100	4.42	9.17	22.24	9.40	33.26	1.05	2.12	17.27	0.89	12.87	184.2	3	97	0	0	68	27.04	-30.24		5.00	Jun-99
100	4.50	9.35	22.33	9.49	33.48	1.05	2.12	17.25	0.89	12.88	184.2	3	97	0	0	68	26.93	-30.24		1.00	Jun-99
	4.59	9.57	22.96	11.16	36.81	1.23	1.62	17.21	0.89	14.35	184.2	3	97	0	0	68	27.23	-30.19			Feb-12
	4.72	9.78	23.53	12.81	40.15	1.55	1.12	17.27	0.89	14.79	184.2	3	97	0	0	68	27.71	-29.97			Jun-99
100	6.33	15.17	35.84	45.89	121.37	0	1.24	13.42	1.14	13.91	391.9	3	97	0	0	58	26.1	-12.95	5.50		Jun-00
100	6.13	14.72	34.78	42.62	113.22	0	1.99	13.41	1.14	11.42	391.9	3	97	0	0	58	25.51	-13.21		5.00	Jun-00
100	6.13	14.73	34.82	42.66	113.12	0	1.99	13.4	1.14	11.41	391.9	3	97	0	0	58	25.51	-13.11		1.00	Jun-00
	6.37	15.25	36.19	47.00	123.95	0	0.99	13.43	1.14	14.82	391.9	3	97	0	0	58	26.31	-12.8			May-12
	6.36	15.30	36.21	46.99	124.01	0	0.99	13.44	1.15	14.85	391.9	3	97	0	0	58	26.31	-12.8			Jun-00
100	2.91	6.59	18.52	15.10		1.4	1.5	10.67	0.7	13.39	71.8	2	98	0	0				5.50		Sep-13
100	2.72	6.14	17.56	12.57		0.87	2.25	10.61	0.7	13.3	71.8	2	98	0	0					1.00	Sep-13
	2.94	6.69	18.83	16.06			1.25	10.63	0.7	13.39	71.8	2	98	0	0						Dec-16
	2.94	6.69	18.80	16.03		1.62	1.25	10.62	0.7	13.39	71.8	2	98	0	0						Sep-13
100	5.37	16.77	42.97	52.23	108.88	0	1.2	13.49	1.06	21.16	584.4	2	98	0	0	79			5.50		Mar-12
100	5.14	16.32	41.93	48.82	101.19	0	1.95	13.49	1.06	20.24	584.4	2	98	0	0	79				1.00	Mar-12
	5.49	16.95	43.46	53.82	112.17	0	0.84	13.52	1.07	21.52	584.4	2	98	0	0	79					Dec-14
	5.45	16.94	43.35	53.28	111.42	0	0.95	13.51	1.07	21.46	584.4	2	98	0	0	79					Mar-12
100	7.13	16.26	36.36	47.58	127.94	0	1.04	12.68	1.11	36.21	4,586	1	99	0	0	54	27.01	-14	5.50		Nov-95
100	6.88	15.79	35.36	44.40	119.96	0	1.95	12.68	1.11	29.12	4,586	1	99	0	0	54	26.57	-14.26		5.00	Nov-95
100	6.93	15.83	35.41	44.49	120.19	0	1.71	12.66	1.11	29.2	4,586	1	99	0	0	54	26.52	-14.24		1.00	Nov-95
	7.27	16.41	36.54	47.77	128.23		0.6	12.68	1.11	38.95	4,586	1	99	0	0	54	27.01	-14			Sep-17
	7.07	16.15	36.12	46.67	125.68	0	1.22	12.66	1.11	31.84	4,586	1	99	0	0	54	26.97	-14.11			Dec-04
	7.14	16.27	36.37	47.60	127.96		1.1	12.68	1.11	38.93	4,586	1	99	0	0	54	27.01	-14			Nov-17
	7.14	16.27	36.38	47.60	127.96		0.85	12.68	1.11	38.94	4,586	1	99	0	0	54	27.01	-14			Nov-17
	7.21	16.46	36.78	48.92	131.46	0	0.68	12.67	1.11	38.94	4,586	1	99	0	0	54	27.29	-13.92			Apr-96
	1.86	7.09	30.73	16.56	149.54	0	1.37	21.44	1.51	44.11	2,301	3	96	0	0	25	31.8	-14.52			Feb-12
100	1.92	7.20	31.00	17.24	151.98	0	1.17	21.44	1.51	44.81	2,301	3	96	0	0	25	32.14	-14.36	5.50		Jun-99
100	1.72	6.80	30.05	14.79	143.29	0	1.87	21.41	1.51	34.31	2,301	3	96	0	0	25	31.59	-14.59		5.00	Jun-99
100	1.75	6.81	30.11	14.80	143.37	0	1.87	21.43	1.51	34.3	2,301	3	96	0	0	25	31.65	-14.63		1.00	Jun-99
	2.01	7.39	31.49	18.51	156.25	0	0.75	21.45	1.51	49.35	2,301	3	96	0	0	25	32.36	-14.25			Jan-16
	1.99	7.36	31.39	18.31	155.81	0	0.87	21.44	1.51	49.26	2,301	3	96	0	0	25	32.36	-14.25			Jun-99
100	5.72	19.57	49.06	38.46	54.37	0	1.26	14.55	1	17.53	63.9	1	99	0	0	69			5.50		Jun-12
100	5.58	19.20	47.93	35.42	48.81	0	1.98	14.53	1	16.82	63.9	1	99	0	0	69				1.00	Jun-12
	5.82	19.84	49.55	39.75	56.51	0.21	0.84	14.55	1	17.7	63.9	1	99	0	0	69					Dec-15
	5.66	19.36	48.39	36.42	50.50		1.5	14.57	1	17.63	63.9	1	99	0	0	69					Nov-17
	5.91	19.86	49.58	39.58	56.31	0.16	0.86	14.58	1	17.71	63.9	1	99	0	0	69					Jun-12
100	5.25	9.62	22.27	22.74	75.17	0	1.08	10.59	0.92	35.27	7,052	4	96	0	0	34	27.24	-17.26	5.50		Dec-96
100	5.00	9.16	21.34	20.08	68.98	0	1.99	10.58	0.92	27.43	7,052	4	96	0	0	34	26.75	-17.52		5.00	Dec-96
100	5.07	9.27	21.45	20.23	69.13	0	1.72	10.59	0.92	27.47	7,052	4	96	0	0	34	26.7	-17.51		1.00	Dec-96
	5.38	9.90	22.87	24.50	79.34	0	0.58	10.59	0.92	38.49	7,052	4	96	0	0	34	27.58	-17.1			Jan-11
	5.19	9.51	22.03	22.03	73.44	0	1.26	10.6	0.92	34.08	7,052	4	96	0	0	34	27.05	-17.32			Jun-05
	5.33	9.78	22.66	23.87	77.80	0	0.79	10.6	0.92	38.06	7,052	4	96	0	0	34	27.45	-17.17			Dec-96
100	-1.08	-2.31	-4.51	-21.26		6.67	3.27	19.26	0.93	7.34	433.5	2	94	0	0	37			5.50		Dec-13
100	-1.39	-2.65	-5.27	-23.03		6.89	4.02	19.26	0.92	7.09	433.5	2	94	0	0	37				1.00	Dec-13
	-1.20	-2.28	-4.35	-20.72		6.59	3.02	19.26	0.92	7.42	433.5	2	94	0	0	37					Dec-13

	MARKET		FUND TYPE, CATEGORY & OBJECTIVE		RATINGS					MINIMUMS
Fund Name	Ticker Symbol	Traded On	Fund Type	Category and (Prospectus Objective)	Overall Rating	Reward Rating	Risk Rating	Recent Up/ Downgrade	Open to New Investors	Min Initial Investment
Prudential Jennison Natural Resources Fund Class A	PGNAX	NAS CM	Open End	Natl Resources Sec Equity (Natl Res)	C	C	C-	Up	Y	2,500
Prudential Jennison Natural Resources Fund Class B	PRGNX	NAS CM	Open End	Natl Resources Sec Equity (Natl Res)	C	C	C-	Up		2,500
Prudential Jennison Natural Resources Fund Class C	PNRCX	NAS CM	Open End	Natl Resources Sec Equity (Natl Res)	C	C	C-	Up	Y	2,500
Prudential Jennison Natural Resources Fund Class Q	PJNQX	NAS CM	Open End	Natl Resources Sec Equity (Natl Res)	C	C	C-	Up	Y	5,000,000
Prudential Jennison Natural Resources Fund Class R	JNRRX	NAS CM	Open End	Natl Resources Sec Equity (Natl Res)	C	C	C-	Up	Y	0
Prudential Jennison Natural Resources Fund Class Z	PNRZX	NAS CM	Open End	Natl Resources Sec Equity (Natl Res)	C	C	C-	Up	Y	5,000,000
Prudential Jennison Rising Dividend Fund Class A	PJDAX	NAS CM	Open End	US Equity Large Cap Blend (Equity-Income)	B-	B-	B-	Down	Y	2,500
Prudential Jennison Rising Dividend Fund Class C	PJDCX	NAS CM	Open End	US Equity Large Cap Blend (Equity-Income)	B-	B-	B-	Down	Y	2,500
Prudential Jennison Rising Dividend Fund Class Q	PJDQX	NAS CM	Open End	US Equity Large Cap Blend (Equity-Income)	B-	B-	B-		Y	5,000,000
Prudential Jennison Rising Dividend Fund Class Z	PJDZX	NAS CM	Open End	US Equity Large Cap Blend (Equity-Income)	B-	B-	B-	Down	Y	5,000,000
Prudential Jennison Small Company Fund Class A	PGOAX	NAS CM	Open End	US Equity Small Cap (Small Company)	B	B	B	Up	Y	2,500
Prudential Jennison Small Company Fund Class B	CHNDX	NAS CM	Open End	US Equity Small Cap (Small Company)	B	B	B	Up		2,500
Prudential Jennison Small Company Fund Class C	PSCCX	NAS CM	Open End	US Equity Small Cap (Small Company)	B	B	B	Up	Y	2,500
Prudential Jennison Small Company Fund Class Q	PJSQX	NAS CM	Open End	US Equity Small Cap (Small Company)	B	B	B	Up	Y	5,000,000
Prudential Jennison Small Company Fund Class R	JSCRX	NAS CM	Open End	US Equity Small Cap (Small Company)	B	B	B	Up	Y	0
Prudential Jennison Small Company Fund Class R2	PSCHX	NAS CM	Open End	US Equity Small Cap (Small Company)	B	B	B		Y	0
Prudential Jennison Small Company Fund Class R4	PSCJX	NAS CM	Open End	US Equity Small Cap (Small Company)	B	B	B		Y	0
Prudential Jennison Small Company Fund Class Z	PSCZX	NAS CM	Open End	US Equity Small Cap (Small Company)	B	B	B	Up	Y	5,000,000
Prudential Jennison Small-Cap Core Equity Fund Class Q	PQJCX	NAS CM	Open End	US Equity Small Cap (Small Company)	D	D+	B+		Y	0
Prudential Jennison Utility Fund Class A	PRUAX	NAS CM	Open End	Utilities Sector Equity (Utility)	C+	B-	C+	Down	Y	2,500
Prudential Jennison Utility Fund Class B	PRUTX	NAS CM	Open End	Utilities Sector Equity (Utility)	C+	C+	C+	Down		2,500
Prudential Jennison Utility Fund Class C	PCUFX	NAS CM	Open End	Utilities Sector Equity (Utility)	C+	C+	C+	Down	Y	2,500
Prudential Jennison Utility Fund Class R	JDURX	NAS CM	Open End	Utilities Sector Equity (Utility)	C+	C+	C+	Down	Y	0
Prudential Jennison Utility Fund Class Z	PRUZX	NAS CM	Open End	Utilities Sector Equity (Utility)	C+	B-	C+	Down	Y	5,000,000
Prudential Jennison Value Fund Class A	PBEAX	NAS CM	Open End	US Equity Large Cap Value (Growth)	C+	C+	C+	Down	Y	2,500
Prudential Jennison Value Fund Class B	PBQIX	NAS CM	Open End	US Equity Large Cap Value (Growth)	C+	C+	C+			2,500
Prudential Jennison Value Fund Class C	PEICX	NAS CM	Open End	US Equity Large Cap Value (Growth)	C+	C+	C+		Y	2,500
Prudential Jennison Value Fund Class Q	PJVQX	NAS CM	Open End	US Equity Large Cap Value (Growth)	C+	C+	C	Down	Y	5,000,000
Prudential Jennison Value Fund Class R	JDVRX	NAS CM	Open End	US Equity Large Cap Value (Growth)	C+	C+	C+	Down	Y	0
Prudential Jennison Value Fund Class Z	PEIZX	NAS CM	Open End	US Equity Large Cap Value (Growth)	C+	C+	C+	Down	Y	5,000,000
Prudential Moderate Allocation Fund Class A	JDTAX	NAS CM	Open End	Moderate Alloc (Balanced)	B-	C+	B	Down	Y	2,500
Prudential Moderate Allocation Fund Class B	JDMBX	NAS CM	Open End	Moderate Alloc (Balanced)	B-	C+	B-	Down		2,500
Prudential Moderate Allocation Fund Class C	JDMCX	NAS CM	Open End	Moderate Alloc (Balanced)	B-	C+	B-	Down	Y	2,500
Prudential Moderate Allocation Fund Class Q	JDTQX	NAS CM	Open End	Moderate Alloc (Balanced)	B-	C+	B-		Y	5,000,000
Prudential Moderate Allocation Fund Class R	JMARX	NAS CM	Open End	Moderate Alloc (Balanced)	B-	C+	B	Down	Y	0
Prudential Moderate Allocation Fund Class Z	JDMZX	NAS CM	Open End	Moderate Alloc (Balanced)	B-	C+	B	Down	Y	5,000,000
Prudential QMA Defensive Equity Fund Class A	PAMGX	NAS CM	Open End	US Equity Large Cap Blend (Growth)	B-	B-	B	Down	Y	2,500
Prudential QMA Defensive Equity Fund Class B	DMGBX	NAS CM	Open End	US Equity Large Cap Blend (Growth)	B-	C+	B	Down		2,500
Prudential QMA Defensive Equity Fund Class C	PIMGX	NAS CM	Open End	US Equity Large Cap Blend (Growth)	B-	C+	B	Down	Y	2,500
Prudential QMA Defensive Equity Fund Class Q	PAMQX	NAS CM	Open End	US Equity Large Cap Blend (Growth)	B-	B-	B	Down	Y	5,000,000
Prudential QMA Defensive Equity Fund Class Retirement	SPMRX	NAS CM	Open End	US Equity Large Cap Blend (Growth)	B-	B-	B	Down	Y	0
Prudential QMA Defensive Equity Fund Class Z	PDMZX	NAS CM	Open End	US Equity Large Cap Blend (Growth)	B-	B-	B	Down	Y	5,000,000
Prudential QMA Emerging Markets Equity Fund Class Q	PQEMX	NAS CM	Open End	Emerging Markets Equity (Div Emerging Mkts)	D	D+	B+		Y	0
Prudential QMA Global Tactical Allocation Fund Class A	PTALX	NAS CM	Open End	Multialternative (Asset Alloc)	C+	C	B	Up	Y	2,500
Prudential QMA Global Tactical Allocation Fund Class C	PTCLX	NAS CM	Open End	Multialternative (Asset Alloc)	C+	C	B	Up	Y	2,500
Prudential QMA Global Tactical Allocation Fund Class Q	PTQLX	NAS CM	Open End	Multialternative (Asset Alloc)	C+	C	B	Up	Y	5,000,000
Prudential QMA Global Tactical Allocation Fund Class Z	PTZLX	NAS CM	Open End	Multialternative (Asset Alloc)	B-	C	B	Up	Y	5,000,000
Prudential QMA Intl Developed Mkts Index Fund Cls Q	PQDMX	NAS CM	Open End	Global Equity Large Cap (Growth & Income)	D	D+	A		Y	0
Prudential QMA International Equity Fund Class A	PJRAX	NAS CM	Open End	Global Equity Large Cap (Foreign Stock)	B-	B-	B-	Up	Y	2,500
Prudential QMA International Equity Fund Class B	PJRBX	NAS CM	Open End	Global Equity Large Cap (Foreign Stock)	C+	C+	C+	Up		2,500
Prudential QMA International Equity Fund Class C	PJRCX	NAS CM	Open End	Global Equity Large Cap (Foreign Stock)	C+	C+	C+	Up	Y	2,500
Prudential QMA International Equity Fund Class Q	PJRQX	NAS CM	Open End	Global Equity Large Cap (Foreign Stock)	B-	B-	B-	Up	Y	5,000,000

★ Expanded analysis of this fund is included in Section II.

Min Additional Investment	3-Month Total Return	6-Month Total Return	1-Year Total Return	3-Year Total Return	5-Year Total Return	Dividend Yield (TTM)	Expense Ratio	3-Yr Std Deviation	3-Year Beta	NAV	Total Assets (MIL)	%Cash	%Stocks	%Bonds	%Other	Turnover Ratio	Last Bull Market Total Return	Last Bear Market Total Return	Front End Fee (%)	Back End Fee (%)	Inception Date
TOTAL RETURNS						PERFORMANCE				ASSETS		ASSET ALLOCATION & TURNOVER					BULL & BEAR		FEES		
100	8.82	18.56	4.95	-0.99	-10.36	0.85	1.25	22.36	1.2	38.95	1,517	4	95	0	1	32	17.35	-32.96	5.50		Jan-90
100	8.56	18.05	4.19	-3.11	-13.49	1.06	1.95	22.35	1.2	31.32	1,517	4	95	0	1	32	16.88	-33.15		5.00	Sep-87
100	8.59	18.13	4.22	-3.08	-13.48	1.06	1.95	22.35	1.2	31.34	1,517	4	95	0	1	32	16.85	-33.14		1.00	Aug-94
	8.92	18.80	5.44	0.42	-8.30	1.2	0.77	22.37	1.2	40.88	1,517	4	95	0	1	32	17.65	-32.83			Dec-10
	8.71	18.39	4.70	-1.63	-11.31	0.87	1.45	22.36	1.2	38.3	1,517	4	95	0	1	32	17.21	-33.01			Aug-06
	8.90	18.71	5.29	-0.09	-9.01	1.04	0.95	22.37	1.2	40.59	1,517	4	95	0	1	32	17.55	-32.86			Sep-96
100	5.13	9.70	17.25	24.13		1.01	1.24	10.19	0.98	13.31	13.8	2	98	0	0	67			5.50		Mar-14
100	4.92	9.37	16.39	21.49		0.35	1.99	10.23	0.98	13.32	13.8	2	98	0	0	67				1.00	Mar-14
	5.20	9.84	17.53	25.14			0.99	10.19	0.98	13.32	13.8	2	98	0	0	67					Sep-17
	5.20	9.84	17.53	25.14		1.23	0.99	10.19	0.98	13.32	13.8	2	98	0	0	67					Mar-14
100	4.86	9.26	19.45	29.26	91.37	0.51	1.15	11.91	0.92	24.94	3,704	4	96	0	0	41	25.94	-23.87	5.50		Jan-90
100	4.55	8.77	18.49	26.32	84.66	0.53	2.04	11.94	0.92	13.55	3,704	4	96	0	0	41	25.19	-24		5.00	Nov-80
100	4.61	8.77	18.51	26.41	84.34	0.52	1.85	11.93	0.92	13.79	3,704	4	96	0	0	41	25.4	-24.05		1.00	Aug-94
	4.97	9.51	20.03	31.11	95.73	0.81	0.68	11.91	0.92	26.41	3,704	4	96	0	0	41	26.51	-25.37			Nov-10
	4.81	9.15	19.26	28.57	89.48	0.38	1.33	11.87	0.92	24.3	3,704	4	96	0	0	41	25.74	-23.85			May-04
	4.75	8.98	18.72	26.57	85.02		1.18	11.94	0.92	26.42	3,704	4	96	0	0	41	25.19	-24			Nov-17
	4.78	9.00	18.75	26.60	85.06		0.93	11.94	0.92	26.42	3,704	4	96	0	0	41	25.19	-24			Nov-17
	4.84	9.30	19.67	30.26	93.89	0.69	0.81	11.92	0.92	26.83	3,704	4	96	0	0	41	26	-23.63			Mar-96
	4.55	8.94	19.28			0.14	0.95			11.98	13.9	3	97	0	0						Nov-16
100	1.19	4.46	13.78	13.51	77.52	1.45	0.85	10.95	0.63	14.11	3,412	2	97	0	1	47	19.6	-12.16	5.50		Jan-90
100	1.05	4.14	13.04	11.15	71.48	0.86	1.55	11	0.63	14.07	3,412	2	97	0	1	47	19.11	-12.49		5.00	Aug-81
100	1.04	4.14	12.97	11.09	71.45	0.86	1.55	10.99	0.63	14.05	3,412	2	97	0	1	47	19.23	-12.5		1.00	Aug-94
	1.15	4.37	13.57	12.77	75.84	1.28	1.05	11	0.63	14.1	3,412	2	97	0	1	47	19.5	-12.26			Aug-06
	1.32	4.67	14.19	14.58	80.35	1.71	0.55	10.99	0.63	14.13	3,412	2	97	0	1	47	19.78	-12.1			Mar-96
100	6.13	10.05	16.24	16.37	73.46	1.01	1.09	11.62	1.09	20.3	524.4	0	99	0	1	15	19.96	-23.22	5.50		Jan-90
100	5.90	9.56	15.36	13.83	67.37	0.49	2.06	11.57	1.08	19.64	524.4	0	99	0	1	15	19.49	-23.47		5.00	Jan-87
100	5.95	9.67	15.42	13.89	67.38	0.49	1.9	11.59	1.08	19.63	524.4	0	99	0	1	15	19.41	-23.42		1.00	Aug-94
	6.22	10.25	16.75	17.83	77.13	1.36	0.7	11.58	1.08	20.29	524.4	0	99	0	1	15	20.19	-23.47			Oct-11
	6.04	9.92	16.00	15.61	71.57	0.85	1.47	11.57	1.08	20.26	524.4	0	99	0	1	15	19.74	-23.21			Jun-05
	6.21	10.24	16.61	17.42	76.00	1.24	0.78	11.58	1.08	20.32	524.4	0	99	0	1	15	20.05	-23.07			Mar-96
100	4.03	8.30	15.92	20.31	49.36	1.02	1.34	6.71		15.15	171.0	2	59	17	21	19	14.8	-13.62	5.50		Mar-04
100	3.88	7.90	15.04	17.68	43.91	0.4	2.09	6.7		15.07	171.0	2	59	17	21	19	14.22	-13.86		5.00	Mar-04
100	3.88	7.90	15.05	17.60	43.94	0.4	2.09	6.73		15.06	171.0	2	59	17	21	19	14.33	-13.93		1.00	Mar-04
	4.20	8.48	16.27	21.28	51.42		1.09	6.7		15.16	171.0	2	59	17	21	19	14.99	-13.55			Nov-17
	4.07	8.15	15.72	19.28	47.20	0.81	1.59	6.78		15.08	171.0	2	59	17	21	19	14.65	-13.73			Jan-07
	4.13	8.40	16.19	21.19	51.31	1.23	1.09	6.7		15.15	171.0	2	59	17	21	19	14.99	-13.55			Mar-04
100	5.86	9.46	16.31	25.61	70.08	1.07	1.3	9.07	0.86	14.8	235.6	5	95	0	0		15.16	-12.33	5.50		Nov-98
100	5.56	9.02	15.36	22.69	63.75	0.44	2.05	9.02	0.86	14.75	235.6	5	95	0	0		14.65	-12.55		5.00	Nov-98
100	5.60	9.06	15.40	22.74	63.83	0.44	2.05	9.05	0.86	14.75	235.6	5	95	0	0		14.65	-12.55		1.00	Nov-98
	5.86	9.60	16.69	26.53	72.36		0.9	9.04	0.86	14.83	235.6	5	95	0	0		15.33	-12.23			Dec-16
	6.94	10.59	17.34	26.01	69.82	0.85	1.55	9.07	0.86	14.96	235.6	5	95	0	0		14.99	-12.43			Oct-04
	5.85	9.59	16.60	26.44	72.23	1.27	1.05	9.04	0.86	14.82	235.6	5	95	0	0		15.33	-12.23			Nov-98
	6.44	14.72	37.34			0.27	1.2			12.84	28.8	0	99	0	0						Nov-16
100	4.51	6.88	11.59			0.54	1.5			9.88	33.4	83	17	0	0	0			5.50		Apr-15
100	4.36	6.65	10.92			0.55	2.25			9.75	33.4	83	17	0	0	0				1.00	Apr-15
	4.61	7.09	11.88			0.71	1.25			9.91	33.4	83	17	0	0	0					Apr-15
	4.60	7.08	11.88			0.71	1.25			9.91	33.4	83	17	0	0	0					Apr-15
	3.74	9.12	25.33			0.07	0.3			12.51	31.4	5	95	0	0	7					Nov-16
100	3.96	11.07	28.27	21.53	41.79	1.59	1.56	11.81	0.95	7.97	283.9	0	100	0	0		15.61	-24.12	5.50		Mar-00
100	3.58	10.37	27.05	18.81	36.63	1.13	2.53	11.77	0.94	7.65	283.9	0	100	0	0		15.15	-24.27		5.00	Mar-00
100	3.71	10.51	27.21	18.96	36.81	1.13	2.33	11.73	0.94	7.65	283.9	0	100	0	0		15.15	-24.27		1.00	Mar-00
	4.12	11.32	28.97	22.99	44.23		0.78	11.82	0.95	8.02	283.9	0	100	0	0		15.87	-23.98			Dec-16

	MARKET			FUND TYPE, CATEGORY & OBJECTIVE	RATINGS					MINIMUMS
Fund Name	Ticker Symbol	Traded On	Fund Type	Category and (Prospectus Objective)	Overall Rating	Reward Rating	Risk Rating	Recent Up/ Downgrade	Open to New Investors	Min Initial Investment
Prudential QMA International Equity Fund Class Z	PJIZX	NAS CM	Open End	Global Equity Large Cap (Foreign Stock)	B-	B-	B-	Up	Y	5,000,000
Prudential QMA Large-Cap Core Equity Class Q	PTMQX	NAS CM	Open End	US Equity Large Cap Blend (Growth)	B	B	B		Y	5,000,000
Prudential QMA Large-Cap Core Equity Fund Class A	PTMAX	NAS CM	Open End	US Equity Large Cap Blend (Growth)	B	B	B-		Y	2,500
Prudential QMA Large-Cap Core Equity Fund Class B	PTMBX	NAS CM	Open End	US Equity Large Cap Blend (Growth)	B	B	B-			2,500
Prudential QMA Large-Cap Core Equity Fund Class C	PTMCX	NAS CM	Open End	US Equity Large Cap Blend (Growth)	B	B	B-		Y	2,500
Prudential QMA Large-Cap Core Equity Fund Class Z	PTEZX	NAS CM	Open End	US Equity Large Cap Blend (Growth)	B	B	B		Y	5,000,000
Prudential QMA Large-Cap Core Equity Plus Fund Class A	PQMAX	NAS CM	Open End	US Equity Large Cap Blend (Growth)	U	U	U		Y	2,500
Prudential QMA Large-Cap Core Equity Plus Fund Class C	PQMCX	NAS CM	Open End	US Equity Large Cap Blend (Growth)	U	U	U		Y	2,500
Prudential QMA Large-Cap Core Equity Plus Fund Class Q	PQMQX	NAS CM	Open End	US Equity Large Cap Blend (Growth)	U	U	U		Y	5,000,000
Prudential QMA Large-Cap Core Equity Plus Fund Class Z	PQMZX	NAS CM	Open End	US Equity Large Cap Blend (Growth)	U	U	U		Y	5,000,000
Prudential QMA Long-Short Equity Fund Class A	PLHAX	NAS CM	Open End	Long/Short Equity (Equity-Income)	B	C+	A+	Up	Y	2,500
Prudential QMA Long-Short Equity Fund Class C	PLHCX	NAS CM	Open End	Long/Short Equity (Equity-Income)	B	C+	A-	Up	Y	2,500
Prudential QMA Long-Short Equity Fund Class Q	PLHQX	NAS CM	Open End	Long/Short Equity (Equity-Income)	B	C+	A-	Up	Y	5,000,000
Prudential QMA Long-Short Equity Fund Class Z	PLHZX	NAS CM	Open End	Long/Short Equity (Equity-Income)	B	C+	A-	Up	Y	5,000,000
Prudential QMA Mid-Cap Core Equity Fund Class Q	PQCCX	NAS CM	Open End	US Equity Mid Cap (Growth & Income)	D	D+	B+		Y	0
Prudential QMA Mid-Cap Value Fund Class A	SPRAX	NAS CM	Open End	US Equity Mid Cap (Growth)	B-	B-	B	Up	Y	2,500
Prudential QMA Mid-Cap Value Fund Class B	SVUBX	NAS CM	Open End	US Equity Mid Cap (Growth)	B-	C+	B	Up		2,500
Prudential QMA Mid-Cap Value Fund Class C	NCBVX	NAS CM	Open End	US Equity Mid Cap (Growth)	B-	C+	B	Up	Y	2,500
Prudential QMA Mid-Cap Value Fund Class Q	PMVQX	NAS CM	Open End	US Equity Mid Cap (Growth)	B	B-	B	Up	Y	5,000,000
Prudential QMA Mid-Cap Value Fund Class R	SDVRX	NAS CM	Open End	US Equity Mid Cap (Growth)	B-	B-	B	Up	Y	0
Prudential QMA Mid-Cap Value Fund Class Z	SPVZX	NAS CM	Open End	US Equity Mid Cap (Growth)	B	B-	B	Up	Y	5,000,000
Prudential QMA Small-Cap Value Fund Class A	TSVAX	NAS CM	Open End	US Equity Small Cap (Small Company)	B	A-	B-	Up	Y	2,500
Prudential QMA Small-Cap Value Fund Class C	TRACX	NAS CM	Open End	US Equity Small Cap (Small Company)	B	B+	B-	Up	Y	2,500
Prudential QMA Small-Cap Value Fund Class Q	TSVQX	NAS CM	Open End	US Equity Small Cap (Small Company)	B+	A-	B-	Up	Y	5,000,000
Prudential QMA Small-Cap Value Fund Class Retirement	TSVRX	NAS CM	Open End	US Equity Small Cap (Small Company)	B	B+	B-	Up	Y	0
Prudential QMA Small-Cap Value Fund Class Z	TASVX	NAS CM	Open End	US Equity Small Cap (Small Company)	B	A-	B-	Up	Y	5,000,000
Prudential QMA Stock Index Fund Class A	PSIAX	NAS CM	Open End	US Equity Large Cap Blend (Growth)	B	B	B		Y	2,500
Prudential QMA Stock Index Fund Class C	PSICX	NAS CM	Open End	US Equity Large Cap Blend (Growth)	B-	B-	B	Down	Y	2,500
Prudential QMA Stock Index Fund Class I	PDSIX	NAS CM	Open End	US Equity Large Cap Blend (Growth)	B	B	B		Y	0
Prudential QMA Stock Index Fund Class Q	PQSIX	NAS CM	Open End	US Equity Large Cap Blend (Growth)	B	B	B		Y	5,000,000
Prudential QMA Stock Index Fund Class Z	PSIFX	NAS CM	Open End	US Equity Large Cap Blend (Growth)	B	B	B		Y	5,000,000
Prudential QMA Strategic Value Fund Class A	SUVAX	NAS CM	Open End	US Equity Large Cap Value (Growth)	B	B	B	Up	Y	2,500
Prudential QMA Strategic Value Fund Class B	SUVBX	NAS CM	Open End	US Equity Large Cap Value (Growth)	B-	B	B-	Down		2,500
Prudential QMA Strategic Value Fund Class C	SUVCX	NAS CM	Open End	US Equity Large Cap Value (Growth)	B-	B	B-	Down	Y	2,500
Prudential QMA Strategic Value Fund Class Q	SUVQX	NAS CM	Open End	US Equity Large Cap Value (Growth)	B	B	B	Up	Y	5,000,000
Prudential QMA Strategic Value Fund Class R	PRVRX	NAS CM	Open End	US Equity Large Cap Value (Growth)	B	B	B-	Up	Y	0
Prudential QMA Strategic Value Fund Class Z	SUVZX	NAS CM	Open End	US Equity Large Cap Value (Growth)	B	B	B	Up	Y	5,000,000
Prudential QMA US Broad Market Index Fund Class Q	PQBMX	NAS CM	Open End	US Equity Large Cap Blend (Growth & Income)	D	D+	A-		Y	0
Prudential Real Assets Fund Class A	PUDAX	NAS CM	Open End	Moderate Alloc (Growth & Income)	C	C	C	Up	Y	2,500
Prudential Real Assets Fund Class B	PUDBX	NAS CM	Open End	Moderate Alloc (Growth & Income)	C	C-	C	Up		2,500
Prudential Real Assets Fund Class C	PUDCX	NAS CM	Open End	Moderate Alloc (Growth & Income)	C	C-	C	Up	Y	2,500
Prudential Real Assets Fund Class Q	PUDQX	NAS CM	Open End	Moderate Alloc (Growth & Income)	C	C	C	Up	Y	5,000,000
Prudential Real Assets Fund Class Z	PUDZX	NAS CM	Open End	Moderate Alloc (Growth & Income)	C	C	C	Up	Y	5,000,000
Prudential Real Estate Income Fund Class A	PRKAX	NAS CM	Open End	Real Estate Sector Equity (Real Estate)	C	C	B	Up	Y	2,500
Prudential Real Estate Income Fund Class C	PRKCX	NAS CM	Open End	Real Estate Sector Equity (Real Estate)	C	C	B	Up	Y	2,500
Prudential Real Estate Income Fund Class Q	PRKQX	NAS CM	Open End	Real Estate Sector Equity (Real Estate)	C	C	B	Up	Y	5,000,000
Prudential Real Estate Income Fund Class Z	PRKZX	NAS CM	Open End	Real Estate Sector Equity (Real Estate)	C	C	B	Up	Y	5,000,000
Prudential Select Real Estate Fund Class A	SREAX	NAS CM	Open End	Real Estate Sector Equity (Real Estate)	B	C+	A-	Up	Y	2,500
Prudential Select Real Estate Fund Class C	SRECX	NAS CM	Open End	Real Estate Sector Equity (Real Estate)	B-	C+	B+	Up	Y	2,500
Prudential Select Real Estate Fund Class Q	SREQX	NAS CM	Open End	Real Estate Sector Equity (Real Estate)	B	C+	A-	Up	Y	5,000,000
Prudential Select Real Estate Fund Class Z	SREZX	NAS CM	Open End	Real Estate Sector Equity (Real Estate)	B	C+	A-	Up	Y	5,000,000
Prudential US Real Estate Fund Class A	PJEAX	NAS CM	Open End	Real Estate Sector Equity (Real Estate)	B-	C+	B	Up	Y	2,500

★ Expanded analysis of this fund is included in Section II.

Min Additional Investment	3-Month Total Return	6-Month Total Return	1-Year Total Return	3-Year Total Return	5-Year Total Return	Dividend Yield (TTM)	Expense Ratio	3-Yr Std Deviation	3-Year Beta	NAV	Total Assets (MIL)	%Cash	%Stocks	%Bonds	%Other	Turnover Ratio	Last Bull Market Total Return	Last Bear Market Total Return	Front End Fee (%)	Back End Fee (%)	Inception Date
	TOTAL RETURNS					PERFORMANCE				ASSETS		ASSET ALLOCATION & TURNOVER					BULL & BEAR		FEES		
	3.96	11.15	28.60	22.64	43.82	1.81	1.16	11.81	0.94	8.02	283.9	0	100	0	0		15.87	-23.98			Mar-00
	7.62	13.89	23.59	35.87	112.51		0.35	10.4	1.02	17.04	269.8	2	98	0	0	89	26.82	-17.67			Dec-16
100	7.47	13.62	23.07	34.63	109.55	0.77	0.73	10.4	1.02	16.62	269.8	2	98	0	0	89	26.67	-17.7	5.50		Mar-99
100	7.21	13.12	22.12	31.54	101.68	0.26	1.48	10.38	1.02	15.14	269.8	2	98	0	0	89	26.05	-17.98		5.00	Mar-99
100	7.31	13.21	22.21	31.72	101.87	0.26	1.48	10.4	1.02	15.17	269.8	2	98	0	0	89	26.02	-17.9		1.00	Mar-99
	7.55	13.77	23.39	35.65	112.16	0.94	0.48	10.4	1.02	17.02	269.8	2	98	0	0	89	26.82	-17.67			Mar-99
100	7.27						1.2			10.72	21.2								5.50		Sep-17
100	7.05						1.95			10.72	21.2									1.00	Sep-17
	7.24						0.95			10.72	21.2										Sep-17
	7.04						0.95			10.7	21.2										Sep-17
100	3.15	6.96	8.69	22.21		0	1.5	5.19	0.32	12.75	418.4	59	41	0	0	83			5.50		May-14
100	2.98	6.52	7.91	19.55		0	2.25	5.23	0.33	12.41	418.4	59	41	0	0	83				1.00	May-14
	3.29	7.07	9.06	23.21			1.25	5.17	0.33	12.87	418.4	59	41	0	0	83					May-17
	3.29	7.07	8.97	23.11		0	1.25	5.17	0.33	12.87	418.4	59	41	0	0	83					May-14
	5.57	9.60	16.25			0.09	0.85			11.73	9.9	0	99	0	1						Nov-16
100	6.93	9.74	12.33	25.50	103.35	1.09	1.2	11.74	1.07	22.39	960.8	0	100	0	0	112	21.78	-21.15	5.50		Apr-04
100	6.73	9.33	11.52	22.75	95.79	0.69	1.95	11.77	1.07	19.34	960.8	0	100	0	0	112	21.21	-21.42		5.00	Apr-04
100	6.72	9.33	11.52	22.73	95.85	0.69	1.95	11.72	1.07	19.25	960.8	0	100	0	0	112	21.18	-21.36		1.00	Aug-98
	7.00	9.94	12.77	27.05	107.25	1.4	0.8	11.74	1.07	22.54	960.8	0	100	0	0	112	22.08	-21			Jan-11
	6.90	9.64	12.11	24.60	98.83	0.89	1.45	11.73	1.07	22.58	960.8	0	100	0	0	112	21.18	-21.36			Dec-14
	6.98	9.86	12.63	26.45	105.85	1.27	0.95	11.73	1.07	22.6	960.8	0	100	0	0	112	21.93	-21.06			Nov-05
100	3.42	7.99	6.00	30.15	91.10	1.29	1.06	16.18	1.12	20.25	1,634	0	100	0	0	95	25.44	-21.88	5.50		Feb-14
100	3.21	7.58	5.20	27.20	84.11	0.71	1.88	16.18	1.12	20.34	1,634	0	100	0	0	95	24.94	-22.11		1.00	Jun-15
	3.55	8.28	6.42	31.54	94.25	1.53	0.64	16.19	1.12	20.23	1,634	0	100	0	0	95	25.66	-21.78			Sep-14
	3.37	7.91	5.74	29.19	88.96	1.12	1.25	16.18	1.12	20	1,634	0	100	0	0	95	25.32	-21.95			Aug-06
	3.48	8.16	6.31	31.18	93.69	1.48	0.7	16.2	1.13	20.21	1,634	0	100	0	0	95	25.66	-21.78			Jan-93
100	6.52	11.14	21.20	34.86	106.45	1.33	0.53	10.09	1	51.92	1,148	2	98	0	0	4	24.79	-16.46	3.25		Nov-99
100	6.34	10.80	20.43	32.28	99.95	0.83	1.18	10.09	1	51.55	1,148	2	98	0	0	4	24.29	-16.64		1.00	Nov-99
	6.60	11.34	21.62	36.21	109.89	1.59	0.18	10.09	1	52.07	1,148	2	98	0	0	4	25	-16.33			Aug-97
	6.60	11.30	21.55	36.00	109.38		0.18	10.09	1	52.08	1,148	2	98	0	0	4	24.98	-16.34			Nov-17
	6.59	11.29	21.54	35.99	109.37	1.54	0.24	10.09	1	52.08	1,148	2	98	0	0	4	24.98	-16.34			Nov-92
100	6.78	11.17	15.42	30.98	103.11	1.31	1.07	11.41	1.06	14.53	402.7	0	100	0	0	126	20.65	-18.34	5.50		Mar-01
100	6.55	10.66	14.53	28.00	95.55	0.81	1.82	11.41	1.06	13.51	402.7	0	100	0	0	126	20.16	-18.59		5.00	Mar-01
100	6.61	10.73	14.51	28.07	95.73	0.81	1.82	11.41	1.06	13.5	402.7	0	100	0	0	126	20.16	-18.59		1.00	Mar-01
	6.87	11.31	15.75	32.11	105.85		0.8	11.43	1.07	14.88	402.7	0	100	0	0	126	20.79	-18.16			Apr-17
	6.73	11.01	15.11	29.90	99.40	1.08	1.32	11.41	1.06	14.89	402.7	0	100	0	0	126	20.27	-18.42			Jun-15
	6.87	11.39	15.76	32.12	105.86	1.48	0.82	11.43	1.07	14.88	402.7	0	100	0	0	126	20.79	-18.16			Mar-01
	6.46	11.23	20.89			0.17	0.2			12.21	27.3	5	95	0	0						Nov-16
100	3.39	5.86	5.83	1.00	4.87	1.65	1.18	6.26		9.69	166.2	2	59	23	16	96	8.11	-7.94	5.50		Dec-10
100	3.14	5.43	5.05	-1.29	1.01	0.93	1.93	6.3		9.65	166.2	2	59	23	16	96	7.56	-8.17		5.00	Dec-10
100	3.29	5.46	5.08	-1.16	1.05	0.93	1.93	6.27		9.65	166.2	2	59	23	16	96	7.57	-8.18		1.00	Dec-10
	3.44	6.00	6.20	1.95	6.41	1.98	0.85	6.28		9.7	166.2	2	59	23	16	96	8.22	-7.8			Jan-15
	3.51	6.04	6.22	1.81	6.25	1.9	0.93	6.28		9.71	166.2	2	59	23	16	96	8.22	-7.8			Dec-10
100	0.87	2.28	7.60			4.9	1.35			9.59	11.2	3	71	0	6	137			5.50		Jun-15
100	0.64	1.96	6.72			4.17	2.1			9.59	11.2	3	71	0	6	137				1.00	Jun-15
	0.87	2.45	7.85				1.1			9.59	11.2	3	71	0	6	137					Dec-16
	0.87	2.45	7.85			5.15	1.1			9.59	11.2	3	71	0	6	137					Jun-15
100	3.79	6.47	11.13	16.18		1.05	1.3	10.7	0.93	10.8	6.6	3	93	0	4	142			5.50		Aug-14
100	3.59	6.10	10.19	13.56		0.53	2.05	10.65	0.92	10.7	6.6	3	93	0	4	142				1.00	Aug-14
	3.86	6.64	11.32	17.05		1.29	1.05	10.68	0.93	10.66	6.6	3	93	0	4	142					Aug-14
	3.80	6.64	11.36	17.10		1.27	1.05	10.71	0.93	10.82	6.6	3	93	0	4	142					Aug-14
100	1.89	3.43	5.32	10.95	49.90	0.95	1.25	12.57	0.94	11.96	23.6	0	100	0	0	122	31	-18.24	5.50		Dec-10

	MARKET			FUND TYPE, CATEGORY & OBJECTIVE	RATINGS					MINIMUMS
Fund Name	Ticker Symbol	Traded On	Fund Type	Category and (Prospectus Objective)	Overall Rating	Reward Rating	Risk Rating	Recent Up/ Downgrade	Open to New Investors	Min Initial Investment
Prudential US Real Estate Fund Class B	PJEBX	NAS CM	Open End	Real Estate Sector Equity (Real Estate)	B-	C+	B	Up		2,500
Prudential US Real Estate Fund Class C	PJECX	NAS CM	Open End	Real Estate Sector Equity (Real Estate)	B-	C+	B	Up	Y	2,500
Prudential US Real Estate Fund Class Q	PJEQX	NAS CM	Open End	Real Estate Sector Equity (Real Estate)	B	C+	B	Up	Y	5,000,000
Prudential US Real Estate Fund Class Z	PJEZX	NAS CM	Open End	Real Estate Sector Equity (Real Estate)	B-	C+	B		Y	5,000,000
PSG Tactical Growth Fund	PSGTX	NAS CM	Open End	Moderate Alloc (Growth & Income)	C	C	C	Up	Y	2,500
PSI All Asset Fund Class A Shares	FXMAX	NAS CM	Open End	Long/Short Equity (Growth & Income)	C+	C	C+	Up	Y	2,500
PSI Opportunistic Fund Class A Shares	FXCAX	NAS CM	Open End	Moderate Alloc (Growth)	C+	C	B	Up	Y	2,500
PSI Strategic Growth Fund Class A Shares	FXSAX	NAS CM	Open End	Moderate Alloc (Growth)	C+	C	B-	Up	Y	2,500
PSI Tactical Growth Fund Class A Shares	FXTAX	NAS CM	Open End	Moderate Alloc (Growth & Income)	C+	C	B-	Up	Y	2,500
Putnam Absolute Return 500 Fund Class A	PJMDX	NAS CM	Open End	Multialternative (Income)	B-	C	B	Up	Y	0
Putnam Absolute Return 500 Fund Class B	PJMBX	NAS CM	Open End	Multialternative (Income)	C+	C	B		Y	0
Putnam Absolute Return 500 Fund Class C	PJMCX	NAS CM	Open End	Multialternative (Income)	C+	C	B		Y	0
Putnam Absolute Return 500 Fund Class M	PJMMX	NAS CM	Open End	Multialternative (Income)	C+	C	B		Y	0
Putnam Absolute Return 500 Fund Class P	US99018R9125		Open End	Multialternative (Income)	B-	C	B	Up		0
Putnam Absolute Return 500 Fund Class R	PJMRX	NAS CM	Open End	Multialternative (Income)	C+	C	B		Y	0
Putnam Absolute Return 500 Fund Class R6	PJMEX	NAS CM	Open End	Multialternative (Income)	B-	C	B	Up	Y	0
Putnam Absolute Return 500 Fund Class Y	PJMYX	NAS CM	Open End	Multialternative (Income)	B-	C	B	Up	Y	0
Putnam Absolute Return 700 Fund Class A	PDMAX	NAS CM	Open End	Multialternative (Income)	B-	C	B	Up	Y	0
Putnam Absolute Return 700 Fund Class B	PDMBX	NAS CM	Open End	Multialternative (Income)	C+	C	B		Y	0
Putnam Absolute Return 700 Fund Class C	PDMCX	NAS CM	Open End	Multialternative (Income)	C+	C	B		Y	0
Putnam Absolute Return 700 Fund Class M	PDMMX	NAS CM	Open End	Multialternative (Income)	B-	C	B	Up	Y	0
Putnam Absolute Return 700 Fund Class P	US99020R9006		Open End	Multialternative (Income)	B-	C+	B	Up		0
Putnam Absolute Return 700 Fund Class R	PDMRX	NAS CM	Open End	Multialternative (Income)	B-	C	B	Up	Y	0
Putnam Absolute Return 700 Fund Class R6	PDMEX	NAS CM	Open End	Multialternative (Income)	B-	C+	B	Up	Y	0
Putnam Absolute Return 700 Fund Class Y	PDMYX	NAS CM	Open End	Multialternative (Income)	B-	C+	B	Up	Y	0
Putnam Capital Opportunities Fund Class A	PCOAX	NAS CM	Open End	US Equity Small Cap (Growth)	B-	C+	B	Up	Y	0
Putnam Capital Opportunities Fund Class B	POPBX	NAS CM	Open End	US Equity Small Cap (Growth)	B-	C+	B	Up	Y	0
Putnam Capital Opportunities Fund Class C	PCOCX	NAS CM	Open End	US Equity Small Cap (Growth)	B-	C+	B	Up	Y	0
Putnam Capital Opportunities Fund Class M	POPMX	NAS CM	Open End	US Equity Small Cap (Growth)	B-	C+	B	Up	Y	0
Putnam Capital Opportunities Fund Class R	PCORX	NAS CM	Open End	US Equity Small Cap (Growth)	B-	C+	B	Up	Y	0
Putnam Capital Opportunities Fund Class R5	POPDX	NAS CM	Open End	US Equity Small Cap (Growth)	B-	C+	B	Up	Y	0
Putnam Capital Opportunities Fund Class R6	PCOEX	NAS CM	Open End	US Equity Small Cap (Growth)	B-	C+	B	Up	Y	0
Putnam Capital Opportunities Fund Class Y	PYCOX	NAS CM	Open End	US Equity Small Cap (Growth)	B-	C+	B	Up	Y	0
Putnam Capital Spectrum Fund Class A	PVSAX	NAS CM	Open End	Aggressive Alloc (Growth & Income)	C-	C-	C	Down	Y	0
Putnam Capital Spectrum Fund Class B	PVSBX	NAS CM	Open End	Aggressive Alloc (Growth & Income)	C-	C-	C-	Down	Y	0
Putnam Capital Spectrum Fund Class C	PVSCX	NAS CM	Open End	Aggressive Alloc (Growth & Income)	C-	C-	C-	Down	Y	0
Putnam Capital Spectrum Fund Class M	PVSMX	NAS CM	Open End	Aggressive Alloc (Growth & Income)	C-	C-	C-	Down	Y	0
Putnam Capital Spectrum Fund Class R	PVSRX	NAS CM	Open End	Aggressive Alloc (Growth & Income)	C-	C-	C	Down	Y	0
Putnam Capital Spectrum Fund Class Y	PVSYX	NAS CM	Open End	Aggressive Alloc (Growth & Income)	C-	C-	C	Down	Y	0
Putnam Convertible Securities Fund Class A	PCONX	NAS CM	Open End	Convertibles (Growth & Income)	C+	C+	C+	Down	Y	0
Putnam Convertible Securities Fund Class B	PCNBX	NAS CM	Open End	Convertibles (Growth & Income)	C+	C+	C+	Down	Y	0
Putnam Convertible Securities Fund Class C	PRCCX	NAS CM	Open End	Convertibles (Growth & Income)	C+	C+	C+	Down	Y	0
Putnam Convertible Securities Fund Class M	PCNMX	NAS CM	Open End	Convertibles (Growth & Income)	C+	C+	C+	Down	Y	0
Putnam Convertible Securities Fund Class R	PCVRX	NAS CM	Open End	Convertibles (Growth & Income)	C+	C+	C+	Down	Y	0
Putnam Convertible Securities Fund Class Y	PCGYX	NAS CM	Open End	Convertibles (Growth & Income)	C+	C+	C+	Down	Y	0
Putnam Dynamic Asset Allocation Balanced Fund Class A	PABAX	NAS CM	Open End	Moderate Alloc (Asset Alloc)	B-	C+	B	Down	Y	0
Putnam Dynamic Asset Allocation Balanced Fund Class B	PABBX	NAS CM	Open End	Moderate Alloc (Asset Alloc)	B-	C+	B	Down	Y	0
Putnam Dynamic Asset Allocation Balanced Fund Class C	AABCX	NAS CM	Open End	Moderate Alloc (Asset Alloc)	B-	C+	B	Down	Y	0
Putnam Dynamic Asset Allocation Balanced Fund Class M	PABMX	NAS CM	Open End	Moderate Alloc (Asset Alloc)	B-	C+	B	Down	Y	0
Putnam Dynamic Asset Allocation Balanced Fund Class P	US7464449005		Open End	Moderate Alloc (Asset Alloc)	B-	C+	B	Down		0
Putnam Dynamic Asset Allocation Balanced Fund Class R	PAARX	NAS CM	Open End	Moderate Alloc (Asset Alloc)	B-	C+	B	Down	Y	0
Putnam Dynamic Asset Allocation Balanced Fund Class R5	PAADX	NAS CM	Open End	Moderate Alloc (Asset Alloc)	B-	C+	B	Down	Y	0

★Expanded analysis of this fund is included in Section II.

Min Additional Investment	TOTAL RETURNS 3-Month Total Return	6-Month Total Return	1-Year Total Return	3-Year Total Return	5-Year Total Return	PERFORMANCE Dividend Yield (TTM)	Expense Ratio	3-Yr Std Deviation	3-Year Beta	ASSETS NAV	Total Assets (MIL)	ASSET ALLOCATION & TURNOVER %Cash	%Stocks	%Bonds	%Other	Turnover Ratio	BULL & BEAR Last Bull Market Total Return	Last Bear Market Total Return	FEES Front End Fee (%)	Back End Fee (%)	Inception Date
100	1.73	3.11	4.59	8.54	44.51	0.48	2	12.59	0.94	11.75	23.6	0	100	0	0	122	30.37	-18.46		5.00	Dec-10
100	1.73	3.11	4.59	8.56	44.47	0.48	2	12.57	0.94	11.73	23.6	0	100	0	0	122	30.44	-18.56		1.00	Dec-10
	1.92	3.62	5.68	11.88	51.91		1	12.63	0.94	11.97	23.6	0	100	0	0	122	31.16	-18.14			May-17
	1.92	3.53	5.60	11.79	51.79	1.11	1	12.62	0.94	11.97	23.6	0	100	0	0	122	31.16	-18.14			Dec-10
250	1.87	3.02	5.96	-3.85	4.28	0.56	2.22	7.18	1.67	9.93	19.1	28	46	11	6	120					Apr-12
500	-0.67	1.96	6.13	5.37	0.34	0	2.21	9.13	0.3	8.82	19.9	66	-4	36	2	7,042	-2.22	-7.58	5.75		Aug-10
500	3.47	3.69	7.43	3.18		0	2.14	7.1	0.5	10.11	4.2	-24	69	58	-2	1,576			5.75		Oct-13
500	7.08	9.53	18.08	14.45	20.64	0	2.31	7.14	0.02	11.38	22.7	69	26	6	0	5,910	11.34	-18.58	5.75		Aug-10
500	3.80	7.64	13.26	3.24	15.16	0	2.43	6.55	0.15	10.01	18.1	4	57	39	0	5,656	6.17	-13.73	5.75		Aug-10
	1.98	3.99	7.17	7.48	17.45	0	1.07	3.11	-3.77	11.19	940.7	61	21	30	-13	522	8.42	-6.5	5.75		Dec-08
	1.82	3.69	6.42	5.06	13.20	0	1.82	3.12	-3.82	11.03	940.7	61	21	30	-13	522	8.02	-6.83		5.00	Dec-08
	1.80	3.58	6.42	5.00	13.09	0	1.82	3.1	-3.41	10.98	940.7	61	21	30	-13	522	7.97	-6.83		1.00	Dec-08
	1.87	3.83	6.65	5.85	14.58	0	1.57	3.17	-4.12	11.06	940.7	61	21	30	-13	522	8.08	-6.72	3.50		Dec-08
	2.11	4.21	7.57	8.45	19.15	0	0.7	3.09	-3.49	11.25	940.7	61	21	30	-13	522	8.65	-6.4			Aug-16
	1.90	3.87	6.99	6.75	16.04	0	1.32	3.11	-3.9	11.44	940.7	61	21	30	-13	522	8.22	-6.62			Dec-08
	2.06	4.24	7.60	8.55	19.50	0	0.74	3.15	-3.97	11.28	940.7	61	21	30	-13	522	8.65	-6.4			Jul-12
	2.00	4.09	7.45	8.24	18.91	0	0.82	3.1	-3.44	11.24	940.7	61	21	30	-13	522	8.65	-6.4			Dec-08
	2.62	5.39	9.74	10.49	24.93	0	1.21	4.55	-4.58	12.2	1,199	52	30	39	-21	578	9.88	-7.85	5.75		Dec-08
	2.48	5.15	8.94	8.07	20.38	0	1.96	4.53	-4.36	11.91	1,199	52	30	39	-21	578	9.32	-8.1		5.00	Dec-08
	2.39	5.07	8.96	8.03	20.40	0	1.96	4.52	-4.84	11.87	1,199	52	30	39	-21	578	9.35	-8.1		1.00	Dec-08
	2.54	5.19	9.23	8.93	21.90	0	1.71	4.56	-4.86	11.98	1,199	52	30	39	-21	578	9.5	-8	3.50		Dec-08
	2.66	5.59	10.11	11.52	26.79	0	0.82	4.51	-4.46	12.24	1,199	52	30	39	-21	578	10.03	-7.76			Aug-16
	2.60	5.32	9.43	9.67	23.39	0	1.46	4.53	-4.72	12.03	1,199	52	30	39	-21	578	9.69	-7.99			Dec-08
	2.78	5.70	10.13	11.69	27.21	0	0.86	4.54	-5.18	12.29	1,199	52	30	39	-21	578	10.03	-7.76			Jul-12
	2.71	5.64	10.08	11.39	26.64	0	0.96	4.52	-4.48	12.24	1,199	52	30	39	-21	578	10.03	-7.76			Dec-08
	0.91	4.25	8.04	14.50	68.02	0.59	1.37	12.45	0.97	13.49	312.4	3	97	0	0	167	32.21	-28.35	5.75		Jun-98
	0.78	3.86	7.22	12.06	61.79	0.05	2.12	12.47	0.97	11.08	312.4	3	97	0	0	167	31.73	-28.58		5.00	Jun-98
	0.69	3.79	7.18	11.97	61.68	0.07	2.12	12.48	0.97	11.28	312.4	3	97	0	0	167	31.71	-28.58		1.00	Jul-99
	0.81	3.98	7.53	12.82	63.89	0.27	1.87	12.5	0.97	11.98	312.4	3	97	0	0	167	31.87	-28.49	3.50		Jun-98
	0.88	4.12	7.79	13.74	65.87	0.35	1.62	12.43	0.97	13.03	312.4	3	97	0	0	167	32.04	-28.39			Jan-03
	1.02	4.42	7.30	14.51	69.16	0.87	1.05	12.46	0.97	13.88	312.4	3	97	0	0	167	32.21	-28.35			Jul-12
	1.00	4.43	8.44	15.96	71.78	0.95	0.95	12.46	0.97	14.07	312.4	3	97	0	0	167	32.21	-28.35			Jul-12
	1.01	4.32	8.27	15.39	70.07	0.78	1.12	12.47	0.97	14.01	312.4	3	97	0	0	167	32.47	-28.3			Oct-00
	-3.08	-7.66	4.26	-3.14	49.23	0	0.95	10.9		34.19	3,271	6	87	2	0	9	26.04	-14.18	5.75		May-09
	-3.26	-8.01	3.49	-5.33	43.71	0	1.7	10.92		32.61	3,271	6	87	2	0	9	25.48	-14.43		5.00	May-09
	-3.26	-8.00	3.49	-5.29	43.71	0	1.7	10.9		32.54	3,271	6	87	2	0	9	25.47	-14.43		1.00	May-09
	-3.23	-7.91	3.72	-4.62	45.48	0	1.45	10.89		33.15	3,271	6	87	2	0	9	25.66	-14.35	3.50		May-09
	-3.16	-7.77	4.01	-3.88	47.34	0	1.2	10.91		33.67	3,271	6	87	2	0	9	25.81	-14.23			May-09
	-3.02	-7.54	4.53	-2.41	51.12	0	0.7	10.91		34.58	3,271	6	87	2	0	9	26.21	-14.09			May-09
	1.80	6.26	14.93	16.54	54.64	1.83	1.09	8.23	1.03	25.49	716.0	3	3	1	1	49	12.34	-16	5.75		Jun-72
	1.65	5.86	14.10	13.96	48.94	1.16	1.84	8.23	1.03	24.98	716.0	3	3	1	1	49	11.77	-16.26		5.00	Jul-93
	1.63	5.88	14.09	13.98	48.99	1.13	1.84	8.23	1.03	25.21	716.0	3	3	1	1	49	11.84	-16.27		1.00	Jul-99
	1.65	5.97	14.32	14.77	50.79	1.39	1.59	8.23	1.03	25.22	716.0	3	3	1	1	49	11.93	-16.14	3.50		Mar-95
	1.73	6.09	14.60	15.63	52.71	1.61	1.34	8.25	1.04	25.38	716.0	3	3	1	1	49	12.19	-16.12			Dec-03
	1.87	6.39	15.23	17.45	56.64	2.07	0.84	8.26	1.04	25.48	716.0	3	3	1	1	49	12.49	-15.93			Dec-98
	4.19	8.07	15.18	22.64	62.53	1.34	1	6.73	0.64	15.3	2,727	14	55	30	0	200	16.93	-13.77	5.75		Feb-94
	4.01	7.63	14.30	19.84	56.46	0.65	1.75	6.7	0.64	15.23	2,727	14	55	30	0	200	16.36	-14.02		5.00	Feb-94
	3.98	7.70	14.40	19.89	56.48	0.71	1.75	6.72	0.64	14.88	2,727	14	55	30	0	200	16.32	-13.96		1.00	Sep-94
	4.11	7.80	14.62	20.85	58.44	0.89	1.5	6.73	0.64	15.27	2,727	14	55	30	0	200	16.48	-13.94	3.50		Feb-95
	4.28	8.26	15.65	22.80	62.74	1.69	0.6	6.74	0.64	15.34	2,727	14	55	30	0	200	16.93	-13.77			Aug-16
	4.09	7.87	14.89	21.68	60.37	1.14	1.25	6.72	0.64	15.17	2,727	14	55	30	0	200	16.69	-13.81			Jan-03
	4.25	8.20	15.49	23.56	64.52	1.54	0.74	6.72	0.64	15.33	2,727	14	55	30	0	200	16.93	-13.77			Jul-12

Fund Name	Ticker Symbol	Traded On	Fund Type	Category and (Prospectus Objective)	Overall Rating	Reward Rating	Risk Rating	Recent Up/ Downgrade	Open to New Investors	Min Initial Investment
	MARKET		FUND TYPE, CATEGORY & OBJECTIVE		RATINGS				MINIMUMS	
Putnam Dynamic Asset Allocation Balanced Fund Class R6	PAAEX	NAS CM	Open End	Moderate Alloc (Asset Alloc)	B-	C+	B	Down	Y	0
Putnam Dynamic Asset Allocation Balanced Fund Class Y	PABYX	NAS CM	Open End	Moderate Alloc (Asset Alloc)	B-	C+	B	Down	Y	0
Putnam Dynamic Asset Allocation Conservative Fund Class A	PACAX	NAS CM	Open End	Moderate Alloc (Asset Alloc)	B-	C+	B	Up	Y	0
Putnam Dynamic Asset Allocation Conservative Fund Class B	PACBX	NAS CM	Open End	Moderate Alloc (Asset Alloc)	B-	C+	B	Up	Y	0
Putnam Dynamic Asset Allocation Conservative Fund Class C	PACCX	NAS CM	Open End	Moderate Alloc (Asset Alloc)	B-	C+	B	Up	Y	0
Putnam Dynamic Asset Allocation Conservative Fund Class M	PACMX	NAS CM	Open End	Moderate Alloc (Asset Alloc)	B	C+	A-	Up	Y	0
Putnam Dynamic Asset Allocation Conservative Fund Class P	US9981459087		Open End	Moderate Alloc (Asset Alloc)	B-	C+	B	Up		0
Putnam Dynamic Asset Allocation Conservative Fund Class R	PACRX	NAS CM	Open End	Moderate Alloc (Asset Alloc)	B-	C+	B	Up	Y	0
Putnam Dynamic Asset Allocation Conservative Fund Class R5	PACDX	NAS CM	Open End	Moderate Alloc (Asset Alloc)	B-	C+	B	Up	Y	0
Putnam Dynamic Asset Allocation Conservative Fund Class R6	PCCEX	NAS CM	Open End	Moderate Alloc (Asset Alloc)	B-	C+	B	Up	Y	0
Putnam Dynamic Asset Allocation Conservative Fund Class Y	PACYX	NAS CM	Open End	Moderate Alloc (Asset Alloc)	B-	C+	B	Up	Y	0
Putnam Dynamic Asset Allocation Equity Fund Class A	US7467641749		Open End	US Equity Large Cap Blend (Asset Alloc)	B-	B-	B-	Down	Y	0
Putnam Dynamic Asset Allocation Equity Fund Class P			Open End	US Equity Large Cap Blend (Asset Alloc)	B-	B-	B-	Down		0
Putnam Dynamic Asset Allocation Growth Fund Class A	PAEAX	NAS CM	Open End	Aggressive Alloc (Asset Alloc)	B-	B-	B	Down	Y	0
Putnam Dynamic Asset Allocation Growth Fund Class B	PAEBX	NAS CM	Open End	Aggressive Alloc (Asset Alloc)	B-	B-	B-	Down	Y	0
Putnam Dynamic Asset Allocation Growth Fund Class C	PAECX	NAS CM	Open End	Aggressive Alloc (Asset Alloc)	B-	B-	B-	Down	Y	0
Putnam Dynamic Asset Allocation Growth Fund Class M	PAGMX	NAS CM	Open End	Aggressive Alloc (Asset Alloc)	B-	B-	B	Down	Y	0
Putnam Dynamic Asset Allocation Growth Fund Class P	US9981439030		Open End	Aggressive Alloc (Asset Alloc)	B-	B-	B	Down		0
Putnam Dynamic Asset Allocation Growth Fund Class R	PASRX	NAS CM	Open End	Aggressive Alloc (Asset Alloc)	B-	B-	B	Down	Y	0
Putnam Dynamic Asset Allocation Growth Fund Class R5	PADEX	NAS CM	Open End	Aggressive Alloc (Asset Alloc)	B-	B-	B	Down	Y	0
Putnam Dynamic Asset Allocation Growth Fund Class R6	PAEEX	NAS CM	Open End	Aggressive Alloc (Asset Alloc)	B-	B-	B	Down	Y	0
Putnam Dynamic Asset Allocation Growth Fund Class Y	PAGYX	NAS CM	Open End	Aggressive Alloc (Asset Alloc)	B-	B-	B	Down	Y	0
Putnam Dynamic Risk Allocation Fund Class A	PDREX	NAS CM	Open End	Cautious Alloc (Growth & Income)	C+	C+	B-	Down	Y	0
Putnam Dynamic Risk Allocation Fund Class B	PDRBX	NAS CM	Open End	Cautious Alloc (Growth & Income)	C+	C+	C+		Y	0
Putnam Dynamic Risk Allocation Fund Class C	PDRFX	NAS CM	Open End	Cautious Alloc (Growth & Income)	C+	C+	C+		Y	0
Putnam Dynamic Risk Allocation Fund Class M	PDRTX	NAS CM	Open End	Cautious Alloc (Growth & Income)	C+	C+	C+	Down	Y	0
Putnam Dynamic Risk Allocation Fund Class R	PDRRX	NAS CM	Open End	Cautious Alloc (Growth & Income)	C+	C+	C+	Down	Y	0
Putnam Dynamic Risk Allocation Fund Class R6	PDRGX	NAS CM	Open End	Cautious Alloc (Growth & Income)	C+	C+	B-	Down	Y	0
Putnam Dynamic Risk Allocation Fund Class Y	PDRYX	NAS CM	Open End	Cautious Alloc (Growth & Income)	C+	C+	B-	Down	Y	0
Putnam Emerging Markets Equity Fund Class A	PEMMX	NAS CM	Open End	Emerging Markets Equity (Div Emerging Mkts)	B-	B	C	Up	Y	0
Putnam Emerging Markets Equity Fund Class B	PEMBX	NAS CM	Open End	Emerging Markets Equity (Div Emerging Mkts)	B-	B	C	Up	Y	0
Putnam Emerging Markets Equity Fund Class C	PEMZX	NAS CM	Open End	Emerging Markets Equity (Div Emerging Mkts)	B-	B	C	Up	Y	0
Putnam Emerging Markets Equity Fund Class M	PEMAX	NAS CM	Open End	Emerging Markets Equity (Div Emerging Mkts)	B-	B	C	Up	Y	0
Putnam Emerging Markets Equity Fund Class R	PEMLX	NAS CM	Open End	Emerging Markets Equity (Div Emerging Mkts)	B-	B	C	Up	Y	0
Putnam Emerging Markets Equity Fund Class Y	PEMYX	NAS CM	Open End	Emerging Markets Equity (Div Emerging Mkts)	B	B	C	Up	Y	0
Putnam Equity Income Fund Class A	PEYAX	NAS CM	Open End	US Equity Large Cap Value (Equity-Income)	B	B-	B	Up	Y	0
Putnam Equity Income Fund Class B	PEQNX	NAS CM	Open End	US Equity Large Cap Value (Equity-Income)	B	B-	B	Up	Y	0
Putnam Equity Income Fund Class C	PEQCX	NAS CM	Open End	US Equity Large Cap Value (Equity-Income)	B	B-	B	Up	Y	0
Putnam Equity Income Fund Class M	PEIMX	NAS CM	Open End	US Equity Large Cap Value (Equity-Income)	B-	B-	B-	Down	Y	0
Putnam Equity Income Fund Class R	PEQRX	NAS CM	Open End	US Equity Large Cap Value (Equity-Income)	B-	B-	B-	Down	Y	0
Putnam Equity Income Fund Class R5	PEQLX	NAS CM	Open End	US Equity Large Cap Value (Equity-Income)	B-	B-	B-	Down	Y	0
Putnam Equity Income Fund Class R6	PEQSX	NAS CM	Open End	US Equity Large Cap Value (Equity-Income)	B-	B	B-	Down	Y	0
Putnam Equity Income Fund Class Y	PEIYX	NAS CM	Open End	US Equity Large Cap Value (Equity-Income)	B	B-	B	Up	Y	0
Putnam Equity Spectrum Fund Class A	PYSAX	NAS CM	Open End	US Equity Mid Cap (Growth)	C-	C-	C-	Down	Y	0
Putnam Equity Spectrum Fund Class B	PYSOX	NAS CM	Open End	US Equity Mid Cap (Growth)	C-	D+	C-	Down	Y	0
Putnam Equity Spectrum Fund Class C	PYSCX	NAS CM	Open End	US Equity Mid Cap (Growth)	C-	D+	C-	Down	Y	0
Putnam Equity Spectrum Fund Class M	PYSMX	NAS CM	Open End	US Equity Mid Cap (Growth)	C-	C-	C-	Down	Y	0
Putnam Equity Spectrum Fund Class R	PYSRX	NAS CM	Open End	US Equity Mid Cap (Growth)	C-	C-	C-	Down	Y	0
Putnam Equity Spectrum Fund Class Y	PYSYX	NAS CM	Open End	US Equity Mid Cap (Growth)	C-	C-	C-	Down	Y	0
Putnam Europe Equity Fund Class A	PEUGX	NAS CM	Open End	Europe Equity Large Cap (Europe Stock)	C+	C+	C+	Up	Y	0
Putnam Europe Equity Fund Class B	PEUBX	NAS CM	Open End	Europe Equity Large Cap (Europe Stock)	C+	C+	C+	Up	Y	0
Putnam Europe Equity Fund Class C	PEECX	NAS CM	Open End	Europe Equity Large Cap (Europe Stock)	C+	C+	C+	Up	Y	0

★ Expanded analysis of this fund is included in Section II.

	TOTAL RETURNS					PERFORMANCE				ASSETS		ASSET ALLOCATION & TURNOVER					BULL & BEAR		FEES		
Min Additional Investment	3-Month Total Return	6-Month Total Return	1-Year Total Return	3-Year Total Return	5-Year Total Return	Dividend Yield (TTM)	Expense Ratio	3-Yr Std Deviation	3-Year Beta	NAV	Total Assets (MIL)	%Cash	%Stocks	%Bonds	%Other	Turnover Ratio	Last Bull Market Total Return	Last Bear Market Total Return	Front End Fee (%)	Back End Fee (%)	Inception Date
	4.27	8.24	15.63	23.94	65.44	1.66	0.64	6.72	0.64	15.33	2,727	14	55	30	0	200	16.93	-13.77			Jul-12
	4.25	8.19	15.44	23.51	64.52	1.57	0.75	6.68	0.63	15.33	2,727	14	55	30	0	200	17.06	-13.65			Jul-94
	2.52	5.00	9.72	14.84	37.04	1.52	1.04	4	0.35	10.94	1,140	9	39	51	0	327	9.9	-7.04	5.75		Feb-94
	2.25	4.53	8.86	12.32	31.92	0.81	1.79	3.96	0.33	10.85	1,140	9	39	51	0	327	9.47	-7.28		5.00	Feb-94
	2.27	4.57	8.93	12.35	32.10	0.83	1.79	3.92	0.34	10.8	1,140	9	39	51	0	327	9.4	-7.29		1.00	Sep-94
	2.32	4.69	9.15	13.11	33.62	1.03	1.54	3.96	0.34	10.81	1,140	9	39	51	0	327	9.54	-7.19	3.50		Feb-95
	2.52	5.09	10.12	14.78	36.97	1.88	0.63	4.05	0.38	10.97	1,140	9	39	51	0	327	9.9	-7.04			Aug-16
	2.39	4.74	9.37	13.90	35.24	1.24	1.29	3.96	0.33	11.24	1,140	9	39	51	0	327	9.74	-7.09			Jan-03
	2.59	5.12	10.07	15.92	39.13	1.76	0.74	3.98	0.35	10.98	1,140	9	39	51	0	327	9.9	-7.04			Jul-12
	2.50	5.15	10.05	16.14	39.51	1.84	0.67	3.95	0.32	10.98	1,140	9	39	51	0	327	9.9	-7.04			Jul-12
	2.57	5.09	10.03	15.73	38.69	1.73	0.79	3.97	0.35	10.98	1,140	9	39	51	0	327	10.03	-6.82			Jul-94
	6.05	12.00	22.70	30.60	92.41	1.04	0.87	10.51	1	13.19	84.5	19	80	0	0	106	25.04	-21.59	5.75		Jan-09
	6.04	12.14	23.05	29.35	90.56	0	0.63	10.5	1	13.2	84.5	19	80	0	0	106	25.04	-21.59			Aug-16
	5.33	10.47	19.85	27.99	78.23	0.31	1.11	8.88	0.85	17.04	2,929	15	66	18	0	124	21.42	-19.23	5.75		Feb-94
	5.15	10.03	18.99	25.12	71.76	0	1.86	8.86	0.85	16.67	2,929	15	66	18	0	124	20.94	-19.57		5.00	Feb-94
	5.11	10.03	18.94	25.09	71.63	0	1.86	8.82	0.84	16.01	2,929	15	66	18	0	124	20.9	-19.53		1.00	Sep-94
	5.21	10.16	19.28	26.08	73.81	0	1.61	8.86	0.84	16.65	2,929	15	66	18	0	124	21.15	-19.46	3.50		Feb-95
	5.44	10.71	20.36	28.72	79.25	0.4	0.68	8.88	0.85	17.24	2,929	15	66	18	0	124	21.42	-19.23			Aug-16
	5.23	10.28	19.55	26.96	76.03	0.19	1.36	8.84	0.84	16.65	2,929	15	66	18	0	124	21.31	-19.39			Jan-03
	5.34	10.62	20.13	28.91	80.63	0.51	0.82	8.86	0.84	17.2	2,929	15	66	18	0	124	21.42	-19.23			Jul-12
	5.40	10.67	20.32	29.35	81.57	0.63	0.72	8.87	0.85	17.24	2,929	15	66	18	0	124	21.42	-19.23			Jul-12
	5.36	10.57	20.08	28.89	80.47	0.44	0.86	8.83	0.84	17.21	2,929	15	66	18	0	124	21.59	-19.22			Jul-94
	4.21	8.43	12.68	14.25	23.16	2.13	1.14	6.28		11.47	163.4	15	45	38	1	299	12.1		5.75		Sep-11
	3.93	8.03	11.80	11.62	18.56	1.4	1.89	6.29		11.29	163.4	15	45	38	1	299	11.49			5.00	Sep-11
	4.05	8.04	11.81	11.65	18.65	1.32	1.89	6.27		11.32	163.4	15	45	38	1	299	11.51			1.00	Sep-11
	4.02	8.15	12.08	12.48	20.01	1.76	1.64	6.29		11.47	163.4	15	45	38	1	299	11.7		3.50		Sep-11
	4.05	8.18	12.33	13.22	21.53	1.55	1.39	6.29		11.43	163.4	15	45	38	1	299	11.91				Sep-11
	4.25	8.57	13.05	15.38	25.33	2.5	0.76	6.28		11.42	163.4	15	45	38	1	299	12.26				Jul-12
	4.20	8.60	12.95	15.08	24.69	2.37	0.89	6.28		11.48	163.4	15	45	38	1	299	12.26				Sep-11
	7.28	19.98	42.29	33.77	35.60	0.67	1.69	14.41	0.87	12.77	77.0	4	95	0	1	137	21.98	-34.33	5.75		Sep-08
	7.13	19.51	41.33	30.83	30.55	0.18	2.44	14.37	0.87	12.31	77.0	4	95	0	1	137	21.58	-34.58		5.00	Sep-08
	7.07	19.49	41.24	30.82	30.56	0.2	2.44	14.32	0.86	12.26	77.0	4	95	0	1	137	21.47	-34.56		1.00	Sep-08
	7.20	19.61	41.72	31.75	32.16	0.31	2.19	14.38	0.87	12.5	77.0	4	95	0	1	137	21.66	-34.47	3.50		Sep-08
	7.25	19.88	42.12	32.80	33.83	0.68	1.94	14.41	0.87	12.72	77.0	4	95	0	1	137	21.85	-34.39			Sep-08
	7.40	20.18	42.73	34.82	37.32	0.85	1.44	14.33	0.86	12.9	77.0	4	95	0	1	137	22.18	-34.2			Sep-08
	6.26	11.68	18.68	29.19	96.36	1.6	0.94	9.94	0.94	24.51	12,342	2	97	0	0	15	25.6	-19.66	5.75		Jun-77
	6.10	11.26	17.80	26.30	89.10	0.96	1.69	9.92	0.94	24.22	12,342	2	97	0	0	15	25.12	-19.93		5.00	Sep-93
	6.06	11.27	17.77	26.32	89.07	0.94	1.69	9.94	0.94	24.22	12,342	2	97	0	0	15	25.11	-19.93		1.00	Feb-99
	6.13	11.43	18.12	27.26	91.49	1.19	1.44	9.92	0.94	24.19	12,342	2	97	0	0	15	25.21	-19.81	3.50		Dec-94
	6.20	11.53	18.40	28.20	93.94	1.35	1.19	9.94	0.94	24.32	12,342	2	97	0	0	15	25.44	-19.73			Jan-03
	6.32	11.80	18.96	30.32	99.60	1.78	0.66	9.94	0.94	24.52	12,342	2	97	0	0	15	25.6	-19.66			Jul-12
	6.40	11.92	19.13	30.77	100.61	1.91	0.56	9.94	0.94	24.52	12,342	2	97	0	0	15	25.6	-19.66			Jul-12
	6.33	11.81	18.94	30.13	98.76	1.79	0.69	9.91	0.94	24.51	12,342	2	97	0	0	15	25.76	-19.55			Oct-98
	-2.97	-8.02	6.26	-5.25	48.44	0	0.31	12.89	0.94	37.82	1,101	5	88	0	5	11	28.73	-14.43	5.75		May-09
	-3.15	-8.36	5.47	-7.37	42.96	0	1.06	12.88	0.94	35.62	1,101	5	88	0	5	11	28.15	-14.68		5.00	May-09
	-3.15	-8.35	5.48	-7.38	42.96	0	1.06	12.88	0.95	35.55	1,101	5	88	0	5	11	28.11	-14.65		1.00	May-09
	-3.08	-8.24	5.72	-6.67	44.76	0	0.81	12.88	0.95	36.39	1,101	5	88	0	5	11	28.31	-14.58	3.50		May-09
	-3.02	-8.13	5.99	-5.97	46.58	0	0.56	12.88	0.95	37.13	1,101	5	88	0	5	11	28.52	-14.51			May-09
	-2.90	-7.89	6.53	-4.53	50.33	0	0.06	12.88	0.95	38.49	1,101	5	88	0	5	11	28.92	-14.33			May-09
	0.44	6.21	21.14	16.28	44.67	2.3	1.29	12.28	0.92	27.44	220.7	1	94	0	0	47	20.34	-27.78	5.75		Sep-90
	0.22	5.77	20.18	13.69	39.32	1.73	2.04	12.28	0.93	26.2	220.7	1	94	0	0	47	19.84	-28.01		5.00	Feb-94
	0.26	5.82	20.21	13.72	39.35	1.6	2.04	12.28	0.93	26.7	220.7	1	94	0	0	47	19.81	-28.02		1.00	Jul-99

	MARKET			FUND TYPE, CATEGORY & OBJECTIVE	RATINGS				MINIMUMS	
Fund Name	Ticker Symbol	Traded On	Fund Type	Category and (Prospectus Objective)	Overall Rating	Reward Rating	Risk Rating	Recent Up/ Downgrade	Open to New Investors	Min Initial Investment
Putnam Europe Equity Fund Class M	PEUMX	NAS CM	Open End	Europe Equity Large Cap (Europe Stock)	C+	C+	C+	Up	Y	0
Putnam Europe Equity Fund Class R	PEERX	NAS CM	Open End	Europe Equity Large Cap (Europe Stock)	C+	C+	C+	Up	Y	0
Putnam Europe Equity Fund Class Y	PEUYX	NAS CM	Open End	Europe Equity Large Cap (Europe Stock)	C+	C+	B-	Up	Y	0
Putnam Global Consumer Fund Class A	PGCOX	NAS CM	Open End	Consumer Goods Sec Equity ()	B	B-	A-		Y	0
Putnam Global Consumer Fund Class B	PGCKX	NAS CM	Open End	Consumer Goods Sec Equity ()	B	B-	A-	Up	Y	0
Putnam Global Consumer Fund Class C	PGCNX	NAS CM	Open End	Consumer Goods Sec Equity ()	B	B-	A-	Up	Y	0
Putnam Global Consumer Fund Class M	PGCMX	NAS CM	Open End	Consumer Goods Sec Equity ()	B	B-	A-	Up	Y	0
Putnam Global Consumer Fund Class R	PGCIX	NAS CM	Open End	Consumer Goods Sec Equity ()	B	B-	A-	Up	Y	0
Putnam Global Consumer Fund Class Y	PGCYX	NAS CM	Open End	Consumer Goods Sec Equity ()	B	B-	A		Y	0
Putnam Global Equity Fund Class A	PEQUX	NAS CM	Open End	Global Equity (World Stock)	B-	B-	B	Up	Y	0
Putnam Global Equity Fund Class B	PEQBX	NAS CM	Open End	Global Equity (World Stock)	B-	B-	B	Up	Y	0
Putnam Global Equity Fund Class C	PUGCX	NAS CM	Open End	Global Equity (World Stock)	B-	B-	B	Up	Y	0
Putnam Global Equity Fund Class M	PEQMX	NAS CM	Open End	Global Equity (World Stock)	B-	B-	B	Up	Y	0
Putnam Global Equity Fund Class R	PGLRX	NAS CM	Open End	Global Equity (World Stock)	B-	B-	B	Up	Y	0
Putnam Global Equity Fund Class R6	PGLEX	NAS CM	Open End	Global Equity (World Stock)	B-	B-	B	Up	Y	0
Putnam Global Equity Fund Class Y	PEQYX	NAS CM	Open End	Global Equity (World Stock)	B-	B-	B	Up	Y	0
Putnam Global Financial Fund Class A	PGFFX	NAS CM	Open End	Financials Sector Equity (Financial)	C+	B-	C+	Up	Y	0
Putnam Global Financial Fund Class B	PGFOX	NAS CM	Open End	Financials Sector Equity (Financial)	C+	C+	C+	Up	Y	0
Putnam Global Financial Fund Class C	PGFDX	NAS CM	Open End	Financials Sector Equity (Financial)	B-	C+	B	Up	Y	0
Putnam Global Financial Fund Class M	PGFMX	NAS CM	Open End	Financials Sector Equity (Financial)	C+	B-	C+	Up	Y	0
Putnam Global Financial Fund Class R	PGFRX	NAS CM	Open End	Financials Sector Equity (Financial)	C+	B-	C+	Up	Y	0
Putnam Global Financial Fund Class Y	PGFYX	NAS CM	Open End	Financials Sector Equity (Financial)	B-	B-	C+	Up	Y	0
Putnam Global Health Care Fund Class A	PHSTX	NAS CM	Open End	Healthcare Sector Equity (Health)	C+	C	B-	Down	Y	0
Putnam Global Health Care Fund Class B	PHSBX	NAS CM	Open End	Healthcare Sector Equity (Health)	C	C	B-	Down	Y	0
Putnam Global Health Care Fund Class C	PCHSX	NAS CM	Open End	Healthcare Sector Equity (Health)	C	C	B-	Down	Y	0
Putnam Global Health Care Fund Class M	PHLMX	NAS CM	Open End	Healthcare Sector Equity (Health)	C	C	B-	Down	Y	0
Putnam Global Health Care Fund Class R	PHSRX	NAS CM	Open End	Healthcare Sector Equity (Health)	C+	C	B-	Down	Y	0
Putnam Global Health Care Fund Class Y	PHSYX	NAS CM	Open End	Healthcare Sector Equity (Health)	C+	C	B-	Down	Y	0
Putnam Global Industrial Fund Class A	PGIAX	NAS CM	Open End	Industrials Sector Equity ()	B+	A	B-	Up	Y	0
Putnam Global Industrial Fund Class B	PGIVX	NAS CM	Open End	Industrials Sector Equity ()	B+	A-	B-	Up	Y	0
Putnam Global Industrial Fund Class C	PGIEX	NAS CM	Open End	Industrials Sector Equity ()	B+	A-	B-	Up	Y	0
Putnam Global Industrial Fund Class M	PGIHX	NAS CM	Open End	Industrials Sector Equity ()	B+	A	B-	Up	Y	0
Putnam Global Industrial Fund Class R	PGIOX	NAS CM	Open End	Industrials Sector Equity ()	B+	A	B-	Up	Y	0
Putnam Global Industrial Fund Class Y	PGILX	NAS CM	Open End	Industrials Sector Equity ()	B+	A	B-	Up	Y	0
Putnam Global Natural Resources Trust Class A	EBERX	NAS CM	Open End	Natl Resources Sec Equity (Natl Res)	C-	C-	D+	Up	Y	0
Putnam Global Natural Resources Trust Class B	PNRBX	NAS CM	Open End	Natl Resources Sec Equity (Natl Res)	D+	C-	D+	Up	Y	0
Putnam Global Natural Resources Trust Class C	PGLCX	NAS CM	Open End	Natl Resources Sec Equity (Natl Res)	D+	C-	D+	Up	Y	0
Putnam Global Natural Resources Trust Class M	PGLMX	NAS CM	Open End	Natl Resources Sec Equity (Natl Res)	C-	C-	D+	Up	Y	0
Putnam Global Natural Resources Trust Class R	PGNRX	NAS CM	Open End	Natl Resources Sec Equity (Natl Res)	C-	C-	D+	Up	Y	0
Putnam Global Natural Resources Trust Class Y	PGRYX	NAS CM	Open End	Natl Resources Sec Equity (Natl Res)	C-	C-	D+	Up	Y	0
Putnam Global Sector Fund Class A	PPGAX	NAS CM	Open End	Global Equity (World Stock)	B-	B-	B-	Down	Y	0
Putnam Global Sector Fund Class B	PPGBX	NAS CM	Open End	Global Equity (World Stock)	B-	B-	B-	Up	Y	0
Putnam Global Sector Fund Class C	PPGCX	NAS CM	Open End	Global Equity (World Stock)	B	B-	B	Up	Y	0
Putnam Global Sector Fund Class M	PPGMX	NAS CM	Open End	Global Equity (World Stock)	B-	B-	B-	Up	Y	0
Putnam Global Sector Fund Class R	PPGSX	NAS CM	Open End	Global Equity (World Stock)	B-	B-	B-	Up	Y	0
Putnam Global Sector Fund Class Y	PPGYX	NAS CM	Open End	Global Equity (World Stock)	B-	B-	B-	Down	Y	0
Putnam Global Technology Fund Class A	PGTAX	NAS CM	Open End	Technology Sector Equity (Technology)	A	A+	A-	Up	Y	0
Putnam Global Technology Fund Class B	PGTPX	NAS CM	Open End	Technology Sector Equity (Technology)	A	A+	A-	Up	Y	0
Putnam Global Technology Fund Class C	PGTDX	NAS CM	Open End	Technology Sector Equity (Technology)	A	A+	A-	Up	Y	0
Putnam Global Technology Fund Class M	PGTMX	NAS CM	Open End	Technology Sector Equity (Technology)	A	A+	A-	Up	Y	0
Putnam Global Technology Fund Class R	PGTRX	NAS CM	Open End	Technology Sector Equity (Technology)	A	A+	A-	Up	Y	0
Putnam Global Technology Fund Class Y	PGTYX	NAS CM	Open End	Technology Sector Equity (Technology)	A	A+	A-	Up	Y	0

★ Expanded analysis of this fund is included in Section II.

Min Additional Investment	TOTAL RETURNS 3-Month Total Return	6-Month Total Return	1-Year Total Return	3-Year Total Return	5-Year Total Return	PERFORMANCE Dividend Yield (TTM)	Expense Ratio	3-Yr Std Deviation	3-Year Beta	ASSETS NAV	Total Assets (MIL)	ASSET ALLOCATION & TURNOVER %Cash	%Stocks	%Bonds	%Other	Turnover Ratio	BULL & BEAR Last Bull Market Total Return	Last Bear Market Total Return	FEES Front End Fee (%)	Back End Fee (%)	Inception Date
	0.30	5.92	20.51	14.52	41.06	1.9	1.79	12.26	0.92	27.21	220.7	1	94	0	0	47	20.02	-27.93	3.50		Dec-94
	0.34	6.04	20.78	15.42	42.83	2.16	1.54	12.28	0.93	27.13	220.7	1	94	0	0	47	20.2	-27.87			Dec-03
	0.51	6.33	21.42	17.18	46.49	2.56	1.04	12.3	0.93	27.52	220.7	1	94	0	0	47	20.49	-27.7			Oct-05
	3.57	5.14	24.91	37.02	94.24	0.83	1.31	11.14		21.57	58.8	3	97	0	0	41	25.45	-17.72	5.75		Dec-08
	3.34	4.76	24.03	33.94	87.14	0.32	2.06	11.15		20.76	58.8	3	97	0	0	41	24.99	-17.97		5.00	Dec-08
	3.39	4.77	24.06	34.00	87.13	0.26	2.06	11.1		20.68	58.8	3	97	0	0	41	24.92	-18.01		1.00	Dec-08
	3.42	4.87	24.33	35.00	89.52	0.47	1.81	11.14		21.22	58.8	3	97	0	0	41	25.15	-17.91	3.50		Dec-08
	3.50	5.03	24.63	36.07	91.88	0	1.56	11.12		21.49	58.8	3	97	0	0	41	25.34	-17.85			Dec-08
	3.64	5.30	25.26	38.02	96.74	1.03	1.06	11.12		21.67	58.8	3	97	0	0	41	25.69	-17.67			Dec-08
	5.15	12.57	28.08	25.93	72.22	1.26	1.17	10.53	0.96	15.75	846.0	1	96	0	1	48	23.85	-23.36	5.75		Jul-94
	4.99	12.19	27.19	23.15	65.83	0.75	1.92	10.53	0.96	14.08	846.0	1	96	0	1	48	23.37	-23.63		5.00	Jul-94
	4.95	12.18	27.20	23.15	65.89	0.73	1.92	10.51	0.96	14.82	846.0	1	96	0	1	48	23.43	-23.62		1.00	Feb-99
	5.01	12.29	27.49	24.00	67.97	0.93	1.67	10.5	0.95	15.07	846.0	1	96	0	1	48	23.52	-23.5	3.50		Jul-95
	5.11	12.42	27.83	24.98	70.13	0.96	1.42	10.53	0.96	15.65	846.0	1	96	0	1	48	23.74	-23.49			Jan-03
	5.22	12.81	28.64	27.39	76.05	1.54	0.75	10.52	0.96	16.3	846.0	1	96	0	1	48	23.85	-23.36			Jul-12
	5.22	12.69	28.45	26.81	74.44	1.42	0.92	10.49	0.95	16.26	846.0	1	96	0	1	48	23.96	-23.24			Sep-02
	4.41	9.76	20.56	22.55	59.57	1.43	1.31	14.28	0.98	13.52	26.9	2	97	0	2	40	26.25	-32.05	5.75		Dec-08
	4.23	9.31	19.59	19.76	53.65	0.9	2.06	14.26	0.98	13.13	26.9	2	97	0	2	40	25.74	-32.35		5.00	Dec-08
	4.23	9.37	19.57	19.76	53.53	1	2.06	14.27	0.98	12.97	26.9	2	97	0	2	40	25.72	-32.32		1.00	Dec-08
	4.30	9.46	19.87	20.73	55.65	1.08	1.81	14.21	0.98	13.37	26.9	2	97	0	2	40	25.93	-32.25	3.50		Dec-08
	4.36	9.60	20.22	21.60	57.52	1.22	1.56	14.24	0.98	13.37	26.9	2	97	0	2	40	26.07	-32.2			Dec-08
	4.42	9.91	20.76	23.42	61.46	1.6	1.06	14.23	0.98	13.59	26.9	2	97	0	2	40	26.43	-32.05			Dec-08
	-2.18	0.27	15.27	8.70	99.93	0.41	1.09	13.45	1.08	49.34	1,432	1	96	0	0	53	18.21	-19.36	5.75		May-82
	-2.36	-0.10	14.39	6.28	92.55	0	1.84	13.45	1.08	29.3	1,432	1	96	0	0	53	17.67	-19.6		5.00	Mar-93
	-2.37	-0.11	14.39	6.27	92.54	0	1.84	13.44	1.08	36.99	1,432	1	96	0	0	53	17.67	-19.6		1.00	Jul-99
	-2.30	0.03	14.71	7.09	95.01	0.05	1.59	13.44	1.08	38.51	1,432	1	96	0	0	53	17.84	-19.49	3.50		Jul-95
	-2.27	0.13	14.94	7.86	97.38	0.15	1.34	13.45	1.08	46.12	1,432	1	96	0	0	53	18	-19.42			Jan-03
	-2.13	0.38	15.55	9.51	102.42	0.61	0.84	13.45	1.08	52.88	1,432	1	96	0	0	53	18.35	-19.25			Apr-00
	7.97	15.52	27.76	47.77	113.87	1.83	1.29	10.23	0.84	22.34	85.8	2	98	0	0	275	27.83	-30.67	5.75		Dec-08
	7.79	15.10	26.82	44.55	105.94	1.69	2.04	10.22	0.84	21.22	85.8	2	98	0	0	275	27.29	-30.9		5.00	Dec-08
	7.78	15.08	26.77	44.48	106.01	1.74	2.04	10.17	0.83	21.25	85.8	2	98	0	0	275	27.37	-30.94		1.00	Dec-08
	7.89	15.26	27.10	45.67	108.66	1.55	1.79	10.19	0.83	21.93	85.8	2	98	0	0	275	27.56	-30.88	3.50		Dec-08
	7.91	15.35	27.46	46.77	111.24	1.7	1.54	10.18	0.83	22.17	85.8	2	98	0	0	275	27.71	-30.77			Dec-08
	8.09	15.69	28.09	48.99	116.63	1.94	1.04	10.2	0.83	22.55	85.8	2	98	0	0	275	28.05	-30.58			Dec-08
	3.57	14.41	3.32	-12.29	-13.46	0	1.27	19.2	1.14	16.72	161.9	2	98	0	0	119	22.93	-32.61	5.75		Jul-80
	3.41	13.95	2.53	-14.22	-16.64	0	2.02	19.21	1.14	14.5	161.9	2	98	0	0	119	22.44	-32.84		5.00	Feb-94
	3.37	13.84	2.44	-14.30	-16.71	0	2.02	19.18	1.14	14.8	161.9	2	98	0	0	119	22.36	-32.81		1.00	Jul-99
	3.41	14.04	2.73	-13.60	-15.60	0	1.77	19.18	1.14	15.6	161.9	2	98	0	0	119	22.59	-32.76	3.50		Jul-95
	3.48	14.19	3.02	-12.95	-14.55	0	1.52	19.2	1.14	16.25	161.9	2	98	0	0	119	22.77	-32.7			Dec-03
	3.65	14.50	3.53	-11.63	-12.35	0	1.02	19.18	1.14	16.92	161.9	2	98	0	0	119	23.14	-32.57			Oct-05
	2.17	7.88	21.22	26.62	72.45	0.99	1.25	10.96	1.03	11.98	26.4	3	96	0	1	44	22.9	-24.28	5.75		Mar-10
	2.56	8.04	20.98	24.54	67.05	0.33	2	10.93	1.02	11.75	26.4	3	96	0	1	44	22.44	-24.58		5.00	Mar-10
	2.48	7.97	20.93	24.51	66.94	0.48	2	10.98	1.03	11.72	26.4	3	96	0	1	44	22.5	-24.58		1.00	Mar-10
	2.34	7.96	21.06	25.22	68.72	0.1	1.75	10.96	1.02	12	26.4	3	96	0	1	44	22.56	-24.43	3.50		Mar-10
	2.50	8.14	21.40	26.21	70.94	0.74	1.5	11	1.03	12.01	26.4	3	96	0	1	44	22.92	-24.45			Mar-10
	2.08	7.85	21.47	27.52	74.53	1.16	1	10.97	1.03	12.03	26.4	3	96	0	1	44	23.14	-24.23			Mar-10
	5.52	16.11	46.68	80.37	162.86	0.44	1.3	14.43	0.96	34.41	247.7	4	96	0	0	61	24.54	-15.48	5.75		Dec-08
	5.34	15.68	45.61	76.40	153.17	0.09	2.05	14.41	0.96	32.03	247.7	4	96	0	0	61	23.97	-15.73		5.00	Dec-08
	5.34	15.69	45.58	76.36	153.28	0.11	2.05	14.42	0.96	32.01	247.7	4	96	0	0	61	23.97	-15.67		1.00	Dec-08
	5.40	15.80	45.96	77.69	156.30	0.2	1.8	14.41	0.96	32.83	247.7	4	96	0	0	61	24.16	-15.63	3.50		Dec-08
	5.45	15.94	46.33	79.09	159.53	0.37	1.55	14.41	0.96	33.65	247.7	4	96	0	0	61	24.35	-15.53			Dec-08
	5.60	16.26	47.04	81.76	166.11	0.56	1.05	14.42	0.96	35.19	247.7	4	96	0	0	61	24.69	-15.35			Dec-08

	MARKET		FUND TYPE, CATEGORY & OBJECTIVE		RATINGS				MINIMUMS	
Fund Name	Ticker Symbol	Traded On	Fund Type	Category and (Prospectus Objective)	Overall Rating	Reward Rating	Risk Rating	Recent Up/ Downgrade	Open to New Investors	Min Initial Investment
Putnam Global Telecommunication Fund Class A	PGBZX	NAS CM	Open End	Communications Sector Equity (Comm)	B	C+	B+	Up	Y	0
Putnam Global Telecommunication Fund Class B	PGBBX	NAS CM	Open End	Communications Sector Equity (Comm)	B-	C	B	Up	Y	0
Putnam Global Telecommunication Fund Class C	PGBNX	NAS CM	Open End	Communications Sector Equity (Comm)	B-	C	B	Up	Y	0
Putnam Global Telecommunication Fund Class M	PGBMX	NAS CM	Open End	Communications Sector Equity (Comm)	B-	C+	B	Up	Y	0
Putnam Global Telecommunication Fund Class R	PGBTX	NAS CM	Open End	Communications Sector Equity (Comm)	B-	C+	B+	Up	Y	0
Putnam Global Telecommunication Fund Class Y	PGBYX	NAS CM	Open End	Communications Sector Equity (Comm)	B	C+	B+	Up	Y	0
Putnam Global Utilities Fund Class A	PUGIX	NAS CM	Open End	Utilities Sector Equity (Utility)	C+	C+	C+		Y	0
Putnam Global Utilities Fund Class B	PUTBX	NAS CM	Open End	Utilities Sector Equity (Utility)	C+	C+	C+		Y	0
Putnam Global Utilities Fund Class C	PUTCX	NAS CM	Open End	Utilities Sector Equity (Utility)	C+	C+	C+		Y	0
Putnam Global Utilities Fund Class M	PUTMX	NAS CM	Open End	Utilities Sector Equity (Utility)	C+	C+	C+		Y	0
Putnam Global Utilities Fund Class R	PULRX	NAS CM	Open End	Utilities Sector Equity (Utility)	C+	C+	C+		Y	0
Putnam Global Utilities Fund Class Y	PUTYX	NAS CM	Open End	Utilities Sector Equity (Utility)	C+	B-	C+		Y	0
Putnam Growth Opportunities Fund Class A	POGAX	NAS CM	Open End	US Equity Large Cap Growth (Growth)	B+	A-	B-	Up	Y	0
Putnam Growth Opportunities Fund Class B	POGBX	NAS CM	Open End	US Equity Large Cap Growth (Growth)	B	A-	B-		Y	0
Putnam Growth Opportunities Fund Class C	POGCX	NAS CM	Open End	US Equity Large Cap Growth (Growth)	B	A-	B-		Y	0
Putnam Growth Opportunities Fund Class M	PGOMX	NAS CM	Open End	US Equity Large Cap Growth (Growth)	B	A-	B-	Down	Y	0
Putnam Growth Opportunities Fund Class R	PGORX	NAS CM	Open End	US Equity Large Cap Growth (Growth)	B	A-	B-	Down	Y	0
Putnam Growth Opportunities Fund Class R5	PGODX	NAS CM	Open End	US Equity Large Cap Growth (Growth)	B+	A-	B-	Up	Y	0
Putnam Growth Opportunities Fund Class R6	PGOEX	NAS CM	Open End	US Equity Large Cap Growth (Growth)	B+	A-	B-	Up	Y	0
Putnam Growth Opportunities Fund Class Y	PGOYX	NAS CM	Open End	US Equity Large Cap Growth (Growth)	B+	A-	B-	Up	Y	0
Putnam High Income Securities Fund	PCF	NYSE	Closed End	Convertibles (Convertible Bond)	B-	C+	B-	Up	Y	
Putnam International Capital Opportunities Fund Class A	PNVAX	NAS CM	Open End	Global Equity Mid/Small Cap (Foreign Stock)	B	B	B	Up	Y	0
Putnam International Capital Opportunities Fund Class B	PVNBX	NAS CM	Open End	Global Equity Mid/Small Cap (Foreign Stock)	B	B-	B	Up	Y	0
Putnam International Capital Opportunities Fund Class C	PUVCX	NAS CM	Open End	Global Equity Mid/Small Cap (Foreign Stock)	B	B-	B	Up	Y	0
Putnam International Capital Opportunities Fund Class M	PIVMX	NAS CM	Open End	Global Equity Mid/Small Cap (Foreign Stock)	B	B	B	Up	Y	0
Putnam International Capital Opportunities Fund Class R	PICRX	NAS CM	Open End	Global Equity Mid/Small Cap (Foreign Stock)	B	B	B	Up	Y	0
Putnam International Capital Opportunities Fund Class Y	PIVYX	NAS CM	Open End	Global Equity Mid/Small Cap (Foreign Stock)	B	B	B	Up	Y	0
Putnam International Equity Fund Class A	POVSX	NAS CM	Open End	Global Equity Large Cap (Foreign Stock)	B-	C+	B	Up	Y	0
Putnam International Equity Fund Class B	POVBX	NAS CM	Open End	Global Equity Large Cap (Foreign Stock)	B-	C+	B-	Up	Y	0
Putnam International Equity Fund Class C	PIGCX	NAS CM	Open End	Global Equity Large Cap (Foreign Stock)	B-	C+	B-	Up	Y	0
Putnam International Equity Fund Class M	POVMX	NAS CM	Open End	Global Equity Large Cap (Foreign Stock)	B-	C+	B-	Up	Y	0
Putnam International Equity Fund Class R	PIERX	NAS CM	Open End	Global Equity Large Cap (Foreign Stock)	B-	C+	B	Up	Y	0
Putnam International Equity Fund Class R5	POVDX	NAS CM	Open End	Global Equity Large Cap (Foreign Stock)	B-	B-	B	Up	Y	0
Putnam International Equity Fund Class R6	POVEX	NAS CM	Open End	Global Equity Large Cap (Foreign Stock)	B-	B-	B	Up	Y	0
Putnam International Equity Fund Class Y	POVYX	NAS CM	Open End	Global Equity Large Cap (Foreign Stock)	B-	B-	B	Up	Y	0
Putnam International Growth Fund Class A	PINOX	NAS CM	Open End	Global Equity Large Cap (Growth)	B-	B-	B	Up	Y	0
Putnam International Growth Fund Class B	PINWX	NAS CM	Open End	Global Equity Large Cap (Growth)	B-	C+	B	Up	Y	0
Putnam International Growth Fund Class C	PIOCX	NAS CM	Open End	Global Equity Large Cap (Growth)	B-	C+	B	Up	Y	0
Putnam International Growth Fund Class M	PINMX	NAS CM	Open End	Global Equity Large Cap (Growth)	B-	B-	B	Up	Y	0
Putnam International Growth Fund Class R	PNPRX	NAS CM	Open End	Global Equity Large Cap (Growth)	B-	B-	B	Up	Y	0
Putnam International Growth Fund Class Y	PINYX	NAS CM	Open End	Global Equity Large Cap (Growth)	B-	B-	B	Up	Y	0
Putnam International Value Fund Class A	PNGAX	NAS CM	Open End	Global Equity Large Cap (Growth)	B-	C+	B	Up	Y	0
Putnam International Value Fund Class B	PGNBX	NAS CM	Open End	Global Equity Large Cap (Growth)	B-	C+	B-	Up	Y	0
Putnam International Value Fund Class C	PIGRX	NAS CM	Open End	Global Equity Large Cap (Growth)	B-	C+	B-	Up	Y	0
Putnam International Value Fund Class M	PIGMX	NAS CM	Open End	Global Equity Large Cap (Growth)	B-	C+	B-	Up	Y	0
Putnam International Value Fund Class R	PIIRX	NAS CM	Open End	Global Equity Large Cap (Growth)	C+	C+	C+	Up	Y	0
Putnam International Value Fund Class R6	PIGWX	NAS CM	Open End	Global Equity Large Cap (Growth)	B-	C+	B	Up	Y	0
Putnam International Value Fund Class Y	PNGYX	NAS CM	Open End	Global Equity Large Cap (Growth)	B-	C+	B	Up	Y	0
Putnam Investors Fund Class A	PINVX	NAS CM	Open End	US Equity Large Cap Blend (Growth)	B	B	B-	Up	Y	0
Putnam Investors Fund Class B	PNVBX	NAS CM	Open End	US Equity Large Cap Blend (Growth)	B-	B-	B-	Down	Y	0
Putnam Investors Fund Class C	PCINX	NAS CM	Open End	US Equity Large Cap Blend (Growth)	B-	B-	B-	Down	Y	0
Putnam Investors Fund Class M	PNVMX	NAS CM	Open End	US Equity Large Cap Blend (Growth)	B-	B	B-	Down	Y	0

★Expanded analysis of this fund is included in Section II.

Min Additional Investment	TOTAL RETURNS: 3-Month Total Return	6-Month Total Return	1-Year Total Return	3-Year Total Return	5-Year Total Return	PERFORMANCE: Dividend Yield (TTM)	Expense Ratio	3-Yr Std Deviation	3-Year Beta	ASSETS: NAV	Total Assets (MIL)	ASSET ALLOCATION & TURNOVER: %Cash	%Stocks	%Bonds	%Other	Turnover Ratio	BULL & BEAR: Last Bull Market Total Return	Last Bear Market Total Return	FEES: Front End Fee (%)	Back End Fee (%)	Inception Date
	2.10	5.24	14.07	22.95	64.53	3.62	1.31	10.69	0.73	16.01	25.1	3	92	0	0	55	14.67	-13.56	5.75		Dec-08
	1.90	4.80	13.24	20.15	58.42	3.15	2.06	10.72	0.73	15.48	25.1	3	92	0	0	55	14.18	-13.8		5.00	Dec-08
	1.91	4.81	13.26	20.21	58.39	2.88	2.06	10.69	0.73	15.46	25.1	3	92	0	0	55	14.26	-13.8		1.00	Dec-08
	1.99	4.96	13.60	21.14	60.56	2.84	1.81	10.68	0.73	15.87	25.1	3	92	0	0	55	14.39	-13.76	3.50		Dec-08
	2.01	5.04	13.81	21.99	62.41	1.21	1.56	10.67	0.73	16.23	25.1	3	92	0	0	55	14.52	-13.57			Dec-08
	2.16	5.36	14.39	23.88	66.66	3.85	1.06	10.73	0.73	16.07	25.1	3	92	0	0	55	14.9	-13.46			Dec-08
	1.27	8.06	22.07	10.46	46.37	1.58	1.22	11.68	0.96	13.61	179.7	3	97	0	0	43	7	-10.58	5.75		Nov-90
	1.00	7.59	21.12	7.94	40.90	0.92	1.97	11.64	0.95	13.57	179.7	3	97	0	0	43	6.62	-10.88		5.00	Apr-92
	1.09	7.63	21.24	7.95	41.02	0.91	1.97	11.66	0.96	13.51	179.7	3	97	0	0	43	6.55	-10.82		1.00	Jul-99
	1.08	7.72	21.50	8.81	42.65	1.16	1.72	11.6	0.95	13.6	179.7	3	97	0	0	43	6.73	-10.82	3.50		Mar-95
	1.14	7.86	21.81	9.56	44.44	1.38	1.47	11.64	0.95	13.6	179.7	3	97	0	0	43	6.9	-10.71			Dec-03
	1.34	8.12	22.39	11.30	48.11	1.79	0.97	11.66	0.96	13.6	179.7	3	97	0	0	43	7.23	-10.55			Oct-05
	6.59	13.17	30.96	39.62	122.83	0.01	0.93	11.69	1.07	31.3	4,621	1	98	0	0	70	28.75	-20.3	5.75		Oct-95
	6.37	12.72	29.94	36.48	114.59	0	1.68	11.69	1.07	26.69	4,621	1	98	0	0	70	28.22	-20.58		5.00	Aug-97
	6.38	12.70	30.00	36.49	114.64	0	1.68	11.68	1.06	27.17	4,621	1	98	0	0	70	28.21	-20.55		1.00	Feb-99
	6.42	12.83	30.26	37.46	117.28	0	1.43	11.7	1.07	28.32	4,621	1	98	0	0	70	28.35	-20.48	3.50		Aug-97
	6.52	13.01	30.66	38.53	120.04	0	1.18	11.7	1.07	30.26	4,621	1	98	0	0	70	28.61	-20.44			Jan-03
	6.65	13.30	31.33	40.83	126.55	0	0.63	11.69	1.07	32.81	4,621	1	98	0	0	70	28.75	-20.3			Jul-12
	6.69	13.34	31.45	41.28	127.80	0.07	0.53	11.69	1.07	32.76	4,621	1	98	0	0	70	28.75	-20.3			Jul-12
	6.63	13.27	31.27	40.63	125.63	0.02	0.68	11.69	1.07	32.61	4,621	1	98	0	0	70	28.94	-20.22			Jul-99
	1.39	4.83	11.19	18.84	42.02	3.7		6.7	0.99	9.69	126.3	1	2	41	1	26	11.23	-11.94			Jul-87
	6.37	14.65	34.53	33.28	44.33	1.91	1.26	12.18	0.99	42.28	466.6	3	94	0	1	103	17.42	-27.79	5.75		Dec-95
	6.17	14.20	33.54	30.30	39.01	1.19	2.01	12.16	0.99	42.48	466.6	3	94	0	1	103	16.94	-28.01		5.00	Oct-96
	6.20	14.22	33.55	30.35	39.02	1.25	2.01	12.18	0.99	42.23	466.6	3	94	0	1	103	16.93	-28.03		1.00	Jul-99
	6.23	14.36	33.87	31.31	40.74	1.51	1.76	12.17	0.99	42.19	466.6	3	94	0	1	103	17.12	-27.94	3.50		Oct-96
	6.30	14.49	34.17	32.29	42.53	1.71	1.51	12.18	1	41.78	466.6	3	94	0	1	103	17.27	-27.87			Jan-03
	6.45	14.79	34.84	34.29	46.14	2.12	1.01	12.18	0.99	42.21	466.6	3	94	0	1	103	17.64	-27.73			Feb-00
	3.12	10.31	26.47	22.60	48.65	2.49	1.23	11.82	0.94	26.17	1,008	2	96	0	0	67	18.49	-26.16	5.75		Feb-91
	2.89	9.88	25.50	19.85	43.18	1.87	1.98	11.81	0.94	24.9	1,008	2	96	0	0	67	17.98	-26.39		5.00	Jun-94
	2.93	9.93	25.53	19.87	43.22	1.92	1.98	11.78	0.93	25.22	1,008	2	96	0	0	67	17.88	-26.38		1.00	Jul-99
	2.99	10.06	25.83	20.76	44.95	2.1	1.73	11.8	0.93	25.47	1,008	2	96	0	0	67	18.13	-26.3	3.50		Dec-94
	3.07	10.21	26.13	21.66	46.76	2.36	1.48	11.81	0.94	25.71	1,008	2	96	0	0	67	18.23	-26.19			Jan-03
	3.19	10.50	26.83	23.73	51.10	2.73	0.89	11.83	0.94	26.58	1,008	2	96	0	0	67	18.49	-26.16			Jul-12
	3.22	10.56	26.99	24.15	52.04	2.82	0.79	11.82	0.94	26.55	1,008	2	96	0	0	67	18.49	-26.16			Jul-12
	3.16	10.44	26.75	23.50	50.46	2.69	0.98	11.81	0.94	26.45	1,008	2	96	0	0	67	18.62	-26.07			Jul-96
	4.43	13.56	35.04	26.74	48.34	1.41	1.5	11.92	0.94	22.85	308.5	1	97	0	2	121	19.29	-27.82	5.75		Jan-95
	4.27	13.14	34.09	23.95	42.92	0.91	2.25	11.89	0.94	20.49	308.5	1	97	0	2	121	18.75	-28.07		5.00	Jul-95
	4.27	13.16	34.05	23.97	42.91	0.92	2.25	11.93	0.94	20.98	308.5	1	97	0	2	121	18.73	-28.07		1.00	Feb-99
	4.36	13.30	34.40	24.90	44.73	1.12	2	11.93	0.94	21.29	308.5	1	97	0	2	121	18.88	-27.99	3.50		Jul-95
	4.39	13.40	34.65	25.75	46.43	1.28	1.75	11.91	0.94	22.34	308.5	1	97	0	2	121	19.1	-27.93			Dec-03
	4.52	13.68	35.32	27.69	50.22	1.6	1.25	11.91	0.94	23.1	308.5	1	97	0	2	121	19.48	-27.75			Oct-05
	2.45	8.77	24.08	22.08	36.36	1.83	1.36	11.88	0.87	12.21	163.2	2	97	0	0	16	16.55	-24.83	5.75		Aug-96
	2.31	8.36	23.16	19.34	31.42	1.08	2.11	11.91	0.87	12.24	163.2	2	97	0	0	16	16.1	-25.04		5.00	Aug-96
	2.29	8.38	23.15	19.45	31.45	1.18	2.11	11.84	0.87	12.16	163.2	2	97	0	0	16	16.11	-25.06		1.00	Feb-99
	2.34	8.46	23.44	20.19	32.92	1.43	1.86	11.93	0.87	12.25	163.2	2	97	0	0	16	16.25	-25.02	3.50		Aug-96
	2.46	8.67	23.78	21.13	34.75	1.8	1.61	11.89	0.87	12.07	163.2	2	97	0	0	16	16.48	-24.9			Dec-03
	2.55	9.02	24.66	23.60	38.61	2.18	0.92	11.95	0.88	12.24	163.2	2	97	0	0	16	16.55	-24.83			Dec-13
	2.55	8.87	24.43	23.04	38.16	2.06	1.11	11.84	0.87	12.2	163.2	2	97	0	0	16	16.74	-24.7			Oct-00
	7.46	13.95	22.88	32.93	109.66	0.85	1.04	10.9	1.06	28.4	2,054	1	97	0	1	52	27.16	-18.85	5.75		Dec-25
	7.27	13.52	21.98	29.93	101.93	0.36	1.79	10.9	1.06	25.44	2,054	1	97	0	1	52	26.46	-19.04		5.00	Mar-93
	7.28	13.53	21.93	29.96	101.99	0.34	1.79	10.91	1.06	26.76	2,054	1	97	0	1	52	26.55	-19.1		1.00	Jul-99
	7.31	13.66	22.24	30.89	104.42	0.48	1.54	10.91	1.06	26.72	2,054	1	97	0	1	52	26.71	-19.04	3.50		Dec-94

Fund Name	MARKET Ticker Symbol	Traded On	FUND TYPE, CATEGORY & OBJECTIVE Fund Type	Category and (Prospectus Objective)	RATINGS Overall Rating	Reward Rating	Risk Rating	Recent Up/ Downgrade	MINIMUMS Open to New Investors	Min Initial Investment
Putnam Investors Fund Class R	PIVRX	NAS CM	Open End	US Equity Large Cap Blend (Growth)	B-	B	B-	Down	Y	0
Putnam Investors Fund Class R6	PIVEX	NAS CM	Open End	US Equity Large Cap Blend (Growth)	B	B	B-	Up	Y	0
Putnam Investors Fund Class Y	PNVYX	NAS CM	Open End	US Equity Large Cap Blend (Growth)	B	B	B-	Up	Y	0
Putnam Low Volatility Equity Fund Class A	PLVEX	NAS CM	Open End	US Equity Large Cap Blend (Growth)	B-	C+	B	Down	Y	0
Putnam Low Volatility Equity Fund Class B	PLVFX	NAS CM	Open End	US Equity Large Cap Blend (Growth)	B-	C+	B	Down	Y	0
Putnam Low Volatility Equity Fund Class C	PLVGX	NAS CM	Open End	US Equity Large Cap Blend (Growth)	B-	C+	B	Down	Y	0
Putnam Low Volatility Equity Fund Class M	PLVHX	NAS CM	Open End	US Equity Large Cap Blend (Growth)	B-	C+	B	Down	Y	0
Putnam Low Volatility Equity Fund Class Y	PLVKX	NAS CM	Open End	US Equity Large Cap Blend (Growth)	B-	C+	B	Down	Y	0
Putnam Multi-Cap Core Fund Class A	PMYAX	NAS CM	Open End	US Equity Large Cap Blend (Growth)	B	B	C+	Up	Y	0
Putnam Multi-Cap Core Fund Class B	PMYBX	NAS CM	Open End	US Equity Large Cap Blend (Growth)	B-	B	C+	Down	Y	0
Putnam Multi-Cap Core Fund Class C	PMYCX	NAS CM	Open End	US Equity Large Cap Blend (Growth)	B-	B	C+	Down	Y	0
Putnam Multi-Cap Core Fund Class M	PMYMX	NAS CM	Open End	US Equity Large Cap Blend (Growth)	B-	B	C+	Down	Y	0
Putnam Multi-Cap Core Fund Class R	PMYZX	NAS CM	Open End	US Equity Large Cap Blend (Growth)	B-	B	C+	Down	Y	0
Putnam Multi-Cap Core Fund Class Y	PMYYX	NAS CM	Open End	US Equity Large Cap Blend (Growth)	B	B	C+	Up	Y	0
Putnam Multi-Cap Growth Fund Class A	PNOPX	NAS CM	Open End	US Equity Large Cap Growth (Aggr Growth)	B	B+	B-	Down	Y	0
Putnam Multi-Cap Growth Fund Class B	PNOBX	NAS CM	Open End	US Equity Large Cap Growth (Aggr Growth)	B	B+	B-		Y	0
Putnam Multi-Cap Growth Fund Class C	PNOCX	NAS CM	Open End	US Equity Large Cap Growth (Aggr Growth)	B	B+	B-		Y	0
Putnam Multi-Cap Growth Fund Class M	PNOMX	NAS CM	Open End	US Equity Large Cap Growth (Aggr Growth)	B	B+	B-		Y	0
Putnam Multi-Cap Growth Fund Class R	PNORX	NAS CM	Open End	US Equity Large Cap Growth (Aggr Growth)	B	B+	B-	Down	Y	0
Putnam Multi-Cap Growth Fund Class Y	PNOYX	NAS CM	Open End	US Equity Large Cap Growth (Aggr Growth)	B	B+	B-	Down	Y	0
Putnam Multi-Cap Value Fund Class A	PMVAX	NAS CM	Open End	US Equity Mid Cap (Growth & Income)	B-	C+	B	Up	Y	0
Putnam Multi-Cap Value Fund Class B	PMVBX	NAS CM	Open End	US Equity Mid Cap (Growth & Income)	B-	C+	B	Up	Y	0
Putnam Multi-Cap Value Fund Class C	PMPCX	NAS CM	Open End	US Equity Mid Cap (Growth & Income)	B-	C+	B	Up	Y	0
Putnam Multi-Cap Value Fund Class M	PMCVX	NAS CM	Open End	US Equity Mid Cap (Growth & Income)	B-	C+	B	Up	Y	0
Putnam Multi-Cap Value Fund Class R	PMVRX	NAS CM	Open End	US Equity Mid Cap (Growth & Income)	B-	C+	B	Up	Y	0
Putnam Multi-Cap Value Fund Class Y	PMVYX	NAS CM	Open End	US Equity Mid Cap (Growth & Income)	B-	C+	B	Up	Y	0
Putnam PanAgora Managed Futures Strategy Class A	PPMFX	NAS CM	Open End	Other Alternative (Income)	U	U	U		Y	0
Putnam PanAgora Managed Futures Strategy Class B	PPFMX	NAS CM	Open End	Other Alternative (Income)	U	U	U		Y	0
Putnam PanAgora Managed Futures Strategy Class C	PPFLX	NAS CM	Open End	Other Alternative (Income)	U	U	U		Y	0
Putnam PanAgora Managed Futures Strategy Class M	PPFVX	NAS CM	Open End	Other Alternative (Income)	U	U	U		Y	0
Putnam PanAgora Managed Futures Strategy Class R	PPFWX	NAS CM	Open End	Other Alternative (Income)	U	U	U		Y	0
Putnam PanAgora Managed Futures Strategy Class R6	PPFRX	NAS CM	Open End	Other Alternative (Income)	U	U	U		Y	0
Putnam PanAgora Managed Futures Strategy Class Y	PPFYX	NAS CM	Open End	Other Alternative (Income)	U	U	U		Y	0
Putnam PanAgora Market Neutral Fund Class A	PPMAX	NAS CM	Open End	Market Neutral (Income)	U	U	U		Y	0
Putnam PanAgora Market Neutral Fund Class B	PPMBX	NAS CM	Open End	Market Neutral (Income)	U	U	U		Y	0
Putnam PanAgora Market Neutral Fund Class C	PPMDX	NAS CM	Open End	Market Neutral (Income)	U	U	U		Y	0
Putnam PanAgora Market Neutral Fund Class M	PPMVX	NAS CM	Open End	Market Neutral (Income)	U	U	U		Y	0
Putnam PanAgora Market Neutral Fund Class R	PPMLX	NAS CM	Open End	Market Neutral (Income)	U	U	U		Y	0
Putnam PanAgora Market Neutral Fund Class R6	PPMRX	NAS CM	Open End	Market Neutral (Income)	U	U	U		Y	0
Putnam PanAgora Market Neutral Fund Class Y	PPMYX	NAS CM	Open End	Market Neutral (Income)	U	U	U		Y	0
Putnam PanAgora Risk Parity Fund Class A	PPRPX	NAS CM	Open End	Moderate Alloc (Growth & Income)	U	U	U		Y	0
Putnam PanAgora Risk Parity Fund Class B	PPRLX	NAS CM	Open End	Moderate Alloc (Growth & Income)	U	U	U		Y	0
Putnam PanAgora Risk Parity Fund Class C	PPRNX	NAS CM	Open End	Moderate Alloc (Growth & Income)	U	U	U		Y	0
Putnam PanAgora Risk Parity Fund Class M	PPRVX	NAS CM	Open End	Moderate Alloc (Growth & Income)	U	U	U		Y	0
Putnam PanAgora Risk Parity Fund Class R	PPROX	NAS CM	Open End	Moderate Alloc (Growth & Income)	U	U	U		Y	0
Putnam PanAgora Risk Parity Fund Class R6	PPRWX	NAS CM	Open End	Moderate Alloc (Growth & Income)	U	U	U		Y	0
Putnam PanAgora Risk Parity Fund Class Y	PPRYX	NAS CM	Open End	Moderate Alloc (Growth & Income)	U	U	U		Y	0
Putnam Research Fund Class A	PNRAX	NAS CM	Open End	US Equity Large Cap Blend (Growth)	B-	B	B-	Down	Y	0
Putnam Research Fund Class B	PRFBX	NAS CM	Open End	US Equity Large Cap Blend (Growth)	B-	B	B-	Down	Y	0
Putnam Research Fund Class C	PRACX	NAS CM	Open End	US Equity Large Cap Blend (Growth)	B-	B	B-	Down	Y	0
Putnam Research Fund Class M	PRFMX	NAS CM	Open End	US Equity Large Cap Blend (Growth)	B-	B	B-	Down	Y	0
Putnam Research Fund Class R	PRSRX	NAS CM	Open End	US Equity Large Cap Blend (Growth)	B-	B	B-	Down	Y	0

★ Expanded analysis of this fund is included in Section II.

	TOTAL RETURNS					PERFORMANCE				ASSETS		ASSET ALLOCATION & TURNOVER					BULL & BEAR		FEES		
Min Additional Investment	3-Month Total Return	6-Month Total Return	1-Year Total Return	3-Year Total Return	5-Year Total Return	Dividend Yield (TTM)	Expense Ratio	3-Yr Std Deviation	3-Year Beta	NAV	Total Assets (MIL)	%Cash	%Stocks	%Bonds	%Other	Turnover Ratio	Last Bull Market Total Return	Last Bear Market Total Return	Front End Fee (%)	Back End Fee (%)	Inception Date
	7.40	13.82	22.57	31.92	107.02	0.17	1.29	10.94	1.06	28.14	2,054	1	97	0	1	52	26.94	-18.95			Jan-03
	7.58	14.20	23.38	34.50	114.38	1.15	0.65	10.91	1.06	28.93	2,054	1	97	0	1	52	27.16	-18.85			Jul-12
	7.53	14.10	23.16	33.93	112.37	1.03	0.79	10.94	1.06	28.8	2,054	1	97	0	1	52	27.25	-18.72			Jan-97
	4.88	8.23	13.25	13.86		1.44	1.2	5.85	0.51	12.04	27.3	1	97	0	1	47			5.75		Mar-13
	4.69	7.80	12.34	11.21		0.71	1.95	5.89	0.51	11.9	27.3	1	97	0	1	47				5.00	Mar-13
	4.69	7.80	12.46	11.33		0.67	1.95	5.83	0.51	11.9	27.3	1	97	0	1	47				1.00	Mar-13
	4.76	7.94	12.77	12.19		1.02	1.7	5.88	0.51	12	27.3	1	97	0	1	47			3.50		Mar-13
	4.98	8.42	13.55	14.68		1.64	0.95	5.91	0.51	12.04	27.3	1	97	0	1	47					Mar-13
	7.11	14.21	23.68	34.56	122.09	0.78	1.03	11.12	1.05	22.84	564.7	1	98	0	1	76	28.49	-20.09	5.75		Sep-10
	6.90	13.80	22.77	31.65	114.02	0.29	1.78	11.1	1.05	22.32	564.7	1	98	0	1	76	27.85	-20.33		5.00	Sep-10
	6.89	13.80	22.78	31.62	114.10	0.19	1.78	11.09	1.05	22.29	564.7	1	98	0	1	76	27.79	-20.31		1.00	Sep-10
	7.01	13.93	23.10	32.65	116.71	0.35	1.53	11.14	1.06	22.61	564.7	1	98	0	1	76	28.04	-20.28	3.50		Sep-10
	7.07	14.09	23.38	33.60	119.46	0.61	1.28	11.13	1.06	22.78	564.7	1	98	0	1	76	28.3	-20.18			Sep-10
	7.19	14.32	24.01	35.56	124.97	0.99	0.78	11.12	1.06	22.91	564.7	1	98	0	1	76	28.66	-20.06			Sep-10
	6.03	12.13	29.05	37.31	117.92	0	1	11.7	1.06	89.45	4,380	1	99	0	0	76	29.81	-22.16	5.75		Aug-90
	5.84	11.69	28.07	34.24	109.91	0	1.75	11.68	1.06	70.49	4,380	1	99	0	0	76	29.21	-22.38		5.00	Mar-93
	5.83	11.71	28.09	34.25	109.89	0	1.75	11.69	1.06	76.52	4,380	1	99	0	0	76	29.23	-22.39		1.00	Jul-99
	5.89	11.83	28.40	35.27	112.52	0	1.5	11.68	1.06	77.85	4,380	1	99	0	0	76	29.43	-22.31	3.50		Dec-94
	5.97	11.98	28.73	36.30	115.23	0	1.25	11.69	1.06	86.72	4,380	1	99	0	0	76	29.6	-22.23			Jan-03
	6.11	12.27	29.38	38.35	120.70	0	0.75	11.7	1.06	95.53	4,380	1	99	0	0	76	29.98	-22.05			Jul-94
	2.77	5.69	10.63	18.59	91.00	0.85	1.08	10.26	0.9	19.91	455.4	3	96	0	0	78	26.95	-22.23	5.75		Nov-99
	2.57	5.27	9.85	15.95	84.02	0.25	1.83	10.26	0.89	18.27	455.4	3	96	0	0	78	26.31	-22.44		5.00	Jan-01
	2.59	5.31	9.86	15.99	84.02	0.31	1.83	10.25	0.9	18.15	455.4	3	96	0	0	78	26.36	-22.48		1.00	Jan-01
	2.59	5.43	10.12	16.80	86.34	0.5	1.58	10.26	0.9	18.9	455.4	3	96	0	0	78	26.6	-22.46	3.50		Jan-01
	2.68	5.57	10.39	17.70	88.71	0.65	1.33	10.27	0.9	19.4	455.4	3	96	0	0	78	26.75	-22.38			Apr-03
	2.86	5.89	10.95	19.52	93.46	1.06	0.83	10.26	0.9	19.98	455.4	3	96	0	0	78	27.1	-22.17			Apr-02
	2.10						1.6			10.09	11.7								5.75		Sep-17
	1.90						2.35			10.07	11.7									5.00	Sep-17
	1.90						2.35			10.07	11.7									1.00	Sep-17
	2.00						2.1			10.08	11.7								3.50		Sep-17
	2.10						1.85			10.09	11.7										Sep-17
	2.20						1.25			10.1	11.7										Sep-17
	2.20						1.35			10.1	11.7										Sep-17
	-0.80						1.9			9.87	10.9								5.75		Sep-17
	-1.00						2.65			9.85	10.9									5.00	Sep-17
	-1.00						2.65			9.85	10.9									1.00	Sep-17
	-0.90						2.4			9.86	10.9								3.50		Sep-17
	-0.90						2.15			9.86	10.9										Sep-17
	-0.70						1.55			9.88	10.9										Sep-17
	-0.70						1.65			9.88	10.9										Sep-17
	3.34						1.35			10.2	29.0								5.75		Sep-17
	3.24						2.1			10.18	29.0									5.00	Sep-17
	3.24						2.1			10.18	29.0									1.00	Sep-17
	3.14						1.85			10.18	29.0								3.50		Sep-17
	3.24						1.6			10.19	29.0										Sep-17
	3.34						1			10.2	29.0										Sep-17
	3.34						1.1			10.2	29.0										Sep-17
	5.52	10.62	23.19	32.31	106.96	0.87	1.15	10.59	1.03	33.09	307.1	3	97	0	0	98	26.72	-19.01	5.75		Oct-95
	5.33	10.18	22.30	29.33	99.33	0.31	1.9	10.56	1.03	30.83	307.1	3	97	0	0	98	26.12	-19.27		5.00	Jun-98
	5.30	10.19	22.27	29.31	99.30	0.36	1.9	10.58	1.03	30.81	307.1	3	97	0	0	98	26.14	-19.26		1.00	Feb-99
	5.40	10.35	22.62	30.32	101.78	0.48	1.65	10.57	1.03	31.66	307.1	3	97	0	0	98	26.4	-19.21	3.50		Jun-98
	5.45	10.46	22.88	31.30	104.43	0.62	1.4	10.58	1.03	32.7	307.1	3	97	0	0	98	26.53	-19.09			Jan-03

	MARKET			FUND TYPE, CATEGORY & OBJECTIVE	RATINGS				MINIMUMS	
Fund Name	Ticker Symbol	Traded On	Fund Type	Category and (Prospectus Objective)	Overall Rating	Reward Rating	Risk Rating	Recent Up/ Downgrade	Open to New Investors	Min Initial Investment
Putnam Research Fund Class R6 Shares	PLJMX	NAS CM	Open End	US Equity Large Cap Blend (Growth)	B	B	B-		Y	0
Putnam Research Fund Class Y	PURYX	NAS CM	Open End	US Equity Large Cap Blend (Growth)	B	B	B-		Y	0
Putnam Retirement Income Fund Lifestyle 1 Class A	PRMAX	NAS CM	Open End	Target Date 2000-2020 (Asset Alloc)	B-	C	B	Up	Y	0
Putnam Retirement Income Fund Lifestyle 1 Class B	PRMLX	NAS CM	Open End	Target Date 2000-2020 (Asset Alloc)	C+	C	B	Up	Y	0
Putnam Retirement Income Fund Lifestyle 1 Class C	PRMCX	NAS CM	Open End	Target Date 2000-2020 (Asset Alloc)	C+	C	B	Up	Y	0
Putnam Retirement Income Fund Lifestyle 1 Class M	PRMMX	NAS CM	Open End	Target Date 2000-2020 (Asset Alloc)	B-	C	B	Up	Y	0
Putnam Retirement Income Fund Lifestyle 1 Class R	PRMKX	NAS CM	Open End	Target Date 2000-2020 (Asset Alloc)	C+	C	B	Up	Y	0
Putnam Retirement Income Fund Lifestyle 1 Class R6	PREWX	NAS CM	Open End	Target Date 2000-2020 (Asset Alloc)	B-	C	B	Up	Y	0
Putnam Retirement Income Fund Lifestyle 1 Class Y	PRMYX	NAS CM	Open End	Target Date 2000-2020 (Asset Alloc)	B-	C	B	Up	Y	0
Putnam RetirementReady 2020 Fund Class A	PRRMX	NAS CM	Open End	Target Date 2000-2020 (Asset Alloc)	B-	C	B	Up	Y	0
Putnam RetirementReady 2020 Fund Class B	US7468596850		Open End	Target Date 2000-2020 (Asset Alloc)	B-	C	B	Up	Y	0
Putnam RetirementReady 2020 Fund Class C	US7468596777		Open End	Target Date 2000-2020 (Asset Alloc)	B-	C	B	Up	Y	0
Putnam RetirementReady 2020 Fund Class M	US7468596694		Open End	Target Date 2000-2020 (Asset Alloc)	B-	C	B	Up	Y	0
Putnam RetirementReady 2020 Fund Class R	US7468596512		Open End	Target Date 2000-2020 (Asset Alloc)	B-	C	B	Up	Y	0
Putnam RetirementReady 2020 Fund Class R6	PMRGX	NAS CM	Open End	Target Date 2000-2020 (Asset Alloc)	B-	C+	B	Up	Y	0
Putnam RetirementReady 2020 Fund Class Y	PRRNX	NAS CM	Open End	Target Date 2000-2020 (Asset Alloc)	B-	C+	B	Up	Y	0
Putnam RetirementReady 2025 Fund Class A	PRROX	NAS CM	Open End	Target Date 2021-2045 (Asset Alloc)	B-	C+	B	Up	Y	0
Putnam RetirementReady 2025 Fund Class B	US7468597437		Open End	Target Date 2021-2045 (Asset Alloc)	B-	C+	B	Up	Y	0
Putnam RetirementReady 2025 Fund Class C	US7468597353		Open End	Target Date 2021-2045 (Asset Alloc)	B-	C+	B	Up	Y	0
Putnam RetirementReady 2025 Fund Class M	US7468597270		Open End	Target Date 2021-2045 (Asset Alloc)	B-	C+	B	Up	Y	0
Putnam RetirementReady 2025 Fund Class R	US7468597197		Open End	Target Date 2021-2045 (Asset Alloc)	B-	C+	B	Up	Y	0
Putnam RetirementReady 2025 Fund Class R6	PRMFX	NAS CM	Open End	Target Date 2021-2045 (Asset Alloc)	B-	C+	B	Up	Y	0
Putnam RetirementReady 2025 Fund Class Y	PRRPX	NAS CM	Open End	Target Date 2021-2045 (Asset Alloc)	B-	C+	B	Up	Y	0
Putnam RetirementReady 2030 Fund Class A	PRRQX	NAS CM	Open End	Target Date 2021-2045 (Asset Alloc)	B-	C+	B	Up	Y	0
Putnam RetirementReady 2030 Fund Class B	US7468597924		Open End	Target Date 2021-2045 (Asset Alloc)	B-	C+	B	Up	Y	0
Putnam RetirementReady 2030 Fund Class C	US7468597841		Open End	Target Date 2021-2045 (Asset Alloc)	B-	C+	B	Up	Y	0
Putnam RetirementReady 2030 Fund Class M	US7468597767		Open End	Target Date 2021-2045 (Asset Alloc)	B-	C+	B	Up	Y	0
Putnam RetirementReady 2030 Fund Class R	US7468597684		Open End	Target Date 2021-2045 (Asset Alloc)	B-	C+	B	Up	Y	0
Putnam RetirementReady 2030 Fund Class R6	PREZX	NAS CM	Open End	Target Date 2021-2045 (Asset Alloc)	B-	C+	B	Up	Y	0
Putnam RetirementReady 2030 Fund Class Y	PRRTX	NAS CM	Open End	Target Date 2021-2045 (Asset Alloc)	B-	C+	B	Up	Y	0
Putnam RetirementReady 2035 Fund Class A	PRRWX	NAS CM	Open End	Target Date 2021-2045 (Asset Alloc)	B-	C+	B	Down	Y	0
Putnam RetirementReady 2035 Fund Class B	US7468598591		Open End	Target Date 2021-2045 (Asset Alloc)	B-	C+	B	Down	Y	0
Putnam RetirementReady 2035 Fund Class C	US7468598427		Open End	Target Date 2021-2045 (Asset Alloc)	B-	C+	B	Down	Y	0
Putnam RetirementReady 2035 Fund Class M	US7468598344		Open End	Target Date 2021-2045 (Asset Alloc)	B-	C+	B	Down	Y	0
Putnam RetirementReady 2035 Fund Class R	US7468598260		Open End	Target Date 2021-2045 (Asset Alloc)	B-	C+	B	Down	Y	0
Putnam RetirementReady 2035 Fund Class R6	PREGX	NAS CM	Open End	Target Date 2021-2045 (Asset Alloc)	B-	C+	B	Down	Y	0
Putnam RetirementReady 2035 Fund Class Y	PRRYX	NAS CM	Open End	Target Date 2021-2045 (Asset Alloc)	B-	C+	B	Down	Y	0
Putnam RetirementReady 2040 Fund Class A	PRRZX	NAS CM	Open End	Target Date 2021-2045 (Asset Alloc)	B-	B-	B	Down	Y	0
Putnam RetirementReady 2040 Fund Class B	US7468597015		Open End	Target Date 2021-2045 (Asset Alloc)	B-	C+	B	Down	Y	0
Putnam RetirementReady 2040 Fund Class C	US7468598005		Open End	Target Date 2021-2045 (Asset Alloc)	B-	C+	B	Down	Y	0
Putnam RetirementReady 2040 Fund Class M	US7468598831		Open End	Target Date 2021-2045 (Asset Alloc)	B-	C+	B	Down	Y	0
Putnam RetirementReady 2040 Fund Class R	US7468598757		Open End	Target Date 2021-2045 (Asset Alloc)	B-	C+	B	Down	Y	0
Putnam RetirementReady 2040 Fund Class R6	PREHX	NAS CM	Open End	Target Date 2021-2045 (Asset Alloc)	B-	B-	B	Down	Y	0
Putnam RetirementReady 2040 Fund Class Y	PRZZX	NAS CM	Open End	Target Date 2021-2045 (Asset Alloc)	B-	B-	B	Down	Y	0
Putnam RetirementReady 2045 Fund Class A	PRVLX	NAS CM	Open End	Target Date 2021-2045 (Asset Alloc)	B-	B-	B	Down	Y	0
Putnam RetirementReady 2045 Fund Class B	US7468592065		Open End	Target Date 2021-2045 (Asset Alloc)	B-	C+	B-	Down	Y	0
Putnam RetirementReady 2045 Fund Class C	US7468593055		Open End	Target Date 2021-2045 (Asset Alloc)	B-	C+	B-	Down	Y	0
Putnam RetirementReady 2045 Fund Class M	US7468594046		Open End	Target Date 2021-2045 (Asset Alloc)	B-	B-	B-	Down	Y	0
Putnam RetirementReady 2045 Fund Class R	US7468595035		Open End	Target Date 2021-2045 (Asset Alloc)	B-	B-	B	Down	Y	0
Putnam RetirementReady 2045 Fund Class R6	PREKX	NAS CM	Open End	Target Date 2021-2045 (Asset Alloc)	B-	B-	B	Down	Y	0
Putnam RetirementReady 2045 Fund Class Y	PRVYX	NAS CM	Open End	Target Date 2021-2045 (Asset Alloc)	B-	B-	B	Down	Y	0
Putnam RetirementReady 2050 Fund Class A	PRRJX	NAS CM	Open End	Target Date 2046+ (Asset Alloc)	B-	B-	B	Down	Y	0

★ Expanded analysis of this fund is included in Section II.

Min Additional Investment	TOTAL RETURNS 3-Month Total Return	6-Month Total Return	1-Year Total Return	3-Year Total Return	5-Year Total Return	PERFORMANCE Dividend Yield (TTM)	Expense Ratio	3-Yr Std Deviation	3-Year Beta	ASSETS NAV	Total Assets (MIL)	ASSET ALLOCATION & TURNOVER %Cash	%Stocks	%Bonds	%Other	Turnover Ratio	BULL & BEAR Last Bull Market Total Return	Last Bear Market Total Return	FEES Front End Fee (%)	Back End Fee (%)	Inception Date
	5.61	10.84	23.75	33.66	109.07	1.19	0.72	10.61	1.03	33.49	307.1	3	97	0	0	98	26.72	-19.01			Jun-15
	5.57	10.74	23.53	33.29	109.52	1.05	0.9	10.58	1.03	33.38	307.1	3	97	0	0	98	26.94	-18.95			Apr-00
	1.59	3.24	6.80	8.73	20.30	1.13	0.95	2.64	0.14	17.74	95.3	22	24	54	-1	39	6.38	-5.8	4.00		Nov-04
	1.39	2.87	6.01	6.27	15.82	0.81	1.7	2.63	0.14	17.34	95.3	22	24	54	-1	39	5.9	-6.09		5.00	Nov-04
	1.38	2.86	6.00	6.31	15.83	0.8	1.7	2.64	0.13	17.39	95.3	22	24	54	-1	39	5.88	-6.07		1.00	Nov-04
	1.52	3.11	6.47	7.89	18.75	0.9	1.2	2.62	0.14	17.78	95.3	22	24	54	-1	39	6.21	-5.91	3.25		Nov-04
	1.52	3.17	6.55	7.92	18.81	0.89	1.2	2.65	0.14	17.73	95.3	22	24	54	-1	39	6.17	-5.84			Nov-04
	1.68	3.41	7.12	9.65	21.97	1.45	0.61	2.64	0.13	17.8	95.3	22	24	54	-1	39	6.51	-5.68			Sep-16
	1.65	3.36	7.04	9.50	21.80	1.35	0.7	2.64	0.13	17.8	95.3	22	24	54	-1	39	6.51	-5.68			Nov-04
	2.04	4.15	8.42	11.20	31.56	0.96	0.96	3.68	0.33	19.64	204.8	21	30	50	-2	49	11.36	-10.11	5.75		Nov-04
	1.90	3.82	7.66	8.61	26.77	0.28	1.71	3.68	0.33		204.8	21	30	50	-2	49	10.87	-10.37		5.00	Nov-04
	1.90	3.82	7.62	8.59	26.78	0.33	1.71	3.66	0.33		204.8	21	30	50	-2	49	10.86	-10.34		1.00	Nov-04
	1.96	3.95	7.94	9.42	28.38	0.56	1.46	3.67	0.33		204.8	21	30	50	-2	49	11.06	-10.29	3.50		Nov-04
	2.00	4.08	8.20	10.26	30.02	0.72	1.21	3.68	0.33		204.8	21	30	50	-2	49	11.18	-10.21			Nov-04
	2.10	4.31	8.72	12.11	33.31	0.92	0.63	3.67	0.33	22.11	204.8	21	30	50	-2	49	11.5	-10			Sep-16
	2.10	4.31	8.68	12.04	33.23	0.94	0.71	3.67	0.33	22.1	204.8	21	30	50	-2	49	11.5	-10			Nov-04
	2.71	5.45	10.55	14.43	41.98	1.31	1.03	4.76	0.44	22.82	121.3	20	39	43	-2	37	14.42	-13.05	5.75		Nov-04
	2.65	5.18	9.82	11.83	36.98	0.7	1.78	4.77	0.44		121.3	20	39	43	-2	37	13.92	-13.33		5.00	Nov-04
	2.65	5.15	9.81	11.75	36.89	0.8	1.78	4.75	0.44		121.3	20	39	43	-2	37	13.87	-13.3		1.00	Nov-04
	2.70	5.31	10.07	12.64	38.60	1.07	1.53	4.75	0.44		121.3	20	39	43	-2	37	14.09	-13.22	3.50		Nov-04
	2.77	5.40	10.32	13.48	40.37	1.18	1.28	4.77	0.44		121.3	20	39	43	-2	37	14.25	-13.16			Nov-04
	2.76	5.62	10.95	15.45	43.97	1.37	0.65	4.75	0.44	22.97	121.3	20	39	43	-2	37	14.55	-12.94			Sep-16
	2.76	5.58	10.86	15.31	43.80	1.46	0.78	4.74	0.44	22.94	121.3	20	39	43	-2	37	14.55	-12.94			Nov-04
	3.48	6.93	13.21	18.23	52.67	0.62	1.01	6	0.57	23	198.5	19	47	35	-2	41	17.33	-15.97	5.75		Nov-04
	3.45	6.69	12.40	15.44	47.23	0	1.76	6	0.57		198.5	19	47	35	-2	41	16.75	-16.22		5.00	Nov-04
	3.50	6.70	12.46	15.47	47.30	0.03	1.76	6.01	0.57		198.5	19	47	35	-2	41	16.81	-16.19		1.00	Nov-04
	3.54	6.81	12.71	16.33	49.11	0	1.51	6.01	0.57		198.5	19	47	35	-2	41	16.94	-16.12	3.50		Nov-04
	3.58	6.97	13.01	17.17	50.96	0.39	1.26	6	0.57		198.5	19	47	35	-2	41	17.15	-16.03			Nov-04
	3.59	7.13	13.60	19.24	54.69	0.6	0.66	6	0.57	26.47	198.5	19	47	35	-2	41	17.44	-15.83			Sep-16
	3.53	7.07	13.50	19.10	54.50	0.64	0.76	6	0.57	26.44	198.5	19	47	35	-2	41	17.44	-15.83			Nov-04
	4.16	8.34	15.84	21.81	62.76	0.63	1.07	7.22	0.69	23.74	117.2	18	55	28	-2	37	19.6	-17.81	5.75		Nov-04
	4.20	8.15	14.99	18.90	57.12	0	1.82	7.19	0.69		117.2	18	55	28	-2	37	18.98	-18.03		5.00	Nov-04
	4.22	8.13	15.03	18.92	57.10	0.03	1.82	7.21	0.69		117.2	18	55	28	-2	37	19.09	-18.07		1.00	Nov-04
	4.27	8.28	15.30	19.79	59.00	0.22	1.57	7.2	0.69		117.2	18	55	28	-2	37	19.18	-17.99	3.50		Nov-04
	4.31	8.41	15.56	20.70	61.07	0.44	1.32	7.21	0.69		117.2	18	55	28	-2	37	19.42	-17.89			Nov-04
	4.27	8.55	16.26	22.88	65.01	0.59	0.69	7.22	0.69	27.89	117.2	18	55	28	-2	37	19.78	-17.72			Sep-16
	4.22	8.47	16.09	22.67	64.73	0.64	0.82	7.21	0.69	27.85	117.2	18	55	28	-2	37	19.77	-17.72			Nov-04
	5.00	9.71	17.93	24.18	71.17	0.27	1.05	8.16	0.78		152.3	17	63	21	-1	39	21.16	-18.84	5.75		Nov-04
	4.85	9.36	17.13	21.47	64.97	0	1.8	8.14	0.78		152.3	17	63	21	-1	39	20.54	-19.09		5.00	Nov-04
	4.82	9.34	17.10	21.44	64.93	0	1.8	8.14	0.78		152.3	17	63	21	-1	39	20.61	-19.06		1.00	Nov-04
	4.88	9.45	17.42	22.34	67.02	0	1.55	8.16	0.78		152.3	17	63	21	-1	39	20.77	-18.97	3.50		Nov-04
	4.97	9.62	17.68	23.29	69.12	0.03	1.3	8.16	0.78		152.3	17	63	21	-1	39	20.93	-18.93			Nov-04
	5.11	9.94	18.36	25.27	73.52	0.28	0.7	8.15	0.78		152.3	17	63	21	-1	39	21.39	-18.79			Sep-16
	5.08	9.88	18.27	25.13	73.32	0.33	0.8	8.14	0.78		152.3	17	63	21	-1	39	21.39	-18.79			Nov-04
	5.40	10.51	19.29	25.75	75.85	0.46	1.09	8.74	0.84		66.0	14	70	16	-1	37	21.9	-19.35	5.75		Nov-04
	5.20	10.09	18.40	22.92	69.32	0	1.84	8.75	0.84		66.0	14	70	16	-1	37	21.43	-19.63		5.00	Nov-04
	5.19	10.08	18.38	22.93	69.34	0	1.84	8.75	0.84		66.0	14	70	16	-1	37	21.46	-19.69		1.00	Nov-04
	5.24	10.25	18.69	23.87	71.47	0.05	1.59	8.74	0.84		66.0	14	70	16	-1	37	21.6	-19.58	3.50		Nov-04
	5.35	10.38	18.99	24.81	73.67	0.23	1.34	8.75	0.84		66.0	14	70	16	-1	37	21.84	-19.51			Nov-04
	5.48	10.71	19.73	26.88	78.28	0.44	0.7	8.73	0.84		66.0	14	70	16	-1	37	22.12	-19.3			Sep-16
	1.21	6.19	15.06	22.11	70.86	0.49	0.84	8.73	0.84	26.73	66.0	14	70	16	-1	37	22.12	-19.3			Nov-04
	1.04	6.15	15.12	21.48	71.00	0.55	1.08	9.12	0.88	20.03	60.8	14	75	12	-1	37	22.59	-19.82	5.75		May-05

Fund Name	Ticker Symbol	Traded On	Fund Type	Category and (Prospectus Objective)	Overall Rating	Reward Rating	Risk Rating	Recent Up/ Downgrade	Open to New Investors	Min Initial Investment
	MARKET		FUND TYPE, CATEGORY & OBJECTIVE		RATINGS				MINIMUMS	
Putnam RetirementReady 2050 Fund Class B	US7468593626		Open End	Target Date 2046+ (Asset Alloc)	B-	B-	B-	Down	Y	0
Putnam RetirementReady 2050 Fund Class C	US7468593543		Open End	Target Date 2046+ (Asset Alloc)	B-	B-	B-	Down	Y	0
Putnam RetirementReady 2050 Fund Class M	US7468593477		Open End	Target Date 2046+ (Asset Alloc)	B-	B-	B-	Down	Y	0
Putnam RetirementReady 2050 Fund Class R	PRRKX	NAS CM	Open End	Target Date 2046+ (Asset Alloc)	B-	B-	B-	Down	Y	0
Putnam RetirementReady 2050 Fund Class R6	PREUX	NAS CM	Open End	Target Date 2046+ (Asset Alloc)	B-	B-	B	Down	Y	0
Putnam RetirementReady 2050 Fund Class Y	PRRUX	NAS CM	Open End	Target Date 2046+ (Asset Alloc)	B-	B-	B	Down	Y	0
Putnam RetirementReady 2055 Fund Class A	PRRFX	NAS CM	Open End	Target Date 2046+ (Asset Alloc)	B-	B-	B-	Down	Y	0
Putnam RetirementReady 2055 Fund Class B	US7468592974		Open End	Target Date 2046+ (Asset Alloc)	B-	B-	B-	Down	Y	0
Putnam RetirementReady 2055 Fund Class C	US7468592891		Open End	Target Date 2046+ (Asset Alloc)	B-	B-	B-	Down	Y	0
Putnam RetirementReady 2055 Fund Class M	US7468592719		Open End	Target Date 2046+ (Asset Alloc)	B-	B-	B-	Down	Y	0
Putnam RetirementReady 2055 Fund Class R	PRRVX	NAS CM	Open End	Target Date 2046+ (Asset Alloc)	B-	B-	B-	Down	Y	0
Putnam RetirementReady 2055 Fund Class R6	PREVX	NAS CM	Open End	Target Date 2046+ (Asset Alloc)	B-	B-	B-	Down	Y	0
Putnam RetirementReady 2055 Fund Class Y	PRTLX	NAS CM	Open End	Target Date 2046+ (Asset Alloc)	B-	B-	B-	Down	Y	0
Putnam RetirementReady 2060 Fund Class A	PRTFX	NAS CM	Open End	Target Date 2046+ (Asset Alloc)	C	C	B+	Up	Y	0
Putnam RetirementReady 2060 Fund Class B	US7468592305		Open End	Target Date 2046+ (Asset Alloc)	C	C	B+	Up		0
Putnam RetirementReady 2060 Fund Class C	US7468592222		Open End	Target Date 2046+ (Asset Alloc)	C	C	B+	Up	Y	0
Putnam RetirementReady 2060 Fund Class M	US7468592149		Open End	Target Date 2046+ (Asset Alloc)	C	C	B+	Up	Y	0
Putnam RetirementReady 2060 Fund Class R	PRTRX	NAS CM	Open End	Target Date 2046+ (Asset Alloc)	C	C	B+	Up	Y	0
Putnam RetirementReady 2060 Fund Class R6	PEFGX	NAS CM	Open End	Target Date 2046+ (Asset Alloc)	C	C	B+	Up	Y	0
Putnam RetirementReady 2060 Fund Class Y	PRTYX	NAS CM	Open End	Target Date 2046+ (Asset Alloc)	C	C	B+	Up	Y	0
Putnam Small Cap Growth Fund Class A	PNSAX	NAS CM	Open End	US Equity Small Cap (Small Company)	B	B+	B	Up	Y	0
Putnam Small Cap Growth Fund Class B	PNSBX	NAS CM	Open End	US Equity Small Cap (Small Company)	B	B	B-	Up	Y	0
Putnam Small Cap Growth Fund Class C	PNSCX	NAS CM	Open End	US Equity Small Cap (Small Company)	B	B	B-	Up	Y	0
Putnam Small Cap Growth Fund Class M	PSGMX	NAS CM	Open End	US Equity Small Cap (Small Company)	B	B	B-	Up	Y	0
Putnam Small Cap Growth Fund Class R	PSGRX	NAS CM	Open End	US Equity Small Cap (Small Company)	B	B	B	Up	Y	0
Putnam Small Cap Growth Fund Class R6	PLKGX	NAS CM	Open End	US Equity Small Cap (Small Company)	B	B+	B	Up	Y	0
Putnam Small Cap Growth Fund Class Y	PSYGX	NAS CM	Open End	US Equity Small Cap (Small Company)	B	B+	B	Up	Y	0
Putnam Small Cap Value Fund Class A	PSLAX	NAS CM	Open End	US Equity Small Cap (Small Company)	B	B	B	Up	Y	0
Putnam Small Cap Value Fund Class B	PSLBX	NAS CM	Open End	US Equity Small Cap (Small Company)	B	B	B	Up	Y	0
Putnam Small Cap Value Fund Class C	PSLCX	NAS CM	Open End	US Equity Small Cap (Small Company)	B	B	B	Up	Y	0
Putnam Small Cap Value Fund Class M	PSLMX	NAS CM	Open End	US Equity Small Cap (Small Company)	B	B	B	Up	Y	0
Putnam Small Cap Value Fund Class R	PSCRX	NAS CM	Open End	US Equity Small Cap (Small Company)	B	B	B	Up	Y	0
Putnam Small Cap Value Fund Class R5	PSLRX	NAS CM	Open End	US Equity Small Cap (Small Company)	B	B	B	Up	Y	0
Putnam Small Cap Value Fund Class R6	PSCMX	NAS CM	Open End	US Equity Small Cap (Small Company)	B	B	B	Up	Y	0
Putnam Small Cap Value Fund Class Y	PYSVX	NAS CM	Open End	US Equity Small Cap (Small Company)	B	B	B	Up	Y	0
Pzena Emerging Markets Value Fund Institutional	PZIEX	NAS CM	Open End	Emerging Markets Equity (Div Emerging Mkts)	B-	B	C	Up	Y	1,000,000
Pzena Emerging Markets Value Fund Investor	PZVEX	NAS CM	Open End	Emerging Markets Equity (Div Emerging Mkts)	C+	B	C	Up	Y	5,000
Pzena Long/Short Value Fund Institutional Class	PZILX	NAS CM	Open End	Long/Short Equity (Growth)	B-	C+	B	Up	Y	1,000,000
Pzena Long/Short Value Fund Investor Class	PZVLX	NAS CM	Open End	Long/Short Equity (Growth)	B-	C+	B	Up	Y	5,000
Pzena Mid Cap Value Fund Institutional Class	PZIMX	NAS CM	Open End	US Equity Mid Cap (Growth)	B+	A-	B	Up	Y	1,000,000
Pzena Mid Cap Value Fund Investor Class	PZVMX	NAS CM	Open End	US Equity Mid Cap (Growth)	B+	A-	B	Up	Y	5,000
Pzena Small Cap Value Fund Institutional Class	PZISX	NAS CM	Open End	US Equity Small Cap (Small Company)	D+	C-	B	Up	Y	1,000,000
Pzena Small Cap Value Fund Investor Class	PZVSX	NAS CM	Open End	US Equity Small Cap (Small Company)	D+	C-	B	Up	Y	5,000
QCI Balanced Fund Institutional Class	QCIBX	NAS CM	Open End	Cautious Alloc (Balanced)	B-	C+	B	Up	Y	25,000
QS Conservative Growth Fund Class A	SBBAX	NAS CM	Open End	Moderate Alloc (Balanced)	B-	C+	B	Up	Y	1,000
QS Conservative Growth Fund Class C	SCBCX	NAS CM	Open End	Moderate Alloc (Balanced)	B-	C+	B	Up	Y	1,000
QS Conservative Growth Fund Class I	LMEIX	NAS CM	Open End	Moderate Alloc (Balanced)	B-	C+	B	Up	Y	1,000,000
QS Conservative Growth Fund Class R	LLARX	NAS CM	Open End	Moderate Alloc (Balanced)	B-	C+	B	Up	Y	0
QS Defensive Growth Fund Class A	SBCPX	NAS CM	Open End	Cautious Alloc (Growth & Income)	B	C+	A-	Up	Y	1,000
QS Defensive Growth Fund Class C	LWLAX	NAS CM	Open End	Cautious Alloc (Growth & Income)	B-	C	B+	Up	Y	1,000
QS Defensive Growth Fund Class C1	SBCLX	NAS CM	Open End	Cautious Alloc (Growth & Income)	B-	C+	B+	Up		1,000
QS Defensive Growth Fund Class I	LMGIX	NAS CM	Open End	Cautious Alloc (Growth & Income)	B	C+	A-	Up	Y	1,000,000

★Expanded analysis of this fund is included in Section II.

	TOTAL RETURNS					PERFORMANCE				ASSETS		ASSET ALLOCATION & TURNOVER					BULL & BEAR		FEES		
Min Additional Investment	3-Month Total Return	6-Month Total Return	1-Year Total Return	3-Year Total Return	5-Year Total Return	Dividend Yield (TTM)	Expense Ratio	3-Yr Std Deviation	3-Year Beta	NAV	Total Assets (MIL)	%Cash	%Stocks	%Bonds	%Other	Turnover Ratio	Last Bull Market Total Return	Last Bear Market Total Return	Front End Fee (%)	Back End Fee (%)	Inception Date
	5.40	10.47	19.05	23.50	72.08	0	1.83	9.12	0.88		60.8	14	75	12	-1	37	22.04	-20.02		5.00	May-05
	5.40	10.51	19.05	23.51	72.11	0	1.83	9.07	0.87		60.8	14	75	12	-1	37	22.1	-20.13		1.00	May-05
	5.47	10.65	19.35	24.45	74.21	0.21	1.58	9.07	0.87		60.8	14	75	12	-1	37	22.28	-19.98	3.50		May-05
	1.15	6.16	15.04	20.75	69.19	0.34	1.33	9.12	0.88	19.82	60.8	14	75	12	-1	37	22.47	-19.95			May-05
	5.71	11.12	20.43	27.47	81.11	0.61	0.7	9.1	0.88		60.8	14	75	12	-1	37	22.89	-19.82			Sep-16
	5.62	11.04	20.29	27.25	80.81	0.67	0.83	9.09	0.88		60.8	14	75	12	-1	37	22.89	-19.82			May-05
	4.02	9.38	18.87	25.31	77.07	0.68	1.11	9.34	0.9	12.26	20.3	19	73	9	-1	30	22.31	-20.58	5.75		Nov-10
	5.52	10.82	19.59	23.98	73.36	0.06	1.86	9.33	0.9		20.3	19	73	9	-1	30	21.72	-20.82		5.00	Nov-10
	5.51	10.78	19.52	23.93	73.43	0.11	1.86	9.37	0.9		20.3	19	73	9	-1	30	21.84	-20.82		1.00	Nov-10
	5.65	11.01	19.85	25.01	75.72	0.3	1.61	9.34	0.9		20.3	19	73	9	-1	30	21.99	-20.8	3.50		Nov-10
	1.70	6.87	15.97	21.74	71.12	0.49	1.36	9.35	0.9	12.23	20.3	19	73	9	-1	30	22.19	-20.69			Nov-10
	4.14	9.63	19.37	26.58	79.83	0.73	0.69	9.34	0.9	12.37	20.3	19	73	9	-1	30	22.62	-20.56			Sep-16
	4.10	9.51	19.15	26.33	79.48	0.81	0.86	9.34	0.9	12.35	20.3	19	73	9	-1	30	22.61	-20.56			Nov-10
	3.97	9.33	18.85			0.73	1.05			11.4	0.49	19	74	8	-1	15			5.75		Nov-15
	5.63	10.91	19.66			0.13	1.8				0.49	19	74	8	-1	15				5.00	Nov-15
	5.65	10.94	19.67			0.35	1.8				0.49	19	74	8	-1	15				1.00	Nov-15
	5.61	11.07	20.01			0.27	1.55				0.49	19	74	8	-1	15			3.50		Nov-15
	5.69	11.15	20.23			0.46	1.3				0.49	19	74	8	-1	15					Nov-15
	4.14	9.58	19.33			0.77	0.69			11.45	0.49	19	74	8	-1	15					Sep-16
	3.98	9.42	19.16			0.84	0.8			11.43	0.49	19	74	8	-1	15					Nov-15
	6.48	11.09	20.19	26.22	94.94	0	1.21	15.09	1	37.74	164.3	2	98	0	0	127	29.92	-27.54	5.75		Dec-97
	6.26	10.67	19.29	23.39	87.68	0	1.96	15.07	0.99	33.39	164.3	2	98	0	0	127	29.75	-27.77		5.00	Mar-02
	6.29	10.67	19.29	23.40	87.75	0	1.96	15.08	1	33.27	164.3	2	98	0	0	127	29.33	-27.79		1.00	Mar-02
	6.32	10.82	19.58	24.33	90.06	0	1.71	15.1	1	34.8	164.3	2	98	0	0	127	29.54	-27.72	3.50		Mar-02
	6.41	10.98	19.88	25.28	92.55	0	1.46	15.1	1	36.47	164.3	2	98	0	0	127	29.74	-27.64			Dec-03
	6.59	11.36	20.71	27.58	97.04	0.34	0.77	15.1	1	39.1	164.3	2	98	0	0	127	29.92	-27.54			Jun-15
	6.55	11.26	20.51	27.19	97.37	0.19	0.96	15.1	1	39.01	164.3	2	98	0	0	127	30.04	-27.47			Nov-03
	3.07	5.73	7.90	30.52	90.84	0.62	1.42	13.28	0.92	13.54	397.9	11	88	0	1	63	28.51	-24.84	5.75		Apr-99
	2.84	5.30	7.08	27.66	83.81	0.22	2.17	13.22	0.91	10.59	397.9	11	88	0	1	63	27.86	-25.02		5.00	May-99
	2.82	5.22	7.01	27.59	83.74	0.24	2.17	13.25	0.92	10.53	397.9	11	88	0	1	63	28.09	-25.15		1.00	Jul-99
	2.89	5.43	7.28	28.49	85.93	0.33	1.92	13.22	0.91	11.86	397.9	11	88	0	1	63	28.23	-25.04	3.50		Mar-00
	2.91	5.49	7.51	29.42	88.19	0.46	1.67	13.22	0.91	13.22	397.9	11	88	0	1	63	28.36	-24.93			Mar-07
	3.14	5.92	8.19	31.81	93.49	0.87	1.11	13.24	0.91	14.28	397.9	11	88	0	1	63	28.51	-24.84			Nov-13
	3.13	5.91	8.30	32.16	94.11	0.92	1.01	13.25	0.92	14.27	397.9	11	88	0	1	63	28.51	-24.84			Nov-13
	3.04	5.77	8.10	31.47	93.12	0.79	1.17	13.26	0.92	14.22	397.9	11	88	0	1	63	28.75	-24.76			Jan-01
	4.36	9.56	29.97	30.53		0.78	1.26	17.74	1.07	11.07	43.0	4	94	0	0	29					Mar-14
100	4.29	9.48	29.88	29.67		0.56	1.61	17.73	1.07	11.08	43.0	4	94	0	0	29					Mar-14
	1.89	3.15	3.05	13.49		0	1.75	8.39	0.56	10.78	6.6	53	47	0	0	59					Mar-14
100	1.81	3.09	2.89	12.70		0	2.1	8.37	0.56	10.67	6.6	53	47	0	0	59					Mar-14
	6.24	10.78	14.56	37.20		0.75	0.91	15.42	1.35	13.09	8.3	2	98	0	0	26					Mar-14
100	6.30	10.77	14.36	36.29		0.52	1.26	15.39	1.34	13.09	8.3	2	98	0	0	26					Mar-14
	0.49	7.11	3.52			0	1.21			11.49	14.9	5	95	0	0						Apr-16
100	0.50	6.96	3.28			0	1.56			11.43	14.9	5	95	0	0						Apr-16
250	4.16	6.96	11.11	16.45		0.82	1.02	4.93		12.13	62.4	1	53	45	0	29					Jan-14
50	2.99	5.78	12.73	18.30	43.62	1.8	1.2	6.07	-0.04	14.55	316.7	5	48	44	2	20	15.3	-11.43	5.75		Feb-96
50	2.84	5.37	11.86	15.72	38.50	0.97	1.93	6.04	-0.04	15.15	316.7	5	48	44	2	20	14.77	-11.72		1.00	Feb-96
	3.05	5.91	13.01	19.21	44.93	2.04	0.93	6.06	-0.05	14.54	316.7	5	48	44	2	20	15.3	-11.43			Jan-08
	2.87	5.59	12.34	17.24	41.55	1.31	1.5	6.07	-0.05	14.52	316.7	5	48	44	2	20	15.13	-11.53			Jun-14
50	1.94	3.94	9.69	14.95	30.80	2.2	1.17	4.47	0.35	13.29	134.6	5	28	64	2	18	11.18	-7.33	4.25		Feb-96
50	1.70	3.56	8.83	12.59	25.91	1.45	1.86	4.45	0.33	13.22	134.6	5	28	64	2	18	10.7	-7.62		1.00	Aug-12
50	1.78	3.67	9.13	13.29	27.41	1.62	1.67	4.48	0.34	13.59	134.6	5	28	64	2	18	10.81	-7.55		1.00	Feb-96
	2.00	4.09	10.02	16.00	32.29	2.5	0.88	4.49	0.33	13.26	134.6	5	28	64	2	18	11.18	-7.32			Mar-12

	MARKET		FUND TYPE, CATEGORY & OBJECTIVE		RATINGS				MINIMUMS	
Fund Name	Ticker Symbol	Traded On	Fund Type	Category and (Prospectus Objective)	Overall Rating	Reward Rating	Risk Rating	Recent Up/ Downgrade	Open to New Investors	Min Initial Investment
QS Defensive Growth Fund Class R	LMLRX	NAS CM	Open End	Cautious Alloc (Growth & Income)	B-	C+	B	Up	Y	0
QS Global Dividend Fund Class A	LGDAX	NAS CM	Open End	Global Equity (Equity-Income)	B	C+	A		Y	1,000
QS Global Dividend Fund Class A2	LMQSX	NAS CM	Open End	Global Equity (Equity-Income)	B	C+	A		Y	1,000
QS Global Dividend Fund Class C	LGDCX	NAS CM	Open End	Global Equity (Equity-Income)	B	C+	A-		Y	1,000
QS Global Dividend Fund Class FI	LDIGX	NAS CM	Open End	Global Equity (Equity-Income)	B	C+	A-		Y	0
QS Global Dividend Fund Class I	LTTMX	NAS CM	Open End	Global Equity (Equity-Income)	B	C+	A+		Y	1,000,000
QS Global Dividend Fund Class IS	LDIFX	NAS CM	Open End	Global Equity (Equity-Income)	B	B-	A+		Y	1,000,000
QS Global Equity Fund Class 1	LMPEX	NAS CM	Open End	Global Equity (World Stock)	B	B	B	Up		0
QS Global Equity Fund Class A	CFIPX	NAS CM	Open End	Global Equity (World Stock)	B	B	B	Up	Y	1,000
QS Global Equity Fund Class C	SILLX	NAS CM	Open End	Global Equity (World Stock)	B	B	B-	Up	Y	1,000
QS Global Equity Fund Class I	SMYIX	NAS CM	Open End	Global Equity (World Stock)	B	B	B	Up	Y	1,000,000
QS Global Market Neutral Fund Class A	LNFIX	NAS CM	Open End	Market Neutral (Growth & Income)	C	D+	B	Up	Y	1,000
QS Global Market Neutral Fund Class I	LQNIX	NAS CM	Open End	Market Neutral (Growth & Income)	C	D+	B	Up	Y	1,000,000
QS Global Market Neutral Fund Class IS	LQISX	NAS CM	Open End	Market Neutral (Growth & Income)	C	D+	B	Up	Y	1,000,000
QS Growth Fund Class A	SCHAX	NAS CM	Open End	Aggressive Alloc (Growth)	B-	C+	B-	Down	Y	1,000
QS Growth Fund Class C	SCHCX	NAS CM	Open End	Aggressive Alloc (Growth)	C+	C+	B-	Down	Y	1,000
QS Growth Fund Class I	LANIX	NAS CM	Open End	Aggressive Alloc (Growth)	B-	C+	B-	Down	Y	1,000,000
QS Growth Fund Class R	LLLRX	NAS CM	Open End	Aggressive Alloc (Growth)	C+	C+	B-	Down	Y	0
QS International Dividend Fund Class FI	LTIDX	NAS CM	Open End	Global Equity Large Cap (Equity-Income)	B-	C+	B+	Up	Y	0
QS International Dividend Fund Class IS	LDIVX	NAS CM	Open End	Global Equity Large Cap (Equity-Income)	B-	C+	B+	Up	Y	1,000,000
QS International Equity Fund Class A	LMEAX	NAS CM	Open End	Global Equity Large Cap (Foreign Stock)	B	B-	B	Up	Y	1,000
QS International Equity Fund Class A2	LIATX	NAS CM	Open End	Global Equity Large Cap (Foreign Stock)	B-	B-	C+	Up	Y	1,000
QS International Equity Fund Class C	LMGEX	NAS CM	Open End	Global Equity Large Cap (Foreign Stock)	B-	B-	B	Up	Y	1,000
QS International Equity Fund Class FI	LGFEX	NAS CM	Open End	Global Equity Large Cap (Foreign Stock)	B	B-	B	Up	Y	0
QS International Equity Fund Class I	LGIEX	NAS CM	Open End	Global Equity Large Cap (Foreign Stock)	B	B	B	Up	Y	1,000,000
QS International Equity Fund Class IS	LIESX	NAS CM	Open End	Global Equity Large Cap (Foreign Stock)	B-	B	C+	Up	Y	1,000,000
QS International Equity Fund Class R	LMIRX	NAS CM	Open End	Global Equity Large Cap (Foreign Stock)	B-	B-	B	Up	Y	0
QS Moderate Growth Fund Class A	SCGRX	NAS CM	Open End	Aggressive Alloc (Balanced)	B-	C+	B	Down	Y	1,000
QS Moderate Growth Fund Class C	SCGCX	NAS CM	Open End	Aggressive Alloc (Balanced)	B-	C+	B-	Down	Y	1,000
QS Moderate Growth Fund Class I	LLAIX	NAS CM	Open End	Aggressive Alloc (Balanced)	B-	C+	B	Down	Y	1,000,000
QS Moderate Growth Fund Class R	LLMRX	NAS CM	Open End	Aggressive Alloc (Balanced)	B-	C+	B	Down	Y	0
QS S&P 500 Index Fund Class A	SBSPX	NAS CM	Open End	US Equity Large Cap Blend (Growth)	B	B	B		Y	0
QS S&P 500 Index Fund Class D	SBSDX	NAS CM	Open End	US Equity Large Cap Blend (Growth)	B	B	B		Y	0
QS Strategic Real Return Fund Class A	LRRAX	NAS CM	Open End	Moderate Alloc (Asset Alloc)	C	C	C+	Up	Y	1,000
QS Strategic Real Return Fund Class A2	LSRAX	NAS CM	Open End	Moderate Alloc (Asset Alloc)	C	C	C+	Up	Y	1,000
QS Strategic Real Return Fund Class C	LRRCX	NAS CM	Open End	Moderate Alloc (Asset Alloc)	C	C	C+	Up	Y	1,000
QS Strategic Real Return Fund Class I	LRRIX	NAS CM	Open End	Moderate Alloc (Asset Alloc)	C	C	C+	Up	Y	1,000,000
QS Strategic Real Return Fund Class IS	LRRSX	NAS CM	Open End	Moderate Alloc (Asset Alloc)	C	C	C+	Up	Y	1,000,000
QS U.S. Large Cap Equity Fund Class FI	LMUSX	NAS CM	Open End	US Equity Large Cap Blend (Growth)	B-	B-	B-	Down		0
QS U.S. Large Cap Equity Fund Class I	LMTIX	NAS CM	Open End	US Equity Large Cap Blend (Growth)	B-	B	B-	Down		1,000,000
QS U.S. Large Cap Equity Fund Class IS	LMISX	NAS CM	Open End	US Equity Large Cap Blend (Growth)	B-	B	B-	Down	Y	1,000,000
QS U.S. Small Capitalization Equity Fund Class A	LMBAX	NAS CM	Open End	US Equity Small Cap (Small Company)	B	B	B	Up	Y	1,000
QS U.S. Small Capitalization Equity Fund Class A2	LUSAX	NAS CM	Open End	US Equity Small Cap (Small Company)	B	B	B	Up	Y	1,000
QS U.S. Small Capitalization Equity Fund Class C	LMBCX	NAS CM	Open End	US Equity Small Cap (Small Company)	B	B	B	Up	Y	1,000
QS U.S. Small Capitalization Equity Fund Class FI	LGSCX	NAS CM	Open End	US Equity Small Cap (Small Company)	B	B	B	Up	Y	0
QS U.S. Small Capitalization Equity Fund Class I	LMSIX	NAS CM	Open End	US Equity Small Cap (Small Company)	B	B	B	Up	Y	1,000,000
QS U.S. Small Capitalization Equity Fund Class IS	LMBMX	NAS CM	Open End	US Equity Small Cap (Small Company)	B	B	B	Up	Y	1,000,000
Quaker Event Arbitrage Fund Class A	QEAAX	NAS CM	Open End	Multialternative (Growth)	C+	C+	B-		Y	2,000
Quaker Event Arbitrage Fund Class C	QEACX	NAS CM	Open End	Multialternative (Growth)	C+	C	B-	Up	Y	2,000
Quaker Event Arbitrage Fund Class I	QEAIX	NAS CM	Open End	Multialternative (Growth)	C+	C+	B-		Y	1,000,000
Quaker Global Tactical Allocation Fund Class A	QTRAX	NAS CM	Open End	Global Equity (Growth)	C	C-	C		Y	2,000
Quaker Global Tactical Allocation Fund Class C	QTRCX	NAS CM	Open End	Global Equity (Growth)	C-	D+	C	Down	Y	2,000

★Expanded analysis of this fund is included in Section II.

	TOTAL RETURNS					PERFORMANCE				ASSETS		ASSET ALLOCATION & TURNOVER					BULL & BEAR		FEES		
Min Additional Investment	3-Month Total Return	6-Month Total Return	1-Year Total Return	3-Year Total Return	5-Year Total Return	Dividend Yield (TTM)	Expense Ratio	3-Yr Std Deviation	3-Year Beta	NAV	Total Assets (MIL)	%Cash	%Stocks	%Bonds	%Other	Turnover Ratio	Last Bull Market Total Return	Last Bear Market Total Return	Front End Fee (%)	Back End Fee (%)	Inception Date
	1.87	3.80	9.42	14.08	29.09	1.97	1.43	4.44	0.34	13.26	134.6	5	28	64	2	18	11.02	-7.42			Jun-14
50	4.86	7.01	14.55	27.23		1.91	1.15	7	0.53	13.01	356.0	1	99	0	0	43			5.75		Sep-15
50	4.89	6.87	14.32	26.95		1.77	1.34	7.07	0.54	13.02	356.0	1	99	0	0	43			5.75		Apr-15
50	4.73	6.63	13.76	24.52		1.14	1.88	7	0.53	13.01	356.0	1	99	0	0	43				1.00	Sep-15
	4.92	6.90	14.37	26.85		1.62	1.23	7.06	0.54	13.02	356.0	1	99	0	0	43					Sep-14
	4.93	7.11	14.84	28.16		2.12	0.92	7.03	0.54	12.94	356.0	1	99	0	0	43					Mar-15
	5.03	7.22	14.96	28.57		2.21	0.82	7.03	0.54	12.97	356.0	1	99	0	0	43					Feb-13
	6.45	13.56	23.76	37.27	97.31	1.29	1.26	10.04	0.92	17.36	170.8	1	95	0	4	54	19.83	-20.36			Dec-06
50	6.46	13.54	23.69	37.16	97.21	1.24	1.3	10.07	0.93	17.44	170.8	1	95	0	4	54	19.71	-20.4	5.75		Mar-91
50	6.24	13.02	22.74	34.00	89.90	0.51	2.05	10.03	0.92	17.7	170.8	1	95	0	4	54	19.04	-20.62		1.00	Sep-00
	6.58	13.68	24.12	38.67	100.67	1.51	0.95	10.05	0.93	17.38	170.8	1	95	0	4	54	19.81	-20.14			May-03
50	-0.70	4.28	5.34			0	1.58			10.28	41.5	100	1	0	-1	100			5.75		Nov-15
	-0.68	4.38	5.65			0	1.23			10.32	41.5	100	1	0	-1	100					Nov-15
	-0.68	4.48	5.64			0	1.13			10.33	41.5	100	1	0	-1	100					Nov-15
50	4.57	8.23	16.59	21.65	62.86	0.9	1.36	9.28	-0.74	16.57	779.5	5	85	8	2	20	21.16	-18.57	5.75		Feb-96
50	4.38	7.82	15.79	19.18	57.44	0.39	2.04	9.28	-0.74	15.49	779.5	5	85	8	2	20	20.86	-18.82		1.00	Feb-96
	4.61	8.34	16.95	22.83	65.29	1.15	1.04	9.25	-0.73	16.5	779.5	5	85	8	2	20	21.42	-18.58			Dec-08
	4.49	8.06	16.31	20.80	60.91	0.92	1.62	9.25	-0.73	16.48	779.5	5	85	8	2	20	20.98	-18.66			Jun-14
	2.27	4.62	16.63	18.92		2.4	1.3	8.33	0.6	10.17	4.6	1	96	0	2	36					Sep-16
	2.27	4.78	16.98	19.85		2.74	0.85	8.35	0.6	10.17	4.6	1	96	0	2	36					Feb-13
50	3.15	8.64	24.52	26.44	51.29	1.82	1.29	10.67	0.85	16.52	316.9	3	95	0	3	49	12.94	-23.72	5.75		Feb-09
50	3.09	8.40	24.40	24.91	47.35	2.16	1.14	10.68	0.85	16.45	316.9	3	95	0	3	49	12.46	-23.96	5.75		May-16
50	2.93	8.14	23.58	23.43	45.61	1.06	2.06	10.64	0.85	16.61	316.9	3	95	0	3	49	12.46	-23.96		1.00	Feb-95
	3.14	8.62	24.46	26.25	51.13	1.75	1.3	10.67	0.85	17.16	316.9	3	95	0	3	49	12.93	-23.68			May-03
	3.23	8.78	24.90	27.63	53.72	2.03	0.96	10.7	0.85	17.15	316.9	3	95	0	3	49	13.21	-23.62			May-98
	3.21	8.83	25.00	27.98	54.45	2.12	0.86	10.7	0.85	17.11	316.9	3	95	0	3	49	13.24	-23.57			Aug-08
	3.11	8.47	24.23	25.33	49.26	1.6	1.56	10.67	0.85	17.11	316.9	3	95	0	3	49	12.83	-23.89			Dec-06
50	3.96	7.41	15.34	20.79	55.89	1.3	1.29	7.84	-0.44	16.29	499.9	5	69	24	2	21	18.77	-15.41	5.75		Feb-96
50	3.77	7.04	14.47	18.32	50.52	0.66	1.98	7.87	-0.45	16.61	499.9	5	69	24	2	21	18.3	-15.65		1.00	Feb-96
	4.02	7.56	15.71	21.97	57.98	1.58	0.96	7.85	-0.44	16.15	499.9	5	69	24	2	21	18.96	-15.37			Oct-07
	3.84	7.26	14.90	19.69	53.61	1.32	1.57	7.87	-0.44	16.11	499.9	5	69	24	2	21	18.6	-15.5			Jun-14
	6.48	11.10	21.13	34.58	105.78	1.42	0.59	10.1	1	25.18	269.1	1	99	0	0	2	24.69	-16.47			Jan-98
	6.51	11.23	21.42	35.41	107.85	1.57	0.39	10.11	1	25.35	269.1	1	99	0	0	2	24.86	-16.37			Aug-98
50	3.88	7.77	11.90	2.86	-1.56	0	1.35	7.9	0.68	11.96	107.8	6	36	39	19	42	13.7	-13.05	5.75		Feb-10
50	3.83	7.68	11.66	2.21	-2.49	0	1.55	7.87	0.68	11.79	107.8	6	36	39	19	42	13.72	-13.07	5.75		Oct-12
50	3.63	7.35	11.00	0.47	-5.29	0	2.1	7.88	0.68	11.61	107.8	6	36	39	19	42	13.29	-13.34		1.00	Feb-10
	3.97	7.86	12.19	3.63	-0.28	0	1.1	7.86	0.68	12.21	107.8	6	36	39	19	42	13.89	-12.98			Feb-10
	3.94	7.96	12.26	3.92	0.17	0	1	7.85	0.67	12.05	107.8	6	36	39	19	42	13.89	-12.98			Dec-11
	7.82	12.99	23.11	29.50	101.70	1.18	1.05	10.87	1.06	19.53	696.3	1	99	0	0	25	25.32	-17.57			Apr-08
	7.90	13.16	23.50	30.77	104.74	1.16	0.74	10.91	1.06	19.41	696.3	1	99	0	0	25	25.61	-17.48			May-15
	7.90	13.15	23.49	30.83	104.83	1.16	0.7	10.92	1.07	19.42	696.3	1	99	0	0	25	25.61	-17.48			Apr-08
50	3.49	7.28	8.46	22.41	88.89	0.26	1.19	13.83	0.96	13.55	229.4	2	98	0	0	33	26.97	-25.4	5.75		Feb-09
50	3.50	7.25	8.28	21.63	87.39	0.14	1.46	13.82	0.96	13.39	229.4	2	98	0	0	33	26.97	-25.32	5.75		Oct-12
50	3.27	6.91	7.66	19.63	81.97	0	1.96	13.84	0.97	12.66	229.4	2	98	0	0	33	26.23	-25.61		1.00	Feb-09
	3.55	7.34	8.49	22.35	88.93	0.66	1.24	13.85	0.97	12.96	229.4	2	98	0	0	33	26.89	-25.46			Jan-03
	3.59	7.53	8.77	23.59	92.52	0	0.99	13.87	0.97	13.84	229.4	2	98	0	0	33	27.16	-25.24			Mar-00
	3.65	7.67	9.01	24.09	93.28	0.61	0.76	13.86	0.97	13.54	229.4	2	98	0	0	33	27.15	-25.24			Mar-12
100	1.46	1.93	8.16	12.19	29.78	0.5	1.98	9.22	0.75	12.77	23.3	19	63	13	1	326	10.22	-11.82	5.50		Nov-03
100	1.28	1.53	7.29	9.73	25.00	0.14	2.73	9.22	0.75	12.29	23.3	19	63	13	1	326	9.74	-12.1			Jun-10
	1.55	2.09	8.44	13.06	31.45	0.62	1.73	9.21	0.74	12.87	23.3	19	63	13	1	326	10.37	-11.81			Jun-10
100	1.69	1.88	5.04	-0.91	48.01	0	2.24	10.89	0.94	10.82	6.5	10	43	44	1		16.58	-18.07	5.50		May-08
100	1.51	1.51	4.24	-3.17	42.49	0	2.99	10.8	0.93	10.06	6.5	10	43	44	1		16.23	-18.37			May-08

Fund Name	MARKET Ticker Symbol	Traded On	FUND TYPE, CATEGORY & OBJECTIVE Fund Type	Category and (Prospectus Objective)	RATINGS Overall Rating	Reward Rating	Risk Rating	Recent Up/ Downgrade	MINIMUMS Open to New Investors	Min Initial Investment
Quaker Global Tactical Allocation Fund Class I	QTRIX	NAS CM	Open End	Global Equity (Growth)	C	C-	C+		Y	1,000,000
Quaker Mid-Cap Value Fund Class A	QMCVX	NAS CM	Open End	US Equity Mid Cap (Growth)	B-	B-	B-	Up	Y	2,000
Quaker Mid-Cap Value Fund Class C	QMCCX	NAS CM	Open End	US Equity Mid Cap (Growth)	B-	B-	B-	Up	Y	2,000
Quaker Mid-Cap Value Fund Class Institutional	QMVIX	NAS CM	Open End	US Equity Mid Cap (Growth)	B-	B	B-	Up	Y	1,000,000
Quaker Small-Cap Value Fund Class A	QUSVX	NAS CM	Open End	US Equity Small Cap (Small Company)	B	B-	B	Up	Y	2,000
Quaker Small-Cap Value Fund Class C	QSVCX	NAS CM	Open End	US Equity Small Cap (Small Company)	B-	B-	B	Up	Y	2,000
Quaker Small-Cap Value Fund Class Institutional	QSVIX	NAS CM	Open End	US Equity Small Cap (Small Company)	B	B	B	Up	Y	1,000,000
Quaker Strategic Growth Fund Class A	QUAGX	NAS CM	Open End	US Equity Large Cap Growth (Aggr Growth)	C+	C+	B-		Y	2,000
Quaker Strategic Growth Fund Class C	QAGCX	NAS CM	Open End	US Equity Large Cap Growth (Aggr Growth)	C+	C+	C+		Y	2,000
Quaker Strategic Growth Fund Class Institutional	QAGIX	NAS CM	Open End	US Equity Large Cap Growth (Aggr Growth)	C+	C+	B-		Y	1,000,000
Quantified All-Cap Equity Fund Advisor Class	QACAX	NAS CM	Open End	US Equity Mid Cap (Equity-Income)	B-	B-	B-	Down	Y	10,000
Quantified All-Cap Equity Fund Investor Class	QACFX	NAS CM	Open End	US Equity Mid Cap (Equity-Income)	B-	B-	B-	Down	Y	10,000
Quantified Alternative Investment Fund Advisor Class	QALAX	NAS CM	Open End	Multialternative (Growth)	C+	C	B-	Up	Y	10,000
Quantified Alternative Investment Fund Investor Class	QALTX	NAS CM	Open End	Multialternative (Growth)	C+	C	B-	Up	Y	10,000
Quantified Market Leaders Fund Advisor Class	QMLAX	NAS CM	Open End	US Equity Mid Cap (Growth & Income)	B	B+	B	Up	Y	10,000
Quantified Market Leaders Fund Investor Class	QMLFX	NAS CM	Open End	US Equity Mid Cap (Growth & Income)	B+	A-	B	Up	Y	10,000
Quantified STF Fund Advisor Class	QSTAX	NAS CM	Open End	US Equity Large Cap Growth (Growth & Income)	C	C	C	Up	Y	10,000
Quantified STF Fund Investor Class	QSTFX	NAS CM	Open End	US Equity Large Cap Growth (Growth & Income)	C	C	C	Up	Y	10,000
Queens Road Small Cap Value Fund	QRSVX	NAS CM	Open End	US Equity Small Cap (Small Company)	B	C+	B+	Up	Y	2,500
Queens Road Value Fund	QRVLX	NAS CM	Open End	US Equity Large Cap Value (Growth)	B-	B-	B-	Down	Y	2,500
Rainier Small/Mid Cap Equity Fund Institutional Shares	RAISX	NAS CM	Open End	US Equity Mid Cap (Growth)	B	B-	B	Up		100,000
Rainier Small/Mid Cap Equity Fund Original Shares	RIMSX	NAS CM	Open End	US Equity Mid Cap (Growth)	B	B-	B	Up		2,500
RAISE Core Tactical Fund Class I	KRCTX	NAS CM	Open End	Long/Short Equity (Growth)	C-	C-	C		Y	10,000
Ranger Quest For Income & Growth Fund Institutional Cls	RFIDX	NAS CM	Open End	Global Equity (Growth & Income)	C+	C+	C+	Down	Y	250,000
Ranger Quest for Income and Growth Investor	RFTDX	NAS CM	Open End	Global Equity (Growth & Income)	C+	C+	C+	Down	Y	25,000
Ranger Small Cap Fund Institutional Class	RFISX	NAS CM	Open End	US Equity Small Cap (Small Company)	B+	B+	B+	Up	Y	250,000
RARE Global Infrastructure Value Fund Class A	RGAVX	NAS CM	Open End	Other Sector Equity (Utility)	D+	C-	B-	Up	Y	1,000
RARE Global Infrastructure Value Fund Class I	RGIVX	NAS CM	Open End	Other Sector Equity (Utility)	D+	C-	B-	Up	Y	1,000,000
RARE Global Infrastructure Value Fund Class IS	RGSVX	NAS CM	Open End	Other Sector Equity (Utility)	D+	C-	B-	Up	Y	1,000,000
Rareview Longevity Income Generation Fund Inst Cls	RVIGX	NAS CM	Open End	Moderate Alloc (Growth & Income)	D	D+	B+		Y	1,000,000
Rareview Longevity Income Generation Fund Retail Class	RLIGX	NAS CM	Open End	Moderate Alloc (Growth & Income)	D	D+	B+		Y	2,500
Rational Dividend Capture Fund Class A	HDCAX	NAS CM	Open End	US Equity Large Cap Value (Equity-Income)	D+	D+	C	Down	Y	1,000
Rational Dividend Capture Fund Class C	HDCEX	NAS CM	Open End	US Equity Large Cap Value (Equity-Income)	D+	D	C-	Down	Y	1,000
Rational Dividend Capture Fund Class Institutional	HDCTX	NAS CM	Open End	US Equity Large Cap Value (Equity-Income)	C-	D+	C	Down	Y	1,000
Rational Dynamic Brands Fund Class A	HSUAX	NAS CM	Open End	US Equity Small Cap (Growth)	C+	C+	B-	Up	Y	1,000
Rational Dynamic Brands Fund Class C	HSUCX	NAS CM	Open End	US Equity Small Cap (Growth)	C+	C+	B-	Up	Y	1,000
Rational Dynamic Brands Fund Institutional Class	HSUTX	NAS CM	Open End	US Equity Small Cap (Growth)	C+	C+	B-	Up	Y	1,000
Rational Dynamic Momentum Fund Class A	RDMAX	NAS CM	Open End	Other Alternative (Growth)	C-	D+	C	Up	Y	1,000
Rational Dynamic Momentum Fund Class C	RDMCX	NAS CM	Open End	Other Alternative (Growth)	C-	D+	C	Up	Y	1,000
Rational Dynamic Momentum Fund Class I	RDMIX	NAS CM	Open End	Other Alternative (Growth)	C-	D+	C	Up	Y	1,000
Rational Hedged Return Fund Class A	HRSAX	NAS CM	Open End	Natl Resources Sec Equity (Growth & Income)	C	C-	C	Up	Y	1,000
Rational Hedged Return Fund Class C	HRSFX	NAS CM	Open End	Natl Resources Sec Equity (Growth & Income)	C	C-	C	Up	Y	1,000
Rational Hedged Return Fund Class Institutional	HRSTX	NAS CM	Open End	Natl Resources Sec Equity (Growth & Income)	C	C-	C	Up	Y	1,000
Rational Iron Horse Fund Class A	IRHAX	NAS CM	Open End	Long/Short Equity (Growth & Income)	B-	C	B	Up	Y	1,000
Rational Iron Horse Fund Class C	IRHCX	NAS CM	Open End	Long/Short Equity (Growth & Income)	C+	C	B	Down	Y	1,000
Rational Iron Horse Fund Class I	IRHIX	NAS CM	Open End	Long/Short Equity (Growth & Income)	B-	C	B	Up	Y	1,000
Rational Risk Managed Emerging Markets Fund Class A	HGSAX	NAS CM	Open End	Emerging Markets Equity (Div Emerging Mkts)	B-	B-	B	Up	Y	1,000
Rational Risk Managed Emerging Markets Fund Class C	HGSCX	NAS CM	Open End	Emerging Markets Equity (Div Emerging Mkts)	B-	C+	B-	Up	Y	1,000
Rational Risk Managed Emerging Mkts Fund Cls Inst	HGSIX	NAS CM	Open End	Emerging Markets Equity (Div Emerging Mkts)	B-	B-	B	Up	Y	1,000
Rational Strategic Allocation Fund Class A	HBAFX	NAS CM	Open End	Moderate Alloc (Growth & Income)	B-	C+	B	Up	Y	1,000
Rational Strategic Allocation Fund Class C	RHSCX	NAS CM	Open End	Moderate Alloc (Growth & Income)	B-	C+	B	Up	Y	1,000
Rational Strategic Allocation Fund Class Institutional	RHSIX	NAS CM	Open End	Moderate Alloc (Growth & Income)	B-	C+	B	Up	Y	1,000

★ Expanded analysis of this fund is included in Section II.

	TOTAL RETURNS					PERFORMANCE				ASSETS		ASSET ALLOCATION & TURNOVER					BULL & BEAR		FEES		
Min Additional Investment	3-Month Total Return	6-Month Total Return	1-Year Total Return	3-Year Total Return	5-Year Total Return	Dividend Yield (TTM)	Expense Ratio	3-Yr Std Deviation	3-Year Beta	NAV	Total Assets (MIL)	%Cash	%Stocks	%Bonds	%Other	Turnover Ratio	Last Bull Market Total Return	Last Bear Market Total Return	Front End Fee (%)	Back End Fee (%)	Inception Date
	1.70	2.03	5.29	-0.15	49.94	0	1.99	10.86	0.93	12.52	6.5	10	43	44	1		16.78	-18.03			Jul-08
100	6.45	11.65	16.42	25.26	93.39	0	2.39	12.15	1.12	31.33	7.2	2	98	0	0	28	28.07	-22.99	5.50		Dec-97
100	6.22	11.22	15.55	22.48	86.18	0	3.14	12.13	1.12	26.96	7.2	2	98	0	0	28	27.49	-23.22			Jul-00
	6.50	11.79	16.71	26.20	95.79	0	2.14	12.12	1.12	33.09	7.2	2	98	0	0	28	28.27	-22.93			Nov-00
100	2.80	8.26	9.30	21.28	81.44	0	2.22	13.52	0.93	22.44	30.0	1	99	0	0	146	28.41	-24.14	5.50		Nov-96
100	2.62	7.83	8.50	18.55	74.76	0	2.97	13.5	0.92	17.13	30.0	1	99	0	0	146	27.83	-24.34			Jul-00
	2.87	8.40	9.56	22.19	83.70	0	1.97	13.52	0.93	23.95	30.0	1	99	0	0	146	28.62	-24.1			Sep-00
100	5.80	9.97	16.32	19.26	86.60	0	2.22	10.86	0.98	30.64	70.1	0	99	0	1	185	21.78	-19.31	5.50		Nov-96
100	5.60	9.55	15.40	16.57	79.75	0	2.97	10.88	0.98	26.37	70.1	0	99	0	1	185	21.27	-19.55			Jul-00
	5.87	10.13	16.57	20.15	88.98	0	1.97	10.87	0.98	32.07	70.1	0	99	0	1	185	21.96	-19.3			Jul-00
1,000	5.31	9.05	17.95	24.62		0	2.11	7.93	0.65	10.52	10.0	-10	110	0	0	1,018					Mar-16
1,000	5.51	9.41	18.83	27.22		0	1.51	7.92	0.64	10.63	10.0	-10	110	0	0	1,018					Aug-13
1,000	4.88	8.89	14.73	6.69		0.02	2.7	6.32	0.49	10	9.9	21	75	3	1	625					Mar-16
1,000	5.10	9.20	15.53	8.82		0.03	2.1	6.34	0.49	10.05	9.9	21	75	3	1	625					Aug-13
1,000	5.52	14.94	16.12	24.77		2.18	2.29	12.68		11.06	98.8	17	78	0	4	558					Mar-16
1,000	5.69	15.32	16.82	27.32		1.93	1.69	12.7		11.18	98.8	17	78	0	4	558					Aug-13
1,000	13.11	25.80	67.83			0.06	2.29			10.08	108.5	42	1	57	0	41					Nov-15
1,000	13.24	26.16	68.91			0	1.69			10.22	108.5	42	1	57	0	41					Nov-15
1,000	3.75	5.29	5.85	21.25	70.29	0	1.28	8.8	0.57	27.15	143.4	24	75	0	1	27	10.01	-14.63			Jun-02
1,000	6.26	10.22	20.31	30.67	92.23	1.33	0.96	8.11	0.72	23.28	46.7	6	93	0	1	8	14.54	-10.33			Jun-02
1,000	5.09	9.85	20.06	25.36	80.49	0	1.07	11.93	0.9	39.73	266.1	4	96	0	0	122	33.15	-25.13			May-02
250	5.05	9.70	19.64	24.14	77.61	0	1.39	11.93	0.9	36.98	266.1	4	96	0	0	122	32.98	-25.23			May-94
1,000	1.56	-0.51	-0.51			0	1.3			7.8	34.9	99	0	0	1						Aug-15
	3.83	8.25	15.69	13.37	35.45	4	1.27	8.89	0.74	12.84	16.4	3	96	0	0	91	15.95				Sep-11
5,000	3.70	8.14	15.11	12.22	33.30	3.94	1.52	8.91	0.74	12.73	16.4	3	96	0	0	91	15.78				Jun-13
	4.42	7.47	15.31	41.29	103.42	0	1.1	13.7	0.85	17.71	25.1	3	97	0	0	64	39.46				Sep-11
50	-1.54	1.93	17.86			1.51	1.5			11.28	29.7	5	94	0	0	37			5.75		Mar-16
	-1.47	2.06	18.01			1.71	1.15			11.28	29.7	5	94	0	0	37					Mar-16
	-1.45	2.21	18.24			1.71	1.05			11.3	29.7	5	94	0	0	37					Mar-16
1,000	0.69	2.24	10.66			3.04	3.32			10.55	16.6	12	29	52	2						Nov-16
500	0.65	2.14	10.43			2.88	3.57			10.56	16.6	12	29	52	2						Nov-16
50	0.73	-1.35	-2.23	-1.09	33.13	3.86	1.26	8.63	0.63	8.01	36.5	2	95	0	0	159	17.64	-11.85	4.75		Mar-01
50	0.61	-1.59	-2.67	-2.54	29.72	3.39	1.76	8.63	0.63	7.99	36.5	2	95	0	0	159	17.24	-12.13		1.00	Jan-14
500	0.68	-1.21	-1.99	-0.24	34.91	4.11	1.01	8.67	0.62	8.02	36.5	2	95	0	0	159	17.93	-11.76			Mar-01
50	6.89	13.51	14.29	11.15	43.66	1.01	1.25	11.04	0.92	2.47	17.4	1	99	0	0	178	30.28	-23.06	4.75		Sep-02
50	6.92	13.19	14.02	9.65	39.92	0.41	1.75	11.06	0.92	2.26	17.4	1	99	0	0	178	29.71	-23.31		1.00	Jan-14
500	7.01	13.75	14.65	12.23	45.73	1.02	1	11	0.92	3.49	17.4	1	99	0	0	178	30.51	-23			Sep-02
50	6.77	6.10	3.56	5.55	40.29	0	2.34			25.15	16.3	94	6	0	0		3.68	-22.82	5.75		Oct-16
50	6.60	5.74	2.82	3.27	35.23	0	3.09			24.96	16.3	94	6	0	0		3.23	-23.06		1.00	Oct-16
500	6.88	6.25	3.85	6.43	42.17	0	2.09			25.25	16.3	94	6	0	0		3.84	-22.74			Sep-16
50	1.20	13.28	3.58	-6.88	-12.22	13.06	2.24	12.8	0.6	5.04	2.7	3	97	0	0	246	15.36	-24.34	4.75		May-07
50	1.43	13.16	3.01	-9.02	-15.66	12.97	2.99	12.89	0.6	5.06	2.7	3	97	0	0	246	14.69	-24.54		1.00	May-16
500	1.06	13.23	3.49	-6.86	-11.93	13.45	1.99	12.94	0.59	4.99	2.7	3	97	0	0	246	15.35	-24.22			May-07
50	1.78	4.16	8.61	11.19	38.74	0.09	1.95	4.77	0.39	10.57	17.1	12	88	0	0	323	16.37		5.75		Jul-11
50	1.69	3.88	7.74	8.67	33.58		2.7	4.77	0.39	10.54	17.1	12	88	0	0	323	15.86			1.00	Apr-17
500	1.87	4.28	8.83	12.15	40.68	0.21	1.7	4.74	0.38	10.58	17.1	12	88	0	0	323	16.38				Nov-11
50	7.99	17.33	38.12	30.73	41.97	0.71	1.53	11.03	0.59	7.22	10.3	4	96	0	0		12.37	-23.7	4.75		Dec-09
50	7.77	17.00	37.18	27.67	36.59	0.57	2.28	11.1	0.59	7.14	10.3	4	96	0	0		11.82	-23.94		1.00	May-16
500	8.09	17.37	38.51	31.53	43.54	0.91	1.28	11.08	0.59	7.27	10.3	4	96	0	0		12.47	-23.62			Dec-09
50	3.01	6.66	11.61	18.04	37.73	1.37	1.65	5.5	0.51	10.05	13.3	4	64	31	1		13.18	-11.08	4.75		Jul-09
50	2.79	6.27	10.80	15.46	32.72	0.78	2.4	5.53	0.52	10.03	13.3	4	64	31	1		12.69	-11.36		1.00	May-16
500	3.09	6.82	11.94	18.51	38.28	1.8	1.4	5.52	0.52	10.02	13.3	4	64	31	1		13.18	-11.08			May-16

Fund Name	MARKET Ticker Symbol	Traded On	FUND TYPE, CATEGORY & OBJECTIVE Fund Type	Category and (Prospectus Objective)	RATINGS Overall Rating	Reward Rating	Risk Rating	Recent Up/ Downgrade	MINIMUMS Open to New Investors	Min Initial Investment
RBB Free Market U.S. Equity Fund Institutional Class	FMUEX	NAS CM	Open End	US Equity Mid Cap (Growth)	B	B	B	Up	Y	0
RBC Emerging Markets Equity Fund Class A	REEAX	NAS CM	Open End	Emerging Markets Equity (Div Emerging Mkts)	B-	B	C+	Up	Y	1,000
RBC Emerging Markets Equity Fund Class I	REEIX	NAS CM	Open End	Emerging Markets Equity (Div Emerging Mkts)	B-	B	C+	Up	Y	250,000
RBC Emerging Markets Equity Fund Class R6	RREMX	NAS CM	Open End	Emerging Markets Equity (Div Emerging Mkts)	B-	B	C+	Up	Y	250,000
RBC Emerging Markets Small Cap Equity Fund Class A	RSMAX	NAS CM	Open End	Emerging Markets Equity (Small Company)	C+	C+	C	Up	Y	1,000
RBC Emerging Markets Small Cap Equity Fund Class I	RESIX	NAS CM	Open End	Emerging Markets Equity (Small Company)	C+	C+	C		Y	250,000
RBC Enterprise Fund Class A	TETAX	NAS CM	Open End	US Equity Small Cap (Small Company)	B	B	C+	Up	Y	1,000
RBC Enterprise Fund Class I	TETIX	NAS CM	Open End	US Equity Small Cap (Small Company)	B	B	C+	Up	Y	250,000
RBC Global Opportunities Fund Class I	RGOIX	NAS CM	Open End	Global Equity (Growth)	B-	C+	B	Up	Y	250,000
RBC Global Opportunities Fund Class R6	RGORX	NAS CM	Open End	Global Equity (Growth)	B-	C+	B	Up	Y	250,000
RBC International Opportunities Fund Class I	RIOIX	NAS CM	Open End	Global Equity Large Cap (Growth)	C+	C+	C+	Up	Y	250,000
RBC International Opportunities Fund Class R6	RIORX	NAS CM	Open End	Global Equity Large Cap (Growth)	C+	C+	C+	Up	Y	250,000
RBC Microcap Value Fund Class A	TMVAX	NAS CM	Open End	US Equity Small Cap (Growth)	B	B+	B	Up	Y	1,000
RBC Microcap Value Fund Class I	RMVIX	NAS CM	Open End	US Equity Small Cap (Growth)	B	B+	B	Up	Y	250,000
RBC Small Cap Core Fund Class A	TEEAX	NAS CM	Open End	US Equity Small Cap (Small Company)	B	B+	B-	Up	Y	1,000
RBC Small Cap Core Fund Class I	RCSIX	NAS CM	Open End	US Equity Small Cap (Small Company)	B	A-	B-	Up	Y	250,000
RBC Small Cap Core Fund Class R6	RBRCX	NAS CM	Open End	US Equity Small Cap (Small Company)	B	A-	B-	Up	Y	250,000
RBC Small Cap Value Fund Class I	RSVIX	NAS CM	Open End	US Equity Small Cap (Small Company)	B-	C+	B-	Up	Y	250,000
RBC Small Cap Value Fund Class R6	RRSVX	NAS CM	Open End	US Equity Small Cap (Small Company)	B-	C+	B-	Up	Y	250,000
RBC SMID Cap Growth Fund Class A	TMCAX	NAS CM	Open End	US Equity Mid Cap (Growth)	B	B	B+	Up	Y	1,000
RBC SMID Cap Growth Fund Class I	TMCIX	NAS CM	Open End	US Equity Mid Cap (Growth)	B	B	B+		Y	250,000
RBC SMID Cap Growth Fund Class R6	RSMRX	NAS CM	Open End	US Equity Mid Cap (Growth)	B	B	B+		Y	250,000
Reaves Utilities & Energy Infrastructure Fund Cls Inst	RSRFX	NAS CM	Open End	Other Sector Equity (Growth & Income)	B-	B-	B-	Down	Y	1,000
Reaves Utility Income Trust	UTG	AMEX	Closed End	Utilities Sector Equity (Utility)	C+	C	B	Down	Y	
Recurrent Natural Resources Fund Class I	RNRGX	NAS CM	Open End	Natl Resources Sec Equity (Natl Res)	U	U	U		Y	2,500
Red Oak Technology Select Fund	ROGSX	NAS CM	Open End	Technology Sector Equity (Technology)	A-	A+	B	Up	Y	2,000
Redwood AlphaFactor Core Equity Fund Class I	RWAIX	NAS CM	Open End	US Equity Large Cap Blend (Growth & Income)	U	U	U		Y	250,000
Redwood AlphaFactor Core Equity Fund Class N	RWANX	NAS CM	Open End	US Equity Large Cap Blend (Growth & Income)	U	U	U		Y	10,000
Redwood AlphaFactor Tactical Core Fund Class I	RWTIX	NAS CM	Open End	US Equity Large Cap Blend (Growth & Income)	U	U	U		Y	250,000
Redwood AlphaFactor Tactical Core Fund Class N	RWTNX	NAS CM	Open End	US Equity Large Cap Blend (Growth & Income)	U	U	U		Y	10,000
Regal Total Return Fund Class A	RTRTX	NAS CM	Open End	Moderate Alloc (Growth & Income)	C+	C+	B-	Down	Y	1,000
Reinhart Mid Cap PMV Fund Advisor Class	RPMVX	NAS CM	Open End	US Equity Mid Cap (Growth)	B-	C+	B		Y	5,000
Reinhart Mid Cap PMV Fund Institutional Class	RPMNX	NAS CM	Open End	US Equity Mid Cap (Growth)	B-	C+	B		Y	1,000,000
Reinhart Mid Cap PMV Fund Investor Class	RPMMX	NAS CM	Open End	US Equity Mid Cap (Growth)	B-	C+	B		Y	5,000
Relative Value Fund CIA Class Shares	US75943J1007		Closed End	Multialternative (Growth & Income)	U	U	U		Y	1,000
REMS Intl Real Estate Value-Opp Fund Founders Shares	REIFX	NAS CM	Open End	Real Estate Sector Equity (Real Estate)	B	B-	B	Up	Y	50,000
REMS Real Estate Income 50/50 Fund Class Platform Shares	RREFX	NAS CM	Open End	Real Estate Sector Equity (Real Estate)	B	C+	A-	Up	Y	2,500
REMS Real Estate Income 50/50 Fund Institutional Shares	RREIX	NAS CM	Open End	Real Estate Sector Equity (Real Estate)	B	C+	A-	Up	Y	50,000
REMS Real Estate Value Opportunity Fund Institutional Cls	HLRRX	NAS CM	Open End	Real Estate Sector Equity (Real Estate)	C+	C	B-	Down	Y	50,000
REMS Real Estate Value-Opportunity Fund, P Class	HLPPX	NAS CM	Open End	Real Estate Sector Equity (Real Estate)	C	C	B-	Down	Y	2,500
RENN Global Entrepreneurs Fund, Inc.	RCG	AMEX	Closed End	Moderate Alloc (Growth & Income)	D	D	D		Y	
Resource Real Estate Diversified Income Fund Class A	RREDX	NAS CM	Closed End	Real Estate Sector Equity (Real Estate)	B	C+	B+	Up	Y	2,500
Resource Real Estate Diversified Income Fund Class C	CRREX	NAS CM	Closed End	Real Estate Sector Equity (Real Estate)	B	C+	B+	Up	Y	2,500
Resource Real Estate Diversified Income Fund Class D	DRREX	NAS CM	Closed End	Real Estate Sector Equity (Real Estate)	B	C+	B+	Up	Y	2,500
Resource Real Estate Diversified Income Fund Class I	IRREX	NAS CM	Closed End	Real Estate Sector Equity (Real Estate)	B	C+	B+	Up	Y	1,000,000
Resource Real Estate Diversified Income Fund Class L	US76123K8009		Closed End	Real Estate Sector Equity (Real Estate)	B	C+	B+		Y	2,500
Resource Real Estate Diversified Income Fund Class T	RRETX	NAS CM	Closed End	Real Estate Sector Equity (Real Estate)	B	C+	B+	Up	Y	2,500
Resource Real Estate Diversified Income Fund Class U	URREX	NAS CM	Closed End	Real Estate Sector Equity (Real Estate)	B	C+	A-	Up	Y	2,500
Resource Real Estate Diversified Income Fund Cls W Shares	WRREX	NAS CM	Closed End	Real Estate Sector Equity (Real Estate)	B	C+	B+	Up	Y	2,500
RESQ Dynamic Allocation Fund Class A	RQEAX	NAS CM	Open End	Moderate Alloc (Growth)	C	C	C	Up	Y	1,000
RESQ Dynamic Allocation Fund Class C	RQECX	NAS CM	Open End	Moderate Alloc (Growth)	C	C	C	Up	Y	1,000
RESQ Dynamic Allocation Fund Class I	RQEIX	NAS CM	Open End	Moderate Alloc (Growth)	C	C	C	Up	Y	100,000

★Expanded analysis of this fund is included in Section II.

	TOTAL RETURNS					PERFORMANCE				ASSETS		ASSET ALLOCATION & TURNOVER					BULL & BEAR		FEES		
Min Additional Investment	3-Month Total Return	6-Month Total Return	1-Year Total Return	3-Year Total Return	5-Year Total Return	Dividend Yield (TTM)	Expense Ratio	3-Yr Std Deviation	3-Year Beta	NAV	Total Assets (MIL)	%Cash	%Stocks	%Bonds	%Other	Turnover Ratio	Last Bull Market Total Return	Last Bear Market Total Return	Front End Fee (%)	Back End Fee (%)	Inception Date
	4.78	10.23	13.44	30.55	99.40	0.74	0.9	12.49	0.98	18.78	3,032	1	99	0	0	5	26.99	-24.07			Dec-07
	6.83	13.71	34.74	26.91		0.56	1.13	12.56	0.76	13.16	575.0	4	93	0	0	19			5.75		Dec-13
	6.94	13.79	35.12	27.76		0.62	0.88	12.56	0.76	13.36	575.0	4	93	0	0	19					Dec-13
	6.92	13.84	35.06	27.64		0.26	0.88	12.56	0.76	13.42	575.0	4	93	0	0	19					Nov-16
100	6.20	8.73	25.46	19.26		3.64	1.7	11.62	0.7	11.13	6.1	0	93	3	3	38			5.75		Dec-13
	6.24	8.77	25.76	20.06		3.85	1.45	11.66	0.7	11.12	6.1	0	93	3	3	38					Dec-13
	0.80	10.28	14.29	23.66	73.20	0.02	1.33	16.15	0.94	22.07	91.0	0	100	0	0	26	28.45	-21.97	5.75		Apr-04
	0.88	10.44	14.60	24.60	75.39	0.2	1.08	16.16	0.94	22.98	91.0	0	100	0	0	26	28.63	-21.96			Sep-04
	7.26	15.47	34.26	43.52		0.56	0.86			13.51	10.0	0	95	0	2	36					Dec-14
	7.21	15.45	34.32	43.63		0	0.81			13.58	10.0	0	95	0	2	36					Nov-16
	7.67	15.89	33.12	25.82		0.4	0.89			11.69	53.3	0	96	0	0	38					Dec-14
	7.66	15.95	33.24	25.90		0.03	0.84			11.74	53.3	0	96	0	0	38					Nov-16
	0.68	6.26	5.22	24.74	93.04	0.2	1.34	13.88	0.88	30.03	150.1	1	98	0	0	9	27.5	-20.42	5.75		Apr-04
	0.73	6.37	5.46	25.65	95.55	0.43	1.09	13.89	0.88	30.02	150.1	1	98	0	0	9	27.69	-20.3			Sep-87
	5.04	11.80	10.71	28.41	89.80	0	1.15	15.95	1.08	39.67	295.0	1	99	0	0	29	28.22	-23.98	5.75		Apr-04
	5.09	11.93	10.97	29.38	92.17	0.15	0.9	15.96	1.08	41.33	295.0	1	99	0	0	29	28.47	-23.91			Aug-91
0	5.11	11.97	11.01	29.42	92.22	0.07	0.87	15.96	1.08	41.39	295.0	1	99	0	0	29	28.47	-23.91			Nov-16
	3.70	9.32	10.80	41.90		0.38	0.95			13.56	82.6	5	95	0	0	35					Dec-14
0	3.69	9.44	10.91	42.12		0	0.9			13.64	82.6	5	95	0	0	35					Nov-16
	3.57	6.31	16.73	28.59	81.75	0	1.07	10.76	0.77	12.15	79.4	1	99	0	0		27.8	-17.8	5.75		Jun-94
	3.67	6.42	17.06	29.53	84.11	0	0.82	10.77	0.77	13.76	79.4	1	99	0	0		27.94	-17.69			Jun-94
0	3.66	6.41	17.13	29.53	84.10	0	0.77	10.77	0.77	13.77	79.4	1	99	0	0		27.95	-17.7			Nov-16
	3.32	5.69	10.80	23.09	72.71	2.05	1.47	8.45	0.5	10.21	47.5	2	98	0	0	45	14.73	-10			Dec-04
	-1.43	1.63	10.06	25.28	99.96	2.62		12	0.5	33.43	1,651	1	99	0	0	34	16.55	-6.7			Feb-04
500	8.70						1.25			21.91	0.43										Oct-17
25	7.83	15.31	31.09	63.40	176.50	0.32	1.09	13.78	0.96	24.56	494.1	3	97	0	0	6	25	-15.58			Dec-98
1,000	6.61	9.80					0.8			17.01	59.1	0	99	0	1						Mar-17
1,000	6.60	9.78					1.05			17.01	59.1	0	99	0	1						Mar-17
1,000	6.57	9.63					1.2			16.99	66.3	0	99	0	1						Mar-17
1,000	6.52	9.57					1.45			16.99	66.3	0	99	0	1						Mar-17
100	4.55	7.27	11.52	14.98		0.31	1.64	6.2	0.93	11.34	30.7	18	68	18	-4	104			5.75		May-14
100	5.15	5.81	10.72	28.10	82.41	0.47	1.06	10.88	0.95	15.51	196.2	6	94	0	0	62					Jun-12
	5.19	5.85	10.76	28.14	82.48		0.91	10.89	0.95	15.51	196.2	6	94	0	0	62					Sep-17
100	5.10	5.69	10.47	27.25	80.27	0.27	1.31	10.89	0.95	15.5	196.2	6	94	0	0	62					Jun-12
1,000	1.45	2.83					3.15			25.63	--	40	41	10	8						Jun-17
5,000	4.78	9.84	27.11	24.58		0.74	1.56	10.22	0.71	11.72	54.5	13	86	0	0	40					May-14
100	0.25	1.68	3.34	14.51	43.94	4.08	0.96	8.16	0.55	12.24	74.9	7	45	0	0	29	16.47	-9.38			Mar-06
5,000	0.30	1.86	3.64	15.40	45.94	4.27	0.71	8.14	0.55	12.39	74.9	7	45	0	0	29	16.74	-9.26			Apr-11
5,000	-0.33	-1.32	-1.35	6.40	47.62	1.96	1.25	11.2	0.68	12.75	180.1	7	79	0	0	34	37.37	-24.05			Dec-02
100	-0.39	-1.46	-1.56	5.62	45.75	1.74	1.5	11.14	0.67	12.6	180.1	7	79	0	0	34	37.12	-24.14			Dec-09
	-4.54	1.37	8.88	-35.24	-39.25	0	0	31.24	-0.17	1.47	6.7	36	36	0	-1	72	15.38	-16.42			Jan-94
1,000	1.19	1.59	6.48	18.16		5.92	2.01	6.35		10.11	--	6	69	-8	11				5.75		Mar-13
1,000	1.00	1.21	5.68	15.63		5.16	2.76	6.3		10.11	--	6	69	-8	11				1.50		Aug-14
2,500	1.07	1.36	5.94	16.55		5.41	2.51			10.27	--	6	69	-8	11						Feb-15
	1.17	1.68	6.53	16.59		6.17	1.76	6.3		10.53	--	6	69	-8	11						Aug-14
1,000	1.02	1.46	6.35	18.01			2.26			10.11	--	6	69	-8	11				4.25		Jul-17
2,500	1.00	1.20	5.68	15.51		5.16	2.76			10.09	--	6	69	-8	11				1.50	1.00	Feb-15
2,500	1.19	1.59	6.48	18.27		5.91	2.01			10.12	--	6	69	-8	11				6.50		Feb-15
1,000	1.29	1.61	6.48	17.09		5.79	2.01	6.29		10.27	--	6	69	-8	11						Nov-14
	2.64	6.88	11.36	-8.09		0	2.64	10.67	0.61	9.31	43.8	2	97	0	1	1,060			5.75		Dec-13
	2.57	6.64	10.77	-9.58		0	3.24	10.68	0.6	9.15	43.8	2	97	0	1	1,060				1.00	Oct-14
	2.82	7.12	11.93	-6.88		0	2.24	10.67	0.61	9.47	43.8	2	97	0	1	1,060					Dec-13

	MARKET			FUND TYPE, CATEGORY & OBJECTIVE	RATINGS				MINIMUMS	
Fund Name	Ticker Symbol	Traded On	Fund Type	Category and (Prospectus Objective)	Overall Rating	Reward Rating	Risk Rating	Recent Up/ Downgrade	Open to New Investors	Min Initial Investment
RESQ Strategic Income Fund Class A	RQIAX	NAS CM	Open End	Cautious Alloc (Income)	C-	C-	C	Up	Y	1,000
RESQ Strategic Income Fund Class C	RQICX	NAS CM	Open End	Cautious Alloc (Income)	C-	D+	C	Up	Y	1,000
RESQ Strategic Income Fund Class I	RQIIX	NAS CM	Open End	Cautious Alloc (Income)	C	C-	C	Up	Y	100,000
Reynolds Blue Chip Growth Fund	RBCGX	NAS CM	Open End	US Equity Large Cap Growth (Growth)	B-	C+	B	Up	Y	1,000
Rice Hall James Micro Cap Portfolio Institutional Class	RHJSX	NAS CM	Open End	US Equity Small Cap (Small Company)	B+	A-	B	Up	Y	2,500
Rice Hall James Small Cap Portfolio Institutional Class	RHJMX	NAS CM	Open End	US Equity Small Cap (Small Company)	B-	C+	B	Up	Y	2,500
Rice Hall James Smid Cap Portfolio Investor	RHJVX	NAS CM	Open End	US Equity Mid Cap (Growth)	B-	C+	B	Up	Y	2,500
River Oak Discovery Fund	RIVSX	NAS CM	Open End	US Equity Small Cap (Growth)	B	B	B	Up	Y	2,000
Riverbridge Eco Leaders® Fund Institutional Class	RIVEX	NAS CM	Open End	US Equity Mid Cap (Growth)	B-	C+	B	Up		1,000,000
Riverbridge Eco Leaders® Fund Investor Class	ECOLX	NAS CM	Open End	US Equity Mid Cap (Growth)	B-	C+	B	Up		2,500
Riverbridge Growth Fund Institutional Class	RIVBX	NAS CM	Open End	US Equity Mid Cap (Growth)	B	B	A-	Up	Y	1,000,000
Riverbridge Growth Fund Investor Class	RIVRX	NAS CM	Open End	US Equity Mid Cap (Growth)	B	B	A-	Up	Y	2,500
RiverFront Conservative Income Builder Fund Class C	RCCBX	NAS CM	Open End	Cautious Alloc (Income)	B-	C	B	Up	Y	2,500
RiverFront Conservative Income Builder Fund Class I	RCIBX	NAS CM	Open End	Cautious Alloc (Income)	B-	C+	B	Up	Y	100,000
RiverFront Conservative Income Builder Fund Class Investor	RCABX	NAS CM	Open End	Cautious Alloc (Income)	B-	C+	B	Up	Y	2,500
RiverFront Dynamic Equity Income Fund Class C	RLGCX	NAS CM	Open End	Alloc (Growth & Income)	C+	C+	B-	Down	Y	2,500
RiverFront Dynamic Equity Income Fund Class I	RLIIX	NAS CM	Open End	Alloc (Growth & Income)	B-	B-	B-	Down	Y	100,000
RiverFront Dynamic Equity Income Fund Class Investor	RLGAX	NAS CM	Open End	Alloc (Growth & Income)	B-	C+	B-	Down	Y	2,500
RiverFront Global Allocation Fund Class C	RMGCX	NAS CM	Open End	Global Equity (Growth)	C+	C+	C+	Down	Y	2,500
RiverFront Global Allocation Fund Class I	RMGIX	NAS CM	Open End	Global Equity (Growth)	C+	C+	C+	Down	Y	100,000
RiverFront Global Allocation Fund Class Investor	RMGAX	NAS CM	Open End	Global Equity (Growth)	C+	C+	C+	Down	Y	2,500
RiverFront Global Growth Fund Class C	RLTCX	NAS CM	Open End	Global Equity (Growth)	C+	C+	C+	Down	Y	2,500
RiverFront Global Growth Fund Class I	RLFIX	NAS CM	Open End	Global Equity (Growth)	C+	B-	C+	Down	Y	100,000
RiverFront Global Growth Fund Class Investor	RLTAX	NAS CM	Open End	Global Equity (Growth)	C+	B-	C+	Down	Y	2,500
RiverFront Global Growth Fund Class Investor II shares	RLTSX	NAS CM	Open End	Global Equity (Growth)	C+	B-	C+	Down	Y	2,500
RiverFront Global Growth Fund Class L	RLTIX	NAS CM	Open End	Global Equity (Growth)	C+	B-	C+	Down	Y	1,000,000
RiverFront Moderate Growth & Income Fund Class C	RMICX	NAS CM	Open End	Moderate Alloc (Growth & Income)	B-	C+	B	Up	Y	2,500
RiverFront Moderate Growth & Income Fund Class I	RMIIX	NAS CM	Open End	Moderate Alloc (Growth & Income)	B-	C+	B	Up	Y	100,000
RiverFront Moderate Growth & Income Fund Class Investor	RMIAX	NAS CM	Open End	Moderate Alloc (Growth & Income)	B-	C+	B	Up	Y	2,500
RiverNorth Core Opportunity Fund Class I	RNCIX	NAS CM	Open End	Moderate Alloc (Growth & Income)	B-	B-	C+	Down	Y	5,000,000
RiverNorth Core Opportunity Fund Class R	RNCOX	NAS CM	Open End	Moderate Alloc (Growth & Income)	C+	B-	C+	Down	Y	5,000
RiverNorth Opportunities	RIV	NYSE	Closed End	Moderate Alloc (Growth & Income)	C-	C-	B+	Up	Y	
RiverNorth/DoubleLine Strategic Opportunity Fund	OPP	NYSE	Closed End	Moderate Alloc (Growth & Income)	D	C-	B+		Y	
RiverPark Focused Value Fund Institutional Class	RFVIX	NAS CM	Open End	US Equity Large Cap Blend (Growth)	C	C	C		Y	100,000
RiverPark Focused Value Fund Retail Class	RFVFX	NAS CM	Open End	US Equity Large Cap Blend (Growth)	C	C	C		Y	1,000
RiverPark Large Growth Fund Class Institutional	RPXIX	NAS CM	Open End	US Equity Large Cap Growth (Growth)	B	B	C+	Up	Y	100,000
RiverPark Large Growth Fund Class Retail	RPXFX	NAS CM	Open End	US Equity Large Cap Growth (Growth)	B	B	C+	Up	Y	1,000
RiverPark Long/Short Opportunity Fund Institutional Class	RLSIX	NAS CM	Open End	Long/Short Equity (Growth)	B-	C+	B-	Down	Y	100,000
RiverPark Long/Short Opportunity Fund Retail Class	RLSFX	NAS CM	Open End	Long/Short Equity (Growth)	B-	C+	B-	Down	Y	1,000
RiverPark/Wedgewood Fund Class Institutional	RWGIX	NAS CM	Open End	US Equity Large Cap Growth (Growth)	B-	C+	B		Y	100,000
RiverPark/Wedgewood Fund Class Retail	RWGFX	NAS CM	Open End	US Equity Large Cap Growth (Growth)	B-	C+	B		Y	1,000
RMB Fund Class A	RMBHX	NAS CM	Open End	US Equity Large Cap Growth (Growth)	B-	C+	B	Down	Y	2,500
RMB Fund Class C	RMBJX	NAS CM	Open End	US Equity Large Cap Growth (Growth)	B-	C+	B-	Down	Y	2,500
RMB Fund Class I	RMBGX	NAS CM	Open End	US Equity Large Cap Growth (Growth)	B-	B-	B	Down	Y	100,000
RMB Mendon Financial Long/Short Fund Class A	RMBFX	NAS CM	Open End	Long/Short Equity (Financial)	B-	C+	B		Y	2,500
RMB Mendon Financial Long/Short Fund Class C	RMBCX	NAS CM	Open End	Long/Short Equity (Financial)	B-	C+	B		Y	2,500
RMB Mendon Financial Long/Short Fund Class I	RMBIX	NAS CM	Open End	Long/Short Equity (Financial)	B-	B-	B			100,000
RMB Mendon Financial Services Fund Class A	RMBKX	NAS CM	Open End	Financials Sector Equity (Financial)	A	A	A-	Up	Y	2,500
RMB Mendon Financial Services Fund Class C	RMBNX	NAS CM	Open End	Financials Sector Equity (Financial)	A	A	A-	Up	Y	2,500
RMB Mendon Financial Services Fund Class I	RMBLX	NAS CM	Open End	Financials Sector Equity (Financial)	A	A	A-	Up	Y	100,000
RMR Real Estate Income Fund	RIF	AMEX	Closed End	Real Estate Sector Equity (Real Estate)	B-	C+	B	Up	Y	
RNC Genter Dividend Income Fund	GDIIX	NAS CM	Open End	US Equity Large Cap Value (Equity-Income)	B	B-	B	Up	Y	2,500

★ Expanded analysis of this fund is included in Section II.

Min Additional Investment	TOTAL RETURNS 3-Month Total Return	6-Month Total Return	1-Year Total Return	3-Year Total Return	5-Year Total Return	PERFORMANCE Dividend Yield (TTM)	Expense Ratio	3-Yr Std Deviation	3-Year Beta	ASSETS NAV	Total Assets (MIL)	ASSET ALLOCATION & TURNOVER %Cash	%Stocks	%Bonds	%Other	Turnover Ratio	BULL & BEAR Last Bull Market Total Return	Last Bear Market Total Return	FEES Front End Fee (%)	Back End Fee (%)	Inception Date
	0.00	2.60	3.75	-5.21		0.48	2.75	4.92	0.67	9.62	41.6	17	24	22	-3	935			4.75		Dec-13
	-0.09	2.26	3.03	-6.92		0.01	3.35	5.01	0.69	9.51	41.6	17	24	22	-3	935				1.00	Oct-14
	0.09	2.79	4.13	-4.06		0.89	2.35	4.94	0.68	9.65	41.6	17	24	22	-3	935					Dec-13
100	6.30	11.44	24.71	20.04	72.58	0	1.86	10.08	0.86	56.38	72.0	2	98	0	0	343	26.64	-22.87			Aug-88
100	-1.48	6.32	12.86	31.91	95.17	0	1.25	13.44	0.81	33.09	51.6	3	97	0	0	54	35.87	-23.73			Jul-94
100	4.99	5.18	12.05	16.27	68.60	0	1	12.63	0.81	10.93	47.1	4	96	0	0	54	21.14	-18.97			Nov-96
100	3.43	5.28	13.42	13.71	64.45	0	1	11.55	0.9	22.3	4.5	6	94	0	0	49	24.12	-25.49			Jul-04
25	4.32	8.49	11.30	21.71	79.78	0	1.35	12.51	0.74	16.72	14.7	6	94	0	0	21	27.99	-26			Jun-05
	7.71	9.23	23.98	35.17		0	0.95			13.13	2.7	2	100	0	-2	24					Dec-14
100	7.76	9.12	23.71	34.26		0	1.2			13.04	2.7	2	100	0	-2	24					Dec-14
	7.97	9.94	25.41	37.21	96.21	0	1.01	10.29	0.87	18.07	85.0	2	98	0	0	21					Dec-12
100	7.94	9.80	25.10	36.29	93.94	0	1.26	10.33	0.87	17.85	85.0	2	98	0	0	21					Dec-12
	1.93	4.00	7.60	10.36	22.22	0.8	2.13	4.36	0.28	11.01	11.4	5	38	56	0	137				1.00	Sep-12
	2.10	4.48	8.57	13.54	28.30	1.46	1.13	4.4	0.28	10.96	11.4	5	38	56	0	137					Sep-12
	2.13	4.37	8.37	12.90	26.84	1.32	1.38	4.39	0.26	11.14	11.4	5	38	56	0	137			5.50		Sep-12
	3.67	7.85	16.46	21.18	48.11	0.76	2.2	8.84	0.78	14.03	79.4	4	80	16	0	129	15.16	-16.28		1.00	Aug-10
	3.91	8.36	17.58	24.87	55.79	1.24	1.2	8.8	0.78	14.29	79.4	4	80	16	0	129	16	-16.02			Aug-10
	3.85	8.19	17.31	23.92	53.71	1.08	1.45	8.78	0.78	14.35	79.4	4	80	16	0	129	15.76	-16.03	5.50		Aug-10
	3.88	8.40	18.52	19.73	46.39	1.12	2.21	9.85	0.88	13.74	33.4	2	91	7	0	124	15.46	-19.32		1.00	Aug-10
	4.21	8.92	19.72	23.39	53.83	1.24	1.21	9.85	0.88	13.99	33.4	2	91	7	0	124	16.1	-18.91			Aug-10
	4.11	8.82	19.36	22.41	52.03	1.19	1.46	9.87	0.88	14.18	33.4	2	91	7	0	124	15.87	-19.03	5.50		Aug-10
	4.21	9.24	20.19	22.08	52.11	1.08	2.21	10.4	0.92	15.43	61.7	2	98	0	0	113	18.23	-22.37		1.00	Sep-10
	4.51	9.84	21.51	25.68	59.83	1.17	1.21	10.44	0.92	16.15	61.7	2	98	0	0	113	18.86	-22.01			Sep-10
	4.45	9.69	21.19	24.77	57.92	1.15	1.46	10.43	0.92	15.98	61.7	2	98	0	0	113	18.74	-22.1	5.50		Sep-10
	4.48	9.74	21.15	24.84	57.96	1.15	1.46	10.45	0.92	15.89	61.7	2	98	0	0	113	18.74	-22.07			Oct-08
	4.45	9.78	21.46	25.73	59.88	1.17	1.21	10.46	0.92	16.12	61.7	2	98	0	0	113	18.9	-22.04			Oct-08
	2.81	5.75	11.09	14.91	35.93	0.81	2.16	6.52	0.6	11.91	95.8	4	60	36	0	132	11.88	-10.95		1.00	Aug-10
	3.11	6.22	12.20	18.34	42.90	1.43	1.16	6.49	0.6	12.05	95.8	4	60	36	0	132	12.61	-10.57			Aug-10
	2.98	6.08	11.91	17.42	41.12	1.27	1.41	6.54	0.6	12.04	95.8	4	60	36	0	132	12.46	-10.59	5.50		Aug-10
100	3.77	8.29	18.08	25.18	55.07	4.63	2.56	8.97	0.78	10.81	323.2	21	49	25	3	39	17.13	-13.93			Aug-14
100	3.69	8.13	17.76	24.20	53.76	4.39	2.81	9	0.79	10.81	323.2	21	49	25	3	39	17.13	-13.93			Dec-06
	1.85	4.70	13.02			4.7	3.72			20.04	75.0	5	32	51	2						Dec-15
	0.81	2.63	8.35			7.44	2.94			19.78	217.5	3	2	87	1						Sep-16
100	4.90	8.55	23.14			0.72	1			9.88	44.1	4	96	0	0	36					Mar-15
100	4.87	8.41	22.69			0.49	1.25			9.88	44.1	4	96	0	0	36					Mar-15
100	6.58	12.60	30.19	33.38	96.12	0.41	0.9	12.87	1.12	22.11	49.8	1	99	0	0	13	30.12	-13.39			Sep-10
100	6.48	12.41	29.82	32.41	93.63	0.18	1.11	12.86	1.12	21.83	49.8	1	99	0	0	13	29.98	-13.48			Sep-10
100	2.15	7.36	22.09	20.11	31.21	0	1.77	10.1	0.81	12.48	89.5	52	64	0	-16	24	29.8	-6.2			Mar-12
100	2.17	7.34	21.89	19.44	30.00	0	1.96	10.13	0.81	12.38	89.5	52	64	0	-16	24	29.8	-6.2			Mar-12
100	8.70	13.74	19.90	15.67	69.07	0.14	0.82	11.17	0.93	17.64	573.0	1	99	0	0	31	29.35	-10.41			Sep-10
100	8.65	13.66	19.64	15.34	67.81	0	1.08	11.1	0.92	17.5	573.0	1	99	0	0	31	29.12	-10.51			Sep-10
500	3.99	9.55	22.48	24.82	72.48	0.21	1.55	11.68	1.02	23.56	87.1	0	100	0	0	51	28.05	-13.35	5.00		Jun-75
500	3.76	9.10	21.57	22.00	66.12	0	2.3	11.66	1.02	19.87	87.1	0	100	0	0	51	27.49	-13.64		1.00	Apr-04
25,000	4.05	9.71	22.79	25.14	72.92		1.3	11.68	1.02	23.56	87.1	0	100	0	0	51	28.05	-13.35			Feb-17
500	-1.22	0.34	-3.07	21.36	71.47	0	1.68	12.89	0.54	17.67	249.5	4	70	0	26	61	23.48	-24	5.00		Apr-04
500	-1.38	0.00	-3.75	18.72	65.38	0	2.38	12.89	0.54	16.39	249.5	4	70	0	26	61	22.89	-24.22		1.00	Apr-04
25,000	-1.16	0.50	-2.78	22.31	72.81	0	1.39	12.89	0.54	17.82	249.5	4	70	0	26	61	23.48	-24			Aug-15
500	2.50	7.84	11.99	73.97	167.36	0	1.41	15.18		43.4	641.1	2	96	0	2	71	19.63	-20.1	5.00		Jun-99
500	2.30	7.44	11.17	70.16	157.49	0	2.16	15.17		39.76	641.1	2	96	0	2	71	19.15	-20.41		1.00	Apr-05
25,000	2.57	7.98	12.23	74.35	167.94		1.16	15.18		43.87	641.1	2	96	0	2	71	19.63	-20.1			Feb-17
	0.28	0.17	3.75	15.53	60.63	5.57		14.29	1.03	23.28	241.7	5	70	1	0	10	29.85	-15.58			Dec-03
500	6.75	13.17	17.09	32.77	79.47	1.72	1.25	10.76	0.99	18.34	16.8	2	98	0	-1	25	20.52	-12.2			Dec-08

	MARKET		FUND TYPE, CATEGORY & OBJECTIVE		RATINGS					MINIMUMS
Fund Name	Ticker Symbol	Traded On	Fund Type	Category and (Prospectus Objective)	Overall Rating	Reward Rating	Risk Rating	Recent Up/ Downgrade	Open to New Investors	Min Initial Investment
Rock Oak Core Growth Fund	RCKSX	NAS CM	Open End	US Equity Mid Cap (Growth)	B-	B	C	Up	Y	2,000
Rockefeller Equity Allocation Fund Institutional Class	ROCKX	NAS CM	Open End	Aggressive Alloc (Growth & Income)	C+	C+	B-	Up	Y	1,000,000
Rondure New World Fund Institutional Class	RNWIX	NAS CM	Open End	Global Equity Large Cap (Foreign Stock)	U	U	U		Y	2,000
Rondure New World Fund Investor Class	RNWOX	NAS CM	Open End	Global Equity Large Cap (Foreign Stock)	U	U	U		Y	2,000
Rondure Overseas Fund Institutional Class	ROSIX	NAS CM	Open End	Global Equity Large Cap (Foreign Stock)	U	U	U		Y	2,000
Rondure Overseas Fund Investor Class	ROSOX	NAS CM	Open End	Global Equity Large Cap (Foreign Stock)	U	U	U		Y	2,000
Roumell Opportunistic Value Fund Institutional Class	RAMSX	NAS CM	Open End	Moderate Alloc (Growth)	C+	C+	C	Up	Y	2,500
Royce Dividend Value Fund Consultant Class	RDVCX	NAS CM	Open End	US Equity Mid Cap (Growth & Income)	B-	B-	C+	Up	Y	2,000
Royce Dividend Value Fund Institutional Shares	RDIIX	NAS CM	Open End	US Equity Mid Cap (Growth & Income)	B	B	C+	Up	Y	1,000,000
Royce Dividend Value Fund Investment Class	RDVIX	NAS CM	Open End	US Equity Mid Cap (Growth & Income)	B	B	C+	Up	Y	2,000
Royce Dividend Value Fund Service Class	RYDVX	NAS CM	Open End	US Equity Mid Cap (Growth & Income)	B-	B	C+		Y	2,000
Royce Global Financial Services Fund Institutional Class	RGFIX	NAS CM	Open End	Financials Sector Equity (Financial)	B	B	B	Up	Y	1,000,000
Royce Global Financial Services Fund Service Class	RYFSX	NAS CM	Open End	Financials Sector Equity (Financial)	B	B	B	Up	Y	2,000
Royce Global Value Trust	RGT	NYSE	Closed End	Global Equity Mid/Small Cap (World Stock)	B	B	C+	Up	Y	
Royce International Micro-Cap Fund Service Class	ROIMX	NAS CM	Open End	Global Equity Mid/Small Cap (Foreign Stock)	B	B-	B	Up	Y	2,000
Royce International Premier Fund Consultant Class	RINPX	NAS CM	Open End	Global Equity Mid/Small Cap (Foreign Stock)	A	A	A-	Up	Y	2,000
Royce International Premier Fund Investment Class	RIPNX	NAS CM	Open End	Global Equity Mid/Small Cap (Foreign Stock)	A	A	A-	Up	Y	2,000
Royce International Premier Fund R Class	RINRX	NAS CM	Open End	Global Equity Mid/Small Cap (Foreign Stock)	A	A	A-	Up	Y	0
Royce International Premier Fund Service Class	RYIPX	NAS CM	Open End	Global Equity Mid/Small Cap (Foreign Stock)	A	A	A-	Up	Y	2,000
Royce Low-Priced Stock Fund Class R	RLPRX	NAS CM	Open End	US Equity Small Cap (Small Company)	C+	C+	C	Up	Y	0
Royce Low-Priced Stock Fund Institutional Class	RLPIX	NAS CM	Open End	US Equity Small Cap (Small Company)	C+	C+	C	Up	Y	1,000,000
Royce Low-Priced Stock Fund Investment Class	RLPHX	NAS CM	Open End	US Equity Small Cap (Small Company)	C+	C+	C	Up	Y	2,000
Royce Low-Priced Stock Fund Service Class	RYLPX	NAS CM	Open End	US Equity Small Cap (Small Company)	C+	C+	C	Up	Y	2,000
Royce Micro Cap Trust	RMT	NYSE	Closed End	US Equity Small Cap (Small Company)	B-	B	C+	Up		
Royce Micro-Cap Fund Consultant Class	RYMCX	NAS CM	Open End	US Equity Small Cap (Small Company)	C+	C+	C	Up	Y	2,000
Royce Micro-Cap Fund Investment Class	RYOTX	NAS CM	Open End	US Equity Small Cap (Small Company)	C+	C+	C	Up	Y	2,000
Royce Micro-Cap Fund Service Class	RMCFX	NAS CM	Open End	US Equity Small Cap (Small Company)	C+	C+	C	Up	Y	2,000
Royce Micro-Cap Opportunity Fund Investment Class	ROSFX	NAS CM	Open End	US Equity Small Cap (Small Company)	B	A-	C+	Up	Y	2,000
Royce Micro-Cap Opportunity Fund Service Class	ROSSX	NAS CM	Open End	US Equity Small Cap (Small Company)	B	A-	C+	Up	Y	2,000
Royce Opportunity Fund Class K	ROFKX	NAS CM	Open End	US Equity Small Cap (Small Company)	B+	A	C+	Up	Y	0
Royce Opportunity Fund Consultant Class	ROFCX	NAS CM	Open End	US Equity Small Cap (Small Company)	B	A	C+	Up	Y	2,000
Royce Opportunity Fund Institutional Class	ROFIX	NAS CM	Open End	US Equity Small Cap (Small Company)	B+	A	C+	Up	Y	1,000,000
Royce Opportunity Fund Investment Class	RYPNX	NAS CM	Open End	US Equity Small Cap (Small Company)	B+	A	C+	Up	Y	2,000
Royce Opportunity Fund Retirement Class	ROFRX	NAS CM	Open End	US Equity Small Cap (Small Company)	B+	A	C+	Up	Y	0
Royce Opportunity Fund Service Class	RYOFX	NAS CM	Open End	US Equity Small Cap (Small Company)	B+	A	C+	Up	Y	2,000
Royce Pennsylvania Mutual Fund Class K	RPMKX	NAS CM	Open End	US Equity Small Cap (Small Company)	B	B	C+	Up	Y	0
Royce Pennsylvania Mutual Fund Consultant Class	RYPCX	NAS CM	Open End	US Equity Small Cap (Small Company)	B-	B	C+	Up	Y	2,000
Royce Pennsylvania Mutual Fund Institutional Class	RPMIX	NAS CM	Open End	US Equity Small Cap (Small Company)	B	B+	C+	Up	Y	1,000,000
Royce Pennsylvania Mutual Fund Investment Class	PENNX	NAS CM	Open End	US Equity Small Cap (Small Company)	B	B	C+	Up	Y	2,000
Royce Pennsylvania Mutual Fund Retirement Class	RPMRX	NAS CM	Open End	US Equity Small Cap (Small Company)	B	B	C+	Up	Y	0
Royce Pennsylvania Mutual Fund Service Class	RYPFX	NAS CM	Open End	US Equity Small Cap (Small Company)	B	B	C+	Up	Y	2,000
Royce Premier Fund Class W	RPRWX	NAS CM	Open End	US Equity Small Cap (Small Company)	B	B+	C+	Up		1,000,000
Royce Premier Fund Consultant Class	RPRCX	NAS CM	Open End	US Equity Small Cap (Small Company)	B	B	C+	Up		2,000
Royce Premier Fund Institutional Class	RPFIX	NAS CM	Open End	US Equity Small Cap (Small Company)	B	B+	C+	Up		1,000,000
Royce Premier Fund Investment Class	RYPRX	NAS CM	Open End	US Equity Small Cap (Small Company)	B	B+	C+	Up		2,000
Royce Premier Fund Retirement Class	RPRRX	NAS CM	Open End	US Equity Small Cap (Small Company)	B	B	C+	Up		0
Royce Premier Fund Service Class	RPFFX	NAS CM	Open End	US Equity Small Cap (Small Company)	B	B+	C+	Up		2,000
Royce Small/Mid-Cap Premier Fund Class R	RHFRX	NAS CM	Open End	US Equity Mid Cap (Small Company)	B	B	B	Up	Y	0
Royce Small/Mid-Cap Premier Fund Consultant Class	RYGCX	NAS CM	Open End	US Equity Mid Cap (Small Company)	B-	B-	B-		Y	2,000
Royce Small/Mid-Cap Premier Fund Investment Class	RHFHX	NAS CM	Open End	US Equity Mid Cap (Small Company)	B	B	B	Up	Y	2,000
Royce Small/Mid-Cap Premier Fund Service Class	RGFAX	NAS CM	Open End	US Equity Mid Cap (Small Company)	B	B	B	Up	Y	2,000
Royce Small-Cap Leaders Fund Class R	ROHRX	NAS CM	Open End	US Equity Small Cap (Small Company)	C+	C+	C+		Y	0

★ Expanded analysis of this fund is included in Section II.

Min Additional Investment	3-Month Total Return	6-Month Total Return	1-Year Total Return	3-Year Total Return	5-Year Total Return	Dividend Yield (TTM)	Expense Ratio	3-Yr Std Deviation	3-Year Beta	NAV	Total Assets (MIL)	%Cash	%Stocks	%Bonds	%Other	Turnover Ratio	Last Bull Market Total Return	Last Bear Market Total Return	Front End Fee (%)	Back End Fee (%)	Inception Date
	TOTAL RETURNS					PERFORMANCE				ASSETS		ASSET ALLOCATION & TURNOVER					BULL & BEAR		FEES		
25	5.75	11.60	22.68	26.70	91.34	0.57	1.25	12.16	1.11	15.63	9.4	0	99	0	1	11	24.58	-21.58			Dec-04
10,000	4.89	9.28	25.25			0.78	1.31			12.46	122.2	2	93	3	0	59					Feb-15
	7.69	12.52					1.1			11.28	91.4	5	94	0	1						May-17
	7.65	12.36					1.35			11.28	91.4	5	94	0	1						May-17
	4.95	11.61					0.85			11.48	15.4	15	85	0	0						May-17
	4.82	11.37					1.1			11.5	15.4	15	85	0	0						May-17
100	2.20	3.77	18.32	9.57	18.39	0.13	1.33	12.08		9.45	70.5	23	49	14	0	112	1.82	-13.09			Dec-10
50	6.41	12.46	20.70	29.45	67.02	0.24	2.09	11.68	0.74	8.87	189.3	6	90	0	4	21	24.38	-22.33	0.00	1.00	Mar-14
	6.69	13.10	22.21	33.62	76.51	1.29	0.89	11.64	0.74	7.46	189.3	6	90	0	4	21	24.92	-22.09			Aug-12
50	6.61	13.07	21.91	33.45	75.97	1.03	1.08	11.69	0.74	7.56	189.3	6	90	0	4	21	25.08	-21.92			Sep-07
50	6.54	12.93	21.65	32.49	73.59	0.69	1.34	11.67	0.74	7.76	189.3	6	90	0	4	21	24.92	-22.09			May-04
	7.00	11.67	23.00	32.40	97.64	0.63	1.15	12.96	0.77	13.58	54.9	2	94	0	4	37	22.95	-23.52			Jan-16
50	6.92	11.49	22.45	31.21	95.87	0.45	1.6	12.98	0.77	10.57	54.9	2	94	0	4	37	22.95	-23.52			Dec-03
	6.00	12.74	30.90	39.22		1.13	1.58	11.98		12.48	129.0	-3	102	0	2	59					Oct-13
50	6.40	10.84	27.72	34.04	57.05	1.3	1.64	11.17	0.92	12.57	7.8	8	91	0	1	113	15.21	-26.52			Dec-10
50	5.99	13.85	38.72	57.00	69.47	1.03	2.19	11.83	0.95	16.99	139.5	4	95	0	2	67	16.44	-22.03		1.00	Feb-16
50	6.21	14.38	40.07	61.78	77.46	2.17	1.19	11.74	0.94	13.07	139.5	4	95	0	2	67	16.95	-21.79	0.00	0.00	Jan-14
	6.08	14.14	39.33	59.23	73.59	2.01	1.74	11.8	0.94	12.53	139.5	4	95	0	2	67	16.78	-21.87			Feb-16
50	6.10	14.28	39.80	60.46	75.80	1.67	1.44	11.79	0.94	15.6	139.5	4	95	0	2	67	16.95	-21.79			Dec-10
	2.33	8.31	9.14	12.47	24.93	0.13	1.94	14.74	0.96	7.99	280.9	3	92	0	5	34	17.96	-27.5			May-07
	2.58	8.72	9.77	14.78	29.09	0.58	1.31	14.76	0.97	8.52	280.9	3	92	0	5	34	18.42	-27.28			Jan-06
50	2.53	8.67	9.85	14.47	28.66	0.6	1.34	14.73	0.96	8.49	280.9	3	92	0	5	34	18.43	-27.31			Mar-07
50	2.56	8.61	9.66	13.80	27.18	0.41	1.59	14.81	0.97	8.46	280.9	3	92	0	5	34	18.26	-27.4			Dec-93
	2.74	10.71	16.70	21.34	81.13	0.32		14		10.48	410.2	-3	98	0	4	26	24.22	-24.41			Dec-93
50	-1.52	2.81	4.23	5.95	23.28	0	2.62	14.11	0.93	9.09	214.0	4	91	0	5	38	19.36	-27.32	0.00	1.00	May-98
50	-1.28	3.34	5.42	9.42	29.88	0.41	1.57	14.12	0.93	11.64	214.0	4	91	0	5	38	20.01	-27.04			Dec-91
50	-1.35	3.28	5.22	8.93	29.08	0.32	1.7	14.11	0.93	11.4	214.0	4	91	0	5	38	19.94	-27.07			Aug-02
50	4.60	13.85	24.98	29.58	83.61	0	1.24	17.72	1.04	19.77	48.1	5	90	0	5	83	32.35	-32.45			Aug-10
50	4.57	13.70	24.73	28.75	81.58	0	1.49	17.71	1.04	9.94	48.1	5	90	0	5	83	32.16	-32.52	0.00		Mar-14
	3.34	12.29	21.08	34.02	94.85	0	1.75	16.52	1.11	11.13	1,646	8	89	0	3	26	35.91	-31.61			May-08
50	3.24	12.02	20.49	31.82	88.81	0	2.28	16.51	1.11	11.19	1,646	8	89	0	3	26	35.29	-31.81	0.00	1.00	Mar-06
	3.50	12.71	22.02	36.61	100.68	0	1.07	16.57	1.11	13.84	1,646	8	89	0	3	26	36.21	-31.42			Dec-01
50	3.51	12.67	21.87	36.19	99.53	0	1.19	16.54	1.11	13.58	1,646	8	89	0	3	26	36.16	-31.54			Nov-96
	3.34	12.21	21.06	33.61	93.15	0	1.82	16.56	1.11	12.25	1,646	8	89	0	3	26	35.62	-31.64			May-07
50	3.39	12.47	21.46	34.92	96.46	0	1.49	16.58	1.11	12.66	1,646	8	89	0	3	26	36.01	-31.59			May-00
	3.78	10.33	15.06	26.06	72.42	0	1.82	13.72	0.92	8.66	2,239	1	96	0	3	18	24.2	-24.4			May-08
50	3.85	10.46	15.06	25.43	69.59	0	1.95	13.75	0.92	8.46	2,239	1	96	0	3	18	23.92	-24.49	0.00	1.00	Jun-97
	4.25	11.10	16.43	29.74	79.51	0.36	0.84	13.73	0.92	10.55	2,239	1	96	0	3	18	24.67	-24.21			Jun-11
50	4.06	10.90	16.24	29.31	78.44	0.29	0.93	13.73	0.92	10.52	2,239	1	96	0	3	18	24.72	-24.23			Oct-72
	3.81	10.49	15.25	26.35	72.26	0	1.64	13.7	0.92	9.94	2,239	1	96	0	3	18	24.13	-24.37			May-07
50	4.00	10.76	15.88	28.12	75.70	0.08	1.27	13.69	0.92	10.56	2,239	1	96	0	3	18	24.44	-24.26			Nov-05
	6.28	14.01	23.83	35.96	76.80	0	1.17	13.53	0.89	16.69	2,443	9	91	0	0	15	23.58	-21.51			May-05
50	6.05	13.30	22.48	31.60	67.68	0	2.22	13.52	0.89	13.21	2,443	9	91	0	0	15	22.87	-21.89	0.00	1.00	Jun-03
	6.27	13.91	23.84	36.16	77.46	0.27	1.07	13.54	0.89	16.82	2,443	9	91	0	0	15	23.67	-21.53			Sep-02
50	6.23	13.86	23.77	35.80	76.56	0.2	1.16	13.54	0.89	16.6	2,443	9	91	0	0	15	23.58	-21.56			Dec-91
	6.02	13.39	22.87	33.02	70.81	0	1.84	13.52	0.89	15.39	2,443	9	91	0	0	15	23.14	-21.73			May-07
50	6.13	13.69	23.31	34.50	73.96	0	1.49	13.52	0.89	16.15	2,443	9	91	0	0	15	23.42	-21.66			Sep-02
	8.03	14.48	20.60	30.72	65.12	0	1.69	12.11	0.79	10.15	210.5	14	85	0	1	67	24.98	-26.96			May-08
50	7.90	14.19	20.09	29.21	61.50	0	2.09	12.11	0.79	11.06	210.5	14	85	0	1	67	24.59	-27.08	0.00	1.00	Dec-01
50	8.16	14.87	21.46	33.51	71.29	0.32	0.96	12.1	0.79	15.66	210.5	14	85	0	1	67	25.37	-26.72			Mar-07
50	8.10	14.68	21.20	32.62	69.08	0.15	1.3	12.1	0.79	15.61	210.5	14	85	0	1	67	25.18	-26.8			Dec-95
	4.34	8.69	9.81	19.05	53.32	0.09	1.84	14.35	0.95	9.13	90.1	7	93	0	0	65	28.06	-27.16			May-08

	MARKET		FUND TYPE, CATEGORY & OBJECTIVE		RATINGS				MINIMUMS	
Fund Name	Ticker Symbol	Traded On	Fund Type	Category and (Prospectus Objective)	Overall Rating	Reward Rating	Risk Rating	Recent Up/ Downgrade	Open to New Investors	Min Initial Investment
Royce Small-Cap Leaders Fund Investment Class	ROHHX	NAS CM	Open End	US Equity Small Cap (Small Company)	C+	B-	C+		Y	2,000
Royce Small-Cap Leaders Fund Service Class	RYOHX	NAS CM	Open End	US Equity Small Cap (Small Company)	C+	B-	C+		Y	2,000
Royce Small-Cap Value Fund Class K	RVFKX	NAS CM	Open End	US Equity Small Cap (Small Company)	C+	C+	C+	Up	Y	0
Royce Small-Cap Value Fund Class R	RVVRX	NAS CM	Open End	US Equity Small Cap (Small Company)	C+	C+	C+	Up	Y	0
Royce Small-Cap Value Fund Consultant Class	RVFCX	NAS CM	Open End	US Equity Small Cap (Small Company)	C+	C+	C	Up	Y	2,000
Royce Small-Cap Value Fund Institutional Class	RVFIX	NAS CM	Open End	US Equity Small Cap (Small Company)	C+	C+	C+	Up	Y	1,000,000
Royce Small-Cap Value Fund Investment Class	RVVHX	NAS CM	Open End	US Equity Small Cap (Small Company)	C+	C+	C+	Up	Y	2,000
Royce Small-Cap Value Fund Service Class	RYVFX	NAS CM	Open End	US Equity Small Cap (Small Company)	C+	C+	C+	Up	Y	2,000
Royce Smaller-Companies Growth Fund Class R	RVPRX	NAS CM	Open End	US Equity Small Cap (Small Company)	B	B	B	Up	Y	0
Royce Smaller-Companies Growth Fund Consultant Class	RVPCX	NAS CM	Open End	US Equity Small Cap (Small Company)	B	B	B	Up	Y	2,000
Royce Smaller-Companies Growth Fund Institutional Class	RVPIX	NAS CM	Open End	US Equity Small Cap (Small Company)	B	B	B	Up	Y	1,000,000
Royce Smaller-Companies Growth Fund Investment Class	RVPHX	NAS CM	Open End	US Equity Small Cap (Small Company)	B	B	B	Up	Y	2,000
Royce Smaller-Companies Growth Fund Service Class	RYVPX	NAS CM	Open End	US Equity Small Cap (Small Company)	B	B	B	Up	Y	2,000
Royce Special Equity Fund Consultant Class	RSQCX	NAS CM	Open End	US Equity Small Cap (Small Company)	B-	B-	B-			2,000
Royce Special Equity Fund Institutional Class	RSEIX	NAS CM	Open End	US Equity Small Cap (Small Company)	B	B	B-	Up		1,000,000
Royce Special Equity Fund Investment Class	RYSEX	NAS CM	Open End	US Equity Small Cap (Small Company)	B	B	B-	Up		2,000
Royce Special Equity Fund Service Class	RSEFX	NAS CM	Open End	US Equity Small Cap (Small Company)	B-	B	B-	Down		2,000
Royce Special Equity Multi-Cap Fund Consultant Class	RSMLX	NAS CM	Open End	US Equity Large Cap Value (Growth)	C+	C+	C+	Down	Y	2,000
Royce Special Equity Multi-Cap Fund Institutional Class	RMUIX	NAS CM	Open End	US Equity Large Cap Value (Growth)	C+	C+	C+	Down	Y	1,000,000
Royce Special Equity Multi-Cap Fund Investment Class	RSMCX	NAS CM	Open End	US Equity Large Cap Value (Growth)	C+	C+	C+	Down	Y	2,000
Royce Special Equity Multi-Cap Fund Service Class	RSEMX	NAS CM	Open End	US Equity Large Cap Value (Growth)	C+	C+	C+	Down	Y	2,000
Royce Total Return Fund Class K	RTRKX	NAS CM	Open End	US Equity Small Cap (Growth & Income)	B	B	B	Up	Y	0
Royce Total Return Fund Class W	RTRWX	NAS CM	Open End	US Equity Small Cap (Growth & Income)	B	B	B	Up	Y	1,000,000
Royce Total Return Fund Consultant Class	RYTCX	NAS CM	Open End	US Equity Small Cap (Growth & Income)	B	B	B	Up	Y	2,000
Royce Total Return Fund Institutional Class	RTRIX	NAS CM	Open End	US Equity Small Cap (Growth & Income)	B	B	B	Up	Y	1,000,000
Royce Total Return Fund Investment Class	RYTRX	NAS CM	Open End	US Equity Small Cap (Growth & Income)	B	B	B	Up	Y	2,000
Royce Total Return Fund Retirement Class	RTRRX	NAS CM	Open End	US Equity Small Cap (Growth & Income)	B	B	B	Up	Y	0
Royce Total Return Fund Service Class	RYTFX	NAS CM	Open End	US Equity Small Cap (Growth & Income)	B	B	B	Up	Y	2,000
Royce Value Trust	RVT	NYSE	Closed End	US Equity Small Cap (Growth)	B+	A-	B-	Up	Y	
RQSI Small Cap Hedged Equity Fund Institutional Shares	RQSIX	NAS CM	Open End	US Equity Small Cap (Small Company)	C	C	B	Up	Y	1,000,000
RQSI Small Cap Hedged Equity Fund Retail Shares	RQSAX	NAS CM	Open End	US Equity Small Cap (Small Company)	C	C	B	Up	Y	2,500
RSQ International Equity Fund Institutional Class	RSQIX	NAS CM	Open End	Global Equity Large Cap (World Stock)	C+	C+	B-	Up	Y	1,000,000
RSQ International Equity Fund Investor Class	RSQVX	NAS CM	Open End	Global Equity Large Cap (World Stock)	C+	C+	B-	Up	Y	2,500
Russell Investments Commodity Strategies Fund Class A	RCSAX	NAS CM	Open End	Commodities Broad Basket (Growth & Income)	D+	C-	D+	Up	Y	0
Russell Investments Commodity Strategies Fund Class C	RCSCX	NAS CM	Open End	Commodities Broad Basket (Growth & Income)	D	D	D		Y	0
Russell Investments Commodity Strategies Fund Class E	RCSEX	NAS CM	Open End	Commodities Broad Basket (Growth & Income)	D+	C-	D+	Up	Y	0
Russell Investments Commodity Strategies Fund Class M	RCOTX	NAS CM	Open End	Commodities Broad Basket (Growth & Income)	D+	C-	D+	Up	Y	0
Russell Investments Commodity Strategies Fund Class S	RCCSX	NAS CM	Open End	Commodities Broad Basket (Growth & Income)	D+	C-	D+	Up	Y	0
Russell Investments Commodity Strategies Fund Class Y	RCSYX	NAS CM	Open End	Commodities Broad Basket (Growth & Income)	D+	C-	D+	Up	Y	10,000,000
Russell Investments Emerging Markets Fund Class A	REMAX	NAS CM	Open End	Emerging Markets Equity (Div Emerging Mkts)	C+	B-	C	Up	Y	0
Russell Investments Emerging Markets Fund Class C	REMCX	NAS CM	Open End	Emerging Markets Equity (Div Emerging Mkts)	C+	B-	C	Up	Y	0
Russell Investments Emerging Markets Fund Class E	REMEX	NAS CM	Open End	Emerging Markets Equity (Div Emerging Mkts)	C+	B-	C	Up	Y	0
Russell Investments Emerging Markets Fund Class M	RMMTX	NAS CM	Open End	Emerging Markets Equity (Div Emerging Mkts)	C+	B-	C	Up	Y	0
Russell Investments Emerging Markets Fund Class R6	REGRX	NAS CM	Open End	Emerging Markets Equity (Div Emerging Mkts)	C+	B-	C	Up	Y	0
Russell Investments Emerging Markets Fund Class S	REMSX	NAS CM	Open End	Emerging Markets Equity (Div Emerging Mkts)	C+	B-	C	Up	Y	0
Russell Investments Emerging Markets Fund Class Y	REMYX	NAS CM	Open End	Emerging Markets Equity (Div Emerging Mkts)	B-	B-	C	Up	Y	10,000,000
Russell Investments Global Equity Fund Class A	RGEAX	NAS CM	Open End	Global Equity (World Stock)	B-	B	B-	Down	Y	0
Russell Investments Global Equity Fund Class C	RGECX	NAS CM	Open End	Global Equity (World Stock)	B-	B-	C+	Down	Y	0
Russell Investments Global Equity Fund Class E	RGEEX	NAS CM	Open End	Global Equity (World Stock)	B-	B-	B-	Up	Y	0
Russell Investments Global Equity Fund Class M	RGDTX	NAS CM	Open End	Global Equity (World Stock)	B-	B	B-	Up	Y	0
Russell Investments Global Equity Fund Class S	RGESX	NAS CM	Open End	Global Equity (World Stock)	B-	B	B-	Up	Y	0
Russell Investments Global Equity Fund Class Y	RLGYX	NAS CM	Open End	Global Equity (World Stock)	B-	B	B-	Down	Y	10,000,000

★Expanded analysis of this fund is included in Section II.

	TOTAL RETURNS					PERFORMANCE				ASSETS		ASSET ALLOCATION & TURNOVER					BULL & BEAR		FEES		
Min Additional Investment	3-Month Total Return	6-Month Total Return	1-Year Total Return	3-Year Total Return	5-Year Total Return	Dividend Yield (TTM)	Expense Ratio	3-Yr Std Deviation	3-Year Beta	NAV	Total Assets (MIL)	%Cash	%Stocks	%Bonds	%Other	Turnover Ratio	Last Bull Market Total Return	Last Bear Market Total Return	Front End Fee (%)	Back End Fee (%)	Inception Date
50	4.45	9.08	10.46	21.20	58.29	0.67	1.23	14.32	0.95	6.67	90.1	7	93	0	0	65	28.65	-27			Mar-07
50	4.35	8.90	10.14	20.27	55.95	0.47	1.49	14.36	0.95	6.59	90.1	7	93	0	0	65	28.39	-27.01			Jun-03
	4.41	9.62	4.71	10.46	44.55	0.13	1.95	14.53	0.85	7	259.5	11	89	0	0	56	21.62	-26.03			May-08
	4.48	9.70	4.80	10.62	44.46	0.26	1.85	14.53	0.85	9.75	259.5	11	89	0	0	56	21.39	-26.05			Sep-07
50	4.32	9.56	4.44	9.18	41.23	0	2.28	14.52	0.85	9.06	259.5	11	89	0	0	56	21.13	-26.21	0.00	1.00	Mar-06
	4.63	11.26	6.72	14.40	51.51	0.85	1.08	14.77	0.86	10.32	259.5	11	89	0	0	56	21.88	-25.8			Jun-06
50	4.65	10.10	5.49	12.67	48.92	0.73	1.24	14.55	0.85	10.16	259.5	11	89	0	0	56	21.84	-25.82			Mar-07
50	4.53	9.89	5.26	11.82	47.02	0.51	1.49	14.55	0.85	10.12	259.5	11	89	0	0	56	21.66	-25.93			Jun-01
	1.45	5.71	17.44	24.79	74.34	0	1.84	14.58	0.94	9.95	384.8	9	87	0	4	59	25.86	-26.5			Sep-07
50	1.25	5.52	16.92	23.26	70.65	0	2.24	14.62	0.95	9.28	384.8	9	87	0	4	59	25.5	-26.6	0.00	1.00	Mar-06
	1.57	6.07	18.22	27.32	80.78	0	1.15	14.66	0.95	11.06	384.8	9	87	0	4	59	26.41	-26.28			May-06
50	1.55	6.10	18.20	27.21	79.46	0	1.15	14.62	0.94	10.93	384.8	9	87	0	4	59	26.29	-26.28			Mar-07
50	1.48	5.88	17.80	26.14	77.62	0	1.49	14.63	0.95	10.69	384.8	9	87	0	4	59	26.11	-26.35			Jun-01
50	4.33	7.73	6.77	20.48	58.32	0.18	2.2	13.08	0.82	19.86	1,581	10	90	0	0	29	24.35	-18.36	0.00	1.00	Jun-03
	4.60	8.30	7.96	24.59	67.44	0.91	1.07	13.09	0.82	21.61	1,581	10	90	0	0	29	25.26	-18.01			Jul-03
50	4.59	8.26	7.86	24.23	66.61	0.83	1.17	13.08	0.83	21.79	1,581	10	90	0	0	29	25.15	-18.04			May-98
50	4.57	8.20	7.66	23.44	64.66	0.68	1.39	13.09	0.82	21.76	1,581	10	90	0	0	29	25.03	-18.12			Oct-03
50	7.65	8.55	14.50	9.79	64.84	0.79	1.99	12.46	1.06	10.19	112.2	16	84	0	0	50	23.26	-12.41	0.00	1.00	Jan-14
	7.95	9.20	15.88	13.53	74.28	1.1	0.89	12.48	1.06	15.62	112.2	16	84	0	0	50	23.8	-12.13			Apr-12
50	7.92	9.09	15.77	13.18	73.44	1.01	1.02	12.5	1.06	15.63	112.2	16	84	0	0	50	23.8	-12.13			Feb-12
50	7.84	8.93	15.41	12.37	71.22	0.8	1.24	12.46	1.06	15.69	112.2	16	84	0	0	50	23.8	-12.13			Dec-10
	4.35	10.43	13.29	30.28	78.47	1.03	1.57	12.36	0.83	9.02	2,534	2	96	0	2	16	21.03	-19.57			May-08
	4.41	10.63	13.59	31.59	81.50	1.28	1.22	12.4	0.83	13.56	2,534	2	96	0	2	16	21.26	-19.41			May-05
50	4.16	10.10	12.52	27.79	72.86	0	2.18	12.42	0.83	13.95	2,534	2	96	0	2	16	20.56	-19.81	0.00	1.00	Oct-01
	4.47	10.68	13.79	32.16	82.77	1.55	1.07	12.38	0.83	13.4	2,534	2	96	0	2	16	21.25	-19.41			Mar-03
50	4.40	10.58	13.65	31.67	81.67	1.34	1.21	12.39	0.83	13.58	2,534	2	96	0	2	16	21.26	-19.44			Dec-93
	4.25	10.30	12.96	29.24	76.19	0.51	1.8	12.37	0.83	13.99	2,534	2	96	0	2	16	20.86	-19.65			May-07
50	4.32	10.43	13.23	30.54	79.07	0.97	1.48	12.39	0.83	13.88	2,534	2	96	0	2	16	20.99	-19.54			Jan-02
	3.70	10.94	18.46	33.79	80.92	0.48	0	13.53	0.92	17.5	1,492	-1	97	0	3	28	27.89	-29.67			Nov-86
	3.39	6.98	10.29			1.17	1.35			10.93	82.4	11	89	0	0	178					Sep-15
	3.37	6.85	10.04			0.92	1.7			10.98	82.4	11	89	0	0	178					Sep-15
	4.45	9.10	25.92	16.18		1.26	1.11	9.86	0.74	9.85	31.8	3	89	0	8	219					Nov-13
	4.34	8.88	25.55	15.18		1.07	1.36	9.81	0.73	9.83	31.8	3	89	0	8	219					Nov-13
	4.87	8.69	1.30	-17.44	-38.97	0	1.44	12	0.92	5.6	691.9	80	0	0	20		-0.42	-19.53	5.75		Jun-10
	4.68	8.47	0.58	-19.16	-41.20	0	2.19	12	0.92	5.38	691.9	80	0	0	20		-0.82	-19.8			Jun-10
	4.99	8.82	1.43	-17.34	-38.89	0	1.44	11.96	0.91	5.67	691.9	80	0	0	20		-0.37	-19.54			Jun-10
	5.09	8.87	1.59	-16.38	-37.64		1.09	11.95	0.91	5.66	691.9	80	0	0	20		-0.07	-19.41			Mar-17
	5.09	9.07	1.74	-16.65	-38.13	0	1.19	11.99	0.92	5.68	691.9	80	0	0	20		-0.26	-19.49			Jun-10
	5.05	8.98	1.74	-16.25	-37.55	0	1	11.96	0.91	5.73	691.9	80	0	0	20		-0.07	-19.41			Jun-10
	5.42	13.19	35.12	26.42	21.89	0.63	1.72	15.35	0.98	21.01	2,498	7	92	0	1	68	19.66	-26.46	5.75		Mar-07
	5.19	12.75	34.12	23.54	17.42	0.09	2.47	15.36	0.98	19.57	2,498	7	92	0	1	68	19.16	-26.71			Jan-99
	5.45	13.25	35.11	26.43	21.95	0.62	1.72	15.35	0.98	21.13	2,498	7	92	0	1	68	19.62	-26.48			Sep-98
	5.51	13.46	35.52	27.47	23.52		1.37	15.35	0.98	21.13	2,498	7	92	0	1	68	19.81	-26.4			Mar-17
	5.51	13.44	35.71	27.71	23.75	0.95	1.32	15.37	0.98	21.16	2,498	7	92	0	1	68	19.81	-26.4			Mar-16
	5.51	13.39	35.44	27.40	23.45	0.82	1.47	15.35	0.98	21.15	2,498	7	92	0	1	68	19.81	-26.4			Jan-93
	5.52	13.45	35.64	28.08	24.60	0.96	1.29	15.38	0.98	21.16	2,498	7	92	0	1	68	20	-26.36			Sep-08
	5.56	10.25	22.84	29.85	76.68	0.97	1.5	11.02	1.04	10.75	2,200	6	93	0	2	46	17.76	-21.99	5.75		Feb-07
	5.29	9.83	21.91	26.94	70.05	0.36	2.25	10.97	1.04	10.62	2,200	6	93	0	2	46	17.31	-22.31			Feb-07
	5.57	10.35	22.93	29.78	76.57	1	1.5	10.96	1.04	10.83	2,200	6	93	0	2	46	17.66	-21.96			Feb-07
	5.62	10.58	23.27	30.94	79.03		1.15	10.98	1.04	10.78	2,200	6	93	0	2	46	17.9	-21.92			Mar-17
	5.63	10.49	23.18	30.84	78.89	1.19	1.25	10.98	1.04	10.8	2,200	6	93	0	2	46	17.9	-21.92			Feb-07
	5.73	10.59	23.51	31.59	80.73	1.35	1.05	10.99	1.04	10.8	2,200	6	93	0	2	46	18.09	-21.9			Sep-08

	MARKET		FUND TYPE, CATEGORY & OBJECTIVE		RATINGS				MINIMUMS	
Fund Name	Ticker Symbol	Traded On	Fund Type	Category and (Prospectus Objective)	Overall Rating	Reward Rating	Risk Rating	Recent Up/ Downgrade	Open to New Investors	Min Initial Investment
Russell Investments Global Infrastructure Fund Class A	RGIAX	NAS CM	Open End	Other Sector Equity (World Stock)	B-	C+	B-		Y	0
Russell Investments Global Infrastructure Fund Class C	RGCIX	NAS CM	Open End	Other Sector Equity (World Stock)	C+	C+	C+	Down	Y	0
Russell Investments Global Infrastructure Fund Class E	RGIEX	NAS CM	Open End	Other Sector Equity (World Stock)	B-	C+	B-		Y	0
Russell Investments Global Infrastructure Fund Class M	RGFTX	NAS CM	Open End	Other Sector Equity (World Stock)	B-	C+	B-		Y	0
Russell Investments Global Infrastructure Fund Class S	RGISX	NAS CM	Open End	Other Sector Equity (World Stock)	B-	C+	B-		Y	0
Russell Investments Global Infrastructure Fund Class Y	RGIYX	NAS CM	Open End	Other Sector Equity (World Stock)	B-	C+	B-		Y	10,000,000
Russell Inv Global Real Estate Securities Fund Cls A	RREAX	NAS CM	Open End	Real Estate Sector Equity (Real Estate)	B-	C+	B	Up	Y	0
Russell Inv Global Real Estate Securities Fund Cls C	RRSCX	NAS CM	Open End	Real Estate Sector Equity (Real Estate)	B-	C	B	Up	Y	0
Russell Inv Global Real Estate Securities Fund Cls E	RREEX	NAS CM	Open End	Real Estate Sector Equity (Real Estate)	B-	C+	B	Up	Y	0
Russell Inv Global Real Estate Securities Fund Cls M	RETTX	NAS CM	Open End	Real Estate Sector Equity (Real Estate)	B-	C+	B	Up	Y	0
Russell Inv Global Real Estate Securities Fund Cls R6	RRSRX	NAS CM	Open End	Real Estate Sector Equity (Real Estate)	B-	C+	B	Up	Y	0
Russell Inv Global Real Estate Securities Fund Cls S	RRESX	NAS CM	Open End	Real Estate Sector Equity (Real Estate)	B-	C+	B	Up	Y	0
Russell Inv Global Real Estate Securities Fund Cls Y	RREYX	NAS CM	Open End	Real Estate Sector Equity (Real Estate)	B-	C+	B	Up	Y	10,000,000
Russell Investments Intl Developed Mkts Fund Cls A	RLNAX	NAS CM	Open End	Global Equity Large Cap (Foreign Stock)	B-	B-	B	Up	Y	0
Russell Investments Intl Developed Mkts Fund Cls C	RLNCX	NAS CM	Open End	Global Equity Large Cap (Foreign Stock)	B-	C+	B	Up	Y	0
Russell Investments Intl Developed Mkts Fund Cls E	RIFEX	NAS CM	Open End	Global Equity Large Cap (Foreign Stock)	B-	B-	B	Up	Y	0
Russell Investments Intl Developed Mkts Fund Cls M	RNTTX	NAS CM	Open End	Global Equity Large Cap (Foreign Stock)	B-	B-	B	Up	Y	0
Russell Investments Intl Developed Mkts Fund Cls S	RINTX	NAS CM	Open End	Global Equity Large Cap (Foreign Stock)	B-	B-	B	Up	Y	0
Russell Investments Intl Developed Mkts Fund Cls Y	RINYX	NAS CM	Open End	Global Equity Large Cap (Foreign Stock)	B	B-	B	Up	Y	10,000,000
Russell Inv LifePoints Balanced Strategy Fund Cls A	RBLAX	NAS CM	Open End	Moderate Alloc (Balanced)	B-	C+	B	Up	Y	0
Russell Inv LifePoints Balanced Strategy Fund Cls C	RBLCX	NAS CM	Open End	Moderate Alloc (Balanced)	B-	C+	B	Up	Y	0
Russell Inv LifePoints Balanced Strategy Fund Cls E	RBLEX	NAS CM	Open End	Moderate Alloc (Balanced)	B-	C+	B	Up	Y	0
Russell Inv LifePoints Balanced Strategy Fund Cls R1	RBLRX	NAS CM	Open End	Moderate Alloc (Balanced)	B-	C+	B	Up	Y	0
Russell Inv LifePoints Balanced Strategy Fund Cls R4	RBLUX	NAS CM	Open End	Moderate Alloc (Balanced)	B-	C+	B	Up	Y	0
Russell Inv LifePoints Balanced Strategy Fund Cls R5	RBLVX	NAS CM	Open End	Moderate Alloc (Balanced)	B-	C+	B	Up	Y	0
Russell Inv LifePoints Balanced Strategy Fund Cls S	RBLSX	NAS CM	Open End	Moderate Alloc (Balanced)	B-	C+	B	Up	Y	0
Russell Inv LifePoints Balanced Strategy Fund Cls T	RBSAX	NAS CM	Open End	Moderate Alloc (Balanced)	B-	C+	B		Y	0
Russell Inv LifePoints Conservative Strategy Fund Cls A	RCLAX	NAS CM	Open End	Cautious Alloc (Growth & Income)	B-	C	A-	Up	Y	0
Russell Inv LifePoints Conservative Strategy Fund Cls C	RCLCX	NAS CM	Open End	Cautious Alloc (Growth & Income)	B-	C	B+	Up	Y	0
Russell Inv LifePoints Conservative Strategy Fund Cls E	RCLEX	NAS CM	Open End	Cautious Alloc (Growth & Income)	B-	C	A-	Up	Y	0
Russell Inv LifePoints Conservative Strategy Fund Cls R1	RCLRX	NAS CM	Open End	Cautious Alloc (Growth & Income)	B	C	A-	Up	Y	0
Russell Inv LifePoints Conservative Strategy Fund Cls R4	RCLUX	NAS CM	Open End	Cautious Alloc (Growth & Income)	B-	C	A-	Up	Y	0
Russell Inv LifePoints Conservative Strategy Fund Cls R5	RCLVX	NAS CM	Open End	Cautious Alloc (Growth & Income)	B-	C	A-	Up	Y	0
Russell Inv LifePoints Conservative Strategy Fund Cls S	RCLSX	NAS CM	Open End	Cautious Alloc (Growth & Income)	B	C	A-	Up	Y	0
Russell Inv LifePoints Eq Growth Strategy Fund Cls A	REAAX	NAS CM	Open End	Aggressive Alloc (Growth & Income)	C+	B-	C+	Down	Y	0
Russell Inv LifePoints Eq Growth Strategy Fund Cls C	RELCX	NAS CM	Open End	Aggressive Alloc (Growth & Income)	C+	C+	C+	Down	Y	0
Russell Inv LifePoints Eq Growth Strategy Fund Cls E	RELEX	NAS CM	Open End	Aggressive Alloc (Growth & Income)	C+	B-	C+	Down	Y	0
Russell Inv LifePoints Eq Growth Strategy Fund Cls R1	RELRX	NAS CM	Open End	Aggressive Alloc (Growth & Income)	B-	B-	C+	Up	Y	0
Russell Inv LifePoints Eq Growth Strategy Fund Cls R4	RELUX	NAS CM	Open End	Aggressive Alloc (Growth & Income)	C+	B-	C+	Down	Y	0
Russell Inv LifePoints Eq Growth Strategy Fund Cls R5	RELVX	NAS CM	Open End	Aggressive Alloc (Growth & Income)	C+	C+	C+	Down	Y	0
Russell Inv LifePoints Eq Growth Strategy Fund Cls S	RELSX	NAS CM	Open End	Aggressive Alloc (Growth & Income)	B-	B-	C+	Down	Y	0
Russell Inv LifePoints Eq Growth Strategy Fund Cls T	RQTAX	NAS CM	Open End	Aggressive Alloc (Growth & Income)	C+	C+	C+	Down	Y	0
Russell Investments LifePoints Growth Strategy Fund Cls A	RALAX	NAS CM	Open End	Aggressive Alloc (Growth)	C+	C+	B-	Down	Y	0
Russell Investments LifePoints Growth Strategy Fund Cls C	RALCX	NAS CM	Open End	Aggressive Alloc (Growth)	C+	C+	C+	Down	Y	0
Russell Investments LifePoints Growth Strategy Fund Cls E	RALEX	NAS CM	Open End	Aggressive Alloc (Growth)	C+	C+	B-	Down	Y	0
Russell Investments LifePoints Growth Strategy Fund Cls R1	RALRX	NAS CM	Open End	Aggressive Alloc (Growth)	C+	C+	B-	Down	Y	0
Russell Investments LifePoints Growth Strategy Fund Cls R4	RALUX	NAS CM	Open End	Aggressive Alloc (Growth)	C+	C+	B-	Down	Y	0
Russell Investments LifePoints Growth Strategy Fund Cls R5	RALVX	NAS CM	Open End	Aggressive Alloc (Growth)	C+	C+	B-	Down	Y	0
Russell Investments LifePoints Growth Strategy Fund Cls S	RALSX	NAS CM	Open End	Aggressive Alloc (Growth)	C+	C+	B-	Down	Y	0
Russell Investments LifePoints Growth Strategy Fund Cls T	RGTAX	NAS CM	Open End	Aggressive Alloc (Growth)	C+	C+	B-	Down	Y	0
Russell Inv LifePoints Moderate Strategy Fund Cls A	RMLAX	NAS CM	Open End	Cautious Alloc (Growth & Income)	B	C+	B+	Up	Y	0
Russell Inv LifePoints Moderate Strategy Fund Cls C	RMLCX	NAS CM	Open End	Cautious Alloc (Growth & Income)	B-	C+	B+	Up	Y	0

★ Expanded analysis of this fund is included in Section II.

	TOTAL RETURNS					PERFORMANCE				ASSETS		ASSET ALLOCATION & TURNOVER					BULL & BEAR		FEES		
Min Additional Investment	3-Month Total Return	6-Month Total Return	1-Year Total Return	3-Year Total Return	5-Year Total Return	Dividend Yield (TTM)	Expense Ratio	3-Yr Std Deviation	3-Year Beta	NAV	Total Assets (MIL)	%Cash	%Stocks	%Bonds	%Other	Turnover Ratio	Last Bull Market Total Return	Last Bear Market Total Return	Front End Fee (%)	Back End Fee (%)	Inception Date
	1.11	3.64	18.45	18.20	53.75	1.91	1.38	9.96	0.94	11.43	948.0	5	95	0	0	102	16.18	-16.06	5.75		Sep-10
	0.96	3.31	17.66	15.56	48.22	1.4	2.13	9.92	0.94	11.36	948.0	5	95	0	0	102	15.73	-16.39			Sep-10
	1.21	3.74	18.56	18.20	53.81	1.85	1.38	9.96	0.94	11.45	948.0	5	95	0	0	102	16.18	-16.07			Sep-10
	1.23	3.85	18.98	19.66	57.15		1.03	9.92	0.94	11.44	948.0	5	95	0	0	102	16.5	-15.89			Mar-17
	1.15	3.82	18.80	19.05	55.81	2.12	1.13	9.9	0.94	11.45	948.0	5	95	0	0	102	16.38	-16.01			Sep-10
	1.25	3.88	19.02	19.69	57.19	2.28	0.95	9.91	0.94	11.45	948.0	5	95	0	0	102	16.5	-15.89			Sep-10
	4.31	5.79	11.30	12.34	34.91	3.05	1.38	10.87	0.98	33.09	1,027	2	98	0	0	79	24.27	-20.69	5.75		Mar-07
	4.07	5.37	10.44	9.84	29.90	2.46	2.13	10.86	0.98	31.86	1,027	2	98	0	0	79	23.73	-20.97			Jan-99
	4.28	5.78	11.31	12.37	34.90	2.97	1.38	10.89	0.98	33.18	1,027	2	98	0	0	79	24.29	-20.7			Nov-96
	4.36	5.93	11.63	13.28	36.68		1.03	10.88	0.98	33.93	1,027	2	98	0	0	79	24.44	-20.61			Mar-17
	4.39	6.00	11.77	13.53	36.99	3.36	0.96	10.88	0.98	33.96	1,027	2	98	0	0	79	24.44	-20.61			Mar-16
	4.35	5.92	11.57	13.22	36.61	3.19	1.13	10.88	0.98	33.97	1,027	2	98	0	0	79	24.44	-20.61			Jul-89
	4.41	6.03	11.77	13.85	37.92	3.38	0.93	10.88	0.98	33.95	1,027	2	98	0	0	79	24.58	-20.56			Sep-08
	3.89	9.97	24.67	25.39	45.77	1.69	1.22	11.35	0.93	41.18	2,908	10	87	0	2	68	13.64	-24.6	5.75		Sep-08
	3.69	9.54	23.71	22.57	40.39	1.03	1.97	11.34	0.93	41.43	2,908	10	87	0	2	68	13.31	-24.87			Sep-08
	3.88	9.94	24.62	25.34	45.73	1.7	1.22	11.36	0.93	41.51	2,908	10	87	0	2	68	13.75	-24.58			May-99
	3.97	10.16	24.98	25.70	46.14		0.83	11.37	0.93	41.17	2,908	10	87	0	2	68	13.75	-24.58			Mar-17
	3.96	10.15	25.00	26.38	47.67	1.9	0.93	11.36	0.93	41.2	2,908	10	87	0	2	68	13.95	-24.54			Sep-08
	4.01	10.22	25.22	27.07	49.08	2.06	0.77	11.36	0.93	41.2	2,908	10	87	0	2	68	13.85	-24.47			Mar-00
	1.37	4.14	10.26	16.84	38.16	2.12	1.22	6.14	-0.02	11.3	2,131	14	51	33	1	16	13.41	-13.55	5.75		Mar-03
	1.11	3.72	9.43	14.18	32.97	1.79	1.97	6.16	-0.01	11.05	2,131	14	51	33	1	16	12.85	-13.82			Jan-99
	1.25	4.06	10.21	16.31	37.64	2.02	1.32	6.11	-0.01	11.36	2,131	14	51	33	1	16	13.47	-13.57			Sep-97
	1.41	4.27	10.58	17.45	40.09	2.22	1.01	6.17	-0.01	11.45	2,131	14	51	33	1	16	13.67	-13.35			Jun-06
	1.35	4.10	10.28	16.66	38.30	2.06	1.26	6.16	-0.02	11.34	2,131	14	51	33	1	16	13.54	-13.47			Mar-06
	1.20	3.92	9.91	15.68	36.55	1.94	1.51	6.21	-0.02	11.35	2,131	14	51	33	1	16	13.3	-13.53			Mar-98
	1.31	4.17	10.45	17.27	39.33	2.19	1.07	6.11	-0.01	11.44	2,131	14	51	33	1	16	13.51	-13.39			Jan-00
	1.27	3.48	9.78	18.88	37.13		1.22	6.11	-0.01		2,131	14	51	33	1	16	13.47	-13.57	2.50		Jun-17
	0.55	1.79	5.43	8.97	16.52	2.21	1.12	3.36	0.51	9.74	286.8	16	16	64	1	18	6.94	-4.23	5.75		Mar-03
	0.48	1.54	4.80	6.61	12.34	1.5	1.87	3.33	0.52	9.65	286.8	16	16	64	1	18	6.51	-4.53			Feb-99
	0.55	1.78	5.51	9.03	16.62	2.19	1.12	3.33	0.52	9.79	286.8	16	16	64	1	18	6.91	-4.27			Nov-97
	0.64	2.07	5.90	10.28	18.92	2.56	0.74	3.35	0.51	9.81	286.8	16	16	64	1	18	7.14	-4.11			Dec-06
	0.61	1.89	5.67	9.50	17.54	2.33	0.99	3.39	0.53	9.76	286.8	16	16	64	1	18	6.97	-4.17			Mar-06
	0.58	1.78	5.34	8.66	16.02	2.07	1.24	3.34	0.52	9.85	286.8	16	16	64	1	18	6.92	-4.32			Mar-98
	0.67	1.97	5.76	9.83	18.09	2.43	0.87	3.38	0.52	9.82	286.8	16	16	64	1	18	7.09	-4.15			Feb-00
	2.95	7.07	15.86	22.46	53.65	1.44	1.39	8.95	0.83	13.38	642.3	11	81	7	1	16	18.85	-20.82	5.75		Mar-03
	2.77	6.63	14.93	19.79	47.91	1.29	2.14	8.98	0.84	11.97	642.3	11	81	7	1	16	18.26	-20.97			Feb-99
	2.94	6.99	15.77	22.46	53.52	1.47	1.39	8.94	0.83	13.07	642.3	11	81	7	1	16	18.88	-20.86			Sep-97
	3.02	7.19	16.21	23.73	56.29	1.58	1.06	8.98	0.83	13.47	642.3	11	81	7	1	16	19.14	-20.62			May-06
	2.96	6.99	15.87	22.70	54.38	1.5	1.31	8.93	0.83	13.11	642.3	11	81	7	1	16	18.93	-20.74			Mar-06
	2.85	6.85	15.56	21.80	52.40	1.42	1.56	8.93	0.83	12.94	642.3	11	81	7	1	16	18.71	-20.8			Mar-98
	3.01	7.19	16.12	23.43	55.44	1.54	1.14	8.95	0.83	13.44	642.3	11	81	7	1	16	19.08	-20.72			Jan-00
	2.88	6.02	14.44	25.09	50.80		1.39	8.94	0.83		642.3	11	81	7	1	16	18.71	-20.94	2.50		Jun-17
	2.52	6.02	13.72	19.40	45.71	1.78	1.33	7.94	0.73	12.6	1,459	12	72	14	1	14	16.36	-17.96	5.75		Mar-03
	2.33	5.69	12.83	16.77	40.33	1.5	2.08	7.93	0.74	12.16	1,459	12	72	14	1	14	15.79	-18.19			Jan-99
	2.51	6.08	13.75	19.47	45.79	1.77	1.33	7.95	0.74	12.66	1,459	12	72	14	1	14	16.3	-17.89			Sep-97
	2.64	6.28	14.17	20.63	48.33	1.89	1.03	7.96	0.74	12.78	1,459	12	72	14	1	14	16.65	-17.81			May-06
	2.60	6.18	13.88	19.65	46.53	1.79	1.28	7.99	0.74	12.66	1,459	12	72	14	1	14	16.39	-17.78			Mar-06
	2.46	6.04	13.55	18.76	44.64	1.68	1.53	7.93	0.73	12.65	1,459	12	72	14	1	14	16.26	-18			Mar-98
	2.63	6.18	14.06	20.38	47.67	1.87	1.08	7.97	0.74	12.77	1,459	12	72	14	1	14	16.56	-17.85			Feb-00
	2.39	5.14	12.67	21.69	43.33		1.33	7.95	0.74		1,459	12	72	14	1	14	16.13	-17.97	2.50		Jun-17
	0.83	3.09	8.40	14.09	27.57	2.53	1.15	4.28	0.41	10.41	494.9	15	33	50	1	34	10.05	-8.64	5.75		Mar-03
	0.64	2.70	7.64	11.53	22.99	2.1	1.9	4.31	0.42	10.27	494.9	15	33	50	1	34	9.51	-8.87			Feb-99

	MARKET		FUND TYPE, CATEGORY & OBJECTIVE		RATINGS				MINIMUMS	
Fund Name	Ticker Symbol	Traded On	Fund Type	Category and (Prospectus Objective)	Overall Rating	Reward Rating	Risk Rating	Recent Up/ Downgrade	Open to New Investors	Min Initial Investment
Russell Inv LifePoints Moderate Strategy Fund Cls E	RMLEX	NAS CM	Open End	Cautious Alloc (Growth & Income)	B	C+	B+	Up	Y	0
Russell Inv LifePoints Moderate Strategy Fund Cls R1	RMLRX	NAS CM	Open End	Cautious Alloc (Growth & Income)	B-	C+	B	Up	Y	0
Russell Inv LifePoints Moderate Strategy Fund Cls R4	RMLUX	NAS CM	Open End	Cautious Alloc (Growth & Income)	B	C+	B+	Up	Y	0
Russell Inv LifePoints Moderate Strategy Fund Cls R5	RMLVX	NAS CM	Open End	Cautious Alloc (Growth & Income)	B-	C+	B+	Up	Y	0
Russell Inv LifePoints Moderate Strategy Fund Cls S	RMLSX	NAS CM	Open End	Cautious Alloc (Growth & Income)	B-	C+	B	Up	Y	0
Russell Investments Multi-Asset Growth Strategy Fund Cls A	US78250F5961		Open End	Alloc (Multi-Asset Global)	U	U	U		Y	0
Russell Investments Multi-Asset Growth Strategy Fund Cls C	US78250F5888		Open End	Alloc (Multi-Asset Global)	U	U	U		Y	0
Russell Investments Multi-Asset Growth Strategy Fund Cls M	RMATX	NAS CM	Open End	Alloc (Multi-Asset Global)	U	U	U		Y	0
Russell Investments Multi-Asset Growth Strategy Fund Cls S	RMGSX	NAS CM	Open End	Alloc (Multi-Asset Global)	U	U	U		Y	0
Russell Investments Multi-Asset Growth Strategy Fund Cls Y	RMGYX	NAS CM	Open End	Alloc (Multi-Asset Global)	U	U	U		Y	0
Russell Investments Multifactor Intl Equity Fund Cls M	RTITX	NAS CM	Open End	Global Equity Large Cap (Growth)	B-	C+	B-	Up	Y	0
Russell Investments Multifactor Intl Equity Fund Cls R6	RTIRX	NAS CM	Open End	Global Equity Large Cap (Growth)	C+	C+	C	Up	Y	0
Russell Investments Multifactor Intl Equity Fund Cls S	RTISX	NAS CM	Open End	Global Equity Large Cap (Growth)	B-	C+	B-	Up	Y	0
Russell Investments Multifactor Intl Equity Fund Cls Y	RTIYX	NAS CM	Open End	Global Equity Large Cap (Growth)	C+	C+	C	Up	Y	10,000,000
Russell Investments Multifactor U.S. Equity Fund Class M	RTDTX	NAS CM	Open End	US Equity Large Cap Blend (Growth)	B	B	B	Up	Y	0
Russell Investments Multifactor U.S. Equity Fund Class R6	RTDRX	NAS CM	Open End	US Equity Large Cap Blend (Growth)	B	B	B	Up	Y	0
Russell Investments Multifactor U.S. Equity Fund Class S	RTDSX	NAS CM	Open End	US Equity Large Cap Blend (Growth)	B	B	B	Up	Y	0
Russell Investments Multifactor U.S. Equity Fund Class Y	RTDYX	NAS CM	Open End	US Equity Large Cap Blend (Growth)	B	B	B	Up	Y	10,000,000
Russell Investments Multi-Strategy Income Fund Class A	RMYAX	NAS CM	Open End	Cautious Alloc (Income)	B-	C	B	Up	Y	0
Russell Investments Multi-Strategy Income Fund Class C	RMYCX	NAS CM	Open End	Cautious Alloc (Income)	C+	C	B	Up	Y	0
Russell Investments Multi-Strategy Income Fund Class E	RMYEX	NAS CM	Open End	Cautious Alloc (Income)	B-	C	B	Up	Y	0
Russell Investments Multi-Strategy Income Fund Class M	RGYTX	NAS CM	Open End	Cautious Alloc (Income)	B-	C	B	Up	Y	0
Russell Investments Multi-Strategy Income Fund Class S	RMYSX	NAS CM	Open End	Cautious Alloc (Income)	B-	C	B	Up	Y	0
Russell Investments Multi-Strategy Income Fund Class T	RGYAX	NAS CM	Open End	Cautious Alloc (Income)	B-	C	B	Up	Y	0
Russell Investments Multi-Strategy Income Fund Class Y	RMYYX	NAS CM	Open End	Cautious Alloc (Income)	B-	C	B	Up	Y	10,000,000
Russell Investments Strategic Call Overwriting Fund Cls S	ROWSX	NAS CM	Open End	Long/Short Equity (Growth)	B	B-	B+		Y	0
Russell Investments Tax-Managed Intl Equity Fund Cls A	RTNAX	NAS CM	Open End	Global Equity Large Cap (Foreign Stock)	C	C+	B-	Up	Y	0
Russell Investments Tax-Managed Intl Equity Fund Cls C	RTNCX	NAS CM	Open End	Global Equity Large Cap (Foreign Stock)	C	C+	B-	Up	Y	0
Russell Investments Tax-Managed Intl Equity Fund Cls E	RTNEX	NAS CM	Open End	Global Equity Large Cap (Foreign Stock)	C	C+	B-	Up	Y	0
Russell Investments Tax-Managed Intl Equity Fund Cls M	RTIUX	NAS CM	Open End	Global Equity Large Cap (Foreign Stock)	C	C+	B-	Up	Y	0
Russell Investments Tax-Managed Intl Equity Fund Cls S	RTNSX	NAS CM	Open End	Global Equity Large Cap (Foreign Stock)	C	C+	B-	Up	Y	0
Russell Investments Tax-Managed U.S. Large Cap Fund Cls A	RTLAX	NAS CM	Open End	US Equity Large Cap Growth (Growth & Income)	B-	B-	B	Down	Y	0
Russell Investments Tax-Managed U.S. Large Cap Fund Cls C	RTLCX	NAS CM	Open End	US Equity Large Cap Growth (Growth & Income)	B-	B-	B-	Down	Y	0
Russell Investments Tax-Managed U.S. Large Cap Fund Cls E	RTLEX	NAS CM	Open End	US Equity Large Cap Growth (Growth & Income)	B-	B-	B	Down	Y	0
Russell Investments Tax-Managed U.S. Large Cap Fund Cls M	RTMTX	NAS CM	Open End	US Equity Large Cap Growth (Growth & Income)	B-	B-	B	Down	Y	0
Russell Investments Tax-Managed U.S. Large Cap Fund Cls S	RETSX	NAS CM	Open End	US Equity Large Cap Growth (Growth & Income)	B-	B-	B	Down	Y	0
Russell Inv Tax-Managed U.S. Mid & Small Cap Fund Cls A	RTSAX	NAS CM	Open End	US Equity Small Cap (Growth)	B	B-	B	Up	Y	0
Russell Inv Tax-Managed U.S. Mid & Small Cap Fund Cls C	RTSCX	NAS CM	Open End	US Equity Small Cap (Growth)	B-	B-	B	Up	Y	0
Russell Inv Tax-Managed U.S. Mid & Small Cap Fund Cls E	RTSEX	NAS CM	Open End	US Equity Small Cap (Growth)	B	B-	B	Up	Y	0
Russell Inv Tax-Managed U.S. Mid & Small Cap Fund Cls M	RTOUX	NAS CM	Open End	US Equity Small Cap (Growth)	B	B	B	Up	Y	0
Russell Inv Tax-Managed U.S. Mid & Small Cap Fund Cls S	RTSSX	NAS CM	Open End	US Equity Small Cap (Growth)	B	B	B	Up	Y	0
Russell Investments U.S. Core Equity Fund Class A	RSQAX	NAS CM	Open End	US Equity Large Cap Blend (Growth & Income)	B-	B-	B-	Down	Y	0
Russell Investments U.S. Core Equity Fund Class C	REQSX	NAS CM	Open End	US Equity Large Cap Blend (Growth & Income)	B-	B-	B-	Down	Y	0
Russell Investments U.S. Core Equity Fund Class E	REAEX	NAS CM	Open End	US Equity Large Cap Blend (Growth & Income)	B-	B-	B-	Down	Y	0
Russell Investments U.S. Core Equity Fund Class S	RLISX	NAS CM	Open End	US Equity Large Cap Blend (Growth & Income)	B	B	B		Y	0
Russell Investments U.S. Core Equity Fund Class Y	REAYX	NAS CM	Open End	US Equity Large Cap Blend (Growth & Income)	B	B	B-		Y	10,000,000
Russell Investments U.S. Defensive Equity Fund Class A	REQAX	NAS CM	Open End	US Equity Large Cap Blend (Growth & Income)	B	B-	B+		Y	0
Russell Investments U.S. Defensive Equity Fund Class C	REQCX	NAS CM	Open End	US Equity Large Cap Blend (Growth & Income)	B	B-	B+		Y	0
Russell Investments U.S. Defensive Equity Fund Class E	REQEX	NAS CM	Open End	US Equity Large Cap Blend (Growth & Income)	B	B-	B+		Y	0
Russell Investments U.S. Defensive Equity Fund Class S	REQTX	NAS CM	Open End	US Equity Large Cap Blend (Growth & Income)	B	B-	B+	Down	Y	0
Russell Investments U.S. Defensive Equity Fund Class Y	REUYX	NAS CM	Open End	US Equity Large Cap Blend (Growth & Income)	B	B-	B+	Down	Y	10,000,000
Russell Investments U.S. Dynamic Equity Fund Class A	RSGAX	NAS CM	Open End	US Equity Large Cap Blend (Asset Alloc)	B	B	B-	Up	Y	0

★ Expanded analysis of this fund is included in Section II.

Min Additional Investment	TOTAL RETURNS 3-Month Total Return	6-Month Total Return	1-Year Total Return	3-Year Total Return	5-Year Total Return	PERFORMANCE Dividend Yield (TTM)	Expense Ratio	3-Yr Std Deviation	3-Year Beta	ASSETS NAV	Total Assets (MIL)	ASSET ALLOCATION & TURNOVER %Cash	%Stocks	%Bonds	%Other	Turnover Ratio	BULL & BEAR Last Bull Market Total Return	Last Bear Market Total Return	FEES Front End Fee (%)	Back End Fee (%)	Inception Date
	0.90	3.04	8.40	13.85	27.44	2.46	1.23	4.3	0.41	10.45	494.9	15	33	50	1	34	10.04	-8.67			Oct-97
	0.89	3.19	8.66	14.93	29.58	2.69	0.9	4.27	0.42	10.47	494.9	15	33	50	1	34	10.26	-8.41			Oct-06
	0.83	3.08	8.48	14.06	27.97	2.52	1.15	4.28	0.42	10.43	494.9	15	33	50	1	34	10.08	-8.57			Mar-06
	0.76	2.94	8.23	13.28	26.48	2.34	1.4	4.27	0.41	10.49	494.9	15	33	50	1	34	10.04	-8.71			Mar-98
	0.96	3.16	8.71	14.68	28.94	2.64	0.98	4.28	0.41	10.47	494.9	15	33	50	1	34	10.12	-8.47			Jan-00
	1.26	2.92					0.91			10.51	1,675	36	33	26	4				5.75		Sep-17
	1.08	2.55					2.08			10.51	1,675	36	33	26	4						Sep-17
	1.35	3.12					0.83			10.5	1,675	36	33	26	4						Mar-17
	1.40	3.07					0.93			10.5	1,675	36	33	26	4						Mar-17
	1.38	3.15					0.73			10.5	1,675	36	33	26	4						Aug-17
	3.85	10.19	25.09	22.13		1.88	0.54	11.46	0.94	10.37	933.3	1	97	0	2	57					Jan-15
	3.86	10.21	25.12	22.27		1.93	0.52	11.48	0.94	10.36	933.3	1	97	0	2	57					Mar-16
	3.84	10.20	24.83	21.56		1.83	0.69	11.47	0.94	10.36	933.3	1	97	0	2	57					Jan-15
	3.87	10.22	25.14	22.31		1.94	0.49	11.48	0.94	10.36	933.3	1	97	0	2	57					Jul-14
	7.25	11.75	21.51	37.48		1.53	0.44	10.1	0.99	13.1	689.6	4	96	0	0	9					Jan-15
	7.28	11.85	21.54	37.45		1.54	0.42	10.07	0.99	13.1	689.6	4	96	0	0	9					Mar-16
	7.19	11.73	21.32	36.79		1.43	0.59	10.1	0.99	13.08	689.6	4	96	0	0	9					Jan-15
	7.20	11.79	21.59	37.55		1.57	0.39	10.08	0.99	13.09	689.6	4	96	0	0	9					Jul-14
	1.39	3.50	9.86			3.06	1.03			10.16	1,330	17	24	48	2	67			5.75		May-15
	1.21	3.04	8.98			2.34	1.78			10.13	1,330	17	24	48	2	67					May-15
	1.47	3.44	9.88			2.05	1.03			10.28	1,330	17	24	48	2	67					May-15
	1.50	3.60	10.18				0.68			10.16	1,330	17	24	48	2	67					Mar-17
	1.43	3.50	10.02			3.3	0.78			10.17	1,330	17	24	48	2	67					May-15
	1.19	3.26	10.27				1.03				1,330	17	24	48	2	67			2.50		Jun-17
	1.52	3.63	10.32			3.47	0.58			10.18	1,330	17	24	48	2	67					May-15
	4.58	8.08	15.90	31.99	50.06	0.96	0.97	8.15	1.15	13.94	101.8	4	96	0	0	4					Aug-12
	4.19	10.84	27.94			1.7	1.34			11.32	1,130	8	91	0	1	85			5.75		Jun-15
	4.03	10.51	27.12			1.18	2.09			11.27	1,130	8	91	0	1	85					Jun-15
	4.00	10.74	27.94			1.6	1.34			11.45	1,130	8	91	0	1	85					Jun-15
	4.22	11.06	28.39				0.99			11.35	1,130	8	91	0	1	85					Mar-17
	4.17	11.01	28.21			1.79	1.09			11.35	1,130	8	91	0	1	85					Jun-15
	6.65	10.63	21.23	31.65	97.56	0.52	1.23	10.4	1.02	40.56	2,510	8	92	0	0	23	28.1	-18.34	5.75		May-10
	6.43	10.23	20.31	28.68	90.19	0	1.98	10.4	1.02	38.57	2,510	8	92	0	0	23	27.62	-18.61			Dec-99
	6.65	10.64	21.22	31.65	97.51	0.51	1.23	10.41	1.03	40.96	2,510	8	92	0	0	23	28.17	-18.35			Nov-99
	6.73	10.85	21.59	32.72	100.09		0.88	10.41	1.03	40.91	2,510	8	92	0	0	23	28.3	-18.24			Mar-17
	6.70	10.76	21.50	32.62	99.94	0.7	0.98	10.41	1.03	40.93	2,510	8	92	0	0	23	28.3	-18.24			Oct-96
	4.89	9.18	14.39	23.13	83.79	0	1.53	11.84	0.95	25.5	571.6	7	93	0	0	70	28.39	-22.96	5.75		May-10
	4.74	8.83	13.60	20.52	77.24	0	2.25	11.82	0.94	21.87	571.6	7	93	0	0	70	27.84	-23.23			Dec-99
	4.88	9.16	14.35	23.19	83.99	0	1.5	11.85	0.95	25.55	571.6	7	93	0	0	70	28.46	-23.01			Nov-99
	4.99	9.36	14.79	24.27	86.56		1.15	11.85	0.95	26.67	571.6	7	93	0	0	70	28.58	-22.92			Mar-17
	4.96	9.32	14.71	24.18	86.42	0	1.25	11.85	0.95	26.65	571.6	7	93	0	0	70	28.58	-22.92			Nov-99
	6.64	10.67	20.73	32.95	99.89	0.69	1.09	10.48	1.03	32.41	605.0	6	94	0	0	73	25.36	-19.62	5.75		Sep-08
	6.45	10.26	19.87	30.00	92.58	0.14	1.84	10.48	1.03	31.63	605.0	6	94	0	0	73	24.83	-19.9			Sep-08
	6.65	10.63	20.72	32.93	99.85	0.66	1.09	10.47	1.02	32.47	605.0	6	94	0	0	73	25.39	-19.59			May-99
	6.75	10.83	21.10	34.01	102.51	0.96	0.8	10.48	1.03	32.32	605.0	6	94	0	0	73	25.54	-19.53			Sep-08
	6.75	10.91	21.14	33.40	100.55		0.64	10.48	1.03	32.28	605.0	6	94	0	0	73	25.39	-19.59			Mar-00
	6.21	9.71	17.94	31.06	96.74	0.51	1.11	8.59	0.92	51.44	598.7	10	90	0	0	94	26.02	-16.68	5.75		Sep-08
	6.02	9.29	17.06	28.13	89.48	0.05	1.86	8.57	0.92	51.05	598.7	10	90	0	0	94	25.51	-16.97			Sep-08
	6.21	9.69	17.93	31.03	96.70	0.46	1.11	8.59	0.92	51.55	598.7	10	90	0	0	94	26.1	-16.67			May-99
	6.28	9.86	18.27	32.07	99.24	0.76	0.82	8.58	0.92	51.5	598.7	10	90	0	0	94	26.24	-16.61			Sep-08
	6.32	9.94	18.45	32.80	101.16	0.91	0.66	8.58	0.92	51.4	598.7	10	90	0	0	94	26.36	-16.55			Mar-00
	6.97	12.00	20.32	35.01	104.26	0.18	1.36	12.38	1.03	8.35	163.6	4	96	0	0	118	28.1	-17.4	5.75		Aug-12

	MARKET			FUND TYPE, CATEGORY & OBJECTIVE	RATINGS				MINIMUMS	
Fund Name	Ticker Symbol	Traded On	Fund Type	Category and (Prospectus Objective)	Overall Rating	Reward Rating	Risk Rating	Recent Up/ Downgrade	Open to New Investors	Min Initial Investment
Russell Investments U.S. Dynamic Equity Fund Class C	RSGCX	NAS CM	Open End	US Equity Large Cap Blend (Asset Alloc)	B	B	B-	Up	Y	0
Russell Investments U.S. Dynamic Equity Fund Class E	RSGEX	NAS CM	Open End	US Equity Large Cap Blend (Asset Alloc)	B	B	B-	Up	Y	0
Russell Investments U.S. Dynamic Equity Fund Class S	RSGSX	NAS CM	Open End	US Equity Large Cap Blend (Asset Alloc)	B	B	B-	Up	Y	0
Russell Investments U.S. Dynamic Equity Fund Class Y	RSGTX	NAS CM	Open End	US Equity Large Cap Blend (Asset Alloc)	B	B	B-	Up	Y	10,000,000
Russell Investments U.S. Large Cap Equity Fund Class A	RLCZX	NAS CM	Open End	US Equity Large Cap Blend (Growth)	B-	B-	B-	Down	Y	0
Russell Investments U.S. Large Cap Equity Fund Class C	RLCCX	NAS CM	Open End	US Equity Large Cap Blend (Growth)	B-	B-	B-	Down	Y	0
Russell Investments U.S. Large Cap Equity Fund Class S	RLCSX	NAS CM	Open End	US Equity Large Cap Blend (Growth)	B-	B-	B	Down	Y	0
Russell Investments U.S. Mid Cap Equity Fund Class A	RMCAX	NAS CM	Open End	US Equity Mid Cap (Growth)	B	B-	B	Up	Y	0
Russell Investments U.S. Mid Cap Equity Fund Class C	RMCCX	NAS CM	Open End	US Equity Mid Cap (Growth)	B	B-	B	Up	Y	0
Russell Investments U.S. Mid Cap Equity Fund Class S	RMCSX	NAS CM	Open End	US Equity Mid Cap (Growth)	B	B-	B	Up	Y	0
Russell Investments U.S. Small Cap Equity Fund Class A	RLACX	NAS CM	Open End	US Equity Small Cap (Small Company)	B	B+	B	Up	Y	0
Russell Investments U.S. Small Cap Equity Fund Class C	RLECX	NAS CM	Open End	US Equity Small Cap (Small Company)	B	B+	B	Up	Y	0
Russell Investments U.S. Small Cap Equity Fund Class E	REBEX	NAS CM	Open End	US Equity Small Cap (Small Company)	B	B+	B	Up	Y	0
Russell Investments U.S. Small Cap Equity Fund Class M	RUNTX	NAS CM	Open End	US Equity Small Cap (Small Company)	B	B+	B	Up	Y	0
Russell Investments U.S. Small Cap Equity Fund Class R6	RSCRX	NAS CM	Open End	US Equity Small Cap (Small Company)	B	B+	B	Up	Y	0
Russell Investments U.S. Small Cap Equity Fund Class S	RLESX	NAS CM	Open End	US Equity Small Cap (Small Company)	B	B+	B	Up	Y	0
Russell Investments U.S. Small Cap Equity Fund Class Y	REBYX	NAS CM	Open End	US Equity Small Cap (Small Company)	B+	A-	B	Up	Y	10,000,000
Russell Investments U.S. Strategic Equity Fund Class A	RSEAX	NAS CM	Open End	US Equity Large Cap Blend (Growth)	B	B	B-	Up	Y	0
Russell Investments U.S. Strategic Equity Fund Class C	RSECX	NAS CM	Open End	US Equity Large Cap Blend (Growth)	B-	B-	B-	Down	Y	0
Russell Investments U.S. Strategic Equity Fund Class E	RSEEX	NAS CM	Open End	US Equity Large Cap Blend (Growth)	B	B	B-	Up	Y	0
Russell Investments U.S. Strategic Equity Fund Class M	RUSTX	NAS CM	Open End	US Equity Large Cap Blend (Growth)	B	B	B-	Up	Y	0
Russell Investments U.S. Strategic Equity Fund Class S	RSESX	NAS CM	Open End	US Equity Large Cap Blend (Growth)	B	B	B-	Up	Y	0
RWC Global Emerging Equity Fund Class I	RWCIX	NAS CM	Open End	Emerging Markets Equity (Div Emerging Mkts)	D-	D+	B+		Y	250,000
RWC Global Emerging Equity Fund Institutional Class	RWCEX	NAS CM	Open End	Emerging Markets Equity (Div Emerging Mkts)	D-	D+	B+		Y	10,000,000
Rydex Banking Fund Class A	RYBKX	NAS CM	Open End	Financials Sector Equity (Financial)	B	A-	B-	Up	Y	2,500
Rydex Banking Fund Class C	RYKCX	NAS CM	Open End	Financials Sector Equity (Financial)	B	A-	B-	Up	Y	2,500
Rydex Banking Fund Class H	RYKAX	NAS CM	Open End	Financials Sector Equity (Financial)	B	A-	B-	Up	Y	2,500
Rydex Banking Fund Class Investor	RYKIX	NAS CM	Open End	Financials Sector Equity (Financial)	B	A-	B-	Up	Y	2,500
Rydex Basic Materials Fund Class A	RYBMX	NAS CM	Open End	Natl Resources Sec Equity ()	B-	B	C	Up	Y	2,500
Rydex Basic Materials Fund Class C	RYBCX	NAS CM	Open End	Natl Resources Sec Equity ()	B-	B	C	Up	Y	2,500
Rydex Basic Materials Fund Class H	RYBAX	NAS CM	Open End	Natl Resources Sec Equity ()	B-	B	C	Up	Y	2,500
Rydex Basic Materials Fund Class Investor	RYBIX	NAS CM	Open End	Natl Resources Sec Equity ()	B	B	C	Up	Y	2,500
Rydex Biotechnology Fund Class A	RYBOX	NAS CM	Open End	Healthcare Sector Equity (Technology)	C+	B-	C		Y	2,500
Rydex Biotechnology Fund Class C	RYCFX	NAS CM	Open End	Healthcare Sector Equity (Technology)	C+	B-	C	Up	Y	2,500
Rydex Biotechnology Fund Class H	RYOAX	NAS CM	Open End	Healthcare Sector Equity (Technology)	C+	B-	C		Y	2,500
Rydex Biotechnology Fund Class Investor	RYOIX	NAS CM	Open End	Healthcare Sector Equity (Technology)	B-	B-	C	Up	Y	2,500
Rydex Commodities Fund Class A	RYMEX	NAS CM	Open End	Commodities Broad Basket (Growth)	D	D+	D		Y	2,500
Rydex Commodities Fund Class C	RYMJX	NAS CM	Open End	Commodities Broad Basket (Growth)	D	D+	D	Up	Y	2,500
Rydex Commodities Fund Class H	RYMBX	NAS CM	Open End	Commodities Broad Basket (Growth)	D	D+	D		Y	2,500
Rydex Consumer Products Fund Class A	RYPDX	NAS CM	Open End	Consumer Goods Sec Equity ()	B	C+	A-		Y	2,500
Rydex Consumer Products Fund Class C	RYCPX	NAS CM	Open End	Consumer Goods Sec Equity ()	B	C+	A-		Y	2,500
Rydex Consumer Products Fund Class H	RYCAX	NAS CM	Open End	Consumer Goods Sec Equity ()	B	C+	A-		Y	2,500
Rydex Consumer Products Fund Class Investor	RYCIX	NAS CM	Open End	Consumer Goods Sec Equity ()	B	C+	A-		Y	2,500
Rydex Dow 2x Strategy Fund Class A	RYLDX	NAS CM	Open End	Trading Tools (Growth)	B+	A+	C	Up	Y	2,500
Rydex Dow 2x Strategy Fund Class C	RYCYX	NAS CM	Open End	Trading Tools (Growth)	B+	A+	C	Up	Y	2,500
Rydex Dow 2x Strategy Fund Class H	RYCVX	NAS CM	Open End	Trading Tools (Growth)	B+	A+	C	Up	Y	2,500
Rydex Dow Jones Industrial Average® Fund Class A	RYDAX	NAS CM	Open End	US Equity Large Cap Value (Growth)	C	C	B+	Up	Y	2,500
Rydex Dow Jones Industrial Average® Fund Class C	RYDKX	NAS CM	Open End	US Equity Large Cap Value (Growth)	C	C	B+	Up	Y	2,500
Rydex Dow Jones Industrial Average® Fund Class H	RYDHX	NAS CM	Open End	US Equity Large Cap Value (Growth)	C	C	B+	Up	Y	2,500
Rydex Electronics Fund Class A	RYELX	NAS CM	Open End	Technology Sector Equity (Technology)	A-	A+	B	Up	Y	2,500
Rydex Electronics Fund Class C	RYSCX	NAS CM	Open End	Technology Sector Equity (Technology)	A-	A+	B	Up	Y	2,500
Rydex Electronics Fund Class H	RYSAX	NAS CM	Open End	Technology Sector Equity (Technology)	A-	A+	B	Up	Y	2,500

★Expanded analysis of this fund is included in Section II.

Min Additional Investment	3-Month Total Return	6-Month Total Return	1-Year Total Return	3-Year Total Return	5-Year Total Return	Dividend Yield (TTM)	Expense Ratio	3-Yr Std Deviation	3-Year Beta	NAV	Total Assets (MIL)	%Cash	%Stocks	%Bonds	%Other	Turnover Ratio	Last Bull Market Total Return	Last Bear Market Total Return	Front End Fee (%)	Back End Fee (%)	Inception Date
	TOTAL RETURNS					PERFORMANCE				ASSETS		ASSET ALLOCATION & TURNOVER					BULL & BEAR		FEES		
	6.73	11.63	19.35	31.99	96.79	0	2.11	12.43	1.03	6.19	163.6	4	96	0	0	118	28.1	-17.4			Jan-01
	6.94	11.96	20.26	34.87	104.00	0.17	1.36	12.44	1.04	8.38	163.6	4	96	0	0	118	28.82	-17.19			Jan-01
	6.98	12.11	20.59	35.95	106.57	0.34	1.07	12.38	1.03	8.98	163.6	4	96	0	0	118	28.89	-17.1			Jan-01
	7.05	12.25	20.78	36.76	108.64	0.48	0.91	12.44	1.04	9.16	163.6	4	96	0	0	118	28.1	-17.4			Aug-12
	6.34	10.39	19.58	31.03	96.95	1.12	1.12	10.76	1.06	11.05	137.9	4	96	0	0	92			5.75		Feb-12
	6.11	9.97	18.68	28.06	89.75	0.47	1.87	10.77	1.06	11	137.9	4	96	0	0	92					Feb-12
	6.38	10.47	19.81	31.98	99.39	1.27	0.87	10.82	1.07	11.1	137.9	4	96	0	0	92					Feb-12
	5.41	7.47	14.86	26.28	93.57	0.29	1.22	11.3	1.06	11.82	170.7	5	95	0	0	127			5.75		Feb-12
	5.28	7.14	14.09	23.56	86.50	0.05	1.97	11.26	1.05	11.44	170.7	5	95	0	0	127					Feb-12
	5.51	7.72	15.27	27.31	95.95	0.51	0.97	11.26	1.05	11.87	170.7	5	95	0	0	127					Feb-12
	4.05	9.42	14.00	28.57	96.49	0.24	1.25	13.8	0.97	31.55	2,045	5	95	0	0	98	29.49	-24.62	5.75		Sep-08
	3.87	9.01	13.17	25.68	89.26	0	2	13.79	0.97	29.64	2,045	5	95	0	0	98	28.95	-24.91			Sep-08
	4.06	9.40	13.99	28.57	96.47	0.19	1.25	13.81	0.97	31.74	2,045	5	95	0	0	98	29.54	-24.62			May-99
	4.16	9.64	14.34	28.96	97.07		0.86	13.81	0.97	31.85	2,045	5	95	0	0	98	29.54	-24.62			Mar-17
	4.18	9.63	14.46	29.55	97.97	0.58	0.83	13.83	0.97	31.87	2,045	5	95	0	0	98	29.54	-24.62			Mar-16
	4.14	9.56	14.32	29.57	99.05	0.42	0.96	13.8	0.97	31.87	2,045	5	95	0	0	98	29.71	-24.58			Sep-08
	4.20	9.68	14.52	30.32	100.92	0.59	0.8	13.8	0.97	31.88	2,045	5	95	0	0	98	29.77	-24.5			Mar-00
	7.24	11.81	20.76	32.18	98.63	0.78	0.99	10.35	1.01	13.63	3,109	5	95	0	0	75			5.75		Aug-12
	7.00	11.37	19.89	29.20	91.42	0.15	1.74	10.4	1.02	13.59	3,109	5	95	0	0	75					Aug-12
	7.17	11.81	20.78	32.09	98.59	0.64	0.99	10.36	1.01	13.67	3,109	5	95	0	0	75					Aug-12
	7.36	12.12	21.30	33.32	101.46		0.64	10.36	1.01	13.65	3,109	5	95	0	0	75					Mar-17
	7.36	11.99	21.20	33.22	101.30	1	0.74	10.36	1.01	13.66	3,109	5	95	0	0	75					Aug-12
	7.43	19.13	41.05				1.4			13.9	97.7	3	91	3	2	47					Sep-17
	7.54	19.26	41.20				1.25			13.91	97.7	3	91	3	2	47					Dec-16
	5.09	9.60	12.20	33.95	82.53	0	1.63	18.7	1.25	78.69	58.7	3	99	0	-2	907	30.77	-30.07	4.75		Sep-04
	4.90	9.19	11.37	30.96	75.78	0	2.37	18.7	1.25	71.08	58.7	3	99	0	-2	907	30.19	-30.3		1.00	Mar-01
	5.10	9.61	12.19	33.91	81.70	0	1.63	18.71	1.25	76.67	58.7	3	99	0	-2	907	30.56	-30.15			Apr-98
	5.16	9.72	12.47	34.89	84.74	0	1.38	18.7	1.25	86.09	58.7	3	99	0	-2	907	30.95	-29.98			Apr-98
	6.49	12.85	21.52	30.07	33.25	0	1.62	18.27	1.27	59.65	116.9	3	99	0	-2	361	16.21	-27.24	4.75		Sep-04
	6.30	12.44	20.60	27.17	28.36	0	2.37	18.26	1.27	53.08	116.9	3	99	0	-2	361	15.73	-27.48		1.00	May-01
	6.51	12.86	21.52	29.89	32.41	0	1.62	18.29	1.27	57.85	116.9	3	99	0	-2	361	16.05	-27.32			Apr-98
	6.56	12.98	21.81	31.05	34.94	0	1.37	18.28	1.27	63.53	116.9	3	99	0	-2	361	16.39	-27.18			Apr-98
	-1.23	7.03	29.40	12.57	135.14	0	1.61	24.59	1.47	80.68	329.0	4	100	0	-4	207	36	-14.54	4.75		Sep-04
	-1.42	6.64	28.44	10.07	126.50	0	2.36	24.57	1.46	72.39	329.0	4	100	0	-4	207	35.38	-14.79		1.00	Mar-01
	-1.22	7.05	29.43	12.41	133.66	0	1.61	24.59	1.47	78.39	329.0	4	100	0	-4	207	35.81	-14.63			Apr-98
	-1.17	7.17	29.72	13.42	138.10	0	1.37	24.6	1.47	87.26	329.0	4	100	0	-4	207	36.18	-14.46			Apr-98
	9.47	16.75	4.67	-24.68	-51.53	0	1.67	20.59	1.02	88.34	8.1	61	0	5	34	208	14.35	-23.99	4.75		May-05
	9.27	16.31	3.80	-26.37	-53.28	0	2.4	20.52	1.01	79.88	8.1	61	0	5	34	208	13.83	-24.2		1.00	May-05
	9.49	16.77	4.64	-24.79	-51.50	0	1.64	20.6	1.02	88.4	8.1	61	0	5	34	208	14.28	-24.03			May-05
	6.37	5.19	11.69	23.79	83.99	0	1.62	8.83	0.54	59.33	252.5	3	100	0	-3	75	14.94	-4.68	4.75		Sep-04
	6.17	4.80	10.85	21.04	77.23	0	2.36	8.83	0.54	51.41	252.5	3	100	0	-3	75	14.47	-5.03		1.00	Jul-01
	6.35	5.17	11.66	23.60	82.80	0	1.61	8.83	0.54	57.15	252.5	3	100	0	-3	75	14.77	-4.8			Aug-98
	6.43	5.32	11.96	24.73	86.33	0	1.36	8.84	0.54	64.58	252.5	3	100	0	-3	75	15.12	-4.62			Jul-98
	21.93	34.58	57.84	92.27	277.50	0	1.86	22.48		88.46	63.8	9	83	0	8	350	45.6	-28.71	4.75		Sep-04
	21.70	34.10	56.70	88.07	264.04	0	2.6	22.45		78.7	63.8	9	83	0	8	350	44.78	-28.93		1.00	Feb-04
	21.93	34.56	57.87	92.25	277.73	0	1.86	22.47		88.18	63.8	9	83	0	8	350	45.4	-28.74			Feb-04
	10.53	16.26	26.16			0	1.57			67.6	80.3	9	80	2	9	668			4.75		Dec-15
	10.32	15.84	25.24			0	2.33			66.5	80.3	9	80	2	9	668				1.00	Dec-15
	10.52	16.27	26.16			0	1.58			67.64	80.3	9	80	2	9	668					Dec-15
	6.12	17.95	31.29	66.27	180.97	0	1.63	17.55	1.21	122.88	56.4	4	100	0	-4	643	16.5	-28.38	4.75		Sep-04
	5.92	17.51	30.32	62.57	170.33	0	2.38	17.56	1.21	111.35	56.4	4	100	0	-4	643	15.95	-28.64		1.00	Mar-01
	6.12	17.94	31.28	65.93	178.71	0	1.63	17.54	1.21	119.66	56.4	4	100	0	-4	643	16.39	-28.43			Apr-98

	MARKET			FUND TYPE, CATEGORY & OBJECTIVE	RATINGS				MINIMUMS	
Fund Name	Ticker Symbol	Traded On	Fund Type	Category and (Prospectus Objective)	Overall Rating	Reward Rating	Risk Rating	Recent Up/ Downgrade	Open to New Investors	Min Initial Investment
Rydex Electronics Fund Class Investor	RYSIX	NAS CM	Open End	Technology Sector Equity (Technology)	A-	A+	B	Up	Y	2,500
Rydex Emerging Markets 2x Strategy Fund A Class	RYWTX	NAS CM	Open End	Trading Tools (Div Emerging Mkts)	C	B-	C-		Y	2,500
Rydex Emerging Markets 2x Strategy Fund C Class	RYWUX	NAS CM	Open End	Trading Tools (Div Emerging Mkts)	C	C+	C-		Y	2,500
Rydex Emerging Markets 2x Strategy Fund H Class	RYWVX	NAS CM	Open End	Trading Tools (Div Emerging Mkts)	C	B-	C-		Y	2,500
Rydex Energy Fund Class A	RYENX	NAS CM	Open End	Energy Sector Equity (Natl Res)	D+	D+	D	Up	Y	2,500
Rydex Energy Fund Class C	RYECX	NAS CM	Open End	Energy Sector Equity (Natl Res)	D	D	D		Y	2,500
Rydex Energy Fund Class H	RYEAX	NAS CM	Open End	Energy Sector Equity (Natl Res)	D+	D+	D	Up	Y	2,500
Rydex Energy Fund Class Investor	RYEIX	NAS CM	Open End	Energy Sector Equity (Natl Res)	D+	D+	D	Up	Y	2,500
Rydex Energy Services Fund Class A	RYESX	NAS CM	Open End	Energy Sector Equity (Natl Res)	D	D	D	Down	Y	2,500
Rydex Energy Services Fund Class C	RYVCX	NAS CM	Open End	Energy Sector Equity (Natl Res)	D	D	D	Down	Y	2,500
Rydex Energy Services Fund Class H	RYVAX	NAS CM	Open End	Energy Sector Equity (Natl Res)	D	D	D	Down	Y	2,500
Rydex Energy Services Fund Class Investor	RYVIX	NAS CM	Open End	Energy Sector Equity (Natl Res)	D	D	D	Down	Y	2,500
Rydex Europe Advantage Fund Class A	RYAEX	NAS CM	Open End	Trading Tools (Europe Stock)	C+	C+	C+	Up	Y	2,500
Rydex Europe Advantage Fund Class C	RYCEX	NAS CM	Open End	Trading Tools (Europe Stock)	C+	C+	C	Up	Y	2,500
Rydex Europe Advantage Fund Class H	RYEUX	NAS CM	Open End	Trading Tools (Europe Stock)	C+	C+	C	Up	Y	2,500
Rydex Financial Services Fund Class A	RYFNX	NAS CM	Open End	Financials Sector Equity (Financial)	B	B	B	Up	Y	2,500
Rydex Financial Services Fund Class C	RYFCX	NAS CM	Open End	Financials Sector Equity (Financial)	B	B-	B	Up	Y	2,500
Rydex Financial Services Fund Class H	RYFAX	NAS CM	Open End	Financials Sector Equity (Financial)	B	B	B	Up	Y	2,500
Rydex Financial Services Fund Class Investor	RYFIX	NAS CM	Open End	Financials Sector Equity (Financial)	B	B	B	Up	Y	2,500
Rydex Government Long Bond 1.2x Strategy Fund Class A	RYABX	NAS CM	Open End	Trading Tools (Govt Bond - Treasury)	C	C	C-	Up	Y	2,500
Rydex Government Long Bond 1.2x Strategy Fund Class C	RYCGX	NAS CM	Open End	Trading Tools (Govt Bond - Treasury)	C-	C-	C-	Down	Y	2,500
Rydex Government Long Bond 1.2x Strategy Fund Class H	RYHBX	NAS CM	Open End	Trading Tools (Govt Bond - Treasury)	C	C	C-	Up	Y	2,500
Rydex Government Long Bond 1.2x Strategy Fund Investor Cls	RYGBX	NAS CM	Open End	Trading Tools (Govt Bond - Treasury)	C	C	C-	Up	Y	2,500
Rydex Health Care Fund Class A	RYHEX	NAS CM	Open End	Healthcare Sector Equity (Health)	B-	C+	B-	Up	Y	2,500
Rydex Health Care Fund Class C	RYHCX	NAS CM	Open End	Healthcare Sector Equity (Health)	C+	C+	B-	Up	Y	2,500
Rydex Health Care Fund Class H	RYHAX	NAS CM	Open End	Healthcare Sector Equity (Health)	B-	C+	B-	Up	Y	2,500
Rydex Health Care Fund Class Investor	RYHIX	NAS CM	Open End	Healthcare Sector Equity (Health)	B-	C+	B-	Up	Y	2,500
Rydex Internet Fund Class A	RYINX	NAS CM	Open End	Technology Sector Equity (Technology)	A-	A-	B	Up	Y	2,500
Rydex Internet Fund Class C	RYICX	NAS CM	Open End	Technology Sector Equity (Technology)	B+	A-	B	Up	Y	2,500
Rydex Internet Fund Class H	RYIAX	NAS CM	Open End	Technology Sector Equity (Technology)	A-	A-	B	Up	Y	2,500
Rydex Internet Fund Class Investor	RYIIX	NAS CM	Open End	Technology Sector Equity (Technology)	A-	A-	B	Up	Y	2,500
Rydex Inverse Dow 2x Strategy Fund Class A	RYIDX	NAS CM	Open End	Trading Tools (Growth)	E+	E+	E+	Down	Y	2,500
Rydex Inverse Dow 2x Strategy Fund Class C	RYCZX	NAS CM	Open End	Trading Tools (Growth)	E+	E+	E+	Down	Y	2,500
Rydex Inverse Dow 2x Strategy Fund Class H	RYCWX	NAS CM	Open End	Trading Tools (Growth)	E+	E+	E+	Down	Y	2,500
Rydex Inverse Emerging Markets 2x Strategy Fund A Class	RYWWX	NAS CM	Open End	Trading Tools (Div Emerging Mkts)	D-	E+	D-	Down	Y	2,500
Rydex Inverse Emerging Markets 2x Strategy Fund C Class	RYWZX	NAS CM	Open End	Trading Tools (Div Emerging Mkts)	D-	E+	D-	Down	Y	2,500
Rydex Inverse Emerging Markets 2x Strategy Fund H Class	RYWYX	NAS CM	Open End	Trading Tools (Div Emerging Mkts)	D-	E+	D-	Down	Y	2,500
Rydex Inverse Government Long Bond Strategy Fund Class A	RYAQX	NAS CM	Open End	Trading Tools (Govt Bond - Treasury)	D	D	D+	Down	Y	2,500
Rydex Inverse Government Long Bond Strategy Fund Class C	RYJCX	NAS CM	Open End	Trading Tools (Govt Bond - Treasury)	D	D	D+	Down	Y	2,500
Rydex Inverse Government Long Bond Strategy Fund Class H	RYHJX	NAS CM	Open End	Trading Tools (Govt Bond - Treasury)	D	D	D+	Down	Y	2,500
Rydex Inverse Government Long Bond Strategy Fund Inv Cls	RYJUX	NAS CM	Open End	Trading Tools (Govt Bond - Treasury)	D	D	D+	Down	Y	2,500
Rydex Inverse High Yield Strategy Fund Class A	RYILX	NAS CM	Open End	Trading Tools (Corporate Bond - High Yield)	D	D	D+		Y	2,500
Rydex Inverse High Yield Strategy Fund Class C	RYIYX	NAS CM	Open End	Trading Tools (Corporate Bond - High Yield)	D	D	D		Y	2,500
Rydex Inverse High Yield Strategy Fund Class H	RYIHX	NAS CM	Open End	Trading Tools (Corporate Bond - High Yield)	D	D	D+		Y	2,500
Rydex Inverse Mid-Cap Strategy Fund Class A	RYAGX	NAS CM	Open End	Other Alternative (Growth)	D-	D-	D-	Down	Y	2,500
Rydex Inverse Mid-Cap Strategy Fund Class C	RYCLX	NAS CM	Open End	Other Alternative (Growth)	D-	D-	D-	Down	Y	2,500
Rydex Inverse Mid-Cap Strategy Fund Class H	RYMHX	NAS CM	Open End	Other Alternative (Growth)	D-	D-	D-	Down	Y	2,500
Rydex Inverse NASDAQ-100® 2x Strategy Fund Class A	RYVTX	NAS CM	Open End	Other Alternative (Growth)	E+	E+	E+	Down	Y	2,500
Rydex Inverse NASDAQ-100® 2x Strategy Fund Class C	RYCDX	NAS CM	Open End	Other Alternative (Growth)	E+	E+	E+	Down	Y	2,500
Rydex Inverse NASDAQ-100® 2x Strategy Fund Class H	RYVNX	NAS CM	Open End	Other Alternative (Growth)	E+	E+	E+	Down	Y	2,500
Rydex Inverse NASDAQ-100® Strategy Fund Class A	RYAPX	NAS CM	Open End	Other Alternative (Growth)	D-	D-	D-	Down	Y	2,500
Rydex Inverse NASDAQ-100® Strategy Fund Class C	RYACX	NAS CM	Open End	Other Alternative (Growth)	D-	D-	D-	Down	Y	2,500

★ Expanded analysis of this fund is included in Section II.

	TOTAL RETURNS					PERFORMANCE				ASSETS		ASSET ALLOCATION & TURNOVER					BULL & BEAR		FEES		
Min Additional Investment	3-Month Total Return	6-Month Total Return	1-Year Total Return	3-Year Total Return	5-Year Total Return	Dividend Yield (TTM)	Expense Ratio	3-Yr Std Deviation	3-Year Beta	NAV	Total Assets (MIL)	%Cash	%Stocks	%Bonds	%Other	Turnover Ratio	Last Bull Market Total Return	Last Bear Market Total Return	Front End Fee (%)	Back End Fee (%)	Inception Date
	6.18	18.09	31.62	67.45	184.35	0	1.38	17.55	1.21	131.44	56.4	4	100	0	-4	643	16.7	-28.31			Apr-98
	3.73	25.28	74.71	32.45	7.24	0	1.76	36.99		83.25	17.0	21	80	0	-2	2,568	28.03	-47.85	4.75		Oct-10
	3.54	24.83	73.38	29.45	3.72	0	2.5	36.98		79.93	17.0	21	80	0	-2	2,568	27.65	-47.5		1.00	Oct-10
	3.73	25.27	74.69	32.22	6.84	0	1.76	37.01		83.26	17.0	21	80	0	-2	2,568	28.19	-47.72			Oct-10
	6.82	14.58	-6.39	-15.12	-12.31	0	1.62	24.62	1.34	73.7	28.1	6	100	0	-6	996	22.97	-31.23	4.75		Sep-04
	6.62	14.17	-7.08	-17.14	-15.62	0	2.37	24.62	1.34	65.52	28.1	6	100	0	-6	996	22.53	-31.46		1.00	Apr-01
	6.82	14.58	-6.41	-15.43	-13.00	0	1.63	24.6	1.34	71.5	28.1	6	100	0	-6	996	22.92	-31.33			May-98
	6.89	14.73	-6.16	-14.62	-11.27	0	1.37	24.65	1.34	78.75	28.1	6	100	0	-6	996	23.22	-31.16			Apr-98
	3.52	10.27	-19.06	-32.65	-39.05	0	1.62	31.11	1.44	26.6	11.3	13	100	0	-13	1,830	24.57	-34.83	4.75		Sep-04
	3.31	9.85	-19.70	-34.19	-41.32	0	2.37	31.07	1.44	23.85	11.3	13	100	0	-13	1,830	24.06	-35.07		1.00	Mar-01
	3.51	10.22	-19.18	-32.94	-39.62	0	1.62	31.13	1.44	25.76	11.3	13	100	0	-13	1,830	24.4	-34.92			Apr-98
	3.60	10.45	-18.85	-32.15	-38.29	0	1.38	31.08	1.44	28.29	11.3	13	100	0	-13	1,830	24.74	-34.78			Apr-98
	1.30	7.41	28.13	9.89	22.78	0	1.74	15.9		98.79	10.9	12	82	0	6	1,616	18.21	-31.91	4.75		Mar-04
	1.09	6.98	27.17	7.56	17.11	0	2.51	15.9		85.57	10.9	12	82	0	6	1,616	17.97	-32.27		1.00	May-01
	1.28	7.40	28.14	10.14	21.76	0	1.75	15.89		98.09	10.9	12	82	0	6	1,616	18.31	-31.91			May-00
	5.15	9.23	15.44	26.70	85.36	0	1.64	12.19	1.04	68.86	45.9	1	99	0	0	389	27.75	-26.56	4.75		Sep-04
	4.95	8.82	14.58	23.87	78.62	0	2.39	12.18	1.04	61.54	45.9	1	99	0	0	389	27.25	-26.8		1.00	Apr-01
	5.16	9.24	15.49	26.59	84.30	0	1.65	12.19	1.04	66.88	45.9	1	99	0	0	389	27.55	-26.62			Apr-98
	5.75	9.92	16.32	28.30	88.65	0	1.4	12.2	1.04	73.17	45.9	1	99	0	0	389	27.94	-26.47			Apr-98
	3.22	3.03	9.67	4.98	17.61	1.21	1.25	15.86		54.63	96.6	23	0	69	7	2,490	-1.73	40.2	4.75		Mar-04
	3.02	2.63	8.82	2.61	12.99	0.47	1.98	15.86		54.24	96.6	23	0	69	7	2,490	-2.22	39.78		1.00	May-01
	3.20	3.01	9.60	5.05	17.33	1.21	1.23	15.86		54.65	96.6	23	0	69	7	2,490	-1.74	40.18			Sep-14
	3.29	3.16	9.91	5.58	18.52	1.45	0.99	15.89		54.2	96.6	23	0	69	7	2,490	-1.59	40.33			Jan-94
	1.77	3.57	23.16	14.73	107.12	0	1.62	14.79	1.01	26.07	66.3	2	99	0	-1	699	20.32	-14.57	4.75		Sep-04
	1.61	3.23	22.30	12.20	99.69	0	2.37	14.8	1.01	22.58	66.3	2	99	0	-1	699	19.81	-14.85		1.00	Mar-01
	1.80	3.58	23.16	14.58	105.93	0	1.62	14.8	1.01	25.12	66.3	2	99	0	-1	699	20.19	-14.69			May-98
	1.82	3.71	23.47	15.61	109.87	0	1.37	14.8	1.01	28.66	66.3	2	99	0	-1	699	20.46	-14.51			Apr-98
	5.36	12.36	34.10	50.90	138.48	0	1.62	14.42	1.23	108.85	65.8	4	100	0	-3	518	25.36	-25.04	4.75		Sep-04
	5.16	11.95	33.09	47.55	129.62	0	2.37	14.41	1.23	97.13	65.8	4	100	0	-3	518	24.84	-25.28		1.00	Apr-01
	5.37	12.37	34.10	50.74	136.83	0	1.62	14.42	1.23	105.73	65.8	4	100	0	-3	518	25.22	-25.14			Apr-00
	5.43	12.51	34.42	52.06	141.51	0	1.37	14.41	1.23	115.83	65.8	4	100	0	-3	518	25.57	-24.96			Apr-00
	-18.70	-26.95	-39.15	-60.92	-83.36	0	1.85	20.38		11.95	9.5	52	-5	53	-1	0	-38.43	23.34	4.75		Sep-04
	-18.86	-27.29	-39.59	-61.74	-83.99	0	2.62	20.37		10.71	9.5	52	-5	53	-1	0	-38.69	22.91		1.00	Feb-04
	-18.71	-26.97	-39.16	-60.90	-83.25	0	1.85	20.38		11.99	9.5	52	-5	53	-1	0	-38.62	23.31			Feb-04
	-5.88	-23.13	-47.98	-57.01	-61.05	0	1.75	34.21		43.35	0.68	104	-3	0	-1	1,085	-35.74	51.9	4.75		Oct-10
	-6.02	-23.41	-48.36	-58.00	-62.48	0	2.48	34.19		43.67	0.68	104	-3	0	-1	1,085	-34.16	54.85		1.00	Oct-10
	-6.03	-23.27	-48.11	-57.20	-61.34	0	1.76	34.16		42.98	0.68	104	-3	0	-1	1,085	-35.74	51.98			Oct-10
	-3.08	-3.35	-9.16	-12.80	-21.73	0	1.63	13.1		32.01	102.5	106	0	-20	14	1,436	-1.43	-27.18	4.75		Mar-04
	-3.26	-3.69	-9.84	-14.74	-24.63	0	2.43	13.08		28.11	102.5	106	0	-20	14	1,436	-1.79	-27.45		1.00	Mar-01
	-3.10	-3.42	-9.19	-12.55	-21.59	0	1.68	13.06		32.1	102.5	106	0	-20	14	1,436	-1.43	-27.21			Sep-14
	-3.05	-3.25	-8.97	-12.17	-20.87	0	1.43	13.09		33.27	102.5	106	0	-20	14	1,436	-1.29	-27.13			Mar-95
	-0.73	-2.32	-5.87	-20.55	-37.72	0	1.53	4.1		63.3	14.8	96	0	2	2	480	-15.3	5.78	4.75		Apr-07
	-0.92	-2.69	-6.65	-22.09	-39.62	0	2.28	4.14		58.93	14.8	96	0	2	2	480	-15.54	5.41		1.00	Apr-07
	-0.73	-2.58	-5.62	-19.18	-36.28	0	1.53	4.26		64.91	14.8	96	0	2	2	480	-15.25	5.77			Apr-07
	-5.83	-8.65	-14.21	-30.99	-57.10	0	1.7	10.55		22.26	0.72	70	-2	6	25	120	-24.99	22.48	4.75		Mar-04
	-6.03	-9.03	-14.93	-32.62	-58.76	0	2.44	10.56		19.93	0.72	70	-2	6	25	120	-25.31	22		1.00	Feb-04
	-5.84	-8.62	-14.19	-30.90	-57.07	0	1.69	10.54		22.25	0.72	70	-2	6	25	120	-24.98	22.45			Feb-04
	-13.21	-23.23	-44.29	-65.97	-89.43	0	1.93	24.94		41.32	14.8	18	-1	83	1	0	-43.94	12.53	4.75		Sep-04
	-13.40	-23.49	-44.65	-66.43	-89.76	0	2.56	24.9		36.51	14.8	18	-1	83	1	0	-44.58	12.64		1.00	Mar-01
	-13.21	-23.22	-44.27	-65.88	-89.42	0	1.83	24.97		41.39	14.8	18	-1	83	1	0	-43.82	12.84			May-00
	-6.68	-12.05	-24.66	-38.56	-65.72	0	1.72	12.89		63.82	12.7	66	0	7	28	486	-24.34	7.77	4.75		Mar-04
	-6.85	-12.38	-25.21	-40.75	-67.49	0	2.48	12.91		54.74	12.7	66	0	7	28	486	-24.64	7.43		1.00	Mar-01

Fund Name	Ticker Symbol	Traded On	Fund Type	Category and (Prospectus Objective)	Overall Rating	Reward Rating	Risk Rating	Recent Up/ Downgrade	Open to New Investors	Min Initial Investment
	MARKET		FUND TYPE, CATEGORY & OBJECTIVE		RATINGS				MINIMUMS	
Rydex Inverse NASDAQ-100® Strategy Fund Class H	RYALX	NAS CM	Open End	Other Alternative (Growth)	D-	D-	D-	Down	Y	2,500
Rydex Inverse NASDAQ-100® Strategy Fund Investor Class	RYAIX	NAS CM	Open End	Other Alternative (Growth)	D-	D-	D-	Down	Y	2,500
Rydex Inverse Russell 2000 2x Strategy Fund Class A	RYIUX	NAS CM	Open End	Other Alternative (Growth)	E+	E+	E+	Down	Y	2,500
Rydex Inverse Russell 2000 2x Strategy Fund Class C	RYIZX	NAS CM	Open End	Other Alternative (Growth)	E+	E+	E+	Down	Y	2,500
Rydex Inverse Russell 2000 2x Strategy Fund Class H	RYIRX	NAS CM	Open End	Other Alternative (Growth)	E+	E+	E+	Down	Y	2,500
Rydex Inverse Russell 2000® Strategy Fund Class A	RYAFX	NAS CM	Open End	Other Alternative (Growth)	D-	D-	D-	Down	Y	2,500
Rydex Inverse Russell 2000® Strategy Fund Class C	RYCQX	NAS CM	Open End	Other Alternative (Growth)	D-	D-	D-	Down	Y	2,500
Rydex Inverse Russell 2000® Strategy Fund Class H	RYSHX	NAS CM	Open End	Other Alternative (Growth)	D-	D-	D-	Down	Y	2,500
Rydex Inverse S&P 500 2x Strategy Fund Class A	RYTMX	NAS CM	Open End	Other Alternative (Growth)	E+	E+	D-	Down	Y	2,500
Rydex Inverse S&P 500 2x Strategy Fund Class C	RYCBX	NAS CM	Open End	Other Alternative (Growth)	E+	E+	D-	Down	Y	2,500
Rydex Inverse S&P 500 2x Strategy Fund Class H	RYTPX	NAS CM	Open End	Other Alternative (Growth)	E+	E+	D-	Down	Y	2,500
Rydex Inverse S&P 500® Strategy Fund Class A	RYARX	NAS CM	Open End	Other Alternative (Growth)	D-	D-	D	Down	Y	2,500
Rydex Inverse S&P 500® Strategy Fund Class C	RYUCX	NAS CM	Open End	Other Alternative (Growth)	D-	D-	D-	Down	Y	2,500
Rydex Inverse S&P 500® Strategy Fund Class H	RYUHX	NAS CM	Open End	Other Alternative (Growth)	D-	D-	D	Down	Y	2,500
Rydex Inverse S&P 500® Strategy Fund Investor Class	RYURX	NAS CM	Open End	Other Alternative (Growth)	D-	D-	D	Down	Y	2,500
Rydex Japan 2x Strategy Fund Class A	RYJSX	NAS CM	Open End	Trading Tools (Pacific Stock)	B+	A+	C+	Up	Y	2,500
Rydex Japan 2x Strategy Fund Class C	RYJTX	NAS CM	Open End	Trading Tools (Pacific Stock)	B+	A+	C+	Up	Y	2,500
Rydex Japan 2x Strategy Fund Class H	RYJHX	NAS CM	Open End	Trading Tools (Pacific Stock)	B+	A+	C+	Up	Y	2,500
Rydex Leisure Fund Class A	RYLSX	NAS CM	Open End	Consumer Goods Sec Equity ()	B	B-	B+		Y	2,500
Rydex Leisure Fund Class C	RYLCX	NAS CM	Open End	Consumer Goods Sec Equity ()	B	B-	B+		Y	2,500
Rydex Leisure Fund Class Investor	RYLIX	NAS CM	Open End	Consumer Goods Sec Equity ()	B	B-	B+		Y	2,500
Rydex Leisure Fund H Class	RYLAX	NAS CM	Open End	Consumer Goods Sec Equity ()	B	B-	B+		Y	2,500
Rydex Mid-Cap 1.5x Strategy Fund Class A	RYAHX	NAS CM	Open End	Trading Tools (Growth)	B+	A	B-	Up	Y	2,500
Rydex Mid-Cap 1.5x Strategy Fund Class C	RYDCX	NAS CM	Open End	Trading Tools (Growth)	B+	A	B-	Up	Y	2,500
Rydex Mid-Cap 1.5x Strategy Fund Class H	RYMDX	NAS CM	Open End	Trading Tools (Growth)	B+	A	B-	Up	Y	2,500
Rydex Monthly Rebalance NASDAQ-100® 2x Strategy Fund Cls A	RMQAX	NAS CM	Open End	Trading Tools (Aggr Growth)	B	B	B-	Up	Y	2,500
Rydex Monthly Rebalance NASDAQ-100® 2x Strategy Fund Cls C	RMQCX	NAS CM	Open End	Trading Tools (Aggr Growth)	B	B	B-	Up	Y	2,500
Rydex Monthly Rebalance NASDAQ-100® 2x Strategy Fund Cls H	RMQHX	NAS CM	Open End	Trading Tools (Aggr Growth)	B	B	B-	Up	Y	2,500
Rydex NASDAQ-100® 2x Strategy Fund Class A	RYVLX	NAS CM	Open End	Trading Tools (Growth)	A-	A+	B-	Up	Y	2,500
Rydex NASDAQ-100® 2x Strategy Fund Class C	RYCCX	NAS CM	Open End	Trading Tools (Growth)	A-	A+	B-	Up	Y	2,500
Rydex NASDAQ-100® 2x Strategy Fund Class H	RYVYX	NAS CM	Open End	Trading Tools (Growth)	A-	A+	B-	Up	Y	2,500
Rydex NASDAQ-100® Fund Class A	RYATX	NAS CM	Open End	US Equity Large Cap Growth (Growth)	B+	A-	B	Down	Y	2,500
Rydex NASDAQ-100® Fund Class C	RYCOX	NAS CM	Open End	US Equity Large Cap Growth (Growth)	B+	A-	B	Down	Y	2,500
Rydex NASDAQ-100® Fund Class H	RYHOX	NAS CM	Open End	US Equity Large Cap Growth (Growth)	B+	A-	B	Down	Y	2,500
Rydex NASDAQ-100® Fund Investor Class	RYOCX	NAS CM	Open End	US Equity Large Cap Growth (Growth)	B+	A-	B	Down	Y	2,500
Rydex Nova Fund Class A	RYANX	NAS CM	Open End	Trading Tools (Aggr Growth)	B+	A	B-	Up	Y	2,500
Rydex Nova Fund Class C	RYNCX	NAS CM	Open End	Trading Tools (Aggr Growth)	B	A-	C+		Y	2,500
Rydex Nova Fund Class H	RYNHX	NAS CM	Open End	Trading Tools (Aggr Growth)	B+	A	B-	Up	Y	2,500
Rydex Nova Fund Investor Class	RYNVX	NAS CM	Open End	Trading Tools (Aggr Growth)	B+	A	B-	Up	Y	2,500
Rydex Precious Metals Fund Class A	RYMNX	NAS CM	Open End	Precious Metals Sector Equity (Precious Metals)	D+	C-	D	Down	Y	2,500
Rydex Precious Metals Fund Class C	RYZCX	NAS CM	Open End	Precious Metals Sector Equity (Precious Metals)	D+	C-	D	Down	Y	2,500
Rydex Precious Metals Fund Class H	RYMPX	NAS CM	Open End	Precious Metals Sector Equity (Precious Metals)	D+	C-	D	Down	Y	2,500
Rydex Precious Metals Fund Class Investor	RYPMX	NAS CM	Open End	Precious Metals Sector Equity (Precious Metals)	D+	C-	D	Down	Y	2,500
Rydex Real Estate Fund Class A	RYREX	NAS CM	Open End	Real Estate Sector Equity (Real Estate)	B-	C+	B		Y	2,500
Rydex Real Estate Fund Class C	RYCRX	NAS CM	Open End	Real Estate Sector Equity (Real Estate)	B-	C+	B	Up	Y	2,500
Rydex Real Estate Fund Class H	RYHRX	NAS CM	Open End	Real Estate Sector Equity (Real Estate)	B-	C+	B		Y	2,500
Rydex Retailing Fund Class A	RYRTX	NAS CM	Open End	Consumer Goods Sec Equity ()	C+	C	B	Up	Y	2,500
Rydex Retailing Fund Class C	RYRCX	NAS CM	Open End	Consumer Goods Sec Equity ()	C+	C	B	Up	Y	2,500
Rydex Retailing Fund Class H	RYRAX	NAS CM	Open End	Consumer Goods Sec Equity ()	C+	C	B	Up	Y	2,500
Rydex Retailing Fund Class Investor	RYRIX	NAS CM	Open End	Consumer Goods Sec Equity ()	C+	C	B	Up	Y	2,500
Rydex Russell 2000 1.5x Strategy Fund Class A	RYAKX	NAS CM	Open End	Trading Tools (Growth)	B+	A	C+	Up	Y	2,500
Rydex Russell 2000 1.5x Strategy Fund Class C	RYCMX	NAS CM	Open End	Trading Tools (Growth)	B+	A	C+	Up	Y	2,500

★ Expanded analysis of this fund is included in Section II.

Min Additional Investment	TOTAL RETURNS 3-Month Total Return	6-Month Total Return	1-Year Total Return	3-Year Total Return	5-Year Total Return	PERFORMANCE Dividend Yield (TTM)	Expense Ratio	3-Yr Std Deviation	3-Year Beta	ASSETS NAV	Total Assets (MIL)	ASSET ALLOCATION & TURNOVER %Cash	%Stocks	%Bonds	%Other	Turnover Ratio	BULL & BEAR Last Bull Market Total Return	Last Bear Market Total Return	FEES Front End Fee (%)	Back End Fee (%)	Inception Date
	-6.66	-12.04	-24.67	-39.43	-66.06	0	1.72	12.95		62.92	12.7	66	0	7	28	486	-24.28	7.83			Sep-14
	-6.61	-11.94	-24.47	-38.99	-65.65	0	1.48	12.91		65.67	12.7	66	0	7	28	486	-24.17	7.95			Sep-98
	-6.58	-17.01	-26.62	-55.68	-84.04	0	1.73	27.09		48.83	11.8	34	15	43	9	0	-48.94	49.38	4.75		May-06
	-6.75	-17.31	-27.14	-56.64	-84.63	0	2.76	27.1		44.59	11.8	34	15	43	9	0	-49.05	49.45		1.00	May-06
	-6.58	-16.99	-26.61	-55.71	-83.96	0	1.84	27.09		48.64	11.8	34	15	43	9	0	-49.11	49.56			May-06
	-3.31	-8.61	-13.54	-31.23	-57.98	0	1.72	13.74		21	11.6	84	-3	10	8	58	-26.44	25.05	4.75		Mar-04
	-3.46	-8.99	-14.19	-32.76	-59.46	0	2.48	13.74		18.92	11.6	84	-3	10	8	58	-26.76	24.66		1.00	Feb-04
	-3.21	-8.59	-13.54	-31.24	-57.91	0	1.73	13.75		21.06	11.6	84	-3	10	8	58	-26.43	25.03			Feb-04
	-11.77	-19.08	-32.51	-53.36	-82.43	0	1.8	18.75		45.11	33.0	52	-3	52	0	78	-40.71	28.42	4.75		Sep-04
	-11.96	-19.42	-33.05	-54.46	-83.10	0	2.54	18.74		39.65	33.0	52	-3	52	0	78	-40.97	28.05		1.00	Mar-01
	-11.79	-19.10	-32.54	-53.37	-82.44	0	1.8	18.78		45.23	33.0	52	-3	52	0	78	-40.65	28.61			May-00
	-6.01	-9.87	-17.57	-30.44	-57.35	0	1.68	9.56		57.01	73.9	38	-2	51	13	114	-22.38	14.92	4.75		Mar-04
	-6.20	-10.23	-18.19	-32.00	-58.95	0	2.43	9.58		51.57	73.9	38	-2	51	13	114	-22.72	14.55		1.00	Mar-01
	-6.01	-9.87	-17.57	-30.49	-57.38	0	1.68	9.57		57.01	73.9	38	-2	51	13	114	-22.38	14.89			Sep-14
	-5.96	-9.76	-17.37	-29.90	-56.81	0	1.43	9.56		61.61	73.9	38	-2	51	13	114	-22.27	15.01			Jan-94
	22.49	26.17	50.96	84.46	143.16	0	1.54	22.35		136.77	6.8	69	21	6	4	1,225	10.86	-20.48	4.75		Feb-08
	22.26	25.70	49.82	80.42	135.37	0	2.29	22.33		127.54	6.8	69	21	6	4	1,225	10.44	-20.78		1.00	Feb-08
	22.48	26.23	51.06	85.05	144.28	0	1.54	22.35		137.81	6.8	69	21	6	4	1,225	10.83	-20.49			Feb-08
	6.00	6.11	20.21	31.49	106.57	0	1.62	10.67	0.96	67.75	19.3	5	100	0	-5	352	30.93	-18.67	4.75		Sep-04
	5.79	5.71	19.32	28.58	98.93	0	2.37	10.68	0.96	61.01	19.3	5	100	0	-5	352	30.41	-18.9		1.00	May-01
	6.05	6.22	20.51	32.50	109.17	0	1.38	10.68	0.96	73.28	19.3	5	100	0	-5	352	31.15	-18.58			Apr-98
	6.00	6.11	20.22	31.37	105.40	0	1.63	10.68	0.96	65.95	19.3	5	100	0	-5	352	30.77	-18.74			Jun-98
	8.89	13.57	22.59	46.96	156.34	0	1.69	16.68		92.37	373.5	9	89	1	1	1,216	40.92	-33.74	4.75		Mar-04
	8.69	13.14	21.71	43.70	146.98	0	2.43	16.67		80.88	373.5	9	89	1	1	1,216	40.31	-33.94		1.00	Aug-01
	8.88	13.55	22.67	47.33	157.08	0	1.69	16.66		92.74	373.5	9	89	1	1	1,216	41.13	-33.72			Aug-01
	13.84	27.05	69.79	122.43		0	1.35	26.82		108.28	51.3	16	77	1	6	259			4.75		Nov-14
	13.63	26.58	68.51	117.08		0	2.1	26.82		105.61	51.3	16	77	1	6	259				1.00	Nov-14
	13.84	27.05	69.79	127.83		0	1.35	26.53		110.91	51.3	16	77	1	6	259					Nov-14
	13.69	26.57	68.94	104.91	436.88	0	1.83	27.9		123.53	444.1	20	78	2	-1	167	58.36	-23.43	4.75		Sep-04
	13.46	26.09	67.63	100.27	416.85	0	2.58	27.88		99.48	444.1	20	78	2	-1	167	57.69	-23.69		1.00	Nov-00
	13.68	26.56	68.90	104.85	436.76	0	1.83	27.9		123.48	444.1	20	78	2	-1	167	58.35	-23.43			May-00
	6.87	12.98	30.91	48.04	142.12	0	1.53	13.6	1	31.37	1,111	2	89	8	1	72	26.94	-11.07	4.75		Mar-04
	6.61	12.53	29.90	44.84	133.39	0	2.28	13.56	1	27.58	1,111	2	89	8	1	72	26.46	-11.37		1.00	Mar-01
	6.84	12.98	30.92	48.06	141.92	0	1.54	13.59	1	31.36	1,111	2	89	8	1	72	26.96	-11.09			Sep-14
	6.91	13.12	31.20	49.30	145.30	0	1.29	13.58	1	33.99	1,111	2	89	8	1	72	27.15	-10.99			Feb-94
	9.37	15.99	30.70	47.10	169.95	0	1.53	15.34		66.28	514.1	13	82	3	3	1,288	37.76	-25.08	4.75		Mar-04
	9.18	15.62	29.93	43.94	160.17	0	2.27	15.33		59.27	514.1	13	82	3	3	1,288	37.12	-25.29		1.00	Mar-01
	9.38	16.06	30.95	47.27	170.19	0	1.52	15.34		66.37	514.1	13	82	3	3	1,288	37.68	-25.03			Sep-14
	9.44	16.23	31.18	48.26	173.29	0	1.28	15.34		71.28	514.1	13	82	3	3	1,288	37.88	-24.96			Jul-93
	1.31	3.72	6.78	21.01	-45.00	0	1.52	43.96	0.03	27.95	59.5	6	100	0	-6	508	-8.65	-22.58	4.75		Sep-04
	1.11	3.34	5.97	18.47	-46.96	0	2.27	43.96	0.02	24.09	59.5	6	100	0	-6	508	-9.03	-22.82		1.00	Apr-01
	1.28	3.69	6.69	20.74	-45.39	0	1.52	43.98	0.03	27.06	59.5	6	100	0	-6	508	-8.77	-22.66			Aug-03
	1.39	3.84	7.07	22.10	-44.23	0	1.27	43.98	0.02	29.25	59.5	6	100	0	-6	508	-8.51	-22.48			Dec-93
	1.74	2.35	6.26	11.32	42.51	0	1.63	11.9	0.7	38.76	28.5	2	99	0	-1	1,060	28.76	-19.69	4.75		Sep-04
	1.56	1.98	5.49	8.84	37.19	0	2.38	11.89	0.7	34.13	28.5	2	99	0	-1	1,060	28.13	-19.98		1.00	Feb-04
	1.72	2.39	6.25	11.29	42.37	0	1.62	11.9	0.7	38.65	28.5	2	99	0	-1	1,060	28.76	-19.71			Feb-04
	8.90	11.53	12.60	11.22	69.45	0	1.62	12.18	0.89	28.14	22.6	6	100	0	-5	887	27.86	-11.08	4.75		Sep-04
	8.65	11.11	11.75	8.70	63.02	0	2.37	12.15	0.89	25.1	22.6	6	100	0	-5	887	27.27	-11.31		1.00	May-01
	8.88	11.53	12.58	11.08	68.39	0	1.62	12.14	0.89	27.46	22.6	6	100	0	-5	887	27.56	-11.13			Apr-98
	8.92	11.62	12.81	11.96	71.18	0	1.37	12.17	0.89	29.66	22.6	6	100	0	-5	887	28.04	-10.94			Apr-98
	4.33	12.78	20.19	40.21	142.04	0	1.74	21.19		65.17	90.3	77	17	1	5	1,315	40.25	-37.27	4.75		Mar-04
	4.14	12.35	19.29	37.07	133.08	0	2.48	21.18		55.82	90.3	77	17	1	5	1,315	39.66	-37.46		1.00	Jan-01

	MARKET		FUND TYPE, CATEGORY & OBJECTIVE		RATINGS				MINIMUMS	
Fund Name	Ticker Symbol	Traded On	Fund Type	Category and (Prospectus Objective)	Overall Rating	Reward Rating	Risk Rating	Recent Up/ Downgrade	Open to New Investors	Min Initial Investment
Rydex Russell 2000 1.5x Strategy Fund Class H	RYMKX	NAS CM	Open End	Trading Tools (Growth)	B+	A	C+	Up	Y	2,500
Rydex Russell 2000 2x Strategy Fund Class A	RYRUX	NAS CM	Open End	Trading Tools (Growth)	B+	A+	C	Up	Y	2,500
Rydex Russell 2000 2x Strategy Fund Class C	RYRLX	NAS CM	Open End	Trading Tools (Growth)	B+	A+	C	Up	Y	2,500
Rydex Russell 2000 2x Strategy Fund Class H	RYRSX	NAS CM	Open End	Trading Tools (Growth)	B+	A+	C	Up	Y	2,500
Rydex Russell 2000 Fund Class A	RYRRX	NAS CM	Open End	US Equity Small Cap (Growth)	B	B	B	Up	Y	2,500
Rydex Russell 2000 Fund Class C	RYROX	NAS CM	Open End	US Equity Small Cap (Growth)	B	B	B	Up	Y	2,500
Rydex Russell 2000 Fund Class H	RYRHX	NAS CM	Open End	US Equity Small Cap (Growth)	B	B	B	Up	Y	2,500
Rydex S&P 500 2x Strategy Fund Class A	RYTTX	NAS CM	Open End	Trading Tools (Growth)	B+	A+	C+	Up	Y	2,500
Rydex S&P 500 2x Strategy Fund Class C	RYCTX	NAS CM	Open End	Trading Tools (Growth)	B+	A+	C+	Up	Y	2,500
Rydex S&P 500 2x Strategy Fund Class H	RYTNX	NAS CM	Open End	Trading Tools (Growth)	B+	A+	C+	Up	Y	2,500
Rydex S&P 500 Fund Class A	RYSOX	NAS CM	Open End	US Equity Large Cap Blend (Growth)	B-	B-	B	Down	Y	2,500
Rydex S&P 500 Fund Class C	RYSYX	NAS CM	Open End	US Equity Large Cap Blend (Growth)	B-	B-	B-	Down	Y	2,500
Rydex S&P 500 Fund Class H	RYSPX	NAS CM	Open End	US Equity Large Cap Blend (Growth)	B-	B-	B	Down	Y	2,500
Rydex S&P 500 Pure Growth Fund Class A	RYLGX	NAS CM	Open End	US Equity Large Cap Growth (Growth)	B	B	B+	Up	Y	2,500
Rydex S&P 500 Pure Growth Fund Class C	RYGRX	NAS CM	Open End	US Equity Large Cap Growth (Growth)	B	B-	B	Up	Y	2,500
Rydex S&P 500 Pure Growth Fund Class H	RYAWX	NAS CM	Open End	US Equity Large Cap Growth (Growth)	B	B	B+	Up	Y	2,500
Rydex S&P 500 Pure Value Fund Class A	RYLVX	NAS CM	Open End	US Equity Large Cap Value (Growth)	C+	B-	C+	Down	Y	2,500
Rydex S&P 500 Pure Value Fund Class C	RYVVX	NAS CM	Open End	US Equity Large Cap Value (Growth)	C+	C+	C+	Down	Y	2,500
Rydex S&P 500 Pure Value Fund Class H	RYZAX	NAS CM	Open End	US Equity Large Cap Value (Growth)	C+	B-	C+	Down	Y	2,500
Rydex S&P MidCap 400 Pure Growth Fund Class A	RYMGX	NAS CM	Open End	US Equity Mid Cap (Growth)	B-	C+	B	Up	Y	2,500
Rydex S&P MidCap 400 Pure Growth Fund Class C	RYCKX	NAS CM	Open End	US Equity Mid Cap (Growth)	B-	C+	B	Up	Y	2,500
Rydex S&P MidCap 400 Pure Growth Fund Class H	RYBHX	NAS CM	Open End	US Equity Mid Cap (Growth)	B-	C+	B	Up	Y	2,500
Rydex S&P MidCap 400 Pure Value Fund Class A	RYMVX	NAS CM	Open End	US Equity Small Cap (Growth)	B	B	B-	Up	Y	2,500
Rydex S&P MidCap 400 Pure Value Fund Class C	RYMMX	NAS CM	Open End	US Equity Small Cap (Growth)	B-	B	C+	Up	Y	2,500
Rydex S&P MidCap 400 Pure Value Fund Class H	RYAVX	NAS CM	Open End	US Equity Small Cap (Growth)	B	B	B-	Up	Y	2,500
Rydex S&P SmallCap 600 Pure Growth Fund Class A	RYSGX	NAS CM	Open End	US Equity Small Cap (Small Company)	B+	A-	B	Up	Y	2,500
Rydex S&P SmallCap 600 Pure Growth Fund Class C	RYWCX	NAS CM	Open End	US Equity Small Cap (Small Company)	B+	A-	B	Up	Y	2,500
Rydex S&P SmallCap 600 Pure Growth Fund Class H	RYWAX	NAS CM	Open End	US Equity Small Cap (Small Company)	B+	A-	B	Up	Y	2,500
Rydex S&P SmallCap 600 Pure Value Fund Class A	RYSVX	NAS CM	Open End	US Equity Small Cap (Small Company)	C	C+	C	Up	Y	2,500
Rydex S&P SmallCap 600 Pure Value Fund Class C	RYYCX	NAS CM	Open End	US Equity Small Cap (Small Company)	C	C+	C	Up	Y	2,500
Rydex S&P SmallCap 600 Pure Value Fund Class H	RYAZX	NAS CM	Open End	US Equity Small Cap (Small Company)	C+	C+	C	Up	Y	2,500
Rydex Strengthening Dollar 2x Strategy Fund Class A	RYSDX	NAS CM	Open End	Trading Tools (Growth)	D+	D+	D+	Down	Y	2,500
Rydex Strengthening Dollar 2x Strategy Fund Class C	RYSJX	NAS CM	Open End	Trading Tools (Growth)	D+	D	D+	Down	Y	2,500
Rydex Strengthening Dollar 2x Strategy Fund Class H	RYSBX	NAS CM	Open End	Trading Tools (Growth)	D+	D+	D+	Down	Y	2,500
Rydex Technology Fund Class A	RYTHX	NAS CM	Open End	Technology Sector Equity (Technology)	B+	A	B-	Down	Y	2,500
Rydex Technology Fund Class C	RYCHX	NAS CM	Open End	Technology Sector Equity (Technology)	B+	A	B-	Down	Y	2,500
Rydex Technology Fund Class H	RYTAX	NAS CM	Open End	Technology Sector Equity (Technology)	B+	A	B-	Up	Y	2,500
Rydex Technology Fund Class Investor	RYTIX	NAS CM	Open End	Technology Sector Equity (Technology)	B+	A	B-	Down	Y	2,500
Rydex Telecommunications Fund Class A	RYTLX	NAS CM	Open End	Communications Sector Equity (Comm)	C+	C+	C+	Down	Y	2,500
Rydex Telecommunications Fund Class C	RYCSX	NAS CM	Open End	Communications Sector Equity (Comm)	C+	C	C+		Y	2,500
Rydex Telecommunications Fund Class H	RYMAX	NAS CM	Open End	Communications Sector Equity (Comm)	C+	C+	C+	Down	Y	2,500
Rydex Telecommunications Fund Class Investor	RYMIX	NAS CM	Open End	Communications Sector Equity (Comm)	C+	C+	C+	Down	Y	2,500
Rydex Transportation Fund Class A	RYTSX	NAS CM	Open End	Industrials Sector Equity ()	B	B	B-	Up	Y	2,500
Rydex Transportation Fund Class C	RYCNX	NAS CM	Open End	Industrials Sector Equity ()	B-	B-	B-	Up	Y	2,500
Rydex Transportation Fund Class H	RYPAX	NAS CM	Open End	Industrials Sector Equity ()	B-	B	B-	Up	Y	2,500
Rydex Transportation Fund Class Investor	RYPIX	NAS CM	Open End	Industrials Sector Equity ()	B	B	B-	Up	Y	2,500
Rydex Utilities Fund Class A	RYUTX	NAS CM	Open End	Utilities Sector Equity (Utility)	B-	B-	B	Down	Y	2,500
Rydex Utilities Fund Class C	RYCUX	NAS CM	Open End	Utilities Sector Equity (Utility)	B-	B-	B-	Down	Y	2,500
Rydex Utilities Fund Class H	RYAUX	NAS CM	Open End	Utilities Sector Equity (Utility)	B-	B-	B	Down	Y	2,500
Rydex Utilities Fund Class Investor	RYUIX	NAS CM	Open End	Utilities Sector Equity (Utility)	B	B	B	Down	Y	2,500
Rydex Weakening Dollar 2x Strategy Fund Class A	RYWDX	NAS CM	Open End	Trading Tools (Growth)	C-	C-	D+	Up	Y	2,500
Rydex Weakening Dollar 2x Strategy Fund Class C	RYWJX	NAS CM	Open End	Trading Tools (Growth)	C-	C-	D+	Up	Y	2,500

★ Expanded analysis of this fund is included in Section II.

	TOTAL RETURNS					PERFORMANCE				ASSETS		ASSET ALLOCATION & TURNOVER					BULL & BEAR		FEES		
Min Additional Investment	3-Month Total Return	6-Month Total Return	1-Year Total Return	3-Year Total Return	5-Year Total Return	Dividend Yield (TTM)	Expense Ratio	3-Yr Std Deviation	3-Year Beta	NAV	Total Assets (MIL)	%Cash	%Stocks	%Bonds	%Other	Turnover Ratio	Last Bull Market Total Return	Last Bear Market Total Return	Front End Fee (%)	Back End Fee (%)	Inception Date
	4.20	12.61	20.06	39.94	141.70	0	1.74	21.15		64.92	90.3	77	17	1	5	1,315	40.3	-37.27			Nov-00
	5.65	16.65	25.59	49.14	203.99	0	1.82	28.48		146.14	47.7	36	21	31	11	810	52.36	-47.76	4.75		May-06
	5.46	16.21	24.65	45.86	193.03	0	2.58	28.48		132.51	47.7	36	21	31	11	810	51.73	-47.89		1.00	May-06
	5.64	16.64	25.56	49.07	203.66	0	1.85	28.48		145.81	47.7	36	21	31	11	810	52.3	-47.77			May-06
	2.89	8.34	12.91	25.27	81.39	0	1.62	14.12	1	43.89	49.9	8	83	12	-3	203	27.33	-25.54	4.75		May-06
	2.71	7.93	12.06	22.53	74.53	0	2.38	14.1	1	39.53	49.9	8	83	12	-3	203	26.71	-25.82		1.00	May-06
	2.89	8.33	12.89	25.24	81.06	0	1.63	14.14	1	43.78	49.9	8	83	12	-3	203	27.31	-25.56			May-06
	12.65	21.75	43.02	64.36	265.48	0	1.79	20.62		108.58	163.6	21	77	0	2	411	50.93	-33.02	4.75		Sep-04
	12.45	21.30	41.94	60.69	251.92	0	2.54	20.59		93.82	163.6	21	77	0	2	411	50.4	-33.19		1.00	Nov-00
	12.66	21.76	43.00	64.31	265.16	0	1.8	20.61		108.44	163.6	21	77	0	2	411	50.98	-33.06			May-00
	6.21	10.51	19.84	30.29	94.74	0.1	1.57	10.06	1	49.28	266.2	18	82	0	0	133	23.95	-16.83	4.75		May-06
	6.00	10.11	18.95	27.34	87.55	0.11	2.33	10.06	1	44.59	266.2	18	82	0	0	133	23.39	-17.15		1.00	May-06
	6.19	10.51	19.85	30.23	94.70	0.1	1.58	10.06	1	49.27	266.2	18	82	0	0	133	24.01	-16.8			May-06
	4.55	10.93	24.69	28.02	109.19	0	1.53	10.71	1	63.68	148.8	1	100	0	0	184	23.27	-17.95	4.75		Sep-04
	4.35	10.51	23.77	25.17	101.46	0	2.27	10.7	1	56.7	148.8	1	100	0	0	184	22.76	-18.21		1.00	Feb-04
	4.55	10.93	24.69	28.03	109.22	0	1.52	10.71	1	63.67	148.8	1	100	0	0	184	23.28	-17.93			Feb-04
	7.71	11.64	15.94	21.85	102.45	0	1.53	13.42	1	85.47	94.3	1	100	0	0	321	22.91	-22.15	4.75		Sep-04
	7.51	11.22	15.08	19.13	94.99	0	2.28	13.41	1	74.53	94.3	1	100	0	0	321	22.39	-22.39		1.00	Feb-04
	7.70	11.64	15.93	21.84	102.44	0	1.53	13.42	1	85.79	94.3	1	100	0	0	321	22.91	-22.15			Feb-04
	6.52	9.59	18.94	22.90	67.91	0	1.52	11.72	0.99	53.96	126.2	2	100	0	-2	127	22.48	-18.48	4.75		Sep-04
	6.33	9.18	18.07	20.16	61.74	0	2.27	11.72	0.99	46.88	126.2	2	100	0	-2	127	21.93	-18.73		1.00	Feb-04
	6.52	9.58	18.94	22.89	67.89	0	1.53	11.73	0.99	54.02	126.2	2	100	0	-2	127	22.45	-18.48			Feb-04
	7.88	10.51	13.14	26.09	87.50	0	1.53	17.01	1	56.49	34.1	5	100	0	-4	628	28.11	-24.86	4.75		Sep-04
	7.68	10.11	12.31	23.31	80.58	0	2.28	17	1	50.26	34.1	5	100	0	-4	628	27.51	-25.1		1.00	Feb-04
	7.87	10.50	13.11	26.10	87.39	0	1.53	17.02	1	56.42	34.1	5	100	0	-4	628	28.08	-24.84			Feb-04
	3.00	9.77	16.15	35.99	97.55	0	1.52	14.83	1	71.11	18.7	5	99	0	-4	818	25.65	-20.41	4.75		Sep-04
	2.79	9.35	15.26	32.94	90.23	0	2.28	14.82	1	63.93	18.7	5	99	0	-4	818	25.14	-20.69		1.00	Feb-04
	2.98	9.74	16.14	35.98	97.44	0	1.53	14.84	1	71.09	18.7	5	99	0	-4	818	25.69	-20.46			Feb-04
	4.12	9.43	-0.92	12.12	64.34	0	1.53	20.44	0.99	28.76	14.8	3	99	0	-2	1,449	27.54	-26.21	4.75		Sep-04
	3.88	8.99	-1.70	9.56	58.28	0	2.28	20.46	0.99	24.85	14.8	3	99	0	-2	1,449	26.88	-26.49		1.00	Feb-04
	4.13	9.66	-0.72	12.32	64.65	0	1.53	20.45	0.99	28.7	14.8	3	99	0	-2	1,449	27.39	-26.27			Feb-04
	-1.28	-6.18	-18.13	-0.15	18.64	0	1.74	14.91		45.36	13.3	84	0	1	14	142	-5.04	13.38	4.75		May-05
	-1.46	-6.52	-18.75	-2.37	14.26	0	2.49	14.9		40.94	13.3	84	0	1	14	142	-5.4	12.87		1.00	May-05
	-1.28	-6.18	-18.13	-0.15	18.64	0	1.74	14.89		45.18	13.3	84	0	1	14	142	-5	13.37			May-05
	5.77	14.22	32.72	47.81	125.34	0	1.63	13.94	1.22	83.43	118.4	4	100	0	-3	320	23.38	-22.02	4.75		Sep-04
	5.55	13.78	31.74	44.54	117.03	0	2.37	13.93	1.22	75.69	118.4	4	100	0	-3	320	22.79	-22.29		1.00	Apr-01
	5.76	14.21	32.73	47.57	123.87	0	1.63	13.94	1.22	81.67	118.4	4	100	0	-3	320	23.08	-22.05			Apr-98
	5.83	14.36	33.07	48.91	128.23	0	1.38	13.94	1.22	89.24	118.4	4	100	0	-3	320	23.66	-21.94			Apr-98
	3.88	5.57	5.55	13.79	39.38	0	1.62	11.86	0.98	43.98	2.6	4	99	0	-3	605	12.54	-23.1	4.75		Sep-04
	3.70	5.18	4.78	11.33	35.44	0	2.37	11.86	0.98	39.38	2.6	4	99	0	-3	605	12.23	-23.44		1.00	Apr-01
	3.86	5.56	5.58	13.69	38.50	0	1.62	11.86	0.98	42.79	2.6	4	99	0	-3	605	12.35	-23.23			Apr-98
	3.96	5.71	5.82	14.88	41.43	0	1.38	11.87	0.98	47.79	2.6	4	99	0	-3	605	12.62	-23.04			Apr-98
	5.71	12.41	22.10	20.26	127.67	0	1.63	15.13	1.19	57.26	40.1	4	99	0	-4	676	24.43	-25.98	4.75		Sep-04
	5.53	12.01	21.21	17.57	119.25	0	2.38	15.13	1.19	52.74	40.1	4	99	0	-4	676	23.82	-26.13		1.00	May-01
	5.72	12.40	22.10	20.10	126.21	0	1.63	15.13	1.19	55.66	40.1	4	99	0	-4	676	24.25	-26.02			Jun-98
	5.79	12.57	22.42	21.17	130.50	0	1.38	15.13	1.19	62.14	40.1	4	99	0	-4	676	24.61	-25.92			Apr-98
	0.24	3.21	11.04	17.64	69.36	0	1.63	11.9	0.27	37.2	50.6	0	99	0	0	507	9.47	-2.13	4.75		Sep-04
	0.06	2.85	10.24	15.07	63.15	0	2.37	11.89	0.28	31.48	50.6	0	99	0	0	507	9.01	-2.51		1.00	Apr-01
	0.27	3.25	11.12	17.60	68.37	0	1.62	11.92	0.27	35.84	50.6	0	99	0	0	507	9.35	-2.21			Apr-00
	0.31	3.37	11.36	18.52	71.50	0	1.38	11.92	0.27	40.34	50.6	0	99	0	0	507	9.68	-2.03			Apr-00
	0.83	5.40	18.86	-11.51	-32.44	0	1.73	14.75		74.91	3.3	51	0	34	15	77	1.17	-14.55	4.75		May-05
	0.62	4.99	17.98	-13.51	-34.93	0	2.48	14.75		67.3	3.3	51	0	34	15	77	0.84	-14.82		1.00	May-05

	MARKET			FUND TYPE, CATEGORY & OBJECTIVE	RATINGS				MINIMUMS	
Fund Name	Ticker Symbol	Traded On	Fund Type	Category and (Prospectus Objective)	Overall Rating	Reward Rating	Risk Rating	Recent Up/ Downgrade	Open to New Investors	Min Initial Investment
Rydex Weakening Dollar 2x Strategy Fund Class H	RYWBX	NAS CM	Open End	Trading Tools (Growth)	C-	C-	D+	Up	Y	2,500
SA Emerging Markets Value Fund Investor Class	SAEMX	NAS CM	Open End	Emerging Markets Equity (Div Emerging Mkts)	C+	B-	C	Up	Y	0
SA Emerging Markets Value Fund Select Class	SAELX	NAS CM	Open End	Emerging Markets Equity (Div Emerging Mkts)	C+	B-	C	Up	Y	100,000
SA International Small Company Fund Investor Class	SAISX	NAS CM	Open End	Global Equity Mid/Small Cap (Foreign Stock)	B	B	B+	Up	Y	0
SA International Small Company Fund Select Class	SACLX	NAS CM	Open End	Global Equity Mid/Small Cap (Foreign Stock)	B+	B	B+	Up	Y	100,000
SA International Value Fund Investor Class	SAHMX	NAS CM	Open End	Global Equity Large Cap (Foreign Stock)	B-	B-	B-	Up	Y	0
SA International Value Fund Select Class	SATLX	NAS CM	Open End	Global Equity Large Cap (Foreign Stock)	C+	B-	C	Up	Y	100,000
SA Real Estate Securities Fund Investor Class	SAREX	NAS CM	Open End	Real Estate Sector Equity (Real Estate)	B-	C+	B		Y	0
SA Real Estate Securities Fund Select Class	SARLX	NAS CM	Open End	Real Estate Sector Equity (Real Estate)	B-	C+	B		Y	100,000
SA U.S. Core Market Fund Investor Class	SAMKX	NAS CM	Open End	US Equity Large Cap Blend (Growth)	B	B	B		Y	0
SA U.S. Core Market Fund Select Class	SAALX	NAS CM	Open End	US Equity Large Cap Blend (Growth)	B	B	B		Y	100,000
SA U.S. Small Company Fund Investor Class	SAUMX	NAS CM	Open End	US Equity Small Cap (Small Company)	B	B+	B	Up	Y	0
SA U.S. Small Company Fund Select Class	SASLX	NAS CM	Open End	US Equity Small Cap (Small Company)	B	B+	B	Up	Y	100,000
SA U.S. Value Fund Investor Class	SABTX	NAS CM	Open End	US Equity Large Cap Value (Growth)	B	B	B	Up	Y	0
SA U.S. Value Fund Select Class	SAVLX	NAS CM	Open End	US Equity Large Cap Value (Growth)	B	B	B		Y	100,000
SA Worldwide Moderate Growth Fund	SAWMX	NAS CM	Open End	Moderate Alloc (Growth & Income)	C	C+	B	Up	Y	5,000
Salient Adaptive Balanced Fund Class A	AOGAX	NAS CM	Open End	Moderate Alloc (Growth)	C	C	B-	Up	Y	2,500
Salient Adaptive Balanced Fund Class C	AGGGX	NAS CM	Open End	Moderate Alloc (Growth)	C	C	B-	Up	Y	2,500
Salient Adaptive Balanced Fund Institutional Class	ACGAX	NAS CM	Open End	Moderate Alloc (Growth)	C+	C	B-	Up	Y	100,000
Salient Adaptive Balanced Fund Investor Class	AGALX	NAS CM	Open End	Moderate Alloc (Growth)	C	C	B-	Up	Y	2,500
Salient Adaptive Growth Fund Class A	SRPAX	NAS CM	Open End	Moderate Alloc (Growth & Income)	B-	B-	B-	Up	Y	2,500
Salient Adaptive Growth Fund Class C	SRPCX	NAS CM	Open End	Moderate Alloc (Growth & Income)	C+	C+	B-	Up	Y	2,500
Salient Adaptive Growth Fund Class I	SRPFX	NAS CM	Open End	Moderate Alloc (Growth & Income)	B-	B-	B-	Up	Y	1,000,000
Salient Adaptive Income Fund Class A	AILAX	NAS CM	Open End	Moderate Alloc (Multisector Bond)	C+	C	B-	Up	Y	2,500
Salient Adaptive Income Fund Class C	AIACX	NAS CM	Open End	Moderate Alloc (Multisector Bond)	C+	C	B-	Up	Y	2,500
Salient Adaptive Income Fund Institutional Class	AIAAX	NAS CM	Open End	Moderate Alloc (Multisector Bond)	C+	C	B-	Up	Y	100,000
Salient Adaptive Income Fund Investor Class	AIAIX	NAS CM	Open End	Moderate Alloc (Multisector Bond)	C+	C	B-	Up	Y	2,500
Salient Adaptive US Equity Fund Institutional Class	ASMCX	NAS CM	Open End	US Equity Large Cap Blend (Growth)	B	B	B+	Up	Y	100,000
Salient Adaptive US Equity Fund Investor Class	ACSIX	NAS CM	Open End	US Equity Large Cap Blend (Growth)	B	B	B+	Up	Y	2,500
Salient EM Infrastructure Fund Class A	KGIAX	NAS CM	Open End	Other Sector Equity (Utility)	C+	C	B-	Up	Y	2,500
Salient EM Infrastructure Fund Class C	KGICX	NAS CM	Open End	Other Sector Equity (Utility)	C	C	C+		Y	2,500
Salient EM Infrastructure Fund Institutional Class	KGIYX	NAS CM	Open End	Other Sector Equity (Utility)	C+	C	B-	Up	Y	100,000
Salient EM Infrastructure Fund Investor Class	FGLRX	NAS CM	Open End	Other Sector Equity (Utility)	C+	C	B-	Up	Y	2,500
Salient International Dividend Signal Fund Class A	FFDAX	NAS CM	Open End	Global Equity Large Cap (Foreign Stock)	C+	C+	B-	Up	Y	2,500
Salient International Dividend Signal Fund Class C	FINCX	NAS CM	Open End	Global Equity Large Cap (Foreign Stock)	C+	C+	B-	Up	Y	2,500
Salient International Dividend Signal Fund Class Investor	FFINX	NAS CM	Open End	Global Equity Large Cap (Foreign Stock)	C+	C+	B-	Up	Y	2,500
Salient Intl Dividend Signal Fund Inst Cls	FFIEX	NAS CM	Open End	Global Equity Large Cap (Foreign Stock)	C+	C+	B-	Up	Y	100,000
Salient International Real Estate Fund Class A	KIRAX	NAS CM	Open End	Real Estate Sector Equity (Real Estate)	C+	C+	B-	Up	Y	2,500
Salient International Real Estate Fund Class C	KIRCX	NAS CM	Open End	Real Estate Sector Equity (Real Estate)	C+	C+	B-	Up	Y	2,500
Salient International Real Estate Fund Institutional Class	KIRYX	NAS CM	Open End	Real Estate Sector Equity (Real Estate)	B-	C+	B-	Up	Y	100,000
Salient International Real Estate Fund Investor Class	FFIRX	NAS CM	Open End	Real Estate Sector Equity (Real Estate)	C+	C+	B-	Up	Y	2,500
Salient International Small Cap Fund Class Investor	PISRX	NAS CM	Open End	Global Equity Mid/Small Cap (Foreign Stock)	A-	A-	A-	Up	Y	2,500
Salient International Small Cap Fund Institutional Class	PTSCX	NAS CM	Open End	Global Equity Mid/Small Cap (Foreign Stock)	A-	A-	A-	Up	Y	100,000
Salient Midstream & MLP Fund	SMM	NYSE	Closed End	Energy Sector Equity (Natl Res)	D	D	D	Down	Y	
Salient MLP & Energy Infrastructure Fund Class A	SMAPX	NAS CM	Open End	Energy Sector Equity (Utility)	D	D	D	Down	Y	2,500
Salient MLP & Energy Infrastructure Fund Class C	SMFPX	NAS CM	Open End	Energy Sector Equity (Utility)	D	D	D	Down	Y	2,500
Salient MLP & Energy Infrastructure Fund Class I	SMLPX	NAS CM	Open End	Energy Sector Equity (Utility)	D	D+	D	Down	Y	1,000,000
Salient MLP & Energy Infrastructure Fund R6 Shares	SMRPX	NAS CM	Open End	Energy Sector Equity (Utility)	D	D	D	Down	Y	1,000,000
Salient Real Estate Fund Class A	KREAX	NAS CM	Open End	Real Estate Sector Equity (Real Estate)	C	C	C+	Down	Y	2,500
Salient Real Estate Fund Class C	KRECX	NAS CM	Open End	Real Estate Sector Equity (Real Estate)	C	C	C	Down	Y	2,500
Salient Real Estate Fund Institutional Class	FPREX	NAS CM	Open End	Real Estate Sector Equity (Real Estate)	C	C	B-	Down	Y	100,000
Salient Real Estate Fund Investor Class	FFREX	NAS CM	Open End	Real Estate Sector Equity (Real Estate)	C	C	C+	Down	Y	2,500

★Expanded analysis of this fund is included in Section II.

	TOTAL RETURNS					PERFORMANCE				ASSETS		ASSET ALLOCATION & TURNOVER					BULL & BEAR		FEES		
Min Additional Investment	3-Month Total Return	6-Month Total Return	1-Year Total Return	3-Year Total Return	5-Year Total Return	Dividend Yield (TTM)	Expense Ratio	3-Yr Std Deviation	3-Year Beta	NAV	Total Assets (MIL)	%Cash	%Stocks	%Bonds	%Other	Turnover Ratio	Last Bull Market Total Return	Last Bear Market Total Return	Front End Fee (%)	Back End Fee (%)	Inception Date
	0.82	5.39	18.87	-11.48	-32.40	0	1.72	14.72		74.83	3.3	51	0	34	15	77	1.22	-14.56			May-05
	7.97	13.39	31.23	22.80	9.78	0.97	1.4	17.64	1.03	10.7	217.2	0	98	0	1	21	13.89	-30.15			Apr-07
	8.15	13.58	31.46	23.01	9.97		1.2	17.64	1.03	10.71	217.2	0	98	0	1	21	13.89	-30.15			Jul-17
	4.38	11.37	29.01	41.33	67.18	1.46	1.49	11.03	0.93	23.58	371.7	1	95	0	3	0	13.75	-23.71			Aug-99
	4.42	11.52	29.73	44.83	74.77		1.29	11.02	0.93	23.57	371.7	1	95	0	3	0	14.39	-23.36			Jul-17
	5.52	14.09	25.03	24.45	42.39	2.38	1.13	14.34	1.09	12.47	758.5	0	98	0	2	17	10.05	-26.29			Aug-99
	5.57	14.14	25.09	24.50	42.45		0.93	14.34	1.09	12.47	758.5	0	98	0	2	17	10.05	-26.29			Jul-17
	1.88	2.60	4.53	13.17	51.91	2.95	1	13.46	0.99	11.34	173.8	0	100	0	0	7	30.61	-16.56			Apr-07
	1.93	2.74	4.67	13.33	52.12		0.8	13.46	0.99	11.34	173.8	0	100	0	0	7	30.61	-16.56			Jul-17
	7.13	12.12	22.19	34.50	104.92	1.04	0.95	10.09	0.98	23.39	780.5	0	100	0	0	8	24.68	-17.73			Aug-99
	7.18	12.16	22.24	34.55	105.01		0.75	10.1	0.98	23.37	780.5	0	100	0	0	8	24.68	-17.73			Jul-17
	3.64	9.40	11.34	29.17	94.76	0.27	1.2	13.63	0.95	26.12	430.9	0	100	0	0	12	27.75	-24.55			Aug-99
	3.72	9.52	11.47	29.31	94.97		1	13.63	0.95	26.13	430.9	0	100	0	0	12	27.75	-24.55			Jul-17
	7.22	11.97	18.37	33.60	108.00	1.19	1	11.87	1.13	18.79	607.9	0	100	0	0	16	25.41	-24.32			Aug-99
	7.30	12.11	18.52	33.76	108.26		0.8	11.88	1.13	18.79	607.9	0	100	0	0	16	25.41	-24.32			Jul-17
2,500	4.49	8.78	15.56			1.25	1.03			11.36	33.8	0	75	24	1	11					Jul-15
100	5.75	8.36	14.25	3.90	15.20	4.62	1.67	7.63	0.58	13.12	34.9	-44	80	52	10	100	15.96	-18.3	5.75		Sep-03
100	5.54	7.99	13.46	1.88	11.39	4.02	2.32	7.66	0.58	12.99	34.9	-44	80	52	10	100	15.47	-18.5		1.00	Dec-02
	5.81	8.51	14.60	5.05	17.15	4.97	1.32	7.62	0.58	13.12	34.9	-44	80	52	10	100	16.14	-18.13			Dec-00
100	5.70	8.27	14.06	3.47	14.22	4.47	1.82	7.65	0.58	13.13	34.9	-44	80	52	10	100	15.87	-18.32			Dec-00
100	7.67	11.58	16.81	18.01	28.56	2.29	1.64	11.95	0.56	7.12	52.0	-162	72	144	46				5.50		Nov-12
100	7.54	11.16	15.90	14.92	23.33	1.57	2.39	11.92	0.56	6.77	52.0	-162	72	144	46					1.00	Oct-12
	7.83	11.69	17.18	18.97	30.33	2.4	1.39	11.96	0.56	7.23	52.0	-162	72	144	46						Jul-12
100	2.25	5.20	9.37	7.73	19.05	3.11	1.69	5.42	0.38	13.86	12.8	6	38	46	1	127	4.67	0.5	3.75		Sep-03
100	1.99	4.76	8.52	5.27	14.63	2.5	2.44	5.38	0.37	13.74	12.8	6	38	46	1	127	4.16	0.27		1.00	Dec-02
	2.31	5.33	9.69	8.46	20.49	3.31	1.44	5.42	0.38	13.88	12.8	6	38	46	1	127	4.81	0.62			Dec-00
100	2.19	5.00	9.13	6.88	17.57	2.9	1.94	5.37	0.36	13.83	12.8	6	38	46	1	127	4.44	0.48			Dec-00
	9.14	15.98	24.50	34.29	103.17	1.07	0.92	10.94	0.95	38.99	18.7	-76	176	0	0	359	28.2	-26.69			Aug-92
100	9.04	15.71	23.97	32.69	99.39	0.83	1.37	10.94	0.95	35	18.7	-76	176	0	0	359	27.91	-26.82			Jun-98
100	2.93	6.30	16.91	9.99	23.82	4.18	1.6	12.21	0.71	22.94	29.1	5	91	1	2	105	20.15	-21.8	5.75		Jun-07
100	2.79	6.03	16.26	8.18	20.37	3.67	2.15	12.2	0.71	22.82	29.1	5	91	1	2	105	19.66	-22.06		1.00	Jun-07
	3.00	6.51	17.38	11.48	26.49	4.5	1.2	12.22	0.71	23.03	29.1	5	91	1	2	105	20.33	-21.68			Jun-07
100	2.93	6.38	16.91	10.22	24.21	4.25	1.55	12.2	0.71	23.08	29.1	5	91	1	2	105	20.1	-21.83			May-11
100	4.76	9.78	24.31	15.08	23.98	3.44	1.49	10.16	0.8	8.84	102.6	-2	94	3	3	90	17.62	-20.31	5.75		May-13
100	4.53	9.56	23.67	13.56	21.33	3.01	1.94	10.17	0.8	8.82	102.6	-2	94	3	3	90	17.34	-20.44		1.00	Jul-12
100	4.67	9.86	24.48	15.51	24.78	3.54	1.34	10.2	0.8	8.84	102.6	-2	94	3	3	90	17.68	-20.28			Oct-98
	4.93	10.23	24.89	16.87	27.12	4.76	0.99	10.18	0.8	7.08	102.6	-2	94	3	3	90	17.99	-20.27			May-07
100	6.53	9.95	21.30	16.39	15.11	5.45	2.32	11.51	0.92	14.74	22.1	2	98	0	0	80	40.33	-26.54	5.75		Apr-06
100	6.46	9.64	20.73	14.44	12.06	5.08	2.87	11.47	0.92	14.73	22.1	2	98	0	0	80	39.78	-26.79		1.00	Apr-06
	6.69	10.20	21.88	17.80	17.55	5.75	1.92	11.48	0.92	14.68	22.1	2	98	0	0	80	40.73	-26.49			Apr-06
100	6.68	10.08	21.43	16.69	15.65	5.46	2.27	11.5	0.92	14.81	22.1	2	98	0	0	80	40.22	-26.58			May-11
100	8.13	14.01	34.28	45.48	72.75	2.88	1.56	11.16	0.9	21.74	118.9	4	95	0	0	63	16.17	-26.76			Mar-02
	8.23	14.29	34.80	47.08	75.84	3.22	1.21	11.17	0.91	21.7	118.9	4	95	0	0	63	16.39	-26.65			Feb-96
	-2.09	-2.36	-14.28	-40.18	-7.24	0.32	2.59	34.34		11.98	199.0	-37	137	0	0	93					May-12
100	-0.47	0.67	-6.91	-26.44	8.01	6.23	1.44	24.66	1.13	8.18	1,292	0	99	0	0				5.50		Dec-12
100	-0.69	0.20	-7.68	-28.19	3.82	5.43	2.23	24.61	1.13	8.13	1,292	0	99	0	0					1.00	Jan-13
	-0.42	0.67	-6.76	-26.08	9.10	6.46	1.26	24.66	1.13	8.15	1,292	0	99	0	0						Sep-12
	-0.52	0.72	-6.69	-25.98	9.24	6.54	1.13	24.64	1.13	8.15	1,292	0	99	0	0						Jan-16
100	-0.96	-2.59	-4.01	6.95	44.05	1.58	1.92	13.37	0.94	10.91	31.1	9	91	0	0	81	32.17	-19.56	5.75		Jun-09
100	-1.01	-2.77	-4.45	5.24	40.22	1.1	2.47	13.37	0.94	11.07	31.1	9	91	0	0	81	31.59	-19.82		1.00	Jun-09
	-0.85	-2.33	-3.63	8.31	47.10	2.26	1.52	13.35	0.94	8.73	31.1	9	91	0	0	81	32.22	-19.42			May-08
100	-0.85	-2.53	-3.91	7.08	44.35	1.6	1.87	13.37	0.94	11.08	31.1	9	91	0	0	81	31.99	-19.61			May-99

		MARKET		FUND TYPE, CATEGORY & OBJECTIVE	RATINGS					MINIMUMS
Fund Name	Ticker Symbol	Traded On	Fund Type	Category and (Prospectus Objective)	Overall Rating	Reward Rating	Risk Rating	Recent Up/ Downgrade	Open to New Investors	Min Initial Investment
Salient Select Income Fund Class A	KIFAX	NAS CM	Open End	US Fixed Income (Real Estate)	B-	C	B+	Down	Y	2,500
Salient Select Income Fund Class C	KIFCX	NAS CM	Open End	US Fixed Income (Real Estate)	B-	C	B	Down	Y	2,500
Salient Select Income Fund Institutional Class	KIFYX	NAS CM	Open End	US Fixed Income (Real Estate)	B-	C	B+	Down	Y	100,000
Salient Select Income Fund Investor Class	FFSLX	NAS CM	Open End	US Fixed Income (Real Estate)	B-	C	B+	Down	Y	2,500
Salient Select Opportunity Fund Class A	FSONX	NAS CM	Open End	Moderate Alloc (Growth & Income)	C+	C+	C+	Up	Y	2,500
Salient Select Opportunity Fund Class C	FSOCX	NAS CM	Open End	Moderate Alloc (Growth & Income)	C+	C+	C+	Up	Y	2,500
Salient Select Opportunity Fund Institutional Class	FSOTX	NAS CM	Open End	Moderate Alloc (Growth & Income)	C+	C+	C+	Up	Y	100,000
Salient Select Opportunity Fund Investor Class	FSORX	NAS CM	Open End	Moderate Alloc (Growth & Income)	C+	C+	C+	Up	Y	2,500
Salient Tactical Growth Fund Class A	FTAGX	NAS CM	Open End	Long/Short Equity (Growth)	B-	C	B	Up	Y	2,500
Salient Tactical Growth Fund Class C	FTGOX	NAS CM	Open End	Long/Short Equity (Growth)	B-	C	B	Up	Y	2,500
Salient Tactical Growth Fund Institutional Class	FTGWX	NAS CM	Open End	Long/Short Equity (Growth)	B-	C+	B		Y	100,000
Salient Tactical Growth Fund Investor Class	FFTGX	NAS CM	Open End	Long/Short Equity (Growth)	B-	C+	B	Up	Y	2,500
Salient Tactical Muni & Credit Fund Class A	FLSLX	NAS CM	Open End	Other Alternative (Growth & Income)	B	C	A	Up	Y	2,500
Salient Tactical Muni & Credit Fund Class C	FLSFX	NAS CM	Open End	Other Alternative (Growth & Income)	B-	C	A-	Up	Y	2,500
Salient Tactical Muni & Credit Fund Institutional Class	FLSIX	NAS CM	Open End	Other Alternative (Growth & Income)	B	C+	A	Up	Y	100,000
Salient Tactical Muni & Credit Fund Investor Class	FLSRX	NAS CM	Open End	Other Alternative (Growth & Income)	B	C	A	Up	Y	2,500
Salient Tactical Plus Fund Class A	SBTAX	NAS CM	Open End	Long/Short Equity (Growth & Income)	B-	C	B		Y	2,500
Salient Tactical Plus Fund Class C	SBTCX	NAS CM	Open End	Long/Short Equity (Growth & Income)	C+	C	B	Down	Y	2,500
Salient Tactical Plus Fund Class F	BTPIX	NAS CM	Open End	Long/Short Equity (Growth & Income)	B-	C+	B	Up	Y	0
Salient Tactical Plus Fund Class I	SBTIX	NAS CM	Open End	Long/Short Equity (Growth & Income)	B-	C+	B	Down	Y	1,000,000
Salient Tactical Real Estate Fund Class A	KSRAX	NAS CM	Open End	Real Estate Sector Equity (Real Estate)	C	C	B-	Down	Y	2,500
Salient Tactical Real Estate Fund Class C	KSRCX	NAS CM	Open End	Real Estate Sector Equity (Real Estate)	C	C	B-	Down	Y	2,500
Salient Tactical Real Estate Fund Institutional Class	KSRYX	NAS CM	Open End	Real Estate Sector Equity (Real Estate)	C	C	B-	Down	Y	100,000
Salient Tactical Real Estate Fund Investor Class	FFSRX	NAS CM	Open End	Real Estate Sector Equity (Real Estate)	C	C	B-	Down	Y	2,500
Salient Trend Fund Class A	SPTAX	NAS CM	Open End	Other Alternative (Growth & Income)	D	D	D	Down	Y	2,500
Salient Trend Fund Class C	SPTCX	NAS CM	Open End	Other Alternative (Growth & Income)	D	D	D	Down	Y	2,500
Salient Trend Fund Class I	SPTIX	NAS CM	Open End	Other Alternative (Growth & Income)	D	D	D	Down	Y	1,000,000
Salient US Dividend Signal Fund Class A	FDYAX	NAS CM	Open End	US Equity Large Cap Blend (Growth & Income)	B-	B-	B	Down	Y	2,500
Salient US Dividend Signal Fund Institutional Class	FDYTX	NAS CM	Open End	US Equity Large Cap Blend (Growth & Income)	B	B	B+		Y	100,000
Salient US Dividend Signal Fund Investor Class	FDYRX	NAS CM	Open End	US Equity Large Cap Blend (Growth & Income)	B	B-	B+		Y	2,500
Sands Capital Global Growth Fund Institutional Shares	SCMGX	NAS CM	Open End	Global Equity (World Stock)	B	B+	B	Up	Y	1,000,000
Sands Capital Global Growth Fund Investor Shares	SCGVX	NAS CM	Open End	Global Equity (World Stock)	B	B+	B	Up	Y	100,000
Saratoga Energy & Basic Materials Portfolio Fund Class A	SBMBX	NAS CM	Open End	Natl Resources Sec Equity (Natl Res)	C	C	C		Y	250
Saratoga Energy & Basic Materials Portfolio Fund Class C	SEPCX	NAS CM	Open End	Natl Resources Sec Equity (Natl Res)	C	C	C		Y	250
Saratoga Energy & Basic Materials Portfolio Fund Cls Inst	SEPIX	NAS CM	Open End	Natl Resources Sec Equity (Natl Res)	C	C	C		Y	250
Saratoga Financial Service Portfolio Fund Class A	SFPAX	NAS CM	Open End	Financials Sector Equity (Financial)	B	B	B-		Y	250
Saratoga Financial Service Portfolio Fund Class C	SFPCX	NAS CM	Open End	Financials Sector Equity (Financial)	B-	B	C+	Down	Y	250
Saratoga Financial Service Portfolio Fund Cls Inst	SFPIX	NAS CM	Open End	Financials Sector Equity (Financial)	B	B	B-		Y	250
Saratoga Health & Biotechnology Portfolio Fund Class A	SHPAX	NAS CM	Open End	Healthcare Sector Equity (Health)	C+	C	B	Down	Y	250
Saratoga Health & Biotechnology Portfolio Fund Class C	SHPCX	NAS CM	Open End	Healthcare Sector Equity (Health)	C+	C	B	Down	Y	250
Saratoga Health & Biotechnology Portfolio Fund Cls Inst	SBHIX	NAS CM	Open End	Healthcare Sector Equity (Health)	C+	C	B	Down	Y	250
Saratoga International Equity Fund Class A	SIEYX	NAS CM	Open End	Global Equity Large Cap (Foreign Stock)	C+	C	B-	Up	Y	250
Saratoga International Equity Fund Class C	SIECX	NAS CM	Open End	Global Equity Large Cap (Foreign Stock)	C+	C	B-	Up	Y	250
Saratoga International Equity Fund Class Institutional	SIEPX	NAS CM	Open End	Global Equity Large Cap (Foreign Stock)	C+	C	B-	Up	Y	250
Saratoga Large Capitalization Growth Portfolio Fund Cls A	SLGYX	NAS CM	Open End	US Equity Large Cap Growth (Growth)	A-	A-	A	Up	Y	250
Saratoga Large Capitalization Growth Portfolio Fund Cls C	SLGCX	NAS CM	Open End	US Equity Large Cap Growth (Growth)	A-	B+	A	Up	Y	250
Saratoga Large Capitalization Growth Port Fund Cls Inst	SLCGX	NAS CM	Open End	US Equity Large Cap Growth (Growth)	A	A-	A	Up	Y	250
Saratoga Large Capitalization Value Fund Class A	SLVYX	NAS CM	Open End	US Equity Large Cap Blend (Growth & Income)	C+	C+	B-		Y	250
Saratoga Large Capitalization Value Fund Class C	SLVCX	NAS CM	Open End	US Equity Large Cap Blend (Growth & Income)	C+	C+	B-		Y	250
Saratoga Large Capitalization Value Fund Cls Institutional	SLCVX	NAS CM	Open End	US Equity Large Cap Blend (Growth & Income)	C+	C+	B-	Down	Y	250
Saratoga Mid Capitalization Portfolio Fund Class A	SPMAX	NAS CM	Open End	US Equity Mid Cap (Growth)	C+	C+	B	Up	Y	250
Saratoga Mid Capitalization Portfolio Fund Class C	SPMCX	NAS CM	Open End	US Equity Mid Cap (Growth)	C+	C+	B-	Up	Y	250

★ Expanded analysis of this fund is included in Section II.

	TOTAL RETURNS					PERFORMANCE				ASSETS		ASSET ALLOCATION & TURNOVER					BULL & BEAR		FEES		
Min Additional Investment	3-Month Total Return	6-Month Total Return	1-Year Total Return	3-Year Total Return	5-Year Total Return	Dividend Yield (TTM)	Expense Ratio	3-Yr Std Deviation	3-Year Beta	NAV	Total Assets (MIL)	%Cash	%Stocks	%Bonds	%Other	Turnover Ratio	Last Bull Market Total Return	Last Bear Market Total Return	Front End Fee (%)	Back End Fee (%)	Inception Date
100	-1.04	-0.44	1.45	13.56	39.14	4.59	1.75	6.84		22.18	888.5	9	29	1	0	46	13.6	-5.4	5.75		Mar-01
100	-1.21	-0.72	0.86	11.68	35.34	4.18	2.3	6.84		21.55	888.5	9	29	1	0	46	13.13	-5.67		1.00	Mar-01
	-0.94	-0.23	1.84	14.96	42.05	5.02	1.35	6.83		22.13	888.5	9	29	1	0	46	13.81	-5.28			Apr-06
100	-1.04	-0.41	1.44	13.68	39.49	4.63	1.7	6.81		22.1	888.5	9	29	1	0	46	13.52	-5.4			Oct-11
100	-0.81	-0.57	5.50	7.97		2.46	2.27	13.09	0.83	24.77	8.7	14	68	7	0	30			5.75		Jul-13
100	-0.94	-0.82	5.02	6.44		2.02	2.72	13.1	0.82	24.75	8.7	14	68	7	0	30				1.00	Feb-14
	-0.66	-0.29	6.04	9.62		2.9	1.77	13.1	0.83	24.79	8.7	14	68	7	0	30					Jul-13
100	-0.79	-0.51	5.65	8.46		2.6	2.12	13.1	0.82	24.8	8.7	14	68	7	0	30					Jun-14
100	3.91	5.96	10.39	10.83	31.97	0	2.08	6.45	0.57	26.15	398.0	28	72	0	0	837	3.25	-6.97	5.75		Mar-10
100	3.79	5.71	9.91	9.34	29.04	0	2.53	6.46	0.57	25.04	398.0	28	72	0	0	837	3	-7.16		1.00	Sep-09
	4.03	6.23	10.90	12.48	35.32	0	1.58	6.45	0.57	27.41	398.0	28	72	0	0	837	3.57	-6.77			Sep-09
100	3.97	6.06	10.57	11.35	32.99	0	1.93	6.47	0.57	26.56	398.0	28	72	0	0	837	3.36	-6.95			Sep-09
100	1.70	3.43	8.30	14.07	6.15	2.52	1.7	3.68	1.03	7.88	80.0	24	0	76	0	276	7.79	5.82	5.75		Sep-10
100	1.59	3.31	7.90	12.49	3.73	2.03	2.15	3.66	1.02	7.93	80.0	24	0	76	0	276	7.5	5.59		1.00	Jun-09
	1.84	3.70	8.87	15.75	8.85	2.99	1.2	3.69	1.03	7.85	80.0	24	0	76	0	276	8.19	5.98			May-08
100	1.86	3.61	8.66	14.65	6.92	2.62	1.55	3.69	1.04	7.93	80.0	24	0	76	0	276	7.83	5.89			May-08
100	6.81	8.30	8.30	10.82	37.36	0	2.43	9.8	0.78	11.4	29.9	-72	172	0	0				5.50		Dec-14
100	6.62	7.85	7.47	8.23	32.16	0	3.18	9.83	0.78	11.1	29.9	-72	172	0	0					1.00	Dec-14
	6.97	8.63	8.91	12.55	40.19	0	1.87	9.79	0.78	11.6	29.9	-72	172	0	0						Dec-12
	6.86	8.44	8.54	11.43	38.80	0	2.18	9.83	0.78	11.47	29.9	-72	172	0	0						Dec-14
100	-1.78	-3.24	-5.24	6.77	37.99	1.6	1.94	11.18	0.77	34.02	56.3	18	82	0	0	82	32.99	-19.36	5.75		Sep-99
100	-1.92	-3.49	-5.76	5.06	34.22	1.04	2.49	11.16	0.77	33.7	56.3	18	82	0	0	82	32.48	-19.64		1.00	Sep-99
	-1.70	-3.05	-4.88	8.06	40.75	1.96	1.54	11.16	0.77	35.09	56.3	18	82	0	0	82	33.31	-19.28			Apr-06
100	-1.80	-3.23	-5.22	6.93	38.33	1.68	1.89	11.17	0.77	33.96	56.3	18	82	0	0	82	32.96	-19.4			May-11
100	10.23	2.07	5.93	-16.26	14.32	6.9	1.69	16.39	1.69	8.52	20.6	-107	131	57	19				5.50		Mar-13
100	9.94	1.55	4.93	-18.12	9.97	5.57	2.44	16.31	1.76	8.46	20.6	-107	131	57	19					1.00	Mar-13
	10.31	2.16	6.02	-15.64	15.69	7.2	1.44	16.36	1.69	8.52	20.6	-107	131	57	19						Jan-13
100	7.34	9.96	21.13	34.40		1.04	1.49	8.43	0.69	32.95	7.1	6	94	0	0	30			5.75		Jul-13
	7.47	10.21	21.75	36.42		1.39	0.99	8.44	0.69	33.14	7.1	6	94	0	0	30					Jul-13
100	7.39	10.03	21.36	34.95		1.14	1.34	8.43	0.69	33.04	7.1	6	94	0	0	30					Dec-14
	4.90	12.21	38.70	39.32	88.86	0	0.99	13.89	1.15	24.7	1,287	4	94	0	2	20	26.32	-17.36			Mar-10
	4.86	12.12	38.37	38.29	86.48	0	1.24	13.88	1.15	24.41	1,287	4	94	0	2	20	26.12	-17.47			Mar-10
	7.61	16.91	8.43	-1.77	-0.07	0	3.4	20.21	1.27	12.72	2.1	1	99	0	0	54	24.86	-34.9	5.75		Oct-97
	7.47	16.66	7.80	-3.49	-2.95	0	4	20.23	1.27	10.5	2.1	1	99	0	0	54	24.47	-35.12		1.00	Jan-03
	7.60	17.15	8.79	-0.64	1.91	0	3	20.23	1.27	13.86	2.1	1	99	0	0	54	25.17	-34.81			Jan-03
	8.06	12.93	19.27	26.65	81.61	0	3.4	15.25	1.19	11.26	2.2	2	98	0	0	55	25.97	-26.73	5.75		Aug-00
	7.90	12.54	18.57	24.34	76.28	0	4	15.22	1.19	9.96	2.2	2	98	0	0	55	25.61	-26.92		1.00	Aug-00
	8.19	13.18	19.83	28.28	85.49	0	3	15.25	1.19	12.02	2.2	2	98	0	0	55	26.33	-26.59			Jan-03
	1.45	-0.96	11.94	16.32	92.68	0	2.29	11.74	0.84	23.55	18.7	2	98	0	0	12	14.61	-10.18	5.75		Jul-99
	1.30	-1.29	11.25	14.22	87.03	0	2.9	11.73	0.84	19.54	18.7	2	98	0	0	12	14.17	-10.42		1.00	Jan-00
	1.51	-0.79	12.36	17.69	96.53	0	1.9	11.74	0.84	25.79	18.7	2	98	0	0	12	14.87	-10.02			Jan-03
	3.44	8.07	18.19	10.35	10.83	0.01	3.06	13.86	1.07	11.11	4.8	1	97	0	0	69	11.73	-28.04	5.75		Feb-06
	3.41	7.76	17.39	8.35	7.42	0	3.82	13.89	1.07	9.99	4.8	1	97	0	0	69	11.27	-28.2		1.00	Jan-99
	3.57	8.32	18.62	11.57	13.02	0.54	2.74	13.9	1.07	11.1	4.8	1	97	0	0	69	11.81	-27.9			Sep-94
	8.20	16.84	29.84	40.43	117.20	0.46	1.62	11.42	1.02	24.93	39.5	1	99	0	0	97	20.36	-13.35	5.75		Feb-06
	8.11	16.55	29.07	37.98	110.91	0.51	2.22	11.42	1.02	19.35	39.5	1	99	0	0	97	19.91	-13.52		1.00	Jan-99
	8.34	17.07	30.35	42.19	121.67	0.77	1.21	11.42	1.02	26.61	39.5	1	99	0	0	97	20.6	-13.2			Sep-94
	0.58	4.01	8.23	8.66	73.62	0	1.65	13.71	1.13	21.67	17.8	4	96	0	0	65	26.31	-25.33	5.75		Feb-06
	0.43	3.70	7.60	6.69	68.57	0	2.25	13.72	1.13	18.52	17.8	4	96	0	0	65	25.76	-25.43		1.00	Jan-99
	0.70	4.24	8.66	9.95	77.09	0	1.25	13.73	1.14	22.52	17.8	4	96	0	0	65	26.64	-25.19			Sep-94
	4.87	8.85	12.93	12.87	80.32	0	2.24	12.48	1.11	11.66	13.9	2	98	0	0	43	24.12	-25.24	5.75		Jun-02
	4.72	8.52	12.24	10.85	75.44	0	2.85	12.5	1.11	9.81	13.9	2	98	0	0	43	23.66	-25.41		1.00	Jun-02

Fund Name	Ticker Symbol	Traded On	Fund Type	Category and (Prospectus Objective)	Overall Rating	Reward Rating	Risk Rating	Recent Up/ Downgrade	Open to New Investors	Min Initial Investment
	MARKET		FUND TYPE, CATEGORY & OBJECTIVE		RATINGS				MINIMUMS	
Saratoga Mid Capitalization Portfolio Fund Cls Inst	SMIPX	NAS CM	Open End	US Equity Mid Cap (Growth)	B-	C+	B	Up	Y	250
Saratoga Small Capitalization Portfolio Fund Class A	SSCYX	NAS CM	Open End	US Equity Small Cap (Small Company)	C+	B-	C+	Up	Y	250
Saratoga Small Capitalization Portfolio Fund Class C	SSCCX	NAS CM	Open End	US Equity Small Cap (Small Company)	C+	C+	C+	Up	Y	250
Saratoga Small Capitalization Portfolio Fund Cls Inst	SSCPX	NAS CM	Open End	US Equity Small Cap (Small Company)	C+	B-	C+	Down	Y	250
Saratoga Technology & Communications Portfolio Class A	STPAX	NAS CM	Open End	Technology Sector Equity (Technology)	A	A	A	Up	Y	250
Saratoga Technology & Communications Portfolio Class C	STPCX	NAS CM	Open End	Technology Sector Equity (Technology)	A	A	A	Up	Y	250
Saratoga Technology & Communications Portfolio Cls Inst	STPIX	NAS CM	Open End	Technology Sector Equity (Technology)	A	A	A	Up	Y	250
Sarofim Equity Fund	SRFMX	NAS CM	Open End	US Equity Large Cap Blend (Growth & Income)	B-	B-	B-	Down	Y	2,500
Satuit Capital U.S. Emerging Companies Fund Class A	SATMX	NAS CM	Open End	US Equity Small Cap (Small Company)	C+	C+	B-	Up	Y	1,000
Satuit Capital U.S. Emerging Companies Fund Class C	SACMX	NAS CM	Open End	US Equity Small Cap (Small Company)	C+	C+	C+	Up	Y	1,000
Saturna Sustainable Equity Fund	SEEFX	NAS CM	Open End	Global Equity (Growth)	C+	C+	B	Up	Y	10,000
Savos Dynamic Hedging Fund	SVDHX	NAS CM	Open End	Moderate Alloc (Growth & Income)	C	C+	B	Up	Y	0
Scharf Alpha Opportunity Fund Retail Class	HEDJX	NAS CM	Open End	Long/Short Equity (Growth)	C-	D+	C	Up	Y	10,000
Scharf Balanced Opportunity Fund Institutional Class	LOGOX	NAS CM	Open End	Moderate Alloc (Balanced)	B	C+	A-	Up	Y	5,000,000
Scharf Balanced Opportunity Fund Retail Class	LOGBX	NAS CM	Open End	Moderate Alloc (Balanced)	B	C+	A-	Up	Y	10,000
Scharf Fund Institutional Class	LOGIX	NAS CM	Open End	US Equity Large Cap Blend (Growth)	B	C+	A-	Up	Y	5,000,000
Scharf Fund Retail Class	LOGRX	NAS CM	Open End	US Equity Large Cap Blend (Growth)	B	C+	B+	Up	Y	10,000
Scharf Global Opportunity Fund Retail Class	WRLDX	NAS CM	Open End	Global Equity (Growth)	C+	C+	B	Down	Y	10,000
Schneider Small Cap Value Fund	SCMVX	NAS CM	Open End	US Equity Small Cap (Small Company)	B	A	C	Up	Y	20,000
Schroder Emerging Markets Small Cap Fund Investor Shares	SMLNX	NAS CM	Open End	Emerging Markets Equity (Div Emerging Mkts)	C	C+	B	Up	Y	250,000
Schroder Emerging Markets Small Cap Fund R6 Shares	SMLRX	NAS CM	Open End	Emerging Markets Equity (Div Emerging Mkts)	C	C+	B	Up	Y	5,000,000
Schroder North American Equity Fund Class Investor	SNAEX	NAS CM	Open End	US Equity Large Cap Blend (Growth)	B	B	B		Y	250,000
Schwab 1000 Index® Fund	SNXFX	NAS CM	Open End	US Equity Large Cap Blend (Growth & Income)	B	B	B		Y	0
Schwab Balanced Fund™	SWOBX	NAS CM	Open End	Moderate Alloc (Balanced)	B-	C+	B	Up	Y	100
Schwab Core Equity Fund™	SWANX	NAS CM	Open End	US Equity Large Cap Blend (Growth)	B	B	B-	Up	Y	100
Schwab Dividend Equity Fund™	SWDSX	NAS CM	Open End	US Equity Large Cap Value (Equity-Income)	B-	B-	B	Down	Y	100
Schwab Fundamental Emerging Mkts Large Company Index Fund	SFENX	NAS CM	Open End	Emerging Markets Equity (Div Emerging Mkts)	B-	B	C	Up	Y	0
Schwab Fundamental Global Real Estate Index Fund	SFREX	NAS CM	Open End	Real Estate Sector Equity (Real Estate)	C+	C+	B-	Down	Y	0
Schwab Fundamental International Large Company Index Fund	SFNNX	NAS CM	Open End	Global Equity Large Cap (Foreign Stock)	C+	B-	C	Up	Y	0
Schwab Fundamental International Small Company Index Fund	SFILX	NAS CM	Open End	Global Equity Mid/Small Cap (Foreign Stock)	B+	B	B+	Up	Y	0
Schwab Fundamental US Large Company Index Fund	SFLNX	NAS CM	Open End	US Equity Large Cap Value (Growth & Income)	B	B-	B		Y	0
Schwab Fundamental US Small Company Index Fund	SFSNX	NAS CM	Open End	US Equity Small Cap (Small Company)	B	B+	B	Up	Y	0
Schwab Global Real Estate Fund™	SWASX	NAS CM	Open End	Real Estate Sector Equity (Real Estate)	B	C+	B	Up	Y	100
Schwab Health Care Fund™	SWHFX	NAS CM	Open End	Healthcare Sector Equity (Health)	B-	C+	B	Up	Y	100
Schwab Hedged Equity Fund™	SWHEX	NAS CM	Open End	Long/Short Equity (Growth)	B	C+	A+		Y	100
Schwab International Index Fund®	SWISX	NAS CM	Open End	Global Equity Large Cap (Foreign Stock)	B-	C+	B	Up	Y	0
Schwab Large-Cap Growth Fund™	SWLSX	NAS CM	Open End	US Equity Large Cap Growth (Growth)	B	B	B	Down	Y	100
Schwab MarketTrack All Equity Portfolio™	SWEGX	NAS CM	Open End	Aggressive Alloc (Growth)	B-	B	B-	Down	Y	100
Schwab MarketTrack Balanced Portfolio™	SWBGX	NAS CM	Open End	Moderate Alloc (Asset Alloc)	B-	C+	B	Up	Y	100
Schwab MarketTrack Conservative Portfolio™	SWCGX	NAS CM	Open End	Cautious Alloc (Asset Alloc)	B-	C+	B	Up	Y	100
Schwab MarketTrack Growth Portfolio™	SWHGX	NAS CM	Open End	Aggressive Alloc (Asset Alloc)	B-	B-	B	Down	Y	100
Schwab Small Cap Index Fund®	SWSSX	NAS CM	Open End	US Equity Small Cap (Small Company)	B+	A-	B	Up	Y	0
Schwab Small-Cap Equity Fund™	SWSCX	NAS CM	Open End	US Equity Small Cap (Small Company)	B	B+	B	Up	Y	100
Schwab Target 2010 Fund	SWBRX	NAS CM	Open End	Target Date 2000-2020 (Asset Alloc)	B	C+	A-	Up	Y	100
Schwab Target 2010 Index Fund	SWYAX	NAS CM	Open End	Target Date 2000-2020 (Asset Alloc)	D	D+	B+	Up	Y	0
Schwab Target 2015 Fund	SWGRX	NAS CM	Open End	Target Date 2000-2020 (Asset Alloc)	B	C+	A-	Up	Y	100
Schwab Target 2015 Index Fund	SWYBX	NAS CM	Open End	Target Date 2000-2020 (Asset Alloc)	D	C-	B+	Up	Y	0
Schwab Target 2020 Fund	SWCRX	NAS CM	Open End	Target Date 2000-2020 (Asset Alloc)	B-	C+	B	Up	Y	100
Schwab Target 2020 Index Fund	SWYLX	NAS CM	Open End	Target Date 2000-2020 (Asset Alloc)	D	C-	B+	Up	Y	0
Schwab Target 2025 Fund	SWHRX	NAS CM	Open End	Target Date 2021-2045 (Asset Alloc)	B-	C+	B	Up	Y	100
Schwab Target 2025 Index Fund	SWYDX	NAS CM	Open End	Target Date 2021-2045 (Asset Alloc)	D	C-	B+	Up	Y	0
Schwab Target 2030 Fund	SWDRX	NAS CM	Open End	Target Date 2021-2045 (Asset Alloc)	B-	C+	B	Down	Y	100

★Expanded analysis of this fund is included in Section II.

Min Additional Investment	TOTAL RETURNS: 3-Month Total Return	6-Month Total Return	1-Year Total Return	3-Year Total Return	5-Year Total Return	PERFORMANCE: Dividend Yield (TTM)	Expense Ratio	3-Yr Std Deviation	3-Year Beta	ASSETS: NAV	Total Assets (MIL)	ASSET ALLOCATION & TURNOVER: %Cash	%Stocks	%Bonds	%Other	Turnover Ratio	BULL & BEAR: Last Bull Market Total Return	Last Bear Market Total Return	FEES: Front End Fee (%)	Back End Fee (%)	Inception Date
	4.88	9.06	13.30	14.19	83.99	0	1.84	12.48	1.11	12.93	13.9	2	98	0	0	43	24.39	-25.15			Jan-03
	2.58	10.67	15.21	15.66	60.25	0	2.13	13.36	0.9	6.74	7.9	3	97	0	0	127	24.25	-23	5.75		Feb-06
	2.34	10.44	14.42	13.63	55.52	0	2.81	13.46	0.9	3.49	7.9	3	97	0	0	127	23.75	-23.17		1.00	Jan-99
	2.68	10.82	15.58	16.92	63.34	0	1.75	13.45	0.9	7.27	7.9	3	97	0	0	127	24.55	-22.85			Sep-94
	7.53	13.13	27.77	54.84	133.30	0	2.24	13.05	1.13	19.05	52.6	2	98	0	0	16	27.35	-24.17	5.75		Oct-97
	7.29	12.73	26.94	52.05	126.28	0	2.84	13.05	1.13	15.54	52.6	2	98	0	0	16	26.84	-24.38		1.00	Jan-00
	7.62	13.31	28.21	56.74	138.05	0	1.84	13.05	1.13	20.93	52.6	2	98	0	0	16	27.64	-24.06			Jan-03
100	7.24	11.85	25.92	29.46		1.21	0.7	9.84	0.94	11.93	94.2	0	100	0	0	5					Jan-14
250	-1.32	5.67	11.17	8.32	43.26	0	1.95	15.31	0.92	30.55	25.4	0	100	0	0	90	26.38	-26.08	5.75		Dec-00
250	-1.51	5.26	10.34	5.92	38.02	0	2.7	15.3	0.92	29.98	25.4	0	100	0	0	90	25.83	-26.31		1.00	Jul-15
25	4.63	8.57	22.81			0.47	0.75			11.52	5.0	10	90	0	0	48					Mar-15
	6.27	10.98	19.97			0	1.57			12.01	112.2	14	54	31	0	35					Jul-15
500	-0.93	-3.02	2.18			0	1.01			23.51	23.8	67	34	0	0	27					Dec-15
	2.01	2.80	10.35	14.52	53.54	0.62	1.01	6.87	0.64	32.22	63.0	21	59	15	0	30					Dec-12
500	1.94	2.67	10.05	13.64	51.59	0.53	1.26	6.86	0.64	32.16	63.0	21	59	15	0	30					Jan-16
	2.82	3.55	13.30	18.67	79.21	0.15	1.11	9.25	0.86	44.1	571.2	17	83	0	0	22					Dec-11
500	2.75	3.39	12.98	17.81	77.02	0	1.36	9.24	0.86	43.94	571.2	17	83	0	0	22					Jan-15
500	4.26	4.43	18.43	26.33		0.45	0.66	11.71	1.02	29.22	30.8	8	92	0	0	76					Oct-14
2,500	4.56	11.18	12.25	38.35	64.04	0	1.15	27.73	1.59	14.98	46.8	8	92	0	0	138	40.62	-37.25			Sep-98
1,000	8.93	11.80	29.15			0.61	1.5			12.07	2.2	3	93	0	0	41					Aug-15
	9.02	11.89	29.14			0.66	1.35			12.08	2.2	3	93	0	0	41					Aug-15
1,000	7.73	12.19	20.09	34.49	104.61	1.62	0.34	10.26	1.01	16.94	1,056	2	96	0	2	70	24.21	-16.47			Sep-03
	6.60	11.35	21.67	35.37	107.98	1.48	0.05	10.1	1	62.61	7,915	0	99	0	0	3	25.29	-17.17			Apr-91
	4.00	7.43	15.51	22.09	59.76	1.3	0.62	6.61	0.63	15.47	388.2	6	60	34	0	19	16.38	-10.26			Nov-96
	6.62	11.94	24.16	32.03	104.87	1.36	0.73	11.04	1.07	22.71	2,404	1	99	0	0	80	25.2	-19.06			Jul-96
	5.23	10.19	15.66	22.36	84.54	1.22	0.89	11.28	1.07	16.33	1,495	1	99	0	0	74	22.96	-15.07			Sep-03
	5.72	13.42	26.34	33.80	16.85	1.77	0.39	19.54	0.98	9.43	556.8	0	97	0	1	20	16.32	-27.15			Jan-08
	3.15	9.15	21.08	26.92		3.25	0.39	11.11	0.97	11.81	123.8	0	99	0	1	23					Oct-14
	4.03	10.99	23.91	25.94	50.62	2.63	0.25	11.9	0.93	9.53	1,391	1	98	0	1	18	10.42	-26.25			Apr-07
	5.26	11.99	29.07	47.44	78.20	1.94	0.39	10.35	0.91	14.51	773.2	1	98	0	1	40	10.39	-19.44			Jan-08
	7.00	11.83	17.05	30.82	102.29	1.87	0.25	10.13	1	17.26	5,492	0	99	0	0	11	23.3	-18.45			Apr-07
	5.03	9.87	12.75	31.12	101.77	1.08	0.25	12.82	1	14.93	1,785	1	99	0	0	30	27.98	-25.46			Apr-07
	2.00	5.52	15.34	21.94	42.63	4.12	1.05	10.58	0.94	7.74	289.4	2	94	0	4	105	23.71	-21.34			May-07
	-0.34	4.08	20.19	23.61	114.40	0.78	0.8	12.61	1.04	24.22	859.3	0	100	0	0	54	18	-9.61			Jul-00
	2.72	6.88	7.77	20.89	56.47	0	1.33	7.19	0.6	17.13	254.0	41	59	0	0	142	14.71	-13.99			Sep-02
	3.76	9.15	25.28	24.90	45.57	2.58	0.06	11.47	0.93	20.88	4,197	1	99	0	0	4	14.07	-23.87			May-97
	7.15	12.91	28.94	38.74	113.95	0.85	0.99	10.87	0.99	17.91	262.0	1	98	0	1	84	28.44	-18.82			Oct-05
	5.15	10.48	19.82	31.23	83.11	1.52	0.55	10.32	0.99	18.76	675.7	1	98	0	0	6	21.8	-20.5			May-98
	3.34	6.66	12.69	20.58	50.35	1.52	0.51	6.03	0.57	18.57	555.3	7	60	32	0	15	14.09	-10.89			Nov-95
	2.30	4.70	9.33	15.01	34.31	1.69	0.52	4.07	0.37	16.09	254.0	8	40	51	0	10	9.94	-5.95			Nov-95
	4.31	8.62	16.09	25.95	67.46	1.48	0.53	8.19	0.79	23.04	818.9	6	79	14	0		18.18	-15.74			Nov-95
	3.35	9.20	14.68	32.08	97.76	1.18	0.05	14.12	1	30.64	3,656	0	100	0	0	17	27.24	-23.72			May-97
	3.28	8.74	10.03	30.22	104.87	0.37	1.1	14.35	0.99	21.02	656.9	1	99	0	0	85	29.07	-24.33			Jul-03
	2.21	4.65	10.24	14.95	33.90	1.64	0.33	4.05		13.33	59.3	9	37	54	0	14	10.84	-6.67			Jul-05
	2.32	4.40	9.47			0.69	0.08			10.69	10.9	10	37	53	0	2			0.00		Aug-16
	2.34	4.85	10.75	15.34	37.76	1.71	0.35	4.23		11.74	100.9	8	39	52	0	14	13.38	-9.47			Mar-08
	2.39	4.66	9.84			0.71	0.08			10.71	12.2	9	39	52	0	15					Aug-16
	2.81	5.86	13.04	18.00	46.94	1.58	0.42	5.6		14.19	584.7	7	49	43	1	9	15.69	-11.76			Jul-05
	2.89	5.62	12.10			0.6	0.08			11.01	44.2	8	48	43	0	17					Aug-16
	3.41	7.01	15.56	21.28	55.92	1.48	0.5	6.68		14.5	530.2	6	60	33	1	5	17.68	-13.59			Mar-08
	3.53	6.82	14.52			0.7	0.08			11.28	57.0	6	61	33	0	6					Aug-16
	3.86	8.00	17.53	23.67	62.92	1.42	0.57	7.55		15.75	984.9	6	69	25	1	5	19.14	-15.25			Jul-05

	MARKET			FUND TYPE, CATEGORY & OBJECTIVE	RATINGS					MINIMUMS
Fund Name	Ticker Symbol	Traded On	Fund Type	Category and (Prospectus Objective)	Overall Rating	Reward Rating	Risk Rating	Recent Up/ Downgrade	Open to New Investors	Min Initial Investment
Schwab Target 2030 Index Fund	SWYEX	NAS CM	Open End	Target Date 2021-2045 (Asset Alloc)	D	C-	B+	Up	Y	0
Schwab Target 2035 Fund	SWIRX	NAS CM	Open End	Target Date 2021-2045 (Asset Alloc)	B-	B-	B	Down	Y	100
Schwab Target 2035 Index Fund	SWYFX	NAS CM	Open End	Target Date 2021-2045 (Asset Alloc)	D	C-	B+	Up	Y	0
Schwab Target 2040 Fund	SWERX	NAS CM	Open End	Target Date 2021-2045 (Asset Alloc)	B-	B-	B	Down	Y	100
Schwab Target 2040 Index Fund	SWYGX	NAS CM	Open End	Target Date 2021-2045 (Asset Alloc)	D	C	B+	Up	Y	0
Schwab Target 2045 Fund	SWMRX	NAS CM	Open End	Target Date 2021-2045 (Asset Alloc)	B-	B-	B-	Down	Y	100
Schwab Target 2045 Index Fund	SWYHX	NAS CM	Open End	Target Date 2021-2045 (Asset Alloc)	D	C	B	Up	Y	0
Schwab Target 2050 Fund	SWNRX	NAS CM	Open End	Target Date 2046+ (Asset Alloc)	B-	B-	B-	Down	Y	100
Schwab Target 2050 Index Fund	SWYMX	NAS CM	Open End	Target Date 2046+ (Asset Alloc)	D	C	B	Up	Y	0
Schwab Target 2055 Fund	SWORX	NAS CM	Open End	Target Date 2046+ (Asset Alloc)	B-	B-	B-	Down	Y	100
Schwab Target 2055 Index Fund	SWYJX	NAS CM	Open End	Target Date 2046+ (Asset Alloc)	D	C	B+	Up	Y	0
Schwab Target 2060 Fund	SWPRX	NAS CM	Open End	Target Date 2046+ (Asset Alloc)	D	C	B+	Up	Y	100
Schwab Target 2060 Index Fund	SWYNX	NAS CM	Open End	Target Date 2046+ (Asset Alloc)	D	C	B+	Up	Y	0
Schwab Total Stock Market Index Fund®	SWTSX	NAS CM	Open End	US Equity Large Cap Blend (Growth & Income)	B	B	B		Y	0
Schwab® International Core Equity Fund	SICNX	NAS CM	Open End	Global Equity Large Cap (Foreign Stock)	B-	B-	B-	Up	Y	100
Schwab® Monthly Income Fund - Enhanced Payout	SWKRX	NAS CM	Open End	Cautious Alloc (Asset Alloc)	B	C	A-	Up	Y	100
Schwab® Monthly Income Fund - Maximum Payout	SWLRX	NAS CM	Open End	Cautious Alloc (Asset Alloc)	B	C	A-	Up	Y	100
Schwab® Monthly Income Fund - Moderate Payout	SWJRX	NAS CM	Open End	Cautious Alloc (Asset Alloc)	B-	C+	B	Up	Y	100
Schwab® S&P 500 Index Fund	SWPPX	NAS CM	Open End	US Equity Large Cap Blend (Growth & Income)	B	B	B		Y	0
Schwartz Value Focused Fund	RCMFX	NAS CM	Open End	US Equity Mid Cap (Growth)	C+	C+	C+	Up	Y	2,500
SCM Shelton Intl Select Equity Fund Inst Cls	SISEX	NAS CM	Open End	Global Equity Large Cap (Foreign Stock)	C	C	C		Y	500,000
SCM Shelton International Select Equity Fund Investor Cls	SISLX	NAS CM	Open End	Global Equity Large Cap (Foreign Stock)	C	C	C	Up	Y	1,000
Seafarer Overseas Growth & Income Fund Institutional Cls	SIGIX	NAS CM	Open End	Emerging Markets Equity (Growth & Income)	B	B	B-	Up	Y	25,000
Seafarer Overseas Growth and Income Fund Investor Class	SFGIX	NAS CM	Open End	Emerging Markets Equity (Growth & Income)	B-	B	B-	Up	Y	2,500
Seafarer Overseas Value Fund Institutional Class	SIVLX	NAS CM	Open End	Emerging Markets Equity (Foreign Stock)	D+	C	A-	Up	Y	25,000
Seafarer Overseas Value Fund Investor Class	SFVLX	NAS CM	Open End	Emerging Markets Equity (Foreign Stock)	D+	C	A-	Up	Y	2,500
Sector Rotation Fund	NAVFX	NAS CM	Open End	Moderate Alloc (Growth)	B-	B-	B-	Down	Y	2,500
Segall Bryant & Hamill All Cap Fund	SBHAX	NAS CM	Open End	US Equity Large Cap Growth (Growth)	B	B-	B	Up	Y	2,500
Segall Bryant & Hamill Emerging Markets Fund Class A	SBHEX	NAS CM	Open End	Emerging Markets Equity (Div Emerging Mkts)	B-	B	C	Up	Y	2,500
Segall Bryant & Hamill Emerging Markets Fund Class I	SBEMX	NAS CM	Open End	Emerging Markets Equity (Div Emerging Mkts)	B-	B	C	Up	Y	1,000,000
Segall Bryant & Hamill International Small Cap Fund Cls A	SBHSX	NAS CM	Open End	Global Equity Mid/Small Cap (Small Company)	B+	B+	B+	Up	Y	2,500
Segall Bryant & Hamill International Small Cap Fund Cls I	SBSIX	NAS CM	Open End	Global Equity Mid/Small Cap (Small Company)	B+	B+	B+	Up	Y	1,000,000
Segall Bryant & Hamill Small Cap Value Fund	SBHVX	NAS CM	Open End	US Equity Small Cap (Small Company)	B	B	B	Up	Y	2,500
SEI Asset Allocation Trust Aggressive Strategy Fund Cls D	SASDX	NAS CM	Open End	Alloc (Growth)	B-	C+	B-	Down	Y	150,000
SEI Asset Allocation Trust Aggressive Strategy Fund Cls F	SSGAX	NAS CM	Open End	Alloc (Growth)	B-	C+	B	Down	Y	100,000
SEI Asset Allocation Trust Aggressive Strategy Fund Cls I	SEAIX	NAS CM	Open End	Alloc (Growth)	B-	C+	B-	Down	Y	100,000
SEI Asset Alloc Trust Conservative Strat Alloc Fund Cls F	SMGAX	NAS CM	Open End	Moderate Alloc (Growth & Income)	B-	C+	B	Up	Y	100,000
SEI Asset Alloc Trust Conservative Strategy Fund Cls D	SSTDX	NAS CM	Open End	Cautious Alloc (Growth)	C+	C	B	Up	Y	150,000
SEI Asset Alloc Trust Conservative Strategy Fund Cls F	SVSAX	NAS CM	Open End	Cautious Alloc (Growth)	B	C	A	Up	Y	100,000
SEI Asset Alloc Trust Conservative Strategy Fund Cls I	SICIX	NAS CM	Open End	Cautious Alloc (Growth)	B-	C	B	Up	Y	100,000
SEI Asset Alloc Trust Core Mkt Strategy Alloc Fund Cls F	SKTAX	NAS CM	Open End	Aggressive Alloc (Growth & Income)	B-	B-	B-	Down	Y	100,000
SEI Asset Allocation Trust Core Market Strategy Fund Cls F	SOKAX	NAS CM	Open End	Cautious Alloc (Growth)	B-	C+	B+	Up	Y	100,000
SEI Asset Allocation Trust Core Market Strategy Fund Cls I	SCMSX	NAS CM	Open End	Cautious Alloc (Growth)	B-	C+	B+	Up	Y	100,000
SEI Asset Alloc Trust Defensive Strategy Alloc Fund Cls F	STDAX	NAS CM	Open End	Moderate Alloc (Growth & Income)	B-	C+	B	Up	Y	100,000
SEI Asset Allocation Trust Defensive Strategy Fund Class F	SNSAX	NAS CM	Open End	Cautious Alloc (Growth & Income)	B-	C	A	Up	Y	100,000
SEI Asset Allocation Trust Defensive Strategy Fund Class I	SEDIX	NAS CM	Open End	Cautious Alloc (Growth & Income)	B-	C	B+	Up	Y	100,000
SEI Asset Alloc Trust Mkt Growth Strategy Alloc Fund Cls F	SGOAX	NAS CM	Open End	Aggressive Alloc (Growth & Income)	B-	B-	B-	Down	Y	100,000
SEI Asset Allocation Trust Mkt Growth Strategy Fund Cls D	SMKDX	NAS CM	Open End	Cautious Alloc (Growth)	C+	C+	B-	Down	Y	150,000
SEI Asset Allocation Trust Mkt Growth Strategy Fund Cls F	SRWAX	NAS CM	Open End	Cautious Alloc (Growth)	B-	C+	B	Down	Y	100,000
SEI Asset Allocation Trust Mkt Growth Strategy Fund Cls I	SMGSX	NAS CM	Open End	Cautious Alloc (Growth)	B-	C+	B-	Down	Y	100,000
SEI Asset Alloc Trust Moderate Strategy Alloc Fund Cls F	SXMAX	NAS CM	Open End	Aggressive Alloc (Growth & Income)	B-	B-	B	Down	Y	100,000
SEI Asset Allocation Trust Moderate Strategy Fund Class D	SMSDX	NAS CM	Open End	Cautious Alloc (Growth)	B-	C	B	Up	Y	150,000

★Expanded analysis of this fund is included in Section II.

Min Additional Investment	TOTAL RETURNS 3-Month Total Return	6-Month Total Return	1-Year Total Return	3-Year Total Return	5-Year Total Return	PERFORMANCE Dividend Yield (TTM)	Expense Ratio	3-Yr Std Deviation	3-Year Beta	ASSETS NAV	Total Assets (MIL)	ASSET ALLOCATION & TURNOVER %Cash	%Stocks	%Bonds	%Other	Turnover Ratio	BULL & BEAR Last Bull Market Total Return	Last Bear Market Total Return	FEES Front End Fee (%)	Back End Fee (%)	Inception Date
	4.02	7.69	16.21			0.89	0.08			11.46	65.1	5	69	25	0	7					Aug-16
	4.24	8.69	19.12	25.59	69.24	1.36	0.62	8.27		15.5	448.4	5	76	18	1	3	20.39	-16.49			Mar-08
	4.39	8.41	17.83			0.85	0.08			11.64	41.1	3	77	19	1	13					Aug-16
	4.55	9.34	20.46	27.33	74.36	1.32	0.66	8.96		16.95	1,017	4	83	12	1	4	21.4	-17.45			Jul-05
	4.71	9.01	19.11			0.96	0.08			11.79	44.1	3	83	13	1	8					Aug-16
	4.80	9.77	21.38	28.55		1.23	0.69	9.27		13.96	125.2	4	87	8	1	1					Jan-13
	5.03	9.51	20.07			0.88	0.08			11.91	28.2	2	88	10	1	8					Aug-16
	4.88	9.96	21.87	29.24		1.2	0.71	9.51		14.13	107.1	4	90	5	1	1					Jan-13
	5.21	9.78	20.48			1.03	0.08			11.95	19.6	1	91	7	1	4					Aug-16
	5.06	10.29	22.46	29.85		1.17	0.73	9.77		14.26	62.4	4	92	3	1	1					Jan-13
	5.32	10.07	21.00			1.04	0.08			12.01	10.4	1	94	5	1	14					Aug-16
	5.05	10.38	22.60			0.92	0.75			12.1	6.6	3	94	2	1						Aug-16
	5.29	10.14	21.18			1.03	0.08			12.03	13.4	1	94	4	1	0					Aug-16
	6.27	11.10	21.06	35.53	108.69	1.54	0.03	10.23	1	47.25	7,020	1	99	0	1	1	25.64	-17.46			Jun-99
	2.38	6.99	25.45	31.53	58.15	2.01	0.86	10.94	0.87	11.12	1,249	2	97	0	1	90	15.65	-21.3			May-08
	1.62	3.91	8.19	11.90	25.44	2.03	0.56	3.44	0.28	11.38	94.5	6	32	61	0	6	7.06	-1.83			Mar-08
	1.01	2.50	5.64	8.81	16.80	2.18	0.46	2.45	0.13	10.15	48.4	7	18	75	0	9	3.96	0.61			Mar-08
	2.32	5.44	10.79	15.18	34.56	1.89	0.65	4.76	0.43	11.09	47.9	6	47	47	1	9	10.35	-5.89			Mar-08
	6.64	11.40	21.79	36.53	110.72	1.65	0.03	10.07	1	41.19	31,173	1	99	0	0	2	24.95	-16.17			May-97
0	5.72	11.92	13.71	13.03	37.03	0	1.27	10.6	0.8	26.44	22.8	7	93	0	0	48	17.75	-11.23			Dec-83
2,500	7.23	15.98	35.30	6.27	12.50	2.98	0.99			21.34	46.2	1	97	0	2	41	21.76	-28.97			Dec-08
1,000	7.19	15.86	34.93	7.03	12.73	2.67	1.24			21.3	46.2	1	97	0	2	41	21.54	-29.03	5.75		Jul-09
100	7.02	9.12	26.04	32.18	39.62	1.6	0.92	13.44	0.8	13.63	2,968	4	84	5	3	14					Feb-12
100	6.98	9.00	25.82	31.54	38.65	1.54	1.02	13.44	0.8	13.59	2,968	4	84	5	3	14					Feb-12
100	1.89	5.86	23.15			1.02	1.05			12.09	18.9	12	88	0	0	0					May-16
100	1.81	5.68	22.92			0.84	1.15			12.08	18.9	12	88	0	0	0					May-16
100	5.94	11.62	20.30	26.79	67.00	0	2.38	9.28	0.85	12.99	24.0	-9	108	0	0	333	14.77	-14.76			Dec-09
500	6.46	8.30	18.68	31.53		0.02	0.98	9.66	0.88	14.4	72.5	9	91	0	0	38					Jul-13
500	6.40	14.36	35.77	31.28	22.52	1.44	1.48	16.33	1.01	9.34	35.7	0	99	0	0	84	23.99		5.75		Jun-14
1,000	6.47	14.39	36.07	32.21	23.50	1.58	1.23	16.45	1.02	9.37	35.7	0	99	0	0	84	24.16		0.80		Jun-11
500	2.83	12.19	28.36	43.60	87.73	1.28	1.28	11.64	0.96	14.05	340.4	2	96	0	2	94	15.99		5.75		Jun-14
1,000	2.89	12.32	28.81	44.49	89.85	1.46	1.03	11.67	0.96	14.06	340.4	2	96	0	2	94	16.16		0.50		May-11
500	4.51	9.66	10.94	26.39		0.05	0.99	12.94	0.85	12.5	83.6	5	95	0	0	70					Jul-13
1,000	4.41	9.03	17.97	21.07	49.27	1.4	1.97	8.01	0.73	15.09	252.8	8	66	26	1	19	21.16	-17.79			Mar-11
1,000	4.65	9.44	18.79	23.88	55.16	1.88	1.23	8.02	0.73	15.22	252.8	8	66	26	1	19	21.74	-17.52			Nov-03
1,000	4.51	9.27	18.42	22.92	53.20	1.7	1.48	8.04	0.74	14.82	252.8	8	66	26	1	19	21.55	-17.52			Nov-03
1,000	3.30	5.26	9.88	22.15	63.57	3.34	1.11	6.62	0.52	13.54	43.9	2	66	30	0	23	18.67	-10.15			Nov-03
1,000	1.18	2.11	4.53	7.02	13.23	1.17	1.58	2.28	0.38	10.64	89.2	21	23	54	2	55	4.96	-2.43			Mar-11
1,000	1.36	2.50	5.23	9.37	17.90	1.92	0.84	2.25	0.37	10.63	89.2	21	23	54	2	55	5.49	-1.94			Nov-03
1,000	1.36	2.40	5.12	8.63	16.61	1.64	1.09	2.25	0.39	10.83	89.2	21	23	54	2	55	5.33	-2.07			Nov-03
1,000	5.74	10.61	20.07	26.39	74.43	1.16	1.14	9.53	0.91	19.04	29.4	4	84	11	0	15	22.42	-18.66			Nov-03
1,000	2.99	6.13	11.75	16.10	31.22	2.48	1.13	5.2	0.48	11.88	109.2	7	38	52	3	23	14.05	-8.99			Nov-03
1,000	2.95	6.03	11.49	17.51	32.11	2.06	1.36	5.18	0.44	12.91	109.2	7	38	52	3	23	13.83	-9.08			Nov-03
1,000	3.00	5.08	9.69	21.95	59.70	3.79	1.1	6.3	0.5	14.49	8.3	2	60	36	0	30	17.95	-9.7			Nov-03
1,000	0.67	1.43	2.80	5.17	8.36	1.36	0.68	1.25	0.27	9.83	29.3	31	13	53	2	69	2.52	0.02			Nov-03
1,000	0.67	1.34	2.55	4.39	6.96	1.07	0.93	1.25	0.28	9.67	29.3	31	13	53	2	69	2.39	-0.24			Nov-03
1,000	5.74	10.61	20.11	26.31	74.52	1.15	1.14	9.52	0.91	23.67	138.3	4	84	11	0	9	22.56	-18.54			Nov-03
1,000	3.44	7.01	13.47	16.00	32.97	1.59	1.93	6.29	0.54	13.19	303.7	7	49	41	3	20	17.37	-13.96			Mar-11
1,000	3.64	7.38	14.28	18.67	38.26	2.22	1.19	6.28	0.54	13.24	303.7	7	49	41	3	20	17.92	-13.58			Nov-03
1,000	3.64	7.29	14.03	17.88	36.47	2.02	1.44	6.32	0.55	13.05	303.7	7	49	41	3	20	17.72	-13.63			Nov-03
1,000	4.46	7.45	14.31	25.02	74.47	2.19	1.12	7.1	0.66	20.72	98.6	3	80	16	0	16	19.04	-12.44			Nov-03
1,000	2.27	3.91	7.63	11.67	23.38	1.68	1.75	3.66	0.54	12.15	209.4	11	35	52	2	30	8.28	-4.15			Mar-11

	MARKET		FUND TYPE, CATEGORY & OBJECTIVE		RATINGS					MINIMUMS
Fund Name	Ticker Symbol	Traded On	Fund Type	Category and (Prospectus Objective)	Overall Rating	Reward Rating	Risk Rating	Recent Up/ Downgrade	Open to New Investors	Min Initial Investment
SEI Asset Allocation Trust Moderate Strategy Fund Class F	SMOAX	NAS CM	Open End	Cautious Alloc (Growth)	B-	C+	B	Up	Y	100,000
SEI Asset Allocation Trust Moderate Strategy Fund Class I	SMSIX	NAS CM	Open End	Cautious Alloc (Growth)	B-	C+	B	Up	Y	100,000
SEI Asset Alloc Trust Tax-Managed Aggress Strat Fund Cls F	SISAX	NAS CM	Open End	Aggressive Alloc (Growth)	B-	B-	B-	Down	Y	100,000
SEI Catholic Values Trust Catholic Values Eq Fund Cls F	CAVAX	NAS CM	Open End	US Equity Large Cap Blend (Growth)	C+	C+	B-	Up	Y	500
SEI Catholic Values Trust Catholic Values Eq Fund Cls Y	CAVYX	NAS CM	Open End	US Equity Large Cap Blend (Growth)	C+	C+	B-	Up	Y	500
SEI Inst Intl Trust Emerging Mkts Equity Fund Cls F	SIEMX	NAS CM	Open End	Emerging Markets Equity (Div Emerging Mkts)	B-	B	C	Up	Y	100,000
SEI Inst Intl Trust Emerging Mkts Equity Fund Cls Y	SEQFX	NAS CM	Open End	Emerging Markets Equity (Div Emerging Mkts)	B-	B	C	Up	Y	100,000
SEI Inst Intl Trust Intl Equity Fund Cls F	SEITX	NAS CM	Open End	Global Equity Large Cap (Foreign Stock)	B	B-	B	Up	Y	100,000
SEI Inst Intl Trust Intl Equity Fund Cls I	SEEIX	NAS CM	Open End	Global Equity Large Cap (Foreign Stock)	B-	B-	B	Up	Y	100,000
SEI Inst Intl Trust Intl Equity Fund Cls Y	SEFCX	NAS CM	Open End	Global Equity Large Cap (Foreign Stock)	B	B-	B	Up	Y	100,000
SEI Inst Inv Trust Dynamic Asset Alloc Fund Cls A	SDLAX	NAS CM	Open End	US Equity Large Cap Blend (Asset Alloc)	B	B	B		Y	100,000
SEI Inst Investments Trust Emerging Mkts Equity Fund Cls A	SMQFX	NAS CM	Open End	Emerging Markets Equity (Div Emerging Mkts)	C+	C+	C	Up	Y	100,000
SEI Inst Investments Trust Extended Mkt Index Fund Cls A	SMXAX	NAS CM	Open End	US Equity Mid Cap (Growth)	B	B	C+	Up	Y	100,000
SEI Inst Inv Trust Global Managed Vol Fund Cls A	SGMAX	NAS CM	Open End	Global Equity (World Stock)	C-	C-	A-	Up	Y	100,000
SEI Inst Inv Trust Large Cap Disciplined Eq Fund Cls A	SCPAX	NAS CM	Open End	US Equity Large Cap Blend (Growth)	B	B-	B+		Y	100,000
SEI Institutional Investments Trust Large Cap Fund Class A	SLCAX	NAS CM	Open End	US Equity Large Cap Blend (Growth & Income)	B-	B-	B-	Down	Y	100,000
SEI Inst Investments Trust Large Cap Index Fund Cls A	LCIAX	NAS CM	Open End	US Equity Large Cap Blend (Growth)	B	B	B		Y	100,000
SEI Inst Inv Trust Multi-Asset Real Return Fund Cls A	SEIAX	NAS CM	Open End	Cautious Alloc (Growth & Income)	C-	D+	C	Up	Y	100,000
SEI Inst Investments Trust S&P 500 Index Fund Cls A	SPINX	NAS CM	Open End	US Equity Large Cap Blend (Growth)	B	B	B		Y	100,000
SEI Inst Inv Trust Screened World Eq Ex-US Fund Cls A	SSEAX	NAS CM	Open End	Global Equity Large Cap (Growth)	B	B+	B-	Up	Y	100,000
SEI Institutional Investments Trust Small Cap Fund Class A	SLPAX	NAS CM	Open End	US Equity Small Cap (Small Company)	B	B	B	Up	Y	100,000
SEI Inst Investments Trust Small Cap II Fund Cls A	SECAX	NAS CM	Open End	US Equity Small Cap (Small Company)	B	B	B	Up	Y	100,000
SEI Inst Investments Trust Small/Mid Cap Equity Fund Cls A	SSMAX	NAS CM	Open End	US Equity Small Cap (Growth)	B	B	B	Up	Y	100,000
SEI Inst Inv Trust U.S. Managed Vol Fund Cls A	SVYAX	NAS CM	Open End	US Equity Large Cap Value (Growth)	B	B-	B		Y	100,000
SEI Inst Investments Trust World Equity Ex-US Fund Cls A	WEUSX	NAS CM	Open End	Global Equity Large Cap (Growth)	B-	B-	B-	Up	Y	100,000
SEI Inst Managed Trust Dynamic Asset Allocation Fund Cls F	SDYAX	NAS CM	Open End	US Equity Large Cap Blend (Asset Alloc)	C	C+	B+	Up	Y	100,000
SEI Inst Managed Trust Dynamic Asset Allocation Fund Cls Y	SDYYX	NAS CM	Open End	US Equity Large Cap Blend (Asset Alloc)	C	C+	B+	Up	Y	100,000
SEI Inst Managed Trust Global Managed Vol Fund Cls F	SVTAX	NAS CM	Open End	Global Equity (Growth)	B	B-	A+		Y	100,000
SEI Inst Managed Trust Global Managed Vol Fund Cls I	SGMIX	NAS CM	Open End	Global Equity (Growth)	B	B-	A+		Y	100,000
SEI Inst Managed Trust Global Managed Vol Fund Cls Y	SGLYX	NAS CM	Open End	Global Equity (Growth)	B	B-	B+		Y	100,000
SEI Institutional Managed Trust Large Cap Fund Class F	SLGAX	NAS CM	Open End	US Equity Large Cap Blend (Growth & Income)	B-	B-	B-	Down	Y	100,000
SEI Institutional Managed Trust Large Cap Fund Class Y	SLYCX	NAS CM	Open End	US Equity Large Cap Blend (Growth & Income)	B-	B	B-	Down	Y	100,000
SEI Inst Managed Trust Large Cap Growth Fund Cls F	SELCX	NAS CM	Open End	US Equity Large Cap Growth (Growth & Income)	B	B	A-	Up	Y	100,000
SEI Inst Managed Trust Large Cap Growth Fund Cls I	SPGIX	NAS CM	Open End	US Equity Large Cap Growth (Growth & Income)	B	B	B+	Up	Y	100,000
SEI Inst Managed Trust Large Cap Growth Fund Cls Y	SLRYX	NAS CM	Open End	US Equity Large Cap Growth (Growth & Income)	B+	B	A-	Up	Y	100,000
SEI Institutional Managed Trust Large Cap Value Fund Cls F	TRMVX	NAS CM	Open End	US Equity Large Cap Value (Growth & Income)	B-	B-	B	Up	Y	100,000
SEI Institutional Managed Trust Large Cap Value Fund Cls I	SEUIX	NAS CM	Open End	US Equity Large Cap Value (Growth & Income)	B-	B-	B	Up	Y	100,000
SEI Institutional Managed Trust Large Cap Value Fund Cls Y	SVAYX	NAS CM	Open End	US Equity Large Cap Value (Growth & Income)	B-	B-	B	Down	Y	100,000
SEI Inst Managed Trust Long/Short Alternative Fund Cls F	SNAAX	NAS CM	Open End	Multialternative (Growth)	C+	C	B	Up	Y	100,000
SEI Inst Managed Trust Long/Short Alternative Fund Cls Y	SLSFX	NAS CM	Open End	Multialternative (Growth)	C+	C	B	Up	Y	100,000
SEI Institutional Managed Trust Mid-Cap Fund Class Y	SFDYX	NAS CM	Open End	US Equity Mid Cap (Growth)	B	B	B-		Y	100,000
SEI Inst Managed Trust Mid-Cap Portfolio Fund Cls F	SEMCX	NAS CM	Open End	US Equity Mid Cap (Growth)	B	B	B+		Y	100,000
SEI Inst Managed Trust Mid-Cap Portfolio Fund Cls I	SIPIX	NAS CM	Open End	US Equity Mid Cap (Growth)	B	B	B-		Y	100,000
SEI Inst Managed Trust Multi-Asset Accumulation Fund Cls F	SAAAX	NAS CM	Open End	Moderate Alloc (Growth & Income)	C+	C+	B-		Y	100,000
SEI Inst Managed Trust Multi-Asset Accumulation Fund Cls Y	SMOYX	NAS CM	Open End	Moderate Alloc (Growth & Income)	C+	C+	B		Y	100,000
SEI Inst Managed Trust Multi-Asset Capital Stability Cls F	SCLAX	NAS CM	Open End	Cautious Alloc (Growth & Income)	B-	C	A	Up	Y	100,000
SEI Inst Managed Trust Multi-Asset Capital Stability Cls Y	SMLYX	NAS CM	Open End	Cautious Alloc (Growth & Income)	B-	C	A	Up	Y	100,000
SEI Inst Managed Trust Multi-Asset Income Fund Cls F	SIOAX	NAS CM	Open End	Moderate Alloc (Income)	B-	C+	B+	Down	Y	100,000
SEI Inst Managed Trust Multi-Asset Income Fund Cls Y	SLIYX	NAS CM	Open End	Moderate Alloc (Income)	B-	C+	B	Down	Y	100,000
SEI Inst Managed Trust Multi-Asset Inflation Managed Cls F	SIFAX	NAS CM	Open End	Cautious Alloc (Income)	D+	D	C		Y	100,000
SEI Inst Managed Trust Multi-Asset Inflation Managed Cls Y	SLFYX	NAS CM	Open End	Cautious Alloc (Income)	D+	D	C		Y	100,000
SEI Inst Managed Trust Multi-Strat Alternative Fund Cls F	SMSAX	NAS CM	Open End	Multialternative (Balanced)	C+	C	B		Y	100,000

★ Expanded analysis of this fund is included in Section II.

Min Additional Investment	TOTAL RETURNS: 3-Month Total Return	6-Month Total Return	1-Year Total Return	3-Year Total Return	5-Year Total Return	PERFORMANCE: Dividend Yield (TTM)	Expense Ratio	3-Yr Std Deviation	3-Year Beta	ASSETS: NAV	Total Assets (MIL)	ASSET ALLOCATION & TURNOVER: %Cash	%Stocks	%Bonds	%Other	Turnover Ratio	BULL & BEAR: Last Bull Market Total Return	Last Bear Market Total Return	FEES: Front End Fee (%)	Back End Fee (%)	Inception Date
1,000	2.46	4.32	8.45	14.19	28.48	2.41	1.01	3.66	0.55	12.16	209.4	11	35	52	2	30	8.81	-3.78			Nov-03
1,000	2.44	4.26	8.29	13.39	26.89	2.09	1.26	3.68	0.54	12.5	209.4	11	35	52	2	30	8.63	-3.94			Nov-03
1,000	5.75	10.62	20.13	26.35	74.55	1.15	1.14	9.5	0.91	21.67	74.9	4	84	11	0	11	22.59	-18.85			Nov-03
100	6.20	11.71	23.68			0.75	0.86			12.38	242.3	5	95	0	0						Apr-15
100	6.20	11.82	23.81			0.9	0.76			12.36	242.3	5	95	0	0						May-15
1,000	6.29	16.19	37.27	32.29	26.49	0.6	1.76	15.57	0.98	12.93	1,989	2	97	0	1	66	16.66	-28.57			Jan-95
1,000	6.27	16.35	37.57	33.30	27.45	0.79	1.52	15.6	0.98	12.93	1,989	2	97	0	1	66	16.66	-28.57			Dec-14
1,000	4.44	10.82	26.65	27.37	47.86	0.94	1.27	10.98	0.89	11.64	4,245	5	94	0	1	57	12.8	-24.29			Dec-89
1,000	4.45	10.74	26.31	26.43	45.95	0.67	1.52	10.9	0.88	11.66	4,245	5	94	0	1	57	12.55	-24.32			Jan-02
1,000	4.49	10.96	26.94	28.25	48.88	1.12	1.02	10.92	0.88	11.64	4,245	5	94	0	1	57	12.8	-24.29			Dec-14
1,000	5.32	9.78	19.77	39.73	119.09	1.34	0.08	9.62	0.92	19.77	2,594	3	97	0	0	8	14.07	-9.21			Jul-10
1,000	7.02	14.49	33.50	29.76		1.67	0.67	13.51	1	11.5	1,231	4	93	0	2	84					Oct-14
1,000	4.90	10.11	18.26	32.25		1.18	0.06	12.23	1	15.19	912.3	3	97	0	0	20					Feb-13
1,000	5.24	8.30	17.64			2.04	0.25			12.14	1,921					36					Feb-16
1,000	5.26	10.46	19.83	34.60	107.85	1.51	0.19	9.89	0.98	13.41	3,437	4	96	0	0	104	26.04	-17.29			Aug-03
1,000	6.61	12.06	21.10	30.16	101.46	1.24	0.2	10.4	1	18.83	1,776	4	96	0	0	97	26.8	-17.64			Jun-96
1,000	6.56	11.30	21.59	36.10	110.67	1.54	0.03	10.12	1	197.01	2,369	2	98	0	0	12	25.45	-17.03			Apr-02
1,000	0.82	1.82	-1.12	-1.72	-10.16	1.76	0.38	4.17	1.57	8.06	872.5	-27	0	88	37	58	3.48				Jul-11
1,000	6.59	11.41	21.73	36.65		1.58	0.06	10.07	1	14.69	4,312	2	98	0	0	8					Dec-13
1,000	5.75	13.13	32.96	36.04	55.29	1.32	0.35	11.66	0.94	11.58	95.1	4	95	0	1	52	15.7	-24.86			Jun-08
1,000	2.25	7.10	9.44	23.90	85.68	0.62	0.44	13.12	0.92	17.74	499.3	4	96	0	0	114	29.25	-26.09			Jun-96
1,000	3.59	8.52	12.09	25.14	88.52	0.46	0.44	13.49	0.95	12.31	447.8	6	94	0	0	111					Apr-12
1,000	4.03	8.42	13.65	25.95	93.48	0.68	0.44	12.4	1	13.07	1,783	5	95	0	0	84	28.44	-24.22			Dec-03
1,000	5.81	8.81	15.31	31.48	105.32	1.86	0.24	7.42	0.62	14.57	1,644	4	94	0	2	40	18.02	-9.7			Dec-08
1,000	5.38	12.27	29.50	25.94	47.09	1.58	0.32	11.76	0.95	13.94	8,453	5	94	0	1	71	16.57	-24.18			Mar-05
1,000	5.15	9.40	19.02			0.78	0.77			12.53	812.0	3	97	0	0	3					Jul-15
1,000	5.21	9.45	19.28			0.96	0.52			12.53	812.0	3	97	0	0	3					Jul-15
1,000	4.63	6.68	17.17	31.88	81.07	2.5	1.14	7.2	0.58	11.69	1,508	3	97	0	1	61	9.73	-4.04			Jul-06
1,000	4.58	6.58	16.86	30.91	78.81	2.24	1.39	7.25	0.59	11.46	1,508	3	97	0	1	61	9.47	-4.19			Jun-07
1,000	2.96	5.07	15.39	30.68	79.43	2.71	0.89	7.23	0.59	11.71	1,508	3	97	0	1	61	9.73	-4.05			Dec-14
1,000	7.67	13.05	22.54	30.45	98.43	0.79	0.92	10.49	1.02	14.74	2,664	5	95	0	0	100	26.3	-17.99			Sep-09
1,000	7.72	13.16	22.83	31.40	99.88	1.01	0.67	10.5	1.02	14.74	2,664	5	95	0	0	100	26.3	-17.99			Dec-14
1,000	7.00	12.91	28.39	31.70	98.19	0.17	0.91	11.26	1	34.22	1,553	3	97	0	0	95	28.32	-16.58			Dec-94
1,000	6.92	12.79	28.08	30.83	95.98	0.03	1.13	11.24	1	33.48	1,553	3	97	0	0	95	28.15	-16.67			Aug-01
1,000	7.03	13.00	28.65	32.39	99.24	0.5	0.66	11.25	1	34.23	1,553	3	97	0	0	95	28.32	-16.58			Oct-15
1,000	7.49	11.92	17.39	25.03	92.43	1.25	0.91	11.89	1.12	25.46	1,444	5	95	0	0	76	25.47	-19.82			Apr-87
1,000	7.44	11.79	17.13	24.21	90.31	1.03	1.13	11.9	1.12	25.49	1,444	5	95	0	0	76	25.3	-19.88			Aug-01
1,000	7.57	12.04	17.68	25.67	93.43	1.48	0.66	11.89	1.12	25.45	1,444	5	95	0	0	76	25.47	-19.82			Oct-15
1,000	1.67	3.77	10.72	10.39		0	1.19			10.03	34.8	75	13	6	6	111					Dec-14
1,000	1.69	3.88	10.93	10.93		0	0.94			10.06	34.8	75	13	6	6	111					Apr-15
1,000	7.26	12.74	20.60	36.77	114.29	0.78	0.78	11.09	1.04	27.66	122.0	5	95	0	0	112	29.09	-23.76			Oct-15
1,000	7.18	12.59	20.33	35.99	113.06	0.56	1.01	11.12	1.04	27.65	122.0	5	95	0	0	112	29.09	-23.76			Feb-93
1,000	7.12	12.46	20.08	35.14	110.72	0.36	1.24	11.1	1.04	27.63	122.0	5	95	0	0	112	28.95	-23.85			Oct-07
1,000	4.71	8.28	13.07	14.34	27.83	0.68	1.26	7.29	0.37	9.98	2,814	22	27	50	1	28					Apr-12
1,000	6.85	10.59	15.58	17.48	31.34	0.87	1.01	7.29	0.37	10.03	2,814	22	27	50	1	28					Dec-14
1,000	1.13	1.93	3.87	4.87	7.30	0.15	0.64	1.76	1.15	9.99	748.9	49	16	35	0	159					Apr-12
1,000	1.23	2.13	4.07	5.27	7.71	0.24	0.54	1.76	1.13	10.01	748.9	49	16	35	0	159					Dec-14
1,000	0.89	2.56	6.76	17.95	32.05	3.55	0.82	2.68	0.2	10.8	979.9	10	14	71	2	77					Apr-12
1,000	0.92	2.61	6.87	18.29	32.43	3.65	0.72	2.66	0.2	10.8	979.9	10	14	71	2	77					Dec-14
1,000	0.68	1.39	-1.95	-3.12	-12.80	1.18	0.92	4.1	1.52	8.46	888.6	-5	14	65	25	68					Apr-12
1,000	0.81	1.52	-1.72	-2.37	-12.14	1.47	0.67	4.08	1.51	8.46	888.6	-5	14	65	25	68					Dec-14
1,000	1.30	2.41	5.25	6.16	12.88	0.07	1.62	3.08	-2.93	10.02	514.3	57	26	14	2	37	2.17	-5.15			Mar-10

	MARKET			FUND TYPE, CATEGORY & OBJECTIVE	RATINGS				MINIMUMS	
Fund Name	Ticker Symbol	Traded On	Fund Type	Category and (Prospectus Objective)	Overall Rating	Reward Rating	Risk Rating	Recent Up/ Downgrade	Open to New Investors	Min Initial Investment
SEI Inst Managed Trust Multi-Strat Alternative Fund Cls Y	SMUYX	NAS CM	Open End	Multialternative (Balanced)	C+	C	B		Y	100,000
SEI Institutional Managed Trust Real Estate Fund Class F	SETAX	NAS CM	Open End	Real Estate Sector Equity (Real Estate)	B	C+	B+	Up	Y	100,000
SEI Institutional Managed Trust Real Estate Fund Class I	SEIRX	NAS CM	Open End	Real Estate Sector Equity (Real Estate)	B	C+	B+	Up	Y	100,000
SEI Institutional Managed Trust Real Estate Fund Class Y	SREYX	NAS CM	Open End	Real Estate Sector Equity (Real Estate)	B	B-	B+	Up	Y	100,000
SEI Institutional Managed Trust S&P 500 Index Fund Class E	TRQIX	NAS CM	Open End	US Equity Large Cap Blend (Growth)	B	B	B		Y	5,000,000
SEI Institutional Managed Trust S&P 500 Index Fund Class F	SSPIX	NAS CM	Open End	US Equity Large Cap Blend (Growth)	B	B	B		Y	100,000
SEI Institutional Managed Trust S&P 500 Index Fund Class I	SPIIX	NAS CM	Open End	US Equity Large Cap Blend (Growth)	B	B-	B		Y	100,000
SEI Institutional Managed Trust S&P 500 Index Fund Class Y	SETYX	NAS CM	Open End	US Equity Large Cap Blend (Growth)	B	B	B		Y	100,000
SEI Institutional Managed Trust Small Cap Fund Class F	SLLAX	NAS CM	Open End	US Equity Small Cap (Small Company)	B-	C+	B	Up	Y	100,000
SEI Institutional Managed Trust Small Cap Fund Class Y	SMYFX	NAS CM	Open End	US Equity Small Cap (Small Company)	B-	B-	B	Up	Y	100,000
SEI Inst Managed Trust Small Cap Growth Fund Cls F	SSCGX	NAS CM	Open End	US Equity Small Cap (Small Company)	B	B	B	Up	Y	100,000
SEI Inst Managed Trust Small Cap Growth Fund Cls I	SPWIX	NAS CM	Open End	US Equity Small Cap (Small Company)	B	B	B	Up	Y	100,000
SEI Inst Managed Trust Small Cap Growth Fund Cls Y	SMAYX	NAS CM	Open End	US Equity Small Cap (Small Company)	B	B	B	Up	Y	100,000
SEI Institutional Managed Trust Small Cap Value Fund Cls F	SESVX	NAS CM	Open End	US Equity Small Cap (Small Company)	B	B	B	Up	Y	100,000
SEI Institutional Managed Trust Small Cap Value Fund Cls I	SMVIX	NAS CM	Open End	US Equity Small Cap (Small Company)	B	B-	B	Up	Y	100,000
SEI Institutional Managed Trust Small Cap Value Fund Cls Y	SPVYX	NAS CM	Open End	US Equity Small Cap (Small Company)	B	B	B	Up	Y	100,000
SEI Inst Managed Trust Tax Managed Large Cap Fund Cls Y	STLYX	NAS CM	Open End	US Equity Large Cap Blend (Growth)	B-	B-	B-	Down	Y	100,000
SEI Inst Managed Trust Tax-Managed Intl Managed Vol Cls F	SMINX	NAS CM	Open End	Global Equity Large Cap (Foreign Stock)	D	D+	A		Y	100,000
SEI Inst Managed Trust Tax-Managed Intl Managed Vol Cls Y	SIMYX	NAS CM	Open End	Global Equity Large Cap (Foreign Stock)	D	D+	A		Y	100,000
SEI Inst Managed Trust Tax-Managed Large Cap Fund Cls F	TMLCX	NAS CM	Open End	US Equity Large Cap Blend (Growth)	B-	B-	B-	Down	Y	100,000
SEI Inst Managed Trust Tax-Managed Managed Vol Fund Cls Y	STVYX	NAS CM	Open End	US Equity Large Cap Value (Asset Alloc)	B	B-	B+	Down	Y	100,000
SEI Inst Managed Trust Tax-Managed Small/Mid Cap Cls F	STMSX	NAS CM	Open End	US Equity Small Cap (Growth & Income)	B	B	B	Up	Y	100,000
SEI Inst Managed Trust Tax-Managed Small/Mid Cap Cls Y	STMPX	NAS CM	Open End	US Equity Small Cap (Growth & Income)	B	B	B	Up	Y	100,000
SEI Inst Managed Trust Tax-Managed Volatility Fund Cls F	TMMAX	NAS CM	Open End	US Equity Large Cap Value (Asset Alloc)	B	B-	B+		Y	100,000
SEI Inst Managed Trust U.S. Managed Volatility Fund Cls F	SVOAX	NAS CM	Open End	US Equity Large Cap Value (Growth)	B-	B-	B	Down	Y	100,000
SEI Inst Managed Trust U.S. Managed Volatility Fund Cls I	SEVIX	NAS CM	Open End	US Equity Large Cap Value (Growth)	B-	B-	B	Down	Y	100,000
SEI Inst Managed Trust U.S. Managed Volatility Fund Cls Y	SUSYX	NAS CM	Open End	US Equity Large Cap Value (Growth)	B-	B-	B	Down	Y	100,000
SEI World Select Equity Fund Class A	SWSAX	NAS CM	Open End	Global Equity Large Cap (World Stock)	U	U	U		Y	100,000
Select Value Real Estate Securities Fund Z Shares	SVREX	NAS CM	Open End	Real Estate Sector Equity (Real Estate)	U	U	U		Y	100,000,000
Selected American Shares Fund Class D	SLADX	NAS CM	Open End	US Equity Large Cap Blend (Growth & Income)	B	B	B	Up	Y	10,000
Selected American Shares Fund Class S	SLASX	NAS CM	Open End	US Equity Large Cap Blend (Growth & Income)	B	B	B	Up	Y	1,000
Selected International Fund Class D	SLSDX	NAS CM	Open End	Global Equity Large Cap (Foreign Stock)	B	B+	B	Up	Y	10,000
Selected International Fund Class S	SLSSX	NAS CM	Open End	Global Equity Large Cap (Foreign Stock)	B	B+	B	Up	Y	1,000
Selective Opportunity Fund	SLCTX	NAS CM	Open End	US Equity Large Cap Blend (Growth & Income)	U	U	U		Y	10,000
Sequoia Fund	SEQUX	NAS CM	Open End	US Equity Large Cap Growth (Growth)	C	C	C	Down		5,000
Sextant Core Fund	SCORX	NAS CM	Open End	Moderate Alloc (Growth)	B-	C+	B	Up	Y	1,000
Sextant Global High Income Fund	SGHIX	NAS CM	Open End	Alloc (Income)	C+	C+	C+		Y	1,000
Sextant Growth Fund	SGZFX	NAS CM	Open End	US Equity Large Cap Growth (Growth)	C+	C+	B-	Down	Y	1,000
Sextant Growth Fund	SSGFX	NAS CM	Open End	US Equity Large Cap Growth (Growth)	C+	C+	B-	Down	Y	1,000
Sextant International Fund	SSIFX	NAS CM	Open End	Global Equity Large Cap (Foreign Stock)	B-	B-	B-	Up	Y	1,000
Sextant International Fund Z Shares	SIFZX	NAS CM	Open End	Global Equity Large Cap (Foreign Stock)	B-	B-	B-	Up	Y	1,000
SFG Futures Strategy Fund Class A	EFSAX	NAS CM	Open End	Other Alternative (Growth)	D+	D	C-		Y	2,500
SFG Futures Strategy Fund Class C	EFSCX	NAS CM	Open End	Other Alternative (Growth)	D+	D	C-		Y	1,000
SFG Futures Strategy Fund Class I	EFSIX	NAS CM	Open End	Other Alternative (Growth)	D+	D	C-		Y	500,000
SFG Futures Strategy Fund Class N	EFSNX	NAS CM	Open End	Other Alternative (Growth)	D+	D	C-		Y	2,500
SGA International Equity Fund Institutional Shares	SGLCX	NAS CM	Open End	Global Equity Large Cap (Growth & Income)	D	C	B		Y	1,000,000
SGA International Equity Fund Investor Shares	SGNLX	NAS CM	Open End	Global Equity Large Cap (Growth & Income)	D	C	B		Y	10,000
SharesPost 100 Fund	PRIVX	NAS CM	Closed End	Other Sector Equity (Equity-Income)	C	C-	B	Up	Y	2,500
Shelton BDC Income Fund Institutional Class	LOAIX	NAS CM	Open End	Financials Sector Equity (Income)	C+	C	B	Down	Y	500,000
Shelton BDC Income Fund Investor Class	LOANX	NAS CM	Open End	Financials Sector Equity (Income)	C+	C	B	Down	Y	1,000
Shelton Capital Management Core Value Fund Class K	EQTKX	NAS CM	Open End	US Equity Large Cap Value (Equity-Income)	B	C+	B	Up	Y	1,000
Shelton Capital Management Core Value Fund Direct Shares	EQTIX	NAS CM	Open End	US Equity Large Cap Value (Equity-Income)	B	C+	B+		Y	1,000

★ Expanded analysis of this fund is included in Section II.

	TOTAL RETURNS					PERFORMANCE				ASSETS		ASSET ALLOCATION & TURNOVER					BULL & BEAR		FEES		
Min Additional Investment	3-Month Total Return	6-Month Total Return	1-Year Total Return	3-Year Total Return	5-Year Total Return	Dividend Yield (TTM)	Expense Ratio	3-Yr Std Deviation	3-Year Beta	NAV	Total Assets (MIL)	%Cash	%Stocks	%Bonds	%Other	Turnover Ratio	Last Bull Market Total Return	Last Bear Market Total Return	Front End Fee (%)	Back End Fee (%)	Inception Date
1,000	1.34	2.56	5.51	6.86	13.62	0.32	1.41	3.12	-2.58	10.01	514.3	57	26	14	2	37	2.17	-5.15			Apr-15
1,000	3.20	4.16	5.20	14.66	55.95	1.84	1.16	13.13	0.99	16.82	154.1	3	97	0	0	67	29.77	-16.4			Nov-03
1,000	3.21	4.11	4.98	13.98	54.34	1.64	1.38	13.14	0.99	16.82	154.1	3	97	0	0	67	29.68	-16.49			Oct-07
1,000	3.34	4.36	5.48	15.56	57.16	2.07	0.92	13.16	0.99	16.82	154.1	3	97	0	0	67	29.77	-16.4			Dec-14
1,000	6.59	11.29	21.55	35.95	109.29	1.51	0.27	10.08	1	63.55	832.4	2	98	0	0	21	25.02	-16.36			Jul-85
1,000	6.53	11.19	21.30	35.21	107.39	1.36	0.45	10.08	1	63.12	832.4	2	98	0	0	21	24.89	-16.44			Feb-96
1,000	6.48	11.06	21.06	34.31	105.12	1.16	0.67	10.08	1	63.52	832.4	2	98	0	0	21	24.73	-16.5			Jun-02
1,000	6.58	11.29	21.52	35.93	109.25	1.52	0.28	10.08	1	63.1	832.4	2	98	0	0	21	25.02	-16.36			Oct-15
1,000	3.66	7.55	9.70	18.01	77.06	0.13	1.17	13.72	0.96	12.81	654.4	6	94	0	0	135	29.05	-26.67			Sep-09
1,000	3.67	7.63	9.86	18.81	78.25	0.29	0.92	13.72	0.96	12.87	654.4	6	94	0	0	135	29.05	-26.67			Dec-14
1,000	3.00	8.72	18.37	25.67	95.77	0	1.14	14.09	0.94	35.33	344.9	4	95	0	0	116	31.12	-26.87			Apr-92
1,000	2.94	8.58	18.06	24.71	93.32	0	1.39	14.1	0.94	33.96	344.9	4	95	0	0	116	31.04	-27.03			Aug-01
1,000	3.07	8.86	18.64	26.39	96.88	0	0.89	14.1	0.94	35.53	344.9	4	95	0	0	116	31.12	-26.87			Oct-15
1,000	3.42	7.45	7.61	22.87	74.97	0.5	1.18	13.13	0.91	24.81	388.5	5	95	0	0	123	28.26	-24.56			Dec-94
1,000	3.35	7.32	7.33	22.04	73.04	0.35	1.4	13.12	0.91	24.59	388.5	5	95	0	0	123	28.16	-24.65			Feb-02
1,000	3.46	7.55	7.87	23.54	75.92	0.73	0.93	13.13	0.91	24.81	388.5	5	95	0	0	123	28.26	-24.56			Oct-15
1,000	7.29	12.12	21.46	28.83	98.00	0.92	0.67	10.61	1.02	25.46	3,924	4	96	0	0	88	26.84	-18.01			Dec-14
1,000	3.14	6.84	20.81			0	1.11			11.63	363.8	4	96	0	0	51					Oct-16
1,000	3.19	6.89	21.07			0.04	0.86			11.63	363.8	4	96	0	0	51					Oct-16
1,000	7.25	11.96	21.16	27.88	96.54	0.7	0.92	10.58	1.02	25.46	3,924	4	96	0	0	88	26.84	-18.01			Mar-98
1,000	5.12	8.03	15.47	30.94	99.97	1.62	0.77	7.22	0.57	16.21	1,107	3	97	0	0	22	16.47	-9.42			Apr-15
1,000	5.58	10.59	15.88	25.91	89.58	0.31	1.14	12.05	0.97	22.9	911.6	6	95	0	0	151	27.46	-23.58			Oct-00
1,000	5.69	10.75	16.17	26.77	90.88	0.45	0.92	12.07	0.97	22.92	911.6	6	95	0	0	151	27.46	-23.58			Dec-14
1,000	5.06	7.97	15.18	30.14	98.74	1.4	1.02	7.2	0.56	16.22	1,107	3	97	0	0	22	16.47	-9.42			Dec-07
1,000	5.25	7.66	14.03	27.50	96.72	1.35	1.02	7.37	0.61	17.72	1,895	1	98	0	0	48	17.94	-10.1			Oct-04
1,000	5.13	7.50	13.70	26.52	94.33	1.09	1.27	7.36	0.61	17.72	1,895	1	98	0	0	48	17.74	-10.24			Jun-07
1,000	5.32	7.80	14.32	28.45	98.19	1.58	0.77	7.38	0.61	17.72	1,895	1	98	0	0	48	17.94	-10.1			Dec-14
1,000	4.96	13.05					0.35			11.12	1,155										Jun-17
	0.09						0.85			10.02	54.0										Oct-17
25	7.10	12.15	22.18	42.06	105.55	0.91	0.65	12.09	1.09	40.59	2,369	2	97	0	0	19	22.9	-19.64			May-04
25	7.00	11.97	21.77	40.67	102.18	0.64	0.97	12.11	1.09	40.53	2,369	2	97	0	0	19	22.66	-19.76			Feb-33
25	5.30	14.30	38.90	38.52	72.03	0.29	0.87	14.88	1.08	14.53	100.0	16	83	0	1	49	19.79	-32.59			May-04
25	5.20	14.00	38.22	36.73	67.92	0	1.3	14.84	1.08	14.44	100.0	16	83	0	1	49	19.29	-32.71			Jan-39
	8.41	11.25					1.94			11.47	39.7	29	71	0	0						Jan-17
	5.56	9.47	20.05	3.24	51.49	0	1.07	12.66	0.4	169.56	4,283	10	90	0	0	16	25.23	-11.48			Jul-70
25	1.99	5.58	13.07	12.37	33.72	1.32	0.8	6.14	0.94	12.91	13.0	6	57	38	0	39	11.88	-9.78			Mar-07
25	-1.38	4.52	12.32	16.57	31.81	4.01	0.75	9.52	0.67	10.98	9.4	8	42	48	0	26					Mar-12
25	7.14	10.89	22.30	18.24	80.05		0.51	11.33	1.06		38.0	3	97	0	0	25	22.65	-16.86			Jun-17
25	6.20	9.28	22.03	17.83	78.55	0.32	0.76	11.33	1.06	26.25	38.0	3	97	0	0	25	22.65	-16.86			Apr-87
25	4.17	12.48	25.76	25.13	33.07	1.13	1	11.27	0.86		67.2	4	96	0	0	0	10.31	-15.6			Sep-95
25	4.27	12.72	25.95	25.32	33.28		0.75	11.28	0.86		67.2	4	96	0	0	0	10.31	-15.6			Jun-17
250	3.16	3.39	-0.21	-6.10	4.33	3.91	2.1	7.94	-17.09	9.13	27.9	68	1	1	24	19			4.50		Dec-11
100	3.06	3.06	-0.79	-8.15	0.48	3.58	2.85	7.92	-17.46	8.75	27.9	68	1	1	24	19					Dec-11
10,000	3.20	3.56	0.22	-5.36	5.59	4.52	1.85	7.91	-16.68	9.01	27.9	68	1	1	24	19					Dec-11
100	3.16	3.39	-0.21	-6.10	4.33	3.91	2.1	7.97	-17.59	9.13	27.9	68	1	1	24	19					Dec-11
	3.58	8.58	24.24			0	0.95			11.76	2.0					145					Sep-16
	3.48	8.67	24.13			0	1.2			11.74	2.0					145					Sep-16
	4.35	4.63	0.07	9.27		0	2.5	5.67		26.85	--	23	36	0	8	2			5.75		Mar-14
2,000	-2.88	-1.57	3.94	15.97		5.58	10.39	11.53	0.71	8.92	15.5	9	80	0	4						May-14
1,000	-2.90	-1.64	3.73	16.59		5.66	10.64	11.47	0.72	9.01	15.5	9	80	0	4				4.50		May-14
100	4.99	8.88	12.15	20.95	83.26	2.13	1.28	9.92	0.93	23.76	172.0	12	88	0	0	9	21.71	-16.83			Oct-03
100	5.10	9.12	12.70	22.76	87.82	2.49	0.78	9.9	0.93	24.06	172.0	12	88	0	0	9	22.14	-16.66			Sep-96

Fund Name	MARKET Ticker Symbol	Traded On	FUND TYPE, CATEGORY & OBJECTIVE Fund Type	Category and (Prospectus Objective)	RATINGS Overall Rating	Reward Rating	Risk Rating	Recent Up/ Downgrade	Open to New Investors	MINIMUMS Min Initial Investment
Shelton Capital Mgmt European Growth & Income Fund Cls K	EUGKX	NAS CM	Open End	Europe Equity Large Cap (Europe Stock)	C+	C+	C		Y	1,000
Shelton Capital Mgmt European Growth & Inc Direct Shares	EUGIX	NAS CM	Open End	Europe Equity Large Cap (Europe Stock)	B-	C+	B-	Up	Y	1,000
Shelton Capital Management Nasdaq-100 Index Fund Class K	NDXKX	NAS CM	Open End	US Equity Large Cap Growth (Growth)	B+	B+	B	Down	Y	1,000
Shelton Capital Mgmt Nasdaq-100 Index Fund Direct Shares	NASDX	NAS CM	Open End	US Equity Large Cap Growth (Growth)	B+	A-	B	Down	Y	1,000
Shelton Capital Management S&P 500 Index Fund Class K	SPXKX	NAS CM	Open End	US Equity Large Cap Blend (Growth & Income)	B	B-	B		Y	1,000
Shelton Capital Mgmt S&P 500 Index Fund Direct Shares	SPFIX	NAS CM	Open End	US Equity Large Cap Blend (Growth & Income)	B	B	B		Y	1,000
Shelton Capital Management S&P Midcap Index Fund Class K	MIDKX	NAS CM	Open End	US Equity Mid Cap (Growth)	B	B	B	Up	Y	1,000
Shelton Capital Mgmt S&P Midcap Index Fund Direct Shares	SPMIX	NAS CM	Open End	US Equity Mid Cap (Growth)	B	B	B		Y	1,000
Shelton Capital Management S&P Smallcap Index Fund Class K	SMLKX	NAS CM	Open End	US Equity Small Cap (Small Company)	B+	A-	B	Up	Y	1,000
Shelton Capital Mgmt S&P Smallcap Index Fund Direct Shares	SMCIX	NAS CM	Open End	US Equity Small Cap (Small Company)	A-	A-	B	Up	Y	1,000
Shelton Greater China Fund	SGCFX	NAS CM	Open End	Greater China Equity (Pacific Stock)	B	A-	C+	Up	Y	1,000
Shelton Green Alpha Fund	NEXTX	NAS CM	Open End	US Equity Mid Cap (Growth)	B	B	B-	Up	Y	1,000
Shelton Real Estate Income Fund Institutional Class	RENIX	NAS CM	Open End	Real Estate Sector Equity (Real Estate)	B-	C+	B+	Down	Y	500,000
Shelton Real Estate Income Fund Investor Class	RENTX	NAS CM	Open End	Real Estate Sector Equity (Real Estate)	B-	C+	B+	Down	Y	1,000
Shelton Tactical Credit Fund Institutional Class	DEBIX	NAS CM	Open End	Other Alternative (Growth & Income)	B-	C	A-	Up	Y	500,000
Shelton Tactical Credit Fund Investor Class	DEBTX	NAS CM	Open End	Other Alternative (Growth & Income)	B-	C	A-	Up	Y	1,000
Sierra Total Return Fund Class T	US82653M4069		Closed End	Cautious Alloc (Growth & Income)	U	U	U		Y	2,500
SilverPepper Commodity Strat Global Macro Fund Adv Cls	SPCAX	NAS CM	Open End	Commodities Broad Basket (Growth & Income)	D+	D	C-	Up	Y	5,000
SilverPepper Commodity Strat Global Macro Fund Inst Cls	SPCIX	NAS CM	Open End	Commodities Broad Basket (Growth & Income)	D+	D	C-	Up	Y	5,000
SilverPepper Merger Arbitrage Fund Advisor Class	SPABX	NAS CM	Open End	Market Neutral (Growth & Income)	B	C	A+	Up	Y	5,000
SilverPepper Merger Arbitrage Fund Institutional Class	SPAIX	NAS CM	Open End	Market Neutral (Growth & Income)	B	C	A+	Up	Y	5,000
Sims Total Return Fund	SIMFX	NAS CM	Open End	US Equity Large Cap Value (Growth & Income)	C+	C	B-		Y	500
Sirius S&P Strategic Large-Cap Allocation Fund	SSPLX	NAS CM	Open End	Long/Short Equity (Growth & Income)	D+	D+	C-	Down	Y	2,500
Sit Balanced Fund	SIBAX	NAS CM	Open End	Moderate Alloc (Balanced)	B	C+	A-		Y	5,000
Sit Developing Markets Growth Fund	SDMGX	NAS CM	Open End	Emerging Markets Equity (Div Emerging Mkts)	C+	B-	C	Up	Y	5,000
Sit Dividend Growth Fund Class I	SDVGX	NAS CM	Open End	US Equity Large Cap Blend (Equity-Income)	B	B-	B		Y	100,000
Sit Dividend Growth Fund Class S	SDVSX	NAS CM	Open End	US Equity Large Cap Blend (Equity-Income)	B-	B-	B	Down	Y	5,000
Sit ESG Growth Fund Class I	IESGX	NAS CM	Open End	US Equity Large Cap Growth (Growth)	D	C	B		Y	100,000
Sit ESG Growth Fund Class S	SESGX	NAS CM	Open End	US Equity Large Cap Growth (Growth)	D	C	B		Y	5,000
Sit Global Dividend Growth Fund Class I	GDGIX	NAS CM	Open End	Global Equity (Equity-Income)	B-	C+	B-	Down	Y	100,000
Sit Global Dividend Growth Fund Class S	GDGSX	NAS CM	Open End	Global Equity (Equity-Income)	B-	C+	B-	Down	Y	5,000
Sit International Growth Fund	SNGRX	NAS CM	Open End	Global Equity Large Cap (Foreign Stock)	B-	C+	B	Up	Y	5,000
Sit Large Cap Growth Fund	SNIGX	NAS CM	Open End	US Equity Large Cap Growth (Growth)	B	B	B+	Down	Y	5,000
Sit Mid Cap Growth Fund	NBNGX	NAS CM	Open End	US Equity Mid Cap (Growth)	B-	C+	B	Up	Y	5,000
Sit Small Cap Dividend Growth Fund Class I	SSCDX	NAS CM	Open End	US Equity Small Cap (Small Company)	B-	C+	B-	Up	Y	100,000
Sit Small Cap Dividend Growth Fund Class S	SDFSX	NAS CM	Open End	US Equity Small Cap (Small Company)	C+	C+	B-	Up	Y	5,000
Sit Small Cap Growth Fund	SSMGX	NAS CM	Open End	US Equity Mid Cap (Small Company)	B-	C+	B-	Up	Y	5,000
SkyBridge Dividend Value Fund Class A	SKYAX	NAS CM	Open End	US Equity Large Cap Value (Equity-Income)	B	C+	A-	Up	Y	1,000
SkyBridge Dividend Value Fund Class C	SKYCX	NAS CM	Open End	US Equity Large Cap Value (Equity-Income)	B-	C+	B	Up	Y	1,000
SkyBridge Dividend Value Fund Class I	SKYIX	NAS CM	Open End	US Equity Large Cap Value (Equity-Income)	B	C+	A-	Up	Y	50,000
Small Cap Value Fund	SCAPX	NAS CM	Open End	US Equity Small Cap (Small Company)	B	A	C	Up	Y	100,000
Small/Mid Cap Growth Fund Institutional Class	TRSMX	NAS CM	Open End	US Equity Mid Cap (Growth)	C+	C+	C+	Down	Y	1,000,000
Smead Value Fund Class A	SVFAX	NAS CM	Open End	US Equity Large Cap Blend (Growth)	B	B	A-		Y	3,000
Smead Value Fund Class I1	SVFFX	NAS CM	Open End	US Equity Large Cap Blend (Growth)	B	B	A-		Y	1,000,000
Smead Value Fund Class R1	SVFDX	NAS CM	Open End	US Equity Large Cap Blend (Growth)	B	B-	A-		Y	25,000
Smead Value Fund Class R2	SVFKX	NAS CM	Open End	US Equity Large Cap Blend (Growth)	B	B-	A-		Y	25,000
Smead Value Fund Class Y	SVFYX	NAS CM	Open End	US Equity Large Cap Blend (Growth)	B	B	A-		Y	10,000,000
Smead Value Fund Investor Class	SMVLX	NAS CM	Open End	US Equity Large Cap Blend (Growth)	B	B	A-		Y	3,000
SMI 50/40/10 Fund	SMIRX	NAS CM	Open End	Aggressive Alloc (Growth & Income)	C+	C+	B-	Up	Y	500
SMI Conservative Allocation Fund	SMILX	NAS CM	Open End	Moderate Alloc (Growth & Income)	C	C	C+	Up	Y	500
SMI Dynamic Allocation Fund	SMIDX	NAS CM	Open End	Moderate Alloc (Growth & Income)	C+	C	B-	Up	Y	500
Smith Group Large Cap Core Growth Fund Institutional Class	BSLGX	NAS CM	Open End	US Equity Large Cap Blend (Growth)	B	B+	B		Y	25,000

★Expanded analysis of this fund is included in Section II.

TOTAL RETURNS						PERFORMANCE				ASSETS		ASSET ALLOCATION & TURNOVER					BULL & BEAR		FEES		
Min Additional Investment	3-Month Total Return	6-Month Total Return	1-Year Total Return	3-Year Total Return	5-Year Total Return	Dividend Yield (TTM)	Expense Ratio	3-Yr Std Deviation	3-Year Beta	NAV	Total Assets (MIL)	%Cash	%Stocks	%Bonds	%Other	Turnover Ratio	Last Bull Market Total Return	Last Bear Market Total Return	Front End Fee (%)	Back End Fee (%)	Inception Date
100	-0.41	4.63	20.79	15.26	31.37	1.82	1.5	12.52	0.79	9.55	10.8	1	99	0	0	0	11.8	-27.13			Oct-03
100	-0.30	4.91	21.28	17.04	34.67	2.13	1	12.52	0.79	9.52	10.8	1	99	0	0	0	12.1	-26.91			Jan-00
100	6.36	12.72	30.57	48.59	147.36	0.21	0.99	13.35	0.98	15.59	497.1	1	99	0	0	4	27.96	-10.97			Oct-03
100	6.57	13.05	31.25	50.98	154.01	0.55	0.49	13.32	0.98	16.04	497.1	1	99	0	0	4	28.5	-10.83			Jan-00
100	6.64	11.16	20.92	34.02	104.10	1.11	0.86	10.11	1	51.4	172.2	-1	101	0	0	5	24.41	-16.28			Oct-03
100	6.79	11.46	21.53	36.04	109.27	1.48	0.36	10.1	1	51.42	172.2	-1	101	0	0	5	24.72	-16.08			Apr-92
100	6.14	9.52	15.14	33.42	97.62	0.35	1.08	11.03	1	26.34	121.5	-4	104	0	0	34	26.99	-22.53			Oct-03
100	6.26	9.78	15.69	35.42	102.63	0.72	0.58	11.04	1	26.68	121.5	-4	104	0	0	34	27.34	-22.37			Apr-92
100	3.25	8.89	11.77	36.03	104.09	0.09	1.24	13.28	0.96	21.98	65.6	-8	108	0	0	31	29.62	-21.81			Oct-03
100	3.38	9.18	12.33	38.11	109.35	0.39	0.74	13.29	0.96	22.52	65.6	-8	108	0	0	31	29.94	-21.67			Oct-96
1,000	5.35	13.86	34.85	28.80	44.42	2.11	1.98	16.45	0.96	9.05	8.9	0	100	0	0	11	7.76	-26.25			May-89
100	2.78	7.24	29.51	24.65		0	1.31	14.02	1.12	17.76	42.5	6	94	0	0	24					Mar-13
2,000	0.92	2.14	3.98	13.80		7.05	1.17	8.54	0.6	8.64	10.2	9	55	2	0						Jun-13
1,000	0.79	1.93	3.71	13.17		5.18	1.42	8.56	0.6	8.88	10.2	9	55	2	0				4.50		Jun-13
100	0.68	1.76	3.65	22.10		5.71	1.44			10.36	26.5	5	5	90	0	246					Dec-14
100	0.52	1.53	3.33	21.11		5.7	1.69			10.31	26.5	5	5	90	0	246			5.75		Dec-14
1,000	0.83	1.11					3.36			24.94	--								2.00		Jun-17
100	0.68	5.62	-2.86	-5.86		0	2.05	4.72	0.24		136.1	72	22	0	6	26					Oct-13
100	0.74	5.53	-2.88	-5.46		0	1.98	4.74	0.25		136.1	72	22	0	6	26					Oct-13
100	0.48	0.39	1.58	14.25		0	2.24	1.95	0.03	11.01	66.7	65	34	0	1	317					Oct-13
100	0.57	0.39	1.66	15.25		0	1.99	1.92	0.02		66.7	65	34	0	1	317					Oct-13
500	2.36	4.95	6.24	7.66	30.14	0	2.8	9.58	0.75	10.91	7.7	18	82	0	0	165	16.28	-13.41			Sep-86
100	-1.70	-2.33	-0.75	-6.37		0	1.95	5.38	0.16	9.22	22.2	143	-46	3	0	574					Oct-14
100	4.60	8.12	17.73	25.21	64.19	1.05	1.02	6.26	-0.06	23.39	27.1	3	63	34	0	50	16.15	-9.35			Dec-93
100	6.11	14.54	43.22	24.72	17.19	0.19	1.43	15.69	0.95	17.19	11.1	6	94	0	0	20	16.64	-24.42			Jul-94
100	6.89	10.71	20.24	32.51	95.00	1.24	0.7	9.37	0.92	16.8	1,079	1	98	0	1	61	23.2	-15.98			Dec-03
100	6.79	10.54	19.87	31.48	92.58	1.03	0.95	9.39	0.92	16.73	1,079	1	98	0	1	61	23.04	-16			Mar-06
100	6.73	11.55	23.71			0.17	1.01			12.48	5.6	4	96	0	0	28					Jul-16
100	6.70	11.53	23.47			0.07	1.26			12.47	5.6	4	96	0	0	28					Jul-16
100	6.14	10.79	19.75	23.58	59.57	1.39	1	9.26	0.86	15.92	33.3	4	95	0	1	32	21.04	-19.2			Sep-08
100	6.08	10.66	19.54	22.72	57.69	1.17	1.25	9.24	0.86	15.92	33.3	4	95	0	1	32	20.86	-19.26			Sep-08
100	2.01	7.66	24.01	20.69	32.72	0.41	1.51	11.23	0.88	17.33	23.9	2	98	0	0	39	19.32	-24.38			Nov-91
100	6.74	11.85	27.83	38.12	103.14	0.4	1	10.4	0.95	40.56	121.4	1	99	0	0	18	25.21	-15.52			Sep-82
100	3.27	5.95	19.00	19.04	72.89	0	1.25	10.8	0.94	18.36	162.7	3	97	0	0	23	32.46	-22.79			Sep-82
100	4.71	9.22	13.69			0.81	1.07			12.44	18.5	4	97	0	0	20					Mar-15
100	4.67	9.12	13.42			0.59	1.32			12.44	18.5	4	97	0	0	20					Mar-15
100	2.72	7.63	15.70	15.87	63.29	0	1.5	12.25	0.79	54.62	97.3	2	98	0	0	29	30.28	-22			Jul-94
50	6.51	7.31	8.45	27.72		2.68	1.25	11.98	0.89	11.51	308.2	-1	101	0	0	73			5.75		Jun-14
50	6.28	6.86	7.59	24.73		2.09	2	11.94	0.88	11.42	308.2	-1	101	0	0	73				1.00	Oct-14
0	6.61	7.48	8.67	28.61		2.88	1	11.89	0.88	11.51	308.2	-1	101	0	0	73					Apr-14
100	8.66	20.31	26.26	36.75	90.35	0.34	0.95	22.04		49.04	21.7	1	99	0	0	78	26.04	-21.96			Dec-05
100	5.82	11.76	21.91	23.50		0	1.01			12.35	5.0	4	96	0	0	40					Dec-14
100	8.06	13.34	25.06	30.16	109.61	0.54	1.26	11.7	1.04	46.3	1,233	3	97	0	0	24	29.88	-15.39	5.75		Jan-14
100	8.09	13.41	25.29	31.04	112.25	0.73	0.99	11.71	1.04	46.48	1,233	3	97	0	0	24	30.13	-15.31			Dec-09
100	7.99	13.16	24.68	28.96	106.76	0.51	1.59	11.7	1.04	45.94	1,233	3	97	0	0	24	29.69	-15.47			Nov-14
100	7.96	13.16	24.74	29.32	107.40	0.4	1.44	11.7	1.04	46.08	1,233	3	97	0	0	24	29.69	-15.47			Nov-14
100	8.16	13.50	25.48	31.66	112.26	0.84	0.84	11.72	1.04	46.5	1,233	3	97	0	0	24	29.88	-15.39			Nov-14
100	8.02	13.27	24.97	30.01	109.54	0.4	1.26	11.71	1.04	46.62	1,233	3	97	0	0	24	29.88	-15.39			Jan-08
50	4.97	10.49	18.61			0.23	1.95			11.03	22.7	6	78	16	0	146					Apr-15
50	2.55	4.15	9.50	1.20	28.19	0.83	1.3	5.62	0.2	9.89	14.6	1	40	59	-1	203	13.59	-13.23			Dec-10
50	3.87	6.54	14.10	1.93		0.22	1.29	8.06	0.26	11.94	162.1	1	70	29	0	152					Feb-13
100	8.00	15.59	24.90	37.37	112.86	0.9	0.79	10.64	0.99	9.52	50.9	2	98	0	0	88	27.07	-19.11			Jun-07

	MARKET			FUND TYPE, CATEGORY & OBJECTIVE	RATINGS				MINIMUMS	
Fund Name	Ticker Symbol	Traded On	Fund Type	Category and (Prospectus Objective)	Overall Rating	Reward Rating	Risk Rating	Recent Up/ Downgrade	Open to New Investors	Min Initial Investment
Smith Group Large Cap Core Growth Fund Investor Class	BSLNX	NAS CM	Open End	US Equity Large Cap Blend (Growth)	B	B	B		Y	2,500
Snow Capital Dividend Plus Fund Class A	SDPAX	NAS CM	Open End	US Equity Large Cap Value (Equity-Income)	C+	C+	C+	Up	Y	2,500
Snow Capital Dividend Plus Fund Institutional Class	SDPIX	NAS CM	Open End	US Equity Large Cap Value (Equity-Income)	C+	B-	C+	Up	Y	1,000,000
Snow Capital Focused Value Fund Class A	SFOAX	NAS CM	Open End	US Equity Large Cap Value (Growth)	C	C+	C	Down	Y	2,500
Snow Capital Focused Value Fund Institutional Class	SFOIX	NAS CM	Open End	US Equity Large Cap Value (Growth)	C	C+	C	Down	Y	1,000,000
Snow Capital Opportunity Fund Class A	SNOAX	NAS CM	Open End	US Equity Mid Cap (Growth)	C	C+	C		Y	2,500
Snow Capital Opportunity Fund Class C	SNOCX	NAS CM	Open End	US Equity Mid Cap (Growth)	C	C	C		Y	2,500
Snow Capital Opportunity Fund Class Institutional	SNOIX	NAS CM	Open End	US Equity Mid Cap (Growth)	C	C+	C		Y	1,000,000
Snow Capital Small Cap Value Fund Class A	SNWAX	NAS CM	Open End	US Equity Small Cap (Small Company)	C	C+	C		Y	2,500
Snow Capital Small Cap Value Fund Class C	SNWCX	NAS CM	Open End	US Equity Small Cap (Small Company)	C	C	C		Y	2,500
Snow Capital Small Cap Value Fund Institutional Class	SNWIX	NAS CM	Open End	US Equity Small Cap (Small Company)	C	C+	C		Y	1,000,000
Sound Mind Investing Fund	SMIFX	NAS CM	Open End	Aggressive Alloc (Asset Alloc)	C+	B-	C+	Down	Y	500
Sound Shore Fund Institutional Class	SSHVX	NAS CM	Open End	US Equity Large Cap Value (Growth)	B-	B-	C+		Y	1,000,000
Sound Shore Fund Investor Class	SSHFX	NAS CM	Open End	US Equity Large Cap Value (Growth)	B-	B-	C+		Y	10,000
Soundwatch Core Hedged Equity Fund Institutional Class	BHHEX	NAS CM	Open End	Long/Short Equity (Growth)	D	D+	A		Y	2,500,000
Source Capital Inc	SOR	NYSE	Closed End	Moderate Alloc (Growth & Income)	B-	C+	B-	Up	Y	
Sparrow Growth Fund Class A	SGFFX	NAS CM	Open End	US Equity Mid Cap (Growth)	B-	B	C	Up	Y	1,000
Sparrow Growth Fund Class C	SGFCX	NAS CM	Open End	US Equity Mid Cap (Growth)	B-	B	B-	Up	Y	1,000
Sparrow Growth Fund No-Load Class	SGNFX	NAS CM	Open End	US Equity Mid Cap (Growth)	B-	B	C	Up	Y	2,500
Special Opportunities Fund	SPE	NYSE	Closed End	Moderate Alloc (Municipal Bond - Natl)	B-	C+	B-	Up	Y	
Spectrum Advisors Preferred Fund Investor Class	SAPEX	NAS CM	Open End	Multialternative (Growth)	C+	C+	B	Up	Y	1,000
Spirit of America Energy Fund Class A	SOAEX	NAS CM	Open End	Energy Sector Equity (Growth & Income)	D	D+	D	Down	Y	500
Spirit of America Energy Fund Class C	SACEX	NAS CM	Open End	Energy Sector Equity (Growth & Income)	D	D	D	Down	Y	500
Spirit of America Income & Opportunity Fund Class A	SOAOX	NAS CM	Open End	Cautious Alloc (Growth & Income)	C+	C	B-		Y	500
Spirit of America Income & Opportunity Fund Class C	SACOX	NAS CM	Open End	Cautious Alloc (Growth & Income)	C+	C	B-		Y	500
Spirit of America Large Cap Value Fund A	SOAVX	NAS CM	Open End	US Equity Large Cap Blend (Growth & Income)	B-	B-	B-	Down	Y	500
Spirit of America Large Cap Value Fund Class C	SACVX	NAS CM	Open End	US Equity Large Cap Blend (Growth & Income)	B-	B-	B-	Down	Y	500
Spirit of America Real Estate Income & Growth Fund Class A	SOAAX	NAS CM	Open End	Real Estate Sector Equity (Real Estate)	B-	C+	B		Y	500
Spirit of America Real Estate Income & Growth Fund Class C	SACRX	NAS CM	Open End	Real Estate Sector Equity (Real Estate)	B-	C+	B		Y	500
Spouting Rock/Convex Global Dynamic Risk Fund Advisor Cls	CVXAX	NAS CM	Open End	Multialternative (Income)	C+	C	B	Up	Y	2,500
Spouting Rock/Convex Global Dynamic Risk Fund Inst Cls	CVXIX	NAS CM	Open End	Multialternative (Income)	C+	C	B	Up	Y	100,000
Sprott Focus Trust Inc.	FUND	NAS CM	Closed End	US Equity Mid Cap (World Stock)	B-	B	C+	Up	Y	
SSgA Dynamic Small Cap Fund Class A	SSSDX	NAS CM	Open End	US Equity Small Cap (Small Company)	B+	B+	B+	Up	Y	2,000
SSgA Dynamic Small Cap Fund Class I	SSSJX	NAS CM	Open End	US Equity Small Cap (Small Company)	B+	B+	B+	Up	Y	1,000,000
SSgA Dynamic Small Cap Fund Class K	SSSKX	NAS CM	Open End	US Equity Small Cap (Small Company)	B+	A-	B+	Up	Y	10,000,000
SSgA Dynamic Small Cap Fund N Class	SVSCX	NAS CM	Open End	US Equity Small Cap (Small Company)	B+	B+	B+	Up		1,000
SSgA International Stock Selection Fund Class A	SSILX	NAS CM	Open End	Global Equity Large Cap (Foreign Stock)	C+	B-	C+	Up	Y	2,000
SSgA International Stock Selection Fund Class I	SSIPX	NAS CM	Open End	Global Equity Large Cap (Foreign Stock)	B-	B-	B	Up	Y	1,000,000
SSgA International Stock Selection Fund Class K	SSIQX	NAS CM	Open End	Global Equity Large Cap (Foreign Stock)	B-	B-	C+	Up	Y	10,000,000
SSgA International Stock Selection Fund N Class	SSAIX	NAS CM	Open End	Global Equity Large Cap (Foreign Stock)	B-	B-	B	Up		1,000
SSgA S&P 500 Index Fund N Class	SVSPX	NAS CM	Open End	US Equity Large Cap Blend (Growth)	B	B	B		Y	10,000
STAAR International Fund	SITIX	NAS CM	Open End	Global Equity Large Cap (Foreign Stock)	C+	C+	C+	Up	Y	1,000
STAAR Investment Trust - Alternative Categories Fund	SITAX	NAS CM	Open End	Global Equity (Multi-Asset Global)	C+	C	C+	Up	Y	1,000
STAAR Larger Company Stock Fund	SITLX	NAS CM	Open End	US Equity Large Cap Growth (Growth)	B-	C+	B	Down	Y	1,000
STAAR Smaller Company Stock Fund	SITSX	NAS CM	Open End	US Equity Small Cap (Small Company)	B-	C+	B-	Up	Y	1,000
Stadion Alternative Income Fund Class A	TACFX	NAS CM	Open End	Long/Short Equity (Growth & Income)	C+	C	B	Up	Y	1,000
Stadion Alternative Income Fund Class C	TACCX	NAS CM	Open End	Long/Short Equity (Growth & Income)	C	C-	C+	Down	Y	1,000
Stadion Alternative Income Fund Class I	TACSX	NAS CM	Open End	Long/Short Equity (Growth & Income)	C+	C	B	Up	Y	0
Stadion Alternative Income Fund Class T	TACRX	NAS CM	Open End	Long/Short Equity (Growth & Income)	C	C	B		Y	1,000
Stadion Tactical Defensive Fund Class A	ETFRX	NAS CM	Open End	Moderate Alloc (Growth)	C+	C+	B-	Down	Y	1,000
Stadion Tactical Defensive Fund Class C	ETFZX	NAS CM	Open End	Moderate Alloc (Growth)	C+	C+	C+		Y	1,000
Stadion Tactical Defensive Fund Class I	ETFWX	NAS CM	Open End	Moderate Alloc (Growth)	B-	C+	B-	Up	Y	0

★ Expanded analysis of this fund is included in Section II.

	TOTAL RETURNS					PERFORMANCE				ASSETS		ASSET ALLOCATION & TURNOVER					BULL & BEAR		FEES		
Min Additional Investment	3-Month Total Return	6-Month Total Return	1-Year Total Return	3-Year Total Return	5-Year Total Return	Dividend Yield (TTM)	Expense Ratio	3-Yr Std Deviation	3-Year Beta	NAV	Total Assets (MIL)	%Cash	%Stocks	%Bonds	%Other	Turnover Ratio	Last Bull Market Total Return	Last Bear Market Total Return	Front End Fee (%)	Back End Fee (%)	Inception Date
100	8.08	15.55	24.71	36.65	110.55	0.59	1.04	10.61	0.99	9.53	50.9	2	98	0	0	88	26.88	-19.2			Feb-14
	4.76	6.18	9.36	18.31		0.54	1.2	13.42	1.18	20.93	3.4	2	87	2	0	81			5.25		Mar-13
	4.84	6.31	9.63	19.18		0.74	0.95	13.4	1.18	23.41	3.4	2	87	2	0	81					Mar-13
	6.49	10.36	16.24	5.76		0.22	1.2	16.64	1.44	22.12	2.2	1	99	0	0	92			5.25		Mar-13
	6.56	10.52	16.51	6.60		0.42	0.95	16.64	1.44	23.57	2.2	1	99	0	0	92					Mar-13
	5.24	7.50	12.50	2.65	63.89	0	1.34	15.78	1.16	27.3	198.4	24	74	2	0	84	25.14	-26.88	5.25		Apr-06
	5.03	7.12	11.69	0.37	58.02	0	2.09	15.78	1.16	25.46	198.4	24	74	2	0	84	24.65	-27.03		1.00	Apr-06
	5.30	7.65	12.78	3.43	65.98	0.32	1.09	15.8	1.16	27.58	198.4	24	74	2	0	84	25.25	-26.8			Apr-06
	7.86	11.37	6.30	5.56	57.75	0	1.5	18.56	1.22	32.9	41.5	0	100	0	0	74	33.83	-28.42	5.25		Nov-10
	7.63	10.94	5.51	3.25	51.92	0	2.25	18.58	1.22	31.02	41.5	0	100	0	0	74	33.29	-28.67		1.00	Nov-10
	7.91	11.53	6.57	6.35	59.72	0	1.25	18.59	1.22	33.54	41.5	0	100	0	0	74	34.04	-28.36			Nov-10
50	4.28	10.67	17.47	21.80	75.73	0	1.97	9.77	0.92	11.65	196.4	3	95	1	1	131	18.04	-21.26			Dec-05
	4.31	7.46	16.40	25.85	104.34	0.99	0.75	12.17	1.15	46.06	2,168	4	96	0	0	46	26.27	-22.68			Dec-13
	4.26	7.38	16.22	25.24	102.97	0.92	0.91	12.17	1.15	45.89	2,168	4	96	0	0	46	26.27	-22.68			May-85
	5.60	9.28	18.17			0.45	0.99			17.76	81.7	4	97	0	0						Nov-16
	3.67	6.91	13.97	18.15	81.57	0.59	0	8.83	0.52	45.06	384.3	8	58	31	3	35	32.5	-26.52			Oct-68
50	4.87	16.72	31.27	23.52	74.74	0	2.45	12.17	0.91	20.9	12.4	0	100	0	0	256	29.55	-15.96	5.75		Oct-98
50	4.72	16.45	30.58	21.70	70.50	0	2.93	12.14	0.91	19.79	12.4	0	100	0	0	256	29.24	-16.13			Jan-12
100	4.93	16.90	31.62	24.44	76.99	0	2.18	12.17	0.91	20.21	12.4	0	100	0	0	256	29.89	-15.86			Nov-00
	3.57	6.08	15.69	19.87	46.54	3.09	0	6.47	0.55	16.6725	151.9	24	94	3	8	49	14.02	-9.4			Jun-93
500	3.86	7.62	15.32			1.8	2.5			21.89	7.7	34	38	27	1	260					May-15
50	-0.24	-0.73	-4.08	-23.41		18.61	1.44	19.7	1.31	4.19	653.3	2	98	0	0	18			5.75		Jul-14
50	-0.48	-0.98	-4.76	-25.21		18.94	2.17	19.65	1.31	4.12	653.3	2	98	0	0	18				1.00	Mar-16
50	1.45	3.57	8.39	9.97		4.18	1.25	6.1	1.21	9.87	54.0	3	33	43	0	12			4.75		Jul-13
50	1.28	3.10	7.59	7.23		3.53	2	6.04	1.19	9.85	54.0	3	33	43	0	12				1.00	Mar-16
50	6.72	10.93	20.21	25.40	82.36	3.43	1.57	10.24	1	21.59	99.7	1	95	0	0	24	25.17	-17.32	5.25		Aug-02
50	6.47	10.56	19.36	22.77	76.07	2.6	2.27	10.23	1	21.62	99.7	1	95	0	0	24	24.66	-17.57		1.00	Mar-16
50	1.42	3.25	6.78	9.05	49.52	5.35	1.54	12.06	0.88	11.65	108.2	0	96	1	0	10	29.14	-20.36	5.25		Jan-98
50	1.22	2.87	6.10	6.63	44.18	5.11	2.24	12.06	0.88	11.56	108.2	0	96	1	0	10	28.61	-20.6		1.00	Mar-16
100	3.57	6.56	12.97	14.05		0.06	2	7.29	-2.25	10.98	4.7	21	61	18	0	248					Nov-14
1,000	3.68	6.86	13.29	14.93		0.21	1.6	7.3	-3.72	11.02	4.7	21	61	18	0	248					Nov-14
	4.62	10.78	17.52	26.89	55.36	2.19		13.06	0.64	8.93	228.1	15	92	0	-7	35	16.21	-25.91			Mar-88
	1.84	7.31	8.75	28.75	97.14	0.17	1.3	12.79	0.87	48.53	31.3	0	100	0	0	94	32.33	-23.3	5.25		Jul-14
	1.92	7.46	9.04	29.73	98.89	0.21	1.05	12.79	0.87	48.78	31.3	0	100	0	0	94	32.33	-23.3			Jul-14
	1.93	7.47	9.07	30.31	99.90	0.37	0.85	12.79	0.87	48.87	31.3	0	100	0	0	94	32.33	-23.3			Jul-14
100	1.85	7.31	8.79	29.32	98.21	0.18	1.1	12.78	0.87	48.8	31.3	0	100	0	0	94	32.33	-23.3			Jul-92
	1.79	6.88	22.34	21.85	47.11	2.06	1.2	11.31	0.91	11.75	302.4	0	98	1	1	94	12.24	-26.03	5.25		Jul-14
	1.77	6.93	22.56	22.78	48.38	2.31	0.95	11.32	0.91	11.78	302.4	0	98	1	1	94	12.24	-26.03			Jul-14
	1.72	6.97	22.60	23.16	49.01	2.49	0.75	11.29	0.9	11.78	302.4	0	98	1	1	94	12.24	-26.03			Jul-14
100	1.72	6.78	22.24	22.39	47.89	2.26	1	11.3	0.91	11.8	302.4	0	98	1	1	94	12.24	-26.03			Mar-95
100	6.64	11.35	21.67	36.31	110.03	1.59	0.16	10.08	1	37.75	1,668	1	99	0	0	3	25.37	-16.41			Dec-92
50	3.13	8.50	23.02	12.46	14.10	0	3.07	10.93	0.86		2.1	8	90	0	2	11	12.83	-23.97			Apr-96
50	3.35	6.42	12.34	8.08	36.06	0	2.75	9.37	0.84		2.8	8	91	0	1	20	15.28	-20.43			Apr-96
50	5.75	8.73	22.80	17.05	60.57	0	2.78	9.1	0.89		2.8	7	92	0	0	9	19.2	-17.94			Apr-96
50	4.32	9.35	10.62	19.78	61.07	0	2.97	11.71	0.81		3.1	4	96	0	0	6	21.21	-23.24			Apr-96
250	0.26	1.12	-1.22	8.23	7.72	3.72	1.41	4.22	0.69	9.73	21.0	1	99	0	0	40			5.75		Dec-12
250	0.16	0.76	-1.89	5.87	3.81	3.33	2.16	4.16	0.68	9.64	21.0	1	99	0	0	40				1.00	Aug-15
	0.34	1.20	-1.06	9.00	8.98	3.98	1.16	4.17	0.66	9.7	21.0	1	99	0	0	40					Feb-13
250	0.27	1.11	-1.23	8.21	7.71		1.4	4.22	0.69	9.73	21.0	1	99	0	0	40			2.50		Aug-17
250	5.29	8.31	15.25	13.74	40.67	0.17	2.11	7.21	0.75	13.38	106.0	1	99	0	0	196	6.68	-12.21	5.75		Sep-06
250	5.06	7.90	14.26	11.05	35.31	0	2.87	7.16	0.75	12.51	106.0	1	99	0	0	196	6.29	-12.53		1.00	Oct-09
	5.36	8.39	15.50	14.48	42.15	0.22	1.87	7.21	0.75	13.61	106.0	1	99	0	0	196	6.85	-12.18			May-10

Fund Name	Ticker Symbol	Traded On	Fund Type	Category and (Prospectus Objective)	Overall Rating	Reward Rating	Risk Rating	Recent Up/ Downgrade	Open to New Investors	Min Initial Investment
	MARKET		FUND TYPE, CATEGORY & OBJECTIVE		RATINGS				MINIMUMS	
Stadion Tactical Defensive Fund Class T	ETFHX	NAS CM	Open End	Moderate Alloc (Growth)	C+	C+	B-		Y	1,000
Stadion Tactical Growth Fund Class A Shares	ETFAX	NAS CM	Open End	Moderate Alloc (Growth)	C+	C+	B-	Down	Y	1,000
Stadion Tactical Growth Fund Class C Shares	ETFCX	NAS CM	Open End	Moderate Alloc (Growth)	B-	C+	B	Down	Y	1,000
Stadion Tactical Growth Fund Class I Shares	ETFOX	NAS CM	Open End	Moderate Alloc (Growth)	C+	C+	B-	Down	Y	0
Stadion Tactical Growth Fund Class T	ETFDX	NAS CM	Open End	Moderate Alloc (Growth)	C+	C+	B-		Y	1,000
Stadion Trilogy Alternative Return Fund Class A Shares	STTGX	NAS CM	Open End	Multialternative (Growth & Income)	B	C	A-	Up	Y	1,000
Stadion Trilogy Alternative Return Fund Class C Shares	STTCX	NAS CM	Open End	Multialternative (Growth & Income)	B-	C	A-	Up	Y	1,000
Stadion Trilogy Alternative Return Fund Class I Shares	STTIX	NAS CM	Open End	Multialternative (Growth & Income)	B	C	A-	Up	Y	0
Stadion Trilogy Alternative Return Fund Class T	STTHX	NAS CM	Open End	Multialternative (Growth & Income)	B	C	A-		Y	1,000
State Farm Balanced Fund	STFBX	NAS CM	Open End	Moderate Alloc (Balanced)	B-	C+	B	Down	Y	250
State Farm Equity & Bond Fund Class A	NBSAX	NAS CM	Open End	Moderate Alloc (Balanced)	B-	C+	B	Up	Y	1,000
State Farm Equity & Bond Fund Class B	NBSBX	NAS CM	Open End	Moderate Alloc (Balanced)	B-	C+	B	Up	Y	1,000
State Farm Equity & Bond Fund Class R1	REBOX	NAS CM	Open End	Moderate Alloc (Balanced)	B-	C+	B	Up	Y	0
State Farm Equity & Bond Fund Class R2	REBTX	NAS CM	Open End	Moderate Alloc (Balanced)	B-	C+	B	Up	Y	0
State Farm Equity & Bond Fund Class R3	REBHX	NAS CM	Open End	Moderate Alloc (Balanced)	B	C+	B+	Up	Y	0
State Farm Equity & Bond Fund Premier Shares	SLBAX	NAS CM	Open End	Moderate Alloc (Balanced)	B-	C+	B	Up	Y	1,000
State Farm Equity and Bond Fund Class Institutional	SEBIX	NAS CM	Open End	Moderate Alloc (Balanced)	B	C+	B+	Up	Y	1,000
State Farm Equity and Bond Fund Legacy Class B	SLBBX	NAS CM	Open End	Moderate Alloc (Balanced)	B-	C+	B	Up	Y	1,000
State Farm Equity Fund Class A	SNEAX	NAS CM	Open End	US Equity Large Cap Blend (Growth)	B	B	B	Up	Y	1,000
State Farm Equity Fund Class B	SNEBX	NAS CM	Open End	US Equity Large Cap Blend (Growth)	B	B	B-	Up	Y	1,000
State Farm Equity Fund Class B Legacy	SLEBX	NAS CM	Open End	US Equity Large Cap Blend (Growth)	B	B	B	Up	Y	1,000
State Farm Equity Fund Class Institutional	SLEIX	NAS CM	Open End	US Equity Large Cap Blend (Growth)	B	B	B	Up	Y	1,000
State Farm Equity Fund Class R1	SREOX	NAS CM	Open End	US Equity Large Cap Blend (Growth)	B	B	B	Up	Y	0
State Farm Equity Fund Class R2	SRETX	NAS CM	Open End	US Equity Large Cap Blend (Growth)	B	B	B	Up	Y	0
State Farm Equity Fund Class R3	SREHX	NAS CM	Open End	US Equity Large Cap Blend (Growth)	B	B	B	Up	Y	0
State Farm Equity Fund Premier Shares	SLEAX	NAS CM	Open End	US Equity Large Cap Blend (Growth)	B	B	B	Up	Y	1,000
State Farm Growth Fund	STFGX	NAS CM	Open End	US Equity Large Cap Blend (Growth)	B-	B-	B-	Down	Y	250
State Farm International Equity Fund Class A	SNIAX	NAS CM	Open End	Global Equity Large Cap (Foreign Stock)	B-	B-	B	Up	Y	1,000
State Farm International Equity Fund Class B	SNIBX	NAS CM	Open End	Global Equity Large Cap (Foreign Stock)	B-	B-	B	Up	Y	1,000
State Farm International Equity Fund Class B Legacy	SFFBX	NAS CM	Open End	Global Equity Large Cap (Foreign Stock)	B-	B-	B	Up	Y	1,000
State Farm International Equity Fund Class Institutional	SFIIX	NAS CM	Open End	Global Equity Large Cap (Foreign Stock)	B-	B-	B	Up	Y	1,000
State Farm International Equity Fund Class R1	RIEOX	NAS CM	Open End	Global Equity Large Cap (Foreign Stock)	B-	B-	B	Up	Y	0
State Farm International Equity Fund Class R2	RIETX	NAS CM	Open End	Global Equity Large Cap (Foreign Stock)	B-	B-	B	Up	Y	0
State Farm International Equity Fund Class R3	RIEHX	NAS CM	Open End	Global Equity Large Cap (Foreign Stock)	B-	B-	B	Up	Y	0
State Farm International Equity Fund Premier Shares	SFFAX	NAS CM	Open End	Global Equity Large Cap (Foreign Stock)	B-	B-	B	Up	Y	1,000
State Farm International Index Fund Class A	NFSAX	NAS CM	Open End	Global Equity Large Cap (Foreign Stock)	B-	C+	B	Up	Y	1,000
State Farm International Index Fund Class B	NFSBX	NAS CM	Open End	Global Equity Large Cap (Foreign Stock)	B-	C+	B-	Up	Y	1,000
State Farm International Index Fund Class B Legacy	SIIBX	NAS CM	Open End	Global Equity Large Cap (Foreign Stock)	B-	C+	B	Up	Y	1,000
State Farm International Index Fund Class Institutional	SFFFX	NAS CM	Open End	Global Equity Large Cap (Foreign Stock)	B-	C+	B	Up	Y	1,000
State Farm International Index Fund Class R1	RIIOX	NAS CM	Open End	Global Equity Large Cap (Foreign Stock)	B-	C+	B	Up	Y	0
State Farm International Index Fund Class R2	RIITX	NAS CM	Open End	Global Equity Large Cap (Foreign Stock)	B-	C+	B	Up	Y	0
State Farm International Index Fund Class R3	RIIHX	NAS CM	Open End	Global Equity Large Cap (Foreign Stock)	B-	C+	B	Up	Y	0
State Farm International Index Fund Premier Shares	SIIAX	NAS CM	Open End	Global Equity Large Cap (Foreign Stock)	B-	C+	B	Up	Y	1,000
State Farm LifePath 2020 Fund Class A	NLWAX	NAS CM	Open End	Target Date 2000-2020 (Asset Alloc)	B-	C+	B+	Up	Y	1,000
State Farm LifePath 2020 Fund Class B	NLWBX	NAS CM	Open End	Target Date 2000-2020 (Asset Alloc)	B-	C+	B+	Up	Y	1,000
State Farm LifePath 2020 Fund Class Institutional	SAWIX	NAS CM	Open End	Target Date 2000-2020 (Asset Alloc)	B	C+	B+	Up	Y	1,000
State Farm LifePath 2020 Fund Class R1	RAWOX	NAS CM	Open End	Target Date 2000-2020 (Asset Alloc)	B-	C+	B+	Up	Y	0
State Farm LifePath 2020 Fund Class R2	RAWTX	NAS CM	Open End	Target Date 2000-2020 (Asset Alloc)	B-	C+	B+	Up	Y	0
State Farm LifePath 2020 Fund Class R3	RAWHX	NAS CM	Open End	Target Date 2000-2020 (Asset Alloc)	B	C+	B+	Up	Y	0
State Farm LifePath 2020 Fund Legacy Class B	SAWBX	NAS CM	Open End	Target Date 2000-2020 (Asset Alloc)	B-	C+	B+	Up	Y	1,000
State Farm LifePath 2020 Fund Premier Shares	SAWAX	NAS CM	Open End	Target Date 2000-2020 (Asset Alloc)	B-	C+	B+	Up	Y	1,000
State Farm LifePath 2030 Fund Class A	NLHAX	NAS CM	Open End	Target Date 2021-2045 (Asset Alloc)	B	C+	B+	Up	Y	1,000

★Expanded analysis of this fund is included in Section II.

Min Additional Investment	TOTAL RETURNS: 3-Month Total Return	6-Month Total Return	1-Year Total Return	3-Year Total Return	5-Year Total Return	PERFORMANCE: Dividend Yield (TTM)	Expense Ratio	3-Yr Std Deviation	3-Year Beta	ASSETS: NAV	Total Assets (MIL)	ASSET ALLOCATION & TURNOVER: %Cash	%Stocks	%Bonds	%Other	Turnover Ratio	BULL & BEAR: Last Bull Market Total Return	Last Bear Market Total Return	FEES: Front End Fee (%)	Back End Fee (%)	Inception Date
250	5.30	8.31	15.24	13.73	40.67		2.09	7.2	0.75	13.37	106.0	1	99	0	0	196	6.68	-12.21	2.50		Aug-17
250	5.17	8.49	11.94	17.31	59.51	0.01	1.77	8.24	0.89	12	418.8	3	90	7	0	96	20.22	-15.62	5.75		Apr-13
250	4.86	8.08	11.07	14.67	53.57	0	2.52	8.28	0.9	11.63	418.8	3	90	7	0	96	19.7	-15.88		1.00	Apr-13
	5.21	8.60	12.26	18.21	61.58	0.03	1.52	8.27	0.9	12.11	418.8	3	90	7	0	96	20.4	-15.53			Apr-04
250	5.12	8.47	11.98	17.33	59.58		1.77	8.27	0.9	12.1	418.8	3	90	7	0	96	20.22	-15.62	2.50		Aug-17
250	0.97	2.90	4.62	11.24	16.27	0.84	1.74	3.03	0.11	11.42	118.1	6	52	41	0	18			5.75		Apr-12
250	0.73	2.36	3.78	8.64	11.74	0.31	2.49	3.07	0.12	11.2	118.1	6	52	41	0	18				1.00	Apr-12
	1.04	2.96	4.90	11.93	17.50	1.01	1.49	3.05	0.14	11.45	118.1	6	52	41	0	18					Apr-12
250	0.93	2.79	4.60	11.06	16.00		1.74	3.05	0.14	11.4	118.1	6	52	41	0	18			2.50		Aug-17
50	4.41	6.72	11.39	19.77	52.68	2.37	0.13	5.89	0.55	68.69	1,951	1	63	35	0	4	11.71	-9.09			Mar-68
50	4.67	8.33	15.20	22.64	62.51	1.12	0.95	5.58		12.14	399.4	2	61	37	0	2	15.81	-10.19	5.00		May-06
50	4.75	8.41	15.09	20.82	58.25	0.66	1.65	5.64		12.16	399.4	2	61	37	0	2	15.25	-10.39		5.00	May-06
	4.70	8.32	15.07	21.66	60.35	0.91	1.27	5.68		11.97	399.4	2	61	37	0	2	15.54	-10.24			Sep-04
	4.77	8.39	15.20	22.33	61.71	1.03	1.07	5.64		12	399.4	2	61	37	0	2	15.62	-10.12			Sep-04
	4.68	8.29	15.26	23.12	63.77	1.25	0.77	5.6		12.02	399.4	2	61	37	0	2	15.77	-10.09			Sep-04
50	4.78	8.40	15.39	22.89	62.85	1.11	0.85	5.65		12.3	399.4	2	61	37	0	2	15.65	-10.12	5.00		Dec-00
50	4.74	8.40	15.33	23.37	64.32	1.29	0.7	5.6		12.17	399.4	2	61	37	0	2	15.93	-10.08			Feb-02
50	4.69	8.30	15.07	21.52	59.79	0.84	1.35	5.57		12.31	399.4	2	61	37	0	2	15.52	-10.31		3.00	Dec-00
50	7.74	13.37	23.88	33.31	108.32	0.37	1.15	9.62	0.92	10.66	649.7	1	99	0	0	57	26.02	-19.39	5.00		May-06
50	7.66	13.47	23.71	31.30	102.38	0	1.85	9.65	0.92	10.56	649.7	1	99	0	0	57	25.63	-19.61		5.00	May-06
50	7.65	13.45	23.74	32.13	104.72	0	1.55	9.66	0.92	11.19	649.7	1	99	0	0	57	25.78	-19.47		3.00	Dec-00
50	7.67	13.37	23.94	34.09	110.54	0.58	0.9	9.6	0.92	10.72	649.7	1	99	0	0	57	26.38	-19.33			Nov-01
	7.74	13.38	23.76	32.28	105.28	0.14	1.47	9.64	0.92	10.67	649.7	1	99	0	0	57	26.04	-19.58			Sep-04
	7.60	13.34	23.75	32.82	106.94	0.26	1.27	9.64	0.92	10.63	649.7	1	99	0	0	57	26.13	-19.46			Sep-04
	7.66	13.35	23.91	33.78	109.78	0.55	0.97	9.56	0.92	10.73	649.7	1	99	0	0	57	26.28	-19.33			Sep-04
50	7.76	13.45	23.95	33.52	108.62	0.42	1.05	9.63	0.92	11.2	649.7	1	99	0	0	57	26.14	-19.32	5.00		Dec-00
50	6.69	10.30	16.57	28.32	86.50	2.2	0.12	9.19	0.87	80.15	4,960	1	99	0	0	0	19.37	-17.29			Mar-68
50	3.79	10.96	33.67	25.06	39.94	0	1.5	12.84	0.97	13	163.7	3	91	0	6	103	20.97	-25.61	5.00		May-06
50	3.77	10.96	33.45	23.18	36.45	0	2.2	12.88	0.97	12.66	163.7	3	91	0	6	103	20.42	-25.85		5.00	May-06
50	3.84	11.00	33.58	24.04	37.68	0	1.9	12.87	0.97	12.88	163.7	3	91	0	6	103	20.68	-25.68		3.00	Dec-00
50	3.81	10.99	33.78	25.76	41.49	0.06	1.25	12.85	0.97	13.15	163.7	3	91	0	6	103	20.98	-25.44			Feb-02
	3.79	10.95	33.52	24.22	38.09	0	1.82	12.9	0.97	12.88	163.7	3	91	0	6	103	20.73	-25.64			Sep-04
	3.73	10.92	33.55	24.63	39.15	0	1.62	12.82	0.96	12.97	163.7	3	91	0	6	103	20.9	-25.63			Sep-04
	3.80	10.90	33.69	25.49	41.00	0.01	1.32	12.86	0.97	13.13	163.7	3	91	0	6	103	21.02	-25.47			Sep-04
50	3.78	11.04	33.74	25.28	40.24	0	1.4	12.86	0.97	13.14	163.7	3	91	0	6	103	20.89	-25.51	5.00		Dec-00
50	3.98	9.37	24.98	22.53	40.42	1.99	0.85	11.72	0.95	13.17	298.9	0	91	0	9	6	12.64	-23.5	5.00		May-06
50	3.99	9.39	24.77	20.55	36.68	1.44	1.55	11.74	0.95	13.19	298.9	0	91	0	9	6	12.36	-23.79		5.00	May-06
50	3.96	9.34	24.87	21.39	37.95	1.68	1.25	11.73	0.95	13.23	298.9	0	91	0	9	6	12.37	-23.6		3.00	Dec-00
50	4.05	9.35	25.03	23.20	41.88	2.21	0.6	11.68	0.95	13.19	298.9	0	91	0	9	6	12.9	-23.46			Feb-02
	3.93	9.32	24.80	21.54	38.41	1.76	1.17	11.74	0.95	13.19	298.9	0	91	0	9	6	12.58	-23.62			Sep-04
	4.00	9.33	24.86	22.19	39.56	1.88	0.97	11.72	0.95	13.14	298.9	0	91	0	9	6	12.64	-23.56			Sep-04
	4.02	9.32	24.98	22.99	41.41	2.17	0.67	11.74	0.95	13.2	298.9	0	91	0	9	6	12.81	-23.44			Sep-04
50	4.02	9.43	25.08	22.74	40.57	2.1	0.75	11.71	0.95	13.14	298.9	0	91	0	9	6	12.63	-23.54	5.00		Dec-00
50	2.77	5.38	11.42	15.08	33.36	1.65	0.91	5.27	0.48	14.97	2,168	2	48	50	0	9	13.34	-9.97	5.00		May-06
50	2.75	5.37	11.21	13.32	29.37	1.02	1.61	5.25	0.47	14.9	2,168	2	48	50	0	9	12.85	-10.26		5.00	May-06
50	2.77	5.37	11.47	15.77	34.71	1.98	0.66	5.26	0.47	15	2,168	2	48	50	0	9	13.56	-9.94			May-03
	2.74	5.29	11.28	14.21	31.43	1.47	1.23	5.29	0.48	14.89	2,168	2	48	50	0	9	13.21	-10.1			Sep-04
	2.78	5.33	11.32	14.80	32.59	1.66	1.03	5.3	0.48	14.89	2,168	2	48	50	0	9	13.25	-10			Sep-04
	2.71	5.31	11.42	15.51	34.22	1.92	0.73	5.28	0.48	14.97	2,168	2	48	50	0	9	13.47	-9.91			Sep-04
50	2.77	5.37	11.38	14.09	31.10	1.25	1.31	5.26	0.47	15.06	2,168	2	48	50	0	9	13.07	-10.11		3.00	May-03
50	2.84	5.46	11.53	15.38	33.56	1.92	0.81	5.25	0.47	14.89	2,168	2	48	50	0	9	13.27	-9.94	5.00		May-03
50	3.85	7.29	15.46	20.00	45.04	1.68	0.93	7.24	0.68	16.43	2,460	1	71	28	0	7	16.36	-13.69	5.00		May-06

Fund Name	MARKET Ticker Symbol	MARKET Traded On	FUND TYPE, CATEGORY & OBJECTIVE Fund Type	Category and (Prospectus Objective)	RATINGS Overall Rating	Reward Rating	Risk Rating	Recent Up/ Downgrade	MINIMUMS Open to New Investors	Min Initial Investment
State Farm LifePath 2030 Fund Class B	NLHBX	NAS CM	Open End	Target Date 2021-2045 (Asset Alloc)	B-	C+	B-	Down	Y	1,000
State Farm LifePath 2030 Fund Class Institutional	SAYIX	NAS CM	Open End	Target Date 2021-2045 (Asset Alloc)	B-	C+	B	Down	Y	1,000
State Farm LifePath 2030 Fund Class R1	RAYOX	NAS CM	Open End	Target Date 2021-2045 (Asset Alloc)	B-	C+	B	Down	Y	0
State Farm LifePath 2030 Fund Class R2	RAYTX	NAS CM	Open End	Target Date 2021-2045 (Asset Alloc)	B-	C+	B	Down	Y	0
State Farm LifePath 2030 Fund Class R3	RAYHX	NAS CM	Open End	Target Date 2021-2045 (Asset Alloc)	B	C+	B+	Up	Y	0
State Farm LifePath 2030 Fund Legacy Class B	SAYBX	NAS CM	Open End	Target Date 2021-2045 (Asset Alloc)	B-	C+	B	Down	Y	1,000
State Farm LifePath 2030 Fund Premier Shares	SAYAX	NAS CM	Open End	Target Date 2021-2045 (Asset Alloc)	B-	C+	B	Down	Y	1,000
State Farm LifePath 2040 Fund Class A	NLOAX	NAS CM	Open End	Target Date 2021-2045 (Asset Alloc)	B-	B-	B-	Down	Y	1,000
State Farm LifePath 2040 Fund Class B	NLBOX	NAS CM	Open End	Target Date 2021-2045 (Asset Alloc)	B-	C+	B-	Down	Y	1,000
State Farm LifePath 2040 Fund Class Institutional	SAUIX	NAS CM	Open End	Target Date 2021-2045 (Asset Alloc)	B-	B-	B-	Down	Y	1,000
State Farm LifePath 2040 Fund Class R1	RAUOX	NAS CM	Open End	Target Date 2021-2045 (Asset Alloc)	B-	C+	B-	Down	Y	0
State Farm LifePath 2040 Fund Class R2	RAUTX	NAS CM	Open End	Target Date 2021-2045 (Asset Alloc)	B-	B-	B-	Down	Y	0
State Farm LifePath 2040 Fund Class R3	RAUHX	NAS CM	Open End	Target Date 2021-2045 (Asset Alloc)	B-	B-	B	Down	Y	0
State Farm LifePath 2040 Fund Legacy Class B	SAUBX	NAS CM	Open End	Target Date 2021-2045 (Asset Alloc)	B-	C+	B-	Down	Y	1,000
State Farm LifePath 2040 Fund Premier Shares	SAUAX	NAS CM	Open End	Target Date 2021-2045 (Asset Alloc)	B-	B-	B-	Down	Y	1,000
State Farm LifePath 2050 Fund Class A	NLPAX	NAS CM	Open End	Target Date 2046+ (Asset Alloc)	B-	B-	B-	Down	Y	1,000
State Farm LifePath 2050 Fund Class R1	RAVRX	NAS CM	Open End	Target Date 2046+ (Asset Alloc)	B-	B-	B-	Down	Y	0
State Farm LifePath 2050 Fund Class R2	RAVSX	NAS CM	Open End	Target Date 2046+ (Asset Alloc)	B-	B-	B-	Down	Y	0
State Farm LifePath 2050 Fund Premier shares	NLPPX	NAS CM	Open End	Target Date 2046+ (Asset Alloc)	B-	B-	B-	Down	Y	1,000
State Farm LifePath Retirement Fund Class A	NILAX	NAS CM	Open End	Target Date 2000-2020 (Asset Alloc)	B	C+	B+	Up	Y	1,000
State Farm LifePath Retirement Fund Class B	NILBX	NAS CM	Open End	Target Date 2000-2020 (Asset Alloc)	B-	C	B+	Up	Y	1,000
State Farm LifePath Retirement Fund Class Institutional	SLRIX	NAS CM	Open End	Target Date 2000-2020 (Asset Alloc)	B	C+	A-	Up	Y	1,000
State Farm LifePath Retirement Fund Class R1	RLROX	NAS CM	Open End	Target Date 2000-2020 (Asset Alloc)	B-	C+	B+	Up	Y	0
State Farm LifePath Retirement Fund Class R2	RLRTX	NAS CM	Open End	Target Date 2000-2020 (Asset Alloc)	B-	C+	B+	Up	Y	0
State Farm LifePath Retirement Fund Class R3	RLRHX	NAS CM	Open End	Target Date 2000-2020 (Asset Alloc)	B	C+	B+	Up	Y	0
State Farm LifePath Retirement Fund Legacy Class B	SLRBX	NAS CM	Open End	Target Date 2000-2020 (Asset Alloc)	B-	C+	B+	Up	Y	1,000
State Farm LifePath Retirement Fund Premier Shares	SLRAX	NAS CM	Open End	Target Date 2000-2020 (Asset Alloc)	B	C+	B+	Up	Y	1,000
State Farm S&P 500 Index Fund Class A	SNPAX	NAS CM	Open End	US Equity Large Cap Blend (Growth)	B	B	B		Y	1,000
State Farm S&P 500 Index Fund Class B	SNPBX	NAS CM	Open End	US Equity Large Cap Blend (Growth)	B-	B-	B	Down	Y	1,000
State Farm S&P 500 Index Fund Class B Legacy	SLIBX	NAS CM	Open End	US Equity Large Cap Blend (Growth)	B	B-	B		Y	1,000
State Farm S&P 500 Index Fund Class Institutional	SFXIX	NAS CM	Open End	US Equity Large Cap Blend (Growth)	B	B	B		Y	1,000
State Farm S&P 500 Index Fund Class R1	RSPOX	NAS CM	Open End	US Equity Large Cap Blend (Growth)	B	B-	B		Y	0
State Farm S&P 500 Index Fund Class R2	RSPTX	NAS CM	Open End	US Equity Large Cap Blend (Growth)	B	B-	B		Y	0
State Farm S&P 500 Index Fund Class R3	RSPHX	NAS CM	Open End	US Equity Large Cap Blend (Growth)	B	B	B		Y	0
State Farm S&P 500 Index Fund Premier Shares	SLIAX	NAS CM	Open End	US Equity Large Cap Blend (Growth)	B	B	B		Y	1,000
State Farm Small Cap Index Fund Class A	SNRAX	NAS CM	Open End	US Equity Small Cap (Small Company)	B+	A-	B	Up	Y	1,000
State Farm Small Cap Index Fund Class B	SNRBX	NAS CM	Open End	US Equity Small Cap (Small Company)	B	B+	B	Up	Y	1,000
State Farm Small Cap Index Fund Class B Legacy	SMIBX	NAS CM	Open End	US Equity Small Cap (Small Company)	B	B+	B	Up	Y	1,000
State Farm Small Cap Index Fund Class Institutional	SMIIX	NAS CM	Open End	US Equity Small Cap (Small Company)	B+	A-	B	Up	Y	1,000
State Farm Small Cap Index Fund Class R1	RSIOX	NAS CM	Open End	US Equity Small Cap (Small Company)	B	B+	B	Up	Y	0
State Farm Small Cap Index Fund Class R2	RSITX	NAS CM	Open End	US Equity Small Cap (Small Company)	B+	B+	B	Up	Y	0
State Farm Small Cap Index Fund Class R3	RSIHX	NAS CM	Open End	US Equity Small Cap (Small Company)	B+	A-	B	Up	Y	0
State Farm Small Cap Index Fund Premier Shares	SMIAX	NAS CM	Open End	US Equity Small Cap (Small Company)	B+	A-	B	Up	Y	1,000
State Farm Small/Mid Cap Equity Fund Class A	SSNAX	NAS CM	Open End	US Equity Small Cap (Small Company)	B-	C+	B	Up	Y	1,000
State Farm Small/Mid Cap Equity Fund Class B	SSNBX	NAS CM	Open End	US Equity Small Cap (Small Company)	B-	C+	B	Up	Y	1,000
State Farm Small/Mid Cap Equity Fund Class B Legacy	SFSBX	NAS CM	Open End	US Equity Small Cap (Small Company)	B-	C+	B	Up	Y	1,000
State Farm Small/Mid Cap Equity Fund Class Institutional	SFEIX	NAS CM	Open End	US Equity Small Cap (Small Company)	B-	C+	B	Up	Y	1,000
State Farm Small/Mid Cap Equity Fund Class R1	RSEOX	NAS CM	Open End	US Equity Small Cap (Small Company)	B-	C+	B	Up	Y	0
State Farm Small/Mid Cap Equity Fund Class R2	RSETX	NAS CM	Open End	US Equity Small Cap (Small Company)	B-	C+	B	Up	Y	0
State Farm Small/Mid Cap Equity Fund Class R3	RSEHX	NAS CM	Open End	US Equity Small Cap (Small Company)	B-	C+	B	Up	Y	0
State Farm Small/Mid Cap Equity Fund Premier Shares	SFSAX	NAS CM	Open End	US Equity Small Cap (Small Company)	B-	C+	B	Up	Y	1,000
State Street Asia Pacific Value Spotlight Fund Class K	SIDKX	NAS CM	Open End	Asia Equity (Growth)	D	C	B		Y	10,000,000

★ Expanded analysis of this fund is included in Section II.

Min Additional Investment	TOTAL RETURNS: 3-Month Total Return	6-Month Total Return	1-Year Total Return	3-Year Total Return	5-Year Total Return	PERFORMANCE: Dividend Yield (TTM)	Expense Ratio	3-Yr Std Deviation	3-Year Beta	ASSETS: NAV	Total Assets (MIL)	ASSET ALLOCATION & TURNOVER: %Cash	%Stocks	%Bonds	%Other	Turnover Ratio	BULL & BEAR: Last Bull Market Total Return	Last Bear Market Total Return	FEES: Front End Fee (%)	Back End Fee (%)	Inception Date
50	3.83	7.29	15.42	19.01	41.83	1.51	1.13	7.26	0.68	16.38	2,460	1	71	28	0	7	15.93	-13.92		5.00	May-06
50	3.83	7.25	15.51	20.62	46.57	1.95	0.68	7.2	0.68	16.54	2,460	1	71	28	0	7	16.61	-13.62			May-03
	3.77	7.24	15.31	19.06	42.93	1.49	1.25	7.23	0.68	16.33	2,460	1	71	28	0	7	16.24	-13.85			Sep-04
	3.79	7.18	15.37	19.53	44.16	1.67	1.05	7.22	0.68	16.38	2,460	1	71	28	0	7	16.31	-13.72			Sep-04
	3.83	7.25	15.43	20.42	46.02	1.92	0.75	7.22	0.68	16.55	2,460	1	71	28	0	7	16.59	-13.64			Sep-04
50	3.88	7.30	15.35	18.95	42.59	1.26	1.33	7.23	0.68	16.56	2,460	1	71	28	0	7	16.16	-13.84		3.00	May-03
50	3.90	7.34	15.58	20.22	45.27	1.9	0.83	7.21	0.68	16.44	2,460	1	71	28	0	7	16.4	-13.69	5.00		May-03
50	4.73	8.90	18.92	24.01	55.11	1.57	0.96	8.96	0.85	17.7	1,899	1	90	9	0	6	19.03	-16.71	5.00		May-06
50	4.72	8.90	18.88	23.04	51.75	1.35	1.16	8.99	0.85	17.65	1,899	1	90	9	0	6	18.53	-16.95		5.00	May-06
50	4.76	8.88	19.02	24.79	56.70	1.78	0.7	8.95	0.85	17.87	1,899	1	90	9	0	6	19.15	-16.66			May-03
	4.73	8.85	18.85	23.15	53.00	1.28	1.27	8.96	0.85	17.63	1,899	1	90	9	0	6	18.79	-16.8			Sep-04
	4.72	8.89	18.93	23.68	54.31	1.53	1.07	8.98	0.85	17.69	1,899	1	90	9	0	6	18.89	-16.72			Sep-04
	4.69	8.82	18.92	24.50	56.14	1.72	0.77	8.96	0.85	18.07	1,899	1	90	9	0	6	19.15	-16.66			Sep-04
50	4.78	8.90	18.90	22.99	52.53	1.09	1.36	8.95	0.85	17.91	1,899	1	90	9	0	6	18.7	-16.87		3.00	May-03
50	4.77	8.98	19.11	24.33	55.49	1.67	0.86	8.96	0.85	17.78	1,899	1	90	9	0	6	18.95	-16.68	5.00		May-03
50	5.15	9.63	20.39	25.77	61.63	1.56	0.99	9.53	0.9	12.4	463.5	1	99	1	0	5	21.25	-19.17	5.00		Jul-08
	5.11	9.48	20.21	24.75	59.17	1.37	1.3	9.56	0.91	12.42	463.5	1	99	1	0	5	21.14	-19.33			Jul-08
	5.06	9.51	20.24	25.20	60.55	1.52	1.11	9.51	0.9	12.43	463.5	1	99	1	0	5	21.15	-19.21			Jul-08
50	5.19	9.67	20.58	25.97	61.89	1.8	0.89	9.53	0.9	12.37	463.5	1	99	1	0	5	21.25	-19.17	5.00		May-16
50	2.41	4.78	9.94	13.46	26.39	1.55	0.91	4.29	0.37	13.15	1,245	2	41	57	0	7	9.94	-5.5	5.00		May-06
50	2.39	4.74	9.71	11.59	23.17	1.22	1.61	4.29	0.36	13.23	1,245	2	41	57	0	7	9.51	-5.73		5.00	May-06
50	2.43	4.74	10.02	14.07	27.76	1.62	0.65	4.25	0.36	13.46	1,245	2	41	57	0	7	10.05	-5.36			May-03
	2.38	4.71	9.84	12.56	24.62	1.34	1.22	4.28	0.36	13.2	1,245	2	41	57	0	7	9.75	-5.57			Sep-04
	2.40	4.69	9.92	13.10	25.68	1.42	1.02	4.29	0.37	13.5	1,245	2	41	57	0	7	9.74	-5.45			Sep-04
	2.41	4.71	9.96	13.84	27.28	1.55	0.72	4.27	0.37	13.44	1,245	2	41	57	0	7	10.03	-5.4			Sep-04
50	2.41	4.79	9.93	12.42	24.28	1.28	1.31	4.28	0.36	13.55	1,245	2	41	57	0	7	9.64	-5.6		3.00	May-03
50	2.38	4.80	10.06	13.58	26.47	1.59	0.81	4.27	0.36	13.45	1,245	2	41	57	0	7	9.83	-5.41	5.00		May-03
50	6.54	11.16	21.20	34.26	104.67	1.24	0.66	10.13	1	19.76	1,540	2	98	0	0	3	24.55	-16.53	5.00		May-06
50	6.53	11.18	21.01	32.20	98.46	0.59	1.36	10.12	1	19.93	1,540	2	98	0	0	3	24.04	-16.79		5.00	May-06
50	6.53	11.19	21.14	33.08	101.15	0.79	1.06	10.1	1	20.13	1,540	2	98	0	0	3	24.31	-16.74		3.00	Dec-00
50	6.54	11.18	21.33	35.06	106.73	1.44	0.41	10.12	1	19.95	1,540	2	98	0	0	3	24.75	-16.5			Feb-02
	6.52	11.19	21.13	33.25	101.70	1	0.98	10.06	1	19.85	1,540	2	98	0	0	3	24.42	-16.69			Sep-04
	6.53	11.15	21.14	33.89	103.47	1.15	0.78	10.1	1	19.74	1,540	2	98	0	0	3	24.51	-16.65			Sep-04
	6.29	10.92	21.01	34.42	105.43	1.42	0.48	10.1	1	19.91	1,540	2	98	0	0	3	24.76	-16.52			Sep-04
50	6.55	11.26	21.39	34.45	104.88	1.32	0.56	10.08	1	19.88	1,540	2	98	0	0	3	24.54	-16.56	5.00		Dec-00
50	2.49	8.20	13.28	28.24	88.58	0.55	0.73	14.16	1	18.04	549.4	1	99	0	0	19	27.11	-25.37	5.00		May-06
50	3.27	8.93	13.99	27.47	85.27	0.12	1.28	14.12	1	17.53	549.4	1	99	0	0	19	26.63	-25.66		5.00	May-06
50	3.20	8.91	14.00	27.98	86.75	0.23	1.13	14.14	1	17.39	549.4	1	99	0	0	19	26.88	-25.57		3.00	Dec-00
50	3.22	8.91	14.18	29.83	91.88	0.7	0.48	14.13	1	18.19	549.4	1	99	0	0	19	27.37	-25.33			Feb-02
	3.22	8.93	13.99	28.20	87.26	0.3	1.05	14.12	1	17.99	549.4	1	99	0	0	19	26.94	-25.5			Sep-04
	3.21	8.90	14.01	28.73	88.78	0.42	0.85	14.12	1	18.04	549.4	1	99	0	0	19	27.05	-25.41			Sep-04
	3.20	8.89	14.09	29.55	91.31	0.65	0.55	14.11	1	18.21	549.4	1	99	0	0	19	27.37	-25.39			Sep-04
50	3.27	9.00	14.24	29.37	90.22	0.56	0.63	14.12	1	17.86	549.4	1	99	0	0	19	27.13	-25.37	5.00		Dec-00
50	4.53	8.85	11.66	18.67	70.00	0	1.14	12.53	0.99	11.86	311.1	1	99	0	0	104	28.77	-24.13	5.00		May-06
50	4.55	8.89	11.45	16.94	65.60	0	1.84	12.48	0.99	10.78	311.1	1	99	0	0	104	28.28	-24.37		5.00	May-06
50	4.47	8.82	11.44	17.64	66.96	0	1.54	12.57	1	10.45	311.1	1	99	0	0	104	28.49	-24.25		3.00	Dec-00
50	4.53	8.89	11.71	19.47	71.84	0.07	0.89	12.51	0.99	12.26	311.1	1	99	0	0	104	29	-24.09			Feb-02
	4.46	8.77	11.46	17.86	67.58	0	1.46	12.52	0.99	11.09	311.1	1	99	0	0	104	28.57	-24.3			Sep-04
	4.48	8.75	11.54	18.30	68.83	0	1.26	12.52	0.99	11.48	311.1	1	99	0	0	104	28.64	-24.24			Sep-04
	4.48	8.81	11.56	19.17	71.18	0.02	0.96	12.48	0.99	12.09	311.1	1	99	0	0	104	28.93	-24.06			Sep-04
50	4.51	8.83	11.70	18.85	70.21	0	1.04	12.51	0.99	11.56	311.1	1	99	0	0	104	28.77	-24.16	5.00		Dec-00
	5.24	8.85	24.87			0.14	0.75			12.05	2.5	0	96	4	0						Sep-16

	MARKET			FUND TYPE, CATEGORY & OBJECTIVE	RATINGS				MINIMUMS	
Fund Name	Ticker Symbol	Traded On	Fund Type	Category and (Prospectus Objective)	Overall Rating	Reward Rating	Risk Rating	Recent Up/ Downgrade	Open to New Investors	Min Initial Investment
State Street Disciplined Emerging Mkts Equity Fund Cls A	SSELX	NAS CM	Open End	Emerging Markets Equity (Div Emerging Mkts)	C+	C+	C	Up	Y	2,000
State Street Disciplined Emerging Mkts Equity Fund Cls I	SSEOX	NAS CM	Open End	Emerging Markets Equity (Div Emerging Mkts)	C+	C+	C	Up	Y	1,000,000
State Street Disciplined Emerging Mkts Equity Fund Cls K	SSEQX	NAS CM	Open End	Emerging Markets Equity (Div Emerging Mkts)	C+	C+	C	Up	Y	10,000,000
State Street Disciplined Emerging Mkts Equity Fund Cls N	SSEMX	NAS CM	Open End	Emerging Markets Equity (Div Emerging Mkts)	C+	C+	C	Up		1,000
State Street Disciplined Global Equity Fund Class I	SSGMX	NAS CM	Open End	Global Equity (Growth & Income)	C-	C	B+	Up	Y	1,000,000
State Street Disciplined Global Equity Portfolio	US78470P1012		Open End	Global Equity (Growth)	C-	C	B+	Up	Y	0
State Street Disciplined International Equity Fund Class I	SSZIX	NAS CM	Open End	Global Equity Large Cap (Growth)	C-	C	B	Up	Y	1,000,000
State Street Disciplined U.S. Equity Fund Class I	SSJIX	NAS CM	Open End	US Equity Large Cap Value (Growth)	C-	C	B+	Up	Y	1,000,000
State Street Emerging Markets Equity Index Fund Class K	SSKEX	NAS CM	Open End	Emerging Markets Equity (Div Emerging Mkts)	C-	C	B+	Up	Y	10,000,000
State Street Equity 500 Index Fund Administrative Shares	STFAX	NAS CM	Open End	US Equity Large Cap Blend (Growth & Income)	B	B	B		Y	25,000,000
State Street Equity 500 Index Fund Class A	SSSVX	NAS CM	Open End	US Equity Large Cap Blend (Growth & Income)	B	B	B		Y	2,000
State Street Equity 500 Index Fund Class I	SSSWX	NAS CM	Open End	US Equity Large Cap Blend (Growth & Income)	B	B	B		Y	1,000,000
State Street Equity 500 Index Fund Class K	SSSYX	NAS CM	Open End	US Equity Large Cap Blend (Growth & Income)	B	B	B		Y	10,000,000
State Street Equity 500 Index Fund Class R Shares	SSFRX	NAS CM	Open End	US Equity Large Cap Blend (Growth & Income)	B	B-	B		Y	25,000,000
State Street Equity 500 Index Fund Service Shares	STBIX	NAS CM	Open End	US Equity Large Cap Blend (Growth & Income)	B	B	B		Y	25,000,000
State Street Equity 500 Index II Portfolio	SSEYX	NAS CM	Open End	US Equity Large Cap Blend (Growth & Income)	B	B	B	Up	Y	0
State Street European Value Spotlight Fund Class K	SIBKX	NAS CM	Open End	Europe Equity Large Cap (Growth)	D	C	B		Y	10,000,000
State Street Global Equity ex-U.S. Index Fund Class A	SSGHX	NAS CM	Open End	Global Equity Large Cap (Growth & Income)	B-	B-	B-	Up	Y	2,000
State Street Global Equity ex-U.S. Index Fund Class I	SSGJX	NAS CM	Open End	Global Equity Large Cap (Growth & Income)	B-	B-	B-	Up	Y	1,000,000
State Street Global Equity ex-U.S. Index Fund Class K	SSGLX	NAS CM	Open End	Global Equity Large Cap (Growth & Income)	B-	B-	B-	Up	Y	10,000,000
State Street Global Equity ex-U.S. Index Portfolio	SSGVX	NAS CM	Open End	Global Equity Large Cap (Growth & Income)	B-	B-	B-	Up	Y	0
State Street Global Value Spotlight Fund Class K	SIAKX	NAS CM	Open End	Global Equity (Growth)	D	C	B		Y	10,000,000
State Street Hedged Intl Developed Equity Index Fund Cls K	SSHQX	NAS CM	Open End	Global Equity Large Cap (Foreign Stock)	C+	C+	B-	Up	Y	10,000,000
State Street Inst Intl Equity Fund Investment Cls	SIEIX	NAS CM	Open End	Global Equity Large Cap (Foreign Stock)	B-	C+	B-	Up	Y	5,000,000
State Street Inst Intl Equity Fund Service Cls	SIESX	NAS CM	Open End	Global Equity Large Cap (Foreign Stock)	B-	C+	B-	Up	Y	5,000,000
State Street Inst Premier Growth Eq Fund Inv Cls	SSPGX	NAS CM	Open End	US Equity Large Cap Growth (Growth)	B	B	B+		Y	5,000,000
State Street Inst Premier Growth Equity Fund Service Cls	SSPSX	NAS CM	Open End	US Equity Large Cap Growth (Growth)	B	B	B+		Y	5,000,000
State Street Inst Small-Cap Equity Fund Investment Cls	SIVIX	NAS CM	Open End	US Equity Small Cap (Small Company)	B	B	B	Up	Y	5,000,000
State Street Inst Small-Cap Equity Fund Service Cls	SSQSX	NAS CM	Open End	US Equity Small Cap (Small Company)	B	B	B	Up	Y	5,000,000
State Street Institutional U.S. Equity Fund Investment Cls	SUSIX	NAS CM	Open End	US Equity Large Cap Blend (Growth)	B-	B-	B-	Down	Y	5,000,000
State Street Institutional U.S. Equity Fund Service Class	SUSSX	NAS CM	Open End	US Equity Large Cap Blend (Growth)	B-	B-	B-	Down	Y	5,000,000
State Street International Value Spotlight Fund Class K	SIVSX	NAS CM	Open End	Global Equity Large Cap (Growth)	D	C	B+		Y	10,000,000
State Street Small/Mid Cap Equity Index Fund Class A	SSMJX	NAS CM	Open End	US Equity Small Cap (Growth & Income)	C	C+	B	Up	Y	2,000
State Street Small/Mid Cap Equity Index Fund Class I	SSMLX	NAS CM	Open End	US Equity Small Cap (Growth & Income)	C	C+	B-	Up	Y	1,000,000
State Street Small/Mid Cap Equity Index Fund Class K	SSMKX	NAS CM	Open End	US Equity Small Cap (Growth & Income)	C	C+	B-	Up	Y	10,000,000
State Street Small/Mid Cap Equity Index Portfolio	SSMHX	NAS CM	Open End	US Equity Small Cap (Growth & Income)	C	C+	B-	Up	Y	0
State Street Target Retirement 2015 Fund Class A	SSBBX	NAS CM	Open End	Target Date 2000-2020 (Asset Alloc)	C+	C	B	Up	Y	2,000
State Street Target Retirement 2015 Fund Class I	SSBFX	NAS CM	Open End	Target Date 2000-2020 (Asset Alloc)	B-	C	B	Up	Y	1,000,000
State Street Target Retirement 2015 Fund Class K	SSBHX	NAS CM	Open End	Target Date 2000-2020 (Asset Alloc)	C+	C	B	Up	Y	10,000,000
State Street Target Retirement 2020 Fund Class A	SSBJX	NAS CM	Open End	Target Date 2000-2020 (Asset Alloc)	C+	C	B	Down	Y	2,000
State Street Target Retirement 2020 Fund Class I	SSBNX	NAS CM	Open End	Target Date 2000-2020 (Asset Alloc)	C+	C	B	Down	Y	1,000,000
State Street Target Retirement 2020 Fund Class K	SSBOX	NAS CM	Open End	Target Date 2000-2020 (Asset Alloc)	C+	C	B	Down	Y	10,000,000
State Street Target Retirement 2025 Fund Class A	SSBPX	NAS CM	Open End	Target Date 2021-2045 (Asset Alloc)	C+	C+	B	Down	Y	2,000
State Street Target Retirement 2025 Fund Class I	SSBRX	NAS CM	Open End	Target Date 2021-2045 (Asset Alloc)	C+	C+	B	Down	Y	1,000,000
State Street Target Retirement 2025 Fund Class K	SSBSX	NAS CM	Open End	Target Date 2021-2045 (Asset Alloc)	C+	C+	B	Down	Y	10,000,000
State Street Target Retirement 2030 Fund Class A	SSBUX	NAS CM	Open End	Target Date 2021-2045 (Asset Alloc)	C+	C+	B	Down	Y	2,000
State Street Target Retirement 2030 Fund Class I	SSBWX	NAS CM	Open End	Target Date 2021-2045 (Asset Alloc)	C+	C+	B	Down	Y	1,000,000
State Street Target Retirement 2030 Fund Class K	SSBYX	NAS CM	Open End	Target Date 2021-2045 (Asset Alloc)	B-	C+	B	Up	Y	10,000,000
State Street Target Retirement 2035 Fund Class A	SSBZX	NAS CM	Open End	Target Date 2021-2045 (Asset Alloc)	C+	C+	B-	Down	Y	2,000
State Street Target Retirement 2035 Fund Class I	SSCJX	NAS CM	Open End	Target Date 2021-2045 (Asset Alloc)	C+	C+	B	Down	Y	1,000,000
State Street Target Retirement 2035 Fund Class K	SSCKX	NAS CM	Open End	Target Date 2021-2045 (Asset Alloc)	B-	C+	B	Up	Y	10,000,000
State Street Target Retirement 2040 Fund Class A	SSCLX	NAS CM	Open End	Target Date 2021-2045 (Asset Alloc)	C+	C+	B-	Down	Y	2,000

★ Expanded analysis of this fund is included in Section II.

	TOTAL RETURNS					PERFORMANCE				ASSETS		ASSET ALLOCATION & TURNOVER					BULL & BEAR		FEES		
Min Additional Investment	3-Month Total Return	6-Month Total Return	1-Year Total Return	3-Year Total Return	5-Year Total Return	Dividend Yield (TTM)	Expense Ratio	3-Yr Std Deviation	3-Year Beta	NAV	Total Assets (MIL)	%Cash	%Stocks	%Bonds	%Other	Turnover Ratio	Last Bull Market Total Return	Last Bear Market Total Return	Front End Fee (%)	Back End Fee (%)	Inception Date
	4.76	10.34	28.52	10.36	0.21	1.35	1.45	13.88	0.86	8.44	88.3	1	99	0	0	38	18.62	-27.77	5.25		Jul-14
	4.88	10.57	28.84	11.24	1.13	1.28	1.2	13.88	0.86	8.5	88.3	1	99	0	0	38	18.62	-27.77			Jul-14
	4.78	10.45	28.80	11.60	1.53	1.46	1	13.91	0.86	8.52	88.3	1	99	0	0	38	18.62	-27.77			Jul-14
100	4.73	10.42	28.48	10.88	0.75	1.22	1.25	13.91	0.86	8.5	88.3	1	99	0	0	38	18.62	-27.77			Mar-94
	4.23	7.88	21.26			2.43	0.95			12.48	5.1	2	98	0	1	38					Feb-16
	4.31	8.12	21.90			2.14	0			12.47	5.0	2	98	0	1						Feb-16
	3.34	7.52	25.19			1.9	1.05			11.97	3.7	1	97	0	2						Feb-16
	6.65	9.61	20.22			1.3	0.85			12.58	4.0	0	99	1	0						Feb-16
	7.40	15.87	37.18			1.49	0.18			14.46	591.2	3	95	0	1	14					Dec-15
	6.54	11.32	21.42	35.76	108.96	1.25	0.21	10.12	1	21.62	764.0	1	99	0	0	5	25.07	-16.4			Apr-01
	0.98	5.40	14.86	27.64	95.96	1	0.51	10.11	1	21.63	764.0	1	99	0	0	5	25	-16.44	5.25		Sep-14
	0.79	5.30	14.80	28.28	97.42	1.21	0.26	10.12	1	21.63	764.0	1	99	0	0	5	25.07	-16.4			Sep-14
	2.90	7.55	17.43	31.66	102.72	1.38	0.06	10.12	1	21.62	764.0	1	99	0	0	5	25.07	-16.4			Sep-14
	6.46	11.09	20.95	33.98	104.24	0.87	0.66	10.11	1	21.61	764.0	1	99	0	0	5	24.7	-16.6			Jun-05
	6.49	11.27	21.33	35.38	107.93	1.17	0.31	10.11	1	21.6	764.0	1	99	0	0	5	24.99	-16.5			Mar-03
	6.59	11.42	21.65	36.78		1.32	0.03	10.09	1	13.07	2,020	2	98	0	0	5					Aug-14
	2.45	7.08	22.77			0.07	0.76			12.16	1.3	5	95	0	0						Sep-16
	3.50	9.74	25.05	22.15		1.02	0.6	11.84	0.96	10.67	499.7	1	98	0	0	8			5.25		Sep-14
	3.57	9.90	25.37	23.08		1.22	0.35	11.86	0.96	10.67	499.7	1	98	0	0	8					Sep-14
	3.56	10.00	25.48	23.19		1.22	0.15	11.86	0.96	10.68	499.7	1	98	0	0	8					Sep-14
	4.97	11.50	27.19	25.07		1.25	0.08	11.88	0.96	10.81	1,359	0	99	0	0	8					Sep-14
	9.01	10.28	26.46			0.32	0.76			12.05	2.6	7	93	0	0						Sep-16
	3.94	7.80	16.85			1.83	0.2			10.4	2,851	42	58	0	0	1					May-15
	4.40	9.29	22.69	19.84	37.42	1.54	0.57	12.87	1.04	13.82	1,246	3	97	0	0	30	16.31	-25.76			Nov-97
	4.31	9.05	22.38	18.97	35.69	1.37	0.82	12.85	1.03	13.75	1,246	3	97	0	0	30	16.1	-25.86			Jan-01
	4.31	10.29	28.77	35.99	116.43	0.69	0.38	13.16	1.19	15.25	382.2	3	97	0	0	24	28.91	-16.75			Oct-99
	4.27	10.18	28.51	34.97	113.84	0.51	0.63	13.18	1.19	15.06	382.2	3	97	0	0	24	28.7	-16.78			Jan-01
	2.68	7.32	13.07	33.95	96.14	0.18	0.89	13	0.9	19.51	1,498	7	93	0	0	34	28.78	-21.71			Aug-98
	2.59	7.23	12.78	32.95	93.86	0.04	1.14	13	0.9	19.54	1,498	7	93	0	0	34	28.55	-21.73			Sep-05
	4.49	8.86	20.45	28.48	100.68	1.31	0.37	11.28	1.1	12.31	477.8	2	98	0	0	80	26.16	-18.65			Nov-97
	4.40	8.74	20.17	27.48	99.35	1.01	0.62	11.26	1.09	13.19	477.8	2	98	0	0	80	25.87	-18.66			Jan-01
	5.76	6.74	22.87			0.14	0.76			12.56	2.7	6	94	0	0						Jul-16
	-0.41	4.54	11.99			0.89	0.53			11.95	23.0	2	98	0	0	21			5.25		Oct-15
	-0.58	4.36	11.99			1.1	0.28			11.95	23.0	2	98	0	0	21					Oct-15
	-0.58	4.36	11.99			1.1	0.08			11.95	23.0	2	98	0	0	21					Aug-15
	4.90	10.13	18.20			0.75	0.03			12.1	355.0	2	98	0	0	21					Aug-15
	2.22	4.72	10.02	14.76		1.22	0.58	4.94	0.43	10.84	149.7	1	40	58	0	49			4.50		Sep-14
	2.37	4.98	10.39	15.73		1.45	0.33	4.94	0.43	10.85	149.7	1	40	58	0	49					Sep-14
	2.37	4.88	10.39	15.73		1.45	0.13	4.94	0.43	10.85	149.7	1	40	58	0	49					Sep-14
	3.15	6.26	13.08	18.51		1.26	0.58	6.07	0.55	11.35	569.1	2	53	46	0	28			4.50		Sep-14
	3.23	6.43	13.37	19.30		1.49	0.33	6.08	0.55	11.34	569.1	2	53	46	0	28					Sep-14
	3.23	6.34	13.37	19.34		1.48	0.13	6.08	0.55	11.34	569.1	2	53	46	0	28					Sep-14
	3.96	7.69	16.24	21.98		1.16	0.58	7.02	0.65	11.74	618.2	2	64	34	0	21			4.50		Sep-14
	4.04	7.87	16.53	22.91		1.37	0.33	7.01	0.65	11.74	618.2	2	64	34	0	21					Sep-14
	4.04	7.86	16.52	23.03		1.37	0.13	7	0.65	11.75	618.2	2	64	34	0	21					Sep-14
	4.47	8.54	17.94	24.17		1.11	0.58	7.59	0.71	12	608.3	2	72	26	0	18			4.50		Sep-14
	4.47	8.63	18.27	24.90		1.33	0.33	7.6	0.71	11.98	608.3	2	72	26	0	18					Sep-14
	4.46	8.71	18.35	25.06		1.33	0.13	7.6	0.71	12	608.3	2	72	26	0	18					Sep-14
	4.78	9.28	19.33	25.81		1.05	0.58	8.19	0.77	12.2	447.4	2	79	19	0	18			4.50		Sep-14
	4.87	9.38	19.55	26.56		1.26	0.33	8.19	0.77	12.18	447.4	2	79	19	0	18					Sep-14
	4.86	9.45	19.73	26.85		1.26	0.13	8.2	0.77	12.21	447.4	2	79	19	0	18					Sep-14
	5.03	9.73	20.28	26.78		1.08	0.58	8.7	0.82	12.26	365.9	2	84	14	0	16			4.50		Sep-14

	MARKET			FUND TYPE, CATEGORY & OBJECTIVE	RATINGS				MINIMUMS	
Fund Name	Ticker Symbol	Traded On	Fund Type	Category and (Prospectus Objective)	Overall Rating	Reward Rating	Risk Rating	Recent Up/ Downgrade	Open to New Investors	Min Initial Investment
State Street Target Retirement 2040 Fund Class I	SSCNX	NAS CM	Open End	Target Date 2021-2045 (Asset Alloc)	C+	C+	B-	Down	Y	1,000,000
State Street Target Retirement 2040 Fund Class K	SSCQX	NAS CM	Open End	Target Date 2021-2045 (Asset Alloc)	C+	C+	B-	Down	Y	10,000,000
State Street Target Retirement 2045 Fund Class A	SSCUX	NAS CM	Open End	Target Date 2021-2045 (Asset Alloc)	C+	C+	B-	Down	Y	2,000
State Street Target Retirement 2045 Fund Class I	SSDDX	NAS CM	Open End	Target Date 2021-2045 (Asset Alloc)	C+	C+	B-	Down	Y	1,000,000
State Street Target Retirement 2045 Fund Class K	SSDEX	NAS CM	Open End	Target Date 2021-2045 (Asset Alloc)	C+	C+	B-	Down	Y	10,000,000
State Street Target Retirement 2050 Fund Class A	SSDFX	NAS CM	Open End	Target Date 2046+ (Asset Alloc)	C+	C+	B-	Down	Y	2,000
State Street Target Retirement 2050 Fund Class I	SSDJX	NAS CM	Open End	Target Date 2046+ (Asset Alloc)	C+	C+	B-	Down	Y	1,000,000
State Street Target Retirement 2050 Fund Class K	SSDLX	NAS CM	Open End	Target Date 2046+ (Asset Alloc)	C+	C+	B-	Down	Y	10,000,000
State Street Target Retirement 2055 Fund Class A	SSDMX	NAS CM	Open End	Target Date 2046+ (Asset Alloc)	C+	C+	B-	Down	Y	2,000
State Street Target Retirement 2055 Fund Class I	SSDOX	NAS CM	Open End	Target Date 2046+ (Asset Alloc)	C+	C+	B-	Down	Y	1,000,000
State Street Target Retirement 2055 Fund Class K	SSDQX	NAS CM	Open End	Target Date 2046+ (Asset Alloc)	C+	C+	B-	Down	Y	10,000,000
State Street Target Retirement 2060 Fund Class A	SSDTX	NAS CM	Open End	Target Date 2046+ (Asset Alloc)	C+	C+	B-	Down	Y	2,000
State Street Target Retirement 2060 Fund Class I	SSDWX	NAS CM	Open End	Target Date 2046+ (Asset Alloc)	C+	C+	B-	Down	Y	1,000,000
State Street Target Retirement 2060 Fund Class K	SSDYX	NAS CM	Open End	Target Date 2046+ (Asset Alloc)	C+	C+	B-	Down	Y	10,000,000
State Street Target Retirement Fund Class A	SSFLX	NAS CM	Open End	Target Date 2000-2020 (Asset Alloc)	C+	C	B	Up	Y	2,000
State Street Target Retirement Fund Class I	SSFNX	NAS CM	Open End	Target Date 2000-2020 (Asset Alloc)	C+	C	B	Up	Y	1,000,000
State Street Target Retirement Fund Class K	SSFOX	NAS CM	Open End	Target Date 2000-2020 (Asset Alloc)	C+	C	B	Up	Y	10,000,000
State Street U.S. Value Spotlight Fund Class K	SIEKX	NAS CM	Open End	US Equity Large Cap Value (Growth)	D	C-	B		Y	10,000,000
Steben Managed Futures Strategy Fund Class A	SKLAX	NAS CM	Open End	Other Alternative (Income)	C	C	C	Up	Y	2,500
Steben Managed Futures Strategy Fund Class C	SKLCX	NAS CM	Open End	Other Alternative (Income)	C	C	C	Up	Y	2,500
Steben Managed Futures Strategy Fund Class I	SKLIX	NAS CM	Open End	Other Alternative (Income)	C	C	C	Up	Y	1,000,000
Steben Managed Futures Strategy Fund Class N	SKLNX	NAS CM	Open End	Other Alternative (Income)	C	C	C	Up	Y	2,500
Steinberg Select Fund Institutional Shares	STMIX	NAS CM	Open End	US Equity Mid Cap (Growth)	C+	C+	B-	Up	Y	100,000
Sterling Capital Behavioral Intl Equity Fund Cls A	SBIAX	NAS CM	Open End	Global Equity Large Cap (Foreign Stock)	C+	C+	C+	Up	Y	1,000
Sterling Capital Behavioral Intl Equity Fund Cls C	SBIDX	NAS CM	Open End	Global Equity Large Cap (Foreign Stock)	C+	C+	C+	Up	Y	1,000
Sterling Capital Behavioral Intl Equity Fund Inst Shares	SBIIX	NAS CM	Open End	Global Equity Large Cap (Foreign Stock)	C+	C+	C+	Up	Y	1,000,000
Sterling Capital Behavioral Large Cap Value Equity Fund A	BBTGX	NAS CM	Open End	US Equity Large Cap Value (Growth & Income)	B	B-	B	Up	Y	1,000
Sterling Capital Behavioral Large Cap Value Equity Fund C	BCVCX	NAS CM	Open End	US Equity Large Cap Value (Growth & Income)	B	B-	B	Up	Y	1,000
Sterling Capital Behavioral Large Cap Value Eq Fund Inst	BBISX	NAS CM	Open End	US Equity Large Cap Value (Growth & Income)	B	B-	B	Up	Y	1,000,000
Sterling Capital Behavioral Small Cap Value Eq Fund Cls A	SPSAX	NAS CM	Open End	US Equity Small Cap (Small Company)	B+	B+	B	Up	Y	1,000
Sterling Capital Behavioral Small Cap Value Eq Fund Cls C	SPSDX	NAS CM	Open End	US Equity Small Cap (Small Company)	B	B	B	Up	Y	1,000
Sterling Capital Behavioral Small Cap Value Eq Fund Cls R	SPSRX	NAS CM	Open End	US Equity Small Cap (Small Company)	B	B+	B	Up	Y	1,000
Sterling Capital Behavioral Small Cap Value Eq Inst Shares	SPSCX	NAS CM	Open End	US Equity Small Cap (Small Company)	B+	A-	B	Up	Y	1,000,000
Sterling Capital Diversified Income Fund Class A	BCGAX	NAS CM	Open End	Cautious Alloc (Asset Alloc)	B-	C	B+	Up	Y	1,000
Sterling Capital Diversified Income Fund Class C	BCCCX	NAS CM	Open End	Cautious Alloc (Asset Alloc)	B-	C	B+	Up	Y	1,000
Sterling Capital Diversified Income Fund Inst Shares	BMGTX	NAS CM	Open End	Cautious Alloc (Asset Alloc)	B	C+	A-	Up	Y	1,000,000
Sterling Capital Equity Income Fund Class A	BAEIX	NAS CM	Open End	US Equity Large Cap Value (Equity-Income)	B-	B-	B-	Down	Y	1,000
Sterling Capital Equity Income Fund Class C	BCEGX	NAS CM	Open End	US Equity Large Cap Value (Equity-Income)	B-	B-	B-	Down	Y	1,000
Sterling Capital Equity Income Fund Class R	BAERX	NAS CM	Open End	US Equity Large Cap Value (Equity-Income)	B-	B-	B-	Down	Y	1,000
Sterling Capital Equity Income Fund Institutional Shares	BEGIX	NAS CM	Open End	US Equity Large Cap Value (Equity-Income)	B-	B	B-	Down	Y	1,000,000
Sterling Capital Long/Short Equity Fund Class A	SLSAX	NAS CM	Open End	Long/Short Equity (Growth)	C	C	C	Up	Y	1,000
Sterling Capital Long/Short Equity Fund Class C	SLSCX	NAS CM	Open End	Long/Short Equity (Growth)	C	C-	C	Up	Y	1,000
Sterling Capital Long/Short Equity Fund Inst Shares	SLSIX	NAS CM	Open End	Long/Short Equity (Growth)	C	C	C	Up	Y	1,000,000
Sterling Capital Mid Value Fund Class A	OVEAX	NAS CM	Open End	US Equity Mid Cap (Growth)	B	B-	B	Up	Y	1,000
Sterling Capital Mid Value Fund Class C	OVECX	NAS CM	Open End	US Equity Mid Cap (Growth)	B	B-	B	Up	Y	1,000
Sterling Capital Mid Value Fund Class R	OVERX	NAS CM	Open End	US Equity Mid Cap (Growth)	B	B-	B	Up	Y	1,000
Sterling Capital Mid Value Fund Institutional Shares	OVEIX	NAS CM	Open End	US Equity Mid Cap (Growth)	B	B-	B	Up	Y	1,000,000
Sterling Capital SMID Opportunities Fund A Shares	SMDPX	NAS CM	Open End	US Equity Mid Cap (Growth)	D	C-	B		Y	1,000
Sterling Capital SMID Opportunities Fund C Shares	SMDQX	NAS CM	Open End	US Equity Mid Cap (Growth)	D	C-	B		Y	1,000
Sterling Capital SMID Opp Fund Inst Shares	SMDOX	NAS CM	Open End	US Equity Mid Cap (Growth)	D	C-	B		Y	1,000,000
Sterling Capital Special Opportunities Fund Class A	BOPAX	NAS CM	Open End	US Equity Large Cap Growth (Growth)	B	B-	B+	Up	Y	1,000
Sterling Capital Special Opportunities Fund Class C	BOPCX	NAS CM	Open End	US Equity Large Cap Growth (Growth)	B	B-	B+	Up	Y	1,000

★Expanded analysis of this fund is included in Section II.

TOTAL RETURNS						PERFORMANCE				ASSETS		ASSET ALLOCATION & TURNOVER					BULL & BEAR		FEES		
Min Additional Investment	3-Month Total Return	6-Month Total Return	1-Year Total Return	3-Year Total Return	5-Year Total Return	Dividend Yield (TTM)	Expense Ratio	3-Yr Std Deviation	3-Year Beta	NAV	Total Assets (MIL)	%Cash	%Stocks	%Bonds	%Other	Turnover Ratio	Last Bull Market Total Return	Last Bear Market Total Return	Front End Fee (%)	Back End Fee (%)	Inception Date
	5.12	9.91	20.58	27.73		1.29	0.33	8.7	0.82	12.26	365.9	2	84	14	0	16					Sep-14
	5.12	9.90	20.68	27.84		1.29	0.13	8.7	0.82	12.27	365.9	2	84	14	0	16					Sep-14
	5.20	10.09	21.14	27.85		1.05	0.58	9	0.85	12.29	239.7	2	88	10	0	17			4.50		Sep-14
	5.29	10.27	21.45	28.81		1.26	0.33	9	0.85	12.29	239.7	2	88	10	0	17					Sep-14
	5.29	10.37	21.45	28.81		1.26	0.13	9	0.85	12.29	239.7	2	88	10	0	17					Sep-14
	5.30	10.21	21.19	27.66		1.04	0.58	8.97	0.85	12.26	177.5	2	88	10	0	16			4.50		Sep-14
	5.31	10.31	21.30	28.42		1.25	0.33	8.98	0.85	12.24	177.5	2	88	10	0	16					Sep-14
	5.31	10.31	21.41	28.42		1.25	0.13	8.97	0.85	12.24	177.5	2	88	10	0	16					Sep-14
	5.19	10.20	21.19	27.60		1.04	0.58	8.99	0.85	12.24	66.2	2	88	10	0	14			4.50		Sep-14
	5.36	10.37	21.60	28.67		1.24	0.33	9	0.85	12.25	66.2	2	88	10	0	14					Sep-14
	5.28	10.29	21.52	28.46		1.25	0.13	8.99	0.85	12.23	66.2	2	88	10	0	14					Sep-14
	5.27	10.21	21.24	27.50		0.97	0.58	9.08	0.86	11.92	9.5	2	88	10	0	55			4.50		Sep-14
	5.27	10.29	21.44	28.35		1.18	0.33	9.08	0.86	11.91	9.5	2	88	10	0	55					Sep-14
	5.27	10.30	21.57	28.36		1.18	0.13	9.08	0.86	11.91	9.5	2	88	10	0	55					Sep-14
	1.99	4.12	8.65	12.94		1.35	0.58	3.91	0.38	10.73	94.1	2	35	63	0	37			4.50		Sep-14
	2.06	4.28	8.92	13.79		1.58	0.33	3.92	0.38	10.73	94.1	2	35	63	0	37					Sep-14
	1.97	4.09	8.83	13.63		1.59	0.13	3.91	0.38	10.71	94.1	2	35	63	0	37					Sep-14
	7.02	11.98	17.98			0.29	0.66			11.75	1.2	9	91	0	0						Sep-16
100	5.73	7.51	3.26	2.05		0	2.24	8.23	16.93	9.3	75.5	-1	38	51	11	38			5.75		Apr-14
100	5.47	7.07	2.52	-0.19		0	2.99	8.22	17.12	9.02	75.5	-1	38	51	11	38				1.00	Apr-14
25,000	5.74	7.62	3.60	2.81		0	1.99	8.2	17.11	9.39	75.5	-1	38	51	11	38					Apr-14
100	5.68	7.46	3.32	2.03		0	2.24	8.17	16.51	9.3	75.5	-1	38	51	11	38					Apr-14
	4.57	8.02	15.17	10.66		0.38	0.75	12.79	0.96	10.29	36.1	6	94	0	0	32					Oct-13
0	3.46	12.46	26.76	28.77		1.19	1	11.92	0.94	11.73	82.9	1	99	0	0	92			5.75		Nov-14
0	3.30	11.96	25.77	25.89		0.8	1.75	11.9	0.94	11.68	82.9	1	99	0	0	92				1.00	Nov-14
0	3.52	12.51	26.94	29.37		1.38	0.75	11.87	0.94	11.72	82.9	1	99	0	0	92					Nov-14
0	6.58	12.66	18.46	26.25	90.59	1.36	0.9	10.96	1.01	21.68	318.6	1	99	0	0	145	24.14	-19.93	5.75		Oct-92
0	6.42	12.25	17.60	23.50	83.58	0.73	1.65	10.92	1	21.07	318.6	1	99	0	0	145	23.66	-20.21		1.00	Feb-01
0	6.70	12.83	18.81	27.22	93.09	1.58	0.65	10.93	1	21.81	318.6	1	99	0	0	145	24.37	-19.87			Oct-92
0	3.25	9.50	8.62	29.44	91.83	0.44	1.09	13.09	0.9	18.22	229.1	1	99	0	0	109	23.73	-25.63	5.75		Feb-10
0	3.06	9.10	7.81	26.56	84.82	0.3	1.84	13.07	0.9	17.58	229.1	1	99	0	0	109	23.18	-25.86		1.00	Feb-10
0	3.21	9.43	8.42	28.36	89.52	0.39	1.34	12.99	0.89	18.13	229.1	1	99	0	0	109	24.01	-25.53			Feb-10
0	3.37	9.69	8.88	30.39	94.33	0.49	0.84	13.1	0.9	18.36	229.1	1	99	0	0	109	23.96	-25.53			Jan-97
0	1.71	2.70	6.38	12.64	30.17	3.92	1.39	4.48		10.86	24.0	5	34	47	10	44	10.21	-8.59	5.75		Jan-98
0	1.54	2.34	5.66	10.31	25.35	3.21	2.14	4.49		10.77	24.0	5	34	47	10	44	9.77	-8.89		1.00	Feb-01
0	1.85	2.89	6.76	13.61	31.85	4.12	1.14	4.46		11	24.0	5	34	47	10	44	10.35	-8.5			Oct-97
0	7.24	12.61	20.64	33.64	75.45	1.69	1.07	10.3	0.93	20.29	1,635	2	98	0	0	17	19.39	-10.26	5.75		Jun-04
0	7.01	12.14	19.71	30.60	68.93	1.03	1.82	10.3	0.93	20.09	1,635	2	98	0	0	17	18.89	-10.54		1.00	Jun-04
0	7.12	12.41	20.31	32.58	73.18	1.53	1.32	10.3	0.93	20.13	1,635	2	98	0	0	17	19.27	-10.3			Feb-10
0	7.28	12.72	20.95	34.57	77.62	1.92	0.82	10.28	0.93	20.34	1,635	2	98	0	0	17	19.65	-10.19			Jun-04
0	4.42	9.51	9.26	0.56		0	2.24	9.86	1.6	9.67	34.0	35	64	0	0				5.75		Dec-13
0	4.22	9.06	8.31	-1.71		0	2.99	9.88	1.59	9.38	34.0	35	64	0	0					1.00	Dec-13
0	4.59	9.76	9.51	1.38		0	1.99	9.91	1.6	9.78	34.0	35	64	0	0						Dec-13
0	5.47	6.49	13.86	28.56	101.93	0	1.24	14.01	1.24	18.89	753.8	4	96	0	0	25	26.25	-23.71	5.75		Aug-96
0	5.21	6.03	12.96	25.64	94.48	0	1.99	14.01	1.24	16.78	753.8	4	96	0	0	25	25.77	-23.97		1.00	Jul-01
0	5.42	6.30	13.62	27.49	97.72	0	1.49	13.92	1.23	18.28	753.8	4	96	0	0	25	26.05	-23.75			Feb-10
0	5.49	6.56	14.14	29.50	104.41	0.06	0.99	14.03	1.24	19.18	753.8	4	96	0	0	25	26.52	-23.66			Aug-96
0	1.28	1.62	13.88			0.06	1.04			11.72	9.5	7	93	0	0	38			5.75		Sep-16
0	1.11	1.29	13.03			0	1.79			11.62	9.5	7	93	0	0	38				1.00	Sep-16
0	1.36	1.71	14.06			0.11	0.79			11.75	9.5	7	93	0	0	38					Sep-16
0	5.16	7.31	19.33	33.81	101.39	0	1.14	9.94	0.88	23.81	1,174	3	97	0	0	19	21.66	-18.05	5.75		Jun-03
0	4.96	6.90	18.39	30.80	93.92	0	1.89	9.93	0.88	19.95	1,174	3	97	0	0	19	21.17	-18.31		1.00	Jun-03

	MARKET			FUND TYPE, CATEGORY & OBJECTIVE	RATINGS				MINIMUMS	
Fund Name	Ticker Symbol	Traded On	Fund Type	Category and (Prospectus Objective)	Overall Rating	Reward Rating	Risk Rating	Recent Up/ Downgrade	Open to New Investors	Min Initial Investment
Sterling Capital Special Opportunities Fund Class R	BOPRX	NAS CM	Open End	US Equity Large Cap Growth (Growth)	B	B-	B+	Up	Y	1,000
Sterling Capital Special Opp Fund Inst Shares	BOPIX	NAS CM	Open End	US Equity Large Cap Growth (Growth)	B	B-	B+	Up	Y	1,000,000
Sterling Capital Strategic Allocation Balanced Fund Cls A	BAMGX	NAS CM	Open End	Moderate Alloc (Balanced)	B-	C+	B	Up	Y	1,000
Sterling Capital Strategic Allocation Balanced Fund Cls C	BCMCX	NAS CM	Open End	Moderate Alloc (Balanced)	B-	C+	B	Up	Y	1,000
Sterling Capital Strategic Alloc Balanced Fund Inst Shares	BCGTX	NAS CM	Open End	Moderate Alloc (Balanced)	B-	C+	B	Up	Y	1,000,000
Sterling Capital Strategic Allocation Growth Fund Class A	BCMAX	NAS CM	Open End	Aggressive Alloc (Asset Alloc)	B-	C+	B	Down	Y	1,000
Sterling Capital Strategic Allocation Growth Fund Class C	BCGCX	NAS CM	Open End	Aggressive Alloc (Asset Alloc)	B-	C+	B-	Up	Y	1,000
Sterling Capital Strategic Alloc Growth Fund Inst Shares	BCMTX	NAS CM	Open End	Aggressive Alloc (Asset Alloc)	B-	C+	B	Up	Y	1,000,000
Sterling Capital Stratton Mid Cap Value Fund A Shares	STRLX	NAS CM	Open End	US Equity Mid Cap (Growth)	B	B	B	Up	Y	1,000
Sterling Capital Stratton Mid Cap Value Fund C Shares	STRNX	NAS CM	Open End	US Equity Mid Cap (Growth)	B	B	B	Up	Y	1,000
Sterling Capital Stratton Mid Cap Value Fund Inst Shares	STRGX	NAS CM	Open End	US Equity Mid Cap (Growth)	B	B	B	Up	Y	1,000,000
Sterling Capital Stratton Real Estate Fund A Shares	STMMX	NAS CM	Open End	Real Estate Sector Equity (Real Estate)	B	B-	B	Up	Y	1,000
Sterling Capital Stratton Real Estate Fund C Shares	STMOX	NAS CM	Open End	Real Estate Sector Equity (Real Estate)	B-	C+	B		Y	1,000
Sterling Capital Stratton Real Estate Fund Inst Shares	STMDX	NAS CM	Open End	Real Estate Sector Equity (Real Estate)	B	B-	B	Up	Y	1,000,000
Sterling Capital Stratton Small Cap Value Fund A Shares	STSNX	NAS CM	Open End	US Equity Small Cap (Small Company)	B+	A-	B	Up	Y	1,000
Sterling Capital Stratton Small Cap Value Fund C Shares	STSOX	NAS CM	Open End	US Equity Small Cap (Small Company)	B	B	B	Up	Y	1,000
Sterling Capital Stratton Small Cap Value Fund Inst Shares	STSCX	NAS CM	Open End	US Equity Small Cap (Small Company)	B+	A-	B	Up	Y	1,000,000
Steward Global Equity Income Fund Class A	SGIDX	NAS CM	Open End	Global Equity (Equity-Income)	B	B	B		Y	2,000
Steward Global Equity Income Fund Class Institutional	SGISX	NAS CM	Open End	Global Equity (Equity-Income)	B	B	B		Y	100,000
Steward International Enhanced Index Fund Class A	SNTKX	NAS CM	Open End	Global Equity Large Cap (Foreign Stock)	C+	C+	C+	Up	Y	2,000
Steward Intl Enhanced Index Fund Cls Inst	SNTCX	NAS CM	Open End	Global Equity Large Cap (Foreign Stock)	C+	C+	C+	Up	Y	100,000
Steward Large Cap Enhanced Index Fund Class A	SEEKX	NAS CM	Open End	US Equity Large Cap Blend (Growth)	B-	B-	B-	Down	Y	2,000
Steward Large Cap Enhanced Index Fund Class Institutional	SEECX	NAS CM	Open End	US Equity Large Cap Blend (Growth)	B	B	B-	Up	Y	100,000
Steward Small-Mid Cap Enhanced Index Fund Class Individual	TRDFX	NAS CM	Open End	US Equity Small Cap (Growth)	B+	B+	B	Up	Y	200
Steward Small-Mid Cap Enhanced Index Fund Cls Inst	SCECX	NAS CM	Open End	US Equity Small Cap (Growth)	B+	B+	B	Up	Y	100,000
Stock Dividend Fund	SDIVX	NAS CM	Open End	US Equity Large Cap Value (Equity-Income)	B	B+	C	Up	Y	100,000
Stone Harbor 500 Plus Fund Institutional Class	SHERX	NAS CM	Open End	US Equity Large Cap Blend (Growth & Income)	U	U	U		Y	1,000,000
Stone Ridge Elements U.S. Portfolio	ELUSX	NAS CM	Open End	US Equity Large Cap Blend (Growth)	U	U	U		Y	0
Stone Ridge Elements U.S. Small Cap Portfolio	ELSMX	NAS CM	Open End	US Equity Small Cap (Small Company)	U	U	U		Y	0
Stralem Equity Fund	STEFX	NAS CM	Open End	US Equity Large Cap Blend (Growth)	B-	B-	B	Down	Y	25,000
Strategic Advisers® Core Fund	FCSAX	NAS CM	Open End	US Equity Large Cap Blend (Growth)	B	B	B-		Y	0
Strategic Advisers® Core Multi-Manager Fund	FLAUX	NAS CM	Open End	US Equity Large Cap Blend (Growth)	B	B-	B		Y	0
Strategic Advisers® Core Multi-Manager Fund Class L	FQAPX	NAS CM	Open End	US Equity Large Cap Blend (Growth)	B	B-	B		Y	0
Strategic Advisers® Core Multi-Manager Fund Class N	FQAQX	NAS CM	Open End	US Equity Large Cap Blend (Growth)	B-	B-	B	Down	Y	0
Strategic Advisers® Emerging Markets Fund	FSAMX	NAS CM	Open End	Emerging Markets Equity (Div Emerging Mkts)	B-	B	C	Up	Y	0
Strategic Advisers® Emerging Markets Fund of Funds	FLILX	NAS CM	Open End	Emerging Markets Equity (Div Emerging Mkts)	B-	B-	C	Up	Y	0
Strategic Advisers® Emerging Markets Fund of Funds Class L	FQAAX	NAS CM	Open End	Emerging Markets Equity (Div Emerging Mkts)	B-	B-	C	Up	Y	0
Strategic Advisers® Emerging Markets Fund of Funds Class N	FQABX	NAS CM	Open End	Emerging Markets Equity (Div Emerging Mkts)	C+	B-	C	Up	Y	0
Strategic Advisers® Growth Fund	FSGFX	NAS CM	Open End	US Equity Large Cap Growth (Growth)	B+	B+	B	Up	Y	0
Strategic Advisers® Growth Multi-Manager Fund	FMELX	NAS CM	Open End	US Equity Large Cap Growth (Growth)	B+	B+	B	Up	Y	0
Strategic Advisers® Growth Multi-Manager Fund Class L	FQACX	NAS CM	Open End	US Equity Large Cap Growth (Growth)	B+	B+	B	Up	Y	0
Strategic Advisers® Growth Multi-Manager Fund Class N	FQAEX	NAS CM	Open End	US Equity Large Cap Growth (Growth)	B+	B+	B	Up	Y	0
Strategic Advisers® International Fund	FILFX	NAS CM	Open End	Global Equity Large Cap (Foreign Stock)	B-	B-	B	Up	Y	0
Strategic Advisers® International II Fund	FUSIX	NAS CM	Open End	Global Equity Large Cap (Foreign Stock)	B	B-	B	Up	Y	0
Strategic Advisers® International Multi-Manager Fund	FMJDX	NAS CM	Open End	Global Equity Large Cap (Foreign Stock)	B-	B-	B	Up	Y	0
Strategic Advisers® International Multi-Manager Fund Cls L	FQAHX	NAS CM	Open End	Global Equity Large Cap (Foreign Stock)	B-	B-	B	Up	Y	0
Strategic Advisers® International Multi-Manager Fund Cls N	FQAIX	NAS CM	Open End	Global Equity Large Cap (Foreign Stock)	B-	C+	B	Up	Y	0
Strategic Advisers® Small-Mid Cap Fund	FSCFX	NAS CM	Open End	US Equity Small Cap (Growth)	B	B	C+	Up	Y	0
Strategic Advisers® Small-Mid Cap Multi-Manager Fund	FNAPX	NAS CM	Open End	US Equity Small Cap (Growth)	B	B	B	Up	Y	0
Strategic Advisers® Small-Mid Cap Multi-Manager Fund Cls L	FQAJX	NAS CM	Open End	US Equity Small Cap (Growth)	B	B	C+	Up	Y	0
Strategic Advisers® Small-Mid Cap Multi-Manager Fund Cls N	FQAKX	NAS CM	Open End	US Equity Small Cap (Growth)	B	B	B	Up	Y	0
Strategic Advisers® Value Fund	FVSAX	NAS CM	Open End	US Equity Large Cap Value (Growth)	B	B	B	Up	Y	0

★Expanded analysis of this fund is included in Section II.

	TOTAL RETURNS					PERFORMANCE				ASSETS		ASSET ALLOCATION & TURNOVER					BULL & BEAR		FEES		
Min Additional Investment	3-Month Total Return	6-Month Total Return	1-Year Total Return	3-Year Total Return	5-Year Total Return	Dividend Yield (TTM)	Expense Ratio	3-Yr Std Deviation	3-Year Beta	NAV	Total Assets (MIL)	%Cash	%Stocks	%Bonds	%Other	Turnover Ratio	Last Bull Market Total Return	Last Bear Market Total Return	Front End Fee (%)	Back End Fee (%)	Inception Date
0	5.06	7.18	19.04	32.85	98.90	0	1.39	9.93	0.88	24.08	1,174	3	97	0	0	19	21.51	-18.12			Feb-10
0	5.24	7.46	19.66	34.85	103.99	0.05	0.89	9.96	0.88	25	1,174	3	97	0	0	19	21.81	-17.93			Jun-03
0	1.93	6.14	13.34	17.92	43.50	1.3	1.38	6.34		12.12	30.8	6	62	32	0	1	14.06	-15.09	5.75		Jan-98
0	1.88	5.89	12.69	15.50	38.49	0.64	2.13	6.33		11.89	30.8	6	62	32	0	1	13.49	-15.33		1.00	Feb-01
0	3.34	7.65	15.14	20.33	47.22	1.52	1.13	6.32		12.21	30.8	6	62	32	0	1	14.11	-14.9			Oct-97
0	2.43	7.49	15.79	20.52	52.79	0.96	1.52	7.86		12.19	24.2	8	75	16	0	2	16.71	-18.65	5.75		Jan-98
0	3.74	8.67	16.66	19.60	49.24	0.53	2.27	7.93		11.74	24.2	8	75	16	0	2	16.24	-18.94		1.00	Feb-01
0	2.43	7.54	16.07	21.37	54.51	1.18	1.27	7.89		12.22	24.2	8	75	16	0	2	16.96	-18.61			Oct-97
0	6.74	13.22	21.45	31.28	99.31	0.05	1.23	11.5	1.04	68.23	70.1	4	96	0	0	12	24.05	-25.54	5.75		Nov-15
0	6.55	12.76	20.54	28.41	92.07	0	1.98	11.49	1.04	67.37	70.1	4	96	0	0	12	23.51	-25.77		1.00	Nov-15
0	6.81	13.35	21.75	32.28	101.83	0.11	0.98	11.51	1.04	68.38	70.1	4	96	0	0	12	24.23	-25.46			Sep-72
0	3.19	3.24	7.53	16.14	58.63	2.72	1.1	12.91	1.01	37.01	98.8	1	99	0	0	14	28.33	-16.68	5.75		Nov-15
0	3.01	2.87	6.76	13.61	52.88	1.95	1.85	12.93	1.01	36.81	98.8	1	99	0	0	14	27.77	-16.94		1.00	Nov-15
0	3.24	3.33	7.80	17.01	60.62	2.96	0.85	12.92	1.01	37.09	98.8	1	99	0	0	14	28.52	-16.59			May-80
0	4.53	10.52	12.90	33.62	96.38	0.05	1.34	13.11	0.89	86.12	1,245	4	96	0	0	7	22.99	-21.27	5.75		Nov-15
0	4.34	10.11	12.07	30.67	89.20	0	2.09	13.1	0.89	84.84	1,245	4	96	0	0	7	22.46	-21.52		1.00	Nov-15
0	4.61	10.67	13.19	34.58	98.79	0.14	1.09	13.12	0.89	86.33	1,245	4	96	0	0	7	23.17	-21.19			Apr-93
1,000	6.38	10.80	21.93	35.09	80.56	1.68	0.99	8.77	0.82	33.05	270.5	1	99	0	0	48	19.52	-13.07			Apr-08
50,000	6.46	10.97	22.30	36.41	83.57	1.92	0.66	8.78	0.82	33.12	270.5	1	99	0	0	48	19.75	-12.97			Apr-08
1,000	3.32	10.96	22.98	16.72	22.33	1.93	1.01	12.79	1.03	22.9	143.4	1	99	0	0	16	12.88	-24.26			Feb-06
50,000	3.38	11.13	23.31	17.89	24.45	2.21	0.67	12.81	1.04	22.96	143.4	1	99	0	0	16	13.1	-24.14			Mar-06
1,000	6.34	11.39	20.98	29.59	104.52	1	0.82	10.54	1.04	41.76	390.7	0	100	0	0	25	23.98	-17.83			Oct-04
50,000	6.44	11.55	21.33	30.86	107.97	1.19	0.5	10.54	1.04	41.59	390.7	0	100	0	0	25	24.22	-17.71			Oct-04
	5.10	9.61	13.79	33.36	97.73	0.38	0.85	13.01	1.1	15.84	235.2	1	99	0	0	33	27.53	-22.36			Jan-52
1,000	5.09	9.76	14.04	34.49	100.48	0.63	0.57	13	1.1	16.06	235.2	1	99	0	0	33	27.79	-22.3			Apr-06
100	11.80	24.05	23.02	36.82	77.45	1.96	0.85	14.92	1.12	29.93	29.6	0	98	0	2	30	22.4	-13.54			Dec-04
250,000	6.78	11.55	18.44				0.61			10.49	2.4	9	53	38	0	20					Jan-17
	2.50						0.45				614.4										Mar-17
	1.30						0.65				422.8										Mar-17
100	3.40	6.17	16.67	26.82	79.26	1.41	0.95	9.31	0.88	10.06	139.3	3	97	0	0	8	20.23	-11.35			Jan-00
	6.62	11.64	22.54	34.71	105.80	1.16	0.49	10.42	1.02	18.03	24,519	2	98	0	0	100	25.06	-18.78			Dec-09
	6.59	11.22	21.15	34.13	102.35	0.72	0.91	10.16	1	13.05	64.2	5	95	0	0	151					Nov-11
	6.59	11.22	21.15	34.13	102.35	0.72	0.91	10.15	1	13.05	64.2	5	95	0	0	151					Nov-13
	6.53	11.05	20.78	33.07	99.77	0.51	1.16	10.16	1	13.04	64.2	5	95	0	0	151					Nov-13
	7.00	15.86	38.37	29.44	24.89	0.87	1.07	14.89	0.93	11.46	5,041	4	95	0	0	23	17.83	-24.81			Sep-10
	6.89	16.14	38.40	28.67	25.20	0.75	1.36	14.86	0.93	12.11	14.7	1	97	0	1	49					May-12
	6.79	16.03	38.40	28.53	25.08	0.75	1.36	14.9	0.93	12.11	14.7	1	97	0	1	49					Nov-13
	6.79	15.94	38.02	27.63	23.66	0.6	1.61	14.87	0.93	12.1	14.7	1	97	0	1	49					Nov-13
	6.89	13.08	29.44	41.27	119.11	0.67	0.44	11.01	1.01	18.68	11,813	2	97	0	0	38	26	-17.56			Jun-10
	7.20	13.87	30.18	40.77	117.81	0.36	0.85	10.84	1	14.86	72.0	6	94	0	0	52					Nov-11
	7.28	13.89	30.21	40.84	117.83	0.36	0.85	10.87	1	14.85	72.0	6	94	0	0	52					Nov-13
	7.13	13.71	29.82	39.74	115.07	0.16	1.1	10.81	0.99	14.84	72.0	6	94	0	0	52					Nov-13
	4.49	10.13	26.22	27.13	49.40	1.54	0.76	11.01	0.88	11.48	17,503	5	94	0	1	28	15.67	-22.74			Mar-06
	4.37	9.95	27.72	27.12	52.63	1.22	0.9	10.82	0.86	10.69	4,477	7	92	0	0	14	15.86	-24.58			Mar-07
	4.87	10.30	26.24	26.27	49.29	1.25	1.01	10.59	0.85	13.56	70.1	5	95	0	0	50					May-12
	4.88	10.23	26.17	26.21	49.30	1.25	1.01	10.56	0.84	13.54	70.1	5	95	0	0	50					Nov-13
	4.84	10.11	25.89	25.27	47.43	1.06	1.26	10.6	0.85	13.53	70.1	5	95	0	0	50					Nov-13
	6.21	11.33	19.27	31.80	91.86	0.32	0.77	12.39	1	14.94	7,605	6	94	0	0	82	27.42	-24.07			Jun-05
	5.75	10.56	19.19	31.52	90.71	0.03	1.16	12.67	1.02	10.3	15.5	6	94	0	0	120					Dec-11
	5.76	10.57	19.21	31.56	90.78	0.03	1.16	12.69	1.02	10.29	15.5	6	94	0	0	120					Nov-13
	5.69	10.42	18.98	30.56	88.39	0	1.41	12.63	1.02	10.23	15.5	6	94	0	0	120					Nov-13
	6.93	11.95	18.13	31.77	102.69	1.68	0.46	10.96	1.04	20.42	11,606	2	98	0	0	32	24.54	-18.6			Dec-08

	MARKET			FUND TYPE, CATEGORY & OBJECTIVE	RATINGS					MINIMUMS
Fund Name	Ticker Symbol	Traded On	Fund Type	Category and (Prospectus Objective)	Overall Rating	Reward Rating	Risk Rating	Recent Up/ Downgrade	Open to New Investors	Min Initial Investment
Strategic Advisers® Value Multi-Manager Fund	FKMOX	NAS CM	Open End	US Equity Large Cap Value (Growth)	B	B	B	Up	Y	0
Strategic Advisers® Value Multi-Manager Fund Class L	FQALX	NAS CM	Open End	US Equity Large Cap Value (Growth)	B	B	B	Up	Y	0
Strategic Advisers® Value Multi-Manager Fund Class N	FQAMX	NAS CM	Open End	US Equity Large Cap Value (Growth)	B	B	B	Up	Y	0
Strategic Global Long/Short Fund Class A Shares	SGFAX	NAS CM	Open End	Long/Short Equity (Growth & Income)	C-	D+	C+	Up	Y	1,000
Stringer Growth Fund Class A Shares	SRGAX	NAS CM	Open End	Aggressive Alloc (Growth)	B-	C+	B-	Down	Y	5,000
Stringer Growth Fund Class C Shares	SRGCX	NAS CM	Open End	Aggressive Alloc (Growth)	C+	C+	B-	Down	Y	5,000
Stringer Growth Fund Institutional Class Shares	SRGIX	NAS CM	Open End	Aggressive Alloc (Growth)	B-	C+	B-	Down	Y	1,000,000
Stringer Moderate Growth Fund Class A	SRQAX	NAS CM	Open End	Moderate Alloc (Growth)	C+	C	B	Up	Y	5,000
Stringer Moderate Growth Fund Class C	SRQCX	NAS CM	Open End	Moderate Alloc (Growth)	C+	C	B	Up	Y	5,000
Stringer Moderate Growth Fund Institutional Class	SRQIX	NAS CM	Open End	Moderate Alloc (Growth)	C+	C	B	Up	Y	1,000,000
Summit Global Investments Global Low Volatility Fund Cls I	DWUGX	NAS CM	Open End	Global Equity (Growth)	B-	C+	B	Up	Y	25,000
Summit Global Inv Small Cap Low Vol Fund Cls C	SMLVX	NAS CM	Open End	US Equity Small Cap (Small Company)	D+	C-	B+	Up	Y	2,500
Summit Global Inv Small Cap Low Vol Fund Cls I	SCLVX	NAS CM	Open End	US Equity Small Cap (Small Company)	D+	C	B+	Up	Y	1,000,000
Summit Global Inv Small Cap Low Vol Fund Cls Retail	LVSMX	NAS CM	Open End	US Equity Small Cap (Small Company)	D+	C	B+	Up	Y	2,500
Summit Global Inv U.S. Low Vol Eq Fund Cls A	LVOLX	NAS CM	Open End	US Equity Large Cap Blend (Growth)	B	B-	B+		Y	2,500
Summit Global Inv U.S. Low Vol Eq Fund Cls C	SGICX	NAS CM	Open End	US Equity Large Cap Blend (Growth)	B	C+	B+		Y	2,500
Summit Global Inv U.S. Low Vol Eq Fund Cls I	SILVX	NAS CM	Open End	US Equity Large Cap Blend (Growth)	B	B-	B+		Y	1,000,000
Superfund Managed Futures Strategy Fund Class A	SUPRX	NAS CM	Open End	Other Alternative (Growth & Income)	C+	C+	C+	Up	Y	2,500
Superfund Managed Futures Strategy Fund Class I	SUPIX	NAS CM	Open End	Other Alternative (Growth & Income)	C+	C+	C+	Up	Y	100,000
Swan Defined Risk Emerging Markets Fund Class A	SDFAX	NAS CM	Open End	Long/Short Equity (Growth & Income)	C+	C+	C+	Up	Y	2,500
Swan Defined Risk Emerging Markets Fund Class C	SDFCX	NAS CM	Open End	Long/Short Equity (Growth & Income)	C+	C+	C+	Up	Y	2,500
Swan Defined Risk Emerging Markets Fund Class I	SDFIX	NAS CM	Open End	Long/Short Equity (Growth & Income)	C+	C+	C+	Up	Y	100,000
Swan Defined Risk Foreign Developed Fund Class A	SDJAX	NAS CM	Open End	Long/Short Equity (Foreign Stock)	C-	C-	B	Up	Y	2,500
Swan Defined Risk Foreign Developed Fund Class C	SDJCX	NAS CM	Open End	Long/Short Equity (Foreign Stock)	C-	C-	B	Up	Y	2,500
Swan Defined Risk Foreign Developed Fund Class I	SDJIX	NAS CM	Open End	Long/Short Equity (Foreign Stock)	C-	C-	B	Up	Y	100,000
Swan Defined Risk Fund Class A Shares	SDRAX	NAS CM	Open End	Long/Short Equity (Growth)	C+	C+	B-	Up	Y	2,500
Swan Defined Risk Fund Class C Shares	SDRCX	NAS CM	Open End	Long/Short Equity (Growth)	C+	C	B-	Up	Y	2,500
Swan Defined Risk Fund Class I Shares	SDRIX	NAS CM	Open End	Long/Short Equity (Growth)	C+	C+	B-	Up	Y	100,000
Swan Defined Risk U.S. Small Cap Fund Class A	SDCAX	NAS CM	Open End	Long/Short Equity (Small Company)	C-	C-	A-	Up	Y	2,500
Swan Defined Risk U.S. Small Cap Fund Class C	SDCCX	NAS CM	Open End	Long/Short Equity (Small Company)	C-	C-	B+	Up	Y	2,500
Swan Defined Risk U.S. Small Cap Fund Class I	SDCIX	NAS CM	Open End	Long/Short Equity (Small Company)	C-	C-	A-	Up	Y	100,000
Swiss Helvetia Fund Inc	SWZ	NYSE	Closed End	Other Equity (Europe Stock)	B-	C+	B	Up	Y	
Symons Value Institutional Fund	SAVIX	NAS CM	Open End	US Equity Large Cap Value (Growth)	B-	C+	B	Up	Y	5,000
T. Rowe Price Africa & Middle East Fund	TRAMX	NAS CM	Open End	Other Equity (Foreign Stock)	C	C	C	Up	Y	2,500
T. Rowe Price Africa & Middle East Fund I Class	PRAMX	NAS CM	Open End	Other Equity (Foreign Stock)	C	C	C	Up	Y	1,000,000
T. Rowe Price Asia Opportunities Fund	TRAOX	NAS CM	Open End	Asia ex-Japan Equity (Pacific Stock)	B+	A	B-	Up	Y	2,500
T. Rowe Price Asia Opportunities Fund Advisor Class	PAAOX	NAS CM	Open End	Asia ex-Japan Equity (Pacific Stock)	B+	A	B-	Up	Y	2,500
T. Rowe Price Asia Opportunities Fund I Class	TRASX	NAS CM	Open End	Asia ex-Japan Equity (Pacific Stock)	B+	A	B-	Up	Y	1,000,000
T. Rowe Price Balanced Fund	RPBAX	NAS CM	Open End	Moderate Alloc (Balanced)	B	B-	A-	Up	Y	2,500
T. Rowe Price Balanced I Class	RBAIX	NAS CM	Open End	Moderate Alloc (Balanced)	B-	B-	B	Down	Y	1,000,000
T. Rowe Price Blue Chip Growth Fund	TRBCX	NAS CM	Open End	US Equity Large Cap Growth (Growth)	A-	A	B	Up	Y	2,500
T. Rowe Price Blue Chip Growth Fund Advisor Class	PABGX	NAS CM	Open End	US Equity Large Cap Growth (Growth)	A-	A	B	Up	Y	2,500
T. Rowe Price Blue Chip Growth Fund Class R	RRBGX	NAS CM	Open End	US Equity Large Cap Growth (Growth)	A-	A	B	Up	Y	2,500
T. Rowe Price Blue Chip Growth Fund I Class	TBCIX	NAS CM	Open End	US Equity Large Cap Growth (Growth)	A-	A	B	Up	Y	1,000,000
T. Rowe Price Capital Appreciation Fund	PRWCX	NAS CM	Open End	Moderate Alloc (Growth)	B	B-	A-	Down		2,500
T. Rowe Price Capital Appreciation Fund Advisor Class	PACLX	NAS CM	Open End	Moderate Alloc (Growth)	B	B-	A-			2,500
T. Rowe Price Capital Appreciation Fund I Class	TRAIX	NAS CM	Open End	Moderate Alloc (Growth)	B	B-	A-	Down	Y	1,000,000
T. Rowe Price Capital Opportunity Fund	PRCOX	NAS CM	Open End	US Equity Large Cap Blend (Growth)	B	B	B+	Down	Y	2,500
T. Rowe Price Capital Opportunity Fund Advisor Class	PACOX	NAS CM	Open End	US Equity Large Cap Blend (Growth)	B	B	B+	Down	Y	2,500
T. Rowe Price Capital Opportunity Fund Class R	RRCOX	NAS CM	Open End	US Equity Large Cap Blend (Growth)	B	B	B+	Down	Y	2,500
T. Rowe Price Capital Opportunity Fund I Class	PCCOX	NAS CM	Open End	US Equity Large Cap Blend (Growth)	B	B	B+	Down	Y	1,000,000
T. Rowe Price Diversified Mid Cap Growth Fund	PRDMX	NAS CM	Open End	US Equity Mid Cap (Growth)	B	B	B-	Up	Y	2,500

★ Expanded analysis of this fund is included in Section II.

	TOTAL RETURNS					PERFORMANCE				ASSETS		ASSET ALLOCATION & TURNOVER					BULL & BEAR		FEES		
Min Additional Investment	3-Month Total Return	6-Month Total Return	1-Year Total Return	3-Year Total Return	5-Year Total Return	Dividend Yield (TTM)	Expense Ratio	3-Yr Std Deviation	3-Year Beta	NAV	Total Assets (MIL)	%Cash	%Stocks	%Bonds	%Other	Turnover Ratio	Last Bull Market Total Return	Last Bear Market Total Return	Front End Fee (%)	Back End Fee (%)	Inception Date
	6.78	11.65	18.97	31.05	99.46	1.21	0.91	11.34	1.08	16.37	21.1	6	94	0	0	27					Nov-11
	6.78	11.65	18.97	31.05	99.47	1.21	0.91	11.34	1.08	16.37	25.9	6	94	0	0	27					Nov-13
	6.71	11.47	18.62	30.02	96.90	1	1.16	11.31	1.08	16.36	25.9	6	94	0	0	27					Nov-13
100	-1.29	0.00	0.40			0	1.95			9.94	12.1	54	30	16	0	257			5.00		Feb-16
250	4.39	8.39	17.79	21.36		0.79	1.62	7.94	0.71	12.65	44.1	7	82	4	1	79			5.50		Mar-13
250	4.22	8.00	16.96	18.71		0.01	2.37	7.93	0.71	12.57	44.1	7	82	4	1	79			1.00	1.00	Mar-13
5,000	4.49	8.56	18.15	22.30		1.02	1.37	7.95	0.72	12.68	44.1	7	82	4	1	79					Mar-13
250	3.13	6.05	13.00			0.94	1.61			10.74	7.3	9	56	28	1	84			5.50		Mar-15
250	3.01	5.74	12.26			0.25	2.36			10.73	7.3	9	56	27	1	84				1.00	Mar-15
5,000	3.22	6.24	13.30			1.1	1.36			10.75	7.3	9	56	27	1	84					Mar-15
	4.82	9.97	23.56	20.11	86.14	0	0.84	13.13	0.98		22.5	1	99	0	0	247	27.97	-14.29			Apr-09
	0.38	5.40	7.66			0	2.23			11.95	21.2	4	96	0	0	95					Mar-16
	0.68	6.00	8.70			0.35	1.23			12.07	21.2	4	96	0	0	95					Mar-16
	0.68	5.85	8.54			0.24	1.48			12.08	21.2	4	96	0	0	95					Mar-16
	7.13	10.10	16.06	28.69	92.13	0.8	1.23	8.38	0.7	15.66	104.8	2	98	0	0	31			5.25		Nov-15
	6.97	9.69	15.40	25.24	84.21	0.65	1.98	8.25	0.69	15.39	104.8	2	98	0	0	31					Dec-15
	7.24	10.20	16.40	29.64	94.51	0.95	0.98	8.36	0.7	15.62	104.8	2	98	0	0	31					Feb-12
500	13.80	19.95	27.43	10.09		4.59	3.42	11.33	-38.74	9.11	5.6	80	0	0	20	0			5.75		Dec-13
1,000	13.83	20.09	27.70	10.87		4.79	3.17	11.32	-39.24	9.16	5.6	80	0	0	20	0					Dec-13
500	3.64	10.18	21.64	13.60		0	2.31			10.79	47.4	4	96	0	0	3			5.50		Dec-14
500	3.41	9.72	20.77	11.10		0	3.06			10.59	47.4	4	96	0	0	3				1.00	Dec-14
500	3.72	10.34	22.03	14.41		0	2.06			10.85	47.4	4	96	0	0	3					Dec-14
500	1.94	6.37	14.58			0.73	1.96			10.96	42.7	3	97	0	0	0			5.50		Dec-15
500	1.77	5.92	13.69			0.32	2.71			10.88	42.7	3	97	0	0	0				1.00	Dec-15
500	1.97	6.49	14.81			0.87	1.71			10.97	42.7	3	97	0	0	0					Dec-15
500	3.57	6.88	9.94	11.46	36.41	1.13	1.55	5.33	0.43	12.98	3,115	2	98	0	0	6			5.50		Jul-12
500	3.39	6.48	9.12	8.98	31.51	0.6	2.29	5.38	0.44	12.8	3,115	2	98	0	0	6				1.00	Oct-12
500	3.54	6.92	10.24	12.31	38.13	1.3	1.3	5.37	0.43	13.02	3,115	2	98	0	0	6					Jul-12
500	1.84	5.02	7.91			0.01	1.84			12.13	35.3	3	97	0	0	0			5.50		Dec-15
500	1.61	4.54	7.07			0	2.59			11.96	35.3	3	97	0	0	0				1.00	Dec-15
500	1.92	5.09	8.17			0.08	1.59			12.17	35.3	3	97	0	0	0					Dec-15
	1.36	2.24	22.06	20.05	51.08	0.93	1.06	11.63	0.84	14.1	354.1	0	95	0	4	19	10.79	-20.92			Aug-87
250	5.19	5.39	9.85	15.49	51.30	1.4	1.23	7.76	0.43	10.41	73.5	14	86	0	0	83	13.04	-7.34			Dec-06
100	11.23	12.64	23.64	5.13	44.36	1.64	1.56	14.64		9.62	142.7	0	100	0	0	60	18.48	-17.11			Sep-07
	11.23	12.64	23.62	5.12	44.34		1.09	14.64		9.61	142.7	0	100	0	0	60	18.48	-17.11			Mar-17
100	8.36	14.43	43.23	48.39		0.95	1.15	13.94	0.87	14.87	94.6	0	96	0	4	52					May-14
100	8.31	14.32	43.06	47.65		0.95	1.25	13.95	0.88	14.83	94.6	0	96	0	4	52					May-14
	8.42	14.57	43.40	48.57			0.84	13.94	0.87	14.89	94.6	0	96	0	4	52					Mar-17
100	3.61	7.57	18.00	25.14	60.45	1.75	0.64	7.01	1.12	24.33	4,030	0	63	33	3	58	17	-11.83			Dec-39
	3.65	7.65	18.19	25.57	61.00	1.9	0.46	7	1.12	24.34	4,030	0	63	33	3	58	17	-11.83			Dec-15
100	7.00	14.41	36.54	52.24	141.88	0.05	0.72	12.33	1.06	96.31	45,560	0	100	0	0	32	31.15	-14.81			Jun-93
100	6.93	14.25	36.16	51.01	138.70	0	0.98	12.33	1.06	95.02	45,560	0	100	0	0	32	30.97	-14.89			Mar-00
100	6.86	14.11	35.81	49.83	135.58	0	1.25	12.33	1.06	91.63	45,560	0	100	0	0	32	30.8	-15.02			Sep-02
	7.03	14.48	36.71	52.65	142.52	0.15	0.58	12.33	1.06	96.33	45,560	0	100	0	0	32	31.15	-14.81			Dec-15
100	2.95	5.69	15.37	30.92	82.44	1.34	0.7	6.44	0.6	28.28	29,649	1	61	20	14	62	19.66	-12.48			Jun-86
100	2.88	5.50	14.97	29.70	79.67	1.05	1	6.44	0.6	27.99	29,649	1	61	20	14	62	19.45	-12.56			Dec-04
	2.98	5.71	15.47	31.18	82.80	1.4	0.6	6.43	0.6	28.29	29,649	1	61	20	14	62	19.66	-12.48			Dec-15
100	6.51	11.36	23.71	38.96	112.61	0.96	0.7	10.38	1.02	26.06	608.7	0	100	0	0	47	25.56	-16.51			Nov-94
100	6.40	11.14	23.32	37.70	109.48	0.8	0.97	10.39	1.02	25.99	608.7	0	100	0	0	47	25.33	-16.7			Dec-04
100	6.34	11.01	23.04	36.54	106.41	0.52	1.3	10.37	1.02	25.94	608.7	0	100	0	0	47	25.09	-16.73			Dec-04
	6.51	11.39	23.85	39.11	112.85	0.96	0.54	10.39	1.02	26.05	608.7	0	100	0	0	47	25.56	-16.51			Nov-16
100	5.89	10.61	24.72	35.90	109.01	0.16	0.87	11.54	1.04	29.4	841.7	0	100	0	0	21	28.51	-22.88			Dec-03

Fund Name	MARKET Ticker Symbol	MARKET Traded On	FUND TYPE, CATEGORY & OBJECTIVE Fund Type	FUND TYPE, CATEGORY & OBJECTIVE Category and (Prospectus Objective)	RATINGS Overall Rating	RATINGS Reward Rating	RATINGS Risk Rating	RATINGS Recent Up/ Downgrade	MINIMUMS Open to New Investors	MINIMUMS Min Initial Investment
T. Rowe Price Diversified Mid Cap Growth Fund I Class	RPTTX	NAS CM	Open End	US Equity Mid Cap (Growth)	B	B	B-		Y	1,000,000
T. Rowe Price Dividend Growth Fund	PRDGX	NAS CM	Open End	US Equity Large Cap Blend (Equity-Income)	B	B-	B+		Y	2,500
T. Rowe Price Dividend Growth Fund Advisor Class	TADGX	NAS CM	Open End	US Equity Large Cap Blend (Equity-Income)	B	B-	B+		Y	2,500
T. Rowe Price Dividend Growth Fund I Class	PDGIX	NAS CM	Open End	US Equity Large Cap Blend (Equity-Income)	B	B-	B+		Y	1,000,000
T. Rowe Price Emerging Europe Fund	TREMX	NAS CM	Open End	Other Equity (Foreign Stock)	C+	C+	C	Up	Y	2,500
T. Rowe Price Emerging Europe Fund I Class	TTEEX	NAS CM	Open End	Other Equity (Foreign Stock)	C+	C+	C	Up	Y	1,000,000
T. Rowe Price Emerging Markets Stock Fund	PRMSX	NAS CM	Open End	Emerging Markets Equity (Div Emerging Mkts)	B	A	C	Up	Y	2,500
T. Rowe Price Emerging Markets Stock Fund I Class	PRZIX	NAS CM	Open End	Emerging Markets Equity (Div Emerging Mkts)	B	A	C	Up	Y	1,000,000
T. Rowe Price Emerging Markets Value Stock Fund	PRIJX	NAS CM	Open End	Emerging Markets Equity (Div Emerging Mkts)	C	C+	B	Up	Y	2,500
T. Rowe Price Emerging Mkts Value Stock Fund Adv Cls	PAIJX	NAS CM	Open End	Emerging Markets Equity (Div Emerging Mkts)	C	C+	B	Up	Y	2,500
T. Rowe Price Emerging Markets Value Stock Fund I Class	REVIX	NAS CM	Open End	Emerging Markets Equity (Div Emerging Mkts)	C	C+	B	Up	Y	1,000,000
T. Rowe Price Equity Income Fund	PRFDX	NAS CM	Open End	US Equity Large Cap Value (Equity-Income)	B-	B-	B-	Down	Y	2,500
T. Rowe Price Equity Income Fund Advisor Class	PAFDX	NAS CM	Open End	US Equity Large Cap Value (Equity-Income)	B-	B-	C+	Down	Y	0
T. Rowe Price Equity Income Fund Class R	RRFDX	NAS CM	Open End	US Equity Large Cap Value (Equity-Income)	B-	B-	C+	Down	Y	0
T. Rowe Price Equity Income Fund I Class	REIPX	NAS CM	Open End	US Equity Large Cap Value (Equity-Income)	B-	B	C+	Down	Y	1,000,000
T. Rowe Price Equity Index 500 Fund	PREIX	NAS CM	Open End	US Equity Large Cap Blend (Growth & Income)	B	B	B		Y	2,500
T. Rowe Price Equity Index 500 Fund I Class	PRUIX	NAS CM	Open End	US Equity Large Cap Blend (Growth & Income)	B	B	B		Y	1,000,000
T. Rowe Price European Stock Fund	PRESX	NAS CM	Open End	Europe Equity Large Cap (Europe Stock)	C+	C+	C	Up	Y	2,500
T. Rowe Price European Stock Fund I Class	TEUIX	NAS CM	Open End	Europe Equity Large Cap (Europe Stock)	C+	C+	C	Up	Y	1,000,000
T. Rowe Price Extended Equity Market Index Fund	PEXMX	NAS CM	Open End	US Equity Mid Cap (Growth)	B	B	B	Up	Y	2,500
T. Rowe Price Financial Services Fund	PRISX	NAS CM	Open End	Financials Sector Equity (Financial)	B+	A-	B	Up	Y	2,500
T. Rowe Price Financial Services Fund I Class	TFIFX	NAS CM	Open End	Financials Sector Equity (Financial)	B+	A-	B	Up	Y	1,000,000
T. Rowe Price Global Allocation Fund	RPGAX	NAS CM	Open End	Alloc (Growth & Income)	B-	C+	B	Down	Y	2,500
T. Rowe Price Global Allocation Fund Advisor Class	PAFGX	NAS CM	Open End	Alloc (Growth & Income)	B	C+	B+	Up	Y	2,500
T. Rowe Price Global Allocation Fund I Class	TGAFX	NAS CM	Open End	Alloc (Growth & Income)	B-	C+	B	Down	Y	1,000,000
T. Rowe Price Global Consumer Fund	PGLOX	NAS CM	Open End	Consumer Goods Sec Equity (Growth)	D	C-	B-		Y	2,500
T. Rowe Price Global Growth Stock Fund	RPGEX	NAS CM	Open End	Global Equity (Growth)	B	B	B	Up	Y	2,500
T. Rowe Price Global Growth Stock Fund Advisor Class	PAGLX	NAS CM	Open End	Global Equity (Growth)	B	B	B	Up	Y	2,500
T. Rowe Price Global Growth Stock Fund I Class	RGGIX	NAS CM	Open End	Global Equity (Growth)	B	B	B	Up	Y	1,000,000
T. Rowe Price Global Industrials Fund	RPGIX	NAS CM	Open End	Industrials Sector Equity (Growth)	B	B+	C+	Up	Y	2,500
T. Rowe Price Global Industrials Fund I Class	TRGAX	NAS CM	Open End	Industrials Sector Equity (Growth)	B	B+	C+		Y	1,000,000
T. Rowe Price Global Real Estate Fund	TRGRX	NAS CM	Open End	Real Estate Sector Equity (Real Estate)	B-	C	B	Up	Y	2,500
T. Rowe Price Global Real Estate Fund Advisor Class	PAGEX	NAS CM	Open End	Real Estate Sector Equity (Real Estate)	B-	C	B	Up	Y	2,500
T. Rowe Price Global Real Estate Fund I Class	TIRGX	NAS CM	Open End	Real Estate Sector Equity (Real Estate)	B-	C	B	Up	Y	1,000,000
T. Rowe Price Global Stock Fund	PRGSX	NAS CM	Open End	Global Equity (World Stock)	B+	B+	B+	Down	Y	2,500
T. Rowe Price Global Stock Fund Advisor Class	PAGSX	NAS CM	Open End	Global Equity (World Stock)	B+	B+	B+	Up	Y	2,500
T. Rowe Price Global Stock Fund I Class	TRGLX	NAS CM	Open End	Global Equity (World Stock)	B+	A-	B+	Down	Y	1,000,000
T. Rowe Price Global Technology Fund	PRGTX	NAS CM	Open End	Technology Sector Equity (Technology)	A	A+	B+	Up	Y	2,500
T. Rowe Price Global Technology Fund I Class	PGTIX	NAS CM	Open End	Technology Sector Equity (Technology)	A	A+	B+	Up	Y	1,000,000
T. Rowe Price Growth and Income Fund	PRGIX	NAS CM	Open End	US Equity Large Cap Blend (Growth & Income)	B	B-	B+		Y	2,500
T. Rowe Price Growth and Income Fund I Class	TGTIX	NAS CM	Open End	US Equity Large Cap Blend (Growth & Income)	B	B-	B+		Y	1,000,000
T. Rowe Price Growth Stock Fund	PRGFX	NAS CM	Open End	US Equity Large Cap Growth (Growth)	B+	B+	B	Down	Y	2,500
T. Rowe Price Growth Stock Fund Advisor Class	TRSAX	NAS CM	Open End	US Equity Large Cap Growth (Growth)	B+	B+	B	Down	Y	2,500
T. Rowe Price Growth Stock Fund I Class	PRUFX	NAS CM	Open End	US Equity Large Cap Growth (Growth)	B+	B+	B	Down	Y	1,000,000
T. Rowe Price Growth Stock Fund R Class	RRGSX	NAS CM	Open End	US Equity Large Cap Growth (Growth)	B+	B+	B	Down	Y	2,500
T. Rowe Price Health Sciences Fund	PRHSX	NAS CM	Open End	Healthcare Sector Equity (Health)	B	B	B	Up		2,500
T. Rowe Price Health Sciences Fund I Class	THISX	NAS CM	Open End	Healthcare Sector Equity (Health)	B	B	B	Up	Y	1,000,000
T. Rowe Price Institutional Africa & Middle East Fund	TRIAX	NAS CM	Open End	Other Equity (Foreign Stock)	C	C	C	Up	Y	1,000,000
T. Rowe Price Institutional Emerging Markets Equity Fund	IEMFX	NAS CM	Open End	Emerging Markets Equity (Div Emerging Mkts)	B	A	C	Up	Y	1,000,000
T. Rowe Price Institutional Frontier Markets Equity Fund	PRFFX	NAS CM	Open End	Emerging Markets Equity (Growth)	C+	C+	C	Up	Y	1,000,000
T. Rowe Price Inst Global Focused Growth Equity Fund	TRGSX	NAS CM	Open End	Global Equity (World Stock)	B+	B+	B+	Down	Y	1,000,000
T. Rowe Price Institutional Global Growth Equity Fund	RPIGX	NAS CM	Open End	Global Equity (Growth)	B	B+	B	Up	Y	1,000,000

★Expanded analysis of this fund is included in Section II.

	TOTAL RETURNS					PERFORMANCE				ASSETS		ASSET ALLOCATION & TURNOVER					BULL & BEAR		FEES		
Min Additional Investment	3-Month Total Return	6-Month Total Return	1-Year Total Return	3-Year Total Return	5-Year Total Return	Dividend Yield (TTM)	Expense Ratio	3-Yr Std Deviation	3-Year Beta	NAV	Total Assets (MIL)	%Cash	%Stocks	%Bonds	%Other	Turnover Ratio	Last Bull Market Total Return	Last Bear Market Total Return	Front End Fee (%)	Back End Fee (%)	Inception Date
	5.92	10.67	24.88	36.08	109.29		0.69	11.54	1.04	29.41	841.7	0	100	0	0	21	28.51	-22.88			May-17
100	5.82	9.04	19.32	35.13	102.40	1.37	0.64	9.26	0.9	43.38	8,771	0	95	0	5	11	23.59	-15.25			Dec-92
100	5.78	8.93	19.02	34.07	99.72	1.13	0.91	9.26	0.9	43.34	8,771	0	95	0	5	11	23.4	-15.37			Dec-05
	5.87	9.15	19.47	35.45	102.88	1.46	0.51	9.27	0.9	43.37	8,771	0	95	0	5	11	23.59	-15.25			Dec-15
100	2.35	14.21	19.73	29.26	-11.59	0.92	1.75	18.58	0.86	15.64	181.3	1	98	0	1	40	18.76	-34.24			Aug-00
	2.41	14.42	20.12	29.69	-11.30		1.09	18.6	0.86	15.65	181.3	1	98	0	1	40	18.76	-34.24			Mar-17
100	7.39	18.74	42.85	41.22	38.29	0.36	1.26	15.41	0.94	44.99	11,106	0	89	0	5	31	17.68	-26.02			Mar-95
	7.41	18.83	43.03	41.67	38.74	0.55	1.09	15.43	0.94	44.96	11,106	0	89	0	5	31	17.68	-26.02			Aug-15
100	5.35	14.10	34.11			1.15	1.5			13.62	42.9	3	95	2	0	64					Sep-15
100	5.21	13.96	33.76			1.01	1.65			13.59	42.9	3	95	2	0	64					Sep-15
	5.42	14.24	34.38				1.09			13.63	42.9	3	95	2	0	64					Mar-17
100	5.44	10.05	16.17	28.09	83.09	2	0.66	10.99	1.02	33.34	22,563	0	96	0	2	19	23.56	-18.08			Oct-85
	5.33	9.84	15.83	26.99	80.51	1.73	0.94	10.98	1.02	33.26	22,563	0	96	0	2	19	23.35	-18.18			Mar-00
	5.28	9.74	15.52	25.96	78.15	1.47	1.21	11	1.03	33.2	22,563	0	96	0	2	19	23.19	-18.29			Sep-02
	5.46	10.11	16.30	28.36	83.47	2.07	0.54	11	1.03	33.35	22,563	0	96	0	2	19	23.56	-18.08			Dec-15
100	6.59	11.31	21.54	35.88	109.01	1.67	0.21	10.08	1	71.71	29,685	0	100	0	0	9	24.92	-16.37			Mar-90
	6.62	11.39	21.72	36.34	109.72	1.79	0.06	10.09	1	71.72	29,685	0	100	0	0	9	24.92	-16.37			Aug-15
100	1.21	6.35	25.71	12.61	45.85	2.44	0.96	12.33	0.91	20.7	1,174	0	95	0	2	48	21.42	-27.29			Feb-90
	1.20	6.40	25.83	12.72	45.99		0.84	12.34	0.91	20.7	1,174	0	95	0	2	48	21.42	-27.29			Mar-17
100	4.58	9.82	17.95	31.28	100.68	0.94	0.35	12.44	1.01	28.2	859.2	0	98	0	2	22	28.84	-23.93			Jan-98
100	5.04	10.13	19.09	37.65	112.51	0.75	0.93	15.33	1.15	28	789.9	0	98	0	2	42	32.83	-27.62			Sep-96
	5.07	10.20	19.25	37.84	112.80	0.75	0.74	15.33	1.15	27.99	789.9	0	98	0	2	42	32.83	-27.62			Nov-16
100	3.07	6.92	17.01	23.77		1.01	1.15	6.8	0.99	12.68	329.0	0	54	26	20	36					May-13
100	3.01	6.78	16.68	23.32		0.94	1.25	6.81	0.99	12.64	329.0	0	54	26	20	36					May-13
	3.07	6.99	17.16	24.37		1.16	0.84	6.79	0.99	12.7	329.0	0	54	26	20	36					Mar-16
100	5.99	7.49	20.80			0.33	1.05			11.97	14.1	0	98	0	2	28					Jun-16
100	6.37	12.46	34.25	38.78	84.03	0.35	1	11.67	1.06	25.5	473.1	0	99	0	0	70	23.39	-22.44			Oct-08
100	6.28	12.36	34.06	38.39	83.03	0.28	1.1	11.64	1.05	25.35	473.1	0	99	0	0	70	23.27	-22.48			Oct-08
	6.35	12.58	34.45	38.98	84.30		0.69	11.67	1.06	25.51	473.1	0	99	0	0	70	23.39	-22.44			Mar-17
100	4.10	10.45	25.91	35.46		0.55	1.05	11.69	0.94	13.05	24.9	0	97	0	3	55					Oct-13
	4.17	10.52	26.10	35.66			0.74	11.7	0.94	13.05	24.9	0	97	0	3	55					May-17
100	4.24	4.56	7.59	11.18	31.60	2.16	1.05	10.88	0.97	20.48	185.5	0	97	0	3	18	24.54	-17.87			Oct-08
100	4.22	4.49	7.48	10.80	30.84	2.08	1.15	10.9	0.97	20.34	185.5	0	97	0	3	18	24.51	-17.9			Oct-08
	4.25	4.67	7.86	11.46	31.93	2.45	0.74	10.89	0.97	20.47	185.5	0	97	0	3	18	24.54	-17.87			Nov-16
100	7.60	11.72	33.08	50.26	116.52	0.48	0.89	12.64	1.12	38.07	906.8	0	98	0	2	96	21.89	-22.7			Dec-95
100	7.51	11.53	32.65	49.00	113.63	0.24	1.15	12.63	1.12	37.75	906.8	0	98	0	2	96	21.7	-22.82			Apr-06
	7.65	11.80	33.22	50.42	116.74		0.69	12.65	1.12	38.08	906.8	0	98	0	2	96	21.89	-22.7			Mar-17
100	6.22	14.75	47.04	88.90	236.63	0	0.9	16.1	1.04	16.83	6,279	0	100	0	0	171	29.67	-20.38			Sep-00
	6.26	14.85	47.15	89.19	237.15	0	0.77	16.08	1.04	16.84	6,279	0	100	0	0	171	29.67	-20.38			Nov-16
100	6.15	8.74	21.04	33.94	105.99	0.85	0.67	9.48	0.9	28.44	1,912	0	95	0	5	82	23.7	-16.61			Dec-82
	6.15	8.82	21.18	34.07	106.21	0.88	0.59	9.48	0.9	28.45	1,912	0	95	0	5	82	23.7	-16.61			Nov-16
100	6.04	11.81	33.63	49.33	132.13	0.06	0.68	12.17	1.04	62.65	53,389	0	99	0	1	44	31.05	-16.52			Apr-50
100	5.98	11.68	33.31	48.24	129.27	0	0.93	12.16	1.04	61.26	53,389	0	99	0	1	44	30.83	-16.58			Dec-01
	6.10	11.91	33.84	49.92	133.03	0.18	0.52	12.17	1.04	62.7	53,389	0	99	0	1	44	31.05	-16.52			Aug-15
100	5.91	11.53	32.97	47.12	126.40	0	1.18	12.18	1.04	59.26	53,389	0	99	0	1	44	30.64	-16.69			Sep-02
100	1.65	7.02	27.94	28.88	162.57	0	0.77	15.79	0.98	70.35	11,913	0	99	0	0	25	31.05	-14.4			Dec-95
	1.68	7.09	28.08	29.12	163.07	0	0.66	15.78	0.98	70.34	11,913	0	99	0	0	25	31.05	-14.4			Mar-16
	11.09	12.57	23.75	5.86	47.01	1.9	1.21	14.54		6.64	182.6	0	100	0	0	56	18.68	-16.95			Apr-08
	7.39	18.86	42.87	41.54	38.81	0.5	1.1	15.38	0.94	41.08	1,668	0	90	0	4	20	18.17	-25.99			Oct-02
	7.71	11.92	31.68	25.96		1.43	1.35	10.03	0.8	10.86	65.6	0	98	0	2	58					Sep-14
	7.69	11.79	33.26	50.59	116.32	1.41	0.75	12.65	1.12	11.93	45.2	0	97	0	1	106	21.68	-22.42			Jun-06
	6.49	12.69	34.61	39.91	86.05	0.56	0.75	11.62	1.05	27.62	443.5	0	99	0	0	84	23.87	-22.52			Oct-08

	MARKET		FUND TYPE, CATEGORY & OBJECTIVE		RATINGS				MINIMUMS	
Fund Name	Ticker Symbol	Traded On	Fund Type	Category and (Prospectus Objective)	Overall Rating	Reward Rating	Risk Rating	Recent Up/ Downgrade	Open to New Investors	Min Initial Investment
T. Rowe Price Institutional Global Value Equity Fund	PRIGX	NAS CM	Open End	Global Equity (World Stock)	B-	B-	B-	Down	Y	1,000,000
T. Rowe Price Inst Intl Concentrated Equity Fund	RPICX	NAS CM	Open End	Global Equity Large Cap (Foreign Stock)	B-	B-	B	Up	Y	1,000,000
T. Rowe Price Institutional International Core Equity Fund	TRCEX	NAS CM	Open End	Global Equity Large Cap (World Stock)	B	B	B	Up	Y	1,000,000
T. Rowe Price Inst Intl Growth Equity Fund	PRFEX	NAS CM	Open End	Global Equity Large Cap (Foreign Stock)	B	B	B	Up	Y	1,000,000
T. Rowe Price Institutional Large Cap Core Growth Fund	TPLGX	NAS CM	Open End	US Equity Large Cap Growth (Growth)	A-	A	B	Up	Y	1,000,000
T. Rowe Price Institutional Large Cap Growth Fund	TRLGX	NAS CM	Open End	US Equity Large Cap Growth (Growth)	A-	A	B	Up	Y	1,000,000
T. Rowe Price Institutional Large Cap Value Fund	TILCX	NAS CM	Open End	US Equity Large Cap Value (Growth)	B-	B	B-	Down	Y	1,000,000
T. Rowe Price Institutional Mid-Cap Equity Growth Fund	PMEGX	NAS CM	Open End	US Equity Mid Cap (Growth)	B	B	B	Down		1,000,000
T. Rowe Price Institutional Small-Cap Stock Fund	TRSSX	NAS CM	Open End	US Equity Small Cap (Small Company)	B	B+	B	Up		1,000,000
T. Rowe Price Institutional U.S. Structured Research Fund	TRISX	NAS CM	Open End	US Equity Large Cap Blend (Growth)	B	B	B+	Down	Y	1,000,000
T. Rowe Price International Concentrated Equity Fund	PRCNX	NAS CM	Open End	Global Equity Large Cap (Foreign Stock)	B-	B-	B	Up	Y	2,500
T. Rowe Price Intl Concentrated Equity Fund Adv Cls	PRNCX	NAS CM	Open End	Global Equity Large Cap (Foreign Stock)	B-	C+	B	Up	Y	2,500
T. Rowe Price International Concentrated Equity Fund I Cls	RICIX	NAS CM	Open End	Global Equity Large Cap (Foreign Stock)	B-	B-	B	Up	Y	1,000,000
T. Rowe Price International Discovery Fund	PRIDX	NAS CM	Open End	Global Equity Mid/Small Cap (Foreign Stock)	A	A	A-	Up	Y	2,500
T. Rowe Price International Discovery Fund I Class	TIDDX	NAS CM	Open End	Global Equity Mid/Small Cap (Foreign Stock)	A	A	A-	Up	Y	1,000,000
T. Rowe Price International Equity Index Fund	PIEQX	NAS CM	Open End	Global Equity Large Cap (Growth)	B-	B-	B	Up	Y	2,500
T. Rowe Price International Stock Fund	PRITX	NAS CM	Open End	Global Equity Large Cap (Foreign Stock)	B	B	B	Up	Y	2,500
T. Rowe Price International Stock Fund Advisor Class	PAITX	NAS CM	Open End	Global Equity Large Cap (Foreign Stock)	B	B-	B	Up	Y	2,500
T. Rowe Price International Stock Fund Class R	RRITX	NAS CM	Open End	Global Equity Large Cap (Foreign Stock)	B-	B-	B	Up	Y	2,500
T. Rowe Price International Stock Fund I Class	PRIUX	NAS CM	Open End	Global Equity Large Cap (Foreign Stock)	B	B	B	Up	Y	1,000,000
T. Rowe Price International Value Equity Fund	TRIGX	NAS CM	Open End	Global Equity Large Cap (Foreign Stock)	B-	C+	B-	Up	Y	2,500
T. Rowe Price International Value Equity Fund Advisor Cls	PAIGX	NAS CM	Open End	Global Equity Large Cap (Foreign Stock)	B-	C+	B-	Up	Y	2,500
T. Rowe Price International Value Equity Fund Class I	TRTIX	NAS CM	Open End	Global Equity Large Cap (Foreign Stock)	B-	C+	B-	Up	Y	1,000,000
T. Rowe Price International Value Equity Fund Class R	RRIGX	NAS CM	Open End	Global Equity Large Cap (Foreign Stock)	C+	C+	B-	Up	Y	2,500
T. Rowe Price Japan Fund	PRJPX	NAS CM	Open End	Japan Equity (Pacific Stock)	A	A	A	Up	Y	2,500
T. Rowe Price Japan Fund I Class	RJAIX	NAS CM	Open End	Japan Equity (Pacific Stock)	A	A	A	Up	Y	1,000,000
T. Rowe Price Latin America Fund	PRLAX	NAS CM	Open End	Latin America Equity (Foreign Stock)	C	C	C		Y	2,500
T. Rowe Price Latin America Fund I Class	RLAIX	NAS CM	Open End	Latin America Equity (Foreign Stock)	C	C	C		Y	1,000,000
T. Rowe Price Media and Telecommunications Fund	PRMTX	NAS CM	Open End	Communications Sector Equity (Comm)	B+	B+	A-	Up	Y	2,500
T. Rowe Price Media and Telecommunications Fund I Class	TTMIX	NAS CM	Open End	Communications Sector Equity (Comm)	B+	B+	A-	Up	Y	1,000,000
T. Rowe Price Mid-Cap Growth Fund	RPMGX	NAS CM	Open End	US Equity Mid Cap (Growth)	B	B	B	Down		2,500
T. Rowe Price Mid-Cap Growth Fund Advisor Class	PAMCX	NAS CM	Open End	US Equity Mid Cap (Growth)	B	B	B	Down		2,500
T. Rowe Price Mid-Cap Growth Fund I Class	RPTIX	NAS CM	Open End	US Equity Mid Cap (Growth)	B	B	B	Down	Y	1,000,000
T. Rowe Price Mid-Cap Growth Fund R Class	RRMGX	NAS CM	Open End	US Equity Mid Cap (Growth)	B	B	B	Down		2,500
T. Rowe Price Mid-Cap Value Fund	TRMCX	NAS CM	Open End	US Equity Mid Cap (Growth)	B	B-	B	Up		2,500
T. Rowe Price Mid-Cap Value Fund Advisor Class	TAMVX	NAS CM	Open End	US Equity Mid Cap (Growth)	B	B-	B	Up		2,500
T. Rowe Price Mid-Cap Value Fund I Class	TRMIX	NAS CM	Open End	US Equity Mid Cap (Growth)	B	B-	B	Up	Y	1,000,000
T. Rowe Price Mid-Cap Value Fund R Class	RRMVX	NAS CM	Open End	US Equity Mid Cap (Growth)	B	B-	B	Up		2,500
T. Rowe Price New America Growth Fund	PRWAX	NAS CM	Open End	US Equity Large Cap Growth (Growth)	B+	B+	B+	Down	Y	2,500
T. Rowe Price New America Growth Fund Advisor Class	PAWAX	NAS CM	Open End	US Equity Large Cap Growth (Growth)	B+	B+	B	Down	Y	0
T. Rowe Price New America Growth Fund I Class	PNAIX	NAS CM	Open End	US Equity Large Cap Growth (Growth)	B+	B+	B	Down	Y	1,000,000
T. Rowe Price New Asia Fund	PRASX	NAS CM	Open End	Asia ex-Japan Equity (Pacific Stock)	B	B+	C+	Up	Y	2,500
T. Rowe Price New Asia Fund I Class	PNSIX	NAS CM	Open End	Asia ex-Japan Equity (Pacific Stock)	B	B+	C+	Up	Y	1,000,000
T. Rowe Price New Era Fund	PRNEX	NAS CM	Open End	Natl Resources Sec Equity (Natl Res)	C	C+	C	Up	Y	2,500
T. Rowe Price New Era Fund I Class	TRNEX	NAS CM	Open End	Natl Resources Sec Equity (Natl Res)	C	C+	C	Up	Y	1,000,000
T. Rowe Price New Horizons Fund	PRNHX	NAS CM	Open End	US Equity Small Cap (Aggr Growth)	B+	A-	B+	Up		2,500
T. Rowe Price New Horizons Fund I Class	PRJIX	NAS CM	Open End	US Equity Small Cap (Aggr Growth)	B+	A-	B+	Up	Y	1,000,000
T. Rowe Price Overseas Stock Fund	TROSX	NAS CM	Open End	Global Equity Large Cap (Growth)	B	B-	B	Up	Y	2,500
T. Rowe Price Overseas Stock Fund Advisor Class	PAEIX	NAS CM	Open End	Global Equity Large Cap (Growth)	B-	B-	B	Up	Y	2,500
T. Rowe Price Overseas Stock Fund I Class	TROIX	NAS CM	Open End	Global Equity Large Cap (Growth)	B-	B	C+	Up	Y	1,000,000
T. Rowe Price Personal Strategy Balanced Fund	TRPBX	NAS CM	Open End	Moderate Alloc (Balanced)	B	C+	A-	Up	Y	2,500
T. Rowe Price Personal Strategy Balanced Fund I Class	TPPAX	NAS CM	Open End	Moderate Alloc (Balanced)	B	B-	A-	Up	Y	1,000,000

★ Expanded analysis of this fund is included in Section II.

Min Additional Investment	TOTAL RETURNS 3-Month Total Return	6-Month Total Return	1-Year Total Return	3-Year Total Return	5-Year Total Return	PERFORMANCE Dividend Yield (TTM)	Expense Ratio	3-Yr Std Deviation	3-Year Beta	ASSETS NAV	Total Assets (MIL)	ASSET ALLOCATION & TURNOVER %Cash	%Stocks	%Bonds	%Other	Turnover Ratio	BULL & BEAR Last Bull Market Total Return	Last Bear Market Total Return	FEES Front End Fee (%)	Back End Fee (%)	Inception Date
	4.19	8.37	19.58	28.42	85.07	1.62	0.75	9.57	0.89	13.34	11.6	0	95	0	3	84					Jul-12
	1.90	5.00	21.68	27.37	53.90	1.25	0.75	10.53	0.82	12.99	531.0	0	93	0	7	112	16.84	-18.69			Jul-10
	3.21	10.27	27.96	27.30	50.20	1.85	0.75	11.52	0.92	13.94	183.6	0	99	0	1	12	17.05	-23.43			Oct-10
	3.50	8.50	28.34	29.92	49.60	1.26	0.75	11.83	0.93	24.88	57.8	0	96	0	2	35	19.27	-23.72			Sep-89
	7.01	14.43	36.49	52.64	142.34	0.18	0.57	12.29	1.06	37.43	3,054	0	100	0	0	40	31	-14.79			Sep-03
	7.29	15.20	37.82	55.13	150.21	0.17	0.56	12.6	1.1	36.91	15,923	0	98	0	2	37	29.76	-16.72			Oct-01
	5.50	9.31	16.82	29.86	101.93	1.82	0.57	11.01	1.05	23.38	3,957	0	97	0	2	26	23.79	-20.44			Mar-00
	4.63	9.40	26.02	43.06	130.19	0.15	0.61	11.08	0.98	54.48	7,137	0	98	0	2	36	25.84	-20.61			Jul-96
	3.36	8.79	15.45	32.27	103.55	0.24	0.67	12.73	0.89	23.72	4,260	0	98	0	2	42	32.48	-24.06			Mar-00
	6.51	11.37	23.81	39.34	113.71	1.22	0.55	10.36	1.02	12.92	648.5	0	99	0	1	34	25.66	-16.39			Oct-07
100	1.37	4.50	21.05	26.19		1.36	0.9	10.59	0.83	10.63	25.8	0	93	0	7	118					Aug-14
100	1.37	4.41	20.83	26.24		1.45	1	10.55	0.82	10.63	25.8	0	93	0	7	118					Aug-14
	1.46	4.59	21.27	26.42			0.69	10.6	0.83	10.64	25.8	0	93	0	7	118					Mar-17
100	6.06	15.90	39.00	53.89	92.59	0.42	1.2	10.67	0.85	71.41	7,842	0	94	0	5	22	20.32	-21.75			Dec-88
	6.08	15.97	39.16	54.27	93.05	0.51	1.08	10.67	0.86	71.45	7,842	0	94	0	5	22	20.32	-21.75			Dec-15
100	4.23	9.62	26.44	26.59	45.15	2.32	0.45	11.55	0.93	14.45	612.3	0	97	0	1	8	14.19	-24.21			Nov-00
100	3.53	8.58	28.18	29.53	49.22	0.98	0.84	11.84	0.93	18.67	15,754	0	97	0	1	31	19.24	-23.53			May-80
100	3.53	8.46	27.88	28.89	47.81	0.46	1.08	11.82	0.93	18.74	15,754	0	97	0	1	31	19.14	-23.61			Mar-00
100	3.39	8.30	27.51	27.45	45.13	0.47	1.4	11.82	0.93	18.57	15,754	0	97	0	1	31	18.97	-23.7			Sep-02
	3.58	8.63	28.39	30.08	49.85	1.24	0.68	11.81	0.93	18.66	15,754	0	97	0	1	31	19.24	-23.53			Aug-15
100	1.39	6.48	20.78	17.12	38.33	2.22	0.85	11.15	0.89	15.12	13,844	0	98	0	2	50	15.56	-24.46			Dec-98
100	1.37	6.39	20.52	16.32	36.75	2.06	1.08	11.16	0.89	15.39	13,844	0	98	0	2	50	15.43	-24.59			Sep-02
	1.39	6.56	20.97	17.66	38.97	2.61	0.67	11.14	0.89	15.09	13,844	0	98	0	2	50	15.56	-24.46			Aug-15
100	1.25	6.19	20.12	15.28	34.85	1.89	1.36	11.16	0.89	15.19	13,844	0	98	0	2	50	15.18	-24.66			Sep-02
100	8.16	14.76	32.66	68.56	102.76	0.46	1.02	10.45	0.72	15.11	750.1	0	98	0	2	13	6.94	-6.84			Dec-91
	8.15	14.75	32.64	68.54	102.73		0.84	10.46	0.72	15.11	750.1	0	98	0	2	13	6.94	-6.84			Mar-17
100	-2.37	13.01	29.54	23.25	-8.82	1.15	1.38	22.98	0.9	24.56	675.3	0	96	0	4	28	13.11	-29.34			Dec-93
	-2.33	13.10	29.69	23.40	-8.71		1.09	22.98	0.9	24.56	675.3	0	96	0	4	28	13.11	-29.34			Mar-17
100	4.99	10.97	32.98	58.95	139.20	0.02	0.79	13.12	1.06	96.47	4,829	0	99	0	1	16	24.55	-16.87			Oct-93
	5.01	11.02	33.12	59.24	139.63	0.02	0.67	13.12	1.06	96.54	4,829	0	99	0	1	16	24.55	-16.87			Mar-16
100	4.43	8.92	24.85	40.41	122.90	0	0.77	10.76	0.96	87.02	30,423	0	94	0	6	29	25.27	-20.15			Jun-92
100	4.36	8.78	24.53	39.31	120.07	0	1.02	10.76	0.96	84.5	30,423	0	94	0	6	29	25.11	-20.24			Mar-00
	4.46	9.00	25.02	40.83	123.57	0	0.63	10.77	0.96	87.01	30,423	0	94	0	6	29	25.27	-20.15			Aug-15
100	4.30	8.66	24.20	38.27	117.29	0	1.28	10.76	0.96	82.06	30,423	0	94	0	6	29	24.92	-20.33			Sep-02
100	5.16	8.28	11.64	32.86	98.08	0.8	0.8	10.51	0.97	30.4	14,034	0	91	0	9	50	20.73	-19.44			Jun-96
100	5.09	8.16	11.33	31.85	95.59	0.59	1.05	10.53	0.98	30.28	14,034	0	91	0	9	50	20.56	-19.5			Sep-02
	5.19	8.39	11.78	33.25	98.67	0.94	0.66	10.5	0.97	30.39	14,034	0	91	0	9	50	20.73	-19.44			Aug-15
100	4.49	7.48	10.49	30.22	92.11	0.39	1.3	10.5	0.97	29.82	14,034	0	91	0	9	50	20.4	-19.62			Sep-02
100	7.10	12.06	34.56	47.37	127.64	0.04	0.8	13.07	1.16	48.03	4,429	0	94	0	6	93	21.8	-16.67			Sep-85
	7.05	11.93	34.21	46.20	124.66	0	1.07	13.07	1.16	47.03	4,429	0	94	0	6	93	21.63	-16.74			Dec-05
	7.16	12.14	34.76	47.75	128.23	0.16	0.66	13.07	1.16	48.02	4,429	0	94	0	6	93	21.8	-16.67			Dec-15
100	8.00	13.60	41.33	35.18	45.27	0.62	0.95	14.12	0.9	19.56	3,172	0	95	0	4	71	20.01	-19.4			Sep-90
	8.05	13.70	41.51	35.52	45.64	0.67	0.84	14.11	0.9	19.58	3,172	0	95	0	4	71	20.01	-19.4			Dec-15
100	6.61	13.26	10.57	11.41	22.33	1.19	0.67	15.25	1.02	36.5	3,829	0	98	0	1	66	17.09	-30.95			Jan-69
	6.64	13.32	10.69	11.71	22.65	1.3	0.56	15.25	1.02	36.5	3,829	0	98	0	1	66	17.09	-30.95			Dec-15
100	4.62	11.60	31.49	47.70	138.62	0	0.79	12.06	0.76	52.57	22,021	0	95	0	5	42	31.94	-18.11			Jun-60
	4.65	11.68	31.67	48.18	139.40	0	0.65	12.05	0.76	52.63	22,021	0	95	0	5	42	31.94	-18.11			Aug-15
100	3.04	9.82	27.02	26.68	49.33	1.58	0.84	11.2	0.89	11.31	15,748	0	96	0	3	13	16.86	-23.21			Dec-06
100	3.07	9.81	26.75	25.80	47.55	1.86	1.1	11.16	0.89	11.22	15,748	0	96	0	3	13	16.69	-23.29			Aug-15
	3.14	9.95	27.22	27.16	49.89	2.02	0.67	11.17	0.89	11.28	15,748	0	96	0	3	13	16.86	-23.21			Aug-15
100	3.37	7.37	17.30	25.04	58.00	1.42	0.74	6.85	1.1	24.09	2,363	3	58	33	6	63	18.19	-13.12			Jul-94
	3.37	7.45	17.45	25.31	58.34	1.54	0.62	6.85	1.1	24.09	2,363	3	58	33	6	63	18.19	-13.12			Mar-16

Fund Name	Ticker Symbol	Traded On	Fund Type	Category and (Prospectus Objective)	Overall Rating	Reward Rating	Risk Rating	Recent Up/ Downgrade	Open to New Investors	Min Initial Investment
	MARKET			FUND TYPE, CATEGORY & OBJECTIVE	RATINGS				MINIMUMS	
T. Rowe Price Personal Strategy Growth Fund	TRSGX	NAS CM	Open End	Aggressive Alloc (Asset Alloc)	B-	B-	B	Down	Y	2,500
T. Rowe Price Personal Strategy Growth Fund I Class	TGIPX	NAS CM	Open End	Aggressive Alloc (Asset Alloc)	B-	B-	B	Down	Y	1,000,000
T. Rowe Price Personal Strategy Income Fund	PRSIX	NAS CM	Open End	Cautious Alloc (Asset Alloc)	B	C+	A-	Up	Y	2,500
T. Rowe Price Personal Strategy Income Fund I Class	PPIPX	NAS CM	Open End	Cautious Alloc (Asset Alloc)	B	C+	A-	Up	Y	1,000,000
T. Rowe Price QM Global Equity Fund	TQGEX	NAS CM	Open End	Global Equity (Growth)	D+	C	A-	Up	Y	2,500
T. Rowe Price QM Global Equity Fund Advisor Class	TQGAX	NAS CM	Open End	Global Equity (Growth)	D+	C	B+	Up	Y	2,500
T. Rowe Price QM Global Equity Fund I Class	TQGIX	NAS CM	Open End	Global Equity (Growth)	D+	C	B+	Up	Y	1,000,000
T. Rowe Price QM U.S. Small & Mid-Cap Core Equity Fund	TQSMX	NAS CM	Open End	US Equity Mid Cap (Growth)	C-	C	B+	Up	Y	2,500
T. Rowe Price QM U.S. Small & Mid-Cap Core Eq Fund Adv Cls	TQSAX	NAS CM	Open End	US Equity Mid Cap (Growth)	C-	C	B+	Up	Y	2,500
T. Rowe Price QM U.S. Small & Mid-Cap Core Eq Fund I Cls	TQSIX	NAS CM	Open End	US Equity Mid Cap (Growth)	C-	C	B+	Up	Y	1,000,000
T. Rowe Price QM U.S. Small-Cap Growth Equity Fund	PRDSX	NAS CM	Open End	US Equity Small Cap (Small Company)	B+	B+	B	Up	Y	2,500
T. Rowe Price QM U.S. Small-Cap Growth Equity Fund Adv Cls	TQAAX	NAS CM	Open End	US Equity Small Cap (Small Company)	B+	B+	B	Up	Y	2,500
T. Rowe Price QM U.S. Small-Cap Growth Equity Fund I Class	TQAIX	NAS CM	Open End	US Equity Small Cap (Small Company)	B+	B+	B	Up	Y	1,000,000
T. Rowe Price QM U.S. Value Equity Fund	TQMVX	NAS CM	Open End	US Equity Large Cap Value (Growth)	C-	C-	B+	Up	Y	2,500
T. Rowe Price QM U.S. Value Equity Fund Advisor Class	TQVAX	NAS CM	Open End	US Equity Large Cap Value (Growth)	C-	C-	B+	Up	Y	2,500
T. Rowe Price QM U.S. Value Equity Fund I Class	TQVIX	NAS CM	Open End	US Equity Large Cap Value (Growth)	C-	C	B+	Up	Y	1,000,000
T. Rowe Price Real Assets Fund	PRAFX	NAS CM	Open End	Natl Resources Sec Equity (Real Estate)	C+	C+	C	Up	Y	2,500
T. Rowe Price Real Assets Fund I Class	PRIKX	NAS CM	Open End	Natl Resources Sec Equity (Real Estate)	C+	C+	C	Up	Y	1,000,000
T. Rowe Price Real Estate Fund	TRREX	NAS CM	Open End	Real Estate Sector Equity (Real Estate)	B	B-	B+	Up	Y	2,500
T. Rowe Price Real Estate Fund Advisor Class	PAREX	NAS CM	Open End	Real Estate Sector Equity (Real Estate)	B	C+	B+	Up	Y	2,500
T. Rowe Price Real Estate Fund I Class	TIRRX	NAS CM	Open End	Real Estate Sector Equity (Real Estate)	B	B-	B+	Up	Y	1,000,000
T. Rowe Price Retirement 2005 Fund	TRRFX	NAS CM	Open End	Target Date 2000-2020 (Asset Alloc)	B	C+	A-	Up	Y	2,500
T. Rowe Price Retirement 2005 Fund Advisor Class	PARGX	NAS CM	Open End	Target Date 2000-2020 (Asset Alloc)	B	C+	A-	Up	Y	0
T. Rowe Price Retirement 2005 Fund Class R	RRTLX	NAS CM	Open End	Target Date 2000-2020 (Asset Alloc)	B	C+	B+	Up	Y	0
T. Rowe Price Retirement 2010 Fund	TRRAX	NAS CM	Open End	Target Date 2000-2020 (Asset Alloc)	B	C+	A-	Up	Y	2,500
T. Rowe Price Retirement 2010 Fund Advisor Class	PARAX	NAS CM	Open End	Target Date 2000-2020 (Asset Alloc)	B	C+	A-	Up	Y	0
T. Rowe Price Retirement 2010 Fund Class R	RRTAX	NAS CM	Open End	Target Date 2000-2020 (Asset Alloc)	B	C+	B+	Up	Y	0
T. Rowe Price Retirement 2015 Fund	TRRGX	NAS CM	Open End	Target Date 2000-2020 (Asset Alloc)	B-	C+	B	Up	Y	2,500
T. Rowe Price Retirement 2015 Fund Advisor Class	PARHX	NAS CM	Open End	Target Date 2000-2020 (Asset Alloc)	B	C+	A-	Up	Y	0
T. Rowe Price Retirement 2015 Fund Class R	RRTMX	NAS CM	Open End	Target Date 2000-2020 (Asset Alloc)	B-	C+	B	Up	Y	0
T. Rowe Price Retirement 2020 Fund	TRRBX	NAS CM	Open End	Target Date 2000-2020 (Asset Alloc)	B-	C+	B	Down	Y	2,500
T. Rowe Price Retirement 2020 Fund Advisor Class	PARBX	NAS CM	Open End	Target Date 2000-2020 (Asset Alloc)	B	C+	B+	Up	Y	0
T. Rowe Price Retirement 2020 Fund Class R	RRTBX	NAS CM	Open End	Target Date 2000-2020 (Asset Alloc)	B	C+	B+	Up	Y	0
T. Rowe Price Retirement 2025 Fund	TRRHX	NAS CM	Open End	Target Date 2021-2045 (Asset Alloc)	B-	B-	B	Down	Y	2,500
T. Rowe Price Retirement 2025 Fund Advisor Class	PARJX	NAS CM	Open End	Target Date 2021-2045 (Asset Alloc)	B-	C+	B	Down	Y	0
T. Rowe Price Retirement 2025 Fund Class R	RRTNX	NAS CM	Open End	Target Date 2021-2045 (Asset Alloc)	B-	C+	B	Down	Y	0
T. Rowe Price Retirement 2030 Fund	TRRCX	NAS CM	Open End	Target Date 2021-2045 (Asset Alloc)	B-	B-	B	Down	Y	2,500
T. Rowe Price Retirement 2030 Fund Advisor Class	PARCX	NAS CM	Open End	Target Date 2021-2045 (Asset Alloc)	B-	B-	B	Down	Y	0
T. Rowe Price Retirement 2030 Fund Class R	RRTCX	NAS CM	Open End	Target Date 2021-2045 (Asset Alloc)	B	B-	B+	Up	Y	0
T. Rowe Price Retirement 2035 Fund	TRRJX	NAS CM	Open End	Target Date 2021-2045 (Asset Alloc)	B-	B-	B	Down	Y	2,500
T. Rowe Price Retirement 2035 Fund Advisor Class	PARKX	NAS CM	Open End	Target Date 2021-2045 (Asset Alloc)	B-	B-	B	Down	Y	0
T. Rowe Price Retirement 2035 Fund Class R	RRTPX	NAS CM	Open End	Target Date 2021-2045 (Asset Alloc)	B-	B-	B	Down	Y	0
T. Rowe Price Retirement 2040 Fund	TRRDX	NAS CM	Open End	Target Date 2021-2045 (Asset Alloc)	B-	B-	B-	Down	Y	2,500
T. Rowe Price Retirement 2040 Fund Advisor Class	PARDX	NAS CM	Open End	Target Date 2021-2045 (Asset Alloc)	B-	B-	B-	Down	Y	0
T. Rowe Price Retirement 2040 Fund Class R	RRTDX	NAS CM	Open End	Target Date 2021-2045 (Asset Alloc)	B-	B-	B-	Down	Y	0
T. Rowe Price Retirement 2045 Fund	TRRKX	NAS CM	Open End	Target Date 2021-2045 (Asset Alloc)	B-	B-	B-	Down	Y	2,500
T. Rowe Price Retirement 2045 Fund Advisor Class	PARLX	NAS CM	Open End	Target Date 2021-2045 (Asset Alloc)	B-	B-	B-	Down	Y	0
T. Rowe Price Retirement 2045 Fund Class R	RRTRX	NAS CM	Open End	Target Date 2021-2045 (Asset Alloc)	B-	B-	B-	Down	Y	0
T. Rowe Price Retirement 2050 Fund	TRRMX	NAS CM	Open End	Target Date 2046+ (Asset Alloc)	B-	B-	B-	Down	Y	2,500
T. Rowe Price Retirement 2050 Fund Advisor Class	PARFX	NAS CM	Open End	Target Date 2046+ (Asset Alloc)	B-	B-	B-	Down	Y	0
T. Rowe Price Retirement 2050 Fund Class R	RRTFX	NAS CM	Open End	Target Date 2046+ (Asset Alloc)	B-	B-	B-	Down	Y	0
T. Rowe Price Retirement 2055 Fund	TRRNX	NAS CM	Open End	Target Date 2046+ (Asset Alloc)	B-	B-	B-	Down	Y	2,500

★ Expanded analysis of this fund is included in Section II.

Min Additional Investment	3-Month Total Return	6-Month Total Return	1-Year Total Return	3-Year Total Return	5-Year Total Return	Dividend Yield (TTM)	Expense Ratio	3-Yr Std Deviation	3-Year Beta	NAV	Total Assets (MIL)	%Cash	%Stocks	%Bonds	%Other	Turnover Ratio	Last Bull Market Total Return	Last Bear Market Total Return	Front End Fee (%)	Back End Fee (%)	Inception Date
	TOTAL RETURNS					PERFORMANCE				ASSETS		ASSET ALLOCATION & TURNOVER					BULL & BEAR		FEES		
100	4.30	9.34	21.91	30.11	75.33	1.15	0.78	8.7	1.05	33.94	2,227	0	77	16	7	58	22.31	-16.94			Jul-94
	4.33	9.39	22.04	30.42	75.75	1.24	0.66	8.71	1.05	33.96	2,227	0	77	16	7	58	22.31	-16.94			Mar-16
100	2.35	5.40	12.79	19.47	41.13	1.7	0.6	5.03	1.18	19.54	2,137	9	38	46	6	61	13.89	-9.48			Jul-94
	2.46	5.52	12.97	19.66	41.37	1.8	0.53	5.03	1.18	19.54	2,137	9	38	46	6	61	13.89	-9.48			Mar-16
100	5.31	10.74	24.90			1.1	0.68			12.72	17.6	0	99	0	0	12					Apr-16
100	5.24	10.49	24.51			0.86	1.04			12.72	17.6	0	99	0	0	12					Apr-16
	5.30	10.73	25.12			1.17	0.59			12.71	17.6	0	99	0	0	12					Apr-16
100	5.65	9.92	15.93			0.49	0.8			14.31	52.9	0	98	0	2	11					Feb-16
100	5.59	9.78	15.60			0.21	1.14			14.3	52.9	0	98	0	2	11					Feb-16
	5.72	9.99	16.09			0.55	0.69			14.31	52.9	0	98	0	2	11					Feb-16
100	5.89	10.31	22.11	38.18	117.59	0	0.81	12.01	0.85	34.89	5,856	0	99	0	1	10	30.19	-23.8			Jun-97
100	5.84	10.16	21.77	37.05	114.74	0	1.04	12.01	0.85	34.79	5,856	0	99	0	1	10	30	-23.88			Jul-16
	5.91	10.35	22.26	38.54	118.16	0	0.66	12.02	0.85	34.94	5,856	0	99	0	1	10	30.19	-23.8			Mar-16
100	6.66	10.96	15.90			0.93	0.69			13.55	19.7	0	99	0	1	22					Feb-16
100	6.60	10.90	15.57			0.72	0.99			13.54	19.7	0	99	0	1	22					Feb-16
	6.73	11.11	16.06			1	0.54			13.55	19.7	0	99	0	1	22					Feb-16
100	5.46	9.45	10.47	12.90	16.30	1.83	0.84	13.1	0.91	11.69	3,302	0	97	0	2	49	17.15	-25.21			Jul-10
	5.56	9.55	10.67	13.21	16.62	2	0.66	13.12	0.92	11.68	3,302	0	97	0	2	49	17.15	-25.21			Aug-15
100	3.27	4.19	4.42	14.25	57.16	2.42	0.74	12.66	0.94	28.7	6,309	0	96	0	4	6	32.33	-16.36			Oct-97
100	3.23	4.07	4.11	13.44	55.25	2.06	1.02	12.65	0.94	29.07	6,309	0	96	0	4	6	32.2	-16.46			Dec-04
	3.34	4.30	4.56	14.57	57.60	2.49	0.61	12.65	0.94	28.71	6,309	0	96	0	4	6	32.33	-16.36			Dec-15
100	2.16	4.64	10.66	16.86	35.60	1.68	0.58	4.72	1.4	13.65	1,747	2	36	60	2	16	13	-9.33			Feb-04
	2.03	4.51	10.38	15.95	33.88	1.48	0.83	4.68	1.39	13.6	1,747	2	36	60	2	16	12.84	-9.44			May-07
	1.94	4.34	10.00	15.10	32.17	0.91	1.08	4.67	1.39	13.68	1,747	2	36	60	2	16	12.63	-9.51			May-07
100	2.34	5.11	11.66	18.22	40.58	1.78	0.57	5.17	1.24	18.28	5,233	2	41	55	2	12	14.72	-11.09			Sep-02
	2.30	4.98	11.35	17.40	38.78	1.54	0.82	5.17	1.24	18.2	5,233	2	41	55	2	12	14.57	-11.15			Oct-03
	2.20	4.84	11.06	16.45	37.03	1.29	1.07	5.16	1.24	18.1	5,233	2	41	55	2	12	14.43	-11.27			Oct-03
100	2.69	5.73	13.34	20.42	48.14	1.67	0.59	5.96	1.19	14.98	8,885	2	48	47	2	13	16.77	-12.97			Feb-04
	2.64	5.63	13.10	19.52	46.32	1.49	0.84	5.97	1.19	14.94	8,885	2	48	47	2	13	16.64	-13.09			May-07
	2.61	5.55	12.85	18.72	44.52	1.25	1.09	5.94	1.18	14.81	8,885	2	48	47	2	13	16.46	-13.17			May-07
100	3.10	6.64	15.73	23.26	56.19	1.59	0.63	6.83	1.18	22.54	25,234	2	58	38	2	14	18.62	-14.71			Sep-02
	3.09	6.56	15.49	22.40	54.25	1.35	0.88	6.84	1.18	22.39	25,234	2	58	38	2	14	18.38	-14.74			Oct-03
	2.98	6.39	15.17	21.46	52.29	1.11	1.13	6.84	1.18	22.19	25,234	2	58	38	2	14	18.31	-14.85			Oct-03
100	3.46	7.36	17.68	25.63	63.51	1.46	0.67	7.59	1.16	17.59	21,665	2	66	30	2	16	20.04	-16.08			Feb-04
	3.37	7.22	17.37	24.70	61.43	1.2	0.92	7.61	1.16	17.5	21,665	2	66	30	2	16	19.93	-16.22			May-07
	3.35	7.12	17.06	23.79	59.50	1.05	1.17	7.58	1.16	17.34	21,665	2	66	30	2	16	19.76	-16.31			May-07
100	3.82	8.03	19.44	27.82	70.03	1.32	0.69	8.25	1.14	25.92	27,637	2	73	23	2	16	21.5	-17.37			Sep-02
	3.74	7.90	19.15	26.85	67.94	1.15	0.94	8.25	1.14	25.71	27,637	2	73	23	2	16	21.39	-17.53			Oct-03
	3.70	7.76	18.84	25.90	65.78	0.93	1.19	8.26	1.14	25.51	27,637	2	73	23	2	16	21.24	-17.63			Oct-03
100	4.07	8.54	20.87	29.43	74.90	1.2	0.72	8.82	1.12	18.97	16,788	2	79	17	2	16	22.42	-18.29			Feb-04
	4.04	8.42	20.59	28.47	72.80	1	0.97	8.83	1.12	18.89	16,788	2	79	17	2	16	22.2	-18.41			May-07
	3.98	8.29	20.30	27.53	70.66	0.81	1.22	8.85	1.13	18.69	16,788	2	79	17	2	16	22.17	-18.54			May-07
100	4.31	9.01	22.02	30.68	78.42	1.11	0.74	9.31	1.12	27.24	19,593	2	84	12	2	18	22.82	-18.65			Sep-02
	4.20	8.82	21.67	29.67	76.13	0.91	0.99	9.3	1.12	27	19,593	2	84	12	2	18	22.7	-18.73			Oct-03
	4.16	8.68	21.36	28.67	73.99	0.7	1.24	9.3	1.12	26.83	19,593	2	84	12	2	18	22.53	-18.82			Oct-03
100	4.36	9.13	22.40	31.14	79.03	1.08	0.74	9.33	1.07	18.47	10,668	1	86	10	2	14	22.77	-18.49			May-05
	4.34	9.02	22.07	30.18	76.94	0.88	0.99	9.32	1.07	18.36	10,668	1	86	10	2	14	22.55	-18.56			May-07
	4.29	8.89	21.78	29.29	74.78	0.73	1.24	9.32	1.07	18.17	10,668	1	86	10	2	14	22.4	-18.68			May-07
100	4.41	9.16	22.37	31.27	79.24	1.1	0.74	9.33	1.03	15.52	8,650	1	86	10	2	16	22.77	-18.52			Dec-06
	4.32	9.04	22.08	30.25	76.95	0.86	0.99	9.33	1.03	15.39	8,650	1	86	10	2	16	22.53	-18.61			Dec-06
	4.23	8.84	21.71	29.23	74.64	0.68	1.24	9.32	1.03	15.26	8,650	1	86	10	2	16	22.28	-18.62			Dec-06
100	4.40	9.14	22.32	31.23	78.96	1.1	0.74	9.34	1.01	15.58	3,790	2	86	10	2	14	22.72	-18.45			Dec-06

	MARKET		FUND TYPE, CATEGORY & OBJECTIVE		RATINGS				MINIMUMS	
Fund Name	Ticker Symbol	Traded On	Fund Type	Category and (Prospectus Objective)	Overall Rating	Reward Rating	Risk Rating	Recent Up/ Downgrade	Open to New Investors	Min Initial Investment
T. Rowe Price Retirement 2055 Fund Advisor Class	PAROX	NAS CM	Open End	Target Date 2046+ (Asset Alloc)	B-	B-	B-	Down	Y	0
T. Rowe Price Retirement 2055 Fund Class R	RRTVX	NAS CM	Open End	Target Date 2046+ (Asset Alloc)	B-	B-	B-	Down	Y	0
T. Rowe Price Retirement 2060 Fund	TRRLX	NAS CM	Open End	Target Date 2046+ (Asset Alloc)	B-	B-	B-	Up	Y	2,500
T. Rowe Price Retirement 2060 Fund Advisor Class	TRRYX	NAS CM	Open End	Target Date 2046+ (Asset Alloc)	B-	B-	B-	Up	Y	0
T. Rowe Price Retirement 2060 Fund R Class	TRRZX	NAS CM	Open End	Target Date 2046+ (Asset Alloc)	B-	B-	B-	Up	Y	0
T. Rowe Price Retirement Balanced Fund	TRRIX	NAS CM	Open End	Cautious Alloc (Asset Alloc)	B-	C+	B	Up	Y	2,500
T. Rowe Price Retirement Balanced Fund Advisor Class	PARIX	NAS CM	Open End	Cautious Alloc (Asset Alloc)	B-	C+	B	Up	Y	0
T. Rowe Price Retirement Balanced Fund Class R	RRTIX	NAS CM	Open End	Cautious Alloc (Asset Alloc)	B	C+	B+	Up	Y	0
T. Rowe Price Retirement Balanced I Fund I Class	TRPTX	NAS CM	Open End	Cautious Alloc (Asset Alloc)	C	C	B	Up	Y	1,000,000
T. Rowe Price Retirement I 2005 Fund I Class	TRPFX	NAS CM	Open End	Target Date 2000-2020 (Asset Alloc)	C	C	B	Up	Y	1,000,000
T. Rowe Price Retirement I 2010 Fund I Class	TRPAX	NAS CM	Open End	Target Date 2000-2020 (Asset Alloc)	C	C	B	Up	Y	1,000,000
T. Rowe Price Retirement I 2015 Fund I Class	TRFGX	NAS CM	Open End	Target Date 2000-2020 (Asset Alloc)	C	C	B	Up	Y	1,000,000
T. Rowe Price Retirement I 2020 Fund I Class	TRBRX	NAS CM	Open End	Target Date 2000-2020 (Asset Alloc)	C	C+	B	Up	Y	1,000,000
T. Rowe Price Retirement I 2025 Fund I Class	TRPHX	NAS CM	Open End	Target Date 2021-2045 (Asset Alloc)	C	C+	B	Up	Y	1,000,000
T. Rowe Price Retirement I 2030 Fund I Class	TRPCX	NAS CM	Open End	Target Date 2021-2045 (Asset Alloc)	C	C+	B	Up	Y	1,000,000
T. Rowe Price Retirement I 2035 Fund I Class	TRPJX	NAS CM	Open End	Target Date 2021-2045 (Asset Alloc)	C	C+	B	Up	Y	1,000,000
T. Rowe Price Retirement I 2040 Fund I Class	TRPDX	NAS CM	Open End	Target Date 2021-2045 (Asset Alloc)	C	C+	B	Up	Y	1,000,000
T. Rowe Price Retirement I 2045 Fund I Class	TRPKX	NAS CM	Open End	Target Date 2021-2045 (Asset Alloc)	C	C+	B	Up	Y	1,000,000
T. Rowe Price Retirement I 2050 Fund I Class	TRPMX	NAS CM	Open End	Target Date 2046+ (Asset Alloc)	C	C+	B	Up	Y	1,000,000
T. Rowe Price Retirement I 2055 Fund I Class	TRPNX	NAS CM	Open End	Target Date 2046+ (Asset Alloc)	C	C+	B	Up	Y	1,000,000
T. Rowe Price Retirement I 2060 Fund I Class	TRPLX	NAS CM	Open End	Target Date 2046+ (Asset Alloc)	C	C+	B	Up	Y	1,000,000
T. Rowe Price Retirement Income 2020 Fund	TRLAX	NAS CM	Open End	Target Date 2000-2020 (Asset Alloc)	U	U	U		Y	25,000
T. Rowe Price Science and Technology Fund	PRSCX	NAS CM	Open End	Technology Sector Equity (Technology)	A	A+	B+	Up	Y	2,500
T. Rowe Price Science and Technology Fund Advisor Class	PASTX	NAS CM	Open End	Technology Sector Equity (Technology)	A	A+	B+	Up	Y	2,500
T. Rowe Price Science and Technology Fund I Class	TSNIX	NAS CM	Open End	Technology Sector Equity (Technology)	A	A+	B+	Up	Y	1,000,000
T. Rowe Price Small-Cap Stock Fund	OTCFX	NAS CM	Open End	US Equity Small Cap (Small Company)	B	B+	B	Up		2,500
T. Rowe Price Small-Cap Stock Fund Advisor Class	PASSX	NAS CM	Open End	US Equity Small Cap (Small Company)	B	B	B	Up		2,500
T. Rowe Price Small-Cap Stock Fund I Class	OTIIX	NAS CM	Open End	US Equity Small Cap (Small Company)	B	B+	B	Up	Y	1,000,000
T. Rowe Price Small-Cap Value Fund	PRSVX	NAS CM	Open End	US Equity Small Cap (Small Company)	A-	A	B	Up	Y	2,500
T. Rowe Price Small-Cap Value Fund Advisor Class	PASVX	NAS CM	Open End	US Equity Small Cap (Small Company)	B+	A-	B	Up	Y	2,500
T. Rowe Price Small-Cap Value Fund I Class	PRVIX	NAS CM	Open End	US Equity Small Cap (Small Company)	A-	A	B	Up	Y	1,000,000
T. Rowe Price Spectrum Growth Fund	PRSGX	NAS CM	Open End	US Equity Large Cap Growth (Growth)	B-	B	B-	Down	Y	2,500
T. Rowe Price Spectrum International Fund	PSILX	NAS CM	Open End	Global Equity Large Cap (Asset Alloc)	B-	B-	B	Up	Y	2,500
T. Rowe Price Target 2005 Fund	TRARX	NAS CM	Open End	Target Date 2000-2020 (Asset Alloc)	B	C+	A-	Up	Y	2,500
T. Rowe Price Target 2005 Fund Advisor Class	PANRX	NAS CM	Open End	Target Date 2000-2020 (Asset Alloc)	B	C+	A-	Up	Y	0
T. Rowe Price Target 2005 Fund I Class	TFRRX	NAS CM	Open End	Target Date 2000-2020 (Asset Alloc)	B	C+	A-	Up	Y	1,000,000
T. Rowe Price Target 2010 Fund	TRROX	NAS CM	Open End	Target Date 2000-2020 (Asset Alloc)	B-	C+	B	Up	Y	2,500
T. Rowe Price Target 2010 Fund Advisor Class	PAERX	NAS CM	Open End	Target Date 2000-2020 (Asset Alloc)	B-	C+	B	Up	Y	0
T. Rowe Price Target 2010 Fund I Class	TORFX	NAS CM	Open End	Target Date 2000-2020 (Asset Alloc)	B	C+	A-	Up	Y	1,000,000
T. Rowe Price Target 2015 Fund	TRRTX	NAS CM	Open End	Target Date 2000-2020 (Asset Alloc)	B	C+	A-	Up	Y	2,500
T. Rowe Price Target 2015 Fund Advisor Class	PAHRX	NAS CM	Open End	Target Date 2000-2020 (Asset Alloc)	B	C+	A-	Up	Y	0
T. Rowe Price Target 2015 Fund I Class	TTRTX	NAS CM	Open End	Target Date 2000-2020 (Asset Alloc)	B-	C+	B	Up	Y	1,000,000
T. Rowe Price Target 2020 Fund	TRRUX	NAS CM	Open End	Target Date 2000-2020 (Asset Alloc)	B-	C+	B	Up	Y	2,500
T. Rowe Price Target 2020 Fund Advisor Class	PAIRX	NAS CM	Open End	Target Date 2000-2020 (Asset Alloc)	B	C+	A-	Up	Y	0
T. Rowe Price Target 2020 Fund I Class	TTURX	NAS CM	Open End	Target Date 2000-2020 (Asset Alloc)	B	C+	A-	Up	Y	1,000,000
T. Rowe Price Target 2025 Fund	TRRVX	NAS CM	Open End	Target Date 2021-2045 (Asset Alloc)	B-	C+	B	Up	Y	2,500
T. Rowe Price Target 2025 Fund Advisor Class	PAJRX	NAS CM	Open End	Target Date 2021-2045 (Asset Alloc)	B-	C+	B	Up	Y	0
T. Rowe Price Target 2025 Fund I Class	TRVVX	NAS CM	Open End	Target Date 2021-2045 (Asset Alloc)	B-	C+	B	Up	Y	1,000,000
T. Rowe Price Target 2030 Fund	TRRWX	NAS CM	Open End	Target Date 2021-2045 (Asset Alloc)	B-	C+	B	Down	Y	2,500
T. Rowe Price Target 2030 Fund Advisor Class	PAKRX	NAS CM	Open End	Target Date 2021-2045 (Asset Alloc)	B-	C+	B	Down	Y	0
T. Rowe Price Target 2030 Fund I Class	TWRRX	NAS CM	Open End	Target Date 2021-2045 (Asset Alloc)	B-	C+	B	Down	Y	1,000,000
T. Rowe Price Target 2035 Fund	RPGRX	NAS CM	Open End	Target Date 2021-2045 (Asset Alloc)	B-	B-	B	Down	Y	2,500

★Expanded analysis of this fund is included in Section II.

Min Additional Investment	TOTAL RETURNS 3-Month Total Return	6-Month Total Return	1-Year Total Return	3-Year Total Return	5-Year Total Return	PERFORMANCE Dividend Yield (TTM)	Expense Ratio	3-Yr Std Deviation	3-Year Beta	ASSETS NAV	Total Assets (MIL)	ASSET ALLOCATION & TURNOVER %Cash	%Stocks	%Bonds	%Other	Turnover Ratio	BULL & BEAR Last Bull Market Total Return	Last Bear Market Total Return	FEES Front End Fee (%)	Back End Fee (%)	Inception Date
	4.30	9.00	22.06	30.21	76.83	0.86	0.99	9.36	1.01	15.49	3,790	2	86	10	2	14	22.56	-18.59			May-07
	4.27	8.92	21.79	29.28	74.62	0.74	1.24	9.33	1.01	15.41	3,790	2	86	10	2	14	22.48	-18.63			May-07
100	4.37	9.15	22.29	31.13		0.96	0.74	9.37	1.01	12.06	390.6	1	86	10	2	19					Jun-14
	4.31	9.01	22.05	30.26		0.8	0.99	9.29	1	12.02	390.6	1	86	10	2	19					Jun-14
	4.25	8.88	21.75	29.17		0.73	1.24	9.34	1.01	11.97	390.6	1	86	10	2	19					Jun-14
100	2.16	4.64	10.35	16.32	33.14	1.46	0.56	4.55	1.34	15.39	2,730	2	38	58	2	12	11.7	-8.39			Sep-02
	2.09	4.57	10.07	15.45	31.48	1.22	0.81	4.58	1.35	15.4	2,730	2	38	58	2	12	11.46	-8.48			Oct-03
	2.03	4.38	9.80	14.58	29.85	0.99	1.06	4.55	1.34	15.39	2,730	2	38	58	2	12	11.39	-8.58			Oct-03
	2.27	4.75	10.52			1.63	0.42			11.35	213.7	2	38	58	2	28					Sep-15
	2.12	4.65	10.74			1.1	0.43			11.46	111.6	2	36	60	2	31					Sep-15
	2.42	5.19	11.81			1.25	0.42			11.72	390.6	2	41	55	2	19					Sep-15
	2.66	5.83	13.52			1.18	0.45			11.91	693.0	2	48	47	2	20					Sep-15
	3.21	6.76	15.90			1.23	0.49			12.35	2,421	2	58	38	2	12					Sep-15
	3.49	7.42	17.81			1.16	0.52			12.65	2,082	2	66	30	2	13					Sep-15
	3.83	8.05	19.51			1.21	0.55			12.9	2,982	2	73	23	2	12					Sep-15
	4.16	8.67	21.02			1.15	0.58			13.13	1,767	2	79	17	2	13					Sep-15
	4.34	9.07	22.10			1.1	0.59			13.29	2,296	2	84	12	2	11					Sep-15
	4.40	9.21	22.55			1.1	0.6			13.36	1,179	1	86	10	2	11					Sep-15
	4.40	9.21	22.55			1.1	0.6			13.36	1,253	1	86	10	2	9					Sep-15
	4.48	9.22	22.57			1.1	0.6			13.37	449.7	1	86	10	2	11					Sep-15
	4.35	9.20	22.53			1.14	0.6			13.23	74.6	1	86	10	2	13					Sep-15
100	3.43	6.00					0.74				18.8	1	58	38	3						May-17
100	7.62	15.01	39.22	68.25	178.86	0	0.83	14.52	1.24	45.48	5,439	0	90	1	10	81	20.99	-19			Sep-87
100	7.52	14.84	38.84	67.02	175.73	0	1.06	14.52	1.24	44.92	5,439	0	90	1	10	81	20.84	-19.05			Mar-00
	7.63	15.07	39.39	68.63	179.49	0	0.68	14.52	1.24	45.47	5,439	0	90	1	10	81	20.99	-19			Mar-16
100	3.43	8.80	15.27	31.46	98.50	0.11	0.9	12.46	0.87	47.7	9,755	0	97	0	3	38	32.01	-23.84			Jun-56
100	3.34	8.63	14.95	30.38	95.71	0	1.15	12.46	0.87	47.25	9,755	0	97	0	3	38	31.84	-23.93			Mar-00
	3.47	8.86	15.42	31.88	99.13	0.23	0.75	12.47	0.87	47.71	9,755	0	97	0	3	38	32.01	-23.84			Aug-15
100	3.29	9.39	13.37	38.45	88.98	0.75	0.93	12.41	0.86	49.06	10,514	0	99	0	1	22	28.42	-21.85			Jun-88
100	3.15	9.15	12.94	37.01	85.96	0.51	1.29	12.41	0.86	48.81	10,514	0	99	0	1	22	28.23	-21.92			Mar-00
	3.36	9.47	13.55	38.90	89.59	0.85	0.78	12.4	0.86	49.06	10,514	0	99	0	1	22	28.42	-21.85			Aug-15
100	4.99	10.59	25.52	35.44	88.18	0.91	0.8	10.34	0.96	24.36	3,864	0	97	0	2	11	24.65	-19.4			Jun-90
100	3.81	9.61	28.53	26.72	47.23	1.4	0.94	11.26	0.89	14.61	1,539	1	96	0	2	11	18.13	-23.53			Dec-96
100	1.86	4.30	9.84	15.91		1.79	0.58	4.4	1.31	11.44	33.4	2	33	62	2	33					Aug-13
	1.86	4.21	9.65	15.07		1.54	0.83	4.37	1.3	11.45	33.4	2	33	62	2	33					Aug-13
	2.04	4.48	10.03	16.12		1.87	0.48	4.4	1.31	11.45	33.4	2	33	62	2	33					Feb-16
100	2.02	4.53	10.24	16.29		1.68	0.58	4.45	1.07	11.52	66.9	2	34	61	2	22					Aug-13
	1.94	4.36	9.88	15.48		1.52	0.83	4.48	1.07	11.51	66.9	2	34	61	2	22					Aug-13
	2.10	4.52	10.33	16.47		1.76	0.47	4.45	1.07	11.53	66.9	2	34	61	2	22					Feb-16
100	2.20	4.76	10.99	17.32		1.57	0.57	4.91	0.97	11.71	193.7	2	38	58	2	19					Aug-13
	2.03	4.60	10.65	16.32		1.32	0.86	4.87	0.97	11.69	193.7	2	38	58	2	19					Aug-13
	2.20	4.85	11.10	17.43		1.65	0.49	4.9	0.97	11.7	193.7	2	38	58	2	19					Feb-16
100	2.48	5.35	12.63	19.15		1.36	0.64	5.48	0.94	12.02	268.8	2	45	51	2	18					Aug-13
	2.41	5.21	12.30	18.28		1.21	0.89	5.5	0.94	11.99	268.8	2	45	51	2	18					Aug-13
	2.48	5.44	12.81	19.45		1.44	0.51	5.51	0.94	12.03	268.8	2	45	51	2	18					Feb-16
100	2.75	5.93	14.34	21.23		1.33	0.67	6.23	0.95	12.29	228.8	2	52	44	2	18					Aug-13
	2.77	5.87	14.08	20.33		1.02	0.92	6.22	0.95	12.27	228.8	2	52	44	2	18					Aug-13
	2.84	6.10	14.52	21.53		1.41	0.54	6.24	0.95	12.29	228.8	2	52	44	2	18					Feb-16
100	3.16	6.71	16.21	23.72		1.37	0.7	6.95	0.96	12.63	233.2	2	59	36	2	17					Aug-13
	3.09	6.56	15.98	22.85		1.14	0.95	6.95	0.96	12.6	233.2	2	59	36	2	17					Aug-13
	3.16	6.78	16.39	24.02		1.44	0.57	6.94	0.96	12.63	233.2	2	59	36	2	17					Feb-16
100	3.44	7.29	17.90	25.79		1.34	0.72	7.66	0.97	12.82	146.3	2	66	30	2	16					Aug-13

	MARKET		FUND TYPE, CATEGORY & OBJECTIVE		RATINGS				MINIMUMS	
Fund Name	Ticker Symbol	Traded On	Fund Type	Category and (Prospectus Objective)	Overall Rating	Reward Rating	Risk Rating	Recent Up/ Downgrade	Open to New Investors	Min Initial Investment
T. Rowe Price Target 2035 Fund Advisor Class	PATVX	NAS CM	Open End	Target Date 2021-2045 (Asset Alloc)	B-	B-	B	Down	Y	0
T. Rowe Price Target 2035 Fund I Class	TPGPX	NAS CM	Open End	Target Date 2021-2045 (Asset Alloc)	B-	B-	B	Down	Y	1,000,000
T. Rowe Price Target 2040 Fund	TRHRX	NAS CM	Open End	Target Date 2021-2045 (Asset Alloc)	B-	B-	B	Down	Y	2,500
T. Rowe Price Target 2040 Fund Advisor Class	PAHHX	NAS CM	Open End	Target Date 2021-2045 (Asset Alloc)	B-	B-	B	Down	Y	0
T. Rowe Price Target 2040 Fund I Class	TRXRX	NAS CM	Open End	Target Date 2021-2045 (Asset Alloc)	B-	B-	B	Down	Y	1,000,000
T. Rowe Price Target 2045 Fund	RPTFX	NAS CM	Open End	Target Date 2021-2045 (Asset Alloc)	B-	B-	B	Down	Y	2,500
T. Rowe Price Target 2045 Fund Advisor Class	PAFFX	NAS CM	Open End	Target Date 2021-2045 (Asset Alloc)	B-	B-	B	Down	Y	0
T. Rowe Price Target 2045 Fund I Class	TRFWX	NAS CM	Open End	Target Date 2021-2045 (Asset Alloc)	B-	B-	B	Down	Y	1,000,000
T. Rowe Price Target 2050 Fund	TRFOX	NAS CM	Open End	Target Date 2046+ (Asset Alloc)	B-	B-	B	Down	Y	2,500
T. Rowe Price Target 2050 Fund Advisor Class	PAOFX	NAS CM	Open End	Target Date 2046+ (Asset Alloc)	B-	B-	B-	Down	Y	0
T. Rowe Price Target 2050 Fund I Class	TOORX	NAS CM	Open End	Target Date 2046+ (Asset Alloc)	B-	B-	B	Down	Y	1,000,000
T. Rowe Price Target 2055 Fund	TRFFX	NAS CM	Open End	Target Date 2046+ (Asset Alloc)	B-	B-	B-	Down	Y	2,500
T. Rowe Price Target 2055 Fund Advisor Class	PAFTX	NAS CM	Open End	Target Date 2046+ (Asset Alloc)	B-	B-	B-	Down	Y	0
T. Rowe Price Target 2055 Fund I Class	TRPPX	NAS CM	Open End	Target Date 2046+ (Asset Alloc)	B-	B-	B-	Down	Y	1,000,000
T. Rowe Price Target 2060 Fund	TRTFX	NAS CM	Open End	Target Date 2046+ (Asset Alloc)	B-	B-	B-	Up	Y	2,500
T. Rowe Price Target 2060 Fund Advisor Class	TRTGX	NAS CM	Open End	Target Date 2046+ (Asset Alloc)	B-	B-	B-	Up	Y	0
T. Rowe Price Target 2060 Fund I Class	TTOIX	NAS CM	Open End	Target Date 2046+ (Asset Alloc)	B-	B-	B-	Up	Y	1,000,000
T. Rowe Price Tax-Efficient Equity Fund	PREFX	NAS CM	Open End	US Equity Large Cap Growth (Growth)	B+	B	B+	Up	Y	2,500
T. Rowe Price Tax-Efficient Equity Fund I Class	TEEFX	NAS CM	Open End	US Equity Large Cap Growth (Growth)	B	B	B	Down	Y	1,000,000
T. Rowe Price Total Equity Market Index Fund	POMIX	NAS CM	Open End	US Equity Large Cap Blend (Growth)	B	B	B		Y	2,500
T. Rowe Price U.S. Large-Cap Core Fund	TRULX	NAS CM	Open End	US Equity Large Cap Blend (Growth)	B	B-	B+		Y	2,500
T. Rowe Price U.S. Large-Cap Core Fund Advisor Class	PAULX	NAS CM	Open End	US Equity Large Cap Blend (Growth)	B	B-	B+		Y	2,500
T. Rowe Price U.S. Large-Cap Core Fund I Class	RCLIX	NAS CM	Open End	US Equity Large Cap Blend (Growth)	B	B-	B+		Y	1,000,000
T. Rowe Price Value Fund	TRVLX	NAS CM	Open End	US Equity Large Cap Value (Growth & Income)	B-	B	B-	Down	Y	2,500
T. Rowe Price Value Fund Advisor Class	PAVLX	NAS CM	Open End	US Equity Large Cap Value (Growth & Income)	B-	B-	B-	Down	Y	2,500
T. Rowe Price Value Fund I Class	TRPIX	NAS CM	Open End	US Equity Large Cap Value (Growth & Income)	B-	B	B-	Down	Y	1,000,000
Taiwan Fund Inc	TWN	NYSE	Closed End	Greater China Equity (Pacific Stock)	C+	C+	B-	Up	Y	
Tanaka Growth Fund	TGFRX	NAS CM	Open End	US Equity Large Cap Growth (Growth)	C+	C+	C+	Up	Y	2,000
Tarkio Fund	TARKX	NAS CM	Open End	US Equity Mid Cap (Growth)	B+	A+	C	Up	Y	2,500
Taylor Frigon Core Growth Fund	TFCGX	NAS CM	Open End	US Equity Large Cap Growth (Growth)	D-	D+	B+		Y	5,000
TCM Small Cap Growth Fund	TCMSX	NAS CM	Open End	US Equity Small Cap (Growth)	A-	A	B	Up	Y	2,500
TCW I Gargoyle Dynamic 500 Fund I Class	TFDIX	NAS CM	Open End	Long/Short Equity (Growth)	C	C-	A-	Up	Y	100,000
TCW I Gargoyle Dynamic 500 Fund N Class	TFDNX	NAS CM	Open End	Long/Short Equity (Growth)	C	C-	A-	Up	Y	5,000
TCW I Gargoyle Hedged Value Fund I Class	TFHIX	NAS CM	Open End	Long/Short Equity (Growth)	C+	C	B-	Up	Y	100,000
TCW I Gargoyle Hedged Value Fund N Class	TFHVX	NAS CM	Open End	Long/Short Equity (Growth)	C+	C	B-	Up	Y	5,000
TCW I Gargoyle Systematic Value Fund I Class	TFVSX	NAS CM	Open End	US Equity Mid Cap (Growth)	C	C-	B	Up	Y	100,000
TCW I Gargoyle Systematic Value Fund N Class	TFSNX	NAS CM	Open End	US Equity Mid Cap (Growth)	C	C-	B	Up	Y	5,000
TCW Artificial Intelligence Equity Fund Class I	TGFTX	NAS CM	Open End	Technology Sector Equity (Growth)	U	U	U		Y	2,000
TCW Artificial Intelligence Equity Fund Class N	TGJNX	NAS CM	Open End	Technology Sector Equity (Growth)	U	U	U		Y	2,000
TCW Conservative Allocation Fund Class Institutional	TGPCX	NAS CM	Open End	Cautious Alloc (Income)	B	C	A-	Up	Y	2,000
TCW Conservative Allocation Fund Class N	TGPNX	NAS CM	Open End	Cautious Alloc (Income)	B	C	A-	Up	Y	2,000
TCW Developing Markets Equity Fund Class I	TGDMX	NAS CM	Open End	Emerging Markets Equity (Growth)	C	C+	B-	Up	Y	2,000
TCW Developing Markets Equity Fund Class N	TGDPX	NAS CM	Open End	Emerging Markets Equity (Growth)	C	C+	B-	Up	Y	2,000
TCW Emerging Mkts Multi-Asset Opp Fund I Share Cls	TGMAX	NAS CM	Open End	Emerging Markets Equity (Div Emerging Mkts)	C+	B-	C+	Up	Y	2,000
TCW Emerging Mkts Multi-Asset Opp Fund N Share Cls	TGMEX	NAS CM	Open End	Emerging Markets Equity (Div Emerging Mkts)	C+	B-	C+	Up	Y	2,000
TCW Enhanced Commodity Strategy Fund Class I	TGGWX	NAS CM	Open End	Commodities Broad Basket (Growth)	C-	C-	D+	Up	Y	2,000
TCW Enhanced Commodity Strategy Fund Class N	TGABX	NAS CM	Open End	Commodities Broad Basket (Growth)	C-	C-	D+	Up	Y	2,000
TCW Focused Equities Fund Class Institutional	TGFFX	NAS CM	Open End	US Equity Large Cap Blend (Growth)	B-	C+	B	Up	Y	2,000
TCW Focused Equities Fund Class N	TGFVX	NAS CM	Open End	US Equity Large Cap Blend (Growth)	B-	C+	B	Up	Y	2,000
TCW Global Real Estate Fund Class I	TGREX	NAS CM	Open End	Real Estate Sector Equity (Real Estate)	C+	C	B-	Up	Y	2,000
TCW Global Real Estate Fund Class N	TGRYX	NAS CM	Open End	Real Estate Sector Equity (Real Estate)	C+	C	B-	Up	Y	2,000
TCW High Dividend Equities Fund Class I	TGHDX	NAS CM	Open End	US Equity Large Cap Value (Growth & Income)	C	C	C	Down		2,000

★ Expanded analysis of this fund is included in Section II.

	TOTAL RETURNS					PERFORMANCE				ASSETS		ASSET ALLOCATION & TURNOVER					BULL & BEAR		FEES		
Min Additional Investment	3-Month Total Return	6-Month Total Return	1-Year Total Return	3-Year Total Return	5-Year Total Return	Dividend Yield (TTM)	Expense Ratio	3-Yr Std Deviation	3-Year Beta	NAV	Total Assets (MIL)	%Cash	%Stocks	%Bonds	%Other	Turnover Ratio	Last Bull Market Total Return	Last Bear Market Total Return	Front End Fee (%)	Back End Fee (%)	Inception Date
	3.37	7.15	17.66	24.88		1.2	0.97	7.64	0.97	12.8	146.3	2	66	30	2	16					Aug-13
	3.51	7.46	18.08	26.09		1.42	0.6	7.65	0.97	12.83	146.3	2	66	30	2	16					Feb-16
100	3.76	7.98	19.42	27.62		1.31	0.74	8.16	0.98	13.06	122.4	2	72	24	2	20					Aug-13
	3.70	7.77	19.12	26.66		1.1	0.99	8.16	0.98	13.02	122.4	2	72	24	2	20					Aug-13
	3.75	7.98	19.51	27.82		1.38	0.62	8.16	0.98	13.06	122.4	2	72	24	2	20					Feb-16
100	3.89	8.32	20.37	28.86		1.29	0.74	8.62	0.99	13.29	86.3	2	77	19	2	20					Aug-13
	3.91	8.18	20.15	27.86		1.08	0.99	8.59	0.99	13.27	86.3	2	77	19	2	20					Aug-13
	4.04	8.47	20.64	29.25		1.36	0.63	8.65	1	13.31	86.3	2	77	19	2	20					Feb-16
100	4.18	8.73	21.41	29.93		1.13	0.75	9.04	1	13.47	62.0	1	81	15	2	26					Aug-13
	4.05	8.53	21.03	28.87		1	1	8.96	0.99	13.42	62.0	1	81	15	2	26					Aug-13
	4.18	8.73	21.41	30.04		1.2	0.63	9.01	1	13.46	62.0	1	81	15	2	26					Feb-16
100	4.27	9.02	22.03	30.66		1.13	0.75	9.31	1.01	13.44	35.3	1	85	12	2	25					Aug-13
	4.22	8.90	21.74	29.70		0.92	1	9.32	1.01	13.4	35.3	1	85	12	2	25					Aug-13
	4.35	9.09	22.21	30.96		1.2	0.63	9.29	1	13.44	35.3	1	85	12	2	25					Feb-16
100	4.39	9.13	22.23	30.88		1.15	0.75	9.34	1.01	11.55	10.4	1	86	10	2	56					Jun-14
	4.30	8.94	21.88	29.98		0.82	1	9.32	1.01	11.57	10.4	1	86	10	2	56					Jun-14
	4.37	9.20	22.41	31.20		1.14	0.64	9.32	1.01	11.57	10.4	1	86	10	2	56					Feb-16
100	6.33	11.76	29.12	39.64	112.65	0.17	0.83	11.48	1.04	28.87	286.1	0	100	0	0	17	26.78	-17.65			Dec-00
	6.37	11.84	29.21	39.74	112.80		0.69	11.48	1.04	28.88	286.1	0	100	0	0	17	26.78	-17.65			Jul-17
100	6.21	10.83	20.79	35.24	108.68	1.34	0.3	10.27	1	30.13	1,715	0	97	0	3	7	25.56	-17.93			Jan-98
100	6.16	8.75	20.92	38.80	109.78	0.78	0.81	9.27	0.88	23.81	519.7	0	95	0	5	80	24.35	-17.74			Jun-09
100	6.10	8.60	20.63	37.76	108.06	0.49	1.1	9.29	0.88	23.81	519.7	0	95	0	5	80	24.38	-17.77			Jun-09
	6.15	8.78	21.12	39.02	110.12	0.77	0.59	9.27	0.88	23.82	519.7	0	95	0	5	80	24.35	-17.74			Nov-16
100	6.02	9.56	18.94	28.23	105.20	1.38	0.82	10.41	1.01	37.32	27,030	0	99	0	1	107	24.92	-20.63			Sep-94
100	5.95	9.40	18.64	27.32	102.90	1.21	1.04	10.39	1	36.77	27,030	0	99	0	1	107	24.77	-20.7			Mar-00
	6.07	9.63	19.15	28.73	106.00	1.53	0.64	10.42	1.01	37.32	27,030	0	99	0	1	107	24.92	-20.64			Aug-15
	2.42	7.00	28.56	34.94	53.72	0	0	12.56	0.82	23.26	195.5	0	97	0	3	89	2.74	-19.59			Dec-86
500	0.66	2.08	7.27	14.17	64.07	0	2.31	15.84	1.22	22.56	14.4	2	98	0	0	77	25.02	-24.85			Dec-98
100	5.46	12.19	29.03	50.80	135.07	0.03	1	15.12	1.23	21.64	101.2	1	99	0	0	10	25.69				Jun-11
100	3.41	8.21	21.93				1.45			12.12	6.1	8	92	0	0						Dec-16
500	3.81	11.30	24.70	42.50	133.01	0	0.96	13.12	0.83	33.56	387.5	3	96	0	0	139	32.17	-28.14			Oct-04
25,000	2.98	6.30	13.08			0.59	1.09			11.77	7.6	1	99	0	1						Nov-15
0	2.97	6.11	12.88			0.37	1.34			11.76	7.6	1	99	0	1						Nov-15
25,000	6.14	9.92	14.11	8.57	49.10	1.13	1.25	9.51	0.7	10.19	38.4	0	100	0	0	57	13.76	-15.2			Apr-12
0	6.12	9.76	13.79	7.77	47.46	0.67	1.5	9.57	0.7	10.23	38.4	0	100	0	0	57	13.6	-15.29			Apr-12
25,000	6.17	11.40	17.28			0.85	0.9			11.73	1.5	0	100	0	0						Nov-15
0	6.12	11.25	17.02			0.64	1.15			11.73	1.5	0	100	0	0						Nov-15
250	5.99						1.05			10.65	1.2	3	97	0	0						Aug-17
250	5.99						1.05			10.65	1.2	3	97	0	0						Aug-17
250	2.23	4.04	8.95	11.24	31.56	2.24	1	4.33			30.8	8	38	51	2	38	10.72	-8.15			Nov-06
250	2.07	3.88	8.50	9.55	28.25	1.55	1.55	4.26			30.8	8	38	51	2	38	10.66	-8.15			Nov-06
250	8.58	19.88	35.66			0.76	1.25			11.69	6.2	1	99	0	0	155					Jun-15
250	8.58	19.88	35.66			0.76	1.25			11.69	6.2	1	99	0	0	155					Jun-15
250	6.14	14.44	26.75	26.14		3.2	1.23	9.28		11.88	86.3	3	68	28	1	228					Jun-13
250	6.16	14.50	26.86	26.23		3.21	1.23	9.29		11.84	86.3	3	68	28	1	228					Jun-13
250	4.80	8.21	4.03	-13.03	-30.16	2.1	0.7	13.07	1	5.32	1.3	42	0	34	23	2	3.66	-20.7			Mar-11
250	4.80	7.99	3.83	-13.20	-30.22	2.1	0.75	13.21	1.01	5.32	1.3	42	0	34	23	2	3.66	-20.78			Mar-11
250	4.97	8.69	13.95	12.49	88.06	1.13	1.09	11.05	1	22.28	10.0	0	100	0	0	48	27.41	-24.88			Oct-04
250	4.98	8.69	13.94	12.46	88.07	1.14	1.09	11.06	1	22.04	10.0	0	100	0	0	48	26.89	-25.33			Feb-01
250	2.45	3.93	11.05	11.10		2.63	1.46	9.94	0.79	10.18	3.5	1	99	0	0	69					Nov-14
250	2.45	3.93	11.05	11.11		2.63	1.46	9.94	0.79	10.18	3.5	1	99	0	0	69					Nov-14
250	3.56	2.92	7.62	7.15		2.11	1.35	8.98	0.69	9.82	3.6	16	84	0	0	93					Nov-14

	MARKET		FUND TYPE, CATEGORY & OBJECTIVE		RATINGS				MINIMUMS	
Fund Name	Ticker Symbol	Traded On	Fund Type	Category and (Prospectus Objective)	Overall Rating	Reward Rating	Risk Rating	Recent Up/ Downgrade	Open to New Investors	Min Initial Investment
TCW High Dividend Equities Fund Class N	TGDEX	NAS CM	Open End	US Equity Large Cap Value (Growth & Income)	C	C	C	Down	Y	2,000
TCW High Dividend Equities Long/Short Fund I Class	TFDEX	NAS CM	Open End	Long/Short Equity (Equity-Income)	C-	D+	C+	Up	Y	100,000
TCW High Dividend Equities Long/Short Fund N Class	TFENX	NAS CM	Open End	Long/Short Equity (Equity-Income)	C-	D+	C	Up	Y	5,000
TCW International Small Cap Fund Class I	TGICX	NAS CM	Open End	Global Equity Mid/Small Cap (Growth)	B	B	B	Up	Y	2,000
TCW International Small Cap Fund Class N	TGNIX	NAS CM	Open End	Global Equity Mid/Small Cap (Growth)	B	B	B	Up	Y	2,000
TCW Long/Short Fundamental Value Fund I Class	TFFSX	NAS CM	Open End	Long/Short Equity (Growth)	U	U	U		Y	100,000
TCW Long/Short Fundamental Value Fund N Class	TFFNX	NAS CM	Open End	Long/Short Equity (Growth)	U	U	U		Y	5,000
TCW New America Premier Equities Fund Class I	TGUSX	NAS CM	Open End	US Equity Large Cap Blend (Growth)	C-	C	B+	Up	Y	2,000
TCW New America Premier Equities Fund Class N	TGUNX	NAS CM	Open End	US Equity Large Cap Blend (Growth)	C-	C	B+	Up	Y	2,000
TCW Relative Value Dividend Appreciation Fund Class I	TGDFX	NAS CM	Open End	US Equity Large Cap Value (Equity-Income)	B-	C+	B	Down	Y	2,000
TCW Relative Value Dividend Appreciation Fund Class N	TGIGX	NAS CM	Open End	US Equity Large Cap Value (Equity-Income)	B-	C+	B	Down	Y	2,000
TCW Relative Value Large Cap Fund Class Institutional	TGDIX	NAS CM	Open End	US Equity Large Cap Value (Growth)	B-	B-	C+	Down	Y	2,000
TCW Relative Value Large Cap Fund Class N	TGDVX	NAS CM	Open End	US Equity Large Cap Value (Growth)	B	B-	B	Up	Y	2,000
TCW Relative Value Mid Cap Fund Class I	TGVOX	NAS CM	Open End	US Equity Mid Cap (Growth)	B	B+	B-	Up	Y	2,000
TCW Relative Value Mid Cap Fund Class N	TGVNX	NAS CM	Open End	US Equity Mid Cap (Growth)	B	B+	B-	Up	Y	2,000
TCW Select Equities Fund Class I	TGCEX	NAS CM	Open End	US Equity Large Cap Growth (Growth)	B	B	B+		Y	2,000
TCW Select Equities Fund Class N	TGCNX	NAS CM	Open End	US Equity Large Cap Growth (Growth)	B	B	B+		Y	2,000
TCW/Gargoyle Dynamic 500 Collar Fund I Class	TFCSX	NAS CM	Open End	Long/Short Equity (Growth)	U	U	U		Y	100,000
TCW/Gargoyle Dynamic 500 Collar Fund N Class	TFCNX	NAS CM	Open End	Long/Short Equity (Growth)	U	U	U		Y	5,000
TCW/Gargoyle Dynamic 500 Market-Neutral Fund I Class	TFMSX	NAS CM	Open End	Long/Short Equity (Growth)	U	U	U		Y	100,000
TCW/Gargoyle Dynamic 500 Market-Neutral Fund N Class	TFMNX	NAS CM	Open End	Long/Short Equity (Growth)	U	U	U		Y	5,000
TD Global Low Volatility Equity Fund Advisor Class	TDGVX	NAS CM	Open End	Global Equity (Growth)	B	C+	A-	Up	Y	100,000
TD Global Low Volatility Equity Fund Institutional Class	TDLVX	NAS CM	Open End	Global Equity (Growth)	B-	B-	B	Down	Y	1,000,000
Teberg Fund	TEBRX	NAS CM	Open End	Moderate Alloc (Growth & Income)	C+	C+	C	Up	Y	2,000
Tekla Healthcare Investors	HQH	NYSE	Closed End	Healthcare Sector Equity (Health)	C-	D+	C-	Down	Y	
Tekla Healthcare Opportunities Fund	THQ	NYSE	Closed End	Healthcare Sector Equity (Health)	C+	C	B-	Down	Y	
Tekla Life Sciences Investors	HQL	NYSE	Closed End	Healthcare Sector Equity (Health)	C	C-	C	Up	Y	
Tekla World Healthcare Fund	THW	NYSE	Closed End	Healthcare Sector Equity (Growth & Income)	C-	C-	C	Down	Y	
Templeton China World Fund Class A	TCWAX	NAS CM	Open End	Greater China Equity (Growth)	B	B	C+	Up	Y	1,000
Templeton China World Fund Class Advisor	TACWX	NAS CM	Open End	Greater China Equity (Growth)	B	B	C+	Up	Y	100,000
Templeton China World Fund Class C	TCWCX	NAS CM	Open End	Greater China Equity (Growth)	B-	B	C+	Up	Y	1,000
Templeton China World Fund Class R6	FCWRX	NAS CM	Open End	Greater China Equity (Growth)	B	B	C+	Up	Y	1,000,000
Templeton Developing Markets Trust Class A	TEDMX	NAS CM	Open End	Emerging Markets Equity (Growth)	B	B+	C	Up	Y	1,000
Templeton Developing Markets Trust Class Advisor	TDADX	NAS CM	Open End	Emerging Markets Equity (Growth)	B	B+	C	Up	Y	0
Templeton Developing Markets Trust Class C	TDMTX	NAS CM	Open End	Emerging Markets Equity (Growth)	B-	B	C	Up	Y	1,000
Templeton Developing Markets Trust Class R6	FDEVX	NAS CM	Open End	Emerging Markets Equity (Growth)	B	B+	C	Up	Y	1,000,000
Templeton Developing Markets Trust Class Retirement	TDMRX	NAS CM	Open End	Emerging Markets Equity (Growth)	B-	B	C	Up	Y	1,000
Templeton Dragon Fund Inc	TDF	NYSE	Closed End	Greater China Equity (Pacific Stock)	B	A-	C+	Up	Y	
Templeton Emerging Markets Balanced Fund Advisor Class	TZEMX	NAS CM	Open End	Emerging Markets Equity (Growth & Income)	C+	B-	C		Y	100,000
Templeton Emerging Markets Balanced Fund Class A	TAEMX	NAS CM	Open End	Emerging Markets Equity (Growth & Income)	C+	B-	C		Y	1,000
Templeton Emerging Markets Balanced Fund Class C	US88019R5679		Open End	Emerging Markets Equity (Growth & Income)	C+	B-	C	Up	Y	1,000
Templeton Emerging Markets Balanced Fund Class R	US88019R5596		Open End	Emerging Markets Equity (Growth & Income)	C+	B-	C		Y	1,000
Templeton Emerging Markets Balanced Fund Class R6	FEBQX	NAS CM	Open End	Emerging Markets Equity (Growth & Income)	C+	B-	C		Y	0
Templeton Emerging Markets Fund Inc.	EMF	NYSE	Closed End	Emerging Markets Equity (World Stock)	B	B+	C	Up	Y	
Templeton Emerging Markets Small Cap Fund Class A	TEMMX	NAS CM	Open End	Emerging Markets Equity (Growth)	B-	B-	B-	Up	Y	1,000
Templeton Emerging Markets Small Cap Fund Class Advisor	TEMZX	NAS CM	Open End	Emerging Markets Equity (Growth)	B-	B-	B-	Up	Y	100,000
Templeton Emerging Markets Small Cap Fund Class C	TCEMX	NAS CM	Open End	Emerging Markets Equity (Growth)	C+	C+	B-	Up	Y	1,000
Templeton Emerging Markets Small Cap Fund Class R6	FTEQX	NAS CM	Open End	Emerging Markets Equity (Growth)	B-	B-	B-		Y	0
Templeton Emerging Markets Small Cap Fund Class Retirement	FTESX	NAS CM	Open End	Emerging Markets Equity (Growth)	B-	C+	B-	Up	Y	1,000
Templeton Foreign Fund Class A	TEMFX	NAS CM	Open End	Global Equity Large Cap (Foreign Stock)	C+	C+	B-	Up	Y	1,000
Templeton Foreign Fund Class Advisor	TFFAX	NAS CM	Open End	Global Equity Large Cap (Foreign Stock)	C+	C+	B-	Up	Y	100,000
Templeton Foreign Fund Class C	TEFTX	NAS CM	Open End	Global Equity Large Cap (Foreign Stock)	C+	C+	B-	Up	Y	1,000

★ Expanded analysis of this fund is included in Section II.

Min Additional Investment	TOTAL RETURNS: 3-Month Total Return	6-Month Total Return	1-Year Total Return	3-Year Total Return	5-Year Total Return	PERFORMANCE: Dividend Yield (TTM)	Expense Ratio	3-Yr Std Deviation	3-Year Beta	ASSETS: NAV	Total Assets (MIL)	ASSET ALLOCATION & TURNOVER: %Cash	%Stocks	%Bonds	%Other	Turnover Ratio	BULL & BEAR: Last Bull Market Total Return	Last Bear Market Total Return	FEES: Front End Fee (%)	Back End Fee (%)	Inception Date
250	3.67	2.92	7.62	7.15		2.11	1.35	8.97	0.69	9.82	3.6	16	84	0	0	93					Nov-14
25,000	0.56	-2.11	1.16			1.18	2.16			10.21	1.3	23	77	0	0						Nov-15
0	0.51	-2.26	0.90			0.95	2.41			10.21	1.3	23	77	0	0						Nov-15
250	8.03	20.41	38.91	43.17	58.52	0.26	1.44	10.66	0.79	11.03	10.1	4	96	0	0	129	17.77	-29.8			Feb-11
250	8.02	20.39	38.86	43.12	58.34	0.26	1.44	10.65	0.78	11.04	10.1	4	96	0	0	129	17.72	-29.87			Feb-11
25,000	4.50						2			10.45	1.0										Sep-17
0	4.40						2.25			10.44	1.0										Sep-17
250	8.46	12.88	38.04			0.35	1.04			14.95	19.4	12	88	0	0						Jan-16
250	8.38	12.89	37.94			0.35	1.04			14.94	19.4	12	88	0	0						Jan-16
250	3.58	7.22	11.16	21.87	85.66	2.34	0.77	11.56	1.09	19.13	630.2	0	100	0	0	19	29.37	-21.39			Oct-04
250	3.57	7.10	10.91	20.93	83.32	2.13	1	11.55	1.08	19.46	630.2	0	100	0	0	19	29.22	-21.52			Sep-86
250	4.04	8.64	15.27	25.21	94.70	1.58	0.78	11.82	1.09	21.76	501.5	1	99	0	0	15	29.05	-23.45			Dec-03
250	3.97	8.44	14.97	24.30	92.26	1.4	1	11.82	1.08	21.71	501.5	1	99	0	0	15	28.84	-23.57			Dec-97
250	6.12	12.99	19.70	31.57	94.40	0.48	0.98	15.11	1.32	25.16	106.6	2	98	0	0	18	33.08	-25.98			Oct-97
250	6.12	12.94	19.51	30.77	92.25	0.33	1.16	15.1	1.32	24.5	106.6	2	98	0	0	18	32.92	-26.14			Oct-00
250	5.43	11.68	32.80	35.87	93.91	0	0.89	13.69	1.15	24.93	922.7	3	97	0	0	14	23.84	-12.32			Feb-93
250	5.39	11.55	32.51	34.89	91.45	0	1.16	13.68	1.15	22.66	922.7	3	97	0	0	14	23.65	-12.45			Feb-99
25,000	1.91	3.12					1			10.28	1.1	1	99	0	1						Feb-17
0	1.80	3.02					1.25			10.28	1.1	1	99	0	1						Feb-17
25,000	-0.59	0.57					1			9.92	1.1	1	99	0	1						Feb-17
0	-0.70	0.46					1.25			9.92	1.1	1	99	0	1						Feb-17
	3.97	5.37	13.19	26.01		1.79	1.15	6.76	0.5	12.33	39.6	2	98	0	1	28					Mar-13
	4.09	5.50	13.52	26.50		1.87	0.9	6.75	0.5	12.33	39.6	2	98	0	1	28					Mar-13
100	3.89	8.48	15.24	4.84	35.51	0	2.15	13.55	1.23	11.18	30.3	3	69	27	0	101	10.55	-6.45			Apr-02
	-5.05	-1.48	15.86	0.21	108.65	0	0	19.27	0.8	24.17	967.4	2	95	0	1	29	31.92	-12.09			Apr-87
	-2.55	0.31	19.82	14.51		1.94	1.44	14.87	0.58	19.27	836.3	6	104	13	-26	36					Jul-14
	-5.77	-0.06	19.34	6.45	117.44	0	1.66	22.13	0.92	19.93	423.9	3	94	0	1	43	38.67	-12.53			May-92
	-3.41	-1.74	12.41			2.33	1.86			14.67	447.5	4	104	17	-24	58					Jun-15
	2.61	12.59	33.69	25.00	20.17	0.71	1.91	16.98	0.96	21.64	314.2	0	99	0	1	8	20.64	-23.09	5.75		Sep-93
	2.67	12.67	33.96	25.94	21.80	0.95	1.66	17	0.97	21.77	314.2	0	99	0	1	8	20.82	-22.97			Aug-03
	2.41	12.12	32.68	22.21	15.86	0	2.66	16.97	0.96	21.46	314.2	0	99	0	1	8	20.16	-23.32		1.00	Sep-93
	2.73	12.85	34.28	26.84	22.86	1.18	1.42	16.98	0.96	21.7	314.2	0	99	0	1	8	20.64	-23.09			May-13
	7.01	15.52	40.20	32.87	20.87	0.9	1.58	15.52	0.95	21.98	1,625	0	99	1	1	27	17.42	-24.75	5.75		Oct-91
	7.05	15.66	40.58	33.92	22.49	1.08	1.33	15.48	0.95	21.86	1,625	0	99	1	1	27	17.64	-24.68			Jan-97
	6.77	15.08	39.19	29.94	16.50	0.41	2.33	15.49	0.95	21.34	1,625	0	99	1	1	27	16.92	-24.99		1.00	May-95
	7.12	15.73	40.87	34.71	23.39	1.22	1.09	15.49	0.95	21.82	1,625	0	99	1	1	27	17.42	-24.75			May-13
	6.93	15.35	39.89	31.91	19.49	0.69	1.83	15.47	0.95	21.61	1,625	0	99	1	1	27	17.31	-24.84			Jan-02
	4.94	14.36	38.07	31.32	35.69	1.35		18.13	1.01	24.5052	820.1	0	93	0	6	47	20.6	-18.7			Sep-94
	3.56	10.51	28.59	26.29	9.98	2.01	1.25	11.73	0.71	11.27	41.2	10	54	34	1	26					Oct-11
	3.48	10.35	28.31	25.29	8.50	1.79	1.5	11.79	0.71	11.26	41.2	10	54	34	1	26			5.75		Oct-11
	3.37	10.01	27.45	22.61	4.63	1.2	2.25	11.71	0.7	11.17	41.2	10	54	34	1	26				1.00	Oct-11
	3.51	10.23	28.08	24.41	7.31	1.6	1.75	11.75	0.71	11.24	41.2	10	54	34	1	26					Oct-11
	3.59	10.57	28.67	26.36	10.04		1.17	11.73	0.71	11.27	41.2	10	54	34	1	26					Aug-17
	6.51	17.42	41.60	32.01	21.63	1.02		17.41	1.06	18.4432	344.9	1	92	0	3	20	15.33	-26.83			Feb-87
	5.59	9.02	31.30	26.67	36.25	1.38	1.97	12.08	0.76	15.1	1,000	3	96	1	0	21	14.85	-28.92	5.75		Oct-06
	5.59	9.21	31.60	27.61	38.10	1.58	1.72	12.07	0.76	15.26	1,000	3	96	1	0	21	14.94	-28.79			Oct-06
	5.40	8.65	30.35	23.94	31.49	0.81	2.72	12.06	0.76	14.43	1,000	3	96	1	0	21	14.26	-29.07		1.00	Oct-06
	5.65	9.35	31.76	27.77	38.28		1.56	12.07	0.76	15.25	1,000	3	96	1	0	21	14.94	-28.79			Aug-17
	5.49	8.95	30.97	25.80	34.78	1.2	2.22	12.08	0.75	14.97	1,000	3	96	1	0	21	14.6	-28.92			Oct-06
	2.68	5.45	17.07	21.77	39.16	1.64	1.22	13.59	1.06	8.07	7,405	3	97	0	0	43	11.11	-25.03	5.75		Oct-82
	2.78	5.73	17.57	22.72	41.22	1.93	0.97	13.62	1.06	7.95	7,405	3	97	0	0	43	11.21	-24.9			Jan-97
	2.48	5.05	16.27	19.07	34.23	1.01	1.97	13.63	1.06	7.9	7,405	3	97	0	0	43	10.52	-25.22		1.00	May-95

	MARKET		FUND TYPE, CATEGORY & OBJECTIVE		RATINGS					MINIMUMS
Fund Name	Ticker Symbol	Traded On	Fund Type	Category and (Prospectus Objective)	Overall Rating	Reward Rating	Risk Rating	Recent Up/ Downgrade	Open to New Investors	Min Initial Investment
Templeton Foreign Fund Class R	TEFRX	NAS CM	Open End	Global Equity Large Cap (Foreign Stock)	C+	C+	B-	Up	Y	1,000
Templeton Foreign Fund Class R6	FTFGX	NAS CM	Open End	Global Equity Large Cap (Foreign Stock)	C+	C+	B-	Up	Y	1,000,000
Templeton Foreign Smaller Companies Fund Class A	FINEX	NAS CM	Open End	Global Equity Mid/Small Cap (Foreign Stock)	B	B	B	Up		1,000
Templeton Foreign Smaller Companies Fund Class Advisor	FTFAX	NAS CM	Open End	Global Equity Mid/Small Cap (Foreign Stock)	B	B	B	Up		100,000
Templeton Foreign Smaller Companies Fund Class Advisor C	FCFSX	NAS CM	Open End	Global Equity Mid/Small Cap (Foreign Stock)	B	B	B	Up		1,000
Templeton Foreign Smaller Companies Fund Class R6	US88019R4680		Open End	Global Equity Mid/Small Cap (Foreign Stock)	B	B	B	Up		1,000,000
Templeton Frontier Markets Fund Class A	TFMAX	NAS CM	Open End	Emerging Markets Equity (Growth)	C	C	C	Up		1,000
Templeton Frontier Markets Fund Class Adv	FFRZX	NAS CM	Open End	Emerging Markets Equity (Growth)	C	C	C	Up		100,000
Templeton Frontier Markets Fund Class C	FFRMX	NAS CM	Open End	Emerging Markets Equity (Growth)	C	C	C	Up		1,000
Templeton Frontier Markets Fund Class R	US88019R6586		Open End	Emerging Markets Equity (Growth)	C	C	C	Up		1,000
Templeton Frontier Markets Fund Class R6	FFMRX	NAS CM	Open End	Emerging Markets Equity (Growth)	C	C	C	Up		0
Templeton Global Balanced Fund Class A	TAGBX	NAS CM	Open End	Alloc (Balanced)	C+	C+	C+	Up	Y	1,000
Templeton Global Balanced Fund Class A1	TINCX	NAS CM	Open End	Alloc (Balanced)	C+	C+	C+	Up		1,000
Templeton Global Balanced Fund Class Advisor	TZINX	NAS CM	Open End	Alloc (Balanced)	C+	C+	C+	Up	Y	0
Templeton Global Balanced Fund Class C	FCGBX	NAS CM	Open End	Alloc (Balanced)	C+	C+	C+	Up	Y	1,000
Templeton Global Balanced Fund Class C1	TCINX	NAS CM	Open End	Alloc (Balanced)	C+	C+	C+	Up		1,000
Templeton Global Balanced Fund Class R6	US88019R5182		Open End	Alloc (Balanced)	C+	C+	C+	Up	Y	1,000,000
Templeton Global Balanced Fund Class Retirement	US88019R7733		Open End	Alloc (Balanced)	C+	C+	C+	Up	Y	1,000
Templeton Global Opportunities Trust Class A	TEGOX	NAS CM	Open End	Global Equity (World Stock)	C+	C+	C	Up	Y	1,000
Templeton Global Opportunities Trust Class C	TEGPX	NAS CM	Open End	Global Equity (World Stock)	C+	C+	C	Up	Y	1,000
Templeton Global Opportunities Trust Fund Advisor Class	FGOZX	NAS CM	Open End	Global Equity (World Stock)	C+	B-	C	Up	Y	100,000
Templeton Global Smaller Companies Fund Class A	TEMGX	NAS CM	Open End	Global Equity Mid/Small Cap (World Stock)	B-	B-	C	Up	Y	1,000
Templeton Global Smaller Companies Fund Class Advisor	TGSAX	NAS CM	Open End	Global Equity Mid/Small Cap (World Stock)	B-	B	C	Up	Y	100,000
Templeton Global Smaller Companies Fund Class C	TESGX	NAS CM	Open End	Global Equity Mid/Small Cap (World Stock)	C+	B-	C	Down	Y	1,000
Templeton Global Smaller Companies Fund Class R6	FBOGX	NAS CM	Open End	Global Equity Mid/Small Cap (World Stock)	B-	B	C	Up	Y	1,000,000
Templeton Growth Fund Class R6	FTGFX	NAS CM	Open End	Global Equity (World Stock)	C+	C+	C	Up	Y	1,000,000
Templeton Growth Fund, Inc. Class A	TEPLX	NAS CM	Open End	Global Equity (World Stock)	B-	C+	B-	Up	Y	1,000
Templeton Growth Fund, Inc. Class Advisor	TGADX	NAS CM	Open End	Global Equity (World Stock)	C+	C+	C	Up	Y	100,000
Templeton Growth Fund, Inc. Class C	TEGTX	NAS CM	Open End	Global Equity (World Stock)	C+	C+	B-	Up	Y	1,000
Templeton Growth Fund, Inc. Class Retirement	TEGRX	NAS CM	Open End	Global Equity (World Stock)	C+	C+	C	Up	Y	1,000
Templeton Inst Foreign Smaller Companies Series Adv	TFSCX	NAS CM	Open End	Global Equity Mid/Small Cap (Foreign Stock)	B	B+	B	Up		100,000
Templeton Inst Fund Emerging Mkts Series Fund Adv	TEEMX	NAS CM	Open End	Emerging Markets Equity (Div Emerging Mkts)	B	A	C	Up	Y	100,000
Templeton Inst Fund Intl Equity Series Primary Shares	TFEQX	NAS CM	Open End	Global Equity Large Cap (Foreign Stock)	C+	C+	C	Up	Y	100,000
Templeton Inst Fund Intl Equity Series Service Shares	TFESX	NAS CM	Open End	Global Equity Large Cap (Foreign Stock)	C+	C+	C	Up	Y	1,000,000
Templeton Institutional Global Equity Fund Class Advisor	TGESX	NAS CM	Open End	Global Equity (Growth)	C+	C+	C+	Up	Y	100,000
Templeton World Fund Class A	TEMWX	NAS CM	Open End	Global Equity (World Stock)	C+	C+	B-	Up	Y	1,000
Templeton World Fund Class Advisor	TWDAX	NAS CM	Open End	Global Equity (World Stock)	B-	C+	B-	Up	Y	100,000
Templeton World Fund Class C	TEWTX	NAS CM	Open End	Global Equity (World Stock)	C+	C+	B-	Up	Y	1,000
Templeton World Fund Class R6	FTWRX	NAS CM	Open End	Global Equity (World Stock)	B-	C+	B-	Up	Y	1,000,000
TETON Convertible Securities Fund Class A	WEIAX	NAS CM	Open End	Convertibles (Growth & Income)	C+	C+	C+	Down	Y	1,000
TETON Convertible Securities Fund Class AAA	WESRX	NAS CM	Open End	Convertibles (Growth & Income)	C+	C+	C+	Down	Y	1,000
TETON Convertible Securities Fund Class C	WEICX	NAS CM	Open End	Convertibles (Growth & Income)	C+	C+	C+	Down	Y	1,000
TETON Convertible Securities Fund Institutional Class	WESIX	NAS CM	Open End	Convertibles (Growth & Income)	C+	C+	C+	Down	Y	100,000
TETON Westwood Balanced Fund Class A	WEBCX	NAS CM	Open End	Moderate Alloc (Balanced)	B-	C+	B	Up	Y	1,000
TETON Westwood Balanced Fund Class AAA	WEBAX	NAS CM	Open End	Moderate Alloc (Balanced)	B-	C+	B	Up	Y	1,000
TETON Westwood Balanced Fund Class C	WBCCX	NAS CM	Open End	Moderate Alloc (Balanced)	B-	C+	B	Up	Y	1,000
TETON Westwood Balanced Fund Class Institutional	WBBIX	NAS CM	Open End	Moderate Alloc (Balanced)	B-	C+	B	Up	Y	500,000
TETON Westwood Equity Fund Class A	WEECX	NAS CM	Open End	US Equity Large Cap Blend (Growth)	B-	B-	B-	Down	Y	1,000
TETON Westwood Equity Fund Class AAA	WESWX	NAS CM	Open End	US Equity Large Cap Blend (Growth)	B-	B-	B	Down	Y	1,000
TETON Westwood Equity Fund Class C	WEQCX	NAS CM	Open End	US Equity Large Cap Blend (Growth)	B-	B-	B-	Down	Y	1,000
TETON Westwood Equity Fund Institutional Class	WEEIX	NAS CM	Open End	US Equity Large Cap Blend (Growth)	B-	B-	B	Down	Y	500,000
TETON Westwood Mid-Cap Equity Fund Class A Shares	WMCAX	NAS CM	Open End	US Equity Mid Cap (Growth & Income)	B-	C+	B	Up	Y	1,000

★Expanded analysis of this fund is included in Section II.

Min Additional Investment	3-Month Total Return	6-Month Total Return	1-Year Total Return	3-Year Total Return	5-Year Total Return	Dividend Yield (TTM)	Expense Ratio	3-Yr Std Deviation	3-Year Beta	NAV	Total Assets (MIL)	%Cash	%Stocks	%Bonds	%Other	Turnover Ratio	Last Bull Market Total Return	Last Bear Market Total Return	Front End Fee (%)	Back End Fee (%)	Inception Date
	TOTAL RETURNS					PERFORMANCE				ASSETS		ASSET ALLOCATION & TURNOVER					BULL & BEAR		FEES		
	2.69	5.39	16.91	20.90	37.60	1.46	1.47	13.69	1.06	7.92	7,405	3	97	0	0	43	10.83	-25.03			Jan-02
	2.86	5.81	17.83	23.60	42.23	2.14	0.72	13.67	1.06	7.94	7,405	3	97	0	0	43	11.11	-25.03			May-13
	5.52	11.35	34.07	33.78	47.54	1.18	1.86	11.9	0.97	20.39	101.6	5	94	0	0	28	12.88	-25.96	5.75		Sep-91
	5.58	11.48	34.39	34.76	49.31	1.34	1.62	11.91	0.97	20.31	101.6	5	94	0	0	28	12.96	-25.86			Dec-96
	5.33	10.91	33.02	30.77	41.98	0.69	2.62	11.91	0.97	19.65	101.6	5	94	0	0	28	12.39	-26.17		1.00	Jul-98
	5.68	11.59	34.66	35.75	51.06	0.78	1.34	11.91	0.97	20.5	101.6	5	94	0	0	28	12.88	-25.96			May-13
	-3.79	4.23	22.82	0.92	0.38	0.52	1.99	15.44	1.06	13.29	111.4	1	92	4	2	29	15.77	-19.55	5.75		Oct-08
	-3.69	4.37	23.10	1.58	1.57	0.58	1.75	15.39	1.06	13.36	111.4	1	92	4	2	29	15.94	-19.46			Oct-08
	-3.98	3.85	21.84	-1.26	-3.27	0	2.75	15.43	1.07	13.04	111.4	1	92	4	2	29	15.33	-19.81		1.00	Oct-08
	-3.86	4.05	22.42	0.18	-0.82	0.37	2.25	15.45	1.06	13.19	111.4	1	92	4	2	29	15.6	-19.61			Oct-08
	-3.66	4.43	23.24	2.29	2.42	0.98	1.62	15.41	1.06	13.33	111.4	1	92	4	2	29	15.94	-19.46			May-13
	1.10	3.85	12.17	15.07	35.54	2.17	1.16	9.13	0.79	3.18	1,789	13	64	20	3	17	15.66	-17.46	5.75		Sep-11
	1.10	3.52	12.17	15.05	35.40	2.17	1.16	9.11	0.8	3.18	1,789	13	64	20	3	17	16.09	-17.54	4.25		Jul-05
	1.19	3.66	12.41	15.89	37.03	2.4	0.91	9.08	0.79	3.19	1,789	13	64	20	3	17	16.17	-17.37			Jul-05
	0.86	3.08	11.03	12.73	30.32	1.45	1.91	9.26	0.8	3.16	1,789	13	64	20	3	17	15.73	-17.7		1.00	Jul-11
	1.28	3.60	11.70	13.74	32.80	1.77	1.56	9.18	0.8	3.18	1,789	13	64	20	3	17	15.85	-17.44		1.00	Jul-05
	1.56	4.08	12.56	16.69	37.77	2.5	0.8	9.02	0.79	3.19	1,789	13	64	20	3	17	16.17	-17.38			May-13
	1.33	3.68	11.84	14.57	33.71	1.9	1.41	9.14	0.8	3.19	1,789	13	64	20	3	17	15.88	-17.32			Jul-05
	5.64	10.00	22.03	24.12	51.44	2.24	1.32	12.6	1.12	22.73	445.6	1	99	0	0	23	15.57	-23.42	5.75		Feb-90
	5.42	9.58	21.06	21.36	45.83	1.68	2.07	12.6	1.12	22.11	445.6	1	99	0	0	23	15.13	-23.68		1.00	May-95
	5.70	10.10	22.29	25.03	53.32	2.46	1.07	12.6	1.12	22.68	445.6	1	99	0	0	23	15.76	-23.36			May-09
	6.92	12.03	25.72	28.76	66.59	0.28	1.41	11.5	1	10.56	1,314	5	95	0	0	23	18.8	-27.3	5.75		Jun-81
	7.09	12.19	26.11	29.87	68.62	0.53	1.16	11.52	1	10.61	1,314	5	95	0	0	23	18.83	-27.23			Jan-97
	6.74	11.65	24.76	25.95	60.56	0	2.16	11.45	0.99	10.03	1,314	5	95	0	0	23	18.11	-27.54		1.00	May-95
	7.03	12.34	26.29	30.55	70.24	0.65	0.94	11.48	1	10.59	1,288	5	95	0	0	23	18.8	-27.3			May-13
	3.12	6.68	18.20	21.04	57.66	1.55	0.7	12.62	1.14	27.22	14,089	5	95	1	0	29	17.72	-22.83			May-13
	3.01	6.45	17.79	19.72	55.09	1.24	1.07	12.64	1.14	27.26	14,089	5	95	1	0	29	17.73	-22.83	5.75		Nov-54
	3.08	6.59	18.07	20.64	57.04	1.46	0.82	12.63	1.14	27.28	14,089	5	95	1	0	29	17.9	-22.77			Jan-97
	2.84	6.09	16.92	17.06	49.36	0.62	1.82	12.64	1.14	26.62	14,089	5	95	1	0	29	17.28	-23.11		1.00	May-95
	2.97	6.32	17.52	18.84	53.13	1.03	1.32	12.63	1.14	27.03	14,089	5	95	1	0	29	17.56	-22.9			Jan-02
	5.44	11.70	34.17	35.79	61.06	1.57	0.98	11.58	0.94	25.08	1,038	5	94	0	0	21	18.37	-19.78			Oct-02
	7.32	16.44	42.84	38.70	28.97	1.41	1.31	15.76	0.97	6.06	55.7	2	97	1	0	18	19.05	-21.07			Apr-93
	3.63	8.54	22.91	21.79	35.98	2.35	0.78	12.21	0.96	21.99	4,475	3	97	0	0	15	13.57	-24.51			Oct-90
	3.58	8.47	22.72	21.26	34.99	2.18	0.93	12.22	0.96	22.07	4,475	3	97	0	0	15	13.4	-24.5			Sep-06
	3.75	8.50	20.87	22.43	57.74	1.57	0.84	12.15	1.07	10.59	321.0	4	96	0	0	28	19.17	-18.99			Mar-08
	2.89	5.31	12.87	18.91	51.84	3.18	1.07	12.54	1.19	16.92	4,638	6	93	1	0	31	18.04	-20.39	5.75		Jan-78
	2.97	5.45	13.17	19.83	53.76	3.4	0.82	12.59	1.2	16.88	4,638	6	93	1	0	31	18.31	-20.32			May-06
	2.72	4.99	12.07	16.30	46.35	2.64	1.82	12.57	1.2	16.13	4,638	6	93	1	0	31	17.55	-20.65		1.00	May-95
	3.01	5.49	13.30	20.16	54.25	3.49	0.72	12.57	1.2	16.86	4,638	6	93	1	0	31	18.04	-20.39			May-13
	3.43	8.11	17.34	14.82	58.86	1.71	1.4	11.46	1.36	13.19	14.9	1	0	0	0	40	15.63	-12.61	4.00		May-01
	3.44	8.31	17.56	15.69	60.90	1.96	1.15	11.45	1.36	12.79	14.9	1	0	0	0	40	15.71	-12.57			Sep-97
	3.25	7.81	16.71	13.10	54.91	1.14	1.9	11.45	1.36	14.05	14.9	1	0	0	0	40	15.2	-12.81		1.00	Nov-01
	3.57	8.43	18.01	16.66	62.94	2.2	0.9	11.42	1.36	12.83	14.9	1	0	0	0	40	15.99	-12.46			Jan-08
	5.11	7.88	13.76	20.00	53.28	0.84	1.6	6.07	-0.22	12.09	66.7	1	69	30	0	23	15.39	-12.1	4.00		Apr-93
	5.21	8.01	14.08	20.89	55.24	1.12	1.35	6.09	-0.22	12.02	66.7	1	69	30	0	23	15.5	-11.96			Oct-91
	4.98	7.60	13.22	18.21	49.57	0.15	2.1	6.11	-0.22	12.28	66.7	1	69	30	0	23	15.07	-12.31		1.00	Sep-01
	5.20	8.12	14.26	21.74	57.15	1.42	1.1	6.08	-0.22	12	66.7	1	69	30	0	23	15.76	-11.92			Jan-08
	7.57	11.49	19.87	29.26	90.17	0.12	1.88	9.58	0.91	13.13	64.2	1	99	0	0	28	24.69	-20.36	4.00		Jan-94
	7.66	11.74	20.22	30.30	92.57	0.43	1.63	9.6	0.91	13.15	64.2	1	99	0	0	28	24.9	-20.3			Jan-87
	7.43	11.29	19.29	27.37	85.50	0	2.38	9.55	0.91	12.41	64.2	1	99	0	0	28	24.2	-20.5		1.00	Feb-01
	7.71	11.81	20.51	31.20	94.53	0.67	1.38	9.6	0.91	13.09	64.2	1	99	0	0	28	24.95	-20.18			Jan-08
	4.60	6.63	19.81	21.34		0	1.3	12.41	1.08	13.18	3.1	9	91	0	0	34			4.00		May-13

	MARKET		FUND TYPE, CATEGORY & OBJECTIVE		RATINGS					MINIMUMS
Fund Name	Ticker Symbol	Traded On	Fund Type	Category and (Prospectus Objective)	Overall Rating	Reward Rating	Risk Rating	Recent Up/ Downgrade	Open to New Investors	Min Initial Investment
TETON Westwood Mid-Cap Equity Fund Class AAA Shares	WMCEX	NAS CM	Open End	US Equity Mid Cap (Growth & Income)	B-	B-	B	Up	Y	1,000
TETON Westwood Mid-Cap Equity Fund Class C Shares	WMCCX	NAS CM	Open End	US Equity Mid Cap (Growth & Income)	B-	C+	B	Up	Y	1,000
TETON Westwood Mid-Cap Equity Fund Class I Shares	WMCRX	NAS CM	Open End	US Equity Mid Cap (Growth & Income)	B-	B-	B	Up	Y	500,000
TETON Westwood Mighty Mites Class Institutional	WEIMX	NAS CM	Open End	US Equity Small Cap (Small Company)	B+	A-	B	Up	Y	500,000
TETON Westwood Mighty Mites Fund Class A	WMMAX	NAS CM	Open End	US Equity Small Cap (Small Company)	B	B+	B	Up	Y	1,000
TETON Westwood Mighty Mites Fund Class AAA	WEMMX	NAS CM	Open End	US Equity Small Cap (Small Company)	B+	B+	B	Up	Y	1,000
TETON Westwood Mighty Mites Fund Class C	WMMCX	NAS CM	Open End	US Equity Small Cap (Small Company)	B	B	B	Up	Y	1,000
TETON Westwood Mighty Mites Fund T	WETMX	NAS CM	Open End	US Equity Small Cap (Small Company)	B+	B+	B	Up	Y	1,000
TETON Westwood SmallCap Equity Fund Class A	WWSAX	NAS CM	Open End	US Equity Small Cap (Small Company)	B+	A	B	Up	Y	1,000
TETON Westwood SmallCap Equity Fund Class AAA	WESCX	NAS CM	Open End	US Equity Small Cap (Small Company)	A-	A	B	Up	Y	1,000
TETON Westwood SmallCap Equity Fund Class C	WWSCX	NAS CM	Open End	US Equity Small Cap (Small Company)	B+	A	B	Up	Y	1,000
TETON Westwood SmallCap Equity Fund Class Institutional	WWSIX	NAS CM	Open End	US Equity Small Cap (Small Company)	A-	A	B	Up	Y	500,000
TETON Westwood SmallCap Equity Fund T	WWSTX	NAS CM	Open End	US Equity Small Cap (Small Company)	A-	A	B	Up	Y	1,000
Thai Fund Inc	TTF	NYSE	Closed End	Other Equity (Pacific Stock)	B-	B	C	Up	Y	
The Arbitrage Credit Opportunities Fund Class A	AGCAX	NAS CM	Open End	Other Alternative (Growth & Income)	C+	C	B	Up	Y	2,000
The Arbitrage Event-Driven Fund Class A	AGEAX	NAS CM	Open End	Market Neutral (Growth)	C	C	C	Up	Y	2,000
The Arbitrage Event-Driven Fund Class C	AEFCX	NAS CM	Open End	Market Neutral (Growth)	C-	C-	C	Down	Y	2,000
The Arbitrage Event-Driven Fund Class I	AEDNX	NAS CM	Open End	Market Neutral (Growth)	C	C	C		Y	100,000
The Arbitrage Event-Driven Fund ClassR	AEDFX	NAS CM	Open End	Market Neutral (Growth)	C	C	C		Y	2,000
The Arbitrage Fund Class A	ARGAX	NAS CM	Open End	Market Neutral (Growth)	B-	C	B+	Up	Y	2,000
The Arbitrage Fund Class C	ARBCX	NAS CM	Open End	Market Neutral (Growth)	C+	C	B	Up	Y	2,000
The Arbitrage Fund Class Institutional	ARBNX	NAS CM	Open End	Market Neutral (Growth)	B	C	A	Up	Y	100,000
The Arbitrage Fund Class R	ARBFX	NAS CM	Open End	Market Neutral (Growth)	B-	C	A	Up	Y	2,000
The Arbitrage Tactical Equity Fund Class A	ATQAX	NAS CM	Open End	Market Neutral (Growth)	C	C	B-		Y	2,000
The Arbitrage Tactical Equity Fund Class C	ATQCX	NAS CM	Open End	Market Neutral (Growth)	C	C	B-		Y	2,000
The Arbitrage Tactical Equity Fund Class I	ATQIX	NAS CM	Open End	Market Neutral (Growth)	C	C	B-		Y	100,000
The Arbitrage Tactical Equity Fund Class R	ATQFX	NAS CM	Open End	Market Neutral (Growth)	C	C	B-		Y	2,000
The Asia Tigers Fund Inc	GRR	NYSE	Closed End	Asia ex-Japan Equity (Pacific Stock)	C+	C+	C	Up	Y	
The BeeHive Fund	BEEHX	NAS CM	Open End	US Equity Large Cap Growth (Growth)	B-	C+	B	Down	Y	2,500
The BeeHive Fund	CEE	NYSE	Closed End	Other Equity (Europe Stock)	B-	B-	C+	Up	Y	
The Cook & Bynum Fund	COBYX	NAS CM	Open End	US Equity Large Cap Blend (World Stock)	B-	C+	B		Y	5,000
The Covered Bridge Fund Class A	TCBAX	NAS CM	Open End	Long/Short Equity (Growth & Income)	B-	C+	B	Down	Y	5,000
The Covered Bridge Fund Class I	TCBIX	NAS CM	Open End	Long/Short Equity (Growth & Income)	B-	C+	B	Down	Y	1,000,000
The Cushing® Energy Income Fund Common	SRF	NYSE	Closed End	Energy Sector Equity (Income)	D	D	D	Down	Y	
The Cushing® Renaissance Fund Common	SZC	NYSE	Closed End	Energy Sector Equity (Growth & Income)	C	C	C	Up	Y	
The Delafield Fund	DEFIX	NAS CM	Open End	US Equity Mid Cap (Growth)	C+	C+	C	Up	Y	1,000
The Disciplined Growth Investors Fund	DGIFX	NAS CM	Open End	Aggressive Alloc (Balanced)	B	B-	B+	Up	Y	10,000
The European Equity Fund Inc	EEA	NYSE	Closed End	Europe Equity Large Cap (Europe Stock)	B	B	B	Up	Y	
The Gabelli Global Rising Income and Dividend Fund AAA	GAGCX	NAS CM	Open End	Moderate Alloc (Growth & Income)	B-	B-	B	Down	Y	1,000
The Gabelli Global Small & Mid Cap Value Trust	GGZ	NYSE	Closed End	Global Equity Mid/Small Cap (World Stock)	B	C	A-	Up	Y	
The Gabelli Multimedia Trust Inc.	GGT	NYSE	Closed End	US Equity Large Cap Growth (Comm)	B	B-	B	Up	Y	
The Gold Bullion Strategy Fund Advisor Class	QGLCX	NAS CM	Open End	Commodities Precious Metals (Precious Metals)	C-	C-	D+	Up	Y	1,000
The Gold Bullion Strategy Fund Investor Class	QGLDX	NAS CM	Open End	Commodities Precious Metals (Precious Metals)	C-	C-	C-		Y	1,000
The Gold Bullion Strategy Portfolio	US00771F8068		Open End	Commodities Precious Metals (Precious Metals)	C-	C-	C-		Y	0
The Hartford Balanced Fund Class F	ITTFX	NAS CM	Open End	Moderate Alloc (Balanced)	B-	C+	B	Down	Y	1,000,000
The Hartford Balanced Income Fund Class A	HBLAX	NAS CM	Open End	Cautious Alloc (Balanced)	B-	C+	B		Y	2,000
The Hartford Balanced Income Fund Class C	HBLCX	NAS CM	Open End	Cautious Alloc (Balanced)	B-	C+	B	Up	Y	2,000
The Hartford Balanced Income Fund Class F	HBLFX	NAS CM	Open End	Cautious Alloc (Balanced)	B-	C+	B		Y	1,000,000
The Hartford Balanced Income Fund Class I	HBLIX	NAS CM	Open End	Cautious Alloc (Balanced)	B-	C+	B		Y	2,000
The Hartford Balanced Income Fund Class R3	HBLRX	NAS CM	Open End	Cautious Alloc (Balanced)	B-	C+	B	Up	Y	0
The Hartford Balanced Income Fund Class R4	HBLSX	NAS CM	Open End	Cautious Alloc (Balanced)	B-	C+	B		Y	0
The Hartford Balanced Income Fund Class R5	HBLTX	NAS CM	Open End	Cautious Alloc (Balanced)	B-	C+	B		Y	0

★ Expanded analysis of this fund is included in Section II.

	TOTAL RETURNS					PERFORMANCE				ASSETS		ASSET ALLOCATION & TURNOVER					BULL & BEAR		FEES		
Min Additional Investment	3-Month Total Return	6-Month Total Return	1-Year Total Return	3-Year Total Return	5-Year Total Return	Dividend Yield (TTM)	Expense Ratio	3-Yr Std Deviation	3-Year Beta	NAV	Total Assets (MIL)	%Cash	%Stocks	%Bonds	%Other	Turnover Ratio	Last Bull Market Total Return	Last Bear Market Total Return	Front End Fee (%)	Back End Fee (%)	Inception Date
	4.55	6.72	20.07	22.21		0	1.05	12.44	1.08	13.33	3.1	9	91	0	0	34					May-13
	4.39	6.29	19.21	19.51		0	1.8	12.45	1.08	12.85	3.1	9	91	0	0	34				1.00	May-13
	4.64	6.86	20.36	23.42		0	0.8	12.45	1.08	13.52	3.1	9	91	0	0	34					May-13
	1.52	9.62	15.66	32.56	92.85	0	1.17	12.14	0.75	28.68	1,382	12	82	5	0	8	19.8	-19.15			Jan-08
	1.35	9.31	15.03	30.58	87.97	0	1.67	12.12	0.75	27.01	1,382	12	82	5	0	8	19.48	-19.32	4.00		Nov-01
	1.44	9.48	15.37	31.62	90.48	0	1.42	12.12	0.75	28.05	1,382	12	82	5	0	8	19.7	-19.24			May-98
	1.24	9.06	14.49	28.63	83.36	0	2.17	12.09	0.75	23.76	1,382	12	82	5	0	8	19.17	-19.49		1.00	Aug-01
	1.44	9.44	15.32	31.57	90.40		1.42	12.12	0.75	28.05	1,382	12	82	5	0	8	19.7	-19.24	2.50		Jul-17
	4.03	12.31	15.34	42.46	96.82	0	1.5	14.52	0.98	19.48	32.6	1	99	0	0	38	26.4	-28.89	4.00		Nov-01
	4.16	12.47	15.63	43.56	99.45	0	1.25	14.53	0.98	20.41	32.6	1	99	0	0	38	26.53	-28.8			Apr-97
	3.92	12.06	14.81	40.40	92.05	0	2	14.54	0.98	16.9	32.6	1	99	0	0	38	26.02	-29.02		1.00	Nov-01
	4.17	12.60	15.89	44.59	101.90	0	1	14.53	0.98	21.11	32.6	1	99	0	0	38	26.85	-28.79			Jan-08
	4.16	12.47	15.63	43.56	99.45		1.25	14.53	0.98	20.41	32.6	1	99	0	0	38	26.53	-28.8	2.50		Jul-17
	7.27	16.50	33.63	29.62	43.17	1.42	1.76	11.73	0.77	10.99	131.9	1	96	0	3	31	39.55	-12.8			Feb-88
	0.27	0.37	1.20	4.69	11.26	3.06	1.52	1.79	0.01	9.61	53.6	31	-6	50	2	211			3.25		May-13
	0.51	1.05	3.59	-0.18	4.04	0	1.72	3.52	0.06	9.45	144.1	28	50	20	0	409	8.57	-4.38	3.25		May-13
	0.32	0.65	2.88	-2.44	0.07	0	2.47	3.45	0.04	9.28	144.1	28	50	20	0	409	8.1	-4.68		1.00	Jun-12
	0.72	1.25	3.89	0.58	5.30	0	1.47	3.48	0.05	9.52	144.1	28	50	20	0	409	8.73	-4.28			Oct-10
	0.59	1.13	3.67	-0.23	4.02	0	1.72	3.46	0.06	9.45	144.1	28	50	20	0	409	8.53	-4.19			Oct-10
	0.07	0.30	2.57	6.67	9.74	0	1.51	1.9	0.05	12.69	1,866	15	70	12	2	363	1.67	1.64	2.50		May-13
	-0.10	-0.02	1.83	4.34	5.67	0	2.26	1.85	0.06	12.21	1,866	15	70	12	2	363	1.22	1.32		1.00	Jun-12
	0.13	0.50	2.86	7.53	11.07	0	1.26	1.83	0.05	13.08	1,866	15	70	12	2	363	1.87	1.69			Oct-03
	0.09	0.32	2.59	6.78	9.77	0	1.51	1.91	0.06	12.71	1,866	15	70	12	2	363	1.67	1.64			Sep-00
	1.39	1.60	5.83	2.47		0	1.72			10.15	2.1					449			3.25		Dec-14
	1.39	1.60	5.83	2.47		0	2.47			10.15	2.1					449				1.00	Dec-14
	1.39	1.60	5.83	2.47		0	1.47			10.15	2.1					449					Dec-14
	1.39	1.60	5.83	2.47		0	1.72			10.15	2.1					449					Dec-14
	5.43	7.20	28.98	15.93	15.22	0.49		14.2	0.89	13.64	47.7	2	90	0	1	14	13.86	-24.1			Nov-93
500	-0.38	1.46	11.06	15.03	72.16	0.84	0.99	12.19	1.14	15.23	132.2	7	93	0	0	15	20.8	-21.6			Sep-08
	0.83	14.47	18.29	29.26	-13.11	1.16		18.87	0.79	27.44	132.2	0	94	9	-3	77	17.34	-34.89			Mar-90
1,000	2.93	4.19	15.12	14.09	36.10	0	1.49	6.65	0.38	16.69	152.8	31	58	0	0	9	11.7	-2.47			Jul-09
1,000	3.01	6.32	9.45	19.77		0.72	1.66	8.16	0.76	10.14	62.9	12	88	0	0	222			5.25		Oct-13
1,000	3.14	6.42	9.68	20.65		1.04	1.41	8.11	0.76	10.11	62.9	12	88	0	0	222					Oct-13
	7.90	15.19	-2.74	-61.82	-81.15	0	1.75	39.03		10.78	25.3	7	82	9	0	53					Feb-12
	7.34	16.86	12.71	7.23	25.58	8.21		17.72		20.8	116.9	6	72	22	0	227					Sep-12
100	0.22	2.83	7.21	7.03	35.73	0	1.26	16.48	1.03	22.63	372.1	26	74	0	0	39	35.75	-27.43			Nov-93
	6.21	8.44	14.88	23.29	72.43	0.46	0.78	7.88	0.66	19.12	193.6	4	70	25	0	16	24.51				Aug-11
	2.75	8.00	26.26	21.68	46.43	0.97		11.16	0.73	10.97	87.3	0	98	1	1	64	14.7	-33.34			Jul-86
	3.79	7.55	20.90	27.90	49.18	0.85	1.61	6.59	0.59	27.2	68.7	28	70	0	0	52	2.99	-11.1			Feb-94
	-3.49	2.59	16.38	24.22		0.23	1.65	8.06		14.63	120.5	10	89	0	0	77					Jun-14
	3.73	7.13	26.50	27.48	90.59	0.25	1.7	13.16	1.15	9.34	229.0	16	83	1	0	10	20.89	-26.76			Nov-94
250	0.85	3.63	10.70	1.15		1.92	2.2	15.72	-0.38	22.52	53.1	31	0	59	10	203					Apr-16
1,000	1.00	3.94	11.39	3.23		1.9	1.6	15.73	-0.38	22.62	53.1	31	0	59	10	203					Jul-13
	0.86	3.72	11.25	2.80		0	1.76	15.78	-0.39	23.42	4.4	17	0	73	10	430					Nov-13
	4.54	7.46	15.10	21.40	63.99		0.74	7.16		24.16	954.9	3	66	32	0	26	18.17	-11.99			Feb-17
50	3.34	6.34	11.49	22.92	49.24	2.35	0.96	5.42		14.62	12,232	3	47	50	0	36	14.09	-5.43	5.50		Jul-06
50	3.20	5.97	10.70	20.21	43.96	1.7	1.69	5.4		14.42	12,232	3	47	50	0	36	13.7	-5.79		1.00	Jul-06
	3.42	6.58	11.81	24.16	51.86		0.62	5.37		14.63	12,232	3	47	50	0	36	14.61	-5.26			Feb-17
50	3.40	6.46	11.75	23.83	51.24	2.57	0.7	5.42		14.62	12,232	3	47	50	0	36	14.33	-5.42			Feb-10
	3.25	6.15	11.11	21.78	47.17	2.06	1.25	5.38		14.67	12,232	3	47	50	0	36	13.99	-5.59			May-10
	3.32	6.38	11.42	22.91	49.44	2.33	0.95	5.38		14.68	12,232	3	47	50	0	36	14.15	-5.45			May-10
	3.38	6.43	11.68	23.79	51.23	2.56	0.7	5.38		14.69	12,232	3	47	50	0	36	14.26	-5.31			May-10

	MARKET			FUND TYPE, CATEGORY & OBJECTIVE	RATINGS				MINIMUMS	
Fund Name	Ticker Symbol	Traded On	Fund Type	Category and (Prospectus Objective)	Overall Rating	Reward Rating	Risk Rating	Recent Up/ Downgrade	Open to New Investors	Min Initial Investment
The Hartford Balanced Income Fund Class R6	HBLVX	NAS CM	Open End	Cautious Alloc (Balanced)	B-	C+	B		Y	0
The Hartford Balanced Income Fund Class Y	HBLYX	NAS CM	Open End	Cautious Alloc (Balanced)	B-	C+	B		Y	250,000
The Hartford Capital Appreciation Fund Class A	ITHAX	NAS CM	Open End	US Equity Large Cap Blend (Growth)	B-	B-	B-	Down	Y	2,000
The Hartford Capital Appreciation Fund Class C	HCACX	NAS CM	Open End	US Equity Large Cap Blend (Growth)	B-	B-	B-	Down	Y	2,000
The Hartford Capital Appreciation Fund Class F	HCAFX	NAS CM	Open End	US Equity Large Cap Blend (Growth)	B-	B-	B-	Down	Y	1,000,000
The Hartford Capital Appreciation Fund Class I	ITHIX	NAS CM	Open End	US Equity Large Cap Blend (Growth)	B-	B-	B-	Down	Y	2,000
The Hartford Capital Appreciation Fund Class R3	ITHRX	NAS CM	Open End	US Equity Large Cap Blend (Growth)	B-	B-	B-	Down	Y	0
The Hartford Capital Appreciation Fund Class R4	ITHSX	NAS CM	Open End	US Equity Large Cap Blend (Growth)	B-	B-	B-	Down	Y	0
The Hartford Capital Appreciation Fund Class R5	ITHTX	NAS CM	Open End	US Equity Large Cap Blend (Growth)	B-	B-	B-	Down	Y	0
The Hartford Capital Appreciation Fund Class R6	ITHVX	NAS CM	Open End	US Equity Large Cap Blend (Growth)	B-	B-	B-	Down	Y	0
The Hartford Capital Appreciation Fund Class Y	HCAYX	NAS CM	Open End	US Equity Large Cap Blend (Growth)	B-	B-	B-	Down	Y	250,000
The Hartford Dividend and Growth Fund Class A	IHGIX	NAS CM	Open End	US Equity Large Cap Value (Equity-Income)	B	B	B-		Y	2,000
The Hartford Dividend and Growth Fund Class C	HDGCX	NAS CM	Open End	US Equity Large Cap Value (Equity-Income)	B-	B-	B-	Down	Y	2,000
The Hartford Dividend and Growth Fund Class F	HDGFX	NAS CM	Open End	US Equity Large Cap Value (Equity-Income)	B	B	B-		Y	1,000,000
The Hartford Dividend and Growth Fund Class I	HDGIX	NAS CM	Open End	US Equity Large Cap Value (Equity-Income)	B	B	B-		Y	2,000
The Hartford Dividend and Growth Fund Class R3	HDGRX	NAS CM	Open End	US Equity Large Cap Value (Equity-Income)	B-	B-	B-	Down	Y	0
The Hartford Dividend and Growth Fund Class R4	HDGSX	NAS CM	Open End	US Equity Large Cap Value (Equity-Income)	B	B	B-		Y	0
The Hartford Dividend and Growth Fund Class R5	HDGTX	NAS CM	Open End	US Equity Large Cap Value (Equity-Income)	B	B	B-		Y	0
The Hartford Dividend and Growth Fund Class R6	HDGVX	NAS CM	Open End	US Equity Large Cap Value (Equity-Income)	B	B	B-		Y	0
The Hartford Dividend and Growth Fund Class Y	HDGYX	NAS CM	Open End	US Equity Large Cap Value (Equity-Income)	B	B	B-		Y	250,000
The Hartford Equity Income Fund Class A	HQIAX	NAS CM	Open End	US Equity Large Cap Value (Equity-Income)	B	B-	B		Y	2,000
The Hartford Equity Income Fund Class C	HQICX	NAS CM	Open End	US Equity Large Cap Value (Equity-Income)	B-	B-	B-	Down	Y	2,000
The Hartford Equity Income Fund Class F	HQIFX	NAS CM	Open End	US Equity Large Cap Value (Equity-Income)	B	B	B		Y	1,000,000
The Hartford Equity Income Fund Class I	HQIIX	NAS CM	Open End	US Equity Large Cap Value (Equity-Income)	B	B	B		Y	2,000
The Hartford Equity Income Fund Class R3	HQIRX	NAS CM	Open End	US Equity Large Cap Value (Equity-Income)	B-	B-	B	Down	Y	0
The Hartford Equity Income Fund Class R4	HQISX	NAS CM	Open End	US Equity Large Cap Value (Equity-Income)	B-	B-	B	Down	Y	0
The Hartford Equity Income Fund Class R5	HQITX	NAS CM	Open End	US Equity Large Cap Value (Equity-Income)	B	B	B		Y	0
The Hartford Equity Income Fund Class R6	HQIVX	NAS CM	Open End	US Equity Large Cap Value (Equity-Income)	B	B	B		Y	0
The Hartford Equity Income Fund Class Y	HQIYX	NAS CM	Open End	US Equity Large Cap Value (Equity-Income)	B	B	B		Y	250,000
The Hartford Global All-Asset Fund Class A	HLAAX	NAS CM	Open End	Alloc (Asset Alloc)	B-	C+	B	Down	Y	5,000
The Hartford Global All-Asset Fund Class Y	HLAYX	NAS CM	Open End	Alloc (Asset Alloc)	B-	C+	B	Down	Y	250,000
The Hartford Global Real Asset Fund Class C	HRLCX	NAS CM	Open End	Alloc (Asset Alloc)	C	C	C	Up	Y	5,000
The Hartford Growth Opportunities Fund Class A	HGOAX	NAS CM	Open End	US Equity Large Cap Growth (Growth)	A-	A-	B+	Up	Y	2,000
The Hartford Growth Opportunities Fund Class C	HGOCX	NAS CM	Open End	US Equity Large Cap Growth (Growth)	B+	A-	B+	Up	Y	2,000
The Hartford Growth Opportunities Fund Class F	HGOFX	NAS CM	Open End	US Equity Large Cap Growth (Growth)	A-	A-	B+	Up	Y	1,000,000
The Hartford Growth Opportunities Fund Class I	HGOIX	NAS CM	Open End	US Equity Large Cap Growth (Growth)	A-	A-	B+	Up	Y	2,000
The Hartford Growth Opportunities Fund Class R3	HGORX	NAS CM	Open End	US Equity Large Cap Growth (Growth)	B+	A-	B+	Up	Y	0
The Hartford Growth Opportunities Fund Class R4	HGOSX	NAS CM	Open End	US Equity Large Cap Growth (Growth)	A-	A-	B+	Up	Y	0
The Hartford Growth Opportunities Fund Class R5	HGOTX	NAS CM	Open End	US Equity Large Cap Growth (Growth)	A-	A-	B+	Up	Y	0
The Hartford Growth Opportunities Fund Class R6	HGOVX	NAS CM	Open End	US Equity Large Cap Growth (Growth)	A-	A-	B+	Up	Y	0
The Hartford Growth Opportunities Fund Class Y	HGOYX	NAS CM	Open End	US Equity Large Cap Growth (Growth)	A-	A-	B+	Up	Y	250,000
The Hartford Healthcare Fund Class A	HGHAX	NAS CM	Open End	Healthcare Sector Equity (Health)	B-	C+	B	Down	Y	2,000
The Hartford Healthcare Fund Class C	HGHCX	NAS CM	Open End	Healthcare Sector Equity (Health)	B-	C+	B	Down	Y	2,000
The Hartford Healthcare Fund Class F	HGHFX	NAS CM	Open End	Healthcare Sector Equity (Health)	B-	C+	B	Down	Y	1,000,000
The Hartford Healthcare Fund Class I	HGHIX	NAS CM	Open End	Healthcare Sector Equity (Health)	B-	C+	B	Down	Y	2,000
The Hartford Healthcare Fund Class R3	HGHRX	NAS CM	Open End	Healthcare Sector Equity (Health)	B-	C+	B	Down	Y	0
The Hartford Healthcare Fund Class R4	HGHSX	NAS CM	Open End	Healthcare Sector Equity (Health)	B-	C+	B	Down	Y	0
The Hartford Healthcare Fund Class R5	HGHTX	NAS CM	Open End	Healthcare Sector Equity (Health)	B-	C+	B	Down	Y	0
The Hartford Healthcare Fund Class Y	HGHYX	NAS CM	Open End	Healthcare Sector Equity (Health)	B-	C+	B	Down	Y	250,000
The Hartford International Opportunities Fund Class A	IHOAX	NAS CM	Open End	Global Equity Large Cap (Foreign Stock)	B	B-	B	Up	Y	2,000
The Hartford International Opportunities Fund Class C	HIOCX	NAS CM	Open End	Global Equity Large Cap (Foreign Stock)	B-	C+	B	Up	Y	2,000
The Hartford International Opportunities Fund Class F	IHOFX	NAS CM	Open End	Global Equity Large Cap (Foreign Stock)	B	B-	B	Up	Y	1,000,000

★ Expanded analysis of this fund is included in Section II.

Min Additional Investment	3-Month Total Return	6-Month Total Return	1-Year Total Return	3-Year Total Return	5-Year Total Return	Dividend Yield (TTM)	Expense Ratio	3-Yr Std Deviation	3-Year Beta	NAV	Total Assets (MIL)	%Cash	%Stocks	%Bonds	%Other	Turnover Ratio	Last Bull Market Total Return	Last Bear Market Total Return	Front End Fee (%)	Back End Fee (%)	Inception Date
	TOTAL RETURNS					PERFORMANCE				ASSETS		ASSET ALLOCATION & TURNOVER					BULL & BEAR		FEES		
	3.46	6.52	11.88	24.13	51.82	2.63	0.62	5.36		14.77	12,232	3	47	50	0	36	14.61	-5.26			Nov-14
	3.37	6.49	11.76	24.11	51.79	2.61	0.65	5.37		14.77	12,232	3	47	50	0	36	14.61	-5.26			Jul-06
50	4.94	7.40	21.25	27.04	97.80	0.34	1.1	11.42	1.07	37.55	8,327	2	95	0	1	88	23.42	-25.61	5.50		Jul-96
50	4.76	7.00	20.36	24.31	90.80	0	1.82	11.4	1.07	29.23	8,327	2	95	0	1	88	22.91	-25.82		1.00	Jul-98
	5.04	7.60	21.72	28.51	101.75		0.7	11.42	1.07	37.65	8,327	2	95	0	1	88	23.76	-25.46			Feb-17
50	5.04	7.56	21.60	28.16	100.93	0.6	0.79	11.41	1.07	37.67	8,327	2	95	0	1	88	23.68	-25.55			Aug-06
	4.86	7.22	20.89	25.85	94.85	0.03	1.4	11.4	1.07	41.39	8,327	2	95	0	1	88	23.26	-25.7			Dec-06
	4.95	7.39	21.25	27.00	97.85	0.14	1.1	11.42	1.07	42.59	8,327	2	95	0	1	88	23.45	-25.6			Dec-06
	5.02	7.56	21.63	28.16	100.78	0.53	0.8	11.41	1.07	43.34	8,327	2	95	0	1	88	23.71	-25.5			Dec-06
	5.03	7.60	21.71	28.46	101.66	0.6	0.7	11.41	1.07	43.56	8,327	2	95	0	1	88	23.76	-25.46			Nov-14
	5.02	7.57	21.68	28.47	101.69	0.6	0.75	11.42	1.07	43.55	8,327	2	95	0	1	88	23.76	-25.46			Jul-96
50	5.97	10.35	17.78	31.33	97.71	1.31	1.03	10.28	1	25.79	8,559	2	98	0	0	22	22.11	-17.37	5.50		Jul-96
50	5.79	9.97	16.94	28.43	90.51	0.71	1.77	10.28	1	24.93	8,559	2	98	0	0	22	21.57	-17.59		1.00	Jul-98
	6.05	10.55	18.19	32.74	101.45		0.66	10.3	1	25.65	8,559	2	98	0	0	22	22.41	-17.22			Feb-17
50	6.07	10.54	18.09	32.17	99.85	1.46	0.83	10.3	1	25.67	8,559	2	98	0	0	22	22.3	-17.29			Aug-06
	5.89	10.16	17.36	29.98	94.49	0.98	1.36	10.29	1	26.13	8,559	2	98	0	0	22	21.9	-17.47			Dec-06
	5.96	10.33	17.73	31.16	97.50	1.24	1.06	10.28	1	26.3	8,559	2	98	0	0	22	22.11	-17.34			Dec-06
	6.05	10.49	18.10	32.34	100.51	1.5	0.76	10.3	1	26.4	8,559	2	98	0	0	22	22.37	-17.27			Dec-06
	6.08	10.55	18.22	32.63	101.28	1.59	0.66	10.29	1	26.4	8,559	2	98	0	0	22	22.41	-17.22			Nov-14
	6.07	10.56	18.18	32.72	101.42	1.57	0.71	10.29	1	26.41	8,559	2	98	0	0	22	22.41	-17.22			Jul-96
50	5.60	9.95	17.52	32.75	91.41	1.48	1.02	9.65	0.91	20.32	4,421	2	98	0	0	14	24.53	-14.05	5.50		Aug-03
50	5.39	9.54	16.63	29.86	84.52	0.83	1.75	9.62	0.91	20.22	4,421	2	98	0	0	14	23.99	-14.31		1.00	Aug-03
	5.66	10.13	17.95	34.21	94.85		0.66	9.61	0.91	20.21	4,421	2	98	0	0	14	24.87	-13.93			Feb-17
50	5.64	10.07	17.76	33.73	93.92	1.68	0.77	9.65	0.91	20.21	4,421	2	98	0	0	14	24.71	-13.96			Aug-06
	5.49	9.73	17.13	31.41	88.22	1.16	1.36	9.64	0.91	20.35	4,421	2	98	0	0	14	24.34	-14.19			Dec-06
	5.57	9.89	17.40	32.56	91.03	1.43	1.06	9.62	0.91	20.37	4,421	2	98	0	0	14	24.46	-14.01			Dec-06
	5.62	10.00	17.79	33.72	93.91	1.68	0.76	9.66	0.91	20.46	4,421	2	98	0	0	14	24.77	-13.98			Dec-06
	5.68	10.09	17.92	34.18	94.81	1.77	0.66	9.63	0.91	20.51	4,421	2	98	0	0	14	24.87	-13.93			Nov-14
	5.61	10.06	17.88	34.13	94.74	1.75	0.71	9.61	0.91	20.51	4,421	2	98	0	0	14	24.87	-13.93			Aug-03
50	3.06	6.57	16.88	22.97	39.55	1.43	1.24	6.9		10.73	311.1	18	43	33	4	95	11.51	-15.63	5.50		May-10
	3.22	6.89	17.40	24.30	42.22	1.76	0.89	6.92		10.78	311.1	18	43	33	4	95	11.72	-15.51			May-10
50	4.79	11.56	8.50	5.61	-9.56	0	2.01	11.84		9.29	288.6	2	67	10	21	115	7.54	-20.47		1.00	May-10
50	5.13	10.98	30.20	41.68	120.99	0	1.13	11.92	1.01	42.76	4,761	0	95	0	1	117	26.92	-23.05	5.50		Feb-02
50	4.93	10.54	29.25	38.56	113.09	0	1.88	11.92	1.01	27.53	4,761	0	95	0	1	117	26.39	-23.25		1.00	Feb-02
	5.24	11.17	30.67	43.21	125.36		0.75	11.93	1.01	44.66	4,761	0	95	0	1	117	27.27	-22.88			Feb-17
50	5.20	11.10	30.52	42.58	123.62	0	0.92	11.93	1.01	44.61	4,761	0	95	0	1	117	27.06	-22.93			Aug-06
	5.06	10.77	29.77	40.26	117.62	0	1.45	11.92	1.01	42.97	4,761	0	95	0	1	117	26.71	-23.13			Dec-06
	5.12	10.96	30.16	41.53	120.94	0	1.15	11.93	1.01	45.1	4,761	0	95	0	1	117	26.94	-23			Dec-06
	5.21	11.12	30.57	42.82	124.26	0	0.85	11.93	1.01	46.94	4,761	0	95	0	1	117	27.14	-22.9			Dec-06
	5.23	11.17	30.67	43.14	125.23	0	0.75	11.92	1.01	47.54	4,761	0	95	0	1	117	27.27	-22.88			Nov-14
	5.23	11.14	30.65	43.19	125.33	0	0.8	11.93	1.01	47.56	4,761	0	95	0	1	117	27.27	-22.88			Feb-02
50	-1.55	-0.10	21.59	24.67	139.49	0	1.32	15.51	1.2	33.53	1,511	2	98	0	0	35	22.44	-12.92	5.50		May-00
50	-1.70	-0.43	20.73	21.96	130.89	0	2.05	15.49	1.2	27.46	1,511	2	98	0	0	35	21.98	-13.19		1.00	May-00
	-1.43	0.08	22.02	26.14	144.25		0.91	15.52	1.2	35.17	1,511	2	98	0	0	35	22.78	-12.72			Feb-17
50	-1.46	0.03	21.93	25.69	142.79	0	1.05	15.52	1.2	35.14	1,511	2	98	0	0	35	22.74	-12.81			Aug-06
	-1.62	-0.26	21.23	23.54	135.89	0	1.61	15.51	1.2	34.54	1,511	2	98	0	0	35	22.37	-13.01			Dec-06
	-1.54	-0.09	21.57	24.66	139.42	0	1.31	15.51	1.2	36.21	1,511	2	98	0	0	35	22.56	-12.89			Dec-06
	-1.46	0.05	21.95	25.76	143.11	0	1.01	15.51	1.2	37.78	1,511	2	98	0	0	35	22.82	-12.81			Dec-06
	-1.42	0.08	22.03	26.16	144.27	0	0.96	15.52	1.2	38.21	1,511	2	98	0	0	35	22.78	-12.72			May-00
50	3.49	8.81	24.23	25.91	47.13	0.84	1.2	10.61	0.83	16.96	3,548	4	93	0	3	82	18.13	-23.19	5.50		Jul-96
50	3.29	8.39	23.33	23.23	41.88	0.38	1.93	10.56	0.83	14.83	3,548	4	93	0	3	82	17.67	-23.47		1.00	Jul-98
	3.53	9.00	24.71	27.61	50.55		0.74	10.59	0.83	16.84	3,548	4	93	0	3	82	18.51	-23.04			Feb-17

	MARKET			FUND TYPE, CATEGORY & OBJECTIVE	RATINGS				MINIMUMS	
Fund Name	Ticker Symbol	Traded On	Fund Type	Category and (Prospectus Objective)	Overall Rating	Reward Rating	Risk Rating	Recent Up/ Downgrade	Open to New Investors	Min Initial Investment
The Hartford International Opportunities Fund Class I	IHOIX	NAS CM	Open End	Global Equity Large Cap (Foreign Stock)	B	B-	B	Up	Y	2,000
The Hartford International Opportunities Fund Class R3	IHORX	NAS CM	Open End	Global Equity Large Cap (Foreign Stock)	B-	B-	B	Up	Y	0
The Hartford International Opportunities Fund Class R4	IHOSX	NAS CM	Open End	Global Equity Large Cap (Foreign Stock)	B	B-	B	Up	Y	0
The Hartford International Opportunities Fund Class R5	IHOTX	NAS CM	Open End	Global Equity Large Cap (Foreign Stock)	B	B-	B	Up	Y	0
The Hartford International Opportunities Fund Class R6	IHOVX	NAS CM	Open End	Global Equity Large Cap (Foreign Stock)	B	B-	B	Up	Y	0
The Hartford International Opportunities Fund Class Y	HAOYX	NAS CM	Open End	Global Equity Large Cap (Foreign Stock)	B	B-	B	Up	Y	250,000
The Hartford International Value Fund Class Y	HILYX	NAS CM	Open End	Global Equity Large Cap (Foreign Stock)	B	B	C+	Up		250,000
The Hartford MidCap Fund Class A	HFMCX	NAS CM	Open End	US Equity Mid Cap (Growth)	B	B+	B	Up	Y	2,000
The Hartford MidCap Fund Class C	HMDCX	NAS CM	Open End	US Equity Mid Cap (Growth)	B	B	B-	Up	Y	2,000
The Hartford MidCap Fund Class F	HMDFX	NAS CM	Open End	US Equity Mid Cap (Growth)	B+	B+	B	Up	Y	1,000,000
The Hartford MidCap Fund Class I	HFMIX	NAS CM	Open End	US Equity Mid Cap (Growth)	B	B+	B	Up	Y	2,000
The Hartford MidCap Fund Class R3	HFMRX	NAS CM	Open End	US Equity Mid Cap (Growth)	B	B+	B-	Up	Y	0
The Hartford MidCap Fund Class R4	HFMSX	NAS CM	Open End	US Equity Mid Cap (Growth)	B	B+	B	Up	Y	0
The Hartford MidCap Fund Class R5	HFMTX	NAS CM	Open End	US Equity Mid Cap (Growth)	B	B+	B	Up	Y	0
The Hartford MidCap Fund Class R6	HFMVX	NAS CM	Open End	US Equity Mid Cap (Growth)	B+	B+	B	Up	Y	0
The Hartford MidCap Fund Class Y	HMDYX	NAS CM	Open End	US Equity Mid Cap (Growth)	B+	B+	B	Up	Y	250,000
The Hartford Small Company Fund Class A	IHSAX	NAS CM	Open End	US Equity Small Cap (Small Company)	C+	C+	C+	Up	Y	2,000
The Hartford Small Company Fund Class C	HSMCX	NAS CM	Open End	US Equity Small Cap (Small Company)	C+	C+	C+	Up	Y	2,000
The Hartford Small Company Fund Class F	IHSFX	NAS CM	Open End	US Equity Small Cap (Small Company)	C+	B-	C	Up	Y	1,000,000
The Hartford Small Company Fund Class I	IHSIX	NAS CM	Open End	US Equity Small Cap (Small Company)	C+	C+	B-	Up	Y	2,000
The Hartford Small Company Fund Class R3	IHSRX	NAS CM	Open End	US Equity Small Cap (Small Company)	C+	C+	C+	Up	Y	0
The Hartford Small Company Fund Class R4	IHSSX	NAS CM	Open End	US Equity Small Cap (Small Company)	C+	C+	C+	Up	Y	0
The Hartford Small Company Fund Class R5	IHSUX	NAS CM	Open End	US Equity Small Cap (Small Company)	C+	B-	C	Up	Y	0
The Hartford Small Company Fund Class R6	IHSVX	NAS CM	Open End	US Equity Small Cap (Small Company)	C+	B-	C	Up	Y	0
The Hartford Small Company Fund Class Y	HSCYX	NAS CM	Open End	US Equity Small Cap (Small Company)	C+	B-	C	Up	Y	250,000
The India Fund Inc	IFN	NYSE	Closed End	India Equity (Pacific Stock)	B-	B-	B-	Up	Y	
The Investment House Growth Fund	TIHGX	NAS CM	Open End	US Equity Large Cap Growth (Growth)	B+	A-	B	Up	Y	1,000
The Merger Fund® Institutional Class	MERIX	NAS CM	Open End	Market Neutral (Growth)	B-	C	A-	Up	Y	1,000,000
The Merger Fund® Investor Class	MERFX	NAS CM	Open End	Market Neutral (Growth)	C+	C	B	Down	Y	2,000
The MP 63 Fund	DRIPX	NAS CM	Open End	US Equity Large Cap Blend (Growth)	B-	B-	B-	Down	Y	0
The Texas Fund Class I	BIGTX	NAS CM	Open End	US Equity Mid Cap (Growth)	C	C	C	Up	Y	50,000
Third Avenue International Value Fund Institutional Class	TAVIX	NAS CM	Open End	Global Equity Mid/Small Cap (Foreign Stock)	B-	B	C	Up	Y	100,000
Third Avenue International Value Fund Investor Class	TVIVX	NAS CM	Open End	Global Equity Mid/Small Cap (Foreign Stock)	B-	B	C	Up	Y	2,500
Third Avenue Real Estate Value Fund Institutional Class	TAREX	NAS CM	Open End	Real Estate Sector Equity (Real Estate)	B-	C+	B	Up	Y	100,000
Third Avenue Real Estate Value Fund Investor Class	TVRVX	NAS CM	Open End	Real Estate Sector Equity (Real Estate)	B-	C+	B	Up	Y	2,500
Third Avenue Small Cap Value Fund Institutional Class	TASCX	NAS CM	Open End	US Equity Small Cap (Small Company)	B	B	B	Up	Y	100,000
Third Avenue Small-Cap Value Fund Investor Class	TVSVX	NAS CM	Open End	US Equity Small Cap (Small Company)	B	B	B	Up	Y	2,500
Third Avenue Value Fund Institutional Class	TAVFX	NAS CM	Open End	Global Equity (Growth)	C+	C+	C+	Down	Y	100,000
Third Avenue Value Fund Investor Class	TVFVX	NAS CM	Open End	Global Equity (Growth)	C+	C+	C+	Down	Y	2,500
Thomas White American Opportunities Fund Investor Class	TWAOX	NAS CM	Open End	US Equity Mid Cap (Growth)	B	B-	B+	Up	Y	2,500
Thomas White Emerging Markets Fund Class I	TWIIX	NAS CM	Open End	Emerging Markets Equity (Div Emerging Mkts)	C+	C+	C	Up	Y	1,000,000
Thomas White Emerging Markets Fund Investor Class	TWEMX	NAS CM	Open End	Emerging Markets Equity (Div Emerging Mkts)	C+	C+	C	Up	Y	2,500
Thomas White International Fund Class I	TWWIX	NAS CM	Open End	Global Equity Large Cap (Foreign Stock)	B-	C+	B-	Up	Y	1,000,000
Thomas White International Fund Investor Class	TWWDX	NAS CM	Open End	Global Equity Large Cap (Foreign Stock)	B-	C+	B-	Up	Y	2,500
Thompson LargeCap Fund	THPGX	NAS CM	Open End	US Equity Large Cap Blend (Growth)	B-	B	B-	Down	Y	250
Thompson MidCap Fund	THPMX	NAS CM	Open End	US Equity Mid Cap (Growth)	B-	B-	B-	Up	Y	250
Thomson Horstmann & Bryant Microcap Fund Inst Cls Shares	THBIX	NAS CM	Open End	US Equity Small Cap (Small Company)	B	A	C+	Up	Y	100,000
Thomson Horstmann & Bryant Microcap Fund Inv Cls Shares	THBVX	NAS CM	Open End	US Equity Small Cap (Small Company)	B	A	C+	Up	Y	100
Thornburg Better World International Fund Class A	TBWAX	NAS CM	Open End	Global Equity Large Cap (Growth)	C	C+	B	Up	Y	5,000
Thornburg Better World International Fund Class C	TBWCX	NAS CM	Open End	Global Equity Large Cap (Growth)	C	C+	B	Up	Y	5,000
Thornburg Better World International Fund Class I	TBWIX	NAS CM	Open End	Global Equity Large Cap (Growth)	C	C+	B	Up	Y	2,500,000
Thornburg Core Growth Fund Class A	THCGX	NAS CM	Open End	US Equity Large Cap Growth (Growth)	B-	B-	B	Up	Y	5,000

★ Expanded analysis of this fund is included in Section II.

Min Additional Investment	TOTAL RETURNS					PERFORMANCE				ASSETS		ASSET ALLOCATION & TURNOVER					BULL & BEAR		FEES		
	3-Month Total Return	6-Month Total Return	1-Year Total Return	3-Year Total Return	5-Year Total Return	Dividend Yield (TTM)	Expense Ratio	3-Yr Std Deviation	3-Year Beta	NAV	Total Assets (MIL)	%Cash	%Stocks	%Bonds	%Other	Turnover Ratio	Last Bull Market Total Return	Last Bear Market Total Return	Front End Fee (%)	Back End Fee (%)	Inception Date
50	3.50	8.91	24.53	27.10	49.56	1.18	0.88	10.6	0.83	16.84	3,548	4	93	0	3	82	18.33	-23.07			May-08
	3.33	8.62	23.85	24.93	45.24	0.72	1.45	10.53	0.83	17.24	3,548	4	93	0	3	82	18.02	-23.22			Dec-06
	3.44	8.78	24.23	26.02	47.49	0.91	1.14	10.59	0.83	17.53	3,548	4	93	0	3	82	18.21	-23.15			Dec-06
	3.52	8.99	24.57	27.24	49.78	1.13	0.84	10.59	0.83	17.68	3,548	4	93	0	3	82	18.45	-23.05			Dec-06
	3.57	9.02	24.76	27.57	50.51	1.2	0.74	10.6	0.83	17.77	3,548	4	93	0	3	82	18.51	-23.04			Nov-14
	3.60	9.05	24.71	27.61	50.55	1.2	0.79	10.59	0.83	17.78	3,548	4	93	0	3	82	18.51	-23.04			Jul-96
	3.86	10.49	24.90	43.72	80.02	1.83	0.94	12.29	0.91	17.63	2,769	5	94	0	0	32	14.54	-22.48			May-10
50	7.34	10.86	23.93	38.96	118.71	0	1.16	11.72	1	30.02	10,481	0	100	0	0	8	29.28	-25.59	5.50		Dec-97
50	7.13	10.46	23.04	35.94	110.88	0	1.88	11.71	1	22.03	10,481	0	100	0	0	8	28.78	-25.83		1.00	Jul-98
	7.46	11.08	24.40	40.59	123.05		0.76	11.71	1	30.86	10,481	0	100	0	0	8	29.71	-25.48			Feb-17
50	7.43	11.06	24.28	39.90	121.34	0	0.87	11.71	1	30.83	10,481	0	100	0	0	8	29.49	-25.56			Feb-09
	7.24	10.68	23.53	37.57	115.23	0	1.47	11.7	1	33.39	10,481	0	100	0	0	8	29.15	-25.72			May-09
	7.30	10.87	23.92	38.85	118.57	0	1.17	11.71	1	34.59	10,481	0	100	0	0	8	29.31	-25.6			May-09
	7.40	11.05	24.30	40.16	121.96	0	0.86	11.7	1	35.46	10,481	0	100	0	0	8	29.6	-25.53			May-09
	7.42	11.08	24.42	40.55	123.07	0	0.76	11.7	1	35.78	10,481	0	100	0	0	8	29.71	-25.48			Nov-14
	7.43	11.05	24.35	40.53	122.96	0	0.76	11.71	1	35.76	10,481	0	100	0	0	8	29.71	-25.48			Dec-97
50	6.08	11.70	25.08	16.12	81.36	0	1.41	14.88	0.96	21.09	483.9	5	93	0	1	81	26.36	-24.9	5.50		Jul-96
50	5.91	11.34	24.27	13.62	74.97	0	2.13	14.88	0.96	15.41	483.9	5	93	0	1	81	25.85	-25.12		1.00	Jul-98
	6.24	12.00	25.73	17.82	85.95		0.89	14.89	0.96	22.11	483.9	5	93	0	1	81	26.74	-24.71			Feb-17
50	6.15	11.86	25.46	16.96	83.59	0	1.16	14.86	0.96	22.07	483.9	5	93	0	1	81	26.52	-24.79			Aug-06
	6.09	11.65	24.93	15.51	79.73	0	1.56	14.89	0.96	22.8	483.9	5	93	0	1	81	26.24	-24.94			Dec-06
	6.10	11.78	25.26	16.53	82.35	0	1.26	14.89	0.96	24	483.9	5	93	0	1	81	26.43	-24.83			Dec-06
	6.21	11.93	25.64	17.57	85.17	0	0.96	14.88	0.96	25.13	483.9	5	93	0	1	81	26.69	-24.74			Dec-06
	6.22	11.99	25.70	17.85	85.92	0	0.89	14.9	0.96	25.58	483.9	5	93	0	1	81	26.74	-24.71			Nov-14
	6.27	12.04	25.76	17.85	85.98	0	0.91	14.89	0.96	25.58	483.9	5	93	0	1	81	26.74	-24.71			Jul-96
	8.02	8.69	34.97	31.65	76.77	0	1.33	17.04	0.96	29.5	886.5	0	100	0	0	12	-5.14	-20.8			Feb-94
100	6.49	12.09	34.05	44.64	119.22	0	1.45	12.41	1.09	32.63	100.6	1	99	0	0	7	33.64	-15.66			Dec-01
500	0.03	0.41	2.73	5.06	11.27	0.88	1.16	2.65	0.58	15.83	2,408	41	50	7	2	182	4.35	-4.06			Aug-13
	-0.03	0.27	2.38	4.06	9.91	0.31	1.49	2.67	1.18	15.94	2,408	41	50	7	2	182	4.35	-4.06			Jan-89
	7.80	10.46	18.51	29.60	99.96	1.7	0.77	9.49	0.88	21.53	67.4	1	99	0	0	4	24.1	-16.92			Mar-99
	8.00	12.39	11.58	8.55		0	1.67	12.54	0.83	10.79	11.1	1	97	0	1	40					Sep-13
1,000	1.67	14.37	24.98	25.07	33.26	3.91	1.4	16.9	1.2	19.25	131.5	11	87	2	0	37	9.76	-22.78			Dec-01
1,000	1.57	14.20	24.55	24.07	31.55	3.74	1.65	16.86	1.2	19.36	131.5	11	87	2	0	37	9.59	-22.81			Dec-09
1,000	6.42	10.72	22.17	23.81	65.41	0.71	1.13	11.32	0.81	34.33	1,989	8	92	0	0	7	27.72	-22.46			Sep-98
1,000	6.35	10.60	21.87	22.92	63.37	0.46	1.38	11.31	0.81	34.16	1,989	8	92	0	0	7	27.52	-22.53			Dec-09
1,000	1.50	6.21	8.85	27.13	77.56	0.49	1.15	13.3	0.9	20.8	297.8	4	96	0	0	32	18.41	-19.64			Apr-97
1,000	1.47	6.09	8.60	26.22	75.38	0.25	1.4	13.28	0.9	20.54	297.8	4	96	0	0	32	18.3	-19.71			Dec-09
1,000	2.45	5.40	14.15	17.69	49.15	0.74	1.15	13.68	1.14	53.26	1,152	9	90	0	1	18	17.95	-26.9			Nov-90
1,000	2.38	5.27	13.86	16.79	47.26	0.49	1.4	13.68	1.14	53.29	1,152	9	90	0	1	18	17.8	-26.98			Dec-09
100	6.76	10.49	16.99	25.56	92.04	0.78	1.2	9.76	0.88	17.21	42.9	0	100	0	0	60	25.52	-19.66			Mar-99
100	8.13	12.58	28.95	14.76	5.06	1.78	1.1	13.94	0.84	11.84	46.3	2	89	0	0	57	20.8	-27.1			Aug-12
100	8.14	12.43	28.78	13.89	3.73	1.44	1.35	13.97	0.84	11.75	46.3	2	89	0	0	57	20.8	-27.1			Jun-10
100	4.59	11.32	28.48	20.44	24.91	2.24	0.99	11.22	0.86	18.24	320.9	0	100	0	0	60	18.48	-23.85			Aug-12
100	4.44	11.08	28.24	19.55	23.36	1.54	1.24	11.26	0.86	18.32	320.9	0	100	0	0	60	18.48	-23.85			Jun-94
50	6.50	10.27	18.23	27.07	103.07	0.69	1.1	13.47	1.22	67.2	129.1	0	100	0	0	32	27.58	-21.59			Feb-92
50	6.89	7.62	17.06	25.61	95.20	0.05	1.2	14.08	1.26	13.15	50.9	0	100	0	0	34	27.23	-23.04			Mar-08
2,500	2.01	7.04	10.97	33.44	92.05	0	1.25	14.94	0.9	16.34	83.1	1	99	0	0	65					Mar-12
	1.95	6.79	10.46	31.42	87.50	0	1.75	14.95	0.9	15.89	83.1	1	99	0	0	65					Mar-12
100	6.96	10.14	21.88			0.82	1.83			14.73	73.2	10	89	0	1	106			4.50		Sep-15
100	6.80	9.78	21.20			0.5	2.38			14.59	73.2	10	89	0	1	106				1.00	Sep-15
100	7.07	10.48	22.87			1.05	1.09			14.96	73.2	10	89	0	1	106					Sep-15
100	4.74	8.10	23.90	23.77	81.04	0	1.4	12.87	1.06	34	642.8	5	95	0	0	72	37.95	-20.98	4.50		Dec-00

	MARKET		FUND TYPE, CATEGORY & OBJECTIVE		RATINGS					MINIMUMS
Fund Name	Ticker Symbol	Traded On	Fund Type	Category and (Prospectus Objective)	Overall Rating	Reward Rating	Risk Rating	Recent Up/ Downgrade	Open to New Investors	Min Initial Investment
Thornburg Core Growth Fund Class C	TCGCX	NAS CM	Open End	US Equity Large Cap Growth (Growth)	B-	C+	B	Up	Y	5,000
Thornburg Core Growth Fund Class I	THIGX	NAS CM	Open End	US Equity Large Cap Growth (Growth)	B	B-	B	Up	Y	2,500,000
Thornburg Core Growth Fund Class R3	THCRX	NAS CM	Open End	US Equity Large Cap Growth (Growth)	B-	B-	B	Up	Y	0
Thornburg Core Growth Fund Class R4	TCGRX	NAS CM	Open End	US Equity Large Cap Growth (Growth)	B-	B-	B	Up	Y	0
Thornburg Core Growth Fund Class R5	THGRX	NAS CM	Open End	US Equity Large Cap Growth (Growth)	B	B-	B	Up	Y	0
Thornburg Developing World Fund Class A	THDAX	NAS CM	Open End	Emerging Markets Equity (Growth)	C+	B-	C	Up	Y	5,000
Thornburg Developing World Fund Class C	THDCX	NAS CM	Open End	Emerging Markets Equity (Growth)	C+	C+	C	Up	Y	5,000
Thornburg Developing World Fund Class I	THDIX	NAS CM	Open End	Emerging Markets Equity (Growth)	C+	B-	C	Up	Y	2,500,000
Thornburg Developing World Fund Class R5	THDRX	NAS CM	Open End	Emerging Markets Equity (Growth)	C+	B-	C	Up	Y	0
Thornburg Developing World Fund Class R6	TDWRX	NAS CM	Open End	Emerging Markets Equity (Growth)	C+	B-	C	Up	Y	0
Thornburg Global Opportunities Fund Class A	THOAX	NAS CM	Open End	Global Equity (Growth)	B	B-	B	Up	Y	5,000
Thornburg Global Opportunities Fund Class C	THOCX	NAS CM	Open End	Global Equity (Growth)	B-	B-	B	Up	Y	5,000
Thornburg Global Opportunities Fund Class I	THOIX	NAS CM	Open End	Global Equity (Growth)	B	B-	B	Up	Y	2,500,000
Thornburg Global Opportunities Fund Class R3	THORX	NAS CM	Open End	Global Equity (Growth)	B	B-	B	Up	Y	0
Thornburg Global Opportunities Fund Class R4	THOVX	NAS CM	Open End	Global Equity (Growth)	B	B-	B	Up	Y	0
Thornburg Global Opportunities Fund Class R5	THOFX	NAS CM	Open End	Global Equity (Growth)	B	B-	B	Up	Y	0
Thornburg Global Opportunities Fund Class R6	THOGX	NAS CM	Open End	Global Equity (Growth)	B	B-	B	Up	Y	0
Thornburg International Growth Fund Class A	TIGAX	NAS CM	Open End	Global Equity Mid/Small Cap (Growth)	B	B	B+	Up	Y	5,000
Thornburg International Growth Fund Class C	TIGCX	NAS CM	Open End	Global Equity Mid/Small Cap (Growth)	B	B	B	Up	Y	5,000
Thornburg International Growth Fund Class I	TINGX	NAS CM	Open End	Global Equity Mid/Small Cap (Growth)	B	B	B+	Up	Y	2,500,000
Thornburg International Growth Fund Class R3	TIGVX	NAS CM	Open End	Global Equity Mid/Small Cap (Growth)	B	B	B+	Up	Y	0
Thornburg International Growth Fund Class R4	TINVX	NAS CM	Open End	Global Equity Mid/Small Cap (Growth)	B	B	B+	Up	Y	0
Thornburg International Growth Fund Class R5	TINFX	NAS CM	Open End	Global Equity Mid/Small Cap (Growth)	B	B	B+	Up	Y	0
Thornburg International Growth Fund Class R6	THGIX	NAS CM	Open End	Global Equity Mid/Small Cap (Growth)	B	B	B+	Up	Y	0
Thornburg International Value Fund Class A	TGVAX	NAS CM	Open End	Global Equity Large Cap (Multi-Asset Global)	B	B	B	Up	Y	5,000
Thornburg International Value Fund Class C	THGCX	NAS CM	Open End	Global Equity Large Cap (Multi-Asset Global)	B-	B-	B	Up	Y	5,000
Thornburg International Value Fund Class I	TGVIX	NAS CM	Open End	Global Equity Large Cap (Multi-Asset Global)	B	B	B	Up	Y	2,500,000
Thornburg International Value Fund Class R3	TGVRX	NAS CM	Open End	Global Equity Large Cap (Multi-Asset Global)	B	B	B	Up	Y	0
Thornburg International Value Fund Class R4	THVRX	NAS CM	Open End	Global Equity Large Cap (Multi-Asset Global)	B	B	B	Up	Y	0
Thornburg International Value Fund Class R5	TIVRX	NAS CM	Open End	Global Equity Large Cap (Multi-Asset Global)	B	B	B	Up	Y	0
Thornburg International Value Fund Class R6	TGIRX	NAS CM	Open End	Global Equity Large Cap (Multi-Asset Global)	B	B	B	Up	Y	0
Thornburg Investment Income Builder Fund Class A	TIBAX	NAS CM	Open End	Alloc (Equity-Income)	C+	C+	C+	Down	Y	5,000
Thornburg Investment Income Builder Fund Class C	TIBCX	NAS CM	Open End	Alloc (Equity-Income)	C+	C+	C+	Down	Y	5,000
Thornburg Investment Income Builder Fund Class I	TIBIX	NAS CM	Open End	Alloc (Equity-Income)	C+	C+	C+	Down	Y	2,500,000
Thornburg Investment Income Builder Fund Class R3	TIBRX	NAS CM	Open End	Alloc (Equity-Income)	C+	C+	C+	Down	Y	0
Thornburg Investment Income Builder Fund Class R4	TIBGX	NAS CM	Open End	Alloc (Equity-Income)	C+	C+	C+	Down	Y	0
Thornburg Investment Income Builder Fund Class R5	TIBMX	NAS CM	Open End	Alloc (Equity-Income)	C+	C+	C+	Down	Y	0
Thornburg Investment Income Builder Fund Class R6	TIBOX	NAS CM	Open End	Alloc (Equity-Income)	C+	C+	C+	Down	Y	0
Thornburg Long/Short Equity Fund Class I	THLSX	NAS CM	Open End	Long/Short Equity (Growth)	B	B	B-	Up	Y	2,500,000
Thornburg Value Fund Class A	TVAFX	NAS CM	Open End	US Equity Large Cap Blend (Growth)	B-	B	B-	Down	Y	5,000
Thornburg Value Fund Class C	TVCFX	NAS CM	Open End	US Equity Large Cap Blend (Growth)	B-	B-	B-	Down	Y	5,000
Thornburg Value Fund Class I	TVIFX	NAS CM	Open End	US Equity Large Cap Blend (Growth)	B	B	B-		Y	2,500,000
Thornburg Value Fund Class R3	TVRFX	NAS CM	Open End	US Equity Large Cap Blend (Growth)	B	B	B-	Up	Y	0
Thornburg Value Fund Class R4	TVIRX	NAS CM	Open End	US Equity Large Cap Blend (Growth)	B	B	B-		Y	0
Thornburg Value Fund Class R5	TVRRX	NAS CM	Open End	US Equity Large Cap Blend (Growth)	B	B	B-		Y	0
Thrivent Aggressive Allocation Fund Class A	TAAAX	NAS CM	Open End	Aggressive Alloc (Asset Alloc)	B-	B-	B-	Down	Y	2,000
Thrivent Aggressive Allocation Fund Class S	TAAIX	NAS CM	Open End	Aggressive Alloc (Asset Alloc)	B-	B-	B-	Down	Y	2,000
Thrivent Balanced Income Plus Fund Class A	AABFX	NAS CM	Open End	Moderate Alloc (Balanced)	B-	C+	B	Up	Y	2,000
Thrivent Balanced Income Plus Fund Class S	IBBFX	NAS CM	Open End	Moderate Alloc (Balanced)	B-	C+	B	Up	Y	2,000
Thrivent Balanced Income Plus Portfolio			Open End	Moderate Alloc (Balanced)	B-	C+	B	Up	Y	0
Thrivent Diversified Income Plus Fund Class A	AAHYX	NAS CM	Open End	Cautious Alloc (Growth & Income)	B-	C+	B	Up	Y	2,000
Thrivent Diversified Income Plus Fund Class S	THYFX	NAS CM	Open End	Cautious Alloc (Growth & Income)	B-	C+	B	Up	Y	2,000

★ Expanded analysis of this fund is included in Section II.

Min Additional Investment	3-Month Total Return	6-Month Total Return	1-Year Total Return	3-Year Total Return	5-Year Total Return	Dividend Yield (TTM)	Expense Ratio	3-Yr Std Deviation	3-Year Beta	NAV	Total Assets (MIL)	%Cash	%Stocks	%Bonds	%Other	Turnover Ratio	Last Bull Market Total Return	Last Bear Market Total Return	Front End Fee (%)	Back End Fee (%)	Inception Date
	TOTAL RETURNS					PERFORMANCE				ASSETS		ASSET ALLOCATION & TURNOVER					BULL & BEAR		FEES		
100	4.53	7.68	22.96	20.96	74.31	0	2.16	12.84	1.05	29.72	642.8	5	95	0	0	72	37.23	-21.21		1.00	Dec-00
100	4.84	8.31	24.40	25.25	84.79	0	0.99	12.86	1.06	36.35	642.8	5	95	0	0	72	38.32	-20.77			Nov-03
	4.70	8.05	23.79	23.38	80.08	0	1.5	12.88	1.06	33.82	642.8	5	95	0	0	72	37.95	-20.98			Jul-03
	4.72	8.10	23.88	23.74	81.06	0	1.4	12.87	1.06	34.13	642.8	5	95	0	0	72	37.99	-20.93			Feb-07
	4.85	8.35	24.42	25.28	84.83	0	0.99	12.86	1.06	36.32	642.8	5	95	0	0	72	38.38	-20.84			Oct-05
100	6.54	15.59	35.31	17.28	32.33	0.49	1.57	12.44	0.74	21.16	1,081	4	93	0	2	78	25.19	-25.32	4.50		Dec-09
100	6.39	15.16	34.35	14.66	27.40	0.19	2.34	12.43	0.74	20.14	1,081	4	93	0	2	78	24.73	-25.57		1.00	Dec-09
100	6.67	15.80	35.86	18.85	35.18	0.76	1.09	12.41	0.73	21.56	1,081	4	93	0	2	78	25.75	-25.19			Dec-09
	6.70	15.86	35.84	18.91	35.03	0.76	1.09	12.44	0.74	21.49	1,081	4	93	0	2	78	25.75	-25.19			Feb-13
	6.72	15.88	35.96	19.24	35.71	0.79	0.99	12.42	0.74	21.57	1,081	4	93	0	2	78	25.75	-25.19			Feb-13
100	2.85	6.53	21.64	27.12	95.40	0.31	1.35	11.65	0.83	31.79	2,497	7	92	0	0	44	18.44	-23.6	4.50		Jul-06
100	2.63	6.07	20.68	24.21	88.02	0.04	2.09	11.62	0.83	30.65	2,497	7	92	0	0	44	17.85	-23.78		1.00	Jul-06
100	2.93	6.71	22.02	28.44	99.08	0.63	0.99	11.64	0.83	31.87	2,497	7	92	0	0	44	18.8	-23.43			Jul-06
	2.76	6.40	21.36	26.44	94.00	0.24	1.5	11.66	0.83	31.45	2,497	7	92	0	0	44	18.41	-23.58			Feb-08
	2.77	6.45	21.49	26.77	94.93	0.29	1.4	11.66	0.83	31.48	2,497	7	92	0	0	44	18.55	-23.54			Feb-08
	2.88	6.64	21.96	28.37	98.98	0.61	0.99	11.64	0.83	31.9	2,497	7	92	0	0	44	18.79	-23.41			Feb-08
	2.95	6.78	22.05	28.47	99.13		0.85	11.63	0.83	31.97	2,497	7	92	0	0	44	18.8	-23.43			Apr-17
100	2.36	10.30	34.32	35.23	62.62	0.03	1.39	13.43	0.97	23.57	1,472	8	90	0	1	61	14.59	-12.44	4.50		Feb-07
100	2.19	9.85	33.37	32.14	56.60	0	2.15	13.42	0.97	22.15	1,472	8	90	0	1	61	13.98	-12.67		1.00	Feb-07
100	2.46	10.47	34.92	36.85	65.96	0.25	0.99	13.41	0.97	24.24	1,472	8	90	0	1	61	14.82	-12.18			Feb-07
	2.34	10.21	34.22	34.80	61.77	0	1.5	13.41	0.97	23.37	1,472	8	90	0	1	61	14.49	-12.4			Feb-08
	2.33	10.23	34.39	35.17	62.60	0.01	1.4	13.44	0.97	23.44	1,472	8	90	0	1	61	14.63	-12.31			Feb-08
	2.50	10.49	34.91	36.93	65.93	0.23	0.99	13.4	0.97	24.31	1,472	8	90	0	1	61	14.86	-12.16			Feb-08
	2.49	10.54	35.03	37.29	66.74	0.34	0.89	13.41	0.97	24.36	1,472	8	90	0	1	61	14.82	-12.18			Feb-13
100	3.51	7.45	24.98	28.40	40.56	0.69	1.28	11.99	0.93	24.5	5,640	1	97	0	2	87	15.19	-24.25	4.50		May-98
100	3.31	7.08	24.06	25.60	35.46	0.42	2.02	11.99	0.93	21.73	5,640	1	97	0	2	87	14.66	-24.49		1.00	May-98
100	3.60	7.66	25.47	29.88	43.21	0.95	0.9	11.98	0.93	25.28	5,640	1	97	0	2	87	15.44	-24.14			Mar-01
	3.48	7.41	24.78	27.77	39.33	0.61	1.45	11.99	0.93	24.49	5,640	1	97	0	2	87	15.04	-24.3			Jul-03
	3.50	7.47	25.05	28.55	40.70	0.72	1.25	11.98	0.93	24.31	5,640	1	97	0	2	87	15.2	-24.24			Feb-07
	3.59	7.61	25.37	29.62	42.67	0.88	0.95	12	0.93	25.26	5,640	1	97	0	2	87	15.36	-24.17			Feb-05
	3.65	7.74	25.59	30.44	44.27	1.09	0.79	12	0.93	25.18	5,640	1	97	0	2	87	15.19	-24.25			May-12
100	3.33	7.60	14.77	18.37	45.45	3.87	1.39	8.46		21.94	16,112	2	88	7	2	37	11.07	-12.08	4.50		Dec-02
100	3.16	7.18	13.99	15.80	40.38	3.21	2.11	8.46		21.92	16,112	2	88	7	2	37	10.59	-12.35		1.00	Dec-02
100	3.45	7.78	15.17	19.51	47.82	4.16	1.07	8.44		22.1	16,112	2	88	7	2	37	11.29	-12			Nov-03
	3.31	7.45	14.49	17.28	43.31	3.58	1.71	8.44		21.94	16,112	2	88	7	2	37	10.9	-12.24			Feb-05
	3.33	7.48	14.58	17.58	44.02	3.68	1.61	8.46		21.97	16,112	2	88	7	2	37	11.01	-12.22			Feb-08
	3.37	7.67	14.97	19.01	46.83	4.04	1.2	8.44		22.08	16,112	2	88	7	2	37	11.15	-12.04			Feb-07
	3.42	7.77	14.84	18.43	45.53		1.01	8.46		22.02	16,112	2	88	7	2	37	11.07	-12.08			Apr-17
100	4.79	7.29	16.86	20.87	57.93		1.5			11.32	103.6	68	31	0	1	62	15.8	-4.19			Dec-16
100	4.07	7.75	23.32	35.63	114.56	0.03	1.39	9.69	0.9	67.56	1,004	8	91	0	0	44	17.68	-25.1	4.50		Oct-95
100	3.88	7.34	22.40	32.61	106.63	0	2.14	9.68	0.9	61.95	1,004	8	91	0	0	44	17.18	-25.34		1.00	Oct-95
100	4.17	7.97	23.81	37.25	118.82	0.35	0.99	9.68	0.9	69.48	1,004	8	91	0	0	44	17.97	-25			Nov-98
	4.07	7.76	23.35	35.76	114.94	0.05	1.35	9.69	0.9	67.16	1,004	8	91	0	0	44	17.66	-25.14			Jul-03
	4.10	7.82	23.48	36.18	116.04	0.13	1.25	9.68	0.9	67.87	1,004	8	91	0	0	44	17.7	-25.08			Feb-07
	4.16	7.96	23.80	37.23	118.85	0.35	0.99	9.69	0.9	69.38	1,004	8	91	0	0	44	17.89	-25.02			Feb-05
50	4.72	9.73	20.92	30.63	78.98	0.43	1.25	10.17	0.97	15.53	1,144	5	90	5	0	57	20.5	-19.91	4.50		Jun-05
50	4.75	9.86	21.21	31.97	82.39	0.71	0.88	10.16	0.97	15.66	1,144	5	90	5	0	57	20.79	-19.8			Jun-05
50	2.87	5.11	11.37	17.37	51.17	1.97	1.11	6.02	0.56	13.27	351.2	7	47	43	0	120	18.02	-15.43	4.50		Dec-97
50	2.96	5.29	11.67	18.59	54.15	2.29	0.74	5.96	0.55	13.24	351.2	7	47	43	0	120	18.32	-15.24			Dec-97
	2.99	5.33	11.67	18.89	51.05	2.27	0.7	5.88	0.54	15.3685	400.6	4	46	46	0	140	17.04	-9.51			Jun-95
50	1.78	3.78	8.97	15.29	32.69	2.85	1.07	4.14	0.37	7.41	861.0	5	27	61	2	91	13.54	-9.03	4.50		Jan-97
50	1.87	3.81	9.20	16.28	34.63	3.14	0.8	4.12	0.37	7.34	861.0	5	27	61	2	91	13.69	-8.93			Dec-97

Fund Name	MARKET Ticker Symbol	Traded On	FUND TYPE, CATEGORY & OBJECTIVE Fund Type	Category and (Prospectus Objective)	RATINGS Overall Rating	Reward Rating	Risk Rating	Recent Up/ Downgrade	Open to New Investors	MINIMUMS Min Initial Investment
Thrivent Growth and Income Plus Fund Class A	TEIAX	NAS CM	Open End	Aggressive Alloc (Growth & Income)	B-	C+	B	Down	Y	2,000
Thrivent Growth and Income Plus Fund Class S	TEIIX	NAS CM	Open End	Aggressive Alloc (Growth & Income)	B-	C+	B	Down	Y	2,000
Thrivent Growth and Income Plus Portfolio			Open End	Aggressive Alloc (Growth & Income)	B-	C+	B	Down	Y	0
Thrivent Large Cap Growth Fund Class A	AAAGX	NAS CM	Open End	US Equity Large Cap Growth (Growth)	B+	B	A-	Up	Y	2,000
Thrivent Large Cap Growth Fund Class S	THLCX	NAS CM	Open End	US Equity Large Cap Growth (Growth)	B+	B	A-	Up	Y	2,000
Thrivent Large Cap Stock Fund Class A	AALGX	NAS CM	Open End	Global Equity (Growth)	B-	B-	B-	Down	Y	2,000
Thrivent Large Cap Stock Fund Class S	IILGX	NAS CM	Open End	Global Equity (Growth)	B-	B-	B-	Down	Y	2,000
Thrivent Large Cap Value Fund Class A	AAUTX	NAS CM	Open End	US Equity Large Cap Value (Growth)	B	B	B	Up	Y	2,000
Thrivent Large Cap Value Fund Class S	TLVIX	NAS CM	Open End	US Equity Large Cap Value (Growth)	B	B	B	Up	Y	2,000
Thrivent Low Volatility Equity Fund Class S	TLVOX	NAS CM	Open End	Global Equity (World Stock)	U	U	U		Y	2,000
Thrivent Mid Cap Stock Fund Class A	AASCX	NAS CM	Open End	US Equity Mid Cap (Growth)	B+	B+	B+	Up	Y	2,000
Thrivent Mid Cap Stock Fund Class S	TMSIX	NAS CM	Open End	US Equity Mid Cap (Growth)	B+	B+	B+	Up	Y	2,000
Thrivent Moderate Allocation Fund Class A	THMAX	NAS CM	Open End	Moderate Alloc (Asset Alloc)	B-	C+	B	Down	Y	2,000
Thrivent Moderate Allocation Fund Class S	TMAIX	NAS CM	Open End	Moderate Alloc (Asset Alloc)	B-	C+	B	Down	Y	2,000
Thrivent Moderately Aggressive Allocation Fund Class A	TMAAX	NAS CM	Open End	Aggressive Alloc (Asset Alloc)	B-	B-	B	Down	Y	2,000
Thrivent Moderately Aggressive Allocation Fund Class S	TMAFX	NAS CM	Open End	Aggressive Alloc (Asset Alloc)	B-	B-	B	Down	Y	2,000
Thrivent Moderately Conservative Allocation Fund Class A	TCAAX	NAS CM	Open End	Cautious Alloc (Asset Alloc)	B-	C+	B	Up	Y	2,000
Thrivent Moderately Conservative Allocation Fund Class S	TCAIX	NAS CM	Open End	Cautious Alloc (Asset Alloc)	B-	C+	B	Up	Y	2,000
Thrivent Multidimensional Income Fund Class S	TMLDX	NAS CM	Open End	Cautious Alloc (Growth & Income)	U	U	U		Y	2,000
Thrivent Partner Emerging Markets Equity Fund Cls A Shares	TPEAX	NAS CM	Open End	Emerging Markets Equity (Div Emerging Mkts)	C+	C+	C	Up	Y	2,000
Thrivent Partner Emerging Markets Equity Fund Class S	TPEIX	NAS CM	Open End	Emerging Markets Equity (Div Emerging Mkts)	C+	C+	C	Up	Y	2,000
Thrivent Partner Healthcare Portfolio Class A			Open End	Healthcare Sector Equity (Health)	C	C	C	Down	Y	0
Thrivent Partner Worldwide Allocation Fund Class A	TWAAX	NAS CM	Open End	Alloc (Multi-Asset Global)	B-	C+	B	Up	Y	2,000
Thrivent Partner Worldwide Allocation Fund Class S	TWAIX	NAS CM	Open End	Alloc (Multi-Asset Global)	B-	B-	B	Up	Y	2,000
Thrivent Partner Worldwide Allocation Portfolio			Open End	Alloc (Asset Alloc)	B-	B-	B	Up	Y	0
Thrivent Series Aggressive Allocation Portfolio			Open End	Aggressive Alloc (Asset Alloc)	B-	B-	B-	Down	Y	0
Thrivent Series Diversified Income Plus Portfolio			Open End	Cautious Alloc (Income)	B-	C+	B	Up	Y	0
Thrivent Series Large Cap Growth Portfolio			Open End	US Equity Large Cap Growth (Growth)	B+	B+	A-	Up	Y	0
Thrivent Series Large Cap Index Portfolio			Open End	US Equity Large Cap Blend (Growth & Income)	B	B	B		Y	0
Thrivent Series Large Cap Stock Portfolio			Open End	Global Equity (Growth)	B-	B-	B-	Down	Y	0
Thrivent Series Large Cap Value Portfolio			Open End	US Equity Large Cap Value (Growth)	B	B	B	Up	Y	0
Thrivent Series Mid Cap Index Portfolio			Open End	US Equity Mid Cap (Growth)	B	B	B		Y	0
Thrivent Series Mid Cap Stock Portfolio			Open End	US Equity Mid Cap (Growth)	B+	B+	B+	Up	Y	0
Thrivent Series Moderate Allocation Portfolio			Open End	Moderate Alloc (Growth)	B-	C+	B	Down	Y	0
Thrivent Series Moderately Aggressive Allocation Portfolio			Open End	Aggressive Alloc (Growth)	B-	B-	B	Down	Y	0
Thrivent Series Moderately Conservative Alloc Port			Open End	Cautious Alloc (Growth)	B-	C+	B	Up	Y	0
Thrivent Series Partner All Cap Portfolio			Open End	US Equity Large Cap Growth (Growth)	B	B-	B+	Up	Y	0
Thrivent Series Partner Emerging Mkts Eq Port Cls A			Open End	Emerging Markets Equity (Div Emerging Mkts)	C+	C+	C	Up	Y	0
Thrivent Series Partner Growth Stock Portfolio			Open End	US Equity Large Cap Growth (Growth & Income)	B+	B+	B	Down	Y	0
Thrivent Series Real Estate Securities Portfolio			Open End	Real Estate Sector Equity (Real Estate)	B	C+	B+	Up	Y	0
Thrivent Series Small Cap Index Portfolio			Open End	US Equity Small Cap (Small Company)	A-	A-	B	Up	Y	0
Thrivent Series Small Cap Stock Portfolio			Open End	US Equity Small Cap (Small Company)	A-	A	B	Up	Y	0
Thrivent Small Cap Stock Fund Class A	AASMX	NAS CM	Open End	US Equity Small Cap (Small Company)	A-	A	B	Up	Y	2,000
Thrivent Small Cap Stock Fund Class S	TSCSX	NAS CM	Open End	US Equity Small Cap (Small Company)	A-	A	B	Up	Y	2,000
TIAA-CREF Emerging Markets Equity Fund Advisor Class	TEMHX	NAS CM	Open End	Emerging Markets Equity (Div Emerging Mkts)	B	B	C	Up	Y	0
TIAA-CREF Emerging Markets Equity Fund Institutional Class	TEMLX	NAS CM	Open End	Emerging Markets Equity (Div Emerging Mkts)	B	B	C	Up	Y	2,000,000
TIAA-CREF Emerging Markets Equity Fund Premier Class	TEMPX	NAS CM	Open End	Emerging Markets Equity (Div Emerging Mkts)	B	B	C	Up	Y	0
TIAA-CREF Emerging Markets Equity Fund Retail Class	TEMRX	NAS CM	Open End	Emerging Markets Equity (Div Emerging Mkts)	B-	B	C	Up	Y	2,500
TIAA-CREF Emerging Markets Equity Fund Retirement Class	TEMSX	NAS CM	Open End	Emerging Markets Equity (Div Emerging Mkts)	B-	B	C	Up	Y	0
TIAA-CREF Emerging Markets Equity Index Fund Advisor Class	TEQHX	NAS CM	Open End	Emerging Markets Equity (Div Emerging Mkts)	B-	B	C	Up	Y	0
TIAA-CREF Emerging Mkts Equity Index Fund Inst Cls	TEQLX	NAS CM	Open End	Emerging Markets Equity (Div Emerging Mkts)	B-	B	C	Up	Y	10,000,000
TIAA-CREF Emerging Markets Equity Index Fund Premier Class	TEQPX	NAS CM	Open End	Emerging Markets Equity (Div Emerging Mkts)	B-	B	C	Up	Y	0

★ Expanded analysis of this fund is included in Section II.

Min Additional Investment	3-Month Total Return	6-Month Total Return	1-Year Total Return	3-Year Total Return	5-Year Total Return	Dividend Yield (TTM)	Expense Ratio	3-Yr Std Deviation	3-Year Beta	NAV	Total Assets (MIL)	%Cash	%Stocks	%Bonds	%Other	Turnover Ratio	Last Bull Market Total Return	Last Bear Market Total Return	Front End Fee (%)	Back End Fee (%)	Inception Date
	TOTAL RETURNS					PERFORMANCE				ASSETS		ASSET ALLOCATION & TURNOVER					BULL & BEAR		FEES		
50	3.71	6.20	13.57	18.82	49.41	1.61	1.13	7.68	0.72	11.05	89.3	7	65	26	0	114	20.37	-19.49	4.50		Feb-08
50	3.77	6.33	13.86	19.96	51.98	1.87	0.83	7.74	0.72	11.07	89.3	7	65	26	0	114	20.55	-19.33			Feb-08
	3.83	6.40	14.00	19.96	51.36	1.88	0.83	7.62	0.71	11.4066	97.6	7	66	25	0	129	20.64	-19.39			Apr-08
50	6.37	11.21	27.70	35.74	106.93	0	1.2	12.17	1.08	10.24	884.3	4	96	0	0	67	27.18	-20.07	4.50		Oct-99
50	6.45	11.38	28.21	37.30	111.12	0	0.82	12.26	1.09	11.27	884.3	4	96	0	0	67	27.53	-19.96			Oct-99
50	3.84	9.08	20.82	28.81	79.29	0.94	1.03	10.78	1.01	27.12	1,876	2	98	0	0	62	24.78	-20.82	4.50		Jul-87
50	3.93	9.28	21.27	30.34	82.95	1.24	0.64	10.79	1.01	27.34	1,876	2	98	0	0	62	25.11	-20.66			Dec-97
50	5.89	11.58	17.22	30.92	91.36	1	0.93	12.37	1.15	22.68	1,017	3	97	0	0	22	25.11	-21.59	4.50		Oct-99
50	5.98	11.79	17.70	32.47	95.47	1.3	0.53	12.35	1.15	22.8	1,017	3	97	0	0	22	25.47	-21.4			Oct-99
50	4.69	7.93					1.2			10.94	6.7	3	97	0	0						Feb-17
50	7.26	10.66	18.51	51.03	133.40	0.08	1.09	12.32	1.06	25.3	1,783	5	95	0	0	21	25.34	-25.91	4.50		Jun-93
50	7.35	10.88	18.93	52.74	138.14	0.31	0.72	12.32	1.06	28.49	1,783	5	95	0	0	21	25.75	-25.75			Dec-97
50	2.90	6.00	12.29	20.17	47.75	1.19	1.07	6.18	0.58	13.69	2,240	5	52	40	2	138	14.4	-13.16	4.50		Jun-05
50	2.89	6.13	12.56	21.26	50.11	1.44	0.75	6.18	0.58	13.72	2,240	5	52	40	2	138	14.68	-12.97			Jun-05
50	3.84	7.87	16.16	25.54	63.68	0.85	1.14	8.36	0.8	14.79	2,522	5	72	22	1	90	17.99	-17.07	4.50		Jun-05
50	3.93	8.00	16.48	26.75	66.43	1.11	0.81	8.33	0.79	14.9	2,522	5	72	22	1	90	18.23	-16.97			Jun-05
50	2.05	4.36	9.06	15.39	33.01	1.61	1.03	4.21	0.37	12.37	867.7	4	34	59	2	181	10.64	-9.23	4.50		Jun-05
50	2.03	4.40	9.33	16.40	34.96	1.87	0.73	4.19	0.37	12.4	867.7	4	34	59	2	181	10.8	-8.97			Jun-05
50	0.86	2.74					1.4			10.15	20.3	6	8	70	0						Feb-17
50	4.32	8.41	26.32	16.20	-4.95	0.41	1.65	14.34	0.85	9.85	13.4	2	98	0	0	11			4.50		Aug-12
50	4.42	8.67	26.81	17.39	-3.33	0.81	1.32	14.35	0.85	9.76	13.4	2	98	0	0	11					Aug-12
	1.35	-0.49	19.41	4.58	72.98	0.25	0.95	15.3	1.13	17.883	195.3	3	97	0	0	101	19.4	-17.07			Apr-08
50	3.07	8.20	23.11	24.63	38.37	1.65	1.35	10.26	0.82	11.14	910.4	1	90	9	0	107	14.44	-20.41	4.50		Feb-08
50	3.25	8.45	23.70	26.33	41.39	1.97	0.95	10.19	0.81	11.19	910.4	1	90	9	0	107	14.7	-20.35			Feb-08
	3.21	8.49	23.84	26.52	41.25	2.01	0.88	10.19	0.81	11.0226	2,026	1	90	9	0	114	14.73	-20.52			Apr-08
	4.84	9.99	21.51	32.33	82.16	0.68	0.81	10.12	0.96	17.5056	1,298	4	91	5	0	65	20.69	-19.72			Apr-05
	1.93	3.97	9.34	16.92	36.47	3.01	0.58	4.04	0.36	8.2281	669.0	5	27	60	2	103	14	-8.95			Mar-98
	6.34	11.41	28.51	38.77	115.48	0.44	0.44	12.33	1.09	35.5091	1,195	4	96	0	0	68	28.18	-19.88			Jan-87
	6.56	11.25	21.46	35.74	108.21	1.24	0.25	10.08	1	36.9564	929.4	0	100	0	0	3	24.78	-16.4			Jun-95
	4.01	9.32	21.15	30.67	83.01	1.2	0.67	10.72	1	14.3744	1,076	2	98	0	0	66	24.76	-20.37			Mar-01
	6.00	11.79	17.64	31.90	94.43	1.3	0.64	12.46	1.16	18.9699	1,541	3	97	0	0	22	25.43	-21.52			Nov-01
	6.17	9.52	15.97	34.69	100.96	0.82	0.3	11.05	1	18.9856	392.3	0	100	0	0	19	27.56	-22.67			Mar-01
	7.37	10.91	18.99	52.07	136.61	0.32	0.68	12.34	1.06	20.8172	1,740	5	95	0	0	23	25.55	-25.72			Mar-01
	3.00	6.30	12.95	21.85	50.40	1.57	0.64	6.21	0.58	15.0666	10,129	5	53	40	2	159	14.37	-12.67			Apr-05
	3.95	8.13	16.79	27.10	66.38	1.15	0.72	8.36	0.8	16.3984	6,130	4	72	22	1	106	17.96	-16.79			Apr-05
	2.11	4.53	9.51	16.67	34.96	1.75	0.61	4.13	0.36	13.6166	5,112	6	33	58	2	211	10.32	-8.67			Apr-05
	5.53	8.90	20.24	28.99	97.34	0.45	0.84	10.87	1.01	15.5452	111.2	1	99	0	0	64	25.62	-20.62			Nov-01
	4.40	8.87	27.64	22.90	12.60	0.66	1.3	14.41	0.85	14.4391	88.1	2	97	0	0	7	21.11	-18.39			Apr-08
	6.08	11.84	33.61	48.97	130.26	0.08	0.8	12.2	1.07	23.7895	181.6	1	97	1	0	43	30.83	-16.67			Nov-01
	2.52	3.43	5.95	15.17	58.25	1.59	0.9	13.09	1.03	24.2031	184.5	0	99	0	0	17	31.59	-16.3			Apr-03
	3.89	10.06	13.13	38.58	111.19	0.78	0.28	13.77	1	19.1961	497.4	0	100	0	0	21	29.23	-22.12			Jun-95
	5.26	11.88	21.23	46.55	114.54	0.31	0.74	13.03	0.9	21.0077	614.0	2	98	0	0	57	26.54	-27.23			Mar-01
50	5.14	11.74	20.88	45.31	110.93	0.14	1.22	13.07	0.9	21.57	621.5	1	99	0	0	58	26.53	-27.62	4.50		Jul-96
50	5.24	11.90	21.28	47.14	115.71	0.35	0.81	13.06	0.9	25.99	621.5	1	99	0	0	58	26.97	-27.41			Dec-97
	5.50	17.62	45.39	34.08	24.81	0.64	1.02	15.19	0.92	12.56	1,441	2	85	1	10	195	17.87	-27.28			Dec-15
1,000	5.49	17.68	45.44	34.31	25.02	0.65	0.94	15.19	0.92	12.57	1,441	2	85	1	10	195	17.87	-27.28			Aug-10
	5.40	17.50	45.25	33.62	23.94	0.57	1.09	15.22	0.92	12.57	1,441	2	85	1	10	195	17.73	-27.3			Aug-10
100	5.37	17.49	44.97	32.78	22.60	0.36	1.34	15.22	0.92	12.55	1,441	2	85	1	10	195	17.46	-27.35			Aug-10
	5.40	17.53	45.06	33.38	23.41	0.47	1.19	15.24	0.92	12.53	1,441	2	85	1	10	195	17.57	-27.39			Aug-10
	6.73	15.28	37.28	29.95	23.08	1.39	0.32	15.56	0.98	12	2,414	0	89	1	8	30	18.63	-27.25			Dec-15
1,000	6.76	15.42	37.44	30.14	23.26	1.41	0.23	15.55	0.98	12	2,414	0	89	1	8	30	18.63	-27.25			Aug-10
	6.75	15.42	37.37	29.59	22.46	1.32	0.38	15.62	0.99	11.98	2,414	0	89	1	8	30	18.59	-27.33			Aug-10

	MARKET			FUND TYPE, CATEGORY & OBJECTIVE	RATINGS				MINIMUMS	
Fund Name	Ticker Symbol	Traded On	Fund Type	Category and (Prospectus Objective)	Overall Rating	Reward Rating	Risk Rating	Recent Up/ Downgrade	Open to New Investors	Min Initial Investment
TIAA-CREF Emerging Markets Equity Index Fund Retail Class	TEQKX	NAS CM	Open End	Emerging Markets Equity (Div Emerging Mkts)	B-	B	C	Up	Y	2,500
TIAA-CREF Emerging Mkts Equity Index Fund Retmnt Cls	TEQSX	NAS CM	Open End	Emerging Markets Equity (Div Emerging Mkts)	B-	B	C	Up	Y	0
TIAA-CREF Enhanced Intl Equity Index Fund Adv Cls	TEIEX	NAS CM	Open End	Global Equity Large Cap (Foreign Stock)	B-	B-	B	Up	Y	0
TIAA-CREF Enhanced Intl Equity Index Fund Inst Cls	TFIIX	NAS CM	Open End	Global Equity Large Cap (Foreign Stock)	B-	B-	B	Up	Y	2,000,000
TIAA-CREF Enhanced Large-Cap Growth Index Fund Advisor Cls	TECGX	NAS CM	Open End	US Equity Large Cap Growth (Growth & Income)	B+	A-	B+		Y	0
TIAA-CREF Enhanced Large-Cap Growth Index Fund Inst Cls	TLIIX	NAS CM	Open End	US Equity Large Cap Growth (Growth & Income)	B+	A-	B+		Y	2,000,000
TIAA-CREF Enhanced Large-Cap Value Index Fund Advisor Cls	TELCX	NAS CM	Open End	US Equity Large Cap Value (Growth & Income)	B	B-	B	Up	Y	0
TIAA-CREF Enhanced Large-Cap Value Index Fund Inst Cls	TEVIX	NAS CM	Open End	US Equity Large Cap Value (Growth & Income)	B	B-	B	Up	Y	2,000,000
TIAA-CREF Equity Index Fund Advisor Class	TEIHX	NAS CM	Open End	US Equity Large Cap Blend (Growth)	B	B	B		Y	0
TIAA-CREF Equity Index Fund Institutional Class	TIEIX	NAS CM	Open End	US Equity Large Cap Blend (Growth)	B	B	B		Y	10,000,000
TIAA-CREF Equity Index Fund Premier Class	TCEPX	NAS CM	Open End	US Equity Large Cap Blend (Growth)	B	B	B		Y	0
TIAA-CREF Equity Index Fund Retail Class	TINRX	NAS CM	Open End	US Equity Large Cap Blend (Growth)	B	B	B-		Y	2,500
TIAA-CREF Equity Index Fund Retirement Class	TIQRX	NAS CM	Open End	US Equity Large Cap Blend (Growth)	B	B	B-		Y	0
TIAA-CREF Global Natural Resources Fund Advisor Class	TNRHX	NAS CM	Open End	Natl Resources Sec Equity (Natl Res)	C	C	C	Up	Y	0
TIAA-CREF Global Natural Resources Fund Inst Cls Shares	TNRIX	NAS CM	Open End	Natl Resources Sec Equity (Natl Res)	C	C	C	Up	Y	2,000,000
TIAA-CREF Global Natural Resources Fund Premier Cls Shares	TNRPX	NAS CM	Open End	Natl Resources Sec Equity (Natl Res)	C	C	C	Up	Y	0
TIAA-CREF Global Natural Resources Fund Retail Cls Shares	TNRLX	NAS CM	Open End	Natl Resources Sec Equity (Natl Res)	C	C	C	Up	Y	2,500
TIAA-CREF Global Natural Resources Fund Retmnt Cls Shares	TNRRX	NAS CM	Open End	Natl Resources Sec Equity (Natl Res)	C	C	C	Up	Y	0
TIAA-CREF Growth & Income Fund Advisor Class	TGIHX	NAS CM	Open End	US Equity Large Cap Growth (Growth & Income)	B	B	B		Y	0
TIAA-CREF Growth & Income Fund Institutional Class	TIGRX	NAS CM	Open End	US Equity Large Cap Growth (Growth & Income)	B	B	B		Y	2,000,000
TIAA-CREF Growth & Income Fund Premier Class	TRPGX	NAS CM	Open End	US Equity Large Cap Growth (Growth & Income)	B	B	B		Y	0
TIAA-CREF Growth & Income Fund Retail Class	TIIRX	NAS CM	Open End	US Equity Large Cap Growth (Growth & Income)	B	B	B		Y	2,500
TIAA-CREF Growth & Income Fund Retirement Class	TRGIX	NAS CM	Open End	US Equity Large Cap Growth (Growth & Income)	B	B	B		Y	0
TIAA-CREF International Equity Fund Advisor Class	TIEHX	NAS CM	Open End	Global Equity Large Cap (Foreign Stock)	B	B	B	Up	Y	0
TIAA-CREF International Equity Fund Institutional Class	TIIEX	NAS CM	Open End	Global Equity Large Cap (Foreign Stock)	B	B	B	Up	Y	2,000,000
TIAA-CREF International Equity Fund Premier Class	TREPX	NAS CM	Open End	Global Equity Large Cap (Foreign Stock)	B	B	B	Up	Y	0
TIAA-CREF International Equity Fund Retail Class	TIERX	NAS CM	Open End	Global Equity Large Cap (Foreign Stock)	B	B	B	Up	Y	2,500
TIAA-CREF International Equity Fund Retirement Class	TRERX	NAS CM	Open End	Global Equity Large Cap (Foreign Stock)	B	B	B	Up	Y	0
TIAA-CREF International Equity Index Fund Advisor Class	TCIHX	NAS CM	Open End	Global Equity Large Cap (Foreign Stock)	B-	B-	B	Up	Y	0
TIAA-CREF Intl Equity Index Fund Inst Cls	TCIEX	NAS CM	Open End	Global Equity Large Cap (Foreign Stock)	B-	B-	B	Up	Y	10,000,000
TIAA-CREF International Equity Index Fund Premier Class	TRIPX	NAS CM	Open End	Global Equity Large Cap (Foreign Stock)	B-	C+	B	Up	Y	0
TIAA-CREF International Equity Index Fund Retirement Class	TRIEX	NAS CM	Open End	Global Equity Large Cap (Foreign Stock)	B-	C+	B	Up	Y	0
TIAA-CREF International Opportunities Fund Advisor Class	TIOHX	NAS CM	Open End	Global Equity Large Cap (Foreign Stock)	B	B	B	Up	Y	0
TIAA-CREF Intl Opp Fund Inst Cls	TIOIX	NAS CM	Open End	Global Equity Large Cap (Foreign Stock)	B	B+	B	Up	Y	2,000,000
TIAA-CREF International Opportunities Fund Premier Class	TIOPX	NAS CM	Open End	Global Equity Large Cap (Foreign Stock)	B	B	B	Up	Y	0
TIAA-CREF International Opportunities Fund Retail Class	TIOSX	NAS CM	Open End	Global Equity Large Cap (Foreign Stock)	B	B	B	Up	Y	2,500
TIAA-CREF International Opportunities Fund Retirement Cls	TIOTX	NAS CM	Open End	Global Equity Large Cap (Foreign Stock)	B	B	B	Up	Y	0
TIAA-CREF International Small-Cap Equity Fund Advisor Cls	TAISX	NAS CM	Open End	Global Equity Mid/Small Cap (Small Company)	D	D+	A-		Y	0
TIAA-CREF Intl Small-Cap Equity Fund Inst Cls	TIISX	NAS CM	Open End	Global Equity Mid/Small Cap (Small Company)	D	D+	A-		Y	2,000,000
TIAA-CREF International Small-Cap Equity Fund Premier Cls	TPISX	NAS CM	Open End	Global Equity Mid/Small Cap (Small Company)	D	D+	A-		Y	0
TIAA-CREF International Small-Cap Equity Fund Retail Class	TLISX	NAS CM	Open End	Global Equity Mid/Small Cap (Small Company)	D	D+	A-		Y	2,500
TIAA-CREF Intl Small-Cap Equity Fund Retmnt Cls	TTISX	NAS CM	Open End	Global Equity Mid/Small Cap (Small Company)	D	D+	A-		Y	0
TIAA-CREF Large Cap Growth Fund Advisor Class	TILHX	NAS CM	Open End	US Equity Large Cap Growth (Growth)	A-	A	A-	Up	Y	0
TIAA-CREF Large Cap Value Fund Advisor Class	TRLHX	NAS CM	Open End	US Equity Large Cap Value (Growth & Income)	B	B-	B	Up	Y	0
TIAA-CREF Large-Cap Growth Fund Institutional Class	TILGX	NAS CM	Open End	US Equity Large Cap Growth (Growth)	A-	A	A-	Up	Y	2,000,000
TIAA-CREF Large-Cap Growth Fund Premier Class	TILPX	NAS CM	Open End	US Equity Large Cap Growth (Growth)	A-	A	A-	Up	Y	0
TIAA-CREF Large-Cap Growth Fund Retail Class	TIRTX	NAS CM	Open End	US Equity Large Cap Growth (Growth)	A-	A	A-	Up	Y	2,500
TIAA-CREF Large-Cap Growth Fund Retirement Class	TILRX	NAS CM	Open End	US Equity Large Cap Growth (Growth)	A-	A	A-	Up	Y	0
TIAA-CREF Large-Cap Growth Index Fund Advisor Class	TRIHX	NAS CM	Open End	US Equity Large Cap Growth (Growth)	B+	B+	B+	Up	Y	0
TIAA-CREF Large-Cap Growth Index Fund Institutional Class	TILIX	NAS CM	Open End	US Equity Large Cap Growth (Growth)	B+	B+	B+	Up	Y	10,000,000
TIAA-CREF Large-Cap Growth Index Fund Retirement Class	TRIRX	NAS CM	Open End	US Equity Large Cap Growth (Growth)	B+	B+	B+	Up	Y	0
TIAA-CREF Large-Cap Value Fund Institutional Class	TRLIX	NAS CM	Open End	US Equity Large Cap Value (Growth & Income)	B	B-	B	Up	Y	2,000,000

★Expanded analysis of this fund is included in Section II.

	TOTAL RETURNS					PERFORMANCE				ASSETS		ASSET ALLOCATION & TURNOVER					BULL & BEAR		FEES		
Min Additional Investment	3-Month Total Return	6-Month Total Return	1-Year Total Return	3-Year Total Return	5-Year Total Return	Dividend Yield (TTM)	Expense Ratio	3-Yr Std Deviation	3-Year Beta	NAV	Total Assets (MIL)	%Cash	%Stocks	%Bonds	%Other	Turnover Ratio	Last Bull Market Total Return	Last Bear Market Total Return	Front End Fee (%)	Back End Fee (%)	Inception Date
100	6.73	15.31	37.10	28.66	21.05	1.15	0.62	15.53	0.98	11.98	2,414	0	89	1	8	30	18.37	-27.38			Aug-10
	6.67	15.25	37.18	29.19	21.79	1.26	0.48	15.59	0.98	11.96	2,414	0	89	1	8	30	18.58	-27.36			Aug-10
	3.55	9.14	25.80	24.21	50.43	2.22	0.51	11.06	0.88	8.24	1,907	1	91	0	8	100	14.14	-23.44			Dec-15
1,000	3.64	9.38	25.91	24.54	50.82	2.24	0.41	11.11	0.89	8.24	1,907	1	91	0	8	100	14.14	-23.44			Nov-07
	8.06	14.86	29.48	48.12	122.06	1.23	0.43	10.8	1	13.54	2,652	0	99	1	0	121	27.66	-15.01			Dec-15
1,000	8.12	14.91	29.65	48.32	122.37	1.24	0.34	10.76	1	13.55	2,652	0	99	1	0	121	27.66	-15.01			Nov-07
	6.01	9.80	13.87	25.92	90.65	1.95	0.43	10.44	1	10.37	2,530	1	100	1	-1	149	24.87	-18.77			Dec-15
1,000	5.99	9.77	13.96	26.02	90.81	1.96	0.34	10.46	1.01	10.37	2,530	1	100	1	-1	149	24.87	-18.77			Nov-07
	6.25	11.08	20.99	35.72	109.29	1.63	0.14	10.21	1	19.66	16,203	0	100	1	-1	9	25.73	-17.79			Dec-15
1,000	6.29	11.17	21.09	35.85	109.49	1.64	0.05	10.23	1	19.65	16,203	0	100	1	-1	9	25.73	-17.79			Jul-99
	6.28	11.12	20.92	35.20	107.94	1.54	0.2	10.24	1	19.61	16,203	0	100	1	-1	9	25.51	-17.73			Sep-09
100	6.22	11.02	20.74	34.67	106.35	1.39	0.34	10.26	1	20.02	16,203	0	100	1	-1	9	25.34	-17.79			Mar-06
	6.27	11.09	20.85	34.89	107.04	1.43	0.3	10.23	1	19.96	16,203	0	100	1	-1	9	25.53	-17.86			Mar-06
	7.33	17.00	1.01	4.48	-7.70	3.27	0.85	17.8	0.83	8.51	42.6	0	93	0	7	365					Dec-15
1,000	7.33	17.15	1.12	4.66	-7.54	3.3	0.75	17.75	0.83	8.5	42.6	0	93	0	7	365					Nov-11
	7.34	17.02	1.01	4.33	-8.19	3.17	0.9	17.79	0.84	8.51	42.6	0	93	0	7	365					Nov-11
100	7.24	16.94	0.78	3.51	-9.34	3.15	1.14	17.79	0.83	8.5	42.6	0	93	0	7	365					Nov-11
	7.20	17.03	0.88	3.97	-8.66	3.15	1	17.8	0.83	8.5	42.6	0	93	0	7	365					Nov-11
	6.83	12.07	23.91	37.98	111.34	1.01	0.5	10.68	1.03	14.3	6,850	0	99	1	0	83	26.19	-16.09			Dec-15
1,000	6.80	12.18	23.96	38.16	111.61	1.08	0.42	10.67	1.03	14.29	6,850	0	99	1	0	83	26.19	-16.09			Jul-99
	6.83	12.16	23.94	37.59	110.26	0.95	0.57	10.69	1.04	14.31	6,850	0	99	1	0	83	26.09	-16.24			Sep-09
100	6.82	12.09	23.65	36.92	108.54	0.56	0.72	10.66	1.03	19.07	6,850	0	99	1	0	83	25.93	-16.19			Mar-06
	6.84	12.07	23.77	37.13	109.17	0.85	0.67	10.62	1.03	14.54	6,850	0	99	1	0	83	26	-16.24			Oct-02
	4.42	11.98	32.74	31.31	52.03	1.15	0.56	13.16	1.02	13.29	5,124	2	91	0	7	95	18.75	-31.19			Dec-15
1,000	4.47	12.04	32.94	31.53	52.29	1.16	0.49	13.13	1.02	13.29	5,124	2	91	0	7	95	18.75	-31.19			Jul-99
	4.41	11.90	32.68	30.99	51.26	1.04	0.64	13.14	1.02	13.27	5,124	2	91	0	7	95	18.61	-31.25			Sep-09
100	4.33	11.78	32.51	30.33	49.96	1.45	0.78	13.05	1.01	8.79	5,124	2	91	0	7	95	18.53	-31.24			Mar-06
	4.38	11.85	32.61	30.54	50.48	0.92	0.74	13.13	1.02	13.78	5,124	2	91	0	7	95	18.44	-31.19			Oct-02
	3.74	9.09	25.17	25.32	46.96	2.36	0.15	11.5	0.93	20.17	11,766	1	90	1	8	11	13.47	-23.25			Dec-15
1,000	3.75	9.16	25.32	25.51	47.19	2.39	0.06	11.52	0.93	20.17	11,766	1	90	1	8	11	13.47	-23.25			Oct-02
	3.73	9.09	25.14	24.97	46.07	2.27	0.21	11.49	0.93	20.13	11,766	1	90	1	8	11	13.44	-23.28			Sep-09
	3.70	9.05	25.03	24.65	45.39	2.15	0.31	11.5	0.93	20.63	11,766	1	90	1	8	11	13.34	-23.3			Oct-02
	5.05	14.86	35.30	36.09		0.98	0.72	11.6	0.87	13.37	1,463	4	87	6	3	31					Dec-15
1,000	5.07	14.88	35.19	36.37		0.99	0.63	11.62	0.87	13.37	1,463	4	87	6	3	31					Apr-13
	5.02	14.81	35.07	35.73		0.68	0.79	11.61	0.87	13.4	1,463	4	87	6	3	31					Apr-13
100	4.96	14.69	34.74	34.68		0.62	1.09	11.62	0.87	13.37	1,463	4	87	6	3	31					Apr-13
	4.97	14.70	34.89	35.24		0.8	0.88	11.57	0.87	13.34	1,463	4	87	6	3	31					Apr-13
	5.54	14.12	34.78				0.81			12.53	960.2	2	87	3	8						Dec-16
1,000	5.57	14.15	34.93				0.72			12.53	960.2	2	87	3	8						Dec-16
	5.50	14.08	34.73				0.87			12.53	960.2	2	87	3	8						Dec-16
100	5.49	13.90	34.40				1.11			12.52	960.2	2	87	3	8						Dec-16
	5.51	14.00	34.63				0.97			12.52	960.2	2	87	3	8						Dec-16
	7.08	14.75	34.27	44.47	130.59	0.43	0.52	12.08	1.08	19.84	4,903	1	99	1	-1	86	26.63	-15.36			Dec-15
	3.93	8.31	12.45	25.68	88.41	1.58	0.52	11.72	1.11	19.04	7,137	0	100	3	-2	62	26.97	-22.95			Dec-15
1,000	7.09	14.81	34.51	44.58	130.76	0.45	0.43	12.07	1.08	19.84	4,903	1	99	1	-1	86	26.63	-15.36			Mar-06
	7.05	14.72	34.27	43.86	129.04	0.34	0.58	12.09	1.08	19.82	4,903	1	99	1	-1	86	26.5	-15.46			Sep-09
100	6.96	14.64	34.03	43.16	126.78	0.2	0.76	12.1	1.08	19.8	4,903	1	99	1	-1	86	26.29	-15.46			Mar-06
	7.01	14.72	34.11	43.31	127.58	0.18	0.68	12.07	1.08	19.74	4,903	1	99	1	-1	86	26.48	-15.49			Mar-06
	7.79	14.12	29.93	45.52	125.11	1.01	0.15	10.77	1	28.83	5,628	0	100	1	-1	22	26.54	-15.26			Dec-15
1,000	7.82	14.15	30.07	45.72	125.41	1.03	0.06	10.76	1	28.83	5,628	0	100	1	-1	22	26.54	-15.26			Oct-02
	7.76	14.05	29.78	44.59	122.61	0.84	0.31	10.76	1	29.05	5,628	0	100	1	-1	22	26.43	-15.43			Oct-02
1,000	3.94	8.32	12.52	26.06	89.98	1.59	0.41	11.75	1.11	19.04	7,137	0	100	3	-2	62	27.13	-22.87			Oct-02

	MARKET			FUND TYPE, CATEGORY & OBJECTIVE	RATINGS				MINIMUMS	
Fund Name	Ticker Symbol	Traded On	Fund Type	Category and (Prospectus Objective)	Overall Rating	Reward Rating	Risk Rating	Recent Up/ Downgrade	Open to New Investors	Min Initial Investment
TIAA-CREF Large-Cap Value Fund Premier Class	TRCPX	NAS CM	Open End	US Equity Large Cap Value (Growth & Income)	B	B-	B	Up	Y	0
TIAA-CREF Large-Cap Value Fund Retail Class	TCLCX	NAS CM	Open End	US Equity Large Cap Value (Growth & Income)	B-	B-	B	Down	Y	2,500
TIAA-CREF Large-Cap Value Fund Retirement Class	TRLCX	NAS CM	Open End	US Equity Large Cap Value (Growth & Income)	B	B-	B	Up	Y	0
TIAA-CREF Large-Cap Value Index Fund Advisor Class	THCVX	NAS CM	Open End	US Equity Large Cap Value (Growth & Income)	B	B-	B		Y	0
TIAA-CREF Large-Cap Value Index Fund Institutional Class	TILVX	NAS CM	Open End	US Equity Large Cap Value (Growth & Income)	B	B-	B		Y	10,000,000
TIAA-CREF Large-Cap Value Index Fund Retirement Class	TRCVX	NAS CM	Open End	US Equity Large Cap Value (Growth & Income)	B-	B-	B	Down	Y	0
TIAA-CREF Lifecycle 2010 Fund Advisor Class	TCLHX	NAS CM	Open End	Target Date 2000-2020 (Asset Alloc)	B-	C+	B	Up	Y	0
TIAA-CREF Lifecycle 2010 Fund Institutional Class	TCTIX	NAS CM	Open End	Target Date 2000-2020 (Asset Alloc)	B	C+	A-	Up	Y	2,000,000
TIAA-CREF Lifecycle 2010 Fund Premier Class	TCTPX	NAS CM	Open End	Target Date 2000-2020 (Asset Alloc)	B-	C+	B	Up	Y	0
TIAA-CREF Lifecycle 2010 Fund Retirement Class	TCLEX	NAS CM	Open End	Target Date 2000-2020 (Asset Alloc)	B-	C+	B	Up	Y	0
TIAA-CREF Lifecycle 2015 Fund Advisor Class	TCNHX	NAS CM	Open End	Target Date 2000-2020 (Asset Alloc)	B-	C+	B	Up	Y	0
TIAA-CREF Lifecycle 2015 Fund Institutional Class	TCNIX	NAS CM	Open End	Target Date 2000-2020 (Asset Alloc)	B-	C+	B	Up	Y	2,000,000
TIAA-CREF Lifecycle 2015 Fund Premier Class	TCFPX	NAS CM	Open End	Target Date 2000-2020 (Asset Alloc)	B-	C+	B	Up	Y	0
TIAA-CREF Lifecycle 2015 Fund Retirement Class	TCLIX	NAS CM	Open End	Target Date 2000-2020 (Asset Alloc)	B-	C+	B	Up	Y	0
TIAA-CREF Lifecycle 2020 Fund Advisor Class	TCWHX	NAS CM	Open End	Target Date 2000-2020 (Asset Alloc)	B-	C+	B	Up	Y	0
TIAA-CREF Lifecycle 2020 Fund Institutional Class	TCWIX	NAS CM	Open End	Target Date 2000-2020 (Asset Alloc)	B-	C+	B	Up	Y	2,000,000
TIAA-CREF Lifecycle 2020 Fund Premier Class	TCWPX	NAS CM	Open End	Target Date 2000-2020 (Asset Alloc)	B-	C+	B	Up	Y	0
TIAA-CREF Lifecycle 2020 Fund Retirement Class	TCLTX	NAS CM	Open End	Target Date 2000-2020 (Asset Alloc)	B-	C+	B	Up	Y	0
TIAA-CREF Lifecycle 2025 Fund Advisor Class	TCQHX	NAS CM	Open End	Target Date 2021-2045 (Asset Alloc)	B-	C+	B	Down	Y	0
TIAA-CREF Lifecycle 2025 Fund Institutional Class	TCYIX	NAS CM	Open End	Target Date 2021-2045 (Asset Alloc)	B-	C+	B	Down	Y	2,000,000
TIAA-CREF Lifecycle 2025 Fund Premier Class	TCQPX	NAS CM	Open End	Target Date 2021-2045 (Asset Alloc)	B-	C+	B	Down	Y	0
TIAA-CREF Lifecycle 2025 Fund Retirement Class	TCLFX	NAS CM	Open End	Target Date 2021-2045 (Asset Alloc)	B-	C+	B	Down	Y	0
TIAA-CREF Lifecycle 2030 Fund Advisor Class	TCHHX	NAS CM	Open End	Target Date 2021-2045 (Asset Alloc)	B-	B-	B	Down	Y	0
TIAA-CREF Lifecycle 2030 Fund Institutional Class	TCRIX	NAS CM	Open End	Target Date 2021-2045 (Asset Alloc)	B-	B-	B	Down	Y	2,000,000
TIAA-CREF Lifecycle 2030 Fund Premier Class	TCHPX	NAS CM	Open End	Target Date 2021-2045 (Asset Alloc)	B-	B-	B	Down	Y	0
TIAA-CREF Lifecycle 2030 Fund Retirement Class	TCLNX	NAS CM	Open End	Target Date 2021-2045 (Asset Alloc)	B-	B-	B	Down	Y	0
TIAA-CREF Lifecycle 2035 Fund Advisor Class	TCYHX	NAS CM	Open End	Target Date 2021-2045 (Asset Alloc)	B-	B-	B	Down	Y	0
TIAA-CREF Lifecycle 2035 Fund Institutional Class	TCIIX	NAS CM	Open End	Target Date 2021-2045 (Asset Alloc)	B-	B-	B	Down	Y	2,000,000
TIAA-CREF Lifecycle 2035 Fund Premier Class	TCYPX	NAS CM	Open End	Target Date 2021-2045 (Asset Alloc)	B-	B-	B	Down	Y	0
TIAA-CREF Lifecycle 2035 Fund Retirement Class	TCLRX	NAS CM	Open End	Target Date 2021-2045 (Asset Alloc)	B-	B-	B	Down	Y	0
TIAA-CREF Lifecycle 2040 Fund Advisor Class	TCZHX	NAS CM	Open End	Target Date 2021-2045 (Asset Alloc)	B-	B-	B-	Down	Y	0
TIAA-CREF Lifecycle 2040 Fund Institutional Class	TCOIX	NAS CM	Open End	Target Date 2021-2045 (Asset Alloc)	B-	B-	B-	Down	Y	2,000,000
TIAA-CREF Lifecycle 2040 Fund Premier Class	TCZPX	NAS CM	Open End	Target Date 2021-2045 (Asset Alloc)	B-	B-	B-	Down	Y	0
TIAA-CREF Lifecycle 2040 Fund Retirement Class	TCLOX	NAS CM	Open End	Target Date 2021-2045 (Asset Alloc)	B-	B-	B-	Down	Y	0
TIAA-CREF Lifecycle 2045 Fund Advisor Class	TTFHX	NAS CM	Open End	Target Date 2021-2045 (Asset Alloc)	B-	B	B-	Down	Y	0
TIAA-CREF Lifecycle 2045 Fund Institutional Class	TTFIX	NAS CM	Open End	Target Date 2021-2045 (Asset Alloc)	B-	B	B-	Down	Y	2,000,000
TIAA-CREF Lifecycle 2045 Fund Premier Class	TTFPX	NAS CM	Open End	Target Date 2021-2045 (Asset Alloc)	B-	B-	B-	Down	Y	0
TIAA-CREF Lifecycle 2045 Fund Retirement Class	TTFRX	NAS CM	Open End	Target Date 2021-2045 (Asset Alloc)	B-	B-	B-	Down	Y	0
TIAA-CREF Lifecycle 2050 Fund Advisor Class	TFTHX	NAS CM	Open End	Target Date 2046+ (Asset Alloc)	B-	B	B-	Down	Y	0
TIAA-CREF Lifecycle 2050 Fund Institutional Class	TFTIX	NAS CM	Open End	Target Date 2046+ (Asset Alloc)	B-	B	B-	Down	Y	2,000,000
TIAA-CREF Lifecycle 2050 Fund Premier Class	TCLPX	NAS CM	Open End	Target Date 2046+ (Asset Alloc)	B-	B	B-	Down	Y	0
TIAA-CREF Lifecycle 2050 Fund Retirement Class	TLFRX	NAS CM	Open End	Target Date 2046+ (Asset Alloc)	B-	B-	B-	Down	Y	0
TIAA-CREF Lifecycle 2055 Fund Advisor Class	TTRHX	NAS CM	Open End	Target Date 2046+ (Asset Alloc)	B	B	B-	Up	Y	0
TIAA-CREF Lifecycle 2055 Fund Institutional Class	TTRIX	NAS CM	Open End	Target Date 2046+ (Asset Alloc)	B	B	B-	Up	Y	2,000,000
TIAA-CREF Lifecycle 2055 Fund Premier Class	TTRPX	NAS CM	Open End	Target Date 2046+ (Asset Alloc)	B-	B	B-	Down	Y	0
TIAA-CREF Lifecycle 2055 Fund Retirement Class	TTRLX	NAS CM	Open End	Target Date 2046+ (Asset Alloc)	B-	B	B-	Down	Y	0
TIAA-CREF Lifecycle 2060 Fund Advisor Class	TLXHX	NAS CM	Open End	Target Date 2046+ (Asset Alloc)	C+	C+	B-	Down	Y	0
TIAA-CREF Lifecycle 2060 Fund Institutional Class	TLXNX	NAS CM	Open End	Target Date 2046+ (Asset Alloc)	C+	C+	B-	Down	Y	2,000,000
TIAA-CREF Lifecycle 2060 Fund Premier Class	TLXPX	NAS CM	Open End	Target Date 2046+ (Asset Alloc)	C+	C+	B-	Down	Y	0
TIAA-CREF Lifecycle 2060 Fund Retirement Class	TLXRX	NAS CM	Open End	Target Date 2046+ (Asset Alloc)	C+	C+	B-	Down	Y	0
TIAA-CREF Lifecycle Index 2010 Fund Advisor Class	TLTHX	NAS CM	Open End	Target Date 2000-2020 (Asset Alloc)	B-	C+	B	Up	Y	0
TIAA-CREF Lifecycle Index 2010 Fund Institutional Class	TLTIX	NAS CM	Open End	Target Date 2000-2020 (Asset Alloc)	B-	C+	B	Up	Y	10,000,000

★ Expanded analysis of this fund is included in Section II.

Min Additional Investment	TOTAL RETURNS 3-Month Total Return	6-Month Total Return	1-Year Total Return	3-Year Total Return	5-Year Total Return	PERFORMANCE Dividend Yield (TTM)	Expense Ratio	3-Yr Std Deviation	3-Year Beta	ASSETS NAV	Total Assets (MIL)	ASSET ALLOCATION & TURNOVER %Cash	%Stocks	%Bonds	%Other	Turnover Ratio	BULL & BEAR Last Bull Market Total Return	Last Bear Market Total Return	FEES Front End Fee (%)	Back End Fee (%)	Inception Date
	3.89	8.22	12.30	25.47	88.56	1.46	0.56	11.72	1.11	19	7,137	0	100	3	-2	62	26.99	-22.9			Sep-09
100	3.84	8.15	12.13	24.86	86.88	1.4	0.73	11.74	1.11	18.28	7,137	0	100	3	-2	62	26.91	-22.95			Oct-02
	3.85	8.19	12.21	25.13	87.58	1.39	0.66	11.72	1.11	18.98	7,137	0	100	3	-2	62	26.97	-22.95			Oct-02
	5.28	8.46	13.45	26.56	95.07	1.87	0.15	10.32	1	19.59	6,721	0	100	1	0	23	24.25	-18.73			Dec-15
1,000	5.32	8.56	13.62	26.69	95.27	1.88	0.06	10.32	1	19.6	6,721	0	100	1	0	23	24.25	-18.73			Oct-02
	5.20	8.39	13.30	25.70	92.89	1.68	0.31	10.35	1	19.93	6,721	0	100	1	0	23	24.12	-18.8			Oct-02
	2.67	5.88	12.74	19.52	40.82	2.29	0.46	5.08	1.22	11.62	1,260	3	40	53	5	26	13.55	-9.17			Dec-15
1,000	2.69	5.99	12.76	19.88	41.89	2.3	0.38	5.06	1.21	11.62	1,260	3	40	53	5	26	13.72	-9.09			Jan-07
	2.63	5.85	12.52	19.19	40.80	2.18	0.53	5.06	1.22	11.59	1,260	3	40	53	5	26	13.62	-9.1			Sep-09
	2.55	5.76	12.38	18.90	40.10	1.76	0.63	5.08	1.22	13.65	1,260	3	40	53	5	26	13.55	-9.17			Oct-04
	2.91	6.41	13.82	20.90	45.28	2.33	0.47	5.56	1.11	10.01	1,970	2	45	48	5	25	15.04	-11.06			Dec-15
1,000	2.94	6.44	13.85	21.29	46.44	2.34	0.39	5.5	1.1	10.01	1,970	2	45	48	5	25	15.25	-10.9			Jan-07
	2.90	6.42	13.74	20.74	45.41	2.22	0.54	5.53	1.1	9.97	1,970	2	45	48	5	25	15.19	-11.02			Sep-09
	2.87	6.35	13.64	20.41	44.68	1.71	0.64	5.56	1.11	12.33	1,970	2	45	48	5	25	15.04	-11.06			Oct-04
	3.30	7.23	15.46	22.84	51.52	2.19	0.48	6.33	1.09	10.36	3,798	2	52	42	4	21	16.81	-12.98			Dec-15
1,000	3.30	7.23	15.58	23.31	52.81	2.2	0.4	6.25	1.08	10.37	3,798	2	52	42	4	21	16.95	-12.9			Jan-07
	3.26	7.10	15.34	22.71	51.56	2.08	0.55	6.28	1.08	10.34	3,798	2	52	42	4	21	16.86	-13.02			Sep-09
	3.25	7.14	15.20	22.34	50.90	1.57	0.65	6.3	1.09	13.04	3,798	2	52	42	4	21	16.81	-12.98			Oct-04
	3.76	8.16	17.34	25.18	58.33	2.04	0.49	7.1	1.08	10.59	4,254	2	60	34	4	20	18.49	-14.94			Dec-15
1,000	3.81	8.11	17.40	25.46	59.61	2.06	0.41	7.09	1.08	10.59	4,254	2	60	34	4	20	18.62	-14.9			Jan-07
	3.77	8.10	17.18	25.03	58.40	1.95	0.56	7.11	1.09	10.55	4,254	2	60	34	4	20	18.69	-15.03			Sep-09
	3.67	8.06	17.05	24.60	57.61	1.44	0.66	7.1	1.08	13.47	4,254	2	60	34	4	20	18.49	-14.94			Oct-04
	4.25	9.07	19.18	27.36	65.03	1.93	0.5	8	1.11	10.67	4,180	2	68	26	4	20	20.17	-16.79			Dec-15
1,000	4.28	9.10	19.21	27.69	66.32	1.94	0.42	7.96	1.1	10.67	4,180	2	68	26	4	20	20.39	-16.75			Jan-07
	4.25	9.00	19.02	27.15	65.14	1.83	0.57	7.97	1.11	10.62	4,180	2	68	26	4	20	20.19	-16.78			Sep-09
	4.11	8.90	18.85	26.72	64.20	1.33	0.67	8.01	1.11	13.82	4,180	2	68	26	4	20	20.17	-16.79			Oct-04
	4.70	10.00	20.96	29.40	71.42	1.75	0.51	8.76	1.12	10.84	4,246	1	77	18	4	21	21.72	-18.57			Dec-15
1,000	4.73	10.02	21.10	29.77	72.88	1.76	0.43	8.78	1.12	10.85	4,246	1	77	18	4	21	21.94	-18.49			Jan-07
	4.69	10.01	20.88	29.20	71.56	1.65	0.58	8.78	1.12	10.82	4,246	1	77	18	4	21	21.86	-18.62			Sep-09
	4.65	9.87	20.76	28.85	70.68	1.17	0.68	8.74	1.12	14.33	4,246	1	77	18	4	21	21.72	-18.57			Oct-04
	5.03	10.91	22.78	31.37	76.23	1.59	0.52	9.56	1.15	10.96	5,272	1	85	10	4	25	22.24	-18.97			Dec-15
1,000	5.15	10.92	22.91	31.82	77.75	1.6	0.44	9.58	1.16	10.97	5,272	1	85	10	4	25	22.35	-18.83			Jan-07
	5.11	10.91	22.69	31.23	76.38	1.49	0.59	9.57	1.16	10.94	5,272	1	85	10	4	25	22.27	-18.96			Sep-09
	5.06	10.76	22.49	30.82	75.49	1.02	0.69	9.54	1.15	14.8	5,272	1	85	10	4	25	22.24	-18.97			Oct-04
	5.35	11.42	23.70	32.96	79.34	1.07	0.53	9.67	1.12	12.66	2,659	1	89	6	4	23	22.42	-18.94			Dec-15
1,000	5.36	11.35	23.61	32.89	79.24	1.08	0.45	9.68	1.12	12.65	2,659	1	89	6	4	23	22.42	-18.94			Nov-07
	5.33	11.25	23.45	32.39	77.95	0.97	0.6	9.63	1.12	12.6	2,659	1	89	6	4	23	22.2	-18.87			Sep-09
	5.24	11.18	23.40	31.97	77.07	0.9	0.7	9.64	1.12	12.57	2,659	1	89	6	4	23	22.24	-18.93			Nov-07
	5.40	11.55	24.02	33.43	79.94	1.04	0.53	9.67	1.08	12.72	1,707	1	91	5	4	22	22.33	-18.82			Dec-15
1,000	5.41	11.56	24.04	33.46	79.98	1.05	0.45	9.68	1.08	12.72	1,707	1	91	5	4	22	22.33	-18.82			Nov-07
	5.38	11.47	23.76	32.85	78.51	0.95	0.6	9.69	1.08	12.67	1,707	1	91	5	4	22	22.25	-18.84			Sep-09
	5.39	11.41	23.62	32.46	77.71	0.88	0.7	9.71	1.08	12.63	1,707	1	91	5	4	22	22.17	-18.9			Nov-07
	5.44	11.59	24.11	33.75	80.29	1.09	0.53	9.74	1.06	14.42	477.9	1	92	4	4	18	22.58	-18.89			Dec-15
1,000	5.45	11.60	24.23	33.78	80.34	1.1	0.45	9.76	1.06	14.42	477.9	1	92	4	4	18	22.58	-18.9			Apr-11
	5.50	11.59	24.06	33.31	79.14	1.01	0.6	9.73	1.06	14.38	477.9	1	92	4	4	18	22.47	-18.9			Apr-11
	5.40	11.49	23.85	32.88	78.18	0.94	0.7	9.73	1.06	14.38	477.9	1	92	4	4	18	22.54	-19			Apr-11
	5.54	11.75	24.33	34.19		1.1	0.53	9.73	1.04	11.8	62.1	1	93	3	4	79					Dec-15
1,000	5.48	11.69	24.40	34.14		1.11	0.45	9.76	1.05	11.79	62.1	1	93	3	4	79					Sep-14
	5.57	11.69	24.28	33.64		1.02	0.6	9.74	1.05	11.79	62.1	1	93	3	4	79					Sep-14
	5.49	11.61	24.20	33.27		0.97	0.7	9.77	1.05	11.78	62.1	1	93	3	4	79					Sep-14
	2.60	5.12	11.13	17.07	39.22	1.76	0.18	4.57	1.11	15.06	346.9	1	42	57	0	16	12.36	-7.55			Dec-15
1,000	2.55	5.14	11.15	17.12	39.27	1.78	0.1	4.57	1.11	15.05	346.9	1	42	57	0	16	12.36	-7.55			Sep-09

Fund Name	Ticker Symbol	Traded On	Fund Type	Category and (Prospectus Objective)	Overall Rating	Reward Rating	Risk Rating	Recent Up/ Downgrade	Open to New Investors	Min Initial Investment
	MARKET		FUND TYPE, CATEGORY & OBJECTIVE		RATINGS				MINIMUMS	
TIAA-CREF Lifecycle Index 2010 Fund Premier Class	TLTPX	NAS CM	Open End	Target Date 2000-2020 (Asset Alloc)	B-	C+	B	Up	Y	0
TIAA-CREF Lifecycle Index 2010 Fund Retirement Class	TLTRX	NAS CM	Open End	Target Date 2000-2020 (Asset Alloc)	B-	C+	B	Up	Y	0
TIAA-CREF Lifecycle Index 2015 Fund Advisor Class	TLFAX	NAS CM	Open End	Target Date 2000-2020 (Asset Alloc)	B-	C+	B	Up	Y	0
TIAA-CREF Lifecycle Index 2015 Fund Institutional Class	TLFIX	NAS CM	Open End	Target Date 2000-2020 (Asset Alloc)	B-	C+	B	Up	Y	10,000,000
TIAA-CREF Lifecycle Index 2015 Fund Premier Class	TLFPX	NAS CM	Open End	Target Date 2000-2020 (Asset Alloc)	B	C+	A-	Up	Y	0
TIAA-CREF Lifecycle Index 2015 Fund Retirement Class	TLGRX	NAS CM	Open End	Target Date 2000-2020 (Asset Alloc)	B-	C+	B	Up	Y	0
TIAA-CREF Lifecycle Index 2020 Fund Advisor Class	TLWHX	NAS CM	Open End	Target Date 2000-2020 (Asset Alloc)	B-	C+	B	Up	Y	0
TIAA-CREF Lifecycle Index 2020 Fund Institutional Class	TLWIX	NAS CM	Open End	Target Date 2000-2020 (Asset Alloc)	B-	C+	B	Up	Y	10,000,000
TIAA-CREF Lifecycle Index 2020 Fund Premier Class	TLWPX	NAS CM	Open End	Target Date 2000-2020 (Asset Alloc)	B-	C+	B	Up	Y	0
TIAA-CREF Lifecycle Index 2020 Fund Retirement Class	TLWRX	NAS CM	Open End	Target Date 2000-2020 (Asset Alloc)	B-	C+	B	Up	Y	0
TIAA-CREF Lifecycle Index 2025 Fund Advisor Class	TLQHX	NAS CM	Open End	Target Date 2021-2045 (Asset Alloc)	B-	C+	B	Up	Y	0
TIAA-CREF Lifecycle Index 2025 Fund Institutional Class	TLQIX	NAS CM	Open End	Target Date 2021-2045 (Asset Alloc)	B-	C+	B	Up	Y	10,000,000
TIAA-CREF Lifecycle Index 2025 Fund Premier Class	TLVPX	NAS CM	Open End	Target Date 2021-2045 (Asset Alloc)	B-	C+	B	Up	Y	0
TIAA-CREF Lifecycle Index 2025 Fund Retirement Class	TLQRX	NAS CM	Open End	Target Date 2021-2045 (Asset Alloc)	B-	C+	B	Up	Y	0
TIAA-CREF Lifecycle Index 2030 Fund Advisor Class	TLHHX	NAS CM	Open End	Target Date 2021-2045 (Asset Alloc)	B-	C+	B	Down	Y	0
TIAA-CREF Lifecycle Index 2030 Fund Institutional Class	TLHIX	NAS CM	Open End	Target Date 2021-2045 (Asset Alloc)	B-	C+	B	Down	Y	10,000,000
TIAA-CREF Lifecycle Index 2030 Fund Premier Class	TLHPX	NAS CM	Open End	Target Date 2021-2045 (Asset Alloc)	B-	C+	B	Down	Y	0
TIAA-CREF Lifecycle Index 2030 Fund Retirement Class	TLHRX	NAS CM	Open End	Target Date 2021-2045 (Asset Alloc)	B-	C+	B	Down	Y	0
TIAA-CREF Lifecycle Index 2035 Fund Advisor Class	TLYHX	NAS CM	Open End	Target Date 2021-2045 (Asset Alloc)	B-	B-	B	Down	Y	0
TIAA-CREF Lifecycle Index 2035 Fund Institutional Class	TLYIX	NAS CM	Open End	Target Date 2021-2045 (Asset Alloc)	B-	B-	B	Down	Y	10,000,000
TIAA-CREF Lifecycle Index 2035 Fund Premier Class	TLYPX	NAS CM	Open End	Target Date 2021-2045 (Asset Alloc)	B-	B-	B	Down	Y	0
TIAA-CREF Lifecycle Index 2035 Fund Retirement Class	TLYRX	NAS CM	Open End	Target Date 2021-2045 (Asset Alloc)	B-	B-	B	Down	Y	0
TIAA-CREF Lifecycle Index 2040 Fund Advisor Class	TLZHX	NAS CM	Open End	Target Date 2021-2045 (Asset Alloc)	B-	B-	B	Down	Y	0
TIAA-CREF Lifecycle Index 2040 Fund Institutional Class	TLZIX	NAS CM	Open End	Target Date 2021-2045 (Asset Alloc)	B-	B-	B	Down	Y	10,000,000
TIAA-CREF Lifecycle Index 2040 Fund Premier Class	TLPRX	NAS CM	Open End	Target Date 2021-2045 (Asset Alloc)	B-	B-	B	Down	Y	0
TIAA-CREF Lifecycle Index 2040 Fund Retirement Class	TLZRX	NAS CM	Open End	Target Date 2021-2045 (Asset Alloc)	B-	B-	B	Down	Y	0
TIAA-CREF Lifecycle Index 2045 Fund Advisor Class	TLMHX	NAS CM	Open End	Target Date 2021-2045 (Asset Alloc)	B-	B-	B-	Down	Y	0
TIAA-CREF Lifecycle Index 2045 Fund Institutional Class	TLXIX	NAS CM	Open End	Target Date 2021-2045 (Asset Alloc)	B-	B-	B-	Down	Y	10,000,000
TIAA-CREF Lifecycle Index 2045 Fund Premier Class	TLMPX	NAS CM	Open End	Target Date 2021-2045 (Asset Alloc)	B-	B-	B-	Down	Y	0
TIAA-CREF Lifecycle Index 2045 Fund Retirement Class	TLMRX	NAS CM	Open End	Target Date 2021-2045 (Asset Alloc)	B-	B-	B-	Down	Y	0
TIAA-CREF Lifecycle Index 2050 Fund Advisor Class	TLLHX	NAS CM	Open End	Target Date 2046+ (Asset Alloc)	B-	B-	B-	Down	Y	0
TIAA-CREF Lifecycle Index 2050 Fund Institutional Class	TLLIX	NAS CM	Open End	Target Date 2046+ (Asset Alloc)	B-	B-	B-	Down	Y	10,000,000
TIAA-CREF Lifecycle Index 2050 Fund Premier Class	TLLPX	NAS CM	Open End	Target Date 2046+ (Asset Alloc)	B-	B-	B-	Down	Y	0
TIAA-CREF Lifecycle Index 2050 Fund Retirement Class	TLLRX	NAS CM	Open End	Target Date 2046+ (Asset Alloc)	B-	B-	B-	Down	Y	0
TIAA-CREF Lifecycle Index 2055 Fund Advisor Class	TTIHX	NAS CM	Open End	Target Date 2046+ (Asset Alloc)	B-	B-	B-	Down	Y	0
TIAA-CREF Lifecycle Index 2055 Fund Institutional Class	TTIIX	NAS CM	Open End	Target Date 2046+ (Asset Alloc)	B-	B-	B-	Down	Y	10,000,000
TIAA-CREF Lifecycle Index 2055 Fund Premier Class	TTIPX	NAS CM	Open End	Target Date 2046+ (Asset Alloc)	B-	B-	B-	Down	Y	0
TIAA-CREF Lifecycle Index 2055 Fund Retirement Class	TTIRX	NAS CM	Open End	Target Date 2046+ (Asset Alloc)	B-	B-	B-	Down	Y	0
TIAA-CREF Lifecycle Index 2060 Fund Advisor Class	TVIHX	NAS CM	Open End	Target Date 2046+ (Asset Alloc)	B-	C+	B-	Up	Y	0
TIAA-CREF Lifecycle Index 2060 Fund Institutional Class	TVIIX	NAS CM	Open End	Target Date 2046+ (Asset Alloc)	B-	C+	B-	Up	Y	10,000,000
TIAA-CREF Lifecycle Index 2060 Fund Premier Class	TVIPX	NAS CM	Open End	Target Date 2046+ (Asset Alloc)	B-	C+	B-	Up	Y	0
TIAA-CREF Lifecycle Index 2060 Fund Retirement Class	TVITX	NAS CM	Open End	Target Date 2046+ (Asset Alloc)	C+	C+	B-	Down	Y	0
TIAA-CREF Lifecycle Index Retmnt Income Fund Adv Cls	TLIHX	NAS CM	Open End	Target Date 2000-2020 (Asset Alloc)	B-	C+	B	Up	Y	0
TIAA-CREF Lifecycle Index Retmnt Income Fund Inst Cls	TRILX	NAS CM	Open End	Target Date 2000-2020 (Asset Alloc)	B-	C+	B	Up	Y	10,000,000
TIAA-CREF Lifecycle Index Retmnt Income Fund Premier Cls	TLIPX	NAS CM	Open End	Target Date 2000-2020 (Asset Alloc)	B	C+	A-	Up	Y	0
TIAA-CREF Lifecycle Index Retmnt Income Fund Retmnt Cls	TRCIX	NAS CM	Open End	Target Date 2000-2020 (Asset Alloc)	B	C+	A-	Up	Y	0
TIAA-CREF Lifecycle Retirement Income Fund Advisor Class	TLRHX	NAS CM	Open End	Target Date 2000-2020 (Income)	B-	C+	B	Up	Y	0
TIAA-CREF Lifecycle Retmnt Income Fund Inst Cls	TLRIX	NAS CM	Open End	Target Date 2000-2020 (Income)	B-	C+	B	Up	Y	2,000,000
TIAA-CREF Lifecycle Retirement Income Fund Premier Class	TPILX	NAS CM	Open End	Target Date 2000-2020 (Income)	B-	C+	B	Up	Y	0
TIAA-CREF Lifecycle Retirement Income Fund Retail Class	TLRRX	NAS CM	Open End	Target Date 2000-2020 (Income)	B	C+	A-	Up	Y	2,500
TIAA-CREF Lifecycle Retirement Income Fund Retirement Cls	TLIRX	NAS CM	Open End	Target Date 2000-2020 (Income)	B-	C+	B	Up	Y	0
TIAA-CREF Lifestyle Aggressive Growth Fund Advisor Class	TSAHX	NAS CM	Open End	Aggressive Alloc (Asset Alloc)	B	B	B-	Up	Y	0

★ Expanded analysis of this fund is included in Section II.

	TOTAL RETURNS					PERFORMANCE				ASSETS		ASSET ALLOCATION & TURNOVER					BULL & BEAR		FEES		
Min Additional Investment	3-Month Total Return	6-Month Total Return	1-Year Total Return	3-Year Total Return	5-Year Total Return	Dividend Yield (TTM)	Expense Ratio	3-Yr Std Deviation	3-Year Beta	NAV	Total Assets (MIL)	%Cash	%Stocks	%Bonds	%Other	Turnover Ratio	Last Bull Market Total Return	Last Bear Market Total Return	Front End Fee (%)	Back End Fee (%)	Inception Date
	2.56	5.10	11.04	16.60	38.35	1.66	0.25	4.59	1.12	15.02	346.9	1	42	57	0	16	12.28	-7.65			Sep-09
	2.47	5.01	10.82	16.21	37.55	1.6	0.35	4.59	1.12	14.94	346.9	1	42	57	0	16	12.23	-7.66			Sep-09
	2.86	5.70	12.20	18.67	44.09	1.8	0.18	5	1	15.74	673.8	1	47	52	0	14	13.79	-9.37			Dec-15
1,000	2.81	5.65	12.22	18.63	44.05	1.82	0.1	5.04	1.01	15.73	673.8	1	47	52	0	14	13.79	-9.37			Sep-09
	2.83	5.62	12.06	18.14	42.97	1.7	0.25	5.06	1.02	15.68	673.8	1	47	52	0	14	13.61	-9.31			Sep-09
	2.78	5.51	11.97	17.70	42.26	1.64	0.35	5.06	1.02	15.63	673.8	1	47	52	0	14	13.62	-9.4			Sep-09
	3.20	6.32	13.59	20.39	50.21	1.76	0.18	5.77	1	16.6	1,468	1	53	45	0	9	15.35	-11.23			Dec-15
1,000	3.20	6.31	13.66	20.47	50.31	1.76	0.1	5.78	1	16.6	1,468	1	53	45	0	9	15.35	-11.22			Sep-09
	3.16	6.21	13.44	19.92	49.20	1.65	0.25	5.78	1	16.53	1,468	1	53	45	0	9	15.28	-11.33			Sep-09
	3.12	6.19	13.36	19.63	48.46	1.6	0.35	5.78	1	16.48	1,468	1	53	45	0	9	15.06	-11.25			Sep-09
	3.63	7.12	15.25	22.69	57.07	1.75	0.18	6.57	1.01	17.44	1,672	1	61	37	0	9	16.89	-13.11			Dec-15
1,000	3.67	7.16	15.36	22.82	57.25	1.76	0.1	6.56	1.01	17.45	1,672	1	61	37	0	9	16.89	-13.11			Sep-09
	3.62	7.13	15.21	22.27	56.06	1.65	0.25	6.58	1.01	17.39	1,672	1	61	37	0	9	16.81	-13.13			Sep-09
	3.59	7.05	15.09	21.85	55.37	1.61	0.35	6.55	1.01	17.32	1,672	1	61	37	0	9	16.75	-13.22			Sep-09
	4.05	7.90	16.96	24.87	64.10	1.75	0.18	7.37	1.03	18.32	1,729	1	69	29	1	6	18.49	-14.98			Dec-15
1,000	4.09	7.93	17.06	25.00	64.27	1.76	0.1	7.39	1.04	18.32	1,729	1	69	29	1	6	18.49	-14.98			Sep-09
	4.04	7.90	16.85	24.46	63.14	1.66	0.25	7.37	1.03	18.25	1,729	1	69	29	1	6	18.43	-15.01			Sep-09
	4.01	7.83	16.73	24.07	62.21	1.62	0.35	7.33	1.03	18.18	1,729	1	69	29	1	6	18.33	-15.03			Sep-09
	4.51	8.81	18.71	27.12	71.25	1.74	0.18	8.16	1.05	19.17	1,626	1	77	22	1	5	20.16	-16.77			Dec-15
1,000	4.52	8.82	18.72	27.22	71.38	1.75	0.1	8.14	1.05	19.18	1,626	1	77	22	1	5	20.16	-16.77			Sep-09
	4.53	8.73	18.59	26.70	70.02	1.65	0.25	8.16	1.05	19.1	1,626	1	77	22	1	5	20.1	-16.81			Sep-09
	4.44	8.66	18.43	26.25	69.11	1.61	0.35	8.16	1.05	19.02	1,626	1	77	22	1	5	20.01	-16.82			Sep-09
	4.94	9.56	20.27	29.27	76.66	1.74	0.18	8.99	1.1	19.76	1,752	1	85	14	1	5	20.73	-17.19			Dec-15
1,000	4.97	9.65	20.37	29.39	76.81	1.75	0.1	8.99	1.1	19.77	1,752	1	85	14	1	5	20.73	-17.19			Sep-09
	4.97	9.56	20.25	28.87	75.57	1.65	0.25	8.98	1.1	19.69	1,752	1	85	14	1	5	20.67	-17.23			Sep-09
	4.89	9.48	20.07	28.48	74.58	1.61	0.35	8.98	1.09	19.62	1,752	1	85	14	1	5	20.58	-17.31			Sep-09
	5.21	10.01	21.18	30.54	78.24	1.73	0.18	9.11	1.06	19.88	1,080	1	89	10	1	4	20.6	-17.09			Dec-15
1,000	5.22	10.07	21.18	30.63	78.36	1.74	0.1	9.09	1.06	19.88	1,080	1	89	10	1	4	20.6	-17.09			Sep-09
	5.17	9.98	20.99	30.03	76.98	1.64	0.25	9.11	1.06	19.8	1,080	1	89	10	1	4	20.64	-17.26			Sep-09
	5.14	9.91	20.89	29.58	76.20	1.6	0.35	9.1	1.06	19.72	1,080	1	89	10	1	4	20.54	-17.21			Sep-09
	5.29	10.13	21.36	31.01	78.95	1.73	0.18	9.13	1.02	19.95	774.8	1	90	8	1	7	20.72	-17.17			Dec-15
1,000	5.31	10.21	21.51	31.18	79.19	1.74	0.1	9.13	1.02	19.96	774.8	1	90	8	1	7	20.72	-17.17			Sep-09
	5.26	10.12	21.33	30.52	77.88	1.64	0.25	9.14	1.02	19.87	774.8	1	90	8	1	7	20.67	-17.21			Sep-09
	5.24	10.06	21.17	30.18	77.00	1.61	0.35	9.15	1.03	19.79	774.8	1	90	8	1	7	20.56	-17.29			Sep-09
	5.34	10.26	21.71	31.55	79.64	1.68	0.18	9.19	1.01	15.96	252.9	1	91	7	1	11	20.72	-17.2			Dec-15
1,000	5.35	10.34	21.71	31.66	79.80	1.69	0.1	9.15	1	15.97	252.9	1	91	7	1	11	20.72	-17.2			Apr-11
	5.31	10.24	21.54	31.06	78.60	1.6	0.25	9.18	1.01	15.94	252.9	1	91	7	1	11	20.73	-17.3			Apr-11
	5.29	10.15	21.47	30.67	77.56	1.56	0.35	9.18	1.01	15.91	252.9	1	91	7	1	11	20.65	-17.3			Apr-11
	5.46	10.38	21.84	32.14		1.74	0.18	9.19	1	12.3	44.4	1	93	6	1	36					Dec-15
1,000	5.39	10.40	21.88	32.08		1.75	0.1	9.23	1	12.29	44.4	1	93	6	1	36					Sep-14
	5.37	10.29	21.76	31.54		1.62	0.25	9.2	1	12.29	44.4	1	93	6	1	36					Sep-14
	5.31	10.23	21.60	31.10		1.62	0.35	9.24	1	12.27	44.4	1	93	6	1	36					Sep-14
	2.38	4.87	10.49	16.11	34.82	1.85	0.18	4.19	1.26	14.25	174.8	1	40	59	0	40	10.66	-5.3			Dec-15
1,000	2.45	4.87	10.49	16.18	34.92	1.88	0.1	4.18	1.26	14.25	174.8	1	40	59	0	40	10.66	-5.3			Sep-09
	2.35	4.80	10.34	15.59	33.83	1.74	0.25	4.17	1.26	14.24	174.8	1	40	59	0	40	10.49	-5.29			Sep-09
	2.39	4.75	10.24	15.32	33.21	1.65	0.35	4.18	1.26	14.23	174.8	1	40	59	0	40	10.53	-5.33			Sep-09
	2.54	5.65	12.08	18.77	37.54	2.27	0.46	4.66	1.37	11.7	520.0	3	37	55	5	21	11.85	-6.9			Dec-15
1,000	2.54	5.66	12.09	18.84	37.62	2.29	0.38	4.66	1.38	11.7	520.0	3	37	55	5	21	11.85	-6.9			Nov-07
	2.50	5.49	11.83	18.32	36.51	2.15	0.53	4.58	1.35	11.69	520.0	3	37	55	5	21	11.77	-6.96			Sep-09
100	2.39	5.44	11.74	17.88	35.87	2.06	0.63	4.65	1.37	11.68	520.0	3	37	55	5	21	11.68	-6.88			Nov-07
	2.40	5.45	11.75	17.90	35.90	2.06	0.63	4.68	1.38	11.67	520.0	3	37	55	5	21	11.73	-6.94			Nov-07
	5.61	12.07	25.47	34.36	86.52	0.69	0.64	10.55	1.06	16.59	92.1	1	97	1	1	20					Dec-15

	MARKET			FUND TYPE, CATEGORY & OBJECTIVE	RATINGS					MINIMUMS
Fund Name	Ticker Symbol	Traded On	Fund Type	Category and (Prospectus Objective)	Overall Rating	Reward Rating	Risk Rating	Recent Up/ Downgrade	Open to New Investors	Min Initial Investment
TIAA-CREF Lifestyle Aggressive Growth Fund Inst Cls	TSAIX	NAS CM	Open End	Aggressive Alloc (Asset Alloc)	B	B	B-	Up	Y	2,000,000
TIAA-CREF Lifestyle Aggressive Growth Fund Premier Class	TSAPX	NAS CM	Open End	Aggressive Alloc (Asset Alloc)	B	B	B-	Up	Y	0
TIAA-CREF Lifestyle Aggressive Growth Fund Retail Class	TSALX	NAS CM	Open End	Aggressive Alloc (Asset Alloc)	B	B	B-	Up	Y	2,500
TIAA-CREF Lifestyle Aggressive Growth Fund Retirement Cls	TSARX	NAS CM	Open End	Aggressive Alloc (Asset Alloc)	B	B	B-	Up	Y	0
TIAA-CREF Lifestyle Conservative Fund Advisor Class	TLSHX	NAS CM	Open End	Cautious Alloc (Asset Alloc)	B-	C+	B	Up	Y	0
TIAA-CREF Lifestyle Conservative Fund Institutional Class	TCSIX	NAS CM	Open End	Cautious Alloc (Asset Alloc)	B-	C+	B	Up	Y	2,000,000
TIAA-CREF Lifestyle Conservative Fund Premier Class	TLSPX	NAS CM	Open End	Cautious Alloc (Asset Alloc)	B-	C+	B	Up	Y	0
TIAA-CREF Lifestyle Conservative Fund Retail Class	TSCLX	NAS CM	Open End	Cautious Alloc (Asset Alloc)	B	C+	A-	Up	Y	2,500
TIAA-CREF Lifestyle Conservative Fund Retirement Class	TSCTX	NAS CM	Open End	Cautious Alloc (Asset Alloc)	B-	C+	B	Up	Y	0
TIAA-CREF Lifestyle Growth Fund Advisor Class	TSGHX	NAS CM	Open End	Aggressive Alloc (Asset Alloc)	B-	B-	B	Down	Y	0
TIAA-CREF Lifestyle Growth Fund Institutional Class	TSGGX	NAS CM	Open End	Aggressive Alloc (Asset Alloc)	B-	B-	B	Down	Y	2,000,000
TIAA-CREF Lifestyle Growth Fund Premier Class	TSGPX	NAS CM	Open End	Aggressive Alloc (Asset Alloc)	B-	B-	B	Down	Y	0
TIAA-CREF Lifestyle Growth Fund Retail Class	TSGLX	NAS CM	Open End	Aggressive Alloc (Asset Alloc)	B-	B-	B	Down	Y	2,500
TIAA-CREF Lifestyle Growth Fund Retirement Class	TSGRX	NAS CM	Open End	Aggressive Alloc (Asset Alloc)	B-	B-	B	Down	Y	0
TIAA-CREF Lifestyle Income Fund Advisor Class	TSIHX	NAS CM	Open End	Cautious Alloc (Asset Alloc)	B	C	A	Up	Y	0
TIAA-CREF Lifestyle Income Fund Institutional Class	TSITX	NAS CM	Open End	Cautious Alloc (Asset Alloc)	B	C	A	Up	Y	2,000,000
TIAA-CREF Lifestyle Income Fund Premier Class	TSIPX	NAS CM	Open End	Cautious Alloc (Asset Alloc)	B	C	A	Up	Y	0
TIAA-CREF Lifestyle Income Fund Retail Class	TSILX	NAS CM	Open End	Cautious Alloc (Asset Alloc)	B	C	A	Up	Y	2,500
TIAA-CREF Lifestyle Income Fund Retirement Class	TLSRX	NAS CM	Open End	Cautious Alloc (Asset Alloc)	B	C	A	Up	Y	0
TIAA-CREF Lifestyle Moderate Fund Advisor Class	TSMHX	NAS CM	Open End	Moderate Alloc (Asset Alloc)	B-	C+	B	Up	Y	0
TIAA-CREF Lifestyle Moderate Fund Institutional Class	TSIMX	NAS CM	Open End	Moderate Alloc (Asset Alloc)	B-	C+	B	Down	Y	2,000,000
TIAA-CREF Lifestyle Moderate Fund Premier Class	TSMPX	NAS CM	Open End	Moderate Alloc (Asset Alloc)	B-	C+	B	Down	Y	0
TIAA-CREF Lifestyle Moderate Fund Retail Class	TSMLX	NAS CM	Open End	Moderate Alloc (Asset Alloc)	B-	C+	B	Up	Y	2,500
TIAA-CREF Lifestyle Moderate Fund Retirement Class	TSMTX	NAS CM	Open End	Moderate Alloc (Asset Alloc)	B-	C+	B	Down	Y	0
TIAA-CREF Managed Allocation Fund Institutional Class	TIMIX	NAS CM	Open End	Moderate Alloc (Growth)	B-	C+	B	Up	Y	2,000,000
TIAA-CREF Managed Allocation Fund Retail Class	TIMRX	NAS CM	Open End	Moderate Alloc (Growth)	B-	C+	B	Up	Y	2,500
TIAA-CREF Managed Allocation Fund Retirement Class	TITRX	NAS CM	Open End	Moderate Alloc (Growth)	B-	C+	B	Up	Y	0
TIAA-CREF Mid-Cap Growth Fund Advisor Class	TCMHX	NAS CM	Open End	US Equity Mid Cap (Growth & Income)	B-	B	C+	Up	Y	0
TIAA-CREF Mid-Cap Growth Fund Institutional Class	TRPWX	NAS CM	Open End	US Equity Mid Cap (Growth & Income)	B	B	B	Up	Y	2,000,000
TIAA-CREF Mid-Cap Growth Fund Premier Class	TRGPX	NAS CM	Open End	US Equity Mid Cap (Growth & Income)	B	B	B	Up	Y	0
TIAA-CREF Mid-Cap Growth Fund Retail Class	TCMGX	NAS CM	Open End	US Equity Mid Cap (Growth & Income)	B	B	B	Up	Y	2,500
TIAA-CREF Mid-Cap Growth Fund Retirement Class	TRGMX	NAS CM	Open End	US Equity Mid Cap (Growth & Income)	B	B	B	Up	Y	0
TIAA-CREF Mid-Cap Value Fund Advisor Class	TRVHX	NAS CM	Open End	US Equity Mid Cap (Growth & Income)	B-	B-	B	Down	Y	0
TIAA-CREF Mid-Cap Value Fund Institutional Class	TIMVX	NAS CM	Open End	US Equity Mid Cap (Growth & Income)	B-	B-	B	Down	Y	2,000,000
TIAA-CREF Mid-Cap Value Fund Premier Class	TRVPX	NAS CM	Open End	US Equity Mid Cap (Growth & Income)	B-	B-	B	Down	Y	0
TIAA-CREF Mid-Cap Value Fund Retail Class	TCMVX	NAS CM	Open End	US Equity Mid Cap (Growth & Income)	B-	C+	B		Y	2,500
TIAA-CREF Mid-Cap Value Fund Retirement Class	TRVRX	NAS CM	Open End	US Equity Mid Cap (Growth & Income)	B-	C+	B		Y	0
TIAA-CREF Real Estate Securities Fund Advisor Class	TIRHX	NAS CM	Open End	Real Estate Sector Equity (Real Estate)	B	B-	B+	Up	Y	0
TIAA-CREF Real Estate Securities Fund Institutional Class	TIREX	NAS CM	Open End	Real Estate Sector Equity (Real Estate)	B	B-	B+	Up	Y	2,000,000
TIAA-CREF Real Estate Securities Fund Premier Class	TRRPX	NAS CM	Open End	Real Estate Sector Equity (Real Estate)	B	B-	B+	Up	Y	0
TIAA-CREF Real Estate Securities Fund Retail Class	TCREX	NAS CM	Open End	Real Estate Sector Equity (Real Estate)	B	B-	B+	Up	Y	2,500
TIAA-CREF Real Estate Securities Fund Retirement Class	TRRSX	NAS CM	Open End	Real Estate Sector Equity (Real Estate)	B	B-	B+	Up	Y	0
TIAA-CREF S&P 500 Index Fund Advisor Class	TISAX	NAS CM	Open End	US Equity Large Cap Blend (Growth)	B	B	B		Y	0
TIAA-CREF S&P 500 Index Fund Institutional Class	TISPX	NAS CM	Open End	US Equity Large Cap Blend (Growth)	B	B	B		Y	10,000,000
TIAA-CREF S&P 500 Index Fund Retirement Class	TRSPX	NAS CM	Open End	US Equity Large Cap Blend (Growth)	B	B	B		Y	0
TIAA-CREF Small/Mid-Cap Equity Fund Advisor Class	TSMNX	NAS CM	Open End	US Equity Small Cap (Growth)	D	C	B+		Y	0
TIAA-CREF Small/Mid-Cap Equity Fund Institutional Class	TSMWX	NAS CM	Open End	US Equity Small Cap (Growth)	D	C	B+		Y	2,000,000
TIAA-CREF Small/Mid-Cap Equity Fund Premier Class	TSMMX	NAS CM	Open End	US Equity Small Cap (Growth)	D	C	B+		Y	0
TIAA-CREF Small/Mid-Cap Equity Fund Retail Class	TSMEX	NAS CM	Open End	US Equity Small Cap (Growth)	D	C	B+		Y	2,500
TIAA-CREF Small/Mid-Cap Equity Fund Retirement Class	TSMOX	NAS CM	Open End	US Equity Small Cap (Growth)	D	C	B+		Y	0
TIAA-CREF Small-Cap Blend Index Fund Advisor Class	TRHBX	NAS CM	Open End	US Equity Small Cap (Growth)	B+	A-	B	Up	Y	0
TIAA-CREF Small-Cap Blend Index Fund Institutional Class	TISBX	NAS CM	Open End	US Equity Small Cap (Growth)	B+	A-	B	Up	Y	10,000,000

★Expanded analysis of this fund is included in Section II.

Min Additional Investment	TOTAL RETURNS 3-Month Total Return	6-Month Total Return	1-Year Total Return	3-Year Total Return	5-Year Total Return	PERFORMANCE Dividend Yield (TTM)	Expense Ratio	3-Yr Std Deviation	3-Year Beta	ASSETS NAV	Total Assets (MIL)	ASSET ALLOCATION & TURNOVER %Cash	%Stocks	%Bonds	%Other	Turnover Ratio	BULL & BEAR Last Bull Market Total Return	Last Bear Market Total Return	FEES Front End Fee (%)	Back End Fee (%)	Inception Date
1,000	5.63	12.17	25.58	34.49	86.72	0.7	0.56	10.57	1.06	16.6	92.1	1	97	1	1	20					Dec-11
	5.54	12.05	25.32	34.00	85.35	0.4	0.71	10.56	1.06	16.64	92.1	1	97	1	1	20					Dec-11
100	5.52	11.94	25.19	33.21	83.68	0.46	0.88	10.57	1.06	16.54	92.1	1	97	1	1	20					Dec-11
	5.58	11.98	25.23	33.52	84.40	0.52	0.81	10.57	1.06	16.56	92.1	1	97	1	1	20					Dec-11
	2.52	5.61	12.19	18.69	38.31	2.12	0.54	4.61	1.06	12.6	211.3	4	40	54	2	15					Dec-15
1,000	2.44	5.62	12.12	18.67	38.28	2.14	0.46	4.57	1.05	12.59	211.3	4	40	54	2	15					Dec-11
	2.40	5.53	11.94	18.10	37.19	2	0.61	4.58	1.06	12.6	211.3	4	40	54	2	15					Dec-11
100	2.37	5.48	11.93	17.74	36.51	1.9	0.73	4.57	1.05	12.58	211.3	4	40	54	2	15					Dec-11
	2.38	5.49	11.86	17.81	36.54	1.91	0.71	4.58	1.06	12.58	211.3	4	40	54	2	15					Dec-11
	4.56	10.01	21.23	29.61	70.15	1.03	0.61	8.57	1.03	15.52	136.8	2	79	18	1	22					Dec-15
1,000	4.61	10.06	21.38	29.90	70.53	1.05	0.53	8.55	1.03	15.53	136.8	2	79	18	1	22					Dec-11
	4.53	9.98	21.10	29.15	69.04	0.76	0.68	8.62	1.04	15.54	136.8	2	79	18	1	22					Dec-11
100	4.58	9.91	20.99	28.70	68.01	0.83	0.82	8.59	1.04	15.47	136.8	2	79	18	1	22					Dec-11
	4.55	9.94	21.01	28.87	68.26	0.87	0.78	8.61	1.04	15.49	136.8	2	79	18	1	22					Dec-11
	1.34	3.29	7.41	12.76	23.11	2.27	0.51	2.66	0.87	11.14	68.7	5	21	72	2	18					Dec-15
1,000	1.25	3.30	7.43	12.72	23.06	2.28	0.43	2.68	0.87	11.14	68.7	5	21	72	2	18					Dec-11
	1.30	3.22	7.36	12.23	22.17	2.14	0.58	2.64	0.86	11.16	68.7	5	21	72	2	18					Dec-11
100	1.28	3.16	7.14	11.79	21.35	2.02	0.71	2.64	0.86	11.14	68.7	5	21	72	2	18					Dec-11
	1.28	3.17	7.27	11.87	21.53	2.05	0.68	2.66	0.87	11.14	68.7	5	21	72	2	18					Dec-11
	3.49	7.88	16.92	24.63	54.86	1.98	0.58	6.67	1.06	14.12	307.7	2	60	36	2	19					Dec-15
1,000	3.58	7.93	17.00	24.78	55.05	2.04	0.5	6.65	1.06	14.12	307.7	2	60	36	2	19					Dec-11
	3.54	7.82	16.79	24.31	54.00	1.84	0.65	6.65	1.06	14.16	307.7	2	60	36	2	19					Dec-11
100	3.52	7.80	16.71	23.91	53.07	1.8	0.77	6.66	1.07	14.11	307.7	2	60	36	2	19					Dec-11
	3.52	7.81	16.73	23.89	53.12	1.82	0.75	6.64	1.06	14.11	307.7	2	60	36	2	19					Dec-11
1,000	3.66	7.99	17.07	25.35	56.29	2.22	0.4	6.58	1.06	12.85	865.4	2	60	37	1	21	16.67	-12.09			Mar-06
100	3.59	7.83	16.63	24.34	54.17	1.99	0.65	6.57	1.05	12.88	865.4	2	60	37	1	21	16.47	-12.16			Mar-06
	3.60	7.87	16.71	24.35	54.17	2	0.65	6.59	1.06	12.83	865.4	2	60	37	1	21	16.41	-12.12			Mar-06
	5.52	11.65	26.13	27.11	91.64	0.4	0.56	11.81	1.04	22.53	1,638	3	97	3	-3	69	29.96	-24.1			Dec-15
1,000	5.54	11.67	26.21	27.20	91.79	0.41	0.47	11.79	1.04	22.53	1,638	3	97	3	-3	69	29.96	-24.1			Oct-02
	5.54	11.65	26.04	26.65	90.41	0.28	0.62	11.82	1.05	22.41	1,638	3	97	3	-3	69	29.87	-24.15			Sep-09
100	5.48	11.54	25.80	26.02	88.84	0.16	0.78	11.82	1.05	21.89	1,638	3	97	3	-3	69	29.62	-24.17			Oct-02
	5.48	11.58	25.89	26.25	89.50	0.21	0.72	11.82	1.05	21.91	1,638	3	97	3	-3	69	29.8	-24.2			Oct-02
	3.80	6.58	10.94	22.15	87.70	1.55	0.49	10.57	0.99	23.44	4,560	0	99	1	0	43	25.96	-21.16			Dec-15
1,000	3.85	6.71	11.12	22.32	87.96	1.56	0.41	10.56	0.99	23.45	4,560	0	99	1	0	43	25.96	-21.16			Oct-02
	3.81	6.64	10.96	21.74	86.52	1.44	0.56	10.54	0.99	23.41	4,560	0	99	1	0	43	25.83	-21.2			Sep-09
100	3.80	6.56	10.78	21.24	85.16	1.34	0.71	10.56	0.99	22.88	4,560	0	99	1	0	43	25.72	-21.2			Oct-02
	3.76	6.55	10.79	21.38	85.61	1.36	0.66	10.56	0.99	23.32	4,560	0	99	1	0	43	25.74	-21.22			Oct-02
	3.76	5.21	12.16	20.53	61.13	1.7	0.6	12.51	0.97	15.56	2,144	1	98	0	1	52	32.49	-17.14			Dec-15
1,000	3.80	5.30	12.29	20.79	61.48	1.79	0.51	12.49	0.97	15.55	2,144	1	98	0	1	52	32.49	-17.14			Oct-02
	3.70	5.22	12.11	20.23	60.35	1.64	0.66	12.48	0.97	15.56	2,144	1	98	0	1	52	32.37	-17.28			Sep-09
100	3.75	5.18	11.97	19.76	59.11	1.52	0.82	12.5	0.97	15.44	2,144	1	98	0	1	52	32.09	-17.24			Oct-02
	3.72	5.16	12.01	19.88	59.53	1.49	0.76	12.47	0.97	16.19	2,144	1	98	0	1	52	32.28	-17.25			Oct-02
	6.54	11.29	21.59	36.41	110.65	1.59	0.15	10.08	1	29.59	4,838	0	99	0	0	8	25.03	-16.26			Dec-15
1,000	6.62	11.41	21.77	36.64	111.01	1.61	0.05	10.08	1	29.61	4,838	0	99	0	0	8	25.03	-16.26			Oct-02
	6.54	11.24	21.45	35.62	108.35	1.44	0.3	10.07	1	29.44	4,838	0	99	0	0	8	24.77	-16.33			Oct-02
	7.08	12.92	19.65			0.15	0.6			12.17	695.7	0	99	3	-2						Aug-16
1,000	7.08	12.91	19.63			0.18	0.51			12.18	695.7	0	99	3	-2						Aug-16
	7.04	12.78	19.50			0.13	0.66			12.17	695.7	0	99	3	-2						Aug-16
100	7.01	12.66	19.17			0.1	0.9			12.15	695.7	0	99	3	-2						Aug-16
	6.98	12.72	19.33			0.13	0.76			12.16	695.7	0	99	3	-2						Aug-16
	3.36	9.22	14.72	32.76	99.45	1.34	0.15	14.12	1	21.28	2,491	0	99	9	-9	22	27.94	-25.08			Dec-15
1,000	3.36	9.26	14.82	32.89	99.65	1.35	0.06	14.11	1	21.28	2,491	0	99	9	-9	22	27.94	-25.08			Oct-02

	MARKET		FUND TYPE, CATEGORY & OBJECTIVE		RATINGS				MINIMUMS	
Fund Name	Ticker Symbol	Traded On	Fund Type	Category and (Prospectus Objective)	Overall Rating	Reward Rating	Risk Rating	Recent Up/ Downgrade	Open to New Investors	Min Initial Investment
TIAA-CREF Small-Cap Blend Index Fund Retirement Class	TRBIX	NAS CM	Open End	US Equity Small Cap (Growth)	B+	A-	B	Up	Y	0
TIAA-CREF Small-Cap Equity Fund Advisor Class	TSCHX	NAS CM	Open End	US Equity Small Cap (Small Company)	B+	A-	B	Up	Y	0
TIAA-CREF Small-Cap Equity Fund Institutional Class	TISEX	NAS CM	Open End	US Equity Small Cap (Small Company)	B+	A-	B	Up	Y	2,000,000
TIAA-CREF Small-Cap Equity Fund Premier Class	TSRPX	NAS CM	Open End	US Equity Small Cap (Small Company)	B+	A-	B	Up	Y	0
TIAA-CREF Small-Cap Equity Fund Retail Class	TCSEX	NAS CM	Open End	US Equity Small Cap (Small Company)	B+	A-	B	Up	Y	2,500
TIAA-CREF Small-Cap Equity Fund Retirement Class	TRSEX	NAS CM	Open End	US Equity Small Cap (Small Company)	B+	A-	B	Up	Y	0
TIAA-CREF Social Choice Equity Fund Advisor Class	TICHX	NAS CM	Open End	US Equity Large Cap Blend (Growth)	B-	B	B-	Down	Y	0
TIAA-CREF Social Choice Equity Fund Institutional Class	TISCX	NAS CM	Open End	US Equity Large Cap Blend (Growth)	B-	B	B-	Down	Y	2,000,000
TIAA-CREF Social Choice Equity Fund Premier Class	TRPSX	NAS CM	Open End	US Equity Large Cap Blend (Growth)	B-	B	B-	Down	Y	0
TIAA-CREF Social Choice Equity Fund Retail Class	TICRX	NAS CM	Open End	US Equity Large Cap Blend (Growth)	B-	B	B-	Down	Y	2,500
TIAA-CREF Social Choice Equity Fund Retirement Class	TRSCX	NAS CM	Open End	US Equity Large Cap Blend (Growth)	B-	B	B-	Down	Y	0
TIAA-CREF Social Choice Intl Equity Fund Adv Cls	TSOHX	NAS CM	Open End	Global Equity Large Cap (Foreign Stock)	C	C+	B	Up	Y	0
TIAA-CREF Social Choice Intl Equity Fund Inst Cls	TSONX	NAS CM	Open End	Global Equity Large Cap (Foreign Stock)	C	C+	B	Up	Y	2,000,000
TIAA-CREF Social Choice Intl Equity Fund Premier Cls	TSOPX	NAS CM	Open End	Global Equity Large Cap (Foreign Stock)	C	C+	B	Up	Y	0
TIAA-CREF Social Choice Intl Equity Fund Retail Cls	TSORX	NAS CM	Open End	Global Equity Large Cap (Foreign Stock)	C	C+	B	Up	Y	2,500
TIAA-CREF Social Choice Intl Equity Fund Retmnt Cls	TSOEX	NAS CM	Open End	Global Equity Large Cap (Foreign Stock)	C	C+	B	Up	Y	0
TIAA-CREF Social Choice Low Carbon Equity Fund Advisor Cls	TCCHX	NAS CM	Open End	US Equity Large Cap Blend (Growth)	C	C+	B+	Up	Y	0
TIAA-CREF Social Choice Low Carbon Equity Fund Inst Cls	TNWCX	NAS CM	Open End	US Equity Large Cap Blend (Growth)	C	C+	B+	Up	Y	2,000,000
TIAA-CREF Social Choice Low Carbon Equity Fund Premier Cls	TPWCX	NAS CM	Open End	US Equity Large Cap Blend (Growth)	C	C+	B+	Up	Y	0
TIAA-CREF Social Choice Low Carbon Equity Fund Retail Cls	TLWCX	NAS CM	Open End	US Equity Large Cap Blend (Growth)	C	C+	B+	Up	Y	2,500
TIAA-CREF Social Choice Low Carbon Equity Fund Retmnt Cls	TEWCX	NAS CM	Open End	US Equity Large Cap Blend (Growth)	C	C+	B+	Up	Y	0
Timothy Aggressive Growth Fund Class A	TAAGX	NAS CM	Open End	US Equity Mid Cap (Aggr Growth)	C+	C+	C+	Up	Y	1,000
Timothy Aggressive Growth Fund Class C	TCAGX	NAS CM	Open End	US Equity Mid Cap (Aggr Growth)	C+	C+	C+	Up	Y	1,000
Timothy Plan Aggressive Growth Fund Class I	TIAGX	NAS CM	Open End	US Equity Mid Cap (Aggr Growth)	C+	C+	C+	Up	Y	100,000
Timothy Plan Conservative Growth Fund Class A	TCGAX	NAS CM	Open End	Cautious Alloc (Growth)	C+	C	B	Up	Y	1,000
Timothy Plan Conservative Growth Fund Class C	TCVCX	NAS CM	Open End	Cautious Alloc (Growth)	C+	C	B		Y	1,000
Timothy Plan Defensive Strategies Fund Class A	TPDAX	NAS CM	Open End	Moderate Alloc (Growth)	C	C	C	Up	Y	1,000
Timothy Plan Defensive Strategies Fund Class C	TPDCX	NAS CM	Open End	Moderate Alloc (Growth)	C	C	C	Up	Y	1,000
Timothy Plan Defensive Strategies Fund Class I	TPDIX	NAS CM	Open End	Moderate Alloc (Growth)	C	C	C		Y	100,000
Timothy Plan Emerging Markets Class A	TPEMX	NAS CM	Open End	Emerging Markets Equity (Div Emerging Mkts)	C	C+	C		Y	1,000
Timothy Plan Emerging Markets Class C	TPECX	NAS CM	Open End	Emerging Markets Equity (Div Emerging Mkts)	C	C	C		Y	1,000
Timothy Plan Emerging Markets Fund Class I	TIEMX	NAS CM	Open End	Emerging Markets Equity (Div Emerging Mkts)	C	C+	C		Y	100,000
Timothy Plan Growth & Income Fund Class A	TGIAX	NAS CM	Open End	Moderate Alloc (Growth & Income)	C+	C	B	Up	Y	1,000
Timothy Plan Growth & Income Fund Class C	TGCIX	NAS CM	Open End	Moderate Alloc (Growth & Income)	C+	C	B	Up	Y	1,000
Timothy Plan Growth & Income Fund Class I	TIGIX	NAS CM	Open End	Moderate Alloc (Growth & Income)	C+	C	B	Up	Y	100,000
Timothy Plan International Fund Class A	TPIAX	NAS CM	Open End	Global Equity Large Cap (Foreign Stock)	C+	C+	C+	Up	Y	1,000
Timothy Plan International Fund Class C	TPICX	NAS CM	Open End	Global Equity Large Cap (Foreign Stock)	B-	C+	B	Up	Y	1,000
Timothy Plan International Fund Class I	TPIIX	NAS CM	Open End	Global Equity Large Cap (Foreign Stock)	C+	C+	C+	Up	Y	100,000
Timothy Plan Israel Common Values Fund Class A	TPAIX	NAS CM	Open End	Other Equity (Growth)	B	B+	B	Up	Y	1,000
Timothy Plan Israel Common Values Fund Class C	TPCIX	NAS CM	Open End	Other Equity (Growth)	B	B	B	Up	Y	1,000
Timothy Plan Israel Common Values Fund Class I	TICIX	NAS CM	Open End	Other Equity (Growth)	B	B+	B	Up	Y	100,000
Timothy Plan Large/Mid Cap Growth Fund Class A	TLGAX	NAS CM	Open End	US Equity Large Cap Growth (Growth)	B	B-	B	Up	Y	1,000
Timothy Plan Large/Mid Cap Growth Fund Class C	TLGCX	NAS CM	Open End	US Equity Large Cap Growth (Growth)	B-	C+	B	Down	Y	1,000
Timothy Plan Large/Mid Cap Growth Fund Class I	TPLIX	NAS CM	Open End	US Equity Large Cap Growth (Growth)	B	B-	B	Up	Y	100,000
Timothy Plan Large/Mid Cap Value Fund Class A	TLVAX	NAS CM	Open End	US Equity Mid Cap (Growth)	B	C+	B+	Up	Y	1,000
Timothy Plan Large/Mid Cap Value Fund Class C	TLVCX	NAS CM	Open End	US Equity Mid Cap (Growth)	B	C+	B	Up	Y	1,000
Timothy Plan Large/Mid Cap Value Fund Class I	TMVIX	NAS CM	Open End	US Equity Mid Cap (Growth)	B	B-	B+	Up	Y	100,000
Timothy Plan Smal Cap Value Fund Class C	TSVCX	NAS CM	Open End	US Equity Small Cap (Growth)	B	B	B	Up	Y	1,000
Timothy Plan Small Cap Value Fund Class A	TPLNX	NAS CM	Open End	US Equity Small Cap (Growth)	B+	A-	B	Up	Y	1,000
Timothy Plan Small Cap Value Fund Class I	TPVIX	NAS CM	Open End	US Equity Small Cap (Growth)	B+	A-	B	Up	Y	100,000
Timothy Plan Strategic Growth Fund Class A	TSGAX	NAS CM	Open End	Moderate Alloc (Growth)	C+	C+	B-	Up	Y	1,000
Timothy Plan Strategic Growth Fund Class C	TSGCX	NAS CM	Open End	Moderate Alloc (Growth)	B-	C	B	Up	Y	1,000

★ Expanded analysis of this fund is included in Section II.

	TOTAL RETURNS					PERFORMANCE				ASSETS		ASSET ALLOCATION & TURNOVER					BULL & BEAR		FEES		
Min Additional Investment	3-Month Total Return	6-Month Total Return	1-Year Total Return	3-Year Total Return	5-Year Total Return	Dividend Yield (TTM)	Expense Ratio	3-Yr Std Deviation	3-Year Beta	NAV	Total Assets (MIL)	%Cash	%Stocks	%Bonds	%Other	Turnover Ratio	Last Bull Market Total Return	Last Bear Market Total Return	Front End Fee (%)	Back End Fee (%)	Inception Date
	3.30	9.14	14.55	31.92	97.28	1.16	0.31	14.11	1	21.38	2,491	0	99	9	-9	22	27.79	-25.16			Oct-02
	3.97	9.95	14.90	36.99	110.87	0.77	0.51	13.95	0.98	19.08	3,938	2	97	3	-2	86	28.53	-25.74			Dec-15
1,000	4.03	10.01	15.01	37.14	111.10	0.79	0.42	13.94	0.98	19.1	3,938	2	97	3	-2	86	28.53	-25.74			Oct-02
	3.99	9.94	14.85	36.53	109.48	0.68	0.57	13.96	0.98	19	3,938	2	97	3	-2	86	28.43	-25.79			Sep-09
100	3.97	9.87	14.72	35.88	107.64	0.6	0.73	13.92	0.97	18.44	3,938	2	97	3	-2	86	28.15	-25.81			Oct-02
	3.97	9.87	14.74	36.06	108.41	0.62	0.67	13.96	0.98	18.63	3,938	2	97	3	-2	86	28.3	-25.83			Oct-02
	6.22	10.88	20.90	32.67	103.54	1.91	0.28	10.32	1	19.18	2,979	1	98	1	0	16	23.79	-17.52			Dec-15
1,000	6.19	10.85	20.92	32.63	103.48	1.92	0.19	10.31	1	19.18	2,979	1	98	1	0	16	23.79	-17.52			Jul-99
	6.14	10.76	20.79	32.05	101.92	1.81	0.34	10.29	1	19.13	2,979	1	98	1	0	16	23.68	-17.57			Sep-09
100	6.11	10.69	20.57	31.58	100.60	1.75	0.46	10.33	1	17.24	2,979	1	98	1	0	16	23.54	-17.55			Mar-06
	6.12	10.72	20.63	31.70	100.94	1.69	0.44	10.31	1	19.48	2,979	1	98	1	0	16	23.61	-17.67			Oct-02
	3.37	8.79	24.45			2.07	0.48			11.18	53.3	3	90	1	6	13					Dec-15
1,000	3.43	8.85	24.52			2.09	0.4			11.18	53.3	3	90	1	6	13					Aug-15
	3.29	8.71	24.25			1.97	0.55			11.17	53.3	3	90	1	6	13					Aug-15
100	3.27	8.69	24.10			1.8	0.72			11.17	53.3	3	90	1	6	13					Aug-15
	3.34	8.67	24.21			1.94	0.65			11.16	53.3	3	90	1	6	13					Aug-15
	5.66	10.35	20.75			1.84	0.41			12.66	95.0	3	94	0	3	83					Dec-15
1,000	5.66	10.44	20.86			1.86	0.32			12.65	95.0	3	94	0	3	83					Aug-15
	5.59	10.35	20.63			1.56	0.47			12.68	95.0	3	94	0	3	83					Aug-15
100	5.60	10.30	20.49			1.61	0.65			12.64	95.0	3	94	0	3	83					Aug-15
	5.64	10.24	20.55			1.73	0.57			12.63	95.0	3	94	0	3	83					Aug-15
	2.95	9.15	19.11	11.27	63.70	0	1.73	13.41	1.11	8.35	28.3	3	97	0	0	151	31.59	-22.09	5.50		Oct-00
	2.82	8.63	18.08	8.70	57.61	0	2.48	13.37	1.1	6.92	28.3	3	97	0	0	151	31.1	-22.44		1.00	Feb-04
25,000	3.04	9.30	19.49	12.09	65.35	0	1.48	13.44	1.11	8.46	28.3	3	97	0	0	151	31.59	-22.09			Aug-13
	1.99	5.05	8.29	9.46	23.21	0	2.3	4.32	0.65	10.85	54.5	12	49	37	2	27	12.64	-10.75	5.50		Oct-00
	1.77	4.66	7.49	7.10	18.62	0	3.05	4.34	0.66	9.91	54.5	12	49	37	2	27	12.13	-11.01		1.00	Feb-04
	2.68	5.64	4.14	4.01	0.79	0.32	1.49	6.23	0.97	11.69	59.2	8	44	32	16	51	12.68	-7.08	5.50		Nov-09
	2.47	5.16	3.32	1.63	-3.01	0	2.21	6.24	0.97	11.19	59.2	8	44	32	16	51	12.09	-7.35		1.00	Nov-09
25,000	2.71	5.77	4.45	4.79	1.93	0.58	1.32	6.24	0.97	11.67	59.2	8	44	32	16	51	12.68	-7.08			Aug-13
	2.43	11.24	24.43	18.51	8.11	0.4	2.6	18.85	1.09	9.9	20.8	13	86	0	2	31			5.50		Dec-12
	2.21	10.73	23.43	15.90	4.11	0	3.38	18.81	1.09	9.67	20.8	13	86	0	2	31				1.00	Dec-12
25,000	2.49	11.37	24.65	19.40	9.33	0.57	2.44	18.88	1.09	9.95	20.8	13	86	0	2	31					Aug-13
	1.88	6.22	6.29	4.26		0.07	1.6	4.96		11.22	35.9	2	47	50	0	118			5.50		Oct-13
	1.66	5.70	5.50	1.94		0	2.33	4.94		10.9	35.9	2	47	50	0	118				1.00	Oct-13
25,000	1.97	6.37	6.60	5.16		0.26	1.33	4.94		11.29	35.9	2	47	50	0	118					Oct-13
	4.22	11.69	23.64	19.30	43.01	0.87	1.71	9.18	0.7	10.07	98.5	5	95	0	0	42	16.04	-27.17	5.50		May-07
	4.05	11.27	22.67	16.68	37.86	0.13	2.46	9.14	0.7	9.78	98.5	5	95	0	0	42	15.52	-27.38		1.00	May-07
25,000	4.25	11.82	23.92	20.16	44.53	1.08	1.48	9.14	0.7	10.07	98.5	5	95	0	0	42	16.04	-27.17			Aug-13
	5.16	8.13	27.06	42.80	55.63	1.25	1.99	10.29		15.47	48.0	5	94	0	0	10			5.50		Oct-11
	5.00	7.71	26.13	39.52	49.78	0.87	2.74	10.32		14.92	48.0	5	94	0	0	10				1.00	Oct-11
25,000	5.25	8.29	27.48	43.93	57.22	1.42	1.75	10.33		15.52	48.0	5	94	0	0	10					Aug-13
	3.97	9.85	16.89	22.41	81.11	0	1.56	10.03	0.82	8.71	87.5	7	93	0	0	76	28.17	-20.07	5.50		Oct-00
	3.81	9.51	16.05	19.66	74.40	0	2.32	10.01	0.82	7.16	87.5	7	93	0	0	76	27.54	-20.19		1.00	Feb-04
25,000	4.03	9.97	17.24	23.34	83.49	0	1.31	10.02	0.82	8.83	87.5	7	93	0	0	76	28.17	-20.07			Aug-13
	6.89	9.46	17.50	23.80	85.75	0	1.53	7.97	0.69	19.18	217.8	4	96	0	0	39	22.59	-18.8	5.50		Jul-99
	6.72	9.14	16.68	21.08	78.99	0	2.28	7.95	0.69	15.61	217.8	4	96	0	0	39	22.05	-19.06		1.00	Feb-04
25,000	6.97	9.63	17.81	24.78	87.63	0	1.3	7.99	0.69	19.34	217.8	4	96	0	0	39	22.59	-18.8			Aug-13
	3.38	9.66	12.18	27.07	101.89	0	2.27	12.74	0.85	14.28	146.3	3	97	0	0	57	32.51	-24.83		1.00	Feb-04
	3.61	10.05	13.04	30.01	109.51	0	1.52	12.73	0.85	19.45	146.3	3	97	0	0	57	33.17	-24.65	5.50		Mar-94
25,000	3.61	10.15	13.28	30.94	111.69	0	1.3	12.73	0.85	19.65	146.3	3	97	0	0	57	33.17	-24.65			Aug-13
	2.95	7.37	11.54	11.15	33.48	0	2.42	6.2	0.7	9.76	40.5	8	70	19	2	36	18.82	-19.3	5.50		Oct-00
	2.80	7.04	10.67	8.63	28.72	0	3.17	6.16	0.69	8.81	40.5	8	70	19	2	36	18.55	-20.38		1.00	Feb-04

	MARKET			FUND TYPE, CATEGORY & OBJECTIVE	RATINGS				MINIMUMS	
Fund Name	Ticker Symbol	Traded On	Fund Type	Category and (Prospectus Objective)	Overall Rating	Reward Rating	Risk Rating	Recent Up/ Downgrade	Open to New Investors	Min Initial Investment
TOBAM Emerging Markets Fund Class I	TBMIX	NAS CM	Open End	Emerging Markets Equity (Div Emerging Mkts)	U	U	U		Y	500,000
Tocqueville Fund	TOCQX	NAS CM	Open End	US Equity Large Cap Blend (Growth)	B-	B-	B-	Down	Y	1,000
Tocqueville Gold Fund	TGLDX	NAS CM	Open End	Precious Metals Sector Equity (Precious Metals)	D+	C-	D	Down	Y	1,000
Tocqueville International Value Fund	TIVFX	NAS CM	Open End	Global Equity Large Cap (Foreign Stock)	B	B	B+	Up	Y	1,000
Tocqueville Opportunity Fund	TOPPX	NAS CM	Open End	US Equity Mid Cap (Growth)	B	A-	C+	Up	Y	1,000
Tocqueville Select Fund	TSELX	NAS CM	Open End	US Equity Small Cap (Growth)	C	C	C		Y	1,000
Toews Tactical Defensive Alpha Fund	TTDAX	NAS CM	Open End	Long/Short Equity (Growth)	C-	C-	B+	Up	Y	10,000
Toews Tactical Growth Allocation Fund	THGWX	NAS CM	Open End	Moderate Alloc (Growth)	C+	C	B-	Up	Y	10,000
Toews Tactical Monument Fund	THLGX	NAS CM	Open End	Long/Short Equity (Growth)	C	C	C+	Up	Y	10,000
Toews Tactical Oceana Fund	THIDX	NAS CM	Open End	Long/Short Equity (Growth)	C+	C+	B-	Up	Y	10,000
Toews Tactical Opportunity Fund	THSMX	NAS CM	Open End	Long/Short Equity (Growth)	C	C-	C	Up	Y	10,000
TOPS® Aggressive Growth ETF Portfolio Class 1	US66537U7679		Open End	Aggressive Alloc (Aggr Growth)	B-	B	C+	Down	Y	0
TOPS® Aggressive Growth ETF Portfolio Class 2	US66537U7596		Open End	Aggressive Alloc (Aggr Growth)	B-	B-	C+	Down	Y	0
TOPS® Aggressive Growth ETF Portfolio Investor Class	US66537U1482		Open End	Aggressive Alloc (Aggr Growth)	B-	B-	C+	Down	Y	0
TOPS® Balanced ETF Portfolio Class 1	US66537U8339		Open End	Moderate Alloc (Balanced)	B-	C+	B	Up	Y	0
TOPS® Balanced ETF Portfolio Class 2	US66537U8255		Open End	Moderate Alloc (Balanced)	B-	C+	B	Up	Y	0
TOPS® Balanced ETF Portfolio Investor Class	US66537U1714		Open End	Moderate Alloc (Balanced)	B-	C+	B	Up	Y	0
TOPS® Conservative ETF Portfolio Class 1	US66537U8586		Open End	Cautious Alloc (Growth & Income)	B-	C	B	Up	Y	0
TOPS® Conservative ETF Portfolio Class 2	US66537U8412		Open End	Cautious Alloc (Growth & Income)	B-	C	B	Up	Y	0
TOPS® Conservative ETF Portfolio Investor Class	US66537U1896		Open End	Cautious Alloc (Growth & Income)	B-	C	B	Up	Y	0
TOPS® Growth ETF Portfolio Class 1	US66537U7836		Open End	Aggressive Alloc (Growth)	B-	B-	C+	Down	Y	0
TOPS® Growth ETF Portfolio Class 2	US66537U7752		Open End	Aggressive Alloc (Growth)	B-	B-	C+	Down	Y	0
TOPS® Growth ETF Portfolio Investor Class	US66537U1557		Open End	Aggressive Alloc (Growth)	C+	C+	C+	Down	Y	0
TOPS® Managed Risk Balanced ETF Portfolio Class 1	US66537U7422		Open End	Cautious Alloc (Balanced)	C+	C+	B	Up	Y	0
TOPS® Managed Risk Balanced ETF Portfolio Class 2	US66537U7349		Open End	Cautious Alloc (Balanced)	C+	C+	B	Up	Y	0
TOPS® Managed Risk Balanced ETF Portfolio Class 3	US66537U5939		Open End	Cautious Alloc (Balanced)	C+	C+	B	Up	Y	0
TOPS® Managed Risk Balanced ETF Portfolio Class 4	US66537U6432		Open End	Cautious Alloc (Balanced)	C+	C+	B-	Up	Y	0
TOPS® Managed Risk Balanced ETF Portfolio Investor Class	US66537U1300		Open End	Cautious Alloc (Balanced)	C+	C+	B-	Up	Y	0
TOPS® Managed Risk Flex ETF Portfolio	US66537U3389		Open End	Cautious Alloc (Growth & Income)	C+	C+	B-	Up	Y	0
TOPS® Managed Risk Growth ETF Portfolio Class 1	US66537U6929		Open End	Aggressive Alloc (Growth)	C+	C+	C+	Up	Y	0
TOPS® Managed Risk Growth ETF Portfolio Class 2	US66537U6846		Open End	Aggressive Alloc (Growth)	C+	C+	C+	Up	Y	0
TOPS® Managed Risk Growth ETF Portfolio Class 3 Shares	US66537U6358		Open End	Aggressive Alloc (Growth)	C+	C+	C+	Up	Y	0
TOPS® Managed Risk Growth ETF Portfolio Class 4 Shares	US66537U6275		Open End	Aggressive Alloc (Growth)	C+	C+	C+	Up	Y	0
TOPS® Managed Risk Growth ETF Portfolio Investor Class	US66537U1144		Open End	Aggressive Alloc (Growth)	C+	C+	C+	Up	Y	0
TOPS® Managed Risk Moderate Growth ETF Portfolio Class 1	US66537U7265		Open End	Moderate Alloc (Growth)	C+	C+	B-	Up	Y	0
TOPS® Managed Risk Moderate Growth ETF Portfolio Class 2	US66537U7182		Open End	Moderate Alloc (Growth)	C+	C+	B-	Up	Y	0
TOPS® Managed Risk Moderate Growth ETF Port Cls 3 Shares	US66537U6192		Open End	Moderate Alloc (Growth)	C+	C+	B-	Up	Y	0
TOPS® Managed Risk Moderate Growth ETF Port Cls 4 Shares	US66537U5855		Open End	Moderate Alloc (Growth)	C+	C+	B-	Up	Y	0
TOPS® Managed Risk Moderate Growth ETF Portfolio Inv Cls	US66537U1227		Open End	Moderate Alloc (Growth)	C+	C+	B-	Up	Y	0
TOPS® Moderate Growth ETF Portfolio Class 1	US66537U8172		Open End	Moderate Alloc (Growth)	B-	C+	B	Down	Y	0
TOPS® Moderate Growth ETF Portfolio Class 2	US66537U7919		Open End	Moderate Alloc (Growth)	B-	C+	B-	Down	Y	0
TOPS® Moderate Growth ETF Portfolio Investor Class	US66537U1631		Open End	Moderate Alloc (Growth)	B-	C+	B-	Down	Y	0
Topturn OneEighty Fund	TTFOX	NAS CM	Open End	Moderate Alloc (Growth & Income)	C	C	B+	Up	Y	100,000
Toreador Core Fund Institutional Class	TORZX	NAS CM	Open End	US Equity Large Cap Blend (Growth)	B+	A	B	Up	Y	10,000
Toreador Core Fund Investor Class	TORLX	NAS CM	Open End	US Equity Large Cap Blend (Growth)	B	A-	C+	Up	Y	1,000
Toreador Explorer Fund Institutional Shares	TMRZX	NAS CM	Open End	US Equity Small Cap (Growth)	C	C+	B-	Up	Y	10,000
Toreador Explorer Fund Investor Shares	TMRLX	NAS CM	Open End	US Equity Small Cap (Growth)	C	C+	B-	Up	Y	1,000
Toreador International Fund Class Institutional	TMRIX	NAS CM	Open End	Global Equity Large Cap (Growth)	B-	C+	B	Up	Y	100,000
Toreador International Fund Investor Class	TMRFX	NAS CM	Open End	Global Equity Large Cap (Growth)	B-	C+	B	Up	Y	2,500
Toreador Select Fund Institutional Class Shares	TOSZX	NAS CM	Open End	US Equity Large Cap Blend (Growth)	U	U	U		Y	10,000
Toreador Select Fund Investor Class Shares	TOSLX	NAS CM	Open End	US Equity Large Cap Blend (Growth)	U	U	U		Y	1,000
Torray Fund	TORYX	NAS CM	Open End	US Equity Large Cap Value (Growth)	B	B-	B		Y	2,000

★Expanded analysis of this fund is included in Section II.

	TOTAL RETURNS					PERFORMANCE				ASSETS		ASSET ALLOCATION & TURNOVER					BULL & BEAR		FEES		
Min Additional Investment	3-Month Total Return	6-Month Total Return	1-Year Total Return	3-Year Total Return	5-Year Total Return	Dividend Yield (TTM)	Expense Ratio	3-Yr Std Deviation	3-Year Beta	NAV	Total Assets (MIL)	%Cash	%Stocks	%Bonds	%Other	Turnover Ratio	Last Bull Market Total Return	Last Bear Market Total Return	Front End Fee (%)	Back End Fee (%)	Inception Date
100	10.78	21.01					0.85			12.36	50.7	0	100	0	0						Apr-17
100	7.28	12.28	20.34	26.15	94.67	0.96	1.24	11.2	1.07	36.62	297.9	0	99	0	0	12	21.17	-18.2			Jan-87
100	-0.37	1.43	8.91	15.00	-40.52	0	1.4	34.6	-0.19	36.78	1,125	1	85	0	15	15	-7.82	-17.44			Jun-98
100	2.11	8.67	24.17	37.10	62.29	0.82	1.26	11.37	0.89	17.53	1,141	9	89	0	0	26	7.8	-21.65			Aug-94
100	5.71	11.95	34.65	28.48	104.73	0	1.26	18.91	1.27	25.5	79.5	0	100	0	0	108	30.48	-21.27			Aug-94
100	0.56	-0.35	-4.18	-3.40	42.94	0	1.25	18.28	1.33	11.74	48.1	5	95	0	0	32	27.28	-27.47			Sep-08
100	3.59	7.26	15.77			0	1.25			11.17	118.7	24	0	76	0	1,741					Jan-16
100	2.80	5.95	14.09	4.35	26.75	0	1.35	6.28	0.47	10.67	22.0	20	0	78	1	163	0.08	-12.82			Aug-10
100	5.76	9.11	20.32	-0.73	41.92	0	1.25	9.32	0.72	11.01	42.1	23	0	77	0	0	7.1	-13.79			Jun-10
100	2.58	6.95	21.21	14.11	16.45	0	1.25	8.56	0.43	9.54	48.9	23	0	77	0	11	-16.42	-11.31			Jun-10
100	3.52	6.73	11.25	-8.33	24.99	0	1.25	9.75	0.51	9.98	65.5	24	0	75	0	13	7.13	-19.08			Jun-10
	5.50	10.91	20.69	31.15	74.29	1.45	0.36	10.01	0.94	14.94	10.8	3	97	0	0	16	21.82	-22.13			Apr-11
	5.48	10.80	20.39	30.30	71.21	1.29	0.61	10.03	0.95	14.82	10.8	3	97	0	0	16	21.57	-22.13			Apr-11
	5.05	10.04	18.97	27.32	66.47	0	0.86	10.03	0.95	15.99	10.8	3	97	0	0	16	21.39	-22.21			Jul-15
	2.86	5.81	11.20	17.06	35.05	1.54	0.41	5.54	0.5	12.58	12.1	3	49	47	0	32	14.09	-10.7			Apr-11
	2.78	5.67	10.94	16.24	32.78	1.35	0.66	5.52	0.49	12.17	12.1	3	49	47	0	32	13.98	-10.7			Apr-11
	2.60	5.35	10.37	15.00	30.70	0	0.91	5.41	0.48	12.98	12.1	3	49	47	0	32	13.81	-10.79			Jul-15
	1.79	3.67	7.08	11.36	20.36	0.88	0.44	3.64	0.31	11.92	8.5	4	30	66	1	93	10.44	-5.85			Apr-11
	1.71	3.49	6.82	10.48	18.74	0.69	0.69	3.63	0.31	11.85	8.5	4	30	66	1	93	10.34	-5.95			Apr-11
	1.66	3.37	6.62	10.00	17.64	0	0.94	3.58	0.31	12.24	8.5	4	30	66	1	93	10.18	-6.05			Jul-15
	4.77	9.71	18.23	26.82	60.40	1.36	0.4	9.09	0.85	15.35	18.4	3	84	13	0	16	20.22	-13.04			Apr-11
	4.71	9.56	17.93	25.96	58.46	1.23	0.65	9.06	0.84	15.11	18.4	3	84	13	0	16	20.11	-13.53			Apr-11
	4.32	8.81	16.53	23.27	54.31	0	0.9	8.76	0.82	16.42	18.4	3	84	13	0	16	19.93	-13.62			Jul-15
	2.76	5.64	10.90	12.60	27.36	1.74	0.61	5.17	0.46	12.25	620.3	13	45	42	0	16	7.76				Jun-11
	2.69	5.49	10.58	11.79	25.72	1.49	0.86	5.16	0.46	12.18	620.3	13	45	42	0	16	7.55				Jun-11
	2.68	5.51	10.58	11.54	25.01	1.45	0.96	5.2	0.46	12.24	620.3	13	45	42	0	16	7.49				May-12
	2.64	5.37	10.23	10.70	23.51	1.16	1.21	5.19	0.46	12.02	620.3	13	45	42	0	16	7.33				May-12
	2.53	5.20	10.04	10.72	23.89	0	1.11	5.05	0.45	12.93	620.3	13	45	42	0	16	7.4				Jul-15
	2.88	5.89	11.24	10.69		1.02	1.06	5.36	0.48	11.78	124.0	13	49	38	0	14					Aug-13
	4.71	9.54	17.96	13.06	36.24	1.77	0.59	7.11	0.62	12.66	993.2	13	76	11	0	12	7.7	-8.62			Apr-11
	4.56	9.40	17.65	12.18	34.55	1.52	0.84	7.08	0.62	12.59	993.2	13	76	11	0	12	7.59	-8.62			Apr-11
	4.58	9.28	17.45	11.83	34.38	1.47	0.94	7.11	0.62	12.54	993.2	13	76	11	0	12	7.48	-8.75			May-12
	4.57	9.27	17.33	11.05	32.36	1.23	1.19	7.12	0.62	12.57	993.2	13	76	11	0	12	7.32	-8.85			May-12
	4.35	9.02	16.96	11.20	32.66	0	1.09	7.01	0.61	13.17	993.2	13	76	11	0	12	7.38	-8.81			Jul-15
	3.67	7.53	14.17	13.61	34.07	1.81	0.6	6.33	0.56	12.71	1,023	13	58	29	0	13	8.15				Jun-11
	3.60	7.38	13.84	12.76	32.44	1.56	0.85	6.33	0.56	12.66	1,023	13	58	29	0	13	8.03				Jun-11
	3.60	7.35	13.83	12.45	32.09	1.53	0.95	6.3	0.56	12.63	1,023	13	58	29	0	13	7.93				May-12
	3.62	7.20	13.61	11.66	30.26	1.2	1.2	6.35	0.57	12.58	1,023	13	58	29	0	13	7.77				May-12
	3.38	7.00	13.12	11.66	30.46	0	1.1	6.17	0.55	13.45	1,023	13	58	29	0	13	7.83				Jul-15
	3.76	7.63	14.37	22.20	45.87	1.3	0.41	7.05	0.64	12.4	19.6	3	64	32	0	19	16.08	-15.04			Apr-11
	3.72	7.46	14.11	21.12	43.94	1.2	0.66	7.12	0.65	11.99	19.6	3	64	32	0	19	15.96	-15.04			Apr-11
	3.38	6.82	12.87	18.29	39.87	0	0.91	6.73	0.62	13.15	19.6	3	64	32	0	19	15.79	-15.13			Jul-15
	2.63	5.78	10.89			0.26	1.92			11.27	25.8	6	66	22	4	303					Sep-15
100	7.15	17.07	25.66	36.13	121.06	0.69	0.95	12.26	1.11	17.79	170.9	0	100	0	0	71	21.73	-19.02			Sep-09
100	7.11	16.91	25.32	35.03	118.39	0.46	1.2	12.3	1.11	17.77	170.9	0	100	0	0	71	21.58	-19.12			Jun-06
100	6.02	11.93	17.53			0	0.83			12	15.1	1	99	0	0	74					Jun-15
100	6.05	11.90	17.29			0	1.08			11.94	15.1	1	99	0	0	74					Jun-15
10,000	4.76	8.49	22.86	19.76	42.10	0.46	1.64	11.91	0.95	19.99	58.7	0	97	0	3	34	6.25	-31.72			Dec-12
100	4.72	8.27	22.50	18.81	40.31	0.18	1.89	11.92	0.95	18.74	58.7	0	97	0	3	34	6.25	-31.72			Dec-12
100	7.60	16.25					0.75			11.89	7.3	1	99	0	0						Feb-17
100	7.51	16.06	20.93				1			11.88	7.3	1	99	0	0						Feb-17
500	4.81	7.59	12.06	25.25	90.48	1.14	1.1	10.09	0.93	49.6	446.7	10	90	0	0	9	17.75	-12.28			Dec-90

	MARKET		FUND TYPE, CATEGORY & OBJECTIVE		RATINGS				MINIMUMS	
Fund Name	Ticker Symbol	Traded On	Fund Type	Category and (Prospectus Objective)	Overall Rating	Reward Rating	Risk Rating	Recent Up/ Downgrade	Open to New Investors	Min Initial Investment
TorrayResolute Small/Mid Cap Growth Fund Investor Class	TRSDX	NAS CM	Open End	US Equity Mid Cap (Growth)	C+	C+	C	Down	Y	2,500
Tortoise Energy Independence Fund, Inc	NDP	NYSE	Closed End	Energy Sector Equity (Growth & Income)	D+	D+	D		Y	
Tortoise Energy Infrastructure Corporation	TYG	NYSE	Closed End	Energy Sector Equity (Natl Res)	D	D	D	Down	Y	
Tortoise MLP & Pipeline Fund C Class Shares	TORCX	NAS CM	Open End	Energy Sector Equity ()	D+	C-	D	Down	Y	2,500
Tortoise MLP & Pipeline Fund lInstitutional Class	TORIX	NAS CM	Open End	Energy Sector Equity ()	D+	C-	D	Down	Y	1,000,000
Tortoise MLP & Pipeline Fund Investor Class	TORTX	NAS CM	Open End	Energy Sector Equity ()	D+	C-	D	Down	Y	2,500
Tortoise MLP Fund	NTG	NYSE	Closed End	Energy Sector Equity (Natl Res)	D	D	D	Down	Y	
Tortoise Pipeline & Energy Fund	TTP	NYSE	Closed End	Energy Sector Equity (Natl Res)	D	D+	D	Down	Y	
Tortoise Power and Energy Infrastructure Fund	TPZ	NYSE	Closed End	Energy Sector Equity (Natl Res)	D+	D+	D+	Down	Y	
Tortoise Select Opportunity Fund C Class	TOPCX	NAS CM	Open End	Energy Sector Equity (Growth & Income)	D+	D+	D+	Down	Y	2,500
Tortoise Select Opportunity Fund Institutional Class	TOPIX	NAS CM	Open End	Energy Sector Equity (Growth & Income)	D+	D+	C-	Down	Y	1,000,000
Tortoise Select Opportunity Fund Investor Class	TOPTX	NAS CM	Open End	Energy Sector Equity (Growth & Income)	D+	D+	C-	Down	Y	2,500
Total Income+ Real Estate Fund Class A	TIPRX	NAS CM	Closed End	Real Estate Sector Equity (Real Estate)	B	C+	A+	Up	Y	2,500
Total Income+ Real Estate Fund Class C	TIPPX	NAS CM	Closed End	Real Estate Sector Equity (Real Estate)	B	C+	A+	Up	Y	2,500
Total Income+ Real Estate Fund Class I	TIPWX	NAS CM	Closed End	Real Estate Sector Equity (Real Estate)	B	C+	A+	Up	Y	1,000,000
Total Income+ Real Estate Fund Class L	US89154U4076		Closed End	Real Estate Sector Equity (Real Estate)	B	C+	A+	Up	Y	2,500
Touchstone Arbitrage Fund Class A	TMARX	NAS CM	Open End	Market Neutral (Growth)	B-	C	A-	Up	Y	2,500
Touchstone Arbitrage Fund Class C	TMACX	NAS CM	Open End	Market Neutral (Growth)	C+	C	B	Down	Y	2,500
Touchstone Arbitrage Fund Class Y	TMAYX	NAS CM	Open End	Market Neutral (Growth)	B-	C	A	Up	Y	2,500
Touchstone Arbitrage Fund Institutional	TARBX	NAS CM	Open End	Market Neutral (Growth)	B	C	A	Up	Y	500,000
Touchstone Balanced Fund Class A	SEBLX	NAS CM	Open End	Moderate Alloc (Balanced)	B-	C+	B	Down	Y	2,500
Touchstone Balanced Fund Class C	SBACX	NAS CM	Open End	Moderate Alloc (Balanced)	B-	C+	B	Up	Y	2,500
Touchstone Balanced Fund Class Y	SIBLX	NAS CM	Open End	Moderate Alloc (Balanced)	B-	C+	B	Down	Y	2,500
Touchstone Controlled Growth with Income Fund A	TSAAX	NAS CM	Open End	Multialternative (Growth & Income)	B-	C	B	Up	Y	2,500
Touchstone Controlled Growth with Income Fund C	TSACX	NAS CM	Open End	Multialternative (Growth & Income)	C+	C	B	Up	Y	2,500
Touchstone Controlled Growth with Income Fund Y	TSAYX	NAS CM	Open End	Multialternative (Growth & Income)	B-	C	B	Up	Y	2,500
Touchstone Dynamic Diversified Income Fund A	TBAAX	NAS CM	Open End	Cautious Alloc (Income)	B-	C+	B	Up	Y	2,500
Touchstone Dynamic Diversified Income Fund C	TBACX	NAS CM	Open End	Cautious Alloc (Income)	C+	C	B	Up	Y	2,500
Touchstone Dynamic Diversified Income Fund Y	TBAYX	NAS CM	Open End	Cautious Alloc (Income)	B-	C+	B	Up	Y	2,500
Touchstone Dynamic Equity Fund Class A	TDEAX	NAS CM	Open End	Long/Short Equity (Growth)	B	C+	A+		Y	2,500
Touchstone Dynamic Equity Fund Class C	TDECX	NAS CM	Open End	Long/Short Equity (Growth)	B	C+	A+		Y	2,500
Touchstone Dynamic Equity Fund Class Y	TDEYX	NAS CM	Open End	Long/Short Equity (Growth)	B	C+	A+		Y	2,500
Touchstone Dynamic Equity Fund Institutional Class	TDELX	NAS CM	Open End	Long/Short Equity (Growth)	B	C+	A+		Y	500,000
Touchstone Dynamic Global Allocation Fund A	TSMAX	NAS CM	Open End	Alloc (Growth)	C+	C+	B-	Down	Y	2,500
Touchstone Dynamic Global Allocation Fund C	TSMCX	NAS CM	Open End	Alloc (Growth)	B-	C+	B	Up	Y	2,500
Touchstone Dynamic Global Allocation Fund Y	TSMYX	NAS CM	Open End	Alloc (Growth)	C+	C+	B-	Down	Y	2,500
Touchstone Emerging Markets Small Cap Fund Class A	TEMAX	NAS CM	Open End	Emerging Markets Equity (Div Emerging Mkts)	C+	C+	C	Up	Y	2,500
Touchstone Emerging Markets Small Cap Fund Class C	TEFCX	NAS CM	Open End	Emerging Markets Equity (Div Emerging Mkts)	C+	C+	C	Up	Y	2,500
Touchstone Emerging Markets Small Cap Fund Class Y	TEMYX	NAS CM	Open End	Emerging Markets Equity (Div Emerging Mkts)	C+	C+	C	Up	Y	2,500
Touchstone Emerging Mkts Small Cap Fund Inst Cls	TMEIX	NAS CM	Open End	Emerging Markets Equity (Div Emerging Mkts)	C+	C+	C	Up	Y	500,000
Touchstone Focused Fund Class A	TFOAX	NAS CM	Open End	US Equity Large Cap Blend (Growth)	B	B-	B		Y	2,500
Touchstone Focused Fund Class C	TFFCX	NAS CM	Open End	US Equity Large Cap Blend (Growth)	B-	B-	B	Down	Y	2,500
Touchstone Focused Fund Class Y	TFFYX	NAS CM	Open End	US Equity Large Cap Blend (Growth)	B	B-	A		Y	2,500
Touchstone Focused Fund Institutional	TFFIX	NAS CM	Open End	US Equity Large Cap Blend (Growth)	B	B-	A		Y	500,000
Touchstone Global Growth Fund Class A	TGGAX	NAS CM	Open End	Global Equity (Growth)	A-	A	B+	Up	Y	2,500
Touchstone Global Growth Fund Class C	TGGCX	NAS CM	Open End	Global Equity (Growth)	A-	A-	B+	Up	Y	2,500
Touchstone Global Growth Fund Class Y	TYGGX	NAS CM	Open End	Global Equity (Growth)	A-	A	B+	Up	Y	2,500
Touchstone Global Growth Fund Institutional Class	DSMGX	NAS CM	Open End	Global Equity (Growth)	A-	A	B+	Up	Y	500,000
Touchstone Growth Opportunities Fund Class A	TGVFX	NAS CM	Open End	US Equity Large Cap Growth (Growth)	B-	B	C+	Up	Y	2,500
Touchstone Growth Opportunities Fund Class C	TGVCX	NAS CM	Open End	US Equity Large Cap Growth (Growth)	B-	B-	B	Up	Y	2,500
Touchstone Growth Opportunities Fund Class Y	TGVYX	NAS CM	Open End	US Equity Large Cap Growth (Growth)	B-	B	C+	Up	Y	2,500
Touchstone Growth Opportunities Fund Institutional Class	TGVVX	NAS CM	Open End	US Equity Large Cap Growth (Growth)	B-	B	C+	Up	Y	500,000

★ Expanded analysis of this fund is included in Section II.

	TOTAL RETURNS					PERFORMANCE				ASSETS		ASSET ALLOCATION & TURNOVER					BULL & BEAR		FEES		
Min Additional Investment	3-Month Total Return	6-Month Total Return	1-Year Total Return	3-Year Total Return	5-Year Total Return	Dividend Yield (TTM)	Expense Ratio	3-Yr Std Deviation	3-Year Beta	NAV	Total Assets (MIL)	%Cash	%Stocks	%Bonds	%Other	Turnover Ratio	Last Bull Market Total Return	Last Bear Market Total Return	Front End Fee (%)	Back End Fee (%)	Inception Date
100	5.86	11.64	21.84	22.70		0	1.26			12.27	5.0	4	96	0	0	40					Dec-14
	7.87	12.37	-10.11	-16.14	-3.29	0		26.85	1.11	13.4683	187.5	0	98	0	0	47					Jul-12
	7.78	4.37	1.10	-25.03	16.90	8.21	2.13	22.97	1.48	27.851	1,174	-53	184	-32	-2	24	19.7	-10.72			Feb-04
100	0.78	1.08	-1.95	-12.85	25.44	2.34	1.97	19.04	1.08	13.28	3,236	2	98	0	0	25	25.72			1.00	Sep-12
100	0.99	1.59	-1.02	-10.24	31.90	3.28	0.97	19.02	1.08	13.47	3,236	2	98	0	0	25	26.45				May-11
100	0.90	1.50	-1.24	-10.91	30.28	3.05	1.22	19.08	1.08	13.39	3,236	2	98	0	0	25	26.23		5.75		May-11
	3.79	0.65	-3.00	-21.07	9.77	4.41	3.66	20.42		17.7731	752.7	-37	170	-34	-1	35	14.26	-10.72			Jul-10
	-1.17	0.55	-10.64	-25.59	14.27	0.09	2.57	27.92		20.0993	188.5	0	97	0	0	90					Oct-11
	-1.58	-1.15	-4.86	-6.93	18.55	2.61	1.51	16.73		21.89	148.3	-33	58	68	4	41	14.66	-6.4			Jul-09
100	7.26	12.72	-6.15	-3.47		0	2.1	19.62	1.18	9.3	63.9	3	95	0	1	168				1.00	Sep-13
100	7.51	13.35	-5.14	-0.46		0.47	1.1	19.7	1.18	9.59	63.9	3	95	0	1	168					Sep-13
100	7.53	13.27	-5.44	-1.29		0.27	1.35	19.68	1.18	9.56	63.9	3	95	0	1	168			5.75		Sep-13
100	1.91	3.44	6.80	22.28	50.52	5.21	1.95	2.06		29.4	--	5	39	-9	66	35			5.75		Oct-12
100	1.75	3.07	6.01	19.59	46.54	5.23	2.7	2.05		28.61	--	5	39	-9	66	35				1.00	Apr-14
	1.98	3.58	7.04	23.22	52.20	5.2	1.7	2.05		29.74	--	5	39	-9	66	35					Apr-14
100	1.84	3.30	6.65	22.12	50.31		2.14			29.35	--	5	39	-9	66	35			4.25		Jun-17
50	-0.56	-0.66	0.11	7.53		0	1.7	2.28	4.36	9.74	239.1	14	70	11	1	358			5.75		Sep-13
50	-0.68	-0.98	-0.68	5.05		0	2.45	2.31	4.52	9.44	239.1	14	70	11	1	358				1.00	Sep-13
50	-0.46	-0.56	0.30	8.34		0	1.41	2.37	4.65	9.86	239.1	14	70	11	1	358					Sep-13
50	-0.56	-0.46	0.40	8.66		0	1.3	2.32	5.49	9.9	239.1	14	70	11	1	358					Sep-13
50	4.76	7.97	15.67	23.35	59.53	1.1	1.03	6.62	0.65	21.51	332.2	16	64	20	0	45	18.14	-11.36	5.75		Nov-38
50	4.54	7.57	14.79	20.50	53.42	0.4	1.8	6.62	0.65	21.6	332.2	16	64	20	0	45	17.61	-11.66		1.00	May-98
50	4.81	8.06	15.98	24.13	61.43	1.35	0.83	6.63	0.65	21.36	332.2	16	64	20	0	45	18.16	-11.32			Aug-07
50	1.24	2.94	5.22	10.29	21.97	2.17	1.98	2.87	3.56	11.26	45.8	7	51	39	1	41	7.65	-4.71	5.75		Sep-04
50	1.05	2.56	4.51	7.90	17.47	1.41	2.73	2.83	3.28	11.21	45.8	7	51	39	1	41	7.29	-5.06		1.00	Sep-04
50	1.31	3.16	5.59	11.14	23.42	2.42	1.73	2.87	3.31	11.26	45.8	7	51	39	1	41	7.87	-4.65			Dec-05
50	1.46	3.34	7.73	13.79	36.15	4	1.32	5.46	0.18	13.23	56.2	3	31	60	5	32	14.22	-11.21	5.75		Sep-04
50	1.26	2.92	6.93	11.22	31.11	3.2	2.07	5.5	0.17	13.26	56.2	3	31	60	5	32	13.72	-11.41		1.00	Sep-04
50	1.52	3.46	8.06	14.71	38.03	4.24	1.07	5.47	0.17	13.26	56.2	3	31	60	5	32	14.34	-11.07			Dec-05
50	3.16	7.03	7.17	19.30	49.84	0.36	1.56	6.15	0.48	16.05	117.4	2	99	0	-2	245	17.13	-9.85	5.75		Mar-05
50	2.99	6.59	6.37	16.59	44.33	0	2.31	6.12	0.48	14.89	117.4	2	99	0	-2	245	16.7	-10.12		1.00	Mar-05
50	3.30	7.23	7.58	20.49	52.14	0.58	1.23	6.16	0.48	16.32	117.4	2	99	0	-2	245	17.3	-9.73			Jun-78
50	3.28	7.19	7.54	20.38	52.14	0.55	1.2	6.17	0.48	16.38	117.4	2	99	0	-2	245	17.31	-9.72			Dec-05
50	2.80	6.25	13.96	12.92	41.33	2.52	1.29	7.15	0.66	12.56	114.5	3	60	37	0	39	18.04	-15.31	5.75		Sep-04
50	2.58	5.81	13.10	10.36	36.05	1.85	2.04	7.19	0.67	12.28	114.5	3	60	37	0	39	17.55	-15.55		1.00	Sep-04
50	2.84	6.32	14.20	13.73	43.05	2.72	1.04	7.16	0.66	12.67	114.5	3	60	37	0	39	18.3	-15.25			Dec-05
50	6.85	14.83	38.80	16.30	0.43	0	1.69	13.78	0.84	11.77	13.3	1	99	0	0	115	17.07	-20.99	5.75		Sep-09
50	6.57	14.31	37.74	13.77	-3.28	0	2.44	13.74	0.84	11.48	13.3	1	99	0	0	115	16.51	-21.22		1.00	Sep-09
50	6.88	14.92	39.25	17.28	1.80	0	1.44	13.79	0.84	11.8	13.3	1	99	0	0	115	17.28	-20.97			Sep-09
50	6.90	15.01	39.42	17.76	2.41	0	1.29	13.8	0.84	11.7	13.3	1	99	0	0	115	17.35	-20.94			Sep-09
50	4.67	7.61	13.90	29.63	96.96	0.31	1.21	10.12	0.95	42.87	1,245	2	98	0	0	20	26.39	-18.51	5.75		Sep-03
50	4.46	7.18	13.04	26.75	89.80	0.24	1.96	10.11	0.95	40.9	1,245	2	98	0	0	20	25.92	-18.82		1.00	Apr-12
50	4.72	7.75	14.20	30.67	99.62	0.49	0.93	10.12	0.95	43.4	1,245	2	98	0	0	20	26.65	-18.48			Feb-99
50	4.74	7.79	14.27	31.08	100.72	0.57	0.84	10.12	0.95	43.57	1,245	2	98	0	0	20	26.71	-18.43			Dec-06
50	5.11	13.76	43.24	50.00	110.57	0	1.41	13.36	1.1	24.85	28.4	2	98	0	0	72			5.75		Aug-16
50	4.95	13.35	42.17	46.62	102.79	0	2.16	13.35	1.1	24.59	28.4	2	98	0	0	72				1.00	Aug-16
50	5.19	13.94	43.39	50.87	112.85	0	1.16	13.35	1.1	24.89	28.4	2	98	0	0	72					Aug-16
50	5.22	14.00	43.70	51.28	113.44	0	1.06	13.38	1.1	24.96	28.4	2	98	0	0	72					Mar-12
50	5.00	10.62	28.06	25.10	98.30	0	1.24	12.18	1.09	31.96	282.8	1	99	0	0	90	26.53	-23.09	5.75		Sep-95
50	4.79	10.20	27.06	22.28	90.95	0	1.99	12.2	1.09	26.44	282.8	1	99	0	0	90	26.1	-23.35		1.00	Aug-99
50	5.06	10.75	28.35	26.04	100.98	0.08	0.99	12.2	1.09	32.81	282.8	1	99	0	0	90	26.68	-23.02			Feb-09
50	5.07	10.83	28.48	26.42	101.89	0.15	0.89	12.17	1.09	33.18	282.8	1	99	0	0	90	26.78	-22.98			Feb-09

Fund Name	Ticker Symbol	Traded On	Fund Type	Category and (Prospectus Objective)	Overall Rating	Reward Rating	Risk Rating	Recent Up/ Downgrade	Open to New Investors	Min Initial Investment
	MARKET			FUND TYPE, CATEGORY & OBJECTIVE	RATINGS				MINIMUMS	
Touchstone International Equity Fund Class A	SWRLX	NAS CM	Open End	Global Equity Large Cap (Foreign Stock)	B	B	B	Up	Y	2,500
Touchstone International Equity Fund Class C	SWFCX	NAS CM	Open End	Global Equity Large Cap (Foreign Stock)	B	B-	B	Up	Y	2,500
Touchstone International Equity Fund Class Y	SIIEX	NAS CM	Open End	Global Equity Large Cap (Foreign Stock)	B	B	B	Up	Y	2,500
Touchstone International Equity Fund Institutional USD	TOIIX	NAS CM	Open End	Global Equity Large Cap (Foreign Stock)	B	B	B		Y	500,000
Touchstone International Growth Fund Class A	TIAPX	NAS CM	Open End	Global Equity Large Cap (Foreign Stock)	D+	C	B	Up	Y	2,500
Touchstone International Growth Fund Class C	TAGCX	NAS CM	Open End	Global Equity Large Cap (Foreign Stock)	D+	C	B	Up	Y	2,500
Touchstone International Growth Fund Class Y	TSPYX	NAS CM	Open End	Global Equity Large Cap (Foreign Stock)	D+	C	B	Up	Y	2,500
Touchstone International Growth Fund Institutional	TSIGX	NAS CM	Open End	Global Equity Large Cap (Foreign Stock)	D+	C	B	Up	Y	500,000
Touchstone International Small Cap Fund Class A	TNSAX	NAS CM	Open End	Global Equity Mid/Small Cap (Small Company)	B	B	B	Up	Y	2,500
Touchstone International Small Cap Fund Class C	TNSCX	NAS CM	Open End	Global Equity Mid/Small Cap (Small Company)	B	B	B	Up	Y	2,500
Touchstone International Small Cap Fund Class Y	TNSYX	NAS CM	Open End	Global Equity Mid/Small Cap (Small Company)	B	B	B	Up	Y	2,500
Touchstone International Small Cap Fund Institutional	TNSIX	NAS CM	Open End	Global Equity Mid/Small Cap (Small Company)	B	B	B	Up	Y	500,000
Touchstone International Value Fund Class A	FSIEX	NAS CM	Open End	Global Equity Large Cap (Foreign Stock)	C+	C+	C	Up	Y	2,500
Touchstone International Value Fund Class C	FTECX	NAS CM	Open End	Global Equity Large Cap (Foreign Stock)	C+	C+	C	Up	Y	2,500
Touchstone International Value Fund Class Y	FIEIX	NAS CM	Open End	Global Equity Large Cap (Foreign Stock)	C+	C+	C	Up	Y	2,500
Touchstone International Value Fund Institutional Class	FIVIX	NAS CM	Open End	Global Equity Large Cap (Foreign Stock)	C+	C+	C	Up	Y	500,000
Touchstone Large Cap Focused Fund Class A	SENCX	NAS CM	Open End	US Equity Large Cap Blend (Growth & Income)	B	B	B		Y	2,500
Touchstone Large Cap Focused Fund Class C	SCSCX	NAS CM	Open End	US Equity Large Cap Blend (Growth & Income)	B-	B-	B	Down	Y	2,500
Touchstone Large Cap Focused Fund Class Y	SICWX	NAS CM	Open End	US Equity Large Cap Blend (Growth & Income)	B	B	B		Y	2,500
Touchstone Large Cap Focused Fund Institutional Class	SCRLX	NAS CM	Open End	US Equity Large Cap Blend (Growth & Income)	B	B	B		Y	500,000
Touchstone Large Cap Fund Class A	TACLX	NAS CM	Open End	US Equity Large Cap Blend (Growth)	B-	B-	B-	Down	Y	2,500
Touchstone Large Cap Fund Class C	TFCCX	NAS CM	Open End	US Equity Large Cap Blend (Growth)	B-	B-	C+	Down	Y	2,500
Touchstone Large Cap Fund Class Y	TLCYX	NAS CM	Open End	US Equity Large Cap Blend (Growth)	B-	B-	B-	Down	Y	2,500
Touchstone Large Cap Fund Institutional Class	TLCIX	NAS CM	Open End	US Equity Large Cap Blend (Growth)	B-	B-	B-	Down	Y	500,000
Touchstone Large Company Growth Fund Class A	TSAGX	NAS CM	Open End	US Equity Large Cap Growth (Growth)	A-	A-	B+	Up	Y	2,500
Touchstone Large Company Growth Fund Class C	TCGLX	NAS CM	Open End	US Equity Large Cap Growth (Growth)	B+	B+	B+	Up	Y	2,500
Touchstone Large Company Growth Fund Class Institutional	DSMLX	NAS CM	Open End	US Equity Large Cap Growth (Growth)	A-	A-	B+	Up	Y	500,000
Touchstone Large Company Growth Fund Class Y	TLGYX	NAS CM	Open End	US Equity Large Cap Growth (Growth)	A-	A-	B+	Up	Y	2,500
Touchstone Merger Arbitrage Fund Class A	TMGAX	NAS CM	Open End	Market Neutral (Growth)	B	C	A	Up	Y	2,500
Touchstone Merger Arbitrage Fund Class C	TMGCX	NAS CM	Open End	Market Neutral (Growth)	B	C	A+	Up	Y	2,500
Touchstone Merger Arbitrage Fund Class Y	TMGYX	NAS CM	Open End	Market Neutral (Growth)	B	C	A+	Up	Y	2,500
Touchstone Merger Arbitrage Fund Institutional Class	TMGLX	NAS CM	Open End	Market Neutral (Growth)	B	C	A+	Up	Y	500,000
Touchstone Mid Cap Fund Class A	TMAPX	NAS CM	Open End	US Equity Mid Cap (Growth)	B	B	B		Y	2,500
Touchstone Mid Cap Fund Class C	TMCJX	NAS CM	Open End	US Equity Mid Cap (Growth)	B	B-	B		Y	2,500
Touchstone Mid Cap Fund Class Y	TMCPX	NAS CM	Open End	US Equity Mid Cap (Growth)	B	B	B		Y	2,500
Touchstone Mid Cap Fund Class Z	TMCTX	NAS CM	Open End	US Equity Mid Cap (Growth)	B	B	B		Y	2,500
Touchstone Mid Cap Fund Institutional	TMPIX	NAS CM	Open End	US Equity Mid Cap (Growth)	B	B	B		Y	500,000
Touchstone Mid Cap Growth Fund Class A	TEGAX	NAS CM	Open End	US Equity Mid Cap (Growth)	B	B	C+	Up	Y	2,500
Touchstone Mid Cap Growth Fund Class C	TOECX	NAS CM	Open End	US Equity Mid Cap (Growth)	B-	B	C+	Down	Y	2,500
Touchstone Mid Cap Growth Fund Class Y	TEGYX	NAS CM	Open End	US Equity Mid Cap (Growth)	B	B	C+	Up	Y	2,500
Touchstone Mid Cap Growth Fund Institutional Class	TEGIX	NAS CM	Open End	US Equity Mid Cap (Growth)	B	B	B-	Up	Y	500,000
Touchstone Mid Cap Value Class A	TCVAX	NAS CM	Open End	US Equity Mid Cap (Growth)	B	B	B		Y	2,500
Touchstone Mid Cap Value Class C	TMFCX	NAS CM	Open End	US Equity Mid Cap (Growth)	B	B	B		Y	2,500
Touchstone Mid Cap Value Fund Class Y	TCVYX	NAS CM	Open End	US Equity Mid Cap (Growth)	B	B	B		Y	2,500
Touchstone Mid Cap Value Institutional Class	TCVIX	NAS CM	Open End	US Equity Mid Cap (Growth)	B	B	B+		Y	500,000
Touchstone Premium Yield Equity Fund Class A	TPYAX	NAS CM	Open End	US Equity Large Cap Value (Growth & Income)	C+	C+	C+	Down	Y	2,500
Touchstone Premium Yield Equity Fund Class C	TPYCX	NAS CM	Open End	US Equity Large Cap Value (Growth & Income)	C+	C+	C+	Down	Y	2,500
Touchstone Premium Yield Equity Fund Class Y	TPYYX	NAS CM	Open End	US Equity Large Cap Value (Growth & Income)	C+	C+	C+	Down	Y	2,500
Touchstone Sands Capital Emerging Mkts Growth Fund Cls Y	TSEMX	NAS CM	Open End	Emerging Markets Equity (Growth)	B-	B	C	Up	Y	2,500
Touchstone Sands Capital Emerg Mkts Growth Inst Cls	TSEGX	NAS CM	Open End	Emerging Markets Equity (Growth)	B-	B	C	Up	Y	500,000
Touchstone Sands Capital Institutional Growth Fund	CISGX	NAS CM	Open End	US Equity Large Cap Growth (Growth)	B	B	B	Up		500,000
Touchstone Sands Capital Select Growth Fund Class A	TSNAX	NAS CM	Open End	US Equity Large Cap Growth (Growth)	B	B	B	Up		2,500

★ Expanded analysis of this fund is included in Section II.

Min Additional Investment	3-Month Total Return	6-Month Total Return	1-Year Total Return	3-Year Total Return	5-Year Total Return	Dividend Yield (TTM)	Expense Ratio	3-Yr Std Deviation	3-Year Beta	NAV	Total Assets (MIL)	%Cash	%Stocks	%Bonds	%Other	Turnover Ratio	Last Bull Market Total Return	Last Bear Market Total Return	Front End Fee (%)	Back End Fee (%)	Inception Date
	TOTAL RETURNS					PERFORMANCE				ASSETS		ASSET ALLOCATION & TURNOVER					BULL & BEAR		FEES		
50	7.03	10.34	28.62	33.20	59.60	0.53	1.37	12.4	0.92	19.42	199.4	7	93	0	0	36	15.61	-24.11	5.75		Mar-93
50	6.72	9.78	27.26	28.65	49.51	0	2.5	12.37	0.92	18.4	199.4	7	93	0	0	36	14.59	-24.53		1.00	May-98
50	7.17	10.58	29.14	34.70	63.12	0.93	1	12.42	0.92	19.17	199.4	7	93	0	0	36	15.99	-24.01			Aug-07
50	7.14	10.45	28.76	33.34	59.77		0.9	12.4	0.92	19.15	199.4	7	93	0	0	36	15.61	-24.11			Oct-17
50	4.66	11.87	29.73			0.19	1.33			12.91	15.6	2	98	0	0	63			5.75		Mar-16
50	4.47	11.44	28.73			0	2.08			12.8	15.6	2	98	0	0	63				1.00	Mar-16
50	4.73	12.04	30.08			0.35	1.08			12.9	15.6	2	98	0	0	63					Mar-16
50	4.80	12.10	30.13			0.4	0.98			12.92	15.6	2	98	0	0	63					Mar-16
50	5.04	12.67	31.02	30.51	69.52	0.76	1.56	11.24	0.88	18.52	354.8	1	99	0	0	89	18.86	-21.29	5.75		Jul-03
50	4.84	12.22	30.07	27.59	63.30	0	2.31	11.23	0.88	18.26	354.8	1	99	0	0	89	18.22	-21.56		1.00	Apr-12
50	5.11	12.87	31.43	31.54	71.82	1.07	1.31	11.29	0.88	18.9	354.8	1	99	0	0	89	18.91	-21.23			Dec-96
50	5.10	12.87	31.48	31.95	72.89	1.19	1.19	11.28	0.88	18.98	354.8	1	99	0	0	89	19.18	-21.13			Dec-06
50	2.07	8.03	22.51	14.26	32.21	12.75	1.34	11.86	0.88	8.05	24.5	1	99	0	0	23	12.34	-25.02	5.75		Aug-94
50	1.91	7.57	21.59	11.69	27.16	11.92	2.09	11.86	0.88	7.44	24.5	1	99	0	0	23	12	-25.38		1.00	Apr-96
50	2.13	8.15	22.81	15.01	33.89	13.26	1.09	11.78	0.87	8.06	24.5	1	99	0	0	23	12.55	-24.99			Oct-98
50	2.17	8.14	22.92	15.46	34.55	13.77	0.99	11.76	0.87	7.99	24.5	1	99	0	0	23	12.34	-25.02			Sep-12
50	6.92	11.71	23.07	36.33	101.27	0.99	1	10.05	0.99	42.31	1,883	3	97	0	0	8	24.14	-16.97	5.75		Jan-34
50	6.73	11.26	22.10	33.13	93.45	0.35	1.79	10.04	0.99	40.05	1,883	3	97	0	0	8	23.52	-17.26		1.00	May-98
50	7.01	11.86	23.42	37.48	104.18	1.23	0.72	10.04	0.99	42.16	1,883	3	97	0	0	8	24.35	-16.83			May-07
50	7.04	11.94	23.57	37.81	103.50	1.31	0.65	10.04	0.99	42.21	1,883	3	97	0	0	8	24.14	-16.97			Dec-14
50	7.66	12.52	21.24	25.53		0.6	1.12	10.26	0.97	13.41	357.0	2	98	0	0	23			5.75		Jul-14
50	7.47	12.11	20.38	22.92		0.14	1.87	10.29	0.98	13.23	357.0	2	98	0	0	23				1.00	Jul-14
50	7.77	12.71	21.62	26.59		0.78	0.87	10.32	0.98	13.44	357.0	2	98	0	0	23					Jul-14
50	7.69	12.70	21.72	26.97		0.86	0.77	10.3	0.98	13.45	357.0	2	98	0	0	23					Jul-14
50	5.56	13.17	38.04	42.70	117.77	0	1.23	13.26	1.14	39.06	223.2	0	100	0	0	55	29.9	-16.3	5.75		Aug-16
50	5.40	12.77	37.06	39.56	109.82	0	1.98	13.27	1.14	38.65	223.2	0	100	0	0	55	29.33	-16.57		1.00	Aug-16
50	5.67	13.38	38.59	44.01	120.86	0	0.88	13.28	1.14	39.26	223.2	0	100	0	0	55	30.09	-16.22			Aug-09
50	5.65	13.31	38.43	43.80	120.53	0	0.98	13.27	1.14	39.2	223.2	0	100	0	0	55	30.08	-16.22			Aug-16
50	-0.37	-0.37	1.18	6.99	10.59	0	1.74	2.19	6.93	10.37	193.1	21	61	13	1	331	5.64		5.75		Aug-11
50	-0.58	-0.77	0.46	4.52	6.27	0	2.49	2.18	6.98	9.85	193.1	21	61	13	1	331	5.15			1.00	Aug-11
50	-0.37	-0.28	1.44	7.80	11.99	0	1.43	2.2	6.12	10.53	193.1	21	61	13	1	331	5.95				Aug-11
50	-0.28	-0.19	1.62	8.17	12.53	0	1.34	2.16	5.93	10.59	193.1	21	61	13	1	331	5.84				Aug-11
50	6.79	13.13	19.92	29.29	95.71	0.26	1.24	11.59	1.04	32.26	828.7	1	99	0	0	19	22.29	-19.01	5.75		May-07
50	6.55	12.73	19.02	26.42	88.55	0	1.99	11.61	1.04	30.61	828.7	1	99	0	0	19	21.83	-19.3		1.00	May-07
50	6.82	13.26	20.22	30.29	98.22	0.49	0.99	11.62	1.04	32.51	828.7	1	99	0	0	19	22.48	-18.9			Jan-03
50	6.80	13.14	19.93	29.33	95.79	0.24	1.24	11.6	1.04	32.07	828.7	1	99	0	0	19	22.21	-19			Apr-06
50	6.85	13.32	20.32	30.55	98.88	0.55	0.92	11.61	1.04	32.54	828.7	1	99	0	0	19	22.56	-18.9			Jan-12
50	5.29	8.97	24.16	30.09	102.72	0	1.31	11.75	1.03	27.16	753.3	3	97	0	0	95	24.65	-25.99	5.75		Oct-94
50	5.09	8.55	23.24	27.16	95.37	0	2.07	11.78	1.03	17.72	753.3	3	97	0	0	95	24.02	-26.19		1.00	Oct-94
50	5.37	9.09	24.47	31.01	105.32	0	1.07	11.78	1.03	28.13	753.3	3	97	0	0	95	24.81	-25.85			Feb-09
50	5.36	9.13	24.54	31.36	106.38	0	1	11.76	1.03	28.37	753.3	3	97	0	0	95	24.92	-25.88			Apr-11
50	4.25	7.68	13.67	32.61	97.37	0.13	1.27	10.22	0.95	19.02	747.3	3	97	0	0	43	25.37	-23.27	5.75		Sep-09
50	4.05	7.23	12.81	29.62	90.13	0	2.02	10.24	0.96	18.56	747.3	3	97	0	0	43	24.78	-23.5		1.00	Sep-09
50	4.30	7.77	13.91	33.57	99.87	0.37	1.02	10.21	0.95	19.11	747.3	3	97	0	0	43	25.54	-23.23			Sep-09
50	4.36	7.86	14.10	34.17	101.35	0.48	0.89	10.23	0.96	19.21	747.3	3	97	0	0	43	25.74	-23.17			Sep-09
50	3.62	6.07	12.43	17.04	62.33	2.43	1.24	9.99	0.86	9.47	124.6	3	97	0	0	39	20.46	-9.27	5.75		Dec-07
50	3.43	5.67	11.60	14.45	56.37	1.71	1.99	10.01	0.86	9.46	124.6	3	97	0	0	39	19.67	-9.43		1.00	Dec-07
50	3.69	6.22	12.74	17.85	64.57	2.68	0.99	10.06	0.86	9.45	124.6	3	97	0	0	39	20.51	-9.18			Aug-08
50	4.56	12.29	38.34	27.16		0	1.5	14.82	0.82	13.06	465.9	3	97	0	0	49					May-14
50	4.63	12.34	38.47	27.55		0	1.4	14.84	0.82	13.1	465.9	3	97	0	0	49					May-14
50	3.77	10.52	34.74	22.48	93.18	0	0.79	15.11	1.23	20.58	1,940	2	98	0	0	40	35.22	-11.8			Jan-05
50	3.62	10.21	34.15	21.03	89.02	0	1.07	15.14	1.23	13.81	2,528	3	97	0	0	22	34.71	-11.99	5.75		Nov-10

	MARKET			FUND TYPE, CATEGORY & OBJECTIVE	RATINGS				MINIMUMS	
Fund Name	Ticker Symbol	Traded On	Fund Type	Category and (Prospectus Objective)	Overall Rating	Reward Rating	Risk Rating	Recent Up/ Downgrade	Open to New Investors	Min Initial Investment
Touchstone Sands Capital Select Growth Fund Class C	TSNCX	NAS CM	Open End	US Equity Large Cap Growth (Growth)	B-	B-	B	Up		2,500
Touchstone Sands Capital Select Growth Fund Class Y	CFSIX	NAS CM	Open End	US Equity Large Cap Growth (Growth)	B	B	B	Up		2,500
Touchstone Sands Capital Select Growth Fund Class Z	PTSGX	NAS CM	Open End	US Equity Large Cap Growth (Growth)	B	B	B	Up		2,500
Touchstone Small Cap Class A	TSFAX	NAS CM	Open End	US Equity Small Cap (Small Company)	C	C	C+	Down		2,500
Touchstone Small Cap Class C	TSFCX	NAS CM	Open End	US Equity Small Cap (Small Company)	C	C	C+	Down		2,500
Touchstone Small Cap Class Y	TSFYX	NAS CM	Open End	US Equity Small Cap (Small Company)	C+	C	C+	Down		2,500
Touchstone Small Cap Growth Fund Class A	MXCAX	NAS CM	Open End	US Equity Small Cap (Small Company)	C+	C	B-	Up	Y	2,500
Touchstone Small Cap Growth Fund Class C	MXCSX	NAS CM	Open End	US Equity Small Cap (Small Company)	C+	C	B-	Up	Y	2,500
Touchstone Small Cap Growth Fund Class Instl	MXCIX	NAS CM	Open End	US Equity Small Cap (Small Company)	C+	C+	B-	Up	Y	500,000
Touchstone Small Cap Growth Fund Class Y	MXAIX	NAS CM	Open End	US Equity Small Cap (Small Company)	C+	C+	B-	Up	Y	2,500
Touchstone Small Cap Institutional Class	TSFIX	NAS CM	Open End	US Equity Small Cap (Small Company)	C+	C	C+	Down		500,000
Touchstone Small Cap Value Fund Class A	TVOAX	NAS CM	Open End	US Equity Small Cap (Small Company)	B-	B-	C+	Up	Y	2,500
Touchstone Small Cap Value Fund Class C	TVOCX	NAS CM	Open End	US Equity Small Cap (Small Company)	C+	C+	C+	Up	Y	2,500
Touchstone Small Cap Value Fund Class Y	TVOYX	NAS CM	Open End	US Equity Small Cap (Small Company)	B-	B-	C+	Up	Y	2,500
Touchstone Small Cap Value Fund Institutional Class	TVOIX	NAS CM	Open End	US Equity Small Cap (Small Company)	B-	B-	C+	Up	Y	500,000
Touchstone Small Cap Value Opportunities Fund Class A	TSOAX	NAS CM	Open End	US Equity Small Cap (Small Company)	C	C	C	Up	Y	2,500
Touchstone Small Cap Value Opportunities Fund Class C	TSOCX	NAS CM	Open End	US Equity Small Cap (Small Company)	C	C	C	Up	Y	2,500
Touchstone Small Cap Value Opportunities Fund Class Y	TSOYX	NAS CM	Open End	US Equity Small Cap (Small Company)	C	C	C	Up	Y	2,500
Touchstone Small Cap Value Opp Fund Inst	TSOIX	NAS CM	Open End	US Equity Small Cap (Small Company)	C	C	C	Up	Y	500,000
Touchstone Small Company Fund Class A	SAGWX	NAS CM	Open End	US Equity Small Cap (Small Company)	B	B	B	Up	Y	2,500
Touchstone Small Company Fund Class C	SSCOX	NAS CM	Open End	US Equity Small Cap (Small Company)	B	B	B	Up	Y	2,500
Touchstone Small Company Fund Class R6	SSRRX	NAS CM	Open End	US Equity Small Cap (Small Company)	B	B	B	Up	Y	50,000
Touchstone Small Company Fund Class Y	SIGWX	NAS CM	Open End	US Equity Small Cap (Small Company)	B	B	B	Up	Y	2,500
Touchstone Small Company Fund Institutional USD	TICSX	NAS CM	Open End	US Equity Small Cap (Small Company)	B	B	B		Y	500,000
Touchstone Sustainability and Impact Equity Fund Class A	TEQAX	NAS CM	Open End	Global Equity (Growth)	B-	B	C+	Down	Y	2,500
Touchstone Sustainability and Impact Equity Fund Class C	TEQCX	NAS CM	Open End	Global Equity (Growth)	B-	B-	C+	Down	Y	2,500
Touchstone Sustainability and Impact Equity Fund Class Y	TIQIX	NAS CM	Open End	Global Equity (Growth)	B-	B	C+	Down	Y	2,500
Touchstone Sustainability & Impact Equity Fund Inst Cls	TROCX	NAS CM	Open End	Global Equity (Growth)	B-	B	C+	Down	Y	500,000
Touchstone Value Fund Class A	TVLAX	NAS CM	Open End	US Equity Large Cap Value (Growth)	B	C+	B	Up	Y	2,500
Touchstone Value Fund Class C	TVLCX	NAS CM	Open End	US Equity Large Cap Value (Growth)	B-	C+	B	Down	Y	2,500
Touchstone Value Fund Class Y	TVLYX	NAS CM	Open End	US Equity Large Cap Value (Growth)	B	C+	B	Up	Y	2,500
Touchstone Value Fund Institutional	TVLIX	NAS CM	Open End	US Equity Large Cap Value (Growth)	B	B-	B	Up	Y	500,000
Towle Deep Value Fund	TDVFX	NAS CM	Open End	US Equity Small Cap (Growth)	B+	A+	C+	Up	Y	5,000
Transamerica Asset Allocation Conservative Portfolio Adv	TACVX	NAS CM	Open End	Cautious Alloc (Asset Alloc)	B-	C+	B	Up	Y	1,000
Transamerica Asset Allocation Conservative Portfolio Cls A	ICLAX	NAS CM	Open End	Cautious Alloc (Asset Alloc)	B	C+	A-	Up	Y	1,000
Transamerica Asset Allocation Conservative Portfolio Cls B	ICLBX	NAS CM	Open End	Cautious Alloc (Asset Alloc)	B	C	A-	Up		1,000
Transamerica Asset Allocation Conservative Portfolio Cls C	ICLLX	NAS CM	Open End	Cautious Alloc (Asset Alloc)	B	C+	A-	Up	Y	1,000
Transamerica Asset Allocation Conservative Portfolio Cls I	TACIX	NAS CM	Open End	Cautious Alloc (Asset Alloc)	B-	C+	B	Up	Y	1,000,000
Transamerica Asset Allocation Conservative Portfolio Cls R	ICVRX	NAS CM	Open End	Cautious Alloc (Asset Alloc)	B	C+	A-	Up	Y	0
Transamerica Asset Alloc Conservative Port Cls T1	TACQX	NAS CM	Open End	Cautious Alloc (Asset Alloc)	B	C+	A-	Up	Y	1,000
Transamerica Asset Allocation Growth Portfolio Class A	IAAAX	NAS CM	Open End	Aggressive Alloc (Asset Alloc)	B-	B-	B-	Down	Y	1,000
Transamerica Asset Allocation Growth Portfolio Class B	IAABX	NAS CM	Open End	Aggressive Alloc (Asset Alloc)	B-	B-	B-	Down		1,000
Transamerica Asset Allocation Growth Portfolio Class C	IAALX	NAS CM	Open End	Aggressive Alloc (Asset Alloc)	B-	B-	B-	Down	Y	1,000
Transamerica Asset Allocation Growth Portfolio Class I	TAGIX	NAS CM	Open End	Aggressive Alloc (Asset Alloc)	B-	B-	B-	Down	Y	1,000,000
Transamerica Asset Allocation Growth Portfolio Class R	IGWRX	NAS CM	Open End	Aggressive Alloc (Asset Alloc)	B-	B-	B-	Down	Y	0
Transamerica Asset Allocation Growth Portfolio Fund Adv	TAGVX	NAS CM	Open End	Aggressive Alloc (Asset Alloc)	B-	B-	B-	Down	Y	1,000
Transamerica Asset Allocation Growth Portfolio Fund Cls T1	TAGTX	NAS CM	Open End	Aggressive Alloc (Asset Alloc)	B-	B-	B-	Down	Y	1,000
Transamerica Asset Allocation Intermediate Horizon R	TAARX	NAS CM	Open End	Moderate Alloc (Asset Alloc)	B-	C+	B		Y	0
Transamerica Asset Allocation Intermediate Horizon R4	TAAFX	NAS CM	Open End	Moderate Alloc (Asset Alloc)	B-	C+	B	Up	Y	0
Transamerica Asset Allocation Long Horizon R	TALRX	NAS CM	Open End	Aggressive Alloc (Asset Alloc)	B-	B-	B-	Down	Y	0
Transamerica Asset Allocation Long Horizon R4	TALFX	NAS CM	Open End	Aggressive Alloc (Asset Alloc)	B-	B-	B-	Down	Y	0
Transamerica Asset Alloc Moderate Growth Port Cls A	IMLAX	NAS CM	Open End	Moderate Alloc (Asset Alloc)	B-	C+	B	Down	Y	1,000

★ Expanded analysis of this fund is included in Section II.

Min Additional Investment	TOTAL RETURNS: 3-Month Total Return	6-Month Total Return	1-Year Total Return	3-Year Total Return	5-Year Total Return	PERFORMANCE: Dividend Yield (TTM)	Expense Ratio	3-Yr Std Deviation	3-Year Beta	ASSETS: NAV	Total Assets (MIL)	ASSET ALLOCATION & TURNOVER: %Cash	%Stocks	%Bonds	%Other	Turnover Ratio	BULL & BEAR: Last Bull Market Total Return	Last Bear Market Total Return	FEES: Front End Fee (%)	Back End Fee (%)	Inception Date
50	3.48	9.86	33.20	18.43	82.21	0	1.82	15.13	1.23	12.69	2,528	3	97	0	0	22	34.08	-12.22		1.00	Nov-10
50	3.71	10.35	34.44	21.96	91.45	0	0.82	15.15	1.23	14.56	2,528	3	97	0	0	22	34.72	-11.8			Aug-04
50	3.70	10.28	34.22	21.17	89.25	0	1.04	15.19	1.24	13.83	2,528	3	97	0	0	22	34.61	-11.99			Aug-00
50	3.37	8.00	5.93	8.11	45.55	0	1.38	13.7	0.85	14.97	218.5	3	97	0	0	18	34.24	-17.88	5.75		Sep-09
50	3.15	7.53	5.08	5.70	40.13	0	2.13	13.66	0.85	14.27	218.5	3	97	0	0	18	33.66	-18.12		1.00	Sep-09
50	3.42	8.06	6.17	8.90	47.46	0.29	1.13	13.72	0.85	15.13	218.5	3	97	0	0	18	34.46	-17.8			Sep-09
50	4.13	9.45	9.86	11.37	58.81	0	1.45	13.34	0.84	5.79	297.0	3	97	0	0	58	24.64	-21.55	5.75		Aug-01
50	3.72	8.96	8.96	8.77	52.86	0	2.2	13.43	0.85	4.74	297.0	3	97	0	0	58	24.28	-21.75		1.00	Aug-01
50	4.30	9.73	10.28	12.77	62.31	0	1.05	13.48	0.85	6.54	297.0	3	97	0	0	58	24.86	-21.39			Sep-12
50	4.17	9.83	10.01	12.32	60.88	0	1.2	13.48	0.85	6.48	297.0	3	97	0	0	58	24.86	-21.39			Feb-98
50	3.46	8.17	6.28	9.23	48.11	0.38	1.04	13.68	0.85	15.08	218.5	3	97	0	0	18	34.54	-17.7			Sep-09
50	2.72	5.60	7.21	16.96	61.85	0.06	1.39	15.84	1.04	26.77	91.1	2	98	0	0	63	30.36	-22.65	5.75		Mar-02
50	2.49	5.17	6.36	14.33	55.94	0	2.14	15.81	1.04	26.24	91.1	2	98	0	0	63	29.82	-22.92		1.00	Mar-11
50	2.80	5.71	7.48	17.86	63.89	0.17	1.14	15.84	1.04	26.86	91.1	2	98	0	0	63	30.61	-22.41			Mar-11
50	2.82	5.78	7.63	18.36	65.13	0.23	0.99	15.84	1.04	26.84	91.1	2	98	0	0	63	30.76	-22.55			Mar-11
50	3.19	5.84	2.72	5.41	67.68	0	1.43	15.11	1.02	17.74	108.8	2	98	0	0	59	26.2	-22.85	5.75		Jul-03
50	3.01	5.43	1.97	3.02	61.54	0	2.18	15.1	1.02	17.06	108.8	2	98	0	0	59	25.64	-23.11		1.00	Apr-12
50	3.27	5.94	2.94	6.14	69.96	0.04	1.18	15.1	1.02	18.9	108.8	2	98	0	0	59	26.37	-22.78			Jul-03
50	3.28	6.02	3.06	6.47	70.73	0.11	1.1	15.12	1.02	19.19	108.8	2	98	0	0	59	26.48	-22.76			Dec-08
50	6.16	8.59	17.33	36.60	100.38	0	1.23	12.29	0.84	5.22	1,238	19	81	0	0	61	23.66	-20.31	5.75		Mar-93
50	6.05	8.32	16.55	34.01	93.33	0	1.96	12.19	0.83	3.06	1,238	19	81	0	0	61	23.24	-20.59		1.00	Jul-01
50	6.24	8.84	17.93	38.70	103.48	0	0.74	12.1	0.83	5.32	1,238	19	81	0	0	61	23.66	-20.31			Dec-14
50	6.03	8.65	17.58	37.88	103.67	0	0.9	12.2	0.83	5.68	1,238	19	81	0	0	61	23.91	-20.08			May-07
50	6.13	8.56	17.29	36.56	100.32		0.8	12.3	0.84	5.68	1,238	19	81	0	0	61	23.65	-20.31			Oct-17
50	5.32	9.95	25.73	29.97	92.21	0.44	1.25	10.55	0.88	22.4	776.0	2	98	0	0	53	22.05	-10.77	5.75		Dec-97
50	5.10	9.48	24.79	27.07	85.05	0.05	2	10.54	0.88	19.04	776.0	2	98	0	0	53	21.5	-11.03		1.00	Oct-03
50	5.39	10.07	26.05	30.96	94.61	0.6	1	10.55	0.88	23.13	776.0	2	98	0	0	53	22.19	-10.66			Nov-04
50	5.40	10.12	26.14	31.01	93.74	0.65	0.9	10.56	0.89	23.15	776.0	2	98	0	0	53	22.05	-10.77			May-15
50	5.74	7.17	13.93	24.72	85.71	2.02	1.08	10.39	0.98	10.01	393.1	0	100	0	0	29	24.73	-16.53	5.75		Jul-03
50	5.48	6.70	13.02	21.89	78.68	1.11	1.83	10.37	0.98	9.97	393.1	0	100	0	0	29	24.28	-16.86		1.00	Apr-12
50	5.90	7.29	14.30	25.71	88.12	2.32	0.83	10.36	0.97	10.05	393.1	0	100	0	0	29	25.01	-16.52			Sep-98
50	5.84	7.37	14.37	26.20	89.21	2.5	0.68	10.36	0.97	10.02	393.1	0	100	0	0	29	24.89	-16.35			Dec-06
500	4.83	17.91	14.80	47.67	142.74	0	1.2	24.54	1.57	18.75	121.8	3	97	0	0	40					Oct-11
50	1.92	4.36	9.92	15.05	30.78		1.09	4.14	0.28	11.18	1,097	10	35	49	5	4	9.92	-8.33			Mar-17
50	1.89	4.22	9.86	14.99	30.70	2.07	1.22	4.14	0.29	11.12	1,097	10	35	49	5	4	9.92	-8.33	5.50		Mar-02
50	1.64	3.78	8.90	12.12	25.57	1.16	2.04	4.13	0.28	11.08	1,097	10	35	49	5	4	9.48	-8.53		5.00	Mar-02
50	1.72	3.85	9.08	12.54	26.20	1.33	1.96	4.15	0.29	11.03	1,097	10	35	49	5	4	9.53	-8.49		1.00	Nov-02
	1.94	4.41	10.16	15.82	32.39	2.26	1	4.12	0.28	11.15	1,097	10	35	49	5	4	10.15	-8.14			Nov-09
	1.81	4.11	9.56	13.73	28.58	1.67	1.6	4.16	0.28	11.24	1,097	10	35	49	5	4	9.81	-8.45			Jun-06
50	1.82	4.25	9.89	15.02	30.74		1.22	4.14	0.29	11.15	1,097	10	35	49	5	4	9.92	-8.33	2.50		Mar-17
50	4.51	9.11	20.15	28.90	76.86	1.38	1.45	8.97	0.85	15.18	1,540	10	93	-8	5	1	21.27	-20.07	5.50		Mar-02
50	4.33	8.59	19.08	25.63	69.83	0.4	2.29	8.96	0.85	15.08	1,540	10	93	-8	5	1	20.78	-20.29		5.00	Mar-02
50	4.37	8.75	19.34	26.17	70.79	0.78	2.19	9	0.85	14.75	1,540	10	93	-8	5	1	20.83	-20.29		1.00	Nov-02
	4.59	9.20	20.51	29.91	79.42	1.61	1.18	9.02	0.85	15.15	1,540	10	93	-8	5	1	21.5	-19.9			Nov-09
	4.49	8.99	19.86	27.78	74.39	1.14	1.78	8.96	0.85	15.06	1,540	10	93	-8	5	1	21.15	-20.15			Jun-06
50	4.57	9.11	20.23	28.99	76.98		1.27	8.97	0.85	15.23	1,540	10	93	-8	5	1	21.27	-20.07			Mar-17
50	4.56	9.16	20.28	29.04	77.05		1.45	8.97	0.85	15.25	1,540	10	93	-8	5	1	21.27	-20.07	2.50		Mar-17
	3.01	5.51	11.46	17.06	40.52		1.16	5.72	0.54	10.52	445.4	4	49	45	1	45	13.84	-10.53			May-17
	3.19	5.62	11.71	17.91	42.25	1.64	0.91	5.72	0.54	10.52	445.4	4	49	45	1	45	14.01	-10.44			Sep-00
	5.11	8.98	18.18	25.77	68.87		1.27	9.68	0.92	10.94	258.5	2	88	9	1	28	21.83	-19.09			May-17
	5.17	9.11	18.48	26.72	71.00	0.91	1.02	9.69	0.92	10.94	258.5	2	88	9	1	28	22.01	-19.01			Sep-00
50	3.42	7.02	15.86	22.86	57.74	1.62	1.33	7.14	0.66	13.39	2,672	11	68	16	4	1	16.82	-16.28	5.50		Mar-02

Fund Name	Ticker Symbol	Traded On	Fund Type	Category and (Prospectus Objective)	Overall Rating	Reward Rating	Risk Rating	Recent Up/ Downgrade	Open to New Investors	Min Initial Investment
	MARKET		FUND TYPE, CATEGORY & OBJECTIVE		RATINGS				MINIMUMS	
Transamerica Asset Alloc Moderate Growth Port Cls B	IMLBX	NAS CM	Open End	Moderate Alloc (Asset Alloc)	B-	C+	B	Down		1,000
Transamerica Asset Alloc Moderate Growth Port Cls C	IMLLX	NAS CM	Open End	Moderate Alloc (Asset Alloc)	B-	C+	B	Down	Y	1,000
Transamerica Asset Alloc Moderate Growth Port Cls I	TMGIX	NAS CM	Open End	Moderate Alloc (Asset Alloc)	B-	C+	B	Down	Y	1,000,000
Transamerica Asset Alloc Moderate Growth Port Cls R	IMGRX	NAS CM	Open End	Moderate Alloc (Asset Alloc)	B-	C+	B	Down	Y	0
Transamerica Asset Alloc Moderate Growth Port Fund Adv	TMGQX	NAS CM	Open End	Moderate Alloc (Asset Alloc)	B-	C+	B	Down	Y	1,000
Transamerica Asset Alloc Moderate Growth Port Fund Cls T1	TMGUX	NAS CM	Open End	Moderate Alloc (Asset Alloc)	B-	C+	B	Down	Y	1,000
Transamerica Asset Allocation Moderate Portfolio Class A	IMOAX	NAS CM	Open End	Cautious Alloc (Asset Alloc)	B	C+	A-	Up	Y	1,000
Transamerica Asset Allocation Moderate Portfolio Class B	IMOBX	NAS CM	Open End	Cautious Alloc (Asset Alloc)	B	C+	B+	Up		1,000
Transamerica Asset Allocation Moderate Portfolio Class C	IMOLX	NAS CM	Open End	Cautious Alloc (Asset Alloc)	B	C+	A-	Up	Y	1,000
Transamerica Asset Allocation Moderate Portfolio Class I	TMMIX	NAS CM	Open End	Cautious Alloc (Asset Alloc)	B-	C+	B	Up	Y	1,000,000
Transamerica Asset Allocation Moderate Portfolio Class R	IMDRX	NAS CM	Open End	Cautious Alloc (Asset Alloc)	B-	C+	B	Up	Y	0
Transamerica Asset Allocation Moderate Portfolio Fund Adv	TMMVX	NAS CM	Open End	Cautious Alloc (Asset Alloc)	B-	C+	B	Up	Y	1,000
Transamerica Asset Alloc Moderate Port Fund Cls T1	TMMTX	NAS CM	Open End	Cautious Alloc (Asset Alloc)	B-	C+	B	Up	Y	1,000
Transamerica Balanced II I3	TBLTX	NAS CM	Open End	Moderate Alloc (Balanced)	B-	C+	B		Y	0
Transamerica Balanced II R	TBLRX	NAS CM	Open End	Moderate Alloc (Balanced)	B-	C+	B	Down	Y	0
Transamerica Capital Growth Fund Class A	IALAX	NAS CM	Open End	US Equity Large Cap Growth (Growth)	B+	A-	B	Up	Y	1,000
Transamerica Capital Growth Fund Class Advisor	TACGX	NAS CM	Open End	US Equity Large Cap Growth (Growth)	B+	A-	B	Up	Y	1,000
Transamerica Capital Growth Fund Class B	IACBX	NAS CM	Open End	US Equity Large Cap Growth (Growth)	B+	B+	B	Up		1,000
Transamerica Capital Growth Fund Class C	ILLLX	NAS CM	Open End	US Equity Large Cap Growth (Growth)	B+	B+	B	Up	Y	1,000
Transamerica Capital Growth Fund Class I	TFOIX	NAS CM	Open End	US Equity Large Cap Growth (Growth)	B+	A-	B+	Up	Y	1,000,000
Transamerica Capital Growth Fund Class I2	US8935091335		Open End	US Equity Large Cap Growth (Growth)	B+	A-	B+	Up	Y	0
Transamerica Capital Growth Fund Class T1	TFOTX	NAS CM	Open End	US Equity Large Cap Growth (Growth)	B+	A-	B	Up	Y	1,000
Transamerica Concentrated Growth Fund Class A	TORAX	NAS CM	Open End	US Equity Large Cap Growth (Growth)	B	B	B		Y	1,000
Transamerica Concentrated Growth Fund Class Advisor	TACNX	NAS CM	Open End	US Equity Large Cap Growth (Growth)	B	B	B		Y	1,000
Transamerica Concentrated Growth Fund Class C	TCCGX	NAS CM	Open End	US Equity Large Cap Growth (Growth)	B	B-	B		Y	1,000
Transamerica Concentrated Growth Fund Class I	TOREX	NAS CM	Open End	US Equity Large Cap Growth (Growth)	B	B	B+		Y	1,000,000
Transamerica Concentrated Growth Fund Class I2	US89354D8175		Open End	US Equity Large Cap Growth (Growth)	B	B	B		Y	0
Transamerica Concentrated Growth Fund Class T1	TORQX	NAS CM	Open End	US Equity Large Cap Growth (Growth)	B	B	B		Y	1,000
Transamerica Developing Markets Equity Fund Class I2	TDMIX	NAS CM	Open End	Emerging Markets Equity (Div Emerging Mkts)	C+	B-	C	Up	Y	0
Transamerica Dividend Focused Advisor	TADVX	NAS CM	Open End	US Equity Large Cap Value (Growth & Income)	B-	B-	B-	Down	Y	1,000
Transamerica Dividend Focused Class A	TDFAX	NAS CM	Open End	US Equity Large Cap Value (Growth & Income)	B-	B-	B-	Down	Y	1,000
Transamerica Dividend Focused Class C	TDFCX	NAS CM	Open End	US Equity Large Cap Value (Growth & Income)	B-	B-	B	Down	Y	1,000
Transamerica Dividend Focused Class I	TDFIX	NAS CM	Open End	US Equity Large Cap Value (Growth & Income)	B-	B-	B-	Down	Y	1,000,000
Transamerica Dividend Focused Class I2	TRDIX	NAS CM	Open End	US Equity Large Cap Value (Growth & Income)	B-	B-	B-	Down	Y	0
Transamerica Dividend Focused Class R6	TADFX	NAS CM	Open End	US Equity Large Cap Value (Growth & Income)	B-	B-	B-	Down	Y	0
Transamerica Dividend Focused Class T1	TADTX	NAS CM	Open End	US Equity Large Cap Value (Growth & Income)	B	B-	B	Up	Y	1,000
Transamerica Dynamic Allocation Fund Class A	ATTRX	NAS CM	Open End	Moderate Alloc (Growth & Income)	B-	C+	B	Up	Y	1,000
Transamerica Dynamic Allocation Fund Class C	CTTRX	NAS CM	Open End	Moderate Alloc (Growth & Income)	C+	C+	B	Down	Y	1,000
Transamerica Dynamic Allocation Fund Class I	ITTOX	NAS CM	Open End	Moderate Alloc (Growth & Income)	B-	C+	B	Up	Y	1,000,000
Transamerica Dynamic Allocation Fund Class T1	ATTTX	NAS CM	Open End	Moderate Alloc (Growth & Income)	B-	C+	B	Up	Y	1,000
Transamerica Dynamic Income Fund Advisor	IGTVX	NAS CM	Open End	Cautious Alloc (Income)	C+	C	B-	Down	Y	1,000
Transamerica Dynamic Income Fund Class A	IGTAX	NAS CM	Open End	Cautious Alloc (Income)	C+	C	B-		Y	1,000
Transamerica Dynamic Income Fund Class C	IGTCX	NAS CM	Open End	Cautious Alloc (Income)	C+	C	C+		Y	1,000
Transamerica Dynamic Income Fund Class I	IGTIX	NAS CM	Open End	Cautious Alloc (Income)	C+	C	B-		Y	1,000,000
Transamerica Dynamic Income Fund Class T1	IGTTX	NAS CM	Open End	Cautious Alloc (Income)	C+	C	B-		Y	1,000
Transamerica Emerging Markets Equity Fund Advisor	TAEEX	NAS CM	Open End	Emerging Markets Equity (Div Emerging Mkts)	C+	B-	C	Up	Y	1,000
Transamerica Emerging Markets Equity Fund Class A	AEMTX	NAS CM	Open End	Emerging Markets Equity (Div Emerging Mkts)	C+	B-	C	Up	Y	1,000
Transamerica Emerging Markets Equity Fund Class C	CEMTX	NAS CM	Open End	Emerging Markets Equity (Div Emerging Mkts)	C+	B-	C	Up	Y	1,000
Transamerica Emerging Markets Equity Fund Class I	IEMTX	NAS CM	Open End	Emerging Markets Equity (Div Emerging Mkts)	C+	B-	C	Up	Y	1,000,000
Transamerica Emerging Markets Equity Fund Class I2	US89355J8541		Open End	Emerging Markets Equity (Div Emerging Mkts)	C+	B-	C	Up	Y	0
Transamerica Emerging Markets Equity Fund Class T1	AEMQX	NAS CM	Open End	Emerging Markets Equity (Div Emerging Mkts)	C+	B-	C	Up	Y	1,000
Transamerica Event Driven Fund Class Advisor	TAEVX	NAS CM	Open End	Multialternative (Growth)	C+	C	B	Up	Y	1,000

★Expanded analysis of this fund is included in Section II.

	TOTAL RETURNS					PERFORMANCE				ASSETS		ASSET ALLOCATION & TURNOVER					BULL & BEAR		FEES		
Min Additional Investment	3-Month Total Return	6-Month Total Return	1-Year Total Return	3-Year Total Return	5-Year Total Return	Dividend Yield (TTM)	Expense Ratio	3-Yr Std Deviation	3-Year Beta	NAV	Total Assets (MIL)	%Cash	%Stocks	%Bonds	%Other	Turnover Ratio	Last Bull Market Total Return	Last Bear Market Total Return	Front End Fee (%)	Back End Fee (%)	Inception Date
50	3.24	6.64	14.87	19.89	51.49	0.5	2.17	7.12	0.66	13.78	2,672	11	68	16	4	1	16.32	-16.53		5.00	Mar-02
50	3.23	6.62	15.02	20.23	52.13	0.92	2.07	7.09	0.66	13.39	2,672	11	68	16	4	1	16.36	-16.5		1.00	Nov-02
	3.46	7.22	16.19	23.82	59.84	1.84	1.08	7.11	0.66	13.36	2,672	11	68	16	4	1	17.1	-16.2			Nov-09
	3.36	6.90	15.51	21.90	55.81	1.35	1.62	7.11	0.66	13.34	2,672	11	68	16	4	1	16.78	-16.43			Jun-06
50	5.62	8.71	17.12	24.19	59.45		1.17	7.07	0.66	12.1	2,672	11	68	16	4	1	16.82	-16.28			Mar-17
50	3.40	7.01	15.93	22.93	57.83		1.33	7.13	0.66	13.45	2,672	11	68	16	4	1	16.82	-16.28	2.50		Mar-17
50	2.45	5.43	12.45	18.15	41.87	1.76	1.25	5.27	0.47	12.07	1,954	11	49	35	5	2	13.34	-11.77	5.50		Mar-02
50	2.29	4.97	11.45	15.27	36.38	0.7	2.08	5.25	0.47	12.45	1,954	11	49	35	5	2	12.79	-12.07		5.00	Mar-02
50	2.34	5.08	11.62	15.62	36.92	1.02	1.99	5.24	0.47	12.07	1,954	11	49	35	5	2	12.93	-12.06		1.00	Nov-02
	2.61	5.60	12.73	19.00	43.74	1.96	1.02	5.24	0.47	12.05	1,954	11	49	35	5	2	13.47	-11.61			Nov-09
	2.45	5.37	12.22	17.35	40.34	1.51	1.51	5.27	0.47	12.03	1,954	11	49	35	5	2	13.22	-11.83			Jun-06
50	0.76	4.36	11.93	17.61	41.23		1.11	5.37	0.48	13.42	1,954	11	49	35	5	2	13.34	-11.77			Mar-17
50	2.52	5.51	12.52	18.24	41.97		1.25	5.27	0.47	12.13	1,954	11	49	35	5	2	13.34	-11.77	2.50		Mar-17
	4.16	7.11	13.80	21.78	60.53		0.5	5.98	0.58	10.36	148.5	2	57	36	4	37	16.42	-9.27			Sep-17
	4.01	6.96	13.64	21.60	60.29	1.05	1.14	5.98	0.58	10.36	148.5	2	57	36	4	37	16.42	-9.27			Jul-94
50	7.36	12.34	43.89	54.32	148.46	0	1.23	15.11	1.18	23.44	853.5	7	93	0	0	32	20.94	-16.25	5.50		Mar-99
50	7.43	12.44	44.17	54.63	148.96		1.01	15.12	1.18	24.52	853.5	7	93	0	0	32	20.94	-16.25			Dec-16
50	7.13	11.79	42.54	49.89	137.17	0	2.2	15.09	1.18	18.48	853.5	7	93	0	0	32	20.61	-16.52		5.00	Mar-99
50	7.21	11.96	42.90	51.01	140.02	0	1.96	15.11	1.18	18.84	853.5	7	93	0	0	32	20.55	-16.53		1.00	Nov-02
	7.46	12.51	44.32	55.64	152.52	0	0.94	15.13	1.18	24.55	853.5	7	93	0	0	32	21.35	-16.08			Nov-09
	7.46	12.54	44.42	56.10	153.88	0	0.81	15.11	1.18	12.18	853.5	7	93	0	0	32	21.49	-16.25			Sep-11
50	7.44	12.46	44.05	54.49	148.74		1.23	15.12	1.18	23.47	853.5	7	93	0	0	32	20.94	-16.25	2.50		Mar-17
50	4.59	9.65	24.01	27.86	85.53	0.27	1.12	10.21	0.89	17.34	228.5	1	99	0	0	83	25.81	-12.85	5.50		Mar-14
50	4.66	9.80	24.30	28.77	87.67		0.92	10.23	0.9	17.31	228.5	1	99	0	0	83	26	-12.76			Dec-16
50	4.40	9.31	23.14	25.17	78.98	0	1.81	10.21	0.9	16.88	228.5	1	99	0	0	83	25.27	-13.13		1.00	Mar-14
	4.73	9.91	24.46	28.94	87.92	0.55	0.83	10.24	0.9	17.18	228.5	1	99	0	0	83	26	-12.76			Dec-10
	4.70	9.87	24.47	29.26	88.82	0.61	0.72	10.25	0.9	17.39	228.5	1	99	0	0	83	26	-12.76			Mar-14
50	4.65	9.77	24.26	28.08	85.74		1.12	10.24	0.9	17.36	228.5	1	99	0	0	83	25.81	-12.85	2.50		Mar-17
	4.81	13.17	33.36	21.44	23.91	0.08	1.21	14.7	0.87	12.43	1,178	3	96	0	1	27	18.21	-23.15			Dec-05
50	5.38	8.40	16.00	28.36	84.55		0.9	9.59	0.9	11.35	706.9	0	100	0	0	54					Dec-16
50	5.40	8.31	15.90	27.67	82.42	1.77	0.97	9.6	0.9	11.27	706.9	0	100	0	0	54			5.50		Jan-13
50	5.21	7.88	15.01	24.57	75.21	1.05	1.8	9.61	0.9	11.22	706.9	0	100	0	0	54				1.00	Jan-13
	5.37	8.43	16.13	28.22	83.88	1.92	0.81	9.64	0.91	11.26	706.9	0	100	0	0	54					Jan-13
	5.47	8.46	16.21	28.59	84.88	2	0.7	9.6	0.9	11.27	706.9	0	100	0	0	54					Jan-13
	5.47	8.46	16.32	28.60	84.89	2	0.71	9.59	0.9	11.27	706.9	0	100	0	0	54					May-15
50	5.39	8.31	15.89	27.60	82.54		0.97	9.6	0.9	11.31	706.9	0	100	0	0	54			2.50		Mar-17
50	3.69	6.72	12.50	14.64	43.53	1.14	1.32	5.98	0.55	11.95	18.9	2	70	27	1	142			5.50		Oct-12
50	3.55	6.33	11.75	12.09	38.30	0.41	2.07	5.95	0.55	11.85	18.9	2	70	27	1	142				1.00	Oct-12
	3.80	6.85	12.86	15.53	45.46	1.41	1.07	5.98	0.55	11.9	18.9	2	70	27	1	142					Oct-12
50	3.71	6.74	12.57	14.66	43.64		1.32	5.98	0.55	11.97	18.9	2	70	27	1	142			2.50		Mar-17
50	1.29	2.71	7.10	9.96	21.37		1.08	6.85	1.06	9.53	319.1	2	31	67	0	27					Mar-17
50	1.33	2.70	6.97	9.30	20.09	4.26	1.3	6.84	1.06	9.54	319.1	2	31	67	0	27			4.75		Oct-11
50	1.14	2.31	6.06	6.82	15.67	3.5	2.06	6.87	1.07	9.5	319.1	2	31	67	0	27				1.00	Oct-11
	1.40	2.83	7.23	10.08	21.51	4.5	1.06	6.85	1.06	9.54	319.1	2	31	67	0	27					Oct-11
50	1.25	2.64	6.92	9.22	19.96		1.3	6.84	1.06	9.56	319.1	2	31	67	0	27			2.50		Mar-17
50	5.40	13.90	37.57	18.86	19.72		1.39	15.88	0.98	11.49	238.8	2	97	0	1	61					Dec-16
50	5.20	13.68	37.16	17.59	17.74	1.29	1.73	15.88	0.98	11.21	238.8	2	97	0	1	61			5.50		Apr-12
50	5.12	13.45	36.31	15.45	14.05	0.82	2.33	15.92	0.99	11.16	238.8	2	97	0	1	61				1.00	Apr-12
	5.34	14.01	37.61	18.89	19.76	1.5	1.31	15.88	0.98	11.26	238.8	2	97	0	1	61					Apr-12
	5.40	14.06	37.81	19.37	20.45	1.61	1.19	15.84	0.98	11.27	238.8	2	97	0	1	61					Apr-12
50	5.29	13.88	37.40	18.12	18.38		1.73	15.87	0.98	11.24	238.8	2	97	0	1	61			2.50		Mar-17
50	1.34	2.92	5.38				1.4			10.41	89.5	14	39	17	2	579					Dec-16

	MARKET			FUND TYPE, CATEGORY & OBJECTIVE	RATINGS					MINIMUMS
Fund Name	Ticker Symbol	Traded On	Fund Type	Category and (Prospectus Objective)	Overall Rating	Reward Rating	Risk Rating	Recent Up/ Downgrade	Open to New Investors	Min Initial Investment
Transamerica Event Driven Fund Class I	TENIX	NAS CM	Open End	Multialternative (Growth)	C+	C	B	Up	Y	1,000,000
Transamerica Event Driven Fund Class I2	US89354D7425		Open End	Multialternative (Growth)	C+	C	B	Up	Y	0
Transamerica Global Equity Class A	IMNAX	NAS CM	Open End	Global Equity (Growth)	B	B-	B	Up	Y	1,000
Transamerica Global Equity Class Advisor	TAGQX	NAS CM	Open End	Global Equity (Growth)	B-	B-	B-	Down	Y	1,000
Transamerica Global Equity Class B	IMNBX	NAS CM	Open End	Global Equity (Growth)	B-	B-	B-	Down		1,000
Transamerica Global Equity Class C	IMNCX	NAS CM	Open End	Global Equity (Growth)	B-	B-	B-	Down	Y	1,000
Transamerica Global Equity Class I	TMUIX	NAS CM	Open End	Global Equity (Growth)	B-	B	B-	Down	Y	1,000,000
Transamerica Global Equity Class R6	TAGEX	NAS CM	Open End	Global Equity (Growth)	B-	B	B-	Down	Y	0
Transamerica Global Equity Class T1	TMUTX	NAS CM	Open End	Global Equity (Growth)	B-	B-	B-	Down	Y	1,000
Transamerica Global Multifactor Macro Class I2	US89354D7185		Open End	Multialternative (Growth & Income)	D+	D	C-	Up	Y	0
Transamerica Global Real Estate Securities Fund Class I2	TRSIX	NAS CM	Open End	Real Estate Sector Equity (Real Estate)	C+	C	B	Up	Y	0
Transamerica Growth Fund Class I2	TJNIX	NAS CM	Open End	US Equity Large Cap Growth (Growth)	A-	A	B+	Up	Y	0
Transamerica Growth Fund Class R6	TAGOX	NAS CM	Open End	US Equity Large Cap Growth (Growth)	A-	A	B+	Up	Y	0
Transamerica International Equity A	TRWAX	NAS CM	Open End	Global Equity Large Cap (Foreign Stock)	B-	C+	B	Up	Y	1,000
Transamerica International Equity Advisor	TAIQX	NAS CM	Open End	Global Equity Large Cap (Foreign Stock)	B-	C+	B	Up	Y	1,000
Transamerica International Equity C	TRWCX	NAS CM	Open End	Global Equity Large Cap (Foreign Stock)	B-	C+	B	Up	Y	1,000
Transamerica International Equity Class T1	TRWWX	NAS CM	Open End	Global Equity Large Cap (Foreign Stock)	B-	C+	B	Up	Y	1,000
Transamerica International Equity I	TSWIX	NAS CM	Open End	Global Equity Large Cap (Foreign Stock)	B-	B-	B	Up	Y	1,000,000
Transamerica International Equity I2	TRWIX	NAS CM	Open End	Global Equity Large Cap (Foreign Stock)	B-	B-	B	Up	Y	0
Transamerica International Equity I3	TRWTX	NAS CM	Open End	Global Equity Large Cap (Foreign Stock)	B-	B-	B	Up	Y	0
Transamerica Intl Equity Opp Fund Cls I2	US8939616491		Open End	Global Equity Large Cap (Foreign Stock)	B	B-	B	Up	Y	0
Transamerica International Equity R	TRWRX	NAS CM	Open End	Global Equity Large Cap (Foreign Stock)	B-	C+	B	Up	Y	0
Transamerica International Equity R4	TRWFX	NAS CM	Open End	Global Equity Large Cap (Foreign Stock)	B-	C+	B	Up	Y	0
Transamerica International Equity R6	TAINX	NAS CM	Open End	Global Equity Large Cap (Foreign Stock)	B-	B-	B	Up	Y	0
Transamerica International Small Cap Fund Class I2	US8939626136		Open End	Global Equity Mid/Small Cap (Foreign Stock)	A-	A	A-	Up	Y	0
Transamerica International Small Cap Value Class I	TISVX	NAS CM	Open End	Global Equity Mid/Small Cap (Small Company)	B+	B+	A-	Up		1,000,000
Transamerica International Small Cap Value Class I2	US89355J5166		Open End	Global Equity Mid/Small Cap (Small Company)	B+	B+	A-	Up		0
Transamerica Large Cap Value Fund Class A	TWQAX	NAS CM	Open End	US Equity Large Cap Value (Growth)	B	B	B	Up	Y	1,000
Transamerica Large Cap Value Fund Class Advisor	TALPX	NAS CM	Open End	US Equity Large Cap Value (Growth)	B	B	B+	Up	Y	1,000
Transamerica Large Cap Value Fund Class C	TWQCX	NAS CM	Open End	US Equity Large Cap Value (Growth)	B	B	B+	Up	Y	1,000
Transamerica Large Cap Value Fund Class I	TWQIX	NAS CM	Open End	US Equity Large Cap Value (Growth)	B	B	B	Up	Y	1,000,000
Transamerica Large Cap Value Fund Class I2	TWQZX	NAS CM	Open End	US Equity Large Cap Value (Growth)	B	B	B	Up	Y	0
Transamerica Large Cap Value Fund Class R6	TALCX	NAS CM	Open End	US Equity Large Cap Value (Growth)	B	B	B+	Up	Y	0
Transamerica Large Cap Value Fund T1	TWQTX	NAS CM	Open End	US Equity Large Cap Value (Growth)	B	B	B+	Up	Y	1,000
Transamerica Large Core Fund Class I3	TLATX	NAS CM	Open End	US Equity Large Cap Value (Growth & Income)	B-	B	B-	Down	Y	0
Transamerica Large Core Fund Class R	TLARX	NAS CM	Open End	US Equity Large Cap Value (Growth & Income)	B-	B-	B-		Y	0
Transamerica Large Core Fund Class R4	TLAFX	NAS CM	Open End	US Equity Large Cap Value (Growth & Income)	B-	B	B-	Down	Y	0
Transamerica Large Growth Fund Class I3	TGWTX	NAS CM	Open End	US Equity Large Cap Growth (Growth)	B+	A-	B	Down	Y	0
Transamerica Large Growth Fund Class R	TGWRX	NAS CM	Open End	US Equity Large Cap Growth (Growth)	B+	A-	B	Up	Y	0
Transamerica Large Growth Fund Class R4	TGWFX	NAS CM	Open End	US Equity Large Cap Growth (Growth)	A-	A-	A-	Up	Y	0
Transamerica Large Value Opportunities Fund Class I3	TLOTX	NAS CM	Open End	US Equity Large Cap Value (Growth)	B	B-	B	Up	Y	0
Transamerica Large Value Opportunities Fund Class R	TLORX	NAS CM	Open End	US Equity Large Cap Value (Growth)	B-	C+	B	Up	Y	0
Transamerica Large Value Opportunities Fund Class R4	TLOFX	NAS CM	Open End	US Equity Large Cap Value (Growth)	B	C+	B	Up	Y	0
Transamerica Long/Short Strategy Fund Class I2	US8939626623		Open End	Long/Short Equity (Equity-Income)	C+	C	B		Y	0
Transamerica Managed Futures Strategy Fund Class I2	US8935092994		Open End	Other Alternative (Growth & Income)	D	D	D+	Down	Y	0
Transamerica Mid Cap Growth A	MCGAX	NAS CM	Open End	US Equity Mid Cap (Growth)	B	B	B	Up	Y	1,000
Transamerica Mid Cap Growth Advisor	TAMGX	NAS CM	Open End	US Equity Mid Cap (Growth)	B	B	B	Up	Y	1,000
Transamerica Mid Cap Growth C	MGTCX	NAS CM	Open End	US Equity Mid Cap (Growth)	B	B	B	Up	Y	1,000
Transamerica Mid Cap Growth Class T1	IMCTX	NAS CM	Open End	US Equity Mid Cap (Growth)	B	B	B	Up	Y	1,000
Transamerica Mid Cap Growth I	IMCGX	NAS CM	Open End	US Equity Mid Cap (Growth)	B	B	B	Up	Y	1,000,000
Transamerica Mid Cap Growth I2	US89355J3591		Open End	US Equity Mid Cap (Growth)	B	B	B	Up	Y	0
Transamerica Mid Cap Growth I3	TMITX	NAS CM	Open End	US Equity Mid Cap (Growth)	B	B	B	Up	Y	0

★Expanded analysis of this fund is included in Section II.

	TOTAL RETURNS					PERFORMANCE				ASSETS		ASSET ALLOCATION & TURNOVER					BULL & BEAR		FEES		
Min Additional Investment	3-Month Total Return	6-Month Total Return	1-Year Total Return	3-Year Total Return	5-Year Total Return	Dividend Yield (TTM)	Expense Ratio	3-Yr Std Deviation	3-Year Beta	NAV	Total Assets (MIL)	%Cash	%Stocks	%Bonds	%Other	Turnover Ratio	Last Bull Market Total Return	Last Bear Market Total Return	Front End Fee (%)	Back End Fee (%)	Inception Date
	1.34	2.92	5.39			0.21	1.4			10.4	89.5	14	39	17	2	579					Nov-16
	1.36	2.96	5.36			1.53	1.4			10.25	89.5	14	39	17	2	579					Mar-15
50	5.32	10.02	26.54	29.21	53.95	1.99	1.36	10.72	0.96	13.81	126.1	1	99	0	1	63	16.05	-24.31	5.50		Mar-06
50	5.40	10.20	26.87	29.55	54.35		1.11	10.73	0.96	14.22	126.1	1	99	0	1	63	16.05	-24.31			Dec-16
50	5.11	9.61	25.57	26.37	48.17	1.11	2.11	10.68	0.96	13.7	126.1	1	99	0	1	63	15.6	-24.56		5.00	Mar-06
50	5.08	9.52	25.54	26.38	48.19	1.36	2.11	10.73	0.96	13.58	126.1	1	99	0	1	63	15.54	-24.46		1.00	Mar-06
	5.41	10.17	26.88	30.38	56.31	2.37	1.05	10.67	0.96	13.82	126.1	1	99	0	1	63	16.25	-24.15			Nov-09
	5.40	10.17	26.85	30.40	55.38	2.54	0.96	10.74	0.96	13.82	126.1	1	99	0	1	63	16.05	-24.31			May-15
50	5.35	10.04	26.57	29.24	53.99		1.36	10.72	0.96	13.86	126.1	1	99	0	1	63	16.05	-24.31	2.50		Mar-17
	-0.62	0.49	-3.51			0	1.61			8.59	123.0	471	-80	-451	160						Mar-15
	4.44	5.60	10.59	9.12	31.31	3.24	1.22	11.06	1.02	14.28	26.2	1	95	0	4	52	22.37	-18.92			Nov-05
	7.03	16.13	36.28	48.96	131.53	0.06	0.85	12.75	1.12	10.36	356.0	1	99	0	0	36	26.55	-13.8			Nov-05
	7.04	16.13	36.41	48.97	131.54	0.06	0.85	12.76	1.12	10.36	356.0	1	99	0	0	36	26.55	-13.8			May-15
50	4.13	7.80	22.21	22.94	49.07	1.01	1.24	11.75	0.94	19.31	5,530	4	94	0	2	19	17.07	-22.2	5.50		Mar-11
50	4.12	7.91	22.47	24.07	50.50		1	11.81	0.94	19.81	5,530	4	94	0	2	19	17.32	-22.06			Dec-16
50	3.87	7.36	21.26	20.40	44.01	0.43	1.96	11.74	0.94	19.05	5,530	4	94	0	2	19	16.58	-22.35		1.00	Mar-11
50	4.15	7.88	22.47	23.45	49.00		1.24	11.82	0.94	19.42	5,530	4	94	0	2	19	17.15	-22.14	2.50		Mar-17
	4.18	7.98	22.58	24.32	51.69	1.36	0.9	11.78	0.94	19.52	5,530	4	94	0	2	19	17.32	-22.06			Dec-92
	4.20	8.00	22.66	24.68	52.42	1.43	0.81	11.8	0.94	19.53	5,530	4	94	0	2	19	17.39	-22.06			Mar-11
	4.23	8.03	22.77	24.38	50.86	1.36	0.81	11.82	0.94	19.66	5,530	4	94	0	2	19	17.32	-22.06			Dec-92
	3.96	8.49	27.58	26.37	44.67	0.87	0.95	11.55	0.92	9.06	1,374	1	97	0	1	15	18.95	-23.41			Jun-08
	4.09	7.77	22.20	22.56	47.19		1.3	11.81	0.94	19.71	5,530	4	94	0	2	19	16.98	-22.22			Mar-17
	4.10	7.89	22.40	23.39	48.92		1.06	11.82	0.94	19.66	5,530	4	94	0	2	19	17.15	-22.14			Mar-17
	4.22	8.04	22.70	24.67	51.23	1.42	0.81	11.79	0.94	19.72	5,530	4	94	0	2	19	17.32	-22.06			May-15
	5.78	14.23	39.66	48.30	86.24	5.63	1.17	11.91	0.97	6.56	153.5	2	97	0	1	17	17.12	-25.42			Mar-08
	6.09	13.14	30.47	39.15	65.12	1.7	1.12	10.41	0.83	14.05	876.8	1	97	0	2	20					Jan-13
	6.09	13.12	30.63	39.58	65.86	1.78	1.02	10.45	0.83	14.07	876.8	1	97	0	2	20					Jan-13
50	2.69	6.47	12.04	37.80	107.77	1.15	1.05	12.25	1.11	12.43	2,355	4	96	0	0	127	22.86	-19.17	5.50		Nov-10
50	2.73	6.65	12.28	39.13	111.42		0.88	12.28	1.12	12.57	2,355	4	96	0	0	127	23.16	-18.99			Dec-16
50	2.45	6.14	11.30	34.78	100.35	0.6	1.8	12.26	1.11	12.36	2,355	4	96	0	0	127	22.36	-19.38		1.00	Nov-10
	2.77	6.69	12.38	38.98	110.69	1.36	0.79	12.26	1.11	12.51	2,355	4	96	0	0	127	22.99	-19			Nov-10
	2.79	6.74	12.48	39.38	111.79	1.43	0.69	12.29	1.12	12.5	2,355	4	96	0	0	127	23.16	-18.99			Nov-10
	2.79	6.74	12.48	39.39	111.80	1.44	0.69	12.27	1.11	12.5	2,355	4	96	0	0	127	23.16	-18.99			May-15
50	2.74	6.64	12.25	38.40	109.25		1.05	12.28	1.12	12.45	2,355	4	96	0	0	127	22.98	-19.07	2.50		Mar-17
	8.81	14.60	22.85	29.85	109.83		0.65	11.48	1.1	11.13	295.3	1	99	0	0	47	25.89	-16.17			Mar-17
	8.67	14.32	22.32	28.65	106.85		1.15	11.46	1.1	11.13	295.3	1	99	0	0	47	25.7	-16.26			Mar-17
	8.73	14.45	22.61	29.60	109.42	0.91	0.9	11.46	1.1	11.13	295.3	1	99	0	0	47	25.89	-16.18			Sep-00
	7.45	14.37	32.76	44.37	120.99		0.65	12.03	1.09	11.6	851.6	1	99	0	0	36	27.2	-16.9			Mar-17
	7.40	14.09	32.17	43.02	117.83		1.18	12.02	1.09	11.6	851.6	1	99	0	0	36	27.02	-16.98			Mar-17
	7.38	14.22	32.48	44.07	120.53	0.17	0.9	12.02	1.09	11.6	851.6	1	99	0	0	36	27.2	-16.9			Sep-00
	7.28	12.26	15.48	23.90	91.95		0.5	11.85	1.08	11.01	695.0	1	99	0	0	48	25.64	-18.18			May-17
	7.15	11.86	14.96	22.72	89.18		1	11.84	1.08	11.01	695.0	1	99	0	0	48	25.46	-18.27			May-17
	7.21	12.11	15.28	23.68	91.61	1.41	0.75	11.84	1.09	11.01	695.0	1	99	0	0	48	25.64	-18.18			Sep-00
	2.79	5.17	11.36	8.69	28.28	0	1.59	5.05	-11.56	6.18	17.2	70	30	0	0	955	5.82	-7.47			Jan-07
	4.65	4.93	-0.98	-7.95	10.14	1.16	1.46	9.24		7.9	161.2	18	106	-79	55		-4.08	-5.4			Sep-10
50	6.25	9.38	20.85	30.97	86.71	0	1.22	12.59	1.04	14.62	259.4	1	99	0	0	79	23.11	-22.5	5.50		Oct-13
50	6.40	9.50	21.09	32.69	91.63		1	12.66	1.04	14.72	259.4	1	99	0	0	79	23.11	-22.5			Dec-16
50	6.04	8.92	19.85	27.91	79.74	0	2	12.61	1.04	14.22	259.4	1	99	0	0	79	22.58	-22.74		1.00	Oct-13
50	6.31	9.44	21.15	32.75	91.72		1.22	12.67	1.04	14.63	259.4	1	99	0	0	79	23.11	-22.5	2.50		Mar-17
	6.34	9.52	21.10	32.08	88.80	0	0.93	12.58	1.04	14.72	259.4	1	99	0	0	79	23.11	-22.5			Oct-13
	6.34	9.60	21.25	32.43	89.64	0.06	0.81	12.57	1.04	14.75	259.4	1	99	0	0	79	23.11	-22.5			Oct-13
	6.44	9.61	21.34	31.50	87.48	0	0.75	12.59	1.04	14.78	259.4	1	99	0	0	79	23.11	-22.49			Oct-13

Fund Name	Ticker Symbol	Traded On	Fund Type	Category and (Prospectus Objective)	Overall Rating	Reward Rating	Risk Rating	Recent Up/ Downgrade	Open to New Investors	Min Initial Investment
	MARKET		FUND TYPE, CATEGORY & OBJECTIVE		RATINGS				MINIMUMS	
Transamerica Mid Cap Growth R	TMIRX	NAS CM	Open End	US Equity Mid Cap (Growth)	B	B	B	Up	Y	0
Transamerica Mid Cap Value Fund Class I2	US8939615659		Open End	US Equity Mid Cap (Growth)	B	B-	B+			0
Transamerica Mid Cap Value Opportunities A	MCVAX	NAS CM	Open End	US Equity Mid Cap (Growth)	B	C+	A	Up	Y	1,000
Transamerica Mid Cap Value Opportunities Advisor	TAMOX	NAS CM	Open End	US Equity Mid Cap (Growth)	B	C+	A	Up	Y	1,000
Transamerica Mid Cap Value Opportunities C	MCVCX	NAS CM	Open End	US Equity Mid Cap (Growth)	B	C+	A-	Up	Y	1,000
Transamerica Mid Cap Value Opportunities Class T1	MVTTX	NAS CM	Open End	US Equity Mid Cap (Growth)	B	C+	A	Up	Y	1,000
Transamerica Mid Cap Value Opportunities I	MVTIX	NAS CM	Open End	US Equity Mid Cap (Growth)	B	C+	A	Up	Y	1,000,000
Transamerica Mid Cap Value Opportunities I2	US89354D7672		Open End	US Equity Mid Cap (Growth)	B	C+	A	Up	Y	0
Transamerica Mid Cap Value Opportunities I3	TOTTX	NAS CM	Open End	US Equity Mid Cap (Growth)	B	C+	A	Up	Y	0
Transamerica Mid Cap Value Opportunities R	TOTRX	NAS CM	Open End	US Equity Mid Cap (Growth)	B	C+	A-	Up	Y	0
Transamerica Mid Cap Value Opportunities R4	TOTFX	NAS CM	Open End	US Equity Mid Cap (Growth)	B	C+	A	Up	Y	0
Transamerica Mid Cap Value Opportunities R6	MVTRX	NAS CM	Open End	US Equity Mid Cap (Growth)	B	C+	A	Up	Y	0
Transamerica MLP & Energy Income Advisor	TAMLX	NAS CM	Open End	Energy Sector Equity (Growth & Income)	D+	C-	D	Down	Y	1,000
Transamerica MLP & Energy Income Class A	TMLAX	NAS CM	Open End	Energy Sector Equity (Growth & Income)	D+	C-	D	Down	Y	1,000
Transamerica MLP & Energy Income Class C	TMCLX	NAS CM	Open End	Energy Sector Equity (Growth & Income)	D+	C-	D	Down	Y	1,000
Transamerica MLP & Energy Income Class I	TMLPX	NAS CM	Open End	Energy Sector Equity (Growth & Income)	D+	C-	D	Down	Y	1,000,000
Transamerica MLP & Energy Income Class I2	US89355J4821		Open End	Energy Sector Equity (Growth & Income)	D+	C-	D	Down	Y	0
Transamerica MLP & Energy Income Class T1	TMLTX	NAS CM	Open End	Energy Sector Equity (Growth & Income)	D+	C-	D	Down	Y	1,000
Transamerica Multi-Cap Growth Class A	ITSAX	NAS CM	Open End	US Equity Large Cap Growth (Growth)	C	C	C	Down	Y	1,000
Transamerica Multi-Cap Growth Class Advisor	TAMHX	NAS CM	Open End	US Equity Large Cap Growth (Growth)	C	C	C	Down	Y	1,000
Transamerica Multi-Cap Growth Class B	ITCBX	NAS CM	Open End	US Equity Large Cap Growth (Growth)	C	C	C	Down		1,000
Transamerica Multi-Cap Growth Class C	ITSLX	NAS CM	Open End	US Equity Large Cap Growth (Growth)	C	C	C	Down	Y	1,000
Transamerica Multi-Cap Growth Class I	TGPIX	NAS CM	Open End	US Equity Large Cap Growth (Growth)	C	C	C	Down	Y	1,000,000
Transamerica Multi-Cap Growth Class I2	US8939613266		Open End	US Equity Large Cap Growth (Growth)	C	C	C	Down	Y	0
Transamerica Multi-Cap Growth Class T1	TGPTX	NAS CM	Open End	US Equity Large Cap Growth (Growth)	C	C	C	Down	Y	1,000
Transamerica Multi-Managed Balanced Fund Advisor	IBAVX	NAS CM	Open End	Moderate Alloc (Balanced)	B-	C+	B	Down	Y	1,000
Transamerica Multi-Managed Balanced Fund Class A	IBALX	NAS CM	Open End	Moderate Alloc (Balanced)	B-	C+	B	Down	Y	1,000
Transamerica Multi-Managed Balanced Fund Class B	IBABX	NAS CM	Open End	Moderate Alloc (Balanced)	B-	C+	B	Up		1,000
Transamerica Multi-Managed Balanced Fund Class C	IBLLX	NAS CM	Open End	Moderate Alloc (Balanced)	B-	C+	B	Up	Y	1,000
Transamerica Multi-Managed Balanced Fund Class I	TBLIX	NAS CM	Open End	Moderate Alloc (Balanced)	B-	C+	B	Down	Y	1,000,000
Transamerica Multi-Managed Balanced Fund Class R6	TAMMX	NAS CM	Open End	Moderate Alloc (Balanced)	B-	C+	B	Down	Y	0
Transamerica Multi-Managed Balanced Fund Class T1	IBATX	NAS CM	Open End	Moderate Alloc (Balanced)	B-	C+	B	Down	Y	1,000
Transamerica Multi-Mgr Alternative Strat Port Cls A	IMUAX	NAS CM	Open End	Multialternative (Growth)	C	C	C+	Up	Y	1,000
Transamerica Multi-Mgr Alternative Strat Port Cls C	IMUCX	NAS CM	Open End	Multialternative (Growth)	C	C-	C	Up	Y	1,000
Transamerica Multi-Mgr Alternative Strat Port Cls I	TASIX	NAS CM	Open End	Multialternative (Growth)	C+	C	B	Up	Y	1,000,000
Transamerica Multi-Mgr Alternative Strat Port Cls R6	TAMAX	NAS CM	Open End	Multialternative (Growth)	C+	C	B	Up	Y	0
Transamerica Multi-Mgr Alternative Strat Port Cls T1	IMUTX	NAS CM	Open End	Multialternative (Growth)	C	C	C+	Up	Y	1,000
Transamerica Small Cap Core Fund Advisor Class	TASOX	NAS CM	Open End	US Equity Small Cap (Small Company)	C+	C+	C+		Y	1,000
Transamerica Small Cap Core Fund Class A	SCCAX	NAS CM	Open End	US Equity Small Cap (Small Company)	C+	C+	C+		Y	1,000
Transamerica Small Cap Core Fund Class C	SCCCX	NAS CM	Open End	US Equity Small Cap (Small Company)	C+	C+	C+	Up	Y	1,000
Transamerica Small Cap Core Fund Class I	ISMTX	NAS CM	Open End	US Equity Small Cap (Small Company)	B-	B-	B-	Up	Y	1,000,000
Transamerica Small Cap Core Fund Class I2	US89355J3187		Open End	US Equity Small Cap (Small Company)	B-	B-	B-	Up	Y	0
Transamerica Small Cap Core Fund Class I3	TCCTX	NAS CM	Open End	US Equity Small Cap (Small Company)	C+	C+	C+		Y	0
Transamerica Small Cap Core Fund Class R	TCCRX	NAS CM	Open End	US Equity Small Cap (Small Company)	C+	C+	C+	Up	Y	0
Transamerica Small Cap Core Fund Class R4	TCCFX	NAS CM	Open End	US Equity Small Cap (Small Company)	C+	C+	C+		Y	0
Transamerica Small Cap Core Fund Class T1	ISMQX	NAS CM	Open End	US Equity Small Cap (Small Company)	C+	C+	C+		Y	1,000
Transamerica Small Cap Growth A	ASGTX	NAS CM	Open End	US Equity Small Cap (Small Company)	B+	B+	B+	Up	Y	1,000
Transamerica Small Cap Growth Advisor	TASPX	NAS CM	Open End	US Equity Small Cap (Small Company)	B+	B+	B+	Up	Y	1,000
Transamerica Small Cap Growth C	CSGTX	NAS CM	Open End	US Equity Small Cap (Small Company)	B+	B+	B+	Up	Y	1,000
Transamerica Small Cap Growth Class T1	RTSTX	NAS CM	Open End	US Equity Small Cap (Small Company)	B+	B+	B+	Up	Y	1,000
Transamerica Small Cap Growth I	ISCGX	NAS CM	Open End	US Equity Small Cap (Small Company)	B+	B+	B+	Up	Y	1,000,000
Transamerica Small Cap Growth I2	US89355J6560		Open End	US Equity Small Cap (Small Company)	B+	B+	B+	Up	Y	0

★ Expanded analysis of this fund is included in Section II.

	TOTAL RETURNS					PERFORMANCE				ASSETS		ASSET ALLOCATION & TURNOVER					BULL & BEAR		FEES		
Min Additional Investment	3-Month Total Return	6-Month Total Return	1-Year Total Return	3-Year Total Return	5-Year Total Return	Dividend Yield (TTM)	Expense Ratio	3-Yr Std Deviation	3-Year Beta	NAV	Total Assets (MIL)	%Cash	%Stocks	%Bonds	%Other	Turnover Ratio	Last Bull Market Total Return	Last Bear Market Total Return	Front End Fee (%)	Back End Fee (%)	Inception Date
	6.26	9.36	20.87	31.79	89.38		1.3	12.66	1.04	14.76	259.4	1	99	0	0	79	22.93	-22.58			Mar-17
	4.83	7.12	13.80	25.82	96.88	0.72	0.89	9.85	0.91	16.05	220.4	1	99	0	0	23	27.74	-17.55			Nov-05
50	4.59	2.36	9.34	27.74		0.89	1.08	9.03	0.74	11.59	1,673	6	94	0	0	95			5.50		Apr-14
50	4.66	2.47	9.44	27.86			0.94	9.01	0.74	11.77	1,673	6	94	0	0	95					Dec-16
50	4.39	1.88	8.43	24.88		0.53	1.9	9	0.74	11.48	1,673	6	94	0	0	95				1.00	Apr-14
50	4.69	2.47	9.40	27.17			1.08	9	0.74	11.63	1,673	6	94	0	0	95			2.50		Mar-17
	4.64	2.51	9.65	28.66		0.99	0.86	9.03	0.74	11.64	1,673	6	94	0	0	95					Apr-14
	4.74	2.52	9.65	28.99		1.04	0.74	9.02	0.74	11.65	1,673	6	94	0	0	95					Apr-14
	4.76	2.63	9.72	28.18		0.89	0.7	9.01	0.74	11.71	1,673	6	94	0	0	95					Apr-14
	4.62	2.32	9.16	26.26			1.24	9	0.74	11.71	1,673	6	94	0	0	95					Mar-17
	4.63	2.42	9.42	27.20			0.9	9.02	0.74	11.71	1,673	6	94	0	0	95					Mar-17
	4.79	2.59	9.77	28.36		0.46	0.79	9.02	0.74	11.74	1,673	6	94	0	0	95					Jul-16
50	0.24	1.91	-0.14	-18.30			1.35	18.62	1.16	7.71	297.8	1	96	2	0	79					Dec-16
50	0.07	1.82	-0.37	-19.02		5.61	1.57	18.56	1.15	7.6	297.8	1	96	2	0	79			5.50		Apr-13
50	-0.15	1.41	-1.17	-20.91		4.79	2.35	18.61	1.16	7.57	297.8	1	96	2	0	79				1.00	Apr-13
	0.13	1.97	-0.20	-18.35		5.93	1.26	18.62	1.16	7.6	297.8	1	96	2	0	79					Apr-13
	0.16	1.89	-0.10	-18.10		6.03	1.16	18.62	1.15	7.6	297.8	1	96	2	0	79					Apr-13
50	0.10	1.88	-0.34	-18.87			1.57	18.61	1.16	7.69	297.8	1	96	2	0	79			2.50		Mar-17
50	5.29	11.61	22.84	2.09	42.63	0	1.25	12.45	0.98	7.09	264.7	1	99	0	0	101	17.39	-22.22	5.50		Mar-00
50	5.34	11.78	23.14	2.34	42.97		0.96	12.46	0.98	7.88	264.7	1	99	0	0	101	17.39	-22.22			Dec-16
50	5.20	11.12	21.99	-0.36	36.78	0	2	12.42	0.98	5.38	264.7	1	99	0	0	101	17.05	-22.48		5.00	Mar-00
50	5.13	11.16	21.88	-0.20	37.21	0	2	12.42	0.98	5.46	264.7	1	99	0	0	101	17.1	-22.41		1.00	Nov-02
	5.51	11.81	23.36	3.15	45.19	0.05	0.95	12.41	0.98	7.88	264.7	1	99	0	0	101	17.9	-21.91			Nov-09
	5.57	11.91	23.45	3.75	46.52	0.22	0.77	12.38	0.97	8.01	264.7	1	99	0	0	101	17.98	-21.95			Nov-05
50	4.80	11.09	22.27	1.62	41.97		1.25	12.45	0.98	7.1	264.7	1	99	0	0	101	17.39	-22.22	2.50		Mar-17
50	4.04	7.13	13.96	21.52	59.91		0.91	6.12	0.6	28.15	1,082	2	59	35	4	35	16.03	-9.13			Mar-17
50	3.99	7.07	13.84	21.40	59.75	1.13	1.08	6.12	0.6	27.97	1,082	2	59	35	4	35	16.03	-9.13	5.50		Dec-94
50	3.73	6.49	12.57	17.67	52.10	0.09	2.1	6.11	0.6	27.81	1,082	2	59	35	4	35	15.38	-9.4		5.00	Sep-95
50	3.80	6.63	12.93	18.73	54.24	0.43	1.81	6.1	0.6	27.48	1,082	2	59	35	4	35	15.61	-9.31		1.00	Nov-02
	4.07	7.19	14.08	22.32	62.10	1.31	0.82	6.11	0.6	28.1	1,082	2	59	35	4	35	16.33	-8.93			Nov-09
	4.10	7.25	14.20	22.52	61.22	1.4	0.71	6.1	0.6	28.1	1,082	2	59	35	4	35	16.03	-9.13			May-15
50	4.04	7.14	13.92	21.49	59.87		1.08	6.13	0.6	28.04	1,082	2	59	35	4	35	16.03	-9.13	2.50		Mar-17
50	1.42	3.10	4.94	1.16	8.55	1.03	2.01	3.54		9.84	160.2	85	13	-36	31	42	5.68	-8.3	5.50		Dec-06
50	1.33	2.70	4.22	-1.03	4.65	0.14	2.76	3.51		9.81	160.2	85	13	-36	31	42	5.27	-8.55		1.00	Dec-06
	1.56	3.24	5.31	2.14	10.35	1.38	1.69	3.52		9.8	160.2	85	13	-36	31	42	5.96	-8.11			Nov-09
	1.55	3.31	5.47	2.28	9.75	1.49	1.59	3.53		9.93	160.2	85	13	-36	31	42	5.68	-8.3			May-15
50	1.49	3.17	5.01	1.23	8.62		2.01	3.54		9.86	160.2	85	13	-36	31	42	5.68	-8.3	2.50		Mar-17
50	2.83	6.49	6.12	16.91	66.56		1.07	14.25	0.96	11.73	257.6	2	98	0	0	122	24.37	-22.92			Dec-16
50	2.79	6.37	5.91	17.51	66.64	0.13	1.32	14.06	0.94	11.67	257.6	2	98	0	0	122	24.37	-22.92	5.50		Oct-13
50	2.49	5.93	5.01	14.67	60.22	0	2.07	14.06	0.95	11.55	257.6	2	98	0	0	122	23.83	-23.16		1.00	Oct-13
	2.75	6.51	6.14	18.12	68.12	0.2	1.07	14.08	0.95	11.7	257.6	2	98	0	0	122	24.37	-22.92			Oct-13
	2.82	6.58	6.21	18.45	68.73	0.21	1.03	14.05	0.94	11.71	257.6	2	98	0	0	122	24.37	-22.92			Oct-13
	2.92	6.68	6.48	17.31	67.13		0.87	14.24	0.96	11.84	257.6	2	98	0	0	122	24.37	-22.92			Mar-17
	2.74	6.32	5.87	16.06	64.52		1.51	14.24	0.96	11.83	257.6	2	98	0	0	122	24.19	-23			Mar-17
	2.88	6.55	6.26	17.07	66.79	0.18	1.12	14.24	0.96	11.84	257.6	2	98	0	0	122	24.37	-22.92			Sep-00
50	2.81	6.40	6.11	16.90	66.54		1.32	14.25	0.96	11.78	257.6	2	98	0	0	122	24.37	-22.92	2.50		Mar-17
50	4.37	7.39	15.11	40.94	102.53	0	1.33	13.69	0.85	6.36	156.7	2	98	0	0	43			5.50		Aug-12
50	4.38	7.47	15.50	38.75	99.38		1.11	13.7	0.85	6.58	156.7	2	98	0	0	43					Dec-16
50	4.25	7.00	14.35	37.84	95.65	0	2.09	13.67	0.84	5.81	156.7	2	98	0	0	43				1.00	Aug-12
50	4.53	7.56	15.25	37.76	96.97		1.33	13.68	0.85	6.37	156.7	2	98	0	0	43			2.50		Mar-17
	4.54	7.48	15.51	42.05	105.58	0	1.03	13.7	0.85	6.58	156.7	2	98	0	0	43					Aug-12
	4.48	7.70	15.66	42.56	106.56	0	0.92	13.7	0.85	6.67	156.7	2	98	0	0	43					Aug-12

	MARKET		FUND TYPE, CATEGORY & OBJECTIVE		RATINGS				MINIMUMS	
Fund Name	Ticker Symbol	Traded On	Fund Type	Category and (Prospectus Objective)	Overall Rating	Reward Rating	Risk Rating	Recent Up/ Downgrade	Open to New Investors	Min Initial Investment
Transamerica Small Cap Growth I3	TSPTX	NAS CM	Open End	US Equity Small Cap (Small Company)	B+	B+	B+	Up	Y	0
Transamerica Small Cap Growth R	TSPRX	NAS CM	Open End	US Equity Small Cap (Small Company)	B+	B+	B+	Up	Y	0
Transamerica Small Cap Growth R4	TSPFX	NAS CM	Open End	US Equity Small Cap (Small Company)	B+	B+	B+	Up	Y	0
Transamerica Small Cap Growth R6	RTSGX	NAS CM	Open End	US Equity Small Cap (Small Company)	B+	B+	B+	Up	Y	0
Transamerica Small Cap Value A	TSLAX	NAS CM	Open End	US Equity Small Cap (Small Company)	C+	C+	B-	Up	Y	1,000
Transamerica Small Cap Value Advisor	TASLX	NAS CM	Open End	US Equity Small Cap (Small Company)	B	B	B	Up	Y	1,000
Transamerica Small Cap Value C	TSLCX	NAS CM	Open End	US Equity Small Cap (Small Company)	C+	C+	C+	Up	Y	1,000
Transamerica Small Cap Value Class T1	TSLWX	NAS CM	Open End	US Equity Small Cap (Small Company)	B	B	B	Up	Y	1,000
Transamerica Small Cap Value I	TSLIX	NAS CM	Open End	US Equity Small Cap (Small Company)	C+	C+	B-		Y	1,000,000
Transamerica Small Cap Value I2	US89355J7634		Open End	US Equity Small Cap (Small Company)	C+	C+	B-		Y	0
Transamerica Small Cap Value I3	US89360T4269		Open End	US Equity Small Cap (Small Company)	B	B	B	Up	Y	0
Transamerica Small Cap Value R	TRSLX	NAS CM	Open End	US Equity Small Cap (Small Company)	B	B-	B	Up	Y	0
Transamerica Small Cap Value R6	TSLRX	NAS CM	Open End	US Equity Small Cap (Small Company)	B	B	B	Up	Y	0
Transamerica Small/Mid Cap Value Fund Class A	IIVAX	NAS CM	Open End	US Equity Mid Cap (Growth & Income)	B	B	B	Up	Y	1,000
Transamerica Small/Mid Cap Value Fund Class Advisor	TASDX	NAS CM	Open End	US Equity Mid Cap (Growth & Income)	B	B	B	Up	Y	1,000
Transamerica Small/Mid Cap Value Fund Class B	IIVBX	NAS CM	Open End	US Equity Mid Cap (Growth & Income)	B	B	B	Up		1,000
Transamerica Small/Mid Cap Value Fund Class C	IIVLX	NAS CM	Open End	US Equity Mid Cap (Growth & Income)	B	B	B	Up	Y	1,000
Transamerica Small/Mid Cap Value Fund Class I	TSVIX	NAS CM	Open End	US Equity Mid Cap (Growth & Income)	B	B	B	Up	Y	1,000,000
Transamerica Small/Mid Cap Value Fund Class I2	TSMVX	NAS CM	Open End	US Equity Mid Cap (Growth & Income)	B	B	B	Up	Y	0
Transamerica Small/Mid Cap Value Fund Class R6	TASMX	NAS CM	Open End	US Equity Mid Cap (Growth & Income)	B	B	B	Up	Y	0
Transamerica Small/Mid Cap Value Fund Class T1	TASWX	NAS CM	Open End	US Equity Mid Cap (Growth & Income)	B	B	B		Y	1,000
Transamerica Stock Index R	TSTRX	NAS CM	Open End	US Equity Large Cap Blend (Growth & Income)	B	B	B		Y	0
Transamerica Stock Index R4	TSTFX	NAS CM	Open End	US Equity Large Cap Blend (Growth & Income)	B	B	B		Y	0
Transamerica Strategic High Income Fund Class A	TASHX	NAS CM	Open End	Cautious Alloc (Income)	B-	C+	B	Down	Y	1,000
Transamerica Strategic High Income Fund Class Advisor	TASKX	NAS CM	Open End	Cautious Alloc (Income)	B-	C+	B	Down	Y	1,000
Transamerica Strategic High Income Fund Class C	TCSHX	NAS CM	Open End	Cautious Alloc (Income)	B-	C+	B	Down	Y	1,000
Transamerica Strategic High Income Fund Class I	TSHIX	NAS CM	Open End	Cautious Alloc (Income)	B-	C+	B	Down	Y	1,000,000
Transamerica Strategic High Income Fund Class I2	US89354D8829		Open End	Cautious Alloc (Income)	B-	C+	B	Down	Y	0
Transamerica Strategic High Income Fund Class T1	TCSWX	NAS CM	Open End	Cautious Alloc (Income)	B-	C+	B	Down	Y	1,000
Transamerica US Growth Class A	TADAX	NAS CM	Open End	US Equity Large Cap Growth (Growth)	B+	B	A-	Up	Y	1,000
Transamerica US Growth Class Advisor	TAUGX	NAS CM	Open End	US Equity Large Cap Growth (Growth)	B+	B	A-	Up	Y	1,000
Transamerica US Growth Class B	TADBX	NAS CM	Open End	US Equity Large Cap Growth (Growth)	B+	B	A-	Up		1,000
Transamerica US Growth Class C	TADCX	NAS CM	Open End	US Equity Large Cap Growth (Growth)	B+	B	A-	Up	Y	1,000
Transamerica US Growth Class I	TDEIX	NAS CM	Open End	US Equity Large Cap Growth (Growth)	B+	B	A-	Up	Y	1,000,000
Transamerica US Growth Class I2	US8939623737		Open End	US Equity Large Cap Growth (Growth)	B+	B	A-	Up	Y	0
Transamerica US Growth Class T	TWMTX	NAS CM	Open End	US Equity Large Cap Growth (Growth)	B+	B	A-	Up	Y	1,000
Transamerica US Growth Class T1	TJNTX	NAS CM	Open End	US Equity Large Cap Growth (Growth)	B+	B	A-	Up	Y	1,000
Tributary Balanced Fund Class Institutional Plus	FOBPX	NAS CM	Open End	Moderate Alloc (Balanced)	B-	C+	B	Down	Y	5,000,000
Tributary Balanced Fund Institutional Class	FOBAX	NAS CM	Open End	Moderate Alloc (Balanced)	B-	C+	B	Down	Y	1,000
Tributary Growth Opportunities Fund Cls Institutional Plus	FOGPX	NAS CM	Open End	US Equity Mid Cap (Growth)	B	B	B	Up	Y	5,000,000
Tributary Growth Opportunities Fund Institutional Class	FOGRX	NAS CM	Open End	US Equity Mid Cap (Growth)	B	B-	B	Up	Y	1,000
Tributary Small Company Fund Institutional Class	FOSCX	NAS CM	Open End	US Equity Small Cap (Small Company)	B+	B	B+	Up	Y	1,000
Tributary Small Company Fund Institutional Plus Class	FOSBX	NAS CM	Open End	US Equity Small Cap (Small Company)	B+	B	B+	Up	Y	5,000,000
Tri-Continental Corporation	TY	NYSE	Closed End	Aggressive Alloc (Growth & Income)	B-	B-	B	Up	Y	
Trillium Small/Mid Cap Fund Institutional Class	TSMDX	NAS CM	Open End	US Equity Mid Cap (Growth)	C	C+	B	Up	Y	100,000
Triloma EIG Energy Income Fund	US89619L1098		Closed End	Energy Sector Equity (Growth & Income)	C	C	B+	Up	Y	5,000
Triloma EIG Energy Income Fund - Term I	US89620U1060		Closed End	Energy Sector Equity (Growth)	C	C	B+	Up	Y	5,000
TS&W Equity Portfolio Institutional Class Shares	TSWEX	NAS CM	Open End	US Equity Large Cap Value (Growth & Income)	B	C+	B+	Up	Y	2,500
Tweedy, Browne Global Value Fund	TBGVX	NAS CM	Open End	Global Equity Large Cap (Foreign Stock)	B-	C+	B	Down	Y	2,500
Tweedy, Browne Global Value Fund II - Currency Unhedged	TBCUX	NAS CM	Open End	Global Equity Large Cap (Foreign Stock)	B-	C+	B	Up		2,500
Tweedy, Browne Value Fund	TWEBX	NAS CM	Open End	Global Equity (Growth)	C+	C+	C+	Down	Y	2,500
Tweedy, Browne Worldwide High Dividend Yield Value Fund	TBHDX	NAS CM	Open End	Global Equity (Growth)	C+	C+	C+	Up	Y	2,500

★Expanded analysis of this fund is included in Section II.

Min Additional Investment	TOTAL RETURNS: 3-Month Total Return	6-Month Total Return	1-Year Total Return	3-Year Total Return	5-Year Total Return	PERFORMANCE: Dividend Yield (TTM)	Expense Ratio	3-Yr Std Deviation	3-Year Beta	ASSETS: NAV	Total Assets (MIL)	ASSET ALLOCATION & TURNOVER: %Cash	%Stocks	%Bonds	%Other	Turnover Ratio	BULL & BEAR: Last Bull Market Total Return	Last Bear Market Total Return	FEES: Front End Fee (%)	Back End Fee (%)	Inception Date
	4.63	7.69	15.68	38.97	99.69	0	0.9	13.7	0.85	6.68	156.7	2	98	0	0	43					Aug-12
	4.36	7.42	14.91	36.67	94.45		1.41	13.7	0.85	6.64	156.7	2	98	0	0	43					Mar-17
	4.48	7.54	15.28	37.79	97.02		1.15	13.67	0.85	6.66	156.7	2	98	0	0	43					Mar-17
	4.48	7.70	15.66	41.67	103.57	0	0.92	13.71	0.85	6.67	156.7	2	98	0	0	43					Jul-16
50	2.11	6.32	8.70	11.30	60.39	0.64	1.3	13.21	0.9	11.63	314.0	1	99	0	0	89	28.06	-21.39	5.50		Apr-12
50	2.05	6.38	8.83	20.42	76.98		1.05	12.74	0.86	11.78	314.0	1	99	0	0	89	28.25	-21.31			Dec-16
50	1.85	5.90	7.80	8.83	55.05	0.02	2.01	13.17	0.9	11.53	314.0	1	99	0	0	89	27.51	-21.64		1.00	Apr-12
50	2.08	6.38	8.52	19.47	74.72		1.3	12.77	0.87	11.64	314.0	1	99	0	0	89	28.06	-21.39	2.50		Mar-17
	2.14	6.42	8.99	12.12	62.87	0.75	1.03	13.19	0.9	11.69	314.0	1	99	0	0	89	28.25	-21.31			Apr-12
	2.11	6.47	9.03	12.57	63.87	0.86	0.9	13.17	0.89	11.7	314.0	1	99	0	0	89	28.25	-21.31			Apr-12
	2.20	6.57	8.79	20.37	76.92	0.18	0.85	12.75	0.86	11.73	314.0	1	99	0	0	89	28.25	-21.31			Jan-03
	2.00	6.18	8.12	18.44	72.35		1.39	12.74	0.86	11.71	314.0	1	99	0	0	89	27.87	-21.48			Apr-17
	2.10	6.53	8.98	20.37	76.92	0.37	0.9	12.72	0.86	11.76	314.0	1	99	0	0	89	28.25	-21.31			Jul-16
50	5.54	7.56	15.14	33.47	95.11	0.69	1.31	13.02	1.05	27.3	909.6	3	97	0	0	74	29.22	-25.84	5.50		Apr-01
50	5.59	7.71	15.38	33.76	95.53		1.04	13.02	1.05	28.51	909.6	3	97	0	0	74	29.22	-25.84			Dec-16
50	5.33	7.16	14.28	30.50	88.14	0	2.06	13.04	1.05	24.17	909.6	3	97	0	0	74	28.68	-26.05		5.00	Apr-01
50	5.37	7.19	14.32	30.77	88.70	0.25	1.99	13.03	1.05	23.77	909.6	3	97	0	0	74	28.68	-26.01		1.00	Nov-02
	5.63	7.74	15.50	34.86	98.71	0.96	0.95	13.03	1.05	28.19	909.6	3	97	0	0	74	29.53	-25.72			Nov-09
	5.68	7.82	15.61	35.29	99.71	1.03	0.85	13.02	1.05	28.23	909.6	3	97	0	0	74	29.52	-25.65			Nov-05
	5.62	7.78	15.59	35.04	97.41	1.03	0.85	13.03	1.05	28.34	909.6	3	97	0	0	74	29.22	-25.84			May-15
50	5.57	7.63	15.25	33.60	95.30		1.31	13.02	1.05	27.31	909.6	3	97	0	0	74	29.22	-25.84	2.50		Mar-17
	6.53	11.03	21.06	34.59	105.93		0.6	10.11	1	11.25	802.5	1	99	0	0	4	24.72	-16.43			Apr-17
	6.59	11.27	21.48	35.73	108.71	1.56	0.3	10.11	1	11.26	802.5	1	99	0	0	4	24.9	-16.34			Sep-00
50	4.10	6.82	13.29	22.26		3.27	1.2	5.73	0.54	11.13	136.3	0	52	41	1	51			5.50		Mar-14
50	4.19	6.98	13.67	23.20			0.95	5.78	0.54	11.19	136.3	0	52	41	1	51					Dec-16
50	3.83	6.46	12.49	19.50		2.67	1.94	5.75	0.54	11.09	136.3	0	52	41	1	51				1.00	Mar-14
	4.16	7.07	13.70	23.23		3.47	0.95	5.78	0.54	11.14	136.3	0	52	41	1	51					Mar-14
	4.07	6.93	13.65	16.99		3.72	0.91	5.75	0.54	10.68	136.3	0	52	41	1	51					Mar-14
50	4.11	6.96	13.53	22.43			1.2	5.77	0.54	11.23	136.3	0	52	41	1	51			2.50		Mar-17
50	7.94	12.33	28.72	38.92	107.81	0.05	1.2	11.42	1.05	19.42	1,099	1	99	0	0	34	27.2	-20.04	5.50		Nov-09
50	7.97	12.45	29.03	40.39	112.32		0.94	11.43	1.05	19.81	1,099	1	99	0	0	34	27.74	-19.86			Dec-16
50	7.61	11.74	27.48	34.96	98.28	0	2.17	11.41	1.05	18.27	1,099	1	99	0	0	34	26.71	-20.31		5.00	Nov-09
50	7.69	11.88	27.74	35.65	99.66	0	1.99	11.44	1.05	18.35	1,099	1	99	0	0	34	26.67	-20.28		1.00	Nov-09
	8.00	12.49	29.14	40.27	111.42	0.3	0.87	11.46	1.05	19.74	1,099	1	99	0	0	34	27.62	-20			Nov-09
	8.04	12.55	29.32	40.71	112.80	0.41	0.74	11.45	1.05	19.68	1,099	1	99	0	0	34	27.74	-19.86			Nov-09
50	8.01	12.53	29.20	40.42	111.83	0.1	0.82	11.44	1.05	52.01	1,099	1	99	0	0	34	27.72	-19.86	8.50		Feb-12
50	7.97	12.42	29.03	39.69	110.21		1.2	11.45	1.05	19.42	1,099	1	99	0	0	34	27.56	-19.94	2.50		Mar-17
50	4.19	6.71	14.22	20.08	58.01	0.97	0.99	6.68		16.86	78.1	4	65	30	0	22	17.03	-9.92			Oct-11
50	4.09	6.52	13.94	19.35	56.41	0.74	1.18	6.65		16.99	78.1	4	65	30	0	22	17.01	-9.92			Aug-96
50	4.89	9.64	20.85	29.03	90.76	0	0.94	11.73	1.02	16.27	141.0	3	97	0	0	36	29.94	-24.36			Oct-11
50	4.86	9.56	20.66	28.14	88.74	0	1.14	11.74	1.02	15.95	141.0	3	97	0	0	36	29.78	-24.36			Apr-98
50	1.96	4.66	8.48	33.41	95.83	0.21	1.2	13.18	0.89	28.48	726.6	6	94	0	0	33	26.46	-21.38			Jun-96
50	2.02	4.83	8.76	34.24	98.03	0.31	0.99	13.18	0.89	28.61	726.6	6	94	0	0	33	26.67	-21.31			Dec-10
	5.44	10.89	20.13	33.72	91.81	3.36	0.56	9.29	0.9	29.88	1,670	0	69	14	0	82	25.71	-14.7			Jan-29
1,000	6.98	12.11	18.97			0.09	0.98			12.63	14.1	2	98	0	0	27					Aug-15
	2.84	6.06	13.10			6.02	4.57			27.21	--								2.50		Jul-15
	2.77	5.98	12.34			5.6	6.08			27.28	--								5.00		Jul-15
100	3.57	5.55	14.53	22.09	77.46	0.52	1.63	9.74	0.91	12.9	41.7	6	94	0	0	66	22.18	-20.88			Jul-92
200	2.86	4.91	15.43	20.18	45.94	1	1.38	7.52	0.58	28.49	10,248	5	82	6	3	3	14.63	-14.18			Jun-93
200	3.95	7.39	21.59	17.64	34.52	1.28	1.38	9.36	0.72	15.71	376.2	12	82	0	0	4	12.62	-14			Oct-09
200	4.41	8.48	16.45	20.35	55.08	0.77	1.39	8.8	0.83	23.86	607.7	9	87	0	0	8	17.1	-15.19			Dec-93
200	4.55	8.89	22.05	17.71	39.04	1.91	1.38	10.27	0.92	10.33	306.7	14	82	0	0	5	12.4	-11.79			Sep-07

	MARKET		FUND TYPE, CATEGORY & OBJECTIVE		RATINGS				MINIMUMS	
Fund Name	Ticker Symbol	Traded On	Fund Type	Category and (Prospectus Objective)	Overall Rating	Reward Rating	Risk Rating	Recent Up/ Downgrade	Open to New Investors	Min Initial Investment
Two Oaks Diversified Growth & Income Class A Shares	TWOAX	NAS CM	Open End	Aggressive Alloc (Growth & Income)	B	C+	B		Y	2,500
U.S. Global Investors All American Equity Fund	GBTFX	NAS CM	Open End	US Equity Large Cap Blend (Growth)	C	C	C	Down	Y	5,000
U.S. Global Investors China Region Fund Investor Class	USCOX	NAS CM	Open End	Greater China Equity (Pacific Stock)	B	A-	C+	Up	Y	5,000
U.S. Global Investors Emerging Europe Fund	EUROX	NAS CM	Open End	Other Equity (Europe Stock)	C	C+	C	Up	Y	5,000
U.S. Global Investors Global Resources Fund	PSPFX	NAS CM	Open End	Natl Resources Sec Equity (Natl Res)	C	C	C	Up	Y	5,000
U.S. Global Invs Global Resources Fund Inst Cls Shares	PIPFX	NAS CM	Open End	Natl Resources Sec Equity (Natl Res)	C	C	C	Up	Y	1,000,000
U.S. Global Investors Gold and Precious Metals Fund	USERX	NAS CM	Open End	Precious Metals Sector Equity (Precious Metals)	C	C	C-	Up	Y	5,000
U.S. Global Investors Holmes Macro Trends Fund	MEGAX	NAS CM	Open End	US Equity Mid Cap (Growth)	B-	C+	B		Y	5,000
U.S. Global Investors World Precious Minerals Fund	UNWPX	NAS CM	Open End	Precious Metals Sector Equity (Precious Metals)	C-	C	D		Y	5,000
U.S. Global Invs World Precious Minerals Inst Cls Shares	UNWIX	NAS CM	Open End	Precious Metals Sector Equity (Precious Metals)	C-	C	D+		Y	1,000,000
UBS Dynamic Alpha Fund Class A	BNAAX	NAS CM	Open End	Multialternative (Asset Alloc)	C-	C-	C	Down	Y	1,000
UBS Dynamic Alpha Fund Class C	BNACX	NAS CM	Open End	Multialternative (Asset Alloc)	C-	C-	C		Y	1,000
UBS Dynamic Alpha Fund Class P	BNAYX	NAS CM	Open End	Multialternative (Asset Alloc)	C	C-	C	Up	Y	5,000,000
UBS Global Allocation Fund Class A	BNGLX	NAS CM	Open End	Alloc (Asset Alloc)	B-	C+	B+	Down	Y	1,000
UBS Global Allocation Fund Class C	BNPCX	NAS CM	Open End	Alloc (Asset Alloc)	B-	C+	B	Up	Y	1,000
UBS Global Allocation Fund Class P	BPGLX	NAS CM	Open End	Alloc (Asset Alloc)	B	C+	B+	Up	Y	5,000,000
UBS International Sustainable Equity Fund Class A	BNIEX	NAS CM	Open End	Global Equity Large Cap (Foreign Stock)	B	B	B-	Up	Y	1,000
UBS International Sustainable Equity Fund Class C	BNICX	NAS CM	Open End	Global Equity Large Cap (Foreign Stock)	B-	B-	B-	Up	Y	1,000
UBS International Sustainable Equity Fund Class P	BNUEX	NAS CM	Open End	Global Equity Large Cap (Foreign Stock)	B	B	B	Up	Y	5,000,000
UBS U.S. Allocation Fund Class A	PWTAX	NAS CM	Open End	Moderate Alloc (Asset Alloc)	B-	C+	B	Down	Y	1,000
UBS U.S. Allocation Fund Class C	KPAAX	NAS CM	Open End	Moderate Alloc (Asset Alloc)	B-	C+	B	Down	Y	1,000
UBS U.S. Allocation Fund Class P	PWTYX	NAS CM	Open End	Moderate Alloc (Asset Alloc)	B-	C+	B	Down	Y	5,000,000
UBS U.S. Small Cap Growth Fund Class A	BNSCX	NAS CM	Open End	US Equity Small Cap (Small Company)	B	B	C+	Up	Y	1,000
UBS U.S. Small Cap Growth Fund Class C	BNMCX	NAS CM	Open End	US Equity Small Cap (Small Company)	B-	B	C+	Up	Y	1,000
UBS U.S. Small Cap Growth Fund Class P	BISCX	NAS CM	Open End	US Equity Small Cap (Small Company)	B	B	C+	Up	Y	5,000,000
UBS U.S. Sustainable Equity Fund Class A	BNEQX	NAS CM	Open End	US Equity Large Cap Blend (Growth & Income)	B	B-	B		Y	1,000
UBS U.S. Sustainable Equity Fund Class C	BNQCX	NAS CM	Open End	US Equity Large Cap Blend (Growth & Income)	B-	B-	C+	Down	Y	1,000
UBS U.S. Sustainable Equity Fund Class P	BPEQX	NAS CM	Open End	US Equity Large Cap Blend (Growth & Income)	B	B-	B		Y	5,000,000
Undiscovered Managers Behavioral Value Fund Class A	UBVAX	NAS CM	Open End	US Equity Small Cap (Growth)	A-	B+	A-	Up		1,000
Undiscovered Managers Behavioral Value Fund Class C	UBVCX	NAS CM	Open End	US Equity Small Cap (Growth)	B+	B+	A-	Up		1,000
Undiscovered Managers Behavioral Value Fund Class I	UBVSX	NAS CM	Open End	US Equity Small Cap (Growth)	A-	B+	A-	Up	Y	1,000,000
Undiscovered Managers Behavioral Value Fund Class L	UBVLX	NAS CM	Open End	US Equity Small Cap (Growth)	A-	A-	A-	Up	Y	3,000,000
Undiscovered Managers Behavioral Value Fund Class R2	UBVRX	NAS CM	Open End	US Equity Small Cap (Growth)	B+	B+	A-	Up	Y	0
Undiscovered Managers Behavioral Value Fund Class R3	UBVTX	NAS CM	Open End	US Equity Small Cap (Growth)	A-	B+	A-	Up	Y	0
Undiscovered Managers Behavioral Value Fund Class R4	UBVUX	NAS CM	Open End	US Equity Small Cap (Growth)	A-	A-	A-	Up	Y	0
Undiscovered Managers Behavioral Value Fund Class R5	UBVVX	NAS CM	Open End	US Equity Small Cap (Growth)	A-	A-	A-	Up	Y	0
Undiscovered Managers Behavioral Value Fund Class R6	UBVFX	NAS CM	Open End	US Equity Small Cap (Growth)	A-	A-	A-	Up	Y	15,000,000
Union Street Partners Value Fund Advisor Class	USPFX	NAS CM	Open End	US Equity Large Cap Value (Growth)	B	B-	B	Up	Y	2,500
Union Street Partners Value Fund C Class	USPCX	NAS CM	Open End	US Equity Large Cap Value (Growth)	B-	C+	B	Up	Y	2,500
Union Street Partners Value Fund Class A Shares	USPVX	NAS CM	Open End	US Equity Large Cap Value (Growth)	B-	B-	B	Up	Y	2,500
Upright Assets Allocation Plus Fund			Open End	Alloc (Multi-Asset Global)	U	U	U		Y	2,000
Upright Growth & Income Fund			Open End	Aggressive Alloc (Growth & Income)	U	U	U		Y	2,000
Upright Growth Fund	UPUPX	NAS CM	Open End	Technology Sector Equity (Growth)	D	D	D	Down	Y	2,000
USA Mutuals Navigator Fund Institutional Class	UNAVX	NAS CM	Open End	Long/Short Equity (Growth)	U	U	U		Y	2,000
USA Mutuals Vice Fund Class A Shares	VICAX	NAS CM	Open End	US Equity Large Cap Blend (Growth)	B	B	A-		Y	2,000
USA Mutuals Vice Fund Class C Shares	VICCX	NAS CM	Open End	US Equity Large Cap Blend (Growth)	B	B	B+		Y	2,000
USA Mutuals Vice Fund Institutional Class	VICVX	NAS CM	Open End	US Equity Large Cap Blend (Growth)	B+	B	A	Up	Y	2,000
USA Mutuals Vice Fund Investor Class Shares	VICEX	NAS CM	Open End	US Equity Large Cap Blend (Growth)	B	B	A-		Y	2,000
USA Mutuals Wave Front Quantamental Long/Short Opp Inst Cl	QUANX	NAS CM	Open End	Long/Short Equity (Income)	U	U	U		Y	2,000
USAA Aggressive Growth Fund	USAUX	NAS CM	Open End	US Equity Large Cap Growth (Aggr Growth)	B+	B	A-	Up	Y	3,000
USAA Aggressive Growth Fund Institutional Shares	UIAGX	NAS CM	Open End	US Equity Large Cap Growth (Aggr Growth)	B+	B	A-	Up	Y	1,000,000
USAA Capital Growth Fund	USCGX	NAS CM	Open End	Global Equity (Growth)	B	B	B-	Up	Y	3,000

★ Expanded analysis of this fund is included in Section II.

Min Additional Investment	3-Month Total Return	6-Month Total Return	1-Year Total Return	3-Year Total Return	5-Year Total Return	Dividend Yield (TTM)	Expense Ratio	3-Yr Std Deviation	3-Year Beta	NAV	Total Assets (MIL)	%Cash	%Stocks	%Bonds	%Other	Turnover Ratio	Last Bull Market Total Return	Last Bear Market Total Return	Front End Fee (%)	Back End Fee (%)	Inception Date
	TOTAL RETURNS					PERFORMANCE				ASSETS		ASSET ALLOCATION & TURNOVER					BULL & BEAR		FEES		
1,000	4.71	7.00	12.03	27.78	54.83	1.28	1.76	8.77	0.74	13.76	29.0	2	80	12	0	24	16.12	-10.52	5.75		Apr-02
100	1.41	2.54	5.89	0.26	42.56	0.15	1.76	9.24	0.85	24.9	15.9	0	100	0	1	303	26.04	-18.31			Mar-81
100	3.69	22.39	57.67	43.83	54.85	0.11	2.76	19.46	1.01	11.53	33.6	0	99	0	1	165	8.78	-29			Feb-94
100	4.29	14.98	22.72	11.63	-16.71	0	2.33	16.58	0.77	7.29	44.4	1	99	0	0	164	15.06	-32.67			Mar-97
100	8.60	16.46	19.56	-2.90	-28.85	2.95	1.85	16.3	0.97	6.09	92.8	0	81	3	8	255	15.48	-31.76			Aug-83
	8.73	16.94	20.95	-0.58	-26.15	3.62	5.41	16.26	0.98	6.13	92.8	0	81	3	8	255	15.73	-31.55			Mar-10
100	1.40	10.24	13.06	55.29	-29.71	0.85	1.86	35.81	-0.22	7.96	94.3	1	97	0	0	181	-12.37	-18.04			Jul-74
100	9.00	12.08	19.17	27.32	69.95	0	1.68	12	1.03	19.52	41.0	-1	97	0	3	275	23.57	-21.9			Oct-94
100	-5.94	-2.47	-4.16	41.84	-40.71	0.37	2.1	35.85	0.05	4.69	114.5	2	90	0	5	136	-9.38	-28.46			Nov-85
	-5.77	-2.17	-3.71	44.50	-39.34	0.69	2.71	35.98	0.04	4.71	114.5	2	90	0	5	136	-9.1	-28.31			Mar-10
100	-0.90	0.30	4.14	-5.08	3.85	0	1.38	5.22	-0.73	6.54	150.6	8	7	84	1	48	5.43	-2.09	5.50		Jan-05
100	-0.97	0.16	3.40	-7.09	0.18	0	2.13	5.17	-0.7	6.07	150.6	8	7	84	1	48	5.01	-2.52		1.00	Jan-05
0	-0.74	0.45	4.36	-4.30	5.09	0	1.13	5.17	-0.71	6.69	150.6	8	7	84	1	48	5.5	-2.05			Jan-05
100	3.19	7.13	16.64	15.44	36.96	1.86	1.31	7.83	0.69	12.17	342.1	13	47	32	8	56	12.36	-15.98	5.50		Jun-97
100	3.05	6.64	15.84	12.84	31.92	1.04	2.06	7.83	0.7	11.88	342.1	13	47	32	8	56	11.82	-16.31		1.00	Nov-01
0	3.38	7.24	17.08	16.39	38.96	2.07	1.06	7.83	0.69	12.43	342.1	13	47	32	8	56	12.56	-15.86			Aug-92
100	5.86	13.15	30.92	27.05	56.78	1.58	1.25	11.89	0.93	10.72	39.5	0	95	5	0	33	19.69	-27.94	5.50		Jun-97
100	5.69	12.70	29.93	24.19	51.13	0.96	2	11.89	0.93	10.47	39.5	0	95	5	0	33	19.12	-28.09		1.00	Jan-02
0	5.93	13.32	31.21	27.98	58.89	1.79	1	11.87	0.93	10.74	39.5	0	95	5	0	33	19.81	-27.81			Aug-93
100	3.53	6.60	15.43	23.14	67.64	0.37	1.03	7.67	0.73	48.87	261.9	17	54	29	0	253	18.79	-12.16	5.50		May-93
100	3.34	6.20	14.57	20.38	61.43	0	1.78	7.67	0.73	47.1	261.9	17	54	29	0	253	18.27	-12.46		1.00	Jul-92
0	3.61	6.76	15.78	24.15	70.03	0.59	0.75	7.69	0.74	49.71	261.9	17	54	29	0	253	18.99	-12.08			May-93
100	6.14	9.44	19.13	23.16	98.14	0	1.25	16.84	1.09	17.99	109.8	3	97	0	0	50	32.05	-21.63	5.50		Dec-98
100	5.94	9.07	18.25	20.44	90.92	0	2	16.8	1.09	14.26	109.8	3	97	0	0	50	31.55	-21.87		1.00	Nov-01
0	6.25	9.59	19.44	24.10	100.87	0	1	16.81	1.09	19.84	109.8	3	97	0	0	50	32.3	-21.52			Sep-97
100	1.94	6.15	18.79	29.02	106.48	0.85	0.95	12.31	1.11	33	31.2	0	100	0	0	78	24.86	-19.44	5.50		Jun-97
100	1.77	5.79	17.91	26.14	98.85	0.21	1.7	12.29	1.1	31.59	31.2	0	100	0	0	78	24.31	-19.65		1.00	Nov-01
0	2.03	6.29	19.10	29.90	108.96	1.05	0.7	12.3	1.11	33.11	31.2	0	100	0	0	78	25	-19.29			Feb-94
50	7.02	11.76	14.66	40.69	109.04	0.56	1.44	12.4	0.8	68.34	6,256	3	97	0	0	24	43.24	-27.32	5.25		Jun-04
50	5.30	9.85	12.41	36.53	100.88	0.2	1.94	12.4	0.8	64.47	6,256	3	97	0	0	24	42.84	-27.49		1.00	Jun-04
	7.04	11.87	14.91	41.69	111.64	0.75	1.19	12.4	0.8	69.74	6,256	3	97	0	0	24	43.43	-27.3			Apr-13
	7.08	11.94	15.08	42.32	113.11	0.86	1.04	12.39	0.8	69.93	6,256	3	97	0	0	24	43.43	-27.3			Dec-98
	6.95	11.62	14.38	39.63	106.50	0.48	1.69	12.41	0.8	67.81	6,256	3	97	0	0	24	43.01	-27.45			Apr-13
	7.00	11.76	14.67	41.11	110.25		1.44	12.39	0.8	68.08	6,256	3	97	0	0	24	43.22	-27.38			Feb-17
	7.04	11.86	14.93	42.13	112.84		1.19	12.39	0.8	69.64	6,256	3	97	0	0	24	43.43	-27.3			Feb-17
	7.07	11.94	15.06	42.30	113.08		1.04	12.39	0.8	69.91	6,256	3	97	0	0	24	43.43	-27.3			Feb-17
	7.09	11.99	15.18	42.71	114.09	0.93	0.94	12.41	0.8	70.02	6,256	3	97	0	0	24	43.43	-27.3			Apr-13
50	7.80	12.02	9.30	28.65	85.00	0.9	1.35	13.8	1.21	17.8	28.2	0	100	0	0	9	21.44	-18.35			Apr-16
50	7.54	11.46	8.21	25.16	77.42	0	2.35	13.82	1.21	17.28	28.2	0	100	0	0	9	20.94	-18.64		1.00	Apr-11
50	7.70	11.85	9.01	27.96	84.02	0.43	1.6	13.79	1.21	17.83	28.2	0	100	0	0	9	21.43	-18.35	5.75		Dec-10
100	-3.18						1.75			10.04	0.49										Oct-17
100	2.54						1.95			10.46	0.46										Oct-17
100	-10.45	-33.61	-14.45	-8.70	44.10	0	2.19	31.24	0.76	8.51	17.8	9	90	0	1	10	34.71	-20.89			Jan-99
100	4.51						1.99			20.84	21.5										Oct-17
100	7.91	10.92	25.71	40.19	89.58	0.77	1.49	10.56	0.81	32.17	233.0	2	96	0	0	56	30.04	-13.93	5.75		Dec-11
100	7.74	10.50	24.80	37.05	82.59	0.35	2.24	10.6	0.81	31.61	233.0	2	96	0	0	56	29.56	-14.2		1.00	Dec-11
100	8.02	11.06	26.08	41.27	91.40	0.92	1.24	10.57	0.81	32.66	233.0	2	96	0	0	56	30.04	-13.93			Apr-14
100	7.95	10.91	25.71	40.21	89.67	0.77	1.49	10.6	0.81	32.31	233.0	2	96	0	0	56	30.04	-13.93			Aug-02
100	3.42						1.3			10.18	8.5										Oct-17
50	6.14	12.30	30.05	37.55	110.37	0.67	0.81	11.26	1.03	43.76	1,446	3	97	0	0	51	26.56	-18.73			Oct-81
	6.12	12.33	29.98	37.89	111.92	0.73	0.7	11.28	1.03	44.32	1,446	3	97	0	0	51	26.82	-18.55			Aug-08
50	6.44	14.24	23.86	36.32	98.25	1.2	1.21	10.27	0.95	12.39	905.6	0	96	0	3	55	19.28	-22.05			Oct-00

	MARKET			FUND TYPE, CATEGORY & OBJECTIVE	RATINGS					MINIMUMS
Fund Name	Ticker Symbol	Traded On	Fund Type	Category and (Prospectus Objective)	Overall Rating	Reward Rating	Risk Rating	Recent Up/ Downgrade	Open to New Investors	Min Initial Investment
USAA Capital Growth Fund Institutional Shares	UICGX	NAS CM	Open End	Global Equity (Growth)	B	B	B-	Up	Y	1,000,000
USAA Cornerstone Aggressive Fund	UCAGX	NAS CM	Open End	Alloc (Growth)	B-	C+	B-	Up	Y	500
USAA Cornerstone Conservative Fund	USCCX	NAS CM	Open End	Cautious Alloc (Asset Alloc)	B-	C+	B+	Up	Y	500
USAA Cornerstone Equity Fund	UCEQX	NAS CM	Open End	Global Equity (Growth)	B-	B-	C+	Down	Y	500
USAA Cornerstone Moderate Fund	USBSX	NAS CM	Open End	Moderate Alloc (Balanced)	B-	C+	B	Up	Y	500
USAA Cornerstone Moderately Aggressive Fund	USCRX	NAS CM	Open End	Moderate Alloc (Multi-Asset Global)	B-	C+	B	Up	Y	500
USAA Cornerstone Moderately Conservative Fund	UCMCX	NAS CM	Open End	Cautious Alloc (Balanced)	B-	C+	B	Up	Y	500
USAA Emerging Markets Fund	USEMX	NAS CM	Open End	Emerging Markets Equity (Div Emerging Mkts)	C+	B-	C	Up	Y	3,000
USAA Emerging Markets Fund Adviser Shares	UAEMX	NAS CM	Open End	Emerging Markets Equity (Div Emerging Mkts)	C+	B-	C	Up	Y	3,000
USAA Emerging Markets Fund Institutional Shares	UIEMX	NAS CM	Open End	Emerging Markets Equity (Div Emerging Mkts)	C+	B-	C	Up	Y	1,000,000
USAA Extended Market Index Fund	USMIX	NAS CM	Open End	US Equity Mid Cap (Growth)	B	B	B	Up	Y	3,000
USAA First Start Growth Fund	UFSGX	NAS CM	Open End	Aggressive Alloc (Growth)	B-	C+	B	Down	Y	500
USAA Flexible Income Fund Adviser Shares	UAFIX	NAS CM	Open End	US Fixed Income (Growth & Income)	C	C	C	Down	Y	3,000
USAA Flexible Income Fund Fund Shares	USFIX	NAS CM	Open End	US Fixed Income (Growth & Income)	C	C	C	Down	Y	3,000
USAA Flexible Income Fund Institutional Shares	UIFIX	NAS CM	Open End	US Fixed Income (Growth & Income)	C	C	C	Down	Y	1,000,000
USAA Global Equity Income Fund Fund Shares	UGEIX	NAS CM	Open End	Global Equity (Equity-Income)	C	C+	B	Up	Y	3,000
USAA Global Equity Income Fund Institutional Shares	UIGEX	NAS CM	Open End	Global Equity (Equity-Income)	C	C+	B	Up	Y	1,000,000
USAA Global Managed Volatility Fund Fund Shares	UGMVX	NAS CM	Open End	Global Equity (Equity-Income)	C+	C+	C+	Down	Y	3,000
USAA Global Managed Volatility Fund Institutional Shares	UGOFX	NAS CM	Open End	Global Equity (Equity-Income)	C+	C+	C+	Down	Y	1,000,000
USAA Growth & Income Fund	USGRX	NAS CM	Open End	US Equity Large Cap Blend (Growth & Income)	B-	B	B-	Down	Y	3,000
USAA Growth & Income Fund Adviser Shares	USGIX	NAS CM	Open End	US Equity Large Cap Blend (Growth & Income)	B-	B-	B-	Down	Y	3,000
USAA Growth & Income Fund Institutional Shares	UIGIX	NAS CM	Open End	US Equity Large Cap Blend (Growth & Income)	B	B	B+	Up	Y	1,000,000
USAA Growth and Tax Strategy Fund	USBLX	NAS CM	Open End	Cautious Alloc (Asset Alloc)	B	C+	A+	Up	Y	3,000
USAA Growth Fund	USAAX	NAS CM	Open End	US Equity Large Cap Growth (Growth)	B+	B+	A	Up	Y	3,000
USAA Growth Fund Institutional Shares	UIGRX	NAS CM	Open End	US Equity Large Cap Growth (Growth)	B+	B+	A	Up	Y	1,000,000
USAA Income Stock Fund	USISX	NAS CM	Open End	US Equity Large Cap Value (Equity-Income)	B-	B-	B	Down	Y	3,000
USAA Income Stock Fund Institutional Shares	UIISX	NAS CM	Open End	US Equity Large Cap Value (Equity-Income)	B-	B-	B	Down	Y	1,000,000
USAA Income Stock Fund R6 Shares	URISX	NAS CM	Open End	US Equity Large Cap Value (Equity-Income)	B-	B-	B	Down	Y	0
USAA International Fund	USIFX	NAS CM	Open End	Global Equity Large Cap (Foreign Stock)	B	B	B	Up	Y	3,000
USAA International Fund Adviser Shares	UAIFX	NAS CM	Open End	Global Equity Large Cap (Foreign Stock)	B	B	B	Up	Y	3,000
USAA International Fund Institutional Shares	UIIFX	NAS CM	Open End	Global Equity Large Cap (Foreign Stock)	B	B	B	Up	Y	1,000,000
USAA Managed Allocation Fund	UMAFX	NAS CM	Open End	Moderate Alloc (Asset Alloc)	B-	C+	B	Up	Y	0
USAA Nasdaq 100 Index Fund R6 Shares	URNQX	NAS CM	Open End	US Equity Large Cap Growth (Growth)	B+	A-	B	Down	Y	0
USAA NASDAQ-100 Index Fund	USNQX	NAS CM	Open End	US Equity Large Cap Growth (Growth)	B+	A-	B		Y	3,000
USAA Precious Metals and Minerals Fund	USAGX	NAS CM	Open End	Precious Metals Sector Equity (Precious Metals)	D+	C-	D	Down	Y	3,000
USAA Precious Metals and Minerals Fund Adviser Shares	UPMMX	NAS CM	Open End	Precious Metals Sector Equity (Precious Metals)	D+	C-	D	Down	Y	3,000
USAA Precious Metals & Minerals Fund Institutional Shares	UIPMX	NAS CM	Open End	Precious Metals Sector Equity (Precious Metals)	D+	C-	D	Down	Y	1,000,000
USAA Real Return Fund	USRRX	NAS CM	Open End	Cautious Alloc (Growth)	C+	C	B-	Up	Y	3,000
USAA Real Return Fund Institutional Shares	UIRRX	NAS CM	Open End	Cautious Alloc (Growth)	C+	C	B-	Up	Y	1,000,000
USAA S&P 500 Index Fund Member Shares	USSPX	NAS CM	Open End	US Equity Large Cap Blend (Growth & Income)	B	B	B		Y	3,000
USAA S&P 500 Index Fund Reward Shares	USPRX	NAS CM	Open End	US Equity Large Cap Blend (Growth & Income)	B	B	B		Y	100,000
USAA Science & Technology Fund	USSCX	NAS CM	Open End	Technology Sector Equity (Technology)	A-	A	B+	Up	Y	3,000
USAA Science & Technology Fund Adviser Shares	USTCX	NAS CM	Open End	Technology Sector Equity (Technology)	A-	A	B+	Up	Y	3,000
USAA Small Cap Stock Fund	USCAX	NAS CM	Open End	US Equity Small Cap (Small Company)	B	B	B	Up	Y	3,000
USAA Small Cap Stock Fund Institutional Shares	UISCX	NAS CM	Open End	US Equity Small Cap (Small Company)	B	B	B	Up	Y	1,000,000
USAA Target Managed Allocation Fund	UTMAX	NAS CM	Open End	Moderate Alloc (Asset Alloc)	C	C	B	Up	Y	0
USAA Target Retirement 2020 Fund	URTNX	NAS CM	Open End	Target Date 2000-2020 (Growth & Income)	B-	C+	B	Up	Y	500
USAA Target Retirement 2030 Fund	URTRX	NAS CM	Open End	Target Date 2021-2045 (Growth & Income)	B-	C+	B-	Down	Y	500
USAA Target Retirement 2040 Fund	URFRX	NAS CM	Open End	Target Date 2021-2045 (Growth & Income)	B-	B-	B-	Down	Y	500
USAA Target Retirement 2050 Fund	URFFX	NAS CM	Open End	Target Date 2046+ (Growth & Income)	B-	B-	B-	Down	Y	500
USAA Target Retirement 2060 Fund	URSIX	NAS CM	Open End	Target Date 2046+ (Growth & Income)	B-	B-	B-	Down	Y	500
USAA Target Retirement Income Fund	URINX	NAS CM	Open End	Target Date 2000-2020 (Growth & Income)	B-	C+	B	Up	Y	500

★ Expanded analysis of this fund is included in Section II.

Min Additional Investment	3-Month Total Return	6-Month Total Return	1-Year Total Return	3-Year Total Return	5-Year Total Return	Dividend Yield (TTM)	Expense Ratio	3-Yr Std Deviation	3-Year Beta	NAV	Total Assets (MIL)	%Cash	%Stocks	%Bonds	%Other	Turnover Ratio	Last Bull Market Total Return	Last Bear Market Total Return	Front End Fee (%)	Back End Fee (%)	Inception Date
	TOTAL RETURNS					PERFORMANCE				ASSETS		ASSET ALLOCATION & TURNOVER					BULL & BEAR		FEES		
	6.44	14.31	23.92	36.71	98.83	1.1	1.1	10.31	0.95	12.41	905.6	0	96	0	3	55	19.28	-22.05			Aug-15
50	4.69	8.75	17.90	19.58	41.12	1.27	1.22	8.29	0.78	12.86	316.4	2	72	24	1	70					Jun-12
50	1.32	3.10	8.12	13.27	22.42	2.79	0.7	3.59	0.83	10.84	197.0	6	17	70	3	7					Jun-12
50	5.01	10.25	22.58	30.99	62.13	1.22	0.94	9.99	0.93	15.6	176.3	3	95	0	2	7					Jun-12
50	3.00	5.92	13.40	13.73	32.12	1.81	1.07	5.72	0.51	14.98	1,175	1	46	45	4	66	12.47	-13.37			Sep-95
50	3.57	6.85	14.98	14.80	34.64	1.82	1.16	6.56	0.6	25.95	2,507	1	55	38	4	69	10.64	-13.98			Aug-84
50	2.48	4.87	11.46	12.30	27.08	1.85	0.99	4.88	0.87	11.44	213.9	3	37	55	1	55					Jun-12
50	4.81	14.29	33.55	28.47	20.27	0.7	1.51	15.18	0.93	20.15	1,054	5	90	0	4	45	14.97	-28.85			Nov-94
	4.77	14.22	33.36	27.76	18.97	0.6	1.75	15.18	0.93	20.1	1,054	5	90	0	4	45	14.71	-28.97			Aug-10
	4.85	14.42	33.76	29.38	21.68	0.91	1.29	15.16	0.93	20.08	1,054	5	90	0	4	45	15.14	-28.77			Aug-08
50	4.73	9.86	17.71	29.81	96.14	0.84	0.48	12.24	1	18.98	765.4	14	98	0	-12	13	28.3	-23.55			Oct-00
50	3.72	7.20	15.84	18.57	51.27	1.35	1.45	7.26	0.67	13.79	444.3	6	69	23	1	40	15.54	-15.6			Aug-97
	0.56	0.80	6.99	7.92		3	1.24	6.69	1.85	9.22	74.9	23	-1	61	7	17					Jul-13
50	0.62	0.94	7.24	8.59		3.26	0.99	6.73	1.86	9.22	74.9	23	-1	61	7	17					Jul-13
	0.62	0.96	7.29	9.05		3.32	0.89	6.66	1.85	9.24	74.9	23	-1	61	7	17					Jul-13
50	3.44	7.75	16.81			1.92	1.21			11.23	105.0	2	96	0	2	22					Aug-15
	3.40	7.61	16.74			1.89	1.11			11.24	105.0	2	96	0	2	22					Aug-15
50	5.31	9.87	20.94	23.49	37.91	1.02	1.14	9.5	0.89	10.73	822.4	0	95	5	0	9	11.32	-12.57			Jul-13
	5.40	9.91	21.23	24.02	39.34	1.21	0.94	9.51	0.89	10.84	822.4	0	95	5	0	9	11.32	-12.57			Jul-08
50	6.87	9.91	20.64	33.10	106.45	0.83	0.91	11.41	1.08	25.17	1,865	1	98	0	1	21	24.4	-19.56			Jun-93
	6.77	9.74	20.26	32.00	103.42	0.58	1.15	11.4	1.08	25.09	1,865	1	98	0	1	21	24.14	-19.69			Aug-10
	6.89	9.95	20.72	33.30	106.76	0.88	0.85	11.41	1.08	25.15	1,865	1	98	0	1	21	24.4	-19.56			Aug-15
50	3.98	6.81	13.47	21.62	53.92	2.16	0.64	4.57	0.4	19.75	427.9	1	49	50	0	4	14.66	-4.01			Jan-89
50	6.44	12.12	28.42	43.16	128.25	0.16	0.99	11.09	1.01	30.53	2,917	1	99	0	0	17	24.34	-17.28			Apr-71
	6.43	12.16	28.50	43.52	128.80	0.23	0.91	11.08	1.01	30.45	2,917	1	99	0	0	17	24.32	-17.21			Aug-08
50	5.77	9.74	16.63	27.33	91.30	2.02	0.77	9.22	0.84	19.95	2,893	2	97	0	1	23	22.9	-16.68			May-87
	5.78	9.71	16.68	27.53	91.85	2.05	0.73	9.21	0.84	19.93	2,893	2	97	0	1	23	22.9	-16.52			Aug-08
	5.86	9.82	16.79	27.51	91.58		0.65	9.22	0.84	19.94	2,893	2	97	0	1	23	22.9	-16.68			Dec-16
50	4.17	9.77	28.10	30.32	48.29	1.23	1.11	11.61	0.93	33.27	4,320	1	97	0	2	4	18.96	-23.19			Jul-88
	4.08	9.63	27.78	29.34	46.26	1.08	1.35	11.6	0.93	33.16	4,320	1	97	0	2	4	18.71	-23.28			Aug-10
	4.20	9.85	28.20	30.81	49.25	1.35	1	11.61	0.93	33.17	4,320	1	97	0	2	4	19.07	-23.08			Aug-08
	4.77	7.00	16.20	14.84	22.63	2	1.05	7.37	0.55	12.27	808.6	2	97	0	0	199	9.1	-1.59			Feb-10
	7.15	13.62	32.41	52.47	154.21		0.4	13.63	1	17.89	1,609	3	96	0	0	4	27.52	-10.94			Mar-17
50	7.11	13.58	32.28	52.33	153.97	0.38	0.54	13.64	1	17.89	1,609	3	96	0	0	4	27.52	-10.94			Oct-00
50	1.37	4.07	9.65	17.73	-45.82	4.06	1.22	39.48	-0.11	13.29	567.5	1	96	0	4	14	-15.77	-12.02			Aug-84
	1.30	4.03	9.57	17.45	-46.14	4.11	1.3	39.46	-0.1	13.16	567.5	1	96	0	4	14	-15.95	-12.13			Aug-10
	1.50	4.33	10.22	18.96	-45.00	3.99	0.76	39.48	-0.1	13.47	567.5	1	96	0	4	14	-15.68	-11.93			Aug-08
50	3.32	5.87	8.34	7.75	8.40	0	1.31	5.79	0.85	10.58	69.8	8	38	51	3	165	9.19	-6.08			Oct-10
	3.22	5.87	8.45	7.96	9.04	0	1.21	5.73	0.83	10.58	69.8	8	38	51	3	165	9.29	-5.99			Oct-10
50	6.58	11.28	21.53	35.84	108.99	1.58	0.25	10.09	1	38	6,869	0	98	2	0	4	24.94	-16.36			May-96
50	6.60	11.33	21.63	36.26	110.04	1.66	0.15	10.09	1	38.01	6,869	0	98	2	0	4	25.01	-16.31			May-02
50	4.45	11.18	36.00	53.73	166.27	0	1.14	12.73	1.07	26.45	1,353	1	97	0	1	75	24.72	-16.27			Aug-97
	4.35	11.00	35.59	52.45	163.27	0	1.35	12.73	1.07	25.85	1,353	1	97	0	1	75	24.55	-16.38			Aug-10
50	3.52	8.83	10.12	23.05	78.29	0.17	1.09	14.34	1	17.55	1,672	4	96	0	0	53	27.55	-24.05			Aug-99
	3.54	8.93	10.28	23.59	79.85	0.29	0.97	14.34	1	17.7	1,672	4	96	0	0	53	27.79	-23.91			Aug-08
	4.72	8.38	13.52			1.21	0.94			11.36	500.3	20	66	14	1	125					Aug-15
50	2.82	5.57	12.70	17.85	34.51	2.75	0.7	5.4	0.92	12.86	613.5	4	48	46	1	11	11.14	-9.19			Jul-08
50	3.80	7.37	16.12	22.02	45.62	3.25	0.75	7.08	0.98	13.84	1,269	4	66	29	1	8	14.8	-13.31			Jul-08
50	4.51	8.70	18.46	24.81	53.77	3.22	0.78	8.17	0.99	14.25	1,404	4	79	16	1	9	17.79	-17.41			Jul-08
50	4.71	9.13	19.38	26.04	57.31	2.74	0.81	8.51	0.95	14.45	793.7	4	84	11	1	6	19.59	-19.48			Jul-08
50	4.74	9.15	19.50	25.90		2.27	0.86	8.54	0.92	12.74	75.3	4	85	10	1	4					Jul-13
50	1.94	3.93	8.65	13.02	24.19	2.15	0.67	3.8	1.11	11.69	348.2	4	31	63	1	14	8.18	-5.72			Jul-08

Fund Name	Ticker Symbol	Traded On	Fund Type	Category and (Prospectus Objective)	Overall Rating	Reward Rating	Risk Rating	Recent Up/ Downgrade	Open to New Investors	Min Initial Investment
	MARKET		**FUND TYPE, CATEGORY & OBJECTIVE**		**RATINGS**				**MINIMUMS**	
USAA Total Return Strategy Fund Institutional Shares	UTRIX	NAS CM	Open End	Aggressive Alloc (Growth & Income)	C-	C-	C-	Up	Y	1,000,000
USAA Total Return Strategy Fund Shares	USTRX	NAS CM	Open End	Aggressive Alloc (Growth & Income)	C-	C-	C-	Up	Y	3,000
USAA Value Fund	UVALX	NAS CM	Open End	US Equity Large Cap Value (Growth)	B	B-	B	Up	Y	3,000
USAA Value Fund Adviser Shares	UAVAX	NAS CM	Open End	US Equity Large Cap Value (Growth)	B	B-	B	Up	Y	3,000
USAA Value Fund Institutional Shares	UIVAX	NAS CM	Open End	US Equity Large Cap Value (Growth)	B	B-	B	Up	Y	1,000,000
USAA World Growth Fund	USAWX	NAS CM	Open End	Global Equity (World Stock)	B	B-	B	Up	Y	3,000
USAA World Growth Fund Adviser Shares	USWGX	NAS CM	Open End	Global Equity (World Stock)	B	B-	B	Up	Y	3,000
USAA World Growth Fund Institutional Shares	UIWGX	NAS CM	Open End	Global Equity (World Stock)	B	B-	B	Up	Y	1,000,000
USCA Shield Fund Institutional Class Shares	SHLDX	NAS CM	Open End	Long/Short Equity (Growth & Income)	D	D+	A		Y	100,000
USCF Commodity Strategy Fund Class A Shares	USCFX	NAS CM	Open End	Commodities Broad Basket (Growth & Income)	U	U	U		Y	1,000
USCF Commodity Strategy Fund Class I Shares	USCIX	NAS CM	Open End	Commodities Broad Basket (Growth & Income)	U	U	U		Y	100,000
USQ Core Real Estate Fund Class I Shares	US90351Y1010		Closed End	Multialternative (Real Estate)	U	U	U		Y	25,000
USQ Core Real Estate Fund Class IS Shares	US90351Y2000		Closed End	Multialternative (Real Estate)	U	U	U		Y	2,500
UTC North American Fund	UTCNX	NAS CM	Open End	Aggressive Alloc (Growth & Income)	B-	C+	B	Up	Y	250
VALIC Company I Asset Allocation Fund	VCAAX	NAS CM	Open End	Moderate Alloc (Asset Alloc)	B-	C+	B	Up	Y	0
VALIC Company I Blue Chip Growth Fund	VCBCX	NAS CM	Open End	US Equity Large Cap Growth (Growth)	A-	A	B	Up	Y	0
VALIC Company I Broad Cap Value Income Fund	VBCVX	NAS CM	Open End	US Equity Large Cap Value (Growth)	B	B	B-	Up	Y	0
VALIC Company I Core Equity Fund	VCCEX	NAS CM	Open End	US Equity Large Cap Blend (Growth)	B	B	B-	Up	Y	0
VALIC Company I Dividend Value Fund	VCIGX	NAS CM	Open End	US Equity Large Cap Value (Growth)	B	B	B		Y	0
VALIC Company I Dynamic Allocation Fund	VDAFX	NAS CM	Open End	Moderate Alloc (Asset Alloc)	B-	C+	B-	Down	Y	0
VALIC Company I Emerging Economies Fund	VCGEX	NAS CM	Open End	Emerging Markets Equity (Div Emerging Mkts)	B	B+	C	Up	Y	0
VALIC Company I Foreign Value Fund	VCFVX	NAS CM	Open End	Global Equity Large Cap (Foreign Stock)	C+	C+	B-	Up	Y	0
VALIC Company I Global Real Estate Fund	VGREX	NAS CM	Open End	Real Estate Sector Equity (Real Estate)	B-	C+	B	Up	Y	0
VALIC Company I Global Social Awareness Fund	VCSOX	NAS CM	Open End	Global Equity (World Stock)	B-	B-	B-	Down	Y	0
VALIC Company I Global Strategy Fund	VGLSX	NAS CM	Open End	Alloc (World Stock)	C+	C+	C+	Up	Y	0
VALIC Company I Growth & Income Fund	VCGAX	NAS CM	Open End	US Equity Large Cap Blend (Growth)	B-	B-	B-	Down	Y	0
VALIC Company I Growth Fund	VCULX	NAS CM	Open End	US Equity Large Cap Growth (Aggr Growth)	B+	B+	B	Up	Y	0
VALIC Company I Health Sciences Fund	VCHSX	NAS CM	Open End	Healthcare Sector Equity (Health)	B	B	B		Y	0
VALIC Company I International Equities Index Fund	VCIEX	NAS CM	Open End	Global Equity Large Cap (Foreign Stock)	B-	B-	B	Up	Y	0
VALIC Company I International Growth Fund	VCINX	NAS CM	Open End	Global Equity Large Cap (Foreign Stock)	B-	B-	B	Up	Y	0
VALIC Company I Large Cap Core Fund	VLCCX	NAS CM	Open End	US Equity Large Cap Blend (Growth)	B	B-	B+		Y	0
VALIC Company I Large Capital Growth Fund	VLCGX	NAS CM	Open End	US Equity Large Cap Growth (Growth)	B	B	A-		Y	0
VALIC Company I Mid Cap Index Fund	VMIDX	NAS CM	Open End	US Equity Mid Cap (Growth)	B	B	B		Y	0
VALIC Company I Mid Cap Strategic Growth Fund	VMSGX	NAS CM	Open End	US Equity Mid Cap (Growth)	B	B	C+	Up	Y	0
VALIC Company I Nasdaq-100 Index Fund	VCNIX	NAS CM	Open End	US Equity Large Cap Growth (Growth)	B+	A-	B	Down	Y	0
VALIC Company I Science & Technology Fund	VCSTX	NAS CM	Open End	Technology Sector Equity (Technology)	A	A+	B+	Up	Y	0
VALIC Company I Small Cap Aggressive Growth Fund	VSAGX	NAS CM	Open End	US Equity Small Cap (Small Company)	B	A	C+	Up	Y	0
VALIC Company I Small Cap Fund	VCSMX	NAS CM	Open End	US Equity Small Cap (Small Company)	B	B	B	Up	Y	0
VALIC Company I Small Cap Index Fund	VCSLX	NAS CM	Open End	US Equity Small Cap (Small Company)	B+	A-	B	Up	Y	0
VALIC Company I Small Cap Special Values Fund	VSSVX	NAS CM	Open End	US Equity Small Cap (Small Company)	B+	A-	B	Up	Y	0
VALIC Company I Small-Mid Growth Fund	VSSGX	NAS CM	Open End	US Equity Mid Cap (Small Company)	B	B	B	Up	Y	0
VALIC Company I Stock Index Fund	VSTIX	NAS CM	Open End	US Equity Large Cap Blend (Growth)	B	B	B		Y	0
VALIC Company I Value Fund	VAVAX	NAS CM	Open End	US Equity Large Cap Value (Growth)	B	B-	B	Up	Y	0
VALIC Company II Aggressive Growth Lifestyle Fund	VAGLX	NAS CM	Open End	Aggressive Alloc (Aggr Growth)	B-	C+	B-	Down	Y	0
VALIC Company II Capital Appreciation Fund	VCCAX	NAS CM	Open End	US Equity Large Cap Growth (Growth)	B	B	B		Y	0
VALIC Company II Conservative Growth Lifestyle Fund	VCGLX	NAS CM	Open End	Cautious Alloc (Growth)	B	C+	A-	Up	Y	0
VALIC Company II International Opportunities Fund	VISEX	NAS CM	Open End	Global Equity Mid/Small Cap (Foreign Stock)	A	A	A-	Up	Y	0
VALIC Company II Large Cap Value Fund	VACVX	NAS CM	Open End	US Equity Large Cap Value (Growth)	B	B-	B	Up	Y	0
VALIC Company II Mid Cap Growth Fund	VAMGX	NAS CM	Open End	US Equity Mid Cap (Growth)	B	B+	C+	Up	Y	0
VALIC Company II Mid Cap Value Fund	VMCVX	NAS CM	Open End	US Equity Mid Cap (Growth)	B	B	B	Up	Y	0
VALIC Company II Moderate Growth Lifestyle Fund	VMGLX	NAS CM	Open End	Moderate Alloc (Growth)	B-	C+	B	Down	Y	0
VALIC Company II Small Cap Growth Fund	VASMX	NAS CM	Open End	US Equity Small Cap (Small Company)	B	A	C	Up	Y	0

★Expanded analysis of this fund is included in Section II.

Min Additional Investment	3-Month Total Return	6-Month Total Return	1-Year Total Return	3-Year Total Return	5-Year Total Return	Dividend Yield (TTM)	Expense Ratio	3-Yr Std Deviation	3-Year Beta	NAV	Total Assets (MIL)	%Cash	%Stocks	%Bonds	%Other	Turnover Ratio	Last Bull Market Total Return	Last Bear Market Total Return	Front End Fee (%)	Back End Fee (%)	Inception Date
	TOTAL RETURNS					PERFORMANCE				ASSETS		ASSET ALLOCATION & TURNOVER					BULL & BEAR		FEES		
	1.53	2.86	6.92	-3.90	-0.86	0.22	1.27	10.88	0.39	8.61	79.6	10	29	47	13	26	10.87	-11.04			Jul-13
50	1.42	2.63	6.59	-4.95	-2.33	0	1.65	10.84	0.38	8.57	79.6	10	29	47	13	26	10.88	-11.04			Jan-05
50	5.02	8.54	15.15	25.96	90.21	1.22	0.98	10.89	1.01	21.68	1,641	2	98	0	0	27	25.94	-20.91			Aug-01
	4.97	8.41	14.86	24.97	87.70	0.97	1.28	10.9	1.01	21.62	1,641	2	98	0	0	27	25.6	-21.1			Aug-10
	5.02	8.59	15.26	26.41	91.40	1.32	0.88	10.92	1.01	21.66	1,641	2	98	0	0	27	26.04	-20.85			Aug-08
50	4.33	7.15	23.92	29.55	74.73	0.61	1.13	10.33	0.96	32.29	1,430	1	96	0	2	12	22.88	-19.73			Oct-92
	4.27	7.02	23.57	28.52	72.64	0.41	1.35	10.33	0.96	32.37	1,430	1	96	0	2	12	22.68	-19.86			Aug-10
	4.32	7.14	23.92	29.68	74.91	0.53	1.1	10.3	0.95	32.21	1,430	1	96	0	2	12	22.88	-19.73			Aug-15
1,000	-1.36	0.37	3.85			0.91	1.18			10.29	16.2	18	80	1	1						Nov-16
250	5.93	10.12					1.3			26.97	2.6	42	0	39	19	1			5.00		Mar-17
	6.03	10.32					0.95			27.04	2.6	42	0	39	19	1					Mar-17
100	1.64						0.96			25.09	--										Sep-17
100	1.64						1.21			25.09	--										Sep-17
100	2.10	3.04	7.17	10.40	42.44	0	2.21	8.85	0.79	10.09	43.6	0	83	17	0	120	14.43	-15.4			May-93
	4.69	7.98	13.24	20.22	49.37	2.14	0.74	6.85		12.04	170.6	8	69	20	3	161	17.25	-11.01			Sep-83
	7.00	14.33	36.20	51.54	139.84	0	0.84	12.34	1.06	19.86	731.6	0	100	0	0	27	30.72	-14.72			Nov-00
	5.00	9.23	18.13	31.46	97.78	1.33	0.85	11.06	1.02	17.63	60.5	0	100	0	0	20	23.79	-18.7			Dec-05
	7.05	12.93	21.03	32.63	104.58	0.95	0.8	11.8	1.13	25.05	260.8	0	100	0	0	36	26.14	-20.5			Apr-94
	5.91	11.02	18.06	35.54	97.19	1.71	0.82	10.13	0.95	13.6	794.6	3	95	0	1	41	21.58	-11.77			Dec-00
	5.78	10.08	20.21	19.47	48.82	1.65	0.92	7.32	0.69	12.99	259.5	3	77	19	0	14					Dec-12
	6.06	16.81	41.26	34.21	24.76	1.2	0.94	15.91	0.99	9.45	800.7	2	97	0	1	69	23.04	-23.59			Dec-05
	2.58	5.51	16.99	21.31	37.25	1.77	0.8	13.41	1	11.1	889.6	3	95	0	2	40	10.58	-24.66			Dec-05
	4.75	6.53	13.83	15.14	37.54	4.01	0.85	10.56	0.93	8.15	388.0	1	93	1	6	47	24.38	-20.95			Mar-08
	5.68	10.41	22.71	29.59	84.49	1.5	0.62	10.05	0.96	26.39	442.8	5	94	0	0	23	19.07	-19.87			Oct-89
	1.64	4.84	13.55	13.38	38.94	0.86	0.66	9.02		12.33	408.5	5	65	26	5	35	14.03	-15.21			Dec-05
	6.41	11.07	21.06	33.14	107.06	1.04	0.85	10.22	1.01	23.06	129.1	1	99	0	0	34	25.43	-19.73			Apr-94
	6.69	12.96	30.23	39.42	107.91	0.67	0.76	10.66	0.98	16.9	1,168	1	99	0	1	71	27.53	-17.31			Dec-05
	1.58	6.92	27.65	27.97	159.62	0	1.07	15.78	1.17	21.78	764.5	0	98	0	0	30	31.23	-14.69			Nov-00
	3.65	9.11	24.35	23.73	41.39	2.34	0.45	11.68	0.94	7.66	1,371	11	89	0	0	11	13.49	-23.64			Oct-89
	3.83	10.12	27.63	22.78	45.36	1.25	1.01	11.47	0.91	14.36	461.0	3	95	0	2	39	18.39	-23.08			Dec-00
	5.35	9.76	21.43	34.62	113.12	0.84	0.83	10.23	0.99	12.59	179.4	3	97	0	0	54	25.46	-19.99			Dec-05
	7.56	11.58	28.54	35.17	104.09	0.61	0.75	10.89	0.98	15.22	439.0	1	99	0	0	23	24.24	-18.87			Dec-04
	6.24	9.53	15.90	34.91	101.70	1.07	0.36	11.06	1	29.42	3,560	4	96	0	0	14	27.72	-22.66			Oct-91
	5.97	11.26	26.28	34.08	96.20	0	0.82	11.22	0.97	15.61	281.4	2	95	0	1	38	20.85	-21.72			Dec-04
	7.10	13.53	32.28	52.52	154.69	0.61	0.53	13.56	1	13.42	432.0	5	95	0	0	4	27.52	-10.87			Oct-00
	7.07	16.08	41.31	62.32	171.42	0	0.99	14	0.94	29.81	1,281	1	95	0	4	92	22.34	-19.41			Apr-94
	6.65	16.95	37.87	41.85	139.39	0	0.99	15.32	0.98	14.9	136.2	5	95	0	0	82	27.94	-25.72			Dec-05
	4.11	9.03	14.71	24.99	87.48	0.26	0.93	13.15	0.92	12.91	323.5	2	97	0	1	82	30.5	-24.89			Dec-00
	3.25	9.08	14.37	31.49	96.32	0.95	0.41	14.16	1	22.81	1,292	4	96	0	0	12	27.61	-25.15			May-92
	5.25	9.60	11.24	37.12	109.26	0.89	0.87	12.75	0.88	14.83	326.3	5	94	0	0	46	28.85	-24.04			Dec-05
	5.12	10.99	27.76	26.45	94.23	0	0.95	12.83	0.92	13.53	116.1	5	95	0	0	61	26.35	-23.2			Dec-05
	6.58	11.25	21.41	35.50	108.11	1.35	0.34	10.11	1	40.81	4,822	2	98	0	0	3	24.84	-16.35			Apr-87
	5.69	8.70	15.33	25.37	87.66	1.55	0.85	11.27	1.08	18.36	114.2	2	98	0	0	15	27.4	-20.63			Dec-01
	4.00	8.24	16.26	24.59	61.48	1.71	0.86	8.41	0.79	11.42	598.2	3	77	18	1	36	19.17	-13.97			Sep-98
	6.73	10.80	23.73	32.22	101.07	0.43	0.85	10.95	1	17.74	96.5	3	97	0	0	66	28.01	-19.41			Sep-98
	2.28	5.02	10.24	15.61	32.11	2.52	0.9	5.04	0.43	12.54	341.3	4	38	55	2	38	12.89	-7.54			Sep-98
	6.03	16.47	39.35	49.71	74.25	1.2	1	10.92	0.86	21.07	722.9	3	93	0	4	62	14.72	-24.2			Sep-98
	6.91	10.61	15.05	29.58	99.57	1.17	0.81	11.35	1.07	22.72	247.2	2	98	0	0	77	24.41	-22.39			Sep-98
	7.36	11.02	31.59	35.65	85.84	0	0.85	12.11	0.94	11.08	147.8	1	99	0	1	162	24.82	-23.55			Sep-98
	4.94	9.05	14.46	27.59	87.85	0.53	1.05	12.05	1.11	23.12	1,084	2	98	0	0	44	31.5	-25.59			Sep-98
	3.36	6.96	13.61	21.35	49.79	2.05	0.87	6.84	0.63	15.06	938.0	3	64	31	1	36	16.62	-11.43			Sep-98
	7.99	17.88	41.45	50.31	126.89	0	1.16	17.03	1.1	19.31	159.5	2	98	0	0	40	30.69	-28.15			Sep-98

	MARKET			FUND TYPE, CATEGORY & OBJECTIVE	RATINGS				MINIMUMS	
Fund Name	Ticker Symbol	Traded On	Fund Type	Category and (Prospectus Objective)	Overall Rating	Reward Rating	Risk Rating	Recent Up/ Downgrade	Open to New Investors	Min Initial Investment
VALIC Company II Small Cap Value Fund	VCSVX	NAS CM	Open End	US Equity Small Cap (Growth)	B	B+	B	Up	Y	0
VALIC Company II Socially Responsible Fund	VCSRX	NAS CM	Open End	US Equity Large Cap Blend (Growth)	B	B	B		Y	0
Value Line Asset Allocation Fund Institutional Class	VLAIX	NAS CM	Open End	Moderate Alloc (Asset Alloc)	B	C+	A		Y	100,000
Value Line Asset Allocation Fund Investor Class	VLAAX	NAS CM	Open End	Moderate Alloc (Asset Alloc)	B	C+	A		Y	1,000
Value Line Income & Growth Fund Institutional Class	VLIIX	NAS CM	Open End	Aggressive Alloc (Growth & Income)	B	B-	B	Up	Y	100,000
Value Line Income & Growth Fund Investor Class	VALIX	NAS CM	Open End	Aggressive Alloc (Growth & Income)	B	B-	B	Up	Y	1,000
Value Line Larger Companies Focused Fund Institutional Cls	VLLIX	NAS CM	Open End	US Equity Large Cap Growth (Growth)	B	B	B+	Up	Y	100,000
Value Line Larger Companies Focused Fund Investor Class	VALLX	NAS CM	Open End	US Equity Large Cap Growth (Growth)	B	B	B+	Up	Y	1,000
Value Line Mid Cap Focused Fund	VLIFX	NAS CM	Open End	US Equity Mid Cap (Growth)	B	B	A		Y	1,000
Value Line Mid Cap Focused Fund Institutional Class	VLMIX	NAS CM	Open End	US Equity Mid Cap (Growth)	B+	B	A		Y	100,000
Value Line Premier Growth Fund	VALSX	NAS CM	Open End	US Equity Mid Cap (Growth)	B	B-	B+		Y	1,000
Value Line Small Cap Opportunities Fund Institutional Cls	VLEIX	NAS CM	Open End	US Equity Small Cap (Small Company)	B+	B+	A-	Up	Y	100,000
Value Line Small Cap Opportunities Fund Investor Class	VLEOX	NAS CM	Open End	US Equity Small Cap (Small Company)	B+	B	A-	Up	Y	1,000
VanEck CM Commodity Index Fund Class A	CMCAX	NAS CM	Open End	Commodities Broad Basket (Growth)	C-	C	D+	Up	Y	1,000
VanEck CM Commodity Index Fund Class I	COMIX	NAS CM	Open End	Commodities Broad Basket (Growth)	C-	C	D+	Up	Y	1,000,000
VanEck CM Commodity Index Fund Class Y	CMCYX	NAS CM	Open End	Commodities Broad Basket (Growth)	C-	C	D+	Up	Y	1,000
VanEck Emerging Markets Fund Class A	GBFAX	NAS CM	Open End	Emerging Markets Equity (Div Emerging Mkts)	B-	B	C	Up	Y	1,000
VanEck Emerging Markets Fund Class C	EMRCX	NAS CM	Open End	Emerging Markets Equity (Div Emerging Mkts)	C+	B-	C	Up	Y	1,000
VanEck Emerging Markets Fund Class I	EMRIX	NAS CM	Open End	Emerging Markets Equity (Div Emerging Mkts)	B-	B	C	Up	Y	1,000,000
VanEck Emerging Markets Fund Class Y	EMRYX	NAS CM	Open End	Emerging Markets Equity (Div Emerging Mkts)	B-	B	C	Up	Y	1,000
VanEck Global Hard Assets Fund Class A	GHAAX	NAS CM	Open End	Natl Resources Sec Equity (Natl Res)	D+	C-	D	Up	Y	1,000
VanEck Global Hard Assets Fund Class C	GHACX	NAS CM	Open End	Natl Resources Sec Equity (Natl Res)	D+	C-	D	Up	Y	1,000
VanEck Global Hard Assets Fund Class I	GHAIX	NAS CM	Open End	Natl Resources Sec Equity (Natl Res)	D+	C-	D	Up	Y	1,000,000
VanEck Global Hard Assets Fund Class Y	GHAYX	NAS CM	Open End	Natl Resources Sec Equity (Natl Res)	D+	C-	D	Up	Y	1,000
VanEck International Investors Gold Fund Class A	INIVX	NAS CM	Open End	Precious Metals Sector Equity (Precious Metals)	D+	C-	D	Down	Y	1,000
VanEck International Investors Gold Fund Class C	IIGCX	NAS CM	Open End	Precious Metals Sector Equity (Precious Metals)	D+	C-	D	Down	Y	1,000
VanEck International Investors Gold Fund Class I	INIIX	NAS CM	Open End	Precious Metals Sector Equity (Precious Metals)	D+	C-	D	Down	Y	1,000,000
VanEck International Investors Gold Fund Class Y	INIYX	NAS CM	Open End	Precious Metals Sector Equity (Precious Metals)	D+	C-	D	Down	Y	1,000
VanEck NDR Managed Allocation Fund Class A	NDRMX	NAS CM	Open End	Moderate Alloc (Asset Alloc)	D+	C-	A-	Up	Y	1,000
VanEck NDR Managed Allocation Fund Class I	NDRUX	NAS CM	Open End	Moderate Alloc (Asset Alloc)	D+	C-	A-	Up	Y	1,000,000
VanEck NDR Managed Allocation Fund Class Y	NDRYX	NAS CM	Open End	Moderate Alloc (Asset Alloc)	D+	C-	A-	Up	Y	1,000
★ Vanguard 500 Index Fund Admiral Shares	VFIAX	NAS CM	Open End	US Equity Large Cap Blend (Growth)	B	B	B		Y	10,000
Vanguard 500 Index Fund Institutional Select Shares	VFFSX	NAS CM	Open End	US Equity Large Cap Blend (Growth)	B	B	B		Y	5 Billion
★ Vanguard 500 Index Fund Investor Shares	VFINX	NAS CM	Open End	US Equity Large Cap Blend (Growth)	B	B	B		Y	3,000
Vanguard Alternative Strategies Fund Investor Shares	VASFX	NAS CM	Open End	Multialternative (Growth & Income)	C	C	C+	Up	Y	250,000
Vanguard Balanced Index Fund Admiral Shares	VBIAX	NAS CM	Open End	Moderate Alloc (Balanced)	B-	C+	B	Down	Y	10,000
Vanguard Balanced Index Fund Institutional Shares	VBAIX	NAS CM	Open End	Moderate Alloc (Balanced)	B-	C+	B	Down	Y	5,000,000
Vanguard Balanced Index Fund Investor Shares	VBINX	NAS CM	Open End	Moderate Alloc (Balanced)	B-	C+	B	Down	Y	3,000
Vanguard Capital Opportunity Fund Admiral Shares	VHCAX	NAS CM	Open End	US Equity Large Cap Growth (Growth)	B	A-	B-	Down		50,000
Vanguard Capital Opportunity Fund Investor Shares	VHCOX	NAS CM	Open End	US Equity Large Cap Growth (Growth)	B	A-	B-	Down		3,000
Vanguard Capital Value Fund Investor Shares	VCVLX	NAS CM	Open End	US Equity Mid Cap (Growth)	C+	C+	C+	Up	Y	3,000
Vanguard Consumer Discretionary Index Fund Admiral Shares	VCDAX	NAS CM	Open End	Consumer Goods Sec Equity ()	B	B	A-		Y	100,000
Vanguard Consumer Staples Index Fund Class Admiral Shares	VCSAX	NAS CM	Open End	Consumer Goods Sec Equity ()	B	C+	A-		Y	100,000
Vanguard Convertible Securities Fund Investor Shares	VCVSX	NAS CM	Open End	Convertibles (Growth & Income)	C+	C+	B-	Down		3,000
★ Vanguard Developed Markets Index Fund Admiral Shares	VTMGX	NAS CM	Open End	Global Equity Large Cap (Foreign Stock)	B	B-	B	Up	Y	10,000
Vanguard Developed Mkts Index Fund Inst Plus Shares	VDIPX	NAS CM	Open End	Global Equity Large Cap (Foreign Stock)	B	B-	B	Up	Y	100,000,000
Vanguard Developed Markets Index Fund Institutional Shares	VTMNX	NAS CM	Open End	Global Equity Large Cap (Foreign Stock)	B	B-	B	Up	Y	5,000,000
★ Vanguard Developed Markets Index Fund Investor Shares	VDVIX	NAS CM	Open End	Global Equity Large Cap (Foreign Stock)	B-	B-	B	Up	Y	3,000
Vanguard Diversified Equity Fund Investor Shares	VDEQX	NAS CM	Open End	US Equity Large Cap Growth (Growth & Income)	B	B	B-	Up	Y	3,000
Vanguard Dividend Appreciation Index Fund Admiral Shares	VDADX	NAS CM	Open End	US Equity Large Cap Blend (Equity-Income)	B	B	B+		Y	10,000
Vanguard Dividend Appreciation Index Fund Investor Shares	VDAIX	NAS CM	Open End	US Equity Large Cap Blend (Equity-Income)	B	B-	B+		Y	3,000
Vanguard Dividend Growth Fund Investor Shares	VDIGX	NAS CM	Open End	US Equity Large Cap Blend (Equity-Income)	B	B-	B+		Y	3,000

★Expanded analysis of this fund is included in Section II.

Min Additional Investment	3-Month Total Return	6-Month Total Return	1-Year Total Return	3-Year Total Return	5-Year Total Return	Dividend Yield (TTM)	Expense Ratio	3-Yr Std Deviation	3-Year Beta	NAV	Total Assets (MIL)	%Cash	%Stocks	%Bonds	%Other	Turnover Ratio	Last Bull Market Total Return	Last Bear Market Total Return	Front End Fee (%)	Back End Fee (%)	Inception Date
	TOTAL RETURNS					PERFORMANCE				ASSETS		ASSET ALLOCATION & TURNOVER					BULL & BEAR		FEES		
	1.74	6.79	4.93	26.47	86.94	0.83	0.95	14.86	1.04	15.71	589.0	2	98	0	0	79	27.34	-28.13			Sep-98
	6.64	11.33	20.65	33.54	114.80	1.24	0.56	10.38	1.02	22	807.3	6	94	0	0	0	24.76	-16.44			Sep-98
100	3.89	6.20	15.19	22.79	60.83	0.27	0.88	6.33	0.57	31.61	328.9	5	68	27	0	17	20.19	-10.9			Oct-15
100	3.80	6.04	14.93	22.15	59.99	0.22	1.13	6.31	0.57	31.54	328.9	5	68	27	0	17	20.19	-10.9			Aug-93
100	2.29	8.56	24.31	25.25	68.07	0.29	0.9	9.74	0.84	9.9	400.3	4	85	12	0	53	13.68	-12.81			Oct-15
100	2.13	8.37	23.86	25.56	68.48	0.29	1.16	9.66	0.83	9.95	400.3	4	85	12	0	53	13.68	-12.81			Sep-52
100	1.74	10.05	33.96	46.24	118.68	0	0.9	13.35	1.05	28.65	275.4	0	99	0	1	47	24.04	-18.36			Oct-15
100	1.74	9.98	33.79	46.21	118.63	0	1.15	13.29	1.04	28.65	275.4	0	99	0	1	47	24.04	-18.36			Mar-72
100	4.32	6.89	19.83	35.66	96.30	0	1.21	8.86	0.76	19.19	150.4	2	98	0	0	20	22.18	-13.59			Mar-50
100	4.31	6.95	19.89	35.73	96.40		0.96	8.86	0.76	19.2	150.4	2	98	0	0	20	22.18	-13.59			Aug-17
100	5.47	8.67	22.31	30.05	79.89	0	1.21	9.38	0.88	33.11	345.2	1	99	0	0	7	26.62	-16.14			May-56
100	5.68	9.99	17.95	36.57	102.69	0	0.96	10.59	0.7	52.09	507.9	2	98	0	0	21	27.45	-16.57			Oct-15
100	5.59	9.85	17.63	35.79	101.53	0	1.21	10.59	0.7	51.77	507.9	2	98	0	0	21	27.45	-16.57			Jun-93
100	6.35	11.98	6.57	-9.02	-32.22	9.53	0.95	14		4.87	369.5	80	0	0	20	0	5.51	-17.64	5.75		Dec-10
	6.50	12.26	6.94	-8.15	-31.10	9.3	0.65	14.13		4.98	369.5	80	0	0	20	0	5.75	-17.52	0.00		Dec-10
100	6.49	12.02	6.71	-8.36	-31.37	9.34	0.7	14.06		4.96	369.5	80	0	0	20	0	5.62	-17.52	0.00		Dec-10
100	8.26	19.39	49.70	30.07	45.50	0.09	1.53	15.94	0.96	18.44	1,871	3	96	0	0	51	21.4	-29.65	5.75		Dec-93
100	8.09	18.97	48.56	27.01	39.48	0.1	2.32	15.96	0.96	16.55	1,871	3	96	0	0	51	21.05	-29.92		1.00	Oct-03
	8.37	19.65	50.39	32.01	49.06	0.09	1	15.97	0.96	19.46	1,871	3	96	0	0	51	21.81	-29.48			Dec-07
100	8.38	19.62	50.32	31.68	47.88	0.09	1.1	15.93	0.96	18.73	1,871	3	96	0	0	51	21.72	-29.67			Apr-10
100	8.70	17.80	-1.49	-6.54	-13.96	0.03	1.38	23.41	1.16	36.32	2,073	2	98	0	0	36	14.32	-29.5	5.75		Nov-94
100	8.49	17.32	-2.24	-8.73	-17.33	0.04	2.15	23.4	1.16	31.28	2,073	2	98	0	0	36	13.84	-29.74		1.00	Nov-94
	8.82	18.06	-1.06	-5.44	-12.29	0.03	0.95	23.42	1.16	38.1	2,073	2	98	0	0	36	14.61	-29.4			May-06
100	8.78	17.94	-1.22	-5.86	-12.89	0.03	1.13	23.42	1.16	37.01	2,073	2	98	0	0	36	14.5	-29.45			Apr-10
100	1.80	2.55	13.02	30.77	-35.41	6.09	1.35	40.76	0.94	9.38	673.6	0	100	0	0	28	-15.18	-16.5	5.75		Feb-56
100	1.67	2.16	12.23	27.83	-37.79	6.94	2.1	40.72	0.94	8.25	673.6	0	100	0	0	28	-15.59	-16.77		1.00	Oct-03
	1.94	2.78	13.55	32.60	-33.93	4.77	1	40.69	0.94	12.05	673.6	0	100	0	0	28	-15	-16.42			Oct-06
100	1.80	2.65	13.28	32.03	-34.42	5.97	1.1	40.72	0.94	9.55	673.6	0	100	0	0	28	-15.1	-16.44			Apr-10
100	4.01	6.91	15.14			0.85	1.38			29.31	35.5	2	85	13	0				5.75		May-16
	4.08	7.08	15.48			0.84	1.08			29.41	35.5	2	85	13	0						May-16
100	4.08	7.04	15.44			0.85	1.13			29.39	35.5	2	85	13	0						May-16
1	6.63	11.41	21.78	36.74	111.30	1.84	0.04	10.09	1	246.82	383,897	0	100	0	0	4	25.08	-16.27			Nov-00
1	6.64	11.42	21.83	36.59	110.56	1.87	0.01	10.09	1	130.79	383,897	0	100	0	0	4	24.99	-16.31			Jun-16
1	6.60	11.35	21.66	36.32	110.14	1.76	0.14	10.09	1	246.82	383,897	0	100	0	0	4	24.99	-16.31			Aug-76
1	-0.17	0.61	0.35			0.44	0.36			20.18	290.9	30	61	1	8	120					Aug-15
1	3.96	7.10	13.89	23.79	63.23	1.97	0.07	5.95		34.72	36,658	2	60	38	0	44	16.1	-8.96			Nov-00
1	3.96	7.10	13.85	23.82	63.30	1.97	0.06	5.95		34.72	36,658	2	60	38	0	44	16.1	-8.96			Dec-00
1	3.93	7.03	13.75	23.32	62.14	1.86	0.19	5.95		34.72	36,658	2	60	38	0	44	15.97	-9.03			Nov-92
1	6.10	11.80	29.19	45.90	153.26	0.58	0.38	12.36	1.03	153.61	16,526	3	97	0	0	9	20.61	-21.72			Nov-01
1	6.08	11.76	29.09	45.58	152.37	0.52	0.45	12.35	1.03	66.5	16,526	3	97	0	0	9	20.56	-21.75			Aug-95
1	4.70	7.69	12.98	13.38	76.24	1.5	0.25	14.75	1.31	13.31	915.0	0	98	0	2	41	28.41	-29.64			Dec-01
1	9.07	10.57	22.83	38.79	123.32	1.37	0.1	11.37	1	80.68	2,508	1	99	0	0	6	32.24	-15.14			Jul-05
1	6.11	4.85	11.79	24.48	89.00	2.5	0.1	9.4	1	71.97	4,585	0	100	0	0	5	16.23	-4.25			Jan-04
1	1.84	4.46	8.84	14.22	40.59	1.34	0.34	6.44	0.78	13.44	1,292	6	1	1	4	103	14.09	-16.7			Jun-86
1	4.45	10.18	26.39	28.62	50.17	2.5	0.07	11.46	0.95	14.41	104,114	3	96	0	1	11	13.27	-23.3			Aug-99
1	4.45	10.24	26.49	28.76	50.37	2.52	0.05	11.46	0.95	22.56	104,114	3	96	0	1	11	13.27	-23.3			Apr-14
1	4.45	10.25	26.46	28.72	50.31	2.5	0.06	11.45	0.95	14.43	104,114	3	96	0	1	11	13.31	-23.28			Jan-01
1	4.40	10.23	26.30	28.23	49.40	2.4	0.17	11.44	0.94	11.16	104,114	3	96	0	1	11	13.21	-23.33			Dec-13
1	6.02	11.03	22.69	32.90	105.13	1.08	0.36	10.73	1.04	34.94	1,472	3	97	0	0	9	27.14	-19.21			Jun-05
1	8.07	11.11	22.22	32.73	92.79	1.92	0.08	9.23	1	27.66	33,549	0	100	0	0	19	21.1	-14.22			Dec-13
1	8.10	11.12	22.14	32.45	92.00	1.85	0.17	9.24	1	40.79	33,549	0	100	0	0	19	21.03	-14.25			Apr-06
1	5.62	8.54	19.33	30.50	96.07	1.87	0.3	9.1	0.84	26.55	33,269	1	97	0	2	27	20.46	-10.03			May-92

	MARKET			FUND TYPE, CATEGORY & OBJECTIVE	RATINGS				MINIMUMS	
Fund Name	Ticker Symbol	Traded On	Fund Type	Category and (Prospectus Objective)	Overall Rating	Reward Rating	Risk Rating	Recent Up/ Downgrade	Open to New Investors	Min Initial Investment
Vanguard Emerging Mkts Select Stock Fund Inv Shares	VMMSX	NAS CM	Open End	Emerging Markets Equity (Div Emerging Mkts)	B-	B	C	Up	Y	3,000
Vanguard Emerging Markets Stock Index Fund Admiral Shares	VEMAX	NAS CM	Open End	Emerging Markets Equity (Div Emerging Mkts)	C+	B-	C	Up	Y	10,000
Vanguard Emerging Mkts Stock Index Fund Inst Plus Shares	VEMRX	NAS CM	Open End	Emerging Markets Equity (Div Emerging Mkts)	C+	B-	C	Up	Y	100,000,000
Vanguard Emerging Mkts Stock Index Fund Inst Shares	VEMIX	NAS CM	Open End	Emerging Markets Equity (Div Emerging Mkts)	C+	B-	C	Up	Y	5,000,000
Vanguard Emerging Markets Stock Index Fund Investor Shares	VEIEX	NAS CM	Open End	Emerging Markets Equity (Div Emerging Mkts)	C+	B-	C	Up	Y	3,000
Vanguard Energy Fund Admiral Shares	VGELX	NAS CM	Open End	Energy Sector Equity (Natl Res)	C	C	C	Up	Y	50,000
Vanguard Energy Fund Investor Shares	VGENX	NAS CM	Open End	Energy Sector Equity (Natl Res)	C	C	C	Up	Y	3,000
Vanguard Energy Index Fund Admiral Shares	VENAX	NAS CM	Open End	Energy Sector Equity (Natl Res)	C-	D+	C		Y	100,000
Vanguard Equity-Income Fund Admiral Shares	VEIRX	NAS CM	Open End	US Equity Large Cap Value (Equity-Income)	B	B-	B		Y	50,000
Vanguard Equity-Income Fund Investor Shares	VEIPX	NAS CM	Open End	US Equity Large Cap Value (Equity-Income)	B	B-	B		Y	3,000
Vanguard European Stock Index Fund Admiral Shares	VEUSX	NAS CM	Open End	Europe Equity Large Cap (Europe Stock)	B-	B-	B	Up	Y	10,000
Vanguard European Stock Index Fund Inst Plus Shares	VEUPX	NAS CM	Open End	Europe Equity Large Cap (Europe Stock)	B-	B-	B	Up	Y	100,000,000
Vanguard European Stock Index Fund Institutional Shares	VESIX	NAS CM	Open End	Europe Equity Large Cap (Europe Stock)	B-	B-	B	Up	Y	5,000,000
Vanguard European Stock Index Fund Investor Shares	VEURX	NAS CM	Open End	Europe Equity Large Cap (Europe Stock)	B-	B-	B-	Up	Y	3,000
Vanguard Explorer Fund Admiral Shares	VEXRX	NAS CM	Open End	US Equity Small Cap (Growth)	B	B+	B	Up	Y	50,000
Vanguard Explorer Fund Investor Class	VEXPX	NAS CM	Open End	US Equity Small Cap (Growth)	B	B+	B	Up	Y	3,000
Vanguard Explorer Value Fund Investor Shares	VEVFX	NAS CM	Open End	US Equity Small Cap (Growth)	B	B+	B	Up	Y	3,000
Vanguard Extended Market Index Fund Admiral Shares	VEXAX	NAS CM	Open End	US Equity Mid Cap (Growth)	B	B	B	Up	Y	10,000
Vanguard Extended Mkt Index Fund Inst Plus Shares	VEMPX	NAS CM	Open End	US Equity Mid Cap (Growth)	B	B	B	Up	Y	100,000,000
Vanguard Extended Mkt Index Fund Inst Select Shares	VSEMX	NAS CM	Open End	US Equity Mid Cap (Growth)	B	B	B	Up	Y	3 Billion
Vanguard Extended Market Index Fund Institutional Shares	VIEIX	NAS CM	Open End	US Equity Mid Cap (Growth)	B	B	B	Up	Y	5,000,000
Vanguard Extended Market Index Fund Investor Shares	VEXMX	NAS CM	Open End	US Equity Mid Cap (Growth)	B	B	B	Up	Y	3,000
Vanguard Financials Index Fund Admiral Shares	VFAIX	NAS CM	Open End	Financials Sector Equity (Financial)	A-	A	B	Up	Y	100,000
Vanguard FTSE All-World ex-US Index Fund Admiral Shares	VFWAX	NAS CM	Open End	Global Equity Large Cap (Foreign Stock)	B-	B-	B-	Up	Y	10,000
Vanguard FTSE All-World ex-US Index Fund Inst Plus Shares	VFWPX	NAS CM	Open End	Global Equity Large Cap (Foreign Stock)	B-	B-	B-	Up	Y	100,000,000
Vanguard FTSE All-World ex-US Index Fund Inst Shares	VFWSX	NAS CM	Open End	Global Equity Large Cap (Foreign Stock)	B-	B-	B-	Up	Y	5,000,000
Vanguard FTSE All-World ex-US Index Fund Investor Shares	VFWIX	NAS CM	Open End	Global Equity Large Cap (Foreign Stock)	B-	B-	B-	Up	Y	3,000
Vanguard FTSE All-World ex-US Small Capital Ind Inv Shares	VFSVX	NAS CM	Open End	Global Equity Mid/Small Cap (Foreign Stock)	B	B	B	Up	Y	3,000
Vanguard FTSE All-World ex-US Small-Cap Ind Inst Shares	VFSNX	NAS CM	Open End	Global Equity Mid/Small Cap (Foreign Stock)	B	B	B	Up	Y	5,000,000
Vanguard FTSE Social Index Fund Institutional Shares	VFTNX	NAS CM	Open End	US Equity Large Cap Blend (Growth)	B	B	B		Y	5,000,000
Vanguard FTSE Social Index Fund Investor Shares	VFTSX	NAS CM	Open End	US Equity Large Cap Blend (Growth)	B	B	B		Y	3,000
Vanguard Global Equity Fund Investor Shares	VHGEX	NAS CM	Open End	Global Equity (World Stock)	B	B	B	Up	Y	3,000
Vanguard Global ex-U.S. Real Est Ind Admiral Shares	VGRLX	NAS CM	Open End	Real Estate Sector Equity (Real Estate)	B-	B-	B	Up	Y	10,000
Vanguard Global ex-U.S. Real Estate Index Fund Inst Shares	VGRNX	NAS CM	Open End	Real Estate Sector Equity (Real Estate)	B-	B-	B	Up	Y	5,000,000
Vanguard Global ex-U.S. Real Estate Index Fund Inv Shares	VGXRX	NAS CM	Open End	Real Estate Sector Equity (Real Estate)	B-	B-	B	Up	Y	3,000
Vanguard Global Minimum Volatility Fund Admiral Shares	VMNVX	NAS CM	Open End	Global Equity Mid/Small Cap (World Stock)	B	B-	B+		Y	50,000
Vanguard Global Minimum Volatility Fund Investor Shares	VMVFX	NAS CM	Open End	Global Equity Mid/Small Cap (World Stock)	B	B-	A+		Y	3,000
Vanguard Global Wellesley Income Fund Admiral Shares	VGYAX	NAS CM	Open End	Cautious Alloc (Income)	U	U	U		Y	50,000
Vanguard Global Wellesley Income Fund Investor Shares	VGWIX	NAS CM	Open End	Cautious Alloc (Income)	U	U	U		Y	3,000
Vanguard Global Wellington Fund Admiral Shares	VGWAX	NAS CM	Open End	Moderate Alloc (Growth)	U	U	U		Y	50,000
Vanguard Global Wellington Fund Investor Shares	VGWLX	NAS CM	Open End	Moderate Alloc (Growth)	U	U	U		Y	3,000
Vanguard Growth and Income Fund Admiral Shares	VGIAX	NAS CM	Open End	US Equity Large Cap Blend (Growth & Income)	B	B	B+		Y	50,000
Vanguard Growth and Income Fund Investor Shares	VQNPX	NAS CM	Open End	US Equity Large Cap Blend (Growth & Income)	B	B	B+		Y	3,000
Vanguard Growth Index Fund Admiral Shares	VIGAX	NAS CM	Open End	US Equity Large Cap Growth (Growth)	B+	B	A-	Up	Y	10,000
Vanguard Growth Index Fund Institutional Shares	VIGIX	NAS CM	Open End	US Equity Large Cap Growth (Growth)	B	B	B	Down	Y	5,000,000
Vanguard Growth Index Fund Investor Shares	VIGRX	NAS CM	Open End	US Equity Large Cap Growth (Growth)	B+	B	A-	Up	Y	3,000
Vanguard Health Care Fund Admiral Shares	VGHAX	NAS CM	Open End	Healthcare Sector Equity (Health)	B-	C+	B	Up	Y	50,000
Vanguard Health Care Fund Investor Shares	VGHCX	NAS CM	Open End	Healthcare Sector Equity (Health)	B-	C+	B	Up	Y	0
Vanguard Health Care Index Fund Admiral Shares	VHCIX	NAS CM	Open End	Healthcare Sector Equity (Health)	B	B	B	Up	Y	100,000
Vanguard High Dividend Yield Index Fund Investor Shares	VHDYX	NAS CM	Open End	US Equity Large Cap Value (Equity-Income)	B-	B-	B	Down	Y	3,000
Vanguard Industrials Index Fund Admiral Shares	VINAX	NAS CM	Open End	Industrials Sector Equity ()	B	B+	B-		Y	100,000
Vanguard Information Technology Index Fund Admiral Shares	VITAX	NAS CM	Open End	Technology Sector Equity ()	A-	A+	B	Up	Y	100,000

★ Expanded analysis of this fund is included in Section II.

Min Additional Investment	TOTAL RETURNS: 3-Month Total Return	6-Month Total Return	1-Year Total Return	3-Year Total Return	5-Year Total Return	PERFORMANCE: Dividend Yield (TTM)	Expense Ratio	3-Yr Std Deviation	3-Year Beta	ASSETS: NAV	Total Assets (MIL)	ASSET ALLOCATION & TURNOVER: %Cash	%Stocks	%Bonds	%Other	Turnover Ratio	BULL & BEAR: Last Bull Market Total Return	Last Bear Market Total Return	FEES: Front End Fee (%)	Back End Fee (%)	Inception Date
1	5.32	13.36	31.99	30.84	24.70	1.12	0.9	16.08	1.01	22.78	660.6	6	91	1	3	46	20.13				Jun-11
1	6.29	14.55	31.37	24.33	19.94	2.28	0.14	15.32	0.97	38.18	89,216	2	97	0	0	13	18.73	-27.19			Jun-06
1	6.30	14.57	31.45	24.53	20.26	2.32	0.09	15.32	0.97	96.59	89,216	2	97	0	0	13	18.81	-27.16			Dec-10
1	6.26	14.52	31.42	24.44	20.13	2.31	0.11	15.33	0.97	29.03	89,216	2	97	0	0	13	18.79	-27.16			Jun-00
1	6.23	14.42	31.15	23.66	18.87	2.1	0.32	15.31	0.97	29.08	89,216	2	97	0	0	13	18.65	-27.23			May-94
1	6.45	14.59	3.26	7.46	11.47	1.98	0.33	18.91	1.05	100.82	9,447	4	94	0	2	29	19.32	-27.57			Nov-01
1	6.43	14.53	3.17	7.23	11.10	1.88	0.41	18.91	1.05	53.74	9,447	4	94	0	2	29	19.28	-27.59			May-84
1	6.42	13.76	-2.38	-4.03	12.00	3.01	0.1	19.54	0.99	49.42	4,591	0	100	0	0	11	22.63	-26.89			Oct-04
1	6.34	11.11	18.49	35.82	101.68	2.5	0.17	9.34	0.87	77.95	30,939	2	97	0	1	28	23.56	-12.06			Aug-01
1	6.30	11.04	18.38	35.44	100.74	2.42	0.26	9.34	0.87	37.19	30,939	2	97	0	1	28	23.5	-12.12			Mar-88
1	2.05	8.64	27.05	23.21	45.95	2.57	0.1	12.53	0.96	74.01	24,631	1	98	0	1	6	15.27	-27.18			Aug-01
1	2.09	8.70	27.13	23.39	45.71	2.6	0.07	12.53	0.96	141.01	24,631	1	98	0	1	6	15.16	-27.21			Dec-14
1	2.05	8.65	27.05	23.30	46.11	2.59	0.08	12.55	0.96	31.56	24,631	1	98	0	1	6	15.33	-27.17			May-00
1	2.00	8.53	26.82	22.63	44.83	2.43	0.26	12.51	0.96	31.78	24,631	1	98	0	1	6	15.16	-27.21			Jun-90
1	6.02	10.76	23.09	31.77	103.41	0.4	0.34	13.12	0.98	88.41	13,418	5	95	0	0	66	28.24	-23.24			Nov-01
1	5.98	10.70	22.95	31.28	101.99	0.29	0.46	13.11	0.98	95.01	13,418	5	95	0	0	66	28.12	-23.29			Dec-67
1	4.47	10.22	13.27	31.88	95.94	0.81	0.55	12.89	1.04	36.66	661.5	7	93	0	0	33	27.77	-22.89			Mar-10
1	4.82	10.02	18.10	31.68	101.14	1.25	0.08	12.28	1	84.76	62,586	3	97	0	0	14	28.84	-23.87			Nov-00
1	4.82	10.03	18.12	31.82	101.48	1.27	0.05	12.28	1	209.16	62,586	3	97	0	0	14	28.89	-23.87			Jan-11
1	4.82	10.04	18.17	31.54	100.35	1.3	0.02	12.28	1	136.19	62,586	3	97	0	0	14	28.75	-23.91			Jun-16
1	4.81	10.01	18.12	31.76	101.30	1.27	0.06	12.28	1	84.75	62,586	3	97	0	0	14	28.86	-23.87			Jul-97
1	4.77	9.94	17.94	31.16	99.78	1.12	0.21	12.28	1	84.8	62,586	3	97	0	0	14	28.75	-23.91			Dec-87
1	7.68	13.10	20.05	47.25	128.88	1.42	0.1	14.79	1	35.08	7,594	0	100	0	0	5	31.67	-26.3			Feb-04
1	4.71	10.93	27.21	26.60	40.94	2.53	0.11	11.63	0.95	33.96	36,769	2	98	0	0	5	14.74	-24.47			Sep-11
1	4.74	10.96	27.29	26.77	41.28	2.56	0.07	11.62	0.94	114.02	36,769	2	98	0	0	5	14.79	-24.45			Dec-10
1	4.74	10.94	27.25	26.66	41.10	2.54	0.1	11.62	0.94	107.67	36,769	2	98	0	0	5	14.76	-24.46			Apr-07
1	4.71	10.88	27.07	26.17	40.04	2.41	0.23	11.61	0.94	21.56	36,769	2	98	0	0	5	14.58	-24.5			Mar-07
1	5.63	12.57	30.12	35.04	52.38	2.3	0.27	11	0.95	45.35	5,799	6	93	0	1	14	13.89	-25.86			Apr-09
1	5.68	12.63	30.30	35.63	53.69	2.41	0.12	11	0.95	227.19	5,799	6	93	0	1	14	14.04	-25.77			Apr-09
1	6.84	11.92	24.18	37.41	123.75	1.52	0.12	10.7	1	17.49	3,811	0	100	0	0	11	23.22	-15.62			Jan-03
1	6.82	11.89	24.11	36.97	122.63	1.45	0.2	10.72	1	17.48	3,811	0	100	0	0	11	23.1	-15.74			May-00
1	5.78	11.55	27.78	34.94	83.02	1.19	0.51	10.22	0.93	31.31	5,661	4	95	0	0	47	20.05	-22.16			Aug-95
1	5.42	11.49	26.50	26.47	35.79	3.45	0.15	11.39	0.95	36.68	6,133	2	96	0	2	7	19.43	-21.55			Feb-11
1	5.43	11.50	26.52	26.54	35.95	3.46	0.13	11.41	0.95	122.2	6,133	2	96	0	2	7	19.47	-21.55			Apr-11
1	5.37	11.37	26.25	25.72	34.64	3.31	0.35	11.4	0.95	24.21	6,133	2	96	0	2	7	19.36	-21.65			Nov-10
1	4.00	6.35	16.03	32.62		2.44	0.17	6.18	0.52	27.06	2,340	1	97	0	2	58					Dec-13
1	3.99	6.39	15.92	32.38		2.35	0.25	6.16	0.52	13.53	2,340	1	97	0	2	58					Dec-13
1	1.66						0.32			25.17	344.6										Oct-17
1	1.64						0.42			20.13	344.6										Oct-17
1	2.56						0.35			25.42	517.3										Oct-17
1	2.58						0.45			20.34	517.3										Oct-17
1	6.70	11.91	20.80	36.70	113.02	1.66	0.23	9.9	0.98	77.11	10,531	2	98	0	0	96	26.15	-16.43			May-01
1	6.67	11.84	20.67	36.22	111.80	1.56	0.34	9.89	0.98	47.24	10,531	2	98	0	0	96	26.1	-16.5			Dec-86
1	6.22	11.37	27.80	38.81	114.70	1.19	0.06	11.07	1	72.35	72,657	1	99	0	0	11	27.48	-15.16			Nov-00
1	6.22	11.38	27.81	38.84	114.79	1.19	0.05	11.07	1	72.35	72,657	1	99	0	0	11	27.49	-15.15			May-98
1	6.19	11.31	27.64	38.27	113.22	1.08	0.18	11.07	1	72.36	72,657	1	99	0	0	11	27.39	-15.2			Nov-92
1	0.56	1.55	19.66	21.84	128.46	0.89	0.32	12.47	1.01	86.68	47,587	2	97	0	1	12	14.6	-7.49			Nov-01
	0.54	1.52	19.61	21.67	127.90	0.83	0.37	12.47	1.01	205.54	47,587	2	97	0	1	12	14.57	-7.5			May-84
1	1.53	5.28	23.35	26.70	131.69	1.27	0.1	13.1	1	77.09	8,277	0	100	0	0	4	20.86	-11.28			Feb-04
1	6.25	11.07	16.37	34.63	103.86	2.76	0.15	9.46	1	33.89	28,812	0	100	0	0	7	21.84	-11.22			Nov-06
1	6.45	11.82	21.50	39.65	121.44	1.62	0.1	12.17	1	73.09	3,805	0	100	0	0	5	30.04	-25.06			May-06
1	8.55	17.52	37.07	61.96	158.43	0.98	0.1	14.32	1	84.31	17,977	0	100	0	0	6	29.16	-14.12			Mar-04

Fund Name	MARKET Ticker Symbol	MARKET Traded On	FUND TYPE Fund Type	Category and (Prospectus Objective)	RATINGS Overall Rating	Reward Rating	Risk Rating	Recent Up/ Downgrade	MINIMUMS Open to New Investors	Min Initial Investment
Vanguard Inst Index Fund Inst Plus Shares	VIIIX	NAS CM	Open End	US Equity Large Cap Blend (Growth & Income)	B	B	B		Y	100,000,000
Vanguard Institutional Index Fund Institutional Shares	VINIX	NAS CM	Open End	US Equity Large Cap Blend (Growth & Income)	B	B	B		Y	5,000,000
Vanguard Inst Target Retmnt 2015 Fund Inst Shares	VITVX	NAS CM	Open End	Target Date 2000-2020 (Asset Alloc)	C	C	B+	Up	Y	100,000,000
Vanguard Inst Target Retmnt 2020 Fund Inst Shares	VITWX	NAS CM	Open End	Target Date 2000-2020 (Asset Alloc)	C	C	B	Up	Y	100,000,000
Vanguard Inst Target Retmnt 2025 Fund Inst Shares	VRIVX	NAS CM	Open End	Target Date 2021-2045 (Asset Alloc)	C	C+	B	Up	Y	100,000,000
Vanguard Inst Target Retmnt 2030 Fund Inst Shares	VTTWX	NAS CM	Open End	Target Date 2021-2045 (Asset Alloc)	C	C+	B	Up	Y	100,000,000
Vanguard Inst Target Retmnt 2035 Fund Inst Shares	VITFX	NAS CM	Open End	Target Date 2021-2045 (Asset Alloc)	C	C+	B	Up	Y	100,000,000
Vanguard Inst Target Retmnt 2040 Fund Inst Shares	VIRSX	NAS CM	Open End	Target Date 2021-2045 (Asset Alloc)	C	C+	B	Up	Y	100,000,000
Vanguard Inst Target Retmnt 2045 Fund Inst Shares	VITLX	NAS CM	Open End	Target Date 2021-2045 (Asset Alloc)	C	C+	B	Up	Y	100,000,000
Vanguard Inst Target Retmnt 2050 Fund Inst Shares	VTRLX	NAS CM	Open End	Target Date 2046+ (Asset Alloc)	C	C+	B	Up	Y	100,000,000
Vanguard Inst Target Retmnt 2055 Fund Inst Shares	VIVLX	NAS CM	Open End	Target Date 2046+ (Asset Alloc)	C	C+	B	Up	Y	100,000,000
Vanguard Inst Target Retmnt 2060 Fund Inst Shares	VILVX	NAS CM	Open End	Target Date 2046+ (Asset Alloc)	C	C+	B	Up	Y	100,000,000
Vanguard Inst Target Retmnt 2065 Fund Inst Shares	VSXFX	NAS CM	Open End	Target Date 2046+ (Asset Alloc)	U	U	U		Y	100,000,000
Vanguard Inst Target Retmnt Income Fund Inst Shares	VITRX	NAS CM	Open End	Target Date 2000-2020 (Asset Alloc)	C	C	B+	Up	Y	100,000,000
Vanguard Inst Total Stock Mkt Index Fund Inst Plus Shares	VITPX	NAS CM	Open End	US Equity Large Cap Blend (Growth)	B	B	B		Y	100,000,000
Vanguard Inst Total Stock Mkt Index Fund Inst Shares	VITNX	NAS CM	Open End	US Equity Large Cap Blend (Growth)	B	B	B		Y	5,000,000
Vanguard Intl Div Appreciation Index Fund Admiral Shares	VIAAX	NAS CM	Open End	Global Equity Large Cap (Foreign Stock)	C-	C	B-	Up	Y	10,000
Vanguard Intl Dividend Appreciation Index Fund Inv Shares	VIAIX	NAS CM	Open End	Global Equity Large Cap (Foreign Stock)	C-	C	B-	Up	Y	3,000
Vanguard International Explorer Fund Investor Shares	VINEX	NAS CM	Open End	Global Equity Mid/Small Cap (Foreign Stock)	A-	A-	A-	Up	Y	3,000
Vanguard International Growth Fund Admiral Shares	VWILX	NAS CM	Open End	Global Equity Large Cap (Foreign Stock)	B+	A	B-	Up	Y	50,000
Vanguard International Growth Fund Investor Shares	VWIGX	NAS CM	Open End	Global Equity Large Cap (Foreign Stock)	B+	A	B-	Up	Y	3,000
Vanguard Intl High Div Yield Index Fund Admiral Shares	VIHAX	NAS CM	Open End	Global Equity Large Cap (Foreign Stock)	C-	C	B+	Up	Y	10,000
Vanguard Intl High Dividend Yield Index Fund Inv Shares	VIHIX	NAS CM	Open End	Global Equity Large Cap (Foreign Stock)	C-	C	B+	Up	Y	3,000
Vanguard International Value Fund Investor Shares	VTRIX	NAS CM	Open End	Global Equity Large Cap (Foreign Stock)	B-	B-	B-	Up	Y	3,000
Vanguard Large Cap Index Fund Admiral Shares	VLCAX	NAS CM	Open End	US Equity Large Cap Blend (Growth)	B	B	B		Y	10,000
Vanguard Large Cap Index Fund Institutional Shares	VLISX	NAS CM	Open End	US Equity Large Cap Blend (Growth)	B	B	B		Y	5,000,000
Vanguard Large Cap Index Fund Investor Shares	VLACX	NAS CM	Open End	US Equity Large Cap Blend (Growth)	B	B	B		Y	3,000
Vanguard LifeStrategy Conservative Growth Fund Inv Shares	VSCGX	NAS CM	Open End	Cautious Alloc (Asset Alloc)	B	C+	A-	Up	Y	3,000
Vanguard LifeStrategy Growth Fund Investor Shares	VASGX	NAS CM	Open End	Aggressive Alloc (Asset Alloc)	B-	B-	B	Down	Y	3,000
Vanguard LifeStrategy Income Fund Investor Shares	VASIX	NAS CM	Open End	Cautious Alloc (Asset Alloc)	B	C	A-	Up	Y	3,000
Vanguard LifeStrategy Moderate Growth Fund Investor Shares	VSMGX	NAS CM	Open End	Moderate Alloc (Asset Alloc)	B-	C+	B	Up	Y	3,000
Vanguard Managed Payout Fund Investor Shares	VPGDX	NAS CM	Open End	Moderate Alloc (Growth & Income)	B-	C+	B	Up	Y	25,000
Vanguard Market Neutral Fund Institutional Shares	VMNIX	NAS CM	Open End	Market Neutral (Growth & Income)	C-	D+	C	Down	Y	5,000,000
Vanguard Market Neutral Fund Investor Shares	VMNFX	NAS CM	Open End	Market Neutral (Growth & Income)	C-	D+	C		Y	250,000
Vanguard Materials Index Fund Admiral Shares	VMIAX	NAS CM	Open End	Natl Resources Sec Equity ()	B	A-	C+	Up	Y	100,000
Vanguard Mega Cap Growth Index Fund Institutional Shares	VMGAX	NAS CM	Open End	US Equity Large Cap Growth (Growth)	B	B	B	Down	Y	5,000,000
Vanguard Mega Cap Index Fund Institutional Shares	VMCTX	NAS CM	Open End	US Equity Large Cap Blend (Growth)	B	B	B		Y	5,000,000
Vanguard Mega Cap Value Index Fund Institutional Shares	VMVLX	NAS CM	Open End	US Equity Large Cap Value (Growth & Income)	B	B	B+		Y	5,000,000
Vanguard Mid-Cap Growth Fund Investor Shares	VMGRX	NAS CM	Open End	US Equity Mid Cap (Growth)	B-	B-	C+	Up	Y	3,000
Vanguard Mid-Cap Growth Index Fund Admiral Shares	VMGMX	NAS CM	Open End	US Equity Mid Cap (Growth)	B-	B	C+	Down	Y	10,000
Vanguard Mid-Cap Growth Index Fund Investor Shares	VMGIX	NAS CM	Open End	US Equity Mid Cap (Growth)	B-	B	C+	Down	Y	3,000
Vanguard Mid-Cap Index Fund Admiral Shares	VIMAX	NAS CM	Open End	US Equity Mid Cap (Growth)	B-	B-	B-	Down	Y	10,000
Vanguard Mid-Cap Index Fund Institutional Plus Shares	VMCPX	NAS CM	Open End	US Equity Mid Cap (Growth)	B-	B-	B-	Down	Y	100,000,000
Vanguard Mid-Cap Index Fund Institutional Shares	VMCIX	NAS CM	Open End	US Equity Mid Cap (Growth)	B-	B-	B-	Down	Y	5,000,000
Vanguard Mid-Cap Index Fund Investor Shares	VIMSX	NAS CM	Open End	US Equity Mid Cap (Growth)	B-	B-	B-	Down	Y	3,000
Vanguard Mid-Cap Value Index Fund Admiral Shares	VMVAX	NAS CM	Open End	US Equity Mid Cap (Growth)	B	B	B+		Y	10,000
Vanguard Mid-Cap Value Index Fund Investor Shares	VMVIX	NAS CM	Open End	US Equity Mid Cap (Growth)	B-	B	B-	Down	Y	3,000
Vanguard Morgan™ Growth Fund Admiral™ Shares	VMRAX	NAS CM	Open End	US Equity Large Cap Growth (Growth)	B+	B+	B	Up	Y	50,000
Vanguard Morgan™ Growth Fund Investor Shares	VMRGX	NAS CM	Open End	US Equity Large Cap Growth (Growth)	B+	B+	B	Up	Y	3,000
Vanguard Pacific Stock Index Fund Admiral Shares	VPADX	NAS CM	Open End	Asia Equity (Pacific Stock)	B	B	B	Up	Y	10,000
Vanguard Pacific Stock Index Fund Institutional Shares	VPKIX	NAS CM	Open End	Asia Equity (Pacific Stock)	B	B	B	Up	Y	5,000,000
Vanguard Pacific Stock Index Fund Investor Shares	VPACX	NAS CM	Open End	Asia Equity (Pacific Stock)	B	B	B	Up	Y	3,000

★ Expanded analysis of this fund is included in Section II.

	TOTAL RETURNS					PERFORMANCE				ASSETS		ASSET ALLOCATION & TURNOVER					BULL & BEAR		FEES		
Min Additional Investment	3-Month Total Return	6-Month Total Return	1-Year Total Return	3-Year Total Return	5-Year Total Return	Dividend Yield (TTM)	Expense Ratio	3-Yr Std Deviation	3-Year Beta	NAV	Total Assets (MIL)	%Cash	%Stocks	%Bonds	%Other	Turnover Ratio	Last Bull Market Total Return	Last Bear Market Total Return	Front End Fee (%)	Back End Fee (%)	Inception Date
1	6.64	11.42	21.81	36.84	111.60	1.86	0.02	10.09	1	243.48	233,655	0	100	0	0	5	25.1	-16.26			Jul-97
1	6.63	11.40	21.78	36.76	111.39	1.84	0.04	10.09	1	243.46	233,655	0	100	0	0	5	25.08	-16.26			Jul-90
1	2.72	5.42	11.49			1.71	0.09			21.99	7,825	2	43	54	1	10					Jun-15
1	3.39	6.66	14.12			1.72	0.09			22.53	18,601	2	54	43	1	6					Jun-15
1	3.80	7.49	15.93			1.7	0.09			22.86	23,039	2	63	35	1	4					Jun-15
1	4.25	8.27	17.56			1.69	0.09			23.12	20,522	2	70	28	1	4					Jun-15
1	4.59	8.99	19.13			1.67	0.09			23.37	18,877	2	77	20	0	4					Jun-15
1	4.99	9.72	20.73			1.65	0.09			23.62	16,054	2	85	13	0	5					Jun-15
1	5.23	10.15	21.46			1.62	0.09			23.8	13,080	2	88	10	0	5					Jun-15
1	5.19	10.11	21.46			1.59	0.09			23.82	8,720	2	88	10	0	5					Jun-15
1	5.17	10.13	21.47			1.5	0.09			23.86	3,597	2	88	10	0	6					Jun-15
1	5.16	10.07	21.41			1.5	0.09			23.86	926.3	2	88	10	0	7					Jun-15
1	5.22	7.92					0.09			21.72	13.8	2	88	10	0	133					Jul-17
1	2.04	4.08	8.54			1.84	0.09			21.5	5,193	3	30	67	1	7					Jun-15
1	6.33	11.18	21.13	35.91	110.17	1.76	0.02	10.22	1	59.47	43,361	0	99	0	0	8	25.85	-17.66			May-01
1	6.34	11.16	21.13	35.85	109.94	1.74	0.04	10.22	1	59.47	43,361	0	99	0	0	8	25.84	-17.67			Aug-01
1	4.38	8.57	27.82			1.58	0.25			32.19	868.2	2	97	0	1	8					Mar-16
1	4.34	8.51	27.70			1.49	0.35			26.49	868.2	2	97	0	1	8					Mar-16
1	5.49	13.93	38.76	47.95	88.67	1.45	0.41	11.62	0.96	21.29	4,070	8	92	0	1	37	15.1	-25.66			Nov-96
1	4.12	15.24	43.15	44.30	70.47	1	0.32	14.24	1.1	95.58	33,542	2	95	0	2	15	19.77	-25.55			Aug-01
1	4.06	15.14	42.96	43.76	69.34	0.89	0.45	14.21	1.1	30.04	33,542	2	95	0	2	15	19.73	-25.6			Sep-81
1	2.78	8.81	22.39			2.97	0.32			32.36	839.6	1	95	0	3	6					Mar-16
1	2.76	8.76	22.29			2.89	0.42			26.73	839.6	1	95	0	3	6					Feb-16
1	4.90	11.95	27.96	24.57	43.96	1.82	0.43	12.39	0.99	39.88	10,162	4	94	1	2	30	15.06	-24.2			May-83
1	6.61	11.37	22.02	36.29	110.62	1.76	0.06	10.1	1	61.86	18,396	0	100	0	0	5	25.36	-16.74			Feb-04
1	6.61	11.39	22.03	36.33	110.70	1.77	0.05	10.1	1	254.61	18,396	0	100	0	0	5	25.39	-16.75			Jun-05
1	6.59	11.32	21.89	35.79	109.24	1.66	0.18	10.1	1	49.48	18,396	0	100	0	0	5	25.26	-16.81			Jan-04
1	2.60	5.18	10.92	17.01	37.53	2.08	0.13	4.21	0.43	19.96	9,469	2	40	57	1	9	10.32	-7.41			Sep-94
1	4.66	9.05	19.21	26.83	67.65	1.98	0.15	8.03	0.75	33.67	14,790	2	79	19	0	5	18.14	-16.17			Sep-94
1	1.59	3.27	6.98	12.05	23.86	2.14	0.12	2.93	0.73	15.56	4,246	3	20	76	1	4	6.3	-2.5			Sep-94
1	3.62	7.09	15.04	21.99	52.13	2.01	0.14	6.02	0.14	27.14	15,968	2	59	38	1	9	14.1	-11.41			Sep-94
1	3.51	6.84	13.29	20.44	49.89	5.59	0.34	5.56	0.5	19.11	2,066	9	67	17	7	19	14.98	-12.59			May-08
1	-0.15	-0.41	-4.82	2.77	17.31	0.5	0.14	5.62	-17.05	11.61	1,851	58	42	0	0	64	-0.09	2.59			Oct-98
1	-0.13	-0.47	-4.89	2.51	16.82	0.4	0.22	5.58	-17.04	11.66	1,851	58	42	0	0	64	-0.19	2.58			Nov-98
1	6.67	13.26	23.67	33.53	82.14	1.65	0.1	16.63	1	69.58	2,638	0	100	0	0	5	29.14	-28.04			Feb-04
1	6.58	11.99	29.48	41.54	119.26	1.22	0.06	11.31	1	220.86	3,438	0	100	0	0	8	27.58	-13.66			Apr-08
1	6.80	11.80	22.56	37.71	111.88	1.86	0.06	10.14	1	180.74	1,478	0	100	0	0	6	25.18	-15.74			Feb-08
1	6.97	11.59	16.80	34.52	106.23	2.4	0.06	10.02	1	151.33	2,020	0	100	0	0	8	22.7	-17.81			Mar-08
1	5.97	10.46	22.00	21.89	85.63	0.55	0.36	11.35	0.99	26.41	4,340	5	95	0	0	91	28.63	-18.47			Dec-97
1	5.04	8.97	21.82	27.81	96.76	0.78	0.07	11.09	1	54.96	11,298	0	100	0	0	21	26.99	-21.74			Sep-11
1	5.01	8.91	21.71	27.38	95.55	0.68	0.19	11.08	1	50.21	11,298	0	100	0	0	21	26.87	-21.78			Aug-06
1	5.64	9.27	19.25	29.71	104.73	1.36	0.06	10.58	1	191.55	93,725	0	100	0	0	15	26.38	-21.36			Nov-01
1	5.64	9.28	19.28	29.80	104.99	1.37	0.04	10.58	1	208.69	93,725	0	100	0	0	15	26.41	-21.34			Dec-10
1	5.66	9.29	19.29	29.76	104.90	1.37	0.05	10.58	1	42.32	93,725	0	100	0	0	15	26.43	-21.37			May-98
1	5.61	9.21	19.11	29.23	103.40	1.25	0.18	10.59	1	42.23	93,725	0	100	0	0	15	26.27	-21.4			May-98
1	6.14	9.47	17.04	31.11	111.33	1.83	0.07	10.42	1	57.74	16,764	0	100	0	0	20	25.77	-20.99			Sep-11
1	6.13	9.41	16.91	30.67	109.96	1.72	0.19	10.43	1	43.89	16,764	0	100	0	0	20	25.66	-21			Aug-06
1	6.11	13.05	30.00	42.33	119.08	0.72	0.28	10.96	1	90.71	13,694	4	96	0	0	48	27.3	-18.57			May-01
1	6.08	13.01	29.85	41.87	117.77	0.64	0.38	10.97	1	29.26	13,694	4	96	0	0	48	27.18	-18.64			Dec-68
1	8.27	12.62	28.61	38.05	56.95	2.29	0.1	11.56	0.9	89.97	8,471	2	97	0	0	4	10.23	-15.25			Aug-01
1	8.25	12.57	28.54	38.14	57.11	2.31	0.08	11.57	0.9	13.76	8,471	2	97	0	0	4	10.34	-15.24			May-00
1	8.23	12.55	28.38	37.45	55.85	2.14	0.26	11.56	0.9	13.87	8,471	2	97	0	0	4	10.18	-15.32			Jun-90

Fund Name	Ticker Symbol	Traded On	Fund Type	Category and (Prospectus Objective)	Overall Rating	Reward Rating	Risk Rating	Recent Up/ Downgrade	Open to New Investors	Min Initial Investment
	MARKET		FUND TYPE, CATEGORY & OBJECTIVE		RATINGS				MINIMUMS	
Vanguard Precious Metals And Mining Fund Investor Shares	VGPMX	NAS CM	Open End	Precious Metals Sector Equity (Precious Metals)	C-	C	D		Y	3,000
Vanguard PRIMECAP Core Fund Investor Shares	VPCCX	NAS CM	Open End	US Equity Large Cap Growth (Growth)	B	B+	B-	Down		3,000
Vanguard PRIMECAP Fund Admiral Shares	VPMAX	NAS CM	Open End	US Equity Large Cap Growth (Growth)	B+	A-	B-	Up		50,000
Vanguard PRIMECAP Fund Investor Shares	VPMCX	NAS CM	Open End	US Equity Large Cap Growth (Growth)	B+	A-	B-	Up		3,000
Vanguard REIT II Index Fund	VRTPX	NAS CM	Open End	Real Estate Sector Equity (Real Estate)	U	U	U		Y	100,000,000
Vanguard REIT Index Fund Admiral Shares	VGSLX	NAS CM	Open End	Real Estate Sector Equity (Real Estate)	B-	C+	B		Y	10,000
Vanguard REIT Index Fund Institutional Shares	VGSNX	NAS CM	Open End	Real Estate Sector Equity (Real Estate)	B-	C+	B		Y	5,000,000
Vanguard REIT Index Fund Investor Shares	VGSIX	NAS CM	Open End	Real Estate Sector Equity (Real Estate)	B-	C+	B		Y	3,000
Vanguard Russell 1000 Growth Index Fund Inst Shares	VRGWX	NAS CM	Open End	US Equity Large Cap Growth (Growth)	B+	B+	B+	Up	Y	5,000,000
Vanguard Russell 1000 Index Fund Institutional Shares	VRNIX	NAS CM	Open End	US Equity Large Cap Blend (Growth)	B	B	B		Y	5,000,000
Vanguard Russell 1000 Value Index Fund Inst Shares	VRVIX	NAS CM	Open End	US Equity Large Cap Value (Growth & Income)	B	B-	B		Y	5,000,000
Vanguard Russell 2000 Growth Index Fund Inst Shares	VRTGX	NAS CM	Open End	US Equity Small Cap (Small Company)	B+	A-	B	Up	Y	5,000,000
Vanguard Russell 2000 Index Fund Institutional Shares	VRTIX	NAS CM	Open End	US Equity Small Cap (Small Company)	B+	A-	B	Up	Y	5,000,000
Vanguard Russell 2000 Value Index Fund Inst Shares	VRTVX	NAS CM	Open End	US Equity Small Cap (Small Company)	B	A-	B	Up	Y	5,000,000
Vanguard Russell 3000 Index Fund Institutional Shares	VRTTX	NAS CM	Open End	US Equity Large Cap Blend (Growth)	B	B	B		Y	5,000,000
Vanguard S&P 500 Value Index Fund Institutional Shares	VSPVX	NAS CM	Open End	US Equity Large Cap Value (Growth & Income)	B	B-	B		Y	5,000,000
Vanguard S&P Mid-Cap 400 Growth Index Fund Inst Shares	VMFGX	NAS CM	Open End	US Equity Mid Cap (Growth & Income)	B+	B+	B+	Up	Y	5,000,000
Vanguard S&P Mid-Cap 400 Index Fund Institutional Shares	VSPMX	NAS CM	Open End	US Equity Mid Cap (Growth & Income)	B	B	B		Y	5,000,000
Vanguard S&P Mid-Cap 400 Value Index Fund Inst Shares	VMFVX	NAS CM	Open End	US Equity Mid Cap (Growth & Income)	B	B	B	Up	Y	5,000,000
Vanguard S&P Small-Cap 600 Index Fund Institutional Shares	VSMSX	NAS CM	Open End	US Equity Small Cap (Growth & Income)	A-	A	B	Up	Y	5,000,000
Vanguard S&P Small-Cap 600 Value Index Fund Inst Shares	VSMVX	NAS CM	Open End	US Equity Small Cap (Growth & Income)	B+	A-	B	Up	Y	5,000,000
Vanguard Selected Value Fund Investor Shares	VASVX	NAS CM	Open End	US Equity Mid Cap (Growth & Income)	B	B	B	Up	Y	3,000
Vanguard Small Cap Value Index Fund Admiral Shares	VSIAX	NAS CM	Open End	US Equity Small Cap (Small Company)	B	B	B	Up	Y	10,000
Vanguard Small Capitalization Growth Index Fund Inv Shares	VISGX	NAS CM	Open End	US Equity Small Cap (Small Company)	B	B	B	Up	Y	3,000
Vanguard Small Capitalization Index Fund Investor Shares	NAESX	NAS CM	Open End	US Equity Small Cap (Small Company)	B	B	B	Up	Y	3,000
Vanguard Small Capitalization Value Index Fund Inv Shares	VISVX	NAS CM	Open End	US Equity Small Cap (Small Company)	B	B	B	Up	Y	3,000
Vanguard Small-Cap Growth Index Fund Admiral Shares	VSGAX	NAS CM	Open End	US Equity Small Cap (Small Company)	B	B	B	Up	Y	10,000
Vanguard Small-Cap Growth Index Fund Institutional Shares	VSGIX	NAS CM	Open End	US Equity Small Cap (Small Company)	B	B	B	Up	Y	5,000,000
Vanguard Small-Cap Index Fund Admiral Shares	VSMAX	NAS CM	Open End	US Equity Small Cap (Small Company)	B	B	B	Up	Y	10,000
Vanguard Small-Cap Index Fund Institutional Plus Shares	VSCPX	NAS CM	Open End	US Equity Small Cap (Small Company)	B	B	B	Up	Y	100,000,000
Vanguard Small-Cap Index Fund Institutional Shares	VSCIX	NAS CM	Open End	US Equity Small Cap (Small Company)	B	B	B	Up	Y	5,000,000
Vanguard Small-Cap Value Index Fund Institutional Shares	VSIIX	NAS CM	Open End	US Equity Small Cap (Small Company)	B	B	B	Up	Y	5,000,000
Vanguard Star Fund Investor Shares	VGSTX	NAS CM	Open End	Moderate Alloc (Balanced)	B	B-	A-	Up	Y	1,000
Vanguard Strategic Equity Fund Investor Shares	VSEQX	NAS CM	Open End	US Equity Mid Cap (Aggr Growth)	B	B	B	Up	Y	3,000
Vanguard Strategic Small-Cap Equity Fund Investor Shares	VSTCX	NAS CM	Open End	US Equity Small Cap (Small Company)	B	B	B	Up	Y	3,000
Vanguard Target Retirement 2015 Fund Investor Shares	VTXVX	NAS CM	Open End	Target Date 2000-2020 (Growth & Income)	B	C+	A-	Up	Y	1,000
Vanguard Target Retirement 2020 Fund Investor Shares	VTWNX	NAS CM	Open End	Target Date 2000-2020 (Growth & Income)	B-	C+	B	Up	Y	1,000
Vanguard Target Retirement 2025 Fund Investor Shares	VTTVX	NAS CM	Open End	Target Date 2021-2045 (Growth & Income)	B-	C+	B	Up	Y	1,000
Vanguard Target Retirement 2030 Fund Investor Shares	VTHRX	NAS CM	Open End	Target Date 2021-2045 (Growth & Income)	B-	B-	B	Down	Y	1,000
Vanguard Target Retirement 2035 Fund Investor Shares	VTTHX	NAS CM	Open End	Target Date 2021-2045 (Growth & Income)	B-	B-	B	Down	Y	1,000
Vanguard Target Retirement 2040 Fund Investor Shares	VFORX	NAS CM	Open End	Target Date 2021-2045 (Growth & Income)	B-	B-	B-	Down	Y	1,000
Vanguard Target Retirement 2045 Fund Investor Shares	VTIVX	NAS CM	Open End	Target Date 2021-2045 (Growth & Income)	B-	B-	B-	Down	Y	1,000
Vanguard Target Retirement 2050 Fund Investor Shares	VFIFX	NAS CM	Open End	Target Date 2046+ (Growth & Income)	B-	B-	B-	Down	Y	1,000
Vanguard Target Retirement 2055 Fund Investor Shares	VFFVX	NAS CM	Open End	Target Date 2046+ (Growth & Income)	B-	B-	B-	Down	Y	1,000
Vanguard Target Retirement 2060 Fund Investor Shares	VTTSX	NAS CM	Open End	Target Date 2046+ (Growth & Income)	B-	B-	B-	Down	Y	1,000
Vanguard Target Retirement 2065 Fund Investor Shares	VLXVX	NAS CM	Open End	Target Date 2046+ (Growth & Income)	U	U	U		Y	1,000
Vanguard Target Retirement Income Fund Investor Shares	VTINX	NAS CM	Open End	Target Date 2000-2020 (Growth & Income)	B	C+	A-	Up	Y	1,000
Vanguard Tax-Managed Balanced Fund Admiral Shares	VTMFX	NAS CM	Open End	Cautious Alloc (Balanced)	B	C+	A-	Up	Y	10,000
Vanguard Tax-Managed Capital Appreciation Admiral Shares	VTCLX	NAS CM	Open End	US Equity Large Cap Blend (Growth)	B	B	B		Y	10,000
Vanguard Tax-Managed Capital Appreciation Fund Inst Shares	VTCIX	NAS CM	Open End	US Equity Large Cap Blend (Growth)	B	B	B		Y	5,000,000
Vanguard Tax-Managed Small Cap Fund Admiral Shares	VTMSX	NAS CM	Open End	US Equity Small Cap (Small Company)	A-	A-	B	Up	Y	10,000
Vanguard Tax-Managed Small-Cap Fund Institutional Shares	VTSIX	NAS CM	Open End	US Equity Small Cap (Small Company)	A-	A-	B	Up	Y	5,000,000

★Expanded analysis of this fund is included in Section II.

	TOTAL RETURNS					PERFORMANCE				ASSETS		ASSET ALLOCATION & TURNOVER					BULL & BEAR		FEES		
Min Additional Investment	3-Month Total Return	6-Month Total Return	1-Year Total Return	3-Year Total Return	5-Year Total Return	Dividend Yield (TTM)	Expense Ratio	3-Yr Std Deviation	3-Year Beta	NAV	Total Assets (MIL)	%Cash	%Stocks	%Bonds	%Other	Turnover Ratio	Last Bull Market Total Return	Last Bear Market Total Return	Front End Fee (%)	Back End Fee (%)	Inception Date
1	2.59	4.80	13.74	21.07	-28.99	0.02	0.43	33.99	0.39	10.69	2,434	6	93	0	0	29	-1	-25.25			May-84
1	6.33	11.62	26.22	42.16	135.93	0.97	0.46	11.03	1.03	26.9	10,705	3	97	0	0	9	18.7	-17.64			Dec-04
1	7.30	13.13	29.60	46.20	148.19	1.04	0.33	11.17	1.04	133.61	61,536	6	94	0	0	8	20.42	-18.36			Nov-01
1	7.28	13.09	29.50	45.90	147.25	0.98	0.39	11.17	1.04	128.89	61,536	6	94	0	0	8	20.34	-18.38			Nov-84
1	1.41						0.08			20.01	6,408	0	100	0	0						Sep-17
1	1.38	2.28	4.93	14.66	57.29	3.84	0.12	13.47	1	117.55	64,780	0	100	0	0	7	31.27	-16.26			Nov-01
1	1.38	2.26	4.92	14.70	57.47	4.69	0.1	13.48	1	18.19	64,780	0	100	0	0	7	31.24	-16.24			Dec-03
1	1.36	2.22	4.82	14.21	56.19	3.7	0.26	13.47	1	27.56	64,780	0	100	0	0	7	31.21	-16.32			May-96
1	7.84	14.19	30.11	45.68	125.44	1.23	0.08	10.76	1	265.2	4,157	0	100	0	0	21	26.6	-15.4			Dec-10
1	6.57	11.31	21.58	35.73	109.80	1.74	0.08	10.14	1	237.15	2,893	0	100	0	0	11	25.48	-17.08			Oct-10
1	5.32	8.58	13.59	26.45	95.01	2.31	0.08	10.32	1	211.75	2,869	0	100	0	0	22	24.35	-18.82			Dec-10
1	4.61	11.15	22.28	34.03	108.76	0.81	0.08	14.83	1	257.96	657.3	2	98	0	0	34	28.12	-25.44			May-11
1	3.37	9.26	14.77	32.38	98.47	1.23	0.08	14.13	1	233.92	1,876	2	98	0	0	23	27.77	-25.08			Dec-10
1	2.06	7.30	7.91	30.35	87.97	1.68	0.08	14.16	1	215.2	352.6	1	99	0	0	36	27.35	-24.77			Jul-12
1	6.30	11.15	21.03	35.48	108.93	1.71	0.08	10.24	1	236.93	1,164	1	99	0	0	16	25.64	-17.76			Nov-10
1	6.30	9.99	15.28	29.54	96.60	2.18	0.08	10.44	1	240.96	862.0	0	100	0	0	16	25.79	-19.65			Mar-15
1	7.07	10.47	19.86	38.75	103.36	0.95	0.08	10.51	1	265.15	1,000	1	99	0	0	40	25.63	-20.97			Mar-11
1	6.24	9.65	16.18	35.62	103.84	1.24	0.08	11.05	1	254.85	2,112	1	99	0	0	13	27.88	-22.61			Mar-11
1	5.35	8.77	12.26	31.02	101.94	1.27	0.08	12.4	1	243.78	844.3	1	99	0	0	39	30.21	-24.19			Nov-10
1	3.96	10.18	13.37	39.57	113.86	0.87	0.08	13.78	1	280.11	1,579	1	99	0	0	22	29.45	-22.07			Apr-11
1	4.02	10.57	11.63	35.64	108.63	1.37	0.08	14.68	1	276.63	272.9	1	99	0	0	46	31.25	-22.71			Nov-14
1	5.34	10.56	19.51	32.63	105.69	1.44	0.35	11.84	1.04	31.27	10,803	6	94	0	0	27	23.1	-19.11			Feb-96
1	4.55	9.14	11.79	31.70	104.35	1.74	0.07	12.56	1	57.02	29,416	1	99	0	0	18	28.1	-23.97			Sep-11
1	5.73	10.72	21.78	30.30	91.95	0.75	0.19	12.43	1	45.24	21,153	2	98	0	0	27	29.39	-25.13			May-98
1	5.07	9.84	16.10	30.93	98.80	1.22	0.18	12.22	1	70.76	83,745	2	98	0	0	14	28.67	-24.56			Oct-60
1	4.53	9.11	11.67	31.25	103.09	1.63	0.19	12.57	1	31.82	29,416	1	99	0	0	18	27.94	-23.97			May-98
1	5.75	10.79	21.91	30.74	93.22	0.86	0.07	12.43	1	56.55	21,153	2	98	0	0	27	29.48	-25.13			Sep-11
1	5.76	10.81	21.94	30.78	93.28	0.87	0.06	12.44	1	45.29	21,153	2	98	0	0	27	29.55	-25.08			May-00
1	5.10	9.90	16.23	31.39	100.12	1.33	0.06	12.22	1	70.78	83,745	2	98	0	0	14	28.76	-24.5			Nov-00
1	5.09	9.92	16.26	31.49	100.38	1.35	0.04	12.22	1	204.3	83,745	2	98	0	0	14	28.79	-24.5			Dec-10
1	5.10	9.92	16.24	31.43	100.22	1.34	0.05	12.22	1	70.78	83,745	2	98	0	0	14	28.75	-24.5			Jul-97
1	4.55	9.16	11.80	31.72	104.51	1.75	0.06	12.56	1	31.87	29,416	1	99	0	0	18	28.1	-23.96			Dec-99
1	3.92	8.03	18.33	25.33	60.44	1.77	0.32	6.89		26.8	21,531	4	61	35	1	12	15.79	-11.43			Mar-85
1	5.56	8.64	13.78	30.97	117.09	1.37	0.18	12.17	1.03	33.97	7,344	1	99	0	0	81	29.14	-22.23			Aug-95
1	2.90	7.74	10.33	27.83	105.63	1.23	0.29	13.15	0.98	35.63	1,708	2	98	0	0	91	27.99	-24.06			Apr-06
1	2.72	5.40	11.50	17.36	42.83	1.77	0.14	4.91	0.26	15.33	17,413	2	43	54	1	7	13.57	-9.63			Oct-03
1	3.36	6.61	14.08	20.66	51.63	1.75	0.14	5.92	0.54	31.38	32,239	2	54	43	1	9	15.15	-11.62			Jun-06
1	3.87	7.52	15.94	22.96	57.94	1.73	0.14	6.67	0.61	18.5	38,749	2	63	34	1	10	16.65	-13.45			Oct-03
1	4.21	8.25	17.52	24.71	63.72	1.69	0.15	7.41	0.69	33.63	32,283	2	70	27	1	9	18.22	-15.23			Jun-06
1	4.61	8.98	19.12	26.56	69.77	1.69	0.15	8.22	0.77	20.69	31,221	2	78	20	0	9	19.76	-16.99			Oct-03
1	5.00	9.74	20.71	28.26	74.39	1.66	0.16	8.97	0.84	35.77	23,438	2	85	13	0	8	20.19	-17.37			Jun-06
1	5.21	10.11	21.42	29.21	75.58	1.65	0.16	9.07	0.85	22.5	21,569	2	88	10	0	8	20.17	-17.34			Oct-03
1	5.19	10.09	21.39	29.14	75.60	1.61	0.16	9.06	0.85	36.2	14,237	2	88	10	0	6	20.15	-17.4			Jun-06
1	5.17	10.10	21.37	28.99	75.36	1.66	0.16	9.06	0.85	39.23	6,095	2	88	10	0	5	20.27	-17.27			Aug-10
1	5.19	10.09	21.39	28.98	75.34	1.65	0.16	9.08	0.85	34.64	2,308	2	88	10	0	4					Jan-12
1	5.19	7.67					0.16			21.7	37.6	2	88	10	0	29					Jul-17
1	2.03	4.03	8.47	13.79	27.66	1.86	0.13	3.35	0.47	13.55	16,864	3	30	67	1	8	8.71	-3			Oct-03
1	3.27	6.12	12.60	21.55	54.55	2.03	0.09	4.62	0.43	30.72	3,858	1	49	51	0	11	14.31	-6.48			Sep-94
1	6.62	11.68	22.39	38.02	113.19	1.6	0.09	10.27	1.01	137.3	9,065	0	100	0	0	8	25.84	-17.39			Nov-01
1	6.64	11.71	22.43	38.17	113.55	1.62	0.06	10.28	1.01	68.23	9,065	0	100	0	0	8	25.88	-17.38			Feb-99
1	3.92	10.13	13.05	38.50	113.05	1.02	0.09	13.64	0.99	61.63	5,940	0	100	0	0	45	29.56	-21.87			Mar-99
1	3.92	10.14	13.07	38.62	113.46	1.05	0.06	13.63	0.99	61.77	5,940	0	100	0	0	45	29.64	-21.89			Apr-99

	MARKET			FUND TYPE, CATEGORY & OBJECTIVE	RATINGS					MINIMUMS
Fund Name	Ticker Symbol	Traded On	Fund Type	Category and (Prospectus Objective)	Overall Rating	Reward Rating	Risk Rating	Recent Up/ Downgrade	Open to New Investors	Min Initial Investment
Vanguard Telecommunication Services Index Fund Admiral Cls	VTCAX	NAS CM	Open End	Communications Sector Equity (Comm)	C	C	C+		Y	100,000
★ Vanguard Total Intl Stock Index Fund Admiral Shares	VTIAX	NAS CM	Open End	Global Equity Large Cap (Foreign Stock)	B-	B-	B-	Up	Y	10,000
Vanguard Total Intl Stock Index Fund Inst Plus Shares	VTPSX	NAS CM	Open End	Global Equity Large Cap (Foreign Stock)	B-	B-	B-	Up	Y	100,000,000
Vanguard Total Intl Stock Index Fund Inst Shares	VTSNX	NAS CM	Open End	Global Equity Large Cap (Foreign Stock)	B-	B-	B-	Up	Y	5,000,000
★ Vanguard Total Intl Stock Index Fund Inv Shares	VGTSX	NAS CM	Open End	Global Equity Large Cap (Foreign Stock)	B-	B-	B-	Up	Y	3,000
Vanguard Total Intl Stock Idx Fund Inst Select Shares	VTISX	NAS CM	Open End	Global Equity Large Cap (Foreign Stock)	B-	B-	B-	Up	Y	3 Billion
★ Vanguard Total Stock Market Index Fund Admiral Shares	VTSAX	NAS CM	Open End	US Equity Large Cap Blend (Growth)	B	B	B		Y	10,000
Vanguard Total Stock Mkt Index Fund Inst Plus Shares	VSMPX	NAS CM	Open End	US Equity Large Cap Blend (Growth)	B	B	B		Y	100,000,000
Vanguard Total Stock Mkt Index Fund Inst Select Shares	VSTSX	NAS CM	Open End	US Equity Large Cap Blend (Growth)	B	B	B		Y	5 Billion
Vanguard Total Stock Mkt Index Fund Inst Shares	VITSX	NAS CM	Open End	US Equity Large Cap Blend (Growth)	B	B	B		Y	5,000,000
★ Vanguard Total Stock Market Index Fund Investor Shares	VTSMX	NAS CM	Open End	US Equity Large Cap Blend (Growth)	B	B	B		Y	3,000
Vanguard Total World Stock Index Fund Institutional Shares	VTWIX	NAS CM	Open End	Global Equity (World Stock)	B-	B-	C+	Down	Y	5,000,000
Vanguard Total World Stock Index Investor Shares	VTWSX	NAS CM	Open End	Global Equity (World Stock)	B-	B-	C+	Down	Y	3,000
Vanguard U.S. Growth Fund Admiral™ Shares	VWUAX	NAS CM	Open End	US Equity Large Cap Growth (Growth)	A-	A-	A-	Up	Y	50,000
Vanguard U.S. Growth Portfolio Fund Investor Shares	VWUSX	NAS CM	Open End	US Equity Large Cap Growth (Growth)	A-	A-	A-	Up	Y	3,000
Vanguard U.S. Value Fund Investor Shares	VUVLX	NAS CM	Open End	US Equity Large Cap Value (Growth & Income)	B	B	B	Up	Y	3,000
Vanguard Utilities Index Fund Admiral Shares	VUIAX	NAS CM	Open End	Utilities Sector Equity (Utility)	B	B	B		Y	100,000
Vanguard Value Index Fund Admiral Shares	VVIAX	NAS CM	Open End	US Equity Large Cap Value (Growth)	B	B	B+		Y	10,000
Vanguard Value Index Fund Institutional Shares	VIVIX	NAS CM	Open End	US Equity Large Cap Value (Growth)	B	B	B+		Y	5,000,000
Vanguard Value Index Fund Investor Shares	VIVAX	NAS CM	Open End	US Equity Large Cap Value (Growth)	B	B	B+		Y	3,000
Vanguard Wellesley® Income Fund Admiral™ Shares	VWIAX	NAS CM	Open End	Cautious Alloc (Income)	B	C+	A+	Up	Y	50,000
Vanguard Wellesley® Income Fund Investor Shares	VWINX	NAS CM	Open End	Cautious Alloc (Income)	B	C+	A+	Up	Y	3,000
★ Vanguard Wellington™ Fund Admiral™ Shares	VWENX	NAS CM	Open End	Moderate Alloc (Growth & Income)	B-	B-	B	Down		50,000
★ Vanguard Wellington™ Fund Investor Shares	VWELX	NAS CM	Open End	Moderate Alloc (Growth & Income)	B-	B-	B	Down		3,000
Vanguard Windsor™ Fund Admiral™ Shares	VWNEX	NAS CM	Open End	US Equity Large Cap Value (Growth & Income)	B-	B	C+	Down	Y	50,000
Vanguard Windsor™ Fund Investor Share	VWNDX	NAS CM	Open End	US Equity Large Cap Value (Growth & Income)	B-	B	C+	Down	Y	3,000
Vanguard Windsor™ II Fund Admiral™ Shares	VWNAX	NAS CM	Open End	US Equity Large Cap Value (Growth & Income)	B	B-	B	Up	Y	50,000
Vanguard Windsor™ II Fund Investor Share	VWNFX	NAS CM	Open End	US Equity Large Cap Value (Growth & Income)	B	B-	B	Up	Y	3,000
Vericimetry U.S. Small Cap Value Fund	VYSVX	NAS CM	Open End	US Equity Small Cap (Small Company)	B	B	B	Up	Y	0
Versus Capital Multi-Mgr Real Estate Income Fund LLC Cls F	VCMRX	NAS CM	Closed End	Real Estate Sector Equity (Real Estate)	B	C+	A+	Up	Y	2,000
Versus Capital Multi-Mgr Real Estate Income Fund LLC Cls I	VCMIX	NAS CM	Closed End	Real Estate Sector Equity (Real Estate)	B	C+	A+	Up	Y	1,000,000
Versus Capital Real Assets Fund	US92535N1000		Closed End	Alloc (Growth & Income)	U	U	U		Y	10,000,000
Vert Global Sustainable Real Estate Fund Institutional Cls	VGSRX	NAS CM	Open End	Real Estate Sector Equity (Real Estate)	U	U	U		Y	10,000
Victory CEMP Market Neutral Income Fund Class A	CBHAX	NAS CM	Open End	Market Neutral (Income)	B-	C	B+	Up	Y	2,500
Victory CEMP Market Neutral Income Fund Class C	CBHCX	NAS CM	Open End	Market Neutral (Income)	B-	C	A-	Up	Y	2,500
Victory CEMP Market Neutral Income Fund Class I	CBHIX	NAS CM	Open End	Market Neutral (Income)	B	C	A+	Up	Y	2,000,000
Victory CEMP US 500 Enhanced Vol Wtd Index Fund Cls A	CUHAX	NAS CM	Open End	US Equity Large Cap Blend (Growth & Income)	B	B	B-		Y	2,500
Victory CEMP US 500 Enhanced Vol Wtd Index Fund Cls C	CUHCX	NAS CM	Open End	US Equity Large Cap Blend (Growth & Income)	B	B	B-		Y	2,500
Victory CEMP US 500 Enhanced Vol Wtd Index Fund Cls I	CUHIX	NAS CM	Open End	US Equity Large Cap Blend (Growth & Income)	B	B	B-		Y	2,000,000
Victory Diversified Stock Fund Class A	SRVEX	NAS CM	Open End	US Equity Large Cap Blend (Growth)	B-	B-	B	Down	Y	2,500
Victory Diversified Stock Fund Class C	VDSCX	NAS CM	Open End	US Equity Large Cap Blend (Growth)	B-	B-	B-	Down	Y	2,500
Victory Diversified Stock Fund Class I	VDSIX	NAS CM	Open End	US Equity Large Cap Blend (Growth)	B-	B-	B	Down	Y	2,000,000
Victory Diversified Stock Fund Class R	GRINX	NAS CM	Open End	US Equity Large Cap Blend (Growth)	B-	B-	B-	Down	Y	0
Victory Diversified Stock Fund Class R6	VDSRX	NAS CM	Open End	US Equity Large Cap Blend (Growth)	B-	B-	B	Down	Y	0
Victory Diversified Stock Fund Class Y	VDSYX	NAS CM	Open End	US Equity Large Cap Blend (Growth)	B-	B-	B	Down	Y	1,000,000
Victory Expedition Emerging Markets Small Cap Fund Class A	VAEMX	NAS CM	Open End	Emerging Markets Equity (Div Emerging Mkts)	C	C	C	Up	Y	2,500
Victory Expedition Emerging Markets Small Cap Fund Class I	VIEMX	NAS CM	Open End	Emerging Markets Equity (Div Emerging Mkts)	C	C	C	Up	Y	2,000,000
Victory Global Natural Resources Fund Class A	RSNRX	NAS CM	Open End	Natl Resources Sec Equity (Natl Res)	D+	C-	D	Down	Y	2,500
Victory Global Natural Resources Fund Class C	RGNCX	NAS CM	Open End	Natl Resources Sec Equity (Natl Res)	D+	C-	D	Down	Y	2,500
Victory Global Natural Resources Fund Class R	RSNKX	NAS CM	Open End	Natl Resources Sec Equity (Natl Res)	D+	C-	D	Down	Y	0
Victory Global Natural Resources Fund Class Y	RSNYX	NAS CM	Open End	Natl Resources Sec Equity (Natl Res)	D+	C-	D+	Down	Y	1,000,000
Victory INCORE Investment Grade Convertible Fund Class A	SBFCX	NAS CM	Open End	Convertibles (Convertible Bond)	B-	B-	B	Down	Y	2,500

★ Expanded analysis of this fund is included in Section II.

Min Additional Investment	TOTAL RETURNS: 3-Month Total Return	6-Month Total Return	1-Year Total Return	3-Year Total Return	5-Year Total Return	PERFORMANCE: Dividend Yield (TTM)	Expense Ratio	3-Yr Std Deviation	3-Year Beta	ASSETS: NAV	Total Assets (MIL)	ASSET ALLOCATION & TURNOVER: %Cash	%Stocks	%Bonds	%Other	Turnover Ratio	BULL & BEAR: Last Bull Market Total Return	Last Bear Market Total Return	FEES: Front End Fee (%)	Back End Fee (%)	Inception Date
1	-0.20	1.11	-5.55	17.82	55.94	3.46	0.1	12.2	1	46.35	1,370	4	96	0	0	18	10.49	-13.47			Mar-05
1	4.88	11.12	27.55	27.38	42.40	2.5	0.11	11.51	0.94	30.52	321,185	3	96	0	1	3	14.52	-24.32			Nov-10
1	4.87	11.13	27.57	27.52	42.64	2.54	0.07	11.52	0.95	122.05	321,185	3	96	0	1	3	14.61	-24.32			Nov-10
1	4.87	11.12	27.55	27.43	42.49	2.52	0.09	11.52	0.95	122.03	321,185	3	96	0	1	3	14.59	-24.32			Nov-10
1	4.79	11.04	27.39	27.08	41.78	2.45	0.18	11.5	0.94	18.24	321,185	3	96	0	1	3	14.58	-24.35			Apr-96
1	4.87	11.15	27.60	27.33	42.06	2.55	0.05	11.52	0.95	128.52	321,185	3	96	0	1	3	14.58	-24.35			Jun-16
1	6.33	11.17	21.16	35.72	109.49	1.76	0.04	10.23	1	66.72	656,961	0	99	0	1	4	25.82	-17.71			Nov-00
1	6.33	11.17	21.19	35.73	109.03	1.77	0.02	10.23	1	125.14	656,961	0	99	0	1	4	25.72	-17.74			Apr-15
1	6.34	11.18	21.20	35.55	108.74	1.78	0.01	10.23	1	131.31	656,961	0	99	0	1	4	25.72	-17.74			Jun-16
1	6.33	11.16	21.17	35.75	109.58	1.76	0.04	10.24	1	66.73	656,961	0	99	0	1	4	25.82	-17.68			Jul-97
1	6.31	11.11	21.05	35.28	108.33	1.66	0.15	10.23	1	66.7	656,961	0	99	0	1	4	25.72	-17.74			Apr-92
1	5.63	11.19	24.20	31.65	71.76	2.09	0.1	10.25	0.97	151.44	14,145	2	98	0	0	15	19.31	-21.1			Oct-08
1	5.60	11.13	24.06	31.24	70.77	2	0.21	10.23	0.97	30.22	14,145	2	98	0	0	15	19.18	-21.14			Jun-08
1	6.09	13.60	31.75	41.19	122.78	0.43	0.3	11.13	0.99	94.6	8,396	4	95	0	1	27	29.16	-17.31			Aug-01
1	6.07	13.52	31.60	40.64	121.29	0.31	0.43	11.12	0.99	36.52	8,396	4	95	0	1	27	29.03	-17.34			Jan-59
1	5.37	10.49	12.97	27.82	102.21	1.86	0.23	10.88	1.01	19.15	1,728	1	99	0	0	95	25.88	-18.36			Jun-00
1	0.60	3.67	12.49	23.54	86.17	2.98	0.1	12.38	1	58.48	3,728	0	100	0	0	4	8.77	1.41			Apr-04
1	6.96	11.40	17.13	34.23	107.42	2.36	0.06	10.08	1	41.41	63,566	0	100	0	0	7	23.26	-18.39			Nov-00
1	6.96	11.41	17.14	34.27	107.52	2.37	0.05	10.08	1	41.41	63,566	0	100	0	0	7	23.28	-18.38			Jul-98
1	6.93	11.34	16.98	33.70	106.06	2.25	0.18	10.07	1	41.42	63,566	0	100	0	0	7	23.17	-18.46			Nov-92
1	3.11	5.46	10.25	20.50	43.21	2.9	0.15	4.11	0.64	65.3	55,459	3	38	58	0	22	11.06	-1.88			May-01
1	3.05	5.38	10.15	20.24	42.68	2.84	0.22	4.1	0.64	26.95	55,459	3	38	58	0	22	11.01	-1.9			Jul-70
1	4.53	8.11	14.81	26.93	69.42	2.41	0.16	6.79	0.66	72.58	105,558	4	65	30	1	31	16.35	-10.37			May-01
1	4.52	8.06	14.72	26.62	68.76	2.33	0.25	6.8	0.66	42.03	105,558	4	65	30	1	31	16.28	-10.37			Jul-29
1	5.52	9.57	19.20	28.78	101.41	1.85	0.2	12.16	1.13	78.98	20,074	3	97	0	0	26	26.57	-21.09			Nov-01
1	5.50	9.50	19.09	28.37	100.39	1.76	0.3	12.17	1.13	23.42	20,074	3	97	0	0	26	26.51	-21.14			Oct-58
1	5.91	8.39	16.88	27.22	89.78	2.11	0.25	10.55	1	67.12	50,094	2	98	0	0	33	25.42	-17.14			May-01
1	5.88	8.34	16.77	26.92	89.04	2.04	0.33	10.56	1	37.83	50,094	2	98	0	0	33	25.37	-17.18			Jun-85
	2.96	9.74	8.97	26.08	91.80	0.56	0.61	13.62	0.95	20.14	309.5	3	97	0	0	42					Dec-11
1,000	1.77	2.68	5.74	20.97	34.99	4.29	1.58	1.75		27.76	--					40					Dec-11
	1.84	2.82	6.07	22.24	38.37	4.57	1.28	1.77		27.84	--					40					Jul-12
	0.68						1.6			25.15	--										Sep-17
	3.48						0.5			10.32	3.3										Oct-17
50	1.59	3.92	6.77	10.88	9.08	2.76	0.9	3.49	-11.62	9.63	56.4	11	89	0	0				5.75		Nov-12
50	1.28	3.47	5.88	8.28	4.86	2.16	1.65	3.54	-11.1	9.55	56.4	11	89	0	0					1.00	Nov-12
	1.56	3.92	6.99	11.58	10.47	2.98	0.65	3.52	-11.21	9.66	56.4	11	89	0	0						Nov-12
50	7.14	11.15	21.52	35.14	102.46	0.62	0.99	9.96	1	16.31	132.9	1	99	0	0				5.75		Nov-12
50	7.00	10.73	20.70	32.15	95.06	0.08	1.74	9.99	1.01	16.01	132.9	1	99	0	0					1.00	Nov-12
	7.21	11.27	21.86	36.18	104.93	0.83	0.74	9.97	1	16.32	132.9	1	99	0	0						Nov-12
50	9.81	17.73	27.32	27.01	93.26	0.74	1.07	10.4	0.97	19.04	515.4	1	99	0	0	74	26.59	-22.59	5.75		Oct-89
50	9.55	17.26	26.26	23.87	85.47	0.18	1.9	10.39	0.97	18.06	515.4	1	99	0	0	74	26	-22.9		1.00	Feb-02
	9.88	17.90	27.60	28.02	95.69	0.95	0.8	10.39	0.97	19	515.4	1	99	0	0	74	26.89	-22.53			Aug-07
	9.69	17.55	26.89	25.93	90.45	0.53	1.36	10.4	0.97	18.7	515.4	1	99	0	0	74	26.38	-22.67			Mar-99
	9.87	17.90	27.62	28.11	95.42	0.97	0.78	10.41	0.97	19	515.4	1	99	0	0	74	26.59	-22.59			Mar-14
	9.85	17.82	27.55	27.82	95.29	0.9	0.86	10.39	0.97	19.03	515.4	1	99	0	0	74	26.59	-22.59			Jan-13
50	2.09	6.32	6.42	-5.60		0.17	1.8	11.66	0.66		25.6	2	98	0	0	111			5.75		Apr-14
	4.90	9.54	20.87	2.14		0.15	1.5	11.68	0.66	10.02	26.0	2	98	0	0	111					Apr-14
50	-0.66	12.14	1.02	-4.27	-25.18	0	1.48	29.69	1.47	23.73	1,416	8	92	0	0	29	18.82	-25.21	5.75		Nov-95
50	-0.87	11.71	0.23	-6.52	-28.04	0	2.28	29.67	1.47	21.64	1,416	8	92	0	0	29	18.35	-25.44		1.00	May-07
	-0.79	11.90	0.62	-5.21	-26.45	0	1.74	29.69	1.47	22.56	1,416	8	92	0	0	29	18.55	-25.34			Dec-06
100	-0.56	12.37	1.35	-3.33	-23.93	0	1.15	29.7	1.47	24.61	1,416	8	92	0	0	29	19.08	-25.1			May-07
50	3.69	8.42	18.47	22.79	67.81	1.51	1.39	7.29		16.11	118.2	6	0	0	1	22	9.86	-12.18	2.00		Apr-88

Fund Name	Ticker Symbol	Traded On	Fund Type	Category and (Prospectus Objective)	Overall Rating	Reward Rating	Risk Rating	Recent Up/ Downgrade	Open to New Investors	Min Initial Investment
	MARKET		FUND TYPE, CATEGORY & OBJECTIVE		RATINGS				MINIMUMS	
Victory INCORE Investment Grade Convertible Fund Class I	VICIX	NAS CM	Open End	Convertibles (Convertible Bond)	B-	B-	B	Down	Y	2,000,000
Victory Institutional Diversified Stock Fund	VIDSX	NAS CM	Open End	US Equity Large Cap Blend (Growth)	B-	B-	B	Down	Y	10,000,000
Victory Integrity Discovery Fund Class A	MMEAX	NAS CM	Open End	US Equity Small Cap (Small Company)	A-	A	B	Up	Y	2,500
Victory Integrity Discovery Fund Class C	MMECX	NAS CM	Open End	US Equity Small Cap (Small Company)	B+	A	B	Up	Y	2,500
Victory Integrity Discovery Fund Class R	MMERX	NAS CM	Open End	US Equity Small Cap (Small Company)	A-	A	B	Up	Y	0
Victory Integrity Discovery Fund Class Y	MMEYX	NAS CM	Open End	US Equity Small Cap (Small Company)	A-	A	B	Up	Y	1,000,000
Victory Integrity Mid-Cap Value Fund Class A	MAIMX	NAS CM	Open End	US Equity Mid Cap (Growth)	B	B	B	Up	Y	2,500
Victory Integrity Mid-Cap Value Fund Class R6	MRIMX	NAS CM	Open End	US Equity Mid Cap (Growth)	B	B	B	Up	Y	0
Victory Integrity Mid-Cap Value Fund Class Y	MYIMX	NAS CM	Open End	US Equity Mid Cap (Growth)	B	B	B	Up	Y	1,000,000
Victory Integrity Small/Mid-Cap Value Fund Class A	MAISX	NAS CM	Open End	US Equity Mid Cap (Growth)	B	B	B-	Up	Y	2,500
Victory Integrity Small/Mid-Cap Value Fund Class R6	MIRSX	NAS CM	Open End	US Equity Mid Cap (Growth)	B	B	B-	Up	Y	0
Victory Integrity Small/Mid-Cap Value Fund Class Y	MYISX	NAS CM	Open End	US Equity Mid Cap (Growth)	B	B	B-	Up	Y	1,000,000
Victory Integrity Small-Cap Value Fund Class A	VSCVX	NAS CM	Open End	US Equity Small Cap (Small Company)	B	B+	B	Up	Y	2,500
Victory Integrity Small-Cap Value Fund Class C	MCVSX	NAS CM	Open End	US Equity Small Cap (Small Company)	B	B	B	Up	Y	2,500
Victory Integrity Small-Cap Value Fund Class R	MRVSX	NAS CM	Open End	US Equity Small Cap (Small Company)	B	B+	B	Up	Y	0
Victory Integrity Small-Cap Value Fund Class R6	MVSSX	NAS CM	Open End	US Equity Small Cap (Small Company)	B+	A-	B	Up	Y	0
Victory Integrity Small-Cap Value Fund Class Y	VSVIX	NAS CM	Open End	US Equity Small Cap (Small Company)	B+	A-	B	Up	Y	1,000,000
Victory Munder Mid-Cap Core Growth Fund Class A	MGOAX	NAS CM	Open End	US Equity Mid Cap (Growth)	B-	B-	C+	Up	Y	2,500
Victory Munder Mid-Cap Core Growth Fund Class C	MGOTX	NAS CM	Open End	US Equity Mid Cap (Growth)	C+	B-	C	Down	Y	2,500
Victory Munder Mid-Cap Core Growth Fund Class R	MMSRX	NAS CM	Open End	US Equity Mid Cap (Growth)	B-	B-	C+	Up	Y	0
Victory Munder Mid-Cap Core Growth Fund Class R6	MGOSX	NAS CM	Open End	US Equity Mid Cap (Growth)	B-	B	C+	Up	Y	0
Victory Munder Mid-Cap Core Growth Fund Class Y	MGOYX	NAS CM	Open End	US Equity Mid Cap (Growth)	B-	B	C+	Up	Y	1,000,000
Victory Munder Multi-Cap Fund Class A	MNNAX	NAS CM	Open End	US Equity Large Cap Growth (Growth)	B+	B+	B	Up	Y	2,500
Victory Munder Multi-Cap Fund Class C	MNNCX	NAS CM	Open End	US Equity Large Cap Growth (Growth)	B	B	B	Up	Y	2,500
Victory Munder Multi-Cap Fund Class R	MNNRX	NAS CM	Open End	US Equity Large Cap Growth (Growth)	B	B	B	Up	Y	0
Victory Munder Multi-Cap Fund Class Y	MNNYX	NAS CM	Open End	US Equity Large Cap Growth (Growth)	B+	A-	B	Up	Y	1,000,000
Victory Munder Small Cap Growth Fund Class A	MASCX	NAS CM	Open End	US Equity Small Cap (Growth)	C+	C+	C+	Up	Y	2,500
Victory Munder Small Cap Growth Fund Class I	MIGSX	NAS CM	Open End	US Equity Small Cap (Growth)	C+	C+	C+	Up	Y	2,000,000
Victory Munder Small Cap Growth Fund Class Y	MYSGX	NAS CM	Open End	US Equity Small Cap (Growth)	C+	C+	C+	Up	Y	1,000,000
Victory NewBridge Large Cap Growth Fund Class A	VFGAX	NAS CM	Open End	US Equity Large Cap Growth (Growth)	B	B	B+		Y	2,500
Victory NewBridge Large Cap Growth Fund Class C	VFGCX	NAS CM	Open End	US Equity Large Cap Growth (Growth)	B	B-	B+		Y	2,500
Victory NewBridge Large Cap Growth Fund Class I	VFGIX	NAS CM	Open End	US Equity Large Cap Growth (Growth)	B	B	B+		Y	2,000,000
Victory NewBridge Large Cap Growth Fund Class R	VFGRX	NAS CM	Open End	US Equity Large Cap Growth (Growth)	B	B	B+		Y	0
Victory NewBridge Large Cap Growth Fund Class Y	VFGYX	NAS CM	Open End	US Equity Large Cap Growth (Growth)	B	B	B+		Y	1,000,000
Victory RS Global Fund Class A	RSGGX	NAS CM	Open End	Global Equity (Growth)	B	B	B	Up	Y	2,500
Victory RS Global Fund Class C	RGGCX	NAS CM	Open End	Global Equity (Growth)	B-	B-	B	Down	Y	2,500
Victory RS Global Fund Class R	RGGKX	NAS CM	Open End	Global Equity (Growth)	B	B	B		Y	0
Victory RS Global Fund Class Y	RGGYX	NAS CM	Open End	Global Equity (Growth)	B	B	B	Up	Y	1,000,000
Victory RS Growth Fund Class A	RSGRX	NAS CM	Open End	US Equity Large Cap Growth (Growth)	A-	B+	A-	Up	Y	2,500
Victory RS Growth Fund Class C	RGWCX	NAS CM	Open End	US Equity Large Cap Growth (Growth)	B+	B+	B+	Up	Y	2,500
Victory RS Growth Fund Class R	RSGKX	NAS CM	Open End	US Equity Large Cap Growth (Growth)	B+	B+	A-	Up	Y	0
Victory RS Growth Fund Class Y	RGRYX	NAS CM	Open End	US Equity Large Cap Growth (Growth)	A-	A-	A-	Up	Y	1,000,000
Victory RS International Fund Class A	GUBGX	NAS CM	Open End	Global Equity Large Cap (Foreign Stock)	B	B-	B	Up	Y	2,500
Victory RS International Fund Class C	RIGCX	NAS CM	Open End	Global Equity Large Cap (Foreign Stock)	B-	B-	B	Up	Y	2,500
Victory RS International Fund Class R	RIGKX	NAS CM	Open End	Global Equity Large Cap (Foreign Stock)	B	B-	B	Up	Y	0
Victory RS International Fund Class Y	RSIGX	NAS CM	Open End	Global Equity Large Cap (Foreign Stock)	B	B	B	Up	Y	1,000,000
Victory RS Investors Fund Class A	RSINX	NAS CM	Open End	US Equity Mid Cap (Growth)	B-	B-	B		Y	2,500
Victory RS Investors Fund Class C	RIVCX	NAS CM	Open End	US Equity Mid Cap (Growth)	B-	C+	B		Y	2,500
Victory RS Investors Fund Class R	RSIKX	NAS CM	Open End	US Equity Mid Cap (Growth)	B-	C+	B		Y	0
Victory RS Investors Fund Class Y	RSIYX	NAS CM	Open End	US Equity Mid Cap (Growth)	B-	B-	B		Y	1,000,000
Victory RS Large Cap Alpha Fund Class A	GPAFX	NAS CM	Open End	US Equity Large Cap Blend (Growth)	B	B-	B	Up	Y	2,500
Victory RS Large Cap Alpha Fund Class C	RCOCX	NAS CM	Open End	US Equity Large Cap Blend (Growth)	B-	B-	B	Down	Y	2,500

★ Expanded analysis of this fund is included in Section II.

	TOTAL RETURNS					PERFORMANCE				ASSETS		ASSET ALLOCATION & TURNOVER					BULL & BEAR		FEES		
Min Additional Investment	3-Month Total Return	6-Month Total Return	1-Year Total Return	3-Year Total Return	5-Year Total Return	Dividend Yield (TTM)	Expense Ratio	3-Yr Std Deviation	3-Year Beta	NAV	Total Assets (MIL)	%Cash	%Stocks	%Bonds	%Other	Turnover Ratio	Last Bull Market Total Return	Last Bear Market Total Return	Front End Fee (%)	Back End Fee (%)	Inception Date
	3.87	8.64	18.91	24.36	71.49	1.81	0.99	7.31		16.1	118.2	6	0	0	1	22	10.22	-12.07			Aug-07
	10.05	18.04	27.72	27.88	95.88	0.79	0.68	10.37	0.97	10.59	88.9	1	99	0	0	68	26.41	-22.04			Jun-05
250	2.45	8.77	10.74	41.88	117.64	0	1.57	15.81	1.01	40.17	158.7	4	96	0	0		36.13	-24.84	5.75		Dec-96
250	2.29	8.36	9.92	38.57	109.46	0	2.38	15.8	1.01	29.9	158.7	4	96	0	0		35.55	-25.1		1.00	Mar-97
	2.33	8.50	10.20	39.85	113.41	0	2.1	15.79	1	38.41	158.7	4	96	0	0		35.9	-24.92			Jul-04
	2.53	8.93	11.02	42.98	120.41	0	1.4	15.8	1.01	43.61	158.7	4	96	0	0		36.33	-24.78			Dec-96
250	6.49	11.67	16.07	29.07	100.60	0	1.1	11.79	1.1	19.23	64.3	2	98	0	0		29.63		5.75		Jul-11
	6.59	11.85	16.44	30.11	103.34	0.3	0.8	11.83	1.1	19.34	64.3	2	98	0	0		29.93				Dec-15
	6.56	11.75	16.32	30.14	103.39	0.39	0.85	11.8	1.1	19.37	64.3	2	98	0	0		29.92				Jul-11
250	7.58	14.49	18.10	29.83	91.16	0	1.13	13.38	1.09	18.12	78.2	3	97	0	0		30.85		5.75		Jul-11
	7.62	14.66	18.46	30.99	93.77	0	0.83	13.39	1.09	18.3	78.2	3	97	0	0		31.15				Mar-15
	7.59	14.64	18.38	30.75	93.41	0.09	0.88	13.4	1.09	18.26	78.2	3	97	0	0		31.15				Jul-11
50	5.47	11.59	11.95	27.93	97.91	0	1.5	14.7	1.02	39.72	2,705	2	98	0	0	58	27.41	-25.04	5.75		Mar-04
50	5.33	11.26	11.26	25.32	91.02	0	2.16	14.71	1.02	35.21	2,705	2	98	0	0	58	26.82	-25.26		1.00	May-11
	5.42	11.48	11.69	27.00	95.50	0	1.75	14.72	1.02	38.74	2,705	2	98	0	0	58	27.21	-25.11			May-11
	5.63	11.91	12.58	29.94	102.62	0.31	0.96	14.72	1.02	41.05	2,705	2	98	0	0	58	27.41	-25.04			Jun-12
	5.59	11.82	12.35	29.33	101.05	0.23	1.15	14.72	1.02	40.83	2,705	2	98	0	0	58	27.56	-24.97			Jul-05
50	5.95	11.81	24.16	25.72	89.40	0	1.31	11.24	1.03	34.48	4,105	0	99	0	1		27.54	-18.99	5.75		Jul-00
50	5.76	11.43	23.32	23.21	82.85	0	1.97	11.24	1.02	28.02	4,105	0	99	0	1		26.98	-19.27		1.00	Jul-00
	5.92	11.71	23.85	24.81	87.07	0	1.57	11.24	1.02	32.89	4,105	0	99	0	1		27.38	-19.09			Jul-04
	6.07	12.08	24.72	27.45	93.62	0	0.85	11.25	1.03	37.2	4,105	0	99	0	1		27.73	-18.92			Jun-12
	5.99	11.98	24.50	26.71	91.84	0	1.04	11.25	1.03	36.66	4,105	0	99	0	1		27.73	-18.92			Jun-98
250	9.66	17.35	28.38	38.14	114.56	0	1.38	10.9	1.01	46.57	465.8	2	98	0	0		26.51	-20.71	5.75		Aug-96
250	9.43	16.88	27.34	34.77	106.19	0	2.21	10.92	1.01	38.25	465.8	2	98	0	0		25.92	-20.92		1.00	Nov-98
	9.50	17.02	27.65	36.20	110.41	0	1.88	10.9	1.01	44.22	465.8	2	98	0	0		26.27	-20.77			Jul-04
	9.79	17.59	28.82	39.79	118.25	0	1.01	10.91	1.01	50.02	465.8	2	98	0	0		26.66	-20.61			Jun-98
50	5.14	9.10	20.22			0	1.4			12.08	6.8	1	99	0	0				5.75		May-15
	5.19	9.23	20.51			0	1.15			12.17	6.8	1	99	0	0						May-15
	5.20	9.25	20.46			0	1.25			12.14	6.8	1	99	0	0						May-15
50	4.41	7.87	24.86	27.19	84.95	0	1.3	11.36	0.99	7.37	31.2	3	97	0	0	52	25.94	-18.2	5.75		Dec-03
50	4.19	7.54	23.82	24.15	77.61	0	2.1	11.36	0.99	4.67	31.2	3	97	0	0	52	25.29	-18.48		1.00	Dec-03
	4.52	8.15	25.35	28.75	88.37	0	0.88	11.34	0.99	7.86	31.2	3	97	0	0	52	26.15	-18.14			Mar-11
	4.31	7.83	24.52	25.95	81.82	0	1.65	11.35	0.99	6.23	31.2	3	97	0	0	52	25.69	-18.34			Dec-03
	4.51	8.12	25.29	28.37	87.48	0	1.02	11.36	0.99	7.63	31.2	3	97	0	0	52	25.94	-18.2			Jan-13
50	5.88	12.48	24.48	37.07	88.54	0.17	1.09	9.28	0.85	12.75	27.3	1	99	0	1	184	21.27		5.75		May-11
50	5.70	12.01	23.47	33.91	81.36	0	1.84	9.23	0.85	12.38	27.3	1	99	0	1	184	20.61			1.00	May-11
	5.76	12.29	24.08	66.53	127.12	1.4	1.34	13.1	0.83	15.76	27.3	1	99	0	1	184	20.95				May-11
	5.94	12.52	24.75	38.31	91.21	1.55	0.84	9.26	0.85	12.63	27.3	1	99	0	1	184	21.51				May-11
50	6.17	13.51	31.74	38.32	124.46	0	1.1	10.69	0.95	20.6	256.5	2	98	0	0	123	25.55	-15.95	5.75		May-92
50	5.91	13.05	30.57	34.87	115.04	0	1.93	10.65	0.95	17.9	256.5	2	98	0	0	123	24.37	-16.34		1.00	Jun-07
	6.00	13.22	30.91	35.86	117.78	0	1.71	10.69	0.95	19.22	256.5	2	98	0	0	123	25.25	-16.14			Nov-06
	6.24	13.72	32.04	39.41	127.38	0	0.83	10.67	0.95	21.23	256.5	2	98	0	0	123	25.75	-15.86			May-07
50	4.45	10.93	25.25	28.95	42.48	1.43	1.13	10	0.79	12.12	25.2	1	95	0	0	103	18.6	-25.14	5.75		Feb-93
50	4.28	10.54	24.24	25.93	35.92	1.43	1.88	9.92	0.78	8.89	25.2	1	95	0	0	103	18.12	-25.37		1.00	Aug-00
	4.38	10.80	24.85	27.56	39.32	1.21	1.38	9.95	0.79	11.35	25.2	1	95	0	0	103	18.23	-25.26			May-01
	4.52	11.11	25.56	29.85	44.75	1.56	0.88	9.96	0.79	11.93	25.2	1	95	0	0	103	18.86	-25.05			Mar-09
50	2.33	8.41	16.28	21.44	89.81	0	1.33	10.5	0.95	13.86	60.7	6	94	0	0	92	31.07	-23.97	5.75		Nov-05
50	2.16	8.01	15.48	18.84	82.87	0	2.07	10.55	0.95	12.69	60.7	6	94	0	0	92	30.44	-24.17		1.00	Jul-07
	2.13	8.01	15.50	19.41	84.67	0	1.92	10.55	0.95	12.81	60.7	6	94	0	0	92	30.6	-23.99			Jan-07
	2.36	8.50	16.59	22.49	92.23	0.04	1.05	10.52	0.95	14.1	60.7	6	94	0	0	92	31.19	-23.86			May-07
50	6.10	10.97	18.31	24.93	100.02	0.67	0.89	10.82	0.99	56.61	610.9	2	98	0	0	79	25.1	-24.79	5.75		Jun-72
50	5.88	10.52	17.36	21.98	92.11	0.06	1.69	10.81	0.99	49.5	610.9	2	98	0	0	79	24.5	-25.02		1.00	Aug-00

Fund Name	MARKET Ticker Symbol	Traded On	FUND TYPE, CATEGORY & OBJECTIVE Fund Type	Category and (Prospectus Objective)	RATINGS Overall Rating	Reward Rating	Risk Rating	Recent Up/ Downgrade	MINIMUMS Open to New Investors	Min Initial Investment
Victory RS Large Cap Alpha Fund Class R	RCEKX	NAS CM	Open End	US Equity Large Cap Blend (Growth)	B	B-	B	Up	Y	0
Victory RS Large Cap Alpha Fund Class Y	RCEYX	NAS CM	Open End	US Equity Large Cap Blend (Growth)	B	B-	B	Up	Y	1,000,000
Victory RS Mid Cap Growth Fund Class A	RSMOX	NAS CM	Open End	US Equity Mid Cap (Growth)	B	B	B	Up	Y	2,500
Victory RS Mid Cap Growth Fund Class C	RMOCX	NAS CM	Open End	US Equity Mid Cap (Growth)	B	B-	B	Up	Y	2,500
Victory RS Mid Cap Growth Fund Class R	RSMKX	NAS CM	Open End	US Equity Mid Cap (Growth)	B	B-	B	Up	Y	0
Victory RS Mid Cap Growth Fund Class R6	RMORX	NAS CM	Open End	US Equity Mid Cap (Growth)	B	B	B	Up	Y	0
Victory RS Mid Cap Growth Fund Class Y	RMOYX	NAS CM	Open End	US Equity Mid Cap (Growth)	B	B	B	Up	Y	1,000,000
Victory RS Partners Fund Class A	RSPFX	NAS CM	Open End	US Equity Small Cap (Small Company)	B-	B-	C+	Up		2,500
Victory RS Partners Fund Class R	RSPKX	NAS CM	Open End	US Equity Small Cap (Small Company)	B-	B-	C+	Up		0
Victory RS Partners Fund Class Y	RSPYX	NAS CM	Open End	US Equity Small Cap (Small Company)	B-	B	C+	Up		1,000,000
Victory RS Science and Technology Fund Class A	RSIFX	NAS CM	Open End	Technology Sector Equity (Technology)	A-	A+	B	Up	Y	2,500
Victory RS Science and Technology Fund Class C	RINCX	NAS CM	Open End	Technology Sector Equity (Technology)	A-	A+	B	Up	Y	2,500
Victory RS Science and Technology Fund Class R	RIFKX	NAS CM	Open End	Technology Sector Equity (Technology)	A-	A+	B	Up	Y	0
Victory RS Science and Technology Fund Class Y	RIFYX	NAS CM	Open End	Technology Sector Equity (Technology)	A-	A+	B	Up	Y	1,000,000
Victory RS Select Growth Fund Class A	RSDGX	NAS CM	Open End	US Equity Small Cap (Growth)	B	B	B	Up	Y	2,500
Victory RS Select Growth Fund Class C	RSGFX	NAS CM	Open End	US Equity Small Cap (Growth)	B	B-	B	Up	Y	2,500
Victory RS Select Growth Fund Class R	RSDKX	NAS CM	Open End	US Equity Small Cap (Growth)	B	B-	B	Up	Y	0
Victory RS Select Growth Fund Class R6	RSSRX	NAS CM	Open End	US Equity Small Cap (Growth)	B	B	B	Up	Y	0
Victory RS Select Growth Fund Class Y	RSSYX	NAS CM	Open End	US Equity Small Cap (Growth)	B	B	B	Up	Y	1,000,000
Victory RS Small Cap Equity Fund Class A	GPSCX	NAS CM	Open End	US Equity Small Cap (Small Company)	B	A	C	Up		2,500
Victory RS Small Cap Equity Fund Class C	RSCCX	NAS CM	Open End	US Equity Small Cap (Small Company)	B	A	C	Up		2,500
Victory RS Small Cap Equity Fund Class R	RSCKX	NAS CM	Open End	US Equity Small Cap (Small Company)	B	A	C	Up		0
Victory RS Small Cap Equity Fund Class Y	RSCYX	NAS CM	Open End	US Equity Small Cap (Small Company)	B	A	C	Up		1,000,000
Victory RS Small Cap Growth Fund Class A	RSEGX	NAS CM	Open End	US Equity Small Cap (Small Company)	B	A	C	Up		2,500
Victory RS Small Cap Growth Fund Class C	REGWX	NAS CM	Open End	US Equity Small Cap (Small Company)	B	A	C	Up		2,500
Victory RS Small Cap Growth Fund Class R	RSEKX	NAS CM	Open End	US Equity Small Cap (Small Company)	B	A	C	Up		0
Victory RS Small Cap Growth Fund Class R6	RSEJX	NAS CM	Open End	US Equity Small Cap (Small Company)	B	A	C	Up	Y	0
Victory RS Small Cap Growth Fund Class Y	RSYEX	NAS CM	Open End	US Equity Small Cap (Small Company)	B	A	C	Up		1,000,000
Victory RS Value Fund Class A	RSVAX	NAS CM	Open End	US Equity Mid Cap (Growth)	B-	B-	B	Up	Y	2,500
Victory RS Value Fund Class C	RVACX	NAS CM	Open End	US Equity Mid Cap (Growth)	B-	C+	B	Up	Y	2,500
Victory RS Value Fund Class R	RSVKX	NAS CM	Open End	US Equity Mid Cap (Growth)	B-	C+	B	Up	Y	0
Victory RS Value Fund Class Y	RSVYX	NAS CM	Open End	US Equity Mid Cap (Growth)	B-	B-	B	Up	Y	1,000,000
Victory S&P 500 Index Fund Class A	MUXAX	NAS CM	Open End	US Equity Large Cap Blend (Growth)	B	B	B		Y	2,500
Victory S&P 500 Index Fund Class R	MUXRX	NAS CM	Open End	US Equity Large Cap Blend (Growth)	B-	B-	B	Down	Y	0
Victory S&P 500 Index Fund Class Y	MUXYX	NAS CM	Open End	US Equity Large Cap Blend (Growth)	B	B	B		Y	1,000,000
Victory Sophus Emerging Markets Fund Class A	GBEMX	NAS CM	Open End	Emerging Markets Equity (Div Emerging Mkts)	B	B+	C	Up	Y	2,500
Victory Sophus Emerging Markets Fund Class C	REMGX	NAS CM	Open End	Emerging Markets Equity (Div Emerging Mkts)	B-	B	C	Up	Y	2,500
Victory Sophus Emerging Markets Fund Class R	REMKX	NAS CM	Open End	Emerging Markets Equity (Div Emerging Mkts)	B	B	C	Up	Y	0
Victory Sophus Emerging Markets Fund Class R6	RSERX	NAS CM	Open End	Emerging Markets Equity (Div Emerging Mkts)	B	B+	C	Up	Y	0
Victory Sophus Emerging Markets Fund Class Y	RSENX	NAS CM	Open End	Emerging Markets Equity (Div Emerging Mkts)	B	B+	C	Up	Y	1,000,000
Victory Sophus Emerging Markets Small Cap Fund Class A	RSMSX	NAS CM	Open End	Emerging Markets Equity (Div Emerging Mkts)	B	B	B-	Up	Y	2,500
Victory Sophus Emerging Markets Small Cap Fund Class C	RSMGX	NAS CM	Open End	Emerging Markets Equity (Div Emerging Mkts)	B-	B-	C+	Up	Y	2,500
Victory Sophus Emerging Markets Small Cap Fund Class Y	RSMYX	NAS CM	Open End	Emerging Markets Equity (Div Emerging Mkts)	B	B	B-	Up	Y	1,000,000
Victory Special Value Fund Class A	SSVSX	NAS CM	Open End	US Equity Large Cap Blend (Growth & Income)	B-	B-	B-	Down	Y	2,500
Victory Special Value Fund Class C	VSVCX	NAS CM	Open End	US Equity Large Cap Blend (Growth & Income)	B-	C+	B-	Down	Y	2,500
Victory Special Value Fund Class I	VSPIX	NAS CM	Open End	US Equity Large Cap Blend (Growth & Income)	B-	B-	B-	Down	Y	2,000,000
Victory Special Value Fund Class R	VSVGX	NAS CM	Open End	US Equity Large Cap Blend (Growth & Income)	B-	B-	B-	Down	Y	0
Victory Special Value Fund Class Y	VSVYX	NAS CM	Open End	US Equity Large Cap Blend (Growth & Income)	B-	B-	B-	Down	Y	1,000,000
Victory Strategic Allocation Fund Class A	SBALX	NAS CM	Open End	Multialternative (Balanced)	B	C+	B+	Up	Y	2,500
Victory Strategic Allocation Fund Class C	VBFCX	NAS CM	Open End	Multialternative (Balanced)	B-	C+	B	Up	Y	2,500
Victory Strategic Allocation Fund Class I	VBFIX	NAS CM	Open End	Multialternative (Balanced)	B	C+	B+	Up	Y	2,000,000
Victory Strategic Allocation Fund Class R	VBFGX	NAS CM	Open End	Multialternative (Balanced)	B-	C+	B	Up	Y	0

★ Expanded analysis of this fund is included in Section II.

	TOTAL RETURNS					PERFORMANCE				ASSETS		ASSET ALLOCATION & TURNOVER					BULL & BEAR		FEES		
Min Additional Investment	3-Month Total Return	6-Month Total Return	1-Year Total Return	3-Year Total Return	5-Year Total Return	Dividend Yield (TTM)	Expense Ratio	3-Yr Std Deviation	3-Year Beta	NAV	Total Assets (MIL)	%Cash	%Stocks	%Bonds	%Other	Turnover Ratio	Last Bull Market Total Return	Last Bear Market Total Return	Front End Fee (%)	Back End Fee (%)	Inception Date
	6.01	10.77	17.87	23.59	96.33	0.34	1.23	10.81	0.99	56.35	610.9	2	98	0	0	79	24.77	-24.91			May-01
	6.16	11.10	18.56	25.70	102.35	0.89	0.68	10.82	0.99	56.39	610.9	2	98	0	0	79	25.28	-24.68			May-07
50	5.74	10.17	20.87	27.07	101.01	0	1.2	10.6	0.89	25.77	449.1	3	98	0	0	138	30.29	-18.96	5.75		Jul-95
50	5.54	9.68	19.81	23.70	92.37	0	2.11	10.59	0.89	23.22	449.1	3	98	0	0	138	29.69	-19.34		1.00	May-07
	5.64	9.87	20.20	25.06	95.86	0	1.69	10.61	0.89	24.15	449.1	3	98	0	0	138	29.89	-19.14			Dec-06
	5.86	10.30	21.23	27.44	101.60	0	0.94	10.61	0.89	26.55	449.1	3	98	0	0	138	30.29	-18.96			Nov-16
	5.86	10.30	21.18	28.02	103.52	0	0.95	10.57	0.89	26.54	449.1	3	98	0	0	138	30.45	-18.88			May-07
50	3.25	8.37	14.20	25.24	75.29	0	1.45	12.22	0.79	29.21	626.2	2	98	0	0	60	24.61	-24.41	5.75		Jul-95
	3.18	8.21	13.80	23.92	72.20	0	1.81	12.2	0.79	27.1	626.2	2	98	0	0	60	24.26	-24.61			Oct-06
	3.35	8.56	14.59	26.44	78.15	0	1.12	12.21	0.79	30.67	626.2	2	98	0	0	60	24.84	-24.35			May-07
50	5.17	18.12	44.73	73.16	172.58	0	1.49	16	0.85	21.56	191.0	1	99	0	0	114	24.1	-26.76	5.75		Nov-95
50	5.02	17.73	43.70	69.18	161.94	0	2.28	16.03	0.86	17.74	191.0	1	99	0	0	114	23.52	-26.98		1.00	May-07
	5.05	17.85	44.04	70.94	166.39	0	1.91	16	0.85	18.99	191.0	1	99	0	0	114	23.68	-26.96			Jan-07
	5.23	18.31	45.10	74.42	176.22	0	1.24	16.02	0.85	22.9	191.0	1	99	0	0	114	24.27	-26.64			May-07
50	5.24	7.74	17.09	23.71	77.52	0	1.4	11.33	0.81	46.03	464.9	2	98	0	0	89	28.7	-19.38	5.75		Aug-96
50	5.06	7.34	16.18	20.85	70.69	0	2.18	11.32	0.81	40.81	464.9	2	98	0	0	89	28.2	-19.88		1.00	Nov-07
	5.10	7.46	16.50	21.95	73.11	0	1.82	11.33	0.81	41.06	464.9	2	98	0	0	89	28.3	-19.68			Feb-07
	5.34	7.94	17.48	24.17	78.18	0	1.06	11.34	0.81	47.53	464.9	2	98	0	0	89	28.7	-19.38			Nov-16
	5.32	7.90	17.39	24.69	79.85	0	1.14	11.33	0.81	47.48	464.9	2	98	0	0	89	28.95	-19.3			May-09
50	6.63	16.95	37.56	39.42	135.08	0	1.35	15.52	0.99	18.88	76.4	1	99	0	0	86	28.64	-25.68	5.75		May-97
50	6.38	16.35	36.34	36.03	125.66	0	2.1	15.5	0.99	9.61	76.4	1	99	0	0	86	27.87	-25.96		1.00	Aug-00
	6.46	16.67	36.84	37.67	130.58	0	1.7	15.52	0.99	16.08	76.4	1	99	0	0	86	28.33	-25.77			May-01
	6.63	16.97	37.78	39.61	136.84	0	1.1	15.54	0.99	19.2	76.4	1	99	0	0	86	28.78	-25.56			May-07
50	6.32	16.41	36.85	37.55	130.27	0	1.4	15.35	0.98	80.97	1,703	2	98	0	0	91	27.99	-25.07	5.75		Nov-87
50	6.13	15.97	35.84	34.47	121.37	0	2.16	15.34	0.98	71.71	1,703	2	98	0	0	91	26.41	-25.47		1.00	Sep-07
	6.20	16.12	36.23	36.04	125.55	0	1.7	15.33	0.98	75.56	1,703	2	98	0	0	91	27.56	-25.28			Jan-07
	6.42	16.58	37.05	37.75	130.60		1.06	15.35	0.98	83.67	1,703	2	98	0	0	91	27.99	-25.07			Jul-17
	6.39	16.55	37.23	38.67	133.44	0.01	1.13	15.34	0.98	83.64	1,703	2	98	0	0	91	28.23	-24.98			May-07
50	3.54	8.90	17.40	21.12	91.05	0.36	1.3	9.97	0.89	26.21	518.3	3	97	0	0	67	24.37	-26.03	5.75		Jun-93
50	3.30	8.48	16.53	18.28	83.79	0	2.07	9.97	0.89	23.76	518.3	3	97	0	0	67	23.81	-26.25		1.00	May-07
	3.44	8.70	16.95	19.64	87.26	0	1.69	9.97	0.89	25.06	518.3	3	97	0	0	67	24.03	-26.13			Dec-06
	3.55	9.02	17.70	21.91	93.30	0	1.06	9.99	0.89	26.77	518.3	3	97	0	0	67	24.52	-25.94			May-07
250	6.53	11.13	21.10	34.57	105.48	1.35	0.58	10.08	1	21.17	238.8	0	99	0	1		24.6	-16.52	2.50		Dec-92
	6.40	10.92	20.56	32.84	101.36	0.97	1.03	10.1	1	21.12	238.8	0	99	0	1		24.33	-16.64			Jul-04
	6.53	11.22	21.28	35.34	107.25	1.46	0.4	10.1	1	21.3	238.8	0	99	0	1		24.68	-16.46			Nov-91
50	7.50	17.76	42.08	37.25	27.63	0.69	1.34	15.44	0.96	22.53	226.3	1	98	0	1	120	24.88	-27.86	5.75		May-97
50	7.28	17.33	40.95	33.97	22.64	0.64	2.14	15.42	0.96	17.08	226.3	1	98	0	1	120	24.26	-28.11		1.00	Aug-00
	7.39	17.59	41.69	36.15	25.92	0.68	1.58	15.43	0.96	21.18	226.3	1	98	0	1	120	24.58	-28			May-01
	7.61	18.01	42.77	37.96	28.29	0.17	0.89	15.46	0.96	22.81	226.3	1	98	0	1	120	24.88	-27.86			Nov-16
	7.54	17.96	42.58	38.60	29.86	0.65	0.99	15.45	0.96	22.64	226.3	1	98	0	1	120	24.92	-27.81			Mar-09
50	8.15	16.69	42.54	35.19		0	1.75	13.04	0.84	10.13	7.2	1	98	0	1	141			5.75		Jan-14
50	8.02	16.38	41.67	29.73		0	2.5	13.11	0.84	9.51	7.2	1	98	0	1	141				1.00	Jan-14
	8.26	16.88	43.02	36.45		0.5	1.5	13.08	0.85	10.08	7.2	1	98	0	1	141					Jan-14
50	9.64	17.46	26.14	25.17	78.67	0.89	1.3	10.48	0.98	27.71	91.5	1	99	0	0	76	26.68	-26.94	5.75		Dec-93
50	9.41	16.89	24.96	21.80	70.71	0.21	2.19	10.52	0.99	24.98	91.5	1	99	0	0	76	26.03	-27.21		1.00	Feb-03
	9.72	17.45	26.14	25.63	80.31	1	1.15	10.49	0.98	27.99	91.5	1	99	0	0	76	27	-26.86			Aug-07
	9.54	17.24	25.76	24.09	76.11	0.72	1.56	10.49	0.98	26.63	91.5	1	99	0	0	76	26.49	-27.04			Dec-99
	9.73	17.56	26.43	26.15	80.95	1.11	1.03	10.5	0.99	27.83	91.5	1	99	0	0	76	26.68	-26.94			Jan-13
50	3.79	7.38	14.55	17.32	56.61	2.35	1.19	6.71	0.59	16.46	38.1	7	79	13	0	192	16.98	-14.01	5.75		Dec-93
50	3.64	7.00	13.78	14.89	51.16	2	1.94	6.71	0.59	16.23	38.1	7	79	13	0	192	16.45	-14.25		1.00	Feb-03
	3.83	7.50	14.83	18.18	58.49	2.5	0.94	6.74	0.59	16.53	38.1	7	79	13	0	192	17.18	-13.87			Aug-07
	3.76	7.26	14.30	16.32	54.32	2.18	1.44	6.72	0.59	16.43	38.1	7	79	13	1	192	16.8	-14.13			Dec-99

	MARKET			FUND TYPE, CATEGORY & OBJECTIVE	RATINGS				MINIMUMS	
Fund Name	Ticker Symbol	Traded On	Fund Type	Category and (Prospectus Objective)	Overall Rating	Reward Rating	Risk Rating	Recent Up/ Downgrade	Open to New Investors	Min Initial Investment
Victory Sycamore Established Value Fund Class A	VETAX	NAS CM	Open End	US Equity Mid Cap (Growth)	B+	B	A	Up	Y	2,500
Victory Sycamore Established Value Fund Class C	VEVCX	NAS CM	Open End	US Equity Mid Cap (Growth)	B	B	A-		Y	2,500
Victory Sycamore Established Value Fund Class I	VEVIX	NAS CM	Open End	US Equity Mid Cap (Growth)	B+	B	A	Up	Y	2,000,000
Victory Sycamore Established Value Fund Class R	GETGX	NAS CM	Open End	US Equity Mid Cap (Growth)	B+	B	A	Up	Y	0
Victory Sycamore Established Value Fund Class R6	VEVRX	NAS CM	Open End	US Equity Mid Cap (Growth)	B+	B	A	Up	Y	0
Victory Sycamore Established Value Fund Class Y	VEVYX	NAS CM	Open End	US Equity Mid Cap (Growth)	B+	B	A	Up	Y	1,000,000
Victory Sycamore Small Company Opportunity Fund Class A	SSGSX	NAS CM	Open End	US Equity Small Cap (Small Company)	A-	A	A-	Up	Y	2,500
Victory Sycamore Small Company Opportunity Fund Class I	VSOIX	NAS CM	Open End	US Equity Small Cap (Small Company)	A-	A	A-	Up	Y	2,000,000
Victory Sycamore Small Company Opportunity Fund Class R	GOGFX	NAS CM	Open End	US Equity Small Cap (Small Company)	A-	A	A-	Up	Y	0
Victory Sycamore Small Company Opportunity Fund Class Y	VSOYX	NAS CM	Open End	US Equity Small Cap (Small Company)	A-	A	A-	Up	Y	1,000,000
Victory Sycamore Small Company Opportunity Fund R6	VSORX	NAS CM	Open End	US Equity Small Cap (Small Company)	A-	A	A-	Up	Y	0
Victory Trivalent Emerging Markets Small-Cap Fund Class A	MAEMX	NAS CM	Open End	Emerging Markets Equity (Div Emerging Mkts)	B	B	C+	Up	Y	2,500
Victory Trivalent Emerging Markets Small-Cap Fund Class Y	MYEMX	NAS CM	Open End	Emerging Markets Equity (Div Emerging Mkts)	B	B	C+	Up	Y	1,000,000
Victory Trivalent International Fund-Core Equity Class A	MAICX	NAS CM	Open End	Global Equity Large Cap (Growth)	B-	B-	B-	Up	Y	2,500
Victory Trivalent International Fund-Core Equity Class C	MICCX	NAS CM	Open End	Global Equity Large Cap (Growth)	B-	B-	B-	Up	Y	2,500
Victory Trivalent International Fund-Core Equity Class I	MICIX	NAS CM	Open End	Global Equity Large Cap (Growth)	B-	B-	B	Up	Y	2,000,000
Victory Trivalent International Fund-Core Equity Class R6	MAIRX	NAS CM	Open End	Global Equity Large Cap (Growth)	B-	B-	B	Up	Y	0
Victory Trivalent International Fund-Core Equity Class Y	MICYX	NAS CM	Open End	Global Equity Large Cap (Growth)	B-	B-	B-	Up	Y	1,000,000
Victory Trivalent International Small-Cap Fund Class A	MISAX	NAS CM	Open End	Global Equity Mid/Small Cap (Small Company)	A-	A-	B+	Up	Y	2,500
Victory Trivalent International Small-Cap Fund Class C	MCISX	NAS CM	Open End	Global Equity Mid/Small Cap (Small Company)	B+	A-	B	Up	Y	2,500
Victory Trivalent International Small-Cap Fund Class I	MISIX	NAS CM	Open End	Global Equity Mid/Small Cap (Small Company)	A-	A-	B+	Up	Y	2,000,000
Victory Trivalent International Small-Cap Fund Class R6	MSSIX	NAS CM	Open End	Global Equity Mid/Small Cap (Small Company)	A-	A-	B+	Up	Y	0
Victory Trivalent International Small-Cap Fund Class Y	MYSIX	NAS CM	Open End	Global Equity Mid/Small Cap (Small Company)	A-	A-	B+	Up	Y	1,000,000
Villere Balanced Fund Investor Class	VILLX	NAS CM	Open End	Moderate Alloc (Balanced)	C+	C	B-	Up	Y	2,000
Villere Equity Fund	VLEQX	NAS CM	Open End	US Equity Mid Cap (Growth)	C	C	C+	Down	Y	2,000
Virtus Aviva Multi-Strategy Target Return Fund Class A	VMSAX	NAS CM	Open End	Multialternative (Growth & Income)	C-	D+	C		Y	2,500
Virtus Aviva Multi-Strategy Target Return Fund Class C	VCMSX	NAS CM	Open End	Multialternative (Growth & Income)	D+	D	C	Down	Y	2,500
Virtus Aviva Multi-Strategy Target Return Fund Class I	VMSIX	NAS CM	Open End	Multialternative (Growth & Income)	C-	C-	C		Y	100,000
Virtus Aviva Multi-Strategy Target Return Fund Class R6	VMSRX	NAS CM	Open End	Multialternative (Growth & Income)	C-	C-	C		Y	0
Virtus Ceredex Large-Cap Value Equity Fund Class A	SVIIX	NAS CM	Open End	US Equity Large Cap Value (Growth)	B-	B-	B	Down	Y	2,500
Virtus Ceredex Large-Cap Value Equity Fund Class C	SVIFX	NAS CM	Open End	US Equity Large Cap Value (Growth)	B-	B-	B-	Down	Y	2,500
Virtus Ceredex Large-Cap Value Equity Fund Class I	STVTX	NAS CM	Open End	US Equity Large Cap Value (Growth)	B-	B-	B-	Down	Y	100,000
Virtus Ceredex Large-Cap Value Equity Fund Class R6	STVZX	NAS CM	Open End	US Equity Large Cap Value (Growth)	B-	B-	B-	Down	Y	0
Virtus Ceredex Mid-Cap Value Equity Fund Class A	SAMVX	NAS CM	Open End	US Equity Mid Cap (Growth)	B-	B-	B-		Y	2,500
Virtus Ceredex Mid-Cap Value Equity Fund Class C	SMVFX	NAS CM	Open End	US Equity Mid Cap (Growth)	B-	C+	B-		Y	2,500
Virtus Ceredex Mid-Cap Value Equity Fund Class I	SMVTX	NAS CM	Open End	US Equity Mid Cap (Growth)	B-	B-	B-		Y	100,000
Virtus Ceredex Mid-Cap Value Equity Fund Class R6	SMVZX	NAS CM	Open End	US Equity Mid Cap (Growth)	B-	B-	B	Down	Y	0
Virtus Ceredex Small-Cap Value Equity Fund Class A	SASVX	NAS CM	Open End	US Equity Small Cap (Small Company)	B	B	B	Up		2,500
Virtus Ceredex Small-Cap Value Equity Fund Class C	STCEX	NAS CM	Open End	US Equity Small Cap (Small Company)	B	B	B	Up		2,500
Virtus Ceredex Small-Cap Value Equity Fund Class I	SCETX	NAS CM	Open End	US Equity Small Cap (Small Company)	B	B	B	Up		100,000
Virtus Conservative Allocation Strategy Fund Class A	SVCAX	NAS CM	Open End	Cautious Alloc (Asset Alloc)	B	C	A-	Up	Y	2,500
Virtus Conservative Allocation Strategy Fund Class C	SCCLX	NAS CM	Open End	Cautious Alloc (Asset Alloc)	B-	C	A-	Up	Y	2,500
Virtus Conservative Allocation Strategy Fund Class I	SCCTX	NAS CM	Open End	Cautious Alloc (Asset Alloc)	B	C	A-	Up	Y	100,000
Virtus Contrarian Value Fund Class A	FMIVX	NAS CM	Open End	US Equity Mid Cap (Growth)	C	C+	C	Down	Y	2,500
Virtus Contrarian Value Fund Class C	FMICX	NAS CM	Open End	US Equity Mid Cap (Growth)	C	C+	C	Down	Y	2,500
Virtus Contrarian Value Fund Class I	PIMVX	NAS CM	Open End	US Equity Mid Cap (Growth)	C+	C+	C		Y	100,000
Virtus Contrarian Value Fund Class R6	VMVRX	NAS CM	Open End	US Equity Mid Cap (Growth)	C+	C+	C		Y	0
Virtus DFA 2015 Target Date Retirement Income Fund Class A	VARTX	NAS CM	Open End	Target Date 2000-2020 (Asset Alloc)	C-	D+	B+	Up	Y	2,500
Virtus DFA 2015 Target Date Retirement Income Fund Class I	VDFIX	NAS CM	Open End	Target Date 2000-2020 (Asset Alloc)	C-	D+	B+	Up	Y	100,000
Virtus DFA 2015 Target Date Retirement Income Fund Cls R6	VDFRX	NAS CM	Open End	Target Date 2000-2020 (Asset Alloc)	C-	D+	B+	Up	Y	0
Virtus DFA 2020 Target Date Retirement Income Fund Class A	VATDX	NAS CM	Open End	Target Date 2000-2020 (Asset Alloc)	C-	D+	B+	Up	Y	2,500
Virtus DFA 2020 Target Date Retirement Income Fund Class I	VDTIX	NAS CM	Open End	Target Date 2000-2020 (Asset Alloc)	C-	D+	B+	Up	Y	100,000

★ Expanded analysis of this fund is included in Section II.

	TOTAL RETURNS					PERFORMANCE				ASSETS		ASSET ALLOCATION & TURNOVER					BULL & BEAR		FEES		
Min Additional Investment	3-Month Total Return	6-Month Total Return	1-Year Total Return	3-Year Total Return	5-Year Total Return	Dividend Yield (TTM)	Expense Ratio	3-Yr Std Deviation	3-Year Beta	NAV	Total Assets (MIL)	%Cash	%Stocks	%Bonds	%Other	Turnover Ratio	Last Bull Market Total Return	Last Bear Market Total Return	Front End Fee (%)	Back End Fee (%)	Inception Date
50	5.73	9.82	15.66	39.14	114.48	0.51	0.95	10.7	0.96	40.58	10,865	4	96	0	0	40	26.28	-20.78	5.75		May-00
50	5.52	9.40	14.75	36.09	106.92	0.1	1.8	10.7	0.96	39.78	10,865	4	96	0	0	40	25.79	-21		1.00	Mar-16
	5.81	9.98	16.01	40.44	118.06	0.76	0.69	10.72	0.96	40.59	10,865	4	96	0	0	40	26.56	-20.66			Mar-10
	5.68	9.74	15.43	38.36	112.49	0.35	1.13	10.71	0.96	40.09	10,865	4	96	0	0	40	26.16	-20.84			Aug-83
	5.86	10.05	16.07	40.70	116.96	0.82	0.59	10.71	0.96	40.61	10,865	4	96	0	0	40	26.16	-20.84			Mar-14
	5.82	10.01	16.01	40.16	116.74	0.77	0.72	10.72	0.97	40.59	10,865	4	96	0	0	40	26.16	-20.84			Jan-13
50	3.08	10.30	11.47	42.07	106.59	0.23	1.26	12.96	0.89	46.72	5,201	4	96	0	0	59	26.83	-20.81	5.75		Mar-99
	3.19	10.50	11.87	43.49	110.13	0.45	0.96	12.95	0.89	47.13	5,201	4	96	0	0	59	27.08	-20.69			Aug-07
	3.03	10.16	11.25	41.17	104.28	0.1	1.48	12.95	0.89	43.98	5,201	4	96	0	0	59	26.63	-20.87			Aug-83
	3.13	10.35	11.58	42.55	107.95	0.33	1.15	12.95	0.89	46.88	5,201	4	96	0	0	59	26.63	-20.87			Jan-13
	3.18	10.48	11.87	42.62	106.37	0.46	0.98	12.96	0.89	47.06	5,201	4	96	0	0	59	26.63	-20.87			Dec-15
250	8.45	19.26	42.60	37.31		0.64	1.76	14.79	0.97	14.36	5.8	1	98	0	0				5.75		Jul-13
	8.57	19.45	43.02	38.34		0.79	1.51	14.8	0.97	14.35	5.8	1	98	0	0						Jul-13
50	4.21	11.59	26.90	26.08	49.58	1.56	1.15	10.99	0.87	7.54	26.2	1	93	0	4		17.1	-27.05	5.75		Aug-07
50	4.11	11.24	25.82	23.47	44.13	0.96	1.9	10.95	0.87	7.52	26.2	1	93	0	4		16.52	-27.43		1.00	Aug-07
	4.27	11.92	27.26	27.92	53.57	1.94	0.78	11.04	0.88	7.55	26.2	1	93	0	4		17.3	-27.01			Aug-07
	4.33	11.98	27.50	28.16	53.86	2.01	0.76	11.01	0.87	7.57	26.2	1	93	0	4		17.3	-27.01			Mar-15
	4.19	11.72	27.07	26.94	51.15	1.76	0.9	11	0.87	7.52	26.2	1	93	0	4		17.21	-27.05			Aug-07
250	6.85	15.32	36.54	45.20	92.95	0.87	1.36	12.02	1	14.61	1,389	1	98	0	1		19.63	-23.11	5.75		Aug-07
250	6.65	14.88	35.57	41.97	85.91	0.26	2.11	12	1	14.32	1,389	1	98	0	1		19.11	-23.34		1.00	Aug-07
	6.88	15.54	37.13	46.91	96.96	1.17	0.96	12.07	1	14.7	1,389	1	98	0	1		20.14	-23			Aug-07
	6.95	15.50	36.96	46.31	95.72	1.06	1.11	12.05	1	14.78	1,389	1	98	0	1		20.14	-23			Jun-12
	6.86	15.47	36.89	46.31	95.43	1.07	1.11	12.04	1	14.65	1,389	1	98	0	1		19.91	-23.08			Aug-07
500	1.24	1.06	9.13	9.53	33.12	0.83	0.98	10.76	0.8	22.12	284.5	10	67	23	0	18	22.09	-12.82			Sep-99
500	0.91	0.09	7.33	4.53		0.1	1.26	13.08	1	10.97	37.9	15	85	0	0	25					May-13
100	-0.58	-0.89	-2.29			0.33	1.74			9.64	100.9	71	5	24	0	129			5.75		Jul-15
100	-0.70	-1.22	-3.03			0	2.49			9.52	100.9	71	5	24	0	129				1.00	Jul-15
	-0.52	-0.82	-2.13			0.62	1.49			9.67	100.9	71	5	24	0	129					Jul-15
	-0.51	-0.81	-2.02			0.63	1.43			9.67	100.9	71	5	24	0	129					Nov-16
100	5.88	9.74	15.89	25.67	91.05	1.52	1.25	10.89	1.03	16.2	2,031	3	97	0	0	77	24.72	-19.48	5.75		Feb-93
100	5.74	9.45	15.37	23.92	86.66	1.04	1.73	10.88	1.03	15.78	2,031	3	97	0	0	77	24.15	-19.65		1.00	Jun-95
	6.00	9.91	16.22	26.70	93.89	1.81	0.98	10.9	1.03	16.35	2,031	3	97	0	0	77	24.85	-19.34			Feb-93
	6.05	10.03	16.53	27.76	95.62	2.09	0.73	10.92	1.03	16.41	2,031	3	97	0	0	77	24.85	-19.34			Aug-14
100	4.74	4.41	11.22	23.82	84.16	0.86	1.38	11.78	1.08	12.5	2,979	4	96	0	0	108	29.68	-27.84	5.75		Oct-03
100	4.66	4.17	10.81	22.35	80.54	0.47	1.8	11.77	1.08	12.18	2,979	4	96	0	0	108	29.28	-28.05		1.00	Nov-01
	4.94	4.68	11.68	25.05	87.06	1.17	1.09	11.75	1.07	12.66	2,979	4	96	0	0	108	30.01	-27.77			Nov-01
	4.94	4.82	11.97	26.16	88.96	1.51	0.8	11.8	1.08	12.67	2,979	4	96	0	0	108	30.01	-27.77			Aug-14
100	7.17	11.39	10.04	31.69	85.51	0.67	1.48	12.64	0.79	11.53	821.9	1	99	0	0	29	23.01	-20.87	5.75		Oct-03
100	6.93	11.08	9.61	30.10	82.02	0.45	1.9	12.65	0.79	10.31	821.9	1	99	0	0	29	22.57	-21.14		1.00	Jun-97
	7.16	11.50	10.28	32.80	88.23	0.91	1.23	12.64	0.79	11.97	821.9	1	99	0	0	29	23.25	-20.78			Jan-97
100	1.97	4.09	9.03	11.16	27.66	2.13	1.02	3.98	0.34	11.84	38.1	5	34	60	0	14	9.67	-5.3	5.75		Nov-03
100	1.82	3.71	8.24	8.91	23.32	1.4	1.72	3.98	0.35	11.7	38.1	5	34	60	0	14	9.18	-5.57		1.00	Apr-05
	2.01	4.25	9.37	12.20	29.64	2.65	0.72	3.96	0.34	11.83	38.1	5	34	60	0	14	9.81	-5.16			Nov-03
100	4.80	10.72	12.44	7.90	53.54	1.04	1.43	13.44	1.16	38.04	154.7	1	99	0	0		34.93	-22.79	5.75		Dec-97
100	4.61	10.32	11.63	5.50	47.96	0.15	2.14	13.45	1.16	36.47	154.7	1	99	0	0		34.37	-23.04		1.00	Oct-04
	4.86	10.86	12.75	8.72	55.54	1.31	1.11	13.46	1.16	37.97	154.7	1	99	0	0		35.14	-22.69			Mar-08
	4.90	10.93	12.91	9.25	55.47	1.45	0.99	13.48	1.16	37.95	154.7	1	99	0	0		34.93	-22.79			Nov-14
100	2.87	4.76	7.98			1.3	1			11.21	1.4	1	25	74	0				5.75		Jan-16
	2.98	4.97	8.32			1.48	0.75			11.22	1.4	1	25	74	0						Jan-16
	3.06	5.14	8.59			1.47	0.55			11.27	1.4	1	25	74	0						Jan-16
100	3.81	6.13	10.17			1.34	1.02			11.58	1.4	0	31	68	1				5.75		Jan-16
	3.88	6.19	10.46			1.51	0.77			11.59	1.4	0	31	68	1						Jan-16

	MARKET			FUND TYPE, CATEGORY & OBJECTIVE	RATINGS					MINIMUMS
Fund Name	Ticker Symbol	Traded On	Fund Type	Category and (Prospectus Objective)	Overall Rating	Reward Rating	Risk Rating	Recent Up/ Downgrade	Open to New Investors	Min Initial Investment
Virtus DFA 2020 Target Date Retirement Income Fund Cls R6	VDRRX	NAS CM	Open End	Target Date 2000-2020 (Asset Alloc)	C-	D+	B+	Up	Y	0
Virtus DFA 2025 Target Date Retirement Income Fund Class A	VDAAX	NAS CM	Open End	Target Date 2021-2045 (Asset Alloc)	C-	C-	B+	Up	Y	2,500
Virtus DFA 2025 Target Date Retirement Income Fund Class I	VITDX	NAS CM	Open End	Target Date 2021-2045 (Asset Alloc)	C-	C-	B+	Up	Y	100,000
Virtus DFA 2025 Target Date Retirement Income Fund Cls R6	VRDFX	NAS CM	Open End	Target Date 2021-2045 (Asset Alloc)	C-	C-	B+	Up	Y	0
Virtus DFA 2030 Target Date Retirement Income Fund Class A	VDFAX	NAS CM	Open End	Target Date 2021-2045 (Asset Alloc)	C-	C-	B+	Up	Y	2,500
Virtus DFA 2030 Target Date Retirement Income Fund Class I	VRITX	NAS CM	Open End	Target Date 2021-2045 (Asset Alloc)	C-	C-	A-	Up	Y	100,000
Virtus DFA 2030 Target Date Retirement Income Fund Cls R6	VRRDX	NAS CM	Open End	Target Date 2021-2045 (Asset Alloc)	C-	C-	A-	Up	Y	0
Virtus DFA 2035 Target Date Retirement Income Fund Class A	VRTAX	NAS CM	Open End	Target Date 2021-2045 (Asset Alloc)	C-	C-	A-	Up	Y	2,500
Virtus DFA 2035 Target Date Retirement Income Fund Class I	VTDIX	NAS CM	Open End	Target Date 2021-2045 (Asset Alloc)	C-	C-	A-	Up	Y	100,000
Virtus DFA 2035 Target Date Retirement Income Fund Cls R6	VRRTX	NAS CM	Open End	Target Date 2021-2045 (Asset Alloc)	C-	C-	A-	Up	Y	0
Virtus DFA 2040 Target Date Retirement Income Fund Class A	VTARX	NAS CM	Open End	Target Date 2021-2045 (Asset Alloc)	C-	C	A-	Up	Y	2,500
Virtus DFA 2040 Target Date Retirement Income Fund Class I	VIDFX	NAS CM	Open End	Target Date 2021-2045 (Asset Alloc)	C-	C	A-	Up	Y	100,000
Virtus DFA 2040 Target Date Retirement Income Fund Cls R6	VRTRX	NAS CM	Open End	Target Date 2021-2045 (Asset Alloc)	C-	C	A-	Up	Y	0
Virtus DFA 2045 Target Date Retirement Income Fund Class A	VTATX	NAS CM	Open End	Target Date 2021-2045 (Asset Alloc)	C-	C	B+	Up	Y	2,500
Virtus DFA 2045 Target Date Retirement Income Fund Class I	VTIDX	NAS CM	Open End	Target Date 2021-2045 (Asset Alloc)	C-	C	B+	Up	Y	100,000
Virtus DFA 2045 Target Date Retirement Income Fund Cls R6	VTDRX	NAS CM	Open End	Target Date 2021-2045 (Asset Alloc)	C-	C	B+	Up	Y	0
Virtus DFA 2050 Target Date Retirement Income Fund Class A	VTDAX	NAS CM	Open End	Target Date 2046+ (Asset Alloc)	C-	C	B+	Up	Y	2,500
Virtus DFA 2050 Target Date Retirement Income Fund Class I	VTIRX	NAS CM	Open End	Target Date 2046+ (Asset Alloc)	C-	C	B+	Up	Y	100,000
Virtus DFA 2050 Target Date Retirement Income Fund Cls R6	VTRTX	NAS CM	Open End	Target Date 2046+ (Asset Alloc)	C-	C	B+	Up	Y	0
Virtus DFA 2055 Target Date Retirement Income Fund Class A	VTRAX	NAS CM	Open End	Target Date 2046+ (Asset Alloc)	C-	C	B+	Up	Y	2,500
Virtus DFA 2055 Target Date Retirement Income Fund Class I	VTITX	NAS CM	Open End	Target Date 2046+ (Asset Alloc)	C-	C	B+	Up	Y	100,000
Virtus DFA 2055 Target Date Retirement Income Fund Cls R6	VRDTX	NAS CM	Open End	Target Date 2046+ (Asset Alloc)	C-	C	B+	Up	Y	0
Virtus DFA 2060 Target Date Retirement Income Fund Class A	VTTAX	NAS CM	Open End	Target Date 2046+ (Asset Alloc)	C-	C	B+	Up	Y	2,500
Virtus DFA 2060 Target Date Retirement Income Fund Class I	VTTIX	NAS CM	Open End	Target Date 2046+ (Asset Alloc)	C-	C	B+	Up	Y	100,000
Virtus DFA 2060 Target Date Retirement Income Fund Cls R6	VTTRX	NAS CM	Open End	Target Date 2046+ (Asset Alloc)	C-	C	B+	Up	Y	0
Virtus Duff & Phelps Global Infrastructure Fund Class A	PGUAX	NAS CM	Open End	Other Sector Equity (Growth & Income)	C+	C+	C+	Down	Y	2,500
Virtus Duff & Phelps Global Infrastructure Fund Class C	PGUCX	NAS CM	Open End	Other Sector Equity (Growth & Income)	C+	C+	C+	Down	Y	2,500
Virtus Duff & Phelps Global Infrastructure Fund Class I	PGIUX	NAS CM	Open End	Other Sector Equity (Growth & Income)	C+	C+	C+	Down	Y	100,000
Virtus Duff & Phelps Global Real Estate Sec Fund Cls A	VGSAX	NAS CM	Open End	Real Estate Sector Equity (Real Estate)	B-	C+	B	Up	Y	2,500
Virtus Duff & Phelps Global Real Estate Sec Fund Cls C	VGSCX	NAS CM	Open End	Real Estate Sector Equity (Real Estate)	B-	C+	B	Up	Y	2,500
Virtus Duff & Phelps Global Real Estate Sec Fund Cls I	VGISX	NAS CM	Open End	Real Estate Sector Equity (Real Estate)	B-	C+	B		Y	100,000
Virtus Duff & Phelps Global Real Estate Sec Fund Cls R6	VRGEX	NAS CM	Open End	Real Estate Sector Equity (Real Estate)	B-	C+	B		Y	0
Virtus Duff & Phelps International Equity Fund Class A	VIEAX	NAS CM	Open End	Global Equity Large Cap (Foreign Stock)	C+	C	B-	Up	Y	2,500
Virtus Duff & Phelps International Equity Fund Class C	VIECX	NAS CM	Open End	Global Equity Large Cap (Foreign Stock)	C+	C	B-	Up	Y	2,500
Virtus Duff & Phelps International Equity Fund Class I	VIIEX	NAS CM	Open End	Global Equity Large Cap (Foreign Stock)	C+	C+	B	Up	Y	100,000
Virtus Duff & Phelps Intl Real Estate Sec Fund Cls A	PXRAX	NAS CM	Open End	Real Estate Sector Equity (Real Estate)	B-	C+	B	Up	Y	2,500
Virtus Duff & Phelps Intl Real Estate Sec Fund Cls C	PXRCX	NAS CM	Open End	Real Estate Sector Equity (Real Estate)	C+	C+	B-	Up	Y	2,500
Virtus Duff & Phelps Intl Real Estate Sec Fund Cls I	PXRIX	NAS CM	Open End	Real Estate Sector Equity (Real Estate)	B-	C+	B	Up	Y	100,000
Virtus Duff & Phelps Real Estate Securities Fund Class A	PHRAX	NAS CM	Open End	Real Estate Sector Equity (Real Estate)	B	C+	B+	Up	Y	2,500
Virtus Duff & Phelps Real Estate Securities Fund Class C	PHRCX	NAS CM	Open End	Real Estate Sector Equity (Real Estate)	B-	C+	B		Y	2,500
Virtus Duff & Phelps Real Estate Securities Fund Class I	PHRIX	NAS CM	Open End	Real Estate Sector Equity (Real Estate)	B	B-	B+	Up	Y	100,000
Virtus Duff & Phelps Real Estate Securities Fund Class R6	VRREX	NAS CM	Open End	Real Estate Sector Equity (Real Estate)	B	B-	B+	Up	Y	0
Virtus Duff & Phelps Select MLP and Energy Fund Class A	VLPAX	NAS CM	Open End	Energy Sector Equity (Growth & Income)	C-	C-	C	Up	Y	2,500
Virtus Duff & Phelps Select MLP and Energy Fund Class C	VLPCX	NAS CM	Open End	Energy Sector Equity (Growth & Income)	C-	C-	C-	Up	Y	2,500
Virtus Duff & Phelps Select MLP and Energy Fund Class I	VLPIX	NAS CM	Open End	Energy Sector Equity (Growth & Income)	C-	C-	C	Up	Y	100,000
Virtus Global Dividend & Income Fund Inc.	ZTR	NYSE	Closed End	Aggressive Alloc (Growth)	B-	C+	B	Up	Y	
Virtus Growth Allocation Strategy Fund Class A	SGIAX	NAS CM	Open End	Aggressive Alloc (Asset Alloc)	B-	C+	B	Down	Y	2,500
Virtus Growth Allocation Strategy Fund Class C	SGILX	NAS CM	Open End	Aggressive Alloc (Asset Alloc)	B-	C+	B	Down	Y	2,500
Virtus Growth Allocation Strategy Fund Class I	CLVGX	NAS CM	Open End	Aggressive Alloc (Asset Alloc)	B-	C+	B	Down	Y	100,000
Virtus Herzfeld Fund Class A	VHFAX	NAS CM	Open End	Moderate Alloc (Growth & Income)	B-	B-	C+	Down	Y	2,500
Virtus Herzfeld Fund Class C	VHFCX	NAS CM	Open End	Moderate Alloc (Growth & Income)	C+	B-	C+	Down	Y	2,500
Virtus Herzfeld Fund Class I	VHFIX	NAS CM	Open End	Moderate Alloc (Growth & Income)	B-	B-	B-	Down	Y	100,000

★Expanded analysis of this fund is included in Section II.

	TOTAL RETURNS					PERFORMANCE				ASSETS		ASSET ALLOCATION & TURNOVER					BULL & BEAR		FEES		
Min Additional Investment	3-Month Total Return	6-Month Total Return	1-Year Total Return	3-Year Total Return	5-Year Total Return	Dividend Yield (TTM)	Expense Ratio	3-Yr Std Deviation	3-Year Beta	NAV	Total Assets (MIL)	%Cash	%Stocks	%Bonds	%Other	Turnover Ratio	Last Bull Market Total Return	Last Bear Market Total Return	Front End Fee (%)	Back End Fee (%)	Inception Date
	3.97	6.37	10.73			1.5	0.57			11.64	1.4	0	31	68	1						Jan-16
100	4.74	7.75	13.30			1.31	1.04			12.24	2.1	0	44	55	1				5.75		Jan-16
	4.87	7.97	13.54			1.46	0.79			12.25	2.1	0	44	55	1						Jan-16
	4.94	8.03	13.79			1.45	0.59			12.3	2.1	0	44	55	1						Jan-16
100	5.13	8.62	15.64			1.17	1.06			12.58	1.6	0	57	41	2				5.75		Jan-16
	5.09	8.77	15.80			1.32	0.81			12.58	1.6	0	57	41	2						Jan-16
	5.17	8.83	16.06			1.32	0.61			12.63	1.6	0	57	41	2						Jan-16
100	4.73	8.68	17.05			0.97	1.07			12.8	1.9	0	70	28	2				5.75		Jan-16
	4.77	8.81	17.41			1.12	0.82			12.81	1.9	0	70	28	2						Jan-16
	5.00	9.03	17.83			1.12	0.62			12.88	1.9	0	70	28	2						Jan-16
100	4.85	9.30	19.17			0.93	1.07			13.22	1.5	0	82	15	2				5.75		Jan-16
	4.91	9.45	19.48			1.1	0.82			13.22	1.5	0	82	15	2						Jan-16
	4.98	9.59	19.70			1.09	0.62			13.28	1.5	0	82	15	2						Jan-16
100	5.53	10.53	21.40			0.95	1.08			13.62	1.6	1	93	5	2				5.75		Jan-16
	5.50	10.58	21.69			1.1	0.83			13.62	1.6	1	93	5	2						Jan-16
	5.65	10.81	21.91			1.1	0.63			13.68	1.6	1	93	5	2						Jan-16
100	5.56	10.56	21.46			0.95	1.08			13.6	1.6	1	93	5	2				5.75		Jan-16
	5.61	10.61	21.75			1.11	0.83			13.6	1.6	1	93	5	2						Jan-16
	5.59	10.75	21.98			1.1	0.63			13.65	1.6	1	93	5	2						Jan-16
100	5.47	10.47	21.39			0.93	1.08			13.58	1.4	1	93	5	2	10			5.75		Jan-16
	5.59	10.59	21.65			1.09	0.83			13.58	1.4	1	93	5	2	10					Jan-16
	5.64	10.72	21.97			1.08	0.63			13.64	1.4	1	93	5	2	10					Jan-16
100	5.54	10.54	21.43			0.94	1.08			13.63	1.5	1	93	5	2				5.75		Jan-16
	5.64	10.64	21.78			1.1	0.83			13.64	1.5	1	93	5	2						Jan-16
	5.64	10.80	22.04			1.1	0.63			13.69	1.5	1	93	5	2						Jan-16
100	1.58	3.83	17.80	16.59	51.58	1.76	1.32	9.85	0.95	15	120.6	1	99	0	0	56	16.3	-9.58	5.75		Dec-04
100	1.39	3.43	16.90	14.02	46.01	1.08	2.07	9.84	0.95	14.94	120.6	1	99	0	0	56	15.91	-9.95		1.00	Dec-04
	1.72	3.97	18.11	17.49	53.59	2.01	1.07	9.84	0.95	15.01	120.6	1	99	0	0	56	16.45	-9.54			Jun-08
100	5.17	8.08	12.78	17.77	48.98	2.42	1.4	11.37	1.01	29.66	198.5	1	98	0	1	36	25.75	-18.06	5.75		Mar-09
100	4.94	7.66	11.87	15.06	43.47	1.62	2.15	11.37	1.01	29.03	198.5	1	98	0	1	36	25.22	-18.28		1.00	Mar-09
	5.24	8.18	13.02	18.60	50.81	2.93	1.15	11.38	1.02	29.63	198.5	1	98	0	1	36	25.93	-17.93			Mar-09
	5.26	8.31	13.19	18.78	51.04	2.99	1.04	11.38	1.02	29.64	198.5	1	98	0	1	36	25.93	-17.93			Nov-16
100	1.51	8.42	15.39	10.82	23.87	0.78	1.5	11.01	0.83	11.08	3.8	2	98	0	0	98	12.95	-14.91	5.75		Sep-10
100	1.42	8.08	14.60	8.51	19.38	0	2.25	10.97	0.82	10.88	3.8	2	98	0	0	98	12.37	-15.25		1.00	Sep-10
	1.61	8.56	15.69	11.70	25.40	1.06	1.25	10.96	0.82	11.01	3.8	2	98	0	0	98	12.91	-14.92			Sep-10
100	8.13	12.01	21.45	21.20	37.38	6.06	1.5	11.51	0.96	7.37	25.8	2	97	0	2	24	18.47	-20.99	5.75		Oct-07
100	7.96	11.69	20.56	18.48	32.38	5.41	2.25	11.57	0.97	7.38	25.8	2	97	0	2	24	17.96	-21.33		1.00	Oct-07
	8.14	12.18	21.83	21.97	39.11	6.26	1.25	11.5	0.96	7.34	25.8	2	97	0	2	24	18.79	-20.99			Oct-07
100	2.56	4.26	5.84	13.46	53.43	1.54	1.38	13.28	0.99	26.61	930.0	0	100	0	0	20	32.69	-16.45	5.75		Mar-95
100	2.34	3.88	5.01	10.95	47.79	0.88	2.13	13.27	0.99	26.52	930.0	0	100	0	0	20	32.13	-16.69		1.00	Jul-03
	2.61	4.43	6.11	14.35	55.37	1.77	1.13	13.28	0.99	26.56	930.0	0	100	0	0	20	32.91	-16.34			Dec-06
	2.68	4.50	6.27	14.96	55.51	1.9	0.96	13.28	0.99	26.57	930.0	0	100	0	0	20	32.69	-16.45			Nov-14
100	2.42	4.11	-1.42			2.1	1.57			9.86	5.5	2	95	0	2	33			5.75		Sep-15
100	2.19	3.57	-2.16			1.31	2.32			9.84	5.5	2	95	0	2	33				1.00	Sep-15
	2.48	4.18	-1.15			2.32	1.32			9.86	5.5	2	95	0	2	33					Sep-15
	3.53	6.82	18.16	14.57	47.04	3.78	1.15	7.37		13.04	312.4	0	63	36	0	178	12.2	-8.19			Sep-88
100	3.93	7.70	15.86	19.27	56.16	0.94	1.33	7.96	0.76	9.49	85.7	4	73	23	0	20	18.02	-15.44	5.75		Nov-03
100	3.84	7.40	15.30	17.08	51.51	0.49	1.94	7.91	0.76	9.19	85.7	4	73	23	0	20	17.58	-15.66		1.00	Apr-05
	4.11	7.88	16.13	19.98	57.58	1.14	1.14	7.94	0.76	9.57	85.7	4	73	23	0	20	18.25	-15.34			Jun-97
100	3.75	7.77	17.36	27.64	52.15	2.94	2.68	8.91		12.45	66.9	19	62	5	-1	44			5.75		Sep-12
100	3.48	7.32	16.49	24.78	46.52	2.29	3.43	8.9		12.39	66.9	19	62	5	-1	44				1.00	Sep-12
	3.73	7.82	17.66	28.59	54.03	3.2	2.43	8.94		12.46	66.9	19	62	5	-1	44					Sep-12

Fund Name	Ticker Symbol	Traded On	Fund Type	Category and (Prospectus Objective)	Overall Rating	Reward Rating	Risk Rating	Recent Up/ Downgrade	Open to New Investors	Min Initial Investment
	MARKET		FUND TYPE, CATEGORY & OBJECTIVE		RATINGS				MINIMUMS	
Virtus Horizon International Wealth Masters Fund Class A	VIWAX	NAS CM	Open End	Global Equity Large Cap (Growth)	C+	C+	B-	Down	Y	2,500
Virtus Horizon International Wealth Masters Fund Class C	VIWCX	NAS CM	Open End	Global Equity Large Cap (Growth)	C+	C+	B-	Down	Y	2,500
Virtus Horizon International Wealth Masters Fund Class I	VWIIX	NAS CM	Open End	Global Equity Large Cap (Growth)	C+	C+	B-	Down	Y	100,000
Virtus Horizon Wealth Masters Fund Class A	VWMAX	NAS CM	Open End	US Equity Mid Cap (Growth)	B-	B-	B-	Up	Y	2,500
Virtus Horizon Wealth Masters Fund Class C	VWMCX	NAS CM	Open End	US Equity Mid Cap (Growth)	B-	C+	B-	Up	Y	2,500
Virtus Horizon Wealth Masters Fund Class I	VWMIX	NAS CM	Open End	US Equity Mid Cap (Growth)	B-	B-	B-	Up	Y	100,000
Virtus KAR Capital Growth Fund Class A	PSTAX	NAS CM	Open End	US Equity Large Cap Growth (Growth)	A-	A-	B+	Up	Y	2,500
Virtus KAR Capital Growth Fund Class C	SSTFX	NAS CM	Open End	US Equity Large Cap Growth (Growth)	B+	A-	B+	Up	Y	2,500
Virtus KAR Capital Growth Fund Class I	PLXGX	NAS CM	Open End	US Equity Large Cap Growth (Growth)	A-	A-	A-	Up	Y	100,000
Virtus KAR Emerging Markets Small-Cap Fund Class A	VAESX	NAS CM	Open End	Emerging Markets Equity (Small Company)	C+	B-	C		Y	2,500
Virtus KAR Emerging Markets Small-Cap Fund Class C	VCESX	NAS CM	Open End	Emerging Markets Equity (Small Company)	C+	B-	C		Y	2,500
Virtus KAR Emerging Markets Small-Cap Fund Class I	VIESX	NAS CM	Open End	Emerging Markets Equity (Small Company)	C+	B-	C		Y	100,000
Virtus KAR Global Quality Dividend Fund Class A	PPTAX	NAS CM	Open End	Global Equity Large Cap (Growth)	B-	C+	B	Down	Y	2,500
Virtus KAR Global Quality Dividend Fund Class C	PPTCX	NAS CM	Open End	Global Equity Large Cap (Growth)	B-	C+	B	Down	Y	2,500
Virtus KAR Global Quality Dividend Fund Class I	PIPTX	NAS CM	Open End	Global Equity Large Cap (Growth)	B-	C+	B	Down	Y	100,000
Virtus KAR International Small-Cap Fund Class A	VISAX	NAS CM	Open End	Global Equity Mid/Small Cap (Growth)	B	B+	C	Up	Y	2,500
Virtus KAR International Small-Cap Fund Class C	VCISX	NAS CM	Open End	Global Equity Mid/Small Cap (Growth)	B	B	C	Up	Y	2,500
Virtus KAR International Small-Cap Fund Class I	VIISX	NAS CM	Open End	Global Equity Mid/Small Cap (Growth)	B	B+	C	Up	Y	100,000
Virtus KAR International Small-Cap Fund Class R6	VRISX	NAS CM	Open End	Global Equity Mid/Small Cap (Growth)	B	B+	C	Up	Y	0
Virtus KAR Mid-Cap Core Fund Class A	VMACX	NAS CM	Open End	US Equity Mid Cap (Growth)	B+	A-	B+	Up	Y	2,500
Virtus KAR Mid-Cap Core Fund Class C	VMCCX	NAS CM	Open End	US Equity Mid Cap (Growth)	B+	B+	B+	Up	Y	2,500
Virtus KAR Mid-Cap Core Fund Class I	VIMCX	NAS CM	Open End	US Equity Mid Cap (Growth)	B	A-	B-		Y	100,000
Virtus KAR Mid-Cap Growth Fund Class A	PHSKX	NAS CM	Open End	US Equity Mid Cap (Growth)	B+	A-	B	Up	Y	2,500
Virtus KAR Mid-Cap Growth Fund Class C	PSKCX	NAS CM	Open End	US Equity Mid Cap (Growth)	B+	B+	B	Up	Y	2,500
Virtus KAR Mid-Cap Growth Fund Class I	PICMX	NAS CM	Open End	US Equity Mid Cap (Growth)	B+	A-	B	Up	Y	100,000
Virtus KAR Small-Cap Core Fund Class A	PKSAX	NAS CM	Open End	US Equity Small Cap (Small Company)	B+	A	B-	Up	Y	2,500
Virtus KAR Small-Cap Core Fund Class C	PKSCX	NAS CM	Open End	US Equity Small Cap (Small Company)	B+	A	B-	Up	Y	2,500
Virtus KAR Small-Cap Core Fund Class I	PKSFX	NAS CM	Open End	US Equity Small Cap (Small Company)	A-	A	B	Up	Y	100,000
Virtus KAR Small-Cap Core Fund Class R6	VSCRX	NAS CM	Open End	US Equity Small Cap (Small Company)	A-	A	B	Up	Y	0
Virtus KAR Small-Cap Growth Fund Class A	PSGAX	NAS CM	Open End	US Equity Small Cap (Small Company)	A-	A+	B-	Up	Y	2,500
Virtus KAR Small-Cap Growth Fund Class C	PSGCX	NAS CM	Open End	US Equity Small Cap (Small Company)	B+	A+	B-	Up	Y	2,500
Virtus KAR Small-Cap Growth Fund Class I	PXSGX	NAS CM	Open End	US Equity Small Cap (Small Company)	A-	A+	B-	Up	Y	100,000
Virtus KAR Small-Cap Value Fund Class A	PQSAX	NAS CM	Open End	US Equity Small Cap (Small Company)	B+	A	B	Up	Y	2,500
Virtus KAR Small-Cap Value Fund Class C	PQSCX	NAS CM	Open End	US Equity Small Cap (Small Company)	A-	A	B+	Up	Y	2,500
Virtus KAR Small-Cap Value Fund Class I	PXQSX	NAS CM	Open End	US Equity Small Cap (Small Company)	B+	A	B	Up	Y	100,000
Virtus KAR Small-Cap Value Fund Class R6	VQSRX	NAS CM	Open End	US Equity Small Cap (Small Company)	B+	A	B	Up	Y	0
Virtus Rampart Alternatives Diversifier Fund Class A	PDPAX	NAS CM	Open End	Multialternative (Growth)	C+	C	C+	Up	Y	2,500
Virtus Rampart Alternatives Diversifier Fund Class C	PDPCX	NAS CM	Open End	Multialternative (Growth)	C	C	C+	Up	Y	2,500
Virtus Rampart Alternatives Diversifier Fund Class I	VADIX	NAS CM	Open End	Multialternative (Growth)	C+	C	C+	Up	Y	100,000
Virtus Rampart Enhanced Core Equity Fund Class A	PDIAX	NAS CM	Open End	US Equity Large Cap Blend (Growth & Income)	B	B	B+	Down	Y	2,500
Virtus Rampart Enhanced Core Equity Fund Class C	PGICX	NAS CM	Open End	US Equity Large Cap Blend (Growth & Income)	B	B	B+	Down	Y	2,500
Virtus Rampart Enhanced Core Equity Fund Class I	PXIIX	NAS CM	Open End	US Equity Large Cap Blend (Growth & Income)	B	B	B+	Down	Y	100,000
Virtus Rampart Equity Trend Fund Class A	VAPAX	NAS CM	Open End	US Equity Large Cap Blend (Growth)	C+	C+	C+	Up	Y	2,500
Virtus Rampart Equity Trend Fund Class C	VAPCX	NAS CM	Open End	US Equity Large Cap Blend (Growth)	C+	C	C+	Up	Y	2,500
Virtus Rampart Equity Trend Fund Class I	VAPIX	NAS CM	Open End	US Equity Large Cap Blend (Growth)	C+	C+	C+	Up	Y	100,000
Virtus Rampart Equity Trend Fund Class R6	VRPAX	NAS CM	Open End	US Equity Large Cap Blend (Growth)	C+	C+	C+	Up	Y	0
Virtus Rampart Global Equity Trend Fund Class A	VGPAX	NAS CM	Open End	Global Equity (Growth)	C+	C+	C+	Up	Y	2,500
Virtus Rampart Global Equity Trend Fund Class C	VGPCX	NAS CM	Open End	Global Equity (Growth)	C+	C	C+	Up	Y	2,500
Virtus Rampart Global Equity Trend Fund Class I	VGPIX	NAS CM	Open End	Global Equity (Growth)	C+	C+	C+	Up	Y	100,000
Virtus Rampart Low Volatility Equity Fund Class A	VLVAX	NAS CM	Open End	Long/Short Equity (Growth)	B-	C	B+	Up	Y	2,500
Virtus Rampart Low Volatility Equity Fund Class C	VLVCX	NAS CM	Open End	Long/Short Equity (Growth)	B-	C	B+	Up	Y	2,500
Virtus Rampart Low Volatility Equity Fund Class I	VLVIX	NAS CM	Open End	Long/Short Equity (Growth)	B-	C	A-	Up	Y	100,000

★ Expanded analysis of this fund is included in Section II.

	TOTAL RETURNS					PERFORMANCE				ASSETS		ASSET ALLOCATION & TURNOVER					BULL & BEAR		FEES		
Min Additional Investment	3-Month Total Return	6-Month Total Return	1-Year Total Return	3-Year Total Return	5-Year Total Return	Dividend Yield (TTM)	Expense Ratio	3-Yr Std Deviation	3-Year Beta	NAV	Total Assets (MIL)	%Cash	%Stocks	%Bonds	%Other	Turnover Ratio	Last Bull Market Total Return	Last Bear Market Total Return	Front End Fee (%)	Back End Fee (%)	Inception Date
100	3.99	9.50	26.54	29.29		1.13	1.55	12.32	0.96	12.05	6.4	0	99	0	0	27			5.75		Nov-14
100	3.72	9.05	25.59	26.33		0.41	2.3	12.29	0.95	12.04	6.4	0	99	0	0	27				1.00	Nov-14
	3.99	9.58	26.84	30.24		1.27	1.3	12.34	0.96	12.05	6.4	0	99	0	0	27					Nov-14
100	5.66	11.13	18.04	24.90	87.06	0.57	1.45	13.38	1	17.89	72.5	0	100	0	0	30			5.75		Sep-12
100	5.56	10.82	17.25	22.12	80.29	0	2.2	13.36	1	17.43	72.5	0	100	0	0	30				1.00	Sep-12
	5.76	11.35	18.34	25.82	89.44	0.9	1.2	13.42	1	17.96	72.5	0	100	0	0	30					Sep-12
100	5.50	12.45	35.14	44.20	112.88	0	1.3	12.61	1.11	16.21	493.0	1	99	0	0		30.45	-23.26	5.75		Oct-95
100	5.26	12.03	34.14	40.90	105.01	0	2.11	12.58	1.1	12.73	493.0	1	99	0	0		29.95	-23.58		1.00	Nov-97
	5.57	12.66	35.52	45.32	115.74	0	1.06	12.64	1.11	16.76	493.0	1	99	0	0		30.83	-23.26			Sep-06
100	6.73	6.15	30.72	25.96		1.52	1.85	14.05	0.87	11.62	13.7	9	91	0	0	28			5.75		Dec-13
100	6.57	5.70	29.66	23.21		1.08	2.6	14.01	0.87	11.67	13.7	9	91	0	0	28				1.00	Dec-13
	6.81	6.23	31.01	26.90		1.6	1.6	14.03	0.87	11.64	13.7	9	91	0	0	28					Dec-13
100	3.40	4.95	14.24	18.30	74.90	1.54	1.35	10.22	0.86	14.86	55.7	1	99	0	0		23.75	-16.97	5.75		Jul-05
100	3.27	4.59	13.41	15.66	68.44	0.77	2.1	10.25	0.86	14.48	55.7	1	99	0	0		23.21	-17.25		1.00	Jul-05
	3.51	5.06	14.53	19.20	77.26	1.81	1.1	10.21	0.86	14.87	55.7	1	99	0	0		23.9	-16.86			Jun-08
100	3.30	8.17	28.19	53.24	92.94	1.78	1.6	12.91	1	16.51	292.4	12	88	0	0	27			5.75		Sep-12
100	3.12	7.76	27.24	49.86	86.06	1.45	2.35	12.91	1	16.34	292.4	12	88	0	0	27				1.00	Sep-12
	3.33	8.32	28.47	54.40	95.37	1.87	1.35	12.96	1	16.56	292.4	12	88	0	0	27					Sep-12
	3.43	8.36	28.67	54.82	96.04	1.92	1.24	12.94	1	16.56	292.4	12	88	0	0	27					Nov-14
100	8.65	13.74	24.63	40.11	110.57	0	1.2	10.77	0.96	30.37	126.8	6	94	0	0		24.22	-16.33	5.75		Jun-09
100	8.45	13.30	23.65	37.00	102.81	0	1.95	10.76	0.96	28.61	126.8	6	94	0	0		23.63	-16.6		1.00	Jun-09
	8.75	13.90	24.94	41.16	113.24	0	0.95	10.75	0.96	30.81	126.8	6	94	0	0		24.42	-16.25			Jun-09
100	5.44	11.64	33.52	38.60	83.57	0	1.4	13.14	1.11	27.69	97.5	0	100	0	0		31.22	-26.82	5.75		Dec-75
100	5.23	11.20	32.47	35.49	76.84	0	2.15	13.14	1.11	22.16	97.5	0	100	0	0		30.64	-27.07		1.00	Jan-01
	5.51	11.79	33.80	39.58	85.88	0	1.15	13.13	1.11	28.5	97.5	0	100	0	0		31.41	-26.73			Sep-07
100	9.99	19.40	34.62	57.54	117.44	0	1.37	11.7	0.72	30.81	775.6	7	93	0	0		22.39	-14.04	5.75		Aug-02
100	9.76	18.97	33.64	54.04	109.45	0	2.11	11.7	0.72	26.19	775.6	7	93	0	0		21.88	-14.28		1.00	Aug-02
	10.03	19.57	34.98	58.75	120.16	0	1.1	11.72	0.73	32.35	775.6	7	93	0	0		22.49	-13.87			Oct-96
	10.07	19.59	35.06	59.22	120.89	0	1	11.7	0.72	32.45	775.6	7	93	0	0		22.49	-13.87			Nov-14
100	7.23	17.64	36.62	70.96	151.98	0	1.49	12.44	0.68	27.27	1,638	13	87	0	0		21.34	-8.26	5.75		Jun-06
100	7.05	17.24	35.61	67.19	142.70	0	2.25	12.45	0.67	24.75	1,638	13	87	0	0		20.69	-8.57		1.00	Jun-06
	7.31	17.79	36.99	72.26	155.12	0	1.25	12.44	0.68	27.74	1,638	13	87	0	0		21.43	-8.17			Jun-06
100	4.51	11.47	18.57	43.82	108.59	1.05	1.34	12.25	0.78	18.93	470.9	6	94	0	0		20.84	-16.19	5.75		Jun-06
100	4.34	11.10	17.75	40.70	101.00	0.67	2.06	12.26	0.78	18.56	470.9	6	94	0	0		20.34	-16.45		1.00	Jun-06
	4.58	11.61	18.89	44.93	111.23	1.27	1.05	12.27	0.78	18.94	470.9	6	94	0	0		21.18	-16.15			Jun-06
	4.59	11.68	19.04	45.05	111.40	1.34	0.96	12.28	0.78	18.95	470.9	6	94	0	0		21.18	-16.15			Nov-16
100	4.42	8.14	8.14	6.83	11.72	1.74	1.65	6.88	0.47	11.43	43.9	14	66	13	7	4	12.87	-14.86	5.75		Nov-05
100	4.21	7.74	7.37	4.44	7.64	0.38	2.4	6.92	0.47	11.37	43.9	14	66	13	7	4	12.35	-15.03		1.00	Nov-05
	4.47	8.30	8.38	7.68	13.14	2.24	1.4	6.93	0.47	11.4	43.9	14	66	13	7	4	13.02	-14.76			Oct-09
100	6.83	12.44	22.54	39.47	109.59	0.51	1.21	9.91	0.91	20.29	192.2	0	100	0	0		26.86	-20.05	5.75		Sep-97
100	6.64	12.05	21.62	36.45	101.91	0.09	1.96	9.9	0.91	18.14	192.2	0	100	0	0		26.28	-20.34		1.00	Sep-97
	6.87	12.61	22.83	40.53	112.22	0.67	0.96	9.9	0.91	20.23	192.2	0	100	0	0		27.13	-20.02			Nov-07
100	8.08	10.85	20.59	7.61	45.77	0	1.61	8.45	0.7	14.7	531.6	0	100	0	0	92	11.8	-11.57	5.75		Jul-10
100	7.93	10.46	19.71	5.36	40.58	0	2.36	8.43	0.7	14.15	531.6	0	100	0	0	92	11.26	-11.8		1.00	Jul-10
	8.16	10.92	20.86	8.24	47.47	0	1.36	8.5	0.71	14.83	531.6	0	100	0	0	92	11.91	-11.48			Jul-10
	8.20	11.02	21.03	8.75	48.16	0	1.27	8.46	0.7	14.9	531.6	0	100	0	0	92	11.91	-11.48			Nov-14
100	6.15	8.82	20.70	8.71	27.40	0	1.86	7.69	0.61	11.72	13.9	1	98	0	0	126	7.83	-13.01	5.75		Mar-11
100	5.89	8.32	19.78	6.29	22.86	0	2.61	7.72	0.61	11.32	13.9	1	98	0	0	126	7.56	-13.36		1.00	Mar-11
	6.19	8.93	20.96	9.53	29.04	0	1.61	7.71	0.61	11.83	13.9	1	98	0	0	126	8.09	-12.98			Mar-11
100	2.37	3.45	7.86	7.65		0.16	1.75	7.87	1.02	11.41	2.5	0	100	0	0	847			5.75		Jun-13
100	2.31	3.16	7.09	5.33		0	2.5	7.83	1.01	11.13	2.5	0	100	0	0	847				1.00	Jun-13
	2.48	3.66	8.17	8.53		0.96	1.5	7.86	1.02	11.39	2.5	0	100	0	0	847					Jun-13

Fund Name	MARKET Ticker Symbol	Traded On	FUND TYPE, CATEGORY & OBJECTIVE Fund Type	Category and (Prospectus Objective)	RATINGS Overall Rating	Reward Rating	Risk Rating	Recent Up/ Downgrade	MINIMUMS Open to New Investors	Min Initial Investment
Virtus Rampart Multi-Asset Trend Fund Class A	VAAAX	NAS CM	Open End	Moderate Alloc (Growth)	C+	C	B-	Up	Y	2,500
Virtus Rampart Multi-Asset Trend Fund Class C	VAACX	NAS CM	Open End	Moderate Alloc (Growth)	C+	C	B-	Up	Y	2,500
Virtus Rampart Multi-Asset Trend Fund Class I	VAISX	NAS CM	Open End	Moderate Alloc (Growth)	C+	C	B	Up	Y	100,000
Virtus Rampart Sector Trend Fund Class A	PWBAX	NAS CM	Open End	US Equity Large Cap Blend (Growth)	C+	C+	B-		Y	2,500
Virtus Rampart Sector Trend Fund Class C	PWBCX	NAS CM	Open End	US Equity Large Cap Blend (Growth)	C+	C+	B-	Up	Y	2,500
Virtus Rampart Sector Trend Fund Class I	VARIX	NAS CM	Open End	US Equity Large Cap Blend (Growth)	C+	C+	B-		Y	100,000
Virtus Silvant Large-Cap Growth Stock Fund Class A	STCIX	NAS CM	Open End	US Equity Large Cap Growth (Growth)	B	B	B+	Up	Y	2,500
Virtus Silvant Large-Cap Growth Stock Fund Class C	STCFX	NAS CM	Open End	US Equity Large Cap Growth (Growth)	B	B	B+	Up	Y	2,500
Virtus Silvant Large-Cap Growth Stock Fund Class I	STCAX	NAS CM	Open End	US Equity Large Cap Growth (Growth)	B	B	B+	Up	Y	100,000
Virtus Silvant Large-Cap Growth Stock Fund Class R6	STCZX	NAS CM	Open End	US Equity Large Cap Growth (Growth)	B	B	B	Up	Y	0
Virtus Silvant Small-Cap Growth Stock Fund Class A	SCGIX	NAS CM	Open End	US Equity Small Cap (Small Company)	B	B	B	Up	Y	2,500
Virtus Silvant Small-Cap Growth Stock Fund Class C	SSCFX	NAS CM	Open End	US Equity Small Cap (Small Company)	B-	B-	B	Up	Y	2,500
Virtus Silvant Small-Cap Growth Stock Fund Class I	SSCTX	NAS CM	Open End	US Equity Small Cap (Small Company)	B	B	B	Up	Y	100,000
Virtus Strategic Allocation Fund Class A	PHBLX	NAS CM	Open End	Moderate Alloc (Balanced)	B-	C+	B	Up	Y	2,500
Virtus Strategic Allocation Fund Class C	PSBCX	NAS CM	Open End	Moderate Alloc (Balanced)	B-	C+	B	Up	Y	2,500
Virtus Tactical Allocation Fund Class A	NAINX	NAS CM	Open End	Moderate Alloc (Asset Alloc)	B-	C+	B	Up	Y	2,500
Virtus Tactical Allocation Fund Class C	POICX	NAS CM	Open End	Moderate Alloc (Asset Alloc)	B-	C+	B	Up	Y	2,500
Virtus Vontobel Emerging Markets Opportunities Fund Cls A	HEMZX	NAS CM	Open End	Emerging Markets Equity (Div Emerging Mkts)	C+	B-	C	Up	Y	2,500
Virtus Vontobel Emerging Markets Opportunities Fund Cls C	PICEX	NAS CM	Open End	Emerging Markets Equity (Div Emerging Mkts)	C+	C+	C	Up	Y	2,500
Virtus Vontobel Emerging Markets Opportunities Fund Cls I	HIEMX	NAS CM	Open End	Emerging Markets Equity (Div Emerging Mkts)	C+	B-	C	Up	Y	100,000
Virtus Vontobel Emerging Markets Opportunities Fund Cls R6	VREMX	NAS CM	Open End	Emerging Markets Equity (Div Emerging Mkts)	C+	B-	C	Up	Y	0
Virtus Vontobel Foreign Opportunities Fund Class A	JVIAX	NAS CM	Open End	Global Equity Large Cap (Foreign Stock)	B	B	B	Up	Y	2,500
Virtus Vontobel Foreign Opportunities Fund Class C	JVICX	NAS CM	Open End	Global Equity Large Cap (Foreign Stock)	B	B-	B	Up	Y	2,500
Virtus Vontobel Foreign Opportunities Fund Class I	JVXIX	NAS CM	Open End	Global Equity Large Cap (Foreign Stock)	B	B	B	Up	Y	100,000
Virtus Vontobel Foreign Opportunities Fund Class R6	VFOPX	NAS CM	Open End	Global Equity Large Cap (Foreign Stock)	B	B	B	Up	Y	0
Virtus Vontobel Global Opportunities Fund Class A	NWWOX	NAS CM	Open End	Global Equity (World Stock)	B+	B	A	Up	Y	2,500
Virtus Vontobel Global Opportunities Fund Class C	WWOCX	NAS CM	Open End	Global Equity (World Stock)	B	B	A		Y	2,500
Virtus Vontobel Global Opportunities Fund Class I	WWOIX	NAS CM	Open End	Global Equity (World Stock)	B+	B	A	Up	Y	100,000
Virtus Vontobel Greater European Opportunities Fund Cls A	VGEAX	NAS CM	Open End	Europe Equity Large Cap (Europe Stock)	B-	C+	B-	Up	Y	2,500
Virtus Vontobel Greater European Opportunities Fund Cls C	VGECX	NAS CM	Open End	Europe Equity Large Cap (Europe Stock)	C+	C+	B-	Down	Y	2,500
Virtus Vontobel Greater European Opportunities Fund Cls I	VGEIX	NAS CM	Open End	Europe Equity Large Cap (Europe Stock)	B-	B-	B-	Up	Y	100,000
Virtus WCM International Equity Fund Class A	SCIIX	NAS CM	Open End	Global Equity Large Cap (Foreign Stock)	B	B	B	Up	Y	2,500
Virtus WCM International Equity Fund Class I	STITX	NAS CM	Open End	Global Equity Large Cap (Foreign Stock)	B	B	B	Up	Y	100,000
Virtus WCM International Equity Fund Class R6	SCIZX	NAS CM	Open End	Global Equity Large Cap (Foreign Stock)	B	B	B	Up	Y	0
Virtus Zevenbergen Innovative Growth Stock Fund Class A	SAGAX	NAS CM	Open End	US Equity Large Cap Growth (Aggr Growth)	B	B	B	Up	Y	2,500
Virtus Zevenbergen Innovative Growth Stock Fund Class I	SCATX	NAS CM	Open End	US Equity Large Cap Growth (Aggr Growth)	B	B	B	Up	Y	100,000
Vivaldi Merger Arbitrage Fund Class A	VARAX	NAS CM	Open End	Market Neutral (Growth)	B-	C	A-	Up	Y	1,000
Vivaldi Merger Arbitrage Fund Class I	VARBX	NAS CM	Open End	Market Neutral (Growth)	B-	C	A	Up	Y	500,000
Vivaldi Multi-Strategy Fund Class A	OMOAX	NAS CM	Open End	Multialternative (Growth)	B	C	A+	Up	Y	5,000
Vivaldi Multi-Strategy Fund Class I	OMOIX	NAS CM	Open End	Multialternative (Growth)	B	C	A+	Up	Y	100,000
Vivaldi Opportunities Fund	US92853C1080		Closed End	Multialternative (Growth & Income)	U	U	U		Y	1,500
Volumetric Fund	VOLMX	NAS CM	Open End	US Equity Mid Cap (Growth)	B-	B-	B-	Down	Y	500
Vontobel Global Emerging Mkts Equity Inst Fund Cls I	VTGIX	NAS CM	Open End	Emerging Markets Equity (Div Emerging Mkts)	C+	C+	C	Up		1,000,000
Vontobel Global Equity Institutional Fund Class I	VTEIX	NAS CM	Open End	Global Equity (Growth)	B-	C+	B	Up	Y	1,000,000
Vontobel International Equity Institutional Fund Class I	VTIIX	NAS CM	Open End	Global Equity Large Cap (Growth)	C+	C+	B-	Down	Y	1,000,000
Voya Asia Pacific High Dividend Equity Income Fund	IAE	NYSE	Closed End	Asia ex-Japan Equity (Pacific Stock)	C+	C+	C	Up	Y	
Voya Australia Index Portfolio Class I	IAIIX	NAS CM	Open End	Other Equity (Pacific Stock)	C+	C+	C	Up	Y	0
Voya Balanced Portfolio Class I	IBPIX	NAS CM	Open End	Moderate Alloc (Balanced)	B-	C+	B	Down	Y	0
Voya Balanced Portfolio Class S	IBPSX	NAS CM	Open End	Moderate Alloc (Balanced)	B-	C+	B	Down	Y	0
Voya CBRE Global Infrastructure Fund Class A	VCRAX	NAS CM	Open End	Other Sector Equity (Growth & Income)	B-	B-	B-		Y	1,000
Voya CBRE Global Infrastructure Fund Class I	VCRIX	NAS CM	Open End	Other Sector Equity (Growth & Income)	B-	B-	B	Down	Y	1,000,000
Voya CBRE Long/Short Fund Class A	VCRLX	NAS CM	Open End	Long/Short Equity (Growth & Income)	C	C	C+	Up	Y	1,000

★ Expanded analysis of this fund is included in Section II.

	TOTAL RETURNS					PERFORMANCE				ASSETS		ASSET ALLOCATION & TURNOVER					BULL & BEAR		FEES		
Min Additional Investment	3-Month Total Return	6-Month Total Return	1-Year Total Return	3-Year Total Return	5-Year Total Return	Dividend Yield (TTM)	Expense Ratio	3-Yr Std Deviation	3-Year Beta	NAV	Total Assets (MIL)	%Cash	%Stocks	%Bonds	%Other	Turnover Ratio	Last Bull Market Total Return	Last Bear Market Total Return	Front End Fee (%)	Back End Fee (%)	Inception Date
100	3.78	5.63	12.49	5.92	18.87	0	1.73	5.14	0.65	11.25	85.9	3	63	30	3	167	6.77	-8.58	5.75		Mar-11
100	3.70	5.30	11.65	3.60	14.63	0	2.48	5.16	0.65	10.92	85.9	3	63	30	3	167	6.27	-8.78		1.00	Mar-11
	3.85	5.79	12.74	6.67	20.33	0	1.48	5.17	0.66	11.32	85.9	3	63	30	3	167	6.84	-8.39			Mar-11
100	5.69	9.93	16.91	10.17	60.64	1.13	1.07	7.22	0.55	12.78	274.1	1	99	0	0	259	12.84	-11.09	5.75		Aug-03
100	5.55	9.49	16.04	7.78	54.88	0.42	1.82	7.21	0.55	12.6	274.1	1	99	0	0	259	12.34	-11.29		1.00	Aug-03
	5.81	10.05	17.25	11.10	62.76	1.36	0.82	7.23	0.55	12.75	274.1	1	99	0	0	259	12.89	-10.9			Oct-09
100	7.65	13.16	26.86	30.83	96.76	0	1.23	12.24	1.1	5.49	135.5	3	97	0	0	42	29.58	-16.87	5.75		Jun-92
100	7.65	12.92	26.34	28.48	90.65	0	1.9	12.14	1.09	2.42	135.5	3	97	0	0	42	29.08	-17.12		1.00	Jun-95
	7.84	13.46	27.32	31.75	99.16	0	0.97	12.19	1.09	7.53	135.5	3	97	0	0	42	29.79	-16.73			Jul-92
	8.09	13.82	27.67	32.52	99.74	0	0.9	12.16	1.09	7.59	135.5	3	97	0	0	42	29.58	-16.87			Aug-14
100	4.12	7.62	14.33	20.33	70.63	0	1.42	13.78	0.9	6.92	32.9	1	99	0	0	56	29.13	-25.63	5.75		Dec-99
100	4.20	7.58	13.83	18.16	65.46	0	2.08	13.71	0.9	2.58	32.9	1	99	0	0	56	28.58	-25.85		1.00	Oct-98
	4.19	7.72	14.57	20.67	71.39	0	1.3	13.74	0.9	8.78	32.9	1	99	0	0	56	29.3	-25.51			Oct-98
100	3.19	7.96	19.72	14.92	41.03	1.01	1.15	7.14	0.16	14.59	483.7	1	64	34	0	24	18.45	-12.28	5.75		Dec-75
100	2.95	7.55	18.81	12.34	35.84	0.42	1.93	7.11	0.15	14.45	483.7	1	64	34	0	24	17.88	-12.56		1.00	Apr-05
100	3.06	8.04	19.84	15.49	43.95	1.52	1.36	7.92	0.05	9.17	147.7	1	63	34	0		18.02	-12.03	5.75		Sep-40
100	2.99	7.73	19.00	13.01	38.68	0.8	2.13	7.87	0.03	9.43	147.7	1	63	34	0		17.5	-12.38		1.00	Aug-99
100	5.53	9.27	34.10	23.77	22.54	0.43	1.58	12.57	0.65	11.69	8,548	5	95	0	0	27	19.92	-12.73	5.75		Aug-99
100	5.29	8.82	33.09	21.02	17.95	0	2.33	12.6	0.66	11.34	8,548	5	95	0	0	27	19.28	-13.02		1.00	Jun-06
	5.55	9.45	34.46	24.76	24.08	0.66	1.33	12.6	0.66	12.08	8,548	5	95	0	0	27	20.07	-12.66			Oct-97
	5.59	9.50	34.54	25.15	24.48	0.85	1.2	12.59	0.66	12.07	8,548	5	95	0	0	27	20.07	-12.66			Nov-14
100	4.73	8.53	32.32	29.94	41.82	0.5	1.43	11.28	0.79	35.49	1,501	3	95	0	0	31	19.61	-14.03	5.75		Jul-90
100	4.52	8.12	31.36	27.09	36.61	0.33	2.18	11.26	0.79	34.85	1,501	3	95	0	0	31	19.13	-14.32		1.00	Oct-03
	4.81	8.71	32.69	30.98	43.64	0.56	1.18	11.29	0.79	35.49	1,501	3	95	0	0	31	19.8	-13.92			May-06
	4.82	8.71	32.82	31.38	43.42	0.58	1.08	11.3	0.79	35.49	1,501	3	95	0	0	31	19.61	-14.03			Nov-14
100	6.11	9.13	29.21	39.92	75.85	0.26	1.47	9.69	0.8	16.3	232.3	4	94	0	0	37	21.61	-9.08	5.75		May-60
100	5.90	8.76	28.25	36.85	69.43	0	2.22	9.68	0.8	13.98	232.3	4	94	0	0	37	21.22	-9.41		1.00	Dec-98
	6.17	9.27	29.47	40.91	78.05	0.4	1.22	9.7	0.8	16.27	232.3	4	94	0	0	37	21.61	-9.08			Aug-12
100	3.45	5.00	25.47	25.08	35.63	1.35	1.45	11.16	0.78	16.23	13.2	0	94	0	0	42	20.4	-15.41	5.75		Apr-09
100	3.24	4.64	24.59	22.28	30.69	1.13	2.2	11.17	0.78	15.9	13.2	0	94	0	0	42	19.93	-15.7		1.00	Apr-09
	3.44	5.11	25.74	25.95	37.25	1.65	1.2	11.18	0.78	16.22	13.2	0	94	0	0	42	20.56	-15.3			Apr-09
100	5.12	9.66	31.30	33.69	52.04	0.36	1.43	10.95	0.79	11.9	97.7	7	93	0	0	37	16.34	-25.57	5.75		Jan-96
	5.22	9.74	31.57	34.50	53.13	0.44	1.21	11.04	0.8	12.09	97.7	7	93	0	0	37	16.58	-25.52			Jan-95
	5.21	9.84	31.67	34.84	53.53	0.51	1.11	11	0.8	12.11	97.7	7	93	0	0	37	16.58	-25.52			Sep-15
100	3.84	7.47	33.97	39.40	132.91	0	1.5	14.86	1.19	19.96	23.5	0	100	0	0	64	23.82	-26.21	5.75		Feb-04
	3.88	7.58	34.29	40.27	135.01	0	1.24	14.86	1.19	21.1	23.5	0	100	0	0	64	24.14	-26.11			Feb-04
50	-0.86	-0.11	2.11	8.61	21.60	0	1.84			10.36	524.8	22	61	0	18	478	1.79	0.69	5.75		Oct-15
0	-0.76	0.07	2.39	9.57	23.29	0	1.53			10.44	524.8	22	61	0	18	478	1.94	0.79			Oct-15
	0.02	2.49	1.41	11.55	16.40	0	2.54	2.49	4.21	26.12	151.3	25	32	9	32				5.00		Apr-12
	0.09	2.64	1.72	12.61	18.26	0	2.24	2.49	4.1	26.62	151.3	25	32	9	32						Apr-12
500	0.41						1.86			15.01	--										Oct-17
200	5.65	9.80	17.54	23.77	70.95	0	1.93	9.26	0.85	21.03	35.4	15	85	0	0	87	13.88	-16.65			Jan-79
	5.54	9.76	34.26	22.12		0	0.99	12.31	0.62	11.15	17.4	3	96	0	0						May-13
	6.16	9.51	29.75	41.53		0.94	0.91			13.42	48.0	3	97	0	0						Jan-15
	4.60	8.58	32.17	32.05		1.44	0.96			12.68	29.7	6	94	0	0						Jan-15
	4.44	7.62	25.38	20.87	19.62	2.34	1.5	14.06		11.75	141.2	3	97	0	0	29	22.26	-24.97			Mar-07
	6.28	9.41	20.26	20.03	18.51	3.35	0.48	14.82	0.95	9.3	100.7	1	99	0	0	36	22	-26.47			Mar-11
	3.79	6.78	14.72	20.73	51.98	2.46	0.73	6.85	1.08	16.69	430.8	11	46	42	0	184	15.37	-12.96			Apr-89
	3.68	6.61	14.36	19.79	50.11	2.22	0.98	6.87	1.08	16.59	430.8	11	46	42	0	184	15.17	-13.03			May-03
	2.96	5.76	20.00	24.40		0.99	1.35	10.01	0.97	10.77	38.9	2	98	0	0	88			5.75		Oct-13
	3.09	5.90	20.48	25.74		1.2	1.1	10.04	0.98	10.77	38.9	2	98	0	0	88					Jun-13
	5.42	4.88	4.12	0.38	15.55	0	1.73	7.62	0.49	10.1	229.4	0	100	0	0	196	10.14	-3.6	5.75		Dec-11

	MARKET			FUND TYPE, CATEGORY & OBJECTIVE	RATINGS				MINIMUMS	
Fund Name	Ticker Symbol	Traded On	Fund Type	Category and (Prospectus Objective)	Overall Rating	Reward Rating	Risk Rating	Recent Up/ Downgrade	Open to New Investors	Min Initial Investment
Voya CBRE Long/Short Fund Class I	VCRSX	NAS CM	Open End	Long/Short Equity (Growth & Income)	C	C	B-		Y	250,000
Voya Corporate Leaders 100 Fund Class A	IACLX	NAS CM	Open End	US Equity Large Cap Blend (Growth)	B-	B-	B-	Down	Y	1,000
Voya Corporate Leaders 100 Fund Class C	ICCLX	NAS CM	Open End	US Equity Large Cap Blend (Growth)	B-	B-	B-	Down	Y	1,000
Voya Corporate Leaders 100 Fund Class I	IICLX	NAS CM	Open End	US Equity Large Cap Blend (Growth)	B-	B-	B-	Down	Y	250,000
Voya Corporate Leaders 100 Fund Class O	IOCLX	NAS CM	Open End	US Equity Large Cap Blend (Growth)	B-	B-	B-	Down	Y	1,000
Voya Corporate Leaders 100 Fund Class R	IRCLX	NAS CM	Open End	US Equity Large Cap Blend (Growth)	B-	B-	B-	Down	Y	0
Voya Corporate Leaders 100 Fund Class R6	VCLRX	NAS CM	Open End	US Equity Large Cap Blend (Growth)	B-	B-	B-	Down	Y	1,000,000
Voya Corporate Leaders 100 Fund Class W	IWCLX	NAS CM	Open End	US Equity Large Cap Blend (Growth)	B-	B-	B-	Down	Y	1,000
Voya Corporate Leaders Trust Fund Series B	LEXCX	NAS CM	Open End	US Equity Large Cap Value (Growth & Income)	C+	B-	C+	Down	Y	1,000
Voya Emerging Markets High Dividend Equity Fund	IHD	NYSE	Closed End	Emerging Markets Equity (Equity-Income)	C+	C+	C	Up	Y	
Voya Emerging Markets Index Portfolio Class I	IEPIX	NAS CM	Open End	Emerging Markets Equity (Div Emerging Mkts)	C+	B-	C	Up	Y	0
Voya Emerging Markets Index Portfolio Class P2	VPEPX	NAS CM	Open End	Emerging Markets Equity (Div Emerging Mkts)	C+	B-	C		Y	0
Voya Emerging Markets Index Portfolio Class S	IEPSX	NAS CM	Open End	Emerging Markets Equity (Div Emerging Mkts)	C+	B-	C	Up	Y	0
Voya Euro STOXX 50® Index Portfolio Class A	IDJAX	NAS CM	Open End	Europe Equity Large Cap (Europe Stock)	C+	B-	C	Up	Y	0
Voya Euro STOXX 50® Index Portfolio Class I	IDJIX	NAS CM	Open End	Europe Equity Large Cap (Europe Stock)	C+	B-	C	Up	Y	0
Voya FTSE 100 Index® Portfolio Class A	IAFPX	NAS CM	Open End	Other Equity (Europe Stock)	C+	C	B-	Up	Y	0
Voya FTSE 100 Index® Portfolio Class I	IIFPX	NAS CM	Open End	Other Equity (Europe Stock)	C+	C+	B-	Up	Y	0
Voya Global Advantage and Premium Opportunity Fund	IGA	NYSE	Closed End	Global Equity (World Stock)	B-	B-	B-	Up	Y	
Voya Global Corporate Leaders® 100 Fund Class A	VGDAX	NAS CM	Open End	Global Equity (Growth)	D	D+	A		Y	1,000
Voya Global Corporate Leaders® 100 Fund Class I	VGDIX	NAS CM	Open End	Global Equity (Growth)	D	D+	A		Y	250,000
Voya Global Equity Dividend and Premium Opportunity Fund	IGD	NYSE	Closed End	Global Equity (World Stock)	C+	C+	B-		Y	
Voya Global Equity Dividend Fund Class A	IAGEX	NAS CM	Open End	Global Equity (Equity-Income)	C+	C+	C+	Down	Y	1,000
Voya Global Equity Dividend Fund Class C	ICGEX	NAS CM	Open End	Global Equity (Equity-Income)	C+	C+	C+	Down	Y	1,000
Voya Global Equity Dividend Fund Class I	IGEIX	NAS CM	Open End	Global Equity (Equity-Income)	C+	C+	C+	Down	Y	250,000
Voya Global Equity Dividend Fund Class O	IDGEX	NAS CM	Open End	Global Equity (Equity-Income)	C+	C+	C+	Down	Y	1,000
Voya Global Equity Dividend Fund Class W	IGEWX	NAS CM	Open End	Global Equity (Equity-Income)	C+	C+	C+	Down	Y	1,000
Voya Global Equity Fund Class A	NAWGX	NAS CM	Open End	Global Equity (World Stock)	C+	B-	C+	Down	Y	1,000
Voya Global Equity Fund Class C	NAWCX	NAS CM	Open End	Global Equity (World Stock)	C+	B-	C+	Down	Y	1,000
Voya Global Equity Fund Class I	NAWIX	NAS CM	Open End	Global Equity (World Stock)	B-	B-	C+	Up	Y	250,000
Voya Global Equity Fund Class W	IGVWX	NAS CM	Open End	Global Equity (World Stock)	B-	B-	C+	Up	Y	1,000
Voya Global Equity Portfolio Class A	IGHAX	NAS CM	Open End	Global Equity (Equity-Income)	C+	B-	C+	Down	Y	0
Voya Global Equity Portfolio Class I	IIGZX	NAS CM	Open End	Global Equity (Equity-Income)	B-	B-	C+	Down	Y	0
Voya Global Equity Portfolio Class S	IGHSX	NAS CM	Open End	Global Equity (Equity-Income)	C+	B-	C+	Down	Y	0
Voya Global Equity Portfolio Class S2	IWTTX	NAS CM	Open End	Global Equity (Equity-Income)	C+	B-	C+	Down	Y	0
Voya Global Equity Portfolio Class T	VGVTX	NAS CM	Open End	Global Equity (Equity-Income)	C+	B-	C+	Down	Y	0
Voya Global High Dividend Low Volatility Fund Class A	VGLAX	NAS CM	Open End	Global Equity (Growth & Income)	D	D+	A		Y	1,000
Voya Global High Dividend Low Volatility Fund Class I	VGLIX	NAS CM	Open End	Global Equity (Growth & Income)	D	D+	A		Y	250,000
Voya Global Multi-Asset Fund Class A	ATLAX	NAS CM	Open End	Alloc (Asset Alloc)	B-	C+	B	Down	Y	1,000
Voya Global Multi-Asset Fund Class C	ACLGX	NAS CM	Open End	Alloc (Asset Alloc)	B-	C+	B-	Down	Y	1,000
Voya Global Multi-Asset Fund Class I	ALEGX	NAS CM	Open End	Alloc (Asset Alloc)	B-	C+	B	Down	Y	250,000
Voya Global Multi-Asset Fund Class O	IDSIX	NAS CM	Open End	Alloc (Asset Alloc)	B-	C+	B-	Down	Y	1,000
Voya Global Multi-Asset Fund Class W	IAFWX	NAS CM	Open End	Alloc (Asset Alloc)	B-	C+	B	Down	Y	1,000
Voya Global Multi-Asset Fund R6	VGMRX	NAS CM	Open End	Alloc (Asset Alloc)	B-	C+	B		Y	1,000,000
Voya Global Perspectives Fund Class A	IAPVX	NAS CM	Open End	Alloc (Growth & Income)	B-	C+	B	Up	Y	1,000
Voya Global Perspectives Fund Class C	ICPVX	NAS CM	Open End	Alloc (Growth & Income)	B-	C+	B	Up	Y	1,000
Voya Global Perspectives Fund Class I	IIPVX	NAS CM	Open End	Alloc (Growth & Income)	B-	C+	B	Up	Y	250,000
Voya Global Perspectives Fund Class R	IRPVX	NAS CM	Open End	Alloc (Growth & Income)	B-	C+	B	Up	Y	0
Voya Global Perspectives Fund Class W	IWPVX	NAS CM	Open End	Alloc (Growth & Income)	B-	C+	B	Up	Y	1,000
Voya Global Perspectives Portfolio Class A	IPARX	NAS CM	Open End	Alloc (Growth & Income)	B-	C+	B	Up	Y	0
Voya Global Perspectives Portfolio Class I	IPIRX	NAS CM	Open End	Alloc (Growth & Income)	B-	C+	B	Up	Y	0
Voya Global Perspectives Portfolio Class S	IPSRX	NAS CM	Open End	Alloc (Growth & Income)	B-	C+	B	Up	Y	0
Voya Global Real Estate Fund Class A	IGLAX	NAS CM	Open End	Real Estate Sector Equity (Real Estate)	C+	C	B	Up	Y	1,000

★ Expanded analysis of this fund is included in Section II.

	TOTAL RETURNS					PERFORMANCE				ASSETS		ASSET ALLOCATION & TURNOVER					BULL & BEAR		FEES		
Min Additional Investment	3-Month Total Return	6-Month Total Return	1-Year Total Return	3-Year Total Return	5-Year Total Return	Dividend Yield (TTM)	Expense Ratio	3-Yr Std Deviation	3-Year Beta	NAV	Total Assets (MIL)	%Cash	%Stocks	%Bonds	%Other	Turnover Ratio	Last Bull Market Total Return	Last Bear Market Total Return	Front End Fee (%)	Back End Fee (%)	Inception Date
	5.54	5.11	4.46	1.29	17.01	0	1.5	7.62	0.5	10.19	229.4	0	100	0	0	196	10.11	-3.5			Dec-11
	5.94	10.78	18.90	29.21	100.51	1.29	0.81	10.66	1.04	21.9	1,075	1	99	0	0	19	25.09	-16.52	5.75		Jun-08
	5.77	10.48	18.27	27.04	95.33	0.84	1.41	10.68	1.04	21.79	1,075	1	99	0	0	19	24.68	-16.82		1.00	Jun-08
	6.07	11.02	19.35	30.50	103.89	1.56	0.49	10.66	1.04	21.89	1,075	1	99	0	0	19	25.04	-16.41			Jun-08
	5.97	10.82	18.89	29.05	100.30	1.25	0.9	10.66	1.04	21.88	1,075	1	99	0	0	19	24.89	-16.5			Mar-12
	5.89	10.66	18.58	28.04	98.00	1.09	1.15	10.68	1.04	21.78	1,075	1	99	0	0	19	24.73	-16.59			Mar-12
	6.03	10.98	19.29	30.47	103.94	1.57	0.48	10.64	1.04	21.89	1,075	1	99	0	0	19	25.04	-16.41			Oct-14
	6.05	10.99	19.24	30.23	103.01	1.51	0.56	10.64	1.04	21.92	1,075	1	99	0	0	19	25.21	-16.4			Jun-08
50	8.26	13.59	16.61	22.09	79.91	3.45	0.59	11.63	0.95	37.75	954.7	0	100	0	0	0	24.85	-16.36			Nov-35
	3.30	8.20	23.23	13.30	8.41	1.78	1.42	15.35	0.96	9.77	184.2	4	96	0	0	39	15.03	-22.49			Apr-11
	6.81	15.35	36.65	27.77	17.56	1.44	0.55	15.54	0.98	12.85	705.4	2	94	0	0	34					Dec-11
	6.88	15.51	36.84	27.95	17.73		0.15	15.55	0.98	12.88	705.4	2	94	0	0	34					May-17
	6.69	15.16	36.34	27.48	16.76	0.75	0.8	15.62	0.99	12.91	705.4	2	94	0	0	34					Dec-11
	-1.30	6.65	23.82	17.59	35.81	2.97	0.94	14.46	0.96	11.38	397.3	2	97	0	0	37	7.41	-33.53			Aug-09
	-1.20	6.88	24.34	19.24	39.13	3.45	0.44	14.52	0.96	11.49	397.3	2	97	0	0	37	7.71	-33.43			Aug-09
	5.12	9.81	21.60	10.85	24.36	3.12	0.92	12.46	0.96	9.85	274.0	2	98	0	0	22	19.48	-20.94			Aug-09
	5.18	10.19	22.24	12.59	27.54	3.64	0.42	12.54	0.96	9.94	274.0	2	98	0	0	22	19.81	-20.79			Aug-09
	3.99	9.78	18.13	26.71	54.78	3.08	0	8.34		12.23	227.0	4	96	0	0	98	17.32	-13.78			Oct-05
	5.44	10.49	22.70				0.91			12	3.9	0	100	0	0				5.75		Dec-16
	5.49	10.63	23.07				0.56			12.01	3.9	0	100	0	0						Dec-16
	1.63	6.61	15.55	20.45	44.29	2.66	0	9.46	0.85	8.24	807.7	7	93	0	0	31	8.99	-12.81			Mar-05
	3.21	8.10	17.39	20.87	53.15	2.12	1.25	11.11	1.02	14.87	80.7	7	93	0	0	29	15.53	-16.92	5.75		Sep-03
	3.02	7.75	16.50	18.14	47.58	1.41	2	11.08	1.02	14.79	80.7	7	93	0	0	29	14.99	-17.09		1.00	Oct-03
	3.26	8.28	17.64	21.70	55.30	2.34	1	11.1	1.02	14.89	80.7	7	93	0	0	29	15.52	-16.65			Aug-07
	3.22	8.12	17.34	20.81	53.15	2.13	1.25	11.13	1.03	14.84	80.7	7	93	0	0	29	15.43	-16.86			Nov-06
	3.30	8.29	17.72	21.78	55.16	2.1	1	11.11	1.02	16.55	80.7	7	93	0	0	29	15.41	-16.71			Feb-08
	5.58	9.25	24.31	25.87	51.03	1.12	1.37	10.29	0.95	36.03	287.1	5	95	0	0	92	-1.89	-15.06	5.75		Apr-93
	5.40	8.84	23.38	23.07	45.43	0.56	2.12	10.28	0.94	33.61	287.1	5	95	0	0	92	-2.31	-15.32		1.00	Apr-93
	5.66	9.36	24.60	26.80	52.90	1.33	1.12	10.28	0.94	36.34	287.1	5	95	0	0	92	-1.72	-14.93			Sep-06
	5.67	9.38	24.63	26.82	52.94	1.34	1.12	10.3	0.95	36.32	287.1	5	95	0	0	92	-1.76	-14.93			Jun-09
	5.65	9.32	23.09	25.22	51.51	1.71	1.11	10.32	0.95	11.02	714.5	4	96	0	0	101	11.89	-19.88			Jan-08
	5.79	9.65	23.73	27.06	54.42	2.17	0.61	10.38	0.96	11.13	714.5	4	96	0	0	101	12.09	-19.75			Mar-15
	5.80	9.55	23.43	26.22	53.39	1.93	0.86	10.33	0.95	11.12	714.5	4	96	0	0	101	12.09	-19.75			Jan-08
	5.69	9.50	23.28	25.60	52.18	1.93	1.01	10.33	0.95	10.95	714.5	4	96	0	0	101	11.99	-19.8			Mar-15
	5.69	9.38	22.94	24.74	50.09	1.59	1.21	10.36	0.96	10.96	714.5	4	96	0	0	101	11.76	-19.92			Mar-15
	4.71	8.63	19.99				0.85			11.55	9.8	1	98	0	0				5.75		Dec-16
	4.85	8.77	20.36				0.6			11.56	9.8	1	98	0	0						Dec-16
	4.88	8.87	17.40	21.48	43.65	1.61	1.15	7.13	1.13	11.97	163.0	6	64	29	1	102	14.4	-13.12	5.75		Jan-97
	4.72	8.51	16.53	18.88	38.29	0.9	1.9	7.13	1.13	12.08	163.0	6	64	29	1	102	13.93	-13.39		1.00	Jun-98
	4.97	9.00	17.73	22.40	45.42	1.81	0.9	7.11	1.12	12.14	163.0	6	64	29	1	102	14.66	-13.05			Jan-95
	4.91	8.93	17.41	21.57	43.64	1.63	1.15	7.08	1.12	11.9	163.0	6	64	29	1	102	14.5	-13.18			Nov-06
	5.04	9.08	17.72	22.58	45.53	1.87	0.9	7.14	1.13	12.13	163.0	6	64	29	1	102	14.64	-13.05			Aug-11
	4.93	8.96	17.69	22.36	45.37		0.9	7.11	1.12	12.13	163.0	4	64	31	2	102	14.66	-13.05			Sep-17
	3.24	6.80	14.81	17.36		2.01	1.23	5.22	0.8	11.65	45.5	4	60	36	0	20			5.75		Mar-13
	3.08	6.49	14.05	14.80		1.42	1.98	5.28	0.81	11.54	45.5	3	59	37	1	20				1.00	Mar-13
	3.23	6.97	15.09	18.11		2.26	0.98	5.21	0.8	11.66	45.5	4	60	36	0	20					Mar-13
	3.19	6.77	14.60	16.45		1.82	1.48	5.21	0.8	11.62	45.5	4	60	36	0	20					Mar-13
	3.31	6.95	15.16	18.17		2.23	0.98	5.22	0.81	11.68	45.5	3	59	37	1	20					Mar-13
	3.52	6.79	14.60	17.02		2.49	1.09	5.31	0.81	11.46	132.1	3	60	36	0	52					May-13
	3.58	6.91	14.98	18.15		2.81	0.81	5.24	0.8	11.55	132.1	3	60	36	0	52					May-13
	3.51	6.81	14.71	17.16		2.6	1.06	5.25	0.8	11.48	132.1	3	58	37	2	52					May-13
	4.75	5.93	10.13	6.97	28.65	3.3	1.3	11.34	1.02	17.52	1,962	1	99	0	0	34	22.07	-18.48	5.75		Nov-01

	MARKET			FUND TYPE, CATEGORY & OBJECTIVE	RATINGS					MINIMUMS
Fund Name	Ticker Symbol	Traded On	Fund Type	Category and (Prospectus Objective)	Overall Rating	Reward Rating	Risk Rating	Recent Up/ Downgrade	Open to New Investors	Min Initial Investment
Voya Global Real Estate Fund Class C	IGCAX	NAS CM	Open End	Real Estate Sector Equity (Real Estate)	C	C	C+		Y	1,000
Voya Global Real Estate Fund Class I	IGLIX	NAS CM	Open End	Real Estate Sector Equity (Real Estate)	C+	C	B	Up	Y	250,000
Voya Global Real Estate Fund Class O	IDGTX	NAS CM	Open End	Real Estate Sector Equity (Real Estate)	C+	C	B	Up	Y	1,000
Voya Global Real Estate Fund Class R	IGARX	NAS CM	Open End	Real Estate Sector Equity (Real Estate)	C+	C	B-	Up	Y	0
Voya Global Real Estate Fund Class R6	VGRQX	NAS CM	Open End	Real Estate Sector Equity (Real Estate)	C+	C	B	Up	Y	1,000,000
Voya Global Real Estate Fund Class W	IRGWX	NAS CM	Open End	Real Estate Sector Equity (Real Estate)	C+	C	B	Up	Y	1,000
Voya Global Target Payment Fund Class A	IGPAX	NAS CM	Open End	Alloc (Growth & Income)	B-	C+	B	Up	Y	1,000
Voya Global Target Payment Fund Class C	IGPCX	NAS CM	Open End	Alloc (Growth & Income)	B-	C+	B	Up	Y	1,000
Voya Global Target Payment Fund Class I	IGPIX	NAS CM	Open End	Alloc (Growth & Income)	B-	C+	B	Up	Y	250,000
Voya Global Target Payment Fund Class R	IGPRX	NAS CM	Open End	Alloc (Growth & Income)	B-	C+	B	Up	Y	0
Voya Global Target Payment Fund Class W	IGPWX	NAS CM	Open End	Alloc (Growth & Income)	B-	C+	B	Up	Y	1,000
Voya Growth and Income Portfolio Class A	IAVGX	NAS CM	Open End	US Equity Large Cap Blend (Growth & Income)	B	B-	B	Up	Y	0
Voya Growth and Income Portfolio Class I	IIVGX	NAS CM	Open End	US Equity Large Cap Blend (Growth & Income)	B	B-	B	Up	Y	0
Voya Growth and Income Portfolio Class S	ISVGX	NAS CM	Open End	US Equity Large Cap Blend (Growth & Income)	B-	B-	B-	Down	Y	0
Voya Growth and Income Portfolio Class S2	IGISX	NAS CM	Open End	US Equity Large Cap Blend (Growth & Income)	B	B-	B	Up	Y	0
Voya Hang Seng Index Portfolio Class A	IHSPX	NAS CM	Open End	Greater China Equity (Pacific Stock)	B	A-	C+	Up	Y	0
Voya Hang Seng Index Portfolio Class I	IHPIX	NAS CM	Open End	Greater China Equity (Pacific Stock)	B	A-	C+	Up	Y	0
Voya Hang Seng Index Portfolio Class S	IHPSX	NAS CM	Open End	Greater China Equity (Pacific Stock)	B	A-	C+	Up	Y	0
Voya Index Plus LargeCap Portfolio Class I	IPLIX	NAS CM	Open End	US Equity Large Cap Blend (Growth)	B	B	B		Y	0
Voya Index Plus LargeCap Portfolio Class S	IPLSX	NAS CM	Open End	US Equity Large Cap Blend (Growth)	B	B	B		Y	0
Voya Index Plus MidCap Portfolio Class I	IPMIX	NAS CM	Open End	US Equity Mid Cap (Growth)	B	B	B	Up	Y	0
Voya Index Plus MidCap Portfolio Class S	IPMSX	NAS CM	Open End	US Equity Mid Cap (Growth)	B	B	B	Up	Y	0
Voya Index Plus SmallCap Portfolio Class I	IPSIX	NAS CM	Open End	US Equity Small Cap (Small Company)	B+	B+	B	Up	Y	0
Voya Index Plus SmallCap Portfolio Class S	IPSSX	NAS CM	Open End	US Equity Small Cap (Small Company)	B+	B+	B	Up	Y	0
Voya Index Solution 2020 Portfolio Class ADV	IDXAX	NAS CM	Open End	Target Date 2000-2020 (Asset Alloc)	B-	C+	B	Up	Y	0
Voya Index Solution 2020 Portfolio Class I	IDXBX	NAS CM	Open End	Target Date 2000-2020 (Asset Alloc)	B-	C+	B	Up	Y	0
Voya Index Solution 2020 Portfolio Class S	IDXCX	NAS CM	Open End	Target Date 2000-2020 (Asset Alloc)	B-	C+	B	Up	Y	0
Voya Index Solution 2020 Portfolio Class S2	IDXDX	NAS CM	Open End	Target Date 2000-2020 (Asset Alloc)	B-	C+	B	Up	Y	0
Voya Index Solution 2020 Portfolio Class Z	VSZAX	NAS CM	Open End	Target Date 2000-2020 (Asset Alloc)	B-	C+	B	Up	Y	0
Voya Index Solution 2025 Portfolio Class ADV	ISDAX	NAS CM	Open End	Target Date 2021-2045 (Asset Alloc)	B-	C+	B	Up	Y	0
Voya Index Solution 2025 Portfolio Class I	ISDIX	NAS CM	Open End	Target Date 2021-2045 (Asset Alloc)	B-	C+	B	Up	Y	0
Voya Index Solution 2025 Portfolio Class S	ISDSX	NAS CM	Open End	Target Date 2021-2045 (Asset Alloc)	B-	C+	B	Up	Y	0
Voya Index Solution 2025 Portfolio Class S2	IXXVX	NAS CM	Open End	Target Date 2021-2045 (Asset Alloc)	B-	C+	B	Up	Y	0
Voya Index Solution 2025 Portfolio Class Z	VSZBX	NAS CM	Open End	Target Date 2021-2045 (Asset Alloc)	B-	C+	B	Up	Y	0
Voya Index Solution 2030 Portfolio Class ADV	IDXFX	NAS CM	Open End	Target Date 2021-2045 (Asset Alloc)	B-	C+	B	Down	Y	0
Voya Index Solution 2030 Portfolio Class I	IDXGX	NAS CM	Open End	Target Date 2021-2045 (Asset Alloc)	B-	C+	B	Down	Y	0
Voya Index Solution 2030 Portfolio Class S	IDXHX	NAS CM	Open End	Target Date 2021-2045 (Asset Alloc)	B-	C+	B	Down	Y	0
Voya Index Solution 2030 Portfolio Class S2	IDXIX	NAS CM	Open End	Target Date 2021-2045 (Asset Alloc)	B-	C+	B	Down	Y	0
Voya Index Solution 2030 Portfolio Class Z	VSZCX	NAS CM	Open End	Target Date 2021-2045 (Asset Alloc)	B-	C+	B	Down	Y	0
Voya Index Solution 2035 Portfolio Class ADV	ISEAX	NAS CM	Open End	Target Date 2021-2045 (Asset Alloc)	B-	C+	B-	Down	Y	0
Voya Index Solution 2035 Portfolio Class I	ISEIX	NAS CM	Open End	Target Date 2021-2045 (Asset Alloc)	B-	B-	B	Down	Y	0
Voya Index Solution 2035 Portfolio Class S	ISESX	NAS CM	Open End	Target Date 2021-2045 (Asset Alloc)	B-	B-	B-	Down	Y	0
Voya Index Solution 2035 Portfolio Class S2	IXISX	NAS CM	Open End	Target Date 2021-2045 (Asset Alloc)	B-	C+	B-	Down	Y	0
Voya Index Solution 2035 Portfolio Class Z	VSZDX	NAS CM	Open End	Target Date 2021-2045 (Asset Alloc)	B-	B-	B	Down	Y	0
Voya Index Solution 2040 Portfolio Class ADV	IDXKX	NAS CM	Open End	Target Date 2021-2045 (Asset Alloc)	B-	B-	B-	Down	Y	0
Voya Index Solution 2040 Portfolio Class I	IDXLX	NAS CM	Open End	Target Date 2021-2045 (Asset Alloc)	B-	B-	B-	Down	Y	0
Voya Index Solution 2040 Portfolio Class S	IDXMX	NAS CM	Open End	Target Date 2021-2045 (Asset Alloc)	B-	B-	B-	Down	Y	0
Voya Index Solution 2040 Portfolio Class S2	IDXNX	NAS CM	Open End	Target Date 2021-2045 (Asset Alloc)	B-	B-	B-	Down	Y	0
Voya Index Solution 2040 Portfolio Class Z	VSZEX	NAS CM	Open End	Target Date 2021-2045 (Asset Alloc)	B-	B-	B-	Down	Y	0
Voya Index Solution 2045 Portfolio Class ADV	ISJAX	NAS CM	Open End	Target Date 2021-2045 (Asset Alloc)	B-	B-	B-	Down	Y	0
Voya Index Solution 2045 Portfolio Class I	ISJIX	NAS CM	Open End	Target Date 2021-2045 (Asset Alloc)	B-	B-	B-	Down	Y	0
Voya Index Solution 2045 Portfolio Class S	ISJSX	NAS CM	Open End	Target Date 2021-2045 (Asset Alloc)	B-	B-	B-	Down	Y	0

★ Expanded analysis of this fund is included in Section II.

	TOTAL RETURNS					PERFORMANCE				ASSETS		ASSET ALLOCATION & TURNOVER					BULL & BEAR		FEES		
Min Additional Investment	3-Month Total Return	6-Month Total Return	1-Year Total Return	3-Year Total Return	5-Year Total Return	Dividend Yield (TTM)	Expense Ratio	3-Yr Std Deviation	3-Year Beta	NAV	Total Assets (MIL)	%Cash	%Stocks	%Bonds	%Other	Turnover Ratio	Last Bull Market Total Return	Last Bear Market Total Return	Front End Fee (%)	Back End Fee (%)	Inception Date
	4.52	5.52	9.30	4.63	23.89	3.21	2.05	11.35	1.02	14.51	1,962	1	99	0	0	34	21.6	-18.76		1.00	Jan-02
	4.81	6.02	10.43	7.91	30.46	3.62	1.01	11.37	1.02	17.49	1,962	1	99	0	0	34	22.3	-18.4			Jun-05
	4.72	5.91	10.12	6.97	28.67	3.35	1.3	11.33	1.02	17.5	1,962	1	99	0	0	34	22.07	-18.48			Nov-06
	4.64	5.76	9.80	6.14	27.05	3.11	1.55	11.36	1.02	17.44	1,962	1	99	0	0	34	21.91	-18.6			Aug-11
	4.83	6.14	10.61	8.36	30.52	3.78	0.87	11.36	1.02	17.49	1,962	1	99	0	0	34	22.07	-18.48			Jul-14
	4.83	6.03	10.43	7.78	30.31	3.58	1.05	11.34	1.02	17.54	1,962	1	99	0	0	34	22.26	-18.44			Feb-08
	2.80	5.60	12.10	16.24	34.80	5.48	1.3	5.46	0.86	8.49	505.6	6	60	34	0	57	13.76	-13.97	5.75		Jul-08
	2.57	5.12	11.32	13.57	29.84	4.75	2.05	5.43	0.86	8.78	505.6	6	60	34	0	57	13.31	-14.22		1.00	Aug-08
	2.89	5.64	12.47	17.22	36.71	5.78	0.99	5.38	0.85	8.46	505.6	6	60	34	0	57	14.1	-13.89			Jul-08
	2.85	5.58	11.93	15.53	33.30	5.2	1.55	5.43	0.86	8.49	505.6	6	60	34	0	57	13.61	-14.06			Aug-11
	2.89	5.66	12.36	17.08	36.43	5.8	1.05	5.41	0.85	8.44	505.6	6	60	34	0	57	13.98	-13.91			Jul-08
	6.08	8.56	19.79	27.05	87.53	1.33	1.03	9.96	0.96	28.94	3,501	1	99	0	0	98	26.8	-18.17			Dec-06
	6.21	8.80	20.33	28.82	91.80	1.7	0.58	9.96	0.96	29.37	3,501	1	99	0	0	98	27.07	-17.98			Dec-79
	6.16	8.67	20.06	27.86	89.47	1.51	0.83	9.96	0.96	28.97	3,501	1	99	0	0	98	26.95	-18.09			Jun-03
	6.10	8.60	19.89	27.27	88.05	1.42	0.98	9.95	0.96	28.65	3,501	1	99	0	0	98	26.94	-18.18			Feb-09
	7.65	17.11	38.96	35.50	47.12	0.47	1.01	16.82	0.97	17.59	74.6	1	99	0	0	17	21.9	-26.23			May-09
	7.73	17.39	39.60	37.44	50.77	0.94	0.51	16.84	0.97	17.68	74.6	1	99	0	0	17	22.32	-26.11			May-09
	7.75	17.27	39.32	36.46	48.97	0.73	0.76	16.85	0.97	17.65	74.6	1	99	0	0	17	22.1	-26.17			May-09
	7.65	13.44	24.63	37.13	113.23	1.46	0.49	10.34	1.02	29.11	873.1	1	99	0	0	96	24.3	-17.55			Sep-96
	7.60	13.30	24.30	36.05	110.54	1.24	0.74	10.36	1.02	28.87	873.1	1	99	0	0	96	24.15	-17.64			Jul-01
	6.06	7.65	13.57	30.40	97.39	1.24	0.54	10.97	0.98	22.95	653.8	1	99	0	0	99	28.3	-22.34			Dec-97
	5.96	7.48	13.28	29.40	94.92	1.01	0.79	10.98	0.98	22.59	653.8	1	99	0	0	99	28.07	-22.43			Jul-01
	3.15	7.55	9.91	34.33	107.55	0.84	0.55	13.35	0.96	26.78	304.5	1	99	0	0	60	27.02	-22.97			Dec-97
	3.07	7.38	9.60	33.31	104.94	0.61	0.8	13.37	0.96	26.47	304.5	1	99	0	0	60	26.87	-23.03			Jul-01
	2.94	5.70	11.77	17.86	42.73	0.41	0.89	5.28	0.9	13.27	234.3	3	49	44	3	75					Oct-11
	3.11	6.02	12.41	19.20	45.88	0.67	0.39	5.34	0.92	13.59	234.3	3	49	44	3	75					Oct-11
	3.04	5.83	12.05	18.48	43.95	0.56	0.64	5.32	0.91	13.54	234.3	3	49	44	3	75					Oct-11
	2.98	5.76	11.92	17.95	43.20	0.54	0.79	5.35	0.92	13.46	234.3	3	49	44	3	75					Oct-11
	3.17	6.16	12.63	19.72	46.51	0.67	0.2	5.31	0.91	13.65	234.3	3	49	44	3	75					May-15
	3.59	6.96	14.32	19.06	48.90	1.23	0.89	6.7	1.03	10.94	822.4	2	64	32	1	44	15.28	-14.02			Mar-08
	3.70	7.22	14.84	20.88	52.69	1.67	0.39	6.72	1.04	11.21	822.4	2	64	32	1	44	15.65	-13.86			Mar-08
	3.64	7.03	14.61	19.90	50.86	1.45	0.64	6.67	1.03	11.09	822.4	2	64	32	1	44	15.53	-13.95			Mar-08
	3.61	7.02	14.40	19.37	49.70	1.35	0.79	6.71	1.03	10.9	822.4	2	64	32	1	44	15.34	-14			May-09
	3.77	7.29	14.99	21.38	53.32	1.67	0.19	6.7	1.03	11.26	822.4	2	64	32	1	44	15.65	-13.86			May-15
	4.30	8.11	16.62	23.32	56.41	0.3	0.89	7.41	1.04	15.28	286.5	2	71	22	4	64					Oct-11
	4.40	8.38	17.13	24.88	60.10	0.45	0.39	7.46	1.04	15.65	286.5	2	71	22	4	64					Oct-11
	4.35	8.28	16.90	24.07	58.04	0.38	0.64	7.47	1.04	15.56	286.5	2	71	22	4	64					Oct-11
	4.34	8.14	16.68	23.25	56.55	0.3	0.79	7.4	1.03	15.37	286.5	2	71	22	4	64					Oct-11
	4.46	8.51	17.34	25.20	60.51	0.45	0.19	7.4	1.03	15.69	286.5	2	71	22	4	64					May-15
	4.70	8.89	17.95	23.68	62.28	1.16	0.89	8.5	1.1	11.34	739.5	2	83	15	1	41	18.72	-17.4			Mar-08
	4.86	9.15	18.65	25.58	66.34	1.57	0.39	8.45	1.09	11.65	739.5	2	83	15	1	41	19.05	-17.22			Mar-08
	4.82	9.00	18.38	24.57	64.34	1.35	0.64	8.51	1.1	11.51	739.5	2	83	15	1	41	18.95	-17.4			Mar-08
	4.71	8.94	18.13	23.96	63.07	1.28	0.79	8.49	1.1	11.32	739.5	2	83	15	1	41	18.85	-17.37			May-09
	4.92	9.29	18.87	26.25	67.24	1.56	0.19	8.53	1.1	11.72	739.5	2	83	15	1	41	19.05	-17.22			May-15
	4.91	9.37	19.05	24.97	66.45	0.32	0.89	8.85	1.08	16	181.5	2	82	10	5	52					Oct-11
	5.14	9.68	19.68	26.68	70.46	0.46	0.39	8.78	1.07	16.36	181.5	2	82	10	5	52					Oct-11
	5.01	9.48	19.38	25.76	68.41	0.39	0.64	8.84	1.08	16.33	181.5	2	82	10	5	52					Oct-11
	5.01	9.44	19.20	25.20	66.95	0.38	0.79	8.83	1.08	16.13	181.5	2	82	10	5	52					Oct-11
	5.12	9.71	19.85	27.05	70.95	0.45	0.18	8.82	1.08	16.42	181.5	2	82	10	5	52					May-15
	5.17	9.76	19.96	25.58	68.24	1.03	0.89	9.23	1.08	11.79	493.2	2	91	7	0	41	19.99	-19.25			Mar-08
	5.27	9.94	20.48	27.33	72.32	1.44	0.39	9.26	1.08	12.17	493.2	2	91	7	0	41	20.25	-19.04			Mar-08
	5.26	9.85	20.20	26.43	70.27	1.25	0.64	9.24	1.08	12	493.2	2	91	7	0	41	20.18	-19.22			Mar-08

	MARKET			FUND TYPE, CATEGORY & OBJECTIVE	RATINGS					MINIMUMS
Fund Name	Ticker Symbol	Traded On	Fund Type	Category and (Prospectus Objective)	Overall Rating	Reward Rating	Risk Rating	Recent Up/ Downgrade	Open to New Investors	Min Initial Investment
Voya Index Solution 2045 Portfolio Class S2	ISVLX	NAS CM	Open End	Target Date 2021-2045 (Asset Alloc)	B-	B-	B-	Down	Y	0
Voya Index Solution 2045 Portfolio Class Z	VSZFX	NAS CM	Open End	Target Date 2021-2045 (Asset Alloc)	B-	B-	B-	Down	Y	0
Voya Index Solution 2050 Portfolio Class ADV	IDXPX	NAS CM	Open End	Target Date 2046+ (Asset Alloc)	B-	B-	B-	Down	Y	0
Voya Index Solution 2050 Portfolio Class I	IDXQX	NAS CM	Open End	Target Date 2046+ (Asset Alloc)	B-	B-	B-	Down	Y	0
Voya Index Solution 2050 Portfolio Class S	IDXRX	NAS CM	Open End	Target Date 2046+ (Asset Alloc)	B-	B-	B-	Down	Y	0
Voya Index Solution 2050 Portfolio Class S2	IDXSX	NAS CM	Open End	Target Date 2046+ (Asset Alloc)	B-	B-	B-	Down	Y	0
Voya Index Solution 2050 Portfolio Class Z	VSZGX	NAS CM	Open End	Target Date 2046+ (Asset Alloc)	B-	B-	B-	Down	Y	0
Voya Index Solution 2055 Portfolio Class ADV	IISAX	NAS CM	Open End	Target Date 2046+ (Asset Alloc)	B-	B-	B-	Down	Y	0
Voya Index Solution 2055 Portfolio Class I	IISNX	NAS CM	Open End	Target Date 2046+ (Asset Alloc)	B-	B-	B-	Down	Y	0
Voya Index Solution 2055 Portfolio Class S	IISSX	NAS CM	Open End	Target Date 2046+ (Asset Alloc)	B-	B-	B-	Down	Y	0
Voya Index Solution 2055 Portfolio Class S2	IISTX	NAS CM	Open End	Target Date 2046+ (Asset Alloc)	B-	B-	B-	Down	Y	0
Voya Index Solution 2055 Portfolio Class Z	VSZHX	NAS CM	Open End	Target Date 2046+ (Asset Alloc)	B-	B-	B-	Down	Y	0
Voya Index Solution 2060 Portfolio Class ADV	VPSAX	NAS CM	Open End	Target Date 2046+ (Asset Alloc)	C+	C+	B-	Up	Y	0
Voya Index Solution 2060 Portfolio Class I	VISPX	NAS CM	Open End	Target Date 2046+ (Asset Alloc)	C+	C+	B-	Up	Y	0
Voya Index Solution 2060 Portfolio Class S	VPISX	NAS CM	Open End	Target Date 2046+ (Asset Alloc)	C+	C+	B-	Up	Y	0
Voya Index Solution 2060 Portfolio Class S2	VPSSX	NAS CM	Open End	Target Date 2046+ (Asset Alloc)	C+	C+	B-	Up	Y	0
Voya Index Solution 2060 Portfolio Class Z	VSZIX	NAS CM	Open End	Target Date 2046+ (Asset Alloc)	C+	C+	B-	Up	Y	0
Voya Index Solution Income Portfolio Class ADV	ISKAX	NAS CM	Open End	Target Date 2000-2020 (Asset Alloc)	B	C	A-	Up	Y	0
Voya Index Solution Income Portfolio Class I	ISKIX	NAS CM	Open End	Target Date 2000-2020 (Asset Alloc)	B	C+	A-	Up	Y	0
Voya Index Solution Income Portfolio Class S	ISKSX	NAS CM	Open End	Target Date 2000-2020 (Asset Alloc)	B	C+	A-	Up	Y	0
Voya Index Solution Income Portfolio Class S2	IIIPX	NAS CM	Open End	Target Date 2000-2020 (Asset Alloc)	B	C+	A-	Up	Y	0
Voya Index Solution Income Portfolio Class Z	VSZJX	NAS CM	Open End	Target Date 2000-2020 (Asset Alloc)	B	C+	A-	Up	Y	0
Voya Infrastructure Industrials and Materials Fund	IDE	NYSE	Closed End	Industrials Sector Equity (Growth)	C+	B-	C+	Up	Y	
Voya International High Dividend Equity Income Fund	IID	NYSE	Closed End	Global Equity Large Cap (Foreign Stock)	C+	C+	B-	Up	Y	
Voya International Index Portfolio Class A	IIIAX	NAS CM	Open End	Global Equity Large Cap (Foreign Stock)	B-	C+	B	Up	Y	0
Voya International Index Portfolio Class I	IIIIX	NAS CM	Open End	Global Equity Large Cap (Foreign Stock)	B-	C+	B	Up	Y	0
Voya International Index Portfolio Class P2	VIPPX	NAS CM	Open End	Global Equity Large Cap (Foreign Stock)	B-	C+	B	Up	Y	0
Voya International Index Portfolio Class S	INTIX	NAS CM	Open End	Global Equity Large Cap (Foreign Stock)	B-	C+	B	Up	Y	0
Voya International Index Portfolio Class S2	ISIIX	NAS CM	Open End	Global Equity Large Cap (Foreign Stock)	B-	C+	B	Up	Y	0
Voya International Real Estate Fund Class A	IIRAX	NAS CM	Open End	Real Estate Sector Equity (Real Estate)	C+	C+	B-	Up	Y	1,000
Voya International Real Estate Fund Class C	IIRCX	NAS CM	Open End	Real Estate Sector Equity (Real Estate)	C+	C	B-	Up	Y	1,000
Voya International Real Estate Fund Class I	IIRIX	NAS CM	Open End	Real Estate Sector Equity (Real Estate)	C+	C+	B	Up	Y	250,000
Voya International Real Estate Fund Class W	IIRWX	NAS CM	Open End	Real Estate Sector Equity (Real Estate)	C+	C+	B	Up	Y	1,000
Voya Japan TOPIX Index® Portfolio Class A	IJIAX	NAS CM	Open End	Japan Equity (Pacific Stock)	A-	A-	B+	Up	Y	0
Voya Japan TOPIX Index® Portfolio Class I	IJIIX	NAS CM	Open End	Japan Equity (Pacific Stock)	A-	A-	B+	Up	Y	0
Voya Large Cap Growth Portfolio Class A	IEOPX	NAS CM	Open End	US Equity Large Cap Growth (Growth)	B	B	B	Down	Y	0
Voya Large Cap Growth Portfolio Class I	IEOHX	NAS CM	Open End	US Equity Large Cap Growth (Growth)	B	B	B	Down	Y	0
Voya Large Cap Growth Portfolio Class R6	VRLCX	NAS CM	Open End	US Equity Large Cap Growth (Growth)	B	B	B	Down	Y	0
Voya Large Cap Growth Portfolio Class S	IEOSX	NAS CM	Open End	US Equity Large Cap Growth (Growth)	B	B	B	Down	Y	0
Voya Large Cap Growth Portfolio Class S2	IEOTX	NAS CM	Open End	US Equity Large Cap Growth (Growth)	B	B	B	Down	Y	0
Voya Large Cap Value Fund Class A	IEDAX	NAS CM	Open End	US Equity Large Cap Value (Equity-Income)	C+	C+	C+	Down	Y	1,000
Voya Large Cap Value Fund Class C	IEDCX	NAS CM	Open End	US Equity Large Cap Value (Equity-Income)	B-	C+	B	Down	Y	1,000
Voya Large Cap Value Fund Class I	IEDIX	NAS CM	Open End	US Equity Large Cap Value (Equity-Income)	B-	C+	B	Down	Y	250,000
Voya Large Cap Value Fund Class O	ILVOX	NAS CM	Open End	US Equity Large Cap Value (Equity-Income)	C+	C+	C+	Down	Y	1,000
Voya Large Cap Value Fund Class R	IEDRX	NAS CM	Open End	US Equity Large Cap Value (Equity-Income)	B-	C+	B	Down	Y	0
Voya Large Cap Value Fund Class R6	IEDZX	NAS CM	Open End	US Equity Large Cap Value (Equity-Income)	B-	C+	B	Down	Y	1,000,000
Voya Large Cap Value Fund Class W	IWEDX	NAS CM	Open End	US Equity Large Cap Value (Equity-Income)	B-	C+	B	Down	Y	1,000
Voya Large Cap Value Portfolio Class A	IPEAX	NAS CM	Open End	US Equity Large Cap Value (Equity-Income)	B-	C+	B	Down	Y	0
Voya Large Cap Value Portfolio Class I	IPEIX	NAS CM	Open End	US Equity Large Cap Value (Equity-Income)	B-	C+	B	Down	Y	0
Voya Large Cap Value Portfolio Class S	IPESX	NAS CM	Open End	US Equity Large Cap Value (Equity-Income)	C+	C+	C+	Down	Y	0
Voya Large Cap Value Portfolio Class S2	IPETX	NAS CM	Open End	US Equity Large Cap Value (Equity-Income)	B-	C+	B	Down	Y	0
Voya Large Cap Value Portfolio R6	VLCRX	NAS CM	Open End	US Equity Large Cap Value (Equity-Income)	C+	C+	C+	Down	Y	0

★ Expanded analysis of this fund is included in Section II.

	TOTAL RETURNS					PERFORMANCE				ASSETS		ASSET ALLOCATION & TURNOVER					BULL & BEAR		FEES		
Min Additional Investment	3-Month Total Return	6-Month Total Return	1-Year Total Return	3-Year Total Return	5-Year Total Return	Dividend Yield (TTM)	Expense Ratio	3-Yr Std Deviation	3-Year Beta	NAV	Total Assets (MIL)	%Cash	%Stocks	%Bonds	%Other	Turnover Ratio	Last Bull Market Total Return	Last Bear Market Total Return	Front End Fee (%)	Back End Fee (%)	Inception Date
	5.16	9.78	19.96	25.90	68.93	1.14	0.79	9.29	1.08	11.8	493.2	2	91	7	0	41	20.11	-19.26			May-09
	5.42	10.17	20.80	27.91	73.10	1.43	0.17	9.26	1.08	12.24	493.2	2	91	7	0	41	20.25	-19.04			May-15
	5.24	9.89	20.11	26.18	68.62	0.26	0.89	9.2	1.03	16.26	109.4	2	88	5	5	49					Oct-11
	5.41	10.15	20.74	28.20	73.08	0.4	0.39	9.21	1.03	16.55	109.4	2	88	5	5	49					Oct-11
	5.29	9.97	20.46	27.34	71.09	0.34	0.64	9.22	1.03	16.51	109.4	2	88	5	5	49					Oct-11
	5.22	9.92	20.21	26.57	69.50	0.32	0.79	9.22	1.03	16.3	109.4	2	88	5	5	49					Oct-11
	5.46	10.27	21.02	28.70	73.75	0.4	0.18	9.22	1.03	16.6	109.4	2	88	5	5	49					May-15
	5.27	9.97	20.36	25.80	69.02	0.89	0.89	9.4	1.03	15.18	173.1	2	88	5	5	42	19.93	-19.21			Mar-10
	5.42	10.24	21.02	27.71	73.20	1.25	0.39	9.38	1.03	15.54	173.1	2	88	5	5	42	20.3	-19.09			Mar-10
	5.27	10.01	20.63	26.70	71.06	1.09	0.64	9.41	1.03	15.36	173.1	2	88	5	5	42	20.06	-19.17			Mar-10
	5.32	9.97	20.49	26.19	69.76	0.99	0.79	9.39	1.03	15.24	173.1	2	88	5	5	42	19.91	-19.2			Mar-10
	5.46	10.34	21.26	28.24	73.92	1.24	0.16	9.39	1.03	15.62	173.1	2	88	5	5	42	20.3	-19.09			May-15
	5.31	9.94	20.44			0.25	0.89			12.49	22.7	2	88	5	5	63					Feb-15
	5.41	10.16	21.10			0.39	0.39			12.65	22.7	2	88	5	5	63					Feb-15
	5.36	10.08	20.76			0.34	0.64			12.56	22.7	2	88	5	5	63					Feb-15
	5.30	9.96	20.53			0.36	0.79			12.51	22.7	2	88	5	5	63					Feb-15
	5.48	10.31	21.24			0.39	0.17			12.7	22.7	2	88	5	5	63					May-15
	2.17	4.29	8.69	12.04	28.25	1.56	0.89	3.98	1.2	10.34	477.3	3	36	60	2	45	8.65	-4.56			Mar-08
	2.41	4.53	9.36	13.70	31.55	2.05	0.39	3.95	1.19	10.62	477.3	3	36	60	2	45	9.13	-4.5			Mar-08
	2.23	4.39	9.05	12.86	29.77	1.8	0.64	3.94	1.19	10.51	477.3	3	36	60	2	45	8.89	-4.52			Mar-08
	2.28	4.35	8.89	12.36	28.91	1.71	0.79	3.96	1.2	10.29	477.3	3	36	60	2	45	8.79	-4.6			May-09
	2.39	4.61	9.53	14.22	32.14	2.04	0.19	3.95	1.2	10.67	477.3	3	36	60	2	45	9.13	-4.5			May-15
	3.79	9.25	21.36	27.76	46.68	1.11		9.31		16.63	323.9	1	99	0	0	32	25.53	-27.88			Jan-10
	3.49	7.72	22.63	16.85	28.27	2.49	1.25	11.02	0.76	7.24	60.7	2	98	0	0	43	18.4	-23.54			Sep-07
	3.44	8.68	24.19	22.33	40.63	1.82	0.94	11.51	0.93	10.51	1,673	3	97	0	0	3	13.03	-23.39			Mar-08
	3.66	8.92	24.87	24.14	44.28	2.24	0.45	11.5	0.93	10.74	1,673	3	97	0	0	3	13.35	-23.28			Mar-08
	3.76	9.12	25.11	24.37	44.54		0.15	11.51	0.93	10.76	1,673	3	97	0	0	3	13.35	-23.28			May-17
	3.59	8.77	24.50	23.18	42.39	2.02	0.7	11.52	0.93	10.66	1,673	3	97	0	0	3	13.28	-23.38			Mar-08
	3.59	8.78	24.44	22.67	41.40	1.63	0.85	11.5	0.93	10.65	1,673	3	97	0	0	3	12.94	-23.3			Feb-09
	0.91	3.90	13.25	8.66	19.66	8.78	1.45	11.02	0.95	8.57	232.8	1	98	0	1	89	15.5	-20.66	5.75		Feb-06
	0.84	3.76	12.66	6.37	15.39	8.09	2.2	11.04	0.96	8.54	232.8	1	98	0	1	89	15.01	-20.89		1.00	Feb-06
	6.26	9.20	20.60	15.04	27.87	9.04	1.13	11.04	0.96		232.8	1	98	0	1	89	15.67	-20.57			Feb-06
	6.24	9.32	20.65	14.96	27.61	9.01	1.2	11.04	0.96		232.8	1	98	0	1	89	15.68	-20.62			Feb-08
	7.89	12.33	25.40	41.90	69.79	1.28	0.93	10.92	0.84	12.57	310.6	0	100	0	0	1	3.19	-7			Aug-09
	7.98	12.57	25.92	43.92	74.06	1.86	0.43	10.91	0.84	12.71	310.6	0	100	0	0	1	3.57	-6.86			Aug-09
	7.79	13.23	29.01	39.68	111.59	0.06	1.27	10.94	1	19.36	6,331	1	99	0	0	74	26.65	-14.51			Dec-06
	7.93	13.56	29.74	42.21	117.60	0.58	0.67	10.95	1	20.8	6,331	1	99	0	0	74	27.15	-14.35			May-05
	7.99	13.55	29.79	41.91	116.02	0.58	0.67	10.99	1.01	20.81	6,331	1	99	0	0	74	26.91	-14.37			Nov-15
	7.85	13.37	29.41	41.10	114.79	0.37	0.92	10.95	1	20.32	6,331	1	99	0	0	74	26.91	-14.37			May-04
	7.85	13.35	29.21	40.51	113.24	0.23	1.07	10.96	1.01	20.18	6,331	1	99	0	0	74	26.81	-14.48			May-04
	4.60	6.64	13.29	20.76	76.53	1.6	1.1	10.15	0.96	12.34	961.4	2	98	0	0	80	22.91	-15.74	5.75		Dec-07
	4.38	6.22	12.37	18.08	70.12	0.89	1.85	10.12	0.96	12.32	961.4	2	98	0	0	80	22.4	-15.97		1.00	Feb-08
	4.65	6.80	13.58	21.98	79.62	1.79	0.76	10.14	0.96	13.33	961.4	2	98	0	0	80	23.07	-15.56			Mar-10
	4.53	6.58	13.22	20.72	76.50	1.61	1.1	10.13	0.96	12.32	961.4	2	98	0	0	80	22.91	-15.74			Jan-13
	4.41	6.46	12.95	19.78	74.49	1.37	1.35	10.13	0.96	12.32	961.4	2	98	0	0	80	22.79	-15.81			Aug-11
	4.67	6.82	13.62	22.09	79.53	1.81	0.74	10.13	0.96	13.32	961.4	2	98	0	0	80	22.91	-15.74			May-13
	4.62	6.74	13.53	21.66	78.74	1.72	0.85	10.12	0.96	13.29	961.4	2	98	0	0	80	23.06	-15.6			Jun-09
	4.47	6.43	12.84	19.90	75.13	1.73	1.24	10.16	0.96	13.06	1,308	1	99	0	0	118	23.14	-15.8			May-07
	4.61	6.78	13.54	22.18	80.53	2.21	0.64	10.17	0.96	13.3	1,308	1	99	0	0	118	23.66	-15.62			May-07
	4.55	6.58	13.23	21.24	78.31	2.01	0.89	10.17	0.96	13.14	1,308	1	99	0	0	118	23.44	-15.72			May-07
	4.50	6.53	13.09	20.70	77.15	1.87	1.04	10.19	0.97	13.15	1,308	1	99	0	0	118	23.37	-15.76			Sep-13
	4.70	6.79	13.56	22.11	80.42	2.21	0.64	10.15	0.96	13.29	1,308	1	99	0	0	118	23.66	-15.62			Nov-15

Fund Name	MARKET Ticker Symbol	Traded On	FUND TYPE, CATEGORY & OBJECTIVE Fund Type	Category and (Prospectus Objective)	RATINGS Overall Rating	Reward Rating	Risk Rating	Recent Up/ Downgrade	MINIMUMS Open to New Investors	Min Initial Investment
Voya Large-Cap Growth Fund Class A	NLCAX	NAS CM	Open End	US Equity Large Cap Growth (Growth)	B	B	B	Down	Y	1,000
Voya Large-Cap Growth Fund Class C	NLCCX	NAS CM	Open End	US Equity Large Cap Growth (Growth)	B+	B	A-	Up	Y	1,000
Voya Large-Cap Growth Fund Class I	PLCIX	NAS CM	Open End	US Equity Large Cap Growth (Growth)	B	B	B	Down	Y	250,000
Voya Large-Cap Growth Fund Class R	VGORX	NAS CM	Open End	US Equity Large Cap Growth (Growth)	B	B	B	Down	Y	0
Voya Large-Cap Growth Fund Class R6	VGOSX	NAS CM	Open End	US Equity Large Cap Growth (Growth)	B	B	B	Down	Y	1,000,000
Voya Large-Cap Growth Fund Class W	IGOWX	NAS CM	Open End	US Equity Large Cap Growth (Growth)	B	B	B	Down	Y	1,000
Voya Mid Cap Research Enhanced Index Fund Class A	AIMAX	NAS CM	Open End	US Equity Mid Cap (Growth & Income)	B-	B-	B-	Up	Y	1,000
Voya Mid Cap Research Enhanced Index Fund Class C	APMCX	NAS CM	Open End	US Equity Mid Cap (Growth & Income)	B-	C+	B-	Up	Y	1,000
Voya Mid Cap Research Enhanced Index Fund Class I	AIMIX	NAS CM	Open End	US Equity Mid Cap (Growth & Income)	B-	B-	B-		Y	250,000
Voya Mid Cap Research Enhanced Index Fund Class O	IDMOX	NAS CM	Open End	US Equity Mid Cap (Growth & Income)	B-	B-	B-	Up	Y	1,000
Voya Mid Cap Research Enhanced Index Fund Class R	AIMRX	NAS CM	Open End	US Equity Mid Cap (Growth & Income)	B-	C+	B-	Up	Y	0
Voya Mid Cap Research Enhanced Index Fund Class W	AIMWX	NAS CM	Open End	US Equity Mid Cap (Growth & Income)	B-	B-	B-		Y	1,000
Voya MidCap Opportunities Fund Class A	NMCAX	NAS CM	Open End	US Equity Mid Cap (Growth)	B	B	B+	Up	Y	1,000
Voya MidCap Opportunities Fund Class C	NMCCX	NAS CM	Open End	US Equity Mid Cap (Growth)	B	B	B	Up	Y	1,000
Voya MidCap Opportunities Fund Class I	NMCIX	NAS CM	Open End	US Equity Mid Cap (Growth)	B	B	B+		Y	250,000
Voya MidCap Opportunities Fund Class O	NMCOX	NAS CM	Open End	US Equity Mid Cap (Growth)	B	B	B+	Up	Y	1,000
Voya MidCap Opportunities Fund Class R	IMORX	NAS CM	Open End	US Equity Mid Cap (Growth)	B	B	B+	Up	Y	0
Voya MidCap Opportunities Fund Class R6	IMOZX	NAS CM	Open End	US Equity Mid Cap (Growth)	B	B	B+		Y	1,000,000
Voya MidCap Opportunities Fund Class W	IMOWX	NAS CM	Open End	US Equity Mid Cap (Growth)	B	B	B+		Y	1,000
Voya MidCap Opportunities Portfolio Class A	IAMOX	NAS CM	Open End	US Equity Mid Cap (Growth)	B	B	B+	Up	Y	0
Voya MidCap Opportunities Portfolio Class I	IIMOX	NAS CM	Open End	US Equity Mid Cap (Growth)	B	B	B+		Y	0
Voya MidCap Opportunities Portfolio Class S	ISMOX	NAS CM	Open End	US Equity Mid Cap (Growth)	B	B	B+		Y	0
Voya MidCap Opportunities Portfolio Class S2	IMOPX	NAS CM	Open End	US Equity Mid Cap (Growth)	B	B	B+	Up	Y	0
Voya MidCap Opportunities Portfolio R6	VMCRX	NAS CM	Open End	US Equity Mid Cap (Growth)	B	B	B+		Y	0
Voya Multi-Manager Emerging Markets Equity Fund Class A	IEMHX	NAS CM	Open End	Emerging Markets Equity (Div Emerging Mkts)	B-	B	C	Up	Y	1,000
Voya Multi-Manager Emerging Markets Equity Fund Class C	IEMJX	NAS CM	Open End	Emerging Markets Equity (Div Emerging Mkts)	C+	B	C	Up	Y	1,000
Voya Multi-Manager Emerging Markets Equity Fund Class I	IEMGX	NAS CM	Open End	Emerging Markets Equity (Div Emerging Mkts)	B-	B	C	Up	Y	250,000
Voya Multi-Manager Emerging Markets Equity Fund Class R	IEMKX	NAS CM	Open End	Emerging Markets Equity (Div Emerging Mkts)	B-	B	C	Up	Y	0
Voya Multi-Manager Emerging Markets Equity Fund Class W	IEMLX	NAS CM	Open End	Emerging Markets Equity (Div Emerging Mkts)	B-	B	C	Up	Y	1,000
Voya Multi-Manager International Equity Fund Class I	IIGIX	NAS CM	Open End	Global Equity Large Cap (Foreign Stock)	B-	C+	B	Up	Y	250,000
Voya Multi-Manager International Factors Fund Class I	IICFX	NAS CM	Open End	Global Equity Large Cap (Foreign Stock)	B	B-	B	Up	Y	250,000
Voya Multi-Manager International Factors Fund Class W	IICWX	NAS CM	Open End	Global Equity Large Cap (Foreign Stock)	B	B-	B	Up	Y	1,000
Voya Multi-Manager International Small Cap Fund Class A	NTKLX	NAS CM	Open End	Global Equity Mid/Small Cap (Small Company)	A-	A-	A-	Up	Y	1,000
Voya Multi-Manager International Small Cap Fund Class C	NARCX	NAS CM	Open End	Global Equity Mid/Small Cap (Small Company)	A-	B+	A-	Up	Y	1,000
Voya Multi-Manager International Small Cap Fund Class I	NAPIX	NAS CM	Open End	Global Equity Mid/Small Cap (Small Company)	A-	A-	A-	Up	Y	250,000
Voya Multi-Manager International Small Cap Fund Class O	NAPOX	NAS CM	Open End	Global Equity Mid/Small Cap (Small Company)	A-	A-	A-	Up	Y	1,000
Voya Multi-Manager International Small Cap Fund Class W	ISCWX	NAS CM	Open End	Global Equity Mid/Small Cap (Small Company)	A-	A-	A-	Up	Y	1,000
Voya Multi-Manager Large Cap Core Portfolio Class A	IPFAX	NAS CM	Open End	US Equity Large Cap Blend (Growth & Income)	B-	B-	B-	Down	Y	0
Voya Multi-Manager Large Cap Core Portfolio Class I	IPPIX	NAS CM	Open End	US Equity Large Cap Blend (Growth & Income)	B-	B	B-	Down	Y	0
Voya Multi-Manager Large Cap Core Portfolio Class R6	VPMMX	NAS CM	Open End	US Equity Large Cap Blend (Growth & Income)	B-	B-	B-	Down	Y	0
Voya Multi-Manager Large Cap Core Portfolio Class S	IPPSX	NAS CM	Open End	US Equity Large Cap Blend (Growth & Income)	B-	B-	B-	Down	Y	0
Voya Multi-Manager Mid Cap Value Fund Class I	IMCVX	NAS CM	Open End	US Equity Mid Cap (Growth)	B	B-	B	Up	Y	250,000
Voya Natural Resources Equity Income Fund	IRR	NYSE	Closed End	Energy Sector Equity (Natl Res)	C-	C-	C	Up	Y	
Voya Real Estate Fund Class A	CLARX	NAS CM	Open End	Real Estate Sector Equity (Real Estate)	B-	C+	B	Up	Y	1,000
Voya Real Estate Fund Class C	CRCRX	NAS CM	Open End	Real Estate Sector Equity (Real Estate)	C+	C	B		Y	1,000
Voya Real Estate Fund Class I	CRARX	NAS CM	Open End	Real Estate Sector Equity (Real Estate)	B-	C+	B	Up	Y	250,000
Voya Real Estate Fund Class O	IDROX	NAS CM	Open End	Real Estate Sector Equity (Real Estate)	B-	C+	B	Up	Y	1,000
Voya Real Estate Fund Class R	CRWRX	NAS CM	Open End	Real Estate Sector Equity (Real Estate)	B-	C+	B	Up	Y	0
Voya Real Estate Fund Class R6	VREQX	NAS CM	Open End	Real Estate Sector Equity (Real Estate)	B-	C+	B	Up	Y	1,000,000
Voya Real Estate Fund Class W	IREWX	NAS CM	Open End	Real Estate Sector Equity (Real Estate)	B-	C+	B	Up	Y	1,000
Voya Retirement Conservative Portfolio Class A	IRCAX	NAS CM	Open End	Cautious Alloc (Asset Alloc)	B	C	A-	Up	Y	0
Voya Retirement Conservative Portfolio Class I	IRCPX	NAS CM	Open End	Cautious Alloc (Asset Alloc)	B	C	A-	Up	Y	0

★ Expanded analysis of this fund is included in Section II.

Min Additional Investment	3-Month Total Return	6-Month Total Return	1-Year Total Return	3-Year Total Return	5-Year Total Return	Dividend Yield (TTM)	Expense Ratio	3-Yr Std Deviation	3-Year Beta	NAV	Total Assets (ML)	%Cash	%Stocks	%Bonds	%Other	Turnover Ratio	Last Bull Market Total Return	Last Bear Market Total Return	Front End Fee (%)	Back End Fee (%)	Inception Date
	TOTAL RETURNS					PERFORMANCE				ASSETS		ASSET ALLOCATION & TURNOVER					BULL & BEAR		FEES		
	7.88	13.39	29.20	40.22	109.01	0.09	1.04	10.9	1	37.12	682.5	1	99	0	0	76	28.76	-14.56	5.75		Jul-97
	7.66	12.96	28.25	37.21	101.98	0	1.79	10.9	1	31.63	682.5	1	99	0	0	76	28.3	-14.82		1.00	Jul-97
	7.97	13.61	29.66	41.71	112.84	0.45	0.66	10.91	1	41.01	682.5	1	99	0	0	76	29.02	-14.44			Jan-02
	7.80	13.23	28.83	39.35	106.87	0	1.29	10.9	1	40.61	682.5	1	99	0	0	76	28.66	-14.62			May-14
	8.00	13.63	29.69	41.68	112.67	0.46	0.58	10.92	1	41.01	682.5	1	99	0	0	76	29.03	-14.45			Jun-15
	7.94	13.54	29.48	41.34	112.15	0.4	0.79	10.91	1	39.98	682.5	1	99	0	0	76	29.03	-14.45			Jul-97
	5.95	7.43	13.07	19.71	76.76	0.74	0.99	11.32	1	17.22	164.5	0	100	0	0	90	27.67	-22.56	5.75		Feb-98
	5.81	7.13	12.53	17.89	72.45	0.38	1.49	11.29	1	15.99	164.5	0	100	0	0	90	27.29	-22.69		1.00	Jun-98
	6.02	7.58	13.34	20.57	79.27	0.9	0.74	11.33	1	17.69	164.5	0	100	0	0	90	27.84	-22.47			Feb-98
	5.95	7.42	13.11	19.67	76.73	0.73	0.99	11.31	1	17.28	164.5	0	100	0	0	90	27.7	-22.57			Aug-01
	5.85	7.22	12.80	18.78	74.50	0.55	1.24	11.32	1	16.95	164.5	0	100	0	0	90	27.49	-22.62			Oct-03
	6.02	7.58	13.42	20.64	79.04	0.91	0.74	11.33	1	17.66	164.5	0	100	0	0	90	27.92	-22.47			Aug-11
	7.64	10.63	24.46	31.98	92.01	0	1.29	10.57	0.94	22.35	1,401	1	99	0	0	88	27.61	-19.96	5.75		Aug-98
	7.44	10.23	23.57	28.98	84.95	0	2.04	10.58	0.94	16.79	1,401	1	99	0	0	88	27.1	-20.24		1.00	Aug-98
	7.72	10.79	24.84	33.28	95.36	0	0.98	10.58	0.94	25.61	1,401	1	99	0	0	88	27.99	-19.82			Aug-98
	7.63	10.63	24.46	31.95	91.98	0	1.29	10.57	0.94	22.25	1,401	1	99	0	0	88	27.64	-19.96			Jun-08
	7.59	10.54	24.17	31.00	89.71	0	1.54	10.58	0.94	21.84	1,401	1	99	0	0	88	27.45	-19.99			Aug-11
	7.72	10.82	24.95	33.65	96.22	0	0.88	10.57	0.94	25.75	1,401	1	99	0	0	88	27.99	-19.82			May-13
	7.71	10.78	24.76	32.97	94.33	0	1.04	10.56	0.94	25.23	1,401	1	99	0	0	88	27.78	-19.86			Jun-09
	7.69	10.69	24.48	31.96	92.23	0	1.16	10.56	0.94	13.44	2,232	1	99	0	0	91	27.63	-20.07			Dec-06
	7.77	10.96	25.08	33.98	97.10	0.13	0.66	10.58	0.94	14.56	2,232	1	99	0	0	91	27.99	-19.87			May-00
	7.66	10.77	24.76	32.93	94.56	0	0.91	10.59	0.94	13.77	2,232	1	99	0	0	91	27.77	-19.96			May-01
	7.72	10.77	24.56	32.38	93.18	0	1.06	10.58	0.94	13.66	2,232	1	99	0	0	91	27.7	-20.07			Feb-09
	7.77	10.96	25.08	33.88	96.95	0.13	0.66	10.59	0.94	14.56	2,232	1	99	0	0	91	27.99	-19.87			Nov-15
	5.86	17.77	44.01	30.93	24.71	0.58	1.59	16.69	1.03	13.36	314.1	2	94	0	0	47			5.75		Oct-11
	5.66	17.41	42.95	28.04	20.12	0.03	2.34	16.69	1.03	13.35	314.1	2	94	0	0	47				1.00	Oct-11
	6.02	18.11	44.52	32.48	26.92	0.83	1.24	16.68	1.03	13.38	314.1	2	94	0	0	47					Oct-11
	5.79	17.66	43.64	29.93	23.13	0.45	1.84	16.73	1.04	13.41	314.1	2	94	0	0	47					Oct-11
	5.93	17.92	44.32	31.99	26.29	0.77	1.34	16.7	1.03	13.36	314.1	2	94	0	0	47					Oct-11
	4.41	9.57	25.23	24.09	41.51	1.48	0.96	11.52	0.92	12.34	519.4	2	98	0	0	39	18.13	-22.86			Jan-11
	3.95	9.71	25.31	27.29	47.38	1.25	0.76	10.47	0.83	10.61	394.5	0	99	0	1	84	17.39	-24.26			Feb-11
	3.95	9.72	25.32	27.28	47.36	1.25	0.76	10.55	0.84	10.61	394.5	0	99	0	1	84	17.39	-24.26			Aug-12
	5.28	13.63	34.92	44.28	76.15	0.43	1.65	11.28	0.94	64.16	213.7	0	99	0	0	64	16.92	-24.72	5.75		Aug-94
	5.10	13.25	34.06	41.51	70.52	0	2.3	11.27	0.94	59.76	213.7	0	99	0	0	64	16.5	-24.95		1.00	Aug-94
	5.39	13.88	35.51	46.23	80.26	0.8	1.22	11.28	0.94	63.89	213.7	0	99	0	0	64	17.2	-24.6			Dec-05
	5.31	13.67	35.08	44.72	77.06	0.52	1.55	11.26	0.94	63.32	213.7	0	99	0	0	64	16.99	-24.68			Jun-08
	5.37	13.83	35.41	45.83	79.27	0.6	1.3	11.29	0.94	77.09	213.7	0	99	0	0	64	17.15	-24.62			Feb-08
	6.43	10.91	21.03	28.37	96.00	0.59	1.32	10.11	0.99	16.76	338.9	2	98	0	0	41	21.24	-20.44			Dec-06
	6.55	11.27	21.73	30.74	102.05	1.09	0.72	10.09	0.99	16.88	338.9	2	98	0	0	41	21.68	-20.24			Apr-05
	6.56	11.20	21.66	30.75	102.07	1.09	0.72	10.09	0.99	16.87	338.9	2	98	0	0	41	21.68	-20.24			May-16
	6.46	11.10	21.38	29.67	99.41	0.87	0.97	10.09	0.99	16.9	338.9	2	98	0	0	41	21.47	-20.32			May-05
	5.48	10.02	14.98	25.85	93.37	1.08	0.84	11.25	1.03	11.91	233.9	1	99	0	0	24					Oct-11
	5.79	11.51	0.00	-3.24	-4.14	1.35	1.25	16.32	0.98	6.47	143.3	1	99	0	0	41	3.24	-12.61			Oct-06
	2.52	2.74	4.78	9.81	49.56	2.48	1.27	13.96	1.03	15.24	871.1	1	99	0	0	53	31.86	-15.95	5.75		Dec-02
	2.29	2.29	3.93	7.49	43.43	1.58	2.02	13.62	1.01	16.3	871.1	1	99	0	0	53	31.28	-16.17		1.00	Jan-03
	2.58	2.88	5.11	11.26	51.42	2.62	0.9	13.47	1	16.85	871.1	1	99	0	0	53	32.02	-15.78			Dec-96
	2.54	2.71	4.75	9.79	49.51	2.51	1.27	13.94	1.03	15.2	871.1	1	99	0	0	53	31.83	-15.92			Sep-04
	2.48	2.58	4.50	8.97	47.80	2.27	1.52	13.96	1.03	15.16	871.1	1	99	0	0	53	31.59	-15.97			Aug-11
	2.67	2.93	5.23	11.51	51.71	2.68	0.86	13.45	0.99	16.86	871.1	1	99	0	0	53	32.02	-15.78			Jul-14
	2.58	2.80	4.99	11.19	49.02	2.17	1.02	12.75	0.94	19.8	871.1	1	99	0	0	53	32.06	-15.85			Dec-07
	1.98	3.78	7.75	11.66	24.05	1.39	0.91	3.51	0.92	9.24	460.6	2	31	65	1	23	8.24	-2.83			Oct-07
	2.06	3.90	7.81	12.22	25.00	1.63	0.66	3.53	0.93	9.38	460.6	2	31	65	1	23	8.45	-2.61			Oct-07

	MARKET			FUND TYPE, CATEGORY & OBJECTIVE	RATINGS					MINIMUMS
Fund Name	Ticker Symbol	Traded On	Fund Type	Category and (Prospectus Objective)	Overall Rating	Reward Rating	Risk Rating	Recent Up/ Downgrade	Open to New Investors	Min Initial Investment
Voya Retirement Growth Portfolio Class A	IRGPX	NAS CM	Open End	Aggressive Alloc (Asset Alloc)	B-	C+	B	Down	Y	0
Voya Retirement Growth Portfolio Class I	IIRGX	NAS CM	Open End	Aggressive Alloc (Asset Alloc)	B-	C+	B	Down	Y	0
Voya Retirement Moderate Growth Portfolio Class A	IRMGX	NAS CM	Open End	Moderate Alloc (Asset Alloc)	B	C+	B+	Up	Y	0
Voya Retirement Moderate Growth Portfolio Class I	IRGMX	NAS CM	Open End	Moderate Alloc (Asset Alloc)	B-	C+	B	Up	Y	0
Voya Retirement Moderate Portfolio Class A	IRMPX	NAS CM	Open End	Cautious Alloc (Asset Alloc)	B	C+	B+	Up	Y	0
Voya Retirement Moderate Portfolio Class I	IRMIX	NAS CM	Open End	Cautious Alloc (Asset Alloc)	B-	C+	B	Up	Y	0
Voya Russell Large Cap Growth Index Portfolio Class A	IRLAX	NAS CM	Open End	US Equity Large Cap Growth (Growth & Income)	B+	A-	B+	Down	Y	0
Voya Russell Large Cap Growth Index Portfolio Class I	IRLNX	NAS CM	Open End	US Equity Large Cap Growth (Growth & Income)	B+	A-	B+	Down	Y	0
Voya Russell Large Cap Growth Index Portfolio Class S	IRLSX	NAS CM	Open End	US Equity Large Cap Growth (Growth & Income)	B+	A-	B+	Down	Y	0
Voya Russell Large Cap Index Portfolio Class A	IRLIX	NAS CM	Open End	US Equity Large Cap Blend (Growth & Income)	B	B	B		Y	0
Voya Russell Large Cap Index Portfolio Class I	IIRLX	NAS CM	Open End	US Equity Large Cap Blend (Growth & Income)	B	B	B+		Y	0
Voya Russell Large Cap Index Portfolio Class S	IRLCX	NAS CM	Open End	US Equity Large Cap Blend (Growth & Income)	B	B	B+		Y	0
Voya Russell Large Cap Index Portfolio Class S2	IRLUX	NAS CM	Open End	US Equity Large Cap Blend (Growth & Income)	B	B	B		Y	0
Voya Russell Large Cap Value Index Portfolio Class A	IRVAX	NAS CM	Open End	US Equity Large Cap Value (Growth & Income)	B-	B-	B	Down	Y	0
Voya Russell Large Cap Value Index Portfolio Class I	IRVIX	NAS CM	Open End	US Equity Large Cap Value (Growth & Income)	B-	B-	B	Down	Y	0
Voya Russell Large Cap Value Index Portfolio Class S	IRVSX	NAS CM	Open End	US Equity Large Cap Value (Growth & Income)	B-	B-	B	Down	Y	0
Voya Russell Mid Cap Growth Index Portfolio Class I	IRGJX	NAS CM	Open End	US Equity Mid Cap (Growth & Income)	B	B	B-	Up	Y	0
Voya Russell Mid Cap Growth Index Portfolio Class S	IRGUX	NAS CM	Open End	US Equity Mid Cap (Growth & Income)	B	B	B-	Up	Y	0
Voya Russell Mid Cap Growth Index Portfolio Class S2	IRGVX	NAS CM	Open End	US Equity Mid Cap (Growth & Income)	B	B	B-	Up	Y	0
Voya Russell Mid Cap Index Portfolio Class A	IRMAX	NAS CM	Open End	US Equity Mid Cap (Growth & Income)	B-	B-	C+	Down	Y	0
Voya Russell Mid Cap Index Portfolio Class I	IIRMX	NAS CM	Open End	US Equity Mid Cap (Growth & Income)	B-	B	B-	Down	Y	0
Voya Russell Mid Cap Index Portfolio Class P2	VRMPX	NAS CM	Open End	US Equity Mid Cap (Growth & Income)	B-	B	B-	Down	Y	0
Voya Russell Mid Cap Index Portfolio Class S	IRMCX	NAS CM	Open End	US Equity Mid Cap (Growth & Income)	B-	B-	C+	Down	Y	0
Voya Russell Mid Cap Index Portfolio Class S2	IRMTX	NAS CM	Open End	US Equity Mid Cap (Growth & Income)	B	B-	B	Up	Y	0
Voya Russell Small Cap Index Portfolio Class A	IRSIX	NAS CM	Open End	US Equity Small Cap (Small Company)	B+	B+	B	Up	Y	0
Voya Russell Small Cap Index Portfolio Class I	IIRSX	NAS CM	Open End	US Equity Small Cap (Small Company)	B+	A-	B	Up	Y	0
Voya Russell Small Cap Index Portfolio Class P2	VRSPX	NAS CM	Open End	US Equity Small Cap (Small Company)	B+	A-	B	Up	Y	0
Voya Russell Small Cap Index Portfolio Class S	IRSSX	NAS CM	Open End	US Equity Small Cap (Small Company)	B+	A-	B	Up	Y	0
Voya Russell Small Cap Index Portfolio Class S2	IRCIX	NAS CM	Open End	US Equity Small Cap (Small Company)	B+	A-	B	Up	Y	0
Voya Russia Fund Class A	LETRX	NAS CM	Open End	Other Equity (Europe Stock)	B	A-	C+	Up	Y	1,000
Voya Russia Fund Class I	IIRFX	NAS CM	Open End	Other Equity (Europe Stock)	B	A-	C+	Up	Y	250,000
Voya Russia Fund Class W	IWRFX	NAS CM	Open End	Other Equity (Europe Stock)	B	A-	C+	Up	Y	1,000
Voya Small Company Fund Class A	AESAX	NAS CM	Open End	US Equity Small Cap (Small Company)	B	B	B	Up	Y	1,000
Voya Small Company Fund Class C	ASCCX	NAS CM	Open End	US Equity Small Cap (Small Company)	B	B	B	Up	Y	1,000
Voya Small Company Fund Class I	AESGX	NAS CM	Open End	US Equity Small Cap (Small Company)	B	B+	B	Up	Y	250,000
Voya Small Company Fund Class O	ISCOX	NAS CM	Open End	US Equity Small Cap (Small Company)	B	B	B	Up	Y	1,000
Voya Small Company Fund Class R	VSMRX	NAS CM	Open End	US Equity Small Cap (Small Company)	B	B	B	Up	Y	0
Voya Small Company Fund Class R6	ISMZX	NAS CM	Open End	US Equity Small Cap (Small Company)	B	B+	B	Up	Y	1,000,000
Voya Small Company Fund Class W	ISMWX	NAS CM	Open End	US Equity Small Cap (Small Company)	B	B+	B	Up	Y	1,000
Voya Small Company Portfolio Class A	IASCX	NAS CM	Open End	US Equity Small Cap (Small Company)	B	B+	B	Up	Y	0
Voya Small Company Portfolio Class I	IVCSX	NAS CM	Open End	US Equity Small Cap (Small Company)	B+	B+	B	Up	Y	0
Voya Small Company Portfolio Class S	IVPSX	NAS CM	Open End	US Equity Small Cap (Small Company)	B	B+	B	Up	Y	0
Voya Small Company Portfolio R6	VSPRX	NAS CM	Open End	US Equity Small Cap (Small Company)	B+	B+	B	Up	Y	0
Voya SmallCap Opportunities Fund Class A	NSPAX	NAS CM	Open End	US Equity Small Cap (Small Company)	B	B	B	Up	Y	1,000
Voya SmallCap Opportunities Fund Class C	NSPCX	NAS CM	Open End	US Equity Small Cap (Small Company)	B	B	B	Up	Y	1,000
Voya SmallCap Opportunities Fund Class I	NSPIX	NAS CM	Open End	US Equity Small Cap (Small Company)	B	B	B	Up	Y	250,000
Voya SmallCap Opportunities Fund Class R	ISORX	NAS CM	Open End	US Equity Small Cap (Small Company)	B	B	B	Up	Y	0
Voya SmallCap Opportunities Fund Class R6	ISOZX	NAS CM	Open End	US Equity Small Cap (Small Company)	B	B	B	Up	Y	1,000,000
Voya SmallCap Opportunities Fund Class W	ISOWX	NAS CM	Open End	US Equity Small Cap (Small Company)	B	B	B	Up	Y	1,000
Voya SmallCap Opportunities Portfolio Class A	ISOPX	NAS CM	Open End	US Equity Small Cap (Small Company)	B	B	B	Up	Y	0
Voya SmallCap Opportunities Portfolio Class I	IVSOX	NAS CM	Open End	US Equity Small Cap (Small Company)	B	B+	B	Up	Y	0
Voya SmallCap Opportunities Portfolio Class S	IVPOX	NAS CM	Open End	US Equity Small Cap (Small Company)	B	B	B	Up	Y	0

★Expanded analysis of this fund is included in Section II.

Min Additional Investment	TOTAL RETURNS: 3-Month Total Return	6-Month Total Return	1-Year Total Return	3-Year Total Return	5-Year Total Return	PERFORMANCE: Dividend Yield (TTM)	Expense Ratio	3-Yr Std Deviation	3-Year Beta	ASSETS: NAV	Total Assets (MIL)	ASSET ALLOCATION & TURNOVER: %Cash	%Stocks	%Bonds	%Other	Turnover Ratio	BULL & BEAR: Last Bull Market Total Return	Last Bear Market Total Return	FEES: Front End Fee (%)	Back End Fee (%)	Inception Date
	4.09	8.00	16.66	22.02	54.93	1.67	1.06	7.63	0.93	13.99	3,145	2	75	23	1	17	16.05	-14.6			Apr-06
	4.22	8.23	17.10	23.47	58.34	2.1	0.64	7.61	0.93	14.07	3,145	2	75	23	1	17	16.28	-14.42			Apr-06
	3.56	6.94	14.55	19.78	48.68	1.69	1.03	6.62	1.06	12.8	2,166	2	62	32	3	16	14.22	-12.02			Apr-06
	3.74	7.21	15.05	21.23	51.61	2.11	0.64	6.58	1.05	12.73	2,166	2	65	32	1	16	14.37	-11.87			Apr-06
	2.87	5.67	11.82	16.05	35.66	1.58	1	5.24	1.16	11.79	1,205	2	51	46	1	15	11.44	-8.23			Apr-06
	2.93	5.84	12.20	17.23	38.11	1.93	0.66	5.27	1.16	11.93	1,205	2	51	46	1	15	11.73	-8.18			Apr-06
	7.94	14.28	30.60	47.02	123.31	0.66	0.93	10.98	1	35.05	709.4	1	99	0	0	19	25.6	-13.17			Jul-15
	8.07	14.54	31.26	49.04	128.65	1	0.43	10.99	1	35.35	709.4	1	99	0	0	19	25.96	-12.99			May-09
	8.02	14.42	30.92	47.92	125.82	0.82	0.68	10.97	1	35.15	709.4	1	99	0	0	19	25.91	-13.11			May-09
	6.57	11.53	21.95	35.36	105.39	1.11	0.87	10.26	1	20.6	911.5	1	99	0	0	5	24.48	-15.74			Mar-08
	6.71	11.82	22.57	37.36	110.62	1.49	0.37	10.28	1	20.99	911.5	1	99	0	0	5	24.99	-15.46			Mar-08
	6.65	11.68	22.26	36.35	107.90	1.29	0.62	10.28	1	20.84	911.5	1	99	0	0	5	24.65	-15.63			Mar-08
	6.58	11.58	22.08	35.78	106.37	1.16	0.77	10.25	1	21.38	911.5	1	99	0	0	5	24.6	-15.65			Feb-09
	5.04	8.59	13.05	23.49	86.19	1.58	0.89	10.61	1	23.13	429.4	0	100	0	0	16	23.39	-18.16			Jul-15
	5.13	8.81	13.45	25.17	90.62	1.97	0.39	10.61	1	23.34	429.4	0	100	0	0	16	23.75	-17.99			May-09
	5.07	8.67	13.19	24.22	88.19	1.76	0.64	10.62	1	23.17	429.4	0	100	0	0	16	23.55	-18.07			May-09
	6.69	12.20	24.66	31.82	103.54	0.83	0.43	11.04	1	35.21	311.2	0	100	0	0	27	27.43	-21.03			May-09
	6.62	12.06	24.35	30.82	101.01	0.61	0.68	11.05	1	35.11	311.2	0	100	0	0	27	27.3	-21.14			May-09
	6.59	12.01	24.18	30.25	99.60	0.52	0.83	11.04	1	35.05	311.2	0	100	0	0	27	27.2	-21.19			May-09
	5.83	9.27	17.38	26.94	95.38	1.01	0.93	10.5	1	15.79	1,954	0	100	0	0	20	25.91	-21.27			Mar-08
	5.92	9.48	17.97	28.82	100.17	1.37	0.43	10.54	1	16.28	1,954	0	100	0	0	20	26.18	-21.06			Mar-08
	6.04	9.68	18.27	29.14	100.68		0.15	10.54	1	16.31	1,954	0	100	0	0	20	26.18	-21.06			May-17
	5.85	9.38	17.66	27.83	97.76	1.16	0.68	10.52	1	16.09	1,954	0	100	0	0	20	26.03	-21.11			Mar-08
	5.86	9.28	17.47	27.32	96.28	1.03	0.83	10.5	1	15.89	1,954	0	100	0	0	20	25.94	-21.18			Feb-09
	3.06	8.75	13.64	29.16	91.41	0.66	0.95	14.11	1	15.15	968.1	1	99	0	0	11	27.16	-25.11			Mar-08
	3.23	9.05	14.26	31.13	96.28	1	0.45	14.15	1	15.66	968.1	1	99	0	0	11	27.47	-24.95			Mar-08
	3.35	9.25	14.47	31.37	96.64		0.15	14.15	1	15.7	968.1	1	99	0	0	11	27.47	-24.95			May-17
	3.19	8.91	13.96	30.14	93.81	0.79	0.7	14.12	1	15.51	968.1	1	99	0	0	11	27.34	-25.03			Mar-08
	3.11	8.85	13.76	29.56	92.49	0.69	0.85	14.14	1	15.24	968.1	1	99	0	0	11	27.23	-25.04			Feb-09
	3.22	19.94	11.70	54.45	2.24	1.46	2.01	21.28	0.73	29.79	87.9	0	96	0	0	34	17.28	-34.93	5.75		Jul-96
	3.30	20.06	11.94	55.40	3.18	1.69	1.74	21.26	0.73	29.88	87.9	0	96	0	0	34	17.56	-34.73			Sep-09
	3.37	20.35	12.25	55.78	3.61	1.65	1.76	21.28	0.73	29.82	87.9	0	96	0	0	34	17.44	-34.9			Aug-11
	3.08	7.44	10.73	33.19	98.04	0	1.36	13.04	0.91	14.24	779.2	2	98	0	0	69	30.07	-23.99	5.75		Apr-94
	2.89	7.04	9.88	30.25	90.72	0	2.11	13.05	0.91	11.25	779.2	2	98	0	0	69	29.38	-24.17		1.00	Jun-98
	3.14	7.62	11.01	34.46	101.01	0.18	1.05	13.07	0.91	16.99	779.2	2	98	0	0	69	30.28	-23.82			Jan-94
	3.07	7.50	10.73	33.22	98.05	0	1.36	13.08	0.91	14.22	779.2	2	98	0	0	69	29.98	-23.94			Jun-08
	3.01	7.32	10.47	32.37	95.92	0.16	1.61	13.06	0.91	14.16	779.2	2	98	0	0	69	29.91	-23.98			Oct-16
	3.15	7.69	11.14	34.80	101.80	0.23	0.97	13.04	0.91	17.01	779.2	2	98	0	0	69	30.28	-23.82			May-13
	3.18	7.62	11.01	34.29	100.51	0.14	1.11	13.06	0.91	16.95	779.2	2	98	0	0	69	30.17	-23.87			Jun-09
	3.10	7.50	10.68	34.15	100.07	0	1.39	13.11	0.91	20.95	748.4	1	99	0	0	71	30.08	-23.83			Dec-08
	3.29	7.84	11.28	36.27	105.28	0.31	0.89	13.12	0.91	22.01	748.4	1	99	0	0	71	30.52	-23.68			Dec-96
	3.23	7.68	11.00	35.23	102.69	0.12	1.14	13.12	0.91	21.46	748.4	1	99	0	0	71	30.35	-23.79			Nov-01
	3.29	7.79	11.23	36.27	105.28	0.31	0.89	13.06	0.91	22.01	748.4	1	99	0	0	71	30.52	-23.68			Nov-15
	3.30	7.64	17.99	29.69	91.77	0	1.41	14.15	0.94	58.43	1,459	3	97	0	0	79	30.94	-22.51	5.75		Jun-95
	3.13	7.29	17.13	26.82	84.73	0	2.16	14.14	0.94	44.83	1,459	3	97	0	0	79	30.4	-22.73		1.00	Jun-95
	3.34	7.77	18.30	30.81	94.69	0	1.12	14.15	0.94	63.8	1,459	3	97	0	0	79	31.26	-22.36			Apr-99
	3.23	7.51	17.70	28.72	89.43	0	1.66	14.14	0.94	57.21	1,459	3	97	0	0	79	30.72	-22.6			Aug-11
	3.40	7.87	18.48	31.40	95.48	0	0.97	14.15	0.94	64.23	1,459	3	97	0	0	79	30.94	-22.51			May-13
	3.34	7.78	18.26	30.67	94.21	0	1.16	14.16	0.94	62.94	1,459	3	97	0	0	79	31.15	-22.41			Dec-07
	3.29	7.71	18.11	30.54	94.67	0	1.38	14.13	0.94	26.04	410.6	2	98	0	0	73	30.95	-22.39			Nov-08
	3.42	8.02	18.72	32.51	99.62	0.07	0.88	14.17	0.94	28.72	410.6	2	98	0	0	73	31.3	-22.22			May-94
	3.37	7.89	18.44	31.55	97.19	0	1.13	14.17	0.94	26.98	410.6	2	98	0	0	73	31.14	-22.28			May-01

Fund Name	Ticker Symbol	Traded On	Fund Type	Category and (Prospectus Objective)	Overall Rating	Reward Rating	Risk Rating	Recent Up/ Downgrade	Open to New Investors	Min Initial Investment
	MARKET			FUND TYPE, CATEGORY & OBJECTIVE	RATINGS				MINIMUMS	
Voya SmallCap Opportunities Portfolio Class S2	ISCTX	NAS CM	Open End	US Equity Small Cap (Small Company)	B	B	B	Up	Y	0
Voya SmallCap Opportunities Portfolio R6	VRSCX	NAS CM	Open End	US Equity Small Cap (Small Company)	B	B+	B	Up	Y	0
Voya SMID Cap Growth Fund Class A	VGROX	NAS CM	Open End	US Equity Mid Cap (Growth)	D	D+	B+		Y	1,000
Voya SMID Cap Growth Fund Class I	VSMDX	NAS CM	Open End	US Equity Mid Cap (Growth)	D	D+	B+		Y	250,000
Voya SMID Cap Growth Fund Class R6	VSGRX	NAS CM	Open End	US Equity Mid Cap (Growth)	D	D+	B+		Y	1,000,000
Voya Solution 2020 Portfolio Class ADV	ISNAX	NAS CM	Open End	Target Date 2000-2020 (Asset Alloc)	B-	C+	B	Up	Y	0
Voya Solution 2020 Portfolio Class I	ISNBX	NAS CM	Open End	Target Date 2000-2020 (Asset Alloc)	B-	C+	B	Up	Y	0
Voya Solution 2020 Portfolio Class S	ISNCX	NAS CM	Open End	Target Date 2000-2020 (Asset Alloc)	B-	C+	B	Up	Y	0
Voya Solution 2020 Portfolio Class S2	ISNDX	NAS CM	Open End	Target Date 2000-2020 (Asset Alloc)	B-	C+	B	Up	Y	0
Voya Solution 2020 Portfolio Class T	ISNEX	NAS CM	Open End	Target Date 2000-2020 (Asset Alloc)	B-	C+	B	Up	Y	0
Voya Solution 2025 Portfolio Class ADV	ISZAX	NAS CM	Open End	Target Date 2021-2045 (Asset Alloc)	B-	C+	B	Up	Y	0
Voya Solution 2025 Portfolio Class I	ISZIX	NAS CM	Open End	Target Date 2021-2045 (Asset Alloc)	B-	C+	B	Up	Y	0
Voya Solution 2025 Portfolio Class S	ISZSX	NAS CM	Open End	Target Date 2021-2045 (Asset Alloc)	B-	C+	B	Up	Y	0
Voya Solution 2025 Portfolio Class S2	ISPBX	NAS CM	Open End	Target Date 2021-2045 (Asset Alloc)	B-	C+	B	Up	Y	0
Voya Solution 2025 Portfolio Class T	ISZTX	NAS CM	Open End	Target Date 2021-2045 (Asset Alloc)	B-	C+	B	Up	Y	0
Voya Solution 2030 Portfolio Class ADV	ISNFX	NAS CM	Open End	Target Date 2021-2045 (Asset Alloc)	B-	C+	B	Down	Y	0
Voya Solution 2030 Portfolio Class I	ISNGX	NAS CM	Open End	Target Date 2021-2045 (Asset Alloc)	B-	B-	B	Down	Y	0
Voya Solution 2030 Portfolio Class S	ISNHX	NAS CM	Open End	Target Date 2021-2045 (Asset Alloc)	B-	C+	B	Down	Y	0
Voya Solution 2030 Portfolio Class S2	ISNIX	NAS CM	Open End	Target Date 2021-2045 (Asset Alloc)	B-	C+	B	Down	Y	0
Voya Solution 2030 Portfolio Class T	ISNJX	NAS CM	Open End	Target Date 2021-2045 (Asset Alloc)	B-	C+	B	Down	Y	0
Voya Solution 2035 Portfolio Class ADV	ISQAX	NAS CM	Open End	Target Date 2021-2045 (Asset Alloc)	B-	B-	B	Down	Y	0
Voya Solution 2035 Portfolio Class I	ISQIX	NAS CM	Open End	Target Date 2021-2045 (Asset Alloc)	B-	B-	B	Down	Y	0
Voya Solution 2035 Portfolio Class S	ISQSX	NAS CM	Open End	Target Date 2021-2045 (Asset Alloc)	B-	B-	B	Down	Y	0
Voya Solution 2035 Portfolio Class S2	ISPCX	NAS CM	Open End	Target Date 2021-2045 (Asset Alloc)	B-	B-	B	Down	Y	0
Voya Solution 2035 Portfolio Class T	ISQTX	NAS CM	Open End	Target Date 2021-2045 (Asset Alloc)	B-	C+	B	Down	Y	0
Voya Solution 2040 Portfolio Class ADV	ISNKX	NAS CM	Open End	Target Date 2021-2045 (Asset Alloc)	B-	B-	B-	Down	Y	0
Voya Solution 2040 Portfolio Class I	ISNLX	NAS CM	Open End	Target Date 2021-2045 (Asset Alloc)	B-	B-	B	Down	Y	0
Voya Solution 2040 Portfolio Class S	ISNMX	NAS CM	Open End	Target Date 2021-2045 (Asset Alloc)	B-	B-	B-	Down	Y	0
Voya Solution 2040 Portfolio Class S2	ISNNX	NAS CM	Open End	Target Date 2021-2045 (Asset Alloc)	B-	B-	B-	Down	Y	0
Voya Solution 2040 Portfolio Class T	ISNOX	NAS CM	Open End	Target Date 2021-2045 (Asset Alloc)	B-	B-	B-	Down	Y	0
Voya Solution 2045 Portfolio Class ADV	ISRAX	NAS CM	Open End	Target Date 2021-2045 (Asset Alloc)	B-	B-	B-	Down	Y	0
Voya Solution 2045 Portfolio Class I	ISRIX	NAS CM	Open End	Target Date 2021-2045 (Asset Alloc)	B-	B-	B-	Down	Y	0
Voya Solution 2045 Portfolio Class S	ISRSX	NAS CM	Open End	Target Date 2021-2045 (Asset Alloc)	B-	B-	B-	Down	Y	0
Voya Solution 2045 Portfolio Class S2	ISPDX	NAS CM	Open End	Target Date 2021-2045 (Asset Alloc)	B-	B-	B-	Down	Y	0
Voya Solution 2045 Portfolio Class T	ISRTX	NAS CM	Open End	Target Date 2021-2045 (Asset Alloc)	B-	B-	B-	Down	Y	0
Voya Solution 2050 Portfolio Class ADV	ISNPX	NAS CM	Open End	Target Date 2046+ (Asset Alloc)	B-	B-	B-	Down	Y	0
Voya Solution 2050 Portfolio Class I	ISNQX	NAS CM	Open End	Target Date 2046+ (Asset Alloc)	B-	B-	B-	Down	Y	0
Voya Solution 2050 Portfolio Class S	ISNRX	NAS CM	Open End	Target Date 2046+ (Asset Alloc)	B-	B-	B-	Down	Y	0
Voya Solution 2050 Portfolio Class S2	ISNSX	NAS CM	Open End	Target Date 2046+ (Asset Alloc)	B-	B-	B-	Down	Y	0
Voya Solution 2050 Portfolio Class T	ISNTX	NAS CM	Open End	Target Date 2046+ (Asset Alloc)	B-	B-	B-	Down	Y	0
Voya Solution 2055 Portfolio Class ADV	IASPX	NAS CM	Open End	Target Date 2046+ (Asset Alloc)	B-	B-	B-	Down	Y	0
Voya Solution 2055 Portfolio Class I	IISPX	NAS CM	Open End	Target Date 2046+ (Asset Alloc)	B-	B-	B-	Down	Y	0
Voya Solution 2055 Portfolio Class S	ISSPX	NAS CM	Open End	Target Date 2046+ (Asset Alloc)	B-	B-	B-	Down	Y	0
Voya Solution 2055 Portfolio Class S2	ITSPX	NAS CM	Open End	Target Date 2046+ (Asset Alloc)	B-	B-	B-	Down	Y	0
Voya Solution 2055 Portfolio Class T	ISTPX	NAS CM	Open End	Target Date 2046+ (Asset Alloc)	B-	B-	B-	Down	Y	0
Voya Solution 2060 Portfolio Class ADV	VSPAX	NAS CM	Open End	Target Date 2046+ (Growth & Income)	C+	C+	B-	Up	Y	0
Voya Solution 2060 Portfolio Class I	VSIPX	NAS CM	Open End	Target Date 2046+ (Growth & Income)	C+	C+	B-	Up	Y	0
Voya Solution 2060 Portfolio Class S	VSPSX	NAS CM	Open End	Target Date 2046+ (Growth & Income)	C+	C+	B-	Up	Y	0
Voya Solution 2060 Portfolio Class S2	VSSPX	NAS CM	Open End	Target Date 2046+ (Growth & Income)	C+	C+	B-	Up	Y	0
Voya Solution 2060 Portfolio Class T	VSPTX	NAS CM	Open End	Target Date 2046+ (Growth & Income)	C+	C+	B-	Up	Y	0
Voya Solution Aggressive Portfolio Class A	IAVAX	NAS CM	Open End	Aggressive Alloc (Aggr Growth)	B-	B-	B-	Down	Y	0
Voya Solution Aggressive Portfolio Class I	IAVIX	NAS CM	Open End	Aggressive Alloc (Aggr Growth)	B-	B-	B-	Down	Y	0

★ Expanded analysis of this fund is included in Section II.

	TOTAL RETURNS					PERFORMANCE				ASSETS		ASSET ALLOCATION & TURNOVER					BULL & BEAR		FEES		
Min Additional Investment	3-Month Total Return	6-Month Total Return	1-Year Total Return	3-Year Total Return	5-Year Total Return	Dividend Yield (TTM)	Expense Ratio	3-Yr Std Deviation	3-Year Beta	NAV	Total Assets (MIL)	%Cash	%Stocks	%Bonds	%Other	Turnover Ratio	Last Bull Market Total Return	Last Bear Market Total Return	Front End Fee (%)	Back End Fee (%)	Inception Date
	3.32	7.77	18.25	30.92	95.68	0	1.28	14.14	0.94	26.39	410.6	2	98	0	0	73	31.03	-22.34			Feb-09
	3.45	8.02	18.73	32.52	99.64	0.07	0.88	14.17	0.94	28.72	410.6	2	98	0	0	73	31.3	-22.22			Nov-15
	5.42	8.63	18.82				1.2			11.16	3.6	4	96	0	0	33			5.75		Dec-16
	5.50	8.70	19.12				0.95			11.19	3.6	4	96	0	0	33					Dec-16
	5.50	8.70	19.12				0.93			11.19	3.6	4	96	0	0	33					Dec-16
	2.95	5.81	12.43	18.87	44.13	1.01	1.22	5.42	0.93	13.23	31.1	4	50	43	2	84					Oct-11
	3.12	6.06	13.01	20.57	47.99	1.26	0.72	5.46	0.94	13.51	31.1	4	50	43	2	84					Oct-11
	3.06	5.98	12.77	19.75	46.15	1.09	0.97	5.37	0.92	13.46	31.1	4	50	43	2	84					Oct-11
	3.01	5.87	12.54	19.16	45.06	1.02	1.12	5.41	0.93	13.32	31.1	4	50	43	2	84					Oct-11
	2.95	5.70	12.22	18.12	43.33	0.84	1.42	5.43	0.93	13.24	31.1	4	50	43	2	84					Oct-11
	3.62	6.99	15.02	20.50	49.30	1.63	1.28	6.67	1.02	11.72	923.6	4	62	32	2	43	17.66	-16.08			Apr-05
	3.79	7.28	15.62	22.28	53.17	2.11	0.78	6.68	1.02	12.04	923.6	4	62	32	2	43	18.03	-15.91			Apr-05
	3.65	7.17	15.29	21.40	51.22	1.87	1.03	6.66	1.02	11.9	923.6	4	62	32	2	43	17.87	-15.95			Apr-05
	3.58	7.03	15.07	20.84	50.12	1.68	1.18	6.65	1.02	11.56	923.6	4	62	32	2	43	17.68	-15.96			May-09
	3.55	6.88	14.78	19.77	47.95	1.33	1.48	6.61	1.01	12.23	923.6	4	62	32	2	43	17.6	-16.13			Aug-05
	4.31	8.21	17.21	23.50	58.96	0.72	1.29	7.6	1.06	15.96	30.6	3	75	19	2	67					Oct-11
	4.46	8.48	17.86	25.43	63.26	0.88	0.79	7.59	1.06	16.36	30.6	3	75	19	2	67					Oct-11
	4.42	8.34	17.58	24.61	60.89	0.78	1.04	7.61	1.06	16.28	30.6	3	75	19	2	67					Oct-11
	4.34	8.25	17.37	23.93	59.38	0.62	1.19	7.63	1.06	16.08	30.6	3	75	19	2	67					Oct-11
	4.29	8.15	17.05	22.64	57.82	0.5	1.49	7.64	1.06	16.02	30.6	3	75	19	2	67					Oct-11
	4.78	9.12	19.21	24.64	60.73	1.25	1.33	8.45	1.08	12.27	927.4	2	83	13	2	44	20.95	-18.9			Apr-05
	4.91	9.36	19.82	26.46	64.73	1.72	0.83	8.46	1.09	12.59	927.4	2	83	13	2	44	21.28	-18.75			Apr-05
	4.88	9.28	19.43	25.52	62.64	1.49	1.08	8.51	1.09	12.45	927.4	2	83	13	2	44	21.12	-18.8			Apr-05
	4.80	9.18	19.27	24.99	61.50	1.39	1.23	8.45	1.08	12	927.4	2	83	13	2	44	20.98	-18.85			May-09
	4.75	9.04	19.02	23.85	59.15	1	1.53	8.44	1.08	12.79	927.4	2	83	13	2	44	20.73	-18.86			Aug-05
	5.03	9.61	20.23	26.57	68.52	0.48	1.33	8.87	1.08	17.11	23.3	2	87	9	1	72					Oct-11
	5.22	9.90	20.84	28.55	73.05	0.7	0.83	8.9	1.08	17.53	23.3	2	87	9	1	72					Oct-11
	5.13	9.75	20.52	27.64	70.45	0.63	1.08	8.89	1.08	17.4	23.3	2	87	9	1	72					Oct-11
	5.07	9.66	20.31	26.77	69.11	0.62	1.23	8.89	1.08	17.18	23.3	2	87	9	1	72					Oct-11
	5.04	9.49	20.04	25.72	66.88	0.37	1.53	8.88	1.08	17.08	23.3	2	87	9	1	72					Oct-11
	5.35	10.14	20.92	25.96	67.68	0.79	1.36	9.27	1.08	12.4	689.9	2	91	6	0	45	21.9	-19.77			Apr-05
	5.45	10.41	21.53	27.90	71.92	1.25	0.86	9.29	1.08	12.75	689.9	2	91	6	0	45	22.1	-19.6			Apr-05
	5.36	10.19	21.24	26.85	69.74	1.03	1.11	9.29	1.08	12.57	689.9	2	91	6	0	45	21.98	-19.67			Apr-05
	5.33	10.12	21.02	26.30	68.46	0.91	1.26	9.28	1.08	12.25	689.9	2	91	6	0	45	21.82	-19.72			May-09
	5.36	10.03	20.68	25.26	66.01	0.71	1.56	9.3	1.08	12.77	689.9	2	91	6	0	45	21.61	-19.78			Aug-05
	5.47	10.32	21.30	27.45	70.99	0.37	1.36	9.25	1.04	17.33	16.7	2	93	4	0	70					Oct-11
	5.63	10.64	21.99	29.61	75.81	0.54	0.86	9.26	1.04	17.81	16.7	2	93	4	0	70					Oct-11
	5.56	10.44	21.63	28.41	73.09	0.47	1.11	9.24	1.03	17.65	16.7	2	93	4	0	70					Oct-11
	5.50	10.38	21.47	27.82	71.51	0.42	1.26	9.22	1.03	17.43	16.7	2	93	4	0	70					Oct-11
	5.39	10.20	21.15	26.57	69.77	0.13	1.56	9.25	1.03	17.39	16.7	2	93	4	0	70					Oct-11
	5.45	10.25	21.40	26.39	68.75	0.67	1.36	9.44	1.03	14.49	180.3	2	93	4	0	58	21.77	-19.76			Mar-10
	5.57	10.61	21.93	28.37	73.06	1.08	0.86	9.43	1.03	14.78	180.3	2	93	4	0	58	22.15	-19.59			Mar-10
	5.55	10.49	21.65	27.39	71.01	0.88	1.11	9.42	1.03	14.62	180.3	2	93	4	0	58	21.91	-19.67			Mar-10
	5.51	10.39	21.51	26.88	69.65	0.75	1.26	9.44	1.03	14.54	180.3	2	93	4	0	58	21.85	-19.73			Mar-10
	5.36	10.15	21.07	25.76	67.35	0.66	1.56	9.45	1.03	14.73	180.3	2	93	4	0	58	21.69	-19.81			Mar-10
	5.44	10.31	21.42			0.33	1.37			12.39	7.9	2	93	4	0	82					Feb-15
	5.64	10.65	22.14			0.47	0.87			12.53	7.9	2	93	4	0	82					Feb-15
	5.53	10.45	21.80			0.46	1.12			12.4	7.9	2	93	4	0	82					Feb-15
	5.44	10.33	21.55			0.35	1.27			12.4	7.9	2	93	4	0	82					Feb-15
	5.38	10.17	21.24			0	1.57			12.33	7.9	2	93	4	0	82					Feb-15
	5.44	10.41	21.62	26.76		0.34	1.39	9.99	1.21	13.55	13.4	2	95	2	0	61					May-13
	5.64	10.70	22.19	28.64		0.7	0.89	9.99	1.21	13.84	13.4	2	95	2	0	61					May-13

	MARKET			FUND TYPE, CATEGORY & OBJECTIVE	RATINGS					MINIMUMS
Fund Name	Ticker Symbol	Traded On	Fund Type	Category and (Prospectus Objective)	Overall Rating	Reward Rating	Risk Rating	Recent Up/ Downgrade	Open to New Investors	Min Initial Investment
Voya Solution Aggressive Portfolio Class R6	VYRMX	NAS CM	Open End	Aggressive Alloc (Aggr Growth)	B-	B-	B-	Down	Y	0
Voya Solution Aggressive Portfolio Class S	IAVSX	NAS CM	Open End	Aggressive Alloc (Aggr Growth)	B-	B-	B-	Down	Y	0
Voya Solution Aggressive Portfolio Class S2	IAVTX	NAS CM	Open End	Aggressive Alloc (Aggr Growth)	B-	B-	B-	Down	Y	0
Voya Solution Balanced Portfolio Class A	ISGAX	NAS CM	Open End	Moderate Alloc (Asset Alloc)	B-	C+	B	Up	Y	0
Voya Solution Balanced Portfolio Class I	ISGJX	NAS CM	Open End	Moderate Alloc (Asset Alloc)	B-	C+	B	Up	Y	0
Voya Solution Balanced Portfolio Class R6	VYRLX	NAS CM	Open End	Moderate Alloc (Asset Alloc)	B-	C+	B	Up	Y	0
Voya Solution Balanced Portfolio Class S	ISGKX	NAS CM	Open End	Moderate Alloc (Asset Alloc)	B-	C+	B	Up	Y	0
Voya Solution Balanced Portfolio Class S2	ISGTX	NAS CM	Open End	Moderate Alloc (Asset Alloc)	B-	C+	B	Up	Y	0
Voya Solution Conservative Portfolio Class A	ICGAX	NAS CM	Open End	Cautious Alloc (Asset Alloc)	B-	C	B	Up	Y	0
Voya Solution Conservative Portfolio Class I	ICGIX	NAS CM	Open End	Cautious Alloc (Asset Alloc)	B	C+	A-	Up	Y	0
Voya Solution Conservative Portfolio Class R6	VYRPX	NAS CM	Open End	Cautious Alloc (Asset Alloc)	B-	C+	B	Up	Y	0
Voya Solution Conservative Portfolio Class S	ICGSX	NAS CM	Open End	Cautious Alloc (Asset Alloc)	B-	C	B	Up	Y	0
Voya Solution Conservative Portfolio Class S2	ICGTX	NAS CM	Open End	Cautious Alloc (Asset Alloc)	B-	C	B	Up	Y	0
Voya Solution Income Portfolio Class ADV	ISWAX	NAS CM	Open End	Target Date 2000-2020 (Asset Alloc)	B-	C+	B	Up	Y	0
Voya Solution Income Portfolio Class I	ISWIX	NAS CM	Open End	Target Date 2000-2020 (Asset Alloc)	B	C+	A-	Up	Y	0
Voya Solution Income Portfolio Class S	ISWSX	NAS CM	Open End	Target Date 2000-2020 (Asset Alloc)	B-	C+	B	Up	Y	0
Voya Solution Income Portfolio Class S2	IJKBX	NAS CM	Open End	Target Date 2000-2020 (Asset Alloc)	B	C+	A-	Up	Y	0
Voya Solution Income Portfolio Class T	ISWTX	NAS CM	Open End	Target Date 2000-2020 (Asset Alloc)	B	C	A-	Up	Y	0
Voya Solution Moderately Aggressive Portfolio Class A	IAGAX	NAS CM	Open End	Aggressive Alloc (Asset Alloc)	B-	C+	B-	Down	Y	0
Voya Solution Moderately Aggressive Portfolio Class I	IAGIX	NAS CM	Open End	Aggressive Alloc (Asset Alloc)	B-	C+	B-	Down	Y	0
Voya Solution Moderately Aggressive Portfolio Class R6	VYROX	NAS CM	Open End	Aggressive Alloc (Asset Alloc)	B-	C+	B-	Down	Y	0
Voya Solution Moderately Aggressive Portfolio Class S	IAGSX	NAS CM	Open End	Aggressive Alloc (Asset Alloc)	B-	C+	B-	Down	Y	0
Voya Solution Moderately Aggressive Portfolio Class S2	IAGTX	NAS CM	Open End	Aggressive Alloc (Asset Alloc)	B-	C+	B-	Down	Y	0
Voya Solution Moderately Conservative Portfolio Class A	ISPGX	NAS CM	Open End	Cautious Alloc (Asset Alloc)	B-	C+	B	Up	Y	0
Voya Solution Moderately Conservative Portfolio Class I	ISPRX	NAS CM	Open End	Cautious Alloc (Asset Alloc)	B-	C+	B	Up	Y	0
Voya Solution Moderately Conservative Portfolio Class R6	VYRNX	NAS CM	Open End	Cautious Alloc (Asset Alloc)	B-	C+	B	Up	Y	0
Voya Solution Moderately Conservative Portfolio Class S	ISPSX	NAS CM	Open End	Cautious Alloc (Asset Alloc)	B-	C+	B	Up	Y	0
Voya Solution Moderately Conservative Portfolio Class S2	ISPTX	NAS CM	Open End	Cautious Alloc (Asset Alloc)	B-	C+	B	Up	Y	0
Voya Strategic Allocation Conservative Portfolio Class I	ISAIX	NAS CM	Open End	Cautious Alloc (Asset Alloc)	B-	C+	B	Up	Y	0
Voya Strategic Allocation Conservative Portfolio Class S	ISCVX	NAS CM	Open End	Cautious Alloc (Asset Alloc)	B-	C+	B	Up	Y	0
Voya Strategic Allocation Growth Portfolio Class I	ISAGX	NAS CM	Open End	Aggressive Alloc (Asset Alloc)	B-	C+	B-	Down	Y	0
Voya Strategic Allocation Growth Portfolio Class S	ISGRX	NAS CM	Open End	Aggressive Alloc (Asset Alloc)	B-	C+	B-	Down	Y	0
Voya Strategic Allocation Moderate Portfolio Class I	IIMDX	NAS CM	Open End	Moderate Alloc (Asset Alloc)	B-	C+	B	Up	Y	0
Voya Strategic Allocation Moderate Portfolio Class S	ISMDX	NAS CM	Open End	Moderate Alloc (Asset Alloc)	B-	C+	B	Up	Y	0
Voya Target In-Retirement Fund Class A	VTRVX	NAS CM	Open End	Target Date 2000-2020 (Asset Alloc)	B-	C+	B	Up	Y	1,000
Voya Target In-Retirement Fund Class I	ISOLX	NAS CM	Open End	Target Date 2000-2020 (Asset Alloc)	B	C+	A-	Up	Y	250,000
Voya Target In-Retirement Fund Class R6	VTRWX	NAS CM	Open End	Target Date 2000-2020 (Asset Alloc)	B	C+	A-	Up	Y	1,000,000
Voya Target Retirement 2020 Fund Class A	VFTRX	NAS CM	Open End	Target Date 2000-2020 (Asset Alloc)	B-	C+	B	Up	Y	1,000
Voya Target Retirement 2020 Fund Class I	IRSJX	NAS CM	Open End	Target Date 2000-2020 (Asset Alloc)	B-	C+	B	Up	Y	250,000
Voya Target Retirement 2020 Fund Class R6	VTRBX	NAS CM	Open End	Target Date 2000-2020 (Asset Alloc)	B-	C+	B	Up	Y	1,000,000
Voya Target Retirement 2025 Fund Class A	VTRCX	NAS CM	Open End	Target Date 2021-2045 (Asset Alloc)	B-	C+	B	Up	Y	1,000
Voya Target Retirement 2025 Fund Class I	IRSLX	NAS CM	Open End	Target Date 2021-2045 (Asset Alloc)	B-	C+	B	Up	Y	250,000
Voya Target Retirement 2025 Fund Class R6	VTRDX	NAS CM	Open End	Target Date 2021-2045 (Asset Alloc)	B-	C+	B	Up	Y	1,000,000
Voya Target Retirement 2030 Fund Class A	VTREX	NAS CM	Open End	Target Date 2021-2045 (Asset Alloc)	B-	C+	B	Down	Y	1,000
Voya Target Retirement 2030 Fund Class I	IRSMX	NAS CM	Open End	Target Date 2021-2045 (Asset Alloc)	B-	C+	B	Down	Y	250,000
Voya Target Retirement 2030 Fund Class R6	VTRFX	NAS CM	Open End	Target Date 2021-2045 (Asset Alloc)	B-	C+	B	Down	Y	1,000,000
Voya Target Retirement 2035 Fund Class A	VTRGX	NAS CM	Open End	Target Date 2021-2045 (Asset Alloc)	B-	C+	B-	Down	Y	1,000
Voya Target Retirement 2035 Fund Class I	IRSNX	NAS CM	Open End	Target Date 2021-2045 (Asset Alloc)	B-	B-	B	Down	Y	250,000
Voya Target Retirement 2035 Fund Class R6	VTRHX	NAS CM	Open End	Target Date 2021-2045 (Asset Alloc)	B-	B-	B	Down	Y	1,000,000
Voya Target Retirement 2040 Fund Class A	VTRJX	NAS CM	Open End	Target Date 2021-2045 (Asset Alloc)	B-	B-	B-	Down	Y	1,000
Voya Target Retirement 2040 Fund Class I	IRSOX	NAS CM	Open End	Target Date 2021-2045 (Asset Alloc)	B-	B-	B-	Down	Y	250,000
Voya Target Retirement 2040 Fund Class R6	VTRKX	NAS CM	Open End	Target Date 2021-2045 (Asset Alloc)	B-	B-	B-	Down	Y	1,000,000

★Expanded analysis of this fund is included in Section II.

Min Additional Investment	TOTAL RETURNS: 3-Month Total Return	6-Month Total Return	1-Year Total Return	3-Year Total Return	5-Year Total Return	PERFORMANCE: Dividend Yield (TTM)	Expense Ratio	3-Yr Std Deviation	3-Year Beta	ASSETS: NAV	Total Assets (MIL)	ASSET ALLOCATION & TURNOVER: %Cash	%Stocks	%Bonds	%Other	Turnover Ratio	BULL & BEAR: Last Bull Market Total Return	Last Bear Market Total Return	FEES: Front End Fee (%)	Back End Fee (%)	Inception Date
	5.56	10.70	22.19	28.53		0.7	0.89	10.01	1.21	13.84	13.4	2	95	2	0	61					May-16
	5.55	10.51	21.91	27.75		0.52	1.14	9.94	1.2	13.69	13.4	2	95	2	0	61					May-13
	5.54	10.48	21.70	27.10		0.53	1.29	9.93	1.2	13.52	13.4	2	95	2	0	61					May-13
	3.60	6.90	14.34	19.85	48.84	1.12	1.3	6.82	1.07	10.07	60.5	4	64	29	2	78	17.86	-15.22			Jul-07
	3.77	7.13	14.88	21.67	52.63	1.61	0.8	6.81	1.07	10.45	60.5	4	64	29	2	78	18.28	-14.98			Jul-07
	3.77	7.13	15.01	21.67	52.63	1.61	0.8	6.81	1.07	10.45	60.5	4	64	29	2	78	18.28	-14.99			May-16
	3.76	7.05	14.75	20.76	50.87	1.42	1.05	6.8	1.07	10.21	60.5	4	64	29	2	78	18.07	-15.21			Jul-07
	3.67	6.93	14.52	20.10	49.71	1.48	1.2	6.87	1.08	10.16	60.5	4	64	29	2	78	17.89	-15.28			Apr-10
	1.65	3.26	7.06	12.17	23.85	1.96	1.16	3.34	0.87	11.06	16.1	5	26	67	2	58	10.88	-8.23			Apr-10
	1.72	3.45	7.50	13.75	26.85	2.43	0.66	3.37	0.87	11.2	16.1	5	26	67	2	58	11.19	-7.97			Apr-10
	1.72	3.45	7.50	13.75	26.85	2.43	0.66	3.36	0.87	11.2	16.1	5	26	67	2	58	11.19	-7.97			May-16
	1.73	3.42	7.30	13.04	25.38	2.12	0.91	3.34	0.86	11.13	16.1	5	26	67	2	58	11.04	-8.11			Apr-10
	1.65	3.30	7.10	12.46	24.38	2.17	1.06	3.36	0.87	11.03	16.1	5	26	67	2	58	10.96	-8.13			Apr-10
	2.15	4.27	9.05	13.17	28.21	1.97	1.18	3.87	1.16	11.84	435.6	5	36	57	2	46	10.73	-8.23			Apr-05
	2.36	4.51	9.65	14.93	31.56	2.5	0.68	3.84	1.15	12.13	435.6	5	36	57	2	46	11.02	-8.05			Apr-05
	2.21	4.41	9.31	14.01	29.91	2.22	0.93	3.86	1.16	12.02	435.6	5	36	57	2	46	10.8	-8.11			Apr-05
	2.26	4.38	9.22	13.56	28.97	2.05	1.08	3.83	1.15	11.72	435.6	5	36	57	2	46	10.71	-8.19			May-09
	2.18	4.13	8.84	12.57	27.09	1	1.38	3.9	1.17	12.6	435.6	5	36	57	2	46	10.62	-8.24			Aug-05
	4.61	8.55	17.79	22.24	59.31	1.09	1.38	8.67	1.05	13.38	715.9	3	81	15	1	52	20.97	-19.15			Apr-10
	4.76	8.92	18.49	24.16	63.48	1.55	0.88	8.7	1.06	13.64	715.9	3	81	15	1	52	21.34	-18.99			Apr-10
	4.76	8.93	18.51	24.08	63.36	1.55	0.88	8.71	1.06	13.63	715.9	3	81	15	1	52	21.34	-18.99			May-16
	4.65	8.66	18.13	23.22	61.36	1.33	1.13	8.69	1.05	13.49	715.9	3	81	15	1	52	21.09	-19.06			Apr-10
	4.58	8.58	17.95	22.63	60.10	1.32	1.28	8.7	1.06	13.46	715.9	3	81	15	1	52	20.99	-19.17			Apr-10
	2.56	4.86	10.08	15.15	33.64	1.77	1.24	4.77	1.03	9.99	31.4	4	43	50	2	65	14.15	-11.39			Jul-07
	2.66	5.06	10.62	16.96	36.93	2.47	0.74	4.74	1.02	10.41	31.4	4	43	50	2	65	14.5	-11.16			Jul-07
	2.66	5.11	10.57	16.80	36.75	2.42	0.74	4.74	1.02	10.4	31.4	4	43	50	2	65	14.49	-11.16			May-16
	2.62	4.95	10.29	15.99	35.29	2.21	0.99	4.72	1.02	10.18	31.4	4	43	50	2	65	14.28	-11.3			Jul-07
	2.54	4.93	10.21	15.50	34.39	2.17	1.14	4.76	1.03	10.07	31.4	4	43	50	2	65	14.22	-11.38			Apr-10
	2.73	5.13	10.53	16.21	40.23	2.47	0.71	4.77	0.19	13.51	69.3	5	43	51	1	76	11.58	-7.91			Jul-95
	2.68	5.01	10.18	15.38	38.47	2.25	0.96	4.8	0.19	13.39	69.3	5	43	51	1	76	11.35	-7.94			Aug-05
	4.70	8.60	17.88	23.74	64.56	1.64	0.77	8.6	0.82	16.03	144.6	3	81	16	0	56	18.55	-16.67			Jul-95
	4.61	8.39	17.56	22.74	62.45	1.45	1.02	8.59	0.81	15.88	144.6	3	81	16	0	56	18.36	-16.74			Aug-05
	3.93	7.09	14.48	20.74	52.52	1.83	0.75	6.72	0.63	14.8	145.9	4	64	31	1	65	14.85	-12.39			Jul-95
	3.88	6.98	14.29	19.80	50.60	1.6	1	6.68	0.63	14.71	145.9	4	64	31	1	65	14.6	-12.42			Jun-05
	2.50	4.56	9.22	13.65	30.86	1.32	0.95	3.9	1.17		3.7	5	36	58	0	74			5.75		Dec-15
	2.45	4.70	9.49	14.60	32.37	1.48	0.7	3.88	1.17	10.98	3.7	2	36	61	1	74					Dec-12
	2.49	4.74	9.51	14.56	32.57	1.5	0.65	3.88	1.17		3.7	2	36	61	1	74					Dec-15
	3.19	6.04	12.27	17.17	42.84	1.12	0.95	5.51	0.96		5.2	2	52	44	1	105			5.75		Dec-15
	3.20	6.14	12.53	18.43	44.73	1.23	0.7	5.46	0.95	11.7	5.2	4	53	42	0	105					Dec-12
	3.35	6.28	12.65	18.19	44.80	1.23	0.65	5.53	0.96		5.2	4	53	42	0	105					Dec-15
	3.93	7.45	15.04	20.31	50.06	1.15	0.95	6.54	1		6.7	4	65	31	0	76			5.75		Dec-15
	3.77	7.28	15.26	21.36	51.62	1.32	0.7	6.57	1.01	12.1	6.7	2	64	33	1	76					Dec-12
	4.00	7.52	15.30	21.21	51.94	1.38	0.65	6.53	1		6.7	2	64	33	1	76					Dec-15
	4.68	8.72	17.10	22.47	57.61	1.19	0.95	7.47	1.04		5.6	2	75	22	1	68			5.75		Dec-15
	4.50	8.52	17.34	23.78	59.43	1.33	0.7	7.48	1.05	12.36	5.6	3	75	21	0	68					Dec-12
	4.75	8.96	17.41	23.53	59.77	1.38	0.65	7.52	1.05		5.6	3	75	21	0	68					Dec-15
	5.10	9.56	18.84	24.07	61.23	1.12	0.95	8.45	1.09		4.8	2	83	14	0	66			5.75		Dec-15
	4.94	9.37	19.15	25.56	63.17	1.3	0.7	8.43	1.08	12.42	4.8	1	83	15	1	66					Dec-12
	5.17	9.71	19.16	25.05	63.32	1.32	0.65	8.41	1.08		4.8	1	83	15	1	66					Dec-15
	5.34	10.10	19.97	25.62	66.93	1.3	0.95	8.85	1.08		2.7	1	87	10	1	43			5.75		Dec-15
	5.11	9.84	20.17	26.87	68.62	1.45	0.7	8.88	1.08	12.68	2.7	2	88	10	0	43					Dec-12
	5.48	10.33	20.28	26.70	69.22	1.51	0.65	8.88	1.08		2.7	2	88	10	0	43					Dec-15

	MARKET		FUND TYPE, CATEGORY & OBJECTIVE		RATINGS				MINIMUMS	
Fund Name	Ticker Symbol	Traded On	Fund Type	Category and (Prospectus Objective)	Overall Rating	Reward Rating	Risk Rating	Recent Up/ Downgrade	Open to New Investors	Min Initial Investment
Voya Target Retirement 2045 Fund Class A	VTRMX	NAS CM	Open End	Target Date 2021-2045 (Asset Alloc)	B-	B-	B-	Down	Y	1,000
Voya Target Retirement 2045 Fund Class I	IRSPX	NAS CM	Open End	Target Date 2021-2045 (Asset Alloc)	B-	B-	B-	Down	Y	250,000
Voya Target Retirement 2045 Fund Class R6	VTRNX	NAS CM	Open End	Target Date 2021-2045 (Asset Alloc)	B-	B-	B-	Down	Y	1,000,000
Voya Target Retirement 2050 Fund Class A	VTROX	NAS CM	Open End	Target Date 2046+ (Asset Alloc)	B-	B-	B-	Down	Y	1,000
Voya Target Retirement 2050 Fund Class I	IRSQX	NAS CM	Open End	Target Date 2046+ (Asset Alloc)	B-	B-	B-	Down	Y	250,000
Voya Target Retirement 2050 Fund Class R6	VTRPX	NAS CM	Open End	Target Date 2046+ (Asset Alloc)	B-	B-	B-	Down	Y	1,000,000
Voya Target Retirement 2055 Fund Class A	VTRQX	NAS CM	Open End	Target Date 2046+ (Asset Alloc)	B-	B-	B-	Down	Y	1,000
Voya Target Retirement 2055 Fund Class I	IRSVX	NAS CM	Open End	Target Date 2046+ (Asset Alloc)	B-	B-	B-	Down	Y	250,000
Voya Target Retirement 2055 Fund Class R6	VTRRX	NAS CM	Open End	Target Date 2046+ (Asset Alloc)	B-	B-	B-	Down	Y	1,000,000
Voya Target Retirement 2060 Fund Class A	VTRSX	NAS CM	Open End	Target Date 2046+ (Asset Alloc)	C-	C	B+	Up	Y	1,000
Voya Target Retirement 2060 Fund Class I	VRSAX	NAS CM	Open End	Target Date 2046+ (Asset Alloc)	C-	C	B+	Up	Y	250,000
Voya Target Retirement 2060 Fund Class R6	VTRUX	NAS CM	Open End	Target Date 2046+ (Asset Alloc)	C-	C	B+	Up	Y	1,000,000
Voya U.S. High Dividend Low Volatility Fund Class A	VHDAX	NAS CM	Open End	US Equity Large Cap Value (Equity-Income)	D	D+	A		Y	1,000
Voya U.S. High Dividend Low Volatility Fund Class I	VHDIX	NAS CM	Open End	US Equity Large Cap Value (Equity-Income)	D	D+	A		Y	250,000
Voya U.S. Stock Index Portfolio Class A	ISIVX	NAS CM	Open End	US Equity Large Cap Blend (Growth)	B	B-	B		Y	0
Voya U.S. Stock Index Portfolio Class I	INGIX	NAS CM	Open End	US Equity Large Cap Blend (Growth)	B	B	B		Y	0
Voya U.S. Stock Index Portfolio Class S	ISJBX	NAS CM	Open End	US Equity Large Cap Blend (Growth)	B	B	B		Y	0
Voya U.S. Stock Index Portfolio Class S2	ISIPX	NAS CM	Open End	US Equity Large Cap Blend (Growth)	B	B-	B		Y	0
Voya U.S. Stock Index Portfolio P2	VPSPX	NAS CM	Open End	US Equity Large Cap Blend (Growth)	B	B	B		Y	0
Vulcan Value Partners Fund	VVPLX	NAS CM	Open End	US Equity Large Cap Blend (Growth)	C+	C+	C+	Down		5,000
Vulcan Value Partners Small Cap Fund	VVPSX	NAS CM	Open End	US Equity Small Cap (Small Company)	B-	B-	B			5,000
VY® American Century Small-Mid Cap Value Portfolio Class A	IASAX	NAS CM	Open End	US Equity Mid Cap (Growth)	B	B	B+		Y	0
VY® American Century Small-Mid Cap Value Portfolio Class I	IACIX	NAS CM	Open End	US Equity Mid Cap (Growth)	B	B	B+		Y	0
VY® American Century Small-Mid Cap Value Portfolio Class S	IASSX	NAS CM	Open End	US Equity Mid Cap (Growth)	B	B	B+		Y	0
VY® American Century Small-Mid Cap Value Portfolio Cls S2	ISMSX	NAS CM	Open End	US Equity Mid Cap (Growth)	B	B	B+		Y	0
VY® Baron Growth Portfolio Class A	IBSAX	NAS CM	Open End	US Equity Mid Cap (Small Company)	B	B	B	Up	Y	0
VY® Baron Growth Portfolio Class I	IBGIX	NAS CM	Open End	US Equity Mid Cap (Small Company)	B	B	B	Up	Y	0
VY® Baron Growth Portfolio Class R6	VYRBX	NAS CM	Open End	US Equity Mid Cap (Small Company)	B	B	B	Up	Y	0
VY® Baron Growth Portfolio Class S	IBSSX	NAS CM	Open End	US Equity Mid Cap (Small Company)	B	B	B	Up	Y	0
VY® Baron Growth Portfolio Class S2	IBCGX	NAS CM	Open End	US Equity Mid Cap (Small Company)	B	B	B	Up	Y	0
VY® Clarion Global Real Estate Portfolio Class A	ICRNX	NAS CM	Open End	Real Estate Sector Equity (Real Estate)	C+	C	B	Up	Y	0
VY® Clarion Global Real Estate Portfolio Class I	IRGIX	NAS CM	Open End	Real Estate Sector Equity (Real Estate)	C+	C	B	Up	Y	0
VY® Clarion Global Real Estate Portfolio Class S	IRGTX	NAS CM	Open End	Real Estate Sector Equity (Real Estate)	C+	C	B	Up	Y	0
VY® Clarion Global Real Estate Portfolio Class S2	IRGSX	NAS CM	Open End	Real Estate Sector Equity (Real Estate)	C+	C	B	Up	Y	0
VY® Clarion Real Estate Portfolio Class A	ICRPX	NAS CM	Open End	Real Estate Sector Equity (Real Estate)	B-	C+	B	Up	Y	0
VY® Clarion Real Estate Portfolio Class I	IVRIX	NAS CM	Open End	Real Estate Sector Equity (Real Estate)	B-	C+	B	Up	Y	0
VY® Clarion Real Estate Portfolio Class S	IVRSX	NAS CM	Open End	Real Estate Sector Equity (Real Estate)	B-	C+	B	Up	Y	0
VY® Clarion Real Estate Portfolio Class S2	IVRTX	NAS CM	Open End	Real Estate Sector Equity (Real Estate)	B-	C+	B	Up	Y	0
VY® Columbia Contrarian Core Portfolio Class A	ISBAX	NAS CM	Open End	US Equity Large Cap Blend (Growth)	B	B-	B		Y	0
VY® Columbia Contrarian Core Portfolio Class I	ISFIX	NAS CM	Open End	US Equity Large Cap Blend (Growth)	B	B-	B+	Down	Y	0
VY® Columbia Contrarian Core Portfolio Class S	ISCSX	NAS CM	Open End	US Equity Large Cap Blend (Growth)	B	B-	B+		Y	0
VY® Columbia Small Cap Value II Portfolio Class A	ICSAX	NAS CM	Open End	US Equity Small Cap (Small Company)	B+	B+	B	Up	Y	0
VY® Columbia Small Cap Value II Portfolio Class I	ICISX	NAS CM	Open End	US Equity Small Cap (Small Company)	B+	A-	B	Up	Y	0
VY® Columbia Small Cap Value II Portfolio Class R6	VYRDX	NAS CM	Open End	US Equity Small Cap (Small Company)	B+	A-	B	Up	Y	0
VY® Columbia Small Cap Value II Portfolio Class S	ICSSX	NAS CM	Open End	US Equity Small Cap (Small Company)	B+	A-	B	Up	Y	0
VY® Columbia Small Cap Value II Portfolio Class S2	ICVPX	NAS CM	Open End	US Equity Small Cap (Small Company)	B+	B+	B	Up	Y	0
VY® Franklin Income Portfolio Class A	IIFAX	NAS CM	Open End	Moderate Alloc (Income)	C+	C+	B-	Down	Y	0
VY® Franklin Income Portfolio Class I	IIFIX	NAS CM	Open End	Moderate Alloc (Income)	B-	C+	B-		Y	0
VY® Franklin Income Portfolio Class S	IIFSX	NAS CM	Open End	Moderate Alloc (Income)	C+	C+	B-	Down	Y	0
VY® Franklin Income Portfolio Class S2	IIFTX	NAS CM	Open End	Moderate Alloc (Income)	C+	C+	B-	Down	Y	0
VY® Invesco Comstock Portfolio Class A	IVKAX	NAS CM	Open End	US Equity Large Cap Value (Growth & Income)	B	B	B-	Up	Y	0
VY® Invesco Comstock Portfolio Class I	IVKIX	NAS CM	Open End	US Equity Large Cap Value (Growth & Income)	B	B	B-	Up	Y	0

★ Expanded analysis of this fund is included in Section II.

	TOTAL RETURNS					PERFORMANCE				ASSETS		ASSET ALLOCATION & TURNOVER					BULL & BEAR		FEES		
Min Additional Investment	3-Month Total Return	6-Month Total Return	1-Year Total Return	3-Year Total Return	5-Year Total Return	Dividend Yield (TTM)	Expense Ratio	3-Yr Std Deviation	3-Year Beta	NAV	Total Assets (MIL)	%Cash	%Stocks	%Bonds	%Other	Turnover Ratio	Last Bull Market Total Return	Last Bear Market Total Return	Front End Fee (%)	Back End Fee (%)	Inception Date
	5.59	10.57	20.59	26.26	69.20	1.12	0.95	9.19	1.07		3.4	1	91	7	1	48			5.75		Dec-15
	5.26	10.12	20.78	27.54	70.96	1.29	0.7	9.19	1.07	12.87	3.4	1	91	7	1	48					Dec-12
	5.57	10.62	20.93	27.36	71.54	1.34	0.65	9.19	1.07		3.4	2	92	6	0	48					Dec-15
	5.58	10.73	20.87	26.46	69.56	1.18	0.95	9.15	1.02		2.2	1	93	5	1	45			5.75		Dec-15
	5.38	10.33	21.01	27.84	71.31	1.36	0.7	9.16	1.02	12.82	2.2	1	93	5	1	45					Dec-12
	5.72	10.86	21.21	27.58	71.92	1.4	0.65	9.17	1.03		2.2	1	93	5	1	45					Dec-15
	5.63	10.67	20.98	26.73	70.26	1.16	0.95	9.37	1.03		2.4	1	93	5	1	44			5.75		Dec-15
	3.41	8.33	18.98	25.51	68.67	1.34	0.7	9.39	1.03	12.92	2.4	1	93	5	1	44					Dec-12
	5.70	10.82	21.34	27.75	72.49	1.38	0.65	9.35	1.02		2.4	1	93	5	1	44					Dec-15
	5.64	10.71	20.91			1.09	0.95				1.6	1	93	5	1	36			5.75		Dec-15
	5.70	10.86	21.31			1.26	0.7				1.6	1	93	5	1	36					Dec-15
	5.70	10.86	21.26			1.3	0.65				1.6	1	93	5	1	36					Dec-15
	6.44	9.68	17.49				0.8			11.47	21.0	1	99	0	0	16			5.75		Dec-16
	6.53	9.86	17.99				0.55			11.51	21.0	1	99	0	0	16					Dec-16
	6.41	10.95	20.81	33.56	103.43	1.18	0.8	10.1	1	15.19	5,089	1	99	0	0	5	24.52	-16.55			May-09
	6.53	11.29	21.46	35.73	108.89	1.57	0.27	10.14	1	15.69	5,089	1	99	0	0	5	24.9	-16.36			May-04
	6.50	11.15	21.22	34.71	106.39	1.42	0.51	10.09	1	15.57	5,089	1	99	0	0	5	24.76	-16.45			Apr-07
	6.47	11.10	21.03	34.19	104.73	1.27	0.67	10.1	1	15.39	5,089	1	99	0	0	5	24.6	-16.45			Aug-07
	6.59	11.35	21.53	35.81	109.01		0.15	10.13	1	15.71	5,089	1	99	0	0	5	24.9	-16.36			May-17
500	3.37	5.41	16.74	16.41	84.87	1.12	1.07	11.73	1.04	20.49	1,331	4	96	0	0	49	30.52	-13.63			Dec-09
500	3.97	3.71	11.45	24.27	81.81	0.29	1.27	12.51	0.76	19.63	1,206	23	77	0	0	52	29.7	-21.28			Dec-09
	3.94	6.98	10.89	33.22	100.64	0.9	1.37	10.92	0.9	12.66	378.0	2	97	0	0	68	23.11	-19.89			May-02
	4.10	7.31	11.44	35.25	105.87	1.21	0.87	10.91	0.89	13.44	378.0	2	97	0	0	68	23.53	-19.72			May-02
	4.00	7.10	11.11	34.13	103.17	1.03	1.12	10.97	0.9	13.25	378.0	2	97	0	0	68	23.27	-19.71			May-02
	4.03	7.12	10.95	33.61	101.79	0.94	1.27	10.92	0.89	12.64	378.0	2	97	0	0	68	23.23	-19.83			Feb-09
	5.12	8.71	27.86	26.38	86.03	0.52	1.48	10.78	0.62	27.88	780.7	3	97	0	0	4	24.02	-19.48			May-02
	5.26	9.00	28.52	28.31	90.85	0.9	0.98	10.78	0.62	30.58	780.7	3	97	0	0	4	24.35	-19.32			May-02
	5.22	9.00	28.51	28.35	90.89	0.9	0.98	10.78	0.62	30.59	780.7	3	97	0	0	4	24.35	-19.32			May-16
	5.20	8.88	28.20	27.39	88.48	0.71	1.23	10.78	0.62	29.31	780.7	3	97	0	0	4	24.24	-19.39			May-02
	5.16	8.80	28.01	26.79	87.07	0.35	1.38	10.79	0.62	28.1	780.7	3	97	0	0	4	24.07	-19.44			Feb-09
	4.74	5.92	10.20	7.09	28.19	3.19	1.49	11.28	1.02	12.17	318.2	0	100	0	0	49	21.8	-18.52			Apr-06
	4.88	6.23	10.77	9.01	32.04	3.78	0.89	11.27	1.02	12.49	318.2	0	100	0	0	49	22.18	-18.28			Jan-06
	4.82	6.04	10.50	8.24	30.35	3.51	1.14	11.26	1.01	12.43	318.2	0	100	0	0	49	22.04	-18.4			Jan-06
	4.78	5.99	10.42	7.72	29.43	3.32	1.29	11.27	1.02	12.52	318.2	0	100	0	0	49	21.94	-18.45			May-06
	2.59	2.76	4.81	9.94	48.68	1.82	1.31	13.52	1.01	36.01	496.2	1	99	0	0	43	31.71	-16.19			Apr-06
	2.77	3.11	5.47	11.96	53.23	2.38	0.71	13.53	1.01	37.76	496.2	1	99	0	0	43	32.16	-15.95			May-03
	2.69	2.95	5.17	11.12	51.27	2.07	0.96	13.53	1.01	37.67	496.2	1	99	0	0	43	31.98	-16.06			Jan-89
	2.63	2.87	5.02	10.62	50.15	1.9	1.11	13.53	1.01	37.44	496.2	1	99	0	0	43	31.89	-16.12			Sep-02
	5.31	9.54	21.32	33.43	106.48	0.8	1.21	10.19	0.98	23.4	325.5	3	97	0	0	53	22.26	-20.1			Dec-01
	5.44	9.85	21.95	35.43	111.91	1.16	0.71	10.22	0.98	24.58	325.5	3	97	0	0	53	22.67	-19.98			Dec-01
	5.38	9.68	21.57	34.40	109.09	0.93	0.96	10.2	0.98	24.08	325.5	3	97	0	0	53	22.45	-20.01			Dec-01
	3.32	9.34	10.64	31.12	96.08	0.16	1.36	13.57	0.94	19.57	219.1	1	99	0	0	61	30.11	-27.17			Dec-06
	3.43	9.59	11.20	33.09	100.96	0.52	0.86	13.58	0.94	20.2	219.1	1	99	0	0	61	30.4	-26.95			Apr-06
	3.48	9.59	11.20	33.07	100.93	0.52	0.86	13.55	0.94	20.21	219.1	1	99	0	0	61	30.4	-26.95			May-16
	3.39	9.41	10.91	32.04	98.44	0.28	1.11	13.58	0.94	20.1	219.1	1	99	0	0	61	30.31	-27.02			May-06
	3.38	9.34	10.77	31.54	97.06	0.18	1.26	13.56	0.94	19.52	219.1	1	99	0	0	61	30.19	-27.15			Feb-09
	1.54	5.17	10.03	17.54	42.33	4.37	1.26	7.78	0.67	11.18	463.1	3	49	37	4	42	12.43	-11.2			Dec-06
	1.56	5.50	10.56	19.29	46.10	4.7	0.66	7.8	0.66	11.65	463.1	3	49	37	4	42	12.92	-10.98			Apr-06
	1.57	5.34	10.32	18.74	44.80	4.46	0.91	7.8	0.67	11.59	463.1	3	49	37	4	42	12.77	-11.07			Apr-06
	1.49	5.26	10.16	18.13	43.59	4.29	1.06	7.84	0.67	11.56	463.1	3	49	37	4	42	12.69	-11.18			May-06
	7.32	13.70	17.31	28.07	92.89	2.03	1.23	13.2	1.23	20.14	503.4	2	98	0	0	18	24.82	-20.39			May-02
	7.53	13.97	17.95	30.13	97.84	2.42	0.73	13.21	1.23	20.32	503.4	2	98	0	0	18	25.08	-20.16			May-02

	MARKET			FUND TYPE, CATEGORY & OBJECTIVE	RATINGS					MINIMUMS
Fund Name	Ticker Symbol	Traded On	Fund Type	Category and (Prospectus Objective)	Overall Rating	Reward Rating	Risk Rating	Recent Up/ Downgrade	Open to New Investors	Min Initial Investment
VY® Invesco Comstock Portfolio Class S	IVKSX	NAS CM	Open End	US Equity Large Cap Value (Growth & Income)	B	B	B-	Up	Y	0
VY® Invesco Equity and Income Portfolio Class A	IUAAX	NAS CM	Open End	Moderate Alloc (Equity-Income)	B	C+	B+	Up	Y	0
VY® Invesco Equity and Income Portfolio Class I	IUAIX	NAS CM	Open End	Moderate Alloc (Equity-Income)	B	C+	B+	Up	Y	0
VY® Invesco Equity and Income Portfolio Class S	IUASX	NAS CM	Open End	Moderate Alloc (Equity-Income)	B	C+	B+	Up	Y	0
VY® Invesco Equity and Income Portfolio Class S2	IVIPX	NAS CM	Open End	Moderate Alloc (Equity-Income)	B	C+	B+	Up	Y	0
VY® Invesco Growth and Income Portfolio Class A	IVGAX	NAS CM	Open End	US Equity Large Cap Value (Growth & Income)	B	B	B	Up	Y	0
VY® Invesco Growth and Income Portfolio Class I	IVGIX	NAS CM	Open End	US Equity Large Cap Value (Growth & Income)	B	B	B	Up	Y	0
VY® Invesco Growth and Income Portfolio Class S	IVGSX	NAS CM	Open End	US Equity Large Cap Value (Growth & Income)	B	B	B	Up	Y	0
VY® Invesco Growth and Income Portfolio Class S2	IVITX	NAS CM	Open End	US Equity Large Cap Value (Growth & Income)	B	B	B	Up	Y	0
VY® JPMorgan Emerging Markets Equity Portfolio Class A	IJEAX	NAS CM	Open End	Emerging Markets Equity (Div Emerging Mkts)	B	B	C	Up	Y	0
VY® JPMorgan Emerging Markets Equity Portfolio Class I	IJEMX	NAS CM	Open End	Emerging Markets Equity (Div Emerging Mkts)	B	B+	C	Up	Y	0
VY® JPMorgan Emerging Markets Equity Portfolio Class S	IJPIX	NAS CM	Open End	Emerging Markets Equity (Div Emerging Mkts)	B	B+	C	Up	Y	0
VY® JPMorgan Emerging Markets Equity Portfolio Class S2	IJPTX	NAS CM	Open End	Emerging Markets Equity (Div Emerging Mkts)	B	B	C	Up	Y	0
VY® JPMorgan Mid Cap Value Portfolio Class A	IJMAX	NAS CM	Open End	US Equity Mid Cap (Growth)	B	B-	B			0
VY® JPMorgan Mid Cap Value Portfolio Class I	IJMIX	NAS CM	Open End	US Equity Mid Cap (Growth)	B	B-	B+			0
VY® JPMorgan Mid Cap Value Portfolio Class S	IJMSX	NAS CM	Open End	US Equity Mid Cap (Growth)	B	B-	B			0
VY® JPMorgan Mid Cap Value Portfolio Class S2	IJPMX	NAS CM	Open End	US Equity Mid Cap (Growth)	B-	B-	B-	Down		0
VY® JPMorgan Small Cap Core Equity Portfolio Class A	IJSAX	NAS CM	Open End	US Equity Small Cap (Small Company)	B+	A-	B	Up	Y	0
VY® JPMorgan Small Cap Core Equity Portfolio Class I	IJSIX	NAS CM	Open End	US Equity Small Cap (Small Company)	B+	A-	B	Up	Y	0
VY® JPMorgan Small Cap Core Equity Portfolio Class R6	VPRSX	NAS CM	Open End	US Equity Small Cap (Small Company)	B+	A-	B	Up	Y	0
VY® JPMorgan Small Cap Core Equity Portfolio Class S	IJSSX	NAS CM	Open End	US Equity Small Cap (Small Company)	B+	A-	B	Up	Y	0
VY® JPMorgan Small Cap Core Equity Portfolio Class S2	IJSTX	NAS CM	Open End	US Equity Small Cap (Small Company)	B+	A-	B	Up	Y	0
VY® Morgan Stanley Global Franchise Portfolio Class A	IGFAX	NAS CM	Open End	Global Equity (World Stock)	B	B	A		Y	0
VY® Morgan Stanley Global Franchise Portfolio Class R6	VPRDX	NAS CM	Open End	Global Equity (World Stock)	B+	B	A	Up	Y	0
VY® Morgan Stanley Global Franchise Portfolio Class S	IVGTX	NAS CM	Open End	Global Equity (World Stock)	B	B	A	Down	Y	0
VY® Morgan Stanley Global Franchise Portfolio Class S2	IGFSX	NAS CM	Open End	Global Equity (World Stock)	B	B	A		Y	0
VY® Oppenheimer Global Portfolio Class A	IGMAX	NAS CM	Open End	Global Equity (World Stock)	B	B+	C+	Up	Y	0
VY® Oppenheimer Global Portfolio Class I	IGMIX	NAS CM	Open End	Global Equity (World Stock)	B+	A-	B	Up	Y	0
VY® Oppenheimer Global Portfolio Class S	IGMSX	NAS CM	Open End	Global Equity (World Stock)	B	B+	C+	Up	Y	0
VY® Oppenheimer Global Portfolio Class S2	IOGPX	NAS CM	Open End	Global Equity (World Stock)	B+	B+	B	Up	Y	0
VY® T. Rowe Price Capital Appreciation Portfolio Class A	ITRAX	NAS CM	Open End	Moderate Alloc (Growth & Income)	B	B-	A-		Y	0
VY® T. Rowe Price Capital Appreciation Portfolio Class I	ITRIX	NAS CM	Open End	Moderate Alloc (Growth & Income)	B	B-	A-	Down	Y	0
VY® T. Rowe Price Capital Appreciation Portfolio Class R6	VPRAX	NAS CM	Open End	Moderate Alloc (Growth & Income)	B	B-	A-	Down	Y	0
VY® T. Rowe Price Capital Appreciation Portfolio Class S	ITCSX	NAS CM	Open End	Moderate Alloc (Growth & Income)	B	B-	A-		Y	0
VY® T. Rowe Price Capital Appreciation Portfolio Class S2	ITCTX	NAS CM	Open End	Moderate Alloc (Growth & Income)	B	B-	A-		Y	0
VY® T. Rowe Price Diversified Mid Cap Growth Port Cls A	IAXAX	NAS CM	Open End	US Equity Mid Cap (Aggr Growth)	B	B	B-	Up	Y	0
VY® T. Rowe Price Diversified Mid Cap Growth Port Cls I	IAXIX	NAS CM	Open End	US Equity Mid Cap (Aggr Growth)	B	B	B-	Up	Y	0
VY® T. Rowe Price Diversified Mid Cap Growth Port Cls R6	VYRIX	NAS CM	Open End	US Equity Mid Cap (Aggr Growth)	B	B	B-	Up	Y	0
VY® T. Rowe Price Diversified Mid Cap Growth Port Cls S	IAXSX	NAS CM	Open End	US Equity Mid Cap (Aggr Growth)	B	B	B-	Up	Y	0
VY® T. Rowe Price Diversified Mid Cap Growth Port Cls S2	IAXTX	NAS CM	Open End	US Equity Mid Cap (Aggr Growth)	B	B	B-	Up	Y	0
VY® T. Rowe Price Equity Income Portfolio Class A	ITEAX	NAS CM	Open End	US Equity Large Cap Value (Equity-Income)	B-	B-	C+	Down	Y	0
VY® T. Rowe Price Equity Income Portfolio Class I	ITEIX	NAS CM	Open End	US Equity Large Cap Value (Equity-Income)	B-	B	C+	Down	Y	0
VY® T. Rowe Price Equity Income Portfolio Class S	IRPSX	NAS CM	Open End	US Equity Large Cap Value (Equity-Income)	B-	B-	C+	Down	Y	0
VY® T. Rowe Price Equity Income Portfolio Class S2	ITETX	NAS CM	Open End	US Equity Large Cap Value (Equity-Income)	B-	B-	C+	Down	Y	0
VY® T. Rowe Price Growth Equity Portfolio Class A	IGEAX	NAS CM	Open End	US Equity Large Cap Growth (Growth)	B+	B+	B	Down	Y	0
VY® T. Rowe Price Growth Equity Portfolio Class I	ITGIX	NAS CM	Open End	US Equity Large Cap Growth (Growth)	B+	B+	B	Down	Y	0
VY® T. Rowe Price Growth Equity Portfolio Class S	ITGSX	NAS CM	Open End	US Equity Large Cap Growth (Growth)	B+	B+	B	Down	Y	0
VY® T. Rowe Price Growth Equity Portfolio Class S2	ITRGX	NAS CM	Open End	US Equity Large Cap Growth (Growth)	B+	B+	B	Down	Y	0
VY® T. Rowe Price International Stock Portfolio Class A	IMIOX	NAS CM	Open End	Global Equity Large Cap (Foreign Stock)	B-	B-	B	Up	Y	0
VY® T. Rowe Price International Stock Portfolio Class I	IMASX	NAS CM	Open End	Global Equity Large Cap (Foreign Stock)	B	B	B	Up	Y	0
VY® T. Rowe Price International Stock Portfolio Class S	IMISX	NAS CM	Open End	Global Equity Large Cap (Foreign Stock)	B	B-	B	Up	Y	0
VY® Templeton Foreign Equity Portfolio Class A	IFTAX	NAS CM	Open End	Global Equity Large Cap (Foreign Stock)	B-	C+	B-	Up	Y	0

★ Expanded analysis of this fund is included in Section II.

Min Additional Investment	TOTAL RETURNS 3-Month Total Return	6-Month Total Return	1-Year Total Return	3-Year Total Return	5-Year Total Return	PERFORMANCE Dividend Yield (TTM)	Expense Ratio	3-Yr Std Deviation	3-Year Beta	ASSETS NAV	Total Assets (MIL)	ASSET ALLOCATION & TURNOVER %Cash	%Stocks	%Bonds	%Other	Turnover Ratio	BULL & BEAR Last Bull Market Total Return	Last Bear Market Total Return	FEES Front End Fee (%)	Back End Fee (%)	Inception Date
	7.43	13.82	17.67	29.08	95.24	2.21	0.98	13.17	1.22	20.3	503.4	2	98	0	0	18	25.05	-20.28			May-02
	3.06	6.09	10.32	22.48	67.87	1.38	1.15	8.4	0.79	46.81	1,684	5	64	21	0	134	17.08	-15.4			Dec-01
	3.19	6.37	10.89	24.35	72.17	2.19	0.65	8.39	0.78	47.51	1,684	5	64	21	0	134	17.38	-15.19			Dec-01
	3.14	6.24	10.61	23.44	70.03	1.72	0.9	8.4	0.79	47.22	1,684	5	64	21	0	134	17.25	-15.32			Dec-01
	3.10	6.16	10.47	22.94	68.86	1.51	1.03	8.39	0.78	46.59	1,684	5	64	21	0	134	17.15	-15.36			Feb-09
	4.44	8.86	13.46	29.90	94.90	1.76	1.24	12.08	1.12	27.94	571.4	2	98	0	0	23	23.54	-20.18			Feb-04
	4.59	9.16	14.13	32.23	100.76	2.17	0.64	12.07	1.12	28.23	571.4	2	98	0	0	23	24.03	-20			Apr-06
	4.56	9.07	13.88	31.29	98.30	1.94	0.89	12.04	1.12	28.43	571.4	2	98	0	0	23	23.81	-20.07			Oct-93
	4.52	8.94	13.67	30.67	96.82	1.78	1.04	12.04	1.12	28.19	571.4	2	98	0	0	23	23.67	-20.1			Sep-02
	7.21	16.54	42.55	34.34	28.43	0.23	1.85	15.19	0.89	20.52	600.8	2	97	0	1	24	19.64	-25.64			Mar-06
	7.38	16.89	43.45	36.78	32.29	0.61	1.25	15.2	0.89	21.52	600.8	2	97	0	1	24	20.04	-25.46			Dec-05
	7.32	16.69	43.11	35.78	30.70	0.41	1.5	15.18	0.89	21.4	600.8	2	97	0	1	24	19.85	-25.53			Feb-98
	7.24	16.63	42.85	35.17	29.69	0.25	1.65	15.17	0.89	21.17	600.8	2	97	0	1	24	19.7	-25.55			Sep-02
	4.67	6.82	13.41	24.29	91.57	0.41	1.37	10.02	0.93	19.78	584.8	3	97	0	0	19	27.15	-17.89			May-02
	4.83	7.09	14.03	26.22	96.44	0.81	0.87	10.02	0.93	20.3	584.8	3	97	0	0	19	27.48	-17.71			May-02
	4.77	6.95	13.72	25.26	93.97	0.6	1.12	10	0.93	20.1	584.8	3	97	0	0	19	27.36	-17.81			May-02
	4.69	6.85	13.51	24.65	92.42	0.49	1.27	10.02	0.93	19.72	584.8	3	97	0	0	19	27.24	-17.81			Feb-09
	3.65	9.11	15.17	32.80	103.94	0.21	1.45	13.04	0.92	20.12	774.4	2	98	0	0	40	29.96	-24.13			Aug-04
	3.84	9.48	15.85	35.20	110.23	0.65	0.85	13.02	0.91	21.35	774.4	2	98	0	0	40	30.5	-24.01			May-04
	3.84	9.49	15.86	34.71	108.40	0.65	0.85	13.07	0.92	21.34	774.4	2	98	0	0	40	30.27	-24.08			May-16
	3.74	9.28	15.55	34.15	107.54	0.43	1.1	13.06	0.92	21.07	774.4	2	98	0	0	40	30.26	-24.08			May-02
	3.73	9.26	15.42	33.58	106.05	0.29	1.25	13	0.91	20.85	774.4	2	98	0	0	40	30.12	-24.12			Sep-02
	7.80	7.85	25.46	38.66	74.41	0.95	1.54	11.26	0.85	16.98	412.3	2	98	0	0	26	17.72	-6.85			Dec-06
	7.99	8.18	26.16	40.68	78.22	1.35	0.94	11.28	0.85	17.96	412.3	2	98	0	0	26	18.03	-6.75			May-16
	7.86	7.96	25.81	40.02	77.38	1.1	1.19	11.27	0.85	17.97	412.3	2	98	0	0	26	18.03	-6.75			May-02
	7.86	7.97	25.69	39.51	76.22	0.96	1.34	11.29	0.85	17.83	412.3	2	98	0	0	26	17.99	-6.82			Sep-02
	7.10	13.48	35.82	39.25	82.89	0.61	1.25	12.98	1.13	21.42	1,738	2	98	0	0	6	17.76	-22.99			May-02
	7.25	13.80	36.48	41.38	87.50	0.98	0.75	12.98	1.13	22.33	1,738	2	98	0	0	6	18.09	-22.93			May-02
	7.16	13.65	36.13	40.30	85.14	0.81	1	12.98	1.13	21.53	1,738	2	98	0	0	6	17.9	-22.96			May-02
	7.09	13.54	35.91	39.69	83.80	0.75	1.15	12.97	1.13	20.97	1,738	2	98	0	0	6	17.9	-23.06			Feb-09
	2.74	5.35	14.71	28.79	77.88	1.08	1.24	6.45	0.6	26.53	6,462	1	62	19	14	69	19.2	-12.92			Dec-03
	2.91	5.68	15.38	31.08	83.27	1.48	0.64	6.44	0.6	27.64	6,462	1	62	19	14	69	19.65	-12.72			May-03
	2.94	5.72	15.46	30.71	81.81	1.48	0.64	6.45	0.6	27.66	6,462	1	62	19	14	69	19.45	-12.8			May-16
	2.83	5.53	15.09	30.12	81.00	1.27	0.89	6.45	0.6	27.65	6,462	1	62	19	14	69	19.45	-12.8			Jan-89
	2.82	5.46	14.96	29.54	79.65	1.14	1.04	6.45	0.6	27.47	6,462	1	62	19	14	69	19.35	-12.86			Sep-02
	5.84	10.42	24.11	33.79	105.30	0.22	1.27	11.47	0.95	10.5	1,016	0	98	0	1	26	27.7	-22.86			Dec-01
	5.95	10.68	24.80	35.87	110.35	0.58	0.77	11.47	0.96	11.56	1,016	0	98	0	1	26	27.99	-22.71			Dec-01
	5.86	10.58	24.80	35.99	110.54	0.58	0.77	11.45	0.95	11.56	1,016	0	98	0	1	26	27.99	-22.71			May-16
	5.88	10.46	24.45	34.78	107.75	0.42	1.02	11.44	0.95	11.15	1,016	0	98	0	1	26	27.8	-22.8			Dec-01
	5.82	10.39	24.27	34.15	106.29	0.31	1.17	11.48	0.96	10.54	1,016	0	98	0	1	26	27.74	-22.83			Feb-09
	5.45	9.92	15.88	25.92	78.78	1.75	1.24	11.14	1.04	14.34	981.5	0	96	0	2	26	23.42	-18.44			Jan-04
	5.57	10.18	16.47	28.22	84.25	2.21	0.64	11.15	1.04	14.59	981.5	0	96	0	2	26	23.83	-18.2			May-03
	5.51	10.12	16.23	27.21	81.94	2	0.89	11.16	1.04	14.62	981.5	0	96	0	2	26	23.59	-18.27			Jan-89
	5.45	9.97	16.07	26.66	80.50	1.9	1.04	11.13	1.04	14.42	981.5	0	96	0	2	26	23.52	-18.32			Sep-02
	5.89	11.52	32.91	47.16	126.30	0	1.23	12.17	1.04	86.22	1,760	0	97	1	1	40	30.54	-16.68			Dec-01
	6.03	11.80	33.58	49.37	132.03	0.05	0.73	12.18	1.04	93.19	1,760	0	97	1	1	40	30.96	-16.51			Nov-97
	5.96	11.67	33.24	48.26	129.14	0	0.98	12.17	1.04	89.69	1,760	0	97	1	1	40	30.75	-16.58			Dec-01
	5.92	11.59	33.05	47.60	127.46	0	1.13	12.17	1.04	87.3	1,760	0	97	1	1	40	30.65	-16.65			Feb-09
	3.39	8.28	27.42	27.29	45.06	0.82	1.38	11.78	0.93	16.16	242.0	1	99	0	1	33	19.48	-24.06			Jan-06
	3.57	8.63	28.20	29.65	49.45	1.28	0.78	11.76	0.93	16.22	242.0	1	99	0	1	33	19.89	-23.81			Apr-05
	3.52	8.49	27.86	28.67	47.56	1.06	1.03	11.8	0.93	16.15	242.0	1	99	0	1	33	19.63	-23.88			May-05
	2.27	7.11	21.65	18.45	33.74	1.49	1.41	12.28	0.96	13.06	638.6	1	99	0	0	15	13.43	-25.08			Dec-06

	MARKET			FUND TYPE, CATEGORY & OBJECTIVE	RATINGS				MINIMUMS	
Fund Name	Ticker Symbol	Traded On	Fund Type	Category and (Prospectus Objective)	Overall Rating	Reward Rating	Risk Rating	Recent Up/ Downgrade	Open to New Investors	Min Initial Investment
VY® Templeton Foreign Equity Portfolio Class I	IFTIX	NAS CM	Open End	Global Equity Large Cap (Foreign Stock)	C+	C+	C	Up	Y	0
VY® Templeton Foreign Equity Portfolio Class S	IFTSX	NAS CM	Open End	Global Equity Large Cap (Foreign Stock)	B-	C+	B-	Up	Y	0
VY® Templeton Foreign Equity Portfolio Class S2	ITFEX	NAS CM	Open End	Global Equity Large Cap (Foreign Stock)	C+	C+	C	Up	Y	0
VY® Templeton Global Growth Portfolio Class A	IGGAX	NAS CM	Open End	Global Equity (World Stock)	C+	C+	C	Up	Y	0
VY® Templeton Global Growth Portfolio Class I	IIGGX	NAS CM	Open End	Global Equity (World Stock)	C+	C+	C	Up	Y	0
VY® Templeton Global Growth Portfolio Class S	ISGGX	NAS CM	Open End	Global Equity (World Stock)	C+	C+	C	Up	Y	0
VY® Templeton Global Growth Portfolio Class S2	ICGGX	NAS CM	Open End	Global Equity (World Stock)	C+	C+	C	Up	Y	0
Waddell & Reed Advisor Accumulative Fund Class A	UNACX	NAS CM	Open End	US Equity Large Cap Growth (Growth)	B	C+	B+	Up	Y	750
Waddell & Reed Advisor Accumulative Fund Class B	WAABX	NAS CM	Open End	US Equity Large Cap Growth (Growth)	B-	C+	B+	Up		750
Waddell & Reed Advisor Accumulative Fund Class C	WAACX	NAS CM	Open End	US Equity Large Cap Growth (Growth)	B-	C+	B+	Up	Y	750
Waddell & Reed Advisor Accumulative Fund Class Y	WAAYX	NAS CM	Open End	US Equity Large Cap Growth (Growth)	B	C+	A-	Up	Y	0
Waddell & Reed Advisor Continental Income Fund Class A	UNCIX	NAS CM	Open End	Moderate Alloc (Balanced)	B-	C+	B+	Down	Y	750
Waddell & Reed Advisor Continental Income Fund Class B	WACBX	NAS CM	Open End	Moderate Alloc (Balanced)	B-	C	B+	Up		750
Waddell & Reed Advisor Continental Income Fund Class C	WACCX	NAS CM	Open End	Moderate Alloc (Balanced)	B-	C	B+	Up	Y	750
Waddell & Reed Advisor Continental Income Fund Class Y	WACYX	NAS CM	Open End	Moderate Alloc (Balanced)	B	C+	B+	Up	Y	0
Waddell & Reed Advisor New Concepts Fund Class A	UNECX	NAS CM	Open End	US Equity Mid Cap (Growth)	B-	B-	C	Up	Y	750
Waddell & Reed Advisor New Concepts Fund Class B	UNEBX	NAS CM	Open End	US Equity Mid Cap (Growth)	C+	B-	C	Down		750
Waddell & Reed Advisor New Concepts Fund Class C	WNCCX	NAS CM	Open End	US Equity Mid Cap (Growth)	C+	B-	C	Down	Y	750
Waddell & Reed Advisor New Concepts Fund Class Y	UNEYX	NAS CM	Open End	US Equity Mid Cap (Growth)	B-	B	C	Up	Y	0
Waddell & Reed Advisor Science and Technology Fund Class A	UNSCX	NAS CM	Open End	Technology Sector Equity (Technology)	B	A-	C	Up	Y	750
Waddell & Reed Advisor Science and Technology Fund Class B	USTBX	NAS CM	Open End	Technology Sector Equity (Technology)	B	B	C	Up		750
Waddell & Reed Advisor Science and Technology Fund Class C	WCSTX	NAS CM	Open End	Technology Sector Equity (Technology)	B	B+	C	Up	Y	750
Waddell & Reed Advisor Science and Technology Fund Class Y	USTFX	NAS CM	Open End	Technology Sector Equity (Technology)	B	A-	C	Up	Y	0
Waddell & Reed Advisor Small Cap Fund Class A	UNSAX	NAS CM	Open End	US Equity Small Cap (Small Company)	B+	B+	B	Up	Y	750
Waddell & Reed Advisor Small Cap Fund Class B	WRSBX	NAS CM	Open End	US Equity Small Cap (Small Company)	B	B+	B	Up		750
Waddell & Reed Advisor Small Cap Fund Class C	WSCCX	NAS CM	Open End	US Equity Small Cap (Small Company)	B	B+	B	Up	Y	750
Waddell & Reed Advisor Small Cap Fund Class Y	WRSYX	NAS CM	Open End	US Equity Small Cap (Small Company)	B+	B+	B	Up	Y	0
Waddell & Reed Advisors Global Growth Fund Class A	UNCGX	NAS CM	Open End	Global Equity (World Stock)	B-	C+	B	Up	Y	750
Waddell & Reed Advisors Global Growth Fund Class B	WAIBX	NAS CM	Open End	Global Equity (World Stock)	B-	C+	B	Up		750
Waddell & Reed Advisors Global Growth Fund Class C	WAICX	NAS CM	Open End	Global Equity (World Stock)	B-	C+	B	Up	Y	750
Waddell & Reed Advisors Global Growth Fund Class Y	WAIYX	NAS CM	Open End	Global Equity (World Stock)	B	B-	B	Up	Y	0
Waddell & Reed Advisors Vanguard Fund Class A	UNVGX	NAS CM	Open End	US Equity Large Cap Growth (Growth)	A-	A-	A-	Up	Y	750
Waddell & Reed Advisors Vanguard Fund Class B	WRVBX	NAS CM	Open End	US Equity Large Cap Growth (Growth)	B+	B+	A-	Up		750
Waddell & Reed Advisors Vanguard Fund Class C	WAVCX	NAS CM	Open End	US Equity Large Cap Growth (Growth)	B+	B+	B	Up	Y	750
Waddell & Reed Advisors Vanguard Fund Class Y	WAVYX	NAS CM	Open End	US Equity Large Cap Growth (Growth)	A-	A-	A-	Up	Y	0
Waddell & Reed Advs Wilshire Global Allocation Fund Cls A	UNASX	NAS CM	Open End	Alloc (Growth & Income)	C+	C	B-	Up	Y	750
Waddell & Reed Advs Wilshire Global Allocation Fund Cls B	WBASX	NAS CM	Open End	Alloc (Growth & Income)	C	C	B-	Up		750
Waddell & Reed Advs Wilshire Global Allocation Fund Cls C	WCASX	NAS CM	Open End	Alloc (Growth & Income)	C	C	B-	Up	Y	750
Waddell & Reed Advs Wilshire Global Allocation Fund Cls Y	WYASX	NAS CM	Open End	Alloc (Growth & Income)	C+	C	B-	Up	Y	0
Walden Asset Management Fund	WSBFX	NAS CM	Open End	Aggressive Alloc (Balanced)	B	C+	B+		Y	100,000
Walden Equity Fund	WSEFX	NAS CM	Open End	US Equity Large Cap Blend (Growth)	B	B	B		Y	100,000
Walden International Equity Fund	WIEFX	NAS CM	Open End	Global Equity Large Cap (Growth)	C	C+	B	Up	Y	1,000,000
Walden Midcap Fund	WAMFX	NAS CM	Open End	US Equity Mid Cap (Growth)	B	B	B+		Y	100,000
Walden Small Cap Fund	WASOX	NAS CM	Open End	US Equity Small Cap (Small Company)	B	B+	B	Up		100,000
Walden SMID Cap Fund	WASMX	NAS CM	Open End	US Equity Small Cap (Growth)	B	B	B		Y	100,000
Walthausen Select Value Fund Class Retail	WSVRX	NAS CM	Open End	US Equity Small Cap (Growth)	B-	B-	B-	Up	Y	2,500
Walthausen Select Value Fund Institutional Class	WSVIX	NAS CM	Open End	US Equity Small Cap (Growth)	B-	B-	B-	Up	Y	100,000
Walthausen Select Value Fund R6 Class	WRSIX	NAS CM	Open End	US Equity Small Cap (Growth)	B-	B-	B-	Up	Y	0
Walthausen Small Cap Value Fund	WSCVX	NAS CM	Open End	US Equity Small Cap (Small Company)	B	B+	C+	Up		2,500
Wanger International	WSCAX	NAS CM	Open End	Global Equity Mid/Small Cap (Foreign Stock)	U	U	U		Y	0
Wanger International Select	WAFFX	NAS CM	Open End	Global Equity Large Cap (Foreign Stock)	U	U	U		Y	0
Wanger Select	WATWX	NAS CM	Open End	US Equity Mid Cap (Growth)	U	U	U		Y	0

★ Expanded analysis of this fund is included in Section II.

	TOTAL RETURNS					PERFORMANCE				ASSETS		ASSET ALLOCATION & TURNOVER					BULL & BEAR		FEES		
Min Additional Investment	3-Month Total Return	6-Month Total Return	1-Year Total Return	3-Year Total Return	5-Year Total Return	Dividend Yield (TTM)	Expense Ratio	3-Yr Std Deviation	3-Year Beta	NAV	Total Assets (MIL)	%Cash	%Stocks	%Bonds	%Other	Turnover Ratio	Last Bull Market Total Return	Last Bear Market Total Return	Front End Fee (%)	Back End Fee (%)	Inception Date
	2.48	7.42	22.34	20.24	37.16	1.91	0.91	12.28	0.96	13.21	638.6	1	99	0	0	15	13.79	-24.91			Jan-06
	2.41	7.28	21.99	19.35	35.37	1.67	1.16	12.25	0.96	13.12	638.6	1	99	0	0	15	13.63	-25.02			Jan-06
	2.35	7.19	21.89	18.88	34.49	1.4	1.31	12.28	0.96	13.05	638.6	1	99	0	0	15	13.43	-24.99			Feb-09
	2.91	6.34	17.75	19.11	53.20	1.34	1.43	12.69	1.16	10.96	183.9	2	97	1	0	23	18.06	-22.55			Dec-06
	2.99	6.72	18.45	21.34	57.92	1.77	0.83	12.73	1.16	11.35	183.9	2	97	1	0	23	18.58	-22.29			Apr-06
	3.06	6.69	18.22	20.48	56.02	1.51	1.08	12.73	1.16	11.45	183.9	2	97	1	0	23	18.4	-22.35			Oct-92
	3.00	6.52	18.04	19.91	54.91	1.4	1.23	12.71	1.16	11.33	183.9	2	97	1	0	23	18.31	-22.44			Sep-02
	4.64	5.57	15.04	22.11	89.64	0.31	1.11	10.58	1	9.9	1,390	0	99	0	1	102	24.96	-17.57	5.75		Oct-40
	4.39	5.00	13.85	17.95	78.63	0	2.29	10.57	1	8.25	1,390	0	99	0	1	102	24.09	-18.1		5.00	Oct-99
	4.38	4.98	13.88	18.55	80.45	0	2.07	10.6	1	8.46	1,390	0	99	0	1	102	24.3	-18.04		1.00	Oct-99
	4.72	5.64	15.29	22.90	91.78	0.4	0.87	10.62	1	9.96	1,390	0	99	0	1	102	25.44	-17.65			Jul-95
	3.84	5.22	11.38	12.70	51.89	1.75	1.12	7.55	0.7	9.64	1,392	0	62	24	2	52	19.86	-12.28	5.75		Jun-70
	3.58	4.61	10.02	8.89	43.48	0.69	2.29	7.52	0.7	9.49	1,392	0	62	24	2	52	19.13	-12.64		5.00	Oct-99
	3.68	4.76	10.36	9.85	45.58	0.94	2.01	7.56	0.7	9.58	1,392	0	62	24	2	52	19.36	-12.66		1.00	Oct-99
	3.94	5.45	11.63	13.57	54.05	1.92	0.88	7.57	0.7	9.65	1,392	0	62	24	2	52	20.17	-12.25			Jan-96
	7.21	12.57	27.06	26.01	80.67	0	1.33	12.18	1.06	11.27	1,716	0	99	0	0	26	25.97	-21.17	5.75		Jun-83
	6.83	11.89	25.55	21.67	70.60	0	2.53	12.1	1.06	7.36	1,716	0	99	0	0	26	25.1	-21.59		5.00	Oct-99
	6.88	12.00	25.71	22.24	72.22	0	2.34	12.13	1.06	7.76	1,716	0	99	0	0	26	25.24	-21.43		1.00	Oct-99
	7.21	12.69	27.28	27.05	83.67	0	1.04	12.09	1.05	12.76	1,716	0	99	0	0	26	26.34	-21.04			Sep-95
	3.54	13.82	32.01	28.48	112.45	0	1.25	15.15	0.91	16.48	3,748	4	96	1	0	22	22.35	-20.9	5.75		May-50
	3.20	13.15	30.51	24.16	100.98	0	2.42	15.14	0.91	10.87	3,748	4	96	1	0	22	21.54	-21.27		5.00	Oct-99
	3.32	13.36	30.76	24.74	102.31	0	2.31	15.12	0.91	11.13	3,748	4	96	1	0	22	21.67	-21.22		1.00	Oct-99
	3.59	13.98	32.30	29.38	115.24	0	1.03	15.12	0.91	18.79	3,748	4	96	1	0	22	22.59	-20.78			Feb-96
	5.44	9.33	23.74	36.86	104.94	0	1.38	13.29	0.86	16.51	941.6	0	95	0	5	53	24.35	-25.28	5.75		Oct-99
	5.07	8.65	22.20	32.15	93.65	0	2.55	13.3	0.86	11.05	941.6	0	95	0	5	53	23.48	-25.63		5.00	Oct-99
	5.13	8.82	22.57	33.31	96.31	0	2.28	13.31	0.86	12.18	941.6	0	95	0	5	53	23.78	-25.52		1.00	Oct-99
	5.48	9.47	24.06	38.24	108.70	0	1.1	13.29	0.86	19.17	941.6	0	95	0	5	53	24.83	-25.17			Oct-99
	5.66	12.07	25.83	25.56	53.78	0	1.42	10.91	0.96	12.83	551.5	0	99	0	1	83	20.46	-22.24	5.75		Jun-70
	5.46	11.35	24.22	20.35	43.33	0	2.86	10.91	0.96	11.04	551.5	0	99	0	1	83	19.26	-22.63		5.00	Oct-99
	5.51	11.57	24.59	21.55	45.65	0	2.57	10.93	0.96	11.69	551.5	0	99	0	1	83	19.72	-22.61		1.00	Oct-99
	5.66	12.17	26.13	26.74	56.38	0	1.06	10.89	0.96	12.92	551.5	0	99	0	1	83	20.8	-22.1			Sep-95
	6.11	14.24	29.15	38.55	114.36	0	1.13	11.33	1.01	11.05	1,720	0	98	0	2	47	27.39	-14.82	5.75		Oct-69
	5.85	13.48	27.62	33.67	101.93	0	2.31	11.39	1.01	7.47	1,720	0	98	0	2	47	26.47	-15.38		5.00	Oct-99
	5.78	13.58	27.80	34.43	104.04	0	2.12	11.34	1	7.75	1,720	0	98	0	2	47	26.65	-15.24		1.00	Oct-99
	6.17	14.34	29.32	39.47	117.30	0	0.87	11.35	1.01	11.89	1,720	0	98	0	2	47	27.6	-14.76			Sep-95
	3.28	7.01	15.91	2.70	25.11	0	1.14	8.52	0.73	8.55	1,704	4	63	31	2	156	22.29	-22.14	5.75		Mar-95
	2.98	6.43	14.67	-0.59	18.90	0	2.01	8.56	0.73	8.06	1,704	4	63	31	1	156	21.66	-22.51		5.00	Oct-99
	3.07	6.61	14.93	0.10	19.96	0	1.91	8.54	0.73	8.14	1,704	4	63	31	1	156	21.84	-22.45		1.00	Oct-99
	3.36	7.17	16.25	3.59	27.05	0	0.83	8.57	0.73	8.64	1,704	4	63	31	1	156	22.55	-22.04			Sep-95
1,000	5.80	7.82	14.87	24.15	65.13	0.91	1	7.02	0.68	17.76	119.8	1	74	25	0	10	17.84	-11.54			Jun-99
1,000	8.17	11.14	20.76	33.15	95.16	0.77	1	9.94	0.96	21.61	197.6	0	100	0	0	10	24.65	-16.43			Jun-99
1,000	3.23	6.67	19.91			1.52	1.15			11.07	38.4	0	100	0	0	5					Jun-15
1,000	7.80	9.94	19.09	31.65	93.96	0.65	1	9.76	0.89	17.24	46.6	2	98	0	0	13	25.91				Aug-11
1,000	5.28	7.98	11.49	31.74	76.62	0.82	1	12.26	0.82	19.41	95.4	1	99	0	0	15	25.36	-21.59			Oct-08
1,000	7.85	9.16	16.94	35.66	87.92	0.77	1	11.67	0.91	16.69	45.9	1	99	0	0	21					Jun-12
100	4.52	8.56	17.12	22.40	82.65	0.16	1.36	13.04	1.02	18.42	85.4	2	98	0	0	62	27.59	-22.86			Dec-10
1,000	4.62	8.80	17.50	23.36	84.94	0.35	1.11	13.04	1.02	18.64	85.4	2	98	0	0	62	27.76	-22.74			Dec-10
	4.63	8.79	17.54	23.40	85.00	0.18	0.99	13.04	1.02	18.7	85.4	2	98	0	0	62	27.76	-22.74			Nov-16
100	1.56	8.07	10.58	25.72	81.06	0.05	1.28	16.97	1.15	23.63	659.4	2	98	0	0	39	28.93	-24.9			Feb-08
	-7.89	-10.32	-9.12	4.60	12.26	1.52	1.05	10.96	0.85		547.7	0	99	0	1	28	17.26	-21.76			May-95
	-7.95	-8.39	-9.41	-2.12	6.66	1.59	1.43	11.11	0.75		16.7	0	99	0	0	61	15.18	-18.72			Feb-99
	-14.34	-13.87	-10.39	16.28	19.28	0.01	0.73	11.91	0.94		122.7	0	100	0	0	18	26.66	-27.78			Feb-99

	MARKET		FUND TYPE, CATEGORY & OBJECTIVE		RATINGS					MINIMUMS
Fund Name	Ticker Symbol	Traded On	Fund Type	Category and (Prospectus Objective)	Overall Rating	Reward Rating	Risk Rating	Recent Up/ Downgrade	Open to New Investors	Min Initial Investment
Wanger USA	WUSAX	NAS CM	Open End	US Equity Small Cap (Aggr Growth)	U	U	U		Y	0
Wasatch Core Growth Fund	WGROX	NAS CM	Open End	US Equity Small Cap (Growth)	A-	A-	B+	Up	Y	2,000
Wasatch Core Growth Fund Institutional Class Shares	WIGRX	NAS CM	Open End	US Equity Small Cap (Growth)	A-	A-	B+	Up	Y	100,000
Wasatch Emerging India Fund® Institutional Class	WIINX	NAS CM	Open End	India Equity (Foreign Stock)	B	B+	B	Down	Y	100,000
Wasatch Emerging India Fund® Investor Class	WAINX	NAS CM	Open End	India Equity (Foreign Stock)	B	B	B	Down	Y	2,000
Wasatch Emerging Mkts Select Fund Inst Cls Shares	WIESX	NAS CM	Open End	Emerging Markets Equity (Div Emerging Mkts)	C	C+	C	Up	Y	100,000
Wasatch Emerging Markets Select Fund Investor Class Shares	WAESX	NAS CM	Open End	Emerging Markets Equity (Div Emerging Mkts)	C	C+	C	Up	Y	2,000
Wasatch Emerging Markets Small Cap Fund® Institutional Cls	WIEMX	NAS CM	Open End	Emerging Markets Equity (Div Emerging Mkts)	C+	C+	C	Up	Y	100,000
Wasatch Emerging Markets Small Cap Fund® Investor Class	WAEMX	NAS CM	Open End	Emerging Markets Equity (Div Emerging Mkts)	C+	C+	C	Up		2,000
Wasatch Frontier Emerg Small Countries Inv Cls Shares	WAFMX	NAS CM	Open End	Emerging Markets Equity (Growth)	C	C-	C	Up		2,000
Wasatch Frontier Emerging Small Countries Fund® Inst Cls	WIFMX	NAS CM	Open End	Emerging Markets Equity (Growth)	C	C-	C	Up	Y	100,000
Wasatch Global Opportunities Fund® Institutional Class	WIGOX	NAS CM	Open End	Global Equity Mid/Small Cap (World Stock)	B	B	B	Up	Y	100,000
Wasatch Global Opportunities Fund® Investor Class	WAGOX	NAS CM	Open End	Global Equity Mid/Small Cap (World Stock)	B	B	B	Up	Y	2,000
Wasatch Global Value Fund™ Institutional Class Shares	WILCX	NAS CM	Open End	US Equity Large Cap Value (Growth)	B-	B-	B		Y	100,000
Wasatch Global Value Fund™ Investor Class Shares	FMIEX	NAS CM	Open End	US Equity Large Cap Value (Growth)	B-	B-	B		Y	2,000
Wasatch International Growth Fund® Institutional Class	WIIGX	NAS CM	Open End	Global Equity Mid/Small Cap (Foreign Stock)	B	B	B+	Up		100,000
Wasatch International Growth Fund® Investor Class	WAIGX	NAS CM	Open End	Global Equity Mid/Small Cap (Foreign Stock)	B	B	B+	Up		2,000
Wasatch Intl Opp Fund® Inst Cls	WIIOX	NAS CM	Open End	Global Equity Mid/Small Cap (Foreign Stock)	B	B	A-	Down		100,000
Wasatch International Opportunities Fund® Investor Class	WAIOX	NAS CM	Open End	Global Equity Mid/Small Cap (Foreign Stock)	B	B	A-	Down	Y	2,000
Wasatch Long/Short Fund Institutional Class Shares	WILSX	NAS CM	Open End	Long/Short Equity (Aggr Growth)	C-	C-	C-	Down	Y	100,000
Wasatch Long/Short Fund Investor Class	FMLSX	NAS CM	Open End	Long/Short Equity (Aggr Growth)	C-	D+	C-	Down	Y	2,000
Wasatch Micro Cap Fund	WMICX	NAS CM	Open End	US Equity Small Cap (Growth & Income)	B+	A	B	Up	Y	2,000
Wasatch Micro Cap Value Fund	WAMVX	NAS CM	Open End	US Equity Small Cap (Growth & Income)	A-	A	B	Up	Y	2,000
Wasatch Small Cap Growth Fund® Institutional Class	WIAEX	NAS CM	Open End	US Equity Small Cap (Small Company)	B	B	B	Up		100,000
Wasatch Small Cap Growth Fund® Investor Class	WAAEX	NAS CM	Open End	US Equity Small Cap (Small Company)	B	B	B	Up		2,000
Wasatch Small Cap Value Fund	WMCVX	NAS CM	Open End	US Equity Small Cap (Small Company)	B+	A-	B	Up	Y	2,000
Wasatch Small Cap Value Fund Institutional Class Shares	WICVX	NAS CM	Open End	US Equity Small Cap (Small Company)	B+	A-	B	Up	Y	100,000
Wasatch Strategic Income Fund	WASIX	NAS CM	Open End	US Equity Mid Cap (Income)	C	C+	C	Down	Y	2,000
Wasatch Ultra Growth Fund	WAMCX	NAS CM	Open End	US Equity Small Cap (Growth)	B+	A	B	Up	Y	2,000
Wasatch World Innovators Fund® Institutional Class	WIGTX	NAS CM	Open End	Global Equity Mid/Small Cap (World Stock)	B+	B+	A-	Up	Y	100,000
Wasatch World Innovators Fund® Investor Class	WAGTX	NAS CM	Open End	Global Equity Mid/Small Cap (World Stock)	B+	B	A-	Up	Y	2,000
WBI Tactical BA Fund Institutional Class	WBBAX	NAS CM	Open End	Moderate Alloc (Balanced)	C+	C	B			250,000
WBI Tactical BA Fund No Load Class	WBADX	NAS CM	Open End	Moderate Alloc (Balanced)	C+	C	B	Up	Y	2,500
WBI Tactical BP Fund Institutional Class	WBBPX	NAS CM	Open End	Moderate Alloc (Balanced)	C+	C	B-	Up		250,000
WBI Tactical BP Fund No Load Class	WBPNX	NAS CM	Open End	Moderate Alloc (Balanced)	C+	C	B-	Up	Y	2,500
WBI Tactical DG Fund Institutional Class	WBDGX	NAS CM	Open End	Moderate Alloc (Growth & Income)	C	C	C+	Down		250,000
WBI Tactical DG Fund No Load Class	WBIDX	NAS CM	Open End	Moderate Alloc (Growth & Income)	C	C	C+	Down	Y	2,500
WCM Alternatives: Event-Driven Fund Institutional Class	WCEIX	NAS CM	Open End	Multialternative (Growth)	B-	C	B+	Up	Y	1,000,000
WCM Alternatives: Event-Driven Fund Investor Class	WCERX	NAS CM	Open End	Multialternative (Growth)	C+	C	B	Up	Y	2,000
WCM Focused Emerging Markets Fund Institutional Class	WCMEX	NAS CM	Open End	Emerging Markets Equity (Div Emerging Mkts)	C+	B-	C	Up	Y	100,000
WCM Focused Emerging Markets Fund Investor Class	WFEMX	NAS CM	Open End	Emerging Markets Equity (Div Emerging Mkts)	C+	B-	C	Up	Y	1,000
WCM Focused Global Growth Fund Institutional Class	WCMGX	NAS CM	Open End	Global Equity (Growth)	B+	B	A-	Up	Y	100,000
WCM Focused Global Growth Fund Investor Class	WFGGX	NAS CM	Open End	Global Equity (Growth)	B+	B	A-	Up	Y	1,000
WCM Focused International Growth Fund Institutional Class	WCMIX	NAS CM	Open End	Global Equity Large Cap (Foreign Stock)	B+	B	A-	Up	Y	100,000
WCM Focused International Growth Fund Investor Class	WCMRX	NAS CM	Open End	Global Equity Large Cap (Foreign Stock)	B	B	B+	Up	Y	1,000
WCM International Small Cap Growth Fund Institutional Cls	WCMSX	NAS CM	Open End	Global Equity Mid/Small Cap (Small Company)	C	C	B	Up	Y	100,000
Weiss Alternative Balanced Risk Fund Class K	WEIKX	NAS CM	Open End	Multialternative (Balanced)	C	D+	A-	Up	Y	2,000,000
Weiss Alternative Balanced Risk Fund Investor Class	WEIZX	NAS CM	Open End	Multialternative (Balanced)	C-	D+	A-	Up	Y	5,000
Weitz Balanced Fund	WBALX	NAS CM	Open End	Cautious Alloc (Balanced)	B-	C+	B	Up	Y	2,500
Weitz Funds Hickory Fund	WEHIX	NAS CM	Open End	US Equity Mid Cap (Growth)	C+	C	B-	Down	Y	2,500
Weitz Partners III Opportunity Fund Institutional Class	WPOPX	NAS CM	Open End	Long/Short Equity (Growth)	C	C-	C	Down	Y	1,000,000
Weitz Partners III Opportunity Fund Investor Class	WPOIX	NAS CM	Open End	Long/Short Equity (Growth)	C	C-	C	Down	Y	2,500

★ Expanded analysis of this fund is included in Section II.

	TOTAL RETURNS					PERFORMANCE				ASSETS		ASSET ALLOCATION & TURNOVER					BULL & BEAR		FEES		
Min Additional Investment	3-Month Total Return	6-Month Total Return	1-Year Total Return	3-Year Total Return	5-Year Total Return	Dividend Yield (TTM)	Expense Ratio	3-Yr Std Deviation	3-Year Beta	NAV	Total Assets (MIL)	%Cash	%Stocks	%Bonds	%Other	Turnover Ratio	Last Bull Market Total Return	Last Bear Market Total Return	Front End Fee (%)	Back End Fee (%)	Inception Date
	-18.56	-19.32	-16.87	10.19	32.49	0	0.96	14.3	0.94		621.5	0	100	0	0	14	28.11	-24.29			May-95
100	7.66	13.77	24.29	42.15	99.76	0	1.21	11.32	0.73	68.35	1,709	2	98	0	0	26	22.67	-14.49			Dec-86
5,000	7.71	13.87	24.47	42.66	100.75	0.04	1.05	11.32	0.73	68.78	1,709	2	98	0	0	26	22.7	-14.49			Jan-12
5,000	12.72	14.39	53.54	62.23	132.34	0	1.5	16.98	0.84	4.49	246.8	1	97	0	2	17	0.94	-8.5			Feb-16
100	12.79	14.48	53.40	61.54	131.35	0	1.75	16.95	0.84	4.47	246.8	1	97	0	2	17	0.93	-8.5			Apr-11
5,000	5.56	9.17	37.97	9.27	11.33	0	1.2	14.02	0.73	11.19	45.2	0	98	0	0	55					Dec-12
100	5.54	8.98	37.65	8.44	9.53	0	1.5	13.94	0.73	11.04	45.2	0	98	0	0	55					Dec-12
5,000	7.66	15.35	38.03	21.44	18.52	0	1.8	13.13	0.79	3.23	641.6	0	98	0	1	58	22.68	-17.86			Feb-16
100	7.69	14.99	38.19	21.06	18.15	0	1.95	13.16	0.79	3.22	641.6	0	98	0	1	58	22.68	-17.87			Oct-07
100	6.17	8.14	21.15	-5.64	13.65	0	2.25	8.14	0.55	2.92	194.2	3	92	0	2	59					Jan-12
5,000	6.52	8.48	21.48	-5.36	13.99	0	2.05	8.12	0.54	2.94	194.2	3	92	0	2	59					Feb-16
5,000	8.34	13.47	38.10	36.31	71.68	0.32	1.35	13.03	0.96	3.67	108.4	0	99	0	1	27	20.88	-22.03			Feb-16
100	8.34	13.48	37.63	35.93	71.22	0.12	1.53	13.02	0.96	3.67	108.4	0	99	0	1	27	20.88	-22.03			Nov-08
5,000	3.11	6.98	11.50	24.93	70.84	1.95	0.95	10.75	1	8.9	179.1	3	97	0	0	44	20.82	-21.06			Jan-12
100	3.07	6.90	11.20	24.38	69.81	1.81	1.1	10.77	1	8.91	179.1	3	97	0	0	44	20.8	-21.06			Sep-96
5,000	4.50	11.62	33.14	40.21	62.84	0.07	1.35	12.23	0.86	34.48	1,518	0	99	0	1	31	23.12	-21.37			Feb-16
100	4.48	11.56	33.00	39.94	62.53	0	1.48	12.24	0.86	34.43	1,518	0	99	0	1	31	23.12	-21.37			Jun-02
5,000	7.30	10.13	27.73	46.23	81.26	0	1.95	10.56	0.69	3.51	508.0	1	96	0	2	59	17.76	-19.99			Feb-16
100	7.36	10.22	27.58	45.62	80.51	0	2.22	10.54	0.69	3.48	508.0	1	96	0	2	59	17.76	-19.99			Jan-05
5,000	3.63	5.38	-1.79	-3.05	15.57	0	1.15	10.95	0.78	13.12	98.7	56	44	0	0	40	14.51	-13.85			Dec-12
100	3.49	5.16	-2.10	-3.85	14.33	0	1.42	10.99	0.78	13.02	98.7	56	44	0	0	40	14.51	-13.85			Aug-03
100	6.96	16.44	36.05	45.38	113.64	0.06	1.67	13.87	0.76	7.64	329.2	0	98	0	2	31	28.63	-24.26			Jun-95
100	6.42	14.66	26.40	52.31	119.84	0.05	1.84	10.39	0.6	3.43	234.3	7	91	0	2	57	22.76	-22.22			Jul-03
5,000	5.95	10.93	21.95	27.10	74.15	0	1.06	13	0.82	43.56	1,724	2	95	0	2	19	26.45	-17.83			Feb-16
100	5.91	10.83	21.73	26.60	73.47	0	1.3	13	0.82	43.36	1,724	2	95	0	2	19	26.45	-17.83			Dec-86
100	6.75	13.16	19.55	42.32	115.83	0.06	1.45	12.52	0.79	7.95	390.8	1	99	0	0	37	23.39	-21.8			Dec-97
5,000	6.89	13.42	19.80	43.06	116.57	0.19	1.26	12.52	0.79	7.99	390.8	1	99	0	0	37	23.06	-21.8			Jan-12
100	3.32	6.79	14.32	8.49	67.94	0.99	1.67	10.88	0.96	12.01	47.9	16	84	0	0	34	22.9	-14.78			Feb-06
100	5.19	12.08	31.55	47.26	108.43	0.43	1.43	15.7	0.98	20.51	116.5	1	95	0	3	34	19.86	-19.62			Aug-92
5,000	8.56	14.84	33.35	44.33	90.37	0	1.55	11.15	0.92	21.49	207.7	16	84	0	1	91	22.84	-13.21			Feb-16
100	8.47	14.67	32.95	43.61	89.42	0	1.78	11.14	0.92	21.35	207.7	16	84	0	1	91	22.84	-13.21			Dec-00
250	2.61	3.27	5.94	3.91	11.93	0.83	1.38	4.77	0.28	10.97	21.1	2	47	47	0	355	10.23	-8.72			Dec-10
250	2.56	3.16	5.59	2.99	10.27	0.56	1.63	4.8	0.29	10.91	21.1	2	47	47	0	355	10.11	-8.73			Dec-10
250	2.88	4.77	8.71	5.34		1.42	1.46	5.42	0.36	10.74	24.2	2	51	43	0	389					Jun-13
250	2.88	4.70	8.46	4.77		1.22	1.71	5.44	0.37	10.73	24.2	2	51	43	0	389					Jun-13
250	6.20	4.78	9.81	2.50	26.12	0.8	1.36	9.17	0.67	11.91	14.8	1	99	0	0	377	22.94	-20.92			Dec-10
250	6.16	4.67	9.52	1.76	24.39	0.51	1.61	9.13	0.66	11.86	14.8	1	99	0	0	377	22.79	-20.92			Dec-10
500	0.51	0.51	4.71	5.36		0.84	1.91	3.85	2.34	10.17	98.0	27	48	18	5	217					Jan-14
	0.51	0.51	4.55	4.67			2.16	3.86	2.51	10.16	98.0	27	48	18	5	217					Mar-17
5,000	7.50	13.38	40.89	28.95		0.56	1.41	15.49	0.83	12.33	28.0	3	97	0	0	50					Jun-13
100	7.62	13.43	40.92	28.76		0.56	1.66	15.45	0.83	12.29	28.0	3	97	0	0	50					Jun-13
5,000	4.90	9.48	27.51	46.10		1.58	1.16	11.41	0.95	14.8	22.3	6	95	0	-1	46					Jun-13
100	4.85	9.30	27.29	45.53		1.58	1.41	11.4	0.95	14.71	22.3	6	95	0	-1	46					Jun-13
5,000	5.14	9.66	31.23	39.04	70.65	0.39	1.03	11.51	0.82	15.74	5,070	4	95	0	0	21	17.61				May-11
100	5.09	9.55	30.88	38.02	68.52	0.23	1.28	11.51	0.82	15.69	5,070	4	95	0	0	21	17.49				Aug-11
5,000	7.69	15.16	42.34			0	1.41			14.13	2.2	4	97	0	-1	59					Nov-15
1,000	2.09	3.69	7.58			0.48	1.63			10.41	57.4	40	24	36	0						Dec-15
1,000	2.09	3.59	7.34				1.98			10.39	57.4	40	24	36	0					1.00	Feb-17
25	1.81	4.39	11.14	13.88	37.82	0.12	0.95	5.19	0.47	14.19	123.2	6	48	45	0	26	15.96	-10.19			Oct-03
25	-1.66	0.97	8.00	9.25	45.30	0	1.25	10.76	0.72	52.32	261.4	19	78	3	0	7	23.99	-18.31			Apr-93
25	-2.38	-0.38	5.44	3.52	45.95	0	1.17	9.64	0.7	14.43	664.5	41	59	0	0	23	20.5	-14.35			Dec-05
25	-2.51	-0.60	4.98	2.14	43.17	0	1.67	9.62	0.7	14.05	664.5	41	59	0	0	23	20.22	-14.35			Aug-11

	MARKET			FUND TYPE, CATEGORY & OBJECTIVE	RATINGS				MINIMUMS	
Fund Name	Ticker Symbol	Traded On	Fund Type	Category and (Prospectus Objective)	Overall Rating	Reward Rating	Risk Rating	Recent Up/ Downgrade	Open to New Investors	Min Initial Investment
Weitz Partners Value Fund Institutional Class	WPVIX	NAS CM	Open End	US Equity Large Cap Blend (Growth)	C+	C+	B-	Down	Y	1,000,000
Weitz Partners Value Fund Investor Class	WPVLX	NAS CM	Open End	US Equity Large Cap Blend (Growth)	C+	C	B-	Down	Y	2,500
Weitz Value Fund Institutional Class	WVAIX	NAS CM	Open End	US Equity Large Cap Growth (Growth)	C+	C+	C+	Down	Y	1,000,000
Weitz Value Fund Investor Class	WVALX	NAS CM	Open End	US Equity Large Cap Growth (Growth)	C+	C+	C+	Down	Y	2,500
Wellington Shields All-Cap Fund Class A	WSCMX	NAS CM	Open End	US Equity Large Cap Growth (Growth)	C+	C	B-	Down	Y	1,000
Wells Fargo Absolute Return Fund - Class A	WARAX	NAS CM	Open End	Alloc (Growth & Income)	C+	C	B	Up	Y	1,000
Wells Fargo Absolute Return Fund - Class Admin	WARDX	NAS CM	Open End	Alloc (Growth & Income)	B-	C	B	Up	Y	1,000,000
Wells Fargo Absolute Return Fund - Class C	WARCX	NAS CM	Open End	Alloc (Growth & Income)	C+	C	B	Up	Y	1,000
Wells Fargo Absolute Return Fund - Class Inst	WABIX	NAS CM	Open End	Alloc (Growth & Income)	B-	C	B	Up	Y	1,000,000
Wells Fargo Absolute Return Fund - Class R	WARHX	NAS CM	Open End	Alloc (Growth & Income)	B-	C	B	Up	Y	0
Wells Fargo Absolute Return Fund - Class R6	WARRX	NAS CM	Open End	Alloc (Growth & Income)	B-	C+	B	Up	Y	0
Wells Fargo Alternative Strategies Fund - Class A	WALTX	NAS CM	Open End	Multialternative (Growth)	C+	C	B	Up	Y	1,000
Wells Fargo Alternative Strategies Fund - Class Admin	WADTX	NAS CM	Open End	Multialternative (Growth)	C+	C	B	Up	Y	1,000,000
Wells Fargo Alternative Strategies Fund - Class C	WACTX	NAS CM	Open End	Multialternative (Growth)	C+	C	B	Up	Y	1,000
Wells Fargo Alternative Strategies Fund - Class Inst	WAITX	NAS CM	Open End	Multialternative (Growth)	B-	C	B+	Up	Y	1,000,000
Wells Fargo Asia Pacific Fund - Class A	WFAAX	NAS CM	Open End	Asia Equity (Pacific Stock)	B	B	B-	Up	Y	1,000
Wells Fargo Asia Pacific Fund - Class Admin	WFADX	NAS CM	Open End	Asia Equity (Pacific Stock)	B	B+	B-	Up	Y	1,000,000
Wells Fargo Asia Pacific Fund - Class C	WFCAX	NAS CM	Open End	Asia Equity (Pacific Stock)	B	B	B-	Up	Y	1,000
Wells Fargo Asia Pacific Fund - Class Inst	WFPIX	NAS CM	Open End	Asia Equity (Pacific Stock)	B	B+	B-	Up	Y	1,000,000
Wells Fargo Asset Allocation Fund - Class A	EAAFX	NAS CM	Open End	Alloc (Multi-Asset Global)	B-	C+	B	Up	Y	1,000
Wells Fargo Asset Allocation Fund - Class Admin	EAIFX	NAS CM	Open End	Alloc (Multi-Asset Global)	B-	C+	B	Up	Y	1,000,000
Wells Fargo Asset Allocation Fund - Class C	EACFX	NAS CM	Open End	Alloc (Multi-Asset Global)	C+	C+	B	Down	Y	1,000
Wells Fargo Asset Allocation Fund - Class Inst	EAAIX	NAS CM	Open End	Alloc (Multi-Asset Global)	B-	C+	B	Up	Y	1,000,000
Wells Fargo Asset Allocation Fund - Class R	EAXFX	NAS CM	Open End	Alloc (Multi-Asset Global)	B-	C+	B	Up	Y	0
Wells Fargo C&B Large Cap Value Fund - Class A	CBEAX	NAS CM	Open End	US Equity Large Cap Value (Growth)	B-	B-	B-	Down	Y	1,000
Wells Fargo C&B Large Cap Value Fund - Class Admin	CBLLX	NAS CM	Open End	US Equity Large Cap Value (Growth)	B-	B-	B-	Down	Y	1,000,000
Wells Fargo C&B Large Cap Value Fund - Class C	CBECX	NAS CM	Open End	US Equity Large Cap Value (Growth)	B-	B-	B-	Down	Y	1,000
Wells Fargo C&B Large Cap Value Fund - Class Inst	CBLSX	NAS CM	Open End	US Equity Large Cap Value (Growth)	B-	B-	B-	Down	Y	1,000,000
Wells Fargo C&B Large Cap Value Fund Class R6	CBEJX	NAS CM	Open End	US Equity Large Cap Value (Growth)	B-	B-	B-	Down	Y	0
Wells Fargo C&B Mid Cap Value Fund - Class A	CBMAX	NAS CM	Open End	US Equity Mid Cap (Growth)	B	B	B		Y	1,000
Wells Fargo C&B Mid Cap Value Fund - Class Admin	CBMIX	NAS CM	Open End	US Equity Mid Cap (Growth)	B	B	B		Y	1,000,000
Wells Fargo C&B Mid Cap Value Fund - Class C	CBMCX	NAS CM	Open End	US Equity Mid Cap (Growth)	B	B	B	Up	Y	1,000
Wells Fargo C&B Mid Cap Value Fund - Class Inst	CBMSX	NAS CM	Open End	US Equity Mid Cap (Growth)	B	B	B		Y	1,000,000
Wells Fargo Capital Growth Fund - Class A	WFCGX	NAS CM	Open End	US Equity Large Cap Growth (Growth)	B+	B+	B	Up	Y	1,000
Wells Fargo Capital Growth Fund - Class Admin	WFCDX	NAS CM	Open End	US Equity Large Cap Growth (Growth)	B+	B+	B+	Up	Y	1,000,000
Wells Fargo Capital Growth Fund - Class C	WFCCX	NAS CM	Open End	US Equity Large Cap Growth (Growth)	B	B	B	Up	Y	1,000
Wells Fargo Capital Growth Fund - Class Inst	WWCIX	NAS CM	Open End	US Equity Large Cap Growth (Growth)	B+	B+	B+	Up	Y	1,000,000
Wells Fargo Capital Growth Fund - Class R6	WFCRX	NAS CM	Open End	US Equity Large Cap Growth (Growth)	B+	B+	B+	Up	Y	0
Wells Fargo Common Stock Fund - Class A	SCSAX	NAS CM	Open End	US Equity Mid Cap (Growth)	B	B	B	Up	Y	1,000
Wells Fargo Common Stock Fund - Class Admin	SCSDX	NAS CM	Open End	US Equity Mid Cap (Growth)	B	B	B	Up	Y	1,000,000
Wells Fargo Common Stock Fund - Class C	STSAX	NAS CM	Open End	US Equity Mid Cap (Growth)	B	B	B	Up	Y	1,000
Wells Fargo Common Stock Fund - Class Inst	SCNSX	NAS CM	Open End	US Equity Mid Cap (Growth)	B	B	B	Up	Y	1,000,000
Wells Fargo Common Stock Fund - Class R6	SCSRX	NAS CM	Open End	US Equity Mid Cap (Growth)	B	B	B	Up	Y	0
Wells Fargo Disciplined U.S. Core Fund - Class A	EVSAX	NAS CM	Open End	US Equity Large Cap Blend (Growth)	B	B	B+		Y	1,000
Wells Fargo Disciplined U.S. Core Fund - Class Admin	EVSYX	NAS CM	Open End	US Equity Large Cap Blend (Growth)	B	B	B+		Y	1,000,000
Wells Fargo Disciplined U.S. Core Fund - Class C	EVSTX	NAS CM	Open End	US Equity Large Cap Blend (Growth)	B	B	B		Y	1,000
Wells Fargo Disciplined U.S. Core Fund - Class Inst	EVSIX	NAS CM	Open End	US Equity Large Cap Blend (Growth)	B	B	B+		Y	1,000,000
Wells Fargo Disciplined U.S. Core Fund - Class R	EVSHX	NAS CM	Open End	US Equity Large Cap Blend (Growth)	B	B	B+		Y	0
Wells Fargo Disciplined U.S. Core Fund - Class R6	EVSRX	NAS CM	Open End	US Equity Large Cap Blend (Growth)	B	B	B+		Y	0
Wells Fargo Discovery Fund - Class A	WFDAX	NAS CM	Open End	US Equity Mid Cap (Growth)	B+	A-	B	Up	Y	1,000
Wells Fargo Discovery Fund - Class Admin	WFDDX	NAS CM	Open End	US Equity Mid Cap (Growth)	B+	A-	B	Up	Y	1,000,000
Wells Fargo Discovery Fund - Class C	WDSCX	NAS CM	Open End	US Equity Mid Cap (Growth)	B	B+	B	Up	Y	1,000

★ Expanded analysis of this fund is included in Section II.

Min Additional Investment	TOTAL RETURNS 3-Month Total Return	6-Month Total Return	1-Year Total Return	3-Year Total Return	5-Year Total Return	PERFORMANCE Dividend Yield (TTM)	Expense Ratio	3-Yr Std Deviation	3-Year Beta	ASSETS NAV	Total Assets (MIL)	ASSET ALLOCATION & TURNOVER %Cash	%Stocks	%Bonds	%Other	Turnover Ratio	BULL & BEAR Last Bull Market Total Return	Last Bear Market Total Return	FEES Front End Fee (%)	Back End Fee (%)	Inception Date
25	1.84	3.90	11.74	7.43	54.65	0	0.99	9.66	0.8	31.71	694.1	14	83	2	2	16	22.48	-16.13			Jul-14
25	1.79	3.80	11.45	6.73	53.51	0	1.27	9.65	0.8	31.46	694.1	14	83	2	2	16	22.48	-16.13			Jun-83
25	3.04	6.50	15.79	13.52	66.92	0	0.99	9.07	0.78	43	813.1	11	86	2	1	24	22.24	-12.09			Jul-14
25	2.99	6.37	15.54	12.81	65.73	0	1.24	9.07	0.78	42.66	813.1	11	86	2	1	24	22.24	-12.09			May-86
500	3.42	7.64	13.66	22.27		0	1.52			12.39	9.1	0	99	0	1	69					Dec-14
100	2.49	4.62	12.11	9.12	21.23	0.69	1.55	6.17	0.53	11.39	5,696	10	40	38	10	2	8.53	-4.02	5.75		Mar-12
	2.57	4.70	12.28	9.62	22.07	0.83	1.44	6.16	0.53	11.42	5,696	10	40	38	10	2	8.53	-4.02			Mar-12
100	2.34	4.22	11.29	6.79	16.72	0	2.3	6.19	0.53	11.21	5,696	10	40	38	10	2	8.02	-4.31		1.00	Mar-12
	2.64	4.76	12.56	10.36	23.64	1.06	1.2	6.16	0.53	11.39	5,696	10	40	38	10	2	8.49	-4.01			Nov-12
	2.42	4.47	11.90	8.96	22.28	0.89	1.8	6.15	0.53	11.37	5,696	10	40	38	10	2	8.33	-4.11			Oct-15
	2.64	4.86	12.77	10.76	24.87	1.13	1.12	6.14	0.53	11.39	5,696	10	40	38	10	2	8.49	-4.01			Oct-14
100	1.23	2.20	6.82	5.50		0	2.21	3.57	0.02	10.64	164.9	55	45	0	0	237			5.75		Apr-14
	1.22	2.28	6.85	6.48		0	2.1	3.6	-0.03	10.75	164.9	55	45	0	0	237					Apr-14
100	0.97	1.87	6.04	3.14		0	2.96	3.58	0.02	10.35	164.9	55	45	0	0	237				1.00	Apr-14
	1.22	2.38	7.07	6.27		0	2	3.58	0.03	10.74	164.9	55	45	0	0	237					Apr-14
100	9.37	15.46	35.69	34.53	59.89	1	1.6	12.87	0.97	15.5	166.1	1	93	0	7	52	17.2	-19.4	5.75		Jul-07
	9.45	15.56	35.86	35.05	61.12	0.86	1.5	12.88	0.97	15.28	166.1	1	93	0	7	52	17.31	-19.36			Jul-10
100	9.19	15.08	34.67	31.57	54.00	0.23	2.35	12.86	0.97	14.72	166.1	1	93	0	7	52	16.69	-19.63		1.00	Jul-07
	9.49	15.70	36.23	36.07	62.70	1.33	1.25	12.85	0.97	15.17	166.1	1	93	0	7	52	17.44	-19.26			Jul-10
100	3.20	6.18	14.80	13.89	28.38	1.39	1.35	6.74	0.22	14.47	3,288	7	55	35	1	0	9.17	-8.23	5.75		Jul-96
	3.19	6.28	14.97	14.51	29.57	1.49	1.19	6.76	0.22	14.63	3,288	7	55	35	1	0	9.27	-8.11			Oct-02
100	2.93	5.77	13.86	11.31	23.67	0.68	2.1	6.73	0.22	14.04	3,288	7	55	35	1	0	8.67	-8.5		1.00	Oct-02
	3.30	6.42	15.21	15.22	31.12	1.73	0.99	6.74	0.23	14.49	3,288	7	55	35	1	0	9.17	-8.23			Nov-12
	3.15	6.16	14.52	13.17	26.87	1.16	1.6	6.73	0.23	14.36	3,288	7	55	35	1	0	8.91	-8.3			Oct-03
100	4.23	6.24	19.03	32.21	103.13	0.47	1.08	10.69	0.99	14.42	391.7	5	94	0	1	89	21.08	-15.57	5.75		Jul-04
	4.23	6.31	19.18	32.78	105.03	0.5	1	10.68	0.99	14.42	391.7	5	94	0	1	89	21.36	-15.47			Jul-04
100	4.05	5.86	18.10	29.25	95.62	0	1.83	10.69	0.99	14.3	391.7	5	94	0	1	89	20.63	-15.75		1.00	Jul-04
	4.27	6.40	19.35	33.63	107.37	0.75	0.75	10.67	0.98	14.44	391.7	5	94	0	1	89	21.31	-15.3			Jul-04
	4.34	6.48	19.51	33.84	107.69	0.76	0.65	10.67	0.98	14.45	391.7	5	94	0	1	89	21.31	-15.3			Nov-16
100	4.71	6.97	14.90	36.79	101.50	0.06	1.25	11.91	1.04	36.72	258.5	6	91	0	2	54	28.05	-19.79	5.75		Jul-04
	4.74	7.03	15.04	37.14	102.22	0.11	1.15	11.9	1.04	37.15	258.5	6	91	0	2	54	28.1	-19.75			Jul-04
100	4.52	6.58	14.06	33.77	94.16	0	2	11.92	1.04	34.62	258.5	6	91	0	2	54	27.52	-20.05		1.00	Jul-04
	4.81	7.14	15.30	38.17	104.83	0.28	0.9	11.92	1.04	36.99	258.5	6	91	0	2	54	28.24	-19.69			Jul-04
100	7.05	12.64	34.41	36.89	108.62	0.1	1.11	11.33	1	16.59	192.3	4	96	0	1	59	29.61	-21.14	5.75		Jul-07
	7.19	12.81	34.66	37.60	110.67	0.12	0.94	11.35	1	18.05	192.3	4	96	0	1	59	29.75	-21.06			Jun-03
100	6.87	12.24	33.42	33.87	101.05	0	1.86	11.29	1	14.37	192.3	4	96	0	1	59	29.03	-21.39		1.00	Jul-07
	7.23	12.92	34.96	38.54	113.34	0.2	0.7	11.32	1	18.69	192.3	4	96	0	1	59	29.88	-20.95			Apr-05
	7.26	12.98	35.10	38.90	114.00	0.23	0.6	11.31	1	18.78	192.3	4	96	0	1	59	29.75	-21.06			Nov-12
100	6.22	11.21	17.55	30.37	82.85	0	1.26	12.64	0.99	22.98	1,297	2	93	0	5	35	27.41	-22.39	5.75		Nov-00
	6.29	11.35	17.71	30.98	84.26	0	1.11	12.64	0.99	23.38	1,297	2	93	0	5	35	27.54	-22.33			Jul-10
100	6.00	10.78	16.64	27.46	76.09	0	2.01	12.62	0.99	17.3	1,297	2	93	0	5	35	26.88	-22.63		1.00	Nov-00
	6.35	11.44	17.97	31.94	86.51	0	0.86	12.64	0.99	23.98	1,297	2	93	0	5	35	27.64	-22.24			Jul-10
	6.33	11.45	18.03	32.03	86.48	0	0.83	12.64	0.99	24.04	1,297	2	93	0	5	35	27.41	-22.39			Jun-13
100	6.37	11.42	20.46	35.92	114.70	0.84	0.85	9.74	0.96	17.08	1,298	1	99	0	0	60	25.84	-16.77	5.75		Feb-90
	6.41	11.54	20.59	36.47	116.17	0.88	0.74	9.74	0.96	17.53	1,298	1	99	0	0	60	26.01	-16.78			Feb-95
100	6.13	11.02	19.52	32.85	106.70	0.57	1.6	9.75	0.96	15.78	1,298	1	99	0	0	60	25.29	-17.08		1.00	Jun-99
	6.45	11.70	20.87	37.46	119.04	1.13	0.48	9.75	0.96	17.32	1,298	1	99	0	0	60	26.13	-16.63			Jul-10
	6.28	11.34	20.17	34.96	112.11	1.15	1.1	9.74	0.96	17.28	1,298	1	99	0	0	60	25.66	-16.86			Sep-15
	6.46	11.72	20.96	37.27	116.83	1.16	0.42	9.78	0.96	17.49	1,298	1	99	0	0	60	25.84	-16.77			Sep-15
100	6.07	11.77	29.03	35.44	98.98	0	1.2	12.38	0.9	32.57	2,600	2	94	0	4	73	33.96	-22.85	5.75		Jul-07
	6.10	11.83	29.14	35.79	99.99	0	1.12	12.37	0.9	33.61	2,600	2	94	0	4	73	34	-22.77			Apr-05
100	5.89	11.39	28.10	32.44	91.68	0	1.95	12.36	0.9	28.82	2,600	2	94	0	4	73	33.38	-23.09		1.00	Jul-07

	MARKET		FUND TYPE, CATEGORY & OBJECTIVE		RATINGS					MINIMUMS
Fund Name	Ticker Symbol	Traded On	Fund Type	Category and (Prospectus Objective)	Overall Rating	Reward Rating	Risk Rating	Recent Up/ Downgrade	Open to New Investors	Min Initial Investment
Wells Fargo Discovery Fund - Class Inst	WFDSX	NAS CM	Open End	US Equity Mid Cap (Growth)	B+	A-	B	Up	Y	1,000,000
Wells Fargo Discovery Fund - Class R6	WFDRX	NAS CM	Open End	US Equity Mid Cap (Growth)	B+	A-	B	Up	Y	0
Wells Fargo Diversified Capital Builder Fund - Class A	EKBAX	NAS CM	Open End	Aggressive Alloc (Growth)	B	B	B-		Y	1,000
Wells Fargo Diversified Capital Builder Fund - Class Admin	EKBDX	NAS CM	Open End	Aggressive Alloc (Growth)	B	B	B-		Y	1,000,000
Wells Fargo Diversified Capital Builder Fund - Class C	EKBCX	NAS CM	Open End	Aggressive Alloc (Growth)	B-	B-	B-	Down	Y	1,000
Wells Fargo Diversified Capital Builder Fund - Class Inst	EKBYX	NAS CM	Open End	Aggressive Alloc (Growth)	B	B	B-		Y	1,000,000
Wells Fargo Diversified Equity Fund - Class A	NVDAX	NAS CM	Open End	US Equity Large Cap Growth (Growth)	B-	B-	B-	Down	Y	1,000
Wells Fargo Diversified Equity Fund - Class Admin	NVDEX	NAS CM	Open End	US Equity Large Cap Growth (Growth)	B-	B-	B-	Down	Y	1,000,000
Wells Fargo Diversified Equity Fund - Class C	WFDEX	NAS CM	Open End	US Equity Large Cap Growth (Growth)	B-	B-	B-	Down	Y	1,000
Wells Fargo Diversified Income Builder Fund - Class A	EKSAX	NAS CM	Open End	Cautious Alloc (Growth & Income)	B-	C+	B	Down	Y	1,000
Wells Fargo Diversified Income Builder Fund - Class Admin	EKSDX	NAS CM	Open End	Cautious Alloc (Growth & Income)	B-	C+	B	Down	Y	1,000,000
Wells Fargo Diversified Income Builder Fund - Class C	EKSCX	NAS CM	Open End	Cautious Alloc (Growth & Income)	B-	C+	B	Down	Y	1,000
Wells Fargo Diversified Income Builder Fund - Class Inst	EKSYX	NAS CM	Open End	Cautious Alloc (Growth & Income)	B-	C+	B	Down	Y	1,000,000
Wells Fargo Diversified International Fund - Class A	SILAX	NAS CM	Open End	Global Equity Large Cap (Foreign Stock)	B-	C+	B-	Up	Y	1,000
Wells Fargo Diversified International Fund - Class Admin	WFIEX	NAS CM	Open End	Global Equity Large Cap (Foreign Stock)	B-	C+	B-	Up	Y	1,000,000
Wells Fargo Diversified International Fund - Class C	WFECX	NAS CM	Open End	Global Equity Large Cap (Foreign Stock)	B-	C+	B-	Up	Y	1,000
Wells Fargo Diversified International Fund - Class Inst	WFISX	NAS CM	Open End	Global Equity Large Cap (Foreign Stock)	B-	C+	B-	Up	Y	1,000,000
Wells Fargo Diversified International Fund - Class R6	WDIRX	NAS CM	Open End	Global Equity Large Cap (Foreign Stock)	B-	C+	B-	Up	Y	0
Wells Fargo Dynamic Target 2015 Fund Class A	WDTAX	NAS CM	Open End	Target Date 2000-2020 (Asset Alloc)	C	C-	A-	Up	Y	1,000
Wells Fargo Dynamic Target 2015 Fund Class C	WDTCX	NAS CM	Open End	Target Date 2000-2020 (Asset Alloc)	C	C-	A-	Up	Y	1,000
Wells Fargo Dynamic Target 2015 Fund Class R4	WDTYX	NAS CM	Open End	Target Date 2000-2020 (Asset Alloc)	C	C-	A-	Up	Y	0
Wells Fargo Dynamic Target 2015 Fund Class R6	WDTZX	NAS CM	Open End	Target Date 2000-2020 (Asset Alloc)	C	C-	A-	Up	Y	0
Wells Fargo Dynamic Target 2020 Fund Class A	WDTDX	NAS CM	Open End	Target Date 2000-2020 (Asset Alloc)	C	C-	A-	Up	Y	1,000
Wells Fargo Dynamic Target 2020 Fund Class C	WDTEX	NAS CM	Open End	Target Date 2000-2020 (Asset Alloc)	C	C-	A-	Up	Y	1,000
Wells Fargo Dynamic Target 2020 Fund Class R4	WDTGX	NAS CM	Open End	Target Date 2000-2020 (Asset Alloc)	C	C-	A-	Up	Y	0
Wells Fargo Dynamic Target 2020 Fund Class R6	WDTHX	NAS CM	Open End	Target Date 2000-2020 (Asset Alloc)	C	C-	A-	Up	Y	0
Wells Fargo Dynamic Target 2025 Fund Class A	WDTIX	NAS CM	Open End	Target Date 2021-2045 (Asset Alloc)	C	C-	A-	Up	Y	1,000
Wells Fargo Dynamic Target 2025 Fund Class C	WDTJX	NAS CM	Open End	Target Date 2021-2045 (Asset Alloc)	C	C-	A-	Up	Y	1,000
Wells Fargo Dynamic Target 2025 Fund Class R4	WDTLX	NAS CM	Open End	Target Date 2021-2045 (Asset Alloc)	C	C-	A-	Up	Y	0
Wells Fargo Dynamic Target 2025 Fund Class R6	WDTMX	NAS CM	Open End	Target Date 2021-2045 (Asset Alloc)	C	C-	A-	Up	Y	0
Wells Fargo Dynamic Target 2030 Fund Class A	WDTNX	NAS CM	Open End	Target Date 2021-2045 (Asset Alloc)	C	C-	A-	Up	Y	1,000
Wells Fargo Dynamic Target 2030 Fund Class C	WDTOX	NAS CM	Open End	Target Date 2021-2045 (Asset Alloc)	C	C-	A-	Up	Y	1,000
Wells Fargo Dynamic Target 2030 Fund Class R4	WDTQX	NAS CM	Open End	Target Date 2021-2045 (Asset Alloc)	C	C-	A-	Up	Y	0
Wells Fargo Dynamic Target 2030 Fund Class R6	WDTSX	NAS CM	Open End	Target Date 2021-2045 (Asset Alloc)	C	C-	A-	Up	Y	0
Wells Fargo Dynamic Target 2035 Fund Class A	WDTTX	NAS CM	Open End	Target Date 2021-2045 (Asset Alloc)	C	C	B+	Up	Y	1,000
Wells Fargo Dynamic Target 2035 Fund Class C	WDCTX	NAS CM	Open End	Target Date 2021-2045 (Asset Alloc)	C	C	B+	Up	Y	1,000
Wells Fargo Dynamic Target 2035 Fund Class R4	WDTVX	NAS CM	Open End	Target Date 2021-2045 (Asset Alloc)	C	C	B+	Up	Y	0
Wells Fargo Dynamic Target 2035 Fund Class R6	WDTWX	NAS CM	Open End	Target Date 2021-2045 (Asset Alloc)	C	C	B+	Up	Y	0
Wells Fargo Dynamic Target 2040 Fund Class A	WTDAX	NAS CM	Open End	Target Date 2021-2045 (Asset Alloc)	C	C	B+	Up	Y	1,000
Wells Fargo Dynamic Target 2040 Fund Class C	WTDCX	NAS CM	Open End	Target Date 2021-2045 (Asset Alloc)	C	C	B+	Up	Y	1,000
Wells Fargo Dynamic Target 2040 Fund Class R4	WTDEX	NAS CM	Open End	Target Date 2021-2045 (Asset Alloc)	C	C	B+	Up	Y	0
Wells Fargo Dynamic Target 2040 Fund Class R6	WTDFX	NAS CM	Open End	Target Date 2021-2045 (Asset Alloc)	C	C	B+	Up	Y	0
Wells Fargo Dynamic Target 2045 Fund Class A	WTDGX	NAS CM	Open End	Target Date 2021-2045 (Asset Alloc)	C	C	B+	Up	Y	1,000
Wells Fargo Dynamic Target 2045 Fund Class C	WTDHX	NAS CM	Open End	Target Date 2021-2045 (Asset Alloc)	C	C	B+	Up	Y	1,000
Wells Fargo Dynamic Target 2045 Fund Class R4	WTDJX	NAS CM	Open End	Target Date 2021-2045 (Asset Alloc)	C	C	B+	Up	Y	0
Wells Fargo Dynamic Target 2045 Fund Class R6	WTDKX	NAS CM	Open End	Target Date 2021-2045 (Asset Alloc)	C	C	B+	Up	Y	0
Wells Fargo Dynamic Target 2050 Fund Class A	WTDLX	NAS CM	Open End	Target Date 2046+ (Asset Alloc)	C	C	B+	Up	Y	1,000
Wells Fargo Dynamic Target 2050 Fund Class C	WTDMX	NAS CM	Open End	Target Date 2046+ (Asset Alloc)	C	C	B+	Up	Y	1,000
Wells Fargo Dynamic Target 2050 Fund Class R4	WTDOX	NAS CM	Open End	Target Date 2046+ (Asset Alloc)	C	C	B+	Up	Y	0
Wells Fargo Dynamic Target 2050 Fund Class R6	WTDPX	NAS CM	Open End	Target Date 2046+ (Asset Alloc)	C	C	B+	Up	Y	0
Wells Fargo Dynamic Target 2055 Fund Class A	WTDQX	NAS CM	Open End	Target Date 2046+ (Asset Alloc)	C	C	B+	Up	Y	1,000
Wells Fargo Dynamic Target 2055 Fund Class C	WTDRX	NAS CM	Open End	Target Date 2046+ (Asset Alloc)	C	C	B+	Up	Y	1,000

★ Expanded analysis of this fund is included in Section II.

Min Additional Investment	TOTAL RETURNS: 3-Month Total Return	6-Month Total Return	1-Year Total Return	3-Year Total Return	5-Year Total Return	PERFORMANCE: Dividend Yield (TTM)	Expense Ratio	3-Yr Std Deviation	3-Year Beta	ASSETS: NAV	Total Assets (MIL)	ASSET ALLOCATION & TURNOVER: %Cash	%Stocks	%Bonds	%Other	Turnover Ratio	BULL & BEAR: Last Bull Market Total Return	Last Bear Market Total Return	FEES: Front End Fee (%)	Back End Fee (%)	Inception Date
	6.15	11.98	29.47	36.86	102.64	0	0.87	12.39	0.9	35.07	2,600	2	94	0	4	73	34.25	-22.69			Aug-06
	6.21	12.05	29.61	37.21	103.10	0	0.77	12.37	0.9	35.23	2,600	2	94	0	4	73	34	-22.77			Jun-13
100	3.65	7.73	14.40	34.00	96.69	1.24	1.14	8.35		10.16	983.2	0	84	16	0	54	21.35	-23.2	5.75		Jan-98
	3.59	7.88	14.46	34.61	98.43	1.26	1.05	8.36		10.17	983.2	0	84	16	0	54	21.45	-23.09			Jul-10
100	3.40	7.37	13.43	31.00	89.55	0.82	1.89	8.38		10.14	983.2	0	84	16	0	54	20.71	-23.43		1.00	Jan-98
	3.64	7.96	14.75	35.53	100.62	1.46	0.78	8.32		10.09	983.2	0	84	16	0	54	21.7	-23.1			Jan-98
100	5.75	10.77	22.59	28.07	85.89	0.65	1.25	10.45		25.84	180.5	2	96	0	2	90	24.74	-19.56	5.75		May-96
	5.83	10.92	22.94	29.07	88.27	0.84	1	10.45		25.93	180.5	2	96	0	2	90	24.89	-19.49			Nov-94
100	5.58	10.41	21.77	25.30	79.12	0.06	2	10.46		23.08	180.5	2	96	0	2	90	24.18	-19.81		1.00	Oct-98
100	1.51	4.15	9.39	22.94	43.74	3.24	1.08	5.06		6.37	781.3	1	28	70	1	29	14	-10.82	5.75		Apr-87
	1.39	4.11	9.32	23.41	44.79	3.38	0.9	5		6.23	781.3	1	28	70	1	29	14.13	-10.8			Jul-10
100	1.16	3.60	8.40	20.20	38.42	2.51	1.83	5.02		6.38	781.3	1	28	70	1	29	13.49	-11.23		1.00	Feb-93
	1.60	4.21	9.71	24.34	46.50	3.56	0.71	5.04		6.23	781.3	1	28	70	1	29	14.06	-10.74			Jan-97
100	3.80	9.77	25.64	21.84	44.58	1.61	1.36	11.68	0.93	13.4	124.8	-1	100	0	1	50	17.76	-24.3	5.75		Sep-97
	3.89	9.85	25.85	22.25	45.56	1.69	1.26	11.71	0.93	13.65	124.8	-1	100	0	1	50	17.88	-24.17			Nov-99
100	3.71	9.48	24.80	19.14	39.37	1.1	2.11	11.71	0.93	12.35	124.8	-1	100	0	1	50	17.24	-24.53		1.00	Apr-98
	3.88	9.95	26.17	23.27	47.52	1.91	1	11.67	0.92	12.72	124.8	-1	100	0	1	50	18.18	-24.17			Aug-06
	3.96	10.05	26.24	23.17	46.16	1.91	0.9	11.7	0.93	13.71	124.8	-1	100	0	1	50	17.76	-24.3			Sep-15
100	2.89	5.84	13.16			0.38	0.97			11.03	6.1	8	57	32	1	81			5.75		Nov-15
100	2.82	5.50	12.51			0.2	1.72			11.02	6.1	8	57	32	1	81				1.00	Nov-15
	3.07	6.03	13.59			0.45	0.69			11.03	6.1	8	57	32	1	81					Nov-15
	3.12	6.08	13.75			0.49	0.54			11.03	6.1	8	57	32	1	81					Nov-15
100	3.39	6.63	14.89			1.05	0.99			11.13	6.2	7	65	24	1	69			5.75		Nov-15
100	3.15	6.20	13.90			0.32	1.74			11.13	6.2	7	65	24	1	69				1.00	Nov-15
	3.43	6.76	15.12			1.14	0.71			11.15	6.2	7	65	24	1	69					Nov-15
	3.58	6.91	15.38			1.27	0.56			11.16	6.2	7	65	24	1	69					Nov-15
100	3.90	7.51	16.68			0.98	1.01			11.29	6.6	6	73	18	1	58			5.75		Nov-15
100	3.65	7.07	15.78			0.29	1.76			11.29	6.6	6	73	18	1	58				1.00	Nov-15
	3.98	7.68	16.95			1.08	0.73			11.32	6.6	6	73	18	1	58					Nov-15
	3.94	7.73	17.12			1.2	0.58			11.32	6.6	6	73	18	1	58					Nov-15
100	4.28	8.26	18.26			0.95	1.03			11.41	6.7	5	81	10	1	46			5.75		Nov-15
100	4.18	7.88	17.41			0.2	1.78			11.43	6.7	5	81	10	1	46				1.00	Nov-15
	4.43	8.40	18.60			1.02	0.75			11.45	6.7	5	81	10	1	46					Nov-15
	4.38	8.45	18.77			1.14	0.6			11.45	6.7	5	81	10	1	46					Nov-15
100	4.65	8.91	19.73			0.91	1.04			11.51	6.4	5	87	4	1	39			5.75		Nov-15
100	4.48	8.56	18.80			0.18	1.79			11.52	6.4	5	87	4	1	39				1.00	Nov-15
	4.72	9.07	20.00			0.99	0.76			11.54	6.4	5	87	4	1	39					Nov-15
	4.87	9.21	20.27			1.11	0.61			11.55	6.4	5	87	4	1	39					Nov-15
100	4.92	9.27	20.46			0.87	1.05			11.57	6.5	4	91	1	1	33			5.75		Nov-15
100	4.69	8.85	19.56			0.16	1.8			11.59	6.5	4	91	1	1	33				1.00	Nov-15
	4.94	9.37	20.76			0.97	0.77			11.61	6.5	4	91	1	1	33					Nov-15
	4.99	9.51	21.03			1.09	0.62			11.62	6.5	4	91	1	1	33					Nov-15
100	5.01	9.55	20.86			0.85	1.05			11.62	6.3	4	93	-1	1	31			5.75		Nov-15
100	4.70	9.05	19.88			0.16	1.8			11.61	6.3	4	93	-1	1	31				1.00	Nov-15
	5.04	9.66	21.19			0.96	0.77			11.64	6.3	4	93	-1	1	31					Nov-15
	5.18	9.80	21.34			1.08	0.62			11.65	6.3	4	93	-1	1	31					Nov-15
100	5.02	9.55	20.85			0.77	1.05			11.62	6.2	4	94	-2	1	31			5.75		Nov-15
100	4.76	9.11	19.94			0.17	1.8			11.61	6.2	4	94	-2	1	31				1.00	Nov-15
	5.09	9.71	21.25			0.97	0.77			11.64	6.2	4	94	-2	1	31					Nov-15
	5.05	9.76	21.42			1.09	0.62			11.64	6.2	4	94	-2	1	31					Nov-15
100	5.05	9.49	20.91			0.77	1.05			11.62	6.2	4	94	-2	1	31			5.75		Nov-15
100	4.87	9.13	19.97			0.17	1.8			11.61	6.2	4	94	-2	1	31				1.00	Nov-15

	MARKET		FUND TYPE, CATEGORY & OBJECTIVE		RATINGS					MINIMUMS
Fund Name	Ticker Symbol	Traded On	Fund Type	Category and (Prospectus Objective)	Overall Rating	Reward Rating	Risk Rating	Recent Up/ Downgrade	Open to New Investors	Min Initial Investment
Wells Fargo Dynamic Target 2055 Fund Class R4	WTDTX	NAS CM	Open End	Target Date 2046+ (Asset Alloc)	C	C	B+	Up	Y	0
Wells Fargo Dynamic Target 2055 Fund Class R6	WTDUX	NAS CM	Open End	Target Date 2046+ (Asset Alloc)	C	C	B+	Up	Y	0
Wells Fargo Dynamic Target 2060 Fund Class A	WTDVX	NAS CM	Open End	Target Date 2046+ (Asset Alloc)	C	C	B+	Up	Y	1,000
Wells Fargo Dynamic Target 2060 Fund Class C	WTDWX	NAS CM	Open End	Target Date 2046+ (Asset Alloc)	C	C	B+	Up	Y	1,000
Wells Fargo Dynamic Target 2060 Fund Class R4	WTDZX	NAS CM	Open End	Target Date 2046+ (Asset Alloc)	C	C	B+	Up	Y	0
Wells Fargo Dynamic Target 2060 Fund Class R6	WTSZX	NAS CM	Open End	Target Date 2046+ (Asset Alloc)	C	C	B+	Up	Y	0
Wells Fargo Dynamic Target Today Fund Class A	WDYAX	NAS CM	Open End	Target Date 2000-2020 (Asset Alloc)	C	C-	A-	Up	Y	1,000
Wells Fargo Dynamic Target Today Fund Class C	WDYCX	NAS CM	Open End	Target Date 2000-2020 (Asset Alloc)	C	C-	A-	Up	Y	1,000
Wells Fargo Dynamic Target Today Fund Class R4	WDYYX	NAS CM	Open End	Target Date 2000-2020 (Asset Alloc)	C	C-	A-	Up	Y	0
Wells Fargo Dynamic Target Today Fund Class R6	WDYZX	NAS CM	Open End	Target Date 2000-2020 (Asset Alloc)	C	C-	A-	Up	Y	0
Wells Fargo Emerging Growth Fund - Class A	WEMAX	NAS CM	Open End	US Equity Small Cap (Growth)	B	A-	B-	Up		1,000
Wells Fargo Emerging Growth Fund - Class Admin	WFGDX	NAS CM	Open End	US Equity Small Cap (Growth)	B	A-	B-	Up		1,000,000
Wells Fargo Emerging Growth Fund - Class C	WEMCX	NAS CM	Open End	US Equity Small Cap (Growth)	B	A-	C+	Up		1,000
Wells Fargo Emerging Growth Fund - Class Inst	WEMIX	NAS CM	Open End	US Equity Small Cap (Growth)	B	A-	B-	Up		1,000,000
Wells Fargo Emerging Markets Equity Fund - Class A	EMGAX	NAS CM	Open End	Emerging Markets Equity (Div Emerging Mkts)	B-	B	C	Up		1,000
Wells Fargo Emerging Markets Equity Fund - Class Admin	EMGYX	NAS CM	Open End	Emerging Markets Equity (Div Emerging Mkts)	B-	B	C	Up		1,000,000
Wells Fargo Emerging Markets Equity Fund - Class C	EMGCX	NAS CM	Open End	Emerging Markets Equity (Div Emerging Mkts)	C+	B-	C	Up		1,000
Wells Fargo Emerging Markets Equity Fund - Class Inst	EMGNX	NAS CM	Open End	Emerging Markets Equity (Div Emerging Mkts)	B-	B	C	Up		1,000,000
Wells Fargo Emerging Markets Equity Fund - Class R6	EMGDX	NAS CM	Open End	Emerging Markets Equity (Div Emerging Mkts)	B-	B	C	Up		0
Wells Fargo Emerging Markets Equity Income Fund - Class A	EQIAX	NAS CM	Open End	Emerging Markets Equity (Div Emerging Mkts)	C+	C+	C+	Up	Y	1,000
Wells Fargo Emerging Mkts Equity Income Fund - Cls Admin	EQIDX	NAS CM	Open End	Emerging Markets Equity (Div Emerging Mkts)	C+	C+	C+	Up	Y	1,000,000
Wells Fargo Emerging Markets Equity Income Fund - Class C	EQICX	NAS CM	Open End	Emerging Markets Equity (Div Emerging Mkts)	C+	C+	C+	Up	Y	1,000
Wells Fargo Emerging Markets Equity Income Fund - Cls Inst	EQIIX	NAS CM	Open End	Emerging Markets Equity (Div Emerging Mkts)	C+	C+	C+	Up	Y	1,000,000
Wells Fargo Emerging Markets Equity Income Fund - Class R	EQIHX	NAS CM	Open End	Emerging Markets Equity (Div Emerging Mkts)	C+	C+	C+	Up	Y	0
Wells Fargo Emerging Markets Equity Income Fund - Class R6	EQIRX	NAS CM	Open End	Emerging Markets Equity (Div Emerging Mkts)	C+	C+	C+	Up	Y	0
Wells Fargo Endeavor Select Fund - Class A	STAEX	NAS CM	Open End	US Equity Large Cap Growth (Growth)	B+	B+	B+	Up	Y	1,000
Wells Fargo Endeavor Select Fund - Class Admin	WECDX	NAS CM	Open End	US Equity Large Cap Growth (Growth)	B+	B+	A-	Up	Y	1,000,000
Wells Fargo Endeavor Select Fund - Class C	WECCX	NAS CM	Open End	US Equity Large Cap Growth (Growth)	B+	B+	B+	Up	Y	1,000
Wells Fargo Endeavor Select Fund - Class Inst	WFCIX	NAS CM	Open End	US Equity Large Cap Growth (Growth)	B+	B+	A-	Up	Y	1,000,000
Wells Fargo Enterprise Fund - Class A	SENAX	NAS CM	Open End	US Equity Mid Cap (Growth)	B	B	C+	Up	Y	1,000
Wells Fargo Enterprise Fund - Class Admin	SEPKX	NAS CM	Open End	US Equity Mid Cap (Growth)	B	B	C+	Up	Y	1,000,000
Wells Fargo Enterprise Fund - Class C	WENCX	NAS CM	Open End	US Equity Mid Cap (Growth)	B	B	B	Up	Y	1,000
Wells Fargo Enterprise Fund - Class Inst	WFEIX	NAS CM	Open End	US Equity Mid Cap (Growth)	B	B	C+	Up	Y	1,000,000
Wells Fargo Enterprise Fund - Class R6	WENRX	NAS CM	Open End	US Equity Mid Cap (Growth)	B	B	B	Up	Y	0
Wells Fargo Factor Enhanced Emerging Markets Fund	WEEMX	NAS CM	Open End	Emerging Markets Equity (Div Emerging Mkts)	U	U	U		Y	0
Wells Fargo Factor Enhanced International Fund	WINTX	NAS CM	Open End	Global Equity Large Cap (Foreign Stock)	U	U	U		Y	0
Wells Fargo Factor Enhanced International Fund	WLECX	NAS CM	Open End	US Equity Large Cap Blend (Growth)	U	U	U		Y	0
Wells Fargo Factor Enhanced Small Cap Fund	WFESX	NAS CM	Open End	US Equity Small Cap (Small Company)	U	U	U		Y	0
Wells Fargo Global Dividend Opportunity Fund	EOD	NYSE	Closed End	Alloc (World Stock)	C	C	C+		Y	
Wells Fargo Global Small Cap Fund Class A	EKGAX	NAS CM	Open End	Global Equity Mid/Small Cap (World Stock)	B	A-	B-	Up	Y	1,000
Wells Fargo Global Small Cap Fund Class Admin	EKGYX	NAS CM	Open End	Global Equity Mid/Small Cap (World Stock)	B	A-	B-	Up	Y	1,000,000
Wells Fargo Global Small Cap Fund Class C	EKGCX	NAS CM	Open End	Global Equity Mid/Small Cap (World Stock)	B	B+	B-	Up	Y	1,000
Wells Fargo Global Small Cap Fund Class Inst	EKGIX	NAS CM	Open End	Global Equity Mid/Small Cap (World Stock)	B+	A-	B-	Up	Y	1,000,000
Wells Fargo Growth Balanced Fund - Class A	WFGBX	NAS CM	Open End	Moderate Alloc (Balanced)	B-	C+	B	Down	Y	1,000
Wells Fargo Growth Balanced Fund - Class Admin	NVGBX	NAS CM	Open End	Moderate Alloc (Balanced)	B-	C+	B	Down	Y	1,000,000
Wells Fargo Growth Balanced Fund - Class C	WFGWX	NAS CM	Open End	Moderate Alloc (Balanced)	B-	C+	B	Down	Y	1,000
Wells Fargo Growth Fund - Class A	SGRAX	NAS CM	Open End	US Equity Large Cap Growth (Growth)	B+	A-	B	Up		1,000
Wells Fargo Growth Fund - Class Admin	SGRKX	NAS CM	Open End	US Equity Large Cap Growth (Growth)	B+	A-	B	Up		1,000,000
Wells Fargo Growth Fund - Class C	WGFCX	NAS CM	Open End	US Equity Large Cap Growth (Growth)	B	B+	B	Up		1,000
Wells Fargo Growth Fund - Class Inst	SGRNX	NAS CM	Open End	US Equity Large Cap Growth (Growth)	B+	A-	B	Up		1,000,000
Wells Fargo Growth Fund - Class R6	SGRHX	NAS CM	Open End	US Equity Large Cap Growth (Growth)	A-	A-	B	Up	Y	0
Wells Fargo Index Asset Allocation Fund - Class A	SFAAX	NAS CM	Open End	Moderate Alloc (Asset Alloc)	B	C+	B+	Up	Y	1,000

★ Expanded analysis of this fund is included in Section II.

Min Additional Investment	3-Month Total Return	6-Month Total Return	1-Year Total Return	3-Year Total Return	5-Year Total Return	Dividend Yield (TTM)	Expense Ratio	3-Yr Std Deviation	3-Year Beta	NAV	Total Assets (MIL)	%Cash	%Stocks	%Bonds	%Other	Turnover Ratio	Last Bull Market Total Return	Last Bear Market Total Return	Front End Fee (%)	Back End Fee (%)	Inception Date
	TOTAL RETURNS					PERFORMANCE				ASSETS		ASSET ALLOCATION & TURNOVER					BULL & BEAR		FEES		
	5.02	9.64	21.17			0.97	0.77			11.63	6.2	4	94	-2	1	31					Nov-15
	5.16	9.78	21.44			1.09	0.62			11.64	6.2	4	94	-2	1	31					Nov-15
100	4.97	9.50	20.80			0.77	1.05			11.61	6.3	4	94	-2	1	30			5.75		Nov-15
100	4.80	9.15	19.99			0.17	1.8			11.62	6.3	4	94	-2	1	30				1.00	Nov-15
	5.13	9.75	21.30			0.97	0.77			11.65	6.3	4	94	-2	1	30					Nov-15
	5.09	9.80	21.46			1.09	0.62			11.65	6.3	4	94	-2	1	30					Nov-15
100	2.36	4.66	10.77			0.37	0.91			10.83	5.8	9	44	43	1	97			5.75		Nov-15
100	2.13	4.24	9.94			0.18	1.66			10.8	5.8	9	44	43	1	97				1.00	Nov-15
	2.38	4.87	11.01			0.45	0.67			10.81	5.8	9	44	43	1	97					Nov-15
	2.43	4.92	11.17			0.48	0.52			10.81	5.8	9	44	43	1	97					Nov-15
100	3.77	9.37	25.68	29.86	94.83	0	1.35	17.02	1.08	14.61	760.1	1	93	0	5	115	32.13	-23.48	5.75		Mar-08
	3.73	9.40	25.91	30.43	96.42	0	1.2	17.06	1.08	15.03	760.1	1	93	0	5	115	32.24	-23.38			Jan-07
100	3.52	8.98	24.79	26.98	87.73	0	2.1	17.02	1.08	13.07	760.1	1	93	0	5	115	31.47	-23.65		1.00	Mar-08
	3.84	9.57	26.27	31.62	99.27	0	0.9	17.05	1.08	15.66	760.1	1	93	0	5	115	32.41	-23.26			Mar-08
100	3.78	11.77	34.41	30.06	21.25	0.51	1.58	15.35	0.94	25.38	4,116	6	90	0	4	8	11.66	-20.4	5.75		Sep-94
	3.81	11.85	34.51	30.50	22.03	0.61	1.46	15.36	0.94	26.58	4,116	6	90	0	4	8	11.84	-20.36			Sep-94
100	3.58	11.35	33.37	27.11	16.76	0	2.33	15.33	0.94	21.38	4,116	6	90	0	4	8	11.21	-20.65		1.00	Sep-94
	3.87	11.95	34.88	31.56	23.69	0.83	1.19	15.33	0.94	26.42	4,116	6	90	0	4	8	11.94	-20.24			Jul-10
	3.93	12.02	34.96	31.80	23.85	0.87	1.15	15.34	0.94	26.42	4,116	6	90	0	4	8	11.84	-20.36			Jun-13
100	5.40	10.24	24.46	17.38	20.65	1.68	1.65	12.28	0.76	12.01	605.3	7	88	0	4	64			5.75		May-12
	5.47	10.31	24.66	18.20	22.03	1.75	1.48	12.32	0.76	12.1	605.3	7	88	0	4	64					May-12
100	5.24	9.78	23.53	14.75	16.38	1.02	2.4	12.29	0.76	11.96	605.3	7	88	0	4	64				1.00	May-12
	5.56	10.49	24.96	18.82	23.18	2.05	1.25	12.31	0.76	12.04	605.3	7	88	0	4	64					May-12
	5.41	10.08	24.15	16.80	20.47	1.48	1.9	12.26	0.76	12.04	605.3	7	88	0	4	64					Sep-15
	5.59	10.45	25.10	18.95	23.31	2.15	1.2	12.3	0.76	12.03	605.3	7	88	0	4	64					Sep-15
100	7.13	13.44	35.18	38.53	103.86	0	1.2	11.32	0.99	8.16	163.3	2	98	0	0	59	29.22	-19.92	5.75		Dec-00
	7.14	13.45	35.33	39.38	106.15	0	1	11.32	1	8.74	163.3	2	98	0	0	59	29.48	-19.83			Apr-05
100	6.96	12.95	34.04	35.42	96.20	0	1.95	11.26	0.99	5.61	163.3	2	98	0	0	59	28.71	-20.16		1.00	Dec-00
	7.31	13.64	35.83	40.24	108.11	0.05	0.8	11.36	1	9.12	163.3	2	98	0	0	59	29.51	-19.74			Apr-05
100	5.36	9.86	28.51	31.22	95.51	0	1.18	12.09	1.04	46.18	718.6	1	97	0	2	75	32.55	-24.89	5.75		Feb-00
	5.39	9.91	28.61	31.71	96.61	0	1.1	12.08	1.04	48.64	718.6	1	97	0	2	75	32.57	-24.83			Aug-02
100	5.15	9.43	27.52	28.26	88.31	0	1.93	12.08	1.04	40.98	718.6	1	97	0	2	75	31.95	-25.1		1.00	Mar-08
	5.46	10.06	28.95	32.54	98.83	0	0.85	12.09	1.04	50.74	718.6	1	97	0	2	75	32.78	-24.76			Jun-03
	5.47	10.08	29.00	32.73	97.93	0	0.8	12.1	1.04	50.84	718.6	1	97	0	2	75	32.55	-24.89			Oct-14
	7.07						0			10.57	0.01	6	88	0	5						Aug-17
	3.92						0			10.53	0.01	3	90	0	6						Aug-17
	6.32						0			10.8	0.01	2	98	0	0						Aug-17
	3.53						0			10.85	0.01										Aug-17
	-0.88	3.08	12.35	1.80	25.57	8.88		9.54		6.43	306.2	6	60	19	0	134	9.68	-17.34			Mar-07
100	5.22	12.49	24.04	44.63	87.96	0.68	1.56	10.57	0.92	42.4	265.5	6	86	0	8	70	22.03	-29.06	5.75		Mar-88
	5.24	12.54	24.17	45.23	89.36	0.73	1.41	10.58	0.92	44.39	265.5	6	86	0	8	70	22.13	-29			Jan-97
100	5.04	12.07	23.11	41.39	81.03	0.19	2.31	10.56	0.92	29.91	265.5	6	86	0	8	70	21.49	-29.27		1.00	Feb-93
	5.31	12.69	24.53	46.38	91.77	0.95	1.16	10.57	0.92	44.2	265.5	6	86	0	8	70	22.33	-28.92			Jul-10
100	3.67	7.14	15.39	21.83	65.27	0.9	1.2	6.87		46.92	246.3	2	62	33	2	114	20.33	-16.42	5.75		Oct-98
	3.72	7.27	15.67	22.76	67.32	1.26	0.95	6.88		41.81	246.3	2	62	33	2	114	20.51	-16.32			Nov-94
100	3.48	6.75	14.53	19.12	59.22	0.46	1.95	6.86		40.81	246.3	2	62	33	2	114	19.82	-16.7		1.00	Oct-98
100	6.73	14.05	34.59	36.06	92.52	0	1.16	12.45	1.06	33.54	4,617	2	93	0	5	42	31.01	-16.26	5.75		Feb-00
	6.80	14.19	34.88	36.90	94.58	0	0.96	12.45	1.06	38.03	4,617	2	93	0	5	42	31.17	-16.16			Aug-02
100	6.54	13.63	33.62	32.99	85.40	0	1.91	12.45	1.06	26.42	4,617	2	93	0	5	42	30.44	-16.5		1.00	Dec-02
	6.84	14.28	35.13	37.73	96.56	0	0.75	12.45	1.06	41.03	4,617	2	93	0	5	42	31.34	-16.11			Feb-00
	6.88	14.33	35.23	37.95	96.88	0	0.7	12.45	1.06	41.12	4,617	2	93	0	5	42	31.34	-16.11			Sep-15
100	3.75	6.34	12.24	21.16	73.80	0.82	1.1	5.63		32.93	1,337	1	67	31	0	9	18.56	-8.89	5.75		Nov-86

Fund Name	Ticker Symbol	Traded On	Fund Type	Category and (Prospectus Objective)	Overall Rating	Reward Rating	Risk Rating	Recent Up/ Downgrade	Open to New Investors	Min Initial Investment
	MARKET		FUND TYPE, CATEGORY & OBJECTIVE		RATINGS				MINIMUMS	
Wells Fargo Index Asset Allocation Fund - Class Admin	WFAIX	NAS CM	Open End	Moderate Alloc (Asset Alloc)	B	C+	A-	Up	Y	1,000,000
Wells Fargo Index Asset Allocation Fund - Class C	WFALX	NAS CM	Open End	Moderate Alloc (Asset Alloc)	B-	C+	B	Up	Y	1,000
Wells Fargo Index Asset Allocation Fund Institutional Cls	WFATX	NAS CM	Open End	Moderate Alloc (Asset Alloc)	B	C+	B+	Up	Y	1,000,000
Wells Fargo Index Fund - Class A	WFILX	NAS CM	Open End	US Equity Large Cap Blend (Growth)	B	B	B		Y	1,000
Wells Fargo Index Fund - Class Admin	WFIOX	NAS CM	Open End	US Equity Large Cap Blend (Growth)	B	B	B		Y	1,000,000
Wells Fargo Index Fund - Class C	WFINX	NAS CM	Open End	US Equity Large Cap Blend (Growth)	B-	B-	B	Down	Y	1,000
Wells Fargo International Equity Fund - Class A	WFEAX	NAS CM	Open End	Global Equity Large Cap (Foreign Stock)	B	B	C+	Up	Y	1,000
Wells Fargo International Equity Fund - Class Admin	WFEDX	NAS CM	Open End	Global Equity Large Cap (Foreign Stock)	B	B	C+	Up	Y	1,000,000
Wells Fargo International Equity Fund - Class C	WFEFX	NAS CM	Open End	Global Equity Large Cap (Foreign Stock)	B-	B	C+	Up	Y	1,000
Wells Fargo International Equity Fund - Class Inst	WFENX	NAS CM	Open End	Global Equity Large Cap (Foreign Stock)	B	B	C+	Up	Y	1,000,000
Wells Fargo International Equity Fund - Class R	WFERX	NAS CM	Open End	Global Equity Large Cap (Foreign Stock)	B	B	C+	Up	Y	0
Wells Fargo International Equity Fund - Class R6	WFEHX	NAS CM	Open End	Global Equity Large Cap (Foreign Stock)	B	B	C+	Up	Y	0
Wells Fargo International Value Fund - Class A	WFFAX	NAS CM	Open End	Global Equity Large Cap (Foreign Stock)	C+	C+	C	Up	Y	1,000
Wells Fargo International Value Fund - Class Admin	WFVDX	NAS CM	Open End	Global Equity Large Cap (Foreign Stock)	C+	C+	C	Up	Y	1,000,000
Wells Fargo International Value Fund - Class C	WFVCX	NAS CM	Open End	Global Equity Large Cap (Foreign Stock)	C+	C+	C	Up	Y	1,000
Wells Fargo International Value Fund - Class Inst	WFVIX	NAS CM	Open End	Global Equity Large Cap (Foreign Stock)	C+	B-	C	Up	Y	1,000,000
Wells Fargo Intrinsic Small Cap Value Fund - Class A	WFSMX	NAS CM	Open End	US Equity Small Cap (Small Company)	B	B	B	Up	Y	1,000
Wells Fargo Intrinsic Small Cap Value Fund - Class Admin	WFSDX	NAS CM	Open End	US Equity Small Cap (Small Company)	B	B	B	Up	Y	1,000,000
Wells Fargo Intrinsic Small Cap Value Fund - Class C	WSCDX	NAS CM	Open End	US Equity Small Cap (Small Company)	B	B	B-	Up	Y	1,000
Wells Fargo Intrinsic Small Cap Value Fund - Class Inst	WFSSX	NAS CM	Open End	US Equity Small Cap (Small Company)	B	B	B	Up	Y	1,000,000
Wells Fargo Intrinsic Value Fund - Class A	EIVAX	NAS CM	Open End	US Equity Large Cap Blend (Growth)	B-	C+	B-	Down	Y	1,000
Wells Fargo Intrinsic Value Fund - Class Admin	EIVDX	NAS CM	Open End	US Equity Large Cap Blend (Growth)	B-	C+	B-	Down	Y	1,000,000
Wells Fargo Intrinsic Value Fund - Class C	EIVCX	NAS CM	Open End	US Equity Large Cap Blend (Growth)	C+	C+	B-	Down	Y	1,000
Wells Fargo Intrinsic Value Fund - Class Inst	EIVIX	NAS CM	Open End	US Equity Large Cap Blend (Growth)	B-	C+	B-	Down	Y	1,000,000
Wells Fargo Intrinsic Value Fund - Class R	EIVTX	NAS CM	Open End	US Equity Large Cap Blend (Growth)	B-	C+	B-	Down	Y	0
Wells Fargo Intrinsic Value Fund - Class R6	EIVFX	NAS CM	Open End	US Equity Large Cap Blend (Growth)	B-	C+	B-	Down	Y	0
Wells Fargo Intrinsic World Equity Fund - Class A	EWEAX	NAS CM	Open End	Global Equity (World Stock)	B-	B	B-	Up	Y	1,000
Wells Fargo Intrinsic World Equity Fund - Class Admin	EWEIX	NAS CM	Open End	Global Equity (World Stock)	B-	B	B-	Up	Y	1,000,000
Wells Fargo Intrinsic World Equity Fund - Class C	EWECX	NAS CM	Open End	Global Equity (World Stock)	B-	B-	B-	Up	Y	1,000
Wells Fargo Intrinsic World Equity Fund - Class Inst	EWENX	NAS CM	Open End	Global Equity (World Stock)	B-	B	B-	Up	Y	1,000,000
Wells Fargo Large Cap Core Fund - Class A	EGOAX	NAS CM	Open End	US Equity Large Cap Blend (Growth)	B	B	B-	Up	Y	1,000
Wells Fargo Large Cap Core Fund - Class Admin	WFLLX	NAS CM	Open End	US Equity Large Cap Blend (Growth)	B	B	B-	Up	Y	1,000,000
Wells Fargo Large Cap Core Fund - Class C	EGOCX	NAS CM	Open End	US Equity Large Cap Blend (Growth)	B	B	B-	Up	Y	1,000
Wells Fargo Large Cap Core Fund - Class Inst	EGOIX	NAS CM	Open End	US Equity Large Cap Blend (Growth)	B	B+	B-	Up	Y	1,000,000
Wells Fargo Large Cap Core Fund - Class R	EGOHX	NAS CM	Open End	US Equity Large Cap Blend (Growth)	B	B	B-	Up	Y	0
Wells Fargo Large Cap Core Fund - Class R6	EGORX	NAS CM	Open End	US Equity Large Cap Blend (Growth)	B	A-	B-		Y	0
Wells Fargo Large Cap Growth Fund - Class A	STAFX	NAS CM	Open End	US Equity Large Cap Growth (Growth)	B+	B	B+	Up	Y	1,000
Wells Fargo Large Cap Growth Fund - Class Admin	STDFX	NAS CM	Open End	US Equity Large Cap Growth (Growth)	B+	B+	B+	Up	Y	1,000,000
Wells Fargo Large Cap Growth Fund - Class C	STOFX	NAS CM	Open End	US Equity Large Cap Growth (Growth)	B	B	B+	Up	Y	1,000
Wells Fargo Large Cap Growth Fund - Class Inst	STNFX	NAS CM	Open End	US Equity Large Cap Growth (Growth)	B+	B+	B+	Up	Y	1,000,000
Wells Fargo Large Cap Growth Fund - Class R	STMFX	NAS CM	Open End	US Equity Large Cap Growth (Growth)	B+	B	B+	Up	Y	0
Wells Fargo Large Cap Growth Fund - Class R4	SLGRX	NAS CM	Open End	US Equity Large Cap Growth (Growth)	B+	B+	B+	Up	Y	0
Wells Fargo Large Cap Growth Fund - Class R6	STFFX	NAS CM	Open End	US Equity Large Cap Growth (Growth)	B+	B+	B+	Up	Y	0
Wells Fargo Large Company Value Fund - Class A	WLCAX	NAS CM	Open End	US Equity Large Cap Value (Growth)	B-	B-	B	Down	Y	1,000
Wells Fargo Large Company Value Fund - Class Admin	WWIDX	NAS CM	Open End	US Equity Large Cap Value (Growth)	B-	B-	B	Down	Y	1,000,000
Wells Fargo Large Company Value Fund - Class C	WFLVX	NAS CM	Open End	US Equity Large Cap Value (Growth)	B-	C+	B		Y	1,000
Wells Fargo Large Company Value Fund - Class Inst	WLCIX	NAS CM	Open End	US Equity Large Cap Value (Growth)	B-	B-	B	Down	Y	1,000,000
Wells Fargo Large Company Value Fund Class R6	WTLVX	NAS CM	Open End	US Equity Large Cap Value (Growth)	B-	B-	B	Down	Y	0
Wells Fargo Low Vol U.S. Eq Fund Administrator Cls	WLVDX	NAS CM	Open End	US Equity Large Cap Blend (Growth)	D	D+	A-		Y	1,000,000
Wells Fargo Low Volatility U.S. Equity Fund Class A	WLVLX	NAS CM	Open End	US Equity Large Cap Blend (Growth)	D	D+	A-		Y	1,000
Wells Fargo Low Volatility U.S. Equity Fund Class C	WLVKX	NAS CM	Open End	US Equity Large Cap Blend (Growth)	D	D+	A-		Y	1,000
Wells Fargo Low Volatility U.S. Equity Fund Class R6	WLVJX	NAS CM	Open End	US Equity Large Cap Blend (Growth)	D	D+	A-		Y	0

★ Expanded analysis of this fund is included in Section II.

Min Additional Investment	3-Month Total Return	6-Month Total Return	1-Year Total Return	3-Year Total Return	5-Year Total Return	Dividend Yield (TTM)	Expense Ratio	3-Yr Std Deviation	3-Year Beta	NAV	Total Assets (MIL)	%Cash	%Stocks	%Bonds	%Other	Turnover Ratio	Last Bull Market Total Return	Last Bear Market Total Return	Front End Fee (%)	Back End Fee (%)	Inception Date
	TOTAL RETURNS					PERFORMANCE				ASSETS		ASSET ALLOCATION & TURNOVER					BULL & BEAR		FEES		
	3.75	6.43	12.40	21.89	75.73	1.04	0.9	5.64		32.93	1,337	1	67	31	0	9	18.69	-8.75			Nov-99
100	3.53	5.93	11.34	18.39	67.33	0.04	1.85	5.63		20.02	1,337	1	67	31	0	9	18.03	-9.19		1.00	Apr-98
	3.82	6.51	12.58	21.60	74.43	1.27	0.75	5.64		32.89	1,337	1	67	31	0	9	18.56	-8.89			Oct-16
100	6.53	11.17	21.29	34.97	106.45	1.46	0.45	10.09	1	62.21	1,903	1	99	0	0	9	24.64	-16.4	5.75		Nov-98
	6.58	11.28	21.53	35.90	109.19	1.59	0.25	10.09	1	62.84	1,903	1	99	0	0	9	24.85	-16.28			Feb-85
100	6.32	10.75	20.39	31.97	98.85	0.91	1.2	10.08	1	62.72	1,903	1	99	0	0	9	24.1	-16.67		1.00	Apr-99
100	4.67	10.81	24.07	31.62	53.24	2.42	1.15	12.67	0.94	13.35	479.0	-4	102	0	2	65	14.53	-26	5.75		Jan-98
	4.74	10.81	24.10	31.66	53.26	2.37	1.15	12.6	0.94	13.12	479.0	-4	102	0	2	65	14.43	-25.97			Jul-10
100	4.49	10.31	23.11	28.67	47.54	1.74	1.9	12.56	0.94	13.11	479.0	-4	102	0	2	65	13.98	-26.26		1.00	Mar-98
	4.69	10.85	24.36	32.61	55.13	2.66	0.9	12.59	0.94	13.29	479.0	-4	102	0	2	65	14.78	-25.94			Mar-98
	4.66	10.64	23.79	30.74	51.37	2.18	1.4	12.62	0.94	13.54	479.0	-4	102	0	2	65	14.41	-26.13			Oct-03
	4.75	10.90	24.49	32.34	54.08	2.54	0.85	12.66	0.94	13.33	479.0	-4	102	0	2	65	14.53	-26			Sep-15
100	3.19	9.54	24.64	24.86	40.87	1.88	1.35	12.23	0.91	16.1	797.5	1	97	0	2	41	10.83	-22.95	5.75		Oct-03
	3.17	9.59	24.61	24.95	41.61	1.51	1.25	12.27	0.92	16.17	797.5	1	97	0	2	41	11	-22.88			Apr-05
100	3.01	9.12	23.54	21.99	35.56	1.02	2.1	12.24	0.92	15.69	797.5	1	97	0	2	41	10.36	-23.2		1.00	Apr-05
	3.30	9.77	24.90	26.18	43.56	1.94	1	12.22	0.91	15.87	797.5	1	97	0	2	41	11.08	-22.84			Aug-06
100	3.51	9.03	9.80	26.29	86.82	0.42	1.36	14.79	1	31.25	82.2	3	93	0	4	142	31.17	-28	5.75		Mar-08
	3.57	9.11	9.94	26.88	88.58	0.5	1.21	14.8	1	31.84	82.2	3	93	0	4	142	31.35	-27.93			Apr-05
100	3.33	8.60	8.96	23.45	79.88	0	2.11	14.79	1	29.16	82.2	3	93	0	4	142	30.47	-28.21		1.00	Mar-08
	3.63	9.22	10.15	27.62	90.47	0.69	1.01	14.8	1	32.21	82.2	3	93	0	4	142	31.42	-27.85			Apr-05
100	5.56	9.34	15.65	21.78	78.61	0.99	1.11	10.37	0.96	12.36	940.8	1	96	0	4	27	23.6	-19.49	5.75		Aug-06
	5.65	9.52	15.85	22.44	80.24	1.12	0.95	10.35	0.96	12.95	940.8	1	96	0	4	27	23.67	-19.41			Jul-10
100	5.42	8.94	14.77	19.08	72.01	0.28	1.86	10.38	0.96	12.07	940.8	1	96	0	4	27	22.86	-19.7		1.00	Aug-06
	5.77	9.62	16.21	23.35	82.57	1.33	0.7	10.36	0.96	12.42	940.8	1	96	0	4	27	23.75	-19.33			Aug-06
	5.57	9.24	15.40	20.87	76.81	0.78	1.36	10.37	0.96	12.47	940.8	1	96	0	4	27	23.57	-19.41			Mar-13
	5.82	9.74	16.24	23.60	82.17	1.37	0.65	10.39	0.97	12.21	940.8	1	96	0	4	27	23.75	-19.33			Nov-12
100	4.67	10.34	25.16	30.26	64.55	0.94	1.35	11.87	1.11	22.13	163.7	1	99	0	0	23	26.67	-17.25	5.75		Apr-96
	4.70	10.40	25.31	30.92	66.23	0.97	1.25	11.85	1.1	22.01	163.7	1	99	0	0	23	26.87	-17.19			May-07
100	4.44	9.92	24.21	27.34	58.47	0.34	2.1	11.87	1.11	21.28	163.7	1	99	0	0	23	26.18	-17.52		1.00	May-07
	4.76	10.54	25.64	31.90	68.19	1.26	0.95	11.87	1.11	22.05	163.7	1	99	0	0	23	27.02	-17.12			Jul-10
100	7.56	14.17	23.22	32.52	116.68	0.62	1.08	11.76	1.07	19.71	1,120	1	97	0	2	50	30.38	-19.74	5.75		Dec-07
	7.64	14.31	23.41	33.14	118.76	0.02	0.97	11.74	1.07	19.92	1,120	1	97	0	2	50	30.42	-19.5			Jul-10
100	7.42	13.83	22.33	29.62	108.78	0	1.83	11.75	1.07	19.44	1,120	1	97	0	2	50	29.83	-19.91		1.00	Dec-07
	7.69	14.45	23.77	34.34	121.72	1	0.67	11.76	1.07	19.79	1,120	1	97	0	2	50	30.74	-19.5			Dec-07
	7.52	14.12	22.99	32.07	116.89	0.5	1.33	11.71	1.07	19.74	1,120	1	97	0	2	50	30.55	-19.59			Sep-15
	7.73	14.45	23.78	38.37	128.36	3.66	0.65	11.84	1.07	19.76	1,120	1	97	0	2	50	30.74	-19.5			Sep-15
100	8.36	15.63	32.91	34.32	103.11	0	1.07	11.68	1.05	45.67	1,076	2	98	0	0	40	28.5	-14.14	5.75		Jul-10
	8.39	15.71	33.08	34.81	104.34	0.02	0.95	11.69	1.05	46.1	1,076	2	98	0	0	40	28.63	-14.06			Jul-10
100	8.15	15.18	31.89	31.31	95.59	0	1.82	11.68	1.05	42.3	1,076	2	98	0	0	40	27.99	-14.44		1.00	Jul-10
	8.44	15.84	33.34	35.74	106.99	0.09	0.75	11.69	1.05	46.73	1,076	2	98	0	0	40	28.82	-14.01			Jul-10
	8.29	15.50	32.55	33.28	100.55	0	1.32	11.68	1.05	44.75	1,076	2	98	0	0	40	28.63	-14.1			Jun-12
	8.42	15.79	33.29	35.53	106.24	0.08	0.8	11.69	1.05	46.67	1,076	2	98	0	0	40	28.82	-14.01			Nov-12
	8.45	15.86	33.43	36.08	107.69	0.13	0.65	11.69	1.05	46.85	1,076	2	98	0	0	40	28.82	-14.01			Nov-12
100	5.56	9.49	15.28	22.28	81.38	0.88	0.83	10.91	1.02	14.29	266.2	2	98	0	0	221	23.84	-19.18	5.75		Mar-08
	5.53	9.46	15.30	22.82	83.06	0.94	0.75	10.95	1.02	14.41	266.2	2	98	0	0	221	24.09	-19.12			Dec-01
100	5.30	9.02	14.41	19.53	74.67	0.14	1.58	10.88	1.02	14.68	266.2	2	98	0	0	221	23.39	-19.49		1.00	Mar-08
	5.61	9.65	15.63	23.74	85.07	1.19	0.5	10.91	1.02	14.39	266.2	2	98	0	0	221	24.14	-18.98			Mar-08
	5.63	9.66	15.58	23.12	83.52		0.4	10.94	1.02	14.39	266.2	2	98	0	0	221	24.09	-19.13			Apr-17
	4.51	5.64	12.30			0.38	0.75			11.39	40.2	2	98	0	0	39					Oct-16
100	4.47	5.60	12.26			0.34	0.83			11.4	40.2	2	98	0	0	39			5.75		Oct-16
100	4.34	5.28	11.41			0.25	1.58			11.39	40.2	2	98	0	0	39				1.00	Oct-16
	4.57	5.79	12.67			0.43	0.4			11.39	40.2	2	98	0	0	39					Oct-16

	MARKET		FUND TYPE, CATEGORY & OBJECTIVE		RATINGS				MINIMUMS	
Fund Name	Ticker Symbol	Traded On	Fund Type	Category and (Prospectus Objective)	Overall Rating	Reward Rating	Risk Rating	Recent Up/ Downgrade	Open to New Investors	Min Initial Investment
Wells Fargo Low Volatility U.S. Equity Fund Inst Cls	WLVOX	NAS CM	Open End	US Equity Large Cap Blend (Growth)	D	D+	A-		Y	1,000,000
Wells Fargo Moderate Balanced Fund - Class A	WFMAX	NAS CM	Open End	Cautious Alloc (Balanced)	B-	C+	B	Up	Y	1,000
Wells Fargo Moderate Balanced Fund - Class Admin	NVMBX	NAS CM	Open End	Cautious Alloc (Balanced)	B-	C+	B	Up	Y	1,000,000
Wells Fargo Moderate Balanced Fund - Class C	WFBCX	NAS CM	Open End	Cautious Alloc (Balanced)	B-	C+	B	Up	Y	1,000
Wells Fargo Omega Growth Fund - Class A	EKOAX	NAS CM	Open End	US Equity Large Cap Growth (Growth)	B	B	B	Up	Y	1,000
Wells Fargo Omega Growth Fund - Class Admin	EOMYX	NAS CM	Open End	US Equity Large Cap Growth (Growth)	B	B+	B	Up	Y	1,000,000
Wells Fargo Omega Growth Fund - Class C	EKOCX	NAS CM	Open End	US Equity Large Cap Growth (Growth)	B	B	B	Up	Y	1,000
Wells Fargo Omega Growth Fund - Class Inst	EKONX	NAS CM	Open End	US Equity Large Cap Growth (Growth)	B+	B+	B	Up	Y	1,000,000
Wells Fargo Omega Growth Fund - Class R	EKORX	NAS CM	Open End	US Equity Large Cap Growth (Growth)	B	B	B	Up	Y	0
Wells Fargo Opportunity Fund - Class A	SOPVX	NAS CM	Open End	US Equity Large Cap Growth (Growth)	B	B	B	Up	Y	1,000
Wells Fargo Opportunity Fund - Class Admin	WOFDX	NAS CM	Open End	US Equity Large Cap Growth (Growth)	B	B	B	Up	Y	1,000,000
Wells Fargo Opportunity Fund - Class C	WFOPX	NAS CM	Open End	US Equity Large Cap Growth (Growth)	B	B-	B	Up	Y	1,000
Wells Fargo Opportunity Fund - Class Inst	WOFNX	NAS CM	Open End	US Equity Large Cap Growth (Growth)	B	B	B	Up	Y	1,000,000
Wells Fargo Precious Metals Fund - Class A	EKWAX	NAS CM	Open End	Precious Metals Sector Equity (Precious Metals)	D+	C-	D	Down	Y	1,000
Wells Fargo Precious Metals Fund - Class Admin	EKWDX	NAS CM	Open End	Precious Metals Sector Equity (Precious Metals)	D+	C-	D	Down	Y	1,000,000
Wells Fargo Precious Metals Fund - Class C	EKWCX	NAS CM	Open End	Precious Metals Sector Equity (Precious Metals)	D+	C-	D	Down	Y	1,000
Wells Fargo Precious Metals Fund - Class Inst	EKWYX	NAS CM	Open End	Precious Metals Sector Equity (Precious Metals)	D+	C-	D	Down	Y	1,000,000
Wells Fargo Premier Large Company Growth Fund - Class A	EKJAX	NAS CM	Open End	US Equity Large Cap Growth (Growth)	B	B	B	Up	Y	1,000
Wells Fargo Premier Large Company Growth Fund - Cls Admin	WFPDX	NAS CM	Open End	US Equity Large Cap Growth (Growth)	B	B	B	Up	Y	1,000,000
Wells Fargo Premier Large Company Growth Fund - Class C	EKJCX	NAS CM	Open End	US Equity Large Cap Growth (Growth)	B	B	B	Up	Y	1,000
Wells Fargo Premier Large Company Growth Fund - Class Inst	EKJYX	NAS CM	Open End	US Equity Large Cap Growth (Growth)	B	B	B	Up	Y	1,000,000
Wells Fargo Premier Large Company Growth Fund - Class R4	EKJRX	NAS CM	Open End	US Equity Large Cap Growth (Growth)	B	B	B	Up	Y	0
Wells Fargo Premier Large Company Growth Fund - Class R6	EKJFX	NAS CM	Open End	US Equity Large Cap Growth (Growth)	B	B	B	Up	Y	0
Wells Fargo Small Cap Core Fund Administrator Class	WNSCX	NAS CM	Open End	US Equity Small Cap (Small Company)	B	B	B	Up	Y	1,000,000
Wells Fargo Small Cap Core Fund Class A	WOSCX	NAS CM	Open End	US Equity Small Cap (Small Company)	B	B	B	Up	Y	1,000
Wells Fargo Small Cap Core Fund Class C	WCSCX	NAS CM	Open End	US Equity Small Cap (Small Company)	B	B	B	Up	Y	1,000
Wells Fargo Small Cap Core Fund Class R6	WRSCX	NAS CM	Open End	US Equity Small Cap (Small Company)	B	B	B	Up	Y	0
Wells Fargo Small Cap Core Fund Institutional Class	WYSCX	NAS CM	Open End	US Equity Small Cap (Small Company)	B	B	B	Up	Y	1,000,000
Wells Fargo Small Cap Opportunities Fund - Class Admin	NVSOX	NAS CM	Open End	US Equity Small Cap (Small Company)	B	B	B+	Up	Y	1,000,000
Wells Fargo Small Cap Opportunities Fund - Class Inst	WSCOX	NAS CM	Open End	US Equity Small Cap (Small Company)	B	B	B+	Up	Y	1,000,000
Wells Fargo Small Cap Opportunities Fund Class R6	WSCJX	NAS CM	Open End	US Equity Small Cap (Small Company)	B	B	B+	Up	Y	0
Wells Fargo Small Cap Value Fund - Class A	SMVAX	NAS CM	Open End	US Equity Small Cap (Small Company)	B	A-	C+	Up	Y	1,000
Wells Fargo Small Cap Value Fund - Class Admin	SMVDX	NAS CM	Open End	US Equity Small Cap (Small Company)	B	A-	C+	Up	Y	1,000,000
Wells Fargo Small Cap Value Fund - Class C	SMVCX	NAS CM	Open End	US Equity Small Cap (Small Company)	B	B+	C+	Up	Y	1,000
Wells Fargo Small Cap Value Fund - Class Inst	WFSVX	NAS CM	Open End	US Equity Small Cap (Small Company)	B	A-	C+	Up	Y	1,000,000
Wells Fargo Small Cap Value Fund - Class R6	SMVRX	NAS CM	Open End	US Equity Small Cap (Small Company)	B	A	C+	Up	Y	0
Wells Fargo Small Company Growth Fund - Class A	WFSAX	NAS CM	Open End	US Equity Small Cap (Small Company)	B	B	B-	Up	Y	1,000
Wells Fargo Small Company Growth Fund - Class Admin	NVSCX	NAS CM	Open End	US Equity Small Cap (Small Company)	B	B	B-	Up	Y	1,000,000
Wells Fargo Small Company Growth Fund - Class C	WSMCX	NAS CM	Open End	US Equity Small Cap (Small Company)	B-	B-	B-	Up	Y	1,000
Wells Fargo Small Company Growth Fund - Class Inst	WSCGX	NAS CM	Open End	US Equity Small Cap (Small Company)	B	B	B-	Up	Y	1,000,000
Wells Fargo Small Company Growth Fund - Class R6	WSCRX	NAS CM	Open End	US Equity Small Cap (Small Company)	B	B	B-	Up	Y	0
Wells Fargo Small Company Value Fund - Class A	SCVAX	NAS CM	Open End	US Equity Small Cap (Small Company)	B+	A-	B	Up	Y	1,000
Wells Fargo Small Company Value Fund - Class Admin	SCVIX	NAS CM	Open End	US Equity Small Cap (Small Company)	B+	A-	B	Up	Y	1,000,000
Wells Fargo Small Company Value Fund - Class C	SCVFX	NAS CM	Open End	US Equity Small Cap (Small Company)	B	B+	B	Up	Y	1,000
Wells Fargo Small Company Value Fund - Class Inst	SCVNX	NAS CM	Open End	US Equity Small Cap (Small Company)	B+	A-	B	Up	Y	1,000,000
Wells Fargo Small Company Value Fund Class R6	SCVJX	NAS CM	Open End	US Equity Small Cap (Small Company)	B+	A-	B	Up	Y	0
Wells Fargo Special Mid Cap Value Fund - Class A	WFPAX	NAS CM	Open End	US Equity Mid Cap (Growth)	B	B-	B		Y	1,000
Wells Fargo Special Mid Cap Value Fund - Class Admin	WFMDX	NAS CM	Open End	US Equity Mid Cap (Growth)	B	B-	B		Y	1,000,000
Wells Fargo Special Mid Cap Value Fund - Class C	WFPCX	NAS CM	Open End	US Equity Mid Cap (Growth)	B	B-	B	Up	Y	1,000
Wells Fargo Special Mid Cap Value Fund - Class Inst	WFMIX	NAS CM	Open End	US Equity Mid Cap (Growth)	B	B-	B+		Y	1,000,000
Wells Fargo Special Mid Cap Value Fund - Class R	WFHHX	NAS CM	Open End	US Equity Mid Cap (Growth)	B	B-	B	Up	Y	0
Wells Fargo Special Mid Cap Value Fund - Class R6	WFPRX	NAS CM	Open End	US Equity Mid Cap (Growth)	B	B-	B+		Y	0

★ Expanded analysis of this fund is included in Section II.

	TOTAL RETURNS					PERFORMANCE				ASSETS		ASSET ALLOCATION & TURNOVER					BULL & BEAR		FEES		
Min Additional Investment	3-Month Total Return	6-Month Total Return	1-Year Total Return	3-Year Total Return	5-Year Total Return	Dividend Yield (TTM)	Expense Ratio	3-Yr Std Deviation	3-Year Beta	NAV	Total Assets (MIL)	%Cash	%Stocks	%Bonds	%Other	Turnover Ratio	Last Bull Market Total Return	Last Bear Market Total Return	Front End Fee (%)	Back End Fee (%)	Inception Date
	4.61	5.83	12.60			0.41	0.5			11.4	40.2	2	98	0	0	39					Oct-16
100	2.44	4.75	10.32	15.95	42.25	1.17	1.15	4.34		22.69	159.2	4	36	59	1	114	13.3	-9.72	5.75		Jan-04
	2.50	4.87	10.59	16.76	43.97	1.38	0.9	4.34		22.88	159.2	4	36	59	1	114	13.51	-9.61			Nov-94
100	2.21	4.34	9.46	13.32	36.92	0.57	1.9	4.34		22.23	159.2	4	36	59	1	114	12.87	-10.02		1.00	Jan-04
100	7.62	13.64	34.33	34.80	99.62	0	1.28	11.84	1.04	47.93	769.4	1	98	0	0	76	32.36	-22.96	5.75		Apr-68
	7.67	13.73	34.57	35.62	101.79	0	1.1	11.84	1.04	51.93	769.4	1	98	0	0	76	32.53	-22.86			Jan-97
100	7.41	13.19	33.30	31.80	92.22	0	2.03	11.81	1.04	33.42	769.4	1	98	0	0	76	31.77	-23.2		1.00	Aug-93
	7.73	13.88	34.90	36.65	104.38	0	0.85	11.84	1.04	53.34	769.4	1	98	0	0	76	32.7	-22.79			Jul-10
	7.53	13.47	33.99	33.77	97.08	0	1.53	11.84	1.04	45.5	769.4	1	98	0	0	76	32.15	-23.04			Oct-03
100	6.60	10.48	20.00	28.81	89.12	0.25	1.21	11.39	1.07	42.87	1,832	2	97	0	1	43	23.75	-22.99	5.75		Feb-00
	6.63	10.59	20.25	29.61	91.17	0.34	1	11.38	1.07	46.67	1,832	2	97	0	1	43	23.92	-22.91			Aug-02
100	6.38	10.05	19.10	25.91	82.12	0	1.96	11.38	1.07	40.42	1,832	2	97	0	1	43	23.22	-23.23		1.00	Mar-08
	6.70	10.73	20.53	30.59	93.52	0.48	0.75	11.38	1.07	47.5	1,832	2	97	0	1	43	24.1	-22.87			Jul-10
100	1.00	2.65	9.66	20.28	-40.92	1.07	1.09	38.3	0.9	35.94	335.1	1	95	0	4	21	-13.28	-11.64	5.75		Jan-98
	1.04	2.74	9.83	20.77	-40.50	1.19	0.95	38.32	0.9	36.24	335.1	1	95	0	4	21	-13.22	-11.57			Jul-10
100	0.80	2.27	8.86	17.59	-43.09	0.18	1.84	38.27	0.9	31.93	335.1	1	95	0	4	21	-13.66	-11.9		1.00	Jan-98
	1.08	2.82	10.00	21.29	-40.06	1.42	0.79	38.51	0.91	36.46	335.1	1	95	0	4	21	-13.11	-11.49			Feb-00
100	7.41	14.12	33.92	31.14	94.30	0	1.11	11.72	1.04	13.21	2,478	1	99	0	1	65	30.37	-14.97	5.75		Jan-98
	7.44	14.23	34.10	31.59	95.80	0	1	11.77	1.04	13.42	2,478	1	99	0	1	65	30.45	-14.96			Jul-10
100	7.26	13.70	32.97	28.18	87.27	0	1.86	11.74	1.04	10.43	2,478	1	99	0	1	65	29.8	-15.27		1.00	Jan-98
	7.53	14.32	34.43	32.67	98.41	0	0.7	11.75	1.04	13.8	2,478	1	99	0	1	65	30.61	-14.84			Jun-99
	7.53	14.35	34.41	32.38	97.47	0	0.8	11.74	1.04	13.7	2,478	1	99	0	1	65	30.37	-14.97			Nov-12
	7.53	14.37	34.55	32.97	98.85	0	0.65	11.74	1.04	13.84	2,478	1	99	0	1	65	30.37	-14.97			Nov-12
	0.74	4.16	5.07	22.55	91.02	0.19	1.25	13.08	0.86	21.53	76.4	1	99	0	0	25	26.38	-24.8			May-16
100	0.70	4.11	4.98	22.38	90.76	0.2	1.35	13.09	0.86	21.5	76.4	1	99	0	0	25	26.38	-24.8	5.75		May-16
100	0.51	3.75	4.21	19.72	83.84	0.13	2.1	13.08	0.86	21.26	76.4	1	99	0	0	25	25.83	-25.03		1.00	May-16
	0.83	4.33	5.45	23.27	92.14	0.22	0.9	13.1	0.86	21.65	76.4	1	99	0	0	25	26.38	-24.8			May-16
	0.79	4.29	5.36	23.10	91.87	0.22	1	13.09	0.86	21.62	76.4	1	99	0	0	25	26.38	-24.8			Sep-05
	3.98	7.47	14.84	34.30	101.75	0.24	1.27	11.25	0.78	22.94	302.6	7	86	0	7	73	23.81	-22.83			Aug-93
	4.08	7.61	15.17	35.39	103.44	0.47	0.96	11.27	0.78	23.01	302.6	7	86	0	7	73	23.81	-22.83			Oct-14
	4.09	7.65	15.27	34.85	102.58	0.48	0.92	11.26	0.78	23.03	302.6	7	86	0	7	73	23.8	-22.83			Nov-16
100	3.06	7.97	13.85	34.13	63.63	0	1.28	14.04	0.87	17.43	609.6	2	98	0	0	31	20.62	-22.31	5.75		Nov-00
	3.07	8.06	14.04	34.92	65.22	0	1.08	14.05	0.87	18.69	609.6	2	98	0	0	31	20.79	-22.25			Jul-10
100	2.89	7.61	13.01	31.13	57.58	0	2.03	14.04	0.87	11.82	609.6	2	98	0	0	31	20.12	-22.57		1.00	Nov-00
	3.15	8.22	14.28	35.73	66.91	0	0.88	14.04	0.87	18.84	609.6	2	98	0	0	31	20.88	-22.18			Jul-07
	3.10	8.21	14.32	35.90	66.91	0	0.83	14.08	0.87	18.87	609.6	2	98	0	0	31	20.62	-22.31			Jun-13
100	4.96	10.05	20.17	22.28	96.88	0	1.33	15.08	0.99	50.15	1,820	3	86	0	10	82	30.26	-26.79	5.75		Jan-04
	5.00	10.13	20.31	22.86	98.68	0	1.2	15.08	0.99	52.06	1,820	3	86	0	10	82	30.48	-26.73			Nov-94
100	4.77	9.63	19.27	19.57	89.63	0	2.08	15.06	0.98	44.73	1,820	3	86	0	10	82	29.7	-27.02		1.00	Jan-04
	5.05	10.25	20.60	23.71	101.10	0	0.95	15.08	0.99	53.2	1,820	3	86	0	10	82	30.64	-26.64			Mar-08
	5.06	10.28	20.67	23.90	100.45	0	0.9	15.09	0.99	53.28	1,820	3	86	0	10	82	30.48	-26.73			Oct-14
100	5.45	10.27	11.57	30.88	90.00	0.04	1.35	15.02	1.04	27.21	141.5	2	89	0	8	110	33.54	-26.17	5.75		Jan-02
	5.50	10.34	11.76	31.54	91.74	0.16	1.2	15.02	1.04	27.79	141.5	2	89	0	8	110	33.84	-26.15			Jan-02
100	5.25	9.84	10.79	27.94	82.93	0	2.1	14.98	1.03	24.22	141.5	2	89	0	8	110	33.03	-26.41		1.00	Aug-02
	5.56	10.45	11.99	32.30	93.57	0.33	1	15.01	1.04	27.93	141.5	2	89	0	8	110	33.88	-26.05			Jul-10
	5.57	10.50	12.09	31.99	92.40	0.32	0.9	15.02	1.04	27.95	141.5	2	89	0	8	110	33.84	-26.15			Oct-16
100	3.97	6.90	10.83	28.92	104.84	0.49	1.2	9.8	0.89	37.41	8,420	5	94	0	1	46	26.09	-22.26	5.75		Jul-07
	3.97	6.94	10.89	29.26	105.89	0.55	1.12	9.8	0.89	38.02	8,420	5	94	0	1	46	26.18	-22.2			Apr-05
100	3.77	6.49	10.00	26.03	97.27	0.01	1.95	9.8	0.89	36.04	8,420	5	94	0	1	46	25.51	-22.46		1.00	Jul-07
	4.05	7.08	11.16	30.22	108.59	0.82	0.87	9.79	0.89	38.32	8,420	5	94	0	1	46	26.37	-22.11			Apr-05
	3.90	6.79	10.54	28.31	104.51	0.65	1.45	9.78	0.89	37.97	8,420	5	94	0	1	46	26.19	-22.19			Sep-15
	4.08	7.14	11.27	30.59	109.30	0.87	0.77	9.82	0.89	38.35	8,420	5	94	0	1	46	26.37	-22.11			Jun-13

	MARKET		FUND TYPE, CATEGORY & OBJECTIVE		RATINGS				MINIMUMS	
Fund Name	Ticker Symbol	Traded On	Fund Type	Category and (Prospectus Objective)	Overall Rating	Reward Rating	Risk Rating	Recent Up/ Downgrade	Open to New Investors	Min Initial Investment
Wells Fargo Special Small Cap Value Fund - Class A	ESPAX	NAS CM	Open End	US Equity Small Cap (Small Company)	B+	A-	B	Up	Y	1,000
Wells Fargo Special Small Cap Value Fund - Class Admin	ESPIX	NAS CM	Open End	US Equity Small Cap (Small Company)	B+	A-	B	Up	Y	1,000,000
Wells Fargo Special Small Cap Value Fund - Class C	ESPCX	NAS CM	Open End	US Equity Small Cap (Small Company)	B	B+	B	Up	Y	1,000
Wells Fargo Special Small Cap Value Fund - Class Inst	ESPNX	NAS CM	Open End	US Equity Small Cap (Small Company)	B+	A-	B	Up	Y	1,000,000
Wells Fargo Special Small Cap Value Fund - Class R	ESPHX	NAS CM	Open End	US Equity Small Cap (Small Company)	B+	A-	B	Up	Y	0
Wells Fargo Special Small Cap Value Fund - Class R6	ESPRX	NAS CM	Open End	US Equity Small Cap (Small Company)	B+	A-	B	Up	Y	0
Wells Fargo Specialized Technology Fund - Class A	WFSTX	NAS CM	Open End	Technology Sector Equity (Technology)	A-	A+	B+	Up	Y	1,000
Wells Fargo Specialized Technology Fund - Class Admin	WFTDX	NAS CM	Open End	Technology Sector Equity (Technology)	A-	A+	B+	Up	Y	1,000,000
Wells Fargo Specialized Technology Fund - Class C	WFTCX	NAS CM	Open End	Technology Sector Equity (Technology)	A-	A	B+	Up	Y	1,000
Wells Fargo Specialized Technology Fund Institutional Cls	WFTIX	NAS CM	Open End	Technology Sector Equity (Technology)	A-	A+	B+	Up	Y	1,000,000
Wells Fargo Target 2010 Fund - Class A	STNRX	NAS CM	Open End	Target Date 2000-2020 (Asset Alloc)	B-	C	B+	Up	Y	1,000
Wells Fargo Target 2010 Fund - Class Admin	WFLGX	NAS CM	Open End	Target Date 2000-2020 (Asset Alloc)	B-	C	B+	Up	Y	1,000,000
Wells Fargo Target 2010 Fund - Class C	WFOCX	NAS CM	Open End	Target Date 2000-2020 (Asset Alloc)	C+	C	B		Y	1,000
Wells Fargo Target 2010 Fund - Class R	WFARX	NAS CM	Open End	Target Date 2000-2020 (Asset Alloc)	B-	C	B+	Up	Y	0
Wells Fargo Target 2010 Fund - Class R4	WFORX	NAS CM	Open End	Target Date 2000-2020 (Asset Alloc)	B-	C	A-	Up	Y	0
Wells Fargo Target 2010 Fund - Class R6	WFOAX	NAS CM	Open End	Target Date 2000-2020 (Asset Alloc)	B-	C	A-	Up	Y	0
Wells Fargo Target 2015 Fund - Class A	WFACX	NAS CM	Open End	Target Date 2000-2020 (Asset Alloc)	B-	C	B+	Up	Y	1,000
Wells Fargo Target 2015 Fund - Class Admin	WFFFX	NAS CM	Open End	Target Date 2000-2020 (Asset Alloc)	B-	C	B+	Up	Y	1,000,000
Wells Fargo Target 2015 Fund - Class R	WFBRX	NAS CM	Open End	Target Date 2000-2020 (Asset Alloc)	B-	C	B+	Up	Y	0
Wells Fargo Target 2015 Fund - Class R4	WFSRX	NAS CM	Open End	Target Date 2000-2020 (Asset Alloc)	B-	C	A-	Up	Y	0
Wells Fargo Target 2015 Fund - Class R6	WFSCX	NAS CM	Open End	Target Date 2000-2020 (Asset Alloc)	B-	C	A-	Up	Y	0
Wells Fargo Target 2020 Fund - Class A	STTRX	NAS CM	Open End	Target Date 2000-2020 (Asset Alloc)	B-	C	B+	Up	Y	1,000
Wells Fargo Target 2020 Fund - Class Admin	WFLPX	NAS CM	Open End	Target Date 2000-2020 (Asset Alloc)	B-	C	B+	Up	Y	1,000,000
Wells Fargo Target 2020 Fund - Class C	WFLAX	NAS CM	Open End	Target Date 2000-2020 (Asset Alloc)	B-	C	B+	Up	Y	1,000
Wells Fargo Target 2020 Fund - Class R	WFURX	NAS CM	Open End	Target Date 2000-2020 (Asset Alloc)	B-	C	B+	Up	Y	0
Wells Fargo Target 2020 Fund - Class R4	WFLRX	NAS CM	Open End	Target Date 2000-2020 (Asset Alloc)	B	C+	A-	Up	Y	0
Wells Fargo Target 2020 Fund - Class R6	WFOBX	NAS CM	Open End	Target Date 2000-2020 (Asset Alloc)	B	C+	A-	Up	Y	0
Wells Fargo Target 2025 Fund - Class A	WFAYX	NAS CM	Open End	Target Date 2021-2045 (Asset Alloc)	B	C+	B+	Up	Y	1,000
Wells Fargo Target 2025 Fund - Class Admin	WFTRX	NAS CM	Open End	Target Date 2021-2045 (Asset Alloc)	B	C+	B+	Up	Y	1,000,000
Wells Fargo Target 2025 Fund - Class R	WFHRX	NAS CM	Open End	Target Date 2021-2045 (Asset Alloc)	B-	C+	B+	Up	Y	0
Wells Fargo Target 2025 Fund - Class R4	WFGRX	NAS CM	Open End	Target Date 2021-2045 (Asset Alloc)	B	C+	B+	Up	Y	0
Wells Fargo Target 2025 Fund - Class R6	WFTYX	NAS CM	Open End	Target Date 2021-2045 (Asset Alloc)	B	C+	A-	Up	Y	0
Wells Fargo Target 2030 Fund - Class A	STHRX	NAS CM	Open End	Target Date 2021-2045 (Asset Alloc)	B	C+	B+	Up	Y	1,000
Wells Fargo Target 2030 Fund - Class Admin	WFLIX	NAS CM	Open End	Target Date 2021-2045 (Asset Alloc)	B	C+	B+	Up	Y	1,000,000
Wells Fargo Target 2030 Fund - Class C	WFDMX	NAS CM	Open End	Target Date 2021-2045 (Asset Alloc)	B-	C+	B+	Up	Y	1,000
Wells Fargo Target 2030 Fund - Class R	WFJRX	NAS CM	Open End	Target Date 2021-2045 (Asset Alloc)	B	C+	B+	Up	Y	0
Wells Fargo Target 2030 Fund - Class R4	WTHRX	NAS CM	Open End	Target Date 2021-2045 (Asset Alloc)	B	C+	B+	Up	Y	0
Wells Fargo Target 2030 Fund - Class R6	WFOOX	NAS CM	Open End	Target Date 2021-2045 (Asset Alloc)	B	C+	B+	Up	Y	0
Wells Fargo Target 2035 Fund - Class A	WFQBX	NAS CM	Open End	Target Date 2021-2045 (Asset Alloc)	B-	C+	B	Down	Y	1,000
Wells Fargo Target 2035 Fund - Class Admin	WFQWX	NAS CM	Open End	Target Date 2021-2045 (Asset Alloc)	B-	C+	B	Down	Y	1,000,000
Wells Fargo Target 2035 Fund - Class R	WFKRX	NAS CM	Open End	Target Date 2021-2045 (Asset Alloc)	B-	C+	B-	Down	Y	0
Wells Fargo Target 2035 Fund - Class R4	WTTRX	NAS CM	Open End	Target Date 2021-2045 (Asset Alloc)	B-	C+	B	Down	Y	0
Wells Fargo Target 2035 Fund - Class R6	WFQRX	NAS CM	Open End	Target Date 2021-2045 (Asset Alloc)	B-	C+	B	Down	Y	0
Wells Fargo Target 2040 Fund - Class A	STFRX	NAS CM	Open End	Target Date 2021-2045 (Asset Alloc)	B-	C+	B-	Down	Y	1,000
Wells Fargo Target 2040 Fund - Class Admin	WFLWX	NAS CM	Open End	Target Date 2021-2045 (Asset Alloc)	B-	C+	B-	Down	Y	1,000,000
Wells Fargo Target 2040 Fund - Class C	WFOFX	NAS CM	Open End	Target Date 2021-2045 (Asset Alloc)	B-	C+	B-	Down	Y	1,000
Wells Fargo Target 2040 Fund - Class R	WFMRX	NAS CM	Open End	Target Date 2021-2045 (Asset Alloc)	B-	C+	B-	Down	Y	0
Wells Fargo Target 2040 Fund - Class R4	WTFRX	NAS CM	Open End	Target Date 2021-2045 (Asset Alloc)	B-	B-	B-	Down	Y	0
Wells Fargo Target 2040 Fund - Class R6	WFOSX	NAS CM	Open End	Target Date 2021-2045 (Asset Alloc)	B-	B-	B-	Down	Y	0
Wells Fargo Target 2045 Fund - Class A	WFQVX	NAS CM	Open End	Target Date 2021-2045 (Asset Alloc)	B-	B-	B-	Down	Y	1,000
Wells Fargo Target 2045 Fund - Class Admin	WFQYX	NAS CM	Open End	Target Date 2021-2045 (Asset Alloc)	B-	B-	B-	Down	Y	1,000,000
Wells Fargo Target 2045 Fund - Class R	WFNRX	NAS CM	Open End	Target Date 2021-2045 (Asset Alloc)	B-	B-	B-	Down	Y	0

★ Expanded analysis of this fund is included in Section II.

	TOTAL RETURNS					PERFORMANCE				ASSETS		ASSET ALLOCATION & TURNOVER					BULL & BEAR		FEES		
Min Additional Investment	3-Month Total Return	6-Month Total Return	1-Year Total Return	3-Year Total Return	5-Year Total Return	Dividend Yield (TTM)	Expense Ratio	3-Yr Std Deviation	3-Year Beta	NAV	Total Assets (MIL)	%Cash	%Stocks	%Bonds	%Other	Turnover Ratio	Last Bull Market Total Return	Last Bear Market Total Return	Front End Fee (%)	Back End Fee (%)	Inception Date
100	5.23	9.56	11.05	35.46	106.17	0.48	1.33	12.61	0.87	34.86	2,220	6	90	0	4	51	29.92	-22.37	5.75		May-93
	5.24	9.59	11.15	36.07	108.05	0.6	1.21	12.63	0.87	35.66	2,220	6	90	0	4	51	30.09	-22.28			Jul-96
100	5.04	9.15	10.23	32.45	98.55	0	2.08	12.6	0.87	31.67	2,220	6	90	0	4	51	29.34	-22.61		1.00	Dec-00
	5.32	9.76	11.45	37.05	110.19	0.76	0.95	12.63	0.87	35.69	2,220	6	90	0	4	51	30.2	-22.22			Jul-10
	5.14	9.39	10.76	34.55	103.78	0.64	1.58	12.62	0.87	35.41	2,220	6	90	0	4	51	29.73	-22.45			Sep-15
	5.35	9.77	11.52	37.23	109.01	0.78	0.9	12.63	0.87	35.67	2,220	6	90	0	4	51	29.92	-22.37			Oct-14
100	6.80	17.30	42.99	55.73	157.23	0	1.41	14.78	1	12.74	425.0	1	95	0	3	131	20.66	-21.45	5.75		Sep-00
	6.77	17.28	43.05	56.22	158.97	0	1.31	14.79	1	12.96	425.0	1	95	0	3	131	20.75	-21.31			Jul-10
100	6.64	16.90	41.87	52.38	147.69	0	2.16	14.79	1	10.32	425.0	1	95	0	3	131	20.03	-21.62		1.00	Sep-00
	6.83	17.44	43.36	56.29	158.16	0	1.06	14.79	1	12.99	425.0	1	95	0	3	131	20.66	-21.45			Nov-16
100	1.91	3.36	6.41	7.41	13.56	0.17	0.65	2.74	0.14	10.91	164.2	3	33	63	1	41	5.83	-2.49	5.75		Mar-94
	1.89	3.41	6.50	7.73	14.31	0.19	0.54	2.76	0.14	11.05	164.2	3	33	63	1	41	5.9	-2.43			Nov-99
100	1.62	2.90	5.64	4.96	9.35	0	1.4	2.78	0.14	11.02	164.2	3	33	63	1	41	5.36	-2.81		1.00	Dec-98
	1.87	3.25	6.23	6.64	12.12	0.11	0.9	2.79	0.15	10.83	164.2	3	33	63	1	41	5.68	-2.59			Jun-13
	1.92	3.44	6.71	8.41	15.53	0.25	0.34	2.75	0.14	11.04	164.2	3	33	63	1	41	5.83	-2.49			Nov-12
	1.98	3.58	6.94	8.97	16.42	0.31	0.19	2.76	0.15	11.03	164.2	3	33	63	1	41	6.18	-2.34			Jun-04
100	2.12	3.71	7.68	9.49	19.15	0.44	0.65	3.5	0.2	8.02	184.5	3	38	58	1	41	7.86	-4.53	5.75		Nov-12
	2.09	3.75	7.89	9.94	19.96	0.49	0.54	3.51	0.2	8.21	184.5	3	38	58	1	41	7.69	-4.74			Jun-07
	2.00	3.56	7.31	8.53	17.92	0.2	0.9	3.48	0.2	8.16	184.5	3	38	58	1	41	7.7	-4.63			Jun-13
	2.21	3.89	8.01	10.46	21.18	0.66	0.34	3.47	0.2	8.08	184.5	3	38	58	1	41	7.86	-4.53			Nov-12
	2.11	3.90	8.10	10.85	21.95	0.8	0.19	3.51	0.2	8.07	184.5	3	38	58	1	41	7.85	-4.53			Jun-07
100	2.57	4.53	9.64	12.07	26.77	0.39	0.65	4.09	0.3	12.74	959.0	3	46	49	1	39	9.78	-7.48	5.75		Mar-94
	2.58	4.57	9.69	12.35	27.55	0.41	0.54	4.1	0.3	12.99	959.0	3	46	49	1	39	9.94	-7.47			Nov-99
100	2.41	4.18	8.88	9.56	22.16	0.19	1.4	4.07	0.3	12.51	959.0	3	46	49	1	39	9.38	-7.82		1.00	Dec-98
	2.44	4.40	9.46	11.28	25.29	0.32	0.9	4.11	0.3	12.65	959.0	3	46	49	1	39	9.63	-7.58			Jun-13
	2.65	4.70	10.01	13.10	28.99	0.46	0.34	4.08	0.3	13.08	959.0	3	46	49	1	39	9.78	-7.48			Nov-12
	2.62	4.73	10.12	13.56	29.80	0.5	0.19	4.11	0.3	13.08	959.0	3	46	49	1	39	10.18	-7.34			Jun-04
100	3.20	5.60	11.72	15.19	35.81	0.62	0.65	5.02	0.42	6.49	516.4	3	56	40	1	36	12.8	-10.42	5.75		Nov-12
	3.16	5.64	11.94	15.73	36.71	0.64	0.54	5.03	0.42	6.56	516.4	3	56	40	1	36	12.69	-10.64			Jun-07
	3.11	5.53	10.60	13.45	33.46	0.56	0.9	4.94	0.42	6.43	516.4	3	56	40	1	36	12.63	-10.51			Jun-13
	3.26	5.74	12.06	16.30	38.03	0.7	0.34	5	0.42	6.53	516.4	3	56	40	1	36	12.8	-10.42			Nov-12
	3.11	5.79	12.12	16.71	38.91	0.75	0.19	5	0.42	6.51	516.4	3	56	40	1	36	12.8	-10.42			Jun-07
100	3.62	6.63	13.92	18.58	45.17	1.67	0.65	6.21	0.56	13.66	1,135	3	66	30	1	31	15.11	-13.77	5.75		Mar-94
	3.64	6.67	14.06	18.98	46.15	1.71	0.54	6.24	0.56	13.93	1,135	3	66	30	1	31	15.22	-13.7			Mar-94
100	3.44	6.23	13.08	15.88	39.77	1.17	1.4	6.2	0.56	13.15	1,135	3	66	30	1	31	14.59	-13.99		1.00	Dec-98
	3.55	6.52	13.48	17.50	43.33	1.49	0.9	6.21	0.56	13.69	1,135	3	66	30	1	31	15.05	-13.79			Jun-13
	3.75	6.83	14.29	19.69	47.74	1.87	0.34	6.22	0.56	13.94	1,135	3	66	30	1	31	15.22	-13.7			Nov-12
	3.73	6.82	14.42	20.19	48.70	2	0.19	6.23	0.56	13.91	1,135	3	66	30	1	31	15.5	-13.55			Jun-04
100	4.08	7.59	15.98	21.18	53.67	0.87	0.65	7.44	0.69	8.42	475.4	3	75	21	1	27	17.59	-15.96	5.75		Nov-12
	4.11	7.60	16.08	21.61	54.33	0.91	0.54	7.45	0.69	8.48	475.4	3	75	21	1	27	17.47	-16.16			Jun-07
	4.10	7.50	15.82	20.30	51.96	0.71	0.9	7.47	0.69	8.5	475.4	3	75	21	1	27	17.42	-16.05			Jun-13
	4.25	7.75	16.41	22.37	56.08	1.07	0.34	7.43	0.69	8.44	475.4	3	75	21	1	27	17.59	-15.96			Nov-12
	4.27	7.87	16.51	22.98	57.29	1.18	0.19	7.43	0.69	8.43	475.4	3	75	21	1	27	17.59	-15.96			Jun-07
100	4.44	8.23	17.58	23.37	60.13	0.49	0.65	8.4	0.79	16.14	992.2	3	81	15	1	24	18.75	-17.81	5.75		Mar-94
	4.44	8.25	17.71	23.73	61.09	0.5	0.54	8.42	0.79	16.59	992.2	3	81	15	1	24	18.86	-17.82			Nov-99
100	4.23	7.83	16.71	20.58	54.18	0.35	1.4	8.41	0.79	14.74	992.2	3	81	15	1	24	18.24	-18.08		1.00	Jul-98
	4.41	8.11	17.36	22.52	58.31	0.43	0.9	8.42	0.79	16.15	992.2	3	81	15	1	24	18.58	-17.9			Jun-13
	4.53	8.38	17.95	24.55	62.78	0.55	0.34	8.42	0.79	16.63	992.2	3	81	15	1	24	18.75	-17.81			Nov-12
	4.59	8.51	18.15	25.08	64.07	0.59	0.19	8.43	0.79	16.62	992.2	3	81	15	1	24	19.1	-17.64			Jun-04
100	4.72	8.80	18.82	24.88	64.26	0.9	0.65	9.08	0.86	9.25	307.2	3	85	10	1	22	19.68	-18.3	5.75		Nov-12
	4.73	8.78	18.83	25.28	65.15	0.94	0.54	9.09	0.86	9.36	307.2	3	85	10	1	22	19.53	-18.47			Jun-07
	4.61	8.56	18.41	23.94	62.50	0.73	0.9	9.06	0.85	9.4	307.2	3	85	10	1	22	19.51	-18.39			Jun-13

Fund Name	MARKET Ticker Symbol	MARKET Traded On	FUND TYPE Fund Type	CATEGORY & OBJECTIVE Category and (Prospectus Objective)	RATINGS Overall Rating	RATINGS Reward Rating	RATINGS Risk Rating	Recent Up/ Downgrade	Open to New Investors	MINIMUMS Min Initial Investment
Wells Fargo Target 2045 Fund - Class R4	WFFRX	NAS CM	Open End	Target Date 2021-2045 (Asset Alloc)	B-	B-	B-	Down	Y	0
Wells Fargo Target 2045 Fund - Class R6	WFQPX	NAS CM	Open End	Target Date 2021-2045 (Asset Alloc)	B-	B-	B-	Down	Y	0
Wells Fargo Target 2050 Fund - Class A	WFQAX	NAS CM	Open End	Target Date 2046+ (Asset Alloc)	B-	B-	B-	Down	Y	1,000
Wells Fargo Target 2050 Fund - Class Admin	WFQDX	NAS CM	Open End	Target Date 2046+ (Asset Alloc)	B-	B-	B-	Down	Y	1,000,000
Wells Fargo Target 2050 Fund - Class C	WFQCX	NAS CM	Open End	Target Date 2046+ (Asset Alloc)	B-	C+	B-	Down	Y	1,000
Wells Fargo Target 2050 Fund - Class R	WFWRX	NAS CM	Open End	Target Date 2046+ (Asset Alloc)	B-	B-	B-	Down	Y	0
Wells Fargo Target 2050 Fund - Class R4	WQFRX	NAS CM	Open End	Target Date 2046+ (Asset Alloc)	B-	B-	B-	Down	Y	0
Wells Fargo Target 2050 Fund - Class R6	WFQFX	NAS CM	Open End	Target Date 2046+ (Asset Alloc)	B-	B-	B-	Down	Y	0
Wells Fargo Target 2055 Fund - Class A	WFQZX	NAS CM	Open End	Target Date 2046+ (Asset Alloc)	B-	B-	B-	Down	Y	1,000
Wells Fargo Target 2055 Fund - Class Admin	WFLHX	NAS CM	Open End	Target Date 2046+ (Asset Alloc)	B-	B-	B-	Down	Y	1,000,000
Wells Fargo Target 2055 Fund - Class R	WFYRX	NAS CM	Open End	Target Date 2046+ (Asset Alloc)	B-	B-	B-	Down	Y	0
Wells Fargo Target 2055 Fund - Class R4	WFVRX	NAS CM	Open End	Target Date 2046+ (Asset Alloc)	B-	B-	B-	Down	Y	0
Wells Fargo Target 2055 Fund - Class R6	WFQUX	NAS CM	Open End	Target Date 2046+ (Asset Alloc)	B-	B-	B-	Down	Y	0
Wells Fargo Target 2060 Fund - Class A	WFAFX	NAS CM	Open End	Target Date 2046+ (Asset Alloc)	C	C+	B	Up	Y	1,000
Wells Fargo Target 2060 Fund - Class Admin	WFDFX	NAS CM	Open End	Target Date 2046+ (Asset Alloc)	C	C+	B	Up	Y	1,000,000
Wells Fargo Target 2060 Fund - Class C	WFCFX	NAS CM	Open End	Target Date 2046+ (Asset Alloc)	C	C+	B	Up	Y	1,000
Wells Fargo Target 2060 Fund - Class R	WFRFX	NAS CM	Open End	Target Date 2046+ (Asset Alloc)	C	C+	B	Up	Y	0
Wells Fargo Target 2060 Fund - Class R4	WFSFX	NAS CM	Open End	Target Date 2046+ (Asset Alloc)	C	C+	B	Up	Y	0
Wells Fargo Target 2060 Fund - Class R6	WFUFX	NAS CM	Open End	Target Date 2046+ (Asset Alloc)	C	C+	B	Up	Y	0
Wells Fargo Target Today Fund - Class A	STWRX	NAS CM	Open End	Target Date 2000-2020 (Asset Alloc)	B-	C	B+	Up	Y	1,000
Wells Fargo Target Today Fund - Class Admin	WFLOX	NAS CM	Open End	Target Date 2000-2020 (Asset Alloc)	B-	C	A-	Up	Y	1,000,000
Wells Fargo Target Today Fund - Class C	WFODX	NAS CM	Open End	Target Date 2000-2020 (Asset Alloc)	C+	C	B		Y	1,000
Wells Fargo Target Today Fund - Class R	WFRRX	NAS CM	Open End	Target Date 2000-2020 (Asset Alloc)	B-	C	B+	Up	Y	0
Wells Fargo Target Today Fund - Class R4	WOTRX	NAS CM	Open End	Target Date 2000-2020 (Asset Alloc)	B-	C	A-	Up	Y	0
Wells Fargo Target Today Fund - Class R6	WOTDX	NAS CM	Open End	Target Date 2000-2020 (Asset Alloc)	B-	C	A-	Up	Y	0
Wells Fargo Traditional Small Cap Growth Fund - Class A	EGWAX	NAS CM	Open End	US Equity Small Cap (Growth)	B-	B	C	Up	Y	1,000
Wells Fargo Traditional Small Cap Growth Fund - Cls Admin	EGWDX	NAS CM	Open End	US Equity Small Cap (Growth)	B-	B	C	Down	Y	1,000,000
Wells Fargo Traditional Small Cap Growth Fund - Class C	EGWCX	NAS CM	Open End	US Equity Small Cap (Growth)	B-	B	C	Up	Y	1,000
Wells Fargo Traditional Small Cap Growth Fund - Class Inst	EGRYX	NAS CM	Open End	US Equity Small Cap (Growth)	B	B	C	Up	Y	1,000,000
Wells Fargo Utilities and High Income Fund	ERH	AMEX	Closed End	Moderate Alloc (Balanced)	B-	C+	B	Up	Y	
Wells Fargo Utility and Telecommunications Fund - Class A	EVUAX	NAS CM	Open End	Utilities Sector Equity (Utility)	B	B	B		Y	1,000
Wells Fargo Utility & Telecommunications Fund - Cls Admin	EVUDX	NAS CM	Open End	Utilities Sector Equity (Utility)	B	B	B		Y	1,000,000
Wells Fargo Utility and Telecommunications Fund - Class C	EVUCX	NAS CM	Open End	Utilities Sector Equity (Utility)	B-	B-	B	Down	Y	1,000
Wells Fargo Utility & Telecommunications Fund - Cls Inst	EVUYX	NAS CM	Open End	Utilities Sector Equity (Utility)	B	B	B		Y	1,000,000
Wells Fargo WealthBuilder Conservative Alloc Fund Cls A	WCAFX	NAS CM	Open End	Cautious Alloc (Income)	B-	C	A-	Up	Y	1,000
Wells Fargo WealthBuilder Equity Fund Class A	WEAFX	NAS CM	Open End	Aggressive Alloc (Growth)	B-	B-	B-	Down	Y	1,000
Wells Fargo WealthBuilder Growth Allocation Fund Class A	WGAFX	NAS CM	Open End	Aggressive Alloc (Growth)	B-	B-	B-	Down	Y	1,000
Wells Fargo WealthBuilder Growth Balanced Fund Class A	WGBAX	NAS CM	Open End	Moderate Alloc (Balanced)	B-	C+	B	Down	Y	1,000
Wells Fargo WealthBuilder Moderate Balanced Fund Class A	WMBGX	NAS CM	Open End	Cautious Alloc (Balanced)	B-	C+	B	Up	Y	1,000
WesMark Balanced Fund	WMBLX	NAS CM	Open End	Moderate Alloc (Balanced)	B-	C+	B	Up	Y	1,000
WesMark Growth Fund	WMKGX	NAS CM	Open End	US Equity Large Cap Growth (Growth)	B-	B-	C+	Up	Y	1,000
WesMark Small Company Growth Fund	WMKSX	NAS CM	Open End	US Equity Small Cap (Small Company)	B	B-	B	Up	Y	1,000
WesMark Tactical Opportunity Fund	WMKTX	NAS CM	Open End	Moderate Alloc (Growth)	U	U	U		Y	1,000
West Loop Realty Fund Class A Shares	REIAX	NAS CM	Open End	Real Estate Sector Equity (Real Estate)	B	B-	B+	Up	Y	2,500
West Loop Realty Fund Class C Shares	REICX	NAS CM	Open End	Real Estate Sector Equity (Real Estate)	B	B-	B+	Up	Y	2,500
West Loop Realty Fund Institutional Class Shares	REIIX	NAS CM	Open End	Real Estate Sector Equity (Real Estate)	B	B-	B+	Up	Y	1,000,000
Westcore Global Large-Cap Dividend Fund Institutional Cls	WIMVX	NAS CM	Open End	Global Equity (Growth & Income)	B	B-	B		Y	250,000
Westcore Global Large-Cap Dividend Fund Retail Class	WTMVX	NAS CM	Open End	Global Equity (Growth & Income)	B	B-	B		Y	2,500
Westcore International Small-Cap Fund Institutional Class	WIIFX	NAS CM	Open End	Global Equity Mid/Small Cap (Growth)	B	B	C+	Up	Y	250,000
Westcore International Small-Cap Fund Retail Class	WTIFX	NAS CM	Open End	Global Equity Mid/Small Cap (Growth)	B	B	C+	Up		2,500
Westcore Large-Cap Dividend Fund Institutional Class	WILGX	NAS CM	Open End	US Equity Large Cap Value (Growth)	B	C+	A-	Up	Y	250,000
Westcore Large-Cap Dividend Fund Retail Class	WTEIX	NAS CM	Open End	US Equity Large Cap Value (Growth)	B	C+	A-	Up	Y	2,500

★ Expanded analysis of this fund is included in Section II.

Min Additional Investment	3-Month Total Return	6-Month Total Return	1-Year Total Return	3-Year Total Return	5-Year Total Return	Dividend Yield (TTM)	Expense Ratio	3-Yr Std Deviation	3-Year Beta	NAV	Total Assets (MIL)	%Cash	%Stocks	%Bonds	%Other	Turnover Ratio	Last Bull Market Total Return	Last Bear Market Total Return	Front End Fee (%)	Back End Fee (%)	Inception Date
TOTAL RETURNS						PERFORMANCE				ASSETS		ASSET ALLOCATION & TURNOVER					BULL & BEAR		FEES		
	4.79	8.95	19.09	26.11	67.14	1.1	0.34	9.11	0.86	9.3	307.2	3	85	10	1	22	19.68	-18.3			Nov-12
	4.71	8.96	19.22	26.54	68.09	1.21	0.19	9.07	0.86	9.26	307.2	3	85	10	1	22	19.68	-18.3			Jun-07
100	4.75	8.83	19.09	25.46	65.36	1.04	0.65	9.29	0.88	8.67	542.1	3	86	9	1	21	19.75	-18.33	5.75		Nov-12
	4.66	8.83	19.24	25.86	66.34	1.1	0.54	9.29	0.88	8.68	542.1	3	86	9	1	21	19.58	-18.42			Jun-07
100	4.55	8.46	18.22	22.63	59.24	0.57	1.4	9.26	0.88	8.63	542.1	3	86	9	1	21	19.23	-18.59		1.00	Nov-12
	4.64	8.71	18.92	24.58	63.70	0.87	0.9	9.33	0.88	8.7	542.1	3	86	9	1	21	19.58	-18.42			Jun-13
	4.81	9.06	19.58	26.71	68.20	1.24	0.34	9.32	0.88	8.72	542.1	3	86	9	1	21	19.75	-18.33			Nov-12
	4.91	9.17	19.68	27.33	69.52	1.34	0.19	9.31	0.88	8.71	542.1	3	86	9	1	21	19.75	-18.33			Jun-07
100	4.76	8.84	19.19	25.47	65.32	1.05	0.65	9.3	0.88	12.82	90.5	3	86	9	1	21	19.48		5.75		Nov-12
	4.74	8.89	19.28	25.78	66.17	1.11	0.54	9.26	0.88	12.82	90.5	3	86	9	1	21	19.26				Jul-11
	4.62	8.66	18.83	24.40	63.49	0.89	0.9	9.3	0.88	12.65	90.5	3	86	9	1	21	19.3				Jun-13
	4.79	9.01	19.52	26.60	67.90	1.26	0.34	9.28	0.88	12.85	90.5	3	86	9	1	21	19.48				Nov-12
	4.89	9.12	19.75	27.19	69.28	1.39	0.19	9.33	0.88	12.82	90.5	3	86	9	1	21	19.48				Jul-11
100	4.69	8.76	19.08			0.68	0.65			11.91	23.6	3	86	9	1	21			5.75		Jun-15
	4.74	8.88	19.22			0.71	0.54			11.98	23.6	3	86	9	1	21					Jun-15
100	4.56	8.42	18.27			0.13	1.4			11.95	23.6	3	86	9	1	21				1.00	Jun-15
	4.68	8.72	18.83			0.49	0.9			11.75	23.6	3	86	9	1	21					Jun-15
	4.79	8.98	19.50			0.82	0.34			12.14	23.6	3	86	9	1	21					Jun-15
	4.80	9.00	19.63			0.91	0.19			12.1	23.6	3	86	9	1	21					Jun-15
100	1.70	3.11	5.98	6.82	10.85	1.59	0.65	2.53	0.13	9.14	145.3	3	29	67	1	41	4.47	-0.65	5.75		Mar-94
	1.68	3.11	6.02	7.10	11.51	1.7	0.54	2.52	0.12	9.37	145.3	3	29	67	1	41	4.62	-0.6			Nov-99
100	1.51	2.70	5.11	4.39	6.65	0.41	1.4	2.51	0.12	9.36	145.3	3	29	67	1	41	4.03	-1		1.00	Dec-98
	1.53	2.87	5.64	5.94	9.38	1.28	0.9	2.52	0.13	9.1	145.3	3	29	67	1	41	4.32	-0.75			Jun-13
	1.76	2.92	5.91	7.47	12.36	1.9	0.34	2.48	0.12	9.37	145.3	3	29	67	1	41	4.47	-0.65			Nov-12
	1.79	3.24	6.36	8.28	13.44	2.45	0.19	2.51	0.12	9.35	145.3	3	29	67	1	41	4.72	-0.46			Jun-04
100	2.46	8.92	21.70	22.27	83.65	0	1.33	13.47	0.87	15.07	95.7	3	89	0	8	113	30.55	-27.64	5.75		Jun-95
	2.56	9.01	21.87	23.00	85.35	0	1.2	13.49	0.87	16.86	95.7	3	89	0	8	113	30.7	-27.57			Jul-10
100	2.26	8.51	20.77	19.54	76.91	0	2.08	13.48	0.87	13.74	95.7	3	89	0	8	113	29.97	-27.85		1.00	Jul-10
	2.56	9.07	22.06	23.52	86.75	0	0.98	13.49	0.87	17.23	95.7	3	89	0	8	113	30.83	-27.52			Nov-97
	1.13	4.37	13.92	16.82	57.59	6.52		8.52	0.78	13.12	127.7	10	56	27	0	73	11.62	-11.75			Apr-04
100	0.75	4.12	13.65	15.98	63.84	1.45	1.14	10.14	0.7	21.16	411.5	2	97	0	0	22	15.24	-5.23	5.75		Jan-94
	0.76	4.23	13.86	16.60	65.42	1.59	0.95	10.17	0.7	21.18	411.5	2	97	0	0	22	15.34	-5.13			Jul-10
100	0.52	3.73	12.77	13.37	57.84	0.75	1.89	10.15	0.7	21.17	411.5	2	97	0	0	22	14.72	-5.53		1.00	Sep-94
	0.81	4.33	14.07	17.26	66.66	1.77	0.78	10.17	0.7	21.15	411.5	2	97	0	0	22	15.43	-5.11			Feb-94
100	-3.39	-1.76	1.88	3.32	10.74		1.29	3.04		10.22	371.4	5	22	69	2	175	8.02	-5.74	5.75		Feb-17
100	-10.34	-5.80	5.63	10.14	47.05		1.52	10.63		20.45	539.0	2	84	0	13	30	25.33	-20.15	5.75		Feb-17
100	-8.13	-4.15	5.25	9.62	43.58		1.5	8.98		13.86	403.6	3	75	8	12	58	24.11	-20.94	5.75		Feb-17
100	-7.53	-4.24	3.30	7.15	34.68		1.43	6.99		13.33	835.6	4	57	28	10	102	20.84	-18.21	5.75		Feb-17
100	-5.87	-3.49	2.11	5.11	21.67		1.35	4.94		11.18	645.1	5	42	49	3	136	13.76	-11.65	5.75		Feb-17
100	2.85	7.05	10.76	18.47	46.90	1.59	1.24	5.87	0.55	13.05	117.8	2	63	35	0	49	16.31	-7.8			Apr-98
100	5.81	11.16	24.21	21.34	85.63	0.17	1.17	11.61	1.12	20	362.9	3	96	0	1	61	25.31	-22.71			Apr-97
100	3.61	9.88	13.18	21.79	80.32	0.25	1.24	12.73	0.87	13.9	106.9	5	94	0	0	41	23.6	-24.05			Dec-93
100	2.68	5.58					2.08			10.62	22.6	11	59	26	5						Mar-17
100	5.13	6.60	7.02	18.69		1.16	1.35	12.69	0.92	13.84	98.1	2	98	0	0	24			5.75		Dec-13
100	4.98	6.17	6.25	16.11		0.48	2.1	12.65	0.92	13.78	98.1	2	98	0	0	24				1.00	Dec-13
100,000	5.38	6.84	7.48	19.72		1.38	1.1	12.72	0.92	13.85	98.1	2	98	0	0	24					Dec-13
	6.30	8.51	19.78	28.59	72.00	1.6	0.82	8.9	0.76	11.04	55.5	1	99	0	0	61	22.75	-13.11			Sep-07
25	6.23	8.52	19.55	27.99	70.57	1.52	1	8.9	0.76	11.12	55.5	1	99	0	0	61	22.69	-13.1			Jun-88
	6.56	16.14	33.88	37.33	37.51	1.08	1.25	13.16	0.98	20.83	77.6	2	98	0	0	44	23.24	-19.2			Apr-16
25	6.51	16.02	33.63	36.86	37.03	3.81	1.5	13.16	0.98	19.76	77.6	2	98	0	0	44	23.24	-19.2			Dec-99
	6.22	10.45	17.09	21.36	77.73	1.01	0.67	11	1	6.12	10.7	0	100	0	0	112	25.51	-15.8			Sep-07
25	6.17	10.22	16.72	20.38	75.62	0.82	0.89	11.07	1	6.01	10.7	0	100	0	0	112	25.43	-15.91			Jun-88

	MARKET		FUND TYPE, CATEGORY & OBJECTIVE		RATINGS				MINIMUMS	
Fund Name	Ticker Symbol	Traded On	Fund Type	Category and (Prospectus Objective)	Overall Rating	Reward Rating	Risk Rating	Recent Up/ Downgrade	Open to New Investors	Min Initial Investment
Westcore Micro-Cap Opportunity Fund Retail Class	WTMIX	NAS CM	Open End	US Equity Small Cap (Growth)	B	B+	B	Up	Y	2,500
Westcore Mid-Cap Value Dividend Fund II Institutional Cls	WIMGX	NAS CM	Open End	US Equity Mid Cap (Growth)	C-	D+	C	Up	Y	250,000
Westcore Mid-Cap Value Dividend Fund II Retail Class	WTMGX	NAS CM	Open End	US Equity Mid Cap (Growth)	C-	D+	C	Up	Y	2,500
Westcore Mid-Cap Value Dividend Fund Institutional Class	WIMCX	NAS CM	Open End	US Equity Mid Cap (Growth)	B	B-	B	Up	Y	250,000
Westcore Mid-Cap Value Dividend Fund Retail Class	WTMCX	NAS CM	Open End	US Equity Mid Cap (Growth)	B	B-	B	Up	Y	2,500
Westcore Small-Cap Growth Fund II Institutional Class	WTSLX	NAS CM	Open End	US Equity Small Cap (Growth)	C+	C+	C+	Up	Y	2,500
Westcore Small-Cap Growth Fund Institutional Class	WISGX	NAS CM	Open End	US Equity Small Cap (Small Company)	B	A-	C	Up	Y	250,000
Westcore Small-Cap Growth Fund Retail Class	WTSGX	NAS CM	Open End	US Equity Small Cap (Small Company)	B	A-	C	Up	Y	2,500
Westcore Small-Cap Value Dividend Fund Institutional Class	WISVX	NAS CM	Open End	US Equity Small Cap (Small Company)	B-	C+	B	Up		250,000
Westcore Small-Cap Value Dividend Fund Retail Class	WTSVX	NAS CM	Open End	US Equity Small Cap (Small Company)	B-	C+	B	Up		2,500
Westcore Smid-Cap Value Dividend Fund Institutional Class	WISDX	NAS CM	Open End	US Equity Small Cap (Equity-Income)	D-	D+	B		Y	250,000
Westcore Smid-Cap Value Dividend Fund Retail Class	WTSDX	NAS CM	Open End	US Equity Small Cap (Equity-Income)	D-	D+	B-		Y	2,500
Westfield Capital Dividend Growth Fund Institutional Class	WDIVX	NAS CM	Open End	US Equity Large Cap Blend (Equity-Income)	B-	B-	B-	Down	Y	50,000
Westfield Capital Dividend Growth Fund Investor Class	WCDGX	NAS CM	Open End	US Equity Large Cap Blend (Equity-Income)	B-	B-	B-	Down	Y	2,500
Westfield Capital Large Cap Growth Fund Inst Cls Shares	WCLGX	NAS CM	Open End	US Equity Large Cap Growth (Growth)	B	B	B-	Down	Y	50,000
Westfield Capital Large Cap Growth Fund Inv Cls Shares	WCLCX	NAS CM	Open End	US Equity Large Cap Growth (Growth)	B	B	B-		Y	2,500
Westwood Emerging Markets Fund A Class Shares	WWEAX	NAS CM	Open End	Emerging Markets Equity (Div Emerging Mkts)	C+	C+	C	Up	Y	5,000
Westwood Emerging Markets Fund Institutional Shares	WWEMX	NAS CM	Open End	Emerging Markets Equity (Div Emerging Mkts)	C+	C+	C	Up	Y	100,000
Westwood Global Equity Fund Institutional Shares	WWGEX	NAS CM	Open End	Global Equity (World Stock)	B-	B-	B	Up	Y	5,000
Westwood Income Opportunity Fund A Class	WWIAX	NAS CM	Open End	Moderate Alloc (Income)	B-	C+	B	Up	Y	5,000
Westwood Income Opportunity Fund Institutional Class	WHGIX	NAS CM	Open End	Moderate Alloc (Income)	B-	C+	B	Up	Y	100,000
Westwood LargeCap Value Fund A Class	WWLAX	NAS CM	Open End	US Equity Large Cap Blend (Growth)	B-	B-	B	Down	Y	5,000
Westwood LargeCap Value Fund Institutional Class	WHGLX	NAS CM	Open End	US Equity Large Cap Blend (Growth)	B-	B-	B	Down	Y	100,000
Westwood Low Volatility Equity Fund Institutional Class	WLVIX	NAS CM	Open End	US Equity Large Cap Blend (Growth & Income)	B	C+	B+	Up	Y	5,000
Westwood Market Neutral Income Fund Institutional Shares	WMNIX	NAS CM	Open End	Market Neutral (Convertible Bond)	C+	C-	B	Up	Y	5,000
Westwood Market Neutral Income Fund Ultra Shares	WMNUX	NAS CM	Open End	Market Neutral (Convertible Bond)	C+	C-	B+	Up	Y	250,000
Westwood MLP & Strategic Energy Fund Institutional Shares	WMLPX	NAS CM	Open End	Energy Sector Equity (Growth & Income)	D+	D+	D	Down	Y	5,000
Westwood SmallCap Fund Institutional Class	WHGSX	NAS CM	Open End	US Equity Small Cap (Growth)	B+	A-	B	Up	Y	5,000
Westwood SMidCap Fund Institutional Class	WHGMX	NAS CM	Open End	US Equity Mid Cap (Growth)	B-	C+	B	Up	Y	5,000
Westwood SMidCap Plus Fund Institutional Class	WHGPX	NAS CM	Open End	US Equity Mid Cap (Growth)	B-	C+	B	Up	Y	5,000
Westwood Strategic Convertibles Fund Institutional Shares	WSCIX	NAS CM	Open End	Convertibles (Convertible Bond)	C+	C	B	Up	Y	5,000
Westwood Worldwide Income Opp Fund Inst Shares	WWIOX	NAS CM	Open End	Alloc (Equity-Income)	B-	C	B	Up	Y	5,000
White Oak Select Growth Fund	WOGSX	NAS CM	Open End	US Equity Large Cap Growth (Growth)	B+	B	A-	Up	Y	2,000
Wildermuth Endowment Strategy Fund Class A	WESFX	NAS CM	Closed End	Alloc (Growth & Income)	B-	C	B	Up	Y	2,500
Wildermuth Endowment Strategy Fund Class C	US96812D2062		Closed End	Alloc (Growth & Income)	B-	C	B	Up	Y	2,500
Wildermuth Endowment Strategy Fund Class I	US96812D3052		Closed End	Alloc (Growth & Income)	B-	C+	B	Up	Y	1,000,000
William Blair Emerging Markets Fund Class N	WBENX	NAS CM	Open End	Emerging Markets Equity (Div Emerging Mkts)	B-	B	C	Up		2,500
William Blair Emerging Markets Growth Fund Class I	WBEIX	NAS CM	Open End	Emerging Markets Equity (Div Emerging Mkts)	B-	B	C	Up		500,000
William Blair Emerging Mkts Growth Fund Cls Inst	BIEMX	NAS CM	Open End	Emerging Markets Equity (Div Emerging Mkts)	B-	B	C	Up		5,000,000
William Blair Emerging Markets Leaders Fund Class I	WBELX	NAS CM	Open End	Emerging Markets Equity (Div Emerging Mkts)	C+	B-	C	Up	Y	500,000
William Blair Emerging Markets Leaders Fund Class N	WELNX	NAS CM	Open End	Emerging Markets Equity (Div Emerging Mkts)	C+	B-	C	Up	Y	2,500
William Blair Emerging Mkts Leaders Fund Inst Cls	WELIX	NAS CM	Open End	Emerging Markets Equity (Div Emerging Mkts)	C+	B-	C	Up	Y	5,000,000
William Blair Emerging Markets Small Cap Growth Fund Cls I	BESIX	NAS CM	Open End	Emerging Markets Equity (Div Emerging Mkts)	B-	B-	C+	Up		500,000
William Blair Emerging Markets Small Cap Growth Fund Cls N	WESNX	NAS CM	Open End	Emerging Markets Equity (Div Emerging Mkts)	B-	B-	C+	Up		2,500
William Blair Emerging Mkts Small Cap Growth Fund Inst Cls	WESJX	NAS CM	Open End	Emerging Markets Equity (Div Emerging Mkts)	B-	B-	C+	Up		5,000,000
William Blair Global Leaders Fund Class I	WGFIX	NAS CM	Open End	Global Equity (World Stock)	B	B	B	Up	Y	500,000
William Blair Global Leaders Fund Class N	WGGNX	NAS CM	Open End	Global Equity (World Stock)	B	B	B	Up	Y	2,500
William Blair Global Leaders Fund Institutional Class	BGGIX	NAS CM	Open End	Global Equity (World Stock)	B	B	B	Up	Y	5,000,000
William Blair Growth Fund Class I	BGFIX	NAS CM	Open End	US Equity Large Cap Growth (Growth)	B	B	A-	Up	Y	500,000
William Blair Growth Fund Class N	WBGSX	NAS CM	Open End	US Equity Large Cap Growth (Growth)	B	B-	A-	Up	Y	2,500
William Blair Inst Intl Developed Plus Fund Cls Inst	WIIEX	NAS CM	Open End	Global Equity Large Cap (Foreign Stock)	B	B-	B	Up	Y	5,000,000
William Blair Institutional International Growth Fund	WBIIX	NAS CM	Open End	Global Equity Large Cap (Foreign Stock)	B	B-	B	Up		5,000,000

★ Expanded analysis of this fund is included in Section II.

Min Additional Investment	TOTAL RETURNS 3-Month Total Return	6-Month Total Return	1-Year Total Return	3-Year Total Return	5-Year Total Return	PERFORMANCE Dividend Yield (TTM)	Expense Ratio	3-Yr Std Deviation	3-Year Beta	ASSETS NAV	Total Assets (MIL)	ASSET ALLOCATION & TURNOVER %Cash	%Stocks	%Bonds	%Other	Turnover Ratio	BULL & BEAR Last Bull Market Total Return	Last Bear Market Total Return	FEES Front End Fee (%)	Back End Fee (%)	Inception Date
25	1.10	5.58	5.69	25.02	91.30	0.31	1.3	13.38	0.8	17.24	14.4	1	99	0	0	43	28.18	-24.2			Jun-08
	4.32	5.67	6.82	-5.00	47.95	0.04	0.93	13.82	1.16	4.87	32.1	1	99	0	0	158	24.95	-26.77			Sep-07
25	4.26	5.64	6.82	-5.45	46.67	0.04	1.12	13.82	1.15	4.74	32.1	1	99	0	0	158	24.71	-26.87			Aug-86
	4.28	5.10	6.23	27.26	92.41	0.36	0.91	10.72	0.98	27.3	84.3	1	99	0	0	78	19.64	-17.84			Apr-16
25	4.23	5.02	6.01	26.77	91.67	1.36	1.16	10.71	0.98	26.87	84.3	1	99	0	0	78	19.64	-17.84			Oct-98
25	3.34	9.86	33.25	5.33	65.12	0	1.15	14.72	0.86	26.85	45.5	2	98	0	0	182	19.54	-29.32			Oct-99
	2.42	8.67	25.93	31.66		0	0.99	14.68	0.95	12.88	5.8	2	98	0	0	81					Dec-13
25	2.38	8.70	25.97	30.64		0	1.24	14.73	0.96	12.72	5.8	2	98	0	0	81					Dec-13
	0.08	0.82	-1.67	16.57	74.23	1.59	1.09	14.15	0.95	10.7	202.0	5	95	0	0	96	23.87	-20			Sep-07
25	0.07	0.73	-1.84	15.94	72.71	1.36	1.31	14.19	0.96	10.68	202.0	5	95	0	0	96	23.86	-20.06			Dec-04
	2.04	2.35	1.73				1.09			9.88	0.82	7	93	0	0	2					Dec-16
25	2.04	2.25	1.53				1.22			9.92	0.82	7	93	0	0	2					Dec-16
	7.96	12.42	21.51	28.79	77.27	1.72	0.95	9.5	0.9	11.3	114.6	1	99	0	0	112	20.25	-14.14			Jul-13
	7.91	12.36	21.18	27.94	76.24	1.56	1.2	9.54	0.9	11.35	114.6	1	99	0	0	112	20.25	-14.14			Jul-13
	5.75	11.86	30.57	36.08	112.93	0.33	0.85	11.7	1.05	10.81	107.5	1	99	0	0	63	24.59				Jul-11
	5.59	11.71	30.18	35.00	110.13	0.15	1.1	11.7	1.05	10.96	107.5	1	99	0	0	63	24.58				Jul-11
	6.20	9.14	27.90	17.20	6.35	0.69	1.45	14.87	0.9	10.22	351.4	3	89	0	1	47			5.00		Dec-12
	6.34	9.28	28.35	18.12	7.79	0.9	1.2	14.9	0.9	10.22	351.4	3	89	0	1	47					Dec-12
	4.05	9.23	19.73	26.68	45.61	1.2	1	10.52	0.94	13.68	18.0	0	98	0	0	17					Dec-12
	3.28	4.62	10.68	13.81	43.45	1.21	1.11	5.7	-0.22	15.8	2,724	15	51	15	0	22	12.93	-6.64	5.00		Dec-07
	3.35	4.76	10.96	14.69	45.22	1.45	0.86	5.74	-0.22	15.81	2,724	15	51	15	0	22	13.04	-6.52			Dec-05
	7.65	11.90	20.54	31.22	94.72	0.75	0.9	9.52	0.89	13.08	214.0	3	97	0	0	39	24.72	-19.96	5.00		Dec-07
	7.70	12.05	20.84	32.11	97.07	0.95	0.65	9.55	0.9	13.01	214.0	3	97	0	0	39	24.79	-19.85			Jun-06
	3.65	4.88	12.76	18.92	77.91	1.1	0.75	8.5	0.81	10.54	45.5	2	72	0	1	39	21.02	-14.13			Aug-01
	-1.53	-1.33	0.56			0.82	1.2			9.94	30.8	20	-19	0	0	99					May-15
	-1.41	-1.22	0.71			0.9	1.05			9.94	30.8	20	-19	0	0	99					May-15
	0.89	3.11	-2.33	-21.11		3.37	1			7.24	14.4	1	96	0	0	44					Dec-14
	3.39	9.63	12.36	34.28	118.76	0.45	0.99	14.48	0.99	17.29	245.7	4	96	0	0	65	33.68	-23.74			Apr-07
	3.60	7.18	10.39	18.42	70.36	0.39	0.88	11.61	0.9	15.78	350.8	0	100	0	0	82	26.27	-24.21			Dec-05
	3.20	6.23	11.51	18.27	73.58	0.5	0.81	10.29	0.78	15.88	161.2	2	98	0	0	54	23.66	-22.44			Mar-11
	1.25	3.03	10.82			1.02	0.85			10.17	6.4	7	0	4	2	118					May-15
	2.66	5.57	11.80			1.2	1			10.4	5.0	13	57	18	0	54					May-15
25	7.12	10.91	19.75	43.58	108.45	0.86	1.06	13.24	1.21	85.76	293.7	0	100	0	1	14	21.3	-16.2			Aug-92
100	3.24	7.16	13.21	37.42		1.47	3.23			12.92	--	16	58	4	17	55			5.75		Dec-14
100	2.96	6.74	12.35	34.93		1.49	3.98			12.73	--	16	58	4	17	55				1.00	Mar-16
	3.23	7.65	13.73	37.51			2.98			12.98	--	16	58	4	17	55					Apr-17
1,000	6.96	19.75	48.52	28.18	34.63	0.14	1.65	15.1	0.92	16.2	1,351	1	99	0	0	105	21.11	-22.94			Jun-05
	6.99	19.79	48.82	29.04	36.27	0.31	1.41	15.08	0.92	16.36	1,351	1	99	0	0	105	21.26	-22.86			Jun-05
	7.03	19.89	49.06	29.36	37.26	0.36	1.19	15.11	0.92	16.49	1,351	1	99	0	0	105	21.44	-22.79			Jun-05
	6.45	17.92	41.89	24.25	27.03	0.1	1.4	14.85	0.89	11.09	463.2	3	97	0	0	135	20.12	-23.03			Mar-08
1,000	6.49	17.91	41.68	23.17	25.31	0	1.65	14.9	0.89	11.06	463.2	3	97	0	0	135	19.96	-23.15			May-10
	6.51	17.98	42.15	24.43	27.73	0.13	1.25	14.88	0.89	11.09	463.2	3	97	0	0	135	20.2	-23.01			Mar-08
	9.39	17.49	40.53	26.14	68.69	1.97	1.4	12.01	0.7	18.73	450.3	1	95	0	4	157					Oct-11
1,000	9.28	17.35	40.08	24.96	66.23	1.71	1.65	12	0.7	18.66	450.3	1	95	0	4	157					Oct-11
	9.37	17.52	40.62	26.38	69.45	2	1.25	12.02	0.7	18.76	450.3	1	95	0	4	157					Dec-12
	7.24	14.52	30.69	34.72	73.26	0.21	1.15	11.59	1.04	14.56	209.6	2	96	0	1	75	27.07	-18.8			Oct-07
1,000	7.12	14.34	30.31	33.48	70.68	0	1.4	11.58	1.04	14.53	209.6	2	96	0	1	75	26.97	-18.93			Oct-07
	7.24	14.60	30.77	34.97	73.92	0.25	1	11.61	1.05	14.56	209.6	2	96	0	1	75	27.07	-18.8			Dec-12
	7.17	11.90	24.64	29.82	93.18	0.18	0.9	10.84	0.96	11.51	375.6	0	100	0	0	79	25.68	-17.02			Oct-99
1,000	7.07	11.80	24.34	28.71	90.36	0	1.2	10.88	0.96	10.27	375.6	0	100	0	0	79	25.54	-17.2			Mar-46
	3.76	10.71	24.27	25.58	47.21	1.68	0.9	11.03	0.88	14.55	19.1	4	94	0	3	75	17.57	-23			Dec-04
	4.59	13.12	29.53	25.80	47.64	0.9	0.98	11.17	0.88	18.08	2,337	2	96	0	2	105	20.71	-21.77			Jul-02

	MARKET			FUND TYPE, CATEGORY & OBJECTIVE	RATINGS					MINIMUMS
Fund Name	Ticker Symbol	Traded On	Fund Type	Category and (Prospectus Objective)	Overall Rating	Reward Rating	Risk Rating	Recent Up/ Downgrade	Open to New Investors	Min Initial Investment
William Blair Intl Developed Plus Fund Cls Inst	WIEIX	NAS CM	Open End	Global Equity Large Cap (Foreign Stock)	B	B-	B	Up	Y	500,000
William Blair International Developed Plus Fund Class N	WIENX	NAS CM	Open End	Global Equity Large Cap (Foreign Stock)	B	B-	B	Up	Y	2,500
William Blair International Growth Fund Class I	BIGIX	NAS CM	Open End	Global Equity Large Cap (Foreign Stock)	B	B-	B	Up		500,000
William Blair International Growth Fund Class N	WBIGX	NAS CM	Open End	Global Equity Large Cap (Foreign Stock)	B-	B-	B	Up		2,500
William Blair International Leaders Fund Class I Shares	WILIX	NAS CM	Open End	Global Equity Large Cap (Growth)	B+	A-	B	Up	Y	500,000
William Blair International Leaders Fund Class N Shares	WILNX	NAS CM	Open End	Global Equity Large Cap (Growth)	B+	A-	B	Up	Y	2,500
William Blair Intl Leaders Fund Inst Cls Shares	WILJX	NAS CM	Open End	Global Equity Large Cap (Growth)	B+	A-	B	Up	Y	5,000,000
William Blair International Small Cap Growth Fund Class I	WISIX	NAS CM	Open End	Global Equity Mid/Small Cap (Foreign Stock)	A-	B+	A-	Up		500,000
William Blair Intl Small Cap Growth Fund Cls Inst	WIISX	NAS CM	Open End	Global Equity Mid/Small Cap (Foreign Stock)	A-	B+	A-	Up		5,000,000
William Blair International Small Cap Growth Fund Class N	WISNX	NAS CM	Open End	Global Equity Mid/Small Cap (Foreign Stock)	A-	B+	A-	Up		2,500
William Blair Large Cap Growth Fund Class I	LCGFX	NAS CM	Open End	US Equity Large Cap Growth (Growth)	A-	A-	A-	Up	Y	500,000
William Blair Large Cap Growth Fund Class N	LCGNX	NAS CM	Open End	US Equity Large Cap Growth (Growth)	A-	A-	A-	Up	Y	2,500
William Blair Macro Allocation Fund Class I	WMCIX	NAS CM	Open End	Multialternative (Asset Alloc)	C	C	C		Y	500,000
William Blair Macro Allocation Fund Class N	WMCNX	NAS CM	Open End	Multialternative (Asset Alloc)	C	C	C		Y	2,500
William Blair Macro Allocation Fund Institutional Class	WMCJX	NAS CM	Open End	Multialternative (Asset Alloc)	C	C	C		Y	5,000,000
William Blair Mid Cap Growth Fund Class I	WCGIX	NAS CM	Open End	US Equity Mid Cap (Growth)	B-	C+	B	Down	Y	500,000
William Blair Mid Cap Growth Fund Class N	WCGNX	NAS CM	Open End	US Equity Mid Cap (Growth)	B-	C+	B	Up	Y	2,500
William Blair Small Cap Growth Fund Class I	WBSIX	NAS CM	Open End	US Equity Small Cap (Small Company)	B	A-	C	Down	Y	500,000
William Blair Small Cap Growth Fund Class N	WBSNX	NAS CM	Open End	US Equity Small Cap (Small Company)	B	A-	C	Down	Y	2,500
William Blair Small Cap Value Fund Class I	BVDIX	NAS CM	Open End	US Equity Small Cap (Small Company)	B+	B+	B	Up	Y	500,000
William Blair Small Cap Value Fund Class N	WBVDX	NAS CM	Open End	US Equity Small Cap (Small Company)	B	B+	B	Up	Y	2,500
William Blair Small-Mid Cap Growth Fund Class I	WSMDX	NAS CM	Open End	US Equity Mid Cap (Small Company)	B+	A-	B	Up	Y	500,000
William Blair Small-Mid Cap Growth Fund Class N	WSMNX	NAS CM	Open End	US Equity Mid Cap (Small Company)	B	A-	B-	Down	Y	2,500
William Blair Small-Mid Cap Value Fund Class I	WSMIX	NAS CM	Open End	US Equity Small Cap (Growth)	B	B	B	Up	Y	500,000
William Blair Small-Mid Cap Value Fund Class N	BSMNX	NAS CM	Open End	US Equity Small Cap (Growth)	B	B	B	Up	Y	2,500
Williston Basin/Mid-North America Stock Fund Class A	ICPAX	NAS CM	Open End	Energy Sector Equity (Growth)	D+	D+	D+	Down	Y	1,000
Williston Basin/Mid-North America Stock Fund Class C	ICPUX	NAS CM	Open End	Energy Sector Equity (Growth)	D+	D+	D+	Down	Y	1,000
Williston Basin/Mid-North America Stock Fund Class I	ICWIX	NAS CM	Open End	Energy Sector Equity (Growth)	D+	D+	D+	Down	Y	1,000
Wilmington Diversified Income Fund Class A	ARBAX	NAS CM	Open End	Moderate Alloc (Balanced)	B	C+	B+	Up	Y	1,000
Wilmington Diversified Income Fund Class I	ARGIX	NAS CM	Open End	Moderate Alloc (Balanced)	B-	C+	B	Up	Y	1,000,000
Wilmington Global Alpha Equities Fund Class A	WRAAX	NAS CM	Open End	Multialternative (Growth)	C+	C	B	Up	Y	1,000
Wilmington Global Alpha Equities Fund Class I	WRAIX	NAS CM	Open End	Multialternative (Growth)	C+	C	B	Up	Y	1,000,000
Wilmington International Fund Class A	GVIEX	NAS CM	Open End	Global Equity Large Cap (Foreign Stock)	B-	B-	B-	Up	Y	1,000
Wilmington International Fund Class Institutional	MVIEX	NAS CM	Open End	Global Equity Large Cap (Foreign Stock)	B-	B-	B-	Up	Y	1,000,000
Wilmington Large-Cap Strategy Fund Class Institutional	WMLIX	NAS CM	Open End	US Equity Large Cap Blend (Growth)	B	B	B		Y	1,000,000
Wilmington Real Asset Fund Class A	WMMRX	NAS CM	Open End	Alloc (Growth & Income)	C+	C	B-	Up	Y	1,000
Wilmington Real Asset Fund Class Institutional	WMRIX	NAS CM	Open End	Alloc (Growth & Income)	C+	C	B-	Up	Y	1,000,000
Wilshire 5000 Index Portfolio Class Institutional	WINDX	NAS CM	Open End	US Equity Large Cap Blend (Growth)	B	B	B		Y	250,000
Wilshire 5000 Index Portfolio Investment Class Shares	WFIVX	NAS CM	Open End	US Equity Large Cap Blend (Growth)	B	B	B		Y	1,000
Wilshire Intl Equity Fund Inst Cls Shares	WLTTX	NAS CM	Open End	Global Equity Large Cap (Foreign Stock)	B-	B-	B	Up	Y	250,000
Wilshire International Equity Fund Investment Class Shares	WLCTX	NAS CM	Open End	Global Equity Large Cap (Foreign Stock)	B-	B-	B	Up	Y	2,500
Wilshire Large Company Growth Portfolio Fund Cls Inst	WLCGX	NAS CM	Open End	US Equity Large Cap Growth (Growth)	A-	B+	A	Up	Y	250,000
Wilshire Large Company Growth Port Inv Cls Shares	DTLGX	NAS CM	Open End	US Equity Large Cap Growth (Growth)	B+	B+	A	Up	Y	2,500
Wilshire Large Company Value Portfolio Fund Cls Inst	WLCVX	NAS CM	Open End	US Equity Large Cap Value (Growth)	B-	B-	B	Down	Y	250,000
Wilshire Large Company Value Port Inv Cls Shares	DTLVX	NAS CM	Open End	US Equity Large Cap Value (Growth)	B-	B-	B	Down	Y	2,500
Wilshire Small Company Growth Portfolio Fund Cls Inst	WSMGX	NAS CM	Open End	US Equity Small Cap (Small Company)	B+	A-	B+	Up	Y	250,000
Wilshire Small Company Growth Port Inv Cls Shares	DTSGX	NAS CM	Open End	US Equity Small Cap (Small Company)	B+	A-	B+	Up	Y	2,500
Wilshire Small Company Value Fund Class Institutional	WSMVX	NAS CM	Open End	US Equity Small Cap (Small Company)	B+	A-	B	Up	Y	250,000
Wilshire Small Company Value Port Inv Cls Shares	DTSVX	NAS CM	Open End	US Equity Small Cap (Small Company)	B+	A-	B	Up	Y	2,500
Wintergreen Fund Institutional Class	WGRIX	NAS CM	Open End	Global Equity (Growth)	C+	C+	B-	Up	Y	100,000
Wintergreen Fund Investor Class	WGRNX	NAS CM	Open End	Global Equity (Growth)	C+	C+	B-	Up	Y	10,000
Wireless Fund	WIREX	NAS CM	Open End	Technology Sector Equity (Comm)	B	B+	B-		Y	5,000

★Expanded analysis of this fund is included in Section II.

		TOTAL RETURNS				PERFORMANCE				ASSETS		ASSET ALLOCATION & TURNOVER					BULL & BEAR		FEES		
Min Additional Investment	3-Month Total Return	6-Month Total Return	1-Year Total Return	3-Year Total Return	5-Year Total Return	Dividend Yield (TTM)	Expense Ratio	3-Yr Std Deviation	3-Year Beta	NAV	Total Assets (MIL)	%Cash	%Stocks	%Bonds	%Other	Turnover Ratio	Last Bull Market Total Return	Last Bear Market Total Return	Front End Fee (%)	Back End Fee (%)	Inception Date
	3.67	10.51	23.72	25.20	47.76	0.98	1.05	10.99	0.87	16.76	119.5	2	95	0	3	70	17.07	-23.31			May-04
1,000	3.65	10.36	23.42	24.26	45.92	0.79	1.3	10.99	0.87	16.6	119.5	2	95	0	3	70	16.84	-23.37			May-04
	4.59	13.13	29.48	25.42	46.92	1.41	1.13	11.19	0.88	31.13	3,172	2	97	0	2	101	20.45	-22.14			Oct-99
1,000	4.53	12.92	29.10	24.31	44.71	1.19	1.43	11.21	0.88	30.41	3,172	2	97	0	2	101	20.3	-22.3			Oct-92
	5.21	12.68	30.04	38.69	63.56	0.79	1.1	11.78	0.9	16.44	369.8	1	98	0	1	59					Aug-12
1,000	5.08	12.52	29.64	37.75	61.61	0.74	1.35	11.74	0.9	16.37	369.8	1	98	0	1	59					Aug-12
	5.16	12.71	30.07	39.12	64.49	0.84	0.95	11.77	0.9	16.43	369.8	1	98	0	1	59					Nov-12
	4.86	13.56	32.70	38.76	63.28	0.27	1.3	10.88	0.86	15.65	594.0	1	95	0	4	73	16.34	-20.9			Nov-05
	4.86	13.51	32.70	39.07	64.31	0.33	1.07	10.9	0.86	15.73	594.0	1	95	0	4	73	16.5	-20.8			Nov-05
1,000	4.80	13.32	32.16	37.50	60.84	0.04	1.59	10.86	0.86	15.49	594.0	1	95	0	4	73	16.15	-21.05			Nov-05
	10.26	16.58	31.29	42.76	124.73	0.23	0.8	11.04	0.98	13.97	203.6	0	100	0	0	44	31.15	-17.63			Dec-99
1,000	10.15	16.46	30.87	41.63	121.78	0.05	1.05	11.01	0.98	13.35	203.6	0	100	0	0	44	31.08	-17.78			Dec-99
	0.63	2.52	5.49	1.73	18.33	2.16	1.25	5.49	-0.22	11.88	1,423	23	35	40	1	50					Nov-11
1,000	0.54	2.26	5.06	0.81	16.65	1.75	1.5	5.49	0.26	11.84	1,423	23	35	40	1	50					Nov-11
	0.65	2.53	5.50	1.92	18.81	2.23	1.04	5.47	-0.51	11.89	1,423	23	35	40	1	50					Oct-13
	5.54	9.81	21.18	20.93	72.43	0	1.05	10.21	0.89	11.57	79.7	2	98	0	0	60	24.68	-17.72			Feb-06
1,000	5.48	9.69	20.88	20.07	70.26	0	1.3	10.19	0.88	10.92	79.7	2	98	0	0	60	24.47	-17.78			Feb-06
	4.89	9.90	26.98	44.44	133.57	0	1.25	13.42	0.84	29.61	493.1	2	98	0	0	90	28.8	-25.75			Dec-99
1,000	4.81	9.74	26.69	43.37	130.69	0	1.5	13.42	0.84	26.87	493.1	2	98	0	0	90	28.62	-25.84			Dec-99
	1.83	8.37	7.84	27.73	90.85	0.37	1.25	13.1	0.91	20.7	714.9	1	99	0	0	33	25.59	-24.22			Oct-99
1,000	1.77	8.21	7.57	26.76	88.41	0.16	1.5	13.13	0.91	20.15	714.9	1	99	0	0	33	25.37	-24.29			Dec-96
	5.58	10.99	28.89	42.97	125.93	0	1.1	10.93	0.79	24.48	1,821	3	97	0	0	66	23.99	-20.8			Dec-03
1,000	5.53	10.89	28.56	41.91	123.06	0	1.35	10.88	0.79	23.36	1,821	3	97	0	0	66	23.97	-20.91			Dec-03
	5.32	9.38	9.83	27.79	88.23	0.68	1.1	11.58	0.95	14.24	3.5	0	100	0	0	45					Dec-11
1,000	5.31	9.28	9.58	26.82	85.90	0.08	1.35	11.59	0.95	14.31	3.5	0	100	0	0	45					Dec-11
50	7.99	12.42	-7.48	-5.21	15.17	0.2	1.47	20.58	1.09	5.48	433.3	0	100	0	0	64	30.02	-32.64	5.00		Apr-99
50	7.95	12.19	-7.80	-6.58	12.52	0	1.97	20.47	1.09	5.43	433.3	0	100	0	0	64	29.64	-32.78		1.00	May-14
50	8.25	12.68	-6.92	-4.56	15.96	0.71	0.97	20.56	1.09	5.47	433.3	0	100	0	0	64	30.02	-32.64			Aug-16
25	2.67	6.43	14.52	17.89	37.16	1.22	0.75	6.32	0.52	10.64	44.2	7	59	33	0	9	14.16	-15.14	5.50		Feb-99
25	2.72	6.55	14.78	18.78	38.97	1.45	0.5	6.33	0.52	10.65	44.2	7	59	33	0	9	14.35	-15.05			Jun-10
25	1.55	3.63	9.54	6.78	15.52	0.22	1.5	4.11	0.52	11.02	150.9	11	89	0	0				5.50		Jan-12
25	1.60	3.67	9.75	7.64	16.98	0.27	1.25	4.14	0.53	11.1	150.9	11	89	0	0						Jan-12
25	5.27	12.61	33.38	28.46	42.49	0.99	1.05	11.74	0.93	9.13	582.2	3	97	0	0	177	12.56	-25.11	5.50		Dec-05
25	5.38	12.71	33.56	29.09	43.55	1.07	0.92	11.77	0.93	9.2	582.2	3	97	0	0	177	12.62	-24.94			Jun-98
25	6.67	11.65	21.98	36.62	110.93	1.57	0.25	10.81	1.06	22.09	551.1	0	100	0	0	18	25.78	-17.05			Jul-03
25	3.77	6.89	11.54	8.03	8.96	0.37	1.1	6.52	1.25	14.58	317.5	6	67	24	4	593	10.95	-10.44	5.50		Dec-05
25	3.87	7.03	11.80	8.82	10.39	0.48	0.85	6.5	1.25	14.72	317.5	6	67	24	4	593	11.17	-10.38			Jul-03
100,000	6.40	11.08	20.57	35.15	106.97	1.73	0.36	10.15	1	20.83	186.5	1	99	0	0	5	24.97	-17.6			Feb-99
100	6.33	10.96	20.20	34.00	104.38	1.45	0.67	10.16	1	20.83	186.5	1	99	0	0	5	24.82	-17.69			Feb-99
100,000	4.55	10.38	25.91	26.31	44.21	1.46	1.27	10.65	0.84	11.04	343.6	1	99	0	0	79	24.61	-19.45			Nov-07
100	4.45	10.21	25.53	25.35	42.43	1.33	1.52	10.67	0.84	11.19	343.6	1	99	0	0	79	24.41	-19.56			Nov-07
100,000	5.80	11.00	27.35	39.49	102.80	0.32	1.04	10.66	0.97	42.53	237.4	1	99	0	0	75	27.7	-17.85			Jul-96
100	5.74	10.82	26.93	38.22	99.72	0.03	1.32	10.65	0.97	39.53	237.4	1	99	0	0	75	27.4	-17.93			Sep-92
100,000	6.25	9.66	14.98	25.20	95.50	1.73	1.04	11.54	1.1	20.95	158.7	0	100	0	0	174	26.04	-21.48			Jul-96
100	6.16	9.54	14.64	24.43	93.26	0.6	1.26	11.55	1.1	21.18	158.7	0	100	0	0	174	25.85	-21.65			Sep-92
100,000	3.37	8.05	13.96	40.38	111.55	0	1.12	13.01	0.84	27.14	48.7	2	98	0	0	114	25.97	-25.09			Jul-96
100	3.33	7.91	13.66	39.25	108.86	0	1.36	13.01	0.84	25.05	48.7	2	98	0	0	114	25.72	-25.21			Oct-92
100,000	3.72	9.69	8.97	30.58	105.61	0.62	1.12	14.03	0.97	23.49	42.6	5	95	0	0	99	26.77	-25.15			Jul-96
100	3.62	9.52	8.64	29.49	102.78	0.27	1.36	14.03	0.97	22.99	42.6	5	95	0	0	99	26.43	-25.42			Sep-92
1,000	3.70	2.78	14.17	13.58	31.77	3.18	1.75	9.67	0.66	13.61	405.5	0	88	12	0	8	14.36	-13.38			Dec-11
1,000	3.70	2.71	14.00	12.84	30.24	2.85	2	9.71	0.67	13.63	405.5	0	88	12	0	8	14.36	-13.38			Oct-05
100	6.44	14.13	29.76	42.11	98.67	0	1.97	12.23	0.84	10.9	4.2	4	96	0	0	16	14.85	-20.86			Apr-00

	MARKET		FUND TYPE, CATEGORY & OBJECTIVE		RATINGS				MINIMUMS	
Fund Name	Ticker Symbol	Traded On	Fund Type	Category and (Prospectus Objective)	Overall Rating	Reward Rating	Risk Rating	Recent Up/ Downgrade	Open to New Investors	Min Initial Investment
WOA All Asset I Class I Shares	WOAIX	NAS CM	Open End	Moderate Alloc (Growth & Income)	B-	C+	B	Up	Y	1,000,000
WP Intl Companies Income Plus Fund Inst Cls	WPITX	NAS CM	Open End	Global Equity Large Cap (Equity-Income)	C-	C	B+	Up	Y	2,000
WP Large Cap Income Plus Fund Institutional Class	WPLCX	NAS CM	Open End	US Equity Large Cap Value (Growth)	B	B+	C+	Up	Y	2,000
WP Smaller Companies Income Plus Fund Institutional Class	WPSMX	NAS CM	Open End	US Equity Small Cap (Small Company)	C-	C-	B+	Up	Y	2,000
WPG Partners Small/Micro Cap Value Fund	WPGTX	NAS CM	Open End	US Equity Small Cap (Small Company)	C	C+	C		Y	100,000
Wright International Blue Chip Equities Fund	WIBCX	NAS CM	Open End	Global Equity Large Cap (Foreign Stock)	C+	C+	C+	Up	Y	1,000
Wright Major Blue Chip Equities Fund	WQCEX	NAS CM	Open End	US Equity Large Cap Blend (Growth & Income)	B	B	B-		Y	1,000
Wright Selected Blue Chip Equities Fund	WSBEX	NAS CM	Open End	US Equity Mid Cap (Growth & Income)	B	B-	B	Up	Y	1,000
WSTCM Sector Select Risk - Managed Fund Inst Shares	WSTIX	NAS CM	Open End	Aggressive Alloc (Growth & Income)	B-	C	B	Up	Y	100,000
WSTCM Sector Select Risk - Managed Fund Investor Shares	WSTEX	NAS CM	Open End	Aggressive Alloc (Growth & Income)	B-	C	B	Up	Y	1,000
WV Concentrated Equities Fund Class A Shares	WVCAX	NAS CM	Open End	US Equity Mid Cap (Growth)	U	U	U		Y	1,000
WV Concentrated Equities Fund Class I Shares	WVCIX	NAS CM	Open End	US Equity Mid Cap (Growth)	U	U	U		Y	500,000
YCG Enhanced Fund	YCGEX	NAS CM	Open End	US Equity Large Cap Blend (Growth)	B	B-	B+		Y	2,500
Yorktown Capital Income Fund Class A	APIGX	NAS CM	Open End	Global Equity (Growth & Income)	C+	C+	C+	Down		1,000
Yorktown Capital Income Fund Class Institutional	AFAAX	NAS CM	Open End	Global Equity (Growth & Income)	C+	C+	B-	Down	Y	1,000,000
Yorktown Capital Income Fund Class L	AFDDX	NAS CM	Open End	Global Equity (Growth & Income)	C+	C+	C+	Down	Y	1,000
Yorktown Growth Fund Class A	AFGGX	NAS CM	Open End	Global Equity (Growth)	B	B	B	Up	Y	1,000
Yorktown Growth Fund Class Institutional	APGRX	NAS CM	Open End	Global Equity (Growth)	B	B	B	Up	Y	1,000,000
Yorktown Growth Fund Class L	APITX	NAS CM	Open End	Global Equity (Growth)	B	B-	B	Up	Y	1,000
Yorktown Master Allocation Fund Class A	APIFX	NAS CM	Open End	US Equity Mid Cap (Asset Alloc)	C+	C+	C+	Down	Y	1,000
Yorktown Master Allocation Fund Class Institutional	APMAX	NAS CM	Open End	US Equity Mid Cap (Asset Alloc)	C+	C+	C+	Down	Y	1,000,000
Yorktown Master Allocation Fund Class L	APILX	NAS CM	Open End	US Equity Mid Cap (Asset Alloc)	B-	C+	B	Up	Y	1,000
Yorktown Mid-Cap Fund Class A	YWBAX	NAS CM	Open End	US Equity Mid Cap (Growth)	D+	D+	B	Up	Y	1,000
Yorktown Mid-Cap Fund Class L	YWBLX	NAS CM	Open End	US Equity Mid Cap (Growth)	D+	D+	B	Up	Y	1,000
Yorktown Mid-Cap Fund Institutional Class	YWBIX	NAS CM	Open End	US Equity Mid Cap (Growth)	D+	D+	B	Up	Y	1,000,000
Yorktown Multi-Asset Income Fund Class A	APIUX	NAS CM	Open End	Cautious Alloc (Income)	C+	C+	B-	Down	Y	1,000
Yorktown Multi-Asset Income Fund Class C	AFFCX	NAS CM	Open End	Cautious Alloc (Income)	C+	C+	C+		Y	1,000
Yorktown Multi-Asset Income Fund Class Institutional	APIIX	NAS CM	Open End	Cautious Alloc (Income)	C+	C+	B-		Y	1,000,000
Yorktown Multi-Asset Income Fund Class L	AFFIX	NAS CM	Open End	Cautious Alloc (Income)	C+	C+	C+		Y	1,000
Yorktown Small-Cap Fund Class A	YOVAX	NAS CM	Open End	US Equity Small Cap (Small Company)	D+	C-	B+	Up	Y	1,000
Yorktown Small-Cap Fund Class L	YOVLX	NAS CM	Open End	US Equity Small Cap (Small Company)	D+	C-	B+	Up	Y	1,000
Yorktown Small-Cap Fund Institutional Class	YOVIX	NAS CM	Open End	US Equity Small Cap (Small Company)	D+	C-	B+	Up	Y	1,000,000
Zacks All-Cap Core Fund Class C	CZOCX	NAS CM	Open End	US Equity Large Cap Blend (Growth & Income)	B-	B-	B-	Down	Y	2,500
Zacks All-Cap Core Fund Investor Class	CZOVX	NAS CM	Open End	US Equity Large Cap Blend (Growth & Income)	B-	B-	B-	Down	Y	2,500
Zacks Dividend Fund Institutional Class Shares	ZDIIX	NAS CM	Open End	US Equity Large Cap Value (Equity-Income)	B	B-	B		Y	5,000
Zacks Dividend Fund Investor Class	ZDIVX	NAS CM	Open End	US Equity Large Cap Value (Equity-Income)	B-	B-	B-	Down	Y	2,500
Zacks Market Neutral Fund Institutional Class	ZMNIX	NAS CM	Open End	Market Neutral (Growth & Income)	C	C-	B-	Up	Y	5,000
Zacks Market Neutral Fund Investor Class	ZMNVX	NAS CM	Open End	Market Neutral (Growth & Income)	C	C-	B-	Up	Y	2,500
Zacks Small-Cap Core Fund Institutional Class	ZSCIX	NAS CM	Open End	US Equity Small Cap (Small Company)	A-	A	B+	Up	Y	5,000
Zacks Small-Cap Core Fund Investor Class	ZSCCX	NAS CM	Open End	US Equity Small Cap (Small Company)	A-	A	B	Up	Y	2,500
Zevenbergen Genea Fund Institutional Class	ZVGIX	NAS CM	Open End	US Equity Large Cap Growth (Technology)	C	B-	B	Up	Y	250,000
Zevenbergen Genea Fund Investor Class	ZVGNX	NAS CM	Open End	US Equity Large Cap Growth (Technology)	C	B-	B	Up	Y	2,500
Zevenbergen Growth Fund Institutional Class	ZVNIX	NAS CM	Open End	US Equity Large Cap Growth (Growth)	C	C+	B	Up	Y	250,000
Zevenbergen Growth Fund Investor Class	ZVNBX	NAS CM	Open End	US Equity Large Cap Growth (Growth)	C	C+	B	Up	Y	2,500

★ Expanded analysis of this fund is included in Section II.

	TOTAL RETURNS					PERFORMANCE				ASSETS		ASSET ALLOCATION & TURNOVER					BULL & BEAR		FEES		
Min Additional Investment	3-Month Total Return	6-Month Total Return	1-Year Total Return	3-Year Total Return	5-Year Total Return	Dividend Yield (TTM)	Expense Ratio	3-Yr Std Deviation	3-Year Beta	NAV	Total Assets (MIL)	%Cash	%Stocks	%Bonds	%Other	Turnover Ratio	Last Bull Market Total Return	Last Bear Market Total Return	Front End Fee (%)	Back End Fee (%)	Inception Date
25,000	3.00	6.41	13.85	18.17	29.69	0.65	1.52	8.37	0.75	11.94	222.5	2	63	34	0	162					Mar-12
100	2.04	7.38	24.19			0	3.25			12.6	9.0	4	96	0	0	0					Dec-15
100	6.57	12.77	23.72	44.67		0.15	3.05	17.69	1.48	13.79	32.6	1	96	3	0	3					Oct-13
100	0.06	5.57	13.14			0	3.12			12.95	5.6	3	97	0	0	0					Dec-15
5,000	3.96	7.84	5.68	8.73	52.08	0.4	1.1	15.33	1.03	16.74	33.3	3	97	0	0	78	31.34	-28.94			Mar-72
	3.62	8.60	19.53	15.67	30.83	1.43	1.85	11.35	0.92	16.54	10.8	0	100	0	0	49	13.9	-25.36			Sep-89
	8.21	15.21	27.66	34.30	110.35	0.72	1.4	10.92	1.06	23.43	13.7	0	100	0	0	44	23.38	-19.01			Jul-85
	6.61	10.11	16.45	21.89	88.88	0.38	1.17	10.5	0.89	12.65	31.9	1	99	0	0	24	28.93	-22.8			Jan-83
1,000	4.74	8.27	13.48	6.26		0.19	1.56	6.51	0.36	11.5	16.5	1	89	4	5	346					Dec-13
250	4.67	8.12	13.24	5.47		0.12	1.81	6.48	0.36	11.43	16.5	1	89	4	5	346					Dec-13
50	2.38	3.30					1.42			24.73	214.4	15	73	0	11				5.75		Apr-17
	2.42	3.38					1.17			24.76	214.4	15	73	0	11						Apr-17
100	5.98	8.71	22.79	33.59	89.48	0.46	1.19	9.56	0.88	16.29	142.1	0	91	8	0	24					Dec-12
100	3.92	7.33	16.53	20.05	50.73	1.69	1.63	8.9	0.82	40.98	39.1	3	97	0	0	67	18.29	-15.81	5.75		Apr-88
100,000	3.98	7.47	16.85	21.58	54.20	1.95	1.38	8.89	0.82	42	39.1	3	97	0	0	67	18.63	-15.64			Jun-04
100	3.70	6.91	15.68	17.96	46.67	1.16	2.38	8.89	0.82	39.48	39.1	3	97	0	0	67	17.94	-16			Jun-04
100	6.01	12.34	27.50	32.16	82.52	0	1.48	10.51	0.95	17.62	65.9	1	99	0	0	37	26.23	-21.52	5.75		Jul-04
100,000	6.05	12.33	27.50	32.28	81.75	0	1.48	10.5	0.95	18.55	65.9	1	99	0	0	37	25.55	-21.9			May-13
100	5.80	11.81	26.24	28.31	73.59	0	2.48	10.44	0.95	14.96	65.9	1	99	0	0	37	25.55	-21.9			Jun-85
100	4.70	8.85	16.12	17.31	54.26	0	2.6	10.08	0.93	29.13	28.3	6	94	0	0	27	20.91	-20.64	5.75		Mar-09
100,000	4.76	9.00	16.42	18.81	57.51	0	2.35	10.08	0.93	31.05	28.3	6	94	0	0	27	20.91	-20.64			May-13
100	4.52	8.44	15.28	15.29	50.14	0	3.35	10.08	0.93	27.43	28.3	6	94	0	0	27	20.52	-20.82			Mar-09
100	6.00	8.04	6.81			0.01	1.5			11.03	21.2	4	96	0	0	44			5.75		May-16
100	5.76	7.71	6.26			0	2.25			10.92	21.2	4	96	0	0	44					May-16
100,000	6.07	8.21	7.28			0.11	1.25			11.08	21.2	4	96	0	0	44					May-16
100	1.73	4.40	10.03	19.43	26.90	5.53	1.17	7.9	1.95	10.53	803.5	1	36	51	1	102	13.1	-12.74	5.75		Jul-97
100	1.53	4.09	9.46	17.62	23.74	5.57	1.67	7.89	1.93	9.79	803.5	1	36	51	1	102	12.77	-12.92		1.00	May-16
100,000	1.87	4.65	10.57	21.25	30.16	5.71	0.67	7.86	1.93	11.02	803.5	1	36	51	1	102	13.52	-12.4			Apr-10
100	1.59	4.09	9.46	17.55	23.70	5.42	1.67	7.86	1.93	9.96	803.5	1	36	51	1	102	12.79	-12.72			Jul-04
100	4.40	9.30	8.84			0.22	1.4			11.09	21.4	5	95	0	0	41			5.75		May-16
100	4.17	8.83	7.92			0	2.15			10.95	21.4	5	95	0	0	41					May-16
100,000	4.47	9.36	8.99			0.25	1.15			11.13	21.4	5	95	0	0	41					May-16
100	6.06	11.96	21.08	26.16	82.74	0	2.37	9.83	0.93	22.34	40.8	1	99	0	0	51	21.82	-17.36		1.00	Dec-05
100	6.31	12.37	22.02	29.11	89.88	0.14	1.62	9.83	0.93	24.97	40.8	1	99	0	0	51	22.27	-17.06	5.75		Dec-05
1,000	5.39	10.31	16.48	29.16			1.05	10.45	1	20.56	47.3	1	99	0	0	15					Jan-17
100	5.33	10.18	16.21	28.86		1.28	1.3	10.44	1	20.56	47.3	1	99	0	0	15					Jan-14
1,000	1.36	2.13	-2.90	5.18	3.87	0	1.4	4.87	5.63	13.39	20.1	100	0	0	0	179	3.18	2.7		1.00	Jul-08
100	1.28	2.01	-3.20	6.21	6.53	0	1.65	4.87	9.45	14.19	20.1	100	0	0	0	179	3.63	3.04	5.75		Jul-08
1,000	0.15	9.76	14.38	37.11	108.91	0	1.14	13.56	0.88	28.2	178.3	1	95	0	4	147	28.69				Feb-14
100	0.12	9.64	14.15	35.99	106.79	0	1.39	13.54	0.88	27.87	178.3	1	95	0	4	147	28.69				Jun-11
500	4.63	10.48	52.21			0	1.1			15.8	8.6	2	98	0	0	68					Aug-15
100	4.66	10.56	51.69			0	1.4			15.7	8.6	2	98	0	0	68					Aug-15
500	3.45	6.81	33.97			0	1			13.17	7.9	0	100	0	0	26					Aug-15
100	3.47	6.68	33.70			0	1.3			13.09	7.9	0	100	0	0	26					Aug-15

Section II:
Analysis of 100 Largest Stock Mutual Funds

Detailed analysis of the 100 Largest Open End and Closed End Stock Mutual Funds. Funds are listed by their asset size.

Section II: Contents

This section contains an expanded analysis of the 100 Largest Stock Mutual Funds, with current and historical Weiss Investment Ratings, key rating factors, summary financial data and performance charts. Funds are listed by their asset size.

TOP ROW

Fund Name

Describes the fund's assets, regions of investments and investment strategies. Many funds have similar names, so you want to make sure the fund you look up is really the one you are interested in evaluating.

Overall Rating

The Weiss rating measured on a scale from A to E based on each fund's risk and performance. See the preceding section, "What Our Ratings Mean," for an explanation of each letter grade rating.

BUY-HOLD-SELL Indicator

Funds that are rated in the A or B range are, in our opinion, a potential BUY. Funds in the C range will indicate a HOLD status. Funds in the D or E range will indicate a SELL status.

Ticker Symbol

An arrangement of characters (usually letters) representing a particular security listed on an exchange or otherwise traded publicly. When a company issues securities to the public marketplace, it selects an available ticker symbol for its securities which investors use to place trade orders. Every listed security has a unique ticker symbol, facilitating the vast array of trade orders that flow through the financial markets every day. If a ticker symbol is not assigned to a particular fund, the International Securities Identification Number (ISIN) is displayed.

Traded On (Exchange)

The stock exchange on which the fund is listed. The core function of a stock exchange is to ensure fair and orderly trading, as well as efficient dissemination of price information. Exchanges such as: NYSE (New York Stock Exchange), AMEX (American Stock Exchange), NNM (NASDAQ National Market), and NASQ (NASDAQ Small Cap) give companies, governments and other groups a platform to sell securities to the investing public. NASDAQ CM is abbreviated as NAS in this section.

NAV (Net Asset Value)

A fund's price per share. The value is calculated by dividing the total value of all the securities in the portfolio, less any liabilities, by the number of fund shares outstanding.

Total Assets ($)

The total of all assets listed on the institution's balance sheet. This figure primarily consists of loans, investments, and fixed assets. Total Assets are displayed in dollars.

Dividend Yield (TTM)
Trailing twelve months dividends paid out relative to the share price. Expressed as a percentage and measures how much cash flow an investor is getting for each invested dollar. **Trailing Twelve Months** (TTM) is a representation of a fund's financial performance over the most recent 12 months. TTM uses the latest available financial data from a company's interim, quarterly or annual reports.

Turnover Ratio
The percentage of a mutual fund or other investment vehicle's holdings that have been replaced with other holdings in a given year. Generally, low turnover ratio is favorable, because high turnover equates to higher brokerage transaction fees, which reduce fund returns.

Expense Ratio
A measure of what it costs an investment company to operate a mutual fund. An expense ratio is determined through an annual calculation, where a fund's operating expenses are divided by the average dollar value of its assets under management. Operating expenses may include money spent on administration and management of the fund, advertising, etc. An expense ratio of 1 percent per annum means that each year 1 percent of the fund's total assets will be used to cover expenses.

LEFT COLUMN

Ratings

Reward Rating
This is based on the total return over a period of up to five years, including net asset value and price growth. The total return figure is stated net of the expenses and fees charged by the fund. Based on proprietary modeling the individual components of the risk and reward ratings are calculated and weighted and the final rating is generated.

Risk Rating
This is includes the risk ratings of component stocks where applicable and also includes the financial stability of the fund, turnover where applicable, together with the level of volatility as measured by the fund's daily returns over a period of up to five years. Funds with greater stability are considered less risky and receive a higher risk rating. Funds with greater volatility are considered riskier, and will receive a lower risk rating. In addition to considering the fund's volatility, the risk rating also considers an assessment of the valuation and quality of a fund's holdings.

Fund Information

Fund Type
Describes the fund's assets, regions of investments and investment strategies.

Open End Fund

A type of mutual fund that does not have restrictions on the amount of shares the fund will issue. If demand is high enough, the fund will continue to issue shares no matter how many investors there are. Open-end funds also buy back shares when investors wish to sell.

Closed End Fund

They are launched through an Initial Public Offering in order to raise money and then trade in the open market just like a stock or an ETF. They only issue a set amount of shares and, although their value is also based on the Net Asset Value, the actual price of the fund is affected by supply and demand, allowing it to trade at prices above or below its real value.

Category

Identifies funds according to their actual investment styles as measured by their portfolio holdings. This categorization allows investors to spread their money around in a mix of funds with a variety of risk and return characteristics.

Sub-Category

A subdivision of funds, usually with common characteristics as the category.

Prospectus Objective

Gives a general idea of a fund's overall investment approach and goals.

Inception Date

The date on which the fund began its operations. The commencement date indicates when a fund began investing in the market. Many investors prefer funds with longer operating histories. Funds with longer histories have longer track records and can thereby provide investors with a more long-standing picture of their performance.

Open to New Investments

Indicates whether the fund accepts investments from those who are not existing investors. A "Y" in this column identifies that the fund accepts new investors. No data in this column indicates that the fund is closed to new investors. The fund may be closed to new investors because the fund's asset base is getting too large to effectively execute its investing style. Although, the fund may be closed, in most cases, existing investors are able to add to their holdings.

Minimum Initial Investment

The smallest investment amount a fund will accept to establish a new account. This amount could be $0 or any other number set by the fund.

Minimum Subsequent Investment

The smallest additional investment amount a fund will accept in an existing account.

Front End Fee
A commission or sales charge applied at the time of the initial purchase of an investment. The fee percentage is generally based on the amount of the investment. Larger investments, both initial and cumulative, generally receive percentage discounts based on the dollar value invested. Fees are displayed as a percent.

Back End Fee
A fee that investors pay when withdrawing money from an investment within a specified number of years, usually five to 10 years. The back-end load is designed to discourage withdrawals and typically declines for each year that a shareholder remains in a fund. The fee is a percentage of the value of the share being sold. Fees are displayed as a percent.

Total Returns (%)

3-Month Total Return
The rate of return on an investment over three months that includes interest, capital gains, dividends and distributions realized.

6-Month Total Return
The rate of return on an investment over six months that includes interest, capital gains, dividends and distributions realized.

1-Year Total Return
The rate of return on an investment over one year that includes interest, capital gains, dividends and distributions realized.

3-Year Total Return
The rate of return on an investment over three years that includes interest, capital gains, dividends and distributions realized.

5-Year Total Return
The rate of return on an investment over five years that includes interest, capital gains, dividends and distributions realized.

Last Bull Market Total Return
The fund's total return (the rate of return on an investment over a period of time that includes interest, capital gains, dividends and distributions realized) during the last market upswing. A **Bull Market** is a financial market condition in which prices are rising or are expected to rise. Bull markets are characterized by optimism, investor confidence and expectations that strong results will continue.

Last Bear Market Total Return
The fund's total return (the rate of return on an investment over a period of time that includes interest, capital gains, dividends and distributions realized) during the last market downturn. A **Bear Market** is a financial market condition in which the prices of securities are falling, investors anticipate losses, and selling of securities increases.

3-Year Standard Deviation

A statistical measurement of dispersion about an average, which depicts how widely the returns varied over the past three years. Investors use the standard deviation of historical performance to try to predict the range of returns that are most likely for a given fund. When a fund has a high standard deviation, the predicted range of performance is wide, implying greater volatility. Standard deviation is most appropriate for measuring risk if it is for a fund that is an investor's only holding. The figure cannot be combined for more than one fund because the standard deviation for a portfolio of multiple funds is a function of not only the individual standard deviations, but also of the degree of correlation among the funds' returns. If a fund's returns follow a normal distribution, then approximately 68 percent of the time they will fall within one standard deviation of the mean return for the fund, and 95 percent of the time within two standard deviations.

3-Year Beta

A three year measure of volatility, or systematic risk, of a security in comparison to the market as a whole. A beta of less than 1 means that the security will be less volatile than the market, a beta larger than 1 means more volatility. Beta value cannot be calculated if less than 24 months of pricing is available.

Company Information

Provider

The legal company that issues the fund.

Manager/Tenure (Years)

The name of the manager and the number of years spent managing the fund.

Website

The company's web address.

Address

The company’s street address.

Phone Number

The company's phone number.

RIGHT COLUMN

Performance Chart

A graphical representation of the fund’s total returns over the past year.

Ratings History

Indicates the fund's Overall, Risk and Reward Ratings for the previous three years. Ratings are listed as of December 31, 2017 (Q4-17), September 30, 2017 (Q3-17), June 30, 2017 (Q2-17), March 31, 2017 (Q1-17), December 31, 2016 (Q4-16), and December 31, 2015 (Q4-15).

Overall Rating

The Weiss rating measured on a scale from A to E based on each fund's risk and performance. See the preceding section, "What Our Ratings Mean," for an explanation of each letter grade rating.

Risk Rating

This is includes the risk ratings of component stocks where applicable and also includes the financial stability of the fund, turnover where applicable, together with the level of volatility as measured by the fund's daily returns over a period of up to five years. Funds with greater stability are considered less risky and receive a higher risk rating. Funds with greater volatility are considered riskier, and will receive a lower risk rating. In addition to considering the fund's volatility, the risk rating also considers an assessment of the valuation and quality of a fund's holdings.

Reward Rating

This is based on the total return over a period of up to five years, including net asset value and price growth. The total return figure is stated net of the expenses and fees charged by the fund. Based on proprietary modeling the individual components of the risk and reward ratings are calculated and weighted and the final rating is generated.

Asset & Performance History

Indicates the fund's NAV (Net Asset Value) and 1-Year Total Return for the previous 6 years.

NAV (Net Asset Value)

A fund's price per share. The value is calculated by dividing the total value of all the securities in the portfolio, less any liabilities, by the number of fund shares outstanding.

1-Year Total Return

The rate of return on an investment over one year that includes interest, capital gains, dividends and distributions realized.

Total Assets ($)

The total of all assets listed on the institution's balance sheet. This figure primarily consists of loans, investments, and fixed assets. Total Assets are displayed in dollars.

Asset Allocation

Indicates the percentage of assets in each category. Used as an investment strategy that attempts to balance risk versus reward by adjusting the percentage of each asset in an investment portfolio according to the investor's risk tolerance, goals and investment time frame. Allocation percentages may not add up to 100%. Negative values reflect short positions.

%Cash

The percentage of the fund's assets invested in short-term obligations, usually less than 90 days, that provide a return in the form of interest payments. This type of investment generally offers a low return compared to other investments but has a low risk level.

%Stocks

The percentage of the fund's assets invested in stock.

%US Stocks

The percentage of the fund's assets invested in US stock.

%Bonds

The percentage of the fund's assets invested in bonds. A bond is an unsecured debt security issued by companies, municipalities, states and sovereign governments to raise funds. When a company issues a bond it borrows money from the bondholder to boost the business, in exchange the bondholder receives the principal amount back plus the interest on the determined maturity date.

%US Bonds

The percentage of the fund's assets invested in US bonds.

%Other

The percentage of the fund's assets invested in other financial instruments.

Services Offered

Services offered by the fund provider. Such services can include:

Systematic Withdrawal Plan

A plan offered by mutual funds that pays specific amounts to shareholders at predetermined intervals.

Institutional Only

This indicates if the fund is offered to institutional clients only (pension funds, mutual funds, money managers, insurance companies, investment banks, commercial trusts, endowment funds, hedge funds, and some hedge fund investors).

Phone Exchange

This indicates that investors can move money between different funds within the same fund family over the phone.

Wire Redemption

This indicates whether or not investors can redeem electronically.

Qualified Investment

Under a qualified plan, an investor may invest in the variable annuity with pretax dollars through an employee pension plan, such as a 401(k) or 403(b). Money builds up on a tax-deferred basis, and when the qualified investor makes a withdrawal or annuitizes, all contributions received are taxable income.

Investment Strategy

A set of rules, behaviors or procedures, designed to guide an investor's selection of an investment portfolio. Individuals have different profit objectives, and their individual skills make different tactics and strategies appropriate.

Top Holdings

The highest amount of publicly traded assets held by a fund. These publicly traded assets may include company stock, mutual funds or other investment vehicles.

Vanguard Total Stock Market Index Fund Investor Shares B BUY

Ticker	Traded On	NAV	Total Assets ($)	Dividend Yield (TTM)	Turnover Ratio	Expense Ratio
VTSMX	NAS CM	66.7	$656,960,692,801	1.66	4	0.15

Ratings

Reward	B
Risk	B

Fund Information

Fund Type	Open End
Category	US Equity Large Cap Blend
Sub-Category	Large Blend
Prospectus Objective	Growth
Inception Date	Apr-92
Open to New Investments	Y
Minimum Initial Investment	3,000
Minimum Subsequent Investment	1
Front End Fee	
Back End Fee	

Total Returns (%)

3-Month	6-Month	1-Year	3-Year	5-Year
6.31	11.11	21.05	35.28	108.33

Last Bull Market	25.72
Last Bear Market	-17.74
3-Year Standard Deviation	10.23
3-Year Beta	1

Company Information

Provider	Vanguard
Manager/Tenure	Gerard C. O'Reilly (22), Walter Nejman (1)
Website	http://www.vanguard.com
Address	Vanguard 100 Vanguard Boulevard Malvern PA 19355 United States
Phone Number	877-662-7447

Ratings History

Date	Overall Rating	Risk Rating	Reward Rating
Q4-17	B	B	B
Q3-17	B	A-	B
Q2-17	B	B	B
Q1-17	B	C+	B
Q4-16	B	B	B
Q4-15	C+	B-	C

Asset & Performance History

Date	NAV	1-Year Total Return
2016	56.06	12.53
2015	50.78	0.29
2014	51.58	12.42
2013	46.67	33.34
2012	35.64	16.25
2011	31.29	0.96

Total Assets: $656,960,692,801

Asset Allocation

Asset	%
Cash	0%
Stocks	99%
US Stocks	98%
Bonds	0%
US Bonds	0%
Other	1%

Services Offered: Systematic Withdrawal Plan, Automatic Investment Plan, Phone Exchange, Wire Redemption

Investment Strategy: The investment seeks to track the performance of a benchmark index that measures the investment return of the overall stock market. The fund employs an indexing investment approach designed to track the performance of the CRSP US Total Market Index, which represents approximately 100% of the investable U.S. stock market and includes large-, mid-, small-, and micro-cap stocks regularly traded on the New York Stock Exchange and Nasdaq. It invests by sampling the index, meaning that it holds a broadly diversified collection of securities that, in the aggregate, approximates the full index in terms of key characteristics. **Top Holdings:** Apple Inc Microsoft Corp Amazon.com Inc Facebook Inc A Johnson & Johnson

Vanguard Total Stock Market Index Fund Admiral Shares B BUY

Ticker	Traded On	NAV	Total Assets ($)	Dividend Yield (TTM)	Turnover Ratio	Expense Ratio
VTSAX	NAS CM	66.72	$656,960,692,801	1.76	4	0.04

Ratings

Reward	B
Risk	B

Fund Information

Fund Type	Open End
Category	US Equity Large Cap Blend
Sub-Category	Large Blend
Prospectus Objective	Growth
Inception Date	Nov-00
Open to New Investments	Y
Minimum Initial Investment	10,000
Minimum Subsequent Investment	1
Front End Fee	
Back End Fee	

Total Returns (%)

3-Month	6-Month	1-Year	3-Year	5-Year
6.33	11.17	21.16	35.72	109.49

Last Bull Market	25.82
Last Bear Market	-17.71
3-Year Standard Deviation	10.23
3-Year Beta	1

Company Information

Provider	Vanguard
Manager/Tenure	Gerard C. O'Reilly (22), Walter Nejman (1)
Website	http://www.vanguard.com
Address	Vanguard 100 Vanguard Boulevard Malvern PA 19355 United States
Phone Number	877-662-7447

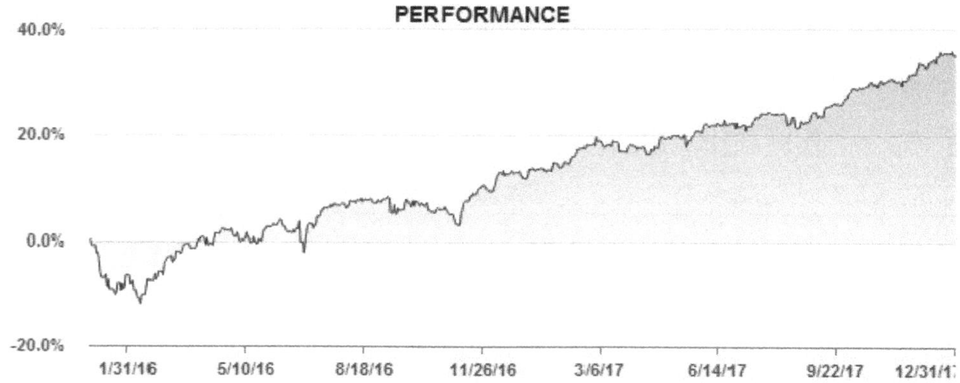

Ratings History

Date	Overall Rating	Risk Rating	Reward Rating
Q4-17	B	B	B
Q3-17	B	A-	B
Q2-17	B	B	B
Q1-17	B	C+	B
Q4-16	B	B	B
Q4-15	C+	B-	C

Asset & Performance History

Date	NAV	1-Year Total Return
2016	56.08	12.66
2015	50.79	0.38
2014	51.6	12.55
2013	46.69	33.52
2012	35.65	16.38
2011	31.3	1.08

Total Assets: $656,960,692,801

Asset Allocation

Asset	%
Cash	0%
Stocks	99%
US Stocks	98%
Bonds	0%
US Bonds	0%
Other	1%

Services Offered: Systematic Withdrawal Plan, Automatic Investment Plan, Phone Exchange, Wire Redemption

Investment Strategy: The investment seeks to track the performance of a benchmark index that measures the investment return of the overall stock market. The fund employs an indexing investment approach designed to track the performance of the CRSP US Total Market Index, which represents approximately 100% of the investable U.S. stock market and includes large-, mid-, small-, and micro-cap stocks regularly traded on the New York Stock Exchange and Nasdaq. It invests by sampling the index, meaning that it holds a broadly diversified collection of securities that, in the aggregate, approximates the full index in terms of key characteristics. **Top Holdings:** Apple Inc Microsoft Corp Amazon.com Inc Facebook Inc A Johnson & Johnson

Vanguard 500 Index Fund Admiral Shares

B BUY

Ticker	Traded On	NAV	Total Assets ($)	Dividend Yield (TTM)	Turnover Ratio	Expense Ratio
VFIAX	NAS CM	246.82	$383,897,193,155	1.84	4	0.04

Ratings

Reward	B
Risk	B

Fund Information

Fund Type	Open End
Category	US Equity Large Cap Blend
Sub-Category	Large Blend
Prospectus Objective	Growth
Inception Date	Nov-00
Open to New Investments	Y
Minimum Initial Investment	10,000
Minimum Subsequent Investment	1
Front End Fee	
Back End Fee	

Total Returns (%)

3-Month	6-Month	1-Year	3-Year	5-Year
6.63	11.41	21.78	36.74	111.30

Last Bull Market	25.08
Last Bear Market	-16.27
3-Year Standard Deviation	10.09
3-Year Beta	1

Company Information

Provider	Vanguard
Manager/Tenure	Donald M. Butler (1), Michelle Louie (0)
Website	http://www.vanguard.com
Address	Vanguard 100 Vanguard Boulevard Malvern PA 19355 United States
Phone Number	877-662-7447

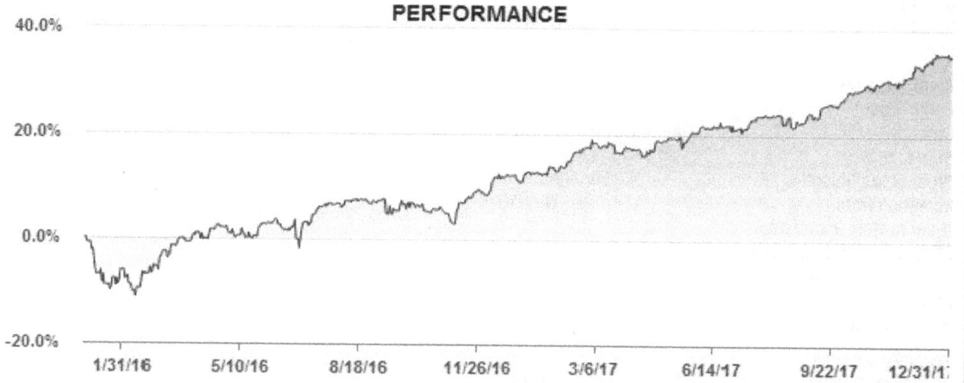

Ratings History

Date	Overall Rating	Risk Rating	Reward Rating
Q4-17	B	B	B
Q3-17	B	A-	B
Q2-17	B	B+	B
Q1-17	B	B-	B
Q4-16	B	B	B
Q4-15	C+	C+	C

Asset & Performance History

Date	NAV	1-Year Total Return
2016	206.57	11.92
2015	188.48	1.36
2014	189.89	13.64
2013	170.36	32.33
2012	131.37	15.96
2011	115.8	2.08

Total Assets: $383,897,193,155

Asset Allocation

Asset	%
Cash	0%
Stocks	100%
US Stocks	99%
Bonds	0%
US Bonds	0%
Other	0%

Services Offered: Systematic Withdrawal Plan, Automatic Investment Plan, Phone Exchange, Wire Redemption

Investment Strategy: The investment seeks to track the performance of a benchmark index that measures the investment return of large-capitalization stocks. The fund employs an indexing investment approach designed to track the performance of the Standard & Poor's 500 Index, a widely recognized benchmark of U.S. stock market performance that is dominated by the stocks of large U.S. companies. The advisor attempts to replicate the target index by investing all, or substantially all, of its assets in the stocks that make up the index, holding each stock in approximately the same proportion as its weighting in the index. **Top Holdings:** Apple Inc Microsoft Corp Amazon.com Inc Facebook Inc A Johnson & Johnson

Vanguard 500 Index Fund Investor Shares

B BUY

Ticker	Traded On	NAV	Total Assets ($)	Dividend Yield (TTM)	Turnover Ratio	Expense Ratio
VFINX	NAS CM	246.82	$383,897,193,155	1.76	4	0.14

Ratings

Reward	B
Risk	B

Fund Information

Fund Type	Open End
Category	US Equity Large Cap Blend
Sub-Category	Large Blend
Prospectus Objective	Growth
Inception Date	Aug-76
Open to New Investments	Y
Minimum Initial Investment	3,000
Minimum Subsequent Investment	1
Front End Fee	
Back End Fee	

Total Returns (%)

3-Month	6-Month	1-Year	3-Year	5-Year
6.60	11.35	21.66	36.32	110.14

Last Bull Market	24.99
Last Bear Market	-16.31
3-Year Standard Deviation	10.09
3-Year Beta	1

Company Information

Provider	Vanguard
Manager/Tenure	Donald M. Butler (1), Michelle Louie (0)
Website	http://www.vanguard.com
Address	Vanguard 100 Vanguard Boulevard Malvern PA 19355 United States
Phone Number	877-662-7447

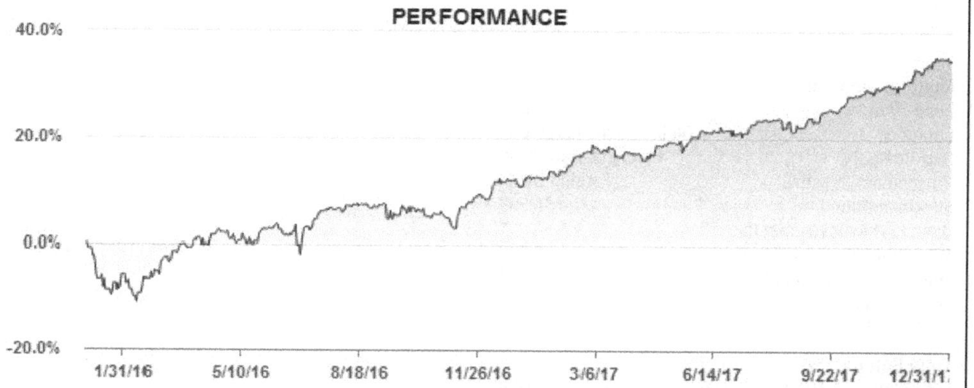

Ratings History

Date	Overall Rating	Risk Rating	Reward Rating
Q4-17	B	B	B
Q3-17	B	A-	B
Q2-17	B	B+	B
Q1-17	B	B-	B
Q4-16	B	B	B
Q4-15	C+	C+	C

Asset & Performance History

Date	NAV	1-Year Total Return
2016	206.57	11.81
2015	188.48	1.24
2014	189.89	13.5
2013	170.36	32.17
2012	131.37	15.82
2011	115.8	1.96

Total Assets: $383,897,193,155

Asset Allocation

Asset	%
Cash	0%
Stocks	100%
US Stocks	99%
Bonds	0%
US Bonds	0%
Other	0%

Services Offered: Systematic Withdrawal Plan, Automatic Investment Plan, Phone Exchange, Wire Redemption

Investment Strategy: The investment seeks to track the performance of a benchmark index that measures the investment return of large-capitalization stocks. The fund employs an indexing investment approach designed to track the performance of the Standard & Poor's 500 Index, a widely recognized benchmark of U.S. stock market performance that is dominated by the stocks of large U.S. companies. The advisor attempts to replicate the target index by investing all, or substantially all, of its assets in the stocks that make up the index, holding each stock in approximately the same proportion as its weighting in the index. **Top Holdings:** Apple Inc Microsoft Corp Amazon.com Inc Facebook Inc A Johnson & Johnson

Vanguard Total International Stock Index Fund Admiral Shares B- BUY

Ticker	Traded On	NAV	Total Assets ($)	Dividend Yield (TTM)	Turnover Ratio	Expense Ratio
VTIAX	NAS CM	30.52	$321,184,618,012	2.5	3	0.11

Ratings

Reward	B-
Risk	B-

Fund Information

Fund Type	Open End
Category	Global Equity Large Cap
Sub-Category	Foreign Large Blend
Prospectus Objective	Foreign Stock
Inception Date	Nov-10
Open to New Investments	Y
Minimum Initial Investment	10,000
Minimum Subsequent Investment	1
Front End Fee	
Back End Fee	

Total Returns (%)

3-Month	6-Month	1-Year	3-Year	5-Year
4.88	11.12	27.55	27.38	42.40

Last Bull Market	14.52
Last Bear Market	-24.32
3-Year Standard Deviation	11.51
3-Year Beta	0.94

Company Information

Provider	Vanguard
Manager/Tenure	Michael Perre (9), Christine D. Franquin (0)
Website	http://www.vanguard.com
Address	Vanguard 100 Vanguard Boulevard Malvern PA 19355 United States
Phone Number	877-662-7447

Ratings History

Date	Overall Rating	Risk Rating	Reward Rating
Q4-17	B-	B-	B-
Q3-17	B-	B	C+
Q2-17	C	C	C+
Q1-17	C	C-	C+
Q4-16	C-	C	D+
Q4-15	C	B	C-

Asset & Performance History

Date	NAV	1-Year Total Return
2016	24.63	4.67
2015	24.24	-4.25
2014	26	-4.17
2013	28.01	15.14
2012	25.05	18.2
2011	21.84	-14.52

Total Assets: $321,184,618,012

Asset Allocation

Asset	%
Cash	3%
Stocks	96%
US Stocks	1%
Bonds	0%
US Bonds	0%
Other	1%

Services Offered: Systematic Withdrawal Plan, Automatic Investment Plan, Phone Exchange, Wire Redemption

Investment Strategy: The investment seeks to track the performance of a benchmark index that measures the investment return of stocks issued by companies located in developed and emerging markets, excluding the United States. The fund employs an indexing investment approach designed to track the performance of the FTSE Global All Cap ex US Index, a float-adjusted market-capitalization-weighted index designed to measure equity market performance of companies located in developed and emerging markets, excluding the United States. The index includes approximately 5,800 stocks of companies located in over 45 countries. **Top Holdings:** Nestle SA Tencent Holdings Ltd Samsung Electronics Co Ltd HSBC Holdings PLC Novartis AG

Vanguard Total International Stock Index Fund Investor Shares B- BUY

Ticker	Traded On	NAV	Total Assets ($)	Dividend Yield (TTM)	Turnover Ratio	Expense Ratio
VGTSX	NAS CM	18.24	$321,184,618,012	2.45	3	0.18

Ratings

Reward	B-
Risk	B-

Fund Information

Fund Type	Open End
Category	Global Equity Large Cap
Sub-Category	Foreign Large Blend
Prospectus Objective	Foreign Stock
Inception Date	Apr-96
Open to New Investments	Y
Minimum Initial Investment	3,000
Minimum Subsequent Investment	1
Front End Fee	
Back End Fee	

Total Returns (%)

3-Month	6-Month	1-Year	3-Year	5-Year
4.79	11.04	27.39	27.08	41.78

Last Bull Market	14.58
Last Bear Market	-24.35
3-Year Standard Deviation	11.5
3-Year Beta	0.94

Company Information

Provider	Vanguard
Manager/Tenure	Michael Perre (9), Christine D. Franquin (0)
Website	http://www.vanguard.com
Address	Vanguard 100 Vanguard Boulevard Malvern PA 19355 United States
Phone Number	877-662-7447

Ratings History

Date	Overall Rating	Risk Rating	Reward Rating
Q4-17	B-	B-	B-
Q3-17	C+	B	C+
Q2-17	C	C	C+
Q1-17	C	C-	C+
Q4-16	C-	C	D+
Q4-15	C	B	C-

Asset & Performance History

Date	NAV	1-Year Total Return
2016	14.73	4.65
2015	14.49	-4.37
2014	15.55	-4.23
2013	16.75	15.04
2012	14.98	18.14
2011	13.06	-14.56

Total Assets: $321,184,618,012

Asset Allocation

Asset	%
Cash	3%
Stocks	96%
US Stocks	1%
Bonds	0%
US Bonds	0%
Other	1%

Services Offered: Systematic Withdrawal Plan, Automatic Investment Plan, Phone Exchange, Wire Redemption

Investment Strategy: The investment seeks to track the performance of a benchmark index that measures the investment return of stocks issued by companies located in developed and emerging markets, excluding the United States. The fund employs an indexing investment approach designed to track the performance of the FTSE Global All Cap ex US Index, a float-adjusted market-capitalization-weighted index designed to measure equity market performance of companies located in developed and emerging markets, excluding the United States. The index includes approximately 5,800 stocks of companies located in over 45 countries. **Top Holdings:** Nestle SA Tencent Holdings Ltd Samsung Electronics Co Ltd HSBC Holdings PLC Novartis AG

American Funds The Growth Fund of America® Class 529-F

B BUY

Ticker	Traded On	NAV	Total Assets ($)	Dividend Yield (TTM)	Turnover Ratio	Expense Ratio
CGFFX	NAS CM	48.91	$176,789,886,629	0.59	25	0.49

Ratings

Reward	B
Risk	B

Fund Information

Fund Type	Open End
Category	US Equity Large Cap Growth
Sub-Category	Large Growth
Prospectus Objective	Growth
Inception Date	Sep-02
Open to New Investments	Y
Minimum Initial Investment	250
Minimum Subsequent Investment	50
Front End Fee	
Back End Fee	

Total Returns (%)

3-Month	6-Month	1-Year	3-Year	5-Year
6.95	12.35	26.30	43.76	115.60

Last Bull Market	24.26
Last Bear Market	-18.95
3-Year Standard Deviation	10.66
3-Year Beta	0.99

Company Information

Provider	American Funds
Manager/Tenure	Donald D. O'Neal (24), Michael T. Kerr (19), J. Blair Frank (16), 9 others
Website	http://www.americanfunds.com
Address	American Funds 333 South Hope Street Los Angeles CA 90071-1406 United States
Phone Number	800-421-4225

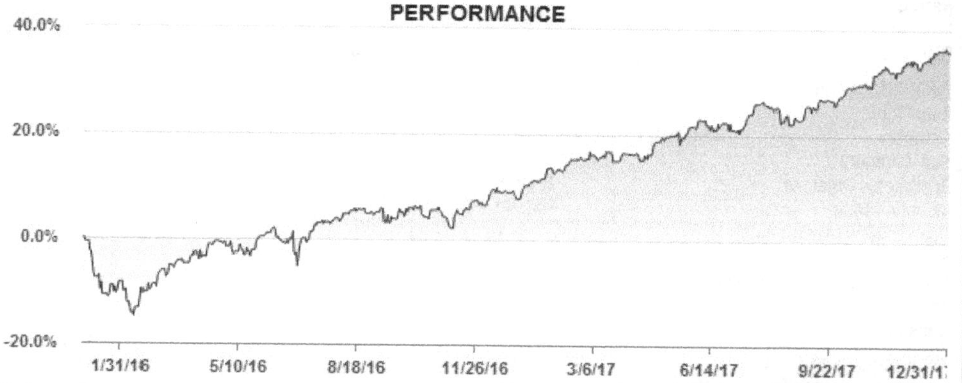

Ratings History

Date	Overall Rating	Risk Rating	Reward Rating
Q4-17	B	B	B
Q3-17	B+	B+	B
Q2-17	B	B	B
Q1-17	B	B-	B
Q4-16	B	B	B
Q4-15	C+	C+	C+

Asset & Performance History

Date	NAV	1-Year Total Return
2016	41.55	8.61
2015	40.84	5.48
2014	42.26	9.45
2013	42.62	33.99
2012	34.06	20.69
2011	28.5	-4.72

Total Assets: $176,789,886,629

Asset Allocation

Asset	%
Cash	4%
Stocks	91%
US Stocks	76%
Bonds	2%
US Bonds	2%
Other	2%

Services Offered: Systematic Withdrawal Plan, Automatic Investment Plan, Qualified Investment, Phone Exchange, Retirement Investment

Investment Strategy: The investment seeks growth of capital. The fund invests primarily in common stocks and seeks to invest in companies that appear to offer superior opportunities for growth of capital. It may invest up to 25% of its assets in securities of issuers domiciled outside the United States. The investment adviser uses a system of multiple portfolio managers in managing the fund's assets. Under this approach, the portfolio of the fund is divided into segments managed by individual managers who decide how their respective segments will be invested. **Top Holdings:** Amazon.com Inc Broadcom Ltd Microsoft Corp Netflix Inc Alphabet Inc C

American Funds The Growth Fund of America® Class F-2

B BUY

Ticker	Traded On	NAV	Total Assets ($)	Dividend Yield (TTM)	Turnover Ratio	Expense Ratio
GFFFX	NAS CM	49.42	$176,789,886,629	0.64	25	0.43

Ratings

Reward	B
Risk	B

Fund Information

Fund Type	Open End
Category	US Equity Large Cap Growth
Sub-Category	Large Growth
Prospectus Objective	Growth
Inception Date	Aug-08
Open to New Investments	Y
Minimum Initial Investment	250
Minimum Subsequent Investment	50
Front End Fee	
Back End Fee	

Total Returns (%)

3-Month	6-Month	1-Year	3-Year	5-Year
6.95	12.39	26.38	44.08	116.59

Last Bull Market	24.36
Last Bear Market	-18.91
3-Year Standard Deviation	10.67
3-Year Beta	0.99

Company Information

Provider	American Funds
Manager/Tenure	Donald D. O'Neal (24), Michael T. Kerr (19), J. Blair Frank (16), 9 others
Website	http://www.americanfunds.com
Address	American Funds 333 South Hope Street Los Angeles CA 90071-1406 United States
Phone Number	800-421-4225

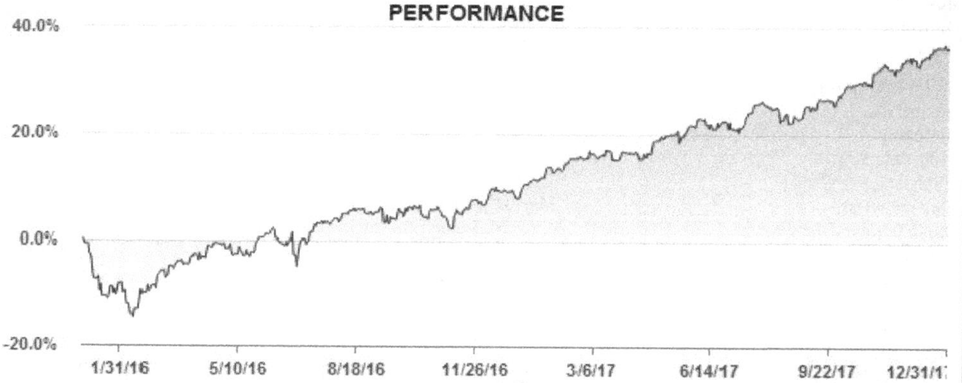

Ratings History

Date	Overall Rating	Risk Rating	Reward Rating
Q4-17	B	B	B
Q3-17	B+	B+	B
Q2-17	B	B	B
Q1-17	B	B-	B
Q4-16	B	B	B
Q4-15	C+	C+	C+

Asset & Performance History

Date	NAV	1-Year Total Return
2016	41.95	8.69
2015	41.21	5.6
2014	42.6	9.53
2013	42.95	34.15
2012	34.3	20.85
2011	28.7	-4.63

Total Assets: $176,789,886,629

Asset Allocation

Asset	%
Cash	4%
Stocks	91%
US Stocks	76%
Bonds	2%
US Bonds	2%
Other	2%

Services Offered: Systematic Withdrawal Plan, Automatic Investment Plan, Qualified Investment, Phone Exchange, Retirement Investment

Investment Strategy: The investment seeks growth of capital. The fund invests primarily in common stocks and seeks to invest in companies that appear to offer superior opportunities for growth of capital. It may invest up to 25% of its assets in securities of issuers domiciled outside the United States. The investment adviser uses a system of multiple portfolio managers in managing the fund's assets. Under this approach, the portfolio of the fund is divided into segments managed by individual managers who decide how their respective segments will be invested. **Top Holdings:** Amazon.com Inc Broadcom Ltd Microsoft Corp Netflix Inc Alphabet Inc C

American Funds The Growth Fund of America® Class R-6 B BUY

Ticker	Traded On	NAV	Total Assets ($)	Dividend Yield (TTM)	Turnover Ratio	Expense Ratio
RGAGX	NAS CM	49.56	$176,789,886,629	0.71	25	0.33

Ratings

Reward	B
Risk	B

Fund Information

Fund Type	Open End
Category	US Equity Large Cap Growth
Sub-Category	Large Growth
Prospectus Objective	Growth
Inception Date	May-09
Open to New Investments	Y
Minimum Initial Investment	250
Minimum Subsequent Investment	50
Front End Fee	
Back End Fee	

Total Returns (%)

3-Month	6-Month	1-Year	3-Year	5-Year
7.00	12.45	26.52	44.54	117.67

Last Bull Market	24.41
Last Bear Market	-18.89
3-Year Standard Deviation	10.67
3-Year Beta	0.99

Company Information

Provider	American Funds
Manager/Tenure	Donald D. O'Neal (24), Michael T. Kerr (19), J. Blair Frank (16), 9 others
Website	http://www.americanfunds.com
Address	American Funds 333 South Hope Street Los Angeles CA 90071-1406 United States
Phone Number	800-421-4225

PERFORMANCE

Ratings History

Date	Overall Rating	Risk Rating	Reward Rating
Q4-17	B	B	B
Q3-17	B+	B+	B
Q2-17	B	B	B
Q1-17	B	B-	B
Q4-16	B	B	B
Q4-15	B-	B+	C+

Asset & Performance History

Date	NAV	1-Year Total Return
2016	42.05	8.81
2015	41.29	5.69
2014	42.68	9.63
2013	43.01	34.29
2012	34.34	20.98
2011	28.72	-4.53

Total Assets: $176,789,886,629

Asset Allocation

Asset	%
Cash	4%
Stocks	91%
US Stocks	76%
Bonds	2%
US Bonds	2%
Other	2%

Services Offered: Automatic Investment Plan, Qualified Investment, Phone Exchange

Investment Strategy: The investment seeks growth of capital. The fund invests primarily in common stocks and seeks to invest in companies that appear to offer superior opportunities for growth of capital. It may invest up to 25% of its assets in securities of issuers domiciled outside the United States. The investment adviser uses a system of multiple portfolio managers in managing the fund's assets. Under this approach, the portfolio of the fund is divided into segments managed by individual managers who decide how their respective segments will be invested. **Top Holdings:** Amazon.com Inc Broadcom Ltd Microsoft Corp Netflix Inc Alphabet Inc C

American Funds The Growth Fund of America® Class F-1 B BUY

Ticker	Traded On	NAV	Total Assets ($)	Dividend Yield (TTM)	Turnover Ratio	Expense Ratio
GFAFX	NAS CM	49.22	$176,789,886,629	0.42	25	0.7

Ratings

Reward	B
Risk	B

Fund Information

Fund Type	Open End
Category	US Equity Large Cap Growth
Sub-Category	Large Growth
Prospectus Objective	Growth
Inception Date	Mar-01
Open to New Investments	Y
Minimum Initial Investment	250
Minimum Subsequent Investment	50
Front End Fee	
Back End Fee	

Total Returns (%)

3-Month	6-Month	1-Year	3-Year	5-Year
6.90	12.25	26.07	42.94	113.65

Last Bull Market	24.17
Last Bear Market	-18.97
3-Year Standard Deviation	10.66
3-Year Beta	0.99

Company Information

Provider	American Funds
Manager/Tenure	Donald D. O'Neal (24), Michael T. Kerr (19), J. Blair Frank (16), 9 others
Website	http://www.americanfunds.com
Address	American Funds 333 South Hope Street Los Angeles CA 90071-1406 United States
Phone Number	800-421-4225

PERFORMANCE

Ratings History

Date	Overall Rating	Risk Rating	Reward Rating
Q4-17	B	B	B
Q3-17	B+	B+	B
Q2-17	B	B	B
Q1-17	B	B-	B
Q4-16	B	B	B
Q4-15	B-	B+	C+

Asset & Performance History

Date	NAV	1-Year Total Return
2016	41.77	8.37
2015	41.05	5.33
2014	42.44	9.23
2013	42.74	33.79
2012	34.14	20.52
2011	28.56	-4.83

Total Assets: $176,789,886,629

Asset Allocation

Asset	%
Cash	4%
Stocks	91%
US Stocks	76%
Bonds	2%
US Bonds	2%
Other	2%

Services Offered: Systematic Withdrawal Plan, Automatic Investment Plan, Qualified Investment, Phone Exchange, Retirement Investment

Investment Strategy: The investment seeks growth of capital. The fund invests primarily in common stocks and seeks to invest in companies that appear to offer superior opportunities for growth of capital. It may invest up to 25% of its assets in securities of issuers domiciled outside the United States. The investment adviser uses a system of multiple portfolio managers in managing the fund's assets. Under this approach, the portfolio of the fund is divided into segments managed by individual managers who decide how their respective segments will be invested. **Top Holdings:** Amazon.com Inc Broadcom Ltd Microsoft Corp Netflix Inc Alphabet Inc C

American Funds The Growth Fund of America® Class R-1 **B BUY**

Ticker	Traded On	NAV	Total Assets ($)	Dividend Yield (TTM)	Turnover Ratio	Expense Ratio
RGAAX	NAS CM	46.65	$176,789,886,629	0	25	1.44

Ratings

Reward	B
Risk	B

Fund Information

Fund Type	Open End
Category	US Equity Large Cap Growth
Sub-Category	Large Growth
Prospectus Objective	Growth
Inception Date	Jun-02
Open to New Investments	Y
Minimum Initial Investment	250
Minimum Subsequent Investment	50
Front End Fee	
Back End Fee	

Total Returns (%)

3-Month	6-Month	1-Year	3-Year	5-Year
6.68	11.83	25.15	39.86	106.06

Last Bull Market	23.63
Last Bear Market	-19.26
3-Year Standard Deviation	10.65
3-Year Beta	0.99

Company Information

Provider	American Funds
Manager/Tenure	Donald D. O'Neal (24), Michael T. Kerr (19), J. Blair Frank (16), 9 others
Website	http://www.americanfunds.com
Address	American Funds 333 South Hope Street Los Angeles CA 90071-1406 United States
Phone Number	800-421-4225

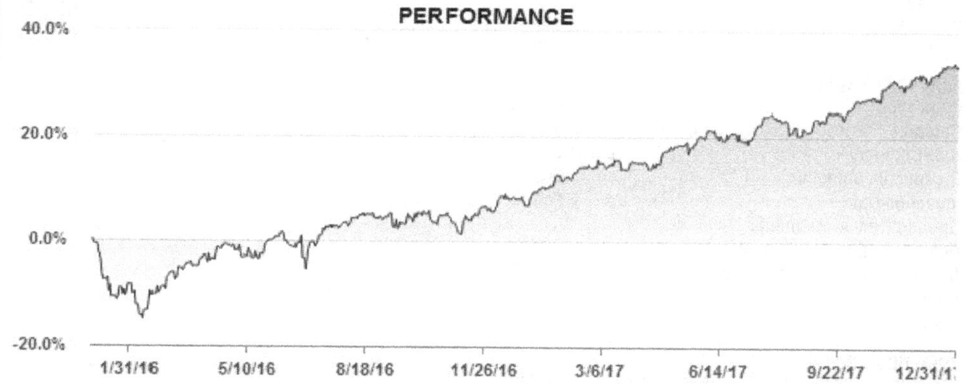

Ratings History

Date	Overall Rating	Risk Rating	Reward Rating
Q4-17	B	B	B
Q3-17	B	B+	B
Q2-17	B	B	B
Q1-17	B	B-	B
Q4-16	B	B	B
Q4-15	C+	C+	C+

Asset & Performance History

Date	NAV	1-Year Total Return
2016	39.86	7.6
2015	39.36	4.55
2014	40.9	8.44
2013	41.54	32.8
2012	33.4	19.66
2011	27.92	-5.57

Total Assets: $176,789,886,629

Asset Allocation

Asset	%
Cash	4%
Stocks	91%
US Stocks	76%
Bonds	2%
US Bonds	2%
Other	2%

Services Offered: Automatic Investment Plan, Qualified Investment, Phone Exchange

Investment Strategy: The investment seeks growth of capital. The fund invests primarily in common stocks and seeks to invest in companies that appear to offer superior opportunities for growth of capital. It may invest up to 25% of its assets in securities of issuers domiciled outside the United States. The investment adviser uses a system of multiple portfolio managers in managing the fund's assets. Under this approach, the portfolio of the fund is divided into segments managed by individual managers who decide how their respective segments will be invested. **Top Holdings:** Amazon.com Inc Broadcom Ltd Microsoft Corp Netflix Inc Alphabet Inc C

American Funds The Growth Fund of America® Class A **B BUY**

Ticker	Traded On	NAV	Total Assets ($)	Dividend Yield (TTM)	Turnover Ratio	Expense Ratio
AGTHX	NAS CM	49.54	$176,789,886,629	0.46	25	0.64

Ratings

Reward	B
Risk	B

Fund Information

Fund Type	Open End
Category	US Equity Large Cap Growth
Sub-Category	Large Growth
Prospectus Objective	Growth
Inception Date	Nov-73
Open to New Investments	Y
Minimum Initial Investment	250
Minimum Subsequent Investment	50
Front End Fee	5.75
Back End Fee	

Total Returns (%)

3-Month	6-Month	1-Year	3-Year	5-Year
6.91	12.27	26.13	43.20	114.21

Last Bull Market	24.15
Last Bear Market	-19.01
3-Year Standard Deviation	10.66
3-Year Beta	0.99

Company Information

Provider	American Funds
Manager/Tenure	Donald D. O'Neal (24), Michael T. Kerr (19), J. Blair Frank (16), 9 others
Website	http://www.americanfunds.com
Address	American Funds 333 South Hope Street Los Angeles CA 90071-1406 United States
Phone Number	800-421-4225

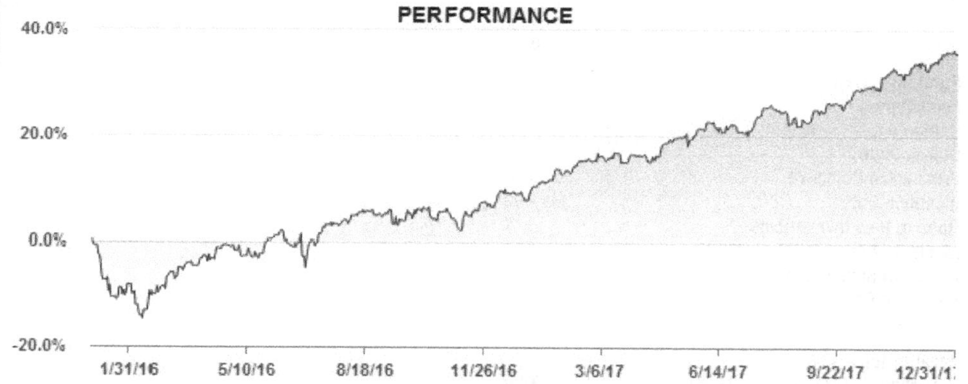

Ratings History

Date	Overall Rating	Risk Rating	Reward Rating
Q4-17	B	B	B
Q3-17	B+	B+	B
Q2-17	B	B	B
Q1-17	B	B-	B
Q4-16	B	B	B
Q4-15	C+	C+	C+

Asset & Performance History

Date	NAV	1-Year Total Return
2016	42.04	8.45
2015	41.29	5.36
2014	42.68	9.3
2013	43	33.79
2012	34.35	20.54
2011	28.73	-4.89

Total Assets: $176,789,886,629

Asset Allocation

Asset	%
Cash	4%
Stocks	91%
US Stocks	76%
Bonds	2%
US Bonds	2%
Other	2%

Services Offered: Systematic Withdrawal Plan, Automatic Investment Plan, Phone Exchange, Retirement Investment

Investment Strategy: The investment seeks growth of capital. The fund invests primarily in common stocks and seeks to invest in companies that appear to offer superior opportunities for growth of capital. It may invest up to 25% of its assets in securities of issuers domiciled outside the United States. The investment adviser uses a system of multiple portfolio managers in managing the fund's assets. Under this approach, the portfolio of the fund is divided into segments managed by individual managers who decide how their respective segments will be invested. **Top Holdings:** Amazon.com Inc Broadcom Ltd Microsoft Corp Netflix Inc Alphabet Inc C

American Funds The Growth Fund of America® Class 529-C — B BUY

Ticker	Traded On	NAV	Total Assets ($)	Dividend Yield (TTM)	Turnover Ratio	Expense Ratio
CGFCX	NAS CM	46.1	$176,789,886,629	0	25	1.49

Ratings

Reward	B
Risk	B

Fund Information

Fund Type	Open End
Category	US Equity Large Cap Growth
Sub-Category	Large Growth
Prospectus Objective	Growth
Inception Date	Feb-02
Open to New Investments	Y
Minimum Initial Investment	250
Minimum Subsequent Investment	50
Front End Fee	
Back End Fee	1.00

Total Returns (%)

3-Month	6-Month	1-Year	3-Year	5-Year
6.67	11.80	25.06	39.55	105.22

Last Bull Market	23.54
Last Bear Market	-19.3
3-Year Standard Deviation	10.65
3-Year Beta	0.99

Company Information

Provider	American Funds
Manager/Tenure	Donald D. O'Neal (24), Michael T. Kerr (19), J. Blair Frank (16), 9 others
Website	http://www.americanfunds.com
Address	American Funds 333 South Hope Street Los Angeles CA 90071-1406 United States
Phone Number	800-421-4225

Ratings History

Date	Overall Rating	Risk Rating	Reward Rating
Q4-17	B	B	B
Q3-17	B	B+	B
Q2-17	B	B	B
Q1-17	B	C+	B
Q4-16	B	B	B
Q4-15	C+	C+	C+

Asset & Performance History

Date	NAV	1-Year Total Return
2016	39.45	7.54
2015	39	4.47
2014	40.59	8.34
2013	41.29	32.68
2012	33.24	19.46
2011	27.84	-5.65

Total Assets: $176,789,886,629

Asset Allocation

Asset	%
Cash	4%
Stocks	91%
US Stocks	76%
Bonds	2%
US Bonds	2%
Other	2%

Services Offered: Systematic Withdrawal Plan, Automatic Investment Plan, Qualified Investment, Phone Exchange, Retirement Investment

Investment Strategy: The investment seeks growth of capital. The fund invests primarily in common stocks and seeks to invest in companies that appear to offer superior opportunities for growth of capital. It may invest up to 25% of its assets in securities of issuers domiciled outside the United States. The investment adviser uses a system of multiple portfolio managers in managing the fund's assets. Under this approach, the portfolio of the fund is divided into segments managed by individual managers who decide how their respective segments will be invested. **Top Holdings:** Amazon.com Inc Broadcom Ltd Microsoft Corp Netflix Inc Alphabet Inc C

American Funds The Growth Fund of America® Class R-5 — B BUY

Ticker	Traded On	NAV	Total Assets ($)	Dividend Yield (TTM)	Turnover Ratio	Expense Ratio
RGAFX	NAS CM	49.49	$176,789,886,629	0.66	25	0.38

Ratings

Reward	B
Risk	B

Fund Information

Fund Type	Open End
Category	US Equity Large Cap Growth
Sub-Category	Large Growth
Prospectus Objective	Growth
Inception Date	May-02
Open to New Investments	Y
Minimum Initial Investment	250
Minimum Subsequent Investment	50
Front End Fee	
Back End Fee	

Total Returns (%)

3-Month	6-Month	1-Year	3-Year	5-Year
6.97	12.43	26.43	44.33	117.12

Last Bull Market	24.39
Last Bear Market	-18.89
3-Year Standard Deviation	10.66
3-Year Beta	0.99

Company Information

Provider	American Funds
Manager/Tenure	Donald D. O'Neal (24), Michael T. Kerr (19), J. Blair Frank (16), 9 others
Website	http://www.americanfunds.com
Address	American Funds 333 South Hope Street Los Angeles CA 90071-1406 United States
Phone Number	800-421-4225

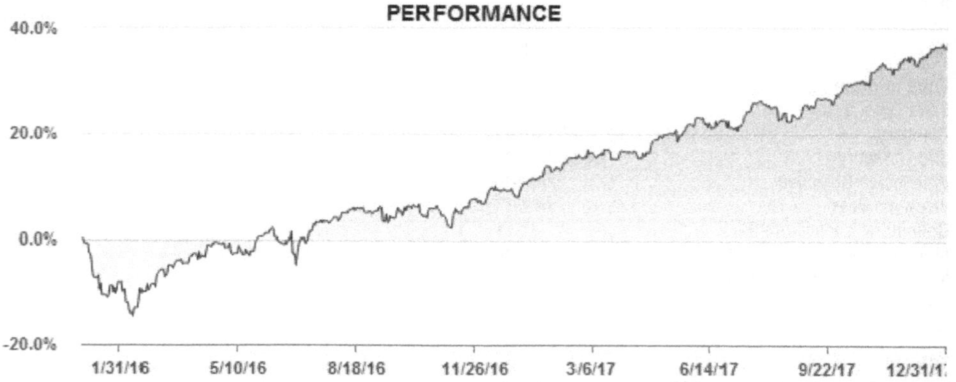

Ratings History

Date	Overall Rating	Risk Rating	Reward Rating
Q4-17	B	B	B
Q3-17	B+	B+	B
Q2-17	B	B	B
Q1-17	B	B-	B
Q4-16	B	B	B
Q4-15	C+	C+	C+

Asset & Performance History

Date	NAV	1-Year Total Return
2016	42	8.75
2015	41.24	5.65
2014	42.63	9.6
2013	42.95	34.2
2012	34.3	20.92
2011	28.68	-4.59

Total Assets: $176,789,886,629

Asset Allocation

Asset	%
Cash	4%
Stocks	91%
US Stocks	76%
Bonds	2%
US Bonds	2%
Other	2%

Services Offered: Automatic Investment Plan, Qualified Investment, Phone Exchange

Investment Strategy: The investment seeks growth of capital. The fund invests primarily in common stocks and seeks to invest in companies that appear to offer superior opportunities for growth of capital. It may invest up to 25% of its assets in securities of issuers domiciled outside the United States. The investment adviser uses a system of multiple portfolio managers in managing the fund's assets. Under this approach, the portfolio of the fund is divided into segments managed by individual managers who decide how their respective segments will be invested. **Top Holdings:** Amazon.com Inc Broadcom Ltd Microsoft Corp Netflix Inc Alphabet Inc C

American Funds The Growth Fund of America® Class R-2 B BUY

Ticker	Traded On	NAV	Total Assets ($)	Dividend Yield (TTM)	Turnover Ratio	Expense Ratio
RGABX	NAS CM	47.13	$176,789,886,629	0	25	1.42

Ratings

Reward	B
Risk	B

Fund Information

Fund Type	Open End
Category	US Equity Large Cap Growth
Sub-Category	Large Growth
Prospectus Objective	Growth
Inception Date	May-02
Open to New Investments	Y
Minimum Initial Investment	250
Minimum Subsequent Investment	50
Front End Fee	
Back End Fee	

Total Returns (%)

3-Month	6-Month	1-Year	3-Year	5-Year
6.71	11.85	25.16	40.01	106.50

Last Bull Market	23.64
Last Bear Market	-19.22
3-Year Standard Deviation	10.66
3-Year Beta	0.99

Company Information

Provider	American Funds
Manager/Tenure	Donald D. O'Neal (24), Michael T. Kerr (19), J. Blair Frank (16), 9 others
Website	http://www.americanfunds.com
Address	American Funds 333 South Hope Street Los Angeles CA 90071-1406 United States
Phone Number	800-421-4225

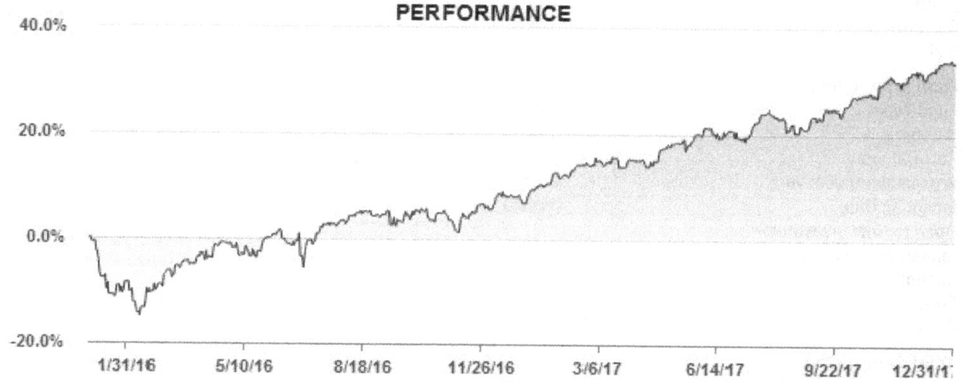

Ratings History

Date	Overall Rating	Risk Rating	Reward Rating
Q4-17	B	B	B
Q3-17	B	B+	B
Q2-17	B	B	B
Q1-17	B	B-	B
Q4-16	B	B	B
Q4-15	C+	C+	C+

Asset & Performance History

Date	NAV	1-Year Total Return
2016	40.24	7.64
2015	39.7	4.62
2014	41.2	8.48
2013	41.8	32.9
2012	33.57	19.72
2011	28.08	-5.55

Total Assets: $176,789,886,629

Asset Allocation

Asset	%
Cash	4%
Stocks	91%
US Stocks	76%
Bonds	2%
US Bonds	2%
Other	2%

Services Offered: Automatic Investment Plan, Qualified Investment, Phone Exchange

Investment Strategy: The investment seeks growth of capital. The fund invests primarily in common stocks and seeks to invest in companies that appear to offer superior opportunities for growth of capital. It may invest up to 25% of its assets in securities of issuers domiciled outside the United States. The investment adviser uses a system of multiple portfolio managers in managing the fund's assets. Under this approach, the portfolio of the fund is divided into segments managed by individual managers who decide how their respective segments will be invested. **Top Holdings:** Amazon.com Inc Broadcom Ltd Microsoft Corp Netflix Inc Alphabet Inc C

American Funds The Growth Fund of America® Class C B BUY

Ticker	Traded On	NAV	Total Assets ($)	Dividend Yield (TTM)	Turnover Ratio	Expense Ratio
GFACX	NAS CM	45.95	$176,789,886,629	0	25	1.44

Ratings

Reward	B
Risk	B

Fund Information

Fund Type	Open End
Category	US Equity Large Cap Growth
Sub-Category	Large Growth
Prospectus Objective	Growth
Inception Date	Mar-01
Open to New Investments	Y
Minimum Initial Investment	250
Minimum Subsequent Investment	50
Front End Fee	
Back End Fee	1.00

Total Returns (%)

3-Month	6-Month	1-Year	3-Year	5-Year
6.69	11.84	25.12	39.78	105.78

Last Bull Market	23.6
Last Bear Market	-19.27
3-Year Standard Deviation	10.65
3-Year Beta	0.99

Company Information

Provider	American Funds
Manager/Tenure	Donald D. O'Neal (24), Michael T. Kerr (19), J. Blair Frank (16), 9 others
Website	http://www.americanfunds.com
Address	American Funds 333 South Hope Street Los Angeles CA 90071-1406 United States
Phone Number	800-421-4225

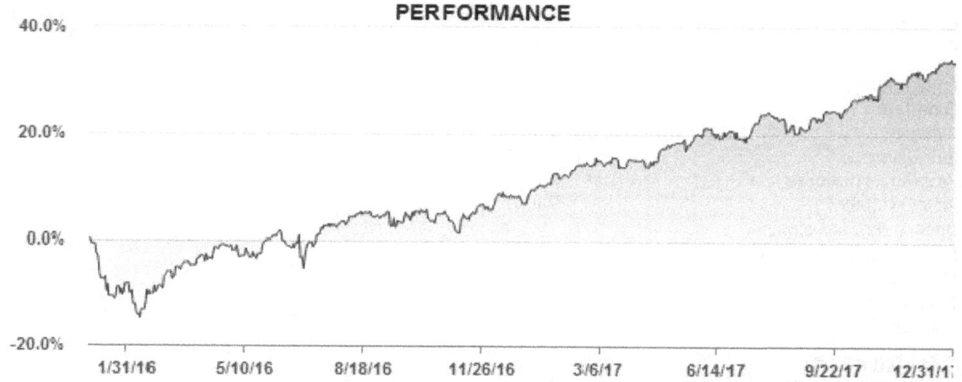

Ratings History

Date	Overall Rating	Risk Rating	Reward Rating
Q4-17	B	B	B
Q3-17	B	B+	B
Q2-17	B	B	B
Q1-17	B	B-	B
Q4-16	B	B	B
Q4-15	C+	C+	C+

Asset & Performance History

Date	NAV	1-Year Total Return
2016	39.31	7.6
2015	38.85	4.51
2014	40.43	8.43
2013	41.11	32.74
2012	33.09	19.58
2011	27.68	-5.62

Total Assets: $176,789,886,629

Asset Allocation

Asset	%
Cash	4%
Stocks	91%
US Stocks	76%
Bonds	2%
US Bonds	2%
Other	2%

Services Offered: Systematic Withdrawal Plan, Automatic Investment Plan, Phone Exchange, Retirement Investment

Investment Strategy: The investment seeks growth of capital. The fund invests primarily in common stocks and seeks to invest in companies that appear to offer superior opportunities for growth of capital. It may invest up to 25% of its assets in securities of issuers domiciled outside the United States. The investment adviser uses a system of multiple portfolio managers in managing the fund's assets. Under this approach, the portfolio of the fund is divided into segments managed by individual managers who decide how their respective segments will be invested. **Top Holdings:** Amazon.com Inc Broadcom Ltd Microsoft Corp Netflix Inc Alphabet Inc C

American Funds The Growth Fund of America® Class R-5E B BUY

Ticker	Traded On	NAV	Total Assets ($)	Dividend Yield (TTM)	Turnover Ratio	Expense Ratio
RGAHX	NAS CM	49.18	$176,789,886,629	0.74	25	0.46

Ratings

Reward	B
Risk	B

Fund Information

Fund Type	Open End
Category	US Equity Large Cap Growth
Sub-Category	Large Growth
Prospectus Objective	Growth
Inception Date	Nov-15
Open to New Investments	Y
Minimum Initial Investment	250
Minimum Subsequent Investment	50
Front End Fee	
Back End Fee	

Total Returns (%)

3-Month	6-Month	1-Year	3-Year	5-Year
6.95	12.36	26.35	43.61	114.83

Last Bull Market	24.15
Last Bear Market	-19
3-Year Standard Deviation	10.67
3-Year Beta	0.99

Company Information

Provider	American Funds
Manager/Tenure	Donald D. O'Neal (24), Michael T. Kerr (19), J. Blair Frank (16), 9 others
Website	http://www.americanfunds.com
Address	American Funds 333 South Hope Street Los Angeles CA 90071-1406 United States
Phone Number	800-421-4225

PERFORMANCE

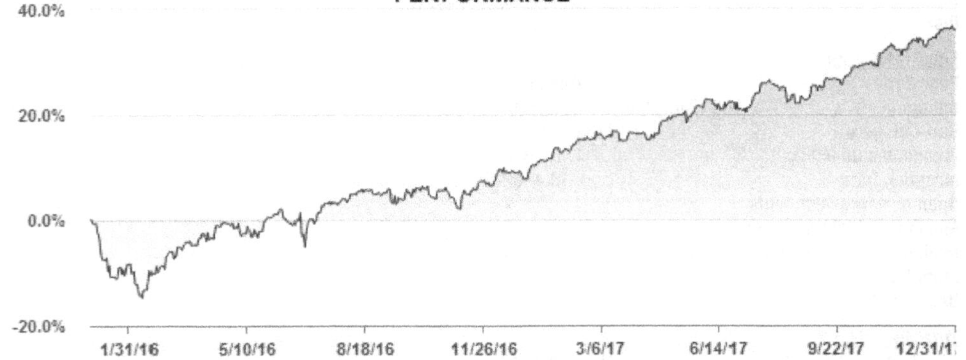

Ratings History

Date	Overall Rating	Risk Rating	Reward Rating
Q4-17	B	B	B
Q3-17	B+	B+	B
Q2-17	B	B	B
Q1-17	B	B-	B
Q4-16	B	B	B
Q4-15			

Asset & Performance History

Date	NAV	1-Year Total Return
2016	41.77	8.56
2015	41.14	5.37
2014		9.3
2013		33.79
2012		20.54
2011		-4.89

Total Assets: $176,789,886,629

Asset Allocation

Asset	%
Cash	4%
Stocks	91%
US Stocks	76%
Bonds	2%
US Bonds	2%
Other	2%

Services Offered: Automatic Investment Plan, Qualified Investment, Phone Exchange

Investment Strategy: The investment seeks growth of capital. The fund invests primarily in common stocks and seeks to invest in companies that appear to offer superior opportunities for growth of capital. It may invest up to 25% of its assets in securities of issuers domiciled outside the United States. The investment adviser uses a system of multiple portfolio managers in managing the fund's assets. Under this approach, the portfolio of the fund is divided into segments managed by individual managers who decide how their respective segments will be invested. **Top Holdings:** Amazon.com Inc Broadcom Ltd Microsoft Corp Netflix Inc Alphabet Inc C

American Funds The Growth Fund of America® Class 529-E B BUY

Ticker	Traded On	NAV	Total Assets ($)	Dividend Yield (TTM)	Turnover Ratio	Expense Ratio
CGFEX	NAS CM	48.55	$176,789,886,629	0.23	25	0.94

Ratings

Reward	B
Risk	B

Fund Information

Fund Type	Open End
Category	US Equity Large Cap Growth
Sub-Category	Large Growth
Prospectus Objective	Growth
Inception Date	Mar-02
Open to New Investments	Y
Minimum Initial Investment	250
Minimum Subsequent Investment	50
Front End Fee	
Back End Fee	

Total Returns (%)

3-Month	6-Month	1-Year	3-Year	5-Year
6.81	12.10	25.73	41.80	110.72

Last Bull Market	23.94
Last Bear Market	-19.13
3-Year Standard Deviation	10.66
3-Year Beta	0.99

Company Information

Provider	American Funds
Manager/Tenure	Donald D. O'Neal (24), Michael T. Kerr (19), J. Blair Frank (16), 9 others
Website	http://www.americanfunds.com
Address	American Funds 333 South Hope Street Los Angeles CA 90071-1406 United States
Phone Number	800-421-4225

PERFORMANCE

Ratings History

Date	Overall Rating	Risk Rating	Reward Rating
Q4-17	B	B	B
Q3-17	B+	B+	B
Q2-17	B	B	B
Q1-17	B	B-	B
Q4-16	B	B	B
Q4-15	C+	C+	C+

Asset & Performance History

Date	NAV	1-Year Total Return
2016	41.27	8.11
2015	40.59	5.03
2014	42.01	8.91
2013	42.4	33.38
2012	33.91	20.14
2011	28.38	-5.17

Total Assets: $176,789,886,629

Asset Allocation

Asset	%
Cash	4%
Stocks	91%
US Stocks	76%
Bonds	2%
US Bonds	2%
Other	2%

Services Offered: Systematic Withdrawal Plan, Automatic Investment Plan, Qualified Investment, Phone Exchange, Retirement Investment

Investment Strategy: The investment seeks growth of capital. The fund invests primarily in common stocks and seeks to invest in companies that appear to offer superior opportunities for growth of capital. It may invest up to 25% of its assets in securities of issuers domiciled outside the United States. The investment adviser uses a system of multiple portfolio managers in managing the fund's assets. Under this approach, the portfolio of the fund is divided into segments managed by individual managers who decide how their respective segments will be invested. **Top Holdings:** Amazon.com Inc Broadcom Ltd Microsoft Corp Netflix Inc Alphabet Inc C

American Funds The Growth Fund of America® Class R-4 — B BUY

Ticker	Traded On	NAV	Total Assets ($)	Dividend Yield (TTM)	Turnover Ratio	Expense Ratio
RGAEX	NAS CM	49.1	$176,789,886,629	0.45	25	0.68

Ratings

Reward	B
Risk	B

Fund Information

Fund Type	Open End
Category	US Equity Large Cap Growth
Sub-Category	Large Growth
Prospectus Objective	Growth
Inception Date	May-02
Open to New Investments	Y
Minimum Initial Investment	250
Minimum Subsequent Investment	50
Front End Fee	
Back End Fee	

Total Returns (%)

3-Month	6-Month	1-Year	3-Year	5-Year
6.90	12.27	26.08	43.07	113.95

Last Bull Market	24.14
Last Bear Market	-19
3-Year Standard Deviation	10.65
3-Year Beta	0.99

Company Information

Provider	American Funds
Manager/Tenure	Donald D. O'Neal (24), Michael T. Kerr (19), J. Blair Frank (16), 9 others
Website	http://www.americanfunds.com
Address	American Funds 333 South Hope Street Los Angeles CA 90071-1406 United States
Phone Number	800-421-4225

PERFORMANCE

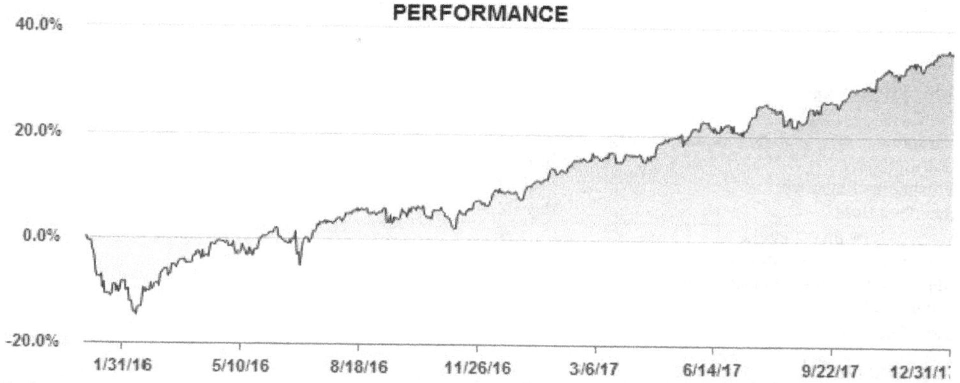

Ratings History

Date	Overall Rating	Risk Rating	Reward Rating
Q4-17	B	B	B
Q3-17	B+	B+	B
Q2-17	B	B	B
Q1-17	B	B-	B
Q4-16	B	B	B
Q4-15	C+	C+	C+

Asset & Performance History

Date	NAV	1-Year Total Return
2016	41.69	8.43
2015	40.97	5.33
2014	42.37	9.25
2013	42.72	33.82
2012	34.13	20.55
2011	28.52	-4.86

Total Assets: $176,789,886,629

Asset Allocation

Asset	%
Cash	4%
Stocks	91%
US Stocks	76%
Bonds	2%
US Bonds	2%
Other	2%

Services Offered: Automatic Investment Plan, Qualified Investment, Phone Exchange

Investment Strategy: The investment seeks growth of capital. The fund invests primarily in common stocks and seeks to invest in companies that appear to offer superior opportunities for growth of capital. It may invest up to 25% of its assets in securities of issuers domiciled outside the United States. The investment adviser uses a system of multiple portfolio managers in managing the fund's assets. Under this approach, the portfolio of the fund is divided into segments managed by individual managers who decide how their respective segments will be invested. **Top Holdings:** Amazon.com Inc Broadcom Ltd Microsoft Corp Netflix Inc Alphabet Inc C

American Funds The Growth Fund of America® Class 529-A — B BUY

Ticker	Traded On	NAV	Total Assets ($)	Dividend Yield (TTM)	Turnover Ratio	Expense Ratio
CGFAX	NAS CM	49.03	$176,789,886,629	0.41	25	0.72

Ratings

Reward	B
Risk	B

Fund Information

Fund Type	Open End
Category	US Equity Large Cap Growth
Sub-Category	Large Growth
Prospectus Objective	Growth
Inception Date	Feb-02
Open to New Investments	Y
Minimum Initial Investment	250
Minimum Subsequent Investment	50
Front End Fee	5.75
Back End Fee	

Total Returns (%)

3-Month	6-Month	1-Year	3-Year	5-Year
6.88	12.25	26.05	42.84	113.34

Last Bull Market	24.13
Last Bear Market	-19.02
3-Year Standard Deviation	10.67
3-Year Beta	0.99

Company Information

Provider	American Funds
Manager/Tenure	Donald D. O'Neal (24), Michael T. Kerr (19), J. Blair Frank (16), 9 others
Website	http://www.americanfunds.com
Address	American Funds 333 South Hope Street Los Angeles CA 90071-1406 United States
Phone Number	800-421-4225

PERFORMANCE

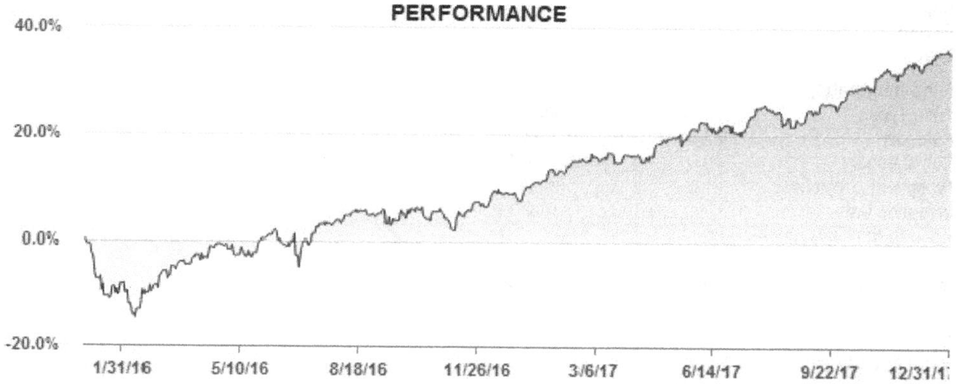

Ratings History

Date	Overall Rating	Risk Rating	Reward Rating
Q4-17	B	B	B
Q3-17	B+	B+	B
Q2-17	B	B	B
Q1-17	B	B-	B
Q4-16	B	B	B
Q4-15	C+	C+	C+

Asset & Performance History

Date	NAV	1-Year Total Return
2016	41.65	8.35
2015	40.94	5.29
2014	42.34	9.19
2013	42.7	33.69
2012	34.13	20.44
2011	28.56	-4.92

Total Assets: $176,789,886,629

Asset Allocation

Asset	%
Cash	4%
Stocks	91%
US Stocks	76%
Bonds	2%
US Bonds	2%
Other	2%

Services Offered: Systematic Withdrawal Plan, Automatic Investment Plan, Qualified Investment, Phone Exchange, Retirement Investment

Investment Strategy: The investment seeks growth of capital. The fund invests primarily in common stocks and seeks to invest in companies that appear to offer superior opportunities for growth of capital. It may invest up to 25% of its assets in securities of issuers domiciled outside the United States. The investment adviser uses a system of multiple portfolio managers in managing the fund's assets. Under this approach, the portfolio of the fund is divided into segments managed by individual managers who decide how their respective segments will be invested. **Top Holdings:** Amazon.com Inc Broadcom Ltd Microsoft Corp Netflix Inc Alphabet Inc C

American Funds The Growth Fund of America® Class R-3 B BUY

Ticker	Traded On	NAV	Total Assets ($)	Dividend Yield (TTM)	Turnover Ratio	Expense Ratio
RGACX	NAS CM	48.63	$176,789,886,629	0.19	25	0.98

Ratings

Reward	B
Risk	B

Fund Information

Fund Type	Open End
Category	US Equity Large Cap Growth
Sub-Category	Large Growth
Prospectus Objective	Growth
Inception Date	May-02
Open to New Investments	Y
Minimum Initial Investment	250
Minimum Subsequent Investment	50
Front End Fee	
Back End Fee	

Total Returns (%)

3-Month	6-Month	1-Year	3-Year	5-Year
6.83	12.09	25.70	41.77	110.79

Last Bull Market	23.96
Last Bear Market	-19.09
3-Year Standard Deviation	10.66
3-Year Beta	0.99

Company Information

Provider	American Funds
Manager/Tenure	Donald D. O'Neal (24), Michael T. Kerr (19), J. Blair Frank (16), 9 others
Website	http://www.americanfunds.com
Address	American Funds 333 South Hope Street Los Angeles CA 90071-1406 United States
Phone Number	800-421-4225

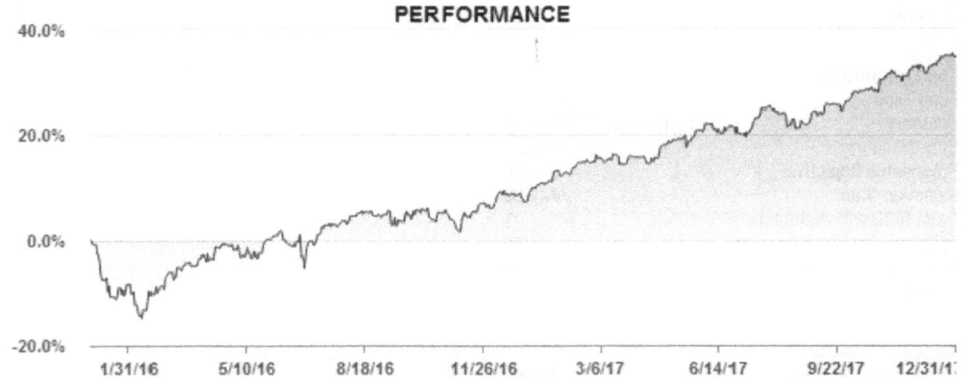

Ratings History

Date	Overall Rating	Risk Rating	Reward Rating
Q4-17	B	B	B
Q3-17	B+	B+	B
Q2-17	B	B	B
Q1-17	B	B-	B
Q4-16	B	B	B
Q4-15	C+	C+	C+

Asset & Performance History

Date	NAV	1-Year Total Return
2016	41.32	8.11
2015	40.62	5.03
2014	42.02	8.94
2013	42.39	33.42
2012	33.89	20.19
2011	28.33	-5.14

Total Assets: $176,789,886,629

Asset Allocation

Asset	%
Cash	4%
Stocks	91%
US Stocks	76%
Bonds	2%
US Bonds	2%
Other	2%

Services Offered: Automatic Investment Plan, Qualified Investment, Phone Exchange

Investment Strategy: The investment seeks growth of capital. The fund invests primarily in common stocks and seeks to invest in companies that appear to offer superior opportunities for growth of capital. It may invest up to 25% of its assets in securities of issuers domiciled outside the United States. The investment adviser uses a system of multiple portfolio managers in managing the fund's assets. Under this approach, the portfolio of the fund is divided into segments managed by individual managers who decide how their respective segments will be invested. **Top Holdings:** Amazon.com Inc Broadcom Ltd Microsoft Corp Netflix Inc Alphabet Inc C

American Funds The Growth Fund of America® Class R-2E B BUY

Ticker	Traded On	NAV	Total Assets ($)	Dividend Yield (TTM)	Turnover Ratio	Expense Ratio
RGEBX	NAS CM	48.73	$176,789,886,629	0.32	25	1.12

Ratings

Reward	B
Risk	B

Fund Information

Fund Type	Open End
Category	US Equity Large Cap Growth
Sub-Category	Large Growth
Prospectus Objective	Growth
Inception Date	Aug-14
Open to New Investments	Y
Minimum Initial Investment	250
Minimum Subsequent Investment	50
Front End Fee	
Back End Fee	

Total Returns (%)

3-Month	6-Month	1-Year	3-Year	5-Year
6.78	12.02	25.52	41.37	110.31

Last Bull Market	23.89
Last Bear Market	-19.13
3-Year Standard Deviation	10.64
3-Year Beta	0.99

Company Information

Provider	American Funds
Manager/Tenure	Donald D. O'Neal (24), Michael T. Kerr (19), J. Blair Frank (16), 9 others
Website	http://www.americanfunds.com
Address	American Funds 333 South Hope Street Los Angeles CA 90071-1406 United States
Phone Number	800-421-4225

Ratings History

Date	Overall Rating	Risk Rating	Reward Rating
Q4-17	B	B	B
Q3-17	B+	B+	B
Q2-17	B	B	B
Q1-17	B	B-	B
Q4-16	B	B	B
Q4-15	C+	C+	C+

Asset & Performance History

Date	NAV	1-Year Total Return
2016	41.48	7.98
2015	40.88	4.97
2014	42.57	9.09
2013		33.31
2012		20.11
2011		-5.23

Total Assets: $176,789,886,629

Asset Allocation

Asset	%
Cash	4%
Stocks	91%
US Stocks	76%
Bonds	2%
US Bonds	2%
Other	2%

Services Offered: Automatic Investment Plan, Qualified Investment, Phone Exchange

Investment Strategy: The investment seeks growth of capital. The fund invests primarily in common stocks and seeks to invest in companies that appear to offer superior opportunities for growth of capital. It may invest up to 25% of its assets in securities of issuers domiciled outside the United States. The investment adviser uses a system of multiple portfolio managers in managing the fund's assets. Under this approach, the portfolio of the fund is divided into segments managed by individual managers who decide how their respective segments will be invested. **Top Holdings:** Amazon.com Inc Broadcom Ltd Microsoft Corp Netflix Inc Alphabet Inc C

American Funds The Growth Fund of America® Class F-3

B **BUY**

Ticker	Traded On	NAV	Total Assets ($)	Dividend Yield (TTM)	Turnover Ratio	Expense Ratio
GAFFX	NAS CM	49.53	$176,789,886,629		25	0.33

Ratings

Reward	B
Risk	B

Fund Information

Fund Type	Open End
Category	US Equity Large Cap Growth
Sub-Category	Large Growth
Prospectus Objective	Growth
Inception Date	Jan-17
Open to New Investments	Y
Minimum Initial Investment	250
Minimum Subsequent Investment	50
Front End Fee	
Back End Fee	

Total Returns (%)

3-Month	6-Month	1-Year	3-Year	5-Year
6.98	12.45	26.47	43.57	114.77

Last Bull Market	24.15
Last Bear Market	-19.01
3-Year Standard Deviation	10.66
3-Year Beta	0.99

Company Information

Provider	American Funds
Manager/Tenure	Donald D. O'Neal (24), Michael T. Kerr (19), J. Blair Frank (16), 9 others
Website	http://www.americanfunds.com
Address	American Funds 333 South Hope Street Los Angeles CA 90071-1406 United States
Phone Number	800-421-4225

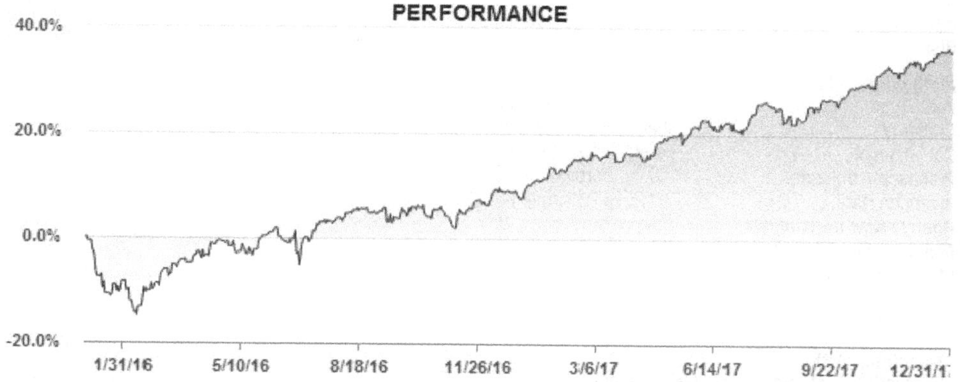

Ratings History

Date	Overall Rating	Risk Rating	Reward Rating
Q4-17	B	B	B
Q3-17	B+	B+	B
Q2-17	B		B
Q1-17	B	B-	B
Q4-16			
Q4-15			

Asset & Performance History

Date	NAV	1-Year Total Return
2016		
2015		5.36
2014		9.3
2013		33.79
2012		20.54
2011		-4.89

Total Assets: $176,789,886,629

Asset Allocation

Asset	%
Cash	4%
Stocks	91%
US Stocks	76%
Bonds	2%
US Bonds	2%
Other	2%

Services Offered: Systematic Withdrawal Plan, Automatic Investment Plan, Qualified Investment, Phone Exchange, Retirement Investment

Investment Strategy: The investment seeks growth of capital. The fund invests primarily in common stocks and seeks to invest in companies that appear to offer superior opportunities for growth of capital. It may invest up to 25% of its assets in securities of issuers domiciled outside the United States. The investment adviser uses a system of multiple portfolio managers in managing the fund's assets. Under this approach, the portfolio of the fund is divided into segments managed by individual managers who decide how their respective segments will be invested. **Top Holdings:** Amazon.com Inc Broadcom Ltd Microsoft Corp Netflix Inc Alphabet Inc C

American Funds EuroPacific Growth Fund® Class F-3

B **BUY**

Ticker	Traded On	NAV	Total Assets ($)	Dividend Yield (TTM)	Turnover Ratio	Expense Ratio
FEUPX	NAS CM	56.19	$160,340,414,689		36	0.51

Ratings

Reward	B
Risk	B

Fund Information

Fund Type	Open End
Category	Global Equity Large Cap
Sub-Category	Foreign Large Growth
Prospectus Objective	Foreign Stock
Inception Date	Jan-17
Open to New Investments	Y
Minimum Initial Investment	250
Minimum Subsequent Investment	50
Front End Fee	
Back End Fee	

Total Returns (%)

3-Month	6-Month	1-Year	3-Year	5-Year
4.22	11.36	31.12	30.25	54.48

Last Bull Market	16.84
Last Bear Market	-24.03
3-Year Standard Deviation	11.15
3-Year Beta	0.86

Company Information

Provider	American Funds
Manager/Tenure	Mark E. Denning (25), Carl M. Kawaja (16), Nicholas J. Grace (15), 6 others
Website	http://www.americanfunds.com
Address	American Funds 333 South Hope Street Los Angeles CA 90071-1406 United States
Phone Number	800-421-4225

Ratings History

Date	Overall Rating	Risk Rating	Reward Rating
Q4-17	B	B	B
Q3-17	C+	B-	C+
Q2-17	C		C+
Q1-17	C	C	C+
Q4-16			
Q4-15			

Asset & Performance History

Date	NAV	1-Year Total Return
2016		
2015		-0.82
2014		-2.64
2013		20.15
2012		19.21
2011		-13.58

Total Assets: $160,340,414,689

Asset Allocation

Asset	%
Cash	2%
Stocks	91%
US Stocks	1%
Bonds	1%
US Bonds	1%
Other	4%

Services Offered: Systematic Withdrawal Plan, Automatic Investment Plan, Qualified Investment, Phone Exchange, Retirement Investment

Investment Strategy: The investment seeks long-term growth of capital. The fund invests primarily in common stocks of issuers in Europe and the Pacific Basin that the investment adviser believes have the potential for growth. Growth stocks are stocks that the investment adviser believes have the potential for above-average capital appreciation. It normally will invest at least 80% of its net assets in securities of issuers in Europe and the Pacific Basin. The fund may invest a portion of its assets in common stocks and other securities of companies in emerging markets. **Top Holdings:** Samsung Electronics Co Ltd Alibaba Group Holding Ltd ADR British American Tobacco PLC AIA Group Ltd Taiwan Semiconductor Manufacturing Co Ltd

American Funds EuroPacific Growth Fund® Class R-2E B BUY

Ticker	Traded On	NAV	Total Assets ($)	Dividend Yield (TTM)	Turnover Ratio	Expense Ratio
REEBX	NAS CM	55.39	$160,340,414,689	1.04	36	1.28

Ratings

Reward	B-
Risk	B

Fund Information

Fund Type	Open End
Category	Global Equity Large Cap
Sub-Category	Foreign Large Growth
Prospectus Objective	Foreign Stock
Inception Date	Aug-14
Open to New Investments	Y
Minimum Initial Investment	250
Minimum Subsequent Investment	50
Front End Fee	
Back End Fee	

Total Returns (%)

3-Month	6-Month	1-Year	3-Year	5-Year
4.01	10.92	30.13	28.29	51.14

Last Bull Market	16.59
Last Bear Market	-24.14
3-Year Standard Deviation	11.12
3-Year Beta	0.86

Company Information

Provider	American Funds
Manager/Tenure	Mark E. Denning (25), Carl M. Kawaja (16), Nicholas J. Grace (15), 6 others
Website	http://www.americanfunds.com
Address	American Funds 333 South Hope Street Los Angeles CA 90071-1406 United States
Phone Number	800-421-4225

PERFORMANCE

Ratings History

Date	Overall Rating	Risk Rating	Reward Rating
Q4-17	B	B	B-
Q3-17	C+	C+	C+
Q2-17	C	C	C+
Q1-17	C	C-	C
Q4-16	C	C+	C-
Q4-15	C	C	C

Asset & Performance History

Date	NAV	1-Year Total Return
2016	44.51	0.28
2015	44.9	-1.19
2014	46.96	-2.94
2013		19.72
2012		18.78
2011		-13.89

Total Assets: $160,340,414,689

Asset Allocation

Asset	%
Cash	2%
Stocks	91%
US Stocks	1%
Bonds	1%
US Bonds	1%
Other	4%

Services Offered: Automatic Investment Plan, Qualified Investment, Phone Exchange

Investment Strategy: The investment seeks long-term growth of capital. The fund invests primarily in common stocks of issuers in Europe and the Pacific Basin that the investment adviser believes have the potential for growth. Growth stocks are stocks that the investment adviser believes have the potential for above-average capital appreciation. It normally will invest at least 80% of its net assets in securities of issuers in Europe and the Pacific Basin. The fund may invest a portion of its assets in common stocks and other securities of companies in emerging markets. **Top Holdings:** Samsung Electronics Co Ltd Alibaba Group Holding Ltd ADR British American Tobacco PLC AIA Group Ltd Taiwan Semiconductor Manufacturing Co Ltd

American Funds EuroPacific Growth Fund® Class R-6 B BUY

Ticker	Traded On	NAV	Total Assets ($)	Dividend Yield (TTM)	Turnover Ratio	Expense Ratio
RERGX	NAS CM	56.14	$160,340,414,689	1.55	36	0.5

Ratings

Reward	B
Risk	B

Fund Information

Fund Type	Open End
Category	Global Equity Large Cap
Sub-Category	Foreign Large Growth
Prospectus Objective	Foreign Stock
Inception Date	May-09
Open to New Investments	Y
Minimum Initial Investment	250
Minimum Subsequent Investment	50
Front End Fee	
Back End Fee	

Total Returns (%)

3-Month	6-Month	1-Year	3-Year	5-Year
4.22	11.37	31.17	31.19	56.68

Last Bull Market	17.06
Last Bear Market	-23.91
3-Year Standard Deviation	11.15
3-Year Beta	0.86

Company Information

Provider	American Funds
Manager/Tenure	Mark E. Denning (25), Carl M. Kawaja (16), Nicholas J. Grace (15), 6 others
Website	http://www.americanfunds.com
Address	American Funds 333 South Hope Street Los Angeles CA 90071-1406 United States
Phone Number	800-421-4225

PERFORMANCE

Ratings History

Date	Overall Rating	Risk Rating	Reward Rating
Q4-17	B	B	B
Q3-17	B-	B-	C+
Q2-17	C	C	C+
Q1-17	C	C	C+
Q4-16	C	C+	C-
Q4-15	C	C	C

Asset & Performance History

Date	NAV	1-Year Total Return
2016	45.04	1.01
2015	45.32	-0.48
2014	47.09	-2.29
2013	49.03	20.57
2012	41.18	19.63
2011	35.13	-13.3

Total Assets: $160,340,414,689

Asset Allocation

Asset	%
Cash	2%
Stocks	91%
US Stocks	1%
Bonds	1%
US Bonds	1%
Other	4%

Services Offered: Automatic Investment Plan, Qualified Investment, Phone Exchange

Investment Strategy: The investment seeks long-term growth of capital. The fund invests primarily in common stocks of issuers in Europe and the Pacific Basin that the investment adviser believes have the potential for growth. Growth stocks are stocks that the investment adviser believes have the potential for above-average capital appreciation. It normally will invest at least 80% of its net assets in securities of issuers in Europe and the Pacific Basin. The fund may invest a portion of its assets in common stocks and other securities of companies in emerging markets. **Top Holdings:** Samsung Electronics Co Ltd Alibaba Group Holding Ltd ADR British American Tobacco PLC AIA Group Ltd Taiwan Semiconductor Manufacturing Co Ltd

American Funds EuroPacific Growth Fund® Class A

B BUY

Ticker	Traded On	NAV	Total Assets ($)	Dividend Yield (TTM)	Turnover Ratio	Expense Ratio
AEPGX	NAS CM	56.22	$160,340,414,689	1.18	36	0.85

Ratings

Reward	B
Risk	B

Fund Information

Fund Type	Open End
Category	Global Equity Large Cap
Sub-Category	Foreign Large Growth
Prospectus Objective	Foreign Stock
Inception Date	Apr-84
Open to New Investments	Y
Minimum Initial Investment	250
Minimum Subsequent Investment	50
Front End Fee	5.75
Back End Fee	

Total Returns (%)

3-Month	6-Month	1-Year	3-Year	5-Year
4.15	11.19	30.72	29.85	54.01

Last Bull Market	16.84
Last Bear Market	-24.03
3-Year Standard Deviation	11.14
3-Year Beta	0.86

Company Information

Provider	American Funds
Manager/Tenure	Mark E. Denning (25), Carl M. Kawaja (16), Nicholas J. Grace (15), 6 others
Website	http://www.americanfunds.com
Address	American Funds 333 South Hope Street Los Angeles CA 90071-1406 United States
Phone Number	800-421-4225

PERFORMANCE

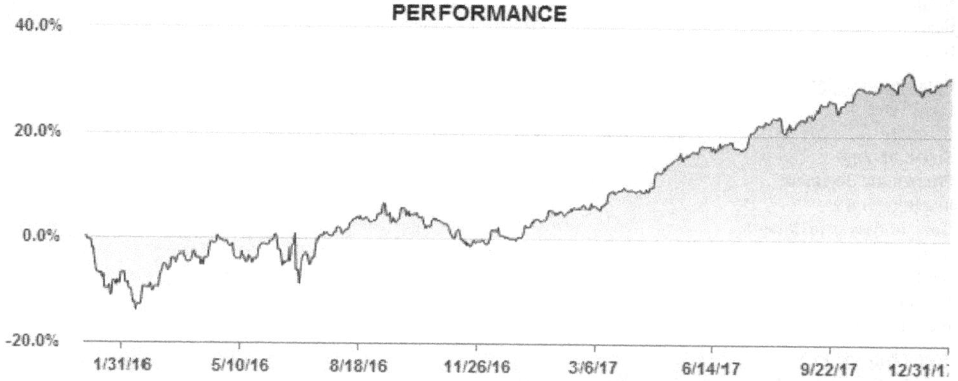

Ratings History

Date	Overall Rating	Risk Rating	Reward Rating
Q4-17	B	B	B
Q3-17	C+	B-	C+
Q2-17	C	C	C+
Q1-17	C	C	C+
Q4-16	C	C+	C-
Q4-15	C	C	C

Asset & Performance History

Date	NAV	1-Year Total Return
2016	45.11	0.66
2015	45.37	-0.82
2014	47.13	-2.64
2013	49.07	20.15
2012	41.22	19.21
2011	35.16	-13.58

Total Assets: $160,340,414,689

Asset Allocation

Asset	%
Cash	2%
Stocks	91%
US Stocks	1%
Bonds	1%
US Bonds	1%
Other	4%

Services Offered: Systematic Withdrawal Plan, Automatic Investment Plan, Phone Exchange, Retirement Investment

Investment Strategy: The investment seeks long-term growth of capital. The fund invests primarily in common stocks of issuers in Europe and the Pacific Basin that the investment adviser believes have the potential for growth. Growth stocks are stocks that the investment adviser believes have the potential for above-average capital appreciation. It normally will invest at least 80% of its net assets in securities of issuers in Europe and the Pacific Basin. The fund may invest a portion of its assets in common stocks and other securities of companies in emerging markets. **Top Holdings:** Samsung Electronics Co Ltd Alibaba Group Holding Ltd ADR British American Tobacco PLC AIA Group Ltd Taiwan Semiconductor Manufacturing Co Ltd

American Funds EuroPacific Growth Fund® Class F-1

B BUY

Ticker	Traded On	NAV	Total Assets ($)	Dividend Yield (TTM)	Turnover Ratio	Expense Ratio
AEGFX	NAS CM	55.96	$160,340,414,689	1.15	36	0.87

Ratings

Reward	B
Risk	B

Fund Information

Fund Type	Open End
Category	Global Equity Large Cap
Sub-Category	Foreign Large Growth
Prospectus Objective	Foreign Stock
Inception Date	Mar-01
Open to New Investments	Y
Minimum Initial Investment	250
Minimum Subsequent Investment	50
Front End Fee	
Back End Fee	

Total Returns (%)

3-Month	6-Month	1-Year	3-Year	5-Year
4.13	11.16	30.68	29.74	53.80

Last Bull Market	16.84
Last Bear Market	-24.04
3-Year Standard Deviation	11.14
3-Year Beta	0.86

Company Information

Provider	American Funds
Manager/Tenure	Mark E. Denning (25), Carl M. Kawaja (16), Nicholas J. Grace (15), 6 others
Website	http://www.americanfunds.com
Address	American Funds 333 South Hope Street Los Angeles CA 90071-1406 United States
Phone Number	800-421-4225

PERFORMANCE

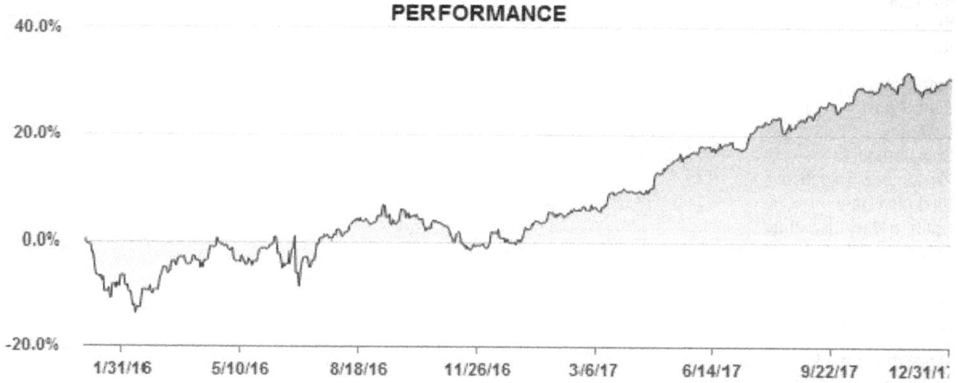

Ratings History

Date	Overall Rating	Risk Rating	Reward Rating
Q4-17	B	B	B
Q3-17	C+	B-	C+
Q2-17	C	C	C+
Q1-17	C	C	C+
Q4-16	C	C+	C-
Q4-15	C	C	C

Asset & Performance History

Date	NAV	1-Year Total Return
2016	44.91	0.65
2015	45.16	-0.85
2014	46.91	-2.66
2013	48.8	20.13
2012	40.99	19.19
2011	34.98	-13.59

Total Assets: $160,340,414,689

Asset Allocation

Asset	%
Cash	2%
Stocks	91%
US Stocks	1%
Bonds	1%
US Bonds	1%
Other	4%

Services Offered: Systematic Withdrawal Plan, Automatic Investment Plan, Qualified Investment, Phone Exchange, Retirement Investment

Investment Strategy: The investment seeks long-term growth of capital. The fund invests primarily in common stocks of issuers in Europe and the Pacific Basin that the investment adviser believes have the potential for growth. Growth stocks are stocks that the investment adviser believes have the potential for above-average capital appreciation. It normally will invest at least 80% of its net assets in securities of issuers in Europe and the Pacific Basin. The fund may invest a portion of its assets in common stocks and other securities of companies in emerging markets. **Top Holdings:** Samsung Electronics Co Ltd Alibaba Group Holding Ltd ADR British American Tobacco PLC AIA Group Ltd Taiwan Semiconductor Manufacturing Co Ltd

American Funds EuroPacific Growth Fund® Class R-3 — B BUY

Ticker	Traded On	NAV	Total Assets ($)	Dividend Yield (TTM)	Turnover Ratio	Expense Ratio
RERCX	NAS CM	55.09	$160,340,414,689	0.89	36	1.14

Ratings

Reward	B
Risk	B

Fund Information

Fund Type	Open End
Category	Global Equity Large Cap
Sub-Category	Foreign Large Growth
Prospectus Objective	Foreign Stock
Inception Date	May-02
Open to New Investments	Y
Minimum Initial Investment	250
Minimum Subsequent Investment	50
Front End Fee	
Back End Fee	

Total Returns (%)

3-Month	6-Month	1-Year	3-Year	5-Year
4.07	11.02	30.31	28.71	51.74

Last Bull Market	16.64
Last Bear Market	-24.13
3-Year Standard Deviation	11.13
3-Year Beta	0.86

Company Information

Provider	American Funds
Manager/Tenure	Mark E. Denning (25), Carl M. Kawaja (16), Nicholas J. Grace (15), 6 others
Website	http://www.americanfunds.com
Address	American Funds 333 South Hope Street Los Angeles CA 90071-1406 United States
Phone Number	800-421-4225

Ratings History

Date	Overall Rating	Risk Rating	Reward Rating
Q4-17	B	B	B
Q3-17	C+	C+	C+
Q2-17	C	C	C+
Q1-17	C	C-	C
Q4-16	C	C+	C-
Q4-15	C	C	C

Asset & Performance History

Date	NAV	1-Year Total Return
2016	44.25	0.38
2015	44.5	-1.12
2014	46.24	-2.91
2013	48.13	19.78
2012	40.45	18.88
2011	34.52	-13.85

Total Assets: $160,340,414,689

Asset Allocation

Asset	%
Cash	2%
Stocks	91%
US Stocks	1%
Bonds	1%
US Bonds	1%
Other	4%

Services Offered: Automatic Investment Plan, Qualified Investment, Phone Exchange

Investment Strategy: The investment seeks long-term growth of capital. The fund invests primarily in common stocks of issuers in Europe and the Pacific Basin that the investment adviser believes have the potential for growth. Growth stocks are stocks that the investment adviser believes have the potential for above-average capital appreciation. It normally will invest at least 80% of its net assets in securities of issuers in Europe and the Pacific Basin. The fund may invest a portion of its assets in common stocks and other securities of companies in emerging markets. **Top Holdings:** Samsung Electronics Co Ltd Alibaba Group Holding Ltd ADR British American Tobacco PLC AIA Group Ltd Taiwan Semiconductor Manufacturing Co Ltd

American Funds EuroPacific Growth Fund® Class 529-E — B BUY

Ticker	Traded On	NAV	Total Assets ($)	Dividend Yield (TTM)	Turnover Ratio	Expense Ratio
CEUEX	NAS CM	55.11	$160,340,414,689	0.94	36	1.13

Ratings

Reward	B
Risk	B

Fund Information

Fund Type	Open End
Category	Global Equity Large Cap
Sub-Category	Foreign Large Growth
Prospectus Objective	Foreign Stock
Inception Date	Mar-02
Open to New Investments	Y
Minimum Initial Investment	250
Minimum Subsequent Investment	50
Front End Fee	
Back End Fee	

Total Returns (%)

3-Month	6-Month	1-Year	3-Year	5-Year
4.06	11.03	30.33	28.72	51.70

Last Bull Market	16.64
Last Bear Market	-24.14
3-Year Standard Deviation	11.13
3-Year Beta	0.86

Company Information

Provider	American Funds
Manager/Tenure	Mark E. Denning (25), Carl M. Kawaja (16), Nicholas J. Grace (15), 6 others
Website	http://www.americanfunds.com
Address	American Funds 333 South Hope Street Los Angeles CA 90071-1406 United States
Phone Number	800-421-4225

Ratings History

Date	Overall Rating	Risk Rating	Reward Rating
Q4-17	B	B	B
Q3-17	C+	C+	C+
Q2-17	C	C	C+
Q1-17	C	C-	C
Q4-16	C	C+	C-
Q4-15	C	C	C

Asset & Performance History

Date	NAV	1-Year Total Return
2016	44.28	0.38
2015	44.55	-1.13
2014	46.31	-2.92
2013	48.22	19.78
2012	40.53	18.82
2011	34.6	-13.86

Total Assets: $160,340,414,689

Asset Allocation

Asset	%
Cash	2%
Stocks	91%
US Stocks	1%
Bonds	1%
US Bonds	1%
Other	4%

Services Offered: Systematic Withdrawal Plan, Automatic Investment Plan, Qualified Investment, Phone Exchange, Retirement Investment

Investment Strategy: The investment seeks long-term growth of capital. The fund invests primarily in common stocks of issuers in Europe and the Pacific Basin that the investment adviser believes have the potential for growth. Growth stocks are stocks that the investment adviser believes have the potential for above-average capital appreciation. It normally will invest at least 80% of its net assets in securities of issuers in Europe and the Pacific Basin. The fund may invest a portion of its assets in common stocks and other securities of companies in emerging markets. **Top Holdings:** Samsung Electronics Co Ltd Alibaba Group Holding Ltd ADR British American Tobacco PLC AIA Group Ltd Taiwan Semiconductor Manufacturing Co Ltd

American Funds EuroPacific Growth Fund® Class R-4 — B BUY

Ticker	Traded On	NAV	Total Assets ($)	Dividend Yield (TTM)	Turnover Ratio	Expense Ratio
REREX	NAS CM	55.09	$160,340,414,689	1.21	36	0.85

Ratings

Reward	B
Risk	B

Fund Information

Fund Type	Open End
Category	Global Equity Large Cap
Sub-Category	Foreign Large Growth
Prospectus Objective	Foreign Stock
Inception Date	Jun-02
Open to New Investments	Y
Minimum Initial Investment	250
Minimum Subsequent Investment	50
Front End Fee	
Back End Fee	

Total Returns (%)

3-Month	6-Month	1-Year	3-Year	5-Year
4.13	11.19	30.70	29.84	54.00

Last Bull Market	16.84
Last Bear Market	-24.05
3-Year Standard Deviation	11.14
3-Year Beta	0.86

Company Information

Provider	American Funds
Manager/Tenure	Mark E. Denning (25), Carl M. Kawaja (16), Nicholas J. Grace (15), 6 others
Website	http://www.americanfunds.com
Address	American Funds 333 South Hope Street Los Angeles CA 90071-1406 United States
Phone Number	800-421-4225

Ratings History

Date	Overall Rating	Risk Rating	Reward Rating
Q4-17	B	B	B
Q3-17	C+	B-	C+
Q2-17	C	C	C+
Q1-17	C	C	C+
Q4-16	C	C+	C-
Q4-15	C	C	C

Asset & Performance History

Date	NAV	1-Year Total Return
2016	44.25	0.68
2015	44.51	-0.82
2014	46.26	-2.65
2013	48.18	20.16
2012	40.48	19.21
2011	34.55	-13.6

Total Assets: $160,340,414,689

Asset Allocation

Asset	%
Cash	2%
Stocks	91%
US Stocks	1%
Bonds	1%
US Bonds	1%
Other	4%

Services Offered: Automatic Investment Plan, Qualified Investment, Phone Exchange

Investment Strategy: The investment seeks long-term growth of capital. The fund invests primarily in common stocks of issuers in Europe and the Pacific Basin that the investment adviser believes have the potential for growth. Growth stocks are stocks that the investment adviser believes have the potential for above-average capital appreciation. It normally will invest at least 80% of its net assets in securities of issuers in Europe and the Pacific Basin. The fund may invest a portion of its assets in common stocks and other securities of companies in emerging markets. **Top Holdings:** Samsung Electronics Co Ltd Alibaba Group Holding Ltd ADR British American Tobacco PLC AIA Group Ltd Taiwan Semiconductor Manufacturing Co Ltd

American Funds EuroPacific Growth Fund® Class C — B- BUY

Ticker	Traded On	NAV	Total Assets ($)	Dividend Yield (TTM)	Turnover Ratio	Expense Ratio
AEPCX	NAS CM	55	$160,340,414,689	0.33	36	1.63

Ratings

Reward	B-
Risk	B

Fund Information

Fund Type	Open End
Category	Global Equity Large Cap
Sub-Category	Foreign Large Growth
Prospectus Objective	Foreign Stock
Inception Date	Mar-01
Open to New Investments	Y
Minimum Initial Investment	250
Minimum Subsequent Investment	50
Front End Fee	
Back End Fee	1.00

Total Returns (%)

3-Month	6-Month	1-Year	3-Year	5-Year
3.94	10.76	29.70	26.82	48.12

Last Bull Market	16.33
Last Bear Market	-24.28
3-Year Standard Deviation	11.14
3-Year Beta	0.86

Company Information

Provider	American Funds
Manager/Tenure	Mark E. Denning (25), Carl M. Kawaja (16), Nicholas J. Grace (15), 6 others
Website	http://www.americanfunds.com
Address	American Funds 333 South Hope Street Los Angeles CA 90071-1406 United States
Phone Number	800-421-4225

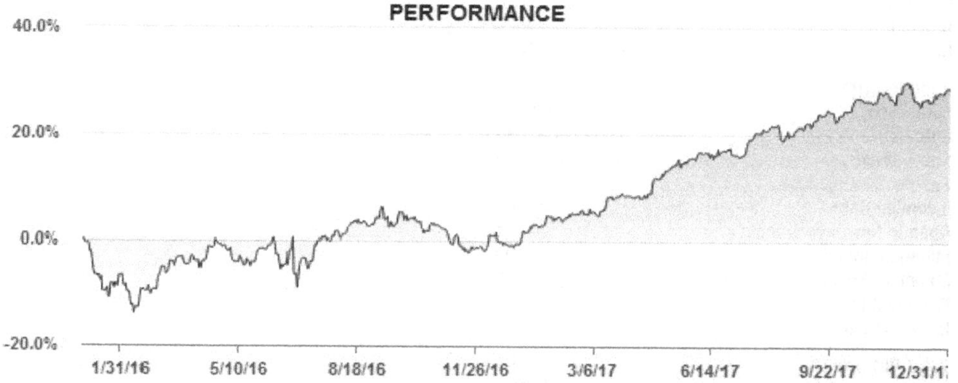

Ratings History

Date	Overall Rating	Risk Rating	Reward Rating
Q4-17	B-	B	B-
Q3-17	C+	C+	C+
Q2-17	C	C	C
Q1-17	C	C-	C
Q4-16	C-	C	D+
Q4-15	C	C	C

Asset & Performance History

Date	NAV	1-Year Total Return
2016	44.19	-0.11
2015	44.4	-1.59
2014	46.13	-3.39
2013	48.01	19.22
2012	40.35	18.29
2011	34.42	-14.24

Total Assets: $160,340,414,689

Asset Allocation

Asset	%
Cash	2%
Stocks	91%
US Stocks	1%
Bonds	1%
US Bonds	1%
Other	4%

Services Offered: Systematic Withdrawal Plan, Automatic Investment Plan, Phone Exchange, Retirement Investment

Investment Strategy: The investment seeks long-term growth of capital. The fund invests primarily in common stocks of issuers in Europe and the Pacific Basin that the investment adviser believes have the potential for growth. Growth stocks are stocks that the investment adviser believes have the potential for above-average capital appreciation. It normally will invest at least 80% of its net assets in securities of issuers in Europe and the Pacific Basin. The fund may invest a portion of its assets in common stocks and other securities of companies in emerging markets. **Top Holdings:** Samsung Electronics Co Ltd Alibaba Group Holding Ltd ADR British American Tobacco PLC AIA Group Ltd Taiwan Semiconductor Manufacturing Co Ltd

American Funds EuroPacific Growth Fund® Class F-2 — B BUY

Ticker	Traded On	NAV	Total Assets ($)	Dividend Yield (TTM)	Turnover Ratio	Expense Ratio
AEPFX	NAS CM	56.04	$160,340,414,689	1.46	36	0.6

Ratings

Reward	B
Risk	B

Fund Information

Fund Type	Open End
Category	Global Equity Large Cap
Sub-Category	Foreign Large Growth
Prospectus Objective	Foreign Stock
Inception Date	Aug-08
Open to New Investments	Y
Minimum Initial Investment	250
Minimum Subsequent Investment	50
Front End Fee	
Back End Fee	

Total Returns (%)

3-Month	6-Month	1-Year	3-Year	5-Year
4.19	11.30	31.02	30.79	55.88

Last Bull Market	17.03
Last Bear Market	-23.96
3-Year Standard Deviation	11.14
3-Year Beta	0.86

Company Information

Provider	American Funds
Manager/Tenure	Mark E. Denning (25), Carl M. Kawaja (16), Nicholas J. Grace (15), 6 others
Website	http://www.americanfunds.com
Address	American Funds 333 South Hope Street Los Angeles CA 90071-1406 United States
Phone Number	800-421-4225

Ratings History

Date	Overall Rating	Risk Rating	Reward Rating
Q4-17	B	B	B
Q3-17	C+	B-	C+
Q2-17	C	C	C+
Q1-17	C	C	C+
Q4-16	C	C+	C-
Q4-15	C	C	C

Asset & Performance History

Date	NAV	1-Year Total Return
2016	44.97	0.91
2015	45.25	-0.57
2014	47.02	-2.4
2013	48.98	20.44
2012	41.15	19.54
2011	35.11	-13.35

Total Assets: $160,340,414,689

Asset Allocation

Asset	%
Cash	2%
Stocks	91%
US Stocks	1%
Bonds	1%
US Bonds	1%
Other	4%

Services Offered: Systematic Withdrawal Plan, Automatic Investment Plan, Qualified Investment, Phone Exchange, Retirement Investment

Investment Strategy: The investment seeks long-term growth of capital. The fund invests primarily in common stocks of issuers in Europe and the Pacific Basin that the investment adviser believes have the potential for growth. Growth stocks are stocks that the investment adviser believes have the potential for above-average capital appreciation. It normally will invest at least 80% of its net assets in securities of issuers in Europe and the Pacific Basin. The fund may invest a portion of its assets in common stocks and other securities of companies in emerging markets. **Top Holdings:** Samsung Electronics Co Ltd Alibaba Group Holding Ltd ADR British American Tobacco PLC AIA Group Ltd Taiwan Semiconductor Manufacturing Co Ltd

American Funds EuroPacific Growth Fund® Class 529-A — B BUY

Ticker	Traded On	NAV	Total Assets ($)	Dividend Yield (TTM)	Turnover Ratio	Expense Ratio
CEUAX	NAS CM	55.57	$160,340,414,689	1.16	36	0.91

Ratings

Reward	B
Risk	B

Fund Information

Fund Type	Open End
Category	Global Equity Large Cap
Sub-Category	Foreign Large Growth
Prospectus Objective	Foreign Stock
Inception Date	Feb-02
Open to New Investments	Y
Minimum Initial Investment	250
Minimum Subsequent Investment	50
Front End Fee	5.75
Back End Fee	

Total Returns (%)

3-Month	6-Month	1-Year	3-Year	5-Year
4.13	11.17	30.65	29.64	53.59

Last Bull Market	16.82
Last Bear Market	-24.05
3-Year Standard Deviation	11.13
3-Year Beta	0.86

Company Information

Provider	American Funds
Manager/Tenure	Mark E. Denning (25), Carl M. Kawaja (16), Nicholas J. Grace (15), 6 others
Website	http://www.americanfunds.com
Address	American Funds 333 South Hope Street Los Angeles CA 90071-1406 United States
Phone Number	800-421-4225

Ratings History

Date	Overall Rating	Risk Rating	Reward Rating
Q4-17	B	B	B
Q3-17	C+	B-	C+
Q2-17	C	C	C+
Q1-17	C	C	C+
Q4-16	C	C+	C-
Q4-15	C	C	C

Asset & Performance History

Date	NAV	1-Year Total Return
2016	44.63	0.62
2015	44.9	-0.9
2014	46.67	-2.66
2013	48.59	20.08
2012	40.83	19.13
2011	34.85	-13.61

Total Assets: $160,340,414,689

Asset Allocation

Asset	%
Cash	2%
Stocks	91%
US Stocks	1%
Bonds	1%
US Bonds	1%
Other	4%

Services Offered: Systematic Withdrawal Plan, Automatic Investment Plan, Qualified Investment, Phone Exchange, Retirement Investment

Investment Strategy: The investment seeks long-term growth of capital. The fund invests primarily in common stocks of issuers in Europe and the Pacific Basin that the investment adviser believes have the potential for growth. Growth stocks are stocks that the investment adviser believes have the potential for above-average capital appreciation. It normally will invest at least 80% of its net assets in securities of issuers in Europe and the Pacific Basin. The fund may invest a portion of its assets in common stocks and other securities of companies in emerging markets. **Top Holdings:** Samsung Electronics Co Ltd Alibaba Group Holding Ltd ADR British American Tobacco PLC AIA Group Ltd Taiwan Semiconductor Manufacturing Co Ltd

American Funds EuroPacific Growth Fund® Class R-2 B BUY

Ticker	Traded On	NAV	Total Assets ($)	Dividend Yield (TTM)	Turnover Ratio	Expense Ratio
RERBX	NAS CM	54.61	$160,340,414,689	0.45	36	1.6

Ratings

Reward	B-
Risk	B

Fund Information

Fund Type	Open End
Category	Global Equity Large Cap
Sub-Category	Foreign Large Growth
Prospectus Objective	Foreign Stock
Inception Date	May-02
Open to New Investments	Y
Minimum Initial Investment	250
Minimum Subsequent Investment	50
Front End Fee	
Back End Fee	

Total Returns (%)

3-Month	6-Month	1-Year	3-Year	5-Year
3.95	10.75	29.72	26.99	48.41

Last Bull Market	16.33
Last Bear Market	-24.29
3-Year Standard Deviation	11.13
3-Year Beta	0.86

Company Information

Provider	American Funds
Manager/Tenure	Mark E. Denning (25), Carl M. Kawaja (16), Nicholas J. Grace (15), 6 others
Website	http://www.americanfunds.com
Address	American Funds 333 South Hope Street Los Angeles CA 90071-1406 United States
Phone Number	800-421-4225

Ratings History

Date	Overall Rating	Risk Rating	Reward Rating
Q4-17	B	B	B-
Q3-17	C+	C+	C+
Q2-17	C	C	C
Q1-17	C	C-	C
Q4-16	C-	C	D+
Q4-15	C	C	C

Asset & Performance History

Date	NAV	1-Year Total Return
2016	43.9	-0.06
2015	44.15	-1.52
2014	45.87	-3.37
2013	47.75	19.26
2012	40.14	18.31
2011	34.26	-14.23

Total Assets: $160,340,414,689

Asset Allocation

Asset	%
Cash	2%
Stocks	91%
US Stocks	1%
Bonds	1%
US Bonds	1%
Other	4%

Services Offered: Automatic Investment Plan, Qualified Investment, Phone Exchange

Investment Strategy: The investment seeks long-term growth of capital. The fund invests primarily in common stocks of issuers in Europe and the Pacific Basin that the investment adviser believes have the potential for growth. Growth stocks are stocks that the investment adviser believes have the potential for above-average capital appreciation. It normally will invest at least 80% of its net assets in securities of issuers in Europe and the Pacific Basin. The fund may invest a portion of its assets in common stocks and other securities of companies in emerging markets. **Top Holdings:** Samsung Electronics Co Ltd Alibaba Group Holding Ltd ADR British American Tobacco PLC AIA Group Ltd Taiwan Semiconductor Manufacturing Co Ltd

American Funds EuroPacific Growth Fund® Class R-5E B BUY

Ticker	Traded On	NAV	Total Assets ($)	Dividend Yield (TTM)	Turnover Ratio	Expense Ratio
RERHX	NAS CM	55.82	$160,340,414,689	1.57	36	0.62

Ratings

Reward	B
Risk	B

Fund Information

Fund Type	Open End
Category	Global Equity Large Cap
Sub-Category	Foreign Large Growth
Prospectus Objective	Foreign Stock
Inception Date	Nov-15
Open to New Investments	Y
Minimum Initial Investment	250
Minimum Subsequent Investment	50
Front End Fee	
Back End Fee	

Total Returns (%)

3-Month	6-Month	1-Year	3-Year	5-Year
4.19	11.29	30.98	30.34	54.59

Last Bull Market	16.84
Last Bear Market	-24.03
3-Year Standard Deviation	11.15
3-Year Beta	0.86

Company Information

Provider	American Funds
Manager/Tenure	Mark E. Denning (25), Carl M. Kawaja (16), Nicholas J. Grace (15), 6 others
Website	http://www.americanfunds.com
Address	American Funds 333 South Hope Street Los Angeles CA 90071-1406 United States
Phone Number	800-421-4225

Ratings History

Date	Overall Rating	Risk Rating	Reward Rating
Q4-17	B	B	B
Q3-17	C+	B-	C+
Q2-17	C	C	C+
Q1-17	C	C	C+
Q4-16	C	C+	C-
Q4-15			

Asset & Performance History

Date	NAV	1-Year Total Return
2016	44.84	0.81
2015	45.21	-0.79
2014		-2.64
2013		20.15
2012		19.21
2011		-13.58

Total Assets: $160,340,414,689

Asset Allocation

Asset	%
Cash	2%
Stocks	91%
US Stocks	1%
Bonds	1%
US Bonds	1%
Other	4%

Services Offered: Automatic Investment Plan, Qualified Investment, Phone Exchange

Investment Strategy: The investment seeks long-term growth of capital. The fund invests primarily in common stocks of issuers in Europe and the Pacific Basin that the investment adviser believes have the potential for growth. Growth stocks are stocks that the investment adviser believes have the potential for above-average capital appreciation. It normally will invest at least 80% of its net assets in securities of issuers in Europe and the Pacific Basin. The fund may invest a portion of its assets in common stocks and other securities of companies in emerging markets. **Top Holdings:** Samsung Electronics Co Ltd Alibaba Group Holding Ltd ADR British American Tobacco PLC AIA Group Ltd Taiwan Semiconductor Manufacturing Co Ltd

American Funds EuroPacific Growth Fund® Class 529-F-1 B BUY

Ticker	Traded On	NAV	Total Assets ($)	Dividend Yield (TTM)	Turnover Ratio	Expense Ratio
CEUFX	NAS CM	55.53	$160,340,414,689	1.38	36	0.68

Ratings

Reward	B
Risk	B

Fund Information

Fund Type	Open End
Category	Global Equity Large Cap
Sub-Category	Foreign Large Growth
Prospectus Objective	Foreign Stock
Inception Date	Sep-02
Open to New Investments	Y
Minimum Initial Investment	250
Minimum Subsequent Investment	50
Front End Fee	
Back End Fee	

Total Returns (%)

3-Month	6-Month	1-Year	3-Year	5-Year
4.19	11.29	30.92	30.47	55.24

Last Bull Market	16.95
Last Bear Market	-23.96
3-Year Standard Deviation	11.14
3-Year Beta	0.86

Company Information

Provider	American Funds
Manager/Tenure	Mark E. Denning (25), Carl M. Kawaja (16), Nicholas J. Grace (15), 6 others
Website	http://www.americanfunds.com
Address	American Funds 333 South Hope Street Los Angeles CA 90071-1406 United States
Phone Number	800-421-4225

Ratings History

Date	Overall Rating	Risk Rating	Reward Rating
Q4-17	B	B	B
Q3-17	C+	B-	C+
Q2-17	C	C	C+
Q1-17	C	C	C+
Q4-16	C	C+	C-
Q4-15	C	C	C

Asset & Performance History

Date	NAV	1-Year Total Return
2016	44.59	0.82
2015	44.87	-0.65
2014	46.63	-2.49
2013	48.57	20.36
2012	40.8	19.39
2011	34.82	-13.45

Total Assets: $160,340,414,689

Asset Allocation

Asset	%
Cash	2%
Stocks	91%
US Stocks	1%
Bonds	1%
US Bonds	1%
Other	4%

Services Offered: Systematic Withdrawal Plan, Automatic Investment Plan, Qualified Investment, Phone Exchange, Retirement Investment

Investment Strategy: The investment seeks long-term growth of capital. The fund invests primarily in common stocks of issuers in Europe and the Pacific Basin that the investment adviser believes have the potential for growth. Growth stocks are stocks that the investment adviser believes have the potential for above-average capital appreciation. It normally will invest at least 80% of its net assets in securities of issuers in Europe and the Pacific Basin. The fund may invest a portion of its assets in common stocks and other securities of companies in emerging markets. **Top Holdings:** Samsung Electronics Co Ltd Alibaba Group Holding Ltd ADR British American Tobacco PLC AIA Group Ltd Taiwan Semiconductor Manufacturing Co Ltd

American Funds EuroPacific Growth Fund® Class R-1 B- BUY

Ticker	Traded On	NAV	Total Assets ($)	Dividend Yield (TTM)	Turnover Ratio	Expense Ratio
RERAX	NAS CM	54.14	$160,340,414,689	0.49	36	1.61

Ratings

Reward	B-
Risk	B

Fund Information

Fund Type	Open End
Category	Global Equity Large Cap
Sub-Category	Foreign Large Growth
Prospectus Objective	Foreign Stock
Inception Date	Jun-02
Open to New Investments	Y
Minimum Initial Investment	250
Minimum Subsequent Investment	50
Front End Fee	
Back End Fee	

Total Returns (%)

3-Month	6-Month	1-Year	3-Year	5-Year
3.94	10.76	29.70	26.90	48.23

Last Bull Market	16.33
Last Bear Market	-24.28
3-Year Standard Deviation	11.13
3-Year Beta	0.86

Company Information

Provider	American Funds
Manager/Tenure	Mark E. Denning (25), Carl M. Kawaja (16), Nicholas J. Grace (15), 6 others
Website	http://www.americanfunds.com
Address	American Funds 333 South Hope Street Los Angeles CA 90071-1406 United States
Phone Number	800-421-4225

Ratings History

Date	Overall Rating	Risk Rating	Reward Rating
Q4-17	B-	B	B-
Q3-17	C+	C+	C+
Q2-17	C	C	C
Q1-17	C	C-	C
Q4-16	C-	C	D+
Q4-15	C	C	C

Asset & Performance History

Date	NAV	1-Year Total Return
2016	43.54	-0.08
2015	43.82	-1.57
2014	45.55	-3.37
2013	47.43	19.25
2012	39.85	18.29
2011	34.02	-14.24

Total Assets: $160,340,414,689

Asset Allocation

Asset	%
Cash	2%
Stocks	91%
US Stocks	1%
Bonds	1%
US Bonds	1%
Other	4%

Services Offered: Automatic Investment Plan, Qualified Investment, Phone Exchange

Investment Strategy: The investment seeks long-term growth of capital. The fund invests primarily in common stocks of issuers in Europe and the Pacific Basin that the investment adviser believes have the potential for growth. Growth stocks are stocks that the investment adviser believes have the potential for above-average capital appreciation. It normally will invest at least 80% of its net assets in securities of issuers in Europe and the Pacific Basin. The fund may invest a portion of its assets in common stocks and other securities of companies in emerging markets. **Top Holdings:** Samsung Electronics Co Ltd Alibaba Group Holding Ltd ADR British American Tobacco PLC AIA Group Ltd Taiwan Semiconductor Manufacturing Co Ltd

American Funds EuroPacific Growth Fund® Class R-5 B BUY

Ticker	Traded On	NAV	Total Assets ($)	Dividend Yield (TTM)	Turnover Ratio	Expense Ratio
RERFX	NAS CM	56.09	$160,340,414,689	1.5	36	0.54

Ratings

Reward	B
Risk	B

Fund Information

Fund Type	Open End
Category	Global Equity Large Cap
Sub-Category	Foreign Large Growth
Prospectus Objective	Foreign Stock
Inception Date	May-02
Open to New Investments	Y
Minimum Initial Investment	250
Minimum Subsequent Investment	50
Front End Fee	
Back End Fee	

Total Returns (%)

3-Month	6-Month	1-Year	3-Year	5-Year
4.22	11.34	31.08	31.02	56.33

Last Bull Market	17.05
Last Bear Market	-23.93
3-Year Standard Deviation	11.13
3-Year Beta	0.86

Company Information

Provider	American Funds
Manager/Tenure	Mark E. Denning (25), Carl M. Kawaja (16), Nicholas J. Grace (15), 6 others
Website	http://www.americanfunds.com
Address	American Funds 333 South Hope Street Los Angeles CA 90071-1406 United States
Phone Number	800-421-4225

Ratings History

Date	Overall Rating	Risk Rating	Reward Rating
Q4-17	B	B	B
Q3-17	C+	B-	C+
Q2-17	C	C	C+
Q1-17	C	C	C+
Q4-16	C	C+	C-
Q4-15	C	C	C

Asset & Performance History

Date	NAV	1-Year Total Return
2016	45.01	1
2015	45.27	-0.53
2014	47.04	-2.35
2013	48.98	20.53
2012	41.13	19.57
2011	35.09	-13.33

Total Assets: $160,340,414,689

Asset Allocation

Asset	%
Cash	2%
Stocks	91%
US Stocks	1%
Bonds	1%
US Bonds	1%
Other	4%

Services Offered: Automatic Investment Plan, Qualified Investment, Phone Exchange

Investment Strategy: The investment seeks long-term growth of capital. The fund invests primarily in common stocks of issuers in Europe and the Pacific Basin that the investment adviser believes have the potential for growth. Growth stocks are stocks that the investment adviser believes have the potential for above-average capital appreciation. It normally will invest at least 80% of its net assets in securities of issuers in Europe and the Pacific Basin. The fund may invest a portion of its assets in common stocks and other securities of companies in emerging markets. **Top Holdings:** Samsung Electronics Co Ltd Alibaba Group Holding Ltd ADR British American Tobacco PLC AIA Group Ltd Taiwan Semiconductor Manufacturing Co Ltd

American Funds EuroPacific Growth Fund® Class 529-C B- BUY

Ticker	Traded On	NAV	Total Assets ($)	Dividend Yield (TTM)	Turnover Ratio	Expense Ratio
CEUCX	NAS CM	54.47	$160,340,414,689	0.4	36	1.68

Ratings

Reward	B-
Risk	B

Fund Information

Fund Type	Open End
Category	Global Equity Large Cap
Sub-Category	Foreign Large Growth
Prospectus Objective	Foreign Stock
Inception Date	Feb-02
Open to New Investments	Y
Minimum Initial Investment	250
Minimum Subsequent Investment	50
Front End Fee	
Back End Fee	1.00

Total Returns (%)

3-Month	6-Month	1-Year	3-Year	5-Year
3.93	10.72	29.64	26.62	47.69

Last Bull Market	16.27
Last Bear Market	-24.31
3-Year Standard Deviation	11.13
3-Year Beta	0.86

Company Information

Provider	American Funds
Manager/Tenure	Mark E. Denning (25), Carl M. Kawaja (16), Nicholas J. Grace (15), 6 others
Website	http://www.americanfunds.com
Address	American Funds 333 South Hope Street Los Angeles CA 90071-1406 United States
Phone Number	800-421-4225

Ratings History

Date	Overall Rating	Risk Rating	Reward Rating
Q4-17	B-	B	B-
Q3-17	C+	C+	C+
Q2-17	C	C	C
Q1-17	C	C-	C
Q4-16	C-	C	D+
Q4-15	C	C	C

Asset & Performance History

Date	NAV	1-Year Total Return
2016	43.77	-0.17
2015	44.04	-1.65
2014	45.78	-3.46
2013	47.68	19.14
2012	40.1	18.21
2011	34.24	-14.31

Total Assets: $160,340,414,689

Asset Allocation

Asset	%
Cash	2%
Stocks	91%
US Stocks	1%
Bonds	1%
US Bonds	1%
Other	4%

Services Offered: Systematic Withdrawal Plan, Automatic Investment Plan, Qualified Investment, Phone Exchange, Retirement Investment

Investment Strategy: The investment seeks long-term growth of capital. The fund invests primarily in common stocks of issuers in Europe and the Pacific Basin that the investment adviser believes have the potential for growth. Growth stocks are stocks that the investment adviser believes have the potential for above-average capital appreciation. It normally will invest at least 80% of its net assets in securities of issuers in Europe and the Pacific Basin. The fund may invest a portion of its assets in common stocks and other securities of companies in emerging markets. **Top Holdings:** Samsung Electronics Co Ltd Alibaba Group Holding Ltd ADR British American Tobacco PLC AIA Group Ltd Taiwan Semiconductor Manufacturing Co Ltd

Fidelity® 500 Index Fund Premium Class — B BUY

Ticker	Traded On	NAV	Total Assets ($)	Dividend Yield (TTM)	Turnover Ratio	Expense Ratio
FUSVX	NAS CM	93.45	$136,826,694,466	1.78	5	0.04

Ratings

Reward	B
Risk	B

Fund Information

Fund Type	Open End
Category	US Equity Large Cap Blend
Sub-Category	Large Blend
Prospectus Objective	Growth & Income
Inception Date	Oct-05
Open to New Investments	Y
Minimum Initial Investment	10,000
Minimum Subsequent Investment	
Front End Fee	
Back End Fee	

Total Returns (%)

3-Month	6-Month	1-Year	3-Year	5-Year
6.63	11.40	21.79	36.73	111.29

Last Bull Market	25.06
Last Bear Market	-16.29
3-Year Standard Deviation	10.09
3-Year Beta	1

Company Information

Provider	Fidelity Investments
Manager/Tenure	Patrick Waddell (13), Louis Bottari (8), Peter Matthew (5), 3 others
Website	http://www.institutional.fidelity.com
Address	Fidelity Investments 82 Devonshire Street Boston MA 2109 United States
Phone Number	617-563-7000

Ratings History

Date	Overall Rating	Risk Rating	Reward Rating
Q4-17	B	B	B
Q3-17	B	A-	B
Q2-17	B	B+	B
Q1-17	B	B-	B
Q4-16	B	B	B
Q4-15	C+	B-	C

Asset & Performance History

Date	NAV	1-Year Total Return
2016	78.34	11.92
2015	71.8	1.35
2014	72.85	13.62
2013	65.49	32.33
2012	50.49	15.96
2011	44.49	2.06

Total Assets: $136,826,694,466

Asset Allocation

Asset	%
Cash	0%
Stocks	100%
US Stocks	99%
Bonds	0%
US Bonds	0%
Other	0%

Services Offered: Qualified Investment, Phone Exchange

Investment Strategy: The investment seeks to provide investment results that correspond to the total return performance of common stocks publicly traded in the United States. The fund normally invests at least 80% of assets in common stocks included in the S&P 500® Index, which broadly represents the performance of common stocks publicly traded in the United States. It lends securities to earn income. **Top Holdings:** Apple Inc Microsoft Corp Amazon.com Inc Facebook Inc A Johnson & Johnson

Fidelity® 500 Index Fund Investor Class — B BUY

Ticker	Traded On	NAV	Total Assets ($)	Dividend Yield (TTM)	Turnover Ratio	Expense Ratio
FUSEX	NAS CM	93.44	$136,826,694,466	1.74	5	0.09

Ratings

Reward	B
Risk	B

Fund Information

Fund Type	Open End
Category	US Equity Large Cap Blend
Sub-Category	Large Blend
Prospectus Objective	Growth & Income
Inception Date	Feb-88
Open to New Investments	Y
Minimum Initial Investment	2,500
Minimum Subsequent Investment	
Front End Fee	
Back End Fee	

Total Returns (%)

3-Month	6-Month	1-Year	3-Year	5-Year
6.62	11.38	21.72	36.52	110.78

Last Bull Market	25.04
Last Bear Market	-16.29
3-Year Standard Deviation	10.09
3-Year Beta	1

Company Information

Provider	Fidelity Investments
Manager/Tenure	Patrick Waddell (13), Louis Bottari (8), Peter Matthew (5), 3 others
Website	http://www.institutional.fidelity.com
Address	Fidelity Investments 82 Devonshire Street Boston MA 2109 United States
Phone Number	617-563-7000

Ratings History

Date	Overall Rating	Risk Rating	Reward Rating
Q4-17	B	B	B
Q3-17	B	A-	B
Q2-17	B	B+	B
Q1-17	B	B-	B
Q4-16	B	B	B
Q4-15	C+	B-	C

Asset & Performance History

Date	NAV	1-Year Total Return
2016	78.34	11.87
2015	71.8	1.3
2014	72.85	13.58
2013	65.48	32.25
2012	50.49	15.92
2011	44.49	2.03

Total Assets: $136,826,694,466

Asset Allocation

Asset	%
Cash	0%
Stocks	100%
US Stocks	99%
Bonds	0%
US Bonds	0%
Other	0%

Services Offered: Phone Exchange, Retirement Investment

Investment Strategy: The investment seeks to provide investment results that correspond to the total return performance of common stocks publicly traded in the United States. The fund normally invests at least 80% of assets in common stocks included in the S&P 500® Index, which broadly represents the performance of common stocks publicly traded in the United States. It lends securities to earn income. **Top Holdings:** Apple Inc Microsoft Corp Amazon.com Inc Facebook Inc A Johnson & Johnson

Fidelity® Contrafund® Fund Class K

A- BUY

Ticker	Traded On	NAV	Total Assets ($)	Dividend Yield (TTM)	Turnover Ratio	Expense Ratio
FCNKX	NAS CM	122.39	$124,619,002,771	0.3	41	0.58

Ratings

Reward	A-
Risk	A-

Fund Information

Fund Type	Open End
Category	US Equity Large Cap Growth
Sub-Category	Large Growth
Prospectus Objective	Growth
Inception Date	May-08
Open to New Investments	Y
Minimum Initial Investment	0
Minimum Subsequent Investment	
Front End Fee	
Back End Fee	

Total Returns (%)

3-Month	6-Month	1-Year	3-Year	5-Year
6.77	13.31	32.38	44.75	118.81

Last Bull Market	24.41
Last Bear Market	-14.38
3-Year Standard Deviation	10.12
3-Year Beta	0.9

Company Information

Provider	Fidelity Investments
Manager/Tenure	William Danoff (27)
Website	http://www.institutional.fidelity.com
Address	Fidelity Investments 82 Devonshire Street Boston MA 2109 United States
Phone Number	617-563-7000

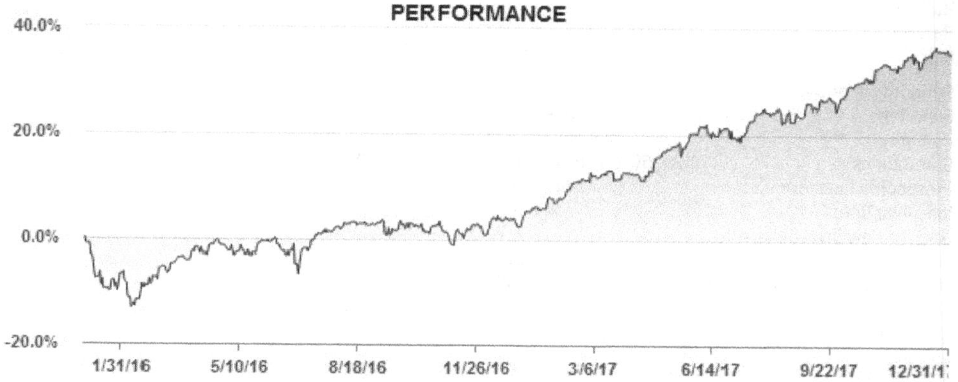

Ratings History

Date	Overall Rating	Risk Rating	Reward Rating
Q4-17	A-	A-	A-
Q3-17	A-	B+	A-
Q2-17	B	B+	B+
Q1-17	B	B-	B
Q4-16	B	B	B-
Q4-15	B	A	C+

Asset & Performance History

Date	NAV	1-Year Total Return
2016	98.38	3.47
2015	98.84	6.55
2014	97.9	9.67
2013	96.07	34.29
2012	77.51	16.39
2011	67.4	-0.02

Total Assets: $124,619,002,771

Asset Allocation

Asset	%
Cash	2%
Stocks	96%
US Stocks	88%
Bonds	0%
US Bonds	0%
Other	0%

Services Offered: Qualified Investment, Phone Exchange

Investment Strategy: The investment seeks capital appreciation. The fund normally invests primarily in common stocks. It invests in securities of companies whose value the advisor believes is not fully recognized by the public. The fund invests in domestic and foreign issuers. It invests in either "growth" stocks or "value" stocks or both. The fund uses fundamental analysis of factors such as each issuer's financial condition and industry position, as well as market and economic conditions to select investments. **Top Holdings:** Facebook Inc A Berkshire Hathaway Inc A Amazon.com Inc Alphabet Inc A Apple Inc

Fidelity® Contrafund® Fund

A- BUY

Ticker	Traded On	NAV	Total Assets ($)	Dividend Yield (TTM)	Turnover Ratio	Expense Ratio
FCNTX	NAS CM	122.47	$124,619,002,771	0.22	41	0.68

Ratings

Reward	A-
Risk	A-

Fund Information

Fund Type	Open End
Category	US Equity Large Cap Growth
Sub-Category	Large Growth
Prospectus Objective	Growth
Inception Date	May-67
Open to New Investments	Y
Minimum Initial Investment	2,500
Minimum Subsequent Investment	
Front End Fee	
Back End Fee	

Total Returns (%)

3-Month	6-Month	1-Year	3-Year	5-Year
6.74	13.25	32.26	44.32	117.69

Last Bull Market	24.33
Last Bear Market	-14.42
3-Year Standard Deviation	10.12
3-Year Beta	0.9

Company Information

Provider	Fidelity Investments
Manager/Tenure	William Danoff (27)
Website	http://www.institutional.fidelity.com
Address	Fidelity Investments 82 Devonshire Street Boston MA 2109 United States
Phone Number	617-563-7000

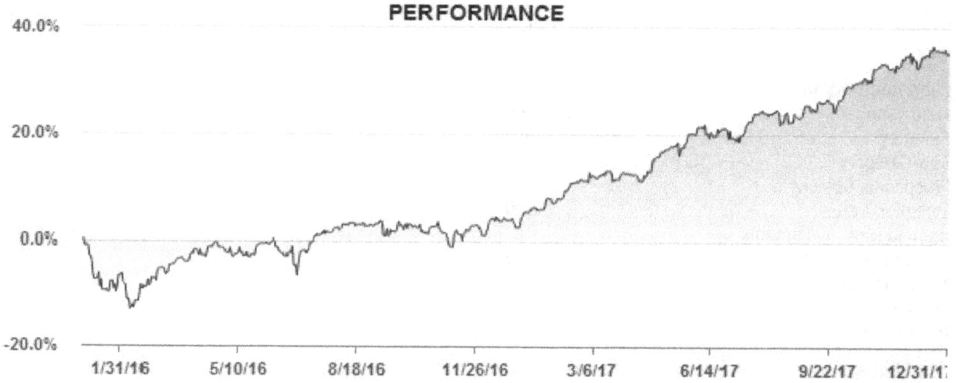

Ratings History

Date	Overall Rating	Risk Rating	Reward Rating
Q4-17	A-	A-	A-
Q3-17	A-	B+	A-
Q2-17	B	B	B
Q1-17	B	B-	B
Q4-16	B	B	B-
Q4-15	B	A	C+

Asset & Performance History

Date	NAV	1-Year Total Return
2016	98.45	3.37
2015	98.92	6.46
2014	97.97	9.55
2013	96.14	34.14
2012	77.57	16.25
2011	67.45	-0.13

Total Assets: $124,619,002,771

Asset Allocation

Asset	%
Cash	2%
Stocks	96%
US Stocks	88%
Bonds	0%
US Bonds	0%
Other	0%

Services Offered: Phone Exchange, Wire Redemption, Retirement Investment

Investment Strategy: The investment seeks capital appreciation. The fund normally invests primarily in common stocks. It invests in securities of companies whose value the advisor believes is not fully recognized by the public. The fund invests in domestic and foreign issuers. It invests in either "growth" stocks or "value" stocks or both. The fund uses fundamental analysis of factors such as each issuer's financial condition and industry position, as well as market and economic conditions to select investments. **Top Holdings:** Facebook Inc A Berkshire Hathaway Inc A Amazon.com Inc Alphabet Inc A Apple Inc

American Funds American Balanced Fund® Class R-1 B BUY

Ticker	Traded On	NAV	Total Assets ($)	Dividend Yield (TTM)	Turnover Ratio	Expense Ratio
RLBAX	NAS CM	26.96	$123,184,871,331	0.81	79	1.38

Ratings

Reward	C+
Risk	B+

Fund Information

Fund Type	Open End
Category	Moderate Alloc
Sub-Category	Alloc--50% to 70% Equity
Prospectus Objective	Balanced
Inception Date	May-02
Open to New Investments	Y
Minimum Initial Investment	250
Minimum Subsequent Investment	50
Front End Fee	
Back End Fee	

Total Returns (%)

3-Month	6-Month	1-Year	3-Year	5-Year
4.29	7.80	14.55	23.76	64.01

Last Bull Market	16.93
Last Bear Market	-10.27
3-Year Standard Deviation	6.46
3-Year Beta	0.62

Company Information

Provider	American Funds
Manager/Tenure	John H. Smet (20), Hilda L. Applbaum (18), Gregory D. Johnson (14), 6 others
Website	http://www.americanfunds.com
Address	American Funds 333 South Hope Street Los Angeles CA 90071-1406 United States
Phone Number	800-421-4225

PERFORMANCE

Ratings History

Date	Overall Rating	Risk Rating	Reward Rating
Q4-17	B	B+	C+
Q3-17	B-	B-	B-
Q2-17	B	A	B-
Q1-17	B	B	B-
Q4-16	B	B+	B-
Q4-15	C+	B-	C

Asset & Performance History

Date	NAV	1-Year Total Return
2016	24.64	7.74
2015	23.68	0.88
2014	24.61	8.05
2013	24.28	20.76
2012	20.29	13.27
2011	18.12	3.08

Total Assets: $123,184,871,331

Asset Allocation

Asset	%
Cash	3%
Stocks	59%
US Stocks	52%
Bonds	36%
US Bonds	32%
Other	2%

Services Offered: Automatic Investment Plan, Qualified Investment, Phone Exchange

Investment Strategy: The investment seeks conservation of capital, current income and long-term growth of capital and income. The fund uses a balanced approach to invest in a broad range of securities, including common stocks and investment-grade bonds. It also invests in securities issued and guaranteed by the U.S. government and by federal agencies and instrumentalities. In addition, the fund may invest a portion of its assets in common stocks, most of which have a history of paying dividends, bonds and other securities of issuers domiciled outside the United States. **Top Holdings:** Microsoft Corp The Home Depot Inc Berkshire Hathaway Inc A UnitedHealth Group Inc Comcast Corp Class A

American Funds American Balanced Fund® Class 529-C B BUY

Ticker	Traded On	NAV	Total Assets ($)	Dividend Yield (TTM)	Turnover Ratio	Expense Ratio
CLBCX	NAS CM	27.11	$123,184,871,331	0.79	79	1.44

Ratings

Reward	C+
Risk	B

Fund Information

Fund Type	Open End
Category	Moderate Alloc
Sub-Category	Alloc--50% to 70% Equity
Prospectus Objective	Balanced
Inception Date	Feb-02
Open to New Investments	Y
Minimum Initial Investment	250
Minimum Subsequent Investment	50
Front End Fee	
Back End Fee	1.00

Total Returns (%)

3-Month	6-Month	1-Year	3-Year	5-Year
4.30	7.83	14.54	23.58	63.55

Last Bull Market	16.81
Last Bear Market	-10.27
3-Year Standard Deviation	6.48
3-Year Beta	0.62

Company Information

Provider	American Funds
Manager/Tenure	John H. Smet (20), Hilda L. Applbaum (18), Gregory D. Johnson (14), 6 others
Website	http://www.americanfunds.com
Address	American Funds 333 South Hope Street Los Angeles CA 90071-1406 United States
Phone Number	800-421-4225

PERFORMANCE

Ratings History

Date	Overall Rating	Risk Rating	Reward Rating
Q4-17	B	B	C+
Q3-17	B-	B-	B-
Q2-17	B	A	B-
Q1-17	B	B	B-
Q4-16	B	B+	B-
Q4-15	C+	B-	C

Asset & Performance History

Date	NAV	1-Year Total Return
2016	24.75	7.63
2015	23.79	0.88
2014	24.7	7.89
2013	24.38	20.67
2012	20.37	13.18
2011	18.19	2.99

Total Assets: $123,184,871,331

Asset Allocation

Asset	%
Cash	3%
Stocks	59%
US Stocks	52%
Bonds	36%
US Bonds	32%
Other	2%

Services Offered: Systematic Withdrawal Plan, Automatic Investment Plan, Qualified Investment, Phone Exchange, Retirement Investment

Investment Strategy: The investment seeks conservation of capital, current income and long-term growth of capital and income. The fund uses a balanced approach to invest in a broad range of securities, including common stocks and investment-grade bonds. It also invests in securities issued and guaranteed by the U.S. government and by federal agencies and instrumentalities. In addition, the fund may invest a portion of its assets in common stocks, most of which have a history of paying dividends, bonds and other securities of issuers domiciled outside the United States. **Top Holdings:** Microsoft Corp The Home Depot Inc Berkshire Hathaway Inc A UnitedHealth Group Inc Comcast Corp Class A

American Funds American Balanced Fund® Class R-6 B BUY

Ticker	Traded On	NAV	Total Assets ($)	Dividend Yield (TTM)	Turnover Ratio	Expense Ratio
RLBGX	NAS CM	27.16	$123,184,871,331	1.81	79	0.29

Ratings

Reward	B-
Risk	A-

Fund Information

Fund Type	Open End
Category	Moderate Alloc
Sub-Category	Alloc--50% to 70% Equity
Prospectus Objective	Balanced
Inception Date	May-09
Open to New Investments	Y
Minimum Initial Investment	250
Minimum Subsequent Investment	50
Front End Fee	
Back End Fee	

Total Returns (%)

3-Month	6-Month	1-Year	3-Year	5-Year
4.59	8.42	15.84	27.92	73.27

Last Bull Market	17.71
Last Bear Market	-9.86
3-Year Standard Deviation	6.44
3-Year Beta	0.62

Company Information

Provider	American Funds
Manager/Tenure	John H. Smet (20), Hilda L. Applbaum (18), Gregory D. Johnson (14), 6 others
Website	http://www.americanfunds.com
Address	American Funds 333 South Hope Street Los Angeles CA 90071-1406 United States
Phone Number	800-421-4225

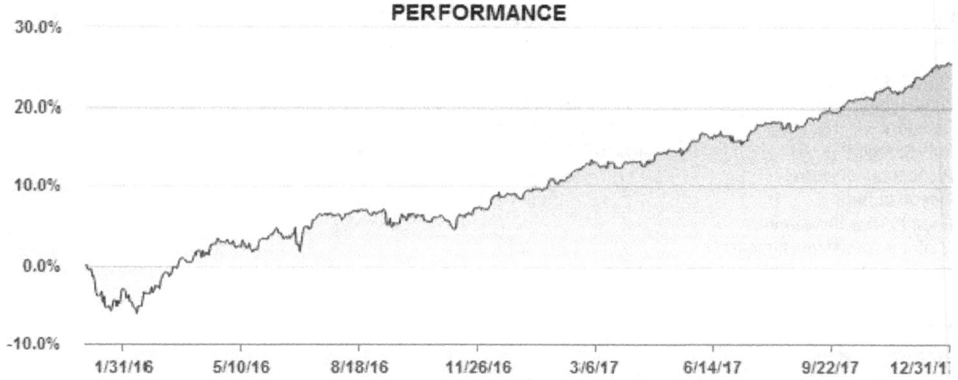

Ratings History

Date	Overall Rating	Risk Rating	Reward Rating
Q4-17	B	A-	B-
Q3-17	B	A+	B-
Q2-17	B	A	B-
Q1-17	B	B+	B
Q4-16	B	B+	B-
Q4-15	C+	B-	C

Asset & Performance History

Date	NAV	1-Year Total Return
2016	24.81	8.89
2015	23.84	2.02
2014	24.76	9.21
2013	24.42	22.11
2012	20.4	14.56
2011	18.21	4.15

Total Assets: $123,184,871,331

Asset Allocation

Asset	%
Cash	3%
Stocks	59%
US Stocks	52%
Bonds	36%
US Bonds	32%
Other	2%

Services Offered: Automatic Investment Plan, Qualified Investment, Phone Exchange

Investment Strategy: The investment seeks conservation of capital, current income and long-term growth of capital and income. The fund uses a balanced approach to invest in a broad range of securities, including common stocks and investment-grade bonds. It also invests in securities issued and guaranteed by the U.S. government and by federal agencies and instrumentalities. In addition, the fund may invest a portion of its assets in common stocks, most of which have a history of paying dividends, bonds and other securities of issuers domiciled outside the United States. **Top Holdings:** Microsoft Corp The Home Depot Inc Berkshire Hathaway Inc A UnitedHealth Group Inc Comcast Corp Class A

American Funds American Balanced Fund® Class 529-F B BUY

Ticker	Traded On	NAV	Total Assets ($)	Dividend Yield (TTM)	Turnover Ratio	Expense Ratio
CLBFX	NAS CM	27.09	$123,184,871,331	1.69	79	0.44

Ratings

Reward	B-
Risk	A-

Fund Information

Fund Type	Open End
Category	Moderate Alloc
Sub-Category	Alloc--50% to 70% Equity
Prospectus Objective	Balanced
Inception Date	Sep-02
Open to New Investments	Y
Minimum Initial Investment	250
Minimum Subsequent Investment	50
Front End Fee	
Back End Fee	

Total Returns (%)

3-Month	6-Month	1-Year	3-Year	5-Year
4.56	8.37	15.68	27.32	71.86

Last Bull Market	17.57
Last Bear Market	-9.91
3-Year Standard Deviation	6.46
3-Year Beta	0.62

Company Information

Provider	American Funds
Manager/Tenure	John H. Smet (20), Hilda L. Applbaum (18), Gregory D. Johnson (14), 6 others
Website	http://www.americanfunds.com
Address	American Funds 333 South Hope Street Los Angeles CA 90071-1406 United States
Phone Number	800-421-4225

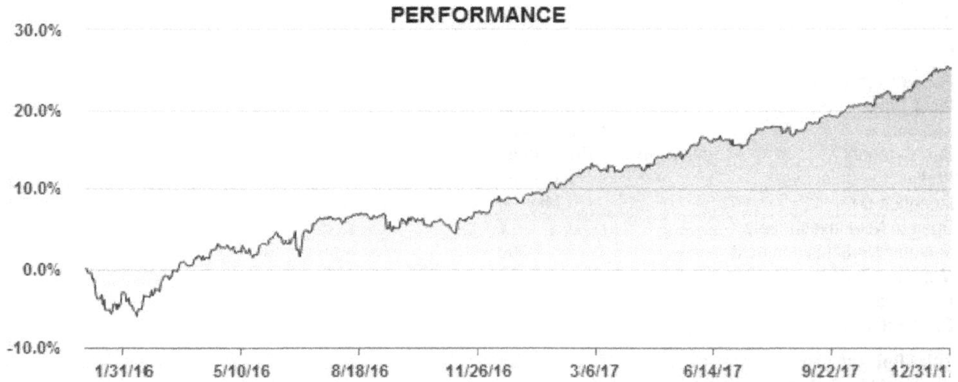

Ratings History

Date	Overall Rating	Risk Rating	Reward Rating
Q4-17	B	A-	B-
Q3-17	B	A+	B-
Q2-17	B	A	B-
Q1-17	B	B+	B
Q4-16	B	B+	B-
Q4-15	C+	B-	C

Asset & Performance History

Date	NAV	1-Year Total Return
2016	24.75	8.74
2015	23.78	1.81
2014	24.71	9.05
2013	24.37	21.88
2012	20.36	14.32
2011	18.18	3.97

Total Assets: $123,184,871,331

Asset Allocation

Asset	%
Cash	3%
Stocks	59%
US Stocks	52%
Bonds	36%
US Bonds	32%
Other	2%

Services Offered: Systematic Withdrawal Plan, Automatic Investment Plan, Qualified Investment, Phone Exchange, Retirement Investment

Investment Strategy: The investment seeks conservation of capital, current income and long-term growth of capital and income. The fund uses a balanced approach to invest in a broad range of securities, including common stocks and investment-grade bonds. It also invests in securities issued and guaranteed by the U.S. government and by federal agencies and instrumentalities. In addition, the fund may invest a portion of its assets in common stocks, most of which have a history of paying dividends, bonds and other securities of issuers domiciled outside the United States. **Top Holdings:** Microsoft Corp The Home Depot Inc Berkshire Hathaway Inc A UnitedHealth Group Inc Comcast Corp Class A

American Funds American Balanced Fund® Class R-2E — B BUY

Ticker	Traded On	NAV	Total Assets ($)	Dividend Yield (TTM)	Turnover Ratio	Expense Ratio
RAMHX	NAS CM	27.05	$123,184,871,331	1.13	79	1.08

Ratings

Reward	C+
Risk	A-

Fund Information

Fund Type	Open End
Category	Moderate Alloc
Sub-Category	Alloc--50% to 70% Equity
Prospectus Objective	Balanced
Inception Date	Aug-14
Open to New Investments	Y
Minimum Initial Investment	250
Minimum Subsequent Investment	50
Front End Fee	
Back End Fee	

Total Returns (%)

3-Month	6-Month	1-Year	3-Year	5-Year
4.39	7.98	14.88	25.42	68.00

Last Bull Market	17.22
Last Bear Market	-10.09
3-Year Standard Deviation	6.43
3-Year Beta	0.61

Company Information

Provider	American Funds
Manager/Tenure	John H. Smet (20), Hilda L. Applbaum (18), Gregory D. Johnson (14), 6 others
Website	http://www.americanfunds.com
Address	American Funds 333 South Hope Street Los Angeles CA 90071-1406 United States
Phone Number	800-421-4225

Ratings History

Date	Overall Rating	Risk Rating	Reward Rating
Q4-17	B	A-	C+
Q3-17	B	A	B-
Q2-17	B	A	B-
Q1-17	B	B+	B
Q4-16	B	B+	B-
Q4-15	C+	B-	C

Asset & Performance History

Date	NAV	1-Year Total Return
2016	24.74	8.1
2015	23.77	1.6
2014	24.75	8.67
2013		21.29
2012		13.78
2011		3.45

Total Assets: $123,184,871,331

Asset Allocation

Asset	%
Cash	3%
Stocks	59%
US Stocks	52%
Bonds	36%
US Bonds	32%
Other	2%

Services Offered: Automatic Investment Plan, Qualified Investment, Phone Exchange

Investment Strategy: The investment seeks conservation of capital, current income and long-term growth of capital and income. The fund uses a balanced approach to invest in a broad range of securities, including common stocks and investment-grade bonds. It also invests in securities issued and guaranteed by the U.S. government and by federal agencies and instrumentalities. In addition, the fund may invest a portion of its assets in common stocks, most of which have a history of paying dividends, bonds and other securities of issuers domiciled outside the United States. **Top Holdings:** Microsoft Corp The Home Depot Inc Berkshire Hathaway Inc A UnitedHealth Group Inc Comcast Corp Class A

American Funds American Balanced Fund® Class R-5 — B BUY

Ticker	Traded On	NAV	Total Assets ($)	Dividend Yield (TTM)	Turnover Ratio	Expense Ratio
RLBFX	NAS CM	27.18	$123,184,871,331	1.76	79	0.34

Ratings

Reward	B-
Risk	A-

Fund Information

Fund Type	Open End
Category	Moderate Alloc
Sub-Category	Alloc--50% to 70% Equity
Prospectus Objective	Balanced
Inception Date	May-02
Open to New Investments	Y
Minimum Initial Investment	250
Minimum Subsequent Investment	50
Front End Fee	
Back End Fee	

Total Returns (%)

3-Month	6-Month	1-Year	3-Year	5-Year
4.61	8.39	15.77	27.71	72.84

Last Bull Market	17.67
Last Bear Market	-9.88
3-Year Standard Deviation	6.47
3-Year Beta	0.62

Company Information

Provider	American Funds
Manager/Tenure	John H. Smet (20), Hilda L. Applbaum (18), Gregory D. Johnson (14), 6 others
Website	http://www.americanfunds.com
Address	American Funds 333 South Hope Street Los Angeles CA 90071-1406 United States
Phone Number	800-421-4225

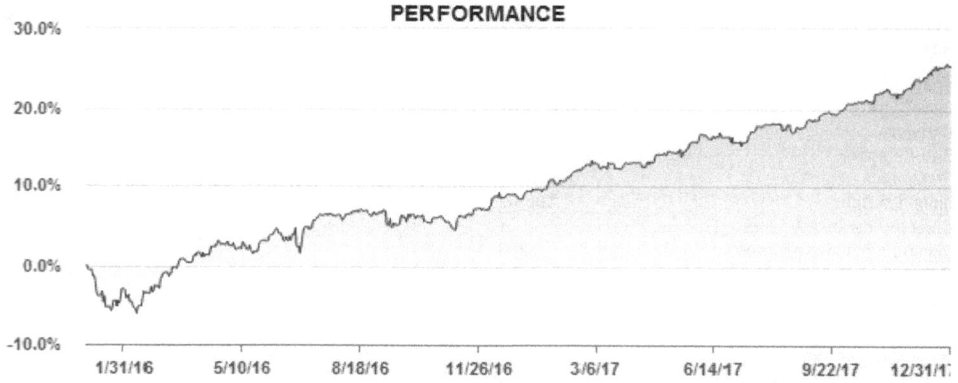

Ratings History

Date	Overall Rating	Risk Rating	Reward Rating
Q4-17	B	A-	B-
Q3-17	B	A+	B-
Q2-17	B	A	B-
Q1-17	B	B+	B
Q4-16	B	B+	B-
Q4-15	C+	B-	C

Asset & Performance History

Date	NAV	1-Year Total Return
2016	24.83	8.87
2015	23.85	1.97
2014	24.77	9.15
2013	24.43	22.04
2012	20.41	14.5
2011	18.22	4.1

Total Assets: $123,184,871,331

Asset Allocation

Asset	%
Cash	3%
Stocks	59%
US Stocks	52%
Bonds	36%
US Bonds	32%
Other	2%

Services Offered: Automatic Investment Plan, Qualified Investment, Phone Exchange

Investment Strategy: The investment seeks conservation of capital, current income and long-term growth of capital and income. The fund uses a balanced approach to invest in a broad range of securities, including common stocks and investment-grade bonds. It also invests in securities issued and guaranteed by the U.S. government and by federal agencies and instrumentalities. In addition, the fund may invest a portion of its assets in common stocks, most of which have a history of paying dividends, bonds and other securities of issuers domiciled outside the United States. **Top Holdings:** Microsoft Corp The Home Depot Inc Berkshire Hathaway Inc A UnitedHealth Group Inc Comcast Corp Class A

American Funds American Balanced Fund® Class A

B BUY

Ticker	Traded On	NAV	Total Assets ($)	Dividend Yield (TTM)	Turnover Ratio	Expense Ratio
ABALX	NAS CM	27.15	$123,184,871,331	1.55	79	0.6

Ratings

Reward	B-
Risk	A-

Fund Information

Fund Type	Open End
Category	Moderate Alloc
Sub-Category	Alloc--50% to 70% Equity
Prospectus Objective	Balanced
Inception Date	Jul-75
Open to New Investments	Y
Minimum Initial Investment	250
Minimum Subsequent Investment	50
Front End Fee	5.75
Back End Fee	

Total Returns (%)

3-Month	6-Month	1-Year	3-Year	5-Year
4.51	8.27	15.47	26.76	70.72

Last Bull Market	17.46
Last Bear Market	-9.96
3-Year Standard Deviation	6.46
3-Year Beta	0.62

Company Information

Provider	American Funds
Manager/Tenure	John H. Smet (20), Hilda L. Applbaum (18), Gregory D. Johnson (14), 6 others
Website	http://www.americanfunds.com
Address	American Funds 333 South Hope Street Los Angeles CA 90071-1406 United States
Phone Number	800-421-4225

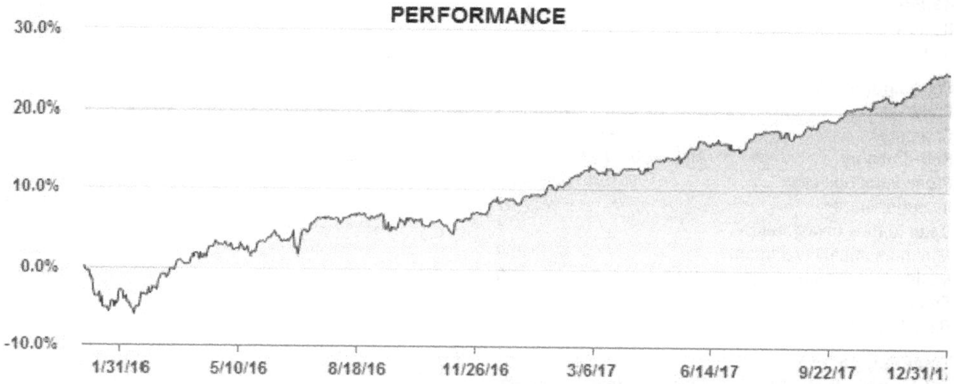

Ratings History

Date	Overall Rating	Risk Rating	Reward Rating
Q4-17	B	A-	B-
Q3-17	B	A+	B-
Q2-17	B	A	B-
Q1-17	B	B+	B
Q4-16	B	B+	B-
Q4-15	C+	B-	C

Asset & Performance History

Date	NAV	1-Year Total Return
2016	24.81	8.61
2015	23.83	1.72
2014	24.75	8.84
2013	24.42	21.73
2012	20.4	14.19
2011	18.21	3.82

Total Assets: $123,184,871,331

Asset Allocation

Asset	%
Cash	3%
Stocks	59%
US Stocks	52%
Bonds	36%
US Bonds	32%
Other	2%

Services Offered: Systematic Withdrawal Plan, Automatic Investment Plan, Phone Exchange, Retirement Investment

Investment Strategy: The investment seeks conservation of capital, current income and long-term growth of capital and income. The fund uses a balanced approach to invest in a broad range of securities, including common stocks and investment-grade bonds. It also invests in securities issued and guaranteed by the U.S. government and by federal agencies and instrumentalities. In addition, the fund may invest a portion of its assets in common stocks, most of which have a history of paying dividends, bonds and other securities of issuers domiciled outside the United States. **Top Holdings:** Microsoft Corp The Home Depot Inc Berkshire Hathaway Inc A UnitedHealth Group Inc Comcast Corp Class A

American Funds American Balanced Fund® Class F-2

B BUY

Ticker	Traded On	NAV	Total Assets ($)	Dividend Yield (TTM)	Turnover Ratio	Expense Ratio
AMBFX	NAS CM	27.13	$123,184,871,331	1.72	79	0.39

Ratings

Reward	B-
Risk	A-

Fund Information

Fund Type	Open End
Category	Moderate Alloc
Sub-Category	Alloc--50% to 70% Equity
Prospectus Objective	Balanced
Inception Date	Aug-08
Open to New Investments	Y
Minimum Initial Investment	250
Minimum Subsequent Investment	50
Front End Fee	
Back End Fee	

Total Returns (%)

3-Month	6-Month	1-Year	3-Year	5-Year
4.56	8.33	15.69	27.47	72.31

Last Bull Market	17.66
Last Bear Market	-9.91
3-Year Standard Deviation	6.48
3-Year Beta	0.62

Company Information

Provider	American Funds
Manager/Tenure	John H. Smet (20), Hilda L. Applbaum (18), Gregory D. Johnson (14), 6 others
Website	http://www.americanfunds.com
Address	American Funds 333 South Hope Street Los Angeles CA 90071-1406 United States
Phone Number	800-421-4225

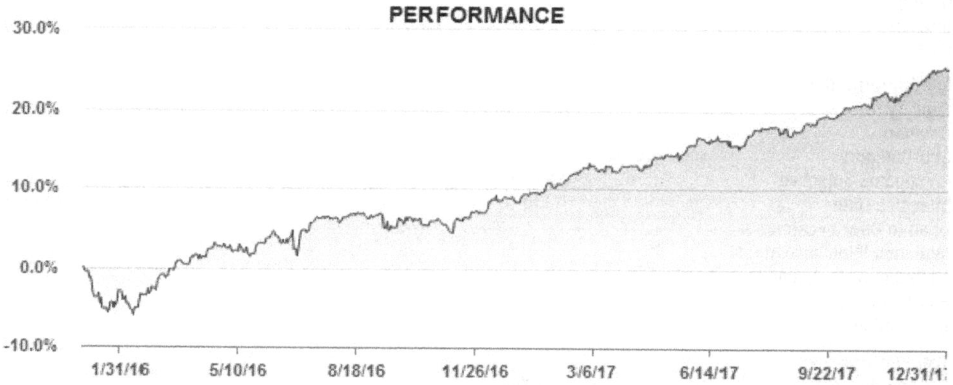

Ratings History

Date	Overall Rating	Risk Rating	Reward Rating
Q4-17	B	A-	B-
Q3-17	B	A+	B-
Q2-17	B	A	B-
Q1-17	B	B+	B
Q4-16	B	B+	B-
Q4-15	C+	B-	C

Asset & Performance History

Date	NAV	1-Year Total Return
2016	24.79	8.8
2015	23.82	1.92
2014	24.74	9.07
2013	24.41	21.98
2012	20.39	14.39
2011	18.21	4.11

Total Assets: $123,184,871,331

Asset Allocation

Asset	%
Cash	3%
Stocks	59%
US Stocks	52%
Bonds	36%
US Bonds	32%
Other	2%

Services Offered: Systematic Withdrawal Plan, Automatic Investment Plan, Qualified Investment, Phone Exchange, Retirement Investment

Investment Strategy: The investment seeks conservation of capital, current income and long-term growth of capital and income. The fund uses a balanced approach to invest in a broad range of securities, including common stocks and investment-grade bonds. It also invests in securities issued and guaranteed by the U.S. government and by federal agencies and instrumentalities. In addition, the fund may invest a portion of its assets in common stocks, most of which have a history of paying dividends, bonds and other securities of issuers domiciled outside the United States. **Top Holdings:** Microsoft Corp The Home Depot Inc Berkshire Hathaway Inc A UnitedHealth Group Inc Comcast Corp Class A

American Funds American Balanced Fund® Class F-1

B BUY

Ticker	Traded On	NAV	Total Assets ($)	Dividend Yield (TTM)	Turnover Ratio	Expense Ratio
BALFX	NAS CM	27.13	$123,184,871,331	1.48	79	0.66

Ratings

Reward	B-
Risk	A-

Fund Information

Fund Type	Open End
Category	Moderate Alloc
Sub-Category	Alloc--50% to 70% Equity
Prospectus Objective	Balanced
Inception Date	Mar-01
Open to New Investments	Y
Minimum Initial Investment	250
Minimum Subsequent Investment	50
Front End Fee	
Back End Fee	

Total Returns (%)

3-Month	6-Month	1-Year	3-Year	5-Year
4.49	8.23	15.39	26.52	70.13

Last Bull Market	17.4
Last Bear Market	-9.96
3-Year Standard Deviation	6.46
3-Year Beta	0.62

Company Information

Provider	American Funds
Manager/Tenure	John H. Smet (20), Hilda L. Applbaum (18), Gregory D. Johnson (14), 6 others
Website	http://www.americanfunds.com
Address	American Funds 333 South Hope Street Los Angeles CA 90071-1406 United States
Phone Number	800-421-4225

PERFORMANCE

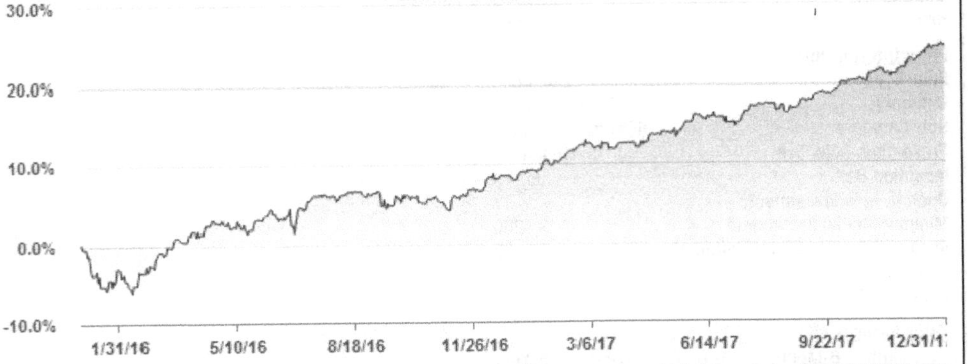

Ratings History

Date	Overall Rating	Risk Rating	Reward Rating
Q4-17	B	A-	B-
Q3-17	B	A+	B-
Q2-17	B	A	B-
Q1-17	B	B+	B
Q4-16	B	B+	B-
Q4-15	C+	B-	C

Asset & Performance History

Date	NAV	1-Year Total Return
2016	24.79	8.5
2015	23.82	1.66
2014	24.74	8.79
2013	24.41	21.7
2012	20.39	14.13
2011	18.21	3.87

Total Assets: $123,184,871,331

Asset Allocation

Asset	%
Cash	3%
Stocks	59%
US Stocks	52%
Bonds	36%
US Bonds	32%
Other	2%

Services Offered: Systematic Withdrawal Plan, Automatic Investment Plan, Qualified Investment, Phone Exchange, Retirement Investment

Investment Strategy: The investment seeks conservation of capital, current income and long-term growth of capital and income. The fund uses a balanced approach to invest in a broad range of securities, including common stocks and investment-grade bonds. It also invests in securities issued and guaranteed by the U.S. government and by federal agencies and instrumentalities. In addition, the fund may invest a portion of its assets in common stocks, most of which have a history of paying dividends, bonds and other securities of issuers domiciled outside the United States. **Top Holdings:** Microsoft Corp The Home Depot Inc Berkshire Hathaway Inc A UnitedHealth Group Inc Comcast Corp Class A

American Funds American Balanced Fund® Class R-3

B BUY

Ticker	Traded On	NAV	Total Assets ($)	Dividend Yield (TTM)	Turnover Ratio	Expense Ratio
RLBCX	NAS CM	27.01	$123,184,871,331	1.23	79	0.93

Ratings

Reward	C+
Risk	A-

Fund Information

Fund Type	Open End
Category	Moderate Alloc
Sub-Category	Alloc--50% to 70% Equity
Prospectus Objective	Balanced
Inception Date	Jun-02
Open to New Investments	Y
Minimum Initial Investment	250
Minimum Subsequent Investment	50
Front End Fee	
Back End Fee	

Total Returns (%)

3-Month	6-Month	1-Year	3-Year	5-Year
4.40	8.08	15.05	25.43	67.80

Last Bull Market	17.22
Last Bear Market	-10.05
3-Year Standard Deviation	6.48
3-Year Beta	0.62

Company Information

Provider	American Funds
Manager/Tenure	John H. Smet (20), Hilda L. Applbaum (18), Gregory D. Johnson (14), 6 others
Website	http://www.americanfunds.com
Address	American Funds 333 South Hope Street Los Angeles CA 90071-1406 United States
Phone Number	800-421-4225

PERFORMANCE

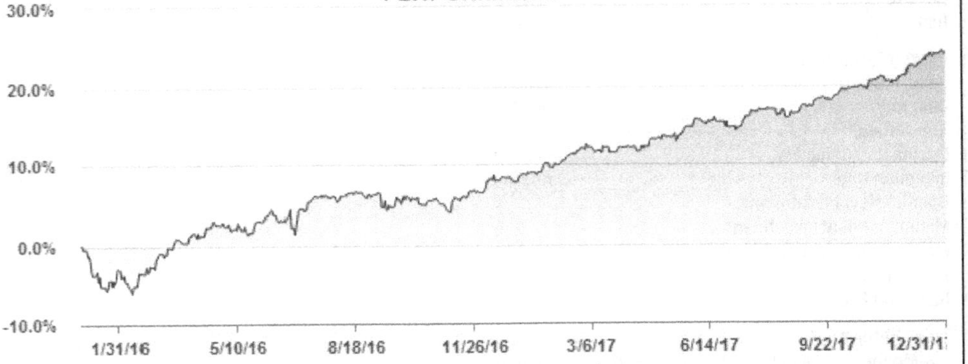

Ratings History

Date	Overall Rating	Risk Rating	Reward Rating
Q4-17	B	A-	C+
Q3-17	B	A	B-
Q2-17	B	A	B-
Q1-17	B	B+	B
Q4-16	B	B+	B-
Q4-15	C+	B-	C

Asset & Performance History

Date	NAV	1-Year Total Return
2016	24.69	8.24
2015	23.72	1.33
2014	24.65	8.51
2013	24.32	21.32
2012	20.32	13.83
2011	18.14	3.49

Total Assets: $123,184,871,331

Asset Allocation

Asset	%
Cash	3%
Stocks	59%
US Stocks	52%
Bonds	36%
US Bonds	32%
Other	2%

Services Offered: Automatic Investment Plan, Qualified Investment, Phone Exchange

Investment Strategy: The investment seeks conservation of capital, current income and long-term growth of capital and income. The fund uses a balanced approach to invest in a broad range of securities, including common stocks and investment-grade bonds. It also invests in securities issued and guaranteed by the U.S. government and by federal agencies and instrumentalities. In addition, the fund may invest a portion of its assets in common stocks, most of which have a history of paying dividends, bonds and other securities of issuers domiciled outside the United States. **Top Holdings:** Microsoft Corp The Home Depot Inc Berkshire Hathaway Inc A UnitedHealth Group Inc Comcast Corp Class A

American Funds American Balanced Fund® Class C — B BUY

Ticker	Traded On	NAV	Total Assets ($)	Dividend Yield (TTM)	Turnover Ratio	Expense Ratio
BALCX	NAS CM	26.98	$123,184,871,331	0.84	79	1.38

Ratings

Reward C+
Risk B+

Fund Information

Fund Type	Open End
Category	Moderate Alloc
Sub-Category	Alloc--50% to 70% Equity
Prospectus Objective	Balanced
Inception Date	Mar-01
Open to New Investments	Y
Minimum Initial Investment	250
Minimum Subsequent Investment	50
Front End Fee	
Back End Fee	1.00

Total Returns (%)

3-Month	6-Month	1-Year	3-Year	5-Year
4.30	7.81	14.58	23.80	64.06

Last Bull Market	16.89
Last Bear Market	-10.23
3-Year Standard Deviation	6.46
3-Year Beta	0.62

Company Information

Provider	American Funds
Manager/Tenure	John H. Smet (20), Hilda L. Applbaum (18), Gregory D. Johnson (14), 6 others
Website	http://www.americanfunds.com
Address	American Funds 333 South Hope Street Los Angeles CA 90071-1406 United States
Phone Number	800-421-4225

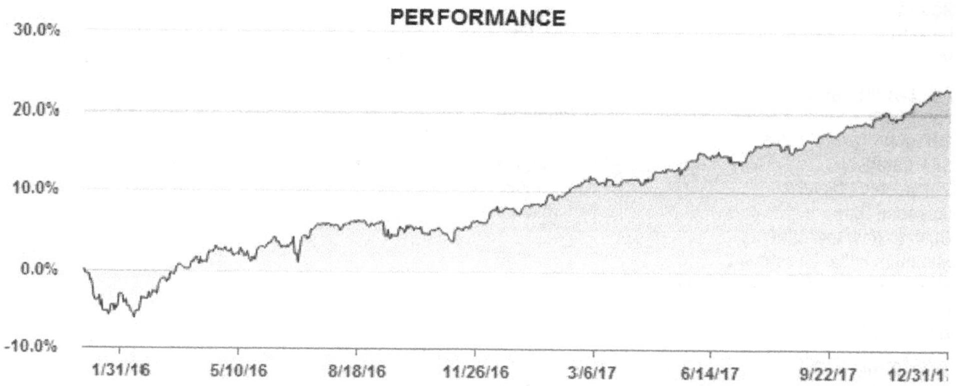

Ratings History

Date	Overall Rating	Risk Rating	Reward Rating
Q4-17	B	B+	C+
Q3-17	B-	B-	B-
Q2-17	B	A	B-
Q1-17	B	B	B-
Q4-16	B	B+	B-
Q4-15	C+	B-	C

Asset & Performance History

Date	NAV	1-Year Total Return
2016	24.66	7.69
2015	23.71	0.93
2014	24.63	8.03
2013	24.3	20.72
2012	20.31	13.3
2011	18.13	3

Total Assets: $123,184,871,331

Asset Allocation

Asset	%
Cash	3%
Stocks	59%
US Stocks	52%
Bonds	36%
US Bonds	32%
Other	2%

Services Offered: Systematic Withdrawal Plan, Automatic Investment Plan, Phone Exchange, Retirement Investment

Investment Strategy: The investment seeks conservation of capital, current income and long-term growth of capital and income. The fund uses a balanced approach to invest in a broad range of securities, including common stocks and investment-grade bonds. It also invests in securities issued and guaranteed by the U.S. government and by federal agencies and instrumentalities. In addition, the fund may invest a portion of its assets in common stocks, most of which have a history of paying dividends, bonds and other securities of issuers domiciled outside the United States. **Top Holdings:** Microsoft Corp The Home Depot Inc Berkshire Hathaway Inc A UnitedHealth Group Inc Comcast Corp Class A

American Funds American Balanced Fund® Class R-5E — B BUY

Ticker	Traded On	NAV	Total Assets ($)	Dividend Yield (TTM)	Turnover Ratio	Expense Ratio
RLEFX	NAS CM	27.12	$123,184,871,331	1.74	79	0.42

Ratings

Reward B-
Risk A-

Fund Information

Fund Type	Open End
Category	Moderate Alloc
Sub-Category	Alloc--50% to 70% Equity
Prospectus Objective	Balanced
Inception Date	Nov-15
Open to New Investments	Y
Minimum Initial Investment	250
Minimum Subsequent Investment	50
Front End Fee	
Back End Fee	

Total Returns (%)

3-Month	6-Month	1-Year	3-Year	5-Year
4.56	8.39	15.70	27.14	71.24

Last Bull Market	17.46
Last Bear Market	-9.96
3-Year Standard Deviation	6.46
3-Year Beta	0.62

Company Information

Provider	American Funds
Manager/Tenure	John H. Smet (20), Hilda L. Applbaum (18), Gregory D. Johnson (14), 6 others
Website	http://www.americanfunds.com
Address	American Funds 333 South Hope Street Los Angeles CA 90071-1406 United States
Phone Number	800-421-4225

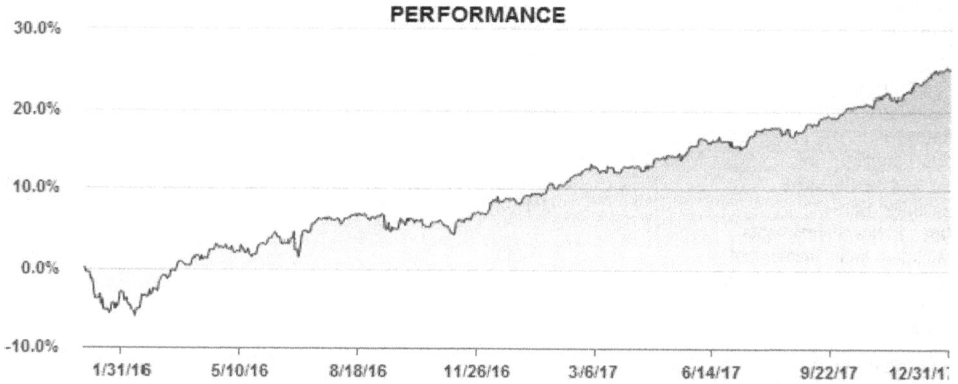

Ratings History

Date	Overall Rating	Risk Rating	Reward Rating
Q4-17	B	A-	B-
Q3-17	B	A+	B-
Q2-17	B	A	B-
Q1-17	B	B+	B
Q4-16	B	B+	B-
Q4-15			

Asset & Performance History

Date	NAV	1-Year Total Return
2016	24.78	8.65
2015	23.82	1.79
2014		8.84
2013		21.73
2012		14.19
2011		3.82

Total Assets: $123,184,871,331

Asset Allocation

Asset	%
Cash	3%
Stocks	59%
US Stocks	52%
Bonds	36%
US Bonds	32%
Other	2%

Services Offered: Automatic Investment Plan, Qualified Investment, Phone Exchange

Investment Strategy: The investment seeks conservation of capital, current income and long-term growth of capital and income. The fund uses a balanced approach to invest in a broad range of securities, including common stocks and investment-grade bonds. It also invests in securities issued and guaranteed by the U.S. government and by federal agencies and instrumentalities. In addition, the fund may invest a portion of its assets in common stocks, most of which have a history of paying dividends, bonds and other securities of issuers domiciled outside the United States. **Top Holdings:** Microsoft Corp The Home Depot Inc Berkshire Hathaway Inc A UnitedHealth Group Inc Comcast Corp Class A

American Funds American Balanced Fund® Class R-2 B BUY

Ticker	Traded On	NAV	Total Assets ($)	Dividend Yield (TTM)	Turnover Ratio	Expense Ratio
RLBBX	NAS CM	26.98	$123,184,871,331	0.83	79	1.37

Ratings
Reward C+
Risk B+

Fund Information
Fund Type Open End
Category Moderate Alloc
Sub-Category Alloc--50% to 70% Equity
Prospectus Objective Balanced
Inception Date May-02
Open to New Investments Y
Minimum Initial Investment 250
Minimum Subsequent Investment 50
Front End Fee
Back End Fee

Total Returns (%)

3-Month	6-Month	1-Year	3-Year	5-Year
4.29	7.85	14.57	23.89	64.29

Last Bull Market 16.93
Last Bear Market -10.26
3-Year Standard Deviation 6.47
3-Year Beta 0.62

Company Information
Provider American Funds
Manager/Tenure John H. Smet (20), Hilda L. Applbaum (18), Gregory D. Johnson (14), 6 others
Website http://www.americanfunds.com
Address American Funds 333 South Hope Street Los Angeles CA 90071-1406 United States
Phone Number 800-421-4225

PERFORMANCE

Ratings History

Date	Overall Rating	Risk Rating	Reward Rating
Q4-17	B	B+	C+
Q3-17	B-	B-	B-
Q2-17	B	A	B-
Q1-17	B	B	B-
Q4-16	B	B+	B-
Q4-15	C+	B-	C

Asset & Performance History

Date	NAV	1-Year Total Return
2016	24.66	7.74
2015	23.7	0.97
2014	24.62	8.03
2013	24.3	20.86
2012	20.3	13.31
2011	18.13	3.04

Total Assets: $123,184,871,331
Asset Allocation

Asset	%
Cash	3%
Stocks	59%
US Stocks	52%
Bonds	36%
US Bonds	32%
Other	2%

Services Offered: Automatic Investment Plan, Qualified Investment, Phone Exchange

Investment Strategy: The investment seeks conservation of capital, current income and long-term growth of capital and income. The fund uses a balanced approach to invest in a broad range of securities, including common stocks and investment-grade bonds. It also invests in securities issued and guaranteed by the U.S. government and by federal agencies and instrumentalities. In addition, the fund may invest a portion of its assets in common stocks, most of which have a history of paying dividends, bonds and other securities of issuers domiciled outside the United States. **Top Holdings:** Microsoft Corp The Home Depot Inc Berkshire Hathaway Inc A UnitedHealth Group Inc Comcast Corp Class A

American Funds American Balanced Fund® Class 529-E B BUY

Ticker	Traded On	NAV	Total Assets ($)	Dividend Yield (TTM)	Turnover Ratio	Expense Ratio
CLBEX	NAS CM	27.09	$123,184,871,331	1.27	79	0.91

Ratings
Reward C+
Risk A-

Fund Information
Fund Type Open End
Category Moderate Alloc
Sub-Category Alloc--50% to 70% Equity
Prospectus Objective Balanced
Inception Date Mar-02
Open to New Investments Y
Minimum Initial Investment 250
Minimum Subsequent Investment 50
Front End Fee
Back End Fee

Total Returns (%)

3-Month	6-Month	1-Year	3-Year	5-Year
4.44	8.08	15.10	25.55	67.90

Last Bull Market 17.24
Last Bear Market -10.14
3-Year Standard Deviation 6.46
3-Year Beta 0.62

Company Information
Provider American Funds
Manager/Tenure John H. Smet (20), Hilda L. Applbaum (18), Gregory D. Johnson (14), 6 others
Website http://www.americanfunds.com
Address American Funds 333 South Hope Street Los Angeles CA 90071-1406 United States
Phone Number 800-421-4225

PERFORMANCE

Ratings History

Date	Overall Rating	Risk Rating	Reward Rating
Q4-17	B	A-	C+
Q3-17	B	A	B-
Q2-17	B	A	B-
Q1-17	B	B+	B
Q4-16	B	B+	B-
Q4-15	C+	B-	C

Asset & Performance History

Date	NAV	1-Year Total Return
2016	24.76	8.24
2015	23.79	1.38
2014	24.71	8.49
2013	24.38	21.3
2012	20.37	13.83
2011	18.18	3.47

Total Assets: $123,184,871,331
Asset Allocation

Asset	%
Cash	3%
Stocks	59%
US Stocks	52%
Bonds	36%
US Bonds	32%
Other	2%

Services Offered: Systematic Withdrawal Plan, Automatic Investment Plan, Qualified Investment, Phone Exchange, Retirement Investment

Investment Strategy: The investment seeks conservation of capital, current income and long-term growth of capital and income. The fund uses a balanced approach to invest in a broad range of securities, including common stocks and investment-grade bonds. It also invests in securities issued and guaranteed by the U.S. government and by federal agencies and instrumentalities. In addition, the fund may invest a portion of its assets in common stocks, most of which have a history of paying dividends, bonds and other securities of issuers domiciled outside the United States. **Top Holdings:** Microsoft Corp The Home Depot Inc Berkshire Hathaway Inc A UnitedHealth Group Inc Comcast Corp Class A

American Funds American Balanced Fund® Class R-4 — B BUY

Ticker	Traded On	NAV	Total Assets ($)	Dividend Yield (TTM)	Turnover Ratio	Expense Ratio
RLBEX	NAS CM	27.1	$123,184,871,331	1.51	79	0.64

Ratings

Reward	B-
Risk	A-

Fund Information

Fund Type	Open End
Category	Moderate Alloc
Sub-Category	Alloc--50% to 70% Equity
Prospectus Objective	Balanced
Inception Date	Jun-02
Open to New Investments	Y
Minimum Initial Investment	250
Minimum Subsequent Investment	50
Front End Fee	
Back End Fee	

Total Returns (%)

3-Month	6-Month	1-Year	3-Year	5-Year
4.50	8.21	15.43	26.57	70.25

Last Bull Market	17.41
Last Bear Market	-9.98
3-Year Standard Deviation	6.46
3-Year Beta	0.62

Company Information

Provider	American Funds
Manager/Tenure	John H. Smet (20), Hilda L. Applbaum (18), Gregory D. Johnson (14), 6 others
Website	http://www.americanfunds.com
Address	American Funds 333 South Hope Street Los Angeles CA 90071-1406 United States
Phone Number	800-421-4225

PERFORMANCE

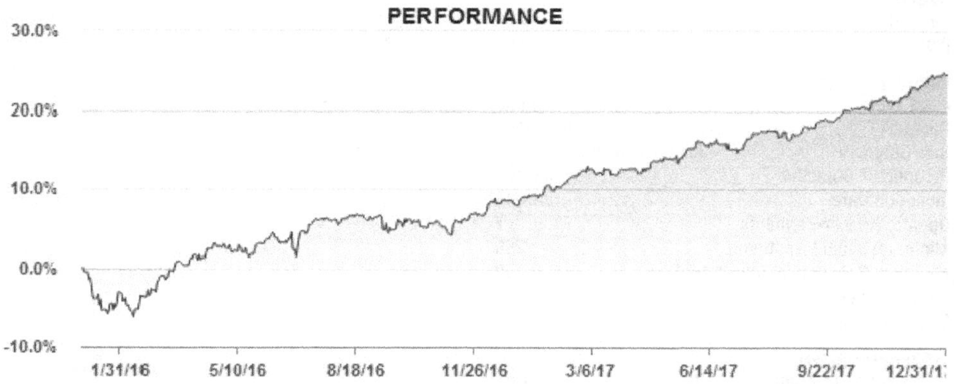

Ratings History

Date	Overall Rating	Risk Rating	Reward Rating
Q4-17	B	A-	B-
Q3-17	B	A+	B-
Q2-17	B	A	B-
Q1-17	B	B+	B
Q4-16	B	B+	B-
Q4-15	C+	B-	C

Asset & Performance History

Date	NAV	1-Year Total Return
2016	24.76	8.49
2015	23.8	1.67
2014	24.72	8.85
2013	24.38	21.68
2012	20.37	14.14
2011	18.19	3.8

Total Assets: $123,184,871,331

Asset Allocation

Asset	%
Cash	3%
Stocks	59%
US Stocks	52%
Bonds	36%
US Bonds	32%
Other	2%

Services Offered: Automatic Investment Plan, Qualified Investment, Phone Exchange

Investment Strategy: The investment seeks conservation of capital, current income and long-term growth of capital and income. The fund uses a balanced approach to invest in a broad range of securities, including common stocks and investment-grade bonds. It also invests in securities issued and guaranteed by the U.S. government and by federal agencies and instrumentalities. In addition, the fund may invest a portion of its assets in common stocks, most of which have a history of paying dividends, bonds and other securities of issuers domiciled outside the United States. **Top Holdings:** Microsoft Corp The Home Depot Inc Berkshire Hathaway Inc A UnitedHealth Group Inc Comcast Corp Class A

American Funds American Balanced Fund® Class 529-A — B BUY

Ticker	Traded On	NAV	Total Assets ($)	Dividend Yield (TTM)	Turnover Ratio	Expense Ratio
CLBAX	NAS CM	27.11	$123,184,871,331	1.48	79	0.68

Ratings

Reward	B-
Risk	A-

Fund Information

Fund Type	Open End
Category	Moderate Alloc
Sub-Category	Alloc--50% to 70% Equity
Prospectus Objective	Balanced
Inception Date	Feb-02
Open to New Investments	Y
Minimum Initial Investment	250
Minimum Subsequent Investment	50
Front End Fee	5.75
Back End Fee	

Total Returns (%)

3-Month	6-Month	1-Year	3-Year	5-Year
4.51	8.25	15.42	26.49	69.97

Last Bull Market	17.38
Last Bear Market	-10.01
3-Year Standard Deviation	6.48
3-Year Beta	0.62

Company Information

Provider	American Funds
Manager/Tenure	John H. Smet (20), Hilda L. Applbaum (18), Gregory D. Johnson (14), 6 others
Website	http://www.americanfunds.com
Address	American Funds 333 South Hope Street Los Angeles CA 90071-1406 United States
Phone Number	800-421-4225

PERFORMANCE

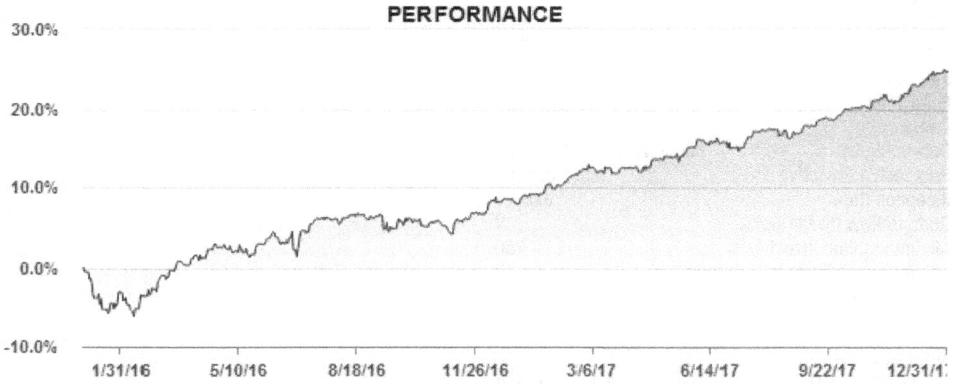

Ratings History

Date	Overall Rating	Risk Rating	Reward Rating
Q4-17	B	A-	B-
Q3-17	B	A+	B-
Q2-17	B	A	B-
Q1-17	B	B+	B
Q4-16	B	B+	B-
Q4-15	C+	B-	C

Asset & Performance History

Date	NAV	1-Year Total Return
2016	24.77	8.49
2015	23.8	1.62
2014	24.72	8.76
2013	24.39	21.59
2012	20.38	14.11
2011	18.19	3.74

Total Assets: $123,184,871,331

Asset Allocation

Asset	%
Cash	3%
Stocks	59%
US Stocks	52%
Bonds	36%
US Bonds	32%
Other	2%

Services Offered: Systematic Withdrawal Plan, Automatic Investment Plan, Qualified Investment, Phone Exchange, Retirement Investment

Investment Strategy: The investment seeks conservation of capital, current income and long-term growth of capital and income. The fund uses a balanced approach to invest in a broad range of securities, including common stocks and investment-grade bonds. It also invests in securities issued and guaranteed by the U.S. government and by federal agencies and instrumentalities. In addition, the fund may invest a portion of its assets in common stocks, most of which have a history of paying dividends, bonds and other securities of issuers domiciled outside the United States. **Top Holdings:** Microsoft Corp The Home Depot Inc Berkshire Hathaway Inc A UnitedHealth Group Inc Comcast Corp Class A

American Funds American Balanced Fund® Class F-3 — B — BUY

Ticker	Traded On	NAV	Total Assets ($)	Dividend Yield (TTM)	Turnover Ratio	Expense Ratio
AFMBX	NAS CM	27.14	$123,184,871,331		79	0.29

Ratings

Reward	B-
Risk	A-

Fund Information

Fund Type	Open End
Category	Moderate Alloc
Sub-Category	Alloc--50% to 70% Equity
Prospectus Objective	Balanced
Inception Date	Jan-17
Open to New Investments	Y
Minimum Initial Investment	250
Minimum Subsequent Investment	50
Front End Fee	
Back End Fee	

Total Returns (%)

3-Month	6-Month	1-Year	3-Year	5-Year
4.59	8.43	15.81	27.14	71.23

Last Bull Market	17.46
Last Bear Market	-9.96
3-Year Standard Deviation	6.47
3-Year Beta	0.62

Company Information

Provider	American Funds
Manager/Tenure	John H. Smet (20), Hilda L. Applbaum (18), Gregory D. Johnson (14), 6 others
Website	http://www.americanfunds.com
Address	American Funds 333 South Hope Street Los Angeles CA 90071-1406 United States
Phone Number	800-421-4225

PERFORMANCE

Ratings History

Date	Overall Rating	Risk Rating	Reward Rating
Q4-17	B	A-	B-
Q3-17	B	A+	B-
Q2-17	B		B-
Q1-17	B	B+	B
Q4-16			
Q4-15			

Asset & Performance History

Date	NAV	1-Year Total Return
2016		
2015		1.72
2014		8.84
2013		21.73
2012		14.19
2011		3.82

Total Assets: $123,184,871,331

Asset Allocation

Asset	%
Cash	3%
Stocks	59%
US Stocks	52%
Bonds	36%
US Bonds	32%
Other	2%

Services Offered: Systematic Withdrawal Plan, Automatic Investment Plan, Qualified Investment, Phone Exchange, Retirement Investment

Investment Strategy: The investment seeks conservation of capital, current income and long-term growth of capital and income. The fund uses a balanced approach to invest in a broad range of securities, including common stocks and investment-grade bonds. It also invests in securities issued and guaranteed by the U.S. government and by federal agencies and instrumentalities. In addition, the fund may invest a portion of its assets in common stocks, most of which have a history of paying dividends, bonds and other securities of issuers domiciled outside the United States. **Top Holdings:** Microsoft Corp The Home Depot Inc Berkshire Hathaway Inc A UnitedHealth Group Inc Comcast Corp Class A

American Funds The Income Fund of America® Class F-3 — B- — BUY

Ticker	Traded On	NAV	Total Assets ($)	Dividend Yield (TTM)	Turnover Ratio	Expense Ratio
FIFAX	NAS CM	23.36	$110,348,505,468		42	0.29

Ratings

Reward	C+
Risk	B

Fund Information

Fund Type	Open End
Category	Aggressive Alloc
Sub-Category	Alloc--70% to 85% Equity
Prospectus Objective	Income
Inception Date	Jan-17
Open to New Investments	Y
Minimum Initial Investment	250
Minimum Subsequent Investment	50
Front End Fee	
Back End Fee	

Total Returns (%)

3-Month	6-Month	1-Year	3-Year	5-Year
3.55	7.47	13.64	22.95	60.03

Last Bull Market	14.52
Last Bear Market	-10.07
3-Year Standard Deviation	7.12
3-Year Beta	0.66

Company Information

Provider	American Funds
Manager/Tenure	Dina N. Perry (25), John H. Smet (25), Hilda L. Applbaum (20), 6 others
Website	http://www.americanfunds.com
Address	American Funds 333 South Hope Street Los Angeles CA 90071-1406 United States
Phone Number	800-421-4225

PERFORMANCE

Ratings History

Date	Overall Rating	Risk Rating	Reward Rating
Q4-17	B-	B	C+
Q3-17	B	A	C+
Q2-17	B		B-
Q1-17	B-	B-	B
Q4-16			
Q4-15			

Asset & Performance History

Date	NAV	1-Year Total Return
2016		
2015		-1.47
2014		8.39
2013		18.25
2012		11.95
2011		5.58

Total Assets: $110,348,505,468

Asset Allocation

Asset	%
Cash	1%
Stocks	72%
US Stocks	51%
Bonds	22%
US Bonds	20%
Other	3%

Services Offered: Systematic Withdrawal Plan, Automatic Investment Plan, Qualified Investment, Phone Exchange, Retirement Investment

Investment Strategy: The investment seeks to provide investors with current income while secondarily striving for capital growth. Normally the fund invests primarily in income-producing securities. These include equity securities, such as dividend-paying common stocks, and debt securities, such as interest-paying bonds. Generally at least 60% of the fund's assets will be invested in common stocks and other equity-type securities. The fund may also invest up to 25% of its assets in equity securities of issuers domiciled outside the United States, including issuers in developing countries. **Top Holdings:** Microsoft Corp Lockheed Martin Corp Intel Corp McDonald's Corp DowDuPont Inc

American Funds The Income Fund of America® Class A B- BUY

Ticker	Traded On	NAV	Total Assets ($)	Dividend Yield (TTM)	Turnover Ratio	Expense Ratio
AMECX	NAS CM	23.37	$110,348,505,468	2.83	42	0.56

Ratings

Reward	C+
Risk	B

Fund Information

Fund Type	Open End
Category	Aggressive Alloc
Sub-Category	Alloc--70% to 85% Equity
Prospectus Objective	Income
Inception Date	Nov-73
Open to New Investments	Y
Minimum Initial Investment	250
Minimum Subsequent Investment	50
Front End Fee	5.75
Back End Fee	

Total Returns (%)

3-Month	6-Month	1-Year	3-Year	5-Year
3.48	7.32	13.37	22.66	59.65

Last Bull Market	14.52
Last Bear Market	-10.07
3-Year Standard Deviation	7.12
3-Year Beta	0.66

Company Information

Provider	American Funds
Manager/Tenure	Dina N. Perry (25), John H. Smet (25), Hilda L. Applbaum (20), 6 others
Website	http://www.americanfunds.com
Address	American Funds 333 South Hope Street Los Angeles CA 90071-1406 United States
Phone Number	800-421-4225

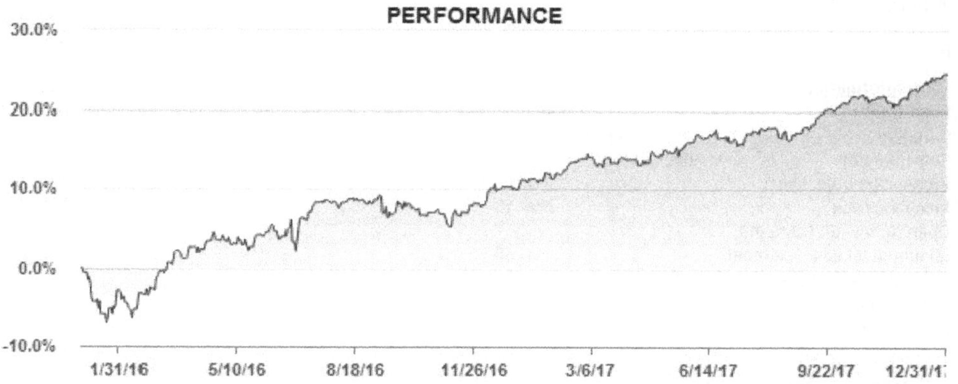

Ratings History

Date	Overall Rating	Risk Rating	Reward Rating
Q4-17	B-	B	C+
Q3-17	B	A	C+
Q2-17	B	A-	B-
Q1-17	B-	B-	B-
Q4-16	B-	B	B-
Q4-15	B-	B+	C

Asset & Performance History

Date	NAV	1-Year Total Return
2016	21.67	10.57
2015	20.23	-1.47
2014	21.58	8.39
2013	20.65	18.25
2012	18.06	11.95
2011	16.76	5.58

Total Assets: $110,348,505,468

Asset Allocation

Asset	%
Cash	1%
Stocks	72%
US Stocks	51%
Bonds	22%
US Bonds	20%
Other	3%

Services Offered: Systematic Withdrawal Plan, Automatic Investment Plan, Phone Exchange, Retirement Investment

Investment Strategy: The investment seeks to provide investors with current income while secondarily striving for capital growth. Normally the fund invests primarily in income-producing securities. These include equity securities, such as dividend-paying common stocks, and debt securities, such as interest-paying bonds. Generally at least 60% of the fund's assets will be invested in common stocks and other equity-type securities. The fund may also invest up to 25% of its assets in equity securities of issuers domiciled outside the United States, including issuers in developing countries. **Top Holdings:** Microsoft Corp Lockheed Martin Corp Intel Corp McDonald's Corp DowDuPont Inc

American Funds The Income Fund of America® Class F-1 B- BUY

Ticker	Traded On	NAV	Total Assets ($)	Dividend Yield (TTM)	Turnover Ratio	Expense Ratio
IFAFX	NAS CM	23.31	$110,348,505,468	2.75	42	0.65

Ratings

Reward	C+
Risk	B

Fund Information

Fund Type	Open End
Category	Aggressive Alloc
Sub-Category	Alloc--70% to 85% Equity
Prospectus Objective	Income
Inception Date	Mar-01
Open to New Investments	Y
Minimum Initial Investment	250
Minimum Subsequent Investment	50
Front End Fee	
Back End Fee	

Total Returns (%)

3-Month	6-Month	1-Year	3-Year	5-Year
3.46	7.24	13.24	22.28	58.90

Last Bull Market	14.52
Last Bear Market	-10.11
3-Year Standard Deviation	7.1
3-Year Beta	0.66

Company Information

Provider	American Funds
Manager/Tenure	Dina N. Perry (25), John H. Smet (25), Hilda L. Applbaum (20), 6 others
Website	http://www.americanfunds.com
Address	American Funds 333 South Hope Street Los Angeles CA 90071-1406 United States
Phone Number	800-421-4225

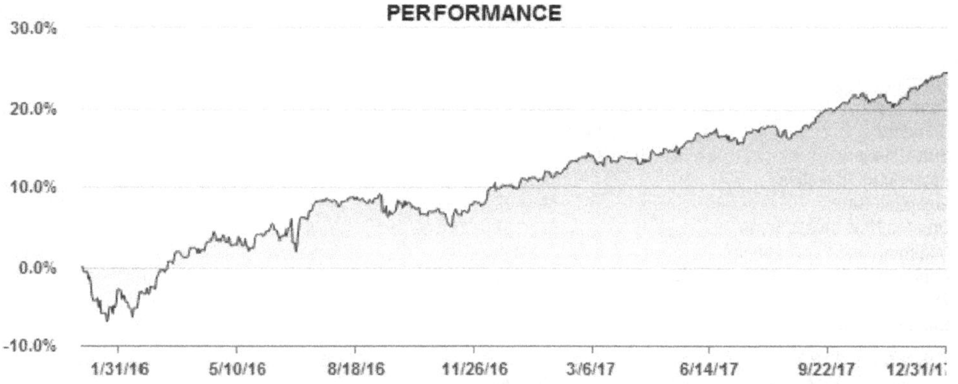

Ratings History

Date	Overall Rating	Risk Rating	Reward Rating
Q4-17	B-	B	C+
Q3-17	B	A	C+
Q2-17	B	A-	B-
Q1-17	B-	B-	B-
Q4-16	B-	B	B-
Q4-15	B-	B+	C

Asset & Performance History

Date	NAV	1-Year Total Return
2016	21.62	10.5
2015	20.18	-1.55
2014	21.53	8.31
2013	20.6	18.09
2012	18.03	11.92
2011	16.73	5.54

Total Assets: $110,348,505,468

Asset Allocation

Asset	%
Cash	1%
Stocks	72%
US Stocks	51%
Bonds	22%
US Bonds	20%
Other	3%

Services Offered: Systematic Withdrawal Plan, Automatic Investment Plan, Qualified Investment, Phone Exchange, Retirement Investment

Investment Strategy: The investment seeks to provide investors with current income while secondarily striving for capital growth. Normally the fund invests primarily in income-producing securities. These include equity securities, such as dividend-paying common stocks, and debt securities, such as interest-paying bonds. Generally at least 60% of the fund's assets will be invested in common stocks and other equity-type securities. The fund may also invest up to 25% of its assets in equity securities of issuers domiciled outside the United States, including issuers in developing countries. **Top Holdings:** Microsoft Corp Lockheed Martin Corp Intel Corp McDonald's Corp DowDuPont Inc

American Funds The Income Fund of America® Class R-5E B- BUY

Ticker	Traded On	NAV	Total Assets ($)	Dividend Yield (TTM)	Turnover Ratio	Expense Ratio
RIDHX	NAS CM	23.34	$110,348,505,468	2.95	42	0.44

Ratings

Reward	C+
Risk	B

Fund Information

Fund Type	Open End
Category	Aggressive Alloc
Sub-Category	Alloc--70% to 85% Equity
Prospectus Objective	Income
Inception Date	Nov-15
Open to New Investments	Y
Minimum Initial Investment	250
Minimum Subsequent Investment	50
Front End Fee	
Back End Fee	

Total Returns (%)

3-Month	6-Month	1-Year	3-Year	5-Year
3.48	7.35	13.46	22.85	59.89

Last Bull Market	14.52
Last Bear Market	-10.07
3-Year Standard Deviation	7.12
3-Year Beta	0.66

Company Information

Provider	American Funds
Manager/Tenure	Dina N. Perry (25), John H. Smet (25), Hilda L. Applbaum (20), 6 others
Website	http://www.americanfunds.com
Address	American Funds 333 South Hope Street Los Angeles CA 90071-1406 United States
Phone Number	800-421-4225

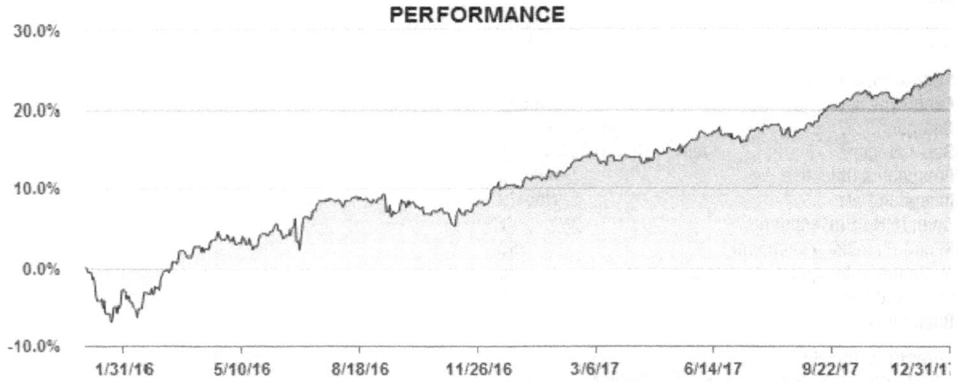

Ratings History

Date	Overall Rating	Risk Rating	Reward Rating
Q4-17	B-	B	C+
Q3-17	B	A	C+
Q2-17	B	A-	B-
Q1-17	B-	B-	B
Q4-16	B-	B	B-
Q4-15			

Asset & Performance History

Date	NAV	1-Year Total Return
2016	21.66	10.64
2015	20.22	-1.46
2014		8.39
2013		18.25
2012		11.95
2011		5.58

Total Assets: $110,348,505,468

Asset Allocation

Asset	%
Cash	1%
Stocks	72%
US Stocks	51%
Bonds	22%
US Bonds	20%
Other	3%

Services Offered: Automatic Investment Plan, Qualified Investment, Phone Exchange

Investment Strategy: The investment seeks to provide investors with current income while secondarily striving for capital growth. Normally the fund invests primarily in income-producing securities. These include equity securities, such as dividend-paying common stocks, and debt securities, such as interest-paying bonds. Generally at least 60% of the fund's assets will be invested in common stocks and other equity-type securities. The fund may also invest up to 25% of its assets in equity securities of issuers domiciled outside the United States, including issuers in developing countries. **Top Holdings:** Microsoft Corp Lockheed Martin Corp Intel Corp McDonald's Corp DowDuPont Inc

American Funds The Income Fund of America® Class R-5 B- BUY

Ticker	Traded On	NAV	Total Assets ($)	Dividend Yield (TTM)	Turnover Ratio	Expense Ratio
RIDFX	NAS CM	23.36	$110,348,505,468	3.04	42	0.34

Ratings

Reward	C+
Risk	B

Fund Information

Fund Type	Open End
Category	Aggressive Alloc
Sub-Category	Alloc--70% to 85% Equity
Prospectus Objective	Income
Inception Date	May-02
Open to New Investments	Y
Minimum Initial Investment	250
Minimum Subsequent Investment	50
Front End Fee	
Back End Fee	

Total Returns (%)

3-Month	6-Month	1-Year	3-Year	5-Year
3.49	7.39	13.56	23.44	61.39

Last Bull Market	14.72
Last Bear Market	-9.97
3-Year Standard Deviation	7.1
3-Year Beta	0.66

Company Information

Provider	American Funds
Manager/Tenure	Dina N. Perry (25), John H. Smet (25), Hilda L. Applbaum (20), 6 others
Website	http://www.americanfunds.com
Address	American Funds 333 South Hope Street Los Angeles CA 90071-1406 United States
Phone Number	800-421-4225

Ratings History

Date	Overall Rating	Risk Rating	Reward Rating
Q4-17	B-	B	C+
Q3-17	B	A	C+
Q2-17	B	A-	B-
Q1-17	B	B-	B
Q4-16	B-	B	B-
Q4-15	C+	C+	C

Asset & Performance History

Date	NAV	1-Year Total Return
2016	21.67	10.88
2015	20.22	-1.29
2014	21.58	8.68
2013	20.64	18.47
2012	18.06	12.21
2011	16.76	5.82

Total Assets: $110,348,505,468

Asset Allocation

Asset	%
Cash	1%
Stocks	72%
US Stocks	51%
Bonds	22%
US Bonds	20%
Other	3%

Services Offered: Automatic Investment Plan, Qualified Investment, Phone Exchange

Investment Strategy: The investment seeks to provide investors with current income while secondarily striving for capital growth. Normally the fund invests primarily in income-producing securities. These include equity securities, such as dividend-paying common stocks, and debt securities, such as interest-paying bonds. Generally at least 60% of the fund's assets will be invested in common stocks and other equity-type securities. The fund may also invest up to 25% of its assets in equity securities of issuers domiciled outside the United States, including issuers in developing countries. **Top Holdings:** Microsoft Corp Lockheed Martin Corp Intel Corp McDonald's Corp DowDuPont Inc

American Funds The Income Fund of America® Class R-2 — B- BUY

Ticker	Traded On	NAV	Total Assets ($)	Dividend Yield (TTM)	Turnover Ratio	Expense Ratio
RIDBX	NAS CM	23.11	$110,348,505,468	2.09	42	1.4

Ratings

Reward	C+
Risk	B

Fund Information

Fund Type	Open End
Category	Aggressive Alloc
Sub-Category	Alloc--70% to 85% Equity
Prospectus Objective	Income
Inception Date	May-02
Open to New Investments	Y
Minimum Initial Investment	250
Minimum Subsequent Investment	50
Front End Fee	
Back End Fee	

Total Returns (%)

3-Month	6-Month	1-Year	3-Year	5-Year
3.26	6.87	12.45	19.71	53.27

Last Bull Market	13.99
Last Bear Market	-10.37
3-Year Standard Deviation	7.1
3-Year Beta	0.66

Company Information

Provider	American Funds
Manager/Tenure	Dina N. Perry (25), John H. Smet (25), Hilda L. Applbaum (20), 6 others
Website	http://www.americanfunds.com
Address	American Funds 333 South Hope Street Los Angeles CA 90071-1406 United States
Phone Number	800-421-4225

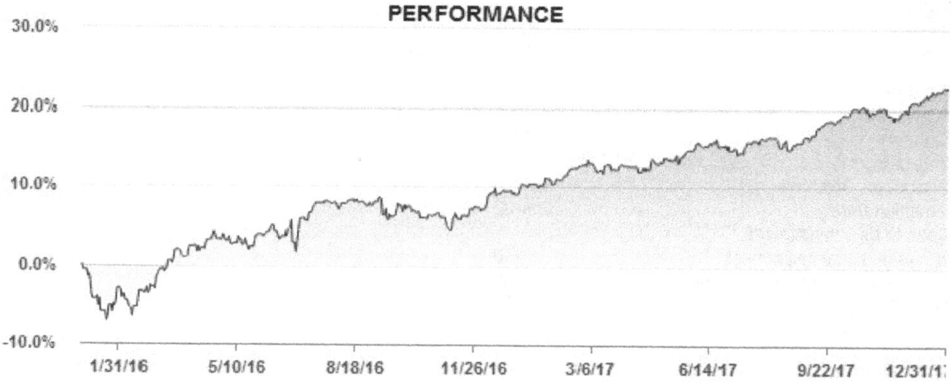

Ratings History

Date	Overall Rating	Risk Rating	Reward Rating
Q4-17	B-	B	C+
Q3-17	B	A	C+
Q2-17	B	B+	C+
Q1-17	B-	B-	B-
Q4-16	B-	B	C+
Q4-15	B-	B+	C

Asset & Performance History

Date	NAV	1-Year Total Return
2016	21.44	9.69
2015	20.02	-2.27
2014	21.37	7.51
2013	20.46	17.33
2012	17.9	11.05
2011	16.62	4.69

Total Assets: $110,348,505,468

Asset Allocation

Asset	%
Cash	1%
Stocks	72%
US Stocks	51%
Bonds	22%
US Bonds	20%
Other	3%

Services Offered: Automatic Investment Plan, Qualified Investment, Phone Exchange

Investment Strategy: The investment seeks to provide investors with current income while secondarily striving for capital growth. Normally the fund invests primarily in income-producing securities. These include equity securities, such as dividend-paying common stocks, and debt securities, such as interest-paying bonds. Generally at least 60% of the fund's assets will be invested in common stocks and other equity-type securities. The fund may also invest up to 25% of its assets in equity securities of issuers domiciled outside the United States, including issuers in developing countries. **Top Holdings:** Microsoft Corp Lockheed Martin Corp Intel Corp McDonald's Corp DowDuPont Inc

American Funds The Income Fund of America® Class 529-A — B- BUY

Ticker	Traded On	NAV	Total Assets ($)	Dividend Yield (TTM)	Turnover Ratio	Expense Ratio
CIMAX	NAS CM	23.32	$110,348,505,468	2.77	42	0.65

Ratings

Reward	C+
Risk	B

Fund Information

Fund Type	Open End
Category	Aggressive Alloc
Sub-Category	Alloc--70% to 85% Equity
Prospectus Objective	Income
Inception Date	Feb-02
Open to New Investments	Y
Minimum Initial Investment	250
Minimum Subsequent Investment	50
Front End Fee	5.75
Back End Fee	

Total Returns (%)

3-Month	6-Month	1-Year	3-Year	5-Year
3.43	7.25	13.27	22.33	58.90

Last Bull Market	14.49
Last Bear Market	-10.13
3-Year Standard Deviation	7.14
3-Year Beta	0.66

Company Information

Provider	American Funds
Manager/Tenure	Dina N. Perry (25), John H. Smet (25), Hilda L. Applbaum (20), 6 others
Website	http://www.americanfunds.com
Address	American Funds 333 South Hope Street Los Angeles CA 90071-1406 United States
Phone Number	800-421-4225

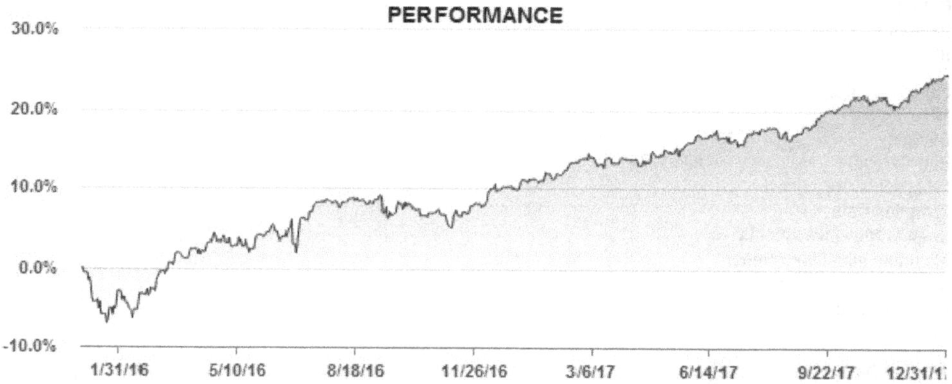

Ratings History

Date	Overall Rating	Risk Rating	Reward Rating
Q4-17	B-	B	C+
Q3-17	B	A	C+
Q2-17	B	A-	B-
Q1-17	B-	B-	B-
Q4-16	B-	B	B-
Q4-15	B-	B+	C

Asset & Performance History

Date	NAV	1-Year Total Return
2016	21.63	10.5
2015	20.19	-1.57
2014	21.54	8.3
2013	20.61	18.11
2012	18.03	11.8
2011	16.74	5.49

Total Assets: $110,348,505,468

Asset Allocation

Asset	%
Cash	1%
Stocks	72%
US Stocks	51%
Bonds	22%
US Bonds	20%
Other	3%

Services Offered: Systematic Withdrawal Plan, Automatic Investment Plan, Qualified Investment, Phone Exchange, Retirement Investment

Investment Strategy: The investment seeks to provide investors with current income while secondarily striving for capital growth. Normally the fund invests primarily in income-producing securities. These include equity securities, such as dividend-paying common stocks, and debt securities, such as interest-paying bonds. Generally at least 60% of the fund's assets will be invested in common stocks and other equity-type securities. The fund may also invest up to 25% of its assets in equity securities of issuers domiciled outside the United States, including issuers in developing countries. **Top Holdings:** Microsoft Corp Lockheed Martin Corp Intel Corp McDonald's Corp DowDuPont Inc

American Funds The Income Fund of America® Class R-1 B- BUY

Ticker	Traded On	NAV	Total Assets ($)	Dividend Yield (TTM)	Turnover Ratio	Expense Ratio
RIDAX	NAS CM	23.23	$110,348,505,468	2.07	42	1.39

Ratings

Reward	C+
Risk	B

Fund Information

Fund Type	Open End
Category	Aggressive Alloc
Sub-Category	Alloc--70% to 85% Equity
Prospectus Objective	Income
Inception Date	Jun-02
Open to New Investments	Y
Minimum Initial Investment	250
Minimum Subsequent Investment	50
Front End Fee	
Back End Fee	

Total Returns (%)

3-Month	6-Month	1-Year	3-Year	5-Year
3.24	6.87	12.42	19.65	53.20

Last Bull Market	14
Last Bear Market	-10.38
3-Year Standard Deviation	7.13
3-Year Beta	0.66

Company Information

Provider	American Funds
Manager/Tenure	Dina N. Perry (25), John H. Smet (25), Hilda L. Applbaum (20), 6 others
Website	http://www.americanfunds.com
Address	American Funds 333 South Hope Street Los Angeles CA 90071-1406 United States
Phone Number	800-421-4225

PERFORMANCE

Ratings History

Date	Overall Rating	Risk Rating	Reward Rating
Q4-17	B-	B	C+
Q3-17	B	A	C+
Q2-17	B	B+	C+
Q1-17	B-	B-	B-
Q4-16	B-	B	C+
Q4-15	B-	B+	C

Asset & Performance History

Date	NAV	1-Year Total Return
2016	21.55	9.68
2015	20.12	-2.29
2014	21.47	7.56
2013	20.54	17.21
2012	17.98	11.05
2011	16.69	4.74

Total Assets: $110,348,505,468

Asset Allocation

Asset	%
Cash	1%
Stocks	72%
US Stocks	51%
Bonds	22%
US Bonds	20%
Other	3%

Services Offered: Automatic Investment Plan, Qualified Investment, Phone Exchange

Investment Strategy: The investment seeks to provide investors with current income while secondarily striving for capital growth. Normally the fund invests primarily in income-producing securities. These include equity securities, such as dividend-paying common stocks, and debt securities, such as interest-paying bonds. Generally at least 60% of the fund's assets will be invested in common stocks and other equity-type securities. The fund may also invest up to 25% of its assets in equity securities of issuers domiciled outside the United States, including issuers in developing countries. **Top Holdings:** Microsoft Corp Lockheed Martin Corp Intel Corp McDonald's Corp DowDuPont Inc

American Funds The Income Fund of America® Class 529-C B- BUY

Ticker	Traded On	NAV	Total Assets ($)	Dividend Yield (TTM)	Turnover Ratio	Expense Ratio
CIMCX	NAS CM	23.25	$110,348,505,468	2.05	42	1.41

Ratings

Reward	C+
Risk	B

Fund Information

Fund Type	Open End
Category	Aggressive Alloc
Sub-Category	Alloc--70% to 85% Equity
Prospectus Objective	Income
Inception Date	Feb-02
Open to New Investments	Y
Minimum Initial Investment	250
Minimum Subsequent Investment	50
Front End Fee	
Back End Fee	1.00

Total Returns (%)

3-Month	6-Month	1-Year	3-Year	5-Year
3.24	6.86	12.40	19.51	52.84

Last Bull Market	13.96
Last Bear Market	-10.41
3-Year Standard Deviation	7.12
3-Year Beta	0.66

Company Information

Provider	American Funds
Manager/Tenure	Dina N. Perry (25), John H. Smet (25), Hilda L. Applbaum (20), 6 others
Website	http://www.americanfunds.com
Address	American Funds 333 South Hope Street Los Angeles CA 90071-1406 United States
Phone Number	800-421-4225

PERFORMANCE

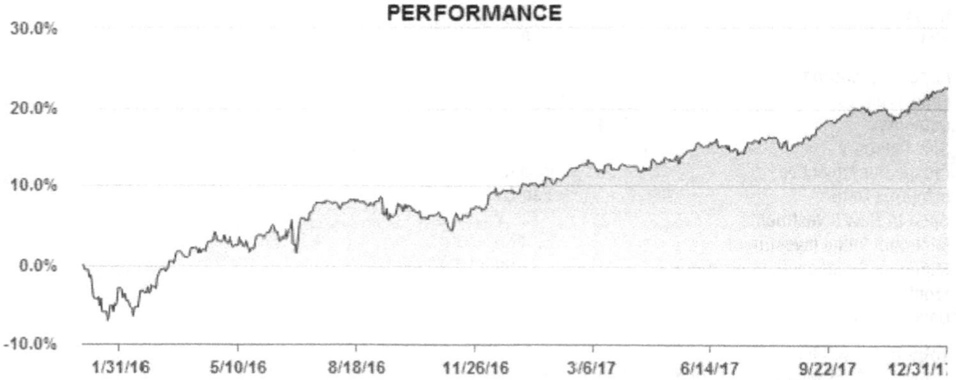

Ratings History

Date	Overall Rating	Risk Rating	Reward Rating
Q4-17	B-	B	C+
Q3-17	B	A	C+
Q2-17	B	B+	C+
Q1-17	B-	B-	B-
Q4-16	B-	B	C+
Q4-15	B-	B+	C

Asset & Performance History

Date	NAV	1-Year Total Return
2016	21.55	9.64
2015	20.12	-2.35
2014	21.47	7.45
2013	20.55	17.2
2012	17.98	10.98
2011	16.69	4.69

Total Assets: $110,348,505,468

Asset Allocation

Asset	%
Cash	1%
Stocks	72%
US Stocks	51%
Bonds	22%
US Bonds	20%
Other	3%

Services Offered: Systematic Withdrawal Plan, Automatic Investment Plan, Qualified Investment, Phone Exchange, Retirement Investment

Investment Strategy: The investment seeks to provide investors with current income while secondarily striving for capital growth. Normally the fund invests primarily in income-producing securities. These include equity securities, such as dividend-paying common stocks, and debt securities, such as interest-paying bonds. Generally at least 60% of the fund's assets will be invested in common stocks and other equity-type securities. The fund may also invest up to 25% of its assets in equity securities of issuers domiciled outside the United States, including issuers in developing countries. **Top Holdings:** Microsoft Corp Lockheed Martin Corp Intel Corp McDonald's Corp DowDuPont Inc

American Funds The Income Fund of America® Class 529-E

B- BUY

Ticker	Traded On	NAV	Total Assets ($)	Dividend Yield (TTM)	Turnover Ratio	Expense Ratio
CIMEX	NAS CM	23.25	$110,348,505,468	2.55	42	0.87

Ratings

Reward	C+
Risk	B

Fund Information

Fund Type	Open End
Category	Aggressive Alloc
Sub-Category	Alloc--70% to 85% Equity
Prospectus Objective	Income
Inception Date	Feb-02
Open to New Investments	Y
Minimum Initial Investment	250
Minimum Subsequent Investment	50
Front End Fee	
Back End Fee	

Total Returns (%)

3-Month	6-Month	1-Year	3-Year	5-Year
3.37	7.14	12.98	21.41	56.96

Last Bull Market	14.32
Last Bear Market	-10.21
3-Year Standard Deviation	7.13
3-Year Beta	0.66

Company Information

Provider	American Funds
Manager/Tenure	Dina N. Perry (25), John H. Smet (25), Hilda L. Applbaum (20), 6 others
Website	http://www.americanfunds.com
Address	American Funds 333 South Hope Street Los Angeles CA 90071-1406 United States
Phone Number	800-421-4225

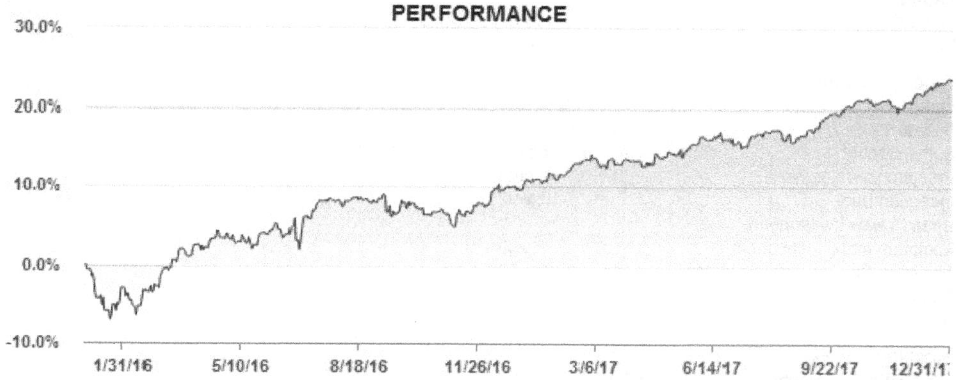

Ratings History

Date	Overall Rating	Risk Rating	Reward Rating
Q4-17	B-	B	C+
Q3-17	B	A	C+
Q2-17	B	A-	B-
Q1-17	B-	B-	B-
Q4-16	B-	B	C+
Q4-15	B-	B+	C

Asset & Performance History

Date	NAV	1-Year Total Return
2016	21.57	10.27
2015	20.13	-1.82
2014	21.48	8.01
2013	20.56	17.81
2012	17.99	11.55
2011	16.7	5.23

Total Assets: $110,348,505,468

Asset Allocation

Asset	%
Cash	1%
Stocks	72%
US Stocks	51%
Bonds	22%
US Bonds	20%
Other	3%

Services Offered: Systematic Withdrawal Plan, Automatic Investment Plan, Qualified Investment, Phone Exchange, Retirement Investment

Investment Strategy: The investment seeks to provide investors with current income while secondarily striving for capital growth. Normally the fund invests primarily in income-producing securities. These include equity securities, such as dividend-paying common stocks, and debt securities, such as interest-paying bonds. Generally at least 60% of the fund's assets will be invested in common stocks and other equity-type securities. The fund may also invest up to 25% of its assets in equity securities of issuers domiciled outside the United States, including issuers in developing countries. **Top Holdings:** Microsoft Corp Lockheed Martin Corp Intel Corp McDonald's Corp DowDuPont Inc

American Funds The Income Fund of America® Class R-4

B- BUY

Ticker	Traded On	NAV	Total Assets ($)	Dividend Yield (TTM)	Turnover Ratio	Expense Ratio
RIDEX	NAS CM	23.33	$110,348,505,468	2.77	42	0.64

Ratings

Reward	C+
Risk	B

Fund Information

Fund Type	Open End
Category	Aggressive Alloc
Sub-Category	Alloc--70% to 85% Equity
Prospectus Objective	Income
Inception Date	Jun-02
Open to New Investments	Y
Minimum Initial Investment	250
Minimum Subsequent Investment	50
Front End Fee	
Back End Fee	

Total Returns (%)

3-Month	6-Month	1-Year	3-Year	5-Year
3.47	7.29	13.31	22.38	59.04

Last Bull Market	14.43
Last Bear Market	-10.06
3-Year Standard Deviation	7.11
3-Year Beta	0.66

Company Information

Provider	American Funds
Manager/Tenure	Dina N. Perry (25), John H. Smet (25), Hilda L. Applbaum (20), 6 others
Website	http://www.americanfunds.com
Address	American Funds 333 South Hope Street Los Angeles CA 90071-1406 United States
Phone Number	800-421-4225

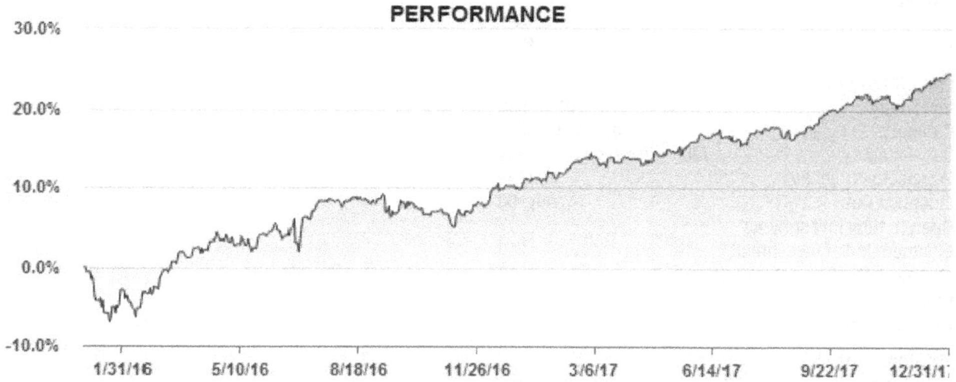

Ratings History

Date	Overall Rating	Risk Rating	Reward Rating
Q4-17	B-	B	C+
Q3-17	B	A	C+
Q2-17	B	A-	B-
Q1-17	B-	B-	B-
Q4-16	B-	B	B-
Q4-15	B-	B+	C

Asset & Performance History

Date	NAV	1-Year Total Return
2016	21.63	10.52
2015	20.19	-1.6
2014	21.55	8.32
2013	20.62	18.14
2012	18.04	11.9
2011	16.74	5.5

Total Assets: $110,348,505,468

Asset Allocation

Asset	%
Cash	1%
Stocks	72%
US Stocks	51%
Bonds	22%
US Bonds	20%
Other	3%

Services Offered: Automatic Investment Plan, Qualified Investment, Phone Exchange

Investment Strategy: The investment seeks to provide investors with current income while secondarily striving for capital growth. Normally the fund invests primarily in income-producing securities. These include equity securities, such as dividend-paying common stocks, and debt securities, such as interest-paying bonds. Generally at least 60% of the fund's assets will be invested in common stocks and other equity-type securities. The fund may also invest up to 25% of its assets in equity securities of issuers domiciled outside the United States, including issuers in developing countries. **Top Holdings:** Microsoft Corp Lockheed Martin Corp Intel Corp McDonald's Corp DowDuPont Inc

American Funds The Income Fund of America® Class 529-F-1 B- BUY

Ticker	Traded On	NAV	Total Assets ($)	Dividend Yield (TTM)	Turnover Ratio	Expense Ratio
CIMFX	NAS CM	23.31	$110,348,505,468	2.98	42	0.41

Ratings

Reward	C+
Risk	B

Fund Information

Fund Type	Open End
Category	Aggressive Alloc
Sub-Category	Alloc--70% to 85% Equity
Prospectus Objective	Income
Inception Date	Sep-02
Open to New Investments	Y
Minimum Initial Investment	250
Minimum Subsequent Investment	50
Front End Fee	
Back End Fee	

Total Returns (%)

3-Month	6-Month	1-Year	3-Year	5-Year
3.48	7.37	13.52	23.12	60.64

Last Bull Market	14.61
Last Bear Market	-10.03
3-Year Standard Deviation	7.11
3-Year Beta	0.66

Company Information

Provider	American Funds
Manager/Tenure	Dina N. Perry (25), John H. Smet (25), Hilda L. Applbaum (20), 6 others
Website	http://www.americanfunds.com
Address	American Funds 333 South Hope Street Los Angeles CA 90071-1406 United States
Phone Number	800-421-4225

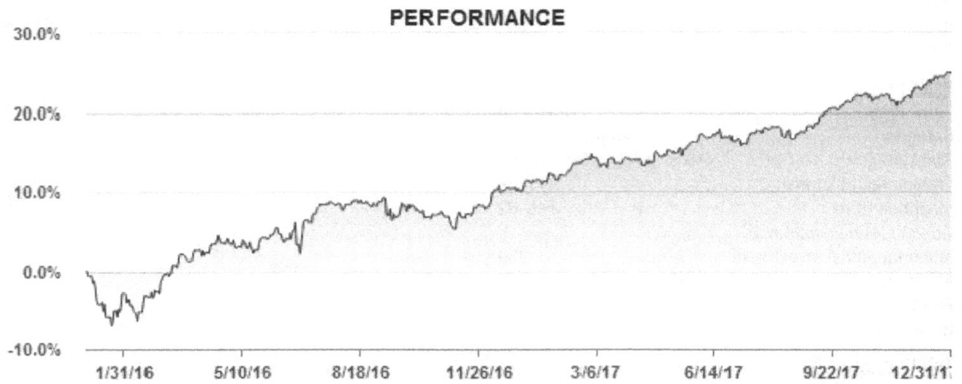

Ratings History

Date	Overall Rating	Risk Rating	Reward Rating
Q4-17	B-	B	C+
Q3-17	B	A	C+
Q2-17	B	A-	B-
Q1-17	B	B-	B
Q4-16	B-	B	B-
Q4-15	C	C	C

Asset & Performance History

Date	NAV	1-Year Total Return
2016	21.62	10.76
2015	20.18	-1.4
2014	21.54	8.54
2013	20.61	18.37
2012	18.03	12.11
2011	16.73	5.73

Total Assets: $110,348,505,468

Asset Allocation

Asset	%
Cash	1%
Stocks	72%
US Stocks	51%
Bonds	22%
US Bonds	20%
Other	3%

Services Offered: Systematic Withdrawal Plan, Automatic Investment Plan, Qualified Investment, Phone Exchange, Retirement Investment

Investment Strategy: The investment seeks to provide investors with current income while secondarily striving for capital growth. Normally the fund invests primarily in income-producing securities. These include equity securities, such as dividend-paying common stocks, and debt securities, such as interest-paying bonds. Generally at least 60% of the fund's assets will be invested in common stocks and other equity-type securities. The fund may also invest up to 25% of its assets in equity securities of issuers domiciled outside the United States, including issuers in developing countries. **Top Holdings:** Microsoft Corp Lockheed Martin Corp Intel Corp McDonald's Corp DowDuPont Inc

American Funds The Income Fund of America® Class F-2 B- BUY

Ticker	Traded On	NAV	Total Assets ($)	Dividend Yield (TTM)	Turnover Ratio	Expense Ratio
AMEFX	NAS CM	23.35	$110,348,505,468	2.99	42	0.39

Ratings

Reward	C+
Risk	B

Fund Information

Fund Type	Open End
Category	Aggressive Alloc
Sub-Category	Alloc--70% to 85% Equity
Prospectus Objective	Income
Inception Date	Aug-08
Open to New Investments	Y
Minimum Initial Investment	250
Minimum Subsequent Investment	50
Front End Fee	
Back End Fee	

Total Returns (%)

3-Month	6-Month	1-Year	3-Year	5-Year
3.53	7.41	13.57	23.25	60.99

Last Bull Market	14.63
Last Bear Market	-10
3-Year Standard Deviation	7.14
3-Year Beta	0.66

Company Information

Provider	American Funds
Manager/Tenure	Dina N. Perry (25), John H. Smet (25), Hilda L. Applbaum (20), 6 others
Website	http://www.americanfunds.com
Address	American Funds 333 South Hope Street Los Angeles CA 90071-1406 United States
Phone Number	800-421-4225

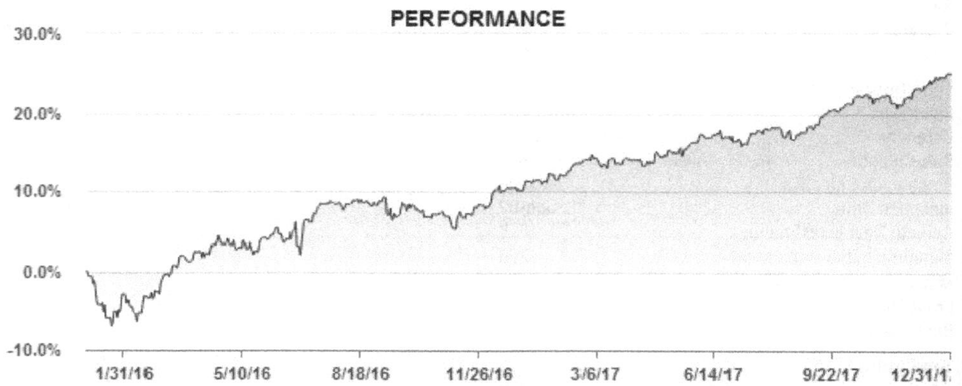

Ratings History

Date	Overall Rating	Risk Rating	Reward Rating
Q4-17	B-	B	C+
Q3-17	B	A	C+
Q2-17	B	A-	B-
Q1-17	B	B-	B
Q4-16	B-	B	B-
Q4-15	C	C	C

Asset & Performance History

Date	NAV	1-Year Total Return
2016	21.65	10.78
2015	20.21	-1.35
2014	21.57	8.64
2013	20.63	18.4
2012	18.05	12.16
2011	16.75	5.77

Total Assets: $110,348,505,468

Asset Allocation

Asset	%
Cash	1%
Stocks	72%
US Stocks	51%
Bonds	22%
US Bonds	20%
Other	3%

Services Offered: Systematic Withdrawal Plan, Automatic Investment Plan, Qualified Investment, Phone Exchange, Retirement Investment

Investment Strategy: The investment seeks to provide investors with current income while secondarily striving for capital growth. Normally the fund invests primarily in income-producing securities. These include equity securities, such as dividend-paying common stocks, and debt securities, such as interest-paying bonds. Generally at least 60% of the fund's assets will be invested in common stocks and other equity-type securities. The fund may also invest up to 25% of its assets in equity securities of issuers domiciled outside the United States, including issuers in developing countries. **Top Holdings:** Microsoft Corp Lockheed Martin Corp Intel Corp McDonald's Corp DowDuPont Inc

American Funds The Income Fund of America® Class C B- BUY

Ticker	Traded On	NAV	Total Assets ($)	Dividend Yield (TTM)	Turnover Ratio	Expense Ratio
IFACX	NAS CM	23.08	$110,348,505,468	2.11	42	1.35

Ratings

Reward	C+
Risk	B

Fund Information

Fund Type	Open End
Category	Aggressive Alloc
Sub-Category	Alloc--70% to 85% Equity
Prospectus Objective	Income
Inception Date	Mar-01
Open to New Investments	Y
Minimum Initial Investment	250
Minimum Subsequent Investment	50
Front End Fee	
Back End Fee	1.00

Total Returns (%)

3-Month	6-Month	1-Year	3-Year	5-Year
3.27	6.88	12.48	19.76	53.37

Last Bull Market	13.95
Last Bear Market	-10.32
3-Year Standard Deviation	7.13
3-Year Beta	0.66

Company Information

Provider	American Funds
Manager/Tenure	Dina N. Perry (25), John H. Smet (25), Hilda L. Applbaum (20), 6 others
Website	http://www.americanfunds.com
Address	American Funds 333 South Hope Street Los Angeles CA 90071-1406 United States
Phone Number	800-421-4225

PERFORMANCE

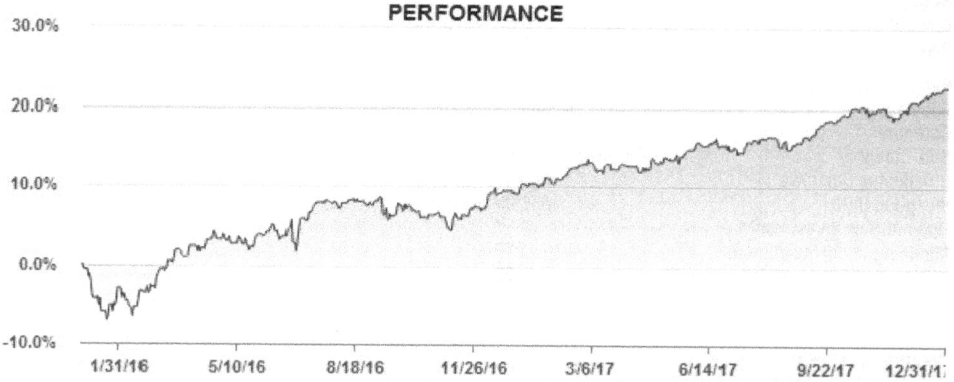

Ratings History

Date	Overall Rating	Risk Rating	Reward Rating
Q4-17	B-	B	C+
Q3-17	B	A	C+
Q2-17	B	B+	C+
Q1-17	B-	B-	B-
Q4-16	B-	B	C+
Q4-15	B-	B+	C

Asset & Performance History

Date	NAV	1-Year Total Return
2016	21.41	9.67
2015	20	-2.24
2014	21.34	7.52
2013	20.43	17.27
2012	17.88	11.06
2011	16.6	4.78

Total Assets: $110,348,505,468

Asset Allocation

Asset	%
Cash	1%
Stocks	72%
US Stocks	51%
Bonds	22%
US Bonds	20%
Other	3%

Services Offered: Systematic Withdrawal Plan, Automatic Investment Plan, Phone Exchange, Retirement Investment

Investment Strategy: The investment seeks to provide investors with current income while secondarily striving for capital growth. Normally the fund invests primarily in income-producing securities. These include equity securities, such as dividend-paying common stocks, and debt securities, such as interest-paying bonds. Generally at least 60% of the fund's assets will be invested in common stocks and other equity-type securities. The fund may also invest up to 25% of its assets in equity securities of issuers domiciled outside the United States, including issuers in developing countries. **Top Holdings:** Microsoft Corp Lockheed Martin Corp Intel Corp McDonald's Corp DowDuPont Inc

American Funds The Income Fund of America® Class R-3 B- BUY

Ticker	Traded On	NAV	Total Assets ($)	Dividend Yield (TTM)	Turnover Ratio	Expense Ratio
RIDCX	NAS CM	23.28	$110,348,505,468	2.49	42	0.95

Ratings

Reward	C+
Risk	B

Fund Information

Fund Type	Open End
Category	Aggressive Alloc
Sub-Category	Alloc--70% to 85% Equity
Prospectus Objective	Income
Inception Date	Jun-02
Open to New Investments	Y
Minimum Initial Investment	250
Minimum Subsequent Investment	50
Front End Fee	
Back End Fee	

Total Returns (%)

3-Month	6-Month	1-Year	3-Year	5-Year
3.35	7.09	12.94	21.27	56.65

Last Bull Market	14.29
Last Bear Market	-10.22
3-Year Standard Deviation	7.11
3-Year Beta	0.66

Company Information

Provider	American Funds
Manager/Tenure	Dina N. Perry (25), John H. Smet (25), Hilda L. Applbaum (20), 6 others
Website	http://www.americanfunds.com
Address	American Funds 333 South Hope Street Los Angeles CA 90071-1406 United States
Phone Number	800-421-4225

PERFORMANCE

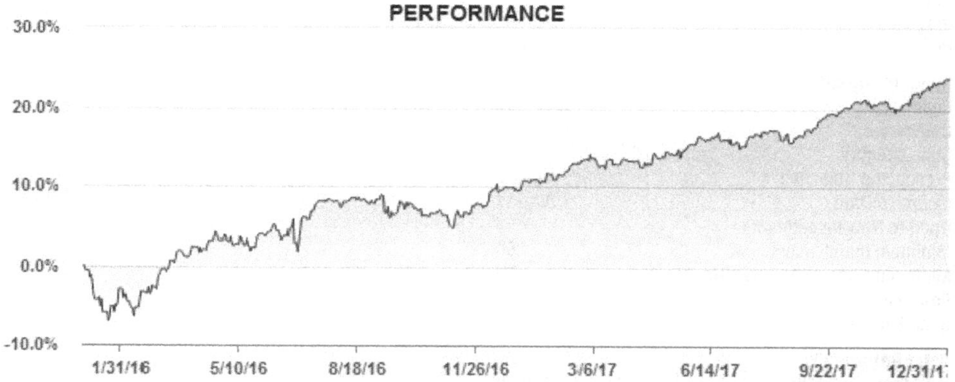

Ratings History

Date	Overall Rating	Risk Rating	Reward Rating
Q4-17	B-	B	C+
Q3-17	B	A	C+
Q2-17	B	A-	B-
Q1-17	B-	B-	B-
Q4-16	B-	B	C+
Q4-15	B-	B+	C

Asset & Performance History

Date	NAV	1-Year Total Return
2016	21.59	10.16
2015	20.16	-1.85
2014	21.51	8.01
2013	20.58	17.76
2012	18.01	11.58
2011	16.71	5.19

Total Assets: $110,348,505,468

Asset Allocation

Asset	%
Cash	1%
Stocks	72%
US Stocks	51%
Bonds	22%
US Bonds	20%
Other	3%

Services Offered: Automatic Investment Plan, Qualified Investment, Phone Exchange

Investment Strategy: The investment seeks to provide investors with current income while secondarily striving for capital growth. Normally the fund invests primarily in income-producing securities. These include equity securities, such as dividend-paying common stocks, and debt securities, such as interest-paying bonds. Generally at least 60% of the fund's assets will be invested in common stocks and other equity-type securities. The fund may also invest up to 25% of its assets in equity securities of issuers domiciled outside the United States, including issuers in developing countries. **Top Holdings:** Microsoft Corp Lockheed Martin Corp Intel Corp McDonald's Corp DowDuPont Inc

American Funds The Income Fund of America® Class R-6 — B- BUY

Ticker	Traded On	NAV	Total Assets ($)	Dividend Yield (TTM)	Turnover Ratio	Expense Ratio
RIDGX	NAS CM	23.37	$110,348,505,468	3.09	42	0.29

Ratings

Reward	C+
Risk	B

Fund Information

Fund Type	Open End
Category	Aggressive Alloc
Sub-Category	Alloc--70% to 85% Equity
Prospectus Objective	Income
Inception Date	May-09
Open to New Investments	Y
Minimum Initial Investment	250
Minimum Subsequent Investment	50
Front End Fee	
Back End Fee	

Total Returns (%)

3-Month	6-Month	1-Year	3-Year	5-Year
3.50	7.42	13.67	23.62	61.77

Last Bull Market	14.74
Last Bear Market	-9.94
3-Year Standard Deviation	7.12
3-Year Beta	0.66

Company Information

Provider	American Funds
Manager/Tenure	Dina N. Perry (25), John H. Smet (25), Hilda L. Applbaum (20), 6 others
Website	http://www.americanfunds.com
Address	American Funds 333 South Hope Street Los Angeles CA 90071-1406 United States
Phone Number	800-421-4225

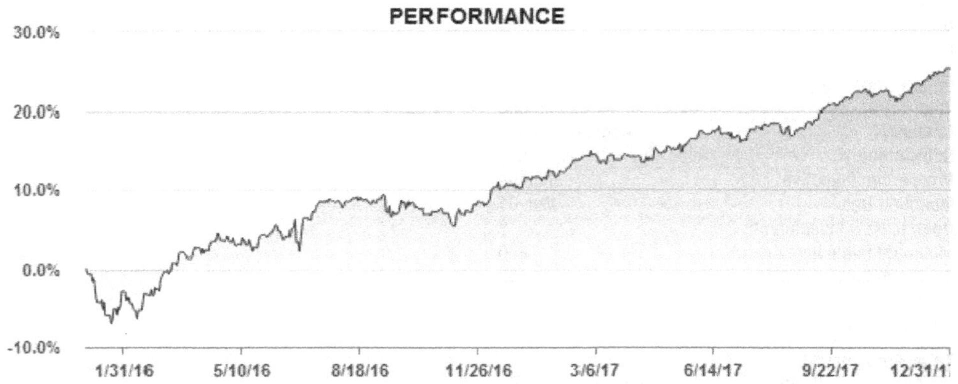

Ratings History

Date	Overall Rating	Risk Rating	Reward Rating
Q4-17	B-	B	C+
Q3-17	B	A	C+
Q2-17	B	A-	B-
Q1-17	B	B-	B
Q4-16	B-	B	B-
Q4-15	C+	C+	C

Asset & Performance History

Date	NAV	1-Year Total Return
2016	21.67	10.88
2015	20.23	-1.24
2014	21.59	8.73
2013	20.65	18.52
2012	18.07	12.26
2011	16.77	5.93

Total Assets: $110,348,505,468

Asset Allocation

Asset	%
Cash	1%
Stocks	72%
US Stocks	51%
Bonds	22%
US Bonds	20%
Other	3%

Services Offered: Automatic Investment Plan, Qualified Investment, Phone Exchange

Investment Strategy: The investment seeks to provide investors with current income while secondarily striving for capital growth. Normally the fund invests primarily in income-producing securities. These include equity securities, such as dividend-paying common stocks, and debt securities, such as interest-paying bonds. Generally at least 60% of the fund's assets will be invested in common stocks and other equity-type securities. The fund may also invest up to 25% of its assets in equity securities of issuers domiciled outside the United States, including issuers in developing countries. **Top Holdings:** Microsoft Corp Lockheed Martin Corp Intel Corp McDonald's Corp DowDuPont Inc

American Funds The Income Fund of America® Class R-2E — B- BUY

Ticker	Traded On	NAV	Total Assets ($)	Dividend Yield (TTM)	Turnover Ratio	Expense Ratio
RIEBX	NAS CM	23.31	$110,348,505,468	2.39	42	1.09

Ratings

Reward	C+
Risk	B

Fund Information

Fund Type	Open End
Category	Aggressive Alloc
Sub-Category	Alloc--70% to 85% Equity
Prospectus Objective	Income
Inception Date	Aug-14
Open to New Investments	Y
Minimum Initial Investment	250
Minimum Subsequent Investment	50
Front End Fee	
Back End Fee	

Total Returns (%)

3-Month	6-Month	1-Year	3-Year	5-Year
3.31	7.02	12.75	20.87	56.44

Last Bull Market	14.28
Last Bear Market	-10.2
3-Year Standard Deviation	7.09
3-Year Beta	0.66

Company Information

Provider	American Funds
Manager/Tenure	Dina N. Perry (25), John H. Smet (25), Hilda L. Applbaum (20), 6 others
Website	http://www.americanfunds.com
Address	American Funds 333 South Hope Street Los Angeles CA 90071-1406 United States
Phone Number	800-421-4225

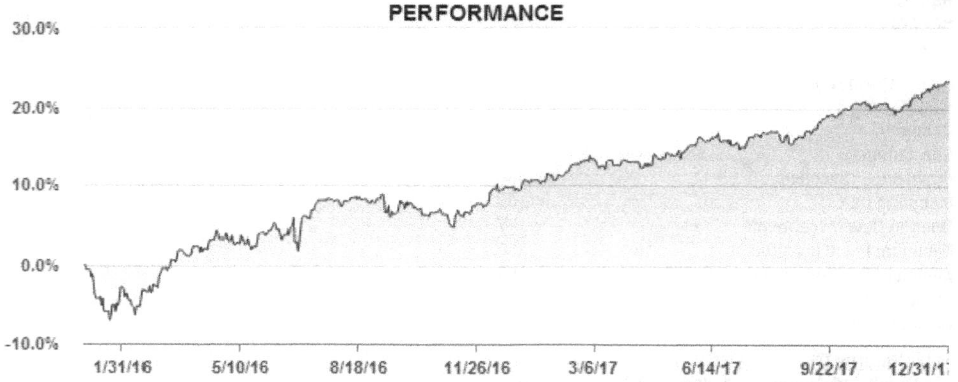

Ratings History

Date	Overall Rating	Risk Rating	Reward Rating
Q4-17	B-	B	C+
Q3-17	B	A	C+
Q2-17	B	A-	B-
Q1-17	B-	B-	B-
Q4-16	B-	B	C+
Q4-15	B-	B+	C

Asset & Performance History

Date	NAV	1-Year Total Return
2016	21.63	10.06
2015	20.2	-1.92
2014	21.57	8.15
2013		17.83
2012		11.55
2011		5.2

Total Assets: $110,348,505,468

Asset Allocation

Asset	%
Cash	1%
Stocks	72%
US Stocks	51%
Bonds	22%
US Bonds	20%
Other	3%

Services Offered: Automatic Investment Plan, Qualified Investment, Phone Exchange

Investment Strategy: The investment seeks to provide investors with current income while secondarily striving for capital growth. Normally the fund invests primarily in income-producing securities. These include equity securities, such as dividend-paying common stocks, and debt securities, such as interest-paying bonds. Generally at least 60% of the fund's assets will be invested in common stocks and other equity-type securities. The fund may also invest up to 25% of its assets in equity securities of issuers domiciled outside the United States, including issuers in developing countries. **Top Holdings:** Microsoft Corp Lockheed Martin Corp Intel Corp McDonald's Corp DowDuPont Inc

American Funds Capital Income Builder® Class R-3

B- **BUY**

Ticker	Traded On	NAV	Total Assets ($)	Dividend Yield (TTM)	Turnover Ratio	Expense Ratio
RIRCX	NAS CM	62.82	$108,816,328,721	2.86	47	0.96

Ratings

Reward	C+
Risk	B

Fund Information

Fund Type	Open End
Category	Alloc
Sub-Category	World Alloc
Prospectus Objective	Equity-Income
Inception Date	Jun-02
Open to New Investments	Y
Minimum Initial Investment	250
Minimum Subsequent Investment	50
Front End Fee	
Back End Fee	

Total Returns (%)

3-Month	6-Month	1-Year	3-Year	5-Year
2.33	5.47	13.82	16.45	43.56

Last Bull Market	12.55
Last Bear Market	-10.1
3-Year Standard Deviation	7.54
3-Year Beta	0.63

Company Information

Provider	American Funds
Manager/Tenure	James B. Lovelace (25), Joyce E. Gordon (17), David A. Hoag (13), 10 others
Website	http://www.americanfunds.com
Address	American Funds 333 South Hope Street Los Angeles CA 90071-1406 United States
Phone Number	800-421-4225

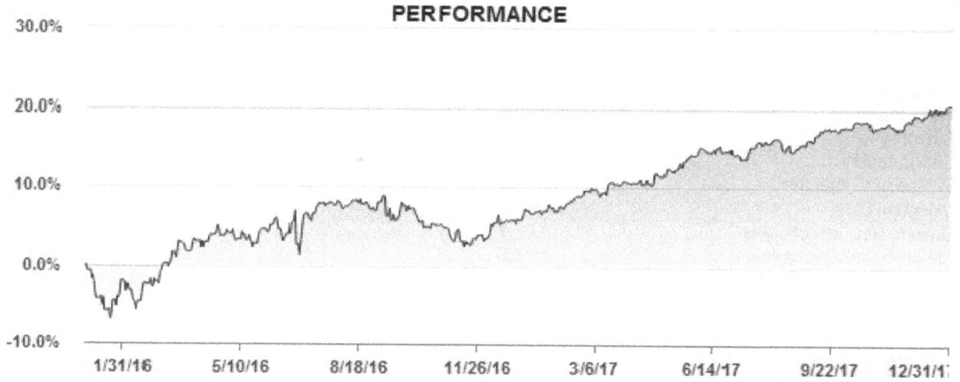

Ratings History

Date	Overall Rating	Risk Rating	Reward Rating
Q4-17	B-	B	C+
Q3-17	B	B+	C+
Q2-17	B-	B+	C+
Q1-17	C+	C+	C+
Q4-16	C+	B	C
Q4-15	B-	B+	C

Asset & Performance History

Date	NAV	1-Year Total Return
2016	57.65	6.54
2015	55.85	-3.28
2014	59.58	6.22
2013	58.55	14.5
2012	52.77	11.41
2011	49.22	2.46

Total Assets: $108,816,328,721

Asset Allocation

Asset	%
Cash	1%
Stocks	70%
US Stocks	33%
Bonds	25%
US Bonds	23%
Other	2%

Services Offered: Automatic Investment Plan, Qualified Investment, Phone Exchange

Investment Strategy: The investment seeks a level of current income and a growing stream of income over years; growth of capital is the secondary objective. The fund normally will invest at least 90% of its assets in income-producing securities (with at least 50% of its assets in common stocks and other equity securities). It invests primarily in a broad range of income-producing securities, including common stocks and bonds. In seeking to provide the investors with a level of current income that exceeds the average yield on U.S. stocks, the fund generally looks to the average yield on stocks of companies listed on the S&P 500 Index. **Top Holdings:** AbbVie Inc Philip Morris International Inc Verizon Communications Inc Sampo Oyj A Novartis AG

American Funds Capital Income Builder® Class 529-E

B- **BUY**

Ticker	Traded On	NAV	Total Assets ($)	Dividend Yield (TTM)	Turnover Ratio	Expense Ratio
CIREX	NAS CM	62.81	$108,816,328,721	2.9	47	0.92

Ratings

Reward	C+
Risk	B

Fund Information

Fund Type	Open End
Category	Alloc
Sub-Category	World Alloc
Prospectus Objective	Equity-Income
Inception Date	Mar-02
Open to New Investments	Y
Minimum Initial Investment	250
Minimum Subsequent Investment	50
Front End Fee	
Back End Fee	

Total Returns (%)

3-Month	6-Month	1-Year	3-Year	5-Year
2.33	5.49	13.88	16.58	43.80

Last Bull Market	12.54
Last Bear Market	-10.09
3-Year Standard Deviation	7.55
3-Year Beta	0.63

Company Information

Provider	American Funds
Manager/Tenure	James B. Lovelace (25), Joyce E. Gordon (17), David A. Hoag (13), 10 others
Website	http://www.americanfunds.com
Address	American Funds 333 South Hope Street Los Angeles CA 90071-1406 United States
Phone Number	800-421-4225

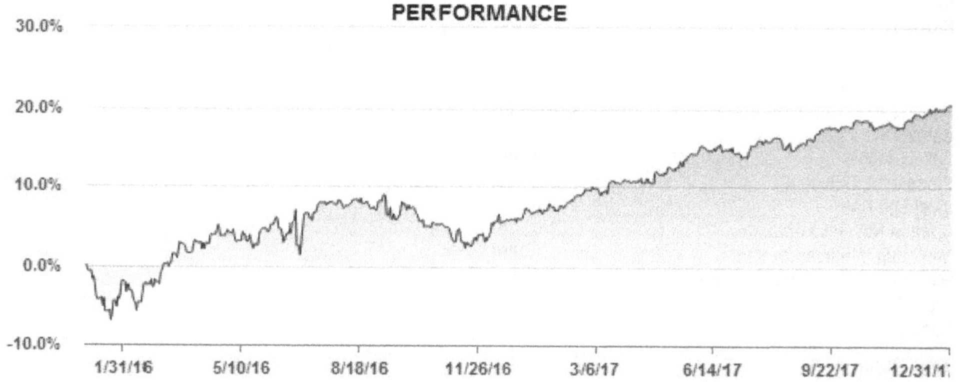

Ratings History

Date	Overall Rating	Risk Rating	Reward Rating
Q4-17	B-	B	C+
Q3-17	B	B+	C+
Q2-17	B	B+	C+
Q1-17	C+	C+	C+
Q4-16	C+	B	C
Q4-15	B-	B+	C

Asset & Performance History

Date	NAV	1-Year Total Return
2016	57.64	6.59
2015	55.84	-3.25
2014	59.57	6.26
2013	58.54	14.5
2012	52.77	11.44
2011	49.22	2.5

Total Assets: $108,816,328,721

Asset Allocation

Asset	%
Cash	1%
Stocks	70%
US Stocks	33%
Bonds	25%
US Bonds	23%
Other	2%

Services Offered: Systematic Withdrawal Plan, Automatic Investment Plan, Qualified Investment, Phone Exchange, Retirement Investment

Investment Strategy: The investment seeks a level of current income and a growing stream of income over years; growth of capital is the secondary objective. The fund normally will invest at least 90% of its assets in income-producing securities (with at least 50% of its assets in common stocks and other equity securities). It invests primarily in a broad range of income-producing securities, including common stocks and bonds. In seeking to provide the investors with a level of current income that exceeds the average yield on U.S. stocks, the fund generally looks to the average yield on stocks of companies listed on the S&P 500 Index. **Top Holdings:** AbbVie Inc Philip Morris International Inc Verizon Communications Inc Sampo Oyj A Novartis AG

American Funds Capital Income Builder® Class F-1 B- BUY

Ticker	Traded On	NAV	Total Assets ($)	Dividend Yield (TTM)	Turnover Ratio	Expense Ratio
CIBFX	NAS CM	62.81	$108,816,328,721	3.12	47	0.67

Ratings

Reward	C+
Risk	B

Fund Information

Fund Type	Open End
Category	Alloc
Sub-Category	World Alloc
Prospectus Objective	Equity-Income
Inception Date	Mar-01
Open to New Investments	Y
Minimum Initial Investment	250
Minimum Subsequent Investment	50
Front End Fee	
Back End Fee	

Total Returns (%)

3-Month	6-Month	1-Year	3-Year	5-Year
2.39	5.61	14.13	17.43	45.62

Last Bull Market	12.75
Last Bear Market	-9.97
3-Year Standard Deviation	7.54
3-Year Beta	0.63

Company Information

Provider	American Funds
Manager/Tenure	James B. Lovelace (25), Joyce E. Gordon (17), David A. Hoag (13), 10 others
Website	http://www.americanfunds.com
Address	American Funds 333 South Hope Street Los Angeles CA 90071-1406 United States
Phone Number	800-421-4225

PERFORMANCE

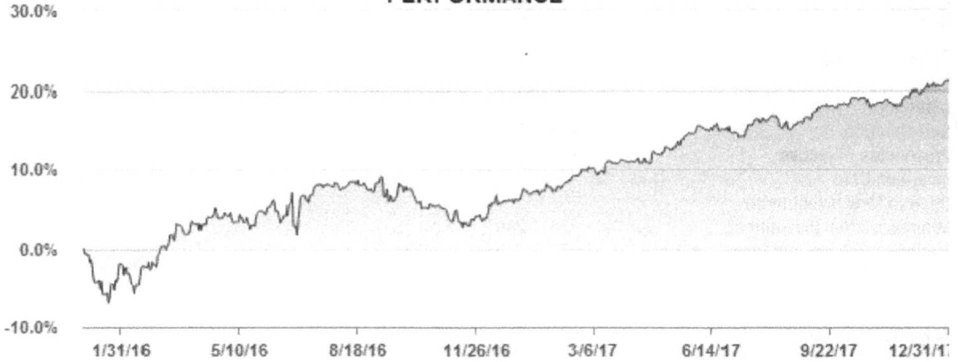

Ratings History

Date	Overall Rating	Risk Rating	Reward Rating
Q4-17	B-	B	C+
Q3-17	B	A-	C+
Q2-17	B	B+	C+
Q1-17	C+	C+	B-
Q4-16	C+	B	C
Q4-15	C+	B-	C

Asset & Performance History

Date	NAV	1-Year Total Return
2016	57.64	6.83
2015	55.85	-2.99
2014	59.59	6.55
2013	58.55	14.82
2012	52.78	11.8
2011	49.22	2.8

Total Assets: $108,816,328,721

Asset Allocation

Asset	%
Cash	1%
Stocks	70%
US Stocks	33%
Bonds	25%
US Bonds	23%
Other	2%

Services Offered: Systematic Withdrawal Plan, Automatic Investment Plan, Qualified Investment, Phone Exchange, Retirement Investment

Investment Strategy: The investment seeks a level of current income and a growing stream of income over years; growth of capital is the secondary objective. The fund normally will invest at least 90% of its assets in income-producing securities (with at least 50% of its assets in common stocks and other equity securities). It invests primarily in a broad range of income-producing securities, including common stocks and bonds. In seeking to provide the investors with a level of current income that exceeds the average yield on U.S. stocks, the fund generally looks to the average yield on stocks of companies listed on the S&P 500 Index. **Top Holdings:** AbbVie Inc Philip Morris International Inc Verizon Communications Inc Sampo Oyj A Novartis AG

American Funds Capital Income Builder® Class R-2E B- BUY

Ticker	Traded On	NAV	Total Assets ($)	Dividend Yield (TTM)	Turnover Ratio	Expense Ratio
RCEEX	NAS CM	62.6	$108,816,328,721	2.77	47	1.11

Ratings

Reward	C+
Risk	B

Fund Information

Fund Type	Open End
Category	Alloc
Sub-Category	World Alloc
Prospectus Objective	Equity-Income
Inception Date	Aug-14
Open to New Investments	Y
Minimum Initial Investment	250
Minimum Subsequent Investment	50
Front End Fee	
Back End Fee	

Total Returns (%)

3-Month	6-Month	1-Year	3-Year	5-Year
2.29	5.39	13.67	16.09	43.17

Last Bull Market	12.54
Last Bear Market	-10.1
3-Year Standard Deviation	7.53
3-Year Beta	0.63

Company Information

Provider	American Funds
Manager/Tenure	James B. Lovelace (25), Joyce E. Gordon (17), David A. Hoag (13), 10 others
Website	http://www.americanfunds.com
Address	American Funds 333 South Hope Street Los Angeles CA 90071-1406 United States
Phone Number	800-421-4225

PERFORMANCE

Ratings History

Date	Overall Rating	Risk Rating	Reward Rating
Q4-17	B-	B	C+
Q3-17	B	B+	C+
Q2-17	B-	B+	C+
Q1-17	C+	C+	C+
Q4-16	C+	B	C
Q4-15	B-	B+	C

Asset & Performance History

Date	NAV	1-Year Total Return
2016	57.47	6.41
2015	55.71	-3.33
2014	59.52	6.26
2013		14.49
2012		11.41
2011		2.49

Total Assets: $108,816,328,721

Asset Allocation

Asset	%
Cash	1%
Stocks	70%
US Stocks	33%
Bonds	25%
US Bonds	23%
Other	2%

Services Offered: Automatic Investment Plan, Qualified Investment, Phone Exchange

Investment Strategy: The investment seeks a level of current income and a growing stream of income over years; growth of capital is the secondary objective. The fund normally will invest at least 90% of its assets in income-producing securities (with at least 50% of its assets in common stocks and other equity securities). It invests primarily in a broad range of income-producing securities, including common stocks and bonds. In seeking to provide the investors with a level of current income that exceeds the average yield on U.S. stocks, the fund generally looks to the average yield on stocks of companies listed on the S&P 500 Index. **Top Holdings:** AbbVie Inc Philip Morris International Inc Verizon Communications Inc Sampo Oyj A Novartis AG

American Funds Capital Income Builder® Class R-5E B- BUY

Ticker	Traded On	NAV	Total Assets ($)	Dividend Yield (TTM)	Turnover Ratio	Expense Ratio
RIRHX	NAS CM	62.74	$108,816,328,721	3.38	47	0.46

Ratings

Reward	C+
Risk	B

Fund Information

Fund Type	Open End
Category	Alloc
Sub-Category	World Alloc
Prospectus Objective	Equity-Income
Inception Date	Nov-15
Open to New Investments	Y
Minimum Initial Investment	250
Minimum Subsequent Investment	50
Front End Fee	
Back End Fee	

Total Returns (%)

3-Month	6-Month	1-Year	3-Year	5-Year
2.45	5.75	14.40	17.99	46.50

Last Bull Market	12.77
Last Bear Market	-9.97
3-Year Standard Deviation	7.54
3-Year Beta	0.63

Company Information

Provider	American Funds
Manager/Tenure	James B. Lovelace (25), Joyce E. Gordon (17), David A. Hoag (13), 10 others
Website	http://www.americanfunds.com
Address	American Funds 333 South Hope Street Los Angeles CA 90071-1406 United States
Phone Number	800-421-4225

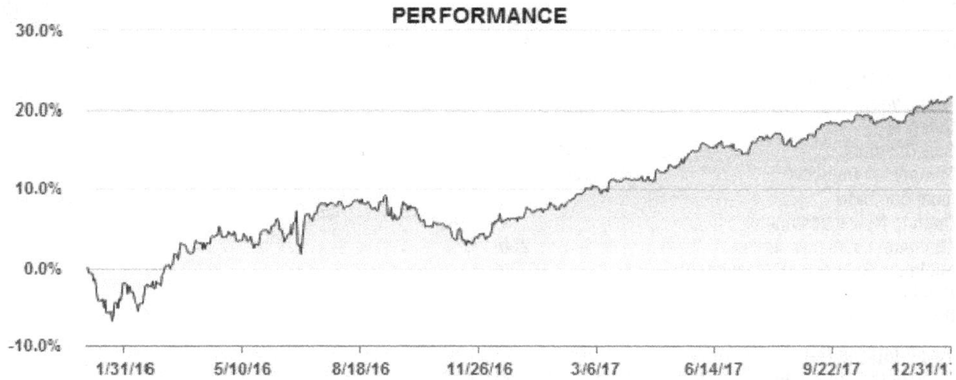

Ratings History

Date	Overall Rating	Risk Rating	Reward Rating
Q4-17	B-	B	C+
Q3-17	B	A-	C+
Q2-17	B	B+	C+
Q1-17	B-	C+	B-
Q4-16	C+	B	C
Q4-15			

Asset & Performance History

Date	NAV	1-Year Total Return
2016	57.58	6.99
2015	55.82	-2.91
2014		6.61
2013		14.9
2012		11.81
2011		2.85

Total Assets: $108,816,328,721

Asset Allocation

Asset	%
Cash	1%
Stocks	70%
US Stocks	33%
Bonds	25%
US Bonds	23%
Other	2%

Services Offered: Automatic Investment Plan, Qualified Investment, Phone Exchange

Investment Strategy: The investment seeks a level of current income and a growing stream of income over years; growth of capital is the secondary objective. The fund normally will invest at least 90% of its assets in income-producing securities (with at least 50% of its assets in common stocks and other equity securities). It invests primarily in a broad range of income-producing securities, including common stocks and bonds. In seeking to provide the investors with a level of current income that exceeds the average yield on U.S. stocks, the fund generally looks to the average yield on stocks of companies listed on the S&P 500 Index. **Top Holdings:** AbbVie Inc Philip Morris International Inc Verizon Communications Inc Sampo Oyj A Novartis AG

American Funds Capital Income Builder® Class 529-A B- BUY

Ticker	Traded On	NAV	Total Assets ($)	Dividend Yield (TTM)	Turnover Ratio	Expense Ratio
CIRAX	NAS CM	62.79	$108,816,328,721	3.12	47	0.71

Ratings

Reward	C+
Risk	B

Fund Information

Fund Type	Open End
Category	Alloc
Sub-Category	World Alloc
Prospectus Objective	Equity-Income
Inception Date	Feb-02
Open to New Investments	Y
Minimum Initial Investment	250
Minimum Subsequent Investment	50
Front End Fee	5.75
Back End Fee	

Total Returns (%)

3-Month	6-Month	1-Year	3-Year	5-Year
2.40	5.61	14.13	17.38	45.48

Last Bull Market	12.73
Last Bear Market	-10.01
3-Year Standard Deviation	7.54
3-Year Beta	0.63

Company Information

Provider	American Funds
Manager/Tenure	James B. Lovelace (25), Joyce E. Gordon (17), David A. Hoag (13), 10 others
Website	http://www.americanfunds.com
Address	American Funds 333 South Hope Street Los Angeles CA 90071-1406 United States
Phone Number	800-421-4225

Ratings History

Date	Overall Rating	Risk Rating	Reward Rating
Q4-17	B-	B	C+
Q3-17	B	A-	C+
Q2-17	B	B+	C+
Q1-17	C+	C+	C+
Q4-16	C+	B	C
Q4-15	C+	B-	C

Asset & Performance History

Date	NAV	1-Year Total Return
2016	57.63	6.83
2015	55.83	-3.03
2014	59.57	6.51
2013	58.54	14.8
2012	52.76	11.71
2011	49.21	2.75

Total Assets: $108,816,328,721

Asset Allocation

Asset	%
Cash	1%
Stocks	70%
US Stocks	33%
Bonds	25%
US Bonds	23%
Other	2%

Services Offered: Systematic Withdrawal Plan, Automatic Investment Plan, Qualified Investment, Phone Exchange, Retirement Investment

Investment Strategy: The investment seeks a level of current income and a growing stream of income over years; growth of capital is the secondary objective. The fund normally will invest at least 90% of its assets in income-producing securities (with at least 50% of its assets in common stocks and other equity securities). It invests primarily in a broad range of income-producing securities, including common stocks and bonds. In seeking to provide the investors with a level of current income that exceeds the average yield on U.S. stocks, the fund generally looks to the average yield on stocks of companies listed on the S&P 500 Index. **Top Holdings:** AbbVie Inc Philip Morris International Inc Verizon Communications Inc Sampo Oyj A Novartis AG

American Funds Capital Income Builder® Class 529-F — B- BUY

Ticker	Traded On	NAV	Total Assets ($)	Dividend Yield (TTM)	Turnover Ratio	Expense Ratio
CIRFX	NAS CM	62.8	$108,816,328,721	3.34	47	0.46

Ratings

Reward	C+
Risk	B

Fund Information

Fund Type	Open End
Category	Alloc
Sub-Category	World Alloc
Prospectus Objective	Equity-Income
Inception Date	Sep-02
Open to New Investments	Y
Minimum Initial Investment	250
Minimum Subsequent Investment	50
Front End Fee	
Back End Fee	

Total Returns (%)

3-Month	6-Month	1-Year	3-Year	5-Year
2.45	5.74	14.40	18.17	47.13

Last Bull Market	12.84
Last Bear Market	-9.91
3-Year Standard Deviation	7.55
3-Year Beta	0.63

Company Information

Provider	American Funds
Manager/Tenure	James B. Lovelace (25), Joyce E. Gordon (17), David A. Hoag (13), 10 others
Website	http://www.americanfunds.com
Address	American Funds 333 South Hope Street Los Angeles CA 90071-1406 United States
Phone Number	800-421-4225

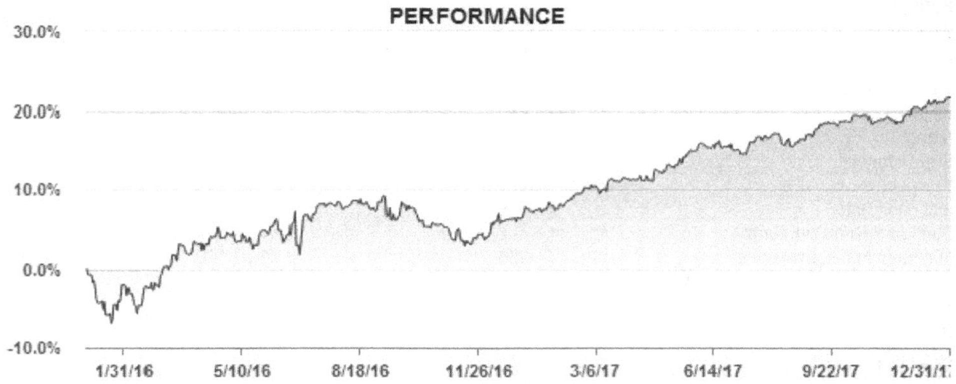

Ratings History

Date	Overall Rating	Risk Rating	Reward Rating
Q4-17	B-	B	C+
Q3-17	B	A-	C+
Q2-17	B	B+	C+
Q1-17	B-	C+	B-
Q4-16	C+	B	C
Q4-15	C+	B-	C

Asset & Performance History

Date	NAV	1-Year Total Return
2016	57.63	7.06
2015	55.84	-2.79
2014	59.57	6.74
2013	58.54	15.05
2012	52.76	11.95
2011	49.21	2.98

Total Assets: $108,816,328,721

Asset Allocation

Asset	%
Cash	1%
Stocks	70%
US Stocks	33%
Bonds	25%
US Bonds	23%
Other	2%

Services Offered: Systematic Withdrawal Plan, Automatic Investment Plan, Qualified Investment, Phone Exchange, Retirement Investment

Investment Strategy: The investment seeks a level of current income and a growing stream of income over years; growth of capital is the secondary objective. The fund normally will invest at least 90% of its assets in income-producing securities (with at least 50% of its assets in common stocks and other equity securities). It invests primarily in a broad range of income-producing securities, including common stocks and bonds. In seeking to provide the investors with a level of current income that exceeds the average yield on U.S. stocks, the fund generally looks to the average yield on stocks of companies listed on the S&P 500 Index. **Top Holdings:** AbbVie Inc Philip Morris International Inc Verizon Communications Inc Sampo Oyj A Novartis AG

American Funds Capital Income Builder® Class R-6 — B- BUY

Ticker	Traded On	NAV	Total Assets ($)	Dividend Yield (TTM)	Turnover Ratio	Expense Ratio
RIRGX	NAS CM	62.8	$108,816,328,721	3.47	47	0.3

Ratings

Reward	C+
Risk	B

Fund Information

Fund Type	Open End
Category	Alloc
Sub-Category	World Alloc
Prospectus Objective	Equity-Income
Inception Date	May-09
Open to New Investments	Y
Minimum Initial Investment	250
Minimum Subsequent Investment	50
Front End Fee	
Back End Fee	

Total Returns (%)

3-Month	6-Month	1-Year	3-Year	5-Year
2.48	5.81	14.56	18.72	48.33

Last Bull Market	12.97
Last Bear Market	-9.85
3-Year Standard Deviation	7.55
3-Year Beta	0.63

Company Information

Provider	American Funds
Manager/Tenure	James B. Lovelace (25), Joyce E. Gordon (17), David A. Hoag (13), 10 others
Website	http://www.americanfunds.com
Address	American Funds 333 South Hope Street Los Angeles CA 90071-1406 United States
Phone Number	800-421-4225

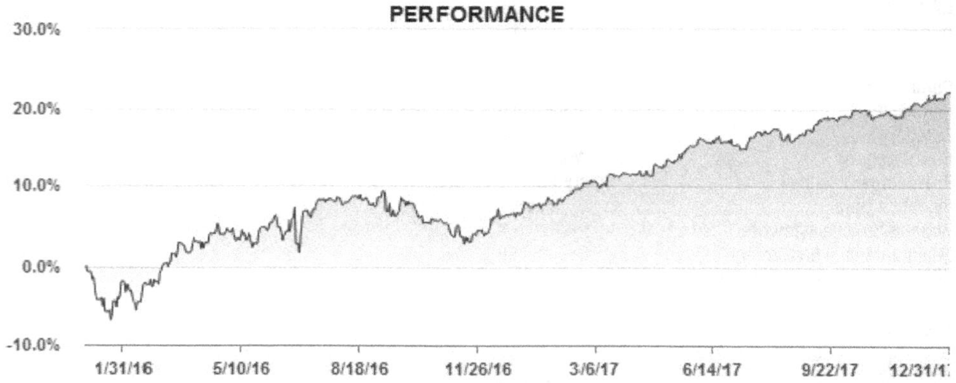

Ratings History

Date	Overall Rating	Risk Rating	Reward Rating
Q4-17	B-	B	C+
Q3-17	B	A-	C+
Q2-17	B	B+	C+
Q1-17	B-	B-	B-
Q4-16	C+	B	C
Q4-15	C+	B-	C

Asset & Performance History

Date	NAV	1-Year Total Return
2016	57.63	7.22
2015	55.84	-2.63
2014	59.57	6.92
2013	58.54	15.24
2012	52.77	12.18
2011	49.21	3.14

Total Assets: $108,816,328,721

Asset Allocation

Asset	%
Cash	1%
Stocks	70%
US Stocks	33%
Bonds	25%
US Bonds	23%
Other	2%

Services Offered: Automatic Investment Plan, Qualified Investment, Phone Exchange

Investment Strategy: The investment seeks a level of current income and a growing stream of income over years; growth of capital is the secondary objective. The fund normally will invest at least 90% of its assets in income-producing securities (with at least 50% of its assets in common stocks and other equity securities). It invests primarily in a broad range of income-producing securities, including common stocks and bonds. In seeking to provide the investors with a level of current income that exceeds the average yield on U.S. stocks, the fund generally looks to the average yield on stocks of companies listed on the S&P 500 Index. **Top Holdings:** AbbVie Inc Philip Morris International Inc Verizon Communications Inc Sampo Oyj A Novartis AG

American Funds Capital Income Builder® Class 529-C

B- BUY

Ticker	Traded On	NAV	Total Assets ($)	Dividend Yield (TTM)	Turnover Ratio	Expense Ratio
CIRCX	NAS CM	62.86	$108,816,328,721	2.39	47	1.46

Ratings

Reward	C+
Risk	B

Fund Information

Fund Type	Open End
Category	Alloc
Sub-Category	World Alloc
Prospectus Objective	Equity-Income
Inception Date	Feb-02
Open to New Investments	Y
Minimum Initial Investment	250
Minimum Subsequent Investment	50
Front End Fee	
Back End Fee	1.00

Total Returns (%)

3-Month	6-Month	1-Year	3-Year	5-Year
2.20	5.22	13.26	14.71	39.96

Last Bull Market	12.2
Last Bear Market	-10.3
3-Year Standard Deviation	7.54
3-Year Beta	0.63

Company Information

Provider	American Funds
Manager/Tenure	James B. Lovelace (25), Joyce E. Gordon (17), David A. Hoag (13), 10 others
Website	http://www.americanfunds.com
Address	American Funds 333 South Hope Street Los Angeles CA 90071-1406 United States
Phone Number	800-421-4225

Ratings History

Date	Overall Rating	Risk Rating	Reward Rating
Q4-17	B-	B	C+
Q3-17	B	B+	C+
Q2-17	B-	C	C+
Q1-17	C+	C+	C+
Q4-16	C	B-	C
Q4-15	B-	B+	C

Asset & Performance History

Date	NAV	1-Year Total Return
2016	57.65	6.02
2015	55.84	-3.78
2014	59.57	5.69
2013	58.54	13.89
2012	52.77	10.85
2011	49.22	1.94

Total Assets: $108,816,328,721

Asset Allocation

Asset	%
Cash	1%
Stocks	70%
US Stocks	33%
Bonds	25%
US Bonds	23%
Other	2%

Services Offered: Systematic Withdrawal Plan, Automatic Investment Plan, Qualified Investment, Phone Exchange, Retirement Investment

Investment Strategy: The investment seeks a level of current income and a growing stream of income over years; growth of capital is the secondary objective. The fund normally will invest at least 90% of its assets in income-producing securities (with at least 50% of its assets in common stocks and other equity securities). It invests primarily in a broad range of income-producing securities, including common stocks and bonds. In seeking to provide the investors with a level of current income that exceeds the average yield on U.S. stocks, the fund generally looks to the average yield on stocks of companies listed on the S&P 500 Index. **Top Holdings:** AbbVie Inc Philip Morris International Inc Verizon Communications Inc Sampo Oyj A Novartis AG

American Funds Capital Income Builder® Class R-2

B- BUY

Ticker	Traded On	NAV	Total Assets ($)	Dividend Yield (TTM)	Turnover Ratio	Expense Ratio
RIRBX	NAS CM	62.84	$108,816,328,721	2.43	47	1.4

Ratings

Reward	C+
Risk	B

Fund Information

Fund Type	Open End
Category	Alloc
Sub-Category	World Alloc
Prospectus Objective	Equity-Income
Inception Date	May-02
Open to New Investments	Y
Minimum Initial Investment	250
Minimum Subsequent Investment	50
Front End Fee	
Back End Fee	

Total Returns (%)

3-Month	6-Month	1-Year	3-Year	5-Year
2.22	5.23	13.31	14.95	40.53

Last Bull Market	12.26
Last Bear Market	-10.27
3-Year Standard Deviation	7.54
3-Year Beta	0.63

Company Information

Provider	American Funds
Manager/Tenure	James B. Lovelace (25), Joyce E. Gordon (17), David A. Hoag (13), 10 others
Website	http://www.americanfunds.com
Address	American Funds 333 South Hope Street Los Angeles CA 90071-1406 United States
Phone Number	800-421-4225

Ratings History

Date	Overall Rating	Risk Rating	Reward Rating
Q4-17	B-	B	C+
Q3-17	B	B+	C+
Q2-17	B-	C	C+
Q1-17	C+	C+	C+
Q4-16	C+	B	C
Q4-15	B-	B+	C

Asset & Performance History

Date	NAV	1-Year Total Return
2016	57.67	6.09
2015	55.86	-3.68
2014	59.59	5.77
2013	58.56	14.03
2012	52.78	10.94
2011	49.23	2.02

Total Assets: $108,816,328,721

Asset Allocation

Asset	%
Cash	1%
Stocks	70%
US Stocks	33%
Bonds	25%
US Bonds	23%
Other	2%

Services Offered: Automatic Investment Plan, Qualified Investment, Phone Exchange

Investment Strategy: The investment seeks a level of current income and a growing stream of income over years; growth of capital is the secondary objective. The fund normally will invest at least 90% of its assets in income-producing securities (with at least 50% of its assets in common stocks and other equity securities). It invests primarily in a broad range of income-producing securities, including common stocks and bonds. In seeking to provide the investors with a level of current income that exceeds the average yield on U.S. stocks, the fund generally looks to the average yield on stocks of companies listed on the S&P 500 Index. **Top Holdings:** AbbVie Inc Philip Morris International Inc Verizon Communications Inc Sampo Oyj A Novartis AG

American Funds Capital Income Builder® Class F-2 B- BUY

Ticker	Traded On	NAV	Total Assets ($)	Dividend Yield (TTM)	Turnover Ratio	Expense Ratio
CAIFX	NAS CM	62.77	$108,816,328,721	3.37	47	0.4

Ratings

Reward	C+
Risk	B

Fund Information

Fund Type	Open End
Category	Alloc
Sub-Category	World Alloc
Prospectus Objective	Equity-Income
Inception Date	Aug-08
Open to New Investments	Y
Minimum Initial Investment	250
Minimum Subsequent Investment	50
Front End Fee	
Back End Fee	

Total Returns (%)

3-Month	6-Month	1-Year	3-Year	5-Year
2.46	5.76	14.44	18.36	47.54

Last Bull Market	12.92
Last Bear Market	-9.88
3-Year Standard Deviation	7.55
3-Year Beta	0.63

Company Information

Provider	American Funds
Manager/Tenure	James B. Lovelace (25), Joyce E. Gordon (17), David A. Hoag (13), 10 others
Website	http://www.americanfunds.com
Address	American Funds 333 South Hope Street Los Angeles CA 90071-1406 United States
Phone Number	800-421-4225

PERFORMANCE

Ratings History

Date	Overall Rating	Risk Rating	Reward Rating
Q4-17	B-	B	C+
Q3-17	B	A-	C+
Q2-17	B	B+	C+
Q1-17	B-	C+	B-
Q4-16	C+	B	C
Q4-15	C+	B-	C

Asset & Performance History

Date	NAV	1-Year Total Return
2016	57.6	7.12
2015	55.81	-2.75
2014	59.55	6.83
2013	58.52	15.12
2012	52.74	12.06
2011	49.19	3.05

Total Assets: $108,816,328,721

Asset Allocation

Asset	%
Cash	1%
Stocks	70%
US Stocks	33%
Bonds	25%
US Bonds	23%
Other	2%

Services Offered: Systematic Withdrawal Plan, Automatic Investment Plan, Qualified Investment, Phone Exchange, Retirement Investment

Investment Strategy: The investment seeks a level of current income and a growing stream of income over years; growth of capital is the secondary objective. The fund normally will invest at least 90% of its assets in income-producing securities (with at least 50% of its assets in common stocks and other equity securities). It invests primarily in a broad range of income-producing securities, including common stocks and bonds. In seeking to provide the investors with a level of current income that exceeds the average yield on U.S. stocks, the fund generally looks to the average yield on stocks of companies listed on the S&P 500 Index. **Top Holdings:** AbbVie Inc Philip Morris International Inc Verizon Communications Inc Sampo Oyj A Novartis AG

American Funds Capital Income Builder® Class R-1 B- BUY

Ticker	Traded On	NAV	Total Assets ($)	Dividend Yield (TTM)	Turnover Ratio	Expense Ratio
RIRAX	NAS CM	62.84	$108,816,328,721	2.42	47	1.4

Ratings

Reward	C+
Risk	B

Fund Information

Fund Type	Open End
Category	Alloc
Sub-Category	World Alloc
Prospectus Objective	Equity-Income
Inception Date	Jun-02
Open to New Investments	Y
Minimum Initial Investment	250
Minimum Subsequent Investment	50
Front End Fee	
Back End Fee	

Total Returns (%)

3-Month	6-Month	1-Year	3-Year	5-Year
2.20	5.22	13.29	14.88	40.40

Last Bull Market	12.24
Last Bear Market	-10.27
3-Year Standard Deviation	7.54
3-Year Beta	0.63

Company Information

Provider	American Funds
Manager/Tenure	James B. Lovelace (25), Joyce E. Gordon (17), David A. Hoag (13), 10 others
Website	http://www.americanfunds.com
Address	American Funds 333 South Hope Street Los Angeles CA 90071-1406 United States
Phone Number	800-421-4225

PERFORMANCE

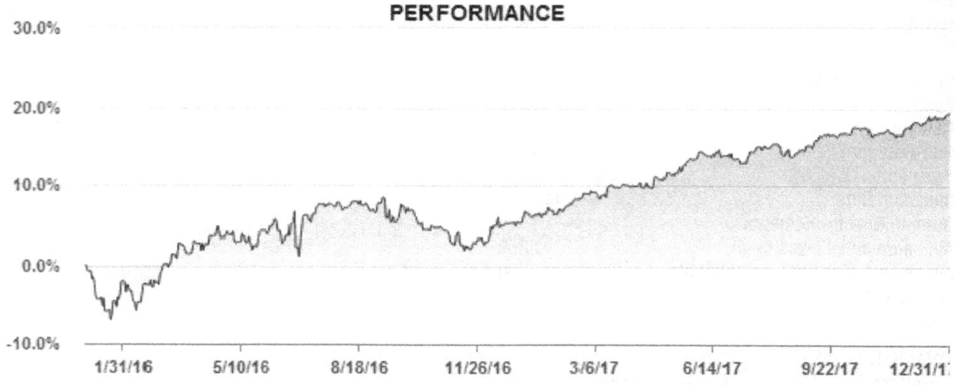

Ratings History

Date	Overall Rating	Risk Rating	Reward Rating
Q4-17	B-	B	C+
Q3-17	B	B+	C+
Q2-17	B-	C	C+
Q1-17	C+	C+	C+
Q4-16	C+	B	C
Q4-15	B-	B+	C

Asset & Performance History

Date	NAV	1-Year Total Return
2016	57.67	6.06
2015	55.87	-3.69
2014	59.59	5.76
2013	58.56	13.99
2012	52.78	10.96
2011	49.22	2

Total Assets: $108,816,328,721

Asset Allocation

Asset	%
Cash	1%
Stocks	70%
US Stocks	33%
Bonds	25%
US Bonds	23%
Other	2%

Services Offered: Automatic Investment Plan, Qualified Investment, Phone Exchange

Investment Strategy: The investment seeks a level of current income and a growing stream of income over years; growth of capital is the secondary objective. The fund normally will invest at least 90% of its assets in income-producing securities (with at least 50% of its assets in common stocks and other equity securities). It invests primarily in a broad range of income-producing securities, including common stocks and bonds. In seeking to provide the investors with a level of current income that exceeds the average yield on U.S. stocks, the fund generally looks to the average yield on stocks of companies listed on the S&P 500 Index. **Top Holdings:** AbbVie Inc Philip Morris International Inc Verizon Communications Inc Sampo Oyj A Novartis AG

American Funds Capital Income Builder® Class R-5

B- BUY

Ticker	Traded On	NAV	Total Assets ($)	Dividend Yield (TTM)	Turnover Ratio	Expense Ratio
RIRFX	NAS CM	62.83	$108,816,328,721	3.42	47	0.37

Ratings

Reward	C+
Risk	B

Fund Information

Fund Type	Open End
Category	Alloc
Sub-Category	World Alloc
Prospectus Objective	Equity-Income
Inception Date	May-02
Open to New Investments	Y
Minimum Initial Investment	250
Minimum Subsequent Investment	50
Front End Fee	
Back End Fee	

Total Returns (%)

3-Month	6-Month	1-Year	3-Year	5-Year
2.49	5.78	14.49	18.56	47.97

Last Bull Market	12.94
Last Bear Market	-9.85
3-Year Standard Deviation	7.55
3-Year Beta	0.63

Company Information

Provider	American Funds
Manager/Tenure	James B. Lovelace (25), Joyce E. Gordon (17), David A. Hoag (13), 10 others
Website	http://www.americanfunds.com
Address	American Funds 333 South Hope Street Los Angeles CA 90071-1406 United States
Phone Number	800-421-4225

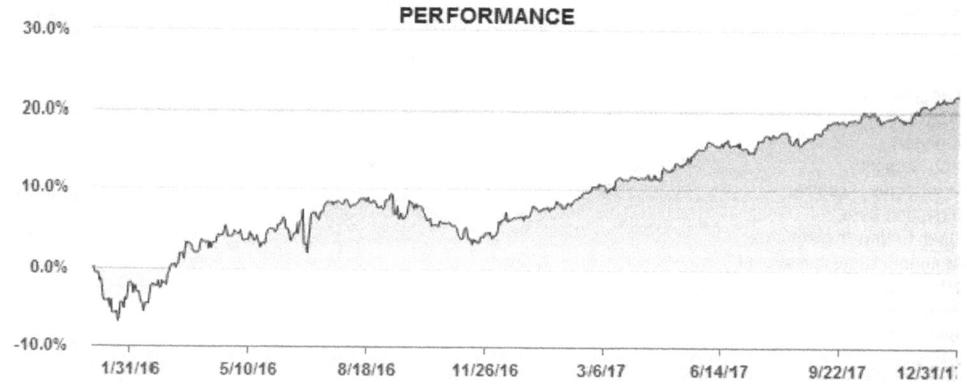

Ratings History

Date	Overall Rating	Risk Rating	Reward Rating
Q4-17	B-	B	C+
Q3-17	B	A-	C+
Q2-17	B	B+	C+
Q1-17	B-	B-	B-
Q4-16	C+	B	C
Q4-15	C+	B-	C

Asset & Performance History

Date	NAV	1-Year Total Return
2016	57.66	7.19
2015	55.85	-2.7
2014	59.59	6.86
2013	58.56	15.19
2012	52.78	12.12
2011	49.22	3.09

Total Assets: $108,816,328,721

Asset Allocation

Asset	%
Cash	1%
Stocks	70%
US Stocks	33%
Bonds	25%
US Bonds	23%
Other	2%

Services Offered: Automatic Investment Plan, Qualified Investment, Phone Exchange

Investment Strategy: The investment seeks a level of current income and a growing stream of income over years; growth of capital is the secondary objective. The fund normally will invest at least 90% of its assets in income-producing securities (with at least 50% of its assets in common stocks and other equity securities). It invests primarily in a broad range of income-producing securities, including common stocks and bonds. In seeking to provide the investors with a level of current income that exceeds the average yield on U.S. stocks, the fund generally looks to the average yield on stocks of companies listed on the S&P 500 Index. **Top Holdings:** AbbVie Inc Philip Morris International Inc Verizon Communications Inc Sampo Oyj A Novartis AG

American Funds Capital Income Builder® Class R-4

B- BUY

Ticker	Traded On	NAV	Total Assets ($)	Dividend Yield (TTM)	Turnover Ratio	Expense Ratio
RIREX	NAS CM	62.79	$108,816,328,721	3.14	47	0.65

Ratings

Reward	C+
Risk	B

Fund Information

Fund Type	Open End
Category	Alloc
Sub-Category	World Alloc
Prospectus Objective	Equity-Income
Inception Date	May-02
Open to New Investments	Y
Minimum Initial Investment	250
Minimum Subsequent Investment	50
Front End Fee	
Back End Fee	

Total Returns (%)

3-Month	6-Month	1-Year	3-Year	5-Year
2.40	5.63	14.14	17.50	45.76

Last Bull Market	12.73
Last Bear Market	-9.97
3-Year Standard Deviation	7.55
3-Year Beta	0.63

Company Information

Provider	American Funds
Manager/Tenure	James B. Lovelace (25), Joyce E. Gordon (17), David A. Hoag (13), 10 others
Website	http://www.americanfunds.com
Address	American Funds 333 South Hope Street Los Angeles CA 90071-1406 United States
Phone Number	800-421-4225

Ratings History

Date	Overall Rating	Risk Rating	Reward Rating
Q4-17	B-	B	C+
Q3-17	B	A-	C+
Q2-17	B	B+	C+
Q1-17	C+	C+	B-
Q4-16	C+	B	C
Q4-15	C+	B-	C

Asset & Performance History

Date	NAV	1-Year Total Return
2016	57.63	6.86
2015	55.84	-2.97
2014	59.57	6.55
2013	58.54	14.85
2012	52.76	11.78
2011	49.21	2.78

Total Assets: $108,816,328,721

Asset Allocation

Asset	%
Cash	1%
Stocks	70%
US Stocks	33%
Bonds	25%
US Bonds	23%
Other	2%

Services Offered: Automatic Investment Plan, Qualified Investment, Phone Exchange

Investment Strategy: The investment seeks a level of current income and a growing stream of income over years; growth of capital is the secondary objective. The fund normally will invest at least 90% of its assets in income-producing securities (with at least 50% of its assets in common stocks and other equity securities). It invests primarily in a broad range of income-producing securities, including common stocks and bonds. In seeking to provide the investors with a level of current income that exceeds the average yield on U.S. stocks, the fund generally looks to the average yield on stocks of companies listed on the S&P 500 Index. **Top Holdings:** AbbVie Inc Philip Morris International Inc Verizon Communications Inc Sampo Oyj A Novartis AG

American Funds Capital Income Builder® Class A — B- BUY

Ticker	Traded On	NAV	Total Assets ($)	Dividend Yield (TTM)	Turnover Ratio	Expense Ratio
CAIBX	NAS CM	62.82	$108,816,328,721	3.19	47	0.61

Ratings

Reward	C+
Risk	B

Fund Information

Fund Type	Open End
Category	Alloc
Sub-Category	World Alloc
Prospectus Objective	Equity-Income
Inception Date	Jul-87
Open to New Investments	Y
Minimum Initial Investment	250
Minimum Subsequent Investment	50
Front End Fee	5.75
Back End Fee	

Total Returns (%)

3-Month	6-Month	1-Year	3-Year	5-Year
2.42	5.65	14.24	17.71	46.15

Last Bull Market	12.77
Last Bear Market	-9.97
3-Year Standard Deviation	7.54
3-Year Beta	0.63

Company Information

Provider	American Funds
Manager/Tenure	James B. Lovelace (25), Joyce E. Gordon (17), David A. Hoag (13), 10 others
Website	http://www.americanfunds.com
Address	American Funds 333 South Hope Street Los Angeles CA 90071-1406 United States
Phone Number	800-421-4225

PERFORMANCE

Ratings History

Date	Overall Rating	Risk Rating	Reward Rating
Q4-17	B-	B	C+
Q3-17	B	A-	C+
Q2-17	B	B+	C+
Q1-17	C+	C+	B-
Q4-16	C+	B	C
Q4-15	C+	B-	C

Asset & Performance History

Date	NAV	1-Year Total Return
2016	57.64	6.9
2015	55.85	-2.92
2014	59.58	6.61
2013	58.55	14.9
2012	52.77	11.81
2011	49.22	2.85

Total Assets: $108,816,328,721

Asset Allocation

Asset	%
Cash	1%
Stocks	70%
US Stocks	33%
Bonds	25%
US Bonds	23%
Other	2%

Services Offered: Systematic Withdrawal Plan, Automatic Investment Plan, Phone Exchange, Retirement Investment

Investment Strategy: The investment seeks a level of current income and a growing stream of income over years; growth of capital is the secondary objective. The fund normally will invest at least 90% of its assets in income-producing securities (with at least 50% of its assets in common stocks and other equity securities). It invests primarily in a broad range of income-producing securities, including common stocks and bonds. In seeking to provide the investors with a level of current income that exceeds the average yield on U.S. stocks, the fund generally looks to the average yield on stocks of companies listed on the S&P 500 Index. **Top Holdings:** AbbVie Inc Philip Morris International Inc Verizon Communications Inc Sampo Oyj A Novartis AG

American Funds Capital Income Builder® Class C — B- BUY

Ticker	Traded On	NAV	Total Assets ($)	Dividend Yield (TTM)	Turnover Ratio	Expense Ratio
CIBCX	NAS CM	62.9	$108,816,328,721	2.42	47	1.4

Ratings

Reward	C+
Risk	B

Fund Information

Fund Type	Open End
Category	Alloc
Sub-Category	World Alloc
Prospectus Objective	Equity-Income
Inception Date	Mar-01
Open to New Investments	Y
Minimum Initial Investment	250
Minimum Subsequent Investment	50
Front End Fee	
Back End Fee	1.00

Total Returns (%)

3-Month	6-Month	1-Year	3-Year	5-Year
2.20	5.24	13.32	14.91	40.40

Last Bull Market	12.25
Last Bear Market	-10.26
3-Year Standard Deviation	7.54
3-Year Beta	0.63

Company Information

Provider	American Funds
Manager/Tenure	James B. Lovelace (25), Joyce E. Gordon (17), David A. Hoag (13), 10 others
Website	http://www.americanfunds.com
Address	American Funds 333 South Hope Street Los Angeles CA 90071-1406 United States
Phone Number	800-421-4225

PERFORMANCE

Ratings History

Date	Overall Rating	Risk Rating	Reward Rating
Q4-17	B-	B	C+
Q3-17	B	B+	C+
Q2-17	B-	C	C+
Q1-17	C+	C+	C+
Q4-16	C+	B	C
Q4-15	B-	B+	C

Asset & Performance History

Date	NAV	1-Year Total Return
2016	57.71	6.07
2015	55.9	-3.71
2014	59.63	5.77
2013	58.59	13.99
2012	52.8	10.91
2011	49.25	2.03

Total Assets: $108,816,328,721

Asset Allocation

Asset	%
Cash	1%
Stocks	70%
US Stocks	33%
Bonds	25%
US Bonds	23%
Other	2%

Services Offered: Systematic Withdrawal Plan, Automatic Investment Plan, Phone Exchange, Retirement Investment

Investment Strategy: The investment seeks a level of current income and a growing stream of income over years; growth of capital is the secondary objective. The fund normally will invest at least 90% of its assets in income-producing securities (with at least 50% of its assets in common stocks and other equity securities). It invests primarily in a broad range of income-producing securities, including common stocks and bonds. In seeking to provide the investors with a level of current income that exceeds the average yield on U.S. stocks, the fund generally looks to the average yield on stocks of companies listed on the S&P 500 Index. **Top Holdings:** AbbVie Inc Philip Morris International Inc Verizon Communications Inc Sampo Oyj A Novartis AG

American Funds Capital Income Builder® Class F-3 — B- BUY

Ticker	Traded On	NAV	Total Assets ($)	Dividend Yield (TTM)	Turnover Ratio	Expense Ratio
CFIHX	NAS CM	62.8	$108,816,328,721		47	0.3

Ratings

Reward	C+
Risk	B

Fund Information

Fund Type	Open End
Category	Alloc
Sub-Category	World Alloc
Prospectus Objective	Equity-Income
Inception Date	Jan-17
Open to New Investments	Y
Minimum Initial Investment	250
Minimum Subsequent Investment	50
Front End Fee	
Back End Fee	

Total Returns (%)

3-Month	6-Month	1-Year	3-Year	5-Year
2.50	5.81	14.53	18.00	46.51

Last Bull Market	12.77
Last Bear Market	-9.97
3-Year Standard Deviation	7.55
3-Year Beta	0.63

Company Information

Provider	American Funds
Manager/Tenure	James B. Lovelace (25), Joyce E. Gordon (17), David A. Hoag (13), 10 others
Website	http://www.americanfunds.com
Address	American Funds 333 South Hope Street Los Angeles CA 90071-1406 United States
Phone Number	800-421-4225

PERFORMANCE

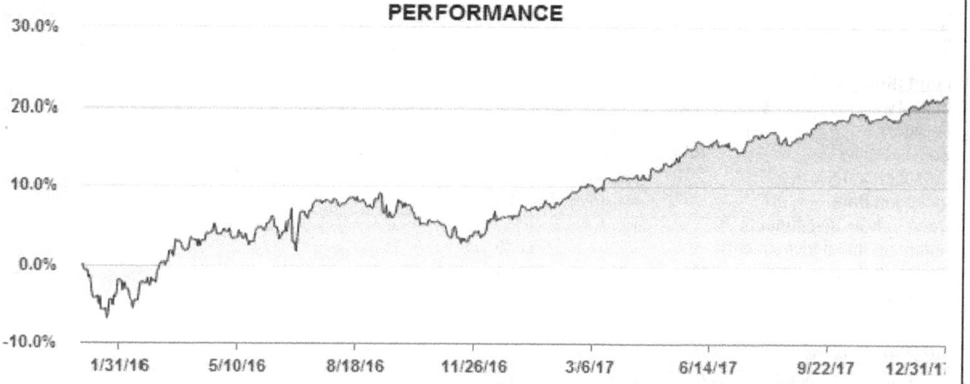

Ratings History

Date	Overall Rating	Risk Rating	Reward Rating
Q4-17	B-	B	C+
Q3-17	B	A-	C+
Q2-17	B		C+
Q1-17	C+	C+	B-
Q4-16			
Q4-15			

Asset & Performance History

Date	NAV	1-Year Total Return
2016		
2015		-2.92
2014		6.61
2013		14.9
2012		11.81
2011		2.85

Total Assets: $108,816,328,721

Asset Allocation

Asset	%
Cash	1%
Stocks	70%
US Stocks	33%
Bonds	25%
US Bonds	23%
Other	2%

Services Offered: Systematic Withdrawal Plan, Automatic Investment Plan, Qualified Investment, Phone Exchange, Retirement Investment

Investment Strategy: The investment seeks a level of current income and a growing stream of income over years; growth of capital is the secondary objective. The fund normally will invest at least 90% of its assets in income-producing securities (with at least 50% of its assets in common stocks and other equity securities). It invests primarily in a broad range of income-producing securities, including common stocks and bonds. In seeking to provide the investors with a level of current income that exceeds the average yield on U.S. stocks, the fund generally looks to the average yield on stocks of companies listed on the S&P 500 Index. **Top Holdings:** AbbVie Inc Philip Morris International Inc Verizon Communications Inc Sampo Oyj A Novartis AG

Vanguard Wellington™ Fund Investor Shares — B- BUY

Ticker	Traded On	NAV	Total Assets ($)	Dividend Yield (TTM)	Turnover Ratio	Expense Ratio
VWELX	NAS CM	42.03	$105,557,742,930	2.33	31	0.25

Ratings

Reward	B-
Risk	B

Fund Information

Fund Type	Open End
Category	Moderate Alloc
Sub-Category	Alloc--50% to 70% Equity
Prospectus Objective	Growth & Income
Inception Date	Jul-29
Open to New Investments	
Minimum Initial Investment	3,000
Minimum Subsequent Investment	1
Front End Fee	
Back End Fee	

Total Returns (%)

3-Month	6-Month	1-Year	3-Year	5-Year
4.52	8.06	14.72	26.62	68.76

Last Bull Market	16.28
Last Bear Market	-10.37
3-Year Standard Deviation	6.8
3-Year Beta	0.66

Company Information

Provider	Vanguard
Manager/Tenure	Edward P. Bousa (14), John C. Keogh (11), Loren L. Moran (0), 1 other
Website	http://www.vanguard.com
Address	Vanguard 100 Vanguard Boulevard Malvern PA 19355 United States
Phone Number	877-662-7447

PERFORMANCE

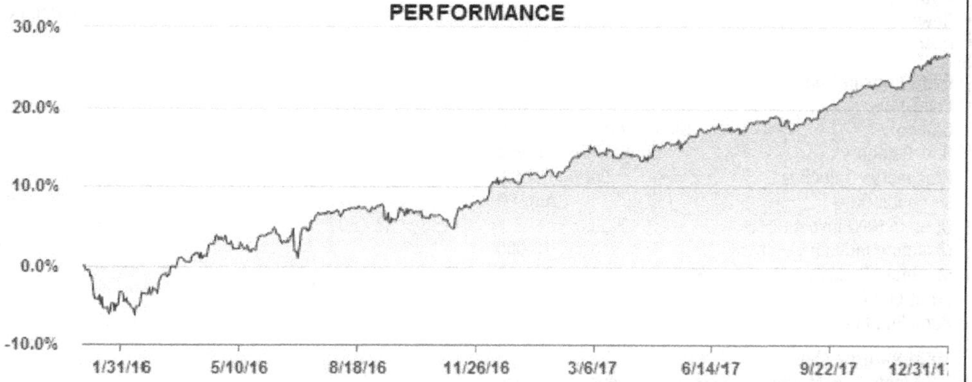

Ratings History

Date	Overall Rating	Risk Rating	Reward Rating
Q4-17	B-	B	B-
Q3-17	B	A	B-
Q2-17	B	A	B-
Q1-17	B	B	B
Q4-16	B	B+	B-
Q4-15	C+	B-	C

Asset & Performance History

Date	NAV	1-Year Total Return
2016	39.06	11.01
2015	36.79	0.05
2014	39.15	9.82
2013	37.94	19.66
2012	33.84	12.57
2011	31.34	3.85

Total Assets: $105,557,742,930

Asset Allocation

Asset	%
Cash	4%
Stocks	65%
US Stocks	53%
Bonds	30%
US Bonds	24%
Other	1%

Services Offered: Systematic Withdrawal Plan, Automatic Investment Plan, Phone Exchange, Wire Redemption

Investment Strategy: The investment seeks to provide long-term capital appreciation and moderate current income. The fund invests 60% to 70% of its assets in dividend-paying and, to a lesser extent, non-dividend-paying common stocks of established large companies. The remaining 30% to 40% of the fund's assets are invested mainly in fixed income securities that the advisor believes will generate a moderate level of current income. These securities include investment-grade corporate bonds, with some exposure to U.S. Treasury and government agency bonds, and mortgage-backed securities. **Top Holdings:** Microsoft Corp JPMorgan Chase & Co Chevron Corp Bank of America Corporation Alphabet Inc A

Vanguard Wellington™ Fund Admiral™ Shares — B- BUY

Ticker	Traded On	NAV	Total Assets ($)	Dividend Yield (TTM)	Turnover Ratio	Expense Ratio
VWENX	NAS CM	72.58	$105,557,742,930	2.41	31	0.16

Ratings

Reward	B-
Risk	B

Fund Information

Fund Type	Open End
Category	Moderate Alloc
Sub-Category	Alloc--50% to 70% Equity
Prospectus Objective	Growth & Income
Inception Date	May-01
Open to New Investments	
Minimum Initial Investment	50,000
Minimum Subsequent Investment	1
Front End Fee	
Back End Fee	

Total Returns (%)

3-Month	6-Month	1-Year	3-Year	5-Year
4.53	8.11	14.81	26.93	69.42

Last Bull Market	16.35
Last Bear Market	-10.37
3-Year Standard Deviation	6.79
3-Year Beta	0.66

Company Information

Provider	Vanguard
Manager/Tenure	Edward P. Bousa (14), John C. Keogh (11), Loren L. Moran (0), 1 other
Website	http://www.vanguard.com
Address	Vanguard 100 Vanguard Boulevard Malvern PA 19355 United States
Phone Number	877-662-7447

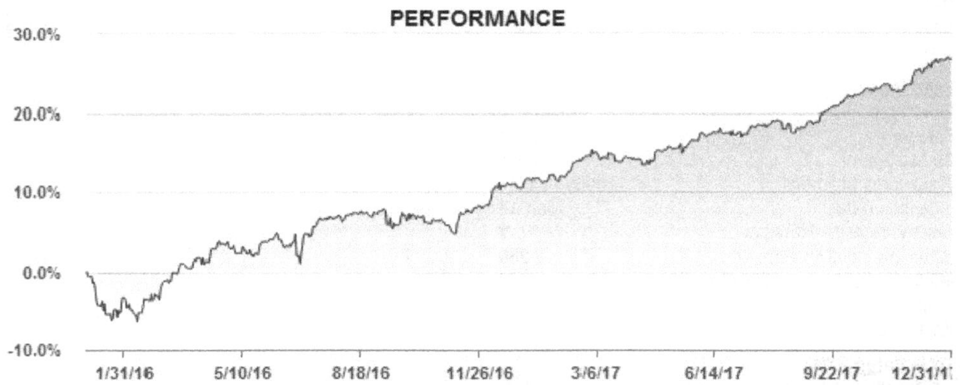

Ratings History

Date	Overall Rating	Risk Rating	Reward Rating
Q4-17	B-	B	B-
Q3-17	B	A	B-
Q2-17	B	A	B-
Q1-17	B	B	B
Q4-16	B	B+	B-
Q4-15	C+	B-	C

Asset & Performance History

Date	NAV	1-Year Total Return
2016	67.45	11.09
2015	63.54	0.14
2014	67.61	9.89
2013	65.53	19.75
2012	58.45	12.66
2011	54.13	3.94

Total Assets: $105,557,742,930

Asset Allocation

Asset	%
Cash	4%
Stocks	65%
US Stocks	53%
Bonds	30%
US Bonds	24%
Other	1%

Services Offered: Systematic Withdrawal Plan, Automatic Investment Plan, Phone Exchange, Wire Redemption

Investment Strategy: The investment seeks to provide long-term capital appreciation and moderate current income. The fund invests 60% to 70% of its assets in dividend-paying and, to a lesser extent, non-dividend-paying common stocks of established large companies. The remaining 30% to 40% of the fund's assets are invested mainly in fixed income securities that the advisor believes will generate a moderate level of current income. These securities include investment-grade corporate bonds, with some exposure to U.S. Treasury and government agency bonds, and mortgage-backed securities. **Top Holdings:** Microsoft Corp JPMorgan Chase & Co Chevron Corp Bank of America Corporation Alphabet Inc A

Vanguard Developed Markets Index Fund Admiral Shares — B BUY

Ticker	Traded On	NAV	Total Assets ($)	Dividend Yield (TTM)	Turnover Ratio	Expense Ratio
VTMGX	NAS CM	14.41	$104,113,909,938	2.5	11	0.07

Ratings

Reward	B-
Risk	B

Fund Information

Fund Type	Open End
Category	Global Equity Large Cap
Sub-Category	Foreign Large Blend
Prospectus Objective	Foreign Stock
Inception Date	Aug-99
Open to New Investments	Y
Minimum Initial Investment	10,000
Minimum Subsequent Investment	1
Front End Fee	
Back End Fee	

Total Returns (%)

3-Month	6-Month	1-Year	3-Year	5-Year
4.45	10.18	26.39	28.62	50.17

Last Bull Market	13.27
Last Bear Market	-23.3
3-Year Standard Deviation	11.46
3-Year Beta	0.95

Company Information

Provider	Vanguard
Manager/Tenure	Christine D. Franquin (4), Michael Perre (0)
Website	http://www.vanguard.com
Address	Vanguard 100 Vanguard Boulevard Malvern PA 19355 United States
Phone Number	877-662-7447

Ratings History

Date	Overall Rating	Risk Rating	Reward Rating
Q4-17	B	B	B-
Q3-17	C+	B-	C+
Q2-17	C	C	C+
Q1-17	C	C	C+
Q4-16	C-	C	D+
Q4-15	C-	C	C-

Asset & Performance History

Date	NAV	1-Year Total Return
2016	11.74	2.45
2015	11.82	-0.18
2014	12.17	-5.66
2013	13.35	22.06
2012	11.26	18.56
2011	9.79	-12.51

Total Assets: $104,113,909,938

Asset Allocation

Asset	%
Cash	3%
Stocks	96%
US Stocks	1%
Bonds	0%
US Bonds	0%
Other	1%

Services Offered: Systematic Withdrawal Plan, Automatic Investment Plan, Phone Exchange, Wire Redemption

Investment Strategy: The investment seeks to track the performance of the FTSE Developed All Cap ex US Index. The fund employs an indexing investment approach designed to track the performance of the FTSE Developed All Cap ex US Index, a market-capitalization-weighted index that is made up of approximately 3,700 common stocks of large-, mid-, and small-cap companies located in Canada and the major markets of Europe and the Pacific region. The adviser attempts to replicate the target index by investing all, or substantially all, of its assets in the stocks that make up the index, holding each stock in approximately the same proportion as its weighting in the index. **Top Holdings:** Nestle SA Samsung Electronics Co Ltd HSBC Holdings PLC Novartis AG Toyota Motor Corp

Vanguard Developed Markets Index Fund Investor Shares — B- BUY

Ticker	Traded On	NAV	Total Assets ($)	Dividend Yield (TTM)	Turnover Ratio	Expense Ratio
VDVIX	NAS CM	11.16	$104,113,909,938	2.4	11	0.17

Ratings

Reward	B-
Risk	B

Fund Information

Fund Type	Open End
Category	Global Equity Large Cap
Sub-Category	Foreign Large Blend
Prospectus Objective	Foreign Stock
Inception Date	Dec-13
Open to New Investments	Y
Minimum Initial Investment	3,000
Minimum Subsequent Investment	1
Front End Fee	
Back End Fee	

Total Returns (%)

3-Month	6-Month	1-Year	3-Year	5-Year
4.40	10.23	26.30	28.23	49.40

Last Bull Market	13.21
Last Bear Market	-23.33
3-Year Standard Deviation	11.44
3-Year Beta	0.94

Company Information

Provider	Vanguard
Manager/Tenure	Christine D. Franquin (4), Michael Perre (0)
Website	http://www.vanguard.com
Address	Vanguard 100 Vanguard Boulevard Malvern PA 19355 United States
Phone Number	877-662-7447

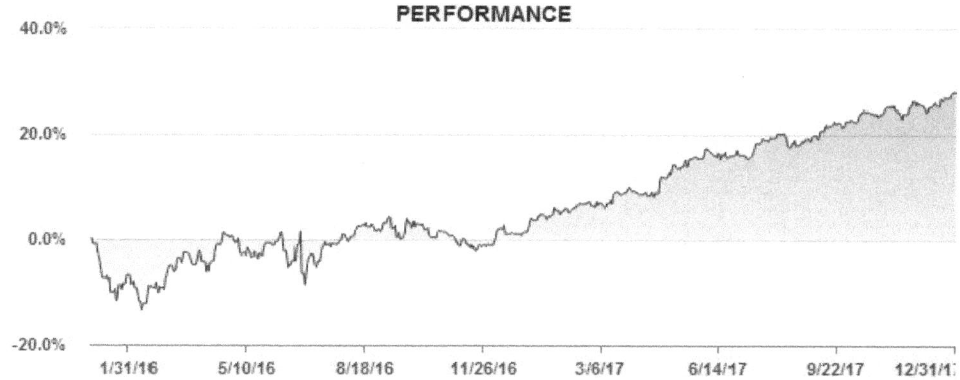

Ratings History

Date	Overall Rating	Risk Rating	Reward Rating
Q4-17	B-	B	B-
Q3-17	C+	B-	C+
Q2-17	C	C	C+
Q1-17	C	C	C+
Q4-16	C-	C	D+
Q4-15	C-	C	C-

Asset & Performance History

Date	NAV	1-Year Total Return
2016	9.09	2.35
2015	9.15	-0.28
2014	9.42	-5.82
2013	10.34	21.96
2012		18.46
2011		-12.58

Total Assets: $104,113,909,938

Asset Allocation

Asset	%
Cash	3%
Stocks	96%
US Stocks	1%
Bonds	0%
US Bonds	0%
Other	1%

Services Offered: Systematic Withdrawal Plan, Automatic Investment Plan, Phone Exchange, Wire Redemption

Investment Strategy: The investment seeks to track the performance of the FTSE Developed All Cap ex US Index. The fund employs an indexing investment approach designed to track the performance of the FTSE Developed All Cap ex US Index, a market-capitalization-weighted index that is made up of approximately 3,700 common stocks of large-, mid-, and small-cap companies located in Canada and the major markets of Europe and the Pacific region. The adviser attempts to replicate the target index by investing all, or substantially all, of its assets in the stocks that make up the index, holding each stock in approximately the same proportion as its weighting in the index. **Top Holdings:** Nestle SA Samsung Electronics Co Ltd HSBC Holdings PLC Novartis AG Toyota Motor Corp

American Funds Washington Mutual Investors Fund Class F-3 — B BUY

Ticker	Traded On	NAV	Total Assets ($)	Dividend Yield (TTM)	Turnover Ratio	Expense Ratio
FWMIX	NAS CM	45.63	$100,165,179,129		21	0.3

Ratings

Reward	B
Risk	B

Fund Information

Fund Type	Open End
Category	US Equity Large Cap Value
Sub-Category	Large Value
Prospectus Objective	Growth & Income
Inception Date	Jan-17
Open to New Investments	Y
Minimum Initial Investment	250
Minimum Subsequent Investment	50
Front End Fee	
Back End Fee	

Total Returns (%)

3-Month	6-Month	1-Year	3-Year	5-Year
6.52	12.56	20.48	35.08	102.91

Last Bull Market	20.97
Last Bear Market	-12.51
3-Year Standard Deviation	9.76
3-Year Beta	0.95

Company Information

Provider	American Funds
Manager/Tenure	Alan N. Berro (20), Jeffrey T. Lager (13), J. David Carpenter (7), 4 others
Website	http://www.americanfunds.com
Address	American Funds 333 South Hope Street Los Angeles CA 90071-1406 United States
Phone Number	800-421-4225

Ratings History

Date	Overall Rating	Risk Rating	Reward Rating
Q4-17	B	B	B
Q3-17	B	A-	B
Q2-17	B		B
Q1-17	B	B	B
Q4-16			
Q4-15			

Asset & Performance History

Date	NAV	1-Year Total Return
2016		
2015		-0.16
2014		11.22
2013		31.9
2012		12.49
2011		7.04

Total Assets: $100,165,179,129

Asset Allocation

Asset	%
Cash	2%
Stocks	96%
US Stocks	87%
Bonds	0%
US Bonds	0%
Other	2%

Services Offered: Systematic Withdrawal Plan, Automatic Investment Plan, Qualified Investment, Phone Exchange, Retirement Investment

Investment Strategy: The investment seeks to produce income and to provide an opportunity for growth of principal consistent with sound common stock investing. The fund invests primarily in common stocks of established companies that are listed on, or meet the financial listing requirements of, the New York Stock Exchange and have a strong record of earnings and dividends. Its advisor strives to maintain a fully invested, diversified portfolio, consisting primarily of high-quality common stocks. **Top Holdings:** Microsoft Corp The Home Depot Inc Boeing Co Lockheed Martin Corp Comcast Corp Class A

Section III:
Best All-Around Stock Mutual Funds

Investment Ratings and analysis of the Best All-Around Stock Mutual Funds. Funds are listed in order by their one-year returns and overall rating.

Section III: Contents

This section contains Weiss Investment Ratings, key rating factors, and summary financial data for our selections for "Best All-Around Stock Mutual Funds." We have selected funds with better returns, lower expense and with a maximum initial investment of $5,000 or less required. Funds are listed in order by their one-year returns and overall rating.

Fund Name

Describes the fund's assets, regions of investments and investment strategies. Many funds have similar names, so you want to make sure the fund you look up is really the one you are interested in evaluating.

Ticker Symbol

An arrangement of characters (usually letters) representing a particular security listed on an exchange or otherwise traded publicly. When a company issues securities to the public marketplace, it selects an available ticker symbol for its securities which investors use to place trade orders. Every listed security has a unique ticker symbol, facilitating the vast array of trade orders that flow through the financial markets every day. If a ticker symbol is not assigned to a particular fund, the International Securities Identification Number (ISIN) is displayed.

RATINGS

Overall Rating

The Weiss rating measured on a scale from A to E based on each fund's risk and performance. See the preceding section, "What Our Ratings Mean," for an explanation of each letter grade rating.

Reward Rating

This is based on the total return over a period of up to five years, including net asset value and price growth. The total return figure is stated net of the expenses and fees charged by the fund. Based on proprietary modeling the individual components of the risk and reward ratings are calculated and weighted and the final rating is generated.

Risk Rating

This is includes the risk ratings of component stocks where applicable and also includes the financial stability of the fund, turnover where applicable, together with the level of volatility as measured by the fund's daily returns over a period of up to five years. Funds with greater stability are considered less risky and receive a higher risk rating. Funds with greater volatility are considered riskier, and will receive a lower risk rating. In addition to considering the fund's volatility, the risk rating also considers an assessment of the valuation and quality of a fund's holdings.

Recent Upgrade/Downgrade

An "Up" or "Down" indicates that the Weiss Mutual Fund rating has changed since the publication of the last print edition. If a fund has had a rating change since September 30, 2017, the change is identified with an "Up" or "Down."

TOTAL RETURNS & PERFORMANCE

3-Month Total Return
The rate of return on an investment over three months that includes interest, capital gains, dividends and distributions realized.

6-Month Total Return
The rate of return on an investment over six months that includes interest, capital gains, dividends and distributions realized.

1-Year Total Return
The rate of return on an investment over one year that includes interest, capital gains, dividends and distributions realized.

3-Year Total Return
The rate of return on an investment over three years that includes interest, capital gains, dividends and distributions realized.

5-Year Total Return
The rate of return on an investment over five years that includes interest, capital gains, dividends and distributions realized.

ASSETS

NAV (Net Asset Value)
A fund's price per share. The value is calculated by dividing the total value of all the securities in the portfolio, less any liabilities, by the number of fund shares outstanding.

Total Assets (MIL)
The total of all assets listed on the institution's balance sheet. This figure primarily consists of loans, investments, and fixed assets. Total Assets are displayed in millions.

NEW INVESTORS

Telephone
The company's phone number.

Open to New Investors
Indicates whether the fund accepts investments from those who are not existing investors. A "Y" in this column identifies that the fund accepts new investors. No data in this column indicates that the fund is closed to new investors. The fund may be closed to new investors because the fund's asset base is getting too large to effectively execute its investing style. Although, the fund may be closed, in most cases, existing investors are able to add to their holdings.

Fund Name	Ticker Symbol	Overall Rating	Reward Rating	Risk Rating	Recent Up/ Downgrade	3-Month Total Return	6-Month Total Return	1-Year Total Return	3-Year Total Return	5-Year Total Return	NAV	Total Assets (MIL)	Telephone	Open to New Investors
		RATINGS				TOTAL RETURNS & PERFORMANCE					ASSETS		NEW INVESTORS	
Oppenheimer Global Opportunities Fund Class Y	OGIYX	A	A+	B+	Up	14.38	22.43	52.93	93.33	169.70	69.34	6,911	800-225-5677	Y
Oppenheimer Global Opportunities Fund Class A	OPGIX	A	A+	B+	Up	14.29	22.25	52.52	91.92	166.36	68.54	6,911	800-225-5677	Y
Vanguard International Growth Fund Investor Shares	VWIGX	B+	A	B-	Up	4.06	15.14	42.96	43.76	69.34	30.04	33,542	877-662-7447	Y
Baron Fifth Avenue Growth Fund Retail Class	BFTHX	A-	A	B	Up	5.94	12.59	40.64	45.37	118.25	25.47	199.5	800-992-2766	Y
Matthews Pacific Tiger Fund Investor Class	MAPTX	B	B	B-	Up	11.23	16.43	39.96	38.01	61.69	31.66	9,228	800-789-2742	Y
Plumb Equity Fund	PLBEX	B+	A	B-	Up	9.97	15.55	39.70	45.59	119.62	27.45	26.0		Y
Transamerica International Small Cap Fund Class I2	US8939626136	A-	A	A-	Up	5.78	14.23	39.66	48.30	86.24	6.56	153.5	888-233-4339	Y
Voya Hang Seng Index Portfolio Class I	IHPIX	B	A-	C+	Up	7.73	17.39	39.60	37.44	50.77	17.68	74.6	800-366-0066	Y
Matthews Asia Growth Fund Investor Class	MPACX	B	B+	B-	Up	9.64	17.12	39.38	40.06	72.20	27.25	801.5	800-789-2742	Y
Franklin DynaTech Fund Class A	FKDNX	A-	A	B+	Up	5.44	13.44	39.30	51.86	133.26	65.39	4,467	650-312-2000	Y
Franklin DynaTech Fund Class R	FDNRX	A-	A	B+	Up	5.39	13.29	38.96	50.73	130.40	63.67	4,467	650-312-2000	Y
Goldman Sachs Technology Opportunities Fund Investor Class	GISTX	A-	A	B+	Up	6.57	14.64	38.35	57.39	130.43	24.74	473.5	800-526-7384	Y
JNL/Mellon Capital Information Technology Sector Cls I	US47760W7873	A-	A+	B	Up	8.48	17.40	36.62	60.58	153.40	15.6	2,369		Y
Oppenheimer Global Fund Class Fund Class Y	OGLYX	B+	B+	B	Up	7.18	13.76	36.56	41.81	87.47	96.05	11,177	800-225-5677	Y
VY® Oppenheimer Global Portfolio Class I	IGMIX	B+	A-	B	Up	7.25	13.80	36.48	41.38	87.50	22.33	1,738	800-366-0066	Y
JNL/Oppenheimer Global Growth Fund Class I	US46644W3025	B+	B+	B	Up	7.39	13.89	36.39	41.29	86.12	18.89	2,577		Y
JNL/Mellon Capital Information Technology Sector Cls A	US47760W7956	A-	A	B	Up	8.42	17.20	36.31	59.61	150.48	15.31	2,369		Y
Oppenheimer Global Fund Class A	OPPAX	B+	B+	B	Up	7.12	13.61	36.24	40.82	85.20	95.98	11,177	800-225-5677	Y
JNL/Oppenheimer Global Growth Fund Class A	US46644W2035	B+	B+	B	Up	7.27	13.72	36.15	40.47	84.25	18.57	2,577		Y
VY® Oppenheimer Global Portfolio Class S	IGMSX	B	B+	C+	Up	7.16	13.65	36.13	40.30	85.14	21.53	1,738	800-366-0066	Y
EQ/Oppenheimer Global Portfolio Class IB	US2689547329	B	B+	B	Up	7.52	13.74	36.00	38.52	82.38		271.8	877-222-2144	Y
EQ/Oppenheimer Global Portfolio Class IA	US2689547402	B	B+	C+	Up	7.52	13.73	35.98	38.49	82.47		271.8	877-222-2144	Y
VY® Oppenheimer Global Portfolio Class S2	IOGPX	B+	B+	B	Up	7.09	13.54	35.91	39.69	83.80	20.97	1,738	800-366-0066	Y
Matthews India Fund Investor Class	MINDX	B	B	B	Up	10.04	11.13	35.78	36.56	110.88	34.31	2,300	800-789-2742	Y
DFA Japanese Small Company Portfolio Institutional Class	DFJSX	A	A	A-	Up	8.34	16.69	35.68	68.83	106.82	29.14	664.3	512-306-7400	Y
Fidelity® International Small Cap Opportunities Fund	FSCOX	A-	B+	A	Up	6.89	12.68	35.68	47.58	84.12	19.34	1,149	617-563-7000	Y
Fidelity Advisor® Intl Small Cap Opp Fund I Cls	FOPIX	A-	B+	A	Up	6.83	12.63	35.66	47.62	84.10	19.31	1,149	617-563-7000	Y
DFA Continental Small Company Portfolio Institutional Cls	DFCSX	B+	B+	A	Up	2.09	9.74	35.13	58.44	106.46	28.59	649.7	512-306-7400	Y
AXA/Loomis Sayles Growth Portfolio Class K	US26883L4648	A-	A-	A	Up	6.77	13.77	34.97	59.96	125.96		690.7	877-222-2144	Y
AXA/Loomis Sayles Growth Portfolio Class IA	US2689402368	A-	A-	A	Up	6.79	13.67	34.67	59.10	124.72		690.7	877-222-2144	Y
AXA/Loomis Sayles Growth Portfolio Class IB	US29364E6032	A-	A-	A	Up	6.88	13.73	34.61	59.15	124.82		690.7	877-222-2144	Y
Ivy Science and Technology Fund Class I	ISTIX	B	A	C	Up	3.52	13.94	33.13	30.85	114.47	69.87	4,284	800-777-6472	Y
T. Rowe Price Media and Telecommunications Fund	PRMTX	B+	B+	A-	Up	4.99	10.97	32.98	58.95	139.20	96.47	4,829	410-345-2000	Y
TCW Select Equities Fund Class I	TGCEX	B	B	B+		5.43	11.68	32.80	35.87	93.91	24.93	922.7	213-244-0000	Y
Oppenheimer International Diversified Fund Class Y	OIDYX	B	B	B	Up	4.75	11.54	32.75	34.75	59.75	18.45	3,860	800-225-5677	Y
T. Rowe Price Japan Fund	PRJPX	A	A	A	Up	8.16	14.76	32.66	68.56	102.76	15.11	750.1	410-345-2000	Y
TCW Select Equities Fund Class N	TGCNX	B	B	B+		5.39	11.55	32.51	34.89	91.45	22.66	922.7	213-244-0000	Y
JNL/Franklin Templeton Intl Small Cap Growth Fund Cls I	US46648M3916	B	B	B	Up	3.37	10.51	32.49	36.53	66.04	11.63	734.0		Y
USAA Nasdaq 100 Index Fund R6 Shares	URNQX	B+	A-	B	Down	7.15	13.62	32.41	52.47	154.21	17.89	1,609	800-531-8722	Y
American Century Ultra® Fund R6 Class	AULDX	B+	A-	B	Up	6.70	13.66	32.39	46.33	127.78	44.82	10,546	800-444-4015	Y
Loomis Sayles Growth Fund Class A	LGRRX	A-	A-	A	Up	6.19	12.69	32.29	51.91	133.14	14.57	7,788	800-862-4863	Y
VALIC Company I Nasdaq-100 Index Fund	VCNIX	B+	A-	B	Down	7.10	13.53	32.28	52.52	154.69	13.42	432.0		Y
USAA NASDAQ-100 Index Fund	USNQX	B+	A-	B		7.11	13.58	32.28	52.33	153.97	17.89	1,609	800-531-8722	Y
American Century Ultra® Fund Y Class	AULYX	B+	A-	B	Up	6.71	13.64	32.22	45.13	124.79	44.87	10,546	800-444-4015	Y
MFS® International New Discovery Fund Class R6	MIDLX	B	B	B+	Up	6.68	12.22	32.15	36.71	60.97	35.74	6,233	877-960-6077	Y
American Century Ultra® Fund R5 Class	AULGX	B+	A-	B	Up	6.64	13.55	32.08	44.98	124.55	44.87	10,546	800-444-4015	Y
PRIMECAP Odyssey Growth Fund	POGRX	A-	A	B+	Up	9.17	15.44	32.05	51.26	145.05	37.25	10,362	800-729-2307	Y
MFS® International New Discovery Fund Class I	MWNIX	B	B	B+	Up	6.63	12.14	32.04	36.21	60.01	35.72	6,233	877-960-6077	Y
MFS® International New Discovery Fund Class R4	MIDJX	B	B	B+	Up	6.63	12.13	32.02	36.21	59.99	34.67	6,233	877-960-6077	Y
American Century Ultra® Fund Investor Class	TWCUX	B+	A-	B	Up	6.59	13.45	31.89	44.77	124.23	43.42	10,546	800-444-4015	Y
DF Dent Premier Growth Fund Investor Shares	DFDPX	A-	A-	B+	Up	6.18	12.91	31.83	36.18	97.16	29.03	158.7		Y
Voya Russell Large Cap Growth Index Portfolio Class I	IRLNX	B+	A-	B+	Down	8.07	14.54	31.26	49.04	128.65	35.35	709.4	800-366-0066	Y

		RATINGS				TOTAL RETURNS & PERFORMANCE					ASSETS		NEW INVESTORS	
Fund Name	Ticker Symbol	Overall Rating	Reward Rating	Risk Rating	Recent Up/ Downgrade	3-Month Total Return	6-Month Total Return	1-Year Total Return	3-Year Total Return	5-Year Total Return	NAV	Total Assets (MIL)	Telephone	Open to New Investors
Shelton Capital Mgmt Nasdaq-100 Index Fund Direct Shares	NASDX	B+	A-	B	Down	6.57	13.05	31.25	50.98	154.01	16.04	497.1	800-955-9988	Y
Red Oak Technology Select Fund	ROGSX	A-	A+	B	Up	7.83	15.31	31.09	63.40	176.50	24.56	494.1	888-462-5386	Y
Voya Russell Large Cap Growth Index Portfolio Class S	IRLSX	B+	A-	B+	Down	8.02	14.42	30.92	47.92	125.82	35.15	709.4	800-366-0066	Y
Voya Russell Large Cap Growth Index Portfolio Class A	IRLAX	B+	A-	B+	Down	7.94	14.28	30.60	47.02	123.31	35.05	709.4	800-366-0066	Y
Shelton Capital Management Nasdaq-100 Index Fund Class K	NDXKX	B+	B+	B	Down	6.36	12.72	30.57	48.59	147.36	15.59	497.1	800-955-9988	Y
Frost Growth Equity Fund Investor Class Shares	FACEX	B	B	B	Down	7.17	12.29	30.39	37.56	106.64	12.49	310.8		Y
John Hancock Funds II Intl Small Company Fund Cls NAV	JHATX	B+	B	B+	Up	4.42	11.74	30.32	43.97	72.90	12.99	640.7	800-225-5913	Y
MFS® International Diversification Fund Class I	MDIJX	B	B	B	Up	5.84	10.90	30.28	33.12	51.92	19.88	9,950	877-960-6077	Y
DFA Intl Small Company Portfolio Inst Cls	DFISX	B+	B	B+	Up	4.60	11.90	30.24	45.68	76.15	21.27	13,645	512-306-7400	Y
MFS® International Diversification Fund Class R4	MDITX	B	B	B	Up	5.81	10.88	30.24	33.10	51.85	19.81	9,950	877-960-6077	Y
MFS® International Diversification Fund Class R6	MDIZX	B	B	B		5.82	10.87	30.24	33.09	51.88	19.87	9,950	877-960-6077	Y
Fidelity Advisor® Japan Fund Class I	FJPIX	B+	A-	B	Up	8.95	12.57	30.16	44.42	65.69	15.41	405.1	617-563-7000	Y
Fidelity® Japan Fund	FJPNX	B+	A-	B	Up	8.96	12.58	30.15	44.34	65.50	15.45	405.1	617-563-7000	Y
Vanguard FTSE All-World ex-US Small Capital Ind Inv Shares	VFSVX	B	B	B	Up	5.63	12.57	30.12	35.04	52.38	45.35	5,799	877-662-7447	Y
Fidelity Advisor® Japan Fund Class A	FPJAX	B+	A-	B	Up	8.92	12.47	29.85	43.17	62.94	15.43	405.1	617-563-7000	Y
RiverPark Large Growth Fund Class Retail	RPXFX	B	B	C+	Up	6.48	12.41	29.82	32.41	93.63	21.83	49.8	888-564-4517	Y
Fidelity® Worldwide Fund	FWWFX	B	B	B	Up	6.09	13.32	29.54	32.43	78.87	26.41	1,761	617-563-7000	Y
Fidelity Advisor® Worldwide Fund I Class	FWIFX	B	B	B	Up	6.13	13.31	29.53	32.33	78.60	26.29	1,761	617-563-7000	Y
EQ/Large Cap Growth Index Portfolio Class K	US26883L5553	B+	B+	B+	Up	8.29	14.80	29.38	43.74	122.08		1,412	877-222-2144	Y
Provident Trust Strategy Fund	PROVX	A-	A-	B+	Up	9.08	15.93	29.37	48.23	101.74	14.73	148.8	855-739-9950	Y
American Century Select Fund R6 Class	ASDEX	B+	B+	B	Up	6.62	13.64	29.35	46.62	118.15	71.13	2,939	800-444-4015	Y
Buffalo International Fund	BUFIX	B	B	B	Up	2.49	7.73	29.33	32.28	56.20	14.91	252.7	800-492-8332	Y
Fidelity® NASDAQ Composite Index® Fund	FNCMX	B+	A-	B	Down	6.39	12.79	29.24	48.86	145.36	90.63	4,896	617-563-7000	Y
American Century Select Fund Y Class	ASLWX	B+	B+	B	Up	6.62	13.64	29.22	45.42	115.31	71.2	2,939	800-444-4015	Y
T. Rowe Price Tax-Efficient Equity Fund	PREFX	B+	B	B+	Up	6.33	11.76	29.12	39.64	112.65	28.87	286.1	410-345-2000	Y
EQ/Large Cap Growth Index Portfolio Class IA	US2689405171	B+	B+	B+	Up	8.28	14.64	29.10	42.70	119.33		1,412	877-222-2144	Y
American Century Select Fund R5 Class	ASLGX	B+	B+	B	Up	6.56	13.54	29.08	45.25	115.06	71.23	2,939	800-444-4015	Y
Archer Balanced Fund	ARCHX	B-	C+	B	Down	17.23	21.06	29.07	34.80	86.21	13.02	35.6		Y
EQ/Large Cap Growth Index Portfolio Class IB	US2689404919	B+	B+	B+	Up	8.23	14.59	29.06	42.73	119.25		1,412	877-222-2144	Y
Tarkio Fund	TARKX	B+	A+	C	Up	5.46	12.19	29.03	50.80	135.07	21.64	101.2	406-541-0130	Y
American Funds Global Growth Portfolio Class R-6	RGGGX	B	B	B	Up	5.27	11.34	29.02	34.45	77.07	16.87	2,670	800-421-4225	Y
American Funds Global Growth Portfolio Class F-3	PGXFX	B	B	B	Up	5.32	11.37	29.00	34.33	76.76	16.73	2,670	800-421-4225	Y
American Funds Global Growth Portfolio Class R-5E	RGTFX	B	B	B	Up	5.30	11.30	28.99	34.05	76.39	16.69	2,670	800-421-4225	Y
Amana Mutual Funds Trust Growth Fund Investor	AMAGX	B	B+	B		6.89	12.96	28.97	36.93	96.48	34.96	1,693	888-732-6262	Y
American Funds Global Growth Portfolio Class F-2	PGWFX	B	B	B	Up	5.29	11.26	28.95	34.08	76.30	16.77	2,670	800-421-4225	Y
DFA Intl Vector Equity Portfolio Inst Cls	DFVQX	B	B	C+	Up	4.84	12.60	28.94	37.25	62.34	13.57	2,555	512-306-7400	Y
American Century Select Fund Investor Class	TWCIX	B+	B+	B	Up	6.52	13.45	28.93	45.08	114.82	70.1	2,939	800-444-4015	Y
American Funds Global Growth Portfolio Class R-5	RGGFX	B	B	B	Up	5.30	11.25	28.93	34.27	76.67	16.84	2,670	800-421-4225	Y
American Funds Global Growth Portfolio Class 529-F-1	CGGFX	B	B	B	Up	5.31	11.29	28.84	33.77	75.62	16.75	2,670	800-421-4225	Y
American Funds Global Growth Portfolio Class R-4	RGGEX	B	B	B	Up	5.20	11.14	28.62	33.07	74.15	16.7	2,670	800-421-4225	Y
American Funds Global Growth Portfolio Class A	PGGAX	B	B	B	Up	5.22	11.14	28.61	33.20	74.43	16.72	2,670	800-421-4225	Y
American Funds Global Growth Portfolio Class F-1	PGGFX	B	B	B	Up	5.21	11.13	28.56	33.04	73.91	16.74	2,670	800-421-4225	Y
American Funds Global Growth Portfolio Class 529-A	CPGAX	B	B	B	Up	5.21	11.14	28.53	33.00	73.93	16.7	2,670	800-421-4225	Y
USAA Growth Fund	USAAX	B+	B+	A	Up	6.44	12.12	28.42	43.16	128.25	30.53	2,917	800-531-8722	Y
Vanguard Pacific Stock Index Fund Investor Shares	VPACX	B	B	B	Up	8.23	12.55	28.38	37.45	55.85	13.87	8,471	877-662-7447	Y
American Funds Global Growth Portfolio Class 529-E	CGGEX	B	B-	B	Up	5.14	10.97	28.24	31.90	71.58	16.63	2,670	800-421-4225	Y
American Funds Global Growth Portfolio Class R-3	RGLCX	B	B-	B	Up	5.17	11.00	28.19	31.88	71.41	16.63	2,670	800-421-4225	Y
DFA International Core Equity Portfolio Institutional Cls	DFIEX	B	B	B	Up	4.69	11.94	28.05	34.03	58.13	14.54	25,849	512-306-7400	Y
DFA Intl Small Cap Value Portfolio Inst Cls	DISVX	B	B	B-	Up	3.83	11.72	27.97	43.42	82.85	22.97	16,235	512-306-7400	Y
Sit Large Cap Growth Fund	SNIGX	B	B	B+	Down	6.74	11.85	27.83	38.12	103.14	40.56	121.4	800-332-5580	Y
JNL/Mellon Capital Dow Index Fund Class I	US47760W8038	B	B+	B-		10.93	16.93	27.78	45.27	113.16	27.69	797.4		Y
Free Market International Equity Fund Institutional Class	FMNEX	B-	B	C	Up	4.80	12.39	27.73	33.76	56.21	11.41	2,294		Y

		RATINGS				TOTAL RETURNS & PERFORMANCE					ASSETS		NEW INVESTORS	
Fund Name	Ticker Symbol	Overall Rating	Reward Rating	Risk Rating	Recent Up/ Downgrade	3-Month Total Return	6-Month Total Return	1-Year Total Return	3-Year Total Return	5-Year Total Return	NAV	Total Assets (MIL)	Telephone	Open to New Investors
DFA Intl Social Core Equity Portfolio Inst Cls Shares	DSCLX	B-	B	C+	Up	4.47	11.91	27.65	34.09	54.99	13.99	845.5	512-306-7400	Y
Vanguard Growth Index Fund Investor Shares	VIGRX	B+	B	A-	Up	6.19	11.31	27.64	38.27	113.22	72.36	72,657	877-662-7447	Y
Dreyfus Worldwide Growth Fund Class I	DPWRX	B	B	B		5.79	9.93	27.37	33.01	69.94	53.81	669.7	800-645-6561	Y
Dreyfus Worldwide Growth Fund Class A	PGROX	B	B	B		5.70	9.78	27.03	31.94	67.71	53.52	669.7	800-645-6561	Y
Dreyfus Appreciation Fund, Inc. Class I	DGIGX	B-	B	B-	Down	7.45	12.19	26.90	31.44	77.07	35.89	2,003	800-645-6561	Y
Franklin Growth Series Class A	FKGRX	B	B	B	Down	6.04	11.61	26.82	38.92	111.37	94.51	14,695	650-312-2000	Y
Janus Henderson Enterprise Fund Class N	JDMNX	B	B+	B	Down	5.52	11.00	26.64	46.03	119.73	118.59	16,122	877-335-2687	Y
Dreyfus Appreciation Fund, Inc. Class Investor	DGAGX	B-	B-	B-	Down	7.42	12.08	26.64	31.07	76.57	36.07	2,003	800-645-6561	Y
Franklin Growth Series Class R	FGSRX	B	B	B	Down	5.98	11.46	26.49	37.87	108.73	94.17	14,695	650-312-2000	Y
Dreyfus Core Equity Fund Class I	DPERX	B-	B-	B-	Down	7.56	12.11	26.48	30.40	75.08	18.44	182.0	800-645-6561	Y
Janus Henderson Enterprise Fund Class T	JAENX	B	B+	B	Down	5.45	10.87	26.34	44.96	117.07	116.99	16,122	877-335-2687	Y
Deutsche Capital Growth Fund Class R6	SDGZX	B	B	B	Down	5.96	10.77	26.33	40.82	119.23	77.41	1,521	201-593-8273	Y
Natixis Funds Trust I U.S. Equity Opportunities Fund Cls A	NEFSX	B	B	B	Down	5.70	11.62	26.28	48.23	133.24	36.9	999.0	800-862-4863	Y
Deutsche Capital Growth Fund Class S	SCGSX	B	B	B	Down	5.96	10.73	26.26	41.01	119.43	77.75	1,521	201-593-8273	Y
Janus Henderson Enterprise Fund Class A	JDMAX	B	B+	B-	Down	5.40	10.74	26.07	44.03	114.80	115.08	16,122	877-335-2687	Y
Janus Henderson Enterprise Fund Class S	JGRTX	B	B+	B-	Down	5.38	10.72	26.02	43.86	114.38	114.58	16,122	877-335-2687	Y
PRIMECAP Odyssey Stock Fund	POSKX	B	B+	B		7.19	12.64	25.96	43.43	126.04	31.91	9,094	800-729-2307	Y
Deutsche Capital Growth Fund Class A	SDGAX	B	B	B	Down	5.89	10.61	25.93	39.93	116.65	77.03	1,521	201-593-8273	Y
Voya Japan TOPIX Index® Portfolio Class I	IJIIX	A-	A-	B+	Up	7.98	12.57	25.92	43.92	74.06	12.71	310.6	800-366-0066	Y
Fidelity® Select Retailing Portfolio	FSRPX	A-	A-	A-	Up	13.11	15.72	25.82	55.57	155.67	133.17	1,923	617-563-7000	Y
Elfun Trusts	ELFNX	B	B	B+		5.00	10.70	25.61	34.12	110.46	60.36	2,772	800-242-0134	Y
American Funds Growth Portfolio Class F-3	GWPDX	B	B	B-	Up	6.07	11.82	25.58	36.84	92.57	18.09	5,887	800-421-4225	Y
DFA U.S. Large Cap Growth Portfolio Institutional Class	DUSLX	B	B	B		8.74	13.87	25.53	38.59	113.73	19.17	1,747	512-306-7400	Y
T. Rowe Price Spectrum Growth Fund	PRSGX	B-	B	B-	Down	4.99	10.59	25.52	35.44	88.18	24.36	3,864	410-345-2000	Y
American Funds Growth Portfolio Class R-6	RGWGX	B	B	B-	Up	5.98	11.77	25.49	36.86	92.89	18.16	5,887	800-421-4225	Y
American Funds Growth Portfolio Class R-5E	RGSFX	B	B	B-	Up	6.00	11.76	25.49	36.49	92.08	18.04	5,887	800-421-4225	Y
ClearBridge Large Cap Growth Fund Class O	LCMMX	B	B	B+	Down	7.05	12.73	25.47	45.95	132.94	45.02	9,321	877-721-1926	Y
American Funds Growth Portfolio Class R-5	RGWFX	B	B	B-	Up	5.98	11.76	25.45	36.70	92.37	18.2	5,887	800-421-4225	Y
Voya Japan TOPIX Index® Portfolio Class A	IJIAX	A-	A-	B+	Up	7.89	12.33	25.40	41.90	69.79	12.57	310.6	800-366-0066	Y
Fidelity Advisor® Stock Selector All Cap Fund Class K	FSSKX	B	B	B-		5.83	11.49	25.37	36.59	108.86	43.94	8,710	617-563-7000	Y
Fidelity Advisor® Stock Selector All Cap Fund Class Z	FZAPX	B	B	B-		5.83	11.50	25.35	36.60	108.70	43.84	8,710	617-563-7000	Y
American Funds Growth Portfolio Class F-2	GWPEX	B	B	B-	Up	5.97	11.70	25.35	36.41	91.87	18.13	5,887	800-421-4225	Y
American Funds Growth Portfolio Class 529-F-1	CGPFX	B	B	B-	Up	5.99	11.67	25.33	36.17	91.16	18.11	5,887	800-421-4225	Y
Fidelity® Stock Selector All Cap Fund	FDSSX	B	B	B-	Up	5.81	11.45	25.26	36.23	107.85	43.94	8,710	617-563-7000	Y
Fidelity Advisor® Stock Selector All Cap Fund I Class	FBRNX	B	B	B-	Up	5.79	11.43	25.20	36.00	107.24	43.97	8,710	617-563-7000	Y
American Funds Growth Portfolio Class A	GWPAX	B	B	B-	Up	5.96	11.59	25.11	35.70	90.09	18.08	5,887	800-421-4225	Y
American Funds Growth Portfolio Class F-1	GWPFX	B	B	B-	Up	5.92	11.62	25.08	35.37	89.47	18.07	5,887	800-421-4225	Y
American Funds Growth Portfolio Class R-4	RGWEX	B	B	B-	Up	5.95	11.59	25.06	35.55	89.73	18.05	5,887	800-421-4225	Y
ClearBridge Large Cap Growth Fund Class A	SBLGX	B	B	B+	Down	6.96	12.51	25.04	44.44	130.50	40.64	9,321	877-721-1926	Y
American Funds Growth Portfolio Class 529-A	CGPAX	B	B	B-	Up	5.94	11.58	25.03	35.39	89.49	18.06	5,887	800-421-4225	Y
Janus Henderson Growth And Income Fund Class N	JDNNX	B	B	B		9.05	14.31	24.96	41.72	113.89	55.07	5,178	877-335-2687	Y
Fidelity Advisor® Stock Selector All Cap Fund Class A	FMAMX	B	B	B-	Up	5.71	11.27	24.86	34.88	104.43	44	8,710	617-563-7000	Y
Janus Henderson Growth And Income Fund Class T	JAGIX	B	B	B		8.99	14.20	24.77	41.33	112.94	55.08	5,178	877-335-2687	Y
American Funds Growth Portfolio Class 529-E	CGPEX	B	B	B-	Up	5.87	11.48	24.77	34.37	86.80	17.96	5,887	800-421-4225	Y
Janus Henderson Growth And Income Fund Class A	JDNAX	B	B	B		8.99	14.18	24.70	41.02	112.08	55.07	5,178	877-335-2687	Y
American Funds Growth Portfolio Class R-3	RGPCX	B	B	B-	Up	5.84	11.44	24.70	34.24	86.59	17.98	5,887	800-421-4225	Y
Fidelity Advisor® Stock Selector All Cap Fund Class M	FSJHX	B	B	B-	Up	5.65	11.13	24.55	33.85	101.80	44.01	8,710	617-563-7000	Y
Janus Henderson Growth And Income Fund Class S	JADGX	B	B	B		8.92	14.05	24.45	40.23	110.20	55.03	5,178	877-335-2687	Y
The Hartford MidCap Fund Class R6	HFMVX	B+	B+	B	Up	7.42	11.08	24.42	40.55	123.07	35.78	10,481	888-843-7824	Y
The Hartford MidCap Fund Class R5	HFMTX	B	B+	B	Up	7.40	11.05	24.30	40.16	121.96	35.46	10,481	888-843-7824	Y
The Hartford MidCap Fund Class I	HFMIX	B	B+	B	Up	7.43	11.06	24.28	39.90	121.34	30.83	10,481	888-843-7824	Y
Vanguard FTSE Social Index Fund Investor Shares	VFTSX	B	B	B		6.82	11.89	24.11	36.97	122.63	17.48	3,811	877-662-7447	Y

Fund Name	Ticker Symbol	RATINGS: Overall Rating	Reward Rating	Risk Rating	Recent Up/ Downgrade	TOTAL RETURNS & PERFORMANCE: 3-Month Total Return	6-Month Total Return	1-Year Total Return	3-Year Total Return	5-Year Total Return	ASSETS: NAV	Total Assets (MIL)	NEW INVESTORS: Telephone	Open to New Investors
TIAA-CREF Lifecycle 2055 Fund Advisor Class	TTRHX	B	B	B-	Up	5.44	11.59	24.11	33.75	80.29	14.42	477.9	877-518-9161	Y
TIAA-CREF Lifecycle 2055 Fund Premier Class	TTRPX	B-	B	B-	Down	5.50	11.59	24.06	33.31	79.14	14.38	477.9	877-518-9161	Y
Vanguard Total World Stock Index Investor Shares	VTWSX	B-	B-	C+	Down	5.60	11.13	24.06	31.24	70.77	30.22	14,145	877-662-7447	Y
MFS® Global Equity Fund Class R6	MWEMX	B	B-	B+	Up	4.40	7.28	24.03	30.49	76.85	44.67	3,386	877-960-6077	Y
The Hartford MidCap Fund Class A	HFMCX	B	B+	B	Up	7.34	10.86	23.93	38.96	118.71	30.02	10,481	888-843-7824	Y
The Hartford MidCap Fund Class R4	HFMSX	B	B+	B	Up	7.30	10.87	23.92	38.85	118.57	34.59	10,481	888-843-7824	Y
MFS® Massachusetts Investors Trust Class R6	MITJX	B	B	B		6.72	10.47	23.92	34.86	103.51	31.28	6,571	877-960-6077	Y
MFS® Global Equity Fund Class R4	MWELX	B	B-	B+	Up	4.37	7.21	23.91	30.15	76.07	43.67	3,386	877-960-6077	Y
MFS® Global Equity Fund Class I	MWEIX	B	B-	B+	Up	4.39	7.22	23.90	30.12	76.15	44.66	3,386	877-960-6077	Y
TIAA-CREF Lifecycle 2055 Fund Retirement Class	TTRLX	B-	B	B-	Down	5.40	11.49	23.85	32.88	78.18	14.38	477.9	877-518-9161	Y
MFS® Massachusetts Investors Trust Class R4	MITDX	B	B	B		6.69	10.42	23.83	34.49	102.67	32.42	6,571	877-960-6077	Y
MFS® Massachusetts Investors Trust Class I	MITIX	B	B	B		6.69	10.40	23.79	34.46	102.58	31.26	6,571	877-960-6077	Y
MFS® Massachusetts Investors Trust Class A	MITTX	B	B	B		6.63	10.32	23.56	33.57	100.30	32.15	6,571	877-960-6077	Y
MFS® Massachusetts Investors Trust Class R3	MITHX	B	B	B		6.63	10.28	23.50	33.48	100.09	31.87	6,571	877-960-6077	Y
MFS® Massachusetts Investors Trust Class 529A	EAMTX	B	B-	B		6.60	10.26	23.47	33.37	99.88	31.38	6,571	877-960-6077	Y
Touchstone Large Cap Focused Fund Class Y	SICWX	B	B	B		7.01	11.86	23.42	37.48	104.18	42.16	1,883	800-543-0407	Y
MFS® Aggressive Growth Allocation Fund Class R4	MAALX	B	B-	B+	Up	5.59	9.91	23.26	31.65	76.49	23.16	1,775	877-960-6077	Y
MFS® Aggressive Growth Allocation Fund Class I	MIAGX	B-	B-	B-	Down	5.56	9.87	23.22	31.63	76.49	23.46	1,775	877-960-6077	Y
Jensen Quality Growth Fund Class J	JENSX	B	B	B+	Down	7.72	9.81	23.21	38.87	109.80	46.65	6,644	800-992-4144	Y
MFS® Massachusetts Investors Trust Class R2	MIRTX	B-	B-	B	Down	6.56	10.13	23.18	32.47	97.60	30.69	6,571	877-960-6077	Y
Touchstone Large Cap Focused Fund Class A	SENCX	B	B	B		6.92	11.71	23.07	36.33	101.27	42.31	1,883	800-543-0407	Y
MFS® Aggressive Growth Allocation Fund Class A	MAAGX	B	B-	B+	Up	5.49	9.73	22.91	30.64	74.23	23.1	1,775	877-960-6077	Y
MFS® Aggressive Growth Allocation Fund Class R3	MAAHX	B	B-	B+	Up	5.49	9.76	22.88	30.63	74.21	22.91	1,775	877-960-6077	Y
MFS® Aggressive Growth Allocation Fund Class 529A	EAGTX	B	B-	B+	Up	5.50	9.76	22.86	30.54	73.99	22.95	1,775	877-960-6077	Y
Buffalo Growth Fund	BUFGX	B	B	B+	Up	6.14	9.66	22.81	30.92	98.49	29.13	235.9	800-492-8332	Y
Vanguard Diversified Equity Fund Investor Shares	VDEQX	B	B	B-	Up	6.02	11.03	22.69	32.90	105.13	34.94	1,472	877-662-7447	Y
American Funds 2055 Target Date Retirement Fund® Class F-3	FCJTX	B-	B-	B	Down	5.18	10.55	22.63	32.71	83.13	18.81	2,616	800-421-4225	Y
American Funds 2055 Target Date Retirement Fund® Class R-6	RFKTX	B-	B-	B	Down	5.14	10.54	22.62	32.70	83.12	18.94	2,616	800-421-4225	Y
American Funds 2050 Target Date Retirement Fund® Class R-6	RFITX	B-	B-	B	Down	5.19	10.58	22.60	32.74	83.21	15.16	5,563	800-421-4225	Y
Columbia Capital Alloc Aggressive Port Inst 2 Cls	CPANX	B-	B-	B	Down	5.29	10.67	22.60	30.63	73.88	13.16	748.6	800-345-6611	Y
USAA Cornerstone Equity Fund	UCEQX	B-	B-	C+	Down	5.01	10.25	22.58	30.99	62.13	15.6	176.3	800-531-8722	Y
Voya Russell Large Cap Index Portfolio Class I	IIRLX	B	B	B+		6.71	11.82	22.57	37.36	110.62	20.99	911.5	800-366-0066	Y
American Funds 2050 Target Date Retirement Fund® Class F-3	DITFX	B-	B-	B	Down	5.21	10.61	22.57	32.57	83.02	15.11	5,563	800-421-4225	Y
Columbia Capital Allocation Aggressive Portfolio Inst Cls	CPAZX	B-	B-	B	Down	5.25	10.63	22.57	30.42	73.23	13.37	748.6	800-345-6611	Y
Fidelity Freedom® 2050 Fund Class K6	FZTKX	B-	B-	B-	Down	5.20	10.30	22.56	31.95	73.20	12.18	10,884	617-563-7000	Y
American Funds 2050 Target Date Retirement Fund® Class R-5	REITX	B-	B-	B	Down	5.20	10.57	22.55	32.55	82.99	15.21	5,563	800-421-4225	Y
Columbia Capital Allocation Aggressive Portfolio Adv Cls	CPDAX	B-	B-	B	Down	5.25	10.72	22.54	30.39	73.19	13.17	748.6	800-345-6611	Y
American Funds 2055 Target Date Retirement Fund® Class R-5	REKTX	B-	B-	B	Down	5.16	10.50	22.52	32.50	82.76	18.92	2,616	800-421-4225	Y
American Funds 2055 Target Date Retirement Fund® Class F-2	FBJTX	B-	B-	B	Down	5.18	10.50	22.52	32.39	82.34	18.8	2,616	800-421-4225	Y
Fidelity Freedom® 2045 Fund Class K6	FJTKX	B-	B-	B-	Down	5.14	10.26	22.50	31.90	72.76	12.11	12,978	617-563-7000	Y
American Funds 2050 Target Date Retirement Fund® Class F-2	FBITX	B-	B-	B	Down	5.09	10.49	22.48	32.30	82.53	15.08	5,563	800-421-4225	Y
American Funds 2055 Target Date Retirement Fund® Cls R-5E	RHJTX	B-	B-	B	Down	5.13	10.52	22.44	32.31	82.59	18.74	2,616	800-421-4225	Y
JNL/Mellon Capital Consumer Discretionary Sector Cls I	US47760W4078	B	B	A-		8.99	10.38	22.43	37.66	120.86	21.21	1,109		Y
American Funds 2045 Target Date Retirement Fund® Class R-6	RFHTX	B-	B-	B	Down	5.10	10.44	22.43	32.49	82.89	15.49	6,946	800-421-4225	Y
Fidelity Freedom® 2040 Fund Class K6	FHTKX	B-	B-	B-	Down	5.18	10.23	22.41	31.86	71.90	10.69	22,091	617-563-7000	Y
American Funds 2050 Target Date Retirement Fund® Cls R-5E	RHITX	B-	B-	B	Down	5.07	10.48	22.40	32.24	82.57	15.05	5,563	800-421-4225	Y
T. Rowe Price Retirement 2045 Fund	TRRKX	B-	B-	B-	Down	4.36	9.13	22.40	31.14	79.03	18.47	10,668	410-345-2000	Y
Fidelity Freedom® 2055 Fund Class K6	FCTKX	B-	B-	B-	Down	5.10	10.20	22.39	31.71	74.21	13.72	4,031	617-563-7000	Y
T. Rowe Price Retirement 2050 Fund	TRRMX	B-	B-	B-	Down	4.41	9.16	22.37	31.27	79.24	15.52	8,650	410-345-2000	Y
T. Rowe Price Retirement 2055 Fund	TRRNX	B-	B-	B-	Down	4.40	9.14	22.32	31.23	78.96	15.58	3,790	410-345-2000	Y
Value Line Premier Growth Fund	VALSX	B	B-	B+		5.47	8.67	22.31	30.05	79.89	33.11	345.2	800-243-2729	Y
Fidelity Freedom® 2055 Fund	FDEEX	B-	B-	B-	Down	5.11	10.12	22.31	31.62	74.09	13.74	4,031	617-563-7000	Y

Fund Name	Ticker Symbol	RATINGS: Overall Rating	Reward Rating	Risk Rating	Recent Up/ Downgrade	TOTAL RETURNS & PERFORMANCE: 3-Month Total Return	6-Month Total Return	1-Year Total Return	3-Year Total Return	5-Year Total Return	ASSETS: NAV	Total Assets (MIL)	NEW INVESTORS: Telephone	Open to New Investors
American Funds 2045 Target Date Retirement Fund® Class F-2	FBHTX	B-	B-	B	Down	5.07	10.42	22.29	32.09	82.03	15.43	6,946	800-421-4225	Y
American Funds 2045 Target Date Retirement Fund® Class R-5	REHTX	B-	B-	B	Down	5.03	10.34	22.28	32.18	82.46	15.54	6,946	800-421-4225	Y
Fidelity Freedom® 2050 Fund	FFFHX	B-	B-	B-	Down	5.05	10.04	22.28	31.64	72.79	12.19	10,884	617-563-7000	Y
American Funds 2045 Target Date Retirement Fund® Cls R-5E	RHHTX	B-	B-	B	Down	5.07	10.36	22.27	31.93	82.12	15.37	6,946	800-421-4225	Y
Voya Russell Large Cap Index Portfolio Class S	IRLCX	B	B	B+		6.65	11.68	22.26	36.35	107.90	20.84	911.5	800-366-0066	Y
Fidelity Freedom® 2040 Fund	FFFFX	B-	B-	B-	Down	5.04	10.08	22.25	31.69	71.67	10.7	22,091	617-563-7000	Y
American Funds 2045 Target Date Retirement Fund® Class F-3	FCHTX	B-	B-	B	Down	5.06	10.41	22.24	32.14	82.40	15.42	6,946	800-421-4225	Y
Fidelity Freedom® 2045 Fund	FFFGX	B-	B-	B-	Down	5.07	10.00	22.20	31.59	72.34	12.12	12,978	617-563-7000	Y
SA U.S. Core Market Fund Investor Class	SAMKX	B	B	B		7.13	12.12	22.19	34.50	104.92	23.39	780.5		Y
JNL/American Funds Growth-Income Fund Class I	US46644W3108	B	B	B		5.64	11.40	22.18	36.57	105.30	22.47	5,732		Y
American Funds 2055 Target Date Retirement Fund® Class A	AAMTX	B-	B-	B	Down	5.07	10.39	22.18	31.41	80.37	18.8	2,616	800-421-4225	Y
American Funds 2050 Target Date Retirement Fund® Class A	AALTX	B-	B-	B	Down	5.06	10.31	22.17	31.42	80.33	15.1	5,563	800-421-4225	Y
Homestead Funds Value Fund	HOVLX	B	B	B		8.00	14.53	22.16	34.19	112.76	55.26	1,107		Y
AXA Large Cap Core Managed Volatility Portfolio Class K	US26883L5637	B	B-	B		6.39	11.37	22.16	34.07	104.38		2,735	877-222-2144	Y
Eaton Vance Tax-Managed Growth 1.2 Fund Class A	EXTGX	B	B	B		7.51	12.18	22.15	33.97	102.73	23.06	768.8		Y
American Funds 2050 Target Date Retirement Fund® Class F-1	FAITX	B-	B-	B	Down	5.05	10.32	22.15	31.33	80.31	15.02	5,563	800-421-4225	Y
American Funds 2050 Target Date Retirement Fund® Class R-4	RDITX	B-	B-	B	Down	5.01	10.35	22.15	31.33	80.12	15.06	5,563	800-421-4225	Y
American Funds 2055 Target Date Retirement Fund® Class R-4	RDJTX	B-	B-	B	Down	5.07	10.33	22.15	31.32	79.96	18.76	2,616	800-421-4225	Y
Davis New York Venture Fund Class A	NYVTX	B	B	B	Up	7.22	12.17	22.14	39.97	105.19	34.25	11,581	800-279-0279	Y
Vanguard Dividend Appreciation Index Fund Investor Shares	VDAIX	B	B-	B+		8.10	11.12	22.14	32.45	92.00	40.79	33,549	877-662-7447	Y
American Funds 2055 Target Date Retirement Fund® Class F-1	FAJTX	B-	B-	B	Down	5.09	10.37	22.14	31.29	80.30	18.71	2,616	800-421-4225	Y
Davis New York Venture Fund Class T	DNVTX	B	B	B		7.20	12.16	22.12	39.91	105.07	34.27	11,581	800-279-0279	Y
T. Rowe Price QM U.S. Small-Cap Growth Equity Fund	PRDSX	B+	B+	B	Up	5.89	10.31	22.11	38.18	117.59	34.89	5,856	410-345-2000	Y
JNL/Mellon Capital Consumer Discretionary Sector Cls A	US47760W3088	B	B	A-		8.89	10.22	22.10	36.73	118.62	20.81	1,109		Y
Voya Russell Large Cap Index Portfolio Class S2	IRLUX	B	B	B		6.58	11.58	22.08	35.78	106.37	21.38	911.5	800-366-0066	Y
T. Rowe Price Retirement 2050 Fund Advisor Class	PARFX	B-	B-	B-	Down	4.32	9.04	22.08	30.25	76.95	15.39	8,650	410-345-2000	Y
T. Rowe Price Retirement 2045 Fund Advisor Class	PARLX	B-	B-	B-	Down	4.34	9.02	22.07	30.18	76.94	18.36	10,668	410-345-2000	Y
T. Rowe Price Retirement 2055 Fund Advisor Class	PAROX	B-	B-	B-	Down	4.30	9.00	22.06	30.21	76.83	15.49	3,790	410-345-2000	Y
T. Rowe Price Retirement 2040 Fund	TRRDX	B-	B-	B-	Down	4.31	9.01	22.02	30.68	78.42	27.24	19,593	410-345-2000	Y
American Funds 2045 Target Date Retirement Fund® Class A	AAHTX	B-	B-	B	Down	5.04	10.25	22.01	31.20	79.93	15.43	6,946	800-421-4225	Y
Fidelity® Series 100 Index Fund	FOHIX	B	B	B+		6.98	11.98	22.00	37.90	107.92	17.36	3,541	617-563-7000	Y
American Funds 2045 Target Date Retirement Fund® Class F-1	FATTX	B-	B-	B	Down	4.96	10.27	21.99	31.10	79.79	15.35	6,946	800-421-4225	Y
American Funds 2045 Target Date Retirement Fund® Class R-4	RDHTX	B-	B-	B	Down	4.98	10.20	21.98	31.10	79.68	15.39	6,946	800-421-4225	Y
American Funds 2040 Target Date Retirement Fund® Class R-6	RFGTX	B-	B-	B	Down	4.97	10.21	21.97	31.78	81.93	15.25	10,103	800-421-4225	Y
Voya Russell Large Cap Index Portfolio Class A	IRLIX	B	B	B		6.57	11.53	21.95	35.36	105.39	20.6	911.5	800-366-0066	Y
American Funds 2040 Target Date Retirement Fund® Class F-3	FCGTX	B-	B-	B	Down	4.98	10.25	21.94	31.61	81.36	15.2	10,103	800-421-4225	Y
Fidelity Advisor Freedom® 2040 Fund Class Z6	FKGLX	B-	B-	B-	Down	4.92	9.82	21.93	30.25	68.65	15.82	2,167	617-563-7000	Y
American Funds 2040 Target Date Retirement Fund® Class R-5	REGTX	B-	B-	B	Down	4.97	10.20	21.92	31.58	81.33	15.3	10,103	800-421-4225	Y
Vanguard Large Cap Index Fund Investor Shares	VLACX	B	B	B		6.59	11.32	21.89	35.79	109.24	49.48	18,396	877-662-7447	Y
AXA Large Cap Core Managed Volatility Portfolio Class IA	US2689405742	B-	B-	B	Down	6.24	11.22	21.89	33.08	101.87		2,735	877-222-2144	Y
AXA Large Cap Core Managed Volatility Portfolio Class IB	US2689405668	B-	B-	B	Down	6.24	11.22	21.88	33.08	101.85		2,735	877-222-2144	Y
JNL/American Funds Growth-Income Fund Class A	US46644W3280	B	B	B		5.55	11.26	21.87	35.71	103.24	22.23	5,732		Y
American Funds 2040 Target Date Retirement Fund® Class F-2	FBGTX	B-	B-	B	Down	4.93	10.13	21.84	31.42	80.88	15.18	10,103	800-421-4225	Y
Schwab® S&P 500 Index Fund	SWPPX	B	B	B		6.64	11.40	21.79	36.53	110.72	41.19	31,173	877-824-5615	Y
American Funds 2055 Target Date Retirement Fund® Class R-3	RCMTX	B-	B-	B	Down	4.96	10.20	21.79	30.09	77.09	18.63	2,616	800-421-4225	Y
T. Rowe Price QM U.S. Small-Cap Growth Equity Fund Adv Cls	TQAAX	B+	B+	B	Up	5.84	10.16	21.77	37.05	114.74	34.79	5,856	410-345-2000	Y
Selected American Shares Fund Class S	SLASX	B	B	B	Up	7.00	11.97	21.77	40.67	102.18	40.53	2,369	800-243-1575	Y
American Funds 2040 Target Date Retirement Fund® Cls R-5E	RHGTX	B-	B-	B	Down	4.91	10.12	21.77	31.27	80.90	15.14	10,103	800-421-4225	Y
DFA U.S. Large Company Portfolio	DFUSX	B	B	B		6.60	11.36	21.73	36.66	110.85	20.71	8,252	512-306-7400	Y
Fidelity® 500 Index Fund Investor Class	FUSEX	B	B	B		6.62	11.38	21.72	36.52	110.78	93.44	136,827	617-563-7000	Y
MM S&P 500® Index Fund Class I	MMIZX	B	B	B		6.67	11.41	21.72	36.40	110.68	18.55	3,367		Y
American Funds 2050 Target Date Retirement Fund® Class R-3	RCITX	B-	B-	B	Down	4.98	10.13	21.72	30.09	77.20	14.95	5,563	800-421-4225	Y

		RATINGS				TOTAL RETURNS & PERFORMANCE					ASSETS		NEW INVESTORS	
Fund Name	Ticker Symbol	Overall Rating	Reward Rating	Risk Rating	Recent Up/ Downgrade	3-Month Total Return	6-Month Total Return	1-Year Total Return	3-Year Total Return	5-Year Total Return	NAV	Total Assets (ML)	Telephone	Open to New Investors
TIAA-CREF Lifecycle Index 2055 Fund Advisor Class	TTIHX	B-	B-	B-	Down	5.34	10.26	21.71	31.55	79.64	15.96	252.9	877-518-9161	Y
Northern Stock Index Fund	NOSIX	B	B	B		6.61	11.38	21.70	36.46	110.66	31.75	8,114	800-595-9111	Y
Schwab 1000 Index® Fund	SNXFX	B	B	B		6.60	11.35	21.67	35.37	107.98	62.61	7,915	877-824-5615	Y
Vanguard 500 Index Fund Investor Shares	VFINX	B	B	B		6.60	11.35	21.66	36.32	110.14	246.82	383,897	877-662-7447	Y
GuideStone Funds Equity Index Fund Investor Class	GEQZX	B	B	B		6.74	11.62	21.65	35.58	108.46	29.45	962.8	214-720-1171	Y
Principal LargeCap S&P 500 Index Fund Institutional Class	PLFIX	B	B	B		6.62	11.31	21.64	36.19	109.84	17.51	5,749	800-222-5852	Y
Great-West S&P 500® Index Fund Institutional Class	MXKWX	B	B	B		7.18	12.08	21.64	35.69	108.57		3,261		Y
Prudential QMA Stock Index Fund Class I	PDSIX	B	B	B		6.60	11.34	21.62	36.21	109.89	52.07	1,148	800-225-1852	Y
American Funds 2040 Target Date Retirement Fund® Class F-1	FAUTX	B-	B-	B	Down	4.90	10.04	21.62	30.43	78.75	15.12	10,103	800-421-4225	Y
American Funds 2040 Target Date Retirement Fund® Class A	AAGTX	B-	B-	B	Down	4.90	10.09	21.61	30.54	78.97	15.2	10,103	800-421-4225	Y
Columbia Large Cap Index Fund Institutional Class	NINDX	B	B	B		6.59	11.32	21.60	36.10	109.66	49.79	3,855	800-345-6611	Y
TIAA-CREF S&P 500 Index Fund Advisor Class	TISAX	B	B	B		6.54	11.29	21.59	36.41	110.65	29.59	4,838	877-518-9161	Y
Columbia Large Cap Index Fund Institutional 2 Class	CLXRX	B	B	B		6.60	11.32	21.59	36.12	109.67	50.48	3,855	800-345-6611	Y
MM S&P 500® Index Fund Class R5	MIEZX	B	B	B		6.58	11.32	21.59	36.00	109.42	18.6	3,367		Y
American Funds 2040 Target Date Retirement Fund® Class R-4	RDGTX	B-	B-	B	Down	4.91	10.04	21.59	30.46	78.80	15.16	10,103	800-421-4225	Y
Dreyfus Institutional S&P 500 Stock Index Fund Class I	DSPIX	B	B	B		6.57	11.31	21.58	36.06	109.68	53.49	2,623	800-645-6561	Y
iShares S&P 500 Index Fund Service Shares	BSPSX	B	B	B		6.59	11.30	21.54	35.93	109.04	318.3	12,674	800-441-7762	Y
T. Rowe Price Equity Index 500 Fund	PREIX	B	B	B		6.59	11.31	21.54	35.88	109.01	71.71	29,685	410-345-2000	Y
TIAA-CREF Lifecycle Index 2055 Fund Premier Class	TTIPX	B-	B-	B-	Down	5.31	10.24	21.54	31.06	78.60	15.94	252.9	877-518-9161	Y
Shelton Capital Mgmt S&P 500 Index Fund Direct Shares	SPFIX	B	B	B		6.79	11.46	21.53	36.04	109.27	51.42	172.2	800-955-9988	Y
Voya U.S. Stock Index Portfolio P2	VPSPX	B	B	B		6.59	11.35	21.53	35.81	109.01	15.71	5,089	800-366-0066	Y
USAA S&P 500 Index Fund Member Shares	USSPX	B	B	B		6.58	11.28	21.53	35.84	108.99	38	6,869	800-531-8722	Y
Transamerica Stock Index R4	TSTFX	B	B	B		6.59	11.27	21.48	35.73	108.71	11.26	802.5	888-233-4339	Y
JNL/Mellon Capital S&P 500 Index Fund Class I	US46648M6497	B	B	B		6.60	11.26	21.48	35.30	107.71	22.45	7,748		Y
TIAA-CREF Lifecycle Index 2055 Fund Retirement Class	TTIRX	B-	B-	B-	Down	5.29	10.15	21.47	30.67	77.56	15.91	252.9	877-518-9161	Y
Voya U.S. Stock Index Portfolio Class I	INGIX	B	B	B		6.53	11.29	21.46	35.73	108.89	15.69	5,089	800-366-0066	Y
Deutsche Equity 500 Index Fund Class R6	BTIRX	B	B	B		6.56	11.30	21.46	35.74	108.71	220.83	774.5	201-593-8273	Y
Thrivent Series Large Cap Index Portfolio		B	B	B		6.56	11.25	21.46	35.74	108.21	36.9564	929.4		Y
TIAA-CREF S&P 500 Index Fund Retirement Class	TRSPX	B	B	B		6.54	11.24	21.45	35.62	108.35	29.44	4,838	877-518-9161	Y
Invesco S&P 500 Index Fund Class Y	SPIDX	B	B	B		6.56	11.24	21.45	35.52	108.23	29.21	1,167	800-659-1005	Y
DFA Tax Managed U.S. Equity Portfolio	DTMEX	B	B	B		6.55	11.44	21.43	36.11	110.10	29.02	3,414	512-306-7400	Y
QS S&P 500 Index Fund Class D	SBSDX	B	B	B		6.51	11.23	21.42	35.41	107.85	25.35	269.1	877-721-1926	Y
EQ/Equity 500 Index Portfolio Class K	US26883L6700	B	B	B		7.09	11.94	21.42	35.27	108.57		5,594	877-222-2144	Y
Deutsche Equity 500 Index Fund Class S	BTIEX	B	B	B		6.55	11.26	21.41	35.55	108.18	217.91	774.5	201-593-8273	Y
VALIC Company I Stock Index Fund	VSTIX	B	B	B		6.58	11.25	21.41	35.50	108.11	40.81	4,822		Y
State Farm S&P 500 Index Fund Premier Shares	SLIAX	B	B	B		6.55	11.26	21.39	34.45	104.88	19.88	1,540		Y
iShares S&P 500 Index Fund Investor A Shares	BSPAX	B	B	B		6.55	11.22	21.38	35.39	107.71	318.24	12,674	800-441-7762	Y
Deutsche S&P 500 Index Fund Class S	SCPIX	B	B	B		6.54	11.22	21.37	35.38	107.77	30.56	1,011	201-593-8273	Y
MM S&P 500® Index Fund Class Service Class	MMIEX	B	B	B		6.56	11.24	21.37	35.35	107.68	18.64	3,367		Y
Deutsche S&P 500 Index Fund Class R6	SXPRX	B	B	B		6.54	11.25	21.36	35.63	108.54	30.55	1,011	201-593-8273	Y
TIAA-CREF Lifecycle Index 2050 Fund Advisor Class	TLLHX	B-	B-	B-	Down	5.29	10.13	21.36	31.01	78.95	19.95	774.8	877-518-9161	Y
State Farm S&P 500 Index Fund Class Institutional	SFXIX	B	B	B		6.54	11.18	21.33	35.06	106.73	19.95	1,540		Y
Principal LargeCap S&P 500 Index Fund Class J	PSPJX	B	B	B		6.55	11.21	21.33	35.20	106.76	17.35	5,749	800-222-5852	Y
TIAA-CREF Lifecycle Index 2050 Fund Premier Class	TLLPX	B-	B-	B-	Down	5.26	10.12	21.33	30.52	77.88	19.87	774.8	877-518-9161	Y
MM S&P 500® Index Fund Class Administrative Class	MIEYX	B	B	B		6.52	11.21	21.30	34.96	106.88	18.33	3,367		Y
Columbia Large Cap Index Fund Class A	NEIAX	B	B	B		6.52	11.19	21.29	35.11	107.08	49.55	3,855	800-345-6611	Y
Wells Fargo Index Fund - Class A	WFILX	B	B	B		6.53	11.17	21.29	34.97	106.45	62.21	1,903	800-222-8222	Y
Principal LargeCap S&P 500 Index Fund R-5 Class	PLFPX	B	B	B		6.51	11.14	21.25	35.14	107.24	17.75	5,749	800-222-5852	Y
Dreyfus S&P 500 Index Fund	PEOPX	B	B	B		6.52	11.16	21.24	34.83	106.54	54.05	2,716	800-645-6561	Y
Great-West S&P 500® Index Fund Investor Class	MXVIX	B	B	B		7.06	11.91	21.24	34.47	106.69		3,261		Y
Principal LargeCap S&P 500 Index Fund Class A	PLSAX	B	B-	B		6.52	11.14	21.23	34.89	106.32	17.53	5,749	800-222-5852	Y
Voya U.S. Stock Index Portfolio Class S	ISJBX	B	B	B		6.50	11.15	21.22	34.71	106.39	15.57	5,089	800-366-0066	Y

		RATINGS				TOTAL RETURNS & PERFORMANCE					ASSETS		NEW INVESTORS	
Fund Name	Ticker Symbol	Overall Rating	Reward Rating	Risk Rating	Recent Up/ Downgrade	3-Month Total Return	6-Month Total Return	1-Year Total Return	3-Year Total Return	5-Year Total Return	NAV	Total Assets (MIL)	Telephone	Open to New Investors
Prudential QMA Stock Index Fund Class A	PSIAX	B	B	B		6.52	11.14	21.20	34.86	106.45	51.92	1,148	800-225-1852	Y
State Farm S&P 500 Index Fund Class A	SNPAX	B	B	B		6.54	11.16	21.20	34.26	104.67	19.76	1,540		Y
TIAA-CREF Lifecycle Index 2045 Fund Advisor Class	TLMHX	B-	B-	B-	Down	5.21	10.01	21.18	30.54	78.24	19.88	1,080	877-518-9161	Y
Fidelity® Total Market Index Fund Class F	FFSMX	B	B	B		6.32	11.19	21.17	35.83	109.47	76.37	48,089	617-563-7000	Y
Principal LargeCap S&P 500 Index Fund R-4 Class	PLFSX	B	B	B		6.46	11.12	21.17	34.67	105.88	17.6	5,749	800-222-5852	Y
American Funds 2035 Target Date Retirement Fund® Class F-3	FDFTX	B-	B-	B	Down	4.77	9.75	21.17	30.58	79.09	14.84	11,498	800-421-4225	Y
TIAA-CREF Lifecycle Index 2050 Fund Retirement Class	TLLRX	B-	B-	B-	Down	5.24	10.06	21.17	30.18	77.00	19.79	774.8	877-518-9161	Y
Homestead Stock Index Fund	HSTIX	B	B	B		6.47	11.09	21.16	34.63	106.01	20.02	144.5		Y
JNL/Mellon Capital S&P 500 Index Fund Class A	US46648M6562	B	B	B		6.50	11.09	21.16	34.69	106.08	21.94	7,748		Y
iShares Russell 1000 Large-Cap Index Fund Inv A Shares	BRGAX	B	B	B		6.46	11.10	21.15	34.60	106.56	17.72	205.4	800-441-7762	Y
AXA 500 Managed Volatility Portfolio Class K	US26883L8862	B	B-	B		7.04	11.82	21.15	34.20	105.98		8,905	877-222-2144	Y
Oakmark Fund Investor Class	OAKMX	B	B	B	Up	5.98	12.08	21.14	36.50	113.99	84.33	19,380	641-219-558	Y
State Farm S&P 500 Index Fund Class R2	RSPTX	B	B-	B		6.53	11.15	21.14	33.89	103.47	19.74	1,540		Y
State Farm S&P 500 Index Fund Class B Legacy	SLIBX	B	B-	B		6.53	11.19	21.14	33.08	101.15	20.13	1,540		Y
QS S&P 500 Index Fund Class A	SBSPX	B	B	B		6.48	11.10	21.13	34.58	105.78	25.18	269.1	877-721-1926	Y
State Farm S&P 500 Index Fund Class R1	RSPOX	B	B-	B		6.52	11.19	21.13	33.25	101.70	19.85	1,540		Y
Invesco S&P 500 Index Fund Class A	SPIAX	B	B	B		6.48	11.09	21.12	34.53	105.65	28.88	1,167	800-659-1005	Y
Nationwide S&P 500 Index Fund Class A	GRMAX	B	B	B		6.49	11.10	21.09	34.45	105.65	16.01	2,942	800-848-0920	Y
Deutsche S&P 500 Index Fund Class A	SXPAX	B	B	B		6.48	11.09	21.09	34.28	104.92	30.5	1,011	201-593-8273	Y
EQ/Equity 500 Index Portfolio Class IA	US4049925476	B	B-	B		7.02	11.79	21.09	34.36	106.13		5,594	877-222-2144	Y
EQ/Equity 500 Index Portfolio Class IB	US4049925542	B	B-	B		7.03	11.80	21.09	34.34	106.06		5,594	877-222-2144	Y
ATM Large Cap Managed Volatility Portfolio Class K	US26883L8789	B	B-	B		6.98	11.78	21.09	33.96	105.70		3,662	877-222-2144	Y
Fidelity® Total Market Index Fund Investor Class	FSTMX	B	B	B		6.30	11.15	21.08	35.57	108.77	76.37	48,089	617-563-7000	Y
MM S&P 500® Index Fund Class R4	MIEAX	B	B	B		6.46	11.08	21.07	34.36	105.16	18.13	3,367		Y
Schwab Total Stock Market Index Fund®	SWTSX	B	B	B		6.27	11.10	21.06	35.53	108.69	47.25	7,020	877-824-5615	Y
Transamerica Stock Index R	TSTRX	B	B	B		6.53	11.03	21.06	34.59	105.93	11.25	802.5	888-233-4339	Y
American Funds 2035 Target Date Retirement Fund® Class R-5	REFTX	B-	B-	B	Down	4.68	9.71	21.06	30.46	78.92	14.94	11,498	800-421-4225	Y
Vanguard Total Stock Market Index Fund Investor Shares	VTSMX	B	B	B		6.31	11.11	21.05	35.28	108.33	66.7	656,961	877-662-7447	Y
Voya U.S. Stock Index Portfolio Class S2	ISIPX	B	B-	B		6.47	11.10	21.03	34.19	104.73	15.39	5,089	800-366-0066	Y
Principal Equity Income Fund Institutional Class	PEIIX	B	B	B-		7.23	12.10	21.03	33.26	95.10	31.47	6,859	800-222-5852	Y
American Funds 2035 Target Date Retirement Fund® Class R-6	RFFTX	B-	B-	B	Down	4.69	9.73	21.03	30.57	79.41	14.88	11,498	800-421-4225	Y
State Farm S&P 500 Index Fund Class R3	RSPHX	B	B	B		6.29	10.92	21.01	34.42	105.43	19.91	1,540		Y
MainStay S&P 500 Index Fund Investor Class	MYSPX	B	B-	B		6.46	11.06	21.01	34.11	104.56	48.03	1,321	800-624-6782	Y
TIAA-CREF Equity Index Fund Advisor Class	TEIHX	B	B	B		6.25	11.08	20.99	35.72	109.29	19.66	16,203	877-518-9161	Y
TIAA-CREF Lifecycle Index 2045 Fund Premier Class	TLMPX	B-	B-	B-	Down	5.17	9.98	20.99	30.03	76.98	19.8	1,080	877-518-9161	Y
MM S&P 500® Index Fund Class A	MMFFX	B	B-	B		6.42	11.02	20.98	33.94	104.34	18.02	3,367		Y
Principal LargeCap S&P 500 Index Fund R-3 Class	PLFMX	B	B-	B		6.42	11.04	20.96	33.92	104.06	17.56	5,749	800-222-5852	Y
American Funds 2035 Target Date Retirement Fund® Class F-2	FBFTX	B-	B-	B	Down	4.72	9.70	20.95	30.23	78.55	14.83	11,498	800-421-4225	Y
Great-West S&P 500® Index Fund Class L	MXVJX	B	B-	B		7.01	11.74	20.94	33.50	104.05		3,261		Y
TIAA-CREF Equity Index Fund Premier Class	TCEPX	B	B	B		6.28	11.12	20.92	35.20	107.94	19.61	16,203	877-518-9161	Y
Shelton Capital Management S&P 500 Index Fund Class K	SPXKX	B	B-	B		6.64	11.16	20.92	34.02	104.10	51.4	172.2	800-955-9988	Y
TIAA-CREF Social Choice Equity Fund Advisor Class	TICHX	B-	B	B-	Down	6.22	10.88	20.90	32.67	103.54	19.18	2,979	877-518-9161	Y
DFA U.S. Core Equity 1 Portfolio Institutional Class	DFEOX	B	B	B-		6.90	12.06	20.89	35.62	110.27	22.78	21,603	512-306-7400	Y
American Funds 2035 Target Date Retirement Fund® Cls R-5E	RHFTX	B-	B-	B	Down	4.63	9.62	20.89	30.22	78.60	14.79	11,498	800-421-4225	Y
Columbia Dividend Income Fund Institutional 2 Class	CDDRX	B	B	B		6.95	11.61	20.88	36.82	103.72	22.39	11,269	800-345-6611	Y
TIAA-CREF Equity Index Fund Retirement Class	TIQRX	B	B	B-		6.27	11.09	20.85	34.89	107.04	19.96	16,203	877-518-9161	Y
Oakmark Fund Service Class	OARMX	B	B	B	Up	5.89	11.93	20.82	35.19	110.75	84.08	19,380	641-219-558	Y
AXA 500 Managed Volatility Portfolio Class IB	US26884M2061	B-	B-	B	Down	6.94	11.66	20.82	33.16	103.43		8,905	877-222-2144	Y
Voya U.S. Stock Index Portfolio Class A	ISIVX	B	B-	B		6.41	10.95	20.81	33.56	103.43	15.19	5,089	800-366-0066	Y
Columbia Dividend Income Fund Advisor Class	CVIRX	B	B	B		6.92	11.61	20.80	36.29	102.48	22.41	11,269	800-345-6611	Y
T. Rowe Price Total Equity Market Index Fund	POMIX	B	B	B		6.21	10.83	20.79	35.24	108.68	30.13	1,715	410-345-2000	Y
TIAA-CREF Social Choice Equity Fund Premier Class	TRPSX	B-	B	B-	Down	6.14	10.76	20.79	32.05	101.92	19.13	2,979	877-518-9161	Y

		RATINGS				TOTAL RETURNS & PERFORMANCE					ASSETS		NEW INVESTORS	
Fund Name	Ticker Symbol	Overall Rating	Reward Rating	Risk Rating	Recent Up/ Downgrade	3-Month Total Return	6-Month Total Return	1-Year Total Return	3-Year Total Return	5-Year Total Return	NAV	Total Assets (MIL)	Telephone	Open to New Investors
Fidelity® Low-Priced Stock Fund Class K	FLPKX	B-	B-	B	Down	6.67	12.04	20.79	30.41	92.16	54.47	39,445	617-563-7000	Y
MM S&P 500® Index Fund Class R3	MMINX	B	B-	B		6.44	10.94	20.78	33.42	102.53	17.71	3,367		Y
Natixis Funds Trust II Oakmark Fund Class A	NEFOX	B	B	B	Up	5.84	11.84	20.74	35.50	111.36	24.72	311.4	800-862-4863	Y
Columbia Dividend Income Fund Institutional Class	GSFTX	B	B	B		6.93	11.59	20.74	36.32	102.42	22.06	11,269	800-345-6611	Y
TIAA-CREF Equity Index Fund Retail Class	TINRX	B	B	B-		6.22	11.02	20.74	34.67	106.35	20.02	16,203	877-518-9161	Y
Nationwide S&P 500 Index Fund Class R	GRMRX	B	B-	B		6.40	10.94	20.74	33.37	102.63	15.96	2,942	800-848-0920	Y
Principal Equity Income Fund R-5 Class	PEIQX	B-	B	B-	Down	7.16	11.97	20.71	32.24	92.63	31.44	6,859	800-222-5852	Y
TOPS® Aggressive Growth ETF Portfolio Class 1	US66537U7679	B-	B	C+	Down	5.50	10.91	20.69	31.15	74.29	14.94	10.8	855-572-5945	Y
Fidelity® Low-Priced Stock Fund	FLPSX	B-	B-	B	Down	6.63	11.99	20.66	30.03	91.20	54.52	39,445	617-563-7000	Y
VALIC Company II Socially Responsible Fund	VCSRX	B	B	B		6.64	11.33	20.65	33.54	114.80	22	807.3		Y
Principal LargeCap S&P 500 Index Fund R-2 Class	PLFNX	B	B-	B		6.38	10.85	20.64	33.10	102.16	17.63	5,749	800-222-5852	Y
Sterling Capital Equity Income Fund Class A	BAEIX	B-	B-	B-	Down	7.24	12.61	20.64	33.64	75.45	20.29	1,635	800-228-1872	Y
Alger Growth & Income Fund Class A	ALBAX	B	B-	B		6.37	10.27	20.63	33.28	97.99	40.56	120.2	800-992-3863	Y
TIAA-CREF Social Choice Equity Fund Retirement Class	TRSCX	B-	B	B-	Down	6.12	10.72	20.63	31.70	100.94	19.48	2,979	877-518-9161	Y
EQ/Common Stock Index Portfolio Class IB	US4049925138	B-	B-	B-	Down	6.80	11.60	20.58	33.22	104.06		5,955	877-222-2144	Y
EQ/Common Stock Index Portfolio Class IA	US4049925054	B-	B-	B-	Down	6.79	11.60	20.57	33.23	104.10		5,955	877-222-2144	Y
TIAA-CREF Social Choice Equity Fund Retail Class	TICRX	B-	B	B-	Down	6.11	10.69	20.57	31.58	100.60	17.24	2,979	877-518-9161	Y
Carillon Eagle Growth & Income Fund Class R6	HIGUX	B-	B-	B-	Down	7.89	11.58	20.57	30.13	89.19	20.94	625.0	800-421-4184	Y
Principal LargeCap S&P 500 Index Fund R-1 Class	PLPIX	B	B-	B		6.32	10.83	20.55	32.67	100.79	17.5	5,749	800-222-5852	Y
JNL/DFA U.S. Core Equity Fund Class I	US46649B7414	B	B	B-	Up	6.92	11.94	20.54	33.90	104.70	14.52	1,189		Y
Principal Equity Income Fund R-4 Class	PEIPX	B-	B	B-	Down	7.10	11.84	20.54	31.71	91.49	31.39	6,859	800-222-5852	Y
Principal Equity Income Fund Class A	PQIAX	B-	B	B-	Down	7.10	11.87	20.54	31.70	91.41	31.43	6,859	800-222-5852	Y
iShares S&P 500 Index Fund Investor C1 Shares	BSPZX	B-	B-	B	Down	6.36	10.83	20.51	32.49	100.39	318.76	12,674	800-441-7762	Y
Consulting Group Large Cap Equity Fund	TLGUX	B-	B-	B	Down	6.14	10.58	20.48	31.71	102.05	19.42	1,788	855-332-5306	Y
Columbia Dividend Income Fund Class T	CDVWX	B	B	B		6.87	11.47	20.47	35.29	99.75	22.03	11,269	800-345-6611	Y
Columbia Dividend Income Fund Class A	LBSAX	B	B	B		6.87	11.41	20.46	35.27	99.78	22.04	11,269	800-345-6611	Y
Columbia Select Large-Cap Value Fund Institutional 2 Class	SLVIX	B	B	B-	Up	7.84	13.50	20.44	36.13	115.02	27.2	1,001	800-345-6611	Y
Prudential QMA Stock Index Fund Class C	PSICX	B-	B-	B	Down	6.34	10.80	20.43	32.28	99.95	51.55	1,148	800-225-1852	Y
Wells Fargo Index Fund - Class C	WFINX	B-	B-	B	Down	6.32	10.75	20.39	31.97	98.85	62.72	1,903	800-222-8222	Y
TOPS® Aggressive Growth ETF Portfolio Class 2	US66537U7596	B-	B-	C+	Down	5.48	10.80	20.39	30.30	71.21	14.82	10.8	855-572-5945	Y
Principal Equity Income Fund R-3 Class	PEIOX	B-	B-	B-	Down	7.10	11.79	20.37	31.01	89.75	31.34	6,859	800-222-5852	Y
Columbia Select Large-Cap Value Fund Institutional Class	CSVZX	B	B	B-	Up	7.84	13.51	20.36	35.80	114.06	27.2	1,001	800-345-6611	Y
Columbia Select Large-Cap Value Fund Advisor Class	CSERX	B	B	B-	Up	7.86	13.50	20.36	35.78	114.14	27.55	1,001	800-345-6611	Y
1290 VT Socially Responsible Portfolio Class IA	US2689404265	B	B-	B	Up	6.40	11.45	20.33	31.74	107.45		149.8	877-222-2144	Y
1290 VT Socially Responsible Portfolio Class IB	US2689404182	B-	B-	B	Down	6.44	11.40	20.32	31.81	107.43		149.8	877-222-2144	Y
Queens Road Value Fund	QRVLX	B-	B-	B-	Down	6.26	10.22	20.31	30.67	92.23	23.28	46.7	888-353-0261	Y
Franklin Rising Dividends Fund Class A	FRDPX	B	B	B-		6.70	11.89	20.28	31.46	90.96	61.16	19,377	650-312-2000	Y
Touchstone Mid Cap Fund Class Y	TMCPX	B	B	B		6.82	13.26	20.22	30.29	98.22	32.51	828.7	800-543-0407	Y
JNL/DFA U.S. Core Equity Fund Class A	US46649B7588	B	B	B-	Up	6.77	11.74	20.22	33.03	102.70	13.72	1,189		Y
Wilshire 5000 Index Portfolio Investment Class Shares	WFIVX	B	B	B		6.33	10.96	20.20	34.00	104.38	20.83	186.5	888-200-6796	Y
Columbia Select Large-Cap Value Fund Class A	SLVAX	B	B	B-	Up	7.77	13.37	20.05	34.75	111.37	26.23	1,001	800-345-6611	Y
Columbia Select Large-Cap Value Fund Class T	CSVWX	B	B	C+	Up	7.78	13.32	20.04	34.70	111.07	26.06	1,001	800-345-6611	Y
Franklin Rising Dividends Fund Class R	FRDRX	B-	B	B-	Down	6.64	11.73	19.98	30.48	88.54	60.97	19,377	650-312-2000	Y
Schwab MarketTrack All Equity Portfolio™	SWEGX	B-	B	B-	Down	5.15	10.48	19.82	31.23	83.11	18.76	675.7	877-824-5615	Y
White Oak Select Growth Fund	WOGSX	B+	B	A-	Up	7.12	10.91	19.75	43.58	108.45	85.76	293.7	888-462-5386	Y
TCW Relative Value Mid Cap Fund Class I	TGVOX	B	B+	B-	Up	6.12	12.99	19.70	31.57	94.40	25.16	106.6	213-244-0000	Y
Government Street Mid-Cap Fund	GVMCX	B	B	B		4.54	8.66	19.53	36.20	97.17	26.34	50.6		Y
TCW Relative Value Mid Cap Fund Class N	TGVNX	B	B+	B-	Up	6.12	12.94	19.51	30.77	92.25	24.5	106.6	213-244-0000	Y
ClearBridge Appreciation Fund Class A	SHAPX	B	B-	B+		6.50	10.50	19.51	30.94	92.21	23.6	6,159	877-721-1926	Y
ClearBridge Appreciation Fund Class FI	LMPIX	B	B-	B+		6.47	10.44	19.46	30.89	92.08	23.72	6,159	877-721-1926	Y
ClearBridge Dividend Strategy Fund Class 1	LCBOX	B-	B-	B	Down	5.70	10.17	19.44	30.46	90.17	23.53	6,226	877-721-1926	Y
Sterling Capital Special Opportunities Fund Class A	BOPAX	B	B-	B+	Up	5.16	7.31	19.33	33.81	101.39	23.81	1,174	800-228-1872	Y

		RATINGS				TOTAL RETURNS & PERFORMANCE					ASSETS		NEW INVESTORS	
Fund Name	Ticker Symbol	Overall Rating	Reward Rating	Risk Rating	Recent Up/ Downgrade	3-Month Total Return	6-Month Total Return	1-Year Total Return	3-Year Total Return	5-Year Total Return	NAV	Total Assets (MIL)	Telephone	Open to New Investors
T. Rowe Price Dividend Growth Fund	PRDGX	B	B-	B+		5.82	9.04	19.32	35.13	102.40	43.38	8,771	410-345-2000	Y
Davis Financial Fund Class A	RPFGX	B+	B	B+	Up	6.31	10.55	19.26	38.19	109.97	51.94	1,332	800-279-0279	Y
Voya Corporate Leaders 100 Fund Class W	IWCLX	B-	B-	B-	Down	6.05	10.99	19.24	30.23	103.01	21.92	1,075	800-366-0066	Y
Putnam Equity Income Fund Class R6	PEQSX	B-	B	B-	Down	6.40	11.92	19.13	30.77	100.61	24.52	12,342	617-292-1000	Y
T. Rowe Price Dividend Growth Fund Advisor Class	TADGX	B	B-	B+		5.78	8.93	19.02	34.07	99.72	43.34	8,771	410-345-2000	Y
DFA U.S. Social Core Equity 2 Portfolio	DFUEX	B	B	C+	Up	7.02	12.11	18.98	32.42	101.47	16.08	997.7	512-306-7400	Y
DFA U.S. Large Cap Value Portfolio Institutional Class	DFLVX	B	B	B	Up	7.46	12.42	18.96	35.07	114.95	39.12	24,727	512-306-7400	Y
Putnam Equity Income Fund Class R5	PEQLX	B-	B-	B-	Down	6.32	11.80	18.96	30.32	99.60	24.52	12,342	617-292-1000	Y
Putnam Equity Income Fund Class Y	PEIYX	B	B-	B	Up	6.33	11.81	18.94	30.13	98.76	24.51	12,342	617-292-1000	Y
DFA U.S. Core Equity II Portfolio Institutional Class	DFQTX	B	B	B-	Up	6.66	11.82	18.93	33.17	106.11	21.56	23,310	512-306-7400	Y
DFA T.A. U.S. Core Equity 2 Portfolio Institutional Class	DFTCX	B	B	B	Up	6.54	11.60	18.81	33.48	106.72	18.12	8,570	512-306-7400	Y
Bridgeway Blue Chip 35 Index Fund	BRLIX	B	B-	B+		7.29	11.60	18.42	35.43	104.00	14.57	571.4	800-661-3550	Y
SA U.S. Value Fund Investor Class	SABTX	B	B	B	Up	7.22	11.97	18.37	33.60	108.00	18.79	607.9		Y
Dodge & Cox Stock Fund	DODGX	B	B	B	Up	5.74	10.78	18.32	35.77	116.29	203.61	69,876	415-981-1710	Y
Fidelity® Extended Market Index Fund Investor Class	FSEMX	B	B	B	Up	4.85	10.08	18.14	31.56	100.84	62.05	21,493	617-563-7000	Y
Invesco Comstock Fund Class Y	ACSDX	B	B	B-	Up	7.55	14.05	18.10	30.29	98.28	26.86	12,696	800-659-1005	Y
American Funds American Mutual Fund® Class R-6	RMFGX	B-	B-	B	Down	5.15	10.39	17.99	30.32	93.23	40.81	48,494	800-421-4225	Y
VY® Invesco Comstock Portfolio Class I	IVKIX	B	B	B-	Up	7.53	13.97	17.95	30.13	97.84	20.32	503.4	800-366-0066	Y
Vanguard Extended Market Index Fund Investor Shares	VEXMX	B	B	B	Up	4.77	9.94	17.94	31.16	99.78	84.8	62,586	877-662-7447	Y
American Funds American Mutual Fund® Class R-5	RMFFX	B-	B-	B	Down	5.11	10.34	17.93	30.14	92.71	40.8	48,494	800-421-4225	Y
The Hartford Equity Income Fund Class R6	HQIVX	B	B	B		5.68	10.09	17.92	34.18	94.81	20.51	4,421	888-843-7824	Y
MFS® Value Fund Class R6	MEIKX	B	B	B		5.03	7.96	17.86	32.83	104.34	40.56	47,021	877-960-6077	Y
Cutler Equity Fund	CALEX	B-	B-	B	Down	10.02	14.47	17.82	30.66	89.45	20.64	157.6		Y
The Hartford Equity Income Fund Class R5	HQITX	B	B	B		5.62	10.00	17.79	33.72	93.91	20.46	4,421	888-843-7824	Y
The Hartford Equity Income Fund Class I	HQIIX	B	B	B		5.64	10.07	17.76	33.73	93.92	20.21	4,421	888-843-7824	Y
MFS® Value Fund Class I	MEIIX	B	B	B		4.99	7.88	17.76	32.43	103.24	40.79	47,021	877-960-6077	Y
MFS® Value Fund Class R4	MEIJX	B	B	B		4.97	7.90	17.74	32.41	103.28	40.56	47,021	877-960-6077	Y
JPMorgan Equity Income Fund Class R5	OIERX	B	B	B		6.99	11.36	17.72	31.30	102.20	17.41	16,369	800-480-4111	Y
The Hartford Equity Income Fund Class A	HQIAX	B	B-	B		5.60	9.95	17.52	32.75	91.41	20.32	4,421	888-843-7824	Y
JPMorgan Equity Income Fund Class R4	OIEQX	B-	B-	B-	Down	6.96	11.22	17.51	30.46	100.13	17.39	16,369	800-480-4111	Y
MFS® Value Fund Class R3	MEIHX	B-	B-	B	Down	4.92	7.77	17.46	31.42	100.74	40.42	47,021	877-960-6077	Y
MFS® Value Fund Class A	MEIAX	B	B-	B		4.90	7.76	17.44	31.42	100.68	40.57	47,021	877-960-6077	Y
MFS® Value Fund Class 529A	EAVLX	B	B-	B		4.91	7.74	17.43	31.40	100.72	40.24	47,021	877-960-6077	Y
The Hartford Equity Income Fund Class R4	HQISX	B-	B-	B	Down	5.57	9.89	17.40	32.56	91.03	20.37	4,421	888-843-7824	Y
MFS® Value Fund Class R2	MVRRX	B-	B-	B	Down	4.85	7.62	17.15	30.43	98.20	40.16	47,021	877-960-6077	Y
Schwab Fundamental US Large Company Index Fund	SFLNX	B	B-	B		7.00	11.83	17.05	30.82	102.29	17.26	5,492	877-824-5615	Y
FAM Value Fund Investor Class	FAMVX	B	B	B+		6.43	11.03	17.00	31.95	102.73	73.52	1,262		Y
DFA Tax-Managed U.S. Marketwide Value Portfolio	DTMMX	B	B	B	Up	6.54	11.01	17.00	31.95	109.67	30.92	5,038	512-306-7400	Y
Vanguard Value Index Fund Investor Shares	VIVAX	B	B	B+		6.93	11.34	16.98	33.70	106.06	41.42	63,566	877-662-7447	Y
JNL/American Funds Blue Chip Income & Gr Fund Cls I	US46644W3934	B	B-	B		7.19	10.63	16.88	32.98	108.39	22.36	3,371		Y
JNL/American Funds Blue Chip Income & Gr Fund Cls A	US46644W4197	B	B-	B		7.06	10.48	16.60	32.09	106.22	22.12	3,371		Y
1290 VT GAMCO Small Company Value Portfolio Class K	US26883L6395	B+	A-	B	Up	4.29	12.71	16.59	34.87	100.95		3,492	877-222-2144	Y
Vanguard High Dividend Yield Index Fund Investor Shares	VHDYX	B-	B-	B	Down	6.25	11.07	16.37	34.63	103.86	33.89	28,812	877-662-7447	Y
1290 VT GAMCO Small Company Value Portfolio Class IA	US2689545596	B+	A-	B	Up	4.22	12.58	16.30	33.88	98.50		3,492	877-222-2144	Y
1290 VT GAMCO Small Company Value Portfolio Class IB	US29364E2072	B+	A-	B	Up	4.21	12.58	16.28	33.84	98.43		3,492	877-222-2144	Y
Vanguard Small Capitalization Index Fund Investor Shares	NAESX	B	B	B	Up	5.07	9.84	16.10	30.93	98.80	70.76	83,745	877-662-7447	Y
Northern Mid Cap Index Fund	NOMIX	B	B	B		6.18	9.60	16.03	35.14	102.71	19.32	2,409	800-595-9111	Y
Columbia Mid Cap Index Fund Institutional 2 Class	CPXRX	B	B	B		6.20	9.57	15.99	35.00	102.49	16.8	4,925	800-345-6611	Y
Thrivent Series Mid Cap Index Portfolio		B	B	B		6.17	9.52	15.97	34.69	100.96	18.9856	392.3		Y
Columbia Mid Cap Index Fund Institutional Class	NMPAX	B	B	B		6.20	9.57	15.96	34.96	102.24	16.47	4,925	800-345-6611	Y
Principal MidCap S&P 400 Index Fund Institutional Class	MPSIX	B	B	B		6.25	9.59	15.96	34.86	102.04	21.42	1,463	800-222-5852	Y
Principal MidCap S&P 400 Index Fund Class R-6	PMAPX	B	B	B		6.25	9.60	15.96	34.30	100.24	21.4	1,463	800-222-5852	Y

		RATINGS				TOTAL RETURNS & PERFORMANCE					ASSETS		NEW INVESTORS	
Fund Name	Ticker Symbol	Overall Rating	Reward Rating	Risk Rating	Recent Up/ Downgrade	3-Month Total Return	6-Month Total Return	1-Year Total Return	3-Year Total Return	5-Year Total Return	NAV	Total Assets (MIL)	Telephone	Open to New Investors
VALIC Company I Mid Cap Index Fund	VMIDX	B	B	B		6.24	9.53	15.90	34.91	101.70	29.42	3,560		Y
Russell Investments Strategic Call Overwriting Fund Cls S	ROWSX	B	B-	B+		4.58	8.08	15.90	31.99	50.06	13.94	101.8	800-426-7969	Y
Parnassus Mid Cap Fund	PARMX	B	B-	B		4.07	6.52	15.78	31.98	92.81	32.07	2,805	999-350-5	Y
Principal MidCap S&P 400 Index Fund Class J	PMFJX	B	B	B		6.18	9.45	15.74	33.78	98.69	20.85	1,463	800-222-5852	Y
Principal MidCap S&P 400 Index Fund R-5 Class	PMFPX	B	B	B		6.16	9.47	15.71	33.96	99.74	22.04	1,463	800-222-5852	Y
Columbia Mid Cap Index Fund Class A	NTIAX	B	B	B		6.15	9.44	15.68	33.99	99.85	16.55	4,925	800-345-6611	Y
Principal MidCap S&P 400 Index Fund R-4 Class	PMFSX	B	B	B		6.14	9.37	15.60	33.48	98.62	21.87	1,463	800-222-5852	Y
Nationwide Mid Cap Market Index Fund Class A	GMXAX	B	B	B		6.08	9.33	15.43	33.11	97.88	17.74	1,283	800-848-0920	Y
Fidelity® Select Insurance Portfolio	FSPCX	B+	B+	A-	Up	4.18	7.30	15.38	39.47	125.71	79.5	372.2	617-563-7000	Y
Principal MidCap S&P 400 Index Fund R-3 Class	PMFMX	B	B	B	Up	6.07	9.26	15.33	32.76	96.71	21.81	1,463	800-222-5852	Y
Principal MidCap S&P 400 Index Fund R-2 Class	PMFNX	B	B	B	Up	6.06	9.19	15.18	32.08	94.97	21.91	1,463	800-222-5852	Y
Pin Oak Equity Fund	POGSX	B	B	A-		6.75	8.94	15.15	42.23	117.12	65.86	219.2	888-462-5386	Y
Federated Strategic Value Dividend Fund Class R6	SVALX	B	B-	A	Up	3.18	6.00	15.15	30.50	81.03	6.15	14,186	800-341-7400	Y
Nationwide Mid Cap Market Index Fund Class R	GMXRX	B	B	B	Up	5.97	9.12	15.08	32.00	95.51	17.51	1,283	800-848-0920	Y
Principal MidCap S&P 400 Index Fund R-1 Class	PMSSX	B	B	B	Up	6.00	9.11	14.99	31.53	93.67	21.25	1,463	800-222-5852	Y
EQ/Small Company Index Class K	US26883L4234	B+	A-	B	Up	4.06	9.88	14.79	31.64	96.83		1,203	877-222-2144	Y
Fidelity® Small Cap Index Fund Investor Class	FSSPX	B+	A-	B	Up	3.36	9.22	14.70	32.28	98.03	20.3	4,095	617-563-7000	Y
Schwab Small Cap Index Fund®	SWSSX	B+	A-	B	Up	3.35	9.20	14.68	32.08	97.76	30.64	3,656	877-824-5615	Y
DFA U.S. Vector Equity Portfolio Institutional Class	DFVEX	B	B	B	Up	5.39	10.78	14.63	30.64	100.42	19.17	4,856	512-306-7400	Y
Northern Small Cap Index Fund	NSIDX	B+	A-	B	Up	3.32	9.15	14.58	31.54	96.36	13.62	1,275	800-595-9111	Y
EQ/Small Company Index Portfolio Class IB	US2689406328	B+	B+	B	Up	3.97	9.70	14.50	30.62	94.49		1,203	877-222-2144	Y
Invesco Growth and Income Fund Class Y	ACGMX	B	B	B	Up	4.71	9.32	14.48	32.17	100.66	26.98	8,263	800-659-1005	Y
Voya Russell Small Cap Index Portfolio Class P2	VRSPX	B+	A-	B	Up	3.35	9.25	14.47	31.37	96.64	15.7	968.1	800-366-0066	Y
EQ/Small Company Index Portfolio Class IA	US2689406401	B+	A-	B	Up	3.98	9.70	14.42	30.65	94.38		1,203	877-222-2144	Y
VALIC Company I Small Cap Index Fund	VCSLX	B+	A-	B	Up	3.25	9.08	14.37	31.49	96.32	22.81	1,292		Y
Voya Russell Small Cap Index Portfolio Class I	IIRSX	B+	A-	B	Up	3.23	9.05	14.26	31.13	96.28	15.66	968.1	800-366-0066	Y
Invesco Growth and Income Fund Class A	ACGIX	B	B	B	Up	4.69	9.19	14.20	31.24	98.22	26.97	8,263	800-659-1005	Y
Nationwide Small Cap Index Fund Class A	GMRAX	B+	A-	B	Up	3.17	8.90	13.97	30.20	93.38	13.76	595.6	800-848-0920	Y
Voya Russell Small Cap Index Portfolio Class S	IRSSX	B+	A-	B	Up	3.19	8.91	13.96	30.14	93.81	15.51	968.1	800-366-0066	Y
Invesco Growth and Income Fund Class R	ACGLX	B	B	B	Up	4.62	9.08	13.91	30.23	95.81	27	8,263	800-659-1005	Y
Royce Total Return Fund Investment Class	RYTRX	B	B	B	Up	4.40	10.58	13.65	31.67	81.67	13.58	2,534	800-221-4268	Y
RBB Free Market U.S. Equity Fund Institutional Class	FMUEX	B	B	B	Up	4.78	10.23	13.44	30.55	99.40	18.78	3,032		Y
Columbia Small Cap Index Fund Institutional 2 Class	CXXRX	A-	A-	B	Up	3.89	10.05	13.09	38.53	111.68	25.37	4,151	800-345-6611	Y
Columbia Small Cap Index Fund Institutional Class	NMSCX	A-	A-	B	Up	3.88	10.04	13.09	38.51	111.55	24.84	4,151	800-345-6611	Y
Columbia Small Cap Index Fund Class A	NMSAX	B+	A-	B	Up	3.87	9.92	12.80	37.51	108.94	24.71	4,151	800-345-6611	Y
Columbia Small Cap Index Fund Class T	CSMWX	B+	A-	B	Up	3.82	9.88	12.79	37.47	108.96	24.47	4,151	800-345-6611	Y
Delaware Small Cap Value Fund Class R6	DVZRX	B+	A-	B	Up	5.17	9.04	12.19	36.53	95.92	69.5	4,547		Y
Delaware Small Cap Value Fund Institutional Class	DEVIX	B+	A-	B	Up	5.14	8.94	11.99	36.65	97.06	69.49	4,547		Y
DFA Tax Managed U.S. Small Cap Portfolio	DFTSX	B+	A-	B	Up	3.92	9.89	11.87	32.98	103.76	44.07	3,026	512-306-7400	Y
Vanguard Small Capitalization Value Index Fund Inv Shares	VISVX	B	B	B	Up	4.53	9.11	11.67	31.25	103.09	31.82	29,416	877-662-7447	Y
DFA U.S. Small Cap Portfolio Institutional Class	DFSTX	B+	A-	B	Up	3.79	9.42	11.52	32.21	101.97	35.94	17,435	512-306-7400	Y
DFA U.S. Micro Cap Portfolio Institutional Class	DFSCX	B+	A-	B	Up	2.70	9.42	11.17	33.92	105.34	22.03	6,474	512-306-7400	Y

Section IV: Consistent Return BUY Stock Mutual Funds

Investment Ratings and analysis of the Consistent Return BUY Stock Mutual Funds. Funds are listed in order by their five-year returns and overall rating.

Section IV: Contents

This section contains Weiss Investment Ratings, key rating factors, and summary financial data for our selections for "Consistent Return BUY Stock Mutual Funds." If your priority is to achieve a consistent return over at least a five-year period, including the last three months then check out this listing. We have selected the highest rated funds with excellent five-year returns with a size of invested assets to give them a substantial base. At the same time, we have looked for the smallest initial investment we could find. Funds are listed in order by their five-year returns and overall rating.

Fund Name

Describes the fund's assets, regions of investments and investment strategies. Many funds have similar names, so you want to make sure the fund you look up is really the one you are interested in evaluating.

Ticker Symbol

An arrangement of characters (usually letters) representing a particular security listed on an exchange or otherwise traded publicly. When a company issues securities to the public marketplace, it selects an available ticker symbol for its securities which investors use to place trade orders. Every listed security has a unique ticker symbol, facilitating the vast array of trade orders that flow through the financial markets every day. If a ticker symbol is not assigned to a particular fund, the International Securities Identification Number (ISIN) is displayed.

RATINGS

Overall Rating

The Weiss rating measured on a scale from A to E based on each fund's risk and performance. See the preceding section, "What Our Ratings Mean," for an explanation of each letter grade rating.

Reward Rating

This is based on the total return over a period of up to five years, including net asset value and price growth. The total return figure is stated net of the expenses and fees charged by the fund. Based on proprietary modeling the individual components of the risk and reward ratings are calculated and weighted and the final rating is generated.

Risk Rating

This is includes the risk ratings of component stocks where applicable and also includes the financial stability of the fund, turnover where applicable, together with the level of volatility as measured by the fund's daily returns over a period of up to five years. Funds with greater stability are considered less risky and receive a higher risk rating. Funds with greater volatility are considered riskier, and will receive a lower risk rating. In addition to considering the fund's volatility, the risk rating also considers an assessment of the valuation and quality of a fund's holdings.

Recent Upgrade/Downgrade

An "Up" or "Down" indicates that the Weiss Mutual Fund rating has changed since the publication of the last print edition. If a fund has had a rating change since September 30, 2017, the change is identified with an "Up" or "Down."

TOTAL RETURNS & PERFORMANCE

3-Month Total Return

The rate of return on an investment over three months that includes interest, capital gains, dividends and distributions realized.

6-Month Total Return

The rate of return on an investment over six months that includes interest, capital gains, dividends and distributions realized.

1-Year Total Return

The rate of return on an investment over one year that includes interest, capital gains, dividends and distributions realized.

3-Year Total Return

The rate of return on an investment over three years that includes interest, capital gains, dividends and distributions realized.

5-Year Total Return

The rate of return on an investment over five years that includes interest, capital gains, dividends and distributions realized.

ASSETS

NAV (Net Asset Value)

A fund's price per share. The value is calculated by dividing the total value of all the securities in the portfolio, less any liabilities, by the number of fund shares outstanding.

Total Assets (MIL)

The total of all assets listed on the institution's balance sheet. This figure primarily consists of loans, investments, and fixed assets. Total Assets are displayed in millions.

NEW INVESTORS

Telephone

The company's phone number.

Open to New Investors

Indicates whether the fund accepts investments from those who are not existing investors. A "Y" in this column identifies that the fund accepts new investors. No data in this column indicates that the fund is closed to new investors. The fund may be closed to new investors because the fund's asset base is getting too large to effectively execute its investing style. Although, the fund may be closed, in most cases, existing investors are able to add to their holdings.

		RATINGS				TOTAL RETURNS & PERFORMANCE					ASSETS		NEW INVESTORS	
Fund Name	Ticker Symbol	Overall Rating	Reward Rating	Risk Rating	Recent Up/ Downgrade	3-Month Total Return	6-Month Total Return	1-Year Total Return	3-Year Total Return	5-Year Total Return	NAV	Total Assets (MIL)	Telephone	Open to New Investors
Fidelity® OTC Portfolio Class K	FOCKX	A-	A	B	Up	6.04	12.26	38.75	57.84	177.99	111.27	17,435	617-563-7000	Y
Morgan Stanley Inst Fund, Inc. Global Opp Portfolio Cls A	MGGPX	A	A+	A-	Up	6.56	17.79	49.02	76.04	173.72	22.28	1,720	855-332-5306	Y
VALIC Company I Science & Technology Fund	VCSTX	A	A+	B+	Up	7.07	16.08	41.31	62.32	171.42	29.81	1,281		Y
Oppenheimer Global Opportunities Fund Class Y	OGIYX	A	A+	B+	Up	14.38	22.43	52.93	93.33	169.70	69.34	6,911	800-225-5677	Y
Oppenheimer Global Opportunities Fund Class A	OPGIX	A	A+	B+	Up	14.29	22.25	52.52	91.92	166.36	68.54	6,911	800-225-5677	Y
AllianzGI Technology Fund Class A	RAGTX	A	A+	B+	Up	7.73	18.79	46.69	59.66	164.94	61.24	1,600	800-498-5413	Y
Morgan Stanley Inst Fund, Inc. Global Opp Portfolio Cls C	MSOPX	A	A	B+	Up	6.35	17.39	47.91	72.51	164.76	21.64	1,720	855-332-5306	Y
Oppenheimer Global Opportunities Fund Class R	OGINX	A	A+	B+	Up	14.23	22.11	52.16	90.44	162.74	65.97	6,911	800-225-5677	Y
Janus Henderson Global Technology Fund Class N	JATNX	A	A+	B+	Up	7.85	17.07	44.93	70.80	158.84	30.73	2,353	877-335-2687	Y
Multimanager Technology Portfolio Class K	US00247C4298	A-	A+	B		8.39	17.43	39.07	60.59	158.29		1,085	877-222-2144	Y
Oppenheimer Global Opportunities Fund Class C	OGICX	A	A+	B+	Up	14.08	21.80	51.39	87.59	156.47	60.62	6,911	800-225-5677	Y
AllianzGI Technology Fund Class C	RCGTX	A	A+	B+	Up	7.55	18.34	45.62	56.09	155.22	47.49	1,600	800-498-5413	Y
Multimanager Technology Portfolio Class IA	US00247C8414	A-	A	B		8.34	17.30	38.77	59.52	154.24		1,085	877-222-2144	Y
Multimanager Technology Portfolio Class IB	US00247C8331	A	A	B+	Up	8.34	17.25	38.69	59.45	154.22		1,085	877-222-2144	Y
USAA Nasdaq 100 Index Fund R6 Shares	URNQX	B+	A-	B	Down	7.15	13.62	32.41	52.47	154.21	17.89	1,609	800-531-8722	Y
JNL/Mellon Capital Information Technology Sector Cls I	US47760W7873	A-	A+	B	Up	8.48	17.40	36.62	60.58	153.40	15.6	2,369		Y
Morgan Stanley Inst Fund, Inc. Growth Portfolio Cls A	MSEGX	B+	A-	B+	Up	7.32	12.48	43.44	55.27	151.22	39.77	4,194	855-332-5306	Y
JNL/Mellon Capital Information Technology Sector Cls A	US47760W7956	A-	A	B	Up	8.42	17.20	36.31	59.61	150.48	15.31	2,369		Y
JNL/Mellon Capital Nasdaq® 100 Index Fund Class I	US47760W8525	B+	A-	B	Down	7.17	13.65	32.42	44.17	149.12	15.08	2,155		Y
JNL/Mellon Capital Nasdaq® 100 Index Fund Class A	US47760W8608	B+	A-	B	Down	7.06	13.46	32.09	43.20	146.48	22.87	2,155		Y
JPMorgan Growth Advantage Fund Class R5	JGVRX	A-	A	B	Up	7.25	14.49	35.68	49.23	143.56	20.56	8,056	800-480-4111	Y
MassMutual Select Blue Chip Growth Fund Class I	MBCZX	A-	A	A-	Up	6.74	13.81	35.08	52.40	142.09	20.2	2,372		Y
Morgan Stanley Inst Fund, Inc. Growth Portfolio Cls C	MSGUX	B+	A-	B+	Up	7.13	12.07	42.37	51.87	141.91	37.76	4,194	855-332-5306	Y
Fidelity® Blue Chip Growth Fund Class K	FBGKX	A-	A	B+	Up	7.16	14.00	36.20	46.45	141.69	87.86	23,260	617-563-7000	Y
MassMutual Select Blue Chip Growth Fund Class R5	MBCSX	A-	A	A-	Up	6.70	13.79	35.00	52.00	141.19	20.18	2,372		Y
Eventide Gilead Class N	ETGLX	B	A-	B-	Up	7.29	14.20	32.85	31.06	140.98	34.25	1,522		Y
John Hancock Funds II Blue Chip Growth Fund Class NAV	JHBCX	A-	A	B	Up	6.96	14.35	36.32	51.82	140.44	36.25	2,733	800-225-5913	Y
Eventide Gilead Class A	ETAGX	B	A-	C	Up	7.25	14.18	32.80	30.86	140.31	34.13	1,522		Y
MassMutual Select Blue Chip Growth Fund Service Class	MBCYX	A-	A	A-	Up	6.67	13.70	34.85	51.52	140.04	20	2,372		Y
John Hancock Funds II Blue Chip Growth Fund Class 1	JIBCX	A-	A	B	Up	6.94	14.33	36.24	51.55	139.77	36.21	2,733	800-225-5913	Y
JPMorgan Growth Advantage Fund Class R4	JGTUX	A-	A	B	Up	7.22	14.39	35.40	47.70	139.47	20.21	8,056	800-480-4111	Y
AB Large Cap Growth Fund Advisor Class	APGYX	A-	B+	A	Up	7.05	12.70	31.66	49.01	139.38	51.89	5,860	212-969-1000	Y
Glenmede Large Cap Growth Portfolio	GTLLX	B+	A-	B+	Up	7.79	14.98	27.81	41.35	139.23	32.31	4,017	800-442-8299	Y
JPMorgan Growth Advantage Fund Class R3	JGTTX	A-	A	B	Up	7.19	14.30	35.25	47.53	139.19	19.68	8,056	800-480-4111	Y
JPMorgan Growth Advantage Fund Class A	VHIAX	A-	A	B	Up	7.14	14.25	35.18	47.46	139.08	19.67	8,056	800-480-4111	Y
MassMutual Select Blue Chip Growth Fund Administrative Cls	MBCLX	A-	A-	A-	Up	6.65	13.66	34.69	51.03	138.54	19.74	2,372		Y
MassMutual Select Blue Chip Growth Fund Class R4	MBGFX	A-	A-	A-	Up	6.60	13.54	34.42	50.39	137.44	18.89	2,372		Y
Thrivent Series Mid Cap Stock Portfolio		B+	B+	B+	Up	7.37	10.91	18.99	52.07	136.61	20.8172	1,740		Y
John Hancock Funds II Blue Chip Growth Fund Class A	JBGAX	A-	A	B	Up	6.87	14.12	35.80	50.28	136.58	35.87	2,733	800-225-5913	Y
JPMorgan Growth Advantage Fund Class R2	JGRJX	A-	A	B		7.24	14.27	35.04	46.57	136.44	19.65	8,056	800-480-4111	Y
AB Large Cap Growth Fund Class K	ALCKX	A-	B+	A	Up	6.97	12.52	31.27	47.69	135.92	48.63	5,860	212-969-1000	Y
MassMutual Select Blue Chip Growth Fund Class A	MBCGX	A-	A-	A-	Up	6.55	13.47	34.31	49.93	135.85	18.94	2,372		Y
Lord Abbett Growth Leaders Fund Class R6	LGLVX	A-	A-	A-	Up	7.57	14.68	31.63	41.12	135.31	28.37	3,095	201-827-2000	Y
Goldman Sachs Large Cap Growth Insights Fund Investor Cls	GLCTX	B+	A-	B	Up	7.13	14.28	29.51	42.73	135.31	29.54	1,944	800-526-7384	Y
Lord Abbett Growth Leaders Fund Class F3	LGLOX	A-	A-	A-	Up	7.57	14.68	31.59	40.90	134.94	28.37	3,095	201-827-2000	Y
Lord Abbett Growth Leaders Fund Class R5	LGLUX	A-	A-	A-	Up	7.54	14.62	31.58	40.89	134.93	28.32	3,095	201-827-2000	Y
Lord Abbett Growth Leaders Fund Class F	LGLFX	A-	A-	A-	Up	7.55	14.62	31.51	40.54	133.76	28.16	3,095	201-827-2000	Y
MassMutual Select Blue Chip Growth Fund Class R3	MBCNX	A-	A-	A-	Up	6.53	13.44	34.11	49.32	133.62	17.74	2,372		Y
Franklin DynaTech Fund Class A	FKDNX	A-	A	B+	Up	5.44	13.44	39.30	51.86	133.26	65.39	4,467	650-312-2000	Y
JPMorgan Growth Advantage Fund Class C	JGACX	A-	A	B	Up	7.03	13.99	34.52	45.41	133.16	17.39	8,056	800-480-4111	Y
JNL/T. Rowe Price Established Growth Fund Class I	US46648L6092	B+	B+	B	Down	6.14	11.90	33.89	50.03	133.09	45.26	8,763		Y
ClearBridge Large Cap Growth Fund Class O	LCMMX	B	B	B+	Down	7.05	12.73	25.47	45.95	132.94	45.02	9,321	877-721-1926	Y

		RATINGS				TOTAL RETURNS & PERFORMANCE					ASSETS		NEW INVESTORS	
Fund Name	Ticker Symbol	Overall Rating	Reward Rating	Risk Rating	Recent Up/ Downgrade	3-Month Total Return	6-Month Total Return	1-Year Total Return	3-Year Total Return	5-Year Total Return	NAV	Total Assets (MIL)	Telephone	Open to New Investors
BlackRock Mid-Cap Growth Equity Portfolio Inv A Shares	BMGAX	A-	A-	B	Up	5.34	11.04	34.20	46.10	132.75	19.63	1,021	800-441-7762	Y
Goldman Sachs Large Cap Growth Insights Fund Class A	GLCGX	B+	A-	B	Up	7.07	14.13	29.20	41.65	132.46	29.95	1,944	800-526-7384	Y
AB Large Cap Growth Fund Class R	ABPRX	A-	B+	A	Up	6.87	12.36	30.87	46.35	132.38	45.94	5,860	212-969-1000	Y
Fidelity Advisor® Small Cap Growth Fund Class Z	FIDGX	A-	A	B	Up	5.01	14.26	29.17	50.98	132.17	24.81	3,744	617-563-7000	Y
VY® T. Rowe Price Growth Equity Portfolio Class I	ITGIX	B+	B+	B	Down	6.03	11.80	33.58	49.37	132.03	93.19	1,760	800-366-0066	Y
EQ/T. Rowe Price Growth Stock Portfolio Class K	US26883L4150	B+	B+	B	Down	6.77	12.65	33.50	49.27	131.99		1,349	877-222-2144	Y
Lord Abbett Growth Leaders Fund Class R4	LGLSX	A-	A-	A-	Up	7.47	14.48	31.23	39.75	131.86	27.86	3,095	201-827-2000	Y
Goldman Sachs Large Cap Growth Insights Fund Service Class	GSCLX	B+	B+	B	Up	7.00	14.04	29.06	41.28	131.36	29.47	1,944	800-526-7384	Y
John Hancock Funds II Capital Appreciation Fund Class NAV	JHCPX	A-	A	B+	Up	6.98	16.16	36.68	49.05	131.28	16.02	1,796	800-225-5913	Y
Eventide Gilead Class C	ETCGX	B	B+	C	Up	7.06	13.72	31.76	27.92	131.28	31.98	1,522		Y
John Hancock Funds II Capital Appreciation Fund Class 1	JICPX	A-	A	B+	Up	6.95	16.14	36.63	48.77	130.70	15.98	1,796	800-225-5913	Y
JNL/T. Rowe Price Established Growth Fund Class A	US46648L5003	B+	B+	B	Down	6.05	11.77	33.62	49.13	130.69	43.98	8,763		Y
Oppenheimer International Small-Mid Company Fund Class A	OSMAX	A-	B+	A	Up	6.17	12.93	37.92	57.36	130.64	49.55	10,129	800-225-5677	Y
Victory RS Small Cap Growth Fund Class R6	RSEJX	B	A	C	Up	6.42	16.58	37.05	37.75	130.60	83.67	1,703	800-539-3863	Y
TIAA-CREF Large Cap Growth Fund Advisor Class	TILHX	A-	A	A-	Up	7.08	14.75	34.27	44.47	130.59	19.84	4,903	877-518-9161	Y
ClearBridge Large Cap Growth Fund Class A	SBLGX	B	B	B+	Down	6.96	12.51	25.04	44.44	130.50	40.64	9,321	877-721-1926	Y
Franklin DynaTech Fund Class R	FDNRX	A-	A	B+	Up	5.39	13.29	38.96	50.73	130.40	63.67	4,467	650-312-2000	Y
BlackRock Mid-Cap Growth Equity Portfolio Class R	BMRRX	B+	A-	B	Up	5.31	10.91	33.89	45.06	129.83	19.36	1,021	800-441-7762	Y
Goldman Sachs Large Cap Growth Insights Fund Class R	GLCRX	B+	B+	B	Up	6.99	13.97	28.90	40.64	129.57	29.28	1,944	800-526-7384	Y
Fidelity® Series Opportunistic Insights Fund	FVWSX	A-	A-	A-	Up	6.81	13.73	33.03	43.13	129.47	17.33	6,392	617-563-7000	Y
Glenmede Large Cap Core Portfolio	GTLOX	B	B	B		7.45	13.71	24.76	39.45	129.39	28.2	2,775	800-442-8299	Y
VY® T. Rowe Price Growth Equity Portfolio Class S	ITGSX	B+	B+	B	Down	5.96	11.67	33.24	48.26	129.14	89.69	1,760	800-366-0066	Y
EQ/T. Rowe Price Growth Stock Portfolio Class IA	US2689545752	B+	B+	B	Down	6.71	12.52	33.20	48.17	129.11		1,349	877-222-2144	Y
EQ/T. Rowe Price Growth Stock Portfolio Class IB	US29364E1082	B+	B+	B	Down	6.72	12.53	33.20	48.18	129.07		1,349	877-222-2144	Y
TIAA-CREF Large-Cap Growth Fund Premier Class	TILPX	A-	A	A-	Up	7.05	14.72	34.27	43.86	129.04	19.82	4,903	877-518-9161	Y
JPMorgan Intrepid Growth Fund Class R5	JGIRX	A-	A	B	Up	8.21	15.67	32.14	41.84	128.96	55.94	1,148	800-480-4111	Y
Lord Abbett Growth Leaders Fund Class R3	LGLRX	A-	A-	A-	Up	7.44	14.34	30.90	38.68	128.94	27.55	3,095	201-827-2000	Y
Lord Abbett Growth Leaders Fund Class R2	LGLQX	A-	A-	B+	Up	7.41	14.28	30.76	38.31	128.89	27.65	3,095	201-827-2000	Y
Wells Fargo Large Cap Core Fund - Class R6	EGORX	B	A-	B-		7.73	14.45	23.78	38.37	128.36	19.76	1,120	800-222-8222	Y
Hartford Growth Opportunities HLS Fund Class IA	HAGOX	A-	A-	B+	Up	5.28	11.21	30.44	44.26	128.22	38.42	1,526	888-843-7824	Y
John Hancock Funds II Blue Chip Growth Fund Class C	JBGCX	A-	A	B	Up	6.69	13.71	34.80	46.97	128.17	34.96	2,733	800-225-5913	Y
Prudential Jennison Growth Fund Class R4	PJFPX	A-	A	B+		7.14	16.27	36.38	47.60	127.96	38.94	4,586	800-225-1852	Y
Prudential Jennison Growth Fund Class R2	PJFOX	A-	A	B+		7.14	16.27	36.37	47.60	127.96	38.93	4,586	800-225-1852	Y
Putnam Growth Opportunities Fund Class R6	PGOEX	B+	A-	B-	Up	6.69	13.34	31.45	41.28	127.80	32.76	4,621	617-292-1000	Y
American Century Ultra® Fund R6 Class	AULDX	B+	A-	B	Up	6.70	13.66	32.39	46.33	127.78	44.82	10,546	800-444-4015	Y
TIAA-CREF Large-Cap Growth Fund Retirement Class	TILRX	A-	A	A-	Up	7.01	14.72	34.11	43.31	127.58	19.74	4,903	877-518-9161	Y
VY® T. Rowe Price Growth Equity Portfolio Class S2	ITRGX	B+	B+	B	Down	5.92	11.59	33.05	47.60	127.46	87.3	1,760	800-366-0066	Y
Fidelity® Growth Discovery Fund Class K	FGDKX	A-	B+	A-	Up	5.19	12.01	34.83	44.81	127.12	32.57	1,725	617-563-7000	Y
ClearBridge Large Cap Growth Fund Class R	LMPLX	B	B	B+	Down	6.87	12.37	24.66	43.29	127.07	39.08	9,321	877-721-1926	Y
Putnam Growth Opportunities Fund Class R5	PGODX	B+	A-	B-	Up	6.65	13.30	31.33	40.83	126.55	32.81	4,621	617-292-1000	Y
AllianzGI Focused Growth Fund Class A	PGWAX	A-	A	A-	Up	7.84	14.87	31.45	45.81	126.38	52.85	1,038	800-498-5413	Y
VY® T. Rowe Price Growth Equity Portfolio Class A	IGEAX	B+	B+	B	Down	5.89	11.52	32.91	47.16	126.30	86.22	1,760	800-366-0066	Y
Fidelity Advisor® Equity Growth Fund Class Z	FZAFX	A-	A-	A-	Up	5.26	12.28	35.37	45.11	126.20	120.12	3,134	617-563-7000	Y
JNL/Mellon Capital Financial Sector Fund Class I	US47760W7469	A-	A	B	Up	7.62	12.87	19.60	45.55	125.88	13.97	1,439		Y
Prudential Jennison Growth Fund Class R	PJGRX	A-	A	B+	Up	7.07	16.15	36.12	46.67	125.68	31.84	4,586	800-225-1852	Y
Janus Henderson VIT Enterprise Portfolio Institutional Cls	JAAGX	B+	A-	B	Up	5.71	11.45	27.41	47.79	125.63	70.65	1,155	877-335-2687	Y
Putnam Growth Opportunities Fund Class Y	PGOYX	B+	A-	B-	Up	6.63	13.27	31.27	40.63	125.63	32.61	4,621	617-292-1000	Y
Hartford Growth Opportunities HLS Fund Class IB	HBGOX	A-	A-	B+	Up	5.18	11.05	30.13	43.14	125.31	36.91	1,526	888-843-7824	Y
The Hartford Growth Opportunities Fund Class R6	HGOVX	A-	A-	B+	Up	5.23	11.17	30.67	43.14	125.23	47.54	4,761	888-843-7824	Y
JPMorgan Small Cap Growth Fund Class R5	JGSVX	B	A	C	Up	8.07	18.03	41.77	49.32	125.17	18.23	1,542	800-480-4111	Y
TIAA-CREF Large-Cap Growth Index Fund Advisor Class	TRIHX	B+	B+	B+	Up	7.79	14.12	29.93	45.52	125.11	28.83	5,628	877-518-9161	Y
American Century Ultra® Fund Y Class	AULYX	B+	A-	B	Up	6.71	13.64	32.22	45.13	124.79	44.87	10,546	800-444-4015	Y

		RATINGS				TOTAL RETURNS & PERFORMANCE					ASSETS		NEW INVESTORS	
Fund Name	Ticker Symbol	Overall Rating	Reward Rating	Risk Rating	Recent Up/ Downgrade	3-Month Total Return	6-Month Total Return	1-Year Total Return	3-Year Total Return	5-Year Total Return	NAV	Total Assets (MIL)	Telephone	Open to New Investors
Franklin DynaTech Fund Class C	FDYNX	A-	A	B+	Up	5.26	13.01	38.27	48.49	124.70	55.15	4,467	650-312-2000	Y
T. Rowe Price New America Growth Fund Advisor Class	PAWAX	B+	B+	B	Down	7.05	11.93	34.21	46.20	124.66	47.03	4,429	410-345-2000	Y
American Century Ultra® Fund R5 Class	AULGX	B+	A-	B	Up	6.64	13.55	32.08	44.98	124.55	44.87	10,546	800-444-4015	Y
Optimum Large Cap Growth Fund Institutional Class	OILGX	B	B	B	Down	6.51	12.25	32.47	43.58	124.55	17.98	1,704		Y
JPMorgan Small Cap Growth Fund Class R4	JGLYX	B	A	C		8.04	17.96	41.34	48.75	124.30	16.1	1,542	800-480-4111	Y
The Hartford Growth Opportunities Fund Class R5	HGOTX	A-	A-	B+	Up	5.21	11.12	30.57	42.82	124.26	46.94	4,761	888-843-7824	Y
BlackRock Mid-Cap Growth Equity Portfolio Inv C Shares	BMGCX	B+	A-	B	Up	5.12	10.59	33.22	42.87	124.20	15.51	1,021	800-441-7762	Y
JPMorgan Small Cap Growth Fund Class R3	JGRQX	B	A	C		7.98	17.82	41.18	48.57	124.04	16.08	1,542	800-480-4111	Y
Goldman Sachs Large Cap Growth Insights Fund Class C	GLCCX	B+	B+	B	Up	6.86	13.70	28.25	38.55	123.95	26.96	1,944	800-526-7384	Y
Fidelity Advisor® Growth Opportunities Fund Class Z	FZAHX	B+	B+	B+	Up	6.64	12.28	35.21	41.95	123.88	69.64	3,029	617-563-7000	Y
JPMorgan Intrepid Growth Fund Class A	JIGAX	B+	A-	B	Up	8.09	15.44	31.54	39.96	123.86	55.84	1,148	800-480-4111	Y
Hartford MidCap HLS Fund Class IA	HIMCX	B	B+	B	Up	7.42	11.07	24.46	40.50	123.83	40.1	2,185	888-843-7824	Y
JNL/Mellon Capital Financial Sector Fund Class A	US47760W7535	A-	A	B	Up	7.47	12.69	19.32	44.60	123.62	13.94	1,439		Y
AllianzGI Focused Growth Fund Class R	PPGRX	A-	A-	A-	Up	7.76	14.71	31.09	44.72	123.49	40.54	1,038	800-498-5413	Y
Great-West T. Rowe Price Mid Cap Growth Fund Inst Cls	MXYKX	B	B	B	Down	4.98	9.85	25.10	40.99	123.41		1,401		Y
Hartford Growth Opportunities HLS Fund Class IC	HCGOX	A-	A-	B+	Up	5.12	10.92	29.80	42.09	123.37	37.71	1,526	888-843-7824	Y
AllianzGI Focused Growth Fund R6	AFGFX	A-	A	A-	Up	7.95	15.10	31.93	45.90	123.15	48.78	1,038	800-498-5413	Y
The Hartford MidCap Fund Class R6	HFMVX	B+	B+	B	Up	7.42	11.08	24.42	40.55	123.07	35.78	10,481	888-843-7824	Y
Putnam Growth Opportunities Fund Class A	POGAX	B+	A-	B-	Up	6.59	13.17	30.96	39.62	122.83	31.3	4,621	617-292-1000	Y
Janus Henderson VIT Enterprise Portfolio Service Class	US4710217179	B	A-	B	Down	5.64	11.32	27.08	46.67	122.80	66.67	1,155	877-335-2687	Y
JNL/BlackRock Large Cap Select Growth Fund Class I	US46644W5004	A-	A-	B+	Up	7.72	13.75	33.91	42.33	122.71	37.8	3,082		Y
Carillon Eagle Mid Cap Growth Fund Class R6	HRAUX	B+	A	B-	Up	6.97	12.34	30.43	42.46	122.68	59.82	2,495	800-421-4184	Y
TIAA-CREF Large-Cap Growth Index Fund Retirement Class	TRIRX	B+	B+	B+	Up	7.76	14.05	29.78	44.59	122.61	29.05	5,628	877-518-9161	Y
JNL/T. Rowe Price Mid-Cap Growth Fund Class I	US46648L8072	B	B	B	Down	4.42	8.93	24.75	40.40	122.48	49.29	5,304		Y
Oppenheimer International Small-Mid Company Fund Class C	OSMCX	B+	B+	A	Up	5.99	12.50	36.92	53.87	122.18	45.67	10,129	800-225-5677	Y
ClearBridge Large Cap Growth Fund Class C	SLCCX	B	B	B	Down	6.76	12.11	24.13	41.30	122.16	32.8	9,321	877-721-1926	Y
EQ/Large Cap Growth Index Portfolio Class K	US26883L5553	B+	B+	B+	Up	8.29	14.80	29.38	43.74	122.08		1,412	877-222-2144	Y
TIAA-CREF Enhanced Large-Cap Growth Index Fund Advisor Cls	TECGX	B+	A-	B+		8.06	14.86	29.48	48.12	122.06	13.54	2,652	877-518-9161	Y
The Hartford MidCap Fund Class R5	HFMTX	B	B+	B	Up	7.40	11.05	24.30	40.16	121.96	35.46	10,481	888-843-7824	Y
Optimum Large Cap Growth Fund Class A	OALGX	B	B	B	Down	6.41	12.06	32.15	42.46	121.48	16.78	1,704		Y
Principal LargeCap Growth Fund I Class R-6	PLCGX	A-	A	B	Up	7.72	14.34	33.77	44.86	121.37	14.42	8,131	800-222-5852	Y
Great-West T. Rowe Price Mid Cap Growth Fund Investor Cls	MXMGX	B	B	B	Down	4.86	9.63	24.70	39.70	121.37		1,401		Y
Principal LargeCap Growth Fund I Institutional Class	PLGIX	A-	A	B	Up	7.68	14.29	33.69	44.87	121.36	14.43	8,131	800-222-5852	Y
Carillon Eagle Mid Cap Growth Fund Class R5	HARSX	B+	A	B-	Up	6.94	12.27	30.31	41.84	121.24	59.32	2,495	800-421-4184	Y
AXA Large Cap Growth Managed Vol Portfolio Class K	US26883L5488	B	B	B	Down	7.83	13.79	29.39	41.49	121.18		5,155	877-222-2144	Y
JPMorgan Intrepid Growth Fund Class R2	JIGZX	B+	A-	B	Up	8.03	15.28	31.25	38.95	121.12	54.83	1,148	800-480-4111	Y
Hartford MidCap HLS Fund Class IB	HBMCX	B	B+	B-	Up	7.37	10.92	24.16	39.47	121.01	39.18	2,185	888-843-7824	Y
The Hartford Growth Opportunities Fund Class R4	HGOSX	A-	A-	B+	Up	5.12	10.96	30.16	41.53	120.94	45.1	4,761	888-843-7824	Y
JNL/Mellon Capital Consumer Discretionary Sector Cls I	US47760W4078	B	B	A-		8.99	10.38	22.43	37.66	120.86	21.21	1,109		Y
Putnam Multi-Cap Growth Fund Class Y	PNOYX	B	B+	B-	Down	6.11	12.27	29.38	38.35	120.70	95.53	4,380	617-292-1000	Y
Multimanager Aggressive Equity Portfolio Class K	US00247C5360	B+	A-	B	Up	7.88	14.80	30.54	39.71	120.65		1,184	877-222-2144	Y
JPMorgan Large Cap Growth Fund Class R5	JLGRX	A-	A	B	Up	8.06	14.06	38.22	45.29	120.47	38.61	13,040	800-480-4111	Y
American Funds The New Economy Fund® Class R-6	RNGGX	A-	A	B	Up	5.61	14.65	34.79	43.08	120.41	44.68	18,784	800-421-4225	Y
Hartford Core Equity Fund Class R6	HAITX	B	B	B+		7.76	10.88	22.16	36.65	120.41	29.16	3,288	888-843-7824	Y
JNL/BlackRock Large Cap Select Growth Fund Class A	US46644W4015	B+	A-	B+	Up	7.67	13.65	33.62	41.47	120.39	36.46	3,082		Y
Deutsche Core Equity Fund Class R6	SUWZX	B	B	B		6.48	11.74	21.57	39.72	120.20	27.62	3,680	201-593-8273	Y
Putnam Growth Opportunities Fund Class R	PGORX	B	A-	B-	Down	6.52	13.01	30.66	38.53	120.04	30.26	4,621	617-292-1000	Y
Janus Henderson Forty Fund Class N	JFRNX	B+	B+	A-	Up	4.50	10.40	29.71	48.14	119.92	32.68	11,753	877-335-2687	Y
American Funds The New Economy Fund® Class R-5	RNGFX	A-	A	B	Up	5.59	14.60	34.74	42.89	119.89	44.84	18,784	800-421-4225	Y
Hartford Core Equity Fund Class R5	HGITX	B	B	B+		7.71	10.80	22.02	36.43	119.82	29.05	3,288	888-843-7824	Y
Janus Henderson Enterprise Fund Class N	JDMNX	B	B+	B	Down	5.52	11.00	26.64	46.03	119.73	118.59	16,122	877-335-2687	Y
MassMutual Select Mid Cap Growth Fund Class I	MEFZX	B	B	B	Down	4.41	8.88	24.66	39.28	119.70	21.47	5,628		Y

Fund Name	Ticker Symbol	RATINGS: Overall Rating	RATINGS: Reward Rating	RATINGS: Risk Rating	RATINGS: Recent Up/ Downgrade	TOTAL RETURNS & PERFORMANCE: 3-Month Total Return	TOTAL RETURNS & PERFORMANCE: 6-Month Total Return	TOTAL RETURNS & PERFORMANCE: 1-Year Total Return	TOTAL RETURNS & PERFORMANCE: 3-Year Total Return	TOTAL RETURNS & PERFORMANCE: 5-Year Total Return	ASSETS: NAV	ASSETS: Total Assets (MIL)	NEW INVESTORS: Telephone	NEW INVESTORS: Open to New Investors
EQ/Large Cap Growth Index Portfolio Class IA	US2689405171	B+	B+	B+	Up	8.28	14.64	29.10	42.70	119.33		1,412	877-222-2144	Y
MFS® Growth Fund Class R6	MFEKX	A-	B+	A	Up	6.50	11.89	30.98	43.25	119.30	95.65	16,680	877-960-6077	Y
American Funds The New Economy Fund® Class F-2	NEFFX	A-	A	B	Up	5.56	14.58	34.66	42.63	119.29	44.55	18,784	800-421-4225	Y
EQ/Large Cap Growth Index Portfolio Class IB	US2689404919	B+	B+	B+	Up	8.23	14.59	29.06	42.73	119.25		1,412	877-222-2144	Y
Deutsche Capital Growth Fund Class R6	SDGZX	B	B	B	Down	5.96	10.77	26.33	40.82	119.23	77.41	1,521	201-593-8273	Y
Laudus U.S. Large Cap Growth Fund	LGILX	A-	A-	B+	Up	7.64	13.82	33.90	42.30	119.20	19.35	1,858		Y
Strategic Advisers® Growth Fund	FSGFX	B+	B+	B	Up	6.89	13.08	29.44	41.27	119.11	18.68	11,813	617-563-7000	Y
John Hancock Funds Strategic Growth Fund Class NAV	US47803W8441	B+	B+	B	Up	5.81	12.54	29.28	39.43	119.03	17.54	1,922	800-225-5913	Y
Fidelity® Magellan® Fund Class K	FMGKX	B	B+	B		6.91	14.08	26.62	37.80	118.95	104.41	16,929	617-563-7000	Y
Fidelity® Contrafund® Fund Class K	FCNKX	A-	A-	A-	Up	6.77	13.31	32.38	44.75	118.81	122.39	124,619	617-563-7000	Y
Principal LargeCap Growth Fund I R-5 Class	PPUPX	A-	A	B	Up	7.72	14.24	33.45	44.02	118.72	13.93	8,131	800-222-5852	Y
JNL/Mellon Capital Consumer Discretionary Sector Cls A	US47760W3088	B	B	A-		8.89	10.22	22.10	36.73	118.62	20.81	1,109		Y
MassMutual Select Mid Cap Growth Fund Class R5	MGRFX	B	B	B	Down	4.40	8.86	24.56	38.92	118.58	21.29	5,628		Y
The Hartford MidCap Fund Class R4	HFMSX	B	B+	B	Up	7.30	10.87	23.92	38.85	118.57	34.59	10,481	888-843-7824	Y
Multimanager Aggressive Equity Portfolio Class IA	US4049924719	B+	A-	B	Up	7.81	14.66	30.20	39.06	118.52		1,184	877-222-2144	Y
AXA Large Cap Growth Managed Volatility Portfolio Class IB	US2689407649	B	B	B	Down	7.76	13.67	29.09	40.45	118.47		5,155	877-222-2144	Y
Multimanager Aggressive Equity Portfolio Class IB	US4049924891	B+	A-	B	Up	7.81	14.66	30.20	39.05	118.46		1,184	877-222-2144	Y
AXA Large Cap Growth Managed Volatility Portfolio Class IA	US2689408068	B	B	B	Down	7.75	13.65	29.07	40.43	118.43		5,155	877-222-2144	Y
JPMorgan Intrepid Growth Fund Class C	JCICX	B	A-	B	Down	7.97	15.15	30.93	37.90	118.38	54.94	1,148	800-480-4111	Y
JPMorgan Large Cap Growth Fund Class R4	JLGQX	A-	A	B	Up	8.03	13.96	37.99	44.45	118.31	37.93	13,040	800-480-4111	Y
MFS® Growth Fund Class R4	MFEJX	A-	B+	A	Up	6.47	11.83	30.87	42.85	118.25	92.87	16,680	877-960-6077	Y
MFS® Growth Fund Class I	MFEIX	A-	B+	A	Up	6.47	11.83	30.86	42.84	118.25	95.4	16,680	877-960-6077	Y
Great-West T. Rowe Price Mid Cap Growth Fund Class L	MXTMX	B	B	B	Down	4.74	9.41	24.33	38.53	118.22		1,401		Y
American Funds The New Economy Fund® Class 529-F	CNGFX	A-	A	B	Up	5.53	14.52	34.55	42.21	118.19	44.11	18,784	800-421-4225	Y
American Century Select Fund R6 Class	ASDEX	B+	B+	B	Up	6.62	13.64	29.35	46.62	118.15	71.13	2,939	800-444-4015	Y
AllianzGI Focused Growth Fund Class C	PGWCX	A-	A-	A-	Up	7.64	14.44	30.44	42.57	118.06	36.79	1,038	800-498-5413	Y
Putnam Multi-Cap Growth Fund Class A	PNOPX	B	B+	B-	Down	6.03	12.13	29.05	37.31	117.92	89.45	4,380	617-292-1000	Y
Carillon Eagle Mid Cap Growth Fund Class A	HAGAX	B+	A	C+	Up	6.87	12.12	29.90	40.61	117.87	56.49	2,495	800-421-4184	Y
Carillon Eagle Mid Cap Growth Fund Class Y	HRAYX	B+	A	C+		6.85	12.10	29.88	40.59	117.84	59.46	2,495	800-421-4184	Y
Alger Capital Appreciation Institutional Fund Class I	ALARX	B+	B+	A-	Up	6.56	12.48	31.01	38.83	117.75	32.42	3,685	800-992-3863	Y
American Funds The Growth Fund of America® Class R-6	RGAGX	B	B	B	Down	7.00	12.45	26.52	44.54	117.67	49.56	176,790	800-421-4225	Y
Principal LargeCap Growth Fund I Class J	PLGJX	A-	A	B	Up	7.61	14.14	33.49	43.74	117.64	12	8,131	800-222-5852	Y
The Hartford Growth Opportunities Fund Class R3	HGORX	B+	A-	B+	Up	5.06	10.77	29.77	40.26	117.62	42.97	4,761	888-843-7824	Y
Ivy Large Cap Growth Fund Class I	IYGIX	B+	A-	B	Up	6.16	14.36	29.37	39.37	117.61	22.84	1,889	800-777-6472	Y
Alger Capital Appreciation Fund Class A	ACAAX	B+	B+	A-	Up	6.48	12.58	31.22	38.79	117.60	24.66	2,859	800-992-3863	Y
Voya Large Cap Growth Portfolio Class I	IEOHX	B	B	B	Down	7.93	13.56	29.74	42.21	117.60	20.8	6,331	800-366-0066	Y
American Funds The New Economy Fund® Class R-5E	RNGHX	A-	A	B	Up	5.54	14.57	34.70	42.21	117.56	44.41	18,784	800-421-4225	Y
Multi-Manager Growth Strategies Fund Institutional Class	CZMGX	B	B	B	Down	5.74	10.92	31.90	36.92	117.52	14.54	2,657	800-345-6611	Y
JNL/JPMorgan MidCap Growth Fund Class I	US46648M1100	B	B+	C+	Up	5.80	12.17	29.73	34.24	117.45	35.34	2,102		Y
American Funds The New Economy Fund® Class F-3	FNEFX	A-	A	B	Up	5.58	14.62	34.78	42.12	117.42	44.63	18,784	800-421-4225	Y
Carillon Scout Mid Cap Fund Class R-5	CSMSX	B+	A	B-		7.46	13.57	24.04	47.48	117.42	19.01	1,790	800-421-4184	Y
Carillon Scout Mid Cap Fund Class R-6	CSMUX	B+	A	B-		7.46	13.57	24.04	47.48	117.42	19.01	1,790	800-421-4184	Y
Fidelity® Series Intrinsic Opportunities Fund	FDMLX	B	B	B	Up	6.87	12.10	24.36	40.70	117.37	18.11	13,638	617-563-7000	Y
Federated Kaufmann Fund Class R Shares	KAUFX	B	B+	B	Up	5.40	11.57	27.68	38.96	117.34	5.6	5,697	800-341-7400	Y
Principal LargeCap Growth Fund I R-4 Class	PPUSX	A-	A	B	Up	7.60	14.06	33.23	43.47	117.31	13.44	8,131	800-222-5852	Y
Waddell & Reed Advisors Vanguard Fund Class Y	WAVYX	A-	A-	A-	Up	6.17	14.34	29.32	39.47	117.30	11.89	1,720	888-923-3355	Y
Putnam Growth Opportunities Fund Class M	PGOMX	B	A-	B-	Down	6.42	12.83	30.26	37.46	117.28	28.32	4,621	617-292-1000	Y
American Funds The Growth Fund of America® Class R-5	RGAFX	B	B	B	Down	6.97	12.43	26.43	44.33	117.12	49.49	176,790	800-421-4225	Y
Deutsche Core Equity Fund Class T	SUWUX	B	B	B		6.39	11.45	21.02	38.49	116.99	27.3	3,680	201-593-8273	Y
Wells Fargo Large Cap Core Fund - Class R	EGOHX	B	B	B-	Up	7.52	14.12	22.99	32.07	116.89	19.74	1,120	800-222-8222	Y
Wells Fargo Disciplined U.S. Core Fund - Class R6	EVSRX	B	B	B+		6.46	11.72	20.96	37.27	116.83	17.49	1,298	800-222-8222	Y
American Funds The New Economy Fund® Class A	ANEFX	A-	A	B	Up	5.52	14.44	34.37	41.69	116.77	44.63	18,784	800-421-4225	Y

		RATINGS				TOTAL RETURNS & PERFORMANCE					ASSETS		NEW INVESTORS	
Fund Name	Ticker Symbol	Overall Rating	Reward Rating	Risk Rating	Recent Up/ Downgrade	3-Month Total Return	6-Month Total Return	1-Year Total Return	3-Year Total Return	5-Year Total Return	NAV	Total Assets (MIL)	Telephone	Open to New Investors
Multi-Manager Growth Strategies Fund Class A	CSLGX	B	B	B	Down	5.77	10.88	31.44	36.44	116.76	14.73	2,657	800-345-6611	Y
Alger Spectra Fund Class I	ASPIX	B+	B+	A-	Up	6.62	12.50	31.04	39.04	116.71	20.77	5,947	800-992-3863	Y
Deutsche Core Equity Fund Class A	SUWAX	B	B	B		6.41	11.53	21.12	38.48	116.70	27.31	3,680	201-593-8273	Y
Wells Fargo Large Cap Core Fund - Class A	EGOAX	B	B	B-	Up	7.56	14.17	23.22	32.52	116.68	19.71	1,120	800-222-8222	Y
Alger Spectra Fund Class A	SPECX	B+	B+	A-	Up	6.64	12.52	31.03	39.01	116.66	20.57	5,947	800-992-3863	Y
Deutsche Capital Growth Fund Class A	SDGAX	B	B	B	Down	5.89	10.61	25.93	39.93	116.65	77.03	1,521	201-593-8273	Y
American Funds The New Economy Fund® Class R-4	RNGEX	A-	A	B	Up	5.50	14.43	34.30	41.58	116.63	44.2	18,784	800-421-4225	Y
American Funds The Growth Fund of America® Class F-2	GFFFX	B	B	B	Down	6.95	12.39	26.38	44.08	116.59	49.42	176,790	800-421-4225	Y
JPMorgan Large Cap Growth Fund Class A	OLGAX	A-	A	B	Up	7.95	13.85	37.71	43.77	116.57	37.61	13,040	800-480-4111	Y
Hartford Core Equity Fund Class R4	HGISX	B	B-	B+		7.63	10.62	21.64	35.26	116.53	29.65	3,288	888-843-7824	Y
American Funds The New Economy Fund® Class F-1	ANFFX	A-	A	B	Up	5.48	14.41	34.28	41.44	116.24	44.76	18,784	800-421-4225	Y
John Hancock Funds Strategic Growth Fund Class R4	JHSGX	B+	B+	B	Up	5.72	12.39	29.02	38.28	116.15	17.55	1,922	800-225-5913	Y
Voya Large Cap Growth Portfolio Class R6	VRLCX	B	B	B	Down	7.99	13.55	29.79	41.91	116.02	20.81	6,331	800-366-0066	Y
American Funds The New Economy Fund® Class 529-A	CNGAX	A-	A	B	Up	5.50	14.41	34.29	41.36	115.98	44.18	18,784	800-421-4225	Y
JPMorgan Mid Cap Growth Fund Class R5	JMGFX	B	B+	B	Up	5.70	12.05	29.67	33.32	115.82	33.79	3,490	800-480-4111	Y
Ivy Large Cap Growth Fund Class Y	WLGYX	A-	A-	A-	Up	6.08	14.25	29.15	38.60	115.69	22.31	1,889	800-777-6472	Y
JPMorgan Large Cap Growth Fund Class R3	JLGPX	A-	A	B	Up	7.94	13.82	37.62	43.40	115.64	37.79	13,040	800-480-4111	Y
MFS® Growth Fund Class A	MFEGX	A-	B+	A	Up	6.40	11.69	30.54	41.79	115.60	89.95	16,680	877-960-6077	Y
American Funds The Growth Fund of America® Class 529-F	CGFFX	B	B	B	Down	6.95	12.35	26.30	43.76	115.60	48.91	176,790	800-421-4225	Y
MFS® Growth Fund Class R3	MFEHX	A-	B+	A	Up	6.40	11.69	30.52	41.77	115.58	89.51	16,680	877-960-6077	Y
Thrivent Series Large Cap Growth Portfolio		B+	B+	A-	Up	6.34	11.41	28.51	38.77	115.48	35.5091	1,195		Y
Principal LargeCap Growth Fund I R-3 Class	PPUMX	A-	A	B	Up	7.64	14.04	33.04	42.64	115.36	13.22	8,131	800-222-5852	Y
American Century Select Fund Y Class	ASLWX	B+	B+	B	Up	6.62	13.64	29.22	45.42	115.31	71.2	2,939	800-444-4015	Y
JNL/JPMorgan MidCap Growth Fund Class A	US46648M1282	B	B+	C+	Up	5.69	11.99	29.40	33.35	115.24	34.51	2,102		Y
Putnam Multi-Cap Growth Fund Class R	PNORX	B	B+	B-	Down	5.97	11.98	28.73	36.30	115.23	86.72	4,380	617-292-1000	Y
The Hartford MidCap Fund Class R3	HFMRX	B	B+	B-	Up	7.24	10.68	23.53	37.57	115.23	33.39	10,481	888-843-7824	Y
Dreyfus Opportunistic Small Cap Fund Class I	DOPIX	B+	A-	B	Up	8.55	13.64	24.40	40.05	115.13	36.82	1,092	800-645-6561	Y
Principal LargeCap Growth Fund I Class A	PLGAX	A-	A	A-	Up	7.58	14.02	33.09	42.55	115.08	14.05	8,131	800-222-5852	Y
American Century Select Fund R5 Class	ASLGX	B+	B+	B	Up	6.56	13.54	29.08	45.25	115.06	71.23	2,939	800-444-4015	Y
Columbia Select Large-Cap Value Fund Institutional 2 Class	SLVIX	B	B	B-	Up	7.84	13.50	20.44	36.13	115.02	27.2	1,001	800-345-6611	Y
DFA U.S. Large Cap Value Portfolio Institutional Class	DFLVX	B	B	B	Up	7.46	12.42	18.96	35.07	114.95	39.12	24,727	512-306-7400	Y
Carillon Scout Mid Cap Fund Class A	CSMEX	B+	A	B-		7.41	13.45	23.76	46.45	114.87	19.01	1,790	800-421-4184	Y
Carillon Scout Mid Cap Fund Class Y	CSMZX	B+	A	B-		7.41	13.45	23.76	46.44	114.86	19.01	1,790	800-421-4184	Y
Carillon Eagle Mid Cap Growth Fund Class R3	HAREX	B	A-	C+	Down	6.80	11.95	29.54	39.46	114.84	54.88	2,495	800-421-4184	Y
American Funds The Growth Fund of America® Class R-5E	RGAHX	B	B	B	Down	6.95	12.36	26.35	43.61	114.83	49.18	176,790	800-421-4225	Y
John Hancock Funds Strategic Growth Fund Class R2	JSGRX	B	B+	B	Down	5.63	12.24	28.68	37.43	114.82	17.57	1,922	800-225-5913	Y
Voya Large Cap Growth Portfolio Class S	IEOSX	B	B	B	Down	7.85	13.37	29.41	41.10	114.79	20.32	6,331	800-366-0066	Y
American Funds The Growth Fund of America® Class F-3	GAFFX	B	B	B	Down	6.98	12.45	26.47	43.57	114.77	49.53	176,790	800-421-4225	Y
Columbia Select Large Cap Growth Fund Institutional 2 Cls	CGTRX	B	B	B	Up	5.23	9.16	35.55	33.24	114.77	17.09	4,164	800-345-6611	Y
Ivy Large Cap Growth Fund Class A	WLGAX	B+	A-	B	Up	6.09	14.25	29.03	38.30	114.73	21.76	1,889	800-777-6472	Y
Wells Fargo Disciplined U.S. Core Fund - Class A	EVSAX	B	B	B+		6.37	11.42	20.46	35.92	114.70	17.08	1,298	800-222-8222	Y
Principal Blue Chip Fund Institutional Class	PBCKX	B+	A-	B	Up	6.83	13.28	28.85	46.66	114.68	21.16	2,340	800-222-5852	Y
Ivy Large Cap Growth Fund Class E	ILCEX	A-	A-	A-	Up	6.05	14.21	29.01	38.21	114.67	21.73	1,889	800-777-6472	Y
Putnam Growth Opportunities Fund Class C	POGCX	B	A-	B-		6.38	12.70	30.00	36.49	114.64	27.17	4,621	617-292-1000	Y
Putnam Growth Opportunities Fund Class B	POGBX	B	A-	B-		6.37	12.72	29.94	36.48	114.59	26.69	4,621	617-292-1000	Y
Principal Blue Chip Fund Class R-6	PGBHX	B+	A-	B	Up	6.83	13.28	28.78	46.58	114.56	21.16	2,340	800-222-5852	Y
Putnam Investors Fund Class R6	PIVEX	B	B	B-	Up	7.58	14.20	23.38	34.50	114.38	28.93	2,054	617-292-1000	Y
Waddell & Reed Advisors Vanguard Fund Class A	UNVGX	A-	A-	A-	Up	6.11	14.24	29.15	38.55	114.36	11.05	1,720	888-923-3355	Y
JPMorgan U.S. Equity Fund Class R5	JUSRX	B	B	B-		6.87	11.49	21.58	34.71	114.36	16.3	15,686	800-480-4111	Y
Columbia Contrarian Core Fund Institutional 3 Class	COFYX	B	B-	B+	Down	5.41	9.81	21.88	35.53	114.23	26.28	11,572	800-345-6611	Y
American Funds The Growth Fund of America® Class A	AGTHX	B	B	B	Down	6.91	12.27	26.13	43.20	114.21	49.54	176,790	800-421-4225	Y
JPMorgan Mid Cap Growth Fund Class R4	JMGQX	B	B+	C+	Up	5.67	11.95	29.39	32.67	114.14	33.4	3,490	800-480-4111	Y

Fund Name	Ticker Symbol	RATINGS: Overall Rating	Reward Rating	Risk Rating	Recent Up/ Downgrade	TOTAL RETURNS & PERFORMANCE: 3-Month Total Return	6-Month Total Return	1-Year Total Return	3-Year Total Return	5-Year Total Return	ASSETS: NAV	Total Assets (MIL)	NEW INVESTORS: Telephone	Open to New Investors
John Hancock Funds Strategic Growth Fund Class A	JSGAX	B+	B+	B	Up	5.66	12.32	28.83	37.74	114.00	17.42	1,922	800-225-5913	Y
Oakmark Fund Investor Class	OAKMX	B	B	B	Up	5.98	12.08	21.14	36.50	113.99	84.33	19,380	641-219-558	Y
Neuberger Berman Multi-Cap Opportunities Fund Class A	NMUAX	B	B	B-		6.96	11.53	24.42	37.54	113.96	18.46	2,064	212-476-9000	Y
American Funds The Growth Fund of America® Class R-4	RGAEX	B	B	B	Down	6.90	12.27	26.08	43.07	113.95	49.1	176,790	800-421-4225	Y
Janus Henderson Research Fund Class N	JRANX	B	B	A-	Down	6.92	10.16	26.38	34.54	113.90	46.29	13,532	877-335-2687	Y
Janus Henderson Growth And Income Fund Class N	JDNNX	B	B	B		9.05	14.31	24.96	41.72	113.89	55.07	5,178	877-335-2687	Y
JPMorgan Large Cap Growth Fund Class R2	JLGZX	A-	A	B	Up	7.86	13.67	37.32	42.63	113.82	36.53	13,040	800-480-4111	Y
Principal Blue Chip Fund Class R-5	PGBGX	B+	A-	B	Up	6.77	13.12	28.53	46.04	113.78	21.11	2,340	800-222-5852	Y
DFA U.S. Large Cap Growth Portfolio Institutional Class	DUSLX	B	B	B		8.74	13.87	25.53	38.59	113.73	19.17	1,747	512-306-7400	Y
American Funds The Growth Fund of America® Class F-1	GFAFX	B	B	B	Down	6.90	12.25	26.07	42.94	113.65	49.22	176,790	800-421-4225	Y
American Funds The New Economy Fund® Class R-2E	RNNEX	A-	A	B	Up	5.37	14.18	33.72	40.37	113.62	43.98	18,784	800-421-4225	Y
Optimum Large Cap Growth Fund Class C	OCLGX	B	B	B	Down	6.28	11.69	31.24	39.32	113.57	14.28	1,704		Y
Pioneer Select Mid Cap Growth Fund Class A	PGOFX	B	B+	B-	Up	8.55	15.55	29.78	35.37	113.50	41.99	1,577	617-742-7825	Y
Principal LargeCap Growth Fund I R-2 Class	PPUNX	A-	A	B	Up	7.56	13.87	32.75	41.90	113.45	12.22	8,131	800-222-5852	Y
JPMorgan U.S. Equity Fund Class R4	JUEQX	B	B	B-		6.85	11.44	21.37	34.21	113.43	16.27	15,686	800-480-4111	Y
Hartford Core Equity Fund Class R3	HGIRX	B	B-	A		7.57	10.49	21.34	34.04	113.36	29.25	3,288	888-843-7824	Y
American Funds The Growth Fund of America® Class 529-A	CGFAX	B	B	B	Down	6.88	12.25	26.05	42.84	113.34	49.03	176,790	800-421-4225	Y
American Funds The New Economy Fund® Class 529-E	CNGEX	A-	A	B	Up	5.45	14.29	33.97	40.32	113.30	43.56	18,784	800-421-4225	Y
American Funds The New Economy Fund® Class R-3	RNGCX	A-	A	B	Up	5.42	14.24	33.90	40.29	113.24	43.63	18,784	800-421-4225	Y
Voya Large Cap Growth Portfolio Class S2	IEOTX	B	B	B	Down	7.85	13.35	29.21	40.51	113.24	20.18	6,331	800-366-0066	Y
Principal Blue Chip Fund Class J	PBCJX	B+	A-	B		6.76	13.17	28.63	45.96	113.02	21.14	2,340	800-222-5852	Y
Columbia Disciplined Core Fund Advisor Class	CLCQX	B	B	B		7.81	13.94	24.45	34.23	113.00	12.05	4,356	800-345-6611	Y
JPMorgan Intrepid America Fund Class R5	JIARX	B	B	B-	Up	8.59	14.80	23.52	32.02	113.00	40.88	4,398	800-480-4111	Y
PRINCIPAL MIDCAP FUND Class R-6	PMAQX	B	B	B-		4.94	11.11	25.40	38.76	112.99	27.25	15,667	800-222-5852	Y
Columbia Disciplined Core Fund Institutional 3 Class	CCQYX	B	B	B		7.74	13.99	24.53	34.45	112.97	12.01	4,356	800-345-6611	Y
MFS® Growth Fund Class R2	MEGRX	A-	B+	A	Up	6.33	11.54	30.20	40.71	112.86	85.22	16,680	877-960-6077	Y
Transamerica US Growth Class I2	US8939623737	B+	B	A-	Up	8.04	12.55	29.32	40.71	112.80	19.68	1,099	888-233-4339	Y
Homestead Funds Value Fund	HOVLX	B	B	B		8.00	14.53	22.16	34.19	112.76	55.26	1,107		Y
Principal Blue Chip Fund Class R-4	PGBFX	B+	A-	B	Up	6.73	13.08	28.43	45.61	112.71	21.08	2,340	800-222-5852	Y
JPMorgan Tax Aware Equity Fund Class A	JPEAX	B	B	B-		7.08	11.31	22.83	35.56	112.65	33.29	1,313	800-480-4111	Y
MainStay Large Cap Growth Fund Class R6	MLRSX	B+	B+	B+	Up	5.85	11.90	32.50	36.56	112.64	9.76	12,363	800-624-6782	Y
Alger Capital Appreciation Institutional Fund Class R	ACARX	B+	B+	A-	Up	6.47	12.24	30.47	36.85	112.60	29.08	3,685	800-992-3863	Y
Putnam Multi-Cap Growth Fund Class M	PNOMX	B	B+	B-		5.89	11.83	28.40	35.27	112.52	77.85	4,380	617-292-1000	Y
JNL/Invesco Small Cap Growth Fund Class I	US46648M1936	B	A-	C+	Up	6.73	13.26	25.25	36.79	112.51	25.82	1,913		Y
AIG Focused Dividend Strategy Fund Class A	FDSAX	B	B	B		7.46	13.58	20.24	36.12	112.44	18.75	14,853	800-858-8850	Y
Deutsche Capital Growth Fund Class R	SDGRX	B	B	B	Down	5.76	10.36	25.41	38.26	112.38	76.04	1,521	201-593-8273	Y
MFS® Core Equity Fund Class R6	MRGKX	B	B	B-		6.23	11.60	24.85	37.95	112.37	32.69	1,853	877-960-6077	Y
Putnam Investors Fund Class Y	PNVYX	B	B	B-	Up	7.53	14.10	23.16	33.93	112.37	28.8	2,054	617-292-1000	Y
Columbia Contrarian Core Fund Advisor Class	CORRX	B	B-	B+		5.38	9.75	21.70	34.92	112.36	26.3	11,572	800-345-6611	Y
Transamerica US Growth Class Advisor	TAUGX	B+	B	A-	Up	7.97	12.45	29.03	40.39	112.32	19.81	1,099	888-233-4339	Y
Carillon Scout Mid Cap Fund Class R-3	CSMRX	B+	A	B-		7.31	13.27	23.41	45.31	112.14	19.01	1,790	800-421-4184	Y
Wells Fargo Disciplined U.S. Core Fund - Class R	EVSHX	B	B	B+		6.28	11.34	20.17	34.96	112.11	17.28	1,298	800-222-8222	Y
Principal LargeCap Growth Fund I R-1 Class	PCRSX	A-	A-	A-	Up	7.47	13.81	32.70	41.38	112.09	12.52	8,131	800-222-5852	Y
American Funds AMCAP Fund® Class R-6	RAFGX	B	B	B-	Up	6.06	12.08	22.41	34.40	111.99	31.8	60,672	800-421-4225	Y
American Funds Fundamental Investors® Class R-6	RFNGX	B	B	B+	Down	6.71	12.37	23.72	43.62	111.98	62.22	95,399	800-421-4225	Y
Transamerica US Growth Class T	TWMTX	B+	B	A-	Up	8.01	12.53	29.20	40.42	111.83	52.01	1,099	888-233-4339	Y
Principal Blue Chip Fund Class T	PBLTX	B+	B+	B	Up	6.67	13.01	28.38	45.39	111.76	21.1	2,340	800-222-5852	Y
Deutsche Core Equity Fund Class R	SUWTX	B	B	B	Up	6.30	11.34	20.65	36.98	111.69	27.57	3,680	201-593-8273	Y
Voya Large Cap Growth Portfolio Class A	IEOPX	B	B	B	Down	7.79	13.23	29.01	39.68	111.59	19.36	6,331	800-366-0066	Y
American Funds AMCAP Fund® Class R-5	RAFFX	B	B	B-	Up	6.06	12.08	22.33	34.23	111.51	31.88	60,672	800-421-4225	Y
JPMorgan Mid Cap Growth Fund Class R3	JMGPX	B	B	C+	Up	5.59	11.82	29.04	31.69	111.50	33.28	3,490	800-480-4111	Y
American Funds Fundamental Investors® Class R-5	RFNFX	B	B	B+	Down	6.71	12.34	23.67	43.41	111.48	62.25	95,399	800-421-4225	Y

Fund Name	Ticker Symbol	RATINGS: Overall Rating	Reward Rating	Risk Rating	Recent Up/ Downgrade	TOTAL RETURNS & PERFORMANCE: 3-Month Total Return	6-Month Total Return	1-Year Total Return	3-Year Total Return	5-Year Total Return	ASSETS: NAV	Total Assets (MIL)	NEW INVESTORS: Telephone	Open to New Investors
MFS® Core Equity Fund Class I	MRGRX	B	B	B-		6.21	11.54	24.76	37.58	111.48	32.65	1,853	877-960-6077	Y
MFS® Core Equity Fund Class R4	MRGJX	B	B	B-		6.19	11.55	24.77	37.56	111.46	31.17	1,853	877-960-6077	Y
Franklin Growth Series Class A	FKGRX	B	B	B	Down	6.04	11.61	26.82	38.92	111.37	94.51	14,695	650-312-2000	Y
TIAA-CREF Growth & Income Fund Advisor Class	TGIHX	B	B	B		6.83	12.07	23.91	37.98	111.34	14.3	6,850	877-518-9161	Y
Ivy Large Cap Growth Fund Class R	WLGRX	A-	A-	A-	Up	6.02	14.07	28.67	36.95	111.23	20.95	1,889	800-777-6472	Y
JPMorgan Large Cap Growth Fund Class C	OLGCX	B+	A	B	Up	7.81	13.55	37.01	41.60	111.23	30.38	13,040	800-480-4111	Y
JPMorgan Mid Cap Growth Fund Class A	OSGIX	B	B	B	Up	5.59	11.82	29.06	31.53	111.10	29.13	3,490	800-480-4111	Y
American Funds AMCAP Fund® Class F-2	AMCFX	B	B	B-	Up	6.04	12.06	22.26	33.98	110.92	31.67	60,672	800-421-4225	Y
MFS® Mid Cap Growth Fund Class R6	OTCKX	B+	B+	A-	Up	5.03	10.39	26.38	37.52	110.91	16.98	2,561	877-960-6077	Y
American Funds Fundamental Investors® Class F-2	FINFX	B	B	B+	Down	6.69	12.30	23.57	43.16	110.90	62.19	95,399	800-421-4225	Y
MainStay Large Cap Growth Fund Class R1	MLRRX	B+	B+	B+	Up	5.83	11.82	32.41	35.69	110.89	9.48	12,363	800-624-6782	Y
DFA U.S. Large Company Portfolio	DFUSX	B	B	B		6.60	11.36	21.73	36.66	110.85	20.71	8,252	512-306-7400	Y
Principal Blue Chip Fund Class R-3	PGBEX	B+	B+	B	Up	6.64	12.95	28.09	44.75	110.83	21.01	2,340	800-222-5852	Y
American Century Growth Fund R6 Class	AGRDX	B+	B+	B	Up	7.73	12.71	30.58	41.95	110.80	33.34	8,242	800-444-4015	Y
American Funds The Growth Fund of America® Class R-3	RGACX	B	B	B	Down	6.83	12.09	25.70	41.77	110.79	48.63	176,790	800-421-4225	Y
Oakmark Fund Service Class	OARMX	B	B	B	Up	5.89	11.93	20.82	35.19	110.75	84.08	19,380	641-219-558	Y
JPMorgan U.S. Equity Fund Class R3	JUEPX	B	B	B-		6.76	11.23	21.02	33.18	110.74	16.19	15,686	800-480-4111	Y
American Funds The Growth Fund of America® Class 529-E	CGFEX	B	B	B	Down	6.81	12.10	25.73	41.80	110.72	48.55	176,790	800-421-4225	Y
Schwab® S&P 500 Index Fund	SWPPX	B	B	B		6.64	11.40	21.79	36.53	110.72	41.19	31,173	877-824-5615	Y
MM S&P 500® Index Fund Class I	MMIZX	B	B	B		6.67	11.41	21.72	36.40	110.68	18.55	3,367		Y
TIAA-CREF S&P 500 Index Fund Advisor Class	TISAX	B	B	B		6.54	11.29	21.59	36.41	110.65	29.59	4,838	877-518-9161	Y
VY® T. Rowe Price Diversified Mid Cap Growth Port Cls R6	VYRIX	B	B	B-	Up	5.86	10.58	24.80	35.99	110.54	11.56	1,016	800-366-0066	Y
Goldman Sachs U.S. Tax-Managed Equity Fund Investor Class	GQIRX	B	B	B-		5.94	11.09	20.14	30.10	110.53	22.7	1,456	800-526-7384	Y
Elfun Trusts	ELFNX	B	B	B+		5.00	10.70	25.61	34.12	110.46	60.36	2,772	800-242-0134	Y
JNL/Invesco Small Cap Growth Fund Class A	US46648M2199	B	A-	C+	Up	6.63	13.14	24.96	35.97	110.40	24.91	1,913		Y
VY® T. Rowe Price Diversified Mid Cap Growth Port Cls I	IAXIX	B	B	B-	Up	5.95	10.68	24.80	35.87	110.35	11.56	1,016	800-366-0066	Y
JPMorgan U.S. Equity Fund Class A	JUEAX	B	B	B-		6.73	11.26	21.12	33.15	110.32	16.24	15,686	800-480-4111	Y
American Funds The Growth Fund of America® Class R-2E	RGEBX	B	B	B	Down	6.78	12.02	25.52	41.37	110.31	48.73	176,790	800-421-4225	Y
DFA U.S. Core Equity 1 Portfolio Institutional Class	DFEOX	B	B	B-		6.90	12.06	20.89	35.62	110.27	22.78	21,603	512-306-7400	Y
TIAA-CREF Growth & Income Fund Premier Class	TRPGX	B	B	B		6.83	12.16	23.94	37.59	110.26	14.31	6,850	877-518-9161	Y
Transamerica US Growth Class T1	TJNTX	B+	B	A-	Up	7.97	12.42	29.03	39.69	110.21	19.42	1,099	888-233-4339	Y
Carillon Eagle Mid Cap Growth Fund Class C	HAGCX	B	A-	C+	Up	6.66	11.72	28.98	37.61	110.20	45.39	2,495	800-421-4184	Y
American Funds Fundamental Investors® Class 529-F-1	CFNFX	B	B	B+	Down	6.69	12.29	23.52	42.91	110.16	62.07	95,399	800-421-4225	Y
DFA Tax Managed U.S. Equity Portfolio	DTMEX	B	B	B		6.55	11.44	21.43	36.11	110.10	29.02	3,414	512-306-7400	Y
American Century NT Growth Fund G Class	ACLTX	B+	B+	B	Up	7.93	13.18	30.81	41.01	110.05	17.3	1,371	800-444-4015	Y
MFS® Mid Cap Growth Fund Class R4	OTCJX	B+	B+	A-	Up	4.98	10.28	26.28	37.10	110.03	16.51	2,561	877-960-6077	Y
American Funds AMCAP Fund® Class 529-F-1	CAFFX	B	B	B-	Up	6.01	12.00	22.19	33.64	109.99	31.38	60,672	800-421-4225	Y
Davis Financial Fund Class A	RPFGX	B+	B	B+	Up	6.31	10.55	19.26	38.19	109.97	51.94	1,332	800-279-0279	Y
Fidelity Advisor® Large Cap Fund Class Z	FIDLX	B	B	B	Up	6.04	11.05	18.62	32.84	109.93	34.76	1,387	617-563-7000	Y
Putnam Multi-Cap Growth Fund Class B	PNOBX	B	B+	B-		5.84	11.69	28.07	34.24	109.91	70.49	4,380	617-292-1000	Y
Putnam Multi-Cap Growth Fund Class C	PNOCX	B	B+	B-		5.83	11.71	28.09	34.25	109.89	76.52	4,380	617-292-1000	Y
Prudential QMA Stock Index Fund Class I	PDSIX	B	B	B		6.60	11.34	21.62	36.21	109.89	52.07	1,148	800-225-1852	Y
MFS® Mid Cap Growth Fund Class I	OTCIX	B+	B	A-	Up	4.99	10.31	26.28	37.07	109.84	16.89	2,561	877-960-6077	Y
Principal LargeCap S&P 500 Index Fund Institutional Class	PLFIX	B	B	B		6.62	11.31	21.64	36.19	109.84	17.51	5,749	800-222-5852	Y
Pioneer Select Mid Cap Growth Fund Class R	PGRRX	B	B	B-	Up	8.42	15.29	29.24	33.82	109.79	40.46	1,577	617-742-7825	Y
Dreyfus Institutional S&P 500 Stock Index Fund Class I	DSPIX	B	B	B		6.57	11.31	21.58	36.06	109.68	53.49	2,623	800-645-6561	Y
Columbia Large Cap Index Fund Institutional 2 Class	CLXRX	B	B	B		6.60	11.32	21.59	36.12	109.67	50.48	3,855	800-345-6611	Y
Putnam Investors Fund Class A	PINVX	B	B	B-	Up	7.46	13.95	22.88	32.93	109.66	28.4	2,054	617-292-1000	Y
DFA U.S. Sustainability Core 1 Portfolio	DFSIX	B	B	B-		6.89	11.93	21.35	35.23	109.63	21.11	1,249	512-306-7400	Y
Alger Capital Appreciation Fund Class C	ALCCX	B+	B+	B+	Up	6.31	12.21	30.30	35.70	109.55	19.59	2,859	800-992-3863	Y
Fidelity® Total Market Index Fund Class F	FFSMX	B	B	B		6.32	11.19	21.17	35.83	109.47	76.37	48,089	617-563-7000	Y
MM S&P 500® Index Fund Class R5	MIEZX	B	B	B		6.58	11.32	21.59	36.00	109.42	18.6	3,367		Y

		RATINGS				TOTAL RETURNS & PERFORMANCE					ASSETS		NEW INVESTORS	
Fund Name	Ticker Symbol	Overall Rating	Reward Rating	Risk Rating	Recent Up/ Downgrade	3-Month Total Return	6-Month Total Return	1-Year Total Return	3-Year Total Return	5-Year Total Return	NAV	Total Assets (MIL)	Telephone	Open to New Investors
American Funds AMCAP Fund® Class F-3	FMACX	B	B	B-	Up	6.06	12.10	22.40	33.55	109.34	31.5	60,672	800-421-4225	Y
American Funds Fundamental Investors® Class F-3	FUNFX	B	B	B+	Down	6.71	12.36	23.67	42.70	109.33	62.19	95,399	800-421-4225	Y
American Funds Fundamental Investors® Class R-5E	RFNHX	B	B	B+	Down	6.67	12.29	23.54	42.70	109.33	62.12	95,399	800-421-4225	Y
American Funds AMCAP Fund® Class R-5E	RAEFX	B	B	B-	Up	5.98	11.98	22.26	33.54	109.33	31.52	60,672	800-421-4225	Y
JPMorgan Mid Cap Growth Fund Class R2	JMGZX	B	B	C+	Up	5.54	11.71	28.80	30.87	109.29	31.68	3,490	800-480-4111	Y
TIAA-CREF Equity Index Fund Advisor Class	TEIHX	B	B	B		6.25	11.08	20.99	35.72	109.29	19.66	16,203	877-518-9161	Y
Principal Blue Chip Fund Class A	PBLAX	B+	B+	B	Up	6.73	13.06	28.30	44.36	109.26	20.93	2,340	800-222-5852	Y
TIAA-CREF Growth & Income Fund Retirement Class	TRGIX	B	B	B		6.84	12.07	23.77	37.13	109.17	14.54	6,850	877-518-9161	Y
Voya U.S. Stock Index Portfolio P2	VPSPX	B	B	B		6.59	11.35	21.53	35.81	109.01	15.71	5,089	800-366-0066	Y
Pioneer Disciplined Growth Fund Class A	PINDX	B	B	B		6.13	11.42	26.25	33.70	108.95	18.2	1,245	617-742-7825	Y
Voya U.S. Stock Index Portfolio Class I	INGIX	B	B	B		6.53	11.29	21.46	35.73	108.89	15.69	5,089	800-366-0066	Y
BlackRock Capital Appreciation Fund Investor A Shares	MDFGX	B+	B+	B+	Up	7.49	13.07	32.58	40.05	108.87	25.87	2,963	800-441-7762	Y
Fidelity Advisor® Stock Selector All Cap Fund Class K	FSSKX	B	B	B-		5.83	11.49	25.37	36.59	108.86	43.94	8,710	617-563-7000	Y
Fidelity Advisor® New Insights Fund Class Z	FZANX	B	B	B	Down	6.68	12.77	28.53	39.84	108.85	32.07	28,060	617-563-7000	Y
MFS® Core Equity Fund Class A	MRGAX	B	B	B-		6.15	11.41	24.45	36.55	108.83	30.95	1,853	877-960-6077	Y
American Funds Fundamental Investors® Class A	ANCFX	B	B	B+	Down	6.65	12.21	23.37	42.35	108.82	62.21	95,399	800-421-4225	Y
Wells Fargo Large Cap Core Fund - Class C	EGOCX	B	B	B-	Up	7.42	13.83	22.33	29.62	108.78	19.44	1,120	800-222-8222	Y
MFS® Core Equity Fund Class R3	MRGHX	B	B	B-		6.14	11.38	24.43	36.49	108.77	30.88	1,853	877-960-6077	Y
PACE Large Co Growth Equity Investments Class A	PLAAX	B+	B	A-	Up	5.72	12.19	29.53	35.31	108.75	24.73	1,383	212-882-5586	Y
American Funds AMCAP Fund® Class A	AMCPX	B	B	B-	Up	5.99	11.93	22.04	33.16	108.74	31.49	60,672	800-421-4225	Y
Franklin Growth Series Class R	FGSRX	B	B	B	Down	5.98	11.46	26.49	37.87	108.73	94.17	14,695	650-312-2000	Y
Columbia Select Large-Cap Value Fund Class R	SLVRX	B	B	B-	Up	7.68	13.18	19.75	33.73	108.72	25.83	1,001	800-345-6611	Y
Fidelity Advisor® Stock Selector All Cap Fund Class Z	FZAPX	B	B	B-		5.83	11.50	25.35	36.60	108.70	43.84	8,710	617-563-7000	Y
Schwab Total Stock Market Index Fund®	SWTSX	B	B	B		6.27	11.10	21.06	35.53	108.69	47.25	7,020	877-824-5615	Y
American Funds The New Economy Fund® Class R-2	RNGBX	B+	A-	B	Up	5.31	14.00	33.31	38.40	108.63	41.74	18,784	800-421-4225	Y
Deutsche Core Equity Fund Class C	SUWCX	B	B	B	Up	6.22	11.15	20.21	35.33	108.61	26.13	3,680	201-593-8273	Y
Alger Spectra Fund Class C	ASPCX	B+	B+	B+	Up	6.48	12.10	30.00	35.88	108.59	18.93	5,947	800-992-3863	Y
Great-West S&P 500® Index Fund Institutional Class	MXKWX	B	B	B		7.18	12.08	21.64	35.69	108.57		3,261		Y
EQ/Equity 500 Index Portfolio Class K	US26883L6700	B	B	B		7.09	11.94	21.42	35.27	108.57		5,594	877-222-2144	Y
American Funds The New Economy Fund® Class R-1	RNGAX	B+	A-	B	Up	5.29	14.00	33.32	38.40	108.54	41.49	18,784	800-421-4225	Y
Deutsche S&P 500 Index Fund Class R6	SXPRX	B	B	B		6.54	11.25	21.36	35.63	108.54	30.55	1,011	201-593-8273	Y
PIMCO StocksPLUS® Absolute Return Fund Class D	PSTDX	B-	B	C+	Down	6.50	11.68	23.36	36.14	108.51	10.35	1,626	866-746-2602	Y
MainStay Large Cap Growth Fund Investor Class	MLINX	B+	B	B+	Up	5.71	11.66	31.97	34.80	108.48	8.93	12,363	800-624-6782	Y
PIMCO StocksPLUS® Absolute Return Fund Class A	PTOAX	B-	B	C+	Down	6.39	11.59	23.41	36.16	108.48	10.53	1,626	866-746-2602	Y
American Funds AMCAP Fund® Class R-4	RAFEX	B	B	B-	Up	5.94	11.90	21.97	33.00	108.43	31.21	60,672	800-421-4225	Y
TIAA-CREF S&P 500 Index Fund Retirement Class	TRSPX	B	B	B		6.54	11.24	21.45	35.62	108.35	29.44	4,838	877-518-9161	Y
Invesco Equally-Weighted S&P 500 Fund Class Y	VADDX	B-	B-	B-	Down	6.13	9.88	18.55	30.97	108.32	60.5	8,015	800-659-1005	Y
MainStay Large Cap Growth Fund Class R2	MLRTX	B+	B	B+	Up	5.76	11.66	31.94	34.63	108.30	9.02	12,363	800-624-6782	Y
American Funds Fundamental Investors® Class R-4	RFNEX	B	B	B+	Down	6.61	12.15	23.29	42.11	108.30	62.07	95,399	800-421-4225	Y
Invesco S&P 500 Index Fund Class Y	SPIDX	B	B	B		6.56	11.24	21.45	35.52	108.23	29.21	1,167	800-659-1005	Y
JPMorgan Intrepid America Fund Class A	JIAAX	B	B	B-	Up	8.47	14.55	22.99	30.22	108.19	39.91	4,398	800-480-4111	Y
American Funds The New Economy Fund® Class C	ANFCX	B+	A-	B	Up	5.31	14.00	33.30	38.27	108.17	40.19	18,784	800-421-4225	Y
American Funds Fundamental Investors® Class F-1	AFIFX	B	B	B+	Down	6.61	12.15	23.27	42.03	108.11	62.17	95,399	800-421-4225	Y
VALIC Company I Stock Index Fund	VSTIX	B	B	B		6.58	11.25	21.41	35.50	108.11	40.81	4,822		Y
American Funds AMCAP Fund® Class F-1	AMPFX	B	B	B-	Up	5.97	11.92	21.95	32.91	108.11	31.22	60,672	800-421-4225	Y
American Century Growth Fund Y Class	AGYWX	A-	B+	A-	Up	7.71	12.72	30.39	40.77	108.03	33.38	8,242	800-444-4015	Y
JPMorgan Equity Index Fund Class A	OGEAX	B	B	B		7.15	11.85	21.99	35.81	108.02	40.92	1,892	800-480-4111	Y
Schwab 1000 Index® Fund	SNXFX	B	B	B		6.60	11.35	21.67	35.37	107.98	62.61	7,915	877-824-5615	Y
TIAA-CREF Equity Index Fund Premier Class	TCEPX	B	B	B		6.28	11.12	20.92	35.20	107.94	19.61	16,203	877-518-9161	Y
Fidelity® Series 100 Index Fund	FOHIX	B	B	B+		6.98	11.98	22.00	37.90	107.92	17.36	3,541	617-563-7000	Y
Deutsche Capital Growth Fund Class C	SDGCX	B	B	B	Down	5.65	10.07	24.83	36.45	107.92	66.57	1,521	201-593-8273	Y
VALIC Company I Growth Fund	VCULX	B+	B+	B	Up	6.69	12.96	30.23	39.42	107.91	16.9	1,168		Y

		RATINGS				TOTAL RETURNS & PERFORMANCE					ASSETS		NEW INVESTORS	
Fund Name	Ticker Symbol	Overall Rating	Reward Rating	Risk Rating	Recent Up/ Downgrade	3-Month Total Return	6-Month Total Return	1-Year Total Return	3-Year Total Return	5-Year Total Return	NAV	Total Assets (MIL)	Telephone	Open to New Investors
Goldman Sachs U.S. Tax-Managed Equity Fund Class A	GCTAX	B	B	B-	Up	5.87	10.94	19.87	29.10	107.89	22.37	1,456	800-526-7384	Y
American Funds Fundamental Investors® Class 529-A	CFNAX	B	B	B+	Down	6.63	12.16	23.27	41.99	107.87	62.12	95,399	800-421-4225	Y
Transamerica US Growth Class A	TADAX	B+	B	A-	Up	7.94	12.33	28.72	38.92	107.81	19.42	1,099	888-233-4339	Y
American Century Growth Fund R5 Class	AGWUX	B+	B+	B	Up	7.65	12.63	30.24	40.61	107.79	33.4	8,242	800-444-4015	Y
American Funds AMCAP Fund® Class 529-A	CAFAX	B	B	B-	Up	5.95	11.88	21.92	32.80	107.76	31.15	60,672	800-421-4225	Y
VY® T. Rowe Price Diversified Mid Cap Growth Port Cls S	IAXSX	B	B	B-	Up	5.88	10.46	24.45	34.78	107.75	11.15	1,016	800-366-0066	Y
Columbia Disciplined Core Fund Class R	CLQRX	B	B	B	Up	7.67	13.67	23.79	32.18	107.73	11.94	4,356	800-345-6611	Y
iShares S&P 500 Index Fund Investor A Shares	BSPAX	B	B	B		6.55	11.22	21.38	35.39	107.71	318.24	12,674	800-441-7762	Y
JNL/Mellon Capital S&P 500 Index Fund Class I	US46648M6497	B	B	B		6.60	11.26	21.48	35.30	107.71	22.45	7,748		Y
JPMorgan U.S. Equity Fund Class R2	JUEZX	B-	B	B-	Down	6.72	11.13	20.76	32.21	107.71	16.11	15,686	800-480-4111	Y
Wells Fargo Large Cap Growth Fund - Class R6	STFFX	B+	B+	B+	Up	8.45	15.86	33.43	36.08	107.69	46.85	1,076	800-222-8222	Y
MM S&P 500® Index Fund Class Service Class	MMIEX	B	B	B		6.56	11.24	21.37	35.35	107.68	18.64	3,367		Y
MFS® Growth Fund Class B	MEGBX	B+	B+	A	Up	6.19	11.26	29.56	38.63	107.63	73.18	16,680	877-960-6077	Y
MFS® Growth Fund Class C	MFECX	B+	B+	A	Up	6.19	11.25	29.55	38.60	107.62	72.62	16,680	877-960-6077	Y
MFS® Growth Fund Class R1	MFELX	B+	B+	A	Up	6.19	11.26	29.55	38.59	107.60	72.88	16,680	877-960-6077	Y
American Funds The New Economy Fund® Class 529-C	CNGCX	B+	A-	B	Up	5.29	13.97	33.21	38.04	107.54	40.75	18,784	800-421-4225	Y
GuideStone Funds Growth Equity Fund Investor Class	GGEZX	B+	B+	B+	Up	6.35	12.46	32.06	36.31	107.45	25.11	1,734	214-720-1171	Y
MFS® Mid Cap Growth Fund Class 529A	EAMCX	B+	B	A-	Up	4.96	10.22	25.96	36.12	107.41	15.52	2,561	877-960-6077	Y
MFS® Mid Cap Growth Fund Class R3	OTCHX	B+	B	A-	Up	4.98	10.19	25.99	36.14	107.39	15.89	2,561	877-960-6077	Y
MFS® Mid Cap Growth Fund Class A	OTCAX	B+	B	A-	Up	4.95	10.20	25.99	36.19	107.37	15.99	2,561	877-960-6077	Y
JPMorgan Tax Aware Equity Fund Class C	JPECX	B	B	B-		6.91	11.04	22.21	33.56	107.36	33.01	1,313	800-480-4111	Y
Principal LargeCap S&P 500 Index Fund R-5 Class	PLFPX	B	B	B		6.51	11.14	21.25	35.14	107.24	17.75	5,749	800-222-5852	Y
JNL/S&P Competitive Advantage Fund Class I	US46648L8312	B	B-	A-	Up	12.30	17.49	19.92	28.00	107.21	16.97	2,858		Y
Columbia Contrarian Core Fund Class R	CCCRX	B	B-	B		5.23	9.43	21.11	32.90	107.10	25.72	11,572	800-345-6611	Y
John Hancock Funds Strategic Growth Fund Class C	JSGCX	B	B	B		5.48	11.87	27.79	34.59	107.06	17.23	1,922	800-225-5913	Y
TIAA-CREF Equity Index Fund Retirement Class	TIQRX	B	B	B-		6.27	11.09	20.85	34.89	107.04	19.96	16,203	877-518-9161	Y
Ivy Large Cap Growth Fund Class C	WLGCX	A-	B+	A-	Up	5.89	13.83	28.17	35.33	107.03	18.16	1,889	800-777-6472	Y
Putnam Investors Fund Class R	PIVRX	B-	B	B-	Down	7.40	13.82	22.57	31.92	107.02	28.14	2,054	617-292-1000	Y
Carillon Scout Mid Cap Fund Class C	CSMFX	B+	A	B-		7.21	13.03	22.84	43.21	107.01	19.01	1,790	800-421-4184	Y
Principal SmallCap Growth Fund I Institutional Class	PGRTX	B	A-	C+	Up	5.38	12.54	26.31	39.07	106.91	13.92	1,634	800-222-5852	Y
Fidelity® Growth Strategies Fund Class K	FAGKX	B	B	B+	Up	6.73	10.09	21.68	28.50	106.91	41.4	2,728	617-563-7000	Y
MM S&P 500® Index Fund Class Administrative Class	MIEYX	B	B	B		6.52	11.21	21.30	34.96	106.88	18.33	3,367		Y
Ivy Small Cap Growth Fund Class Institutional	IYSIX	B+	B+	B	Up	5.48	9.53	24.02	37.99	106.84	23.28	1,163	800-777-6472	Y
Goldman Sachs U.S. Tax-Managed Equity Fund Service Class	GCTSX	B	B	B-	Up	5.85	10.89	19.70	28.73	106.84	22.51	1,456	800-526-7384	Y
Principal LargeCap S&P 500 Index Fund Class J	PSPJX	B	B	B		6.55	11.21	21.33	35.20	106.76	17.35	5,749	800-222-5852	Y
State Farm S&P 500 Index Fund Class Institutional	SFXIX	B	B	B		6.54	11.18	21.33	35.06	106.73	19.95	1,540		Y
DFA T.A. U.S. Core Equity 2 Portfolio Institutional Class	DFTCX	B	B	B	Up	6.54	11.60	18.81	33.48	106.72	18.12	8,570	512-306-7400	Y
Wells Fargo Disciplined U.S. Core Fund - Class C	EVSTX	B	B	B		6.13	11.02	19.52	32.85	106.70	15.78	1,298	800-222-8222	Y
Great-West S&P 500® Index Fund Investor Class	MXVIX	B	B	B		7.06	11.91	21.24	34.47	106.69		3,261		Y
Principal SmallCap Growth Fund I Class R-6	PCSMX	B	A-	C+	Up	5.39	12.55	26.36	39.01	106.68	13.9	1,634	800-222-5852	Y
American Funds Investment Company of America® Class R-6	RICGX	B-	B-	B-	Down	6.24	10.80	20.06	35.11	106.55	40.38	93,046	800-421-4225	Y
American Funds The Growth Fund of America® Class R-2	RGABX	B	B	B		6.71	11.85	25.16	40.01	106.50	47.13	176,790	800-421-4225	Y
Wells Fargo Index Fund - Class A	WFILX	B	B	B		6.53	11.17	21.29	34.97	106.45	62.21	1,903	800-222-8222	Y
Voya U.S. Stock Index Portfolio Class S	ISJBX	B	B	B		6.50	11.15	21.22	34.71	106.39	15.57	5,089	800-366-0066	Y
Principal LargeCap S&P 500 Index Fund Class A	PLSAX	B	B-	B		6.52	11.14	21.23	34.89	106.32	17.53	5,749	800-222-5852	Y
MFS® Core Equity Fund Class R2	MRERX	B	B	B-		6.09	11.29	24.18	35.55	106.30	30.23	1,853	877-960-6077	Y
VY® T. Rowe Price Diversified Mid Cap Growth Port Cls S2	IAXTX	B	B	B-	Up	5.82	10.39	24.27	34.15	106.29	10.54	1,016	800-366-0066	Y
Wells Fargo Large Cap Growth Fund - Class R4	SLGRX	B+	B+	B+	Up	8.42	15.79	33.29	35.53	106.24	46.67	1,076	800-222-8222	Y
EQ/Equity 500 Index Portfolio Class IA	US4049925476	B	B-	B		7.02	11.79	21.09	34.36	106.13		5,594	877-222-2144	Y
DFA U.S. Core Equity II Portfolio Institutional Class	DFQTX	B	B	B-	Up	6.66	11.82	18.93	33.17	106.11	21.56	23,310	512-306-7400	Y
BlackRock Capital Appreciation Fund R Shares	MRFGX	B+	B+	B+	Up	7.42	12.94	32.25	38.94	106.10	21.57	2,963	800-441-7762	Y
Principal Capital Appreciation Fund Institutional Class	PWCIX	B	B	B+		6.54	11.29	21.06	34.18	106.09	62.64	2,412	800-222-5852	Y

		RATINGS				TOTAL RETURNS & PERFORMANCE					ASSETS		NEW INVESTORS	
Fund Name	Ticker Symbol	Overall Rating	Reward Rating	Risk Rating	Recent Up/ Downgrade	3-Month Total Return	6-Month Total Return	1-Year Total Return	3-Year Total Return	5-Year Total Return	NAV	Total Assets (MIL)	Telephone	Open to New Investors
JNL/Mellon Capital S&P 500 Index Fund Class A	US46648M6562	B	B	B		6.50	11.09	21.16	34.69	106.08	21.94	7,748		Y
American Funds Investment Company of America® Class R-5	RICFX	B-	B-	B-	Down	6.23	10.77	20.00	34.92	106.07	40.38	93,046	800-421-4225	Y
American Funds The Growth Fund of America® Class R-1	RGAAX	B	B	B		6.68	11.83	25.15	39.86	106.06	46.65	176,790	800-421-4225	Y
EQ/Equity 500 Index Portfolio Class IB	US4049925542	B	B-	B		7.03	11.80	21.09	34.34	106.06		5,594	877-222-2144	Y
AXA 500 Managed Volatility Portfolio Class K	US26883L8862	B	B-	B		7.04	11.82	21.15	34.20	105.98		8,905	877-222-2144	Y
JNL/T. Rowe Price Value Fund Class I	US46648L8569	B-	B	B-	Down	6.06	9.59	18.99	28.50	105.93	18.2	4,963		Y
Principal LargeCap S&P 500 Index Fund R-4 Class	PLFSX	B	B	B		6.46	11.12	21.17	34.67	105.88	17.6	5,749	800-222-5852	Y
JPMorgan Mid Cap Growth Fund Class C	OMGCX	B	B	B	Up	5.46	11.57	28.42	29.62	105.87	23.08	3,490	800-480-4111	Y
MFS® Blended Research Core Equity Fund Class R6	MUEVX	B-	B-	B	Down	6.77	11.13	20.81	31.02	105.84	27.85	1,587	877-960-6077	Y
PIMCO StocksPLUS® Absolute Return Fund Class R	PTORX	B-	B	C+	Down	6.27	11.43	23.08	35.17	105.83	10.46	1,626	866-746-2602	Y
Strategic Advisers® Core Fund	FCSAX	B	B	B-		6.62	11.64	22.54	34.71	105.80	18.03	24,519	617-563-7000	Y
MainStay Large Cap Growth Fund Class R3	MLGRX	B+	B	B+	Up	5.71	11.62	31.69	33.73	105.79	8.59	12,363	800-624-6782	Y
Neuberger Berman Multi-Cap Opportunities Fund Class C	NMUCX	B	B	B-		6.72	11.09	23.52	34.52	105.79	17.69	2,064	212-476-9000	Y
American Funds The Growth Fund of America® Class C	GFACX	B	B	B		6.69	11.84	25.12	39.78	105.78	45.95	176,790	800-421-4225	Y
ATM Large Cap Managed Volatility Portfolio Class K	US26883L8789	B	B-	B		6.98	11.78	21.09	33.96	105.70		3,662	877-222-2144	Y
JPMorgan Intrepid America Fund Class R2	JIAZX	B-	B-	B-	Down	8.40	14.42	22.68	29.28	105.66	39.09	4,398	800-480-4111	Y
Invesco S&P 500 Index Fund Class A	SPIAX	B	B	B		6.48	11.09	21.12	34.53	105.65	28.88	1,167	800-659-1005	Y
AIG Focused Dividend Strategy Fund Class C	FDSTX	B	B	B-		7.26	13.17	19.46	33.45	105.59	18.58	14,853	800-858-8850	Y
AIG Focused Dividend Strategy Fund Class B	FDSBX	B	B	B-		7.25	13.16	19.45	33.40	105.50	18.59	14,853	800-858-8850	Y
American Funds Investment Company of America® Class F-2	ICAFX	B-	B-	B-	Down	6.22	10.75	19.93	34.69	105.45	40.37	93,046	800-421-4225	Y
American Funds Fundamental Investors® Class 529-E	CFNEX	B	B	B+	Down	6.55	12.03	22.96	40.98	105.44	62.06	95,399	800-421-4225	Y
State Farm S&P 500 Index Fund Class R3	RSPHX	B	B	B		6.29	10.92	21.01	34.42	105.43	19.91	1,540		Y
American Funds Washington Mutual Investors Fund Class R-6	RWMGX	B	B	B		6.52	12.55	20.53	35.89	105.35	45.67	100,165	800-421-4225	Y
American Funds AMCAP Fund® Class 529-E	CAFEX	B-	B	B-	Down	5.91	11.76	21.64	31.88	105.35	30.38	60,672	800-421-4225	Y
JPMorgan U.S. Equity Fund Class C	JUECX	B-	B	B-	Down	6.67	11.05	20.49	31.25	105.31	15.77	15,686	800-480-4111	Y
VY® T. Rowe Price Diversified Mid Cap Growth Port Cls A	IAXAX	B	B	B-	Up	5.84	10.42	24.11	33.79	105.30	10.5	1,016	800-366-0066	Y
JNL/American Funds Growth-Income Fund Class I	US46644W3108	B	B	B		5.64	11.40	22.18	36.57	105.30	22.47	5,732		Y
American Funds AMCAP Fund® Class R-3	RAFCX	B-	B	B-	Down	5.86	11.72	21.59	31.78	105.27	30.54	60,672	800-421-4225	Y
JNL/S&P Competitive Advantage Fund Class A	US46648L8494	B	C+	A-	Up	12.25	17.38	19.66	27.30	105.26	16.86	2,858		Y
American Funds The Growth Fund of America® Class 529-C	CGFCX	B	B	B		6.67	11.80	25.06	39.55	105.22	46.1	176,790	800-421-4225	Y
American Funds Fundamental Investors® Class R-3	RFNCX	B	B	B+	Down	6.55	12.01	22.93	40.88	105.22	62.05	95,399	800-421-4225	Y
Davis New York Venture Fund Class A	NYVTX	B	B	B	Up	7.22	12.17	22.14	39.97	105.19	34.25	11,581	800-279-0279	Y
MM S&P 500® Index Fund Class R4	MIEAX	B	B	B		6.46	11.08	21.07	34.36	105.16	18.13	3,367		Y
American Funds Fundamental Investors® Class R-2E	RFEBX	B	B	B+		6.50	11.91	22.73	40.57	105.11	61.92	95,399	800-421-4225	Y
Davis New York Venture Fund Class T	DNVTX	B	B	B		7.20	12.16	22.12	39.91	105.07	34.27	11,581	800-279-0279	Y
American Funds AMCAP Fund® Class R-2E	RAEBX	B-	B	B-	Down	5.86	11.67	21.45	31.53	105.01	31.2	60,672	800-421-4225	Y
Deutsche S&P 500 Index Fund Class A	SXPAX	B	B	B		6.48	11.09	21.09	34.28	104.92	30.5	1,011	201-593-8273	Y
American Funds Washington Mutual Investors Fund Class R-5	RWMFX	B	B	B		6.51	12.53	20.46	35.69	104.91	45.63	100,165	800-421-4225	Y
MFS® Mid Cap Growth Fund Class R2	MCPRX	B	B	B	Up	4.89	10.06	25.61	35.05	104.90	15.11	2,561	877-960-6077	Y
State Farm S&P 500 Index Fund Premier Shares	SLIAX	B	B	B		6.55	11.26	21.39	34.45	104.88	19.88	1,540		Y
Schwab Core Equity Fund™	SWANX	B	B	B-	Up	6.62	11.94	24.16	32.03	104.87	22.71	2,404	877-824-5615	Y
Pioneer Select Mid Cap Growth Fund Class C	GOFCX	B	B	C+	Up	8.31	15.08	28.75	32.16	104.83	30.92	1,577	617-742-7825	Y
American Funds Investment Company of America® class 529-F	CICFX	B-	B-	B-	Down	6.20	10.71	19.87	34.46	104.79	40.24	93,046	800-421-4225	Y
MFS® Blended Research Core Equity Fund Class I	MUSEX	B-	B-	B-	Down	6.71	11.03	20.63	30.53	104.75	27.81	1,587	877-960-6077	Y
MFS® Blended Research Core Equity Fund Class R4	MUEUX	B-	B-	B-	Down	6.72	11.04	20.62	30.54	104.74	27.56	1,587	877-960-6077	Y
Voya U.S. Stock Index Portfolio Class S2	ISIPX	B	B-	B		6.47	11.10	21.03	34.19	104.73	15.39	5,089	800-366-0066	Y
JNL/DFA U.S. Core Equity Fund Class I	US46649B7414	B	B	B-	Up	6.92	11.94	20.54	33.90	104.70	14.52	1,189		Y
State Farm S&P 500 Index Fund Class A	SNPAX	B	B	B		6.54	11.16	21.20	34.26	104.67	19.76	1,540		Y
Principal SmallCap Growth Fund I R-5 Class	PPNPX	B	A-	C+	Up	5.32	12.38	26.00	38.06	104.60	13.09	1,634	800-222-5852	Y
MFS® Massachusetts Investors Growth Stock Fund Class R6	MIGNX	B	B	A-		7.63	11.80	29.13	36.77	104.59	28.58	7,262	877-960-6077	Y
MainStay S&P 500 Index Fund Investor Class	MYSPX	B	B-	B		6.46	11.06	21.01	34.11	104.56	48.03	1,321	800-624-6782	Y
Ivy Small Cap Growth Fund Class Y	WSCYX	B+	B+	B	Up	5.43	9.40	23.74	37.00	104.43	22	1,163	800-777-6472	Y

		RATINGS				TOTAL RETURNS & PERFORMANCE					ASSETS		NEW INVESTORS	
Fund Name	Ticker Symbol	Overall Rating	Reward Rating	Risk Rating	Recent Up/ Downgrade	3-Month Total Return	6-Month Total Return	1-Year Total Return	3-Year Total Return	5-Year Total Return	NAV	Total Assets (MIL)	Telephone	Open to New Investors
Putnam Investors Fund Class M	PNVMX	B-	B	B-	Down	7.31	13.66	22.24	30.89	104.42	26.72	2,054	617-292-1000	Y
AXA Large Cap Core Managed Volatility Portfolio Class K	US26883L5637	B	B-	B		6.39	11.37	22.16	34.07	104.38		2,735	877-222-2144	Y
MM S&P 500® Index Fund Class A	MMFFX	B	B-	B		6.42	11.02	20.98	33.94	104.34	18.02	3,367		Y
Dreyfus/The Boston Company Small/Mid Cap Growth Fund Cls I	SDSCX	B+	A-	B	Up	5.18	11.56	26.52	36.33	104.25	19.7	1,225	800-645-6561	Y
American Funds Washington Mutual Investors Fund Class F-2	WMFFX	B	B	B		6.48	12.49	20.38	35.46	104.25	45.61	100,165	800-421-4225	Y
EQ/Common Stock Index Portfolio Class IA	US4049925054	B-	B-	B-	Down	6.79	11.60	20.57	33.23	104.10		5,955	877-222-2144	Y
American Funds Investment Company of America® Class R-5E	RICHX	B-	B-	B-	Down	6.21	10.70	19.89	34.30	104.10	40.36	93,046	800-421-4225	Y
American Funds Investment Company of America® Class F-3	FFICX	B-	B-	B-	Down	6.24	10.77	20.00	34.30	104.10	40.37	93,046	800-421-4225	Y
Principal LargeCap S&P 500 Index Fund R-3 Class	PLFMX	B	B-	B		6.42	11.04	20.96	33.92	104.06	17.56	5,749	800-222-5852	Y
EQ/Common Stock Index Portfolio Class IB	US4049925138	B-	B-	B-	Down	6.80	11.60	20.58	33.22	104.06		5,955	877-222-2144	Y
Great-West S&P 500® Index Fund Class L	MXVJX	B	B-	B		7.01	11.74	20.94	33.50	104.05		3,261		Y
Waddell & Reed Advisors Vanguard Fund Class C	WAVCX	B+	B+	B	Up	5.78	13.58	27.80	34.43	104.04	7.75	1,720	888-923-3355	Y
JNL/T. Rowe Price Value Fund Class A	US46648L8643	B-	B-	B-	Down	5.94	9.44	18.70	27.73	103.86	17.46	4,963		Y
American Funds Washington Mutual Invs Fund Cls 529-F-1	CWMFX	B	B	B		6.49	12.49	20.34	35.26	103.75	45.44	100,165	800-421-4225	Y
Columbia Dividend Income Fund Institutional 2 Class	CDDRX	B	B	B		6.95	11.61	20.88	36.82	103.72	22.39	11,269	800-345-6611	Y
MFS® Research Fund Class R6	MFRKX	B	B	B		5.95	10.57	23.71	35.29	103.67	42.06	5,567	877-960-6077	Y
American Funds Investment Company of America® Class A	AIVSX	B-	B-	B-	Down	6.17	10.65	19.72	33.99	103.62	40.39	93,046	800-421-4225	Y
Franklin Growth Series Class C	FRGSX	B	B	B	Down	5.85	11.19	25.88	35.82	103.57	86.91	14,695	650-312-2000	Y
MFS® Massachusetts Investors Growth Stock Fund Class I	MGTIX	B	B	A-		7.60	11.73	28.98	36.33	103.55	28.56	7,262	877-960-6077	Y
Principal Capital Appreciation Fund R-5 Class	PCAQX	B	B	B		6.47	11.15	20.78	33.19	103.54	62.3	2,412	800-222-5852	Y
TIAA-CREF Social Choice Equity Fund Advisor Class	TICHX	B-	B	B-	Down	6.22	10.88	20.90	32.67	103.54	19.18	2,979	877-518-9161	Y
MFS® Massachusetts Investors Growth Stock Fund Class R4	MIGKX	B	B	A-		7.61	11.71	28.98	36.31	103.51	27.98	7,262	877-960-6077	Y
MFS® Massachusetts Investors Trust Class R6	MITJX	B	B	B		6.72	10.47	23.92	34.86	103.51	31.28	6,571	877-960-6077	Y
State Farm S&P 500 Index Fund Class R2	RSPTX	B	B-	B		6.53	11.15	21.14	33.89	103.47	19.74	1,540		Y
Principal LargeCap Growth Fund Institutional Class	PGLIX	B+	B	B+	Up	7.63	15.87	34.57	32.98	103.46	9.58	1,083	800-222-5852	Y
Voya U.S. Stock Index Portfolio Class A	ISIVX	B	B-	B		6.41	10.95	20.81	33.56	103.43	15.19	5,089	800-366-0066	Y
AXA 500 Managed Volatility Portfolio Class IB	US26884M2061	B-	B-	B	Down	6.94	11.66	20.82	33.16	103.43		8,905	877-222-2144	Y
Principal SmallCap Growth Fund I R-4 Class	PPNSX	B	A-	C+	Up	5.39	12.38	25.93	37.68	103.39	12.54	1,634	800-222-5852	Y
Oppenheimer Discovery Mid Cap Growth Fund Y	OEGYX	A-	A-	B+	Up	6.73	12.33	28.37	38.53	103.27	22.29	1,053	800-225-5677	Y
JNL/American Funds Growth-Income Fund Class A	US46644W3280	B	B	B		5.55	11.26	21.87	35.71	103.24	22.23	5,732		Y
Ivy Small Cap Growth Fund Class A	WSGAX	B+	B+	B	Up	5.40	9.34	23.69	36.59	103.20	17.82	1,163	800-777-6472	Y
Wells Fargo Large Cap Growth Fund - Class A	STAFX	B+	B	B+	Up	8.36	15.63	32.91	34.32	103.11	45.67	1,076	800-222-8222	Y
Wells Fargo Discovery Fund - Class R6	WFDRX	B+	A-	B	Up	6.21	12.05	29.61	37.21	103.10	35.23	2,600	800-222-8222	Y
JPMorgan Intrepid America Fund Class C	JIACX	B-	B-	B-	Down	8.32	14.24	22.35	28.28	103.10	39.74	4,398	800-480-4111	Y
BlackRock Advantage Large Cap Core Fund Investor A Shares	MDLRX	B	B	B-		5.66	11.33	21.73	32.78	103.07	15.81	1,696	800-441-7762	Y
American Funds Investment Company of America® Class R-4	RICEX	B-	B-	B-	Down	6.16	10.61	19.63	33.75	103.03	40.28	93,046	800-421-4225	Y
Voya Corporate Leaders 100 Fund Class W	IWCLX	B-	B-	B-	Down	6.05	10.99	19.24	30.23	103.01	21.92	1,075	800-366-0066	Y
American Funds Washington Mutual Investors Fund Class F-3	FWMIX	B	B	B		6.52	12.56	20.48	35.08	102.91	45.63	100,165	800-421-4225	Y
American Funds Washington Mutual Investors Fund Class R-5E	RWMHX	B	B	B		6.49	12.48	20.32	35.05	102.86	45.61	100,165	800-421-4225	Y
MFS® Research Fund Class R4	MFRJX	B	B	B		5.94	10.56	23.64	34.98	102.82	42.15	5,567	877-960-6077	Y
MFS® Research Fund Class I	MRFIX	B	B	B		5.93	10.54	23.63	34.97	102.78	43.18	5,567	877-960-6077	Y
Principal SmallCap Growth Fund I Class J	PSIJX	B	A-	C+	Up	5.38	12.33	25.91	37.58	102.75	10.41	1,634	800-222-5852	Y
JNL/DFA U.S. Core Equity Fund Class A	US46649B7588	B	B	B-	Up	6.77	11.74	20.22	33.03	102.70	13.72	1,189		Y
Franklin Growth Opportunities Fund Class A	FGRAX	B	B	B+	Up	5.40	10.80	28.67	31.24	102.67	36.27	3,750	650-312-2000	Y
MFS® Massachusetts Investors Trust Class R4	MITDX	B	B	B		6.69	10.42	23.83	34.49	102.67	32.42	6,571	877-960-6077	Y
American Funds Investment Company of America® Class F-1	AICFX	B-	B-	B-	Down	6.13	10.59	19.59	33.60	102.67	40.29	93,046	800-421-4225	Y
Nationwide S&P 500 Index Fund Class R	GRMRX	B	B-	B		6.40	10.94	20.74	33.37	102.63	15.96	2,942	800-848-0920	Y
MFS® Massachusetts Investors Trust Class I	MITIX	B	B	B		6.69	10.40	23.79	34.46	102.58	31.26	6,571	877-960-6077	Y
American Funds Investment Company of America® Class 529-A	CICAX	B-	B-	B-	Down	6.14	10.60	19.62	33.59	102.57	40.29	93,046	800-421-4225	Y
Ivy Small Cap Growth Fund Class E	ISGEX	B+	B+	B	Up	5.45	9.37	23.62	36.46	102.56	17.66	1,163	800-777-6472	Y
MM S&P 500® Index Fund Class R3	MMINX	B	B-	B		6.44	10.94	20.78	33.42	102.53	17.71	3,367		Y
American Funds Washington Mutual Investors Fund Class A	AWSHX	B	B-	B		6.45	12.40	20.19	34.75	102.42	45.65	100,165	800-421-4225	Y

		RATINGS				TOTAL RETURNS & PERFORMANCE					ASSETS		NEW INVESTORS	
Fund Name	Ticker Symbol	Overall Rating	Reward Rating	Risk Rating	Recent Up/ Downgrade	3-Month Total Return	6-Month Total Return	1-Year Total Return	3-Year Total Return	5-Year Total Return	NAV	Total Assets (MIL)	Telephone	Open to New Investors
Fidelity® Disciplined Equity Fund Class K	FDEKX	B-	B-	B-	Down	6.55	11.62	21.65	28.40	102.41	38.72	1,402	617-563-7000	Y
Principal Capital Appreciation Fund R-4 Class	PCAPX	B	B	B		6.46	11.09	20.64	32.74	102.36	62.12	2,412	800-222-5852	Y
Principal Capital Appreciation Fund Class A	CMNWX	B	B	B		6.44	11.08	20.64	32.73	102.31	61.57	2,412	800-222-5852	Y
MFS® Blended Research Core Equity Fund Class A	MUEAX	B-	B-	B-	Down	6.67	10.92	20.33	29.60	102.24	27.46	1,587	877-960-6077	Y
Selected American Shares Fund Class S	SLASX	B	B	B	Up	7.00	11.97	21.77	40.67	102.18	40.53	2,369	800-243-1575	Y
Principal LargeCap S&P 500 Index Fund R-2 Class	PLFNX	B	B-	B		6.38	10.85	20.64	33.10	102.16	17.63	5,749	800-222-5852	Y
JPMorgan U.S. Research Enhanced Equity Fund Class A	JDEAX	B-	B-	B-	Down	6.46	11.22	21.23	27.84	102.09	28.09	7,921	800-480-4111	Y
Consulting Group Large Cap Equity Fund	TLGUX	B-	B-	B	Down	6.14	10.58	20.48	31.71	102.05	19.42	1,788	855-332-5306	Y
MFS® Blended Research Core Equity Fund Class R3	MUETX	B-	B-	B-	Down	6.64	10.92	20.32	29.54	102.05	27.36	1,587	877-960-6077	Y
Putnam Investors Fund Class C	PCINX	B-	B-	B-	Down	7.28	13.53	21.93	29.96	101.99	26.76	2,054	617-292-1000	Y
Putnam Investors Fund Class B	PNVBX	B-	B-	B-	Down	7.27	13.52	21.98	29.93	101.93	25.44	2,054	617-292-1000	Y
TIAA-CREF Social Choice Equity Fund Premier Class	TRPSX	B-	B	B-	Down	6.14	10.76	20.79	32.05	101.92	19.13	2,979	877-518-9161	Y
AB Discovery Growth Fund Advisor Class	CHCYX	B	A-	C+	Up	9.00	15.43	32.70	38.03	101.89	11.58	2,141	212-969-1000	Y
AXA Large Cap Core Managed Volatility Portfolio Class IA	US2689405742	B-	B-	B	Down	6.24	11.22	21.89	33.08	101.87		2,735	877-222-2144	Y
American Funds Washington Mutual Investors Fund Class R-4	RWMEX	B	B-	B		6.44	12.38	20.11	34.49	101.86	45.42	100,165	800-421-4225	Y
AXA Large Cap Core Managed Volatility Portfolio Class IB	US2689405668	B-	B-	B	Down	6.24	11.22	21.88	33.08	101.85		2,735	877-222-2144	Y
Dreyfus Research Growth Fund, Inc. Class I	DWOIX	B	B	B		6.66	10.71	23.80	33.50	101.84	15.21	1,845	800-645-6561	Y
State Farm S&P 500 Index Fund Class R1	RSPOX	B	B-	B		6.52	11.19	21.13	33.25	101.70	19.85	1,540		Y
American Funds Washington Mutual Investors Fund Class F-1	WSHFX	B	B-	B		6.42	12.34	20.06	34.39	101.62	45.48	100,165	800-421-4225	Y
Dreyfus/The Boston Company Small/Mid Cap Growth Fund Cls A	DBMAX	B	A-	C+	Up	5.08	11.36	26.09	35.22	101.56	19.06	1,225	800-645-6561	Y
Fidelity® Independence Fund Class K	FDFKX	B-	B-	C+	Up	6.50	13.09	26.53	25.08	101.55	37.3	3,919	617-563-7000	Y
American Funds Washington Mutual Investors Fund Cls 529-A	CWMAX	B	B-	B		6.43	12.37	20.09	34.40	101.54	45.55	100,165	800-421-4225	Y
Principal Blue Chip Fund Class C	PBLCX	B+	B+	B	Up	6.51	12.60	27.29	41.08	101.50	20.29	2,340	800-222-5852	Y
Russell Investments U.S. Strategic Equity Fund Class M	RUSTX	B	B	B-	Up	7.36	12.12	21.30	33.32	101.46	13.65	3,109	800-426-7969	Y
Principal SmallCap Growth Fund I R-3 Class	PPNMX	B	A-	C+	Up	5.27	12.17	25.65	36.78	101.41	11.82	1,634	800-222-5852	Y
Fidelity® Mid-Cap Stock Fund Class K	FKMCX	B-	B	B-	Down	5.06	9.93	18.79	31.64	101.32	38.23	8,227	617-563-7000	Y
Russell Investments U.S. Strategic Equity Fund Class S	RSESX	B	B	B-	Up	7.36	11.99	21.20	33.22	101.30	13.66	3,109	800-426-7969	Y
MFS® Core Equity Fund Class C	MRGCX	B	B	B-	Up	5.93	10.98	23.50	33.54	101.20	27.16	1,853	877-960-6077	Y
MFS® Core Equity Fund Class B	MRGBX	B	B	B-	Up	5.94	11.01	23.55	33.53	101.18	27.48	1,853	877-960-6077	Y
MFS® Massachusetts Investors Growth Stock Fund Class A	MIGFX	B	B	A-		7.54	11.62	28.69	35.40	101.15	27.81	7,262	877-960-6077	Y
State Farm S&P 500 Index Fund Class B Legacy	SLIBX	B	B-	B		6.53	11.19	21.14	33.08	101.15	20.13	1,540		Y
MFS® Core Equity Fund Class R1	MRGGX	B	B	B-	Up	5.93	10.99	23.52	33.51	101.10	27.14	1,853	877-960-6077	Y
Principal LargeCap Growth Fund R-5 Class	PDPPX	B	B	B+	Up	7.55	15.82	34.47	32.14	101.06	9.69	1,083	800-222-5852	Y
MFS® Massachusetts Investors Growth Stock Fund Class R3	MIGHX	B	B	A-		7.53	11.57	28.65	35.33	101.05	27.51	7,262	877-960-6077	Y
TIAA-CREF Social Choice Equity Fund Retirement Class	TRSCX	B-	B	B-	Down	6.12	10.72	20.63	31.70	100.94	19.48	2,979	877-518-9161	Y
American Funds Fundamental Investors® Class R-2	RFNBX	B	B	B+		6.42	11.76	22.39	39.06	100.93	61.86	95,399	800-421-4225	Y
MainStay Large Cap Growth Fund Class C	MLACX	B	B	B+	Up	5.63	11.29	31.06	31.88	100.92	7.56	12,363	800-624-6782	Y
American Century Income and Growth Fund R5 Class	AICGX	B-	B-	C+	Down	6.94	12.62	20.80	28.06	100.87	39.35	2,228	800-444-4015	Y
Fidelity® Capital Appreciation Fund Class K	FCAKX	B-	B	B-	Down	5.87	13.14	24.06	29.53	100.86	35.26	7,390	617-563-7000	Y
American Funds AMCAP Fund® Class R-2	RAFBX	B-	B-	B-	Down	5.76	11.47	21.07	30.08	100.85	28.62	60,672	800-421-4225	Y
Ivy Small Cap Growth Fund Class R	WSGRX	B+	B+	B	Up	5.34	9.23	23.28	35.50	100.84	17.49	1,163	800-777-6472	Y
AB Relative Value Fund Advisor Class	CBBYX	B	B	B		6.29	12.59	19.05	33.45	100.82	5.88	1,811	212-969-1000	Y
PIMCO RAE Fundamental PLUS Fund Class D	PIXDX	B	B	B-	Up	7.42	12.90	18.81	30.42	100.81	7.31	1,841	866-746-2602	Y
Principal LargeCap S&P 500 Index Fund R-1 Class	PLPIX	B	B-	B		6.32	10.83	20.55	32.67	100.79	17.5	5,749	800-222-5852	Y
MFS® Massachusetts Investors Growth Stock Fund Class 529A	EISTX	B	B	A-		7.53	11.54	28.63	35.16	100.72	27.4	7,262	877-960-6077	Y
JPMorgan Equity Index Fund Class C	OEICX	B	B-	B		7.01	11.50	21.29	33.03	100.70	40.56	1,892	800-480-4111	Y
American Funds AMCAP Fund® Class R-1	RAFAX	B-	B-	B-	Down	5.76	11.47	21.06	30.02	100.69	28.63	60,672	800-421-4225	Y
American Funds Fundamental Investors® Class R-1	RFNAX	B	B	B		6.42	11.74	22.37	38.96	100.64	61.88	95,399	800-421-4225	Y
BlackRock Capital Appreciation Fund Investor C Shares	MCFGX	B+	B+	B+	Up	7.26	12.60	31.51	36.69	100.61	19.4	2,963	800-441-7762	Y
Putnam Equity Income Fund Class R6	PEQSX	B-	B	B-	Down	6.40	11.92	19.13	30.77	100.61	24.52	12,342	617-292-1000	Y
American Funds Fundamental Investors® Class C	AFICX	B	B	B+		6.42	11.76	22.37	38.97	100.57	61.88	95,399	800-421-4225	Y
Wells Fargo Large Cap Growth Fund - Class R	STMFX	B+	B	B+	Up	8.29	15.50	32.55	33.28	100.55	44.75	1,076	800-222-8222	Y

		RATINGS				TOTAL RETURNS & PERFORMANCE					ASSETS		NEW INVESTORS	
Fund Name	Ticker Symbol	Overall Rating	Reward Rating	Risk Rating	Recent Up/ Downgrade	3-Month Total Return	6-Month Total Return	1-Year Total Return	3-Year Total Return	5-Year Total Return	NAV	Total Assets (MIL)	Telephone	Open to New Investors
PIMCO RAE Fundamental PLUS Fund Class A	PIXAX	B	B	B-	Up	7.40	12.71	18.77	30.19	100.55	7.32	1,841	866-746-2602	Y
PIMCO StocksPLUS® Absolute Return Fund Class C	PSOCX	B-	B	C+	Down	6.17	11.16	22.32	32.97	100.55	9.61	1,626	866-746-2602	Y
Voya Corporate Leaders 100 Fund Class A	IACLX	B-	B-	B-	Down	5.94	10.78	18.90	29.21	100.51	21.9	1,075	800-366-0066	Y
American Funds AMCAP Fund® Class C	AMPCX	B-	B-	B-	Down	5.77	11.50	21.07	29.99	100.47	27.87	60,672	800-421-4225	Y
Principal Capital Appreciation Fund R-3 Class	PCAOX	B	B	B		6.41	10.99	20.42	32.01	100.45	61.67	2,412	800-222-5852	Y
Oppenheimer Discovery Mid Cap Growth Fund A	OEGAX	A-	A-	B+	Up	6.66	12.13	27.98	37.43	100.43	19.94	1,053	800-225-5677	Y
Franklin Growth Opportunities Fund Class R	FKARX	B	B	B+	Up	5.34	10.66	28.36	30.32	100.41	34.75	3,750	650-312-2000	Y
iShares S&P 500 Index Fund Investor C1 Shares	BSPZX	B-	B-	B	Down	6.36	10.83	20.51	32.49	100.39	318.76	12,674	800-441-7762	Y
MFS® Research Fund Class A	MFRFX	B	B	B		5.87	10.41	23.34	33.96	100.33	42.1	5,567	877-960-6077	Y
MFS® Massachusetts Investors Trust Class A	MITTX	B	B	B		6.63	10.32	23.56	33.57	100.30	32.15	6,571	877-960-6077	Y
Voya Corporate Leaders 100 Fund Class O	IOCLX	B-	B-	B-	Down	5.97	10.82	18.89	29.05	100.30	21.88	1,075	800-366-0066	Y
PACE Large Co Growth Equity Investments Class C	PLACX	B+	B	A-	Up	5.47	11.71	28.50	32.07	100.28	19.9	1,383	212-882-5586	Y
Goldman Sachs U.S. Tax-Managed Equity Fund Class C	GCTCX	B-	B-	B-	Down	5.67	10.50	18.92	26.23	100.27	21.24	1,456	800-526-7384	Y
MFS® Research Fund Class R3	MFRHX	B	B	B		5.86	10.40	23.32	33.95	100.26	41.86	5,567	877-960-6077	Y
Pioneer Disciplined Growth Fund Class C	INDCX	B	B	B		5.86	10.91	25.20	30.34	100.22	16.22	1,245	617-742-7825	Y
BlackRock Advantage Large Cap Core Fund R Shares	MRLRX	B	B	B-		5.55	11.21	21.39	31.64	100.22	14.8	1,696	800-441-7762	Y
Fidelity Advisor® Diversified Stock Fund Class Z	FZACX	B-	B	C+	Down	6.16	11.69	19.22	31.04	100.21	26.01	2,130	617-563-7000	Y
American Funds Investment Company of America® class 529-E	CICEX	B-	B-	B-	Down	6.06	10.44	19.33	32.61	100.11	40.16	93,046	800-421-4225	Y
MFS® Massachusetts Investors Trust Class R3	MITHX	B	B	B		6.63	10.28	23.50	33.48	100.09	31.87	6,571	877-960-6077	Y
Russell Investments Tax-Managed U.S. Large Cap Fund Cls M	RTMTX	B-	B-	B	Down	6.73	10.85	21.59	32.72	100.09	40.91	2,510	800-426-7969	Y
Principal LargeCap Growth Fund R-4 Class	PEPPX	B	B	B+	Up	7.54	15.72	34.24	31.62	99.99	9.82	1,083	800-222-5852	Y
Principal LargeCap Growth Fund Class J	PGLJX	B	B	B+	Up	7.62	15.80	34.35	31.77	99.97	8.31	1,083	800-222-5852	Y
Russell Investments Tax-Managed U.S. Large Cap Fund Cls S	RETSX	B-	B-	B	Down	6.70	10.76	21.50	32.62	99.94	40.93	2,510	800-426-7969	Y
American Funds Fundamental Investors® Class 529-C	CFNCX	B	B	B		6.41	11.73	22.32	38.71	99.93	62.08	95,399	800-421-4225	Y
MFS® Mid Cap Growth Fund Class B	OTCBX	B+	B	A-	Up	4.76	9.75	25.01	33.11	99.91	13.33	2,561	877-960-6077	Y
American Funds AMCAP Fund® Class 529-C	CAFCX	B-	B-	B-	Down	5.77	11.48	20.99	29.80	99.89	28.03	60,672	800-421-4225	Y
MFS® Massachusetts Investors Trust Class 529A	EAMTX	B	B-	B		6.60	10.26	23.47	33.37	99.88	31.38	6,571	877-960-6077	Y
Fidelity® Fund Class K	FFDKX	B	B	B	Up	6.86	13.48	23.94	33.37	99.86	45.21	4,666	617-563-7000	Y
American Funds Investment Company of America® Class R-3	RICCX	B-	B-	B-	Down	6.07	10.43	19.27	32.51	99.84	40.24	93,046	800-421-4225	Y
MFS® Mid Cap Growth Fund Class R1	OTCGX	B+	B	A-	Up	4.78	9.80	25.03	33.16	99.70	13.27	2,561	877-960-6077	Y
MFS® Blended Research Core Equity Fund Class R2	MUESX	B-	B-	B-	Down	6.62	10.77	20.04	28.60	99.67	26.39	1,587	877-960-6077	Y
MFS® Mid Cap Growth Fund Class C	OTCCX	B+	B	A-	Up	4.75	9.71	25.00	33.09	99.66	12.93	2,561	877-960-6077	Y
Transamerica US Growth Class C	TADCX	B+	B	A-	Up	7.69	11.88	27.74	35.65	99.66	18.35	1,099	888-233-4339	Y
American Funds Investment Company of America® Class R-2E	RIBEX	B-	B-	B-	Down	6.03	10.37	19.13	32.15	99.62	40.28	93,046	800-421-4225	Y
Putnam Equity Income Fund Class R5	PEQLX	B-	B-	B-	Down	6.32	11.80	18.96	30.32	99.60	24.52	12,342	617-292-1000	Y
Principal SmallCap Growth Fund I R-2 Class	PPNNX	B	A-	C+	Up	5.21	12.11	25.37	36.08	99.57	11.14	1,634	800-222-5852	Y
AXA/AB Small Cap Growth Portfolio Class K	US26883L7617	B+	A-	B	Up	6.87	13.11	23.31	34.47	99.53		2,071	877-222-2144	Y
MFS® Mid Cap Growth Fund Class 529B	EBCGX	B+	B	A-	Up	4.72	9.74	24.94	32.99	99.43	13.01	2,561	877-960-6077	Y
MFS® Mid Cap Growth Fund Class 529C	ECGRX	B+	B	A-	Up	4.70	9.70	24.94	32.86	99.17	12.61	2,561	877-960-6077	Y
Dreyfus Research Growth Fund, Inc. Class A	DWOAX	B	B	B		6.57	10.56	23.44	32.42	99.14	15.18	1,845	800-645-6561	Y
American Funds Washington Mutual Investors Fund Cls 529-E	CWMEX	B	B-	B		6.37	12.24	19.80	33.44	99.08	45.3	100,165	800-421-4225	Y
Wells Fargo Discovery Fund - Class A	WFDAX	B+	A-	B	Up	6.07	11.77	29.03	35.44	98.98	32.57	2,600	800-222-8222	Y
Principal LargeCap Growth Fund Class A	PRGWX	B	B	B+	Up	7.52	15.72	34.16	31.21	98.88	9.02	1,083	800-222-5852	Y
Wells Fargo Premier Large Company Growth Fund - Class R6	EKJFX	B	B	B	Up	7.53	14.37	34.55	32.97	98.85	13.84	2,478	800-222-8222	Y
Wells Fargo Index Fund - Class C	WFINX	B-	B-	B	Down	6.32	10.75	20.39	31.97	98.85	62.72	1,903	800-222-8222	Y
American Funds Washington Mutual Investors Fund Class R-2E	RWEBX	B-	B-	B	Down	6.30	12.10	19.57	33.14	98.83	45.46	100,165	800-421-4225	Y
American Funds Washington Mutual Investors Fund Class R-3	RWMCX	B-	B-	B	Down	6.36	12.20	19.73	33.26	98.80	45.27	100,165	800-421-4225	Y
John Hancock Funds II Mid Cap Stock Fund Class NAV	JHMSX	B	B	B	Up	5.16	9.08	28.40	32.72	98.79	21.57	1,635	800-225-5913	Y
AB Relative Value Fund Class K	CBBKX	B	B	B		6.28	12.32	18.65	32.34	98.79	5.77	1,811	212-969-1000	Y
Pioneer Fund Class A	PIODX	B-	B	B-	Down	6.37	11.49	21.53	31.30	98.77	28.81	5,008	617-742-7825	Y
Putnam Equity Income Fund Class Y	PEIYX	B	B-	B	Up	6.33	11.81	18.94	30.13	98.76	24.51	12,342	617-292-1000	Y
John Hancock Funds Disciplined Value Fund Class NAV	JDVNX	B-	B-	C+	Down	6.93	12.01	19.34	28.23	98.76	21.87	15,171	800-225-5913	Y

		RATINGS				TOTAL RETURNS & PERFORMANCE					ASSETS		NEW INVESTORS	
Fund Name	Ticker Symbol	Overall Rating	Reward Rating	Risk Rating	Recent Up/ Downgrade	3-Month Total Return	6-Month Total Return	1-Year Total Return	3-Year Total Return	5-Year Total Return	NAV	Total Assets (MIL)	Telephone	Open to New Investors
Neuberger Berman Guardian Fund Class A	NGDAX	B-	B-	C+	Down	6.92	11.39	24.89	28.25	98.75	10.27	1,255	212-476-9000	Y
Russell Investments U.S. Strategic Equity Fund Class A	RSEAX	B	B	B-	Up	7.24	11.81	20.76	32.18	98.63	13.63	3,109	800-426-7969	Y
Principal Capital Appreciation Fund R-2 Class	PCANX	B	B-	B		6.34	10.88	20.18	31.26	98.62	61.71	2,412	800-222-5852	Y
Russell Investments U.S. Strategic Equity Fund Class E	RSEEX	B	B	B-	Up	7.17	11.81	20.78	32.09	98.59	13.67	3,109	800-426-7969	Y
State Farm S&P 500 Index Fund Class B	SNPBX	B-	B-	B	Down	6.53	11.18	21.01	32.20	98.46	19.93	1,540		Y
MFS® Massachusetts Investors Growth Stock Fund Class R2	MIRGX	B	B	A-		7.42	11.40	28.29	34.26	98.45	27.04	7,262	877-960-6077	Y
AB Discovery Growth Fund Class K	CHCKX	B	A-	C+	Up	8.87	15.19	32.27	36.51	98.45	10.76	2,141	212-969-1000	Y
First Investors Opportunity Fund Advisor Class	FIVUX	B	B-	B	Up	5.49	9.61	19.00	26.50	98.39	42.38	1,147	800-423-4026	Y
John Hancock Funds Disciplined Value Fund Class R5	JDVVX	B	B-	B	Up	6.92	11.94	19.27	27.97	98.34	21.87	15,171	800-225-5913	Y
American Century NT Equity Growth Fund G Class	ACLEX	B-	B-	B-	Down	6.82	11.98	22.17	27.63	98.31	13.62	1,815	800-444-4015	Y
Invesco S&P 500 Index Fund Class C	SPICX	B-	B-	B	Down	6.32	10.75	20.27	31.61	98.25	27.93	1,167	800-659-1005	Y
John Hancock Funds II Mid Cap Stock Fund Class 1	JIMSX	B	B	B	Up	5.16	9.07	28.37	32.57	98.23	21.37	1,635	800-225-5913	Y
Principal SmallCap Growth Fund I R-1 Class	PNASX	B	A-	C+	Up	5.16	12.06	25.29	35.57	98.22	11.47	1,634	800-222-5852	Y
Principal LargeCap S&P 500 Index Fund Class C	PLICX	B-	B-	B	Down	6.34	10.73	20.30	31.60	98.21	17.19	5,749	800-222-5852	Y
Principal LargeCap Growth Fund R-3 Class	PLGPX	B	B	B+	Up	7.52	15.55	33.97	30.85	98.04	9.85	1,083	800-222-5852	Y
Voya Corporate Leaders 100 Fund Class R	IRCLX	B-	B-	B-	Down	5.89	10.66	18.58	28.04	98.00	21.78	1,075	800-366-0066	Y
Deutsche S&P 500 Index Fund Class C	SXPCX	B-	B-	B	Down	6.27	10.68	20.19	31.51	97.85	30.43	1,011	201-593-8273	Y
MFS® Research Fund Class R2	MSRRX	B	B	B		5.80	10.26	23.04	32.97	97.82	40.83	5,567	877-960-6077	Y
Oppenheimer Discovery Mid Cap Growth Fund R	OEGNX	A-	A-	B+	Up	6.54	11.99	27.64	36.41	97.73	18.67	1,053	800-225-5677	Y
MFS® Massachusetts Investors Trust Class R2	MIRTX	B-	B-	B	Down	6.56	10.13	23.18	32.47	97.60	30.69	6,571	877-960-6077	Y
Russell Investments Tax-Managed U.S. Large Cap Fund Cls A	RTLAX	B-	B-	B	Down	6.65	10.63	21.23	31.65	97.56	40.56	2,510	800-426-7969	Y
Russell Investments Tax-Managed U.S. Large Cap Fund Cls E	RTLEX	B-	B-	B	Down	6.65	10.64	21.22	31.65	97.51	40.96	2,510	800-426-7969	Y
Ivy Small Cap Growth Fund Class T	IYSTX	B+	B+	B	Up	5.49	9.44	23.30	34.50	97.48	17.82	1,163	800-777-6472	Y
Wells Fargo Premier Large Company Growth Fund - Class R4	EKJRX	B	B	B	Up	7.53	14.35	34.41	32.38	97.47	13.7	2,478	800-222-8222	Y
Columbia Dividend Income Fund Class R	CDIRX	B	B-	B		6.80	11.31	20.15	34.31	97.47	22.06	11,269	800-345-6611	Y
Carillon Eagle Small Cap Growth Fund Class R6	HSRUX	B	B+	B	Up	6.05	10.29	23.40	35.02	97.37	63.38	5,195	800-421-4184	Y
Davis New York Venture Fund Class C	NYVCX	B	B	B	Up	7.04	11.78	21.21	36.76	97.34	31.11	11,581	800-279-0279	Y
Principal Capital Appreciation Fund R-1 Class	PCAMX	B	B-	B		6.31	10.80	20.03	30.76	97.31	61.68	2,412	800-222-5852	Y
Fidelity Advisor® Diversified Stock Fund Class A	FDTOX	B-	B	C+	Down	6.13	11.53	18.91	29.81	97.25	24.75	2,130	617-563-7000	Y
AXA/AB Small Cap Growth Portfolio Class IB	US4049927118	B+	A-	B	Up	6.81	13.04	23.09	33.49	97.19		2,071	877-222-2144	Y
AXA/AB Small Cap Growth Portfolio Class IA	US4049927035	B+	A-	B	Up	6.84	13.03	23.11	33.51	97.13		2,071	877-222-2144	Y
American Century Equity Growth Fund R5 Class	AEYGX	B-	B-	B-	Down	6.78	11.95	22.01	27.29	97.11	32.44	3,243	800-444-4015	Y
Voya MidCap Opportunities Portfolio Class I	IIMOX	B	B	B+		7.77	10.96	25.08	33.98	97.10	14.56	2,232	800-366-0066	Y
Hartford Stock HLS Fund Class IA	HSTAX	B	B-	B+		5.75	9.71	19.84	30.98	96.97	79.57	1,527	888-843-7824	Y
Voya MidCap Opportunities Portfolio R6	VMCRX	B	B	B+		7.77	10.96	25.08	33.88	96.95	14.56	2,232	800-366-0066	Y
Wells Fargo Growth Fund - Class R6	SGRHX	A-	A-	B	Up	6.88	14.33	35.23	37.95	96.88	41.12	4,617	800-222-8222	Y
Ivy Small Cap Growth Fund Class C	WRGCX	B	B+	B	Up	5.20	8.97	22.77	33.92	96.63	14.34	1,163	800-777-6472	Y
Lord Abbett Calibrated Dividend Growth Fund Class R6	LAMHX	B-	B-	B-	Down	7.76	11.51	19.48	33.93	96.62	15.57	2,475	201-827-2000	Y
Amana Mutual Funds Trust Growth Fund Investor	AMAGX	B	B+	B		6.89	12.96	28.97	36.93	96.48	34.96	1,693	888-732-6262	Y
Calvert Equity Fund Class A	CSIEX	B+	B	A	Up	6.97	11.66	25.78	32.34	96.47	42.89	2,222	800-368-2745	Y
Fidelity Advisor® Mid Cap II Fund Class Z	FZAMX	B	B	B-	Up	6.24	10.89	20.71	32.30	96.45	21.57	2,632	617-563-7000	Y
Putnam Equity Income Fund Class A	PEYAX	B	B-	B	Up	6.26	11.68	18.68	29.19	96.36	24.51	12,342	617-292-1000	Y
Lord Abbett Calibrated Dividend Growth Fund Class F3	LRMAX	B-	B-	B-	Down	7.76	11.51	19.48	33.71	96.31	15.57	2,475	201-827-2000	Y
Carillon Eagle Small Cap Growth Fund Class R5	HSRSX	B	B+	B	Up	6.03	10.24	23.29	34.60	96.26	62.89	5,195	800-421-4184	Y
Principal LargeCap Growth Fund R-2 Class	PCPPX	B	B	B+	Up	7.46	15.46	33.73	30.05	96.25	8.64	1,083	800-222-5852	Y
Neuberger Berman Guardian Fund Class R3	NGDRX	B-	B-	C+	Down	6.89	11.23	24.64	27.20	96.21	13.65	1,255	212-476-9000	Y
John Hancock Funds Disciplined Value Fund Class R4	JDVFX	B	B-	B	Up	6.88	11.80	19.01	27.22	96.03	21.85	15,171	800-225-5913	Y
Pioneer Core Equity Fund Class A	PIOTX	B	B	B-	Up	5.89	12.46	24.77	31.84	96.02	20.58	1,696	617-742-7825	Y
Lord Abbett Calibrated Dividend Growth Fund Class R5	LAMTX	B-	B-	B-	Down	7.71	11.39	19.36	33.50	96.00	15.52	2,475	201-827-2000	Y
Oppenheimer Capital Appreciation Fund Class Y	OTCYX	B	B	B		5.92	10.03	26.81	27.25	95.93	63.08	5,215	800-225-5677	Y
First Investors Opportunity Fund Class A	FIUSX	B-	B-	B	Up	5.42	9.48	18.66	25.41	95.90	41.64	1,147	800-423-4026	Y
AB Discovery Growth Fund Class R	CHCRX	B	B+	C+	Up	8.78	15.15	31.99	35.44	95.82	10.26	2,141	212-969-1000	Y

		RATINGS				TOTAL RETURNS & PERFORMANCE					ASSETS		NEW INVESTORS	
Fund Name	Ticker Symbol	Overall Rating	Reward Rating	Risk Rating	Recent Up/ Downgrade	3-Month Total Return	6-Month Total Return	1-Year Total Return	3-Year Total Return	5-Year Total Return	NAV	Total Assets (MIL)	Telephone	Open to New Investors
Victory Trivalent International Small-Cap Fund Class R6	MSSIX	A-	A-	B+	Up	6.95	15.50	36.96	46.31	95.72	14.78	1,389	800-539-3863	Y
Davis New York Venture Fund Class B	NYVBX	B	B	B	Up	7.00	11.68	20.97	35.98	95.66	30.22	11,581	800-279-0279	Y
Lord Abbett Alpha Strategy Fund Class R6	ALFVX	B	B	C+	Up	4.92	11.00	21.02	30.49	95.64	27.24	1,144	201-827-2000	Y
Lord Abbett Alpha Strategy Fund Class F	ALFFX	B	B	C+	Up	4.85	10.87	20.75	30.11	95.60	26.75	1,144	201-827-2000	Y
Wells Fargo Large Cap Growth Fund - Class C	STOFX	B	B	B+	Up	8.15	15.18	31.89	31.31	95.59	42.3	1,076	800-222-8222	Y
American Funds Investment Company of America® Class C	AICCX	B-	B-	B-	Down	5.97	10.20	18.77	30.81	95.58	39.98	93,046	800-421-4225	Y
Lord Abbett Alpha Strategy Fund Class R5	ALFTX	B	B	C+	Up	4.89	10.97	20.94	30.42	95.53	27.23	1,144	201-827-2000	Y
American Funds Investment Company of America® Class R-1	RICAX	B-	B-	B-	Down	5.95	10.19	18.73	30.74	95.51	40.07	93,046	800-421-4225	Y
Franklin Growth Opportunities Fund Class C	FKACX	B	B	B	Up	5.21	10.38	27.70	28.34	95.39	30.79	3,750	650-312-2000	Y
Lord Abbett Calibrated Dividend Growth Fund Class F	LAMFX	B-	B-	B-	Down	7.68	11.37	19.27	33.24	95.26	15.38	2,475	201-827-2000	Y
Principal Equity Income Fund Institutional Class	PEIIX	B	B	B-		7.23	12.10	21.03	33.26	95.10	31.47	6,859	800-222-5852	Y
Principal LargeCap Growth Fund R-1 Class	PLSGX	B	B	B+	Up	7.44	15.37	33.59	29.60	95.07	8.4	1,083	800-222-5852	Y
BlackRock Advantage Large Cap Core Fund Investor C Shares	MCLRX	B	B	B-	Up	5.48	10.97	20.80	29.57	95.06	13.64	1,697	800-441-7762	Y
John Hancock Funds Disciplined Value Fund Class A	JVLAX	B	B-	B	Up	6.86	11.80	18.92	26.88	95.01	22.53	15,171	800-225-5913	Y
Pioneer Fund Class R	PIORX	B-	B-	B-	Down	6.24	11.20	20.98	29.73	94.98	28.93	5,008	617-742-7825	Y
Neuberger Berman Mid Cap Growth Fund Class R6	NRMGX	B	B+	C+	Up	7.05	11.96	25.57	33.28	94.86	14.72	1,274	212-476-9000	Y
MFS® Blended Research Core Equity Fund Class R1	MUERX	B-	B-	B-	Down	6.46	10.51	19.45	26.75	94.83	26.32	1,587	877-960-6077	Y
Goldman Sachs Small/Mid Cap Growth Fund Investor Class	GTMTX	B	B	B	Up	5.12	11.07	28.05	26.06	94.81	21.61	2,352	800-526-7384	Y
MFS® Blended Research Core Equity Fund Class B	MUSBX	B-	B-	B-	Down	6.47	10.53	19.43	26.71	94.78	26.59	1,587	877-960-6077	Y
American Funds Washington Mutual Investors Fund Class R-2	RWMBX	B-	B-	B	Down	6.26	11.95	19.21	31.60	94.73	45.02	100,165	800-421-4225	Y
Fidelity® Dividend Growth Fund Class K	FDGKX	B-	B-	B-	Down	7.53	11.89	20.24	28.28	94.72	32.78	7,560	617-563-7000	Y
MFS® Blended Research Core Equity Fund Class C	MUECX	B-	B-	B-	Down	6.45	10.47	19.40	26.68	94.64	26.2	1,587	877-960-6077	Y
Lord Abbett Alpha Strategy Fund Class F3	ALFOX	B	B	C+	Up	4.89	10.97	20.88	29.81	94.62	27.23	1,144	201-827-2000	Y
Voya MidCap Opportunities Portfolio Class S	ISMOX	B	B	B+		7.66	10.77	24.76	32.93	94.56	13.77	2,232	800-366-0066	Y
Nationwide Fund Class R	GNWRX	B	B	B-		5.70	10.25	19.40	31.43	94.52	24.47	1,043	800-848-0920	Y
Hartford Stock HLS Fund Class IB	HIBSX	B	B-	B+		5.68	9.56	19.54	30.00	94.51	79.54	1,527	888-843-7824	Y
American Funds Washington Mutual Investors Fund Class C	WSHCX	B-	B-	B	Down	6.25	11.96	19.25	31.56	94.51	45.08	100,165	800-421-4225	Y
American Funds Washington Mutual Investors Fund Class R-1	RWMAX	B-	B-	B	Down	6.23	11.93	19.19	31.49	94.41	45.17	100,165	800-421-4225	Y
Voya MidCap Opportunities Fund Class W	IMOWX	B	B	B+		7.71	10.78	24.76	32.97	94.33	25.23	1,401	800-366-0066	Y
Wells Fargo Premier Large Company Growth Fund - Class A	EKJAX	B	B	B	Up	7.41	14.12	33.92	31.14	94.30	13.21	2,478	800-222-8222	Y
Lord Abbett Alpha Strategy Fund Class R4	ALFKX	B	B	C+	Up	4.81	10.83	20.62	29.55	94.23	26.56	1,144	201-827-2000	Y
Principal Capital Appreciation Fund Class C	CMNCX	B-	B-	B	Down	6.24	10.64	19.68	29.54	94.12	47.99	2,412	800-222-5852	Y
American Funds Washington Mutual Investors Fund Cls 529-C	CWMCX	B-	B-	B	Down	6.22	11.92	19.19	31.32	93.88	45.28	100,165	800-421-4225	Y
Lord Abbett Calibrated Dividend Growth Fund Class T	LBDTX	B-	B-	B-		7.72	11.36	19.09	32.61	93.73	15.39	2,475	201-827-2000	Y
Lord Abbett Calibrated Dividend Growth Fund Class A	LAMAX	B-	B-	B-	Down	7.65	11.28	19.08	32.55	93.71	15.39	2,475	201-827-2000	Y
Lord Abbett Calibrated Dividend Growth Fund Class R4	LAMSX	B-	B-	B-	Down	7.67	11.31	19.10	32.58	93.68	15.38	2,475	201-827-2000	Y
Fidelity Advisor® Dividend Growth Fund Class Z	FZADX	B-	B-	B-	Down	7.53	11.81	20.07	27.87	93.66	18.66	1,087	617-563-7000	Y
MFS® Massachusetts Investors Growth Stock Fund Class B	MIGBX	B	B	B+		7.31	11.13	27.66	32.29	93.65	24.21	7,262	877-960-6077	Y
MFS® Massachusetts Investors Growth Stock Fund Class R1	MIGMX	B	B	B+		7.33	11.17	27.66	32.27	93.63	23.76	7,262	877-960-6077	Y
Dreyfus/The Boston Company Small/Mid Cap Growth Fund Cls C	DBMCX	B	B+	C+	Up	4.89	10.95	25.18	32.12	93.63	17.02	1,225	800-645-6561	Y
Victory Munder Mid-Cap Core Growth Fund Class R6	MGOSX	B-	B	C+	Up	6.07	12.08	24.72	27.45	93.62	37.2	4,105	800-539-3863	Y
MFS® Massachusetts Investors Growth Stock Fund Class C	MIGDX	B	B	B+		7.31	11.16	27.67	32.26	93.59	24	7,262	877-960-6077	Y
John Hancock Funds Disciplined Value Fund Class R2	JDVPX	B	B-	B	Up	6.84	11.72	18.75	26.27	93.57	21.84	15,171	800-225-5913	Y
Multi-Manager Value Strategies Fund Institutional Class	CZMVX	B-	B	B-	Down	6.52	11.11	19.64	33.69	93.54	13.96	2,633	800-345-6611	Y
Multi-Manager Value Strategies Fund Class A	CDEIX	B-	B	B-	Down	6.54	11.02	19.60	33.64	93.48	14.11	2,633	800-345-6611	Y
Oppenheimer Capital Appreciation Fund Class A	OPTFX	B	B	B	Up	5.86	9.90	26.52	26.38	93.45	58.38	5,215	800-225-5677	Y
MFS® Massachusetts Investors Growth Stock Fund Class 529B	EMIVX	B	B	B+		7.32	11.15	27.67	32.09	93.19	23.54	7,262	877-960-6077	Y
Voya MidCap Opportunities Portfolio Class S2	IMOPX	B	B	B+	Up	7.72	10.77	24.56	32.38	93.18	13.66	2,232	800-366-0066	Y
MFS® Massachusetts Investors Growth Stock Fund Class 529C	EMICX	B	B	B+		7.30	11.11	27.64	32.10	93.16	23.32	7,262	877-960-6077	Y
MFS® Massachusetts Investors Trust Class 529B	EBMTX	B-	B-	B-	Down	6.45	9.87	22.56	30.83	93.10	29.68	6,571	877-960-6077	Y
Oppenheimer Discovery Mid Cap Growth Fund C	OEGCX	B+	B+	B+	Up	6.45	11.69	27.07	34.33	92.96	16.47	1,053	800-225-5677	Y
MFS® Research Fund Class R1	MFRLX	B-	B-	B-	Down	5.67	9.99	22.41	31.00	92.93	37.48	5,567	877-960-6077	Y

		RATINGS				TOTAL RETURNS & PERFORMANCE					ASSETS		NEW INVESTORS	
Fund Name	Ticker Symbol	Overall Rating	Reward Rating	Risk Rating	Recent Up/ Downgrade	3-Month Total Return	6-Month Total Return	1-Year Total Return	3-Year Total Return	5-Year Total Return	NAV	Total Assets (MIL)	Telephone	Open to New Investors
MFS® Research Fund Class C	MFRCX	B-	B-	B-	Down	5.66	10.00	22.43	30.99	92.92	38.1	5,567	877-960-6077	Y
American Funds Growth Portfolio Class R-6	RGWGX	B	B	B-	Up	5.98	11.77	25.49	36.86	92.89	18.16	5,887	800-421-4225	Y
MFS® Research Fund Class B	MFRBX	B-	B-	B-	Down	5.64	9.97	22.38	30.94	92.88	38.4	5,567	877-960-6077	Y
MFS® Massachusetts Investors Trust Class R1	MITGX	B-	B-	B-	Down	6.41	9.89	22.58	30.50	92.81	30.47	6,571	877-960-6077	Y
MFS® Massachusetts Investors Trust Class B	MITBX	B-	B-	B-	Down	6.43	9.87	22.60	30.54	92.80	31.24	6,571	877-960-6077	Y
MFS® Massachusetts Investors Trust Class C	MITCX	B-	B-	B-	Down	6.43	9.89	22.62	30.55	92.78	30.65	6,571	877-960-6077	Y
Principal Equity Income Fund R-5 Class	PEIQX	B-	B	B-	Down	7.16	11.97	20.71	32.24	92.63	31.44	6,859	800-222-5852	Y
American Funds Growth Portfolio Class F-3	GWPDX	B	B	B-	Up	6.07	11.82	25.58	36.84	92.57	18.09	5,887	800-421-4225	Y
Goldman Sachs Small/Mid Cap Growth Fund Class A	GSMAX	B	B	B	Up	5.10	10.94	27.73	25.13	92.43	20.86	2,352	800-526-7384	Y
American Funds Growth Portfolio Class R-5	RGWFX	B	B	B-	Up	5.98	11.76	25.45	36.70	92.37	18.2	5,887	800-421-4225	Y
MFS® Massachusetts Investors Trust Class 529C	ECITX	B-	B-	B-	Down	6.40	9.83	22.53	30.34	92.34	29.28	6,571	877-960-6077	Y
Voya MidCap Opportunities Portfolio Class A	IAMOX	B	B	B+	Up	7.69	10.69	24.48	31.96	92.23	13.44	2,232	800-366-0066	Y
ClearBridge Appreciation Fund Class A	SHAPX	B	B-	B+		6.50	10.50	19.51	30.94	92.21	23.6	6,159	877-721-1926	Y
Fidelity® Low-Priced Stock Fund Class K	FLPKX	B-	B-	B	Down	6.67	12.04	20.79	30.41	92.16	54.47	39,445	617-563-7000	Y
ClearBridge Appreciation Fund Class FI	LMPIX	B	B-	B+		6.47	10.44	19.46	30.89	92.08	23.72	6,159	877-721-1926	Y
American Funds Growth Portfolio Class R-5E	RGSFX	B	B	B-	Up	6.00	11.76	25.49	36.49	92.08	18.04	5,887	800-421-4225	Y
Voya MidCap Opportunities Fund Class A	NMCAX	B	B	B+	Up	7.64	10.63	24.46	31.98	92.01	22.35	1,401	800-366-0066	Y
Voya MidCap Opportunities Fund Class O	NMCOX	B	B	B+	Up	7.63	10.63	24.46	31.95	91.98	22.25	1,401	800-366-0066	Y
John Hancock Funds Disciplined Value Fund Class R3	JDVHX	B-	B-	B	Down	6.75	11.63	18.55	25.69	91.95	21.82	15,171	800-225-5913	Y
American Funds Growth Portfolio Class F-2	GWPEX	B	B	B-	Up	5.97	11.70	25.35	36.41	91.87	18.13	5,887	800-421-4225	Y
Strategic Advisers® Small-Mid Cap Fund	FSCFX	B	B	C+	Up	6.21	11.33	19.27	31.80	91.86	14.94	7,605	617-563-7000	Y
Dreyfus Research Growth Fund, Inc. Class C	DWOCX	B	B-	A-		6.43	10.24	22.66	29.54	91.85	14.02	1,845	800-645-6561	Y
Lord Abbett Alpha Strategy Fund Class R3	ALFRX	B-	B	C+	Up	4.74	10.68	20.29	28.58	91.81	25.9	1,144	201-827-2000	Y
Wells Fargo Discovery Fund - Class C	WDSCX	B	B+	B	Up	5.89	11.39	28.10	32.44	91.68	28.82	2,600	800-222-8222	Y
TIAA-CREF Mid-Cap Growth Fund Advisor Class	TCMHX	B-	B	C+	Up	5.52	11.65	26.13	27.11	91.64	22.53	1,638	877-518-9161	Y
Principal Equity Income Fund R-4 Class	PEIPX	B-	B	B-	Down	7.10	11.84	20.54	31.71	91.49	31.39	6,859	800-222-5852	Y
Goldman Sachs Small/Mid Cap Growth Fund Service Class	GSMQX	B	B	B	Up	5.09	10.90	27.62	24.72	91.43	20.34	2,352	800-526-7384	Y
Russell Investments U.S. Strategic Equity Fund Class C	RSECX	B-	B-	B-	Down	7.00	11.37	19.89	29.20	91.42	13.59	3,109	800-426-7969	Y
Principal Equity Income Fund Class A	PQIAX	B-	B	B-	Down	7.10	11.87	20.54	31.70	91.41	31.43	6,859	800-222-5852	Y
Lord Abbett Calibrated Dividend Growth Fund Class R3	LAMRX	B-	B-	B-	Down	7.56	11.14	18.75	31.55	91.38	15.31	2,475	201-827-2000	Y
Neuberger Berman Guardian Fund Class C	NGDCX	B-	B-	C+	Down	6.72	10.97	23.93	25.36	91.27	13.11	1,255	212-476-9000	Y
American Funds Growth Portfolio Class 529-F-1	CGPFX	B	B	B-	Up	5.99	11.67	25.33	36.17	91.16	18.11	5,887	800-421-4225	Y
Pioneer Fund Class C	PCODX	B-	B-	B-	Down	6.14	11.01	20.57	28.21	91.09	25.17	5,008	617-742-7825	Y
Franklin Rising Dividends Fund Class A	FRDPX	B	B	B-		6.70	11.89	20.28	31.46	90.96	61.16	19,377	650-312-2000	Y
Oppenheimer Capital Appreciation Fund Class R	OTCNX	B	B-	B	Up	5.79	9.76	26.19	25.39	90.95	55.08	5,215	800-225-5677	Y
Columbia Mid Cap Growth Fund Institutional 3 Class	CMGYX	B	B	B	Up	5.05	10.07	23.12	31.99	90.90	27.37	1,916	800-345-6611	Y
Lord Abbett Alpha Strategy Fund Class R2	ALFQX	B-	B	C+	Up	4.70	10.63	20.15	28.19	90.82	25.71	1,144	201-827-2000	Y
Principal LargeCap Growth Fund Class C	PLGCX	B	B	B	Up	7.28	15.24	33.04	27.98	90.71	7.72	1,083	800-222-5852	Y
Neuberger Berman Mid Cap Growth Fund Class A	NMGAX	B	B+	B	Up	6.91	11.70	25.00	31.48	90.53	14.71	1,274	212-476-9000	Y
TIAA-CREF Mid-Cap Growth Fund Premier Class	TRGPX	B	B	B	Up	5.54	11.65	26.04	26.65	90.41	22.41	1,638	877-518-9161	Y
Lord Abbett Calibrated Dividend Growth Fund Class R2	LAMQX	B-	B-	B-	Down	7.56	11.13	18.65	31.16	90.26	15.54	2,475	201-827-2000	Y
Russell Investments Tax-Managed U.S. Large Cap Fund Cls C	RTLCX	B-	B-	B-	Down	6.43	10.23	20.31	28.68	90.19	38.57	2,510	800-426-7969	Y
ClearBridge Dividend Strategy Fund Class 1	LCBOX	B-	B-	B	Down	5.70	10.17	19.44	30.46	90.17	23.53	6,226	877-721-1926	Y
American Funds Growth Portfolio Class A	GWPAX	B	B	B-	Up	5.96	11.59	25.11	35.70	90.09	18.08	5,887	800-421-4225	Y
Goldman Sachs Small/Mid Cap Growth Fund Class R	GTMRX	B	B	B	Up	5.03	10.83	27.48	24.24	90.01	20.15	2,352	800-526-7384	Y
First Investors Growth and Income Fund Advisor Class	FGIPX	B-	B-	B	Down	6.74	10.50	18.51	24.92	89.77	24	1,948	800-423-4026	Y
Principal MidCap Growth Fund III Institutional Class	PPIMX	B-	B	C+	Down	6.30	10.98	24.58	27.04	89.76	11.12	1,127	800-222-5852	Y
Principal Equity Income Fund R-3 Class	PEIOX	B-	B-	B-	Down	7.10	11.79	20.37	31.01	89.75	31.34	6,859	800-222-5852	Y
American Funds Growth Portfolio Class R-4	RGWEX	B	B	B-	Up	5.95	11.59	25.06	35.55	89.73	18.05	5,887	800-421-4225	Y
Voya MidCap Opportunities Fund Class R	IMORX	B	B	B+	Up	7.59	10.54	24.17	31.00	89.71	21.84	1,401	800-366-0066	Y
TIAA-CREF Mid-Cap Growth Fund Retirement Class	TRGMX	B	B	B	Up	5.48	11.58	25.89	26.25	89.50	21.91	1,638	877-518-9161	Y
American Funds Growth Portfolio Class 529-A	CGPAX	B	B	B-	Up	5.94	11.58	25.03	35.39	89.49	18.06	5,887	800-421-4225	Y

		RATINGS				TOTAL RETURNS & PERFORMANCE					ASSETS		NEW INVESTORS	
Fund Name	Ticker Symbol	Overall Rating	Reward Rating	Risk Rating	Recent Up/ Downgrade	3-Month Total Return	6-Month Total Return	1-Year Total Return	3-Year Total Return	5-Year Total Return	NAV	Total Assets (MIL)	Telephone	Open to New Investors
Prudential Jennison Small Company Fund Class R	JSCRX	B	B	B	Up	4.81	9.15	19.26	28.57	89.48	24.3	3,704	800-225-1852	Y
American Funds Growth Portfolio Class F-1	GWPFX	B	B	B-	Up	5.92	11.62	25.08	35.37	89.47	18.07	5,887	800-421-4225	Y
Fidelity® Export and Multinational Fund Class K	FEXKX	B	B-	B+		7.71	11.77	21.07	33.22	89.40	22.16	1,805	617-563-7000	Y
ClearBridge Appreciation Fund Class R	LMPPX	B	B-	B		6.43	10.30	19.16	29.74	89.30	23.56	6,159	877-721-1926	Y
Calvert Equity Fund Class C	CSECX	B	B-	A		6.74	11.22	24.83	29.29	89.26	25.25	2,222	800-368-2745	Y
Wells Fargo Opportunity Fund - Class A	SOPVX	B	B	B	Up	6.60	10.48	20.00	28.81	89.12	42.87	1,832	800-222-8222	Y
Columbia Mid Cap Growth Fund Advisor Class	CPGRX	B	B	B	Up	5.00	9.97	22.93	31.29	89.01	27.96	1,916	800-345-6611	Y
Fidelity Advisor® Stock Selector Mid Cap Fund Class Z	FSLZX	B-	B	C+	Down	5.01	9.91	20.35	27.71	88.87	40.02	2,551	617-563-7000	Y
Franklin Rising Dividends Fund Class R	FRDRX	B-	B	B-	Down	6.64	11.73	19.98	30.48	88.54	60.97	19,377	650-312-2000	Y
Prudential Jennison 20/20 Focus Fund Class R	JTWRX	B	B	B	Up	5.13	12.25	26.25	34.28	88.44	13.86	1,182	800-225-1852	Y
Neuberger Berman Mid Cap Growth Fund Class R3	NMGRX	B	B	C+	Up	6.89	11.61	24.71	30.54	88.33	14.71	1,274	212-476-9000	Y
Brown Advisory Growth Equity Fund Investor Shares	BIAGX	B+	B	A-	Up	7.89	12.98	30.43	34.07	88.29	20.8	1,953	800-540-6807	Y
Goldman Sachs Intl Small Cap Insights Fund Inv Cls	GIRLX	A-	A-	A	Up	4.82	13.18	32.85	49.00	88.11	12.69	2,617	800-526-7384	Y
Pioneer Core Equity Fund Class C	PCOTX	B-	B-	B-	Down	5.70	12.03	23.74	28.75	88.01	18.26	1,696	617-742-7825	Y
Principal Equity Income Fund R-2 Class	PEINX	B-	B-	B-	Down	7.03	11.70	20.12	30.33	88.01	31.44	6,859	800-222-5852	Y
American Century Heritage Fund R6 Class	ATHDX	B	B	B	Up	5.64	9.76	22.27	28.60	87.84	24.07	5,143	800-444-4015	Y
ClearBridge Dividend Strategy Fund Class A	SOPAX	B-	B-	B	Down	5.68	10.02	19.12	29.41	87.73	23.52	6,226	877-721-1926	Y
VY® Oppenheimer Global Portfolio Class I	IGMIX	B+	A-	B	Up	7.25	13.80	36.48	41.38	87.50	22.33	1,738	800-366-0066	Y
Oppenheimer Global Fund Class Fund Class Y	OGLYX	B+	B+	B	Up	7.18	13.76	36.56	41.81	87.47	96.05	11,177	800-225-5677	Y
Principal MidCap Growth Fund III R-5 Class	PPQPX	B-	B-	C+	Up	6.35	10.90	24.37	26.07	87.36	11.21	1,127	800-222-5852	Y
Wells Fargo Premier Large Company Growth Fund - Class C	EKJCX	B	B	B	Up	7.26	13.70	32.97	28.18	87.27	10.43	2,478	800-222-8222	Y
Victory Munder Mid-Cap Core Growth Fund Class R	MMSRX	B-	B-	C+	Up	5.92	11.71	23.85	24.81	87.07	32.89	4,105	800-539-3863	Y
American Funds SMALLCAP World Fund® Class R-6	RLLGX	B	B	B	Up	4.97	10.81	27.27	38.82	87.01	56.69	38,579	800-421-4225	Y
American Funds Growth Portfolio Class R-2E	RBGEX	B	B	B-	Up	5.78	11.34	24.49	34.20	86.82	17.9	5,887	800-421-4225	Y
MainStay MAP Equity Fund Class R1	MAPRX	B-	B-	C+	Down	5.96	10.90	22.65	27.88	86.81	41.13	1,249	800-624-6782	Y
American Funds Growth Portfolio Class 529-E	CGPEX	B	B	B-	Up	5.87	11.48	24.77	34.37	86.80	17.96	5,887	800-421-4225	Y
Principal Equity Income Fund R-1 Class	PIEMX	B-	B-	B-	Down	6.99	11.60	19.96	29.80	86.72	31.32	6,859	800-222-5852	Y
ClearBridge Dividend Strategy Fund Class FI	LBRIX	B-	B-	B	Down	5.63	9.96	19.01	29.27	86.62	23.49	6,226	877-721-1926	Y
American Funds Growth Portfolio Class R-3	RGPCX	B	B	B-	Up	5.84	11.44	24.70	34.24	86.59	17.98	5,887	800-421-4225	Y
American Funds SMALLCAP World Fund® Class R-5	RSLFX	B	B	B	Up	4.96	10.77	27.21	38.61	86.58	57.3	38,579	800-421-4225	Y
Principal MidCap Growth Fund III R-4 Class	PPQSX	B-	B-	C+	Up	6.24	10.87	24.16	25.55	86.24	10.73	1,127	800-222-5852	Y
American Funds New Perspective Fund® Class R-6	RNPGX	B+	B	A-	Up	4.67	10.41	29.29	38.69	86.23	43.17	76,532	800-421-4225	Y
JNL/Oppenheimer Global Growth Fund Class I	US46644W3025	B+	B+	B	Up	7.39	13.89	36.39	41.29	86.12	18.89	2,577		Y
Principal MidCap Growth Fund III Class J	PPQJX	B-	B-	C+	Up	6.33	10.91	24.22	25.67	86.05	9.07	1,127	800-222-5852	Y
American Funds SMALLCAP World Fund® Class F-2	SMCFX	B	B	B	Up	4.95	10.76	27.16	38.39	86.03	56.51	38,579	800-421-4225	Y
Brown Advisory Growth Equity Fund Advisor Shares	BAGAX	B+	B	A-	Up	7.79	12.83	30.12	33.16	86.01	19.81	1,953	800-540-6807	Y
Goldman Sachs International Small Cap Insights Fund Cls A	GICAX	A-	B+	A-	Up	4.84	13.09	32.53	47.92	85.77	12.76	2,617	800-526-7384	Y
American Funds New Perspective Fund® Class R-5	RNPFX	B+	B	A-	Up	4.67	10.38	29.21	38.51	85.77	43.11	76,532	800-421-4225	Y
American Century Heritage Fund Y Class	ATHYX	B	B	B	Up	5.68	9.81	22.20	27.66	85.55	24.08	5,143	800-444-4015	Y
Calamos Growth Fund Class R	CGRRX	B	B-	B	Up	6.52	10.79	26.29	25.60	85.55	30.36	1,686	800-582-6959	Y
ClearBridge Appreciation Fund Class C	SAPCX	B-	B-	B	Down	6.33	10.07	18.65	28.19	85.50	22.78	6,159	877-721-1926	Y
American Century Heritage Fund R5 Class	ATHGX	B	B	B	Up	5.60	9.66	22.05	27.50	85.32	23.87	5,143	800-444-4015	Y
American Funds New Perspective Fund® Class F-2	ANWFX	B+	B	A-	Up	4.64	10.32	29.11	38.26	85.30	43.02	76,532	800-421-4225	Y
Oppenheimer Global Fund Class A	OPPAX	B+	B+	B	Up	7.12	13.61	36.24	40.82	85.20	95.98	11,177	800-225-5677	Y
ClearBridge Dividend Strategy Fund Class R	LMMRX	B-	B-	B-	Down	5.56	9.79	18.75	28.47	85.20	23.37	6,226	877-721-1926	Y
VY® Oppenheimer Global Portfolio Class S	IGMSX	B	B+	C+	Up	7.16	13.65	36.13	40.30	85.14	21.53	1,738	800-366-0066	Y
Voya MidCap Opportunities Fund Class C	NMCCX	B	B	B	Up	7.44	10.23	23.57	28.98	84.95	16.79	1,401	800-366-0066	Y
American Funds SMALLCAP World Fund® Class 529-F	CSPFX	B	B	B	Up	4.92	10.70	26.99	37.87	84.82	55.8	38,579	800-421-4225	Y
Columbia Mid Cap Growth Fund Class R	CMGRX	B	B	B	Up	4.86	9.72	22.29	29.33	84.63	24.45	1,916	800-345-6611	Y
American Funds New Perspective Fund® Class 529-F	CNPFX	B+	B	A-	Up	4.64	10.31	29.07	38.00	84.55	42.55	76,532	800-421-4225	Y
MainStay MAP Equity Fund Class R2	MPRRX	B-	B-	C+	Down	5.91	10.76	22.36	26.92	84.44	41.08	1,249	800-624-6782	Y
Principal MidCap Growth Fund III R-3 Class	PPQMX	B-	B-	C+	Up	6.22	10.77	23.91	24.93	84.43	10.42	1,127	800-222-5852	Y

		RATINGS				TOTAL RETURNS & PERFORMANCE					ASSETS		NEW INVESTORS	
Fund Name	Ticker Symbol	Overall Rating	Reward Rating	Risk Rating	Recent Up/ Downgrade	3-Month Total Return	6-Month Total Return	1-Year Total Return	3-Year Total Return	5-Year Total Return	NAV	Total Assets (MIL)	Telephone	Open to New Investors
Principal Equity Income Fund Class C	PEUCX	B-	B-	B-	Down	6.93	11.47	19.68	28.82	84.42	30.65	6,859	800-222-5852	Y
JNL/Oppenheimer Global Growth Fund Class A	US46644W2035	B+	B+	B	Up	7.27	13.72	36.15	40.47	84.25	18.57	2,577		Y
American Funds SMALLCAP World Fund® Class R-5E	RSLDX	B	B	B	Up	4.94	10.72	27.09	37.83	84.25	55.78	38,579	800-421-4225	Y
Amana Mutual Funds Trust Income Fund Investor	AMANX	B-	B-	B-	Down	6.43	10.69	21.05	27.36	84.24	51.18	1,427	888-732-6262	Y
DFA Global Equity Portfolio Institutional Class	DGEIX	B-	B	C+	Down	6.62	11.84	22.15	33.26	84.19	23.25	6,535	512-306-7400	Y
American Funds SMALLCAP World Fund® Class F-3	SFCWX	B	B	B	Up	4.96	10.81	27.24	37.76	84.16	55.99	38,579	800-421-4225	Y
Franklin Rising Dividends Fund Class C	FRDTX	B-	B-	B-	Down	6.51	11.46	19.40	28.53	83.90	60.08	19,377	650-312-2000	Y
American Funds New Perspective Fund® Class F-3	FNPFX	B+	B	A-	Up	4.66	10.38	29.25	37.82	83.86	43.15	76,532	800-421-4225	Y
Great-West MFS International Value Fund Institutional Cls	MXJVX	B+	B	A-	Up	5.71	9.14	27.08	39.34	83.83		1,285		Y
American Funds SMALLCAP World Fund® Class R-4	RSLEX	B	B	B	Up	4.88	10.62	26.84	37.38	83.81	55.36	38,579	800-421-4225	Y
VY® Oppenheimer Global Portfolio Class S2	IOGPX	B+	B+	B	Up	7.09	13.54	35.91	39.69	83.80	20.97	1,738	800-366-0066	Y
MainStay MAP Equity Fund Investor Class	MSMIX	B-	B-	C+	Down	5.87	10.69	22.25	26.59	83.76	40.87	1,249	800-624-6782	Y
American Funds New Perspective Fund® Class R-5E	RNPHX	B+	B	A-	Up	4.63	10.32	29.08	37.70	83.70	42.92	76,532	800-421-4225	Y
Neuberger Berman Mid Cap Growth Fund Class C	NMGCX	B	B	C+	Up	6.76	11.34	24.10	28.62	83.69	14.7	1,274	212-476-9000	Y
Waddell & Reed Advisor New Concepts Fund Class Y	UNEYX	B-	B	C	Up	7.21	12.69	27.28	27.05	83.67	12.76	1,716	888-923-3355	Y
American Funds SMALLCAP World Fund® Class A	SMCWX	B	B	B	Up	4.88	10.61	26.83	37.32	83.56	55.8	38,579	800-421-4225	Y
Nuveen Santa Barbara Dividend Growth Fund Class R3	NBDRX	B-	B-	B-	Down	6.24	10.39	19.41	27.00	83.49	41.35	3,116	312-917-8146	Y
American Funds SMALLCAP World Fund® Class F-1	SCWFX	B	B	B	Up	4.86	10.59	26.76	37.21	83.43	55.16	38,579	800-421-4225	Y
American Funds New Perspective Fund® Class A	ANWPX	B+	B	A-	Up	4.59	10.23	28.89	37.43	83.35	43.16	76,532	800-421-4225	Y
American Funds 2050 Target Date Retirement Fund® Class R-6	RFITX	B-	B-	B	Down	5.19	10.58	22.60	32.74	83.21	15.16	5,563	800-421-4225	Y
American Funds 2055 Target Date Retirement Fund® Class F-3	FCJTX	B-	B-	B	Down	5.18	10.55	22.63	32.71	83.13	18.81	2,616	800-421-4225	Y
American Funds 2055 Target Date Retirement Fund® Class R-6	RFKTX	B-	B-	B	Down	5.14	10.54	22.62	32.70	83.12	18.94	2,616	800-421-4225	Y
American Funds 2050 Target Date Retirement Fund® Class F-3	DITFX	B-	B-	B	Down	5.21	10.61	22.57	32.57	83.02	15.11	5,563	800-421-4225	Y
American Funds New Perspective Fund® Class R-4	RNPEX	B+	B	A-	Up	4.59	10.21	28.82	37.25	83.01	42.57	76,532	800-421-4225	Y
American Funds 2050 Target Date Retirement Fund® Class R-5	REITX	B-	B-	B	Down	5.20	10.57	22.55	32.55	82.99	15.21	5,563	800-421-4225	Y
Principal MidCap Growth Fund III R-2 Class	PPQNX	B-	B-	C+	Up	6.23	10.70	23.70	24.39	82.95	9.57	1,127	800-222-5852	Y
Columbia Acorn Fund Institutional 2 Class	CRBRX	B	B+	C+	Up	6.00	11.44	25.20	35.10	82.93	16.2	4,848	800-345-6611	Y
American Funds SMALLCAP World Fund® Class 529-A	CSPAX	B	B	B	Up	4.86	10.57	26.75	37.01	82.91	55.17	38,579	800-421-4225	Y
VY® Oppenheimer Global Portfolio Class A	IGMAX	B	B+	C+	Up	7.10	13.48	35.82	39.25	82.89	21.42	1,738	800-366-0066	Y
American Funds 2045 Target Date Retirement Fund® Class R-6	RFHTX	B-	B-	B	Down	5.10	10.44	22.43	32.49	82.89	15.49	6,946	800-421-4225	Y
Oppenheimer Global Fund Class R	OGLNX	B+	B+	B	Up	7.04	13.47	35.88	39.70	82.79	95.56	11,177	800-225-5677	Y
American Funds 2055 Target Date Retirement Fund® Class R-5	REKTX	B-	B-	B	Down	5.16	10.50	22.52	32.50	82.76	18.92	2,616	800-421-4225	Y
American Funds New Perspective Fund® Class F-1	NPFFX	B+	B	A-	Up	4.57	10.20	28.77	37.15	82.75	42.89	76,532	800-421-4225	Y
John Hancock Funds II Strategic Equity Alloc Fund NAV	US47804M7204	B-	B	B-	Down	5.37	10.72	22.11	30.96	82.73	12.89	7,694	800-225-5913	Y
American Funds Growth Portfolio Class C	GWPCX	B-	B-	B-	Down	5.75	11.21	24.17	32.49	82.70	17.83	5,887	800-421-4225	Y
American Funds 2055 Target Date Retirement Fund® Cls R-5E	RHJTX	B-	B-	B	Down	5.13	10.52	22.44	32.31	82.59	18.74	2,616	800-421-4225	Y
American Funds 2050 Target Date Retirement Fund® Cls R-5E	RHITX	B-	B-	B	Down	5.07	10.48	22.40	32.24	82.57	15.05	5,563	800-421-4225	Y
American Funds Growth Portfolio Class R-1	RGWAX	B-	B-	B-	Down	5.75	11.18	24.16	32.47	82.56	17.91	5,887	800-421-4225	Y
American Funds New Perspective Fund® Class 529-A	CNPAX	B+	B	A-	Up	4.55	10.18	28.78	37.07	82.54	42.65	76,532	800-421-4225	Y
American Funds 2050 Target Date Retirement Fund® Class F-2	FBITX	B-	B-	B	Down	5.09	10.49	22.48	32.30	82.53	15.08	5,563	800-421-4225	Y
American Funds 2045 Target Date Retirement Fund® Class R-5	REHTX	B-	B-	B	Down	5.03	10.34	22.28	32.18	82.46	15.54	6,946	800-421-4225	Y
American Funds 2045 Target Date Retirement Fund® Class F-3	FCHTX	B-	B-	B	Down	5.06	10.41	22.24	32.14	82.40	15.42	6,946	800-421-4225	Y
American Funds Growth Portfolio Class R-2	RGWBX	B-	B-	B-	Down	5.74	11.20	24.16	32.43	82.40	17.82	5,887	800-421-4225	Y
Ivy Mid Cap Growth Fund Class I	IYMIX	B-	B	C	Up	7.22	12.73	27.30	26.97	82.40	24.66	2,406	800-777-6472	Y
American Funds 2055 Target Date Retirement Fund® Class F-2	FBJTX	B-	B-	B	Down	5.18	10.50	22.52	32.39	82.34	18.8	2,616	800-421-4225	Y
Great-West MFS International Value Fund Investor Class	MXIVX	B	B	B+		5.65	9.05	26.68	38.10	82.20		1,285		Y
MainStay MAP Equity Fund Class R3	MMAPX	B-	B-	C+	Down	5.83	10.62	22.07	26.01	82.18	40.93	1,249	800-624-6782	Y
Thrivent Series Aggressive Allocation Portfolio		B-	B-	B-	Down	4.84	9.99	21.51	32.33	82.16	17.5056	1,298		Y
Wells Fargo Opportunity Fund - Class C	WFOPX	B	B-	B	Up	6.38	10.05	19.10	25.91	82.12	40.42	1,832	800-222-8222	Y
American Funds 2045 Target Date Retirement Fund® Cls R-5E	RHHTX	B-	B-	B	Down	5.07	10.36	22.27	31.93	82.12	15.37	6,946	800-421-4225	Y
MFS® New Discovery Fund Class R6	MNDKX	B	B+	C	Up	6.65	13.98	26.49	35.14	82.08	30.32	1,213	877-960-6077	Y
American Funds 2045 Target Date Retirement Fund® Class F-2	FBHTX	B-	B-	B	Down	5.07	10.42	22.29	32.09	82.03	15.43	6,946	800-421-4225	Y

Fund Name	Ticker Symbol	Overall Rating	Reward Rating	Risk Rating	Recent Up/ Downgrade	3-Month Total Return	6-Month Total Return	1-Year Total Return	3-Year Total Return	5-Year Total Return	NAV	Total Assets (MIL)	Telephone	Open to New Investors
		RATINGS				TOTAL RETURNS & PERFORMANCE					ASSETS		NEW INVESTORS	
American Funds 2040 Target Date Retirement Fund® Class R-6	RFGTX	B-	B-	B	Down	4.97	10.21	21.97	31.78	81.93	15.25	10,103	800-421-4225	Y
American Funds Growth Portfolio Class 529-C	CGPCX	B-	B-	B-	Down	5.69	11.14	24.03	32.15	81.89	17.81	5,887	800-421-4225	Y
DFA Global Equity Portfolio Class Retirement 2	DGERX	B-	B	C+	Down	6.59	11.72	21.87	32.23	81.84	23.39	6,535	512-306-7400	Y
Putnam Dynamic Asset Allocation Growth Fund Class R6	PAEEX	B-	B-	B	Down	5.40	10.67	20.32	29.35	81.57	17.24	2,929	617-292-1000	Y
American Funds 2040 Target Date Retirement Fund® Class F-3	FCGTX	B-	B-	B	Down	4.98	10.25	21.94	31.61	81.36	15.2	10,103	800-421-4225	Y
American Funds 2040 Target Date Retirement Fund® Class R-5	REGTX	B-	B-	B	Down	4.97	10.20	21.92	31.58	81.33	15.3	10,103	800-421-4225	Y
MFS® New Discovery Fund Class R4	MNDJX	B	B+	C	Up	6.75	14.06	26.46	34.74	81.19	28.64	1,213	877-960-6077	Y
MFS® New Discovery Fund Class I	MNDIX	B	B+	C	Up	6.64	13.94	26.34	34.65	80.99	30.09	1,213	877-960-6077	Y
American Funds SMALLCAP World Fund® Class 529-E	CSPEX	B	B	B	Up	4.83	10.48	26.48	36.14	80.90	53.64	38,579	800-421-4225	Y
American Funds 2040 Target Date Retirement Fund® Cls R-5E	RHGTX	B-	B-	B	Down	4.91	10.12	21.77	31.27	80.90	15.14	10,103	800-421-4225	Y
American Funds 2040 Target Date Retirement Fund® Class F-2	FBGTX	B-	B-	B	Down	4.93	10.13	21.84	31.42	80.88	15.18	10,103	800-421-4225	Y
American Funds SMALLCAP World Fund® Class R-3	RSLCX	B	B	B	Up	4.82	10.46	26.46	36.09	80.87	53.53	38,579	800-421-4225	Y
American Funds SMALLCAP World Fund® Class R-2E	RSEBX	B	B	B	Up	4.77	10.36	26.27	35.94	80.82	55.38	38,579	800-421-4225	Y
Waddell & Reed Advisor New Concepts Fund Class A	UNECX	B-	B-	C	Up	7.21	12.57	27.06	26.01	80.67	11.27	1,716	888-923-3355	Y
Putnam Dynamic Asset Allocation Growth Fund Class R5	PADEX	B-	B-	B	Down	5.34	10.62	20.13	28.91	80.63	17.2	2,929	617-292-1000	Y
Putnam Dynamic Asset Allocation Growth Fund Class Y	PAGYX	B-	B-	B	Down	5.36	10.57	20.08	28.89	80.47	17.21	2,929	617-292-1000	Y
American Funds New Perspective Fund® Class 529-E	CNPEX	B	B	A-	Up	4.51	10.07	28.47	36.12	80.39	42.25	76,532	800-421-4225	Y
American Funds 2055 Target Date Retirement Fund® Class A	AAMTX	B-	B-	B	Down	5.07	10.39	22.18	31.41	80.37	18.8	2,616	800-421-4225	Y
American Funds 2050 Target Date Retirement Fund® Class A	AALTX	B-	B-	B	Down	5.06	10.31	22.17	31.42	80.33	15.1	5,563	800-421-4225	Y
American Funds 2050 Target Date Retirement Fund® Class F-1	FAITX	B-	B-	B	Down	5.05	10.32	22.15	31.33	80.31	15.02	5,563	800-421-4225	Y
American Funds 2055 Target Date Retirement Fund® Class F-1	FAJTX	B-	B-	B	Down	5.09	10.37	22.14	31.29	80.30	18.71	2,616	800-421-4225	Y
American Funds New Perspective Fund® Class R-2E	RPEBX	B	B	A-	Up	4.46	9.95	28.26	35.91	80.29	42.52	76,532	800-421-4225	Y
Ivy Mid Cap Growth Fund Class Y	WMGYX	B-	B	C	Up	7.16	12.59	27.01	26.13	80.26	23.94	2,406	800-777-6472	Y
American Funds New Perspective Fund® Class R-3	RNPCX	B	B	A-	Up	4.49	10.03	28.45	36.02	80.24	42.2	76,532	800-421-4225	Y
American Funds 2050 Target Date Retirement Fund® Class R-4	RDITX	B-	B-	B	Down	5.01	10.35	22.15	31.33	80.12	15.06	5,563	800-421-4225	Y
American Funds 2055 Target Date Retirement Fund® Class R-4	RDJTX	B-	B-	B	Down	5.07	10.33	22.15	31.32	79.96	18.76	2,616	800-421-4225	Y
TIAA-CREF Lifecycle 2050 Fund Advisor Class	TFTHX	B-	B	B-	Down	5.40	11.55	24.02	33.43	79.94	12.72	1,707	877-518-9161	Y
American Funds 2045 Target Date Retirement Fund® Class A	AAHTX	B-	B-	B	Down	5.04	10.25	22.01	31.20	79.93	15.43	6,946	800-421-4225	Y
American Funds 2045 Target Date Retirement Fund® Class F-1	FATTX	B-	B-	B	Down	4.96	10.27	21.99	31.10	79.79	15.35	6,946	800-421-4225	Y
Ivy Mid Cap Growth Fund Class A	WMGAX	B-	B	C	Up	7.16	12.56	26.99	25.91	79.72	22.92	2,406	800-777-6472	Y
American Funds 2045 Target Date Retirement Fund® Class R-4	RDHTX	B-	B-	B	Down	4.98	10.20	21.98	31.10	79.68	15.39	6,946	800-421-4225	Y
Great-West MFS International Value Fund Class L	MXMIX	B	B	B+		5.58	8.91	26.36	36.82	79.44		1,285		Y
American Funds 2035 Target Date Retirement Fund® Class R-6	RFFTX	B-	B-	B	Down	4.69	9.73	21.03	30.57	79.41	14.88	11,498	800-421-4225	Y
TIAA-CREF Lifecycle 2045 Fund Advisor Class	TTFHX	B-	B	B-	Down	5.35	11.42	23.70	32.96	79.34	12.66	2,659	877-518-9161	Y
American Funds 2035 Target Date Retirement Fund® Class F-3	FDFTX	B-	B-	B	Down	4.77	9.75	21.17	30.58	79.09	14.84	11,498	800-421-4225	Y
Russell Investments Global Equity Fund Class M	RGDTX	B-	B	B-	Up	5.62	10.58	23.27	30.94	79.03	10.78	2,200	800-426-7969	Y
American Funds 2040 Target Date Retirement Fund® Class A	AAGTX	B-	B-	B	Down	4.90	10.09	21.61	30.54	78.97	15.2	10,103	800-421-4225	Y
Goldman Sachs International Small Cap Insights Fund Cls C	GICCX	A-	B+	A-	Up	4.68	12.65	31.68	44.62	78.92	12.35	2,617	800-526-7384	Y
American Funds 2035 Target Date Retirement Fund® Class R-5	REFTX	B-	B-	B	Down	4.68	9.71	21.06	30.46	78.92	14.94	11,498	800-421-4225	Y
Russell Investments Global Equity Fund Class S	RGESX	B-	B	B-	Up	5.63	10.49	23.18	30.84	78.89	10.8	2,200	800-426-7969	Y
MFS® New Discovery Fund Class A	MNDAX	B	B+	C	Up	6.59	13.83	26.08	33.65	78.85	27.26	1,213	877-960-6077	Y
American Funds 2040 Target Date Retirement Fund® Class R-4	RDGTX	B-	B-	B	Down	4.91	10.04	21.59	30.46	78.80	15.16	10,103	800-421-4225	Y
American Funds 2040 Target Date Retirement Fund® Class F-1	FAUTX	B-	B-	B	Down	4.90	10.04	21.62	30.43	78.75	15.12	10,103	800-421-4225	Y
MFS® New Discovery Fund Class R3	MNDHX	B	B+	C	Up	6.55	13.81	26.01	33.64	78.72	27.22	1,213	877-960-6077	Y
Janus Henderson Global Select Fund Class N	JSLNX	B-	B	C		5.76	12.77	31.15	28.62	78.61	16.85	2,221	877-335-2687	Y
American Funds 2035 Target Date Retirement Fund® Cls R-5E	RHFTX	B-	B-	B	Down	4.63	9.62	20.89	30.22	78.60	14.79	11,498	800-421-4225	Y
American Funds 2035 Target Date Retirement Fund® Class F-2	FBFTX	B-	B-	B	Down	4.72	9.70	20.95	30.23	78.55	14.83	11,498	800-421-4225	Y
Principal Strat Asset Mgmt Strat Growth Fund Inst Cls	PSWIX	B-	B-	B-	Down	4.84	10.82	22.11	26.14	78.55	20.09	2,007	800-222-5852	Y
TIAA-CREF Lifecycle 2050 Fund Premier Class	TCLPX	B-	B	B-	Down	5.38	11.47	23.76	32.85	78.51	12.67	1,707	877-518-9161	Y
MFS® New Discovery Fund Class 529A	EANDX	B	B+	C	Up	6.57	13.79	25.96	33.53	78.49	26.34	1,213	877-960-6077	Y
Oppenheimer Global Fund Class C	OGLCX	B	B+	B	Up	6.91	13.18	35.19	37.61	78.38	88.5	11,177	800-225-5677	Y
Ivy Mid Cap Growth Fund Class E	IMCEX	B-	B-	C	Up	7.14	12.57	26.99	25.69	78.30	22.36	2,406	800-777-6472	Y

		RATINGS				TOTAL RETURNS & PERFORMANCE					ASSETS		NEW INVESTORS	
Fund Name	Ticker Symbol	Overall Rating	Reward Rating	Risk Rating	Recent Up/ Downgrade	3-Month Total Return	6-Month Total Return	1-Year Total Return	3-Year Total Return	5-Year Total Return	NAV	Total Assets (MIL)	Telephone	Open to New Investors
TIAA-CREF Lifecycle Index 2045 Fund Advisor Class	TLMHX	B-	B-	B-	Down	5.21	10.01	21.18	30.54	78.24	19.88	1,080	877-518-9161	Y
Putnam Dynamic Asset Allocation Growth Fund Class A	PAEAX	B-	B-	B	Down	5.33	10.47	19.85	27.99	78.23	17.04	2,929	617-292-1000	Y
JPMorgan Investor Growth Fund Class C	OGGCX	B-	B-	B-	Down	5.35	10.07	20.35	26.65	78.14	19.37	2,718	800-480-4111	Y
TIAA-CREF Lifecycle 2045 Fund Premier Class	TTFPX	B-	B-	B-	Down	5.33	11.25	23.45	32.39	77.95	12.6	2,659	877-518-9161	Y
Gabelli Asset Fund T	GALTX	B-	B-	C+	Down	5.40	9.92	20.20	25.10	77.91	58.91	2,698	914-921-5135	Y
Gabelli Asset Fund Class A	GATAX	B-	B-	C+	Down	5.37	9.87	20.17	25.07	77.85	58.36	2,698	914-921-5135	Y
Gabelli Asset Fund Class AAA	GABAX	B-	B-	C+	Down	5.36	9.88	20.16	25.06	77.85	58.97	2,698	914-921-5135	Y
JNL Multi-Manager Small Cap Growth Fund Class I	US46644W4684	B	B+	C	Up	5.08	11.99	27.50	28.63	77.74	27.07	1,713		Y
TIAA-CREF Lifecycle 2050 Fund Retirement Class	TLFRX	B-	B-	B-	Down	5.39	11.41	23.62	32.46	77.71	12.63	1,707	877-518-9161	Y
JNL/S&P Managed Aggressive Growth Fund Class I	US46648L6589	B-	B-	B-		5.35	9.99	23.36	29.62	77.55	22.23	2,220		Y
American Funds 2055 Target Date Retirement Fund® Cls R-2E	RBEMX	B-	B-	B	Down	4.95	10.13	21.64	30.04	77.53	18.59	2,616	800-421-4225	Y
American Funds 2050 Target Date Retirement Fund® Cls R-2E	RBHEX	B-	B-	B	Down	4.98	10.15	21.67	30.00	77.51	14.91	5,563	800-421-4225	Y
JNL/S&P Managed Aggressive Growth Fund Class A	US46648L6662	B-	B-	B-	Down	5.26	9.89	23.25	29.50	77.39	22.21	2,220		Y
American Funds 2050 Target Date Retirement Fund® Class R-3	RCITX	B-	B-	B	Down	4.98	10.13	21.72	30.09	77.20	14.95	5,563	800-421-4225	Y
American Funds 2055 Target Date Retirement Fund® Class R-3	RCMTX	B-	B-	B	Down	4.96	10.20	21.79	30.09	77.09	18.63	2,616	800-421-4225	Y
American Funds Global Growth Portfolio Class R-6	RGGGX	B	B	B	Up	5.27	11.34	29.02	34.45	77.07	16.87	2,670	800-421-4225	Y
Dreyfus Appreciation Fund, Inc. Class I	DGIGX	B-	B	B-	Down	7.45	12.19	26.90	31.44	77.07	35.89	2,003	800-645-6561	Y
TIAA-CREF Lifecycle 2045 Fund Retirement Class	TTFRX	B-	B-	B-	Down	5.24	11.18	23.40	31.97	77.07	12.57	2,659	877-518-9161	Y
Transamerica Asset Allocation Growth Portfolio Fund Cls T1	TAGTX	B-	B-	B-	Down	4.56	9.16	20.28	29.04	77.05	15.25	1,540	888-233-4339	Y
American Funds 2045 Target Date Retirement Fund® Cls R-2E	RBHHX	B-	B-	B	Down	4.87	9.99	21.40	29.66	77.00	15.22	6,946	800-421-4225	Y
TIAA-CREF Lifecycle Index 2045 Fund Premier Class	TLMPX	B-	B-	B-	Down	5.17	9.98	20.99	30.03	76.98	19.8	1,080	877-518-9161	Y
Transamerica Asset Allocation Growth Portfolio Fund Adv	TAGVX	B-	B-	B-	Down	4.57	9.11	20.23	28.99	76.98	15.23	1,540	888-233-4339	Y
American Funds SMALLCAP World Fund® Class R-2	RSLBX	B	B	B	Up	4.67	10.20	25.88	34.31	76.92	50.68	38,579	800-421-4225	Y
American Funds 2045 Target Date Retirement Fund® Class R-3	RCHTX	B-	B-	B	Down	4.88	10.07	21.58	29.80	76.92	15.26	6,946	800-421-4225	Y
Transamerica Asset Allocation Growth Portfolio Class A	IAAAX	B-	B-	B-	Down	4.51	9.11	20.15	28.90	76.86	15.18	1,540	888-233-4339	Y
American Funds SMALLCAP World Fund® Class R-1	RSLAX	B	B	B	Up	4.70	10.18	25.86	34.23	76.81	50.66	38,579	800-421-4225	Y
American Funds Global Growth Portfolio Class F-3	PGXFX	B	B	B	Up	5.32	11.37	29.00	34.33	76.76	16.73	2,670	800-421-4225	Y
Russell Investments Global Equity Fund Class A	RGEAX	B-	B	B-	Down	5.56	10.25	22.84	29.85	76.68	10.75	2,200	800-426-7969	Y
American Funds Global Growth Portfolio Class R-5	RGGFX	B	B	B	Up	5.30	11.25	28.93	34.27	76.67	16.84	2,670	800-421-4225	Y
TIAA-CREF Lifecycle Index 2040 Fund Advisor Class	TLZHX	B-	B-	B	Down	4.94	9.56	20.27	29.27	76.66	19.76	1,752	877-518-9161	Y
MFS® New Discovery Fund Class R2	MNDRX	B	B	C	Up	6.54	13.67	25.73	32.67	76.59	25.67	1,213	877-960-6077	Y
Russell Investments Global Equity Fund Class E	RGEEX	B-	B-	B-	Up	5.57	10.35	22.93	29.78	76.57	10.83	2,200	800-426-7969	Y
MFS® Aggressive Growth Allocation Fund Class R4	MAALX	B	B-	B+	Up	5.59	9.91	23.26	31.65	76.49	23.16	1,775	877-960-6077	Y
MFS® Aggressive Growth Allocation Fund Class I	MIAGX	B-	B-	B-	Down	5.56	9.87	23.22	31.63	76.49	23.46	1,775	877-960-6077	Y
American Funds 2035 Target Date Retirement Fund® Class A	AAFTX	B-	B-	B	Down	4.63	9.61	20.67	29.32	76.40	14.84	11,498	800-421-4225	Y
Principal Strat Asset Mgmt Strat Growth Fund R-5 Cls	PSGFX	B-	B-	B-	Down	4.75	10.72	21.84	25.24	76.40	19.94	2,007	800-222-5852	Y
American Funds SMALLCAP World Fund® Class C	SCWCX	B	B	B	Up	4.68	10.17	25.84	34.07	76.39	49.09	38,579	800-421-4225	Y
American Funds Global Growth Portfolio Class R-5E	RGTFX	B	B	B	Up	5.30	11.30	28.99	34.05	76.39	16.69	2,670	800-421-4225	Y
TIAA-CREF Lifecycle 2040 Fund Premier Class	TCZPX	B-	B-	B-	Down	5.11	10.91	22.69	31.23	76.38	10.94	5,272	877-518-9161	Y
American Funds New Perspective Fund® Class R-2	RNPBX	B	B	A-	Up	4.40	9.80	27.89	34.25	76.35	41.53	76,532	800-421-4225	Y
American Funds 2035 Target Date Retirement Fund® Class F-1	FAQTX	B-	B-	B	Down	4.69	9.62	20.63	29.29	76.31	14.77	11,498	800-421-4225	Y
Principal Strategic Asset Mgmt Strategic Growth Fund Cls J	PSWJX	B-	B-	B-	Down	4.78	10.76	21.97	25.38	76.31	19.89	2,007	800-222-5852	Y
American Funds Global Growth Portfolio Class F-2	PGWFX	B	B	B	Up	5.29	11.26	28.95	34.08	76.30	16.77	2,670	800-421-4225	Y
American Funds 2035 Target Date Retirement Fund® Class R-4	RDFTX	B-	B-	B	Down	4.63	9.55	20.63	29.23	76.23	14.8	11,498	800-421-4225	Y
TIAA-CREF Lifecycle 2040 Fund Advisor Class	TCZHX	B-	B-	B-	Down	5.03	10.91	22.78	31.37	76.23	10.96	5,272	877-518-9161	Y
TIAA-CREF Lifecycle Index 2045 Fund Retirement Class	TLMRX	B-	B-	B-	Down	5.14	9.91	20.89	29.58	76.20	19.72	1,080	877-518-9161	Y
DFA Intl Small Company Portfolio Inst Cls	DFISX	B+	B	B+	Up	4.60	11.90	30.24	45.68	76.15	21.27	13,645	512-306-7400	Y
American Funds New Perspective Fund® Class C	NPFCX	B	B	A-	Up	4.40	9.79	27.85	34.17	76.15	41.48	76,532	800-421-4225	Y
Putnam Dynamic Asset Allocation Growth Fund Class R	PASRX	B-	B-	B	Down	5.23	10.28	19.55	26.96	76.03	16.65	2,929	617-292-1000	Y
American Funds 2040 Target Date Retirement Fund® Cls R-2E	RBEKX	B-	B-	B	Down	4.79	9.81	21.08	29.00	75.93	15.01	10,103	800-421-4225	Y
American Funds 2040 Target Date Retirement Fund® Class R-3	RCKTX	B-	B-	B	Down	4.79	9.81	21.23	29.27	75.90	15.06	10,103	800-421-4225	Y
JNL Multi-Manager Small Cap Growth Fund Class A	US46644W4767	B	B+	B-	Up	4.98	11.84	27.23	27.83	75.88	25.88	1,713		Y

		RATINGS				TOTAL RETURNS & PERFORMANCE					ASSETS		NEW INVESTORS	
Fund Name	Ticker Symbol	Overall Rating	Reward Rating	Risk Rating	Recent Up/ Downgrade	3-Month Total Return	6-Month Total Return	1-Year Total Return	3-Year Total Return	5-Year Total Return	NAV	Total Assets (MIL)	Telephone	Open to New Investors
American Funds SMALLCAP World Fund® Class 529-C	CSPCX	B	B	B	Up	4.65	10.14	25.75	33.83	75.84	50	38,579	800-421-4225	Y
John Hancock Funds International Growth Fund Class NAV	JIGHX	A-	A-	B+	Up	4.63	12.73	36.84	39.61	75.64	27.67	7,998	800-225-5913	Y
American Funds Global Growth Portfolio Class 529-F-1	CGGFX	B	B	B	Up	5.31	11.29	28.84	33.77	75.62	16.75	2,670	800-421-4225	Y
Vanguard Target Retirement 2050 Fund Investor Shares	VFIFX	B-	B-	B-	Down	5.19	10.09	21.39	29.14	75.60	36.2	14,237	877-662-7447	Y
Vanguard Target Retirement 2045 Fund Investor Shares	VTIVX	B-	B-	B-	Down	5.21	10.11	21.42	29.21	75.58	22.5	21,569	877-662-7447	Y
TIAA-CREF Lifecycle Index 2040 Fund Premier Class	TLPRX	B-	B-	B	Down	4.97	9.56	20.25	28.87	75.57	19.69	1,752	877-518-9161	Y
TIAA-CREF Lifecycle 2040 Fund Retirement Class	TCLOX	B-	B-	B-	Down	5.06	10.76	22.49	30.82	75.49	14.8	5,272	877-518-9161	Y
John Hancock Funds International Growth Fund Class 1	GOIOX	A-	A-	B+	Up	4.63	12.68	36.72	39.47	75.46	27.67	7,998	800-225-5913	Y
Sterling Capital Equity Income Fund Class A	BAEIX	B-	B-	B-	Down	7.24	12.61	20.64	33.64	75.45	20.29	1,635	800-228-1872	Y
Principal Strategic Asset Mgmt Strategic Growth Fund Cls A	SACAX	B	B-	B	Up	4.71	10.61	21.69	24.79	75.36	20.58	2,007	800-222-5852	Y
Vanguard Target Retirement 2055 Fund Investor Shares	VFFVX	B-	B-	B-	Down	5.17	10.10	21.37	28.99	75.36	39.23	6,095	877-662-7447	Y
Vanguard Target Retirement 2060 Fund Investor Shares	VTTSX	B-	B-	B-	Down	5.19	10.09	21.39	28.98	75.34	34.64	2,308	877-662-7447	Y
John Hancock Funds II Multimgr Lifest Aggress Port Cls 1	JILAX	B-	B-	B-	Down	5.57	10.35	23.30	29.97	75.29	16.45	4,334	800-225-5913	Y
Principal Strat Asset Mgmt Strat Growth Fund R-4 Cls	PSGLX	B-	B-	B-	Down	4.70	10.60	21.66	24.73	75.22	19.99	2,007	800-222-5852	Y
TIAA-CREF Lifecycle Index 2040 Fund Retirement Class	TLZRX	B-	B-	B	Down	4.89	9.48	20.07	28.48	74.58	19.62	1,752	877-518-9161	Y
John Hancock Funds II Multimgr Lifest Aggress Port Cls R5	JTLAX	B-	B-	B-	Down	5.00	10.25	23.24	29.86	74.56	16.48	4,334	800-225-5913	Y
American Funds Global Growth Portfolio Class A	PGGAX	B	B	B	Up	5.22	11.14	28.61	33.20	74.43	16.72	2,670	800-421-4225	Y
GuideStone Funds Aggressive Allocation Fund Investor Class	GGBZX	B-	B-	C+	Down	5.26	11.42	25.48	29.28	74.41	12.24	1,049	214-720-1171	Y
Vanguard Target Retirement 2040 Fund Investor Shares	VFORX	B-	B-	B-	Down	5.00	9.74	20.71	28.26	74.39	35.77	23,438	877-662-7447	Y
Transamerica Asset Allocation Growth Portfolio Class R	IGWRX	B-	B-	B-	Down	4.49	8.99	19.86	27.78	74.39	15.06	1,540	888-233-4339	Y
City National Rochdale Emerging Markets Fund Class Y	CNRYX	B+	A	C+	Up	5.50	15.48	43.61	43.30	74.37	52.08	1,669		Y
Schwab Target 2040 Fund	SWERX	B-	B-	B	Down	4.55	9.34	20.46	27.33	74.36	16.95	1,017	877-824-5615	Y
MFS® Aggressive Growth Allocation Fund Class A	MAAGX	B	B-	B+	Up	5.49	9.73	22.91	30.64	74.23	23.1	1,775	877-960-6077	Y
MFS® Aggressive Growth Allocation Fund Class R3	MAAHX	B	B-	B+	Up	5.49	9.76	22.88	30.63	74.21	22.91	1,775	877-960-6077	Y
Fidelity Freedom® 2055 Fund Class K6	FCTKX	B-	B-	B-	Down	5.10	10.20	22.39	31.71	74.21	13.72	4,031	617-563-7000	Y
American Funds Global Growth Portfolio Class R-4	RGGEX	B	B	B	Up	5.20	11.14	28.62	33.07	74.15	16.7	2,670	800-421-4225	Y
MFS® Aggressive Growth Allocation Fund Class 529A	EAGTX	B	B-	B+	Up	5.50	9.76	22.86	30.54	73.99	22.95	1,775	877-960-6077	Y
American Funds Global Growth Portfolio Class 529-A	CPGAX	B	B	B	Up	5.21	11.14	28.53	33.00	73.93	16.7	2,670	800-421-4225	Y
American Funds Global Growth Portfolio Class F-1	PGGFX	B	B	B	Up	5.21	11.13	28.56	33.04	73.91	16.74	2,670	800-421-4225	Y
American Funds 2050 Target Date Retirement Fund® Class R-2	RBITX	B-	B-	B	Down	4.82	9.94	21.26	28.49	73.85	14.83	5,563	800-421-4225	Y
Putnam Dynamic Asset Allocation Growth Fund Class M	PAGMX	B-	B-	B	Down	5.21	10.16	19.28	26.08	73.81	16.65	2,929	617-292-1000	Y
City National Rochdale Emerging Markets Fund Class N	RIMIX	B+	A	C+	Up	5.42	15.34	43.29	42.78	73.74	51.96	1,669		Y
American Funds 2055 Target Date Retirement Fund® Class R-2	RBMTX	B-	B-	B	Down	4.86	9.96	21.25	28.50	73.72	18.48	2,616	800-421-4225	Y
AXA Aggressive Allocation Portfolio Class K	US00247C5444	B-	B-	B-	Down	5.29	9.94	19.50	27.02	73.69		3,568	877-222-2144	Y
American Funds 2050 Target Date Retirement Fund® Class C	CCITX	B-	B-	B	Down	4.85	9.96	21.25	28.47	73.65	14.86	5,563	800-421-4225	Y
American Funds 2035 Target Date Retirement Fund® Cls R-2E	RBEFX	B-	B-	B	Down	4.55	9.37	20.17	27.90	73.60	14.64	11,498	800-421-4225	Y
American Funds 2055 Target Date Retirement Fund® Class C	CCJTX	B-	B-	B	Down	4.89	9.97	21.23	28.39	73.58	18.55	2,616	800-421-4225	Y
American Funds 2035 Target Date Retirement Fund® Class R-3	RCFTX	B-	B-	B	Down	4.51	9.39	20.26	28.03	73.54	14.7	11,498	800-421-4225	Y
John Hancock Funds International Growth Fund Class R4	JIGIX	B+	A-	B+	Up	4.59	12.60	36.49	38.41	73.43	27.69	7,998	800-225-5913	Y
American Funds 2045 Target Date Retirement Fund® Class R-2	RBHTX	B-	B-	B	Down	4.74	9.76	21.00	28.19	73.39	15.1	6,946	800-421-4225	Y
American Funds 2050 Target Date Retirement Fund® Class R-1	RAITX	B-	B-	B	Down	4.89	9.93	21.24	28.38	73.28	14.84	5,563	800-421-4225	Y
American Funds Capital World Growth & Income Fund® Cls R-6	RWIGX	B	B-	B	Up	5.13	10.50	25.07	30.24	73.22	51.1	97,411	800-421-4225	Y
American Funds 2045 Target Date Retirement Fund® Class C	CCHTX	B-	B-	B	Down	4.75	9.81	21.09	28.13	73.20	15.19	6,946	800-421-4225	Y
Fidelity Freedom® 2050 Fund Class K6	FZTKX	B-	B-	B-	Down	5.20	10.30	22.56	31.95	73.20	12.18	10,884	617-563-7000	Y
Sterling Capital Equity Income Fund Class R	BAERX	B-	B-	B-	Down	7.12	12.41	20.31	32.58	73.18	20.13	1,635	800-228-1872	Y
American Funds 2055 Target Date Retirement Fund® Class R-1	RAMTX	B-	B-	B	Down	4.89	9.93	21.22	28.30	73.13	18.49	2,616	800-421-4225	Y
American Funds 2045 Target Date Retirement Fund® Class R-1	RAHTX	B-	B-	B	Down	4.80	9.79	21.08	28.09	72.81	15.17	6,946	800-421-4225	Y
American Funds Capital World Growth & Income Fund® Cls R-5	RWIFX	B	B-	B	Up	5.11	10.47	25.01	30.07	72.77	51.11	97,411	800-421-4225	Y
Fidelity Freedom® 2045 Fund Class K6	FJTKX	B-	B-	B-	Down	5.14	10.26	22.50	31.90	72.76	12.11	12,978	617-563-7000	Y
American Funds Global Growth Portfolio Class R-2E	REBGX	B	B	B	Up	5.10	10.86	28.02	32.57	72.60	16.63	2,670	800-421-4225	Y
John Hancock Funds II Multimgr Lifest Aggress Port Cls R4	JSLAX	B-	B-	B-	Down	4.94	10.13	22.98	28.99	72.56	16.45	4,334	800-225-5913	Y
American Funds 2040 Target Date Retirement Fund® Class R-2	RBKTX	B-	B-	B	Down	4.64	9.63	20.71	27.69	72.42	14.91	10,103	800-421-4225	Y

Fund Name	Ticker Symbol	RATINGS: Overall Rating	Reward Rating	Risk Rating	Recent Up/ Downgrade	TOTAL RETURNS & PERFORMANCE: 3-Month Total Return	6-Month Total Return	1-Year Total Return	3-Year Total Return	5-Year Total Return	ASSETS: NAV	Total Assets (MIL)	NEW INVESTORS: Telephone	Open to New Investors
American Funds Capital World Growth & Income Fund® Cls F-2	WGIFX	B	B-	B	Up	5.10	10.43	24.92	29.85	72.36	51.05	97,411	800-421-4225	Y
JPMorgan SmartRetirement® 2040 Fund Class R5	SMTIX	B-	B-	B-	Down	5.25	10.43	21.82	27.03	72.26	22.64	6,524	800-480-4111	Y
John Hancock Funds International Growth Fund Class R2	JHIGX	B+	A-	B+	Up	4.52	12.45	36.14	37.45	72.23	27.68	7,998	800-225-5913	Y
MFS® New Discovery Fund Class B	MNDBX	B-	B	C	Up	6.35	13.35	25.05	30.63	72.23	22.09	1,213	877-960-6077	Y
MFS® New Discovery Fund Class C	MNDCX	B-	B	C	Up	6.38	13.37	25.11	30.68	72.22	22.14	1,213	877-960-6077	Y
MFS® New Discovery Fund Class R1	MNDGX	B-	B	C	Up	6.40	13.35	25.07	30.68	72.21	21.93	1,213	877-960-6077	Y
JPMorgan SmartRetirement® 2045 Fund Class R4	JSAQX	B-	B-	B-	Down	5.27	10.49	21.88	27.11	72.16	21.46	4,298	800-480-4111	Y
JPMorgan SmartRetirement® 2050 Fund Class R4	JTSQX	B-	B-	B-	Down	5.27	10.49	21.85	27.08	72.15	21.44	3,605	800-480-4111	Y
American Funds 2040 Target Date Retirement Fund® Class C	CCGTX	B-	B-	B	Down	4.62	9.58	20.60	27.46	72.13	14.97	10,103	800-421-4225	Y
MFS® Aggressive Growth Allocation Fund Class R2	MAWAX	B	B-	B+	Up	5.42	9.65	22.63	29.66	72.07	22.64	1,775	877-960-6077	Y
John Hancock Funds International Growth Fund Class A	GOIGX	B+	A-	B+	Up	4.54	12.52	36.25	37.90	72.02	27.65	7,998	800-225-5913	Y
John Hancock Funds II Multimgr Lifest Aggress Port Cls A	JALAX	B-	B-	B-	Down	4.90	10.07	22.79	28.55	72.00	16.52	4,334	800-225-5913	Y
JPMorgan SmartRetirement® 2040 Fund Class R4	SMTQX	B-	B-	B-	Down	5.24	10.41	21.71	26.79	71.94	22.56	6,524	800-480-4111	Y
MFS® New Discovery Fund Class 529B	EBNDX	B-	B	C	Up	6.38	13.37	25.04	30.52	71.91	21.3	1,213	877-960-6077	Y
Fidelity Freedom® 2040 Fund Class K6	FHTKX	B-	B-	B-	Down	5.18	10.23	22.41	31.86	71.90	10.69	22,091	617-563-7000	Y
Fidelity® Puritan® Fund Class K	FPUKX	B-	B-	B	Down	4.63	9.32	18.85	26.60	71.82	23.41	27,421	617-563-7000	Y
American Funds 2040 Target Date Retirement Fund® Class R-1	RAKTX	B-	B-	B	Down	4.70	9.60	20.65	27.40	71.82	14.96	10,103	800-421-4225	Y
Putnam Dynamic Asset Allocation Growth Fund Class B	PAEBX	B-	B-	B-	Down	5.15	10.03	18.99	25.12	71.76	16.67	2,929	617-292-1000	Y
MFS® New Discovery Fund Class 529C	ECNDX	B-	B	C	Up	6.39	13.37	25.05	30.47	71.73	21.29	1,213	877-960-6077	Y
Putnam Dynamic Asset Allocation Growth Fund Class C	PAECX	B-	B-	B-	Down	5.11	10.03	18.94	25.09	71.63	16.01	2,929	617-292-1000	Y
AXA Premier VIP Aggressive Allocation Fund Class B	US00247C6921	B-	B-	B-	Down	5.23	9.78	19.23	26.11	71.59		3,568	877-222-2144	Y
American Funds Global Growth Portfolio Class 529-E	CGGEX	B	B-	B	Up	5.14	10.97	28.24	31.90	71.58	16.63	2,670	800-421-4225	Y
TIAA-CREF Lifecycle 2035 Fund Premier Class	TCYPX	B-	B-	B	Down	4.69	10.01	20.88	29.20	71.56	10.82	4,246	877-518-9161	Y
American Funds Capital World Growth & Inc Fund® Cls 529-F	CWIFX	B	B-	B	Up	5.08	10.39	24.85	29.52	71.54	50.97	97,411	800-421-4225	Y
Janus Henderson Global Research Fund Class N	JDWNX	B-	B-	B		5.06	10.07	26.93	25.59	71.49	78.6	2,816	877-335-2687	Y
AXA Premier VIP Aggressive Allocation Fund Class A	US00247C7184	B-	B-	B-	Down	5.14	9.79	19.13	26.01	71.46		3,568	877-222-2144	Y
TIAA-CREF Lifecycle 2035 Fund Advisor Class	TCYHX	B-	B-	B	Down	4.70	10.00	20.96	29.40	71.42	10.84	4,246	877-518-9161	Y
American Funds Global Growth Portfolio Class R-3	RGLCX	B	B-	B	Up	5.17	11.00	28.19	31.88	71.41	16.63	2,670	800-421-4225	Y
Fidelity Advisor® Intl Capital Appreciation Fund Cls Z	FIDZX	B	B	B	Up	5.80	12.68	36.03	35.21	71.26	21.08	1,134	617-563-7000	Y
John Hancock Funds II Multimgr Lifest Aggress Port Cls R2	JQLAX	B-	B-	B-	Down	4.90	10.04	22.67	28.12	71.06	16.42	4,334	800-225-5913	Y
Fidelity Freedom® 2035 Fund Class K6	FWTKX	B-	B-	B-	Down	5.09	10.10	22.19	31.56	70.92	15.23	21,304	617-563-7000	Y
American Funds Capital World Growth & Inc Fund® Cls R-5E	RWIHX	B	B-	B	Up	5.10	10.43	24.90	29.36	70.89	51.03	97,411	800-421-4225	Y
Principal LifeTime 2050 Fund Institutional Class	PPLIX	B-	B-	B-	Down	5.06	10.56	22.12	27.11	70.89	15.67	2,598	800-222-5852	Y
American Funds Capital World Growth & Income Fund® Cls F-3	FWGIX	B	B-	B	Up	5.13	10.50	25.03	29.35	70.88	51.09	97,411	800-421-4225	Y
TIAA-CREF Lifecycle 2035 Fund Retirement Class	TCLRX	B-	B-	B	Down	4.65	9.87	20.76	28.85	70.68	14.33	4,246	877-518-9161	Y
BlackRock LifePath® Index 2050 Fund Investor A Shares	LIPAX	B-	B-	B-	Down	5.34	10.04	21.13	28.53	70.43	14.96	1,201	800-441-7762	Y
American Funds Capital World Growth & Income Fund® Cls A	CWGIX	B-	B-	B	Down	5.06	10.32	24.67	28.98	70.39	51.11	97,411	800-421-4225	Y
John Hancock Funds II MultiMgr 2035 Lifetime Port Cls R5	JLHHX	B-	B-	B-	Down	4.51	9.10	20.18	28.01	70.31	12.01	1,100	800-225-5913	Y
John Hancock Funds II MultiMgr 2035 Lifetime Port Cls 1	JLHOX	B-	B-	B-	Down	4.51	9.10	20.17	28.01	70.30	12.01	1,100	800-225-5913	Y
American Funds Capital World Growth & Income Fund® Cls R-4	RWIEX	B-	B-	B	Down	5.05	10.31	24.63	28.90	70.21	50.98	97,411	800-421-4225	Y
American Century Inv One Choice 2050 Port R6 Cls	ARFEX	B-	B-	B	Down	4.46	9.05	18.92	25.73	70.20	12.75	1,250	800-444-4015	Y
American Funds 2035 Target Date Retirement Fund® Class R-2	RBFTX	B-	B-	B	Down	4.44	9.13	19.71	26.51	70.09	14.57	11,498	800-421-4225	Y
Russell Investments Global Equity Fund Class C	RGECX	B-	B-	C+	Down	5.29	9.83	21.91	26.94	70.05	10.62	2,200	800-426-7969	Y
American Funds Capital World Growth & Income Fund® Cls F-1	CWGFX	B-	B-	B	Down	5.04	10.29	24.61	28.81	70.01	51	97,411	800-421-4225	Y
Fidelity Advisor Freedom® 2050 Fund Class Z6	FVGLX	B-	B-	B-	Down	4.89	9.79	21.77	30.12	69.91	12.28	1,051	617-563-7000	Y
American Funds 2035 Target Date Retirement Fund® Class C	CCFTX	B-	B-	B	Down	4.41	9.15	19.78	26.42	69.85	14.63	11,498	800-421-4225	Y
Vanguard Target Retirement 2035 Fund Investor Shares	VTTHX	B-	B-	B	Down	4.61	8.98	19.12	26.56	69.77	20.69	31,221	877-662-7447	Y
Nationwide Investor Destinations Aggressive Fund Class R	GAFRX	B-	B-	B-	Down	4.82	9.50	19.38	26.59	69.71	9.96	1,098	800-848-0920	Y
American Funds Capital World Growth & Inc Fund® Cls 529-A	CWIAX	B-	B-	B	Down	5.05	10.30	24.60	28.68	69.68	50.94	97,411	800-421-4225	Y
Fidelity Advisor Freedom® 2045 Fund Class Z6	FCGLX	B-	B-	B-	Down	4.90	9.78	21.91	30.19	69.57	12.32	1,328	617-563-7000	Y
American Funds 2035 Target Date Retirement Fund® Class R-1	RAFTX	B-	B-	B	Down	4.45	9.15	19.75	26.27	69.50	14.56	11,498	800-421-4225	Y
John Hancock Funds II Multimgr Lifest Aggress Port Cls R3	JRLAX	B-	B-	C+	Down	4.86	9.92	22.58	27.51	69.33	16.48	4,334	800-225-5913	Y

		RATINGS				TOTAL RETURNS & PERFORMANCE					ASSETS		NEW INVESTORS	
Fund Name	Ticker Symbol	Overall Rating	Reward Rating	Risk Rating	Recent Up/ Downgrade	3-Month Total Return	6-Month Total Return	1-Year Total Return	3-Year Total Return	5-Year Total Return	NAV	Total Assets (MIL)	Telephone	Open to New Investors
Principal Strat Asset Mgmt Cons Growth Inst Cls	PCWIX	B-	B-	B	Down	4.46	9.78	19.67	25.51	68.97	17.8	3,267	800-222-5852	Y
American Funds Growth and Income Portfolio Class R-6	RGNGX	B-	B-	B	Down	4.67	8.95	19.46	27.77	68.93	15.16	7,736	800-421-4225	Y
Sterling Capital Equity Income Fund Class C	BCEGX	B-	B-	B-	Down	7.01	12.14	19.71	30.60	68.93	20.09	1,635	800-228-1872	Y
JNL Aggressive Growth Allocation Fund Class I	US46648L5839	B-	B-	B-		4.58	9.15	21.49	27.15	68.76	13	1,509		Y
PNC International Equity Fund Class Institutional	PIUIX	B	B	B	Up	5.43	12.92	33.27	34.75	68.73	24.44	1,227	800-622-3863	Y
American Funds Growth and Income Portfolio Class F-3	GAIHX	B-	B-	B	Down	4.74	8.97	19.48	27.67	68.65	15.14	7,736	800-421-4225	Y
Fidelity Advisor Freedom® 2040 Fund Class Z6	FKGLX	B-	B-	B-	Down	4.92	9.82	21.93	30.25	68.65	15.82	2,167	617-563-7000	Y
JNL Aggressive Growth Allocation Fund Class A	US46648L5912	B-	B-	B-	Down	4.50	9.06	21.40	27.05	68.63	12.99	1,509		Y
American Funds Growth and Income Portfolio Class R-5	RGNFX	B-	B-	B	Down	4.71	8.99	19.46	27.64	68.62	15.19	7,736	800-421-4225	Y
JPMorgan SmartRetirement® 2035 Fund Class R5	SRJIX	B-	B-	B-	Down	4.92	9.78	20.41	25.42	68.58	20.91	6,440	800-480-4111	Y
John Hancock Funds II MultiMgr 2035 Lifetime Port Cls R4	JLHGX	B-	B-	B-	Down	4.40	8.91	19.86	27.28	68.56	12	1,100	800-225-5913	Y
John Hancock Funds II Multimgr Lifest Aggress Port Cls R1	JPLAX	B-	B-	C+	Down	4.87	9.91	22.44	27.12	68.56	16.55	4,334	800-225-5913	Y
Principal LifeTime 2050 Fund R-5 Class	PTEFX	B-	B-	B-	Down	4.96	10.34	21.73	26.13	68.54	15.62	2,598	800-222-5852	Y
WCM Focused International Growth Fund Investor Class	WCMRX	B	B	B+	Up	5.09	9.55	30.88	38.02	68.52	15.69	5,070	949-380-0200	Y
JPMorgan SmartRetirement® 2035 Fund Class R4	SRJQX	B-	B-	B-	Down	4.90	9.73	20.24	25.18	68.26	20.87	6,440	800-480-4111	Y
American Funds Growth and Income Portfolio Class R-5E	RGQFX	B-	B-	B	Down	4.72	8.94	19.44	27.35	68.23	15.13	7,736	800-421-4225	Y
American Funds Growth and Income Portfolio Class F-2	GAIEX	B-	B-	B	Down	4.71	8.90	19.34	27.39	68.17	15.16	7,736	800-421-4225	Y
JNL/S&P Managed Growth Fund Class I	US46648L3859	B-	B-	B		4.89	9.13	21.11	27.24	68.03	18.87	5,685		Y
JNL/S&P Managed Growth Fund Class A	US46648L3933	B-	B-	B	Down	4.83	9.08	21.05	27.17	67.94	18.86	5,685		Y
MFS® Aggressive Growth Allocation Fund Class C	MCAGX	B	B-	B+	Up	5.27	9.32	21.94	27.70	67.87	22.57	1,775	877-960-6077	Y
MFS® Aggressive Growth Allocation Fund Class R1	MAAFX	B	B-	B+	Up	5.30	9.30	21.98	27.73	67.79	22.25	1,775	877-960-6077	Y
MFS® Aggressive Growth Allocation Fund Class B	MBAGX	B	B-	B+	Up	5.28	9.34	21.96	27.69	67.79	22.8	1,775	877-960-6077	Y
Fidelity Advisor Freedom® 2035 Fund Class Z6	FHGLX	B-	B-	B-	Down	4.85	9.63	21.66	29.92	67.76	14.8	2,395	617-563-7000	Y
American Funds Global Growth Portfolio Class C	GGPCX	B	B-	B	Up	4.98	10.72	27.66	30.13	67.74	16.51	2,670	800-421-4225	Y
American Funds Capital World Growth & Inc Fund® Cls 529-E	CWIEX	B-	B-	B	Down	4.97	10.17	24.30	27.80	67.74	50.87	97,411	800-421-4225	Y
American Funds Capital World Growth & Income Fund® Cls R-3	RWICX	B-	B-	B	Down	4.97	10.14	24.29	27.76	67.73	50.77	97,411	800-421-4225	Y
Principal LifeTime 2050 Fund R-4 Class	PTESX	B-	B-	B-	Down	4.97	10.36	21.61	25.71	67.69	15.59	2,598	800-222-5852	Y
Principal LifeTime 2050 Fund Class A	PPEAX	B-	B-	B-	Down	5.02	10.35	21.66	25.74	67.68	15.76	2,598	800-222-5852	Y
Principal LifeTime 2050 Fund Class J	PFLJX	B-	B-	B-	Down	5.00	10.43	21.85	25.92	67.66	15.25	2,598	800-222-5852	Y
American Funds Global Growth Portfolio Class R-1	RGGAX	B	B-	B	Up	5.02	10.73	27.66	30.11	67.62	16.58	2,670	800-421-4225	Y
American Funds Global Growth Portfolio Class R-2	RGGBX	B	B-	B	Up	5.07	10.76	27.66	30.12	67.60	16.47	2,670	800-421-4225	Y
MFS® Aggressive Growth Allocation Fund Class 529C	ECAAX	B	B-	B+	Up	5.31	9.31	21.93	27.60	67.59	22.25	1,775	877-960-6077	Y

Section V:
High Performance Stock Mutual Funds

Investment Ratings and analysis of High Performance Stock Mutual Funds. Funds are listed in order by their five-year returns and overall rating.

Section V: Contents

This section contains Weiss Investment Ratings, key rating factors, and summary financial data for our selections for "High Performance Stock Mutual Funds." If your priority is to achieve the highest return, balanced with the amount of risk we have chosen the top mutual funds with the best financial performance. Not just "Buy" rated these funds have hit our demanding criteria of being in the top 25% of total returns for funds over a number of time-periods. Keep in mind that past performance alone is not always a guide to future performance. Funds are listed in order by their five-year returns and overall rating.

Fund Name

Describes the fund's assets, regions of investments and investment strategies. Many funds have similar names, so you want to make sure the fund you look up is really the one you are interested in evaluating.

Ticker Symbol

An arrangement of characters (usually letters) representing a particular security listed on an exchange or otherwise traded publicly. When a company issues securities to the public marketplace, it selects an available ticker symbol for its securities which investors use to place trade orders. Every listed security has a unique ticker symbol, facilitating the vast array of trade orders that flow through the financial markets every day. If a ticker symbol is not assigned to a particular fund, the International Securities Identification Number (ISIN) is displayed.

RATINGS

Overall Rating

The Weiss rating measured on a scale from A to E based on each fund's risk and performance. See the preceding section, "What Our Ratings Mean," for an explanation of each letter grade rating.

Reward Rating

This is based on the total return over a period of up to five years, including net asset value and price growth. The total return figure is stated net of the expenses and fees charged by the fund. Based on proprietary modeling the individual components of the risk and reward ratings are calculated and weighted and the final rating is generated.

Risk Rating

This is includes the risk ratings of component stocks where applicable and also includes the financial stability of the fund, turnover where applicable, together with the level of volatility as measured by the fund's daily returns over a period of up to five years. Funds with greater stability are considered less risky and receive a higher risk rating. Funds with greater volatility are considered riskier, and will receive a lower risk rating. In addition to considering the fund's volatility, the risk rating also considers an assessment of the valuation and quality of a fund's holdings.

Recent Upgrade/Downgrade
An "Up" or "Down" indicates that the Weiss Mutual Fund rating has changed since the publication of the last print edition. If a fund has had a rating change since September 30, 2017, the change is identified with an "Up" or "Down."

TOTAL RETURNS & PERFORMANCE

3-Month Total Return
The rate of return on an investment over three months that includes interest, capital gains, dividends and distributions realized.

6-Month Total Return
The rate of return on an investment over six months that includes interest, capital gains, dividends and distributions realized.

1-Year Total Return
The rate of return on an investment over one year that includes interest, capital gains, dividends and distributions realized.

3-Year Total Return
The rate of return on an investment over three years that includes interest, capital gains, dividends and distributions realized.

5-Year Total Return
The rate of return on an investment over five years that includes interest, capital gains, dividends and distributions realized.

ASSETS

NAV (Net Asset Value)
A fund's price per share. The value is calculated by dividing the total value of all the securities in the portfolio, less any liabilities, by the number of fund shares outstanding.

Total Assets (MIL)
The total of all assets listed on the institution's balance sheet. This figure primarily consists of loans, investments, and fixed assets. Total Assets are displayed in millions.

NEW INVESTORS

Telephone
The company's phone number.

Open to New Investors
Indicates whether the fund accepts investments from those who are not existing investors. A "Y" in this column identifies that the fund accepts new investors. No data in this column indicates that the fund is closed to new investors. The fund may be closed to new investors because the fund's asset base is getting too large to effectively execute its investing style. Although, the fund may be closed, in most cases, existing investors are able to add to their holdings.

Fund Name	Ticker Symbol	RATINGS: Overall Rating	Reward Rating	Risk Rating	Recent Up/ Downgrade	TOTAL RETURNS & PERFORMANCE: 3-Month Total Return	6-Month Total Return	1-Year Total Return	3-Year Total Return	5-Year Total Return	ASSETS: NAV	Total Assets (MIL)	NEW INVESTORS: Telephone	Open to New Investors
Columbia Seligman Global Technology Fund Advisor Class	CCHRX	A	A+	B+	Up	3.11	13.40	34.82	72.36	179.46	40.62	1,210	800-345-6611	Y
Fidelity® OTC Portfolio Class K	FOCKX	A-	A	B	Up	6.04	12.26	38.75	57.84	177.99	111.27	17,435	617-563-7000	Y
Columbia Seligman Global Technology Fund Inst 3 Cls	CGTYX	A	A+	B+	Up	3.20	13.51	34.90	71.55	176.76	39.97	1,210	800-345-6611	Y
Morgan Stanley Inst Fund, Inc. Global Opp Portfolio Cls A	MGGPX	A	A+	A-	Up	6.56	17.79	49.02	76.04	173.72	22.28	1,720	855-332-5306	Y
Columbia Seligman Communications & Information Inst 2 Cls	SCMIX	A	A+	B+	Up	3.02	13.27	34.43	69.42	172.57	77.3	6,150	800-345-6611	Y
VALIC Company I Science & Technology Fund	VCSTX	A	A+	B+	Up	7.07	16.08	41.31	62.32	171.42	29.81	1,281		Y
Oppenheimer Global Opportunities Fund Class Y	OGIYX	A	A+	B+	Up	14.38	22.43	52.93	93.33	169.70	69.34	6,911	800-225-5677	Y
Oppenheimer Global Opportunities Fund Class A	OPGIX	A	A+	B+	Up	14.29	22.25	52.52	91.92	166.36	68.54	6,911	800-225-5677	Y
AllianzGI Technology Fund Class A	RAGTX	A	A+	B+	Up	7.73	18.79	46.69	59.66	164.94	61.24	1,600	800-498-5413	Y
Morgan Stanley Inst Fund, Inc. Global Opp Portfolio Cls C	MSOPX	A	A	B+	Up	6.35	17.39	47.91	72.51	164.76	21.64	1,720	855-332-5306	Y
Oppenheimer Global Opportunities Fund Class R	OGINX	A	A+	B+	Up	14.23	22.11	52.16	90.44	162.74	65.97	6,911	800-225-5677	Y
Janus Henderson Global Technology Fund Class N	JATNX	A	A+	B+	Up	7.85	17.07	44.93	70.80	158.84	30.73	2,353	877-335-2687	Y
Oppenheimer Global Opportunities Fund Class C	OGICX	A	A+	B+	Up	14.08	21.80	51.39	87.59	156.47	60.62	6,911	800-225-5677	Y
AllianzGI Technology Fund Class C	RCGTX	A	A+	B+	Up	7.55	18.34	45.62	56.09	155.22	47.49	1,600	800-498-5413	Y
JNL/Mellon Capital Information Technology Sector Cls I	US47760W7873	A-	A+	B	Up	8.48	17.40	36.62	60.58	153.40	15.6	2,369		Y
Morgan Stanley Inst Fund, Inc. Growth Portfolio Cls A	MSEGX	B+	A-	B+	Up	7.32	12.48	43.44	55.27	151.22	39.77	4,194	855-332-5306	Y
JNL/Mellon Capital Information Technology Sector Cls A	US47760W7956	A-	A	B	Up	8.42	17.20	36.31	59.61	150.48	15.31	2,369		Y
JPMorgan Growth Advantage Fund Class R5	JGVRX	A-	A	B	Up	7.25	14.49	35.68	49.23	143.56	20.56	8,056	800-480-4111	Y
Morgan Stanley Inst Fund, Inc. Growth Portfolio Cls C	MSGUX	B+	A-	B+	Up	7.13	12.07	42.37	51.87	141.91	37.76	4,194	855-332-5306	Y
Fidelity® Blue Chip Growth Fund Class K	FBGKX	A-	A	B+	Up	7.16	14.00	36.20	46.45	141.69	87.86	23,260	617-563-7000	Y
Eventide Gilead Class N	ETGLX	B	A-	B-	Up	7.29	14.20	32.85	31.06	140.98	34.25	1,522		Y
Miller Opportunity Trust Class A	LGOAX	B-	B-	C+	Up	5.43	4.96	25.94	25.68	140.73	23.88	1,458		Y
Eventide Gilead Class A	ETAGX	B	A-	C	Up	7.25	14.18	32.80	30.86	140.31	34.13	1,522		Y
Miller Opportunity Trust Class FI	LMOFX	B-	B-	C+	Up	5.43	4.94	25.90	25.58	140.08	24.64	1,458		Y
Glenmede Large Cap Growth Portfolio	GTLLX	B+	A-	B+	Up	7.79	14.98	27.81	41.35	139.23	32.31	4,017	800-442-8299	Y
JPMorgan Growth Advantage Fund Class A	VHIAX	A-	A	B	Up	7.14	14.25	35.18	47.46	139.08	19.67	8,056	800-480-4111	Y
Thrivent Series Mid Cap Stock Portfolio		B+	B+	B+	Up	7.37	10.91	18.99	52.07	136.61	20.8172	1,740		Y
Miller Opportunity Trust Class R	LMORX	B-	B-	C+	Up	5.36	4.80	25.54	24.50	136.20	23.98	1,458		Y
JPMorgan Growth Advantage Fund Class C	JGACX	A-	A	B	Up	7.03	13.99	34.52	45.41	133.16	17.39	8,056	800-480-4111	Y
BlackRock Mid-Cap Growth Equity Portfolio Inv A Shares	BMGAX	A-	A-	B	Up	5.34	11.04	34.20	46.10	132.75	19.63	1,021	800-441-7762	Y
Fidelity Advisor® Small Cap Growth Fund Class Z	FIDGX	A-	A	B	Up	5.01	14.26	29.17	50.98	132.17	24.81	3,744	617-563-7000	Y
Miller Opportunity Trust Class C	LMOPX	B-	B-	C+	Up	5.22	4.54	24.99	22.88	131.56	22.55	1,458		Y
Eventide Gilead Class C	ETCGX	B	B+	C	Up	7.06	13.72	31.76	27.92	131.28	31.98	1,522		Y
Oppenheimer International Small-Mid Company Fund Class A	OSMAX	A-	B+	A	Up	6.17	12.93	37.92	57.36	130.64	49.55	10,129	800-225-5677	Y
BlackRock Mid-Cap Growth Equity Portfolio Class R	BMRRX	B+	A-	B	Up	5.31	10.91	33.89	45.06	129.83	19.36	1,021	800-441-7762	Y
Aberdeen U.S. Small Cap Equity Fund Class A	GSXAX	A	A-	A	Up	3.44	9.46	11.02	46.89	128.77	36.65	2,025	866-667-9231	Y
Aberdeen U.S. Small Cap Equity Fund Class R	GNSRX	A-	A-	A	Up	3.38	9.28	10.63	45.72	126.06	33.91	2,025	866-667-9231	Y
JNL/Mellon Capital Financial Sector Fund Class I	US47760W7469	A-	A	B	Up	7.62	12.87	19.60	45.55	125.88	13.97	1,439		Y
JPMorgan Small Cap Growth Fund Class R5	JGSVX	B	A	C	Up	8.07	18.03	41.77	49.32	125.17	18.23	1,542	800-480-4111	Y
BlackRock Mid-Cap Growth Equity Portfolio Inv C Shares	BMGCX	B+	A-	B	Up	5.12	10.59	33.22	42.87	124.20	15.51	1,021	800-441-7762	Y
Fidelity Advisor® Growth Opportunities Fund Class Z	FZAHX	B+	B+	B+	Up	6.64	12.28	35.21	41.95	123.88	69.64	3,029	617-563-7000	Y
JNL/Mellon Capital Financial Sector Fund Class A	US47760W7535	A-	A	B	Up	7.47	12.69	19.32	44.60	123.62	13.94	1,439		Y
Carillon Eagle Mid Cap Growth Fund Class R6	HRAUX	B+	A	B-	Up	6.97	12.34	30.43	42.46	122.68	59.82	2,495	800-421-4184	Y
Oppenheimer International Small-Mid Company Fund Class C	OSMCX	B+	B+	A	Up	5.99	12.50	36.92	53.87	122.18	45.67	10,129	800-225-5677	Y
Carillon Eagle Mid Cap Growth Fund Class R5	HARSX	B+	A	B-	Up	6.94	12.27	30.31	41.84	121.24	59.32	2,495	800-421-4184	Y
Aberdeen U.S. Small Cap Equity Fund Class C	GSXCX	A-	A-	A	Up	3.31	9.08	10.26	43.80	121.05	31.81	2,025	866-667-9231	Y
LSV Value Equity Fund Investor Class	LVAEX	B	B	B	Up	7.21	12.96	17.99	32.98	118.09	28.82	2,181		Y
Carillon Eagle Mid Cap Growth Fund Class A	HAGAX	B+	A	C+	Up	6.87	12.12	29.90	40.61	117.87	56.49	2,495	800-421-4184	Y
JNL/JPMorgan MidCap Growth Fund Class I	US46648M1100	B	B+	C+	Up	5.80	12.17	29.73	34.24	117.45	35.34	2,102		Y
JPMorgan Mid Cap Growth Fund Class R5	JMGFX	B	B+	B	Up	5.70	12.05	29.67	33.32	115.82	33.79	3,490	800-480-4111	Y
Waddell & Reed Advisor Science and Technology Fund Class Y	USTFX	B	A-	C	Up	3.59	13.98	32.30	29.38	115.24	18.79	3,748	888-923-3355	Y
JNL/JPMorgan MidCap Growth Fund Class A	US46648M1282	B	B+	C+	Up	5.69	11.99	29.40	33.35	115.24	34.51	2,102		Y

Fund Name	Ticker Symbol	RATINGS				TOTAL RETURNS & PERFORMANCE					ASSETS		NEW INVESTORS	
		Overall Rating	Reward Rating	Risk Rating	Recent Up/ Downgrade	3-Month Total Return	6-Month Total Return	1-Year Total Return	3-Year Total Return	5-Year Total Return	NAV	Total Assets (MIL)	Telephone	Open to New Investors
Dreyfus Opportunistic Small Cap Fund Class I	DOPIX	B+	A-	B	Up	8.55	13.64	24.40	40.05	115.13	36.82	1,092	800-645-6561	Y
Columbia Select Large-Cap Value Fund Institutional 2 Class	SLVIX	B	B	B-	Up	7.84	13.50	20.44	36.13	115.02	27.2	1,001	800-345-6611	Y
DFA U.S. Large Cap Value Portfolio Institutional Class	DFLVX	B	B	B	Up	7.46	12.42	18.96	35.07	114.95	39.12	24,727	512-306-7400	Y
Carillon Eagle Mid Cap Growth Fund Class R3	HAREX	B	A-	C+	Down	6.80	11.95	29.54	39.46	114.84	54.88	2,495	800-421-4184	Y
Columbia Select Large Cap Growth Fund Institutional 2 Cls	CGTRX	B	B	B	Up	5.23	9.16	35.55	33.24	114.77	17.09	4,164	800-345-6611	Y
Ivy Science and Technology Fund Class I	ISTIX	B	A	C	Up	3.52	13.94	33.13	30.85	114.47	69.87	4,284	800-777-6472	Y
JPMorgan Mid Cap Growth Fund Class R4	JMGQX	B	B+	C+	Up	5.67	11.95	29.39	32.67	114.14	33.4	3,490	800-480-4111	Y
Undiscovered Managers Behavioral Value Fund Class R5	UBVVX	A-	A-	A-	Up	7.07	11.94	15.06	42.30	113.08	69.91	6,256	800-480-4111	Y
Undiscovered Managers Behavioral Value Fund Class R4	UBVUX	A-	A-	A-	Up	7.04	11.86	14.93	42.13	112.84	69.64	6,256	800-480-4111	Y
Delaware Small Cap Core Fund Institutional Class	DCCIX	B+	A-	B	Up	2.72	8.86	14.20	33.13	112.53	24.11	2,828		Y
JNL/Invesco Small Cap Growth Fund Class I	US46648M1936	B	A-	C+	Up	6.73	13.26	25.25	36.79	112.51	25.82	1,913		Y
Waddell & Reed Advisor Science and Technology Fund Class A	UNSCX	B	A-	C	Up	3.54	13.82	32.01	28.48	112.45	16.48	3,748	888-923-3355	Y
Ivy Science And Technology Fund Class Y	WSTYX	B	A	C	Up	3.46	13.81	32.80	29.88	111.80	67.04	4,284	800-777-6472	Y
John Hancock Capital Series Classic Value Fund Class R5	JCVVX	B	B+	B-	Up	7.31	11.47	16.83	32.01	111.75	33.81	2,262	800-225-5913	Y
Columbia Small Cap Index Fund Institutional 2 Class	CXXRX	A-	A-	B	Up	3.89	10.05	13.09	38.53	111.68	25.37	4,151	800-345-6611	Y
JPMorgan Mid Cap Growth Fund Class R3	JMGPX	B	B	C+	Up	5.59	11.82	29.04	31.69	111.50	33.28	3,490	800-480-4111	Y
Ivy Science And Technology Fund Class A	WSTAX	B	A	C	Up	3.46	13.82	32.82	29.73	111.41	63.57	4,284	800-777-6472	Y
Principal SmallCap S&P 600 Index Fund Institutional Class	PSSIX	A-	A-	B	Up	3.90	10.00	13.01	38.40	111.40	27.09	1,360	800-222-5852	Y
JPMorgan Mid Cap Growth Fund Class A	OSGIX	B	B	B	Up	5.59	11.82	29.06	31.53	111.10	29.13	3,490	800-480-4111	Y
Delaware Small Cap Core Fund Class R6	DCZRX	B+	A-	B	Up	1.80	7.92	13.32	32.22	111.08	24.11	2,828		Y
TIAA-CREF Small-Cap Equity Fund Advisor Class	TSCHX	B+	A-	B	Up	3.97	9.95	14.90	36.99	110.87	19.08	3,938	877-518-9161	Y
VY® T. Rowe Price Diversified Mid Cap Growth Port Cls R6	VYRIX	B	B	B-	Up	5.86	10.58	24.80	35.99	110.54	11.56	1,016	800-366-0066	Y
John Hancock Capital Series Classic Value Fund Class R4	JCVFX	B	B+	B-	Up	7.26	11.43	16.72	31.57	110.46	33.78	2,262	800-225-5913	Y
JNL/Invesco Small Cap Growth Fund Class A	US46648M2199	B	A-	C+	Up	6.63	13.14	24.96	35.97	110.40	24.91	1,913		Y
VY® T. Rowe Price Diversified Mid Cap Growth Port Cls I	IAXIX	B	B	B-	Up	5.95	10.68	24.80	35.87	110.35	11.56	1,016	800-366-0066	Y
Undiscovered Managers Behavioral Value Fund Class R3	UBVTX	A-	B+	A-	Up	7.00	11.76	14.67	41.11	110.25	68.08	6,256	800-480-4111	Y
Ivy Science and Technology Fund Class E	ISTEX	B	A-	C	Up	3.44	13.78	32.75	29.40	110.23	63.14	4,284	800-777-6472	Y
Ariel Fund Investor Class	ARGFX	B	B	B	Up	7.86	8.68	15.88	27.46	110.21	69.98	2,255	312-726-0140	Y
Carillon Eagle Mid Cap Growth Fund Class C	HAGCX	B	A-	C+	Up	6.66	11.72	28.98	37.61	110.20	45.39	2,495	800-421-4184	Y
Dreyfus Small Cap Stock Index Fund Class I	DISIX	B+	A-	B	Up	3.85	9.91	12.66	37.73	109.94	31.47	2,469	800-645-6561	Y
Fidelity Advisor® Large Cap Fund Class Z	FIDLX	B	B	B	Up	6.04	11.05	18.62	32.84	109.93	34.76	1,387	617-563-7000	Y
Delaware Small Cap Core Fund Class A	DCCAX	B+	A-	B	Up	2.63	8.67	13.92	32.11	109.89	23.58	2,828		Y
Principal SmallCap S&P 600 Index Fund Class R-6	PSPIX	B+	A-	B	Up	3.92	10.06	13.03	37.86	109.70	27.07	1,360	800-222-5852	Y
DFA Tax-Managed U.S. Marketwide Value Portfolio	DTMMX	B	B	B	Up	6.54	11.01	17.00	31.95	109.67	30.92	5,038	512-306-7400	Y
TIAA-CREF Small-Cap Equity Fund Premier Class	TSRPX	B+	A-	B	Up	3.99	9.94	14.85	36.53	109.48	19	3,938	877-518-9161	Y
Wells Fargo Special Mid Cap Value Fund - Class R6	WFPRX	B	B-	B+		4.08	7.14	11.27	30.59	109.30	38.35	8,420	800-222-8222	Y
JPMorgan Mid Cap Growth Fund Class R2	JMGZX	B	B	C+	Up	5.54	11.71	28.80	30.87	109.29	31.68	3,490	800-480-4111	Y
Principal SmallCap S&P 600 Index Fund R-5 Class	PSSPX	B+	A-	B	Up	3.85	9.90	12.78	37.55	109.22	28.03	1,360	800-222-5852	Y
Wells Fargo Special Small Cap Value Fund - Class R6	ESPRX	B+	A-	B	Up	5.35	9.77	11.52	37.23	109.01	35.67	2,220	800-222-8222	Y
Federated Kaufmann Large Cap Fund Class R6	KLCSX	B-	B	B-	Down	4.60	8.46	23.62	33.00	108.99	24.06	3,311	800-341-7400	Y
Columbia Select Large-Cap Value Fund Class R	SLVRX	B	B	B-	Up	7.68	13.18	19.75	33.73	108.72	25.83	1,001	800-345-6611	Y
Nuveen Small Cap Value Fund Class R3	FSVSX	B+	B+	B	Up	4.34	7.17	5.78	40.22	108.63	25.16	2,066	312-917-8146	Y
PIMCO StocksPLUS® Absolute Return Fund Class D	PSTDX	B-	B	C+	Down	6.50	11.68	23.36	36.14	108.51	10.35	1,626	866-746-2602	Y
PIMCO StocksPLUS® Absolute Return Fund Class A	PTOAX	B-	B	C+	Down	6.39	11.59	23.41	36.16	108.48	10.53	1,626	866-746-2602	Y
TIAA-CREF Small-Cap Equity Fund Retirement Class	TRSEX	B+	A-	B	Up	3.97	9.87	14.74	36.06	108.41	18.63	3,938	877-518-9161	Y
Principal SmallCap S&P 600 Index Fund Class J	PSSJX	B+	A-	B	Up	3.85	9.92	12.76	37.38	108.22	25.71	1,360	800-222-5852	Y
Columbia Select Large Cap Growth Fund Class R	URLGX	B-	B-	B	Down	5.09	8.80	34.74	30.80	108.15	15.05	4,164	800-345-6611	Y
Ivy Science and Technology Fund Class R	WSTRX	B	A-	C	Up	3.37	13.61	32.35	28.54	108.11	62.02	4,284	800-777-6472	Y
John Hancock Classic Value Fund Class A	PZFVX	B	B+	B-	Up	7.22	11.28	16.45	30.75	108.07	33.75	2,262	800-225-5913	Y
Principal SmallCap S&P 600 Index Fund R-4 Class	PSSSX	B+	A-	B	Up	3.79	9.83	12.64	37.06	107.92	27.89	1,360	800-222-5852	Y
VY® T. Rowe Price Diversified Mid Cap Growth Port Cls S	IAXSX	B	B	B-	Up	5.88	10.46	24.45	34.78	107.75	11.15	1,016	800-366-0066	Y
John Hancock Classic Value Fund Class R2	JCVSX	B	B	B-	Up	7.19	11.23	16.29	30.25	107.51	33.71	2,262	800-225-5913	Y

		RATINGS				TOTAL RETURNS & PERFORMANCE					ASSETS		NEW INVESTORS	
Fund Name	Ticker Symbol	Overall Rating	Reward Rating	Risk Rating	Recent Up/ Downgrade	3-Month Total Return	6-Month Total Return	1-Year Total Return	3-Year Total Return	5-Year Total Return	NAV	Total Assets (MIL)	Telephone	Open to New Investors
JPMorgan Market Expansion Enhanced Index Fund Class A	OMEAX	B+	B+	B	Up	5.19	9.94	14.30	35.61	107.35	11.33	1,072	800-480-4111	Y
Delaware Small Cap Core Fund Class R	DCCRX	B+	A-	B	Up	2.54	8.52	13.65	31.13	107.26	22.85	2,828		Y
Principal SmallCap Growth Fund I Institutional Class	PGRTX	B	A-	C+	Up	5.38	12.54	26.31	39.07	106.91	13.92	1,634	800-222-5852	Y
DFA T.A. U.S. Core Equity 2 Portfolio Institutional Class	DFTCX	B	B	B	Up	6.54	11.60	18.81	33.48	106.72	18.12	8,570	512-306-7400	Y
Principal SmallCap Growth Fund I Class R-6	PCSMX	B	A-	C+	Up	5.39	12.55	26.36	39.01	106.68	13.9	1,634	800-222-5852	Y
Undiscovered Managers Behavioral Value Fund Class R2	UBVRX	B+	B+	A-	Up	6.95	11.62	14.38	39.63	106.50	67.81	6,256	800-480-4111	Y
Glenmede Small Cap Equity Portfolio Class Advisor	GTCSX	B+	B+	B	Up	5.10	9.44	15.74	31.56	106.38	30.1	3,588	800-442-8299	Y
Victory Sycamore Small Company Opportunity Fund R6	VSORX	A-	A	A-	Up	3.18	10.48	11.87	42.62	106.37	47.06	5,201	800-539-3863	Y
VY® T. Rowe Price Diversified Mid Cap Growth Port Cls S2	IAXTX	B	B	B-	Up	5.82	10.39	24.27	34.15	106.29	10.54	1,016	800-366-0066	Y
Wells Fargo Special Small Cap Value Fund - Class A	ESPAX	B+	A-	B	Up	5.23	9.56	11.05	35.46	106.17	34.86	2,220	800-222-8222	Y
DFA U.S. Core Equity II Portfolio Institutional Class	DFQTX	B	B	B-	Up	6.66	11.82	18.93	33.17	106.11	21.56	23,310	512-306-7400	Y
Principal SmallCap S&P 600 Index Fund R-3 Class	PSSMX	B+	A-	B	Up	3.76	9.74	12.44	36.28	105.98	27.64	1,360	800-222-5852	Y
JPMorgan Mid Cap Growth Fund Class C	OMGCX	B	B	B	Up	5.46	11.57	28.42	29.62	105.87	23.08	3,490	800-480-4111	Y
PIMCO StocksPLUS® Absolute Return Fund Class R	PTORX	B-	B	C+	Down	6.27	11.43	23.08	35.17	105.83	10.46	1,626	866-746-2602	Y
John Hancock Capital Series Classic Value Fund Class R3	JCVHX	B	B	B-	Up	7.15	11.15	16.17	29.61	105.43	33.71	2,262	800-225-5913	Y
DFA U.S. Micro Cap Portfolio Institutional Class	DFSCX	B+	A-	B	Up	2.70	9.42	11.17	33.92	105.34	22.03	6,474	512-306-7400	Y
VY® T. Rowe Price Diversified Mid Cap Growth Port Cls A	IAXAX	B	B	B-	Up	5.84	10.42	24.11	33.79	105.30	10.5	1,016	800-366-0066	Y
JPMorgan Market Expansion Enhanced Index Fund Class R2	JMEZX	B+	B+	B	Up	5.13	9.85	14.04	34.78	105.02	11.16	1,072	800-480-4111	Y
Wells Fargo Special Mid Cap Value Fund - Class A	WFPAX	B	B-	B		3.97	6.90	10.83	28.92	104.84	37.41	8,420	800-222-8222	Y
Principal SmallCap Growth Fund I R-5 Class	PPNPX	B	A-	C+	Up	5.32	12.38	26.00	38.06	104.60	13.09	1,634	800-222-5852	Y
Wells Fargo Special Mid Cap Value Fund - Class R	WFHHX	B	B-	B	Up	3.90	6.79	10.54	28.31	104.51	37.97	8,420	800-222-8222	Y
Victory Sycamore Small Company Opportunity Fund Class R	GOGFX	A-	A	A-	Up	3.03	10.16	11.25	41.17	104.28	43.98	5,201	800-539-3863	Y
John Hancock Classic Value Fund Class R1	JCVRX	B	B	B-	Up	7.09	11.07	15.99	29.21	104.28	33.84	2,262	800-225-5913	Y
Dreyfus/The Boston Company Small/Mid Cap Growth Fund Cls I	SDSCX	B+	A-	B	Up	5.18	11.56	26.52	36.33	104.25	19.7	1,225	800-645-6561	Y
Principal SmallCap S&P 600 Index Fund R-2 Class	PSSNX	B+	A-	B	Up	3.69	9.60	12.19	35.53	104.11	27.43	1,360	800-222-5852	Y
Wells Fargo Special Small Cap Value Fund - Class R	ESPHX	B+	A-	B	Up	5.14	9.39	10.76	34.55	103.78	35.41	2,220	800-222-8222	Y
DFA Tax Managed U.S. Small Cap Portfolio	DFTSX	B+	A-	B	Up	3.92	9.89	11.87	32.98	103.76	44.07	3,026	512-306-7400	Y
ClearBridge Small Cap Fund Class A	LMSAX	B	B	B	Up	2.27	4.97	11.86	35.66	103.67	40.61	1,053	877-721-1926	Y
DFA Tax-Managed U.S. Targeted Value Portfolio	DTMVX	B+	B+	B	Up	4.29	10.07	11.07	32.01	103.63	37.53	4,885	512-306-7400	Y
Principal SmallCap Growth Fund I R-4 Class	PPNSX	B	A-	C+	Up	5.39	12.38	25.93	37.68	103.39	12.54	1,634	800-222-5852	Y
AB Discovery Value Fund Advisor Class	ABYSX	B	B+	B	Up	5.99	11.50	12.97	31.75	103.33	23.3	2,959	212-969-1000	Y
Oppenheimer Discovery Mid Cap Growth Fund Y	OEGYX	A-	A-	B+	Up	6.73	12.33	28.37	38.53	103.27	22.29	1,053	800-225-5677	Y
Wells Fargo Discovery Fund - Class R6	WFDRX	B+	A-	B	Up	6.21	12.05	29.61	37.21	103.10	35.23	2,600	800-222-8222	Y
Principal SmallCap S&P 600 Index Fund R-1 Class	PSAPX	B+	A-	B	Up	3.69	9.59	12.11	35.04	102.77	26.72	1,360	800-222-5852	Y
Principal SmallCap Growth Fund I Class J	PSIJX	B	A-	C+	Up	5.38	12.33	25.91	37.58	102.75	10.41	1,634	800-222-5852	Y
Victory Integrity Small-Cap Value Fund Class R6	MVSSX	B+	A-	B	Up	5.63	11.91	12.58	29.94	102.62	41.05	2,705	800-539-3863	Y
Columbia Mid Cap Index Fund Institutional 2 Class	CPXRX	B	B	B		6.20	9.57	15.99	35.00	102.49	16.8	4,925	800-345-6611	Y
Waddell & Reed Advisor Science and Technology Fund Class C	WCSTX	B	B+	C	Up	3.32	13.36	30.76	24.74	102.31	11.13	3,748	888-923-3355	Y
JNL/Mellon Capital Small Cap Index Fund Class I	US46648M5994	B+	A-	B	Up	3.93	10.07	13.08	35.36	102.22	20.06	2,375		Y
Delaware Small Cap Core Fund Class C	DCCCX	B+	A-	B	Up	2.45	8.30	13.06	29.23	102.12	21.23	2,828		Y
Principal MidCap S&P 400 Index Fund Institutional Class	MPSIX	B	B	B		6.25	9.59	15.96	34.86	102.04	21.42	1,463	800-222-5852	Y
DFA U.S. Small Cap Portfolio Institutional Class	DFSTX	B+	A-	B	Up	3.79	9.42	11.52	32.21	101.97	35.94	17,435	512-306-7400	Y
AB Discovery Growth Fund Advisor Class	CHCYX	B	A-	C+	Up	9.00	15.43	32.70	38.03	101.89	11.58	2,141	212-969-1000	Y
Federated Kaufmann Large Cap Fund Class R Shares	KLCKX	B-	B	B-	Down	4.40	8.06	22.77	30.20	101.82	22.48	3,311	800-341-7400	Y
Schwab Fundamental US Small Company Index Fund	SFSNX	B	B+	B	Up	5.03	9.87	12.75	31.12	101.77	14.93	1,785	877-824-5615	Y
VALIC Company I Mid Cap Index Fund	VMIDX	B	B	B		6.24	9.53	15.90	34.91	101.70	29.42	3,560		Y
ClearBridge Small Cap Fund Class FI	LGASX	B	B	B	Up	2.23	4.86	11.63	35.13	101.61	57.88	1,053	877-721-1926	Y
Dreyfus/The Boston Company Small/Mid Cap Growth Fund Cls A	DBMAX	B	A-	C+	Up	5.08	11.36	26.09	35.22	101.56	19.06	1,225	800-645-6561	Y
Fidelity® Independence Fund Class K	FDFKX	B-	B-	C+	Up	6.50	13.09	26.53	25.08	101.55	37.3	3,919	617-563-7000	Y
Principal SmallCap Growth Fund I R-3 Class	PPNMX	B	A-	C+	Up	5.27	12.17	25.65	36.78	101.41	11.82	1,634	800-222-5852	Y
Fidelity® Mid-Cap Stock Fund Class K	FKMCX	B-	B	B-	Down	5.06	9.93	18.79	31.64	101.32	38.23	8,227	617-563-7000	Y
PIMCO StocksPLUS® Small Fund Class A	PCKAX	B+	A	B-	Up	3.13	9.85	17.21	34.85	101.29	10.32	1,361	866-746-2602	Y

		RATINGS				TOTAL RETURNS & PERFORMANCE					ASSETS		NEW INVESTORS	
Fund Name	Ticker Symbol	Overall Rating	Reward Rating	Risk Rating	Recent Up/ Downgrade	3-Month Total Return	6-Month Total Return	1-Year Total Return	3-Year Total Return	5-Year Total Return	NAV	Total Assets (MIL)	Telephone	Open to New Investors
EQ/Mid Cap Index Portfolio Class K	US26883L4804	B	B	B		6.75	10.23	16.00	34.34	101.25		2,031	877-222-2144	Y
PIMCO StocksPLUS® Small Fund Class D	PCKDX	B+	A	B-	Up	3.05	9.82	17.10	34.67	101.19	10.24	1,361	866-746-2602	Y
1290 VT GAMCO Small Company Value Portfolio Class K	US26883L6395	B+	A-	B	Up	4.29	12.71	16.59	34.87	100.95		3,492	877-222-2144	Y
JNL/Mellon Capital S&P 400 MidCap Index Fund Class I	US46648M6232	B	B	B		6.21	9.56	15.88	34.20	100.91	22.06	3,143		Y
PIMCO RAE Fundamental PLUS Fund Class D	PIXDX	B	B	B-	Up	7.42	12.90	18.81	30.42	100.81	7.31	1,841	866-746-2602	Y
JPMorgan Market Expansion Enhanced Index Fund Class C	OMECX	B	B+	B	Up	5.06	9.64	13.68	33.16	100.68	9.5	1,072	800-480-4111	Y
Dreyfus Mid Cap Index Fund Class I	DMIDX	B	B	B		6.21	9.57	15.98	34.41	100.59	37.13	3,851	800-645-6561	Y
PIMCO RAE Fundamental PLUS Fund Class A	PIXAX	B	B	B-	Up	7.40	12.71	18.77	30.19	100.55	7.32	1,841	866-746-2602	Y
PIMCO StocksPLUS® Absolute Return Fund Class C	PSOCX	B-	B	C+	Down	6.17	11.16	22.32	32.97	100.55	9.61	1,626	866-746-2602	Y
Wells Fargo Small Company Growth Fund - Class R6	WSCRX	B	B	B-	Up	5.06	10.28	20.67	23.90	100.45	53.28	1,820	800-222-8222	Y
John Hancock Classic Value Fund Class C	JCVCX	B	B	B-	Up	7.02	10.90	15.63	27.80	100.44	33.29	2,262	800-225-5913	Y
Oppenheimer Discovery Mid Cap Growth Fund A	OEGAX	A-	A-	B+	Up	6.66	12.13	27.98	37.43	100.43	19.94	1,053	800-225-5677	Y
JNL/Mellon Capital Small Cap Index Fund Class A	US46648M6158	B+	A-	B	Up	3.84	9.90	12.83	34.62	100.43	19.71	2,375		Y
DFA U.S. Vector Equity Portfolio Institutional Class	DFVEX	B	B	B	Up	5.39	10.78	14.63	30.64	100.42	19.17	4,856	512-306-7400	Y
Principal MidCap S&P 400 Index Fund Class R-6	PMAPX	B	B	B		6.25	9.60	15.96	34.30	100.24	21.4	1,463	800-222-5852	Y
AB Discovery Value Fund Class K	ABSKX	B	B	B	Up	5.91	11.33	12.58	30.49	100.00	22.47	2,959	212-969-1000	Y
ClearBridge Small Cap Fund Class R	LMARX	B	B	B	Up	2.19	4.80	11.63	34.32	99.81	56.63	1,053	877-721-1926	Y
Principal MidCap S&P 400 Index Fund R-5 Class	PMFPX	B	B	B		6.16	9.47	15.71	33.96	99.74	22.04	1,463	800-222-5852	Y
ClearBridge Small Cap Fund Class A2	LBRTX	B	B	B	Up	2.21	4.88	11.63	34.79	99.66	40.31	1,053	877-721-1926	Y
JNL/Mellon Capital S&P 400 MidCap Index Fund Class A	US46648M6315	B	B	B		6.17	9.41	15.66	33.80	99.60	21.66	3,143		Y
Principal SmallCap Growth Fund I R-2 Class	PPNNX	B	A-	C+	Up	5.21	12.11	25.37	36.08	99.57	11.14	1,634	800-222-5852	Y
AXA/AB Small Cap Growth Portfolio Class K	US26883L7617	B+	A-	B	Up	6.87	13.11	23.31	34.47	99.53		2,071	877-222-2144	Y
TIAA-CREF Small-Cap Blend Index Fund Advisor Class	TRHBX	B+	A-	B	Up	3.36	9.22	14.72	32.76	99.45	21.28	2,491	877-518-9161	Y
RBB Free Market U.S. Equity Fund Institutional Class	FMUEX	B	B	B	Up	4.78	10.23	13.44	30.55	99.40	18.78	3,032		Y
Russell Investments U.S. Small Cap Equity Fund Class S	RLESX	B	B+	B	Up	4.14	9.56	14.32	29.57	99.05	31.87	2,045	800-426-7969	Y
Wells Fargo Discovery Fund - Class A	WFDAX	B+	A-	B	Up	6.07	11.77	29.03	35.44	98.98	32.57	2,600	800-222-8222	Y
John Hancock Funds II Mid Cap Stock Fund Class NAV	JHMSX	B	B	B	Up	5.16	9.08	28.40	32.72	98.79	21.57	1,635	800-225-5913	Y
Principal MidCap S&P 400 Index Fund Class J	PMFJX	B	B	B		6.18	9.45	15.74	33.78	98.69	20.85	1,463	800-222-5852	Y
Principal MidCap S&P 400 Index Fund R-4 Class	PMFSX	B	B	B		6.14	9.37	15.60	33.48	98.62	21.87	1,463	800-222-5852	Y
JPMorgan U.S. Small Company Fund Class R5	JUSYX	B	B	B	Up	3.42	8.02	8.90	26.50	98.58	18.65	1,857	800-480-4111	Y
EQ/Mid Cap Index Portfolio Class IA	US2689403192	B	B	B		6.71	10.12	15.66	33.35	98.56		2,031	877-222-2144	Y
PIMCO StocksPLUS® Small Fund Class R	PCKRX	B+	A-	B-	Up	3.02	9.59	16.94	33.72	98.55	10.25	1,361	866-746-2602	Y
Wells Fargo Special Small Cap Value Fund - Class C	ESPCX	B	B+	B	Up	5.04	9.15	10.23	32.45	98.55	31.67	2,220	800-222-8222	Y
EQ/Mid Cap Index Portfolio Class IB	US2689402939	B	B	B		6.67	10.06	15.60	33.22	98.53		2,031	877-222-2144	Y
1290 VT GAMCO Small Company Value Portfolio Class IA	US2689545596	B+	A-	B	Up	4.22	12.58	16.30	33.88	98.50		3,492	877-222-2144	Y
AB Discovery Growth Fund Class K	CHCKX	B	A-	C+	Up	8.87	15.19	32.27	36.51	98.45	10.76	2,141	212-969-1000	Y
1290 VT GAMCO Small Company Value Portfolio Class IB	US29364E2072	B+	A-	B	Up	4.21	12.58	16.28	33.84	98.43		3,492	877-222-2144	Y
First Investors Opportunity Fund Advisor Class	FIVUX	B	B-	B	Up	5.49	9.61	19.00	26.50	98.39	42.38	1,147	800-423-4026	Y
JPMorgan U.S. Small Company Fund Class R4	JUSQX	B	B	B	Up	3.42	7.97	8.79	26.30	98.26	18.64	1,857	800-480-4111	Y
Principal SmallCap Growth Fund I R-1 Class	PNASX	B	A-	C+	Up	5.16	12.06	25.29	35.57	98.22	11.47	1,634	800-222-5852	Y
Russell Investments U.S. Small Cap Equity Fund Class R6	RSCRX	B	B+	B	Up	4.18	9.63	14.46	29.55	97.97	31.87	2,045	800-426-7969	Y
Schwab Small Cap Index Fund®	SWSSX	B+	A-	B	Up	3.35	9.20	14.68	32.08	97.76	30.64	3,656	877-824-5615	Y
Oppenheimer Discovery Mid Cap Growth Fund R	OEGNX	A-	A-	B+	Up	6.54	11.99	27.64	36.41	97.73	18.67	1,053	800-225-5677	Y
Hartford Capital Appreciation HLS Fund Class IA	HIACX	B-	B-	B-	Down	4.98	8.74	22.13	29.27	97.66	48.16	5,083	888-843-7824	Y
Carillon Eagle Small Cap Growth Fund Class R6	HSRUX	B	B+	B	Up	6.05	10.29	23.40	35.02	97.37	63.38	5,195	800-421-4184	Y
TIAA-CREF Small-Cap Blend Index Fund Retirement Class	TRBIX	B+	A-	B	Up	3.30	9.14	14.55	31.92	97.28	21.38	2,491	877-518-9161	Y
AXA/AB Small Cap Growth Portfolio Class IB	US4049927118	B+	A-	B	Up	6.81	13.04	23.09	33.49	97.19		2,071	877-222-2144	Y
AXA/AB Small Cap Growth Portfolio Class IA	US4049927035	B+	A-	B	Up	6.84	13.03	23.11	33.51	97.13		2,071	877-222-2144	Y
Voya MidCap Opportunities Portfolio Class I	IIMOX	B	B	B+		7.77	10.96	25.08	33.98	97.10	14.56	2,232	800-366-0066	Y
Russell Investments U.S. Small Cap Equity Fund Class M	RUNTX	B	B+	B	Up	4.16	9.64	14.34	28.96	97.07	31.85	2,045	800-426-7969	Y
Delaware Small Cap Value Fund Institutional Class	DEVIX	B+	A-	B	Up	5.14	8.94	11.99	36.65	97.06	69.49	4,547		Y
DFA U.S. Targeted Value Portfolio Institutional Class	DFFVX	B	B	B	Up	4.50	9.99	9.58	30.01	97.03	24.89	11,043	512-306-7400	Y

Fund Name	Ticker Symbol	RATINGS: Overall Rating	Reward Rating	Risk Rating	Recent Up/ Downgrade	TOTAL RETURNS & PERFORMANCE: 3-Month Total Return	6-Month Total Return	1-Year Total Return	3-Year Total Return	5-Year Total Return	ASSETS: NAV	Total Assets (MIL)	NEW INVESTORS: Telephone	Open to New Investors
AB Discovery Value Fund Class R	ABSRX	B	B	B	Up	5.80	11.13	12.24	29.28	97.02	22.14	2,959	212-969-1000	Y
Voya MidCap Opportunities Portfolio R6	VMCRX	B	B	B+		7.77	10.96	25.08	33.88	96.95	14.56	2,232	800-366-0066	Y
Wells Fargo Growth Fund - Class R6	SGRHX	A-	A-	B	Up	6.88	14.33	35.23	37.95	96.88	41.12	4,617	800-222-8222	Y
Wells Fargo Small Company Growth Fund - Class A	WFSAX	B	B	B-	Up	4.96	10.05	20.17	22.28	96.88	50.15	1,820	800-222-8222	Y
EQ/Small Company Index Class K	US26883L4234	B+	A-	B	Up	4.06	9.88	14.79	31.64	96.83		1,203	877-222-2144	Y
Principal MidCap S&P 400 Index Fund R-3 Class	PMFMX	B	B	B	Up	6.07	9.26	15.33	32.76	96.71	21.81	1,463	800-222-5852	Y
Russell Investments U.S. Small Cap Equity Fund Class A	RLACX	B	B+	B	Up	4.05	9.42	14.00	28.57	96.49	31.55	2,045	800-426-7969	Y
Russell Investments U.S. Small Cap Equity Fund Class E	REBEX	B	B+	B	Up	4.06	9.40	13.99	28.57	96.47	31.74	2,045	800-426-7969	Y
Ariel Appreciation Fund Investor Class	CAAPX	B-	C+	B		6.34	6.43	15.09	20.53	96.42	47.88	1,677	312-726-0140	Y
VALIC Company I Small Cap Index Fund	VCSLX	B+	A-	B	Up	3.25	9.08	14.37	31.49	96.32	22.81	1,292		Y
Carillon Eagle Small Cap Growth Fund Class R5	HSRSX	B	B+	B	Up	6.03	10.24	23.29	34.60	96.26	62.89	5,195	800-421-4184	Y
DFA U.S. Targeted Value Portfolio Class R1	DFTVX	B	B	B	Up	4.44	9.91	9.50	29.60	96.21	24.88	11,043	512-306-7400	Y
American Beacon Small Cap Value Fund R6 Class	AASRX	B+	B+	B	Up	3.18	8.08	8.70	29.68	96.13	27.41	7,212	800-658-5811	Y
Delaware Small Cap Value Fund Class R6	DVZRX	B+	A-	B	Up	5.17	9.04	12.19	36.53	95.92	69.5	4,547		Y
JPMorgan U.S. Small Company Fund Class R3	JUSPX	B	B	B	Up	3.38	7.85	8.51	25.43	95.91	18.21	1,857	800-480-4111	Y
First Investors Opportunity Fund Class A	FIUSX	B-	B-	B	Up	5.42	9.48	18.66	25.41	95.90	41.64	1,147	800-423-4026	Y
AB Discovery Growth Fund Class R	CHCRX	B	B+	C+	Up	8.78	15.15	31.99	35.44	95.82	10.26	2,141	212-969-1000	Y
ClearBridge Small Cap Fund Class C	LMASX	B	B	B	Up	2.08	4.57	10.99	32.49	95.78	38.5	1,053	877-721-1926	Y
Lord Abbett Alpha Strategy Fund Class R6	ALFVX	B	B	C+	Up	4.92	11.00	21.02	30.49	95.64	27.24	1,144	201-827-2000	Y
Lord Abbett Alpha Strategy Fund Class F	ALFFX	B	B	C+	Up	4.85	10.87	20.75	30.11	95.60	26.75	1,144	201-827-2000	Y
Lord Abbett Alpha Strategy Fund Class R5	ALFTX	B	B	C+	Up	4.89	10.97	20.94	30.42	95.53	27.23	1,144	201-827-2000	Y
Nationwide Mid Cap Market Index Fund Class R	GMXRX	B	B	B	Up	5.97	9.12	15.08	32.00	95.51	17.51	1,283	800-848-0920	Y
Victory Integrity Small-Cap Value Fund Class R	MRVSX	B	B+	B	Up	5.42	11.48	11.69	27.00	95.50	38.74	2,705	800-539-3863	Y
Hartford Capital Appreciation HLS Fund Class IB	HIBCX	B-	B-	B-	Down	4.90	8.57	21.81	28.28	95.17	47.48	5,083	888-843-7824	Y
Principal MidCap S&P 400 Index Fund R-2 Class	PMFNX	B	B	B	Up	6.06	9.19	15.18	32.08	94.97	21.91	1,463	800-222-5852	Y
Royce Opportunity Fund Class K	ROFKX	B+	A	C+	Up	3.34	12.29	21.08	34.02	94.85	11.13	1,646	800-221-4268	Y
ClearBridge Aggressive Growth Fund Class A	SHRAX	B-	C+	B	Up	3.20	5.74	14.27	14.53	94.79	203.41	11,391	877-721-1926	Y
ClearBridge Aggressive Growth Fund Class FI	LMPFX	B-	C+	B	Up	3.19	5.73	14.28	14.52	94.73	204.42	11,391	877-721-1926	Y
Lord Abbett Alpha Strategy Fund Class F3	ALFOX	B	B	C+	Up	4.89	10.97	20.88	29.81	94.62	27.23	1,144	201-827-2000	Y
Delaware Small Cap Value Fund Class A	DEVLX	B+	A-	B	Up	5.07	8.80	11.69	35.62	94.61	65.94	4,547		Y
Voya MidCap Opportunities Portfolio Class S	ISMOX	B	B	B+		7.66	10.77	24.76	32.93	94.56	13.77	2,232	800-366-0066	Y
DFA U.S. Targeted Value Portfolio Class R2	DFTPX	B	B	B-	Up	4.40	9.85	9.31	29.04	94.52	24.75	11,043	512-306-7400	Y
EQ/Small Company Index Portfolio Class IB	US2689406328	B+	B+	B	Up	3.97	9.70	14.50	30.62	94.49		1,203	877-222-2144	Y
EQ/Small Company Index Portfolio Class IA	US2689406401	B+	A-	B	Up	3.98	9.70	14.42	30.65	94.38		1,203	877-222-2144	Y
JPMorgan U.S. Small Company Fund Class A	JTUAX	B	B	B	Up	3.35	7.86	8.52	24.95	94.37	18.31	1,857	800-480-4111	Y
Voya MidCap Opportunities Fund Class W	IMOWX	B	B	B+		7.71	10.78	24.76	32.97	94.33	25.23	1,401	800-366-0066	Y
Lord Abbett Alpha Strategy Fund Class R4	ALFKX	B	B	C+	Up	4.81	10.83	20.62	29.55	94.23	26.56	1,144	201-827-2000	Y
Voya SmallCap Opportunities Fund Class W	ISOWX	B	B	B	Up	3.34	7.78	18.26	30.67	94.21	62.94	1,459	800-366-0066	Y
Principal SmallCap Value Fund II Class R-6	PSMVX	B	B	B	Up	3.01	8.18	6.94	27.54	93.99	13.17	1,257	800-222-5852	Y
Principal SmallCap Value Fund II Institutional Class	PPVIX	B	B	B	Up	2.98	8.15	6.91	27.49	93.89	13.18	1,257	800-222-5852	Y
PIMCO StocksPLUS® Small Fund Class C	PCKCX	B+	A-	B-	Up	2.98	9.45	16.42	31.82	93.80	9.54	1,361	866-746-2602	Y
Principal MidCap S&P 400 Index Fund R-1 Class	PMSSX	B	B	B	Up	6.00	9.11	14.99	31.53	93.67	21.25	1,463	800-222-5852	Y
Dreyfus/The Boston Company Small/Mid Cap Growth Fund Cls C	DBMCX	B	B+	C+	Up	4.89	10.95	25.18	32.12	93.63	17.02	1,225	800-645-6561	Y
Hartford Capital Appreciation HLS Fund Class IC	HCPCX	B-	B-	B-	Down	4.83	8.44	21.50	27.32	93.43	47.76	5,083	888-843-7824	Y
Voya MidCap Opportunities Portfolio Class S2	IMOPX	B	B	B+	Up	7.72	10.77	24.56	32.38	93.18	13.66	2,232	800-366-0066	Y
Royce Opportunity Fund Retirement Class	ROFRX	B+	A	C+	Up	3.34	12.21	21.06	33.61	93.15	12.25	1,646	800-221-4268	Y
PIMCO RAE Fundamental PLUS Fund Class C	PIXCX	B-	B-	C+	Down	7.17	12.33	17.93	27.25	93.05	6.77	1,841	866-746-2602	Y
Oppenheimer Discovery Mid Cap Growth Fund C	OEGCX	B+	B+	B+	Up	6.45	11.69	27.07	34.33	92.96	16.47	1,053	800-225-5677	Y
Carillon Eagle Small Cap Growth Fund Class A	HRSCX	B	B+	B	Up	5.92	10.01	22.82	33.17	92.91	59.6	5,195	800-421-4184	Y
Voya MidCap Opportunities Portfolio Class A	IAMOX	B	B	B+	Up	7.69	10.69	24.48	31.96	92.23	13.44	2,232	800-366-0066	Y
Delaware Small Cap Value Fund Class R	DVLRX	B	B+	B	Up	5.01	8.68	11.43	34.60	92.19	64.01	4,547		Y
Voya MidCap Opportunities Fund Class A	NMCAX	B	B	B+	Up	7.64	10.63	24.46	31.98	92.01	22.35	1,401	800-366-0066	Y

Fund Name	Ticker Symbol	RATINGS Overall Rating	Reward Rating	Risk Rating	Recent Up/ Downgrade	TOTAL RETURNS & PERFORMANCE 3-Month Total Return	6-Month Total Return	1-Year Total Return	3-Year Total Return	5-Year Total Return	ASSETS NAV	Total Assets (MIL)	NEW INVESTORS Telephone	Open to New Investors
Voya MidCap Opportunities Fund Class O	NMCOX	B	B	B+	Up	7.63	10.63	24.46	31.95	91.98	22.25	1,401	800-366-0066	Y
JPMorgan U.S. Small Company Fund Class R2	JSCZX	B	B	B	Up	3.29	7.70	8.25	23.99	91.97	17.98	1,857	800-480-4111	Y
Lord Abbett Alpha Strategy Fund Class R3	ALFRX	B-	B	C+	Up	4.74	10.68	20.29	28.58	91.81	25.9	1,144	201-827-2000	Y
Voya SmallCap Opportunities Fund Class A	NSPAX	B	B	B	Up	3.30	7.64	17.99	29.69	91.77	58.43	1,459	800-366-0066	Y
Wells Fargo Discovery Fund - Class C	WDSCX	B	B+	B	Up	5.89	11.39	28.10	32.44	91.68	28.82	2,600	800-222-8222	Y
Dreyfus Opportunistic Midcap Value Fund Class I	DVLIX	B-	B-	B-	Up	6.71	11.52	15.97	21.64	91.66	33.21	1,106	800-645-6561	Y
Principal SmallCap Value Fund II R-5 Class	PLARX	B	B	B	Up	2.88	8.04	6.62	26.58	91.65	12.98	1,257	800-222-5852	Y
TIAA-CREF Mid-Cap Growth Fund Advisor Class	TCMHX	B-	B	C+	Up	5.52	11.65	26.13	27.11	91.64	22.53	1,638	877-518-9161	Y
Artisan Global Opportunities Fund Investor Class	ARTRX	B	B	B+	Down	4.32	9.83	31.18	46.98	91.18	25.72	2,806	800-344-1770	Y
DFA U.S. Small Cap Value Portfolio Institutional Class	DFSVX	B	B	B-	Up	3.12	9.28	7.21	25.79	91.08	37.92	15,503	512-306-7400	Y
Lord Abbett Alpha Strategy Fund Class R2	ALFQX	B-	B	C+	Up	4.70	10.63	20.15	28.19	90.82	25.71	1,144	201-827-2000	Y
TIAA-CREF Mid-Cap Growth Fund Premier Class	TRGPX	B	B	B	Up	5.54	11.65	26.04	26.65	90.41	22.41	1,638	877-518-9161	Y
Carillon Eagle Small Cap Growth Fund Class R3	HSRRX	B	B+	B	Up	5.86	9.89	22.51	32.18	90.36	57.72	5,195	800-421-4184	Y
Principal SmallCap Value Fund II R-4 Class	PSTWX	B	B	B	Up	2.87	7.92	6.49	26.09	90.27	12.85	1,257	800-222-5852	Y
Principal SmallCap Value Fund II Class A	PSVAX	B	B	B	Up	2.82	7.87	6.38	25.72	90.01	13.06	1,257	800-222-5852	Y
Principal MidCap Growth Fund III Institutional Class	PPIMX	B-	B	C+	Down	6.30	10.98	24.58	27.04	89.76	11.12	1,127	800-222-5852	Y
Voya MidCap Opportunities Fund Class R	IMORX	B	B	B+	Up	7.59	10.54	24.17	31.00	89.71	21.84	1,401	800-366-0066	Y
Wells Fargo Small Company Growth Fund - Class C	WSMCX	B-	B-	B-	Up	4.77	9.63	19.27	19.57	89.63	44.73	1,820	800-222-8222	Y
JPMorgan U.S. Small Company Fund Class C	JTUCX	B	B	B	Up	3.21	7.54	7.97	23.11	89.59	17.51	1,857	800-480-4111	Y
TIAA-CREF Mid-Cap Growth Fund Retirement Class	TRGMX	B	B	B	Up	5.48	11.58	25.89	26.25	89.50	21.91	1,638	877-518-9161	Y
Prudential Jennison Small Company Fund Class R	JSCRX	B	B	B	Up	4.81	9.15	19.26	28.57	89.48	24.3	3,704	800-225-1852	Y
Voya SmallCap Opportunities Fund Class R	ISORX	B	B	B	Up	3.23	7.51	17.70	28.72	89.43	57.21	1,459	800-366-0066	Y
Homestead Small Company Stock Fund	HSCSX	B	B+	B	Up	4.54	10.62	11.99	25.20	89.39	44.11	1,303		Y
Principal SmallCap Value Fund II Class J	PSMJX	B	B	B	Up	2.83	7.87	6.44	25.84	89.32	12.86	1,257	800-222-5852	Y
Russell Investments U.S. Small Cap Equity Fund Class C	RLECX	B	B+	B	Up	3.87	9.01	13.17	25.68	89.26	29.64	2,045	800-426-7969	Y
Dreyfus Opportunistic Midcap Value Fund Class A	DMCVX	B-	C+	B-	Up	6.60	11.33	15.62	20.56	89.02	33.43	1,106	800-645-6561	Y
Prudential QMA Small-Cap Value Fund Class Retirement	TSVRX	B	B+	B-	Up	3.37	7.91	5.74	29.19	88.96	20	1,634	800-225-1852	Y
Virtus Ceredex Mid-Cap Value Equity Fund Class R6	SMVZX	B-	B-	B	Down	4.94	4.82	11.97	26.16	88.96	12.67	2,979	800-243-1574	Y
Principal SmallCap Value Fund II R-3 Class	PJARX	B	B	B	Up	2.83	7.86	6.32	25.50	88.58	12.68	1,257	800-222-5852	Y
First Investors Opportunity Fund Class B	FIMBX	B-	C+	B	Up	5.21	9.04	17.76	22.55	88.51	32.03	1,147	800-423-4026	Y
Oakmark Global Select Fund Investor Class	OAKWX	B	B	B-	Up	2.98	7.83	21.18	34.75	88.29	19.3	2,866	641-219-558	Y
Goldman Sachs Intl Small Cap Insights Fund Inv Cls	GIRLX	A-	A-	A	Up	4.82	13.18	32.85	49.00	88.11	12.69	2,617	800-526-7384	Y
American Century Heritage Fund R6 Class	ATHDX	B	B	B	Up	5.64	9.76	22.27	28.60	87.84	24.07	5,143	800-444-4015	Y
ClearBridge Mid Cap Fund Class A	SBMAX	B	B-	B+	Up	3.48	6.13	12.71	23.95	87.49	33.43	2,414	877-721-1926	Y
Delaware Small Cap Value Fund Class C	DEVCX	B	B+	B	Up	4.87	8.40	10.85	32.59	87.45	54.74	4,547		Y
Principal MidCap Growth Fund III R-5 Class	PPQPX	B-	B-	C+	Up	6.35	10.90	24.37	26.07	87.36	11.21	1,127	800-222-5852	Y
Neuberger Berman Large Cap Value Fund Class A	NPNAX	B-	B-	B-		5.00	8.38	13.16	25.72	87.26	31.28	1,514	212-476-9000	Y
Principal SmallCap Value Fund II R-2 Class	PKARX	B	B	B	Up	2.77	7.71	6.13	24.72	86.79	12.21	1,257	800-222-5852	Y
Principal MidCap Growth Fund III R-4 Class	PPQSX	B-	B-	C+	Up	6.24	10.87	24.16	25.55	86.24	10.73	1,127	800-222-5852	Y
Carillon Eagle Small Cap Growth Fund Class C	HSCCX	B	B+	B	Up	5.73	9.66	21.98	30.39	86.23	44.24	5,195	800-421-4184	Y
Principal MidCap Growth Fund III Class J	PPQJX	B-	B-	C+	Up	6.33	10.91	24.22	25.67	86.05	9.07	1,127	800-222-5852	Y
Goldman Sachs International Small Cap Insights Fund Cls A	GICAX	A-	B+	A-	Up	4.84	13.09	32.53	47.92	85.77	12.76	2,617	800-526-7384	Y
Principal SmallCap Value Fund II R-1 Class	PCPTX	B	B	B	Up	2.73	7.66	5.97	24.25	85.63	12.02	1,257	800-222-5852	Y
American Century Heritage Fund Y Class	ATHYX	B	B	B	Up	5.68	9.81	22.20	27.66	85.55	24.08	5,143	800-444-4015	Y
American Century Heritage Fund R5 Class	ATHGX	B	B	B	Up	5.60	9.66	22.05	27.50	85.32	23.87	5,143	800-444-4015	Y
American Beacon Small Cap Value Fund C Class	ASVCX	B	B	B	Up	2.98	7.50	7.57	25.42	85.05	24.97	7,212	800-658-5811	Y
Fidelity Advisor® Stock Selector Small Cap Fund Class Z	FSSZX	B	B	B	Up	3.88	9.66	11.84	27.93	84.95	26.52	1,608	617-563-7000	Y
Voya MidCap Opportunities Fund Class C	NMCCX	B	B	B	Up	7.44	10.23	23.57	28.98	84.95	16.79	1,401	800-366-0066	Y
Voya SmallCap Opportunities Fund Class C	NSPCX	B	B	B	Up	3.13	7.29	17.13	26.82	84.73	44.83	1,459	800-366-0066	Y
Neuberger Berman Large Cap Value Fund Class R3	NPNRX	B-	B-	C+		4.95	8.21	12.78	24.64	84.67	31.35	1,514	212-476-9000	Y
Principal MidCap Growth Fund III R-3 Class	PPQMX	B-	B-	C+	Up	6.22	10.77	23.91	24.93	84.43	10.42	1,127	800-222-5852	Y
Fidelity Advisor® Value Strategies Fund Class K	FVSKX	B	B-	B	Up	5.10	9.03	19.30	28.55	83.92	42.02	1,118	617-563-7000	Y

		RATINGS				TOTAL RETURNS & PERFORMANCE					ASSETS		NEW INVESTORS	
Fund Name	Ticker Symbol	Overall Rating	Reward Rating	Risk Rating	Recent Up/ Downgrade	3-Month Total Return	6-Month Total Return	1-Year Total Return	3-Year Total Return	5-Year Total Return	NAV	Total Assets (Mil)	Telephone	Open to New Investors
Columbia Acorn Fund Institutional 2 Class	CRBRX	B	B+	C+	Up	6.00	11.44	25.20	35.10	82.93	16.2	4,848	800-345-6611	Y
MFS® New Discovery Fund Class R6	MNDKX	B	B+	C	Up	6.65	13.98	26.49	35.14	82.08	30.32	1,213	877-960-6077	Y
Franklin Small Cap Value Fund Class A	FRVLX	B	B	B	Up	5.96	10.76	10.62	31.14	81.69	55.84	2,633	650-312-2000	Y
MFS® New Discovery Fund Class R4	MNDJX	B	B+	C	Up	6.75	14.06	26.46	34.74	81.19	28.64	1,213	877-960-6077	Y
JPMorgan Small Cap Value Fund Class R5	JSVRX	B	B	B-	Up	1.81	5.87	3.29	23.37	81.03	30.62	2,073	800-480-4111	Y
MFS® New Discovery Fund Class I	MNDIX	B	B+	C	Up	6.64	13.94	26.34	34.65	80.99	30.09	1,213	877-960-6077	Y
Fidelity Advisor® Leveraged Company Stock Fund Class Z	FZAKX	B-	C+	B	Up	5.63	9.59	17.78	20.93	80.22	44.29	2,243	617-563-7000	Y
JPMorgan Small Cap Value Fund Class R4	JSVQX	B	B	B-	Up	1.74	5.75	3.08	22.85	79.94	30.58	2,073	800-480-4111	Y
Franklin Small Cap Value Fund Class R	FVFRX	B	B	B-	Up	5.88	10.62	10.36	30.19	79.67	55.3	2,633	650-312-2000	Y
Goldman Sachs International Small Cap Insights Fund Cls C	GICCX	A-	B+	A-	Up	4.68	12.65	31.68	44.62	78.92	12.35	2,617	800-526-7384	Y
MFS® New Discovery Fund Class A	MNDAX	B	B+	C	Up	6.59	13.83	26.08	33.65	78.85	27.26	1,213	877-960-6077	Y
MFS® New Discovery Fund Class R3	MNDHX	B	B+	C	Up	6.55	13.81	26.01	33.64	78.72	27.22	1,213	877-960-6077	Y
MFS® New Discovery Fund Class 529A	EANDX	B	B+	C	Up	6.57	13.79	25.96	33.53	78.49	26.34	1,213	877-960-6077	Y
Fidelity® Leveraged Company Stock Fund Class K	FLCKX	B-	C+	B	Up	5.81	11.73	21.14	21.26	78.35	33.53	3,092	617-563-7000	Y
JPMorgan Small Cap Value Fund Class A	PSOAX	B	B	B-	Up	1.71	5.64	2.89	22.05	77.83	28.9	2,073	800-480-4111	Y
JPMorgan Small Cap Value Fund Class R3	JSVPX	B	B	B-	Up	1.69	5.63	2.87	21.96	77.75	28.86	2,073	800-480-4111	Y
JNL Multi-Manager Small Cap Growth Fund Class I	US46644W4684	B	B+	C	Up	5.08	11.99	27.50	28.63	77.74	27.07	1,713		Y
MFS® New Discovery Fund Class R2	MNDRX	B	B	C	Up	6.54	13.67	25.73	32.67	76.59	25.67	1,213	877-960-6077	Y
Oakmark Global Fund Service Class	OARGX	B-	B	C	Up	3.85	13.09	26.78	24.81	76.14	32.24	2,732	641-219-558	Y
Cohen & Steers Real Estate Securities Fund, Inc. Class Z	CSZIX	B	B-	B+		2.81	3.56	8.17	23.95	75.93	15.59	4,350	212-832-3232	Y
JNL Multi-Manager Small Cap Growth Fund Class A	US46644W4767	B	B+	B-	Up	4.98	11.84	27.23	27.83	75.88	25.88	1,713		Y
JPMorgan Small Cap Value Fund Class R2	JSVZX	B	B	B-	Up	1.63	5.48	2.57	21.05	75.53	28.64	2,073	800-480-4111	Y
Franklin Small Cap Value Fund Class C	FRVFX	B	B	B-	Up	5.76	10.37	9.81	28.28	75.22	49.63	2,633	650-312-2000	Y
Cohen & Steers Real Estate Securities Fund, Inc. Class A	CSEIX	B	B-	B+	Up	2.80	3.41	7.78	22.77	73.98	14.82	4,350	212-832-3232	Y
JPMorgan Small Cap Value Fund Class C	OSVCX	B	B	B-	Up	1.56	5.38	2.29	19.87	72.53	24	2,073	800-480-4111	Y
Cohen & Steers Real Estate Securities Fund, Inc. Class R	CIRRX	B	B-	B+	Up	2.77	3.32	7.62	22.21	72.46	15.55	4,350	212-832-3232	Y
Invesco Small Cap Equity Fund Class Y	SMEYX	B-	B-	B	Up	3.95	8.48	13.88	19.63	72.46	15.86	1,291	800-659-1005	Y
JNL Multi-Manager Small Cap Value Fund Class I	US46644W4437	B-	B	B-	Up	3.15	8.21	11.25	24.23	72.41	15.35	1,236		Y
MFS® New Discovery Fund Class B	MNDBX	B-	B	C	Up	6.35	13.35	25.05	30.63	72.23	22.09	1,213	877-960-6077	Y
MFS® New Discovery Fund Class C	MNDCX	B-	B	C	Up	6.38	13.37	25.11	30.68	72.22	22.14	1,213	877-960-6077	Y
MFS® New Discovery Fund Class R1	MNDGX	B-	B	C	Up	6.40	13.35	25.07	30.68	72.21	21.93	1,213	877-960-6077	Y
MFS® New Discovery Fund Class 529B	EBNDX	B-	B	C	Up	6.38	13.37	25.04	30.52	71.91	21.3	1,213	877-960-6077	Y
MFS® New Discovery Fund Class 529C	ECNDX	B-	B	C	Up	6.39	13.37	25.05	30.47	71.73	21.29	1,213	877-960-6077	Y
JNL Multi-Manager Small Cap Value Fund Class A	US46644W4502	B-	B	B-	Up	3.09	8.16	11.06	23.52	70.68	15.33	1,236		Y
Invesco Small Cap Equity Fund Class A	SMEAX	B-	B-	B	Up	3.88	8.33	13.57	18.74	70.33	15.35	1,291	800-659-1005	Y
Cohen & Steers Real Estate Securities Fund, Inc. Class C	CSCIX	B	C+	B+	Up	2.62	3.05	7.07	20.32	68.39	13.44	4,350	212-832-3232	Y
Invesco Small Cap Equity Fund Class R	SMERX	B-	C+	B	Up	3.84	8.25	13.31	17.91	68.20	14.44	1,291	800-659-1005	Y
Principal Real Estate Securities Fund Institutional Class	PIREX	B	B-	B+	Up	3.56	4.94	9.02	18.46	67.77	23.76	3,654	800-222-5852	Y
Principal Real Estate Securities Fund R-5 Class	PREPX	B	B-	B+	Up	3.54	4.84	8.85	17.75	66.10	22.96	3,654	800-222-5852	Y
Principal Real Estate Securities Fund Class J	PREJX	B	B-	B+	Up	3.56	4.84	8.87	17.59	65.25	23.07	3,654	800-222-5852	Y
Principal Real Estate Securities Fund R-4 Class	PRETX	B	B-	B+	Up	3.51	4.83	8.73	17.38	65.16	22.92	3,654	800-222-5852	Y
Principal Real Estate Securities Fund Class A	PRRAX	B	B-	B+	Up	3.49	4.73	8.64	17.04	64.42	23.75	3,654	800-222-5852	Y
Invesco Small Cap Equity Fund Class C	SMECX	B-	C+	B	Up	3.73	7.98	12.78	16.13	64.12	12.35	1,291	800-659-1005	Y
Principal Real Estate Securities Fund R-3 Class	PRERX	B	B-	B+	Up	3.46	4.67	8.51	16.69	63.52	23.17	3,654	800-222-5852	Y
Principal Real Estate Securities Fund R-2 Class	PRENX	B	B-	B+	Up	3.41	4.61	8.33	16.04	62.07	22.61	3,654	800-222-5852	Y
TIAA-CREF Real Estate Securities Fund Advisor Class	TIRHX	B	B-	B+	Up	3.76	5.21	12.16	20.53	61.13	15.56	2,144	877-518-9161	Y
Principal Real Estate Securities Fund R-1 Class	PRAEX	B	B-	B+	Up	3.35	4.51	8.18	15.55	60.97	23.46	3,654	800-222-5852	Y
TIAA-CREF Real Estate Securities Fund Premier Class	TRRPX	B	B-	B+	Up	3.70	5.22	12.11	20.23	60.35	15.56	2,144	877-518-9161	Y
TIAA-CREF Real Estate Securities Fund Retirement Class	TRRSX	B	B-	B+	Up	3.72	5.16	12.01	19.88	59.53	16.19	2,144	877-518-9161	Y
DFA Real Estate Securities Portfolio Institutional Class	DFREX	B	C+	B+	Up	2.05	3.13	5.71	16.35	58.99	35.3	8,586	512-306-7400	Y
JPMorgan Realty Income Fund Class R5	JRIRX	B-	C+	B+		2.05	2.85	4.11	10.20	50.03	13.36	2,588	800-480-4111	Y
VanEck Emerging Markets Fund Class Y	EMRYX	B-	B	C	Up	8.38	19.62	50.32	31.68	47.88	18.73	1,871	800-826-1115	Y

		RATINGS				TOTAL RETURNS & PERFORMANCE					ASSETS		NEW INVESTORS	
Fund Name	Ticker Symbol	Overall Rating	Reward Rating	Risk Rating	Recent Up/ Downgrade	3-Month Total Return	6-Month Total Return	1-Year Total Return	3-Year Total Return	5-Year Total Return	NAV	Total Assets (MIL)	Telephone	Open to New Investors
JPMorgan Realty Income Fund Class A	URTAX	B-	C+	B		1.97	2.70	3.67	8.82	46.76	13.14	2,588	800-480-4111	Y
VanEck Emerging Markets Fund Class A	GBFAX	B-	B	C	Up	8.26	19.39	49.70	30.07	45.50	18.44	1,871	800-826-1115	Y
JPMorgan Realty Income Fund Class C	URTCX	B-	C	B		1.81	2.38	3.13	7.20	43.14	12.71	2,588	800-480-4111	Y
PIMCO RealEstateRealReturn Strategy Fund Class A	PETAX	B-	C+	B		1.78	2.32	3.94	16.15	41.36	7.61	2,001	866-746-2602	Y
PIMCO RealEstateRealReturn Strategy Fund Class D	PETDX	B-	C+	B		1.77	2.31	3.91	16.04	41.31	7.65	2,001	866-746-2602	Y
PIMCO RealEstateRealReturn Strategy Fund Class C	PETCX	B-	C+	B	Up	1.70	2.01	3.16	13.57	36.05	6.64	2,001	866-746-2602	Y

Section VI: Low Volatility Stock Mutual Funds

Investment Ratings and analysis of Low Volatility Stock Mutual Funds. Funds are listed in order by their beta (lowest to highest) and overall rating.

Section VI: Contents

This section contains Weiss Investment Ratings, key rating factors, and summary financial data for our selections for "Low Volatility Stock Mutual Funds". If ultimate safety is your top priority, the top recommended mutual funds with the lowest volatility may be your best bet. These funds may have lower performance ratings than some other funds, but can provide a safe place for your savings. Funds are listed in order by their beta (lowest to highest) and overall rating.

Fund Name

Describes the fund's assets, regions of investments and investment strategies. Many funds have similar names, so you want to make sure the fund you look up is really the one you are interested in evaluating.

Ticker Symbol

An arrangement of characters (usually letters) representing a particular security listed on an exchange or otherwise traded publicly. When a company issues securities to the public marketplace, it selects an available ticker symbol for its securities which investors use to place trade orders. Every listed security has a unique ticker symbol, facilitating the vast array of trade orders that flow through the financial markets every day. If a ticker symbol is not assigned to a particular fund, the International Securities Identification Number (ISIN) is displayed.

RATINGS

Overall Rating

The Weiss rating measured on a scale from A to E based on each fund's risk and performance. See the preceding section, "What Our Ratings Mean," for an explanation of each letter grade rating.

Reward Rating

This is based on the total return over a period of up to five years, including net asset value and price growth. The total return figure is stated net of the expenses and fees charged by the fund. Based on proprietary modeling the individual components of the risk and reward ratings are calculated and weighted and the final rating is generated.

Risk Rating

This is includes the risk ratings of component stocks where applicable and also includes the financial stability of the fund, turnover where applicable, together with the level of volatility as measured by the fund's daily returns over a period of up to five years. Funds with greater stability are considered less risky and receive a higher risk rating. Funds with greater volatility are considered riskier, and will receive a lower risk rating. In addition to considering the fund's volatility, the risk rating also considers an assessment of the valuation and quality of a fund's holdings.

Recent Upgrade/Downgrade

An "Up" or "Down" indicates that the Weiss Mutual Fund rating has changed since the publication of the last print edition. If a fund has had a rating change since September 30, 2017, the change is identified with an "Up" or "Down."

TOTAL RETURNS & PERFORMANCE

3-Month Total Return
The rate of return on an investment over three months that includes interest, capital gains, dividends and distributions realized.

6-Month Total Return
The rate of return on an investment over six months that includes interest, capital gains, dividends and distributions realized.

1-Year Total Return
The rate of return on an investment over one year that includes interest, capital gains, dividends and distributions realized.

3-Year Total Return
The rate of return on an investment over three years that includes interest, capital gains, dividends and distributions realized.

5-Year Total Return
The rate of return on an investment over five years that includes interest, capital gains, dividends and distributions realized.

3-Year Beta
A three year measure of volatility, or systematic risk, of a security in comparison to the market as a whole. A beta of less than 1 means that the security will be less volatile than the market, a beta larger than 1 means more volatility. Beta value cannot be calculated if less than 24 months of pricing is available.

ASSETS

NAV (Net Asset Value)
A fund's price per share. The value is calculated by dividing the total value of all the securities in the portfolio, less any liabilities, by the number of fund shares outstanding.

Total Assets (MIL)
The total of all assets listed on the institution's balance sheet. This figure primarily consists of loans, investments, and fixed assets. Total Assets are displayed in millions.

NEW INVESTORS

Telephone
The company's phone number.

Open to New Investors
Indicates whether the fund accepts investments from those who are not existing investors. A "Y" in this column identifies that the fund accepts new investors. No data in this column indicates that the fund is closed to new investors. The fund may be closed to new investors because the fund's asset base is getting too large to effectively execute its investing style. Although, the fund may be closed, in most cases, existing investors are able to add to their holdings.

		RATINGS				TOTAL RETURNS & PERFORMANCE						ASSETS		NEW INVESTORS	
Fund Name	Ticker Symbol	Overall Rating	Reward Rating	Risk Rating	Recent Up/ Downgrade	3-Month Total Return	6-Month Total Return	1-Year Total Return	3-Year Total Return	5-Year Total Return	3-Year Beta	NAV	Total Assets (MIL)	Telephone	Open to New Investors
JPMorgan Investor Balanced Fund Class A	OGIAX	B-	C+	B	Up	3.25	6.36	13.01	18.63	46.30	-0.47	15.39	5,001	800-480-4111	Y
JPMorgan Investor Balanced Fund Class T	JPBTX	B-	C+	B	Up	3.24	6.34	12.99	18.55	46.19	-0.46	15.37	5,001	800-480-4111	Y
JPMorgan Investor Balanced Fund Class C	OGBCX	B-	C+	B	Up	2.09	5.05	11.25	15.50	41.03	-0.45	15.15	5,001	800-480-4111	Y
Calamos Market Neutral Income Fund Class R	CVSRX	B-	C	B	Up	1.00	1.68	4.31	9.58	18.26	-0.15	13.18	4,780	800-582-6959	Y
Calamos Market Neutral Income Class T	CVSTX	B-	C	B+	Up	0.44	1.63	4.34	10.54	18.53	-0.13		4,634	800-582-6959	Y
Litman Gregory Masters Alternative Strategies Fund Inv Cls	MASNX	B-	C	B	Up	0.51	1.88	4.14	9.83	20.92	0	11.7	2,007	800-960-0188	Y
JPMorgan Investor Conservative Growth Fund Class T	JICTX	B-	C+	B	Up	2.02	4.24	8.96	13.17	30.24	0.04	12.77	3,733	800-480-4111	Y
JPMorgan Investor Conservative Growth Fund Class C	OCGCX	B-	C	B	Up	1.30	3.29	7.71	10.57	26.06	0.04	12.71	3,733	800-480-4111	Y
JPMorgan Investor Conservative Growth Fund Class A	OICAX	B-	C+	B	Up	2.04	4.27	8.93	13.14	30.25	0.06	12.77	3,733	800-480-4111	Y
Fidelity Freedom® 2010 Fund Class K6	FOTKX	B-	C+	B	Up	2.67	5.61	12.49	18.99	39.92	0.14	16.03	6,777	617-563-7000	Y
Berwyn Income Fund	BERIX	B-	C	B+	Up	1.13	1.37	3.91	9.02	31.46	0.15	13.42	1,657	610-296-1400	Y
John Hancock Funds II Multimgr Lifest Mod Port Cls 5	JHLMX	B	C+	B+	Up	2.12	4.71	11.13	17.04	35.64	0.16	13.77	3,876	800-225-5913	Y
AXA Premier VIP Conservative Allocation Fund Class B	US00247C7671	B	C	A	Up	0.99	2.18	5.02	7.61	15.78	0.16		1,219	877-222-2144	Y
John Hancock Funds II Multimgr Lifest Mod Port Cls R5	JTLMX	B-	C+	B	Up	2.18	4.68	11.05	16.84	34.85	0.16	13.79	3,876	800-225-5913	Y
BlackRock Multi-Asset Income Portfolio Investor A Shares	BAICX	B-	C+	B	Up	1.61	3.26	8.75	13.72	30.58	0.16	11.07	16,374	800-441-7762	Y
John Hancock Funds II Multimgr Lifest Mod Port Cls R3	JRLMX	B-	C+	B	Up	1.95	4.36	10.39	14.75	30.83	0.16	13.8	3,876	800-225-5913	Y
John Hancock Funds II Multimgr Lifest Mod Port Cls C	JCLMX	B-	C+	B	Up	1.83	4.11	9.86	13.17	28.04	0.16	13.83	3,876	800-225-5913	Y
AXA Conservative Allocation Portfolio Class K	US00247C5857	B	C	A	Up	1.03	2.22	5.29	8.31	17.14	0.17		1,219	877-222-2144	Y
AXA Premier VIP Conservative Allocation Fund Class A	US00247C7754	B	C	A	Up	0.99	2.07	5.02	7.60	15.78	0.17		1,219	877-222-2144	Y
John Hancock Funds II Multimgr Lifest Mod Port Cls R1	JPLMX	B-	C+	B+	Up	2.00	4.31	10.37	14.37	30.19	0.17	13.81	3,876	800-225-5913	Y
John Hancock Funds II Multimgr Lifest Mod Port Cls 1	JILMX	B-	C+	B	Up	2.18	4.68	11.06	16.94	35.36	0.17	13.79	3,876	800-225-5913	Y
John Hancock Funds II Multimgr Lifest Mod Port Cls R4	JSLMX	B	C+	B+	Up	2.13	4.58	10.93	16.16	33.56	0.18	13.78	3,876	800-225-5913	Y
Principal Strat Asset Mgmt Cons Bal Inst Cls	PCCIX	B-	C+	B	Up	2.46	5.46	11.26	16.82	39.03	0.18	12.12	1,814	800-222-5852	Y
Principal Strat Asset Mgmt Cons Bal R-5 Cls	PCBFX	B-	C+	B	Up	2.31	5.32	10.99	15.88	37.26	0.18	12.11	1,814	800-222-5852	Y
Principal Strat Asset Mgmt Cons Bal R-4 Cls	PCBLX	B-	C+	B	Up	2.28	5.27	10.86	15.52	36.52	0.18	12.11	1,814	800-222-5852	Y
John Hancock Funds II Multimgr Lifest Mod Port Cls A	JALMX	B-	C+	B	Up	2.01	4.48	10.64	15.63	32.84	0.18	13.83	3,876	800-225-5913	Y
John Hancock Funds II Multimgr Lifest Mod Port Cls R2	JQLMX	B-	C+	B	Up	2.00	4.45	10.57	15.24	32.05	0.18	13.78	3,876	800-225-5913	Y
BlackRock Multi-Asset Income Portfolio Investor C Shares	BCICX	B-	C	B	Up	1.32	2.88	7.96	11.10	25.66	0.18	11.05	16,374	800-441-7762	Y
Principal Strat Asset Mgmt Cons Bal Cls J	PCBJX	B-	C+	B	Up	2.34	5.40	11.13	16.13	37.48	0.19	12.08	1,814	800-222-5852	Y
Principal Strat Asset Mgmt Cons Bal Cls A	SAIPX	B-	C+	B	Up	2.35	5.24	10.88	15.76	36.87	0.19	12.24	1,814	800-222-5852	Y
Principal Strat Asset Mgmt Cons Bal R-3 Cls	PCBPX	B-	C+	B	Up	2.32	5.18	10.66	14.92	35.20	0.19	12.1	1,814	800-222-5852	Y
Principal Strat Asset Mgmt Cons Bal R-2 Cls	PCNSX	B-	C+	B	Up	0.99	3.79	9.16	12.96	32.46	0.19	12.17	1,814	800-222-5852	Y
Principal Strat Asset Mgmt Cons Bal R-1 Cls	PCSSX	B-	C+	B	Up	2.15	5.01	10.25	13.81	33.06	0.19	12.08	1,814	800-222-5852	Y
Principal Strat Asset Mgmt Cons Bal Cls C	SCIPX	B	C+	B+	Up	1.00	3.68	8.89	11.85	30.41	0.2	12.11	1,814	800-222-5852	Y
American Funds College 2021 Fund Class 529F1	CTOFX	B	C	A	Up	0.01	1.07	3.64	7.90	28.80	0.2	11.15	1,468	800-421-4225	Y
Blackstone Alternative Multi-Strategy Fund Class Y	BXMYX	B	C	A-	Up	0.31	2.00	7.23	12.95		0.21	10.65	5,227		Y
GuideStone Funds Balanced Allocation Fund Investor Class	GGIZX	B-	C+	B	Up	2.67	5.81	12.30	15.68	33.19	0.21	12.16	1,604	214-720-1171	Y
Fidelity Freedom® 2005 Fund Class K6	FITKX	B-	C+	B	Up	2.18	4.67	10.48	16.33	32.33	0.23	12.55	1,036	617-563-7000	Y
Vanguard Target Retirement 2015 Fund Investor Shares	VTXVX	B	C+	A-	Up	2.72	5.40	11.50	17.36	42.83	0.26	15.33	17,413	877-662-7447	Y
Transamerica Asset Allocation Conservative Portfolio Cls R	ICVRX	B	C+	A-	Up	1.81	4.11	9.56	13.73	28.58	0.28	11.24	1,097	888-233-4339	Y
Oppenheimer Capital Income Fund Class Y	OCIYX	B-	C+	B	Down	1.79	3.39	7.24	14.33	32.17	0.28	10.24	2,779	800-225-5677	Y
Oppenheimer Capital Income Fund Class A	OPPEX	B-	C+	B	Up	1.72	3.36	6.97	13.49	30.63	0.28	10.25	2,779	800-225-5677	Y
Transamerica Asset Allocation Conservative Portfolio Adv	TACVX	B-	C+	B	Up	1.92	4.36	9.92	15.05	30.78	0.28	11.18	1,097	888-233-4339	Y
Oppenheimer Capital Income Fund Class R	OCINX	B-	C	B	Up	1.69	3.20	6.73	12.68	28.90	0.28	10.11	2,779	800-225-5677	Y
Oppenheimer Capital Income Fund Class C	OPECX	B-	C	B	Up	1.57	2.96	6.17	10.96	25.64	0.28	9.92	2,779	800-225-5677	Y
Transamerica Asset Alloc Conservative Port Cls T1	TACQX	B	C+	A-	Up	1.82	4.25	9.89	15.02	30.74	0.29	11.15	1,097	888-233-4339	Y
Transamerica Asset Allocation Conservative Portfolio Cls A	ICLAX	B	C+	A-	Up	1.89	4.22	9.86	14.99	30.70	0.29	11.12	1,097	888-233-4339	Y
Transamerica Asset Allocation Conservative Portfolio Cls C	ICLLX	B	C+	A-	Up	1.72	3.85	9.08	12.54	26.20	0.29	11.03	1,097	888-233-4339	Y
Invesco Balanced-Risk Allocation Fund Class Y	ABRYX	B-	C+	B		4.92	7.72	9.94	16.80	26.96	0.3	10.99	4,978	800-659-1005	Y
Invesco Balanced-Risk Allocation Fund Class A	ABRZX	B-	C+	B	Up	4.98	7.63	9.77	15.91	25.43	0.3	10.84	4,978	800-659-1005	Y
Invesco Balanced-Risk Allocation Fund Class R	ABRRX	B-	C+	B	Up	4.87	7.45	9.41	15.06	23.87	0.31	10.66	4,978	800-659-1005	Y
Invesco Balanced-Risk Allocation Fund Class C	ABRCX	B-	C+	B	Up	4.71	7.24	8.82	13.35	20.80	0.31	10.36	4,978	800-659-1005	Y

		RATINGS				TOTAL RETURNS & PERFORMANCE						ASSETS		NEW INVESTORS	
Fund Name	Ticker Symbol	Overall Rating	Reward Rating	Risk Rating	Recent Up/ Downgrade	3-Month Total Return	6-Month Total Return	1-Year Total Return	3-Year Total Return	5-Year Total Return	3-Year Beta	NAV	Total Assets (MIL)	Telephone	Open to New Investors
Putnam Dynamic Asset Allocation Conservative Fund Class R6	PCCEX	B-	C+	B	Up	2.50	5.15	10.05	16.14	39.51	0.32	10.98	1,140	617-292-1000	Y
Putnam Dynamic Asset Allocation Conservative Fund Class R	PACRX	B-	C+	B	Up	2.39	4.74	9.37	13.90	35.24	0.33	11.24	1,140	617-292-1000	Y
Putnam Dynamic Asset Allocation Conservative Fund Class B	PACBX	B-	C+	B	Up	2.25	4.53	8.86	12.32	31.92	0.33	10.85	1,140	617-292-1000	Y
Putnam Dynamic Asset Allocation Conservative Fund Class M	PACMX	B	C+	A-	Up	2.32	4.69	9.15	13.11	33.62	0.34	10.81	1,140	617-292-1000	Y
Putnam Dynamic Asset Allocation Conservative Fund Class C	PACCX	B-	C+	B	Up	2.27	4.57	8.93	12.35	32.10	0.34	10.8	1,140	617-292-1000	Y
Putnam Dynamic Asset Allocation Conservative Fund Class R5	PACDX	B-	C+	B	Up	2.59	5.12	10.07	15.92	39.13	0.35	10.98	1,140	617-292-1000	Y
Putnam Dynamic Asset Allocation Conservative Fund Class Y	PACYX	B-	C+	B	Up	2.57	5.09	10.03	15.73	38.69	0.35	10.98	1,140	617-292-1000	Y
Putnam Dynamic Asset Allocation Conservative Fund Class A	PACAX	B-	C+	B	Up	2.52	5.00	9.72	14.84	37.04	0.35	10.94	1,140	617-292-1000	Y
Fidelity Freedom® Income Fund Class K6	FYTKX	B-	C+	B	Up	1.73	3.72	8.22	13.28	23.44	0.35	11.77	3,795	617-563-7000	Y
MFS® Conservative Allocation Fund Class R4	MACJX	B	C+	A-	Up	2.34	4.63	11.05	16.42	33.25	0.36	15.5	2,981	877-960-6077	Y
MFS® Conservative Allocation Fund Class R2	MCARX	B	C+	A-	Up	2.26	4.35	10.52	14.68	29.92	0.36	15.07	2,981	877-960-6077	Y
American Funds College 2024 Fund Class 529-A	CFTAX	B	C+	A-	Up	1.54	3.69	7.90	12.67	39.82	0.36	11.92	1,338	800-421-4225	Y
State Farm LifePath Retirement Fund Class Institutional	SLRIX	B	C+	A-	Up	2.43	4.74	10.02	14.07	27.76	0.36	13.46	1,245		Y
State Farm LifePath Retirement Fund Premier Shares	SLRAX	B	C+	B+	Up	2.38	4.80	10.06	13.58	26.47	0.36	13.45	1,245		Y
MFS® Conservative Allocation Fund Class 529C	ECACX	B	C+	A-	Up	2.10	4.11	9.97	12.78	26.44	0.36	15.13	2,981	877-960-6077	Y
State Farm LifePath Retirement Fund Class R1	RLROX	B-	C+	B+	Up	2.38	4.71	9.84	12.56	24.62	0.36	13.2	1,245		Y
State Farm LifePath Retirement Fund Legacy Class B	SLRBX	B-	C+	B+	Up	2.41	4.79	9.93	12.42	24.28	0.36	13.55	1,245		Y
State Farm LifePath Retirement Fund Class B	NILBX	B-	C	B+	Up	2.39	4.74	9.71	11.59	23.17	0.36	13.23	1,245		Y
Thrivent Series Moderately Conservative Alloc Port		B-	C+	B	Up	2.11	4.53	9.51	16.67	34.96	0.36	13.6166	5,112		Y
American Funds College 2024 Fund Class 529F1	CTFFX	B-	C+	B	Up	1.57	3.80	8.09	13.38	41.31	0.36	11.95	1,338	800-421-4225	Y
Principal Strat Asset Mgmt Flexible Income Fund Inst Cls	PIFIX	B-	C+	B	Up	1.83	3.91	8.14	13.55	29.89	0.36	12.46	2,772	800-222-5852	Y
American Funds College 2024 Fund Class 529-E	CTFEX	B-	C	B	Up	1.42	3.58	7.61	11.78	37.91	0.36	11.88	1,338	800-421-4225	Y
American Funds College 2024 Fund Class 529-C	CTFCX	B-	C	B	Up	1.34	3.34	7.02	10.04	34.39	0.36	11.81	1,338	800-421-4225	Y
MFS® Conservative Allocation Fund Class I	MACIX	B	C+	A-	Up	2.32	4.59	11.03	16.44	33.23	0.37	15.63	2,981	877-960-6077	Y
MFS® Conservative Allocation Fund Class 529A	ECLAX	B	C+	A-	Up	2.34	4.50	10.81	15.44	31.35	0.37	15.42	2,981	877-960-6077	Y
MFS® Conservative Allocation Fund Class A	MACFX	B	C+	A-	Up	2.33	4.50	10.78	15.56	31.61	0.37	15.5	2,981	877-960-6077	Y
MFS® Conservative Allocation Fund Class R3	MACNX	B	C+	A-	Up	2.28	4.46	10.80	15.53	31.62	0.37	15.37	2,981	877-960-6077	Y
Principal Strat Asset Mgmt Flexible Income Fund R-4 Cls	PFILX	B	C	A-	Up	1.74	3.73	7.76	12.37	27.63	0.37	12.45	2,772	800-222-5852	Y
State Farm LifePath Retirement Fund Class R3	RLRHX	B	C+	B+	Up	2.41	4.71	9.96	13.84	27.28	0.37	13.44	1,245		Y
MFS® Conservative Allocation Fund Class R1	MACKX	B	C+	A-	Up	2.07	4.10	9.96	12.95	26.76	0.37	14.98	2,981	877-960-6077	Y
MFS® Conservative Allocation Fund Class B	MACBX	B	C+	A-	Up	2.13	4.10	10.00	13.03	26.80	0.37	15.42	2,981	877-960-6077	Y
MFS® Conservative Allocation Fund Class 529B	EBCAX	B	C+	A-	Up	2.09	4.02	9.92	12.82	26.42	0.37	15.18	2,981	877-960-6077	Y
State Farm LifePath Retirement Fund Class A	NILAX	B	C+	B+	Up	2.41	4.78	9.94	13.46	26.39	0.37	13.15	1,245		Y
State Farm LifePath Retirement Fund Class R2	RLRTX	B-	C+	B+	Up	2.40	4.69	9.92	13.10	25.68	0.37	13.5	1,245		Y
AXA Conservative Growth Strategy Fund Class IB	US2689543443	B-	C+	B	Up	2.00	3.99	8.03	12.41	30.62	0.37		1,605	877-222-2144	Y
Principal Strat Asset Mgmt Flexible Income Fund R-5 Cls	PFIFX	B-	C+	B	Up	1.78	3.79	7.89	12.72	28.34	0.37	12.44	2,772	800-222-5852	Y
Principal Strat Asset Mgmt Flexible Income Fund R-2 Cls	PFIVX	B-	C	B	Up	1.57	3.45	7.37	11.09	25.24	0.37	12.44	2,772	800-222-5852	Y
MFS® Conservative Allocation Fund Class C	MACVX	B	C+	A-	Up	2.15	4.15	10.03	13.05	26.77	0.38	15.28	2,981	877-960-6077	Y
Principal Strat Asset Mgmt Flexible Income Fund R-3 Cls	PFIPX	B	C	A-	Up	1.70	3.63	7.55	11.72	26.43	0.38	12.44	2,772	800-222-5852	Y
AXA Conservative-Plus Allocation Portfolio Class K	US00247C5774	B-	C+	B	Up	2.28	4.35	9.26	13.67	31.48	0.38		1,391	877-222-2144	Y
AXA Premier VIP Conservative-Plus Alloc Fund Cl B	US00247C7424	B-	C+	B	Up	2.13	4.21	8.89	12.83	29.72	0.38		1,391	877-222-2144	Y
AXA Premier VIP Conservative-Plus Alloc Fund Cl A	US00247C7598	B-	C+	B	Up	2.13	4.21	8.89	12.72	29.59	0.38		1,391	877-222-2144	Y
Principal Strategic Asset Mgmt Flexible Income Fund Cls J	PFIJX	B-	C+	B	Up	1.81	3.86	8.04	12.96	28.43	0.38	12.4	2,772	800-222-5852	Y
Principal Strategic Asset Mgmt Flexible Income Fund Cls C	SCUPX	B-	C	B+	Up	0.92	2.72	6.37	9.34	22.33	0.39	12.38	2,772	800-222-5852	Y
Principal Strat Asset Mgmt Flexible Income Fund R-1 Cls	PFIGX	B-	C	B	Up	1.62	3.49	7.26	10.63	24.44	0.39	12.41	2,772	800-222-5852	Y
BlackRock LifePath® Index Retmnt Fund Inv A Shares	LIRAX	B	C+	A-	Up	2.39	4.96	10.42	15.56	31.94	0.4	12.25	1,210	800-441-7762	Y
Principal Strategic Asset Mgmt Flexible Income Fund Cls A	SAUPX	B-	C+	B	Up	1.76	3.75	7.80	12.54	27.88	0.4	12.5	2,772	800-222-5852	Y
MFS® Diversified Income Fund Class R6	DIFHX	B	C+	A-	Up	1.34	3.74	8.97	15.93	39.01	0.41	12.57	4,106	877-960-6077	Y
MFS® Diversified Income Fund Class R4	DIFGX	B	C+	A-	Up	1.32	3.69	8.78	15.58	38.34	0.41	12.57	4,106	877-960-6077	Y
MFS® Diversified Income Fund Class A	DIFAX	B	C+	A-	Up	1.26	3.57	8.60	14.73	36.64	0.41	12.57	4,106	877-960-6077	Y
MFS® Diversified Income Fund Class R3	DIFFX	B	C+	A-	Up	1.26	3.57	8.51	14.73	36.52	0.41	12.57	4,106	877-960-6077	Y
MFS® Diversified Income Fund Class R2	DIFEX	B	C+	B+	Up	1.20	3.44	8.25	13.88	34.85	0.41	12.56	4,106	877-960-6077	Y

		RATINGS				TOTAL RETURNS & PERFORMANCE						ASSETS		NEW INVESTORS	
Fund Name	Ticker Symbol	Overall Rating	Reward Rating	Risk Rating	Recent Up/ Downgrade	3-Month Total Return	6-Month Total Return	1-Year Total Return	3-Year Total Return	5-Year Total Return	3-Year Beta	NAV	Total Assets (MIL)	Telephone	Open to New Investors
MFS® Diversified Income Fund Class C	DIFCX	B-	C+	B+	Up	1.08	3.19	7.72	12.20	31.54	0.41	12.56	4,106	877-960-6077	Y
MFS® Diversified Income Fund Class R1	DIFDX	B-	C+	B+	Up	1.08	3.19	7.82	12.20	31.56	0.41	12.55	4,106	877-960-6077	Y
MFS® Diversified Income Fund Class I	DIFIX	B	C+	A-	Up	1.40	3.69	8.87	15.58	38.35	0.42	12.57	4,106	877-960-6077	Y
John Hancock Funds II Multimgr Lifest Cons Cls R4	JSLCX	B-	C	B+	Up	1.15	2.81	7.19	11.22	20.83	0.42	13.03	2,945	800-225-5913	Y
American Funds Tax-Advantaged Income Portfolio Class A	TAIAX	B-	C+	B	Up	3.43	6.98	14.24	21.53	50.22	0.42	13.6	1,756	800-421-4225	Y
John Hancock Funds II Multimgr Lifest Cons Cls C	JCLCX	B-	C	B+	Up	0.93	2.36	6.27	8.47	16.05	0.42	13.06	2,945	800-225-5913	Y
American Funds Tax-Advantaged Income Portfolio Class C	TAICX	B	C+	A-	Up	3.17	6.55	13.36	18.95	44.92	0.43	13.52	1,756	800-421-4225	Y
John Hancock Funds II Multimgr Lifest Cons Cls R5	JTLRX	B-	C	A-	Up	1.28	2.91	7.48	11.92	22.28	0.43	13.04	2,945	800-225-5913	Y
American Funds Tax-Advantaged Income Portfolio Class F-3	TYIFX	B-	C+	B		3.46	7.10	14.54	22.68	52.32	0.43	13.6	1,756	800-421-4225	Y
John Hancock Funds II Multimgr Lifest Cons Cls A	JALRX	B-	C	B+	Up	1.19	2.73	7.11	10.84	20.35	0.43	13.06	2,945	800-225-5913	Y
John Hancock Funds II Multimgr Lifest Cons Cls R2	JQLCX	B-	C	B+	Up	1.09	2.68	6.91	10.49	19.72	0.43	13.04	2,945	800-225-5913	Y
American Funds TaxAdvantaged Income Portfolio Class F2	TXIFX	B-	C+	B		3.43	7.04	14.41	22.55	52.15	0.43	13.61	1,756	800-421-4225	Y
American Funds TaxAdvantaged Income Portfolio Class F1	TAIFX	B-	C+	B	Up	3.37	6.92	14.20	21.56	50.32	0.43	13.59	1,756	800-421-4225	Y
John Hancock Funds II Multimgr Lifest Cons Cls R3	JRLCX	B-	C	B+	Up	1.14	2.63	6.91	10.19	18.85	0.43	13.03	2,945	800-225-5913	Y
John Hancock Funds II Multimgr Lifest Cons Cls 1	JILCX	B	C	A-	Up	1.21	2.92	7.42	12.07	22.58	0.44	13.03	2,945	800-225-5913	Y
John Hancock Funds II Multimgr Lifest Cons Cls R1	JPLCX	B-	C	B+	Up	1.10	2.55	6.74	9.67	17.93	0.44	13.05	2,945	800-225-5913	Y
Vanguard Target Retirement Income Fund Investor Shares	VTINX	B	C+	A-	Up	2.03	4.03	8.47	13.79	27.66	0.47	13.55	16,864	877-662-7447	Y
Transamerica Asset Allocation Moderate Portfolio Class A	IMOAX	B	C+	A-	Up	2.45	5.43	12.45	18.15	41.87	0.47	12.07	1,954	888-233-4339	Y
Transamerica Asset Allocation Moderate Portfolio Class C	IMOLX	B	C+	A-	Up	2.34	5.08	11.62	15.62	36.92	0.47	12.07	1,954	888-233-4339	Y
State Farm LifePath 2020 Fund Class Institutional	SAWIX	B	C+	B+	Up	2.77	5.37	11.47	15.77	34.71	0.47	15	2,168		Y
State Farm LifePath 2020 Fund Premier Shares	SAWAX	B-	C+	B+	Up	2.84	5.46	11.53	15.38	33.56	0.47	14.89	2,168		Y
State Farm LifePath 2020 Fund Legacy Class B	SAWBX	B-	C+	B+	Up	2.77	5.37	11.38	14.09	31.10	0.47	15.06	2,168		Y
State Farm LifePath 2020 Fund Class B	NLWBX	B-	C+	B+	Up	2.75	5.37	11.21	13.32	29.37	0.47	14.9	2,168		Y
Transamerica Asset Alloc Moderate Port Fund Cls T1	TMMTX	B-	C+	B	Up	2.52	5.51	12.52	18.24	41.97	0.47	12.13	1,954	888-233-4339	Y
BlackRock LifePath® Index 2020 Fund Investor A Shares	LIQAX	B-	C+	B	Up	2.85	5.62	12.02	17.45	39.64	0.47	12.71	2,371	800-441-7762	Y
Transamerica Asset Allocation Moderate Portfolio Class R	IMDRX	B-	C+	B	Up	2.45	5.37	12.22	17.35	40.34	0.47	12.03	1,954	888-233-4339	Y
State Farm LifePath 2020 Fund Class R3	RAWHX	B	C+	B+	Up	2.71	5.31	11.42	15.51	34.22	0.48	14.97	2,168		Y
State Farm LifePath 2020 Fund Class A	NLWAX	B-	C+	B+	Up	2.77	5.38	11.42	15.08	33.36	0.48	14.97	2,168		Y
State Farm LifePath 2020 Fund Class R2	RAWTX	B-	C+	B+	Up	2.78	5.33	11.32	14.80	32.59	0.48	14.89	2,168		Y
State Farm LifePath 2020 Fund Class R1	RAWOX	B-	C+	B+	Up	2.74	5.29	11.28	14.21	31.43	0.48	14.89	2,168		Y
Transamerica Asset Allocation Moderate Portfolio Fund Adv	TMMVX	B-	C+	B	Up	0.76	4.36	11.93	17.61	41.23	0.48	13.42	1,954	888-233-4339	Y
AXA Balanced Strategy Fund Class IB	US2689543286	B-	C+	B	Up	2.60	5.10	9.90	15.09	38.70	0.48		3,656	877-222-2144	Y
AXA Balanced Strategy Fund Class IA	US2689543369	B-	C+	B	Up	2.67	5.10	9.98	15.10	38.86	0.48		3,656	877-222-2144	Y
American Funds Income Portfolio Class F-2	INPEX	B-	C+	B	Up	2.43	5.65	11.70	19.72	45.54	0.49	12.72	4,631	800-421-4225	Y
AXA Moderate Allocation Portfolio Class K	US00247C5691	B-	C+	B	Up	2.79	5.51	11.40	16.22	38.17	0.49		8,094	877-222-2144	Y
American Funds Income Portfolio Class 529-A	CIPAX	B-	C+	B	Up	2.36	5.51	11.42	18.59	43.36	0.49	12.7	4,631	800-421-4225	Y
AXA Premier VIP Moderate Allocation Fund Class B		B-	C+	B	Up	2.71	5.30	11.07	15.32	36.34	0.49		8,094	877-222-2144	Y
AXA Premier VIP Moderate Allocation Fund Class A	US4049924974	B-	C+	B	Up	2.68	5.26	11.06	15.29	36.39	0.49		8,094	877-222-2144	Y
JPMorgan Income Builder Fund Class A Shares	JNBAX	B-	C+	B	Up	2.86	5.57	11.84	18.70	35.56	0.49	10.75	12,883	800-480-4111	Y
JPMorgan Income Builder Fund Class T	JIBTX	B-	C+	B	Up	2.76	5.55	11.65	18.33	34.85	0.49	10.75	12,883	800-480-4111	Y
American Funds Income Portfolio Class 529-E	CIPEX	B-	C+	B	Up	2.36	5.37	11.15	17.89	41.72	0.49	12.7	4,631	800-421-4225	Y
JPMorgan Income Builder Fund Class C Shares	JNBCX	B-	C+	B	Up	2.64	5.32	11.20	16.95	32.16	0.49	10.72	12,883	800-480-4111	Y
Franklin Conservative Allocation Fund Class A	FTCIX	B-	C+	B	Up	1.80	4.48	10.58	12.59	29.55	0.49	14.86	1,380	650-312-2000	Y
American Funds College 2027 Fund Class 529F1	CTSFX	B	C+	A-	Up	2.40	5.51	12.04	18.02	51.77	0.5	12.69	1,076	800-421-4225	Y
American Funds College 2027 Fund Class 529-A	CSTAX	B	C+	A-	Up	2.37	5.40	11.77	17.23	50.24	0.5	12.65	1,076	800-421-4225	Y
American Funds College 2027 Fund Class 529-E	CTSEX	B	C+	B+	Up	2.30	5.19	11.48	16.41	48.33	0.5	12.58	1,076	800-421-4225	Y
Fidelity Freedom® Index 2015 Fund Inst Premium Cls	FIWFX	B-	C+	B	Up	3.11	6.11	12.66	18.62	39.10	0.5	15.02	1,160	617-563-7000	Y
American Funds Income Portfolio Class R-5E	RGOFX	B-	C+	B	Up	2.52	5.65	11.80	19.74	45.76	0.5	12.7	4,631	800-421-4225	Y
American Funds Income Portfolio Class R-6	RINGX	B-	C+	B	Up	2.46	5.71	11.82	20.07	46.20	0.5	12.72	4,631	800-421-4225	Y
American Funds Income Portfolio Class F-3	INPDX	B-	C+	B	Up	2.47	5.72	11.93	19.97	46.04	0.5	12.7	4,631	800-421-4225	Y
American Funds Income Portfolio Class R-5	RINFX	B-	C+	B	Up	2.45	5.68	11.85	19.88	45.93	0.5	12.73	4,631	800-421-4225	Y
American Funds Income Portfolio Class 529-F-1	CIPFX	B-	C+	B	Up	2.42	5.63	11.65	19.51	44.93	0.5	12.71	4,631	800-421-4225	Y

		RATINGS				TOTAL RETURNS & PERFORMANCE						ASSETS	NEW INVESTORS		
Fund Name	Ticker Symbol	Overall Rating	Reward Rating	Risk Rating	Recent Up/ Downgrade	3-Month Total Return	6-Month Total Return	1-Year Total Return	3-Year Total Return	5-Year Total Return	3-Year Beta	NAV	Total Assets (MIL)	Telephone	Open to New Investors
American Funds Income Portfolio Class A	INPAX	B-	C+	B	Up	2.45	5.54	11.56	18.96	43.89	0.5	12.71	4,631	800-421-4225	Y
American Funds Income Portfolio Class R-2E	RNBEX	B-	C+	B	Up	2.24	5.26	10.93	18.38	42.59	0.5	12.7	4,631	800-421-4225	Y
American Funds Income Portfolio Class R-4	RINEX	B-	C+	B	Up	2.45	5.52	11.46	18.92	43.85	0.5	12.71	4,631	800-421-4225	Y
American Funds Income Portfolio Class F-1	INPFX	B-	C+	B	Up	2.36	5.51	11.42	18.81	43.58	0.5	12.71	4,631	800-421-4225	Y
American Funds Income Portfolio Class R-3	RNCCX	B-	C+	B	Up	2.36	5.37	11.16	17.81	41.57	0.5	12.69	4,631	800-421-4225	Y
American Funds College 2027 Fund Class 529-C	CTSCX	B-	C+	B	Up	2.10	4.92	10.87	14.48	44.30	0.5	12.52	1,076	800-421-4225	Y
American Funds Income Portfolio Class C	INPCX	B-	C+	B	Up	2.24	5.13	10.70	16.22	38.48	0.5	12.65	4,631	800-421-4225	Y
American Funds Income Portfolio Class R-1	RNCAX	B-	C+	B	Up	2.22	5.19	10.73	16.25	38.50	0.5	12.67	4,631	800-421-4225	Y
American Funds Income Portfolio Class R-2	RINBX	B-	C+	B	Up	2.24	5.13	10.70	16.21	38.34	0.5	12.66	4,631	800-421-4225	Y
American Funds Income Portfolio Class 529-C	CIPCX	B-	C+	B	Up	2.18	5.05	10.58	15.97	37.98	0.5	12.66	4,631	800-421-4225	Y
Franklin Conservative Allocation Fund Advisor Class	FTCZX	B-	C+	B	Up	1.87	4.63	10.87	13.50	31.26	0.5	14.86	1,380	650-312-2000	Y
USAA Cornerstone Moderate Fund	USBSX	B-	C+	B	Up	3.00	5.92	13.40	13.73	32.12	0.51	14.98	1,175	800-531-8722	Y
JPMorgan Hedged Equity Fund Class R5	JHQPX	B-	C+	B	Down	3.00	6.36	12.92	22.61		0.53	19.36	1,443	800-480-4111	Y
JPMorgan Hedged Equity Fund Class A	JHQAX	B-	C+	B	Down	2.90	6.16	12.44	21.01		0.53	19.29	1,443	800-480-4111	Y
JPMorgan Hedged Equity Fund Class C	JHQCX	B-	C+	B	Down	2.76	5.92	11.89	19.21		0.53	19.2	1,443	800-480-4111	Y
Vanguard Target Retirement 2020 Fund Investor Shares	VTWNX	B-	C+	B	Up	3.36	6.61	14.08	20.66	51.63	0.54	31.38	32,239	877-662-7447	Y
AXA/Franklin Bal Managed Volatility Portfolio Cls IB	US2689547998	B-	C+	B	Up	2.40	5.46	9.95	16.98	44.64	0.54		1,284	877-222-2144	Y
AXA/Franklin Bal Managed Volatility Portfolio Cls IA	US2689548152	B-	C+	B	Up	2.40	5.46	9.95	16.98	44.80	0.54		1,284	877-222-2144	Y
MFS® Total Return Fund Class R6	MSFKX	B-	C+	B	Down	3.48	5.75	12.52	22.19	60.47	0.55	19.13	8,026	877-960-6077	Y
MFS® Total Return Fund Class I	MTRIX	B-	C+	B	Down	3.46	5.65	12.37	21.82	59.74	0.55	19.12	8,026	877-960-6077	Y
MFS® Total Return Fund Class R4	MSFJX	B-	C+	B	Up	3.40	5.65	12.36	21.79	59.75	0.55	19.14	8,026	877-960-6077	Y
MFS® Total Return Fund Class 529A	EATRX	B-	C+	B	Up	3.34	5.52	12.09	20.74	57.41	0.55	19.07	8,026	877-960-6077	Y
MFS® Total Return Fund Class A	MSFRX	B-	C+	B	Up	3.40	5.58	12.16	20.96	57.84	0.55	19.13	8,026	877-960-6077	Y
MFS® Total Return Fund Class R3	MSFHX	B-	C+	B	Up	3.39	5.57	12.14	20.92	57.75	0.55	19.14	8,026	877-960-6077	Y
MFS® Total Return Fund Class R2	MTRRX	B-	C+	B	Up	3.32	5.37	11.84	20.01	55.81	0.55	19.18	8,026	877-960-6077	Y
State Farm Balanced Fund	STFBX	B-	C+	B	Down	4.41	6.72	11.39	19.77	52.68	0.55	68.69	1,951		Y
MFS® Total Return Fund Class B	MTRBX	B-	C+	B	Up	3.19	5.16	11.29	18.24	51.94	0.55	19.15	8,026	877-960-6077	Y
MFS® Total Return Fund Class C	MTRCX	B-	C+	B	Up	3.17	5.14	11.23	18.16	51.88	0.55	19.24	8,026	877-960-6077	Y
MFS® Total Return Fund Class R1	MSFFX	B-	C+	B	Up	3.20	5.13	11.27	18.18	51.97	0.55	19.1	8,026	877-960-6077	Y
MFS® Total Return Fund Class 529B	EBTRX	B-	C+	B	Up	3.18	5.14	11.24	18.05	51.55	0.55	19.15	8,026	877-960-6077	Y
MFS® Total Return Fund Class 529C	ECTRX	B-	C+	B	Up	3.16	5.12	11.26	18.02	51.57	0.55	19.23	8,026	877-960-6077	Y
AXA/Franklin Balanced Managed Vol Portfolio Class K	US26883L6544	B-	C+	B	Up	2.55	5.62	10.32	17.86	46.65	0.55		1,284	877-222-2144	Y
Fidelity Freedom® Index 2020 Fund Inst Premium Cls	FIWTX	B-	C+	B	Up	3.52	6.76	13.95	20.36	43.19	0.56	15.8	3,828	617-563-7000	Y
AXA/AB Dynamic Moderate Growth Portfolio Class IB	US26884M6518	B-	C+	B	Up	3.35	6.35	12.98	15.59	43.45	0.56		2,779	877-222-2144	Y
Principal Global Multi-Strategy Fund R-6	PGLSX	B-	C	B	Up	1.53	3.24	6.46	9.04	19.31	0.63	11.29	2,814	800-222-5852	Y
Principal Global Multi-Strategy Fund Inst Cls Shares	PSMIX	B-	C	B	Up	1.56	3.36	6.59	9.17	19.46	0.63	11.3	2,814	800-222-5852	Y
Principal Global Diversified Income Fund Class R-6	PGBLX	B	C+	B+	Up	1.66	4.42	10.25	17.90	34.02	0.72	14.14	12,450	800-222-5852	Y
Principal Global Diversified Income Fund Class C	PGDCX	B-	C+	B	Up	1.32	3.79	9.00	14.09	26.92	0.72	14.11	12,450	800-222-5852	Y
Principal Global Diversified Income Fund Institutional Cls	PGDIX	B-	C+	B	Up	1.65	4.40	10.23	17.88	33.99	0.72	14.14	12,450	800-222-5852	Y
Principal Global Diversified Income Fund Class T	PGKTX	B-	C+	B	Up	2.53	5.24	10.97	18.08	33.55	0.72	14.28	12,450	800-222-5852	Y
Principal Global Diversified Income Fund Class A	PGBAX	B-	C+	B	Up	1.57	4.24	9.85	16.78	31.86	0.72	14.2	12,450	800-222-5852	Y
JNL Institutional Alt 50 Fund Class I	US46644W5426	B-	C+	B		3.00	5.27	10.71	12.48	27.96	0.81	17.15	2,911		Y
Principal Preferred Securities Fund Class J	PPSJX	B	C+	A+	Up	0.83	2.20	10.26	19.32	34.36	0.85	10.19	6,014	800-222-5852	Y
Principal Preferred Securities Fund Institutional Class	PPSIX	B	C+	A+	Up	0.86	2.34	10.50	20.27	36.71	0.86	10.39	6,014	800-222-5852	Y
Principal Global Invs Funds Preferred Securities Fund R-6	PPREX	B	C+	A+	Up	0.98	2.39	10.52	20.30	36.74	0.86	10.39	6,014	800-222-5852	Y
Principal Global Invs Funds Preferred Sec Fund Cls T	PPBTX	B	C+	A+	Up	0.88	2.22	10.23	19.38	35.03	0.86	10.39	6,014	800-222-5852	Y
Principal Preferred Securities Fund Class A	PPSAX	B	C+	A+	Up	0.78	2.20	10.22	19.18	34.65	0.86	10.46	6,014	800-222-5852	Y
Principal Preferred Securities Fund R-2 Class	PPRSX	B	C+	A+	Up	0.70	2.03	9.77	17.82	32.11	0.86	10.28	6,014	800-222-5852	Y
Principal Preferred Securities Fund R-4 Class	PQARX	B	C+	A+	Up	0.79	2.20	10.14	19.08	34.58	0.86	10.3	6,014	800-222-5852	Y
Principal Preferred Securities Fund R-5 Class	PPARX	B	C+	A+	Up	0.92	2.27	10.34	19.66	35.50	0.86	10.35	6,014	800-222-5852	Y
Principal Preferred Securities Fund R-1 Class	PUSAX	B	C+	A+	Up	0.66	1.94	9.66	17.36	31.26	0.86	10.34	6,014	800-222-5852	Y
Principal Preferred Securities Fund Class C	PRFCX	B	C+	A+	Up	0.69	1.81	9.40	16.56	29.77	0.86	10.45	6,014	800-222-5852	Y

Fund Name	Ticker Symbol	RATINGS: Overall Rating	RATINGS: Reward Rating	RATINGS: Risk Rating	RATINGS: Recent Up/ Downgrade	TOTAL RETURNS & PERFORMANCE: 3-Month Total Return	6-Month Total Return	1-Year Total Return	3-Year Total Return	5-Year Total Return	3-Year Beta	ASSETS: NAV	Total Assets (MIL)	NEW INVESTORS: Telephone	Open to New Investors
Principal Preferred Securities Fund R-3 Class	PNARX	B	C+	A+	Up	0.74	2.11	9.91	18.48	33.37	0.86	10.32	6,014	800-222-5852	Y
American Funds 2020 Target Date Retirement Fund® Class R-5	RECTX	B-	C+	B	Up	2.84	5.95	12.85	20.39	54.25	0.87	12.64	11,839	800-421-4225	Y
American Funds 2020 Target Date Retirement Fund® Class F-3	FCCTX	B-	C+	B	Up	2.76	5.96	12.89	20.44	54.31	0.87	12.56	11,839	800-421-4225	Y
American Funds 2020 Target Date Retirement Fund® Cls R-5E	RHCTX	B-	C+	B	Up	2.75	5.88	12.65	20.12	53.91	0.87	12.51	11,839	800-421-4225	Y
American Funds 2020 Target Date Retirement Fund® Class F-1	FAOTX	B-	C+	B	Up	2.72	5.77	12.36	19.17	51.93	0.87	12.49	11,839	800-421-4225	Y
American Funds 2020 Target Date Retirement Fund® Class R-4	RDCTX	B-	C+	B	Up	2.70	5.83	12.50	19.23	51.89	0.87	12.54	11,839	800-421-4225	Y
American Funds 2020 Target Date Retirement Fund® Class A	AACTX	B-	C+	B	Up	2.68	5.80	12.45	19.21	51.93	0.87	12.56	11,839	800-421-4225	Y
American Funds 2020 Target Date Retirement Fund® Class R-3	RCCTX	B-	C+	B	Up	2.64	5.62	12.12	18.14	49.61	0.87	12.47	11,839	800-421-4225	Y
American Funds 2020 Target Date Retirement Fund® Cls R-2E	RBEHX	B-	C+	B	Up	2.56	5.55	11.88	17.92	49.52	0.87	12.4	11,839	800-421-4225	Y
American Funds 2020 Target Date Retirement Fund® Class C	CCCTX	B-	C+	B	Up	2.53	5.44	11.59	16.63	46.44	0.87	12.4	11,839	800-421-4225	Y
American Funds 2020 Target Date Retirement Fund® Class R-2	RBCTX	B-	C+	B	Up	2.55	5.38	11.63	16.69	46.74	0.87	12.38	11,839	800-421-4225	Y
American Funds 2020 Target Date Retirement Fund® Class R-1	RACTX	B-	C+	B	Up	2.49	5.40	11.54	16.46	46.06	0.87	12.43	11,839	800-421-4225	Y
American Funds 2015 Target Date Retirement Fund® Cls R-2E	RBEJX	B	C+	A-	Up	2.26	4.91	10.34	15.95	43.09	0.88	11.44	4,471	800-421-4225	Y
American Funds 2020 Target Date Retirement Fund® Class R-6	RRCTX	B-	C+	B	Up	2.83	5.94	12.86	20.53	54.65	0.88	12.6	11,839	800-421-4225	Y
American Funds 2020 Target Date Retirement Fund® Class F-2	FBCTX	B-	C+	B	Up	2.77	5.90	12.75	20.11	53.94	0.88	12.54	11,839	800-421-4225	Y
KP Retirement Path 2025 Fund Institutional Shares	KPRCX	B-	C+	B	Up	3.38	6.99	14.58	21.28		0.88	11.22	1,047		Y
Nuveen Preferred Securities & Income Fund Class R3	NPSTX	B	C+	A+	Up	1.06	2.57	10.64	20.63	36.56	0.89	17.81	3,997	312-917-8146	Y
American Funds 2015 Target Date Retirement Fund® Class R-1	RAJTX	B	C+	B+	Up	2.16	4.64	9.98	14.46	39.53	0.89	11.43	4,471	800-421-4225	Y
American Funds 2015 Target Date Retirement Fund® Class R-6	RFJTX	B-	C+	B	Up	2.43	5.31	11.18	18.41	47.73	0.89	11.61	4,471	800-421-4225	Y
American Funds 2015 Target Date Retirement Fund® Cls R-5E	RHBTX	B-	C+	B	Up	2.42	5.24	11.04	17.95	47.07	0.89	11.54	4,471	800-421-4225	Y
American Funds 2015 Target Date Retirement Fund® Class R-4	RDBTX	B-	C+	B	Up	2.28	5.09	10.77	17.11	45.13	0.89	11.57	4,471	800-421-4225	Y
American Funds 2015 Target Date Retirement Fund® Class A	AABTX	B-	C+	B	Up	2.35	5.06	10.83	17.12	45.07	0.89	11.59	4,471	800-421-4225	Y
American Funds 2015 Target Date Retirement Fund® Class R-3	RCJTX	B-	C+	B	Up	2.32	4.96	10.57	16.17	42.92	0.89	11.52	4,471	800-421-4225	Y
American Funds 2015 Target Date Retirement Fund® Class C	CCBTX	B-	C+	B	Up	2.19	4.76	9.98	14.53	39.92	0.89	11.46	4,471	800-421-4225	Y
American Funds 2015 Target Date Retirement Fund® Class R-2	RBJTX	B	C+	B+	Up	2.15	4.71	10.05	14.66	40.07	0.9	11.44	4,471	800-421-4225	Y
American Funds 2015 Target Date Retirement Fund® Class F-3	FDBTX	B-	C+	B	Up	2.49	5.38	11.26	18.35	47.57	0.9	11.6	4,471	800-421-4225	Y
American Funds 2015 Target Date Retirement Fund® Class R-5	REJTX	B-	C+	B	Up	2.44	5.31	11.16	18.25	47.44	0.9	11.66	4,471	800-421-4225	Y
American Funds 2015 Target Date Retirement Fund® Class F-2	FBBTX	B-	C+	B	Up	2.43	5.23	11.12	18.09	47.15	0.9	11.58	4,471	800-421-4225	Y
American Funds 2015 Target Date Retirement Fund® Class F-1	FAKTX	B-	C+	B	Up	2.35	5.08	10.78	17.11	45.24	0.9	11.53	4,471	800-421-4225	Y
Cohen & Steers Preferred Sec & Income Fund, Inc. Cls F	CPXFX	B	C+	A+	Up	0.99	2.77	11.31	23.54	42.48	0.92	14.16	7,962	212-832-3232	Y
Cohen & Steers Preferred Sec & Income Fund, Inc. Cls Z	CPXZX	B	C+	A+	Up	1.06	2.84	11.41	23.66	42.52	0.92	14.16	7,962	212-832-3232	Y
Cohen & Steers Preferred Sec & Income Fund, Inc. Cls A	CPXAX	B	C+	A+	Up	0.97	2.66	11.04	22.42	40.12	0.92	14.14	7,962	212-832-3232	Y
Cohen & Steers Preferred Sec & Income Fund, Inc. Cls R	CPRRX	B	C+	A+	Up	0.93	2.58	10.85	21.83	39.02	0.92	14.15	7,962	212-832-3232	Y
Cohen & Steers Preferred Sec & Income Fund, Inc. Cls C	CPXCX	B	C+	A+	Up	0.81	2.34	10.30	20.00	35.66	0.92	14.06	7,962	212-832-3232	Y
Goldman Sachs Absolute Return Tracker Fund Investor Class	GSRTX	B-	C	B	Up	1.91	3.96	7.24	9.61	22.88	0.93	9.5	1,621	800-526-7384	Y
American Century Inv One Choice 2025 Port R6 Cls	ARWDX	B-	C+	B	Up	2.87	5.91	12.56	17.91	46.62	0.94	11.79	3,307	800-444-4015	Y
Goldman Sachs Absolute Return Tracker Fund Class A	GARTX	B-	C	B	Up	1.84	3.81	6.92	8.71	21.31	0.94	9.31	1,621	800-526-7384	Y
American Century Inv One Choice 2020 Port R6 Cls	ARBDX	B-	C+	B	Up	2.56	5.29	11.11	16.25	41.86	0.99	11.49	2,272	800-444-4015	Y
JPMorgan SmartRetirement® 2020 Fund Class R4	JTTQX	B	C+	A-	Up	3.20	6.54	13.77	18.93	46.52	1	19.77	7,320	800-480-4111	Y
JPMorgan SmartRetirement® 2020 Fund Class R2	JTTZX	B	C+	A-	Up	3.04	6.25	13.27	17.33	43.10	1	19.67	7,320	800-480-4111	Y
TIAA-CREF Lifecycle Index 2020 Fund Advisor Class	TLWHX	B-	C+	B	Up	3.20	6.32	13.59	20.39	50.21	1	16.6	1,468	877-518-9161	Y
TIAA-CREF Lifecycle Index 2020 Fund Premier Class	TLWPX	B-	C+	B	Up	3.16	6.21	13.44	19.92	49.20	1	16.53	1,468	877-518-9161	Y
TIAA-CREF Lifecycle Index 2020 Fund Retirement Class	TLWRX	B-	C+	B	Up	3.12	6.19	13.36	19.63	48.46	1	16.48	1,468	877-518-9161	Y
JPMorgan SmartRetirement® 2020 Fund Class R5	JTTIX	B-	C+	B	Up	3.23	6.65	13.96	19.18	46.84	1	19.82	7,320	800-480-4111	Y
JPMorgan SmartRetirement® 2020 Fund Class A	JTTAX	B-	C+	B	Up	3.18	6.51	13.72	18.35	45.18	1	19.73	7,320	800-480-4111	Y
JPMorgan SmartRetirement® 2020 Fund Class R3	JTTPX	B-	C+	B	Up	3.15	6.43	13.50	18.05	44.71	1	19.68	7,320	800-480-4111	Y
JPMorgan SmartRetirement® 2020 Fund Class C	JTTCX	B-	C+	B	Up	3.03	6.20	13.04	16.10	40.49	1	19.65	7,320	800-480-4111	Y

Section VII:
BUY Rated Stock Mutual Funds by Category

Investment Ratings and analysis for BUY Rated Stock Mutual Funds by Category. Within Category, funds are listed in alphabetical order.

Section VII: Contents

This section contains Weiss Investment Ratings, key rating factors, and summary financial data for BUY Rated Stock Mutual Funds by Category. Within category, funds are listed in alphabetical order.

Fund Name

Describes the fund's assets, regions of investments and investment strategies. Many funds have similar names, so you want to make sure the fund you look up is really the one you are interested in evaluating.

Ticker Symbol

An arrangement of characters (usually letters) representing a particular security listed on an exchange or otherwise traded publicly. When a company issues securities to the public marketplace, it selects an available ticker symbol for its securities which investors use to place trade orders. Every listed security has a unique ticker symbol, facilitating the vast array of trade orders that flow through the financial markets every day. If a ticker symbol is not assigned to a particular fund, the International Securities Identification Number (ISIN) is displayed.

RATINGS

Overall Rating

The Weiss rating measured on a scale from A to E based on each fund's risk and performance. See the preceding section, "What Our Ratings Mean," for an explanation of each letter grade rating.

Reward Rating

This is based on the total return over a period of up to five years, including net asset value and price growth. The total return figure is stated net of the expenses and fees charged by the fund. Based on proprietary modeling the individual components of the risk and reward ratings are calculated and weighted and the final rating is generated.

Risk Rating

This is includes the risk ratings of component stocks where applicable and also includes the financial stability of the fund, turnover where applicable, together with the level of volatility as measured by the fund's daily returns over a period of up to five years. Funds with greater stability are considered less risky and receive a higher risk rating. Funds with greater volatility are considered riskier, and will receive a lower risk rating. In addition to considering the fund's volatility, the risk rating also considers an assessment of the valuation and quality of a fund's holdings.

Recent Upgrade/Downgrade

An "Up" or "Down" indicates that the Weiss Mutual Fund rating has changed since the publication of the last print edition. If a fund has had a rating change since September 30, 2017, the change is identified with an "Up" or "Down."

TOTAL RETURNS & PERFORMANCE

3-Month Total Return
The rate of return on an investment over three months that includes interest, capital gains, dividends and distributions realized.

6-Month Total Return
The rate of return on an investment over six months that includes interest, capital gains, dividends and distributions realized.

1-Year Total Return
The rate of return on an investment over one year that includes interest, capital gains, dividends and distributions realized.

3-Year Total Return
The rate of return on an investment over three years that includes interest, capital gains, dividends and distributions realized.

5-Year Total Return
The rate of return on an investment over five years that includes interest, capital gains, dividends and distributions realized.

ASSETS

NAV (Net Asset Value)
A fund's price per share. The value is calculated by dividing the total value of all the securities in the portfolio, less any liabilities, by the number of fund shares outstanding.

Total Assets (MIL)
The total of all assets listed on the institution's balance sheet. This figure primarily consists of loans, investments, and fixed assets. Total Assets are displayed in millions.

NEW INVESTORS

Telephone
The company's phone number.

Open to New Investors
Indicates whether the fund accepts investments from those who are not existing investors. A "Y" in this column identifies that the fund accepts new investors. No data in this column indicates that the fund is closed to new investors. The fund may be closed to new investors because the fund's asset base is getting too large to effectively execute its investing style. Although, the fund may be closed, in most cases, existing investors are able to add to their holdings.

Category: Aggressive Allocation

		RATINGS				TOTAL RETURNS & PERFORMANCE					ASSETS		NEW INVESTORS	
Fund Name	Ticker Symbol	Overall Rating	Reward Rating	Risk Rating	Recent Up/ Downgrade	3-Month Total Return	6-Month Total Return	1-Year Total Return	3-Year Total Return	5-Year Total Return	NAV	Total Assets (MIL)	Telephone	Open to New Investors
1789 Growth and Income Fund Class Class C	PSECX	B-	C	B		3.17	3.50	5.16	8.45	41.12	12.92	12.0	617-399-0900	Y
1789 Growth and Income Fund Class P	PSEPX	B-	C	B	Down	3.47	4.06	6.25	11.86	47.41	12.99	12.0	617-399-0900	Y
AllianzGI Equity & Convertible Income Fund	NIE	B-	B-	B-	Up	5.65	10.16	16.78	24.59	71.14	23.15	646.5		Y
American Century Inv One Choice Port®: Aggressive Inv Cls	AOGIX	B-	B-	B	Down	4.27	8.95	19.13	24.96	64.72	16.91	1,282	800-444-4015	Y
American Century Inv One Choice Port®: Aggressive R Cls	AORYX	B-	C+	B-	Down	4.18	8.67	18.59	23.14	60.71	16.93	1,282	800-444-4015	Y
American Century Inv One Choice Port®: Very Aggress Inv Cl	AOVIX	B-	B-	B-	Down	5.13	10.72	22.77	29.12	79.62	18.29	306.4	800-444-4015	Y
American Century Inv One Choice Port®: Very Aggress R Cls	AORVX	B-	B-	B-	Down	5.00	10.47	22.20	27.20	75.20	18.32	306.4	800-444-4015	Y
American Century Strategic Alloc: Aggressive Fund A Cls	ACVAX	B-	B-	B-	Down	4.30	8.75	18.91	23.57	60.48	8.38	976.0	800-444-4015	Y
American Century Strategic Alloc: Aggressive Fund C Cls	ASTAX	B-	C+	B-	Down	3.94	8.23	17.98	20.68	54.55	8.2	976.0	800-444-4015	Y
American Century Strategic Alloc: Aggressive Fund I Cls	AAAIX	B-	B-	B-	Down	4.35	8.99	19.31	25.17	64.11	8.25	976.0	800-444-4015	Y
American Century Strategic Alloc: Aggressive Fund Inv Cls	TWSAX	B-	B-	B-	Down	4.36	8.84	19.23	24.40	62.64	8.31	976.0	800-444-4015	Y
American Century Strategic Alloc: Aggressive Fund R Cls	AAARX	B-	C+	B-	Down	4.16	8.62	18.49	22.53	58.37	8.37	976.0	800-444-4015	Y
American Century Strategic Alloc: Aggressive Fund R5 Cls	ASAUX	B-	B-	B-	Down	4.29	9.05	19.33	24.51	62.78	8.26	976.0	800-444-4015	Y
American Century Strategic Alloc: Aggressive Fund R6 Cls	AAAUX	B-	B-	B	Down	4.40	9.05	19.54	25.81	65.06	8.23	976.0	800-444-4015	Y
American Funds College 2030 Fund Class 529-A	CTHAX	B-	C+	B	Up	3.29	6.81	15.27	21.40	59.85	13.61	1,242	800-421-4225	Y
American Funds College 2030 Fund Class 529-C	CTYCX	B-	C+	B	Up	3.12	6.44	14.43	18.52	53.49	13.46	1,242	800-421-4225	Y
American Funds College 2030 Fund Class 529-E	CTHEX	B-	C+	B	Up	3.18	6.63	14.94	20.36	57.50	13.54	1,242	800-421-4225	Y
American Funds College 2030 Fund Class 529F1	CTHFX	B-	C+	B	Up	3.33	7.00	15.53	22.14	61.35	13.65	1,242	800-421-4225	Y
American Funds College 2033 Fund Class 529-A	CTLAX	B-	C+	B	Up	4.15	8.50	19.33			11.7	561.7	800-421-4225	Y
American Funds College 2033 Fund Class 529-C	CTLCX	B-	C+	B	Up	3.91	8.00	18.29			11.62	561.7	800-421-4225	Y
American Funds College 2033 Fund Class 529-E	CTLEX	B-	C+	B	Up	4.02	8.28	18.90			11.66	561.7	800-421-4225	Y
American Funds College 2033 Fund Class 529-F-1	CTLFX	B-	C+	B	Up	4.24	8.58	19.50			11.73	561.7	800-421-4225	Y
American Funds Growth and Income Portfolio Class 529-A	CGNAX	B-	B-	B	Down	4.57	8.69	18.98	26.31	65.79	15.13	7,736	800-421-4225	Y
American Funds Growth and Income Portfolio Class 529-C	CGNCX	B	C+	B+	Up	4.41	8.33	18.05	23.35	59.36	15.07	7,736	800-421-4225	Y
American Funds Growth and Income Portfolio Class 529-E	CGNEX	B-	B-	B	Down	4.57	8.63	18.73	25.37	63.63	15.11	7,736	800-421-4225	Y
American Funds Growth and Income Portfolio Class 529-F-1	CGNFX	B-	B-	B	Down	4.70	8.87	19.29	27.07	67.50	15.15	7,736	800-421-4225	Y
American Funds Growth and Income Portfolio Class A	GAIOX	B	B-	B+	Up	4.65	8.78	19.12	26.57	66.49	15.14	7,736	800-421-4225	Y
American Funds Growth and Income Portfolio Class C	GAITX	B-	C+	B	Down	4.44	8.39	18.17	23.73	59.98	15.06	7,736	800-421-4225	Y
American Funds Growth and Income Portfolio Class F-1	GAIFX	B-	B-	B	Down	4.64	8.76	19.07	26.39	65.94	15.14	7,736	800-421-4225	Y
American Funds Growth and Income Portfolio Class F-2	GAIEX	B-	B-	B	Down	4.71	8.90	19.34	27.39	68.17	15.16	7,736	800-421-4225	Y
American Funds Growth and Income Portfolio Class F-3	GAIHX	B-	B-	B	Down	4.74	8.97	19.48	27.67	68.65	15.14	7,736	800-421-4225	Y
American Funds Growth and Income Portfolio Class R-1	RGNAX	B	C+	B+	Up	4.44	8.36	18.21	23.66	59.98	15.09	7,736	800-421-4225	Y
American Funds Growth and Income Portfolio Class R-2	RGNBX	B-	C+	B	Down	4.38	8.34	18.13	23.60	59.73	15.04	7,736	800-421-4225	Y
American Funds Growth and Income Portfolio Class R-2E	RBEGX	B	B-	B+	Up	4.53	8.52	18.49	25.48	64.01	15.11	7,736	800-421-4225	Y
American Funds Growth and Income Portfolio Class R-3	RAICX	B-	B-	B	Down	4.50	8.56	18.65	25.27	63.42	15.09	7,736	800-421-4225	Y
American Funds Growth and Income Portfolio Class R-4	RGNEX	B-	B-	B	Down	4.57	8.70	19.02	26.40	66.14	15.13	7,736	800-421-4225	Y
American Funds Growth and Income Portfolio Class R-5	RGNFX	B-	B-	B	Down	4.71	8.99	19.46	27.64	68.62	15.19	7,736	800-421-4225	Y
American Funds Growth and Income Portfolio Class R-5E	RGQFX	B-	B-	B	Down	4.72	8.94	19.44	27.35	68.23	15.13	7,736	800-421-4225	Y
American Funds Growth and Income Portfolio Class R-6	RGNGX	B-	B-	B	Down	4.67	8.95	19.46	27.77	68.93	15.16	7,736	800-421-4225	Y
American Funds The Income Fund of America® Class 529-A	CIMAX	B-	C+	B	Down	3.43	7.25	13.27	22.33	58.90	23.32	110,349	800-421-4225	Y
American Funds The Income Fund of America® Class 529-C	CIMCX	B-	C+	B	Down	3.24	6.86	12.40	19.51	52.84	23.25	110,349	800-421-4225	Y
American Funds The Income Fund of America® Class 529-E	CIMEX	B-	C+	B	Down	3.37	7.14	12.98	21.41	56.96	23.25	110,349	800-421-4225	Y
American Funds The Income Fund of America® Class 529-F-1	CIMFX	B-	C+	B	Down	3.48	7.37	13.52	23.12	60.64	23.31	110,349	800-421-4225	Y
American Funds The Income Fund of America® Class A	AMECX	B-	C+	B	Down	3.48	7.32	13.37	22.66	59.65	23.37	110,349	800-421-4225	Y
American Funds The Income Fund of America® Class C	IFACX	B-	C+	B	Down	3.27	6.88	12.48	19.76	53.37	23.08	110,349	800-421-4225	Y
American Funds The Income Fund of America® Class F-1	IFAFX	B-	C+	B	Down	3.46	7.24	13.24	22.28	58.90	23.31	110,349	800-421-4225	Y
American Funds The Income Fund of America® Class F-2	AMEFX	B-	C+	B	Down	3.53	7.41	13.57	23.25	60.99	23.35	110,349	800-421-4225	Y
American Funds The Income Fund of America® Class F-3	FIFAX	B-	C+	B	Down	3.55	7.47	13.64	22.95	60.03	23.36	110,349	800-421-4225	Y
American Funds The Income Fund of America® Class R-1	RIDAX	B-	C+	B	Down	3.24	6.87	12.42	19.65	53.20	23.23	110,349	800-421-4225	Y
American Funds The Income Fund of America® Class R-2	RIDBX	B-	C+	B	Down	3.26	6.87	12.45	19.71	53.27	23.11	110,349	800-421-4225	Y
American Funds The Income Fund of America® Class R-2E	RIEBX	B-	C+	B	Down	3.31	7.02	12.75	20.87	56.44	23.31	110,349	800-421-4225	Y
American Funds The Income Fund of America® Class R-3	RIDCX	B-	C+	B	Down	3.35	7.09	12.94	21.27	56.65	23.28	110,349	800-421-4225	Y

Category: Aggressive Allocation (con't)

Fund Name	Ticker Symbol	RATINGS: Overall Rating	Reward Rating	Risk Rating	Recent Up/ Downgrade	TOTAL RETURNS & PERFORMANCE: 3-Month Total Return	6-Month Total Return	1-Year Total Return	3-Year Total Return	5-Year Total Return	ASSETS: NAV	Total Assets (MIL)	NEW INVESTORS: Telephone	Open to New Investors
American Funds The Income Fund of America® Class R-4	RIDEX	B-	C+	B	Down	3.47	7.29	13.31	22.38	59.04	23.33	110,349	800-421-4225	Y
American Funds The Income Fund of America® Class R-5	RIDFX	B-	C+	B	Down	3.49	7.39	13.56	23.44	61.39	23.36	110,349	800-421-4225	Y
American Funds The Income Fund of America® Class R-5E	RIDHX	B-	C+	B	Down	3.48	7.35	13.46	22.85	59.89	23.34	110,349	800-421-4225	Y
American Funds The Income Fund of America® Class R-6	RIDGX	B-	C+	B	Down	3.50	7.42	13.67	23.62	61.77	23.37	110,349	800-421-4225	Y
Archer Balanced Fund	ARCHX	B-	C+	B	Down	17.23	21.06	29.07	34.80	86.21	13.02	35.6		Y
AXA Aggressive Allocation Portfolio Class K	US00247C5444	B-	B-	B-	Down	5.29	9.94	19.50	27.02	73.69		3,568	877-222-2144	Y
AXA Aggressive Strategy Portfolio Class IB	US26884M6443	B-	B-	B	Down	4.58	8.46	15.83	23.82	66.61		3,516	877-222-2144	Y
AXA Growth Strategy Fund Class IA	US2689542866	B-	C+	B	Up	3.97	7.38	13.84	20.87	56.96		5,165	877-222-2144	Y
AXA Growth Strategy Fund Class IB	US2689542783	B-	C+	B	Up	3.91	7.31	13.84	20.86	56.91		5,165	877-222-2144	Y
AXA Moderate-Plus Allocation Portfolio Class K	US00247C5519	B-	C+	B	Down	4.01	7.67	15.29	21.68	55.20		9,736	877-222-2144	Y
AXA Premier VIP Aggressive Allocation Fund Class A	US00247C7184	B-	B-	B-	Down	5.14	9.79	19.13	26.01	71.46		3,568	877-222-2144	Y
AXA Premier VIP Aggressive Allocation Fund Class B	US00247C6921	B-	B-	B-	Down	5.23	9.78	19.23	26.11	71.59		3,568	877-222-2144	Y
AXA Premier VIP Moderate-Plus Allocation Fund Class A	US00247C7341	B-	C+	B	Down	3.85	7.52	14.92	20.70	53.18		9,736	877-222-2144	Y
AXA Premier VIP Moderate-Plus Allocation Fund Class B	US00247C7267	B-	C+	B	Down	3.94	7.51	15.02	20.80	53.30		9,736	877-222-2144	Y
AXA/Franklin Templeton Alloc Managed Vol Port Cls IA	US2689545919	B-	C+	B-	Down	3.95	7.36	14.95	21.21	61.32		1,275	877-222-2144	Y
AXA/Franklin Templeton Alloc Managed Vol Port Cls IB	US2689545836	B-	C+	B-	Down	3.95	7.36	14.95	21.21	61.32		1,275	877-222-2144	Y
BlackRock 80/20 Target Allocation Fund Class A	BAAPX	B-	C+	B-	Down	4.77	8.87	17.02	21.35	73.33	12.46	306.2	800-441-7762	Y
BlackRock 80/20 Target Allocation Fund Class C	BCAPX	B-	C+	B-	Down	4.65	8.41	16.25	18.73	66.93	12.1	306.2	800-441-7762	Y
BlackRock 80/20 Target Allocation Fund Class Institutional	BIAPX	B-	C+	B-	Down	4.85	8.95	17.47	22.66	76.31	12.68	306.2	800-441-7762	Y
BlackRock 80/20 Target Allocation Fund Class K	BKAPX	B-	C+	B-	Down	3.49	7.54	15.95	21.08	74.04	12.68	306.2	800-441-7762	Y
BlackRock 80/20 Target Allocation Fund Class R	BRAPX	B-	C+	B-	Down	4.74	8.77	16.87	20.80	72.01	12.38	306.2	800-441-7762	Y
BMO Aggressive Allocation Fund Class I	BDSHX	B-	B-	B-	Down	5.65	10.52	22.01	27.40	80.91	9.46	185.0	800-236-3863	Y
BMO Aggressive Allocation Fund Class R3	BDSRX	B-	B-	C+	Down	5.56	10.21	21.40	25.53	76.41	9.47	185.0	800-236-3863	Y
BMO Aggressive Allocation Fund Class R6	BDSQX	B-	B-	B-	Down	5.67	10.53	22.14	27.97	81.88	9.45	185.0	800-236-3863	Y
BMO Aggressive Allocation Fund Class Y	BDSYX	B-	B-	B-	Down	5.65	10.40	21.73	26.49	79.36	9.48	185.0	800-236-3863	Y
BMO Growth Allocation Fund Class I	BABHX	B-	C+	B-	Down	4.69	8.87	18.70	23.66	66.09	10.12	135.4	800-236-3863	Y
BMO Growth Allocation Fund Class R3	BABRX	B-	C+	B-	Down	4.54	8.61	18.05	21.77	61.88	10.14	135.4	800-236-3863	Y
BMO Growth Allocation Fund Class R6	BABQX	B-	B-	B-	Down	4.75	8.93	18.77	24.14	66.90	10.11	135.4	800-236-3863	Y
BMO Growth Allocation Fund Class Y	BABYX	B-	C+	B-	Down	4.58	8.76	18.33	22.66	64.52	10.13	135.4	800-236-3863	Y
Boston Trust Asset Management Fund	BTBFX	B	B-	A-		5.85	8.45	16.22	26.80	69.25	46.88	490.8	617-814-1215	Y
Buffalo Flexible Income Fund	BUFBX	B-	C+	B	Down	5.49	11.36	13.20	21.12	48.59	15.6	748.2	800-492-8332	Y
Calamos Growth & Income Fund Class A	CVTRX	B	B-	B+		4.68	8.16	16.37	25.80	60.73	32.05	2,078	800-582-6959	Y
Calamos Growth & Income Fund Class C	CVTCX	B-	C+	B	Down	4.46	7.71	15.49	22.87	54.65	32.22	2,078	800-582-6959	Y
Calamos Growth & Income Fund Class R	CGNRX	B	C+	B		4.58	8.00	16.03	24.87	58.73	31.78	2,078	800-582-6959	Y
Calamos Growth & Income Fund Class T	CVTTX	B	C+	B+		2.33	5.92	15.84	26.56	54.83		2,051	800-582-6959	Y
Calamos Growth & Income Fund Institutional Class	CGIIX	B	B-	B+		4.73	8.28	16.64	26.67	62.69	30.82	2,078	800-582-6959	Y
Calamos® Growth & Income Portfolio	US1281161000	B	C+	B+	Up	4.60	7.71	15.51	23.19	56.22	15.54	26.9	800-582-6959	Y
Calvert Aggressive Allocation Fund Class A	CAAAX	B-	B-	B	Down	4.83	9.25	20.25	27.99	76.35	20.13	141.2	800-368-2745	Y
Calvert Aggressive Allocation Fund Class C	CAACX	B-	B-	B-	Down	4.67	8.84	19.41	24.71	67.95	17.32	141.2	800-368-2745	Y
CAN SLIM Select Growth Fund	CANGX	B-	B-	B-	Down	6.85	11.39	20.35	23.60	79.37	14.18	62.4		Y
Cavalier Multi Strategist Fund C Class	CMSYX	B-	C+	B	Up	5.66	9.11	16.10	14.37	43.27	12.83	10.9	800-773-3863	Y
Cavalier Multi Strategist Fund Institutional Class	CMSFX	B-	C+	B	Down	5.84	9.60	17.17	17.64	50.52	13.36	10.9	800-773-3863	Y
Cavanal Hill Opportunistic Fund Class A	AAOPX	B-	C+	B	Up	3.27	5.63	11.84	17.53	54.09	14.97	47.7		Y
Cavanal Hill Opportunistic Fund Class C	AACOX	B-	C+	B+	Up	3.08	5.20	10.96	14.98	48.45	14.64	47.7		Y
Cavanal Hill Opportunistic Fund Institutional	AIOPX	B-	C+	B	Up	3.39	5.81	12.12	18.55	56.13	15.08	47.7		Y
Cavanal Hill Opportunistic Fund Investor	APOPX	B-	C+	B	Up	3.34	5.63	11.86	17.52	53.65	14.92	47.7		Y
CG Core Total Return Fund Institutional Class	CGBNX	B-	B	C+	Up	7.16	13.67	32.11	29.30		13.8	6.5		Y
CGM Mutual Fund	LOMMX	B-	B-	B	Up	5.68	11.65	16.91	21.98	58.35	31.02	412.4	800-343-5678	Y
Columbia Capital Allocation Aggressive Portfolio Adv Cls	CPDAX	B-	B-	B	Down	5.25	10.72	22.54	30.39	73.19	13.17	748.6	800-345-6611	Y
Columbia Capital Allocation Aggressive Portfolio Class A	AXBAX	B-	B-	B	Down	5.24	10.53	22.31	29.49	71.15	13.43	748.6	800-345-6611	Y
Columbia Capital Allocation Aggressive Portfolio Class C	RBGCX	B-	B-	B	Down	5.00	10.16	21.28	26.56	64.77	13.12	748.6	800-345-6611	Y
Columbia Capital Allocation Aggressive Portfolio Class K	CAGRX	B-	B-	B	Down	5.26	10.62	22.38	29.73	71.90	13.47	748.6	800-345-6611	

Category: Aggressive Allocation (con't)

Fund Name	Ticker Symbol	RATINGS: Overall Rating	Reward Rating	Risk Rating	Recent Up/ Downgrade	TOTAL RETURNS & PERFORMANCE: 3-Month Total Return	6-Month Total Return	1-Year Total Return	3-Year Total Return	5-Year Total Return	ASSETS: NAV	Total Assets (MIL)	NEW INVESTORS: Telephone	Open to New Investors
Columbia Capital Allocation Aggressive Portfolio Class R	CPARX	B-	B-	B	Down	5.22	10.46	22.04	28.56	69.07	13.33	748.6	800-345-6611	Y
Columbia Capital Alloc Aggressive Port Inst 2 Cls	CPANX	B-	B-	B	Down	5.29	10.67	22.60	30.63	73.88	13.16	748.6	800-345-6611	Y
Columbia Capital Alloc Aggressive Port Inst 3 Cls	CPDIX	B-	B-	B	Down	5.34	10.73	22.77	30.93	74.32	13.16	748.6	800-345-6611	Y
Columbia Capital Allocation Aggressive Portfolio Inst Cls	CPAZX	B-	B-	B	Down	5.25	10.63	22.57	30.42	73.23	13.37	748.6	800-345-6611	Y
Eaton Vance Tax-Advantaged Dividend Income Fund	EVT	B	B-	B+	Up	6.70	10.59	17.71	31.34	85.48	23.86	1,712		Y
Eaton Vance Tax-Managed Equity Asset Allocation Fund Cls A	EAEAX	B-	B-	B	Down	6.07	10.17	19.14	28.37	83.40	20.15	488.5		Y
Eaton Vance Tax-Managed Equity Asset Allocation Fund Cls B	EBEAX	B-	B-	B	Down	5.87	9.74	18.27	25.50	76.61	19.05	488.5		
Eaton Vance Tax-Managed Equity Asset Allocation Fund Cls C	ECEAX	B-	B-	B	Down	5.86	9.72	18.21	25.48	76.68	18.76	488.5		Y
Eaton Vance Tax-Managed Equity Asset Allocation Fund Cls I	EIEAX	B-	B-	B	Down	6.11	10.27	19.47	29.03	84.34	20.1	488.5		Y
E-Valuator Aggressive RMS Fund R4 Class Shares	EVFGX	B-	B	B-	Down	4.44	9.88	18.52	26.19	71.55	11.67	71.2	888-507-2798	Y
E-Valuator Aggressive RMS Fund Service Class Shares	EVAGX	B-	B	B-	Down	5.53	11.12	20.09	27.94	73.93	11.64	71.2	888-507-2798	Y
E-Valuator Growth RMS Fund R4 Class Shares	EVGRX	B-	B-	B-	Down	5.13	9.94	18.71	25.58	68.60	11.37	226.6	888-507-2798	Y
E-Valuator Growth RMS Fund Service Class Shares	EVGLX	B-	B-	B-	Down	5.17	10.07	19.08	26.13	69.34	11.32	226.6	888-507-2798	Y
Fallen Angels Income Fund	FAINX	B-	C+	B-	Down	4.93	6.89	13.67	20.02	54.87	11.74	10.4		Y
Fidelity Advisor Asset Manager® 85% Fund Class A	FEYAX	B-	B-	B-	Down	4.98	9.83	21.83	28.56	72.53	19.38	2,147	617-563-7000	Y
Fidelity Advisor Asset Manager® 85% Fund Class C	FEYCX	B-	B-	B-	Down	4.78	9.42	20.93	25.64	66.05	19.09	2,147	617-563-7000	Y
Fidelity Advisor Asset Manager® 85% Fund Class M	FEYTX	B-	B-	B-	Down	4.88	9.70	21.53	27.49	70.09	19.29	2,147	617-563-7000	Y
Fidelity Advisor Asset Manager® 85% Fund I Class	FEYIX	B-	B-	B-	Down	5.07	10.01	22.24	29.75	75.08	19.48	2,147	617-563-7000	Y
Fidelity Advisor® Strategic Dividend & Income® Fund Cls A	FASDX	B-	C+	B	Down	3.90	6.45	11.90	23.01	66.20	15.16	5,260	617-563-7000	Y
Fidelity Advisor® Strategic Dividend & Income® Fund Cls C	FCSDX	B-	C+	B	Down	3.71	6.07	11.13	20.29	59.99	15.1	5,260	617-563-7000	Y
Fidelity Advisor® Strategic Dividend & Income® Fund Cls M	FTSDX	B-	C+	B	Down	3.84	6.25	11.66	22.04	64.04	15.15	5,260	617-563-7000	Y
Fidelity Advisor® Strategic Dividend & Income® Fund I Cls	FSIDX	B-	B-	B	Down	3.96	6.57	12.19	24.00	68.39	15.21	5,260	617-563-7000	Y
Fidelity Asset Manager® 85% Fund	FAMRX	B-	B-	B-	Down	5.07	10.00	22.26	29.74	75.23	19.53	2,147	617-563-7000	Y
Fidelity® Four-in-One Index Fund	FFNOX	B-	B-	B	Down	4.79	9.13	19.27	28.48	74.01	44.45	5,671	617-563-7000	Y
Fidelity® Strategic Dividend & Income® Fund	FSDIX	B-	B-	B	Down	3.96	6.57	12.16	23.98	68.43	15.24	5,260	617-563-7000	Y
Franklin Corefolio Allocation Fund Advisor Class	FCAZX	B-	B-	B-	Down	4.16	8.01	20.40	27.82	82.94	19.71	781.0	650-312-2000	Y
Franklin Corefolio Allocation Fund Class A	FTCOX	B-	B-	B-	Down	4.12	7.87	20.06	26.85	80.53	19.68	781.0	650-312-2000	Y
Franklin Corefolio Allocation Fund Class C	FTCLX	B-	B-	B-	Down	3.89	7.46	19.19	24.04	74.03	19.43	781.0	650-312-2000	Y
Franklin Corefolio Allocation Fund Class R	US35472P7520	B-	B-	B-	Down	4.04	7.73	19.78	25.95	78.51	19.68	781.0	650-312-2000	Y
Franklin Corefolio Allocation Fund Class R6	FTLQX	B-	B-	B-		4.25	8.10	20.49	27.92	83.09	19.7	781.0	650-312-2000	Y
Franklin Founding Funds Allocation Fund Class A	FFALX	B-	C+	B-	Up	1.85	4.38	11.20	17.72	52.35	14.54	4,731	650-312-2000	Y
Franklin Founding Funds Allocation Fund Class R6	FFAQX	B-	C+	B		1.99	4.58	11.58	18.69	54.32	14.63	4,731	650-312-2000	Y
Franklin Growth Allocation Fund Advisor Class	FGTZX	B-	B-	B-	Down	3.89	8.48	19.76	24.10	60.84	19.42	1,334	650-312-2000	Y
Franklin Growth Allocation Fund Class A	FGTIX	B-	C+	B-	Down	3.82	8.32	19.44	23.17	58.85	19.34	1,334	650-312-2000	Y
Franklin Growth Allocation Fund Class C	FTGTX	B-	C+	B-	Down	3.60	7.95	18.55	20.40	52.95	18.81	1,334	650-312-2000	Y
Franklin Growth Allocation Fund Class R	FGTRX	B-	C+	B-	Down	3.73	8.23	19.16	22.24	56.84	19.1	1,334	650-312-2000	Y
Franklin Growth Allocation Fund Class R6	US35472P4147	B-	B-	B-	Down	3.89	8.53	19.89	24.60	61.64	19.4	1,334	650-312-2000	Y
Franklin Mutual Beacon Fund Class A	TEBIX	B-	B-	B		2.92	5.02	14.09	25.71	75.05	16.47	4,013	650-312-2000	Y
Franklin Mutual Beacon Fund Class C	TEMEX	B-	C+	B	Up	2.69	4.63	13.24	22.90	68.71	16.34	4,013	650-312-2000	Y
Franklin Mutual Beacon Fund Class R	US3540268584	B-	B-	B		2.81	4.88	13.76	24.81	72.98	16.28	4,013	650-312-2000	Y
Franklin Mutual Beacon Fund Class R6	FMBRX	B-	B-	B		2.98	5.13	14.41	26.97	78.04	16.6	4,013	650-312-2000	Y
Franklin Mutual Beacon Fund Class Z	BEGRX	B-	B-	B		2.96	5.18	14.39	26.71	77.45	16.61	4,013	650-312-2000	Y
Franklin Mutual Shares Fund Class A	TESIX	B-	C+	B	Down	1.94	2.73	8.20	19.12	66.38	28.35	15,462	650-312-2000	Y
Franklin Mutual Shares Fund Class C	TEMTX	B-	C+	B	Down	1.75	2.34	7.37	16.48	60.43	28.04	15,462	650-312-2000	Y
Franklin Mutual Shares Fund Class R	TESRX	B-	C+	B	Down	1.88	2.61	7.95	18.29	64.54	28.21	15,462	650-312-2000	Y
Franklin Mutual Shares Fund Class R6	FMSHX	B-	C+	B		2.06	2.91	8.60	20.50	69.56	28.61	15,462	650-312-2000	Y
Franklin Mutual Shares Fund Class Z	MUTHX	B-	C+	B	Down	2.02	2.87	8.49	20.08	68.64	28.63	15,462	650-312-2000	Y
FundX Upgrader Fund	FUNDX	B	C+	B	Up	4.22	10.42	15.35	21.10	74.09	59.96	225.3	866-455-3863	Y
Goldman Sachs Tax-Advantaged Global Equity Portfolio Cls A	TAGGX	B-	B-	B-	Down	4.51	9.50	18.61	25.60	72.47	15.68	2,400	800-526-7384	Y
Goldman Sachs Tax-Advantaged Global Eq Port Inst Cls	TIGGX	B-	B-	B-	Down	4.62	9.71	19.14	27.17	75.99	15.59	2,400	800-526-7384	Y
Great-West Aggressive Profile Fund Class L	MXEPX	B-	B-	B-	Down	5.81	10.23	20.68	30.86	87.35		803.2		Y
Great-West Aggressive Profile Fund Institutional Class	MXGTX	B-	B-	B-	Down	5.88	10.46	21.30	33.02	91.46		803.2		Y

Category: Aggressive Allocation (con't)

Fund Name	Ticker Symbol	RATINGS: Overall Rating	Reward Rating	Risk Rating	Recent Up/ Downgrade	TOTAL RETURNS & PERFORMANCE: 3-Month Total Return	6-Month Total Return	1-Year Total Return	3-Year Total Return	5-Year Total Return	ASSETS: NAV	Total Assets (MIL)	NEW INVESTORS: Telephone	Open to New Investors
Great-West Aggressive Profile Fund Investor Class	MXAPX	B-	B-	B-	Down	5.83	10.39	20.93	31.82	89.73		803.2		Y
Great-West Moderately Aggressive Profile Fund Class L	MXFPX	B-	C+	B	Down	4.16	7.34	15.29	23.31	61.70		739.5		Y
Great-West Moderately Aggressive Profile Fund Inst Cls	MXHRX	B-	B-	B	Down	4.29	7.70	15.98	25.34	65.19		739.5		Y
Great-West Moderately Aggressive Profile Fund Investor Cls	MXBPX	B-	C+	B	Down	4.18	7.56	15.54	24.25	63.75		739.5		Y
GuidePath® Conservative Allocation Fund Inst Shares	GITTX	B-	C	B	Up	2.43	5.27	12.21	9.39	34.47	9.66	241.6	603-888-5500	Y
GuidePath® Conservative Allocation Fund Service Shares	GPTCX	B-	C	B	Up	2.33	4.85	11.56	7.37	30.35	9.61	241.6	603-888-5500	Y
GuideStone Funds Growth Allocation Fund Institutional Cls	GGRYX	B-	C+	B-	Down	4.04	8.72	18.93	22.16	51.50	12.43	1,243	214-720-1171	Y
GuideStone Funds Growth Allocation Fund Investor Class	GCOZX	B-	C+	B-	Down	3.98	8.58	18.58	21.49	50.67	12.42	1,243	214-720-1171	Y
Hennessy Total Return Fund Investor Class	HDOGX	B	C+	B+		3.66	9.17	11.16	25.65	60.29	13.54	78.2	800-966-4354	Y
ICON Equity Income Fund Class A	IEQAX	B	B-	B+		2.56	5.90	12.35	26.19	75.76	18.01	88.1	303-790-1600	Y
ICON Equity Income Fund Class C	IOECX	B	B-	B		2.59	5.70	11.81	23.64	69.57	18.22	88.1	303-790-1600	Y
ICON Equity Income Fund Class S	IOEZX	B	B-	B+		2.55	6.01	12.65	27.05	77.85	18.06	88.1	303-790-1600	Y
Invesco Growth Allocation Fund Class A	AADAX	B-	C+	B-	Down	3.71	7.89	15.76	19.76	46.38	16.05	1,062	800-659-1005	Y
Invesco Growth Allocation Fund Class R	AADRX	B-	C+	B-	Down	3.65	7.70	15.42	18.87	44.42	16.01	1,062	800-659-1005	Y
Invesco Growth Allocation Fund Class R6	AAESX	B-	C+	B-	Down	3.80	8.09	16.18	21.02	49.01	16.11	1,062	800-659-1005	Y
Invesco Growth Allocation Fund Class S	AADSX	B-	C+	B-	Down	3.75	7.93	15.89	20.07	47.05	16.03	1,062	800-659-1005	Y
Invesco Growth Allocation Fund Class Y	AADYX	B-	C+	B-	Down	3.84	8.10	16.08	20.73	48.19	16.02	1,062	800-659-1005	Y
Invesco Growth Allocation Fund R5 Class	AADIX	B-	C+	B-	Down	3.86	8.16	16.25	21.10	49.11	16.12	1,062	800-659-1005	Y
InvestEd Growth Portfolio	WAGRX	B	B-	B+	Up	4.27	9.56	21.84	25.07	71.54	12.61	135.6	888-923-3355	Y
JNL Aggressive Growth Allocation Fund Class A	US46648L5912	B-	B-	B-	Down	4.50	9.06	21.40	27.05	68.63	12.99	1,509		Y
JNL Aggressive Growth Allocation Fund Class I	US46648L5839	B-	B-	B-		4.58	9.15	21.49	27.15	68.76	13	1,509		Y
JNL Growth Allocation Fund Class A	US46648L5599	B-	B-	B-	Down	3.98	7.87	18.63	24.25	63.13	13.56	2,481		Y
JNL Growth Allocation Fund Class I	US46648L5425	B-	B-	B-		4.06	7.95	18.71	24.34	63.25	13.58	2,481		Y
JNL/American Funds Growth Allocation Fund Class A	US46644W3447	B-	B-	B	Down	4.21	9.08	20.60	29.48	65.36	16.33	2,025		Y
JNL/American Funds Growth Allocation Fund Class I	US46644W3363	B-	B-	B		4.33	9.21	20.75	29.63	65.56	16.35	2,025		Y
JNL/Franklin Templeton Mutual Shares Fund Class A	US46648M3833	B-	C+	B	Down	2.01	2.74	8.10	18.25	66.10	11.66	1,210		Y
JNL/Franklin Templeton Mutual Shares Fund Class I	US46648M3759	B-	C+	B	Up	2.07	2.91	8.41	18.99	67.83	11.78	1,210		Y
JNL/Mellon Capital 10 x 10 Fund Class A	US46648M5739	B-	B-	B-	Down	5.01	10.46	16.21	26.38	78.56	13.83	493.3		Y
JNL/Mellon Capital 10 x 10 Fund Class I	US46648M4419	B-	B-	B-		5.08	10.54	16.30	26.48	78.69	13.84	493.3		Y
JNL/Mellon Capital Index 5 Fund Class A	US46648M5812	B-	B-	B-	Down	4.13	8.05	15.29	26.41	67.98	14.62	1,025		Y
JNL/Mellon Capital Index 5 Fund Class I	US46648M4583	B-	B-	B-		4.20	8.13	15.37	26.50	68.10	14.63	1,025		Y
JNL/S&P Managed Aggressive Growth Fund Class A	US46648L6662	B-	B-	B-	Down	5.26	9.89	23.25	29.50	77.39	22.21	2,220		Y
JNL/S&P Managed Aggressive Growth Fund Class I	US46648L6589	B-	B-	B-		5.35	9.99	23.36	29.62	77.55	22.23	2,220		Y
JNL/S&P Managed Growth Fund Class A	US46648L3933	B-	B-	B	Down	4.83	9.08	21.05	27.17	67.94	18.86	5,685		Y
JNL/S&P Managed Growth Fund Class I	US46648L3859	B-	B-	B		4.89	9.13	21.11	27.24	68.03	18.87	5,685		Y
John Hancock Funds II Multimgr Lifest Aggress Port Cls 1	JILAX	B-	B-	B-	Down	5.57	10.35	23.30	29.97	75.29	16.45	4,334	800-225-5913	Y
John Hancock Funds II Multimgr Lifest Aggress Port Cls A	JALAX	B-	B-	B-	Down	4.90	10.07	22.79	28.55	72.00	16.52	4,334	800-225-5913	Y
John Hancock Funds II Multimgr Lifest Aggress Port Cls B	JBLAX	B-	B-	C+	Up	4.71	9.69	21.97	25.78	65.70	16.55	4,334	800-225-5913	
John Hancock Funds II Multimgr Lifest Aggress Port Cls C	JCLAX	B-	B-	C+	Up	4.77	9.69	22.02	25.83	66.04	16.57	4,334	800-225-5913	Y
John Hancock Funds II Multimgr Lifest Aggress Port Cls I	JTAIX	B-	B-	B-	Down	5.57	10.27	23.20	29.69	74.92	16.47	4,334	800-225-5913	Y
John Hancock Funds II Multimgr Lifest Aggress Port Cls R1	JPLAX	B-	B-	C+	Down	4.87	9.91	22.44	27.12	68.56	16.55	4,334	800-225-5913	Y
John Hancock Funds II Multimgr Lifest Aggress Port Cls R2	JQLAX	B-	B-	B-	Down	4.90	10.04	22.67	28.12	71.06	16.42	4,334	800-225-5913	Y
John Hancock Funds II Multimgr Lifest Aggress Port Cls R3	JRLAX	B-	B-	C+	Down	4.86	9.92	22.58	27.51	69.33	16.48	4,334	800-225-5913	Y
John Hancock Funds II Multimgr Lifest Aggress Port Cls R4	JSLAX	B-	B-	B-	Down	4.94	10.13	22.98	28.99	72.56	16.45	4,334	800-225-5913	Y
John Hancock Funds II Multimgr Lifest Aggress Port Cls R5	JTLAX	B-	B-	B-	Down	5.00	10.25	23.24	29.86	74.56	16.48	4,334	800-225-5913	Y
John Hancock Funds II Multimgr Lifest Aggress Port Cls R6	JULAX	B-	B-	B-	Down	5.05	10.31	23.31	30.19	75.78	16.47	4,334	800-225-5913	Y
John Hancock Funds II Multimgr Lifest Growth Port Cls 1	JILGX	B-	B-	B-	Down	4.10	8.48	19.25	25.71	63.76	16.08	13,119	800-225-5913	Y
John Hancock Funds II Multimgr Lifest Growth Port Cls 5	JHLGX	B-	B-	B-	Down	4.15	8.47	19.33	25.85	64.26	16.06	13,119	800-225-5913	Y
John Hancock Funds II Multimgr Lifest Growth Port Cls A	JALGX	B-	C+	B-	Down	4.04	8.28	18.83	24.34	60.81	16.16	13,119	800-225-5913	Y
John Hancock Funds II Multimgr Lifest Growth Port Cls B	JBLGX	B-	C+	B-	Down	3.79	7.89	17.94	21.72	55.13	16.2	13,119	800-225-5913	
John Hancock Funds II Multimgr Lifest Growth Port Cls C	JCLGX	B-	C+	B-	Down	3.79	7.90	17.96	21.67	55.12	16.18	13,119	800-225-5913	Y
John Hancock Funds II Multimgr Lifest Growth Port Cls I	JTGIX	B-	B-	B-	Down	4.10	8.42	19.20	25.57	63.59	16.07	13,119	800-225-5913	Y

Category: Aggressive Allocation (con't)

Fund Name	Ticker Symbol	RATINGS: Overall Rating	Reward Rating	Risk Rating	Recent Up/ Downgrade	TOTAL RETURNS & PERFORMANCE: 3-Month Total Return	6-Month Total Return	1-Year Total Return	3-Year Total Return	5-Year Total Return	ASSETS: NAV	Total Assets (MIL)	NEW INVESTORS: Telephone	Open to New Investors
John Hancock Funds II Multimgr Lifest Growth Port Cls R1	JPLGX	B-	C+	B-	Down	3.94	8.10	18.45	23.05	57.87	16.23	13,119	800-225-5913	Y
John Hancock Funds II Multimgr Lifest Growth Port Cls R2	JQLGX	B-	C+	B-	Down	3.97	8.24	18.71	23.92	59.92	16.05	13,119	800-225-5913	Y
John Hancock Funds II Multimgr Lifest Growth Port Cls R3	JRLGX	B-	C+	B-	Down	3.94	8.12	18.53	23.42	58.66	16.13	13,119	800-225-5913	Y
John Hancock Funds II Multimgr Lifest Growth Port Cls R4	JSLGX	B-	B-	B-	Down	4.07	8.37	19.03	24.85	61.81	16.14	13,119	800-225-5913	Y
John Hancock Funds II Multimgr Lifest Growth Port Cls R5	JTLGX	B-	B-	B-	Down	4.06	8.42	19.21	25.61	63.44	16.16	13,119	800-225-5913	Y
John Hancock Funds II Multimgr Lifest Growth Port Cls R6	JULGX	B-	B-	B-	Down	4.13	8.51	19.29	25.88	64.18	16.08	13,119	800-225-5913	Y
John Hancock Funds II Strategic Equity Allocation Fund NAV	US47804M7204	B-	B	B-	Down	5.37	10.72	22.11	30.96	82.73	12.89	7,694	800-225-5913	Y
John Hancock Funds Multi-Ind Lifestyle Aggress Port Cls 1	JIIOX	B-	B-	B-	Down	5.47	10.58	21.52	30.33		12.54	280.2	800-225-5913	Y
John Hancock Funds Multi-Ind Lifestyle Aggress Port Cls R6	JIIRX	B-	B-	B-	Down	5.51	10.62	21.57	30.59		12.54	280.2	800-225-5913	Y
John Hancock Funds Multi-Index Lifestyle Growth Port Cls 1	JLGOX	B-	B-	B	Down	4.33	8.50	17.51	25.40		12.12	686.1	800-225-5913	Y
John Hancock Funds Multi-Ind Lifestyle Growth Port Cls R6	JLGSX	B-	B-	B	Down	4.35	8.53	17.53	25.61		12.13	686.1	800-225-5913	Y
JPMorgan Investor Growth & Income Fund Class A	ONGIX	B-	C+	B	Down	2.90	6.76	15.06	21.53	58.67	17.4	3,020	800-480-4111	Y
JPMorgan Investor Growth & Income Fund Class C	ONECX	B-	C+	B	Down	2.88	6.56	14.46	19.65	54.61	16.9	3,020	800-480-4111	Y
JPMorgan Investor Growth & Income Fund Class I	ONGFX	B-	C+	B	Down	2.89	6.81	15.18	22.35	60.62	17.12	3,020	800-480-4111	Y
JPMorgan Investor Growth & Income Fund Class R6	JFBUX	B-	C+	B		4.45	8.46	16.97	24.24	63.11	17.12	3,020	800-480-4111	Y
JPMorgan Investor Growth & Income Fund Class T	JGITX	B-	C+	B	Down	4.63	8.62	16.66	23.12	61.40		3,020	800-480-4111	Y
JPMorgan Investor Growth Fund Class A	ONGAX	B-	B-	B-	Down	3.77	8.55	19.07	26.68	80.01	20.69	2,718	800-480-4111	Y
JPMorgan Investor Growth Fund Class C	OGGCX	B-	B-	B-	Down	5.35	10.07	20.35	26.65	78.14	19.37	2,718	800-480-4111	Y
JPMorgan Investor Growth Fund Class I	ONIFX	B-	B-	B-	Down	3.79	8.64	19.30	27.60	82.25	21.12	2,718	800-480-4111	Y
JPMorgan Investor Growth Fund Class R6	JFTUX	B-	B-	B-		3.84	8.68	19.34	27.64	82.31	21.12	2,718	800-480-4111	Y
JPMorgan Investor Growth Fund Class T	JPITX	B-	B-	B-	Down	3.77	8.54	19.04	26.69	80.05	20.67	2,718	800-480-4111	Y
KL Allocation Fund Advisor Class	GAVAX	B	C+	A		5.09	9.64	15.88	22.88	56.32	15	481.1		Y
KL Allocation Fund Institutional Class	GAVIX	B	C+	A		5.16	9.80	16.13	23.71	58.23	15.18	481.1		Y
Lord Abbett Multi-Asset Focused Growth Fund Class A	LDSAX	B-	C+	B-	Down	4.28	7.51	16.12	22.93	79.01	17.21	239.7	201-827-2000	Y
Lord Abbett Multi-Asset Focused Growth Fund Class B	LDSBX	B-	C+	B	Up	4.09	7.14	15.34	20.26	72.43	17.24	239.7	201-827-2000	
Lord Abbett Multi-Asset Focused Growth Fund Class F	LDSFX	B-	C+	B-	Down	4.33	7.62	16.30	23.45	80.26	17.2	239.7	201-827-2000	Y
Lord Abbett Multi-Asset Focused Growth Fund Class F3	LDSOX	B-	C+	B-	Down	4.33	7.59	16.45	23.87	81.25	17.36	239.7	201-827-2000	Y
Lord Abbett Multi-Asset Focused Growth Fund Class I	LDSYX	B	C+	B+	Up	4.33	7.65	16.45	23.87	81.25	17.37	239.7	201-827-2000	Y
Lord Abbett Multi-Asset Focused Growth Fund Class R2	LDSQX	B-	C+	B	Up	4.22	7.37	15.80	20.33	74.04	17.74	239.7	201-827-2000	Y
Lord Abbett Multi-Asset Focused Growth Fund Class R3	LDSRX	B	C+	B	Up	4.25	7.40	15.90	22.07	76.88	17.01	239.7	201-827-2000	Y
Lord Abbett Multi-Asset Focused Growth Fund Class R4	LDSSX	B-	C+	B-	Down	4.29	7.53	16.16	22.95	79.01	17.14	239.7	201-827-2000	Y
Lord Abbett Multi-Asset Focused Growth Fund Class R5	LDSTX	B-	C+	B-	Down	4.38	7.70	16.51	23.93	81.34	17.38	239.7	201-827-2000	Y
Lord Abbett Multi-Asset Focused Growth Fund Class R6	LDSVX	B-	C+	B-	Down	4.36	7.67	16.55	23.97	81.40	17.37	239.7	201-827-2000	Y
Lord Abbett Multi-Asset Growth Fund Class C	LWSCX	B-	C+	B	Up	2.52	4.96	9.85	14.86	49.38	17.31	1,023	201-827-2000	Y
Lord Abbett Multi-Asset Growth Fund Class R3	LGIRX	B-	C+	B	Down	2.56	5.12	10.28	16.53	52.95	17.42	1,023	201-827-2000	Y
Madison Aggressive Allocation Fund Class A	MAGSX	B-	B-	B	Down	4.44	8.61	18.04	24.76	65.79	12.33	66.5	800-767-0300	Y
Madison Aggressive Allocation Fund Class B	MAGBX	B-	C+	B	Down	4.27	8.18	17.19	21.93	59.63	12.04	66.5	800-767-0300	Y
Madison Aggressive Allocation Fund Class C	MAACX	B-	C+	B	Down	4.26	8.18	17.18	22.01	59.73	12.05	66.5	800-767-0300	Y
MainStay Growth Allocation Fund Class I	MGXIX	B-	B-	C+	Up	5.95	11.55	21.52	25.69	79.86	16.96	401.5	800-624-6782	Y
MainStay Moderate Growth Allocation Class R3	MGDRX	B-	C+	B-	Down	4.75	9.29	17.28	21.27	63.62	15.59	768.2	800-624-6782	Y
MainStay Moderate Growth Allocation Fund Class A	MGDAX	B-	C+	B-	Down	4.89	9.50	17.73	22.35	65.95	15.64	768.2	800-624-6782	Y
MainStay Moderate Growth Allocation Fund Class I	MGDIX	B-	C+	B-	Down	5.02	9.65	18.05	23.39	68.14	15.8	768.2	800-624-6782	Y
MainStay Moderate Growth Allocation Fund Investor Class	MGDNX	B-	C+	B-	Down	4.83	9.37	17.51	21.74	64.53	15.66	768.2	800-624-6782	Y
Manning & Napier Pro-Blend Maximum Term Series Class I	MNHIX	B-	B-	B	Up	5.17	9.71	24.49	23.25	67.87	10.34	486.6	585-325-6880	Y
Manning & Napier Pro-Blend Maximum Term Series Class R	MNHRX	B-	C+	B	Up	5.02	9.39	23.93	21.44	63.83	13.15	486.6	585-325-6880	Y
Manning & Napier Pro-Blend Maximum Term Series Class R2	MNHCX	B-	C+	B-	Up	4.90	9.11	23.23	19.58	59.74	10.93	486.6	585-325-6880	Y
Manning & Napier Pro-Blend Maximum Term Series Class S	EXHAX	B-	B-	B	Up	5.10	9.52	24.19	22.35	65.96	20.8	486.6	585-325-6880	Y
Marsico Flexible Capital Fund	MFCFX	B	C+	B+	Up	5.00	8.79	18.80	17.17	71.09	14.37	246.0	888-860-8686	Y
MassMutual RetireSMART Growth Fund Administrative Class	MRGLX	B-	B-	C+	Up	4.92	9.94	20.83	24.66	65.91	11.68	118.7		Y
MassMutual RetireSMART Growth Fund Class I	MRGUX	B-	B-	B-	Down	5.04	10.16	21.21	25.89	67.97	11.66	118.7		Y
MassMutual RetireSMART Growth Fund Class R5	MRRSX	B-	B-	B-	Down	5.03	10.05	20.96	25.50	67.40	11.67	118.7		Y
MassMutual RetireSMART Growth Fund Service Class	MRGYX	B-	B-	C+	Down	5.00	10.02	20.91	25.10	66.78	11.69	118.7		Y

Category: Aggressive Allocation (con't)

Fund Name	Ticker Symbol	RATINGS: Overall Rating	Reward Rating	Risk Rating	Recent Up/ Downgrade	TOTAL RETURNS & PERFORMANCE: 3-Month Total Return	6-Month Total Return	1-Year Total Return	3-Year Total Return	5-Year Total Return	ASSETS: NAV	Total Assets (MIL)	NEW INVESTORS: Telephone	Open to New Investors
MassMutual RetireSMART Moderate Growth Fund Admin Cls	MRSLX	B-	C+	B-	Down	4.35	8.89	18.40	22.66	57.53	10.78	263.2		Y
MassMutual RetireSMART Moderate Growth Fund Class A	MOGAX	B-	C+	B-	Down	4.36	8.79	18.14	21.78	55.64	10.82	263.2		Y
MassMutual RetireSMART Moderate Growth Fund Class I	MROUX	B-	C+	B-	Down	4.49	9.04	18.71	23.67	59.22	10.74	263.2		Y
MassMutual RetireSMART Moderate Growth Fund Class R3	MROTX	B-	C+	B-	Down	4.30	8.78	17.99	21.31	54.47	10.7	263.2		Y
MassMutual RetireSMART Moderate Growth Fund Class R4	MROZX	B-	C+	B-	Down	4.38	8.84	18.28	22.21	56.42	10.72	263.2		Y
MassMutual RetireSMART Moderate Growth Fund Class R5	MRSSX	B-	C+	B-	Down	4.48	9.04	18.70	23.48	58.83	10.75	263.2		Y
MassMutual RetireSMART Moderate Growth Fund Service Class	MROYX	B-	C+	B-	Down	4.45	8.99	18.62	23.12	58.29	10.79	263.2		Y
Meeder Aggressive Allocation Fund Adviser Class	AGHAX	B-	C+	B	Up	4.80	9.51	13.22	16.06	77.30	10.45	42.0		Y
Meeder Aggressive Allocation Fund Institutional Class	AGHIX	B-	C+	B	Up	4.98	9.80	13.52	16.34	77.72	10.46	42.0		Y
Meeder Aggressive Allocation Fund Retail Class	FLAGX	B-	C+	B	Up	4.70	9.41	12.91	15.60	76.59	10.45	42.0		Y
Meeder Dynamic Allocation Fund Adviser Class	DYGAX	B-	B-	C+	Down	6.03	11.66	21.42	22.48	87.19	10.88	129.4		Y
Meeder Dynamic Allocation Fund Institutional Class	DYGIX	B-	B-	C+	Down	5.98	11.71	21.60	22.56	87.30	10.86	129.4		Y
Meeder Dynamic Allocation Fund Retail Class	FLDGX	B-	B-	C+	Down	5.97	11.50	21.20	22.12	86.64	10.85	129.4		Y
MFS® Aggressive Growth Allocation Fund Class 529A	EAGTX	B	B-	B+	Up	5.50	9.76	22.86	30.54	73.99	22.95	1,775	877-960-6077	Y
MFS® Aggressive Growth Allocation Fund Class 529B	EBAAX	B	B-	B+	Up	5.26	9.31	21.89	27.57	67.49	22.54	1,775	877-960-6077	Y
MFS® Aggressive Growth Allocation Fund Class 529C	ECAAX	B	B-	B+	Up	5.31	9.31	21.93	27.60	67.59	22.25	1,775	877-960-6077	Y
MFS® Aggressive Growth Allocation Fund Class A	MAAGX	B	B-	B+	Up	5.49	9.73	22.91	30.64	74.23	23.1	1,775	877-960-6077	Y
MFS® Aggressive Growth Allocation Fund Class B	MBAGX	B	B-	B+	Up	5.28	9.34	21.96	27.69	67.79	22.8	1,775	877-960-6077	Y
MFS® Aggressive Growth Allocation Fund Class C	MCAGX	B	B-	B+	Up	5.27	9.32	21.94	27.70	67.87	22.57	1,775	877-960-6077	Y
MFS® Aggressive Growth Allocation Fund Class I	MIAGX	B-	B-	B-	Down	5.56	9.87	23.22	31.63	76.49	23.46	1,775	877-960-6077	Y
MFS® Aggressive Growth Allocation Fund Class R1	MAAFX	B	B-	B+	Up	5.30	9.30	21.98	27.73	67.79	22.25	1,775	877-960-6077	Y
MFS® Aggressive Growth Allocation Fund Class R2	MAWAX	B	B-	B+	Up	5.42	9.65	22.63	29.66	72.07	22.64	1,775	877-960-6077	Y
MFS® Aggressive Growth Allocation Fund Class R3	MAAHX	B	B-	B+	Up	5.49	9.76	22.88	30.63	74.21	22.91	1,775	877-960-6077	Y
MFS® Aggressive Growth Allocation Fund Class R4	MAALX	B	B-	B+	Up	5.59	9.91	23.26	31.65	76.49	23.16	1,775	877-960-6077	Y
MFS® Growth Allocation Fund Class 529A	EAGWX	B-	B-	B	Down	4.43	8.07	18.83	25.84	59.45	20.38	5,109	877-960-6077	Y
MFS® Growth Allocation Fund Class 529B	EBGWX	B	C+	B+	Up	4.21	7.62	17.95	22.99	53.54	20.19	5,109	877-960-6077	Y
MFS® Growth Allocation Fund Class 529C	ECGWX	B	C+	B+	Up	4.21	7.67	17.95	23.04	53.57	19.91	5,109	877-960-6077	Y
MFS® Growth Allocation Fund Class A	MAGWX	B	B-	B+	Up	4.42	8.09	18.89	26.01	59.76	20.54	5,109	877-960-6077	Y
MFS® Growth Allocation Fund Class B	MBGWX	B	C+	B+	Up	4.22	7.71	18.01	23.20	53.87	20.39	5,109	877-960-6077	Y
MFS® Growth Allocation Fund Class C	MCGWX	B	C+	B+	Up	4.23	7.70	18.06	23.17	53.92	20.17	5,109	877-960-6077	Y
MFS® Growth Allocation Fund Class I	MGWIX	B	B-	B+	Up	4.49	8.23	19.20	26.99	61.85	20.71	5,109	877-960-6077	Y
MFS® Growth Allocation Fund Class R1	MAGMX	B	C+	B+	Up	4.26	7.69	18.06	23.21	53.87	19.77	5,109	877-960-6077	Y
MFS® Growth Allocation Fund Class R2	MGALX	B	B-	B+	Up	4.34	7.93	18.58	25.01	57.75	20.09	5,109	877-960-6077	Y
MFS® Growth Allocation Fund Class R3	MAGEX	B	B-	B+	Up	4.40	8.10	18.94	25.97	59.80	20.36	5,109	877-960-6077	Y
MFS® Growth Allocation Fund Class R4	MAGJX	B	B-	B+	Up	4.48	8.20	19.21	26.93	61.80	20.51	5,109	877-960-6077	Y
MH Elite Fund of Funds Fund	MHEFX	B-	B-	B-	Down	5.64	10.19	20.43	24.30	76.61	6.92	12.6		Y
MH Elite Small Capital Fund of Funds	MHELX	B-	B-	B	Up	3.54	7.64	12.39	20.79	68.86	7.6	7.0		Y
Morningstar Aggressive Growth ETF Asset Alloc Port Cls I	US00162T8606	B-	B-	B-	Down	5.02	9.97	20.17	29.39	63.84	13.03	99.7	866-759-5679	Y
Morningstar Growth ETF Asset Allocation Portfolio Class I	US00162T8861	B-	B-	B-	Down	4.26	8.53	17.67	25.54	56.46	12.15	227.0	866-759-5679	Y
Nationwide Investor Destinations Aggressive Fund Class A	NDAAX	B-	B-	B-	Down	4.99	9.76	19.88	27.71	72.30	10.2	1,098	800-848-0920	Y
Nationwide Investor Destinations Aggressive Fund Class C	NDACX	B-	B-	B-	Down	4.66	9.27	18.94	24.87	66.20	9.83	1,098	800-848-0920	Y
Nationwide Investor Destinations Aggressive Fund Class R	GAFRX	B-	B-	B-	Down	4.82	9.50	19.38	26.59	69.71	9.96	1,098	800-848-0920	Y
Nationwide Investor Destinations Aggressive Fund Class R6	GAIDX	B-	B-	B-	Down	5.02	9.93	20.24	29.07	75.30	10.34	1,098	800-848-0920	Y
Nationwide Inv Destinations Aggressive Fund Inst Serv Cls	NWWHX	B-	B-	B-	Down	5.05	9.89	20.14	28.76	73.87	10.21	1,098	800-848-0920	Y
Nationwide Inv Destinations Aggressive Fund Service Cls	NDASX	B-	B-	B-	Down	4.86	9.71	19.76	27.58	71.82	10.22	1,098	800-848-0920	Y
Nationwide Inv Destinations Mod Aggress Fund Cls A	NDMAX	B-	B-	B-	Down	4.43	8.79	17.67	24.87	61.68	10.52	1,733	800-848-0920	Y
Nationwide Inv Destinations Mod Aggress Fund Cls C	NDMCX	B-	C+	B-	Down	4.27	8.34	16.74	22.25	55.84	10.21	1,733	800-848-0920	Y
Nationwide Inv Destinations Mod Aggress Fund Cls R	GMARX	B-	C+	B-	Down	4.38	8.58	17.26	23.89	59.24	10.22	1,733	800-848-0920	Y
Nationwide Inv Destinations Mod Aggress Fund Cls R6	GMIAX	B-	B-	B-	Down	4.63	9.00	18.09	26.38	64.62	10.51	1,733	800-848-0920	Y
Nationwide Inv Destinations Mod Aggress Fund Inst Serv Cls	NWWIX	B-	B-	B-	Down	4.62	8.97	18.04	25.91	63.43	10.49	1,733	800-848-0920	Y
Nationwide Inv Destinations Mod Aggress Fund Serv Cls	NDMSX	B-	B-	B-	Down	4.53	8.79	17.64	24.88	61.24	10.5	1,733	800-848-0920	Y
Nuveen Strategy Aggressive Growth Allocation Fund Class A	FAAGX	B-	B-	B-	Down	4.79	9.52	19.53	24.39	63.80	16	76.1	312-917-8146	Y

Category: Aggressive Allocation (con't)

Fund Name	Ticker Symbol	RATINGS: Overall Rating	Reward Rating	Risk Rating	Recent Up/ Downgrade	TOTAL RETURNS & PERFORMANCE: 3-Month Total Return	6-Month Total Return	1-Year Total Return	3-Year Total Return	5-Year Total Return	ASSETS: NAV	Total Assets (MIL)	NEW INVESTORS: Telephone	Open to New Investors
Nuveen Strategy Aggressive Growth Allocation Fund Class I	FSAYX	B-	B-	B-	Down	4.90	9.68	19.84	25.33	65.88	16.04	76.1	312-917-8146	Y
Nuveen Strategy Aggressive Growth Allocation Fund Class R3	FSASX	B-	C+	B-	Down	4.79	9.44	19.26	23.52	61.79	15.8	76.1	312-917-8146	Y
Nuveen Tax-Advantaged Dividend Growth Fund	JTD	B	B-	B	Up	5.66	10.22	25.32	30.28	74.42	18.07	261.7	312-917-8146	Y
Oppenheimer Portfolio Series Active Allocation Fund Cls A	OAAAX	B-	C+	B	Down	4.04	7.93	19.37	22.46	57.63	14.59	2,562	800-225-5677	Y
Oppenheimer Portfolio Series Active Allocation Fund Cls B	OAABX	B-	C+	B-	Down	3.78	7.47	18.43	19.57	51.67	14.52	2,562	800-225-5677	
Oppenheimer Portfolio Series Active Allocation Fund Cls C	OAACX	B	C+	B+	Up	3.82	7.48	18.49	19.71	51.91	14.28	2,562	800-225-5677	Y
Oppenheimer Portfolio Series Active Allocation Fund Cls R	OAANX	B	C+	B+	Up	3.97	7.79	19.01	21.48	55.76	14.51	2,562	800-225-5677	Y
Oppenheimer Portfolio Series Active Allocation Fund Cls Y	OAAYX	B	C+	B+	Up	4.08	7.99	19.58	23.37	59.64	14.74	2,562	800-225-5677	Y
Pacific Funds Optimization Aggress-Growth Adv Cls	POEDX	B-	B-	B-	Down	4.30	9.00	19.40	27.59	63.13	17.17	340.1	800-722-2333	Y
Pacific Funds Port Optimization Aggress-Growth Fund Cls A	POEAX	B-	B-	B-	Down	4.25	8.90	19.15	26.61	61.18	17.14	340.1	800-722-2333	Y
Pacific Funds Port Optimization Aggress-Growth Fund Cls B	POEBX	B-	B-	B-	Down	4.07	8.50	18.25	23.80	56.01	16.76	340.1	800-722-2333	Y
Pacific Funds Port Optimization Aggress-Growth Fund Cls C	POCEX	B-	B-	B-	Down	4.10	8.46	18.23	23.74	56.12	16.73	340.1	800-722-2333	Y
Pacific Funds Optimization Aggress-Growth Retmnt Cls	POERX	B-	B-	B-	Down	4.22	8.76	18.84	25.67	59.43	17.03	340.1	800-722-2333	Y
Pacific Funds Portfolio Optimization Growth Fund Adv Cls	PMADX	B-	B-	B	Down	3.62	7.73	16.59	24.80	56.24	15.64	1,038	800-722-2333	Y
Pacific Funds Portfolio Optimization Growth Fund Class A	PODAX	B-	C+	B	Down	3.58	7.63	16.34	23.91	54.35	15.61	1,038	800-722-2333	Y
Pacific Funds Portfolio Optimization Growth Fund Class B	PODBX	B-	C+	B-	Down	3.38	7.20	15.43	21.16	48.96	15.4	1,038	800-722-2333	Y
Pacific Funds Portfolio Optimization Growth Fund Class C	PODCX	B-	C+	B-	Down	3.32	7.23	15.41	21.17	49.06	15.35	1,038	800-722-2333	Y
Pacific Funds Port Optimization Growth Fund Cls Retmnt	PODRX	B-	C+	B	Down	3.47	7.53	16.01	23.01	52.50	15.57	1,038	800-722-2333	Y
Pacific Funds Port Optimization Growth Fund Cls Retmnt	ATBAX	B-	C+	B	Up	3.93	6.45	10.93	14.19	43.05	13.92	1,038		Y
Pacific Funds Port Optimization Growth Fund Cls Retmnt	ATBTX	B-	C+	B	Up	3.72	6.07	10.16	11.68	37.63	13.58	1,038		Y
Pacific Funds Port Optimization Growth Fund Cls Retmnt	ATBIX	B-	C+	B	Up	3.95	6.54	11.26	15.02	44.88	13.95	1,038		Y
PIMCO StocksPLUS® Long Duration Fund Institutional Class	PSLDX	A-	A	B		8.43	14.65	32.86	53.41	151.15	7.21	727.9	866-746-2602	Y
Pioneer Solutions - Growth Fund Class A	GRAAX	B-	C+	B-	Up	2.72	7.20	16.77	17.84	49.22	13.88	312.6	617-742-7825	Y
Pioneer Solutions - Growth Fund Class C	GRACX	B-	C+	B	Up	3.20	7.57	16.71	16.17	45.02	13.08	312.6	617-742-7825	Y
Pioneer Solutions - Growth Fund Class R	SOGRX	B-	C+	B-	Up	4.13	8.71	18.08	18.27	49.52		312.6	617-742-7825	Y
Pioneer Solutions - Growth Fund Class Y	IBGYX	B-	C+	B-	Down	2.59	7.19	16.83	18.57	50.83	14.18	312.6	617-742-7825	Y
Praxis Genesis Growth Portfolio Class A	MGAFX	B-	C+	B	Down	4.31	8.34	16.70	21.82	58.48	15.09	64.5		Y
Principal Strat Asset Mgmt Conservative Growth Fund Cls A	SAGPX	B-	B-	B	Down	4.39	9.60	19.33	24.20	66.10	18.22	3,267	800-222-5852	Y
Principal Strat Asset Mgmt Conservative Growth Fund Cls C	SCGPX	B	C+	B+	Up	4.17	9.18	18.38	21.41	60.02	16.98	3,267	800-222-5852	Y
Principal Strat Asset Mgmt Conservative Growth Fund Cls J	PCGJX	B-	B-	B	Down	4.38	9.70	19.49	24.69	66.84	17.57	3,267	800-222-5852	Y
Principal Strat Asset Mgmt Cons Growth Inst Cls	PCWIX	B-	B-	B	Down	4.46	9.78	19.67	25.51	68.97	17.8	3,267	800-222-5852	Y
Principal Strat Asset Mgmt Cons Growth R-1 Cls	PCGGX	B-	C+	B	Down	4.22	9.31	18.72	22.29	61.73	17.62	3,267	800-222-5852	Y
Principal Strat Asset Mgmt Cons Growth R-2 Cls	PCGVX	B-	C+	B	Down	4.28	9.36	18.77	22.70	62.72	17.64	3,267	800-222-5852	Y
Principal Strat Asset Mgmt Cons Growth R-3 Cls	PCGPX	B-	B-	B	Down	4.25	9.46	19.02	23.32	64.19	17.58	3,267	800-222-5852	Y
Principal Strat Asset Mgmt Cons Growth R-4 Cls	PCWSX	B-	B-	B	Down	4.31	9.52	19.21	24.02	65.80	17.75	3,267	800-222-5852	Y
Principal Strat Asset Mgmt Cons Growth R-5 Cls	PCWPX	B-	B-	B	Down	4.41	9.65	19.37	24.57	66.82	17.71	3,267	800-222-5852	Y
Principal Strategic Asset Mgmt Strategic Growth Fund Cls A	SACAX	B	B-	B	Up	4.71	10.61	21.69	24.79	75.36	20.58	2,007	800-222-5852	Y
Principal Strategic Asset Mgmt Strategic Growth Fund Cls C	SWHCX	B	B-	B	Up	4.51	10.19	20.80	22.03	68.88	18.8	2,007	800-222-5852	Y
Principal Strategic Asset Mgmt Strategic Growth Fund Cls J	PSWJX	B-	B-	B-	Down	4.78	10.76	21.97	25.38	76.31	19.89	2,007	800-222-5852	Y
Principal Strat Asset Mgmt Strat Growth Fund Inst Cls	PSWIX	B-	B-	B-	Down	4.84	10.82	22.11	26.14	78.55	20.09	2,007	800-222-5852	Y
Principal Strat Asset Mgmt Strat Growth Fund R-1 Cls	PSGGX	B-	B-	B-	Down	4.58	10.31	21.05	22.88	70.91	19.95	2,007	800-222-5852	Y
Principal Strat Asset Mgmt Strat Growth Fund R-2 Cls	PSGVX	B-	B-	B-	Down	4.61	10.37	21.20	23.34	71.99	19.9	2,007	800-222-5852	Y
Principal Strat Asset Mgmt Strat Growth Fund R-3 Cls	PSGPX	B-	B-	B-	Down	4.67	10.55	21.49	24.08	73.59	19.88	2,007	800-222-5852	Y
Principal Strat Asset Mgmt Strat Growth Fund R-4 Cls	PSGLX	B-	B-	B-	Down	4.70	10.60	21.66	24.73	75.22	19.99	2,007	800-222-5852	Y
Principal Strat Asset Mgmt Strat Growth Fund R-5 Cls	PSGFX	B-	B-	B-	Down	4.75	10.72	21.84	25.24	76.40	19.94	2,007	800-222-5852	Y
Prospector Capital Appreciation Fund	PCAFX	B	C+	B	Up	4.64	7.04	11.37	23.56	56.45	17.63	26.6	877-734-7862	Y
Prudential Growth Allocation Fund Class A	JDAAX	B-	B-	C+	Down	5.31	10.96	21.06	25.60	66.44	18.36	109.7	800-225-1852	Y
Prudential Growth Allocation Fund Class Q	JDGQX	B-	B-	C+		5.37	11.14	21.43	26.48	68.48	18.58	109.7	800-225-1852	Y
Prudential Growth Allocation Fund Class R	JGARX	B-	B-	C+	Down	5.27	10.91	20.80	24.74	64.36	18.23	109.7	800-225-1852	Y
Prudential Growth Allocation Fund Class Z	JDGZX	B-	B-	C+	Down	5.37	11.14	21.43	26.47	68.47	18.58	109.7	800-225-1852	Y
Putnam Dynamic Asset Allocation Growth Fund Class A	PAEAX	B-	B-	B	Down	5.33	10.47	19.85	27.99	78.23	17.04	2,929	617-292-1000	Y
Putnam Dynamic Asset Allocation Growth Fund Class B	PAEBX	B-	B-	B-	Down	5.15	10.03	18.99	25.12	71.76	16.67	2,929	617-292-1000	Y

Category: Aggressive Allocation (con't)

Fund Name	Ticker Symbol	RATINGS: Overall Rating	Reward Rating	Risk Rating	Recent Up/ Downgrade	TOTAL RETURNS & PERFORMANCE: 3-Month Total Return	6-Month Total Return	1-Year Total Return	3-Year Total Return	5-Year Total Return	ASSETS: NAV	Total Assets (MIL)	NEW INVESTORS: Telephone	Open to New Investors
Putnam Dynamic Asset Allocation Growth Fund Class C	PAECX	B-	B-	B-	Down	5.11	10.03	18.94	25.09	71.63	16.01	2,929	617-292-1000	Y
Putnam Dynamic Asset Allocation Growth Fund Class M	PAGMX	B-	B-	B	Down	5.21	10.16	19.28	26.08	73.81	16.65	2,929	617-292-1000	Y
Putnam Dynamic Asset Allocation Growth Fund Class P	US9981439030	B-	B-	B	Down	5.44	10.71	20.36	28.72	79.25	17.24	2,929	617-292-1000	
Putnam Dynamic Asset Allocation Growth Fund Class R	PASRX	B-	B-	B	Down	5.23	10.28	19.55	26.96	76.03	16.65	2,929	617-292-1000	Y
Putnam Dynamic Asset Allocation Growth Fund Class R5	PADEX	B-	B-	B	Down	5.34	10.62	20.13	28.91	80.63	17.2	2,929	617-292-1000	Y
Putnam Dynamic Asset Allocation Growth Fund Class R6	PAEEX	B-	B-	B	Down	5.40	10.67	20.32	29.35	81.57	17.24	2,929	617-292-1000	Y
Putnam Dynamic Asset Allocation Growth Fund Class Y	PAGYX	B-	B-	B	Down	5.36	10.57	20.08	28.89	80.47	17.21	2,929	617-292-1000	Y
QS Growth Fund Class A	SCHAX	B-	C+	B-	Down	4.57	8.23	16.59	21.65	62.86	16.57	779.5	877-721-1926	Y
QS Growth Fund Class I	LANIX	B-	C+	B-	Down	4.61	8.34	16.95	22.83	65.29	16.5	779.5	877-721-1926	Y
QS Moderate Growth Fund Class A	SCGRX	B-	C+	B	Down	3.96	7.41	15.34	20.79	55.89	16.29	499.9	877-721-1926	Y
QS Moderate Growth Fund Class C	SCGCX	B-	C+	B-	Down	3.77	7.04	14.47	18.32	50.52	16.61	499.9	877-721-1926	Y
QS Moderate Growth Fund Class I	LLAIX	B-	C+	B	Down	4.02	7.56	15.71	21.97	57.98	16.15	499.9	877-721-1926	Y
QS Moderate Growth Fund Class R	LLMRX	B-	C+	B	Down	3.84	7.26	14.90	19.69	53.61	16.11	499.9	877-721-1926	Y
Russell Inv LifePoints Eq Growth Strategy Fund Cls R1	RELRX	B-	B-	C+	Up	3.02	7.19	16.21	23.73	56.29	13.47	642.3	800-426-7969	Y
Russell Inv LifePoints Eq Growth Strategy Fund Cls S	RELSX	B-	B-	C+	Down	3.01	7.19	16.12	23.43	55.44	13.44	642.3	800-426-7969	Y
Schwab MarketTrack All Equity Portfolio™	SWEGX	B-	B	B-	Down	5.15	10.48	19.82	31.23	83.11	18.76	675.7	877-824-5615	Y
Schwab MarketTrack Growth Portfolio™	SWHGX	B-	B-	B	Down	4.31	8.62	16.09	25.95	67.46	23.04	818.9	877-824-5615	Y
SEI Asset Alloc Trust Core Mkt Strategy Alloc Fund Cls F	SKTAX	B-	B-	B-	Down	5.74	10.61	20.07	26.39	74.43	19.04	29.4	800-342-5734	Y
SEI Asset Alloc Trust Mkt Growth Strategy Alloc Fund Cls F	SGOAX	B-	B-	B-	Down	5.74	10.61	20.11	26.31	74.52	23.67	138.3	800-342-5734	Y
SEI Asset Alloc Trust Moderate Strategy Alloc Fund Cls F	SXMAX	B-	B-	B	Down	4.46	7.45	14.31	25.02	74.47	20.72	98.6	800-342-5734	Y
SEI Asset Alloc Trust Tax-Managed Aggress Strat Fund Cls F	SISAX	B-	B-	B-	Down	5.75	10.62	20.13	26.35	74.55	21.67	74.9	800-342-5734	Y
Sterling Capital Strategic Allocation Growth Fund Class A	BCMAX	B-	C+	B	Down	2.43	7.49	15.79	20.52	52.79	12.19	24.2	800-228-1872	Y
Sterling Capital Strategic Allocation Growth Fund Class C	BCGCX	B-	C+	B-	Up	3.74	8.67	16.66	19.60	49.24	11.74	24.2	800-228-1872	Y
Sterling Capital Strategic Alloc Growth Fund Inst Shares	BCMTX	B-	C+	B	Up	2.43	7.54	16.07	21.37	54.51	12.22	24.2	800-228-1872	Y
Stringer Growth Fund Class A Shares	SRGAX	B-	C+	B-	Down	4.39	8.39	17.79	21.36		12.65	44.1		Y
Stringer Growth Fund Institutional Class Shares	SRGIX	B-	C+	B-	Down	4.49	8.56	18.15	22.30		12.68	44.1		Y
T. Rowe Price Personal Strategy Growth Fund	TRSGX	B-	B-	B	Down	4.30	9.34	21.91	30.11	75.33	33.94	2,227	410-345-2000	Y
T. Rowe Price Personal Strategy Growth Fund I Class	TGIPX	B-	B-	B	Down	4.33	9.39	22.04	30.42	75.75	33.96	2,227	410-345-2000	Y
The Disciplined Growth Investors Fund	DGIFX	B	B-	B+	Up	6.21	8.44	14.88	23.29	72.43	19.12	193.6	855-344-3863	Y
Thrivent Aggressive Allocation Fund Class A	TAAAX	B-	B-	B-	Down	4.72	9.73	20.92	30.63	78.98	15.53	1,144		Y
Thrivent Aggressive Allocation Fund Class S	TAAIX	B-	B-	B-	Down	4.75	9.86	21.21	31.97	82.39	15.66	1,144		Y
Thrivent Growth and Income Plus Fund Class A	TEIAX	B-	C+	B	Down	3.71	6.20	13.57	18.82	49.41	11.05	89.3		Y
Thrivent Growth and Income Plus Fund Class S	TEIIX	B-	C+	B	Down	3.77	6.33	13.86	19.96	51.98	11.07	89.3		Y
Thrivent Growth and Income Plus Portfolio		B-	C+	B	Down	3.83	6.40	14.00	19.96	51.36	11.4066	97.6		Y
Thrivent Moderately Aggressive Allocation Fund Class A	TMAAX	B-	B-	B	Down	3.84	7.87	16.16	25.54	63.68	14.79	2,522		Y
Thrivent Moderately Aggressive Allocation Fund Class S	TMAFX	B-	B-	B	Down	3.93	8.00	16.48	26.75	66.43	14.9	2,522		Y
Thrivent Series Aggressive Allocation Portfolio		B-	B-	B-	Down	4.84	9.99	21.51	32.33	82.16	17.5056	1,298		Y
Thrivent Series Moderately Aggressive Allocation Portfolio		B-	B-	B	Down	3.95	8.13	16.79	27.10	66.38	16.3984	6,130		Y
TIAA-CREF Lifestyle Aggressive Growth Fund Advisor Class	TSAHX	B	B	B-	Up	5.61	12.07	25.47	34.36	86.52	16.59	92.1	877-518-9161	Y
TIAA-CREF Lifestyle Aggressive Growth Fund Inst Cls	TSAIX	B	B	B-	Up	5.63	12.17	25.58	34.49	86.72	16.6	92.1	877-518-9161	Y
TIAA-CREF Lifestyle Aggressive Growth Fund Premier Class	TSAPX	B	B	B-	Up	5.54	12.05	25.32	34.00	85.35	16.64	92.1	877-518-9161	Y
TIAA-CREF Lifestyle Aggressive Growth Fund Retail Class	TSALX	B	B	B-	Up	5.52	11.94	25.19	33.21	83.68	16.54	92.1	877-518-9161	Y
TIAA-CREF Lifestyle Aggressive Growth Fund Retirement Cls	TSARX	B	B	B-	Up	5.58	11.98	25.23	33.52	84.40	16.56	92.1	877-518-9161	Y
TIAA-CREF Lifestyle Growth Fund Advisor Class	TSGHX	B-	B-	B	Down	4.56	10.01	21.23	29.61	70.15	15.52	136.8	877-518-9161	Y
TIAA-CREF Lifestyle Growth Fund Institutional Class	TSGGX	B-	B-	B	Down	4.61	10.06	21.38	29.90	70.53	15.53	136.8	877-518-9161	Y
TIAA-CREF Lifestyle Growth Fund Premier Class	TSGPX	B-	B-	B	Down	4.53	9.98	21.10	29.15	69.04	15.54	136.8	877-518-9161	Y
TIAA-CREF Lifestyle Growth Fund Retail Class	TSGLX	B-	B-	B	Down	4.58	9.91	20.99	28.70	68.01	15.47	136.8	877-518-9161	Y
TIAA-CREF Lifestyle Growth Fund Retirement Class	TSGRX	B-	B-	B	Down	4.55	9.94	21.01	28.87	68.26	15.49	136.8	877-518-9161	Y
TOPS® Aggressive Growth ETF Portfolio Class 1	US66537U7679	B-	B	C+	Down	5.50	10.91	20.69	31.15	74.29	14.94	10.8	855-572-5945	Y
TOPS® Aggressive Growth ETF Portfolio Class 2	US66537U7596	B-	B-	C+	Down	5.48	10.80	20.39	30.30	71.21	14.82	10.8	855-572-5945	Y
TOPS® Aggressive Growth ETF Portfolio Investor Class	US66537U1482	B-	B-	C+	Down	5.05	10.04	18.97	27.32	66.47	15.99	10.8	855-572-5945	Y
TOPS® Growth ETF Portfolio Class 1	US66537U7836	B-	B-	C+	Down	4.77	9.71	18.23	26.82	60.40	15.35	18.4	855-572-5945	Y

Category: Aggressive Allocation (con't)

Fund Name	Ticker Symbol	Overall Rating	Reward Rating	Risk Rating	Recent Up/ Downgrade	3-Month Total Return	6-Month Total Return	1-Year Total Return	3-Year Total Return	5-Year Total Return	NAV	Total Assets (MIL)	Telephone	Open to New Investors
		RATINGS				TOTAL RETURNS & PERFORMANCE					ASSETS		NEW INVESTORS	
TOPS® Growth ETF Portfolio Class 2	US66537U7752	B-	B-	C+	Down	4.71	9.56	17.93	25.96	58.46	15.11	18.4	855-572-5945	Y
Transamerica Asset Allocation Growth Portfolio Class A	IAAAX	B-	B-	B-	Down	4.51	9.11	20.15	28.90	76.86	15.18	1,540	888-233-4339	Y
Transamerica Asset Allocation Growth Portfolio Class B	IAABX	B-	B-	B-	Down	4.33	8.59	19.08	25.63	69.83	15.08	1,540	888-233-4339	
Transamerica Asset Allocation Growth Portfolio Class C	IAALX	B-	B-	B-	Down	4.37	8.75	19.34	26.17	70.79	14.75	1,540	888-233-4339	Y
Transamerica Asset Allocation Growth Portfolio Class I	TAGIX	B-	B-	B-	Down	4.59	9.20	20.51	29.91	79.42	15.15	1,540	888-233-4339	Y
Transamerica Asset Allocation Growth Portfolio Class R	IGWRX	B-	B-	B-	Down	4.49	8.99	19.86	27.78	74.39	15.06	1,540	888-233-4339	Y
Transamerica Asset Allocation Growth Portfolio Fund Adv	TAGVX	B-	B-	B-	Down	4.57	9.11	20.23	28.99	76.98	15.23	1,540	888-233-4339	Y
Transamerica Asset Allocation Growth Portfolio Fund Cls T1	TAGTX	B-	B-	B-	Down	4.56	9.16	20.28	29.04	77.05	15.25	1,540	888-233-4339	Y
Transamerica Asset Allocation Long Horizon R	TALRX	B-	B-	B-	Down	5.11	8.98	18.18	25.77	68.87	10.94	258.5	888-233-4339	Y
Transamerica Asset Allocation Long Horizon R4	TALFX	B-	B-	B-	Down	5.17	9.11	18.48	26.72	71.00	10.94	258.5	888-233-4339	Y
Tri-Continental Corporation	TY	B-	B-	B	Up	5.44	10.89	20.13	33.72	91.81	29.88	1,670	800-345-6611	Y
Two Oaks Diversified Growth & Income Class A Shares	TWOAX	B	C+	B		4.71	7.00	12.03	27.78	54.83	13.76	29.0	888-806-8633	Y
USAA First Start Growth Fund	UFSGX	B-	C+	B	Down	3.72	7.20	15.84	18.57	51.27	13.79	444.3	800-531-8722	Y
UTC North American Fund	UTCNX	B-	C+	B	Up	2.10	3.04	7.17	10.40	42.44	10.09	43.6		Y
VALIC Company II Aggressive Growth Lifestyle Fund	VAGLX	B-	C+	B-	Down	4.00	8.24	16.26	24.59	61.48	11.42	598.2		Y
Value Line Income & Growth Fund Institutional Class	VLIIX	B	B-	B	Up	2.29	8.56	24.31	25.25	68.07	9.9	400.3	800-243-2729	Y
Value Line Income & Growth Fund Investor Class	VALIX	B	B-	B	Up	2.13	8.37	23.86	25.56	68.48	9.95	400.3	800-243-2729	Y
Vanguard LifeStrategy Growth Fund Investor Shares	VASGX	B-	B-	B	Down	4.66	9.05	19.21	26.83	67.65	33.67	14,790	877-662-7447	Y
Virtus Global Dividend & Income Fund Inc.	ZTR	B-	C+	B	Up	3.53	6.82	18.16	14.57	47.04	13.04	312.4		Y
Virtus Growth Allocation Strategy Fund Class A	SGIAX	B-	C+	B	Down	3.93	7.70	15.86	19.27	56.16	9.49	85.7	800-243-1574	Y
Virtus Growth Allocation Strategy Fund Class C	SGILX	B-	C+	B	Down	3.84	7.40	15.30	17.08	51.51	9.19	85.7	800-243-1574	Y
Virtus Growth Allocation Strategy Fund Class I	CLVGX	B-	C+	B	Down	4.11	7.88	16.13	19.98	57.58	9.57	85.7	800-243-1574	Y
Voya Retirement Growth Portfolio Class A	IRGPX	B-	C+	B	Down	4.09	8.00	16.66	22.02	54.93	13.99	3,145	800-366-0066	Y
Voya Retirement Growth Portfolio Class I	IIRGX	B-	C+	B	Down	4.22	8.23	17.10	23.47	58.34	14.07	3,145	800-366-0066	Y
Voya Solution Aggressive Portfolio Class A	IAVAX	B-	B-	B-	Down	5.44	10.41	21.62	26.76		13.55	13.4	800-366-0066	Y
Voya Solution Aggressive Portfolio Class I	IAVIX	B-	B-	B-	Down	5.64	10.70	22.19	28.64		13.84	13.4	800-366-0066	Y
Voya Solution Aggressive Portfolio Class R6	VYRMX	B-	B-	B-	Down	5.56	10.70	22.19	28.53		13.84	13.4	800-366-0066	Y
Voya Solution Aggressive Portfolio Class S	IAVSX	B-	B-	B-	Down	5.55	10.51	21.91	27.75		13.69	13.4	800-366-0066	Y
Voya Solution Aggressive Portfolio Class S2	IAVTX	B-	B-	B-	Down	5.54	10.48	21.70	27.10		13.52	13.4	800-366-0066	Y
Voya Solution Moderately Aggressive Portfolio Class A	IAGAX	B-	C+	B-	Down	4.61	8.55	17.79	22.24	59.31	13.38	715.9	800-366-0066	Y
Voya Solution Moderately Aggressive Portfolio Class I	IAGIX	B-	C+	B-	Down	4.76	8.92	18.49	24.16	63.48	13.64	715.9	800-366-0066	Y
Voya Solution Moderately Aggressive Portfolio Class R6	VYROX	B-	C+	B-	Down	4.76	8.93	18.51	24.08	63.36	13.63	715.9	800-366-0066	Y
Voya Solution Moderately Aggressive Portfolio Class S	IAGSX	B-	C+	B-	Down	4.65	8.66	18.13	23.22	61.36	13.49	715.9	800-366-0066	Y
Voya Solution Moderately Aggressive Portfolio Class S2	IAGTX	B-	C+	B-	Down	4.58	8.58	17.95	22.63	60.10	13.46	715.9	800-366-0066	Y
Voya Strategic Allocation Growth Portfolio Class I	ISAGX	B-	C+	B-	Down	4.70	8.60	17.88	23.74	64.56	16.03	144.6	800-366-0066	Y
Voya Strategic Allocation Growth Portfolio Class S	ISGRX	B-	C+	B-	Down	4.61	8.39	17.56	22.74	62.45	15.88	144.6	800-366-0066	Y
Walden Asset Management Fund	WSBFX	B	C+	B+		5.80	7.82	14.87	24.15	65.13	17.76	119.8	617-814-1215	Y
Wells Fargo Diversified Capital Builder Fund - Class A	EKBAX	B	B	B-		3.65	7.73	14.40	34.00	96.69	10.16	983.2	800-222-8222	Y
Wells Fargo Diversified Capital Builder Fund - Class Admin	EKBDX	B	B	B-		3.59	7.88	14.46	34.61	98.43	10.17	983.2	800-222-8222	Y
Wells Fargo Diversified Capital Builder Fund - Class C	EKBCX	B-	B-	B-	Down	3.40	7.37	13.43	31.00	89.55	10.14	983.2	800-222-8222	Y
Wells Fargo Diversified Capital Builder Fund - Class Inst	EKBYX	B	B	B-		3.64	7.96	14.75	35.53	100.62	10.09	983.2	800-222-8222	Y
Wells Fargo WealthBuilder Equity Fund Class A	WEAFX	B-	B-	B-	Down	-10.34	-5.80	5.63	10.14	47.05	20.45	539.0	800-222-8222	Y
Wells Fargo WealthBuilder Growth Allocation Fund Class A	WGAFX	B-	B-	B-	Down	-8.13	-4.15	5.25	9.62	43.58	13.86	403.6	800-222-8222	Y
WSTCM Sector Select Risk - Managed Fund Inst Shares	WSTIX	B-	C	B	Up	4.74	8.27	13.48	6.26		11.5	16.5	865-243-8000	Y
WSTCM Sector Select Risk - Managed Fund Investor Shares	WSTEX	B-	C	B	Up	4.67	8.12	13.24	5.47		11.43	16.5	865-243-8000	Y

Category: Allocation

Fund Name	Ticker Symbol	RATINGS Overall Rating	Reward Rating	Risk Rating	Recent Up/ Downgrade	TOTAL RETURNS & PERFORMANCE 3-Month Total Return	6-Month Total Return	1-Year Total Return	3-Year Total Return	5-Year Total Return	ASSETS NAV	Total Assets (MIL)	NEW INVESTORS Telephone	Open to New Investors
Aberdeen Dynamic Allocation Fund Class A	GMMAX	B-	C+	B+	Up	2.39	5.48	10.83	11.86	31.86	13.88	15.0	866-667-9231	Y
Aberdeen Dynamic Allocation Fund Class C	GMMCX	B-	C	B	Up	2.26	5.12	10.12	9.61	27.31	13.61	15.0	866-667-9231	Y
Aberdeen Dynamic Allocation Fund Class R	GAGRX	B-	C+	B	Up	2.31	5.22	10.40	10.56	29.21	13.8	15.0	866-667-9231	Y
AIG Global Trends Fund A Share	GTFAX	B-	C	B+	Up	3.64	6.38	9.10	8.94	12.60	12.95	36.5	800-858-8850	Y
AIG Global Trends Fund C Share	GTFCX	B-	C	B+	Up	3.48	5.99	8.37	6.79	9.01	12.38	36.5	800-858-8850	Y
AIG Income Explorer Fund Class A	IEAAX	B-	C+	B		1.77	4.57	14.90	23.12		15.93	44.7	800-858-8850	Y
AIG Income Explorer Fund Class C	IEACX	B-	C+	B		1.63	4.26	14.12	20.74		15.9	44.7	800-858-8850	Y
AIG Income Explorer Fund Class W	IEAWX	B-	C+	B		1.81	4.67	15.14	23.85		15.93	44.7	800-858-8850	Y
AllianzGI Global Allocation Fund Administrative Class	AGAMX	B-	C+	B+	Up	3.35	7.68	16.98	18.43	35.48	11.9	364.7	800-498-5413	Y
AllianzGI Global Allocation Fund Class A	PALAX	B-	C+	B+	Up	3.35	7.60	16.89	18.28	35.31	11.6	364.7	800-498-5413	Y
AllianzGI Global Allocation Fund Class C	PALCX	B-	C+	B	Up	3.19	7.28	16.06	15.67	30.38	11.82	364.7	800-498-5413	Y
AllianzGI Global Allocation Fund Class P	AGAPX	B	C+	B+	Up	3.36	7.69	17.19	19.21	37.02	11.5	364.7	800-498-5413	Y
AllianzGI Global Allocation Fund Class R	AGARX	B-	C+	B+	Up	3.28	7.54	16.63	17.61	34.20	11.47	364.7	800-498-5413	Y
AllianzGI Global Allocation Fund Class R6	AGASX	B	C+	B+	Up	3.35	7.74	17.18	19.11	36.27	11.35	364.7	800-498-5413	Y
AllianzGI Global Allocation Fund Institutional Class	PALLX	B-	C+	B+	Up	3.37	7.69	16.94	18.88	36.75	11.57	364.7	800-498-5413	Y
AllianzGI Global Fundamental Strategy Fund Class A	AZDAX	B-	C+	B+	Up	0.57	4.28	9.77	13.38		15.39	17.2	800-498-5413	Y
AllianzGI Global Fundamental Strategy Fund Class C	AZDCX	B-	C	B	Up	0.43	3.94	8.97	10.85		15.4	17.2	800-498-5413	Y
AllianzGI Global Fundamental Strategy Fund Class P	AZDPX	B-	C+	B+	Up	0.58	4.33	9.87	13.83		15.5	17.2	800-498-5413	Y
AllianzGI Global Fundamental Strategy Fund Inst Cls	AZDIX	B-	C+	B+	Up	0.61	4.42	10.01	14.24		15.56	17.2	800-498-5413	Y
American Funds Capital Income Builder® Class 529-A	CIRAX	B-	C+	B	Down	2.40	5.61	14.13	17.38	45.48	62.79	108,816	800-421-4225	Y
American Funds Capital Income Builder® Class 529-C	CIRCX	B-	C+	B	Down	2.20	5.22	13.26	14.71	39.96	62.86	108,816	800-421-4225	Y
American Funds Capital Income Builder® Class 529-E	CIREX	B-	C+	B	Down	2.33	5.49	13.88	16.58	43.80	62.81	108,816	800-421-4225	Y
American Funds Capital Income Builder® Class 529-F	CIRFX	B-	C+	B	Down	2.45	5.74	14.40	18.17	47.13	62.8	108,816	800-421-4225	Y
American Funds Capital Income Builder® Class A	CAIBX	B-	C+	B	Down	2.42	5.65	14.24	17.71	46.15	62.82	108,816	800-421-4225	Y
American Funds Capital Income Builder® Class C	CIBCX	B-	C+	B	Down	2.20	5.24	13.32	14.91	40.40	62.9	108,816	800-421-4225	Y
American Funds Capital Income Builder® Class F-1	CIBFX	B-	C+	B	Down	2.39	5.61	14.13	17.43	45.62	62.81	108,816	800-421-4225	Y
American Funds Capital Income Builder® Class F-2	CAIFX	B-	C+	B	Down	2.46	5.76	14.44	18.36	47.54	62.77	108,816	800-421-4225	Y
American Funds Capital Income Builder® Class F-3	CFIHX	B-	C+	B	Down	2.50	5.81	14.53	18.00	46.51	62.8	108,816	800-421-4225	Y
American Funds Capital Income Builder® Class R-1	RIRAX	B-	C+	B	Down	2.20	5.22	13.29	14.88	40.40	62.84	108,816	800-421-4225	Y
American Funds Capital Income Builder® Class R-2	RIRBX	B-	C+	B	Down	2.22	5.23	13.31	14.95	40.53	62.84	108,816	800-421-4225	Y
American Funds Capital Income Builder® Class R-2E	RCEEX	B-	C+	B	Down	2.29	5.39	13.67	16.09	43.17	62.6	108,816	800-421-4225	Y
American Funds Capital Income Builder® Class R-3	RIRCX	B-	C+	B	Down	2.33	5.47	13.82	16.45	43.56	62.82	108,816	800-421-4225	Y
American Funds Capital Income Builder® Class R-4	RIREX	B-	C+	B	Down	2.40	5.63	14.14	17.50	45.76	62.79	108,816	800-421-4225	Y
American Funds Capital Income Builder® Class R-5	RIRFX	B-	C+	B	Down	2.49	5.78	14.49	18.56	47.97	62.83	108,816	800-421-4225	Y
American Funds Capital Income Builder® Class R-5E	RIRHX	B-	C+	B	Down	2.45	5.75	14.40	17.99	46.50	62.74	108,816	800-421-4225	Y
American Funds Capital Income Builder® Class R-6	RIRGX	B-	C+	B	Down	2.48	5.81	14.56	18.72	48.33	62.8	108,816	800-421-4225	Y
American Funds Global Balanced Fund Class 529-A	CBFAX	B-	C+	B	Down	2.54	5.69	13.95	16.32	42.60	32.49	14,669	800-421-4225	Y
American Funds Global Balanced Fund Class 529-C	CBFCX	B-	C+	B	Up	2.35	5.30	13.04	13.57	37.06	32.39	14,669	800-421-4225	Y
American Funds Global Balanced Fund Class 529-E	CBFEX	B-	C+	B		2.51	5.60	13.69	15.51	40.95	32.47	14,669	800-421-4225	Y
American Funds Global Balanced Fund Class 529-F-1	CBFFX	B-	C+	B	Down	2.59	5.80	14.18	17.02	44.06	32.5	14,669	800-421-4225	Y
American Funds Global Balanced Fund Class A	GBLAX	B-	C+	B	Down	2.58	5.74	13.98	16.53	43.07	32.51	14,669	800-421-4225	Y
American Funds Global Balanced Fund Class C	GBLCX	B-	C+	B	Up	2.36	5.31	13.10	13.81	37.50	32.44	14,669	800-421-4225	Y
American Funds Global Balanced Fund Class F-1	GBLEX	B-	C+	B	Down	2.57	5.74	13.95	16.39	42.77	32.53	14,669	800-421-4225	Y
American Funds Global Balanced Fund Class F-2	GBLFX	B-	C+	B	Down	2.63	5.89	14.26	17.30	44.64	32.53	14,669	800-421-4225	Y
American Funds Global Balanced Fund Class F-3	GFBLX	B-	C+	B	Down	2.63	5.91	14.36	17.65	45.38	32.5	14,669	800-421-4225	Y
American Funds Global Balanced Fund Class R-1	RGBLX	B-	C+	B	Up	2.36	5.30	13.08	14.00	38.52	32.47	14,669	800-421-4225	Y
American Funds Global Balanced Fund Class R-2	RGBBX	B-	C+	B	Up	2.36	5.33	13.14	13.90	37.66	32.41	14,669	800-421-4225	Y
American Funds Global Balanced Fund Class R-2E	RGGHX	B-	C+	B	Down	2.46	5.49	13.46	15.46	41.16	32.48	14,669	800-421-4225	Y
American Funds Global Balanced Fund Class R-3	RGBCX	B-	C+	B		2.47	5.55	13.61	15.43	40.80	32.46	14,669	800-421-4225	Y
American Funds Global Balanced Fund Class R-4	RGBEX	B-	C+	B	Down	2.58	5.73	13.97	16.45	42.98	32.51	14,669	800-421-4225	Y
American Funds Global Balanced Fund Class R-5	RGBFX	B-	C+	B	Down	2.65	5.88	14.32	17.48	45.03	32.55	14,669	800-421-4225	Y
American Funds Global Balanced Fund Class R-5E	RGBHX	B-	C+	B	Down	2.64	5.90	14.35	17.34	45.00	32.5	14,669	800-421-4225	Y

Category: Allocation (con't)

Fund Name	Ticker Symbol	RATINGS: Overall Rating	Reward Rating	Risk Rating	Recent Up/ Downgrade	TOTAL RETURNS & PERFORMANCE: 3-Month Total Return	6-Month Total Return	1-Year Total Return	3-Year Total Return	5-Year Total Return	ASSETS: NAV	Total Assets (MIL)	NEW INVESTORS: Telephone	Open to New Investors
American Funds Global Balanced Fund Class R-6	RGBGX	B-	C+	B	Down	2.66	5.91	14.38	17.67	45.40	32.53	14,669	800-421-4225	Y
Aristotle/Saul Global Opportunities Fund Class I	ARSOX	B-	B-	B		4.55	7.66	15.28	28.02	42.68	13.29	106.0		Y
Arrow DWA Balanced Fund Class A	DWAFX	B-	C	B	Up	5.21	8.08	12.84	9.72	32.52	12.91	110.8	877-277-6933	Y
Arrow DWA Balanced Fund Class C	DWATX	B-	C	B	Up	4.97	7.66	11.93	7.28	27.51	12.06	110.8	877-277-6933	Y
Arrow DWA Balanced Fund Institutional Class	DWANX	B-	C	B	Up	5.30	8.23	13.13	10.54	34.12	13.07	110.8	877-277-6933	Y
BlackRock Global Allocation Fund, Inc. Class K	MKLOX	B-	C+	B	Down	2.46	5.55	13.70	17.01	38.79	19.8	38,826	800-441-7762	Y
BlackRock Global Allocation Fund, Inc. Class R	MRLOX	B-	C+	B+	Down	2.29	5.19	12.94	14.75	34.44	18.76	38,829	800-441-7762	Y
BlackRock Global Allocation Fund, Inc. Inst Shares	MALOX	B	C+	B+	Up	2.46	5.52	13.60	16.85	38.60	19.81	38,826	800-441-7762	Y
BlackRock Global Allocation Fund, Inc. Investor A Shares	MDLOX	B-	C+	B+	Down	2.39	5.37	13.31	15.92	36.79	19.7	38,826	800-441-7762	Y
BlackRock Global Allocation Fund, Inc. Investor B Shares	MBLOX	B-	C+	B+	Up	2.48	4.41	12.36	12.51	31.20		38,829	800-441-7762	
BlackRock Global Allocation Fund, Inc. Investor C Shares	MCLOX	B-	C+	B+	Down	2.15	4.97	12.45	13.32	31.71	17.78	38,829	800-441-7762	Y
Calamos Global Dynamic Income Fund	CHW	B-	B-	B	Up	4.12	9.62	24.47	28.54	54.35	9.16	545.2	630-245-7234	Y
Calamos Global Growth & Income Fund Class A	CVLOX	B	C+	B+	Up	4.81	9.49	20.05	21.11	41.07	9.47	226.2	800-582-6959	Y
Calamos Global Growth & Income Fund Class C	CVLCX	B-	C+	B+	Up	4.66	9.10	19.06	18.34	35.84	8.43	226.2	800-582-6959	Y
Calamos Global Growth & Income Fund Class I	CGCIX	B	C+	B+	Up	4.89	9.69	20.33	22.05	42.84	9.74	226.2	800-582-6959	Y
Calamos Global Growth & Income Fund Class R	CVLRX	B	C+	B+	Up	4.78	9.43	19.81	20.15	39.32	9.3	226.2	800-582-6959	Y
Calamos Global Growth & Income Fund Class T	CVLTX	B	C+	B+	Up	3.07	7.96	15.22	19.46	37.31		219.5	800-582-6959	Y
Calamos Global Total Return Fund	CGO	B	B-	B	Up	5.63	11.60	24.72	27.90	50.87	13.42	114.4	630-245-7234	Y
Catalyst/MAP Global Balanced Fund Class A	TRXAX	B	C+	A-		3.01	3.92	11.12	10.53	32.67	12.16	23.3	866-447-4228	Y
Catalyst/MAP Global Balanced Fund Class C	TRXCX	B-	C	B+	Down	2.77	3.46	10.27	7.46	27.68	12.05	23.3	866-447-4228	Y
Catalyst/MAP Global Balanced Fund Class I	TRXIX	B	C+	A-		3.00	4.08	11.43	11.46	33.94	12.17	23.3	866-447-4228	Y
Columbia Global Opportunities Fund Advisor Class	CSDRX	B	C+	B+	Up	3.98	8.56	18.42	23.47	42.64	13.82	628.7	800-345-6611	Y
Columbia Global Opportunities Fund Class A	IMRFX	B	C+	B+	Up	3.93	8.45	18.17	22.62	41.08	13.72	628.7	800-345-6611	Y
Columbia Global Opportunities Fund Class C	RSSCX	B-	C+	B+	Down	3.68	7.99	17.28	19.85	35.84	13.23	628.7	800-345-6611	Y
Columbia Global Opportunities Fund Class K	IDRYX	B	C+	B+	Up	3.92	8.50	18.18	22.92	41.81	13.78	628.7	800-345-6611	
Columbia Global Opportunities Fund Class R	CSARX	B	C+	B+	Up	3.82	8.29	17.88	21.62	39.15	13.58	628.7	800-345-6611	Y
Columbia Global Opportunities Fund Class T	CGOPX	B	C+	B+	Up	3.95	8.49	18.16	22.41	40.72	13.66	628.7	800-345-6611	Y
Columbia Global Opportunities Fund Institutional 2 Class	CLNRX	B	C+	B+	Up	4.05	8.61	18.54	23.89	43.65	13.87	628.7	800-345-6611	Y
Columbia Global Opportunities Fund Institutional 3 Class	CGOYX	B	C+	B+	Up	3.99	8.57	18.37	22.83	41.32	13.8	628.7	800-345-6611	Y
Columbia Global Opportunities Fund Institutional Class	CSAZX	B	C+	B+	Up	3.99	8.58	18.47	23.53	42.93	13.79	628.7	800-345-6611	Y
Delaware Enhanced Global Dividend & Income	DEX	B-	B-	B-	Up	2.38	7.02	18.58	25.43	50.76	13.16	207.2		Y
Deutsche Global Income Builder Fund Class A	KTRAX	B-	C+	B-	Up	3.99	8.41	16.30	20.49	41.15	9.58	839.0	201-593-8273	Y
Deutsche Global Income Builder Fund Class R6	KTRZX	B-	C+	B-		4.08	8.62	16.81	21.37	42.16	9.56	839.0	201-593-8273	Y
Deutsche Global Income Builder Fund Class S	KTRSX	B-	C+	B-		4.04	8.52	16.54	21.23	42.59	9.58	839.0	201-593-8273	Y
Deutsche Global Income Builder Fund Institutional Class	KTRIX	B-	C+	B-		3.95	8.44	16.60	21.39	42.67	9.56	839.0	201-593-8273	Y
Deutsche Multi-Asset Global Allocation Fund - Class A	SUPAX	B-	C+	B	Up	2.83	7.05	16.56	11.34	34.41	16.15	100.7	201-593-8273	Y
Deutsche Multi-Asset Global Allocation Fund - Class C	SUPCX	B-	C	B	Up	2.63	6.61	15.73	8.83	29.44	16.1	100.7	201-593-8273	Y
Deutsche Multi-Asset Global Allocation Fund - Class S	SPGRX	B-	C+	B	Up	2.89	7.12	16.86	12.13	36.06	16.14	100.7	201-593-8273	Y
Eaton Vance Global Income Builder Fund Class A	EDIAX	B-	C+	B	Down	3.14	5.74	16.18	22.91	58.62	9.17	358.6		Y
Eaton Vance Global Income Builder Fund Class C	EDICX	B-	C+	B	Down	2.98	5.40	15.34	20.29	52.91	9.08	358.6		Y
Eaton Vance Global Income Builder Fund Class I	EDIIX	B-	C+	B	Down	3.21	5.88	16.52	24.01	60.83	9.16	358.6		Y
Eaton Vance Global Income Builder Fund Class R	EDIRX	B-	C+	B	Down	3.18	5.60	15.91	22.11	56.85	9.15	358.6		Y
Eaton Vance Multi-Strategy All Market Fund Class A	EAAMX	B-	C+	B	Up	2.64	5.06	11.29	18.42	23.80	10.83	39.1		Y
Eaton Vance Multi-Strategy All Market Fund Class C	ECAMX	B-	C+	B+	Up	2.46	4.67	10.50	15.74	19.16	10.79	39.1		Y
Eaton Vance Multi-Strategy All Market Fund Class I	EIAMX	B-	C+	B	Up	2.71	5.11	11.60	19.25	25.22	10.81	39.1		Y
Eaton Vance Tax-Advantaged Global Dividend Income Fund	ETG	B	B-	B	Up	4.91	7.81	24.66	28.98	78.80	18.56	1,399		Y
Eaton Vance Tax-Advantaged Global Dividend Opp Fund	ETO	B	B-	B+	Up	4.90	8.71	24.83	32.68	77.79	24.93	359.2		Y
Federated Global Allocation Fund Class A Shares	FSTBX	B-	C+	B	Up	3.67	8.15	17.05	14.88	43.47	20.16	426.1	800-341-7400	Y
Federated Global Allocation Fund Class B Shares	FSBBX	B-	C+	B	Up	3.45	7.69	16.04	12.08	37.68	19.67	426.1	800-341-7400	Y
Federated Global Allocation Fund Class C Shares	FSBCX	B-	C+	B	Up	3.42	7.75	16.12	12.29	38.08	19.6	426.1	800-341-7400	Y
Federated Global Allocation Fund Class R Shares	FSBKX	B-	C+	B	Up	3.53	7.92	16.48	13.40	40.44	20.02	426.1	800-341-7400	Y
Federated Global Allocation Fund Class R6	FSBLX	B-	C+	B	Up	3.75	8.31	17.33	15.33	44.03	20.16	426.1	800-341-7400	Y

Category: Allocation (con't)

Fund Name	Ticker Symbol	RATINGS: Overall Rating	Reward Rating	Risk Rating	Recent Up/ Downgrade	TOTAL RETURNS & PERFORMANCE: 3-Month Total Return	6-Month Total Return	1-Year Total Return	3-Year Total Return	5-Year Total Return	ASSETS: NAV	Total Assets (MIL)	NEW INVESTORS: Telephone	Open to New Investors
Federated Global Allocation Fund Institutional Shares	SBFIX	B-	C+	B	Up	3.73	8.31	17.35	15.91	45.50	20.27	426.1	800-341-7400	Y
Fidelity Advisor® Global Balanced Fund Class A	FGLAX	B-	C+	B	Up	4.40	8.67	19.57	18.41	37.09	24.72	485.0	617-563-7000	Y
Fidelity Advisor® Global Balanced Fund Class C	FGLCX	B-	C+	B	Up	4.17	8.17	18.61	15.48	31.61	23.9	485.0	617-563-7000	Y
Fidelity Advisor® Global Balanced Fund Class I	FGLIX	B-	C+	B	Up	4.48	8.82	19.94	19.41	38.99	24.97	485.0	617-563-7000	Y
Fidelity Advisor® Global Balanced Fund Class M	FGLTX	B-	C+	B	Up	4.32	8.49	19.23	17.40	35.20	24.48	485.0	617-563-7000	Y
Fidelity Advisor® Global Strategies Fund Class A	FDASX	B	C+	B+	Up	4.59	8.56	19.01	24.41	40.41	9.32	174.9	617-563-7000	Y
Fidelity Advisor® Global Strategies Fund Class C	FDCSX	B	C+	B+	Up	4.42	7.99	18.18	21.58	35.31	9.16	174.9	617-563-7000	Y
Fidelity Advisor® Global Strategies Fund Class M	FDTSX	B	C+	B+	Up	4.46	8.33	18.67	23.43	38.67	9.28	174.9	617-563-7000	Y
Fidelity Advisor® Global Strategies Fund I Class	FDYIX	B	C+	B+	Up	4.61	8.56	19.36	25.28	42.25	9.35	174.9	617-563-7000	Y
Fidelity® Global Balanced Fund	FGBLX	B-	C+	B	Up	4.49	8.82	19.90	19.38	39.06	25.06	485.0	617-563-7000	Y
Fidelity® Global Strategies Fund	FDYSX	B	C+	B+	Up	4.72	8.57	19.37	25.29	42.27	9.35	174.9	617-563-7000	Y
First Eagle Global Fund Class A	SGENX	B	C+	B+		3.21	6.02	13.48	23.52	49.33	59.06	57,793	800-334-2143	Y
First Eagle Global Fund Class C	FESGX	B	C+	B+		3.02	5.62	12.62	20.76	43.79	57.05	57,793	800-334-2143	Y
First Eagle Global Fund Class I	SGIIX	B	C+	B+		3.27	6.16	13.77	24.51	51.28	59.31	57,793	800-334-2143	Y
First Eagle Global Fund Class R6	FEGRX	B	C+	B+		3.30	6.18	13.75	23.81	49.68	59.31	57,793	800-334-2143	Y
First Eagle Global Income Builder Fund Class A	FEBAX	B-	C+	B	Down	2.18	4.47	12.95	21.11	38.47	12.13	1,418	800-334-2143	Y
First Eagle Global Income Builder Fund Class C	FEBCX	B-	C+	B		2.08	4.09	12.14	18.44	33.35	12.1	1,418	800-334-2143	Y
First Eagle Global Income Builder Fund Class I	FEBIX	B-	C+	B	Down	2.24	4.61	13.27	22.09	40.12	12.1	1,418	800-334-2143	Y
First Eagle Global Income Builder Fund Class R6	FEBRX	B-	C+	B	Down	2.34	4.63	13.54	22.38	40.46	12.1	1,418	800-334-2143	Y
Franklin Mutual Quest Fund Class A	TEQIX	B-	C+	B	Up	1.53	4.09	6.94	16.48	52.62	15.66	5,279	650-312-2000	Y
Franklin Mutual Quest Fund Class C	TEMQX	B-	C+	B	Up	1.34	3.68	6.16	13.89	47.23	15.39	5,279	650-312-2000	Y
Franklin Mutual Quest Fund Class R	FMQSX	B-	C+	B	Up	1.51	3.98	6.72	15.66	50.98	15.45	5,279	650-312-2000	Y
Franklin Mutual Quest Fund Class R6	FMQRX	B-	C+	B	Down	1.59	4.25	7.27	17.63	55.13	15.86	5,279	650-312-2000	Y
Franklin Mutual Quest Fund Class Z	MQIFX	B-	C+	B	Down	1.64	4.23	7.25	17.41	54.75	15.88	5,279	650-312-2000	Y
GMO Benchmark-Free Allocation Fund Class III	GBMFX	B-	C+	B	Up	2.74	5.05	13.04	11.66	26.08	27.43	13,414	617-330-7500	Y
GMO Benchmark-Free Allocation Fund Class IV	GBMBX	B-	C+	B	Up	2.73	5.03	13.06	11.80	26.40	27.42	13,414	617-330-7500	Y
GMO Benchmark-Free Allocation Fund Class MF	US3620148052	B-	C+	B	Up	2.73	5.02	13.09	11.85	26.47	27.44	13,414	617-330-7500	Y
GMO Benchmark-Free Allocation Series Fund Class R6	GBMRX	B-	C+	B	Up	2.70	5.01	12.88	11.29	25.26	10.59	323.0	617-330-7500	Y
GMO Benchmark-Free Fund Class III	GBFFX	B-	C+	B	Up	3.74	6.82	17.05	19.20	31.41	20.65	4,381	617-330-7500	Y
GMO Global Asset Allocation Fund Class III	GMWAX	B-	C+	B	Up	3.38	6.63	15.72	16.70	34.31	33.12	2,501	617-330-7500	Y
GMO Global Asset Allocation Series Fund Class R6	GATRX	B-	C+	B	Up	3.32	6.52	15.42	16.10	33.18	9.71	193.3	617-330-7500	Y
GMO Implementation Fund	GIMFX	B-	C+	B	Up	2.98	5.50	14.08	12.41	36.49	13.89	11,384	617-330-7500	Y
GMO Risk Premium Fund Class III	GMRPX	B	B-	B+	Up	1.66	4.72	12.85	32.96	45.15	27.57	150.4	617-330-7500	Y
GMO Risk Premium Fund Class VI	GMOKX	B	B-	B+	Up	1.66	4.78	12.94	33.31	45.80	27.71	150.4	617-330-7500	Y
GMO Strategic Opportunities Allocation Fund Class III	GBATX	B-	C+	B	Up	4.25	8.24	19.30	20.88	49.81	21.89	1,937	617-330-7500	Y
Goldman Sachs Growth Strategy Portfolio Class A	GGSAX	B-	B-	B-	Down	4.48	10.38	21.02	27.96	57.81	15.83	892.1	800-526-7384	Y
Goldman Sachs Growth Strategy Portfolio Class C	GGSCX	B-	B-	B-	Down	4.25	9.88	20.08	25.06	51.86	15.81	892.1	800-526-7384	Y
Goldman Sachs Growth Strategy Portfolio Class R	GGSRX	B-	B-	B-	Down	4.39	10.22	20.67	26.92	55.75	15.42	892.1	800-526-7384	Y
Goldman Sachs Growth Strategy Portfolio Class R6	GGSUX	B-	B-	B-	Down	4.53	10.51	21.50	29.53	60.89	15.81	892.1	800-526-7384	Y
Goldman Sachs Growth Strategy Portfolio Institutional Cls	GGSIX	B-	B-	B-	Down	4.55	10.60	21.52	29.51	60.87	15.81	892.1	800-526-7384	Y
Goldman Sachs Growth Strategy Portfolio Investor Class	GGSTX	B-	B-	B-	Down	4.51	10.50	21.30	28.90	59.78	15.59	892.1	800-526-7384	Y
Goldman Sachs Growth Strategy Portfolio Service Class	GGSSX	B-	B-	B-	Down	4.45	10.30	20.88	27.55	57.08	15.77	892.1	800-526-7384	Y
Goldman Sachs Satellite Strategies Fund Class R6	GXSUX	B-	C+	B	Up	2.62	6.85	14.66	18.12	22.89	8.43	681.4	800-526-7384	Y
Goldman Sachs Satellite Strategies Portfolio Class A	GXSAX	B-	C+	B	Up	2.62	6.72	14.28	16.70	20.41	8.45	681.4	800-526-7384	Y
Goldman Sachs Satellite Strategies Portfolio Class R	GXSRX	B-	C+	B	Up	2.56	6.62	13.94	15.82	18.92	8.41	681.4	800-526-7384	Y
Goldman Sachs Satellite Strategies Portfolio Inst Cls	GXSIX	B-	C+	B	Up	2.74	6.97	14.79	18.08	22.83	8.43	681.4	800-526-7384	Y
Goldman Sachs Satellite Strategies Portfolio Investor Cls	GXSTX	B-	C+	B	Up	2.70	6.89	14.62	17.53	21.90	8.43	681.4	800-526-7384	Y
Goldman Sachs Satellite Strategies Portfolio Service Class	GXSSX	B-	C+	B	Up	2.48	6.54	14.05	16.22	19.83	8.43	681.4	800-526-7384	Y
GuidePath® Multi-Asset Income Alloc Fund Serv Shares	GPMIX	B-	C+	B		1.97	3.84	9.73	13.47	26.79	10.9	120.3	800-664-5345	Y
Hartford Conservative Allocation Fund Class A	HCVAX	B-	C	B	Up	-0.57	1.55	6.85	7.37	8.79	10.44	127.7	888-843-7824	Y
Hartford Conservative Allocation Fund Class F	HCVFX	B-	C	B	Up	-0.76	1.45	6.75	7.26	8.68	10.44	127.7	888-843-7824	Y
Hartford Conservative Allocation Fund Class R3	HCVRX	B-	C	B	Up	-0.28	1.75	6.85	6.80	7.57	10.44	127.7	888-843-7824	Y

Category: Allocation (con't)

		RATINGS				TOTAL RETURNS & PERFORMANCE					ASSETS		NEW INVESTORS	
Fund Name	Ticker Symbol	Overall Rating	Reward Rating	Risk Rating	Recent Up/ Downgrade	3-Month Total Return	6-Month Total Return	1-Year Total Return	3-Year Total Return	5-Year Total Return	NAV	Total Assets (MIL)	Telephone	Open to New Investors
Hartford Conservative Allocation Fund Class R5	HCVTX	B-	C	B	Up	-0.85	1.35	6.84	7.95	10.16	10.46	127.7	888-843-7824	Y
Hartford Global All-Asset Fund Class C	HLACX	B-	C+	B	Down	2.91	6.28	16.06	20.22	34.55	10.61	311.1	888-843-7824	Y
Hartford Global All-Asset Fund Class F	HLAFX	B-	C+	B	Down	3.15	6.82	17.33	24.23	42.14	10.77	311.1	888-843-7824	Y
Hartford Global All-Asset Fund Class I	HLAIX	B	C+	B+	Up	3.17	6.75	17.26	23.92	41.39	10.77	311.1	888-843-7824	Y
Hartford Global All-Asset Fund Class R3	HLARX	B-	C+	B	Down	2.97	6.48	16.57	22.00	37.82	10.74	311.1	888-843-7824	Y
Hartford Global All-Asset Fund Class R4	HLASX	B	C+	B+	Up	3.08	6.63	16.92	23.12	39.97	10.88	311.1	888-843-7824	Y
Hartford Global All-Asset Fund Class R5	HLATX	B	C+	B+	Up	3.14	6.84	17.43	23.45	40.98	10.69	311.1	888-843-7824	Y
Hartford Moderate Allocation Fund Class I	HBAIX	B-	C+	B-	Down	0.75	3.97	11.66	14.05	27.79	12.11	476.8	888-843-7824	Y
Hartford Moderate Allocation Fund Class R5	HBATX	B-	C+	B-	Down	0.83	3.97	11.76	13.97	27.48	12.12	476.8	888-843-7824	Y
IVA Worldwide Fund Class A	IVWAX	B-	C+	B	Up	2.70	5.77	13.54	17.11	42.86	18.87	8,328	866-941-4482	
IVA Worldwide Fund Class C	IVWCX	B-	C+	B	Up	2.52	5.35	12.71	14.50	37.62	18.49	8,328	866-941-4482	
IVA Worldwide Fund Class I	IVWIX	B-	C+	B	Up	2.77	5.94	13.83	17.98	44.73	18.92	8,328	866-941-4482	
Ivy Global Income Allocation Fund Class A	IVBAX	B-	C+	B	Up	3.35	5.68	13.73	17.13	33.17	15.6	686.5	800-777-6472	Y
Janus Henderson All Asset Fund Class A	HGAAX	B-	C+	B+	Up	2.39	5.35	10.95	13.43	25.28	10.51	50.1	877-335-2687	Y
Janus Henderson All Asset Fund Class D	HGADX	B-	C+	B	Up	2.42	5.49	11.22	14.32	26.78	10.44	50.1	877-335-2687	Y
Janus Henderson All Asset Fund Class I	HGAIX	B-	C+	B	Up	2.42	5.49	11.23	14.32	26.79	10.44	50.1	877-335-2687	Y
Janus Henderson All Asset Fund Class N	HGARX	B-	C+	B	Up	2.45	5.53	11.28	14.31	26.78	10.42	50.1	877-335-2687	Y
Janus Henderson All Asset Fund Class T	HGATX	B-	C+	B	Up	2.44	5.51	11.25	14.34	26.81	10.46	50.1	877-335-2687	Y
Janus Henderson Dividend & Income Builder Fund Class A	HDAVX	B-	C+	B	Down	2.62	7.30	17.47	23.47	52.39	13.7	153.8	877-335-2687	Y
Janus Henderson Dividend & Income Builder Fund Class C	HDCVX	B	C+	B+	Up	2.44	6.93	16.60	20.71	46.69	13.55	153.8	877-335-2687	Y
Janus Henderson Dividend & Income Builder Fund Class D	HDDVX	B-	C+	B	Down	2.58	7.39	17.79	24.37	54.11	13.69	153.8	877-335-2687	Y
Janus Henderson Dividend & Income Builder Fund Class I	HDIVX	B-	C+	B	Down	2.65	7.38	17.77	24.35	54.09	13.7	153.8	877-335-2687	Y
Janus Henderson Dividend & Income Builder Fund Class N	HDRVX	B-	C+	B	Down	2.67	7.44	17.66	24.15	53.84	13.67	153.8	877-335-2687	Y
Janus Henderson Dividend & Income Builder Fund Class S	HDQVX	B-	C+	B	Down	2.60	7.23	17.46	23.41	52.16	13.69	153.8	877-335-2687	Y
Janus Henderson Dividend & Income Builder Fund Class T	HDTVX	B-	C+	B	Down	2.58	7.30	17.69	24.26	53.97	13.68	153.8	877-335-2687	Y
Janus Henderson Global Alloc Fund - Conservative Cls A	JCAAX	B-	C+	B+	Up	2.56	5.30	12.74	12.00	29.82	12.67	237.1	877-335-2687	Y
Janus Henderson Global Alloc Fund - Conservative Cls C	JCACX	B-	C	B+	Up	2.36	4.90	11.90	10.47	26.24	12.43	237.1	877-335-2687	Y
Janus Henderson Global Alloc Fund - Conservative Cls D	JMSCX	B-	C+	B+	Up	2.63	5.44	12.87	12.74	31.19	12.71	237.1	877-335-2687	
Janus Henderson Global Alloc Fund - Conservative Cls I	JCAIX	B-	C+	B+	Up	2.61	5.43	12.94	12.86	31.40	12.7	237.1	877-335-2687	Y
Janus Henderson Global Alloc Fund - Conservative Cls S	JCASX	B-	C+	B+	Up	2.50	5.18	12.46	11.51	28.83	12.61	237.1	877-335-2687	Y
Janus Henderson Global Alloc Fund - Conservative Cls T	JSPCX	B-	C+	B+	Up	2.63	5.37	12.80	12.48	30.91	12.69	237.1	877-335-2687	Y
Janus Henderson Global Allocation Fund - Growth Class A	JGCAX	B-	C+	B	Up	4.17	8.35	19.55	20.17	50.25	14.25	262.7	877-335-2687	Y
Janus Henderson Global Allocation Fund - Growth Class C	JGCCX	B-	C+	B	Up	3.98	7.99	18.70	18.15	45.53	14.02	262.7	877-335-2687	Y
Janus Henderson Global Allocation Fund - Growth Class D	JNSGX	B-	C+	B	Down	4.19	8.40	19.71	20.67	51.35	14.34	262.7	877-335-2687	
Janus Henderson Global Allocation Fund - Growth Class I	JGCIX	B-	C+	B	Down	4.22	8.52	19.84	20.98	51.97	14.34	262.7	877-335-2687	Y
Janus Henderson Global Allocation Fund - Growth Class S	JGCSX	B-	C+	B	Up	4.11	8.22	19.29	19.54	48.99	14.18	262.7	877-335-2687	Y
Janus Henderson Global Allocation Fund - Growth Class T	JSPGX	B-	C+	B	Down	4.21	8.43	19.67	20.59	51.09	14.33	262.7	877-335-2687	Y
Janus Henderson Global Allocation Fund - Moderate Class A	JMOAX	B-	C+	B	Down	3.39	6.85	16.03	16.04	39.77	13.11	264.5	877-335-2687	Y
Janus Henderson Global Allocation Fund - Moderate Class C	JMOCX	B-	C+	B	Up	3.20	6.39	15.29	14.10	35.27	12.94	264.5	877-335-2687	Y
Janus Henderson Global Allocation Fund - Moderate Class D	JNSMX	B-	C+	B+	Down	3.41	6.93	16.25	16.73	40.96	13.18	264.5	877-335-2687	
Janus Henderson Global Allocation Fund - Moderate Class I	JMOIX	B-	C+	B+	Down	3.48	6.92	16.34	16.86	41.27	13.17	264.5	877-335-2687	Y
Janus Henderson Global Allocation Fund - Moderate Class S	JMOSX	B-	C+	B	Down	3.30	6.63	15.77	15.41	38.45	13.01	264.5	877-335-2687	Y
Janus Henderson Global Allocation Fund - Moderate Class T	JSPMX	B-	C+	B+	Down	3.43	6.88	16.22	16.56	40.55	13.15	264.5	877-335-2687	Y
Janus Henderson VIT Global Alloc Port - Moderate Inst Cls	JMAPX	B-	C+	B+	Down	3.35	6.93	16.54	17.17	40.79	12.87	7.5	877-335-2687	Y
Janus Henderson VIT Global Alloc Port - Moderate Serv Cls	US4710214283	B-	C+	B	Down	3.33	6.83	16.25	16.36	39.59	12.84	7.5	877-335-2687	Y
JNL/American Funds Balanced Fund Class A	US46644W7992	B	C+	B+	Up	2.93	7.23	16.70	20.98	42.47	11.56	730.3		Y
JNL/American Funds Balanced Fund Class I	US46644W7810	B	C+	B+	Up	3.02	7.38	17.03	21.79	43.86	11.92	730.3		Y
JNL/BlackRock Global Allocation Fund Class A	US46648M8543	B-	C+	B+	Down	2.68	5.75	13.83	16.37	37.20	12.62	4,014		Y
JNL/BlackRock Global Allocation Fund Class I	US46648M8477	B-	C+	B	Down	2.74	5.82	14.12	17.08	38.42	12.72	4,014		Y
JPMorgan Global Allocation Fund Class A	GAOAX	B	C+	B+	Up	3.83	7.28	16.81	21.48	48.50	18.62	2,478	800-480-4111	Y
JPMorgan Global Allocation Fund Class C	GAOCX	B-	C+	B	Down	3.68	6.99	16.21	19.65	44.79	18.4	2,478	800-480-4111	Y
JPMorgan Global Allocation Fund Class I	GAOSX	B-	C+	B	Down	3.87	7.36	17.11	22.34	50.35	18.69	2,478	800-480-4111	Y

Category: Allocation (con't)

Fund Name	Ticker Symbol	RATINGS: Overall Rating	Reward Rating	Risk Rating	Recent Up/ Downgrade	TOTAL RETURNS & PERFORMANCE: 3-Month Total Return	6-Month Total Return	1-Year Total Return	3-Year Total Return	5-Year Total Return	ASSETS: NAV	Total Assets (MIL)	NEW INVESTORS: Telephone	Open to New Investors
JPMorgan Global Allocation Fund Class R2	GAONX	B	C+	B+	Up	3.75	7.08	16.53	20.58	46.57	18.56	2,478	800-480-4111	Y
JPMorgan Global Allocation Fund Class R6	GAOZX	B-	C+	B		3.96	7.46	17.21	22.45	50.49	18.68	2,478	800-480-4111	Y
JPMorgan Global Allocation Fund Class T	JGCTX	B-	C+	B	Down	3.78	7.18	16.76	21.37	48.41	18.6	2,478	800-480-4111	Y
Leuthold Global Fund Class Institutional	GLBIX	B-	C+	B	Up	3.89	8.78	16.71	16.20	43.43	9.65	96.0	800-273-6886	Y
Leuthold Global Fund Class Retail	GLBLX	B-	C+	B+	Up	3.88	8.64	16.52	15.47	41.89	9.54	96.0	800-273-6886	Y
Loomis Sayles Global Allocation Fund Class A	LGMAX	B	B-	A-	Up	4.53	8.65	21.78	28.54	55.90	22.1	1,877	800-862-4863	Y
Loomis Sayles Global Allocation Fund Class C	LGMCX	B	C+	B+	Up	4.32	8.23	20.90	25.63	50.09	21.91	1,877	800-862-4863	Y
Loomis Sayles Global Allocation Fund Class N	LGMNX	B	B-	A-	Up	4.59	8.80	22.06	29.45	57.85	22.19	1,877	800-862-4863	Y
Loomis Sayles Global Allocation Fund Class Y	LSWWX	B	B-	A-	Up	4.58	8.79	22.11	29.50	57.91	22.21	1,877	800-862-4863	Y
MainStay Income Builder Fund Class A	MTRAX	B-	C+	B	Down	2.62	5.21	12.14	17.13	51.34	19.66	1,837	800-624-6782	Y
MainStay Income Builder Fund Class I	MTOIX	B-	C+	B	Down	2.61	5.29	12.36	17.97	53.22	19.83	1,837	800-624-6782	Y
MainStay Income Builder Fund Class R2	MTXRX	B-	C+	B	Down	2.54	5.10	11.98	16.62	47.75	19.64	1,837	800-624-6782	Y
MainStay Income Builder Fund Investor Class	MTINX	B-	C+	B-	Down	2.53	5.07	11.98	16.62	49.94	19.67	1,837	800-624-6782	Y
MassMutual Select BlackRock Global Alloc Fund Admin Cls	MGSLX	B-	C+	B+	Down	2.40	5.43	13.46	15.83	36.45	11.52	610.3		Y
MassMutual Select BlackRock Global Allocation Fund Class A	MGJAX	B-	C+	B+	Down	2.36	5.31	13.08	14.96	34.70	11.14	610.3		Y
MassMutual Select BlackRock Global Allocation Fund Class I	MGJIX	B	C+	B+	Up	2.51	5.63	13.82	16.90	38.50	11.17	610.3		Y
MassMutual Select BlackRock Global Allocation Fund Cls R4	MGJFX	B-	C+	B	Down	2.37	5.34	13.17	15.28	35.68	11.03	610.3		Y
MassMutual Select BlackRock Global Allocation Fund Cls R5	MGSSX	B-	C+	B	Down	2.47	5.55	13.62	16.42	37.65	11.32	610.3		Y
MassMutual Select BlackRock Global Alloc Fund Serv Cls	MGSYX	B-	C+	B	Down	2.40	5.52	13.50	16.17	37.05	11.16	610.3		Y
MFS® Global Total Return Fund Class A	MFWTX	B	C+	B+		2.88	5.91	15.13	18.76	43.95	18.18	2,194	877-960-6077	Y
MFS® Global Total Return Fund Class B	MFWBX	B-	C+	B+	Up	2.71	5.53	14.26	16.16	38.74	18.53	2,194	877-960-6077	Y
MFS® Global Total Return Fund Class C	MFWCX	B-	C+	B+	Up	2.70	5.52	14.30	16.12	38.74	18.27	2,194	877-960-6077	Y
MFS® Global Total Return Fund Class I	MFWIX	B	C+	B+		2.98	6.05	15.45	19.74	45.82	18	2,194	877-960-6077	Y
MFS® Global Total Return Fund Class R1	MFWGX	B-	C+	B+	Up	2.70	5.53	14.30	16.12	38.69	18.2	2,194	877-960-6077	Y
MFS® Global Total Return Fund Class R2	MGBRX	B	C+	B+		2.88	5.81	14.91	17.95	42.20	18	2,194	877-960-6077	Y
MFS® Global Total Return Fund Class R3	MFWHX	B	C+	B+		2.88	5.92	15.18	18.84	44.12	18.13	2,194	877-960-6077	Y
MFS® Global Total Return Fund Class R4	MFWJX	B	C+	B+		3.00	6.09	15.46	19.75	45.84	18.21	2,194	877-960-6077	Y
MFS® Global Total Return Fund Class R6	MFWLX	B	C+	B+		3.01	6.10	15.56	20.08	46.48	18	2,194	877-960-6077	Y
Morgan Stanley Inst Trust Global Strategist Cls A	MBAAX	B-	C+	B-	Up	3.37	6.89	16.26	13.72	36.60	16.85	338.6	855-332-5306	Y
Morgan Stanley Inst Trust Global Strategist Cls Inst	MPBAX	B-	C+	B	Up	3.45	7.13	16.67	14.88	38.76	16.97	338.6	855-332-5306	Y
Neuberger Berman Global Allocation Fund Class A	NGLAX	B-	C+	B	Up	3.39	8.21	17.62	14.89	31.83	11.7	20.3	212-476-9000	Y
Neuberger Berman Global Allocation Fund Class C	NGLCX	B-	C+	B	Up	3.16	7.74	16.62	12.23	26.97	11.4	20.3	212-476-9000	Y
Neuberger Berman Global Allocation Fund Institutional Cls	NGLIX	B-	C+	B	Up	3.52	8.41	17.99	16.10	34.13	11.77	20.3	212-476-9000	Y
Northern Global Tactical Asset Allocation Fund	BBALX	B-	C+	B	Up	3.70	7.52	14.17	21.30	40.19	13.19	91.3	800-595-9111	Y
Nuveen Diversified Dividend and Income Fund	JDD	B	C+	B+	Up	2.95	5.93	12.36	21.98	58.44	12.71	260.0	312-917-8146	Y
Nuveen Real Asset Income Fund Class A	NRIAX	B-	C+	B	Down	0.63	3.30	11.65	18.31	45.61	24.14	2,058	312-917-8146	Y
Nuveen Real Asset Income Fund Class C	NRICX	B-	C+	B	Down	0.49	2.98	10.90	15.67	40.33	24.15	2,058	312-917-8146	Y
Nuveen Real Asset Income Fund Class I	NRIIX	B-	C+	B	Down	0.67	3.41	11.91	19.20	47.34	24.14	2,058	312-917-8146	Y
Nuveen Real Asset Income Fund Class R6	NRIFX	B-	C+	B	Down	0.71	3.45	11.99	19.33	47.50	24.24	2,058	312-917-8146	Y
Nuveen Tax-Advantaged Total Return Strategy Fund	JTA	B-	B-	C+	Up	3.13	7.75	20.15	23.27	79.00	14.22	199.3	312-917-8146	Y
Old Westbury Strategic Opportunities Fund	OWSOX	B-	C+	B	Down	2.63	5.72	13.26	16.83	35.86	7.82	5,572	212-708-9100	Y
Oppenheimer Global Allocation Fund Class A	QVGIX	B	C+	A-	Up	2.29	4.67	14.83	20.49	42.87	19.76	1,640	800-225-5677	Y
Oppenheimer Global Allocation Fund Class B	QGRBX	B	C+	B+	Up	2.05	4.24	13.91	17.73	37.36	18.91	1,640	800-225-5677	
Oppenheimer Global Allocation Fund Class C	QGRCX	B	C+	B+	Up	2.04	4.24	13.97	17.78	37.60	18.92	1,640	800-225-5677	Y
Oppenheimer Global Allocation Fund Class I	QGRIX	B	C+	A-	Up	2.36	4.86	15.28	22.06	46.01	19.72	1,640	800-225-5677	Y
Oppenheimer Global Allocation Fund Class R	QGRNX	B	C+	A-	Up	2.16	4.47	14.53	19.62	41.03	19.38	1,640	800-225-5677	Y
Oppenheimer Global Allocation Fund Class Y	QGRYX	B	C+	A-	Up	2.28	4.78	15.10	21.40	44.83	19.72	1,640	800-225-5677	Y
PIMCO Global Multi-Asset Fund Class C	PGMCX	B-	C+	B	Up	2.97	6.15	13.37	15.14	11.78	12.32	503.2	866-746-2602	Y
PIMCO Global Multi-Asset Fund Class P	PGAPX	B-	C+	B-	Down	3.33	6.77	14.70	19.31	18.72	12.74	503.2	866-746-2602	Y
PIMCO Global Multi-Asset Fund Institutional Class	PGAIX	B-	C+	B-	Down	3.35	6.83	14.78	19.69	19.32	12.76	503.2	866-746-2602	Y
RiverFront Dynamic Equity Income Fund Class I	RLIIX	B-	B-	B-	Down	3.91	8.36	17.58	24.87	55.79	14.29	79.4	866-759-5679	Y
RiverFront Dynamic Equity Income Fund Class Investor	RLGAX	B-	C+	B-	Down	3.85	8.19	17.31	23.92	53.71	14.35	79.4	866-759-5679	Y

Category: Allocation (con't)

Fund Name	Ticker Symbol	RATINGS: Overall Rating	Reward Rating	Risk Rating	Recent Up/ Downgrade	TOTAL RETURNS & PERFORMANCE: 3-Month Total Return	6-Month Total Return	1-Year Total Return	3-Year Total Return	5-Year Total Return	ASSETS: NAV	Total Assets (MIL)	NEW INVESTORS: Telephone	Open to New Investors
SEI Asset Allocation Trust Aggressive Strategy Fund Cls D	SASDX	B-	C+	B-	Down	4.41	9.03	17.97	21.07	49.27	15.09	252.8	800-342-5734	Y
SEI Asset Allocation Trust Aggressive Strategy Fund Cls F	SSGAX	B-	C+	B	Down	4.65	9.44	18.79	23.88	55.16	15.22	252.8	800-342-5734	Y
SEI Asset Allocation Trust Aggressive Strategy Fund Cls I	SEAIX	B-	C+	B-	Down	4.51	9.27	18.42	22.92	53.20	14.82	252.8	800-342-5734	Y
T. Rowe Price Global Allocation Fund	RPGAX	B-	C+	B	Down	3.07	6.92	17.01	23.77		12.68	329.0	410-345-2000	Y
T. Rowe Price Global Allocation Fund Advisor Class	PAFGX	B	C+	B+	Up	3.01	6.78	16.68	23.32		12.64	329.0	410-345-2000	Y
T. Rowe Price Global Allocation Fund I Class	TGAFX	B-	C+	B	Down	3.07	6.99	17.16	24.37		12.7	329.0	410-345-2000	Y
The Hartford Global All-Asset Fund Class A	HLAAX	B-	C+	B	Down	3.06	6.57	16.88	22.97	39.55	10.73	311.1	888-843-7824	Y
The Hartford Global All-Asset Fund Class Y	HLAYX	B-	C+	B	Down	3.22	6.89	17.40	24.30	42.22	10.78	311.1	888-843-7824	Y
Thrivent Partner Worldwide Allocation Fund Class A	TWAAX	B-	C+	B	Up	3.07	8.20	23.11	24.63	38.37	11.14	910.4		Y
Thrivent Partner Worldwide Allocation Fund Class S	TWAIX	B-	B-	B	Up	3.25	8.45	23.70	26.33	41.39	11.19	910.4		Y
Thrivent Partner Worldwide Allocation Portfolio		B-	B-	B	Up	3.21	8.49	23.84	26.52	41.25	11.0226	2,026		Y
Touchstone Dynamic Global Allocation Fund C	TSMCX	B-	C+	B	Up	2.58	5.81	13.10	10.36	36.05	12.28	114.5	800-543-0407	Y
UBS Global Allocation Fund Class A	BNGLX	B-	C+	B+	Down	3.19	7.13	16.64	15.44	36.96	12.17	342.1	212-882-5586	Y
UBS Global Allocation Fund Class C	BNPCX	B-	C+	B	Up	3.05	6.64	15.84	12.84	31.92	11.88	342.1	212-882-5586	Y
UBS Global Allocation Fund Class P	BPGLX	B	C+	B+	Up	3.38	7.24	17.08	16.39	38.96	12.43	342.1	212-882-5586	Y
USAA Cornerstone Aggressive Fund	UCAGX	B-	C+	B-	Up	4.69	8.75	17.90	19.58	41.12	12.86	316.4	800-531-8722	Y
Voya Global Multi-Asset Fund Class A	ATLAX	B-	C+	B	Down	4.88	8.87	17.40	21.48	43.65	11.97	163.0	800-366-0066	Y
Voya Global Multi-Asset Fund Class C	ACLGX	B-	C+	B-	Down	4.72	8.51	16.53	18.88	38.29	12.08	163.0	800-366-0066	Y
Voya Global Multi-Asset Fund Class I	ALEGX	B-	C+	B	Down	4.97	9.00	17.73	22.40	45.42	12.14	163.0	800-366-0066	Y
Voya Global Multi-Asset Fund Class O	IDSIX	B-	C+	B-	Down	4.91	8.93	17.41	21.57	43.64	11.9	163.0	800-366-0066	Y
Voya Global Multi-Asset Fund Class W	IAFWX	B-	C+	B	Down	5.04	9.08	17.72	22.58	45.53	12.13	163.0	800-366-0066	Y
Voya Global Multi-Asset Fund R6	VGMRX	B-	C+	B		4.93	8.96	17.69	22.36	45.37	12.13	163.0	800-366-0066	Y
Voya Global Perspectives Fund Class A	IAPVX	B-	C+	B	Up	3.24	6.80	14.81	17.36		11.65	45.5	800-366-0066	Y
Voya Global Perspectives Fund Class C	ICPVX	B-	C+	B	Up	3.08	6.49	14.05	14.80		11.54	45.5	800-366-0066	Y
Voya Global Perspectives Fund Class I	IIPVX	B-	C+	B	Up	3.23	6.97	15.09	18.11		11.66	45.5	800-366-0066	Y
Voya Global Perspectives Fund Class R	IRPVX	B-	C+	B	Up	3.19	6.77	14.60	16.45		11.62	45.5	800-366-0066	Y
Voya Global Perspectives Fund Class W	IWPVX	B-	C+	B	Up	3.31	6.95	15.16	18.17		11.68	45.5	800-366-0066	Y
Voya Global Perspectives Portfolio Class A	IPARX	B-	C+	B	Up	3.52	6.79	14.60	17.02		11.46	132.1	800-366-0066	Y
Voya Global Perspectives Portfolio Class I	IPIRX	B-	C+	B	Up	3.58	6.91	14.98	18.15		11.55	132.1	800-366-0066	Y
Voya Global Perspectives Portfolio Class S	IPSRX	B-	C+	B	Up	3.51	6.81	14.71	17.16		11.48	132.1	800-366-0066	Y
Voya Global Target Payment Fund Class A	IGPAX	B-	C+	B	Up	2.80	5.60	12.10	16.24	34.80	8.49	505.6	800-366-0066	Y
Voya Global Target Payment Fund Class C	IGPCX	B-	C+	B	Up	2.57	5.12	11.32	13.57	29.84	8.78	505.6	800-366-0066	Y
Voya Global Target Payment Fund Class I	IGPIX	B-	C+	B	Up	2.89	5.64	12.47	17.22	36.71	8.46	505.6	800-366-0066	Y
Voya Global Target Payment Fund Class R	IGPRX	B-	C+	B	Up	2.85	5.58	11.93	15.53	33.30	8.49	505.6	800-366-0066	Y
Voya Global Target Payment Fund Class W	IGPWX	B-	C+	B	Up	2.89	5.66	12.36	17.08	36.43	8.44	505.6	800-366-0066	Y
Wells Fargo Absolute Return Fund - Class Admin	WARDX	B-	C	B	Up	2.57	4.70	12.28	9.62	22.07	11.42	5,696	800-222-8222	Y
Wells Fargo Absolute Return Fund - Class Inst	WABIX	B-	C	B	Up	2.64	4.76	12.56	10.36	23.64	11.39	5,696	800-222-8222	Y
Wells Fargo Absolute Return Fund - Class R	WARHX	B-	C	B	Up	2.42	4.47	11.90	8.96	22.28	11.37	5,696	800-222-8222	Y
Wells Fargo Absolute Return Fund - Class R6	WARRX	B-	C+	B	Up	2.64	4.86	12.77	10.76	24.87	11.39	5,696	800-222-8222	Y
Wells Fargo Asset Allocation Fund - Class A	EAAFX	B-	C+	B	Up	3.20	6.18	14.80	13.89	28.38	14.47	3,288	800-222-8222	Y
Wells Fargo Asset Allocation Fund - Class Admin	EAIFX	B-	C+	B	Up	3.19	6.28	14.97	14.51	29.57	14.63	3,288	800-222-8222	Y
Wells Fargo Asset Allocation Fund - Class Inst	EAAIX	B-	C+	B	Up	3.30	6.42	15.21	15.22	31.12	14.49	3,288	800-222-8222	Y
Wells Fargo Asset Allocation Fund - Class R	EAXFX	B-	C+	B	Up	3.15	6.16	14.52	13.17	26.87	14.36	3,288	800-222-8222	Y
Westwood Worldwide Income Opp Fund Inst Shares	WWIOX	B-	C	B	Up	2.66	5.57	11.80			10.4	5.0		Y
Wildermuth Endowment Strategy Fund Class A	WESFX	B-	C	B	Up	3.24	7.16	13.21	37.42		12.92	--	877-562-0856	Y
Wildermuth Endowment Strategy Fund Class C	US96812D2062	B-	C	B	Up	2.96	6.74	12.35	34.93		12.73	--	877-562-0856	Y
Wildermuth Endowment Strategy Fund Class I	US96812D3052	B-	C+	B	Up	3.23	7.65	13.73	37.51		12.98	--	877-562-0856	Y

Category: Asia Equity

Fund Name	Ticker Symbol	RATINGS				TOTAL RETURNS & PERFORMANCE					ASSETS		NEW INVESTORS	
		Overall Rating	Reward Rating	Risk Rating	Recent Up/ Downgrade	3-Month Total Return	6-Month Total Return	1-Year Total Return	3-Year Total Return	5-Year Total Return	NAV	Total Assets (MIL)	Telephone	Open to New Investors
BlackRock Asian Dragon Fund Class R	MRPCX	B-	B-	B-	Up	6.93	11.14	27.52	27.10	51.62	13.07	238.0	800-441-7762	Y
BlackRock Asian Dragon Fund Institutional Shares	MAPCX	B-	B-	B-	Up	7.15	11.50	28.37	29.74	56.92	17.15	238.0	800-441-7762	Y
BlackRock Asian Dragon Fund Investor A Shares	MDPCX	B-	B-	B-	Up	7.11	11.39	28.15	28.93	55.27	16.94	238.0	800-441-7762	Y
BlackRock Asian Dragon Fund Investor C Shares	MCPCX	B-	B-	B-	Up	6.88	10.91	27.04	25.92	49.23	11.51	238.0	800-441-7762	Y
Columbia Pacific/Asia Fund Advisor Class	CPRAX	B+	A	B	Up	9.18	18.11	41.99	48.57	67.83	11.58	233.1	800-345-6611	Y
Columbia Pacific/Asia Fund Class A	CASAX	B+	A	B	Up	9.10	17.99	41.71	47.40	66.03	11.51	233.1	800-345-6611	Y
Columbia Pacific/Asia Fund Class C	CASCX	B+	A	B	Up	8.92	17.55	40.62	44.18	59.93	11.3	233.1	800-345-6611	Y
Columbia Pacific/Asia Fund Class T	CPAWX	B+	A	B	Up	9.05	17.93	41.64	47.40	65.99	11.5	233.1	800-345-6611	Y
Columbia Pacific/Asia Fund Institutional 3 Class	CPAYX	B+	A	B	Up	9.19	18.23	41.99	48.59	68.11	11.43	233.1	800-345-6611	Y
Columbia Pacific/Asia Fund Institutional Class	USPAX	B+	A	B	Up	9.21	18.16	41.94	48.54	68.05	11.56	233.1	800-345-6611	Y
Fidelity® Pacific Basin Fund	FPBFX	A-	A	B	Up	10.10	16.83	40.06	52.55	97.65	35.48	998.8	617-563-7000	Y
Invesco Pacific Growth Fund Class A	TGRAX	A-	A	B	Up	12.02	21.38	46.88	53.53	70.89	35.59	111.1	800-659-1005	Y
Invesco Pacific Growth Fund Class B	TGRBX	B+	A	B	Up	11.83	20.98	45.77	50.18	64.61	32.8	111.1	800-659-1005	
Invesco Pacific Growth Fund Class C	TGRCX	B+	A	B	Up	11.80	20.93	45.82	50.22	64.63	32.87	111.1	800-659-1005	Y
Invesco Pacific Growth Fund Class R	TGRRX	A-	A	B	Up	11.93	21.23	46.48	52.38	68.61	35.17	111.1	800-659-1005	Y
Invesco Pacific Growth Fund Class R6	TGRUX	A-	A	B	Up	12.10	21.60	46.82	51.25	65.79	36.31	111.1	800-659-1005	Y
Invesco Pacific Growth Fund Class Y	TGRDX	A-	A	B	Up	12.09	21.56	47.23	54.74	72.95	36.25	111.1	800-659-1005	Y
Invesco Pacific Growth Fund R5 Shares	TGRSX	A-	A	B	Up	12.10	21.60	47.36	55.24	74.04	36.31	111.1	800-659-1005	Y
JNL/Mellon Capital Pacific RIM 30 Fund Class A	US46648M6984	B	B	B-	Up	3.91	7.43	23.23	40.96	66.16	16.73	315.5		Y
JNL/Mellon Capital Pacific Rim 30 Fund Class I	US46648M6802	B	B	B-		3.99	7.57	23.48	41.88	67.78	16.9	315.5		Y
Matthews Asia Dividend Fund Institutional Class	MIPIX	B+	A-	B	Up	8.85	13.22	34.77	45.85	63.78	19.73	6,888	800-789-2742	Y
Matthews Asia Dividend Fund Investor Class	MAPIX	B+	A-	B	Up	8.88	13.16	34.69	45.38	62.91	19.74	6,888	800-789-2742	Y
Matthews Asia Growth Fund Institutional Class	MIAPX	B	B+	B-	Up	9.71	17.23	39.64	40.85	73.90	27.45	801.5	800-789-2742	Y
Matthews Asia Growth Fund Investor Class	MPACX	B	B+	B-	Up	9.64	17.12	39.38	40.06	72.20	27.25	801.5	800-789-2742	Y
MS Asia-Pacific Fund, Inc.	APF	B	B	B-	Up	7.70	12.09	35.23	30.67	37.98	21.01	277.1	855-332-5306	Y
Vanguard Pacific Stock Index Fund Admiral Shares	VPADX	B	B	B	Up	8.27	12.62	28.61	38.05	56.95	89.97	8,471	877-662-7447	Y
Vanguard Pacific Stock Index Fund Institutional Shares	VPKIX	B	B	B	Up	8.25	12.57	28.54	38.14	57.11	13.76	8,471	877-662-7447	Y
Vanguard Pacific Stock Index Fund Investor Shares	VPACX	B	B	B	Up	8.23	12.55	28.38	37.45	55.85	13.87	8,471	877-662-7447	Y
Wells Fargo Asia Pacific Fund - Class A	WFAAX	B	B	B-	Up	9.37	15.46	35.69	34.53	59.89	15.5	166.1	800-222-8222	Y
Wells Fargo Asia Pacific Fund - Class Admin	WFADX	B	B+	B-	Up	9.45	15.56	35.86	35.05	61.12	15.28	166.1	800-222-8222	Y
Wells Fargo Asia Pacific Fund - Class C	WFCAX	B	B	B-	Up	9.19	15.08	34.67	31.57	54.00	14.72	166.1	800-222-8222	Y
Wells Fargo Asia Pacific Fund - Class Inst	WFPIX	B	B+	B-	Up	9.49	15.70	36.23	36.07	62.70	15.17	166.1	800-222-8222	Y

Category: Asia ex-Japan Equity

Fund Name	Ticker Symbol	RATINGS				TOTAL RETURNS & PERFORMANCE					ASSETS		NEW INVESTORS	
		Overall Rating	Reward Rating	Risk Rating	Recent Up/ Downgrade	3-Month Total Return	6-Month Total Return	1-Year Total Return	3-Year Total Return	5-Year Total Return	NAV	Total Assets (MIL)	Telephone	Open to New Investors
Aberdeen Asia Pacific (ex-Japan) Equity Fund Class A	APJAX	B-	B-	C	Up	7.92	11.23	37.73	28.03	28.16	13.64	11.6	866-667-9231	Y
Aberdeen Asia Pacific (ex-Japan) Equity Fund Inst Cls	AAPIX	B-	B-	C	Up	8.02	11.39	38.03	28.90	29.68	13.72	11.6	866-667-9231	Y
Aberdeen Asia Pacific (ex-Japan) Eq Fund Inst Serv Cls	AAPEX	B-	B-	C	Up	8.02	11.40	37.81	28.89	29.45	13.7	11.6	866-667-9231	Y
Asia Pacific Fund, Inc	APB	B	A-	B-	Up	8.05	14.32	36.94	34.09	39.44	15.15	158.9	852-288-0926	Y
Columbia Asia Pacific ex-Japan Fund Class A	CAJAX	B	B+	C+	Up	9.52	17.53	43.32	34.87	49.81	14.18	38.8	800-345-6611	Y
Columbia Asia Pacific ex-Japan Fund Class C	CAJCX	B-	B	C+	Up	9.41	17.16	42.16	31.81	44.17	14.03	38.8	800-345-6611	Y
Columbia Asia Pacific ex-Japan Fund Class R	CAJRX	B	B	C+	Up	9.52	17.42	42.90	33.84	47.85	14.07	38.8	800-345-6611	Y
Columbia Asia Pacific ex-Japan Fund Institutional 2 Class	TAPRX	B	B+	C+	Up	9.74	17.82	43.69	36.29	52.51	14.23	38.8	800-345-6611	Y
Columbia Asia Pacific ex-Japan Fund Institutional 3 Class	CAPYX	B	B+	C+	Up	9.64	17.80	43.67	36.27	52.49	14.07	38.8	800-345-6611	Y
Columbia Asia Pacific ex-Japan Fund Institutional Class	CAJZX	B	B+	C+	Up	9.59	17.69	43.49	35.83	51.58	14.18	38.8	800-345-6611	Y
DFA Asia Pacific Small Company Portfolio Institutional Cls	DFRSX	B-	B	B-	Up	7.19	11.71	25.16	32.97	25.68	23.87	335.7	512-306-7400	Y
Fidelity Advisor® Emerging Asia Fund Class A	FEAAX	B+	A	C+	Up	10.26	16.90	46.75	41.62	58.05	41.09	314.6	617-563-7000	Y

Category: Asia ex-Japan Equity (con't)

Fund Name	Ticker Symbol	RATINGS: Overall Rating	Reward Rating	Risk Rating	Recent Up/ Downgrade	TOTAL RETURNS & PERFORMANCE: 3-Month Total Return	6-Month Total Return	1-Year Total Return	3-Year Total Return	5-Year Total Return	ASSETS: NAV	Total Assets (MIL)	NEW INVESTORS: Telephone	Open to New Investors
Fidelity Advisor® Emerging Asia Fund Class C	FERCX	B+	A	C+	Up	10.07	16.47	45.68	38.51	52.27	37.4	314.6	617-563-7000	Y
Fidelity Advisor® Emerging Asia Fund Class M	FEATX	B+	A	C+	Up	10.18	16.76	46.30	40.30	55.66	39.94	314.6	617-563-7000	Y
Fidelity Advisor® Emerging Asia Fund I Class	FERIX	B+	A	C+	Up	10.36	17.08	47.16	42.92	60.46	42.31	314.6	617-563-7000	Y
Fidelity® Emerging Asia Fund	FSEAX	B+	A	C+	Up	10.30	16.76	46.36	42.05	59.73	45.04	1,266	617-563-7000	Y
Goldman Sachs Asia Equity Fund Class A	GSAGX	B+	A	B	Up	11.45	22.92	51.59	49.90	59.78	29.1	86.3	800-526-7384	Y
Goldman Sachs Asia Equity Fund Class C	GSACX	B+	A	B	Up	11.24	22.42	50.39	46.54	53.83	26.52	86.3	800-526-7384	Y
Goldman Sachs Asia Equity Fund Institutional Class	GSAIX	B+	A	B	Up	11.57	23.15	52.15	51.71	62.97	30.8	86.3	800-526-7384	Y
Goldman Sachs Asia Equity Fund Investor Class	GSAEX	B+	A	B	Up	11.52	23.06	51.97	51.01	61.28	30.64	86.3	800-526-7384	Y
Guinness Atkinson Asia Focus Fund	IASMX	B	A	C+	Up	11.38	19.81	47.09	42.24	31.38	22.59	19.8	800-915-6566	Y
Guinness Atkinson Asia Pacific Dividend Builder Fund	GAADX	B+	A	B-	Up	7.82	14.43	36.70	41.88	52.63	17.85	7.4	800-915-6566	Y
Invesco Asia Pacific Growth Fund Class A	ASIAX	B-	B-	C+	Up	5.81	10.10	29.05	28.40	44.79	35.39	970.8	800-659-1005	Y
Invesco Asia Pacific Growth Fund Class R6	ASISX	B-	B-	C+	Up	5.90	10.34	29.43	28.78	45.21	35.41	970.8	800-659-1005	Y
Invesco Asia Pacific Growth Fund Class Y	ASIYX	B-	B-	C+	Up	5.90	10.25	29.35	29.37	46.62	35.44	970.8	800-659-1005	Y
Janus Henderson Asia Equity Fund Class A	JAQAX	B+	A	C+	Up	7.14	11.83	39.25	36.80	47.14	11.94	42.3	877-335-2687	Y
Janus Henderson Asia Equity Fund Class C	JAQCX	B	A	C+	Up	6.93	11.34	38.36	33.96	41.98	11.87	42.3	877-335-2687	Y
Janus Henderson Asia Equity Fund Class D	JAQDX	B+	A	C+	Up	7.10	11.84	39.42	37.62	48.37	12.05	42.3	877-335-2687	
Janus Henderson Asia Equity Fund Class I	JAQIX	B+	A	C+	Up	7.14	11.89	39.64	38.13	49.43	12.04	42.3	877-335-2687	Y
Janus Henderson Asia Equity Fund Class S	JAQSX	B+	A	C+	Up	7.10	11.78	39.25	37.01	47.29	11.98	42.3	877-335-2687	Y
Janus Henderson Asia Equity Fund Class T	JAQTX	B+	A	C+	Up	7.12	11.82	39.49	37.53	48.31	11.91	42.3	877-335-2687	Y
JOHCM Asia Ex-Japan Equity Fund Class I	JOAIX	B	B	B-	Up	4.87	10.75	31.23	28.12		12.66	373.1	866-260-9549	Y
JOHCM Asia Ex-Japan Equity Fund Class II	JOAAX	B	B	B-	Up	4.75	10.63	30.91	27.31		12.62	373.1	866-260-9549	Y
JOHCM Asia Ex-Japan Equity Fund Institutional Shares	JOAMX	B	B	B-	Up	4.80	10.77	31.25	28.39		12.65	373.1	866-260-9549	Y
Matthews Asia Innovators Fund Institutional Class Shares	MITEX	B+	A	B-	Up	9.69	17.58	53.18	45.75	120.14	14.26	200.9	800-789-2742	Y
Matthews Asia Innovators Fund Investor Class Shares	MATFX	B+	A	B-	Up	9.66	17.51	52.88	44.88	118.14	14.19	200.9	800-789-2742	Y
Matthews Emerging Asia Fund Institutional Class	MIASX	B	B	B-	Down	7.25	6.67	18.69	39.14		15.57	457.1	800-789-2742	Y
Matthews Emerging Asia Fund Investor Class	MEASX	B	B	B-	Down	7.12	6.46	18.42	38.08		15.51	457.1	800-789-2742	Y
Matthews Pacific Tiger Fund Institutional Class	MIPTX	B	B	B-	Up	11.26	16.51	40.17	38.74	63.12	31.63	9,228	800-789-2742	Y
Matthews Pacific Tiger Fund Investor Class	MAPTX	B	B	B-	Up	11.23	16.43	39.96	38.01	61.69	31.66	9,228	800-789-2742	Y
Mirae Asset Asia Fund Class A	MALAX	B	B	C+	Up	10.94	19.29	48.28	34.62	66.59	13.79	17.9	212-205-8300	Y
Mirae Asset Asia Fund Class C	MCLAX	B-	B	C+	Up	10.75	18.86	47.16	31.65	60.50	12.98	17.9	212-205-8300	Y
Mirae Asset Asia Fund Class I	MILAX	B	B	C+	Up	11.03	19.40	48.62	35.55	68.61	14.09	17.9	212-205-8300	Y
T. Rowe Price Asia Opportunities Fund	TRAOX	B+	A	B-	Up	8.36	14.43	43.23	48.39		14.87	94.6	410-345-2000	Y
T. Rowe Price Asia Opportunities Fund Advisor Class	PAAOX	B+	A	B-	Up	8.31	14.32	43.06	47.65		14.83	94.6	410-345-2000	Y
T. Rowe Price Asia Opportunities Fund I Class	TRASX	B+	A	B-	Up	8.42	14.57	43.40	48.57		14.89	94.6	410-345-2000	Y
T. Rowe Price New Asia Fund	PRASX	B	B+	C+	Up	8.00	13.60	41.33	35.18	45.27	19.56	3,172	410-345-2000	Y
T. Rowe Price New Asia Fund I Class	PNSIX	B	B+	C+	Up	8.05	13.70	41.51	35.52	45.64	19.58	3,172	410-345-2000	Y

Category: Cautious Allocation

Fund Name	Ticker Symbol	RATINGS: Overall Rating	Reward Rating	Risk Rating	Recent Up/ Downgrade	TOTAL RETURNS & PERFORMANCE: 3-Month Total Return	6-Month Total Return	1-Year Total Return	3-Year Total Return	5-Year Total Return	ASSETS: NAV	Total Assets (MIL)	NEW INVESTORS: Telephone	Open to New Investors
AB All Market Income Portfolio Advisor Class	MRKYX	B-	C	B	Up	1.85	4.53	11.21	23.21		10.25	95.4	212-969-1000	Y
AB All Market Income Portfolio Class A	MRKAX	B-	C	B	Up	1.69	4.41	10.88	22.22		10.23	95.4	212-969-1000	Y
AB All Market Income Portfolio Class C	MRKCX	B-	C	B	Up	1.60	4.04	10.08	19.60		10.24	95.4	212-969-1000	Y
AB Conservative Wealth Strategy Advisor Class	ABPYX	B	C	A-	Up	1.98	3.91	8.55	11.97	24.92	12.18	232.0	212-969-1000	Y
AB Conservative Wealth Strategy Class A	ABPAX	B	C	A-	Up	1.98	3.84	8.32	11.18	23.24	12.14	232.0	212-969-1000	Y
AB Conservative Wealth Strategy Class B	ABPBX	B-	C	B+	Up	1.73	3.34	7.41	8.58	18.70	12.41	232.0	212-969-1000	
AB Conservative Wealth Strategy Class C	ABPCX	B-	C	B+	Up	1.78	3.43	7.50	8.66	18.81	12.13	232.0	212-969-1000	Y
AB Conservative Wealth Strategy Class I	APWIX	B-	C	B	Up	1.93	3.87	8.43	11.84	24.67	12.32	232.0	212-969-1000	Y

Category: Cautious Allocation (con't)

Fund Name	Ticker Symbol	RATINGS: Overall Rating	Reward Rating	Risk Rating	Recent Up/ Downgrade	TOTAL RETURNS & PERFORMANCE: 3-Month Total Return	6-Month Total Return	1-Year Total Return	3-Year Total Return	5-Year Total Return	ASSETS: NAV	Total Assets (MIL)	NEW INVESTORS: Telephone	Open to New Investors
AB Conservative Wealth Strategy Class K	APWKX	B-	C	B	Up	1.91	3.78	8.18	10.85	22.81	12.12	232.0	212-969-1000	Y
AB Conservative Wealth Strategy Class R	APPRX	B-	C	B	Up	1.82	3.60	7.90	9.79	20.84	12.17	232.0	212-969-1000	Y
AB Tax-Managed All Market Income Portfolio Advisor Class	AGIYX	B	C+	A-	Up	1.59	4.57	11.26	13.67	31.91	12.89	128.4	212-969-1000	Y
AB Tax-Managed All Market Income Portfolio Class A	AGIAX	B	C+	A-	Up	1.50	4.41	10.93	12.79	30.15	12.87	128.4	212-969-1000	Y
AB Tax-Managed All Market Income Portfolio Class B	AGIBX	B-	C	B+	Up	1.43	4.08	10.16	10.28	25.41	13.17	128.4	212-969-1000	
AB Tax-Managed All Market Income Portfolio Class C	AGICX	B-	C	B+	Up	1.35	4.03	10.17	10.27	25.48	13.08	128.4	212-969-1000	Y
Aberdeen Diversified Income Fund Class A	GMAAX	B-	C+	B	Down	2.14	4.65	10.62	14.18	28.97	12.62	18.2	866-667-9231	Y
Aberdeen Diversified Income Fund Class I	GMAIX	B-	C+	B	Down	2.22	4.81	11.02	15.33	30.93	12.62	18.2	866-667-9231	Y
Aberdeen Diversified Income Fund Cls Institutional Service	GAMSX	B-	C+	B	Down	2.24	4.85	11.00	15.30	30.91	12.6	18.2	866-667-9231	Y
AdvisorOne CLS Growth and Income Fund Class N	CLERX	B-	C+	B	Up	3.18	6.58	12.18	15.95	32.66	11.36	462.0		Y
AllianzGI Income & Growth Fund Class A	AZNAX	B-	C+	B	Down	3.40	6.54	13.45	20.99	52.58	11.48	3,426	800-498-5413	Y
AllianzGI Income & Growth Fund Class C	AZNCX	B-	C+	B-	Down	3.20	6.18	12.62	18.34	46.99	10.63	3,426	800-498-5413	Y
AllianzGI Income & Growth Fund Class P	AIGPX	B-	C+	B	Down	3.47	6.70	13.79	21.90	54.41	11.74	3,426	800-498-5413	Y
AllianzGI Income & Growth Fund Class R	AIGRX	B-	C+	B	Down	3.34	6.41	13.17	20.07	50.55	11.48	3,426	800-498-5413	Y
AllianzGI Income & Growth Fund Institutional Class	AZNIX	B-	C+	B	Down	3.47	6.69	13.86	22.25	55.15	11.84	3,426	800-498-5413	Y
American Century Inv One Choice Port®: Cons Inv Cls	AOCIX	B	C+	A-	Up	2.51	5.16	11.08	15.23	36.96	13.77	1,269	800-444-4015	Y
American Century Inv One Choice Port®: Conservative R Cls	AORSX	B	C+	A-	Up	2.45	4.97	10.61	13.58	33.66	13.78	1,269	800-444-4015	Y
American Century Inv One Choice Port®: Very Cons Inv Cls	AONIX	B	C	A-	Up	1.59	3.12	6.45	10.97	22.77	12.06	454.3	800-444-4015	Y
American Century Inv One Choice Port®: Very Cons R Cls	AORHX	B-	C	A-	Up	1.45	2.85	5.91	9.30	19.71	12.07	454.3	800-444-4015	Y
American Century Multi-Asset Income Fund R Class	AMJWX	B-	C	B	Up	0.92	3.37	9.25	16.51		10.22	57.6	800-444-4015	Y
American Century Strategic Alloc: Conservative Fund A Cls	ACCAX	B	C+	A-	Up	2.35	4.92	10.36	13.41	32.90	5.77	521.5	800-444-4015	Y
American Century Strategic Alloc: Conservative Fund C Cls	AACCX	B-	C	B+	Up	2.35	4.57	9.74	11.03	28.17	5.7	521.5	800-444-4015	Y
American Century Strategic Alloc: Conservative Fund I Cls	ACCIX	B-	C+	B	Up	2.65	5.16	11.04	15.08	36.05	5.78	521.5	800-444-4015	Y
American Century Strat Alloc: Conservative Fund Inv Cls	TWSCX	B	C+	A-	Up	2.60	5.06	10.82	14.42	34.72	5.78	521.5	800-444-4015	Y
American Century Strategic Alloc: Conservative Fund R Cls	AACRX	B	C+	A-	Up	2.29	4.61	10.10	12.51	31.20	5.76	521.5	800-444-4015	Y
American Century Strategic Alloc: Conservative Fund R5 Cls	AACGX	B-	C+	B	Up	2.65	5.15	10.96	14.56	34.89	5.79	521.5	800-444-4015	Y
American Century Strategic Alloc: Conservative Fund R6 Cls	AACDX	B-	C+	B	Up	2.69	5.24	11.20	15.58	36.84	5.78	521.5	800-444-4015	Y
American Funds College 2021 Fund Class 529-A	CTOAX	B-	C	A-	Up	0.00	1.05	3.44	7.25	27.40	11.13	1,468	800-421-4225	Y
American Funds College 2021 Fund Class 529-C	CTOCX	B-	C	A-	Up	-0.13	0.67	2.70	4.78	22.56	11.04	1,468	800-421-4225	Y
American Funds College 2021 Fund Class 529-E	CTOEX	B-	C	A-	Up	-0.11	0.86	3.16	6.44	25.85	11.09	1,468	800-421-4225	Y
American Funds College 2021 Fund Class 529F1	CTOFX	B	C	A	Up	0.01	1.07	3.64	7.90	28.80	11.15	1,468	800-421-4225	Y
American Funds College 2024 Fund Class 529-A	CFTAX	B	C+	A-	Up	1.54	3.69	7.90	12.67	39.82	11.92	1,338	800-421-4225	Y
American Funds College 2024 Fund Class 529-C	CTFCX	B-	C	B	Up	1.34	3.34	7.02	10.04	34.39	11.81	1,338	800-421-4225	Y
American Funds College 2024 Fund Class 529-E	CTFEX	B-	C	B	Up	1.42	3.58	7.61	11.78	37.91	11.88	1,338	800-421-4225	Y
American Funds College 2024 Fund Class 529F1	CTFFX	B-	C+	B	Up	1.57	3.80	8.09	13.38	41.31	11.95	1,338	800-421-4225	Y
American Funds Tax-Advantaged Income Portfolio Class A	TAIAX	B-	C+	B	Up	3.43	6.98	14.24	21.53	50.22	13.6	1,756	800-421-4225	Y
American Funds Tax-Advantaged Income Portfolio Class C	TAICX	B	C+	A-	Up	3.17	6.55	13.36	18.95	44.92	13.52	1,756	800-421-4225	Y
American Funds TaxAdvantaged Income Portfolio Class F1	TAIFX	B-	C+	B	Up	3.37	6.92	14.20	21.56	50.32	13.59	1,756	800-421-4225	Y
American Funds TaxAdvantaged Income Portfolio Class F2	TXIFX	B-	C+	B		3.43	7.04	14.41	22.55	52.15	13.61	1,756	800-421-4225	Y
American Funds Tax-Advantaged Income Portfolio Class F-3	TYIFX	B-	C+	B		3.46	7.10	14.54	22.68	52.32	13.6	1,756	800-421-4225	Y
AXA Charter Conservative Portfolio Class B	US00248T5048	B-	C	B+	Up	1.47	3.51	7.95	10.93			31.3	877-222-2144	Y
AXA Charter Moderate Portfolio Class B	US00248T5956	B-	C+	B	Up	2.35	5.20	10.88	13.74			33.6	877-222-2144	Y
AXA Conservative Allocation Portfolio Class K	US00247C5857	B	C	A	Up	1.03	2.22	5.29	8.31	17.14		1,219	877-222-2144	Y
AXA Conservative Growth Strategy Fund Class IB	US2689543443	B-	C+	B	Up	2.00	3.99	8.03	12.41	30.62		1,605	877-222-2144	Y
AXA Conservative Growth Strategy Fund Class IB	US2689543690	B-	C	B+	Up	0.74	1.83	4.30	6.79	14.98		1,605	877-222-2144	Y
AXA Conservative-Plus Allocation Portfolio Class K	US00247C5774	B-	C+	B	Up	2.28	4.35	9.26	13.67	31.48		1,391	877-222-2144	Y
AXA Premier VIP Conservative Allocation Fund Class A	US00247C7754	B	C	A	Up	0.99	2.07	5.02	7.60	15.78		1,219	877-222-2144	Y
AXA Premier VIP Conservative Allocation Fund Class B	US00247C7671	B	C	A	Up	0.99	2.18	5.02	7.61	15.78		1,219	877-222-2144	Y
AXA Premier VIP Conservative-Plus Allocation Fund Class A	US00247C7598	B-	C+	B	Up	2.13	4.21	8.89	12.72	29.59		1,391	877-222-2144	Y
AXA Premier VIP Conservative-Plus Allocation Fund Class B	US00247C7424	B-	C+	B	Up	2.13	4.21	8.89	12.83	29.72		1,391	877-222-2144	Y
Berwyn Income Fund	BERIX	B-	C	B+	Up	1.13	1.37	3.91	9.02	31.46	13.42	1,657	610-296-1400	Y
BlackRock 20/80 Target Allocation Fund Class K	BKCPX	B	C	A	Up	1.66	3.80	8.05	12.54	36.03	11.55	330.6	800-441-7762	Y

Category: Cautious Allocation (con't)

		RATINGS				TOTAL RETURNS & PERFORMANCE					ASSETS		NEW INVESTORS	
Fund Name	Ticker Symbol	Overall Rating	Reward Rating	Risk Rating	Recent Up/ Downgrade	3-Month Total Return	6-Month Total Return	1-Year Total Return	3-Year Total Return	5-Year Total Return	NAV	Total Assets (MIL)	Telephone	Open to New Investors
BlackRock 20/80 Target Allocation Fund Inst Shares	BICPX	B	C	A	Up	1.65	3.78	7.94	12.50	35.98	11.55	330.6	800-441-7762	Y
BlackRock 20/80 Target Allocation Fund Investor A Shares	BACPX	B	C	A	Up	1.58	3.56	7.56	11.35	33.48	11.42	330.6	800-441-7762	Y
BlackRock 20/80 Target Allocation Fund Investor C Shares	BCCPX	B	C	A-	Up	1.41	3.23	6.87	8.92	28.65	11.33	330.6	800-441-7762	Y
BlackRock 20/80 Target Allocation Fund R Shares	BRCPX	B	C	A	Up	1.55	3.44	7.27	10.36	31.71	11.38	330.6	800-441-7762	Y
BlackRock 40/60 Target Allocation Fund Class K	BKMPX	B-	C+	B	Up	2.68	5.61	11.68	16.92	50.12	11.94	398.3	800-441-7762	Y
BlackRock 40/60 Target Allocation Fund Class R Shares	BRMPX	B-	C+	B	Up	2.52	5.30	11.13	15.17	46.29	11.81	398.3	800-441-7762	Y
BlackRock 40/60 Target Allocation Fund Institutional	BIMPX	B-	C+	B	Up	2.75	5.59	11.76	16.89	50.08	11.94	398.3	800-441-7762	Y
BlackRock 40/60 Target Allocation Fund Investor A Shares	BAMPX	B-	C+	B	Up	2.60	5.36	11.27	15.70	47.49	11.85	398.3	800-441-7762	Y
BlackRock 40/60 Target Allocation Fund Investor C Shares	BCMPX	B	C+	A-	Up	2.40	5.03	10.50	13.09	41.98	11.73	398.3	800-441-7762	Y
BlackRock Managed Income Fund Class K Shares	BLDRX	B-	C+	B	Up	1.18	2.48	5.44	14.43	14.73	10.05	168.5	800-441-7762	Y
BlackRock Managed Income Fund Institutional Shares	BLDIX	B-	C+	B	Up	1.07	2.35	5.29	14.23	14.19	10.02	168.5	800-441-7762	Y
BlackRock Managed Income Fund Investor A Shares	BLADX	B-	C	B	Up	1.01	2.22	5.02	13.12	12.34	10.02	168.5	800-441-7762	Y
BlackRock Managed Income Fund Investor C Shares	BMICX	B-	C	B	Up	0.82	1.94	4.23	10.99	9.08	10.03	168.5	800-441-7762	Y
BMO Conservative Allocation Fund Class I	BDVIX	B-	C	B	Up	1.46	3.31	7.34	11.44	22.73	8.94	72.5	800-236-3863	Y
BMO Conservative Allocation Fund Class R3	BDVRX	B-	C	B+	Up	1.37	3.12	6.80	9.82	19.69	8.84	72.5	800-236-3863	Y
BMO Conservative Allocation Fund Class R6	BDVSX	B-	C	B	Up	1.50	3.35	7.48	11.93	23.38	8.64	72.5	800-236-3863	Y
BMO Conservative Allocation Fund Class Y	BDVYX	B-	C	B+	Up	1.46	3.21	7.12	10.64	21.67	8.66	72.5	800-236-3863	Y
BMO Moderate Allocation Fund Class I	BMBHX	B-	C+	B	Up	2.60	5.19	11.02	15.52	36.10	9.76	113.2	800-236-3863	Y
BMO Moderate Allocation Fund Class R3	BMBQX	B-	C+	B	Up	2.45	4.93	10.51	13.75	32.65	9.77	113.2	800-236-3863	Y
BMO Moderate Allocation Fund Class R6	BMBTX	B-	C+	B	Up	2.60	5.29	11.24	16.03	36.82	9.74	113.2	800-236-3863	Y
BMO Moderate Allocation Fund Class Y	BMBYX	B-	C+	B	Up	2.43	5.01	10.71	14.55	34.78	9.76	113.2	800-236-3863	Y
Calvert Conservative Allocation Fund Class A	CCLAX	B-	C+	B	Up	2.18	4.15	9.64	15.00	34.41	17.14	186.3	800-368-2745	Y
Calvert Conservative Allocation Fund Class C	CALCX	B-	C+	B	Up	1.96	3.76	8.81	12.12	28.53	16.94	186.3	800-368-2745	Y
Calvert Conservative Allocation Fund Class I	CFAIX	B-	C+	B	Down	2.18	4.31	9.90	15.54	35.04	17.12	186.3	800-368-2745	Y
Columbia Capital Allocation Conservative Portfolio Adv Cls	CPCYX	B	C	A-	Up	1.66	3.55	8.15	12.13	23.23	10.23	256.0	800-345-6611	Y
Columbia Capital Allocation Conservative Portfolio Class A	ABDAX	B	C	A-	Up	1.59	3.50	7.94	11.33	21.94	10.3	256.0	800-345-6611	Y
Columbia Capital Allocation Conservative Portfolio Class C	RPCCX	B-	C	A-	Up	1.41	3.03	7.07	8.80	17.42	10.24	256.0	800-345-6611	Y
Columbia Capital Allocation Conservative Portfolio Class K	CPVRX	B	C	A-	Up	1.61	3.56	7.96	11.54	22.42	10.19	256.0	800-345-6611	
Columbia Capital Allocation Conservative Portfolio Class R	CBVRX	B	C	A-	Up	1.53	3.27	7.57	10.40	20.44	10.29	256.0	800-345-6611	Y
Columbia Capital Alloc Conservative Port Inst 2 Cls	CPAOX	B	C	A-	Up	1.67	3.67	8.19	12.34	23.73	10.23	256.0	800-345-6611	Y
Columbia Capital Alloc Conservative Port Inst 3 Cls	CPDHX	B	C	A-	Up	1.69	3.60	8.15	12.39	23.88	10.21	256.0	800-345-6611	Y
Columbia Capital Alloc Conservative Port Inst Cls	CBVZX	B	C	A-	Up	1.66	3.63	8.10	12.17	23.46	10.29	256.0	800-345-6611	Y
Columbia Capital Alloc Moderate Conservative Port Adv Cls	CHWRX	B-	C+	B	Up	2.46	5.23	11.35	16.52	34.73	11.08	598.1	800-345-6611	Y
Columbia Capital Alloc Moderate Conservative Port Cls A	NLGAX	B	C+	A-	Up	2.37	5.05	10.97	15.60	32.98	11.18	598.1	800-345-6611	Y
Columbia Capital Alloc Moderate Conservative Port Cls C	NIICX	B	C+	A-	Up	2.21	4.73	10.19	13.12	28.13	11.03	598.1	800-345-6611	Y
Columbia Capital Alloc Moderate Conservative Port Cls K	CCAKX	B-	C+	B	Up	2.42	5.06	10.98	15.77	33.43	11	598.1	800-345-6611	
Columbia Capital Alloc Moderate Conservative Port Cls R	CLIRX	B-	C+	B	Up	2.31	4.91	10.78	14.72	31.35	11.2	598.1	800-345-6611	Y
Columbia Capital Alloc Mod Conservative Port Inst 2 Cls	CLRRX	B	C+	A-	Up	2.47	5.16	11.29	16.61	35.11	11.07	598.1	800-345-6611	Y
Columbia Capital Alloc Mod Conservative Port Inst 3 Cls	CPDGX	B-	C+	B	Up	2.42	5.25	11.28	16.76	35.49	10.93	598.1	800-345-6611	Y
Columbia Capital Alloc Moderate Conservative Port Inst Cls	NIPAX	B	C+	A-	Up	2.38	5.16	11.20	16.38	34.59	11.02	598.1	800-345-6611	Y
Columbia Capital Allocation Moderate Portfolio Advisor Cls	CPCZX	B-	C+	B	Up	3.39	7.00	15.13	22.33	48.84	11.51	1,600	800-345-6611	Y
Columbia Capital Allocation Moderate Portfolio Class A	ABUAX	B	C+	A-	Up	3.37	6.87	14.86	21.47	47.13	11.65	1,600	800-345-6611	Y
Columbia Capital Allocation Moderate Portfolio Class C	AMTCX	B-	C+	B	Up	3.11	6.53	14.02	18.71	41.69	11.56	1,600	800-345-6611	Y
Columbia Capital Allocation Moderate Portfolio Class K	CBRRX	B-	C+	B	Up	3.29	6.81	14.82	21.57	47.59	11.63	1,600	800-345-6611	
Columbia Capital Allocation Moderate Portfolio Class R	CBMRX	B-	C+	B	Up	3.31	6.76	14.62	20.51	45.32	11.62	1,600	800-345-6611	Y
Columbia Capital Allocation Moderate Portfolio Inst 2 Cls	CPAMX	B-	C+	B	Up	3.39	7.02	15.18	22.41	49.38	11.5	1,600	800-345-6611	Y
Columbia Capital Allocation Moderate Portfolio Inst 3 Cls	CPDMX	B-	C+	B	Up	3.41	6.95	15.24	22.67	49.80	11.5	1,600	800-345-6611	Y
Columbia Capital Allocation Moderate Portfolio Inst Cls	CBMZX	B-	C+	B	Up	3.35	7.02	15.17	22.30	49.06	11.63	1,600	800-345-6611	Y
Columbia Income Builder Fund Advisor Class	CNMRX	B-	C+	B	Down	1.47	3.63	7.84	16.56	31.20	12.05	1,253	800-345-6611	Y
Columbia Income Builder Fund Class A	RBBAX	B-	C+	B	Down	1.32	3.51	7.50	15.65	29.65	12.01	1,253	800-345-6611	Y
Columbia Income Builder Fund Class C	RBBCX	B-	C+	B		1.21	3.11	6.76	13.12	24.89	12.06	1,253	800-345-6611	Y
Columbia Income Builder Fund Class K	CIPRX	B-	C+	B	Down	1.41	3.52	7.54	16.00	30.09	12.03	1,253	800-345-6611	

Category: Cautious Allocation (con't)

Fund Name	Ticker Symbol	Overall Rating	Reward Rating	Risk Rating	Recent Up/ Downgrade	3-Month Total Return	6-Month Total Return	1-Year Total Return	3-Year Total Return	5-Year Total Return	NAV	Total Assets (MIL)	Telephone	Open to New Investors
		RATINGS				TOTAL RETURNS & PERFORMANCE					ASSETS		NEW INVESTORS	
Columbia Income Builder Fund Class R	CBURX	B-	C+	B	Down	1.33	3.36	7.28	14.80	27.99	12.08	1,253	800-345-6611	Y
Columbia Income Builder Fund Class T	CINDX	B-	C+	B	Up	1.31	3.50	7.48	15.59	29.07	12	1,253	800-345-6611	Y
Columbia Income Builder Fund Institutional 2 Class	CKKRX	B-	C+	B	Down	1.47	3.64	7.85	16.70	31.60	12.06	1,253	800-345-6611	Y
Columbia Income Builder Fund Institutional 3 Class	CIBYX	B-	C+	B	Down	1.48	3.75	7.86	16.35	30.47	12.05	1,253	800-345-6611	Y
Columbia Income Builder Fund Institutional Class	CBUZX	B-	C+	B	Down	1.47	3.73	7.86	16.61	31.27	12.02	1,253	800-345-6611	Y
Columbia Multi-Asset Income Fund Class A	CLNAX	B-	C	B	Up	1.54	3.39	8.91			9.87	136.6	800-345-6611	Y
Columbia Multi-Asset Income Fund Class T	CLNWX	B-	C	B	Up	1.64	3.39	8.91			9.88	136.6	800-345-6611	Y
Columbia Multi-Asset Income Fund Institutional 3 Class	CMUYX	B-	C	B	Up	1.73	3.57	9.28			9.86	136.6	800-345-6611	Y
Columbia Thermostat Fund Advisor Class	CTORX	B	C	A	Up	0.70	2.14	5.49	10.73	28.76	14.5	886.5	800-345-6611	Y
Columbia Thermostat Fund Class A	CTFAX	B	C	A-	Up	0.65	2.01	5.18	9.89	27.10	14.63	886.5	800-345-6611	Y
Columbia Thermostat Fund Class C	CTFDX	B-	C	A-	Up	0.51	1.73	4.47	7.45	22.54	14.74	886.5	800-345-6611	Y
Columbia Thermostat Fund Institutional 2 Class	CQTRX	B	C	A	Up	0.72	2.23	5.50	10.76	28.92	14.52	886.5	800-345-6611	Y
Columbia Thermostat Fund Institutional 3 Class	CYYYX	B	C	A	Up	0.77	2.29	5.63	10.94	29.24	14.5	886.5	800-345-6611	Y
Columbia Thermostat Fund Institutional Class	COTZX	B	C	A	Up	0.77	2.23	5.52	10.78	28.83	14.43	886.5	800-345-6611	Y
Delaware Foundation Conservative Allocation Class A	DFIAX	B	C+	B+	Up	1.92	4.54	9.84	14.02	30.15	9.69	81.3		Y
Delaware Foundation Conservative Allocation Class C	DFICX	B-	C	B	Up	1.82	4.24	9.12	11.46	25.41	9.72	81.3		Y
Delaware Foundation Conservative Allocation Class R	DFIRX	B-	C+	B	Up	1.85	4.52	9.70	13.19	28.67	9.69	81.3		Y
Delaware Foundation Conservative Allocation Inst Cls	DFIIX	B-	C+	B	Up	1.97	4.65	10.09	14.84	31.83	9.71	81.3		Y
Deutsche Multi-Asset Conservative Allocation Fund - Cls A	SPDAX	B-	C+	B	Up	2.21	5.23	10.62	11.97	30.67	13.18	94.5	201-593-8273	Y
Deutsche Multi-Asset Conservative Allocation Fund - Cls C	SPDCX	B-	C	B+	Up	2.02	4.75	9.79	9.55	25.95	13.18	94.5	201-593-8273	Y
Deutsche Multi-Asset Conservative Allocation Fund - Cls S	SPBAX	B-	C+	B	Up	2.20	5.29	10.92	12.83	32.38	13.15	94.5	201-593-8273	Y
DFA Global Allocation 25/75 Portfolio Class R2	DFGPX	B-	C	B	Up	1.79	3.27	6.35	10.62	19.67	13.44	854.9	512-306-7400	Y
DFA Global Allocation 25/75 Portfolio Institutional Class	DGTSX	B-	C	B	Up	1.81	3.43	6.63	11.45	21.63	13.48	854.9	512-306-7400	Y
E-Valuator Conservative RMS Fund R4 Class	EVFCX	B-	C+	B	Up	2.44	4.96	9.52	12.75	30.67	10.61	55.9	888-507-2798	Y
E-Valuator Conservative RMS Fund Service Class	EVCLX	B-	C+	B	Up	2.47	5.09	9.87	13.28	31.29	10.59	55.9	888-507-2798	Y
E-Valuator Very Conservative RMS Fund R4 Class	EVVCX	B-	C	B	Up	1.40	3.26	6.45	8.21	15.92	10.36	16.4	888-507-2798	Y
E-Valuator Very Conservative RMS Fund Service Class	EVVLX	B-	C	A-	Up	1.47	3.33	6.73	9.09	17.46	10.37	16.4	888-507-2798	Y
Federated Muni and Stock Advantage Fund Class A Shares	FMUAX	B-	C+	B	Up	3.90	7.12	11.08	16.39	36.86	13.64	1,609	800-341-7400	Y
Federated Muni and Stock Advantage Fund Class B Shares	FMNBX	B-	C+	B	Up	3.71	6.64	10.26	13.82	31.86	13.63	1,609	800-341-7400	Y
Federated Muni and Stock Advantage Fund Class C Shares	FMUCX	B-	C+	B	Up	3.71	6.72	10.26	13.83	31.89	13.63	1,609	800-341-7400	Y
Federated Muni and Stock Advantage Fund Class F Shares	FMUFX	B-	C+	B	Up	3.90	7.12	11.08	16.40	36.86	13.64	1,609	800-341-7400	Y
Federated Muni & Stock Advantage Fund Institutional Shares	FMUIX	B-	C+	B	Up	3.96	7.26	11.36	17.36	38.56	13.64	1,609	800-341-7400	Y
Fidelity Advisor Asset Manager® 20% Fund Class A	FTAWX	B	C	A-	Up	1.46	3.02	6.65	10.49	20.68	13.41	5,055	617-563-7000	Y
Fidelity Advisor Asset Manager® 20% Fund Class C	FTCWX	B-	C	A-	Up	1.28	2.65	5.87	8.05	16.25	13.34	5,055	617-563-7000	Y
Fidelity Advisor Asset Manager® 20% Fund Class M	FTDWX	B	C	A-	Up	1.45	2.94	6.36	9.64	19.15	13.39	5,055	617-563-7000	Y
Fidelity Advisor Asset Manager® 20% Fund I Class	FTIWX	B	C	A-	Up	1.48	3.18	6.92	11.38	22.30	13.42	5,055	617-563-7000	Y
Fidelity Advisor Asset Manager® 30% Fund Class A	FTAAX	B	C+	A-	Up	2.03	4.16	9.17	13.90	28.94	11.1	1,294	617-563-7000	Y
Fidelity Advisor Asset Manager® 30% Fund Class C	FCANX	B	C	A-	Up	1.79	3.72	8.22	11.20	24.05	11.03	1,294	617-563-7000	Y
Fidelity Advisor Asset Manager® 30% Fund Class M	FTTNX	B	C+	A-	Up	1.86	3.91	8.80	12.85	27.07	11.08	1,294	617-563-7000	Y
Fidelity Advisor Asset Manager® 30% Fund I Class	FTINX	B	C+	A-	Up	2.03	4.21	9.33	14.66	30.36	11.09	1,294	617-563-7000	Y
Fidelity Advisor Asset Manager® 40% Fund Class A	FFNAX	B-	C+	B	Up	2.58	5.19	11.41	16.73	36.72	11.71	1,498	617-563-7000	Y
Fidelity Advisor Asset Manager® 40% Fund Class C	FFNCX	B	C+	B+	Up	2.36	4.78	10.63	14.05	31.44	11.67	1,498	617-563-7000	Y
Fidelity Advisor Asset Manager® 40% Fund Class M	FFNTX	B-	C+	B	Up	2.44	4.98	11.05	15.79	34.80	11.69	1,498	617-563-7000	Y
Fidelity Advisor Asset Manager® 40% Fund I Class	FFNIX	B-	C+	B	Up	2.63	5.31	11.74	17.67	38.39	11.7	1,498	617-563-7000	Y
Fidelity Advisor Asset Manager® 50% Fund Class A	FFAMX	B-	C+	B	Up	3.11	6.25	13.75	19.33	44.11	18.21	8,756	617-563-7000	Y
Fidelity Advisor Asset Manager® 50% Fund Class C	FFCMX	B-	C+	B	Up	2.91	5.82	12.84	16.64	38.76	18.1	8,756	617-563-7000	Y
Fidelity Advisor Asset Manager® 50% Fund Class M	FFTMX	B-	C+	B	Up	3.04	6.12	13.41	18.42	42.21	18.2	8,756	617-563-7000	Y
Fidelity Advisor Asset Manager® 50% Fund I Class	FFIMX	B	C+	A-	Up	3.20	6.41	14.05	20.33	46.04	18.24	8,756	617-563-7000	Y
Fidelity Advisor Managed Retirement 2005 Fund Class A	FIOAX	B-	C+	B	Up	1.74	3.84	8.63	14.38	38.34	58.97	8.4	617-563-7000	Y
Fidelity Advisor Managed Retirement 2005 Fund Class C	FIOCX	B-	C	B	Up	1.56	3.47	7.83	11.82	33.28	58.71	8.4	617-563-7000	Y
Fidelity Advisor Managed Retirement 2005 Fund Class I	FIOIX	B-	C+	B	Up	1.80	3.97	8.89	15.23	40.09	58.95	8.4	617-563-7000	Y
Fidelity Advisor Managed Retirement 2005 Fund Class M	FIOTX	B-	C+	B	Up	1.68	3.73	8.35	13.51	36.65	59.01	8.4	617-563-7000	Y

Category: Cautious Allocation (con't)

Fund Name	Ticker Symbol	RATINGS: Overall Rating	Reward Rating	Risk Rating	Recent Up/ Downgrade	TOTAL RETURNS & PERFORMANCE: 3-Month Total Return	6-Month Total Return	1-Year Total Return	3-Year Total Return	5-Year Total Return	ASSETS: NAV	Total Assets (MIL)	NEW INVESTORS: Telephone	Open to New Investors
Fidelity Advisor Managed Retirement Income Fund Class A	FRAMX	B-	C	B	Up	1.57	3.50	6.81	11.25	30.30	57.89	10.9	617-563-7000	Y
Fidelity Advisor Managed Retirement Income Fund Class C	FRCMX	B-	C	A-	Up	1.38	3.11	6.00	8.78	25.52	57.75	10.9	617-563-7000	Y
Fidelity Advisor Managed Retirement Income Fund Class I	FRIMX	B-	C	B	Up	1.64	3.65	7.08	12.10	31.96	57.85	10.9	617-563-7000	Y
Fidelity Advisor Managed Retirement Income Fund Class M	FRTMX	B-	C	B	Up	1.50	3.37	6.54	10.41	28.74	57.94	10.9	617-563-7000	Y
Fidelity Advisor Simplicity RMD Income Fund Class A	FRNAX	B-	C+	B	Up	1.55	3.50	7.61	12.81	34.69	57.92	11.8	617-563-7000	Y
Fidelity Advisor Simplicity RMD Income Fund Class C	FRNCX	B-	C	B	Up	1.38	3.11	6.82	10.29	29.72	57.69	11.8	617-563-7000	Y
Fidelity Advisor Simplicity RMD Income Fund Class I	FRNIX	B-	C+	B	Up	1.64	3.63	7.89	13.66	36.38	57.91	11.8	617-563-7000	Y
Fidelity Advisor Simplicity RMD Income Fund Class M	FRNTX	B-	C	B	Up	1.51	3.39	7.37	11.98	33.03	57.92	11.8	617-563-7000	Y
Fidelity Asset Manager® 20% Fund	FASIX	B	C	A-	Up	1.57	3.21	6.97	11.59	22.63	13.43	5,055	617-563-7000	Y
Fidelity Asset Manager® 30% Fund	FTANX	B	C+	A-	Up	2.06	4.27	9.43	14.90	30.78	11.09	1,294	617-563-7000	Y
Fidelity Asset Manager® 40% Fund	FFANX	B-	C+	B	Up	2.65	5.34	11.77	17.80	38.65	11.7	1,498	617-563-7000	Y
Fidelity Asset Manager® 50% Fund	FASMX	B	C+	A-	Up	3.15	6.37	14.06	20.44	46.35	18.27	8,756	617-563-7000	Y
Fidelity Managed Retirement 2005 Fund	FIROX	B-	C+	B	Up	1.80	3.99	8.91	15.24	40.11	58.98	8.4	617-563-7000	Y
Fidelity Managed Retirement Income Fund	FIRMX	B-	C	B	Up	1.61	3.63	7.07	12.07	31.95	57.85	10.9	617-563-7000	Y
Fidelity Simplicity RMD Income Fund	FIRNX	B-	C+	B	Up	1.63	3.63	7.90	13.67	36.39	57.91	11.8	617-563-7000	Y
Franklin Conservative Allocation Fund Advisor Class	FTCZX	B-	C+	B	Up	1.87	4.63	10.87	13.50	31.26	14.86	1,380	650-312-2000	Y
Franklin Conservative Allocation Fund Class A	FTCIX	B-	C+	B	Up	1.80	4.48	10.58	12.59	29.55	14.86	1,380	650-312-2000	Y
Franklin Conservative Allocation Fund Class R6	US35472P4303	B-	C+	B	Up	1.91	4.62	10.99	13.71	31.62	14.84	1,380	650-312-2000	Y
Goldman Sachs Income Builder Fund Class R6	GSBUX	B-	C+	B	Up	1.38	3.39	8.38	14.35	39.36	23.29	2,039	800-526-7384	Y
Goldman Sachs Income Builder Fund Institutional Class	GSBIX	B-	C+	B	Up	1.38	3.39	8.37	14.57	40.79	23.29	2,039	800-526-7384	Y
Goldman Sachs Income Builder Fund Investor Class	GKIRX	B-	C+	B	Up	1.35	3.32	8.20	14.11	39.76	23.23	2,039	800-526-7384	Y
Great-West Conservative Profile Fund Class L	MXIPX	B-	C	B	Up	1.61	3.15	7.16	11.79	26.90		719.4		Y
Great-West Conservative Profile Fund Institutional Class	MXKVX	B-	C+	B	Up	1.70	3.46	7.73	13.72	29.86		719.4		Y
Great-West Conservative Profile Fund Investor Class	MXCPX	B-	C+	B	Up	1.76	3.30	7.52	12.62	28.61		719.4		Y
Great-West Moderately Conservative Profile Fund Class L	MXHPX	B-	C+	B	Up	2.49	4.65	9.97	15.76	38.16		388.6		Y
Great-West Moderately Conservative Profile Fund Inst Cls	MXJUX	B-	C+	B	Up	2.59	4.92	10.58	17.66	41.12		388.6		Y
Great-West Moderately Conservative Profile Fund Inv Cls	MXDPX	B-	C+	B	Up	2.55	4.81	10.19	16.65	39.91		388.6		Y
GuidePath® Absolute Return Allocation Fund Inst Shares	GIARX	B-	C+	B	Down	0.47	1.82	5.04	14.64	18.67	10.41	245.8	800-664-5345	Y
GuidePath® Absolute Return Allocation Fund Service Shares	GPARX	B-	C	B	Up	0.34	1.49	4.49	12.56	15.14	10.44	245.8	800-664-5345	Y
GuideStone Funds Balanced Allocation Fund Inst Cls	GBAYX	B-	C+	B	Up	2.74	5.88	12.56	16.28	33.88	12.16	1,604	214-720-1171	Y
GuideStone Funds Balanced Allocation Fund Investor Class	GGIZX	B-	C+	B	Up	2.67	5.81	12.30	15.68	33.19	12.16	1,604	214-720-1171	Y
GuideStone Funds Conservative Allocation Fund Inst Cls	GCAYX	B-	C	B	Up	1.45	3.43	7.33	10.69	16.94	11.47	514.5	214-720-1171	Y
GuideStone Funds Conservative Allocation Fund Investor Cls	GFIZX	B-	C	B	Up	1.42	3.31	7.10	10.17	16.39	11.47	514.5	214-720-1171	Y
Invesco Conservative Allocation Fund Class R6	CNSSX	B-	C+	B	Up	1.63	3.60	8.16	12.18	25.82	11.67	323.5	800-659-1005	Y
Invesco Conservative Allocation Fund Class S	CMASX	B-	C+	B	Up	1.58	3.61	7.97	11.52	24.61	11.64	323.5	800-659-1005	Y
Invesco Conservative Allocation Fund Class Y	CAAYX	B-	C+	B	Up	1.71	3.69	8.14	12.03	25.60	11.62	323.5	800-659-1005	Y
Invesco Conservative Allocation Fund R5 Class	CMAIX	B-	C+	B	Up	1.71	3.69	8.16	12.18	25.82	11.68	323.5	800-659-1005	Y
Invesco Income Allocation Fund Class A	ALAAX	B-	C+	B	Up	1.42	3.23	7.99	16.28	35.08	11.7	618.5	800-659-1005	Y
Invesco Income Allocation Fund Class B	BLIAX	B	C+	A-	Up	1.14	2.84	7.17	13.79	30.21	11.72	618.5	800-659-1005	
Invesco Income Allocation Fund Class C	CLIAX	B-	C+	B	Up	1.14	2.84	7.18	13.69	30.10	11.71	618.5	800-659-1005	Y
Invesco Income Allocation Fund Class R	RLIAX	B	C+	A-	Up	1.27	3.10	7.62	15.41	33.40	11.7	618.5	800-659-1005	Y
Invesco Income Allocation Fund Class R6	IIASX	B-	C+	B	Up	1.39	3.36	8.26	17.16	36.78	11.7	618.5	800-659-1005	Y
Invesco Income Allocation Fund Class Y	ALAYX	B-	C+	B	Up	1.48	3.36	8.26	17.16	36.92	11.7	618.5	800-659-1005	Y
Invesco Income Allocation Fund R5 Class	ILAAX	B	C+	A-	Up	1.39	3.36	8.26	17.16	36.78	11.7	618.5	800-659-1005	Y
James Balanced Golden Rainbow Fund Retail Class	GLRBX	B-	C	A-	Up	2.46	4.61	6.04	9.27	33.99	24.08	3,035	800-995-2637	Y
James Balanced: Golden Rainbow Fund Institutional Class	GLRIX	B-	C	A-	Up	2.51	4.71	6.29	10.07	35.64	23.81	3,035	800-995-2637	Y
JNL Institutional Alt 50 Fund Class I	US46644W5426	B-	C+	B		3.00	5.27	10.71	12.48	27.96	17.15	2,911		Y
JNL/MMRS Conservative Fund Class A	US46648L3107	B-	C+	B+	Up	2.69	4.97	10.78	12.36		11.81	380.6		Y
JNL/MMRS Conservative Fund Class I	US46648L2943	B	C+	B+		2.86	5.15	10.97	12.55		11.83	380.6		Y
JNL/S&P Managed Conservative Fund Class A	US46648L6415	B-	C	B	Up	1.13	2.75	6.84	10.27	19.35	13.42	1,498		Y
JNL/S&P Managed Conservative Fund Class I	US46648L6332	B-	C	B		1.20	2.83	6.92	10.35	19.44	13.43	1,498		Y
JNL/S&P Managed Moderate Fund Class A	US46648L6258	B-	C+	B	Up	2.25	4.68	11.16	15.66	33.99	15.43	3,335		Y

Category: Cautious Allocation (con't)

Fund Name	Ticker Symbol	RATINGS: Overall Rating	Reward Rating	Risk Rating	Recent Up/ Downgrade	TOTAL RETURNS & PERFORMANCE: 3-Month Total Return	6-Month Total Return	1-Year Total Return	3-Year Total Return	5-Year Total Return	ASSETS: NAV	Total Assets (MIL)	NEW INVESTORS: Telephone	Open to New Investors
JNL/S&P Managed Moderate Fund Class I	US46648L6175	B-	C+	B		2.31	4.74	11.23	15.74	34.08	15.44	3,335		Y
John Hancock Funds II Multimgr Lifest Cons Cls 1	JILCX	B	C	A-	Up	1.21	2.92	7.42	12.07	22.58	13.03	2,945	800-225-5913	Y
John Hancock Funds II Multimgr Lifest Cons Cls A	JALRX	B-	C	B+	Up	1.19	2.73	7.11	10.84	20.35	13.06	2,945	800-225-5913	Y
John Hancock Funds II Multimgr Lifest Cons Cls B	JBLCX	B-	C	B+	Up	1.01	2.36	6.35	8.55	16.08	13.07	2,945	800-225-5913	
John Hancock Funds II Multimgr Lifest Cons Cls C	JCLCX	B-	C	B+	Up	0.93	2.36	6.27	8.47	16.05	13.06	2,945	800-225-5913	Y
John Hancock Funds II Multimgr Lifest Cons Cls I	JTOIX	B-	C	A-	Up	1.27	2.89	7.44	11.96	22.46	13.04	2,945	800-225-5913	Y
John Hancock Funds II Multimgr Lifest Cons Cls R1	JPLCX	B-	C	B+	Up	1.10	2.55	6.74	9.67	17.93	13.05	2,945	800-225-5913	Y
John Hancock Funds II Multimgr Lifest Cons Cls R2	JQLCX	B-	C	B+	Up	1.09	2.68	6.91	10.49	19.72	13.04	2,945	800-225-5913	Y
John Hancock Funds II Multimgr Lifest Cons Cls R3	JRLCX	B-	C	B+	Up	1.14	2.63	6.91	10.19	18.85	13.03	2,945	800-225-5913	Y
John Hancock Funds II Multimgr Lifest Cons Cls R4	JSLCX	B-	C	B+	Up	1.15	2.81	7.19	11.22	20.83	13.03	2,945	800-225-5913	Y
John Hancock Funds II Multimgr Lifest Cons Cls R5	JTLRX	B-	C	A-	Up	1.28	2.91	7.48	11.92	22.28	13.04	2,945	800-225-5913	Y
John Hancock Funds II Multimgr Lifest Cons Cls R6	JULCX	B	C	A-	Up	1.29	2.94	7.56	12.24	22.83	13.03	2,945	800-225-5913	Y
John Hancock Funds II Multimgr Lifest Mod Port Cls 1	JILMX	B-	C+	B	Up	2.18	4.68	11.06	16.94	35.36	13.79	3,876	800-225-5913	Y
John Hancock Funds II Multimgr Lifest Mod Port Cls 5	JHLMX	B	C+	B+	Up	2.12	4.71	11.13	17.04	35.64	13.77	3,876	800-225-5913	Y
John Hancock Funds II Multimgr Lifest Mod Port Cls A	JALMX	B-	C+	B	Up	2.01	4.48	10.64	15.63	32.84	13.83	3,876	800-225-5913	Y
John Hancock Funds II Multimgr Lifest Mod Port Cls B	JBLMX	B-	C+	B+	Up	1.91	4.12	9.96	13.19	28.09	13.82	3,876	800-225-5913	
John Hancock Funds II Multimgr Lifest Mod Port Cls C	JCLMX	B-	C+	B	Up	1.83	4.11	9.86	13.17	28.04	13.83	3,876	800-225-5913	Y
John Hancock Funds II Multimgr Lifest Mod Port Cls I	JTMIX	B-	C+	B	Up	2.17	4.66	11.01	16.75	35.14	13.78	3,876	800-225-5913	Y
John Hancock Funds II Multimgr Lifest Mod Port Cls R1	JPLMX	B-	C+	B+	Up	2.00	4.31	10.37	14.37	30.19	13.81	3,876	800-225-5913	Y
John Hancock Funds II Multimgr Lifest Mod Port Cls R2	JQLMX	B-	C+	B	Up	2.00	4.45	10.57	15.24	32.05	13.78	3,876	800-225-5913	Y
John Hancock Funds II Multimgr Lifest Mod Port Cls R3	JRLMX	B-	C+	B	Up	1.95	4.36	10.39	14.75	30.83	13.8	3,876	800-225-5913	Y
John Hancock Funds II Multimgr Lifest Mod Port Cls R4	JSLMX	B	C+	B+	Up	2.13	4.58	10.93	16.16	33.56	13.78	3,876	800-225-5913	Y
John Hancock Funds II Multimgr Lifest Mod Port Cls R5	JTLMX	B-	C+	B	Up	2.18	4.68	11.05	16.84	34.85	13.79	3,876	800-225-5913	Y
John Hancock Funds II Multimgr Lifest Mod Port Cls R6	JULMX	B-	C+	B	Up	2.20	4.71	11.13	17.05	35.58	13.77	3,876	800-225-5913	Y
John Hancock Funds Income Allocation Fund Class I	JIAIX	B-	C	B	Up	1.38	3.36	8.33	13.85		9.98	12.4	800-225-5913	Y
John Hancock Funds Multi-Ind Lifest Cons Cls 1	JLCGX	B	C	A-	Up	1.13	2.74	6.56	11.79		10.63	144.3	800-225-5913	Y
John Hancock Funds Multi-Ind Lifest Cons Cls R6	JLCSX	B	C	A-	Up	1.14	2.76	6.59	11.90		10.63	144.3	800-225-5913	Y
John Hancock Funds Multi-Ind Lifestyle Mod Port Cls 1	JLMOX	B	C+	A-	Up	2.18	4.52	9.96	16.13		11.06	222.8	800-225-5913	Y
John Hancock Funds Multi-Ind Lifestyle Mod Port Cls R6	JLMRX	B-	C+	B	Up	2.18	4.54	9.90	16.25		11.06	222.8	800-225-5913	Y
JPMorgan Income Builder Fund Class A Shares	JNBAX	B-	C+	B	Up	2.86	5.57	11.84	18.70	35.56	10.75	12,883	800-480-4111	Y
JPMorgan Income Builder Fund Class C Shares	JNBCX	B-	C+	B	Up	2.64	5.32	11.20	16.95	32.16	10.72	12,883	800-480-4111	Y
JPMorgan Income Builder Fund Class I Shares	JNBSX	B-	C+	B	Up	2.80	5.64	11.88	19.18	36.50	10.76	12,883	800-480-4111	Y
JPMorgan Income Builder Fund Class R6	JNBZX	B-	C+	B		2.81	5.65	11.89	19.19	36.51	10.76	12,883	800-480-4111	Y
JPMorgan Income Builder Fund Class T	JIBTX	B-	C+	B	Up	2.76	5.55	11.65	18.33	34.85	10.75	12,883	800-480-4111	Y
JPMorgan Insurance Trust Income Builder Portfolio Class 1	US4809067345	B-	C	B	Up	2.68	5.61	11.88	18.38		10.62	49.6	800-480-4111	Y
JPMorgan Insurance Trust Income Builder Portfolio Class 2	US4809067592	B-	C	B	Up	2.69	5.53	11.70	17.58		10.62	49.6	800-480-4111	Y
JPMorgan Investor Conservative Growth Fund Class A	OICAX	B-	C+	B	Up	2.04	4.27	8.93	13.14	30.25	12.77	3,733	800-480-4111	Y
JPMorgan Investor Conservative Growth Fund Class C	OCGCX	B-	C	B	Up	1.30	3.29	7.71	10.57	26.06	12.71	3,733	800-480-4111	Y
JPMorgan Investor Conservative Growth Fund Class I	ONCFX	B-	C+	B	Up	2.17	4.45	9.32	14.11	31.98	12.85	3,733	800-480-4111	Y
JPMorgan Investor Conservative Growth Fund Class R6	JFLJX	B-	C+	B		2.13	4.44	9.30	14.09	31.96	12.84	3,733	800-480-4111	Y
JPMorgan Investor Conservative Growth Fund Class T	JICTX	B-	C+	B	Up	2.02	4.24	8.96	13.17	30.24	12.77	3,733	800-480-4111	Y
Lord Abbett Multi-Asset Income Fund Class A	ISFAX	B-	C+	B	Up	1.82	3.97	8.73	14.56	32.41	14.94	1,659	201-827-2000	Y
Lord Abbett Multi-Asset Income Fund Class F	LIGFX	B-	C+	B	Up	1.84	4.04	8.88	15.07	33.38	14.94	1,659	201-827-2000	Y
Lord Abbett Multi-Asset Income Fund Class F3	ISFOX	B-	C+	B	Up	1.87	4.11	8.96	15.43	34.03	14.86	1,659	201-827-2000	Y
Lord Abbett Multi-Asset Income Fund Class I	ISFYX	B-	C+	B	Up	1.80	4.04	8.89	15.35	33.94	14.85	1,659	201-827-2000	Y
Lord Abbett Multi-Asset Income Fund Class R5	LIXTX	B-	C+	B	Up	1.87	4.11	8.96	15.42	34.02	14.86	1,659	201-827-2000	Y
Lord Abbett Multi-Asset Income Fund Class R6	LIXVX	B-	C+	B	Up	1.87	4.11	9.05	15.47	34.08	14.86	1,659	201-827-2000	Y
Lord Abbett Multi-Asset Income Fund Class T	ISFTX	B-	C+	B		1.82	3.98	8.69	14.57	32.37	14.94	1,659	201-827-2000	Y
Madison Conservative Allocation Fund Class A	MCNAX	B	C+	A-	Up	2.21	4.49	9.67	13.25	29.12	10.79	73.6	800-767-0300	Y
Madison Conservative Allocation Fund Class B	MCNBX	B	C	A-	Up	2.06	4.03	8.74	10.66	24.32	10.88	73.6	800-767-0300	Y
Madison Conservative Allocation Fund Class C	MCOCX	B	C	A-	Up	2.06	4.02	8.84	10.66	24.43	10.89	73.6	800-767-0300	Y
MainStay Conservative Allocation Fund Class A	MCKAX	B-	C+	B	Up	2.55	5.38	10.30	14.38	36.00	12.32	473.0	800-624-6782	Y

Category: Cautious Allocation (con't)

Fund Name	Ticker Symbol	RATINGS: Overall Rating	Reward Rating	Risk Rating	Recent Up/ Downgrade	TOTAL RETURNS & PERFORMANCE: 3-Month Total Return	6-Month Total Return	1-Year Total Return	3-Year Total Return	5-Year Total Return	ASSETS: NAV	Total Assets (MIL)	NEW INVESTORS: Telephone	Open to New Investors
MainStay Conservative Allocation Fund Class I	MCKIX	B-	C+	B	Up	2.67	5.55	10.49	15.28	37.69	12.42	473.0	800-624-6782	Y
MainStay Conservative Allocation Fund Class R3	MCKRX	B-	C+	B	Up	2.50	5.25	9.88	13.40	34.11	12.31	473.0	800-624-6782	Y
MainStay Conservative Allocation Fund Investor Class	MCKNX	B-	C+	B	Up	2.59	5.36	10.20	13.92	35.04	12.33	473.0	800-624-6782	Y
Manning & Napier Pro-Blend Conservative Term Series Cls I	MNCIX	B-	C	B+	Up	1.39	3.60	9.09	10.44	25.05	10.38	933.6	585-325-6880	Y
Manning & Napier Pro-Blend Conservative Term Series Cls R	MNCRX	B-	C	B	Up	1.26	3.26	8.59	8.84	22.03	9.96	933.6	585-325-6880	Y
Manning & Napier Pro-Blend Conservative Term Series Cls S	EXDAX	B-	C	B	Up	1.38	3.53	8.92	9.82	23.89	13.67	933.6	585-325-6880	Y
Manning & Napier Pro-Blend Moderate Term Series Class I	MNMIX	B-	C+	B	Up	1.32	3.95	11.75	10.77	30.68	9.99	697.9	585-325-6880	Y
Manning & Napier Pro-Blend Moderate Term Series Class R	MNMRX	B-	C	B	Up	1.30	3.80	11.28	9.14	27.52	10.56	697.9	585-325-6880	Y
Manning & Napier Pro-Blend Moderate Term Series Class S	EXBAX	B-	C	B	Up	1.35	3.93	11.57	9.98	29.11	13.49	697.9	585-325-6880	Y
Manning & Napier Strat Income Conservative Series Cls I	MSCIX	B-	C+	B	Up	2.13	3.90	7.32	14.34	29.15	10.46	28.5	585-325-6880	Y
Manning & Napier Strat Income Conservative Series Cls S	MSCBX	B-	C+	B	Up	2.05	3.76	7.17	13.49	27.49	10.46	28.5	585-325-6880	Y
MassMutual RetireSMART Conservative Fund Admin Cls	MRCLX	B-	C	B+	Up	1.67	3.74	8.50	11.33	23.57	9.93	219.0		Y
MassMutual RetireSMART Conservative Fund Class A	MCTAX	B-	C	B+	Up	1.68	3.64	8.26	10.43	22.01	9.99	219.0		Y
MassMutual RetireSMART Conservative Fund Class I	MRCUX	B	C	A-	Up	1.78	3.96	8.83	12.27	25.17	9.93	219.0		Y
MassMutual RetireSMART Conservative Fund Class R3	MRCVX	B-	C	B+	Up	1.58	3.57	8.01	9.96	21.15	9.84	219.0		Y
MassMutual RetireSMART Conservative Fund Class R4	MRCZX	B-	C	B+	Up	1.68	3.77	8.33	10.89	22.81	9.86	219.0		Y
MassMutual RetireSMART Conservative Fund Class R5	MRCSX	B	C	A-	Up	1.79	3.86	8.74	12.01	24.74	9.92	219.0		Y
MassMutual RetireSMART Conservative Fund Service Class	MRCYX	B-	C	A-	Up	1.68	3.75	8.50	11.60	24.10	9.92	219.0		Y
MFS Special Value Trust	MFV	B-	C+	B	Up	1.85	4.09	10.70	21.14	43.73	5.98	42.6	877-960-6077	Y
MFS® Conservative Allocation Fund Class 529A	ECLAX	B	C+	A-	Up	2.34	4.50	10.81	15.44	31.35	15.42	2,981	877-960-6077	Y
MFS® Conservative Allocation Fund Class 529B	EBCAX	B	C+	A-	Up	2.09	4.02	9.92	12.82	26.42	15.18	2,981	877-960-6077	Y
MFS® Conservative Allocation Fund Class 529C	ECACX	B	C+	A-	Up	2.10	4.11	9.97	12.78	26.44	15.13	2,981	877-960-6077	Y
MFS® Conservative Allocation Fund Class A	MACFX	B	C+	A-	Up	2.33	4.50	10.78	15.56	31.61	15.5	2,981	877-960-6077	Y
MFS® Conservative Allocation Fund Class B	MACBX	B	C+	A-	Up	2.13	4.10	10.00	13.03	26.80	15.42	2,981	877-960-6077	Y
MFS® Conservative Allocation Fund Class C	MACVX	B	C+	A-	Up	2.15	4.15	10.03	13.05	26.77	15.28	2,981	877-960-6077	Y
MFS® Conservative Allocation Fund Class I	MACIX	B	C+	A-	Up	2.32	4.59	11.03	16.44	33.23	15.63	2,981	877-960-6077	Y
MFS® Conservative Allocation Fund Class R1	MACKX	B	C+	A-	Up	2.07	4.10	9.96	12.95	26.76	14.98	2,981	877-960-6077	Y
MFS® Conservative Allocation Fund Class R2	MCARX	B	C+	A-	Up	2.26	4.35	10.52	14.68	29.92	15.07	2,981	877-960-6077	Y
MFS® Conservative Allocation Fund Class R3	MACNX	B	C+	A-	Up	2.28	4.46	10.80	15.53	31.62	15.37	2,981	877-960-6077	Y
MFS® Conservative Allocation Fund Class R4	MACJX	B	C+	A-	Up	2.34	4.63	11.05	16.42	33.25	15.5	2,981	877-960-6077	Y
MFS® Diversified Income Fund Class A	DIFAX	B	C+	A-	Up	1.26	3.57	8.60	14.73	36.64	12.57	4,106	877-960-6077	Y
MFS® Diversified Income Fund Class C	DIFCX	B-	C+	B+	Up	1.08	3.19	7.72	12.20	31.54	12.56	4,106	877-960-6077	Y
MFS® Diversified Income Fund Class I	DIFIX	B	C+	A-	Up	1.40	3.69	8.87	15.58	38.35	12.57	4,106	877-960-6077	Y
MFS® Diversified Income Fund Class R1	DIFDX	B-	C+	B+	Up	1.08	3.19	7.82	12.20	31.56	12.55	4,106	877-960-6077	Y
MFS® Diversified Income Fund Class R2	DIFEX	B	C+	B+	Up	1.20	3.44	8.25	13.88	34.85	12.56	4,106	877-960-6077	Y
MFS® Diversified Income Fund Class R3	DIFFX	B	C+	A-	Up	1.26	3.57	8.51	14.73	36.52	12.57	4,106	877-960-6077	Y
MFS® Diversified Income Fund Class R4	DIFGX	B	C+	A-	Up	1.32	3.69	8.78	15.58	38.34	12.57	4,106	877-960-6077	Y
MFS® Diversified Income Fund Class R6	DIFHX	B	C+	A-	Up	1.34	3.74	8.97	15.93	39.01	12.57	4,106	877-960-6077	Y
Morningstar Conservative ETF Asset Alloc Port Cls I	US00162T3086	B	C	A-	Up	1.09	2.72	6.45	10.38	17.38	11.16	35.3	866-759-5679	Y
Morningstar Income & Growth ETF Asset Alloc Port Cls I	US00162T5065	B-	C+	B	Up	2.15	4.67	10.11	15.42	29.66	10.26	80.7	866-759-5679	Y
Nationwide Investor Destinations Conservative Fund Class A	NDCAX	B-	C	B	Up	1.48	3.00	5.84	10.33	19.29	10.29	742.6	800-848-0920	Y
Nationwide Investor Destinations Conservative Fund Class C	NDCCX	B-	C	A-	Up	1.30	2.53	4.99	7.90	15.02	10.24	742.6	800-848-0920	Y
Nationwide Investor Destinations Conservative Fund Class R	GCFRX	B	C	A	Up	1.40	2.84	5.51	9.37	17.39	10.27	742.6	800-848-0920	Y
Nationwide Investor Destinations Conservative Fund Cls R6	GIMCX	B-	C	B+	Up	1.66	3.26	6.26	11.59	21.42	10.35	742.6	800-848-0920	Y
Nationwide Inv Destinations Cons Inst Serv Cls	NWWLX	B-	C	B+	Up	1.54	3.12	6.08	11.21	20.25	10.32	742.6	800-848-0920	Y
Nationwide Inv Destinations Conservative Fund Service Cls	NDCSX	B-	C	B	Up	1.56	2.96	5.75	10.28	18.92	10.33	742.6	800-848-0920	Y
Nationwide Inv Destinations Mod Conservative Fund Cls A	NADCX	B-	C+	B	Up	2.49	4.77	9.46	15.22	32.45	10.2	488.6	800-848-0920	Y
Nationwide Inv Destinations Mod Conservative Fund Cls C	NCDCX	B-	C+	B	Up	2.41	4.51	8.78	12.89	27.84	10.16	488.6	800-848-0920	Y
Nationwide Inv Destinations Mod Conservative Fund Cls R	GMMRX	B-	C+	B	Up	2.51	4.71	9.20	14.23	30.46	10.23	488.6	800-848-0920	Y
Nationwide Inv Destinations Mod Conservative Fund Cls R6	GMIMX	B-	C+	B	Up	2.55	5.00	9.82	16.47	34.75	10.32	488.6	800-848-0920	Y
Nationwide Inv Destinations Mod Cons Inst Serv Cls	NWWKX	B-	C+	B	Up	2.64	4.98	9.77	16.19	33.61	10.28	488.6	800-848-0920	Y
Nationwide Inv Destinations Mod Conservative Fund Serv Cls	NSDCX	B-	C+	B	Up	2.55	4.91	9.53	15.14	32.21	10.28	488.6	800-848-0920	Y

Category: Cautious Allocation (con't)

Fund Name	Ticker Symbol	RATINGS: Overall Rating	RATINGS: Reward Rating	RATINGS: Risk Rating	RATINGS: Recent Up/ Downgrade	TOTAL RETURNS & PERFORMANCE: 3-Month Total Return	6-Month Total Return	1-Year Total Return	3-Year Total Return	5-Year Total Return	ASSETS: NAV	Total Assets (MIL)	NEW INVESTORS: Telephone	Open to New Investors
Neuberger Berman Multi-Asset Income Fund Class A	NANAX	B-	C	B	Up	1.92	4.99	11.13			10.26	23.1	212-476-9000	Y
Neuberger Berman Multi-Asset Income Fund Class R6	NRANX	B-	C	B	Up	2.02	5.22	11.61			10.26	23.1	212-476-9000	Y
Neuberger Berman Multi-Asset Income Fund Institutional Cls	NANIX	B-	C	B	Up	2.01	5.18	11.53			10.26	23.1	212-476-9000	Y
New Covenant Balanced Income Fund	NCBIX	B-	C+	B	Up	2.16	4.24	8.69	13.00	29.99	21.25	80.7		Y
Nuveen NWQ Flexible Income Fund Class A	NWQAX	B	C+	A-	Up	0.49	1.59	8.38	20.12	32.47	21.99	716.4	312-917-8146	Y
Nuveen NWQ Flexible Income Fund Class C	NWQCX	B	C+	A-	Up	0.32	1.27	7.66	17.41	27.49	21.94	716.4	312-917-8146	Y
Nuveen NWQ Flexible Income Fund Class I	NWQIX	B	C+	A-	Up	0.49	1.65	8.64	21.03	34.16	22.01	716.4	312-917-8146	Y
Nuveen NWQ Flexible Income Fund Class R6	NQWFX	B	C+	A-	Up	0.53	1.74	8.52	20.95	34.06	22.05	716.4	312-917-8146	Y
Nuveen Strategy Conservative Allocation Fund Class A	FSFIX	B-	C	B+	Up	2.01	4.09	9.28	10.62	23.98	11.73	89.9	312-917-8146	Y
Nuveen Strategy Conservative Allocation Fund Class C	FSJCX	B-	C	B+	Up	1.84	3.65	8.35	8.09	19.34	11.65	89.9	312-917-8146	Y
Nuveen Strategy Conservative Allocation Fund Class I	FSFYX	B-	C	B+	Up	2.08	4.14	9.45	11.40	25.51	11.72	89.9	312-917-8146	Y
Nuveen Strategy Conservative Allocation Fund Class R3	FSJSX	B-	C	B+	Up	1.95	3.97	8.92	9.78	22.44	11.7	89.9	312-917-8146	Y
Oppenheimer Capital Income Fund Class A	OPPEX	B-	C+	B	Up	1.72	3.36	6.97	13.49	30.63	10.25	2,779	800-225-5677	Y
Oppenheimer Capital Income Fund Class B	OPEBX	B-	C	B	Up	1.56	2.90	6.11	10.97	25.42	10.05	2,779	800-225-5677	
Oppenheimer Capital Income Fund Class C	OPECX	B-	C	B	Up	1.57	2.96	6.17	10.96	25.64	9.92	2,779	800-225-5677	Y
Oppenheimer Capital Income Fund Class I	OCIIX	B-	C+	B	Down	1.85	3.59	7.43	14.97	32.91	10.24	2,779	800-225-5677	Y
Oppenheimer Capital Income Fund Class R	OCINX	B-	C	B	Up	1.69	3.20	6.73	12.68	28.90	10.11	2,779	800-225-5677	Y
Oppenheimer Capital Income Fund Class Y	OCIYX	B-	C+	B	Down	1.79	3.39	7.24	14.33	32.17	10.24	2,779	800-225-5677	Y
Oppenheimer Portfolio Series Conservative Inv Fund Cls A	OACIX	B	C	A-	Up	1.95	3.91	9.17	12.22	24.88	9.51	633.7	800-225-5677	Y
Oppenheimer Portfolio Series Conservative Inv Fund Cls B	OBCIX	B-	C	B+	Up	1.81	3.44	8.30	9.62	20.18	9.67	633.7	800-225-5677	
Oppenheimer Portfolio Series Conservative Inv Fund Cls C	OCCIX	B-	C	B+	Up	1.84	3.61	8.44	9.75	20.27	9.41	633.7	800-225-5677	Y
Oppenheimer Portfolio Series Conservative Inv Fund Cls R	ONCIX	B-	C	B+	Up	1.94	3.80	8.82	11.27	23.26	9.49	633.7	800-225-5677	Y
Oppenheimer Portfolio Series Conservative Inv Fund Cls Y	OYCIX	B	C+	A-	Up	2.11	4.06	9.42	13.00	26.41	9.55	633.7	800-225-5677	Y
Pacific Advisors Income and Equity Fund Class A	PADIX	B-	C	B	Up	2.95	5.13	5.25	9.35	33.29	13.01	17.2		Y
Pacific Advisors Income and Equity Fund Class C	PIECX	B-	C	B	Up	2.73	4.64	4.38	6.81	28.27	12.38	17.2		Y
Pacific Funds Port Optimization Conservative Fund Adv Cls	PLCDX	B-	C+	B	Up	1.38	3.55	8.08	12.98	20.09	11.35	320.1	800-722-2333	Y
Pacific Funds Port Optimization Conservative Fund Cls A	POAAX	B-	C	B	Up	1.28	3.36	7.79	12.24	18.87	11.33	320.1	800-722-2333	Y
Pacific Funds Optimization Cons Cls Retmnt	POARX	B-	C	B+	Up	1.22	3.31	7.57	11.41	17.52	11.26	320.1	800-722-2333	Y
Pacific Funds Optimization Mod-Cons Adv Cls	PMCDX	B-	C+	B	Up	1.96	4.81	10.72	16.69	31.42	12.71	475.5	800-722-2333	Y
Pacific Funds Optimization Mod-Cons Cls A	POBAX	B-	C+	B	Up	1.94	4.62	10.45	15.78	30.07	12.68	475.5	800-722-2333	Y
Pacific Funds Optimization Mod-Cons Cls B	POBBX	B-	C+	B	Up	1.77	4.26	9.71	13.32	25.51	12.47	475.5	800-722-2333	Y
Pacific Funds Optimization Mod-Cons Cls C	POBCX	B-	C+	B	Up	1.70	4.27	9.63	13.32	25.47	12.46	475.5	800-722-2333	Y
Pacific Funds Optimization Mod-Cons Cls Retmnt	POBRX	B-	C+	B	Up	1.92	4.54	10.22	14.94	28.59	12.61	475.5	800-722-2333	Y
Pioneer Multi-Asset Income Fund A	PMAIX	B-	B-	B-	Down	2.42	5.94	16.17	25.76	48.52	11.88	988.4	617-742-7825	Y
Pioneer Multi-Asset Income Fund C	PMACX	B-	C+	B-	Down	2.28	5.51	15.26	22.73	42.58	11.84	988.4	617-742-7825	Y
Pioneer Multi-Asset Income Fund Class K	PMFKX	B-	B-	B-	Down	2.44	5.98	16.46	28.22	52.07	12.04	988.4	617-742-7825	Y
Pioneer Multi-Asset Income Fund Class R	PMFRX	B-	C+	B-	Down	2.34	5.64	15.63	24.48	46.17	11.92	988.4	617-742-7825	Y
Pioneer Multi-Asset Income Fund Y	PMFYX	B-	B-	B-	Down	2.46	6.03	16.41	26.39	49.90	11.86	988.4	617-742-7825	Y
Pioneer Solutions - Conservative Fund Class A	PIAVX	B-	C	A-	Up	1.56	3.40	7.93	9.26	23.47	10.61	56.1	617-742-7825	Y
Pioneer Solutions - Conservative Fund Class C	PICVX	B-	C	B+	Up	1.34	3.03	7.15	6.80	19.00	10.3	56.1	617-742-7825	Y
Pioneer Solutions - Conservative Fund Class R	PSMRX	B-	C	A-	Up	1.46	3.30	7.72	8.53	22.04	10.59	56.1	617-742-7825	Y
Pioneer Solutions - Conservative Fund Class Y	IBBCX	B-	C	A-	Up	1.46	3.40	7.88	9.30	22.59	9.97	56.1	617-742-7825	Y
Praxis Genesis Conservative Portfolio Class A	MCONX	B	C	A-	Up	1.15	2.93	7.53	10.94	25.26	11.75	23.0		Y
Principal Global Diversified Income Fund Class A	PGBAX	B-	C+	B	Up	1.57	4.24	9.85	16.78	31.86	14.2	12,450	800-222-5852	Y
Principal Global Diversified Income Fund Class C	PGDCX	B-	C+	B	Up	1.32	3.79	9.00	14.09	26.92	14.11	12,450	800-222-5852	Y
Principal Global Diversified Income Fund Class R-6	PGBLX	B	C+	B+	Up	1.66	4.42	10.25	17.90	34.02	14.14	12,450	800-222-5852	Y
Principal Global Diversified Income Fund Class T	PGKTX	B-	C+	B	Up	2.53	5.24	10.97	18.08	33.55	14.28	12,450	800-222-5852	Y
Principal Global Diversified Income Fund Institutional Cls	PGDIX	B-	C+	B	Up	1.65	4.40	10.23	17.88	33.99	14.14	12,450	800-222-5852	Y
Principal Strat Asset Mgmt Cons Bal Cls A	SAIPX	B-	C+	B	Up	2.35	5.24	10.88	15.76	36.87	12.24	1,814	800-222-5852	Y
Principal Strat Asset Mgmt Cons Bal Cls C	SCIPX	B	C+	B+	Up	1.00	3.68	8.89	11.85	30.41	12.11	1,814	800-222-5852	Y
Principal Strat Asset Mgmt Cons Bal Cls J	PCBJX	B-	C+	B	Up	2.34	5.40	11.13	16.13	37.48	12.08	1,814	800-222-5852	Y
Principal Strat Asset Mgmt Cons Bal Inst Cls	PCCIX	B-	C+	B	Up	2.46	5.46	11.26	16.82	39.03	12.12	1,814	800-222-5852	Y

Category: Cautious Allocation (con't)

		RATINGS				TOTAL RETURNS & PERFORMANCE					ASSETS		NEW INVESTORS	
Fund Name	Ticker Symbol	Overall Rating	Reward Rating	Risk Rating	Recent Up/ Downgrade	3-Month Total Return	6-Month Total Return	1-Year Total Return	3-Year Total Return	5-Year Total Return	NAV	Total Assets (MIL)	Telephone	Open to New Investors
Principal Strat Asset Mgmt Cons Bal R-1 Cls	PCSSX	B-	C+	B	Up	2.15	5.01	10.25	13.81	33.06	12.08	1,814	800-222-5852	Y
Principal Strat Asset Mgmt Cons Bal R-2 Cls	PCNSX	B-	C+	B	Up	0.99	3.79	9.16	12.96	32.46	12.17	1,814	800-222-5852	Y
Principal Strat Asset Mgmt Cons Bal R-3 Cls	PCBPX	B-	C+	B	Up	2.32	5.18	10.66	14.92	35.20	12.1	1,814	800-222-5852	Y
Principal Strat Asset Mgmt Cons Bal R-4 Cls	PCBLX	B-	C+	B	Up	2.28	5.27	10.86	15.52	36.52	12.11	1,814	800-222-5852	Y
Principal Strat Asset Mgmt Cons Bal R-5 Cls	PCBFX	B-	C+	B	Up	2.31	5.32	10.99	15.88	37.26	12.11	1,814	800-222-5852	Y
Principal Strategic Asset Mgmt Flexible Income Fund Cls A	SAUPX	B-	C+	B	Up	1.76	3.75	7.80	12.54	27.88	12.5	2,772	800-222-5852	Y
Principal Strategic Asset Mgmt Flexible Income Fund Cls C	SCUPX	B-	C	B+	Up	0.92	2.72	6.37	9.34	22.33	12.38	2,772	800-222-5852	Y
Principal Strategic Asset Mgmt Flexible Income Fund Cls J	PFIJX	B-	C+	B	Up	1.81	3.86	8.04	12.96	28.43	12.4	2,772	800-222-5852	Y
Principal Strat Asset Mgmt Flexible Income Fund Inst Cls	PIFIX	B-	C+	B	Up	1.83	3.91	8.14	13.55	29.89	12.46	2,772	800-222-5852	Y
Principal Strat Asset Mgmt Flexible Income Fund R-1 Cls	PFIGX	B-	C	B	Up	1.62	3.49	7.26	10.63	24.44	12.41	2,772	800-222-5852	Y
Principal Strat Asset Mgmt Flexible Income Fund R-2 Cls	PFIVX	B-	C	B	Up	1.57	3.45	7.37	11.09	25.24	12.44	2,772	800-222-5852	Y
Principal Strat Asset Mgmt Flexible Income Fund R-3 Cls	PFIPX	B	C	A-	Up	1.70	3.63	7.55	11.72	26.43	12.44	2,772	800-222-5852	Y
Principal Strat Asset Mgmt Flexible Income Fund R-4 Cls	PFILX	B	C	A-	Up	1.74	3.73	7.76	12.37	27.63	12.45	2,772	800-222-5852	Y
Principal Strat Asset Mgmt Flexible Income Fund R-5 Cls	PFIFX	B-	C+	B	Up	1.78	3.79	7.89	12.72	28.34	12.44	2,772	800-222-5852	Y
Prudential Conservative Allocation Fund Class A	JDUAX	B-	C+	B	Up	2.71	5.61	11.17	14.88	31.79	12.99	130.2	800-225-1852	Y
Prudential Conservative Allocation Fund Class B	JDABX	B-	C+	B	Up	2.52	5.15	10.31	12.31	26.85	12.94	130.2	800-225-1852	
Prudential Conservative Allocation Fund Class C	JDACX	B-	C+	B	Up	2.52	5.23	10.31	12.31	26.94	12.95	130.2	800-225-1852	Y
Prudential Conservative Allocation Fund Class Q	JDAQX	B-	C+	B		2.82	5.78	11.39	15.75	33.46	13.04	130.2	800-225-1852	Y
Prudential Conservative Allocation Fund Class R	JDARX	B-	C+	B	Up	2.58	5.40	10.85	13.96	30.04	13.04	130.2	800-225-1852	Y
Prudential Conservative Allocation Fund Class Z	JDAZX	B-	C+	B	Up	2.82	5.77	11.39	15.75	33.46	13.05	130.2	800-225-1852	Y
QCI Balanced Fund Institutional Class	QCIBX	B-	C+	B	Up	4.16	6.96	11.11	16.45		12.13	62.4	252-442-4226	Y
QS Defensive Growth Fund Class A	SBCPX	B	C+	A-	Up	1.94	3.94	9.69	14.95	30.80	13.29	134.6	877-721-1926	Y
QS Defensive Growth Fund Class C	LWLAX	B-	C	B+	Up	1.70	3.56	8.83	12.59	25.91	13.22	134.6	877-721-1926	Y
QS Defensive Growth Fund Class C1	SBCLX	B-	C+	B+	Up	1.78	3.67	9.13	13.29	27.41	13.59	134.6	877-721-1926	
QS Defensive Growth Fund Class I	LMGIX	B	C+	A-	Up	2.00	4.09	10.02	16.00	32.29	13.26	134.6	877-721-1926	Y
QS Defensive Growth Fund Class R	LMLRX	B-	C+	B	Up	1.87	3.80	9.42	14.08	29.09	13.26	134.6	877-721-1926	Y
RiverFront Conservative Income Builder Fund Class C	RCCBX	B-	C	B	Up	1.93	4.00	7.60	10.36	22.22	11.01	11.4	866-759-5679	Y
RiverFront Conservative Income Builder Fund Class I	RCIBX	B-	C+	B	Up	2.10	4.48	8.57	13.54	28.30	10.96	11.4	866-759-5679	Y
RiverFront Conservative Income Builder Fund Class Investor	RCABX	B-	C+	B	Up	2.13	4.37	8.37	12.90	26.84	11.14	11.4	866-759-5679	Y
Russell Inv LifePoints Conservative Strategy Fund Cls A	RCLAX	B-	C	A-	Up	0.55	1.79	5.43	8.97	16.52	9.74	286.8	800-426-7969	Y
Russell Inv LifePoints Conservative Strategy Fund Cls C	RCLCX	B-	C	B+	Up	0.48	1.54	4.80	6.61	12.34	9.65	286.8	800-426-7969	Y
Russell Inv LifePoints Conservative Strategy Fund Cls E	RCLEX	B-	C	A-	Up	0.55	1.78	5.51	9.03	16.62	9.79	286.8	800-426-7969	Y
Russell Inv LifePoints Conservative Strategy Fund Cls R1	RCLRX	B	C	A-	Up	0.64	2.07	5.90	10.28	18.92	9.81	286.8	800-426-7969	Y
Russell Inv LifePoints Conservative Strategy Fund Cls R4	RCLUX	B-	C	A-	Up	0.61	1.89	5.67	9.50	17.54	9.76	286.8	800-426-7969	Y
Russell Inv LifePoints Conservative Strategy Fund Cls R5	RCLVX	B-	C	A-	Up	0.58	1.78	5.34	8.66	16.02	9.85	286.8	800-426-7969	Y
Russell Inv LifePoints Conservative Strategy Fund Cls S	RCLSX	B	C	A-	Up	0.67	1.97	5.76	9.83	18.09	9.82	286.8	800-426-7969	Y
Russell Inv LifePoints Moderate Strategy Fund Cls A	RMLAX	B	C+	B+	Up	0.83	3.09	8.40	14.09	27.57	10.41	494.9	800-426-7969	Y
Russell Inv LifePoints Moderate Strategy Fund Cls C	RMLCX	B-	C+	B+	Up	0.64	2.70	7.64	11.53	22.99	10.27	494.9	800-426-7969	Y
Russell Inv LifePoints Moderate Strategy Fund Cls E	RMLEX	B	C+	B+	Up	0.90	3.04	8.40	13.85	27.44	10.45	494.9	800-426-7969	Y
Russell Inv LifePoints Moderate Strategy Fund Cls R1	RMLRX	B-	C+	B	Up	0.89	3.19	8.66	14.93	29.58	10.47	494.9	800-426-7969	Y
Russell Inv LifePoints Moderate Strategy Fund Cls R4	RMLUX	B	C+	B+	Up	0.83	3.08	8.48	14.06	27.97	10.43	494.9	800-426-7969	Y
Russell Inv LifePoints Moderate Strategy Fund Cls R5	RMLVX	B-	C+	B+	Up	0.76	2.94	8.23	13.28	26.48	10.49	494.9	800-426-7969	Y
Russell Inv LifePoints Moderate Strategy Fund Cls S	RMLSX	B-	C+	B	Up	0.96	3.16	8.71	14.68	28.94	10.47	494.9	800-426-7969	Y
Russell Investments Multi-Strategy Income Fund Class A	RMYAX	B-	C	B	Up	1.39	3.50	9.86			10.16	1,330	800-426-7969	Y
Russell Investments Multi-Strategy Income Fund Class E	RMYEX	B-	C	B	Up	1.47	3.44	9.88			10.28	1,330	800-426-7969	Y
Russell Investments Multi-Strategy Income Fund Class M	RGYTX	B-	C	B	Up	1.50	3.60	10.18			10.16	1,330	800-426-7969	Y
Russell Investments Multi-Strategy Income Fund Class S	RMYSX	B-	C	B	Up	1.43	3.50	10.02			10.17	1,330	800-426-7969	Y
Russell Investments Multi-Strategy Income Fund Class T	RGYAX	B-	C	B	Up	1.19	3.26	10.27				1,330	800-426-7969	Y
Russell Investments Multi-Strategy Income Fund Class Y	RMYYX	B-	C	B	Up	1.52	3.63	10.32			10.18	1,330	800-426-7969	Y
Schwab MarketTrack Conservative Portfolio™	SWCGX	B-	C+	B	Up	2.30	4.70	9.33	15.01	34.31	16.09	254.0	877-824-5615	Y
Schwab® Monthly Income Fund - Enhanced Payout	SWKRX	B	C	A-	Up	1.62	3.91	8.19	11.90	25.44	11.38	94.5	877-824-5615	Y
Schwab® Monthly Income Fund - Maximum Payout	SWLRX	B	C	A-	Up	1.01	2.50	5.64	8.81	16.80	10.15	48.4	877-824-5615	Y

Category: Cautious Allocation (con't)

Fund Name	Ticker Symbol	RATINGS: Overall Rating	Reward Rating	Risk Rating	Recent Up/ Downgrade	TOTAL RETURNS & PERFORMANCE: 3-Month Total Return	6-Month Total Return	1-Year Total Return	3-Year Total Return	5-Year Total Return	ASSETS: NAV	Total Assets (MIL)	NEW INVESTORS: Telephone	Open to New Investors
Schwab® Monthly Income Fund - Moderate Payout	SWJRX	B-	C+	B	Up	2.32	5.44	10.79	15.18	34.56	11.09	47.9	877-824-5615	Y
SEI Asset Alloc Trust Conservative Strategy Fund Cls F	SVSAX	B	C	A	Up	1.36	2.50	5.23	9.37	17.90	10.63	89.2	800-342-5734	Y
SEI Asset Alloc Trust Conservative Strategy Fund Cls I	SICIX	B-	C	B	Up	1.36	2.40	5.12	8.63	16.61	10.83	89.2	800-342-5734	Y
SEI Asset Allocation Trust Core Market Strategy Fund Cls F	SOKAX	B-	C+	B+	Up	2.99	6.13	11.75	16.10	31.22	11.88	109.2	800-342-5734	Y
SEI Asset Allocation Trust Core Market Strategy Fund Cls I	SCMSX	B-	C+	B+	Up	2.95	6.03	11.49	17.51	32.11	12.91	109.2	800-342-5734	Y
SEI Asset Allocation Trust Defensive Strategy Fund Class F	SNSAX	B-	C	A	Up	0.67	1.43	2.80	5.17	8.36	9.83	29.3	800-342-5734	Y
SEI Asset Allocation Trust Defensive Strategy Fund Class I	SEDIX	B-	C	B+	Up	0.67	1.34	2.55	4.39	6.96	9.67	29.3	800-342-5734	Y
SEI Asset Allocation Trust Mkt Growth Strategy Fund Cls F	SRWAX	B-	C+	B	Down	3.64	7.38	14.28	18.67	38.26	13.24	303.7	800-342-5734	Y
SEI Asset Allocation Trust Mkt Growth Strategy Fund Cls I	SMGSX	B-	C+	B-	Down	3.64	7.29	14.03	17.88	36.47	13.05	303.7	800-342-5734	Y
SEI Asset Allocation Trust Moderate Strategy Fund Class D	SMSDX	B-	C	B	Up	2.27	3.91	7.63	11.67	23.38	12.15	209.4	800-342-5734	Y
SEI Asset Allocation Trust Moderate Strategy Fund Class F	SMOAX	B-	C+	B	Up	2.46	4.32	8.45	14.19	28.48	12.16	209.4	800-342-5734	Y
SEI Asset Allocation Trust Moderate Strategy Fund Class I	SMSIX	B-	C+	B	Up	2.44	4.26	8.29	13.39	26.89	12.5	209.4	800-342-5734	Y
SEI Inst Managed Trust Multi-Asset Capital Stability Cls F	SCLAX	B-	C	A	Up	1.13	1.93	3.87	4.87	7.30	9.99	748.9	800-342-5734	Y
SEI Inst Managed Trust Multi-Asset Capital Stability Cls Y	SMLYX	B-	C	A	Up	1.23	2.13	4.07	5.27	7.71	10.01	748.9	800-342-5734	Y
Sterling Capital Diversified Income Fund Class A	BCGAX	B-	C	B+	Up	1.71	2.70	6.38	12.64	30.17	10.86	24.0	800-228-1872	Y
Sterling Capital Diversified Income Fund Class C	BCCCX	B-	C	B+	Up	1.54	2.34	5.66	10.31	25.35	10.77	24.0	800-228-1872	Y
Sterling Capital Diversified Income Fund Inst Shares	BMGTX	B	C+	A-	Up	1.85	2.89	6.76	13.61	31.85	11	24.0	800-228-1872	Y
T. Rowe Price Personal Strategy Income Fund	PRSIX	B	C+	A-	Up	2.35	5.40	12.79	19.47	41.13	19.54	2,137	410-345-2000	Y
T. Rowe Price Personal Strategy Income Fund I Class	PPIPX	B	C+	A-	Up	2.46	5.52	12.97	19.66	41.37	19.54	2,137	410-345-2000	Y
T. Rowe Price Retirement Balanced Fund	TRRIX	B-	C+	B	Up	2.16	4.64	10.35	16.32	33.14	15.39	2,730	410-345-2000	Y
T. Rowe Price Retirement Balanced Fund Advisor Class	PARIX	B-	C+	B	Up	2.09	4.57	10.07	15.45	31.48	15.4	2,730	410-345-2000	Y
T. Rowe Price Retirement Balanced Fund Class R	RRTIX	B	C+	B+	Up	2.03	4.38	9.80	14.58	29.85	15.39	2,730	410-345-2000	Y
TCW Conservative Allocation Fund Class Institutional	TGPCX	B	C	A-	Up	2.23	4.04	8.95	11.24	31.56		30.8	213-244-0000	Y
TCW Conservative Allocation Fund Class N	TGPNX	B	C	A-	Up	2.07	3.88	8.50	9.55	28.25		30.8	213-244-0000	Y
The Hartford Balanced Income Fund Class A	HBLAX	B-	C+	B		3.34	6.34	11.49	22.92	49.24	14.62	12,232	888-843-7824	Y
The Hartford Balanced Income Fund Class C	HBLCX	B-	C+	B	Up	3.20	5.97	10.70	20.21	43.96	14.42	12,232	888-843-7824	Y
The Hartford Balanced Income Fund Class F	HBLFX	B-	C+	B		3.42	6.58	11.81	24.16	51.86	14.63	12,232	888-843-7824	Y
The Hartford Balanced Income Fund Class I	HBLIX	B-	C+	B		3.40	6.46	11.75	23.83	51.24	14.62	12,232	888-843-7824	Y
The Hartford Balanced Income Fund Class R3	HBLRX	B-	C+	B	Up	3.25	6.15	11.11	21.78	47.17	14.67	12,232	888-843-7824	Y
The Hartford Balanced Income Fund Class R4	HBLSX	B-	C+	B		3.32	6.38	11.42	22.91	49.44	14.68	12,232	888-843-7824	Y
The Hartford Balanced Income Fund Class R5	HBLTX	B-	C+	B		3.38	6.43	11.68	23.79	51.23	14.69	12,232	888-843-7824	Y
The Hartford Balanced Income Fund Class R6	HBLVX	B-	C+	B		3.46	6.52	11.88	24.13	51.82	14.77	12,232	888-843-7824	Y
The Hartford Balanced Income Fund Class Y	HBLYX	B-	C+	B		3.37	6.49	11.76	24.11	51.79	14.77	12,232	888-843-7824	Y
Thrivent Diversified Income Plus Fund Class A	AAHYX	B-	C+	B	Up	1.78	3.78	8.97	15.29	32.69	7.41	861.0		Y
Thrivent Diversified Income Plus Fund Class S	THYFX	B-	C+	B	Up	1.87	3.81	9.20	16.28	34.63	7.34	861.0		Y
Thrivent Moderately Conservative Allocation Fund Class A	TCAAX	B-	C+	B	Up	2.05	4.36	9.06	15.39	33.01	12.37	867.7		Y
Thrivent Moderately Conservative Allocation Fund Class S	TCAIX	B-	C+	B	Up	2.03	4.40	9.33	16.40	34.96	12.4	867.7		Y
Thrivent Series Diversified Income Plus Portfolio		B-	C+	B	Up	1.93	3.97	9.34	16.92	36.47	8.2281	669.0		Y
Thrivent Series Moderately Conservative Alloc Port		B-	C+	B	Up	2.11	4.53	9.51	16.67	34.96	13.6166	5,112		Y
TIAA-CREF Lifestyle Conservative Fund Advisor Class	TLSHX	B-	C+	B	Up	2.52	5.61	12.19	18.69	38.31	12.6	211.3	877-518-9161	Y
TIAA-CREF Lifestyle Conservative Fund Institutional Class	TCSIX	B-	C+	B	Up	2.44	5.62	12.12	18.67	38.28	12.59	211.3	877-518-9161	Y
TIAA-CREF Lifestyle Conservative Fund Premier Class	TLSPX	B-	C+	B	Up	2.40	5.53	11.94	18.10	37.19	12.6	211.3	877-518-9161	Y
TIAA-CREF Lifestyle Conservative Fund Retail Class	TSCLX	B	C+	A-	Up	2.37	5.48	11.93	17.74	36.51	12.58	211.3	877-518-9161	Y
TIAA-CREF Lifestyle Conservative Fund Retirement Class	TSCTX	B-	C+	B	Up	2.38	5.49	11.86	17.81	36.54	12.58	211.3	877-518-9161	Y
TIAA-CREF Lifestyle Income Fund Advisor Class	TSIHX	B	C	A	Up	1.34	3.29	7.41	12.76	23.11	11.14	68.7	877-518-9161	Y
TIAA-CREF Lifestyle Income Fund Institutional Class	TSITX	B	C	A	Up	1.25	3.30	7.43	12.72	23.06	11.14	68.7	877-518-9161	Y
TIAA-CREF Lifestyle Income Fund Premier Class	TSIPX	B	C	A	Up	1.30	3.22	7.36	12.23	22.17	11.16	68.7	877-518-9161	Y
TIAA-CREF Lifestyle Income Fund Retail Class	TSILX	B	C	A	Up	1.28	3.16	7.14	11.79	21.35	11.14	68.7	877-518-9161	Y
TIAA-CREF Lifestyle Income Fund Retirement Class	TLSRX	B	C	A	Up	1.28	3.17	7.27	11.87	21.53	11.14	68.7	877-518-9161	Y
TOPS® Conservative ETF Portfolio Class 1	US66537U8586	B-	C	B	Up	1.79	3.67	7.08	11.36	20.36	11.92	8.5	855-572-5945	Y
TOPS® Conservative ETF Portfolio Class 2	US66537U8412	B-	C	B	Up	1.71	3.49	6.82	10.48	18.74	11.85	8.5	855-572-5945	Y
TOPS® Conservative ETF Portfolio Investor Class	US66537U1896	B-	C	B	Up	1.66	3.37	6.62	10.00	17.64	12.24	8.5	855-572-5945	Y

Category: Cautious Allocation (con't)

Fund Name	Ticker Symbol	Overall Rating	Reward Rating	Risk Rating	Recent Up/ Downgrade	3-Month Total Return	6-Month Total Return	1-Year Total Return	3-Year Total Return	5-Year Total Return	NAV	Total Assets (MIL)	Telephone	Open to New Investors
		RATINGS				TOTAL RETURNS & PERFORMANCE					ASSETS		NEW INVESTORS	
Touchstone Dynamic Diversified Income Fund A	TBAAX	B-	C+	B	Up	1.46	3.34	7.73	13.79	36.15	13.23	56.2	800-543-0407	Y
Touchstone Dynamic Diversified Income Fund Y	TBAYX	B-	C+	B	Up	1.52	3.46	8.06	14.71	38.03	13.26	56.2	800-543-0407	Y
Transamerica Asset Allocation Conservative Portfolio Adv	TACVX	B-	C+	B	Up	1.92	4.36	9.92	15.05	30.78	11.18	1,097	888-233-4339	Y
Transamerica Asset Allocation Conservative Portfolio Cls A	ICLAX	B	C+	A-	Up	1.89	4.22	9.86	14.99	30.70	11.12	1,097	888-233-4339	Y
Transamerica Asset Allocation Conservative Portfolio Cls B	ICLBX	B	C	A-	Up	1.64	3.78	8.90	12.12	25.57	11.08	1,097	888-233-4339	
Transamerica Asset Allocation Conservative Portfolio Cls C	ICLLX	B	C+	A-	Up	1.72	3.85	9.08	12.54	26.20	11.03	1,097	888-233-4339	Y
Transamerica Asset Allocation Conservative Portfolio Cls I	TACIX	B-	C+	B	Up	1.94	4.41	10.16	15.82	32.39	11.15	1,097	888-233-4339	Y
Transamerica Asset Allocation Conservative Portfolio Cls R	ICVRX	B	C+	A-	Up	1.81	4.11	9.56	13.73	28.58	11.24	1,097	888-233-4339	Y
Transamerica Asset Alloc Conservative Port Cls T1	TACQX	B	C+	A-	Up	1.82	4.25	9.89	15.02	30.74	11.15	1,097	888-233-4339	Y
Transamerica Asset Allocation Moderate Portfolio Class A	IMOAX	B	C+	A-	Up	2.45	5.43	12.45	18.15	41.87	12.07	1,954	888-233-4339	Y
Transamerica Asset Allocation Moderate Portfolio Class B	IMOBX	B	C+	B+	Up	2.29	4.97	11.45	15.27	36.38	12.45	1,954	888-233-4339	
Transamerica Asset Allocation Moderate Portfolio Class C	IMOLX	B	C+	A-	Up	2.34	5.08	11.62	15.62	36.92	12.07	1,954	888-233-4339	Y
Transamerica Asset Allocation Moderate Portfolio Class I	TMMIX	B-	C+	B	Up	2.61	5.60	12.73	19.00	43.74	12.05	1,954	888-233-4339	Y
Transamerica Asset Allocation Moderate Portfolio Class R	IMDRX	B-	C+	B	Up	2.45	5.37	12.22	17.35	40.34	12.03	1,954	888-233-4339	Y
Transamerica Asset Allocation Moderate Portfolio Fund Adv	TMMVX	B-	C+	B	Up	0.76	4.36	11.93	17.61	41.23	13.42	1,954	888-233-4339	Y
Transamerica Asset Alloc Moderate Port Fund Cls T1	TMMTX	B-	C+	B	Up	2.52	5.51	12.52	18.24	41.97	12.13	1,954	888-233-4339	Y
Transamerica Strategic High Income Fund Class A	TASHX	B-	C+	B	Down	4.10	6.82	13.29	22.26		11.13	136.3	888-233-4339	Y
Transamerica Strategic High Income Fund Class Advisor	TASKX	B-	C+	B	Down	4.19	6.98	13.67	23.20		11.19	136.3	888-233-4339	Y
Transamerica Strategic High Income Fund Class C	TCSHX	B-	C+	B	Down	3.83	6.46	12.49	19.50		11.09	136.3	888-233-4339	Y
Transamerica Strategic High Income Fund Class I	TSHIX	B-	C+	B	Down	4.16	7.07	13.70	23.23		11.14	136.3	888-233-4339	Y
Transamerica Strategic High Income Fund Class I2	US89354D8829	B-	C+	B	Down	4.07	6.93	13.65	16.99		10.68	136.3	888-233-4339	Y
Transamerica Strategic High Income Fund Class T1	TCSWX	B-	C+	B	Down	4.11	6.96	13.53	22.43		11.23	136.3	888-233-4339	Y
USAA Cornerstone Conservative Fund	USCCX	B-	C+	B+	Up	1.32	3.10	8.12	13.27	22.42	10.84	197.0	800-531-8722	Y
USAA Cornerstone Moderately Conservative Fund	UCMCX	B-	C+	B	Up	2.48	4.87	11.46	12.30	27.08	11.44	213.9	800-531-8722	Y
USAA Growth and Tax Strategy Fund	USBLX	B	C+	A+	Up	3.98	6.81	13.47	21.62	53.92	19.75	427.9	800-531-8722	Y
VALIC Company II Conservative Growth Lifestyle Fund	VCGLX	B	C+	A-	Up	2.28	5.02	10.24	15.61	32.11	12.54	341.3		Y
Vanguard LifeStrategy Conservative Growth Fund Inv Shares	VSCGX	B	C+	A-	Up	2.60	5.18	10.92	17.01	37.53	19.96	9,469	877-662-7447	Y
Vanguard LifeStrategy Income Fund Investor Shares	VASIX	B	C	A-	Up	1.59	3.27	6.98	12.05	23.86	15.56	4,246	877-662-7447	Y
Vanguard Tax-Managed Balanced Fund Admiral Shares	VTMFX	B	C+	A-	Up	3.27	6.12	12.60	21.55	54.55	30.72	3,858	877-662-7447	Y
Vanguard Wellesley® Income Fund Admiral™ Shares	VWIAX	B	C+	A+	Up	3.11	5.46	10.25	20.50	43.21	65.3	55,459	877-662-7447	Y
Vanguard Wellesley® Income Fund Investor Shares	VWINX	B	C+	A+	Up	3.05	5.38	10.15	20.24	42.68	26.95	55,459	877-662-7447	Y
Virtus Conservative Allocation Strategy Fund Class A	SVCAX	B	C	A-	Up	1.97	4.09	9.03	11.16	27.66	11.84	38.1	800-243-1574	Y
Virtus Conservative Allocation Strategy Fund Class C	SCCLX	B-	C	A-	Up	1.82	3.71	8.24	8.91	23.32	11.7	38.1	800-243-1574	Y
Virtus Conservative Allocation Strategy Fund Class I	SCCTX	B	C	A-	Up	2.01	4.25	9.37	12.20	29.64	11.83	38.1	800-243-1574	Y
Voya Retirement Conservative Portfolio Class A	IRCAX	B	C	A-	Up	1.98	3.78	7.75	11.66	24.05	9.24	460.6	800-366-0066	Y
Voya Retirement Conservative Portfolio Class I	IRCPX	B	C	A-	Up	2.06	3.90	7.81	12.22	25.00	9.38	460.6	800-366-0066	Y
Voya Retirement Moderate Portfolio Class A	IRMPX	B	C+	B+	Up	2.87	5.67	11.82	16.05	35.66	11.79	1,205	800-366-0066	Y
Voya Retirement Moderate Portfolio Class I	IRMIX	B-	C+	B	Up	2.93	5.84	12.20	17.23	38.11	11.93	1,205	800-366-0066	Y
Voya Solution Conservative Portfolio Class A	ICGAX	B-	C	B	Up	1.65	3.26	7.06	12.17	23.85	11.06	16.1	800-366-0066	Y
Voya Solution Conservative Portfolio Class I	ICGIX	B	C+	A-	Up	1.72	3.45	7.50	13.75	26.85	11.2	16.1	800-366-0066	Y
Voya Solution Conservative Portfolio Class R6	VYRPX	B-	C+	B	Up	1.72	3.45	7.50	13.75	26.85	11.2	16.1	800-366-0066	Y
Voya Solution Conservative Portfolio Class S	ICGSX	B-	C	B	Up	1.73	3.42	7.30	13.04	25.38	11.13	16.1	800-366-0066	Y
Voya Solution Conservative Portfolio Class S2	ICGTX	B-	C	B	Up	1.65	3.30	7.10	12.46	24.38	11.03	16.1	800-366-0066	Y
Voya Solution Moderately Conservative Portfolio Class A	ISPGX	B-	C+	B	Up	2.56	4.86	10.08	15.15	33.64	9.99	31.4	800-366-0066	Y
Voya Solution Moderately Conservative Portfolio Class I	ISPRX	B-	C+	B	Up	2.66	5.06	10.62	16.96	36.93	10.41	31.4	800-366-0066	Y
Voya Solution Moderately Conservative Portfolio Class R6	VYRNX	B-	C+	B	Up	2.66	5.11	10.57	16.80	36.75	10.4	31.4	800-366-0066	Y
Voya Solution Moderately Conservative Portfolio Class S	ISPSX	B-	C+	B	Up	2.62	4.95	10.29	15.99	35.29	10.18	31.4	800-366-0066	Y
Voya Solution Moderately Conservative Portfolio Class S2	ISPTX	B-	C+	B	Up	2.54	4.93	10.21	15.50	34.39	10.07	31.4	800-366-0066	Y
Voya Strategic Allocation Conservative Portfolio Class I	ISAIX	B-	C+	B	Up	2.73	5.13	10.53	16.21	40.23	13.51	69.3	800-366-0066	Y
Voya Strategic Allocation Conservative Portfolio Class S	ISCVX	B-	C+	B	Up	2.68	5.01	10.18	15.38	38.47	13.39	69.3	800-366-0066	Y
Weitz Balanced Fund	WBALX	B-	C+	B	Up	1.81	4.39	11.14	13.88	37.82	14.19	123.2	800-304-9745	Y
Wells Fargo Diversified Income Builder Fund - Class A	EKSAX	B-	C+	B	Down	1.51	4.15	9.39	22.94	43.74	6.37	781.3	800-222-8222	Y

Category: Cautious Allocation (con't)

Fund Name	Ticker Symbol	Overall Rating	Reward Rating	Risk Rating	Recent Up/ Downgrade	3-Month Total Return	6-Month Total Return	1-Year Total Return	3-Year Total Return	5-Year Total Return	NAV	Total Assets (MIL)	Telephone	Open to New Investors
Wells Fargo Diversified Income Builder Fund - Class Admin	EKSDX	B-	C+	B	Down	1.39	4.11	9.32	23.41	44.79	6.23	781.3	800-222-8222	Y
Wells Fargo Diversified Income Builder Fund - Class C	EKSCX	B-	C+	B	Down	1.16	3.60	8.40	20.20	38.42	6.38	781.3	800-222-8222	Y
Wells Fargo Diversified Income Builder Fund - Class Inst	EKSYX	B-	C+	B	Down	1.60	4.21	9.71	24.34	46.50	6.23	781.3	800-222-8222	Y
Wells Fargo Moderate Balanced Fund - Class A	WFMAX	B-	C+	B	Up	2.44	4.75	10.32	15.95	42.25	22.69	159.2	800-222-8222	Y
Wells Fargo Moderate Balanced Fund - Class Admin	NVMBX	B-	C+	B	Up	2.50	4.87	10.59	16.76	43.97	22.88	159.2	800-222-8222	Y
Wells Fargo Moderate Balanced Fund - Class C	WFBCX	B-	C+	B	Up	2.21	4.34	9.46	13.32	36.92	22.23	159.2	800-222-8222	Y
Wells Fargo WealthBuilder Conservative Alloc Fund Cls A	WCAFX	B-	C	A-	Up	-3.39	-1.76	1.88	3.32	10.74	10.22	371.4	800-222-8222	Y
Wells Fargo WealthBuilder Moderate Balanced Fund Class A	WMBGX	B-	C+	B	Up	-5.87	-3.49	2.11	5.11	21.67	11.18	645.1	800-222-8222	Y

Category: Communications Sector Equity

Fund Name	Ticker Symbol	Overall Rating	Reward Rating	Risk Rating	Recent Up/ Downgrade	3-Month Total Return	6-Month Total Return	1-Year Total Return	3-Year Total Return	5-Year Total Return	NAV	Total Assets (MIL)	Telephone	Open to New Investors
Deutsche Communications Fund Class A	TISHX	B-	C+	B+		1.45	5.04	8.32	20.21	59.84	26.96	101.8	201-593-8273	Y
Deutsche Communications Fund Class C	FTICX	B-	C+	B		1.29	4.64	7.53	17.54	53.98	24.77	101.8	201-593-8273	Y
Deutsche Communications Fund Institutional Class	FLICX	B-	C+	B+		1.53	5.19	8.57	21.08	61.94	27.52	101.8	201-593-8273	Y
Fidelity® Select Wireless Portfolio	FWRLX	B-	B	C+	Up	5.45	10.35	25.01	32.48	78.72	10.12	273.8	617-563-7000	Y
Gabelli Global Content & Connectivity Fund Class A	GTCAX	B-	C+	B	Up	1.94	4.59	13.38	12.61	40.96	21.94	96.1	914-921-5135	Y
Gabelli Global Content & Connectivity Fund Class AAA	GABTX	B-	C+	B	Up	1.91	4.57	13.38	12.74	41.16	21.77	96.1	914-921-5135	Y
Gabelli Global Content & Connectivity Fund Class C	GTCCX	B-	C	B	Up	1.71	4.18	12.53	10.26	35.96	21.08	96.1	914-921-5135	Y
Gabelli Global Content & Connectivity Fund Cls Inst	GTTIX	B-	C+	B	Up	2.17	5.03	14.19	14.18	43.63	21.75	96.1	914-921-5135	Y
GAMCO Global Telecommunications Fund T	GGTTX	B-	C+	B	Up	1.91	4.62	13.43	12.79	41.22	21.75	96.1	914-921-5135	Y
JNL/Mellon Capital Telecommunications Sector Fund Class A	US47760W5067	B-	C	B	Up	0.06	2.38	3.53	30.29	70.03	14.55	120.7		Y
JNL/Mellon Capital Telecommunications Sector Fund Class I	US47760W6057	B-	C+	B	Up	0.14	2.47	3.76	30.91	71.80	13.69	120.7		Y
Putnam Global Telecommunication Fund Class A	PGBZX	B	C+	B+	Up	2.10	5.24	14.07	22.95	64.53	16.01	25.1	617-292-1000	Y
Putnam Global Telecommunication Fund Class B	PGBBX	B-	C	B	Up	1.90	4.80	13.24	20.15	58.42	15.48	25.1	617-292-1000	Y
Putnam Global Telecommunication Fund Class C	PGBNX	B-	C	B	Up	1.91	4.81	13.26	20.21	58.39	15.46	25.1	617-292-1000	Y
Putnam Global Telecommunication Fund Class M	PGBMX	B-	C+	B	Up	1.99	4.96	13.60	21.14	60.56	15.87	25.1	617-292-1000	Y
Putnam Global Telecommunication Fund Class R	PGBTX	B-	C+	B+	Up	2.01	5.04	13.81	21.99	62.41	16.23	25.1	617-292-1000	Y
Putnam Global Telecommunication Fund Class Y	PGBYX	B	C+	B+	Up	2.16	5.36	14.39	23.88	66.66	16.07	25.1	617-292-1000	Y
T. Rowe Price Media and Telecommunications Fund	PRMTX	B+	B+	A-	Up	4.99	10.97	32.98	58.95	139.20	96.47	4,829	410-345-2000	Y
T. Rowe Price Media and Telecommunications Fund I Class	TTMIX	B+	B+	A-	Up	5.01	11.02	33.12	59.24	139.63	96.54	4,829	410-345-2000	Y

Category: Consumer Goods Sector Equity

Fund Name	Ticker Symbol	Overall Rating	Reward Rating	Risk Rating	Recent Up/ Downgrade	3-Month Total Return	6-Month Total Return	1-Year Total Return	3-Year Total Return	5-Year Total Return	NAV	Total Assets (MIL)	Telephone	Open to New Investors
Fidelity Advisor® Consumer Discretionary Fund Class A	FCNAX	B	B	A-	Up	10.87	11.51	21.77	31.34	106.74	25.28	274.2	617-563-7000	Y
Fidelity Advisor® Consumer Discretionary Fund Class C	FCECX	B	B-	A-	Up	10.68	11.16	20.95	28.41	98.99	20.61	274.2	617-563-7000	Y
Fidelity Advisor® Consumer Discretionary Fund Class M	FACPX	B	B	A-	Up	10.81	11.39	21.45	30.20	103.75	23.66	274.2	617-563-7000	Y
Fidelity Advisor® Consumer Discretionary Fund I Class	FCNIX	B	B	A-	Up	10.97	11.69	22.18	32.40	109.68	27.21	274.2	617-563-7000	Y
Fidelity® Select Automotive Portfolio	FSAVX	B-	B-	C+	Up	4.38	15.45	23.95	16.49	79.48	37.1	61.6	617-563-7000	Y
Fidelity® Select Consumer Discretionary Portfolio	FSCPX	B	B	A-	Up	11.02	11.85	22.07	33.90	112.98	41.45	717.5	617-563-7000	Y
Fidelity® Select Leisure Portfolio	FDLSX	B+	B+	A-	Up	9.79	11.60	29.05	41.48	121.72	166.01	521.9	617-563-7000	Y
Fidelity® Select Retailing Portfolio	FSRPX	A-	A-	A-	Up	13.11	15.72	25.82	55.57	155.67	133.17	1,923	617-563-7000	Y
ICON Consumer Discretionary Fund Class A	ICCAX	B-	C	B+		4.49	1.97	8.30	13.53	68.19	13.46	27.0	303-790-1600	Y
ICON Consumer Discretionary Fund Class S	ICCCX	B-	C	B+	Down	4.65	2.31	8.94	15.47	72.20	14.12	27.0	303-790-1600	Y
ICON Consumer Staples Fund Class A	ICRAX	B	C+	A		5.32	5.60	11.34	22.67	74.16	6.95	14.8	303-790-1600	Y
ICON Consumer Staples Fund Class S	ICLEX	B	C+	A		5.48	5.76	11.64	23.67	76.34	6.99	14.8	303-790-1600	Y

Category: Consumer Goods Sector Equity (con't)

Fund Name	Ticker Symbol	Overall Rating	Reward Rating	Risk Rating	Recent Up/ Downgrade	3-Month Total Return	6-Month Total Return	1-Year Total Return	3-Year Total Return	5-Year Total Return	NAV	Total Assets (MIL)	Telephone	Open to New Investors
JNL/Mellon Capital Consumer Discretionary Sector Cls A	US47760W3088	B	B	A-		8.89	10.22	22.10	36.73	118.62	20.81	1,109		Y
JNL/Mellon Capital Consumer Discretionary Sector Cls I	US47760W4078	B	B	A-		8.99	10.38	22.43	37.66	120.86	21.21	1,109		Y
Putnam Global Consumer Fund Class A	PGCOX	B	B-	A-		3.57	5.14	24.91	37.02	94.24	21.57	58.8	617-292-1000	Y
Putnam Global Consumer Fund Class B	PGCKX	B	B-	A-	Up	3.34	4.76	24.03	33.94	87.14	20.76	58.8	617-292-1000	Y
Putnam Global Consumer Fund Class C	PGCNX	B	B-	A-	Up	3.39	4.77	24.06	34.00	87.13	20.68	58.8	617-292-1000	Y
Putnam Global Consumer Fund Class M	PGCMX	B	B-	A-	Up	3.42	4.87	24.33	35.00	89.52	21.22	58.8	617-292-1000	Y
Putnam Global Consumer Fund Class R	PGCIX	B	B-	A-	Up	3.50	5.03	24.63	36.07	91.88	21.49	58.8	617-292-1000	Y
Putnam Global Consumer Fund Class Y	PGCYX	B	B-	A		3.64	5.30	25.26	38.02	96.74	21.67	58.8	617-292-1000	Y
Rydex Consumer Products Fund Class A	RYPDX	B	C+	A-		6.37	5.19	11.69	23.79	83.99	59.33	252.5	800-820-0888	Y
Rydex Consumer Products Fund Class C	RYCPX	B	C+	A-		6.17	4.80	10.85	21.04	77.23	51.41	252.5	800-820-0888	Y
Rydex Consumer Products Fund Class H	RYCAX	B	C+	A-		6.35	5.17	11.66	23.60	82.80	57.15	252.5	800-820-0888	Y
Rydex Consumer Products Fund Class Investor	RYCIX	B	C+	A-		6.43	5.32	11.96	24.73	86.33	64.58	252.5	800-820-0888	Y
Rydex Leisure Fund Class A	RYLSX	B	B-	B+		6.00	6.11	20.21	31.49	106.57	67.75	19.3	800-820-0888	Y
Rydex Leisure Fund Class C	RYLCX	B	B-	B+		5.79	5.71	19.32	28.58	98.93	61.01	19.3	800-820-0888	Y
Rydex Leisure Fund Class Investor	RYLIX	B	B-	B+		6.05	6.22	20.51	32.50	109.17	73.28	19.3	800-820-0888	Y
Rydex Leisure Fund H Class	RYLAX	B	B-	B+		6.00	6.11	20.22	31.37	105.40	65.95	19.3	800-820-0888	Y
Vanguard Consumer Discretionary Index Fund Admiral Shares	VCDAX	B	B	A-		9.07	10.57	22.83	38.79	123.32	80.68	2,508	877-662-7447	Y
Vanguard Consumer Staples Index Fund Class Admiral Shares	VCSAX	B	C+	A-		6.11	4.85	11.79	24.48	89.00	71.97	4,585	877-662-7447	Y

Category: Convertibles

Fund Name	Ticker Symbol	Overall Rating	Reward Rating	Risk Rating	Recent Up/ Downgrade	3-Month Total Return	6-Month Total Return	1-Year Total Return	3-Year Total Return	5-Year Total Return	NAV	Total Assets (MIL)	Telephone	Open to New Investors
Bancroft Fund	BCV	B	C+	B+	Up	1.73	5.10	13.12	21.77	58.18	24.12	126.9		Y
Ellsworth Growth and Income Fund Ltd	ECF	B-	C+	B	Up	2.46	4.41	12.66	19.52	58.44	10.32	133.4		Y
Franklin Convertible Securities Fund Advisor Class	FCSZX	B	B-	B+	Up	2.06	6.61	18.23	28.46	68.29	19.48	2,694	650-312-2000	Y
Franklin Convertible Securities Fund Class A	FISCX	B	B-	B+	Up	2.03	6.51	17.93	27.54	66.24	19.49	2,694	650-312-2000	Y
Franklin Convertible Securities Fund Class C	FROTX	B	B-	B+	Up	1.85	6.08	17.07	24.73	60.15	19.21	2,694	650-312-2000	Y
Franklin Convertible Securities Fund Class R6	FCSKX	B	B-	B+	Up	2.14	6.69	18.31	28.93	68.60	19.59	2,694	650-312-2000	Y
Harbor Convertible Securities Fund Administrative Class	HRCSX	B-	C+	B	Up	0.80	2.37	7.97	12.95	30.12	10.24	114.5	800-422-1050	Y
Harbor Convertible Securities Fund Institutional Class	HACSX	B	C+	A-	Up	0.96	2.59	8.24	13.79	31.72	10.25	114.5	800-422-1050	Y
Harbor Convertible Securities Fund Investor Class	HICSX	B	C	A-	Up	0.76	2.30	7.86	12.47	29.26	10.23	114.5	800-422-1050	Y
Harbor Convertible Securities Fund Retirement Class	HNCVX	B	C+	A-	Up	0.88	2.53	8.33	13.81	31.76	10.24	114.5	800-422-1050	Y
MainStay Convertible Fund Class A	MCOAX	B	C+	B	Up	2.38	4.50	10.80	21.27	65.94	16.81	1,199	800-624-6782	Y
MainStay Convertible Fund Class B	MCSVX	B-	C+	B	Down	2.15	3.96	9.79	18.00	58.36	16.74	1,199	800-624-6782	
MainStay Convertible Fund Class C	MCCVX	B-	C+	B	Down	2.15	3.97	9.80	17.96	58.34	16.72	1,199	800-624-6782	Y
MainStay Convertible Fund Class I	MCNVX	B	C+	B+	Up	2.48	4.69	11.23	22.33	68.16	16.84	1,199	800-624-6782	Y
MainStay Convertible Fund Investor Class	MCINX	B	C+	B	Up	2.34	4.41	10.68	20.73	64.44	16.81	1,199	800-624-6782	Y
Miller Convertible Bond Fund Class A	MCFAX	B	C+	A-	Up	2.01	3.92	6.83	15.98	47.14	12.95	974.2	877-441-4434	Y
Miller Convertible Bond Fund Class C	MCFCX	B	C+	A-	Up	1.88	3.59	6.18	14.20	43.46	12.86	974.2	877-441-4434	Y
Miller Convertible Bond Fund Class I	MCIFX	B	C+	A-	Up	2.16	4.13	7.29	17.70	50.88	12.93	974.2	877-441-4434	Y
Putnam High Income Securities Fund	PCF	B-	C+	B-	Up	1.39	4.83	11.19	18.84	42.02	9.69	126.3	617-292-1000	Y
Victory INCORE Investment Grade Convertible Fund Class A	SBFCX	B-	B-	B	Down	3.69	8.42	18.47	22.79	67.81	16.11	118.2	800-539-3863	Y
Victory INCORE Investment Grade Convertible Fund Class I	VICIX	B-	B-	B	Down	3.87	8.64	18.91	24.36	71.49	16.1	118.2	800-539-3863	Y

Category: Emerging Markets Equity

Fund Name	Ticker Symbol	RATINGS: Overall Rating	RATINGS: Reward Rating	RATINGS: Risk Rating	RATINGS: Recent Up/Downgrade	TOTAL RETURNS & PERFORMANCE: 3-Month Total Return	6-Month Total Return	1-Year Total Return	3-Year Total Return	5-Year Total Return	ASSETS: NAV	Total Assets (MIL)	NEW INVESTORS: Telephone	Open to New Investors
AB Emerging Markets Multi-Asset Portfolio Advisor Class	ABYEX	B-	C+	B-		3.98	7.67	20.59	26.80	18.15	9.95	119.8	212-969-1000	Y
AB Emerging Markets Multi-Asset Portfolio Class A	ABAEX	B-	C+	B-	Up	3.90	7.54	20.36	25.81	16.46	9.93	119.8	212-969-1000	Y
AB Emerging Markets Multi-Asset Portfolio Class C	ABCEX	B-	C+	B-	Up	3.74	7.13	19.35	22.94	12.33	9.89	119.8	212-969-1000	Y
AB Emerging Markets Multi-Asset Portfolio Class I	ABIEX	B-	C+	B-	Up	4.02	7.75	20.69	26.73	18.11	9.88	119.8	212-969-1000	Y
AB Emerging Markets Multi-Asset Portfolio Class K	ABKEX	B-	C+	B-	Up	3.99	7.60	20.32	25.82	16.66	9.9	119.8	212-969-1000	Y
AB Emerging Markets Multi-Asset Portfolio Class R	ABREX	B-	C+	B-	Up	3.78	7.37	19.93	24.87	15.18	9.9	119.8	212-969-1000	Y
AB Emerging Markets Multi-Asset Portfolio Class Z	ABZEX	B-	C+	B-		3.99	7.82	20.78	26.82	18.19	9.89	119.8	212-969-1000	Y
AB Emerging Markets Portfolio	SNEMX	B-	B	C	Up	4.75	12.09	32.96	27.07	27.03	32.54	1,335	212-969-1000	Y
Acadian Emerging Markets Portfolio Class I	AEMZX	B-	B	C	Up	6.38	14.83	37.90	28.55	26.76	22.38	1,164		Y
Acadian Emerging Markets Portfolio Class Y	AEMVX	B-	B	C	Up	6.19	14.44	37.64	28.38	26.59	22.35	1,164		Y
Acadian Emerging Markets Portfolio Investor Class	AEMGX	B-	B	C	Up	6.43	14.78	37.62	28.31	26.52	22.39	1,164		
Alger Emerging Markets Fund Class A	AAEMX	B-	B	C+	Up	6.70	15.17	38.70	31.67	31.53	11.33	68.0	800-992-3863	Y
Alger Emerging Markets Fund Class C	ACEMX	B-	B-	C+	Up	6.43	14.70	37.65	28.65	26.61	10.87	68.0	800-992-3863	Y
Alger Emerging Markets Fund Class I	AIEMX	B-	B	C+	Up	6.64	15.16	38.68	31.54	31.40	11.26	68.0	800-992-3863	Y
Alger Emerging Markets Fund Class Y	AYEMX	B-	B	C+	Up	6.73	15.41	39.48	32.62	32.47	11.34	68.0	800-992-3863	Y
Alger Emerging Markets Fund Class Y-2	AEMYX	B-	B	C+	Up	6.81	15.51	39.43	32.72	32.57	11.31	68.0	800-992-3863	Y
Alger Emerging Markets Fund Class Z	AZEMX	B	B	C+	Up	6.70	15.34	39.08	32.97	33.27	11.38	68.0	800-992-3863	Y
AllianzGI NFJ Emerging Markets Value Fund Class A	AZMAX	B	B	C+	Up	6.69	13.97	37.47	40.17	41.07	18.17	81.5	800-498-5413	Y
AllianzGI NFJ Emerging Markets Value Fund Class C	AZMCX	B	B	C+	Up	6.46	13.59	36.44	37.04	35.91	18.38	81.5	800-498-5413	Y
AllianzGI NFJ Emerging Markets Value Fund Class P	AZMPX	B	B+	C+	Up	6.70	14.07	37.69	40.94	42.28	18.14	81.5	800-498-5413	Y
AllianzGI NFJ Emerging Mkts Value Fund Inst Cls	AZMIX	B	B+	C+	Up	6.77	14.17	37.86	41.32	42.93	18.45	81.5	800-498-5413	Y
American Century Emerging Markets Fund A Class	AEMMX	B+	A	C+	Up	5.50	19.03	45.50	43.22	41.77	11.88	1,566	800-444-4015	Y
American Century Emerging Markets Fund C Class	ACECX	B+	A	C+	Up	5.41	18.73	44.56	40.28	36.70	10.9	1,566	800-444-4015	Y
American Century Emerging Markets Fund I Class	AMKIX	B+	A	C+	Up	5.67	19.32	46.24	45.28	44.88	12.66	1,566	800-444-4015	Y
American Century Emerging Markets Fund Investor Class	TWMIX	B+	A	C+	Up	5.65	19.24	45.85	44.29	43.50	12.33	1,566	800-444-4015	Y
American Century Emerging Markets Fund R Class	AEMRX	B+	A	C+	Up	5.46	19.00	45.32	42.21	39.87	11.96	1,566	800-444-4015	Y
American Century Emerging Markets Fund R5 Class	AEGMX	B+	A	C+	Up	5.67	19.32	46.06	44.49	43.71	12.66	1,566	800-444-4015	Y
American Century Emerging Markets Fund R6 Class	AEDMX	B+	A	C+	Up	5.66	19.39	46.35	45.99	45.83	12.68	1,566	800-444-4015	Y
American Century Emerging Markets Fund Y Class	AEYMX	B+	A	C+	Up	5.75	19.49	46.26	44.69	43.90	12.69	1,566	800-444-4015	Y
American Century NT Emerging Markets Fund G Class	ACLKX	B+	A	C+	Up	6.56	20.78	48.36	46.74	45.77	13.46	481.9	800-444-4015	Y
American Funds New World Fund® Class 529-A	CNWAX	B-	B-	C+	Up	5.48	13.10	32.47	28.63	38.00	66.34	34,044	800-421-4225	Y
American Funds New World Fund® Class 529-E	CNWEX	B-	B-	C+	Up	5.40	12.98	32.19	27.80	36.48	65.88	34,044	800-421-4225	Y
American Funds New World Fund® Class 529-F	CNWFX	B-	B-	C+	Up	5.53	13.23	32.74	29.43	39.42	66.3	34,044	800-421-4225	Y
American Funds New World Fund® Class A	NEWFX	B-	B-	C+	Up	5.48	13.13	32.55	28.87	38.44	66.92	34,044	800-421-4225	Y
American Funds New World Fund® Class F-1	NWFFX	B-	B-	C+	Up	5.49	13.13	32.55	28.96	38.60	66.46	34,044	800-421-4225	Y
American Funds New World Fund® Class F-2	NFFFX	B-	B-	C+	Up	5.57	13.28	32.91	29.99	40.47	66.74	34,044	800-421-4225	Y
American Funds New World Fund® Class F-3	FNWFX	B-	B-	C+	Up	5.58	13.35	33.00	29.31	38.90	66.91	34,044	800-421-4225	Y
American Funds New World Fund® Class R-2E	RNEBX	B-	B-	C+	Up	5.38	12.91	32.02	27.50	36.05	66.16	34,044	800-421-4225	Y
American Funds New World Fund® Class R-3	RNWCX	B-	B-	C+	Up	5.42	12.98	32.19	27.82	36.54	65.97	34,044	800-421-4225	Y
American Funds New World Fund® Class R-4	RNWEX	B-	B-	C+	Up	5.50	13.15	32.59	29.05	38.78	66.52	34,044	800-421-4225	Y
American Funds New World Fund® Class R-5	RNWFX	B-	B-	C+	Up	5.56	13.31	32.99	30.22	40.89	67.07	34,044	800-421-4225	Y
American Funds New World Fund® Class R-5E	RNWHX	B-	B-	C+	Up	5.54	13.26	32.85	29.39	38.99	66.31	34,044	800-421-4225	Y
American Funds New World Fund® Class R-6	RNWGX	B-	B-	C+	Up	5.59	13.35	33.06	30.43	41.23	66.88	34,044	800-421-4225	Y
AMG Trilogy Emerging Markets Equity Fund Class I	TLESX	B-	B	C	Up	5.89	16.91	38.10	31.27	21.97	10.33	132.6	800-835-3879	Y
AMG Trilogy Emerging Markets Equity Fund Class N	TLEVX	B-	B	C	Up	5.79	16.80	37.76	29.83	19.78	10.37	132.6	800-835-3879	Y
AMG Trilogy Emerging Markets Equity Fund Class Z	TLEIX	B-	B	C	Up	6.05	17.03	38.53	31.85	22.76	10.28	132.6	800-835-3879	Y
AMG Trilogy Emerging Wealth Equity Fund Class I	TYWSX	B-	B-	C+	Up	8.25	18.88	42.56			12.94	63.0	800-835-3879	Y
AMG Trilogy Emerging Wealth Equity Fund Class N	TYWVX	B-	B-	C+	Up	8.11	18.64	42.12			12.9	63.0	800-835-3879	Y
AMG Trilogy Emerging Wealth Equity Fund Class Z	TYWIX	B-	B-	C+	Up	8.24	18.87	42.67			12.9	63.0	800-835-3879	Y
AQR Emerging Momentum Style Fund Class R6	QEMRX	B-	B-	C	Up	9.31	22.82	44.30	27.48		11.4	13.4	203-742-3600	Y
Artisan Emerging Markets Fund Institutional Class	APHEX	B	A	C	Up	8.32	17.49	39.91	42.05	32.01	16.71	53.9	800-344-1770	Y
Artisan Emerging Markets Fund Investor Class	ARTZX	B	A	C	Up	8.32	17.44	39.94	42.23	31.34	16.79	53.9	800-344-1770	Y

Category: Emerging Markets Equity (con't)

Fund Name	Ticker Symbol	RATINGS: Overall Rating	Reward Rating	Risk Rating	Recent Up/ Downgrade	TOTAL RETURNS & PERFORMANCE: 3-Month Total Return	6-Month Total Return	1-Year Total Return	3-Year Total Return	5-Year Total Return	ASSETS: NAV	Total Assets (MIL)	NEW INVESTORS: Telephone	Open to New Investors
Ashmore Emerging Markets Equity Fund Class A	EMEAX	B	A-	C	Up	8.35	18.83	45.81	36.19	28.73	11.61	10.1	866-876-8294	Y
Ashmore Emerging Markets Equity Fund Class C	EMECX	B	B+	C	Up	8.18	18.49	44.80	33.29	24.20	11.17	10.1	866-876-8294	Y
Ashmore Emerging Markets Equity Fund Institutional Class	EMFIX	B	A	C	Up	8.53	18.98	46.23	37.31	30.51	11.21	10.1	866-876-8294	Y
Ashmore Emerging Markets Small Cap Equity Fund Class A	ESSAX	B	B	C+	Up	4.52	10.11	28.73	34.57	32.21	10.42	40.1	866-876-8294	Y
Ashmore Emerging Markets Small Cap Equity Fund Class C	ESSCX	B	B	C+	Up	4.35	9.86	27.90	31.51	27.14	11.02	40.1	866-876-8294	Y
Ashmore Emerging Mkts Small Cap Equity Fund Inst Cls	ESCIX	B	B	C+	Up	4.59	10.21	28.89	35.59	33.79	13.36	40.1	866-876-8294	
Baillie Gifford The Emerging Markets Fund Class 2	BGEHX	B	A	C	Up	7.51	20.43	53.02	46.05	54.52	22.8204	2,015		Y
Baillie Gifford The Emerging Markets Fund Class 3	BGELX	B	A	C	Up	8.92	22.04	55.10	43.02	51.31	23.0019	2,015		Y
Baillie Gifford The Emerging Markets Fund Class 5	BGEDX	B	A	C	Up	7.55	20.52	53.25	46.53	55.02	23.5479	2,015		Y
Baron Emerging Markets Fund Class R6	BEXUX	B-	B	C	Up	6.15	16.96	40.58	30.50	57.01	15.38	4,592	800-992-2766	Y
Baron Emerging Markets Fund Institutional Shares	BEXIX	B-	B	C	Up	6.16	16.88	40.62	30.41	56.91	15.37	4,592	800-992-2766	Y
Baron Emerging Markets Fund Retail Shares	BEXFX	B-	B	C	Up	6.09	16.76	40.33	29.35	54.91	15.33	4,592	800-992-2766	Y
BlackRock Emerging Mkts Dividend Fund Inst Shares	BICHX	B-	B	C	Up	6.31	13.58	36.85	29.10	26.67	10.17	15.1	800-441-7762	Y
BMO LGM Emerging Markets Equity Fund Class I	MIEMX	B-	B-	C	Up	7.71	10.35	38.18	29.80	30.09	16.96	164.5	800-236-3863	Y
BNY Mellon Emerging Markets Fund Class Investor	MIEGX	B-	B	C	Up	8.43	18.72	42.30	30.58	22.89	12.32	976.5	800-645-6561	Y
BNY Mellon Emerging Markets Fund Class M	MEMKX	B-	B	C	Up	8.41	18.75	42.59	31.47	24.42	11.98	976.5	800-645-6561	Y
Calvert Emerging Markets Equity Fund Class A	CVMAX	B	A	C+	Up	6.66	16.12	44.19	41.12	56.93	17.39	255.1	800-368-2745	Y
Calvert Emerging Markets Equity Fund Class C	CVMCX	B	A-	C	Up	6.48	15.64	43.16	37.86	50.35	17.08	255.1	800-368-2745	Y
Calvert Emerging Markets Equity Fund Class I	CVMIX	B	A	C+	Up	6.77	16.30	44.71	42.60	59.73	17.55	255.1	800-368-2745	Y
Capital Emerging Markets Growth Fund, Inc.	EMRGX	B-	B	C	Up	8.72	16.27	41.30	31.04	24.01	8.44	2,645	213-486-9200	Y
Capital Group Emerging Markets Growth Fund, Inc. Class F-3	EMGEX	B-	B	C		8.71	16.27	41.29	31.03	24.00	8.44	2,645	213-486-9200	Y
Capital Group Emerging Markets Growth Fund, Inc. Class R-6	REFGX	B-	B	C		8.67	16.22	41.23	30.97	23.94	8.44	2,645	213-486-9200	Y
Causeway Emerging Markets Fund Class Institutional	CEMIX	B-	B	C	Up	7.21	16.88	39.58	28.08	28.75	14.17	4,614	866-947-7000	Y
Causeway Emerging Markets Fund Investor Class	CEMVX	B-	B	C	Up	7.16	16.68	39.27	27.12	27.21	14.28	4,614	866-947-7000	Y
City National Rochdale Emerging Markets Fund Class N	RIMIX	B+	A	C+	Up	5.42	15.34	43.29	42.78	73.74	51.96	1,669		Y
City National Rochdale Emerging Markets Fund Class Y	CNRYX	B+	A	C+	Up	5.50	15.48	43.61	43.30	74.37	52.08	1,669		Y
Columbia Emerging Markets Fund Advisor Class	CEMHX	B	A-	C	Up	7.12	19.41	46.81	39.89	35.77	13.9	1,455	800-345-6611	Y
Columbia Emerging Markets Fund Class A	EEMAX	B	A-	C	Up	7.11	19.23	46.52	38.80	34.12	13.68	1,455	800-345-6611	Y
Columbia Emerging Markets Fund Class C	EEMCX	B	B+	C	Up	6.84	18.80	45.50	35.74	29.11	12.95	1,455	800-345-6611	Y
Columbia Emerging Markets Fund Class K	CEKMX	B	A-	C	Up	7.11	19.36	46.66	39.39	35.18	13.75	1,455	800-345-6611	
Columbia Emerging Markets Fund Class R	CEMRX	B	B+	C	Up	7.04	19.11	46.16	37.81	32.41	13.52	1,455	800-345-6611	Y
Columbia Emerging Markets Fund Class T	CEMWX	B	A-	C	Up	7.02	19.24	46.40	38.83	33.99	13.67	1,455	800-345-6611	Y
Columbia Emerging Markets Fund Institutional 2 Class	CEKRX	B	A	C	Up	7.17	19.56	47.03	40.52	36.81	13.89	1,455	800-345-6611	Y
Columbia Emerging Markets Fund Institutional 3 Class	CEKYX	B	A	C	Up	7.16	19.49	47.08	40.73	37.18	13.95	1,455	800-345-6611	Y
Columbia Emerging Markets Fund Institutional Class	UMEMX	B	A-	C	Up	7.17	19.45	46.94	39.97	35.82	13.81	1,455	800-345-6611	Y
Consulting Group Emerging Markets Equity Fund	TEMUX	B-	B	C	Up	7.14	16.56	39.16	34.92	22.63	16.22	504.4	855-332-5306	Y
Delaware Emerging Markets Fund Class A	DEMAX	B	A-	C	Up	2.51	16.23	41.61	43.26	51.24	20.17	4,736		Y
Delaware Emerging Markets Fund Class C	DEMCX	B	B+	C	Up	2.34	15.78	40.58	40.08	45.66	18.84	4,736		Y
Delaware Emerging Markets Fund Class R	DEMRX	B	A-	C	Up	2.46	16.08	41.32	42.18	49.33	20.33	4,736		Y
Delaware Emerging Markets Fund Class R6	DEMZX	B	A-	C	Up	2.59	16.39	42.17	44.59	53.36	20.28	4,736		Y
Delaware Emerging Markets Fund Institutional Class	DEMIX	B	A-	C	Up	2.56	16.31	41.97	44.35	53.11	20.29	4,736		Y
Deutsche Emerging Markets Equity Fund Class A	SEKAX	B-	B	C	Up	8.72	18.06	37.38	31.86	28.82	20.39	89.1	201-593-8273	Y
Deutsche Emerging Markets Equity Fund Class C	SEKCX	B-	B	C	Up	8.56	17.66	36.39	28.97	24.08	18.25	89.1	201-593-8273	Y
Deutsche Emerging Markets Equity Fund Class S	SEMGX	B-	B	C	Up	8.74	18.13	37.70	32.79	30.36	20.65	89.1	201-593-8273	Y
Deutsche Emerging Markets Equity Fund Class T	SEKTX	B-	B	C	Up	8.72	18.06	37.44	31.88	28.82	20.39	89.1	201-593-8273	Y
Deutsche Emerging Markets Equity Fund Institutional Class	SEKIX	B-	B	C	Up	8.77	18.18	37.77	32.86	30.41	20.63	89.1	201-593-8273	Y
DFA Emerging Mkts Core Equity Portfolio Inst Cls	DFCEX	B-	B	C	Up	7.70	14.75	36.55	30.83	27.64	23.22	27,437	512-306-7400	Y
DFA Emerging Markets Portfolio II	DFETX	B-	B	C	Up	7.22	14.14	36.73	29.81	25.56	29.13	83.9	512-306-7400	
DFA Emerging Markets Portfolio Institutional Class	DFEMX	B-	B	C	Up	7.21	14.08	36.57	29.03	24.25	30.47	6,686	512-306-7400	Y
DFA Emerging Markets Small Cap Portfolio Institutional Cls	DEMSX	B	B	C+	Up	8.58	15.17	35.25	37.46	40.66	23.87	7,375	512-306-7400	Y
DFA Emerging Markets Social Core Portfolio	DFESX	B-	B	C	Up	7.33	14.72	37.30	31.53	27.23	14.91	1,368	512-306-7400	Y
Dreyfus Diversified Emerging Markets Fund Class A	DBEAX	B-	B	C	Up	7.40	15.02	39.18	29.06	29.15	25.79	234.0	800-645-6561	Y

Category: Emerging Markets Equity (con't)

Fund Name	Ticker Symbol	RATINGS: Overall Rating	Reward Rating	Risk Rating	Recent Up/ Downgrade	TOTAL RETURNS & PERFORMANCE: 3-Month Total Return	6-Month Total Return	1-Year Total Return	3-Year Total Return	5-Year Total Return	ASSETS: NAV	Total Assets (ML)	NEW INVESTORS: Telephone	Open to New Investors
Dreyfus Diversified Emerging Markets Fund Class I	SBCEX	B-	B	C	Up	7.50	15.28	39.76	30.68	31.50	25.67	234.0	800-645-6561	Y
Dreyfus Diversified Emerging Markets Fund Class Y	SBYEX	B-	B	C	Up	7.53	15.31	39.82	30.98	32.00	25.7	234.0	800-645-6561	Y
Dreyfus Global Emerging Markets Fund Class A	DGEAX	B-	B	C	Up	8.95	15.54	45.58	34.89		18.71	296.5	800-645-6561	Y
Dreyfus Global Emerging Markets Fund Class C	DGECX	B-	B	C	Up	8.74	15.06	44.53	31.89		18.23	296.5	800-645-6561	Y
Dreyfus Global Emerging Markets Fund Class I	DGIEX	B-	B	C	Up	8.98	15.60	46.01	35.76		18.81	296.5	800-645-6561	Y
Dreyfus Global Emerging Markets Fund Class Y	DGEYX	B-	B	C	Up	9.00	15.60	45.95	35.94		18.89	296.5	800-645-6561	Y
Dreyfus Strategic Beta Emerging Markets Equity Fund Cls A	DOFAX	B-	B	C	Up	5.54	11.78	30.72	29.27		13.94	19.5	800-645-6561	Y
Dreyfus Strategic Beta Emerging Markets Equity Fund Cls C	DOFCX	B-	B	C	Up	5.37	11.44	29.42	26.14		13.97	19.5	800-645-6561	Y
Dreyfus Strategic Beta Emerging Markets Equity Fund Cls I	DOFIX	B-	B	C	Up	5.64	11.97	30.60	29.86		13.93	19.5	800-645-6561	Y
Dreyfus Strategic Beta Emerging Markets Equity Fund Cls Y	DOFYX	B-	B	C	Up	5.64	11.96	30.69	29.83		13.94	19.5	800-645-6561	Y
Dreyfus Total Emerging Markets Fund Class A	DTMAX	B	B	C	Up	8.79	18.19	42.36	40.68	32.77	14.89	116.5	800-645-6561	Y
Dreyfus Total Emerging Markets Fund Class C	DTMCX	B-	B	C	Up	8.58	17.72	41.26	37.59	27.88	14.65	116.5	800-645-6561	Y
Dreyfus Total Emerging Markets Fund Class I	DTEIX	B	B+	C	Up	8.85	18.38	42.71	41.87	34.54	14.95	116.5	800-645-6561	Y
Dreyfus Total Emerging Markets Fund Class Y	DTMYX	B	B+	C	Up	8.92	18.36	42.78	42.03	34.80	14.97	116.5	800-645-6561	Y
Driehaus Emerging Markets Growth Fund Institutional Class	DIEMX	B-	B	C+	Up	7.52	19.36	42.61	34.88	40.27	39.61	1,730	877-779-0079	Y
Driehaus Emerging Markets Growth Fund Investor Class	DREGX	B-	B	C+	Up	7.48	19.28	42.52	34.79	40.18	39.64	1,730	877-779-0079	Y
Fidelity Advisor® Emerging Markets Discovery Fund Class A	FEDAX	B	B	C+	Up	6.44	13.39	37.21	37.42	31.66	15.29	427.1	617-563-7000	Y
Fidelity Advisor® Emerging Markets Discovery Fund Class C	FEDGX	B-	B	C+	Up	6.15	12.93	36.11	34.38	26.79	14.93	427.1	617-563-7000	Y
Fidelity Advisor® Emerging Markets Discovery Fund Class M	FEDTX	B	B	C+	Up	6.34	13.24	36.81	36.38	30.00	15.23	427.1	617-563-7000	Y
Fidelity Advisor® Emerging Markets Discovery Fund I Class	FEDIX	B	B	B-	Up	6.49	13.55	37.55	38.50	33.46	15.39	427.1	617-563-7000	Y
Fidelity Advisor® Emerging Markets Fund Class A	FAMKX	B	B	C	Up	8.21	17.90	46.78	34.85	42.52	30.18	644.2	617-563-7000	Y
Fidelity Advisor® Emerging Markets Fund Class C	FMCKX	B-	B	C	Up	7.99	17.43	45.62	31.80	37.21	28.76	644.2	617-563-7000	Y
Fidelity Advisor® Emerging Markets Fund Class M	FTMKX	B	B	C	Up	8.12	17.72	46.33	33.73	40.65	29.96	644.2	617-563-7000	Y
Fidelity Advisor® Emerging Markets Fund Class Z	FZAEX	B	B+	C	Up	8.32	18.16	47.45	36.82	45.96	30.26	644.2	617-563-7000	Y
Fidelity Advisor® Emerging Markets Fund I Class	FIMKX	B	B+	C	Up	8.27	18.10	47.28	36.28	45.01	30.3	644.2	617-563-7000	Y
Fidelity Advisor® Total Emerging Markets Fund Class A	FTEDX	B-	B	B-	Up	5.15	12.29	29.33	34.59	32.53	13.54	749.9	617-563-7000	Y
Fidelity Advisor® Total Emerging Markets Fund Class C	FTEFX	B-	B-	B-	Up	4.91	11.92	28.31	31.59	27.57	13.47	749.9	617-563-7000	Y
Fidelity Advisor® Total Emerging Markets Fund Class M	FTEHX	B-	B-	B-	Up	5.01	12.06	28.81	33.35	30.76	13.55	749.9	617-563-7000	Y
Fidelity Advisor® Total Emerging Markets Fund I Class	FTEJX	B	B	B-	Up	5.13	12.44	29.63	35.54	34.23	13.53	749.9	617-563-7000	Y
Fidelity® Emerging Markets Discovery Fund	FEDDX	B	B	C+	Up	6.49	13.57	37.63	38.56	33.39	15.36	427.1	617-563-7000	Y
Fidelity® Emerging Markets Fund	FEMKX	B	B+	C	Up	8.40	18.29	47.67	36.98	46.06	32.75	5,082	617-563-7000	Y
Fidelity® Emerging Markets Fund Class K	FKEMX	B	B+	C	Up	8.42	18.38	47.89	37.67	47.42	32.76	5,082	617-563-7000	Y
Fidelity® Emerging Markets Index Fund Institutional Class	FPMIX	B-	B	C	Up	7.30	15.72	37.45	29.06	24.48	11.42	1,412	617-563-7000	Y
Fidelity® Emerging Mkts Index Fund Inst Premium Cls	FPADX	B-	B	C	Up	7.32	15.75	37.64	29.15	24.65	11.42	1,412	617-563-7000	Y
Fidelity® Emerging Markets Index Fund Investor Class	FPEMX	B-	B	C	Up	7.20	15.64	37.23	28.23	23.35	11.41	1,412	617-563-7000	Y
Fidelity® Emerging Markets Index Fund Premium Class	FPMAX	B-	B	C	Up	7.27	15.71	37.45	28.78	24.16	11.41	1,412	617-563-7000	Y
Fidelity® Series Emerging Markets Fund	FEMSX	B	B	C	Up	7.03	16.78	40.43	36.20	36.14	21.41	15,789	617-563-7000	
Fidelity® Total Emerging Markets Fund	FTEMX	B	B	B-	Up	5.20	12.42	29.59	35.43	34.19	13.55	749.9	617-563-7000	Y
GMO Emerging Domestic Opportunities Fund Class II	GEDTX	B-	B	B-	Up	8.15	15.80	37.46	31.94	35.98	28.45	2,355	617-330-7500	Y
GMO Emerging Domestic Opportunities Fund Class III	GEDSX	B-	B	B-	Up	8.15	15.84	37.51	32.15	36.41	28.45	2,355	617-330-7500	Y
GMO Emerging Domestic Opportunities Fund Class IV	GEDIX	B-	B	B-	Up	8.21	15.89	37.67	32.39	36.78	28.47	2,355	617-330-7500	Y
GMO Emerging Domestic Opportunities Fund Class V	GEDOX	B-	B	B-	Up	8.20	15.90	37.65	32.50	36.77	28.43	2,355	617-330-7500	Y
GMO Emerging Markets Fund Class III	GMOEX	B-	B-	C	Up	6.74	10.58	32.04	28.83	15.21	35.07	5,203	617-330-7500	Y
GMO Emerging Markets Fund Class IV	GMEFX	B-	B-	C	Up	6.75	10.59	32.08	28.89	15.40	34.73	5,203	617-330-7500	Y
GMO Emerging Markets Fund Class V	GEMVX	B-	B	C	Up	6.73	10.60	32.12	29.03	15.66	34.63	5,203	617-330-7500	Y
GMO Emerging Markets Fund Class VI	GEMMX	B-	B	C	Up	6.76	10.66	32.22	29.20	15.90	34.72	5,203	617-330-7500	Y
GMO Emerging Markets Series Fund Class R6	GECRX	B-	B	C	Up	6.68	10.49	32.94	32.65	18.90	10.47	15.8	617-330-7500	Y
Goldman Sachs Emerging Markets Equity Fund Class A	GEMAX	B+	A	C+	Up	9.26	20.62	47.63	45.32	43.82	22.02	927.6	800-526-7384	Y
Goldman Sachs Emerging Markets Equity Fund Class C	GEMCX	B	A-	C+	Up	9.05	20.16	46.56	42.14	38.56	19.78	927.6	800-526-7384	Y
Goldman Sachs Emerging Markets Equity Fund Class R6	GEMUX	B+	A	C+	Up	9.36	20.88	48.34	47.26	46.80	23.65	927.6	800-526-7384	Y
Goldman Sachs Emerging Mkts Equity Fund Inst Cls	GEMIX	B+	A	C+	Up	9.39	20.91	48.31	47.15	46.69	23.55	927.6	800-526-7384	Y
Goldman Sachs Emerging Markets Equity Fund Investor Class	GIRMX	B+	A	C+	Up	9.35	20.78	48.10	46.40	45.59	23.38	927.6	800-526-7384	Y

Category: Emerging Markets Equity (con't)

Fund Name	Ticker Symbol	RATINGS: Overall Rating	RATINGS: Reward Rating	RATINGS: Risk Rating	RATINGS: Recent Up/Downgrade	TOTAL RETURNS & PERFORMANCE: 3-Month Total Return	6-Month Total Return	1-Year Total Return	3-Year Total Return	5-Year Total Return	NAV	ASSETS: Total Assets (MIL)	NEW INVESTORS: Telephone	Open to New Investors
Goldman Sachs Emerging Markets Equity Fund Service Class	GEMSX	B+	A	C+	Up	9.26	20.58	47.49	44.95	43.09	21.29	927.6	800-526-7384	Y
Goldman Sachs Emerging Markets Equity Insights Fund Cls A	GERAX	B	A-	C+	Up	5.20	17.19	38.76	38.93	33.23	10.75	1,721	800-526-7384	Y
Goldman Sachs Emerging Markets Equity Insights Fund Cls C	GERCX	B	B+	C+	Up	4.97	16.71	37.72	35.78	28.31	10.64	1,721	800-526-7384	Y
Goldman Sachs Emerging Markets Equity Insights Fund Cls R	GRRPX	B	A-	C+	Up	5.09	16.97	38.43	37.90	31.72	10.63	1,721	800-526-7384	Y
Goldman Sachs Emerging Markets Equity Insights Fund Cls R6	GERUX	B+	A	C+	Up	5.25	17.37	39.17	40.58	35.78	10.72	1,721	800-526-7384	Y
Goldman Sachs Emerging Mkts Equity Insights Fund Intl	GERIX	B+	A	C+	Up	5.33	17.33	39.27	40.59	35.79	10.73	1,721	800-526-7384	Y
Goldman Sachs Emerging Mkts Equity Insights Fund Inv Cls	GIRPX	B+	A	C+	Up	5.29	17.30	39.09	40.15	34.97	10.72	1,721	800-526-7384	Y
Grandeur Peak Emerging Mkts Opp Fund Inst Cls	GPEIX	B-	B-	B-	Up	8.41	10.87	28.33	30.49		13.19	449.2	855-377-7325	
Grandeur Peak Emerging Mkts Opp Fund Inv Cls	GPEOX	B-	B-	B-	Up	8.33	10.80	27.97	29.55		13.13	449.2	855-377-7325	
GuideMark® Emerging Markets Fund Service Shares	GMLVX	B+	A	B-	Up	6.42	15.91	38.26	34.98	104.63	16.51	111.1	603-888-5500	
Harding Loevner Emerging Markets Portfolio Advisor Class	HLEMX	B-	B	C	Up	5.69	13.34	35.22	32.41	36.67	59.23	4,057	877-435-8105	Y
Harding Loevner Inst Emerging Mkts Portfolio Cls I	HLMEX	B-	B	C	Up	5.69	13.37	35.32	32.70	36.92	22.61	4,891	877-435-8105	Y
Harding Loevner Inst Emerging Mkts Portfolio Cls II	HLEEX	B-	B	C	Up	5.85	13.55	35.78	33.66	38.03	22.61	4,891	877-435-8105	
Hartford Emerging Markets Equity Fund Class A	HERAX	B	B	C	Up	5.44	15.96	41.43	34.80	32.13	9.97	86.3	888-843-7824	Y
Hartford Emerging Markets Equity Fund Class C	HERCX	B-	B	C	Up	5.38	15.61	40.40	32.05	27.67	9.79	86.3	888-843-7824	Y
Hartford Emerging Markets Equity Fund Class F	HERFX	B	B+	C+	Up	5.58	16.26	42.06	36.60	35.01	9.89	86.3	888-843-7824	Y
Hartford Emerging Markets Equity Fund Class I	HERIX	B	B+	C+	Up	5.62	16.19	41.81	36.36	34.77	9.94	86.3	888-843-7824	Y
Hartford Emerging Markets Equity Fund Class R3	HERRX	B	B	C	Up	5.44	15.84	41.08	33.96	30.78	9.98	86.3	888-843-7824	Y
Hartford Emerging Markets Equity Fund Class R4	HERSX	B	B	C+	Up	5.48	16.08	41.42	34.89	32.47	10.03	86.3	888-843-7824	Y
Hartford Emerging Markets Equity Fund Class R5	HERTX	B	B	C+	Up	5.67	16.30	42.09	35.64	33.97	9.9	86.3	888-843-7824	Y
Hartford Emerging Markets Equity Fund Class Y	HERYX	B	B+	C+	Up	5.61	16.32	42.01	36.73	35.19	9.93	86.3	888-843-7824	Y
Hartford Schroders Emerging Markets Equity Fund Class A	SEMVX	B	B	C	Up	6.87	16.85	40.53	34.75	26.88	16.68	2,799	888-843-7824	Y
Hartford Schroders Emerging Markets Equity Fund Class C	HHHCX	B-	B	C	Up	6.68	16.41	39.50	31.90	22.30	16.53	2,799	888-843-7824	Y
Hartford Schroders Emerging Markets Equity Fund Class F	HHHFX	B	B+	C	Up	7.00	16.99	40.96	35.78	28.44	16.63	2,799	888-843-7824	Y
Hartford Schroders Emerging Markets Equity Fund Class I	SEMNX	B	B+	C	Up	6.93	16.91	40.86	35.69	28.35	16.64	2,799	888-843-7824	Y
Hartford Schroders Emerging Markets Equity Fund Class R3	HHHRX	B	B	C	Up	6.87	16.86	40.61	34.17	25.66	16.61	2,799	888-843-7824	Y
Hartford Schroders Emerging Markets Equity Fund Class R4	HHHSX	B	B	C	Up	6.84	16.75	40.48	34.74	26.82	16.62	2,799	888-843-7824	Y
Hartford Schroders Emerging Markets Equity Fund Class R5	HHHTX	B	B+	C	Up	6.96	16.95	40.91	35.85	28.51	16.64	2,799	888-843-7824	Y
Hartford Schroders Emerging Markets Equity Fund Class SDR	SEMTX	B	B+	C	Up	6.98	17.03	41.09	36.27	28.90	16.66	2,799	888-843-7824	Y
Hartford Schroders Emerging Markets Equity Fund Class Y	HHHYX	B	B+	C	Up	6.97	16.94	41.10	36.07	28.71	16.65	2,799	888-843-7824	Y
ICON Emerging Markets Fund Class A	IPCAX	B-	C+	B	Up	2.98	5.52	24.25	22.01	28.63	16.24	63.5	303-790-1600	Y
ICON Emerging Markets Fund Class S	ICARX	B-	C+	B	Up	3.03	5.62	24.48	22.98	29.89	16.35	63.5	303-790-1600	Y
Invesco Emerging Markets Equity Fund Class A	IEMAX	B	B+	C+	Up	10.43	22.22	47.52	41.71	25.98	9.83	46.4	800-659-1005	Y
Invesco Emerging Markets Equity Fund Class C	IEMCX	B	B	C+	Up	10.15	21.81	46.24	38.60	21.20	9.55	46.4	800-659-1005	Y
Invesco Emerging Markets Equity Fund Class R	IEMRX	B	B	C+	Up	10.30	22.05	47.12	40.54	24.12	9.74	46.4	800-659-1005	Y
Invesco Emerging Markets Equity Fund Class R6	EMEFX	B	B+	C+	Up	10.45	22.37	47.44	42.62	27.22	9.84	46.4	800-659-1005	Y
Invesco Emerging Markets Equity Fund Class Y	IEMYX	B	B+	C+	Up	10.43	22.34	47.80	42.96	27.51	9.85	46.4	800-659-1005	Y
Invesco Emerging Markets Equity Fund R5 Class	IEMIX	B	B+	C+	Up	10.44	22.35	47.81	42.77	27.35	9.85	46.4	800-659-1005	Y
Ivy Emerging Markets Equity Fund Class A	IPOAX	B+	A	C+	Up	5.40	17.51	42.46	37.64	53.69	21.07	2,135	800-777-6472	Y
Ivy Emerging Markets Equity Fund Class B	IPOBX	B	A	C+	Up	5.17	16.98	41.14	33.67	45.77	17.29	2,135	800-777-6472	
Ivy Emerging Markets Equity Fund Class C	IPOCX	B	A	C+	Up	5.22	17.06	41.48	34.29	47.53	18.11	2,135	800-777-6472	Y
Ivy Emerging Markets Equity Fund Class I	IPOIX	B+	A	C+	Up	5.54	17.74	43.10	39.04	56.62	21.73	2,135	800-777-6472	Y
Ivy Emerging Markets Equity Fund Class N	IMEGX	B+	A	C+	Up	5.57	17.83	43.24	39.54	56.07	21.85	2,135	800-777-6472	Y
Ivy Emerging Markets Equity Fund Class R	IYPCX	B	A	C+	Up	5.34	17.35	42.10	36.46	51.80	20.89	2,135	800-777-6472	Y
Ivy Emerging Markets Equity Fund Class T	IPOTX	B+	A	C+	Up	5.43	17.54	42.50	37.68	53.74	21.08	2,135	800-777-6472	Y
Ivy Emerging Markets Equity Fund Class Y	IPOYX	B+	A	C+	Up	5.40	17.51	42.55	37.81	54.37	21.47	2,135	800-777-6472	Y
JNL/American Funds New World Fund Class A	US46644W2787	B-	B-	B-	Up	4.94	12.90	28.89	29.93	34.03	13.16	1,368		Y
JNL/American Funds New World Fund Class I	US46644W2605	B-	B-	B-	Up	4.98	13.01	29.22	30.69	35.35	13.28	1,368		Y
JOHCM Emerging Markets Opportunities Fund Class I	JOEIX	B	B	C+	Up	6.76	14.21	38.64	31.78	37.69	12.31	380.0	866-260-9549	Y
JOHCM Emerging Markets Opportunities Fund Class II Shares	JOEAX	B	B	C+	Up	6.77	14.22	38.53	31.43	36.82	12.31	380.0	866-260-9549	Y
JOHCM Emerging Mkts Opp Fund Inst Shares	JOEMX	B	B+	C+	Up	6.81	14.35	38.90	32.11	38.22	12.34	380.0	866-260-9549	Y
JPMorgan Emerging Economies Fund Class A Shares	JEEAX	B-	B	C	Up	4.83	15.31	36.68	27.01	16.21	14.85	2,032	800-480-4111	Y

Category: Emerging Markets Equity (con't)

Fund Name	Ticker Symbol	Overall Rating	Reward Rating	Risk Rating	Recent Up/ Downgrade	3-Month Total Return	6-Month Total Return	1-Year Total Return	3-Year Total Return	5-Year Total Return	NAV	Total Assets (MIL)	Telephone	Open to New Investors
		RATINGS				TOTAL RETURNS & PERFORMANCE					ASSETS		NEW INVESTORS	
JPMorgan Emerging Economies Fund Class I Shares	JEESX	B-	B	C	Up	4.94	15.45	37.01	28.02	17.72	15.03	2,032	800-480-4111	Y
JPMorgan Emerging Economies Fund Class R5 Shares	JEERX	B-	B	C	Up	4.97	15.55	37.17	28.76	18.78	15.17	2,032	800-480-4111	Y
JPMorgan Emerging Economies Fund Class R6	JEEEX	B-	B	C	Up	5.03	15.60	37.43	29.16	19.14	14.95	2,032	800-480-4111	Y
JPMorgan Emerging Markets Equity Fund Class A	JFAMX	B	B	C	Up	7.29	16.42	42.13	34.17	28.26	29.11	4,585	800-480-4111	Y
JPMorgan Emerging Markets Equity Fund Class C	JEMCX	B-	B	C	Up	7.16	16.18	41.43	32.23	25.09	28.3	4,585	800-480-4111	Y
JPMorgan Emerging Markets Equity Fund Class I	JEMSX	B	B+	C	Up	7.35	16.60	42.49	35.20	29.85	29.79	4,585	800-480-4111	Y
JPMorgan Emerging Markets Equity Fund Class L	JMIEX	B	B+	C	Up	7.39	16.66	42.70	35.82	30.81	29.99	4,585	800-480-4111	Y
JPMorgan Emerging Markets Equity Fund Class R2	JHUJX	B-	B	C		7.21	16.27	41.86	33.68	27.47	29.04	4,585	800-480-4111	Y
JPMorgan Emerging Markets Equity Fund Class R3	JHURX	B	B	C		7.28	16.41	42.21	34.69	29.07	29.04	4,585	800-480-4111	Y
JPMorgan Emerging Markets Equity Fund Class R4	JHUKX	B	B+	C		7.35	16.56	42.56	35.70	30.69	29.76	4,585	800-480-4111	Y
JPMorgan Emerging Markets Equity Fund Class R5	JEMOX	B	B+	C	Up	7.37	16.65	42.68	35.84	30.83	29.95	4,585	800-480-4111	Y
JPMorgan Emerging Markets Equity Fund Class R6	JEMWX	B	B+	C	Up	7.41	16.74	42.84	36.26	31.33	29.93	4,585	800-480-4111	Y
Lazard Developing Mkts Eq Port Institutiona Shares	LDMIX	B	A	C	Up	6.53	18.25	41.14	41.92	23.09	14.48	270.2	800-823-6300	Y
Lazard Developing Markets Equity Portfolio Open Shares	LDMOX	B	A-	C	Up	6.40	18.05	40.56	40.28	20.91	14.45	270.2	800-823-6300	Y
Lazard Emerging Mkts Core Equity Portfolio Inst Shares	ECEIX	B-	B	C+	Up	5.81	16.91	40.34	30.44		12.3	208.4	800-823-6300	Y
Lazard Emerging Markets Core Equity Portfolio Open Shares	ECEOX	B-	B	C+	Up	5.70	16.63	39.80	28.90		12.27	208.4	800-823-6300	Y
Lazard Emerging Mkts Eq Advantage Port Inst Shares	LEAIX	B-	B-	B-	Up	6.46	16.55	42.51			12.27	4.4	800-823-6300	Y
Lazard Emerging Mkts Eq Advantage Port Open Shares	LEAOX	B-	B-	B-	Up	6.32	16.42	42.09			12.27	4.4	800-823-6300	Y
Lazard Emerging Mkts Equity Blend Portfolio Inst Shares	EMBIX	B-	B	C	Up	5.27	14.40	35.97	33.94	22.36	12.93	382.1	800-823-6300	Y
Lazard Emerging Markets Equity Blend Portfolio Open Shares	EMBOX	B-	B	C	Up	5.19	14.13	35.37	32.86	20.69	12.95	382.1	800-823-6300	Y
Macquarie Pooled Trust Emerging Markets Portfolio II	DPEGX	B-	B	C	Up	3.18	16.70	44.46	33.72	39.90	10.42	44.8	215-255-2300	Y
MainStay Emerging Markets Equity Fund Class A	MEOAX	B-	B	C	Up	5.94	14.72	40.13	25.57		10.98	173.8	800-624-6782	Y
MainStay Emerging Markets Equity Fund Class I	MEOIX	B-	B	C	Up	5.94	14.70	40.19	26.25		11	173.8	800-624-6782	Y
Martin Currie Emerging Markets Fund Class FI	MEFIX	B-	B-	B-	Up	7.08	18.87	46.34			13.17	107.1	877-721-1926	Y
Martin Currie Emerging Markets Fund Class I	MCEIX	B-	B-	B-	Up	7.15	19.03	46.80			13.21	107.1	877-721-1926	Y
Martin Currie Emerging Markets Fund Class IS	MCEMX	B-	B-	B-	Up	7.14	19.29	47.09			13.23	107.1	877-721-1926	Y
MFS® Emerging Markets Equity Fund Class A	MEMAX	B-	B-	C	Up	5.84	14.68	37.37	29.69	15.66	35.11	1,318	877-960-6077	Y
MFS® Emerging Markets Equity Fund Class I	MEMIX	B-	B	C	Up	5.95	14.85	37.74	30.64	17.11	36.95	1,318	877-960-6077	Y
MFS® Emerging Markets Equity Fund Class R3	MEMGX	B-	B-	C	Up	5.86	14.71	37.41	29.68	15.69	34.97	1,318	877-960-6077	Y
MFS® Emerging Markets Equity Fund Class R4	MEMHX	B-	B	C	Up	5.94	14.86	37.75	30.63	17.09	34.94	1,318	877-960-6077	Y
MFS® Emerging Markets Equity Fund Class R6	MEMJX	B-	B	C	Up	5.94	14.91	37.86	31.07	17.71	36.94	1,318	877-960-6077	Y
Mirae Asset Emerging Markets Fund Class A	MALGX	B	A-	C	Up	8.73	19.99	45.29	39.70	42.97	13.44	36.4	212-205-8300	Y
Mirae Asset Emerging Markets Fund Class C	MCLGX	B	B+	C	Up	8.54	19.58	44.15	36.41	37.44	12.7	36.4	212-205-8300	Y
Mirae Asset Emerging Markets Fund Class I	MILGX	B	A-	C	Up	8.75	20.14	45.62	40.68	44.53	13.66	36.4	212-205-8300	Y
Morgan Stanley Inst Fund, Inc. Emerging Mkts Port Cls IS	MMMPX	B-	B-	C	Up	5.32	12.64	35.09	29.07	23.96	27.94	1,354	855-332-5306	Y
Neuberger Berman Emerging Markets Equity Fund Class A	NEMAX	B	B	C	Up	7.29	17.63	41.29	36.10	34.21	21.39	1,033	212-476-9000	Y
Neuberger Berman Emerging Markets Equity Fund Class C	NEMCX	B-	B	C	Up	7.06	17.17	40.22	32.98	29.19	20.55	1,033	212-476-9000	Y
Neuberger Berman Emerging Markets Equity Fund Class R3	NEMRX	B-	B	C	Up	7.13	17.32	40.60	34.32	31.37	20.91	1,033	212-476-9000	Y
Neuberger Berman Emerging Markets Equity Fund Class R6	NREMX	B	B+	C	Up	7.35	17.80	41.69	37.35	36.35	21.52	1,033	212-476-9000	Y
Neuberger Berman Emerging Mkts Equity Fund Inst Cls	NEMIX	B	B+	C	Up	7.28	17.73	41.61	37.07	35.82	21.5	1,033	212-476-9000	Y
Northern Emerging Markets Equity Index Fund	NOEMX	B-	B	C	Up	7.01	15.62	37.33	28.67	21.86	12.86	2,979	800-595-9111	Y
Oppenheimer Emerging Markets Innovators Fund Class A	EMIAX	B-	B-	B-	Up	7.76	16.68	40.50	30.36		11.54	382.1	800-225-5677	Y
Oppenheimer Emerging Markets Innovators Fund Class C	EMVCX	B-	B-	C+	Up	7.44	16.20	39.35	27.23		11.26	382.1	800-225-5677	Y
Oppenheimer Emerging Markets Innovators Fund Class I	EMVIX	B-	B-	B-	Up	7.83	16.96	41.14	32.24		11.68	382.1	800-225-5677	Y
Oppenheimer Emerging Markets Innovators Fund Class R	EMIRX	B-	B-	C+	Up	7.58	16.44	39.90	29.17		11.45	382.1	800-225-5677	Y
Oppenheimer Emerging Markets Innovators Fund Class Y	EMIYX	B-	B-	B-	Up	7.71	16.77	40.75	31.39		11.61	382.1	800-225-5677	Y
PIMCO RAE Fundamental Emerging Markets Fund Class A	PEAFX	B-	B	C	Up	6.81	15.40	28.87	22.85	28.27	11.51	1,842	866-746-2602	Y
PIMCO RAE Fundamental Emerging Markets Fund Class P	PEPFX	B-	B	C	Up	6.78	15.39	29.03	23.50	29.59	11.49	1,842	866-746-2602	Y
PIMCO RAE Fundamental Emerging Mkts Fund Inst Cls	PEIFX	B-	B	C	Up	6.91	15.60	29.33	24.17	30.55	11.55	1,842	866-746-2602	Y
PIMCO RAE Fundamental PLUS EMG Fund Administrative Class	PEFAX	B	B+	C	Up	6.73	16.25	31.51	32.49	20.92	11.13	2,030	866-746-2602	Y
PIMCO RAE Fundamental PLUS EMG Fund Class A	PEFFX	B-	B+	C	Up	6.82	16.20	31.30	31.98	20.33	11.12	2,030	866-746-2602	Y
PIMCO RAE Fundamental PLUS EMG Fund Class C	PEFCX	B-	B	C	Up	6.60	15.68	30.37	29.02	15.65	10.81	2,030	866-746-2602	Y

Category: Emerging Markets Equity (con't)

Fund Name	Ticker Symbol	RATINGS Overall Rating	Reward Rating	Risk Rating	Recent Up/ Downgrade	TOTAL RETURNS & PERFORMANCE 3-Month Total Return	6-Month Total Return	1-Year Total Return	3-Year Total Return	5-Year Total Return	ASSETS NAV	Total Assets (MIL)	NEW INVESTORS Telephone	Open to New Investors
PIMCO RAE Fundamental PLUS EMG Fund Class D	PEFDX	B-	B+	C	Up	6.79	16.19	31.46	32.02	19.97	11.08	2,030	866-746-2602	Y
PIMCO RAE Fundamental PLUS EMG Fund Class P	PEFPX	B	B+	C	Up	6.80	16.27	31.65	33.08	21.93	11.24	2,030	866-746-2602	Y
PIMCO RAE Fundamental PLUS EMG Fund Institutional Class	PEFIX	B	B+	C	Up	6.81	16.40	31.83	33.53	22.54	11.25	2,030	866-746-2602	Y
Principal International Emerging Markets Fund Class A	PRIAX	B-	B	C	Up	5.88	17.48	40.73	31.27	20.58	29.96	976.8	800-222-5852	Y
Principal International Emerging Markets Fund Class C	PMKCX	B-	B-	C	Up	5.63	16.88	39.33	27.21	14.60	28.64	976.8	800-222-5852	Y
Principal International Emerging Markets Fund Class J	PIEJX	B-	B	C	Up	5.90	17.52	40.88	31.63	21.23	28.84	976.8	800-222-5852	Y
Principal International Emerging Markets Fund Class R-6	PIIMX	B-	B	C	Up	5.99	17.72	41.22	32.37	22.34	29.63	976.8	800-222-5852	Y
Principal Intl Emerging Mkts Fund Inst Cls	PIEIX	B-	B	C	Up	5.95	17.63	41.17	32.90	23.46	29.63	976.8	800-222-5852	Y
Principal International Emerging Markets Fund R-1 Class	PIXEX	B-	B	C	Up	5.74	17.15	40.03	29.63	18.29	29.62	976.8	800-222-5852	Y
Principal International Emerging Markets Fund R-2 Class	PEASX	B-	B	C	Up	5.82	17.27	40.27	30.15	19.09	29.44	976.8	800-222-5852	Y
Principal International Emerging Markets Fund R-3 Class	PEAPX	B-	B	C	Up	5.84	17.34	40.51	30.82	20.17	29.6	976.8	800-222-5852	Y
Principal International Emerging Markets Fund R-4 Class	PESSX	B-	B	C	Up	5.92	17.50	40.78	31.58	21.35	29.72	976.8	800-222-5852	Y
Principal International Emerging Markets Fund R-5 Class	PEPSX	B-	B	C	Up	5.91	17.56	40.89	32.04	22.03	29.74	976.8	800-222-5852	Y
Putnam Emerging Markets Equity Fund Class A	PEMMX	B-	B	C	Up	7.28	19.98	42.29	33.77	35.60	12.77	77.0	617-292-1000	Y
Putnam Emerging Markets Equity Fund Class B	PEMBX	B-	B	C	Up	7.13	19.51	41.33	30.83	30.55	12.31	77.0	617-292-1000	Y
Putnam Emerging Markets Equity Fund Class C	PEMZX	B-	B	C	Up	7.07	19.49	41.24	30.82	30.56	12.26	77.0	617-292-1000	Y
Putnam Emerging Markets Equity Fund Class M	PEMAX	B-	B	C	Up	7.20	19.61	41.72	31.75	32.16	12.5	77.0	617-292-1000	Y
Putnam Emerging Markets Equity Fund Class R	PEMLX	B-	B	C	Up	7.25	19.88	42.12	32.80	33.83	12.72	77.0	617-292-1000	Y
Putnam Emerging Markets Equity Fund Class Y	PEMYX	B	B	C	Up	7.40	20.18	42.73	34.82	37.32	12.9	77.0	617-292-1000	Y
Pzena Emerging Markets Value Fund Institutional	PZIEX	B-	B	C	Up	4.36	9.56	29.97	30.53		11.07	43.0		Y
Rational Risk Managed Emerging Markets Fund Class A	HGSAX	B-	B-	B	Up	7.99	17.33	38.12	30.73	41.97	7.22	10.3	800-253-0412	Y
Rational Risk Managed Emerging Markets Fund Class C	HGSCX	B-	C+	B-	Up	7.77	17.00	37.18	27.67	36.59	7.14	10.3	800-253-0412	Y
Rational Risk Managed Emerging Mkts Fund Cls Inst	HGSIX	B-	B-	B	Up	8.09	17.37	38.51	31.53	43.54	7.27	10.3	800-253-0412	Y
RBC Emerging Markets Equity Fund Class A	REEAX	B-	B	C+	Up	6.83	13.71	34.74	26.91		13.16	575.0	800-422-2766	Y
RBC Emerging Markets Equity Fund Class I	REEIX	B-	B	C+	Up	6.94	13.79	35.12	27.76		13.36	575.0	800-422-2766	Y
RBC Emerging Markets Equity Fund Class R6	RREMX	B-	B	C+	Up	6.92	13.84	35.06	27.64		13.42	575.0	800-422-2766	Y
Russell Investments Emerging Markets Fund Class Y	REMYX	B-	B-	C	Up	5.52	13.45	35.64	28.08	24.60	21.16	2,498	800-426-7969	Y
Schwab Fundamental Emerging Mkts Large Company Index Fund	SFENX	B-	B	C	Up	5.72	13.42	26.34	33.80	16.85	9.43	556.8	877-824-5615	Y
Seafarer Overseas Growth & Income Fund Institutional Cls	SIGIX	B	B	B-	Up	7.02	9.12	26.04	32.18	39.62	13.63	2,968		Y
Seafarer Overseas Growth and Income Fund Investor Class	SFGIX	B-	B	B-	Up	6.98	9.00	25.82	31.54	38.65	13.59	2,968		Y
Segall Bryant & Hamill Emerging Markets Fund Class A	SBHEX	B-	B	C	Up	6.40	14.36	35.77	31.28	22.52	9.34	35.7	312-474-1222	Y
Segall Bryant & Hamill Emerging Markets Fund Class I	SBEMX	B-	B	C	Up	6.47	14.39	36.07	32.21	23.50	9.37	35.7	312-474-1222	Y
SEI Inst Intl Trust Emerging Mkts Equity Fund Cls F	SIEMX	B-	B	C	Up	6.29	16.19	37.27	32.29	26.49	12.93	1,989	800-342-5734	Y
SEI Inst Intl Trust Emerging Mkts Equity Fund Cls Y	SEQFX	B-	B	C	Up	6.27	16.35	37.57	33.30	27.45	12.93	1,989	800-342-5734	Y
Strategic Advisers® Emerging Markets Fund	FSAMX	B-	B	C	Up	7.00	15.86	38.37	29.44	24.89	11.46	5,041	617-563-7000	Y
Strategic Advisers® Emerging Markets Fund of Funds	FLILX	B-	B-	C	Up	6.89	16.14	38.40	28.67	25.20	12.11	14.7	617-563-7000	Y
Strategic Advisers® Emerging Markets Fund of Funds Class L	FQAAX	B-	B-	C	Up	6.79	16.03	38.40	28.53	25.08	12.11	14.7	617-563-7000	Y
T. Rowe Price Emerging Markets Stock Fund	PRMSX	B	A	C	Up	7.39	18.74	42.85	41.22	38.29	44.99	11,106	410-345-2000	Y
T. Rowe Price Emerging Markets Stock Fund I Class	PRZIX	B	A	C	Up	7.41	18.83	43.03	41.67	38.74	44.96	11,106	410-345-2000	Y
T. Rowe Price Institutional Emerging Markets Equity Fund	IEMFX	B	A	C	Up	7.39	18.86	42.87	41.54	38.81	41.08	1,668	410-345-2000	Y
Templeton Developing Markets Trust Class A	TEDMX	B	B+	C	Up	7.01	15.52	40.20	32.87	20.87	21.98	1,625	650-312-2000	Y
Templeton Developing Markets Trust Class Advisor	TDADX	B	B+	C	Up	7.05	15.66	40.58	33.92	22.49	21.86	1,625	650-312-2000	Y
Templeton Developing Markets Trust Class C	TDMTX	B-	B	C	Up	6.77	15.08	39.19	29.94	16.50	21.34	1,625	650-312-2000	Y
Templeton Developing Markets Trust Class R6	FDEVX	B	B+	C	Up	7.12	15.73	40.87	34.71	23.39	21.82	1,625	650-312-2000	Y
Templeton Developing Markets Trust Class Retirement	TDMRX	B-	B	C	Up	6.93	15.35	39.89	31.91	19.49	21.61	1,625	650-312-2000	Y
Templeton Emerging Markets Fund Inc.	EMF	B	B+	C	Up	6.51	17.42	41.60	32.01	21.63	18.4432	344.9	954-527-7500	Y
Templeton Emerging Markets Small Cap Fund Class A	TEMMX	B-	B-	B-	Up	5.59	9.02	31.30	26.67	36.25	15.1	1,000	650-312-2000	Y
Templeton Emerging Markets Small Cap Fund Class Advisor	TEMZX	B-	B-	B-	Up	5.59	9.21	31.60	27.61	38.10	15.26	1,000	650-312-2000	Y
Templeton Emerging Markets Small Cap Fund Class R6	FTEQX	B-	B-	B-		5.65	9.35	31.76	27.77	38.28	15.25	1,000	650-312-2000	Y
Templeton Emerging Markets Small Cap Fund Class Retirement	FTESX	B-	C+	B-	Up	5.49	8.95	30.97	25.80	34.78	14.97	1,000	650-312-2000	Y
Templeton Inst Fund Emerging Mkts Series Fund Adv	TEEMX	B	A	C	Up	7.32	16.44	42.84	38.70	28.97	6.06	55.7	650-312-2000	Y
TIAA-CREF Emerging Markets Equity Fund Advisor Class	TEMHX	B	B	C	Up	5.50	17.62	45.39	34.08	24.81	12.56	1,441	877-518-9161	Y

Category: Emerging Markets Equity (con't)

		RATINGS				TOTAL RETURNS & PERFORMANCE					ASSETS		NEW INVESTORS	
Fund Name	Ticker Symbol	Overall Rating	Reward Rating	Risk Rating	Recent Up/ Downgrade	3-Month Total Return	6-Month Total Return	1-Year Total Return	3-Year Total Return	5-Year Total Return	NAV	Total Assets (MIL)	Telephone	Open to New Investors
TIAA-CREF Emerging Markets Equity Fund Institutional Class	TEMLX	B	B	C	Up	5.49	17.68	45.44	34.31	25.02	12.57	1,441	877-518-9161	Y
TIAA-CREF Emerging Markets Equity Fund Premier Class	TEMPX	B	B	C	Up	5.40	17.50	45.25	33.62	23.94	12.57	1,441	877-518-9161	Y
TIAA-CREF Emerging Markets Equity Fund Retail Class	TEMRX	B-	B	C	Up	5.37	17.49	44.97	32.78	22.60	12.55	1,441	877-518-9161	Y
TIAA-CREF Emerging Markets Equity Fund Retirement Class	TEMSX	B-	B	C	Up	5.40	17.53	45.06	33.38	23.41	12.53	1,441	877-518-9161	Y
TIAA-CREF Emerging Markets Equity Index Fund Advisor Class	TEQHX	B-	B	C	Up	6.73	15.28	37.28	29.95	23.08	12	2,414	877-518-9161	Y
TIAA-CREF Emerging Mkts Equity Index Fund Inst Cls	TEQLX	B-	B	C	Up	6.76	15.42	37.44	30.14	23.26	12	2,414	877-518-9161	Y
TIAA-CREF Emerging Markets Equity Index Fund Premier Class	TEQPX	B-	B	C	Up	6.75	15.42	37.37	29.59	22.46	11.98	2,414	877-518-9161	Y
TIAA-CREF Emerging Markets Equity Index Fund Retail Class	TEQKX	B-	B	C	Up	6.73	15.31	37.10	28.66	21.05	11.98	2,414	877-518-9161	Y
TIAA-CREF Emerging Mkts Equity Index Fund Retmnt Cls	TEQSX	B-	B	C	Up	6.67	15.25	37.18	29.19	21.79	11.96	2,414	877-518-9161	Y
Touchstone Sands Capital Emerging Mkts Growth Fund Cls Y	TSEMX	B-	B	C	Up	4.56	12.29	38.34	27.16		13.06	465.9	800-543-0407	Y
Touchstone Sands Capital Emerg Mkts Growth Inst Cls	TSEGX	B-	B	C	Up	4.63	12.34	38.47	27.55		13.1	465.9	800-543-0407	Y
VALIC Company I Emerging Economies Fund	VCGEX	B	B+	C	Up	6.06	16.81	41.26	34.21	24.76	9.45	800.7		Y
VanEck Emerging Markets Fund Class A	GBFAX	B-	B	C	Up	8.26	19.39	49.70	30.07	45.50	18.44	1,871	800-826-1115	Y
VanEck Emerging Markets Fund Class I	EMRIX	B-	B	C	Up	8.37	19.65	50.39	32.01	49.06	19.46	1,871	800-826-1115	Y
VanEck Emerging Markets Fund Class Y	EMRYX	B-	B	C	Up	8.38	19.62	50.32	31.68	47.88	18.73	1,871	800-826-1115	Y
Vanguard Emerging Mkts Select Stock Fund Inv Shares	VMMSX	B-	B	C	Up	5.32	13.36	31.99	30.84	24.70	22.78	660.6	877-662-7447	Y
Victory Sophus Emerging Markets Fund Class A	GBEMX	B	B+	C	Up	7.50	17.76	42.08	37.25	27.63	22.53	226.3	800-539-3863	Y
Victory Sophus Emerging Markets Fund Class C	REMGX	B-	B	C	Up	7.28	17.33	40.95	33.97	22.64	17.08	226.3	800-539-3863	Y
Victory Sophus Emerging Markets Fund Class R	REMKX	B	B	C	Up	7.39	17.59	41.69	36.15	25.92	21.18	226.3	800-539-3863	Y
Victory Sophus Emerging Markets Fund Class R6	RSERX	B	B+	C	Up	7.61	18.01	42.77	37.96	28.29	22.81	226.3	800-539-3863	Y
Victory Sophus Emerging Markets Fund Class Y	RSENX	B	B+	C	Up	7.54	17.96	42.58	38.60	29.86	22.64	226.3	800-539-3863	Y
Victory Sophus Emerging Markets Small Cap Fund Class A	RSMSX	B	B	B-	Up	8.15	16.69	42.54	35.19		10.13	7.2	800-539-3863	Y
Victory Sophus Emerging Markets Small Cap Fund Class C	RSMGX	B-	B-	C+	Up	8.02	16.38	41.67	29.73		9.51	7.2	800-539-3863	Y
Victory Sophus Emerging Markets Small Cap Fund Class Y	RSMYX	B	B	B-	Up	8.26	16.88	43.02	36.45		10.08	7.2	800-539-3863	Y
Victory Trivalent Emerging Markets Small-Cap Fund Class A	MAEMX	B	B	C+	Up	8.45	19.26	42.60	37.31		14.36	5.8	800-539-3863	Y
Victory Trivalent Emerging Markets Small-Cap Fund Class Y	MYEMX	B	B	C+	Up	8.57	19.45	43.02	38.34		14.35	5.8	800-539-3863	Y
Voya Multi-Manager Emerging Markets Equity Fund Class A	IEMHX	B-	B	C	Up	5.86	17.77	44.01	30.93	24.71	13.36	314.1	800-366-0066	Y
Voya Multi-Manager Emerging Markets Equity Fund Class I	IEMGX	B-	B	C	Up	6.02	18.11	44.52	32.48	26.92	13.38	314.1	800-366-0066	Y
Voya Multi-Manager Emerging Markets Equity Fund Class R	IEMKX	B-	B	C	Up	5.79	17.66	43.64	29.93	23.13	13.41	314.1	800-366-0066	Y
Voya Multi-Manager Emerging Markets Equity Fund Class W	IEMLX	B-	B	C	Up	5.93	17.92	44.32	31.99	26.29	13.36	314.1	800-366-0066	Y
VY® JPMorgan Emerging Markets Equity Portfolio Class A	IJEAX	B	B	C	Up	7.21	16.54	42.55	34.34	28.43	20.52	600.8	800-366-0066	Y
VY® JPMorgan Emerging Markets Equity Portfolio Class I	IJEMX	B	B+	C	Up	7.38	16.89	43.45	36.78	32.29	21.52	600.8	800-366-0066	Y
VY® JPMorgan Emerging Markets Equity Portfolio Class S	IJPIX	B	B+	C	Up	7.32	16.69	43.11	35.78	30.70	21.4	600.8	800-366-0066	Y
VY® JPMorgan Emerging Markets Equity Portfolio Class S2	IJPTX	B	B	C	Up	7.24	16.63	42.85	35.17	29.69	21.17	600.8	800-366-0066	Y
Wells Fargo Emerging Markets Equity Fund - Class A	EMGAX	B-	B	C	Up	3.78	11.77	34.41	30.06	21.25	25.38	4,116	800-222-8222	
Wells Fargo Emerging Markets Equity Fund - Class Admin	EMGYX	B-	B	C	Up	3.81	11.85	34.51	30.50	22.03	26.58	4,116	800-222-8222	
Wells Fargo Emerging Markets Equity Fund - Class Inst	EMGNX	B-	B	C	Up	3.87	11.95	34.88	31.56	23.69	26.42	4,116	800-222-8222	
Wells Fargo Emerging Markets Equity Fund - Class R6	EMGDX	B-	B	C	Up	3.93	12.02	34.96	31.80	23.85	26.42	4,116	800-222-8222	
William Blair Emerging Markets Fund Class N	WBENX	B-	B	C	Up	6.96	19.75	48.52	28.18	34.63	16.2	1,351	800-621-0687	
William Blair Emerging Markets Growth Fund Class I	WBEIX	B-	B	C	Up	6.99	19.79	48.82	29.04	36.27	16.36	1,351	800-621-0687	
William Blair Emerging Mkts Growth Fund Cls Inst	BIEMX	B-	B	C	Up	7.03	19.89	49.06	29.36	37.26	16.49	1,351	800-621-0687	
William Blair Emerging Markets Small Cap Growth Fund Cls I	BESIX	B-	B-	C+	Up	9.39	17.49	40.53	26.14	68.69	18.73	450.3	800-621-0687	
William Blair Emerging Markets Small Cap Growth Fund Cls N	WESNX	B-	B-	C+	Up	9.28	17.35	40.08	24.96	66.23	18.66	450.3	800-621-0687	
William Blair Emerging Mkts Small Cap Growth Fund Inst Cls	WESJX	B-	B-	C+	Up	9.37	17.52	40.62	26.38	69.45	18.76	450.3	800-621-0687	

Category: Europe Equity Large Cap

Fund Name	Ticker Symbol	RATINGS: Overall Rating	Reward Rating	Risk Rating	Recent Up/ Downgrade	TOTAL RETURNS & PERFORMANCE: 3-Month Total Return	6-Month Total Return	1-Year Total Return	3-Year Total Return	5-Year Total Return	ASSETS: NAV	Total Assets (MIL)	NEW INVESTORS: Telephone	Open to New Investors
Brown Advy WMC Strategic European Equity Fund Adv Shares	BAHAX	B	B	B	Up	2.52	7.74	32.11	35.45		12.8	1,305	800-540-6807	Y
Brown Advy WMC Strategic European Equity Fund Inst Shares	BAFHX	B	B	B	Up	2.62	7.99	32.65	37.12		12.9	1,305	800-540-6807	Y
Brown Advy WMC Strategic European Equity Fund Inv Shares	BIAHX	B	B	B	Up	2.58	7.86	32.35	36.45		12.89	1,305	800-540-6807	Y
Columbia Acorn European Fund Advisor Class	CLOFX	B+	A-	B	Up	4.51	11.80	38.28	39.36	75.00	19.36	96.6	800-345-6611	Y
Columbia Acorn European Fund Class A	CAEAX	B+	A-	B	Up	4.44	11.65	37.89	38.26	72.81	19.27	96.6	800-345-6611	Y
Columbia Acorn European Fund Class C	CAECX	B+	B+	B	Up	4.29	11.21	36.95	35.17	66.42	19.12	96.6	800-345-6611	Y
Columbia Acorn European Fund Institutional 2 Class	CAEEX	B+	A-	B	Up	4.55	11.81	38.32	39.46	74.99	19.46	96.6	800-345-6611	Y
Columbia Acorn European Fund Institutional 3 Class	CAEYX	B+	A-	B	Up	4.54	11.84	38.44	39.42	75.02	19.17	96.6	800-345-6611	Y
Columbia Acorn European Fund Institutional Class	CAEZX	B+	A-	B	Up	4.54	11.81	38.34	39.32	74.90	19.27	96.6	800-345-6611	Y
Columbia European Equity Fund Advisor Class	CADJX	B-	B-	C+	Up	1.37	9.13	25.80	19.27	44.00	7.28	402.0	800-345-6611	Y
Columbia European Equity Fund Institutional 2 Class	CADKX	B-	B-	C+	Up	1.43	9.14	26.11	19.68	44.74	7.33	402.0	800-345-6611	Y
Columbia European Equity Fund Institutional 3 Class	CEEUX	B-	B-	C+	Up	1.51	9.29	26.14	19.41	44.02	7.14	402.0	800-345-6611	Y
Columbia European Equity Fund Institutional Class	CEEZX	B-	B-	C+	Up	1.50	9.12	25.98	19.22	44.27	7.29	402.0	800-345-6611	Y
DFA Continental Small Company Portfolio Institutional Cls	DFCSX	B+	B+	A	Up	2.09	9.74	35.13	58.44	106.46	28.59	649.7	512-306-7400	Y
Fidelity Advisor® Europe Fund Class A	FHJUX	B	B	B	Up	3.80	8.99	28.78	25.48	48.27	42.33	1,263	617-563-7000	Y
Fidelity Advisor® Europe Fund Class C	FHJTX	B-	B-	B	Up	3.59	8.56	27.74	22.51	42.64	42.18	1,263	617-563-7000	Y
Fidelity Advisor® Europe Fund Class M	FHJVX	B	B-	B	Up	3.71	8.82	28.40	24.36	46.21	42.41	1,263	617-563-7000	Y
Fidelity Advisor® Europe Fund I Class	FHJMX	B	B	B	Up	3.86	9.16	29.20	26.81	50.76	42.3	1,263	617-563-7000	Y
Fidelity® Europe Fund	FIEUX	B	B	B	Up	3.87	9.17	29.18	26.69	50.55	42.33	1,263	617-563-7000	Y
Franklin Mutual European Fund Class R6	FMEUX	B-	C+	B	Up	0.36	3.10	10.63	14.81	40.81	20.91	2,582	650-312-2000	Y
Global Strategic Income Fund Class A	VEEEX	B-	C	B	Up	1.63	3.58	12.69	13.95	20.47	26.41	12.6		Y
Invesco European Growth Fund Class A	AEDAX	B	B	B	Up	3.59	10.14	26.89	28.68	50.57	41.26	1,732	800-659-1005	Y
Invesco European Growth Fund Class B	AEDBX	B	B-	B	Up	3.41	9.74	25.93	25.80	45.07	38.41	1,732	800-659-1005	
Invesco European Growth Fund Class C	AEDCX	B	B-	B	Up	3.41	9.73	25.93	25.81	45.05	38.45	1,732	800-659-1005	Y
Invesco European Growth Fund Class R	AEDRX	B	B	B	Up	3.54	9.99	26.57	27.71	48.72	41.13	1,732	800-659-1005	Y
Invesco European Growth Fund Class R6	AEGSX	B	B	B	Up	3.69	10.33	27.22	29.01	50.96	41.27	1,732	800-659-1005	Y
Invesco European Growth Fund Class Y	AEDYX	B	B	B	Up	3.67	10.26	27.19	29.63	52.46	41.29	1,732	800-659-1005	Y
Invesco European Growth Fund Investor Class	EGINX	B	B	B	Up	3.61	10.17	26.94	28.80	50.86	41.14	1,732	800-659-1005	
Invesco European Small Company Fund Class A	ESMAX	B+	B	A	Up	2.73	5.71	28.28	48.85	82.95	16.58	811.8	800-659-1005	
Invesco European Small Company Fund Class B	ESMBX	B+	B	A	Up	2.48	5.26	27.22	45.45	76.11	15.49	811.8	800-659-1005	
Invesco European Small Company Fund Class C	ESMCX	B+	B	A	Up	2.55	5.32	27.26	45.47	76.24	15.52	811.8	800-659-1005	
Invesco European Small Company Fund Class R6	ESMSX	B	B	B+	Down	2.77	5.86	28.43	49.02	83.16	16.64	811.8	800-659-1005	Y
Invesco European Small Company Fund Class Y	ESMYX	B+	B	A	Up	2.73	5.82	28.47	49.86	85.13	16.64	811.8	800-659-1005	
Ivy European Opportunities Fund Class A	IEOAX	B-	B-	C+	Up	0.83	10.05	21.17	21.75	44.32	32.66	253.3	800-777-6472	Y
Ivy European Opportunities Fund Class C	IEOCX	B-	B-	C+	Up	0.71	9.73	20.42	19.45	39.81	30.84	253.3	800-777-6472	Y
Ivy European Opportunities Fund Class I	IEOIX	B-	B	C+	Up	0.99	10.33	21.74	23.46	47.98	32.93	253.3	800-777-6472	Y
Ivy European Opportunities Fund Class N	IEURX	B-	B	C+	Up	1.03	10.39	21.92	24.02	47.41	33.07	253.3	800-777-6472	Y
Ivy European Opportunities Fund Class R	IYEUX	B-	B-	C+	Up	0.82	9.98	21.02	21.29	43.64	32.63	253.3	800-777-6472	Y
Ivy European Opportunities Fund Class Y	IEOYX	B-	B	C+	Up	0.95	10.20	21.54	22.49	46.07	32.9	253.3	800-777-6472	Y
JNL/Mellon Capital European 30 Fund Class A	US46648M7222	B-	C+	B-	Up	0.59	7.34	23.73	18.44	51.60	13.55	477.8		Y
JNL/Mellon Capital European 30 Fund Class I	US46648M7149	B-	C+	B-	Up	0.73	7.53	24.00	19.12	53.20	13.68	477.8		Y
JPMorgan Intrepid European Fund Class A	VEUAX	B-	C+	B-	Up	0.97	6.39	22.26	18.28	52.45	26.59	963.5	800-480-4111	Y
JPMorgan Intrepid European Fund Class I	JFESX	B-	B-	B-	Up	1.01	6.52	22.61	19.40	54.67	27.08	963.5	800-480-4111	Y
JPMorgan Intrepid European Fund Class L	JFEIX	B-	B-	C+	Up	1.05	6.59	22.80	20.04	56.05	27.31	963.5	800-480-4111	Y
Shelton Capital Mgmt European Growth & Inc Direct Shares	EUGIX	B-	C+	B-	Up	-0.30	4.91	21.28	17.04	34.67	9.52	10.8	800-955-9988	Y
The European Equity Fund Inc	EEA	B	B	B	Up	2.75	8.00	26.26	21.68	46.43	10.97	87.3		Y
Vanguard European Stock Index Fund Admiral Shares	VEUSX	B-	B-	B	Up	2.05	8.64	27.05	23.21	45.95	74.01	24,631	877-662-7447	Y
Vanguard European Stock Index Fund Inst Plus Shares	VEUPX	B-	B-	B	Up	2.09	8.70	27.13	23.39	45.71	141.01	24,631	877-662-7447	Y
Vanguard European Stock Index Fund Institutional Shares	VESIX	B-	B-	B	Up	2.05	8.65	27.05	23.30	46.11	31.56	24,631	877-662-7447	Y
Vanguard European Stock Index Fund Investor Shares	VEURX	B-	B-	B-	Up	2.00	8.53	26.82	22.63	44.83	31.78	24,631	877-662-7447	Y
Virtus Vontobel Greater European Opportunities Fund Cls A	VGEAX	B-	C+	B-	Up	3.45	5.00	25.47	25.08	35.63	16.23	13.2	800-243-1574	Y
Virtus Vontobel Greater European Opportunities Fund Cls I	VGEIX	B-	B-	B-	Up	3.44	5.11	25.74	25.95	37.25	16.22	13.2	800-243-1574	Y

Category: Financials Sector Equity

Fund Name	Ticker Symbol	RATINGS: Overall Rating	Reward Rating	Risk Rating	Recent Up/ Downgrade	TOTAL RETURNS & PERFORMANCE: 3-Month Total Return	6-Month Total Return	1-Year Total Return	3-Year Total Return	5-Year Total Return	ASSETS: NAV	Total Assets (MIL)	NEW INVESTORS: Telephone	Open to New Investors
1919 Financial Services Fund Class A	SBFAX	A-	A	B+	Up	4.74	10.45	14.64	53.18	132.73	27.16	248.8		Y
1919 Financial Services Fund Class C	SFSLX	A-	A	B+	Up	4.57	10.03	13.81	50.06	124.99	25.12	248.8		Y
1919 Financial Services Fund Class I	LMRIX	A-	A	B+	Up	4.82	10.55	14.95	54.84	137.23	27.42	248.8		Y
Alpine Financial Services Fund Class A Shares	ADAFX	B+	A	B-	Up	8.36	12.90	19.58	48.56	123.93	17.34	22.5	888-785-5578	Y
Alpine Financial Services Fund Institutional Class	ADFSX	B+	A	B	Up	8.17	12.80	19.65	49.41	126.27	17.45	22.5	888-785-5578	
Davis Financial Fund Class A	RPFGX	B+	B	B+	Up	6.31	10.55	19.26	38.19	109.97	51.94	1,332	800-279-0279	Y
Davis Financial Fund Class C	DFFCX	B	B	B+		6.10	10.11	18.37	34.82	101.12	43.27	1,332	800-279-0279	Y
Davis Financial Fund Class Y	DVFYX	B+	B	B+	Up	6.36	10.68	19.56	39.05	111.99	53.5	1,332	800-279-0279	Y
Diamond Hill Financial Long Short Fund Class A	BANCX	B	B	B	Up	3.52	6.47	11.57	25.53	89.50	24.67	34.3	888-226-5595	Y
Diamond Hill Financial Long Short Fund Class C	BSGCX	B	B	B	Up	3.29	6.07	10.76	22.70	82.36	22.54	34.3	888-226-5595	Y
Diamond Hill Financial Long Short Fund Class I	DHFSX	B	B	B	Up	3.57	6.65	11.90	26.56	92.02	24.74	34.3	888-226-5595	Y
Emerald Banking and Finance Fund Class A	HSSAX	A-	A	B	Up	4.52	10.20	12.57	64.83	157.44	45.41	515.7	855-828-9909	Y
Emerald Banking and Finance Fund Class C	HSSCX	A-	A	B	Up	4.36	9.84	11.82	61.62	149.21	40.38	515.7	855-828-9909	Y
Emerald Banking and Finance Fund Institutional Class	HSSIX	A-	A	B	Up	4.62	10.35	12.92	66.38	161.67	46.28	515.7	855-828-9909	Y
Emerald Banking and Finance Fund Investor Class	FFBFX	A-	A	B	Up	4.51	10.15	12.57	64.83	157.31	43.43	515.7	855-828-9909	Y
Fidelity Advisor® Financial Services Fund Class A	FAFDX	B+	A-	B	Up	8.56	14.38	20.54	35.60	104.75	21.87	431.7	617-563-7000	Y
Fidelity Advisor® Financial Services Fund Class C	FAFCX	B	B+	B		8.39	13.99	19.63	32.58	97.33	20.53	431.7	617-563-7000	Y
Fidelity Advisor® Financial Services Fund Class M	FAFSX	B	A-	B		8.50	14.21	20.23	34.43	101.87	21.66	431.7	617-563-7000	Y
Fidelity Advisor® Financial Services Fund I Class	FFSIX	B+	A-	B	Up	8.64	14.53	20.90	36.85	108.05	22.47	431.7	617-563-7000	Y
Fidelity® Select Banking Portfolio	FSRBX	B+	A	B-	Up	6.37	10.79	12.67	42.36	117.72	35.37	798.9	617-563-7000	Y
Fidelity® Select Brokerage & Invmt Mgmt Portfolio	FSLBX	B	B	C+	Up	9.16	16.21	29.93	24.43	98.77	81.76	441.5	617-563-7000	Y
Fidelity® Select Consumer Finance Portfolio	FSVLX	B	B+	B	Up	8.45	16.10	23.10	32.84	93.34	16.21	98.2	617-563-7000	Y
Fidelity® Select Financial Services Portfolio	FIDSX	B+	A-	B	Up	8.67	14.58	20.94	36.60	106.55	114.22	1,211	617-563-7000	Y
Fidelity® Select Insurance Portfolio	FSPCX	B+	B+	A-	Up	4.18	7.30	15.38	39.47	125.71	79.5	372.2	617-563-7000	Y
Franklin Mutual Financial Services Fund Class A	TFSIX	B	B	B+	Up	3.47	7.50	13.34	36.17	91.75	24.2	705.2	650-312-2000	Y
Franklin Mutual Financial Services Fund Class C	TMFSX	B	B-	B+	Up	3.31	7.10	12.49	33.15	84.94	24.08	705.2	650-312-2000	Y
Franklin Mutual Financial Services Fund Class R6	FMFVX	B	B	B+	Up	3.58	7.73	13.76	37.81	95.62	24.3	705.2	650-312-2000	Y
Franklin Mutual Financial Services Fund Class Z	TEFAX	B	B	B+	Up	3.56	7.65	13.61	37.26	94.33	24.14	705.2	650-312-2000	Y
Hennessy Large Cap Financial Fund Institutional Class	HILFX	B	A-	B-		7.96	14.43	19.73	28.74	102.63	21.74	33.6	800-966-4354	Y
Hennessy Large Cap Financial Fund Investor Class	HLFNX	B	B+	B-		7.98	14.30	19.37	27.42	100.55	21.84	33.6	800-966-4354	Y
Hennessy Small Cap Financial Fund Institutional Class	HISFX	B+	A-	B	Up	0.58	5.15	0.13	49.40	102.71	14.53	210.0	800-966-4354	Y
Hennessy Small Cap Financial Fund Investor Class	HSFNX	B+	A-	B	Up	0.52	4.98	-0.20	47.79	99.11	24.12	210.0	800-966-4354	Y
ICON Financial Fund Class A	ICFAX	B	B	B	Up	8.44	13.33	19.59	28.52	81.39	10.81	44.7	303-790-1600	Y
ICON Financial Fund Class S	ICFSX	B	B+	B	Up	8.57	13.47	20.03	29.84	84.38	10.78	44.7	303-790-1600	Y
JNL/Mellon Capital Financial Sector Fund Class A	US47760W7535	A-	A	B	Up	7.47	12.69	19.32	44.60	123.62	13.94	1,439		Y
JNL/Mellon Capital Financial Sector Fund Class I	US47760W7469	A-	A	B	Up	7.62	12.87	19.60	45.55	125.88	13.97	1,439		Y
John Hancock Financial Industries Fund Class A	FIDAX	B	B+	B	Up	3.62	8.40	13.29	31.56	95.86	19.97	976.3	800-225-5913	Y
John Hancock Financial Industries Fund Class B	FIDBX	B	B+	B	Up	3.46	8.06	12.52	28.78	88.73	18.15	976.3	800-225-5913	
John Hancock Financial Industries Fund Class C	FIDCX	B	B+	B	Up	3.45	8.04	12.49	28.80	88.99	18.18	976.3	800-225-5913	Y
John Hancock Financial Industries Fund Class I	JFIFX	B	B+	B	Up	3.73	8.57	13.65	32.05	96.59	19.93	976.3	800-225-5913	Y
John Hancock Financial Industries Fund Class NAV	US4099058178	B	B+	B	Up	3.74	8.63	13.71	33.17	99.65	19.92	976.3	800-225-5913	Y
John Hancock Financial Industries Fund Class R6	JFDRX	B	B+	B		3.73	8.57	13.46	31.77	96.16	19.92	976.3	800-225-5913	Y
John Hancock Financial Opportunities Fund	BTO	A-	A	B	Up	3.34	8.85	10.20	66.07	155.06	36.94	703.9	800-225-5913	Y
John Hancock Regional Bank Fund Class A	FRBAX	A-	A	B	Up	4.07	8.91	10.49	61.27	150.29	27.63	1,946	800-225-5913	Y
John Hancock Regional Bank Fund Class B	FRBFX	A-	A	B	Up	3.91	8.55	9.76	57.92	141.76	26.21	1,946	800-225-5913	
John Hancock Regional Bank Fund Class C	FRBCX	A-	A	B	Up	3.90	8.53	9.74	57.93	141.78	26.26	1,946	800-225-5913	Y
John Hancock Regional Bank Fund Class I	JRBFX	A-	A	B	Up	4.18	9.07	10.85	59.89	144.77	27.63	1,946	800-225-5913	Y
John Hancock Regional Bank Fund Class R6	JRGRX	A-	A	B		4.21	8.95	10.17	58.51	142.66	27.63	1,946	800-225-5913	Y
Kinetics Market Opportunities Fund Advisor Class A	KMKAX	B+	A	C+	Up	19.41	36.27	46.90	59.82	123.72	26.41	65.1	800-930-3828	Y
Kinetics Market Opportunities Fund Advisor Class C	KMKCX	B+	A	C+	Up	19.22	35.95	46.12	57.45	118.01	25.53	65.1	800-930-3828	Y
Kinetics Market Opportunities Fund Class Institutional	KMKYX	B+	A	C+	Up	19.59	36.68	47.64	62.13	129.11	27.04	65.1	800-930-3828	Y
Kinetics Market Opportunities Fund No Load Class	KMKNX	B+	A	C+	Up	19.47	36.51	47.27	61.03	126.44	26.72	65.1	800-930-3828	Y

Category: Financials Sector Equity (con't)

Fund Name	Ticker Symbol	Overall Rating	Reward Rating	Risk Rating	Recent Up/ Downgrade	3-Month Total Return	6-Month Total Return	1-Year Total Return	3-Year Total Return	5-Year Total Return	NAV	Total Assets (MIL)	Telephone	Open to New Investors
		RATINGS				TOTAL RETURNS & PERFORMANCE					ASSETS		NEW INVESTORS	
Putnam Global Financial Fund Class C	PGFDX	B-	C+	B	Up	4.23	9.37	19.57	19.76	53.53	12.97	26.9	617-292-1000	Y
Putnam Global Financial Fund Class Y	PGFYX	B-	B-	C+	Up	4.42	9.91	20.76	23.42	61.46	13.59	26.9	617-292-1000	Y
RMB Mendon Financial Services Fund Class A	RMBKX	A	A	A-	Up	2.50	7.84	11.99	73.97	167.36	43.4	641.1		Y
RMB Mendon Financial Services Fund Class C	RMBNX	A	A	A-	Up	2.30	7.44	11.17	70.16	157.49	39.76	641.1		Y
RMB Mendon Financial Services Fund Class I	RMBLX	A	A	A-	Up	2.57	7.98	12.23	74.35	167.94	43.87	641.1		Y
Royce Global Financial Services Fund Institutional Class	RGFIX	B	B	B	Up	7.00	11.67	23.00	32.40	97.64	13.58	54.9	800-221-4268	Y
Royce Global Financial Services Fund Service Class	RYFSX	B	B	B	Up	6.92	11.49	22.45	31.21	95.87	10.57	54.9	800-221-4268	Y
Rydex Banking Fund Class A	RYBKX	B	A-	B-	Up	5.09	9.60	12.20	33.95	82.53	78.69	58.7	800-820-0888	Y
Rydex Banking Fund Class C	RYKCX	B	A-	B-	Up	4.90	9.19	11.37	30.96	75.78	71.08	58.7	800-820-0888	Y
Rydex Banking Fund Class H	RYKAX	B	A-	B-	Up	5.10	9.61	12.19	33.91	81.70	76.67	58.7	800-820-0888	Y
Rydex Banking Fund Class Investor	RYKIX	B	A-	B-	Up	5.16	9.72	12.47	34.89	84.74	86.09	58.7	800-820-0888	Y
Rydex Financial Services Fund Class A	RYFNX	B	B	B	Up	5.15	9.23	15.44	26.70	85.36	68.86	45.9	800-820-0888	Y
Rydex Financial Services Fund Class C	RYFCX	B	B-	B	Up	4.95	8.82	14.58	23.87	78.62	61.54	45.9	800-820-0888	Y
Rydex Financial Services Fund Class H	RYFAX	B	B	B	Up	5.16	9.24	15.49	26.59	84.30	66.88	45.9	800-820-0888	Y
Rydex Financial Services Fund Class Investor	RYFIX	B	B	B	Up	5.75	9.92	16.32	28.30	88.65	73.17	45.9	800-820-0888	Y
Saratoga Financial Service Portfolio Fund Class A	SFPAX	B	B	B-		8.06	12.93	19.27	26.65	81.61	11.26	2.2	800-807-3863	Y
Saratoga Financial Service Portfolio Fund Class C	SFPCX	B-	B	C+	Down	7.90	12.54	18.57	24.34	76.28	9.96	2.2	800-807-3863	Y
Saratoga Financial Service Portfolio Fund Cls Inst	SFPIX	B	B	B-		8.19	13.18	19.83	28.28	85.49	12.02	2.2	800-807-3863	Y
T. Rowe Price Financial Services Fund	PRISX	B+	A-	B	Up	5.04	10.13	19.09	37.65	112.51	28	789.9	410-345-2000	Y
T. Rowe Price Financial Services Fund I Class	TFIFX	B+	A-	B	Up	5.07	10.20	19.25	37.84	112.80	27.99	789.9	410-345-2000	Y
Vanguard Financials Index Fund Admiral Shares	VFAIX	A-	A	B	Up	7.68	13.10	20.05	47.25	128.88	35.08	7,594	877-662-7447	Y

Category: Flexible Allocation

Fund Name	Ticker Symbol	Overall Rating	Reward Rating	Risk Rating	Recent Up/ Downgrade	3-Month Total Return	6-Month Total Return	1-Year Total Return	3-Year Total Return	5-Year Total Return	NAV	Total Assets (MIL)	Telephone	Open to New Investors
		RATINGS				TOTAL RETURNS & PERFORMANCE					ASSETS		NEW INVESTORS	
Invesco Balanced-Risk Allocation Fund Class A	ABRZX	B-	C+	B	Up	4.98	7.63	9.77	15.91	25.43	10.84	4,978	800-659-1005	Y
Invesco Balanced-Risk Allocation Fund Class B	ABRBX	B-	C+	B	Up	4.71	7.24	8.93	13.35	20.80	10.36	4,978	800-659-1005	
Invesco Balanced-Risk Allocation Fund Class C	ABRCX	B-	C+	B	Up	4.71	7.24	8.82	13.35	20.80	10.36	4,978	800-659-1005	Y
Invesco Balanced-Risk Allocation Fund Class R	ABRRX	B-	C+	B	Up	4.87	7.45	9.41	15.06	23.87	10.66	4,978	800-659-1005	Y
Invesco Balanced-Risk Allocation Fund Class R6	ALLFX	B-	C+	B		5.00	7.80	10.13	17.26	27.82	11.01	4,978	800-659-1005	Y
Invesco Balanced-Risk Allocation Fund Class Y	ABRYX	B-	C+	B		4.92	7.72	9.94	16.80	26.96	10.99	4,978	800-659-1005	Y
Invesco Balanced-Risk Allocation Fund R5 Class	ABRIX	B-	C+	B		5.00	7.81	10.04	16.92	27.32	11	4,978	800-659-1005	Y
Invesco Multi-Asset Income Fund Class A	PIAFX	B	C+	A-		0.91	3.32	10.71	24.14	31.74	10.93	683.5	800-659-1005	Y
Invesco Multi-Asset Income Fund Class C	PICFX	B	C+	B+		0.72	2.93	9.88	21.37	26.88	10.92	683.5	800-659-1005	Y
Invesco Multi-Asset Income Fund Class R	PIRFX	B	C+	A-		0.85	3.19	10.43	23.21	30.10	10.93	683.5	800-659-1005	Y
Invesco Multi-Asset Income Fund Class R5	IPNFX	B	C+	A-		0.98	3.45	11.08	25.06	33.39	10.94	683.5	800-659-1005	Y
Invesco Multi-Asset Income Fund Class R6	PIFFX	B	C+	A-		0.98	3.36	10.98	24.95	33.39	10.93	683.5	800-659-1005	Y
Invesco Multi-Asset Income Fund Class Y	PIYFX	B	C+	A-		0.98	3.36	10.98	25.07	33.26	10.93	683.5	800-659-1005	Y
Power Momentum Index VIT Fund Class 1 shares	US66537U4031	B-	B-	B-	Down	5.39	11.50	20.92	24.91	89.09	33.82	81.8		Y

Category: Global Equity

Fund Name	Ticker Symbol	RATINGS: Overall Rating	Reward Rating	Risk Rating	Recent Up/ Downgrade	TOTAL RETURNS & PERFORMANCE: 3-Month Total Return	6-Month Total Return	1-Year Total Return	3-Year Total Return	5-Year Total Return	ASSETS: NAV	Total Assets (MIL)	NEW INVESTORS: Telephone	Open to New Investors
1290 SmartBeta Equity Fund Class A	TNBAX	B-	C+	B	Up	5.12	9.50	21.28	28.57		12.28	15.4	212-554-1234	Y
1290 SmartBeta Equity Fund Class I	TNBIX	B-	C+	B	Up	5.17	9.64	21.66	29.55		12.28	15.4	212-554-1234	Y
1290 SmartBeta Equity Fund Class R	TNBRX	B-	C+	B	Up	5.13	9.33	21.10	27.56		12.28	15.4	212-554-1234	Y
1290 SmartBeta Equity Fund Class T	TNBCX	B-	C+	B	Up	5.26	9.64	21.66	29.55		12.28	15.4	212-554-1234	Y
1290 VT Low Volatility Global Equity Portfolio Class IB	US29439V7964	B	B-	B+		4.06	7.40	18.33	26.85			9.4	877-222-2144	Y
1290 VT Low Volatility Global Equity Portfolio Class K	US29439V7881	B	B-	B+		4.14	7.57	18.62	27.82			9.4	877-222-2144	Y
1290 VT SmartBeta Equity Portfolio Class IB	US29439V8046	B	B-	A-		5.56	10.17	21.80	28.75			18.4	877-222-2144	Y
1290 VT SmartBeta Equity Portfolio Class K	US29439V8871	B-	B-	B	Down	5.64	10.34	22.08	29.71			18.4	877-222-2144	Y
AB Sustainable Global Thematic Fund Advisor Class	ATEYX	B+	B+	B	Up	7.14	13.16	37.49	44.64	91.45	124.16	891.9	212-969-1000	Y
AB Sustainable Global Thematic Fund Class A	ALTFX	B+	B+	B	Up	7.07	13.02	37.15	43.55	88.89	117.38	891.9	212-969-1000	Y
AB Sustainable Global Thematic Fund Class B	ATEBX	B	B+	B	Up	6.86	12.57	36.06	40.10	81.53	96.66	891.9	212-969-1000	
AB Sustainable Global Thematic Fund Class C	ATECX	B	B+	B	Up	6.87	12.58	36.09	40.28	81.93	97.25	891.9	212-969-1000	Y
AB Sustainable Global Thematic Fund Class I	AGTIX	B+	B+	B	Up	7.19	13.26	37.74	45.61	93.70	124.52	891.9	212-969-1000	Y
AB Sustainable Global Thematic Fund Class K	ATEKX	B+	B+	B	Up	7.08	13.03	37.20	44.00	90.31	119.92	891.9	212-969-1000	Y
AB Sustainable Global Thematic Fund Class R	ATERX	B+	B+	B	Up	7.01	12.89	36.82	42.70	87.39	116	891.9	212-969-1000	Y
AB Tax-Managed Wealth Appreciation Strategy Advisor Class	ATWYX	B-	B-	B-	Down	5.81	11.22	23.05	27.72	73.90	16.18	726.5	212-969-1000	Y
AB Tax-Managed Wealth Appreciation Strategy Class A	ATWAX	B-	B-	B-	Down	5.72	11.08	22.78	26.70	71.65	16.13	726.5	212-969-1000	Y
AB Tax-Managed Wealth Appreciation Strategy Class B	ATWBX	B-	C+	B-	Up	5.52	10.65	21.84	23.87	65.27	16.06	726.5	212-969-1000	
AB Tax-Managed Wealth Appreciation Strategy Class C	ATWCX	B-	C+	B-	Up	5.55	10.66	21.86	23.94	65.48	15.93	726.5	212-969-1000	Y
AB Wealth Appreciation Strategy Advisor Class	AWAYX	B-	B-	B-	Down	5.78	11.07	21.95	26.01	66.60	16.29	1,383	212-969-1000	Y
AB Wealth Appreciation Strategy Class A	AWAAX	B-	B-	B-	Up	5.70	10.91	21.67	25.05	64.44	16.34	1,383	212-969-1000	Y
AB Wealth Appreciation Strategy Class I	AWAIX	B-	B-	B-	Down	5.75	10.97	21.86	25.86	66.22	16.29	1,383	212-969-1000	Y
AB Wealth Appreciation Strategy Class K	AWAKX	B-	B-	B-	Up	5.66	10.77	21.41	24.55	63.46	16.24	1,383	212-969-1000	Y
AB Wealth Appreciation Strategy Class R	AWARX	B-	C+	B-	Up	5.61	10.66	21.06	23.38	60.89	16.25	1,383	212-969-1000	Y
AdvisorOne CLS Global Aggressive Equity Fund Class N	CLACX	B-	B	C+	Down	5.91	11.28	24.51	34.62	81.31	15.69	172.1		Y
AllianzGI Best Styles Global Equity Fund Class A	ALLGX	B-	B-	C+	Down	4.48	10.58	24.35	28.14		17.16	617.7	800-498-5413	Y
AllianzGI Best Styles Global Equity Fund Class C	ABSGX	B-	B-	C+	Down	4.25	10.14	23.46	25.69		16.85	617.7	800-498-5413	Y
AllianzGI Best Styles Global Equity Fund Cls Institutional	ALLHX	B-	B-	B-	Down	4.51	10.67	24.67	29.33		16.97	617.7	800-498-5413	Y
AllianzGI Best Styles Global Equity Fund Class P	ALGPX	B-	B-	B-	Down	4.48	10.59	24.53	28.96		17.14	617.7	800-498-5413	Y
AllianzGI Best Styles Global Equity Fund Class R6	AGERX	B-	B-	B-	Down	4.51	10.69	24.68	29.54		17.1	617.7	800-498-5413	Y
AllianzGI Global Sustainability Fund Class A	ASUAX	B-	C+	B	Up	4.85	9.93	24.29	30.37		18.18	28.1	800-498-5413	Y
AllianzGI Global Sustainability Fund Class P	ASTPX	B-	C+	B	Up	4.89	9.99	24.46	30.96		18.36	28.1	800-498-5413	Y
AllianzGI Global Sustainability Fund Institutional Class	ASTNX	B-	C+	B	Up	4.87	10.03	24.51	31.28		18.38	28.1	800-498-5413	Y
Alpine Dynamic Dividend Fund Class A Shares	ADAVX	B-	B-	C+	Up	5.69	9.96	23.05	29.84	69.63	4.19	166.1	888-785-5578	Y
Alpine Dynamic Dividend Fund Institutional Class	ADVDX	B-	B-	C+	Up	5.75	10.09	23.35	30.82	71.75	4.19	166.1	888-785-5578	Y
Alpine Global Dynamic Dividend Fund	AGD	B-	B-	C+	Up	5.80	10.26	23.90	30.55	71.31	11.85	146.7	914-251-0880	Y
Alpine Total Dynamic Dividend Fund	AOD	B-	B-	C+	Up	5.53	9.74	22.57	26.78	64.57	10.26	1,091	914-251-0880	Y
American Beacon SGA Global Growth Fund A Class	SGAAX	B+	B	A-	Up	8.67	11.92	32.69	47.91	82.64	18.42	39.7	800-658-5811	Y
American Beacon SGA Global Growth Fund C Class	SGACX	B	B	A-	Up	8.48	11.50	31.68	44.59	75.78	17.79	39.7	800-658-5811	Y
American Beacon SGA Global Growth Fund Institutional Class	SGAGX	B+	B	A-	Up	8.80	12.20	33.25	49.73	86.19	18.78	39.7	800-658-5811	Y
American Beacon SGA Global Growth Fund Investor Class	SGAPX	B+	B	A-	Up	8.72	11.97	32.75	48.03	83.30	18.45	39.7	800-658-5811	Y
American Beacon SGA Global Growth Fund Y Class	SGAYX	B+	B	A-	Up	8.78	12.13	33.11	49.28	85.36	18.69	39.7	800-658-5811	Y
American Century Global Growth Fund A Class	AGGRX	B	B-	B	Up	3.73	9.88	27.32	27.02	72.69	11.85	552.9	800-444-4015	Y
American Century Global Growth Fund C Class	AGLCX	B	B-	B	Up	3.50	9.47	26.43	24.32	66.46	10.3	552.9	800-444-4015	Y
American Century Global Growth Fund I Class	AGGIX	B	B	B	Up	3.87	10.20	27.91	28.91	76.75	12.46	552.9	800-444-4015	Y
American Century Global Growth Fund Investor Class	TWGGX	B	B-	B	Up	3.78	10.04	27.54	28.07	74.95	12.21	552.9	800-444-4015	Y
American Century Global Growth Fund R Class	AGORX	B	B-	B	Up	3.70	9.75	26.96	26.19	70.62	11.68	552.9	800-444-4015	Y
American Century Global Growth Fund R5 Class	AGFGX	B	B-	B	Up	3.87	10.11	27.76	28.29	75.25	12.45	552.9	800-444-4015	Y
American Century Global Growth Fund R6 Class	AGGDX	B	B	B	Up	3.85	10.22	28.02	29.34	77.57	12.52	552.9	800-444-4015	Y
American Century Global Growth Fund Y Class	AGYGX	B	B-	B	Up	3.85	10.22	27.88	28.41	75.41	12.52	552.9	800-444-4015	Y
American Funds Capital World Growth & Inc Fund® Cls 529-A	CWIAX	B-	B-	B	Down	5.05	10.30	24.60	28.68	69.68	50.94	97,411	800-421-4225	Y
American Funds Capital World Growth & Inc Fund® Cls 529-C	CWICX	B-	B-	B	Up	4.82	9.85	23.64	25.71	63.18	50.76	97,411	800-421-4225	Y

Category: Global Equity (con't)

Fund Name	Ticker Symbol	RATINGS: Overall Rating	Reward Rating	Risk Rating	Recent Up/ Downgrade	TOTAL RETURNS & PERFORMANCE: 3-Month Total Return	6-Month Total Return	1-Year Total Return	3-Year Total Return	5-Year Total Return	ASSETS: NAV	Total Assets (MIL)	NEW INVESTORS: Telephone	Open to New Investors
American Funds Capital World Growth & Inc Fund® Cls 529-E	CWIEX	B-	B-	B	Down	4.97	10.17	24.30	27.80	67.74	50.87	97,411	800-421-4225	Y
American Funds Capital World Growth & Inc Fund® Cls 529-F	CWIFX	B	B-	B	Up	5.08	10.39	24.85	29.52	71.54	50.97	97,411	800-421-4225	Y
American Funds Capital World Growth & Income Fund® Cls A	CWGIX	B-	B-	B	Down	5.06	10.32	24.67	28.98	70.39	51.11	97,411	800-421-4225	Y
American Funds Capital World Growth & Income Fund® Cls C	CWGCX	B-	B-	B	Up	4.84	9.88	23.69	25.92	63.70	50.56	97,411	800-421-4225	Y
American Funds Capital World Growth & Income Fund® Cls F-1	CWGFX	B-	B-	B	Down	5.04	10.29	24.61	28.81	70.01	51	97,411	800-421-4225	Y
American Funds Capital World Growth & Income Fund® Cls F-2	WGIFX	B	B-	B	Up	5.10	10.43	24.92	29.85	72.36	51.05	97,411	800-421-4225	Y
American Funds Capital World Growth & Income Fund® Cls F-3	FWGIX	B	B-	B	Up	5.13	10.50	25.03	29.35	70.88	51.09	97,411	800-421-4225	Y
American Funds Capital World Growth & Income Fund® Cls R-1	RWIAX	B-	B-	B	Up	4.84	9.90	23.70	26.04	63.96	50.63	97,411	800-421-4225	Y
American Funds Capital World Growth & Income Fund® Cls R-2	RWIBX	B-	B-	B	Up	4.84	9.89	23.70	26.08	64.14	50.49	97,411	800-421-4225	Y
American Funds Capital World Growth & Inc Fund® Cls R-2E	RWBEX	B-	B-	B	Down	4.92	10.07	24.09	27.25	67.08	50.93	97,411	800-421-4225	Y
American Funds Capital World Growth & Income Fund® Cls R-3	RWICX	B-	B-	B	Down	4.97	10.14	24.29	27.76	67.73	50.77	97,411	800-421-4225	Y
American Funds Capital World Growth & Income Fund® Cls R-4	RWIEX	B-	B-	B	Down	5.05	10.31	24.63	28.90	70.21	50.98	97,411	800-421-4225	Y
American Funds Capital World Growth & Income Fund® Cls R-5	RWIFX	B	B-	B	Up	5.11	10.47	25.01	30.07	72.77	51.11	97,411	800-421-4225	Y
American Funds Capital World Growth & Inc Fund® Cls R-5E	RWIHX	B	B-	B	Up	5.10	10.43	24.90	29.36	70.89	51.03	97,411	800-421-4225	Y
American Funds Capital World Growth & Income Fund® Cls R-6	RWIGX	B	B-	B	Up	5.13	10.50	25.07	30.24	73.22	51.1	97,411	800-421-4225	Y
American Funds Global Growth Portfolio Class 529-A	CPGAX	B	B	B	Up	5.21	11.14	28.53	33.00	73.93	16.7	2,670	800-421-4225	Y
American Funds Global Growth Portfolio Class 529-C	CPGCX	B	B-	B	Up	5.03	10.69	27.53	29.80	67.03	16.52	2,670	800-421-4225	Y
American Funds Global Growth Portfolio Class 529-E	CGGEX	B	B-	B	Up	5.14	10.97	28.24	31.90	71.58	16.63	2,670	800-421-4225	Y
American Funds Global Growth Portfolio Class 529-F-1	CGGFX	B	B	B	Up	5.31	11.29	28.84	33.77	75.62	16.75	2,670	800-421-4225	Y
American Funds Global Growth Portfolio Class A	PGGAX	B	B	B	Up	5.22	11.14	28.61	33.20	74.43	16.72	2,670	800-421-4225	Y
American Funds Global Growth Portfolio Class C	GGPCX	B	B-	B	Up	4.98	10.72	27.66	30.13	67.74	16.51	2,670	800-421-4225	Y
American Funds Global Growth Portfolio Class F-1	PGGFX	B	B	B	Up	5.21	11.13	28.56	33.04	73.91	16.74	2,670	800-421-4225	Y
American Funds Global Growth Portfolio Class F-2	PGWFX	B	B	B	Up	5.29	11.26	28.95	34.08	76.30	16.77	2,670	800-421-4225	Y
American Funds Global Growth Portfolio Class F-3	PGXFX	B	B	B	Up	5.32	11.37	29.00	34.33	76.76	16.73	2,670	800-421-4225	Y
American Funds Global Growth Portfolio Class R-1	RGGAX	B	B-	B	Up	5.02	10.73	27.66	30.11	67.62	16.58	2,670	800-421-4225	Y
American Funds Global Growth Portfolio Class R-2	RGGBX	B	B-	B	Up	5.07	10.76	27.66	30.12	67.60	16.47	2,670	800-421-4225	Y
American Funds Global Growth Portfolio Class R-2E	REBGX	B	B	B	Up	5.10	10.86	28.02	32.57	72.60	16.63	2,670	800-421-4225	Y
American Funds Global Growth Portfolio Class R-3	RGLCX	B	B-	B	Up	5.17	11.00	28.19	31.88	71.41	16.63	2,670	800-421-4225	Y
American Funds Global Growth Portfolio Class R-4	RGGEX	B	B	B	Up	5.20	11.14	28.62	33.07	74.15	16.7	2,670	800-421-4225	Y
American Funds Global Growth Portfolio Class R-5	RGGFX	B	B	B	Up	5.30	11.25	28.93	34.27	76.67	16.84	2,670	800-421-4225	Y
American Funds Global Growth Portfolio Class R-5E	RGTFX	B	B	B	Up	5.30	11.30	28.99	34.05	76.39	16.69	2,670	800-421-4225	Y
American Funds Global Growth Portfolio Class R-6	RGGGX	B	B	B	Up	5.27	11.34	29.02	34.45	77.07	16.87	2,670	800-421-4225	Y
American Funds New Perspective Fund® Class 529-A	CNPAX	B+	B	A-	Up	4.55	10.18	28.78	37.07	82.54	42.65	76,532	800-421-4225	Y
American Funds New Perspective Fund® Class 529-C	CNPCX	B	B	A-	Up	4.37	9.73	27.76	33.90	75.57	41.36	76,532	800-421-4225	Y
American Funds New Perspective Fund® Class 529-E	CNPEX	B	B	A-	Up	4.51	10.07	28.47	36.12	80.39	42.25	76,532	800-421-4225	Y
American Funds New Perspective Fund® Class 529-F	CNPFX	B+	B	A-	Up	4.64	10.31	29.07	38.00	84.55	42.55	76,532	800-421-4225	Y
American Funds New Perspective Fund® Class A	ANWPX	B+	B	A-	Up	4.59	10.23	28.89	37.43	83.35	43.16	76,532	800-421-4225	Y
American Funds New Perspective Fund® Class C	NPFCX	B	B	A-	Up	4.40	9.79	27.85	34.17	76.15	41.48	76,532	800-421-4225	Y
American Funds New Perspective Fund® Class F-1	NPFFX	B+	B	A-	Up	4.57	10.20	28.77	37.15	82.75	42.89	76,532	800-421-4225	Y
American Funds New Perspective Fund® Class F-2	ANWFX	B+	B	A-	Up	4.64	10.32	29.11	38.26	85.30	43.02	76,532	800-421-4225	Y
American Funds New Perspective Fund® Class F-3	FNPFX	B+	B	A-	Up	4.66	10.38	29.25	37.82	83.86	43.15	76,532	800-421-4225	Y
American Funds New Perspective Fund® Class R-1	RNPAX	B	B	A-	Up	4.39	9.79	27.88	34.21	76.21	41.13	76,532	800-421-4225	Y
American Funds New Perspective Fund® Class R-2	RNPBX	B	B	A-	Up	4.40	9.80	27.89	34.25	76.35	41.53	76,532	800-421-4225	Y
American Funds New Perspective Fund® Class R-2E	RPEBX	B	B	A-	Up	4.46	9.95	28.26	35.91	80.29	42.52	76,532	800-421-4225	Y
American Funds New Perspective Fund® Class R-3	RNPCX	B	B	A-	Up	4.49	10.03	28.45	36.02	80.24	42.2	76,532	800-421-4225	Y
American Funds New Perspective Fund® Class R-4	RNPEX	B+	B	A-	Up	4.59	10.21	28.82	37.25	83.01	42.57	76,532	800-421-4225	Y
American Funds New Perspective Fund® Class R-5	RNPFX	B+	B	A-	Up	4.67	10.38	29.21	38.51	85.77	43.11	76,532	800-421-4225	Y
American Funds New Perspective Fund® Class R-5E	RNPHX	B+	B	A-	Up	4.63	10.32	29.08	37.70	83.70	42.92	76,532	800-421-4225	Y
American Funds New Perspective Fund® Class R-6	RNPGX	B+	B	A-	Up	4.67	10.41	29.29	38.69	86.23	43.17	76,532	800-421-4225	Y
AMG Managers Guardian Capital Global Dividend Fund Class I	AGCDX	B-	C+	B-	Up	5.13	9.34	19.43	19.18		11.6	38.2	800-835-3879	Y
AMG Managers Guardian Capital Global Dividend Fund Class N	AGCNX	B-	C+	B-	Up	5.10	9.41	19.34	18.61		11.66	38.2	800-835-3879	Y
AQR Global Equity Fund Class I	AQGIX	B	B	B-	Up	5.40	12.76	25.44	36.55	85.28	8.92	244.6	203-742-3600	Y

Category: Global Equity (con't)

Fund Name	Ticker Symbol	RATINGS: Overall Rating	Reward Rating	Risk Rating	Recent Up/ Downgrade	TOTAL RETURNS & PERFORMANCE: 3-Month Total Return	6-Month Total Return	1-Year Total Return	3-Year Total Return	5-Year Total Return	ASSETS: NAV	Total Assets (MIL)	NEW INVESTORS: Telephone	Open to New Investors
AQR Global Equity Fund Class N	AQGNX	B	B	B-	Up	5.22	12.61	25.02	35.30	82.73	8.88	244.6	203-742-3600	Y
AQR Global Equity Fund Class R6	AQGRX	B	B	B-	Up	5.39	12.82	25.57	37.05	86.01	8.99	244.6	203-742-3600	Y
Ariel Global Fund Institutional Class	AGLYX	B	C+	B	Up	1.16	5.70	15.81	22.20	68.04	15.02	104.8	312-726-0140	Y
Ariel Global Fund Investor Class	AGLOX	B-	C+	B		1.12	5.60	15.60	21.28	65.93	15.52	104.8	312-726-0140	Y
Artisan Global Equity Fund Institutional Shares	APHHX	B	B	B	Up	5.62	14.16	31.59	30.26	77.74	20.63	314.2	800-344-1770	Y
Artisan Global Equity Fund Investor Class	ARTHX	B	B	B	Up	5.53	14.03	31.33	29.54	76.75	20.55	314.2	800-344-1770	Y
Artisan Global Opportunities Fund Advisor Class	APDRX	B	B	B+	Down	4.35	9.90	31.33	47.41	91.75	25.79	2,806	800-344-1770	Y
Artisan Global Opportunities Fund Institutional Class	APHRX	B	B	A-	Down	4.40	9.95	31.49	48.00	93.48	25.98	2,806	800-344-1770	Y
Artisan Global Opportunities Fund Investor Class	ARTRX	B	B	B+	Down	4.32	9.83	31.18	46.98	91.18	25.72	2,806	800-344-1770	Y
Artisan Global Value Fund Advisor Class	APDGX	B-	B	B-	Down	3.75	9.20	21.75	29.28	80.29	18.13	3,192	800-344-1770	
Artisan Global Value Fund Institutional Class	APHGX	B	B	B-	Up	3.82	9.25	21.86	29.73	81.85	18.17	3,192	800-344-1770	Y
Artisan Global Value Fund Investor Class	ARTGX	B-	B	B-	Down	3.75	9.13	21.58	28.80	79.62	18.17	3,192	800-344-1770	Y
Aspiriant Risk-Managed Equity Allocation Fund Adv Shares	RMEAX	B	B-	B+	Up	5.58	8.88	21.77	26.27		13.22	1,004	877-997-9971	Y
Ave Maria World Equity Fund	AVEWX	B-	C+	B	Up	4.90	7.00	17.88	21.02	53.29	15.08	60.6	888-726-9331	Y
AXA Global Equity Managed Volatility Portfolio Class IA	US2689408894	B-	B-	B	Up	5.54	10.99	26.15	27.79	60.39		2,365	877-222-2144	Y
AXA Global Equity Managed Volatility Portfolio Class IB	US2689407565	B-	B-	B	Up	5.55	11.01	26.14	27.77	60.44		2,365	877-222-2144	Y
AXA Global Equity Managed Volatility Portfolio Class K	US26883L6213	B-	B-	C+	Up	5.60	11.11	26.44	28.73	62.39		2,365	877-222-2144	Y
Baillie Gifford The Global Alpha Equity Fund Class 2	BGATX	B+	A-	B-	Up	5.59	13.22	34.56	42.62	108.54	18.8538	786.7		Y
Baillie Gifford The Global Alpha Equity Fund Class 3	BGAEX	B+	A	B-	Up	5.61	13.26	34.65	43.02	96.23	19.2158	786.7		Y
Baillie Gifford The Global Alpha Equity Fund Class I	BGASX	B	B	C	Up	5.62	13.24	34.54	24.98	69.00	18.8367	786.7		Y
Baillie Gifford The Global Alpha Equity Fund Class K	BGAKX	B	B	C	Up	5.56	13.18	34.47	24.91	70.99	18.8247	786.7		Y
Baillie Gifford The Long Term Global Growth Eq Fund Cls 2	BGLTX	A-	A+	B	Up	6.10	17.26	54.06	67.90		17.3341	198.3		Y
Baillie Gifford The Long Term Global Growth Eq Fund Cls 4	BGLFX	A-	A+	B	Up	6.13	17.32	54.21	69.26		19.9887	198.3		Y
Baillie Gifford The Long Term Global Growth Eq Fund Cls I	BSGLX	A-	A+	B	Up	6.11	17.24	53.99	65.30		17.3399	198.3		Y
Baillie Gifford The Long Term Global Growth Eq Fund Cls K	BGLKX	A-	A+	B	Up	6.10	17.24	53.99	65.30		17.3405	198.3		Y
Baron Global Advantage Fund Institutional Shares	BGAIX	B+	A	B-	Up	9.88	18.67	49.81	45.98	103.28	20.78	40.1	800-992-2766	Y
Baron Global Advantage Fund R6 Shares	BGLUX	B+	A	B-	Up	9.88	18.66	49.89	46.05	103.38	20.79	40.1	800-992-2766	Y
Baron Global Advantage Fund Retail Shares	BGAFX	B+	A	B-	Up	9.82	18.49	49.59	45.13	101.16	20.57	40.1	800-992-2766	Y
BBH Global Core Select Fund Class N Shares	BBGNX	B	B-	B+	Up	4.43	8.11	22.50	24.27		13.5	135.9	800-575-1265	Y
BBH Global Core Select Fund Retail Class Shares	BBGRX	B	C+	B+	Up	4.45	7.99	22.33	23.35		13.45	135.9	800-575-1265	Y
BlackRock Enhanced Global Dividend Trust	BOE	B-	C+	B	Up	2.68	4.00	16.36	18.84	41.62	13.2166	995.1	800-441-7762	Y
BlackRock Global Dividend Portfolio Class K	BKBDX	B	B-	A-		3.74	5.59	19.94	29.75	61.52	13.43	3,004	800-441-7762	Y
BlackRock Global Dividend Portfolio Insitutional Shares	BIBDX	B	B-	A-		3.73	5.56	19.80	29.64	61.39	13.41	3,004	800-441-7762	Y
BlackRock Global Dividend Portfolio Investor A Shares	BABDX	B	B-	B+		3.68	5.45	19.53	28.57	59.29	13.37	3,004	800-441-7762	Y
BlackRock Global Dividend Portfolio Investor C Shares	BCBDX	B	C+	B+		3.46	5.04	18.58	25.70	53.36	13.29	3,004	800-441-7762	Y
BlackRock Long-Horizon Equity Fund Class R Shares	MREGX	B-	C+	B	Up	5.25	9.58	24.02	13.21	47.33	13.1	292.7	800-441-7762	Y
BlackRock Long-Horizon Equity Fund Institutional Shares	MAEGX	B-	C+	B	Up	5.41	9.93	24.79	15.56	52.55	13.04	292.7	800-441-7762	Y
BlackRock Long-Horizon Equity Fund Investor A Shares	MDEGX	B-	C+	B	Up	5.39	9.75	24.48	14.65	50.40	13.04	292.7	800-441-7762	Y
BMO Global Low Volatility Equity Fund Class A	BAEGX	B	C+	A-		5.87	8.41	17.51	25.42		13.51	51.9	800-236-3863	Y
BMO Global Low Volatility Equity Fund Class I	BGLBX	B	C+	A-		5.87	8.57	17.76	26.20		13.54	51.9	800-236-3863	Y
Boston Partners Global Equity Institutional Class	BPGIX	B-	B-	B-	Down	5.80	9.62	20.37	30.74	83.68	18.41	640.3	617-832-8200	Y
Brandes Global Equity Fund Class A	BGEAX	B-	C+	B	Up	3.46	6.96	15.92	20.71	61.89	24.61	69.4	800-331-2979	Y
Brandes Global Equity Fund Class C	BGVCX	B-	C+	B	Up	3.25	6.56	15.05	18.03	56.09	24.46	69.4	800-331-2979	Y
Brandes Global Equity Fund Class I	BGVIX	B-	C+	B	Up	3.53	7.09	16.21	21.63	63.96	24.77	69.4	800-331-2979	Y
Calamos Global Equity Fund Class A	CAGEX	B+	B+	B+	Up	6.88	15.95	34.41	38.77	70.50	14.72	134.5	800-582-6959	Y
Calamos Global Equity Fund Class C	CCGEX	B	B	B	Up	6.67	15.48	33.34	35.62	64.13	13.42	134.5	800-582-6959	Y
Calamos Global Equity Fund Class R	CRGEX	B	B	B	Up	6.88	15.82	34.06	37.73	68.48	14.25	134.5	800-582-6959	Y
Calamos Global Equity Fund Class T	CTGEX	B	B-	B+	Up	5.36	14.32	25.74	35.21	62.47		127.9	800-582-6959	Y
Calamos Global Equity Fund Institutional Class	CIGEX	B+	B+	B+	Up	6.99	16.12	34.75	39.83	72.70	15.04	134.5	800-582-6959	Y
Cambiar Global Equity Fund Investor Class	CAMGX	B-	C+	B-	Up	5.08	12.38	17.97	25.31	69.43	13.25	14.4	866-777-8227	Y
Cambiar Global Ultra Focus Fund Investor Class	CAMAX	B-	C+	B	Up	0.86	5.23	6.47	18.72	87.81	19.84	110.2	866-777-8227	Y
Capital Group Global Equity Fund	CGLOX	B	B	B	Up	5.36	10.74	27.73	30.39	74.27	15.31	588.6	213-486-9200	Y

Category: Global Equity (con't)

Fund Name	Ticker Symbol	RATINGS: Overall Rating	Reward Rating	Risk Rating	Recent Up/ Downgrade	TOTAL RETURNS & PERFORMANCE: 3-Month Total Return	6-Month Total Return	1-Year Total Return	3-Year Total Return	5-Year Total Return	ASSETS: NAV	Total Assets (MIL)	NEW INVESTORS: Telephone	Open to New Investors
Catalyst/MAP Global Equity Fund Class A	CAXAX	B-	B-	B		2.49	4.60	17.08	25.98	54.47	14.78	39.9	866-447-4228	Y
Catalyst/MAP Global Equity Fund Class C	CAXCX	B-	C+	B		2.31	4.23	16.11	23.13	48.69	14.62	39.9	866-447-4228	Y
Catalyst/MAP Global Equity Fund Class I	CAXIX	B	B-	B	Up	2.54	4.80	17.30	27.41	56.38	14.75	39.9	866-447-4228	Y
Clough Global Equity Fund	GLQ	B-	C+	B-	Up	5.32	10.58	27.83	14.97	50.64	14.4681	160.1		Y
Columbia Global Strategic Equity Fund Advisor Class	CWPRX	B-	B	B-	Down	5.77	12.57	27.86	31.50	82.65	16.22	690.5	800-345-6611	Y
Columbia Global Strategic Equity Fund Class A	NLGIX	B	B-	B	Up	5.71	12.41	27.46	30.55	80.55	15.53	690.5	800-345-6611	Y
Columbia Global Strategic Equity Fund Class C	NLGCX	B	B-	B	Up	5.44	12.01	26.58	27.73	73.85	13.3	690.5	800-345-6611	Y
Columbia Global Strategic Equity Fund Class K	CGRUX	B-	B-	B-	Down	5.72	12.48	27.57	30.95	81.42	15.93	690.5	800-345-6611	
Columbia Global Strategic Equity Fund Class R	CLGRX	B-	B-	C+	Down	5.61	12.34	27.20	29.65	78.24	15.28	690.5	800-345-6611	Y
Columbia Global Strategic Equity Fund Institutional 2 Cls	CGPRX	B	B	B	Up	5.72	12.58	27.88	31.90	83.84	16.24	690.5	800-345-6611	Y
Columbia Global Strategic Equity Fund Institutional 3 Cls	CGSYX	B-	B	B-	Down	5.74	12.60	27.86	31.67	82.91	16.05	690.5	800-345-6611	Y
Columbia Global Strategic Equity Fund Institutional Class	NGPAX	B	B	B	Up	5.80	12.63	27.81	31.61	82.83	15.97	690.5	800-345-6611	Y
Columbia Select Global Equity Fund Class A	IGLGX	B	B	B+	Up	5.06	8.41	32.22	32.09	73.66	12.89	421.8	800-345-6611	Y
Columbia Select Global Equity Fund Class C	RGCEX	B	B-	B	Up	4.84	7.97	31.26	29.06	67.11	11.51	421.8	800-345-6611	Y
Columbia Select Global Equity Fund Class K	IDGYX	B	B	B+	Up	5.12	8.43	32.30	32.45	74.99	13.03	421.8	800-345-6611	
Columbia Select Global Equity Fund Class R	CGERX	B	B	B+	Up	4.99	8.25	31.91	30.99	71.30	12.86	421.8	800-345-6611	Y
Columbia Select Global Equity Fund Class T	CGEWX	B	B	B+	Up	5.04	8.37	32.19	31.80	73.37	12.94	421.8	800-345-6611	Y
Columbia Select Global Equity Fund Institutional 2 Class	RGERX	B	B	B+	Up	5.12	8.50	32.65	33.46	77.25	13.08	421.8	800-345-6611	Y
Columbia Select Global Equity Fund Institutional 3 Class	CSEYX	B	B	B+	Up	5.15	8.56	32.58	32.45	74.13	12.94	421.8	800-345-6611	Y
Columbia Select Global Equity Fund Institutional Class	CGEZX	B	B	B+	Up	5.14	8.53	32.56	32.98	75.75	13.03	421.8	800-345-6611	Y
Columbia Select Global Growth Fund Advisor Class	CADHX	B	B	B	Up	4.26	8.90	33.99	26.95	87.72	15.41	64.6	800-345-6611	Y
Columbia Select Global Growth Fund Class A	COGAX	B	B-	B	Up	4.14	8.71	33.65	26.00	85.38	15.09	64.6	800-345-6611	Y
Columbia Select Global Growth Fund Class C	COGCX	B-	B-	B	Up	3.96	8.33	32.58	23.18	78.50	14.16	64.6	800-345-6611	Y
Columbia Select Global Growth Fund Class R	COGRX	B	B-	B	Up	4.08	8.59	33.27	25.12	83.12	14.78	64.6	800-345-6611	Y
Columbia Select Global Growth Fund Institutional 2 Class	CADIX	B	B	B	Up	4.18	8.87	33.99	27.25	88.17	15.45	64.6	800-345-6611	Y
Columbia Select Global Growth Fund Institutional 3 Class	CGGYX	B	B-	B	Up	4.22	8.89	34.06	27.00	87.81	15.3	64.6	800-345-6611	Y
Columbia Select Global Growth Fund Institutional Class	COGZX	B	B-	B	Up	4.19	8.82	34.00	26.94	87.71	15.41	64.6	800-345-6611	Y
Cornerstone Advs Global Public Equity Fund Inst Shares	CAGLX	B-	B	B-	Down	4.80	10.91	25.05	32.94	79.24	13.99	1,113		Y
Davis Global Fund Class A	DGFAX	B+	A	B-	Up	7.05	16.77	33.33	50.61	111.25	26.24	999.6	800-279-0279	Y
Davis Global Fund Class C	DGFCX	A-	A	B	Up	6.83	16.29	32.31	47.10	102.36	24.69	999.6	800-279-0279	Y
Davis Global Fund Class Y	DGFYX	B+	A	B-	Up	7.07	16.86	33.59	51.67	113.87	26.3	999.6	800-279-0279	Y
DFA Global Equity Portfolio Class Retirement 2	DGERX	B-	B	C+	Down	6.59	11.72	21.87	32.23	81.84	23.39	6,535	512-306-7400	Y
DFA Global Equity Portfolio Institutional Class	DGEIX	B-	B	C+	Down	6.62	11.84	22.15	33.26	84.19	23.25	6,535	512-306-7400	Y
DFA Selectively Hedged Global Eq Port Inst Cls Shares	DSHGX	B-	B	C+	Down	6.60	11.75	22.65	33.56	76.76	16.65	412.1	512-306-7400	Y
DFA World Core Equity Portfolio Institutional Class	DREIX	B-	B	C+	Down	6.67	12.26	25.08	34.26	82.08	16.57	637.1	512-306-7400	Y
Dodge & Cox Global Stock Fund	DODWX	B-	B	C	Up	3.44	9.55	21.51	29.74	88.86	13.86	9,241	415-981-1710	Y
Dreyfus Global Equity Income Fund Class Y	DEQYX	B	B-	A		3.83	6.55	18.21	32.97	61.23	13.08	457.4	800-645-6561	Y
Dreyfus Global Equity Income Fund Fund Class A	DEQAX	B	B-	A		3.75	6.35	17.83	31.59	58.68	13.71	457.4	800-645-6561	Y
Dreyfus Global Equity Income Fund Fund Class C	DEQCX	B	B-	A-		3.53	5.94	16.94	28.71	52.92	14.13	457.4	800-645-6561	Y
Dreyfus Global Equity Income Fund Fund Class I	DQEIX	B	B-	A		3.84	6.55	18.17	32.68	60.86	13.1	457.4	800-645-6561	Y
Dreyfus Global Stock Fund Class A	DGLAX	B	B-	B+	Up	5.19	9.41	23.04	29.13	59.33	20.11	1,297	800-645-6561	
Dreyfus Global Stock Fund Class C	DGLCX	B	B-	B	Up	5.75	9.77	22.99	27.14	54.50	19.61	1,297	800-645-6561	
Dreyfus Global Stock Fund Class I	DGLRX	B	B-	B+	Up	5.03	9.35	23.11	29.99	61.45	20.37	1,297	800-645-6561	
Dreyfus Global Stock Fund Class Y	DGLYX	B	B-	B+	Up	4.98	9.30	23.15	30.05	61.46	20.34	1,297	800-645-6561	
Dreyfus Worldwide Growth Fund Class A	PGROX	B	B	B		5.70	9.78	27.03	31.94	67.71	53.52	669.7	800-645-6561	Y
Dreyfus Worldwide Growth Fund Class C	PGRCX	B	B-	B	Up	5.51	9.37	26.11	29.06	61.60	47.14	669.7	800-645-6561	Y
Dreyfus Worldwide Growth Fund Class I	DPWRX	B	B	B		5.79	9.93	27.37	33.01	69.94	53.81	669.7	800-645-6561	Y
Dreyfus Worldwide Growth Fund Class Y	DPRIX	B	B	B-		5.82	9.97	27.50	33.35	70.40	53.76	669.7	800-645-6561	Y
Eaton Vance Hexavest Global Equity Fund Class A	EHGAX	B-	B-	B-	Down	4.18	7.06	14.47	26.10	63.01	12.83	106.1		Y
Eaton Vance Hexavest Global Equity Fund Class C	EHGCX	B-	C+	B-	Down	3.99	6.72	13.67	23.38	57.08	12.79	106.1		Y
Eaton Vance Hexavest Global Equity Fund Class I	EHGIX	B-	B-	B-	Down	4.26	7.30	14.81	27.13	65.10	12.85	106.1		Y
Eaton Vance Richard Bernstein Equity Strategy Fund Class A	ERBAX	B-	B-	B-	Down	5.51	11.10	20.70	30.43	77.09	17.09	965.6		Y

Category: Global Equity (con't)

Fund Name	Ticker Symbol	RATINGS: Overall Rating	Reward Rating	Risk Rating	Recent Up/ Downgrade	TOTAL RETURNS & PERFORMANCE: 3-Month Total Return	6-Month Total Return	1-Year Total Return	3-Year Total Return	5-Year Total Return	ASSETS: NAV	Total Assets (MIL)	NEW INVESTORS: Telephone	Open to New Investors
Eaton Vance Richard Bernstein Equity Strategy Fund Class C	ERBCX	B-	B-	B-	Down	5.31	10.70	19.82	27.51	70.58	16.94	965.6		Y
Eaton Vance Richard Bernstein Equity Strategy Fund Class I	ERBIX	B-	B-	B-	Down	5.53	11.24	20.92	31.39	79.24	17.09	965.6		Y
Eaton Vance Tax-Managed Global Dividend Income Fund Cls A	EADIX	B-	C+	B	Down	4.54	7.29	20.01	25.01	58.52	12.8	774.9		Y
Eaton Vance Tax-Managed Global Dividend Income Fund Cls B	EBDIX	B	C+	B+	Up	4.35	6.91	19.14	22.16	52.66	12.77	774.9		
Eaton Vance Tax-Managed Global Dividend Income Fund Cls C	ECDIX	B-	C+	B-	Down	4.36	7.01	19.15	22.20	52.73	12.77	774.9		Y
Eaton Vance Tax-Managed Global Dividend Income Fund Cls I	EIDIX	B-	C+	B	Down	4.68	7.50	20.47	26.03	60.57	12.82	774.9		Y
Epoch Global Equity Shareholder Fund Advisor Class	TDGIX	B-	C+	B		3.32	6.93	16.68	18.28		11.81	9.6		Y
Epoch Global Equity Shareholder Fund Institutional Class	TDGEX	B-	C+	B		3.33	6.94	16.69	18.32		11.81	9.6		Y
EQ/Oppenheimer Global Portfolio Class IA	US2689547402	B	B+	C+	Up	7.52	13.73	35.98	38.49	82.47		271.8	877-222-2144	Y
EQ/Oppenheimer Global Portfolio Class IB	US2689547329	B	B+	B	Up	7.52	13.74	36.00	38.52	82.38		271.8	877-222-2144	Y
Fidelity Advisor® Global Equity Income Fund Class A	FBLYX	B-	B-	B	Down	5.67	10.30	21.29	27.30	70.86	14.83	18.4	617-563-7000	Y
Fidelity Advisor® Global Equity Income Fund Class C	FGTNX	B	C+	B+	Up	5.48	9.90	20.46	24.52	64.60	14.77	18.4	617-563-7000	Y
Fidelity Advisor® Global Equity Income Fund Class M	FGABX	B	B-	B+	Up	5.58	10.08	20.96	26.30	68.68	14.82	18.4	617-563-7000	Y
Fidelity Advisor® Global Equity Income Fund I Class	FBUSX	B	B-	B+	Up	5.75	10.42	21.58	28.29	72.94	14.85	18.4	617-563-7000	Y
Fidelity Advisor® Worldwide Fund Class A	FWAFX	B	B	B	Up	6.00	13.14	29.11	31.18	76.10	26.14	1,761	617-563-7000	Y
Fidelity Advisor® Worldwide Fund Class C	FWCFX	B	B-	B	Up	5.85	12.72	28.15	28.19	69.48	25.58	1,761	617-563-7000	Y
Fidelity Advisor® Worldwide Fund Class M	FWTFX	B	B-	B	Up	5.94	12.98	28.73	30.03	73.58	26.03	1,761	617-563-7000	Y
Fidelity Advisor® Worldwide Fund I Class	FWIFX	B	B	B	Up	6.13	13.31	29.53	32.33	78.60	26.29	1,761	617-563-7000	Y
Fidelity® Global Equity Income Fund	FGILX	B-	B-	B-	Down	5.95	10.67	22.05	28.47	73.87	14.49	82.4	617-563-7000	Y
Fidelity® Worldwide Fund	FWWFX	B	B	B	Up	6.09	13.32	29.54	32.43	78.87	26.41	1,761	617-563-7000	Y
First Investors Global Fund Advisor Class	FIITX	B-	B	B-	Down	5.13	8.84	24.23	28.67	73.65	8.55	602.5	800-423-4026	Y
First Investors Global Fund Class A	FIISX	B-	B-	B-	Up	5.03	8.56	23.73	26.97	70.84	8.36	602.5	800-423-4026	Y
First Investors Global Fund Class B	FIBGX	B-	B-	B-	Up	4.70	8.18	22.66	23.87	63.98	6.49	602.5	800-423-4026	Y
First Investors Global Fund Institutional Class	FIIUX	B-	B	B-	Down	5.12	8.82	24.12	28.61	74.33	8.59	602.5	800-423-4026	Y
FPA Paramount Fund	FPRAX	B	B	C+	Up	4.59	11.00	27.23	35.22	66.36	22.2	179.3	800-982-4372	Y
Franklin Mutual Global Discovery Fund Class A	TEDIX	B-	C+	B	Up	0.99	2.80	9.56	18.34	57.78	31.8	21,893	650-312-2000	Y
Franklin Mutual Global Discovery Fund Class C	TEDSX	B-	C+	B	Up	0.82	2.43	8.77	15.78	52.20	31.44	21,893	650-312-2000	Y
Franklin Mutual Global Discovery Fund Class R	TEDRX	B-	C+	B	Up	0.96	2.70	9.30	17.53	56.06	31.37	21,893	650-312-2000	Y
Franklin Mutual Global Discovery Fund Class R6	FMDRX	B-	C+	B	Up	1.09	2.99	9.97	19.77	61.08	32.41	21,893	650-312-2000	Y
Franklin Mutual Global Discovery Fund Class Z	MDISX	B-	C+	B	Up	1.06	2.96	9.84	19.29	59.98	32.42	21,893	650-312-2000	Y
Gabelli International Small Cap Fund Class A	GOCAX	B	B-	B	Up	6.47	11.24	27.73	28.23	53.86	18.44	11.1	914-921-5135	Y
Gabelli International Small Cap Fund Class AAA	GABOX	B	B-	B	Up	6.70	11.60	28.08	28.62	54.38	18.55	11.1	914-921-5135	Y
Gabelli International Small Cap Fund Class C	GGLCX	B-	C+	B	Up	6.28	10.86	26.78	26.00	48.91	17.26	11.1	914-921-5135	Y
Gabelli International Small Cap Fund Class Institutional	GLOIX	B	B-	B	Up	6.75	11.81	29.02	31.28	58.73	18.93	11.1	914-921-5135	Y
GAMCO Global Growth Fund Class A	GGGAX	B	B-	B	Up	6.36	12.18	28.97	27.96	75.03	33.41	89.0	914-921-5135	Y
GAMCO Global Growth Fund Class AAA	GICPX	B	B-	B	Up	6.39	12.18	29.01	27.97	74.99	33.42	89.0	914-921-5135	Y
GAMCO Global Growth Fund Class C	GGGCX	B	B-	B	Up	6.17	11.75	28.04	25.07	68.52	28.73	89.0	914-921-5135	Y
GAMCO Global Growth Fund Class Institutional	GGGIX	B	B	B	Up	6.53	12.53	29.84	30.60	79.82	33.9	89.0	914-921-5135	Y
GMO Global Equity Allocation Fund Class III	GMGEX	B-	B-	B-	Up	5.82	11.21	26.39	27.74	55.98	26.46	2,494	617-330-7500	Y
Goldman Sachs Equity Growth Strategy Portfolio Class A	GAPAX	B	B	B-	Up	5.31	12.39	25.96	34.74	75.00	18.84	370.4	800-526-7384	Y
Goldman Sachs Equity Growth Strategy Portfolio Class C	GAXCX	B-	B-	B-	Down	5.10	11.94	25.07	31.75	68.64	18.01	370.4	800-526-7384	Y
Goldman Sachs Equity Growth Strategy Portfolio Class R	GAPRX	B	B	B-	Up	5.27	12.22	25.70	33.66	72.86	18.69	370.4	800-526-7384	Y
Goldman Sachs Equity Growth Strategy Portfolio Class R6	GAPUX	B	B	B-	Up	5.41	12.61	26.53	36.36	78.63	19.04	370.4	800-526-7384	Y
Goldman Sachs Equity Growth Strategy Portfolio Inst Cls	GAPIX	B	B	B-	Up	5.43	12.63	26.47	36.33	78.60	19.01	370.4	800-526-7384	Y
Goldman Sachs Equity Growth Strategy Portfolio Inv Cls	GAPTX	B	B	B-	Up	5.38	12.50	26.35	35.76	77.32	18.58	370.4	800-526-7384	Y
Goldman Sachs Equity Growth Strategy Portfolio Service Cls	GAPSX	B	B	B-	Up	5.27	12.33	25.79	34.22	74.15	18.75	370.4	800-526-7384	Y
Guggenheim World Equity Income Fund Class A	SEQAX	B-	C+	B	Down	4.00	8.63	14.70	23.46	57.16	15.4	91.4	212-739-0700	Y
Guggenheim World Equity Income Fund Class C	SFGCX	B-	C+	B	Down	3.77	8.18	13.79	20.62	51.32	13.2	91.4	212-739-0700	Y
Guggenheim World Equity Income Fund Class P	SEQPX	B-	C+	B	Down	3.92	8.60	14.65	24.38	58.34	15.64	91.4	212-739-0700	Y
Guggenheim World Equity Income Fund Institutional Class	SEWIX	B-	C+	B	Down	4.07	8.76	14.98	24.31	59.30	15.3	91.4	212-739-0700	Y
GuidePath® Growth Allocation Fund Service Shares	GPSTX	B-	B-	B	Up	4.97	10.70	21.91	22.63	53.96	11.55	553.9	603-888-5500	Y
GuideStone Funds Aggressive Allocation Fund Inst Cls	GAGYX	B-	B-	C+	Down	5.28	11.51	25.88	29.94	75.30	12.28	1,049	214-720-1171	Y

Category: Global Equity (con't)

Fund Name	Ticker Symbol	RATINGS: Overall Rating	Reward Rating	Risk Rating	Recent Up/ Downgrade	TOTAL RETURNS & PERFORMANCE: 3-Month Total Return	6-Month Total Return	1-Year Total Return	3-Year Total Return	5-Year Total Return	ASSETS: NAV	Total Assets (MIL)	NEW INVESTORS: Telephone	Open to New Investors
GuideStone Funds Aggressive Allocation Fund Investor Class	GGBZX	B-	B-	C+	Down	5.26	11.42	25.48	29.28	74.41	12.24	1,049	214-720-1171	Y
Guinness Atkinson Dividend Builder Fund	GAINX	B-	C+	B	Down	5.70	8.01	21.33	24.15	71.84	18.09	9.0	800-915-6566	Y
Harbor Global Leaders Fund Administrative Class	HRGAX	B	B-	B	Up	5.83	10.99	31.09	26.70	88.52	23.79	47.8	800-422-1050	Y
Harbor Global Leaders Fund Institutional Class	HGGAX	B	B-	B	Up	5.92	11.14	31.43	27.68	90.95	24.15	47.8	800-422-1050	Y
Harbor Global Leaders Fund Investor Class	HGGIX	B	B-	B	Up	5.81	10.97	30.90	26.29	87.49	23.53	47.8	800-422-1050	Y
Harbor Global Leaders Fund Retirement Class	HNGIX	B	B-	B	Up	5.90	11.16	31.50	27.81	91.14	24.16	47.8	800-422-1050	Y
Harding Loevner Global Equity Portfolio Advisor Class	HLMGX	B	B	B+	Up	6.63	11.99	31.84	40.06	80.37	37.17	823.7	877-435-8105	Y
Harding Loevner Global Equity Portfolio Institutional Cls	HLMVX	B	B	B+	Up	6.65	12.09	32.14	41.10	82.69	37.18	823.7	877-435-8105	Y
Harding Loevner Global Equity Portfolio Inst Cls Z	HLGZX	B	B	B+		6.65	12.03	31.88	40.11	80.43	37.15	823.7	877-435-8105	Y
Hartford Global Capital Appreciation Fund Class C	HFCCX	B-	C+	B	Up	3.26	6.29	19.73	19.40	69.92	17.24	1,081	888-843-7824	Y
Hartford Global Capital Appreciation Fund Class R3	HCTRX	B-	C+	B	Up	3.39	6.62	20.48	21.68	75.21	18.52	1,081	888-843-7824	Y
Hartford Global Equity Income Fund Class F	HLEFX	B-	B-	C+	Up	3.04	8.76	20.31	25.71	70.35	12.83	168.1	888-843-7824	Y
Hartford Global Equity Income Fund Class R5	HLETX	B-	B-	C+	Up	3.03	8.74	20.21	25.77	70.22	12.84	168.1	888-843-7824	Y
Hartford Global Equity Income Fund Class Y	HLEYX	B-	B-	C+	Up	3.08	8.78	20.33	25.73	70.38	12.69	168.1	888-843-7824	Y
Hartford Global Growth HLS Fund Class IA	HIALX	B+	B+	A-	Up	5.80	12.32	32.72	44.97	116.10	27.89	520.7	888-843-7824	Y
Hartford Global Growth HLS Fund Class IB	HBGLX	B+	B+	A-	Up	5.74	12.17	32.36	43.92	113.42	27.63	520.7	888-843-7824	Y
Hotchkis & Wiley Global Value Fund Class A	HWGAX	B-	B-	B-	Up	2.89	7.87	16.52	25.96	75.80	13.1	8.6	866-493-8637	Y
Hotchkis & Wiley Global Value Fund Class I	HWGIX	B-	B	B-	Up	2.88	7.94	16.78	26.81	77.81	13.1	8.6	866-493-8637	Y
Invesco Global Core Equity Fund Class A	AWSAX	B-	B-	B	Up	4.92	10.50	22.83	27.38	59.26	16.2	933.5	800-659-1005	Y
Invesco Global Core Equity Fund Class C	AWSCX	B-	B-	B	Up	4.68	10.09	21.97	24.56	53.42	15.44	933.5	800-659-1005	Y
Invesco Global Core Equity Fund Class R6	AWSSX	B-	B-	C+	Up	4.92	10.55	23.00	27.56	59.48	16.41	933.5	800-659-1005	Y
Invesco Global Core Equity Fund Class Y	AWSYX	B	B-	B	Up	4.92	10.63	23.14	28.33	61.19	16.19	933.5	800-659-1005	Y
Invesco Global Core Equity Fund ClassR	AWSRX	B-	B-	B	Up	4.79	10.37	22.53	26.43	57.24	16.19	933.5	800-659-1005	Y
Invesco Global Core Equity Fund R5 Class	AWSIX	B-	B-	C+	Up	4.92	10.62	23.13	28.62	61.80	16.41	933.5	800-659-1005	Y
Invesco Global Growth Fund Class A	AGGAX	B-	C+	B	Up	2.01	5.22	18.63	19.95	60.30	31.98	684.3	800-659-1005	Y
Invesco Global Growth Fund Class B	AGGBX	B-	C+	B	Up	1.85	4.81	17.75	17.31	54.40	29.38	684.3	800-659-1005	
Invesco Global Growth Fund Class C	AGGCX	B-	C+	B	Up	1.82	4.81	17.71	17.31	54.40	29.38	684.3	800-659-1005	Y
Invesco Global Growth Fund Class R5	GGAIX	B-	C+	B	Up	2.12	5.38	19.01	21.29	63.60	31.77	684.3	800-659-1005	Y
Invesco Global Growth Fund Class R6	AGGFX	B-	C+	B	Up	2.12	5.38	19.02	21.30	63.63	31.76	684.3	800-659-1005	Y
Invesco Global Growth Fund Class Y	AGGYX	B-	C+	B	Up	2.07	5.34	18.89	20.87	62.27	32.02	684.3	800-659-1005	Y
Invesco Global Opportunities Fund Class A	IAOPX	B	B	C+	Up	3.13	10.40	27.16	36.88	85.28	16.79	29.8	800-659-1005	Y
Invesco Global Opportunities Fund Class C	ICOPX	B	B	C+	Up	2.92	9.97	26.14	33.87	78.36	16.49	29.8	800-659-1005	Y
Invesco Global Opportunities Fund Class R	IROPX	B	B	C+	Up	3.06	10.30	26.87	35.84	82.88	16.7	29.8	800-659-1005	Y
Invesco Global Opportunities Fund Class R6	IFOPX	B	B	C+	Up	3.23	10.55	27.45	37.97	87.60	16.84	29.8	800-659-1005	Y
Invesco Global Opportunities Fund Class Y	IYOPX	B	B	C+	Up	3.23	10.62	27.55	37.97	87.59	16.84	29.8	800-659-1005	Y
Invesco Global Opportunities Fund R5 Class	IIOPX	B	B	C+	Up	3.17	10.55	27.45	37.97	87.59	16.84	29.8	800-659-1005	Y
Ivy Global Equity Income Fund Class A	IBIAX	B-	C+	B-	Up	3.95	10.15	18.65	23.21	56.50	13.97	297.4	800-777-6472	Y
Ivy Global Equity Income Fund Class I	IBIIX	B-	C+	B-	Up	4.03	10.40	19.01	24.48	59.36	13.98	297.4	800-777-6472	Y
Ivy Global Equity Income Fund Class N	IICNX	B-	B-	B-	Up	4.07	10.50	19.19	24.99	60.11	13.99	297.4	800-777-6472	Y
Ivy Global Equity Income Fund Class R	IYGEX	B-	C+	B-	Up	3.88	10.09	18.32	22.24	54.35	13.98	297.4	800-777-6472	Y
Ivy Global Equity Income Fund Class Y	IBIYX	B-	C+	B-	Up	3.98	10.21	18.77	23.57	57.41	13.97	297.4	800-777-6472	Y
Ivy Global Growth Fund Class A	IVINX	B-	C+	B	Up	4.23	10.57	24.36	23.19	49.82	45.51	439.8	800-777-6472	Y
Ivy Global Growth Fund Class B	IVIBX	B-	C+	B	Up	4.01	10.10	23.06	19.28	42.29	38.53	439.8	800-777-6472	
Ivy Global Growth Fund Class C	IVNCX	B-	C+	B	Up	4.04	10.15	23.47	20.48	44.26	38.95	439.8	800-777-6472	Y
Ivy Global Growth Fund Class I	IGIIX	B-	C+	B	Up	4.30	10.73	24.75	24.50	52.57	46.41	439.8	800-777-6472	Y
Ivy Global Growth Fund Class N	ITGRX	B-	B-	B	Up	4.35	10.82	24.96	25.11	52.47	46.64	439.8	800-777-6472	Y
Ivy Global Growth Fund Class R	IYIGX	B-	C+	B	Up	4.17	10.43	24.06	22.33	48.13	45.2	439.8	800-777-6472	Y
Ivy Global Growth Fund Class Y	IVIYX	B-	C+	B	Up	4.26	10.61	24.44	23.56	50.64	45.73	439.8	800-777-6472	Y
Janus Henderson Global Income Managed Vol Fund Cls A	JGDAX	B	C+	A		2.22	3.81	15.90	30.24	58.15	13.62	246.3	877-335-2687	Y
Janus Henderson Global Income Managed Vol Fund Cls C	JGDCX	B	C+	A		2.00	3.50	15.10	27.36	52.30	13.52	246.3	877-335-2687	Y
Janus Henderson Global Income Managed Vol Fund Cls D	JGDDX	B	B-	A		2.21	3.95	16.16	31.03	59.60	13.58	246.3	877-335-2687	Y
Janus Henderson Global Income Managed Vol Fund Cls I	JGDIX	B	B-	A		2.22	3.97	16.24	31.38	60.42	13.65	246.3	877-335-2687	Y

Category: Global Equity (con't)

		RATINGS				TOTAL RETURNS & PERFORMANCE					ASSETS		NEW INVESTORS	
Fund Name	Ticker Symbol	Overall Rating	Reward Rating	Risk Rating	Recent Up/ Downgrade	3-Month Total Return	6-Month Total Return	1-Year Total Return	3-Year Total Return	5-Year Total Return	NAV	Total Assets (MIL)	Telephone	Open to New Investors
Janus Henderson Global Income Managed Vol Fund Cls N	JGGNX	B	B-	A		2.23	3.99	16.27	31.41	60.46	13.65	246.3	877-335-2687	Y
Janus Henderson Global Income Managed Vol Fund Cls S	JGDSX	B	C+	A		2.22	3.81	15.85	30.14	58.42	13.59	246.3	877-335-2687	Y
Janus Henderson Global Income Managed Vol Fund Cls T	JDGTX	B	B-	A		2.26	3.90	16.03	30.66	59.00	13.6	246.3	877-335-2687	Y
Janus Henderson Global Research Fund Class A	JDWAX	B-	B-	B	Up	4.96	9.86	26.47	24.61	69.51	79.77	2,816	877-335-2687	Y
Janus Henderson Global Research Fund Class C	JWWCX	B-	B-	B	Up	4.78	9.50	25.66	22.03	63.47	78.14	2,816	877-335-2687	Y
Janus Henderson Global Research Fund Class D	JANWX	B-	B-	B	Up	5.03	10.02	26.86	25.53	71.40	78.77	2,816	877-335-2687	
Janus Henderson Global Research Fund Class I	JWWFX	B-	B-	B	Up	5.06	10.06	26.98	25.90	72.18	79.85	2,816	877-335-2687	Y
Janus Henderson Global Research Fund Class N	JDWNX	B-	B-	B		5.06	10.07	26.93	25.59	71.49	78.6	2,816	877-335-2687	Y
Janus Henderson Global Research Fund Class R	JDWRX	B-	B-	B	Up	4.87	9.69	26.12	23.36	66.54	79.16	2,816	877-335-2687	Y
Janus Henderson Global Research Fund Class S	JWGRX	B-	B-	B	Up	4.94	9.83	26.44	24.29	68.67	79.93	2,816	877-335-2687	Y
Janus Henderson Global Research Fund Class T	JAWWX	B-	B-	B	Up	5.01	9.97	26.75	25.26	70.82	78.72	2,816	877-335-2687	Y
Janus Henderson Global Select Fund Class A	JORAX	B-	B	C	Up	5.68	12.65	30.87	27.91	77.24	16.95	2,221	877-335-2687	Y
Janus Henderson Global Select Fund Class D	JANRX	B-	B	C	Up	5.69	12.71	31.08	28.55	78.51	16.83	2,221	877-335-2687	
Janus Henderson Global Select Fund Class I	JORFX	B-	B	C	Up	5.64	12.78	31.20	28.97	79.80	16.88	2,221	877-335-2687	Y
Janus Henderson Global Select Fund Class N	JSLNX	B-	B	C		5.76	12.77	31.15	28.62	78.61	16.85	2,221	877-335-2687	Y
Janus Henderson Global Select Fund Class R	JORRX	B-	B-	C	Up	5.48	12.36	30.34	26.32	73.63	16.78	2,221	877-335-2687	Y
Janus Henderson Global Select Fund Class S	JORIX	B-	B	C	Up	5.61	12.54	30.72	27.38	75.94	17.08	2,221	877-335-2687	Y
Janus Henderson Global Select Fund Class T	JORNX	B-	B	C	Up	5.71	12.72	31.06	28.39	78.14	16.86	2,221	877-335-2687	Y
Janus Henderson Global Value Fund Class A	JPPAX	B-	C+	B	Down	4.46	7.95	18.72	18.85	53.43	15.14	256.3	877-335-2687	Y
Janus Henderson Global Value Fund Class C	JPPCX	B-	C+	B-	Up	4.22	7.49	17.82	16.25	47.81	14.82	256.3	877-335-2687	Y
Janus Henderson Global Value Fund Class D	JNGOX	B-	C+	B	Down	4.50	8.04	18.87	19.40	54.48	15.23	256.3	877-335-2687	
Janus Henderson Global Value Fund Class I	JPPIX	B-	C+	B	Down	4.53	8.05	19.00	19.73	55.46	14.97	256.3	877-335-2687	Y
Janus Henderson Global Value Fund Class N	JPPNX	B-	C+	B	Down	4.51	8.04	19.13	20.03	56.04	14.89	256.3	877-335-2687	Y
Janus Henderson Global Value Fund Class S	JPPSX	B-	C+	B	Down	4.39	7.81	18.50	18.33	52.09	15.4	256.3	877-335-2687	Y
Janus Henderson Global Value Fund Class T	JGVAX	B-	C+	B	Down	4.43	7.97	18.83	19.24	54.08	15.2	256.3	877-335-2687	Y
Janus Henderson VIT Global Research Portfolio Inst Cls	JAWGX	B-	B-	B	Up	5.06	10.09	27.02	25.77	77.75	51.2	747.0	877-335-2687	Y
Janus Henderson VIT Global Research Portfolio Service Cls	US4710216429	B-	B-	B	Up	4.98	9.94	26.68	24.83	75.53	50.17	747.0	877-335-2687	Y
JNL/Franklin Templeton Global Fund Class A	US46644W7737	B-	C+	B-	Up	2.98	6.35	17.56	21.00	57.07	11.74	1,032		Y
JNL/Mellon Capital MSCI World Index Fund Class A	US47760W8863	B-	B-	B	Up	5.43	11.70	21.24	18.96	51.97	28.54	366.5		Y
JNL/Mellon Capital MSCI World Index Fund Class I	US47760W8780	B-	B-	B		5.57	11.85	21.40	19.13	52.18	28.59	366.5		Y
JNL/Oppenheimer Global Growth Fund Class A	US46644W2035	B+	B+	B	Up	7.27	13.72	36.15	40.47	84.25	18.57	2,577		Y
JNL/Oppenheimer Global Growth Fund Class I	US46644W3025	B+	B+	B	Up	7.39	13.89	36.39	41.29	86.12	18.89	2,577		Y
JOHCM Global Equity Fund Institutional Shares	JOGIX	B-	C+	B-	Up	6.42	14.31	25.38	17.73		15.97	518.2	866-260-9549	Y
John Hancock Funds Fundamental Global Franchise Fund Cls A	JFGAX	B	B	A	Up	3.21	8.26	24.29	44.66	84.48	12.54	481.4	800-225-5913	Y
John Hancock Funds Fundamental Global Franchise Fund Cls I	JFGIX	B	B	A	Up	3.28	8.46	24.67	46.03	87.83	12.58	481.4	800-225-5913	Y
John Hancock Funds Fundament Glob Franch Fund Cls NAV	US47804M2585	B	B	A	Up	3.31	8.49	24.80	46.50	88.53	12.58	481.4	800-225-5913	Y
John Hancock Funds Fundament Global Franchise Fund Cls R6	JFGFX	B	B	A	Up	3.37	8.56	24.77	46.15	87.98	12.59	481.4	800-225-5913	Y
John Hancock Funds Global Equity Fund Class A	JHGEX	B-	C+	B	Down	3.69	5.68	16.45	23.93		11.69	859.4	800-225-5913	Y
John Hancock Funds Global Equity Fund Class I	JGEFX	B-	C+	B-	Down	3.82	5.80	16.78	25.06		11.69	859.4	800-225-5913	Y
John Hancock Funds Global Equity Fund Class NAV	US47804M1181	B-	B-	B-	Down	3.85	5.92	16.92	25.63		11.68	859.4	800-225-5913	Y
John Hancock Funds Global Equity Fund Class R2	JGERX	B-	C+	B	Down	3.73	5.71	16.56	24.39		11.72	859.4	800-225-5913	Y
John Hancock Funds Global Equity Fund Class R4	JGETX	B-	C+	B-	Down	3.85	5.84	16.72	25.00		11.69	859.4	800-225-5913	Y
John Hancock Funds Global Equity Fund Class R6	JGEMX	B-	B-	B-	Down	3.82	5.90	16.90	25.60		11.68	859.4	800-225-5913	Y
John Hancock Global Shareholder Yield Fund Class A	JGYAX	B-	C+	B		3.18	6.69	16.49	17.03	55.51	11.75	2,491	800-225-5913	Y
John Hancock Global Shareholder Yield Fund Class C	JGYCX	B-	C+	B-		2.98	6.29	15.61	14.61	50.08	11.77	2,491	800-225-5913	Y
John Hancock Global Shareholder Yield Fund Class I	JGYIX	B-	C+	B		3.23	6.80	16.71	18.10	57.81	11.79	2,491	800-225-5913	Y
John Hancock Global Shareholder Yield Fund Class NAV	US47803U4004	B-	C+	B		3.17	6.86	16.84	18.40	58.84	11.78	2,491	800-225-5913	Y
John Hancock Global Shareholder Yield Fund Class R2	JGSRX	B-	C+	B		3.12	6.58	16.35	16.66	54.54	11.8	2,491	800-225-5913	Y
John Hancock Global Shareholder Yield Fund Class R6	JGRSX	B-	C+	B		3.17	6.77	16.85	18.42	58.62	11.77	2,491	800-225-5913	Y
John Hancock Hedged Equity & Income Fund	HEQ	B-	C+	B	Up	2.42	6.29	15.14	26.09	54.35	17.64	218.8	800-225-5913	Y
John Hancock Tax Advantage Global Shareholder Yield Fund	XHTYX	B-	C+	B	Up	2.26	5.29	14.14	14.95	37.72	8.85	99.6	800-225-5913	Y
JPMorgan Global Research Enhanced Index Fund Class I	JEITX	B-	B-	B-	Down	5.41	10.49	22.30	29.31		22.69	8,890	800-480-4111	Y

Category: Global Equity (con't)

Fund Name	Ticker Symbol	RATINGS: Overall Rating	Reward Rating	Risk Rating	Recent Up/ Downgrade	TOTAL RETURNS & PERFORMANCE: 3-Month Total Return	6-Month Total Return	1-Year Total Return	3-Year Total Return	5-Year Total Return	ASSETS: NAV	Total Assets (MIL)	NEW INVESTORS: Telephone	Open to New Investors
JPMorgan Global Research Enhanced Index Fund Class R6	JEIYX	B-	B-	B-		5.43	10.51	22.32	29.33		22.45	8,890	800-480-4111	Y
JPMorgan Global Unconstrained Equity Fund Class A	JFUAX	B-	B-	B-	Up	8.48	12.40	23.21	29.96	71.92	17.02	3.8	800-480-4111	Y
JPMorgan Global Unconstrained Equity Fund Class C	JFECX	B-	B-	C+	Up	8.43	12.19	22.68	28.04	67.74	16.83	3.8	800-480-4111	Y
JPMorgan Global Unconstrained Equity Fund Class I	JMESX	B-	B-	B-	Up	5.58	9.44	20.18	27.58	69.75	17.15	3.8	800-480-4111	Y
JPMorgan Global Unconstrained Equity Fund Class R5	JFETX	B-	B	B-	Up	8.64	12.68	23.78	31.73	75.81	17.1	3.8	800-480-4111	Y
JPMorgan Global Unconstrained Equity Fund Class R6	JFEUX	B-	B	B-	Up	8.63	12.67	23.87	31.86	76.23	17.08	3.8	800-480-4111	Y
Kinetics Global Fund Class Advisor Class A	KGLAX	B	B+	C	Up	21.68	38.30	50.29	47.29	67.99	7.15	13.2	800-930-3828	Y
Kinetics Global Fund Class Advisor Class C	KGLCX	B-	B	C	Up	21.48	36.52	48.02	43.55	61.88	6.76	13.2	800-930-3828	Y
Kinetics Global No Load Class	WWWEX	B	B+	C	Up	21.73	36.89	49.19	47.07	68.05	7.15	13.2	800-930-3828	Y
Lazard Global Equity Select Portfolio Institutional Shares	GESIX	B	B-	B+	Up	6.47	12.30	28.51	31.38		13.04	54.2	800-823-6300	Y
Lazard Global Equity Select Portfolio Open Shares	GESOX	B	B-	B+	Up	6.40	12.06	28.01	30.20		13.04	54.2	800-823-6300	Y
Lazard Global Strategic Equity Portfolio Inst Shares	LSTIX	B-	C+	B	Up	6.24	10.99	24.19	20.97		2.31	5.7	800-823-6300	Y
Lazard Global Strategic Equity Portfolio Open Shares	LSTOX	B-	C+	B	Up	6.12	10.78	23.71	19.77		2.3	5.7	800-823-6300	Y
Lazard Global Total Return and Income Fund Inc	LGI	B-	B	C	Up	7.07	13.61	33.26	32.81	56.60	19.81	187.5		Y
Lazard Managed Equity Volatility Portfolio Inst Shares	MEVIX	B-	C+	B+	Up	5.75	9.20	20.57			11.57	4.3	800-823-6300	Y
Lazard Managed Equity Volatility Portfolio Open Shares	MEVOX	B-	C+	B+	Up	5.62	8.98	20.11			11.56	4.3	800-823-6300	Y
Leuthold Global Industries Fund Institutional Class	LGIIX	B-	B-	C+	Up	6.09	13.51	25.02	25.12	83.09	17.85	11.8	800-273-6886	Y
Leuthold Global Industries Fund Retail Class	LGINX	B-	B-	C+	Up	6.02	13.34	24.66	24.20	80.78	17.75	11.8	800-273-6886	Y
LMCG Global MultiCap Fund Institutional Shares	GMCIX	B-	B	B-	Down	5.54	11.26	22.47	32.09		12.98	2.3		Y
LMCG Global MultiCap Fund Investor Shares	GMCRX	B-	B	C+	Down	5.41	11.06	22.27	31.18		13	2.3		Y
Longleaf Partners Global Fund	LLGLX	B-	B	C	Up	2.64	5.73	26.33	30.75	58.39	14.94	231.3	800-445-9469	Y
LSV Global Managed Volatility Fund Institutional Class	LSVFX	B-	B-	B-		6.36	9.97	19.03	25.30		11.16	8.2		Y
LSV Global Managed Volatility Fund Investor Class	LVAFX	B-	C+	B		6.17	9.76	18.66	24.32		11.2	8.2		Y
LSV Global Value Fund Institutional Class	LSVGX	B-	B-	C+	Up	5.95	11.97	21.85	28.00		11.77	4.6		Y
Mainstay Epoch Global Choice Fund Class A	EPAPX	B-	B-	B	Up	4.52	10.18	27.86	22.22	62.45	21	206.9	800-624-6782	Y
Mainstay Epoch Global Choice Fund Class C	EPAKX	B-	B-	B	Up	4.25	9.60	26.58	18.64	54.56	19.83	206.9	800-624-6782	Y
Mainstay Epoch Global Choice Fund Class I	EPACX	B-	B-	B	Up	4.54	10.29	28.17	23.16	64.45	21.64	206.9	800-624-6782	Y
Mainstay Epoch Global Choice Fund Investor Class	EPAIX	B-	B-	B	Up	4.43	10.01	27.54	21.31	60.38	20.9	206.9	800-624-6782	Y
MainStay Epoch Global Equity Yield Fund Class A	EPSPX	B-	C+	B		3.22	6.80	16.52	17.69	57.02	20.07	3,967	800-624-6782	Y
MainStay Epoch Global Equity Yield Fund Class C	EPSKX	B-	C+	B-		3.06	6.42	15.68	15.13	51.22	19.94	3,967	800-624-6782	Y
Mainstay Epoch Global Equity Yield Fund Class I	EPSYX	B-	C+	B		3.34	6.95	16.84	18.61	59.09	20.04	3,967	800-624-6782	Y
MainStay Epoch Global Equity Yield Fund Class R2	EPSZX	B-	C+	B		3.25	6.75	16.46	17.42	56.59	20.08	3,967	800-624-6782	Y
MainStay Epoch Global Equity Yield Fund Class R3	EPSHX	B-	C+	B		3.19	6.58	16.15	16.63	54.87	20.06	3,967	800-624-6782	Y
MainStay Epoch Global Equity Yield Fund Class R6	EPSRX	B-	C+	B		3.33	7.04	17.02	19.07	59.89	20.04	3,967	800-624-6782	Y
MainStay Epoch Global Equity Yield Fund Investor Class	EPSIX	B-	C+	B		3.29	6.85	16.66	17.75	56.97	20.04	3,967	800-624-6782	Y
Marsico Global Fund	MGLBX	B+	A-	B	Up	4.36	14.67	40.23	34.43	100.70	14.45	48.5	888-860-8686	Y
MassMutual Premier Global Fund Administrative Class	MGFLX	B	B+	C+	Up	7.12	13.61	35.98	39.60	83.21	15.63	333.8		Y
MassMutual Premier Global Fund Class A	MGFAX	B	B+	C+	Up	7.04	13.46	35.74	38.50	80.83	15.48	333.8		Y
MassMutual Premier Global Fund Class I	MGFZX	B	B+	C+	Up	7.23	13.80	36.40	40.83	85.81	15.62	333.8		Y
MassMutual Premier Global Fund Class R3	MGFNX	B	B+	C+	Up	7.00	13.36	35.50	37.99	79.60	15.42	333.8		Y
MassMutual Premier Global Fund Class R4	MGFRX	B	B+	C+	Up	7.03	13.50	35.83	38.91	82.08	15.3	333.8		Y
MassMutual Premier Global Fund Class R5	MGFSX	B+	B+	B	Up	7.12	13.67	36.34	40.35	85.14	15.63	333.8		Y
MassMutual Premier Global Fund Service Class	MGFYX	B+	B+	B	Up	7.13	13.67	36.14	40.01	84.10	15.5	333.8		Y
Meeder Global Allocation Fund Adviser Class	GBPAX	B-	C+	B-	Up	5.23	11.96	22.84	17.15	57.55	11.54	74.4		Y
Meeder Global Allocation Fund Institutional Class	GBPIX	B-	C+	B-	Up	5.44	12.17	23.06	17.36	57.83	11.55	74.4		Y
MFS® Global Equity Fund Class A	MWEFX	B	B-	B	Up	4.33	7.11	23.62	29.19	73.98	43.57	3,386	877-960-6077	Y
MFS® Global Equity Fund Class B	MWEBX	B	B-	B	Up	4.13	6.69	22.67	26.32	67.54	40.3	3,386	877-960-6077	Y
MFS® Global Equity Fund Class C	MWECX	B	B-	B	Up	4.13	6.69	22.68	26.32	67.56	38.55	3,386	877-960-6077	Y
MFS® Global Equity Fund Class I	MWEIX	B	B-	B+	Up	4.39	7.22	23.90	30.12	76.15	44.66	3,386	877-960-6077	Y
MFS® Global Equity Fund Class R1	MWEGX	B	B-	B	Up	4.13	6.69	22.70	26.31	67.52	39.41	3,386	877-960-6077	Y
MFS® Global Equity Fund Class R2	MEQRX	B	B-	B	Up	4.25	6.94	23.28	28.21	71.77	42.36	3,386	877-960-6077	Y
MFS® Global Equity Fund Class R3	MWEHX	B	B-	B	Up	4.32	7.11	23.62	29.20	73.99	43.28	3,386	877-960-6077	Y

Category: Global Equity (con't)

Fund Name	Ticker Symbol	RATINGS: Overall Rating	Reward Rating	Risk Rating	Recent Up/ Downgrade	TOTAL RETURNS & PERFORMANCE: 3-Month Total Return	6-Month Total Return	1-Year Total Return	3-Year Total Return	5-Year Total Return	ASSETS: NAV	Total Assets (MIL)	NEW INVESTORS: Telephone	Open to New Investors
MFS® Global Equity Fund Class R4	MWELX	B	B-	B+	Up	4.37	7.21	23.91	30.15	76.07	43.67	3,386	877-960-6077	Y
MFS® Global Equity Fund Class R6	MWEMX	B	B-	B+	Up	4.40	7.28	24.03	30.49	76.85	44.67	3,386	877-960-6077	Y
MFS® Global Growth Fund Class A	MWOFX	B	B	B	Up	6.75	11.60	31.38	34.35	72.18	40.71	303.8	877-960-6077	Y
MFS® Global Growth Fund Class B	MWOBX	B	B	B	Up	6.54	11.14	30.38	31.33	65.77	35.64	303.8	877-960-6077	Y
MFS® Global Growth Fund Class C	MWOCX	B	B	B	Up	6.53	11.15	30.39	31.34	65.78	35.21	303.8	877-960-6077	Y
MFS® Global Growth Fund Class I	MWOIX	B	B	B	Up	6.79	11.70	31.68	35.30	74.23	41.66	303.8	877-960-6077	Y
MFS® Global Growth Fund Class R1	MWOGX	B	B	B	Up	6.55	11.15	30.38	31.29	65.78	35.13	303.8	877-960-6077	Y
MFS® Global Growth Fund Class R2	MGWRX	B	B	B	Up	6.69	11.46	31.03	33.32	69.98	39.48	303.8	877-960-6077	Y
MFS® Global Growth Fund Class R3	MWOHX	B	B	B	Up	6.73	11.55	31.35	34.28	72.10	40.49	303.8	877-960-6077	Y
MFS® Global Growth Fund Class R4	MWOJX	B	B	B	Up	6.81	11.71	31.67	35.30	74.25	40.74	303.8	877-960-6077	Y
MFS® Global Growth Fund Class R6	MWOKX	B	B	B	Up	6.83	11.74	31.77	35.65	74.76	41.64	303.8	877-960-6077	Y
MFS® Low Volatility Global Equity Fund Class A	MVGAX	B	B-	B+		4.79	6.90	18.14	25.60		13.33	187.1	877-960-6077	Y
MFS® Low Volatility Global Equity Fund Class B	MVGBX	B	C+	B+		4.60	6.51	17.26	22.62		13.26	187.1	877-960-6077	Y
MFS® Low Volatility Global Equity Fund Class C	MVGCX	B	C+	B+		4.59	6.49	17.26	22.58		13.24	187.1	877-960-6077	Y
MFS® Low Volatility Global Equity Fund Class I	MVGIX	B	B-	B+		4.85	7.02	18.48	26.37		13.33	187.1	877-960-6077	Y
MFS® Low Volatility Global Equity Fund Class R1	MVGJX	B	C+	B+		4.65	6.55	17.26	22.67		13.32	187.1	877-960-6077	Y
MFS® Low Volatility Global Equity Fund Class R2	MVGKX	B	C+	B+		4.70	6.82	17.87	24.50		13.34	187.1	877-960-6077	Y
MFS® Low Volatility Global Equity Fund Class R3	MVGLX	B	C+	B+		4.73	6.84	18.06	25.38		13.34	187.1	877-960-6077	Y
MFS® Low Volatility Global Equity Fund Class R4	MVGMX	B	B-	B+		4.85	7.02	18.48	26.33		13.33	187.1	877-960-6077	Y
MFS® Low Volatility Global Equity Fund Class R6	MVGNX	B	B-	B+		4.80	6.98	18.46	26.52		13.31	187.1	877-960-6077	Y
MH Elite Select Portfolio of Funds Fund	MHESX	B-	C+	B-	Up	4.50	9.23	21.70	18.52	31.40	6.27	5.8		Y
Morgan Stanley Inst Fund, Inc. Global Advantage Port Cls A	MIGPX	B+	B+	B	Up	8.70	14.98	41.02	44.40	91.65	15.21	11.9	855-332-5306	Y
Morgan Stanley Inst Fund, Inc. Global Advantage Port Cls C	MSPTX	B	B	B	Up	8.48	14.49	40.02	41.27	84.96	14.6	11.9	855-332-5306	Y
Morgan Stanley Inst Fund, Inc. Global Advantage Port Cls I	MIGIX	B+	B+	B+	Up	8.79	15.14	41.55	46.06	95.09	15.43	11.9	855-332-5306	Y
Morgan Stanley Inst Fund, Inc. Global Advantage Port Cls L	MIGLX	B	B+	B	Up	8.53	14.57	40.33	42.23	86.96	14.75	11.9	855-332-5306	
Morgan Stanley Inst Fund, Inc. Global Franchise Port Cls A	MSFBX	B	B	A	Down	7.86	7.96	25.58	39.67	76.55	24.21	1,034	855-332-5306	
Morgan Stanley Inst Fund, Inc. Global Franchise Port Cls C	MSGFX	B	B-	A		7.62	7.53	24.62	36.51	70.14	23.82	1,034	855-332-5306	Y
Morgan Stanley Inst Fund, Inc. Global Franchise Port Cls I	MSFAX	B+	B	A	Up	7.89	8.08	25.84	40.68	78.85	24.72	1,034	855-332-5306	
Morgan Stanley Inst Fund, Inc. Global Franch Port Cls IS	MGISX	B+	B	A	Up	7.92	8.15	25.99	40.93	79.17	24.72	1,034	855-332-5306	Y
Morgan Stanley Inst Fund, Inc. Global Franchise Port Cls L	MSFLX	B	B-	A		7.69	7.69	24.97	37.67	72.26	24.18	1,034	855-332-5306	
Morgan Stanley Inst Fund, Inc. Global Opp Portfolio Cls A	MGGPX	A	A+	A-	Up	6.56	17.79	49.02	76.04	173.72	22.28	1,720	855-332-5306	Y
Morgan Stanley Inst Fund, Inc. Global Opp Portfolio Cls C	MSOPX	A	A	B+	Up	6.35	17.39	47.91	72.51	164.76	21.64	1,720	855-332-5306	Y
Morgan Stanley Inst Fund, Inc. Global Opp Portfolio Cls I	MGGIX	A	A+	A-	Up	6.61	17.97	49.44	77.92	178.54	22.94	1,720	855-332-5306	Y
Morgan Stanley Inst Fund, Inc. Global Opp Portfolio Cls IS	MGTSX	A	A+	A-	Up	6.64	18.04	49.54	78.24	179.22	23	1,720	855-332-5306	Y
Morgan Stanley Inst Fund, Inc. Global Opp Portfolio Cls L	MGGLX	A	A+	B+	Up	6.55	17.73	48.91	75.72	172.83	22.01	1,720	855-332-5306	
Morgan Stanley Inst Fund, Inc. Global Quality Port Cls A	MGQAX	B	B-	A		5.77	6.29	22.44	32.55		12.44	10.6	855-332-5306	Y
Morgan Stanley Inst Fund, Inc. Global Quality Port Cls C	MSGQX	B	B-	A		5.52	5.88	21.45	29.40		12.26	10.6	855-332-5306	Y
Morgan Stanley Inst Fund, Inc. Global Quality Port Cls I	MGQIX	B	B-	A		5.81	6.41	22.85	33.81		12.47	10.6	855-332-5306	Y
Morgan Stanley Inst Fund, Inc. Global Quality Port Cls IS	MGQSX	B	B-	A		5.86	6.46	22.91	33.98		12.47	10.6	855-332-5306	Y
Morgan Stanley Inst Fund, Inc. Global Quality Port Cls L	MGQLX	B	B-	A		5.59	6.02	21.79	30.54		12.41	10.6	855-332-5306	
Motley Fool Independence Fund Institutional Shares	FOIIX	B	B	B	Up	6.85	10.27	30.60	31.66	78.75	22.76	429.2		Y
Motley Fool Independence Fund Investor Shares	FOOLX	B	B-	B	Up	6.82	10.19	30.37	31.02	77.77	22.72	429.2		Y
Neuberger Berman Global Equity Fund Class A	NGQAX	B	B-	B	Up	4.13	10.29	25.12	24.85	60.03	7.98	4.9	212-476-9000	Y
Neuberger Berman Global Equity Fund Class C	NGQCX	B-	B-	B	Up	3.96	9.82	24.18	22.12	54.30	7.6	4.9	212-476-9000	Y
Neuberger Berman Global Equity Fund Institutional Class	NGQIX	B	B-	B	Up	4.05	10.43	25.47	25.95	62.79	8.06	4.9	212-476-9000	Y
Northern Global Sustainability Index Fund	NSRIX	B-	B-	B-	Down	4.86	9.99	21.20	28.11	73.97	13.96	371.0	800-595-9111	Y
Nuveen NWQ Global All-Cap Fund Class A	NGEAX	B	B-	B	Up	3.85	7.83	22.40	25.86		24.62	1.7	312-917-8146	Y
Nuveen NWQ Global All-Cap Fund Class C	NGECX	B-	C+	B	Up	3.66	7.43	21.48	23.02		24.51	1.7	312-917-8146	Y
Nuveen NWQ Global All-Cap Fund Class I	NGEIX	B	B-	B	Up	3.88	7.94	22.69	26.78		24.61	1.7	312-917-8146	
Nuveen NWQ Global Equity Income Fund Class A	NQGAX	B-	C+	B-	Up	2.88	7.39	18.43	21.41	69.79	28.99	320.9	312-917-8146	Y
Nuveen NWQ Global Equity Income Fund Class I	NQGIX	B-	C+	B-	Up	2.95	7.52	18.72	22.32	71.96	29	320.9	312-917-8146	Y
Nuveen NWQ Global Equity Income Fund Class R3	NQGRX	B-	C+	B-	Up	2.83	7.23	18.17	20.55	67.80	28.94	320.9	312-917-8146	Y

Category: Global Equity (con't)

Fund Name	Ticker Symbol	RATINGS: Overall Rating	Reward Rating	Risk Rating	Recent Up/ Downgrade	TOTAL RETURNS & PERFORMANCE: 3-Month Total Return	6-Month Total Return	1-Year Total Return	3-Year Total Return	5-Year Total Return	ASSETS: NAV	Total Assets (MIL)	NEW INVESTORS: Telephone	Open to New Investors
Nuveen Santa Barbara Global Dividend Growth Fund Class A	NUGAX	B-	B-	B-	Down	4.37	8.27	19.50	25.37	60.67	27.27	20.4	312-917-8146	Y
Nuveen Santa Barbara Global Dividend Growth Fund Class C	NUGCX	B-	C+	B-	Down	4.23	7.90	18.66	22.62	54.83	27.21	20.4	312-917-8146	Y
Nuveen Santa Barbara Global Dividend Growth Fund Class I	NUGIX	B-	B-	B-	Down	4.47	8.45	19.84	26.32	62.68	27.27	20.4	312-917-8146	Y
Nuveen Santa Barbara Global Dividend Growth Fund Class R3	NUGRX	B-	B-	B-	Down	4.31	8.16	19.25	24.46	58.66	27.21	20.4	312-917-8146	Y
Oakmark Global Fund Class Advisor	OAYGX	B-	B	C	Up	3.95	13.28	27.24	26.25	79.36	33.13	2,732	641-219-558	Y
Oakmark Global Fund Class Institutional	OANGX	B-	B	C	Up	3.96	13.32	27.33	26.34	79.50	33.14	2,732	641-219-558	Y
Oakmark Global Fund Investor Class	OAKGX	B-	B	C	Up	3.90	13.23	27.08	26.04	79.07	33.13	2,732	641-219-558	
Oakmark Global Fund Service Class	OARGX	B-	B	C	Up	3.85	13.09	26.78	24.81	76.14	32.24	2,732	641-219-558	Y
Oakmark Global Select Fund Class Advisor	OAYWX	B	B	B-	Up	2.98	7.88	21.36	34.96	88.57	19.3	2,866	641-219-558	Y
Oakmark Global Select Fund Class Institutional	OANWX	B	B	B-	Up	3.02	7.92	21.40	35.01	88.64	19.3	2,866	641-219-558	Y
Oakmark Global Select Fund Investor Class	OAKWX	B	B	B-	Up	2.98	7.83	21.18	34.75	88.29	19.3	2,866	641-219-558	Y
Old Westbury Large Cap Strategies Fund	OWLSX	B	C+	B	Up	4.84	8.18	19.39	22.63	68.24	14.46	17,483	212-708-9100	Y
Oppenheimer Global Fund Class A	OPPAX	B+	B+	B	Up	7.12	13.61	36.24	40.82	85.20	95.98	11,177	800-225-5677	Y
Oppenheimer Global Fund Class B	OGLBX	B	B+	B	Up	6.90	13.17	35.20	37.60	78.02	87.17	11,177	800-225-5677	
Oppenheimer Global Fund Class C	OGLCX	B	B+	B	Up	6.91	13.18	35.19	37.61	78.38	88.5	11,177	800-225-5677	Y
Oppenheimer Global Fund Class Fund Class Y	OGLYX	B+	B+	B	Up	7.18	13.76	36.56	41.81	87.47	96.05	11,177	800-225-5677	Y
Oppenheimer Global Fund Class I	OGLIX	B+	A-	B	Up	7.21	13.84	36.78	42.59	89.23	96.02	11,177	800-225-5677	Y
Oppenheimer Global Fund Class R	OGLNX	B+	B+	B	Up	7.04	13.47	35.88	39.70	82.79	95.56	11,177	800-225-5677	Y
Oppenheimer Global Value Fund Class A	GLVAX	B	B-	B	Up	0.87	7.22	25.08	22.10	69.61	50.36	561.6	800-225-5677	Y
Oppenheimer Global Value Fund Class C	GLVCX	B-	B-	B	Up	0.69	6.83	24.15	19.35	63.25	47.31	561.6	800-225-5677	Y
Oppenheimer Global Value Fund Class I	GLVIX	B	B	B	Up	0.98	7.46	25.61	23.72	73.34	51.71	561.6	800-225-5677	Y
Oppenheimer Global Value Fund Class R	GLVNX	B	B-	B	Up	0.81	7.09	24.80	21.18	67.38	49.26	561.6	800-225-5677	Y
Oppenheimer Global Value Fund Class Y	GLVYX	B	B	B	Up	0.93	7.35	25.41	23.01	71.79	51.26	561.6	800-225-5677	Y
Oppenheimer Portfolio Series Equity Investor Fund Class A	OAAIX	B	B-	B	Up	4.61	9.66	24.90	28.00	70.38	18.43	918.4	800-225-5677	Y
Oppenheimer Portfolio Series Equity Investor Fund Class B	OBAIX	B	B-	B	Up	4.42	9.26	23.90	25.16	64.04	18.23	918.4	800-225-5677	
Oppenheimer Portfolio Series Equity Investor Fund Class C	OCAIX	B	B-	B	Up	4.47	9.27	24.02	25.24	64.15	17.98	918.4	800-225-5677	Y
Oppenheimer Portfolio Series Equity Investor Fund Class R	ONAIX	B	B-	B	Up	4.58	9.57	24.58	27.12	68.24	18.42	918.4	800-225-5677	Y
Oppenheimer Portfolio Series Equity Investor Fund Class Y	OYAIX	B	B-	B	Up	4.72	9.80	25.21	29.02	72.58	18.52	918.4	800-225-5677	Y
Pax Ellevate Global Women's Index Fund Individual Inv Cls	PXWEX	B-	B-	B-	Down	6.02	11.17	24.86	29.73	74.97	25.02	173.0	800-767-1729	Y
Pax Ellevate Global Women's Index Fund Institutional Class	PXWIX	B-	B-	B-	Down	6.09	11.26	25.14	30.67	77.11	25.13	173.0	800-767-1729	Y
PIMCO Global StocksPLUS and Income Fund	PGP	B	B+	B-	Up	2.69	8.31	30.07	49.89	97.45	11.2	121.1	866-746-2602	Y
Pioneer Global Equity Fund Class A	GLOSX	B-	B-	C+	Up	5.85	13.74	28.44	30.23	84.12	16.3	317.1	617-742-7825	Y
Pioneer Global Equity Fund Class K	PGEKX	B-	B	C+	Down	5.97	13.93	29.00	32.03	86.66	16.27	317.1	617-742-7825	Y
Pioneer Global Equity Fund Class R	PRGEX	B-	B-	C+	Up	5.76	13.48	27.98	29.26	81.83	16.22	317.1	617-742-7825	Y
Pioneer Global Equity Fund Class Y	PGSYX	B-	B	C+	Down	5.94	13.95	29.01	31.98	88.48	16.32	317.1	617-742-7825	Y
Polen Global Growth Fund Institutional Class	PGIIX	B	C+	B+	Up	6.11	10.91	31.51	42.49		14.23	23.6	561-241-2425	Y
Polen Global Growth Fund Investor Class	PGIRX	B	C+	B+	Up	6.08	10.73	31.19	41.33		14.13	23.6	561-241-2425	Y
Portfolio 21 Global Equity Fund Class Institutional	PORIX	B	B	B+	Up	5.60	11.85	28.22	35.28	68.69	42.77	502.3	866-209-1962	Y
Portfolio 21 Global Equity Fund Class R	PORTX	B	B	B+	Up	5.53	11.68	27.86	34.19	66.37	42.98	502.3	866-209-1962	Y
Principal Global Opportunities Fund Class A	PGLAX	B-	C+	B	Up	4.76	9.42	21.60	21.26	57.76	12.52	947.6	800-222-5852	Y
Principal Global Opportunities Fund Class C	PGOCX	B-	C+	B	Up	4.47	8.99	20.69	18.44	51.90	12.43	947.6	800-222-5852	Y
Principal Global Opportunities Fund Institutional Class	PGOIX	B	C+	B	Up	4.81	9.77	22.31	23.55	62.47	12.6	947.6	800-222-5852	Y
Prudential Jennison Global Opportunities Fund Class A	PRJAX	A-	A	B	Up	5.37	16.77	42.97	52.23	108.88	21.16	584.4	800-225-1852	Y
Prudential Jennison Global Opportunities Fund Class C	PRJCX	A-	A	B	Up	5.14	16.32	41.93	48.82	101.19	20.24	584.4	800-225-1852	Y
Prudential Jennison Global Opportunities Fund Class Q	PRJQX	A-	A	B	Up	5.49	16.95	43.46	53.82	112.17	21.52	584.4	800-225-1852	Y
Prudential Jennison Global Opportunities Fund Class Z	PRJZX	A-	A	B	Up	5.45	16.94	43.35	53.28	111.42	21.46	584.4	800-225-1852	Y
Putnam Global Equity Fund Class A	PEQUX	B-	B-	B	Up	5.15	12.57	28.08	25.93	72.22	15.75	846.0	617-292-1000	Y
Putnam Global Equity Fund Class B	PEQBX	B-	B-	B	Up	4.99	12.19	27.19	23.15	65.83	14.08	846.0	617-292-1000	Y
Putnam Global Equity Fund Class C	PUGCX	B-	B-	B	Up	4.95	12.18	27.20	23.15	65.89	14.82	846.0	617-292-1000	Y
Putnam Global Equity Fund Class M	PEQMX	B-	B-	B	Up	5.01	12.29	27.49	24.00	67.97	15.07	846.0	617-292-1000	Y
Putnam Global Equity Fund Class R	PGLRX	B-	B-	B	Up	5.11	12.42	27.83	24.98	70.13	15.65	846.0	617-292-1000	Y
Putnam Global Equity Fund Class R6	PGLEX	B-	B-	B	Up	5.22	12.81	28.64	27.39	76.05	16.3	846.0	617-292-1000	Y

Category: Global Equity (con't)

		RATINGS				TOTAL RETURNS & PERFORMANCE					ASSETS		NEW INVESTORS	
Fund Name	Ticker Symbol	Overall Rating	Reward Rating	Risk Rating	Recent Up/ Downgrade	3-Month Total Return	6-Month Total Return	1-Year Total Return	3-Year Total Return	5-Year Total Return	NAV	Total Assets (MIL)	Telephone	Open to New Investors
Putnam Global Equity Fund Class Y	PEQYX	B-	B-	B	Up	5.22	12.69	28.45	26.81	74.44	16.26	846.0	617-292-1000	Y
Putnam Global Sector Fund Class A	PPGAX	B-	B-	B-	Down	2.17	7.88	21.22	26.62	72.45	11.98	26.4	617-292-1000	Y
Putnam Global Sector Fund Class B	PPGBX	B-	B-	B-	Up	2.56	8.04	20.98	24.54	67.05	11.75	26.4	617-292-1000	Y
Putnam Global Sector Fund Class C	PPGCX	B	B-	B	Up	2.48	7.97	20.93	24.51	66.94	11.72	26.4	617-292-1000	Y
Putnam Global Sector Fund Class M	PPGMX	B-	B-	B-	Up	2.34	7.96	21.06	25.22	68.72	12	26.4	617-292-1000	Y
Putnam Global Sector Fund Class R	PPGSX	B-	B-	B-	Up	2.50	8.14	21.40	26.21	70.94	12.01	26.4	617-292-1000	Y
Putnam Global Sector Fund Class Y	PPGYX	B-	B-	B-	Down	2.08	7.85	21.47	27.52	74.53	12.03	26.4	617-292-1000	Y
QS Global Dividend Fund Class A	LGDAX	B	C+	A		4.86	7.01	14.55	27.23		13.01	356.0	877-721-1926	Y
QS Global Dividend Fund Class A2	LMQSX	B	C+	A		4.89	6.87	14.32	26.95		13.02	356.0	877-721-1926	Y
QS Global Dividend Fund Class C	LGDCX	B	C+	A-		4.73	6.63	13.76	24.52		13.01	356.0	877-721-1926	Y
QS Global Dividend Fund Class FI	LDIGX	B	C+	A-		4.92	6.90	14.37	26.85		13.02	356.0	877-721-1926	Y
QS Global Dividend Fund Class I	LTTMX	B	C+	A+		4.93	7.11	14.84	28.16		12.94	356.0	877-721-1926	Y
QS Global Dividend Fund Class IS	LDIFX	B	B-	A+		5.03	7.22	14.96	28.57		12.97	356.0	877-721-1926	Y
QS Global Equity Fund Class 1	LMPEX	B	B	B	Up	6.45	13.56	23.76	37.27	97.31	17.36	170.8	877-721-1926	
QS Global Equity Fund Class A	CFIPX	B	B	B	Up	6.46	13.54	23.69	37.16	97.21	17.44	170.8	877-721-1926	Y
QS Global Equity Fund Class C	SILLX	B	B	B-	Up	6.24	13.02	22.74	34.00	89.90	17.7	170.8	877-721-1926	Y
QS Global Equity Fund Class I	SMYIX	B	B	B	Up	6.58	13.68	24.12	38.67	100.67	17.38	170.8	877-721-1926	Y
RBC Global Opportunities Fund Class I	RGOIX	B-	C+	B	Up	7.26	15.47	34.26	43.52		13.51	10.0	800-422-2766	Y
RBC Global Opportunities Fund Class R6	RGORX	B-	C+	B	Up	7.21	15.45	34.32	43.63		13.58	10.0	800-422-2766	Y
Russell Investments Global Equity Fund Class A	RGEAX	B-	B	B-	Down	5.56	10.25	22.84	29.85	76.68	10.75	2,200	800-426-7969	Y
Russell Investments Global Equity Fund Class C	RGECX	B-	B-	C+	Down	5.29	9.83	21.91	26.94	70.05	10.62	2,200	800-426-7969	Y
Russell Investments Global Equity Fund Class E	RGEEX	B-	B-	B-	Up	5.57	10.35	22.93	29.78	76.57	10.83	2,200	800-426-7969	Y
Russell Investments Global Equity Fund Class M	RGDTX	B-	B	B-	Up	5.62	10.58	23.27	30.94	79.03	10.78	2,200	800-426-7969	Y
Russell Investments Global Equity Fund Class S	RGESX	B-	B	B-	Up	5.63	10.49	23.18	30.84	78.89	10.8	2,200	800-426-7969	Y
Russell Investments Global Equity Fund Class Y	RLGYX	B-	B	B-	Down	5.73	10.59	23.51	31.59	80.73	10.8	2,200	800-426-7969	Y
Sands Capital Global Growth Fund Institutional Shares	SCMGX	B	B+	B	Up	4.90	12.21	38.70	39.32	88.86	24.7	1,287		Y
Sands Capital Global Growth Fund Investor Shares	SCGVX	B	B+	B	Up	4.86	12.12	38.37	38.29	86.48	24.41	1,287		Y
SEI Inst Managed Trust Global Managed Vol Fund Cls F	SVTAX	B	B-	A+		4.63	6.68	17.17	31.88	81.07	11.69	1,508	800-342-5734	Y
SEI Inst Managed Trust Global Managed Vol Fund Cls I	SGMIX	B	B-	A+		4.58	6.58	16.86	30.91	78.81	11.46	1,508	800-342-5734	Y
SEI Inst Managed Trust Global Managed Vol Fund Cls Y	SGLYX	B	B-	B+		2.96	5.07	15.39	30.68	79.43	11.71	1,508	800-342-5734	Y
Sit Global Dividend Growth Fund Class I	GDGIX	B-	C+	B-	Down	6.14	10.79	19.75	23.58	59.57	15.92	33.3	800-332-5580	Y
Sit Global Dividend Growth Fund Class S	GDGSX	B-	C+	B-	Down	6.08	10.66	19.54	22.72	57.69	15.92	33.3	800-332-5580	Y
Steward Global Equity Income Fund Class A	SGIDX	B	B	B		6.38	10.80	21.93	35.09	80.56	33.05	270.5	800-262-6631	Y
Steward Global Equity Income Fund Class Institutional	SGISX	B	B	B		6.46	10.97	22.30	36.41	83.57	33.12	270.5	800-262-6631	Y
Summit Global Investments Global Low Volatility Fund Cls I	DWUGX	B-	C+	B	Up	4.82	9.97	23.56	20.11	86.14		22.5		Y
T. Rowe Price Global Growth Stock Fund	RPGEX	B	B	B	Up	6.37	12.46	34.25	38.78	84.03	25.5	473.1	410-345-2000	Y
T. Rowe Price Global Growth Stock Fund Advisor Class	PAGLX	B	B	B	Up	6.28	12.36	34.06	38.39	83.03	25.35	473.1	410-345-2000	Y
T. Rowe Price Global Growth Stock Fund I Class	RGGIX	B	B	B	Up	6.35	12.58	34.45	38.98	84.30	25.51	473.1	410-345-2000	Y
T. Rowe Price Global Stock Fund	PRGSX	B+	B+	B+	Down	7.60	11.72	33.08	50.26	116.52	38.07	906.8	410-345-2000	Y
T. Rowe Price Global Stock Fund Advisor Class	PAGSX	B+	B+	B+	Up	7.51	11.53	32.65	49.00	113.63	37.75	906.8	410-345-2000	Y
T. Rowe Price Global Stock Fund I Class	TRGLX	B+	A-	B+	Down	7.65	11.80	33.22	50.42	116.74	38.08	906.8	410-345-2000	Y
T. Rowe Price Inst Global Focused Growth Equity Fund	TRGSX	B+	B+	B+	Down	7.69	11.79	33.26	50.59	116.32	11.93	45.2	410-345-2000	Y
T. Rowe Price Institutional Global Growth Equity Fund	RPIGX	B	B+	B	Up	6.49	12.69	34.61	39.91	86.05	27.62	443.5	410-345-2000	Y
T. Rowe Price Institutional Global Value Equity Fund	PRIGX	B-	B-	B-	Down	4.19	8.37	19.58	28.42	85.07	13.34	11.6	410-345-2000	Y
TD Global Low Volatility Equity Fund Advisor Class	TDGVX	B	C+	A-	Up	3.97	5.37	13.19	26.01		12.33	39.6		Y
TD Global Low Volatility Equity Fund Institutional Class	TDLVX	B-	B-	B	Down	4.09	5.50	13.52	26.50		12.33	39.6		Y
Templeton Growth Fund, Inc. Class A	TEPLX	B-	C+	B-	Up	3.01	6.45	17.79	19.72	55.09	27.26	14,089	650-312-2000	Y
Templeton World Fund Class Advisor	TWDAX	B-	C+	B-	Up	2.97	5.45	13.17	19.83	53.76	16.88	4,638	650-312-2000	Y
Templeton World Fund Class R6	FTWRX	B-	C+	B-	Up	3.01	5.49	13.30	20.16	54.25	16.86	4,638	650-312-2000	Y
Thornburg Global Opportunities Fund Class A	THOAX	B	B-	B	Up	2.85	6.53	21.64	27.12	95.40	31.79	2,497	800-847-0200	Y
Thornburg Global Opportunities Fund Class C	THOCX	B-	B-	B	Up	2.63	6.07	20.68	24.21	88.02	30.65	2,497	800-847-0200	Y
Thornburg Global Opportunities Fund Class I	THOIX	B	B-	B	Up	2.93	6.71	22.02	28.44	99.08	31.87	2,497	800-847-0200	Y

Category: Global Equity (con't)

Fund Name	Ticker Symbol	RATINGS: Overall Rating	Reward Rating	Risk Rating	Recent Up/ Downgrade	TOTAL RETURNS & PERFORMANCE: 3-Month Total Return	6-Month Total Return	1-Year Total Return	3-Year Total Return	5-Year Total Return	ASSETS: NAV	Total Assets (MIL)	NEW INVESTORS: Telephone	Open to New Investors
Thornburg Global Opportunities Fund Class R3	THORX	B	B-	B	Up	2.76	6.40	21.36	26.44	94.00	31.45	2,497	800-847-0200	Y
Thornburg Global Opportunities Fund Class R4	THOVX	B	B-	B	Up	2.77	6.45	21.49	26.77	94.93	31.48	2,497	800-847-0200	Y
Thornburg Global Opportunities Fund Class R5	THOFX	B	B-	B	Up	2.88	6.64	21.96	28.37	98.98	31.9	2,497	800-847-0200	Y
Thornburg Global Opportunities Fund Class R6	THOGX	B	B-	B	Up	2.95	6.78	22.05	28.47	99.13	31.97	2,497	800-847-0200	Y
Thrivent Large Cap Stock Fund Class A	AALGX	B-	B-	B-	Down	3.84	9.08	20.82	28.81	79.29	27.12	1,876		Y
Thrivent Large Cap Stock Fund Class S	IILGX	B-	B-	B-	Down	3.93	9.28	21.27	30.34	82.95	27.34	1,876		Y
Thrivent Series Large Cap Stock Portfolio		B-	B-	B-	Down	4.01	9.32	21.15	30.67	83.01	14.3744	1,076		Y
Touchstone Global Growth Fund Class A	TGGAX	A-	A	B+	Up	5.11	13.76	43.24	50.00	110.57	24.85	28.4	800-543-0407	Y
Touchstone Global Growth Fund Class C	TGGCX	A-	A-	B+	Up	4.95	13.35	42.17	46.62	102.79	24.59	28.4	800-543-0407	Y
Touchstone Global Growth Fund Class Y	TYGGX	A-	A	B+	Up	5.19	13.94	43.39	50.87	112.85	24.89	28.4	800-543-0407	Y
Touchstone Global Growth Fund Institutional Class	DSMGX	A-	A	B+	Up	5.22	14.00	43.70	51.28	113.44	24.96	28.4	800-543-0407	Y
Touchstone Sustainability and Impact Equity Fund Class A	TEQAX	B-	B	C+	Down	5.32	9.95	25.73	29.97	92.21	22.4	776.0	800-543-0407	Y
Touchstone Sustainability and Impact Equity Fund Class C	TEQCX	B-	B-	C+	Down	5.10	9.48	24.79	27.07	85.05	19.04	776.0	800-543-0407	Y
Touchstone Sustainability and Impact Equity Fund Class Y	TIQIX	B-	B	C+	Down	5.39	10.07	26.05	30.96	94.61	23.13	776.0	800-543-0407	Y
Touchstone Sustainability & Impact Equity Fund Inst Cls	TROCX	B-	B	C+	Down	5.40	10.12	26.14	31.01	93.74	23.15	776.0	800-543-0407	Y
Transamerica Global Equity Class A	IMNAX	B	B-	B	Up	5.32	10.02	26.54	29.21	53.95	13.81	126.1	888-233-4339	Y
Transamerica Global Equity Class Advisor	TAGQX	B-	B-	B-	Down	5.40	10.20	26.87	29.55	54.35	14.22	126.1	888-233-4339	Y
Transamerica Global Equity Class B	IMNBX	B-	B-	B-	Down	5.11	9.61	25.57	26.37	48.17	13.7	126.1	888-233-4339	
Transamerica Global Equity Class C	IMNCX	B-	B-	B-	Down	5.08	9.52	25.54	26.38	48.19	13.58	126.1	888-233-4339	Y
Transamerica Global Equity Class I	TMUIX	B-	B	B-	Down	5.41	10.17	26.88	30.38	56.31	13.82	126.1	888-233-4339	Y
Transamerica Global Equity Class R6	TAGEX	B-	B	B-	Down	5.40	10.17	26.85	30.40	55.38	13.82	126.1	888-233-4339	Y
Transamerica Global Equity Class T1	TMUTX	B-	B-	B-	Down	5.35	10.04	26.57	29.24	53.99	13.86	126.1	888-233-4339	Y
USAA Capital Growth Fund	USCGX	B	B	B-	Up	6.44	14.24	23.86	36.32	98.25	12.39	905.6	800-531-8722	Y
USAA Capital Growth Fund Institutional Shares	UICGX	B	B	B-	Up	6.44	14.31	23.92	36.71	98.83	12.41	905.6	800-531-8722	Y
USAA Cornerstone Equity Fund	UCEQX	B-	B-	C+	Down	5.01	10.25	22.58	30.99	62.13	15.6	176.3	800-531-8722	Y
USAA World Growth Fund	USAWX	B	B-	B	Up	4.33	7.15	23.92	29.55	74.73	32.29	1,430	800-531-8722	Y
USAA World Growth Fund Adviser Shares	USWGX	B	B-	B	Up	4.27	7.02	23.57	28.52	72.64	32.37	1,430	800-531-8722	Y
USAA World Growth Fund Institutional Shares	UIWGX	B	B-	B	Up	4.32	7.14	23.92	29.68	74.91	32.21	1,430	800-531-8722	Y
VALIC Company I Global Social Awareness Fund	VCSOX	B-	B-	B-	Down	5.68	10.41	22.71	29.59	84.49	26.39	442.8		Y
Vanguard Global Equity Fund Investor Shares	VHGEX	B	B	B	Up	5.78	11.55	27.78	34.94	83.02	31.31	5,661	877-662-7447	Y
Vanguard Total World Stock Index Fund Institutional Shares	VTWIX	B-	B-	C+	Down	5.63	11.19	24.20	31.65	71.76	151.44	14,145	877-662-7447	Y
Vanguard Total World Stock Index Investor Shares	VTWSX	B-	B-	C+	Down	5.60	11.13	24.06	31.24	70.77	30.22	14,145	877-662-7447	Y
Victory RS Global Fund Class A	RSGGX	B	B	B	Up	5.88	12.48	24.48	37.07	88.54	12.75	27.3	800-539-3863	Y
Victory RS Global Fund Class C	RGGCX	B-	B-	B	Down	5.70	12.01	23.47	33.91	81.36	12.38	27.3	800-539-3863	Y
Victory RS Global Fund Class R	RGGKX	B	B	B		5.76	12.29	24.08	66.53	127.12	15.76	27.3	800-539-3863	Y
Victory RS Global Fund Class Y	RGGYX	B	B	B	Up	5.94	12.52	24.75	38.31	91.21	12.63	27.3	800-539-3863	Y
Virtus Vontobel Global Opportunities Fund Class A	NWWOX	B+	B	A	Up	6.11	9.13	29.21	39.92	75.85	16.3	232.3	800-243-1574	Y
Virtus Vontobel Global Opportunities Fund Class C	WWOCX	B	B	A		5.90	8.76	28.25	36.85	69.43	13.98	232.3	800-243-1574	Y
Virtus Vontobel Global Opportunities Fund Class I	WWOIX	B+	B	A	Up	6.17	9.27	29.47	40.91	78.05	16.27	232.3	800-243-1574	Y
Vontobel Global Equity Institutional Fund Class I	VTEIX	B-	C+	B	Up	6.16	9.51	29.75	41.53		13.42	48.0	212-415-7000	Y
Voya Global Advantage and Premium Opportunity Fund	IGA	B-	B-	B-	Up	3.99	9.78	18.13	26.71	54.78	12.23	227.0		Y
Voya Global Equity Fund Class I	NAWIX	B-	B-	C+	Up	5.66	9.36	24.60	26.80	52.90	36.34	287.1	800-366-0066	Y
Voya Global Equity Fund Class W	IGVWX	B-	B-	C+	Up	5.67	9.38	24.63	26.82	52.94	36.32	287.1	800-366-0066	Y
Voya Global Equity Portfolio Class I	IIGZX	B-	B-	C+	Down	5.79	9.65	23.73	27.06	54.42	11.13	714.5	800-366-0066	Y
VY® Morgan Stanley Global Franchise Portfolio Class A	IGFAX	B	B	A		7.80	7.85	25.46	38.66	74.41	16.98	412.3	800-366-0066	Y
VY® Morgan Stanley Global Franchise Portfolio Class R6	VPRDX	B+	B	A	Up	7.99	8.18	26.16	40.68	78.22	17.96	412.3	800-366-0066	Y
VY® Morgan Stanley Global Franchise Portfolio Class S	IVGTX	B	B	A	Down	7.86	7.96	25.81	40.02	77.38	17.97	412.3	800-366-0066	Y
VY® Morgan Stanley Global Franchise Portfolio Class S2	IGFSX	B	B	A		7.86	7.97	25.69	39.51	76.22	17.83	412.3	800-366-0066	Y
VY® Oppenheimer Global Portfolio Class A	IGMAX	B	B+	C+	Up	7.10	13.48	35.82	39.25	82.89	21.42	1,738	800-366-0066	Y
VY® Oppenheimer Global Portfolio Class I	IGMIX	B+	A-	B	Up	7.25	13.80	36.48	41.38	87.50	22.33	1,738	800-366-0066	Y
VY® Oppenheimer Global Portfolio Class S	IGMSX	B	B+	C+	Up	7.16	13.65	36.13	40.30	85.14	21.53	1,738	800-366-0066	Y
VY® Oppenheimer Global Portfolio Class S2	IOGPX	B+	B+	B	Up	7.09	13.54	35.91	39.69	83.80	20.97	1,738	800-366-0066	Y

Category: Global Equity (con't)

Fund Name	Ticker Symbol	RATINGS: Overall Rating	Reward Rating	Risk Rating	Recent Up/ Downgrade	TOTAL RETURNS & PERFORMANCE: 3-Month Total Return	6-Month Total Return	1-Year Total Return	3-Year Total Return	5-Year Total Return	ASSETS: NAV	Total Assets (MIL)	NEW INVESTORS: Telephone	Open to New Investors
Waddell & Reed Advisors Global Growth Fund Class A	UNCGX	B-	C+	B	Up	5.66	12.07	25.83	25.56	53.78	12.83	551.5	888-923-3355	Y
Waddell & Reed Advisors Global Growth Fund Class B	WAIBX	B-	C+	B	Up	5.46	11.35	24.22	20.35	43.33	11.04	551.5	888-923-3355	
Waddell & Reed Advisors Global Growth Fund Class C	WAICX	B-	C+	B	Up	5.51	11.57	24.59	21.55	45.65	11.69	551.5	888-923-3355	Y
Waddell & Reed Advisors Global Growth Fund Class Y	WAIYX	B	B-	B	Up	5.66	12.17	26.13	26.74	56.38	12.92	551.5	888-923-3355	Y
WCM Focused Global Growth Fund Institutional Class	WCMGX	B+	B	A-	Up	4.90	9.48	27.51	46.10		14.8	22.3	949-380-0200	Y
WCM Focused Global Growth Fund Investor Class	WFGGX	B+	B	A-	Up	4.85	9.30	27.29	45.53		14.71	22.3	949-380-0200	Y
Wells Fargo Intrinsic World Equity Fund - Class A	EWEAX	B-	B	B-	Up	4.67	10.34	25.16	30.26	64.55	22.13	163.7	800-222-8222	Y
Wells Fargo Intrinsic World Equity Fund - Class Admin	EWEIX	B-	B	B-	Up	4.70	10.40	25.31	30.92	66.23	22.01	163.7	800-222-8222	Y
Wells Fargo Intrinsic World Equity Fund - Class C	EWECX	B-	B-	B-	Up	4.44	9.92	24.21	27.34	58.47	21.28	163.7	800-222-8222	Y
Wells Fargo Intrinsic World Equity Fund - Class Inst	EWENX	B-	B	B-	Up	4.76	10.54	25.64	31.90	68.19	22.05	163.7	800-222-8222	Y
Westcore Global Large-Cap Dividend Fund Institutional Cls	WIMVX	B	B-	B		6.30	8.51	19.78	28.59	72.00	11.04	55.5	800-392-2673	Y
Westcore Global Large-Cap Dividend Fund Retail Class	WTMVX	B	B-	B		6.23	8.52	19.55	27.99	70.57	11.12	55.5	800-392-2673	Y
Westwood Global Equity Fund Institutional Shares	WWGEX	B-	B-	B	Up	4.05	9.23	19.73	26.68	45.61	13.68	18.0		Y
William Blair Global Leaders Fund Class I	WGFIX	B	B	B	Up	7.24	14.52	30.69	34.72	73.26	14.56	209.6	800-621-0687	Y
William Blair Global Leaders Fund Class N	WGGNX	B	B	B	Up	7.12	14.34	30.31	33.48	70.68	14.53	209.6	800-621-0687	Y
William Blair Global Leaders Fund Institutional Class	BGGIX	B	B	B	Up	7.24	14.60	30.77	34.97	73.92	14.56	209.6	800-621-0687	Y
Yorktown Growth Fund Class A	AFGGX	B	B	B	Up	6.01	12.34	27.50	32.16	82.52	17.62	65.9	800-544-6060	Y
Yorktown Growth Fund Class Institutional	APGRX	B	B	B	Up	6.05	12.33	27.50	32.28	81.75	18.55	65.9	800-544-6060	Y
Yorktown Growth Fund Class L	APITX	B	B-	B	Up	5.80	11.81	26.24	28.31	73.59	14.96	65.9	800-544-6060	Y

Category: Global Equity Large Cap

Fund Name	Ticker Symbol	RATINGS: Overall Rating	Reward Rating	Risk Rating	Recent Up/ Downgrade	TOTAL RETURNS & PERFORMANCE: 3-Month Total Return	6-Month Total Return	1-Year Total Return	3-Year Total Return	5-Year Total Return	ASSETS: NAV	Total Assets (MIL)	NEW INVESTORS: Telephone	Open to New Investors
AB International Growth Fund Advisor Class	AWPYX	B-	C+	B-	Up	2.79	9.95	34.87	22.81	40.24	19.88	313.0	212-969-1000	Y
AB International Growth Fund Class A	AWPAX	B-	C+	B-	Up	2.68	9.79	34.45	21.89	38.39	19.51	313.0	212-969-1000	Y
AB International Growth Fund Class I	AWPIX	B-	B-	B-	Up	2.80	10.07	35.01	23.34	41.32	19.78	313.0	212-969-1000	Y
AB International Growth Fund Class K	AWPKX	B-	C+	B-	Up	2.69	9.84	34.48	21.94	38.53	19.42	313.0	212-969-1000	Y
AB International Growth Fund Class R	AWPRX	B-	C+	B-	Up	2.66	9.69	34.10	20.83	36.50	19.23	313.0	212-969-1000	Y
AB International Portfolio	SIMTX	B	B-	B	Up	2.96	9.10	26.50	27.93	45.62	18.44	1,331	212-969-1000	Y
AB International Portfolio Class A	AIZAX	B	B-	B	Up	2.95	9.12	26.49	27.95	44.50	18.14	1,331	212-969-1000	Y
AB International Portfolio Class B	AIZBX	B-	C+	B	Up	2.75	8.75	25.62	25.17	39.25	18.63	1,331	212-969-1000	
AB International Portfolio Class C	AIZCX	B-	C+	B	Up	2.74	8.71	25.54	25.10	39.28	18.33	1,331	212-969-1000	Y
AB International Value Fund Advisor Class	ABIYX	B	B-	B	Up	3.00	8.86	25.20	27.15	48.64	15.2	282.7	212-969-1000	Y
AB International Value Fund Class A	ABIAX	B-	B-	B	Up	2.93	8.69	24.82	26.21	46.58	14.86	282.7	212-969-1000	Y
AB International Value Fund Class B	ABIBX	B-	C+	B	Up	2.73	8.30	23.81	23.19	41.10	14.65	282.7	212-969-1000	
AB International Value Fund Class C	ABICX	B-	C+	B	Up	2.73	8.29	23.92	23.40	41.40	14.59	282.7	212-969-1000	Y
AB International Value Fund Class I	AIVIX	B	B-	B	Up	3.06	8.98	25.36	28.01	50.41	14.83	282.7	212-969-1000	Y
AB International Value Fund Class K	AIVKX	B-	B-	B	Up	2.98	8.76	24.95	26.38	47.22	14.82	282.7	212-969-1000	Y
AB International Value Fund Class R	AIVRX	B-	B-	B	Up	2.87	8.53	24.48	25.19	44.92	14.75	282.7	212-969-1000	Y
AB Tax-Managed International Portfolio	SNIVX	B	B-	B	Up	2.97	9.16	26.27	27.71	45.87	18.44	3,322	212-969-1000	Y
AB Tax-Managed International Portfolio Class A	ABXAX	B	B-	B	Up	3.00	9.16	26.31	27.79	45.28	18.18	3,322	212-969-1000	Y
AB Tax-Managed International Portfolio Class B	ABXBX	B-	C+	B	Up	2.75	8.72	25.34	24.95	39.92	18.48	3,322	212-969-1000	
AB Tax-Managed International Portfolio Class C	ABXCX	B-	C+	B	Up	2.79	8.75	25.28	24.86	39.95	18.38	3,322	212-969-1000	Y
AdvisorOne CLS International Equity Fund Class N	CLHAX	B-	B-	B-	Up	3.59	9.62	23.76	25.27	45.52	4.79	50.5		Y
Alger International Growth Fund Class A	ALGAX	B-	C+	B-	Up	3.89	12.27	26.69	20.49	47.62	17.05	179.3	800-992-3863	Y
Alger International Growth Fund Class B	AFGPX	B-	C+	B-	Up	3.71	11.78	25.80	17.90	42.55	14.85	179.3	800-992-3863	
Alger International Growth Fund Class C	ALGCX	B-	C+	B-	Up	3.67	11.80	25.69	17.68	41.95	14.49	179.3	800-992-3863	Y
Alger International Growth Fund Class I	AIGIX	B-	C+	B	Up	3.97	12.32	26.87	21.13	48.54	17.05	179.3	800-992-3863	Y
Alger International Growth Fund Class Z	ALCZX	B-	C+	B	Up	4.01	12.52	27.27	22.12	50.97	17.19	179.3	800-992-3863	Y
AllianzGI International Growth Fund Class A	AIGFX	B-	C+	B-	Up	4.95	13.65	38.69			18.02	19.4	800-498-5413	Y
AllianzGI International Growth Fund Institutional Class	GLIIX	B-	C+	B-	Up	4.99	13.80	39.01			18.4	19.4	800-498-5413	Y

Category: Global Equity Large Cap (con't)

		RATINGS				TOTAL RETURNS & PERFORMANCE					ASSETS		NEW INVESTORS	
Fund Name	Ticker Symbol	Overall Rating	Reward Rating	Risk Rating	Recent Up/ Downgrade	3-Month Total Return	6-Month Total Return	1-Year Total Return	3-Year Total Return	5-Year Total Return	NAV	Total Assets (MIL)	Telephone	Open to New Investors
American Beacon International Equity Fund Advisor Class	AAISX	B-	C+	B-	Up	4.47	10.12	24.31	20.63	40.37	21.21	3,140	800-658-5811	Y
American Beacon International Equity Fund Class A	AIEAX	B-	C+	B-	Up	4.48	10.10	24.37	20.85	40.63	20.71	3,140	800-658-5811	Y
American Beacon International Equity Fund Class R6	AAERX	B-	C+	B-	Up	4.60	10.38	24.92	22.31	43.84	20.89	3,140	800-658-5811	Y
American Beacon International Equity Fund Class Y	ABEYX	B-	C+	B-	Up	4.53	10.26	24.76	21.98	42.95	21.68	3,140	800-658-5811	Y
American Beacon Intl Equity Fund Inst Cls	AAIEX	B-	C+	B-	Up	4.57	10.30	24.83	22.22	43.73	20.88	3,140	800-658-5811	Y
American Beacon International Equity Fund Investor Class	AAIPX	B-	C+	B-	Up	4.45	10.11	24.39	20.94	41.07	20.72	3,140	800-658-5811	Y
American Century International Core Equity Fund Class A	ACIQX	B-	C+	B-	Up	2.78	8.71	25.42	20.01	45.84	9.6	34.6	800-444-4015	Y
American Century Intl Core Equity Fund Inv Cls	ACIMX	B-	C+	B-	Up	2.83	8.89	25.80	20.68	47.39	9.58	34.6	800-444-4015	Y
American Century International Growth Fund A Class	TWGAX	B-	B-	B	Up	4.03	12.43	30.72	22.27	44.35	13.39	1,567	800-444-4015	Y
American Century International Growth Fund C Class	AIWCX	B-	C+	B-	Up	3.77	11.89	29.74	19.53	38.95	13	1,567	800-444-4015	Y
American Century International Growth Fund I Class	TGRIX	B-	B-	B	Up	4.10	12.61	31.31	24.01	47.60	13.18	1,567	800-444-4015	Y
American Century International Growth Fund Investor Class	TWIEX	B-	B-	B	Up	4.10	12.47	31.03	23.25	46.03	13.27	1,567	800-444-4015	Y
American Century International Growth Fund R Class	ATGRX	B-	B-	B	Up	3.89	12.19	30.36	21.29	42.37	13.53	1,567	800-444-4015	Y
American Century International Growth Fund R5 Class	ATGGX	B-	B-	B	Up	4.12	12.54	31.13	23.35	46.15	13.18	1,567	800-444-4015	Y
American Century International Growth Fund R6 Class	ATGDX	B	B-	B	Up	4.11	12.70	31.41	24.45	48.33	13.17	1,567	800-444-4015	Y
American Century International Growth Fund Y Class	ATYGX	B-	B-	B	Up	4.16	12.67	31.28	23.49	46.32	13.18	1,567	800-444-4015	Y
American Century NT International Growth Fund G Class	ACLNX	B-	B-	B	Up	4.29	13.29	31.82	24.04	47.93	12.28	1,041	800-444-4015	Y
American Funds EuroPacific Growth Fund® Class 529-A	CEUAX	B	B	B	Up	4.13	11.17	30.65	29.64	53.59	55.57	160,340	800-421-4225	Y
American Funds EuroPacific Growth Fund® Class 529-C	CEUCX	B-	B-	B	Up	3.93	10.72	29.64	26.62	47.69	54.47	160,340	800-421-4225	Y
American Funds EuroPacific Growth Fund® Class 529-E	CEUEX	B	B	B	Up	4.06	11.03	30.33	28.72	51.70	55.11	160,340	800-421-4225	Y
American Funds EuroPacific Growth Fund® Class 529-F-1	CEUFX	B	B	B	Up	4.19	11.29	30.92	30.47	55.24	55.53	160,340	800-421-4225	Y
American Funds EuroPacific Growth Fund® Class A	AEPGX	B	B	B	Up	4.15	11.19	30.72	29.85	54.01	56.22	160,340	800-421-4225	Y
American Funds EuroPacific Growth Fund® Class C	AEPCX	B-	B-	B	Up	3.94	10.76	29.70	26.82	48.12	55	160,340	800-421-4225	Y
American Funds EuroPacific Growth Fund® Class F-1	AEGFX	B	B	B	Up	4.13	11.16	30.68	29.74	53.80	55.96	160,340	800-421-4225	Y
American Funds EuroPacific Growth Fund® Class F-2	AEPFX	B	B	B	Up	4.19	11.30	31.02	30.79	55.88	56.04	160,340	800-421-4225	Y
American Funds EuroPacific Growth Fund® Class F-3	FEUPX	B	B	B	Up	4.22	11.36	31.12	30.25	54.48	56.19	160,340	800-421-4225	Y
American Funds EuroPacific Growth Fund® Class R-1	RERAX	B-	B-	B	Up	3.94	10.76	29.70	26.90	48.23	54.14	160,340	800-421-4225	Y
American Funds EuroPacific Growth Fund® Class R-2	RERBX	B	B-	B	Up	3.95	10.75	29.72	26.99	48.41	54.61	160,340	800-421-4225	Y
American Funds EuroPacific Growth Fund® Class R-2E	REEBX	B	B-	B	Up	4.01	10.92	30.13	28.29	51.14	55.39	160,340	800-421-4225	Y
American Funds EuroPacific Growth Fund® Class R-3	RERCX	B	B	B	Up	4.07	11.02	30.31	28.71	51.74	55.09	160,340	800-421-4225	Y
American Funds EuroPacific Growth Fund® Class R-4	REREX	B	B	B	Up	4.13	11.19	30.70	29.84	54.00	55.09	160,340	800-421-4225	Y
American Funds EuroPacific Growth Fund® Class R-5	RERFX	B	B	B	Up	4.22	11.34	31.08	31.02	56.33	56.09	160,340	800-421-4225	Y
American Funds EuroPacific Growth Fund® Class R-5E	RERHX	B	B	B	Up	4.19	11.29	30.98	30.34	54.59	55.82	160,340	800-421-4225	Y
American Funds EuroPacific Growth Fund® Class R-6	RERGX	B	B	B	Up	4.22	11.37	31.17	31.19	56.68	56.14	160,340	800-421-4225	Y
AMG Managers Pictet International Fund Class I	APCTX	B	B	B+	Up	3.64	7.71	27.46	38.93		11.32	2,055	800-835-3879	Y
AMG Managers Pictet International Fund Class N	APINX	B	B	B+	Up	3.51	7.56	27.11	37.68		11.31	2,055	800-835-3879	Y
AMG Managers Pictet International Fund Class Z	APCZX	B	B	B+		3.63	7.70	27.45	38.92		11.29	2,055	800-835-3879	Y
AMG Renaissance International Equity Fund Class I	RIESX	B-	C+	B-	Up	2.45	7.80	26.76	22.30		10.55	2.8	800-835-3879	Y
AMG Renaissance International Equity Fund Class N	RIEIX	B-	C+	B-	Up	2.34	7.69	26.38	21.07		10.59	2.8	800-835-3879	Y
AMG Renaissance International Equity Fund Class Z	RIELX	B-	C+	B-	Up	2.51	7.97	26.96	22.77		10.56	2.8	800-835-3879	Y
AQR International Defensive Style Fund Class I	ANDIX	B-	C+	B	Up	3.45	7.25	21.60	23.17	44.63	13.42	194.9	203-742-3600	Y
AQR International Defensive Style Fund Class N	ANDNX	B-	C+	B	Up	3.42	7.13	21.39	22.27	42.74	13.78	194.9	203-742-3600	Y
AQR International Defensive Style Fund Class R6	ANDRX	B-	C+	B	Up	3.47	7.27	21.74	23.51	45.08	13.4	194.9	203-742-3600	Y
AQR International Equity Fund Class I	AQIIX	B	B	B	Up	3.18	9.47	25.71	31.49	53.26	10.96	422.5	203-742-3600	Y
AQR International Equity Fund Class N	AQINX	B	B	B	Up	3.09	9.35	25.35	30.52	51.09	11.23	422.5	203-742-3600	Y
AQR International Equity Fund Class R6	AQIRX	B	B	B	Up	3.09	9.54	25.71	31.79	53.91	11.69	422.5	203-742-3600	Y
AQR International Momentum Style Fund Class I	AIMOX	B-	C+	B	Up	3.51	11.11	25.25	20.38	35.70	15.7	417.5	203-742-3600	Y
AQR International Momentum Style Fund Class N	AIONX	B-	C+	B	Up	3.48	11.02	24.99	19.58	34.10	15.69	417.5	203-742-3600	Y
AQR International Momentum Style Fund Class R6	QIORX	B-	C+	B	Up	3.55	11.23	25.41	20.88	36.23	15.68	417.5	203-742-3600	Y
AQR International Multi-Style Fund Class I	QICLX	B-	C+	B-	Up	3.21	9.05	24.96	19.44		12.04	473.5	203-742-3600	Y
AQR International Multi-Style Fund Class R6	QICRX	B-	C+	B-	Up	3.22	9.16	24.99	19.80		12.02	473.5	203-742-3600	Y
AQR TM International Momentum Style Fund Class I	ATIMX	B-	C+	B	Up	3.52	10.46	25.07	19.71	37.90	13.94	110.9	203-742-3600	Y

Category: Global Equity Large Cap (con't)

Fund Name	Ticker Symbol	RATINGS: Overall Rating	Reward Rating	Risk Rating	Recent Up/ Downgrade	TOTAL RETURNS & PERFORMANCE: 3-Month Total Return	6-Month Total Return	1-Year Total Return	3-Year Total Return	5-Year Total Return	ASSETS: NAV	Total Assets (MIL)	NEW INVESTORS: Telephone	Open to New Investors
AQR TM International Momentum Style Fund Class N	ATNNX	B-	C+	B	Up	3.49	10.37	24.83	19.10	36.39	13.87	110.9	203-742-3600	Y
AQR TM International Momentum Style Fund Class R6	QTIRX	B-	C+	B	Up	3.55	10.50	25.15	20.10	38.40	13.9	110.9	203-742-3600	Y
Ariel International Fund Investor Class	AINTX	B-	C	B	Up	0.15	2.68	16.34	19.53	48.80	14	620.6	312-726-0140	Y
Ariel International Institutional Class	AINIX	B-	C	B	Up	0.27	2.76	16.70	20.38	50.76	13.74	620.6	312-726-0140	Y
Aristotle International Equity Fund Class I	ARSFX	B-	C+	B	Up	3.73	8.59	22.64	20.85		10.74	15.6		Y
Artisan International Value Fund Advisor Class	APDKX	B	B	B	Up	2.73	8.88	23.97	28.05	68.73	38.58	15,140	800-344-1770	
Artisan International Value Fund Institutional Class	APHKX	B	B	B	Up	2.74	8.92	24.06	28.40	69.78	38.73	15,140	800-344-1770	
Artisan International Value Fund Investor Class	ARTKX	B	B	B	Up	2.72	8.81	23.82	27.52	68.03	38.62	15,140	800-344-1770	
ATM International Managed Volatility Portfolio Class K	US26883L8110	B-	C+	B	Up	3.72	8.71	24.63	19.92	39.12		1,693	877-222-2144	Y
AXA International Core Managed Volatility Portfolio Cls IA	US2689404679	B-	C+	B-	Up	3.80	9.24	26.32	19.03	34.24		1,755	877-222-2144	Y
AXA International Core Managed Volatility Portfolio Cls IB	US2689404596	B-	C+	B-	Up	3.80	9.33	26.41	19.12	34.32		1,755	877-222-2144	Y
AXA International Core Managed Volatility Portfolio Cls K	US26883L6130	B-	C+	B-	Up	3.93	9.45	26.78	20.02	36.05		1,755	877-222-2144	Y
AXA International Managed Volatility Portfolio Class IB	US26884M7680	B-	C+	B-	Up	3.60	8.51	24.30	19.08	37.33		2,290	877-222-2144	Y
AXA International Managed Volatility Portfolio Class K	US26883L8292	B-	C+	B	Up	3.74	8.71	24.63	20.03	39.08		2,290	877-222-2144	Y
AXA Intl Value Managed Volatility Portfolio Cls IA	US2689404000	B-	C+	B-	Up	3.05	7.91	23.59	18.14	33.99		1,031	877-222-2144	Y
AXA Intl Value Managed Volatility Portfolio Cls IB	US2689408142	B-	C+	B-	Up	3.05	7.98	23.68	18.23	34.08		1,031	877-222-2144	Y
AXA International Value Managed Volatility Portfolio Cls K	US26883L5892	B-	C+	B-	Up	3.13	8.05	23.90	19.05	35.71		1,031	877-222-2144	Y
Baillie Gifford The EAFE Choice Fund Class 2	BGCWX	B	B	B	Up	4.55	9.74	31.28	34.15	58.27	16.1131	332.3		Y
Baillie Gifford The EAFE Choice Fund Class 3	BGCJX	B	B	B	Up	4.57	9.78	31.37	34.47	60.51	16.2626	332.3		Y
Baillie Gifford The EAFE Fund Class 2	BGETX	B+	A	B-	Up	2.90	16.50	46.09	42.56	74.24	14.3922	2,822		Y
Baillie Gifford The EAFE Fund Class 3	BGEUX	B+	A	B-	Up	2.91	16.53	46.19	42.78	74.88	14.4206	2,822		Y
Baillie Gifford The EAFE Fund Class 4	BGEFX	B+	A	B-	Up	2.92	16.55	46.23	42.75	74.48	14.4301	2,822		Y
Baillie Gifford The EAFE Fund Class 5	BGEVX	B+	A	B-	Up	2.94	16.58	46.31	43.22	75.62	14.4582	2,822		Y
Baillie Gifford The EAFE Pure Fund Class 2	BGPTX	B	B	B	Up	3.76	8.60	28.58	33.45		12.0562	315.8		Y
Baillie Gifford The EAFE Pure Fund Class 3	US0568237848	B	B	B	Up	3.78	8.64	28.65	33.52		12.1734	315.8		Y
Baillie Gifford The EAFE Pure Fund Class I	BSGPX	B	B	B	Up	3.82	8.71	28.59	29.57		12.0555	315.8		Y
Baillie Gifford The EAFE Pure Fund Class K	BGPKX	B	B	B	Up	3.82	8.71	28.59	29.57		12.0555	315.8		Y
Baillie Gifford The International Equity Fund Class 2	BGITX	B	B+	B	Up	5.56	12.37	34.95	38.80	58.12	14.1969	2,100		Y
Baillie Gifford The International Equity Fund Class 3	BGIFX	B	B+	B	Up	5.58	12.41	35.05	39.12	58.74	14.373	2,100		Y
Baillie Gifford The International Equity Fund Class 5	BGIVX	B	B+	B	Up	5.60	12.46	35.16	39.45	62.32	14.8228	2,100		Y
Baron International Growth Fund Institutional Shares	BINIX	B+	A-	B	Up	7.32	16.46	37.33	40.78	70.57	24.19	157.9	800-992-2766	Y
Baron International Growth Fund R6 Shares	BIGUX	B+	A-	B	Up	7.32	16.46	37.33	40.19	68.92	24.19	157.9	800-992-2766	Y
Baron International Growth Fund Retail Shares	BIGFX	B+	B+	B	Up	7.28	16.35	36.94	39.74	68.38	23.9	157.9	800-992-2766	Y
BBH Partner Fund - International Equity Cls Institutional	BBHLX	B-	C+	B	Up	1.78	5.16	20.47	22.02	38.72	15.6	1,421	800-575-1265	Y
BlackRock Advantage Intl Fund Inst Shares	BROIX	B	B-	B	Up	3.98	9.46	24.20	27.94	63.37	17.31	484.2	800-441-7762	Y
BlackRock Advantage International Fund Investor A Shares	BROAX	B	B-	B	Up	3.86	9.32	23.76	26.89	61.17	17.14	484.2	800-441-7762	Y
BlackRock Advantage International Fund Investor C Shares	BROCX	B-	B-	B	Up	3.69	8.88	22.86	23.92	54.75	16.55	484.2	800-441-7762	Y
BlackRock Advantage International Fund R Shares	BGORX	B-	B-	B	Up	3.80	9.14	23.44	25.53	58.16	17.13	484.2	800-441-7762	
BlackRock Enhanced International Dividend Trust	BGY	B-	C+	B	Up	2.95	7.76	20.64	16.64	23.49	7.0803	764.4	800-441-7762	Y
BlackRock International Dividend Fund Institutional Shares	BISIX	B-	C+	B	Up	1.94	4.80	16.71	16.81	29.06	31.12	423.4	800-441-7762	Y
BlackRock International Dividend Fund Investor A Shares	BREAX	B-	C+	B	Up	1.87	4.65	16.39	15.73	27.06	29.14	423.4	800-441-7762	Y
BlackRock International Dividend Fund Service Shares	BRESX	B-	C+	B	Up	1.86	4.66	16.38	15.78	26.96	29.59	423.4	800-441-7762	Y
BlackRock International Fund Class R Shares	BIFRX	B-	B-	B-	Up	5.42	12.30	31.01	25.58	46.32	17.42	611.9	800-441-7762	Y
BlackRock International Fund Institutional Shares	MAILX	B-	B-	B	Up	5.58	12.65	31.86	28.12	51.41	17.76	611.9	800-441-7762	Y
BlackRock International Fund Investor A Shares	MDILX	B-	B-	B	Up	5.46	12.48	31.31	26.67	48.54	17.39	611.9	800-441-7762	Y
BlackRock International Fund Investor C Shares	MCILX	B-	C+	B-	Up	5.24	11.99	30.20	23.01	41.48	16.25	611.9	800-441-7762	Y
BMO Pyrford International Stock Fund Class F3	BISBX	B-	C+	B-		3.24	5.86	18.61	16.43	36.76	13.43	678.3	800-236-3863	Y
BMO Pyrford International Stock Fund Class I	MISNX	B-	C+	B-	Up	3.26	5.80	18.55	16.36	36.68	13.43	678.3	800-236-3863	Y
BMO Pyrford International Stock Fund Class R6	BISGX	B-	C+	B-	Up	3.24	5.86	18.70	16.85	37.36	13.43	678.3	800-236-3863	Y
BNY Mellon International Appreciation Fund Class M Shares	MPPMX	B-	C+	B	Up	3.64	8.85	23.78	23.11	42.51	14.43	80.9	800-645-6561	Y
BNY Mellon International Appreciation Fund Investor Shares	MARIX	B-	C+	B	Up	3.58	8.76	23.50	22.13	40.66	14.32	80.9	800-645-6561	Y
BNY Mellon International Fund Class Investor	MIINX	B-	B-	B	Up	3.92	11.02	27.72	25.71	48.99	14.76	1,153	800-645-6561	Y

Category: Global Equity Large Cap (con't)

Fund Name	Ticker Symbol	RATINGS: Overall Rating	RATINGS: Reward Rating	RATINGS: Risk Rating	RATINGS: Recent Up/ Downgrade	TOTAL RETURNS & PERFORMANCE: 3-Month Total Return	6-Month Total Return	1-Year Total Return	3-Year Total Return	5-Year Total Return	ASSETS: NAV	Total Assets (MIL)	NEW INVESTORS: Telephone	Open to New Investors
BNY Mellon International Fund Class M	MPITX	B-	B-	B	Up	4.00	11.16	27.96	26.67	50.80	13.84	1,153	800-645-6561	Y
Boston Common International Fund	BCAIX	B-	C+	B-	Up	3.03	7.86	26.38	22.06	39.65	30.69	228.6	877-777-6944	Y
Brandes International Equity Fund A	BIEAX	B-	C+	B	Up	1.71	5.83	14.88	21.45	47.88	17.78	625.5	800-331-2979	Y
Brandes International Equity Fund Class C	BIECX	B-	C+	B	Up	1.56	5.46	14.03	18.76	42.51	17.57	625.5	800-331-2979	Y
Brandes International Equity Fund Class I	BIIEX	B-	C+	B	Up	1.76	5.93	15.13	22.16	49.26	17.83	625.5	800-331-2979	Y
Brandes International Equity Fund Class R6	BIERX	B-	C+	B	Up	1.82	5.98	15.27	22.57	49.77	17.88	625.5	800-331-2979	Y
Brown Capital Mgmt Intl Equity Fund Inst Shares	BCISX	B-	C+	B	Up	4.84	8.00	23.88	25.05	57.78	14.19	38.4		Y
Brown Capital Mgmt Intl Equity Fund Inv Shares	BCIIX	B-	C+	B	Up	4.76	7.84	23.61	24.14	56.41	14.18	38.4		Y
Buffalo International Fund	BUFIX	B	B	B	Up	2.49	7.73	29.33	32.28	56.20	14.91	252.7	800-492-8332	Y
Calamos International Growth Fund Class A	CIGRX	B	B	B	Up	6.93	17.74	39.18	33.76	45.01	21.4	293.9	800-582-6959	Y
Calamos International Growth Fund Class C	CIGCX	B	B-	B	Up	6.78	17.32	38.22	30.86	39.65	19.49	293.9	800-582-6959	Y
Calamos International Growth Fund Class R	CIGFX	B	B	B	Up	6.90	17.60	38.89	32.79	43.26	20.88	293.9	800-582-6959	Y
Calamos International Growth Fund Class T	CITGX	B-	B-	B	Up	6.49	17.10	26.87	27.38	40.22		274.1	800-582-6959	Y
Calamos International Growth Fund Institutional Class	CIGIX	B	B	B	Up	7.02	17.85	39.57	34.78	46.80	21.88	293.9	800-582-6959	Y
Calvert International Equity Fund Class I	CWVIX	B-	C+	B	Up	4.42	8.22	21.70	16.69	36.84	18.73	188.9	800-368-2745	Y
Cambiar International Equity Fund Investor Class	CAMIX	B	B-	B	Up	3.73	11.25	21.25	28.16	51.44	28.42	3,618	866-777-8227	Y
Cambiar International Equity Institutional	CAMYX	B-	B-	B-	Up	3.77	11.35	21.38	28.67	52.69	28.48	3,618	866-777-8227	Y
Capital Group International Equity Fund	CNUSX	B	B-	B	Up	3.97	9.86	30.15	25.53	44.59	13.76	1,604	213-486-9200	Y
Carillon ClariVest International Stock Fund Class A	EISAX	B	B	B	Up	4.99	11.47	27.08	29.50		18.94	19.4	800-421-4184	Y
Carillon ClariVest International Stock Fund Class C	EISDX	B-	B-	B-	Up	4.81	11.09	26.21	26.48		18.63	19.4	800-421-4184	Y
Carillon ClariVest International Stock Fund Class I	EISIX	B	B	B-	Up	5.03	11.64	27.56	31.17		18.89	19.4	800-421-4184	Y
Carillon ClariVest International Stock Fund Class R-3	EISRX	B	B-	B	Up	4.91	11.32	26.81	28.86		18.78	19.4	800-421-4184	Y
Carillon ClariVest International Stock Fund Class R-5	EISSX	B	B	B	Up	5.04	11.60	27.42	31.04		18.91	19.4	800-421-4184	Y
Carillon ClariVest International Stock Fund Class R-6	EISVX	B	B	B-	Up	5.08	11.68	27.65	31.51		18.93	19.4	800-421-4184	Y
Carillon Clarivest International Stock Fund Class Y	EISYX	B	B	B		5.04	11.57	27.36	30.56		18.88	19.4	800-421-4184	Y
Carillon Scout International Fund Class A	CSIGX	B-	B-	B-		3.36	9.66	23.11	24.15	36.24	21.47	1,147	800-421-4184	Y
Carillon Scout International Fund Class C	CSIHX	B-	B-	B-		3.18	9.27	22.22	21.42	31.27	21.47	1,147	800-421-4184	Y
Carillon Scout International Fund Class I	UMBWX	B-	B-	B-	Up	3.40	9.78	23.39	25.03	37.86	21.47	1,147	800-421-4184	Y
Carillon Scout International Fund Class R-3	CSIQX	B-	B-	B-		3.28	9.51	22.80	23.21	34.54	21.47	1,147	800-421-4184	Y
Carillon Scout International Fund Class R-5	CSIUX	B-	B-	B-		3.43	9.80	23.42	25.05	37.89	21.47	1,147	800-421-4184	Y
Carillon Scout International Fund Class R-6	CSIWX	B-	B-	B-		3.43	9.80	23.42	25.05	37.89	21.47	1,147	800-421-4184	Y
Carillon Scout International Fund Class Y	CSIZX	B-	B-	B-		3.36	9.66	23.11	24.15	36.24	21.47	1,147	800-421-4184	Y
Causeway Intl Opp Fund Inst Cls	CIOIX	B-	B-	B-	Up	5.61	13.21	29.57	23.49	42.39	14.58	144.0	866-947-7000	Y
Causeway International Opportunities Fund Investor Class	CIOVX	B-	B-	B-	Up	5.64	13.13	29.38	22.54	40.56	14.49	144.0	866-947-7000	Y
Causeway International Value Fund Class Institutional	CIVIX	B-	C+	B-	Up	5.12	12.35	27.18	23.36	45.88	17.32	8,499	866-947-7000	Y
Causeway International Value Fund Class Investor	CIVVX	B-	C+	B-	Up	5.23	12.39	27.07	22.58	44.33	17.21	8,499	866-947-7000	Y
ClearBridge International Growth Fund Class A	LGGAX	B	B	B	Up	3.67	12.70	36.10	29.00	82.35	42.65	228.4	877-721-1926	Y
ClearBridge International Growth Fund Class C	LMGTX	B	B	B	Up	3.45	12.26	35.08	26.15	75.71	40.08	228.4	877-721-1926	Y
ClearBridge International Growth Fund Class FI	LMGFX	B	B	B	Up	3.66	12.69	36.10	29.02	82.38	44.47	228.4	877-721-1926	Y
ClearBridge International Growth Fund Class I	LMGNX	B	B	B	Up	3.70	12.81	36.41	29.95	84.65	46.01	228.4	877-721-1926	Y
ClearBridge International Growth Fund Class R	LMGRX	B	B	B	Up	3.59	12.55	35.79	28.02	80.04	43.21	228.4	877-721-1926	Y
ClearBridge International Value Fund Class A	SBIEX	B-	C+	B-	Up	2.54	7.90	23.23	21.88	37.96	11.82	327.2	877-721-1926	Y
ClearBridge International Value Fund Class I	SBIYX	B-	C+	B-	Up	2.72	8.18	23.68	23.33	40.61	11.63	327.2	877-721-1926	Y
Columbia Acorn International Select Fund Advisor Class	CILRX	B	B	B	Up	6.81	12.77	35.66	35.12	46.95	29.46	129.4	800-345-6611	Y
Columbia Acorn International Select Fund Class A	LAFAX	B	B	B	Up	6.76	12.62	35.30	34.08	45.06	28.89	129.4	800-345-6611	Y
Columbia Acorn International Select Fund Class C	LFFCX	B-	B-	B	Up	6.58	12.20	34.31	31.06	39.58	26.85	129.4	800-345-6611	Y
Columbia Acorn Intl Select Fund Inst 2 Cls	CRIRX	B	B	B	Up	6.84	12.76	35.72	35.40	47.44	29.44	129.4	800-345-6611	Y
Columbia Acorn Intl Select Fund Inst 3 Cls	CSIRX	B	B	B	Up	6.86	12.82	35.81	35.62	47.81	29.42	129.4	800-345-6611	Y
Columbia Acorn International Select Fund Institutional Cls	ACFFX	B	B	B	Up	6.86	12.78	35.70	35.23	47.17	29.25	129.4	800-345-6611	Y
Columbia Overseas Value Fund Advisor Class	COSVX	B	B	B-	Up	4.01	12.82	30.04	36.29	59.07	10.29	945.5	800-345-6611	Y
Columbia Overseas Value Fund Class A	COAVX	B	B	B-	Up	4.00	12.68	29.68	35.24	57.27	10.32	945.5	800-345-6611	Y
Columbia Overseas Value Fund Class C	COCVX	B	B	B-	Up	3.71	12.21	28.79	32.32	51.37	10.27	945.5	800-345-6611	Y

Category: Global Equity Large Cap (con't)

Fund Name	Ticker Symbol	RATINGS: Overall Rating	RATINGS: Reward Rating	RATINGS: Risk Rating	RATINGS: Recent Up/ Downgrade	TOTAL RETURNS & PERFORMANCE: 3-Month Total Return	6-Month Total Return	1-Year Total Return	3-Year Total Return	5-Year Total Return	ASSETS: NAV	Total Assets (MIL)	NEW INVESTORS: Telephone	Open to New Investors
Columbia Overseas Value Fund Class K	COKVX	B	B	B-	Up	4.00	12.79	29.94	36.16	58.70	10.33	945.5	800-345-6611	
Columbia Overseas Value Fund Class R	COVUX	B	B	B-	Up	3.88	12.54	29.34	34.19	55.06	10.08	945.5	800-345-6611	
Columbia Overseas Value Fund Class T	COVWX	B	B	B-	Up	3.89	12.57	29.57	35.14	57.03	10.3	945.5	800-345-6611	Y
Columbia Overseas Value Fund Institutional 2 Class	COSSX	B	B	B-	Up	4.02	12.84	30.22	36.79	59.65	10.28	945.5	800-345-6611	Y
Columbia Overseas Value Fund Institutional 3 Class	COSYX	B	B	B-	Up	4.06	12.87	30.23	36.95	59.84	10.29	945.5	800-345-6611	Y
Columbia Overseas Value Fund Institutional Class	COSZX	B	B	B-	Up	3.99	12.77	30.05	36.20	58.96	10.33	945.5	800-345-6611	
Consulting Group International Equity Fund	TIEUX	B-	B-	B	Up	4.00	10.53	27.14	25.45	38.10	12.98	1,330	855-332-5306	Y
CRM International Opportunity Fund Institutional Class	CRIIX	B	B	A	Up	4.28	9.56	25.77	35.53	40.47	14.09	14.3	800-276-2883	Y
CRM International Opportunity Fund Investor Class	CRMIX	B	B	A	Up	4.20	9.43	25.50	34.49	38.81	14.03	14.3	800-276-2883	Y
Cullen International High Dividend Fund Cls Institutional	CIHIX	B-	C+	B	Up	1.77	4.59	17.99	14.95	23.63	10.65	251.4	800-582-6757	Y
Davis International Fund Class A	DILAX	B	B+	B	Up	4.67	16.07	38.08	36.85	62.56	13.31	200.7	800-279-0279	Y
Davis International Fund Class C	DILCX	B	B	B-	Up	4.34	15.42	36.61	32.46	54.04	12.5	200.7	800-279-0279	Y
Davis International Fund Class Y	DILYX	B+	A-	B	Up	4.70	16.13	38.43	38.00	65.33	13.14	200.7	800-279-0279	Y
Delaware International Value Equity Fund Class A	DEGIX	B	B-	B	Up	2.07	7.53	22.39	28.03	45.69	15.63	319.9		Y
Delaware International Value Equity Fund Class C	DEGCX	B-	C+	B	Up	1.86	7.12	21.53	25.12	40.26	15.42	319.9		Y
Delaware International Value Equity Fund Class R	DIVRX	B-	B-	B	Up	2.03	7.44	22.15	27.06	43.90	15.6	319.9		Y
Delaware International Value Equity Fund Institutional Cls	DEQIX	B	B-	B	Up	2.10	7.69	22.68	28.96	47.56	15.68	319.9		Y
Deutsche EAFE Equity Index Fund Institutional Class	BTAEX	B-	B-	B	Up	4.08	9.63	25.44	24.57	44.61	6.58	60.6	201-593-8273	Y
Deutsche International Growth Fund - Class A	SGQAX	B-	C+	B	Up	3.02	8.14	25.10	22.15	53.73	35.18	629.2	201-593-8273	Y
Deutsche International Growth Fund - Class C	SGQCX	B-	C+	B	Up	2.81	7.71	24.17	19.40	48.01	33.23	629.2	201-593-8273	Y
Deutsche International Growth Fund - Class Institutional	SGQIX	B-	B-	B	Up	3.12	8.33	25.54	23.22	55.87	35.15	629.2	201-593-8273	Y
Deutsche International Growth Fund - Class R	SGQRX	B-	C+	B	Up	2.94	7.97	24.77	21.18	51.71	34.95	629.2	201-593-8273	Y
Deutsche International Growth Fund - Class R6	SGQTX	B-	B-	B	Up	3.11	8.29	25.46	23.06	55.64	35.14	629.2	201-593-8273	Y
Deutsche International Growth Fund - Class S	SCOBX	B-	B-	B	Up	3.10	8.28	25.45	23.09	55.68	35.14	629.2	201-593-8273	Y
DFA CSTG&E International Social Core Equity Portfolio	DFCCX	B-	B	C+	Up	4.47	11.90	27.49	31.87	52.92	10.28	98.0	512-306-7400	
DFA International Core Equity Portfolio Institutional Cls	DFIEX	B	B	B	Up	4.69	11.94	28.05	34.03	58.13	14.54	25,849	512-306-7400	Y
DFA International Large Cap Growth Portfolio	DILRX	B-	B-	B	Up	3.26	8.19	26.42	25.22	49.44	13.19	328.9	512-306-7400	Y
DFA Intl Social Core Equity Portfolio Inst Cls Shares	DSCLX	B-	B	C+	Up	4.47	11.91	27.65	34.09	54.99	13.99	845.5	512-306-7400	Y
DFA International Sustainability Core 1 Portfolio	DFSPX	B	B-	B	Up	3.85	9.90	27.25	29.92	52.26	11.05	794.8	512-306-7400	Y
DFA International Value Portfolio Class R2	DFIPX	B-	B-	B-	Up	5.41	14.09	25.80	26.41	46.92	20.44	9,950	512-306-7400	Y
DFA Large Cap International Portfolio Institutional Class	DFALX	B-	B-	B	Up	4.10	9.99	25.36	24.96	45.41	23.93	4,774	512-306-7400	Y
DFA T.A. World ex U.S. Core Equity Portfolio Inst Cls	DFTWX	B	B	B-	Up	5.53	12.80	30.50	33.18	49.86	11.87	3,447	512-306-7400	Y
DFA Tax Managed International Value Portfolio	DTMIX	B-	B-	B-	Up	5.34	13.99	25.94	26.73	46.66	16.87	3,968	512-306-7400	Y
DFA World ex U.S. Core Equity Portfolio Inst Cls Shares	DFWIX	B	B	B-	Up	5.50	12.76	30.12	32.76		12.49	2,863	512-306-7400	Y
Domini Impact International Equity Fund A Shares	DOMAX	B	B	B	Up	2.75	7.35	24.45	29.55	60.84	9.4	1,226	800-582-6757	Y
Domini Impact Intl Equity Fund Inst Shares	DOMOX	B	B	B	Up	2.85	7.58	24.78	31.17	63.97	8.9	1,226	800-582-6757	Y
Domini Impact International Equity Fund Investor Shares	DOMIX	B	B-	B	Up	2.85	7.45	24.60	29.61	60.83	8.93	1,226	800-582-6757	Y
Dreyfus Diversified International Fund Class A	DFPAX	B-	B-	B	Up	4.70	10.93	27.45	25.70	40.93	13.47	894.8	800-645-6561	Y
Dreyfus Diversified International Fund Class C	DFPCX	B-	C+	B	Up	4.54	10.50	26.47	23.06	35.68	13.46	894.8	800-645-6561	Y
Dreyfus Diversified International Fund Class I	DFPIX	B	B-	B	Up	4.84	11.16	27.82	27.10	43.22	13.47	894.8	800-645-6561	Y
Dreyfus Diversified International Fund Class Y	DDIFX	B	B-	B	Up	4.81	11.13	27.91	27.15	43.29	13.45	894.8	800-645-6561	Y
Dreyfus International Equity Fund Class A	DIEAX	B-	B-	B	Up	3.95	11.18	27.99	26.68	53.62	40.45	722.6	800-645-6561	Y
Dreyfus International Equity Fund Class C	DIECX	B-	B-	B	Up	3.76	10.74	26.99	23.77	47.76	40.97	722.6	800-645-6561	Y
Dreyfus International Equity Fund Class I	DIERX	B	B-	B	Up	4.02	11.32	28.34	27.29	54.71	41.06	722.6	800-645-6561	Y
Dreyfus International Equity Fund Class Y	DIEYX	B	B-	B	Up	4.03	11.33	28.35	27.23	54.64	41.04	722.6	800-645-6561	Y
Dreyfus International Stock Fund Class A	DISAX	B	B	B	Up	4.51	9.51	26.51	29.98	36.35	18.62	4,096	800-645-6561	
Dreyfus International Stock Fund Class C	DISCX	B-	B-	B	Up	4.36	9.13	25.68	27.07	31.36	18.4	4,096	800-645-6561	
Dreyfus International Stock Fund Class I	DISRX	B	B	B	Up	4.57	9.67	27.00	31.29	38.75	18.69	4,096	800-645-6561	
Dreyfus International Stock Fund Class Y	DISYX	B	B	B	Up	4.59	9.75	26.99	31.44	37.45	18.48	4,096	800-645-6561	
Dreyfus International Stock Index Fund Class I	DINIX	B-	B-	B	Up	3.88	9.32	24.71	23.66	43.11	17.91	621.1	800-645-6561	Y
Dreyfus International Stock Index Fund Investor Shares	DIISX	B-	B-	B	Up	3.80	9.18	24.46	23.22	42.60	17.93	621.1	800-645-6561	Y
Dreyfus/Newton International Equity Fund Class A	NIEAX	B-	C+	B	Up	6.43	11.94	28.42	21.74	40.60	22.69	1,214	800-645-6561	Y

Category: Global Equity Large Cap (con't)

Fund Name	Ticker Symbol	RATINGS: Overall Rating	Reward Rating	Risk Rating	Recent Up/ Downgrade	TOTAL RETURNS & PERFORMANCE: 3-Month Total Return	6-Month Total Return	1-Year Total Return	3-Year Total Return	5-Year Total Return	ASSETS: NAV	Total Assets (MIL)	NEW INVESTORS: Telephone	Open to New Investors
Dreyfus/Newton International Equity Fund Class C	NIECX	B-	C+	B	Up	6.24	11.48	27.44	18.76	35.20	22.21	1,214	800-645-6561	Y
Dreyfus/Newton International Equity Fund Class I	SNIEX	B-	C+	B	Up	6.47	12.03	28.68	22.62	42.54	22.46	1,214	800-645-6561	Y
Dreyfus/Newton International Equity Fund Class Y	NIEYX	B-	C+	B	Up	6.47	12.05	28.72	22.78	42.94	22.36	1,214	800-645-6561	Y
Dunham International Stock Fund Class A	DAINX	B-	C+	B-	Up	4.42	10.07	25.36	22.16	44.35	16.97	112.9	800-442-4358	Y
Dunham International Stock Fund Class C	DCINX	B-	C+	B-	Up	4.25	9.62	24.38	19.43	39.00	16.18	112.9	800-442-4358	Y
Dunham International Stock Fund Class N	DNINX	B-	C+	B-	Up	4.47	10.15	25.61	23.08	46.12	17.06	112.9	800-442-4358	Y
Eaton Vance Hexavest International Equity Fund Class A	EHIAX	B-	C+	B	Up	1.84	4.67	16.63	17.75	34.03	11.8	8.0		Y
Eaton Vance Hexavest International Equity Fund Class I	EHIIX	B-	C+	B	Up	1.89	4.89	17.06	18.76	35.69	11.84	8.0		Y
Elfun International Equity Fund	EGLBX	B-	C+	B-	Up	4.37	9.43	22.98	20.60	38.54	22.68	235.8	800-242-0134	Y
EntrepreneurShares Global Fund Institutional Class	ENTIX	B	B+	B-	Up	7.32	13.25	30.13	43.44	83.45	15.34	39.2		Y
EQ/International Equity Index Portfolio Class IA Shares	US4049926615	B-	B-	B	Up	3.50	8.86	23.50	20.80	40.24		1,841	877-222-2144	Y
EQ/MFS International Growth Portfolio Class IA	US2689544359	B	B	B	Up	5.46	10.17	32.03	32.91	46.40		1,546	877-222-2144	Y
EQ/MFS International Growth Portfolio Class IB	US29364E4052	B	B	B	Up	5.45	10.29	32.14	33.02	46.51		1,546	877-222-2144	Y
EQ/MFS International Growth Portfolio Class K	US26883L4986	B	B	B	Up	5.44	10.27	32.33	33.88	48.22		1,546	877-222-2144	Y
FDP BlackRock International Fund Institutional Shares	MAIQX	B-	C+	B-	Up	5.68	10.50	28.53	23.49	38.34	14.14	102.5		Y
FDP BlackRock International Fund Investor A Shares	MDIQX	B-	C+	B-	Up	5.63	10.39	28.32	22.54	36.58	14.05	102.5		Y
FDP BlackRock International Fund Investor C Shares	MCIQX	B-	C+	B-	Up	5.42	9.98	27.29	19.76	31.57	13.99	102.5		Y
Fidelity Advisor® Diversified International Fund Class A	FDVAX	B	B-	B	Up	3.75	9.05	26.56	27.19	56.86	23.66	2,266	617-563-7000	Y
Fidelity Advisor® Diversified International Fund Class C	FADCX	B-	C+	B	Up	3.56	8.60	25.62	24.37	51.09	22.72	2,266	617-563-7000	Y
Fidelity Advisor® Diversified International Fund Class M	FADIX	B	B-	B	Up	3.68	8.88	26.17	26.18	54.81	23.52	2,266	617-563-7000	Y
Fidelity Advisor® Diversified International Fund Class Z	FZABX	B	B-	B	Up	3.85	9.26	27.06	28.86	60.25	23.98	2,266	617-563-7000	Y
Fidelity Advisor® Diversified International Fund I Class	FDVIX	B	B-	B	Up	3.80	9.16	26.87	28.20	59.12	24.01	2,266	617-563-7000	Y
Fidelity Advisor® Intl Capital Appreciation Fund Cls A	FCPAX	B	B	B	Up	5.71	12.51	35.49	33.97	68.95	19.76	1,134	617-563-7000	Y
Fidelity Advisor® Intl Capital Appreciation Fund Cls C	FCPCX	B	B	B	Up	5.49	12.05	34.46	30.93	62.60	17.48	1,134	617-563-7000	Y
Fidelity Advisor® Intl Capital Appreciation Fund Cls M	FIATX	B	B	B	Up	5.64	12.28	35.10	32.96	66.81	19.28	1,134	617-563-7000	Y
Fidelity Advisor® Intl Capital Appreciation Fund Cls Z	FIDZX	B	B	B	Up	5.80	12.68	36.03	35.21	71.26	21.08	1,134	617-563-7000	Y
Fidelity Advisor® Intl Capital Appreciation Fund I Cls	FCPIX	B	B	B	Up	5.78	12.61	35.87	35.05	71.05	21.07	1,134	617-563-7000	Y
Fidelity Advisor® International Discovery Fund Class A	FAIDX	B	B-	B	Up	3.90	11.41	31.24	28.34	52.24	45.41	10,832	617-563-7000	Y
Fidelity Advisor® International Discovery Fund Class C	FCADX	B-	B-	B	Up	3.70	10.98	30.27	25.45	46.59	44.94	10,832	617-563-7000	Y
Fidelity Advisor® International Discovery Fund Class I	FIADX	B	B	B	Up	4.00	11.60	31.69	29.68	54.85	45.55	10,832	617-563-7000	Y
Fidelity Advisor® International Discovery Fund Class M	FTADX	B	B-	B	Up	3.83	11.28	30.94	27.43	50.43	45.18	10,832	617-563-7000	Y
Fidelity Advisor® International Discovery Fund Class Z	FZAIX	B	B	B	Up	4.03	11.67	31.88	30.22	55.81	45.5	10,832	617-563-7000	Y
Fidelity Advisor® International Growth Fund Class A	FIAGX	B	B-	B	Up	4.33	8.39	29.18	28.44	53.38	13.61	2,366	617-563-7000	Y
Fidelity Advisor® International Growth Fund Class C	FIGCX	B-	C+	B	Up	4.19	7.97	28.22	25.51	47.54	13.4	2,366	617-563-7000	Y
Fidelity Advisor® International Growth Fund Class M	FITGX	B	B-	B	Up	4.29	8.27	28.85	27.27	51.12	13.6	2,366	617-563-7000	Y
Fidelity Advisor® International Growth Fund Class Z	FZAJX	B	B-	B	Up	4.47	8.67	29.85	30.18	56.74	13.67	2,366	617-563-7000	Y
Fidelity Advisor® International Growth Fund I Class	FIIIX	B	B-	B	Up	4.44	8.56	29.62	29.60	55.81	13.66	2,366	617-563-7000	Y
Fidelity Advisor® International Value Fund Class A	FIVMX	B-	C+	B	Up	2.08	6.70	19.29	17.38	33.65	9.08	554.5	617-563-7000	Y
Fidelity Advisor® International Value Fund Class M	FIVPX	B-	C+	B	Up	1.89	6.50	18.94	16.29	31.76	9.08	554.5	617-563-7000	Y
Fidelity Advisor® Overseas Fund Class A	FAOAX	B-	B-	B	Up	3.54	9.30	29.64	26.43	53.09	24.85	669.4	617-563-7000	Y
Fidelity Advisor® Overseas Fund Class C	FAOCX	B-	C+	B	Up	3.30	8.85	28.56	23.37	47.15	24.17	669.4	617-563-7000	Y
Fidelity Advisor® Overseas Fund Class I	FAOIX	B	B-	B	Up	3.58	9.44	30.03	27.63	55.60	25.35	669.4	617-563-7000	Y
Fidelity Advisor® Overseas Fund Class M	FAERX	B-	B-	B	Up	3.46	9.14	29.35	25.64	51.61	25.54	669.4	617-563-7000	Y
Fidelity Advisor® Overseas Fund Class Z	FAOSX	B-	B-	B	Up	3.64	9.50	30.05	26.32	52.43	25.34	669.4	617-563-7000	Y
Fidelity Advisor® Total International Equity Fund Class A	FTAEX	B-	B-	B	Up	4.95	10.84	30.06	28.57	42.79	9.29	119.1	617-563-7000	Y
Fidelity Advisor® Total International Equity Fund Class C	FTCEX	B-	B-	B	Up	4.78	10.41	29.01	25.71	37.69	9.32	119.1	617-563-7000	Y
Fidelity Advisor® Total International Equity Fund Class M	FTTEX	B-	B-	B	Up	4.83	10.69	29.64	27.58	41.07	9.33	119.1	617-563-7000	Y
Fidelity Advisor® Total International Equity Fund Class Z	FIEZX	B	B-	B	Up	5.05	11.08	30.37	29.58	44.76	9.28	119.1	617-563-7000	Y
Fidelity Advisor® Total International Equity Fund I Class	FTEIX	B	B-	B	Up	4.95	10.97	30.27	29.48	44.65	9.26	119.1	617-563-7000	Y
Fidelity® Diversified International Fund	FDIVX	B-	B-	B	Up	3.67	8.92	26.65	25.37	53.71	40.02	19,405	617-563-7000	Y
Fidelity® Diversified International Fund Class K	FDIKX	B-	B-	B	Up	3.70	8.98	26.79	25.86	54.69	39.93	19,405	617-563-7000	Y
Fidelity® Global ex U.S. Index Fund Institutional Class	FSGSX	B-	B-	B-	Up	4.74	11.04	27.37	25.26	38.60	13.54	3,166	617-563-7000	Y

Category: Global Equity Large Cap (con't)

		RATINGS				TOTAL RETURNS & PERFORMANCE					ASSETS		NEW INVESTORS	
Fund Name	Ticker Symbol	Overall Rating	Reward Rating	Risk Rating	Recent Up/ Downgrade	3-Month Total Return	6-Month Total Return	1-Year Total Return	3-Year Total Return	5-Year Total Return	NAV	Total Assets (MIL)	Telephone	Open to New Investors
Fidelity® Global ex U.S. Index Fund Inst Premium Cls	FSGGX	B-	B-	B-	Up	4.68	10.97	27.39	25.35	38.79	13.54	3,166	617-563-7000	Y
Fidelity® Global ex U.S. Index Fund Investor Class	FSGUX	B-	B-	B-	Up	4.73	11.03	27.25	24.91	37.96	13.54	3,166	617-563-7000	Y
Fidelity® Global ex U.S. Index Fund Premium Class	FSGDX	B-	B-	B-	Up	4.72	11.02	27.34	25.19	38.38	13.54	3,166	617-563-7000	Y
Fidelity® International Capital Appreciation Fund	FIVFX	B	B	B	Up	5.84	12.75	36.24	35.55	72.16	21.06	2,158	617-563-7000	Y
Fidelity® International Discovery Fund	FIGRX	B	B	B	Up	3.99	11.60	31.70	29.72	54.92	45.66	10,832	617-563-7000	Y
Fidelity® International Discovery Fund Class K	FIDKX	B	B	B	Up	4.03	11.65	31.85	30.18	55.96	45.53	10,832	617-563-7000	Y
Fidelity® International Enhanced Index Fund	FIENX	B-	B	C+	Up	3.60	10.61	27.58	31.29	57.58	10.14	925.2	617-563-7000	Y
Fidelity® International Growth Fund	FIGFX	B	B-	B	Up	4.43	8.54	29.56	29.61	55.63	13.69	2,366	617-563-7000	Y
Fidelity® International Index Fund Institutional Class	FSPNX	B-	B-	B	Up	3.93	9.36	25.33	25.52	46.77	43.18	20,829	617-563-7000	Y
Fidelity® Intl Index Fund Inst Premium Cls	FSPSX	B-	B-	B	Up	3.94	9.39	25.37	25.56	46.84	43.18	20,829	617-563-7000	Y
Fidelity® International Index Fund Investor Class	FSIIX	B-	C+	B	Up	3.93	9.32	25.22	25.05	45.83	43.18	20,829	617-563-7000	Y
Fidelity® International Index Fund Premium Class	FSIVX	B-	B-	B	Up	3.95	9.37	25.35	25.41	46.48	43.18	20,829	617-563-7000	Y
Fidelity® International Value Fund	FIVLX	B-	C+	B	Up	2.13	6.87	19.64	18.60	36.00	9.06	554.5	617-563-7000	Y
Fidelity® Overseas Fund	FOSFX	B	B	A-	Up	3.35	9.30	29.64	38.13	70.58	50.7	8,058	617-563-7000	Y
Fidelity® Overseas Fund Class K	FOSKX	B	B	A-	Up	3.38	9.36	29.80	38.66	71.75	50.58	8,058	617-563-7000	Y
Fidelity® SAI International Minimum Volatility Index Fund	FSKLX	B-	C+	B	Up	4.48	7.60	21.40			10.98	1,903	617-563-7000	Y
Fidelity® Series Global ex U.S. Index Fund	FSGEX	B-	B-	B-	Up	4.74	11.00	27.47	25.26	38.55	13.24	5,095	617-563-7000	Y
Fidelity® Series International Growth Fund	FIGSX	B	B-	B	Up	4.88	9.36	30.21	30.36	56.09	16.15	14,950	617-563-7000	
Fidelity® Total International Equity Fund	FTIEX	B	B-	B	Up	4.90	10.91	30.29	29.63	45.23	9.31	119.1	617-563-7000	Y
First Eagle Overseas Fund Class A	SGOVX	B-	C+	B+		1.94	4.39	14.05	22.54	37.14	24.69	18,411	800-334-2143	
First Eagle Overseas Fund Class C	FESOX	B-	C+	B		1.73	4.02	13.22	19.81	32.11	23.76	18,411	800-334-2143	
First Eagle Overseas Fund Class I	SGOIX	B	C+	B+	Up	2.00	4.53	14.36	23.54	38.92	25.22	18,411	800-334-2143	
First Eagle Overseas Fund Class R6	FEORX	B-	C+	B+		2.02	4.59	14.33	22.84	37.48	25.22	18,411	800-334-2143	
First Investors International Fund Advisor Class	FIIPX	B	B	B	Up	4.72	8.54	32.21	29.36	41.36	16.64	371.0	800-423-4026	Y
First Investors International Fund Class A	FIINX	B	B-	B	Up	4.64	8.37	31.68	27.87	39.14	16.39	371.0	800-423-4026	Y
First Investors International Fund Class B	FIIOX	B-	C+	B	Up	4.37	7.83	30.51	24.68	33.45	15.27	371.0	800-423-4026	Y
First Investors International Fund Institutional Class	FIIQX	B	B	B	Up	4.74	8.55	32.35	29.78	42.47	16.68	371.0	800-423-4026	Y
FMI International Fund	FMIJX	B	B-	B+	Up	2.69	5.52	15.44	30.65	72.84	33.94	8,143	800-811-5311	Y
FMI International Fund Institutional Class	FMIYX	B	B-	B+	Up	2.73	5.62	15.58	30.84	73.09	33.97	8,143	800-811-5311	Y
Franklin International Growth Fund Class A	FNGAX	B+	A-	B	Up	6.19	15.65	36.80	38.46	47.79	14.47	307.2	650-312-2000	Y
Franklin International Growth Fund Class Adv	FNGZX	B+	A-	B	Up	6.23	15.82	37.03	39.55	49.91	14.47	307.2	650-312-2000	Y
Franklin International Growth Fund Class C	US3535337220	B	B+	B	Up	5.93	15.22	35.71	35.45	42.48	14	307.2	650-312-2000	Y
Franklin International Growth Fund Class R	US3535337147	B+	A-	B	Up	6.09	15.56	36.37	37.50	46.19	14.4	307.2	650-312-2000	Y
Franklin International Growth Fund Class R6	FILRX	B+	A-	B	Up	6.23	15.91	37.24	40.36	50.92	14.47	307.2	650-312-2000	Y
GAMCO International Growth Fund Class A	GAIGX	B-	C+	B-	Up	6.08	10.63	29.32	21.41	31.17	24.65	25.1	914-921-5135	Y
GAMCO International Growth Fund Class AAA	GIGRX	B-	C+	B-	Up	6.04	10.59	29.29	21.39	31.08	24.15	25.1	914-921-5135	Y
GAMCO International Growth Fund Class C	GCIGX	B-	C+	B-	Up	5.89	10.25	28.37	18.71	26.36	21.92	25.1	914-921-5135	Y
GAMCO International Growth Fund Class I	GIIGX	B-	B-	B	Up	6.35	11.24	30.78	25.50	36.70	24.45	25.1	914-921-5135	Y
Gerstein Fisher Multi-Factor Intl Growth Equity Fund	GFIGX	B	B	B	Up	4.66	11.65	32.12	30.26	66.05	15.97	239.6		Y
Glenmede Fund International Portfolio	GTCIX	B-	C+	B	Up	3.55	7.80	22.43	21.47	34.07	15.4	464.5	800-442-8299	Y
GMO International Developed Equity Allocation Fund Cls III	GIOTX	B-	C+	B-	Up	4.31	11.16	26.38	21.30	44.17	17.27	671.7	617-330-7500	Y
GMO International Equity Allocation Fund Class III	GIEAX	B-	B-	B-	Up	5.02	11.03	27.79	23.52	37.19	32.18	1,076	617-330-7500	Y
GMO International Equity Allocation Series Fund Class R6	GEARX	B-	B-	B-	Up	4.96	10.94	27.37	23.08	36.40	10.52	253.6	617-330-7500	Y
GMO International Equity Fund Class II	GMICX	B-	C+	B-	Up	4.04	11.14	25.60	19.79	41.64	23.66	5,428	617-330-7500	Y
GMO International Equity Fund Class III	GMOIX	B-	C+	B-	Up	4.05	11.19	25.72	20.05	42.11	23.95	5,428	617-330-7500	Y
GMO International Equity Fund Class IV	GMCFX	B-	C+	B-	Up	4.10	11.25	25.81	20.33	42.62	23.91	5,428	617-330-7500	Y
GMO International Large/Mid Cap Equity Fund Class IV	GMIRX	B-	C+	B-	Up	5.06	11.49	25.03	19.25	40.84	26.32	80.4	617-330-7500	Y
GMO Tax-Managed International Equities Fund Class III	GTMIX	B-	C+	B-	Up	4.11	12.31	28.44	20.50	42.10	17.01	110.9	617-330-7500	Y
Goldman Sachs Enhanced Div Global Eq Port Cls A	GADGX	B-	C+	B-	Down	3.41	7.73	14.67	22.50	56.11	12.07	674.5	800-526-7384	Y
Goldman Sachs Enhanced Div Global Eq Port Cls Inst	GIDGX	B-	C+	B-	Up	3.57	7.89	15.17	23.99	59.37	12.17	674.5	800-526-7384	Y
Goldman Sachs Focused International Equity Fund Class A	GSIFX	B-	C+	B	Up	5.09	9.34	25.29	23.14	39.53	20.28	186.0	800-526-7384	Y
Goldman Sachs Focused International Equity Fund Class C	GSICX	B-	C+	B-	Up	4.89	8.94	24.40	20.44	34.42	18.82	186.0	800-526-7384	Y

Category: Global Equity Large Cap (con't)

Fund Name	Ticker Symbol	Overall Rating	Reward Rating	Risk Rating	Recent Up/ Downgrade	3-Month Total Return	6-Month Total Return	1-Year Total Return	3-Year Total Return	5-Year Total Return	NAV	Total Assets (MIL)	Telephone	Open to New Investors
		RATINGS				TOTAL RETURNS & PERFORMANCE					ASSETS		NEW INVESTORS	
Goldman Sachs Focused International Equity Fund Class R6	GSIWX	B-	C+	B	Up	5.19	9.59	25.86	23.83	40.04	20.61	186.0	800-526-7384	Y
Goldman Sachs Focused Intl Equity Fund Inst Cls	GSIEX	B-	C+	B	Up	5.22	9.63	25.82	24.61	42.39	20.62	186.0	800-526-7384	Y
Goldman Sachs Focused Intl Equity Fund Inv Cls	GIRNX	B-	C+	B	Up	5.17	9.53	25.62	24.10	41.31	20.61	186.0	800-526-7384	Y
Goldman Sachs Focused Intl Equity Fund Service Cls	GSISX	B-	C+	B	Up	5.08	9.33	25.19	22.72	38.78	21.22	186.0	800-526-7384	Y
Goldman Sachs International Equity Insights Fund Class A	GCIAX	B	B	B+	Up	3.78	10.99	29.13	41.04	62.72	13.25	1,482	800-526-7384	Y
Goldman Sachs International Equity Insights Fund Class C	GCICX	B	B	B	Up	3.60	10.49	28.08	37.80	56.71	12.97	1,482	800-526-7384	Y
Goldman Sachs International Equity Insights Fund Class R	GCIRX	B	B	B-	Up	3.72	10.85	28.76	39.92	60.71	12.9	1,482	800-526-7384	Y
Goldman Sachs International Equity Insights Fund Class R6	GCIUX	B	B+	B-	Up	3.93	11.21	29.69	42.58	66.03	13.59	1,482	800-526-7384	Y
Goldman Sachs International Equity Insights Fund Class S	GCISX	B	B	B+	Up	3.75	10.88	28.92	40.47	61.75	13.38	1,482	800-526-7384	Y
Goldman Sachs Intl Equity Insights Fund Inst Cls	GCIIX	B+	B+	B+	Up	3.91	11.19	29.65	42.58	66.03	13.6	1,482	800-526-7384	Y
Goldman Sachs Intl Equity Insights Fund Inv Cls	GCITX	B	B	B-	Up	3.91	11.17	29.48	41.96	64.70	12.99	1,482	800-526-7384	Y
Goldman Sachs International Tax-Managed Equity Fund Cls A	GATMX	B	B	B	Up	4.09	10.96	28.85	34.49	57.27	10.93	622.3	800-526-7384	Y
Goldman Sachs International Tax-Managed Equity Fund Cls C	GCTMX	B	B	B	Up	3.84	10.47	27.85	31.44	51.44	10.59	622.3	800-526-7384	Y
Goldman Sachs Intl Tax-Managed Equity Fund Inst Cls	GHTMX	B	B	B	Up	4.17	11.19	29.42	35.99	60.58	10.85	622.3	800-526-7384	Y
Goldman Sachs Intl Tax-Managed Equity Fund Inv Cls	GITRX	B	B	B	Up	4.16	11.03	29.09	35.29	59.11	10.92	622.3	800-526-7384	Y
Goldman Sachs Strategic International Equity Fund Class A	GSAKX	B-	C+	B	Up	3.81	9.06	26.04	22.13	41.28	14.69	63.2	800-526-7384	Y
Goldman Sachs Strategic International Equity Fund Class C	GSCKX	B-	C+	B-	Up	3.57	8.64	25.06	19.45	36.00	13.2	63.2	800-526-7384	Y
Goldman Sachs Strategic Intl Equity Fund Cls Inst	GSIKX	B-	C+	B	Up	3.90	9.27	26.53	23.58	44.13	15.36	63.2	800-526-7384	Y
Goldman Sachs Strategic International Equity Fund Class R	GSRKX	B-	C+	B	Up	3.81	8.94	25.76	21.30	39.55	14.79	63.2	800-526-7384	Y
Goldman Sachs Strategic International Equity Fund Class R6	GSUKX	B-	C+	B	Up	3.93	9.31	26.48	23.56	44.10	15.35	63.2	800-526-7384	Y
Goldman Sachs Strategic Intl Equity Fund Inv Cls	GSTKX	B-	C+	B	Up	3.88	9.28	26.42	23.19	43.14	14.68	63.2	800-526-7384	Y
Great-West International Index Fund Institutional Class	MXPBX	B-	C+	B	Up	3.74	9.07	25.50	23.29	43.74		965.4		Y
Great-West International Index Fund Investor Class	MXINX	B-	C+	B	Up	3.65	8.91	24.97	22.31	42.59		965.4		Y
Great-West MFS International Growth Fund Institutional Cls	MXHTX	B-	B-	B	Up	3.30	7.41	27.41	25.26	43.78		371.4		Y
Great-West MFS International Growth Fund Investor Class	MXIGX	B-	B-	B	Up	3.29	7.28	26.98	24.58	43.00		371.4		Y
Great-West MFS International Value Fund Class L	MXMIX	B	B	B+		5.58	8.91	26.36	36.82	79.44		1,285		Y
Great-West MFS International Value Fund Institutional Cls	MXJVX	B+	B	A-	Up	5.71	9.14	27.08	39.34	83.83		1,285		Y
Great-West MFS International Value Fund Investor Class	MXIVX	B	B	B+		5.65	9.05	26.68	38.10	82.20		1,285		Y
GuideMark® World ex-US Fund Institutional Shares	GIWEX	B-	B-	B-	Up	4.04	10.54	27.64	23.35	37.87	9.74	200.7	603-888-5500	Y
GuideMark® World ex-US Fund Service Shares	GMWEX	B-	C+	B-	Up	3.81	9.22	25.93	20.11	32.68	9.5	200.7	603-888-5500	Y
GuideStone Funds Intl Equity Fund Inst Cls	GIEYX	B	B	B	Up	3.49	11.24	29.84	30.25	48.14	15.72	1,604	214-720-1171	Y
GuideStone Funds International Equity Fund Investor Class	GIEZX	B	B	B	Up	3.38	11.04	29.50	29.10	46.18	15.74	1,604	214-720-1171	Y
Harbor International Fund Institutional Class	HAINX	B-	C+	B-	Up	2.18	5.87	22.89	18.00	30.51	67.52	31,937	800-422-1050	Y
Harbor International Fund Retirement Class	HNINX	B-	C+	B-	Up	2.20	5.91	22.98	18.12	30.64	67.48	31,937	800-422-1050	Y
Harbor International Growth Fund Administrative Class	HRIGX	B	B	B	Up	4.34	9.27	30.77	32.05	45.95	15.81	403.4	800-422-1050	Y
Harbor International Growth Fund Institutional Class	HAIGX	B	B	B	Up	4.44	9.44	31.06	33.11	47.88	15.81	403.4	800-422-1050	Y
Harbor International Growth Fund Investor Class	HIIGX	B	B	B	Up	4.33	9.21	30.63	31.61	45.13	15.74	403.4	800-422-1050	Y
Harbor International Growth Fund Retirement Class	HNGFX	B	B	B	Up	4.50	9.51	31.34	33.37	48.16	15.82	403.4	800-422-1050	Y
Harding Loevner Intl Equity Portfolio Inst Cls	HLMIX	B	B	B-	Up	4.51	10.76	29.90	33.89	52.50	22.78	12,226	877-435-8105	Y
Harding Loevner Intl Equity Portfolio Inst Cls Z	HLIZX	B	B	B-	Up	3.69	9.99	28.99	32.95	51.43	22.77	12,226	877-435-8105	Y
Harding Loevner Intl Equity Portfolio Inv Cls	HLMNX	B	B	B-	Up	4.46	10.62	29.43	32.59	50.06	22.75	12,226	877-435-8105	Y
Hartford International Equity Fund Class A	HDVAX	B	B	B	Up	3.81	10.89	28.54	32.36	50.16	11.35	56.1	888-843-7824	Y
Hartford International Equity Fund Class C	HDVCX	B-	B-	B	Up	3.59	10.42	27.49	29.49	44.57	11.25	56.1	888-843-7824	Y
Hartford International Equity Fund Class F	HDVFX	B	B	B	Up	3.95	11.07	29.00	33.64	52.86	11.46	56.1	888-843-7824	Y
Hartford International Equity Fund Class I	HDVIX	B	B	B	Up	3.87	11.00	28.80	33.43	52.62	11.43	56.1	888-843-7824	Y
Hartford International Equity Fund Class R3	HDVRX	B	B	B	Up	3.74	10.74	28.16	31.18	48.15	11.32	56.1	888-843-7824	Y
Hartford International Equity Fund Class R4	HDVSX	B	B	B	Up	3.78	10.84	28.47	32.33	50.31	11.36	56.1	888-843-7824	Y
Hartford International Equity Fund Class R5	HDVTX	B	B	B	Up	3.92	11.05	28.89	32.80	51.88	9.97	56.1	888-843-7824	Y
Hartford International Equity Fund Class Y	HDVYX	B	B	B	Up	3.92	11.06	29.02	33.91	53.29	11.41	56.1	888-843-7824	Y
Hartford International Growth Fund Class A	HNCAX	B	B	B	Up	3.76	11.64	33.01	28.14	56.76	15.35	267.3	888-843-7824	Y
Hartford International Growth Fund Class C	HNCCX	B-	B-	B	Up	3.57	11.21	31.90	25.24	51.14	14.18	267.3	888-843-7824	Y
Hartford International Growth Fund Class F	HNCFX	B	B	B	Up	3.91	11.94	33.56	29.69	60.48	15.22	267.3	888-843-7824	Y

Category: Global Equity Large Cap (con't)

Fund Name	Ticker Symbol	RATINGS: Overall Rating	RATINGS: Reward Rating	RATINGS: Risk Rating	RATINGS: Recent Up/ Downgrade	TOTAL RETURNS & PERFORMANCE: 3-Month Total Return	6-Month Total Return	1-Year Total Return	3-Year Total Return	5-Year Total Return	ASSETS: NAV	Total Assets (MIL)	NEW INVESTORS: Telephone	Open to New Investors
Hartford International Growth Fund Class I	HNCJX	B	B	B	Up	3.86	11.82	33.31	29.26	59.38	15.21	267.3	888-843-7824	Y
Hartford International Growth Fund Class R3	HNCRX	B	B-	B	Up	3.74	11.54	32.61	27.10	55.34	15.57	267.3	888-843-7824	Y
Hartford International Growth Fund Class R4	HNCSX	B	B	B	Up	3.77	11.68	32.98	28.29	57.66	15.75	267.3	888-843-7824	Y
Hartford International Growth Fund Class R5	HNCTX	B	B	B	Up	3.85	11.84	33.41	29.47	60.04	15.86	267.3	888-843-7824	Y
Hartford International Growth Fund Class Y	HNCYX	B	B	B	Up	3.88	11.92	33.54	29.68	60.46	15.91	267.3	888-843-7824	Y
Hartford International Opportunities HLS Fund Class IA	HIAOX	B	B	B	Up	3.62	9.18	25.25	28.65	52.89	17.46	1,578	888-843-7824	Y
Hartford International Opportunities HLS Fund Class IB	HBIOX	B	B-	B	Up	3.57	9.06	24.99	27.71	51.00	17.68	1,578	888-843-7824	Y
Hartford International Value Fund Class A	HILAX	B	B	C+	Up	3.79	10.23	24.33	41.77	73.40	17.11	2,769	888-843-7824	
Hartford International Value Fund Class C	HILCX	B	B	C+	Up	3.58	9.90	23.57	39.03	67.81	16.93	2,769	888-843-7824	
Hartford International Value Fund Class F	HILDX	B	B	C+	Up	3.85	10.55	24.86	43.52	76.91	17.27	2,769	888-843-7824	Y
Hartford International Value Fund Class I	HILIX	B	B	C+	Up	3.88	10.45	24.76	43.40	76.76	17.27	2,769	888-843-7824	
Hartford International Value Fund Class R3	HILRX	B	B	C+	Up	3.70	10.09	23.97	40.70	71.30	17.24	2,769	888-843-7824	
Hartford International Value Fund Class R4	HILSX	B	B	C+	Up	3.73	10.26	24.35	41.97	73.97	17.22	2,769	888-843-7824	
Hartford International Value Fund Class R5	HILTX	B	B	C+	Up	3.90	10.52	24.71	43.31	76.68	17.32	2,769	888-843-7824	
Hartford Schroders Intl Multi-Cap Value Fund Cls A	SIDVX	B-	B-	B-	Up	3.57	8.39	22.95	26.05	44.71	10.26	1,441	888-843-7824	Y
Hartford Schroders Intl Multi-Cap Value Fund Cls C	HFYCX	B-	C+	B-	Up	3.34	8.01	22.04	23.34	39.61	10.2	1,441	888-843-7824	Y
Hartford Schroders Intl Multi-Cap Value Fund Cls F	HFYFX	B-	C+	B-	Up	3.57	7.95	21.95	25.72	45.16	10.25	1,441	888-843-7824	Y
Hartford Schroders Intl Multi-Cap Value Fund Cls I	SIDNX	B-	B-	B-	Up	3.54	8.43	23.28	27.09	46.75	10.25	1,441	888-843-7824	Y
Hartford Schroders Intl Multi-Cap Value Fund Cls R3	HFYRX	B-	C+	B-	Up	3.44	8.19	22.50	25.12	43.04	10.23	1,441	888-843-7824	Y
Hartford Schroders Intl Multi-Cap Value Fund Cls R4	HFYSX	B-	B-	B-	Up	3.57	8.38	22.88	26.16	44.94	10.24	1,441	888-843-7824	Y
Hartford Schroders Intl Multi-Cap Value Fund Cls R5	HFYTX	B-	B-	B-	Up	3.54	8.43	23.14	27.07	46.73	10.24	1,441	888-843-7824	Y
Hartford Schroders Intl Multi-Cap Value Fund Cls SDR	SIDRX	B-	B-	B-	Up	3.57	8.49	23.26	27.43	47.31	10.24	1,441	888-843-7824	Y
Hartford Schroders Intl Multi-Cap Value Fund Cls Y	HFYYX	B-	B-	B-	Up	3.66	8.55	23.48	27.45	47.17	10.25	1,441	888-843-7824	Y
Hartford Schroders International Stock Fund Class A	SCVEX	B-	B-	B	Up	3.39	11.47	29.43	26.05	45.49	13.69	204.1	888-843-7824	Y
Hartford Schroders International Stock Fund Class C	HSWCX	B-	B-	B	Up	3.19	11.04	28.56	23.28	40.19	13.15	204.1	888-843-7824	Y
Hartford Schroders International Stock Fund Class F	HSWFX	B	B-	B	Up	3.44	11.71	29.87	27.07	47.40	13.25	204.1	888-843-7824	Y
Hartford Schroders International Stock Fund Class I	SCIEX	B	B-	B	Up	3.45	11.54	29.69	26.88	47.19	13.24	204.1	888-843-7824	Y
Hartford Schroders International Stock Fund Class R3	HSWRX	B-	B-	B	Up	3.35	11.53	29.56	25.46	44.09	13.25	204.1	888-843-7824	Y
Hartford Schroders International Stock Fund Class R4	HSWSX	B-	B-	B	Up	3.41	11.51	29.65	26.19	45.66	13.25	204.1	888-843-7824	Y
Hartford Schroders International Stock Fund Class R5	HSWTX	B	B-	B	Up	3.39	11.56	29.82	27.02	47.34	13.25	204.1	888-843-7824	Y
Hartford Schroders International Stock Fund Class SDR	SCIJX	B	B-	B	Up	3.43	11.69	29.84	27.39	47.77	13.25	204.1	888-843-7824	Y
Hartford Schroders International Stock Fund Class Y	HSWYX	B	B-	B	Up	3.43	11.69	29.97	27.17	47.53	13.26	204.1	888-843-7824	Y
Homestead International Equity Fund	HISIX	B-	B-	B-	Up	4.24	9.85	28.11	29.08	47.47	8.49	73.1		Y
ICON International Equity Fund Class A	IIQAX	B-	C+	B	Up	3.78	7.69	22.64	17.19	19.27	13.43	51.4	303-790-1600	Y
ICON International Equity Fund Class C	IIQCX	B-	C+	B	Up	3.69	7.38	21.91	14.62	15.06	12.07	51.4	303-790-1600	Y
ICON International Equity Fund Class S	ICNEX	B-	C+	B	Up	3.87	7.88	23.02	18.23	21.28	13.68	51.4	303-790-1600	Y
Invesco International Core Equity Fund Class A	IBVAX	B-	C+	B	Up	5.49	12.01	24.46	23.81	38.02	12.68	92.2	800-659-1005	Y
Invesco International Core Equity Fund Class B	IBVBX	B-	C+	B	Up	5.27	11.57	23.56	21.05	32.75	12.78	92.2	800-659-1005	
Invesco International Core Equity Fund Class C	IBVCX	B-	C+	B	Up	5.35	11.64	23.55	21.08	32.86	12.42	92.2	800-659-1005	Y
Invesco International Core Equity Fund Class R	IIBRX	B-	C+	B	Up	5.47	11.89	24.19	22.88	36.27	12.72	92.2	800-659-1005	Y
Invesco International Core Equity Fund Class R5	IBVIX	B-	B-	B	Up	5.60	12.17	24.74	25.24	40.94	12.58	92.2	800-659-1005	Y
Invesco International Core Equity Fund Class R6	IBVFX	B-	B-	B	Up	5.60	12.17	24.87	25.27	41.14	12.58	92.2	800-659-1005	Y
Invesco International Core Equity Fund Class Y	IBVYX	B-	C+	B	Up	5.55	12.15	24.75	24.76	39.65	12.88	92.2	800-659-1005	Y
Invesco International Core Equity Fund Investor Class	IIBCX	B-	C+	B	Up	5.48	12.08	24.45	23.80	37.92	12.89	92.2	800-659-1005	
Invesco International Growth Fund Class A	AIIEX	B-	C+	B	Up	3.07	7.50	22.63	18.14	41.66	36.28	9,060	800-659-1005	
Invesco International Growth Fund Class B	AIEBX	B-	C+	B	Up	2.87	7.08	21.71	15.52	36.47	33.36	9,060	800-659-1005	
Invesco International Growth Fund Class C	AIECX	B-	C+	B	Up	2.86	7.07	21.68	15.50	36.42	33.39	9,060	800-659-1005	
Invesco International Growth Fund Class R	AIERX	B-	C+	B	Up	2.99	7.33	22.32	17.24	39.90	35.86	9,060	800-659-1005	
Invesco International Growth Fund Class R6	IGFRX	B-	C+	B	Up	3.17	7.72	23.16	19.64	44.65	36.79	9,060	800-659-1005	
Invesco International Growth Fund Class Y	AIIYX	B-	C+	B	Up	3.12	7.64	22.94	19.04	43.45	36.34	9,060	800-659-1005	
Invesco International Growth Fund R5 Class	AIEVX	B-	C+	B	Up	3.15	7.67	23.02	19.30	44.08	36.81	9,060	800-659-1005	
iShares MSCI EAFE International Index Fund Class K	BTMKX	B-	C+	B	Up	3.80	9.18	25.17	24.72	44.73	14.18	10,415	800-441-7762	Y

Category: Global Equity Large Cap (con't)

Fund Name	Ticker Symbol	RATINGS: Overall Rating	RATINGS: Reward Rating	RATINGS: Risk Rating	RATINGS: Recent Up/ Downgrade	TOTAL RETURNS & PERFORMANCE: 3-Month Total Return	6-Month Total Return	1-Year Total Return	3-Year Total Return	5-Year Total Return	ASSETS: NAV	Total Assets (MIL)	NEW INVESTORS: Telephone	Open to New Investors
iShares MSCI EAFE Intl Index Fund Inst Shares	MAIIX	B-	C+	B	Up	3.77	9.15	25.24	24.72	44.54	14.18	10,415	800-441-7762	Y
iShares MSCI EAFE Intl Index Fund Inv A Shares	MDIIX	B-	C+	B	Up	3.72	9.05	24.84	23.66	42.58	14.09	10,415	800-441-7762	Y
iShares MSCI Total International Index Fund Class K	BDOKX	B-	B-	B-	Up	4.50	11.02	27.61	24.98	37.57	9.82	607.4	800-441-7762	Y
iShares MSCI Total Intl Index Fund Inst Shares	BDOIX	B-	B-	B-	Up	4.51	10.97	27.56	24.75	37.28	9.54	607.4	800-441-7762	Y
iShares MSCI Total Intl Index Fund Inv A Shares	BDOAX	B-	B-	B-	Up	4.45	10.85	27.32	23.83	35.56	9.52	607.4	800-441-7762	Y
Ivy International Core Equity Fund Class A	IVIAX	B-	C+	B	Up	4.22	7.68	22.74	22.34	56.57	20.23	6,950	800-777-6472	Y
Ivy International Core Equity Fund Class B	IIFBX	B-	C+	B-	Up	3.97	7.12	21.63	19.02	49.80	17.97	6,950	800-777-6472	
Ivy International Core Equity Fund Class C	IVIFX	B-	C+	B-	Up	4.04	7.24	21.88	19.82	51.36	18.02	6,950	800-777-6472	Y
Ivy International Core Equity Fund Class E	IICEX	B-	C+	B	Up	4.20	7.58	22.67	21.96	55.73	20.36	6,950	800-777-6472	Y
Ivy International Core Equity Fund Class I	ICEIX	B-	B-	B	Up	4.29	7.78	23.11	23.52	59.19	20.33	6,950	800-777-6472	Y
Ivy International Core Equity Fund Class N	IINCX	B-	B-	B	Up	4.32	7.85	23.28	24.05	59.09	20.39	6,950	800-777-6472	Y
Ivy International Core Equity Fund Class R	IYITX	B-	C+	B	Up	4.16	7.51	22.43	21.37	54.61	20.23	6,950	800-777-6472	Y
Ivy International Core Equity Fund Class T	IICTX	B-	B-	B	Up	4.32	7.84	22.93	22.53	56.81	20.25	6,950	800-777-6472	Y
Ivy International Core Equity Fund Class Y	IVVYX	B-	B-	B	Up	4.25	7.68	22.78	22.52	57.18	20.36	6,950	800-777-6472	Y
Ivy Managed International Opportunities Fund Class A	IVTAX	B-	B-	B	Up	3.76	9.74	24.43	23.01	44.61	11.89	214.7	800-777-6472	Y
Ivy Managed International Opportunities Fund Class B	IVTBX	B-	C+	B-	Up	3.74	9.58	23.99	20.32	39.31	11.66	214.7	800-777-6472	
Ivy Managed International Opportunities Fund Class C	IVTCX	B-	C+	B-	Up	3.73	9.54	24.02	20.70	39.88	11.69	214.7	800-777-6472	Y
Ivy Managed International Opportunities Fund Class I	IVTIX	B-	B-	B	Up	3.89	9.85	24.71	24.10	46.51	11.94	214.7	800-777-6472	Y
Ivy Managed International Opportunities Fund Class R	IYMGX	B-	C+	B	Up	3.74	9.65	24.24	22.49	43.44	11.86	214.7	800-777-6472	Y
Ivy Managed International Opportunities Fund Class Y	IVTYX	B-	B-	B	Up	3.84	9.82	24.52	23.39	45.29	11.89	214.7	800-777-6472	Y
Janus Henderson Global Equity Income Fund Class A	HFQAX	B-	C+	B-	Up	3.42	8.16	19.13	23.61	47.82	7.97	5,369	877-335-2687	Y
Janus Henderson Global Equity Income Fund Class C	HFQCX	B-	C+	B	Up	3.28	7.86	18.46	21.07	42.45	7.92	5,369	877-335-2687	Y
Janus Henderson Global Equity Income Fund Class D	HFQDX	B-	C+	B-		3.50	8.31	19.30	23.79	48.03	7.96	5,369	877-335-2687	Y
Janus Henderson Global Equity Income Fund Class I	HFQIX	B-	C+	B-	Up	3.63	8.46	19.59	24.69	49.84	7.99	5,369	877-335-2687	Y
Janus Henderson Global Equity Income Fund Class N	HFQRX	B-	C+	B-	Up	3.65	8.49	19.67	24.57	48.97	7.99	5,369	877-335-2687	Y
Janus Henderson Global Equity Income Fund Class S	HFQSX	B-	C+	B		3.42	8.12	19.09	23.57	47.77	7.96	5,369	877-335-2687	Y
Janus Henderson Global Equity Income Fund Class T	HFQTX	B-	C+	B-		3.61	8.44	19.43	23.93	48.20	7.96	5,369	877-335-2687	Y
Janus Henderson Intl Managed Volatility Fund Cls A	JMIAX	B	B-	B	Up	4.67	10.82	28.17	26.70	52.55	9.39	109.4	877-335-2687	Y
Janus Henderson Intl Managed Volatility Fund Cls C	JMICX	B-	C+	B	Up	4.50	10.52	27.51	24.31	50.25	9.17	109.4	877-335-2687	Y
Janus Henderson Intl Managed Volatility Fund Cls D	JIIDX	B	B-	B	Up	4.70	11.04	28.76	27.98	54.96	9.23	109.4	877-335-2687	Y
Janus Henderson Intl Managed Volatility Fund Cls I	JMIIX	B	B-	B	Up	4.67	11.10	28.76	28.15	55.17	9.26	109.4	877-335-2687	Y
Janus Henderson Intl Managed Volatility Fund Cls N	JMRNX	B	B-	B	Up	4.83	11.15	29.02	28.59	55.71	9.25	109.4	877-335-2687	Y
Janus Henderson Intl Managed Volatility Fund Cls S	JMISX	B	B-	B	Up	4.69	10.96	28.45	27.00	53.41	9.37	109.4	877-335-2687	Y
Janus Henderson Intl Managed Volatility Fund Cls T	JRMTX	B	B-	B	Up	4.71	11.05	28.62	27.54	53.42	9.24	109.4	877-335-2687	Y
Janus Henderson International Opportunities Fund Class A	HFOAX	B-	C+	B	Up	3.15	8.21	21.18	18.38	49.77	30.14	4,890	877-335-2687	Y
Janus Henderson International Opportunities Fund Class C	HFOCX	B-	C+	B	Up	2.98	7.81	20.29	15.67	44.09	28.25	4,890	877-335-2687	Y
Janus Henderson International Opportunities Fund Class D	HFODX	B-	C+	B	Up	3.21	8.36	21.35	18.54	49.97	30.04	4,890	877-335-2687	Y
Janus Henderson International Opportunities Fund Class I	HFOIX	B-	C+	B	Up	3.26	8.41	21.53	19.37	51.91	30.03	4,890	877-335-2687	Y
Janus Henderson International Opportunities Fund Class N	HFOQX	B-	C+	B	Up	3.14	8.21	21.18	18.38	49.76	30.02	4,890	877-335-2687	Y
Janus Henderson International Opportunities Fund Class R	HFORX	B-	C+	B	Up	3.06	8.05	20.75	17.20	47.46	29.5	4,890	877-335-2687	Y
Janus Henderson International Opportunities Fund Class S	HFOSX	B-	C+	B	Up	3.27	8.42	21.54	19.07	50.63	30.01	4,890	877-335-2687	Y
Janus Henderson International Opportunities Fund Class T	HFOTX	B-	C+	B	Up	3.20	8.31	21.29	18.49	49.90	30.03	4,890	877-335-2687	Y
Janus Henderson International Value Fund Class A	JIFAX	B-	C+	B	Up	3.77	8.57	22.59	21.50		11.63	52.6	877-335-2687	Y
Janus Henderson International Value Fund Class C	JIFCX	B-	C+	B	Up	3.50	8.22	21.76	18.87		11.61	52.6	877-335-2687	Y
Janus Henderson International Value Fund Class D	JIFDX	B-	C+	B	Up	3.68	8.58	22.76	22.07		11.59	52.6	877-335-2687	
Janus Henderson International Value Fund Class I	JIFIX	B-	C+	B	Up	3.74	8.65	22.85	22.29		11.58	52.6	877-335-2687	Y
Janus Henderson International Value Fund Class N	JIFNX	B-	C+	B	Up	3.76	8.75	23.06	22.65		11.61	52.6	877-335-2687	Y
Janus Henderson International Value Fund Class S	JIFSX	B-	C+	B	Up	3.70	8.49	22.59	21.35		11.65	52.6	877-335-2687	Y
Janus Henderson International Value Fund Class T	JIFTX	B-	C+	B	Up	3.80	8.61	22.68	21.67		11.59	52.6	877-335-2687	Y
JNL/American Funds International Fund Class A	US46644W2944	B-	B-	B-	Up	4.77	11.28	31.63	28.41	52.92	14.92	1,953		Y
JNL/American Funds International Fund Class I	US46644W2860	B-	B	B-	Up	4.79	11.37	31.93	29.15	54.35	15.07	1,953		Y
JNL/Causeway International Value Select Fund Class I	US46648M1365	B-	B-	B-	Up	5.19	12.48	28.74	24.05	38.04	17.63	1,827		Y

Category: Global Equity Large Cap (con't)

Fund Name	Ticker Symbol	RATINGS: Overall Rating	Reward Rating	Risk Rating	Recent Up/ Downgrade	TOTAL RETURNS & PERFORMANCE: 3-Month Total Return	6-Month Total Return	1-Year Total Return	3-Year Total Return	5-Year Total Return	ASSETS: NAV	Total Assets (MIL)	NEW INVESTORS: Telephone	Open to New Investors
JNL/Invesco International Growth Fund Class A	US46648M2355	B-	C+	B	Up	3.44	7.83	23.19	19.07	43.81	14.1	1,475		Y
JNL/Invesco International Growth Fund Class I	US46648M2272	B-	C+	B	Up	3.47	8.04	23.55	19.85	45.21	14.87	1,475		Y
JNL/Mellon Capital International Index Fund Class A	US46648M5408	B-	C+	B	Up	4.00	9.19	25.03	24.00	43.70	15.59	2,054		Y
JNL/Mellon Capital International Index Fund Class I	US46648M5325	B-	C+	B	Up	4.11	9.40	25.45	24.72	45.20	16.21	2,054		Y
JNL/S&P International 5 Fund Class A	US46648L7165	B	B	C+	Up	4.91	10.64	33.09	40.27		11.53	45.4		Y
JNL/S&P International 5 Fund Class I	US46648L6902	B	B	C+		4.81	10.54	32.97	40.14		11.53	45.4		Y
JNL/Vanguard International Fund Class A	US46648L4840	B+	A	B-		3.81	14.48	41.44	39.55	60.90	10.34	57.1		Y
JNL/Vanguard International Fund Class I	US46648L4766	B+	A	B-		3.91	14.68	41.90	40.83	63.35	10.34	57.1		Y
JOHCM International Select Fund Class I Shares	JOHIX	B-	B-	B	Up	4.04	10.02	22.88	23.69	82.24	22.54	6,797	866-260-9549	
JOHCM International Select Fund Class II Shares	JOHAX	B-	B-	B	Up	3.95	9.86	22.56	22.74	79.82	22.59	6,797	866-260-9549	
John Hancock Disciplined Value International Fund Class A	JDIBX	B-	C+	B	Up	4.37	10.36	24.87	25.45	54.31	14.27	1,009	800-225-5913	Y
John Hancock Disciplined Value International Fund Class C	JDICX	B-	C+	B	Up	4.14	9.89	23.95	22.79	49.05	14.27	1,009	800-225-5913	Y
John Hancock Disciplined Value International Fund Class I	JDVIX	B-	B-	B	Up	4.37	10.51	25.23	26.61	56.68	14.27	1,009	800-225-5913	Y
John Hancock Disciplined Value International Fund Cls NAV	JDIVX	B-	B-	B	Up	4.40	10.53	25.37	26.94	57.19	14.26	1,009	800-225-5913	Y
John Hancock Disciplined Value International Fund Class R2	JDISX	B-	C+	B	Up	4.35	10.33	24.81	25.38	54.33	14.3	1,009	800-225-5913	Y
John Hancock Disciplined Value International Fund Class R4	JDITX	B-	B-	B	Up	4.40	10.46	25.18	26.33	55.61	14.28	1,009	800-225-5913	Y
John Hancock Disciplined Value International Fund Class R6	JDIUX	B-	B-	B	Up	4.47	10.61	25.45	27.02	57.30	14.27	1,009	800-225-5913	Y
John Hancock Funds International Growth Fund Class 1	GOIOX	A-	A-	B+	Up	4.63	12.68	36.72	39.47	75.46	27.67	7,998	800-225-5913	Y
John Hancock Funds International Growth Fund Class A	GOIGX	B+	A-	B+	Up	4.54	12.52	36.25	37.90	72.02	27.65	7,998	800-225-5913	Y
John Hancock Funds International Growth Fund Class B	GONBX	B+	B+	B	Up	4.32	12.09	35.30	34.90	65.76	27.25	7,998	800-225-5913	
John Hancock Funds International Growth Fund Class C	GONCX	B+	B+	B	Up	4.33	12.12	35.34	35.00	65.84	27.19	7,998	800-225-5913	Y
John Hancock Funds International Growth Fund Class I	GOGIX	A-	A-	B+	Up	4.61	12.70	36.67	39.17	74.81	27.69	7,998	800-225-5913	Y
John Hancock Funds International Growth Fund Class NAV	JIGHX	A-	A-	B+	Up	4.63	12.73	36.84	39.61	75.64	27.67	7,998	800-225-5913	Y
John Hancock Funds International Growth Fund Class R2	JHIGX	B+	A-	B+	Up	4.52	12.45	36.14	37.45	72.23	27.68	7,998	800-225-5913	Y
John Hancock Funds International Growth Fund Class R4	JIGIX	B+	A-	B+	Up	4.59	12.60	36.49	38.41	73.43	27.69	7,998	800-225-5913	Y
John Hancock Funds International Growth Fund Class R6	JIGTX	A-	A-	B+	Up	4.61	12.74	36.83	39.63	75.66	27.7	7,998	800-225-5913	Y
John Hancock II International Growth Stock Fund Class NAV	JGSNX	B-	C+	B	Up	2.64	7.11	22.03	17.65	42.24	14.17	831.7	800-225-5913	Y
JPMorgan International Equity Fund Class A	JSEAX	B-	B-	B-	Up	5.41	12.07	29.36	27.02	38.72	18.04	4,061	800-480-4111	Y
JPMorgan International Equity Fund Class C	JIECX	B-	B-	B-	Up	5.32	11.80	28.81	25.21	35.32	17.1	4,061	800-480-4111	Y
JPMorgan International Equity Fund Class I	VSIEX	B-	B-	B-	Up	5.51	12.20	29.72	28.04	40.48	18.31	4,061	800-480-4111	Y
JPMorgan International Equity Fund Class R2	JIEZX	B-	B-	B-	Up	5.41	11.91	29.08	26.10	36.97	17.95	4,061	800-480-4111	Y
JPMorgan International Equity Fund Class R5	JIERX	B-	B-	B-	Up	5.53	12.27	29.91	28.69	41.74	18.33	4,061	800-480-4111	Y
JPMorgan International Equity Fund Class R6	JNEMX	B-	B	B-	Up	5.55	12.35	30.04	28.96	42.27	18.33	4,061	800-480-4111	Y
JPMorgan International Equity Income Fund Class A	JEIAX	B-	C+	B	Up	3.50	7.94	19.41	16.47	44.89	16.84	202.0	800-480-4111	Y
JPMorgan International Equity Income Fund Class C	JEICX	B-	C+	B	Up	3.34	7.69	18.86	14.69	41.20	16.72	202.0	800-480-4111	Y
JPMorgan International Equity Income Fund Class I	JEISX	B-	C+	B	Up	3.56	8.16	19.84	17.68	47.04	16.89	202.0	800-480-4111	Y
JPMorgan International Equity Income Fund Class R2	JGEZX	B-	C+	B	Up	3.44	7.81	19.19	15.56	43.00	16.81	202.0	800-480-4111	Y
JPMorgan International Equity Income Fund Class R5	JEIRX	B-	C+	B	Up	3.58	8.20	20.02	17.96	48.06	16.9	202.0	800-480-4111	Y
JPMorgan International Equity Income Fund Class R6	JIEFX	B-	C+	B	Up	3.67	8.25	20.11	18.09	48.22	16.89	202.0	800-480-4111	Y
JPMorgan International Research Enhanced Equity Fund Cls A	OEIAX	B-	B-	B	Up	3.64	8.44	23.34	25.66	45.12	18.75	5,126	800-480-4111	Y
JPMorgan International Research Enhanced Equity Fund Cls I	OIEAX	B-	B-	B	Up	3.71	8.59	23.69	26.70	47.04	18.96	5,126	800-480-4111	Y
JPMorgan Intl Research Enhanced Equity Fund Cls R6	JEIQX	B-	B-	C+		3.69	8.57	23.68	26.68	47.03	18.89	5,126	800-480-4111	Y
JPMorgan International Unconstrained Equity Fund Class A	IUAEX	B	B	B	Up	4.00	10.29	28.01	30.29	45.18	21.39	388.2	800-480-4111	Y
JPMorgan International Unconstrained Equity Fund Class C	IUCEX	B	B	B	Up	3.86	9.99	27.32	28.27	41.43	21.16	388.2	800-480-4111	Y
JPMorgan International Unconstrained Equity Fund Class I	IUESX	B	B	B	Up	4.05	10.49	28.46	31.58	47.31	21.63	388.2	800-480-4111	Y
JPMorgan International Unconstrained Equity Fund Class R2	IUERX	B	B	B	Up	3.92	10.10	27.64	29.23	43.25	21.32	388.2	800-480-4111	Y
JPMorgan International Unconstrained Equity Fund Class R5	IUEFX	B	B	B	Up	4.10	10.49	28.54	31.97	48.34	21.61	388.2	800-480-4111	Y
JPMorgan International Unconstrained Equity Fund Class R6	IUENX	B	B	B	Up	4.13	10.57	28.64	32.26	48.79	21.62	388.2	800-480-4111	Y
JPMorgan Intrepid International Fund Class A	JFTAX	B-	C+	B	Up	3.03	8.88	22.82	23.90	44.28	22.05	3,154	800-480-4111	Y
JPMorgan Intrepid International Fund Class C	JIICX	B-	C+	B	Up	2.85	8.57	22.12	22.01	40.61	22.37	3,154	800-480-4111	Y
JPMorgan Intrepid International Fund Class I	JISIX	B-	B-	B	Up	3.08	9.05	23.19	25.10	46.47	22.91	3,154	800-480-4111	Y
JPMorgan Intrepid International Fund Class R2	JIIZX	B-	C+	B	Up	2.94	8.74	22.46	22.94	42.40	21.78	3,154	800-480-4111	Y

Category: Global Equity Large Cap (con't)

Fund Name	Ticker Symbol	RATINGS				TOTAL RETURNS & PERFORMANCE					ASSETS		NEW INVESTORS	
		Overall Rating	Reward Rating	Risk Rating	Recent Up/ Downgrade	3-Month Total Return	6-Month Total Return	1-Year Total Return	3-Year Total Return	5-Year Total Return	NAV	Total Assets (MIL)	Telephone	Open to New Investors
JPMorgan Intrepid International Fund Class R6	JIFFX	B-	B-	B	Up	3.12	9.13	23.40	25.56	46.21	22.54	3,154	800-480-4111	Y
KP International Equity Fund Institutional Shares	KPIEX	B-	B-	B-	Up	4.96	11.68	28.94	28.58		11.2	1,419		Y
Laudus International MarketMasters Fund™ - Investor Shares	SWOIX	B	B	B	Up	4.76	13.42	33.39	34.34	56.88	26.51	1,754		Y
Laudus International MarketMasters Fund™ - Select Shares®	SWMIX	B	B	B	Up	4.83	13.55	33.65	34.99	58.19	26.47	1,754		Y
Laudus Mondrian International Equity Fund	LIEIX	B-	C+	B	Up	3.44	8.49	21.05	22.13	47.78	6.66	120.9		Y
Lazard International Equity Portfolio Institutional Shares	LZIEX	B-	C+	B	Up	4.49	9.49	22.80	18.74	39.34	19.61	3,855	800-823-6300	Y
Lazard International Equity Portfolio Open Shares	LZIOX	B-	C+	B	Up	4.46	9.34	22.50	17.73	37.39	19.83	3,855	800-823-6300	Y
Lazard International Equity Portfolio R6 Shares	RLIEX	B-	C+	B	Up	4.51	9.51	22.84	18.84	39.46	19.59	3,855	800-823-6300	Y
Lazard Intl Equity Select Portfolio Inst Shares	LZSIX	B-	C+	B-	Up	5.05	11.54	28.30	21.94	36.12	11.02	55.0	800-823-6300	Y
Lazard International Equity Select Portfolio Open Shares	LZESX	B-	C+	B-	Up	4.94	11.42	27.88	20.79	33.78	11.03	55.0	800-823-6300	Y
Lazard Intl Strategic Equity Portfolio Inst Shares	LISIX	B-	C+	B	Up	6.10	12.16	27.85	18.31	47.79	15.7	7,119	800-823-6300	Y
Lazard Intl Strategic Equity Portfolio Open Shares	LISOX	B-	C+	B	Up	6.06	12.00	27.44	17.38	45.93	15.83	7,119	800-823-6300	Y
Lazard International Strategic Equity Portfolio R6 Shares	RLITX	B-	C+	B	Up	6.08	12.14	27.81	17.99	47.40	15.71	7,119	800-823-6300	Y
Lord Abbett International Equity Fund Class A	LICAX	B-	C+	B-	Up	4.54	12.27	25.10	18.69	34.07	14.28	654.5	201-827-2000	Y
Lord Abbett International Equity Fund Class F	LICFX	B-	C+	B-	Up	4.57	12.36	25.28	19.46	35.65	14.18	654.5	201-827-2000	Y
Lord Abbett International Equity Fund Class F3	LICOX	B-	C+	B-	Up	4.69	12.53	25.59	19.90	36.53	14.41	654.5	201-827-2000	Y
Lord Abbett International Equity Fund Class I	LICYX	B-	C+	B-	Up	4.61	12.46	25.52	19.83	36.45	14.38	654.5	201-827-2000	Y
Lord Abbett International Equity Fund Class P	LICPX	B-	C+	B-	Up	4.49	12.22	24.83	18.01	33.12	14.3	654.5	201-827-2000	
Lord Abbett International Equity Fund Class R4	LICSX	B-	C+	B-	Up	4.54	12.22	25.07	18.63	34.42	14.22	654.5	201-827-2000	Y
Lord Abbett International Equity Fund Class R5	LICTX	B-	C+	B-	Up	4.62	12.41	25.28	19.48	36.06	14.34	654.5	201-827-2000	Y
Lord Abbett International Equity Fund Class R6	LICVX	B-	C+	B-	Up	4.69	12.54	25.59	20.04	36.69	14.4	654.5	201-827-2000	Y
LWAS/DFA International High Book To Market Portfolio	DFHBX	B-	B-	B-	Up	5.57	14.29	26.26	27.31	48.40	8.9	58.0	512-306-7400	
Macquarie Pooled Trust Labor Select Intl Equity Portfolio	DELPX	B-	C+	B	Up	2.37	8.04	21.70	19.85	43.68	14.97	493.6	215-255-2300	Y
Madison International Stock Fund Class A	MINAX	B-	C+	B	Up	4.41	9.32	21.98	16.72	35.44	14.31	31.6	800-767-0300	Y
Madison International Stock Fund Class Y	MINYX	B-	C+	B	Up	4.47	9.45	22.31	17.62	37.13	14.32	31.6	800-767-0300	Y
MainStay International Equity Fund Class A	MSEAX	B	B	B	Up	5.58	11.59	32.08	31.09	47.28	16.96	307.6	800-624-6782	Y
MainStay International Equity Fund Class B	MINEX	B	B-	B	Up	5.29	11.01	30.68	26.84	39.48	15.12	307.6	800-624-6782	
MainStay International Equity Fund Class C	MIECX	B	B-	B	Up	5.29	11.01	30.68	26.84	39.35	15.12	307.6	800-624-6782	Y
MainStay International Equity Fund Class I	MSIIX	B	B	B	Up	5.60	11.73	32.33	32.03	49.07	17.02	307.6	800-624-6782	Y
MainStay International Equity Fund Class R1	MIERX	B	B	B	Up	5.60	11.68	32.30	31.70	48.43	16.94	307.6	800-624-6782	Y
MainStay International Equity Fund Class R2	MIRRX	B	B	B	Up	5.53	11.52	31.93	30.64	46.60	17.01	307.6	800-624-6782	Y
MainStay International Equity Fund Class R3	MIFRX	B	B-	B	Up	5.45	11.42	31.59	29.67	44.68	16.9	307.6	800-624-6782	Y
MainStay International Equity Fund Investor Class	MINNX	B	B-	B	Up	5.47	11.38	31.56	29.64	44.75	16.89	307.6	800-624-6782	Y
Mainstay International Opportunities Fund Class I	MYIIX	B-	B-	C+	Up	2.73	9.84	23.19	23.52	58.14	9.66	765.2	800-624-6782	Y
Manning & Napier International Series Class I	MNIIX	B-	B-	B-	Up	3.83	10.60	25.50	26.58	43.17	11.93	541.3	585-325-6880	Y
Manning & Napier International Series Class S Shares	EXITX	B-	C+	B-	Up	3.73	10.38	25.13	25.49	41.29	9.39	541.3	585-325-6880	Y
Manning & Napier Overseas Series Class I	EXOSX	B-	C+	B-	Up	2.71	7.95	23.91	21.57	33.53	24.95	658.7	585-325-6880	Y
Manning & Napier World Opportunities Series Class S	EXWAX	B-	C+	B-	Up	2.61	7.67	23.32	18.33	28.68	8.32	756.9	585-325-6880	Y
Marsico International Opportunities Fund	MIOFX	B	B+	B	Up	4.81	15.33	44.08	32.48	55.41	20.23	65.3	888-860-8686	Y
MassMutual Premier Intl Equity Fund Admin Cls	MIELX	B	B	B	Up	3.57	9.40	26.22	26.14	49.21	13.67	552.7		Y
MassMutual Premier International Equity Fund Class A	MMIAX	B	B-	B	Up	3.52	9.27	25.92	25.21	47.38	13.29	552.7		Y
MassMutual Premier International Equity Fund Class I	MIZIX	B	B	B	Up	3.65	9.61	26.65	27.36	51.29	13.76	552.7		Y
MassMutual Premier International Equity Fund Class R3	MEERX	B	B-	B	Up	3.41	9.12	25.72	24.64	46.49	13.14	552.7		Y
MassMutual Premier International Equity Fund Class R4	MEIRX	B	B-	B	Up	3.50	9.29	26.09	25.55	48.36	13.16	552.7		Y
MassMutual Premier International Equity Fund Class R5	MIEDX	B	B	B	Up	3.55	9.41	26.40	26.83	50.67	13.76	552.7		Y
MassMutual Premier International Equity Fund Service Class	MYIEX	B	B	B	Up	3.63	9.43	26.38	26.57	50.04	13.73	552.7		Y
MassMutual Select Overseas Fund Administrative Class	MOSLX	B-	B-	C	Up	3.25	9.01	26.76	25.92	45.73	9.8	645.3		Y
MassMutual Select Overseas Fund Class A	MOSAX	B-	B-	B-	Up	3.27	8.92	26.44	24.95	44.15	9.61	645.3		Y
MassMutual Select Overseas Fund Class I	MOSZX	B-	B	C	Up	3.37	9.29	27.20	27.11	48.22	9.74	645.3		Y
MassMutual Select Overseas Fund Class R5	MOSSX	B-	B	C	Up	3.26	9.15	26.97	26.57	47.04	9.77	645.3		Y
MassMutual Select Overseas Fund Service Class	MOSYX	B-	B-	C	Up	3.28	9.09	26.85	26.26	46.57	9.72	645.3		Y
McKee International Equity Fund Class Institutional	MKIEX	B-	B-	B-	Up	5.04	11.27	26.23	26.96	43.52	13.87	196.3		Y

Category: Global Equity Large Cap (con't)

Fund Name	Ticker Symbol	RATINGS: Overall Rating	Reward Rating	Risk Rating	Recent Up/ Downgrade	TOTAL RETURNS & PERFORMANCE: 3-Month Total Return	6-Month Total Return	1-Year Total Return	3-Year Total Return	5-Year Total Return	ASSETS: NAV	Total Assets (MIL)	NEW INVESTORS: Telephone	Open to New Investors
MFS® Institutional International Equity Fund	MIEIX	B	B-	B	Up	3.99	8.52	28.02	27.94	47.39	25.46	9,538	877-960-6077	Y
MFS® International Diversification Fund Class A	MDIDX	B	B	B	Up	5.72	10.70	29.93	32.07	49.96	19.69	9,950	877-960-6077	Y
MFS® International Diversification Fund Class B	MDIFX	B-	B-	B	Up	5.55	10.29	28.90	29.16	44.46	19.49	9,950	877-960-6077	Y
MFS® International Diversification Fund Class C	MDIGX	B-	B-	B	Up	5.52	10.31	28.99	29.13	44.53	19.27	9,950	877-960-6077	Y
MFS® International Diversification Fund Class I	MDIJX	B	B	B	Up	5.84	10.90	30.28	33.12	51.92	19.88	9,950	877-960-6077	Y
MFS® International Diversification Fund Class R1	MDIOX	B-	B-	B	Up	5.55	10.29	28.95	29.16	44.44	18.99	9,950	877-960-6077	Y
MFS® International Diversification Fund Class R2	MDIKX	B	B-	B	Up	5.67	10.55	29.55	31.12	48.14	19.37	9,950	877-960-6077	Y
MFS® International Diversification Fund Class R3	MDIHX	B	B	B	Up	5.72	10.74	29.89	32.06	49.97	19.55	9,950	877-960-6077	Y
MFS® International Diversification Fund Class R4	MDITX	B	B	B	Up	5.81	10.88	30.24	33.10	51.85	19.81	9,950	877-960-6077	Y
MFS® International Diversification Fund Class R6	MDIZX	B	B	B		5.82	10.87	30.24	33.09	51.88	19.87	9,950	877-960-6077	Y
MFS® International Growth Fund Class A	MGRAX	B	B	B	Up	5.80	10.87	32.17	34.78	46.76	33.76	5,450	877-960-6077	Y
MFS® International Growth Fund Class B	MGRBX	B	B	B	Up	5.57	10.41	31.12	31.70	41.32	31.69	5,450	877-960-6077	Y
MFS® International Growth Fund Class C	MGRCX	B	B	B	Up	5.58	10.44	31.13	31.73	41.34	30.84	5,450	877-960-6077	Y
MFS® International Growth Fund Class I	MQGIX	B	B	B	Up	5.84	10.98	32.45	35.74	48.60	37.54	5,450	877-960-6077	Y
MFS® International Growth Fund Class R1	MGRRX	B	B	B	Up	5.60	10.44	31.16	31.78	41.33	30.27	5,450	877-960-6077	Y
MFS® International Growth Fund Class R2	MGRQX	B	B	B	Up	5.71	10.71	31.82	33.73	44.92	30.93	5,450	877-960-6077	Y
MFS® International Growth Fund Class R3	MGRTX	B	B	B	Up	5.79	10.85	32.10	34.72	46.73	33.52	5,450	877-960-6077	Y
MFS® International Growth Fund Class R4	MGRVX	B	B	B	Up	5.86	11.01	32.48	35.76	48.58	33.8	5,450	877-960-6077	Y
MFS® International Growth Fund Class R6	MGRDX	B	B	B	Up	5.89	11.04	32.57	36.24	49.41	33.77	5,450	877-960-6077	Y
MFS® International Value Fund Class A	MGIAX	B	B	A-		5.84	9.21	26.82	39.80	82.03	43.18	29,692	877-960-6077	
MFS® International Value Fund Class B	MGIBX	B	B	B+		5.64	8.79	25.85	36.68	75.37	41.18	29,692	877-960-6077	
MFS® International Value Fund Class C	MGICX	B	B	B+		5.65	8.78	25.86	36.69	75.36	39.28	29,692	877-960-6077	
MFS® International Value Fund Class I	MINIX	B+	B	A	Up	5.93	9.34	27.15	40.85	84.34	45.26	29,692	877-960-6077	
MFS® International Value Fund Class R1	MINRX	B	B	B+		5.66	8.80	25.89	36.67	75.33	39.76	29,692	877-960-6077	
MFS® International Value Fund Class R2	MINFX	B	B	B+		5.77	9.05	26.50	38.74	79.76	40.42	29,692	877-960-6077	
MFS® International Value Fund Class R3	MINGX	B	B	A-		5.84	9.20	26.80	39.78	82.07	42.88	29,692	877-960-6077	
MFS® International Value Fund Class R4	MINHX	B+	B	A	Up	5.92	9.33	27.15	40.85	84.35	43.26	29,692	877-960-6077	
MFS® International Value Fund Class R6	MINJX	B+	B	A	Up	5.94	9.37	27.25	41.27	85.20	43.29	29,692	877-960-6077	
MFS® Research International Fund Class 529A	EARSX	B-	C+	B-	Up	5.33	10.18	27.99	23.17	37.99	18.94	7,938	877-960-6077	Y
MFS® Research International Fund Class 529B	EBRIX	B-	C+	B-	Up	5.18	9.80	27.01	20.41	32.85	17.93	7,938	877-960-6077	Y
MFS® Research International Fund Class 529C	ECRIX	B-	C+	B-	Up	5.17	9.81	27.09	20.42	32.83	17.58	7,938	877-960-6077	Y
MFS® Research International Fund Class A	MRSAX	B-	C+	B-	Up	5.36	10.25	28.04	23.32	38.20	19.31	7,938	877-960-6077	Y
MFS® Research International Fund Class B	MRIBX	B-	C+	B-	Up	5.17	9.86	27.07	20.55	33.13	18.68	7,938	877-960-6077	Y
MFS® Research International Fund Class C	MRICX	B-	C+	B-	Up	5.10	9.78	27.06	20.54	33.14	18.19	7,938	877-960-6077	Y
MFS® Research International Fund Class I	MRSIX	B-	C+	B-	Up	5.40	10.41	28.37	24.27	39.97	19.96	7,938	877-960-6077	Y
MFS® Research International Fund Class R1	MRSGX	B-	C+	B-	Up	5.17	9.86	27.07	20.59	33.14	17.92	7,938	877-960-6077	Y
MFS® Research International Fund Class R2	MRSRX	B-	C+	B-	Up	5.25	10.12	27.66	22.36	36.45	18.67	7,938	877-960-6077	Y
MFS® Research International Fund Class R3	MRSHX	B-	C+	B-	Up	5.37	10.24	28.08	23.33	38.20	19.11	7,938	877-960-6077	Y
MFS® Research International Fund Class R4	MRSJX	B-	C+	B-	Up	5.42	10.36	28.38	24.20	39.90	19.33	7,938	877-960-6077	Y
MFS® Research International Fund Class R6	MRSKX	B-	C+	B-	Up	5.41	10.44	28.45	24.59	40.67	19.18	7,938	877-960-6077	Y
MM MSCI EAFE® International Index Fund Administrative Cls	MKRYX	B-	C+	B	Up	3.79	9.03	24.79	23.59	43.57	13.24	232.5		Y
MM MSCI EAFE® International Index Fund Class A	MKRAX	B-	C+	B	Up	3.67	8.84	24.39	22.63	41.68	13.21	232.5		Y
MM MSCI EAFE® International Index Fund Class I	MKRZX	B-	B-	B	Up	3.81	9.19	25.10	24.92	46.09	13.29	232.5		Y
MM MSCI EAFE® International Index Fund Class R3	MKRTX	B-	C+	B	Up	3.58	8.78	24.24	22.18	41.22	13.11	232.5		Y
MM MSCI EAFE® International Index Fund Class R4	MKRFX	B-	C+	B	Up	3.68	8.88	24.52	23.03	42.94	13.14	232.5		Y
MM MSCI EAFE® International Index Fund Class R5	MKRIX	B-	C+	B	Up	3.78	9.08	25.08	24.50	45.39	13.29	232.5		Y
MM MSCI EAFE® International Index Fund Service Cls shares	MKRSX	B-	C+	B	Up	3.75	8.98	24.82	23.95	44.16	13.24	232.5		Y
Mondrian International Equity Fund	DPIEX	B-	C+	B-	Up	2.98	8.42	21.42	20.57	45.48	15.73	576.0	888-832-4386	
Morgan Stanley Inst Fund, Inc. Active Intl Alloc Cls A	MSIBX	B-	C+	B-	Up	3.19	9.21	24.29	19.84	37.35	14.79	226.4	855-332-5306	Y
Morgan Stanley Inst Fund, Inc. Active Intl Alloc Cls I	MSACX	B-	C+	B-	Up	3.33	9.49	24.76	21.13	39.74	14.46	226.4	855-332-5306	Y
Morgan Stanley Inst Fund, Inc. Active Intl Alloc Cls L	MSLLX	B-	C+	B-	Up	3.12	9.03	23.79	17.91	33.79	14.73	226.4	855-332-5306	
Morgan Stanley Inst Fund, Inc. Intl Advantage Port Cls A	MFAPX	A-	A-	A-	Up	4.27	13.46	44.17	61.07	87.78	16.75	281.3	855-332-5306	Y

Category: Global Equity Large Cap (con't)

Fund Name	Ticker Symbol	RATINGS: Overall Rating	Reward Rating	Risk Rating	Recent Up/ Downgrade	TOTAL RETURNS & PERFORMANCE: 3-Month Total Return	6-Month Total Return	1-Year Total Return	3-Year Total Return	5-Year Total Return	ASSETS: NAV	Total Assets (MIL)	NEW INVESTORS: Telephone	Open to New Investors
Morgan Stanley Inst Fund, Inc. Intl Advantage Port Cls C	MSIAX	A-	A-	A-	Up	4.13	13.10	43.16	57.63	81.26	16.3	281.3	855-332-5306	Y
Morgan Stanley Inst Fund, Inc. Intl Advantage Port Cls I	MFAIX	A-	A-	A-	Up	4.42	13.71	44.75	62.70	90.85	16.89	281.3	855-332-5306	Y
Morgan Stanley Inst Fund, Inc. Intl Advantage Port Cls L	MSALX	A-	A-	A-	Up	4.16	13.22	43.41	58.59	83.04	16.43	281.3	855-332-5306	
Morgan Stanley Inst Fund, Inc. Intl Equity Portfolio Cls A	MIQBX	B-	C+	B	Up	3.72	7.13	24.77	21.12	37.92	17.75	4,155	855-332-5306	Y
Morgan Stanley Inst Fund, Inc. Intl Equity Portfolio Cls C	MSECX	B-	C+	B	Up	3.49	6.70	23.77	18.49	33.03	17.51	4,155	855-332-5306	Y
Morgan Stanley Inst Fund, Inc. Intl Equity Portfolio Cls I	MSIQX	B-	C+	B	Up	3.79	7.28	25.16	22.38	40.16	17.97	4,155	855-332-5306	Y
Morgan Stanley Inst Fund, Inc. Intl Eq Port Cls IS	MIQPX	B-	C+	B	Up	3.77	7.32	25.21	22.47	40.29	17.97	4,155	855-332-5306	Y
Morgan Stanley Inst Fund, Inc. Intl Equity Portfolio Cls L	MSQLX	B-	C+	B	Up	3.56	6.80	24.05	19.27	34.40	17.7	4,155	855-332-5306	
Morgan Stanley Inst Fund, Inc. Intl Opp Portfolio Cls A	MIOPX	A-	A	B+	Up	5.52	17.80	53.01	67.15	120.72	22.25	528.6	855-332-5306	Y
Morgan Stanley Inst Fund, Inc. Intl Opp Portfolio Cls C	MSOCX	A-	A	B+	Up	5.32	17.35	51.77	63.45	113.07	21.46	528.6	855-332-5306	Y
Morgan Stanley Inst Fund, Inc. Intl Opp Portfolio Cls I	MIOIX	A	A+	B+	Up	5.60	17.92	53.38	68.78	124.44	22.52	528.6	855-332-5306	Y
Morgan Stanley Inst Fund, Inc. Intl Opp Portfolio Cls IS	MNOPX	A	A+	B+	Up	5.59	17.96	53.41	68.84	124.69	22.54	528.6	855-332-5306	Y
Morgan Stanley Inst Fund, Inc. Intl Opp Portfolio Cls L	MIOLX	A-	A	B+	Up	5.38	17.44	52.10	64.42	114.90	21.63	528.6	855-332-5306	
Nationwide Bailard International Equities Fund Class A	NWHJX	B-	C+	B	Up	3.63	9.53	24.22	21.51	46.08	8.95	506.1	800-848-0920	Y
Nationwide Bailard International Equities Fund Class C	NWHKX	B-	C+	B	Up	3.41	9.09	23.21	18.58	40.65	8.84	506.1	800-848-0920	Y
Nationwide Bailard International Equities Fund Class M	NWHLX	B-	C+	B	Up	3.77	9.65	24.70	22.70	48.52	8.94	506.1	800-848-0920	Y
Nationwide Bailard International Equities Fund Class R6	NWHMX	B-	C+	B	Up	3.76	9.77	24.67	22.84	48.70	8.95	506.1	800-848-0920	Y
Nationwide Bailard Intl Equities Fund Inst Service Cls	NWHNX	B-	C+	B	Up	3.63	9.61	24.44	22.20	47.67	8.93	506.1	800-848-0920	Y
Nationwide International Index Fund Class A	GIIAX	B-	C+	B	Up	3.68	9.01	24.73	23.34	42.78	8.47	1,553	800-848-0920	Y
Nationwide International Index Fund Class C	GIICX	B-	C+	B	Up	3.60	8.57	24.00	20.95	38.08	7.96	1,553	800-848-0920	Y
Nationwide International Index Fund Class R	GIIRX	B-	C+	B	Up	3.60	8.85	24.30	22.29	41.11	8.47	1,553	800-848-0920	Y
Nationwide International Index Fund Class R6	GIXIX	B-	C+	B	Up	3.86	9.15	25.19	24.82	45.52	8.52	1,553	800-848-0920	Y
Natixis Funds Trust I Oakmark International Fund Class A	NOIAX	B	B+	C	Up	1.75	11.01	29.56	32.04	61.47	15.58	1,112	800-862-4863	Y
Natixis Funds Trust I Oakmark International Fund Class C	NOICX	B-	B	C	Up	1.55	10.53	28.55	29.09	55.37	15.3	1,112	800-862-4863	Y
Natixis Funds Trust I Oakmark International Fund Class N	NIONX	B	B+	C	Up	1.88	11.29	29.88	32.36	61.88	15.58	1,112	800-862-4863	Y
Natixis Funds Trust I Oakmark International Fund Class Y	NOIYX	B	B+	C	Up	1.79	11.11	29.77	32.25	61.74	15.56	1,112	800-862-4863	Y
Neuberger Berman Advisers Mgmt Trust Intl Portfolio Cls S	US6412223025	B	B	B	Up	3.58	10.25	26.75	25.79	45.63	13.63	86.4	212-476-9000	Y
Neuberger Berman International Equity Fund Class A	NIQAX	B	B	B	Up	3.58	10.19	26.65	26.46	47.74	28.13	1,949	212-476-9000	Y
Neuberger Berman International Equity Fund Class C	NIQCX	B	B-	B	Up	3.43	9.78	25.78	23.67	42.27	27.37	1,949	212-476-9000	Y
Neuberger Berman International Equity Fund Class R6	NRIQX	B	B	B	Up	3.66	10.45	27.23	28.18	50.91	13.51	1,949	212-476-9000	Y
Neuberger Berman Intl Equity Fund Inst Cls	NBIIX	B	B	B	Up	3.75	10.45	27.16	27.91	50.47	13.4	1,949	212-476-9000	Y
Neuberger Berman International Equity Fund Investor Class	NIQVX	B	B	B	Up	3.65	10.26	27.35	27.54	49.49	25.33	1,949	212-476-9000	Y
Neuberger Berman International Equity Fund Trust Class	NIQTX	B	B	B	Up	3.63	10.23	27.34	27.35	48.97	28.34	1,949	212-476-9000	
Neuberger Berman International Select Fund Class A	NBNAX	B	B-	B	Up	3.24	10.45	27.25	24.60	43.31	13.03	245.5	212-476-9000	Y
Neuberger Berman International Select Fund Class C	NBNCX	B-	B-	B	Up	3.04	9.98	26.21	21.89	38.10	12.9	245.5	212-476-9000	Y
Neuberger Berman Intl Select Fund Cls Inst	NILIX	B	B	B	Up	3.25	10.59	27.54	25.93	45.85	13.08	245.5	212-476-9000	Y
Neuberger Berman International Select Fund Class R3	NBNRX	B	B-	B	Up	3.03	10.20	26.75	23.66	41.41	12.92	245.5	212-476-9000	Y
Neuberger Berman International Select Fund Class R6	NRILX	B	B-	B	Up	3.23	10.56	27.59	25.04	43.64	13.08	245.5	212-476-9000	Y
Neuberger Berman International Select Fund Class Trust	NILTX	B	B-	B	Up	3.23	10.47	27.25	24.71	43.26	13.13	245.5	212-476-9000	
Northern Active M International Equity Fund	NMIEX	B-	C+	B-	Up	4.73	11.40	29.04	20.51	33.19	11.74	1,419	800-595-9111	Y
Northern International Equity Index Fund	NOINX	B-	C+	B	Up	3.82	9.14	25.26	24.81	45.32	12.91	6,046	800-595-9111	Y
Nuveen International Growth Fund Class A	NBQAX	B	B	B-	Up	7.12	17.53	37.52	30.49	69.29	48.31	425.8	312-917-8146	Y
Nuveen International Growth Fund Class C	NBQCX	B-	B-	B-	Up	6.92	17.09	36.49	27.57	63.06	46.04	425.8	312-917-8146	Y
Nuveen International Growth Fund Class I	NBQIX	B	B	B-	Up	7.20	17.68	37.85	31.47	71.37	48.69	425.8	312-917-8146	Y
Nuveen International Growth Fund Class R3	NBQBX	B	B	B-	Up	7.06	17.38	37.19	29.52	67.09	47.73	425.8	312-917-8146	Y
Nuveen International Growth Fund Class R6	NBQFX	B	B	B-	Up	7.21	17.71	37.99	31.69	71.65	48.77	425.8	312-917-8146	Y
Nuveen NWQ International Value Fund Class A	NAIGX	B-	C+	B	Up	4.97	8.00	20.43	25.11	41.94	26.15	289.6	312-917-8146	Y
Nuveen NWQ International Value Fund Class C	NCIGX	B-	C+	B	Up	4.76	7.64	19.54	22.36	36.70	24.97	289.6	312-917-8146	Y
Nuveen NWQ International Value Fund Class I	NGRRX	B-	C+	B	Up	5.00	8.15	20.74	26.00	43.71	26.25	289.6	312-917-8146	Y
Nuveen NWQ International Value Fund Class R3	NTITX	B-	C+	B	Up	4.87	7.88	20.14	24.13	40.12	26.36	289.6	312-917-8146	Y
Nuveen Santa Barbara Intl Dividend Growth Fund Cls A	NUIAX	B-	C+	B	Up	1.99	5.55	19.96	21.00	37.96	27.92	6.0	312-917-8146	Y
Nuveen Santa Barbara Intl Dividend Growth Fund Cls C	NUICX	B-	C+	B	Up	1.84	5.18	19.10	18.33	32.91	27.66	6.0	312-917-8146	Y

Category: Global Equity Large Cap (con't)

		RATINGS				TOTAL RETURNS & PERFORMANCE					ASSETS		NEW INVESTORS	
Fund Name	Ticker Symbol	Overall Rating	Reward Rating	Risk Rating	Recent Up/ Downgrade	3-Month Total Return	6-Month Total Return	1-Year Total Return	3-Year Total Return	5-Year Total Return	NAV	Total Assets (MIL)	Telephone	Open to New Investors
Nuveen Santa Barbara Intl Dividend Growth Fund Cls I	NUIIX	B-	C+	B	Up	2.05	5.68	20.23	21.91	39.66	27.95	6.0	312-917-8146	Y
Nuveen Santa Barbara Intl Dividend Growth Fund Cls R3	NUIRX	B-	C+	B	Up	1.94	5.40	19.63	20.13	36.20	27.82	6.0	312-917-8146	Y
Nuveen Symphony International Equity Fund Class A	NSIAX	B-	B-	B	Up	4.17	11.02	27.67	27.58	49.20	21.25	17.4	312-917-8146	Y
Nuveen Symphony International Equity Fund Class C	NSECX	B-	B-	B-	Up	3.93	10.58	26.66	24.65	43.64	21.05	17.4	312-917-8146	Y
Nuveen Symphony International Equity Fund Class I	NSIEX	B	B	B	Up	4.26	11.23	28.00	28.54	51.08	21.23	17.4	312-917-8146	Y
Nuveen Symphony International Equity Fund Class R3	NSREX	B-	B-	B	Up	4.12	10.90	27.37	26.64	47.32	21.31	17.4	312-917-8146	Y
Oakmark International Fund Class Advisor	OAYIX	B	A-	C	Up	2.38	11.76	29.92	34.04	66.24	28.58	41,961	641-219-558	Y
Oakmark International Fund Class Institutional	OANIX	B	A-	C	Up	2.43	11.82	29.99	34.11	66.33	28.59	41,961	641-219-558	Y
Oakmark International Fund Investor Class	OAKIX	B	A-	C	Up	2.37	11.69	29.75	33.80	65.94	28.57	41,961	641-219-558	
Oakmark International Fund Service Class	OARIX	B	B+	C	Up	2.30	11.56	29.44	32.55	63.22	28.76	41,961	641-219-558	
Oppenheimer International Diversified Fund Class A	OIDAX	B	B	B	Up	4.68	11.42	32.40	33.73	57.75	18.28	3,860	800-225-5677	Y
Oppenheimer International Diversified Fund Class B	OIDBX	B	B	B	Up	4.45	10.95	31.31	30.64	51.65	17.82	3,860	800-225-5677	
Oppenheimer International Diversified Fund Class C	OIDCX	B	B	B	Up	4.46	10.98	31.31	30.69	51.93	17.78	3,860	800-225-5677	Y
Oppenheimer International Diversified Fund Class I	OIDIX	B	B	B	Up	4.80	11.64	32.96	35.46	61.91	18.51	3,860	800-225-5677	Y
Oppenheimer International Diversified Fund Class R	OIDNX	B	B	B	Up	4.58	11.20	31.97	32.63	55.67	18.06	3,860	800-225-5677	Y
Oppenheimer International Diversified Fund Class Y	OIDYX	B	B	B	Up	4.75	11.54	32.75	34.75	59.75	18.45	3,860	800-225-5677	Y
Oppenheimer International Equity Fund Class A	QIVAX	B	B	B	Up	3.86	9.67	31.09	31.83	55.79	22.35	1,838	800-225-5677	Y
Oppenheimer International Equity Fund Class B	QIVBX	B	B	B	Up	3.61	9.16	30.01	28.64	49.80	20.36	1,838	800-225-5677	
Oppenheimer International Equity Fund Class C	QIVCX	B	B	B	Up	3.63	9.26	30.15	28.93	49.99	19.94	1,838	800-225-5677	Y
Oppenheimer International Equity Fund Class I	QIVIX	B	B	B	Up	3.94	9.88	31.61	33.54	59.08	22.21	1,838	800-225-5677	Y
Oppenheimer International Equity Fund Class R	QIVNX	B	B	B	Up	3.75	9.51	30.71	30.82	53.76	22.09	1,838	800-225-5677	Y
Oppenheimer International Equity Fund Class Y	QIVYX	B	B	B	Up	3.89	9.80	31.39	32.82	57.45	22.52	1,838	800-225-5677	Y
Oppenheimer International Growth Fund Class A	OIGAX	B	B	B	Up	3.61	9.52	26.60	27.10	49.76	43.91	27,302	800-225-5677	Y
Oppenheimer International Growth Fund Class B	IGRWX	B	B-	B	Up	3.40	9.10	25.64	24.24	44.20	42.18	27,302	800-225-5677	Y
Oppenheimer International Growth Fund Class C	OIGCX	B	B-	B	Up	3.42	9.10	25.67	24.26	44.26	41.7	27,302	800-225-5677	Y
Oppenheimer International Growth Fund Class I	OIGIX	B	B	B	Up	3.73	9.74	27.15	28.77	53.12	43.63	27,302	800-225-5677	Y
Oppenheimer International Growth Fund Class R	OIGNX	B	B	B	Up	3.54	9.35	26.25	26.12	47.87	43.1	27,302	800-225-5677	Y
Oppenheimer International Growth Fund Class Y	OIGYX	B	B	B	Up	3.66	9.63	26.89	28.04	51.69	43.62	27,302	800-225-5677	Y
Optimum International Fund Class A	OAIEX	B-	B-	B-	Up	3.67	10.78	30.07	30.24	45.54	14.44	641.6		Y
Optimum International Fund Class C	OCIEX	B-	B-	B-	Up	3.51	10.39	29.15	27.37	40.47	14.11	641.6		Y
Optimum International Fund Institutional Class	OIIEX	B	B	B	Up	3.74	10.95	30.45	31.28	47.63	14.54	641.6		Y
PACE International Equity Investments Class A	PWGAX	B-	B-	B	Up	4.42	10.80	25.15	25.65	47.77	17.08	1,207	212-882-5586	Y
PACE International Equity Investments Class C	PWGCX	B-	C+	B	Up	4.25	10.35	24.14	22.76	42.03	16.79	1,207	212-882-5586	Y
PACE International Equity Investments Class P	PCIEX	B-	B-	B	Up	4.48	10.90	25.45	26.71	49.81	16.95	1,207	212-882-5586	Y
PACE International Equity Investments Class Y	PWIYX	B-	B-	B	Up	4.46	10.87	25.46	26.70	49.79	16.99	1,207	212-882-5586	Y
Pacific Financial International Fund Class Institutional	PFGIX	B-	C+	B	Up	2.95	8.50	24.35	16.29	41.52	5.87	94.9	425-451-7722	Y
Pacific Financial International Fund Class Investor	PFLIX	B-	C+	B-	Up	3.13	8.29	23.64	13.99	36.82	5.51	94.9	425-451-7722	Y
Parametric International Equity Fund Class R	ERISX	B	B-	B	Up	3.44	8.57	25.17	28.32	46.78	13.68	255.4		Y
Parametric International Equity Fund Class R6	ESISX	B	B	B	Up	3.53	8.86	25.77	30.24	50.46	13.78	255.4		Y
Parametric International Equity Fund Institutional Class	EIISX	B	B	B	Up	3.56	8.81	25.70	30.12	50.32	13.78	255.4		Y
Parametric International Equity Fund Investor Class	EAISX	B	B-	B	Up	3.46	8.73	25.48	29.23	48.52	13.73	255.4		Y
Parametric Tax-Managed International Equity Fund Class C	ECIGX	B-	C+	B	Up	3.25	8.08	23.86	23.86	40.06	10.67	41.0		
Parametric Tax-Managed Intl Equity Fund Inst Cls	EITIX	B	B-	B	Up	3.50	8.67	25.21	27.70	47.25	11.22	41.0		Y
Parametric Tax-Managed Intl Equity Fund Inv Cls	ETIGX	B	B-	B	Up	3.52	8.59	24.81	26.72	45.46	11.26	41.0		Y
Pax MSCI EAFE ESG Leaders Index Fund Individual Inv Cls	PXINX	B-	C+	B	Up	3.01	7.96	23.00	21.09	43.03	9.36	671.0	800-767-1729	Y
Pax MSCI EAFE ESG Leaders Index Fund Institutional Class	PXNIX	B-	C+	B	Up	3.09	8.14	23.34	22.13	44.80	9.19	671.0	800-767-1729	Y
Pear Tree Polaris Foreign Value Fund Class Institutional	QFVIX	B-	B	C+	Up	4.84	10.12	25.68	30.91	59.66	22.11	2,193	800-326-2151	Y
Pear Tree Polaris Foreign Value Fund Class Ordinary	QFVOX	B-	B	C+	Up	4.71	9.87	25.24	29.82	57.43	22.17	2,193	800-326-2151	Y
Pear Tree Polaris Foreign Value Fund Class R6	QFVRX	B-	B	C+	Up	4.89	10.15	25.64	30.24	57.94	11.86	2,193	800-326-2151	Y
PF International Large-Cap Fund Class P	US69447T1280	B-	B-	B	Up	3.73	8.07	27.55	25.87	43.40	21.1	179.6	800-722-2333	Y
PIMCO RAE Fundamental PLUS International Fund Class A	PTSOX	B-	B	C	Up	4.24	12.80	28.05	27.35	49.11	9.99	1,228	866-746-2602	Y
PIMCO RAE Fundamental PLUS International Fund Class C	PTSKX	B-	B	C	Up	3.91	12.26	26.97	24.33	43.53	9.85	1,228	866-746-2602	Y

Category: Global Equity Large Cap (con't)

		RATINGS				TOTAL RETURNS & PERFORMANCE					ASSETS		NEW INVESTORS	
Fund Name	Ticker Symbol	Overall Rating	Reward Rating	Risk Rating	Recent Up/ Downgrade	3-Month Total Return	6-Month Total Return	1-Year Total Return	3-Year Total Return	5-Year Total Return	NAV	Total Assets (MIL)	Telephone	Open to New Investors
PIMCO RAE Fundamental PLUS International Fund Class D	PTSLX	B-	B	C	Up	4.21	12.73	27.99	27.27	49.01	9.98	1,228	866-746-2602	Y
PIMCO RAE Fundamental PLUS International Fund Class P	PTIPX	B-	B	C	Up	4.18	12.92	28.31	28.10	50.99	9.99	1,228	866-746-2602	Y
PIMCO RAE Fundamental PLUS Intl Fund Inst Cls	PTSIX	B-	B	C	Up	4.20	12.96	28.38	28.49	51.68	10	1,228	866-746-2602	Y
PIMCO RAE Low Volatility PLUS International Fund Class A	PLVBX	B-	B	C	Up	5.65	11.09	23.54	29.54		11.11	672.3	866-746-2602	Y
PIMCO RAE Low Volatility PLUS International Fund Class P	PLVZX	B	B	B	Up	5.71	11.10	23.88	30.40		11.13	672.3	866-746-2602	Y
PIMCO RAE Low Volatility PLUS Intl Fund Inst Cls	PLVTX	B	B	B	Up	5.82	11.22	24.02	30.94		11.16	672.3	866-746-2602	Y
PIMCO StocksPLUS® Intl Fund (U.S. Dollar-Hedged) Cls A	PIPAX	B	B	B-	Up	3.78	8.37	18.32	30.12	69.17	8.07	3,170	866-746-2602	Y
PIMCO StocksPLUS® Intl Fund (U.S. Dollar-Hedged) Cls C	PIPCX	B	B	B-	Up	3.63	7.80	17.33	27.15	62.88	7.45	3,170	866-746-2602	Y
PIMCO StocksPLUS® Intl Fund (U.S. Dollar-Hedged) Cls D	PIPDX	B	B	B-	Up	3.77	8.34	18.27	30.03	68.95	8.08	3,170	866-746-2602	Y
PIMCO StocksPLUS® Intl Fund (U.S. Dollar-Hedged) Cls P	PIUHX	B-	B	C		3.84	8.47	18.61	31.17	71.70	8.4	3,170	866-746-2602	Y
PIMCO StocksPLUS® Intl Fund (U.S. Dollar-Hedged) Cls R	PIRHX	B-	B	C		3.75	8.19	18.00	29.24	66.97	8.02	3,170	866-746-2602	Y
PIMCO StocksPLUS® Intl Fund (U.S. Dollar-Hedged) Inst Cls	PISIX	B	B	B	Up	3.96	8.58	18.84	31.69	72.36	8.47	3,170	866-746-2602	Y
PIMCO StocksPLUS® Intl Fund (Unhedged) Admin Cls	PSKAX	B-	B	C	Up	4.02	10.16	26.55	25.47	45.30	6.83	1,848	866-746-2602	Y
PIMCO StocksPLUS® International Fund (Unhedged) Class A	PPUAX	B-	B	C	Up	3.73	9.88	26.38	24.60	43.81	6.75	1,848	866-746-2602	Y
PIMCO StocksPLUS® International Fund (Unhedged) Class D	PPUDX	B-	B	C	Up	3.86	10.03	26.46	24.62	43.89	6.79	1,848	866-746-2602	Y
PIMCO StocksPLUS® International Fund (Unhedged) Class P	PPLPX	B-	B	C	Up	3.86	10.06	26.55	25.82	46.03	6.96	1,848	866-746-2602	Y
PIMCO StocksPLUS® Intl Fund (Unhedged) Inst Cls	PSKIX	B-	B	C	Up	4.03	10.30	27.11	26.25	47.01	6.95	1,848	866-746-2602	Y
Pioneer International Equity Fund Class A	PIIFX	B-	B-	B	Up	3.76	10.19	27.10	25.07	46.74	24.64	185.4	617-742-7825	Y
Pioneer International Equity Fund Class C	PCITX	B-	C+	B	Up	3.48	9.67	25.88	21.67	40.22	21.53	185.4	617-742-7825	Y
Pioneer International Equity Fund Class Y	INVYX	B-	B-	B	Up	3.83	10.39	27.57	26.52	49.50	24.62	185.4	617-742-7825	Y
PNC International Equity Fund Class A	PMIEX	B	B	B	Up	5.33	12.75	32.86	33.43	66.21	24.23	1,227	800-622-3863	Y
PNC International Equity Fund Class C	PIUCX	B	B	B	Up	5.17	12.38	31.95	30.93	60.94	23.26	1,227	800-622-3863	Y
PNC International Equity Fund Class Institutional	PIUIX	B	B	B	Up	5.43	12.92	33.27	34.75	68.73	24.44	1,227	800-622-3863	Y
Praxis International Index Fund Class A	MPLAX	B-	C+	B-	Up	3.99	9.78	24.97	22.99	34.58	11.69	283.3		Y
Praxis International Index Fund Class I	MPLIX	B-	B-	B-	Up	4.19	10.04	25.67	24.92	38.30	11.75	283.3		Y
Principal Diversified International Fund Class A	PRWLX	B-	B-	B	Up	2.96	11.02	28.08	26.13	46.03	13.99	12,112	800-222-5852	Y
Principal Diversified International Fund Class C	PDNCX	B-	C+	B	Up	2.74	10.63	27.06	23.47	40.81	14.02	12,112	800-222-5852	Y
Principal Diversified International Fund Class J	PIIJX	B-	B-	B	Up	2.94	11.09	28.25	26.71	46.91	13.82	12,112	800-222-5852	Y
Principal Diversified International Fund Institutional Cls	PIIIX	B	B-	B	Up	3.08	11.26	28.66	28.08	49.75	13.9	12,112	800-222-5852	Y
Principal Diversified International Fund R-1 Class	PDVIX	B-	B-	B	Up	2.85	10.86	27.61	24.74	43.39	13.97	12,112	800-222-5852	Y
Principal Diversified International Fund R-2 Class	PINNX	B-	B-	B	Up	2.88	10.83	27.75	25.19	44.27	13.9	12,112	800-222-5852	Y
Principal Diversified International Fund R-3 Class	PINRX	B-	B-	B	Up	2.94	10.95	27.95	25.97	45.52	13.94	12,112	800-222-5852	Y
Principal Diversified International Fund R-4 Class	PINLX	B-	B-	B	Up	3.04	11.11	28.22	26.64	47.02	14.12	12,112	800-222-5852	Y
Principal Diversified International Fund R-5 Class	PINPX	B	B-	B	Up	2.98	11.15	28.31	27.05	47.79	14.08	12,112	800-222-5852	Y
Principal Intl Equity Index Fund Inst Cls	PIDIX	B-	C+	B	Up	3.68	8.93	24.86	23.98	43.77	10.81	1,084	800-222-5852	Y
Principal International Equity Index Fund R-1 Class	PILIX	B-	C+	B	Up	3.37	8.46	23.78	20.79	37.62	10.49	1,084	800-222-5852	Y
Principal International Equity Index Fund R-2 Class	PINEX	B-	C+	B	Up	3.47	8.53	23.91	21.28	38.57	10.8	1,084	800-222-5852	Y
Principal International Equity Index Fund R-3 Class	PIIOX	B-	C+	B	Up	3.51	8.64	24.17	21.91	39.75	10.63	1,084	800-222-5852	Y
Principal International Equity Index Fund R-4 Class	PIIPX	B-	C+	B	Up	3.55	8.73	24.35	22.58	41.11	10.74	1,084	800-222-5852	Y
Principal International Equity Index Fund R-5 Class	PIIQX	B-	C+	B	Up	3.56	8.84	24.58	23.04	42.01	10.76	1,084	800-222-5852	Y
Principal International Equity Index Fund R-6	PFIEX	B-	C+	B	Up	3.60	8.95	24.76	23.88	43.65	10.8	1,084	800-222-5852	Y
Principal International Fund I Class A	PFAFX	B	B	B	Up	6.32	17.21	38.28	31.51	61.72	17.05	466.9	800-222-5852	Y
Principal International Fund I Class R-6	PIIDX	B	B	B	Up	6.38	17.51	38.85	33.29	64.86	17.1	466.9	800-222-5852	Y
Principal International Fund I Institutional Class	PINIX	B	B	B	Up	6.38	17.51	38.83	33.34	64.92	17.12	466.9	800-222-5852	Y
Principal International Fund I R-1 Class	PPISX	B	B	B	Up	6.22	17.01	37.77	30.05	58.27	17.11	466.9	800-222-5852	Y
Principal International Fund I R-2 Class	PSPPX	B	B	B	Up	6.25	17.09	37.90	30.51	59.26	17.15	466.9	800-222-5852	Y
Principal International Fund I R-3 Class	PRPPX	B	B	B	Up	6.31	17.23	38.22	31.31	60.76	17.12	466.9	800-222-5852	Y
Principal International Fund I R-4 Class	PUPPX	B	B	B	Up	6.34	17.33	38.41	32.05	62.20	17.13	466.9	800-222-5852	Y
Principal International Fund I R-5 Class	PTPPX	B	B	B	Up	6.34	17.34	38.57	32.36	63.10	17.09	466.9	800-222-5852	Y
Principal Overseas Fund R-4 Class	PINUX	B-	C+	B-	Up	3.67	10.11	25.03	19.60	38.99	11.4	3,659	800-222-5852	Y
Prudential Jennison International Opportunities Fund Cls A	PWJAX	B+	A-	B-	Up	5.72	19.57	49.06	38.46	54.37	17.53	63.9	800-225-1852	Y
Prudential Jennison International Opportunities Fund Cls C	PWJCX	B	B+	B-	Up	5.58	19.20	47.93	35.42	48.81	16.82	63.9	800-225-1852	Y

Category: Global Equity Large Cap (con't)

Fund Name	Ticker Symbol	RATINGS: Overall Rating	Reward Rating	Risk Rating	Recent Up/ Downgrade	TOTAL RETURNS & PERFORMANCE: 3-Month Total Return	6-Month Total Return	1-Year Total Return	3-Year Total Return	5-Year Total Return	ASSETS: NAV	Total Assets (Mil)	NEW INVESTORS: Telephone	Open to New Investors
Prudential Jennison International Opportunities Fund Cls Q	PWJQX	B+	A	B	Up	5.82	19.84	49.55	39.75	56.51	17.7	63.9	800-225-1852	Y
Prudential Jennison International Opportunities Fund Cls R	PWJRX	B	A-	B-		5.66	19.36	48.39	36.42	50.50	17.63	63.9	800-225-1852	Y
Prudential Jennison International Opportunities Fund Cls Z	PWJZX	B+	A	B	Up	5.91	19.86	49.58	39.58	56.31	17.71	63.9	800-225-1852	Y
Prudential QMA International Equity Fund Class A	PJRAX	B-	B-	B-	Up	3.96	11.07	28.27	21.53	41.79	7.97	283.9	800-225-1852	Y
Prudential QMA International Equity Fund Class Q	PJRQX	B-	B-	B-	Up	4.12	11.32	28.97	22.99	44.23	8.02	283.9	800-225-1852	Y
Prudential QMA International Equity Fund Class Z	PJIZX	B-	B-	B-	Up	3.96	11.15	28.60	22.64	43.82	8.02	283.9	800-225-1852	Y
Putnam International Equity Fund Class A	POVSX	B-	C+	B	Up	3.12	10.31	26.47	22.60	48.65	26.17	1,008	617-292-1000	Y
Putnam International Equity Fund Class B	POVBX	B-	C+	B-	Up	2.89	9.88	25.50	19.85	43.18	24.9	1,008	617-292-1000	Y
Putnam International Equity Fund Class C	PIGCX	B-	C+	B-	Up	2.93	9.93	25.53	19.87	43.22	25.22	1,008	617-292-1000	Y
Putnam International Equity Fund Class M	POVMX	B-	C+	B-	Up	2.99	10.06	25.83	20.76	44.95	25.47	1,008	617-292-1000	Y
Putnam International Equity Fund Class R	PIERX	B-	C+	B	Up	3.07	10.21	26.13	21.66	46.76	25.71	1,008	617-292-1000	Y
Putnam International Equity Fund Class R5	POVDX	B-	B-	B	Up	3.19	10.50	26.83	23.73	51.10	26.58	1,008	617-292-1000	Y
Putnam International Equity Fund Class R6	POVEX	B-	B-	B	Up	3.22	10.56	26.99	24.15	52.04	26.55	1,008	617-292-1000	Y
Putnam International Equity Fund Class Y	POVYX	B-	B-	B	Up	3.16	10.44	26.75	23.50	50.46	26.45	1,008	617-292-1000	Y
Putnam International Growth Fund Class A	PINOX	B-	B-	B	Up	4.43	13.56	35.04	26.74	48.34	22.85	308.5	617-292-1000	Y
Putnam International Growth Fund Class B	PINWX	B-	C+	B	Up	4.27	13.14	34.09	23.95	42.92	20.49	308.5	617-292-1000	Y
Putnam International Growth Fund Class C	PIOCX	B-	C+	B	Up	4.27	13.16	34.05	23.97	42.91	20.98	308.5	617-292-1000	Y
Putnam International Growth Fund Class M	PINMX	B-	B-	B	Up	4.36	13.30	34.40	24.90	44.73	21.29	308.5	617-292-1000	Y
Putnam International Growth Fund Class R	PNPRX	B-	B-	B	Up	4.39	13.40	34.65	25.75	46.43	22.34	308.5	617-292-1000	Y
Putnam International Growth Fund Class Y	PINYX	B-	B-	B	Up	4.52	13.68	35.32	27.69	50.22	23.1	308.5	617-292-1000	Y
Putnam International Value Fund Class A	PNGAX	B-	C+	B	Up	2.45	8.77	24.08	22.08	36.36	12.21	163.2	617-292-1000	Y
Putnam International Value Fund Class B	PGNBX	B-	C+	B-	Up	2.31	8.36	23.16	19.34	31.42	12.24	163.2	617-292-1000	Y
Putnam International Value Fund Class C	PIGRX	B-	C+	B-	Up	2.29	8.38	23.15	19.45	31.45	12.16	163.2	617-292-1000	Y
Putnam International Value Fund Class M	PIGMX	B-	C+	B-	Up	2.34	8.46	23.44	20.19	32.92	12.25	163.2	617-292-1000	Y
Putnam International Value Fund Class R6	PIGWX	B-	C+	B	Up	2.55	9.02	24.66	23.60	38.61	12.24	163.2	617-292-1000	Y
Putnam International Value Fund Class Y	PNGYX	B-	C+	B	Up	2.55	8.87	24.43	23.04	38.16	12.2	163.2	617-292-1000	Y
QS International Dividend Fund Class FI	LTIDX	B-	C+	B+	Up	2.27	4.62	16.63	18.92		10.17	4.6	877-721-1926	Y
QS International Dividend Fund Class IS	LDIVX	B-	C+	B+	Up	2.27	4.78	16.98	19.85		10.17	4.6	877-721-1926	Y
QS International Equity Fund Class A	LMEAX	B	B-	B	Up	3.15	8.64	24.52	26.44	51.29	16.52	316.9	877-721-1926	Y
QS International Equity Fund Class A2	LIATX	B-	B-	C+	Up	3.09	8.40	24.40	24.91	47.35	16.45	316.9	877-721-1926	Y
QS International Equity Fund Class C	LMGEX	B-	B-	B	Up	2.93	8.14	23.58	23.43	45.61	16.61	316.9	877-721-1926	Y
QS International Equity Fund Class FI	LGFEX	B	B-	B	Up	3.14	8.62	24.46	26.25	51.13	17.16	316.9	877-721-1926	Y
QS International Equity Fund Class I	LGIEX	B	B	B	Up	3.23	8.78	24.90	27.63	53.72	17.15	316.9	877-721-1926	Y
QS International Equity Fund Class IS	LIESX	B-	B	C+	Up	3.21	8.83	25.00	27.98	54.45	17.11	316.9	877-721-1926	Y
QS International Equity Fund Class R	LMIRX	B-	B-	B	Up	3.11	8.47	24.23	25.33	49.26	17.11	316.9	877-721-1926	Y
Russell Investments Intl Developed Mkts Fund Cls A	RLNAX	B-	B-	B	Up	3.89	9.97	24.67	25.39	45.77	41.18	2,908	800-426-7969	Y
Russell Investments Intl Developed Mkts Fund Cls C	RLNCX	B-	C+	B	Up	3.69	9.54	23.71	22.57	40.39	41.43	2,908	800-426-7969	Y
Russell Investments Intl Developed Mkts Fund Cls E	RIFEX	B-	B-	B	Up	3.88	9.94	24.62	25.34	45.73	41.51	2,908	800-426-7969	Y
Russell Investments Intl Developed Mkts Fund Cls M	RNTTX	B-	B-	B	Up	3.97	10.16	24.98	25.70	46.14	41.17	2,908	800-426-7969	Y
Russell Investments Intl Developed Mkts Fund Cls S	RINTX	B-	B-	B	Up	3.96	10.15	25.00	26.38	47.67	41.2	2,908	800-426-7969	Y
Russell Investments Intl Developed Mkts Fund Cls Y	RINYX	B	B-	B	Up	4.01	10.22	25.22	27.07	49.08	41.2	2,908	800-426-7969	Y
Russell Investments Multifactor Intl Equity Fund Cls M	RTITX	B-	C+	B-	Up	3.85	10.19	25.09	22.13		10.37	933.3	800-426-7969	Y
Russell Investments Multifactor Intl Equity Fund Cls S	RTISX	B-	C+	B-	Up	3.84	10.20	24.83	21.56		10.36	933.3	800-426-7969	Y
SA International Value Fund Investor Class	SAHMX	B-	B-	B-	Up	5.52	14.09	25.03	24.45	42.39	12.47	758.5		Y
Schwab International Index Fund®	SWISX	B-	C+	B	Up	3.76	9.15	25.28	24.90	45.57	20.88	4,197	877-824-5615	Y
Schwab® International Core Equity Fund	SICNX	B-	B-	B-	Up	2.38	6.99	25.45	31.53	58.15	11.12	1,249	877-824-5615	Y
SEI Inst Intl Trust Intl Equity Fund Cls F	SEITX	B	B-	B	Up	4.44	10.82	26.65	27.37	47.86	11.64	4,245	800-342-5734	Y
SEI Inst Intl Trust Intl Equity Fund Cls I	SEEIX	B-	B-	B	Up	4.45	10.74	26.31	26.43	45.95	11.66	4,245	800-342-5734	Y
SEI Inst Intl Trust Intl Equity Fund Cls Y	SEFCX	B	B-	B	Up	4.49	10.96	26.94	28.25	48.88	11.64	4,245	800-342-5734	Y
SEI Inst Inv Trust Screened World Eq Ex-US Fund Cls A	SSEAX	B	B+	B-	Up	5.75	13.13	32.96	36.04	55.29	11.58	95.1	800-342-5734	Y
SEI Inst Investments Trust World Equity Ex-US Fund Cls A	WEUSX	B-	B-	B-	Up	5.38	12.27	29.50	25.94	47.09	13.94	8,453	800-342-5734	Y
Selected International Fund Class D	SLSDX	B	B+	B	Up	5.30	14.30	38.90	38.52	72.03	14.53	100.0	800-243-1575	Y

Category: Global Equity Large Cap (con't)

Fund Name	Ticker Symbol	Overall Rating	Reward Rating	Risk Rating	Recent Up/ Downgrade	3-Month Total Return	6-Month Total Return	1-Year Total Return	3-Year Total Return	5-Year Total Return	NAV	Total Assets (MIL)	Telephone	Open to New Investors
Selected International Fund Class S	SLSSX	B	B+	B	Up	5.20	14.00	38.22	36.73	67.92	14.44	100.0	800-243-1575	Y
Sextant International Fund	SSIFX	B-	B-	B-	Up	4.17	12.48	25.76	25.13	33.07		67.2		Y
Sextant International Fund Z Shares	SIFZX	B-	B-	B-	Up	4.27	12.72	25.95	25.32	33.28		67.2		Y
Sit International Growth Fund	SNGRX	B-	C+	B	Up	2.01	7.66	24.01	20.69	32.72	17.33	23.9	800-332-5580	Y
SSgA International Stock Selection Fund Class I	SSIPX	B-	B-	B	Up	1.77	6.93	22.56	22.78	48.38	11.78	302.4	617-664-7338	Y
SSgA International Stock Selection Fund Class K	SSIQX	B-	B-	C+	Up	1.72	6.97	22.60	23.16	49.01	11.78	302.4	617-664-7338	Y
SSgA International Stock Selection Fund N Class	SSAIX	B-	B-	B	Up	1.72	6.78	22.24	22.39	47.89	11.8	302.4	617-664-7338	
State Farm International Equity Fund Class A	SNIAX	B-	B-	B	Up	3.79	10.96	33.67	25.06	39.94	13	163.7		Y
State Farm International Equity Fund Class B	SNIBX	B-	B-	B	Up	3.77	10.96	33.45	23.18	36.45	12.66	163.7		
State Farm International Equity Fund Class B Legacy	SFFBX	B-	B-	B	Up	3.84	11.00	33.58	24.04	37.68	12.88	163.7		Y
State Farm International Equity Fund Class Institutional	SFIIX	B-	B-	B	Up	3.81	10.99	33.78	25.76	41.49	13.15	163.7		Y
State Farm International Equity Fund Class R1	RIEOX	B-	B-	B	Up	3.79	10.95	33.52	24.22	38.09	12.88	163.7		Y
State Farm International Equity Fund Class R2	RIETX	B-	B-	B	Up	3.73	10.92	33.55	24.63	39.15	12.97	163.7		Y
State Farm International Equity Fund Class R3	RIEHX	B-	B-	B	Up	3.80	10.90	33.69	25.49	41.00	13.13	163.7		Y
State Farm International Equity Fund Premier Shares	SFFAX	B-	B-	B	Up	3.78	11.04	33.74	25.28	40.24	13.14	163.7		Y
State Farm International Index Fund Class A	NFSAX	B-	C+	B	Up	3.98	9.37	24.98	22.53	40.42	13.17	298.9		Y
State Farm International Index Fund Class B	NFSBX	B-	C+	B-	Up	3.99	9.39	24.77	20.55	36.68	13.19	298.9		
State Farm International Index Fund Class B Legacy	SIIBX	B-	C+	B	Up	3.96	9.34	24.87	21.39	37.95	13.23	298.9		Y
State Farm International Index Fund Class Institutional	SFFFX	B-	C+	B	Up	4.05	9.35	25.03	23.20	41.88	13.19	298.9		Y
State Farm International Index Fund Class R1	RIIOX	B-	C+	B	Up	3.93	9.32	24.80	21.54	38.41	13.19	298.9		Y
State Farm International Index Fund Class R2	RIITX	B-	C+	B	Up	4.00	9.33	24.86	22.19	39.56	13.14	298.9		Y
State Farm International Index Fund Class R3	RIIHX	B-	C+	B	Up	4.02	9.32	24.98	22.99	41.41	13.2	298.9		Y
State Farm International Index Fund Premier Shares	SIIAX	B-	C+	B	Up	4.02	9.43	25.08	22.74	40.57	13.14	298.9		Y
State Street Global Equity ex-U.S. Index Fund Class A	SSGHX	B-	B-	B-	Up	3.50	9.74	25.05	22.15		10.67	499.7	617-664-7338	Y
State Street Global Equity ex-U.S. Index Fund Class I	SSGJX	B-	B-	B-	Up	3.57	9.90	25.37	23.08		10.67	499.7	617-664-7338	Y
State Street Global Equity ex-U.S. Index Fund Class K	SSGLX	B-	B-	B-	Up	3.56	10.00	25.48	23.19		10.68	499.7	617-664-7338	Y
State Street Global Equity ex-U.S. Index Portfolio	SSGVX	B-	B-	B-	Up	4.97	11.50	27.19	25.07		10.81	1,359	617-664-7338	Y
State Street Inst Intl Equity Fund Investment Cls	SIEIX	B-	C+	B-	Up	4.40	9.29	22.69	19.84	37.42	13.82	1,246	617-664-7338	Y
State Street Inst Intl Equity Fund Service Cls	SIESX	B-	C+	B-	Up	4.31	9.05	22.38	18.97	35.69	13.75	1,246	617-664-7338	Y
Strategic Advisers® International Fund	FILFX	B-	B-	B	Up	4.49	10.13	26.22	27.13	49.40	11.48	17,503	617-563-7000	Y
Strategic Advisers® International II Fund	FUSIX	B	B-	B	Up	4.37	9.95	27.72	27.12	52.63	10.69	4,477	617-563-7000	Y
Strategic Advisers® International Multi-Manager Fund	FMJDX	B-	B-	B	Up	4.87	10.30	26.24	26.27	49.29	13.56	70.1	617-563-7000	Y
Strategic Advisers® International Multi-Manager Fund Cls L	FQAHX	B-	B-	B	Up	4.88	10.23	26.17	26.21	49.30	13.54	70.1	617-563-7000	Y
Strategic Advisers® International Multi-Manager Fund Cls N	FQAIX	B-	C+	B	Up	4.84	10.11	25.89	25.27	47.43	13.53	70.1	617-563-7000	Y
T. Rowe Price Inst Intl Concentrated Equity Fund	RPICX	B-	B-	B	Up	1.90	5.00	21.68	27.37	53.90	12.99	531.0	410-345-2000	Y
T. Rowe Price Institutional International Core Equity Fund	TRCEX	B	B	B	Up	3.21	10.27	27.96	27.30	50.20	13.94	183.6	410-345-2000	Y
T. Rowe Price Inst Intl Growth Equity Fund	PRFEX	B	B	B	Up	3.50	8.50	28.34	29.92	49.60	24.88	57.8	410-345-2000	Y
T. Rowe Price International Concentrated Equity Fund	PRCNX	B-	B-	B	Up	1.37	4.50	21.05	26.19		10.63	25.8	410-345-2000	Y
T. Rowe Price Intl Concentrated Equity Fund Adv Cls	PRNCX	B-	C+	B	Up	1.37	4.41	20.83	26.24		10.63	25.8	410-345-2000	Y
T. Rowe Price International Concentrated Equity Fund I Cls	RICIX	B-	B-	B	Up	1.46	4.59	21.27	26.42		10.64	25.8	410-345-2000	Y
T. Rowe Price International Equity Index Fund	PIEQX	B-	B-	B	Up	4.23	9.62	26.44	26.59	45.15	14.45	612.3	410-345-2000	Y
T. Rowe Price International Stock Fund	PRITX	B	B	B	Up	3.53	8.58	28.18	29.53	49.22	18.67	15,754	410-345-2000	Y
T. Rowe Price International Stock Fund Advisor Class	PAITX	B	B-	B	Up	3.53	8.46	27.88	28.89	47.81	18.74	15,754	410-345-2000	Y
T. Rowe Price International Stock Fund Class R	RRITX	B-	B-	B	Up	3.39	8.30	27.51	27.45	45.13	18.57	15,754	410-345-2000	Y
T. Rowe Price International Stock Fund I Class	PRIUX	B	B	B	Up	3.58	8.63	28.39	30.08	49.85	18.66	15,754	410-345-2000	Y
T. Rowe Price International Value Equity Fund	TRIGX	B-	C+	B-	Up	1.39	6.48	20.78	17.12	38.33	15.12	13,844	410-345-2000	Y
T. Rowe Price International Value Equity Fund Advisor Cls	PAIGX	B-	C+	B-	Up	1.37	6.39	20.52	16.32	36.75	15.39	13,844	410-345-2000	Y
T. Rowe Price International Value Equity Fund Class I	TRTIX	B-	C+	B-	Up	1.39	6.56	20.97	17.66	38.97	15.09	13,844	410-345-2000	Y
T. Rowe Price Overseas Stock Fund	TROSX	B	B-	B	Up	3.04	9.82	27.02	26.68	49.33	11.31	15,748	410-345-2000	Y
T. Rowe Price Overseas Stock Fund Advisor Class	PAEIX	B-	B-	B	Up	3.07	9.81	26.75	25.80	47.55	11.22	15,748	410-345-2000	Y
T. Rowe Price Overseas Stock Fund I Class	TROIX	B-	B	C+	Up	3.14	9.95	27.22	27.16	49.89	11.28	15,748	410-345-2000	Y
T. Rowe Price Spectrum International Fund	PSILX	B-	B-	B	Up	3.81	9.61	28.53	26.72	47.23	14.61	1,539	410-345-2000	Y

Category: Global Equity Large Cap (con't)

Fund Name	Ticker Symbol	RATINGS: Overall Rating	Reward Rating	Risk Rating	Recent Up/ Downgrade	TOTAL RETURNS & PERFORMANCE: 3-Month Total Return	6-Month Total Return	1-Year Total Return	3-Year Total Return	5-Year Total Return	ASSETS: NAV	Total Assets (MIL)	NEW INVESTORS: Telephone	Open to New Investors
The Hartford International Opportunities Fund Class A	IHOAX	B	B-	B	Up	3.49	8.81	24.23	25.91	47.13	16.96	3,548	888-843-7824	Y
The Hartford International Opportunities Fund Class C	HIOCX	B-	C+	B	Up	3.29	8.39	23.33	23.23	41.88	14.83	3,548	888-843-7824	Y
The Hartford International Opportunities Fund Class F	IHOFX	B	B-	B	Up	3.53	9.00	24.71	27.61	50.55	16.84	3,548	888-843-7824	Y
The Hartford International Opportunities Fund Class I	IHOIX	B	B-	B	Up	3.50	8.91	24.53	27.10	49.56	16.84	3,548	888-843-7824	Y
The Hartford International Opportunities Fund Class R3	IHORX	B-	B-	B	Up	3.33	8.62	23.85	24.93	45.24	17.24	3,548	888-843-7824	Y
The Hartford International Opportunities Fund Class R4	IHOSX	B	B-	B	Up	3.44	8.78	24.23	26.02	47.49	17.53	3,548	888-843-7824	Y
The Hartford International Opportunities Fund Class R5	IHOTX	B	B-	B	Up	3.52	8.99	24.57	27.24	49.78	17.68	3,548	888-843-7824	Y
The Hartford International Opportunities Fund Class R6	IHOVX	B	B-	B	Up	3.57	9.02	24.76	27.57	50.51	17.77	3,548	888-843-7824	Y
The Hartford International Opportunities Fund Class Y	HAOYX	B	B-	B	Up	3.60	9.05	24.71	27.61	50.55	17.78	3,548	888-843-7824	Y
The Hartford International Value Fund Class Y	HILYX	B	B	C+	Up	3.86	10.49	24.90	43.72	80.02	17.63	2,769	888-843-7824	
Thomas White International Fund Class I	TWWIX	B-	C+	B-	Up	4.59	11.32	28.48	20.44	24.91	18.24	320.9	800-811-0535	Y
Thomas White International Fund Investor Class	TWWDX	B-	C+	B-	Up	4.44	11.08	28.24	19.55	23.36	18.32	320.9	800-811-0535	Y
Thornburg International Value Fund Class A	TGVAX	B	B	B	Up	3.51	7.45	24.98	28.40	40.56	24.5	5,640	800-847-0200	Y
Thornburg International Value Fund Class C	THGCX	B-	B-	B	Up	3.31	7.08	24.06	25.60	35.46	21.73	5,640	800-847-0200	Y
Thornburg International Value Fund Class I	TGVIX	B	B	B	Up	3.60	7.66	25.47	29.88	43.21	25.28	5,640	800-847-0200	Y
Thornburg International Value Fund Class R3	TGVRX	B	B	B	Up	3.48	7.41	24.78	27.77	39.33	24.49	5,640	800-847-0200	Y
Thornburg International Value Fund Class R4	THVRX	B	B	B	Up	3.50	7.47	25.05	28.55	40.70	24.31	5,640	800-847-0200	Y
Thornburg International Value Fund Class R5	TIVRX	B	B	B	Up	3.59	7.61	25.37	29.62	42.67	25.26	5,640	800-847-0200	Y
Thornburg International Value Fund Class R6	TGIRX	B	B	B	Up	3.65	7.74	25.59	30.44	44.27	25.18	5,640	800-847-0200	Y
TIAA-CREF Enhanced Intl Equity Index Fund Adv Cls	TEIEX	B-	B-	B	Up	3.55	9.14	25.80	24.21	50.43	8.24	1,907	877-518-9161	Y
TIAA-CREF Enhanced Intl Equity Index Fund Inst Cls	TFIIX	B-	B-	B	Up	3.64	9.38	25.91	24.54	50.82	8.24	1,907	877-518-9161	Y
TIAA-CREF International Equity Fund Advisor Class	TIEHX	B	B	B	Up	4.42	11.98	32.74	31.31	52.03	13.29	5,124	877-518-9161	Y
TIAA-CREF International Equity Fund Institutional Class	TIIEX	B	B	B	Up	4.47	12.04	32.94	31.53	52.29	13.29	5,124	877-518-9161	Y
TIAA-CREF International Equity Fund Premier Class	TREPX	B	B	B	Up	4.41	11.90	32.68	30.99	51.26	13.27	5,124	877-518-9161	Y
TIAA-CREF International Equity Fund Retail Class	TIERX	B	B	B	Up	4.33	11.78	32.51	30.33	49.96	8.79	5,124	877-518-9161	Y
TIAA-CREF International Equity Fund Retirement Class	TRERX	B	B	B	Up	4.38	11.85	32.61	30.54	50.48	13.78	5,124	877-518-9161	Y
TIAA-CREF International Equity Index Fund Advisor Class	TCIHX	B-	B-	B	Up	3.74	9.09	25.17	25.32	46.96	20.17	11,766	877-518-9161	Y
TIAA-CREF Intl Equity Index Fund Inst Cls	TCIEX	B-	B-	B	Up	3.75	9.16	25.32	25.51	47.19	20.17	11,766	877-518-9161	Y
TIAA-CREF International Equity Index Fund Premier Class	TRIPX	B-	C+	B	Up	3.73	9.09	25.14	24.97	46.07	20.13	11,766	877-518-9161	Y
TIAA-CREF International Equity Index Fund Retirement Class	TRIEX	B-	C+	B	Up	3.70	9.05	25.03	24.65	45.39	20.63	11,766	877-518-9161	Y
TIAA-CREF International Opportunities Fund Advisor Class	TIOHX	B	B	B	Up	5.05	14.86	35.30	36.09		13.37	1,463	877-518-9161	Y
TIAA-CREF Intl Opp Fund Inst Cls	TIOIX	B	B+	B	Up	5.07	14.88	35.19	36.37		13.37	1,463	877-518-9161	Y
TIAA-CREF International Opportunities Fund Premier Class	TIOPX	B	B	B	Up	5.02	14.81	35.07	35.73		13.4	1,463	877-518-9161	Y
TIAA-CREF International Opportunities Fund Retail Class	TIOSX	B	B	B	Up	4.96	14.69	34.74	34.68		13.37	1,463	877-518-9161	Y
TIAA-CREF International Opportunities Fund Retirement Cls	TIOTX	B	B	B	Up	4.97	14.70	34.89	35.24		13.34	1,463	877-518-9161	Y
Timothy Plan International Fund Class C	TPICX	B-	C+	B	Up	4.05	11.27	22.67	16.68	37.86	9.78	98.5	800-662-0201	Y
Tocqueville International Value Fund	TIVFX	B	B	B+	Up	2.11	8.67	24.17	37.10	62.29	17.53	1,141	212-698-0800	Y
Toreador International Fund Class Institutional	TMRIX	B-	C+	B	Up	4.76	8.49	22.86	19.76	42.10	19.99	58.7		Y
Toreador International Fund Investor Class	TMRFX	B-	C+	B	Up	4.72	8.27	22.50	18.81	40.31	18.74	58.7		Y
Touchstone International Equity Fund Class A	SWRLX	B	B	B	Up	7.03	10.34	28.62	33.20	59.60	19.42	199.4	800-543-0407	Y
Touchstone International Equity Fund Class C	SWFCX	B	B-	B	Up	6.72	9.78	27.26	28.65	49.51	18.4	199.4	800-543-0407	Y
Touchstone International Equity Fund Class Y	SIIEX	B	B	B	Up	7.17	10.58	29.14	34.70	63.12	19.17	199.4	800-543-0407	Y
Touchstone International Equity Fund Institutional USD	TOIIX	B	B	B		7.14	10.45	28.76	33.34	59.77	19.15	199.4	800-543-0407	Y
Transamerica International Equity A	TRWAX	B-	C+	B	Up	4.13	7.80	22.21	22.94	49.07	19.31	5,530	888-233-4339	Y
Transamerica International Equity Advisor	TAIQX	B-	C+	B	Up	4.12	7.91	22.47	24.07	50.50	19.81	5,530	888-233-4339	Y
Transamerica International Equity C	TRWCX	B-	C+	B	Up	3.87	7.36	21.26	20.40	44.01	19.05	5,530	888-233-4339	Y
Transamerica International Equity Class T1	TRWWX	B-	C+	B	Up	4.15	7.88	22.47	23.45	49.00	19.42	5,530	888-233-4339	Y
Transamerica International Equity I	TSWIX	B-	B-	B	Up	4.18	7.98	22.58	24.32	51.69	19.52	5,530	888-233-4339	Y
Transamerica International Equity I2	TRWIX	B-	B-	B	Up	4.20	8.00	22.66	24.68	52.42	19.53	5,530	888-233-4339	Y
Transamerica International Equity I3	TRWTX	B-	B-	B	Up	4.23	8.03	22.77	24.38	50.86	19.66	5,530	888-233-4339	Y
Transamerica Intl Equity Opp Fund Cls I2	US8939616491	B	B-	B	Up	3.96	8.49	27.58	26.37	44.67	9.06	1,374	888-233-4339	Y
Transamerica International Equity R	TRWRX	B-	C+	B	Up	4.09	7.77	22.20	22.56	47.19	19.71	5,530	888-233-4339	Y

Category: Global Equity Large Cap (con't)

Fund Name	Ticker Symbol	RATINGS: Overall Rating	Reward Rating	Risk Rating	Recent Up/ Downgrade	TOTAL RETURNS & PERFORMANCE: 3-Month Total Return	6-Month Total Return	1-Year Total Return	3-Year Total Return	5-Year Total Return	ASSETS: NAV	Total Assets (MIL)	NEW INVESTORS: Telephone	Open to New Investors
Transamerica International Equity R4	TRWFX	B-	C+	B	Up	4.10	7.89	22.40	23.39	48.92	19.66	5,530	888-233-4339	Y
Transamerica International Equity R6	TAINX	B-	B-	B	Up	4.22	8.04	22.70	24.67	51.23	19.72	5,530	888-233-4339	Y
Tweedy, Browne Global Value Fund	TBGVX	B-	C+	B	Down	2.86	4.91	15.43	20.18	45.94	28.49	10,248	800-432-4789	Y
Tweedy, Browne Global Value Fund II - Currency Unhedged	TBCUX	B-	C+	B	Up	3.95	7.39	21.59	17.64	34.52	15.71	376.2	800-432-4789	
UBS International Sustainable Equity Fund Class A	BNIEX	B	B	B-	Up	5.86	13.15	30.92	27.05	56.78	10.72	39.5	212-882-5586	Y
UBS International Sustainable Equity Fund Class C	BNICX	B-	B-	B-	Up	5.69	12.70	29.93	24.19	51.13	10.47	39.5	212-882-5586	Y
UBS International Sustainable Equity Fund Class P	BNUEX	B	B	B	Up	5.93	13.32	31.21	27.98	58.89	10.74	39.5	212-882-5586	Y
USAA International Fund	USIFX	B	B	B	Up	4.17	9.77	28.10	30.32	48.29	33.27	4,320	800-531-8722	Y
USAA International Fund Adviser Shares	UAIFX	B	B	B	Up	4.08	9.63	27.78	29.34	46.26	33.16	4,320	800-531-8722	Y
USAA International Fund Institutional Shares	UIIFX	B	B	B	Up	4.20	9.85	28.20	30.81	49.25	33.17	4,320	800-531-8722	Y
VALIC Company I International Equities Index Fund	VCIEX	B-	B-	B	Up	3.65	9.11	24.35	23.73	41.39	7.66	1,371		Y
VALIC Company I International Growth Fund	VCINX	B-	B-	B	Up	3.83	10.12	27.63	22.78	45.36	14.36	461.0		Y
Vanguard Developed Markets Index Fund Admiral Shares	VTMGX	B	B-	B	Up	4.45	10.18	26.39	28.62	50.17	14.41	104,114	877-662-7447	Y
Vanguard Developed Mkts Index Fund Inst Plus Shares	VDIPX	B	B-	B	Up	4.45	10.24	26.49	28.76	50.37	22.56	104,114	877-662-7447	Y
Vanguard Developed Markets Index Fund Institutional Shares	VTMNX	B	B-	B	Up	4.45	10.25	26.46	28.72	50.31	14.43	104,114	877-662-7447	Y
Vanguard Developed Markets Index Fund Investor Shares	VDVIX	B-	B-	B	Up	4.40	10.23	26.30	28.23	49.40	11.16	104,114	877-662-7447	Y
Vanguard FTSE All-World ex-US Index Fund Admiral Shares	VFWAX	B-	B-	B-	Up	4.71	10.93	27.21	26.60	40.94	33.96	36,769	877-662-7447	Y
Vanguard FTSE All-World ex-US Index Fund Inst Plus Shares	VFWPX	B-	B-	B-	Up	4.74	10.96	27.29	26.77	41.28	114.02	36,769	877-662-7447	Y
Vanguard FTSE All-World ex-US Index Fund Inst Shares	VFWSX	B-	B-	B-	Up	4.74	10.94	27.25	26.66	41.10	107.67	36,769	877-662-7447	Y
Vanguard FTSE All-World ex-US Index Fund Investor Shares	VFWIX	B-	B-	B-	Up	4.71	10.88	27.07	26.17	40.04	21.56	36,769	877-662-7447	Y
Vanguard International Growth Fund Admiral Shares	VWILX	B+	A	B-	Up	4.12	15.24	43.15	44.30	70.47	95.58	33,542	877-662-7447	Y
Vanguard International Growth Fund Investor Shares	VWIGX	B+	A	B-	Up	4.06	15.14	42.96	43.76	69.34	30.04	33,542	877-662-7447	Y
Vanguard International Value Fund Investor Shares	VTRIX	B-	B-	B-	Up	4.90	11.95	27.96	24.57	43.96	39.88	10,162	877-662-7447	Y
Vanguard Total Intl Stock Index Fund Admiral Shares	VTIAX	B-	B-	B-	Up	4.88	11.12	27.55	27.38	42.40	30.52	321,185	877-662-7447	Y
Vanguard Total Intl Stock Index Fund Inst Plus Shares	VTPSX	B-	B-	B-	Up	4.87	11.13	27.57	27.52	42.64	122.05	321,185	877-662-7447	Y
Vanguard Total Intl Stock Index Fund Inst Shares	VTSNX	B-	B-	B-	Up	4.87	11.12	27.55	27.43	42.49	122.03	321,185	877-662-7447	Y
Vanguard Total Intl Stock Index Fund Inv Shares	VGTSX	B-	B-	B-	Up	4.79	11.04	27.39	27.08	41.78	18.24	321,185	877-662-7447	Y
Vanguard Total Intl Stock Idx Fund Inst Select Shares	VTISX	B-	B-	B-	Up	4.87	11.15	27.60	27.33	42.06	128.52	321,185	877-662-7447	Y
Victory RS International Fund Class A	GUBGX	B	B-	B	Up	4.45	10.93	25.25	28.95	42.48	12.12	25.2	800-539-3863	Y
Victory RS International Fund Class C	RIGCX	B-	B-	B	Up	4.28	10.54	24.24	25.93	35.92	8.89	25.2	800-539-3863	Y
Victory RS International Fund Class R	RIGKX	B	B-	B	Up	4.38	10.80	24.85	27.56	39.32	11.35	25.2	800-539-3863	Y
Victory RS International Fund Class Y	RSIGX	B	B	B	Up	4.52	11.11	25.56	29.85	44.75	11.93	25.2	800-539-3863	Y
Victory Trivalent International Fund-Core Equity Class A	MAICX	B-	B-	B-	Up	4.21	11.59	26.90	26.08	49.58	7.54	26.2	800-539-3863	Y
Victory Trivalent International Fund-Core Equity Class C	MICCX	B-	B-	B-	Up	4.11	11.24	25.82	23.47	44.13	7.52	26.2	800-539-3863	Y
Victory Trivalent International Fund-Core Equity Class I	MICIX	B-	B-	B	Up	4.27	11.92	27.26	27.92	53.57	7.55	26.2	800-539-3863	Y
Victory Trivalent International Fund-Core Equity Class R6	MAIRX	B-	B-	B	Up	4.33	11.98	27.50	28.16	53.86	7.57	26.2	800-539-3863	Y
Victory Trivalent International Fund-Core Equity Class Y	MICYX	B-	B-	B-	Up	4.19	11.72	27.07	26.94	51.15	7.52	26.2	800-539-3863	Y
Virtus KAR Global Quality Dividend Fund Class A	PPTAX	B-	C+	B	Down	3.40	4.95	14.24	18.30	74.90	14.86	55.7	800-243-1574	Y
Virtus KAR Global Quality Dividend Fund Class C	PPTCX	B-	C+	B	Down	3.27	4.59	13.41	15.66	68.44	14.48	55.7	800-243-1574	Y
Virtus KAR Global Quality Dividend Fund Class I	PIPTX	B-	C+	B	Down	3.51	5.06	14.53	19.20	77.26	14.87	55.7	800-243-1574	Y
Virtus Vontobel Foreign Opportunities Fund Class A	JVIAX	B	B	B	Up	4.73	8.53	32.32	29.94	41.82	35.49	1,501	800-243-1574	Y
Virtus Vontobel Foreign Opportunities Fund Class C	JVICX	B	B-	B	Up	4.52	8.12	31.36	27.09	36.61	34.85	1,501	800-243-1574	Y
Virtus Vontobel Foreign Opportunities Fund Class I	JVXIX	B	B	B	Up	4.81	8.71	32.69	30.98	43.64	35.49	1,501	800-243-1574	Y
Virtus Vontobel Foreign Opportunities Fund Class R6	VFOPX	B	B	B	Up	4.82	8.71	32.82	31.38	43.42	35.49	1,501	800-243-1574	Y
Virtus WCM International Equity Fund Class A	SCIIX	B	B	B	Up	5.12	9.66	31.30	33.69	52.04	11.9	97.7	800-243-1574	Y
Virtus WCM International Equity Fund Class I	STITX	B	B	B	Up	5.22	9.74	31.57	34.50	53.13	12.09	97.7	800-243-1574	Y
Virtus WCM International Equity Fund Class R6	SCIZX	B	B	B	Up	5.21	9.84	31.67	34.84	53.53	12.11	97.7	800-243-1574	Y
Voya International Index Portfolio Class A	IIIAX	B-	C+	B	Up	3.44	8.68	24.19	22.33	40.63	10.51	1,673	800-366-0066	Y
Voya International Index Portfolio Class I	IIIIX	B-	C+	B	Up	3.66	8.92	24.87	24.14	44.28	10.74	1,673	800-366-0066	Y
Voya International Index Portfolio Class P2	VIPPX	B-	C+	B	Up	3.76	9.12	25.11	24.37	44.54	10.76	1,673	800-366-0066	Y
Voya International Index Portfolio Class S	INTIX	B-	C+	B	Up	3.59	8.77	24.50	23.18	42.39	10.66	1,673	800-366-0066	Y
Voya International Index Portfolio Class S2	ISIIX	B-	C+	B	Up	3.59	8.78	24.44	22.67	41.40	10.65	1,673	800-366-0066	Y

Category: Global Equity Large Cap (con't)

Fund Name	Ticker Symbol	RATINGS: Overall Rating	Reward Rating	Risk Rating	Recent Up/ Downgrade	TOTAL RETURNS & PERFORMANCE: 3-Month Total Return	6-Month Total Return	1-Year Total Return	3-Year Total Return	5-Year Total Return	ASSETS: NAV	Total Assets (MIL)	NEW INVESTORS: Telephone	Open to New Investors
Voya Multi-Manager International Equity Fund Class I	IIGIX	B-	C+	B	Up	4.41	9.57	25.23	24.09	41.51	12.34	519.4	800-366-0066	Y
Voya Multi-Manager International Factors Fund Class I	IICFX	B	B-	B	Up	3.95	9.71	25.31	27.29	47.38	10.61	394.5	800-366-0066	Y
Voya Multi-Manager International Factors Fund Class W	IICWX	B	B-	B	Up	3.95	9.72	25.32	27.28	47.36	10.61	394.5	800-366-0066	Y
VY® T. Rowe Price International Stock Portfolio Class A	IMIOX	B-	B-	B	Up	3.39	8.28	27.42	27.29	45.06	16.16	242.0	800-366-0066	Y
VY® T. Rowe Price International Stock Portfolio Class I	IMASX	B	B	B	Up	3.57	8.63	28.20	29.65	49.45	16.22	242.0	800-366-0066	Y
VY® T. Rowe Price International Stock Portfolio Class S	IMISX	B	B-	B	Up	3.52	8.49	27.86	28.67	47.56	16.15	242.0	800-366-0066	Y
VY® Templeton Foreign Equity Portfolio Class A	IFTAX	B-	C+	B-	Up	2.27	7.11	21.65	18.45	33.74	13.06	638.6	800-366-0066	Y
VY® Templeton Foreign Equity Portfolio Class S	IFTSX	B-	C+	B-	Up	2.41	7.28	21.99	19.35	35.37	13.12	638.6	800-366-0066	Y
WCM Focused International Growth Fund Institutional Class	WCMIX	B+	B	A-	Up	5.14	9.66	31.23	39.04	70.65	15.74	5,070	949-380-0200	Y
WCM Focused International Growth Fund Investor Class	WCMRX	B	B	B+	Up	5.09	9.55	30.88	38.02	68.52	15.69	5,070	949-380-0200	Y
Wells Fargo Diversified International Fund - Class A	SILAX	B-	C+	B-	Up	3.80	9.77	25.64	21.84	44.58	13.4	124.8	800-222-8222	Y
Wells Fargo Diversified International Fund - Class Admin	WFIEX	B-	C+	B-	Up	3.89	9.85	25.85	22.25	45.56	13.65	124.8	800-222-8222	Y
Wells Fargo Diversified International Fund - Class C	WFECX	B-	C+	B-	Up	3.71	9.48	24.80	19.14	39.37	12.35	124.8	800-222-8222	Y
Wells Fargo Diversified International Fund - Class Inst	WFISX	B-	C+	B-	Up	3.88	9.95	26.17	23.27	47.52	12.72	124.8	800-222-8222	Y
Wells Fargo Diversified International Fund - Class R6	WDIRX	B-	C+	B-	Up	3.96	10.05	26.24	23.17	46.16	13.71	124.8	800-222-8222	Y
Wells Fargo International Equity Fund - Class A	WFEAX	B	B	C+	Up	4.67	10.81	24.07	31.62	53.24	13.35	479.0	800-222-8222	Y
Wells Fargo International Equity Fund - Class Admin	WFEDX	B	B	C+	Up	4.74	10.81	24.10	31.66	53.26	13.12	479.0	800-222-8222	Y
Wells Fargo International Equity Fund - Class C	WFEFX	B-	B	C+	Up	4.49	10.31	23.11	28.67	47.54	13.11	479.0	800-222-8222	Y
Wells Fargo International Equity Fund - Class Inst	WFENX	B	B	C+	Up	4.69	10.85	24.36	32.61	55.13	13.29	479.0	800-222-8222	Y
Wells Fargo International Equity Fund - Class R	WFERX	B	B	C+	Up	4.66	10.64	23.79	30.74	51.37	13.54	479.0	800-222-8222	Y
Wells Fargo International Equity Fund - Class R6	WFEHX	B	B	C+	Up	4.75	10.90	24.49	32.34	54.08	13.33	479.0	800-222-8222	Y
William Blair Inst Intl Developed Plus Fund Cls Inst	WIIEX	B	B-	B	Up	3.76	10.71	24.27	25.58	47.21	14.55	19.1	800-621-0687	Y
William Blair Institutional International Growth Fund	WBIIX	B	B-	B	Up	4.59	13.12	29.53	25.80	47.64	18.08	2,337	800-621-0687	
William Blair Intl Developed Plus Fund Cls Inst	WIEIX	B	B-	B	Up	3.67	10.51	23.72	25.20	47.76	16.76	119.5	800-621-0687	Y
William Blair International Developed Plus Fund Class N	WIENX	B	B-	B	Up	3.65	10.36	23.42	24.26	45.92	16.6	119.5	800-621-0687	Y
William Blair International Growth Fund Class I	BIGIX	B	B-	B	Up	4.59	13.13	29.48	25.42	46.92	31.13	3,172	800-621-0687	
William Blair International Growth Fund Class N	WBIGX	B-	B-	B	Up	4.53	12.92	29.10	24.31	44.71	30.41	3,172	800-621-0687	
William Blair International Leaders Fund Class I Shares	WILIX	B+	A-	B	Up	5.21	12.68	30.04	38.69	63.56	16.44	369.8	800-621-0687	Y
William Blair International Leaders Fund Class N Shares	WILNX	B+	A-	B	Up	5.08	12.52	29.64	37.75	61.61	16.37	369.8	800-621-0687	Y
William Blair Intl Leaders Fund Inst Cls Shares	WILJX	B+	A-	B	Up	5.16	12.71	30.07	39.12	64.49	16.43	369.8	800-621-0687	Y
Wilmington International Fund Class A	GVIEX	B-	B-	B-	Up	5.27	12.61	33.38	28.46	42.49	9.13	582.2	800-836-2211	Y
Wilmington International Fund Class Institutional	MVIEX	B-	B-	B-	Up	5.38	12.71	33.56	29.09	43.55	9.2	582.2	800-836-2211	Y
Wilshire Intl Equity Fund Inst Cls Shares	WLTTX	B-	B-	B	Up	4.55	10.38	25.91	26.31	44.21	11.04	343.6	888-200-6796	Y
Wilshire International Equity Fund Investment Class Shares	WLCTX	B-	B-	B	Up	4.45	10.21	25.53	25.35	42.43	11.19	343.6	888-200-6796	Y

Category: Global Equity Mid/Small Cap

Fund Name	Ticker Symbol	RATINGS: Overall Rating	Reward Rating	Risk Rating	Recent Up/ Downgrade	TOTAL RETURNS & PERFORMANCE: 3-Month Total Return	6-Month Total Return	1-Year Total Return	3-Year Total Return	5-Year Total Return	ASSETS: NAV	Total Assets (MIL)	NEW INVESTORS: Telephone	Open to New Investors
Aberdeen International Small Cap Fund Class A	WVCCX	B	B	B	Up	5.65	15.11	31.75	34.63	50.86	31.49	79.5	866-667-9231	Y
Aberdeen International Small Cap Fund Class C	CPVCX	B	B	B	Up	5.47	14.75	30.91	31.92	45.84	28.97	79.5	866-667-9231	Y
Aberdeen International Small Cap Fund Class R	WPVAX	B	B	B	Up	5.54	14.91	31.25	33.28	48.62	29.97	79.5	866-667-9231	Y
Aberdeen International Small Cap Fund Institutional Class	ABNIX	B	B	B	Up	5.72	15.32	32.18	35.92	53.24	31.52	79.5	866-667-9231	Y
Aberdeen Intl Small Cap Fund Inst Service Cls	AGISX	B	B	B	Up	5.68	15.20	31.90	35.05	51.66	31.67	79.5	866-667-9231	Y
Acuitas International Small Cap Fund Institutional Shares	AISCX	B	B	B	Up	4.22	9.37	21.24	29.00		10.5	49.2		Y
Advisory Research International Small Cap Value Fund Cls I	ADVLX	B-	B	C+	Up	6.94	15.10	29.52	35.51	64.32	13.65	16.2	312-565-1414	Y
Advy Research Intl Small Cap Value Fund Inv Cls	ADVIX	B-	B	C+	Up	6.88	15.03	29.44	35.44	64.02	13.65	16.2	312-565-1414	Y
AllianzGI Global Small-Cap Fund Class A	RGSAX	B	B	B	Up	6.35	14.05	26.86	30.54	83.74	50.07	205.5	800-498-5413	Y
AllianzGI Global Small-Cap Fund Class C	RGSCX	B	B-	B	Up	6.15	13.63	25.92	27.64	77.00	44.13	205.5	800-498-5413	Y
AllianzGI Global Small-Cap Fund Class P	ARSPX	B	B	B	Up	6.43	14.20	27.19	31.53	86.09	53.1	205.5	800-498-5413	Y
AllianzGI Global Small-Cap Fund Institutional Class	DGSCX	B	B	B	Up	6.45	14.26	27.32	31.93	87.00	53.5	205.5	800-498-5413	Y

Category: Global Equity Mid/Small Cap (con't)

Fund Name	Ticker Symbol	RATINGS: Overall Rating	Reward Rating	Risk Rating	Recent Up/ Downgrade	TOTAL RETURNS & PERFORMANCE: 3-Month Total Return	6-Month Total Return	1-Year Total Return	3-Year Total Return	5-Year Total Return	ASSETS: NAV	Total Assets (MIL)	NEW INVESTORS: Telephone	Open to New Investors
AllianzGI International Small-Cap Fund Class A	AOPAX	B+	A-	B	Up	7.64	18.01	39.03	47.58	81.32	43.4	171.5	800-498-5413	Y
AllianzGI International Small-Cap Fund Class C	AOPCX	B+	A-	B	Up	7.39	17.52	37.89	44.18	74.54	42.18	171.5	800-498-5413	Y
AllianzGI International Small-Cap Fund Class P	ALOPX	B+	A-	B	Up	7.66	18.09	39.22	48.26	82.81	43.32	171.5	800-498-5413	Y
AllianzGI International Small-Cap Fund Class R	ALORX	B+	A-	B	Up	7.55	17.83	38.58	46.32	78.95	42.31	171.5	800-498-5413	Y
AllianzGI International Small-Cap Fund Class R6	AIISX	B+	A-	B	Up	7.72	18.19	39.40	48.75	83.67	44.88	171.5	800-498-5413	Y
AllianzGI International Small-Cap Fund Institutional Class	ALOIX	B+	A-	B	Up	7.68	18.13	39.28	48.54	83.42	44.9	171.5	800-498-5413	Y
AllianzGI NFJ International Small-Cap Value Fund Class A	AJVAX	B-	B-	B	Up	3.25	10.85	27.89	25.17	58.60	20.97	4.5	800-498-5413	Y
AllianzGI NFJ International Small-Cap Value Fund Class C	AJVCX	B-	C+	B	Up	3.04	10.38	26.87	22.37	52.90	20.3	4.5	800-498-5413	Y
AllianzGI NFJ International Small-Cap Value Fund Class P	AJVPX	B-	B-	B	Up	3.32	10.95	28.19	25.85	59.92	20.29	4.5	800-498-5413	Y
AllianzGI NFJ International Small-Cap Value Fund Class R6	AJVSX	B-	B-	B	Up	3.33	10.97	28.28	26.40	60.98	20.13	4.5	800-498-5413	Y
AllianzGI NFJ Intl Small-Cap Value Fund Inst Cls	AJVIX	B-	B-	B	Up	3.31	10.99	28.20	26.19	60.72	20.94	4.5	800-498-5413	Y
ALPS | Red Rocks Listed Private Equity Fund Class C	LPFCX	B	B	B	Up	1.15	5.72	26.11	32.66	87.63	6.79	218.8	866-759-5679	Y
ALPS | Red Rocks Listed Private Equity Fund Class I	LPEIX	B	B	C+	Up	1.36	6.32	27.49	36.67	97.06	7.27	218.8	866-759-5679	Y
ALPS | Red Rocks Listed Private Equity Fund Class Investor	LPEFX	B	B	C+	Up	1.34	6.11	27.04	35.50	93.76	7.15	218.8	866-759-5679	Y
ALPS | Red Rocks Listed Private Equity Fund Class R	LPERX	B-	B	C+	Up	1.28	6.02	26.88	34.68	94.07	6.06	218.8	866-759-5679	Y
American Century International Discovery Fund C Class	TWECX	B+	A-	B	Up	6.57	18.66	39.02	36.90	65.72	16.21	550.8	800-444-4015	Y
American Century International Discovery Fund Class A	ACIDX	B+	A-	B	Up	6.76	19.13	40.10	40.07	71.89	16.56	550.8	800-444-4015	Y
American Century International Discovery Fund I Class	TIDIX	B+	A-	B	Up	6.91	19.46	40.73	41.93	75.94	17.31	550.8	800-444-4015	Y
American Century International Discovery Fund Investor Cls	TWEGX	B+	A-	B	Up	6.89	19.30	40.52	41.17	74.23	17.06	550.8	800-444-4015	Y
American Century International Discovery Fund R Class	TWERX	B+	A-	B	Up	6.75	19.06	39.84	38.99	69.87	16.74	550.8	800-444-4015	Y
American Century International Discovery Fund Y Class	AIYDX	B+	A-	B	Up	6.97	19.51	40.83	41.47	74.60	17.33	550.8	800-444-4015	Y
American Century International Opportunities Fund Class A	AIVOX	A-	A	B+	Up	7.80	18.98	44.76	50.00	82.44	11.15	190.1	800-444-4015	Y
American Century International Opportunities Fund Class C	AIOCX	A-	A-	B+	Up	7.59	18.55	43.63	46.52	75.94	10.77	190.1	800-444-4015	Y
American Century International Opportunities Fund Class R	AIORX	A-	A	B+	Up	7.78	18.85	44.36	48.87	80.16	11.06	190.1	800-444-4015	Y
American Century International Opportunities Fund I Class	ACIOX	A-	A	B+	Up	7.97	19.28	45.27	51.83	86.36	11.34	190.1	800-444-4015	Y
American Century Intl Opp Fund Inv Cls	AIOIX	A-	A	B+	Up	7.92	19.13	45.04	51.06	84.76	11.23	190.1	800-444-4015	Y
American Century NT International Small-Mid Cap Fund G Cls	ANTMX	B-	C+	B-	Up	7.07	17.52	37.19			13.03	249.6	800-444-4015	
American Century NT Intl Small-Mid Cap Fund Inv Cls	ANTSX	B-	C+	B-	Up	6.62	16.67	36.07			12.92	249.6	800-444-4015	Y
American Funds SMALLCAP World Fund® Class 529-A	CSPAX	B	B	B	Up	4.86	10.57	26.75	37.01	82.91	55.17	38,579	800-421-4225	Y
American Funds SMALLCAP World Fund® Class 529-C	CSPCX	B	B	B	Up	4.65	10.14	25.75	33.83	75.84	50	38,579	800-421-4225	Y
American Funds SMALLCAP World Fund® Class 529-E	CSPEX	B	B	B	Up	4.83	10.48	26.48	36.14	80.90	53.64	38,579	800-421-4225	Y
American Funds SMALLCAP World Fund® Class 529-F	CSPFX	B	B	B	Up	4.92	10.70	26.99	37.87	84.82	55.8	38,579	800-421-4225	Y
American Funds SMALLCAP World Fund® Class A	SMCWX	B	B	B	Up	4.88	10.61	26.83	37.32	83.56	55.8	38,579	800-421-4225	Y
American Funds SMALLCAP World Fund® Class C	SCWCX	B	B	B	Up	4.68	10.17	25.84	34.07	76.39	49.09	38,579	800-421-4225	Y
American Funds SMALLCAP World Fund® Class F-1	SCWFX	B	B	B	Up	4.86	10.59	26.76	37.21	83.43	55.16	38,579	800-421-4225	Y
American Funds SMALLCAP World Fund® Class F-2	SMCFX	B	B	B	Up	4.95	10.76	27.16	38.39	86.03	56.51	38,579	800-421-4225	Y
American Funds SMALLCAP World Fund® Class F-3	SFCWX	B	B	B	Up	4.96	10.81	27.24	37.76	84.16	55.99	38,579	800-421-4225	Y
American Funds SMALLCAP World Fund® Class R-1	RSLAX	B	B	B	Up	4.70	10.18	25.86	34.23	76.81	50.66	38,579	800-421-4225	Y
American Funds SMALLCAP World Fund® Class R-2	RSLBX	B	B	B	Up	4.67	10.20	25.88	34.31	76.92	50.68	38,579	800-421-4225	Y
American Funds SMALLCAP World Fund® Class R-2E	RSEBX	B	B	B	Up	4.77	10.36	26.27	35.94	80.82	55.38	38,579	800-421-4225	Y
American Funds SMALLCAP World Fund® Class R-3	RSLCX	B	B	B	Up	4.82	10.46	26.46	36.09	80.87	53.53	38,579	800-421-4225	Y
American Funds SMALLCAP World Fund® Class R-4	RSLEX	B	B	B	Up	4.88	10.62	26.84	37.38	83.81	55.36	38,579	800-421-4225	Y
American Funds SMALLCAP World Fund® Class R-5	RSLFX	B	B	B	Up	4.96	10.77	27.21	38.61	86.58	57.3	38,579	800-421-4225	Y
American Funds SMALLCAP World Fund® Class R-5E	RSLDX	B	B	B	Up	4.94	10.72	27.09	37.83	84.25	55.78	38,579	800-421-4225	Y
American Funds SMALLCAP World Fund® Class R-6	RLLGX	B	B	B	Up	4.97	10.81	27.27	38.82	87.01	56.69	38,579	800-421-4225	Y
AMG TimesSquare International Small Cap Fund Class I	TQTIX	A-	A-	A	Up	4.61	12.31	38.83	55.85	98.98	17.08	578.9	800-835-3879	Y
AMG TimesSquare International Small Cap Fund Class N	TCMPX	A-	A-	A	Up	4.58	12.19	38.62	54.71	97.19	16.99	578.9	800-835-3879	Y
AMG TimesSquare International Small Cap Fund Class Z	TCMIX	A-	A-	A	Up	4.56	12.25	38.85	55.88	99.01	17.08	578.9	800-835-3879	Y
AMG Yacktman Special Opportunities Fund Class I	YASSX	B	A	C	Up	7.85	13.27	34.66	44.71		12.03	35.7	800-835-3879	Y
AMG Yacktman Special Opportunities Fund Class Z	YASLX	B	A	C	Up	7.89	13.30	34.80	45.06		12.05	35.7	800-835-3879	Y
Artisan International Small Cap Fund Institutional Share	APHJX	B-	B-	C	Up	7.05	15.54	33.61	28.84	48.00	23.18	490.1	800-344-1770	Y
Brandes International Small Cap Equity Fund Class A	BISAX	B	C	A		1.09	2.55	11.45	29.06	61.35		1,759	800-331-2979	Y

Category: Global Equity Mid/Small Cap (con't)

Fund Name	Ticker Symbol	RATINGS: Overall Rating	Reward Rating	Risk Rating	Recent Up/ Downgrade	TOTAL RETURNS & PERFORMANCE: 3-Month Total Return	6-Month Total Return	1-Year Total Return	3-Year Total Return	5-Year Total Return	ASSETS: NAV	Total Assets (MIL)	NEW INVESTORS: Telephone	Open to New Investors
Brandes International Small Cap Equity Fund Class C	BINCX	B	C	A	Up	-2.41	-1.43	6.71	22.12	50.60	13.22	1,759	800-331-2979	Y
Brandes International Small Cap Equity Fund Class I	BISMX	B	C	A		1.16	2.65	11.78	29.95	63.26		1,759	800-331-2979	Y
Brandes International Small Cap Equity Fund Class R6	BISRX	B	C	A		1.16	2.67	11.82	29.84	62.33		1,759	800-331-2979	Y
Calvert International Opportunities Fund Class A	CIOAX	B+	A-	B	Up	5.67	14.56	37.90	40.25	73.21	18.52	173.3	800-368-2745	Y
Calvert International Opportunities Fund Class C	COICX	B	B+	B	Up	5.52	14.13	36.88	36.65	65.87	18.14	173.3	800-368-2745	Y
Calvert International Opportunities Fund Class I	COIIX	B+	A-	B	Up	5.79	14.77	38.50	41.94	76.95	18.15	173.3	800-368-2745	Y
Cambiar International Small Cap Fund Institutional Class	CAMFX	B-	C+	B-	Up	6.02	11.25	33.75	40.17		12.43	2.1	866-777-8227	Y
Causeway International Small Cap Fund Institutional Class	CIISX	B-	C+	B-	Up	4.52	15.32	34.72	45.70		13.06	12.4	866-947-7000	Y
Causeway International Small Cap Fund Investor Class	CVISX	B-	C+	B-	Up	4.52	15.23	34.49	44.78		13.07	12.4	866-947-7000	Y
ClearBridge International Small Cap Fund Class A	LCOAX	B	B	B	Up	5.97	13.87	32.27	37.51	69.68	18.99	181.4	877-721-1926	Y
ClearBridge International Small Cap Fund Class A2	LCRNX	B	B	B	Up	5.94	13.75	31.98	36.64	68.53	18.88	181.4	877-721-1926	Y
ClearBridge International Small Cap Fund Class C	LCOCX	B	B	B	Up	5.79	13.46	31.28	34.49	63.37	18.77	181.4	877-721-1926	Y
ClearBridge International Small Cap Fund Class I	LCOIX	B	B	B	Up	6.08	14.03	32.63	38.74	71.97	19.12	181.4	877-721-1926	Y
ClearBridge International Small Cap Fund Class IS	CBISX	B	B	B	Up	6.09	14.11	32.79	39.16	72.49	19.13	181.4	877-721-1926	Y
Columbia Acorn International Fund Advisor Class	CCIRX	B-	B-	B	Up	6.32	11.51	32.21	27.08	50.28	46.95	4,936	800-345-6611	Y
Columbia Acorn International Fund Class A	LAIAX	B-	B-	B	Up	6.27	11.38	31.90	26.28	48.67	46.51	4,936	800-345-6611	Y
Columbia Acorn International Fund Class C	LAICX	B-	C+	B	Up	6.07	10.94	30.92	23.46	43.18	44.57	4,936	800-345-6611	Y
Columbia Acorn International Fund Class R	CACRX	B-	C+	B	Up	6.20	11.22	31.57	25.06	46.10	46.51	4,936	800-345-6611	Y
Columbia Acorn International Fund Institutional 2 Class	CAIRX	B-	B-	B	Up	6.34	11.54	32.27	27.41	51.00	46.54	4,936	800-345-6611	Y
Columbia Acorn International Fund Institutional 3 Class	CCYIX	B-	B-	B	Up	6.36	11.57	32.35	27.60	51.37	46.95	4,936	800-345-6611	Y
Columbia Acorn International Fund Institutional Class	ACINX	B-	B-	B	Up	6.34	11.52	32.23	27.26	50.71	46.57	4,936	800-345-6611	Y
Conductor Global Equity Value Fund Class A	RAALX	B+	A	B-	Up	7.17	15.68	28.55	46.12		14.32	83.4		Y
Conductor Global Equity Value Fund Class C	RACLX	B	A-	B-	Up	6.91	15.24	27.55	42.89		14.15	83.4		Y
Conductor Global Equity Value Fund Class I	RAILX	B+	A	B-	Up	7.16	15.87	28.90	47.15		14.4	83.4		Y
Conductor Global Equity Value Fund Class Y	RAYLX	B+	A	B-	Up	7.41	16.16	29.59	48.46		14.53	83.4		Y
Delaware International Small Cap Fund Class A	DGGAX	B+	A	B	Up	5.47	21.65	46.76	43.23	83.47	7.92	31.7		Y
Delaware International Small Cap Fund Class C	DGGCX	B+	A	B	Up	5.19	21.12	45.70	39.87	76.56	6.71	31.7		Y
Delaware International Small Cap Fund Class R	DGGRX	B+	A	B	Up	5.33	21.47	46.40	41.99	81.04	7.52	31.7		Y
Delaware International Small Cap Fund Class R6	DGRRX	B+	A	B	Up	5.60	21.89	47.31	44.40	85.89	8.29	31.7		Y
Delaware International Small Cap Fund Institutional Class	DGGIX	B+	A	B	Up	5.61	21.75	47.14	44.24	85.68	8.28	31.7		Y
DFA International Small Cap Growth Portfolio	DISMX	A-	B+	A-	Up	5.01	12.57	34.64	50.33	84.79	15.92	181.2	512-306-7400	Y
DFA Intl Small Cap Value Portfolio Inst Cls	DISVX	B	B	B-	Up	3.83	11.72	27.97	43.42	82.85	22.97	16,235	512-306-7400	Y
DFA Intl Small Company Portfolio Inst Cls	DFISX	B+	B	B+	Up	4.60	11.90	30.24	45.68	76.15	21.27	13,645	512-306-7400	Y
DFA Intl Vector Equity Portfolio Inst Cls	DFVQX	B	B	C+	Up	4.84	12.60	28.94	37.25	62.34	13.57	2,555	512-306-7400	Y
DFA World ex U.S. Targeted Value Portfolio Inst Cls Shares	DWUSX	B	B	B	Up	5.13	12.79	31.52	41.91	64.51	15.25	474.6	512-306-7400	Y
Driehaus International Small Cap Growth Fund	DRIOX	A-	A	B	Up	5.65	15.65	41.44	48.20	86.83	11.39	321.6	877-779-0079	
Evermore Global Value Fund Institutional Class	EVGIX	B	B	B+		-0.95	7.58	19.00	51.54	98.35	15.2	580.1	866-383-7667	Y
Evermore Global Value Fund Investor Class	EVGBX	B	B	B+		-1.02	7.42	18.72	50.42	95.99	15.08	580.1	866-383-7667	Y
Federated International Small-Mid Company Fund Class A	ISCAX	B	B	B	Up	5.75	14.41	34.69	35.07	58.86	40.01	166.6	800-341-7400	Y
Federated International Small-Mid Company Fund Class B	ISCBX	B	B	B-	Up	5.54	13.98	33.61	31.89	52.66	31.13	166.6	800-341-7400	
Federated International Small-Mid Company Fund Class C	ISCCX	B	B	B-	Up	5.54	13.96	33.61	31.89	52.68	31.09	166.6	800-341-7400	Y
Federated Intl Small-Mid Company Fund Inst Cls	ISCIX	B	B	B	Up	5.82	14.54	34.95	35.89	60.51	40.86	166.6	800-341-7400	Y
Fidelity Advisor® Global Capital Appreciation Fund Class A	FGEAX	B	B	B	Up	5.60	13.87	30.24	37.69	99.95	18.32	140.8	617-563-7000	Y
Fidelity Advisor® Global Capital Appreciation Fund Class C	FEUCX	B	B	B	Up	5.36	13.41	29.23	34.58	92.58	15.78	140.8	617-563-7000	Y
Fidelity Advisor® Global Capital Appreciation Fund Class M	FGETX	B	B	B	Up	5.49	13.68	29.88	36.61	97.41	17.49	140.8	617-563-7000	Y
Fidelity Advisor® Global Capital Appreciation Fund I Class	FEUIX	B	B	B	Up	5.62	13.97	30.61	38.72	102.73	19.25	140.8	617-563-7000	Y
Fidelity Advisor® International Small Cap Fund Class A	FIASX	B+	B+	B+	Up	5.45	12.05	32.52	51.56	94.30	29.4	1,803	617-563-7000	Y
Fidelity Advisor® International Small Cap Fund Class C	FICSX	B+	B+	B+	Up	5.24	11.62	31.46	48.09	87.10	28.42	1,803	617-563-7000	Y
Fidelity Advisor® International Small Cap Fund Class I	FIXIX	B+	B+	A-	Up	5.51	12.19	32.85	53.00	97.74	30.09	1,803	617-563-7000	Y
Fidelity Advisor® International Small Cap Fund Class M	FTISX	B+	B+	B+	Up	5.37	11.89	32.10	50.19	91.65	29.28	1,803	617-563-7000	Y
Fidelity Advisor® Intl Small Cap Opp Fund Cls A	FOPAX	A-	B+	A	Up	6.76	12.49	35.28	46.22	81.26	19.15	1,149	617-563-7000	Y
Fidelity Advisor® Intl Small Cap Opp Fund Cls C	FOPCX	B+	B	A	Up	6.56	12.02	34.16	42.80	74.55	18.56	1,149	617-563-7000	Y

Category: Global Equity Mid/Small Cap (con't)

Fund Name	Ticker Symbol	RATINGS: Overall Rating	Reward Rating	Risk Rating	Recent Up/ Downgrade	TOTAL RETURNS & PERFORMANCE: 3-Month Total Return	6-Month Total Return	1-Year Total Return	3-Year Total Return	5-Year Total Return	ASSETS: NAV	Total Assets (MIL)	NEW INVESTORS: Telephone	Open to New Investors
Fidelity Advisor® Intl Small Cap Opp Fund Cls M	FOPTX	A-	B+	A	Up	6.68	12.32	34.90	44.92	78.78	19.02	1,149	617-563-7000	Y
Fidelity Advisor® Intl Small Cap Opp Fund I Cls	FOPIX	A-	B+	A	Up	6.83	12.63	35.66	47.62	84.10	19.31	1,149	617-563-7000	Y
Fidelity® International Small Cap Fund	FISMX	B+	B+	A-	Up	5.54	12.19	32.90	52.85	97.10	29.9	1,803	617-563-7000	Y
Fidelity® International Small Cap Opportunities Fund	FSCOX	A-	B+	A	Up	6.89	12.68	35.68	47.58	84.12	19.34	1,149	617-563-7000	Y
Fidelity® Series International Small Cap Fund	FSTSX	B+	B+	A-	Up	6.83	12.74	34.45	43.42	77.12	17.97	3,669	617-563-7000	
FPA International Value Fund	FPIVX	B-	B	C+	Up	2.58	9.14	27.11	30.44	39.34	15.45	262.8	800-982-4372	Y
Franklin International Small Cap Growth Fund Advisor Class	FKSCX	B+	B+	B	Up	1.72	10.64	34.49	39.18	70.89	20.17	1,480	650-312-2000	
Franklin International Small Cap Growth Fund Class A	FINAX	B+	B+	B	Up	1.67	10.45	34.16	38.20	68.78	20.14	1,480	650-312-2000	
Franklin International Small Cap Growth Fund Class C	FCSMX	B	B+	B	Up	1.48	10.04	33.19	35.03	62.62	19.96	1,480	650-312-2000	
Franklin International Small Cap Growth Fund Class R	FISDX	B+	B+	B	Up	1.63	10.34	33.89	37.14	66.65	20.22	1,480	650-312-2000	
Franklin International Small Cap Growth Fund Class R6	FCAPX	B+	B+	B	Up	1.75	10.62	34.61	39.75	71.97	20.15	1,480	650-312-2000	
Free Market International Equity Fund Institutional Class	FMNEX	B-	B	C	Up	4.80	12.39	27.73	33.76	56.21	11.41	2,294		Y
GMO Foreign Small Companies Fund Class III	GMFSX	B	B	B	Up	7.80	13.37	28.16	35.79	58.60	15.57	256.6	617-330-7500	Y
GMO Foreign Small Companies Fund Class IV	GFSFX	B	B	B	Up	7.84	13.42	28.30	36.09	58.95	15.53	256.6	617-330-7500	Y
GMO International Small Companies Fund Class III	GMISX	B	B	B	Up	7.63	15.12	31.22	36.35	68.55	19.79	19.6	617-330-7500	Y
Goldman Sachs International Small Cap Insights Fund Cls A	GICAX	A-	B+	A-	Up	4.84	13.09	32.53	47.92	85.77	12.76	2,617	800-526-7384	Y
Goldman Sachs International Small Cap Insights Fund Cls C	GICCX	A-	B+	A-	Up	4.68	12.65	31.68	44.62	78.92	12.35	2,617	800-526-7384	Y
Goldman Sachs International Small Cap Insights Fund Cls R6	GICUX	A-	A-	A	Up	4.97	13.28	33.20	50.00	90.01	12.78	2,617	800-526-7384	Y
Goldman Sachs Intl Small Cap Insights Fund Inst Cls	GICIX	A-	A-	A	Up	4.88	13.30	33.02	49.57	89.46	12.75	2,617	800-526-7384	Y
Goldman Sachs Intl Small Cap Insights Fund Inv Cls	GIRLX	A-	A-	A	Up	4.82	13.18	32.85	49.00	88.11	12.69	2,617	800-526-7384	Y
Grandeur Peak Global Opportunities Fund Institutional Cls	GPGIX	B+	B+	B	Up	7.70	14.06	32.95	43.98	110.02	4.03	797.8	855-377-7325	
Grandeur Peak Global Opportunities Fund Investor Class	GPGOX	B+	B+	B	Up	7.68	13.81	32.48	42.65	107.13	3.98	797.8	855-377-7325	
Grandeur Peak Global Reach Fund Institutional Class	GPRIX	B	B	B	Up	7.33	13.24	30.77	40.74		16.82	358.5	855-377-7325	
Grandeur Peak Global Reach Fund Investor Class	GPROX	B	B	B	Up	7.28	13.21	30.50	39.63		16.78	358.5	855-377-7325	
Grandeur Peak Intl Opp Fund Inst Cls	GPIIX	B+	A-	B	Up	7.84	14.74	38.81	47.04	102.40	4.16	893.4	855-377-7325	
Grandeur Peak Intl Opp Fund Inv Cls	GPIOX	B+	A-	B	Up	7.72	14.65	38.39	46.11	100.65	4.14	893.4	855-377-7325	
Harding Loevner Intl Small Companies Portfolio Inst	HLMRX	B	B	B	Up	4.84	11.02	34.66	40.64	69.74	17.12	204.6	877-435-8105	Y
Harding Loevner Intl Small Companies Portfolio Inv	HLMSX	B	B	B	Up	4.84	10.93	34.41	39.61	67.74	17.01	204.6	877-435-8105	Y
Hartford International Small Company Fund Class A	HNSAX	B	B	B	Up	6.03	12.38	34.25	37.04	68.15	16.71	393.5	888-843-7824	Y
Hartford International Small Company Fund Class C	HNSCX	B	B	B	Up	5.78	11.99	33.23	34.10	62.18	15.04	393.5	888-843-7824	Y
Hartford International Small Company Fund Class F	HNSFX	B	B+	B	Up	6.14	12.67	34.98	39.12	72.42	16.56	393.5	888-843-7824	Y
Hartford International Small Company Fund Class I	HNSJX	B	B+	B	Up	6.08	12.55	34.74	38.66	71.26	16.55	393.5	888-843-7824	Y
Hartford International Small Company Fund Class R3	HNSRX	B	B	B	Up	5.95	12.26	33.93	36.27	66.67	16.84	393.5	888-843-7824	Y
Hartford International Small Company Fund Class R4	HNSSX	B	B+	B	Up	6.01	12.42	34.33	37.48	69.20	16.9	393.5	888-843-7824	Y
Hartford International Small Company Fund Class R5	HNSTX	B	B+	B	Up	6.11	12.56	34.72	38.68	71.68	16.98	393.5	888-843-7824	Y
Hartford International Small Company Fund Class Y	HNSYX	B	B+	B	Up	6.08	12.59	34.84	38.97	72.23	16.99	393.5	888-843-7824	Y
Intrepid International Fund Investor Class	ICMIX	B-	C	B+	Up	6.67	13.65	14.46	28.38		10.6	23.1		Y
Invesco Global Small & Mid Cap Growth Fund Class A	AGAAX	B-	C+	B	Up	2.52	8.42	24.21	22.56	61.14	19.8	549.1	800-659-1005	Y
Invesco Global Small & Mid Cap Growth Fund Class B	AGABX	B-	C+	B	Up	2.27	7.97	23.22	19.85	55.17	16.08	549.1	800-659-1005	
Invesco Global Small & Mid Cap Growth Fund Class C	AGACX	B-	C+	B	Up	2.28	7.97	23.28	19.82	55.22	16.1	549.1	800-659-1005	Y
Invesco Global Small & Mid Cap Growth Fund Class R5	GAIIX	B-	B-	B	Up	2.52	8.50	24.54	23.87	64.15	19.63	549.1	800-659-1005	Y
Invesco Global Small & Mid Cap Growth Fund Class R6	AGSSX	B-	C+	B	Up	2.59	8.62	24.53	22.87	61.55	19.63	549.1	800-659-1005	Y
Invesco Global Small & Mid Cap Growth Fund Class Y	AGAYX	B-	C+	B	Up	2.57	8.50	24.48	23.48	63.12	19.82	549.1	800-659-1005	Y
Invesco International Small Company Fund Class A	IEGAX	B-	B	C+	Up	3.93	10.33	33.41	31.92	37.99	19.33	322.3	800-659-1005	Y
Invesco International Small Company Fund Class B	IEGBX	B-	B	C+	Up	3.72	9.91	32.45	29.08	32.98	18.38	322.3	800-659-1005	
Invesco International Small Company Fund Class C	IEGCX	B-	B	C+	Up	3.72	9.98	32.45	29.01	32.92	18.38	322.3	800-659-1005	Y
Invesco International Small Company Fund Class R6	IEGFX	B	B	C+	Up	4.01	10.63	34.04	33.71	40.93	19.17	322.3	800-659-1005	Y
Invesco International Small Company Fund Class Y	IEGYX	B	B	C+	Up	4.00	10.50	33.73	32.91	39.75	19.36	322.3	800-659-1005	Y
Invesco International Small Company Fund R5 Class	IEGIX	B	B	C+	Up	4.02	10.57	33.96	33.47	40.49	19.19	322.3	800-659-1005	Y
IVA International Fund Class A	IVIOX	B	C+	B+	Up	2.37	6.08	16.98	20.96	42.34	17.83	4,237	866-941-4482	
IVA International Fund Class C	IVICX	B	C+	B+	Up	2.20	5.67	16.16	18.31	37.18	17.54	4,237	866-941-4482	
IVA International Fund Class I	IVIQX	B	C+	B+	Up	2.44	6.14	17.24	21.84	44.18	17.84	4,237	866-941-4482	

Category: Global Equity Mid/Small Cap (con't)

Fund Name	Ticker Symbol	RATINGS: Overall Rating	Reward Rating	Risk Rating	Recent Up/ Downgrade	TOTAL RETURNS & PERFORMANCE: 3-Month Total Return	6-Month Total Return	1-Year Total Return	3-Year Total Return	5-Year Total Return	ASSETS: NAV	Total Assets (Mil)	NEW INVESTORS: Telephone	Open to New Investors
JNL/American Funds Global Small Capitalization Fund Cls A	US46644W3694	B	B-	B	Up	5.06	11.59	25.52	27.38	68.83	14.31	676.5		Y
JNL/American Funds Global Small Capitalization Fund Cls I	US46644W3512	B	B	B	Up	5.15	11.71	25.77	28.20	70.47	14.48	676.5		Y
JNL/Franklin Templeton Intl Small Cap Growth Fund Cls A	US46648M4179	B	B	B	Up	3.32	10.36	32.28	35.71	64.47	11.51	734.0		Y
JNL/Franklin Templeton Intl Small Cap Growth Fund Cls I	US46648M3916	B	B	B	Up	3.37	10.51	32.49	36.53	66.04	11.63	734.0		Y
JOHCM International Small Cap Equity Fund Class I	JOISX	B	B	B	Up	3.27	6.53	27.35	38.03		13.08	242.7	866-260-9549	Y
JOHCM International Small Cap Equity Fund Class II	JOSAX	B	B	B	Up	3.97	7.23	28.15	38.52		13.16	242.7	866-260-9549	Y
JOHCM Intl Small Cap Equity Fund Inst Shares	JOSMX	B	B	B	Up	4.04	7.33	28.32	39.41		13.06	242.7	866-260-9549	Y
John Hancock Funds II International Small Cap Fund Class 1	JIIMX	B	B	B	Up	5.39	11.47	34.95	32.19	54.61	22.55	627.6	800-225-5913	Y
John Hancock Funds II International Small Cap Fund Cls NAV	JHISX	B	B	B	Up	5.39	11.47	35.03	32.33	55.02	22.54	627.6	800-225-5913	Y
John Hancock Funds II Intl Small Company Fund Cls A	JISAX	B	B	B+	Up	4.35	11.66	29.98	42.32	69.35	13.02	640.7	800-225-5913	Y
John Hancock Funds II Intl Small Company Fund Cls C	JISDX	B	B	B	Up	4.18	11.21	28.95	39.09	63.66	13.06	640.7	800-225-5913	Y
John Hancock Funds II Intl Small Company Fund Cls I	JSCIX	B	B	B+	Up	4.48	11.81	30.17	43.48	72.01	13	640.7	800-225-5913	Y
John Hancock Funds II Intl Small Company Fund Cls NAV	JHATX	B+	B	B+	Up	4.42	11.74	30.32	43.97	72.90	12.99	640.7	800-225-5913	Y
John Hancock Funds II Intl Small Company Fund Cls R6	JHSMX	B+	B	B+		4.49	11.81	30.41	44.06	73.02	13	640.7	800-225-5913	Y
Kopernik Global All-Cap Fund Class A	KGGAX	B	B+	C	Up	1.99	11.60	8.74	43.06		10.58	1,160	855-887-4544	Y
Kopernik Global All-Cap Fund Class I	KGGIX	B	B+	C	Up	2.07	11.71	8.95	44.06		10.53	1,160	855-887-4544	Y
Lazard Intl Small Cap Equity Portfolio Inst Shares	LZISX	B+	A-	B	Up	7.31	16.96	36.66	42.27	81.95	13.79	80.9	800-823-6300	Y
Lazard Intl Small Cap Equity Portfolio Open Shares	LZSMX	B+	A-	B	Up	7.21	16.72	36.29	41.04	79.49	13.82	80.9	800-823-6300	Y
LMCG International Small Cap Fund Institutional Shares	ISMIX	A-	A-	A-	Up	5.56	13.85	32.73	47.27	100.66	12.81	35.0		Y
LMCG International Small Cap Fund Investor shares	ISMRX	A-	A-	A-	Up	5.50	13.61	32.22	46.05	98.01	12.79	35.0		Y
Lord Abbett International Opportunities Fund Clas R4	LINSX	A-	A-	A-	Up	5.80	14.75	37.88	45.61	81.99	20.62	834.3	201-827-2000	Y
Lord Abbett International Opportunities Fund Clas R5	LINTX	A-	A	A-	Up	5.91	14.90	38.31	46.52	83.13	21.23	834.3	201-827-2000	Y
Lord Abbett International Opportunities Fund Clas R6	LINVX	A-	A	A-	Up	5.85	14.92	38.35	46.99	83.72	21.29	834.3	201-827-2000	Y
Lord Abbett International Opportunities Fund Class A	LAIEX	A-	A-	A-	Up	5.82	14.75	37.97	45.65	82.05	20.69	834.3	201-827-2000	Y
Lord Abbett International Opportunities Fund Class B	LINBX	A-	A-	A-	Up	5.61	14.32	36.89	42.41	75.61	19.63	834.3	201-827-2000	
Lord Abbett International Opportunities Fund Class C	LINCX	A-	A-	A-	Up	5.60	14.30	36.95	42.43	75.58	19.29	834.3	201-827-2000	Y
Lord Abbett International Opportunities Fund Class F	LINFX	A-	A	A-	Up	5.82	14.83	38.14	46.27	83.63	20.48	834.3	201-827-2000	Y
Lord Abbett International Opportunities Fund Class F3	LOIEX	A-	A-	A-	Up	5.90	14.92	38.17	45.86	82.31	21.29	834.3	201-827-2000	Y
Lord Abbett International Opportunities Fund Class I	LINYX	A-	A	A-	Up	5.88	14.92	38.25	46.74	84.48	21.23	834.3	201-827-2000	Y
Lord Abbett International Opportunities Fund Class P	LINPX	A-	A-	A-	Up	5.76	14.63	37.64	44.71	80.45	21.13	834.3	201-827-2000	
Lord Abbett International Opportunities Fund Class R2	LINQX	A-	A-	A-	Up	5.76	14.60	37.52	44.11	79.19	20.38	834.3	201-827-2000	Y
Lord Abbett International Opportunities Fund Class R3	LINRX	A-	A-	A-	Up	5.79	14.66	37.65	44.71	80.24	20.34	834.3	201-827-2000	Y
MainStay Epoch International Small Cap Fund Class A	EPIPX	B+	B+	B	Up	5.53	14.07	30.65	35.89	55.20	25.61	38.2	800-624-6782	Y
MainStay Epoch International Small Cap Fund Class C	EPIKX	B	B	B	Up	5.29	13.57	29.44	32.12	47.92	25.05	38.2	800-624-6782	Y
MainStay Epoch International Small Cap Fund Class I	EPIEX	B+	B+	B+	Up	5.64	14.25	30.98	36.92	57.14	26.4	38.2	800-624-6782	Y
MainStay Epoch International Small Cap Fund Investor Class	EPIIX	B	B	B	Up	5.51	13.98	30.41	35.11	53.50	25.56	38.2	800-624-6782	Y
Manning & Napier Rainier Intl Discovery Series Cls I	RAIIX	A-	A	B	Up	6.26	18.26	42.04	53.03	105.76	21.66	316.3	585-325-6880	Y
Manning & Napier Rainier Intl Discovery Series Cls K	RISAX	A-	A	B	Up	6.23	18.16	41.71	51.91	103.44	21.47	316.3	585-325-6880	Y
Manning & Napier Rainier Intl Discovery Series Cls R6	RAIRX	A-	A	B		6.30	18.30	42.09	53.09	105.83	21.66	316.3	585-325-6880	Y
MFS® Global New Discovery Fund Class A	GLNAX	B+	B	B+	Up	6.60	12.83	29.42	40.78	74.73	19.48	41.2	877-960-6077	Y
MFS® Global New Discovery Fund Class B	GLNBX	B	B	B+	Up	6.44	12.49	28.45	37.65	68.27	18.61	41.2	877-960-6077	Y
MFS® Global New Discovery Fund Class C	GLNCX	B	B	B+	Up	6.44	12.49	28.45	37.65	68.41	18.61	41.2	877-960-6077	Y
MFS® Global New Discovery Fund Class I	GLNIX	B+	B	B+	Up	6.69	13.05	29.75	41.90	76.94	19.7	41.2	877-960-6077	Y
MFS® Global New Discovery Fund Class R1	GLNJX	B	B	B+	Up	6.39	12.43	28.46	37.68	68.32	18.6	41.2	877-960-6077	Y
MFS® Global New Discovery Fund Class R2	GLNKX	B+	B	B+	Up	6.58	12.78	29.11	39.75	72.51	19.2	41.2	877-960-6077	Y
MFS® Global New Discovery Fund Class R3	GLNLX	B+	B	B+	Up	6.66	12.90	29.42	40.84	74.81	19.48	41.2	877-960-6077	Y
MFS® Global New Discovery Fund Class R4	GLNMX	B+	B	B+	Up	6.69	13.04	29.80	41.76	76.77	19.72	41.2	877-960-6077	Y
MFS® Global New Discovery Fund Class R6	GLNNX	B+	B+	B+	Up	6.74	13.09	29.86	42.29	77.66	19.73	41.2	877-960-6077	Y
MFS® International New Discovery Fund Class 529A	EAIDX	B	B	B+	Up	6.56	12.01	31.70	35.15	58.03	34.16	6,233	877-960-6077	Y
MFS® International New Discovery Fund Class 529B	EBIDX	B	B	B	Up	6.58	11.97	31.17	33.64	53.79	32.44	6,233	877-960-6077	Y
MFS® International New Discovery Fund Class 529C	ECIDX	B	B	B	Up	6.39	11.58	30.68	32.02	51.96	32.1	6,233	877-960-6077	Y
MFS® International New Discovery Fund Class A	MIDAX	B	B	B+	Up	6.59	12.02	31.75	35.22	58.10	34.74	6,233	877-960-6077	Y

Category: Global Equity Mid/Small Cap (con't)

Fund Name	Ticker Symbol	RATINGS: Overall Rating	RATINGS: Reward Rating	RATINGS: Risk Rating	RATINGS: Recent Up/ Downgrade	TOTAL RETURNS & PERFORMANCE: 3-Month Total Return	6-Month Total Return	1-Year Total Return	3-Year Total Return	5-Year Total Return	ASSETS: NAV	Total Assets (MIL)	NEW INVESTORS: Telephone	Open to New Investors
MFS® International New Discovery Fund Class B	MIDBX	B	B	B	Up	6.39	11.60	30.71	32.17	52.25	33.8	6,233	877-960-6077	Y
MFS® International New Discovery Fund Class C	MIDCX	B	B	B	Up	6.39	11.62	30.74	32.21	52.24	33.18	6,233	877-960-6077	Y
MFS® International New Discovery Fund Class I	MWNIX	B	B	B+	Up	6.63	12.14	32.04	36.21	60.01	35.72	6,233	877-960-6077	Y
MFS® International New Discovery Fund Class R1	MIDGX	B	B	B	Up	6.39	11.60	30.74	32.19	52.21	32.38	6,233	877-960-6077	Y
MFS® International New Discovery Fund Class R2	MIDRX	B	B	B+	Up	6.50	11.87	31.39	34.19	56.08	33.83	6,233	877-960-6077	Y
MFS® International New Discovery Fund Class R3	MIDHX	B	B	B+	Up	6.58	12.02	31.70	35.17	58.07	34.43	6,233	877-960-6077	Y
MFS® International New Discovery Fund Class R4	MIDJX	B	B	B+	Up	6.63	12.13	32.02	36.21	59.99	34.67	6,233	877-960-6077	Y
MFS® International New Discovery Fund Class R6	MIDLX	B	B	B+	Up	6.68	12.22	32.15	36.71	60.97	35.74	6,233	877-960-6077	Y
Morgan Stanley Inst Fund, Inc. Global Discovery Port Cls A	MGDPX	B	B+	C+	Down	2.85	8.84	24.88	61.49	125.61	15.8	113.9	855-332-5306	Y
Morgan Stanley Inst Fund, Inc. Global Discovery Port Cls C	MSPCX	B	B+	C+	Down	2.63	8.39	23.89	57.78	117.51	15.41	113.9	855-332-5306	Y
Morgan Stanley Inst Fund, Inc. Global Discovery Port Cls I	MLDIX	B	B+	C+	Down	2.94	9.04	25.39	63.26	129.58	15.87	113.9	855-332-5306	Y
Morgan Stanley Inst Fund, Inc. Global Discovery Port Cls L	MGDLX	B	B+	C+	Down	2.72	8.56	24.26	59.11	120.00	15.62	113.9	855-332-5306	
Morgan Stanley Inst Fund, Inc. Global Insight Port Cls A	MBPHX	B	B+	C+	Down	3.67	8.92	26.98	54.56	98.92	14.78	13.6	855-332-5306	Y
Morgan Stanley Inst Fund, Inc. Global Insight Port Cls C	MSIZX	B	B+	C+	Down	3.57	8.60	26.08	51.31	92.07	14.46	13.6	855-332-5306	Y
Morgan Stanley Inst Fund, Inc. Global Insight Port Cls I	MBPIX	B	B+	C+	Down	3.76	9.17	27.38	56.12	102.16	14.77	13.6	855-332-5306	Y
Morgan Stanley Inst Fund, Inc. Global Insight Port Cls L	MBPLX	B	B+	C+	Down	3.61	8.67	26.34	52.00	93.83	14.56	13.6	855-332-5306	
Oakmark International Small Cap Fund Class Advisor	OAYEX	B	B-	B	Up	1.63	5.53	26.19	34.78	60.49	17.73	3,029	641-219-558	Y
Oakmark International Small Cap Fund Class Institutional	OANEX	B	B-	B	Up	1.67	5.63	26.31	34.90	60.64	17.74	3,029	641-219-558	Y
Oakmark International Small Cap Fund Investor Class	OAKEX	B	B-	B	Up	1.58	5.48	26.07	34.56	60.23	17.74	3,029	641-219-558	
Oakmark International Small Cap Service Class	OAREX	B-	B-	B	Up	1.55	5.41	25.71	33.45	58.00	17.65	3,029	641-219-558	Y
Oberweis Emerging Growth Fund	OBEGX	B+	A-	B	Up	3.29	14.62	33.29	44.45	111.41	28.36	56.0		Y
Oberweis Emerging Growth Fund Institutional Class	OBGIX	B+	A-	B	Up	3.35	14.77	33.51	44.68	111.75	28.41	56.0		Y
Oberweis International Opportunities Fund	OBIOX	A-	A	B+	Up	7.45	17.24	40.76	52.45	129.98	25.49	927.9		Y
Oberweis International Opportunities Institutional Fund	OBIIX	A-	A	B+	Up	7.48	17.22	40.98	53.20		12.77	1,039		Y
Old Westbury Small & Mid Cap Strategies Fund	OWSMX	B-	B-	B-	Down	3.81	6.89	18.18	29.77	67.55	16.76	6,654	212-708-9100	Y
Oppenheimer Global Opportunities Fund Class A	OPGIX	A	A+	B+	Up	14.29	22.25	52.52	91.92	166.36	68.54	6,911	800-225-5677	Y
Oppenheimer Global Opportunities Fund Class B	OGGIX	A	A+	B+	Up	14.08	21.79	51.36	87.54	155.93	60.53	6,911	800-225-5677	
Oppenheimer Global Opportunities Fund Class C	OGICX	A	A+	B+	Up	14.08	21.80	51.39	87.59	156.47	60.62	6,911	800-225-5677	Y
Oppenheimer Global Opportunities Fund Class I	OGIIX	A	A+	B+	Up	14.43	22.52	53.18	94.38	172.19	69.61	6,911	800-225-5677	Y
Oppenheimer Global Opportunities Fund Class R	OGINX	A	A+	B+	Up	14.23	22.11	52.16	90.44	162.74	65.97	6,911	800-225-5677	Y
Oppenheimer Global Opportunities Fund Class Y	OGIYX	A	A+	B+	Up	14.38	22.43	52.93	93.33	169.70	69.34	6,911	800-225-5677	Y
Oppenheimer International Small-Mid Company Fund Class A	OSMAX	A-	B+	A	Up	6.17	12.93	37.92	57.36	130.64	49.55	10,129	800-225-5677	Y
Oppenheimer International Small-Mid Company Fund Class B	OSMBX	B+	B+	A	Up	5.95	12.48	36.87	53.82	121.96	46.34	10,129	800-225-5677	
Oppenheimer International Small-Mid Company Fund Class C	OSMCX	B+	B+	A	Up	5.99	12.50	36.92	53.87	122.18	45.67	10,129	800-225-5677	Y
Oppenheimer International Small-Mid Company Fund Class I	OSCIX	A-	B+	A	Up	6.28	13.17	38.53	59.41	135.62	49.22	10,129	800-225-5677	
Oppenheimer International Small-Mid Company Fund Class R	OSMNX	A-	B+	A	Up	6.11	12.78	37.62	56.20	127.71	47.37	10,129	800-225-5677	
Oppenheimer International Small-Mid Company Fund Class Y	OSMYX	A-	B+	A	Up	6.24	13.08	38.30	58.52	133.63	49.12	10,129	800-225-5677	
Pax Global Environmental Markets Fund Class A	PXEAX	B	B	B	Up	5.27	9.81	26.45	37.19	79.61	16.09	582.6	800-767-1729	Y
Pax Global Environmental Mkts Fund Individual Inv Cls	PGRNX	B	B	B	Up	5.21	9.81	26.42	37.15	79.43	16.11	582.6	800-767-1729	Y
Pax Global Environmental Markets Fund Institutional Class	PGINX	B	B	B	Up	5.31	9.95	26.78	38.24	81.80	16.22	582.6	800-767-1729	Y
Pear Tree Polaris Foreign Value Small Cap Fund Class R6	QUSRX	B+	A-	B	Up	3.88	12.66	33.44	35.69	81.65	12.31	899.7	800-326-2151	Y
Pear Tree Polaris Foreign Value Small Cap Fund Inst Cls	QUSIX	B+	A-	B	Up	3.84	12.54	33.43	35.68	81.64	16.04	899.7	800-326-2151	Y
Pear Tree Polaris Foreign Value Small Cap Ordinary Cls	QUSOX	B+	A-	B	Up	3.79	12.43	33.05	34.50	79.13	16.03	899.7	800-326-2151	Y
PF International Small-Cap Fund Class P	US69448A7147	B-	C+	B-	Up	4.39	13.18	31.83			11.36	44.3	800-722-2333	Y
Polaris Global Value Fund	PGVFX	B	B	B-	Up	5.49	9.43	20.60	36.18	95.70	27.71	543.8		Y
Principal International Small Company Fund Class A	PICAX	A-	A	A-	Up	5.44	15.31	35.60	46.95		12.61	1,044	800-222-5852	Y
Principal Intl Small Company Fund Inst Cls	PISMX	A-	A	A-	Up	5.57	15.48	35.76	48.48		12.66	1,044	800-222-5852	Y
Principal International Small Company Fund R-6	PFISX	A-	A	A-	Up	5.56	15.53	36.23	47.63		12.7	1,044	800-222-5852	Y
Putnam International Capital Opportunities Fund Class A	PNVAX	B	B	B	Up	6.37	14.65	34.53	33.28	44.33	42.28	466.6	617-292-1000	Y
Putnam International Capital Opportunities Fund Class B	PVNBX	B	B-	B	Up	6.17	14.20	33.54	30.30	39.01	42.48	466.6	617-292-1000	Y
Putnam International Capital Opportunities Fund Class C	PUVCX	B	B-	B	Up	6.20	14.22	33.55	30.35	39.02	42.23	466.6	617-292-1000	Y
Putnam International Capital Opportunities Fund Class M	PIVMX	B	B	B	Up	6.23	14.36	33.87	31.31	40.74	42.19	466.6	617-292-1000	Y

Category: Global Equity Mid/Small Cap (con't)

Fund Name	Ticker Symbol	RATINGS: Overall Rating	Reward Rating	Risk Rating	Recent Up/ Downgrade	TOTAL RETURNS & PERFORMANCE: 3-Month Total Return	6-Month Total Return	1-Year Total Return	3-Year Total Return	5-Year Total Return	ASSETS: NAV	Total Assets (MIL)	NEW INVESTORS: Telephone	Open to New Investors
Putnam International Capital Opportunities Fund Class R	PICRX	B	B	B	Up	6.30	14.49	34.17	32.29	42.53	41.78	466.6	617-292-1000	Y
Putnam International Capital Opportunities Fund Class Y	PIVYX	B	B	B	Up	6.45	14.79	34.84	34.29	46.14	42.21	466.6	617-292-1000	Y
Royce Global Value Trust	RGT	B	B	C+	Up	6.00	12.74	30.90	39.22		12.48	129.0	800-221-4268	Y
Royce International Micro-Cap Fund Service Class	ROIMX	B	B-	B	Up	6.40	10.84	27.72	34.04	57.05	12.57	7.8	800-221-4268	Y
Royce International Premier Fund Consultant Class	RINPX	A	A	A-	Up	5.99	13.85	38.72	57.00	69.47	16.99	139.5	800-221-4268	Y
Royce International Premier Fund Investment Class	RIPNX	A	A	A-	Up	6.21	14.38	40.07	61.78	77.46	13.07	139.5	800-221-4268	Y
Royce International Premier Fund R Class	RINRX	A	A	A-	Up	6.08	14.14	39.33	59.23	73.59	12.53	139.5	800-221-4268	Y
Royce International Premier Fund Service Class	RYIPX	A	A	A-	Up	6.10	14.28	39.80	60.46	75.80	15.6	139.5	800-221-4268	Y
SA International Small Company Fund Investor Class	SAISX	B	B	B+	Up	4.38	11.37	29.01	41.33	67.18	23.58	371.7		Y
SA International Small Company Fund Select Class	SACLX	B+	B	B+	Up	4.42	11.52	29.73	44.83	74.77	23.57	371.7		Y
Salient International Small Cap Fund Class Investor	PISRX	A-	A-	A-	Up	8.13	14.01	34.28	45.48	72.75	21.74	118.9	866-667-9228	Y
Salient International Small Cap Fund Institutional Class	PTSCX	A-	A-	A-	Up	8.23	14.29	34.80	47.08	75.84	21.7	118.9	866-667-9228	Y
Schwab Fundamental International Small Company Index Fund	SFILX	B+	B	B+	Up	5.26	11.99	29.07	47.44	78.20	14.51	773.2	877-824-5615	Y
Segall Bryant & Hamill International Small Cap Fund Cls A	SBHSX	B+	B+	B+	Up	2.83	12.19	28.36	43.60	87.73	14.05	340.4	312-474-1222	Y
Segall Bryant & Hamill International Small Cap Fund Cls I	SBSIX	B+	B+	B+	Up	2.89	12.32	28.81	44.49	89.85	14.06	340.4	312-474-1222	Y
T. Rowe Price International Discovery Fund	PRIDX	A	A	A-	Up	6.06	15.90	39.00	53.89	92.59	71.41	7,842	410-345-2000	Y
T. Rowe Price International Discovery Fund I Class	TIDDX	A	A	A-	Up	6.08	15.97	39.16	54.27	93.05	71.45	7,842	410-345-2000	Y
TCW International Small Cap Fund Class I	TGICX	B	B	B	Up	8.03	20.41	38.91	43.17	58.52	11.03	10.1	213-244-0000	Y
TCW International Small Cap Fund Class N	TGNIX	B	B	B	Up	8.02	20.39	38.86	43.12	58.34	11.04	10.1	213-244-0000	Y
Templeton Foreign Smaller Companies Fund Class A	FINEX	B	B	B	Up	5.52	11.35	34.07	33.78	47.54	20.39	101.6	650-312-2000	
Templeton Foreign Smaller Companies Fund Class Advisor	FTFAX	B	B	B	Up	5.58	11.48	34.39	34.76	49.31	20.31	101.6	650-312-2000	
Templeton Foreign Smaller Companies Fund Class Advisor C	FCFSX	B	B	B	Up	5.33	10.91	33.02	30.77	41.98	19.65	101.6	650-312-2000	
Templeton Foreign Smaller Companies Fund Class R6	US88019R4680	B	B	B	Up	5.68	11.59	34.66	35.75	51.06	20.5	101.6	650-312-2000	
Templeton Global Smaller Companies Fund Class A	TEMGX	B-	B-	C	Up	6.92	12.03	25.72	28.76	66.59	10.56	1,314	650-312-2000	Y
Templeton Global Smaller Companies Fund Class Advisor	TGSAX	B-	B	C	Up	7.09	12.19	26.11	29.87	68.62	10.61	1,314	650-312-2000	Y
Templeton Global Smaller Companies Fund Class R6	FBOGX	B-	B	C	Up	7.03	12.34	26.29	30.55	70.24	10.59	1,288	650-312-2000	Y
Templeton Inst Foreign Smaller Companies Series Adv	TFSCX	B	B+	B	Up	5.44	11.70	34.17	35.79	61.06	25.08	1,038	650-312-2000	
The Gabelli Global Small & Mid Cap Value Trust	GGZ	B	C	A-	Up	-3.49	2.59	16.38	24.22		14.63	120.5		Y
Third Avenue International Value Fund Institutional Class	TAVIX	B-	B	C	Up	1.67	14.37	24.98	25.07	33.26	19.25	131.5	800-443-1021	Y
Third Avenue International Value Fund Investor Class	TVIVX	B-	B	C	Up	1.57	14.20	24.55	24.07	31.55	19.36	131.5	800-443-1021	Y
Thornburg International Growth Fund Class A	TIGAX	B	B	B+	Up	2.36	10.30	34.32	35.23	62.62	23.57	1,472	800-847-0200	Y
Thornburg International Growth Fund Class C	TIGCX	B	B	B	Up	2.19	9.85	33.37	32.14	56.60	22.15	1,472	800-847-0200	Y
Thornburg International Growth Fund Class I	TINGX	B	B	B+	Up	2.46	10.47	34.92	36.85	65.96	24.24	1,472	800-847-0200	Y
Thornburg International Growth Fund Class R3	TIGVX	B	B	B+	Up	2.34	10.21	34.22	34.80	61.77	23.37	1,472	800-847-0200	Y
Thornburg International Growth Fund Class R4	TINVX	B	B	B+	Up	2.33	10.23	34.39	35.17	62.60	23.44	1,472	800-847-0200	Y
Thornburg International Growth Fund Class R5	TINFX	B	B	B+	Up	2.50	10.49	34.91	36.93	65.93	24.31	1,472	800-847-0200	Y
Thornburg International Growth Fund Class R6	THGIX	B	B	B+	Up	2.49	10.54	35.03	37.29	66.74	24.36	1,472	800-847-0200	Y
Touchstone International Small Cap Fund Class A	TNSAX	B	B	B	Up	5.04	12.67	31.02	30.51	69.52	18.52	354.8	800-543-0407	Y
Touchstone International Small Cap Fund Class C	TNSCX	B	B	B	Up	4.84	12.22	30.07	27.59	63.30	18.26	354.8	800-543-0407	Y
Touchstone International Small Cap Fund Class Y	TNSYX	B	B	B	Up	5.11	12.87	31.43	31.54	71.82	18.9	354.8	800-543-0407	Y
Touchstone International Small Cap Fund Institutional	TNSIX	B	B	B	Up	5.10	12.87	31.48	31.95	72.89	18.98	354.8	800-543-0407	Y
Transamerica International Small Cap Fund Class I2	US8939626136	A-	A	A-	Up	5.78	14.23	39.66	48.30	86.24	6.56	153.5	888-233-4339	Y
Transamerica International Small Cap Value Class I	TISVX	B+	B+	A-	Up	6.09	13.14	30.47	39.15	65.12	14.05	876.8	888-233-4339	
Transamerica International Small Cap Value Class I2	US89355J5166	B+	B+	A-	Up	6.09	13.12	30.63	39.58	65.86	14.07	876.8	888-233-4339	
VALIC Company II International Opportunities Fund	VISEX	A	A	A-	Up	6.03	16.47	39.35	49.71	74.25	21.07	722.9		Y
Vanguard FTSE All-World ex-US Small Capital Ind Inv Shares	VFSVX	B	B	B	Up	5.63	12.57	30.12	35.04	52.38	45.35	5,799	877-662-7447	Y
Vanguard FTSE All-World ex-US Small-Cap Ind Inst Shares	VFSNX	B	B	B	Up	5.68	12.63	30.30	35.63	53.69	227.19	5,799	877-662-7447	Y
Vanguard Global Minimum Volatility Fund Admiral Shares	VMNVX	B	B-	B+		4.00	6.35	16.03	32.62		27.06	2,340	877-662-7447	Y
Vanguard Global Minimum Volatility Fund Investor Shares	VMVFX	B	B-	A+		3.99	6.39	15.92	32.38		13.53	2,340	877-662-7447	Y
Vanguard International Explorer Fund Investor Shares	VINEX	A-	A-	A-	Up	5.49	13.93	38.76	47.95	88.67	21.29	4,070	877-662-7447	Y
Victory Trivalent International Small-Cap Fund Class A	MISAX	A-	A-	B+	Up	6.85	15.32	36.54	45.20	92.95	14.61	1,389	800-539-3863	Y
Victory Trivalent International Small-Cap Fund Class C	MCISX	B+	A-	B	Up	6.65	14.88	35.57	41.97	85.91	14.32	1,389	800-539-3863	Y

Category: Global Equity Mid/Small Cap (con't)

Fund Name	Ticker Symbol	RATINGS: Overall Rating	Reward Rating	Risk Rating	Recent Up/ Downgrade	TOTAL RETURNS & PERFORMANCE: 3-Month Total Return	6-Month Total Return	1-Year Total Return	3-Year Total Return	5-Year Total Return	ASSETS: NAV	Total Assets (MIL)	NEW INVESTORS: Telephone	Open to New Investors
Victory Trivalent International Small-Cap Fund Class I	MISIX	A-	A-	B+	Up	6.88	15.54	37.13	46.91	96.96	14.7	1,389	800-539-3863	Y
Victory Trivalent International Small-Cap Fund Class R6	MSSIX	A-	A-	B+	Up	6.95	15.50	36.96	46.31	95.72	14.78	1,389	800-539-3863	Y
Victory Trivalent International Small-Cap Fund Class Y	MYSIX	A-	A-	B+	Up	6.86	15.47	36.89	46.31	95.43	14.65	1,389	800-539-3863	Y
Virtus KAR International Small-Cap Fund Class A	VISAX	B	B+	C	Up	3.30	8.17	28.19	53.24	92.94	16.51	292.4	800-243-1574	Y
Virtus KAR International Small-Cap Fund Class C	VCISX	B	B	C	Up	3.12	7.76	27.24	49.86	86.06	16.34	292.4	800-243-1574	Y
Virtus KAR International Small-Cap Fund Class I	VIISX	B	B+	C	Up	3.33	8.32	28.47	54.40	95.37	16.56	292.4	800-243-1574	Y
Virtus KAR International Small-Cap Fund Class R6	VRISX	B	B+	C	Up	3.43	8.36	28.67	54.82	96.04	16.56	292.4	800-243-1574	Y
Voya Multi-Manager International Small Cap Fund Class A	NTKLX	A-	A-	A-	Up	5.28	13.63	34.92	44.28	76.15	64.16	213.7	800-366-0066	Y
Voya Multi-Manager International Small Cap Fund Class C	NARCX	A-	B+	A-	Up	5.10	13.25	34.06	41.51	70.52	59.76	213.7	800-366-0066	Y
Voya Multi-Manager International Small Cap Fund Class I	NAPIX	A-	A-	A-	Up	5.39	13.88	35.51	46.23	80.26	63.89	213.7	800-366-0066	Y
Voya Multi-Manager International Small Cap Fund Class O	NAPOX	A-	A-	A-	Up	5.31	13.67	35.08	44.72	77.06	63.32	213.7	800-366-0066	Y
Voya Multi-Manager International Small Cap Fund Class W	ISCWX	A-	A-	A-	Up	5.37	13.83	35.41	45.83	79.27	77.09	213.7	800-366-0066	Y
Wasatch Global Opportunities Fund® Institutional Class	WIGOX	B	B	B	Up	8.34	13.47	38.10	36.31	71.68	3.67	108.4	800-551-1700	Y
Wasatch Global Opportunities Fund® Investor Class	WAGOX	B	B	B	Up	8.34	13.48	37.63	35.93	71.22	3.67	108.4	800-551-1700	Y
Wasatch International Growth Fund® Institutional Class	WIIGX	B	B	B+	Up	4.50	11.62	33.14	40.21	62.84	34.48	1,518	800-551-1700	
Wasatch International Growth Fund® Investor Class	WAIGX	B	B	B+	Up	4.48	11.56	33.00	39.94	62.53	34.43	1,518	800-551-1700	
Wasatch Intl Opp Fund® Inst Cls	WIIOX	B	B	A-	Down	7.30	10.13	27.73	46.23	81.26	3.51	508.0	800-551-1700	
Wasatch International Opportunities Fund® Investor Class	WAIOX	B	B	A-	Down	7.36	10.22	27.58	45.62	80.51	3.48	508.0	800-551-1700	Y
Wasatch World Innovators Fund® Institutional Class	WIGTX	B+	B+	A-	Up	8.56	14.84	33.35	44.33	90.37	21.49	207.7	800-551-1700	Y
Wasatch World Innovators Fund® Investor Class	WAGTX	B+	B	A-	Up	8.47	14.67	32.95	43.61	89.42	21.35	207.7	800-551-1700	Y
Wells Fargo Global Small Cap Fund Class A	EKGAX	B	A-	B-	Up	5.22	12.49	24.04	44.63	87.96	42.4	265.5	800-222-8222	Y
Wells Fargo Global Small Cap Fund Class Admin	EKGYX	B	A-	B-	Up	5.24	12.54	24.17	45.23	89.36	44.39	265.5	800-222-8222	Y
Wells Fargo Global Small Cap Fund Class C	EKGCX	B	B+	B-	Up	5.04	12.07	23.11	41.39	81.03	29.91	265.5	800-222-8222	Y
Wells Fargo Global Small Cap Fund Class Inst	EKGIX	B+	A-	B-	Up	5.31	12.69	24.53	46.38	91.77	44.2	265.5	800-222-8222	Y
Westcore International Small-Cap Fund Institutional Class	WIIFX	B	B	C+	Up	6.56	16.14	33.88	37.33	37.51	20.83	77.6	800-392-2673	Y
Westcore International Small-Cap Fund Retail Class	WTIFX	B	B	C+	Up	6.51	16.02	33.63	36.86	37.03	19.76	77.6	800-392-2673	
William Blair International Small Cap Growth Fund Class I	WISIX	A-	B+	A-	Up	4.86	13.56	32.70	38.76	63.28	15.65	594.0	800-621-0687	
William Blair Intl Small Cap Growth Fund Cls Inst	WIISX	A-	B+	A-	Up	4.86	13.51	32.70	39.07	64.31	15.73	594.0	800-621-0687	
William Blair International Small Cap Growth Fund Class N	WISNX	A-	B+	A-	Up	4.80	13.32	32.16	37.50	60.84	15.49	594.0	800-621-0687	

Category: Greater China Equity

Fund Name	Ticker Symbol	RATINGS: Overall Rating	Reward Rating	Risk Rating	Recent Up/ Downgrade	TOTAL RETURNS & PERFORMANCE: 3-Month Total Return	6-Month Total Return	1-Year Total Return	3-Year Total Return	5-Year Total Return	ASSETS: NAV	Total Assets (MIL)	NEW INVESTORS: Telephone	Open to New Investors
Aberdeen China Opportunities Fund Class A	GOPAX	B-	B-	C+	Up	9.00	11.77	35.84	27.44	19.82	23.25	13.6	866-667-9231	Y
Aberdeen China Opportunities Fund Institutional Class	GOPIX	B-	B-	C+	Up	9.33	12.25	36.71	29.00	21.77	23.38	13.6	866-667-9231	Y
Aberdeen China Opp Fund Inst Service Cls	GOPSX	B-	B-	C+	Up	9.28	12.20	36.54	28.62	21.49	23.34	13.6	866-667-9231	Y
Aberdeen Greater China Fund	GCH	B	B	C+	Up	7.89	11.09	35.46	32.25	27.62	13.73	119.7	866-667-9231	Y
AC One China Fund Institutional Class	ACOIX	B	A-	C+	Up	8.17	20.44	45.76	34.33	66.79	17.2	14.8		Y
China Fund, Inc.	CHN	B	A-	C+	Up	8.08	16.71	37.82	31.80	61.91	23.4328	368.7	852-223-8863	Y
Clough China Fund Class C	CHNCX	B	B	C+	Up	6.74	17.67	39.98	22.75	44.96	26.57	61.0	866-759-5679	Y
Clough China Fund Class I	CHNIX	B	A-	C+	Up	7.02	18.28	41.46	26.90	53.10	28.66	61.0	866-759-5679	Y
Clough China Fund Class Investor	CHNAX	B	A-	C+	Up	6.95	18.16	41.08	25.57	50.58	28	61.0	866-759-5679	Y
Columbia Greater China Fund Advisor Class	CGCHX	B+	A	C+	Up	11.96	27.33	61.03	51.06	84.89	56.43	130.0	800-345-6611	Y
Columbia Greater China Fund Class A	NGCAX	B+	A	C+	Up	11.89	27.19	60.65	49.98	82.63	51.12	130.0	800-345-6611	Y
Columbia Greater China Fund Class C	NGCCX	B+	A	C+	Up	11.69	26.70	59.45	46.62	75.91	47.38	130.0	800-345-6611	Y
Columbia Greater China Fund Class T	CGCWX	B+	A	C+	Up	11.91	27.19	60.61	49.90	82.78	51.11	130.0	800-345-6611	Y
Columbia Greater China Fund Institutional 2 Class	CGCRX	B+	A	C+	Up	11.99	27.41	61.20	51.68	86.21	56.56	130.0	800-345-6611	Y
Columbia Greater China Fund Institutional 3 Class	CGCYX	B+	A	C+	Up	12.02	27.45	61.23	51.28	85.16	55.13	130.0	800-345-6611	Y
Columbia Greater China Fund Institutional Class	LNGZX	B+	A	C+	Up	11.99	27.36	61.05	51.12	84.96	55.42	130.0	800-345-6611	Y

Category: Greater China Equity (con't)

Fund Name	Ticker Symbol	RATINGS: Overall Rating	Reward Rating	Risk Rating	Recent Up/ Downgrade	TOTAL RETURNS & PERFORMANCE: 3-Month Total Return	6-Month Total Return	1-Year Total Return	3-Year Total Return	5-Year Total Return	ASSETS: NAV	Total Assets (MIL)	NEW INVESTORS: Telephone	Open to New Investors
Eaton Vance Greater China Growth Fund Class A	EVCGX	B+	A	C+	Up	10.93	20.46	49.38	44.69	68.54	25.35	103.8		Y
Eaton Vance Greater China Growth Fund Class C	ECCGX	B	A	C+	Up	10.72	20.02	48.31	41.66	62.75	23.94	103.8		Y
Eaton Vance Greater China Growth Fund Class I	EICGX	B+	A	C+	Up	10.98	20.63	49.85	45.98	71.03	25.53	103.8		Y
Fidelity Advisor® China Region Fund Class A	FHKAX	B	A	C	Up	9.88	19.97	51.45	37.48	75.38	35.59	1,442	617-563-7000	Y
Fidelity Advisor® China Region Fund Class C	FCHKX	B	A-	C	Up	9.68	19.51	50.36	34.40	68.99	34.78	1,442	617-563-7000	Y
Fidelity Advisor® China Region Fund Class M	FHKTX	B	A	C	Up	9.81	19.75	50.93	36.03	72.61	35.47	1,442	617-563-7000	Y
Fidelity Advisor® China Region Fund I Class	FHKIX	B	A	C	Up	9.96	20.13	51.91	38.73	78.39	35.72	1,442	617-563-7000	Y
Fidelity® China Region Fund	FHKCX	B	A	C	Up	9.98	20.18	51.92	38.75	78.25	35.98	1,442	617-563-7000	Y
Guinness Atkinson China And Hong Kong Fund	ICHKX	B	A	C+	Up	10.74	20.30	48.85	42.17	49.75	26.55	78.4	800-915-6566	Y
Invesco Greater China Fund Class A	AACFX	B+	A	B-	Up	4.98	16.47	42.40	53.33	60.90	29.64	96.6	800-659-1005	Y
Invesco Greater China Fund Class B	ABCFX	B+	A	B-	Up	4.79	16.04	41.33	49.94	55.01	28.86	96.6	800-659-1005	
Invesco Greater China Fund Class C	CACFX	B+	A	B-	Up	4.76	16.07	41.36	49.92	54.99	28.81	96.6	800-659-1005	Y
Invesco Greater China Fund Class R5	IACFX	B+	A	B-	Up	5.06	16.71	42.96	55.40	64.56	29.61	96.6	800-659-1005	Y
Invesco Greater China Fund Class R6	CACSX	B+	A	B-	Up	5.04	16.70	42.94	55.38	64.55	29.6	96.6	800-659-1005	Y
Invesco Greater China Fund Class Y	AMCYX	B+	A	B-	Up	5.01	16.62	42.71	54.44	62.88	29.63	96.6	800-659-1005	Y
John Hancock Greater China Opportunities Fund Class A	JCOAX	B+	A	C+	Up	9.62	25.12	53.77	46.48	71.58	25.59	67.0	800-225-5913	Y
John Hancock Greater China Opportunities Fund Class B	JCOBX	B	A	C+	Up	9.42	24.57	52.52	43.29	64.87	24.52	67.0	800-225-5913	
John Hancock Greater China Opportunities Fund Class C	JCOCX	B	A	C+	Up	9.42	24.62	52.58	43.27	64.94	24.53	67.0	800-225-5913	Y
John Hancock Greater China Opportunities Fund Class I	JCOIX	B+	A	C+	Up	9.73	25.24	54.20	48.02	74.85	25.46	67.0	800-225-5913	Y
John Hancock Greater China Opportunities Fund Class NAV	JGCNX	B+	A	C+	Up	9.75	25.30	54.30	48.23	75.34	25.84	67.0	800-225-5913	Y
Matthews China Dividend Fund Institutional Class	MICDX	B+	A	B-	Up	8.46	17.65	37.87	60.42	86.30	17.61	309.0	800-789-2742	Y
Matthews China Dividend Fund Investor Class	MCDFX	B+	A	B-	Up	8.45	17.57	37.69	59.67	84.49	17.61	309.0	800-789-2742	Y
Matthews China Fund Institutional Class	MICFX	B+	A+	C+	Up	9.64	22.68	59.71	56.82	62.64	22.17	877.1	800-789-2742	Y
Matthews China Fund Investor Class	MCHFX	B+	A+	C+	Up	9.57	22.53	59.37	56.15	61.40	22.2	877.1	800-789-2742	Y
Matthews China Small Companies Fund	MCSMX	B+	A	C+	Up	8.90	24.96	53.87	57.57	98.36	11.89	31.8	800-789-2742	Y
Morgan Stanley China A Share Fund	CAF	B	A	C+	Up	8.35	13.82	41.39	42.62	127.74	28.14	612.7	855-332-5306	Y
Neuberger Berman Greater China Equity Fund Class A	NCEAX	B+	A+	C+	Up	12.53	24.98	65.41	62.88		15.98	140.0	212-476-9000	Y
Neuberger Berman Greater China Equity Fund Class C	NCECX	B+	A+	C+	Up	12.28	24.46	64.06	58.74		15.56	140.0	212-476-9000	Y
Neuberger Berman Greater China Equity Fund Inst Cls	NCEIX	B+	A+	C+	Up	12.62	25.17	66.00	64.05		15.98	140.0	212-476-9000	Y
Oberweis China Opportunities Fund	OBCHX	B	A	C	Up	5.22	24.17	55.04	38.75	112.94	15.95	121.9		Y
Oberweis China Opportunities Fund Institutional Class	OCHIX	B	A	C	Up	5.27	24.31	55.21	38.91	113.17	15.93	121.9		Y
Shelton Greater China Fund	SGCFX	B	A-	C+	Up	5.35	13.86	34.85	28.80	44.42	9.05	8.9	800-955-9988	Y
Templeton China World Fund Class A	TCWAX	B	B	C+	Up	2.61	12.59	33.69	25.00	20.17	21.64	314.2	650-312-2000	Y
Templeton China World Fund Class Advisor	TACWX	B	B	C+	Up	2.67	12.67	33.96	25.94	21.80	21.77	314.2	650-312-2000	Y
Templeton China World Fund Class C	TCWCX	B-	B	C+	Up	2.41	12.12	32.68	22.21	15.86	21.46	314.2	650-312-2000	Y
Templeton China World Fund Class R6	FCWRX	B	B	C+	Up	2.73	12.85	34.28	26.84	22.86	21.7	314.2	650-312-2000	Y
Templeton Dragon Fund Inc	TDF	B	A-	C+	Up	4.94	14.36	38.07	31.32	35.69	24.5052	820.1	954-527-7500	Y
U.S. Global Investors China Region Fund Investor Class	USCOX	B	A-	C+	Up	3.69	22.39	57.67	43.83	54.85	11.53	33.6	800-873-8637	Y
Voya Hang Seng Index Portfolio Class A	IHSPX	B	A-	C+	Up	7.65	17.11	38.96	35.50	47.12	17.59	74.6	800-366-0066	Y
Voya Hang Seng Index Portfolio Class I	IHPIX	B	A-	C+	Up	7.73	17.39	39.60	37.44	50.77	17.68	74.6	800-366-0066	Y
Voya Hang Seng Index Portfolio Class S	IHPSX	B	A-	C+	Up	7.75	17.27	39.32	36.46	48.97	17.65	74.6	800-366-0066	Y

Category: Healthcare Sector Equity

Fund Name	Ticker Symbol	RATINGS: Overall Rating	Reward Rating	Risk Rating	Recent Up/ Downgrade	TOTAL RETURNS & PERFORMANCE: 3-Month Total Return	6-Month Total Return	1-Year Total Return	3-Year Total Return	5-Year Total Return	ASSETS: NAV	Total Assets (MIL)	NEW INVESTORS: Telephone	Open to New Investors
Alger Health Sciences Fund Class A	AHSAX	B-	B	C	Up	1.83	6.37	37.15	34.93	127.54	24.51	157.0	800-992-3863	Y
Alger Health Sciences Fund Class C	AHSCX	B-	B	C	Up	1.62	5.97	36.11	31.80	119.07	19.54	157.0	800-992-3863	Y
Alger Health Sciences Fund Class Z	AHSZX	B-	B+	C	Up	1.91	6.61	37.74	35.03	127.71	24.48	157.0	800-992-3863	Y
BlackRock Health Sciences Opportunities Portfolio Class K	SHSKX	B	B-	B		1.64	4.99	25.30	30.11	146.14	56.18	6,137	800-441-7762	Y

Category: Healthcare Sector Equity (con't)

Fund Name	Ticker Symbol	RATINGS: Overall Rating	Reward Rating	Risk Rating	Recent Up/ Downgrade	TOTAL RETURNS & PERFORMANCE: 3-Month Total Return	6-Month Total Return	1-Year Total Return	3-Year Total Return	5-Year Total Return	ASSETS: NAV	Total Assets (MIL)	NEW INVESTORS: Telephone	Open to New Investors
BlackRock Health Sciences Opportunities Portfolio Class R	BHSRX	B	B-	B		1.47	4.63	24.41	28.14	140.93	52.59	6,137	800-441-7762	Y
BlackRock Health Sciences Opp Portfolio Inst Shares	SHSSX	B	B-	B		1.62	4.93	25.15	30.44	148.15	56.15	6,137	800-441-7762	Y
BlackRock Health Sciences Opp Portfolio Inv A Shares	SHSAX	B	B-	B		1.56	4.80	24.81	29.37	144.73	53.64	6,137	800-441-7762	Y
BlackRock Health Sciences Opp Portfolio Inv B Shares	SHSPX	B	B-	B	Up	2.90	3.57	23.58	25.83	135.29		6,137	800-441-7762	
BlackRock Health Sciences Opp Portfolio Inv C Shares	SHSCX	B	B-	B	Up	1.36	4.42	23.90	26.60	135.99	47.29	6,137	800-441-7762	Y
BlackRock Health Sciences Opp Portfolio Service Shares	SHISX	B	B-	B		1.53	4.78	24.79	29.35	144.62	53.83	6,137	800-441-7762	Y
BlackRock Health Sciences Trust	BME	B	B-	B	Up	2.16	5.07	22.68	28.73	123.25	35.8123	325.2	800-441-7762	Y
Delaware Healthcare Fund Class A	DLHAX	A-	A-	B+	Up	1.26	10.85	31.95	39.84	151.76	22.39	443.2		Y
Delaware Healthcare Fund Class C	DLHCX	B+	A-	B+	Up	1.10	10.46	31.02	36.75	142.51	21.42	443.2		Y
Delaware Healthcare Fund Class I	DLHIX	A-	A-	B+	Up	1.36	10.95	32.32	40.89	154.93	22.48	443.2		Y
Delaware Healthcare Fund Class R	DLRHX	A-	A-	B+	Up	1.23	10.72	31.64	38.84	148.66	22.15	443.2		Y
Deutsche Health and Wellness Fund Class A	SUHAX	B-	C+	B	Up	-0.67	2.05	19.01	12.81	113.75	35.12	303.5	201-593-8273	Y
Deutsche Health and Wellness Fund Class S	SCHLX	B-	C+	B	Up	-0.60	2.18	19.34	13.71	116.53	37.59	303.5	201-593-8273	Y
Deutsche Health and Wellness Fund Institutional Class	SUHIX	B-	C+	B	Up	-0.61	2.19	19.30	13.68	116.47	39.12	303.5	201-593-8273	Y
Eventide Healthcare & Life Sciences Fund Class A Shares	ETAHX	B	A-	C	Up	4.76	24.11	45.51	41.13	194.31	28.57	437.8		Y
Eventide Healthcare & Life Sciences Fund CLASS C SHARES	ETCHX	B	A-	C	Up	4.56	23.60	44.39	37.99	183.61	27.51	437.8		Y
Eventide Healthcare & Life Sciences Fund CLASS I SHARES	ETIHX	B	A-	C	Up	4.81	24.26	45.83	42.17	198.04	28.94	437.8		Y
Eventide Healthcare & Life Sciences Fund CLASS N SHARES	ETNHX	B	A-	C	Up	4.78	24.12	45.57	41.34	195.32	28.67	437.8		Y
Fidelity Advisor® Health Care Fund Class A	FACDX	B-	C+	B-		-1.08	2.52	24.09	17.30	145.95	42.65	2,734	617-563-7000	Y
Fidelity Advisor® Health Care Fund Class C	FHCCX	B-	C+	B-	Up	-1.29	2.11	23.11	14.67	136.86	34.35	2,734	617-563-7000	Y
Fidelity Advisor® Health Care Fund Class M	FACTX	B-	C+	B-		-1.16	2.38	23.72	16.36	142.68	39.95	2,734	617-563-7000	Y
Fidelity Advisor® Health Care Fund I Class	FHCIX	B-	C+	B		-1.03	2.63	24.37	18.22	149.17	46.23	2,734	617-563-7000	Y
Fidelity® Select Health Care Services Portfolio	FSHCX	B	B-	B		6.85	5.60	24.34	33.91	130.16	89.89	807.5	617-563-7000	Y
Fidelity® Select Medical Equipment and Systems Portfolio	FSMEX	B	B	B		1.11	0.24	26.57	46.29	168.59	43.88	4,013	617-563-7000	Y
Hartford Healthcare HLS Fund Class IA	HIAHX	B-	C+	B	Down	-1.44	0.10	22.26	26.21	148.15	22.46	339.4	888-843-7824	Y
Hartford Healthcare HLS Fund Class IB	HBGHX	B-	C+	B	Down	-1.52	0.01	21.96	25.28	145.03	21.35	339.4	888-843-7824	Y
JNL/Mellon Capital Healthcare Sector Fund Class A	US47760W7790	B	B-	B	Up	1.38	5.00	22.63	24.56	124.38	25.63	3,038		Y
JNL/Mellon Capital Healthcare Sector Fund Class I	US47760W7618	B	B-	B	Up	1.49	5.17	22.95	25.37	126.79	25.76	3,038		Y
John Hancock II Health Sciences Fund Class NAV	US47804M7048	B	B	B	Up	1.47	6.07	26.66	26.74	157.53	4.3	325.2	800-225-5913	Y
Live Oak Health Sciences Fund	LOGSX	B-	C	B+		1.94	-0.17	13.40	20.85	105.49	19.42	65.3	888-462-5386	Y
Rydex Biotechnology Fund Class Investor	RYOIX	B-	B-	C	Up	-1.17	7.17	29.72	13.42	138.10	87.26	329.0	800-820-0888	Y
Rydex Health Care Fund Class A	RYHEX	B-	C+	B-	Up	1.77	3.57	23.16	14.73	107.12	26.07	66.3	800-820-0888	Y
Rydex Health Care Fund Class H	RYHAX	B-	C+	B-	Up	1.80	3.58	23.16	14.58	105.93	25.12	66.3	800-820-0888	Y
Rydex Health Care Fund Class Investor	RYHIX	B-	C+	B-	Up	1.82	3.71	23.47	15.61	109.87	28.66	66.3	800-820-0888	Y
Schwab Health Care Fund™	SWHFX	B-	C+	B	Up	-0.34	4.08	20.19	23.61	114.40	24.22	859.3	877-824-5615	Y
T. Rowe Price Health Sciences Fund	PRHSX	B	B	B	Up	1.65	7.02	27.94	28.88	162.57	70.35	11,913	410-345-2000	
T. Rowe Price Health Sciences Fund I Class	THISX	B	B	B	Up	1.68	7.09	28.08	29.12	163.07	70.34	11,913	410-345-2000	Y
The Hartford Healthcare Fund Class A	HGHAX	B-	C+	B	Down	-1.55	-0.10	21.59	24.67	139.49	33.53	1,511	888-843-7824	Y
The Hartford Healthcare Fund Class C	HGHCX	B-	C+	B	Down	-1.70	-0.43	20.73	21.96	130.89	27.46	1,511	888-843-7824	Y
The Hartford Healthcare Fund Class F	HGHFX	B-	C+	B	Down	-1.43	0.08	22.02	26.14	144.25	35.17	1,511	888-843-7824	Y
The Hartford Healthcare Fund Class I	HGHIX	B-	C+	B	Down	-1.46	0.03	21.93	25.69	142.79	35.14	1,511	888-843-7824	Y
The Hartford Healthcare Fund Class R3	HGHRX	B-	C+	B	Down	-1.62	-0.26	21.23	23.54	135.89	34.54	1,511	888-843-7824	Y
The Hartford Healthcare Fund Class R4	HGHSX	B-	C+	B	Down	-1.54	-0.09	21.57	24.66	139.42	36.21	1,511	888-843-7824	Y
The Hartford Healthcare Fund Class R5	HGHTX	B-	C+	B	Down	-1.46	0.05	21.95	25.76	143.11	37.78	1,511	888-843-7824	Y
The Hartford Healthcare Fund Class Y	HGHYX	B-	C+	B	Down	-1.42	0.08	22.03	26.16	144.27	38.21	1,511	888-843-7824	Y
VALIC Company I Health Sciences Fund	VCHSX	B	B	B		1.58	6.92	27.65	27.97	159.62	21.78	764.5		Y
Vanguard Health Care Fund Admiral Shares	VGHAX	B-	C+	B	Up	0.56	1.55	19.66	21.84	128.46	86.68	47,587	877-662-7447	Y
Vanguard Health Care Fund Investor Shares	VGHCX	B-	C+	B	Up	0.54	1.52	19.61	21.67	127.90	205.54	47,587	877-662-7447	Y
Vanguard Health Care Index Fund Admiral Shares	VHCIX	B	B	B	Up	1.53	5.28	23.35	26.70	131.69	77.09	8,277	877-662-7447	Y

Category: India Equity

Fund Name	Ticker Symbol	RATINGS: Overall Rating	Reward Rating	Risk Rating	Recent Up/ Downgrade	TOTAL RETURNS & PERFORMANCE: 3-Month Total Return	6-Month Total Return	1-Year Total Return	3-Year Total Return	5-Year Total Return	ASSETS: NAV	Total Assets (MIL)	NEW INVESTORS: Telephone	Open to New Investors
ALPS | Kotak India Growth Fund Class C	INFCX	B	B	B-	Up	10.49	12.28	38.69	38.75	92.69	14.13	31.8	866-759-5679	Y
ALPS | Kotak India Growth Fund Class I	INDIX	B	B	B-	Up	10.78	12.86	40.17	42.92	102.59	15.21	31.8	866-759-5679	Y
ALPS | Kotak India Growth Fund Class Investor	INDAX	B	B	B-	Up	10.75	12.71	39.73	41.69	99.31	14.84	31.8	866-759-5679	Y
Eaton Vance Greater India Fund Class A	ETGIX	B	B	B-	Up	11.08	14.70	44.79	42.18	78.90	36.83	264.3		Y
Eaton Vance Greater India Fund Class B	EMGIX	B	B	C+	Up	10.89	14.28	43.78	39.20	72.73	32.29	264.3		
Eaton Vance Greater India Fund Class C	ECGIX	B	B	C+	Up	10.91	14.31	43.81	39.23	72.77	32.05	264.3		Y
Eaton Vance Greater India Fund Class I	EGIIX	B	B	B-	Up	11.19	14.88	45.22	43.43	81.57	37.52	264.3		Y
Franklin India Growth Fund Advisor Class	FIGZX	B	B	B-	Up	11.26	11.48	36.49	34.53	84.64	16.39	156.5	650-312-2000	Y
Franklin India Growth Fund Class A	FINGX	B	B	B-	Up	11.13	11.28	36.17	33.52	81.99	15.97	156.5	650-312-2000	Y
Franklin India Growth Fund Class C	FINDX	B-	B	B-	Down	10.86	10.86	35.11	30.52	75.46	14.91	156.5	650-312-2000	Y
Franklin India Growth Fund Class R6	US35361F7336	B	B	B-	Up	11.46	11.75	36.98	35.35	86.27	16.52	156.5	650-312-2000	Y
Matthews India Fund Institutional Class	MIDNX	B	B	B	Up	10.10	11.22	36.04	37.39	112.87	34.51	2,300	800-789-2742	Y
Matthews India Fund Investor Class	MINDX	B	B	B	Up	10.04	11.13	35.78	36.56	110.88	34.31	2,300	800-789-2742	Y
MS India Investment Fund	IIF	B	B+	B	Up	7.46	14.39	44.78	52.18	115.35	37.32	578.9	855-332-5306	Y
The India Fund Inc	IFN	B-	B-	B-	Up	8.02	8.69	34.97	31.65	76.77	29.5	886.5	866-667-9231	Y
Wasatch Emerging India Fund® Institutional Class	WIINX	B	B+	B	Down	12.72	14.39	53.54	62.23	132.34	4.49	246.8	800-551-1700	Y
Wasatch Emerging India Fund® Investor Class	WAINX	B	B	B	Down	12.79	14.48	53.40	61.54	131.35	4.47	246.8	800-551-1700	Y

Category: Industrials Sector Equity

Fund Name	Ticker Symbol	RATINGS: Overall Rating	Reward Rating	Risk Rating	Recent Up/ Downgrade	TOTAL RETURNS & PERFORMANCE: 3-Month Total Return	6-Month Total Return	1-Year Total Return	3-Year Total Return	5-Year Total Return	ASSETS: NAV	Total Assets (MIL)	NEW INVESTORS: Telephone	Open to New Investors
Fidelity Advisor® Industrials Fund Class A	FCLAX	B	B	B		8.01	13.34	19.55	33.87	102.95	41.91	865.8	617-563-7000	Y
Fidelity Advisor® Industrials Fund Class C	FCLCX	B	B	B		7.82	12.91	18.65	30.85	95.43	37.61	865.8	617-563-7000	Y
Fidelity Advisor® Industrials Fund Class M	FCLTX	B	B	B		7.94	13.21	19.23	32.86	100.35	41.01	865.8	617-563-7000	Y
Fidelity Advisor® Industrials Fund I Class	FCLIX	B	B+	B		8.09	13.49	19.87	34.95	105.73	44.02	865.8	617-563-7000	Y
Fidelity® Select Defense & Aerospace Portfolio	FSDAX	B+	A+	C+	Up	6.49	21.19	34.21	62.36	153.73	166.95	2,421	617-563-7000	Y
Fidelity® Select Envir and Alt Energy Portfolio	FSLEX	B+	A-	B	Up	7.52	10.16	25.24	42.85	102.03	26.42	182.9	617-563-7000	Y
Fidelity® Select Industrial Equipment Portfolio	FSCGX	A-	A-	B+	Up	6.42	13.07	19.71	36.89	88.00	43.99	171.8	617-563-7000	Y
Fidelity® Select Industrials Portfolio	FCYIX	B	B+	B		8.14	13.59	20.07	34.84	104.98	36.79	883.6	617-563-7000	Y
Fidelity® Select Portfolios Air Transportation Portfolio	FSAIX	A-	A	B	Up	7.79	14.57	24.32	35.95	167.32	84.29	396.1	617-563-7000	Y
Fidelity® Select Transportation Portfolio	FSRFX	B	B+	C+	Up	7.59	14.26	22.19	24.84	153.45	104.28	539.3	617-563-7000	Y
ICON Industrials Fund Class A	ICIAX	B-	B-	B-	Down	4.19	6.56	15.95	25.18	84.77	15.41	17.1	303-790-1600	Y
ICON Industrials Fund Class S	ICTRX	B-	B-	B-	Down	4.34	6.69	16.22	25.95	86.98	15.62	17.1	303-790-1600	Y
Putnam Global Industrial Fund Class A	PGIAX	B+	A	B-	Up	7.97	15.52	27.76	47.77	113.87	22.34	85.8	617-292-1000	Y
Putnam Global Industrial Fund Class B	PGIVX	B+	A-	B-	Up	7.79	15.10	26.82	44.55	105.94	21.22	85.8	617-292-1000	Y
Putnam Global Industrial Fund Class C	PGIEX	B+	A-	B-	Up	7.78	15.08	26.77	44.48	106.01	21.25	85.8	617-292-1000	Y
Putnam Global Industrial Fund Class M	PGIHX	B+	A	B-	Up	7.89	15.26	27.10	45.67	108.66	21.93	85.8	617-292-1000	Y
Putnam Global Industrial Fund Class R	PGIOX	B+	A	B-	Up	7.91	15.35	27.46	46.77	111.24	22.17	85.8	617-292-1000	Y
Putnam Global Industrial Fund Class Y	PGILX	B+	A	B-	Up	8.09	15.69	28.09	48.99	116.63	22.55	85.8	617-292-1000	Y
Rydex Transportation Fund Class A	RYTSX	B	B	B-	Up	5.71	12.41	22.10	20.26	127.67	57.26	40.1	800-820-0888	Y
Rydex Transportation Fund Class C	RYCNX	B-	B-	B-	Up	5.53	12.01	21.21	17.57	119.25	52.74	40.1	800-820-0888	Y
Rydex Transportation Fund Class H	RYPAX	B-	B	B-	Up	5.72	12.40	22.10	20.10	126.21	55.66	40.1	800-820-0888	Y
Rydex Transportation Fund Class Investor	RYPIX	B	B	B-	Up	5.79	12.57	22.42	21.17	130.50	62.14	40.1	800-820-0888	Y
T. Rowe Price Global Industrials Fund	RPGIX	B	B+	C+	Up	4.10	10.45	25.91	35.46		13.05	24.9	410-345-2000	Y
T. Rowe Price Global Industrials Fund I Class	TRGAX	B	B+	C+		4.17	10.52	26.10	35.66		13.05	24.9	410-345-2000	Y
Vanguard Industrials Index Fund Admiral Shares	VINAX	B	B+	B-		6.45	11.82	21.50	39.65	121.44	73.09	3,805	877-662-7447	Y

Category: Japan Equity

Fund Name	Ticker Symbol	RATINGS: Overall Rating	Reward Rating	Risk Rating	Recent Up/ Downgrade	TOTAL RETURNS & PERFORMANCE: 3-Month Total Return	6-Month Total Return	1-Year Total Return	3-Year Total Return	5-Year Total Return	ASSETS: NAV	Total Assets (MIL)	NEW INVESTORS: Telephone	Open to New Investors
Aberdeen Japan Equity Fund, Inc.	JEQ	B+	A-	B	Up	8.89	11.29	25.65	44.36	89.49	10.14	142.5	866-667-9231	Y
AIG Japan Fund Class A	SAESX	B+	A-	B	Up	7.33	12.28	29.58	41.04	79.16	8.6	31.4	800-858-8850	Y
AIG Japan Fund Class C	SAJCX	B+	A-	B	Up	7.12	11.77	28.51	38.23	73.14	8.15	31.4	800-858-8850	Y
AIG Japan Fund Class W	SAJWX	B+	A-	B	Up	7.31	12.39	29.70	41.17	79.33	8.6	31.4	800-858-8850	Y
Brown Advy - WMC Japan Alpha Opp Fund Adv Shares	BAJAX	B	B	B-	Up	8.36	13.98	27.98	25.43		11.32	1,138	800-540-6807	Y
Brown Advy - WMC Japan Alpha Opp Fund Inst Shares	BAFJX	B	B	B-	Up	8.35	14.12	28.38	26.81		11.45	1,138	800-540-6807	Y
Brown Advy - WMC Japan Alpha Opp Fund Inv Shares	BIAJX	B	B	B-	Up	8.39	14.08	28.27	26.30		11.4	1,138	800-540-6807	Y
Commonwealth Japan Fund	CNJFX	A-	B+	A	Up	7.85	10.25	20.60	31.78	50.18	3.98	5.9	888-345-1898	Y
DFA Japanese Small Company Portfolio Institutional Class	DFJSX	A	A	A-	Up	8.34	16.69	35.68	68.83	106.82	29.14	664.3	512-306-7400	Y
Fidelity Advisor® Japan Fund Class A	FPJAX	B+	A-	B	Up	8.92	12.47	29.85	43.17	62.94	15.43	405.1	617-563-7000	Y
Fidelity Advisor® Japan Fund Class C	FJPCX	B+	A-	B	Up	8.69	12.03	28.86	40.03	57.22	15.31	405.1	617-563-7000	Y
Fidelity Advisor® Japan Fund Class I	FJPIX	B+	A-	B	Up	8.95	12.57	30.16	44.42	65.69	15.41	405.1	617-563-7000	Y
Fidelity Advisor® Japan Fund Class M	FJPTX	B+	A-	B	Up	8.85	12.24	29.37	41.62	60.31	15.43	405.1	617-563-7000	Y
Fidelity® Japan Fund	FJPNX	B+	A-	B	Up	8.96	12.58	30.15	44.34	65.50	15.45	405.1	617-563-7000	Y
Fidelity® Japan Smaller Companies Fund	FJSCX	A	A	A	Up	9.23	17.50	35.70	67.60	138.95	18.96	770.3	617-563-7000	Y
Hennessy Japan Fund Institutional Class	HJPIX	A	A	A-	Up	11.65	16.10	32.60	67.03	128.40	35.8	308.7	800-966-4354	Y
Hennessy Japan Fund Investor Class	HJPNX	A	A	A-	Up	11.50	15.84	32.04	65.30	125.09	34.84	308.7	800-966-4354	Y
Hennessy Japan Small Cap Fund Institutional Class	HJSIX	A	A+	A-	Up	11.83	21.12	50.26	81.34	165.16	15.68	127.5	800-966-4354	Y
Hennessy Japan Small Cap Fund Investor Class	HJPSX	A	A+	A-	Up	11.64	20.86	49.57	79.98	163.17	15.9	127.5	800-966-4354	Y
Japan Smaller Capitalization Fund	JOF	A	A	A-	Up	8.43	18.02	37.23	74.01	126.81	13.44	425.3	813-324-1951	Y
Matthews Japan Fund Institutional Class	MIJFX	A-	A	B+	Up	8.21	16.22	33.22	59.72	113.48	24.16	4,191	800-789-2742	
Matthews Japan Fund Investor Class	MJFOX	A-	A	B+	Up	8.24	16.16	33.13	59.27	112.41	24.12	4,191	800-789-2742	Y
T. Rowe Price Japan Fund	PRJPX	A	A	A	Up	8.16	14.76	32.66	68.56	102.76	15.11	750.1	410-345-2000	Y
T. Rowe Price Japan Fund I Class	RJAIX	A	A	A	Up	8.15	14.75	32.64	68.54	102.73	15.11	750.1	410-345-2000	Y
Voya Japan TOPIX Index® Portfolio Class A	IJIAX	A-	A-	B+	Up	7.89	12.33	25.40	41.90	69.79	12.57	310.6	800-366-0066	Y
Voya Japan TOPIX Index® Portfolio Class I	IJIIX	A-	A-	B+	Up	7.98	12.57	25.92	43.92	74.06	12.71	310.6	800-366-0066	Y

Category: Long/Short Equity

Fund Name	Ticker Symbol	RATINGS: Overall Rating	Reward Rating	Risk Rating	Recent Up/ Downgrade	TOTAL RETURNS & PERFORMANCE: 3-Month Total Return	6-Month Total Return	1-Year Total Return	3-Year Total Return	5-Year Total Return	ASSETS: NAV	Total Assets (MIL)	NEW INVESTORS: Telephone	Open to New Investors
361 Global Long/Short Equity Fund Class I	AGAZX	B	C+	B		2.54	7.40	15.24	24.65		11.65	567.6	866-361-1720	Y
361 Global Long/Short Equity Fund Class Y	AGAWX	B	C+	A		2.56	7.51	15.35	25.00		11.66	567.6	866-361-1720	Y
361 Global Long/Short Equity Fund Investor Class	AGAQX	B	C+	A-		2.51	7.39	14.94	23.62		11.63	567.6	866-361-1720	Y
AB Select US Long/Short Portfolio Advisor Class	ASYLX	B-	C+	B	Down	5.23	8.10	12.54	16.57	47.90	12.79	966.1	212-969-1000	Y
AB Select US Long/Short Portfolio Class A	ASLAX	B-	C+	B	Down	5.13	7.96	12.26	15.72	45.99	12.61	966.1	212-969-1000	Y
AB Select US Long/Short Portfolio Class C	ASCLX	B-	C+	B	Up	5.00	7.56	11.41	13.16	40.69	12.11	966.1	212-969-1000	Y
AB Select US Long/Short Portfolio Class I	ASILX	B-	C+	B	Down	5.30	8.17	12.61	16.83	48.23	12.82	966.1	212-969-1000	Y
AB Select US Long/Short Portfolio Class K	ASLKX	B-	C+	B	Down	5.21	8.04	12.25	15.80	46.11	12.62	966.1	212-969-1000	Y
AB Select US Long/Short Portfolio Class R	ASRLX	B-	C+	B	Up	5.12	7.89	12.04	14.93	44.30	12.45	966.1	212-969-1000	Y
Aberdeen Focused U.S. Equity Fund Class A	MLSAX	B-	C+	B	Up	5.99	7.65	12.81	13.91	27.60	6.64	25.5	866-667-9231	Y
Aberdeen Focused U.S. Equity Fund Class C	MLSCX	B-	B-	B	Up	5.97	7.25	12.14	11.62	23.49	2.12	25.5	866-667-9231	Y
Aberdeen Focused U.S. Equity Fund Class R	GLSRX	B-	C+	B	Up	5.83	7.34	12.46	12.62	25.14	5.96	25.5	866-667-9231	Y
Aberdeen Focused U.S. Equity Fund Institutional Class	GGUIX	B-	C+	B	Up	6.05	7.75	13.21	14.96	29.66	7.09	25.5	866-667-9231	Y
Aberdeen Focused U.S. Equity Fund Inst Service Cls	AELSX	B-	C+	B	Up	5.95	7.69	12.99	14.31	28.40	6.88	25.5	866-667-9231	Y
Alger Dynamic Opportunities Fund Class A	SPEDX	B-	C+	B-	Up	3.04	7.28	16.89	18.36	46.88	13.19	82.6	800-992-3863	Y
Alger Dynamic Opportunities Fund Class Z	ADOZX	B-	C+	B	Up	3.05	7.36	17.25	19.38	49.00	13.48	82.6	800-992-3863	Y
AllianzGI Structured Return Fund Class A	AZIAX	B	C	A-	Up	1.05	2.56	5.19	13.62	25.77	15.83	581.7	800-498-5413	Y
AllianzGI Structured Return Fund Class C	AZICX	B-	C	A-	Up	0.89	2.19	4.40	11.09	21.01	15.36	581.7	800-498-5413	Y
AllianzGI Structured Return Fund Class P	AZIPX	B	C	A-		1.16	2.67	5.44	14.25	26.79	15.79	581.7	800-498-5413	Y
AllianzGI Structured Return Fund Class R6	AZIRX	B	C	A-		1.17	2.75	5.57	14.53	27.36	15.88	581.7	800-498-5413	Y

Category: Long/Short Equity (con't)

Fund Name	Ticker Symbol	RATINGS: Overall Rating	Reward Rating	Risk Rating	Recent Up/ Downgrade	TOTAL RETURNS & PERFORMANCE: 3-Month Total Return	6-Month Total Return	1-Year Total Return	3-Year Total Return	5-Year Total Return	ASSETS: NAV	Total Assets (MIL)	NEW INVESTORS: Telephone	Open to New Investors
AllianzGI Structured Return Fund Institutional Class	AZIIX	B	C	A-		1.10	2.73	5.47	14.41	27.24	15.95	581.7	800-498-5413	Y
AllianzGI U.S. Equity-Hedged Fund Class A	AZUAX	B-	C+	B	Down	4.53	7.68	13.25	13.61	44.61	18.31	2.7	800-498-5413	Y
AllianzGI U.S. Equity-Hedged Fund Class P	AZUPX	B-	C+	B	Down	4.56	7.74	13.38	14.11	45.71	18.05	2.7	800-498-5413	Y
AllianzGI U.S. Equity-Hedged Fund Institutional Class	AZUIX	B-	C+	B	Down	4.57	7.76	13.51	14.41	46.46	18.54	2.7	800-498-5413	Y
AlphaCentric Hedged Market Opportunity Fund Class A	HMXAX	B	C	A-		1.14	2.16	5.02	17.41	49.20	18.63	20.5		Y
AlphaCentric Hedged Market Opportunity Fund Class C	HMXCX	B-	C	B+	Down	0.93	1.74	4.31	14.85	43.79	18.47	20.5		Y
AlphaCentric Hedged Market Opportunity Fund Class I	HMXIX	B	C+	A-		1.24	2.32	5.28	18.38	51.19	18.7	20.5		Y
AMG River Road Long-Short Fund Class I	ALSIX	B	C+	A-	Up	1.11	3.51	9.22	14.34	33.96	12.67	34.1	800-835-3879	Y
AMG River Road Long-Short Fund Class N	ARLSX	B	C+	A-	Up	1.04	3.38	8.87	13.42	32.32	12.51	34.1	800-835-3879	Y
AMG River Road Long-Short Fund Class Z	ARLZX	B-	C+	B		1.11	3.45	8.94	13.49	32.41	12.67	34.1	800-835-3879	Y
AQR Long-Short Equity Fund Class I	QLEIX	B+	B+	B+	Up	3.17	9.76	15.72	49.22		13.88	5,573	203-742-3600	Y
AQR Long-Short Equity Fund Class N	QLENX	B+	B+	B+	Up	3.16	9.64	15.46	48.19		13.8	5,573	203-742-3600	Y
AQR Long-Short Equity Fund Class R6	QLERX	B+	B+	B+	Up	3.23	9.81	15.85	49.72		13.91	5,573	203-742-3600	Y
Arin Large Cap Theta Fund Advisor Class	AVOAX	B-	C	B+	Up	1.21	2.70	4.85	8.14		10.34	10.6	252-442-4226	Y
Arin Large Cap Theta Fund Institutional Class	AVOLX	B-	C	B+	Up	1.31	2.98	5.35	9.38		10.39	10.6	252-442-4226	Y
Balter European L/S Small Cap Fund Institutional Class	BESMX	B-	B	C+	Up	5.46	7.86	25.02	24.61	62.29	11.27	71.6		Y
Balter European L/S Small Cap Fund Investor Class	BESRX	B-	B	C+	Up	5.47	7.77	24.92	24.17	60.91	11.27	71.6		Y
Balter L/S Small Cap Equity Fund Institutional Class	BEQIX	B-	C+	B	Down	3.00	7.16	15.61	24.51		11.4	170.7		Y
Balter L/S Small Cap Equity Fund Investor Class	BEQRX	B-	C+	B		2.96	7.05	15.35	23.60		11.4	170.7		Y
Boston Partners Global Long/Short Fund Institutional Class	BGLSX	B	C+	A-	Up	3.32	5.15	7.55	16.72		11.82	1,054	617-832-8200	Y
Boston Partners Global Long/Short Fund Investor Class	BGRSX	B	C	A-	Up	3.16	5.01	7.22	15.75		11.72	1,054	617-832-8200	Y
Boston Partners Long/Short Equity Fund Institutional Class	BPLSX	B	C+	B+	Up	2.76	7.07	2.76	24.04	41.08	22.28	963.5	617-832-8200	
Boston Partners Long/Short Equity Fund Investor Class	BPLEX	B	C+	B+	Up	2.69	6.93	2.54	23.09	39.34	20.55	963.5	617-832-8200	
Boston Partners Long/Short Research Fund Institutional Cls	BPIRX	B	C+	A+	Up	3.78	6.17	10.09	14.98	47.47	17.01	6,833	617-832-8200	
Boston Partners Long/Short Research Fund Investor Class	BPRRX	B	C+	A+	Up	3.72	6.03	9.79	14.13	45.59	16.7	6,833	617-832-8200	
Bridgeway Managed Volatility Fund	BRBPX	B-	C	B	Up	2.72	4.66	8.17	10.50	28.67	15.39	33.6	800-661-3550	Y
Calamos Hedged Equity Income Fund Class I	CIHEX	B-	C	B	Up	2.37	3.91	8.37	15.14		10.98	13.0	800-582-6959	Y
Calamos Phineus Long/Short Fund Class A	CPLSX	B	C+	A-	Up	2.03	2.44	8.89	20.92	60.78	12.48	497.6	800-582-6959	Y
Calamos Phineus Long/Short Fund Class C	CPCLX	B	C+	A-	Up	1.89	2.14	8.07	18.14	54.77	12.32	497.6	800-582-6959	Y
Calamos Phineus Long/Short Fund Class I	CPLIX	B	C+	A-	Up	2.18	2.68	9.21	22.02	63.06	12.55	497.6	800-582-6959	Y
Calamos Phineus Long/Short Fund Class T	CPLTX	B	C+	A-	Up	0.08	2.49	15.30	25.22	57.38		381.7	800-582-6959	Y
Catalyst/Exceed Defined Shield Fund Class A	SHIEX	B-	C	B	Up	4.69	8.18	14.33			10.16	28.9	866-447-4228	Y
Catalyst/Exceed Defined Shield Fund Class C	SHINX	B-	C	B		4.02	7.57	13.76			10.1	28.9	866-447-4228	Y
Catalyst/Exceed Defined Shield Fund Class I	SHIIX	B-	C	B	Up	3.90	7.45	13.63			10.2	28.9	866-447-4228	Y
Day Hagan Hedged Strategy Fund Class A	DHJAX	B	C	A-	Up	1.36	4.27	7.44	28.59		10.34	27.0		Y
Day Hagan Hedged Strategy Fund Class C	DHJCX	B	C	A-	Up	1.46	4.28	7.27	26.41		10.33	27.0		Y
Day Hagan Hedged Strategy Fund Class I	DHJIX	B	C	A-	Up	1.56	4.38	7.47	29.28		10.34	27.0		Y
Diamond Hill Long Short Fund Class A	DIAMX	B-	C+	B+		2.80	2.16	5.64	13.83	52.23	25.76	4,767	888-226-5595	
Diamond Hill Long Short Fund Class C	DHFCX	B-	C	B		2.59	1.75	4.82	11.26	46.59	23.04	4,767	888-226-5595	
Diamond Hill Long Short Fund Class I	DHLSX	B-	C+	B+		2.91	2.33	5.99	14.82	54.33	26.39	4,767	888-226-5595	
Diamond Hill Long-Short Fund Class Y	DIAYX	B-	C+	B+		2.92	2.37	6.06	15.15	55.28	26.49	4,767	888-226-5595	
Diamond Hill Research Opportunities Fund Class A	DHROX	B-	C+	B	Up	5.91	4.68	12.98	16.70	68.28	23.56	67.3	888-226-5595	Y
Diamond Hill Research Opportunities Fund Class C	DROCX	B-	C+	B	Up	5.69	4.21	12.12	14.05	62.02	22.4	67.3	888-226-5595	Y
Diamond Hill Research Opportunities Fund Class I	DROIX	B-	C+	B	Up	6.03	4.80	13.34	17.69	70.54	23.83	67.3	888-226-5595	Y
Diamond Hill Research Opportunities Fund Class Y	DROYX	B-	C+	B	Up	6.06	4.88	13.47	18.11	71.70	23.88	67.3	888-226-5595	Y
Dreyfus Select Managers Long/Short Fund Class I	DBNIX	B-	C	B+	Up	0.30	1.26	4.15	4.41		12.64	458.6	800-645-6561	Y
Dreyfus Select Managers Long/Short Fund Class Y	DBNYX	B-	C	B+	Up	0.38	1.26	4.15	4.49		12.65	458.6	800-645-6561	Y
Eaton Vance Enhanced Equity Income Fund	EOI	B-	B-	B	Up	6.19	9.64	19.36	26.64	79.30	15.1	585.2		Y
Eaton Vance Enhanced Equity Income Fund II	EOS	B	B-	A-	Up	5.16	8.99	23.82	33.75	94.37	15.77	746.3		Y
Eaton Vance Hedged Stock Fund Class A	EROAX	B-	C	B	Down	2.77	4.20	9.63	12.12	37.67	8.97	41.0		Y
Eaton Vance Hedged Stock Fund Class I	EROIX	B-	C	B+	Down	2.81	4.22	9.78	12.90	39.35	8.98	41.0		Y
Eaton Vance Risk-Managed Diversified Equity Income Fund	ETJ	B-	C	B	Up	3.84	5.30	11.01	11.83	37.58	10.08	638.6		Y

Category: Long/Short Equity (con't)

Fund Name	Ticker Symbol	RATINGS: Overall Rating	Reward Rating	Risk Rating	Recent Up/ Downgrade	TOTAL RETURNS & PERFORMANCE: 3-Month Total Return	6-Month Total Return	1-Year Total Return	3-Year Total Return	5-Year Total Return	ASSETS: NAV	Total Assets (MIL)	NEW INVESTORS: Telephone	Open to New Investors
Eaton Vance Tax-Managed Buy-Write Income Fund	ETB	B	B-	B+	Up	2.63	6.41	14.37	27.29	67.47	16.35	407.8		Y
Eaton Vance Tax-Managed Buy-Write Opportunities Fund	ETV	B	B-	B+	Up	4.48	9.34	17.06	32.10	74.96	15.01	974.3		Y
Eaton Vance Tax-Managed Diversified Equity Income Fund	ETY	B	B-	B+	Up	5.87	8.98	17.99	28.97	75.27	12.35	1,829		Y
Eaton Vance Tax-Managed Global Buy-Write Opp Fund	ETW	B	C+	A	Up	3.01	7.54	19.33	26.36	54.03	11.59	1,234		Y
Eaton Vance Tax-Managed Global Diversified Eq Income Fund	EXG	B	C+	A-	Up	3.43	6.31	18.15	23.38	50.92	9.48	2,837		Y
Equinox EquityHedge U.S. Strategy Fund Class A Shares	EEHAX	B-	B-	B-	Down	5.41	8.87	15.44	25.33		10.36	10.6	609-577-4200	Y
Equinox EquityHedge U.S. Strategy Fund Class C Shares	EEHCX	B	C+	B+		5.31	8.57	14.51	22.55		9.96	10.6	609-577-4200	Y
Equinox EquityHedge U.S. Strategy Fund Class I Shares	EEHIX	B-	B-	B-	Down	5.46	9.00	15.53	26.18		10.45	10.6	609-577-4200	Y
FundX Tactical Upgrader Fund	TACTX	B-	C+	B+	Down	-0.60	3.98	8.14	18.37	32.09	24.79	42.1	866-455-3863	Y
Gateway Equity Call Premium Fund Class A	GCPAX	B-	C	B+	Down	2.68	5.76	11.80	24.34		12.08	84.4	800-862-4863	Y
Gateway Equity Call Premium Fund Class C	GCPCX	B-	C	B+		2.46	5.35	10.95	21.57		12.05	84.4	800-862-4863	Y
Gateway Equity Call Premium Fund Class N	GCPNX	B-	C	B+	Down	2.81	5.97	12.25	25.29		12.09	84.4	800-862-4863	Y
Gateway Equity Call Premium Fund Class Y	GCPYX	B-	C	B+	Down	2.80	6.04	12.21	25.25		12.09	84.4	800-862-4863	Y
Gateway Fund Class A Shares	GATEX	B	C+	A-	Up	1.97	4.48	9.66	17.81	32.99	33.47	8,434	800-862-4863	Y
Gateway Fund Class C Shares	GTECX	B-	C+	B+	Down	1.80	4.12	8.85	15.14	28.01	33.32	8,434	800-862-4863	Y
Gateway Fund Class N	GTENX	B	C+	A-		2.05	4.67	9.83	18.00	33.20	33.46	8,434	800-862-4863	Y
Gateway Fund Class Y Shares	GTEYX	B	C+	A-	Up	2.03	4.65	9.93	18.67	34.62	33.46	8,434	800-862-4863	Y
Glenmede Long/Short Portfolio	GTAPX	B	C+	A-	Up	2.75	5.57	8.78	15.80	39.81	13.06	304.3	800-442-8299	Y
Glenmede Secured Options Portfolio	GTSOX	B	C+	B+	Up	0.79	2.40	5.94	19.53	46.47	12.03	818.8	800-442-8299	Y
Glenmede Secured Options Portfolio Institutional Class	GLSOX	B	C+	B+	Up	0.86	2.55	6.18	19.83	46.84	12.06	818.8	800-442-8299	Y
Gotham Absolute 500 Fund Institutional Class	GFIVX	B-	C+	B		8.32	14.38	16.52	21.11		12.21	12.2	877-974-6852	Y
Gotham Total Return Fund Institutional Class	GTRFX	B-	C+	B	Up	8.98	15.45	18.93			12.6	19.9	877-974-6852	Y
Guggenheim Alpha Opportunity Fund Class A	SAOAX	B-	C+	B	Up	4.50	6.96	7.48	14.90	70.67	20.61	222.8	212-739-0700	Y
Guggenheim Alpha Opportunity Fund Class C	SAOCX	B-	C+	B	Up	4.24	6.55	6.67	12.32	64.35	17.97	222.8	212-739-0700	Y
Guggenheim Alpha Opportunity Fund Class P	SAOSX	B-	C+	B	Up	4.44	6.98	7.71	15.38	71.38	20.69	222.8	212-739-0700	Y
Guggenheim Alpha Opportunity Fund Institutional Class	SAOIX	B-	C+	B	Up	4.65	7.29	8.15	16.56	74.00	29.81	222.8	212-739-0700	Y
Guggenheim Long Short Equity Fund Class A	RYAMX	B-	C+	B+	Up	6.29	11.09	14.87	15.96	42.19	18.23	33.3	212-739-0700	Y
Guggenheim Long Short Equity Fund Class C	RYISX	B-	C+	B	Up	6.03	10.60	13.95	13.31	36.80	16.17	33.3	212-739-0700	Y
Guggenheim Long Short Equity Fund Class P	RYSRX	B-	C+	B+	Up	6.27	10.98	14.82	15.91	42.03	18.28	33.3	212-739-0700	Y
Guggenheim Long Short Equity Fund Institutional Cls Shares	RYQTX	B-	C+	B+	Up	6.34	11.17	15.08	16.89	43.92	18.61	33.3	212-739-0700	Y
Hancock Horizon Quantitative Long/Short Fund Class C	HHQCX	B-	C	B+	Up	2.52	4.47	6.55	7.55	46.97	17.33	158.7	800-990-2434	Y
Hancock Horizon Quantitative Long/Short Fund Inst Cls	HHQTX	B	C	A+	Up	2.79	5.00	7.66	10.82	54.39	19.31	158.7	800-990-2434	Y
Hancock Horizon Quantitative Long/Short Fund Investor Cls	HHQAX	B	C	A	Up	3.02	5.17	7.66	10.32	52.93	18.89	158.7	800-990-2434	Y
Hartford Long/Short Global Equity Fund Class A	HLOAX	B	B-	B+	Up	3.17	8.52	17.08	27.19		11.85	44.4	888-843-7824	Y
Hartford Long/Short Global Equity Fund Class C	HLOCX	B-	C+	B	Up	3.15	8.42	16.91	25.24		11.64	44.4	888-843-7824	Y
Hartford Long/Short Global Equity Fund Class F	HLOFX	B	B-	B+	Up	3.27	8.60	17.21	28.06		11.92	44.4	888-843-7824	Y
Hartford Long/Short Global Equity Fund Class I	HLOIX	B	B-	B+	Up	3.20	8.52	17.13	27.97		11.93	44.4	888-843-7824	Y
Hartford Long/Short Global Equity Fund Class Y	HLOYX	B	B-	B+	Up	3.26	8.67	17.29	28.13		11.93	44.4	888-843-7824	Y
Highland Long/Short Equity Fund Class A	HEOAX	B-	C+	B	Up	4.16	6.63	13.34	11.41	35.48	12.27	390.9	877-665-1287	Y
Highland Long/Short Equity Fund Class C	HEOCX	B-	C	B	Up	4.04	6.31	12.66	9.28	31.15	11.36	390.9	877-665-1287	Y
Invesco Long/Short Equity Fund Class A	LSQAX	B	B	B+	Up	9.62	21.95	18.62	28.48		11.92	75.2	800-659-1005	Y
Invesco Long/Short Equity Fund Class C	LSQCX	B	B-	B+	Up	9.56	21.65	17.85	25.89		11.68	75.2	800-659-1005	Y
Invesco Long/Short Equity Fund Class R	LSQRX	B	B	B+	Up	8.72	20.83	17.41	26.59		11.84	75.2	800-659-1005	Y
Invesco Long/Short Equity Fund Class R5	LSQFX	B	B	B+	Up	9.31	21.71	18.60	29.10		12	75.2	800-659-1005	Y
Invesco Long/Short Equity Fund Class R6	LSQSX	B	B	B+	Up	9.40	21.81	18.71	29.22		12	75.2	800-659-1005	Y
Invesco Long/Short Equity Fund Class Y	LSQYX	B	B	B+	Up	9.12	21.41	18.21	28.79		12	75.2	800-659-1005	Y
JNL/Boston Partners Global Long Short Equity Fund Class A	US46648M8394	B	C	A+	Up	3.36	5.32	7.68	15.77		11.07	623.9		Y
JNL/Boston Partners Global Long Short Equity Fund Class I	US46648M8212	B	C	A+		3.54	5.51	7.87	15.98		11.09	623.9		Y
John Hancock Seaport Fund Class A	JSFBX	B	C+	A-	Up	2.04	3.81	15.43	17.65		11.05	655.8	800-225-5913	Y
John Hancock Seaport Fund Class C	JSFTX	B-	C+	B+	Up	1.91	3.44	14.69	15.33		10.79	655.8	800-225-5913	Y
John Hancock Seaport Fund Class I	JSFDX	B	C+	A-	Up	2.10	3.94	15.85	18.87		11.21	655.8	800-225-5913	Y
John Hancock Seaport Fund Class NAV	US47803P4506	B	C+	A-	Up	2.09	4.00	15.97	19.20		11.28	655.8	800-225-5913	Y

Category: Long/Short Equity (con't)

Fund Name	Ticker Symbol	RATINGS: Overall Rating	Reward Rating	Risk Rating	Recent Up/ Downgrade	TOTAL RETURNS & PERFORMANCE: 3-Month Total Return	6-Month Total Return	1-Year Total Return	3-Year Total Return	5-Year Total Return	ASSETS: NAV	Total Assets (MIL)	NEW INVESTORS: Telephone	Open to New Investors
John Hancock Seaport Fund Class R6	JSFRX	B	C+	A-	Up	2.09	4.00	15.86	19.20		11.28	655.8	800-225-5913	Y
JPMorgan Hedged Equity Fund Class A	JHQAX	B-	C+	B	Down	2.90	6.16	12.44	21.01		19.29	1,443	800-480-4111	Y
JPMorgan Hedged Equity Fund Class C	JHQCX	B-	C+	B	Down	2.76	5.92	11.89	19.21		19.2	1,443	800-480-4111	Y
JPMorgan Hedged Equity Fund Class I	JHEQX	B-	C+	B	Down	2.96	6.28	12.69	21.87		19.33	1,443	800-480-4111	Y
JPMorgan Hedged Equity Fund Class R5	JHQPX	B-	C+	B	Down	3.00	6.36	12.92	22.61		19.36	1,443	800-480-4111	Y
JPMorgan Hedged Equity Fund Class R6	JHQRX	B-	C+	B	Down	2.96	6.39	12.91	22.74		19.35	1,443	800-480-4111	Y
JPMorgan Opportunistic Equity Long/Short Fund Class A	JOELX	B	C+	A+	Up	4.88	4.89	16.27	25.57		18.03	162.9	800-480-4111	Y
JPMorgan Opportunistic Equity Long/Short Fund Class C	JOECX	B	C+	B+	Up	4.79	4.62	15.66	23.68		17.71	162.9	800-480-4111	Y
JPMorgan Opportunistic Equity Long/Short Fund Class I	JOEQX	B	C+	A+	Up	4.26	4.26	15.75	25.59		18.19	162.9	800-480-4111	Y
JPMorgan Opportunistic Equity Long/Short Fund Class R2	JOEZX	B	C+	A+	Up	4.81	4.75	15.93	24.62		17.87	162.9	800-480-4111	Y
JPMorgan Opportunistic Equity Long/Short Fund Class R5	JOEPX	B	C+	B+	Up	4.98	5.10	16.74	27.24		18.33	162.9	800-480-4111	Y
JPMorgan Opportunistic Equity Long/Short Fund Class R6	JOERX	B	C+	A+	Up	5.03	5.15	16.85	27.44		18.36	162.9	800-480-4111	Y
LJM Preservation and Growth Fund Class A	LJMAX	B	B-	B+		1.41	3.65	9.17	35.98		10.6	781.9		Y
LJM Preservation and Growth Fund Class C	LJMCX	B	C+	B+		1.24	3.21	8.42	33.30		10.48	781.9		Y
LJM Preservation and Growth Fund Class I	LJMIX	B	B-	B+		1.57	3.79	9.45	37.01		10.76	781.9		Y
LoCorr Dynamic Equity Fund Class A	LEQAX	B-	C+	B	Up	1.20	2.97	2.37	25.22		11.82	64.7	855-523-8637	Y
LoCorr Dynamic Equity Fund Class I	LEQIX	B-	C+	B	Up	1.18	3.11	2.60	26.12		11.96	64.7	855-523-8637	Y
LS Opportunity Fund	LSOFX	B-	C+	B	Down	3.70	6.55	9.57	18.17	49.96	13.78	37.1		Y
LS Theta Fund Institutional Class	LQTIX	B	C	A-	Up	1.19	2.54	5.75	14.33		53.4	304.8	770-350-8700	Y
LS Theta Fund Investor Class	LQTVX	B	C	A-	Up	1.12	2.40	5.50	13.51		52.89	304.8	770-350-8700	Y
Lyrical U.S. Hedged Value Fund Institutional Class	LYRHX	B-	C+	B	Up	1.64	2.93	9.13	8.53		10.41	1.5	888-884-8099	Y
Lyrical U.S. Hedged Value Fund Investor Class	LYRDX	B-	C+	B	Up	1.65	2.86	8.87	7.72		10.32	1.5	888-884-8099	Y
M.D. Sass Equity Income Plus Fund Institutional Class	MDEIX	B-	C	B	Up	0.99	3.38	7.27	8.27		11.13	61.2		Y
M.D. Sass Equity Income Plus Fund Investor Class	MDEPX	B-	C	B	Up	0.90	3.19	6.99	7.20		11.1	61.2		Y
Madison Covered Call & Equity Income Fund Class A	MENAX	B-	C	B+	Down	2.31	4.25	7.17	13.83	38.99	8.89	129.7	800-767-0300	Y
Madison Covered Call & Equity Income Fund Class C	MENCX	B-	C	B+		2.23	3.90	6.43	11.43	34.07	8.47	129.7	800-767-0300	Y
Madison Covered Call & Equity Income Fund Class R6	MENRX	B-	C+	B+	Down	2.41	4.42	7.62	15.16	41.67	9.15	129.7	800-767-0300	Y
Madison Covered Call & Equity Income Fund Class Y	MENYX	B-	C+	B+	Down	2.43	4.46	7.56	14.77	40.89	9.08	129.7	800-767-0300	Y
MAI Managed Volatility Fund Institutional Class	MAIPX	B-	C+	B	Up	2.54	4.70	8.65	14.16	33.30	11.33	123.3	866-624-9584	Y
MAI Managed Volatility Fund Investor Class	DIVPX	B-	C+	B	Up	2.51	4.61	8.39	13.36	32.01	11.53	123.3	866-624-9584	Y
MFS® Managed Wealth Fund Class A	MNWAX	B-	C	A-	Up	0.69	0.99	6.67	6.49		10.17	23.0	877-960-6077	Y
MFS® Managed Wealth Fund Class B	MNWBX	B-	C	A-	Up	0.50	0.50	5.68	3.71		10.03	23.0	877-960-6077	Y
MFS® Managed Wealth Fund Class C	MNWCX	B-	C	A-	Up	0.40	0.50	5.72	3.72		9.98	23.0	877-960-6077	Y
MFS® Managed Wealth Fund Class I	MNWIX	B-	C	A-	Up	0.64	1.03	6.70	6.82		10.18	23.0	877-960-6077	Y
MFS® Managed Wealth Fund Class R1	MNWRX	B-	C	A-	Up	0.40	0.50	5.68	3.71		10.03	23.0	877-960-6077	Y
MFS® Managed Wealth Fund Class R2	MNWSX	B-	C	A-	Up	0.57	0.77	6.23	5.32		10.14	23.0	877-960-6077	Y
MFS® Managed Wealth Fund Class R3	MNWTX	B-	C	A-	Up	0.62	0.81	6.47	6.03		10.17	23.0	877-960-6077	Y
MFS® Managed Wealth Fund Class R4	MNWUX	B-	C	A-	Up	0.67	1.06	6.73	6.85		10.18	23.0	877-960-6077	Y
MFS® Managed Wealth Fund Class R6	MNWZX	B-	C	A-		0.62	1.01	6.68	6.80		10.18	23.0	877-960-6077	Y
Nationwide Long/Short Equity Fund Class R6	NWLFX	B-	C+	B-	Down	4.72	8.32	16.50	21.85	53.71	14.19	11.2	800-848-0920	Y
Nationwide Long/Short Equity Fund Inst Service Cls	NWLGX	B-	C+	B	Down	4.58	8.19	16.20	21.34	53.06	14.13	11.2	800-848-0920	Y
Natixis ASG Tactical U.S. Market Fund Class A	USMAX	B-	B-	B-	Down	8.31	13.97	25.36	24.79		14.11	97.9	800-862-4863	Y
Natixis ASG Tactical U.S. Market Fund Class C	USMCX	B-	B-	B-	Down	8.11	13.47	24.36	21.83		13.75	97.9	800-862-4863	Y
Natixis ASG Tactical U.S. Market Fund Class Y	USMYX	B-	B-	B-	Down	8.39	14.11	25.67	25.82		14.17	97.9	800-862-4863	Y
Navigator Equity Hedged Fund Class A	NAVAX	B-	C+	B	Up	2.84	7.23	11.76	11.92	28.10	8.82	44.5		Y
Navigator Equity Hedged Fund Class I	NAVIX	B-	C+	B	Up	2.92	7.39	12.02	12.72	29.80	8.74	44.5		Y
Nuveen Dow 30 Dynamic Overwrite Fund	DIAX	B	B	B		8.63	13.32	22.15	36.09	85.72	19.05	686.3	312-917-8146	Y
Nuveen Equity Long/Short Fund Class A	NELAX	B	B-	B+	Up	6.12	12.49	18.99	23.02	80.99	41.14	130.3	312-917-8146	Y
Nuveen Equity Long/Short Fund Class C	NELCX	B	C+	B+	Up	5.90	12.05	18.09	20.28	74.37	38.13	130.3	312-917-8146	Y
Nuveen Equity Long/Short Fund Class I	NELIX	B	B-	B+	Up	6.18	12.64	19.30	23.96	83.27	42.13	130.3	312-917-8146	Y
Nuveen NASDAQ 100 Dynamic Overwrite Fund	QQQX	B+	B+	B	Up	5.45	11.86	24.63	40.31	118.34	22.84	843.9	312-917-8146	Y
Nuveen S&P 500 Buy-Write Income Fund	BXMX	B	B-	B+	Up	2.58	6.04	12.90	28.51	57.62	14.3077	1,501	312-917-8146	Y

Category: Long/Short Equity (con't)

Fund Name	Ticker Symbol	RATINGS Overall Rating	Reward Rating	Risk Rating	Recent Up/ Downgrade	TOTAL RETURNS & PERFORMANCE 3-Month Total Return	6-Month Total Return	1-Year Total Return	3-Year Total Return	5-Year Total Return	ASSETS NAV	Total Assets (MIL)	NEW INVESTORS Telephone	Open to New Investors
Nuveen S&P 500 Dynamic Overwrite Fund	SPXX	B-	B-	B	Up	4.51	8.00	16.77	27.27	62.05	16.447	267.0	312-917-8146	Y
PF Equity Long/Short Fund Class P	US69448A6800	B-	C+	B+	Up	3.60	11.14	18.21			9.71	74.9	800-722-2333	Y
PIMCO EqS® Long/Short Fund Class A	PMHAX	B	C	A-	Up	1.70	1.19	9.66	11.25	48.46	11.55	534.3	866-746-2602	Y
PIMCO EqS® Long/Short Fund Class C	PMHCX	B	C	A-	Up	1.50	0.80	8.74	8.66	43.00	11.1	534.3	866-746-2602	Y
PIMCO EqS® Long/Short Fund Class D	PMHDX	B	C	A-	Up	1.70	1.19	9.54	11.21	48.49	11.57	534.3	866-746-2602	Y
PIMCO EqS® Long/Short Fund Class P	PMHBX	B	C+	A-	Up	1.76	1.26	9.82	12.02	50.30	11.7	534.3	866-746-2602	Y
PIMCO EqS® Long/Short Fund Institutional Class	PMHIX	B-	C+	B	Up	1.75	1.34	9.95	12.39	51.20	11.78	534.3	866-746-2602	Y
PIMCO EqS® Long/Short Fund Institutional Class	PROAX	B-	C+	B	Up	6.15	6.52	15.76	11.14	39.93	10.79	534.3	855-224-7204	Y
PIMCO EqS® Long/Short Fund Institutional Class	PROCX	B-	C+	B	Up	6.07	6.16	14.95	8.73	34.74	10.44	534.3	855-224-7204	Y
Prudential QMA Long-Short Equity Fund Class A	PLHAX	B	C+	A+	Up	3.15	6.96	8.69	22.21		12.75	418.4	800-225-1852	Y
Prudential QMA Long-Short Equity Fund Class C	PLHCX	B	C+	A-	Up	2.98	6.52	7.91	19.55		12.41	418.4	800-225-1852	Y
Prudential QMA Long-Short Equity Fund Class Q	PLHQX	B	C+	A-	Up	3.29	7.07	9.06	23.21		12.87	418.4	800-225-1852	Y
Prudential QMA Long-Short Equity Fund Class Z	PLHZX	B	C+	A-	Up	3.29	7.07	8.97	23.11		12.87	418.4	800-225-1852	Y
Pzena Long/Short Value Fund Institutional Class	PZILX	B-	C+	B	Up	1.89	3.15	3.05	13.49		10.78	6.6		Y
Pzena Long/Short Value Fund Investor Class	PZVLX	B-	C+	B	Up	1.81	3.09	2.89	12.70		10.67	6.6		Y
Rational Iron Horse Fund Class A	IRHAX	B-	C	B	Up	1.78	4.16	8.61	11.19	38.74	10.57	17.1	800-253-0412	Y
Rational Iron Horse Fund Class I	IRHIX	B-	C	B	Up	1.87	4.28	8.83	12.15	40.68	10.58	17.1	800-253-0412	Y
RiverPark Long/Short Opportunity Fund Institutional Class	RLSIX	B-	C+	B-	Down	2.15	7.36	22.09	20.11	31.21	12.48	89.5	888-564-4517	Y
RiverPark Long/Short Opportunity Fund Retail Class	RLSFX	B-	C+	B-	Down	2.17	7.34	21.89	19.44	30.00	12.38	89.5	888-564-4517	Y
RMB Mendon Financial Long/Short Fund Class A	RMBFX	B-	C+	B		-1.22	0.34	-3.07	21.36	71.47	17.67	249.5		Y
RMB Mendon Financial Long/Short Fund Class C	RMBCX	B-	C+	B		-1.38	0.00	-3.75	18.72	65.38	16.39	249.5		Y
RMB Mendon Financial Long/Short Fund Class I	RMBIX	B-	B-	B		-1.16	0.50	-2.78	22.31	72.81	17.82	249.5		
Russell Investments Strategic Call Overwriting Fund Cls S	ROWSX	B	B-	B+		4.58	8.08	15.90	31.99	50.06	13.94	101.8	800-426-7969	Y
Salient Tactical Growth Fund Class A	FTAGX	B-	C	B	Up	3.91	5.96	10.39	10.83	31.97	26.15	398.0	866-667-9228	Y
Salient Tactical Growth Fund Class C	FTGOX	B-	C	B	Up	3.79	5.71	9.91	9.34	29.04	25.04	398.0	866-667-9228	Y
Salient Tactical Growth Fund Institutional Class	FTGWX	B-	C+	B		4.03	6.23	10.90	12.48	35.32	27.41	398.0	866-667-9228	Y
Salient Tactical Growth Fund Investor Class	FFTGX	B-	C+	B	Up	3.97	6.06	10.57	11.35	32.99	26.56	398.0	866-667-9228	Y
Salient Tactical Plus Fund Class A	SBTAX	B-	C	B		6.81	8.30	8.30	10.82	37.36	11.4	29.9	866-667-9228	Y
Salient Tactical Plus Fund Class F	BTPIX	B-	C+	B	Up	6.97	8.63	8.91	12.55	40.19	11.6	29.9	866-667-9228	Y
Salient Tactical Plus Fund Class I	SBTIX	B-	C+	B	Down	6.86	8.44	8.54	11.43	38.80	11.47	29.9	866-667-9228	Y
Schwab Hedged Equity Fund™	SWHEX	B	C+	A+		2.72	6.88	7.77	20.89	56.47	17.13	254.0	877-824-5615	Y
The Covered Bridge Fund Class A	TCBAX	B-	C+	B	Down	3.01	6.32	9.45	19.77		10.14	62.9		Y
The Covered Bridge Fund Class I	TCBIX	B-	C+	B	Down	3.14	6.42	9.68	20.65		10.11	62.9		Y
Thornburg Long/Short Equity Fund Class I	THLSX	B	B	B-	Up	4.79	7.29	16.86	20.87	57.93	11.32	103.6	800-847-0200	Y
Touchstone Dynamic Equity Fund Class A	TDEAX	B	C+	A+		3.16	7.03	7.17	19.30	49.84	16.05	117.4	800-543-0407	Y
Touchstone Dynamic Equity Fund Class C	TDECX	B	C+	A+		2.99	6.59	6.37	16.59	44.33	14.89	117.4	800-543-0407	Y
Touchstone Dynamic Equity Fund Class Y	TDEYX	B	C+	A+		3.30	7.23	7.58	20.49	52.14	16.32	117.4	800-543-0407	Y
Touchstone Dynamic Equity Fund Institutional Class	TDELX	B	C+	A+		3.28	7.19	7.54	20.38	52.14	16.38	117.4	800-543-0407	Y
Virtus Rampart Low Volatility Equity Fund Class A	VLVAX	B-	C	B+	Up	2.37	3.45	7.86	7.65		11.41	2.5	800-243-1574	Y
Virtus Rampart Low Volatility Equity Fund Class C	VLVCX	B-	C	B+	Up	2.31	3.16	7.09	5.33		11.13	2.5	800-243-1574	Y
Virtus Rampart Low Volatility Equity Fund Class I	VLVIX	B-	C	A-	Up	2.48	3.66	8.17	8.53		11.39	2.5	800-243-1574	Y

Category: Market Neutral

Fund Name	Ticker Symbol	RATINGS: Overall Rating	Reward Rating	Risk Rating	Recent Up/ Downgrade	TOTAL RETURNS & PERFORMANCE: 3-Month Total Return	6-Month Total Return	1-Year Total Return	3-Year Total Return	5-Year Total Return	ASSETS: NAV	Total Assets (MIL)	NEW INVESTORS: Telephone	Open to New Investors
1290 VT GAMCO Mergers & Acquisitions Portfolio Class IA	US2689545679	B	C+	A-	Up	1.50	4.13	6.22	16.88	33.12		240.7	877-222-2144	Y
1290 VT GAMCO Mergers & Acquisitions Portfolio Class IB	US29364E7444	B	C+	A-	Up	1.51	4.07	6.16	16.88	33.09		240.7	877-222-2144	Y
1290 VT GAMCO Mergers & Acquisitions Portfolio Class K	US26883L6478	B	C+	A-	Up	1.58	4.26	6.50	17.75	34.80		240.7	877-222-2144	Y
AC Alternatives® Market Neutral Value Fund I Class	ACVKX	B-	C	A-	Up	0.93	1.40	1.88	9.64	15.38	10.62	612.4	800-444-4015	
American Beacon Ionic Strategic Arbitrage Fund Class Y	IONYX	B-	C	A-	Up	0.05	-0.05	-0.25	5.86		8.36	106.3	800-658-5811	Y
AQR Equity Market Neutral Fund Class I	QMNIX	B-	C	B+		0.86	4.70	5.83	31.35		12.25	2,160	203-742-3600	Y
AQR Equity Market Neutral Fund Class N	QMNNX	B-	C	B+		0.75	4.50	5.55	30.28		12.21	2,160	203-742-3600	Y
AQR Equity Market Neutral Fund Class R6	QMNRX	B-	C	B+		0.85	4.68	5.90	31.40		12.25	2,160	203-742-3600	Y
BlackRock Event Driven Equity Fund Institutional Shares	BILPX	B-	C	A-	Up	-0.91	-0.07	7.14	8.78	63.27	9.03	229.3	800-441-7762	Y
BlackRock Event Driven Equity Fund Investor A Shares	BALPX	B-	C	A-	Up	-1.00	-0.25	6.86	7.99	61.04	8.7	229.3	800-441-7762	Y
BlackRock Event Driven Equity Fund Investor C Shares	BCLPX	B-	C	B+	Up	-1.19	-0.60	6.15	5.64	55.35	7.9	229.3	800-441-7762	Y
Calamos Market Neutral Income Class T	CVSTX	B-	C	B+	Up	0.44	1.63	4.34	10.54	18.53		4,634	800-582-6959	Y
Calamos Market Neutral Income Fund Class A	CVSIX	B-	C	B+		1.07	1.82	4.56	10.36	19.71	13.23	4,780	800-582-6959	Y
Calamos Market Neutral Income Fund Class C	CVSCX	B-	C	B	Up	0.86	1.41	3.80	7.86	15.35	13.45	4,780	800-582-6959	Y
Calamos Market Neutral Income Fund Class R	CVSRX	B-	C	B	Up	1.00	1.68	4.31	9.58	18.26	13.18	4,780	800-582-6959	Y
Calamos Market Neutral Income Fund Institutional Class	CMNIX	B-	C	B+		1.07	1.90	4.73	11.09	21.21	13.07	4,780	800-582-6959	Y
Gabelli ABC Fund Class Advisor	GADVX	B-	C	A	Up	0.43	0.82	2.02	7.04	13.38	10.27	1,429	914-921-5135	Y
Gabelli ABC Fund Class Class AAA	GABCX	B	C	A	Up	0.42	0.81	2.20	7.69	14.74	10.38	1,429	914-921-5135	Y
Gabelli Enterprise Mergers and Acquisitions Fund Class A	EMAAX	B	C+	A-	Up	0.63	2.29	5.10	14.56	32.74	14.7	168.1	914-921-5135	Y
Gabelli Enterprise Mergers and Acquisitions Fund Class AAA	EAAAX	B	C+	A-	Up	0.62	2.39	5.32	15.27	34.07	14.93	168.1	914-921-5135	Y
Gabelli Enterprise Mergers and Acquisitions Fund Class C	EMACX	B	C+	A-	Up	0.47	2.04	4.54	12.72	29.12	13.48	168.1	914-921-5135	Y
Gabelli Enterprise Mergers and Acquisitions Fund Class Y	EMAYX	B-	C+	B	Up	0.72	2.54	5.60	16.18	35.73	15.7	168.1	914-921-5135	Y
Gabelli Enterprise Mergers and Acquisitions Fund T	EMATX	B	C+	A-	Up	0.63	2.43	5.36	15.33	34.06	14.72	168.1	914-921-5135	Y
Grant Park Absolute Return Fund Class A	GPHAX	B-	C+	B	Up	6.41	6.41	16.26			11.08	29.7	866-501-4758	Y
Grant Park Absolute Return Fund Class C	GPHCX	B-	C+	B	Up	6.37	6.17	15.40			10.83	29.7	866-501-4758	Y
Grant Park Absolute Return Fund Class I	GPHIX	B-	C+	B	Up	6.58	6.58	16.51			11.14	29.7	866-501-4758	Y
Grant Park Absolute Return Fund Class N	GPHNX	B-	C+	B	Up	6.52	6.52	16.29			11.07	29.7	866-501-4758	Y
Highland Merger Arbitrage Fund Class A	HMEAX	B-	C	A-	Up	-0.35	-0.70	5.14			20.17	37.3	877-665-1287	Y
Highland Merger Arbitrage Fund Class C	HMECX	B-	C	A-	Up	-0.54	-1.07	4.43			20.12	37.3	877-665-1287	Y
Highland Merger Arbitrage Fund Class Z	HMEZX	B-	C	A-	Up	-0.27	-0.52	5.45			20.32	37.3	877-665-1287	Y
Nuveen Equity Market Neutral Fund Class A	NMAEX	B	C+	A-	Up	2.59	6.93	5.07	12.07		23.76	86.2	312-917-8146	Y
Nuveen Equity Market Neutral Fund Class C	NMECX	B-	C	A-	Up	2.41	6.55	4.32	9.61		22.95	86.2	312-917-8146	Y
Nuveen Equity Market Neutral Fund Class I	NIMEX	B	C+	A-	Up	2.60	7.03	5.33	12.95		24.04	86.2	312-917-8146	Y
SilverPepper Merger Arbitrage Fund Advisor Class	SPABX	B	C	A+	Up	0.48	0.39	1.58	14.25		11.01	66.7		Y
SilverPepper Merger Arbitrage Fund Institutional Class	SPAIX	B	C	A+	Up	0.57	0.39	1.66	15.25			66.7		Y
The Arbitrage Fund Class A	ARGAX	B-	C	B+	Up	0.07	0.30	2.57	6.67	9.74	12.69	1,866	800-285-4485	Y
The Arbitrage Fund Class Institutional	ARBNX	B	C	A	Up	0.13	0.50	2.86	7.53	11.07	13.08	1,866	800-285-4485	Y
The Arbitrage Fund Class R	ARBFX	B-	C	A	Up	0.09	0.32	2.59	6.78	9.77	12.71	1,866	800-285-4485	Y
The Merger Fund® Institutional Class	MERIX	B-	C	A-	Up	0.03	0.41	2.73	5.06	11.27	15.83	2,408		Y
Touchstone Arbitrage Fund Class A	TMARX	B-	C	A-	Up	-0.56	-0.66	0.11	7.53		9.74	239.1	800-543-0407	Y
Touchstone Arbitrage Fund Class Y	TMAYX	B-	C	A	Up	-0.46	-0.56	0.30	8.34		9.86	239.1	800-543-0407	Y
Touchstone Arbitrage Fund Institutional	TARBX	B	C	A	Up	-0.56	-0.46	0.40	8.66		9.9	239.1	800-543-0407	Y
Touchstone Merger Arbitrage Fund Class A	TMGAX	B	C	A	Up	-0.37	-0.37	1.18	6.99	10.59	10.37	193.1	800-543-0407	Y
Touchstone Merger Arbitrage Fund Class C	TMGCX	B	C	A+	Up	-0.58	-0.77	0.46	4.52	6.27	9.85	193.1	800-543-0407	Y
Touchstone Merger Arbitrage Fund Class Y	TMGYX	B	C	A+	Up	-0.37	-0.28	1.44	7.80	11.99	10.53	193.1	800-543-0407	Y
Touchstone Merger Arbitrage Fund Institutional Class	TMGLX	B	C	A+	Up	-0.28	-0.19	1.62	8.17	12.53	10.59	193.1	800-543-0407	Y
Victory CEMP Market Neutral Income Fund Class A	CBHAX	B-	C	B+	Up	1.59	3.92	6.77	10.88	9.08	9.63	56.4	800-539-3863	Y
Victory CEMP Market Neutral Income Fund Class C	CBHCX	B-	C	A-	Up	1.28	3.47	5.88	8.28	4.86	9.55	56.4	800-539-3863	Y
Victory CEMP Market Neutral Income Fund Class I	CBHIX	B	C	A+	Up	1.56	3.92	6.99	11.58	10.47	9.66	56.4	800-539-3863	Y
Vivaldi Merger Arbitrage Fund Class A	VARAX	B-	C	A-	Up	-0.86	-0.11	2.11	8.61	21.60	10.36	524.8		Y
Vivaldi Merger Arbitrage Fund Class I	VARBX	B-	C	A	Up	-0.76	0.07	2.39	9.57	23.29	10.44	524.8		Y

Category: Moderate Allocation

Fund Name	Ticker Symbol	RATINGS: Overall Rating	Reward Rating	Risk Rating	Recent Up/ Downgrade	TOTAL RETURNS & PERFORMANCE: 3-Month Total Return	6-Month Total Return	1-Year Total Return	3-Year Total Return	5-Year Total Return	ASSETS: NAV	Total Assets (MIL)	NEW INVESTORS: Telephone	Open to New Investors
1919 Socially Responsive Balanced Fund Class A	SSIAX	B-	C+	B	Down	4.64	9.34	16.35	19.71	57.05	17.94	127.0		Y
1919 Socially Responsive Balanced Fund Class B	SESIX	B-	C+	B	Down	4.45	8.94	15.32	16.63	49.56	17.48	127.0		
1919 Socially Responsive Balanced Fund Class C	SESLX	B-	C+	B	Down	4.46	8.93	15.47	17.09	51.41	18.11	127.0		Y
1919 Socially Responsive Balanced Fund Class I	LMRNX	B-	C+	B	Down	4.74	9.51	16.71	20.61	59.12	17.91	127.0		Y
AB All Market Total Return Portfolio Advisor Class	ABWYX	B-	C+	B	Down	2.29	4.48	11.48	16.00	41.16	14.92	904.9	212-969-1000	Y
AB All Market Total Return Portfolio Class A	ABWAX	B-	C+	B	Down	2.20	4.33	11.21	15.14	39.22	14.83	904.9	212-969-1000	Y
AB All Market Total Return Portfolio Class C	ABWCX	B-	C+	B+	Down	2.04	3.98	10.41	12.57	34.22	14.77	904.9	212-969-1000	Y
AB All Market Total Return Portfolio Class I	ABWIX	B-	C+	B	Down	2.23	4.36	11.38	15.85	40.90	15.07	904.9	212-969-1000	Y
AB All Market Total Return Portfolio Class K	ABWKX	B-	C+	B	Down	2.15	4.29	11.10	14.75	38.69	14.79	904.9	212-969-1000	Y
AB Global Risk Allocation Fund Class A	CABNX	B-	C+	B	Down	3.64	6.58	11.78	15.14	24.13	16.42	282.0	212-969-1000	Y
AB Global Risk Allocation Fund Class B	CABBX	B-	C+	B	Up	3.38	6.11	10.88	12.45	19.44	14.91	282.0	212-969-1000	
AdvisorOne CLS Shelter Fund Class N	CLSHX	B-	B-	B-	Down	6.27	11.12	20.88	28.41	78.37	14.56	171.1		Y
AIG Active Allocation Fund Class A	FBAAX	B-	C+	B	Down	3.52	7.38	14.49	19.55	52.99	17.67	155.3	800-858-8850	Y
AIG Active Allocation Fund Class B	FBABX	B-	C+	B	Down	3.40	7.03	13.71	17.25	47.97	17.52	155.3	800-858-8850	Y
AIG Active Allocation Fund Class C	FBACX	B-	C+	B	Down	3.40	7.03	13.74	17.35	48.23	17.59	155.3	800-858-8850	Y
AIG Active Allocation Fund Class I	US86704B8550	B-	C+	B	Down	3.56	7.34	14.43	19.49	52.85	17.71	155.3	800-858-8850	Y
AIG Multi-Asset Allocation Fund Class A	FASAX	B-	C+	B-	Down	4.03	8.04	13.80	19.92	54.97	18.36	274.7	800-858-8850	Y
AIG Multi-Asset Allocation Fund Class B	FMABX	B-	C+	B-	Down	3.84	7.62	12.96	17.40	49.65	18.36	274.7	800-858-8850	Y
AIG Multi-Asset Allocation Fund Class C	FMATX	B-	C+	B-	Down	3.85	7.63	13.04	17.60	50.08	18.34	274.7	800-858-8850	Y
AIG Multi-Asset Allocation Fund Class I	US86704F1049	B-	C+	B-	Down	4.04	7.93	13.68	19.65	54.46	18.35	274.7	800-858-8850	Y
Alger Balanced Portfolio Class I-2	ABLOX	B	B-	B		4.28	7.38	15.44	26.40	62.26	17.2	47.4	800-992-3863	Y
All Asset Growth – Alt 20 Portfolio Class IA	US26884M6930	B-	C+	B-	Down	4.10	7.86	15.90	21.14	44.26		344.2	877-222-2144	Y
All Asset Growth – Alt 20 Portfolio Class IB	US29364E3062	B-	C+	B	Down	4.14	8.47	15.91	21.15	44.29		344.2	877-222-2144	Y
All Asset Growth – Alt 20 Portfolio Class K	US26883L8037	B-	C+	B-	Down	4.21	8.55	16.14	22.01	46.06		344.2	877-222-2144	Y
AllianzGI Global Dynamic Allocation Fund Admin Cls	AGFAX	B-	C+	B	Up	3.49	7.96	16.73	16.86	37.33	20.26	290.0	800-498-5413	Y
AllianzGI Global Dynamic Allocation Fund Class A	ASGAX	B-	C+	B	Up	3.54	8.01	16.80	16.91	37.33	20.31	290.0	800-498-5413	Y
AllianzGI Global Dynamic Allocation Fund Class C	ASACX	B-	C+	B	Up	3.29	7.58	15.89	14.20	32.03	19.79	290.0	800-498-5413	Y
AllianzGI Global Dynamic Allocation Fund Class P	AGSPX	B-	C+	B	Up	3.59	8.07	17.01	17.49	38.45	20.17	290.0	800-498-5413	Y
AllianzGI Global Dynamic Allocation Fund Class R	ASFRX	B-	C+	B	Up	3.41	7.81	16.33	15.87	35.47	20.15	290.0	800-498-5413	Y
AllianzGI Global Dynamic Allocation Fund Class R6	ADYFX	B-	C+	B+	Down	3.59	8.17	17.09	17.94	39.27	20.23	290.0	800-498-5413	Y
AllianzGI Global Dynamic Allocation Fund Institutional Cls	AGAIX	B-	C+	B+	Down	3.58	8.09	17.04	17.74	39.04	20.3	290.0	800-498-5413	Y
ALPS/Stadion Core ETF Portfolio Class I	US02110B1089	B-	C+	B-	Up	3.41	6.57	13.83	13.82		11.83	9.3	866-759-5679	Y
American Beacon Balanced Fund Advisor Class	ABLSX	B-	C+	B-	Down	3.84	7.01	11.95	18.80	57.82	15.84	356.1	800-658-5811	Y
American Beacon Balanced Fund C Class	ABCCX	B-	C+	B	Down	3.81	6.75	11.34	16.62	52.71	15.09	356.1	800-658-5811	Y
American Beacon Balanced Fund Class A	ABFAX	B-	C+	B-	Down	4.02	7.20	12.20	19.30	58.61	14.92	356.1	800-658-5811	Y
American Beacon Balanced Fund Class Y	ACBYX	B-	C+	B-	Down	3.99	7.28	12.44	20.55	61.44	16.88	356.1	800-658-5811	Y
American Beacon Balanced Fund Institutional Class	AADBX	B-	C+	B-	Down	3.99	7.23	12.49	20.67	61.92	16.79	356.1	800-658-5811	Y
American Beacon Balanced Fund Investor Class	AABPX	B-	C+	B-	Down	3.92	7.11	12.18	19.44	59.23	14.94	356.1	800-658-5811	Y
American Century Balanced Fund I Class	ABINX	B-	C+	B	Up	4.22	7.52	14.27	18.73	55.90	18.83	899.6	800-444-4015	Y
American Century Balanced Fund Investor Class	TWBIX	B-	C+	B	Up	4.11	7.36	14.05	17.97	54.30	18.82	899.6	800-444-4015	Y
American Century Balanced Fund R5 Class	ABGNX	B-	C+	B	Up	4.22	7.53	14.27	18.21	54.61	18.83	899.6	800-444-4015	Y
American Century Inv One Choice Port®: Moderate Inv Cls	AOMIX	B-	C+	B	Down	3.52	7.24	15.43	20.32	51.58	15.85	1,933	800-444-4015	Y
American Century Inv One Choice Port®: Moderate R Cls	AORMX	B-	C+	B	Down	3.39	6.96	14.85	18.59	47.92	15.85	1,933	800-444-4015	Y
American Century Strategic Allocation: Moderate Fund A Cls	ACOAX	B	C+	B+	Up	3.35	7.00	14.88	18.59	47.73	6.85	1,292	800-444-4015	Y
American Century Strategic Allocation: Moderate Fund C Cls	ASTCX	B-	C+	B	Down	3.33	6.65	14.18	16.16	42.49	6.79	1,292	800-444-4015	Y
American Century Strategic Allocation: Moderate Fund I Cls	ASAMX	B-	C+	B	Down	3.60	7.22	15.34	20.25	51.08	6.87	1,292	800-444-4015	Y
American Century Strategic Alloc: Moderate Fund Inv Cls	TWSMX	B-	C+	B	Down	3.56	7.12	15.13	19.54	49.59	6.87	1,292	800-444-4015	Y
American Century Strategic Allocation: Moderate Fund R Cls	ASMRX	B-	C+	B	Down	3.45	6.90	14.55	17.80	45.95	6.82	1,292	800-444-4015	Y
American Century Strategic Alloc: Moderate Fund R5 Cls	ASMUX	B-	C+	B	Down	3.61	7.38	15.29	19.71	49.79	6.88	1,292	800-444-4015	Y
American Century Strategic Alloc: Moderate Fund R6 Cls	ASMDX	B-	C+	B	Down	3.51	7.32	15.54	20.81	51.80	6.86	1,292	800-444-4015	Y
American Funds American Balanced Fund® Class 529-A	CLBAX	B	B-	A-		4.51	8.25	15.42	26.49	69.97	27.11	123,185	800-421-4225	Y
American Funds American Balanced Fund® Class 529-C	CLBCX	B	C+	B	Up	4.30	7.83	14.54	23.58	63.55	27.11	123,185	800-421-4225	Y

Category: Moderate Allocation (con't)

Fund Name	Ticker Symbol	RATINGS: Overall Rating	Reward Rating	Risk Rating	Recent Up/ Downgrade	TOTAL RETURNS & PERFORMANCE: 3-Month Total Return	6-Month Total Return	1-Year Total Return	3-Year Total Return	5-Year Total Return	ASSETS: NAV	Total Assets (MIL)	NEW INVESTORS: Telephone	Open to New Investors
American Funds American Balanced Fund® Class 529-E	CLBEX	B	C+	A-		4.44	8.08	15.10	25.55	67.90	27.09	123,185	800-421-4225	Y
American Funds American Balanced Fund® Class 529-F	CLBFX	B	B-	A-		4.56	8.37	15.68	27.32	71.86	27.09	123,185	800-421-4225	Y
American Funds American Balanced Fund® Class A	ABALX	B	B-	A-		4.51	8.27	15.47	26.76	70.72	27.15	123,185	800-421-4225	Y
American Funds American Balanced Fund® Class C	BALCX	B	C+	B+	Up	4.30	7.81	14.58	23.80	64.06	26.98	123,185	800-421-4225	Y
American Funds American Balanced Fund® Class F-1	BALFX	B	B-	A-		4.49	8.23	15.39	26.52	70.13	27.13	123,185	800-421-4225	Y
American Funds American Balanced Fund® Class F-2	AMBFX	B	B-	A-		4.56	8.33	15.69	27.47	72.31	27.13	123,185	800-421-4225	Y
American Funds American Balanced Fund® Class F-3	AFMBX	B	B-	A-		4.59	8.43	15.81	27.14	71.23	27.14	123,185	800-421-4225	Y
American Funds American Balanced Fund® Class R-1	RLBAX	B	C+	B+	Up	4.29	7.80	14.55	23.76	64.01	26.96	123,185	800-421-4225	Y
American Funds American Balanced Fund® Class R-2	RLBBX	B	C+	B+	Up	4.29	7.85	14.57	23.89	64.29	26.98	123,185	800-421-4225	Y
American Funds American Balanced Fund® Class R-2E	RAMHX	B	C+	A-		4.39	7.98	14.88	25.42	68.00	27.05	123,185	800-421-4225	Y
American Funds American Balanced Fund® Class R-3	RLBCX	B	C+	A-		4.40	8.08	15.05	25.43	67.80	27.01	123,185	800-421-4225	Y
American Funds American Balanced Fund® Class R-4	RLBEX	B	B-	A-		4.50	8.21	15.43	26.57	70.25	27.1	123,185	800-421-4225	Y
American Funds American Balanced Fund® Class R-5	RLBFX	B	B-	A-		4.61	8.39	15.77	27.71	72.84	27.18	123,185	800-421-4225	Y
American Funds American Balanced Fund® Class R-5E	RLEFX	B	B-	A-		4.56	8.39	15.70	27.14	71.24	27.12	123,185	800-421-4225	Y
American Funds American Balanced Fund® Class R-6	RLBGX	B	B-	A-		4.59	8.42	15.84	27.92	73.27	27.16	123,185	800-421-4225	Y
American Funds Balanced Portfolio Class 529-A	CBAAX	B-	C+	B	Up	3.63	7.36	16.63	23.53	57.41	14.81	6,898	800-421-4225	Y
American Funds Balanced Portfolio Class 529-C	CBPCX	B-	C+	B	Up	3.38	6.93	15.72	20.54	51.28	14.75	6,898	800-421-4225	Y
American Funds Balanced Portfolio Class 529-E	CBAEX	B-	C+	B	Up	3.49	7.23	16.36	22.60	55.40	14.78	6,898	800-421-4225	Y
American Funds Balanced Portfolio Class 529-F-1	CBAFX	B-	C+	B	Up	3.61	7.41	16.87	24.32	59.08	14.82	6,898	800-421-4225	Y
American Funds Balanced Portfolio Class A	BLPAX	B-	C+	B	Up	3.63	7.38	16.70	23.71	57.96	14.81	6,898	800-421-4225	Y
American Funds Balanced Portfolio Class C	BLPCX	B-	C+	B	Up	3.43	6.93	15.76	20.87	51.93	14.73	6,898	800-421-4225	Y
American Funds Balanced Portfolio Class F-1	BLPFX	B-	C+	B	Up	3.56	7.37	16.65	23.55	57.60	14.81	6,898	800-421-4225	Y
American Funds Balanced Portfolio Class F-2	BLPEX	B-	C+	B	Up	3.70	7.51	16.93	24.56	59.76	14.83	6,898	800-421-4225	Y
American Funds Balanced Portfolio Class F-3	BLPDX	B-	C+	B	Up	3.73	7.57	17.07	24.81	60.06	14.81	6,898	800-421-4225	Y
American Funds Balanced Portfolio Class R-1	RBAAX	B	C+	A-	Up	3.42	6.97	15.76	20.86	51.88	14.76	6,898	800-421-4225	Y
American Funds Balanced Portfolio Class R-2	RBABX	B-	C+	B	Up	3.44	7.01	15.79	20.92	51.78	14.74	6,898	800-421-4225	Y
American Funds Balanced Portfolio Class R-2E	RBBEX	B-	C+	B	Up	3.40	7.07	16.13	22.62	55.72	14.81	6,898	800-421-4225	Y
American Funds Balanced Portfolio Class R-3	RBACX	B-	C+	B	Up	3.55	7.23	16.30	22.52	55.32	14.78	6,898	800-421-4225	Y
American Funds Balanced Portfolio Class R-4	RBAEX	B-	C+	B	Up	3.63	7.39	16.70	23.66	57.85	14.81	6,898	800-421-4225	Y
American Funds Balanced Portfolio Class R-5	RBAFX	B-	C+	B	Up	3.64	7.46	16.99	24.73	59.95	14.83	6,898	800-421-4225	Y
American Funds Balanced Portfolio Class R-5E	RGPFX	B	C+	A-	Up	3.70	7.50	16.91	24.47	59.62	14.82	6,898	800-421-4225	Y
American Funds Balanced Portfolio Class R-6	RBAGX	B-	C+	B	Up	3.66	7.49	17.04	24.92	60.34	14.83	6,898	800-421-4225	Y
American Funds College 2027 Fund Class 529-A	CSTAX	B	C+	A-	Up	2.37	5.40	11.77	17.23	50.24	12.65	1,076	800-421-4225	Y
American Funds College 2027 Fund Class 529-C	CTSCX	B-	C+	B	Up	2.10	4.92	10.87	14.48	44.30	12.52	1,076	800-421-4225	Y
American Funds College 2027 Fund Class 529-E	CTSEX	B	C+	B+	Up	2.30	5.19	11.48	16.41	48.33	12.58	1,076	800-421-4225	Y
American Funds College 2027 Fund Class 529F1	CTSFX	B	C+	A-	Up	2.40	5.51	12.04	18.02	51.77	12.69	1,076	800-421-4225	Y
American Funds Income Portfolio Class 529-A	CIPAX	B-	C+	B	Up	2.36	5.51	11.42	18.59	43.36	12.7	4,631	800-421-4225	Y
American Funds Income Portfolio Class 529-C	CIPCX	B-	C+	B	Up	2.18	5.05	10.58	15.97	37.98	12.66	4,631	800-421-4225	Y
American Funds Income Portfolio Class 529-E	CIPEX	B-	C+	B	Up	2.36	5.37	11.15	17.89	41.72	12.7	4,631	800-421-4225	Y
American Funds Income Portfolio Class 529-F-1	CIPFX	B-	C+	B	Up	2.42	5.63	11.65	19.51	44.93	12.71	4,631	800-421-4225	Y
American Funds Income Portfolio Class A	INPAX	B-	C+	B	Up	2.45	5.54	11.56	18.96	43.89	12.71	4,631	800-421-4225	Y
American Funds Income Portfolio Class C	INPCX	B-	C+	B	Up	2.24	5.13	10.70	16.22	38.48	12.65	4,631	800-421-4225	Y
American Funds Income Portfolio Class F-1	INPFX	B-	C+	B	Up	2.36	5.51	11.42	18.81	43.58	12.71	4,631	800-421-4225	Y
American Funds Income Portfolio Class F-2	INPEX	B-	C+	B	Up	2.43	5.65	11.70	19.72	45.54	12.72	4,631	800-421-4225	Y
American Funds Income Portfolio Class F-3	INPDX	B-	C+	B	Up	2.47	5.72	11.93	19.97	46.04	12.7	4,631	800-421-4225	Y
American Funds Income Portfolio Class R-1	RNCAX	B-	C+	B	Up	2.22	5.19	10.73	16.25	38.50	12.67	4,631	800-421-4225	Y
American Funds Income Portfolio Class R-2	RINBX	B-	C+	B	Up	2.24	5.13	10.70	16.21	38.34	12.66	4,631	800-421-4225	Y
American Funds Income Portfolio Class R-2E	RNBEX	B-	C+	B	Up	2.24	5.26	10.93	18.38	42.59	12.7	4,631	800-421-4225	Y
American Funds Income Portfolio Class R-3	RNCCX	B-	C+	B	Up	2.36	5.37	11.16	17.81	41.57	12.69	4,631	800-421-4225	Y
American Funds Income Portfolio Class R-4	RINEX	B-	C+	B	Up	2.45	5.52	11.46	18.92	43.85	12.71	4,631	800-421-4225	Y
American Funds Income Portfolio Class R-5	RINFX	B-	C+	B	Up	2.45	5.68	11.85	19.88	45.93	12.73	4,631	800-421-4225	Y
American Funds Income Portfolio Class R-5E	RGOFX	B-	C+	B	Up	2.52	5.65	11.80	19.74	45.76	12.7	4,631	800-421-4225	Y

Category: Moderate Allocation (con't)

Fund Name	Ticker Symbol	RATINGS: Overall Rating	Reward Rating	Risk Rating	Recent Up/ Downgrade	TOTAL RETURNS & PERFORMANCE: 3-Month Total Return	6-Month Total Return	1-Year Total Return	3-Year Total Return	5-Year Total Return	ASSETS: NAV	Total Assets (MIL)	NEW INVESTORS: Telephone	Open to New Investors
American Funds Income Portfolio Class R-6	RINGX	B-	C+	B	Up	2.46	5.71	11.82	20.07	46.20	12.72	4,631	800-421-4225	Y
American Independence JAForlines Global Tact Alloc Cls A	AARMX	B	C+	B+	Up	2.99	7.58	17.01	20.88		11.82	141.6		Y
American Independence JAForlines Global Tact Alloc Cls C	ACRMX	B	C+	B+	Up	2.88	7.27	16.35	18.75		11.64	141.6		Y
American Independence JAForlines Global Tact Alloc Inst Cl	RMAIX	B	C+	B+	Up	3.15	7.83	17.48	22.21		11.87	141.6		Y
AMG Chicago Equity Partners Balanced Fund Class I	MBESX	B	C+	B+	Up	4.65	8.03	15.71	23.37	61.94	17.19	199.6	800-835-3879	Y
AMG Chicago Equity Partners Balanced Fund Class N	MBEAX	B	C+	B+	Up	4.59	7.95	15.53	22.75	60.36	17.03	199.6	800-835-3879	Y
AMG Chicago Equity Partners Balanced Fund Class Z	MBEYX	B	C+	B+	Up	4.68	8.15	15.89	23.72	62.45	17.19	199.6	800-835-3879	Y
AMG FQ Global Risk-Balanced Fund Class I	MMASX	B-	C+	B	Up	3.44	7.74	15.81	24.13	29.82	16.02	63.0	800-835-3879	Y
AMG FQ Global Risk-Balanced Fund Class N	MMAVX	B-	C+	B	Up	3.29	7.53	15.35	22.62	27.21	15.97	63.0	800-835-3879	Y
AMG FQ Global Risk-Balanced Fund Class Z	MMAFX	B-	C+	B	Up	3.45	7.73	15.87	24.39	30.33	16.01	63.0	800-835-3879	Y
AMG Managers Montag & Caldwell Balanced Fund Class I	MOBIX	B	C+	A-		3.67	6.26	15.38	17.54	45.86	22.06	21.6	800-835-3879	Y
AMG Managers Montag & Caldwell Balanced Fund Class N	MOBAX	B	C+	A-		3.63	6.24	15.24	17.25	45.19	22.15	21.6	800-835-3879	Y
Arrow DWA Tactical Fund Class A	DWTFX	B-	C+	B	Up	5.00	9.92	16.04	13.88	56.52	10.48	188.5	877-277-6933	Y
Arrow DWA Tactical Fund Class C	DWTTX	B-	C+	B	Up	4.79	9.55	15.27	11.34	50.79	9.85	188.5	877-277-6933	Y
Arrow DWA Tactical Fund Institutional Class	DWTNX	B-	C+	B	Up	5.05	10.07	16.40	14.65	58.37	10.51	188.5	877-277-6933	Y
Astor Dynamic Allocation Fund Class A	ASTLX	B-	C+	B	Down	5.49	9.58	15.77	19.47	46.27	13.32	142.9	877-738-0333	Y
Astor Dynamic Allocation Fund Class C	ASTZX	B-	C+	B-	Down	5.34	9.16	14.90	16.80	40.86	12.85	142.9	877-738-0333	Y
Astor Dynamic Allocation Fund Class I	ASTIX	B-	C+	B	Down	5.59	9.75	16.09	20.42	48.14	13.34	142.9	877-738-0333	Y
AT Income Opportunities Fund Institutional Class	AWIIX	B-	C+	B-	Up	4.38	7.43	13.78	22.42		11.38	329.4		Y
ATAC Inflation Rotation Fund Investor Class Shares	ATACX	B+	A-	B+	Up	4.72	15.89	26.93	40.42	46.59	32.17	109.3		Y
AXA Balanced Strategy Fund Class IA	US2689543369	B-	C+	B	Up	2.67	5.10	9.98	15.10	38.86		3,656	877-222-2144	Y
AXA Balanced Strategy Fund Class IB	US2689543286	B-	C+	B	Up	2.60	5.10	9.90	15.09	38.70		3,656	877-222-2144	Y
AXA Charter Moderate Growth Portfolio Class B	US00248T6376	B-	C+	B	Down	2.93	6.31	12.93	15.84			24.0	877-222-2144	Y
AXA Moderate Allocation Portfolio Class K	US00247C5691	B-	C+	B	Up	2.79	5.51	11.40	16.22	38.17		8,094	877-222-2144	Y
AXA Moderate Growth Strategy Fund Class IB	US2689542940	B-	C+	B	Up	3.28	6.19	11.86	18.02	47.73		7,537	877-222-2144	Y
AXA Premier VIP Moderate Allocation Fund Class A	US4049924974	B-	C+	B	Up	2.68	5.26	11.06	15.29	36.39		8,094	877-222-2144	Y
AXA Premier VIP Moderate Allocation Fund Class B		B-	C+	B	Up	2.71	5.30	11.07	15.32	36.34		8,094	877-222-2144	Y
AXA/AB Dynamic Growth Portfolio Class IB	US29439V6719	B-	C	B	Up	3.99	7.33	14.89				514.8	877-222-2144	Y
AXA/AB Dynamic Moderate Growth Portfolio Class IB	US26884M6518	B-	C+	B	Up	3.35	6.35	12.98	15.59	43.45		2,779	877-222-2144	Y
AXA/Franklin Balanced Managed Volatility Portfolio Cls IA	US2689548152	B-	C+	B	Up	2.40	5.46	9.95	16.98	44.80		1,284	877-222-2144	Y
AXA/Franklin Balanced Managed Volatility Portfolio Cls IB	US2689547998	B-	C+	B	Up	2.40	5.46	9.95	16.98	44.64		1,284	877-222-2144	Y
AXA/Franklin Balanced Managed Volatility Portfolio Class K	US26883L6544	B-	C+	B	Up	2.55	5.62	10.32	17.86	46.65		1,284	877-222-2144	Y
AXA/Goldman Sachs Strategic Allocation Portfolio Class IB	US29439V6149	B-	C	B	Up	2.85	5.23	10.70				443.1	877-222-2144	Y
BlackRock 60/40 Target Allocation Fund Class K	BKGPX	B-	C+	B	Down	2.87	6.41	13.72	18.04	59.18	13.28	524.3	800-441-7762	Y
BlackRock 60/40 Target Allocation Fund Class R Shares	BRGPX	B-	C+	B	Down	2.67	6.04	12.99	16.76	57.45	13.05	524.3	800-441-7762	Y
BlackRock 60/40 Target Allocation Fund Inst Shares	BIGPX	B-	C+	B	Down	2.85	6.31	13.61	18.74	61.80	13.28	524.3	800-441-7762	Y
BlackRock 60/40 Target Allocation Fund Investor A Shares	BAGPX	B-	C+	B	Down	2.79	6.23	13.26	17.53	58.92	13.09	524.3	800-441-7762	Y
BlackRock 60/40 Target Allocation Fund Investor C Shares	BCGPX	B-	C+	B	Down	3.56	6.77	13.52	15.96	54.64	12.84	524.3	800-441-7762	Y
BlackRock Balanced Capital Fund Institutional Shares	MACPX	B-	B-	B	Down	3.39	7.15	14.61	24.14	68.41	22.7	1,071	800-441-7762	Y
BlackRock Balanced Capital Fund Investor A Shares	MDCPX	B-	C+	B	Down	3.28	6.95	14.24	23.07	65.95	22.62	1,071	800-441-7762	Y
BlackRock Balanced Capital Fund Investor B Shares	MBCPX	B-	C+	B	Up	1.94	4.15	10.36	16.15	53.48		1,071	800-441-7762	
BlackRock Balanced Capital Fund Investor C Shares	MCCPX	B-	C+	B	Up	3.10	6.54	13.34	20.27	59.73	19.78	1,071	800-441-7762	Y
BlackRock Balanced Capital Fund R Shares	MRBPX	B-	C+	B	Up	3.18	6.77	13.81	21.79	63.07	20.89	1,071	800-441-7762	Y
BlackRock Multi-Asset Income Portfolio Class K	BKMIX	B-	C+	B	Up	1.59	3.42	9.07	14.63	32.28	11.07	16,374	800-441-7762	Y
BlackRock Multi-Asset Income Portfolio Inst Shares	BIICX	B-	C+	B	Up	1.67	3.39	9.02	14.57	32.22	11.08	16,374	800-441-7762	Y
BlackRock Multi-Asset Income Portfolio Investor A Shares	BAICX	B-	C+	B	Up	1.61	3.26	8.75	13.72	30.58	11.07	16,374	800-441-7762	Y
BlackRock Multi-Asset Income Portfolio Investor C Shares	BCICX	B-	C	B	Up	1.32	2.88	7.96	11.10	25.66	11.05	16,374	800-441-7762	Y
BMO Balanced Allocation Fund Class I	BGRHX	B-	C+	B	Down	3.65	7.15	14.80	19.52	50.48	9.13	381.7	800-236-3863	Y
BMO Balanced Allocation Fund Class R3	BGRRX	B-	C+	B	Down	3.50	6.79	14.15	17.70	46.68	9.15	381.7	800-236-3863	Y
BMO Balanced Allocation Fund Class R6	BGRQX	B-	C+	B	Down	3.65	7.04	14.92	20.01	51.23	9.12	381.7	800-236-3863	Y
BMO Balanced Allocation Fund Class Y	BGRYX	B-	C+	B	Down	3.55	6.83	14.45	18.56	49.05	9.13	381.7	800-236-3863	Y
BNY Mellon Asset Allocation Fund Class M	MPBLX	B-	C+	B	Down	3.90	8.07	16.30	20.78	49.93	12.61	484.7	800-645-6561	Y

Category: Moderate Allocation (con't)

Fund Name	Ticker Symbol	RATINGS: Overall Rating	Reward Rating	Risk Rating	Recent Up/ Downgrade	TOTAL RETURNS & PERFORMANCE: 3-Month Total Return	6-Month Total Return	1-Year Total Return	3-Year Total Return	5-Year Total Return	ASSETS: NAV	Total Assets (MIL)	NEW INVESTORS: Telephone	Open to New Investors
BNY Mellon Asset Allocation Fund Investor Class	MIBLX	B-	C+	B	Down	3.83	7.97	15.91	19.98	48.12	12.7	484.7	800-645-6561	Y
Bruce Fund	BRUFX	B	C+	A		2.67	4.52	12.46	19.97	63.85	525.14	578.8		Y
Calamos Strategic Total Return Fund	CSQ	B-	B	B-		5.13	9.87	20.97	34.40	86.11	12.89	2,001	630-245-7234	Y
Calvert Balanced Fund Class A	CSIFX	B-	C+	B	Down	3.97	6.21	11.52	16.02	51.67	31.65	672.8	800-368-2745	Y
Calvert Balanced Fund Class I	CBAIX	B-	C+	B	Down	4.07	6.39	11.94	17.40	55.02	32.23	672.8	800-368-2745	Y
Calvert Moderate Allocation Fund Class A	CMAAX	B-	C+	B	Down	3.63	6.90	15.07	21.63	55.13	19.14	273.4	800-368-2745	Y
Calvert Moderate Allocation Fund Class C	CMACX	B-	C+	B	Down	3.49	6.50	14.25	18.93	49.55	18.26	273.4	800-368-2745	Y
Cavalier Dynamic Growth Fund C Class	CADYX	B-	C+	B	Up	0.42	2.20	14.78	17.59	49.03	9.85	21.3	800-773-3863	Y
Cavalier Dynamic Growth Fund Institutional Class	CDYGX	B-	C+	B-	Down	0.67	2.73	15.89	21.26	56.61	10.53	21.3	800-773-3863	Y
Cavalier Global Opportunities Fund C Class	CATDX	B-	B-	C+	Up	7.27	13.74	26.33	29.43	71.36	16.19	30.5	800-773-3863	Y
Cavalier Global Opportunities Fund Institutional Class	CATEX	B-	B	C+	Down	7.56	14.39	27.63	33.54	80.91	16.74	30.5	800-773-3863	Y
Cavalier Tactical Rotation Fund Institutional Class	CTROX	B-	C+	B-	Down	5.34	8.54	16.90	19.59	60.62	13.88	117.9	800-773-3863	Y
Cavanal Hill Active Core Fund Class A	AABAX	B-	C+	B	Up	4.03	6.58	12.07	17.61	48.03	13.63	54.3		Y
Cavanal Hill Active Core Fund Class C	AACBX	B-	C+	B	Up	3.81	6.04	11.21	14.97	42.67	13.63	54.3		Y
Cavanal Hill Active Core Fund Institutional Class	AIBLX	B-	C+	B	Up	4.07	6.68	12.36	18.52	50.09	13.71	54.3		Y
Cavanal Hill Active Core Fund Investor Class	APBAX	B-	C+	B	Up	4.02	6.48	12.03	17.83	48.42	13.67	54.3		Y
Centaur Total Return Fund	TILDX	B-	C+	B	Down	2.89	7.34	13.52	19.79	52.76	12.91	25.6		Y
Clough Global Dividend and Income Fund	GLV	B-	C+	B	Up	3.37	5.70	19.33	12.07	43.06	14.59	103.0		Y
Clough Global Opportunities Fund	GLO	B-	C+	B	Up	5.46	9.78	23.79	12.79	43.73	12.12	389.6		Y
Cohen & Steers REIT & Preferred Income Fund	RNP	B	B-	A-	Up	2.17	3.53	11.97	27.64	73.69	22.8	1,091	212-832-3232	Y
Columbia Adaptive Risk Allocation Fund Advisor Class	CARRX	B-	C+	B	Down	5.03	7.16	13.31	18.18	23.81	10.86	2,643	800-345-6611	Y
Columbia Adaptive Risk Allocation Fund Class A	CRAAX	B-	C+	B	Down	4.93	6.97	13.05	17.30	22.15	10.76	2,643	800-345-6611	Y
Columbia Adaptive Risk Allocation Fund Class C	CRACX	B-	C+	B		4.80	6.59	12.26	14.79	17.65	10.41	2,643	800-345-6611	Y
Columbia Adaptive Risk Allocation Fund Class K	CRFRX	B-	C+	B	Down	5.01	7.05	13.12	17.59	22.71	10.79	2,643	800-345-6611	
Columbia Adaptive Risk Allocation Fund Class R	CRKRX	B-	C+	B		4.98	6.94	12.85	16.48	20.77	10.66	2,643	800-345-6611	Y
Columbia Adaptive Risk Allocation Fund Class T	CRAWX	B-	C+	B	Down	5.02	6.96	13.03	17.38	22.36	10.78	2,643	800-345-6611	Y
Columbia Adaptive Risk Allocation Fund Institutional 2 Cls	CRDRX	B-	C+	B	Down	5.01	7.03	13.28	18.32	24.10	10.87	2,643	800-345-6611	Y
Columbia Adaptive Risk Allocation Fund Institutional 3 Cls	CARYX	B-	C+	B	Down	5.07	7.09	13.43	18.56	24.11	10.89	2,643	800-345-6611	Y
Columbia Adaptive Risk Allocation Fund Institutional Class	CRAZX	B-	C+	B	Down	5.03	7.06	13.31	18.18	23.70	10.85	2,643	800-345-6611	Y
Columbia Balanced Fund Advisor Class	CBDRX	B	C+	A-		3.49	6.46	14.29	23.19	67.50	41.69	7,468	800-345-6611	Y
Columbia Balanced Fund Class A	CBLAX	B	C+	B+		3.43	6.32	14.00	22.27	65.40	41.39	7,468	800-345-6611	Y
Columbia Balanced Fund Class C	CBLCX	B-	C+	B	Down	3.24	5.91	13.16	19.58	59.32	41.3	7,468	800-345-6611	Y
Columbia Balanced Fund Class K	CLRFX	B	C+	B+		3.42	6.34	14.05	22.54	66.10	41.3	7,468	800-345-6611	
Columbia Balanced Fund Class R	CBLRX	B-	C+	B	Down	3.36	6.19	13.72	21.36	63.39	41.4	7,468	800-345-6611	Y
Columbia Balanced Fund Class T	CBDTX	B	C+	B+		3.46	6.35	14.01	22.30	65.41	41.39	7,468	800-345-6611	Y
Columbia Balanced Fund Institutional 2 Class	CLREX	B	C+	A-		3.51	6.46	14.34	23.50	68.33	41.33	7,468	800-345-6611	Y
Columbia Balanced Fund Institutional 3 Class	CBDYX	B	C+	A-		3.51	6.48	14.38	23.68	68.74	41.69	7,468	800-345-6611	Y
Columbia Balanced Fund Institutional Class	CBALX	B	C+	A-		3.50	6.46	14.28	23.20	67.47	41.31	7,468	800-345-6611	Y
Columbia Capital Alloc Moderate Aggressive Port Adv Cls	CGBRX	B-	B-	B	Down	4.30	8.82	18.81	26.42	60.18	13.09	2,241	800-345-6611	Y
Columbia Capital Alloc Moderate Aggressive Port Cls A	NBIAX	B-	B-	B	Down	4.27	8.76	18.58	25.49	58.08	12.99	2,241	800-345-6611	Y
Columbia Capital Alloc Moderate Aggressive Port Cls C	NBICX	B-	C+	B	Down	4.07	8.31	17.62	22.68	52.37	13.02	2,241	800-345-6611	Y
Columbia Capital Alloc Moderate Aggressive Port Cls K	CAMKX	B-	B-	B	Down	4.31	8.77	18.69	25.68	58.83	12.93	2,241	800-345-6611	
Columbia Capital Alloc Moderate Aggressive Port Cls R	CLBRX	B-	C+	B	Down	4.21	8.64	18.31	24.58	56.19	12.98	2,241	800-345-6611	Y
Columbia Capital Alloc Moderate Aggressive Port Cls V	CGGTX	B-	B-	B	Down	4.27	8.76	18.58	25.49	58.07	12.99	2,241	800-345-6611	
Columbia Capital Alloc Moderate Aggressive Port Inst 2 Cls	CLHRX	B-	B-	B	Down	4.32	8.86	18.90	26.67	60.86	13.08	2,241	800-345-6611	Y
Columbia Capital Alloc Moderate Aggressive Port Inst 3 Cls	CPHNX	B-	B-	B	Down	4.43	8.92	19.01	26.93	61.22	12.8	2,241	800-345-6611	Y
Columbia Capital Alloc Moderate Aggressive Port Inst Cls	NBGPX	B-	B-	B	Down	4.35	8.83	18.82	26.39	60.06	12.96	2,241	800-345-6611	Y
Columbia Flexible Capital Income Fund Advisor Class	CFCRX	B-	B-	B-	Down	2.62	6.89	13.63	26.20	57.14	13.11	552.5	800-345-6611	Y
Columbia Flexible Capital Income Fund Class A	CFIAX	B-	B-	B-	Up	2.57	6.81	13.46	25.36	55.27	13.02	552.5	800-345-6611	Y
Columbia Flexible Capital Income Fund Class R	CFIRX	B-	B-	B-	Up	2.51	6.59	13.09	24.34	53.19	13.01	552.5	800-345-6611	Y
Columbia Flexible Capital Income Fund Class T	CFIWX	B-	B-	B-	Down	2.57	6.72	13.37	25.27	55.10	13.02	552.5	800-345-6611	Y
Columbia Flexible Capital Income Fund Institutional 2 Cls	CFXRX	B-	B-	B-	Down	2.62	6.90	13.66	26.53	57.61	13.12	552.5	800-345-6611	Y

Category: Moderate Allocation (con't)

Fund Name	Ticker Symbol	RATINGS: Overall Rating	Reward Rating	Risk Rating	Recent Up/ Downgrade	TOTAL RETURNS & PERFORMANCE: 3-Month Total Return	6-Month Total Return	1-Year Total Return	3-Year Total Return	5-Year Total Return	ASSETS: NAV	Total Assets (MIL)	NEW INVESTORS: Telephone	Open to New Investors
Columbia Flexible Capital Income Fund Institutional 3 Cls	CFCYX	B-	B-	B-	Down	2.59	6.88	13.80	26.36	57.29	12.96	552.5	800-345-6611	Y
Columbia Flexible Capital Income Fund Institutional Class	CFIZX	B-	B-	B-	Down	2.64	6.86	13.65	26.20	57.09	13.01	552.5	800-345-6611	Y
CornerCap Balanced Fund	CBLFX	B-	C+	B	Down	4.22	7.87	13.51	17.67	60.02	14.63	35.8	888-813-8637	Y
Day Hagan Tactical Allocation Fund Class A	DHAAX	B-	C	B	Up	2.72	5.55	8.25	7.85	29.39	11.45	29.1		Y
Day Hagan Tactical Allocation Fund Class I	DHAIX	B-	C	B	Up	2.89	5.70	8.58	8.84	30.82	11.5	29.1		Y
Delaware Foundation Moderate Allocation Class A	DFBAX	B-	C+	B	Up	2.09	5.83	12.74	17.32	40.89	11.62	264.7		Y
Delaware Foundation Moderate Allocation Class C	DFBCX	B-	C+	B	Up	1.90	5.43	11.89	14.69	35.64	11.62	264.7		Y
Delaware Foundation Moderate Allocation Class R	DFBRX	B-	C+	B+	Up	2.03	5.71	12.50	16.38	38.94	11.57	264.7		Y
Delaware Foundation Moderate Allocation Institutional Cls	DFFIX	B-	C+	B	Up	2.24	5.95	13.09	18.14	42.56	11.63	264.7		Y
Delaware Investments Dividend and Income Fund	DDF	B-	B-	B	Up	4.22	8.70	13.48	28.05	85.28	11.92	92.9		Y
Delaware Wealth Builder Fund Class A	DDIAX	B-	C+	B	Down	2.37	4.74	9.13	15.19	51.20	14.71	685.8		Y
Delaware Wealth Builder Fund Class R	DDDRX	B-	C+	B	Down	2.32	4.62	8.86	14.34	49.34	14.71	685.8		Y
Delaware Wealth Builder Fund Institutional Class	DDIIX	B-	C+	B	Down	2.44	4.87	9.40	16.05	53.09	14.71	685.8		Y
Deutsche Multi-Asset Moderate Allocation Fund - Class A	PLUSX	B-	C+	B	Up	3.56	7.20	13.80	14.62	46.16	9.82	32.0	201-593-8273	Y
Deutsche Multi-Asset Moderate Allocation Fund - Class S	PPLSX	B-	C+	B	Up	3.62	7.38	13.98	15.42	47.96	9.8	32.0	201-593-8273	Y
DFA Global Allocation 60/40 Portfolio Class R2	DFPRX	B-	C+	B	Up	3.87	7.11	13.79	20.92	46.79	18.19	3,926	512-306-7400	Y
DFA Global Allocation 60/40 Portfolio Institutional Class	DGSIX	B-	C+	B	Up	3.99	7.25	14.03	21.78	48.54	18.09	3,926	512-306-7400	Y
Direxion Hilton Tactical Income Fund Class A	HCYAX	B-	C+	B	Down	2.28	4.73	8.32	17.98		16.76	107.7	646-572-3390	Y
Direxion Hilton Tactical Income Fund Class C	HCYCX	B-	C+	B	Down	2.10	4.36	7.55	15.38		16.75	107.7	646-572-3390	Y
Direxion Hilton Tactical Income Fund Institutional Class	HCYIX	B-	C+	B	Down	2.34	4.85	8.63	18.90		16.79	107.7	646-572-3390	Y
Dodge & Cox Balanced Fund	DODBX	B	B-	B+	Up	3.61	6.86	12.59	26.70	80.37	107	16,335	415-981-1710	Y
DoubleLine Multi-Asset Growth Fund Class A	DMLAX	B-	C+	B	Down	1.88	4.84	13.73	21.45	29.74	9.57	212.7	877-354-6311	Y
DoubleLine Multi-Asset Growth Fund Class I	DMLIX	B-	C+	B	Down	2.03	5.05	14.06	22.58	31.46	9.61	212.7	877-354-6311	Y
Dreyfus Balanced Opportunity Fund Class A	DBOAX	B	C+	A-	Up	3.67	6.31	10.57	20.12	59.09	22.81	323.0	800-645-6561	Y
Dreyfus Balanced Opportunity Fund Class C	DBOCX	B	C+	A-	Up	4.33	6.76	10.68	18.39	54.45	22.91	323.0	800-645-6561	Y
Dreyfus Balanced Opportunity Fund Class I	DBORX	B-	C+	B	Down	3.53	6.21	10.61	20.74	60.64	22.84	323.0	800-645-6561	Y
Dreyfus Balanced Opportunity Fund Class J	THPBX	B	C+	A-	Up	3.48	6.21	10.61	20.73	60.63	22.84	323.0	800-645-6561	
Dreyfus Balanced Opportunity Fund Class Y	DBOYX	B-	C+	B	Down	5.00	7.77	11.95	22.19	62.92		323.0	800-645-6561	Y
Dreyfus Balanced Opportunity Fund Class Z	DBOZX	B	C+	A-	Up	3.55	6.25	10.62	20.54	60.13	22.71	323.0	800-645-6561	
Dynamic U.S. Opportunity Fund Class I	ICSIX	B-	B-	B	Down	3.75	7.00	15.17	31.21	30.72	12.35	68.3	512-354-7041	Y
Dynamic U.S. Opportunity Fund Class N	ICSNX	B-	B-	B	Down	3.73	6.98	14.95	30.33	29.38	12.37	68.3	512-354-7041	Y
Eaton Vance Balanced Fund Class A	EVIFX	B	C+	A+	Up	4.15	6.63	13.52	21.18	63.58	9.11	841.4		Y
Eaton Vance Balanced Fund Class B	EMIFX	B-	C+	B	Up	3.94	6.19	12.59	18.45	57.45	9.13	841.4		
Eaton Vance Balanced Fund Class C	ECIFX	B	C+	A	Up	3.82	6.08	12.63	18.48	57.40	9.14	841.4		Y
Eaton Vance Balanced Fund Class I	EIIFX	B	C+	A-	Up	4.21	6.77	13.80	22.05	65.57	9.11	841.4		Y
Eaton Vance Balanced Fund Class R	ERIFX	B	C+	B+	Up	4.14	6.45	13.21	20.39	61.69	9.09	841.4		Y
Eaton Vance Balanced Fund Class R6	ESIFX	B	C+	A-	Up	4.23	6.68	13.74	21.69	64.26	9.11	841.4		Y
Eaton Vance Richard Bernstein All Asset Strat Fund Cls A	EARAX	B-	C+	B	Up	3.80	7.73	14.70	20.71	42.66	14.76	657.1		Y
Eaton Vance Richard Bernstein All Asset Strat Fund Cls C	ECRAX	B-	C+	B	Up	3.55	7.32	13.88	18.09	37.35	14.52	657.1		Y
Eaton Vance Richard Bernstein All Asset Strat Fund Cls I	EIRAX	B-	C+	B	Up	3.82	7.88	15.00	21.64	44.45	14.81	657.1		Y
Elfun Diversified Fund	ELDFX	B	C+	B+	Up	3.75	7.42	15.40	19.50	48.71	18.6	211.4	800-242-0134	Y
E-Valuator Moderate RMS Fund R4 Class Shares	EVFMX	B-	C+	B	Up	4.25	8.39	15.83	20.97	51.82	11.2	165.9	888-507-2798	Y
E-Valuator Moderate RMS Fund Service Class Shares	EVMLX	B-	C+	B	Up	4.35	8.60	16.26	21.62	52.63	11.18	165.9	888-507-2798	Y
Federated MDT Balanced Fund Class A Shares	QABGX	B-	C+	B	Down	4.13	8.50	13.86	17.50	58.20	18.64	140.3	800-341-7400	Y
Federated MDT Balanced Fund Class C Shares	QCBGX	B-	C+	B	Down	3.94	8.11	12.98	14.92	52.30	18.46	140.3	800-341-7400	Y
Federated MDT Balanced Fund Class R6 Shares	QKBGX	B-	C+	B	Down	4.22	8.65	14.15	17.42	57.27	18.64	140.3	800-341-7400	Y
Federated MDT Balanced Fund Institutional Shares	QIBGX	B-	C+	B	Down	4.21	8.62	14.11	18.41	60.12	18.67	140.3	800-341-7400	Y
Fidelity Advisor Asset Manager® 60% Fund Class A	FSAAX	B-	C+	B	Down	3.57	7.28	15.99	22.03	51.61	12.53	2,053	617-563-7000	Y
Fidelity Advisor Asset Manager® 60% Fund Class C	FSCNX	B-	C+	B	Down	3.41	6.83	15.13	19.18	45.86	12.35	2,053	617-563-7000	Y
Fidelity Advisor Asset Manager® 60% Fund Class M	FSATX	B-	C+	B	Down	3.61	7.17	15.81	21.07	49.79	12.48	2,053	617-563-7000	Y
Fidelity Advisor Asset Manager® 60% Fund I Class	FSNIX	B-	C+	B	Down	3.65	7.35	16.33	23.00	53.72	12.57	2,053	617-563-7000	Y
Fidelity Advisor Asset Manager® 70% Fund Class A	FAASX	B-	C+	B	Down	4.20	8.29	18.35	24.68	59.58	22.39	5,190	617-563-7000	Y

Category: Moderate Allocation (con't)

Fund Name	Ticker Symbol	RATINGS Overall Rating	Reward Rating	Risk Rating	Recent Up/ Downgrade	TOTAL RETURNS & PERFORMANCE 3-Month Total Return	6-Month Total Return	1-Year Total Return	3-Year Total Return	5-Year Total Return	ASSETS NAV	Total Assets (MIL)	NEW INVESTORS Telephone	Open to New Investors
Fidelity Advisor Asset Manager® 70% Fund Class C	FCASX	B-	C+	B-	Down	4.00	7.91	17.46	21.85	53.69	22.32	5,190	617-563-7000	Y
Fidelity Advisor Asset Manager® 70% Fund Class M	FTASX	B-	C+	B	Down	4.13	8.21	18.08	23.75	57.52	22.41	5,190	617-563-7000	Y
Fidelity Advisor Asset Manager® 70% Fund I Class	FAAIX	B-	B-	B	Down	4.25	8.47	18.65	25.69	61.78	22.41	5,190	617-563-7000	Y
Fidelity Advisor Managed Retirement 2010 Fund Class A	FRQAX	B-	C+	B	Up	2.13	4.62	10.33	16.72	43.48	56.85	10.9	617-563-7000	Y
Fidelity Advisor Managed Retirement 2010 Fund Class C	FRQCX	B-	C+	B	Up	1.97	4.24	9.53	14.15	38.23	56.45	10.9	617-563-7000	Y
Fidelity Advisor Managed Retirement 2010 Fund Class I	FRQIX	B-	C+	B	Up	2.20	4.76	10.63	17.61	45.31	56.85	10.9	617-563-7000	Y
Fidelity Advisor Managed Retirement 2010 Fund Class M	FRQTX	B-	C+	B	Up	2.09	4.50	10.08	15.87	41.70	56.98	10.9	617-563-7000	Y
Fidelity Advisor Managed Retirement 2015 Fund Class A	FARSX	B-	C+	B	Up	2.54	5.39	11.76	18.48	47.17	53.85	4.8	617-563-7000	Y
Fidelity Advisor Managed Retirement 2015 Fund Class C	FCRSX	B-	C+	B	Up	2.35	5.00	10.93	15.84	41.74	53.67	4.8	617-563-7000	Y
Fidelity Advisor Managed Retirement 2015 Fund Class I	FRASX	B-	C+	B	Up	2.62	5.53	12.04	19.38	49.01	53.83	4.8	617-563-7000	Y
Fidelity Advisor Managed Retirement 2015 Fund Class M	FTRSX	B-	C+	B	Up	2.47	5.26	11.53	17.59	45.34	53.95	4.8	617-563-7000	Y
Fidelity Advisor Managed Retirement 2020 Fund Class A	FARVX	B-	C+	B	Up	2.93	6.09	13.01	19.92	50.39	52.2	4.0	617-563-7000	Y
Fidelity Advisor Managed Retirement 2020 Fund Class C	FCRVX	B-	C+	B	Up	2.73	5.69	12.15	17.24	44.85	51.69	4.0	617-563-7000	Y
Fidelity Advisor Managed Retirement 2020 Fund Class I	FIIVX	B-	C+	B	Up	3.00	6.24	13.31	20.84	52.32	52.2	4.0	617-563-7000	Y
Fidelity Advisor Managed Retirement 2020 Fund Class M	FTRVX	B-	C+	B	Up	2.88	5.97	12.73	19.02	48.55	52.17	4.0	617-563-7000	Y
Fidelity Advisor Managed Retirement 2025 Fund Class A	FARFX	B-	C+	B	Up	3.15	6.50	13.94	21.02	53.94	53.83	20.8	617-563-7000	Y
Fidelity Advisor Managed Retirement 2025 Fund Class C	FCRFX	B-	C+	B	Up	2.94	6.10	13.10	18.34	48.29	53.31	20.8	617-563-7000	Y
Fidelity Advisor Managed Retirement 2025 Fund Class M	FITTX	B-	C+	B	Up	3.07	6.36	13.65	20.13	52.04	53.84	20.8	617-563-7000	Y
Fidelity Advisor Managed Retirement 2025 Fund I Class	FIRFX	B-	C+	B	Up	3.21	6.65	14.23	21.96	55.93	53.93	20.8	617-563-7000	Y
Fidelity Advisor Simplicity RMD 2005 Fund Class A	FARPX	B-	C+	B	Up	1.76	3.89	9.16	15.28	40.76	58.33	19.4	617-563-7000	Y
Fidelity Advisor Simplicity RMD 2005 Fund Class C	FCRPX	B-	C+	B	Up	1.57	3.49	8.34	12.70	35.56	58.05	19.4	617-563-7000	Y
Fidelity Advisor Simplicity RMD 2005 Fund Class I	FRAPX	B-	C+	B	Up	1.81	4.00	9.40	16.13	42.52	58.28	19.4	617-563-7000	Y
Fidelity Advisor Simplicity RMD 2005 Fund Class M	FTRPX	B-	C+	B	Up	1.69	3.75	8.88	14.42	39.00	58.29	19.4	617-563-7000	Y
Fidelity Advisor Simplicity RMD 2010 Fund Class A	FIARX	B-	C+	B	Up	2.19	4.72	10.76	17.32	45.10	53.42	6.5	617-563-7000	Y
Fidelity Advisor Simplicity RMD 2010 Fund Class C	FICRX	B-	C+	B	Up	2.01	4.33	9.92	14.68	39.74	53.11	6.5	617-563-7000	Y
Fidelity Advisor Simplicity RMD 2010 Fund Class I	FIIRX	B-	C+	B	Up	2.26	4.84	11.01	18.18	46.90	53.42	6.5	617-563-7000	Y
Fidelity Advisor Simplicity RMD 2010 Fund Class M	FTIRX	B-	C+	B	Up	2.13	4.59	10.46	16.41	43.28	53.46	6.5	617-563-7000	Y
Fidelity Advisor Simplicity RMD 2015 Fund Class A	FURAX	B-	C+	B	Up	2.66	5.60	12.23	19.05	48.56	58.91	9.5	617-563-7000	Y
Fidelity Advisor Simplicity RMD 2015 Fund Class C	FURCX	B-	C+	B	Up	2.47	5.22	11.41	16.40	43.10	58.37	9.5	617-563-7000	Y
Fidelity Advisor Simplicity RMD 2015 Fund Class I	FURIX	B-	C+	B	Up	2.71	5.75	12.52	20.05	50.67	58.97	9.5	617-563-7000	Y
Fidelity Advisor Simplicity RMD 2015 Fund Class M	FURTX	B-	C+	B	Up	2.59	5.48	11.95	18.13	46.72	58.86	9.5	617-563-7000	Y
Fidelity Advisor Simplicity RMD 2020 Fund Class A	FARWX	B-	C+	B	Up	3.12	6.48	13.67	20.68	52.31	59.34	14.0	617-563-7000	Y
Fidelity Advisor Simplicity RMD 2020 Fund Class C	FCRWX	B-	C+	B	Up	2.92	6.06	12.81	17.98	46.70	58.71	14.0	617-563-7000	Y
Fidelity Advisor Simplicity RMD 2020 Fund Class I	FIIWX	B-	C+	B	Up	3.19	6.58	13.94	21.56	54.21	59.24	14.0	617-563-7000	Y
Fidelity Advisor Simplicity RMD 2020 Fund Class M	FTRWX	B-	C+	B	Up	3.05	6.33	13.38	19.76	50.43	59.4	14.0	617-563-7000	Y
Fidelity Advisor® Balanced Fund Class A	FABLX	B-	C+	B	Down	3.49	7.04	16.08	23.45	65.73	20.85	2,879	617-563-7000	Y
Fidelity Advisor® Balanced Fund Class C	FABCX	B-	C+	B	Down	3.31	6.65	15.23	20.68	59.56	20.72	2,879	617-563-7000	Y
Fidelity Advisor® Balanced Fund Class M	FAIGX	B-	C+	B	Down	3.46	6.91	15.78	22.56	63.79	21.09	2,879	617-563-7000	Y
Fidelity Advisor® Balanced Fund Class Z	FZAAX	B-	B-	B	Down	3.57	7.21	16.50	24.89	68.33	21.24	2,879	617-563-7000	Y
Fidelity Advisor® Balanced Fund I Class	FAIOX	B-	B-	B	Down	3.55	7.16	16.35	24.39	67.87	21.24	2,879	617-563-7000	Y
Fidelity Asset Manager® 60% Fund	FSANX	B-	C+	B	Down	3.70	7.40	16.40	23.15	54.00	12.56	2,053	617-563-7000	Y
Fidelity Asset Manager® 70% Fund	FASGX	B-	B-	B	Down	4.24	8.46	18.70	25.76	62.03	22.4	5,190	617-563-7000	Y
Fidelity Managed Retirement 2010 Fund	FIRQX	B-	C+	B	Up	2.20	4.75	10.62	17.60	45.30	56.85	10.9	617-563-7000	Y
Fidelity Managed Retirement 2015 Fund	FIRSX	B-	C+	B	Up	2.63	5.54	12.05	19.39	49.03	53.83	4.8	617-563-7000	Y
Fidelity Managed Retirement 2020 Fund	FIRVX	B-	C+	B	Up	2.99	6.24	13.29	20.82	52.32	52.2	4.0	617-563-7000	Y
Fidelity Managed Retirement 2025 Fund	FIXRX	B-	C+	B	Up	3.21	6.64	14.23	21.96	55.89	53.86	20.8	617-563-7000	Y
Fidelity Simplicity RMD 2005 Fund	FIRPX	B-	C+	B	Up	1.82	4.01	9.43	16.14	42.52	58.28	19.4	617-563-7000	Y
Fidelity Simplicity RMD 2010 Fund	FIRRX	B-	C+	B	Up	2.27	4.85	11.02	18.19	46.91	53.42	6.5	617-563-7000	Y
Fidelity Simplicity RMD 2015 Fund	FIRUX	B-	C+	B	Up	2.72	5.74	12.51	19.93	50.45	58.88	9.5	617-563-7000	Y
Fidelity Simplicity RMD 2020 Fund	FIRWX	B-	C+	B	Up	3.18	6.59	13.93	21.55	54.20	59.26	14.0	617-563-7000	Y
Fidelity® Balanced Fund	FBALX	B-	B-	B	Down	3.60	7.27	16.50	24.47	68.39	23.73	32,486	617-563-7000	Y
Fidelity® Balanced Fund Class K	FBAKX	B-	B-	B	Down	3.64	7.34	16.60	24.81	69.20	23.73	32,486	617-563-7000	Y

Category: Moderate Allocation (con't)

Fund Name	Ticker Symbol	Overall Rating	Reward Rating	Risk Rating	Recent Up/ Downgrade	3-Month Total Return	6-Month Total Return	1-Year Total Return	3-Year Total Return	5-Year Total Return	NAV	Total Assets (MIL)	Telephone	Open to New Investors
		RATINGS				TOTAL RETURNS & PERFORMANCE					ASSETS		NEW INVESTORS	
Fidelity® Puritan® Fund	FPURX	B-	B-	B	Down	4.59	9.25	18.74	26.22	70.91	23.42	27,421	617-563-7000	Y
Fidelity® Puritan® Fund Class K	FPUKX	B-	B-	B	Down	4.63	9.32	18.85	26.60	71.82	23.41	27,421	617-563-7000	Y
First Investors Total Return Fund Advisor Class	FITUX	B-	C+	B	Up	4.27	6.72	12.06	17.10	51.48	20.36	939.1	800-423-4026	Y
First Investors Total Return Fund Institutional Class	FITVX	B-	C+	B	Up	4.26	6.71	12.09	17.14	52.03	20.43	939.1	800-423-4026	Y
First Investors Total Return Series Class A	FITRX	B-	C+	B	Up	4.14	6.47	11.64	15.74	49.19	20.25	939.1	800-423-4026	Y
First Investors Total Return Series Class B	FBTRX	B-	C+	B+	Up	3.97	6.11	10.83	13.09	43.56	19.92	939.1	800-423-4026	Y
FPA Crescent Fund	FPACX	B	C+	B+	Up	2.90	4.85	10.38	18.63	56.13	34.69	17,529	800-982-4372	Y
Franklin Balanced Fund Advisor Class	FBFZX	B-	C+	B	Up	2.79	6.46	9.84	19.49	48.07	12.37	3,540	650-312-2000	Y
Franklin Balanced Fund Class A	FBLAX	B-	C+	B	Up	2.65	6.26	9.51	18.52	45.91	12.34	3,540	650-312-2000	Y
Franklin Balanced Fund Class C	FBMCX	B-	C+	B	Down	2.49	5.92	8.78	15.91	40.81	12.23	3,540	650-312-2000	Y
Franklin Balanced Fund Class R	US3536126663	B-	C+	B+	Down	2.58	6.11	9.30	17.63	44.30	12.37	3,540	650-312-2000	Y
Franklin Balanced Fund Class R6	FBFRX	B-	C+	B	Up	2.81	6.51	9.95	19.73	48.92	12.37	3,529	650-312-2000	Y
Franklin Moderate Allocation Fund Advisor Class	FMTZX	B-	C+	B	Down	2.85	6.55	15.19	18.86	43.79	16.12	2,173	650-312-2000	Y
Franklin Moderate Allocation Fund Class A	FMTIX	B-	C+	B	Down	2.83	6.40	14.98	17.92	41.95	16.11	2,173	650-312-2000	Y
Franklin Moderate Allocation Fund Class C	FTMTX	B-	C+	B	Down	2.65	6.06	14.09	15.38	36.82	15.67	2,173	650-312-2000	Y
Franklin Moderate Allocation Fund Class R	FTMRX	B-	C+	B	Down	2.79	6.31	14.68	17.09	40.24	16.08	2,173	650-312-2000	Y
Franklin Moderate Allocation Fund Class R6	US35472P4220	B-	C+	B	Down	2.96	6.59	15.39	19.23	44.38	16.11	2,173	650-312-2000	Y
FundX Conservative Upgrader Fund	RELAX	B-	C+	B	Up	2.69	6.96	10.97	17.65	49.85	41.49	59.7	866-455-3863	Y
Gabelli Global Rising Income and Dividend Fund Class A	GAGAX	B-	B-	B	Down	3.81	7.57	20.93	27.67	49.12	27.26	68.7	914-921-5135	Y
Gabelli Global Rising Income and Dividend Fund Class C	GACCX	B-	B-	B	Down	3.60	7.13	19.97	24.78	41.99	22.93	68.7	914-921-5135	Y
Gabelli Global Rising Income and Dividend Fund Class I	GAGIX	B	B-	B	Up	4.00	7.91	21.68	29.23	51.76	27.35	68.7	914-921-5135	Y
George Putnam Balanced Fund Class A	PGEOX	B-	C+	B	Down	3.61	7.05	15.02	22.04	61.04	20.01	1,234	617-292-1000	Y
George Putnam Balanced Fund Class B	PGEBX	B-	C+	B	Down	3.39	6.60	14.19	19.29	55.13	19.79	1,234	617-292-1000	Y
George Putnam Balanced Fund Class C	PGPCX	B-	C+	B	Down	3.38	6.64	14.16	19.29	55.10	19.87	1,234	617-292-1000	Y
George Putnam Balanced Fund Class M	PGEMX	B-	C+	B	Down	3.42	6.72	14.44	20.18	57.09	19.73	1,234	617-292-1000	Y
George Putnam Balanced Fund Class R	PGPRX	B-	C+	B	Down	3.52	6.91	14.73	21.12	59.07	19.95	1,234	617-292-1000	Y
George Putnam Balanced Fund Class R5	PGELX	B-	C+	B	Down	3.64	7.19	15.37	23.04	62.80	20.16	1,234	617-292-1000	Y
George Putnam Balanced Fund Class R6	PGEJX	B-	C+	B	Down	3.64	7.17	15.45	23.35	63.39	20.08	1,234	617-292-1000	Y
George Putnam Balanced Fund Class Y	PGEYX	B-	C+	B	Down	3.65	7.16	15.30	22.93	63.09	20.08	1,234	617-292-1000	Y
Goldman Sachs Balanced Strategy Portfolio Class A	GIPAX	B	C+	B+	Up	2.48	5.61	11.19	15.34	29.15	11.55	500.3	800-526-7384	Y
Goldman Sachs Balanced Strategy Portfolio Class C	GIPCX	B-	C+	B+	Up	2.29	5.18	10.29	12.77	24.37	11.55	500.3	800-526-7384	Y
Goldman Sachs Balanced Strategy Portfolio Class R	GIPRX	B-	C+	B+	Up	2.34	5.42	10.81	14.64	27.80	11.5	500.3	800-526-7384	Y
Goldman Sachs Balanced Strategy Portfolio Class R6	GIPUX	B-	C+	B	Up	2.59	5.74	11.53	16.76	31.79	11.55	500.3	800-526-7384	Y
Goldman Sachs Balanced Strategy Portfolio Inst Cls	GIPIX	B-	C+	B	Up	2.59	5.83	11.63	16.74	31.77	11.55	500.3	800-526-7384	Y
Goldman Sachs Balanced Strategy Portfolio Investor Class	GIPTX	B	C+	B+	Up	2.56	5.67	11.41	16.18	30.70	11.5	500.3	312-362-3000	Y
Goldman Sachs Balanced Strategy Portfolio Service Class	GIPSX	B	C+	B+	Up	2.51	5.57	11.03	15.88	29.44	11.68	500.3	800-526-7384	Y
Goldman Sachs Growth and Income Strategy Portfolio Class A	GOIAX	B-	C+	B	Up	3.55	8.02	16.19	21.71	42.72	13.81	960.0	800-526-7384	Y
Goldman Sachs Growth and Income Strategy Portfolio Class C	GOICX	B-	C+	B	Up	3.28	7.54	15.31	18.92	37.36	13.49	960.0	800-526-7384	Y
Goldman Sachs Growth and Income Strategy Portfolio Class R	GPIRX	B-	C+	B	Up	3.43	7.78	15.82	20.65	40.84	13.7	960.0	800-526-7384	Y
Goldman Sachs Growth & Income Strategy Portfolio Cls R6	GOIUX	B-	C+	B	Up	3.65	8.22	16.70	23.13	45.50	13.85	960.0	800-526-7384	Y
Goldman Sachs Growth & Income Strategy Portfolio Inst Cls	GOIIX	B-	C+	B	Up	3.65	8.22	16.59	23.11	45.47	13.85	960.0	800-526-7384	Y
Goldman Sachs Growth & Income Strategy Portfolio Inv Cls	GPITX	B-	C+	B	Up	3.56	8.12	16.39	22.58	44.46	13.74	960.0	800-526-7384	Y
Goldman Sachs Growth & Inc Strategy Port Serv Cls	GOISX	B-	C+	B	Up	3.45	7.90	16.02	21.23	41.97	13.77	960.0	800-526-7384	Y
Great-West Moderate Profile Fund Class L	MXGPX	B-	C+	B	Up	3.43	6.17	12.75	19.87	50.24		1,583		Y
Great-West Moderate Profile Fund Institutional Class	MXITX	B-	C+	B	Up	3.49	6.43	13.39	21.79	53.49		1,583		Y
Great-West Moderate Profile Fund Investor Class	MXMPX	B-	C+	B	Up	3.45	6.29	13.09	20.70	52.12		1,583		Y
Great-West SecureFoundation® Balanced ETF Fund Class A	SFBPX	B-	C+	B	Up	3.68	7.06	13.68	21.82	52.07		46.3		Y
Great-West SecureFoundation® Balanced Fund Class L	MXLDX	B-	C+	B	Up	3.56	6.66	12.71	20.31	50.07		691.4		Y
Great-West SecureFoundation® Balanced Fund Inst Cls	MXCJX	B-	C+	B	Up	3.76	6.93	13.48	22.47	53.52		691.4		Y
Great-West SecureFoundation® Balanced Fund Investor Class	MXSBX	B-	C+	B	Up	3.63	6.78	13.10	21.23	51.97		691.4		Y
Great-West SecureFoundation® Balanced Fund Service Class	MXSHX	B-	C+	B	Up	3.55	6.74	12.91	20.95	51.27		691.4		Y
Green Century Balanced Fund	GCBLX	B-	C+	B	Down	2.95	5.18	12.78	16.51	57.33	26.3	240.0	800-221-5519	Y

Category: Moderate Allocation (con't)

Fund Name	Ticker Symbol	RATINGS: Overall Rating	Reward Rating	Risk Rating	Recent Up/ Downgrade	TOTAL RETURNS & PERFORMANCE: 3-Month Total Return	6-Month Total Return	1-Year Total Return	3-Year Total Return	5-Year Total Return	ASSETS: NAV	Total Assets (MIL)	NEW INVESTORS: Telephone	Open to New Investors
Greenspring Fund	GRSPX	B-	C+	B-	Up	3.90	5.14	7.81	20.79	41.29	24.32	277.2	800-366-3863	Y
GuideStone Funds Defensive Mkt Strategies Fund Inst Cls	GDMYX	B	B-	A-	Up	3.32	6.22	12.73	28.21	70.68	12.68	964.8	214-720-1171	Y
GuideStone Funds Defensive Mkt Strategies Fund Inv Cls	GDMZX	B	B-	A-	Up	3.25	5.98	12.34	27.12	68.41	12.68	964.8	214-720-1171	Y
Hartford Balanced Fund Class A	ITTAX	B-	C+	B	Down	4.43	7.66	15.12	20.40	61.26	24.18	954.9	888-843-7824	Y
Hartford Balanced Fund Class C	HAFCX	B-	C+	B	Down	4.25	7.28	14.30	17.87	55.68	24.18	954.9	888-843-7824	Y
Hartford Balanced Fund Class I	ITTIX	B-	C+	B	Down	4.52	7.83	15.38	21.51	64.15	24.17	954.9	888-843-7824	Y
Hartford Balanced Fund Class R3	ITTRX	B-	C+	B	Down	4.32	7.50	14.74	19.40	59.13	24.42	954.9	888-843-7824	Y
Hartford Balanced Fund Class R4	ITTSX	B-	C+	B	Down	4.42	7.65	15.08	20.48	61.53	24.47	954.9	888-843-7824	Y
Hartford Balanced Fund Class R5	ITTTX	B-	C+	B	Down	4.50	7.80	15.48	21.59	64.08	24.5	954.9	888-843-7824	Y
Hartford Balanced Fund Class Y	IHAYX	B-	C+	B	Down	4.55	7.87	15.49	21.81	64.55	24.51	954.9	888-843-7824	Y
Hartford Balanced HLS Fund Class IA	HADAX	B-	C+	B	Down	4.67	8.36	15.59	22.06	65.04	31.02	2,368	888-843-7824	Y
Hartford Balanced HLS Fund Class IB	HAIBX	B-	C+	B	Down	4.61	8.26	15.29	21.14	63.01	31.48	2,368	888-843-7824	Y
Hartford Checks and Balances Fund Class A	HCKAX	B-	C+	B	Up	0.70	3.24	11.12	18.31	59.49	9.47	1,722	888-843-7824	Y
Hartford Checks and Balances Fund Class C	HCKCX	B-	C+	B	Up	0.71	3.12	10.51	15.87	53.83	9.41	1,722	888-843-7824	Y
Hartford Checks and Balances Fund Class F	HCKFX	B-	C+	B	Up	0.69	2.98	10.48	17.63	58.58	9.48	1,722	888-843-7824	Y
Hartford Checks and Balances Fund Class I	HCKIX	B-	C+	B	Up	0.69	3.31	11.19	18.98	61.18	9.48	1,722	888-843-7824	Y
Hartford Checks and Balances Fund Class R3	HCKRX	B-	C+	B	Up	0.70	3.13	10.72	17.13	56.75	9.43	1,722	888-843-7824	Y
Hartford Checks and Balances Fund Class R4	HCKSX	B-	C+	B	Up	0.70	3.23	10.98	18.16	59.04	9.44	1,722	888-843-7824	Y
Hartford Checks and Balances Fund Class R5	HCKTX	B-	C+	B	Up	0.69	3.31	11.32	19.20	61.49	9.48	1,722	888-843-7824	Y
Hennessy Balanced Fund Investor Class	HBFBX	B-	C+	B	Down	2.56	6.59	8.34	17.18	36.04	12.28	12.4	800-966-4354	Y
Hennessy Equity and Income Fund Institutional Class	HEIIX	B-	C+	B	Down	4.75	7.96	13.87	17.50	53.09	15.11	267.0	800-966-4354	Y
Hennessy Equity and Income Fund Investor Class	HEIFX	B-	C+	B	Down	4.67	7.79	13.50	16.18	50.59	16.01	267.0	800-966-4354	Y
Highland Total Return Fund Class A	HTAAX	B-	C+	B	Down	0.37	0.41	7.87	17.62	43.47	22.85	105.6	877-665-1287	Y
Highland Total Return Fund Class C	HTACX	B-	C	B	Up	0.14	0.01	7.00	14.98	38.15	20.46	105.6	877-665-1287	Y
Highland Total Return Fund Class Y	HTAYX	B-	C+	B	Down	0.41	0.53	8.11	18.43	45.19	23.2	105.6	877-665-1287	Y
Holland Balanced Fund	HOLBX	B	C+	A+		4.85	6.24	9.24	16.58	57.80	20.03	31.6		Y
Horizon Active Asset Allocation Fund Class I	HASIX	B-	B-	C+	Up	4.92	10.11	21.90	21.01	66.11	12.74	427.4		Y
Hotchkis & Wiley Capital Income Fund Class A	HWIAX	B-	C+	B-	Up	1.32	3.50	9.98	21.71	63.55	13.21	39.2	866-493-8637	Y
Hotchkis & Wiley Capital Income Fund Class I	HWIIX	B-	C+	B-		1.36	3.69	10.22	22.49	65.32	12.7	39.2	866-493-8637	Y
Hundredfold Select Alternative Fund Investor Class	HFSAX	B	C+	A		2.21	4.30	9.92	21.13	34.59	22.62	52.4	855-582-8006	Y
Hundredfold Select Alternative Fund Service Class	SFHYX	B	C+	A-	Up	1.98	3.79	8.95	17.90	28.64	21.65	52.4	855-582-8006	Y
ICON Risk-Managed Balanced Fund Class A	IOCAX	B-	C+	B	Up	2.95	5.16	11.45	15.35	42.57	15.57	36.1	303-790-1600	Y
ICON Risk-Managed Balanced Fund Class C	IOCCX	B-	C+	B	Up	1.31	3.31	9.05	11.24	35.38	14.61	36.1	303-790-1600	Y
ICON Risk-Managed Balanced Fund Class S	IOCZX	B-	C+	B	Up	1.39	3.58	9.98	14.40	41.92	15.96	36.1	303-790-1600	Y
Invesco Equity and Income Fund Class A	ACEIX	B	C+	B+	Up	3.25	6.46	10.88	23.50	71.14	10.96	14,928	800-659-1005	Y
Invesco Equity and Income Fund Class B	ACEQX	B-	C+	B	Down	3.11	6.09	10.06	20.71	64.86	10.7	14,928	800-659-1005	
Invesco Equity and Income Fund Class C	ACERX	B-	C+	B	Down	3.10	6.06	10.02	20.76	64.88	10.76	14,928	800-659-1005	Y
Invesco Equity and Income Fund Class R	ACESX	B	C+	B	Up	3.17	6.30	10.55	22.60	68.99	11.02	14,928	800-659-1005	Y
Invesco Equity and Income Fund Class R6	IEIFX	B	B-	B+	Up	3.45	6.68	11.33	25.06	74.74	10.96	14,928	800-659-1005	Y
Invesco Equity and Income Fund Class Y	ACETX	B	C+	B+	Up	3.32	6.60	11.16	24.44	73.30	10.96	14,928	800-659-1005	Y
Invesco Equity and Income Fund R5 Class	ACEKX	B	B-	B+	Up	3.33	6.63	11.23	24.58	73.91	10.96	14,928	800-659-1005	Y
Invesco Macro Allocation Strategy Fund Class A	GMSDX	B-	C+	B	Down	5.13	7.41	7.30	13.53	26.50	9.45	43.5	800-659-1005	Y
Invesco Macro Allocation Strategy Fund Class C	GMSEX	B-	C+	B		4.82	6.99	6.41	11.09	21.97	9.4	43.5	800-659-1005	Y
Invesco Macro Allocation Strategy Fund Class R	GMSJX	B-	C+	B	Down	5.02	7.18	6.95	12.69	25.14	9.45	43.5	800-659-1005	Y
Invesco Macro Allocation Strategy Fund Class R5	GMSKX	B-	C+	B+	Down	5.11	7.61	7.49	14.48	28.33	9.5	43.5	800-659-1005	Y
Invesco Macro Allocation Strategy Fund Class R6	GMSLX	B-	C+	B+	Down	5.11	7.50	7.50	14.38	27.97	9.48	43.5	800-659-1005	Y
Invesco Macro Allocation Strategy Fund Class Y	GMSHX	B-	C+	B+	Down	5.11	7.50	7.50	14.48	28.08	9.49	43.5	800-659-1005	Y
Invesco Moderate Allocation Fund Class A	AMKAX	B-	C+	B-	Up	2.99	6.31	12.66	16.37	35.75	13.62	774.1	800-659-1005	Y
Invesco Moderate Allocation Fund Class R6	AMLSX	B-	C+	B-	Up	3.07	6.46	12.97	17.20	37.42	13.67	774.1	800-659-1005	Y
Invesco Moderate Allocation Fund Class S	AMKSX	B-	C+	B-	Up	3.02	6.37	12.69	16.64	36.39	13.61	774.1	800-659-1005	Y
Invesco Moderate Allocation Fund Class Y	ABKYX	B-	C+	B-	Up	3.06	6.36	12.85	17.15	37.40	13.63	774.1	800-659-1005	Y
Invesco Moderate Allocation Fund R5 Class	AMLIX	B-	C+	B-	Up	3.06	6.45	12.96	17.19	37.41	13.68	774.1	800-659-1005	Y

Category: Moderate Allocation (con't)

Fund Name	Ticker Symbol	RATINGS: Overall Rating	Reward Rating	Risk Rating	Recent Up/ Downgrade	TOTAL RETURNS & PERFORMANCE: 3-Month Total Return	6-Month Total Return	1-Year Total Return	3-Year Total Return	5-Year Total Return	ASSETS: NAV	Total Assets (MIL)	NEW INVESTORS: Telephone	Open to New Investors
InvestEd Balanced Portfolio	WBLAX	B-	C+	B	Down	3.43	8.25	16.60	19.49	51.27	11.65	81.5	888-923-3355	Y
InvestEd Conservative Portfolio	WICAX	B-	C	B	Up	2.37	5.29	8.82	10.50	30.34	10.68	87.7	888-923-3355	Y
Ivy Balanced Fund Class A	IBNAX	B-	C+	B+	Down	3.80	5.15	11.38	12.59	51.64	24.89	1,897	800-777-6472	Y
Ivy Balanced Fund Class B	IBNBX	B-	C	B+	Up	3.64	4.81	10.60	10.22	46.20	24.64	1,897	800-777-6472	
Ivy Balanced Fund Class C	IBNCX	B-	C	B+	Up	3.64	4.77	10.59	10.32	46.47	24.72	1,897	800-777-6472	Y
Ivy Balanced Fund Class I	IYBIX	B	C+	B+	Up	3.91	5.29	11.65	13.51	53.64	24.89	1,897	800-777-6472	Y
Ivy Balanced Fund Class N	IBARX	B	C+	A-	Up	3.94	5.35	11.85	14.00	53.77	24.93	1,897	800-777-6472	Y
Ivy Balanced Fund Class R	IYBFX	B-	C	B+	Up	3.76	5.00	11.02	11.51	49.14	24.86	1,897	800-777-6472	Y
Ivy Balanced Fund Class Y	IBNYX	B-	C+	B+	Down	3.85	5.16	11.38	12.66	51.76	24.9	1,897	800-777-6472	Y
Janus Henderson Balanced Fund Class A	JDBAX	B-	C+	B	Down	5.19	9.20	18.24	23.18	61.61	32.86	13,878	877-335-2687	Y
Janus Henderson Balanced Fund Class C	JABCX	B-	C+	B	Down	5.02	8.84	17.42	20.69	55.98	32.58	13,878	877-335-2687	Y
Janus Henderson Balanced Fund Class D	JANBX	B-	C+	B	Down	5.27	9.34	18.51	23.95	63.29	32.93	13,878	877-335-2687	
Janus Henderson Balanced Fund Class I	JBALX	B-	C+	B	Down	5.29	9.38	18.58	24.24	63.90	32.94	13,878	877-335-2687	Y
Janus Henderson Balanced Fund Class N	JABNX	B-	B-	B	Down	5.32	9.42	18.68	24.52	64.48	32.91	13,878	877-335-2687	Y
Janus Henderson Balanced Fund Class R	JDBRX	B-	C+	B	Down	5.08	8.99	17.79	21.74	58.48	32.68	13,878	877-335-2687	Y
Janus Henderson Balanced Fund Class S	JABRX	B-	C+	B	Down	5.16	9.11	18.05	22.64	60.49	32.84	13,878	877-335-2687	Y
Janus Henderson Balanced Fund Class T	JABAX	B-	C+	B	Down	5.22	9.26	18.38	23.61	62.55	32.89	13,878	877-335-2687	Y
Janus Henderson Value Plus Income Fund Class A	JPVAX	B-	C+	B	Up	2.84	4.63	9.28	17.52	47.00	11.65	59.6	877-335-2687	Y
Janus Henderson Value Plus Income Fund Class C	JPVCX	B-	C+	B	Up	2.64	4.31	8.53	14.87	41.67	11.68	59.6	877-335-2687	Y
Janus Henderson Value Plus Income Fund Class D	JPVDX	B-	C+	B	Up	2.96	4.78	9.50	17.94	48.07	11.66	59.6	877-335-2687	Y
Janus Henderson Value Plus Income Fund Class I	JPVIX	B-	C+	B	Up	2.98	4.81	9.57	18.15	48.69	11.67	59.6	877-335-2687	Y
Janus Henderson Value Plus Income Fund Class N	JPVNX	B-	C+	B		2.90	4.82	9.59	18.17	48.71	11.66	59.6	877-335-2687	Y
Janus Henderson Value Plus Income Fund Class S	JPVSX	B-	C+	B	Up	2.82	4.56	9.15	17.32	46.59	11.66	59.6	877-335-2687	Y
Janus Henderson Value Plus Income Fund Class T	JPVTX	B-	C+	B	Up	2.85	4.72	9.30	17.75	47.75	11.66	59.6	877-335-2687	Y
Janus Henderson VIT Balanced Portfolio Institutional Class	JABLX	B-	C+	B	Down	5.17	9.15	18.42	24.01	64.08	35.27	3,268	877-335-2687	Y
Janus Henderson VIT Balanced Portfolio Service Class	US4710216916	B-	C+	B	Down	5.09	9.02	18.13	23.11	62.00	37.09	3,268	877-335-2687	Y
JNL Institutional Alt 25 Fund Class A	US46644W5913	B-	C+	B	Up	3.39	6.62	14.33	18.01	39.09	17.07	3,311		Y
JNL Institutional Alt 25 Fund Class I	US46644W5830	B-	C+	B		3.45	6.68	14.40	18.08	39.17	17.08	3,311		Y
JNL Moderate Growth Allocation Fund Class A	US46648L5755	B-	C+	B	Up	3.08	6.11	14.53	20.12	50.09	13.71	2,467		Y
JNL Moderate Growth Allocation Fund Class I	US46648L5672	B-	C+	B		3.15	6.19	14.61	20.21	50.20	13.72	2,467		Y
JNL/AB Dynamic Asset Allocation Fund Class A	US46644W2522	B-	C+	B-	Down	3.65	7.12	15.88	17.84		11.64	37.9		Y
JNL/AB Dynamic Asset Allocation Fund Class I	US46644W2456	B-	C+	B-		3.73	7.22	15.98	17.94		11.65	37.9		Y
JNL/American Funds Moderate Growth Allocation Class A	US46644W4353	B	C+	A-	Up	3.18	6.81	15.69	23.60	50.17	14.89	2,198		Y
JNL/American Funds Moderate Growth Allocation Class I	US46644W4270	B	C+	A-		3.18	6.81	15.69	23.60	50.17	14.89	2,198		Y
JNL/S&P Managed Moderate Growth Fund Class A	US46648L6829	B-	C+	B	Down	3.48	6.82	16.00	21.04	48.61	17.54	6,400		Y
JNL/S&P Managed Moderate Growth Fund Class I	US46648L6746	B-	C+	B		3.59	6.94	16.13	21.18	48.78	17.56	6,400		Y
JNL/WMC Balanced Fund Class A	US46649B8818	B-	C+	B	Down	3.98	6.98	12.48	22.62	63.35	24.02	7,674		Y
JNL/WMC Balanced Fund Class I	US46649B8735	B-	C+	B	Down	4.07	7.14	12.74	23.43	65.07	24.75	7,674		Y
John Hancock Balanced Fund Class A	SVBAX	B-	C+	B	Down	4.58	7.40	13.91	20.01	57.62	20.46	1,957	800-225-5913	Y
John Hancock Balanced Fund Class B	SVBBX	B-	C+	B	Down	4.46	7.04	13.09	17.55	52.22	20.43	1,957	800-225-5913	
John Hancock Balanced Fund Class C	SVBCX	B-	C+	B	Down	4.41	7.04	13.09	17.54	52.18	20.44	1,957	800-225-5913	Y
John Hancock Balanced Fund Class I	SVBIX	B-	C+	B	Down	4.66	7.58	14.22	21.15	60.08	20.44	1,957	800-225-5913	Y
John Hancock Balanced Fund Class R1	JBAOX	B-	C+	B	Down	4.47	7.19	13.46	18.76	54.96	20.54	1,957	800-225-5913	Y
John Hancock Balanced Fund Class R2	JBATX	B-	C+	B	Down	4.56	7.36	13.77	19.67	57.40	20.43	1,957	800-225-5913	Y
John Hancock Balanced Fund Class R3	JBAHX	B-	C+	B	Down	4.56	7.25	13.60	19.17	55.78	20.51	1,957	800-225-5913	Y
John Hancock Balanced Fund Class R4	JBAFX	B-	C+	B	Down	4.65	7.51	14.08	20.60	58.94	20.55	1,957	800-225-5913	Y
John Hancock Balanced Fund Class R5	JBAVX	B-	C+	B	Down	4.71	7.62	14.32	21.36	60.54	20.52	1,957	800-225-5913	Y
John Hancock Balanced Fund Class R6	JBAWX	B-	C+	B	Down	4.68	7.62	14.31	21.52	61.05	20.46	1,957	800-225-5913	Y
John Hancock Funds Diversified Strategies Fund Class I	JDSIX	B-	C	B+	Up	0.84	2.77	7.30	9.68	19.28	10.33	43.0	800-225-5913	Y
John Hancock Funds II Multimgr Lifest Balanced Port Cls 1	JILBX	B-	C+	B	Down	3.15	6.64	15.14	21.52	49.18	15.19	12,976	800-225-5913	Y
John Hancock Funds II Multimgr Lifest Balanced Port Cls 5	JHLAX	B-	C+	B	Down	3.22	6.66	15.27	21.69	49.53	15.2	12,976	800-225-5913	Y
John Hancock Funds II Multimgr Lifest Balanced Port Cls A	JALBX	B-	C+	B	Down	3.10	6.40	14.79	20.16	46.41	15.29	12,976	800-225-5913	Y

Category: Moderate Allocation (con't)

Fund Name	Ticker Symbol	RATINGS: Overall Rating	Reward Rating	Risk Rating	Recent Up/ Downgrade	TOTAL RETURNS & PERFORMANCE: 3-Month Total Return	6-Month Total Return	1-Year Total Return	3-Year Total Return	5-Year Total Return	ASSETS: NAV	Total Assets (MIL)	NEW INVESTORS: Telephone	Open to New Investors
John Hancock Funds II Multimgr Lifest Balanced Port Cls B	JBLBX	B-	C+	B	Down	2.92	6.03	13.93	17.64	41.13	15.28	12,976	800-225-5913	
John Hancock Funds II Multimgr Lifest Balanced Port Cls C	JCLBX	B-	C+	B	Down	2.92	6.09	13.99	17.71	41.27	15.3	12,976	800-225-5913	Y
John Hancock Funds II Multimgr Lifest Balanced Port Cls I	JTBIX	B-	C+	B	Down	3.13	6.60	15.14	21.37	49.01	15.2	12,976	800-225-5913	Y
John Hancock Funds II Multimgr Lifest Balanced Port Cls R1	JPLBX	B-	C+	B	Down	3.02	6.24	14.38	18.90	43.64	15.22	12,976	800-225-5913	Y
John Hancock Funds II Multimgr Lifest Balanced Port Cls R2	JQLBX	B-	C+	B	Down	3.03	6.32	14.60	19.74	45.50	15.2	12,976	800-225-5913	Y
John Hancock Funds II Multimgr Lifest Balanced Port Cls R3	JRLBX	B-	C+	B	Down	3.04	6.29	14.46	19.29	44.54	15.25	12,976	800-225-5913	Y
John Hancock Funds II Multimgr Lifest Balanced Port Cls R4	JSLBX	B-	C+	B	Down	3.14	6.49	14.98	20.71	47.53	15.26	12,976	800-225-5913	Y
John Hancock Funds II Multimgr Lifest Balanced Port Cls R5	JTSBX	B-	C+	B	Down	3.19	6.59	15.19	21.46	48.90	15.28	12,976	800-225-5913	Y
John Hancock Funds II Multimgr Lifest Balanced Port Cls R6	JULBX	B-	C+	B	Down	3.23	6.66	15.27	21.69	49.45	15.2	12,976	800-225-5913	Y
John Hancock Funds Multi-Ind Lifestyle Balanced Port Cls 1	JIBOX	B-	C+	B	Up	3.21	6.42	13.55	20.66		11.53	796.3	800-225-5913	Y
John Hancock Funds Multi-Ind Lifest Bal Cls R6	JIBRX	B-	C+	B	Up	3.31	6.53	13.70	20.90		11.54	796.3	800-225-5913	Y
John Hancock II Capital Appreciation Value Fund Class NAV	JCAVX	B	B-	A-	Down	2.87	5.60	15.25	30.41	81.42	11.42	1,907	800-225-5913	Y
John Hancock Tax-Advantaged Dividend Income Fund	HTD	B	B-	A	Up	0.20	1.83	11.38	28.96	80.86	25.23	943.0	800-225-5913	Y
JPMorgan Diversified Fund Class A	JDVAX	B-	C+	B	Down	3.98	8.29	17.35	21.86	54.76	17.69	1,574	800-480-4111	Y
JPMorgan Diversified Fund Class C	JDVCX	B-	C+	B	Down	3.82	8.00	16.72	19.94	50.85	17.56	1,574	800-480-4111	Y
JPMorgan Diversified Fund Class I	JDVSX	B-	C+	B	Down	4.02	8.37	17.60	22.71	56.65	17.78	1,574	800-480-4111	Y
JPMorgan Diversified Fund Class L	JPDVX	B-	C+	B	Down	4.05	8.48	17.88	23.60	58.50	17.75	1,574	800-480-4111	Y
JPMorgan Diversified Fund Class R6	JDVZX	B-	C+	B		4.09	8.52	17.92	23.65	58.56	17.75	1,574	800-480-4111	Y
JPMorgan Investor Balanced Fund Class A	OGIAX	B-	C+	B	Up	3.25	6.36	13.01	18.63	46.30	15.39	5,001	800-480-4111	Y
JPMorgan Investor Balanced Fund Class C	OGBCX	B-	C+	B	Up	2.09	5.05	11.25	15.50	41.03	15.15	5,001	800-480-4111	Y
JPMorgan Investor Balanced Fund Class I	OIBFX	B-	C+	B	Up	3.31	6.47	13.27	19.44	48.03	15.41	5,001	800-480-4111	Y
JPMorgan Investor Balanced Fund Class R6	JFQUX	B-	C+	B		3.35	6.55	13.36	19.53	48.14	15.41	5,001	800-480-4111	Y
JPMorgan Investor Balanced Fund Class T	JPBTX	B-	C+	B	Up	3.24	6.34	12.99	18.55	46.19	15.37	5,001	800-480-4111	Y
Lazard Capital Allocator Opportunistic Strat Inst Shares	LCAIX	B-	C+	B-	Down	3.44	8.45	17.73	18.61	40.91	10.6	156.0	800-823-6300	Y
Lazard Capital Allocator Opportunistic Strat Open Shares	LCAOX	B-	C+	B-	Down	3.43	8.37	17.47	17.05	38.27	10.55	156.0	800-823-6300	Y
Leuthold Core Investment Fund Class Institutional	LCRIX	B-	C+	B	Up	3.14	7.88	15.88	19.59	57.06	20.55	865.9	800-273-6886	Y
Leuthold Core Investment Fund Retail Class	LCORX	B-	C+	B	Up	3.14	7.83	15.76	19.21	56.33	20.53	865.9	800-273-6886	Y
LK Balanced Fund Institutional Class Shares	LKBLX	B-	C+	B	Up	4.46	10.47	14.03	20.06	45.01	48.5	28.0		Y
LKCM Balanced Fund	LKBAX	B-	C+	B	Down	3.80	6.38	12.87	24.08	65.08	22.18	81.3	800-688-5526	Y
Loomis Sayles Multi-Asset Income Fund Class A	IIDPX	B-	C+	B	Up	3.54	6.68	12.41	20.47	46.13	13.87	142.3	800-862-4863	Y
Loomis Sayles Multi-Asset Income Fund Class C	CIDPX	B-	C+	B	Down	3.42	6.30	11.70	17.84	40.77	13.82	142.3	800-862-4863	Y
Loomis Sayles Multi-Asset Income Fund Class N	LMINX	B-	C+	B	Up	3.64	6.81	12.82	21.31	47.14	13.79	142.3	800-862-4863	Y
Loomis Sayles Multi-Asset Income Fund Class Y	YIDPX	B-	C+	B	Up	3.71	6.86	12.76	21.42	47.38	13.8	142.3	800-862-4863	Y
Lord Abbett Multi-Asset Balanced Opportunity Fund Class B	LABBX	B-	C+	B	Up	2.57	4.75	9.42	13.27	41.46	11.81	1,838	201-827-2000	
Lord Abbett Multi-Asset Balanced Opportunity Fund Class C	BFLAX	B-	C+	B	Up	2.62	4.75	9.41	13.28	41.61	11.73	1,838	201-827-2000	Y
Lord Abbett Multi-Asset Balanced Opportunity Fund Class F	BLAFX	B-	C+	B	Down	2.85	5.21	10.35	16.35	47.99	11.8	1,838	201-827-2000	Y
Madison Diversified Income Fund Class A	MBLAX	B-	C+	B	Up	4.49	7.59	12.83	21.86	51.69	16.13	168.2	800-767-0300	Y
Madison Diversified Income Fund Class B	MBLNX	B-	C+	B	Down	4.27	7.14	11.99	19.13	46.13	16.23	168.2	800-767-0300	Y
Madison Diversified Income Fund Class C	MBLCX	B-	C+	B	Down	4.27	7.15	12.00	19.14	46.16	16.22	168.2	800-767-0300	Y
Madison Moderate Allocation Fund Class A	MMDAX	B-	C+	B	Up	3.47	6.75	14.28	19.59	48.37	11.86	149.1	800-767-0300	Y
Madison Moderate Allocation Fund Class B	MMDRX	B-	C+	B	Up	3.23	6.26	13.41	16.87	42.90	11.79	149.1	800-767-0300	Y
Madison Moderate Allocation Fund Class C	MMDCX	B-	C+	B	Up	3.23	6.35	13.40	16.85	42.86	11.8	149.1	800-767-0300	Y
MainStay Balanced Fund Class A	MBNAX	B-	C+	B	Up	3.59	5.84	9.61	16.09	58.54	32.67	770.9	800-624-6782	Y
MainStay Balanced Fund Class B	MBNBX	B-	C+	B+	Up	3.33	5.35	8.58	12.98	51.46	32.54	770.9	800-624-6782	
MainStay Balanced Fund Class C	MBACX	B-	C+	B+	Up	3.33	5.35	8.59	12.99	51.45	32.52	770.9	800-624-6782	Y
MainStay Balanced Fund Class I	MBAIX	B	C+	B+	Up	3.65	5.96	9.86	16.96	60.53	32.74	770.9	800-624-6782	Y
MainStay Balanced Fund Class R1	MBNRX	B-	C+	B	Up	3.63	5.95	9.75	16.62	59.75	32.7	770.9	800-624-6782	Y
MainStay Balanced Fund Class R2	MBCRX	B	C+	B+	Up	3.53	5.78	9.64	15.90	57.96	32.71	770.9	800-624-6782	Y
MainStay Balanced Fund Class R3	MBDRX	B-	C+	B	Up	3.47	5.65	9.20	14.86	55.72	32.64	770.9	800-624-6782	Y
MainStay Balanced Fund Investor Class	MBINX	B-	C+	B	Up	3.51	5.76	9.40	15.53	57.19	32.69	770.9	800-624-6782	Y
MainStay Moderate Allocation Class R3	MMRHX	B-	C+	B	Down	3.66	7.34	14.19	17.70	49.01	13.78	744.2	800-624-6782	Y
MainStay Moderate Allocation Fund Class A	MMRAX	B-	C+	B	Down	3.77	7.53	14.64	18.86	51.16	13.8	744.2	800-624-6782	Y

Category: Moderate Allocation (con't)

Fund Name	Ticker Symbol	RATINGS: Overall Rating	Reward Rating	Risk Rating	Recent Up/ Downgrade	TOTAL RETURNS & PERFORMANCE: 3-Month Total Return	6-Month Total Return	1-Year Total Return	3-Year Total Return	5-Year Total Return	NAV	ASSETS: Total Assets (MIL)	NEW INVESTORS: Telephone	Open to New Investors
MainStay Moderate Allocation Fund Class B	MMRBX	B-	C+	B	Down	3.47	7.03	13.58	15.64	44.43	13.69	744.2	800-624-6782	
MainStay Moderate Allocation Fund Class C	MMRCX	B-	C+	B	Down	3.47	6.96	13.50	15.57	44.33	13.68	744.2	800-624-6782	Y
MainStay Moderate Allocation Fund Class I	MMRIX	B-	C+	B	Down	3.85	7.66	14.91	19.75	53.13	13.88	744.2	800-624-6782	Y
MainStay Moderate Allocation Fund Investor Class	MMRDX	B-	C+	B	Down	3.71	7.46	14.40	18.28	49.94	13.82	744.2	800-624-6782	Y
Mairs & Power Balanced Fund Investor Class	MAPOX	B-	C+	B	Down	4.00	6.07	11.89	20.80	57.53	94.01	985.2	800-304-7404	Y
Manning & Napier Pro-Blend Extended Term Series Class I	MNBIX	B-	C+	B	Up	1.85	5.25	15.09	13.83	41.67	9.29	681.2	585-325-6880	Y
Manning & Napier Pro-Blend Extended Term Series Class R	MNBRX	B-	C+	B	Up	1.79	5.02	14.64	12.12	38.23	10.85	681.2	585-325-6880	Y
Manning & Napier Pro-Blend Extended Term Series Class R2	MNECX	B-	C+	B	Up	1.68	4.74	13.98	10.43	34.77	10.09	681.2	585-325-6880	Y
Manning & Napier Pro-Blend Extended Term Series Class S	MNBAX	B-	C+	B	Up	1.84	5.16	14.86	12.98	39.98	17.3	681.2	585-325-6880	Y
Manning & Napier Strategic Income Moderate Series Class I	MSMAX	B-	C+	B	Up	3.57	6.18	10.66	19.55	44.45	11.27	32.9	585-325-6880	Y
Manning & Napier Strategic Income Moderate Series Class S	MSMSX	B-	C+	B	Up	3.49	6.03	10.39	18.78	42.75	11.27	32.9	585-325-6880	Y
MassMutual Premier Balanced Fund Administrative Class	MMBLX	B-	C+	B	Up	4.68	8.66	15.85	22.81	57.98	12.28	119.7		Y
MassMutual Premier Balanced Fund Class A	MMBDX	B-	C+	B	Up	4.49	8.39	15.55	21.74	55.93	11.94	119.7		Y
MassMutual Premier Balanced Fund Class I	MBBIX	B-	C+	B	Up	4.72	8.80	16.23	23.88	60.49	12.22	119.7		Y
MassMutual Premier Balanced Fund Class R3	MMBRX	B-	C+	B	Up	4.45	8.31	15.33	21.26	55.30	11.81	119.7		Y
MassMutual Premier Balanced Fund Class R4	MBBRX	B-	C+	B	Up	4.54	8.47	15.68	22.14	57.11	11.85	119.7		Y
MassMutual Premier Balanced Fund Class R5	MBLDX	B-	C+	B	Up	4.70	8.69	16.10	23.47	59.86	12.23	119.7		Y
MassMutual Premier Balanced Fund Service Class	MBAYX	B-	C+	B	Up	4.65	8.62	15.97	23.02	58.76	12.85	119.7		Y
MassMutual RetireSMART Moderate Fund Administrative Class	MRMLX	B-	C+	B	Up	3.16	6.46	13.62	17.17	41.12	10.32	307.5		Y
MassMutual RetireSMART Moderate Fund Class A	MRMAX	B-	C+	B	Up	3.07	6.36	13.37	16.32	39.44	10.36	307.5		Y
MassMutual RetireSMART Moderate Fund Class I	MRMUX	B-	C+	B	Up	3.19	6.61	13.91	18.24	42.84	10.28	307.5		Y
MassMutual RetireSMART Moderate Fund Class R3	MRMTX	B-	C+	B	Up	3.05	6.27	13.22	15.95	38.41	10.26	307.5		Y
MassMutual RetireSMART Moderate Fund Class R4	MRMZX	B-	C+	B	Up	3.18	6.40	13.47	16.74	40.08	10.27	307.5		Y
MassMutual RetireSMART Moderate Fund Class R5	MROSX	B-	C+	B	Up	3.20	6.61	13.91	18.05	42.49	10.29	307.5		Y
MassMutual RetireSMART Moderate Fund Service Class	MRMYX	B-	C+	B	Up	3.17	6.57	13.72	17.55	41.84	10.34	307.5		Y
Matisse Discounted Closed-End Fund Strategy Class A Shares	MDCAX	B-	B-	C+	Down	2.05	6.00	19.33	29.04	48.07		117.3	252-442-4226	Y
Matisse Discounted Closed-End Fund Strat Inst Cls Shares	MDCEX	B-	B-	C+	Down	3.23	7.18	20.69	30.66	52.42	11.32	117.3	252-442-4226	Y
Meeder Balanced Fund Adviser Class	BLNAX	B-	C+	B-	Down	4.05	7.78	15.21	14.55	51.73	11.68	230.4		Y
Meeder Balanced Fund Institutional Class	BLNIX	B-	C+	B-	Down	4.09	7.92	15.25	14.66	51.88	11.68	230.4		Y
Meeder Balanced Fund Retail Class	FLDFX	B-	C+	B	Down	3.92	7.66	14.73	14.06	51.09	11.61	230.4		Y
MFS® Moderate Allocation Fund Class 529A	EAMDX	B	C+	A-	Up	3.38	6.34	14.78	20.38	45.21	17.66	5,882	877-960-6077	Y
MFS® Moderate Allocation Fund Class 529B	EBMDX	B	C+	B+	Up	3.18	5.91	13.84	17.67	39.74	17.37	5,882	877-960-6077	Y
MFS® Moderate Allocation Fund Class 529C	ECMAX	B	C+	B+	Up	3.15	5.91	13.84	17.68	39.73	17.25	5,882	877-960-6077	Y
MFS® Moderate Allocation Fund Class A	MAMAX	B	C+	A-	Up	3.43	6.39	14.81	20.55	45.52	17.75	5,882	877-960-6077	Y
MFS® Moderate Allocation Fund Class B	MMABX	B	C+	B+	Up	3.21	5.93	13.94	17.79	40.10	17.55	5,882	877-960-6077	Y
MFS® Moderate Allocation Fund Class C	MMACX	B	C+	B+	Up	3.18	5.92	13.90	17.80	40.08	17.43	5,882	877-960-6077	Y
MFS® Moderate Allocation Fund Class I	MMAIX	B	C+	A-	Up	3.45	6.43	15.08	21.37	47.27	17.98	5,882	877-960-6077	Y
MFS® Moderate Allocation Fund Class R1	MAMFX	B	C+	B+	Up	3.20	5.93	13.89	17.80	40.09	17.07	5,882	877-960-6077	Y
MFS® Moderate Allocation Fund Class R2	MARRX	B	C+	A-	Up	3.32	6.21	14.52	19.61	43.58	17.37	5,882	877-960-6077	Y
MFS® Moderate Allocation Fund Class R3	MAMHX	B	C+	A-	Up	3.40	6.38	14.80	20.50	45.46	17.61	5,882	877-960-6077	Y
MFS® Moderate Allocation Fund Class R4	MAMJX	B	C+	A-	Up	3.50	6.46	15.10	21.48	47.28	17.73	5,882	877-960-6077	Y
MFS® Total Return Fund Class 529A	EATRX	B-	C+	B	Up	3.34	5.52	12.09	20.74	57.41	19.07	8,026	877-960-6077	Y
MFS® Total Return Fund Class 529B	EBTRX	B-	C+	B	Up	3.18	5.14	11.24	18.05	51.55	19.15	8,026	877-960-6077	Y
MFS® Total Return Fund Class 529C	ECTRX	B-	C+	B	Up	3.16	5.12	11.26	18.02	51.57	19.23	8,026	877-960-6077	Y
MFS® Total Return Fund Class A	MSFRX	B-	C+	B	Up	3.40	5.58	12.16	20.96	57.84	19.13	8,026	877-960-6077	Y
MFS® Total Return Fund Class B	MTRBX	B-	C+	B	Up	3.19	5.16	11.29	18.24	51.94	19.15	8,026	877-960-6077	Y
MFS® Total Return Fund Class C	MTRCX	B-	C+	B	Up	3.17	5.14	11.23	18.16	51.88	19.24	8,026	877-960-6077	Y
MFS® Total Return Fund Class I	MTRIX	B-	C+	B	Down	3.46	5.65	12.37	21.82	59.74	19.12	8,026	877-960-6077	Y
MFS® Total Return Fund Class R1	MSFFX	B-	C+	B	Up	3.20	5.13	11.27	18.18	51.97	19.1	8,026	877-960-6077	Y
MFS® Total Return Fund Class R2	MTRRX	B-	C+	B	Up	3.32	5.37	11.84	20.01	55.81	19.18	8,026	877-960-6077	Y
MFS® Total Return Fund Class R3	MSFHX	B-	C+	B	Up	3.39	5.57	12.14	20.92	57.75	19.14	8,026	877-960-6077	Y
MFS® Total Return Fund Class R4	MSFJX	B-	C+	B	Up	3.40	5.65	12.36	21.79	59.75	19.14	8,026	877-960-6077	Y

Category: Moderate Allocation (con't)

Fund Name	Ticker Symbol	RATINGS: Overall Rating	Reward Rating	Risk Rating	Recent Up/ Downgrade	TOTAL RETURNS & PERFORMANCE: 3-Month Total Return	6-Month Total Return	1-Year Total Return	3-Year Total Return	5-Year Total Return	ASSETS: NAV	Total Assets (MIL)	NEW INVESTORS: Telephone	Open to New Investors
MFS® Total Return Fund Class R6	MSFKX	B-	C+	B	Down	3.48	5.75	12.52	22.19	60.47	19.13	8,026	877-960-6077	Y
Morningstar Balanced ETF Asset Allocation Portfolio Cls I	US00162T7046	B-	C+	B	Up	3.21	6.53	13.65	20.45	43.48	11.29	194.6	866-759-5679	Y
Nationwide Investor Destinations Moderate Fund Class A	NADMX	B-	C+	B	Up	3.65	7.01	13.74	20.04	46.43	10.15	1,403	800-848-0920	Y
Nationwide Investor Destinations Moderate Fund Class C	NCDMX	B-	C+	B	Up	3.43	6.54	12.80	17.45	41.23	9.94	1,403	800-848-0920	Y
Nationwide Investor Destinations Moderate Fund Class R	GMDRX	B-	C+	B	Up	3.58	6.84	13.45	19.10	44.26	9.87	1,403	800-848-0920	Y
Nationwide Investor Destinations Moderate Fund Class R6	GMDIX	B-	C+	B	Up	3.67	7.14	14.11	21.36	48.85	10.09	1,403	800-848-0920	Y
Nationwide Investor Destinations Moderate Fund Cls Service	NSDMX	B-	C+	B	Up	3.66	7.02	13.63	20.00	46.15	10.1	1,403	800-848-0920	Y
Nationwide Inv Destinations Moderate Fund Inst Service Cls	NWWJX	B-	C+	B	Up	3.65	7.10	14.05	20.93	47.79	10.08	1,403	800-848-0920	Y
Neiman Balanced Allocation Fund Class A	NBAFX	B-	C+	B	Up	3.73	6.80	12.89	16.13	40.23	13.14	9.3	858-551-4078	Y
New Covenant Balanced Growth Fund	NCBGX	B-	C+	B	Up	3.85	6.91	13.47	18.61	49.18	101.83	295.4		Y
Newfound Multi-Asset Income Fund Class A	NFMAX	B-	C	B	Up	0.56	2.42	7.48	8.52		9.97	85.2		Y
Newfound Multi-Asset Income Fund Class I	NFMIX	B-	C	B	Up	0.72	2.65	7.84	9.40		9.98	85.2		Y
Nuveen Real Asset Income and Growth Fund	JRI	B-	B-	B	Up	1.37	3.93	15.96	22.96	64.62	19.62	539.4	312-917-8146	Y
Nuveen Strategy Balanced Allocation Fund Class A	FSGNX	B	C+	B+	Up	3.00	5.86	12.39	15.87	41.95	10.64	254.1	312-917-8146	Y
Nuveen Strategy Balanced Allocation Fund Class C	FSKCX	B-	C+	B+	Up	2.83	5.43	11.56	13.29	36.61	10.46	254.1	312-917-8146	Y
Nuveen Strategy Balanced Allocation Fund Class I	FSKYX	B-	C+	B	Up	3.07	6.01	12.60	16.67	43.72	10.6	254.1	312-917-8146	Y
Nuveen Strategy Balanced Allocation Fund Class R3	FSKSX	B-	C+	B	Up	2.86	5.68	12.04	14.95	40.06	10.49	254.1	312-917-8146	Y
Nuveen Strategy Growth Allocation Fund Class A	FSNAX	B-	C+	B	Down	4.04	8.10	16.56	21.51	55.52	12.9	138.4	312-917-8146	Y
Nuveen Strategy Growth Allocation Fund Class C	FSNCX	B-	C+	B-	Down	3.92	7.76	15.85	18.90	49.86	12.57	138.4	312-917-8146	Y
Nuveen Strategy Growth Allocation Fund Class I	FSGYX	B-	C+	B	Down	4.12	8.25	16.96	22.43	57.48	12.96	138.4	312-917-8146	Y
Nuveen Strategy Growth Allocation Fund Class R3	FSNSX	B-	C+	B	Down	4.06	8.02	16.40	20.65	53.62	12.73	138.4	312-917-8146	Y
NWM Momentum Fund	MOMOX	B	B-	A+		0.38	5.80	12.17	39.46		10.18	77.8		Y
Oakmark Equity and Income Fund Class Advisor	OAYBX	B-	C+	B	Down	4.25	8.16	14.63	20.61	63.17	32.19	16,501	641-219-558	Y
Oakmark Equity and Income Fund Class Institutional	OANBX	B	C+	B	Up	4.27	8.14	14.65	20.62	63.20	32.19	16,501	641-219-558	Y
Oakmark Equity And Income Fund Investor Class	OAKBX	B-	C+	B	Down	4.21	8.06	14.46	20.38	62.87	32.19	16,501	641-219-558	Y
Oakmark Equity And Income Fund Service Class	OARBX	B-	C+	B	Down	4.14	7.94	14.15	19.30	60.37	32.03	16,501	641-219-558	Y
Oppenheimer Portfolio Series Moderate Investor Fund Cls A	OAMIX	B-	C+	B	Down	3.29	6.37	15.01	18.42	45.54	12.24	1,669	800-225-5677	Y
Oppenheimer Portfolio Series Moderate Investor Fund Cls B	OBMIX	B	C+	B+	Up	3.09	6.02	14.19	15.83	40.16	12.31	1,669	800-225-5677	
Oppenheimer Portfolio Series Moderate Investor Fund Cls C	OCMIX	B	C+	B+	Up	3.12	5.99	14.27	15.85	40.10	12.01	1,669	800-225-5677	Y
Oppenheimer Portfolio Series Moderate Investor Fund Cls R	ONMIX	B-	C+	B	Down	3.16	6.26	14.74	17.54	43.78	12.17	1,669	800-225-5677	Y
Oppenheimer Portfolio Series Moderate Investor Fund Cls Y	OYMIX	B-	C+	B	Down	3.37	6.53	15.43	19.33	47.43	12.31	1,669	800-225-5677	Y
Pacific Funds Portfolio Optimization Moderate Fund Adv Cls	POMDX	B-	C+	B	Up	2.91	6.42	13.77	20.96	43.84	14.4	1,386	800-722-2333	Y
Pacific Funds Portfolio Optimization Moderate Fund Class A	POCAX	B-	C+	B	Up	2.87	6.31	13.50	20.05	42.12	14.38	1,386	800-722-2333	Y
Pacific Funds Portfolio Optimization Moderate Fund Class B	POMBX	B-	C+	B	Down	2.67	5.86	12.60	17.39	37.13	14.21	1,386	800-722-2333	Y
Pacific Funds Portfolio Optimization Moderate Fund Class C	POMCX	B-	C+	B	Up	2.61	5.87	12.54	17.34	37.08	14.18	1,386	800-722-2333	Y
Pacific Funds Port Optimization Moderate Fund Cls Retmnt	POCRX	B-	C+	B	Up	2.85	6.15	13.18	19.16	40.43	14.34	1,386	800-722-2333	Y
Pax Balanced Fund Class Institutional	PAXIX	B-	C+	B	Up	3.88	6.62	13.42	19.24	53.39	23.01	1,989	800-767-1729	Y
Pax Balanced Fund Individual Investor Class	PAXWX	B-	C+	B	Up	3.80	6.48	13.16	18.33	51.41	22.66	1,989	800-767-1729	Y
Pioneer Classic Balanced Fund Class A	AOBLX	B-	C+	B	Down	4.46	8.07	15.00	20.07	60.38	9.52	275.8	617-742-7825	Y
Pioneer Classic Balanced Fund Class C	PCBCX	B-	C+	B	Down	4.30	7.71	14.17	17.51	54.31	9.46	275.8	617-742-7825	Y
Pioneer Classic Balanced Fund Class K	PCBKX	B-	C+	B	Down	4.55	8.39	15.46	21.14	62.63	9.52	275.8	617-742-7825	Y
Pioneer Classic Balanced Fund Class R	CBPRX	B-	C+	B	Down	4.41	8.02	14.84	19.50	58.82	9.53	275.8	617-742-7825	Y
Pioneer Classic Balanced Fund Class Y	AYBLX	B-	C+	B	Down	4.48	8.18	15.19	20.90	62.30	9.58	275.8	617-742-7825	Y
Pioneer Flexible Opportunities Fund Class A	PMARX	B	B-	B	Up	4.51	11.82	23.24	29.77	44.39	13.48	660.5	617-742-7825	Y
Pioneer Flexible Opportunities Fund Class C	PRRCX	B-	C+	B	Up	4.34	11.45	22.44	26.84	39.02	13.27	660.5	617-742-7825	Y
Pioneer Flexible Opportunities Fund Class R	MUARX	B-	C+	B	Up	4.54	11.67	22.78	27.32	41.09	13.42	660.5	617-742-7825	Y
Pioneer Flexible Opportunities Fund Class Y	PMYRX	B	B-	B	Up	4.62	12.00	23.66	30.97	46.55	13.54	660.5	617-742-7825	Y
Pioneer Solutions - Balanced Fund Class A	PIALX	B-	C+	B+	Up	2.57	5.79	12.89	12.63	37.46	12.23	166.2	617-742-7825	Y
Pioneer Solutions - Balanced Fund Class C	PIDCX	B-	C	B+	Up	2.32	5.45	11.97	10.23	32.69	11.26	166.2	617-742-7825	Y
Pioneer Solutions - Balanced Fund Class Y	IMOYX	B-	C+	B+	Up	2.65	5.92	13.13	13.44	39.28	12.39	166.2	617-742-7825	Y
Plumb Balanced Fund	PLBBX	B-	B-	B	Down	5.82	8.80	23.22	27.89	75.49	28.37	39.6		Y
PNC Balanced Allocation Class T	PBTTX	B	C+	A-	Up	3.72	7.49	15.34	20.05	47.98	13.45	22.2	800-622-3863	Y

Category: Moderate Allocation (con't)

Fund Name	Ticker Symbol	RATINGS: Overall Rating	RATINGS: Reward Rating	RATINGS: Risk Rating	RATINGS: Recent Up/ Downgrade	TOTAL RETURNS & PERFORMANCE: 3-Month Total Return	6-Month Total Return	1-Year Total Return	3-Year Total Return	5-Year Total Return	ASSETS: NAV	Total Assets (MIL)	NEW INVESTORS: Telephone	Open to New Investors
PNC Balanced Allocation Fund Class A	PBAAX	B-	C+	B	Up	3.78	7.55	15.36	19.13	47.60	13.33	22.2	800-622-3863	Y
PNC Balanced Allocation Fund Class C	PBCCX	B	C+	A-	Up	3.55	7.13	14.61	16.65	42.51	13.11	22.2	800-622-3863	Y
PNC Balanced Allocation Fund Class I	PBLIX	B	C+	A-	Up	3.87	7.73	15.75	20.19	49.63	13.27	22.2	800-622-3863	Y
Praxis Genesis Balanced Portfolio Class A	MBAPX	B-	C+	B	Up	1.69	4.79	11.51	16.13	43.05	13.71	72.7		Y
Principal Strategic Asset Mgmt Balanced Portfolio Cls A	SABPX	B-	C+	B	Up	2.01	5.80	13.12	18.19	49.30	15.95	4,917	800-222-5852	Y
Principal Strategic Asset Mgmt Balanced Portfolio Cls C	SCBPX	B-	C+	B	Up	3.19	6.89	13.87	17.19	45.82	15.72	4,917	800-222-5852	Y
Principal Strategic Asset Mgmt Balanced Portfolio Cls J	PSAJX	B-	C+	B	Up	2.01	5.83	13.27	18.59	49.85	15.43	4,917	800-222-5852	Y
Principal Strategic Asset Mgmt Balanced Portfolio Inst Cls	PSBIX	B-	C+	B	Up	3.46	7.45	15.03	21.03	53.85	15.7	4,917	800-222-5852	Y
Principal Strategic Asset Mgmt Balanced Portfolio R-1 Cls	PSBGX	B-	C+	B	Up	1.99	5.64	12.63	16.47	45.42	15.67	4,917	800-222-5852	Y
Principal Strategic Asset Mgmt Balanced Portfolio R-2 Cls	PSBVX	B-	C+	B	Up	1.99	5.67	12.75	16.84	46.36	15.62	4,917	800-222-5852	Y
Principal Strategic Asset Mgmt Balanced Portfolio R-3 Cls	PBAPX	B-	C+	B	Up	1.99	5.71	12.95	17.44	47.66	15.66	4,917	800-222-5852	Y
Principal Strategic Asset Mgmt Balanced Portfolio R-4 Cls	PSBLX	B-	C+	B	Up	1.98	5.75	13.08	18.03	48.91	15.68	4,917	800-222-5852	Y
Principal Strategic Asset Mgmt Balanced Portfolio R-5 Cls	PSBFX	B-	C+	B	Up	1.98	5.78	13.19	18.43	49.83	15.68	4,917	800-222-5852	Y
Prudential Balanced Fund Class A	PIBAX	B-	C+	B	Up	4.09	7.84	14.04	23.04	62.27	15.82	589.8	800-225-1852	Y
Prudential Balanced Fund Class B	PBFBX	B-	C+	B	Up	3.89	7.42	13.17	20.42	56.58	15.93	589.8	800-225-1852	
Prudential Balanced Fund Class C	PABCX	B-	C+	B	Up	3.96	7.56	13.24	20.50	56.81	15.93	589.8	800-225-1852	Y
Prudential Balanced Fund Class Q	PIBQX	B-	C+	B		4.16	8.03	14.35	24.13	64.75	15.93	589.8	800-225-1852	Y
Prudential Balanced Fund Class R	PALRX	B-	C+	B	Up	4.02	7.70	13.73	22.28	60.64	15.84	589.8	800-225-1852	Y
Prudential Balanced Fund Class Z	PABFX	B-	C+	B	Down	4.16	8.03	14.35	24.13	64.75	15.93	589.8	800-225-1852	Y
Prudential Moderate Allocation Fund Class A	JDTAX	B-	C+	B	Down	4.03	8.30	15.92	20.31	49.36	15.15	171.0	800-225-1852	Y
Prudential Moderate Allocation Fund Class B	JDMBX	B-	C+	B-	Down	3.88	7.90	15.04	17.68	43.91	15.07	171.0	800-225-1852	
Prudential Moderate Allocation Fund Class C	JDMCX	B-	C+	B-	Down	3.88	7.90	15.05	17.60	43.94	15.06	171.0	800-225-1852	Y
Prudential Moderate Allocation Fund Class Q	JDTQX	B-	C+	B-		4.20	8.48	16.27	21.28	51.42	15.16	171.0	800-225-1852	Y
Prudential Moderate Allocation Fund Class R	JMARX	B-	C+	B	Down	4.07	8.15	15.72	19.28	47.20	15.08	171.0	800-225-1852	Y
Prudential Moderate Allocation Fund Class Z	JDMZX	B-	C+	B	Down	4.13	8.40	16.19	21.19	51.31	15.15	171.0	800-225-1852	Y
Putnam Dynamic Asset Allocation Balanced Fund Class A	PABAX	B-	C+	B	Down	4.19	8.07	15.18	22.64	62.53	15.3	2,727	617-292-1000	Y
Putnam Dynamic Asset Allocation Balanced Fund Class B	PABBX	B-	C+	B	Down	4.01	7.63	14.30	19.84	56.46	15.23	2,727	617-292-1000	Y
Putnam Dynamic Asset Allocation Balanced Fund Class C	AABCX	B-	C+	B	Down	3.98	7.70	14.40	19.89	56.48	14.88	2,727	617-292-1000	Y
Putnam Dynamic Asset Allocation Balanced Fund Class M	PABMX	B-	C+	B	Down	4.11	7.80	14.62	20.85	58.44	15.27	2,727	617-292-1000	Y
Putnam Dynamic Asset Allocation Balanced Fund Class P	US7464449005	B-	C+	B	Down	4.28	8.26	15.65	22.80	62.74	15.34	2,727	617-292-1000	
Putnam Dynamic Asset Allocation Balanced Fund Class R	PAARX	B-	C+	B	Down	4.09	7.87	14.89	21.68	60.37	15.17	2,727	617-292-1000	Y
Putnam Dynamic Asset Allocation Balanced Fund Class R5	PAADX	B-	C+	B	Down	4.25	8.20	15.49	23.56	64.52	15.33	2,727	617-292-1000	Y
Putnam Dynamic Asset Allocation Balanced Fund Class R6	PAAEX	B-	C+	B	Down	4.27	8.24	15.63	23.94	65.44	15.33	2,727	617-292-1000	Y
Putnam Dynamic Asset Allocation Balanced Fund Class Y	PABYX	B-	C+	B	Down	4.25	8.19	15.44	23.51	64.52	15.33	2,727	617-292-1000	Y
Putnam Dynamic Asset Allocation Conservative Fund Class A	PACAX	B-	C+	B	Up	2.52	5.00	9.72	14.84	37.04	10.94	1,140	617-292-1000	Y
Putnam Dynamic Asset Allocation Conservative Fund Class B	PACBX	B-	C+	B	Up	2.25	4.53	8.86	12.32	31.92	10.85	1,140	617-292-1000	Y
Putnam Dynamic Asset Allocation Conservative Fund Class C	PACCX	B-	C+	B	Up	2.27	4.57	8.93	12.35	32.10	10.8	1,140	617-292-1000	Y
Putnam Dynamic Asset Allocation Conservative Fund Class M	PACMX	B	C+	A-	Up	2.32	4.69	9.15	13.11	33.62	10.81	1,140	617-292-1000	Y
Putnam Dynamic Asset Allocation Conservative Fund Class P	US9981459087	B-	C+	B	Up	2.52	5.09	10.12	14.78	36.97	10.97	1,140	617-292-1000	
Putnam Dynamic Asset Allocation Conservative Fund Class R	PACRX	B-	C+	B	Up	2.39	4.74	9.37	13.90	35.24	11.24	1,140	617-292-1000	Y
Putnam Dynamic Asset Allocation Conservative Fund Class R5	PACDX	B-	C+	B	Up	2.59	5.12	10.07	15.92	39.13	10.98	1,140	617-292-1000	Y
Putnam Dynamic Asset Allocation Conservative Fund Class R6	PCCEX	B-	C+	B	Up	2.50	5.15	10.05	16.14	39.51	10.98	1,140	617-292-1000	Y
Putnam Dynamic Asset Allocation Conservative Fund Class Y	PACYX	B-	C+	B	Up	2.57	5.09	10.03	15.73	38.69	10.98	1,140	617-292-1000	Y
QS Conservative Growth Fund Class A	SBBAX	B-	C+	B	Up	2.99	5.78	12.73	18.30	43.62	14.55	316.7	877-721-1926	Y
QS Conservative Growth Fund Class C	SCBCX	B-	C+	B	Up	2.84	5.37	11.86	15.72	38.50	15.15	316.7	877-721-1926	Y
QS Conservative Growth Fund Class I	LMEIX	B-	C+	B	Up	3.05	5.91	13.01	19.21	44.93	14.54	316.7	877-721-1926	Y
QS Conservative Growth Fund Class R	LLARX	B-	C+	B	Up	2.87	5.59	12.34	17.24	41.55	14.52	316.7	877-721-1926	Y
Rational Strategic Allocation Fund Class A	HBAFX	B-	C+	B	Up	3.01	6.66	11.61	18.04	37.73	10.05	13.3	800-253-0412	Y
Rational Strategic Allocation Fund Class C	RHSCX	B-	C+	B	Up	2.79	6.27	10.80	15.46	32.72	10.03	13.3	800-253-0412	Y
Rational Strategic Allocation Fund Class Institutional	RHSIX	B-	C+	B	Up	3.09	6.82	11.94	18.51	38.28	10.02	13.3	800-253-0412	Y
RiverFront Moderate Growth & Income Fund Class C	RMICX	B-	C+	B	Up	2.81	5.75	11.09	14.91	35.93	11.91	95.8	866-759-5679	Y
RiverFront Moderate Growth & Income Fund Class I	RMIIX	B-	C+	B	Up	3.11	6.22	12.20	18.34	42.90	12.05	95.8	866-759-5679	Y

Category: Moderate Allocation (con't)

Fund Name	Ticker Symbol	RATINGS Overall Rating	Reward Rating	Risk Rating	Recent Up/ Downgrade	TOTAL RETURNS & PERFORMANCE 3-Month Total Return	6-Month Total Return	1-Year Total Return	3-Year Total Return	5-Year Total Return	ASSETS NAV	Total Assets (ML)	NEW INVESTORS Telephone	Open to New Investors
RiverFront Moderate Growth & Income Fund Class Investor	RMIAX	B-	C+	B	Up	2.98	6.08	11.91	17.42	41.12	12.04	95.8	866-759-5679	Y
RiverNorth Core Opportunity Fund Class I	RNCIX	B-	B-	C+	Down	3.77	8.29	18.08	25.18	55.07	10.81	323.2	312-832-1440	Y
Russell Inv LifePoints Balanced Strategy Fund Cls A	RBLAX	B-	C+	B	Up	1.37	4.14	10.26	16.84	38.16	11.3	2,131	800-426-7969	Y
Russell Inv LifePoints Balanced Strategy Fund Cls C	RBLCX	B-	C+	B	Up	1.11	3.72	9.43	14.18	32.97	11.05	2,131	800-426-7969	Y
Russell Inv LifePoints Balanced Strategy Fund Cls E	RBLEX	B-	C+	B	Up	1.25	4.06	10.21	16.31	37.64	11.36	2,131	800-426-7969	Y
Russell Inv LifePoints Balanced Strategy Fund Cls R1	RBLRX	B-	C+	B	Up	1.41	4.27	10.58	17.45	40.09	11.45	2,131	800-426-7969	Y
Russell Inv LifePoints Balanced Strategy Fund Cls R4	RBLUX	B-	C+	B	Up	1.35	4.10	10.28	16.66	38.30	11.34	2,131	800-426-7969	Y
Russell Inv LifePoints Balanced Strategy Fund Cls R5	RBLVX	B-	C+	B	Up	1.20	3.92	9.91	15.68	36.55	11.35	2,131	800-426-7969	Y
Russell Inv LifePoints Balanced Strategy Fund Cls S	RBLSX	B-	C+	B	Up	1.31	4.17	10.45	17.27	39.33	11.44	2,131	800-426-7969	Y
Russell Inv LifePoints Balanced Strategy Fund Cls T	RBSAX	B-	C+	B		1.27	3.48	9.78	18.88	37.13		2,131	800-426-7969	Y
Salient Adaptive Growth Fund Class A	SRPAX	B-	B-	B-	Up	7.67	11.58	16.81	18.01	28.56	7.12	52.0	866-667-9228	Y
Salient Adaptive Growth Fund Class I	SRPFX	B-	B-	B-	Up	7.83	11.69	17.18	18.97	30.33	7.23	52.0	866-667-9228	Y
Scharf Balanced Opportunity Fund Institutional Class	LOGOX	B	C+	A-	Up	2.01	2.80	10.35	14.52	53.54	32.22	63.0	831-429-6513	Y
Scharf Balanced Opportunity Fund Retail Class	LOGBX	B	C+	A-	Up	1.94	2.67	10.05	13.64	51.59	32.16	63.0	831-429-6513	Y
Schwab Balanced Fund™	SWOBX	B-	C+	B	Up	4.00	7.43	15.51	22.09	59.76	15.47	388.2	877-824-5615	Y
Schwab MarketTrack Balanced Portfolio™	SWBGX	B-	C+	B	Up	3.34	6.66	12.69	20.58	50.35	18.57	555.3	877-824-5615	Y
Sector Rotation Fund	NAVFX	B-	B-	B-	Down	5.94	11.62	20.30	26.79	67.00	12.99	24.0	252-442-4226	Y
SEI Asset Alloc Trust Conservative Strat Alloc Fund Cls F	SMGAX	B-	C+	B	Up	3.30	5.26	9.88	22.15	63.57	13.54	43.9	800-342-5734	Y
SEI Asset Alloc Trust Defensive Strategy Alloc Fund Cls F	STDAX	B-	C+	B	Up	3.00	5.08	9.69	21.95	59.70	14.49	8.3	800-342-5734	Y
SEI Inst Managed Trust Multi-Asset Income Fund Cls F	SIOAX	B-	C+	B+	Down	0.89	2.56	6.76	17.95	32.05	10.8	979.9	800-342-5734	Y
SEI Inst Managed Trust Multi-Asset Income Fund Cls Y	SLIYX	B-	C+	B	Down	0.92	2.61	6.87	18.29	32.43	10.8	979.9	800-342-5734	Y
Sextant Core Fund	SCORX	B-	C+	B	Up	1.99	5.58	13.07	12.37	33.72	12.91	13.0		Y
Sit Balanced Fund	SIBAX	B	C+	A-		4.60	8.12	17.73	25.21	64.19	23.39	27.1	800-332-5580	Y
Source Capital Inc	SOR	B-	C+	B-	Up	3.67	6.91	13.97	18.15	81.57	45.06	384.3		Y
Special Opportunities Fund	SPE	B-	C+	B-	Up	3.57	6.08	15.69	19.87	46.54	16.6725	151.9	914-747-5262	Y
Stadion Tactical Defensive Fund Class I	ETFWX	B-	C+	B-	Up	5.36	8.39	15.50	14.48	42.15	13.61	106.0	706-353-8737	Y
Stadion Tactical Growth Fund Class C Shares	ETFCX	B-	C+	B	Down	4.86	8.08	11.07	14.67	53.57	11.63	418.8	706-353-8737	Y
State Farm Balanced Fund	STFBX	B-	C+	B	Down	4.41	6.72	11.39	19.77	52.68	68.69	1,951		Y
State Farm Equity & Bond Fund Class A	NBSAX	B-	C+	B	Up	4.67	8.33	15.20	22.64	62.51	12.14	399.4		Y
State Farm Equity & Bond Fund Class B	NBSBX	B-	C+	B	Up	4.75	8.41	15.09	20.82	58.25	12.16	399.4		Y
State Farm Equity & Bond Fund Class R1	REBOX	B-	C+	B	Up	4.70	8.32	15.07	21.66	60.35	11.97	399.4		Y
State Farm Equity & Bond Fund Class R2	REBTX	B-	C+	B	Up	4.77	8.39	15.20	22.33	61.71	12	399.4		Y
State Farm Equity & Bond Fund Class R3	REBHX	B	C+	B+	Up	4.68	8.29	15.26	23.12	63.77	12.02	399.4		Y
State Farm Equity & Bond Fund Premier Shares	SLBAX	B-	C+	B	Up	4.78	8.40	15.39	22.89	62.85	12.3	399.4		Y
State Farm Equity and Bond Fund Class Institutional	SEBIX	B	C+	B+	Up	4.74	8.40	15.33	23.37	64.32	12.17	399.4		Y
State Farm Equity and Bond Fund Legacy Class B	SLBBX	B-	C+	B	Up	4.69	8.30	15.07	21.52	59.79	12.31	399.4		Y
Sterling Capital Strategic Allocation Balanced Fund Cls A	BAMGX	B-	C+	B	Up	1.93	6.14	13.34	17.92	43.50	12.12	30.8	800-228-1872	Y
Sterling Capital Strategic Allocation Balanced Fund Cls C	BCMCX	B-	C+	B	Up	1.88	5.89	12.69	15.50	38.49	11.89	30.8	800-228-1872	Y
Sterling Capital Strategic Alloc Balanced Fund Inst Shares	BCGTX	B-	C+	B	Up	3.34	7.65	15.14	20.33	47.22	12.21	30.8	800-228-1872	Y
T. Rowe Price Balanced Fund	RPBAX	B	B-	A-	Up	3.61	7.57	18.00	25.14	60.45	24.33	4,030	410-345-2000	Y
T. Rowe Price Balanced I Class	RBAIX	B-	B-	B	Down	3.65	7.65	18.19	25.57	61.00	24.34	4,030	410-345-2000	Y
T. Rowe Price Capital Appreciation Fund	PRWCX	B	B-	A-	Down	2.95	5.69	15.37	30.92	82.44	28.28	29,649	410-345-2000	
T. Rowe Price Capital Appreciation Fund Advisor Class	PACLX	B	B-	A-		2.88	5.50	14.97	29.70	79.67	27.99	29,649	410-345-2000	
T. Rowe Price Capital Appreciation Fund I Class	TRAIX	B	B-	A-	Down	2.98	5.71	15.47	31.18	82.80	28.29	29,649	410-345-2000	Y
T. Rowe Price Personal Strategy Balanced Fund	TRPBX	B	C+	A-	Up	3.37	7.37	17.30	25.04	58.00	24.09	2,363	410-345-2000	Y
T. Rowe Price Personal Strategy Balanced Fund I Class	TPPAX	B	B-	A-	Up	3.37	7.45	17.45	25.31	58.34	24.09	2,363	410-345-2000	Y
TETON Westwood Balanced Fund Class A	WEBCX	B-	C+	B	Up	5.11	7.88	13.76	20.00	53.28	12.09	66.7		Y
TETON Westwood Balanced Fund Class AAA	WEBAX	B-	C+	B	Up	5.21	8.01	14.08	20.89	55.24	12.02	66.7		Y
TETON Westwood Balanced Fund Class C	WBCCX	B-	C+	B	Up	4.98	7.60	13.22	18.21	49.57	12.28	66.7		Y
TETON Westwood Balanced Fund Class Institutional	WBBIX	B-	C+	B	Up	5.20	8.12	14.26	21.74	57.15	12	66.7		Y
The Gabelli Global Rising Income and Dividend Fund AAA	GAGCX	B-	B-	B	Down	3.79	7.55	20.90	27.90	49.18	27.2	68.7	914-921-5135	Y
The Hartford Balanced Fund Class F	ITTFX	B-	C+	B	Down	4.54	7.46	15.10	21.40	63.99	24.16	954.9	888-843-7824	Y

Category: Moderate Allocation (con't)

Fund Name	Ticker Symbol	RATINGS: Overall Rating	Reward Rating	Risk Rating	Recent Up/ Downgrade	TOTAL RETURNS & PERFORMANCE: 3-Month Total Return	6-Month Total Return	1-Year Total Return	3-Year Total Return	5-Year Total Return	ASSETS: NAV	Total Assets (MIL)	NEW INVESTORS: Telephone	Open to New Investors
Thrivent Balanced Income Plus Fund Class A	AABFX	B-	C+	B	Up	2.87	5.11	11.37	17.37	51.17	13.27	351.2		Y
Thrivent Balanced Income Plus Fund Class S	IBBFX	B-	C+	B	Up	2.96	5.29	11.67	18.59	54.15	13.24	351.2		Y
Thrivent Balanced Income Plus Portfolio		B-	C+	B	Up	2.99	5.33	11.67	18.89	51.05	15.3685	400.6		Y
Thrivent Moderate Allocation Fund Class A	THMAX	B-	C+	B	Down	2.90	6.00	12.29	20.17	47.75	13.69	2,240		Y
Thrivent Moderate Allocation Fund Class S	TMAIX	B-	C+	B	Down	2.89	6.13	12.56	21.26	50.11	13.72	2,240		Y
Thrivent Series Moderate Allocation Portfolio		B-	C+	B	Down	3.00	6.30	12.95	21.85	50.40	15.0666	10,129		Y
TIAA-CREF Lifestyle Moderate Fund Advisor Class	TSMHX	B-	C+	B	Up	3.49	7.88	16.92	24.63	54.86	14.12	307.7	877-518-9161	Y
TIAA-CREF Lifestyle Moderate Fund Institutional Class	TSIMX	B-	C+	B	Down	3.58	7.93	17.00	24.78	55.05	14.12	307.7	877-518-9161	Y
TIAA-CREF Lifestyle Moderate Fund Premier Class	TSMPX	B-	C+	B	Down	3.54	7.82	16.79	24.31	54.00	14.16	307.7	877-518-9161	Y
TIAA-CREF Lifestyle Moderate Fund Retail Class	TSMLX	B-	C+	B	Up	3.52	7.80	16.71	23.91	53.07	14.11	307.7	877-518-9161	Y
TIAA-CREF Lifestyle Moderate Fund Retirement Class	TSMTX	B-	C+	B	Down	3.52	7.81	16.73	23.89	53.12	14.11	307.7	877-518-9161	Y
TIAA-CREF Managed Allocation Fund Institutional Class	TIMIX	B-	C+	B	Up	3.66	7.99	17.07	25.35	56.29	12.85	865.4	877-518-9161	Y
TIAA-CREF Managed Allocation Fund Retail Class	TIMRX	B-	C+	B	Up	3.59	7.83	16.63	24.34	54.17	12.88	865.4	877-518-9161	Y
TIAA-CREF Managed Allocation Fund Retirement Class	TITRX	B-	C+	B	Up	3.60	7.87	16.71	24.35	54.17	12.83	865.4	877-518-9161	Y
Timothy Plan Strategic Growth Fund Class C	TSGCX	B-	C	B	Up	2.80	7.04	10.67	8.63	28.72	8.81	40.5	800-662-0201	Y
TOPS® Balanced ETF Portfolio Class 1	US66537U8339	B-	C+	B	Up	2.86	5.81	11.20	17.06	35.05	12.58	12.1	855-572-5945	Y
TOPS® Balanced ETF Portfolio Class 2	US66537U8255	B-	C+	B	Up	2.78	5.67	10.94	16.24	32.78	12.17	12.1	855-572-5945	Y
TOPS® Balanced ETF Portfolio Investor Class	US66537U1714	B-	C+	B	Up	2.60	5.35	10.37	15.00	30.70	12.98	12.1	855-572-5945	Y
TOPS® Moderate Growth ETF Portfolio Class 1	US66537U8172	B-	C+	B	Down	3.76	7.63	14.37	22.20	45.87	12.4	19.6	855-572-5945	Y
TOPS® Moderate Growth ETF Portfolio Class 2	US66537U7919	B-	C+	B-	Down	3.72	7.46	14.11	21.12	43.94	11.99	19.6	855-572-5945	Y
TOPS® Moderate Growth ETF Portfolio Investor Class	US66537U1631	B-	C+	B-	Down	3.38	6.82	12.87	18.29	39.87	13.15	19.6	855-572-5945	Y
Touchstone Balanced Fund Class A	SEBLX	B-	C+	B	Down	4.76	7.97	15.67	23.35	59.53	21.51	332.2	800-543-0407	Y
Touchstone Balanced Fund Class C	SBACX	B-	C+	B	Up	4.54	7.57	14.79	20.50	53.42	21.6	332.2	800-543-0407	Y
Touchstone Balanced Fund Class Y	SIBLX	B-	C+	B	Down	4.81	8.06	15.98	24.13	61.43	21.36	332.2	800-543-0407	Y
Transamerica Asset Allocation Intermediate Horizon R	TAARX	B-	C+	B		3.01	5.51	11.46	17.06	40.52	10.52	445.4	888-233-4339	Y
Transamerica Asset Allocation Intermediate Horizon R4	TAAFX	B-	C+	B	Up	3.19	5.62	11.71	17.91	42.25	10.52	445.4	888-233-4339	Y
Transamerica Asset Alloc Moderate Growth Port Cls A	IMLAX	B-	C+	B	Down	3.42	7.02	15.86	22.86	57.74	13.39	2,672	888-233-4339	Y
Transamerica Asset Alloc Moderate Growth Port Cls B	IMLBX	B-	C+	B	Down	3.24	6.64	14.87	19.89	51.49	13.78	2,672	888-233-4339	
Transamerica Asset Alloc Moderate Growth Port Cls C	IMLLX	B-	C+	B	Down	3.23	6.62	15.02	20.23	52.13	13.39	2,672	888-233-4339	Y
Transamerica Asset Alloc Moderate Growth Port Cls I	TMGIX	B-	C+	B	Down	3.46	7.22	16.19	23.82	59.84	13.36	2,672	888-233-4339	Y
Transamerica Asset Alloc Moderate Growth Port Cls R	IMGRX	B-	C+	B	Down	3.36	6.90	15.51	21.90	55.81	13.34	2,672	888-233-4339	Y
Transamerica Asset Alloc Moderate Growth Port Fund Adv	TMGQX	B-	C+	B	Down	5.62	8.71	17.12	24.19	59.45	12.1	2,672	888-233-4339	Y
Transamerica Asset Alloc Moderate Growth Port Fund Cls T1	TMGUX	B-	C+	B	Down	3.40	7.01	15.93	22.93	57.83	13.45	2,672	888-233-4339	Y
Transamerica Balanced II I3	TBLTX	B-	C+	B		4.16	7.11	13.80	21.78	60.53	10.36	148.5	888-233-4339	Y
Transamerica Balanced II R	TBLRX	B-	C+	B	Down	4.01	6.96	13.64	21.60	60.29	10.36	148.5	888-233-4339	Y
Transamerica Dynamic Allocation Fund Class A	ATTRX	B-	C+	B	Up	3.69	6.72	12.50	14.64	43.53	11.95	18.9	888-233-4339	Y
Transamerica Dynamic Allocation Fund Class I	ITTOX	B-	C+	B	Up	3.80	6.85	12.86	15.53	45.46	11.9	18.9	888-233-4339	Y
Transamerica Dynamic Allocation Fund Class T1	ATTTX	B-	C+	B	Up	3.71	6.74	12.57	14.66	43.64	11.97	18.9	888-233-4339	Y
Transamerica Multi-Managed Balanced Fund Advisor	IBAVX	B-	C+	B	Down	4.04	7.13	13.96	21.52	59.91	28.15	1,082	888-233-4339	Y
Transamerica Multi-Managed Balanced Fund Class A	IBALX	B-	C+	B	Down	3.99	7.07	13.84	21.40	59.75	27.97	1,082	888-233-4339	Y
Transamerica Multi-Managed Balanced Fund Class B	IBABX	B-	C+	B	Up	3.73	6.49	12.57	17.67	52.10	27.81	1,082	888-233-4339	
Transamerica Multi-Managed Balanced Fund Class C	IBLLX	B-	C+	B	Up	3.80	6.63	12.93	18.73	54.24	27.48	1,082	888-233-4339	Y
Transamerica Multi-Managed Balanced Fund Class I	TBLIX	B-	C+	B	Down	4.07	7.19	14.08	22.32	62.10	28.1	1,082	888-233-4339	Y
Transamerica Multi-Managed Balanced Fund Class R6	TAMMX	B-	C+	B	Down	4.10	7.25	14.20	22.52	61.22	28.1	1,082	888-233-4339	Y
Transamerica Multi-Managed Balanced Fund Class T1	IBATX	B-	C+	B	Down	4.04	7.14	13.92	21.49	59.87	28.04	1,082	888-233-4339	Y
Tributary Balanced Fund Class Institutional Plus	FOBPX	B-	C+	B	Down	4.19	6.71	14.22	20.08	58.01	16.86	78.1		Y
Tributary Balanced Fund Institutional Class	FOBAX	B-	C+	B	Down	4.09	6.52	13.94	19.35	56.41	16.99	78.1		Y
UBS U.S. Allocation Fund Class A	PWTAX	B-	C+	B	Down	3.53	6.60	15.43	23.14	67.64	48.87	261.9	212-882-5586	Y
UBS U.S. Allocation Fund Class C	KPAAX	B-	C+	B	Down	3.34	6.20	14.57	20.38	61.43	47.1	261.9	212-882-5586	Y
UBS U.S. Allocation Fund Class P	PWTYX	B-	C+	B	Down	3.61	6.76	15.78	24.15	70.03	49.71	261.9	212-882-5586	Y
USAA Cornerstone Moderate Fund	USBSX	B-	C+	B	Up	3.00	5.92	13.40	13.73	32.12	14.98	1,175	800-531-8722	Y
USAA Cornerstone Moderately Aggressive Fund	USCRX	B-	C+	B	Up	3.57	6.85	14.98	14.80	34.64	25.95	2,507	800-531-8722	Y

Category: Moderate Allocation (con't)

Fund Name	Ticker Symbol	RATINGS: Overall Rating	Reward Rating	Risk Rating	Recent Up/ Downgrade	TOTAL RETURNS & PERFORMANCE: 3-Month Total Return	6-Month Total Return	1-Year Total Return	3-Year Total Return	5-Year Total Return	ASSETS: NAV	Total Assets (MIL)	NEW INVESTORS: Telephone	Open to New Investors
USAA Managed Allocation Fund	UMAFX	B-	C+	B	Up	4.77	7.00	16.20	14.84	22.63	12.27	808.6	800-531-8722	Y
VALIC Company I Asset Allocation Fund	VCAAX	B-	C+	B	Up	4.69	7.98	13.24	20.22	49.37	12.04	170.6		Y
VALIC Company I Dynamic Allocation Fund	VDAFX	B-	C+	B-	Down	5.78	10.08	20.21	19.47	48.82	12.99	259.5		Y
VALIC Company II Moderate Growth Lifestyle Fund	VMGLX	B-	C+	B	Down	3.36	6.96	13.61	21.35	49.79	15.06	938.0		Y
Value Line Asset Allocation Fund Institutional Class	VLAIX	B	C+	A		3.89	6.20	15.19	22.79	60.83	31.61	328.9	800-243-2729	Y
Value Line Asset Allocation Fund Investor Class	VLAAX	B	C+	A		3.80	6.04	14.93	22.15	59.99	31.54	328.9	800-243-2729	Y
Vanguard Balanced Index Fund Admiral Shares	VBIAX	B-	C+	B	Down	3.96	7.10	13.89	23.79	63.23	34.72	36,658	877-662-7447	Y
Vanguard Balanced Index Fund Institutional Shares	VBAIX	B-	C+	B	Down	3.96	7.10	13.85	23.82	63.30	34.72	36,658	877-662-7447	Y
Vanguard Balanced Index Fund Investor Shares	VBINX	B-	C+	B	Down	3.93	7.03	13.75	23.32	62.14	34.72	36,658	877-662-7447	Y
Vanguard LifeStrategy Moderate Growth Fund Investor Shares	VSMGX	B-	C+	B	Up	3.62	7.09	15.04	21.99	52.13	27.14	15,968	877-662-7447	Y
Vanguard Managed Payout Fund Investor Shares	VPGDX	B-	C+	B	Up	3.51	6.84	13.29	20.44	49.89	19.11	2,066	877-662-7447	Y
Vanguard Star Fund Investor Shares	VGSTX	B	B-	A-	Up	3.92	8.03	18.33	25.33	60.44	26.8	21,531	877-662-7447	Y
Vanguard Wellington™ Fund Admiral™ Shares	VWENX	B-	B-	B	Down	4.53	8.11	14.81	26.93	69.42	72.58	105,558	877-662-7447	
Vanguard Wellington™ Fund Investor Shares	VWELX	B-	B-	B	Down	4.52	8.06	14.72	26.62	68.76	42.03	105,558	877-662-7447	
Virtus Herzfeld Fund Class A	VHFAX	B-	B-	C+	Down	3.75	7.77	17.36	27.64	52.15	12.45	66.9	800-243-1574	Y
Virtus Herzfeld Fund Class I	VHFIX	B-	B-	B-	Down	3.73	7.82	17.66	28.59	54.03	12.46	66.9	800-243-1574	Y
Virtus Strategic Allocation Fund Class A	PHBLX	B-	C+	B	Up	3.19	7.96	19.72	14.92	41.03	14.59	483.7	800-243-1574	Y
Virtus Strategic Allocation Fund Class C	PSBCX	B-	C+	B	Up	2.95	7.55	18.81	12.34	35.84	14.45	483.7	800-243-1574	Y
Virtus Tactical Allocation Fund Class A	NAINX	B-	C+	B	Up	3.06	8.04	19.84	15.49	43.95	9.17	147.7	800-243-1574	Y
Virtus Tactical Allocation Fund Class C	POICX	B-	C+	B	Up	2.99	7.73	19.00	13.01	38.68	9.43	147.7	800-243-1574	Y
Voya Balanced Portfolio Class I	IBPIX	B-	C+	B	Down	3.79	6.78	14.72	20.73	51.98	16.69	430.8	800-366-0066	Y
Voya Balanced Portfolio Class S	IBPSX	B-	C+	B	Down	3.68	6.61	14.36	19.79	50.11	16.59	430.8	800-366-0066	Y
Voya Retirement Moderate Growth Portfolio Class A	IRMGX	B	C+	B+	Up	3.56	6.94	14.55	19.78	48.68	12.8	2,166	800-366-0066	Y
Voya Retirement Moderate Growth Portfolio Class I	IRGMX	B-	C+	B	Up	3.74	7.21	15.05	21.23	51.61	12.73	2,166	800-366-0066	Y
Voya Solution Balanced Portfolio Class A	ISGAX	B-	C+	B	Up	3.60	6.90	14.34	19.85	48.84	10.07	60.5	800-366-0066	Y
Voya Solution Balanced Portfolio Class I	ISGJX	B-	C+	B	Up	3.77	7.13	14.88	21.67	52.63	10.45	60.5	800-366-0066	Y
Voya Solution Balanced Portfolio Class R6	VYRLX	B-	C+	B	Up	3.77	7.13	15.01	21.67	52.63	10.45	60.5	800-366-0066	Y
Voya Solution Balanced Portfolio Class S	ISGKX	B-	C+	B	Up	3.76	7.05	14.75	20.76	50.87	10.21	60.5	800-366-0066	Y
Voya Solution Balanced Portfolio Class S2	ISGTX	B-	C+	B	Up	3.67	6.93	14.52	20.10	49.71	10.16	60.5	800-366-0066	Y
Voya Strategic Allocation Moderate Portfolio Class I	IIMDX	B-	C+	B	Up	3.93	7.09	14.48	20.74	52.52	14.8	145.9	800-366-0066	Y
Voya Strategic Allocation Moderate Portfolio Class S	ISMDX	B-	C+	B	Up	3.88	6.98	14.29	19.80	50.60	14.71	145.9	800-366-0066	Y
VY® Franklin Income Portfolio Class I	IIFIX	B-	C+	B-		1.56	5.50	10.56	19.29	46.10	11.65	463.1	800-366-0066	Y
VY® Invesco Equity and Income Portfolio Class A	IUAAX	B	C+	B+	Up	3.06	6.09	10.32	22.48	67.87	46.81	1,684	800-366-0066	Y
VY® Invesco Equity and Income Portfolio Class I	IUAIX	B	C+	B+	Up	3.19	6.37	10.89	24.35	72.17	47.51	1,684	800-366-0066	Y
VY® Invesco Equity and Income Portfolio Class S	IUASX	B	C+	B+	Up	3.14	6.24	10.61	23.44	70.03	47.22	1,684	800-366-0066	Y
VY® Invesco Equity and Income Portfolio Class S2	IVIPX	B	C+	B+	Up	3.10	6.16	10.47	22.94	68.86	46.59	1,684	800-366-0066	Y
VY® T. Rowe Price Capital Appreciation Portfolio Class A	ITRAX	B	B-	A-		2.74	5.35	14.71	28.79	77.88	26.53	6,462	800-366-0066	Y
VY® T. Rowe Price Capital Appreciation Portfolio Class I	ITRIX	B	B-	A-	Down	2.91	5.68	15.38	31.08	83.27	27.64	6,462	800-366-0066	Y
VY® T. Rowe Price Capital Appreciation Portfolio Class R6	VPRAX	B	B-	A-	Down	2.94	5.72	15.46	30.71	81.81	27.66	6,462	800-366-0066	Y
VY® T. Rowe Price Capital Appreciation Portfolio Class S	ITCSX	B	B-	A-		2.83	5.53	15.09	30.12	81.00	27.65	6,462	800-366-0066	Y
VY® T. Rowe Price Capital Appreciation Portfolio Class S2	ITCTX	B	B-	A-		2.82	5.46	14.96	29.54	79.65	27.47	6,462	800-366-0066	Y
Waddell & Reed Advisor Continental Income Fund Class A	UNCIX	B-	C+	B+	Down	3.84	5.22	11.38	12.70	51.89	9.64	1,392	888-923-3355	Y
Waddell & Reed Advisor Continental Income Fund Class B	WACBX	B-	C	B+	Up	3.58	4.61	10.02	8.89	43.48	9.49	1,392	888-923-3355	
Waddell & Reed Advisor Continental Income Fund Class C	WACCX	B-	C	B+	Up	3.68	4.76	10.36	9.85	45.58	9.58	1,392	888-923-3355	Y
Waddell & Reed Advisor Continental Income Fund Class Y	WACYX	B	C+	B+	Up	3.94	5.45	11.63	13.57	54.05	9.65	1,392	888-923-3355	Y
Wells Fargo Growth Balanced Fund - Class A	WFGBX	B-	C+	B	Down	3.67	7.14	15.39	21.83	65.27	46.92	246.3	800-222-8222	Y
Wells Fargo Growth Balanced Fund - Class Admin	NVGBX	B-	C+	B	Down	3.72	7.27	15.67	22.76	67.32	41.81	246.3	800-222-8222	Y
Wells Fargo Growth Balanced Fund - Class C	WFGWX	B-	C+	B	Down	3.48	6.75	14.53	19.12	59.22	40.81	246.3	800-222-8222	Y
Wells Fargo Index Asset Allocation Fund - Class A	SFAAX	B	C+	B+	Up	3.75	6.34	12.24	21.16	73.80	32.93	1,337	800-222-8222	Y
Wells Fargo Index Asset Allocation Fund - Class Admin	WFAIX	B	C+	A-	Up	3.75	6.43	12.40	21.89	75.73	32.93	1,337	800-222-8222	Y
Wells Fargo Index Asset Allocation Fund - Class C	WFALX	B-	C+	B	Up	3.53	5.93	11.34	18.39	67.33	20.02	1,337	800-222-8222	Y
Wells Fargo Index Asset Allocation Fund Institutional Cls	WFATX	B	C+	B+	Up	3.82	6.51	12.58	21.60	74.43	32.89	1,337	800-222-8222	Y

Category: Moderate Allocation (con't)

Fund Name	Ticker Symbol	RATINGS: Overall Rating	Reward Rating	Risk Rating	Recent Up/ Downgrade	TOTAL RETURNS & PERFORMANCE: 3-Month Total Return	6-Month Total Return	1-Year Total Return	3-Year Total Return	5-Year Total Return	ASSETS: NAV	Total Assets (MIL)	NEW INVESTORS: Telephone	Open to New Investors
Wells Fargo Utilities and High Income Fund	ERH	B-	C+	B	Up	1.13	4.37	13.92	16.82	57.59	13.12	127.7	877-709-8009	Y
Wells Fargo WealthBuilder Growth Balanced Fund Class A	WGBAX	B-	C+	B	Down	-7.53	-4.24	3.30	7.15	34.68	13.33	835.6	800-222-8222	Y
WesMark Balanced Fund	WMBLX	B-	C+	B	Up	2.85	7.05	10.76	18.47	46.90	13.05	117.8	800-861-1013	Y
Westwood Income Opportunity Fund A Class	WWIAX	B-	C+	B	Up	3.28	4.62	10.68	13.81	43.45	15.8	2,724		Y
Westwood Income Opportunity Fund Institutional Class	WHGIX	B-	C+	B	Up	3.35	4.76	10.96	14.69	45.22	15.81	2,724		Y
Wilmington Diversified Income Fund Class A	ARBAX	B	C+	B+	Up	2.67	6.43	14.52	17.89	37.16	10.64	44.2	800-836-2211	Y
Wilmington Diversified Income Fund Class I	ARGIX	B-	C+	B	Up	2.72	6.55	14.78	18.78	38.97	10.65	44.2	800-836-2211	Y
WOA All Asset I Class I Shares	WOAIX	B-	C+	B	Up	3.00	6.41	13.85	18.17	29.69	11.94	222.5	855-754-7935	Y

Category: Multialternative

Fund Name	Ticker Symbol	RATINGS: Overall Rating	Reward Rating	Risk Rating	Recent Up/ Downgrade	TOTAL RETURNS & PERFORMANCE: 3-Month Total Return	6-Month Total Return	1-Year Total Return	3-Year Total Return	5-Year Total Return	ASSETS: NAV	Total Assets (MIL)	NEW INVESTORS: Telephone	Open to New Investors
ACR Multi-Strategy Quality Return (MQR) Fund Class A	MQRAX	B-	C	B	Up	5.95	9.37	13.23	17.07		11.39	94.8	314-932-7600	Y
ACR Multi-Strategy Quality Return (MQR) Fund Class I	MQRIX	B-	C	B	Up	6.01	9.52	13.49	17.67		11.44	94.8	314-932-7600	Y
AQR Multi-Strategy Alternative Fund Class I	ASAIX	B	C	A-	Up	0.34	3.31	3.09	12.41	25.03	9.05	3,273	203-742-3600	
AQR Multi-Strategy Alternative Fund Class N	ASANX	B	C	A-	Up	0.29	3.16	2.72	11.42	23.47	9	3,273	203-742-3600	
AQR Multi-Strategy Alternative Fund Class R6	QSARX	B	C	A-	Up	0.34	3.40	3.18	12.70	25.45	9.06	3,273	203-742-3600	Y
AQR Style Premia Alternative Fund Class I	QSPIX	B	B	B	Up	5.65	10.59	12.04	21.04		10.39	4,661	203-742-3600	
AQR Style Premia Alternative Fund Class N	QSPNX	B	B	B	Up	5.58	10.33	11.67	19.99		10.35	4,661	203-742-3600	
AQR Style Premia Alternative Fund Class R6	QSPRX	B	B	B	Up	5.72	10.54	12.10	21.27		10.41	4,661	203-742-3600	
AQR Style Premia Alternative LV Fund Class I	QSLIX	B-	C	B+	Up	3.07	5.72	6.74	11.63		10.57	475.2	203-742-3600	
AQR Style Premia Alternative LV Fund Class N	QSLNX	B-	C	B+	Up	2.98	5.54	6.45	10.73		10.53	475.2	203-742-3600	
AQR Style Premia Alternative LV Fund Class R6	QSLRX	B-	C	B+	Up	3.14	5.78	6.90	12.03		10.59	475.2	203-742-3600	
BlackRock Alternative Capital Strategies Fund Inst Shares	BIMBX	B-	C	B	Up	2.50	5.33	9.89			10.14	28.6	800-441-7762	Y
BlackRock Total Factor Fund Class K	BSTKX	B-	C+	B	Down	4.20	5.75	10.23	14.62	22.59	10.19	38.8	800-441-7762	Y
BlackRock Total Factor Fund Institutional Shares	BSTIX	B-	C+	B	Down	4.17	5.72	10.21	14.60	22.56	10.19	38.8	800-441-7762	Y
BlackRock Total Factor Fund Investor A Shares	BSTAX	B-	C+	B	Up	4.14	5.59	9.97	13.80	21.01	10.17	38.8	800-441-7762	Y
BlackRock Total Factor Fund Investor C Shares	BSTCX	B-	C+	B	Up	3.92	5.17	9.10	11.25	16.50	10.14	38.8	800-441-7762	Y
Blackstone Alternative Multi-Strategy Fund Class D	BXMDX	B-	C	A-	Up	0.23	1.82	6.82	11.62		10.72	5,227		Y
Blackstone Alternative Multi-Strategy Fund Class I	BXMIX	B	C	A-	Up	0.22	1.99	7.19	12.49		10.73	5,227		Y
Blackstone Alternative Multi-Strategy Fund Class Y	BXMYX	B	C	A-	Up	0.31	2.00	7.23	12.95		10.65	5,227		Y
Catalyst/Millburn Hedge Strategy Fund Class A	MBXAX	B	B	B+	Up	4.12	9.43	13.66	35.81	72.26	31.59	3,561	866-447-4228	Y
Catalyst/Millburn Hedge Strategy Fund Class C	MBXCX	B	B	B+	Up	3.94	9.01	12.82	32.69	65.82	31.18	3,561	866-447-4228	Y
Catalyst/Millburn Hedge Strategy Fund Class I	MBXIX	B+	B	B+	Up	4.18	9.54	13.96	36.81	74.39	31.71	3,561	866-447-4228	Y
Cornerstone Advs Public Alternatives Fund Inst Shares	CAALX	B-	C	B+	Up	1.90	4.73	4.84	8.15	17.49	9.89	562.6		Y
Credit Suisse Multialternative Strategy Fund Cls A Shares	CSQAX	B-	C	A-	Up	1.70	3.49	3.59	5.61	15.17	10.1	104.0	877-870-2874	Y
Credit Suisse Multialternative Strategy Fund Cls C Shares	CSQCX	B-	C	B+	Up	1.45	3.19	2.88	3.28	10.95	9.77	104.0	877-870-2874	Y
Credit Suisse Multialternative Strategy Fund Cls I Shares	CSQIX	B-	C	A-	Up	1.68	3.66	3.86	6.31	16.64	10.18	104.0	877-870-2874	Y
Deutsche Global Macro Fund Class A	DBISX	B-	C+	B	Up	0.20	0.71	13.33	16.27	40.72	9.86	19.1	201-593-8273	Y
Deutsche Global Macro Fund Class C	DBICX	B-	C+	B	Up	0.10	0.43	12.62	13.86	35.64	9.28	19.1	201-593-8273	Y
Deutsche Global Macro Fund Class R	DBITX	B-	C+	B	Up	0.21	0.63	13.07	15.41	39.09	9.51	19.1	212-454-5624	Y
Deutsche Global Macro Fund Class S	DBIVX	B-	C+	B	Up	0.20	0.83	13.56	17.01	42.03	9.63	19.1	201-593-8273	Y
Deutsche Global Macro Fund Institutional Class	MGINX	B-	C+	B	Up	0.31	0.94	13.64	17.23	42.41	9.66	19.1	201-593-8273	Y
Dreyfus Dynamic Total Return Fund Class A	AVGAX	B-	C	B	Up	2.14	3.79	7.42	6.86	33.00	15.8	1,564	800-645-6561	Y
Dreyfus Dynamic Total Return Fund Class I	AVGRX	B-	C	B	Up	2.20	3.95	7.70	7.69	34.79	16.22	1,564	800-645-6561	Y
Dreyfus Dynamic Total Return Fund Class Y	AVGYX	B-	C	B	Up	2.21	4.01	7.76	7.96	34.87	16.23	1,564	800-645-6561	Y
Dunham Monthly Distribution Fund Class A	DAMDX	B-	C	B	Up	-0.29	1.13	4.08	4.78	14.28	35.22	287.0	800-442-4358	Y
EnTrustPermal Alternative Core Fund Class I	LPTIX	B-	C	B+	Up	-0.14	-0.91	2.29	6.24	25.72	14.04	366.5	877-721-1926	Y

Category: Multialternative (con't)

Fund Name	Ticker Symbol	RATINGS: Overall Rating	Reward Rating	Risk Rating	Recent Up/ Downgrade	TOTAL RETURNS & PERFORMANCE: 3-Month Total Return	6-Month Total Return	1-Year Total Return	3-Year Total Return	5-Year Total Return	ASSETS: NAV	Total Assets (MIL)	NEW INVESTORS: Telephone	Open to New Investors
EnTrustPermal Alternative Core Fund Class IS	LPTSX	B-	C	B+	Up	-0.21	-1.04	2.18	6.18	25.63	14.23	366.5	877-721-1926	Y
GMO SGM Major Markets Fund Class III	GSMFX	B-	C	B	Up	0.09	1.05	3.88	8.63	19.52	32.04	1,482	617-330-7500	Y
GMO SGM Major Markets Fund Class IV	GSMJX	B-	C	B	Up	0.12	1.08	3.96	8.72	19.62	31.93	1,482	617-330-7500	Y
GMO SGM Major Markets Fund Class VI	GSMHX	B-	C	B	Up	0.09	1.08	3.99	8.84	19.75	31.95	1,482	617-330-7500	Y
GMO Special Opportunities Fund Class VI	GSOFX	A-	B	A	Up	9.07	13.75	32.22	41.28		24.42	1,025	617-330-7500	Y
Goldman Sachs Absolute Return Tracker Fund Class A	GARTX	B-	C	B	Up	1.84	3.81	6.92	8.71	21.31	9.31	1,621	800-526-7384	Y
Goldman Sachs Absolute Return Tracker Fund Class R6	GARUX	B-	C	B	Up	1.95	3.98	7.36	9.93	23.71	9.57	1,621	800-526-7384	Y
Goldman Sachs Absolute Return Tracker Fund Inst Cls	GJRTX	B-	C	B	Up	1.93	3.96	7.45	9.96	23.75	9.58	1,621	800-526-7384	Y
Goldman Sachs Absolute Return Tracker Fund Investor Class	GSRTX	B-	C	B	Up	1.91	3.96	7.24	9.61	22.88	9.5	1,621	800-526-7384	Y
Highland Resolute Fund Class I	RMRGX	B	C	A-	Up	2.61	5.45	8.14	10.29	24.09		393.7	855-268-2242	Y
Janus Henderson Diversified Alternatives Fund Class A	JDDAX	B-	C	B	Up	1.17	1.96	3.59	6.84	8.44	10.1	106.6	877-335-2687	Y
Janus Henderson Diversified Alternatives Fund Class D	JDADX	B-	C	B	Up	1.26	2.05	3.78	7.25	9.07	10.14	106.6	877-335-2687	Y
Janus Henderson Diversified Alternatives Fund Class I	JDAIX	B-	C	B	Down	1.24	2.04	3.86	7.58	9.62	10.15	106.6	877-335-2687	Y
Janus Henderson Diversified Alternatives Fund Class N	JDANX	B-	C	B	Down	1.34	2.13	3.95	7.74	9.89	10.18	106.6	877-335-2687	Y
Janus Henderson Diversified Alternatives Fund Class S	JDASX	B-	C	B	Up	1.29	1.89	3.64	6.76	7.93	10.06	106.6	877-335-2687	Y
Janus Henderson Diversified Alternatives Fund Class T	JDATX	B-	C	B		1.19	1.99	3.72	7.30	8.90	10.09	106.6	877-335-2687	Y
KCM Macro Trends Fund Class R-1	KCMTX	B-	B-	B	Up	9.37	18.08	22.53	24.41	77.70	13.25	94.6		Y
KCM Macro Trends Fund Institutional Class	KCMIX	B-	B-	B	Up	9.61	18.34	22.80	24.68	78.09	13.25	94.6		Y
Litman Gregory Masters Alternative Strat Fund Inst Cls	MASFX	B-	C	B	Up	0.67	2.02	4.50	10.63	22.38	11.69	2,007	800-960-0188	Y
Litman Gregory Masters Alternative Strategies Fund Inv Cls	MASNX	B-	C	B	Up	0.51	1.88	4.14	9.83	20.92	11.7	2,007	800-960-0188	Y
Multi-Strategy Growth & Income Fund Class A Shares	MSFDX	B-	C	B+	Up	0.19	1.84	2.73	8.51	30.77	15.11	--	855-601-3841	Y
Multi-Strategy Growth & Income Fund Class C Shares	US62546J4067	B-	C	B	Up	0.02	1.40	1.99	6.10	27.43	14.77	--	855-601-3841	Y
Multi-Strategy Growth & Income Fund Class I Shares	US62546J2087	B-	C	B+	Up	0.27	1.98	3.04	9.92	32.04	15.31	--	855-601-3841	Y
Multi-Strategy Growth & Income Fund Class L Shares	US62546J3077	B-	C	B+	Up	0.10	1.62	2.28	6.92	28.60	14.89	--	855-601-3841	Y
Oppenheimer Fundamental Alternatives Fund A	QVOPX	B-	C	A-	Up	-0.66	-0.59	1.28	4.33	19.52	26.82	1,239	800-225-5677	Y
Oppenheimer Fundamental Alternatives Fund I	QOPIX	B-	C	A	Up	-0.55	-0.38	1.74	5.71	22.06	27.5	1,239	800-225-5677	Y
Oppenheimer Fundamental Alternatives Fund Y	QOPYX	B-	C	A	Up	-0.60	-0.50	1.52	5.04	20.88	27.4	1,239	800-225-5677	Y
Pacific Funds Diversified Alternatives Fund Advisor Class	PLDLX	B-	C+	B	Down	0.89	3.37	7.08	14.01		9.87	24.3	800-722-2333	Y
Pacific Funds Diversified Alternatives Fund Class A	PLALX	B	C+	A-	Up	0.85	3.33	6.83	13.27		9.84	24.3	800-722-2333	Y
Pacific Funds Diversified Alternatives Fund Class C	PLCLX	B-	C	B+	Up	0.62	2.92	6.01	10.73		9.69	24.3	800-722-2333	Y
Principal Global Multi-Strategy Fund Inst Cls Shares	PSMIX	B-	C	B	Up	1.56	3.36	6.59	9.17	19.46	11.3	2,814	800-222-5852	Y
Principal Global Multi-Strategy Fund R-6	PGLSX	B-	C	B	Up	1.53	3.24	6.46	9.04	19.31	11.29	2,814	800-222-5852	Y
Prudential QMA Global Tactical Allocation Fund Class Z	PTZLX	B-	C	B	Up	4.60	7.08	11.88			9.91	33.4	800-225-1852	Y
Putnam Absolute Return 500 Fund Class A	PJMDX	B-	C	B	Up	1.98	3.99	7.17	7.48	17.45	11.19	940.7	617-292-1000	Y
Putnam Absolute Return 500 Fund Class P	US99018R9125	B-	C	B	Up	2.11	4.21	7.57	8.45	19.15	11.25	940.7	617-292-1000	
Putnam Absolute Return 500 Fund Class R6	PJMEX	B-	C	B	Up	2.06	4.24	7.60	8.55	19.50	11.28	940.7	617-292-1000	Y
Putnam Absolute Return 500 Fund Class Y	PJMYX	B-	C	B	Up	2.00	4.09	7.45	8.24	18.91	11.24	940.7	617-292-1000	Y
Putnam Absolute Return 700 Fund Class A	PDMAX	B-	C	B	Up	2.62	5.39	9.74	10.49	24.93	12.2	1,199	617-292-1000	Y
Putnam Absolute Return 700 Fund Class M	PDMMX	B-	C	B	Up	2.54	5.19	9.23	8.93	21.90	11.98	1,199	617-292-1000	Y
Putnam Absolute Return 700 Fund Class P	US99020R9006	B-	C+	B	Up	2.66	5.59	10.11	11.52	26.79	12.24	1,199	617-292-1000	
Putnam Absolute Return 700 Fund Class R	PDMRX	B-	C	B	Up	2.60	5.32	9.43	9.67	23.39	12.03	1,199	617-292-1000	Y
Putnam Absolute Return 700 Fund Class R6	PDMEX	B-	C+	B	Up	2.78	5.70	10.13	11.69	27.21	12.29	1,199	617-292-1000	Y
Putnam Absolute Return 700 Fund Class Y	PDMYX	B-	C+	B	Up	2.71	5.64	10.08	11.39	26.64	12.24	1,199	617-292-1000	Y
Stadion Trilogy Alternative Return Fund Class A Shares	STTGX	B	C	A-	Up	0.97	2.90	4.62	11.24	16.27	11.42	118.1	706-353-8737	Y
Stadion Trilogy Alternative Return Fund Class C Shares	STTCX	B-	C	A-	Up	0.73	2.36	3.78	8.64	11.74	11.2	118.1	706-353-8737	Y
Stadion Trilogy Alternative Return Fund Class I Shares	STTIX	B	C	A-	Up	1.04	2.96	4.90	11.93	17.50	11.45	118.1	706-353-8737	Y
Stadion Trilogy Alternative Return Fund Class T	STTHX	B	C	A-		0.93	2.79	4.60	11.06	16.00	11.4	118.1	706-353-8737	Y
Touchstone Controlled Growth with Income Fund A	TSAAX	B-	C	B	Up	1.24	2.94	5.22	10.29	21.97	11.26	45.8	800-543-0407	Y
Touchstone Controlled Growth with Income Fund Y	TSAYX	B-	C	B	Up	1.31	3.16	5.59	11.14	23.42	11.26	45.8	800-543-0407	Y
Victory Strategic Allocation Fund Class A	SBALX	B	C+	B+	Up	3.79	7.38	14.55	17.32	56.61	16.46	38.1	800-539-3863	Y
Victory Strategic Allocation Fund Class C	VBFCX	B-	C+	B	Up	3.64	7.00	13.78	14.89	51.16	16.23	38.1	800-539-3863	Y
Victory Strategic Allocation Fund Class I	VBFIX	B	C+	B+	Up	3.83	7.50	14.83	18.18	58.49	16.53	38.1	800-539-3863	Y

Category: Multialternative (con't)

Fund Name	Ticker Symbol	RATINGS: Overall Rating	RATINGS: Reward Rating	RATINGS: Risk Rating	RATINGS: Recent Up/ Downgrade	TOTAL RETURNS & PERFORMANCE: 3-Month Total Return	6-Month Total Return	1-Year Total Return	3-Year Total Return	5-Year Total Return	ASSETS: NAV	Total Assets (MIL)	NEW INVESTORS: Telephone	Open to New Investors
Victory Strategic Allocation Fund Class R	VBFGX	B-	C+	B	Up	3.76	7.26	14.30	16.32	54.32	16.43	38.1	800-539-3863	Y
Vivaldi Multi-Strategy Fund Class A	OMOAX	B	C	A+	Up	0.02	2.49	1.41	11.55	16.40	26.12	151.3		Y
Vivaldi Multi-Strategy Fund Class I	OMOIX	B	C	A+	Up	0.09	2.64	1.72	12.61	18.26	26.62	151.3		Y
WCM Alternatives: Event-Driven Fund Institutional Class	WCEIX	B-	C	B+	Up	0.51	0.51	4.71	5.36		10.17	98.0		Y
Wells Fargo Alternative Strategies Fund - Class Inst	WAITX	B-	C	B+	Up	1.22	2.38	7.07	6.27		10.74	164.9	800-222-8222	Y

Category: Natural Resources Sector Equity

Fund Name	Ticker Symbol	RATINGS: Overall Rating	RATINGS: Reward Rating	RATINGS: Risk Rating	RATINGS: Recent Up/ Downgrade	TOTAL RETURNS & PERFORMANCE: 3-Month Total Return	6-Month Total Return	1-Year Total Return	3-Year Total Return	5-Year Total Return	ASSETS: NAV	Total Assets (MIL)	NEW INVESTORS: Telephone	Open to New Investors
AllianzGI Global Water Fund Class A	AWTAX	B	B	B+	Up	3.90	9.34	22.30	27.87	59.45	15.67	668.5	800-498-5413	Y
AllianzGI Global Water Fund Class C	AWTCX	B	B-	B	Up	3.66	8.88	21.35	24.92	53.21	14.98	668.5	800-498-5413	Y
AllianzGI Global Water Fund Class P	AWTPX	B	B	B+	Up	3.99	9.48	22.67	28.91	61.38	15.68	668.5	800-498-5413	Y
AllianzGI Global Water Fund Institutional Class	AWTIX	B	B	B+	Up	3.96	9.46	22.70	28.93	61.81	15.4	668.5	800-498-5413	Y
Fidelity Advisor® Materials Fund Class A	FMFAX	B-	B	C+	Up	6.86	14.53	25.85	26.72	58.02	90.59	1,888	617-563-7000	Y
Fidelity Advisor® Materials Fund Class C	FMFCX	B-	B-	C+	Up	6.67	14.10	24.92	23.91	52.21	87.66	1,888	617-563-7000	Y
Fidelity Advisor® Materials Fund Class I	FMFEX	B-	B	C+	Up	6.94	14.70	26.20	27.80	60.28	90.79	1,888	617-563-7000	Y
Fidelity Advisor® Materials Fund Class M	FMFTX	B-	B	C+	Up	6.79	14.38	25.49	25.57	55.65	89.92	1,888	617-563-7000	Y
Fidelity® Select Chemicals Portfolio	FSCHX	B+	A	C+	Up	6.02	17.24	31.75	46.09	103.76	178.31	1,890	617-563-7000	Y
Fidelity® Select Materials Portfolio	FSDPX	B-	B	C+	Up	6.94	14.69	26.21	27.74	60.16	90.97	1,888	617-563-7000	Y
GMO Resources Fund Class III	GOFIX	B-	B	C	Up	8.56	27.73	28.19	43.29	25.26	20.24	228.2	617-330-7500	Y
GMO Resources Fund Class IV	GOVIX	B-	B	C	Up	8.58	27.77	28.31	43.47	25.48	20.17	228.2	617-330-7500	Y
Rydex Basic Materials Fund Class A	RYBMX	B-	B	C	Up	6.49	12.85	21.52	30.07	33.25	59.65	116.9	800-820-0888	Y
Rydex Basic Materials Fund Class C	RYBCX	B-	B	C	Up	6.30	12.44	20.60	27.17	28.36	53.08	116.9	800-820-0888	Y
Rydex Basic Materials Fund Class H	RYBAX	B-	B	C	Up	6.51	12.86	21.52	29.89	32.41	57.85	116.9	800-820-0888	Y
Rydex Basic Materials Fund Class Investor	RYBIX	B	B	C	Up	6.56	12.98	21.81	31.05	34.94	63.53	116.9	800-820-0888	Y
Vanguard Materials Index Fund Admiral Shares	VMIAX	B	A-	C+	Up	6.67	13.26	23.67	33.53	82.14	69.58	2,638	877-662-7447	Y

Category: Other Alternative

Fund Name	Ticker Symbol	RATINGS: Overall Rating	RATINGS: Reward Rating	RATINGS: Risk Rating	RATINGS: Recent Up/ Downgrade	TOTAL RETURNS & PERFORMANCE: 3-Month Total Return	6-Month Total Return	1-Year Total Return	3-Year Total Return	5-Year Total Return	ASSETS: NAV	Total Assets (MIL)	NEW INVESTORS: Telephone	Open to New Investors
361 Global Managed Futures Strategy Fund Class I	AGFZX	B	C+	B+	Up	1.37	4.47	8.27	23.26		11.05	114.4	866-361-1720	Y
361 Global Managed Futures Strategy Fund Investor Class	AGFQX	B	C+	B+	Up	1.29	4.23	7.96	22.25		10.93	114.4	866-361-1720	Y
Arbitrage Credit Opportunities Fund Class I	ACFIX	B-	C	B+	Up	0.24	0.51	1.35	5.38	12.50	9.6	53.6	800-285-4485	Y
Goldman Sachs Long Short Credit Strat Fund Inst Shares	GSAWX	B-	C	A-	Up	-0.19	0.16	2.60	7.21	10.03	9.27	215.3	800-526-7384	Y
Goldman Sachs Managed Futures Strategy Fund Inst Cls	GMSSX	B-	C	B	Up	2.43	3.03	2.73	12.84	5.09	10.52	261.4	800-526-7384	Y
LoCorr Macro Strategies Fund Class A	LFMAX	B-	C	B	Up	4.53	5.61	2.65	13.30	22.85	8.64	809.2	855-523-8637	Y
LoCorr Macro Strategies Fund Class I	LFMIX	B-	C	B+	Up	4.58	5.77	2.95	14.19	24.44	8.77	809.2	855-523-8637	Y
PIMCO Credit Absolute Return Fund Class A	PZCRX	B-	C	B	Up	0.50	2.51	6.55	11.61	14.13	10.16	461.3	866-746-2602	Y
PIMCO Credit Absolute Return Fund Class D	PDCRX	B-	C	B	Up	0.51	2.56	6.51	11.57	14.21	10.13	461.3	866-746-2602	Y
PIMCO Credit Absolute Return Fund Class P	PPCRX	B-	C+	B	Up	0.60	2.69	6.82	12.57	15.90	10.11	461.3	866-746-2602	Y
PIMCO Credit Absolute Return Fund Institutional	PCARX	B-	C+	B	Up	0.51	2.71	6.94	12.84	16.45	10.14	461.3	866-746-2602	Y
Salient Tactical Muni & Credit Fund Class A	FLSLX	B	C	A	Up	1.70	3.43	8.30	14.07	6.15	7.88	80.0	866-667-9228	Y
Salient Tactical Muni & Credit Fund Class C	FLSFX	B-	C	A-	Up	1.59	3.31	7.90	12.49	3.73	7.93	80.0	866-667-9228	Y
Salient Tactical Muni & Credit Fund Institutional Class	FLSIX	B	C+	A	Up	1.84	3.70	8.87	15.75	8.85	7.85	80.0	866-667-9228	Y
Salient Tactical Muni & Credit Fund Investor Class	FLSRX	B	C	A	Up	1.86	3.61	8.66	14.65	6.92	7.93	80.0	866-667-9228	Y
Shelton Tactical Credit Fund Institutional Class	DEBIX	B-	C	A-	Up	0.68	1.76	3.65	22.10		10.36	26.5	800-955-9988	Y
Shelton Tactical Credit Fund Investor Class	DEBTX	B-	C	A-	Up	0.52	1.53	3.33	21.11		10.31	26.5	800-955-9988	Y

Category: Other Equity

Fund Name	Ticker Symbol	RATINGS: Overall Rating	Reward Rating	Risk Rating	Recent Up/ Downgrade	TOTAL RETURNS & PERFORMANCE: 3-Month Total Return	6-Month Total Return	1-Year Total Return	3-Year Total Return	5-Year Total Return	ASSETS: NAV	Total Assets (MIL)	NEW INVESTORS: Telephone	Open to New Investors
Aberdeen Chile Fund Inc	CH	B	A-	C	Up	8.06	25.29	39.73	42.09	-2.00	9.83	81.9	866-667-9231	Y
Aberdeen Israel Fund Inc	ISL	B-	C+	B-	Up	3.18	4.31	20.50	25.16	64.23	22.21	87.6	866-667-9231	Y
Fidelity® Nordic Fund	FNORX	B	B-	B	Up	2.99	4.15	23.65	33.75	92.03	53.29	344.8	617-563-7000	Y
JNL/Invesco China-India Fund Class A	US46648M2769	B+	A	B-	Up	7.58	18.66	52.32	40.80	54.53	10.5	714.3		Y
JNL/Invesco China-India Fund Class I	US46648M2686	B+	A	B-	Up	7.72	18.84	52.83	41.86	56.18	10.6	714.3		Y
Korea Fund Inc	KF	B	A-	B-	Up	11.38	13.77	40.87	38.49	28.30	46.65	286.7		Y
Matthews Korea Fund Institutional Class	MIKOX	B+	A-	B	Up	9.88	10.20	40.11	51.85	67.69	6.95	225.9	800-789-2742	Y
Matthews Korea Fund Investor Class	MAKOX	B+	A-	B	Up	9.94	10.27	39.88	51.19	66.74	6.91	225.9	800-789-2742	Y
Matthews Korea Fund Investor Class	GF	A	A	A-	Up	8.36	20.72	48.54	67.62	128.19	21.49	225.9		Y
Swiss Helvetia Fund Inc	SWZ	B-	C+	B	Up	1.36	2.24	22.06	20.05	51.08	14.1	354.1	800-730-2932	Y
Thai Fund Inc	TTF	B-	B	C	Up	7.27	16.50	33.63	29.62	43.17	10.99	131.9	855-332-5306	Y
Thai Fund Inc	CEE	B-	B-	C+	Up	0.83	14.47	18.29	29.26	-13.11	27.44	131.9		Y
Timothy Plan Israel Common Values Fund Class A	TPAIX	B	B+	B	Up	5.16	8.13	27.06	42.80	55.63	15.47	48.0	800-662-0201	Y
Timothy Plan Israel Common Values Fund Class C	TPCIX	B	B	B	Up	5.00	7.71	26.13	39.52	49.78	14.92	48.0	800-662-0201	Y
Timothy Plan Israel Common Values Fund Class I	TICIX	B	B+	B	Up	5.25	8.29	27.48	43.93	57.22	15.52	48.0	800-662-0201	Y
Voya Russia Fund Class A	LETRX	B	A-	C+	Up	3.22	19.94	11.70	54.45	2.24	29.79	87.9	800-366-0066	Y
Voya Russia Fund Class I	IIRFX	B	A-	C+	Up	3.30	20.06	11.94	55.40	3.18	29.88	87.9	800-366-0066	Y
Voya Russia Fund Class W	IWRFX	B	A-	C+	Up	3.37	20.35	12.25	55.78	3.61	29.82	87.9	800-366-0066	Y

Category: Other Sector Equity

Fund Name	Ticker Symbol	RATINGS: Overall Rating	Reward Rating	Risk Rating	Recent Up/ Downgrade	TOTAL RETURNS & PERFORMANCE: 3-Month Total Return	6-Month Total Return	1-Year Total Return	3-Year Total Return	5-Year Total Return	ASSETS: NAV	Total Assets (MIL)	NEW INVESTORS: Telephone	Open to New Investors
Alpine Global Infrastructure Fund Institutional Class	AIFRX	B-	B-	C+	Up	2.37	7.09	24.09	21.53	57.67	20.92	137.3	888-785-5578	Y
Cohen & Steers Global Infrastructure Fund, Inc. Class A	CSUAX	B-	C+	B-		3.49	5.62	18.89	17.01	57.38	19.14	252.9	212-832-3232	Y
Cohen & Steers Global Infrastructure Fund, Inc. Class I	CSUIX	B-	C+	B-		3.58	5.81	19.29	18.14	59.91	19.2	252.9	212-832-3232	Y
Cohen & Steers Global Infrastructure Fund, Inc. Class Z	CSUZX	B-	C+	B-		3.58	5.81	19.29	18.29	60.18	19.2	252.9	212-832-3232	Y
Cohen & Steers Infrastructure Fund	UTF	B-	B-	C+	Up	3.06	6.25	24.63	22.83	77.82	25.53	2,239	212-832-3232	Y
Franklin Global Listed Infrastructure Fund Advisor Class	FLGZX	B-	B-	C+		2.75	5.85	23.59	22.10		13.87	67.7	650-312-2000	Y
Franklin Global Listed Infrastructure Fund Class A	FLGIX	B-	B-	C+	Up	2.74	5.81	23.25	21.11		13.85	67.7	650-312-2000	Y
Franklin Global Listed Infrastructure Fund Class R	US3535335992	B-	B-	C+	Up	2.66	5.65	23.00	20.33		13.84	67.7	650-312-2000	Y
Franklin Global Listed Infrastructure Fund Class R6	US3535335810	B-	B-	B-		2.84	6.04	23.87	22.71		13.88	67.7	650-312-2000	Y
Frontier MFG Core Infrastructure Fund Institutional Class	FMGIX	B	B-	B		1.85	4.35	20.24	25.20	67.15	16.25	276.5		Y
Frontier MFG Core Infrastructure Fund Service Class	FCIVX	B	B-	B		1.76	4.24	20.17	25.10	67.02	16.25	276.5		Y
John Hancock Enduring Assets Fund Class I	JEEIX	B-	C	B		-0.20	4.16	17.44	17.86		11.99	114.0	800-225-5913	Y
John Hancock Enduring Assets Fund Class NAV	US47803P4191	B-	C	B		-0.25	4.21	17.62	18.32		12.01	114.0	800-225-5913	Y
John Hancock Enduring Assets Fund Class R6	JEEDX	B-	C	B		-0.17	4.29	17.70	18.40		12.02	114.0	800-225-5913	Y
Lazard Global Listed Infrastructure Portfolio Inst Shares	GLIFX	B+	B	A	Down	0.16	4.11	20.80	43.48	116.43	16	5,458	800-823-6300	Y
Lazard Global Listed Infrastructure Portfolio Open Shares	GLFOX	B+	B	A	Down	0.04	3.97	20.47	42.28	113.61	16.01	5,458	800-823-6300	Y
Nuveen Global Infrastructure Fund Class A	FGIAX	B-	C+	B-		2.36	4.78	19.37	18.73	58.40	10.93	621.7	312-917-8146	Y
Nuveen Global Infrastructure Fund Class I	FGIYX	B-	C+	B-		2.43	4.94	19.61	19.57	60.45	10.89	621.7	312-917-8146	Y
Nuveen Global Infrastructure Fund Class R3	FGNRX	B-	C+	B-		2.30	4.68	19.02	17.87	56.42	11.11	621.7	312-917-8146	Y
Nuveen Global Infrastructure Fund Class R6	FGIWX	B-	C+	B-		2.52	5.13	19.94	19.89	60.89	10.91	621.7	312-917-8146	Y
Reaves Utilities & Energy Infrastructure Fund Cls Inst	RSRFX	B-	B-	B-	Down	3.32	5.69	10.80	23.09	72.71	10.21	47.5		Y
Russell Investments Global Infrastructure Fund Class A	RGIAX	B-	C+	B-		1.11	3.64	18.45	18.20	53.75	11.43	948.0	800-426-7969	Y
Russell Investments Global Infrastructure Fund Class E	RGIEX	B-	C+	B-		1.21	3.74	18.56	18.20	53.81	11.45	948.0	800-426-7969	Y
Russell Investments Global Infrastructure Fund Class M	RGFTX	B-	C+	B-		1.23	3.85	18.98	19.66	57.15	11.44	948.0	800-426-7969	Y
Russell Investments Global Infrastructure Fund Class S	RGISX	B-	C+	B-		1.15	3.82	18.80	19.05	55.81	11.45	948.0	800-426-7969	Y
Russell Investments Global Infrastructure Fund Class Y	RGIYX	B-	C+	B-		1.25	3.88	19.02	19.69	57.19	11.45	948.0	800-426-7969	Y
Voya CBRE Global Infrastructure Fund Class A	VCRAX	B-	B-	B-		2.96	5.76	20.00	24.40		10.77	38.9	800-366-0066	Y
Voya CBRE Global Infrastructure Fund Class I	VCRIX	B-	B-	B	Down	3.09	5.90	20.48	25.74		10.77	38.9	800-366-0066	Y

Category: Real Estate Sector Equity

Fund Name	Ticker Symbol	RATINGS: Overall Rating	Reward Rating	Risk Rating	Recent Up/ Downgrade	TOTAL RETURNS & PERFORMANCE: 3-Month Total Return	6-Month Total Return	1-Year Total Return	3-Year Total Return	5-Year Total Return	ASSETS: NAV	Total Assets (MIL)	NEW INVESTORS: Telephone	Open to New Investors
1290 VT Real Estate Portfolio Class IB	US26884M5114	B-	C+	B	Up	3.48	4.80	11.39	11.64			28.7	877-222-2144	Y
1290 VT Real Estate Portfolio Class K	US26884M4950	B-	C+	B	Up	3.53	4.94	11.72	12.47			28.7	877-222-2144	Y
AB Global Real Estate Investment Fund Advisor Class	ARSYX	B-	C+	B		3.54	5.82	13.66	16.27	43.22	14.41	148.8	212-969-1000	Y
AB Global Real Estate Investment Fund Class A	AREAX	B-	C+	B		3.51	5.71	13.42	15.34	41.28	14.56	148.8	212-969-1000	Y
AB Global Real Estate Investment Fund Class B	AREBX	B-	C+	B	Up	3.30	5.31	12.51	12.66	35.85	14.39	148.8	212-969-1000	
AB Global Real Estate Investment Fund Class C	ARECX	B-	C+	B	Up	3.31	5.31	12.57	12.75	36.14	14.41	148.8	212-969-1000	Y
AB Global Real Estate Investment Fund Class I	AEEIX	B-	C+	B		3.61	5.91	13.83	16.60	43.89	14.51	148.8	212-969-1000	Y
AB Global Real Estate Investment Fund Class K	ARRKX	B-	C+	B		3.54	5.76	13.42	15.39	41.46	14.45	148.8	212-969-1000	Y
AB Global Real Estate Investment Fund Class R	ARRRX	B-	C+	B	Up	3.42	5.58	13.09	14.35	39.28	14.39	148.8	212-969-1000	Y
AB Global Real Estate Investment Fund II Class I	ARIIX	B-	C+	B		3.65	6.14	14.43	17.83	45.81	11.03	334.7	212-969-1000	Y
Alpine Global Premier Property	AWP	B-	B-	B	Up	4.62	8.62	29.41	25.45	40.56	7.42	625.2	914-251-0880	Y
Alpine Realty Income & Growth Fund Class A shares	AIAGX	B	B-	B	Up	1.45	2.35	7.42	17.67	61.85	22.78	111.3	888-785-5578	Y
Alpine Realty Income and Growth Fund Institutional Class	AIGYX	B	B-	B+	Up	1.45	2.45	7.61	18.50	63.66	22.81	111.3	888-785-5578	Y
Altegris/AACA Opportunistic Real Estate Fund A	RAAAX	B+	A-	B	Up	8.93	11.89	23.60	36.61	94.11	16.02	282.7	858-459-7040	Y
Altegris/AACA Opportunistic Real Estate Fund I	RAAIX	B+	A-	B	Up	9.01	12.03	24.01	37.51	96.46	16.06	282.7	858-459-7040	Y
Altegris/AACA Opportunistic Real Estate Fund N	RAANX	B+	A-	B	Up	9.00	11.88	23.68	36.62	94.12	16.02	282.7	858-459-7040	Y
American Century Global Real Estate Fund A Class	ARYMX	B-	C+	B	Up	4.57	7.98	14.11	12.30	34.73	11.89	84.4	800-444-4015	Y
American Century Global Real Estate Fund I Class	ARYNX	B-	C+	B	Up	4.61	8.29	14.65	13.85	37.87	11.87	84.4	800-444-4015	Y
American Century Global Real Estate Fund Investor Class	ARYVX	B-	C+	B	Up	4.57	8.16	14.41	13.16	36.47	11.88	84.4	800-444-4015	Y
American Century Global Real Estate Fund R Class	ARYWX	B-	C+	B	Up	4.39	7.79	13.70	11.44	33.00	11.9	84.4	800-444-4015	Y
American Century Global Real Estate Fund R5 Class	ARYGX	B-	C+	B	Up	4.55	8.14	14.59	13.79	37.80	11.87	84.4	800-444-4015	Y
American Century Global Real Estate Fund R6 Class	ARYDX	B-	C+	B	Up	4.68	8.37	14.73	14.38	38.69	11.86	84.4	800-444-4015	Y
American Century Global Real Estate Fund Y Class	ARYYX	B-	C+	B	Up	4.67	8.27	14.73	13.92	37.96	11.86	84.4	800-444-4015	Y
American Century Real Estate Fund A Class	AREEX	B-	C+	B	Up	2.50	3.21	4.90	11.53	49.92	28.19	1,141	800-444-4015	Y
American Century Real Estate Fund C Class	ARYCX	B-	C+	B	Up	2.30	2.82	4.12	9.04	44.42	27.48	1,141	800-444-4015	Y
American Century Real Estate Fund I Class	REAIX	B-	C+	B	Up	2.61	3.43	5.37	13.05	53.33	28.29	1,141	800-444-4015	Y
American Century Real Estate Fund Investor Class	REACX	B-	C+	B	Up	2.56	3.33	5.18	12.37	51.84	28.22	1,141	800-444-4015	Y
American Century Real Estate Fund R Class	AREWX	B-	C+	B	Up	2.41	3.06	4.64	10.69	48.07	27.99	1,141	800-444-4015	Y
American Century Real Estate Fund R5 Class	ARREX	B-	C+	B	Up	2.61	3.43	5.32	12.52	52.04	28.29	1,141	800-444-4015	Y
American Century Real Estate Fund R6 Class	AREDX	B-	C+	B	Up	2.66	3.55	5.53	13.60	54.21	28.28	1,141	800-444-4015	Y
American Century Real Estate Fund Y Class	ARYEX	B-	C+	B	Up	2.66	3.51	5.43	12.64	52.20	28.28	1,141	800-444-4015	Y
AMG Managers CenterSquare Real Estate Fund Class I	MRASX	B	B-	B+	Up	3.59	4.34	5.53	16.77	61.14	10.43	304.6	800-835-3879	Y
AMG Managers CenterSquare Real Estate Fund Class N	MRESX	B	B-	B+	Up	3.57	4.28	5.40	16.62	60.93	10.43	304.6	800-835-3879	Y
AMG Managers CenterSquare Real Estate Fund Class Z	MREZX	B	B-	B+	Up	3.72	4.49	5.59	16.84	61.23	10.43	304.6	800-835-3879	Y
Baron Real Estate Fund Class R6	BREUX	B-	B-	C+		9.68	13.53	31.41	22.57	87.36	30.01	1,071	800-992-2766	Y
Baron Real Estate Fund Institutional Shares	BREIX	B-	B-	B		9.69	13.53	31.41	22.56	87.34	30.01	1,071	800-992-2766	Y
BlackRock Real Estate Securities Fund Institutional Shares	BIREX	B	C+	B+	Up	2.79	2.67	6.18	16.66	61.91	12.1	24.5	800-441-7762	Y
BlackRock Real Estate Securities Fund Investor A Shares	BAREX	B-	C+	B+		2.83	2.55	5.90	15.77	59.84	12.08	24.5	800-441-7762	Y
BlackRock Real Estate Securities Fund Investor C Shares	BCREX	B-	C+	B		2.53	2.05	5.05	13.13	53.89	12	24.5	800-441-7762	Y
Brookfield Global Listed Real Estate Fund Class A	BLRAX	B-	C+	B	Up	3.73	4.71	9.83	13.34	45.08	13.34	1,942	212-549-8400	Y
Brookfield Global Listed Real Estate Fund Class C	BLRCX	B-	C	B	Up	3.61	4.32	9.07	10.91	39.83	13.28	1,942	212-549-8400	Y
Brookfield Global Listed Real Estate Fund Class I	BLRIX	B-	C+	B		3.81	4.85	10.12	14.19	46.79	13.35	1,942	212-549-8400	Y
Brookfield Global Listed Real Estate Fund Class Y	BLRYX	B-	C+	B		3.88	4.93	10.20	14.26	46.98	13.37	1,942	212-549-8400	Y
CGM Realty Fund	CGMRX	B+	A-	B	Up	12.96	20.97	32.64	31.60	80.39	32.19	990.3	800-343-5678	Y
ClearBridge Real Estate Opportunities Fund Class I	CRENX	B-	C+	B	Up	3.12	3.75	2.82	14.71	55.08	9.04	35.5	877-721-1926	Y
ClearBridge Real Estate Opportunities Fund Class O	CREOX	B-	C+	B	Up	3.25	3.95	3.10	14.86	55.28	9.08	35.5	877-721-1926	Y
Cohen & Steers Global Realty Shares, Inc. Class A	CSFAX	B-	C+	B		3.82	5.21	12.53	17.66	41.60	53.63	579.3	212-832-3232	Y
Cohen & Steers Global Realty Shares, Inc. Class C	CSFCX	B-	C+	B		3.66	4.88	11.82	15.39	37.09	53.31	579.3	212-832-3232	Y
Cohen & Steers Global Realty Shares, Inc. Class I	CSSPX	B-	C+	B		3.90	5.41	12.95	18.90	44.06	53.87	579.3	212-832-3232	Y
Cohen & Steers Global Realty Shares, Inc. Class R	GRSRX	B-	C+	B		3.78	5.15	12.36	17.35	40.76	54.01	579.3	212-832-3232	Y
Cohen & Steers Global Realty Shares, Inc. Class Z	CSFZX	B-	C+	B		3.93	5.42	12.95	18.93	44.09	53.88	579.3	212-832-3232	Y
Cohen & Steers Institutional Global Realty Shares	GRSIX	B-	C+	B		3.86	5.38	12.93	18.92	44.44	27.07	482.3	212-832-3232	Y

Category: Real Estate Sector Equity (con't)

Fund Name	Ticker Symbol	RATINGS: Overall Rating	Reward Rating	Risk Rating	Recent Up/ Downgrade	TOTAL RETURNS & PERFORMANCE: 3-Month Total Return	6-Month Total Return	1-Year Total Return	3-Year Total Return	5-Year Total Return	ASSETS: NAV	Total Assets (MIL)	NEW INVESTORS: Telephone	Open to New Investors
Cohen & Steers Institutional Realty Shares	CSRIX	B	C+	B+	Up	3.02	3.12	7.44	17.93	63.14	43.31	2,827	212-832-3232	Y
Cohen & Steers International Realty Fund Class A	IRFAX	B-	C+	B	Up	6.00	10.29	23.02	19.67	30.23	12.02	638.2	212-832-3232	Y
Cohen & Steers International Realty Fund Class C	IRFCX	B-	C+	B	Up	5.88	10.01	22.27	17.43	26.12	11.92	638.2	212-832-3232	Y
Cohen & Steers International Realty Fund Class I	IRFIX	B-	C+	B	Up	6.06	10.52	23.39	20.97	32.48	12.09	638.2	212-832-3232	Y
Cohen & Steers International Realty Fund Class R	IRFRX	B-	C+	B	Up	5.95	10.20	22.77	19.65	29.73	12.12	638.2	212-832-3232	Y
Cohen & Steers International Realty Fund Class Z	IRFZX	B-	C+	B	Up	6.06	10.52	23.39	21.08	32.60	12.09	638.2	212-832-3232	Y
Cohen & Steers Quality Income Realty Fund	RQI	B	B-	B	Up	2.82	3.35	8.68	21.90	76.79	13.59	1,496	212-832-3232	Y
Cohen & Steers Real Estate Securities Fund, Inc. Class A	CSEIX	B	B-	B+	Up	2.80	3.41	7.78	22.77	73.98	14.82	4,350	212-832-3232	Y
Cohen & Steers Real Estate Securities Fund, Inc. Class C	CSCIX	B	C+	B+	Up	2.62	3.05	7.07	20.32	68.39	13.44	4,350	212-832-3232	Y
Cohen & Steers Real Estate Securities Fund, Inc. Class F	CREFX	B	B-	B+	Up	2.88	3.63	7.97	22.99	74.30	15.59	4,350	212-832-3232	Y
Cohen & Steers Real Estate Securities Fund, Inc. Cls Inst	CSDIX	B	B-	B+		2.86	3.51	8.08	23.71	76.32	15.59	4,350	212-832-3232	Y
Cohen & Steers Real Estate Securities Fund, Inc. Class R	CIRRX	B	B-	B+	Up	2.77	3.32	7.62	22.21	72.46	15.55	4,350	212-832-3232	Y
Cohen & Steers Real Estate Securities Fund, Inc. Class Z	CSZIX	B	B-	B+		2.81	3.56	8.17	23.95	75.93	15.59	4,350	212-832-3232	Y
Cohen & Steers Realty Shares Fund	CSRSX	B	C+	B+	Up	2.96	2.94	7.08	16.93	61.17	64.44	4,656	212-832-3232	Y
Cohen & Steers Total Return Realty	RFI	B	C+	A-	Up	2.40	2.93	7.87	18.37	58.81	13.41	352.6	212-832-3232	Y
Columbia Real Estate Equity Fund Advisor Class	CRERX	B-	C+	B+		1.40	1.65	5.36	14.22	51.61	14.32	365.2	800-345-6611	Y
Columbia Real Estate Equity Fund Class A	CREAX	B-	C+	B+		1.30	1.49	5.06	13.29	49.65	14.02	365.2	800-345-6611	Y
Columbia Real Estate Equity Fund Class C	CRECX	B-	C+	B		1.11	1.10	4.28	10.76	44.20	14.02	365.2	800-345-6611	Y
Columbia Real Estate Equity Fund Class K	CRRFX	B-	C+	B+		1.33	1.55	5.19	13.80	50.82	14.07	365.2	800-345-6611	
Columbia Real Estate Equity Fund Class R	CRSRX	B-	C+	B		1.24	1.36	4.80	12.52	47.82	14.01	365.2	800-345-6611	Y
Columbia Real Estate Equity Fund Class T	CREWX	B-	C+	B+		1.30	1.49	5.06	13.28	49.61	14.03	365.2	800-345-6611	Y
Columbia Real Estate Equity Fund Institutional 2 Class	CRRVX	B-	C+	B+		1.40	1.69	5.48	14.64	52.62	14.01	365.2	800-345-6611	Y
Columbia Real Estate Equity Fund Institutional 3 Class	CREYX	B-	C+	B+		1.40	1.70	5.51	14.39	51.82	14.15	365.2	800-345-6611	Y
Columbia Real Estate Equity Fund Institutional Class	CREEX	B-	C+	B+		1.36	1.61	5.31	14.18	51.53	14.05	365.2	800-345-6611	Y
Davis Real Estate Fund Class A	RPFRX	B	B-	B	Up	2.90	5.33	8.30	19.16	53.20	39.7	206.0	800-279-0279	Y
Davis Real Estate Fund Class C	DRECX	B	B-	B	Up	2.68	4.90	7.40	16.10	46.63	39.69	206.0	800-279-0279	Y
Davis Real Estate Fund Class Y	DREYX	B	B-	B	Up	2.94	5.44	8.56	19.92	54.82	40.25	206.0	800-279-0279	Y
Delaware Global Real Estate Opportunities Fund Class A	DGRPX	B-	C	B	Up	3.06	3.20	8.64	10.86	37.31	7.65	61.4		Y
Delaware Global Real Estate Opportunities Fund Class C	DLPCX	B-	C	B	Up	2.99	2.94	7.83	8.54	32.24	7.65	61.4		Y
Delaware Global Real Estate Opportunities Fund Class R	DLPRX	B-	C	B	Up	3.13	3.20	8.37	10.20	35.60	7.65	61.4		Y
Delaware Global Real Estate Opp Fund Inst Cls	DGROX	B-	C+	B		3.25	3.46	8.91	11.85	39.05	7.65	61.4		Y
Deutsche Global Real Estate Securities Fund Class A	RRGAX	B-	C+	B	Up	4.41	5.92	11.33	13.64	38.03	9.25	860.0	201-593-8273	Y
Deutsche Global Real Estate Securities Fund Class C	RRGCX	B-	C	B	Up	4.14	5.41	10.39	10.86	32.69	9.3	860.0	201-593-8273	Y
Deutsche Global Real Estate Securities Fund Class S	RRGTX	B-	C+	B	Up	4.40	5.91	11.46	13.55	38.43	9.22	860.0	201-593-8273	Y
Deutsche Global Real Estate Securities Fund Class T	RRGUX	B-	C+	B		4.40	5.90	11.44	13.63	38.36	9.24	860.0	201-593-8273	Y
Deutsche Global Real Estate Securities Fund Inst Cls	RRGIX	B-	C+	B		4.47	5.98	11.65	14.42	40.02	9.22	860.0	201-593-8273	Y
Deutsche Global Real Estate Securities Fund R6	RRGRX	B-	C+	B		4.37	5.87	11.54	14.30	39.87	9.22	860.0	201-593-8273	Y
Deutsche Real Estate Securities Fund Class A	RRRAX	B-	C+	B		2.30	2.94	6.11	14.31	53.60	20.39	1,371	201-593-8273	Y
Deutsche Real Estate Securities Fund Class C	RRRCX	B-	C+	B		2.15	2.60	5.42	11.99	48.40	20.65	1,371	201-593-8273	Y
Deutsche Real Estate Securities Fund Class R	RRRSX	B-	C+	B		2.22	2.77	5.76	13.19	51.15	20.39	1,371	201-593-8273	Y
Deutsche Real Estate Securities Fund Class R6	RRRZX	B-	C+	B		2.48	3.19	6.61	15.93	56.92	20.37	1,371	201-593-8273	Y
Deutsche Real Estate Securities Fund Class S	RRREX	B-	C+	B		2.41	3.12	6.42	15.29	55.60	20.52	1,371	201-593-8273	Y
Deutsche Real Estate Securities Fund Class T	RRRTX	B-	C+	B		2.35	2.98	6.21	14.62	54.34	20.4	1,371	201-593-8273	Y
Deutsche Real Estate Securities Fund Institutional Class	RRRRX	B-	C+	B		2.40	3.13	6.49	15.50	56.31	20.36	1,371	201-593-8273	Y
DFA Global Real Estate Securities Portfolio	DFGEX	B-	C+	B		3.71	5.25	9.20	15.66	47.67	10.95	7,025	512-306-7400	Y
DFA Real Estate Securities Portfolio Institutional Class	DFREX	B	C+	B+	Up	2.05	3.13	5.71	16.35	58.99	35.3	8,586	512-306-7400	Y
Dreyfus Global Real Estate Securities Fund Class A	DRLAX	B-	C+	B		3.85	6.05	11.09	14.13	37.13	9.15	763.2	800-645-6561	Y
Dreyfus Global Real Estate Securities Fund Class C	DGBCX	B-	C+	B	Up	3.53	5.53	10.13	11.51	32.20	9	763.2	800-645-6561	Y
Dreyfus Global Real Estate Securities Fund Class I	DRLIX	B-	C+	B		3.88	6.11	11.22	14.96	39.05	9.01	763.2	800-645-6561	Y
Dreyfus Global Real Estate Securities Fund Class Y	DRLYX	B-	C+	B		3.92	6.15	11.39	15.16	39.13	9.02	763.2	800-645-6561	Y
Dunham Real Estate Stock Fund Class A	DAREX	B-	C+	B		2.02	2.67	3.99	10.47	52.29	15.94	44.0	800-442-4358	Y
Dunham Real Estate Stock Fund Class C	DCREX	B-	C	B		1.81	2.29	3.19	7.93	46.69	15.09	44.0	800-442-4358	Y

Category: Real Estate Sector Equity (con't)

Fund Name	Ticker Symbol	RATINGS: Overall Rating	Reward Rating	Risk Rating	Recent Up/ Downgrade	TOTAL RETURNS & PERFORMANCE: 3-Month Total Return	6-Month Total Return	1-Year Total Return	3-Year Total Return	5-Year Total Return	ASSETS: NAV	Total Assets (MIL)	NEW INVESTORS: Telephone	Open to New Investors
Dunham Real Estate Stock Fund Class N	DNREX	B-	C+	B		2.11	2.83	4.23	11.29	54.32	15.8	44.0	800-442-4358	Y
Eaton Vance Real Estate Fund Class A	EAREX	B-	C+	B		2.13	3.09	3.92	14.25	54.51	13.93	49.7		Y
Eaton Vance Real Estate Fund Class I	EIREX	B-	C+	B		2.26	3.30	4.23	15.13	56.47	13.93	49.7		Y
Fidelity Advisor® International Real Estate Fund Class A	FIRAX	B	B-	B	Up	6.17	10.25	26.47	25.40	48.33	11.53	490.3	617-563-7000	Y
Fidelity Advisor® International Real Estate Fund Class C	FIRCX	B-	C+	B	Up	6.00	9.78	25.46	22.62	42.89	11.28	490.3	617-563-7000	Y
Fidelity Advisor® International Real Estate Fund Class I	FIRIX	B	B-	B	Up	6.23	10.44	26.94	26.81	50.76	11.57	490.3	617-563-7000	Y
Fidelity Advisor® International Real Estate Fund Class M	FIRTX	B	C+	B	Up	6.10	10.06	26.13	24.31	46.19	11.45	490.3	617-563-7000	Y
Fidelity Advisor® Real Estate Fund Class A	FHEAX	B-	C+	B		1.66	1.57	3.57	10.86	49.84	21.8	803.9	617-563-7000	Y
Fidelity Advisor® Real Estate Fund Class M	FHETX	B-	C+	B		1.59	1.48	3.34	10.10	48.20	21.79	803.9	617-563-7000	Y
Fidelity Advisor® Real Estate Fund I Class	FHEIX	B-	C+	B+		1.71	1.70	3.85	11.68	51.78	21.99	803.9	617-563-7000	Y
Fidelity Advisor® Real Estate Income Fund Class A	FRINX	B	C+	A-	Up	0.33	1.61	7.03	18.95	39.82	11.93	5,468	617-563-7000	Y
Fidelity Advisor® Real Estate Income Fund Class C	FRIOX	B	C+	A-	Up	0.16	1.26	6.22	16.25	34.67	11.83	5,468	617-563-7000	Y
Fidelity Advisor® Real Estate Income Fund Class I	FRIRX	B	C+	A	Up	0.43	1.78	7.33	19.91	41.66	11.95	5,468	617-563-7000	Y
Fidelity Advisor® Real Estate Income Fund Class M	FRIQX	B	C+	A-	Up	0.41	1.68	7.01	18.84	39.60	11.94	5,468	617-563-7000	Y
Fidelity® International Real Estate Fund	FIREX	B	B-	B	Up	6.24	10.30	26.69	26.20	50.03	11.65	490.3	617-563-7000	Y
Fidelity® Real Estate Income Fund	FRIFX	B	C+	A	Up	0.43	1.77	7.29	19.80	41.41	11.99	5,468	617-563-7000	Y
Fidelity® Real Estate Index Fund Institutional Class	FSRNX	B-	C+	B+		1.94	2.34	3.74	13.61	55.69	15.58	1,080	617-563-7000	Y
Fidelity® Real Estate Index Fund Investor Class	FRXIX	B-	C+	B+		1.96	2.31	3.58	13.02	54.56	15.57	1,080	617-563-7000	Y
Fidelity® Real Estate Index Fund Premium Class	FSRVX	B-	C+	B+		2.00	2.39	3.72	13.53	55.66	15.58	1,080	617-563-7000	Y
Fidelity® Real Estate Investment Portfolio	FRESX	B	C+	B+		1.27	2.04	4.27	17.17	59.24	41.8	4,277	617-563-7000	Y
Fidelity® Series Real Estate Equity Fund	FREDX	B-	C+	B+		1.92	2.09	4.39	12.37	53.12	12.81	1,275	617-563-7000	
Fidelity® Series Real Estate Income Fund	FSREX	B	C+	A+	Up	0.73	2.32	7.44	18.73	38.94	10.92	908.2	617-563-7000	
Franklin Global Real Estate Fund Advisor Class	FVGRX	B-	C+	B	Up	3.64	5.15	10.74	11.37	33.84	9.34	147.7	650-312-2000	Y
Franklin Global Real Estate Fund Class A	FGRRX	B-	C	B	Up	3.60	5.00	10.48	10.49	31.92	9.31	147.7	650-312-2000	Y
Franklin Global Real Estate Fund Class R6	FGGRX	B-	C+	B	Up	3.69	5.19	10.92	11.90	34.69	9.33	147.7	650-312-2000	Y
Franklin Real Estate Securities Fund Advisor Class	FRLAX	B-	C+	B	Up	1.89	2.04	4.17	12.15	53.92	21.21	412.0	650-312-2000	Y
Franklin Real Estate Securities Fund Class A	FREEX	B-	C+	B	Up	1.80	1.91	3.94	11.32	51.97	21	412.0	650-312-2000	Y
Franklin Real Estate Securities Fund Class C	FRRSX	B-	C+	B	Up	1.61	1.53	3.14	8.80	46.34	20.13	412.0	650-312-2000	Y
Franklin Real Estate Securities Fund Class R6	FSERX	B-	C+	B	Up	1.99	2.21	4.45	12.88	55.36	21.22	412.0	650-312-2000	Y
Gerstein Fisher Multi-Factor Global Real Estate Sec Fund	GFMRX	B-	C+	B		2.55	4.01	10.20	17.15		11.17	135.4		Y
Goldman Sachs Intl Real Estate Securities Fund Cls R6	GIRUX	B-	C+	B	Up	5.94	8.44	18.49	13.82	24.45	6.26	125.5	800-526-7384	Y
Goldman Sachs Intl Real Estate Securities Fund Inst Cls	GIRIX	B-	C+	B	Up	5.75	8.43	18.46	13.77	24.39	6.26	125.5	800-526-7384	Y
Goldman Sachs Intl Real Estate Securities Fund Inv Cls	GIRTX	B-	C+	B	Up	5.78	8.39	18.29	13.51	23.67	6.43	125.5	800-526-7384	Y
Goldman Sachs Real Estate Securities Fund Class A	GREAX	B-	C	B	Up	1.38	2.13	2.10	9.29	48.59	15.53	294.2	800-526-7384	Y
Goldman Sachs Real Estate Securities Fund Class R	GRERX	B-	C	B	Up	1.33	2.03	1.92	8.50	46.81	15.39	294.2	800-526-7384	Y
Goldman Sachs Real Estate Securities Fund Class R6	GREUX	B-	C+	B+	Up	1.51	2.41	2.59	10.70	51.67	15.98	294.2	800-526-7384	Y
Goldman Sachs Real Estate Securities Fund Inst Cls	GREIX	B-	C+	B+	Up	1.51	2.35	2.57	10.65	51.61	15.98	294.2	800-526-7384	Y
Goldman Sachs Real Estate Securities Fund Investor Class	GRETX	B-	C+	B+	Up	1.49	2.31	2.41	10.17	50.50	15.65	294.2	800-526-7384	Y
Goldman Sachs Real Estate Securities Fund Service Class	GRESX	B-	C	B	Up	1.37	2.08	2.07	9.01	47.89	15.65	294.2	800-526-7384	Y
Great-West Real Estate Index Fund Institutional Class	MXSFX	B-	C+	B+	Up	2.04	2.15	4.91	12.34	52.35		329.3		Y
Great-West Real Estate Index Fund Investor Class	MXREX	B-	C+	B+	Up	1.89	1.89	4.42	11.16	50.75		329.3		Y
Griffin Institutional Access Real Estate Fund Class A	GIREX	B	C+	A+	Up	2.23	3.58	6.46	22.19		26.82	--	310-469-6100	Y
Griffin Institutional Access Real Estate Fund Class C	US39822J2015	B	C+	A+	Up	2.01	3.20	5.71	20.15		26.36	--	310-469-6100	Y
Griffin Institutional Access Real Estate Fund Class I	US39822J3005	B	C+	A+	Up	2.26	3.69	6.73	22.88		26.98	--	310-469-6100	Y
Griffin Institutional Access Real Estate Fund Class L	US39822J4094	B	C+	A+	Up	2.11	3.51	6.38	22.10		26.79	--	310-469-6100	Y
Griffin Institutional Access Real Estate Fund Class M	US39822J5083	B	C+	A+	Up	2.08	3.31	5.94	21.51		26.67	--	310-469-6100	Y
Guggenheim Risk Managed Real Estate Fund Class A	GURAX	B	B-	A-	Up	-1.07	0.08	5.65	18.29		29.38	144.9	212-739-0700	Y
Guggenheim Risk Managed Real Estate Fund Class C	GURCX	B	C+	B+	Up	-1.15	-0.24	4.98	15.76		29.19	144.9	212-739-0700	Y
Guggenheim Risk Managed Real Estate Fund Class P	GURPX	B	B-	A-	Up	-1.07	0.02	5.64	18.29		29.53	144.9	212-739-0700	Y
Guggenheim Risk Managed Real Estate Fund Institutional	GURIX	B	B-	A-	Up	-1.09	0.06	5.87	19.23		29.71	144.9	212-739-0700	Y
GuideStone Funds Global Real Estate Sec Fund Inst Cls	GREYX	B-	C+	B		4.34	5.88	11.04	14.57	38.44	9.69	227.5	214-720-1171	Y
GuideStone Funds Global Real Estate Sec Fund Inv Cls	GREZX	B-	C+	B		4.20	5.73	10.72	13.85	37.57	9.72	227.5	214-720-1171	Y

Category: Real Estate Sector Equity (con't)

Fund Name	Ticker Symbol	RATINGS: Overall Rating	Reward Rating	Risk Rating	Recent Up/ Downgrade	TOTAL RETURNS & PERFORMANCE: 3-Month Total Return	6-Month Total Return	1-Year Total Return	3-Year Total Return	5-Year Total Return	ASSETS: NAV	Total Assets (MIL)	NEW INVESTORS: Telephone	Open to New Investors
Invesco Global Real Estate Fund Class A	AGREX	B-	C+	B	Up	3.67	6.26	12.65	11.47	32.81	13.5	1,390	800-659-1005	Y
Invesco Global Real Estate Fund Class B	BGREX	B-	C	B	Up	3.48	5.86	11.80	8.99	27.95	13.52	1,390	800-659-1005	
Invesco Global Real Estate Fund Class C	CGREX	B-	C	B	Up	3.55	5.94	11.89	8.99	28.04	13.53	1,390	800-659-1005	Y
Invesco Global Real Estate Fund Class R	RGREX	B-	C+	B	Up	3.60	6.13	12.37	10.64	31.28	13.51	1,390	800-659-1005	Y
Invesco Global Real Estate Fund Class R6	FGREX	B-	C+	B	Up	3.69	6.42	13.03	13.20	36.56	13.46	1,390	800-659-1005	Y
Invesco Global Real Estate Fund Class Y	ARGYX	B-	C+	B	Up	3.81	6.47	13.02	12.39	34.68	13.51	1,390	800-659-1005	Y
Invesco Global Real Estate Fund R5 Class	IGREX	B-	C+	B	Up	3.75	6.45	13.12	13.05	36.25	13.47	1,390	800-659-1005	Y
Invesco Global Real Estate Income Fund Class A	ASRAX	B-	C+	B+		2.35	4.06	8.76	11.73	29.07	9.11	1,123	800-659-1005	Y
Invesco Global Real Estate Income Fund Class B	SARBX	B-	C	B	Up	2.04	3.67	7.95	9.24	24.29	9.1	1,123	800-659-1005	
Invesco Global Real Estate Income Fund Class C	ASRCX	B-	C	B	Up	2.15	3.78	8.07	9.36	24.42	9.11	1,123	800-659-1005	Y
Invesco Global Real Estate Income Fund Class R5	ASRIX	B-	C+	B+	Down	2.43	4.24	9.13	12.95	31.36	9.1	1,123	800-659-1005	Y
Invesco Global Real Estate Income Fund Class R6	ASRFX	B-	C+	B+	Down	2.45	4.28	9.23	13.12	31.91	9.1	1,123	800-659-1005	Y
Invesco Global Real Estate Income Fund Class Y	ASRYX	B-	C+	B+		2.41	4.19	9.05	12.58	30.74	9.08	1,123	800-659-1005	Y
Invesco Real Estate Fund Class A	IARAX	B	B-	B+	Up	3.31	3.92	8.43	14.87	54.01	21.28	1,657	800-659-1005	Y
Invesco Real Estate Fund Class B	AARBX	B	C+	B	Up	3.12	3.53	7.62	12.31	48.32	21.28	1,657	800-659-1005	
Invesco Real Estate Fund Class C	IARCX	B	C+	B	Up	3.13	3.50	7.60	12.32	48.35	21.17	1,657	800-659-1005	Y
Invesco Real Estate Fund Class R	IARRX	B	B-	B+	Up	3.24	3.78	8.15	14.00	52.06	21.31	1,657	800-659-1005	Y
Invesco Real Estate Fund Class R6	IARFX	B	B-	B+	Up	3.42	4.16	8.95	16.44	57.55	21.25	1,657	800-659-1005	Y
Invesco Real Estate Fund Class Y	IARYX	B	B-	B+	Up	3.33	4.00	8.65	15.69	55.88	21.26	1,657	800-659-1005	Y
Invesco Real Estate Fund Investor Class	REINX	B	B-	B+	Up	3.32	3.93	8.51	14.92	54.13	21.23	1,657	800-659-1005	
Invesco Real Estate Fund R5 Class	IARIX	B	B-	B+	Up	3.40	4.11	8.85	16.13	56.92	21.26	1,657	800-659-1005	Y
Ivy Advantus Real Estate Securities Fund Class A	IRSAX	B-	C+	B		2.00	2.15	5.26	12.57	51.27	24.19	554.4	800-777-6472	Y
Ivy Advantus Real Estate Securities Fund Class B	IRSBX	B-	C+	B	Up	1.75	1.68	4.27	9.52	44.18	23.29	554.4	800-777-6472	
Ivy Advantus Real Estate Securities Fund Class C	IRSCX	B-	C+	B	Up	1.78	1.74	4.42	10.09	45.79	23.66	554.4	800-777-6472	Y
Ivy Advantus Real Estate Securities Fund Class E	IREEX	B-	C+	B		2.00	2.15	5.26	12.41	50.60	24.19	554.4	800-777-6472	Y
Ivy Advantus Real Estate Securities Fund Class I	IREIX	B-	C+	B+		2.08	2.32	5.63	13.92	54.67	24.35	554.4	800-777-6472	Y
Ivy Advantus Real Estate Securities Fund Class N	IRSEX	B-	C+	B+		2.12	2.41	5.81	14.47	54.20	24.38	554.4	800-777-6472	Y
Ivy Advantus Real Estate Securities Fund Class R	IRSRX	B-	C+	B	Up	1.93	2.03	4.98	11.86	49.93	24.16	554.4	800-777-6472	Y
Ivy Advantus Real Estate Securities Fund Class Y	IRSYX	B-	C+	B		2.04	2.23	5.43	13.16	52.93	24.22	554.4	800-777-6472	Y
Ivy LaSalle Global Real Estate Fund Class A	IREAX	B-	C	B	Up	3.91	5.10	8.32	7.91		10.8	65.9	800-777-6472	Y
Ivy LaSalle Global Real Estate Fund Class I	IRESX	B-	C	B	Up	4.02	5.31	8.95	8.28		10.82	65.9	800-777-6472	Y
Ivy LaSalle Global Real Estate Fund Class N	IRENX	B-	C	B	Up	4.00	5.29	8.51	8.11		10.83	65.9	800-777-6472	Y
Ivy LaSalle Global Real Estate Fund Class Y	IREYX	B-	C	B	Up	3.87	5.05	8.43	8.44		10.92	65.9	800-777-6472	Y
James Alpha Global Real Estate Inv Port Cls A Shares	JAREX	B	B-	B+	Up	4.77	7.23	16.78	27.03	43.02	18.71	533.2	800-807-3863	Y
James Alpha Global Real Estate Inv Port Cls C Shares	JACRX	B	B-	B	Up	4.64	6.93	16.00	24.46	39.24	18.9	533.2	800-807-3863	Y
James Alpha Global Real Estate Inv Port Cls I Shares	JARIX	B	B-	B+	Up	4.93	7.51	17.32	28.94	47.65	19.22	533.2	800-807-3863	Y
James Alpha Global Real Estate Inv Port Cls S Shares	JARSX	B	B-	B+		5.03	7.57	17.15	27.44	43.48	19.25	533.2	800-807-3863	Y
Janus Henderson Global Real Estate Fund Class A	JERAX	B-	C+	B	Up	4.65	8.24	17.43	18.02	45.06	11.44	222.9	877-335-2687	Y
Janus Henderson Global Real Estate Fund Class C	JERCX	B-	C+	B	Up	4.41	7.86	16.56	15.34	39.71	11.29	222.9	877-335-2687	Y
Janus Henderson Global Real Estate Fund Class D	JNGSX	B-	C+	B	Up	4.67	8.29	17.63	18.42	46.24	11.51	222.9	877-335-2687	
Janus Henderson Global Real Estate Fund Class I	JERIX	B-	C+	B	Up	4.70	8.27	17.71	18.83	46.98	11.49	222.9	877-335-2687	Y
Janus Henderson Global Real Estate Fund Class S	JERSX	B-	C+	B	Up	4.52	8.07	17.18	17.30	43.80	11.41	222.9	877-335-2687	Y
Janus Henderson Global Real Estate Fund Class T	JERTX	B-	C+	B	Up	4.65	8.27	17.55	18.28	45.84	11.5	222.9	877-335-2687	Y
JNL/Invesco Global Real Estate Fund Class A	US46648M1852	B-	C	B	Up	4.07	5.22	10.19	10.55	33.61	9.97	1,967		Y
JNL/Invesco Global Real Estate Fund Class I	US46648M1779	B-	C+	B	Up	4.21	5.44	10.46	11.26	35.06	10.13	1,967		Y
John Hancock Funds II Global Real Estate Fund Class NAV	JHAMX	B-	C+	B		4.31	5.85	11.60	14.85	40.77	9.9	239.9	800-225-5913	Y
John Hancock Funds II Real Estate Equity Fund Class NAV	JHAZX	B	C+	B+	Up	3.28	4.08	4.29	13.66	56.39	10.19	222.5	800-225-5913	Y
John Hancock Funds II Real Estate Securities Fund Class 1	JIREX	B-	C+	B		2.38	3.01	6.22	14.81	54.96	12.39	474.9	800-225-5913	Y
Johnson Realty Fund	JRLTX	B	C+	B+	Up	1.97	2.49	5.93	14.18	52.95	15.93	11.0		Y
JPMorgan Realty Income Fund Class A	URTAX	B-	C+	B		1.97	2.70	3.67	8.82	46.76	13.14	2,588	800-480-4111	Y
JPMorgan Realty Income Fund Class C	URTCX	B-	C	B		1.81	2.38	3.13	7.20	43.14	12.71	2,588	800-480-4111	Y
JPMorgan Realty Income Fund Class I	URTDX	B-	C+	B+		2.05	2.82	4.01	10.03	49.59	13.28	2,588	800-480-4111	Y

Category: Real Estate Sector Equity (con't)

Fund Name	Ticker Symbol	RATINGS: Overall Rating	Reward Rating	Risk Rating	Recent Up/ Downgrade	TOTAL RETURNS & PERFORMANCE: 3-Month Total Return	6-Month Total Return	1-Year Total Return	3-Year Total Return	5-Year Total Return	ASSETS: NAV	Total Assets (MIL)	NEW INVESTORS: Telephone	Open to New Investors
JPMorgan Realty Income Fund Class L	URTLX	B-	C+	B+		2.05	2.87	4.06	10.08	49.66	13.3	2,588	800-480-4111	Y
JPMorgan Realty Income Fund Class R5	JRIRX	B-	C+	B+		2.05	2.85	4.11	10.20	50.03	13.36	2,588	800-480-4111	Y
JPMorgan Realty Income Fund Class R6	JPINX	B-	C+	B+		2.07	2.94	4.22	10.34	50.01	13.31	2,588	800-480-4111	Y
Lazard Global Realty Equity Portfolio Institutional Shares	LITIX	B-	C+	B		4.55	5.79	14.68	17.07	32.98	15.52	5.1	800-823-6300	Y
Lazard Global Realty Equity Portfolio Open Shares	LITOX	B-	C+	B	Up	4.51	5.62	14.36	15.95	30.96	15.5	5.1	800-823-6300	Y
Lazard US Realty Equity Portfolio Institutional Shares	LREIX	B	C+	A-	Up	3.43	2.58	7.92	17.19	53.89	18.85	67.5	800-823-6300	Y
Lazard US Realty Equity Portfolio Open Shares	LREOX	B	C+	A-	Up	3.42	2.47	7.68	16.25	51.90	18.94	67.5	800-823-6300	Y
Manning & Napier Real Estate Series Class I	MNRIX	B	B-	B+		2.13	3.96	8.85	21.31	64.47	6.81	323.3	585-325-6880	Y
Manning & Napier Real Estate Series Class S	MNREX	B	B-	B+	Up	2.08	3.91	8.65	20.46	62.53	14.93	323.3	585-325-6880	Y
MFS® Global Real Estate Fund Class A	MGLAX	B-	C+	B		4.41	5.77	12.64	20.05	47.32	15.65	735.3	877-960-6077	Y
MFS® Global Real Estate Fund Class B	MGLDX	B-	C+	B		4.24	5.32	11.73	17.37	41.76	8.59	735.3	877-960-6077	Y
MFS® Global Real Estate Fund Class C	MGLCX	B-	C+	B		4.27	5.35	11.79	17.33	41.70	8.53	735.3	877-960-6077	Y
MFS® Global Real Estate Fund Class I	MGLIX	B-	C+	B		4.49	5.91	12.93	20.87	48.95	15.69	735.3	877-960-6077	Y
MFS® Global Real Estate Fund Class R1	MGLJX	B-	C+	B		4.18	5.36	11.85	17.44	41.84	8.67	735.3	877-960-6077	Y
MFS® Global Real Estate Fund Class R2	MGLKX	B-	C+	B		4.37	5.68	12.34	19.25	45.47	8.62	735.3	877-960-6077	Y
MFS® Global Real Estate Fund Class R3	MGLLX	B-	C+	B		4.39	5.82	12.61	20.15	47.29	8.63	735.3	877-960-6077	Y
MFS® Global Real Estate Fund Class R4	MGLMX	B-	C+	B		4.57	5.88	12.94	21.04	49.13	8.64	735.3	877-960-6077	Y
MFS® Global Real Estate Fund Class R6	MGLRX	B	C+	B	Up	4.47	5.89	12.97	21.12	49.25	15.71	735.3	877-960-6077	Y
Morgan Stanley Inst Fund, Inc. Global Real Est Cls A	MRLBX	B-	C	B	Up	4.65	5.97	9.43	10.14	32.16	11.1	1,545	855-332-5306	Y
Morgan Stanley Inst Fund, Inc. Global Real Est Cls I	MRLAX	B-	C	B	Up	4.67	5.99	9.73	11.02	34.03	11.13	1,545	855-332-5306	Y
Morgan Stanley Inst Fund, Inc. Global Real Est Cls IS	MGREX	B-	C	B	Up	4.64	6.05	9.80	11.32	34.52	11.13	1,545	855-332-5306	Y
Morgan Stanley Inst Fund, Inc. U.S. Real Estate Port Cls A	MUSDX	B-	C	B	Up	3.87	4.09	2.97	10.19	50.56	14.76	606.3	855-332-5306	Y
Morgan Stanley Inst Fund, Inc. U.S. Real Estate Port Cls I	MSUSX	B-	C+	B	Up	3.94	4.24	3.30	11.19	52.93	15.24	606.3	855-332-5306	Y
Morgan Stanley Inst Fund, Inc. U.S. Real Est Cls IS	MURSX	B-	C+	B	Up	3.96	4.29	3.31	11.47	53.35	15.24	606.3	855-332-5306	Y
Natixis Funds Trust IV AEW Real Estate Fund Class A	NRFAX	B-	C+	B+		1.15	2.08	3.59	12.76	51.82	15.08	156.8	800-862-4863	Y
Natixis Funds Trust IV AEW Real Estate Fund Class C	NRCFX	B-	C+	B		0.93	1.67	2.80	10.20	46.18	15.13	156.8	800-862-4863	Y
Natixis Funds Trust IV AEW Real Estate Fund Class N	NRFNX	B	C+	B+	Up	1.24	2.26	3.93	14.08	54.56	14.06	156.8	800-862-4863	Y
Natixis Funds Trust IV AEW Real Estate Fund Class Y	NRFYX	B	C+	B+	Up	1.23	2.24	3.85	13.62	53.79	14.03	156.8	800-862-4863	Y
Neuberger Berman Real Estate Fund Class A	NREAX	B	B-	B+	Up	3.75	5.19	11.54	17.52	50.04	13.16	507.2	212-476-9000	Y
Neuberger Berman Real Estate Fund Class C	NRECX	B	B-	B	Up	3.62	4.76	10.65	14.92	44.48	13.19	507.2	212-476-9000	Y
Neuberger Berman Real Estate Fund Class R3	NRERX	B	B-	B+	Up	3.69	5.06	11.19	16.68	48.20	13.14	507.2	212-476-9000	Y
Neuberger Berman Real Estate Fund Class R6	NRREX	B	B-	B+	Up	3.85	5.40	11.92	19.04	53.27	13.19	507.2	212-476-9000	Y
Neuberger Berman Real Estate Fund Institutional Class	NBRIX	B	B-	B+	Up	3.83	5.37	11.92	18.77	52.76	13.2	507.2	212-476-9000	Y
Neuberger Berman Real Estate Fund Trust Class	NBRFX	B	B-	B+	Up	3.79	5.20	11.57	18.06	51.23	13.15	507.2	212-476-9000	
Northern Global Real Estate Index Fund	NGREX	B-	C+	B		3.48	6.80	14.36	16.77	37.41	10.76	1,882	800-595-9111	Y
Northern Multi-Manager Global Real Estate Fund	NMMGX	B-	C+	B	Up	3.33	4.07	9.67	12.01	30.20	10.84	153.7	800-595-9111	Y
Nuveen Real Estate Income Fund	JRS	B	B-	B+	Up	3.29	4.82	8.80	19.84	67.60	11.35	333.1	312-917-8146	Y
Nuveen Real Estate Securities Fund Class A	FREAX	B	C+	B+	Up	2.40	2.78	5.34	14.07	54.96	20.23	3,943	312-917-8146	
Nuveen Real Estate Securities Fund Class C	FRLCX	B-	C+	B+	Up	2.20	2.38	4.58	11.55	49.27	19.64	3,943	312-917-8146	
Nuveen Real Estate Securities Fund Class I	FARCX	B	C+	B+	Up	2.39	2.83	5.60	14.89	56.84	20.55	3,943	312-917-8146	
Nuveen Real Estate Securities Fund Class R3	FRSSX	B-	C+	B+		2.31	2.62	5.08	13.23	52.99	20.56	3,943	312-917-8146	
Nuveen Real Estate Securities Fund Class R6	FREGX	B	C+	B+	Up	2.47	2.96	5.77	15.49	58.08	20.75	3,943	312-917-8146	
Oppenheimer Global Real Estate Fund Class I	OIRGX	B-	C+	B	Up	4.52	6.55	12.35	11.62		10.55	50.9	800-225-5677	Y
Oppenheimer Global Real Estate Fund Class Y	OGRYX	B-	C+	B	Up	4.51	6.53	12.18	11.34		10.54	50.9	800-225-5677	Y
Oppenheimer Real Estate Fund Class A	OREAX	B-	C+	B		1.94	2.69	4.06	11.22	54.40	24.71	1,174	800-225-5677	Y
Oppenheimer Real Estate Fund Class B	OREBX	B-	C+	B		1.72	2.25	3.25	8.66	48.63	24.16	1,174	800-225-5677	
Oppenheimer Real Estate Fund Class C	ORECX	B-	C+	B		1.76	2.29	3.28	8.75	48.71	24.05	1,174	800-225-5677	Y
Oppenheimer Real Estate Fund Class I	OREIX	B-	C+	B+		2.03	2.88	4.50	12.66	57.89	24.95	1,174	800-225-5677	Y
Oppenheimer Real Estate Fund Class R	ORENX	B-	C+	B		1.90	2.55	3.80	10.38	52.48	24.59	1,174	800-225-5677	Y
Oppenheimer Real Estate Fund Class Y	OREYX	B-	C+	B		2.05	2.81	4.34	12.07	56.31	24.99	1,174	800-225-5677	Y
PACE Global Real Estate Securities Investments Class A	PREAX	B-	C+	B	Up	3.77	4.73	10.40	11.89	37.73	7.64	140.6	212-882-5586	Y
PACE Global Real Estate Securities Investments Class P	PREQX	B-	C+	B	Up	3.96	4.81	10.70	12.85	39.51	7.35	140.6	212-882-5586	Y

Category: Real Estate Sector Equity (con't)

Fund Name	Ticker Symbol	RATINGS: Overall Rating	Reward Rating	Risk Rating	Recent Up/ Downgrade	TOTAL RETURNS & PERFORMANCE: 3-Month Total Return	6-Month Total Return	1-Year Total Return	3-Year Total Return	5-Year Total Return	ASSETS: NAV	Total Assets (MIL)	NEW INVESTORS: Telephone	Open to New Investors
PACE Global Real Estate Securities Investments Class Y	PREYX	B-	C+	B	Up	3.94	4.79	10.66	12.53	39.20	7.38	140.6	212-882-5586	Y
PF Real Estate Fund Class P	US69447T8392	B-	C+	B	Up	3.87	4.21	3.31	10.49	49.89	12.87	36.9	800-722-2333	Y
Phocas Real Estate Fund	PHREX	B	B-	B	Up	2.66	3.74	7.35	15.14	66.30	32.39	12.8	866-746-2271	Y
PIMCO RealEstateRealReturn Strategy Fund Class A	PETAX	B-	C+	B		1.78	2.32	3.94	16.15	41.36	7.61	2,001	866-746-2602	Y
PIMCO RealEstateRealReturn Strategy Fund Class C	PETCX	B-	C+	B	Up	1.70	2.01	3.16	13.57	36.05	6.64	2,001	866-746-2602	Y
PIMCO RealEstateRealReturn Strategy Fund Class D	PETDX	B-	C+	B		1.77	2.31	3.91	16.04	41.31	7.65	2,001	866-746-2602	Y
PIMCO RealEstateRealReturn Strategy Fund Class P	PETPX	B-	C+	B		1.97	2.53	4.22	17.12	43.53	8.25	2,001	866-746-2602	Y
PIMCO RealEstateRealReturn Strategy Fund Institutional Cls	PRRSX	B-	C+	B		1.96	2.55	4.31	17.57	43.97	8.4	2,001	866-746-2602	Y
Pioneer Real Estate Fund Class A	PWREX	B-	C+	B+		0.95	1.96	3.19	12.45	51.37	24.59	118.9	617-742-7825	Y
Pioneer Real Estate Fund Class C	PCREX	B-	C+	B		0.81	1.61	2.45	9.80	45.27	24.09	118.9	617-742-7825	Y
Pioneer Real Estate Fund Class Y	PYREX	B	C+	B+	Up	1.12	2.18	3.58	13.67	54.44	24.56	118.9	617-742-7825	Y
Principal Global Real Estate Securities Fund Class A	POSAX	B-	C+	B	Up	4.56	7.25	14.30	14.42	42.50	8.88	2,447	800-222-5852	Y
Principal Global Real Estate Securities Fund Class C	POSCX	B-	C+	B	Up	4.40	6.91	13.45	11.78	37.03	8.59	2,447	800-222-5852	Y
Principal Global Real Estate Securities Fund Class R-6	PGRSX	B-	C+	B	Up	4.59	7.44	14.77	15.69	45.54	9.52	2,447	800-222-5852	Y
Principal Global Real Estate Securities Fund Inst Cls	POSIX	B-	C+	B		4.58	7.41	14.72	15.73	45.58	9.52	2,447	800-222-5852	Y
Principal Global Real Estate Securities Fund R-3	PGRKX	B-	C+	B	Up	4.55	7.25	14.22	14.48	43.30	9.52	2,447	800-222-5852	Y
Principal Global Real Estate Securities Fund R-4	PGRVX	B-	C+	B	Up	4.49	7.24	14.26	14.87	44.22	9.51	2,447	800-222-5852	Y
Principal Global Real Estate Securities Fund R-5	PGRUX	B-	C+	B	Up	4.63	7.41	14.63	15.45	45.23	9.53	2,447	800-222-5852	Y
Principal Real Estate Income Fund	PGZ	B	C+	B+	Up	2.41	5.46	15.23	21.59		19.73	135.0	800-222-5852	Y
Principal Real Estate Securities Fund Class A	PRRAX	B	B-	B+	Up	3.49	4.73	8.64	17.04	64.42	23.75	3,654	800-222-5852	Y
Principal Real Estate Securities Fund Class C	PRCEX	B	C+	B+	Up	3.29	4.36	7.79	14.35	58.03	23.34	3,654	800-222-5852	Y
Principal Real Estate Securities Fund Class J	PREJX	B	B-	B+	Up	3.56	4.84	8.87	17.59	65.25	23.07	3,654	800-222-5852	Y
Principal Real Estate Securities Fund Class R-6	PFRSX	B	B-	B+	Up	3.62	4.99	9.08	17.99	66.45	23.76	3,654	800-222-5852	Y
Principal Real Estate Securities Fund Institutional Class	PIREX	B	B-	B+	Up	3.56	4.94	9.02	18.46	67.77	23.76	3,654	800-222-5852	Y
Principal Real Estate Securities Fund R-1 Class	PRAEX	B	B-	B+	Up	3.35	4.51	8.18	15.55	60.97	23.46	3,654	800-222-5852	Y
Principal Real Estate Securities Fund R-2 Class	PRENX	B	B-	B+	Up	3.41	4.61	8.33	16.04	62.07	22.61	3,654	800-222-5852	Y
Principal Real Estate Securities Fund R-3 Class	PRERX	B	B-	B+	Up	3.46	4.67	8.51	16.69	63.52	23.17	3,654	800-222-5852	Y
Principal Real Estate Securities Fund R-4 Class	PRETX	B	B-	B+	Up	3.51	4.83	8.73	17.38	65.16	22.92	3,654	800-222-5852	Y
Principal Real Estate Securities Fund R-5 Class	PREPX	B	B-	B+	Up	3.54	4.84	8.85	17.75	66.10	22.96	3,654	800-222-5852	Y
Prudential Global Real Estate Fund Class A	PURAX	B-	C	B	Up	3.81	5.86	11.05	10.27	33.04	24.14	2,691	800-225-1852	Y
Prudential Global Real Estate Fund Class Q	PGRQX	B-	C+	B	Up	3.92	6.09	11.59	11.79	35.96	24.23	2,691	800-225-1852	Y
Prudential Global Real Estate Fund Class R	PURRX	B-	C	B	Up	3.73	5.73	10.81	9.59	31.66	24.07	2,691	800-225-1852	Y
Prudential Global Real Estate Fund Class Z	PURZX	B-	C+	B	Up	3.88	6.00	11.40	11.27	35.03	24.24	2,691	800-225-1852	Y
Prudential Select Real Estate Fund Class A	SREAX	B	C+	A-	Up	3.79	6.47	11.13	16.18		10.8	6.6	800-225-1852	Y
Prudential Select Real Estate Fund Class C	SRECX	B-	C+	B+	Up	3.59	6.10	10.19	13.56		10.7	6.6	800-225-1852	Y
Prudential Select Real Estate Fund Class Q	SREQX	B	C+	A-	Up	3.86	6.64	11.32	17.05		10.66	6.6	800-225-1852	Y
Prudential Select Real Estate Fund Class Z	SREZX	B	C+	A-	Up	3.80	6.64	11.36	17.10		10.82	6.6	800-225-1852	Y
Prudential US Real Estate Fund Class A	PJEAX	B-	C+	B	Up	1.89	3.43	5.32	10.95	49.90	11.96	23.6	800-225-1852	Y
Prudential US Real Estate Fund Class B	PJEBX	B-	C+	B	Up	1.73	3.11	4.59	8.54	44.51	11.75	23.6	800-225-1852	
Prudential US Real Estate Fund Class C	PJECX	B-	C+	B	Up	1.73	3.11	4.59	8.56	44.47	11.73	23.6	800-225-1852	Y
Prudential US Real Estate Fund Class Q	PJEQX	B	C+	B	Up	1.92	3.62	5.68	11.88	51.91	11.97	23.6	800-225-1852	Y
Prudential US Real Estate Fund Class Z	PJEZX	B-	C+	B		1.92	3.53	5.60	11.79	51.79	11.97	23.6	800-225-1852	Y
REMS Intl Real Estate Value-Opp Fund Founders Shares	REIFX	B	B-	B	Up	4.78	9.84	27.11	24.58		11.72	54.5		Y
REMS Real Estate Income 50/50 Fund Class Platform Shares	RREFX	B	C+	A-	Up	0.25	1.68	3.34	14.51	43.94	12.24	74.9		Y
REMS Real Estate Income 50/50 Fund Institutional Shares	RREIX	B	C+	A-	Up	0.30	1.86	3.64	15.40	45.94	12.39	74.9		Y
Resource Real Estate Diversified Income Fund Class A	RREDX	B	C+	B+	Up	1.19	1.59	6.48	18.16		10.11	--	855-747-9559	Y
Resource Real Estate Diversified Income Fund Class C	CRREX	B	C+	B+	Up	1.00	1.21	5.68	15.63		10.11	--	855-747-9559	Y
Resource Real Estate Diversified Income Fund Class D	DRREX	B	C+	B+	Up	1.07	1.36	5.94	16.55		10.27	--	855-747-9559	Y
Resource Real Estate Diversified Income Fund Class I	IRREX	B	C+	B+	Up	1.17	1.68	6.53	16.59		10.53	--	855-747-9559	Y
Resource Real Estate Diversified Income Fund Class L	US76123K8009	B	C+	B+		1.02	1.46	6.35	18.01		10.11	--	855-747-9559	Y
Resource Real Estate Diversified Income Fund Class T	RRETX	B	C+	B+	Up	1.00	1.20	5.68	15.51		10.09	--	855-747-9559	Y
Resource Real Estate Diversified Income Fund Class U	URREX	B	C+	A-	Up	1.19	1.59	6.48	18.27		10.12	--	855-747-9559	Y

Category: Real Estate Sector Equity (con't)

Fund Name	Ticker Symbol	RATINGS: Overall Rating	RATINGS: Reward Rating	RATINGS: Risk Rating	RATINGS: Recent Up/ Downgrade	TOTAL RETURNS & PERFORMANCE: 3-Month Total Return	6-Month Total Return	1-Year Total Return	3-Year Total Return	5-Year Total Return	ASSETS: NAV	Total Assets (MIL)	NEW INVESTORS: Telephone	Open to New Investors
Resource Real Estate Diversified Income Fund Cls W Shares	WRREX	B	C+	B+	Up	1.29	1.61	6.48	17.09		10.27	--	855-747-9559	Y
RMR Real Estate Income Fund	RIF	B-	C+	B	Up	0.28	0.17	3.75	15.53	60.63	23.28	241.7		Y
Russell Inv Global Real Estate Securities Fund Cls A	RREAX	B-	C+	B	Up	4.31	5.79	11.30	12.34	34.91	33.09	1,027	800-426-7969	Y
Russell Inv Global Real Estate Securities Fund Cls C	RRSCX	B-	C	B	Up	4.07	5.37	10.44	9.84	29.90	31.86	1,027	800-426-7969	Y
Russell Inv Global Real Estate Securities Fund Cls E	RREEX	B-	C+	B	Up	4.28	5.78	11.31	12.37	34.90	33.18	1,027	800-426-7969	Y
Russell Inv Global Real Estate Securities Fund Cls M	RETTX	B-	C+	B	Up	4.36	5.93	11.63	13.28	36.68	33.93	1,027	800-426-7969	Y
Russell Inv Global Real Estate Securities Fund Cls R6	RRSRX	B-	C+	B	Up	4.39	6.00	11.77	13.53	36.99	33.96	1,027	800-426-7969	Y
Russell Inv Global Real Estate Securities Fund Cls S	RRESX	B-	C+	B	Up	4.35	5.92	11.57	13.22	36.61	33.97	1,027	800-426-7969	Y
Russell Inv Global Real Estate Securities Fund Cls Y	RREYX	B-	C+	B	Up	4.41	6.03	11.77	13.85	37.92	33.95	1,027	800-426-7969	Y
Rydex Real Estate Fund Class A	RYREX	B-	C+	B		1.74	2.35	6.26	11.32	42.51	38.76	28.5	800-820-0888	Y
Rydex Real Estate Fund Class C	RYCRX	B-	C+	B	Up	1.56	1.98	5.49	8.84	37.19	34.13	28.5	800-820-0888	Y
Rydex Real Estate Fund Class H	RYHRX	B-	C+	B		1.72	2.39	6.25	11.29	42.37	38.65	28.5	800-820-0888	Y
SA Real Estate Securities Fund Investor Class	SAREX	B-	C+	B		1.88	2.60	4.53	13.17	51.91	11.34	173.8		Y
SA Real Estate Securities Fund Select Class	SARLX	B-	C+	B		1.93	2.74	4.67	13.33	52.12	11.34	173.8		Y
Salient International Real Estate Fund Institutional Class	KIRYX	B-	C+	B-	Up	6.69	10.20	21.88	17.80	17.55	14.68	22.1	866-667-9228	Y
Schwab Global Real Estate Fund™	SWASX	B	C+	B	Up	2.00	5.52	15.34	21.94	42.63	7.74	289.4	877-824-5615	Y
SEI Institutional Managed Trust Real Estate Fund Class F	SETAX	B	C+	B+	Up	3.20	4.16	5.20	14.66	55.95	16.82	154.1	800-342-5734	Y
SEI Institutional Managed Trust Real Estate Fund Class I	SEIRX	B	C+	B+	Up	3.21	4.11	4.98	13.98	54.34	16.82	154.1	800-342-5734	Y
SEI Institutional Managed Trust Real Estate Fund Class Y	SREYX	B	B-	B+	Up	3.34	4.36	5.48	15.56	57.16	16.82	154.1	800-342-5734	Y
Shelton Real Estate Income Fund Institutional Class	RENIX	B-	C+	B+	Down	0.92	2.14	3.98	13.80		8.64	10.2	800-955-9988	Y
Shelton Real Estate Income Fund Investor Class	RENTX	B-	C+	B+	Down	0.79	1.93	3.71	13.17		8.88	10.2	800-955-9988	Y
Spirit of America Real Estate Income & Growth Fund Class A	SOAAX	B-	C+	B		1.42	3.25	6.78	9.05	49.52	11.65	108.2		Y
Spirit of America Real Estate Income & Growth Fund Class C	SACRX	B-	C+	B		1.22	2.87	6.10	6.63	44.18	11.56	108.2		Y
Sterling Capital Stratton Real Estate Fund A Shares	STMMX	B	B-	B	Up	3.19	3.24	7.53	16.14	58.63	37.01	98.8	800-228-1872	Y
Sterling Capital Stratton Real Estate Fund C Shares	STMOX	B-	C+	B		3.01	2.87	6.76	13.61	52.88	36.81	98.8	800-228-1872	Y
Sterling Capital Stratton Real Estate Fund Inst Shares	STMDX	B	B-	B	Up	3.24	3.33	7.80	17.01	60.62	37.09	98.8	800-228-1872	Y
T. Rowe Price Global Real Estate Fund	TRGRX	B-	C	B	Up	4.24	4.56	7.59	11.18	31.60	20.48	185.5	410-345-2000	Y
T. Rowe Price Global Real Estate Fund Advisor Class	PAGEX	B-	C	B	Up	4.22	4.49	7.48	10.80	30.84	20.34	185.5	410-345-2000	Y
T. Rowe Price Global Real Estate Fund I Class	TIRGX	B-	C	B	Up	4.25	4.67	7.86	11.46	31.93	20.47	185.5	410-345-2000	Y
T. Rowe Price Real Estate Fund	TRREX	B	B-	B+	Up	3.27	4.19	4.42	14.25	57.16	28.7	6,309	410-345-2000	Y
T. Rowe Price Real Estate Fund Advisor Class	PAREX	B	C+	B+	Up	3.23	4.07	4.11	13.44	55.25	29.07	6,309	410-345-2000	Y
T. Rowe Price Real Estate Fund I Class	TIRRX	B	B-	B+	Up	3.34	4.30	4.56	14.57	57.60	28.71	6,309	410-345-2000	Y
Third Avenue Real Estate Value Fund Institutional Class	TAREX	B-	C+	B	Up	6.42	10.72	22.17	23.81	65.41	34.33	1,989	800-443-1021	Y
Third Avenue Real Estate Value Fund Investor Class	TVRVX	B-	C+	B	Up	6.35	10.60	21.87	22.92	63.37	34.16	1,989	800-443-1021	Y
Thrivent Series Real Estate Securities Portfolio		B	C+	B+	Up	2.52	3.43	5.95	15.17	58.25	24.2031	184.5		Y
TIAA-CREF Real Estate Securities Fund Advisor Class	TIRHX	B	B-	B+	Up	3.76	5.21	12.16	20.53	61.13	15.56	2,144	877-518-9161	Y
TIAA-CREF Real Estate Securities Fund Institutional Class	TIREX	B	B-	B+	Up	3.80	5.30	12.29	20.79	61.48	15.55	2,144	877-518-9161	Y
TIAA-CREF Real Estate Securities Fund Premier Class	TRRPX	B	B-	B+	Up	3.70	5.22	12.11	20.23	60.35	15.56	2,144	877-518-9161	Y
TIAA-CREF Real Estate Securities Fund Retail Class	TCREX	B	B-	B+	Up	3.75	5.18	11.97	19.76	59.11	15.44	2,144	877-518-9161	Y
TIAA-CREF Real Estate Securities Fund Retirement Class	TRRSX	B	B-	B+	Up	3.72	5.16	12.01	19.88	59.53	16.19	2,144	877-518-9161	Y
Total Income+ Real Estate Fund Class A	TIPRX	B	C+	A+	Up	1.91	3.44	6.80	22.28	50.52	29.4	--		Y
Total Income+ Real Estate Fund Class C	TIPPX	B	C+	A+	Up	1.75	3.07	6.01	19.59	46.54	28.61	--		Y
Total Income+ Real Estate Fund Class I	TIPWX	B	C+	A+	Up	1.98	3.58	7.04	23.22	52.20	29.74	--		Y
Total Income+ Real Estate Fund Class L	US89154U4076	B	C+	A+	Up	1.84	3.30	6.65	22.12	50.31	29.35	--		Y
VALIC Company I Global Real Estate Fund	VGREX	B-	C+	B	Up	4.75	6.53	13.83	15.14	37.54	8.15	388.0		Y
Vanguard Global ex-U.S. Real Est Ind Admiral Shares	VGRLX	B-	B-	B	Up	5.42	11.49	26.50	26.47	35.79	36.68	6,133	877-662-7447	Y
Vanguard Global ex-U.S. Real Estate Index Fund Inst Shares	VGRNX	B-	B-	B	Up	5.43	11.50	26.52	26.54	35.95	122.2	6,133	877-662-7447	Y
Vanguard Global ex-U.S. Real Estate Index Fund Inv Shares	VGXRX	B-	B-	B	Up	5.37	11.37	26.25	25.72	34.64	24.21	6,133	877-662-7447	Y
Vanguard REIT Index Fund Admiral Shares	VGSLX	B-	C+	B		1.38	2.28	4.93	14.66	57.29	117.55	64,780	877-662-7447	Y
Vanguard REIT Index Fund Institutional Shares	VGSNX	B-	C+	B		1.38	2.26	4.92	14.70	57.47	18.19	64,780	877-662-7447	Y
Vanguard REIT Index Fund Investor Shares	VGSIX	B-	C+	B		1.36	2.22	4.82	14.21	56.19	27.56	64,780	877-662-7447	Y
Versus Capital Multi-Mgr Real Estate Income Fund LLC Cls F	VCMRX	B	C+	A+	Up	1.77	2.68	5.74	20.97	34.99	27.76	--		Y

Category: Real Estate Sector Equity (con't)

Fund Name	Ticker Symbol	RATINGS: Overall Rating	Reward Rating	Risk Rating	Recent Up/ Downgrade	TOTAL RETURNS & PERFORMANCE: 3-Month Total Return	6-Month Total Return	1-Year Total Return	3-Year Total Return	5-Year Total Return	ASSETS: NAV	Total Assets (MIL)	NEW INVESTORS: Telephone	Open to New Investors
Versus Capital Multi-Mgr Real Estate Income Fund LLC Cls I	VCMIX	B	C+	A+	Up	1.84	2.82	6.07	22.24	38.37	27.84	--		Y
Virtus Duff & Phelps Global Real Estate Sec Fund Cls A	VGSAX	B-	C+	B	Up	5.17	8.08	12.78	17.77	48.98	29.66	198.5	800-243-1574	Y
Virtus Duff & Phelps Global Real Estate Sec Fund Cls C	VGSCX	B-	C+	B	Up	4.94	7.66	11.87	15.06	43.47	29.03	198.5	800-243-1574	Y
Virtus Duff & Phelps Global Real Estate Sec Fund Cls I	VGISX	B-	C+	B		5.24	8.18	13.02	18.60	50.81	29.63	198.5	800-243-1574	Y
Virtus Duff & Phelps Global Real Estate Sec Fund Cls R6	VRGEX	B-	C+	B		5.26	8.31	13.19	18.78	51.04	29.64	198.5	800-243-1574	Y
Virtus Duff & Phelps Intl Real Estate Sec Fund Cls A	PXRAX	B-	C+	B	Up	8.13	12.01	21.45	21.20	37.38	7.37	25.8	800-243-1574	Y
Virtus Duff & Phelps Intl Real Estate Sec Fund Cls I	PXRIX	B-	C+	B	Up	8.14	12.18	21.83	21.97	39.11	7.34	25.8	800-243-1574	Y
Virtus Duff & Phelps Real Estate Securities Fund Class A	PHRAX	B	C+	B+	Up	2.56	4.26	5.84	13.46	53.43	26.61	930.0	800-243-1574	Y
Virtus Duff & Phelps Real Estate Securities Fund Class C	PHRCX	B-	C+	B		2.34	3.88	5.01	10.95	47.79	26.52	930.0	800-243-1574	Y
Virtus Duff & Phelps Real Estate Securities Fund Class I	PHRIX	B	B-	B+	Up	2.61	4.43	6.11	14.35	55.37	26.56	930.0	800-243-1574	Y
Virtus Duff & Phelps Real Estate Securities Fund Class R6	VRREX	B	B-	B+	Up	2.68	4.50	6.27	14.96	55.51	26.57	930.0	800-243-1574	Y
Voya Real Estate Fund Class A	CLARX	B-	C+	B	Up	2.52	2.74	4.78	9.81	49.56	15.24	871.1	800-366-0066	Y
Voya Real Estate Fund Class I	CRARX	B-	C+	B	Up	2.58	2.88	5.11	11.26	51.42	16.85	871.1	800-366-0066	Y
Voya Real Estate Fund Class O	IDROX	B-	C+	B	Up	2.54	2.71	4.75	9.79	49.51	15.2	871.1	800-366-0066	Y
Voya Real Estate Fund Class R	CRWRX	B-	C+	B	Up	2.48	2.58	4.50	8.97	47.80	15.16	871.1	800-366-0066	Y
Voya Real Estate Fund Class R6	VREQX	B-	C+	B	Up	2.67	2.93	5.23	11.51	51.71	16.86	871.1	800-366-0066	Y
Voya Real Estate Fund Class W	IREWX	B-	C+	B	Up	2.58	2.80	4.99	11.19	49.02	19.8	871.1	800-366-0066	Y
VY® Clarion Real Estate Portfolio Class A	ICRPX	B-	C+	B	Up	2.59	2.76	4.81	9.94	48.68	36.01	496.2	800-366-0066	Y
VY® Clarion Real Estate Portfolio Class I	IVRIX	B-	C+	B	Up	2.77	3.11	5.47	11.96	53.23	37.76	496.2	800-366-0066	Y
VY® Clarion Real Estate Portfolio Class S	IVRSX	B-	C+	B	Up	2.69	2.95	5.17	11.12	51.27	37.67	496.2	800-366-0066	Y
VY® Clarion Real Estate Portfolio Class S2	IVRTX	B-	C+	B	Up	2.63	2.87	5.02	10.62	50.15	37.44	496.2	800-366-0066	Y
West Loop Realty Fund Class A Shares	REIAX	B	B-	B+	Up	5.13	6.60	7.02	18.69		13.84	98.1	800-207-7108	Y
West Loop Realty Fund Class C Shares	REICX	B	B-	B+	Up	4.98	6.17	6.25	16.11		13.78	98.1	800-207-7108	Y
West Loop Realty Fund Institutional Class Shares	REIIX	B	B-	B+	Up	5.38	6.84	7.48	19.72		13.85	98.1	800-207-7108	Y

Category: Target Date 2000-2020

Fund Name	Ticker Symbol	RATINGS: Overall Rating	Reward Rating	Risk Rating	Recent Up/ Downgrade	TOTAL RETURNS & PERFORMANCE: 3-Month Total Return	6-Month Total Return	1-Year Total Return	3-Year Total Return	5-Year Total Return	ASSETS: NAV	Total Assets (MIL)	NEW INVESTORS: Telephone	Open to New Investors
AB Multi-Manager Select 2010 Fund Advisor Class	TDBYX	B-	C	B	Up	2.80	5.72	11.35	16.20		11.1	16.5	212-969-1000	Y
AB Multi-Manager Select 2010 Fund Class A	TDBAX	B-	C	B	Up	2.82	5.63	11.11	15.43		11.18	16.5	212-969-1000	Y
AB Multi-Manager Select 2010 Fund Class I	TDIBX	B-	C	B	Up	2.88	5.72	11.33	16.20		10.58	16.5	212-969-1000	Y
AB Multi-Manager Select 2010 Fund Class K	TDBKX	B-	C	B	Up	2.86	5.70	11.10	15.32		10.6	16.5	212-969-1000	Y
AB Multi-Manager Select 2010 Fund Class Z	TDBZX	B-	C	B	Up	2.86	5.79	11.40	16.30		10.6	16.5	212-969-1000	Y
AB Multi-Manager Select 2015 Fund Advisor Class	TDCYX	B-	C	B	Up	3.25	6.45	12.70	18.51		11.02	43.8	212-969-1000	Y
AB Multi-Manager Select 2015 Fund Class A	TDCAX	B-	C	B	Up	3.14	6.37	12.38	17.60		10.88	43.8	212-969-1000	Y
AB Multi-Manager Select 2015 Fund Class I	TDCIX	B-	C	B	Up	3.23	6.53	12.78	18.45		10.67	43.8	212-969-1000	Y
AB Multi-Manager Select 2015 Fund Class K	TDCKX	B-	C	B	Up	3.15	6.35	12.49	17.66		10.66	43.8	212-969-1000	Y
AB Multi-Manager Select 2015 Fund Class R	TDCRX	B-	C	B	Up	3.10	6.21	12.12	16.66		10.65	43.8	212-969-1000	Y
AB Multi-Manager Select 2015 Fund Class Z	TDCZX	B-	C	B	Up	3.21	6.41	12.66	18.38		10.63	43.8	212-969-1000	Y
AB Multi-Manager Select 2020 Fund Advisor Class	TDDYX	B-	C	B	Up	3.51	7.18	14.04	20.35		11.17	92.8	212-969-1000	Y
AB Multi-Manager Select 2020 Fund Class A	TDDAX	B-	C	B	Up	3.50	7.09	13.85	19.54		11.17	92.8	212-969-1000	Y
AB Multi-Manager Select 2020 Fund Class I	TDDIX	B-	C	B	Up	3.54	7.10	13.98	20.29		11.22	92.8	212-969-1000	Y
AB Multi-Manager Select 2020 Fund Class K	TDDKX	B-	C	B	Up	3.45	7.11	13.89	19.64		10.95	92.8	212-969-1000	Y
AB Multi-Manager Select 2020 Fund Class Z	TDDZX	B-	C	B	Up	3.48	7.23	14.12	20.40		10.93	92.8	212-969-1000	Y
AllianzGI Retirement 2020 Fund Administrative Class	AGLMX	B-	C+	B	Down	2.85	6.32	13.27	18.41	25.88	20.49	54.6	800-498-5413	Y
AllianzGI Retirement 2020 Fund Class A	AGLAX	B-	C+	B	Down	2.86	6.30	13.23	18.31	25.66	20.36	54.6	800-498-5413	Y
AllianzGI Retirement 2020 Fund Class C	ABSCX	B-	C+	B		2.60	5.89	12.35	15.66	20.97	20.32	54.6	800-498-5413	Y
AllianzGI Retirement 2020 Fund Class P	AGLPX	B-	C+	B+	Down	2.92	6.48	13.55	19.41	27.56	20.52	54.6	800-498-5413	Y

Category: Target Date 2000-2020 (con't)

Fund Name	Ticker Symbol	RATINGS Overall Rating	Reward Rating	Risk Rating	Recent Up/ Downgrade	TOTAL RETURNS & PERFORMANCE 3-Month Total Return	6-Month Total Return	1-Year Total Return	3-Year Total Return	5-Year Total Return	ASSETS NAV	Total Assets (MIL.)	NEW INVESTORS Telephone	Open to New Investors
AllianzGI Retirement 2020 Fund Class R	AGLRX	B-	C+	B	Up	2.72	6.16	10.77	14.86	21.14	20.07	54.6	800-498-5413	Y
AllianzGI Retirement 2020 Fund R6 Class	AGNIX	B	C+	B+	Up	2.90	6.51	13.69	19.65	28.10	20.54	54.6	800-498-5413	Y
AllianzGI Retirement Income Fund Administrative Class	ARAMX	B-	C+	B	Down	1.87	3.13	9.66	15.41	21.61	18.57	50.7	800-498-5413	Y
AllianzGI Retirement Income Fund Class A	AGRAX	B-	C+	B+	Down	1.84	3.10	9.57	16.49	22.61	18.27	50.7	800-498-5413	Y
AllianzGI Retirement Income Fund Class C	ARTCX	B-	C+	B		1.64	2.72	8.76	13.89	18.10	18.27	50.7	800-498-5413	Y
AllianzGI Retirement Income Fund Class P	AGRPX	B-	C+	B+	Down	1.95	3.28	9.91	17.55	24.48	18.46	50.7	800-498-5413	Y
AllianzGI Retirement Income Fund Class R	ASRRX	B-	C+	B	Down	1.77	2.89	9.15	15.23	20.43	19.07	50.7	800-498-5413	Y
AllianzGI Retirement Income Fund R6 Class	AVRIX	B	C+	B+	Up	1.96	3.34	10.03	17.89	25.10	18	50.7	800-498-5413	Y
American Century Inv One Choice 2020 Port A Cls	ARBMX	B-	C+	B	Up	2.45	5.04	10.65	14.33	38.26	12.51	2,272	800-444-4015	Y
American Century Inv One Choice 2020 Port C Cls	ARNCX	B-	C+	B	Up	2.32	4.66	9.86	11.81	33.23	12.55	2,272	800-444-4015	Y
American Century Inv One Choice 2020 Port I Cls	ARBSX	B-	C+	B	Up	2.50	5.26	11.15	15.88	41.28	12.51	2,272	800-444-4015	Y
American Century Inv One Choice 2020 Port Inv Cls	ARBVX	B-	C+	B	Up	2.54	5.22	10.92	15.19	39.98	12.52	2,272	800-444-4015	Y
American Century Inv One Choice 2020 Port R Cls	ARBRX	B-	C+	B	Up	2.44	4.95	10.46	13.56	36.52	12.52	2,272	800-444-4015	Y
American Century Inv One Choice 2020 Port R6 Cls	ARBDX	B-	C+	B	Up	2.56	5.29	11.11	16.25	41.86	11.49	2,272	800-444-4015	Y
American Century Inv One Choice In Retmnt Port A Cls	ARTAX	B-	C+	B	Up	2.29	4.67	9.93	13.45	34.62	13.31	1,979	800-444-4015	Y
American Century Inv One Choice In Retmnt Port C Cls	ATTCX	B-	C+	B	Up	2.17	4.37	9.14	10.96	29.74	13.28	1,979	800-444-4015	Y
American Century Inv One Choice In Retmnt Port I Cls	ATTIX	B-	C+	B	Up	2.41	4.92	10.34	14.91	37.58	13.3	1,979	800-444-4015	Y
American Century Inv One Choice In Retmnt Port Inv Cls	ARTOX	B-	C+	B	Up	2.35	4.81	10.21	14.22	36.22	13.3	1,979	800-444-4015	Y
American Century Inv One Choice In Retmnt Port R Cls	ARSRX	B-	C+	B	Up	2.22	4.55	9.58	12.53	32.88	13.29	1,979	800-444-4015	Y
American Century Inv One Choice In Retmnt Port R6 Cls	ARDTX	B-	C+	B	Up	2.40	4.91	10.47	15.33	38.33	11.13	1,979	800-444-4015	Y
American Funds 2010 Target Date Retirement Fund® Class A	AAATX	B-	C+	B	Up	2.13	4.72	9.97	16.02	39.67	10.91	2,764	800-421-4225	Y
American Funds 2010 Target Date Retirement Fund® Class C	CCATX	B-	C+	B	Up	1.99	4.32	9.19	13.44	34.74	10.79	2,764	800-421-4225	Y
American Funds 2010 Target Date Retirement Fund® Class F-1	FAATX	B-	C+	B	Up	2.07	4.66	9.93	15.96	39.79	10.86	2,764	800-421-4225	Y
American Funds 2010 Target Date Retirement Fund® Class F-2	FBATX	B-	C+	B	Up	2.20	4.79	10.26	16.90	41.61	10.89	2,764	800-421-4225	Y
American Funds 2010 Target Date Retirement Fund® Class F-3	DJTFX	B-	C+	B	Up	2.18	4.85	10.32	17.07	41.81	10.9	2,764	800-421-4225	Y
American Funds 2010 Target Date Retirement Fund® Class R-1	RAATX	B-	C+	B	Up	1.94	4.34	9.19	13.35	34.40	10.9	2,764	800-421-4225	Y
American Funds 2010 Target Date Retirement Fund® Class R-2	RBATX	B-	C+	B+	Up	2.00	4.33	9.20	13.61	34.81	10.8	2,764	800-421-4225	Y
American Funds 2010 Target Date Retirement Fund® Cls R-2E	RBEAX	B-	C+	B	Up	2.01	4.42	9.51	14.78	37.61	10.77	2,764	800-421-4225	Y
American Funds 2010 Target Date Retirement Fund® Class R-3	RCATX	B-	C+	B	Up	2.00	4.50	9.67	14.87	37.41	10.85	2,764	800-421-4225	Y
American Funds 2010 Target Date Retirement Fund® Class R-4	RDATX	B-	C+	B	Up	2.13	4.71	9.97	16.01	39.59	10.89	2,764	800-421-4225	Y
American Funds 2010 Target Date Retirement Fund® Class R-5	REATX	B-	C+	B	Up	2.20	4.86	10.31	17.06	41.80	10.96	2,764	800-421-4225	Y
American Funds 2010 Target Date Retirement Fund® Cls R-5E	RHATX	B-	C+	B	Up	2.16	4.75	10.13	16.80	41.49	10.86	2,764	800-421-4225	Y
American Funds 2010 Target Date Retirement Fund® Class R-6	RFTTX	B-	C+	B	Up	2.17	4.84	10.40	17.18	42.13	10.93	2,764	800-421-4225	Y
American Funds 2015 Target Date Retirement Fund® Class A	AABTX	B-	C+	B	Up	2.35	5.06	10.83	17.12	45.07	11.59	4,471	800-421-4225	Y
American Funds 2015 Target Date Retirement Fund® Class C	CCBTX	B-	C+	B	Up	2.19	4.76	9.98	14.53	39.92	11.46	4,471	800-421-4225	Y
American Funds 2015 Target Date Retirement Fund® Class F-1	FAKTX	B-	C+	B	Up	2.35	5.08	10.78	17.11	45.24	11.53	4,471	800-421-4225	Y
American Funds 2015 Target Date Retirement Fund® Class F-2	FBBTX	B-	C+	B	Up	2.43	5.23	11.12	18.09	47.15	11.58	4,471	800-421-4225	Y
American Funds 2015 Target Date Retirement Fund® Class F-3	FDBTX	B-	C+	B	Up	2.49	5.38	11.26	18.35	47.57	11.6	4,471	800-421-4225	Y
American Funds 2015 Target Date Retirement Fund® Class R-1	RAJTX	B	C+	B+	Up	2.16	4.64	9.98	14.46	39.53	11.43	4,471	800-421-4225	Y
American Funds 2015 Target Date Retirement Fund® Class R-2	RBJTX	B	C+	B+	Up	2.15	4.71	10.05	14.66	40.07	11.44	4,471	800-421-4225	Y
American Funds 2015 Target Date Retirement Fund® Cls R-2E	RBEJX	B	C+	A-	Up	2.26	4.91	10.34	15.95	43.09	11.44	4,471	800-421-4225	Y
American Funds 2015 Target Date Retirement Fund® Class R-3	RCJTX	B-	C+	B	Up	2.32	4.96	10.57	16.17	42.92	11.52	4,471	800-421-4225	Y
American Funds 2015 Target Date Retirement Fund® Class R-4	RDBTX	B-	C+	B	Up	2.28	5.09	10.77	17.11	45.13	11.57	4,471	800-421-4225	Y
American Funds 2015 Target Date Retirement Fund® Class R-5	REJTX	B-	C+	B	Up	2.44	5.31	11.16	18.25	47.44	11.66	4,471	800-421-4225	Y
American Funds 2015 Target Date Retirement Fund® Cls R-5E	RHBTX	B-	C+	B	Up	2.42	5.24	11.04	17.95	47.07	11.54	4,471	800-421-4225	Y
American Funds 2015 Target Date Retirement Fund® Class R-6	RFJTX	B-	C+	B	Up	2.43	5.31	11.18	18.41	47.73	11.61	4,471	800-421-4225	Y
American Funds 2020 Target Date Retirement Fund® Class A	AACTX	B-	C+	B	Up	2.68	5.80	12.45	19.21	51.93	12.56	11,839	800-421-4225	Y
American Funds 2020 Target Date Retirement Fund® Class C	CCCTX	B-	C+	B	Up	2.53	5.44	11.59	16.63	46.44	12.4	11,839	800-421-4225	Y
American Funds 2020 Target Date Retirement Fund® Class F-1	FAOTX	B-	C+	B	Up	2.72	5.77	12.36	19.17	51.93	12.49	11,839	800-421-4225	Y
American Funds 2020 Target Date Retirement Fund® Class F-2	FBCTX	B-	C+	B	Up	2.77	5.90	12.75	20.11	53.94	12.54	11,839	800-421-4225	Y
American Funds 2020 Target Date Retirement Fund® Class F-3	FCCTX	B-	C+	B	Up	2.76	5.96	12.89	20.44	54.31	12.56	11,839	800-421-4225	Y
American Funds 2020 Target Date Retirement Fund® Class R-1	RACTX	B-	C+	B	Up	2.49	5.40	11.54	16.46	46.06	12.43	11,839	800-421-4225	Y

Category: Target Date 2000-2020 (con't)

Fund Name	Ticker Symbol	RATINGS: Overall Rating	Reward Rating	Risk Rating	Recent Up/ Downgrade	TOTAL RETURNS & PERFORMANCE: 3-Month Total Return	6-Month Total Return	1-Year Total Return	3-Year Total Return	5-Year Total Return	ASSETS: NAV	Total Assets (MIL)	NEW INVESTORS: Telephone	Open to New Investors
American Funds 2020 Target Date Retirement Fund® Class R-2	RBCTX	B-	C+	B	Up	2.55	5.38	11.63	16.69	46.74	12.38	11,839	800-421-4225	Y
American Funds 2020 Target Date Retirement Fund® Cls R-2E	RBEHX	B-	C+	B	Up	2.56	5.55	11.88	17.92	49.52	12.4	11,839	800-421-4225	Y
American Funds 2020 Target Date Retirement Fund® Class R-3	RCCTX	B-	C+	B	Up	2.64	5.62	12.12	18.14	49.61	12.47	11,839	800-421-4225	Y
American Funds 2020 Target Date Retirement Fund® Class R-4	RDCTX	B-	C+	B	Up	2.70	5.83	12.50	19.23	51.89	12.54	11,839	800-421-4225	Y
American Funds 2020 Target Date Retirement Fund® Class R-5	RECTX	B-	C+	B	Up	2.84	5.95	12.85	20.39	54.25	12.64	11,839	800-421-4225	Y
American Funds 2020 Target Date Retirement Fund® Cls R-5E	RHCTX	B-	C+	B	Up	2.75	5.88	12.65	20.12	53.91	12.51	11,839	800-421-4225	Y
American Funds 2020 Target Date Retirement Fund® Class R-6	RRCTX	B-	C+	B	Up	2.83	5.94	12.86	20.53	54.65	12.6	11,839	800-421-4225	Y
AXA Target 2015 Allocation Fund Class B	US00247C6764	B-	C+	B	Up	2.57	5.23	11.32	14.66	36.84		60.5	877-222-2144	Y
AXA Target 2015 Allocation Portfolio Class K	US00247C4116	B-	C+	B	Up	2.71	5.49	11.71	15.51	38.55		60.5	877-222-2144	Y
BlackRock LifePath® Dynamic 2020 Fund Class K Shares	LPSCX	B	C+	B+	Up	3.22	6.64	13.60	18.75	39.35	15.94	370.7	800-441-7762	Y
BlackRock LifePath® Dynamic 2020 Fund Class R Shares	LPRMX	B	C+	B+	Up	3.04	6.34	12.88	16.34	34.21	15.92	370.7	800-441-7762	Y
BlackRock LifePath® Dynamic 2020 Fund Institutional Shares	STLCX	B	C+	B+	Up	3.21	6.57	13.37	17.91	37.43	16.01	370.7	800-441-7762	Y
BlackRock LifePath® Dynamic 2020 Fund Investor A Shares	LPRCX	B-	C+	B	Up	3.08	6.43	13.04	16.97	35.64	14.75	370.7	800-441-7762	Y
BlackRock LifePath® Dynamic 2020 Fund Investor C Shares	LPCMX	B-	C+	B+	Up	2.91	6.02	12.15	14.29	30.56	15.79	370.7	800-441-7762	Y
BlackRock LifePath® Dynamic Retirement Fund Class K Shares	LPSAX	B	C+	A-	Up	2.77	5.91	11.86	17.04	32.11	10.96	139.2	800-441-7762	Y
BlackRock LifePath® Dynamic Retirement Fund Class R Shares	LPRRX	B	C+	B+	Up	2.61	5.59	11.11	14.55	27.12	10.91	139.2	800-441-7762	Y
BlackRock LifePath® Dynamic Retmnt Fund Inst Shares	STLAX	B	C+	A-	Up	2.70	5.77	11.67	16.13	30.23	11	139.2	800-441-7762	Y
BlackRock LifePath® Dynamic Retmnt Fund Inv A Shares	LPRAX	B	C+	B+	Up	2.69	5.67	11.39	15.37	28.72	9.72	139.2	800-441-7762	Y
BlackRock LifePath® Dynamic Retmnt Fund Inv C Shares	LPCRX	B-	C+	B+	Up	2.54	5.26	10.47	12.75	23.76	10.87	139.2	800-441-7762	Y
BlackRock LifePath® Index 2020 Fund Class K Shares	LIMKX	B	C+	A-	Up	2.93	5.87	12.33	18.45	41.65	12.73	2,371	800-441-7762	Y
BlackRock LifePath® Index 2020 Fund Institutional Shares	LIQIX	B-	C+	B	Up	2.92	5.75	12.28	18.26	41.31	12.73	2,371	800-441-7762	Y
BlackRock LifePath® Index 2020 Fund Investor A Shares	LIQAX	B-	C+	B	Up	2.85	5.62	12.02	17.45	39.64	12.71	2,371	800-441-7762	Y
BlackRock LifePath® Index Retirement Fund Class K Shares	LIRKX	B	C+	A-	Up	2.47	5.03	10.74	16.57	33.77	12.25	1,210	800-441-7762	Y
BlackRock LifePath® Index Retmnt Fund Inst Shares	LIRIX	B	C+	A-	Up	2.46	5.09	10.68	16.36	33.55	12.26	1,210	800-441-7762	Y
BlackRock LifePath® Index Retmnt Fund Inv A Shares	LIRAX	B	C+	A-	Up	2.39	4.96	10.42	15.56	31.94	12.25	1,210	800-441-7762	Y
BlackRock LifePath® Smart Beta 2020 Fund Class K	BIPCX	B	C+	B+	Up	1.94	4.59	12.87	18.44	42.00	11	26.0	800-441-7762	Y
BlackRock LifePath® Smart Beta 2020 Fund Class R Shares	BRPCX	B-	C+	B	Up	1.76	4.26	12.21	16.41	37.78	10.84	26.0	800-441-7762	Y
BlackRock LifePath® Smart Beta 2020 Fund Inst Shares	BLBIX	B-	C+	B	Up	1.92	4.57	12.72	18.10	41.28	11.02	26.0	800-441-7762	Y
BlackRock LifePath® Smart Beta 2020 Fund Investor A Shares	BAPCX	B-	C+	B	Up	1.87	4.45	12.45	17.24	39.58	10.93	26.0	800-441-7762	Y
BlackRock LifePath® Smart Beta Retirement Fund Class K	BIPBX	B-	C+	B	Up	2.13	4.27	11.38	16.19	36.01	10.73	15.9	800-441-7762	Y
BlackRock LifePath® Smart Beta Retmnt Fund Inst Shares	BLAIX	B-	C+	B+	Up	1.99	4.12	11.22	15.92	35.54	10.72	15.9	800-441-7762	Y
BlackRock LifePath® Smart Beta Retmnt Fund Inv A Shares	BAPBX	B-	C+	B	Up	2.07	4.13	10.95	15.08	33.85	10.66	15.9	800-441-7762	Y
BMO In-Retirement Fund Class R3	BTRRX	B-	C+	B	Up	1.97	4.17	9.10	12.81	30.93	8.94	15.2	800-236-3863	Y
BMO In-Retirement Fund Class R6	BTRTX	B-	C+	B	Up	2.29	4.61	9.96	15.15	35.32	8.88	15.2	800-236-3863	Y
BMO In-Retirement Fund Class Y	BTRYX	B-	C+	B	Up	2.09	4.41	9.50	13.70	32.94	8.9	15.2	800-236-3863	Y
BMO Target Retirement 2015 Fund Class R3	BRTCX	B-	C+	B	Up	2.46	5.23	11.35	15.27		11.45	3.9	800-236-3863	Y
BMO Target Retirement 2015 Fund Class R6	BRTDX	B-	C+	B	Up	2.68	5.62	12.14	17.57		11.5	3.9	800-236-3863	Y
BMO Target Retirement 2015 Fund Class Y	BRTAX	B-	C+	B	Up	2.55	5.32	11.54	16.08		11.5	3.9	800-236-3863	Y
BMO Target Retirement 2020 Fund Class R3	BTRFX	B-	C+	B	Down	3.45	6.55	14.29	18.39	47.17	10.35	82.7	800-236-3863	Y
BMO Target Retirement 2020 Fund Class R6	BTRGX	B-	C+	B	Down	3.59	6.89	15.01	20.71	51.96	10.3	82.7	800-236-3863	Y
BMO Target Retirement 2020 Fund Class Y	BTRDX	B-	C+	B	Down	3.46	6.67	14.54	19.19	49.31	10.31	82.7	800-236-3863	Y
ClearTrack 2015 Fund Class R6	TDKTX	B-	C	B	Up	2.65	5.32	11.43			10.64	52.5	888-233-4339	Y
ClearTrack 2020 Fund Class R1	TCHTX	B-	C	B	Up	2.82	5.50	11.75			10.74	77.3	888-233-4339	Y
ClearTrack Retirement Income Fund Class R6	TCJTX	B-	C	B	Up	1.76	3.80	8.35			10.6	97.7	888-233-4339	Y
Fidelity Advisor Freedom® 2005 Fund Class A	FFAVX	B	C+	A-	Up	2.06	4.36	10.02	14.93	29.64	12	204.3	617-563-7000	Y
Fidelity Advisor Freedom® 2005 Fund Class C	FCFVX	B-	C+	B+	Up	1.79	4.01	9.24	12.31	24.80	12	204.3	617-563-7000	Y
Fidelity Advisor Freedom® 2005 Fund Class I	FFIVX	B-	C+	B	Up	2.09	4.47	10.36	15.76	31.26	12.07	204.3	617-563-7000	Y
Fidelity Advisor Freedom® 2005 Fund Class M	FFTVX	B	C+	A-	Up	1.98	4.29	9.78	14.05	27.97	11.99	204.3	617-563-7000	Y
Fidelity Advisor Freedom® 2005 Fund Class Z6	FYGLX	B-	C+	B	Up	2.17	4.55	10.44	15.84	31.36	12.06	204.3	617-563-7000	Y
Fidelity Advisor Freedom® 2010 Fund Class A	FACFX	B-	C+	B	Up	2.44	5.16	11.86	17.31	36.56	12.49	493.9	617-563-7000	Y
Fidelity Advisor Freedom® 2010 Fund Class C	FCFCX	B	C+	B+	Up	2.31	4.89	11.05	14.76	31.65	12.39	493.9	617-563-7000	Y
Fidelity Advisor Freedom® 2010 Fund Class I	FCIFX	B-	C+	B	Up	2.51	5.39	12.24	18.24	38.38	12.54	493.9	617-563-7000	Y

Category: Target Date 2000-2020 (con't)

Fund Name	Ticker Symbol	RATINGS: Overall Rating	Reward Rating	Risk Rating	Recent Up/ Downgrade	TOTAL RETURNS & PERFORMANCE: 3-Month Total Return	6-Month Total Return	1-Year Total Return	3-Year Total Return	5-Year Total Return	ASSETS: NAV	Total Assets (MIL)	NEW INVESTORS: Telephone	Open to New Investors
Fidelity Advisor Freedom® 2010 Fund Class M	FCFTX	B-	C+	B	Up	2.38	5.02	11.56	16.45	34.92	12.45	493.9	617-563-7000	Y
Fidelity Advisor Freedom® 2010 Fund Class Z6	FUGLX	B-	C+	B	Up	2.58	5.46	12.32	18.32	38.47	12.53	493.9	617-563-7000	Y
Fidelity Advisor Freedom® 2015 Fund Class A	FFVAX	B-	C+	B	Up	2.94	6.07	13.78	19.76	40.88	12.66	1,172	617-563-7000	Y
Fidelity Advisor Freedom® 2015 Fund Class C	FFVCX	B	C+	B+	Up	2.68	5.66	12.92	17.12	35.68	12.57	1,172	617-563-7000	Y
Fidelity Advisor Freedom® 2015 Fund Class I	FFVIX	B-	C+	B	Up	2.90	6.16	13.99	20.57	42.63	12.75	1,172	617-563-7000	Y
Fidelity Advisor Freedom® 2015 Fund Class M	FFVTX	B-	C+	B	Up	2.85	5.90	13.45	18.84	39.13	12.64	1,172	617-563-7000	Y
Fidelity Advisor Freedom® 2015 Fund Class Z6	FIGLX	B	C+	A-	Up	2.99	6.25	14.08	20.66	42.74	12.73	1,172	617-563-7000	Y
Fidelity Advisor Freedom® 2020 Fund Class A	FDAFX	B-	C+	B	Down	3.19	6.64	14.96	21.34	44.94	13.79	2,567	617-563-7000	Y
Fidelity Advisor Freedom® 2020 Fund Class C	FDCFX	B	C+	B+	Up	2.97	6.20	14.17	18.58	39.60	13.7	2,567	617-563-7000	Y
Fidelity Advisor Freedom® 2020 Fund Class I	FDIFX	B	C+	B+	Up	3.23	6.73	15.25	22.22	46.66	13.89	2,567	617-563-7000	Y
Fidelity Advisor Freedom® 2020 Fund Class M	FDTFX	B-	C+	B	Up	3.08	6.45	14.69	20.37	43.07	13.79	2,567	617-563-7000	Y
Fidelity Advisor Freedom® 2020 Fund Class Z6	FOGLX	B-	C+	B	Up	3.28	6.85	15.38	22.37	46.83	13.87	2,567	617-563-7000	Y
Fidelity Advisor Freedom® Income Fund Class A	FAFAX	B	C	A-	Up	1.56	3.44	7.80	11.93	21.16	11.1	215.3	617-563-7000	Y
Fidelity Advisor Freedom® Income Fund Class C	FCAFX	B-	C	A-	Up	1.30	2.99	6.90	9.38	16.59	11.07	215.3	617-563-7000	Y
Fidelity Advisor Freedom® Income Fund Class I	FIAFX	B	C	A-	Up	1.55	3.49	8.04	12.82	22.67	11.13	215.3	617-563-7000	Y
Fidelity Advisor Freedom® Income Fund Class M	FTAFX	B	C	A-	Up	1.48	3.30	7.53	11.10	19.65	11.09	215.3	617-563-7000	Y
Fidelity Advisor Freedom® Income Fund Class Z6	FEGLX	B-	C	B	Up	1.53	3.52	8.06	12.85	22.71	11.12	215.3	617-563-7000	Y
Fidelity Freedom® 2005 Fund	FFFVX	B-	C+	B	Up	2.17	4.65	10.47	16.32	32.31	12.56	1,036	617-563-7000	Y
Fidelity Freedom® 2005 Fund Class K6	FITKX	B-	C+	B	Up	2.18	4.67	10.48	16.33	32.33	12.55	1,036	617-563-7000	Y
Fidelity Freedom® 2010 Fund	FFFCX	B-	C+	B	Up	2.65	5.59	12.47	18.97	39.90	16.06	6,777	617-563-7000	Y
Fidelity Freedom® 2010 Fund Class K6	FOTKX	B-	C+	B	Up	2.67	5.61	12.49	18.99	39.92	16.03	6,777	617-563-7000	Y
Fidelity Freedom® 2015 Fund	FFVFX	B-	C+	B	Up	3.07	6.40	14.28	21.52	44.29	13.38	10,472	617-563-7000	Y
Fidelity Freedom® 2015 Fund Class K6	FPTKX	B-	C+	B	Up	3.18	6.52	14.40	21.65	44.45	13.37	10,472	617-563-7000	Y
Fidelity Freedom® 2020 Fund	FFFDX	B-	C+	B	Down	3.39	7.02	15.64	23.18	48.71	16.57	30,350	617-563-7000	Y
Fidelity Freedom® 2020 Fund Class K6	FATKX	B	C+	A-		3.48	7.12	15.74	23.28	48.84	16.56	30,350	617-563-7000	Y
Fidelity Freedom® Income Fund	FFFAX	B	C+	A-	Up	1.68	3.71	8.21	13.27	23.42	11.78	3,795	617-563-7000	Y
Fidelity Freedom® Income Fund Class K6	FYTKX	B-	C+	B	Up	1.73	3.72	8.22	13.28	23.44	11.77	3,795	617-563-7000	Y
Fidelity Freedom® Index 2005 Fund Inst Premium Cls	FFGFX	B-	C+	B	Up	2.19	4.30	8.93	13.44	27.37	13.45	103.9	617-563-7000	Y
Fidelity Freedom® Index 2005 Fund Investor Class	FJIFX	B-	C+	B	Up	2.17	4.27	8.89	13.29	27.21	13.45	103.9	617-563-7000	Y
Fidelity Freedom® Index 2010 Fund Inst Premium Cls	FFWTX	B-	C+	B	Up	2.61	5.20	10.72	16.07	34.51	14.35	532.8	617-563-7000	Y
Fidelity Freedom® Index 2010 Fund Investor Class	FKIFX	B-	C+	B	Up	2.65	5.17	10.67	15.87	34.29	14.35	532.8	617-563-7000	Y
Fidelity Freedom® Index 2015 Fund Inst Premium Cls	FIWFX	B-	C+	B	Up	3.11	6.11	12.66	18.62	39.10	15.02	1,160	617-563-7000	Y
Fidelity Freedom® Index 2015 Fund Investor Class	FLIFX	B-	C+	B	Up	3.14	6.08	12.60	18.42	38.87	15.03	1,160	617-563-7000	Y
Fidelity Freedom® Index 2020 Fund Inst Premium Cls	FIWTX	B-	C+	B	Up	3.52	6.76	13.95	20.36	43.19	15.8	3,828	617-563-7000	Y
Fidelity Freedom® Index 2020 Fund Investor Class	FPIFX	B-	C+	B	Up	3.42	6.72	13.89	20.16	42.95	15.8	3,828	617-563-7000	Y
Fidelity Freedom® Index Income Fund Inst Premium Cls	FFGZX	B	C	A	Up	1.65	3.28	6.72	10.36	18.54	11.94	282.8	617-563-7000	Y
Fidelity Freedom® Index Income Fund Investor Class	FIKFX	B	C	A	Up	1.54	3.15	6.65	10.18	18.36	11.95	282.8	617-563-7000	Y
Goldman Sachs Target Date 2020 Portfolio Class A Shares	GTAHX	B	C+	A-	Up	1.81	3.58	7.88	12.71	34.54	9.31	48.0	800-526-7384	Y
Goldman Sachs Target Date 2020 Portfolio Cls Inst Shares	GTIHX	B-	C+	B	Up	2.03	3.90	8.43	13.92	36.66	9.33	48.0	800-526-7384	Y
Goldman Sachs Target Date 2020 Portfolio Class IR Shares	GTMHX	B-	C+	B	Up	2.00	3.88	8.30	13.72	36.42	9.32	48.0	800-526-7384	Y
Goldman Sachs Target Date 2020 Portfolio Class R Shares	GTRHX	B	C	A-	Up	1.85	3.51	7.70	12.07	33.11	9.32	48.0	800-526-7384	Y
Goldman Sachs Target Date 2020 Portfolio Class R6 Shares	GTZHX	B	C+	A-	Up	2.03	3.90	8.44	13.93	36.67	9.33	48.0	800-526-7384	Y
Goldman Sachs Target Date 2020 Port Cls Serv Shares	GTVHX	B-	C+	B	Up	1.87	3.53	7.83	12.73	34.56	9.32	48.0	800-526-7384	Y
Great-West Lifetime 2015 Fund Class L	MXABX	B-	C+	B	Up	2.55	4.96	10.93	16.20	39.45		1,014		Y
Great-West Lifetime Conservative 2015 Fund Inst Cls	MXMAX	B-	C+	B	Up	2.04	3.53	9.02	14.84	29.66		109.8		Y
Great-West Lifetime Conservative 2015 Fund Investor Class	MXLTX	B-	C+	B	Up	1.85	3.77	8.47	13.70	28.47		109.8		Y
Great-West Lifetime Conservative 2015 Fund Service Class	MXLUX	B-	C+	B	Up	1.78	3.69	8.35	13.38	27.85		109.8		Y
Great-West SecureFoundation® Lifetime 2015 Fund Class L	MXLEX	B-	C+	B	Up	3.31	6.19	12.68	18.98	45.55		102.6		Y
Great-West SecureFoundation® Lifetime 2015 Fund Inv Cls	MXSJX	B-	C+	B	Up	3.26	6.30	12.81	19.73	47.22		102.6		Y
Great-West SecureFoundation® Lifetime 2015 Fund Serv Cls	MXSKX	B-	C+	B	Up	3.27	6.17	12.72	19.32	46.53		102.6		Y
Great-West SecureFoundation® Lifetime 2020 Fund Class L	MXLFX	B-	C+	B	Up	2.08	5.00	11.34	17.46	43.77		81.0		Y
Great-West SecureFoundation® Lifetime 2020 Fund Inv Cls	MXSMX	B-	C+	B	Up	1.85	4.86	11.37	18.03	45.20		81.0		Y

Category: Target Date 2000-2020 (con't)

Fund Name	Ticker Symbol	RATINGS: Overall Rating	Reward Rating	Risk Rating	Recent Up/ Downgrade	TOTAL RETURNS & PERFORMANCE: 3-Month Total Return	6-Month Total Return	1-Year Total Return	3-Year Total Return	5-Year Total Return	ASSETS: NAV	Total Assets (MIL)	NEW INVESTORS: Telephone	Open to New Investors
Great-West SecureFoundation® Lifetime 2020 Fund Serv Cls	MXSPX	B-	C+	B	Up	3.68	6.74	13.28	19.90	47.08		81.0		Y
GuideStone Funds MyDestination 2015 Fund Institutional	GMTYX	B-	C+	B	Up	2.37	5.40	11.81	16.73	35.28	10.37	622.1	214-720-1171	Y
GuideStone Funds MyDestination 2015 Fund Investor Class	GMTZX	B-	C+	B	Up	2.43	5.26	11.66	16.58	35.10	10.38	622.1	214-720-1171	Y
Harbor Target Retirement 2015 Fund Institutional Class	HARGX	B	C+	A-	Up	1.60	3.98	9.50	14.04	26.27	10.8	6.2	800-422-1050	Y
Harbor Target Retirement 2020 Fund Institutional Class	HARJX	B	C+	B+	Up	2.02	4.79	11.69	16.91	31.61	9.74	27.7	800-422-1050	Y
Harbor Target Retirement Income Fund Institutional Class	HARAX	B	C	A-	Up	1.37	3.46	8.41	13.07	21.40	9.12	14.1	800-422-1050	Y
Invesco Balanced-Risk Retirement 2020 Fund Class A	AFTAX	B-	C	B	Up	3.66	5.66	7.24	12.21	20.48	9.05	64.8	800-659-1005	Y
Invesco Balanced-Risk Retirement 2020 Fund Class AX	VRCAX	B-	C	B	Up	3.66	5.66	7.24	12.21	20.48	9.05	64.8	800-659-1005	
Invesco Balanced-Risk Retirement 2020 Fund Class B	AFTBX	B-	C	B	Up	3.33	5.11	6.46	9.71	15.98	8.96	64.8	800-659-1005	
Invesco Balanced-Risk Retirement 2020 Fund Class C	AFTCX	B-	C	B	Up	3.34	5.12	6.35	9.73	16.02	8.94	64.8	800-659-1005	Y
Invesco Balanced-Risk Retirement 2020 Fund Class CX	VRCCX	B-	C	B	Up	3.34	5.24	6.47	9.72	16.01	8.94	64.8	800-659-1005	
Invesco Balanced-Risk Retirement 2020 Fund Class R	ATFRX	B-	C	B	Up	3.52	5.40	6.99	11.35	18.94	9.01	64.8	800-659-1005	Y
Invesco Balanced-Risk Retirement 2020 Fund Class RX	VRCRX	B-	C	B	Up	3.52	5.40	6.86	11.35	18.94	9.01	64.8	800-659-1005	
Invesco Balanced-Risk Retirement 2020 Fund Class Y	AFTYX	B-	C+	B	Up	3.58	5.69	7.52	13.00	21.96	9.04	64.8	800-659-1005	Y
Invesco Balanced-Risk Retirement 2020 Fund R5 Class	AFTSX	B-	C+	B	Up	3.56	5.66	7.47	12.92	21.85	9.09	64.8	800-659-1005	Y
Invesco Balanced-Risk Retirement Now Fund Class A	IANAX	B-	C	B	Up	3.03	4.75	6.10	9.94	15.49	8.47	24.7	800-659-1005	Y
Invesco Balanced-Risk Retirement Now Fund Class AX	VIRAX	B-	C	B	Up	3.03	4.63	5.98	9.82	15.37	8.45	24.7	800-659-1005	
Invesco Balanced-Risk Retirement Now Fund Class R	IANRX	B-	C	B	Up	3.04	4.66	5.83	8.98	13.93	8.37	24.7	800-659-1005	Y
Invesco Balanced-Risk Retirement Now Fund Class RX	VIRRX	B-	C	B	Up	2.92	4.54	5.83	9.10	13.94	8.36	24.7	800-659-1005	
Invesco Balanced-Risk Retirement Now Fund Class Y	IANYX	B-	C	B	Up	3.13	4.84	6.50	10.79	16.92	8.57	24.7	800-659-1005	Y
Invesco Balanced-Risk Retirement Now Fund R5 Class	IANIX	B-	C	B	Up	3.13	4.85	6.38	10.67	16.79	8.56	24.7	800-659-1005	Y
John Hancock Funds II MultiMgr 2010 Lifetime Port Cls 1	JLAOX	B-	C+	B	Up	2.24	4.64	10.89	17.39	37.44	9.17	239.3	800-225-5913	Y
John Hancock Funds II MultiMgr 2010 Lifetime Port Cls A	JLAAX	B-	C+	B	Up	2.11	4.50	10.50	16.20	34.71	9.18	239.3	800-225-5913	Y
John Hancock Funds II MultiMgr 2010 Lifetime Port Cls I	JHRLX	B-	C+	B	Up	2.19	4.69	10.83	17.16	37.17	9.17	239.3	800-225-5913	Y
John Hancock Funds II MultiMgr 2010 Lifetime Port Cls R1	JLADX	B-	C+	B	Up	2.04	4.33	10.10	15.09	32.82	9.15	239.3	800-225-5913	Y
John Hancock Funds II MultiMgr 2010 Lifetime Port Cls R2	JLAEX	B-	C+	B	Up	2.12	4.41	10.29	15.82	34.27	9.17	239.3	800-225-5913	Y
John Hancock Funds II MultiMgr 2010 Lifetime Port Cls R3	JLAFX	B-	C+	B	Up	1.98	4.27	10.15	15.21	33.20	9.15	239.3	800-225-5913	Y
John Hancock Funds II MultiMgr 2010 Lifetime Port Cls R4	JLAGX	B-	C+	B	Up	2.15	4.55	10.56	16.70	35.98	9.16	239.3	800-225-5913	Y
John Hancock Funds II MultiMgr 2010 Lifetime Port Cls R5	JLAHX	B-	C+	B	Up	2.13	4.64	10.77	17.39	37.31	9.16	239.3	800-225-5913	Y
John Hancock Funds II MultiMgr 2010 Lifetime Port Cls R6	JLAIX	B-	C+	B	Up	2.19	4.69	10.94	17.57	37.79	9.17	239.3	800-225-5913	Y
John Hancock Funds II MultiMgr 2015 Lifetime Port Cls 1	JLBOX	B-	C+	B	Up	2.50	5.28	12.15	18.97	42.87	9.62	415.0	800-225-5913	Y
John Hancock Funds II MultiMgr 2015 Lifetime Port Cls A	JLBAX	B-	C+	B	Up	2.34	5.01	11.63	17.62	40.01	9.63	415.0	800-225-5913	Y
John Hancock Funds II MultiMgr 2015 Lifetime Port Cls I	JHREX	B-	C+	B	Up	2.43	5.21	12.08	18.72	42.57	9.62	415.0	800-225-5913	Y
John Hancock Funds II MultiMgr 2015 Lifetime Port Cls R1	JLBDX	B-	C+	B	Up	2.32	4.90	11.29	16.41	37.92	9.61	415.0	800-225-5913	Y
John Hancock Funds II MultiMgr 2015 Lifetime Port Cls R2	JLBKX	B-	C+	B	Up	2.37	4.95	11.47	17.27	39.50	9.59	415.0	800-225-5913	Y
John Hancock Funds II MultiMgr 2015 Lifetime Port Cls R3	JLBFX	B-	C+	B	Up	2.31	4.89	11.40	16.86	38.60	9.61	415.0	800-225-5913	Y
John Hancock Funds II MultiMgr 2015 Lifetime Port Cls R4	JLBGX	B-	C+	B	Up	2.41	5.20	11.84	18.30	41.42	9.6	415.0	800-225-5913	Y
John Hancock Funds II MultiMgr 2015 Lifetime Port Cls R5	JLBHX	B-	C+	B	Up	2.50	5.28	12.15	18.97	42.87	9.62	415.0	800-225-5913	Y
John Hancock Funds II MultiMgr 2015 Lifetime Port Cls R6	JLBJX	B-	C+	B	Up	2.54	5.32	12.19	19.12	43.34	9.62	415.0	800-225-5913	Y
John Hancock Funds II MultiMgr 2020 Lifetime Port Cls 1	JLDOX	B-	C+	B	Up	2.87	6.13	13.89	21.13	50.22	10.44	1,004	800-225-5913	Y
John Hancock Funds II MultiMgr 2020 Lifetime Port Cls A	JLDAX	B-	C+	B	Up	2.90	5.97	13.59	19.89	47.35	10.47	1,004	800-225-5913	Y
John Hancock Funds II MultiMgr 2020 Lifetime Port Cls I	JHRVX	B-	C+	B	Up	3.00	6.17	13.92	21.11	50.19	10.46	1,004	800-225-5913	Y
John Hancock Funds II MultiMgr 2020 Lifetime Port Cls R1	JLDDX	B-	C+	B	Down	2.76	5.83	13.14	18.66	45.20	10.44	1,004	800-225-5913	Y
John Hancock Funds II MultiMgr 2020 Lifetime Port Cls R2	JLDEX	B-	C+	B	Up	2.81	5.89	13.42	19.67	47.02	10.43	1,004	800-225-5913	Y
John Hancock Funds II MultiMgr 2020 Lifetime Port Cls R3	JLDFX	B-	C+	B	Down	2.76	5.83	13.25	19.01	45.75	10.44	1,004	800-225-5913	Y
John Hancock Funds II MultiMgr 2020 Lifetime Port Cls R4	JLDGX	B-	C+	B	Down	2.87	6.05	13.71	20.47	48.88	10.42	1,004	800-225-5913	Y
John Hancock Funds II MultiMgr 2020 Lifetime Port Cls R5	JLDHX	B-	C+	B	Up	2.87	6.13	13.89	21.13	50.22	10.44	1,004	800-225-5913	Y
John Hancock Funds II MultiMgr 2020 Lifetime Port Cls R6	JLDIX	B-	C+	B	Up	2.93	6.20	14.08	21.35	50.67	10.43	1,004	800-225-5913	Y
John Hancock Funds Multi-Index 2010 Lifetime Port Cls 1	JRLDX	B-	C+	B	Up	2.16	4.44	9.85	16.26		10.68	30.9	800-225-5913	Y
John Hancock Funds Multi-Index 2010 Lifetime Port Cls R6	JRLHX	B-	C+	B	Up	2.11	4.49	9.90	16.43		10.68	30.9	800-225-5913	Y
John Hancock Funds Multi-Index 2015 Lifetime Port Cls 1	JRLIX	B-	C+	B	Up	2.40	5.00	10.96	17.75		10.87	46.3	800-225-5913	Y
John Hancock Funds Multi-Index 2015 Lifetime Port Cls R6	JRLLX	B-	C+	B	Up	2.44	5.05	11.01	17.81		10.87	46.3	800-225-5913	Y

Category: Target Date 2000-2020 (con't)

Fund Name	Ticker Symbol	RATINGS: Overall Rating	Reward Rating	Risk Rating	Recent Up/ Downgrade	TOTAL RETURNS & PERFORMANCE: 3-Month Total Return	6-Month Total Return	1-Year Total Return	3-Year Total Return	5-Year Total Return	ASSETS: NAV	Total Assets (MIL)	NEW INVESTORS: Telephone	Open to New Investors
John Hancock Funds Multi-Index 2020 Lifetime Port Cls 1	JRLOX	B-	C+	B	Up	2.89	6.00	12.72	20.18		11.23	146.7	800-225-5913	Y
John Hancock Funds Multi-Index 2020 Lifetime Port Cls R6	JRTAX	B-	C+	B	Up	3.02	6.04	12.86	20.35		11.24	146.7	800-225-5913	Y
John Hancock Funds Multi-Ind 2020 Preserv Port Cls 1	JRWOX	B	C	A-	Up	1.07	2.73	6.67	11.14	25.55	11.66	851.2	800-225-5913	Y
John Hancock Funds Multi-Ind 2020 Preserv Port Cls R1	JRWQX	B-	C	A-	Up	0.87	2.35	5.91	9.32	21.86	11.72	851.2	800-225-5913	Y
John Hancock Funds Multi-Ind 2020 Preserv Port Cls R2	JRWRX	B-	C	A-	Up	0.93	2.41	6.06	9.68	22.77	11.71	851.2	800-225-5913	Y
John Hancock Funds Multi-Ind 2020 Preserv Port Cls R4	JRWPX	B	C	A-	Up	1.01	2.58	6.50	10.68	24.61	11.7	851.2	800-225-5913	Y
John Hancock Funds Multi-Ind 2020 Preserv Port Cls R6	JRWSX	B	C	A-	Up	1.03	2.69	6.62	11.30	25.85	11.66	851.2	800-225-5913	Y
John Hancock Funds Multi-Ind Income Preserv Port Cls 1	JRFOX	B	C	A	Up	0.53	1.59	4.27	7.88	14.56	11.06	482.7	800-225-5913	Y
John Hancock Funds Multi-Ind Income Preserv Port Cls R1	JRFQX	B-	C	A	Up	0.51	1.40	3.78	6.31	11.32	11.12	482.7	800-225-5913	Y
John Hancock Funds Multi-Ind Income Preserv Port Cls R2	JRFNX	B-	C	A	Up	0.53	1.51	3.99	6.95	12.55	11.1	482.7	800-225-5913	Y
John Hancock Funds Multi-Ind Income Preserv Port Cls R4	JRFPX	B	C	A	Up	0.59	1.56	4.14	7.56	13.66	11.08	482.7	800-225-5913	Y
John Hancock Funds Multi-Ind Income Preserv Port Cls R6	JRFSX	B	C	A	Up	0.67	1.74	4.42	8.05	14.85	11.06	482.7	800-225-5913	Y
JPMorgan SmartRetirement® 2020 Fund Class A	JTTAX	B-	C+	B	Up	3.18	6.51	13.72	18.35	45.18	19.73	7,320	800-480-4111	Y
JPMorgan SmartRetirement® 2020 Fund Class C	JTTCX	B-	C+	B	Up	3.03	6.20	13.04	16.10	40.49	19.65	7,320	800-480-4111	Y
JPMorgan SmartRetirement® 2020 Fund Class I	JTTSX	B-	C+	B	Up	3.20	6.60	13.85	18.79	45.89	19.8	7,320	800-480-4111	Y
JPMorgan SmartRetirement® 2020 Fund Class R2	JTTZX	B	C+	A-	Up	3.04	6.25	13.27	17.33	43.10	19.67	7,320	800-480-4111	Y
JPMorgan SmartRetirement® 2020 Fund Class R3	JTTPX	B-	C+	B	Up	3.15	6.43	13.50	18.05	44.71	19.68	7,320	800-480-4111	Y
JPMorgan SmartRetirement® 2020 Fund Class R4	JTTQX	B	C+	A-	Up	3.20	6.54	13.77	18.93	46.52	19.77	7,320	800-480-4111	Y
JPMorgan SmartRetirement® 2020 Fund Class R5	JTTIX	B-	C+	B	Up	3.23	6.65	13.96	19.18	46.84	19.82	7,320	800-480-4111	Y
JPMorgan SmartRetirement® 2020 Fund Class R6	JTTYX	B-	C+	B	Up	3.30	6.71	14.13	19.53	47.26	19.83	7,320	800-480-4111	Y
JPMorgan SmartRetirement® Blend 2020 Fund Class I	JSSRX	B	C+	A-	Up	3.10	6.20	13.07	18.76	43.99	20.02	475.9	800-480-4111	Y
JPMorgan SmartRetirement® Blend 2020 Fund Class R2	JIORX	B-	C+	B	Up	3.02	5.93	12.57	17.21	40.97	20.03	475.9	800-480-4111	Y
JPMorgan SmartRetirement® Blend 2020 Fund Class R3	JSTKX	B	C+	A-	Up	3.04	6.07	12.90	18.55	43.72	20.01	475.9	800-480-4111	Y
JPMorgan SmartRetirement® Blend 2020 Fund Class R4	JSTLX	B-	C+	B	Up	3.10	6.20	13.18	19.44	45.53	20.01	475.9	800-480-4111	Y
JPMorgan SmartRetirement® Blend 2020 Fund Class R5	JBSRX	B	C+	A-	Up	3.14	6.28	13.24	19.42	45.31	20.03	475.9	800-480-4111	Y
JPMorgan SmartRetirement® Blend 2020 Fund Class R6	JSYRX	B-	C+	B	Up	3.21	6.38	13.40	19.67	45.80	20.04	475.9	800-480-4111	Y
JPMorgan SmartRetirement® Blend Inc Fund Class R3	JITLX	B	C+	A-	Up	2.43	4.94	10.27	14.95	29.74	17.89	259.0	800-480-4111	Y
JPMorgan SmartRetirement® Blend Inc Fund Class R4	JITKX	B-	C+	B	Up	2.50	5.07	10.54	15.82	31.37	17.89	259.0	800-480-4111	Y
JPMorgan SmartRetirement® Blend Income Fund Class I	JIJSX	B	C+	A-	Up	2.49	5.06	10.43	15.07	29.86	17.9	259.0	800-480-4111	Y
JPMorgan SmartRetirement® Blend Income Fund Class R2	JIRBX	B	C+	A-	Up	2.37	4.80	9.88	13.53	27.10	17.9	259.0	800-480-4111	Y
JPMorgan SmartRetirement® Blend Income Fund Class R5	JIBBX	B	C+	A-	Up	2.54	5.09	10.54	15.66	31.11	17.9	259.0	800-480-4111	Y
JPMorgan SmartRetirement® Blend Income Fund Class R6	JIYBX	B-	C+	B	Up	2.56	5.19	10.70	15.98	31.56	17.91	259.0	800-480-4111	Y
JPMorgan SmartRetirement® Income Fund Class A	JSRAX	B	C+	A-	Up	2.53	5.26	10.88	14.61	30.44	18.58	4,457	800-480-4111	Y
JPMorgan SmartRetirement® Income Fund Class C	JSRCX	B	C+	B+	Up	2.36	4.92	10.17	12.42	26.26	18.51	4,457	800-480-4111	Y
JPMorgan SmartRetirement® Income Fund Class I	JSRSX	B	C+	A-	Up	2.61	5.36	11.03	15.01	31.18	18.62	4,457	800-480-4111	Y
JPMorgan SmartRetirement® Income Fund Class R2	JSIZX	B-	C+	B	Up	2.42	5.03	10.45	13.60	28.60	18.54	4,457	800-480-4111	Y
JPMorgan SmartRetirement® Income Fund Class R3	JSIPX	B	C+	A-	Up	2.52	5.19	10.68	14.27	30.02	18.53	4,457	800-480-4111	Y
JPMorgan SmartRetirement® Income Fund Class R4	JSIQX	B-	C+	B	Up	2.55	5.29	10.97	15.15	31.68	18.6	4,457	800-480-4111	Y
JPMorgan SmartRetirement® Income Fund Class R5	JSIIX	B-	C+	B	Up	2.62	5.40	11.11	15.42	31.98	18.65	4,457	800-480-4111	Y
JPMorgan SmartRetirement® Income Fund Class R6	JSIYX	B	C+	A-	Up	2.65	5.45	11.22	15.67	32.28	18.65	4,457	800-480-4111	Y
KP Retirement Path 2015 Fund Institutional Shares	KPRAX	B-	C+	B	Up	2.32	4.86	10.02	15.72		10.51	442.7		Y
KP Retirement Path 2020 Fund Institutional Shares	KPRBX	B-	C+	B	Up	2.77	5.85	12.03	18.18		10.9	870.4		Y
MainStay Retirement 2010 Fund Class A	MYRAX	B-	C+	B	Up	2.28	4.66	10.01	14.23	36.28	9.77	38.4	800-624-6782	Y
MainStay Retirement 2010 Fund Class I	MYRIX	B-	C+	B	Up	2.33	4.70	10.22	14.96	37.93	9.83	38.4	800-624-6782	Y
MainStay Retirement 2010 Fund Class R1	MYRRX	B	C+	A-	Up	2.26	4.75	10.13	14.71	37.49	10.14	38.4	800-624-6782	Y
MainStay Retirement 2010 Fund Class R2	MYRWX	B-	C+	B	Up	2.26	4.53	9.83	13.86	35.61	9.83	38.4	800-624-6782	Y
MainStay Retirement 2010 Fund Class R3	MYREX	B-	C+	B	Up	2.22	4.45	9.65	13.07	34.08	10.03	38.4	800-624-6782	Y
MainStay Retirement 2010 Fund Investor Class	MYRDX	B-	C+	B	Up	2.22	4.60	9.91	13.94	35.61	9.84	38.4	800-624-6782	Y
MainStay Retirement 2020 Fund Class A	MYROX	B-	C+	B	Up	3.27	6.57	13.96	18.46	47.96	10.67	125.3	800-624-6782	Y
MainStay Retirement 2020 Fund Class I	MYRTX	B-	C+	B	Up	3.36	6.74	14.21	19.32	49.89	10.72	125.3	800-624-6782	Y
MainStay Retirement 2020 Fund Class R1	MYRUX	B-	C+	B	Up	3.28	6.68	14.07	18.95	49.30	10.99	125.3	800-624-6782	Y
MainStay Retirement 2020 Fund Class R2	MYRVX	B-	C+	B	Up	3.11	6.38	13.71	17.88	46.97	10.74	125.3	800-624-6782	Y

Category: Target Date 2000-2020 (con't)

Fund Name	Ticker Symbol	RATINGS: Overall Rating	RATINGS: Reward Rating	RATINGS: Risk Rating	RATINGS: Recent Up/ Downgrade	TOTAL RETURNS & PERFORMANCE: 3-Month Total Return	6-Month Total Return	1-Year Total Return	3-Year Total Return	5-Year Total Return	NAV	ASSETS: Total Assets (MIL)	NEW INVESTORS: Telephone	Open to New Investors
MainStay Retirement 2020 Fund Class R3	MYRZX	B-	C+	B	Up	3.22	6.37	13.62	17.14	45.36	10.88	125.3	800-624-6782	Y
MainStay Retirement 2020 Fund Investor Class	MYRYX	B-	C+	B	Up	3.18	6.47	13.74	17.95	47.09	10.7	125.3	800-624-6782	Y
Manning & Napier Target 2015 Series Class I	MTJIX	B-	C	B	Up	1.23	3.75	10.69	9.70	29.73	11.2	4.1	585-325-6880	Y
Manning & Napier Target 2015 Series Class K	MTJKX	B-	C	B	Up	1.18	3.52	10.34	8.78	27.99	11.16	4.1	585-325-6880	Y
Manning & Napier Target 2015 Series Class R	MTJRX	B-	C	B	Up	1.13	3.44	10.06	7.94	26.59	11.32	4.1	585-325-6880	Y
Manning & Napier Target 2015 Series R6	MTJZX	B-	C	B		1.17	3.69	10.63	9.64	29.66	11.19	4.1	585-325-6880	Y
Manning & Napier Target 2020 Series Class I	MTNIX	B-	C+	B	Up	1.26	4.03	12.14	10.80	34.08	9.46	114.9	585-325-6880	Y
Manning & Napier Target 2020 Series Class K	MTNKX	B-	C	B	Up	1.24	3.91	11.89	10.10	32.40	9.43	114.9	585-325-6880	Y
Manning & Napier Target 2020 Series Class R	MTNRX	B-	C	B	Up	1.29	3.88	11.69	9.26	30.91	9.31	114.9	585-325-6880	Y
Manning & Napier Target 2020 Series Fund R6	MTNZX	B-	C+	B		1.40	4.18	12.29	10.96	34.27	9.47	114.9	585-325-6880	Y
Manning & Napier Target Income Series Class I	MTDIX	B-	C	B+	Up	1.17	3.37	8.91	10.09	24.51	9.94	102.6	585-325-6880	Y
Manning & Napier Target Income Series Class K	MTDKX	B-	C	B	Up	1.16	3.26	8.58	9.33	22.96	9.91	102.6	585-325-6880	Y
Manning & Napier Target Income Series Class R	MTDRX	B-	C	B	Up	1.14	3.16	8.32	8.43	21.41	9.79	102.6	585-325-6880	Y
Manning & Napier Target Income Series Fund R6	MTDZX	B-	C	B+		1.21	3.41	8.94	10.13	24.55	9.94	102.6	585-325-6880	Y
MassMutual RetireSMART 2010 Fund Administrative Class	MRXYX	B-	C+	B	Up	2.30	4.85	10.35	13.44	31.12	12.41	64.7		Y
MassMutual RetireSMART 2010 Fund Class A	MRXAX	B-	C+	B	Up	2.28	4.77	10.21	12.71	29.52	12.34	64.7		Y
MassMutual RetireSMART 2010 Fund Class I	MRXUX	B-	C+	B	Up	2.43	5.08	10.83	14.60	32.84	12.31	64.7		Y
MassMutual RetireSMART 2010 Fund Class R3	MRXNX	B-	C+	B+	Up	2.20	4.64	9.98	12.09	28.24	12.1	64.7		Y
MassMutual RetireSMART 2010 Fund Class R4	MRXZX	B-	C+	B	Up	2.25	4.84	10.23	13.03	30.28	12.23	64.7		Y
MassMutual RetireSMART 2010 Fund Class R5	MRXTX	B-	C+	B	Up	2.34	4.97	10.57	14.21	32.27	12.4	64.7		Y
MassMutual RetireSMART 2010 Fund Service Class	MRXSX	B-	C+	B+	Up	2.32	4.94	10.53	13.84	31.99	12.45	64.7		Y
MassMutual RetireSMART 2015 Fund Administrative Class	MMJYX	B-	C+	B+	Up	2.53	5.31	11.25	14.54	36.96	11.9	81.0		Y
MassMutual RetireSMART 2015 Fund Class A	MMJAX	B-	C+	B+	Up	2.41	5.12	10.89	13.68	35.15	11.83	81.0		Y
MassMutual RetireSMART 2015 Fund Class I	MMJUX	B-	C+	B	Up	2.60	5.46	11.49	15.59	38.58	11.92	81.0		Y
MassMutual RetireSMART 2015 Fund Class R3	MMJNX	B-	C+	B	Up	2.45	5.18	10.79	13.25	34.28	11.78	81.0		Y
MassMutual RetireSMART 2015 Fund Class R4	MMJZX	B-	C+	B	Up	2.56	5.28	11.09	14.07	35.88	11.78	81.0		Y
MassMutual RetireSMART 2015 Fund Class R5	MMJTX	B-	C+	B	Up	2.59	5.44	11.47	15.29	38.21	11.93	81.0		Y
MassMutual RetireSMART 2015 Fund Service Class	MMJSX	B-	C+	B	Up	2.64	5.41	11.43	15.03	37.71	11.95	81.0		Y
MassMutual RetireSMART 2020 Fund Administrative Class	MRTYX	B-	C+	B	Down	2.96	6.23	13.44	16.93	44.75	13	474.6		Y
MassMutual RetireSMART 2020 Fund Class A	MRTAX	B-	C+	B	Down	3.00	6.21	13.27	16.19	42.84	12.95	474.6		Y
MassMutual RetireSMART 2020 Fund Class I	MRTDX	B-	C+	B	Down	3.14	6.50	13.81	18.10	46.69	12.99	474.6		Y
MassMutual RetireSMART 2020 Fund Class R3	MRTNX	B-	C+	B	Down	2.93	6.05	13.01	15.55	41.40	12.59	474.6		Y
MassMutual RetireSMART 2020 Fund Class R4	MRTHX	B-	C+	B	Down	3.00	6.25	13.40	16.54	43.73	12.77	474.6		Y
MassMutual RetireSMART 2020 Fund Class R5	MRTBX	B-	C+	B	Down	3.14	6.42	13.74	17.78	46.17	12.98	474.6		Y
MassMutual RetireSMART 2020 Fund Service Class	MRTSX	B-	C+	B	Down	3.05	6.31	13.60	17.34	45.50	13.03	474.6		Y
MassMutual RetireSMART In Retmnt Fund Admin Cls	MDRYX	B-	C	B+	Up	1.99	4.25	9.07	11.84	24.82	11.6	83.7		Y
MassMutual RetireSMART In Retirement Fund Class A	MRDAX	B-	C	B+	Up	1.87	4.04	8.79	11.01	23.00	11.52	83.7		Y
MassMutual RetireSMART In Retirement Fund Class I	MDRVX	B-	C+	B	Up	1.97	4.32	9.36	12.74	26.15	11.55	83.7		Y
MassMutual RetireSMART In Retirement Fund Class R3	MDRNX	B-	C	B+	Up	1.82	4.03	8.65	10.56	22.02	11.36	83.7		Y
MassMutual RetireSMART In Retirement Fund Class R4	MDRZX	B-	C	B+	Up	1.94	4.14	9.03	11.45	23.74	11.44	83.7		Y
MassMutual RetireSMART In Retirement Fund Class R5	MDRTX	B-	C+	B+	Up	1.96	4.31	9.24	12.49	25.64	11.57	83.7		Y
MassMutual RetireSMART In Retirement Fund Service Class	MDRSX	B-	C+	B+	Up	2.02	4.28	9.30	12.18	25.35	11.6	83.7		Y
MFS® Lifetime 2020 Fund Class A	MFLAX	B	C+	A-	Up	2.11	4.29	9.65	15.17	34.84	13.09	416.5	877-960-6077	Y
MFS® Lifetime 2020 Fund Class B	MFLBX	B	C+	A-	Up	1.92	3.88	8.82	12.69	29.90	13.03	416.5	877-960-6077	Y
MFS® Lifetime 2020 Fund Class C	MFLCX	B	C+	A-	Up	1.96	3.87	8.88	12.68	29.88	12.85	416.5	877-960-6077	Y
MFS® Lifetime 2020 Fund Class I	MFLIX	B	C+	A-	Up	2.14	4.39	9.97	16.13	36.61	13.17	416.5	877-960-6077	Y
MFS® Lifetime 2020 Fund Class R1	MFLEX	B	C+	A-	Up	1.91	3.86	8.88	12.60	29.87	13.05	416.5	877-960-6077	Y
MFS® Lifetime 2020 Fund Class R2	MFLGX	B	C+	A-	Up	2.03	4.15	9.37	14.36	33.23	13	416.5	877-960-6077	Y
MFS® Lifetime 2020 Fund Class R3	MFLHX	B	C+	A-	Up	2.15	4.33	9.69	15.28	34.95	13.1	416.5	877-960-6077	Y
MFS® Lifetime 2020 Fund Class R4	MFLJX	B	C+	A-	Up	2.18	4.43	10.02	16.10	36.59	13.17	416.5	877-960-6077	Y
MFS® Lifetime 2020 Fund Class R6	MFLKX	B	C+	A-	Up	2.20	4.44	10.03	16.34	36.86	13.15	416.5	877-960-6077	Y
MFS® Lifetime Income Fund Class 529A	MLLQX	B	C	A-	Up	0.90	2.71	7.06	11.36	22.37	10.19	628.2	877-960-6077	Y

Category: Target Date 2000-2020 (con't)

Fund Name	Ticker Symbol	RATINGS: Overall Rating	Reward Rating	Risk Rating	Recent Up/ Downgrade	TOTAL RETURNS & PERFORMANCE: 3-Month Total Return	6-Month Total Return	1-Year Total Return	3-Year Total Return	5-Year Total Return	ASSETS: NAV	Total Assets (MIL)	NEW INVESTORS: Telephone	Open to New Investors
MFS® Lifetime Income Fund Class 529B	MLLRX	B-	C	A-	Up	0.78	2.39	6.33	8.96	17.95	10.19	628.2	877-960-6077	Y
MFS® Lifetime Income Fund Class 529C	MLLSX	B-	C	A-	Up	0.68	2.29	6.23	8.86	17.84	10.18	628.2	877-960-6077	Y
MFS® Lifetime Income Fund Class A	MLLAX	B	C	A-	Up	1.17	2.97	7.40	11.83	22.88	12.41	628.2	877-960-6077	Y
MFS® Lifetime Income Fund Class B	MLLBX	B-	C	A-	Up	0.99	2.59	6.52	9.35	18.38	12.41	628.2	877-960-6077	Y
MFS® Lifetime Income Fund Class C	MLLCX	B-	C	A-	Up	0.91	2.51	6.53	9.27	18.29	12.4	628.2	877-960-6077	Y
MFS® Lifetime Income Fund Class I	MLLIX	B	C+	A-	Up	1.15	3.01	7.58	12.66	24.41	12.41	628.2	877-960-6077	Y
MFS® Lifetime Income Fund Class R1	MLLEX	B-	C	A-	Up	0.90	2.59	6.52	9.35	18.37	12.42	628.2	877-960-6077	Y
MFS® Lifetime Income Fund Class R2	MLLGX	B	C	A-	Up	1.03	2.76	7.05	10.99	21.25	12.41	628.2	877-960-6077	Y
MFS® Lifetime Income Fund Class R3	MLLHX	B	C	A-	Up	1.17	2.97	7.31	11.82	22.88	12.41	628.2	877-960-6077	Y
MFS® Lifetime Income Fund Class R4	MLLJX	B	C+	A-	Up	1.15	3.09	7.58	12.66	24.41	12.41	628.2	877-960-6077	Y
MFS® Lifetime Income Fund Class R6	MLLKX	B	C+	A-	Up	1.25	3.14	7.75	13.16	24.97	12.45	628.2	877-960-6077	Y
Nationwide Destination 2010 Fund Class A	NWDAX	B-	C+	B	Up	2.10	4.17	9.08	14.20	29.50	8.38	21.8	800-848-0920	Y
Nationwide Destination 2010 Fund Class C	NWDCX	B-	C	B	Up	1.97	3.89	8.36	12.00	25.62	8.31	21.8	800-848-0920	Y
Nationwide Destination 2010 Fund Class R	NWDBX	B-	C+	B	Up	2.16	4.04	8.83	13.26	27.79	8.36	21.8	800-848-0920	Y
Nationwide Destination 2010 Fund Class R6	NWDIX	B-	C+	B	Up	2.35	4.56	9.75	15.97	32.78	8.4	21.8	800-848-0920	Y
Nationwide Destination 2010 Fund Institutional Service Cls	NWDSX	B-	C+	B	Up	2.35	4.43	9.72	15.55	32.32	8.39	21.8	800-848-0920	Y
Nationwide Destination 2015 Fund Class A	NWEAX	B-	C+	B	Up	2.66	5.04	10.77	16.27	35.10	8.59	90.1	800-848-0920	Y
Nationwide Destination 2015 Fund Class C	NWECX	B-	C+	B	Up	2.57	4.82	10.26	14.31	31.38	8.54	90.1	800-848-0920	Y
Nationwide Destination 2015 Fund Class R	NWEBX	B-	C+	B	Up	2.51	4.95	10.41	15.20	33.05	8.55	90.1	800-848-0920	Y
Nationwide Destination 2015 Fund Class R6	NWEIX	B-	C+	B	Up	2.82	5.45	11.44	17.93	38.28	8.62	90.1	800-848-0920	Y
Nationwide Destination 2015 Fund Institutional Service Cls	NWESX	B-	C+	B	Up	2.75	5.20	11.05	17.05	36.61	8.6	90.1	800-848-0920	Y
Nationwide Destination 2020 Fund Class A	NWAFX	B-	C+	B	Up	3.18	6.02	12.38	18.09	41.27	9.46	255.8	800-848-0920	Y
Nationwide Destination 2020 Fund Class C	NWFCX	B-	C+	B	Up	3.05	5.77	11.75	15.80	37.00	9.33	255.8	800-848-0920	Y
Nationwide Destination 2020 Fund Class R	NWFTX	B-	C+	B	Up	3.11	5.88	12.09	16.93	39.08	9.43	255.8	800-848-0920	Y
Nationwide Destination 2020 Fund Class R6	NWFIX	B-	C+	B	Up	3.28	6.34	12.95	19.72	44.44	9.52	255.8	800-848-0920	Y
Nationwide Destination 2020 Fund Institutional Service Cls	NWFSX	B-	C+	B	Up	3.23	6.23	12.72	18.77	42.68	9.48	255.8	800-848-0920	Y
PIMCO RealPath Blend 2020 Fund Administrative Class	PBZDX	B-	C	B	Up	3.43	6.64	13.49	19.24		11.1	11.7	866-746-2602	Y
PIMCO RealPath Blend 2020 Fund Class A	PBZAX	B-	C	B	Up	3.41	6.58	13.21	18.50		11.1	11.7	866-746-2602	Y
PIMCO RealPath Blend 2020 Fund Institutional Class	PBZNX	B-	C	B	Up	3.53	6.80	13.79	20.23		11.11	11.7	866-746-2602	Y
PIMCO RealPath Blend Income Fund Administrative Class	PBRDX	B-	C	B	Up	2.96	6.02	12.38	18.55		11.04	8.0	866-746-2602	Y
PIMCO RealPath Blend Income Fund Class A	PBRAX	B-	C	B	Up	2.89	5.87	12.01	17.64		11	8.0	866-746-2602	Y
PIMCO RealPath Blend Income Fund Institutional Class	PBRNX	B-	C	B	Up	3.16	6.25	12.74	19.48		11.04	8.0	866-746-2602	Y
PIMCO RealPath™ 2020 Fund Administrative Class	PFNAX	B-	C+	B	Up	3.22	6.21	12.91	15.73	23.52	8.37	30.4	866-746-2602	Y
PIMCO RealPath™ 2020 Fund Class A	PTYAX	B-	C+	B	Down	3.11	6.04	12.70	14.85	22.06	8.13	30.4	866-746-2602	Y
PIMCO RealPath™ 2020 Fund Institutional Class	PRWIX	B-	C+	B	Up	3.23	6.36	13.06	16.44	24.92	8.15	30.4	866-746-2602	Y
PIMCO RealPath™ Income Fund Administrative Class	PRNAX	B-	C+	B	Down	2.92	5.89	12.22	16.15	22.50	8.24	31.5	866-746-2602	Y
PIMCO RealPath™ Income Fund Institutional Class	PRIEX	B-	C+	B	Down	3.08	6.00	12.43	17.11	24.14	8.23	31.5	866-746-2602	Y
Principal LifeTime 2010 Fund Class A	PENAX	B	C+	A-	Up	2.36	5.07	10.87	14.37	33.36	13.64	1,039	800-222-5852	Y
Principal LifeTime 2010 Fund Class J	PTAJX	B-	C+	B	Up	2.41	5.15	11.09	14.91	34.20	13.49	1,039	800-222-5852	Y
Principal LifeTime 2010 Fund Institutional Class	PTTIX	B-	C+	B	Up	2.42	5.30	11.23	15.55	35.88	13.53	1,039	800-222-5852	Y
Principal LifeTime 2010 Fund R-1 Class	PVASX	B-	C+	B+	Up	2.16	4.74	10.31	12.60	29.98	13.54	1,039	800-222-5852	Y
Principal LifeTime 2010 Fund R-2 Class	PTANX	B-	C+	B	Up	2.23	4.89	10.48	13.03	30.88	13.54	1,039	800-222-5852	Y
Principal LifeTime 2010 Fund R-3 Class	PTAMX	B	C+	A-	Up	2.28	5.03	10.65	13.70	32.12	13.46	1,039	800-222-5852	Y
Principal LifeTime 2010 Fund R-4 Class	PTASX	B	C+	A-	Up	2.31	5.06	10.83	14.33	33.35	13.48	1,039	800-222-5852	Y
Principal LifeTime 2010 Fund R-5 Class	PTAPX	B-	C+	B	Up	2.38	5.12	10.98	14.75	34.15	13.49	1,039	800-222-5852	Y
Principal LifeTime 2015 Fund Institutional Class	LTINX	B-	C+	B	Up	2.80	6.11	13.19	17.68	41.92	10.41	641.5	800-222-5852	Y
Principal LifeTime 2015 Fund R-1 Class	LTSGX	B-	C+	B	Up	2.59	5.68	12.21	14.53	35.89	10.19	641.5	800-222-5852	Y
Principal LifeTime 2015 Fund R-2 Class	LTASX	B	C+	B+	Up	2.68	5.75	12.25	15.01	36.70	10.25	641.5	800-222-5852	Y
Principal LifeTime 2015 Fund R-3 Class	LTAPX	B-	C+	B	Up	2.67	5.85	12.50	15.62	37.95	10.2	641.5	800-222-5852	Y
Principal LifeTime 2015 Fund R-4 Class	LTSLX	B-	C+	B	Up	2.76	6.02	12.74	16.33	39.39	10.28	641.5	800-222-5852	Y
Principal LifeTime 2015 Fund R-5 Class	LTPFX	B-	C+	B	Up	2.84	6.10	12.93	16.77	40.23	10.29	641.5	800-222-5852	Y
Principal LifeTime 2020 Fund Class A	PTBAX	B	C+	B+	Up	3.24	6.90	14.61	18.39	46.02	14.33	5,497	800-222-5852	Y

Category: Target Date 2000-2020 (con't)

Fund Name	Ticker Symbol	RATINGS: Overall Rating	Reward Rating	Risk Rating	Recent Up/ Downgrade	TOTAL RETURNS & PERFORMANCE: 3-Month Total Return	6-Month Total Return	1-Year Total Return	3-Year Total Return	5-Year Total Return	ASSETS: NAV	Total Assets (MIL)	NEW INVESTORS: Telephone	Open to New Investors
Principal LifeTime 2020 Fund Class J	PLFJX	B	C+	B+	Up	3.21	6.98	14.79	18.92	46.88	14.15	5,497	800-222-5852	Y
Principal LifeTime 2020 Fund Institutional Class	PLWIX	B-	C+	B	Up	3.28	7.10	14.96	19.68	48.75	14.22	5,497	800-222-5852	Y
Principal LifeTime 2020 Fund R-1 Class	PWASX	B-	C+	B	Up	3.07	6.55	13.99	16.61	42.36	14.17	5,497	800-222-5852	Y
Principal LifeTime 2020 Fund R-2 Class	PTBNX	B-	C+	B	Up	3.13	6.69	14.15	17.09	43.31	14.15	5,497	800-222-5852	Y
Principal LifeTime 2020 Fund R-3 Class	PTBMX	B	C+	B+	Up	3.14	6.78	14.35	17.67	44.60	14.11	5,497	800-222-5852	Y
Principal LifeTime 2020 Fund R-4 Class	PTBSX	B-	C+	B	Up	3.23	6.86	14.50	18.33	45.93	14.13	5,497	800-222-5852	Y
Principal LifeTime 2020 Fund R-5 Class	PTBPX	B-	C+	B	Up	3.23	6.93	14.64	18.74	46.71	14.16	5,497	800-222-5852	Y
Principal LifeTime Hybrid 2015 Fund Institutional Class	PHTMX	B-	C	B	Up	2.61	5.63	11.77	17.26		10.89	34.2	800-222-5852	Y
Principal LifeTime Hybrid 2015 Fund R-6	PLRRX	B-	C	B	Up	2.61	5.72	11.86	17.35		10.91	34.2	800-222-5852	Y
Principal LifeTime Hybrid 2020 Fund Institutional Class	PHTTX	B-	C	B	Up	3.07	6.62	13.51	19.73		11.15	125.4	800-222-5852	Y
Principal LifeTime Hybrid 2020 Fund R-6	PLTTX	B-	C	B	Up	2.99	6.55	13.53	19.76		11.15	125.4	800-222-5852	Y
Principal LifeTime Strategic Income Fund Class A	PALTX	B	C	A-	Up	1.67	3.86	8.27	11.55	22.56	12.47	570.2	800-222-5852	Y
Principal LifeTime Strategic Income Fund Class J	PLSJX	B	C	A-	Up	1.76	3.99	8.55	11.99	23.19	12.3	570.2	800-222-5852	Y
Principal LifeTime Strategic Income Fund Institutional Cls	PLSIX	B	C+	A-	Up	1.79	4.09	8.72	12.73	24.89	12.35	570.2	800-222-5852	Y
Principal LifeTime Strategic Income Fund R-1 Class	PLAIX	B-	C	A-	Up	1.63	3.67	7.83	9.91	19.61	12.42	570.2	800-222-5852	Y
Principal LifeTime Strategic Income Fund R-2 Class	PLSNX	B-	C	A-	Up	1.58	3.70	7.96	10.28	20.34	12.41	570.2	800-222-5852	Y
Principal LifeTime Strategic Income Fund R-3 Class	PLSMX	B	C	A-	Up	1.61	3.76	8.15	10.88	21.38	12.27	570.2	800-222-5852	Y
Principal LifeTime Strategic Income Fund R-4 Class	PLSSX	B	C	A-	Up	1.79	3.93	8.32	11.57	22.61	12.29	570.2	800-222-5852	Y
Principal LifeTime Strategic Income Fund R-5 Class	PLSPX	B	C	A-	Up	1.74	3.95	8.49	11.96	23.34	12.36	570.2	800-222-5852	Y
Putnam Retirement Income Fund Lifestyle 1 Class A	PRMAX	B-	C	B	Up	1.59	3.24	6.80	8.73	20.30	17.74	95.3	617-292-1000	Y
Putnam Retirement Income Fund Lifestyle 1 Class M	PRMMX	B-	C	B	Up	1.52	3.11	6.47	7.89	18.75	17.78	95.3	617-292-1000	Y
Putnam Retirement Income Fund Lifestyle 1 Class R6	PREWX	B-	C	B	Up	1.68	3.41	7.12	9.65	21.97	17.8	95.3	617-292-1000	Y
Putnam Retirement Income Fund Lifestyle 1 Class Y	PRMYX	B-	C	B	Up	1.65	3.36	7.04	9.50	21.80	17.8	95.3	617-292-1000	Y
Putnam RetirementReady 2020 Fund Class A	PRRMX	B-	C	B	Up	2.04	4.15	8.42	11.20	31.56	19.64	204.8	617-292-1000	Y
Putnam RetirementReady 2020 Fund Class B	US7468596850	B-	C	B	Up	1.90	3.82	7.66	8.61	26.77		204.8	617-292-1000	Y
Putnam RetirementReady 2020 Fund Class C	US7468596777	B-	C	B	Up	1.90	3.82	7.62	8.59	26.78		204.8	617-292-1000	Y
Putnam RetirementReady 2020 Fund Class M	US7468596694	B-	C	B	Up	1.96	3.95	7.94	9.42	28.38		204.8	617-292-1000	Y
Putnam RetirementReady 2020 Fund Class R	US7468596512	B-	C	B	Up	2.00	4.08	8.20	10.26	30.02		204.8	617-292-1000	Y
Putnam RetirementReady 2020 Fund Class R6	PMRGX	B-	C+	B	Up	2.10	4.31	8.72	12.11	33.31	22.11	204.8	617-292-1000	Y
Putnam RetirementReady 2020 Fund Class Y	PRRNX	B-	C+	B	Up	2.10	4.31	8.68	12.04	33.23	22.1	204.8	617-292-1000	Y
Schwab Target 2010 Fund	SWBRX	B	C+	A-	Up	2.21	4.65	10.24	14.95	33.90	13.33	59.3	877-824-5615	Y
Schwab Target 2015 Fund	SWGRX	B	C+	A-	Up	2.34	4.85	10.75	15.34	37.76	11.74	100.9	877-824-5615	Y
Schwab Target 2020 Fund	SWCRX	B-	C+	B	Up	2.81	5.86	13.04	18.00	46.94	14.19	584.7	877-824-5615	Y
State Farm LifePath 2020 Fund Class A	NLWAX	B-	C+	B+	Up	2.77	5.38	11.42	15.08	33.36	14.97	2,168		Y
State Farm LifePath 2020 Fund Class B	NLWBX	B-	C+	B+	Up	2.75	5.37	11.21	13.32	29.37	14.9	2,168		Y
State Farm LifePath 2020 Fund Class Institutional	SAWIX	B	C+	B+	Up	2.77	5.37	11.47	15.77	34.71	15	2,168		Y
State Farm LifePath 2020 Fund Class R1	RAWOX	B-	C+	B+	Up	2.74	5.29	11.28	14.21	31.43	14.89	2,168		Y
State Farm LifePath 2020 Fund Class R2	RAWTX	B-	C+	B+	Up	2.78	5.33	11.32	14.80	32.59	14.89	2,168		Y
State Farm LifePath 2020 Fund Class R3	RAWHX	B	C+	B+	Up	2.71	5.31	11.42	15.51	34.22	14.97	2,168		Y
State Farm LifePath 2020 Fund Legacy Class B	SAWBX	B-	C+	B+	Up	2.77	5.37	11.38	14.09	31.10	15.06	2,168		Y
State Farm LifePath 2020 Fund Premier Shares	SAWAX	B-	C+	B+	Up	2.84	5.46	11.53	15.38	33.56	14.89	2,168		Y
State Farm LifePath Retirement Fund Class A	NILAX	B	C+	B+	Up	2.41	4.78	9.94	13.46	26.39	13.15	1,245		Y
State Farm LifePath Retirement Fund Class B	NILBX	B-	C	B+	Up	2.39	4.74	9.71	11.59	23.17	13.23	1,245		Y
State Farm LifePath Retirement Fund Class Institutional	SLRIX	B	C+	A-	Up	2.43	4.74	10.02	14.07	27.76	13.46	1,245		Y
State Farm LifePath Retirement Fund Class R1	RLROX	B-	C+	B+	Up	2.38	4.71	9.84	12.56	24.62	13.2	1,245		Y
State Farm LifePath Retirement Fund Class R2	RLRTX	B-	C+	B+	Up	2.40	4.69	9.92	13.10	25.68	13.5	1,245		Y
State Farm LifePath Retirement Fund Class R3	RLRHX	B	C+	B+	Up	2.41	4.71	9.96	13.84	27.28	13.44	1,245		Y
State Farm LifePath Retirement Fund Legacy Class B	SLRBX	B-	C+	B+	Up	2.41	4.79	9.93	12.42	24.28	13.55	1,245		Y
State Farm LifePath Retirement Fund Premier Shares	SLRAX	B	C+	B+	Up	2.38	4.80	10.06	13.58	26.47	13.45	1,245		Y
State Street Target Retirement 2015 Fund Class I	SSBFX	B-	C	B	Up	2.37	4.98	10.39	15.73		10.85	149.7	617-664-7338	Y
T. Rowe Price Retirement 2005 Fund	TRRFX	B	C+	A-	Up	2.16	4.64	10.66	16.86	35.60	13.65	1,747	410-345-2000	Y
T. Rowe Price Retirement 2005 Fund Advisor Class	PARGX	B	C+	A-	Up	2.03	4.51	10.38	15.95	33.88	13.6	1,747	410-345-2000	Y

Category: Target Date 2000-2020 (con't)

Fund Name	Ticker Symbol	RATINGS: Overall Rating	Reward Rating	Risk Rating	Recent Up/ Downgrade	TOTAL RETURNS & PERFORMANCE: 3-Month Total Return	6-Month Total Return	1-Year Total Return	3-Year Total Return	5-Year Total Return	ASSETS: NAV	Total Assets (MIL)	NEW INVESTORS: Telephone	Open to New Investors
T. Rowe Price Retirement 2005 Fund Class R	RRTLX	B	C+	B+	Up	1.94	4.34	10.00	15.10	32.17	13.68	1,747	410-345-2000	Y
T. Rowe Price Retirement 2010 Fund	TRRAX	B	C+	A-	Up	2.34	5.11	11.66	18.22	40.58	18.28	5,233	410-345-2000	Y
T. Rowe Price Retirement 2010 Fund Advisor Class	PARAX	B	C+	A-	Up	2.30	4.98	11.35	17.40	38.78	18.2	5,233	410-345-2000	Y
T. Rowe Price Retirement 2010 Fund Class R	RRTAX	B	C+	B+	Up	2.20	4.84	11.06	16.45	37.03	18.1	5,233	410-345-2000	Y
T. Rowe Price Retirement 2015 Fund	TRRGX	B-	C+	B	Up	2.69	5.73	13.34	20.42	48.14	14.98	8,885	410-345-2000	Y
T. Rowe Price Retirement 2015 Fund Advisor Class	PARHX	B	C+	A-	Up	2.64	5.63	13.10	19.52	46.32	14.94	8,885	410-345-2000	Y
T. Rowe Price Retirement 2015 Fund Class R	RRTMX	B-	C+	B	Up	2.61	5.55	12.85	18.72	44.52	14.81	8,885	410-345-2000	Y
T. Rowe Price Retirement 2020 Fund	TRRBX	B-	C+	B	Down	3.10	6.64	15.73	23.26	56.19	22.54	25,234	410-345-2000	Y
T. Rowe Price Retirement 2020 Fund Advisor Class	PARBX	B	C+	B+	Up	3.09	6.56	15.49	22.40	54.25	22.39	25,234	410-345-2000	Y
T. Rowe Price Retirement 2020 Fund Class R	RRTBX	B	C+	B+	Up	2.98	6.39	15.17	21.46	52.29	22.19	25,234	410-345-2000	Y
T. Rowe Price Target 2005 Fund	TRARX	B	C+	A-	Up	1.86	4.30	9.84	15.91		11.44	33.4	410-345-2000	Y
T. Rowe Price Target 2005 Fund Advisor Class	PANRX	B	C+	A-	Up	1.86	4.21	9.65	15.07		11.45	33.4	410-345-2000	Y
T. Rowe Price Target 2005 Fund I Class	TFRRX	B	C+	A-	Up	2.04	4.48	10.03	16.12		11.45	33.4	410-345-2000	Y
T. Rowe Price Target 2010 Fund	TRROX	B-	C+	B	Up	2.02	4.53	10.24	16.29		11.52	66.9	410-345-2000	Y
T. Rowe Price Target 2010 Fund Advisor Class	PAERX	B-	C+	B	Up	1.94	4.36	9.88	15.48		11.51	66.9	410-345-2000	Y
T. Rowe Price Target 2010 Fund I Class	TORFX	B	C+	A-	Up	2.10	4.52	10.33	16.47		11.53	66.9	410-345-2000	Y
T. Rowe Price Target 2015 Fund	TRRTX	B	C+	A-	Up	2.20	4.76	10.99	17.32		11.71	193.7	410-345-2000	Y
T. Rowe Price Target 2015 Fund Advisor Class	PAHRX	B	C+	A-	Up	2.03	4.60	10.65	16.32		11.69	193.7	410-345-2000	Y
T. Rowe Price Target 2015 Fund I Class	TTRTX	B-	C+	B	Up	2.20	4.85	11.10	17.43		11.7	193.7	410-345-2000	Y
T. Rowe Price Target 2020 Fund	TRRUX	B-	C+	B	Up	2.48	5.35	12.63	19.15		12.02	268.8	410-345-2000	Y
T. Rowe Price Target 2020 Fund Advisor Class	PAIRX	B	C+	A-	Up	2.41	5.21	12.30	18.28		11.99	268.8	410-345-2000	Y
T. Rowe Price Target 2020 Fund I Class	TTURX	B	C+	A-	Up	2.48	5.44	12.81	19.45		12.03	268.8	410-345-2000	Y
TIAA-CREF Lifecycle 2010 Fund Advisor Class	TCLHX	B-	C+	B	Up	2.67	5.88	12.74	19.52	40.82	11.62	1,260	877-518-9161	Y
TIAA-CREF Lifecycle 2010 Fund Institutional Class	TCTIX	B	C+	A-	Up	2.69	5.99	12.76	19.88	41.89	11.62	1,260	877-518-9161	Y
TIAA-CREF Lifecycle 2010 Fund Premier Class	TCTPX	B-	C+	B	Up	2.63	5.85	12.52	19.19	40.80	11.59	1,260	877-518-9161	Y
TIAA-CREF Lifecycle 2010 Fund Retirement Class	TCLEX	B-	C+	B	Up	2.55	5.76	12.38	18.90	40.10	13.65	1,260	877-518-9161	Y
TIAA-CREF Lifecycle 2015 Fund Advisor Class	TCNHX	B-	C+	B	Up	2.91	6.41	13.82	20.90	45.28	10.01	1,970	877-518-9161	Y
TIAA-CREF Lifecycle 2015 Fund Institutional Class	TCNIX	B-	C+	B	Up	2.94	6.44	13.85	21.29	46.44	10.01	1,970	877-518-9161	Y
TIAA-CREF Lifecycle 2015 Fund Premier Class	TCFPX	B-	C+	B	Up	2.90	6.42	13.74	20.74	45.41	9.97	1,970	877-518-9161	Y
TIAA-CREF Lifecycle 2015 Fund Retirement Class	TCLIX	B-	C+	B	Up	2.87	6.35	13.64	20.41	44.68	12.33	1,970	877-518-9161	Y
TIAA-CREF Lifecycle 2020 Fund Advisor Class	TCWHX	B-	C+	B	Up	3.30	7.23	15.46	22.84	51.52	10.36	3,798	877-518-9161	Y
TIAA-CREF Lifecycle 2020 Fund Institutional Class	TCWIX	B-	C+	B	Up	3.30	7.23	15.58	23.31	52.81	10.37	3,798	877-518-9161	Y
TIAA-CREF Lifecycle 2020 Fund Premier Class	TCWPX	B-	C+	B	Up	3.26	7.10	15.34	22.71	51.56	10.34	3,798	877-518-9161	Y
TIAA-CREF Lifecycle 2020 Fund Retirement Class	TCLTX	B-	C+	B	Up	3.25	7.14	15.20	22.34	50.90	13.04	3,798	877-518-9161	Y
TIAA-CREF Lifecycle Index 2010 Fund Advisor Class	TLTHX	B-	C+	B	Up	2.60	5.12	11.13	17.07	39.22	15.06	346.9	877-518-9161	Y
TIAA-CREF Lifecycle Index 2010 Fund Institutional Class	TLTIX	B-	C+	B	Up	2.55	5.14	11.15	17.12	39.27	15.05	346.9	877-518-9161	Y
TIAA-CREF Lifecycle Index 2010 Fund Premier Class	TLTPX	B-	C+	B	Up	2.56	5.10	11.04	16.60	38.35	15.02	346.9	877-518-9161	Y
TIAA-CREF Lifecycle Index 2010 Fund Retirement Class	TLTRX	B-	C+	B	Up	2.47	5.01	10.82	16.21	37.55	14.94	346.9	877-518-9161	Y
TIAA-CREF Lifecycle Index 2015 Fund Advisor Class	TLFAX	B-	C+	B	Up	2.86	5.70	12.20	18.67	44.09	15.74	673.8	877-518-9161	Y
TIAA-CREF Lifecycle Index 2015 Fund Institutional Class	TLFIX	B-	C+	B	Up	2.81	5.65	12.22	18.63	44.05	15.73	673.8	877-518-9161	Y
TIAA-CREF Lifecycle Index 2015 Fund Premier Class	TLFPX	B	C+	A-	Up	2.83	5.62	12.06	18.14	42.97	15.68	673.8	877-518-9161	Y
TIAA-CREF Lifecycle Index 2015 Fund Retirement Class	TLGRX	B-	C+	B	Up	2.78	5.51	11.97	17.70	42.26	15.63	673.8	877-518-9161	Y
TIAA-CREF Lifecycle Index 2020 Fund Advisor Class	TLWHX	B-	C+	B	Up	3.20	6.32	13.59	20.39	50.21	16.6	1,468	877-518-9161	Y
TIAA-CREF Lifecycle Index 2020 Fund Institutional Class	TLWIX	B-	C+	B	Up	3.20	6.31	13.66	20.47	50.31	16.6	1,468	877-518-9161	Y
TIAA-CREF Lifecycle Index 2020 Fund Premier Class	TLWPX	B-	C+	B	Up	3.16	6.21	13.44	19.92	49.20	16.53	1,468	877-518-9161	Y
TIAA-CREF Lifecycle Index 2020 Fund Retirement Class	TLWRX	B-	C+	B	Up	3.12	6.19	13.36	19.63	48.46	16.48	1,468	877-518-9161	Y
TIAA-CREF Lifecycle Index Retmnt Income Fund Adv Cls	TLIHX	B-	C+	B	Up	2.38	4.87	10.49	16.11	34.82	14.25	174.8	877-518-9161	Y
TIAA-CREF Lifecycle Index Retmnt Income Fund Inst Cls	TRILX	B-	C+	B	Up	2.45	4.87	10.49	16.18	34.92	14.25	174.8	877-518-9161	Y
TIAA-CREF Lifecycle Index Retmnt Income Fund Premier Cls	TLIPX	B	C+	A-	Up	2.35	4.80	10.34	15.59	33.83	14.24	174.8	877-518-9161	Y
TIAA-CREF Lifecycle Index Retmnt Income Fund Retmnt Cls	TRCIX	B	C+	A-	Up	2.39	4.75	10.24	15.32	33.21	14.23	174.8	877-518-9161	Y
TIAA-CREF Lifecycle Retirement Income Fund Advisor Class	TLRHX	B-	C+	B	Up	2.54	5.65	12.08	18.77	37.54	11.7	520.0	877-518-9161	Y
TIAA-CREF Lifecycle Retmnt Income Fund Inst Cls	TLRIX	B-	C+	B	Up	2.54	5.66	12.09	18.84	37.62	11.7	520.0	877-518-9161	Y

Category: Target Date 2000-2020 (con't)

Fund Name	Ticker Symbol	RATINGS: Overall Rating	Reward Rating	Risk Rating	Recent Up/ Downgrade	TOTAL RETURNS & PERFORMANCE: 3-Month Total Return	6-Month Total Return	1-Year Total Return	3-Year Total Return	5-Year Total Return	ASSETS: NAV	Total Assets (MIL)	NEW INVESTORS: Telephone	Open to New Investors
TIAA-CREF Lifecycle Retirement Income Fund Premier Class	TPILX	B-	C+	B	Up	2.50	5.49	11.83	18.32	36.51	11.69	520.0	877-518-9161	Y
TIAA-CREF Lifecycle Retirement Income Fund Retail Class	TLRRX	B	C+	A-	Up	2.39	5.44	11.74	17.88	35.87	11.68	520.0	877-518-9161	Y
TIAA-CREF Lifecycle Retirement Income Fund Retirement Cls	TLIRX	B-	C+	B	Up	2.40	5.45	11.75	17.90	35.90	11.67	520.0	877-518-9161	Y
USAA Target Retirement 2020 Fund	URTNX	B-	C+	B	Up	2.82	5.57	12.70	17.85	34.51	12.86	613.5	800-531-8722	Y
USAA Target Retirement Income Fund	URINX	B-	C+	B	Up	1.94	3.93	8.65	13.02	24.19	11.69	348.2	800-531-8722	Y
Vanguard Target Retirement 2015 Fund Investor Shares	VTXVX	B	C+	A-	Up	2.72	5.40	11.50	17.36	42.83	15.33	17,413	877-662-7447	Y
Vanguard Target Retirement 2020 Fund Investor Shares	VTWNX	B-	C+	B	Up	3.36	6.61	14.08	20.66	51.63	31.38	32,239	877-662-7447	Y
Vanguard Target Retirement Income Fund Investor Shares	VTINX	B	C+	A-	Up	2.03	4.03	8.47	13.79	27.66	13.55	16,864	877-662-7447	Y
Voya Index Solution 2020 Portfolio Class ADV	IDXAX	B-	C+	B	Up	2.94	5.70	11.77	17.86	42.73	13.27	234.3	800-366-0066	Y
Voya Index Solution 2020 Portfolio Class I	IDXBX	B-	C+	B	Up	3.11	6.02	12.41	19.20	45.88	13.59	234.3	800-366-0066	Y
Voya Index Solution 2020 Portfolio Class S	IDXCX	B-	C+	B	Up	3.04	5.83	12.05	18.48	43.95	13.54	234.3	800-366-0066	Y
Voya Index Solution 2020 Portfolio Class S2	IDXDX	B-	C+	B	Up	2.98	5.76	11.92	17.95	43.20	13.46	234.3	800-366-0066	Y
Voya Index Solution 2020 Portfolio Class Z	VSZAX	B-	C+	B	Up	3.17	6.16	12.63	19.72	46.51	13.65	234.3	800-366-0066	Y
Voya Index Solution Income Portfolio Class ADV	ISKAX	B	C	A-	Up	2.17	4.29	8.69	12.04	28.25	10.34	477.3	800-366-0066	Y
Voya Index Solution Income Portfolio Class I	ISKIX	B	C+	A-	Up	2.41	4.53	9.36	13.70	31.55	10.62	477.3	800-366-0066	Y
Voya Index Solution Income Portfolio Class S	ISKSX	B	C+	A-	Up	2.23	4.39	9.05	12.86	29.77	10.51	477.3	800-366-0066	Y
Voya Index Solution Income Portfolio Class S2	IIIPX	B	C+	A-	Up	2.28	4.35	8.89	12.36	28.91	10.29	477.3	800-366-0066	Y
Voya Index Solution Income Portfolio Class Z	VSZJX	B	C+	A-	Up	2.39	4.61	9.53	14.22	32.14	10.67	477.3	800-366-0066	Y
Voya Solution 2020 Portfolio Class ADV	ISNAX	B-	C+	B	Up	2.95	5.81	12.43	18.87	44.13	13.23	31.1	800-366-0066	Y
Voya Solution 2020 Portfolio Class I	ISNBX	B-	C+	B	Up	3.12	6.06	13.01	20.57	47.99	13.51	31.1	800-366-0066	Y
Voya Solution 2020 Portfolio Class S	ISNCX	B-	C+	B	Up	3.06	5.98	12.77	19.75	46.15	13.46	31.1	800-366-0066	Y
Voya Solution 2020 Portfolio Class S2	ISNDX	B-	C+	B	Up	3.01	5.87	12.54	19.16	45.06	13.32	31.1	800-366-0066	Y
Voya Solution 2020 Portfolio Class T	ISNEX	B-	C+	B	Up	2.95	5.70	12.22	18.12	43.33	13.24	31.1	800-366-0066	Y
Voya Solution Income Portfolio Class ADV	ISWAX	B-	C+	B	Up	2.15	4.27	9.05	13.17	28.21	11.84	435.6	800-366-0066	Y
Voya Solution Income Portfolio Class I	ISWIX	B	C+	A-	Up	2.36	4.51	9.65	14.93	31.56	12.13	435.6	800-366-0066	Y
Voya Solution Income Portfolio Class S	ISWSX	B-	C+	B	Up	2.21	4.41	9.31	14.01	29.91	12.02	435.6	800-366-0066	Y
Voya Solution Income Portfolio Class S2	IJKBX	B	C+	A-	Up	2.26	4.38	9.22	13.56	28.97	11.72	435.6	800-366-0066	Y
Voya Solution Income Portfolio Class T	ISWTX	B	C	A-	Up	2.18	4.13	8.84	12.57	27.09	12.6	435.6	800-366-0066	Y
Voya Target In-Retirement Fund Class A	VTRVX	B-	C+	B	Up	2.50	4.56	9.22	13.65	30.86		3.7	800-366-0066	Y
Voya Target In-Retirement Fund Class I	ISOLX	B	C+	A-	Up	2.45	4.70	9.49	14.60	32.37	10.98	3.7	800-366-0066	Y
Voya Target In-Retirement Fund Class R6	VTRWX	B	C+	A-	Up	2.49	4.74	9.51	14.56	32.57		3.7	800-366-0066	Y
Voya Target Retirement 2020 Fund Class A	VFTRX	B-	C+	B	Up	3.19	6.04	12.27	17.17	42.84		5.2	800-366-0066	Y
Voya Target Retirement 2020 Fund Class I	IRSJX	B-	C+	B	Up	3.20	6.14	12.53	18.43	44.73	11.7	5.2	800-366-0066	Y
Voya Target Retirement 2020 Fund Class R6	VTRBX	B-	C+	B	Up	3.35	6.28	12.65	18.19	44.80		5.2	800-366-0066	Y
Wells Fargo Target 2010 Fund - Class A	STNRX	B-	C	B+	Up	1.91	3.36	6.41	7.41	13.56	10.91	164.2	800-222-8222	Y
Wells Fargo Target 2010 Fund - Class Admin	WFLGX	B-	C	B+	Up	1.89	3.41	6.50	7.73	14.31	11.05	164.2	800-222-8222	Y
Wells Fargo Target 2010 Fund - Class R	WFARX	B-	C	B+	Up	1.87	3.25	6.23	6.64	12.12	10.83	164.2	800-222-8222	Y
Wells Fargo Target 2010 Fund - Class R4	WFORX	B-	C	A-	Up	1.92	3.44	6.71	8.41	15.53	11.04	164.2	800-222-8222	Y
Wells Fargo Target 2010 Fund - Class R6	WFOAX	B-	C	A-	Up	1.98	3.58	6.94	8.97	16.42	11.03	164.2	800-222-8222	Y
Wells Fargo Target 2015 Fund - Class A	WFACX	B-	C	B+	Up	2.12	3.71	7.68	9.49	19.15	8.02	184.5	800-222-8222	Y
Wells Fargo Target 2015 Fund - Class Admin	WFFFX	B-	C	B+	Up	2.09	3.75	7.89	9.94	19.96	8.21	184.5	800-222-8222	Y
Wells Fargo Target 2015 Fund - Class R	WFBRX	B-	C	B+	Up	2.00	3.56	7.31	8.53	17.92	8.16	184.5	800-222-8222	Y
Wells Fargo Target 2015 Fund - Class R4	WFSRX	B-	C	A-	Up	2.21	3.89	8.01	10.46	21.18	8.08	184.5	800-222-8222	Y
Wells Fargo Target 2015 Fund - Class R6	WFSCX	B-	C	A-	Up	2.11	3.90	8.10	10.85	21.95	8.07	184.5	800-222-8222	Y
Wells Fargo Target 2020 Fund - Class A	STTRX	B-	C	B+	Up	2.57	4.53	9.64	12.07	26.77	12.74	959.0	800-222-8222	Y
Wells Fargo Target 2020 Fund - Class Admin	WFLPX	B-	C	B+	Up	2.58	4.57	9.69	12.35	27.55	12.99	959.0	800-222-8222	Y
Wells Fargo Target 2020 Fund - Class C	WFLAX	B-	C	B+	Up	2.41	4.18	8.88	9.56	22.16	12.51	959.0	800-222-8222	Y
Wells Fargo Target 2020 Fund - Class R	WFURX	B-	C	B+	Up	2.44	4.40	9.46	11.28	25.29	12.65	959.0	800-222-8222	Y
Wells Fargo Target 2020 Fund - Class R4	WFLRX	B	C+	A-	Up	2.65	4.70	10.01	13.10	28.99	13.08	959.0	800-222-8222	Y
Wells Fargo Target 2020 Fund - Class R6	WFOBX	B	C+	A-	Up	2.62	4.73	10.12	13.56	29.80	13.08	959.0	800-222-8222	Y
Wells Fargo Target Today Fund - Class A	STWRX	B-	C	B+	Up	1.70	3.11	5.98	6.82	10.85	9.14	145.3	800-222-8222	Y
Wells Fargo Target Today Fund - Class Admin	WFLOX	B-	C	A-	Up	1.68	3.11	6.02	7.10	11.51	9.37	145.3	800-222-8222	Y

Category: Target Date 2000-2020 (con't)

Fund Name	Ticker Symbol	Overall Rating	Reward Rating	Risk Rating	Recent Up/ Downgrade	3-Month Total Return	6-Month Total Return	1-Year Total Return	3-Year Total Return	5-Year Total Return	NAV	Total Assets (MIL)	Telephone	Open to New Investors
Wells Fargo Target Today Fund - Class R	WFRRX	B-	C	B+	Up	1.53	2.87	5.64	5.94	9.38	9.1	145.3	800-222-8222	Y
Wells Fargo Target Today Fund - Class R4	WOTRX	B-	C	A-	Up	1.76	2.92	5.91	7.47	12.36	9.37	145.3	800-222-8222	Y
Wells Fargo Target Today Fund - Class R6	WOTDX	B-	C	A-	Up	1.79	3.24	6.36	8.28	13.44	9.35	145.3	800-222-8222	Y

Category: Target Date 2021-2045

Fund Name	Ticker Symbol	Overall Rating	Reward Rating	Risk Rating	Recent Up/ Downgrade	3-Month Total Return	6-Month Total Return	1-Year Total Return	3-Year Total Return	5-Year Total Return	NAV	Total Assets (MIL)	Telephone	Open to New Investors
AB Multi-Manager Select 2025 Fund Advisor Class	TDGYX	B-	C+	B	Up	4.00	8.11	16.26	23.37		11.5	145.9	212-969-1000	Y
AB Multi-Manager Select 2025 Fund Class A	TDAGX	B-	C+	B	Up	3.95	7.97	15.90	22.35		11.49	145.9	212-969-1000	Y
AB Multi-Manager Select 2025 Fund Class I	TDIGX	B-	C+	B	Up	3.89	8.08	16.18	23.23		11.28	145.9	212-969-1000	Y
AB Multi-Manager Select 2025 Fund Class K	TDGKX	B-	C+	B	Up	3.90	7.91	15.89	22.37		11.25	145.9	212-969-1000	Y
AB Multi-Manager Select 2025 Fund Class R	TDGRX	B-	C+	B	Up	3.84	7.86	15.64	21.40		11.22	145.9	212-969-1000	Y
AB Multi-Manager Select 2025 Fund Class Z	TDGZX	B-	C+	B	Up	3.92	8.11	16.22	23.24		11.24	145.9	212-969-1000	Y
AB Multi-Manager Select 2030 Fund Advisor Class	TDYHX	B-	C+	B	Up	4.14	8.72	17.97	26.68		11.71	112.0	212-969-1000	Y
AB Multi-Manager Select 2030 Fund Class A	TDHAX	B-	C+	B	Up	4.18	8.59	17.73	25.68		11.7	112.0	212-969-1000	Y
AB Multi-Manager Select 2030 Fund Class C	TDHCX	B-	C+	B	Up	3.91	8.17	16.82	23.01		11.63	112.0	212-969-1000	Y
AB Multi-Manager Select 2030 Fund Class I	TDIHX	B-	C+	B	Up	4.12	8.70	18.02	26.68		11.48	112.0	212-969-1000	Y
AB Multi-Manager Select 2030 Fund Class K	TDHKX	B-	C+	B	Up	4.14	8.64	17.75	25.78		11.46	112.0	212-969-1000	Y
AB Multi-Manager Select 2030 Fund Class R	TDHRX	B-	C+	B	Up	4.10	8.41	17.40	24.82		11.44	112.0	212-969-1000	Y
AB Multi-Manager Select 2030 Fund Class Z	TDHZX	B-	C+	B	Up	4.22	8.71	18.04	26.74		11.46	112.0	212-969-1000	Y
AB Multi-Manager Select 2035 Fund Advisor Class	TDMYX	B-	C+	B	Up	4.57	9.64	20.14	29.03		12.02	103.7	212-969-1000	Y
AB Multi-Manager Select 2035 Fund Class A	TDMAX	B-	C+	B	Up	4.43	9.42	19.83	28.01		11.98	103.7	212-969-1000	Y
AB Multi-Manager Select 2035 Fund Class C	TDMCX	B-	C+	B	Up	4.35	9.04	18.99	25.19		11.92	103.7	212-969-1000	Y
AB Multi-Manager Select 2035 Fund Class I	TDIMX	B-	C+	B	Up	4.53	9.44	20.06	28.96		11.85	103.7	212-969-1000	Y
AB Multi-Manager Select 2035 Fund Class K	TDMKX	B-	C+	B	Up	4.46	9.38	19.80	28.09		11.71	103.7	212-969-1000	Y
AB Multi-Manager Select 2035 Fund Class R	TDRMX	B-	C+	B	Up	4.46	9.30	19.51	27.11		11.68	103.7	212-969-1000	Y
AB Multi-Manager Select 2035 Fund Class Z	TDMZX	B-	C+	B	Up	4.54	9.54	20.19	29.04		11.71	103.7	212-969-1000	Y
AB Multi-Manager Select 2040 Fund Advisor Class	TDJYX	B-	C+	B	Up	4.86	10.11	21.31	30.29		12.13	69.9	212-969-1000	Y
AB Multi-Manager Select 2040 Fund Class A	TDJAX	B-	C+	B	Up	4.74	9.91	21.02	29.26		12.09	69.9	212-969-1000	Y
AB Multi-Manager Select 2040 Fund Class C	TDJCX	B-	C+	B	Up	4.50	9.45	20.08	26.49		12.01	69.9	212-969-1000	Y
AB Multi-Manager Select 2040 Fund Class I	TDJIX	B-	C+	B	Up	4.82	10.01	21.26	30.26		11.88	69.9	212-969-1000	Y
AB Multi-Manager Select 2040 Fund Class K	TDJKX	B-	C+	B	Up	4.68	9.87	21.01	29.37		11.81	69.9	212-969-1000	Y
AB Multi-Manager Select 2040 Fund Class R	TDJRX	B-	C+	B	Up	4.69	9.81	20.76	28.46		11.79	69.9	212-969-1000	Y
AB Multi-Manager Select 2040 Fund Class Z	TDJZX	B-	C+	B	Up	4.78	10.06	21.31	30.37		11.81	69.9	212-969-1000	Y
AB Multi-Manager Select 2045 Fund Advisor Class	TDNYX	B-	C+	B	Up	4.88	10.15	21.74	30.62		12.35	58.9	212-969-1000	Y
AB Multi-Manager Select 2045 Fund Class A	TDNAX	B-	C+	B-	Up	4.83	10.13	21.48	29.79		12.28	58.9	212-969-1000	Y
AB Multi-Manager Select 2045 Fund Class I	TDNIX	B-	C+	B	Up	4.90	10.22	21.74	30.59		12.06	58.9	212-969-1000	Y
AB Multi-Manager Select 2045 Fund Class K	TDNKX	B-	C+	B	Up	4.83	10.07	21.48	29.73		11.96	58.9	212-969-1000	Y
AB Multi-Manager Select 2045 Fund Class R	TDNRX	B-	C+	B-	Up	4.75	9.92	21.13	28.64		11.91	58.9	212-969-1000	Y
AB Multi-Manager Select 2045 Fund Class Z	TDNZX	B-	C+	B	Up	4.92	10.26	21.78	30.58		11.95	58.9	212-969-1000	Y
AllianzGI Retirement 2025 Fund Administrative Class	GVDAX	B-	C+	B	Down	3.61	7.79	15.85	22.42	31.32	18.44	67.2	800-498-5413	Y
AllianzGI Retirement 2025 Fund Class A	GVSAX	B-	C+	B	Down	3.56	7.68	15.80	22.21	30.89	18.37	67.2	800-498-5413	Y
AllianzGI Retirement 2025 Fund Class P	GVSPX	B-	C+	B	Down	3.69	7.94	16.15	23.39	33.02	18.34	67.2	800-498-5413	Y
AllianzGI Retirement 2025 Fund Class R	GVSRX	B-	C+	B	Down	3.48	7.53	15.30	20.93	28.58	18.28	67.2	800-498-5413	Y
AllianzGI Retirement 2025 Fund R6 Class	GVSIX	B-	C+	B	Down	3.71	7.95	16.30	23.76	33.65	18.37	67.2	800-498-5413	Y
AllianzGI Retirement 2030 Fund Administrative Class	ABAMX	B-	C+	B	Down	4.04	8.80	18.18	24.47	36.93	22.45	75.2	800-498-5413	Y
AllianzGI Retirement 2030 Fund Class A	ABLAX	B-	C+	B	Down	3.99	8.78	18.12	24.24	36.59	22.17	75.2	800-498-5413	Y
AllianzGI Retirement 2030 Fund Class C	ABLCX	B-	C+	B		3.79	8.33	17.22	21.42	31.43	21.97	75.2	800-498-5413	Y
AllianzGI Retirement 2030 Fund Class P	ABLPX	B-	C+	B	Down	4.09	8.93	18.48	25.34	38.59	22.38	75.2	800-498-5413	Y
AllianzGI Retirement 2030 Fund Class R	ABLRX	B-	C+	B	Down	3.90	8.56	17.70	22.97	34.12	22.17	75.2	800-498-5413	Y
AllianzGI Retirement 2030 Fund R6 Class	ABLIX	B-	B-	B	Down	4.11	8.94	18.58	25.72	39.25	22.44	75.2	800-498-5413	Y

Category: Target Date 2021-2045 (con't)

Fund Name	Ticker Symbol	RATINGS: Overall Rating	Reward Rating	Risk Rating	Recent Up/ Downgrade	TOTAL RETURNS & PERFORMANCE: 3-Month Total Return	6-Month Total Return	1-Year Total Return	3-Year Total Return	5-Year Total Return	ASSETS: NAV	Total Assets (MIL)	NEW INVESTORS: Telephone	Open to New Investors
AllianzGI Retirement 2035 Fund Administrative Class	GVLAX	B-	B-	B	Down	4.23	9.40	19.78	26.42	42.57	19.88	60.6	800-498-5413	Y
AllianzGI Retirement 2035 Fund Class A	GVRAX	B-	B-	B	Down	4.25	9.38	19.79	26.30	42.18	19.72	60.6	800-498-5413	Y
AllianzGI Retirement 2035 Fund Class P	GVPAX	B-	B-	B	Down	4.32	9.54	20.11	27.42	44.40	19.79	60.6	800-498-5413	Y
AllianzGI Retirement 2035 Fund Class R	GVRRX	B-	B-	B	Down	4.16	9.21	19.32	24.94	39.70	19.66	60.6	800-498-5413	Y
AllianzGI Retirement 2035 Fund R6 Class	GVLIX	B-	B-	B	Down	4.36	9.62	20.26	27.84	45.13	19.82	60.6	800-498-5413	Y
AllianzGI Retirement 2040 Fund Administrative Class	AVAMX	B-	B-	B-	Down	4.44	9.87	20.93	27.67	46.86	22.83	56.6	800-498-5413	Y
AllianzGI Retirement 2040 Fund Class A	AVSAX	B-	B-	B-	Down	4.45	9.83	20.88	27.53	46.51	22.84	56.6	800-498-5413	Y
AllianzGI Retirement 2040 Fund Class C	AVSCX	B-	B-	B-	Up	4.25	9.39	19.97	24.71	41.15	22.68	56.6	800-498-5413	Y
AllianzGI Retirement 2040 Fund Class P	AVSPX	B-	B-	B	Down	4.51	10.02	21.28	28.77	48.81	22.92	56.6	800-498-5413	Y
AllianzGI Retirement 2040 Fund Class R	AVSRX	B-	B-	B-	Down	4.39	9.65	20.46	26.26	44.05	22.7	56.6	800-498-5413	Y
AllianzGI Retirement 2040 Fund R6 Class	AVTIX	B-	B-	B	Down	4.55	10.05	21.40	29.16	49.57	22.97	56.6	800-498-5413	Y
AllianzGI Retirement 2045 Fund Administrative Class	GBMAX	B-	B-	B-	Down	4.55	10.14	21.71	28.90	50.33	19.94	35.1	800-498-5413	Y
AllianzGI Retirement 2045 Fund Class A	GBVAX	B-	B-	B-	Down	4.55	10.13	21.71	28.69	50.00	20.02	35.1	800-498-5413	Y
AllianzGI Retirement 2045 Fund Class P	GBVPX	B-	B-	B-	Down	4.62	10.30	22.01	29.94	52.45	20.04	35.1	800-498-5413	Y
AllianzGI Retirement 2045 Fund Class R	GBVRX	B-	B-	B-	Down	4.40	9.91	21.19	27.34	47.43	19.86	35.1	800-498-5413	Y
AllianzGI Retirement 2045 Fund R6 Class	GBVIX	B-	B-	B-	Down	4.66	10.31	22.13	30.37	53.22	20.09	35.1	800-498-5413	Y
American Century Inv One Choice 2025 Port A Cls	ARWAX	B-	C+	B	Up	2.80	5.71	11.98	16.05	42.53	14.86	3,307	800-444-4015	Y
American Century Inv One Choice 2025 Port C Cls	ARWCX	B-	C+	B	Up	2.56	5.25	11.17	13.40	37.23	14.88	3,307	800-444-4015	Y
American Century Inv One Choice 2025 Port I Cls	ARWFX	B-	C+	B	Up	2.85	5.90	12.49	17.55	45.81	14.85	3,307	800-444-4015	Y
American Century Inv One Choice 2025 Port Inv Cls	ARWIX	B-	C+	B	Up	2.78	5.76	12.27	16.85	44.24	14.85	3,307	800-444-4015	Y
American Century Inv One Choice 2025 Port R Cls	ARWRX	B-	C+	B	Up	2.68	5.53	11.71	15.11	40.67	14.85	3,307	800-444-4015	Y
American Century Inv One Choice 2025 Port R6 Cls	ARWDX	B-	C+	B	Up	2.87	5.91	12.56	17.91	46.62	11.79	3,307	800-444-4015	Y
American Century Inv One Choice 2030 Port A Cls	ARCMX	B-	C+	B	Up	3.00	6.29	13.24	17.59	47.47	12.97	2,683	800-444-4015	Y
American Century Inv One Choice 2030 Port C Cls	ARWOX	B-	C+	B	Up	2.84	5.87	12.32	14.97	41.92	13	2,683	800-444-4015	Y
American Century Inv One Choice 2030 Port I Cls	ARCSX	B-	C+	B	Up	3.14	6.51	13.74	19.18	50.79	12.98	2,683	800-444-4015	Y
American Century Inv One Choice 2030 Port Inv Cls	ARCVX	B-	C+	B	Up	3.09	6.46	13.50	18.45	49.38	12.99	2,683	800-444-4015	Y
American Century Inv One Choice 2030 Port R Cls	ARCRX	B-	C+	B	Up	2.98	6.10	12.95	16.70	45.59	12.98	2,683	800-444-4015	Y
American Century Inv One Choice 2030 Port R6 Cls	ARCUX	B-	C+	B	Up	3.12	6.40	13.73	19.41	51.35	11.98	2,683	800-444-4015	Y
American Century Inv One Choice 2035 Port A Cls	ARYAX	B-	C+	B	Down	3.30	6.88	14.42	19.10	52.71	16.21	2,806	800-444-4015	Y
American Century Inv One Choice 2035 Port C Cls	ARLCX	B-	C+	B	Down	3.16	6.47	13.61	16.48	47.15	16.22	2,806	800-444-4015	Y
American Century Inv One Choice 2035 Port I Cls	ARLIX	B-	C+	B	Up	3.45	7.08	14.93	20.72	56.27	16.22	2,806	800-444-4015	Y
American Century Inv One Choice 2035 Port Inv Cls	ARYIX	B-	C+	B	Down	3.37	7.01	14.71	20.00	54.63	16.21	2,806	800-444-4015	Y
American Century Inv One Choice 2035 Port R Cls	ARYRX	B-	C+	B	Down	3.30	6.74	14.13	18.21	50.89	16.22	2,806	800-444-4015	Y
American Century Inv One Choice 2035 Port R6 Cls	ARLDX	B-	C+	B	Down	3.43	7.11	14.92	21.13	57.09	12.19	2,806	800-444-4015	Y
American Century Inv One Choice 2040 Port A Cls	ARDMX	B-	C+	B	Down	3.68	7.56	15.78	20.66	57.98	13.68	1,996	800-444-4015	Y
American Century Inv One Choice 2040 Port C Cls	ARNOX	B-	C+	B	Down	3.42	7.06	14.87	17.91	52.00	13.67	1,996	800-444-4015	Y
American Century Inv One Choice 2040 Port I Cls	ARDSX	B-	C+	B	Down	3.84	7.80	16.30	22.30	61.59	13.68	1,996	800-444-4015	Y
American Century Inv One Choice 2040 Port Inv Cls	ARDVX	B-	C+	B	Down	3.71	7.66	16.07	21.56	59.96	13.68	1,996	800-444-4015	Y
American Century Inv One Choice 2040 Port R Cls	ARDRX	B-	C+	B	Down	3.65	7.37	15.49	19.75	56.01	13.68	1,996	800-444-4015	Y
American Century Inv One Choice 2040 Port R6 Cls	ARDUX	B-	C+	B	Down	3.78	7.79	16.29	22.61	62.42	12.42	1,996	800-444-4015	Y
American Century Inv One Choice 2045 Port A Cls	AROAX	B-	C+	B	Down	4.06	8.19	17.21	22.41	62.91	17.18	2,007	800-444-4015	Y
American Century Inv One Choice 2045 Port C Cls	AROCX	B-	C+	B-	Down	3.82	7.81	16.35	19.67	56.88	17.18	2,007	800-444-4015	Y
American Century Inv One Choice 2045 Port I Cls	AOOIX	B-	B-	B	Down	4.10	8.41	17.72	24.05	66.56	17.19	2,007	800-444-4015	Y
American Century Inv One Choice 2045 Port Inv Cls	AROIX	B-	C+	B	Down	4.08	8.33	17.50	23.33	64.95	17.18	2,007	800-444-4015	Y
American Century Inv One Choice 2045 Port R Cls	ARORX	B-	C+	B	Down	2.75	6.83	15.59	20.10	59.00	17.19	2,007	800-444-4015	Y
American Century Inv One Choice 2045 Port R6 Cls	ARDOX	B-	B-	B	Down	4.20	8.53	17.84	24.60	67.55	12.59	2,007	800-444-4015	Y
American Funds 2025 Target Date Retirement Fund® Class A	AADTX	B-	C+	B	Up	3.30	6.91	14.95	22.03	62.66	13.44	13,886	800-421-4225	Y
American Funds 2025 Target Date Retirement Fund® Class C	CCDTX	B-	C+	B	Up	3.14	6.56	14.05	19.36	56.64	13.25	13,886	800-421-4225	Y
American Funds 2025 Target Date Retirement Fund® Class F-1	FAPTX	B-	C+	B	Up	3.32	6.96	14.96	22.05	62.59	13.36	13,886	800-421-4225	Y
American Funds 2025 Target Date Retirement Fund® Class F-2	FBDTX	B-	C+	B	Up	3.38	7.08	15.14	22.96	64.64	13.42	13,886	800-421-4225	Y
American Funds 2025 Target Date Retirement Fund® Class F-3	FDDTX	B-	C+	B	Up	3.45	7.14	15.27	23.11	65.03	13.44	13,886	800-421-4225	Y
American Funds 2025 Target Date Retirement Fund® Class R-1	RADTX	B-	C+	B	Up	3.14	6.48	13.95	19.20	56.35	13.26	13,886	800-421-4225	Y

Category: Target Date 2021-2045 (con't)

Fund Name	Ticker Symbol	RATINGS: Overall Rating	Reward Rating	Risk Rating	Recent Up/ Downgrade	TOTAL RETURNS & PERFORMANCE: 3-Month Total Return	6-Month Total Return	1-Year Total Return	3-Year Total Return	5-Year Total Return	ASSETS: NAV	Total Assets (MIL)	NEW INVESTORS: Telephone	Open to New Investors
American Funds 2025 Target Date Retirement Fund® Class R-2	RBDTX	B-	C+	B	Up	3.11	6.55	14.06	19.36	56.86	13.2	13,886	800-421-4225	Y
American Funds 2025 Target Date Retirement Fund® Cls R-2E	RBEDX	B-	C+	B	Up	3.18	6.67	14.41	20.70	60.01	13.26	13,886	800-421-4225	Y
American Funds 2025 Target Date Retirement Fund® Class R-3	RCDTX	B-	C+	B	Up	3.26	6.75	14.57	20.90	59.93	13.32	13,886	800-421-4225	Y
American Funds 2025 Target Date Retirement Fund® Class R-4	RDDTX	B-	C+	B	Up	3.31	6.93	14.90	22.04	62.61	13.41	13,886	800-421-4225	Y
American Funds 2025 Target Date Retirement Fund® Class R-5	REDTX	B-	C+	B	Up	3.36	7.03	15.21	23.04	64.94	13.52	13,886	800-421-4225	Y
American Funds 2025 Target Date Retirement Fund® Cls R-5E	RHDTX	B-	C+	B	Up	3.36	6.99	15.15	22.80	64.62	13.39	13,886	800-421-4225	Y
American Funds 2025 Target Date Retirement Fund® Class R-6	RFDTX	B-	C+	B	Up	3.43	7.20	15.32	23.28	65.51	13.49	13,886	800-421-4225	Y
American Funds 2030 Target Date Retirement Fund® Class A	AAETX	B-	B-	B	Down	4.04	8.39	18.10	26.15	71.56	14.42	14,786	800-421-4225	Y
American Funds 2030 Target Date Retirement Fund® Class C	CCETX	B-	C+	B	Down	3.88	7.91	17.17	23.30	65.10	14.21	14,786	800-421-4225	Y
American Funds 2030 Target Date Retirement Fund® Class F-1	FAETX	B-	B-	B	Down	4.03	8.32	17.99	26.02	71.36	14.32	14,786	800-421-4225	Y
American Funds 2030 Target Date Retirement Fund® Class F-2	FBETX	B-	B-	B	Down	4.13	8.49	18.30	27.00	73.59	14.4	14,786	800-421-4225	Y
American Funds 2030 Target Date Retirement Fund® Class F-3	FCETX	B-	B-	B	Down	4.12	8.47	18.43	27.32	74.11	14.41	14,786	800-421-4225	Y
American Funds 2030 Target Date Retirement Fund® Class R-1	RAETX	B-	C+	B	Down	3.80	7.90	17.15	23.14	64.76	14.26	14,786	800-421-4225	Y
American Funds 2030 Target Date Retirement Fund® Class R-2	RBETX	B-	C+	B	Down	3.84	7.97	17.18	23.40	65.36	14.16	14,786	800-421-4225	Y
American Funds 2030 Target Date Retirement Fund® Cls R-2E	RBEEX	B-	C+	B	Down	3.94	8.11	17.53	24.57	68.59	14.24	14,786	800-421-4225	Y
American Funds 2030 Target Date Retirement Fund® Class R-3	RCETX	B-	C+	B	Down	3.93	8.17	17.67	24.93	68.64	14.29	14,786	800-421-4225	Y
American Funds 2030 Target Date Retirement Fund® Class R-4	RDETX	B-	B-	B	Down	4.05	8.34	17.97	26.07	71.22	14.38	14,786	800-421-4225	Y
American Funds 2030 Target Date Retirement Fund® Class R-5	REETX	B-	B-	B	Down	4.11	8.51	18.33	27.22	73.96	14.51	14,786	800-421-4225	Y
American Funds 2030 Target Date Retirement Fund® Cls R-5E	RHETX	B-	B-	B	Down	4.04	8.40	18.23	26.85	73.46	14.36	14,786	800-421-4225	Y
American Funds 2030 Target Date Retirement Fund® Class R-6	RFETX	B-	B-	B	Down	4.11	8.53	18.39	27.32	74.24	14.45	14,786	800-421-4225	Y
American Funds 2035 Target Date Retirement Fund® Class A	AAFTX	B-	B-	B	Down	4.63	9.61	20.67	29.32	76.40	14.84	11,498	800-421-4225	Y
American Funds 2035 Target Date Retirement Fund® Class C	CCFTX	B-	B-	B	Down	4.41	9.15	19.78	26.42	69.85	14.63	11,498	800-421-4225	Y
American Funds 2035 Target Date Retirement Fund® Class F-1	FAQTX	B-	B-	B	Down	4.69	9.62	20.63	29.29	76.31	14.77	11,498	800-421-4225	Y
American Funds 2035 Target Date Retirement Fund® Class F-2	FBFTX	B-	B-	B	Down	4.72	9.70	20.95	30.23	78.55	14.83	11,498	800-421-4225	Y
American Funds 2035 Target Date Retirement Fund® Class F-3	FDFTX	B-	B-	B	Down	4.77	9.75	21.17	30.58	79.09	14.84	11,498	800-421-4225	Y
American Funds 2035 Target Date Retirement Fund® Class R-1	RAFTX	B-	B-	B	Down	4.45	9.15	19.75	26.27	69.50	14.56	11,498	800-421-4225	Y
American Funds 2035 Target Date Retirement Fund® Class R-2	RBFTX	B-	B-	B	Down	4.44	9.13	19.71	26.51	70.09	14.57	11,498	800-421-4225	Y
American Funds 2035 Target Date Retirement Fund® Cls R-2E	RBEFX	B-	B-	B	Down	4.55	9.37	20.17	27.90	73.60	14.64	11,498	800-421-4225	Y
American Funds 2035 Target Date Retirement Fund® Class R-3	RCFTX	B-	B-	B	Down	4.51	9.39	20.26	28.03	73.54	14.7	11,498	800-421-4225	Y
American Funds 2035 Target Date Retirement Fund® Class R-4	RDFTX	B-	B-	B	Down	4.63	9.55	20.63	29.23	76.23	14.8	11,498	800-421-4225	Y
American Funds 2035 Target Date Retirement Fund® Class R-5	REFTX	B-	B-	B	Down	4.68	9.71	21.06	30.46	78.92	14.94	11,498	800-421-4225	Y
American Funds 2035 Target Date Retirement Fund® Cls R-5E	RHFTX	B-	B-	B	Down	4.63	9.62	20.89	30.22	78.60	14.79	11,498	800-421-4225	Y
American Funds 2035 Target Date Retirement Fund® Class R-6	RFFTX	B-	B-	B	Down	4.69	9.73	21.03	30.57	79.41	14.88	11,498	800-421-4225	Y
American Funds 2040 Target Date Retirement Fund® Class A	AAGTX	B-	B-	B	Down	4.90	10.09	21.61	30.54	78.97	15.2	10,103	800-421-4225	Y
American Funds 2040 Target Date Retirement Fund® Class C	CCGTX	B-	B-	B	Down	4.62	9.58	20.60	27.46	72.13	14.97	10,103	800-421-4225	Y
American Funds 2040 Target Date Retirement Fund® Class F-1	FAUTX	B-	B-	B	Down	4.90	10.04	21.62	30.43	78.75	15.12	10,103	800-421-4225	Y
American Funds 2040 Target Date Retirement Fund® Class F-2	FBGTX	B-	B-	B	Down	4.93	10.13	21.84	31.42	80.88	15.18	10,103	800-421-4225	Y
American Funds 2040 Target Date Retirement Fund® Class F-3	FCGTX	B-	B-	B	Down	4.98	10.25	21.94	31.61	81.36	15.2	10,103	800-421-4225	Y
American Funds 2040 Target Date Retirement Fund® Class R-1	RAKTX	B-	B-	B	Down	4.70	9.60	20.65	27.40	71.82	14.96	10,103	800-421-4225	Y
American Funds 2040 Target Date Retirement Fund® Class R-2	RBKTX	B-	B-	B	Down	4.64	9.63	20.71	27.69	72.42	14.91	10,103	800-421-4225	Y
American Funds 2040 Target Date Retirement Fund® Cls R-2E	RBEKX	B-	B-	B	Down	4.79	9.81	21.08	29.00	75.93	15.01	10,103	800-421-4225	Y
American Funds 2040 Target Date Retirement Fund® Class R-3	RCKTX	B-	B-	B	Down	4.79	9.81	21.23	29.27	75.90	15.06	10,103	800-421-4225	Y
American Funds 2040 Target Date Retirement Fund® Class R-4	RDGTX	B-	B-	B	Down	4.91	10.04	21.59	30.46	78.80	15.16	10,103	800-421-4225	Y
American Funds 2040 Target Date Retirement Fund® Class R-5	REGTX	B-	B-	B	Down	4.97	10.20	21.92	31.58	81.33	15.3	10,103	800-421-4225	Y
American Funds 2040 Target Date Retirement Fund® Cls R-5E	RHGTX	B-	B-	B	Down	4.91	10.12	21.77	31.27	80.90	15.14	10,103	800-421-4225	Y
American Funds 2040 Target Date Retirement Fund® Class R-6	RFGTX	B-	B-	B	Down	4.97	10.21	21.97	31.78	81.93	15.25	10,103	800-421-4225	Y
American Funds 2045 Target Date Retirement Fund® Class A	AAHTX	B-	B-	B	Down	5.04	10.25	22.01	31.20	79.93	15.43	6,946	800-421-4225	Y
American Funds 2045 Target Date Retirement Fund® Class C	CCHTX	B-	B-	B	Down	4.75	9.81	21.09	28.13	73.20	15.19	6,946	800-421-4225	Y
American Funds 2045 Target Date Retirement Fund® Class F-1	FATTX	B-	B-	B	Down	4.96	10.27	21.99	31.10	79.79	15.35	6,946	800-421-4225	Y
American Funds 2045 Target Date Retirement Fund® Class F-2	FBHTX	B-	B-	B	Down	5.07	10.42	22.29	32.09	82.03	15.43	6,946	800-421-4225	Y
American Funds 2045 Target Date Retirement Fund® Class F-3	FCHTX	B-	B-	B	Down	5.06	10.41	22.24	32.14	82.40	15.42	6,946	800-421-4225	Y
American Funds 2045 Target Date Retirement Fund® Class R-1	RAHTX	B-	B-	B	Down	4.80	9.79	21.08	28.09	72.81	15.17	6,946	800-421-4225	Y

Category: Target Date 2021-2045 (con't)

Fund Name	Ticker Symbol	RATINGS: Overall Rating	Reward Rating	Risk Rating	Recent Up/ Downgrade	TOTAL RETURNS & PERFORMANCE: 3-Month Total Return	6-Month Total Return	1-Year Total Return	3-Year Total Return	5-Year Total Return	ASSETS: NAV	Total Assets (MIL)	NEW INVESTORS: Telephone	Open to New Investors
American Funds 2045 Target Date Retirement Fund® Class R-2	RBHTX	B-	B-	B	Down	4.74	9.76	21.00	28.19	73.39	15.1	6,946	800-421-4225	Y
American Funds 2045 Target Date Retirement Fund® Cls R-2E	RBHHX	B-	B-	B	Down	4.87	9.99	21.40	29.66	77.00	15.22	6,946	800-421-4225	Y
American Funds 2045 Target Date Retirement Fund® Class R-3	RCHTX	B-	B-	B	Down	4.88	10.07	21.58	29.80	76.92	15.26	6,946	800-421-4225	Y
American Funds 2045 Target Date Retirement Fund® Class R-4	RDHTX	B-	B-	B	Down	4.98	10.20	21.98	31.10	79.68	15.39	6,946	800-421-4225	Y
American Funds 2045 Target Date Retirement Fund® Class R-5	REHTX	B-	B-	B	Down	5.03	10.34	22.28	32.18	82.46	15.54	6,946	800-421-4225	Y
American Funds 2045 Target Date Retirement Fund® Cls R-5E	RHHTX	B-	B-	B	Down	5.07	10.36	22.27	31.93	82.12	15.37	6,946	800-421-4225	Y
American Funds 2045 Target Date Retirement Fund® Class R-6	RFHTX	B-	B-	B	Down	5.10	10.44	22.43	32.49	82.89	15.49	6,946	800-421-4225	Y
AXA Target 2025 Allocation Fund Class B	US00247C6509	B-	C+	B	Down	3.75	7.42	15.38	20.42	52.49		169.8	877-222-2144	Y
AXA Target 2025 Allocation Portfolio Class K	US00247C3951	B-	C+	B	Down	3.90	7.67	15.77	21.43	54.40		169.8	877-222-2144	Y
AXA Target 2035 Allocation Fund Class B	US00247C6350	B-	C+	B-	Down	4.61	8.77	17.84	23.57	61.77		128.7	877-222-2144	Y
AXA Target 2035 Allocation Portfolio Class K	US00247C3878	B-	B-	B	Down	4.67	8.93	18.11	24.48	63.78		128.7	877-222-2144	Y
AXA Target 2045 Allocation Fund Class B	US00247C6194	B-	B-	B-	Down	5.21	9.89	19.77	25.90	69.89		97.5	877-222-2144	Y
AXA Target 2045 Allocation Portfolio Class K	US00247C3795	B-	B-	B-	Down	5.18	9.95	20.06	26.84	71.87		97.5	877-222-2144	Y
BlackRock LifePath® Dynamic 2025 Fund Class K Shares	LPBKX	B-	C+	B	Up	3.86	7.66	15.74	21.21	44.50	13.49	66.2	800-441-7762	Y
BlackRock LifePath® Dynamic 2025 Fund Class R Shares	LPBRX	B	C+	B+	Up	3.76	7.33	15.02	18.77	40.19	13.49	66.2	800-441-7762	Y
BlackRock LifePath® Dynamic 2025 Fund Institutional Shares	LPBIX	B-	C+	B	Up	3.80	7.55	15.44	20.32	43.52	13.52	66.2	800-441-7762	Y
BlackRock LifePath® Dynamic 2025 Fund Investor A Shares	LPBAX	B-	C+	B	Up	3.80	7.50	15.21	19.46	41.74	13.5	66.2	800-441-7762	Y
BlackRock LifePath® Dynamic 2025 Fund Investor C Shares	LPBCX	B-	C+	B	Up	3.59	7.08	14.39	16.76	36.44	13.44	66.2	800-441-7762	Y
BlackRock LifePath® Dynamic 2030 Fund Class K Shares	LPSDX	B-	C+	B	Down	4.52	8.69	17.95	23.87	51.70	14.24	394.0	800-441-7762	Y
BlackRock LifePath® Dynamic 2030 Fund Class R Shares	LPRNX	B-	C+	B	Down	4.29	8.29	17.16	21.21	45.89	14.12	394.0	800-441-7762	Y
BlackRock LifePath® Dynamic 2030 Fund Institutional Shares	STLDX	B-	C+	B	Down	4.38	8.49	17.66	22.89	49.52	14.26	394.0	800-441-7762	Y
BlackRock LifePath® Dynamic 2030 Fund Investor A Shares	LPRDX	B-	C+	B	Down	4.41	8.37	17.42	22.03	47.66	13.72	394.0	800-441-7762	Y
BlackRock LifePath® Dynamic 2030 Fund Investor C Shares	LPCNX	B-	C+	B-	Down	4.17	7.98	16.47	19.18	42.05	14.01	394.0	800-441-7762	Y
BlackRock LifePath® Dynamic 2035 Fund Class K Shares	LPJKX	B-	B-	B-	Down	5.14	9.58	19.76	25.89	57.63	14.68	55.9	800-441-7762	Y
BlackRock LifePath® Dynamic 2035 Fund Class R Shares	LPJRX	B-	C+	B-	Down	4.97	9.24	19.07	23.34	51.15	14.46	55.9	800-441-7762	Y
BlackRock LifePath® Dynamic 2035 Fund Institutional Shares	LPJIX	B-	B-	B-	Down	5.08	9.55	19.51	24.99	54.74	14.48	55.9	800-441-7762	Y
BlackRock LifePath® Dynamic 2035 Fund Investor A Shares	LPJAX	B-	B-	B-	Down	5.01	9.41	19.29	24.12	52.99	14.46	55.9	800-441-7762	Y
BlackRock LifePath® Dynamic 2035 Fund Investor C Shares	LPJCX	B-	C+	B-	Down	4.85	8.99	18.40	21.29	47.16	14.33	55.9	800-441-7762	Y
BlackRock LifePath® Dynamic 2040 Fund Class K Shares	LPSFX	B-	B-	B-	Down	5.65	10.47	21.66	28.07	62.27	18.13	315.1	800-441-7762	Y
BlackRock LifePath® Dynamic 2040 Fund Class R Shares	LPRKX	B-	B-	B-	Down	5.49	10.12	20.85	25.39	56.18	17.89	315.1	800-441-7762	Y
BlackRock LifePath® Dynamic 2040 Fund Institutional Shares	STLEX	B-	B-	B-	Down	5.62	10.34	21.43	27.10	60.01	18.04	315.1	800-441-7762	Y
BlackRock LifePath® Dynamic 2040 Fund Investor A Shares	LPREX	B-	B-	B-	Down	5.56	10.23	21.17	26.21	58.03	16.53	315.1	800-441-7762	Y
BlackRock LifePath® Dynamic 2040 Fund Investor C Shares	LPCKX	B-	C+	B-	Down	4.75	9.18	19.51	22.54	51.24	17.77	315.1	800-441-7762	Y
BlackRock LifePath® Dynamic 2045 Fund Class K Shares	LPHKX	B-	B-	B-	Down	5.84	10.86	22.57	29.07	66.13	15.57	36.2	800-441-7762	Y
BlackRock LifePath® Dynamic 2045 Fund Class R Shares	LPHRX	B-	B-	B-	Down	5.74	10.53	21.80	26.35	59.92	15.37	36.2	800-441-7762	Y
BlackRock LifePath® Dynamic 2045 Fund Institutional Shares	LPHIX	B-	B-	B-	Down	5.84	10.74	22.29	28.08	63.66	15.41	36.2	800-441-7762	Y
BlackRock LifePath® Dynamic 2045 Fund Investor A Shares	LPHAX	B-	B-	B-	Down	5.77	10.67	22.04	27.17	61.79	15.4	36.2	800-441-7762	Y
BlackRock LifePath® Dynamic 2045 Fund Investor C Shares	LPHCX	B-	B-	B-	Down	5.54	10.20	21.09	24.24	55.57	15.2	36.2	800-441-7762	Y
BlackRock LifePath® Index 2025 Fund Class K Shares	LIBKX	B-	C+	B	Up	3.48	6.80	14.43	21.20	48.37	13.31	2,409	800-441-7762	Y
BlackRock LifePath® Index 2025 Fund Institutional Shares	LIBIX	B-	C+	B	Up	3.47	6.86	14.37	21.01	48.05	13.31	2,409	800-441-7762	Y
BlackRock LifePath® Index 2025 Fund Investor A Shares	LILAX	B-	C+	B	Up	3.32	6.64	14.02	20.08	46.23	13.29	2,409	800-441-7762	Y
BlackRock LifePath® Index 2030 Fund Class K Shares	LINKX	B-	C+	B	Down	3.99	7.78	16.36	23.53	54.29	13.61	3,041	800-441-7762	Y
BlackRock LifePath® Index 2030 Fund Institutional Shares	LINIX	B-	C+	B	Down	3.97	7.75	16.29	23.32	53.86	13.62	3,041	800-441-7762	Y
BlackRock LifePath® Index 2030 Fund Investor A Shares	LINAX	B-	C+	B	Down	3.90	7.61	16.00	22.44	52.14	13.62	3,041	800-441-7762	Y
BlackRock LifePath® Index 2035 Fund Class K Shares	LIJKX	B-	B-	B	Down	4.59	8.69	18.29	25.86	60.23	14.07	2,041	800-441-7762	Y
BlackRock LifePath® Index 2035 Fund Institutional Shares	LIJIX	B-	B-	B	Down	4.50	8.65	18.21	25.64	59.83	14.08	2,041	800-441-7762	Y
BlackRock LifePath® Index 2035 Fund Investor A Shares	LIJAX	B	C+	B+	Up	4.44	8.46	17.89	24.62	57.66	14.04	2,041	800-441-7762	Y
BlackRock LifePath® Index 2040 Fund Class K Shares	LIKKX	B-	B-	B-	Down	4.99	9.45	19.94	27.86	65.54	14.39	2,257	800-441-7762	Y
BlackRock LifePath® Index 2040 Fund Institutional Shares	LIKIX	B-	B-	B-	Down	4.98	9.43	19.89	27.65	65.14	14.39	2,257	800-441-7762	Y
BlackRock LifePath® Index 2040 Fund Investor A Shares	LIKAX	B-	B-	B-	Down	4.84	9.31	19.55	26.62	63.02	14.36	2,257	800-441-7762	Y
BlackRock LifePath® Index 2045 Fund Class K Shares	LIHKX	B-	B-	B-	Down	5.23	9.97	21.06	29.19	70.02	14.76	1,333	800-441-7762	Y
BlackRock LifePath® Index 2045 Fund Institutional Shares	LIHIX	B-	B-	B-	Down	5.22	9.95	21.02	29.01	69.53	14.75	1,333	800-441-7762	Y

Category: Target Date 2021-2045 (con't)

		RATINGS				TOTAL RETURNS & PERFORMANCE					ASSETS		NEW INVESTORS	
Fund Name	Ticker Symbol	Overall Rating	Reward Rating	Risk Rating	Recent Up/ Downgrade	3-Month Total Return	6-Month Total Return	1-Year Total Return	3-Year Total Return	5-Year Total Return	NAV	Total Assets (MIL)	Telephone	Open to New Investors
BlackRock LifePath® Index 2045 Fund Investor A Shares	LIHAX	B-	B-	B-	Down	5.24	9.83	20.76	28.06	67.52	14.73	1,333	800-441-7762	Y
BlackRock LifePath® Smart Beta 2025 Fund Class K	BIPDX	B-	C+	B	Down	3.08	6.25	15.62	21.11	49.22	11.12	31.0	800-441-7762	Y
BlackRock LifePath® Smart Beta 2025 Fund Class R Shares	BRPDX	B-	C+	B	Down	2.93	5.95	14.98	19.02	44.78	10.97	31.0	800-441-7762	Y
BlackRock LifePath® Smart Beta 2025 Fund Inst Shares	BLCIX	B-	C+	B	Down	3.08	6.15	15.52	20.69	48.43	11.1	31.0	800-441-7762	Y
BlackRock LifePath® Smart Beta 2025 Fund Investor A Shares	BAPDX	B-	C+	B	Down	3.06	6.16	15.25	19.98	46.65	11.05	31.0	800-441-7762	Y
BlackRock LifePath® Smart Beta 2030 Fund Class K	BIPEX	B-	C+	B-	Down	2.94	6.55	16.31	22.04	52.16	10.65	25.0	800-441-7762	Y
BlackRock LifePath® Smart Beta 2030 Fund Class R Shares	BRPEX	B-	C+	B-	Down	2.89	6.25	15.75	20.06	47.84	10.53	25.0	800-441-7762	Y
BlackRock LifePath® Smart Beta 2030 Fund Inst Shares	BLEIX	B-	C+	B-	Down	2.92	6.54	16.30	21.85	51.57	10.64	25.0	800-441-7762	Y
BlackRock LifePath® Smart Beta 2030 Fund Investor A Shares	BAPEX	B-	C+	B-	Down	2.83	6.38	15.98	20.90	49.62	10.56	25.0	800-441-7762	Y
BlackRock LifePath® Smart Beta 2035 Fund Class K	BIPGX	B-	B-	B-	Down	4.18	8.19	18.54	23.76	56.79	11.5	20.5	800-441-7762	Y
BlackRock LifePath® Smart Beta 2035 Fund Class R Shares	BRPGX	B-	C+	B-	Down	3.99	7.89	17.80	21.60	52.32	11.31	20.5	800-441-7762	Y
BlackRock LifePath® Smart Beta 2035 Fund Inst Shares	BLGIX	B-	B-	B-	Down	4.17	8.19	18.53	23.50	56.22	11.5	20.5	800-441-7762	Y
BlackRock LifePath® Smart Beta 2035 Fund Investor A Shares	BAPGX	B-	C+	B-	Down	4.03	7.99	18.05	22.45	54.17	11.41	20.5	800-441-7762	Y
BlackRock LifePath® Smart Beta 2040 Fund Class K	BIPHX	B-	B-	B-	Down	4.40	8.86	18.64	24.48	60.11	11.22	16.2	800-441-7762	Y
BlackRock LifePath® Smart Beta 2040 Fund Inst Shares	BLHIX	B-	B-	B-	Down	4.48	8.83	18.49	24.19	59.31	11.22	16.2	800-441-7762	Y
BlackRock LifePath® Smart Beta 2040 Fund Investor A Shares	BAPHX	B-	B-	B-	Down	4.40	8.70	18.21	23.38	57.47	11.12	16.2	800-441-7762	Y
BlackRock LifePath® Smart Beta 2045 Fund Class K	BIPJX	B-	B-	C+	Down	5.32	10.09	20.48	26.59	64.01	12.59	13.8	800-441-7762	Y
BlackRock LifePath® Smart Beta 2045 Fund Inst Shares	BLJIX	B-	B-	C+	Down	5.31	10.08	20.38	26.15	63.19	12.57	13.8	800-441-7762	Y
BlackRock LifePath® Smart Beta 2045 Fund Investor A Shares	BAPJX	B-	B-	C+	Down	5.24	9.90	20.02	25.27	61.12	12.39	13.8	800-441-7762	Y
BMO Target Retirement 2025 Fund Class R3	BRTGX	B-	C+	B-	Down	3.94	7.52	16.58	20.43		12.04	22.2	800-236-3863	Y
BMO Target Retirement 2025 Fund Class R6	BRTHX	B-	C+	B	Down	3.97	7.70	17.12	22.60		11.93	22.2	800-236-3863	Y
BMO Target Retirement 2025 Fund Class Y	BRTEX	B-	C+	B	Down	3.87	7.52	16.64	21.22		11.89	22.2	800-236-3863	Y
BMO Target Retirement 2030 Fund Class R3	BTRKX	B-	C+	B-	Down	4.28	8.06	17.97	21.80	59.98	11.67	96.7	800-236-3863	Y
BMO Target Retirement 2030 Fund Class R6	BTRLX	B-	B-	B-	Down	4.42	8.38	18.77	24.15	65.10	11.62	96.7	800-236-3863	Y
BMO Target Retirement 2030 Fund Class Y	BTRHX	B-	C+	B-	Down	4.32	8.19	18.23	22.74	62.29	11.64	96.7	800-236-3863	Y
BMO Target Retirement 2035 Fund Class R3	BRTKX	B-	C+	B-	Down	4.61	8.66	19.46	23.15		11.76	13.1	800-236-3863	Y
BMO Target Retirement 2035 Fund Class R6	BRTLX	B-	B-	B-	Down	4.79	9.07	20.25	25.68		11.71	13.1	800-236-3863	Y
BMO Target Retirement 2035 Fund Class Y	BRTIX	B-	B-	B-	Down	4.68	8.89	19.67	24.09		11.67	13.1	800-236-3863	Y
BMO Target Retirement 2040 Fund Class R3	BTRPX	B-	B-	B-	Down	4.77	9.03	20.29	23.92	67.68	11.29	54.9	800-236-3863	Y
BMO Target Retirement 2040 Fund Class R6	BTRQX	B-	B-	B-	Down	4.95	9.40	21.07	26.41	73.14	11.22	54.9	800-236-3863	Y
BMO Target Retirement 2040 Fund Class Y	BTRMX	B-	B-	B-	Down	4.93	9.20	20.62	24.88	70.19	11.24	54.9	800-236-3863	Y
BMO Target Retirement 2045 Fund Class R3	BRTPX	B-	B-	B-	Down	4.85	9.09	20.51	24.48		12.12	7.8	800-236-3863	Y
BMO Target Retirement 2045 Fund Class R6	BRTQX	B-	B-	B-	Down	5.08	9.47	21.36	26.90		12.03	7.8	800-236-3863	Y
BMO Target Retirement 2045 Fund Class Y	BRTMX	B-	B-	B-	Down	4.97	9.30	20.80	25.46		11.99	7.8	800-236-3863	Y
ClearTrack 2025 Fund Class R6	TDOTX	B-	C	B	Up	3.21	6.29	13.58			11.16	91.2	888-233-4339	Y
ClearTrack 2030 Fund Class R1	TDFTX	B-	C	B	Up	3.38	6.63	14.02			11.3	70.7	888-233-4339	Y
ClearTrack 2030 Fund Class R6	TDHTX	B-	C	B	Up	3.55	6.97	14.65			11.37	70.7	888-233-4339	Y
ClearTrack 2035 Fund Class R1	TCETX	B-	C+	B	Up	3.90	7.51	16.00			11.55	71.5	888-233-4339	Y
ClearTrack 2035 Fund Class R6	TCHDX	B-	C+	B	Up	4.06	7.93	16.83			11.63	71.5	888-233-4339	Y
ClearTrack 2040 Fund Class R6	TCKTX	B-	C+	B	Up	4.54	8.76	18.56			11.84	61.8	888-233-4339	Y
Fidelity Advisor Freedom® 2025 Fund Class A	FATWX	B-	C+	B	Down	3.53	7.17	16.25	22.72	51.65	13.82	3,049	617-563-7000	Y
Fidelity Advisor Freedom® 2025 Fund Class C	FCTWX	B-	C+	B	Down	3.25	6.69	15.26	19.95	45.98	13.64	3,049	617-563-7000	Y
Fidelity Advisor Freedom® 2025 Fund Class I	FITWX	B-	C+	B	Down	3.58	7.26	16.51	23.67	53.45	13.93	3,049	617-563-7000	Y
Fidelity Advisor Freedom® 2025 Fund Class M	FTTWX	B-	C+	B	Down	3.43	6.98	15.95	21.80	49.74	13.85	3,049	617-563-7000	Y
Fidelity Advisor Freedom® 2025 Fund Class Z6	FPGLX	B-	C+	B	Down	3.54	7.38	16.64	23.80	53.62	13.91	3,049	617-563-7000	Y
Fidelity Advisor Freedom® 2030 Fund Class A	FAFEX	B-	B-	B-	Down	4.09	8.36	18.96	26.16	58.14	15.03	2,989	617-563-7000	Y
Fidelity Advisor Freedom® 2030 Fund Class C	FCFEX	B-	C+	B-	Down	3.97	8.00	18.16	23.40	52.33	14.82	2,989	617-563-7000	Y
Fidelity Advisor Freedom® 2030 Fund Class I	FEFIX	B-	B-	B	Down	4.16	8.47	19.27	27.09	60.17	15.11	2,989	617-563-7000	Y
Fidelity Advisor Freedom® 2030 Fund Class M	FTFEX	B-	B-	B-	Down	4.01	8.22	18.70	25.25	56.23	14.97	2,989	617-563-7000	Y
Fidelity Advisor Freedom® 2030 Fund Class Z6	FDGLX	B-	B-	B	Down	4.23	8.62	19.44	27.27	60.40	15.09	2,989	617-563-7000	Y
Fidelity Advisor Freedom® 2035 Fund Class A	FATHX	B-	B-	B-	Down	4.63	9.36	21.19	28.78	65.42	14.72	2,395	617-563-7000	Y
Fidelity Advisor Freedom® 2035 Fund Class C	FCTHX	B-	B-	B-	Down	4.46	8.91	20.23	25.86	59.28	14.38	2,395	617-563-7000	Y

Category: Target Date 2021-2045 (con't)

Fund Name	Ticker Symbol	RATINGS: Overall Rating	RATINGS: Reward Rating	RATINGS: Risk Rating	RATINGS: Recent Up/ Downgrade	TOTAL RETURNS & PERFORMANCE: 3-Month Total Return	6-Month Total Return	1-Year Total Return	3-Year Total Return	5-Year Total Return	ASSETS: NAV	Total Assets (MIL)	NEW INVESTORS: Telephone	Open to New Investors
Fidelity Advisor Freedom® 2035 Fund Class I	FITHX	B-	B-	B-	Down	4.70	9.47	21.49	29.74	67.52	14.81	2,395	617-563-7000	Y
Fidelity Advisor Freedom® 2035 Fund Class M	FTTHX	B-	B-	B-	Down	4.67	9.21	20.94	27.85	63.43	14.61	2,395	617-563-7000	Y
Fidelity Advisor Freedom® 2035 Fund Class Z6	FHGLX	B-	B-	B-	Down	4.85	9.63	21.66	29.92	67.76	14.8	2,395	617-563-7000	Y
Fidelity Advisor Freedom® 2040 Fund Class A	FAFFX	B-	B-	B-	Down	4.74	9.44	21.33	28.99	66.17	15.76	2,167	617-563-7000	Y
Fidelity Advisor Freedom® 2040 Fund Class C	FCFFX	B-	B-	B-	Down	4.60	9.12	20.50	26.17	60.10	15.43	2,167	617-563-7000	Y
Fidelity Advisor Freedom® 2040 Fund Class I	FIFFX	B-	B-	B-	Down	4.81	9.56	21.64	29.94	68.25	15.84	2,167	617-563-7000	Y
Fidelity Advisor Freedom® 2040 Fund Class M	FTFFX	B-	B-	B-	Down	4.66	9.31	21.02	28.00	64.06	15.7	2,167	617-563-7000	Y
Fidelity Advisor Freedom® 2040 Fund Class Z6	FKGLX	B-	B-	B-	Down	4.92	9.82	21.93	30.25	68.65	15.82	2,167	617-563-7000	Y
Fidelity Advisor Freedom® 2045 Fund Class A	FFFZX	B-	B-	B-	Down	4.73	9.54	21.32	29.02	67.12	12.27	1,328	617-563-7000	Y
Fidelity Advisor Freedom® 2045 Fund Class C	FFFJX	B-	B-	B-	Down	4.48	8.99	20.42	26.12	60.99	12.05	1,328	617-563-7000	Y
Fidelity Advisor Freedom® 2045 Fund Class I	FFFIX	B-	B-	B-	Down	4.77	9.55	21.65	29.92	69.22	12.33	1,328	617-563-7000	Y
Fidelity Advisor Freedom® 2045 Fund Class M	FFFTX	B-	B-	B-	Down	4.70	9.36	21.04	28.01	65.10	12.18	1,328	617-563-7000	Y
Fidelity Advisor Freedom® 2045 Fund Class Z6	FCGLX	B-	B-	B-	Down	4.90	9.78	21.91	30.19	69.57	12.32	1,328	617-563-7000	Y
Fidelity Freedom® 2025 Fund	FFTWX	B-	C+	B	Down	3.71	7.56	16.81	24.77	55.68	14.4	26,834	617-563-7000	Y
Fidelity Freedom® 2025 Fund Class K6	FDTKX	B-	C+	B	Down	3.78	7.70	16.97	24.94	55.88	14.4	26,834	617-563-7000	Y
Fidelity Freedom® 2030 Fund	FFFEX	B-	B-	B	Down	4.40	8.86	19.81	28.55	62.95	18.06	31,461	617-563-7000	Y
Fidelity Freedom® 2030 Fund Class K6	FGTKX	B-	B-	B	Down	4.45	9.03	20.00	28.75	63.20	18.05	31,461	617-563-7000	Y
Fidelity Freedom® 2035 Fund	FFTHX	B-	B-	B-	Down	4.99	9.93	22.00	31.36	70.65	15.24	21,304	617-563-7000	Y
Fidelity Freedom® 2035 Fund Class K6	FWTKX	B-	B-	B-	Down	5.09	10.10	22.19	31.56	70.92	15.23	21,304	617-563-7000	Y
Fidelity Freedom® 2040 Fund	FFFFX	B-	B-	B-	Down	5.04	10.08	22.25	31.69	71.67	10.7	22,091	617-563-7000	Y
Fidelity Freedom® 2040 Fund Class K6	FHTKX	B-	B-	B-	Down	5.18	10.23	22.41	31.86	71.90	10.69	22,091	617-563-7000	Y
Fidelity Freedom® 2045 Fund	FFFGX	B-	B-	B-	Down	5.07	10.00	22.20	31.59	72.34	12.12	12,978	617-563-7000	Y
Fidelity Freedom® 2045 Fund Class K6	FJTKX	B-	B-	B-	Down	5.14	10.26	22.50	31.90	72.76	12.11	12,978	617-563-7000	Y
Fidelity Freedom® Index 2025 Fund Inst Premium Cls	FFEDX	B-	C+	B	Up	3.81	7.33	15.19	22.07	50.25	16.79	3,390	617-563-7000	Y
Fidelity Freedom® Index 2025 Fund Investor Class	FQIFX	B-	C+	B	Up	3.78	7.37	15.14	21.88	50.02	16.79	3,390	617-563-7000	Y
Fidelity Freedom® Index 2030 Fund Inst Premium Cls	FFEGX	B-	B-	B	Down	4.48	8.70	18.03	25.77	57.39	17.69	4,182	617-563-7000	Y
Fidelity Freedom® Index 2030 Fund Investor Class	FXIFX	B-	B-	B	Down	4.51	8.67	18.04	25.64	57.24	17.7	4,182	617-563-7000	Y
Fidelity Freedom® Index 2035 Fund Inst Premium Cls	FFEZX	B-	B-	B-	Down	5.17	9.89	20.39	28.93	65.42	18.76	2,663	617-563-7000	Y
Fidelity Freedom® Index 2035 Fund Investor Class	FIHFX	B-	B-	B-	Down	5.19	9.85	20.34	28.74	65.18	18.76	2,663	617-563-7000	Y
Fidelity Freedom® Index 2040 Fund Inst Premium Cls	FFIZX	B-	B-	B-	Down	5.21	10.03	20.56	29.13	66.19	18.89	2,941	617-563-7000	Y
Fidelity Freedom® Index 2040 Fund Investor Class	FBIFX	B-	B-	B-	Down	5.24	9.99	20.57	28.98	66.01	18.9	2,941	617-563-7000	Y
Fidelity Freedom® Index 2045 Fund Inst Premium Cls	FFOLX	B-	B-	B-	Down	5.23	10.01	20.56	29.08	66.92	19.04	1,748	617-563-7000	Y
Fidelity Freedom® Index 2045 Fund Investor Class	FIOFX	B-	B-	B-	Down	5.26	9.98	20.58	28.97	66.77	19.04	1,748	617-563-7000	Y
Franklin LifeSmart™ 2025 Retmnt Target Fund Adv Cls	FLRFX	B-	C+	B-	Down	3.06	6.67	15.29	16.38	48.96	13	129.3	650-312-2000	Y
Franklin LifeSmart™ 2025 Retirement Target Fund Class C	FTTCX	B-	C+	B	Up	2.82	6.17	14.06	12.92	41.66	12.77	129.3	650-312-2000	Y
Franklin LifeSmart™ 2025 Retirement Target Fund Class R6	FTLMX	B-	C+	B-	Down	3.07	6.71	15.33	16.53	49.27	13.01	129.3	650-312-2000	Y
Franklin LifeSmart™ 2030 Retmnt Target Fund Adv Cls	FLRZX	B	C+	B+	Up	3.47	7.47	16.97	18.39		12.73	45.7	650-312-2000	Y
Franklin LifeSmart™ 2030 Retirement Target Fund Class A	FLRSX	B-	C+	B-	Down	3.41	7.40	16.72	17.53		12.7	45.7	650-312-2000	Y
Franklin LifeSmart™ 2030 Retirement Target Fund Class C	FLRTX	B-	C+	B	Up	3.23	7.00	15.89	15.01		12.56	45.7	650-312-2000	Y
Franklin LifeSmart™ 2030 Retirement Target Fund Class R6	FLERX	B-	C+	B-	Down	3.48	7.51	17.01	18.61		12.74	45.7	650-312-2000	Y
Franklin LifeSmart™ 2035 Retmnt Target Fund Adv Cls	FLRHX	B-	C+	B-	Down	3.71	7.94	18.23	19.57	56.45	13.81	115.1	650-312-2000	Y
Franklin LifeSmart™ 2035 Retirement Target Fund Class A	FRTAX	B-	C+	B-	Up	3.57	7.83	17.93	18.61	54.22	13.7	115.1	650-312-2000	Y
Franklin LifeSmart™ 2035 Retirement Target Fund Class R	FLRGX	B-	C+	B-	Up	3.59	7.70	17.70	17.79	52.62	13.69	115.1	650-312-2000	Y
Franklin LifeSmart™ 2035 Retirement Target Fund Class R6	FMTLX	B-	C+	B-	Down	3.76	8.00	18.31	19.71	56.89	13.8	115.1	650-312-2000	Y
Franklin LifeSmart™ 2040 Retmnt Target Fund Adv Cls	FLSHX	B	C+	B+	Up	3.83	8.23	18.87	19.99		13.1	36.5	650-312-2000	Y
Franklin LifeSmart™ 2040 Retirement Target Fund Class A	FLADX	B-	C+	B-	Up	3.76	8.10	18.50	18.95		13.03	36.5	650-312-2000	Y
Franklin LifeSmart™ 2040 Retirement Target Fund Class R6	FLREX	B	C+	B+	Up	3.87	8.27	18.91	20.16		13.11	36.5	650-312-2000	Y
Franklin LifeSmart™ 2045 Retmnt Target Fund Adv Cls	FLRLX	B-	C+	B-	Up	3.87	8.34	19.03	20.38	58.69	13.88	79.3	650-312-2000	Y
Franklin LifeSmart™ 2045 Retirement Target Fund Class A	FTTAX	B-	C+	B-	Up	3.81	8.23	18.71	19.40	56.65	13.78	79.3	650-312-2000	Y
Franklin LifeSmart™ 2045 Retirement Target Fund Class C	FLRIX	B-	C+	B	Up	3.65	7.78	17.92	16.82	51.09	13.44	79.3	650-312-2000	Y
Franklin LifeSmart™ 2045 Retirement Target Fund Class R	FLRJX	B-	C+	B-	Up	3.74	8.10	18.43	18.54	54.87	13.72	79.3	650-312-2000	Y
Franklin LifeSmart™ 2045 Retirement Target Fund Class R6	FMLTX	B-	C+	B-	Down	3.93	8.39	19.10	20.58	59.18	13.88	79.3	650-312-2000	Y

Category: Target Date 2021-2045 (con't)

Fund Name	Ticker Symbol	RATINGS: Overall Rating	Reward Rating	Risk Rating	Recent Up/ Downgrade	TOTAL RETURNS & PERFORMANCE: 3-Month Total Return	6-Month Total Return	1-Year Total Return	3-Year Total Return	5-Year Total Return	ASSETS: NAV	Total Assets (MIL)	NEW INVESTORS: Telephone	Open to New Investors
Goldman Sachs Target Date 2030 Portfolio Class A Shares	GTAJX	B-	C+	B	Up	3.26	6.03	12.89	19.00	51.26	9.44	77.7	800-526-7384	Y
Goldman Sachs Target Date 2030 Portfolio Cls Inst Shares	GTIJX	B-	C+	B	Up	3.51	6.39	13.48	20.35	53.73	9.47	77.7	800-526-7384	Y
Goldman Sachs Target Date 2030 Portfolio Class IR Shares	GTMJX	B-	C+	B	Up	3.39	6.27	13.24	20.04	53.34	9.45	77.7	800-526-7384	Y
Goldman Sachs Target Date 2030 Portfolio Class R Shares	GTRJX	B-	C+	B	Up	3.24	5.92	12.64	18.20	49.50	9.44	77.7	800-526-7384	Y
Goldman Sachs Target Date 2030 Portfolio Class R6 Shares	GTZJX	B-	C+	B	Up	3.41	6.29	13.37	20.25	53.60	9.46	77.7	800-526-7384	Y
Goldman Sachs Target Date 2030 Port Cls Serv Shares	GTVJX	B-	C+	B	Up	3.27	6.04	12.89	19.02	51.28	9.46	77.7	800-526-7384	Y
Goldman Sachs Target Date 2040 Portfolio Class A Shares	GTAMX	B-	C+	B	Up	3.91	7.16	14.94	22.18	60.19	9.22	50.6	800-526-7384	Y
Goldman Sachs Target Date 2040 Portfolio Cls Inst Shares	GTIMX	B-	C+	B	Up	4.05	7.41	15.44	23.24	62.39	9.24	50.6	800-526-7384	Y
Goldman Sachs Target Date 2040 Portfolio Class IR Shares	GTMMX	B-	C+	B	Up	3.91	7.16	15.17	23.02	62.10	9.22	50.6	800-526-7384	Y
Goldman Sachs Target Date 2040 Portfolio Class R Shares	GTRMX	B-	C+	B	Up	3.82	6.97	14.61	21.21	58.13	9.21	50.6	800-526-7384	Y
Goldman Sachs Target Date 2040 Portfolio Class R6 Shares	GTZMX	B-	C+	B	Up	3.94	7.29	15.43	23.24	62.39	9.24	50.6	800-526-7384	Y
Goldman Sachs Target Date 2040 Port Cls Serv Shares	GTVMX	B-	C+	B	Up	3.93	7.08	14.85	22.02	59.98	9.23	50.6	800-526-7384	Y
Great-West Lifetime 2025 Fund Class L	MXANX	B-	C+	B	Down	3.33	6.42	13.91	19.78	53.90		1,864		Y
Great-West Lifetime 2035 Fund Class L	MXAZX	B-	B-	B-	Down	4.48	8.51	18.16	24.78	67.31		1,703		Y
Great-West Lifetime 2045 Fund Class L	MXBHX	B-	B-	B-	Down	5.00	9.56	20.22	27.11	69.53		968.7		Y
Great-West Lifetime Conservative 2025 Fund Inst Cls	MXOZX	B-	C+	B	Up	2.56	4.49	11.25	17.79	39.08		219.4		Y
Great-West Lifetime Conservative 2025 Fund Investor Class	MXALX	B-	C+	B	Up	2.39	4.83	10.74	16.53	37.79		219.4		Y
Great-West Lifetime Conservative 2025 Fund Service Class	MXBLX	B-	C+	B	Up	2.33	4.76	10.65	16.16	37.17		219.4		Y
Great-West Lifetime Conservative 2035 Fund Inst Cls	MXRCX	B-	C+	B	Down	3.62	6.05	14.96	22.25	53.90		185.7		Y
Great-West Lifetime Conservative 2035 Fund Investor Class	MXGLX	B-	C+	B	Down	3.37	6.66	14.50	21.12	52.67		185.7		Y
Great-West Lifetime Conservative 2035 Fund Service Class	MXHLX	B-	C+	B	Down	3.35	6.64	14.43	20.85	51.96		185.7		Y
Great-West Lifetime Conservative 2045 Fund Inst Cls	MXUCX	B-	B-	B	Down	4.52	8.75	18.62	26.71	64.65		114.9		Y
Great-West Lifetime Conservative 2045 Fund Investor Class	MXMLX	B-	B-	B-	Down	4.36	8.46	18.23	25.48	63.04		114.9		Y
Great-West Lifetime Conservative 2045 Fund Service Class	MXNLX	B-	B-	B-	Down	4.36	8.47	18.21	25.16	62.27		114.9		Y
Great-West SecureFoundation® Lifetime 2025 Fund Class L	MXLHX	B-	C+	B	Up	3.24	6.20	12.66	18.71	47.78		82.8		Y
Great-West SecureFoundation® Lifetime 2025 Fund Inv Cls	MXSNX	B-	C+	B	Up	3.21	6.21	12.82	19.62	49.54		82.8		Y
Great-West SecureFoundation® Lifetime 2025 Fund Serv Cls	MXSOX	B-	C+	B	Up	3.27	6.24	12.82	19.27	48.85		82.8		Y
Great-West SecureFoundation® Lifetime 2030 Fund Class L	MXLIX	B-	C+	B	Down	2.42	5.79	12.98	19.48	53.41		111.4		Y
Great-West SecureFoundation® Lifetime 2030 Fund Inv Cls	MXSQX	B-	C+	B	Down	2.14	5.54	12.85	19.90	54.59		111.4		Y
Great-West SecureFoundation® Lifetime 2030 Fund Serv Cls	MXASX	B-	C+	B	Down	2.29	5.68	12.91	19.73	54.11		111.4		Y
Great-West SecureFoundation® Lifetime 2035 Fund Class L	MXLJX	B-	B-	B	Down	4.30	8.29	16.71	24.41	63.49		69.8		Y
Great-West SecureFoundation® Lifetime 2035 Fund Inv Cls	MXSRX	B-	B-	B	Down	4.34	8.38	16.87	24.74	64.65		69.8		Y
Great-West SecureFoundation® Lifetime 2035 Fund Serv Cls	MXSSX	B-	B-	B	Down	4.26	8.26	16.76	24.31	63.67		69.8		Y
Great-West SecureFoundation® Lifetime 2040 Fund Class L	MXLKX	B-	B-	B-	Down	3.24	7.63	16.89	25.15	66.59		86.2		Y
Great-West SecureFoundation® Lifetime 2040 Fund Inv Cls	MXDSX	B-	B-	B-	Down	3.20	7.63	16.89	25.14	66.56		86.2		Y
Great-West SecureFoundation® Lifetime 2040 Fund Serv Cls	MXESX	B-	B-	B-	Down	3.34	7.77	16.92	24.95	66.13		86.2		Y
Great-West SecureFoundation® Lifetime 2045 Fund Class L	MXLNX	B-	B-	B-	Down	5.11	9.81	19.58	27.88	69.91		32.8		Y
Great-West SecureFoundation® Lifetime 2045 Fund Inv Cls	MXSTX	B-	B-	B-	Down	5.10	9.92	19.80	28.39	70.86		32.8		Y
Great-West SecureFoundation® Lifetime 2045 Fund Serv Cls	MXSWX	B-	B-	B-	Down	5.12	9.88	19.78	27.99	69.91		32.8		Y
GuideStone Funds MyDestination 2025 Fund Institutional	GMWYX	B-	C+	B	Down	3.28	7.00	15.07	20.11	45.68	10.25	1,083	214-720-1171	Y
GuideStone Funds MyDestination 2025 Fund Investor Class	GMWZX	B-	C+	B	Down	3.23	6.85	14.91	19.95	45.48	10.26	1,083	214-720-1171	Y
GuideStone Funds MyDestination 2035 Fund Institutional	GMHYX	B-	C+	B-	Down	4.32	8.93	18.80	22.40	55.79	9.95	636.7	214-720-1171	Y
GuideStone Funds MyDestination 2035 Fund Investor Class	GMHZX	B-	C+	B-	Down	4.20	8.80	18.53	22.13	55.45	9.95	636.7	214-720-1171	Y
Harbor Target Retirement 2025 Fund Institutional Class	HARMX	B-	C+	B	Up	2.31	5.39	13.14	18.52	35.61	12.58	21.2	800-422-1050	Y
Harbor Target Retirement 2030 Fund Institutional Class	HARPX	B	C+	B+	Up	2.65	6.01	14.68	20.16	41.24	9.12	28.9	800-422-1050	Y
Harbor Target Retirement 2035 Fund Institutional Class	HARUX	B-	C+	B-	Down	3.10	6.93	16.87	22.53	48.50	14.37	15.3	800-422-1050	Y
Harbor Target Retirement 2040 Fund Institutional Class	HARYX	B	C+	B+	Up	3.60	7.71	18.90	24.89	56.37	9.21	25.2	800-422-1050	Y
Harbor Target Retirement 2045 Fund Institutional Class	HACCX	B-	B-	B-	Down	4.13	8.56	20.95	27.10	63.56	15.32	10.1	800-422-1050	Y
Invesco Balanced-Risk Retirement 2030 Fund Class A	TNAAX	B-	C+	B	Up	5.04	7.94	10.20	17.18	28.05	8.71	72.7	800-659-1005	Y
Invesco Balanced-Risk Retirement 2030 Fund Class AX	VREAX	B-	C+	B	Up	5.15	7.93	10.32	17.16	28.16	8.72	72.7	800-659-1005	
Invesco Balanced-Risk Retirement 2030 Fund Class B	TNABX	B-	C+	B	Up	4.79	7.47	9.34	14.56	23.26	8.62	72.7	800-659-1005	
Invesco Balanced-Risk Retirement 2030 Fund Class C	TNACX	B-	C+	B	Up	4.79	7.47	9.34	14.70	23.41	8.62	72.7	800-659-1005	Y

Category: Target Date 2021-2045 (con't)

Fund Name	Ticker Symbol	RATINGS: Overall Rating	Reward Rating	Risk Rating	Recent Up/ Downgrade	TOTAL RETURNS & PERFORMANCE: 3-Month Total Return	6-Month Total Return	1-Year Total Return	3-Year Total Return	5-Year Total Return	ASSETS: NAV	Total Assets (MIL)	NEW INVESTORS: Telephone	Open to New Investors
Invesco Balanced-Risk Retirement 2030 Fund Class CX	VRECX	B-	C+	B	Up	4.91	7.60	9.47	14.83	23.55	8.63	72.7	800-659-1005	
Invesco Balanced-Risk Retirement 2030 Fund Class R	TNARX	B-	C+	B	Up	5.04	7.84	9.97	16.46	26.67	8.67	72.7	800-659-1005	Y
Invesco Balanced-Risk Retirement 2030 Fund Class R6	TNAFX	B-	C+	B	Up	5.16	8.05	10.43	18.02	29.56	8.75	72.7	800-659-1005	Y
Invesco Balanced-Risk Retirement 2030 Fund Class RX	VRERX	B-	C+	B	Up	5.05	7.72	9.98	16.48	26.55	8.66	72.7	800-659-1005	
Invesco Balanced-Risk Retirement 2030 Fund Class Y	TNAYX	B-	C+	B		5.17	8.07	10.45	18.07	29.64	8.73	72.7	800-659-1005	Y
Invesco Balanced-Risk Retirement 2030 Fund R5 Class	TNAIX	B-	C+	B	Up	5.15	8.17	10.55	18.15	29.70	8.76	72.7	800-659-1005	Y
Invesco Balanced-Risk Retirement 2040 Fund Class A	TNDAX	B-	B-	B		5.76	9.11	11.77	20.04	32.49	7.94	53.2	800-659-1005	Y
Invesco Balanced-Risk Retirement 2040 Fund Class AX	VRGAX	B-	B-	B		5.77	9.13	11.79	20.05	32.36	7.93	53.2	800-659-1005	
Invesco Balanced-Risk Retirement 2040 Fund Class B	TNDBX	B-	C+	B	Up	5.59	8.70	10.93	17.58	27.92	7.86	53.2	800-659-1005	
Invesco Balanced-Risk Retirement 2040 Fund Class C	TNDCX	B-	C+	B-	Up	5.60	8.71	10.94	17.76	27.96	7.85	53.2	800-659-1005	Y
Invesco Balanced-Risk Retirement 2040 Fund Class CX	VRGCX	B-	C+	B	Up	5.60	8.72	10.96	17.64	27.85	7.84	53.2	800-659-1005	
Invesco Balanced-Risk Retirement 2040 Fund Class R	TNDRX	B-	B-	B		5.67	9.04	11.41	19.33	30.96	7.9	53.2	800-659-1005	Y
Invesco Balanced-Risk Retirement 2040 Fund Class R6	TNDFX	B-	B-	B		5.86	9.20	12.00	20.89	34.07	7.97	53.2	800-659-1005	Y
Invesco Balanced-Risk Retirement 2040 Fund Class RX	VRGRX	B-	B-	B		5.67	9.04	11.57	19.18	30.78	7.9	53.2	800-659-1005	
Invesco Balanced-Risk Retirement 2040 Fund Class Y	TNDYX	B-	B-	B		5.87	9.36	12.01	20.92	34.13	7.96	53.2	800-659-1005	Y
Invesco Balanced-Risk Retirement 2040 Fund R5 Class	TNDIX	B-	B-	B		5.99	9.34	12.14	21.04	34.23	7.98	53.2	800-659-1005	Y
John Hancock Funds II MultiMgr 2025 Lifetime Port Cls 1	JLEOX	B-	C+	B	Down	3.45	7.19	16.20	23.81	58.72	11.13	1,376	800-225-5913	Y
John Hancock Funds II MultiMgr 2025 Lifetime Port Cls A	JLEAX	B-	C+	B	Down	3.44	7.08	15.94	22.47	55.66	11.19	1,376	800-225-5913	Y
John Hancock Funds II MultiMgr 2025 Lifetime Port Cls I	JHRNX	B-	C+	B	Down	3.57	7.31	16.34	23.67	58.55	11.14	1,376	800-225-5913	Y
John Hancock Funds II MultiMgr 2025 Lifetime Port Cls R1	JLEDX	B-	C+	B	Down	3.32	6.88	15.45	21.29	53.29	11.13	1,376	800-225-5913	Y
John Hancock Funds II MultiMgr 2025 Lifetime Port Cls R2	JLEEX	B-	C+	B	Down	3.37	6.93	15.72	22.20	55.19	11.12	1,376	800-225-5913	Y
John Hancock Funds II MultiMgr 2025 Lifetime Port Cls R3	JLEFX	B-	C+	B	Down	3.31	6.96	15.64	21.62	53.97	11.14	1,376	800-225-5913	Y
John Hancock Funds II MultiMgr 2025 Lifetime Port Cls R4	JLEGX	B-	C+	B	Down	3.40	7.14	16.03	23.12	57.21	11.15	1,376	800-225-5913	Y
John Hancock Funds II MultiMgr 2025 Lifetime Port Cls R5	JLEHX	B-	C+	B	Down	3.45	7.19	16.20	23.81	58.73	11.13	1,376	800-225-5913	Y
John Hancock Funds II MultiMgr 2025 Lifetime Port Cls R6	JLEIX	B-	C+	B	Down	3.50	7.24	16.38	24.01	59.01	11.12	1,376	800-225-5913	Y
John Hancock Funds II MultiMgr 2030 Lifetime Port Cls 1	JLFOX	B-	B-	B-	Down	4.01	8.22	18.41	26.09	65.46	11.48	1,307	800-225-5913	Y
John Hancock Funds II MultiMgr 2030 Lifetime Port Cls A	JLFAX	B-	B-	B-	Down	3.92	8.02	17.95	24.65	62.04	11.52	1,307	800-225-5913	Y
John Hancock Funds II MultiMgr 2030 Lifetime Port Cls I	JHRGX	B-	B-	B-	Down	3.95	8.15	18.22	25.83	65.12	11.48	1,307	800-225-5913	Y
John Hancock Funds II MultiMgr 2030 Lifetime Port Cls R1	JLFDX	B-	C+	B-	Down	3.86	7.81	17.55	23.43	59.69	11.47	1,307	800-225-5913	Y
John Hancock Funds II MultiMgr 2030 Lifetime Port Cls R2	JLFEX	B-	B-	B-	Down	3.85	7.89	17.75	24.39	61.59	11.45	1,307	800-225-5913	Y
John Hancock Funds II MultiMgr 2030 Lifetime Port Cls R3	JLFFX	B-	C+	B-	Down	3.87	7.90	17.65	23.89	60.59	11.48	1,307	800-225-5913	Y
John Hancock Funds II MultiMgr 2030 Lifetime Port Cls R4	JLFGX	B-	B-	B-	Down	3.99	8.11	18.20	25.36	63.76	11.47	1,307	800-225-5913	Y
John Hancock Funds II MultiMgr 2030 Lifetime Port Cls R5	JLFHX	B-	B-	B-	Down	3.93	8.14	18.32	26.00	65.35	11.47	1,307	800-225-5913	Y
John Hancock Funds II MultiMgr 2030 Lifetime Port Cls R6	JLFIX	B-	B-	B-	Down	4.07	8.19	18.37	26.30	65.94	11.47	1,307	800-225-5913	Y
John Hancock Funds II MultiMgr 2035 Lifetime Port Cls 1	JLHOX	B-	B-	B-	Down	4.51	9.10	20.17	28.01	70.30	12.01	1,100	800-225-5913	Y
John Hancock Funds II MultiMgr 2035 Lifetime Port Cls A	JLHAX	B-	B-	B-	Down	4.35	8.88	19.67	26.54	66.94	11.95	1,100	800-225-5913	Y
John Hancock Funds II MultiMgr 2035 Lifetime Port Cls I	JHRMX	B-	B-	B-	Down	4.45	9.04	20.00	27.76	69.98	12.01	1,100	800-225-5913	Y
John Hancock Funds II MultiMgr 2035 Lifetime Port Cls R1	JLHDX	B-	B-	B-	Down	4.28	8.64	19.33	25.37	64.51	11.93	1,100	800-225-5913	Y
John Hancock Funds II MultiMgr 2035 Lifetime Port Cls R2	JLHEX	B-	B-	B-	Down	4.33	8.84	19.59	26.35	66.55	12	1,100	800-225-5913	Y
John Hancock Funds II MultiMgr 2035 Lifetime Port Cls R3	JLHFX	B-	B-	B-	Down	4.28	8.73	19.30	25.71	65.22	11.94	1,100	800-225-5913	Y
John Hancock Funds II MultiMgr 2035 Lifetime Port Cls R4	JLHGX	B-	B-	B-	Down	4.40	8.91	19.86	27.28	68.56	12	1,100	800-225-5913	Y
John Hancock Funds II MultiMgr 2035 Lifetime Port Cls R5	JLHHX	B-	B-	B-	Down	4.51	9.10	20.18	28.01	70.31	12.01	1,100	800-225-5913	Y
John Hancock Funds II MultiMgr 2035 Lifetime Port Cls R6	JLHIX	B-	B-	B-	Down	4.48	9.16	20.25	28.22	70.78	12	1,100	800-225-5913	Y
John Hancock Funds II MultiMgr 2040 Lifetime Port Cls 1	JLIOX	B-	B-	B-	Down	4.71	9.67	21.37	29.51	72.79	12.13	879.0	800-225-5913	Y
John Hancock Funds II MultiMgr 2040 Lifetime Port Cls A	JLIAX	B-	B-	B-	Down	4.71	9.43	20.94	28.11	69.26	12.09	879.0	800-225-5913	Y
John Hancock Funds II MultiMgr 2040 Lifetime Port Cls I	JHRDX	B-	B-	B-	Down	4.73	9.60	21.29	29.35	72.57	12.14	879.0	800-225-5913	Y
John Hancock Funds II MultiMgr 2040 Lifetime Port Cls R1	JLIDX	B-	B-	B-	Down	4.56	9.20	20.50	26.71	66.68	12.06	879.0	800-225-5913	Y
John Hancock Funds II MultiMgr 2040 Lifetime Port Cls R2	JLIEX	B-	B-	B-	Down	4.62	9.41	20.79	27.73	69.00	12.12	879.0	800-225-5913	Y
John Hancock Funds II MultiMgr 2040 Lifetime Port Cls R3	JLIFX	B-	B-	B-	Down	4.66	9.31	20.64	27.23	67.76	12.05	879.0	800-225-5913	Y
John Hancock Funds II MultiMgr 2040 Lifetime Port Cls R4	JLIGX	B-	B-	B-	Down	4.68	9.40	21.01	28.63	70.93	12.08	879.0	800-225-5913	Y
John Hancock Funds II MultiMgr 2040 Lifetime Port Cls R5	JLIHX	B-	B-	B-	Down	4.70	9.56	21.35	29.36	72.69	12.14	879.0	800-225-5913	Y
John Hancock Funds II MultiMgr 2040 Lifetime Port Cls R6	JLIIX	B-	B-	B-	Down	4.76	9.64	21.45	29.61	73.09	12.12	879.0	800-225-5913	Y

Category: Target Date 2021-2045 (con't)

Fund Name	Ticker Symbol	RATINGS: Overall Rating	RATINGS: Reward Rating	RATINGS: Risk Rating	RATINGS: Recent Up/ Downgrade	TOTAL RETURNS & PERFORMANCE: 3-Month Total Return	6-Month Total Return	1-Year Total Return	3-Year Total Return	5-Year Total Return	ASSETS: NAV	Total Assets (MIL)	NEW INVESTORS: Telephone	Open to New Investors
John Hancock Funds II MultiMgr 2045 Lifetime Port Cls 1	JLJOX	B-	B-	B-	Down	4.81	9.73	21.44	29.61	72.90	11.97	811.4	800-225-5913	Y
John Hancock Funds II MultiMgr 2045 Lifetime Port Cls A	JLJAX	B-	B-	B-	Down	4.75	9.61	21.04	28.24	69.46	11.92	811.4	800-225-5913	Y
John Hancock Funds II MultiMgr 2045 Lifetime Port Cls I	JHROX	B-	B-	B-	Down	4.76	9.68	21.38	29.48	72.72	11.97	811.4	800-225-5913	Y
John Hancock Funds II MultiMgr 2045 Lifetime Port Cls R1	JLJDX	B-	B-	B-	Down	4.68	9.46	20.70	27.06	67.02	11.9	811.4	800-225-5913	Y
John Hancock Funds II MultiMgr 2045 Lifetime Port Cls R2	JLJEX	B-	B-	B-	Down	4.73	9.58	20.97	27.96	69.14	11.96	811.4	800-225-5913	Y
John Hancock Funds II MultiMgr 2045 Lifetime Port Cls R3	JLJFX	B-	B-	B-	Down	4.70	9.38	20.70	27.32	67.81	11.9	811.4	800-225-5913	Y
John Hancock Funds II MultiMgr 2045 Lifetime Port Cls R4	JLJGX	B-	B-	B-	Down	4.78	9.63	21.25	28.92	71.29	11.94	811.4	800-225-5913	Y
John Hancock Funds II MultiMgr 2045 Lifetime Port Cls R5	JLJHX	B-	B-	B-	Down	4.81	9.82	21.52	29.69	72.97	11.99	811.4	800-225-5913	Y
John Hancock Funds II MultiMgr 2045 Lifetime Port Cls R6	JLJIX	B-	B-	B-	Down	4.78	9.79	21.52	29.83	73.22	11.96	811.4	800-225-5913	Y
John Hancock Funds Multi-Index 2025 Lifetime Port Cls 1	JRTBX	B-	C+	B	Down	3.50	7.11	15.02	22.89		11.54	210.3	800-225-5913	Y
John Hancock Funds Multi-Index 2025 Lifetime Port Cls R6	JRTFX	B-	C+	B	Down	3.63	7.24	15.17	23.18		11.55	210.3	800-225-5913	Y
John Hancock Funds Multi-Ind 2025 Preserv Port Cls 1	JREOX	B-	C+	B	Up	2.16	4.78	10.54	16.19	38.81	12.99	1,463	800-225-5913	Y
John Hancock Funds Multi-Ind 2025 Preserv Port Cls R1	JREQX	B-	C+	B	Up	1.99	4.37	9.75	13.79	34.01	13.04	1,463	800-225-5913	Y
John Hancock Funds Multi-Ind 2025 Preserv Port Cls R2	JRERX	B-	C+	B	Up	2.11	4.64	10.30	15.24	36.41	13.04	1,463	800-225-5913	Y
John Hancock Funds Multi-Ind 2025 Preserv Port Cls R4	JREPX	B-	C+	B	Up	2.18	4.72	10.45	15.81	37.85	13.05	1,463	800-225-5913	Y
John Hancock Funds Multi-Ind 2025 Preserv Port Cls R6	JRESX	B-	C+	B	Up	2.21	4.83	10.68	16.37	39.16	12.99	1,463	800-225-5913	Y
John Hancock Funds Multi-Index 2030 Lifetime Port Cls 1	JRTGX	B-	B-	B-	Down	4.10	8.20	17.13	25.46		11.82	218.7	800-225-5913	Y
John Hancock Funds Multi-Index 2030 Lifetime Port Cls R6	JRTJX	B-	B-	B	Down	4.15	8.25	17.29	25.65		11.82	218.7	800-225-5913	Y
John Hancock Funds Multi-Ind 2030 Preserv Port Cls 1	JRHOX	B-	C+	B	Up	3.17	6.70	14.28	20.98	50.46	13.93	1,501	800-225-5913	Y
John Hancock Funds Multi-Ind 2030 Preserv Port Cls R1	JRHQX	B-	C+	B	Up	3.09	6.40	13.61	18.72	45.57	13.99	1,501	800-225-5913	Y
John Hancock Funds Multi-Ind 2030 Preserv Port Cls R2	JRHRX	B-	C+	B	Up	3.07	6.45	13.84	19.33	47.17	13.96	1,501	800-225-5913	Y
John Hancock Funds Multi-Ind 2030 Preserv Port Cls R4	JRHPX	B-	C+	B	Up	3.25	6.70	14.25	20.62	49.42	14.01	1,501	800-225-5913	Y
John Hancock Funds Multi-Ind 2030 Preserv Port Cls R6	JRHSX	B-	C+	B	Up	3.22	6.75	14.42	21.25	50.97	13.93	1,501	800-225-5913	Y
John Hancock Funds Multi-Index 2035 Lifetime Port Cls 1	JRTKX	B-	B-	B-	Down	4.59	9.10	18.85	27.34		12.07	195.5	800-225-5913	Y
John Hancock Funds Multi-Index 2035 Lifetime Port Cls R6	JRTNX	B-	B-	B-	Down	4.63	9.15	19.02	27.65		12.07	195.5	800-225-5913	Y
John Hancock Funds Multi-Ind 2035 Preserv Port Cls 1	JRYOX	B-	C+	B	Down	3.87	7.97	16.76	24.08	57.89	14.48	1,275	800-225-5913	Y
John Hancock Funds Multi-Ind 2035 Preserv Port Cls R1	JRYQX	B-	C+	B-	Down	3.76	7.63	15.95	21.70	52.78	14.55	1,275	800-225-5913	Y
John Hancock Funds Multi-Ind 2035 Preserv Port Cls R2	JRYRX	B-	C+	B	Down	3.77	7.78	16.22	22.48	54.54	14.52	1,275	800-225-5913	Y
John Hancock Funds Multi-Ind 2035 Preserv Port Cls R4	JRYPX	B-	C+	B	Down	3.88	7.96	16.63	23.69	56.76	14.56	1,275	800-225-5913	Y
John Hancock Funds Multi-Ind 2035 Preserv Port Cls R6	JRYSX	B-	B-	B	Down	3.92	8.01	16.80	24.34	58.36	14.49	1,275	800-225-5913	Y
John Hancock Funds Multi-Index 2040 Lifetime Port Cls 1	JRTTX	B-	B-	B-	Down	4.99	9.74	20.20	29.22		12.3	160.3	800-225-5913	Y
John Hancock Funds Multi-Index 2040 Lifetime Port Cls R6	JRTWX	B-	B-	B-	Down	5.04	9.79	20.14	29.29		12.3	160.3	800-225-5913	Y
John Hancock Funds Multi-Ind 2040 Preserv Port Cls 1	JRROX	B-	B-	B-	Down	4.31	8.71	18.17	25.87	62.05	14.81	1,005	800-225-5913	Y
John Hancock Funds Multi-Ind 2040 Preserv Port Cls R1	JRRQX	B-	B-	B-	Down	4.15	8.39	17.47	23.82	57.31	14.86	1,005	800-225-5913	Y
John Hancock Funds Multi-Ind 2040 Preserv Port Cls R2	JRRRX	B-	B-	B-	Down	4.24	8.55	17.75	24.49	58.83	14.84	1,005	800-225-5913	Y
John Hancock Funds Multi-Ind 2040 Preserv Port Cls R4	JRRPX	B-	B-	B-	Down	4.33	8.70	18.04	25.48	60.89	14.89	1,005	800-225-5913	Y
John Hancock Funds Multi-Ind 2040 Preserv Port Cls R6	JRRSX	B-	B-	B-	Down	4.30	8.77	18.17	26.00	62.40	14.79	1,005	800-225-5913	Y
John Hancock Funds Multi-Index 2045 Lifetime Port Cls 1	JRLQX	B-	B-	B-	Down	5.04	9.89	20.29	29.08		12.26	130.4	800-225-5913	Y
John Hancock Funds Multi-Index 2045 Lifetime Port Cls R6	JRLVX	B-	B-	B-	Down	5.08	9.85	20.35	29.27		12.26	130.4	800-225-5913	Y
John Hancock Funds Multi-Ind 2045 Preserv Port Cls 1	JRVOX	B-	B-	B-	Down	4.53	9.04	18.72	26.79	63.63	14.96	778.3	800-225-5913	Y
John Hancock Funds Multi-Ind 2045 Preserv Port Cls R1	JRVQX	B-	B-	B-	Down	4.29	8.58	17.87	24.19	57.97	15	778.3	800-225-5913	Y
John Hancock Funds Multi-Ind 2045 Preserv Port Cls R2	JRVRX	B-	B-	B-	Down	4.40	8.84	18.25	25.21	60.09	15	778.3	800-225-5913	Y
John Hancock Funds Multi-Ind 2045 Preserv Port Cls R4	JRVPX	B-	B-	B-	Down	4.47	8.96	18.59	26.32	62.35	15.03	778.3	800-225-5913	Y
John Hancock Funds Multi-Ind 2045 Preserv Port Cls R6	JRVSX	B-	B-	B-	Down	4.51	9.09	18.87	26.98	64.02	14.96	778.3	800-225-5913	Y
JPMorgan SmartRetirement® 2025 Fund Class A	JNSAX	B-	C+	B	Down	3.75	7.59	15.98	20.71	53.54	19.53	7,833	800-480-4111	Y
JPMorgan SmartRetirement® 2025 Fund Class C	JNSCX	B	C+	B+	Up	2.67	6.26	14.27	17.37	47.32	19.46	7,833	800-480-4111	Y
JPMorgan SmartRetirement® 2025 Fund Class I	JNSSX	B-	C+	B	Down	3.77	7.64	16.14	21.12	54.27	19.57	7,833	800-480-4111	Y
JPMorgan SmartRetirement® 2025 Fund Class R2	JNSZX	B-	C+	B	Down	3.61	7.34	15.55	19.69	51.41	19.46	7,833	800-480-4111	Y
JPMorgan SmartRetirement® 2025 Fund Class R3	JNSPX	B-	C+	B	Down	3.71	7.44	15.78	20.38	53.14	19.47	7,833	800-480-4111	Y
JPMorgan SmartRetirement® 2025 Fund Class R4	JNSQX	B	C+	B+	Up	3.77	7.63	16.07	21.30	55.07	19.55	7,833	800-480-4111	Y
JPMorgan SmartRetirement® 2025 Fund Class R5	JNSIX	B-	C+	B	Down	3.85	7.74	16.31	21.60	55.46	19.6	7,833	800-480-4111	Y
JPMorgan SmartRetirement® 2025 Fund Class R6	JNSYX	B-	C+	B	Down	3.82	7.74	16.43	21.90	55.84	19.6	7,833	800-480-4111	Y

Category: Target Date 2021-2045 (con't)

Fund Name	Ticker Symbol	RATINGS: Overall Rating	RATINGS: Reward Rating	RATINGS: Risk Rating	RATINGS: Recent Up/Downgrade	TOTAL RETURNS & PERFORMANCE: 3-Month Total Return	6-Month Total Return	1-Year Total Return	3-Year Total Return	5-Year Total Return	ASSETS: NAV	Total Assets (MIL)	NEW INVESTORS: Telephone	Open to New Investors
JPMorgan SmartRetirement® 2030 Fund Class A	JSMAX	B-	C+	B	Down	4.49	8.93	18.65	22.96	60.95	21.37	8,612	800-480-4111	Y
JPMorgan SmartRetirement® 2030 Fund Class C	JSMCX	B-	C+	B-	Down	3.28	7.53	16.71	19.38	54.25	21.17	8,612	800-480-4111	Y
JPMorgan SmartRetirement® 2030 Fund Class I	JSMSX	B-	C+	B	Down	4.47	8.97	18.73	23.30	61.65	21.42	8,612	800-480-4111	Y
JPMorgan SmartRetirement® 2030 Fund Class R2	JSMZX	B-	C+	B-	Down	3.31	7.60	16.97	20.59	57.11	21.29	8,612	800-480-4111	Y
JPMorgan SmartRetirement® 2030 Fund Class R3	JSMNX	B-	C+	B	Down	4.43	8.81	18.44	22.63	60.53	21.32	8,612	800-480-4111	Y
JPMorgan SmartRetirement® 2030 Fund Class R4	JSMQX	B-	C+	B	Down	4.47	8.98	18.74	23.49	62.46	21.39	8,612	800-480-4111	Y
JPMorgan SmartRetirement® 2030 Fund Class R5	JSMIX	B-	B-	B	Down	4.53	9.01	18.88	23.76	62.82	21.47	8,612	800-480-4111	Y
JPMorgan SmartRetirement® 2030 Fund Class R6	JSMYX	B-	B-	B	Down	4.56	9.12	19.00	24.06	63.21	21.47	8,612	800-480-4111	Y
JPMorgan SmartRetirement® 2035 Fund Class A	SRJAX	B-	B-	B-	Down	4.83	9.66	20.15	24.51	66.54	20.79	6,440	800-480-4111	Y
JPMorgan SmartRetirement® 2035 Fund Class C	SRJCX	B-	C+	B-	Down	3.63	8.20	18.19	20.89	59.59	20.62	6,440	800-480-4111	Y
JPMorgan SmartRetirement® 2035 Fund Class I	SRJSX	B-	B-	B-	Down	4.84	9.73	20.23	24.92	67.37	20.89	6,440	800-480-4111	Y
JPMorgan SmartRetirement® 2035 Fund Class R2	SRJZX	B-	B-	B-	Down	3.66	8.33	18.46	22.19	62.56	20.73	6,440	800-480-4111	Y
JPMorgan SmartRetirement® 2035 Fund Class R3	SRJPX	B-	B-	B-	Down	4.81	9.57	19.88	24.19	66.09	20.72	6,440	800-480-4111	Y
JPMorgan SmartRetirement® 2035 Fund Class R4	SRJQX	B-	B-	B-	Down	4.90	9.73	20.24	25.18	68.26	20.87	6,440	800-480-4111	Y
JPMorgan SmartRetirement® 2035 Fund Class R5	SRJIX	B-	B-	B-	Down	4.92	9.78	20.41	25.42	68.58	20.91	6,440	800-480-4111	Y
JPMorgan SmartRetirement® 2035 Fund Class R6	SRJYX	B-	B-	B-	Down	4.95	9.84	20.53	25.65	68.89	20.91	6,440	800-480-4111	Y
JPMorgan SmartRetirement® 2040 Fund Class A	SMTAX	B-	B-	B-	Down	3.93	9.02	20.14	24.71	68.22	22.52	6,524	800-480-4111	Y
JPMorgan SmartRetirement® 2040 Fund Class C	SMTCX	B-	B-	B-	Down	5.07	10.00	20.80	23.78	64.76	22.23	6,524	800-480-4111	Y
JPMorgan SmartRetirement® 2040 Fund Class I	SMTSX	B-	B-	B-	Down	3.97	9.07	20.28	25.04	69.01	22.59	6,524	800-480-4111	Y
JPMorgan SmartRetirement® 2040 Fund Class R2	SMTZX	B-	B-	B-	Down	3.96	8.96	19.81	23.73	66.06	22.41	6,524	800-480-4111	Y
JPMorgan SmartRetirement® 2040 Fund Class R3	SMTPX	B-	B-	B-	Down	3.94	8.96	19.96	24.41	67.87	22.47	6,524	800-480-4111	Y
JPMorgan SmartRetirement® 2040 Fund Class R4	SMTQX	B-	B-	B-	Down	5.24	10.41	21.71	26.79	71.94	22.56	6,524	800-480-4111	Y
JPMorgan SmartRetirement® 2040 Fund Class R5	SMTIX	B-	B-	B-	Down	5.25	10.43	21.82	27.03	72.26	22.64	6,524	800-480-4111	Y
JPMorgan SmartRetirement® 2040 Fund Class R6	SMTYX	B-	B-	B-	Down	5.27	10.48	21.94	27.34	72.68	22.64	6,524	800-480-4111	Y
JPMorgan SmartRetirement® 2045 Fund Class A	JSAAX	B-	B-	B-	Down	4.02	9.16	20.32	24.98	68.52	21.42	4,298	800-480-4111	Y
JPMorgan SmartRetirement® 2045 Fund Class C	JSACX	B-	B-	B-	Down	5.08	10.09	20.95	24.02	65.02	21.25	4,298	800-480-4111	Y
JPMorgan SmartRetirement® 2045 Fund Class I	JSASX	B-	B-	B-	Down	4.00	9.15	20.40	25.31	69.31	21.49	4,298	800-480-4111	Y
JPMorgan SmartRetirement® 2045 Fund Class R2	JSAZX	B-	B-	B-	Down	4.03	9.02	20.02	24.00	66.30	21.34	4,298	800-480-4111	Y
JPMorgan SmartRetirement® 2045 Fund Class R3	JSAPX	B-	B-	B-	Down	3.98	9.06	20.16	24.69	68.04	21.36	4,298	800-480-4111	Y
JPMorgan SmartRetirement® 2045 Fund Class R4	JSAQX	B-	B-	B-	Down	5.27	10.49	21.88	27.11	72.16	21.46	4,298	800-480-4111	Y
JPMorgan SmartRetirement® 2045 Fund Class R5	JSAIX	B-	B-	B-	Down	4.00	9.17	20.55	25.77	70.35	21.51	4,298	800-480-4111	Y
JPMorgan SmartRetirement® 2045 Fund Class R6	JSAYX	B-	B-	B-	Down	5.37	10.64	22.17	27.65	72.89	21.51	4,298	800-480-4111	Y
JPMorgan SmartRetirement® Blend 2025 Fund Class I	JBSSX	B-	C+	B	Up	3.65	7.23	15.28	21.44	51.42	21.19	515.3	800-480-4111	Y
JPMorgan SmartRetirement® Blend 2025 Fund Class R2	JBRSX	B-	C+	B	Up	3.49	6.93	14.68	19.77	48.17	21.18	515.3	800-480-4111	Y
JPMorgan SmartRetirement® Blend 2025 Fund Class R3	JBTUX	B-	C+	B	Up	3.54	7.05	15.11	21.24	51.16	21.18	515.3	800-480-4111	Y
JPMorgan SmartRetirement® Blend 2025 Fund Class R4	JBTBX	B-	C+	B	Up	3.60	7.18	15.40	22.15	53.06	21.18	515.3	800-480-4111	Y
JPMorgan SmartRetirement® Blend 2025 Fund Class R5	JBBSX	B-	C+	B	Up	3.64	7.31	15.45	22.05	52.92	21.2	515.3	800-480-4111	Y
JPMorgan SmartRetirement® Blend 2025 Fund Class R6	JBYSX	B-	C+	B	Up	3.66	7.36	15.56	22.32	53.27	21.2	515.3	800-480-4111	Y
JPMorgan SmartRetirement® Blend 2030 Fund Class I	JRBEX	B-	C+	B	Down	4.14	8.15	17.22	23.86	58.27	22.29	547.2	800-480-4111	Y
JPMorgan SmartRetirement® Blend 2030 Fund Class R2	JRBRX	B-	C+	B	Down	3.96	7.83	16.58	22.19	54.89	22.29	547.2	800-480-4111	Y
JPMorgan SmartRetirement® Blend 2030 Fund Class R3	JUTPX	B-	C+	B	Down	4.03	7.97	16.97	23.49	57.67	22.27	547.2	800-480-4111	Y
JPMorgan SmartRetirement® Blend 2030 Fund Class R4	JUTUX	B-	C+	B	Down	4.09	8.10	17.26	24.42	59.65	22.27	547.2	800-480-4111	Y
JPMorgan SmartRetirement® Blend 2030 Fund Class R5	JRBBX	B-	C+	B	Down	4.13	8.18	17.34	24.51	59.76	22.29	547.2	800-480-4111	Y
JPMorgan SmartRetirement® Blend 2030 Fund Class R6	JRBYX	B-	B-	B	Down	4.15	8.22	17.43	24.76	60.17	22.3	547.2	800-480-4111	Y
JPMorgan SmartRetirement® Blend 2035 Fund Class I	JPSRX	B-	B-	B	Down	4.53	8.85	18.63	25.67	63.71	23.17	415.5	800-480-4111	Y
JPMorgan SmartRetirement® Blend 2035 Fund Class R2	JPRRX	B-	C+	B	Down	4.35	8.53	17.99	23.96	60.25	23.17	415.5	800-480-4111	Y
JPMorgan SmartRetirement® Blend 2035 Fund Class R3	JPTLX	B-	B-	B	Down	4.42	8.67	18.39	25.45	63.43	23.16	415.5	800-480-4111	Y
JPMorgan SmartRetirement® Blend 2035 Fund Class R4	JPTKX	B-	B-	B	Down	4.49	8.80	18.69	26.40	65.49	23.16	415.5	800-480-4111	Y
JPMorgan SmartRetirement® Blend 2035 Fund Class R5	JPBRX	B-	B-	B	Down	4.57	8.92	18.79	26.40	65.29	23.19	415.5	800-480-4111	Y
JPMorgan SmartRetirement® Blend 2035 Fund Class R6	JPYRX	B-	B-	B	Down	4.59	8.98	18.90	26.62	65.78	23.19	415.5	800-480-4111	Y
JPMorgan SmartRetirement® Blend 2040 Fund Class I	JOBEX	B-	B-	B-	Down	4.86	9.44	19.96	27.36	67.70	23.78	418.9	800-480-4111	Y
JPMorgan SmartRetirement® Blend 2040 Fund Class R2	JOBRX	B-	B-	B-	Down	4.73	9.21	19.42	25.69	64.10	23.79	418.9	800-480-4111	Y

Category: Target Date 2021-2045 (con't)

Fund Name	Ticker Symbol	RATINGS: Overall Rating	Reward Rating	Risk Rating	Recent Up/ Downgrade	TOTAL RETURNS & PERFORMANCE: 3-Month Total Return	6-Month Total Return	1-Year Total Return	3-Year Total Return	5-Year Total Return	ASSETS: NAV	Total Assets (MIL)	NEW INVESTORS: Telephone	Open to New Investors
JPMorgan SmartRetirement® Blend 2040 Fund Class R3	JNTEX	B-	B-	B-	Down	4.75	9.30	19.75	26.96	67.01	23.77	418.9	800-480-4111	Y
JPMorgan SmartRetirement® Blend 2040 Fund Class R4	JNTNX	B-	B-	B-	Down	4.82	9.44	20.05	27.92	69.11	23.77	418.9	800-480-4111	Y
JPMorgan SmartRetirement® Blend 2040 Fund Class R5	JOBBX	B-	B-	B-	Down	4.90	9.55	20.18	28.05	69.29	23.8	418.9	800-480-4111	Y
JPMorgan SmartRetirement® Blend 2040 Fund Class R6	JOBYX	B-	B-	B-	Down	4.92	9.61	20.29	28.34	69.80	23.8	418.9	800-480-4111	Y
JPMorgan SmartRetirement® Blend 2045 Fund Class I	JMSSX	B-	B-	B-	Down	4.92	9.64	20.16	27.74	67.84	23.75	285.2	800-480-4111	Y
JPMorgan SmartRetirement® Blend 2045 Fund Class R2	JNARX	B-	B-	B-	Down	4.79	9.37	19.57	25.98	64.30	23.75	285.2	800-480-4111	Y
JPMorgan SmartRetirement® Blend 2045 Fund Class R3	JNTOX	B-	B-	B-	Down	4.82	9.47	19.98	27.50	67.65	23.73	285.2	800-480-4111	Y
JPMorgan SmartRetirement® Blend 2045 Fund Class R4	JNTLX	B-	B-	B-	Down	4.92	9.65	20.33	28.52	69.82	23.74	285.2	800-480-4111	Y
JPMorgan SmartRetirement® Blend 2045 Fund Class R5	JMBRX	B-	B-	B-	Down	4.96	9.72	20.39	28.41	69.39	23.76	285.2	800-480-4111	Y
JPMorgan SmartRetirement® Blend 2045 Fund Class R6	JMYAX	B-	B-	B-	Down	4.98	9.76	20.48	28.68	70.03	23.78	285.2	800-480-4111	Y
KP Retirement Path 2025 Fund Institutional Shares	KPRCX	B-	C+	B	Up	3.38	6.99	14.58	21.28		11.22	1,047		Y
KP Retirement Path 2030 Fund Institutional Shares	KPRDX	B-	C+	B	Down	3.83	7.98	16.92	24.20		11.44	994.8		Y
KP Retirement Path 2035 Fund Institutional Shares	KPREX	B-	B-	B	Down	4.38	8.98	18.92	26.79		11.68	1,112		Y
KP Retirement Path 2040 Fund Institutional Shares	KPRFX	B-	B-	B-	Down	4.60	9.55	20.28	28.47		11.83	1,024		Y
KP Retirement Path 2045 Fund Institutional Shares	KPRGX	B-	B-	B-	Down	4.68	9.80	21.00	29.22		11.9	748.3		Y
MainStay Retirement 2030 Fund Class A	MRTTX	B-	C+	B	Down	4.28	8.28	17.51	22.42	60.76	11.44	253.1	800-624-6782	Y
MainStay Retirement 2030 Fund Class I	MRTIX	B-	C+	B	Down	4.34	8.40	17.77	23.20	62.56	11.53	253.1	800-624-6782	Y
MainStay Retirement 2030 Fund Class R1	MRTOX	B-	C+	B	Down	4.29	8.36	17.75	22.92	62.05	11.77	253.1	800-624-6782	Y
MainStay Retirement 2030 Fund Class R2	MRTUX	B-	C+	B	Down	4.08	8.07	17.27	21.87	59.62	11.46	253.1	800-624-6782	Y
MainStay Retirement 2030 Fund Class R3	MRTVX	B-	C+	B	Down	4.15	8.10	17.07	20.99	57.72	11.61	253.1	800-624-6782	Y
MainStay Retirement 2030 Fund Investor Class	MRTFX	B-	C+	B	Down	4.26	8.25	17.46	22.11	60.00	11.48	253.1	800-624-6782	Y
MainStay Retirement 2040 Fund Class A	MSRTX	B-	B-	B-	Down	4.81	9.37	19.91	24.69	68.52	11.95	213.2	800-624-6782	Y
MainStay Retirement 2040 Fund Class I	MSRYX	B-	B-	B-	Down	4.85	9.54	20.30	25.75	70.66	12.09	213.2	800-624-6782	Y
MainStay Retirement 2040 Fund Class R1	MSREX	B-	B-	B-	Down	4.87	9.48	20.13	25.38	70.16	12.32	213.2	800-624-6782	Y
MainStay Retirement 2040 Fund Class R2	MSRQX	B-	B-	B-	Down	4.54	9.17	19.64	24.18	67.43	12.03	213.2	800-624-6782	Y
MainStay Retirement 2040 Fund Class R3	MSRZX	B-	B-	B-	Down	4.68	9.17	19.55	23.40	65.73	12.13	213.2	800-624-6782	Y
MainStay Retirement 2040 Fund Investor Class	MSRUX	B-	B-	B-	Down	4.73	9.36	19.85	24.41	67.80	12.03	213.2	800-624-6782	Y
Manning & Napier Target 2025 Series Class I	MTOAX	B-	C+	B	Up	1.50	4.59	13.66	11.83	40.12	11.97	41.6	585-325-6880	Y
Manning & Napier Target 2025 Series Class K	MTOKX	B-	C+	B	Up	1.47	4.46	13.38	11.01	38.63	12.01	41.6	585-325-6880	Y
Manning & Napier Target 2025 Series Class R	MTORX	B-	C+	B	Up	1.40	4.38	13.16	10.21	36.82	12.05	41.6	585-325-6880	Y
Manning & Napier Target 2025 Series R6	MTOZX	B-	C+	B		1.53	4.62	13.69	11.86	40.16	11.97	41.6	585-325-6880	Y
Manning & Napier Target 2030 Series Class I	MTPIX	B-	C+	B	Up	2.25	5.80	16.32	14.75	47.31	9.7	143.8	585-325-6880	Y
Manning & Napier Target 2030 Series Class K	MTPKX	B-	C+	B	Up	2.14	5.62	15.96	13.87	45.46	9.6	143.8	585-325-6880	Y
Manning & Napier Target 2030 Series Class R	MTPRX	B-	C+	B	Up	2.08	5.47	15.81	13.02	43.62	9.52	143.8	585-325-6880	Y
Manning & Napier Target 2030 Series Fund R6	MTPZX	B-	C+	B		2.28	5.84	16.36	14.79	47.35	9.69	143.8	585-325-6880	Y
Manning & Napier Target 2035 Series Class I	MTQIX	B-	C+	B	Up	3.02	6.85	18.62	17.04	53.73	12.72	27.5	585-325-6880	Y
Manning & Napier Target 2035 Series Class K	MTQKX	B-	C+	B	Up	3.08	6.75	18.43	16.29	51.94	12.68	27.5	585-325-6880	Y
Manning & Napier Target 2035 Series Class R	MTQRX	B-	C+	B	Up	3.01	6.67	18.14	15.36	50.21	12.73	27.5	585-325-6880	Y
Manning & Napier Target 2035 Series R6	MTQZX	B-	C+	B		3.13	6.96	18.75	17.17	53.90	12.73	27.5	585-325-6880	Y
Manning & Napier Target 2040 Series Class I	MTTIX	B-	C+	B	Up	3.95	8.08	21.02	19.49	60.34	10.11	86.8	585-325-6880	Y
Manning & Napier Target 2040 Series Class K	MTTKX	B-	C+	B	Up	3.85	7.90	20.75	18.56	58.29	10.03	86.8	585-325-6880	Y
Manning & Napier Target 2040 Series Class R	MTTRX	B-	C+	B	Up	3.80	7.77	20.48	17.60	56.33	9.95	86.8	585-325-6880	Y
Manning & Napier Target 2040 Series Fund R6	MTTZX	B-	C+	B		3.98	8.12	21.05	19.53	60.39	10.11	86.8	585-325-6880	Y
Manning & Napier Target 2045 Series Class I	MTUIX	B-	C+	B	Up	4.78	9.15	23.35	21.84	65.01	13.1	16.5	585-325-6880	Y
Manning & Napier Target 2045 Series Class K	MTUKX	B-	C+	B	Up	4.74	9.03	23.11	20.95	63.00	13.08	16.5	585-325-6880	Y
Manning & Napier Target 2045 Series Class R	MTURX	B-	C+	B	Up	4.62	8.85	22.73	20.01	60.91	13	16.5	585-325-6880	Y
Manning & Napier Target 2045 Series R6	MTUZX	B-	C+	B		4.89	9.27	23.48	21.97	65.19	13.11	16.5	585-325-6880	Y
MassMutual RetireSMART 2025 Fund Administrative Class	MMIYX	B-	C+	B-	Down	3.61	7.42	15.85	19.89	51.98	13.04	279.0		Y
MassMutual RetireSMART 2025 Fund Class I	MMNUX	B-	C+	B-	Down	3.73	7.62	16.14	21.03	53.76	13.06	279.0		Y
MassMutual RetireSMART 2025 Fund Class R4	MMNZX	B-	C+	B-	Down	3.60	7.38	15.61	19.34	50.71	12.89	279.0		Y
MassMutual RetireSMART 2025 Fund Class R5	MMNTX	B-	C+	B-	Down	3.75	7.55	16.16	20.67	53.31	13.08	279.0		Y
MassMutual RetireSMART 2025 Fund Service Class	MMISX	B-	C+	B-	Down	3.69	7.57	16.00	20.29	52.73	13.08	279.0		Y

Category: Target Date 2021-2045 (con't)

Fund Name	Ticker Symbol	RATINGS: Overall Rating	RATINGS: Reward Rating	RATINGS: Risk Rating	RATINGS: Recent Up/ Downgrade	TOTAL RETURNS & PERFORMANCE: 3-Month Total Return	6-Month Total Return	1-Year Total Return	3-Year Total Return	5-Year Total Return	ASSETS: NAV	Total Assets (MIL)	NEW INVESTORS: Telephone	Open to New Investors
MassMutual RetireSMART 2030 Fund Administrative Class	MRYYX	B-	C+	B-	Down	4.05	8.26	17.42	21.61	55.98	13.4	551.4		Y
MassMutual RetireSMART 2030 Fund Class I	MRYUX	B-	C+	B-	Down	4.14	8.44	17.78	22.75	58.07	13.4	551.4		Y
MassMutual RetireSMART 2030 Fund Class R4	MRYZX	B-	C+	B-	Down	4.00	8.18	17.25	21.04	54.76	13.23	551.4		Y
MassMutual RetireSMART 2030 Fund Class R5	MRYTX	B-	C+	B-	Down	4.06	8.36	17.63	22.39	57.34	13.37	551.4		Y
MassMutual RetireSMART 2030 Fund Service Class	MRYSX	B-	C+	B-	Down	4.07	8.29	17.52	21.96	56.84	13.41	551.4		Y
MassMutual RetireSMART 2035 Fund Administrative Class	MMXYX	B-	C+	B-	Down	4.41	8.82	18.46	22.66	58.90	13.71	211.9		Y
MassMutual RetireSMART 2035 Fund Class A	MMXAX	B-	C+	B-	Down	4.39	8.76	18.20	21.81	56.72	13.62	211.9		Y
MassMutual RetireSMART 2035 Fund Class I	MMXUX	B-	B-	B-	Down	4.43	9.02	18.94	23.89	60.66	13.61	211.9		Y
MassMutual RetireSMART 2035 Fund Class R4	MMXZX	B-	C+	B-	Down	4.34	8.80	18.37	22.16	57.55	13.55	211.9		Y
MassMutual RetireSMART 2035 Fund Class R5	MMXTX	B-	C+	B-	Down	4.38	8.97	18.71	23.37	59.98	13.6	211.9		Y
MassMutual RetireSMART 2035 Fund Service Class	MMXSX	B-	C+	B-	Down	4.41	8.88	18.60	23.03	59.65	13.75	211.9		Y
MassMutual RetireSMART 2040 Fund Administrative Class	MRFYX	B-	C+	B-	Down	4.58	9.13	19.02	23.16	59.89	13.23	333.5		Y
MassMutual RetireSMART 2040 Fund Class I	MRFUX	B-	B-	B-	Down	4.60	9.30	19.29	24.18	61.63	13.23	333.5		Y
MassMutual RetireSMART 2040 Fund Class R3	MFRNX	B-	C+	B-	Down	4.45	8.96	18.51	21.69	56.17	12.87	333.5		Y
MassMutual RetireSMART 2040 Fund Class R4	MRFZX	B-	C+	B-	Down	4.46	8.99	18.80	22.50	58.58	13.04	333.5		Y
MassMutual RetireSMART 2040 Fund Class R5	MRFTX	B-	B-	B-	Down	4.59	9.21	19.19	23.97	61.21	13.23	333.5		Y
MassMutual RetireSMART 2040 Fund Service Class	MFRSX	B-	C+	B-	Down	4.61	9.23	19.11	23.56	60.71	13.26	333.5		Y
MassMutual RetireSMART 2045 Fund Administrative Class	MMKYX	B-	B-	B-	Down	4.63	9.21	19.31	23.45	63.66	13.76	127.4		Y
MassMutual RetireSMART 2045 Fund Class A	MMKAX	B-	C+	B-	Down	4.48	9.10	18.99	22.53	61.30	13.66	127.4		Y
MassMutual RetireSMART 2045 Fund Class I	MMKUX	B-	B-	B-	Down	4.67	9.40	19.68	24.59	65.42	13.79	127.4		Y
MassMutual RetireSMART 2045 Fund Class R3	MMKNX	B-	C+	B-	Up	4.46	9.03	18.77	21.93	60.23	13.57	127.4		Y
MassMutual RetireSMART 2045 Fund Class R4	MMKZX	B-	C+	B-	Down	4.55	9.11	19.13	22.88	62.19	13.59	127.4		Y
MassMutual RetireSMART 2045 Fund Class R5	MMKTX	B-	B-	B-	Down	4.69	9.41	19.59	24.32	64.94	13.81	127.4		Y
MassMutual RetireSMART 2045 Fund Service Class	MMKSX	B-	B-	B-	Down	4.64	9.29	19.46	23.80	64.34	13.79	127.4		Y
MFS® Lifetime 2025 Fund Class A	LTTAX	B	C+	A-	Up	3.07	5.95	13.06	19.83	48.36	12.88	270.2	877-960-6077	Y
MFS® Lifetime 2025 Fund Class B	LTTBX	B-	C+	B	Up	2.87	5.51	12.18	17.08	42.85	12.81	270.2	877-960-6077	Y
MFS® Lifetime 2025 Fund Class C	LTTCX	B	C+	B+	Up	2.88	5.53	12.13	17.13	42.90	12.75	270.2	877-960-6077	Y
MFS® Lifetime 2025 Fund Class I	LTTIX	B-	C+	B	Up	3.03	5.97	13.15	20.61	50.13	12.91	270.2	877-960-6077	Y
MFS® Lifetime 2025 Fund Class R1	LTTRX	B	C+	B+	Up	2.79	5.50	12.13	17.02	42.81	12.84	270.2	877-960-6077	Y
MFS® Lifetime 2025 Fund Class R2	LTTSX	B	C+	A-	Up	3.01	5.73	12.67	18.83	46.52	12.81	270.2	877-960-6077	Y
MFS® Lifetime 2025 Fund Class R3	LTTTX	B-	C+	B	Up	3.01	5.88	12.90	19.71	48.22	12.86	270.2	877-960-6077	Y
MFS® Lifetime 2025 Fund Class R4	LTTUX	B-	C+	B	Up	3.02	5.96	13.24	20.60	49.95	12.92	270.2	877-960-6077	Y
MFS® Lifetime 2025 Fund Class R6	LTTKX	B-	C+	B	Up	3.08	6.02	13.38	20.82	50.38	12.92	270.2	877-960-6077	Y
MFS® Lifetime 2030 Fund Class A	MLTAX	B-	C+	B	Down	4.09	7.79	16.91	25.33	60.44	15.48	594.8	877-960-6077	Y
MFS® Lifetime 2030 Fund Class B	MLTBX	B-	C+	B	Down	3.85	7.32	16.02	22.51	54.52	15.3	594.8	877-960-6077	Y
MFS® Lifetime 2030 Fund Class C	MLTCX	B	C+	B+	Up	3.89	7.38	16.06	22.55	54.53	15.21	594.8	877-960-6077	Y
MFS® Lifetime 2030 Fund Class I	MLTIX	B-	B-	B	Down	4.11	7.87	17.19	25.98	62.02	15.54	594.8	877-960-6077	Y
MFS® Lifetime 2030 Fund Class R1	MLTEX	B-	C+	B	Down	3.86	7.31	15.97	22.49	54.53	15.36	594.8	877-960-6077	Y
MFS® Lifetime 2030 Fund Class R2	MLTGX	B-	C+	B	Down	4.02	7.62	16.56	24.36	58.43	15.34	594.8	877-960-6077	Y
MFS® Lifetime 2030 Fund Class R3	MLTHX	B-	C+	B	Down	4.12	7.83	16.97	25.31	60.49	15.45	594.8	877-960-6077	Y
MFS® Lifetime 2030 Fund Class R4	MLTJX	B-	B-	B	Down	4.11	7.94	17.18	26.26	62.45	15.56	594.8	877-960-6077	Y
MFS® Lifetime 2030 Fund Class R6	MLTKX	B	B-	B+	Up	4.17	7.99	17.32	26.54	62.74	15.55	594.8	877-960-6077	Y
MFS® Lifetime 2035 Fund Class A	LFEAX	B-	B-	B	Down	4.78	8.95	19.13	28.33	67.16	14.59	249.1	877-960-6077	Y
MFS® Lifetime 2035 Fund Class B	LFEBX	B-	B-	B	Down	4.55	8.52	18.18	25.38	60.99	14.5	249.1	877-960-6077	Y
MFS® Lifetime 2035 Fund Class C	LFECX	B-	B-	B	Down	4.57	8.55	18.25	25.44	61.09	14.46	249.1	877-960-6077	Y
MFS® Lifetime 2035 Fund Class I	LFEDX	B-	B-	B	Down	4.80	9.04	19.48	28.94	68.84	14.6	249.1	877-960-6077	Y
MFS® Lifetime 2035 Fund Class R1	LFERX	B-	B-	B	Down	4.54	8.49	18.20	25.45	60.98	14.51	249.1	877-960-6077	Y
MFS® Lifetime 2035 Fund Class R2	LFESX	B-	B-	B	Down	4.70	8.81	18.83	27.34	65.16	14.53	249.1	877-960-6077	Y
MFS® Lifetime 2035 Fund Class R3	LFETX	B-	B-	B	Down	4.71	8.88	19.12	28.25	67.23	14.6	249.1	877-960-6077	Y
MFS® Lifetime 2035 Fund Class R4	LFEUX	B-	B-	B	Down	4.83	9.06	19.47	29.24	69.24	14.65	249.1	877-960-6077	Y
MFS® Lifetime 2035 Fund Class R6	LFEKX	B-	B-	B	Down	4.87	9.18	19.60	29.53	69.62	14.65	249.1	877-960-6077	Y
MFS® Lifetime 2040 Fund Class A	MLFAX	B-	B-	B	Down	5.09	9.52	20.46	29.90	70.66	16.33	465.2	877-960-6077	Y

Category: Target Date 2021-2045 (con't)

Fund Name	Ticker Symbol	Overall Rating	Reward Rating	Risk Rating	Recent Up/ Downgrade	3-Month Total Return	6-Month Total Return	1-Year Total Return	3-Year Total Return	5-Year Total Return	NAV	Total Assets (MIL)	Telephone	Open to New Investors
MFS® Lifetime 2040 Fund Class B	MLFBX	B-	B-	B	Down	4.94	9.14	19.57	26.98	64.47	16.22	465.2	877-960-6077	Y
MFS® Lifetime 2040 Fund Class C	MLFCX	B-	B-	B	Down	4.92	9.16	19.56	27.01	64.48	16.02	465.2	877-960-6077	Y
MFS® Lifetime 2040 Fund Class I	MLFIX	B-	B-	B	Down	5.16	9.71	20.78	30.51	72.46	16.41	465.2	877-960-6077	Y
MFS® Lifetime 2040 Fund Class R1	MLFEX	B-	B-	B	Down	4.96	9.18	19.57	26.99	64.41	16.16	465.2	877-960-6077	Y
MFS® Lifetime 2040 Fund Class R2	MLFGX	B-	B-	B	Down	5.07	9.40	20.17	28.88	68.64	16.21	465.2	877-960-6077	Y
MFS® Lifetime 2040 Fund Class R3	MLFHX	B-	B-	B	Down	5.10	9.54	20.49	29.84	70.73	16.32	465.2	877-960-6077	Y
MFS® Lifetime 2040 Fund Class R4	MLFJX	B-	B-	B	Down	5.22	9.70	20.83	30.85	72.95	16.45	465.2	877-960-6077	Y
MFS® Lifetime 2040 Fund Class R6	MLFKX	B-	B-	B	Down	5.21	9.75	20.88	31.05	73.18	16.44	465.2	877-960-6077	Y
MFS® Lifetime 2045 Fund Class A	LTMAX	B-	B-	B	Down	5.25	9.78	20.87	30.35	71.69	15.1	169.4	877-960-6077	Y
MFS® Lifetime 2045 Fund Class B	LTMBX	B-	B-	B-	Down	5.13	9.40	20.07	27.58	65.19	15.03	169.4	877-960-6077	Y
MFS® Lifetime 2045 Fund Class C	LTMDX	B-	B-	B-	Down	5.15	9.43	20.06	27.53	65.26	14.97	169.4	877-960-6077	Y
MFS® Lifetime 2045 Fund Class I	LTMKX	B-	B-	B	Down	5.36	9.95	21.19	31.52	73.83	15.16	169.4	877-960-6077	Y
MFS® Lifetime 2045 Fund Class R1	LTMRX	B-	B-	B-	Down	5.16	9.40	20.04	27.53	65.20	15.06	169.4	877-960-6077	Y
MFS® Lifetime 2045 Fund Class R2	LTMSX	B-	B-	B	Down	5.20	9.69	20.57	29.36	69.32	15	169.4	877-960-6077	Y
MFS® Lifetime 2045 Fund Class R3	LTMTX	B-	B-	B	Down	5.26	9.79	20.89	30.40	71.48	15.09	169.4	877-960-6077	Y
MFS® Lifetime 2045 Fund Class R4	LTMUX	B-	B-	B	Down	5.32	9.91	21.17	31.39	73.53	15.14	169.4	877-960-6077	Y
MFS® Lifetime 2045 Fund Class R6	LTMLX	B-	B-	B	Down	5.35	9.94	21.29	31.48	73.78	15.13	169.4	877-960-6077	Y
Nationwide Destination 2025 Fund Class A	NWHAX	B-	C+	B	Down	3.61	6.77	13.97	20.23	48.89	9.84	321.4	800-848-0920	Y
Nationwide Destination 2025 Fund Class C	NWHCX	B-	C+	B	Down	3.39	6.42	13.17	18.00	44.55	9.73	321.4	800-848-0920	Y
Nationwide Destination 2025 Fund Class R	NWHBX	B-	C+	B	Down	3.55	6.64	13.57	19.19	46.83	9.81	321.4	800-848-0920	Y
Nationwide Destination 2025 Fund Class R6	NWHIX	B-	C+	B	Down	3.62	6.98	14.42	21.86	52.25	9.9	321.4	800-848-0920	Y
Nationwide Destination 2025 Fund Institutional Service Cls	NWHSX	B-	C+	B	Down	3.57	6.88	14.21	20.94	50.50	9.85	321.4	800-848-0920	Y
Nationwide Destination 2030 Fund Class A	NWIAX	B-	C+	B-	Down	3.97	7.54	15.10	22.20	56.03	9.56	320.4	800-848-0920	Y
Nationwide Destination 2030 Fund Class C	NWICX	B-	C+	B-	Down	3.76	7.10	14.48	20.05	51.87	9.45	320.4	800-848-0920	Y
Nationwide Destination 2030 Fund Class R	NWBIX	B-	C+	B-	Down	3.81	7.33	14.76	21.12	53.91	9.5	320.4	800-848-0920	Y
Nationwide Destination 2030 Fund Class R6	NWIIX	B-	C+	B	Down	4.07	7.75	15.67	23.92	59.80	9.62	320.4	800-848-0920	Y
Nationwide Destination 2030 Fund Institutional Service Cls	NWISX	B-	C+	B	Down	4.03	7.67	15.36	23.02	57.84	9.57	320.4	800-848-0920	Y
Nationwide Destination 2035 Fund Class A	NWLAX	B-	C+	B-	Down	4.18	7.93	16.07	23.51	61.21	10.26	268.9	800-848-0920	Y
Nationwide Destination 2035 Fund Class C	NWLCX	B-	C+	B-	Down	4.00	7.65	15.35	21.20	56.53	10.07	268.9	800-848-0920	Y
Nationwide Destination 2035 Fund Class R	NWLBX	B-	C+	B-	Down	4.13	7.83	15.79	22.58	59.09	10.2	268.9	800-848-0920	Y
Nationwide Destination 2035 Fund Class R6	NWLIX	B-	B-	B-	Down	4.28	8.24	16.61	25.20	65.17	10.33	268.9	800-848-0920	Y
Nationwide Destination 2035 Fund Institutional Service Cls	NWLSX	B-	B-	B-	Down	4.23	8.05	16.30	24.30	63.06	10.27	268.9	800-848-0920	Y
Nationwide Destination 2040 Fund Class A	NWMAX	B-	B-	B-	Down	4.64	8.55	16.99	25.01	65.13	10.05	221.2	800-848-0920	Y
Nationwide Destination 2040 Fund Class C	NWMCX	B-	C+	B-	Down	4.41	8.19	16.36	22.74	60.43	9.99	221.2	800-848-0920	Y
Nationwide Destination 2040 Fund Class R	NWMDX	B-	B-	B-	Down	4.48	8.33	16.72	23.88	62.82	9.99	221.2	800-848-0920	Y
Nationwide Destination 2040 Fund Class R6	NWMHX	B-	B-	B-	Down	4.72	8.74	17.63	26.77	68.97	10.13	221.2	800-848-0920	Y
Nationwide Destination 2040 Fund Institutional Service Cls	NWMSX	B-	B-	B-	Down	4.57	8.52	17.28	25.67	66.79	10.09	221.2	800-848-0920	Y
Nationwide Destination 2045 Fund Class A	NWNAX	B-	B-	B-	Down	4.74	8.86	17.85	26.35	68.32	10.51	172.2	800-848-0920	Y
Nationwide Destination 2045 Fund Class C	NWNCX	B-	B-	B-	Down	4.64	8.52	17.05	24.04	63.24	10.39	172.2	800-848-0920	Y
Nationwide Destination 2045 Fund Class R	NWNBX	B-	B-	B-	Down	4.70	8.67	17.40	25.30	65.90	10.42	172.2	800-848-0920	Y
Nationwide Destination 2045 Fund Class R6	NWNIX	B-	B-	B-	Down	4.94	9.06	18.37	28.14	72.40	10.57	172.2	800-848-0920	Y
Nationwide Destination 2045 Fund Institutional Service Cls	NWNSX	B-	B-	B-	Down	4.81	9.00	18.11	27.17	70.20	10.49	172.2	800-848-0920	Y
PIMCO RealPath Blend 2025 Fund Administrative Class	PPZDX	B-	C+	B	Up	3.90	7.47	15.09	20.69		11.25	11.6	866-746-2602	Y
PIMCO RealPath Blend 2025 Fund Institutional Class	PPZRX	B-	C+	B	Up	3.99	7.61	15.46	21.69		11.27	11.6	866-746-2602	Y
PIMCO RealPath™ 2025 Fund Class A	PENZX	B-	C+	B	Down	3.67	6.97	14.27	16.64	26.09	9.48	35.5	866-746-2602	Y
PIMCO RealPath™ 2025 Fund Institutional Class	PENTX	B-	C+	B	Down	3.69	7.16	14.69	18.33	29.08	9.46	35.5	866-746-2602	Y
PIMCO RealPath™ 2030 Fund Administrative Class	PNLAX	B-	C+	B-	Down	4.05	7.76	16.05	19.56	32.50	7.84	46.1	866-746-2602	Y
Principal LifeTime 2025 Fund Institutional Class	LTSTX	B-	C+	B	Down	3.67	7.85	16.75	21.66	53.86	11.48	1,781	800-222-5852	Y
Principal LifeTime 2025 Fund R-1 Class	LTSNX	B-	C+	B	Down	3.47	7.36	15.74	18.55	47.22	11.26	1,781	800-222-5852	Y
Principal LifeTime 2025 Fund R-2 Class	LTADX	B-	C+	B	Down	3.48	7.46	15.83	19.00	48.18	11.29	1,781	800-222-5852	Y
Principal LifeTime 2025 Fund R-3 Class	LTVPX	B-	C+	B	Down	3.55	7.52	16.12	19.59	49.64	11.28	1,781	800-222-5852	Y
Principal LifeTime 2025 Fund R-4 Class	LTEEX	B-	C+	B	Down	3.55	7.68	16.33	20.26	51.00	11.38	1,781	800-222-5852	Y

Category: Target Date 2021-2045 (con't)

Fund Name	Ticker Symbol	RATINGS: Overall Rating	Reward Rating	Risk Rating	Recent Up/ Downgrade	TOTAL RETURNS & PERFORMANCE: 3-Month Total Return	6-Month Total Return	1-Year Total Return	3-Year Total Return	5-Year Total Return	ASSETS: NAV	Total Assets (MIL)	NEW INVESTORS: Telephone	Open to New Investors
Principal LifeTime 2025 Fund R-5 Class	LTPDX	B-	C+	B	Down	3.71	7.74	16.46	20.80	51.91	11.42	1,781	800-222-5852	Y
Principal LifeTime 2030 Fund Class A	PTCAX	B-	C+	B	Down	4.09	8.58	18.01	22.10	55.82	14.8	6,679	800-222-5852	Y
Principal LifeTime 2030 Fund Class J	PLTJX	B-	C+	B	Down	4.04	8.62	18.21	22.65	56.70	14.7	6,679	800-222-5852	Y
Principal LifeTime 2030 Fund Institutional Class	PMTIX	B-	C+	B	Down	4.12	8.76	18.42	23.51	58.74	14.74	6,679	800-222-5852	Y
Principal LifeTime 2030 Fund R-1 Class	PXASX	B-	C+	B	Down	3.93	8.24	17.40	20.27	51.87	14.67	6,679	800-222-5852	Y
Principal LifeTime 2030 Fund R-2 Class	PTCNX	B-	C+	B	Down	3.93	8.37	17.61	20.78	52.93	14.71	6,679	800-222-5852	Y
Principal LifeTime 2030 Fund R-3 Class	PTCMX	B-	C+	B	Down	3.96	8.48	17.81	21.40	54.26	14.7	6,679	800-222-5852	Y
Principal LifeTime 2030 Fund R-4 Class	PTCSX	B-	C+	B	Down	3.99	8.51	17.95	22.08	55.75	15.19	6,679	800-222-5852	Y
Principal LifeTime 2030 Fund R-5 Class	PTCPX	B-	C+	B	Down	4.06	8.63	18.20	22.57	56.75	14.74	6,679	800-222-5852	Y
Principal LifeTime 2035 Fund Institutional Class	LTIUX	B-	B-	B	Down	4.45	9.39	19.70	24.28	62.81	12.28	1,361	800-222-5852	Y
Principal LifeTime 2035 Fund R-1 Class	LTANX	B-	C+	B	Down	4.27	8.94	18.64	21.19	55.80	12.09	1,361	800-222-5852	Y
Principal LifeTime 2035 Fund R-2 Class	LTVIX	B	C+	B+	Up	4.29	8.96	18.78	21.56	56.81	12.07	1,361	800-222-5852	Y
Principal LifeTime 2035 Fund R-3 Class	LTAOX	B-	C+	B	Down	4.39	9.14	19.04	22.31	58.37	12.12	1,361	800-222-5852	Y
Principal LifeTime 2035 Fund R-4 Class	LTSEX	B-	C+	B	Down	4.39	9.20	19.25	23.06	59.79	12.2	1,361	800-222-5852	Y
Principal LifeTime 2035 Fund R-5 Class	LTPEX	B-	C+	B	Down	4.40	9.27	19.41	23.40	60.75	12.23	1,361	800-222-5852	Y
Principal LifeTime 2040 Fund Class A	PTDAX	B-	B-	B	Down	4.60	9.66	20.24	24.09	63.03	15.43	4,553	800-222-5852	Y
Principal LifeTime 2040 Fund Class J	PTDJX	B-	B-	B	Down	4.69	9.77	20.43	24.53	63.75	15.57	4,553	800-222-5852	Y
Principal LifeTime 2040 Fund Institutional Class	PTDIX	B-	B-	B	Down	4.75	9.87	20.69	25.46	66.18	15.7	4,553	800-222-5852	Y
Principal LifeTime 2040 Fund R-1 Class	PYASX	B-	C+	B-	Down	4.47	9.42	19.64	22.16	58.91	15.59	4,553	800-222-5852	Y
Principal LifeTime 2040 Fund R-2 Class	PTDNX	B-	C+	B-	Down	4.52	9.47	19.77	22.64	59.94	15.58	4,553	800-222-5852	Y
Principal LifeTime 2040 Fund R-3 Class	PTDMX	B-	C+	B-	Down	4.56	9.53	19.95	23.33	61.36	15.52	4,553	800-222-5852	Y
Principal LifeTime 2040 Fund R-4 Class	PTDSX	B-	B-	B	Down	4.59	9.61	20.20	24.06	62.98	15.54	4,553	800-222-5852	Y
Principal LifeTime 2040 Fund R-5 Class	PTDPX	B-	B-	B	Down	4.71	9.78	20.39	24.52	64.04	15.64	4,553	800-222-5852	Y
Principal LifeTime 2045 Fund Institutional Class	LTRIX	B-	B-	B-	Down	4.90	10.23	21.39	26.28	68.55	12.85	946.8	800-222-5852	Y
Principal LifeTime 2045 Fund R-1 Class	LTRGX	B-	C+	B-	Down	4.69	9.82	20.39	23.11	61.39	12.52	946.8	800-222-5852	Y
Principal LifeTime 2045 Fund R-2 Class	LTRSX	B-	B-	B-	Down	4.76	9.80	20.48	23.49	62.45	12.51	946.8	800-222-5852	Y
Principal LifeTime 2045 Fund R-3 Class	LTRVX	B-	B-	B-	Down	4.75	9.93	20.68	24.14	63.90	12.57	946.8	800-222-5852	Y
Principal LifeTime 2045 Fund R-4 Class	LTRLX	B-	B-	B-	Down	4.82	10.06	20.95	24.91	65.49	12.67	946.8	800-222-5852	Y
Principal LifeTime 2045 Fund R-5 Class	LTRDX	B-	B-	B-	Down	4.89	10.13	21.10	25.36	66.53	12.69	946.8	800-222-5852	Y
Principal LifeTime Hybrid 2025 Fund Institutional Class	PHTQX	B-	C+	B	Up	3.50	7.50	15.23	21.97		11.43	92.3	800-222-5852	Y
Principal LifeTime Hybrid 2025 Fund R-6	PLFTX	B-	C+	B	Up	3.41	7.40	15.12	21.84		11.43	92.3	800-222-5852	Y
Principal LifeTime Hybrid 2030 Fund Institutional Class	PHTNX	B-	C+	B	Up	3.86	8.21	16.81	23.94		11.61	125.3	800-222-5852	Y
Principal LifeTime Hybrid 2030 Fund R-6	PLZTX	B-	C+	B	Up	3.88	8.32	16.71	23.96		11.61	125.3	800-222-5852	Y
Principal LifeTime Hybrid 2035 Fund Institutional Class	PHTJX	B-	C+	B	Up	4.24	8.92	18.14	25.67		11.87	74.0	800-222-5852	Y
Principal LifeTime Hybrid 2035 Fund R-6	PLRTX	B-	C+	B	Up	4.15	8.82	18.02	25.67		11.87	74.0	800-222-5852	Y
Principal LifeTime Hybrid 2040 Fund Institutional Class	PLTQX	B-	C+	B	Up	4.45	9.39	19.16	27.04		11.99	90.6	800-222-5852	Y
Principal LifeTime Hybrid 2040 Fund R-6	PLMTX	B-	C+	B	Up	4.45	9.38	19.14	27.14		12	90.6	800-222-5852	Y
Principal LifeTime Hybrid 2045 Fund Institutional Class	PHTYX	B-	C+	B	Up	4.65	9.84	19.82	27.80		12.13	46.1	800-222-5852	Y
Principal LifeTime Hybrid 2045 Fund R-6	PLNTX	B-	C+	B	Up	4.65	9.83	19.91	28.03		12.14	46.1	800-222-5852	Y
Putnam RetirementReady 2025 Fund Class A	PRROX	B-	C+	B	Up	2.71	5.45	10.55	14.43	41.98	22.82	121.3	617-292-1000	Y
Putnam RetirementReady 2025 Fund Class B	US7468597437	B-	C+	B	Up	2.65	5.18	9.82	11.83	36.98		121.3	617-292-1000	Y
Putnam RetirementReady 2025 Fund Class C	US7468597353	B-	C+	B	Up	2.65	5.15	9.81	11.75	36.89		121.3	617-292-1000	Y
Putnam RetirementReady 2025 Fund Class M	US7468597270	B-	C+	B	Up	2.70	5.31	10.07	12.64	38.60		121.3	617-292-1000	Y
Putnam RetirementReady 2025 Fund Class R	US7468597197	B-	C+	B	Up	2.77	5.40	10.32	13.48	40.37		121.3	617-292-1000	Y
Putnam RetirementReady 2025 Fund Class R6	PRMFX	B-	C+	B	Up	2.76	5.62	10.95	15.45	43.97	22.97	121.3	617-292-1000	Y
Putnam RetirementReady 2025 Fund Class Y	PRRPX	B-	C+	B	Up	2.76	5.58	10.86	15.31	43.80	22.94	121.3	617-292-1000	Y
Putnam RetirementReady 2030 Fund Class A	PRRQX	B-	C+	B	Up	3.48	6.93	13.21	18.23	52.67	23	198.5	617-292-1000	Y
Putnam RetirementReady 2030 Fund Class B	US7468597924	B-	C+	B	Up	3.45	6.69	12.40	15.44	47.23		198.5	617-292-1000	Y
Putnam RetirementReady 2030 Fund Class C	US7468597841	B-	C+	B	Up	3.50	6.70	12.46	15.47	47.30		198.5	617-292-1000	Y
Putnam RetirementReady 2030 Fund Class M	US7468597767	B-	C+	B	Up	3.54	6.81	12.71	16.33	49.11		198.5	617-292-1000	Y
Putnam RetirementReady 2030 Fund Class R	US7468597684	B-	C+	B	Up	3.58	6.97	13.01	17.17	50.96		198.5	617-292-1000	Y
Putnam RetirementReady 2030 Fund Class R6	PREZX	B-	C+	B	Up	3.59	7.13	13.60	19.24	54.69	26.47	198.5	617-292-1000	Y

Category: Target Date 2021-2045 (con't)

		RATINGS				TOTAL RETURNS & PERFORMANCE					ASSETS		NEW INVESTORS	
Fund Name	Ticker Symbol	Overall Rating	Reward Rating	Risk Rating	Recent Up/ Downgrade	3-Month Total Return	6-Month Total Return	1-Year Total Return	3-Year Total Return	5-Year Total Return	NAV	Total Assets (MIL)	Telephone	Open to New Investors
Putnam RetirementReady 2030 Fund Class Y	PRRTX	B-	C+	B	Up	3.53	7.07	13.50	19.10	54.50	26.44	198.5	617-292-1000	Y
Putnam RetirementReady 2035 Fund Class A	PRRWX	B-	C+	B	Down	4.16	8.34	15.84	21.81	62.76	23.74	117.2	617-292-1000	Y
Putnam RetirementReady 2035 Fund Class B	US7468598591	B-	C+	B	Down	4.20	8.15	14.99	18.90	57.12		117.2	617-292-1000	Y
Putnam RetirementReady 2035 Fund Class C	US7468598427	B-	C+	B	Down	4.22	8.13	15.03	18.92	57.10		117.2	617-292-1000	Y
Putnam RetirementReady 2035 Fund Class M	US7468598344	B-	C+	B	Down	4.27	8.28	15.30	19.79	59.00		117.2	617-292-1000	Y
Putnam RetirementReady 2035 Fund Class R	US7468598260	B-	C+	B	Down	4.31	8.41	15.56	20.70	61.07		117.2	617-292-1000	Y
Putnam RetirementReady 2035 Fund Class R6	PREGX	B-	C+	B	Down	4.27	8.55	16.26	22.88	65.01	27.89	117.2	617-292-1000	Y
Putnam RetirementReady 2035 Fund Class Y	PRRYX	B-	C+	B	Down	4.22	8.47	16.09	22.67	64.73	27.85	117.2	617-292-1000	Y
Putnam RetirementReady 2040 Fund Class A	PRRZX	B-	B-	B	Down	5.00	9.71	17.93	24.18	71.17		152.3	617-292-1000	Y
Putnam RetirementReady 2040 Fund Class B	US7468597015	B-	C+	B	Down	4.85	9.36	17.13	21.47	64.97		152.3	617-292-1000	Y
Putnam RetirementReady 2040 Fund Class C	US7468598005	B-	C+	B	Down	4.82	9.34	17.10	21.44	64.93		152.3	617-292-1000	Y
Putnam RetirementReady 2040 Fund Class M	US7468598831	B-	C+	B	Down	4.88	9.45	17.42	22.34	67.02		152.3	617-292-1000	Y
Putnam RetirementReady 2040 Fund Class R	US7468598757	B-	C+	B	Down	4.97	9.62	17.68	23.29	69.12		152.3	617-292-1000	Y
Putnam RetirementReady 2040 Fund Class R6	PREHX	B-	B-	B	Down	5.11	9.94	18.36	25.27	73.52		152.3	617-292-1000	Y
Putnam RetirementReady 2040 Fund Class Y	PRZZX	B-	B-	B	Down	5.08	9.88	18.27	25.13	73.32		152.3	617-292-1000	Y
Putnam RetirementReady 2045 Fund Class A	PRVLX	B-	B-	B	Down	5.40	10.51	19.29	25.75	75.85		66.0	617-292-1000	Y
Putnam RetirementReady 2045 Fund Class B	US7468592065	B-	C+	B-	Down	5.20	10.09	18.40	22.92	69.32		66.0	617-292-1000	Y
Putnam RetirementReady 2045 Fund Class C	US7468593055	B-	C+	B-	Down	5.19	10.08	18.38	22.93	69.34		66.0	617-292-1000	Y
Putnam RetirementReady 2045 Fund Class M	US7468594046	B-	B-	B-	Down	5.24	10.25	18.69	23.87	71.47		66.0	617-292-1000	Y
Putnam RetirementReady 2045 Fund Class R	US7468595035	B-	B-	B	Down	5.35	10.38	18.99	24.81	73.67		66.0	617-292-1000	Y
Putnam RetirementReady 2045 Fund Class R6	PREKX	B-	B-	B	Down	5.48	10.71	19.73	26.88	78.28		66.0	617-292-1000	Y
Putnam RetirementReady 2045 Fund Class Y	PRVYX	B-	B-	B	Down	1.21	6.19	15.06	22.11	70.86	26.73	66.0	617-292-1000	Y
Schwab Target 2025 Fund	SWHRX	B-	C+	B	Up	3.41	7.01	15.56	21.28	55.92	14.5	530.2	877-824-5615	Y
Schwab Target 2030 Fund	SWDRX	B-	C+	B	Down	3.86	8.00	17.53	23.67	62.92	15.75	984.9	877-824-5615	Y
Schwab Target 2035 Fund	SWIRX	B-	B-	B	Down	4.24	8.69	19.12	25.59	69.24	15.5	448.4	877-824-5615	Y
Schwab Target 2040 Fund	SWERX	B-	B-	B	Down	4.55	9.34	20.46	27.33	74.36	16.95	1,017	877-824-5615	Y
Schwab Target 2045 Fund	SWMRX	B-	B-	B-	Down	4.80	9.77	21.38	28.55		13.96	125.2	877-824-5615	Y
State Farm LifePath 2030 Fund Class A	NLHAX	B	C+	B+	Up	3.85	7.29	15.46	20.00	45.04	16.43	2,460		Y
State Farm LifePath 2030 Fund Class B	NLHBX	B-	C+	B-	Down	3.83	7.29	15.42	19.01	41.83	16.38	2,460		Y
State Farm LifePath 2030 Fund Class Institutional	SAYIX	B-	C+	B	Down	3.83	7.25	15.51	20.62	46.57	16.54	2,460		Y
State Farm LifePath 2030 Fund Class R1	RAYOX	B-	C+	B	Down	3.77	7.24	15.31	19.06	42.93	16.33	2,460		Y
State Farm LifePath 2030 Fund Class R2	RAYTX	B-	C+	B	Down	3.79	7.18	15.37	19.53	44.16	16.38	2,460		Y
State Farm LifePath 2030 Fund Class R3	RAYHX	B	C+	B+	Up	3.83	7.25	15.43	20.42	46.02	16.55	2,460		Y
State Farm LifePath 2030 Fund Legacy Class B	SAYBX	B-	C+	B	Down	3.88	7.30	15.35	18.95	42.59	16.56	2,460		Y
State Farm LifePath 2030 Fund Premier Shares	SAYAX	B-	C+	B	Down	3.90	7.34	15.58	20.22	45.27	16.44	2,460		Y
State Farm LifePath 2040 Fund Class A	NLOAX	B-	B-	B-	Down	4.73	8.90	18.92	24.01	55.11	17.7	1,899		Y
State Farm LifePath 2040 Fund Class B	NLBOX	B-	C+	B-	Down	4.72	8.90	18.88	23.04	51.75	17.65	1,899		Y
State Farm LifePath 2040 Fund Class Institutional	SAUIX	B-	B-	B-	Down	4.76	8.88	19.02	24.79	56.70	17.87	1,899		Y
State Farm LifePath 2040 Fund Class R1	RAUOX	B-	C+	B-	Down	4.73	8.85	18.85	23.15	53.00	17.63	1,899		Y
State Farm LifePath 2040 Fund Class R2	RAUTX	B-	B-	B-	Down	4.72	8.89	18.93	23.68	54.31	17.69	1,899		Y
State Farm LifePath 2040 Fund Class R3	RAUHX	B-	B-	B	Down	4.69	8.82	18.92	24.50	56.14	18.07	1,899		Y
State Farm LifePath 2040 Fund Legacy Class B	SAUBX	B-	C+	B-	Down	4.78	8.90	18.90	22.99	52.53	17.91	1,899		Y
State Farm LifePath 2040 Fund Premier Shares	SAUAX	B-	B-	B-	Down	4.77	8.98	19.11	24.33	55.49	17.78	1,899		Y
State Street Target Retirement 2030 Fund Class K	SSBYX	B-	C+	B	Up	4.46	8.71	18.35	25.06		12	608.3	617-664-7338	Y
State Street Target Retirement 2035 Fund Class K	SSCKX	B-	C+	B	Up	4.86	9.45	19.73	26.85		12.21	447.4	617-664-7338	Y
T. Rowe Price Retirement 2025 Fund	TRRHX	B-	B-	B	Down	3.46	7.36	17.68	25.63	63.51	17.59	21,665	410-345-2000	Y
T. Rowe Price Retirement 2025 Fund Advisor Class	PARJX	B-	C+	B	Down	3.37	7.22	17.37	24.70	61.43	17.5	21,665	410-345-2000	Y
T. Rowe Price Retirement 2025 Fund Class R	RRTNX	B-	C+	B	Down	3.35	7.12	17.06	23.79	59.50	17.34	21,665	410-345-2000	Y
T. Rowe Price Retirement 2030 Fund	TRRCX	B-	B-	B	Down	3.82	8.03	19.44	27.82	70.03	25.92	27,637	410-345-2000	Y
T. Rowe Price Retirement 2030 Fund Advisor Class	PARCX	B-	B-	B	Down	3.74	7.90	19.15	26.85	67.94	25.71	27,637	410-345-2000	Y
T. Rowe Price Retirement 2030 Fund Class R	RRTCX	B	B-	B+	Up	3.70	7.76	18.84	25.90	65.78	25.51	27,637	410-345-2000	Y
T. Rowe Price Retirement 2035 Fund	TRRJX	B-	B-	B	Down	4.07	8.54	20.87	29.43	74.90	18.97	16,788	410-345-2000	Y

Category: Target Date 2021-2045 (con't)

Fund Name	Ticker Symbol	RATINGS: Overall Rating	Reward Rating	Risk Rating	Recent Up/ Downgrade	TOTAL RETURNS & PERFORMANCE: 3-Month Total Return	6-Month Total Return	1-Year Total Return	3-Year Total Return	5-Year Total Return	ASSETS: NAV	Total Assets (MIL)	NEW INVESTORS: Telephone	Open to New Investors
T. Rowe Price Retirement 2035 Fund Advisor Class	PARKX	B-	B-	B	Down	4.04	8.42	20.59	28.47	72.80	18.89	16,788	410-345-2000	Y
T. Rowe Price Retirement 2035 Fund Class R	RRTPX	B-	B-	B	Down	3.98	8.29	20.30	27.53	70.66	18.69	16,788	410-345-2000	Y
T. Rowe Price Retirement 2040 Fund	TRRDX	B-	B-	B-	Down	4.31	9.01	22.02	30.68	78.42	27.24	19,593	410-345-2000	Y
T. Rowe Price Retirement 2040 Fund Advisor Class	PARDX	B-	B-	B-	Down	4.20	8.82	21.67	29.67	76.13	27	19,593	410-345-2000	Y
T. Rowe Price Retirement 2040 Fund Class R	RRTDX	B-	B-	B-	Down	4.16	8.68	21.36	28.67	73.99	26.83	19,593	410-345-2000	Y
T. Rowe Price Retirement 2045 Fund	TRRKX	B-	B-	B-	Down	4.36	9.13	22.40	31.14	79.03	18.47	10,668	410-345-2000	Y
T. Rowe Price Retirement 2045 Fund Advisor Class	PARLX	B-	B-	B-	Down	4.34	9.02	22.07	30.18	76.94	18.36	10,668	410-345-2000	Y
T. Rowe Price Retirement 2045 Fund Class R	RRTRX	B-	B-	B-	Down	4.29	8.89	21.78	29.29	74.78	18.17	10,668	410-345-2000	Y
T. Rowe Price Target 2025 Fund	TRRVX	B-	C+	B	Up	2.75	5.93	14.34	21.23		12.29	228.8	410-345-2000	Y
T. Rowe Price Target 2025 Fund Advisor Class	PAJRX	B-	C+	B	Up	2.77	5.87	14.08	20.33		12.27	228.8	410-345-2000	Y
T. Rowe Price Target 2025 Fund I Class	TRVVX	B-	C+	B	Up	2.84	6.10	14.52	21.53		12.29	228.8	410-345-2000	Y
T. Rowe Price Target 2030 Fund	TRRWX	B-	C+	B	Down	3.16	6.71	16.21	23.72		12.63	233.2	410-345-2000	Y
T. Rowe Price Target 2030 Fund Advisor Class	PAKRX	B-	C+	B	Down	3.09	6.56	15.98	22.85		12.6	233.2	410-345-2000	Y
T. Rowe Price Target 2030 Fund I Class	TWRRX	B-	C+	B	Down	3.16	6.78	16.39	24.02		12.63	233.2	410-345-2000	Y
T. Rowe Price Target 2035 Fund	RPGRX	B-	B-	B	Down	3.44	7.29	17.90	25.79		12.82	146.3	410-345-2000	Y
T. Rowe Price Target 2035 Fund Advisor Class	PATVX	B-	B-	B	Down	3.37	7.15	17.66	24.88		12.8	146.3	410-345-2000	Y
T. Rowe Price Target 2035 Fund I Class	TPGPX	B-	B-	B	Down	3.51	7.46	18.08	26.09		12.83	146.3	410-345-2000	Y
T. Rowe Price Target 2040 Fund	TRHRX	B-	B-	B	Down	3.76	7.98	19.42	27.62		13.06	122.4	410-345-2000	Y
T. Rowe Price Target 2040 Fund Advisor Class	PAHHX	B-	B-	B	Down	3.70	7.77	19.12	26.66		13.02	122.4	410-345-2000	Y
T. Rowe Price Target 2040 Fund I Class	TRXRX	B-	B-	B	Down	3.75	7.98	19.51	27.82		13.06	122.4	410-345-2000	Y
T. Rowe Price Target 2045 Fund	RPTFX	B-	B-	B	Down	3.89	8.32	20.37	28.86		13.29	86.3	410-345-2000	Y
T. Rowe Price Target 2045 Fund Advisor Class	PAFFX	B-	B-	B	Down	3.91	8.18	20.15	27.86		13.27	86.3	410-345-2000	Y
T. Rowe Price Target 2045 Fund I Class	TRFWX	B-	B-	B	Down	4.04	8.47	20.64	29.25		13.31	86.3	410-345-2000	Y
TIAA-CREF Lifecycle 2025 Fund Advisor Class	TCQHX	B-	C+	B	Down	3.76	8.16	17.34	25.18	58.33	10.59	4,254	877-518-9161	Y
TIAA-CREF Lifecycle 2025 Fund Institutional Class	TCYIX	B-	C+	B	Down	3.81	8.11	17.40	25.46	59.61	10.59	4,254	877-518-9161	Y
TIAA-CREF Lifecycle 2025 Fund Premier Class	TCQPX	B-	C+	B	Down	3.77	8.10	17.18	25.03	58.40	10.55	4,254	877-518-9161	Y
TIAA-CREF Lifecycle 2025 Fund Retirement Class	TCLFX	B-	C+	B	Down	3.67	8.06	17.05	24.60	57.61	13.47	4,254	877-518-9161	Y
TIAA-CREF Lifecycle 2030 Fund Advisor Class	TCHHX	B-	B-	B	Down	4.25	9.07	19.18	27.36	65.03	10.67	4,180	877-518-9161	Y
TIAA-CREF Lifecycle 2030 Fund Institutional Class	TCRIX	B-	B-	B	Down	4.28	9.10	19.21	27.69	66.32	10.67	4,180	877-518-9161	Y
TIAA-CREF Lifecycle 2030 Fund Premier Class	TCHPX	B-	B-	B	Down	4.25	9.00	19.02	27.15	65.14	10.62	4,180	877-518-9161	Y
TIAA-CREF Lifecycle 2030 Fund Retirement Class	TCLNX	B-	B-	B	Down	4.11	8.90	18.85	26.72	64.20	13.82	4,180	877-518-9161	Y
TIAA-CREF Lifecycle 2035 Fund Advisor Class	TCYHX	B-	B-	B	Down	4.70	10.00	20.96	29.40	71.42	10.84	4,246	877-518-9161	Y
TIAA-CREF Lifecycle 2035 Fund Institutional Class	TCIIX	B-	B-	B	Down	4.73	10.02	21.10	29.77	72.88	10.85	4,246	877-518-9161	Y
TIAA-CREF Lifecycle 2035 Fund Premier Class	TCYPX	B-	B-	B	Down	4.69	10.01	20.88	29.20	71.56	10.82	4,246	877-518-9161	Y
TIAA-CREF Lifecycle 2035 Fund Retirement Class	TCLRX	B-	B-	B	Down	4.65	9.87	20.76	28.85	70.68	14.33	4,246	877-518-9161	Y
TIAA-CREF Lifecycle 2040 Fund Advisor Class	TCZHX	B-	B-	B-	Down	5.03	10.91	22.78	31.37	76.23	10.96	5,272	877-518-9161	Y
TIAA-CREF Lifecycle 2040 Fund Institutional Class	TCOIX	B-	B-	B-	Down	5.15	10.92	22.91	31.82	77.75	10.97	5,272	877-518-9161	Y
TIAA-CREF Lifecycle 2040 Fund Premier Class	TCZPX	B-	B-	B-	Down	5.11	10.91	22.69	31.23	76.38	10.94	5,272	877-518-9161	Y
TIAA-CREF Lifecycle 2040 Fund Retirement Class	TCLOX	B-	B-	B-	Down	5.06	10.76	22.49	30.82	75.49	14.8	5,272	877-518-9161	Y
TIAA-CREF Lifecycle 2045 Fund Advisor Class	TTFHX	B-	B	B-	Down	5.35	11.42	23.70	32.96	79.34	12.66	2,659	877-518-9161	Y
TIAA-CREF Lifecycle 2045 Fund Institutional Class	TTFIX	B-	B	B-	Down	5.36	11.35	23.61	32.89	79.24	12.65	2,659	877-518-9161	Y
TIAA-CREF Lifecycle 2045 Fund Premier Class	TTFPX	B-	B-	B-	Down	5.33	11.25	23.45	32.39	77.95	12.6	2,659	877-518-9161	Y
TIAA-CREF Lifecycle 2045 Fund Retirement Class	TTFRX	B-	B-	B-	Down	5.24	11.18	23.40	31.97	77.07	12.57	2,659	877-518-9161	Y
TIAA-CREF Lifecycle Index 2025 Fund Advisor Class	TLQHX	B-	C+	B	Up	3.63	7.12	15.25	22.69	57.07	17.44	1,672	877-518-9161	Y
TIAA-CREF Lifecycle Index 2025 Fund Institutional Class	TLQIX	B-	C+	B	Up	3.67	7.16	15.36	22.82	57.25	17.45	1,672	877-518-9161	Y
TIAA-CREF Lifecycle Index 2025 Fund Premier Class	TLVPX	B-	C+	B	Up	3.62	7.13	15.21	22.27	56.06	17.39	1,672	877-518-9161	Y
TIAA-CREF Lifecycle Index 2025 Fund Retirement Class	TLQRX	B-	C+	B	Up	3.59	7.05	15.09	21.85	55.37	17.32	1,672	877-518-9161	Y
TIAA-CREF Lifecycle Index 2030 Fund Advisor Class	TLHHX	B-	C+	B	Down	4.05	7.90	16.96	24.87	64.10	18.32	1,729	877-518-9161	Y
TIAA-CREF Lifecycle Index 2030 Fund Institutional Class	TLHIX	B-	C+	B	Down	4.09	7.93	17.06	25.00	64.27	18.32	1,729	877-518-9161	Y
TIAA-CREF Lifecycle Index 2030 Fund Premier Class	TLHPX	B-	C+	B	Down	4.04	7.90	16.85	24.46	63.14	18.25	1,729	877-518-9161	Y
TIAA-CREF Lifecycle Index 2030 Fund Retirement Class	TLHRX	B-	C+	B	Down	4.01	7.83	16.73	24.07	62.21	18.18	1,729	877-518-9161	Y
TIAA-CREF Lifecycle Index 2035 Fund Advisor Class	TLYHX	B-	B-	B	Down	4.51	8.81	18.71	27.12	71.25	19.17	1,626	877-518-9161	Y

Category: Target Date 2021-2045 (con't)

Fund Name	Ticker Symbol	Overall Rating	Reward Rating	Risk Rating	Recent Up/ Downgrade	3-Month Total Return	6-Month Total Return	1-Year Total Return	3-Year Total Return	5-Year Total Return	NAV	Total Assets (MIL)	Telephone	Open to New Investors
TIAA-CREF Lifecycle Index 2035 Fund Institutional Class	TLYIX	B-	B-	B	Down	4.52	8.82	18.72	27.22	71.38	19.18	1,626	877-518-9161	Y
TIAA-CREF Lifecycle Index 2035 Fund Premier Class	TLYPX	B-	B-	B	Down	4.53	8.73	18.59	26.70	70.02	19.1	1,626	877-518-9161	Y
TIAA-CREF Lifecycle Index 2035 Fund Retirement Class	TLYRX	B-	B-	B	Down	4.44	8.66	18.43	26.25	69.11	19.02	1,626	877-518-9161	Y
TIAA-CREF Lifecycle Index 2040 Fund Advisor Class	TLZHX	B-	B-	B	Down	4.94	9.56	20.27	29.27	76.66	19.76	1,752	877-518-9161	Y
TIAA-CREF Lifecycle Index 2040 Fund Institutional Class	TLZIX	B-	B-	B	Down	4.97	9.65	20.37	29.39	76.81	19.77	1,752	877-518-9161	Y
TIAA-CREF Lifecycle Index 2040 Fund Premier Class	TLPRX	B-	B-	B	Down	4.97	9.56	20.25	28.87	75.57	19.69	1,752	877-518-9161	Y
TIAA-CREF Lifecycle Index 2040 Fund Retirement Class	TLZRX	B-	B-	B	Down	4.89	9.48	20.07	28.48	74.58	19.62	1,752	877-518-9161	Y
TIAA-CREF Lifecycle Index 2045 Fund Advisor Class	TLMHX	B-	B-	B-	Down	5.21	10.01	21.18	30.54	78.24	19.88	1,080	877-518-9161	Y
TIAA-CREF Lifecycle Index 2045 Fund Institutional Class	TLXIX	B-	B-	B-	Down	5.22	10.07	21.18	30.63	78.36	19.88	1,080	877-518-9161	Y
TIAA-CREF Lifecycle Index 2045 Fund Premier Class	TLMPX	B-	B-	B-	Down	5.17	9.98	20.99	30.03	76.98	19.8	1,080	877-518-9161	Y
TIAA-CREF Lifecycle Index 2045 Fund Retirement Class	TLMRX	B-	B-	B-	Down	5.14	9.91	20.89	29.58	76.20	19.72	1,080	877-518-9161	Y
USAA Target Retirement 2030 Fund	URTRX	B-	C+	B-	Down	3.80	7.37	16.12	22.02	45.62	13.84	1,269	800-531-8722	Y
USAA Target Retirement 2040 Fund	URFRX	B-	B-	B-	Down	4.51	8.70	18.46	24.81	53.77	14.25	1,404	800-531-8722	Y
Vanguard Target Retirement 2025 Fund Investor Shares	VTTVX	B-	C+	B	Up	3.87	7.52	15.94	22.96	57.94	18.5	38,749	877-662-7447	Y
Vanguard Target Retirement 2030 Fund Investor Shares	VTHRX	B-	B-	B	Down	4.21	8.25	17.52	24.71	63.72	33.63	32,283	877-662-7447	Y
Vanguard Target Retirement 2035 Fund Investor Shares	VTTHX	B-	B-	B	Down	4.61	8.98	19.12	26.56	69.77	20.69	31,221	877-662-7447	Y
Vanguard Target Retirement 2040 Fund Investor Shares	VFORX	B-	B-	B-	Down	5.00	9.74	20.71	28.26	74.39	35.77	23,438	877-662-7447	Y
Vanguard Target Retirement 2045 Fund Investor Shares	VTIVX	B-	B-	B-	Down	5.21	10.11	21.42	29.21	75.58	22.5	21,569	877-662-7447	Y
Voya Index Solution 2025 Portfolio Class ADV	ISDAX	B-	C+	B	Up	3.59	6.96	14.32	19.06	48.90	10.94	822.4	800-366-0066	Y
Voya Index Solution 2025 Portfolio Class I	ISDIX	B-	C+	B	Up	3.70	7.22	14.84	20.88	52.69	11.21	822.4	800-366-0066	Y
Voya Index Solution 2025 Portfolio Class S	ISDSX	B-	C+	B	Up	3.64	7.03	14.61	19.90	50.86	11.09	822.4	800-366-0066	Y
Voya Index Solution 2025 Portfolio Class S2	IXXVX	B-	C+	B	Up	3.61	7.02	14.40	19.37	49.70	10.9	822.4	800-366-0066	Y
Voya Index Solution 2025 Portfolio Class Z	VSZBX	B-	C+	B	Up	3.77	7.29	14.99	21.38	53.32	11.26	822.4	800-366-0066	Y
Voya Index Solution 2030 Portfolio Class ADV	IDXFX	B-	C+	B	Down	4.30	8.11	16.62	23.32	56.41	15.28	286.5	800-366-0066	Y
Voya Index Solution 2030 Portfolio Class I	IDXGX	B-	C+	B	Down	4.40	8.38	17.13	24.88	60.10	15.65	286.5	800-366-0066	Y
Voya Index Solution 2030 Portfolio Class S	IDXHX	B-	C+	B	Down	4.35	8.28	16.90	24.07	58.04	15.56	286.5	800-366-0066	Y
Voya Index Solution 2030 Portfolio Class S2	IDXIX	B-	C+	B	Down	4.34	8.14	16.68	23.25	56.55	15.37	286.5	800-366-0066	Y
Voya Index Solution 2030 Portfolio Class Z	VSZCX	B-	C+	B	Down	4.46	8.51	17.34	25.20	60.51	15.69	286.5	800-366-0066	Y
Voya Index Solution 2035 Portfolio Class ADV	ISEAX	B-	C+	B-	Down	4.70	8.89	17.95	23.68	62.28	11.34	739.5	800-366-0066	Y
Voya Index Solution 2035 Portfolio Class I	ISEIX	B-	B-	B	Down	4.86	9.15	18.65	25.58	66.34	11.65	739.5	800-366-0066	Y
Voya Index Solution 2035 Portfolio Class S	ISESX	B-	B-	B-	Down	4.82	9.00	18.38	24.57	64.34	11.51	739.5	800-366-0066	Y
Voya Index Solution 2035 Portfolio Class S2	IXISX	B-	C+	B-	Down	4.71	8.94	18.13	23.96	63.07	11.32	739.5	800-366-0066	Y
Voya Index Solution 2035 Portfolio Class Z	VSZDX	B-	B-	B	Down	4.92	9.29	18.87	26.25	67.24	11.72	739.5	800-366-0066	Y
Voya Index Solution 2040 Portfolio Class ADV	IDXKX	B-	B-	B-	Down	4.91	9.37	19.05	24.97	66.45	16	181.5	800-366-0066	Y
Voya Index Solution 2040 Portfolio Class I	IDXLX	B-	B-	B-	Down	5.14	9.68	19.68	26.68	70.46	16.36	181.5	800-366-0066	Y
Voya Index Solution 2040 Portfolio Class S	IDXMX	B-	B-	B-	Down	5.01	9.48	19.38	25.76	68.41	16.33	181.5	800-366-0066	Y
Voya Index Solution 2040 Portfolio Class S2	IDXNX	B-	B-	B-	Down	5.01	9.44	19.20	25.20	66.95	16.13	181.5	800-366-0066	Y
Voya Index Solution 2040 Portfolio Class Z	VSZEX	B-	B-	B-	Down	5.12	9.71	19.85	27.05	70.95	16.42	181.5	800-366-0066	Y
Voya Index Solution 2045 Portfolio Class ADV	ISJAX	B-	B-	B-	Down	5.17	9.76	19.96	25.58	68.24	11.79	493.2	800-366-0066	Y
Voya Index Solution 2045 Portfolio Class I	ISJIX	B-	B-	B-	Down	5.27	9.94	20.48	27.33	72.32	12.17	493.2	800-366-0066	Y
Voya Index Solution 2045 Portfolio Class S	ISJSX	B-	B-	B-	Down	5.26	9.85	20.20	26.43	70.27	12	493.2	800-366-0066	Y
Voya Index Solution 2045 Portfolio Class S2	ISVLX	B-	B-	B-	Down	5.16	9.78	19.96	25.90	68.93	11.8	493.2	800-366-0066	Y
Voya Index Solution 2045 Portfolio Class Z	VSZFX	B-	B-	B-	Down	5.42	10.17	20.80	27.91	73.10	12.24	493.2	800-366-0066	Y
Voya Solution 2025 Portfolio Class ADV	ISZAX	B-	C+	B	Up	3.62	6.99	15.02	20.50	49.30	11.72	923.6	800-366-0066	Y
Voya Solution 2025 Portfolio Class I	ISZIX	B-	C+	B	Up	3.79	7.28	15.62	22.28	53.17	12.04	923.6	800-366-0066	Y
Voya Solution 2025 Portfolio Class S	ISZSX	B-	C+	B	Up	3.65	7.17	15.29	21.40	51.22	11.9	923.6	800-366-0066	Y
Voya Solution 2025 Portfolio Class S2	ISPBX	B-	C+	B	Up	3.58	7.03	15.07	20.84	50.12	11.56	923.6	800-366-0066	Y
Voya Solution 2025 Portfolio Class T	ISZTX	B-	C+	B	Up	3.55	6.88	14.78	19.77	47.95	12.23	923.6	800-366-0066	Y
Voya Solution 2030 Portfolio Class ADV	ISNFX	B-	C+	B	Down	4.31	8.21	17.21	23.50	58.96	15.96	30.6	800-366-0066	Y
Voya Solution 2030 Portfolio Class I	ISNGX	B-	B-	B	Down	4.46	8.48	17.86	25.43	63.26	16.36	30.6	800-366-0066	Y
Voya Solution 2030 Portfolio Class S	ISNHX	B-	C+	B	Down	4.42	8.34	17.58	24.61	60.89	16.28	30.6	800-366-0066	Y
Voya Solution 2030 Portfolio Class S2	ISNIX	B-	C+	B	Down	4.34	8.25	17.37	23.93	59.38	16.08	30.6	800-366-0066	Y

Category: Target Date 2021-2045 (con't)

Fund Name	Ticker Symbol	RATINGS: Overall Rating	Reward Rating	Risk Rating	Recent Up/ Downgrade	TOTAL RETURNS & PERFORMANCE: 3-Month Total Return	6-Month Total Return	1-Year Total Return	3-Year Total Return	5-Year Total Return	ASSETS: NAV	Total Assets (MIL)	NEW INVESTORS: Telephone	Open to New Investors
Voya Solution 2030 Portfolio Class T	ISNJX	B-	C+	B	Down	4.29	8.15	17.05	22.64	57.82	16.02	30.6	800-366-0066	Y
Voya Solution 2035 Portfolio Class ADV	ISQAX	B-	B-	B	Down	4.78	9.12	19.21	24.64	60.73	12.27	927.4	800-366-0066	Y
Voya Solution 2035 Portfolio Class I	ISQIX	B-	B-	B	Down	4.91	9.36	19.82	26.46	64.73	12.59	927.4	800-366-0066	Y
Voya Solution 2035 Portfolio Class S	ISQSX	B-	B-	B	Down	4.88	9.28	19.43	25.52	62.64	12.45	927.4	800-366-0066	Y
Voya Solution 2035 Portfolio Class S2	ISPCX	B-	B-	B	Down	4.80	9.18	19.27	24.99	61.50	12	927.4	800-366-0066	Y
Voya Solution 2035 Portfolio Class T	ISQTX	B-	C+	B	Down	4.75	9.04	19.02	23.85	59.15	12.79	927.4	800-366-0066	Y
Voya Solution 2040 Portfolio Class ADV	ISNKX	B-	B-	B-	Down	5.03	9.61	20.23	26.57	68.52	17.11	23.3	800-366-0066	Y
Voya Solution 2040 Portfolio Class I	ISNLX	B-	B-	B	Down	5.22	9.90	20.84	28.55	73.05	17.53	23.3	800-366-0066	Y
Voya Solution 2040 Portfolio Class S	ISNMX	B-	B-	B-	Down	5.13	9.75	20.52	27.64	70.45	17.4	23.3	800-366-0066	Y
Voya Solution 2040 Portfolio Class S2	ISNNX	B-	B-	B-	Down	5.07	9.66	20.31	26.77	69.11	17.18	23.3	800-366-0066	Y
Voya Solution 2040 Portfolio Class T	ISNOX	B-	B-	B-	Down	5.04	9.49	20.04	25.72	66.88	17.08	23.3	800-366-0066	Y
Voya Solution 2045 Portfolio Class ADV	ISRAX	B-	B-	B-	Down	5.35	10.14	20.92	25.96	67.68	12.4	689.9	800-366-0066	Y
Voya Solution 2045 Portfolio Class I	ISRIX	B-	B-	B-	Down	5.45	10.41	21.53	27.90	71.92	12.75	689.9	800-366-0066	Y
Voya Solution 2045 Portfolio Class S	ISRSX	B-	B-	B-	Down	5.36	10.19	21.24	26.85	69.74	12.57	689.9	800-366-0066	Y
Voya Solution 2045 Portfolio Class S2	ISPDX	B-	B-	B-	Down	5.33	10.12	21.02	26.30	68.46	12.25	689.9	800-366-0066	Y
Voya Solution 2045 Portfolio Class T	ISRTX	B-	B-	B-	Down	5.36	10.03	20.68	25.26	66.01	12.77	689.9	800-366-0066	Y
Voya Target Retirement 2025 Fund Class A	VTRCX	B-	C+	B	Up	3.93	7.45	15.04	20.31	50.06		6.7	800-366-0066	Y
Voya Target Retirement 2025 Fund Class I	IRSLX	B-	C+	B	Up	3.77	7.28	15.26	21.36	51.62	12.1	6.7	800-366-0066	Y
Voya Target Retirement 2025 Fund Class R6	VTRDX	B-	C+	B	Up	4.00	7.52	15.30	21.21	51.94		6.7	800-366-0066	Y
Voya Target Retirement 2030 Fund Class A	VTREX	B-	C+	B	Down	4.68	8.72	17.10	22.47	57.61		5.6	800-366-0066	Y
Voya Target Retirement 2030 Fund Class I	IRSMX	B-	C+	B	Down	4.50	8.52	17.34	23.78	59.43	12.36	5.6	800-366-0066	Y
Voya Target Retirement 2030 Fund Class R6	VTRFX	B-	C+	B	Down	4.75	8.96	17.41	23.53	59.77		5.6	800-366-0066	Y
Voya Target Retirement 2035 Fund Class A	VTRGX	B-	C+	B-	Down	5.10	9.56	18.84	24.07	61.23		4.8	800-366-0066	Y
Voya Target Retirement 2035 Fund Class I	IRSNX	B-	B-	B	Down	4.94	9.37	19.15	25.56	63.17	12.42	4.8	800-366-0066	Y
Voya Target Retirement 2035 Fund Class R6	VTRHX	B-	B-	B	Down	5.17	9.71	19.16	25.05	63.32		4.8	800-366-0066	Y
Voya Target Retirement 2040 Fund Class A	VTRJX	B-	B-	B-	Down	5.34	10.10	19.97	25.62	66.93		2.7	800-366-0066	Y
Voya Target Retirement 2040 Fund Class I	IRSOX	B-	B-	B-	Down	5.11	9.84	20.17	26.87	68.62	12.68	2.7	800-366-0066	Y
Voya Target Retirement 2040 Fund Class R6	VTRKX	B-	B-	B-	Down	5.48	10.33	20.28	26.70	69.22		2.7	800-366-0066	Y
Voya Target Retirement 2045 Fund Class A	VTRMX	B-	B-	B-	Down	5.59	10.57	20.59	26.26	69.20		3.4	800-366-0066	Y
Voya Target Retirement 2045 Fund Class I	IRSPX	B-	B-	B-	Down	5.26	10.12	20.78	27.54	70.96	12.87	3.4	800-366-0066	Y
Voya Target Retirement 2045 Fund Class R6	VTRNX	B-	B-	B-	Down	5.57	10.62	20.93	27.36	71.54		3.4	800-366-0066	Y
Wells Fargo Target 2025 Fund - Class A	WFAYX	B	C+	B+	Up	3.20	5.60	11.72	15.19	35.81	6.49	516.4	800-222-8222	Y
Wells Fargo Target 2025 Fund - Class Admin	WFTRX	B	C+	B+	Up	3.16	5.64	11.94	15.73	36.71	6.56	516.4	800-222-8222	Y
Wells Fargo Target 2025 Fund - Class R	WFHRX	B-	C+	B+	Up	3.11	5.53	10.60	13.45	33.46	6.43	516.4	800-222-8222	Y
Wells Fargo Target 2025 Fund - Class R4	WFGRX	B	C+	B+	Up	3.26	5.74	12.06	16.30	38.03	6.53	516.4	800-222-8222	Y
Wells Fargo Target 2025 Fund - Class R6	WFTYX	B	C+	A-	Up	3.11	5.79	12.12	16.71	38.91	6.51	516.4	800-222-8222	Y
Wells Fargo Target 2030 Fund - Class A	STHRX	B	C+	B+	Up	3.62	6.63	13.92	18.58	45.17	13.66	1,135	800-222-8222	Y
Wells Fargo Target 2030 Fund - Class Admin	WFLIX	B	C+	B+	Up	3.64	6.67	14.06	18.98	46.15	13.93	1,135	800-222-8222	Y
Wells Fargo Target 2030 Fund - Class C	WFDMX	B-	C+	B+	Up	3.44	6.23	13.08	15.88	39.77	13.15	1,135	800-222-8222	Y
Wells Fargo Target 2030 Fund - Class R	WFJRX	B	C+	B+	Up	3.55	6.52	13.48	17.50	43.33	13.69	1,135	800-222-8222	Y
Wells Fargo Target 2030 Fund - Class R4	WTHRX	B	C+	B+	Up	3.75	6.83	14.29	19.69	47.74	13.94	1,135	800-222-8222	Y
Wells Fargo Target 2030 Fund - Class R6	WFOOX	B	C+	B+	Up	3.73	6.82	14.42	20.19	48.70	13.91	1,135	800-222-8222	Y
Wells Fargo Target 2035 Fund - Class A	WFQBX	B-	C+	B	Down	4.08	7.59	15.98	21.18	53.67	8.42	475.4	800-222-8222	Y
Wells Fargo Target 2035 Fund - Class Admin	WFQWX	B-	C+	B	Down	4.11	7.60	16.08	21.61	54.33	8.48	475.4	800-222-8222	Y
Wells Fargo Target 2035 Fund - Class R	WFKRX	B-	C+	B-	Down	4.10	7.50	15.82	20.30	51.96	8.5	475.4	800-222-8222	Y
Wells Fargo Target 2035 Fund - Class R4	WTTRX	B-	C+	B	Down	4.25	7.75	16.41	22.37	56.08	8.44	475.4	800-222-8222	Y
Wells Fargo Target 2035 Fund - Class R6	WFQRX	B-	C+	B	Down	4.27	7.87	16.51	22.98	57.29	8.43	475.4	800-222-8222	Y
Wells Fargo Target 2040 Fund - Class A	STFRX	B-	C+	B-	Down	4.44	8.23	17.58	23.37	60.13	16.14	992.2	800-222-8222	
Wells Fargo Target 2040 Fund - Class Admin	WFLWX	B-	C+	B-	Down	4.44	8.25	17.71	23.73	61.09	16.59	992.2	800-222-8222	Y
Wells Fargo Target 2040 Fund - Class C	WFOFX	B-	C+	B-	Down	4.23	7.83	16.71	20.58	54.18	14.74	992.2	800-222-8222	Y
Wells Fargo Target 2040 Fund - Class R	WFMRX	B-	C+	B-	Down	4.41	8.11	17.36	22.52	58.31	16.15	992.2	800-222-8222	Y
Wells Fargo Target 2040 Fund - Class R4	WTFRX	B-	B-	B-	Down	4.53	8.38	17.95	24.55	62.78	16.63	992.2	800-222-8222	Y

Category: Target Date 2021-2045 (con't)

Fund Name	Ticker Symbol	Overall Rating	Reward Rating	Risk Rating	Recent Up/ Downgrade	3-Month Total Return	6-Month Total Return	1-Year Total Return	3-Year Total Return	5-Year Total Return	NAV	Total Assets (MIL)	Telephone	Open to New Investors
Wells Fargo Target 2040 Fund - Class R6	WFOSX	B-	B-	B-	Down	4.59	8.51	18.15	25.08	64.07	16.62	992.2	800-222-8222	Y
Wells Fargo Target 2045 Fund - Class A	WFQVX	B-	B-	B-	Down	4.72	8.80	18.82	24.88	64.26	9.25	307.2	800-222-8222	Y
Wells Fargo Target 2045 Fund - Class Admin	WFQYX	B-	B-	B-	Down	4.73	8.78	18.83	25.28	65.15	9.36	307.2	800-222-8222	Y
Wells Fargo Target 2045 Fund - Class R	WFNRX	B-	B-	B-	Down	4.61	8.56	18.41	23.94	62.50	9.4	307.2	800-222-8222	Y
Wells Fargo Target 2045 Fund - Class R4	WFFRX	B-	B-	B-	Down	4.79	8.95	19.09	26.11	67.14	9.3	307.2	800-222-8222	Y
Wells Fargo Target 2045 Fund - Class R6	WFQPX	B-	B-	B-	Down	4.71	8.96	19.22	26.54	68.09	9.26	307.2	800-222-8222	Y

Category: Target Date 2046+

Fund Name	Ticker Symbol	Overall Rating	Reward Rating	Risk Rating	Recent Up/ Downgrade	3-Month Total Return	6-Month Total Return	1-Year Total Return	3-Year Total Return	5-Year Total Return	NAV	Total Assets (MIL)	Telephone	Open to New Investors
AB Multi-Manager Select 2050 Fund Advisor Class	TDLYX	B-	C+	B-	Up	4.91	10.27	22.13	30.91		12.55	22.9	212-969-1000	Y
AB Multi-Manager Select 2050 Fund Class A	TDLAX	B-	C+	B-	Up	4.81	10.11	21.71	29.93		12.5	22.9	212-969-1000	Y
AB Multi-Manager Select 2050 Fund Class I	TDLIX	B-	C+	B-	Up	4.84	10.24	22.05	30.97		12.16	22.9	212-969-1000	Y
AB Multi-Manager Select 2050 Fund Class K	TDLKX	B-	C+	B-	Up	4.77	10.09	21.81	29.91		11.89	22.9	212-969-1000	Y
AB Multi-Manager Select 2050 Fund Class R	TDLRX	B-	C+	B-	Up	4.75	9.99	21.51	29.06		11.87	22.9	212-969-1000	Y
AB Multi-Manager Select 2050 Fund Class Z	TDLZX	B-	C+	B-	Up	4.94	10.35	22.18	31.04		11.91	22.9	212-969-1000	Y
AB Multi-Manager Select 2055 Fund Advisor Class	TDPYX	B-	C+	B-	Up	4.96	10.27	22.11	30.23		12.56	27.6	212-969-1000	Y
AB Multi-Manager Select 2055 Fund Class I	TDIPX	B-	C+	B-	Up	4.89	10.23	22.02	30.23		12.08	27.6	212-969-1000	Y
AB Multi-Manager Select 2055 Fund Class Z	TDPZX	B-	C+	B-	Up	4.92	10.36	22.05	30.31		11.95	27.6	212-969-1000	Y
AllianzGI Retirement 2050 Fund Administrative Class	ANAMX	B-	B-	B-	Down	4.57	10.19	21.82	28.86	51.46	22.28	34.4	800-498-5413	Y
AllianzGI Retirement 2050 Fund Class A	ASNAX	B-	B-	B-	Down	4.57	10.16	21.77	28.63	51.07	22.22	34.4	800-498-5413	Y
AllianzGI Retirement 2050 Fund Class C	ASNCX	B-	B-	B-	Down	4.38	9.76	20.84	25.83	45.52	21.9	34.4	800-498-5413	Y
AllianzGI Retirement 2050 Fund Class P	ASNPX	B-	B-	B-	Down	4.64	10.33	22.10	29.84	53.37	22.37	34.4	800-498-5413	Y
AllianzGI Retirement 2050 Fund Class R	ASNRX	B-	B-	B-	Down	4.49	9.97	21.28	27.24	48.36	22.25	34.4	800-498-5413	Y
AllianzGI Retirement 2050 Fund R6 Class	ASNIX	B-	B-	B-	Down	4.63	10.35	22.19	30.20	54.04	22.45	34.4	800-498-5413	Y
AllianzGI Retirement 2055 Fund Administrative Class	GLRAX	B-	B-	B-	Down	4.53	10.22	21.78	28.32	51.21	19.24	16.3	800-498-5413	Y
AllianzGI Retirement 2055 Fund Class A	GLIAX	B-	B-	B-	Down	4.52	10.16	21.66	28.21	50.84	19.19	16.3	800-498-5413	Y
AllianzGI Retirement 2055 Fund Class P	GLIPX	B-	B-	B-	Down	4.64	10.36	22.07	29.42	53.19	19.33	16.3	800-498-5413	Y
AllianzGI Retirement 2055 Fund Class R	GLLRX	B-	B-	B-	Down	4.45	9.96	21.23	26.91	48.29	19.16	16.3	800-498-5413	Y
AllianzGI Retirement 2055 Fund R6 Class	GBLIX	B-	B-	B-	Down	4.65	10.41	22.21	29.81	54.04	19.41	16.3	800-498-5413	Y
American Century Inv One Choice 2050 Port A Cls	ARFMX	B-	B-	B	Down	4.26	8.67	18.21	23.53	65.35	14.01	1,250	800-444-4015	Y
American Century Inv One Choice 2050 Port C Cls	ARFDX	B-	C+	B-	Down	4.05	8.29	17.32	20.75	59.37	14.02	1,250	800-444-4015	Y
American Century Inv One Choice 2050 Port I Cls	ARFSX	B-	B-	B	Down	4.43	8.98	18.81	25.28	69.33	14.03	1,250	800-444-4015	Y
American Century Inv One Choice 2050 Port Inv Cls	ARFVX	B-	B-	B	Down	4.37	8.93	18.58	24.55	67.56	14.02	1,250	800-444-4015	Y
American Century Inv One Choice 2050 Port R Cls	ARFWX	B-	C+	B-	Down	2.92	7.27	16.50	21.13	61.45	14.02	1,250	800-444-4015	Y
American Century Inv One Choice 2050 Port R6 Cls	ARFEX	B-	B-	B	Down	4.46	9.05	18.92	25.73	70.20	12.75	1,250	800-444-4015	Y
American Century Inv One Choice 2055 Port A Cls	AREMX	B-	B-	B-	Down	3.05	7.65	17.30	22.69	65.47	15.01	651.1	800-444-4015	Y
American Century Inv One Choice 2055 Port C Cls	AREFX	B-	C+	B-	Down	4.20	8.57	17.87	21.43	61.43	14.96	651.1	800-444-4015	Y
American Century Inv One Choice 2055 Port I Cls	ARENX	B-	B-	B	Down	4.52	9.25	19.28	25.90	71.46	15.02	651.1	800-444-4015	Y
American Century Inv One Choice 2055 Port Inv Cls	AREVX	B-	B-	B-	Down	4.45	9.10	19.04	25.14	69.75	15.02	651.1	800-444-4015	Y
American Century Inv One Choice 2055 Port R Cls	AREOX	B-	B-	B-	Down	3.12	7.58	17.03	21.80	63.68	15.03	651.1	800-444-4015	Y
American Century Inv One Choice 2055 Port R6 Cls	AREUX	B-	B-	B	Down	4.52	9.28	19.35	26.32	72.31	13.03	651.1	800-444-4015	Y
American Funds 2050 Target Date Retirement Fund® Class A	AALTX	B-	B-	B	Down	5.06	10.31	22.17	31.42	80.33	15.1	5,563	800-421-4225	Y
American Funds 2050 Target Date Retirement Fund® Class C	CCITX	B-	B-	B	Down	4.85	9.96	21.25	28.47	73.65	14.86	5,563	800-421-4225	Y
American Funds 2050 Target Date Retirement Fund® Class F-1	FAITX	B-	B-	B	Down	5.05	10.32	22.15	31.33	80.31	15.02	5,563	800-421-4225	Y
American Funds 2050 Target Date Retirement Fund® Class F-2	FBITX	B-	B-	B	Down	5.09	10.49	22.48	32.30	82.53	15.08	5,563	800-421-4225	Y
American Funds 2050 Target Date Retirement Fund® Class F-3	DITFX	B-	B-	B	Down	5.21	10.61	22.57	32.57	83.02	15.11	5,563	800-421-4225	Y
American Funds 2050 Target Date Retirement Fund® Class R-1	RAITX	B-	B-	B	Down	4.89	9.93	21.24	28.38	73.28	14.84	5,563	800-421-4225	Y
American Funds 2050 Target Date Retirement Fund® Class R-2	RBITX	B-	B-	B	Down	4.82	9.94	21.26	28.49	73.85	14.83	5,563	800-421-4225	Y
American Funds 2050 Target Date Retirement Fund® Cls R-2E	RBHEX	B-	B-	B	Down	4.98	10.15	21.67	30.00	77.51	14.91	5,563	800-421-4225	Y

Category: Target Date 2046+ (con't)

Fund Name	Ticker Symbol	Overall Rating	Reward Rating	Risk Rating	Recent Up/ Downgrade	3-Month Total Return	6-Month Total Return	1-Year Total Return	3-Year Total Return	5-Year Total Return	NAV	Total Assets (MIL)	Telephone	Open to New Investors
		RATINGS				TOTAL RETURNS & PERFORMANCE					ASSETS		NEW INVESTORS	
American Funds 2050 Target Date Retirement Fund® Class R-3	RCITX	B-	B-	B	Down	4.98	10.13	21.72	30.09	77.20	14.95	5,563	800-421-4225	Y
American Funds 2050 Target Date Retirement Fund® Class R-4	RDITX	B-	B-	B	Down	5.01	10.35	22.15	31.33	80.12	15.06	5,563	800-421-4225	Y
American Funds 2050 Target Date Retirement Fund® Class R-5	REITX	B-	B-	B	Down	5.20	10.57	22.55	32.55	82.99	15.21	5,563	800-421-4225	Y
American Funds 2050 Target Date Retirement Fund® Cls R-5E	RHITX	B-	B-	B	Down	5.07	10.48	22.40	32.24	82.57	15.05	5,563	800-421-4225	Y
American Funds 2050 Target Date Retirement Fund® Class R-6	RFITX	B-	B-	B	Down	5.19	10.58	22.60	32.74	83.21	15.16	5,563	800-421-4225	Y
American Funds 2055 Target Date Retirement Fund® Class A	AAMTX	B-	B-	B	Down	5.07	10.39	22.18	31.41	80.37	18.8	2,616	800-421-4225	Y
American Funds 2055 Target Date Retirement Fund® Class C	CCJTX	B-	B-	B	Down	4.89	9.97	21.23	28.39	73.58	18.55	2,616	800-421-4225	Y
American Funds 2055 Target Date Retirement Fund® Class F-1	FAJTX	B-	B-	B	Down	5.09	10.37	22.14	31.29	80.30	18.71	2,616	800-421-4225	Y
American Funds 2055 Target Date Retirement Fund® Class F-2	FBJTX	B-	B-	B	Down	5.18	10.50	22.52	32.39	82.34	18.8	2,616	800-421-4225	Y
American Funds 2055 Target Date Retirement Fund® Class F-3	FCJTX	B-	B-	B	Down	5.18	10.55	22.63	32.71	83.13	18.81	2,616	800-421-4225	Y
American Funds 2055 Target Date Retirement Fund® Class R-1	RAMTX	B-	B-	B	Down	4.89	9.93	21.22	28.30	73.13	18.49	2,616	800-421-4225	Y
American Funds 2055 Target Date Retirement Fund® Class R-2	RBMTX	B-	B-	B	Down	4.86	9.96	21.25	28.50	73.72	18.48	2,616	800-421-4225	Y
American Funds 2055 Target Date Retirement Fund® Cls R-2E	RBEMX	B-	B-	B	Down	4.95	10.13	21.64	30.04	77.53	18.59	2,616	800-421-4225	Y
American Funds 2055 Target Date Retirement Fund® Class R-3	RCMTX	B-	B-	B	Down	4.96	10.20	21.79	30.09	77.09	18.63	2,616	800-421-4225	Y
American Funds 2055 Target Date Retirement Fund® Class R-4	RDJTX	B-	B-	B	Down	5.07	10.33	22.15	31.32	79.96	18.76	2,616	800-421-4225	Y
American Funds 2055 Target Date Retirement Fund® Class R-5	REKTX	B-	B-	B	Down	5.16	10.50	22.52	32.50	82.76	18.92	2,616	800-421-4225	Y
American Funds 2055 Target Date Retirement Fund® Cls R-5E	RHJTX	B-	B-	B	Down	5.13	10.52	22.44	32.31	82.59	18.74	2,616	800-421-4225	Y
American Funds 2055 Target Date Retirement Fund® Class R-6	RFKTX	B-	B-	B	Down	5.14	10.54	22.62	32.70	83.12	18.94	2,616	800-421-4225	Y
American Funds 2060 Target Date Retirement Fund® Class A	AANTX	B-	C+	B	Up	5.03	10.39	22.20			12.37	547.6	800-421-4225	Y
American Funds 2060 Target Date Retirement Fund® Class C	CCKTX	B-	C+	B	Up	4.85	9.96	21.26			12.27	547.6	800-421-4225	Y
American Funds 2060 Target Date Retirement Fund® Class F-1	FAWTX	B-	C+	B	Up	5.01	10.36	22.04			12.38	547.6	800-421-4225	Y
American Funds 2060 Target Date Retirement Fund® Class F-2	FBKTX	B-	C+	B	Up	5.12	10.46	22.35			12.4	547.6	800-421-4225	Y
American Funds 2060 Target Date Retirement Fund® Class F-3	FCKTX	B-	C+	B	Up	5.18	10.54	22.58			12.37	547.6	800-421-4225	Y
American Funds 2060 Target Date Retirement Fund® Class R-1	RANTX	B-	C+	B	Up	4.94	9.94	21.18			12.32	547.6	800-421-4225	Y
American Funds 2060 Target Date Retirement Fund® Class R-2	RBNTX	B-	C+	B	Up	4.81	9.93	21.10			12.26	547.6	800-421-4225	Y
American Funds 2060 Target Date Retirement Fund® Cls R-2E	RBENX	B-	C+	B	Up	4.98	10.17	21.64			12.32	547.6	800-421-4225	Y
American Funds 2060 Target Date Retirement Fund® Class R-3	RCNTX	B-	C+	B	Up	5.01	10.20	21.80			12.33	547.6	800-421-4225	Y
American Funds 2060 Target Date Retirement Fund® Class R-4	RDKTX	B-	C+	B	Up	5.04	10.39	22.09			12.37	547.6	800-421-4225	Y
American Funds 2060 Target Date Retirement Fund® Class R-5	REMTX	B-	C+	B	Up	5.19	10.52	22.53			12.42	547.6	800-421-4225	Y
American Funds 2060 Target Date Retirement Fund® Cls R-5E	RHKTX	B-	C+	B	Up	5.12	10.47	22.40			12.37	547.6	800-421-4225	Y
American Funds 2060 Target Date Retirement Fund® Class R-6	RFUTX	B-	C+	B	Up	5.16	10.49	22.49			12.42	547.6	800-421-4225	Y
BlackRock LifePath® Dynamic 2050 Fund Class K Shares	LPSGX	B-	B-	B-	Down	6.08	11.19	23.06	29.59	68.91	21.59	119.7	800-441-7762	Y
BlackRock LifePath® Dynamic 2050 Fund Class R Shares	LPRPX	B-	B-	B-	Down	5.91	10.81	22.24	26.83	62.60	21.42	119.7	800-441-7762	Y
BlackRock LifePath® Dynamic 2050 Fund Institutional Shares	STLFX	B-	B-	B-	Down	6.04	11.11	22.85	28.60	66.45	21.54	119.7	800-441-7762	Y
BlackRock LifePath® Dynamic 2050 Fund Investor A Shares	LPRFX	B-	B-	B-	Down	5.95	10.90	22.47	27.65	64.45	21.47	119.7	800-441-7762	Y
BlackRock LifePath® Dynamic 2050 Porfolio Inv C Shares	LPCPX	B-	B-	C+	Up	5.08	9.78	20.75	23.91	57.16	21.26	119.7	800-441-7762	Y
BlackRock LifePath® Dynamic 2055 Fund Class K Shares	LPVKX	B-	B-	B-	Down	5.98	11.09	22.79	29.23	70.90	16.06	19.1	800-441-7762	Y
BlackRock LifePath® Dynamic 2055 Fund Class R Shares	LPVRX	B-	B-	B-	Down	5.82	10.77	21.95	26.45	63.95	15.8	19.1	800-441-7762	Y
BlackRock LifePath® Dynamic 2055 Fund Institutional Shares	LPVIX	B-	B-	B-	Down	5.93	10.98	22.57	28.27	68.00	15.86	19.1	800-441-7762	Y
BlackRock LifePath® Dynamic 2055 Fund Investor A Shares	LPVAX	B-	B-	B-	Down	5.88	10.88	22.23	27.30	65.97	15.81	19.1	800-441-7762	Y
BlackRock LifePath® Dynamic 2055 Fund Investor C Shares	LPVCX	B-	B-	C+	Up	5.05	9.78	20.59	23.65	58.73	15.63	19.1	800-441-7762	Y
BlackRock LifePath® Index 2050 Fund Class K Shares	LIPKX	B-	B-	B-	Down	5.41	10.18	21.43	29.66	72.97	14.99	1,201	800-441-7762	Y
BlackRock LifePath® Index 2050 Fund Institutional Shares	LIPIX	B-	B-	B-	Down	5.39	10.15	21.37	29.45	72.56	14.99	1,201	800-441-7762	Y
BlackRock LifePath® Index 2050 Fund Investor A Shares	LIPAX	B-	B-	B-	Down	5.34	10.04	21.13	28.53	70.43	14.96	1,201	800-441-7762	Y
BlackRock LifePath® Index 2055 Fund Class K Shares	LIVKX	B-	B-	B-	Down	5.40	10.20	21.51	29.78	75.51	15.28	549.4	800-441-7762	Y
BlackRock LifePath® Index 2055 Fund Institutional Shares	LIVIX	B-	B-	B-	Down	5.32	10.10	21.37	29.50	74.99	15.27	549.4	800-441-7762	Y
BlackRock LifePath® Index 2055 Fund Investor A Shares	LIVAX	B-	B-	B-	Down	5.26	9.99	21.05	28.59	72.82	15.24	549.4	800-441-7762	Y
BlackRock LifePath® Smart Beta 2050 Fund Class K	BIPKX	B-	B-	C+	Down	5.42	10.35	20.64	26.69	66.26	11.76	15.0	800-441-7762	Y
BlackRock LifePath® Smart Beta 2050 Fund Inst Shares	BLKIX	B-	B-	C+	Down	5.40	10.24	20.29	26.22	65.26	11.73	15.0	800-441-7762	Y
BlackRock LifePath® Smart Beta 2050 Fund Investor A Shares	BAPKX	B-	B-	C+	Down	5.28	10.07	20.00	25.29	63.09	11.6	15.0	800-441-7762	Y
BlackRock LifePath® Smart Beta 2055 Fund Class K Shares	BIPLX	B-	B-	B-	Down	5.43	10.34	20.48	26.96		12.27	5.2	800-441-7762	Y
BlackRock LifePath® Smart Beta 2055 Fund Class R Shares	BRPLX	B-	B-	C+	Down	5.29	10.06	19.74	24.81		12.14	5.2	800-441-7762	Y

Category: Target Date 2046+ (con't)

Fund Name	Ticker Symbol	RATINGS: Overall Rating	Reward Rating	Risk Rating	Recent Up/ Downgrade	TOTAL RETURNS & PERFORMANCE: 3-Month Total Return	6-Month Total Return	1-Year Total Return	3-Year Total Return	5-Year Total Return	ASSETS: NAV	Total Assets (MIL)	NEW INVESTORS: Telephone	Open to New Investors
BlackRock LifePath® Smart Beta 2055 Fund Inst Shares	BLLIX	B-	B-	C+	Down	5.34	10.24	20.27	26.59		12.25	5.2	800-441-7762	Y
BlackRock LifePath® Smart Beta 2055 Fund Investor A Shares	BAPLX	B-	B-	C+	Down	5.26	10.09	19.94	25.53		12.22	5.2	800-441-7762	Y
BMO Target Retirement 2050 Fund Class R3	BTRWX	B-	B-	B-	Down	4.83	9.13	20.46	24.38	68.85	12.26	40.6	800-236-3863	Y
BMO Target Retirement 2050 Fund Class R6	BTRZX	B-	B-	B-	Down	4.53	8.99	20.73	26.29	72.89	12.23	40.6	800-236-3863	Y
BMO Target Retirement 2050 Fund Class Y	BTRUX	B-	B-	B-	Down	4.92	9.31	20.76	25.29	70.70	12.25	40.6	800-236-3863	Y
BMO Target Retirement 2055 Fund Class R3	BRTTX	B-	B-	B-	Down	4.91	9.18	20.42	24.63		12.27	8.1	800-236-3863	Y
BMO Target Retirement 2055 Fund Class R6	BRTUX	B-	B-	B-	Down	5.05	9.54	21.15	26.98		12.37	8.1	800-236-3863	Y
BMO Target Retirement 2055 Fund Class Y	BRTRX	B-	B-	B-	Down	4.87	9.29	20.59	25.48		12.37	8.1	800-236-3863	Y
Fidelity Advisor Freedom® 2050 Fund Class A	FFFLX	B-	B-	B-	Down	4.77	9.51	21.35	29.06	67.61	12.23	1,051	617-563-7000	Y
Fidelity Advisor Freedom® 2050 Fund Class C	FFFYX	B-	B-	B-	Down	4.60	9.13	20.42	26.15	61.47	12.06	1,051	617-563-7000	Y
Fidelity Advisor Freedom® 2050 Fund Class I	FFFPX	B-	B-	B-	Down	4.87	9.68	21.64	29.99	69.75	12.3	1,051	617-563-7000	Y
Fidelity Advisor Freedom® 2050 Fund Class M	FFFQX	B-	B-	B-	Down	4.63	9.30	20.99	28.00	65.44	12.17	1,051	617-563-7000	Y
Fidelity Advisor Freedom® 2050 Fund Class Z6	FVGLX	B-	B-	B-	Down	4.89	9.79	21.77	30.12	69.91	12.28	1,051	617-563-7000	Y
Fidelity Advisor Freedom® 2055 Fund Class A	FHFAX	B-	B-	B-	Down	4.76	9.52	21.36	29.03	68.70	13.44	506.8	617-563-7000	Y
Fidelity Advisor Freedom® 2055 Fund Class C	FHFCX	B-	B-	B-	Down	4.53	9.07	20.35	26.10	62.43	13.34	506.8	617-563-7000	Y
Fidelity Advisor Freedom® 2055 Fund Class I	FHFIX	B-	B-	B-	Down	4.81	9.63	21.61	29.99	70.87	13.48	506.8	617-563-7000	Y
Fidelity Advisor Freedom® 2055 Fund Class M	FHFTX	B-	B-	B-	Down	4.64	9.33	21.01	28.08	66.60	13.38	506.8	617-563-7000	Y
Fidelity Advisor Freedom® 2055 Fund Class Z6	FBGLX	B-	B-	B-	Down	4.83	9.74	21.73	30.12	71.04	13.46	506.8	617-563-7000	Y
Fidelity Advisor Freedom® 2060 Fund Class A	FDKPX	B-	B-	B-	Up	4.81	9.53	21.34	28.98			77.0	617-563-7000	Y
Fidelity Advisor Freedom® 2060 Fund Class C	FDKSX	B-	B-	B-	Up	4.49	9.09	20.41	26.10			77.0	617-563-7000	Y
Fidelity Advisor Freedom® 2060 Fund Class I	FDKQX	B-	B-	B-	Up	4.78	9.67	21.65	30.00			77.0	617-563-7000	Y
Fidelity Advisor Freedom® 2060 Fund Class M	FDKTX	B-	B-	B-	Up	4.67	9.39	21.01	28.08		11.92	77.0	617-563-7000	Y
Fidelity Advisor Freedom® 2060 Fund Class Z6	FNGLX	B-	B-	B-		4.90	9.80	21.79	30.15		11.94	77.0	617-563-7000	Y
Fidelity Freedom® 2050 Fund	FFFHX	B-	B-	B-	Down	5.05	10.04	22.28	31.64	72.79	12.19	10,884	617-563-7000	Y
Fidelity Freedom® 2050 Fund Class K6	FZTKX	B-	B-	B-	Down	5.20	10.30	22.56	31.95	73.20	12.18	10,884	617-563-7000	Y
Fidelity Freedom® 2055 Fund	FDEEX	B-	B-	B-	Down	5.11	10.12	22.31	31.62	74.09	13.74	4,031	617-563-7000	Y
Fidelity Freedom® 2055 Fund Class K6	FCTKX	B-	B-	B-	Down	5.10	10.20	22.39	31.71	74.21	13.72	4,031	617-563-7000	Y
Fidelity Freedom® 2060 Fund	FDKVX	B-	B-	B-	Up	5.01	10.00	22.10	31.42			633.6	617-563-7000	Y
Fidelity Freedom® 2060 Fund Class K6	FVTKX	B-	B-	B-		5.20	10.20	22.33	31.66		12.23	633.6	617-563-7000	Y
Fidelity Freedom® Index 2050 Fund Inst Premium Cls	FFOPX	B-	B-	B-	Down	5.22	10.03	20.60	29.13	67.46	19.12	1,623	617-563-7000	Y
Fidelity Freedom® Index 2050 Fund Investor Class	FIPFX	B-	B-	B-	Down	5.24	10.00	20.53	28.92	67.18	19.13	1,623	617-563-7000	Y
Fidelity Freedom® Index 2055 Fund Inst Premium Cls	FFLDX	B-	B-	B-	Down	5.20	10.01	20.56	28.96	68.55	15.12	560.5	617-563-7000	Y
Fidelity Freedom® Index 2055 Fund Investor Class	FDEWX	B-	B-	B-	Down	5.17	9.98	20.52	28.86	68.41	15.11	560.5	617-563-7000	Y
Fidelity Freedom® Index 2060 Fund Inst Premium Cls	FFLEX	B-	B-	B-	Up	5.24	9.95	20.62	29.05		12.31	119.0	617-563-7000	Y
Fidelity Freedom® Index 2060 Fund Investor Class	FDKLX	B-	B-	B-	Up	5.22	10.02	20.57	28.92			119.0	617-563-7000	Y
Franklin LifeSmart™ 2050 Retmnt Target Fund Adv Cls	FLSOX	B-	C+	B-	Down	3.97	8.42	19.19	21.08		13.26	30.9	650-312-2000	Y
Franklin LifeSmart™ 2050 Retirement Target Fund Class A	FLSJX	B-	C+	B-	Down	3.85	8.23	18.96	20.22		13.19	30.9	650-312-2000	Y
Franklin LifeSmart™ 2050 Retirement Target Fund Class R	FLSNX	B-	C+	B-	Up	3.84	8.15	18.67	19.31		13.19	30.9	650-312-2000	Y
Franklin LifeSmart™ 2050 Retirement Target Fund Class R6	FRLEX	B-	C+	B-	Down	3.93	8.46	19.35	21.25		13.26	30.9	650-312-2000	Y
Franklin LifeSmart™ 2055 Retmnt Target Fund Adv Cls	FLTKX	B-	C+	B	Up	3.90	8.40	19.16			11.06	9.2	650-312-2000	Y
Franklin LifeSmart™ 2055 Retirement Target Fund Class R	FLSBX	B-	C+	B	Up	3.82	8.14	18.68			11.01	9.2	650-312-2000	Y
Goldman Sachs Target Date 2050 Portfolio Class A Shares	GTASX	B-	B-	B	Down	4.38	8.12	16.95	25.06	69.06	10.33	28.8	800-526-7384	Y
Goldman Sachs Target Date 2050 Portfolio Cls Inst Shares	GTIPX	B-	B-	B	Down	4.51	8.35	17.43	26.27	71.58	10.36	28.8	800-526-7384	Y
Goldman Sachs Target Date 2050 Portfolio Class IR Shares	GTMAX	B-	B-	B	Down	4.50	8.34	17.30	26.07	71.31	10.35	28.8	800-526-7384	Y
Goldman Sachs Target Date 2050 Portfolio Class R Shares	GTRSX	B-	B-	B	Down	4.41	8.06	16.66	24.13	66.93	10.35	28.8	800-526-7384	Y
Goldman Sachs Target Date 2050 Portfolio Class R6 Shares	GTZSX	B-	B-	B	Down	4.52	8.36	17.44	26.29	71.60	10.36	28.8	800-526-7384	Y
Goldman Sachs Target Date 2050 Port Cls Serv Shares	GTVSX	B-	B-	B	Down	4.36	8.10	16.82	24.88	68.81	10.35	28.8	800-526-7384	Y
Great-West Lifetime 2055 Fund Class L	MXBTX	B-	B-	B-	Down	4.99	9.67	20.62	27.05	68.30		366.6		Y
Great-West Lifetime Conservative 2055 Fund Inst Cls	MXXFX	B-	B-	B-	Down	4.82	9.30	19.97	27.75	65.48		44.5		Y
Great-West Lifetime Conservative 2055 Fund Investor Class	MXSLX	B-	B-	B-	Down	4.65	9.03	19.46	26.53	63.90		44.5		Y
Great-West Lifetime Conservative 2055 Fund Service Class	MXTLX	B-	B-	B-	Down	4.63	9.01	19.40	26.18	63.15		44.5		Y
Great-West SecureFoundation® Lifetime 2050 Fund Class L	MXLOX	B-	B-	B-	Down	5.17	10.04	20.05	28.44	70.18		23.6		Y

Category: Target Date 2046+ (con't)

Fund Name	Ticker Symbol	RATINGS: Overall Rating	Reward Rating	Risk Rating	Recent Up/ Downgrade	TOTAL RETURNS & PERFORMANCE: 3-Month Total Return	6-Month Total Return	1-Year Total Return	3-Year Total Return	5-Year Total Return	ASSETS: NAV	Total Assets (MIL)	NEW INVESTORS: Telephone	Open to New Investors
Great-West SecureFoundation® Lifetime 2050 Fund Inv Cls	MXFSX	B-	B-	B-	Down	3.50	8.30	18.33	26.69	67.77		23.6		Y
Great-West SecureFoundation® Lifetime 2050 Fund Serv Cls	MXHSX	B-	B-	B-	Down	5.18	10.08	20.12	28.33	69.72		23.6		Y
Great-West SecureFoundation® Lifetime 2055 Fund Class L	MXLPX	B-	B-	B-	Down	8.08	13.19	23.70	32.18	74.15		8.6		Y
Great-West SecureFoundation® Lifetime 2055 Fund Inv Cls	MXSYX	B-	B-	B-	Down	7.62	12.72	23.25	31.72	73.46		8.6		Y
Great-West SecureFoundation® Lifetime 2055 Fund Serv Cls	MXSZX	B-	B-	B-	Down	5.19	10.17	20.38	28.32	68.62		8.6		Y
Harbor Target Retirement 2050 Fund Institutional Class	HAFFX	B-	B-	B-	Down	4.54	9.46	22.92	29.38	70.73	10.28	23.3	800-422-1050	Y
Invesco Balanced-Risk Retirement 2050 Fund Class A	TNEAX	B	B	B-	Up	6.49	10.24	13.15	22.64	36.83	7.79	38.1	800-659-1005	Y
Invesco Balanced-Risk Retirement 2050 Fund Class AX	VRIAX	B	B	B-	Up	6.48	10.22	13.29	22.61	36.80	7.8	38.1	800-659-1005	
Invesco Balanced-Risk Retirement 2050 Fund Class B	TNEBX	B-	B-	B-		6.37	9.89	12.53	20.32	32.17	7.68	38.1	800-659-1005	
Invesco Balanced-Risk Retirement 2050 Fund Class C	TNECX	B-	B-	B-		6.36	9.87	12.35	20.11	32.08	7.69	38.1	800-659-1005	Y
Invesco Balanced-Risk Retirement 2050 Fund Class CX	VRICX	B-	B-	B-		6.36	9.87	12.51	20.29	32.12	7.69	38.1	800-659-1005	
Invesco Balanced-Risk Retirement 2050 Fund Class R	TNERX	B	B	B-	Up	6.41	10.18	12.96	21.82	35.20	7.75	38.1	800-659-1005	Y
Invesco Balanced-Risk Retirement 2050 Fund Class R5	TNEIX	B	B	B	Up	6.69	10.58	13.65	23.61	38.56	7.83	38.1	800-659-1005	Y
Invesco Balanced-Risk Retirement 2050 Fund Class R6	TNEFX	B	B	B	Up	6.68	10.57	13.63	23.57	38.66	7.84	38.1	800-659-1005	Y
Invesco Balanced-Risk Retirement 2050 Fund Class RX	VRIRX	B	B	B-	Up	6.54	10.17	13.10	21.96	35.33	7.76	38.1	800-659-1005	
Invesco Balanced-Risk Retirement 2050 Fund Class Y	TNEYX	B	B	B	Up	6.70	10.45	13.67	23.63	38.60	7.82	38.1	800-659-1005	Y
John Hancock Funds Multi-Index 2050 Lifetime Port Cls 1	JRLWX	B-	B-	B-	Down	4.98	9.81	20.27	29.14		12.34	89.2	800-225-5913	Y
John Hancock Funds Multi-Index 2050 Lifetime Port Cls R6	JRLZX	B-	B-	B-	Down	5.03	9.86	20.33	29.46		12.34	89.2	800-225-5913	Y
John Hancock Funds Multi-Ind 2050 Preserv Port Cls 1	JRIOX	B-	B-	B-	Down	4.58	9.09	18.91	26.89	63.62	13.3	600.0	800-225-5913	Y
John Hancock Funds Multi-Ind 2050 Preserv Port Cls R1	JRIQX	B-	B-	B-	Down	4.44	8.78	18.17	24.72	58.53	13.35	600.0	800-225-5913	Y
John Hancock Funds Multi-Ind 2050 Preserv Port Cls R2	JRINX	B-	B-	B-	Down	4.39	8.89	18.39	25.65	60.54	13.33	600.0	800-225-5913	Y
John Hancock Funds Multi-Ind 2050 Preserv Port Cls R4	JRIPX	B-	B-	B-	Down	4.46	9.03	18.61	26.34	62.10	13.35	600.0	800-225-5913	Y
John Hancock Funds Multi-Ind 2050 Preserv Port Cls R6	JRISX	B-	B-	B-	Down	4.55	9.14	18.96	27.08	64.01	13.3	600.0	800-225-5913	Y
John Hancock Funds Multi-Index 2055 Lifetime Port Cls 1	JLKZX	B-	B-	B-	Down	5.06	9.93	20.36	29.24		12.22	60.0	800-225-5913	Y
John Hancock Funds Multi-Index 2055 Lifetime Port Cls R6	JLKYX	B-	B-	B-	Down	5.12	9.89	20.33	29.34		12.21	60.0	800-225-5913	Y
John Hancock Funds Multi-Ind 2055 Preserv Port Cls 1	JRIYX	B-	B-	B-	Down	4.50	9.11	18.78	26.79		11.75	226.6	800-225-5913	Y
John Hancock Funds Multi-Ind 2055 Preserv Port Cls R1	JRITX	B-	B-	B-	Down	4.42	8.86	18.29	25.11		11.75	226.6	800-225-5913	Y
John Hancock Funds Multi-Ind 2055 Preserv Port Cls R2	JRIUX	B-	B-	B-	Down	4.47	9.00	18.56	26.01		11.75	226.6	800-225-5913	Y
John Hancock Funds Multi-Ind 2055 Preserv Port Cls R4	JRIVX	B-	B-	B-	Down	4.57	9.10	18.77	26.48		11.76	226.6	800-225-5913	Y
John Hancock Funds Multi-Ind 2055 Preserv Port Cls R6	JRIWX	B-	B-	B-	Down	4.55	9.16	18.94	27.08		11.76	226.6	800-225-5913	Y
John Hancock Funds Multimanager 2050 Lifetime Port Cls 1	JLKOX	B-	B-	B-	Down	4.86	9.76	21.50	29.55	72.96	12.78	389.5	800-225-5913	Y
John Hancock Funds Multimanager 2050 Lifetime Port Cls A	JLKAX	B-	B-	B-	Down	4.76	9.58	21.10	28.15	69.48	12.78	389.5	800-225-5913	Y
John Hancock Funds Multimanager 2050 Lifetime Port Cls I	JHRPX	B-	B-	B-	Down	4.80	9.70	21.32	29.29	72.62	12.78	389.5	800-225-5913	Y
John Hancock Funds Multimanager 2050 Lifetime Port Cls R1	JLKDX	B-	B-	B-	Down	4.60	9.33	20.63	26.85	67.11	12.77	389.5	800-225-5913	Y
John Hancock Funds Multimanager 2050 Lifetime Port Cls R2	JLKEX	B-	B-	B-	Down	4.76	9.58	21.00	27.97	69.24	12.79	389.5	800-225-5913	Y
John Hancock Funds Multimanager 2050 Lifetime Port Cls R3	JLKFX	B-	B-	B-	Down	4.69	9.43	20.74	27.33	68.06	12.77	389.5	800-225-5913	Y
John Hancock Funds Multimanager 2050 Lifetime Port Cls R4	JLKGX	B-	B-	B-	Down	4.76	9.66	21.29	28.90	71.45	12.78	389.5	800-225-5913	Y
John Hancock Funds Multimanager 2050 Lifetime Port Cls R5	JLKHX	B-	B-	B-	Down	4.87	9.85	21.59	29.78	73.27	12.8	389.5	800-225-5913	Y
John Hancock Funds Multimanager 2050 Lifetime Port Cls R6	JLKRX	B-	B-	B-	Down	4.83	9.80	21.54	29.71	73.49	12.79	389.5	800-225-5913	Y
John Hancock Funds Multimanager 2055 Lifetime Port Cls 1	JLKUX	B-	B-	B-	Down	4.88	9.79	21.49	29.42		11.73	159.6	800-225-5913	Y
John Hancock Funds Multimanager 2055 Lifetime Port Cls A	JLKLX	B-	B-	B-	Down	4.72	9.54	21.11	27.94		11.72	159.6	800-225-5913	Y
John Hancock Funds Multimanager 2055 Lifetime Port Cls I	JHRTX	B-	B-	B-	Down	4.83	9.74	21.43	29.19		11.73	159.6	800-225-5913	Y
John Hancock Funds Multimanager 2055 Lifetime Port Cls R1	JLKMX	B-	B-	B-	Down	4.71	9.53	20.88	27.60		11.72	159.6	800-225-5913	Y
John Hancock Funds Multimanager 2055 Lifetime Port Cls R2	JLKNX	B-	B-	B-	Down	4.71	9.53	21.09	28.39		11.72	159.6	800-225-5913	Y
John Hancock Funds Multimanager 2055 Lifetime Port Cls R3	JLKPX	B-	B-	B-	Down	4.76	9.49	20.84	27.53		11.72	159.6	800-225-5913	Y
John Hancock Funds Multimanager 2055 Lifetime Port Cls R4	JLKQX	B-	B-	B-	Down	4.87	9.78	21.37	29.02		11.73	159.6	800-225-5913	Y
John Hancock Funds Multimanager 2055 Lifetime Port Cls R5	JLKSX	B-	B-	B-	Down	4.81	9.72	21.51	29.48		11.73	159.6	800-225-5913	Y
John Hancock Funds Multimanager 2055 Lifetime Port Cls R6	JLKTX	B-	B-	B-	Down	4.84	9.84	21.55	29.61		11.73	159.6	800-225-5913	Y
JPMorgan SmartRetirement® 2050 Fund Class A	JTSAX	B-	B-	B-	Down	4.07	9.18	20.38	24.98	68.47	21.39	3,605	800-480-4111	Y
JPMorgan SmartRetirement® 2050 Fund Class C	JTSCX	B-	B-	B-	Down	5.14	10.11	21.01	24.03	65.00	21.2	3,605	800-480-4111	Y
JPMorgan SmartRetirement® 2050 Fund Class I	JTSSX	B-	B-	B-	Down	4.06	9.22	20.45	25.31	69.26	21.46	3,605	800-480-4111	Y
JPMorgan SmartRetirement® 2050 Fund Class R2	JTSZX	B-	B-	B-	Down	4.04	9.04	19.95	24.01	66.18	21.3	3,605	800-480-4111	Y

Category: Target Date 2046+ (con't)

		RATINGS				TOTAL RETURNS & PERFORMANCE					ASSETS		NEW INVESTORS	
Fund Name	Ticker Symbol	Overall Rating	Reward Rating	Risk Rating	Recent Up/ Downgrade	3-Month Total Return	6-Month Total Return	1-Year Total Return	3-Year Total Return	5-Year Total Return	NAV	Total Assets (MIL)	Telephone	Open to New Investors
JPMorgan SmartRetirement® 2050 Fund Class R3	JTSPX	B-	B-	B-	Down	4.03	9.13	20.13	24.67	68.05	21.33	3,605	800-480-4111	Y
JPMorgan SmartRetirement® 2050 Fund Class R4	JTSQX	B-	B-	B-	Down	5.27	10.49	21.85	27.08	72.15	21.44	3,605	800-480-4111	Y
JPMorgan SmartRetirement® 2050 Fund Class R5	JTSIX	B-	B-	B-	Down	4.10	9.29	20.58	25.81	70.44	21.5	3,605	800-480-4111	Y
JPMorgan SmartRetirement® 2050 Fund Class R6	JTSYX	B-	B-	B-	Down	5.36	10.64	22.12	27.67	72.95	21.5	3,605	800-480-4111	Y
JPMorgan SmartRetirement® 2055 Fund Class A	JFFAX	B-	B-	B-	Down	4.04	9.11	20.27	24.94	68.62	23.88	1,262	800-480-4111	Y
JPMorgan SmartRetirement® 2055 Fund Class C	JFFCX	B-	B-	B-	Down	5.13	10.11	20.95	23.97	65.22	23.78	1,262	800-480-4111	Y
JPMorgan SmartRetirement® 2055 Fund Class I	JFFSX	B-	B-	B-	Down	4.04	9.17	20.37	25.30	69.48	23.92	1,262	800-480-4111	Y
JPMorgan SmartRetirement® 2055 Fund Class R2	JFFRX	B-	B-	B-	Down	4.05	9.01	19.99	23.96	66.55	23.84	1,262	800-480-4111	Y
JPMorgan SmartRetirement® 2055 Fund Class R3	JFFPX	B-	B-	B-	Down	4.01	9.06	20.10	24.64	68.21	23.83	1,262	800-480-4111	Y
JPMorgan SmartRetirement® 2055 Fund Class R4	JFFQX	B-	B-	B-	Down	4.04	9.15	20.39	25.55	70.30	23.91	1,262	800-480-4111	Y
JPMorgan SmartRetirement® 2055 Fund Class R5	JFFIX	B-	B-	B-	Down	4.03	9.19	20.51	25.74	70.56	23.94	1,262	800-480-4111	Y
JPMorgan SmartRetirement® 2055 Fund Class R6	JFFYX	B-	B-	B-	Down	5.34	10.59	22.11	27.65	73.06	23.95	1,262	800-480-4111	Y
JPMorgan SmartRetirement® Blend 2050 Fund Class I	JNEAX	B-	B-	B-	Down	4.91	9.59	20.20	27.68	67.95	23.75	218.7	800-480-4111	Y
JPMorgan SmartRetirement® Blend 2050 Fund Class R2	JNNRX	B-	B-	B-	Down	4.78	9.31	19.61	25.94	64.36	23.75	218.7	800-480-4111	Y
JPMorgan SmartRetirement® Blend 2050 Fund Class R3	JNTKX	B-	B-	B-	Down	4.85	9.45	20.02	27.47	67.63	23.74	218.7	800-480-4111	Y
JPMorgan SmartRetirement® Blend 2050 Fund Class R4	JNTPX	B-	B-	B-	Down	4.92	9.59	20.32	28.43	69.74	23.74	218.7	800-480-4111	Y
JPMorgan SmartRetirement® Blend 2050 Fund Class R5	JNABX	B-	B-	B-	Down	4.95	9.67	20.43	28.37	69.46	23.76	218.7	800-480-4111	Y
JPMorgan SmartRetirement® Blend 2050 Fund Class R6	JNYAX	B-	B-	B-	Down	4.97	9.71	20.53	28.65	70.03	23.77	218.7	800-480-4111	Y
JPMorgan SmartRetirement® Blend 2055 Fund Class I	JPTBX	B-	B-	B-	Down	4.93	9.58	20.14	27.83	67.37	23.37	86.0	800-480-4111	Y
JPMorgan SmartRetirement® Blend 2055 Fund Class R2	JTRBX	B-	B-	B-	Down	4.80	9.31	19.55	26.08	63.83	23.37	86.0	800-480-4111	Y
JPMorgan SmartRetirement® Blend 2055 Fund Class R3	JTTUX	B-	B-	B-	Down	4.82	9.45	19.90	27.60	67.08	23.35	86.0	800-480-4111	Y
JPMorgan SmartRetirement® Blend 2055 Fund Class R4	JTTLX	B-	B-	B	Down	4.93	9.64	20.25	28.62	69.26	23.36	86.0	800-480-4111	Y
JPMorgan SmartRetirement® Blend 2055 Fund Class R5	JTBBX	B-	B-	B-	Down	4.97	9.66	20.31	28.51	69.00	23.38	86.0	800-480-4111	Y
JPMorgan SmartRetirement® Blend 2055 Fund Class R6	JTYBX	B-	B-	B	Down	4.99	9.75	20.41	28.78	69.47	23.39	86.0	800-480-4111	Y
KP Retirement Path 2050 Fund Institutional Shares	KPRHX	B-	B-	B-	Down	4.83	10.12	21.52	29.85		12.01	401.7		Y
KP Retirement Path 2055 Fund Institutional Shares	KPRIX	B-	B-	B-	Down	4.95	10.16	21.59	30.01		12.03	106.6		Y
KP Retirement Path 2060 Fund Institutional Shares	KPRJX	B-	B-	B-	Down	4.90	10.17	21.65	30.05		12	21.5		Y
MainStay Retirement 2050 Fund Class A	MSRLX	B-	B-	B-	Down	5.01	9.95	21.60	26.19	72.11	11.99	115.8	800-624-6782	Y
MainStay Retirement 2050 Fund Class I	MSRMX	B-	B-	B-	Down	5.10	10.10	21.91	27.10	74.23	12.06	115.8	800-624-6782	Y
MainStay Retirement 2050 Fund Class R1	MSROX	B-	B-	B-	Down	5.06	10.04	21.79	26.73	73.57	12.12	115.8	800-624-6782	Y
MainStay Retirement 2050 Fund Class R2	MSRPX	B-	B-	B-	Down	5.16	10.02	21.66	25.89	71.49	12.02	115.8	800-624-6782	Y
MainStay Retirement 2050 Fund Class R3	MSRWX	B-	B-	B-	Down	5.00	9.83	21.17	24.84	69.20	12.08	115.8	800-624-6782	Y
MainStay Retirement 2050 Fund Investor Class	MSRVX	B-	B-	B-	Down	5.06	9.93	21.49	25.71	71.18	11.97	115.8	800-624-6782	Y
Manning & Napier Target 2050 Series Class I	MTYIX	B-	B-	B	Up	5.09	9.61	24.27	22.98	67.42	10.64	37.5	585-325-6880	Y
Manning & Napier Target 2050 Series Class K	MTYKX	B-	B-	B	Up	5.00	9.44	24.06	22.13	65.37	10.56	37.5	585-325-6880	Y
Manning & Napier Target 2050 Series Class R	MTYRX	B-	C+	B	Up	4.97	9.36	23.71	21.19	63.18	10.44	37.5	585-325-6880	Y
Manning & Napier Target 2050 Series Fund R6	MTYZX	B-	B-	B		5.12	9.64	24.31	23.02	67.47	10.64	37.5	585-325-6880	Y
Manning & Napier Target 2055 Series Class I	MTZIX	B-	B-	B	Up	5.06	9.55	24.21	22.94	66.88	12.95	7.5	585-325-6880	Y
Manning & Napier Target 2055 Series Class K	MTZKX	B-	B-	B	Up	4.99	9.42	23.98	22.07	64.59	12.83	7.5	585-325-6880	Y
Manning & Napier Target 2055 Series Class R	MTZRX	B-	C+	B	Up	4.92	9.23	23.65	21.13	62.44	12.68	7.5	585-325-6880	Y
Manning & Napier Target 2055 Series R6	MTZZX	B-	B-	B		5.17	9.66	24.34	23.07	67.06	12.96	7.5	585-325-6880	Y
MassMutual RetireSMART 2050 Fund Administrative Class	MMRYX	B-	B-	B-	Down	4.97	9.81	20.55	24.62	65.16	9.72	176.6		Y
MassMutual RetireSMART 2050 Fund Class A	MMARX	B-	B-	B-	Up	4.78	9.65	20.18	23.57	62.82	9.66	176.6		Y
MassMutual RetireSMART 2050 Fund Class I	MMRUX	B-	B-	B-	Down	5.04	10.00	20.88	25.68	67.04	9.72	176.6		Y
MassMutual RetireSMART 2050 Fund Class R4	MMRZX	B-	B-	B-	Down	4.86	9.75	20.32	23.99	63.88	9.62	176.6		Y
MassMutual RetireSMART 2050 Fund Class R5	MMRTX	B-	B-	B-	Down	4.96	9.91	20.66	25.38	66.44	9.71	176.6		Y
MassMutual RetireSMART 2050 Fund Service Class	MMTSX	B-	B-	B-	Down	4.95	9.90	20.65	24.94	65.83	9.72	176.6		Y
MassMutual RetireSMART 2055 Fund Administrative Class	MMWYX	B-	B-	C+	Down	4.88	9.77	20.59	24.81		11.47	43.8		Y
MassMutual RetireSMART 2055 Fund Class I	MMWZX	B-	B-	C+	Down	4.94	10.02	20.96	25.87		11.49	43.8		Y
MassMutual RetireSMART 2055 Fund Class R4	MMWEX	B-	B-	C+	Down	4.82	9.73	20.35	24.24		11.43	43.8		Y
MassMutual RetireSMART 2055 Fund Class R5	MMWUX	B-	B-	C+	Down	4.91	9.89	20.80	25.48		11.5	43.8		Y
MassMutual RetireSMART 2055 Fund Service Class	MMWSX	B-	B-	C+	Down	4.94	9.91	20.70	25.19		11.52	43.8		Y

Category: Target Date 2046+ (con't)

Fund Name	Ticker Symbol	RATINGS Overall Rating	Reward Rating	Risk Rating	Recent Up/ Downgrade	TOTAL RETURNS & PERFORMANCE 3-Month Total Return	6-Month Total Return	1-Year Total Return	3-Year Total Return	5-Year Total Return	ASSETS NAV	Total Assets (MIL)	NEW INVESTORS Telephone	Open to New Investors
MFS® Lifetime 2050 Fund Class A	MFFSX	B-	B-	B	Down	5.26	9.75	20.86	30.37	71.37	18.24	201.3	877-960-6077	Y
MFS® Lifetime 2050 Fund Class B	MFFRX	B-	B-	B-	Down	5.13	9.43	20.03	27.56	65.16	18.06	201.3	877-960-6077	Y
MFS® Lifetime 2050 Fund Class C	MFFDX	B-	B-	B-	Down	5.09	9.42	20.01	27.50	65.18	17.95	201.3	877-960-6077	Y
MFS® Lifetime 2050 Fund Class I	MFFIX	B-	B-	B	Down	5.36	9.99	21.20	31.49	73.76	18.22	201.3	877-960-6077	Y
MFS® Lifetime 2050 Fund Class R1	MFFMX	B-	B-	B-	Down	5.10	9.35	19.99	27.44	65.11	17.95	201.3	877-960-6077	Y
MFS® Lifetime 2050 Fund Class R2	MFFNX	B-	B-	B	Down	5.21	9.64	20.57	29.36	69.30	18.02	201.3	877-960-6077	Y
MFS® Lifetime 2050 Fund Class R3	MFFOX	B-	B-	B	Down	5.30	9.82	20.93	30.36	71.29	18.12	201.3	877-960-6077	Y
MFS® Lifetime 2050 Fund Class R4	MFFPX	B-	B-	B	Down	5.37	10.00	21.23	31.44	73.58	18.21	201.3	877-960-6077	Y
MFS® Lifetime 2050 Fund Class R6	MFFKX	B-	B-	B	Down	5.41	9.98	21.36	31.55	73.84	18.19	201.3	877-960-6077	Y
MFS® Lifetime 2055 Fund Class A	LFIAX	B-	B-	B	Down	5.28	9.82	20.92	30.41	71.60	15.41	68.3	877-960-6077	Y
MFS® Lifetime 2055 Fund Class B	LFIBX	B-	B-	B	Down	5.12	9.38	20.02	27.53	65.31	15.38	68.3	877-960-6077	Y
MFS® Lifetime 2055 Fund Class C	LFICX	B-	B-	B	Down	5.09	9.37	20.01	27.51	65.27	15.27	68.3	877-960-6077	Y
MFS® Lifetime 2055 Fund Class I	LFIIX	B-	B-	B	Down	5.35	9.89	21.18	30.88	73.00	15.4	68.3	877-960-6077	Y
MFS® Lifetime 2055 Fund Class R1	LFIRX	B-	B-	B	Down	5.06	9.40	19.89	27.39	65.15	15.31	68.3	877-960-6077	Y
MFS® Lifetime 2055 Fund Class R2	LFISX	B-	B-	B	Down	5.20	9.69	20.56	29.43	69.41	15.33	68.3	877-960-6077	Y
MFS® Lifetime 2055 Fund Class R3	LFITX	B-	B-	B	Down	5.25	9.79	20.80	30.29	71.54	15.4	68.3	877-960-6077	Y
MFS® Lifetime 2055 Fund Class R4	LFIUX	B-	B-	B	Down	5.33	9.93	21.08	31.37	73.65	15.46	68.3	877-960-6077	Y
MFS® Lifetime 2055 Fund Class R6	LFIKX	B-	B-	B	Down	5.39	10.06	21.31	31.68	74.05	15.47	68.3	877-960-6077	Y
Nationwide Destination 2050 Fund Class A	NWOAX	B-	B-	B-	Down	4.94	9.00	18.16	26.95	68.92	9.11	133.1	800-848-0920	Y
Nationwide Destination 2050 Fund Class C	NWOCX	B-	B-	B-	Down	4.78	8.64	17.34	24.64	64.37	8.94	133.1	800-848-0920	Y
Nationwide Destination 2050 Fund Class R	NWOBX	B-	B-	B-	Down	4.82	8.85	17.75	25.87	66.77	8.99	133.1	800-848-0920	Y
Nationwide Destination 2050 Fund Class R6	NWOIX	B-	B-	B-	Down	5.06	9.37	18.63	28.78	73.01	9.13	133.1	800-848-0920	Y
Nationwide Destination 2050 Fund Institutional Service Cls	NWOSX	B-	B-	B-	Down	5.01	9.14	18.39	27.77	70.96	9.1	133.1	800-848-0920	Y
Nationwide Destination 2055 Fund Class A	NTDAX	B-	B-	B-	Down	4.97	9.22	18.45	27.30	69.36	13.89	69.9	800-848-0920	Y
Nationwide Destination 2055 Fund Class C	NTDCX	B-	B-	B-	Down	4.90	8.93	17.88	25.20	64.82	13.88	69.9	800-848-0920	Y
Nationwide Destination 2055 Fund Class R	NTDTX	B-	B-	B-	Down	4.91	9.02	18.18	26.25	67.08	13.86	69.9	800-848-0920	Y
Nationwide Destination 2055 Fund Class R6	NTDIX	B-	B-	B-	Down	5.14	9.43	19.06	29.15	73.56	13.96	69.9	800-848-0920	Y
Nationwide Destination 2055 Fund Institutional Service Cls	NTDSX	B-	B-	B-	Down	5.08	9.31	18.80	28.24	71.44	13.95	69.9	800-848-0920	Y
Principal LifeTime 2050 Fund Class A	PPEAX	B-	B-	B-	Down	5.02	10.35	21.66	25.74	67.68	15.76	2,598	800-222-5852	Y
Principal LifeTime 2050 Fund Class J	PFLJX	B-	B-	B-	Down	5.00	10.43	21.85	25.92	67.66	15.25	2,598	800-222-5852	Y
Principal LifeTime 2050 Fund Institutional Class	PPLIX	B-	B-	B-	Down	5.06	10.56	22.12	27.11	70.89	15.67	2,598	800-222-5852	Y
Principal LifeTime 2050 Fund R-1 Class	PZASX	B-	B-	B-	Down	4.85	10.05	20.98	23.76	63.43	15.54	2,598	800-222-5852	Y
Principal LifeTime 2050 Fund R-2 Class	PTENX	B-	B-	B-	Down	4.88	10.15	21.18	24.24	64.50	15.52	2,598	800-222-5852	Y
Principal LifeTime 2050 Fund R-3 Class	PTERX	B-	B-	B-	Down	4.91	10.18	21.39	24.98	66.08	15.51	2,598	800-222-5852	Y
Principal LifeTime 2050 Fund R-4 Class	PTESX	B-	B-	B-	Down	4.97	10.36	21.61	25.71	67.69	15.59	2,598	800-222-5852	Y
Principal LifeTime 2050 Fund R-5 Class	PTEFX	B-	B-	B-	Down	4.96	10.34	21.73	26.13	68.54	15.62	2,598	800-222-5852	Y
Principal LifeTime 2055 Fund Institutional Class	LTFIX	B-	B-	B-	Down	5.13	10.76	22.52	27.74	71.63	13.6	399.5	800-222-5852	Y
Principal LifeTime 2055 Fund R-1 Class	LTFGX	B-	B-	B-	Down	4.93	10.22	21.48	24.48	64.41	13.19	399.5	800-222-5852	Y
Principal LifeTime 2055 Fund R-2 Class	LTFSX	B-	B-	B-	Down	5.00	10.36	21.70	25.00	65.50	13.23	399.5	800-222-5852	Y
Principal LifeTime 2055 Fund R-3 Class	LTFDX	B-	B-	B-	Down	5.02	10.44	21.83	25.61	66.95	13.29	399.5	800-222-5852	Y
Principal LifeTime 2055 Fund R-4 Class	LTFLX	B-	B-	B-	Down	5.11	10.57	22.08	26.38	68.63	13.4	399.5	800-222-5852	Y
Principal LifeTime 2055 Fund R-5 Class	LTFPX	B-	B-	B-	Down	5.14	10.58	22.25	26.81	69.57	13.45	399.5	800-222-5852	Y
Principal LifeTime 2060 Fund Class J	PLTAX	B-	B-	B-	Down	5.13	10.68	22.27	26.53		14.13	264.4	800-222-5852	Y
Principal LifeTime 2060 Fund Class R-1	PLTRX	B-	B-	B-	Down	4.93	10.31	21.65	24.52		13.92	264.4	800-222-5852	Y
Principal LifeTime 2060 Fund Class R-2	PLTBX	B-	B-	B-	Down	4.95	10.40	21.80	24.97		13.96	264.4	800-222-5852	Y
Principal LifeTime 2060 Fund Class R-3	PLTCX	B-	B-	B-	Down	5.08	10.57	22.09	25.69		14.08	264.4	800-222-5852	Y
Principal LifeTime 2060 Fund Class R-4	PLTMX	B-	B-	B-	Down	5.14	10.61	22.33	26.40		14.09	264.4	800-222-5852	Y
Principal LifeTime 2060 Fund Class R-5	PLTOX	B-	B-	B-	Down	5.08	10.62	22.40	26.74		14.12	264.4	800-222-5852	Y
Principal LifeTime 2060 Fund Institutional Class	PLTZX	B-	B-	B-	Down	5.25	10.85	22.69	27.74		14.2	264.4	800-222-5852	Y
Putnam RetirementReady 2050 Fund Class A	PRRJX	B-	B-	B	Down	1.04	6.15	15.12	21.48	71.00	20.03	60.8	617-292-1000	Y
Putnam RetirementReady 2050 Fund Class B	US7468593626	B-	B-	B-	Down	5.40	10.47	19.05	23.50	72.08		60.8	617-292-1000	Y
Putnam RetirementReady 2050 Fund Class C	US7468593543	B-	B-	B-	Down	5.40	10.51	19.05	23.51	72.11		60.8	617-292-1000	Y

Category: Target Date 2046+ (con't)

Fund Name	Ticker Symbol	RATINGS: Overall Rating	Reward Rating	Risk Rating	Recent Up/ Downgrade	TOTAL RETURNS & PERFORMANCE: 3-Month Total Return	6-Month Total Return	1-Year Total Return	3-Year Total Return	5-Year Total Return	ASSETS: NAV	Total Assets (MIL)	NEW INVESTORS: Telephone	Open to New Investors
Putnam RetirementReady 2050 Fund Class M	US7468593477	B-	B-	B-	Down	5.47	10.65	19.35	24.45	74.21		60.8	617-292-1000	Y
Putnam RetirementReady 2050 Fund Class R	PRRKX	B-	B-	B-	Down	1.15	6.16	15.04	20.75	69.19	19.82	60.8	617-292-1000	Y
Putnam RetirementReady 2050 Fund Class R6	PREUX	B-	B-	B	Down	5.71	11.12	20.43	27.47	81.11		60.8	617-292-1000	Y
Putnam RetirementReady 2050 Fund Class Y	PRRUX	B-	B-	B	Down	5.62	11.04	20.29	27.25	80.81		60.8	617-292-1000	Y
Putnam RetirementReady 2055 Fund Class A	PRRFX	B-	B-	B-	Down	4.02	9.38	18.87	25.31	77.07	12.26	20.3	617-292-1000	Y
Putnam RetirementReady 2055 Fund Class B	US7468592974	B-	B-	B-	Down	5.52	10.82	19.59	23.98	73.36		20.3	617-292-1000	Y
Putnam RetirementReady 2055 Fund Class C	US7468592891	B-	B-	B-	Down	5.51	10.78	19.52	23.93	73.43		20.3	617-292-1000	Y
Putnam RetirementReady 2055 Fund Class M	US7468592719	B-	B-	B-	Down	5.65	11.01	19.85	25.01	75.72		20.3	617-292-1000	Y
Putnam RetirementReady 2055 Fund Class R	PRRVX	B-	B-	B-	Down	1.70	6.87	15.97	21.74	71.12	12.23	20.3	617-292-1000	Y
Putnam RetirementReady 2055 Fund Class R6	PREVX	B-	B-	B-	Down	4.14	9.63	19.37	26.58	79.83	12.37	20.3	617-292-1000	Y
Putnam RetirementReady 2055 Fund Class Y	PRTLX	B-	B-	B-	Down	4.10	9.51	19.15	26.33	79.48	12.35	20.3	617-292-1000	Y
Schwab Target 2050 Fund	SWNRX	B-	B-	B-	Down	4.88	9.96	21.87	29.24		14.13	107.1	877-824-5615	Y
Schwab Target 2055 Fund	SWORX	B-	B-	B-	Down	5.06	10.29	22.46	29.85		14.26	62.4	877-824-5615	Y
State Farm LifePath 2050 Fund Class A	NLPAX	B-	B-	B-	Down	5.15	9.63	20.39	25.77	61.63	12.4	463.5		Y
State Farm LifePath 2050 Fund Class R1	RAVRX	B-	B-	B-	Down	5.11	9.48	20.21	24.75	59.17	12.42	463.5		Y
State Farm LifePath 2050 Fund Class R2	RAVSX	B-	B-	B-	Down	5.06	9.51	20.24	25.20	60.55	12.43	463.5		Y
State Farm LifePath 2050 Fund Premier shares	NLPPX	B-	B-	B-	Down	5.19	9.67	20.58	25.97	61.89	12.37	463.5		Y
T. Rowe Price Retirement 2050 Fund	TRRMX	B-	B-	B-	Down	4.41	9.16	22.37	31.27	79.24	15.52	8,650	410-345-2000	Y
T. Rowe Price Retirement 2050 Fund Advisor Class	PARFX	B-	B-	B-	Down	4.32	9.04	22.08	30.25	76.95	15.39	8,650	410-345-2000	Y
T. Rowe Price Retirement 2050 Fund Class R	RRTFX	B-	B-	B-	Down	4.23	8.84	21.71	29.23	74.64	15.26	8,650	410-345-2000	Y
T. Rowe Price Retirement 2055 Fund	TRRNX	B-	B-	B-	Down	4.40	9.14	22.32	31.23	78.96	15.58	3,790	410-345-2000	Y
T. Rowe Price Retirement 2055 Fund Advisor Class	PAROX	B-	B-	B-	Down	4.30	9.00	22.06	30.21	76.83	15.49	3,790	410-345-2000	Y
T. Rowe Price Retirement 2055 Fund Class R	RRTVX	B-	B-	B-	Down	4.27	8.92	21.79	29.28	74.62	15.41	3,790	410-345-2000	Y
T. Rowe Price Retirement 2060 Fund	TRRLX	B-	B-	B-	Up	4.37	9.15	22.29	31.13		12.06	390.6	410-345-2000	Y
T. Rowe Price Retirement 2060 Fund Advisor Class	TRRYX	B-	B-	B-	Up	4.31	9.01	22.05	30.26		12.02	390.6	410-345-2000	Y
T. Rowe Price Retirement 2060 Fund R Class	TRRZX	B-	B-	B-	Up	4.25	8.88	21.75	29.17		11.97	390.6	410-345-2000	Y
T. Rowe Price Target 2050 Fund	TRFOX	B-	B-	B	Down	4.18	8.73	21.41	29.93		13.47	62.0	410-345-2000	Y
T. Rowe Price Target 2050 Fund Advisor Class	PAOFX	B-	B-	B-	Down	4.05	8.53	21.03	28.87		13.42	62.0	410-345-2000	Y
T. Rowe Price Target 2050 Fund I Class	TOORX	B-	B-	B	Down	4.18	8.73	21.41	30.04		13.46	62.0	410-345-2000	Y
T. Rowe Price Target 2055 Fund	TRFFX	B-	B-	B-	Down	4.27	9.02	22.03	30.66		13.44	35.3	410-345-2000	Y
T. Rowe Price Target 2055 Fund Advisor Class	PAFTX	B-	B-	B-	Down	4.22	8.90	21.74	29.70		13.4	35.3	410-345-2000	Y
T. Rowe Price Target 2055 Fund I Class	TRPPX	B-	B-	B-	Down	4.35	9.09	22.21	30.96		13.44	35.3	410-345-2000	Y
T. Rowe Price Target 2060 Fund	TRTFX	B-	B-	B-	Up	4.39	9.13	22.23	30.88		11.55	10.4	410-345-2000	Y
T. Rowe Price Target 2060 Fund Advisor Class	TRTGX	B-	B-	B-	Up	4.30	8.94	21.88	29.98		11.57	10.4	410-345-2000	Y
T. Rowe Price Target 2060 Fund I Class	TTOIX	B-	B-	B-	Up	4.37	9.20	22.41	31.20		11.57	10.4	410-345-2000	Y
TIAA-CREF Lifecycle 2050 Fund Advisor Class	TFTHX	B-	B	B-	Down	5.40	11.55	24.02	33.43	79.94	12.72	1,707	877-518-9161	Y
TIAA-CREF Lifecycle 2050 Fund Institutional Class	TFTIX	B-	B	B-	Down	5.41	11.56	24.04	33.46	79.98	12.72	1,707	877-518-9161	Y
TIAA-CREF Lifecycle 2050 Fund Premier Class	TCLPX	B-	B	B-	Down	5.38	11.47	23.76	32.85	78.51	12.67	1,707	877-518-9161	Y
TIAA-CREF Lifecycle 2050 Fund Retirement Class	TLFRX	B-	B-	B-	Down	5.39	11.41	23.62	32.46	77.71	12.63	1,707	877-518-9161	Y
TIAA-CREF Lifecycle 2055 Fund Advisor Class	TTRHX	B	B	B-	Up	5.44	11.59	24.11	33.75	80.29	14.42	477.9	877-518-9161	Y
TIAA-CREF Lifecycle 2055 Fund Institutional Class	TTRIX	B	B	B-	Up	5.45	11.60	24.23	33.78	80.34	14.42	477.9	877-518-9161	Y
TIAA-CREF Lifecycle 2055 Fund Premier Class	TTRPX	B-	B	B-	Down	5.50	11.59	24.06	33.31	79.14	14.38	477.9	877-518-9161	Y
TIAA-CREF Lifecycle 2055 Fund Retirement Class	TTRLX	B-	B	B-	Down	5.40	11.49	23.85	32.88	78.18	14.38	477.9	877-518-9161	Y
TIAA-CREF Lifecycle Index 2050 Fund Advisor Class	TLLHX	B-	B-	B-	Down	5.29	10.13	21.36	31.01	78.95	19.95	774.8	877-518-9161	Y
TIAA-CREF Lifecycle Index 2050 Fund Institutional Class	TLLIX	B-	B-	B-	Down	5.31	10.21	21.51	31.18	79.19	19.96	774.8	877-518-9161	Y
TIAA-CREF Lifecycle Index 2050 Fund Premier Class	TLLPX	B-	B-	B-	Down	5.26	10.12	21.33	30.52	77.88	19.87	774.8	877-518-9161	Y
TIAA-CREF Lifecycle Index 2050 Fund Retirement Class	TLLRX	B-	B-	B-	Down	5.24	10.06	21.17	30.18	77.00	19.79	774.8	877-518-9161	Y
TIAA-CREF Lifecycle Index 2055 Fund Advisor Class	TTIHX	B-	B-	B-	Down	5.34	10.26	21.71	31.55	79.64	15.96	252.9	877-518-9161	Y
TIAA-CREF Lifecycle Index 2055 Fund Institutional Class	TTIIX	B-	B-	B-	Down	5.35	10.34	21.71	31.66	79.80	15.97	252.9	877-518-9161	Y
TIAA-CREF Lifecycle Index 2055 Fund Premier Class	TTIPX	B-	B-	B-	Down	5.31	10.24	21.54	31.06	78.60	15.94	252.9	877-518-9161	Y
TIAA-CREF Lifecycle Index 2055 Fund Retirement Class	TTIRX	B-	B-	B-	Down	5.29	10.15	21.47	30.67	77.56	15.91	252.9	877-518-9161	Y
TIAA-CREF Lifecycle Index 2060 Fund Advisor Class	TVIHX	B-	C+	B-	Up	5.46	10.38	21.84	32.14		12.3	44.4	877-518-9161	Y

Category: Target Date 2046+ (con't)

Fund Name	Ticker Symbol	RATINGS: Overall Rating	Reward Rating	Risk Rating	Recent Up/ Downgrade	TOTAL RETURNS & PERFORMANCE: 3-Month Total Return	6-Month Total Return	1-Year Total Return	3-Year Total Return	5-Year Total Return	ASSETS: NAV	Total Assets (MIL)	NEW INVESTORS: Telephone	Open to New Investors
TIAA-CREF Lifecycle Index 2060 Fund Institutional Class	TVIIX	B-	C+	B-	Up	5.39	10.40	21.88	32.08		12.29	44.4	877-518-9161	Y
TIAA-CREF Lifecycle Index 2060 Fund Premier Class	TVIPX	B-	C+	B-	Up	5.37	10.29	21.76	31.54		12.29	44.4	877-518-9161	Y
USAA Target Retirement 2050 Fund	URFFX	B-	B-	B-	Down	4.71	9.13	19.38	26.04	57.31	14.45	793.7	800-531-8722	Y
USAA Target Retirement 2060 Fund	URSIX	B-	B-	B-	Down	4.74	9.15	19.50	25.90		12.74	75.3	800-531-8722	Y
Vanguard Target Retirement 2050 Fund Investor Shares	VFIFX	B-	B-	B-	Down	5.19	10.09	21.39	29.14	75.60	36.2	14,237	877-662-7447	Y
Vanguard Target Retirement 2055 Fund Investor Shares	VFFVX	B-	B-	B-	Down	5.17	10.10	21.37	28.99	75.36	39.23	6,095	877-662-7447	Y
Vanguard Target Retirement 2060 Fund Investor Shares	VTTSX	B-	B-	B-	Down	5.19	10.09	21.39	28.98	75.34	34.64	2,308	877-662-7447	Y
Voya Index Solution 2050 Portfolio Class ADV	IDXPX	B-	B-	B-	Down	5.24	9.89	20.11	26.18	68.62	16.26	109.4	800-366-0066	Y
Voya Index Solution 2050 Portfolio Class I	IDXQX	B-	B-	B-	Down	5.41	10.15	20.74	28.20	73.08	16.55	109.4	800-366-0066	Y
Voya Index Solution 2050 Portfolio Class S	IDXRX	B-	B-	B-	Down	5.29	9.97	20.46	27.34	71.09	16.51	109.4	800-366-0066	Y
Voya Index Solution 2050 Portfolio Class S2	IDXSX	B-	B-	B-	Down	5.22	9.92	20.21	26.57	69.50	16.3	109.4	800-366-0066	Y
Voya Index Solution 2050 Portfolio Class Z	VSZGX	B-	B-	B-	Down	5.46	10.27	21.02	28.70	73.75	16.6	109.4	800-366-0066	Y
Voya Index Solution 2055 Portfolio Class ADV	IISAX	B-	B-	B-	Down	5.27	9.97	20.36	25.80	69.02	15.18	173.1	800-366-0066	Y
Voya Index Solution 2055 Portfolio Class I	IISNX	B-	B-	B-	Down	5.42	10.24	21.02	27.71	73.20	15.54	173.1	800-366-0066	Y
Voya Index Solution 2055 Portfolio Class S	IISSX	B-	B-	B-	Down	5.27	10.01	20.63	26.70	71.06	15.36	173.1	800-366-0066	Y
Voya Index Solution 2055 Portfolio Class S2	IISTX	B-	B-	B-	Down	5.32	9.97	20.49	26.19	69.76	15.24	173.1	800-366-0066	Y
Voya Index Solution 2055 Portfolio Class Z	VSZHX	B-	B-	B-	Down	5.46	10.34	21.26	28.24	73.92	15.62	173.1	800-366-0066	Y
Voya Solution 2050 Portfolio Class ADV	ISNPX	B-	B-	B-	Down	5.47	10.32	21.30	27.45	70.99	17.33	16.7	800-366-0066	Y
Voya Solution 2050 Portfolio Class I	ISNQX	B-	B-	B-	Down	5.63	10.64	21.99	29.61	75.81	17.81	16.7	800-366-0066	Y
Voya Solution 2050 Portfolio Class S	ISNRX	B-	B-	B-	Down	5.56	10.44	21.63	28.41	73.09	17.65	16.7	800-366-0066	Y
Voya Solution 2050 Portfolio Class S2	ISNSX	B-	B-	B-	Down	5.50	10.38	21.47	27.82	71.51	17.43	16.7	800-366-0066	Y
Voya Solution 2050 Portfolio Class T	ISNTX	B-	B-	B-	Down	5.39	10.20	21.15	26.57	69.77	17.39	16.7	800-366-0066	Y
Voya Solution 2055 Portfolio Class ADV	IASPX	B-	B-	B-	Down	5.45	10.25	21.40	26.39	68.75	14.49	180.3	800-366-0066	Y
Voya Solution 2055 Portfolio Class I	IISPX	B-	B-	B-	Down	5.57	10.61	21.93	28.37	73.06	14.78	180.3	800-366-0066	Y
Voya Solution 2055 Portfolio Class S	ISSPX	B-	B-	B-	Down	5.55	10.49	21.65	27.39	71.01	14.62	180.3	800-366-0066	Y
Voya Solution 2055 Portfolio Class S2	ITSPX	B-	B-	B-	Down	5.51	10.39	21.51	26.88	69.65	14.54	180.3	800-366-0066	Y
Voya Solution 2055 Portfolio Class T	ISTPX	B-	B-	B-	Down	5.36	10.15	21.07	25.76	67.35	14.73	180.3	800-366-0066	Y
Voya Target Retirement 2050 Fund Class A	VTROX	B-	B-	B-	Down	5.58	10.73	20.87	26.46	69.56		2.2	800-366-0066	Y
Voya Target Retirement 2050 Fund Class I	IRSQX	B-	B-	B-	Down	5.38	10.33	21.01	27.84	71.31	12.82	2.2	800-366-0066	Y
Voya Target Retirement 2050 Fund Class R6	VTRPX	B-	B-	B-	Down	5.72	10.86	21.21	27.58	71.92		2.2	800-366-0066	Y
Voya Target Retirement 2055 Fund Class A	VTRQX	B-	B-	B-	Down	5.63	10.67	20.98	26.73	70.26		2.4	800-366-0066	Y
Voya Target Retirement 2055 Fund Class I	IRSVX	B-	B-	B-	Down	3.41	8.33	18.98	25.51	68.67	12.92	2.4	800-366-0066	Y
Voya Target Retirement 2055 Fund Class R6	VTRRX	B-	B-	B-	Down	5.70	10.82	21.34	27.75	72.49		2.4	800-366-0066	Y
Wells Fargo Target 2050 Fund - Class A	WFQAX	B-	B-	B-	Down	4.75	8.83	19.09	25.46	65.36	8.67	542.1	800-222-8222	Y
Wells Fargo Target 2050 Fund - Class Admin	WFQDX	B-	B-	B-	Down	4.66	8.83	19.24	25.86	66.34	8.68	542.1	800-222-8222	Y
Wells Fargo Target 2050 Fund - Class C	WFQCX	B-	C+	B-	Down	4.55	8.46	18.22	22.63	59.24	8.63	542.1	800-222-8222	Y
Wells Fargo Target 2050 Fund - Class R	WFWRX	B-	B-	B-	Down	4.64	8.71	18.92	24.58	63.70	8.7	542.1	800-222-8222	Y
Wells Fargo Target 2050 Fund - Class R4	WQFRX	B-	B-	B-	Down	4.81	9.06	19.58	26.71	68.20	8.72	542.1	800-222-8222	Y
Wells Fargo Target 2050 Fund - Class R6	WFQFX	B-	B-	B-	Down	4.91	9.17	19.68	27.33	69.52	8.71	542.1	800-222-8222	Y
Wells Fargo Target 2055 Fund - Class A	WFQZX	B-	B-	B-	Down	4.76	8.84	19.19	25.47	65.32	12.82	90.5	800-222-8222	Y
Wells Fargo Target 2055 Fund - Class Admin	WFLHX	B-	B-	B-	Down	4.74	8.89	19.28	25.78	66.17	12.82	90.5	800-222-8222	Y
Wells Fargo Target 2055 Fund - Class R	WFYRX	B-	B-	B-	Down	4.62	8.66	18.83	24.40	63.49	12.65	90.5	800-222-8222	Y
Wells Fargo Target 2055 Fund - Class R4	WFVRX	B-	B-	B-	Down	4.79	9.01	19.52	26.60	67.90	12.85	90.5	800-222-8222	Y
Wells Fargo Target 2055 Fund - Class R6	WFQUX	B-	B-	B-	Down	4.89	9.12	19.75	27.19	69.28	12.82	90.5	800-222-8222	Y

Category: Technology Sector Equity

Fund Name	Ticker Symbol	RATINGS: Overall Rating	Reward Rating	Risk Rating	Recent Up/ Downgrade	TOTAL RETURNS & PERFORMANCE: 3-Month Total Return	6-Month Total Return	1-Year Total Return	3-Year Total Return	5-Year Total Return	ASSETS: NAV	Total Assets (Mil.)	NEW INVESTORS: Telephone	Open to New Investors
AllianzGI Technology Fund Administrative Class	DGTAX	A	A+	B+	Up	7.78	18.85	46.83	60.13	166.29	64.77	1,600	800-498-5413	Y
AllianzGI Technology Fund Class A	RAGTX	A	A+	B+	Up	7.73	18.79	46.69	59.66	164.94	61.24	1,600	800-498-5413	Y
AllianzGI Technology Fund Class C	RCGTX	A	A+	B+	Up	7.55	18.34	45.62	56.09	155.22	47.49	1,600	800-498-5413	Y
AllianzGI Technology Fund Class P	ARTPX	A	A+	B+	Up	7.81	18.94	47.07	60.86	168.30	67.53	1,600	800-498-5413	Y
AllianzGI Technology Fund Institutional Class	DRGTX	A	A+	B+	Up	7.83	19.00	47.21	61.33	169.66	68.65	1,600	800-498-5413	Y
Berkshire Focus Fund	BFOCX	A-	A	B	Up	7.99	17.95	44.07	61.29	136.45	21.47	76.8	877-526-0707	Y
Black Oak Emerging Technology Fund	BOGSX	B	A-	B-	Up	5.82	9.44	19.02	31.53	113.45	5.05	38.4	888-462-5386	Y
BlackRock Science & Technology Opp Portfolio Cls R Shares	BGSRX	A	A+	B+	Up	6.99	19.92	49.40	76.46	184.34	23.99	638.4	800-441-7762	Y
BlackRock Science & Technology Opp Portfolio Inst Shares	BGSIX	A	A+	B+	Up	7.11	20.24	50.15	79.56	192.83	25.44	638.4	800-441-7762	Y
BlackRock Science & Technology Opp Portfolio Inv A Shares	BGSAX	A	A+	B+	Up	7.02	20.06	49.72	77.96	188.10	23.68	638.4	800-441-7762	Y
BlackRock Science & Technology Opp Portfolio Inv C Shares	BGSCX	A	A+	B+	Up	6.91	19.68	48.70	73.92	176.99	20.24	638.4	800-441-7762	Y
BlackRock Science & Technology Opp Port Serv Shares	BSTSX	A	A+	B+	Up	7.09	20.12	49.85	78.30	189.50	24.19	638.4	800-441-7762	Y
BlackRock Science and Technology Trust	BST	B	B-	B	Up	6.68	18.71	45.63	69.59		27.7807	625.1	800-441-7762	Y
Columbia Global Technology Growth Fund Advisor Class	CTYRX	A-	A+	B		7.13	18.52	43.36	77.35	212.73	31.78	953.1	800-345-6611	Y
Columbia Global Technology Growth Fund Class A	CTCAX	A-	A+	B		7.06	18.32	42.93	75.99	208.86	30.22	953.1	800-345-6611	Y
Columbia Global Technology Growth Fund Class C	CTHCX	A-	A+	B		6.84	17.90	41.94	72.20	197.42	27.25	953.1	800-345-6611	Y
Columbia Global Technology Growth Fund Institutional 2 Cls	CTHRX	A-	A+	B		7.15	18.55	43.46	77.99	214.79	31.97	953.1	800-345-6611	Y
Columbia Global Technology Growth Fund Institutional 3 Cls	CGTUX	A-	A+	B		7.14	18.55	43.51	77.76	213.44	32.04	953.1	800-345-6611	Y
Columbia Global Technology Growth Fund Institutional Class	CMTFX	A-	A+	B		7.12	18.49	43.32	77.34	212.70	31.37	953.1	800-345-6611	Y
Columbia Seligman Communications & Information Adv Cls	SCIOX	A	A+	B+	Up	3.01	13.26	34.37	68.94	171.04	68.62	6,150	800-345-6611	Y
Columbia Seligman Communications & Information Fund Cls A	SLMCX	A	A+	B+	Up	2.94	13.12	34.05	67.68	167.69	70.78	6,150	800-345-6611	Y
Columbia Seligman Communications & Information Fund Cls C	SCICX	A	A+	B+	Up	2.76	12.69	33.03	63.94	157.83	48.99	6,150	800-345-6611	Y
Columbia Seligman Communications & Information Fund Cls K	SCIFX	A	A+	B+	Up	2.97	13.14	34.11	68.17	169.17	75.87	6,150	800-345-6611	
Columbia Seligman Communications & Information Fund Cls R	SCIRX	A	A+	B+	Up	2.89	12.98	33.70	66.45	164.40	67.43	6,150	800-345-6611	Y
Columbia Seligman Communications & Information Fund Cls T	CITTX	A	A+	B+	Up	2.94	13.09	34.01	67.63	167.61	71.09	6,150	800-345-6611	Y
Columbia Seligman Communications & Information Inst 2 Cls	SCMIX	A	A+	B+	Up	3.02	13.27	34.43	69.42	172.57	77.3	6,150	800-345-6611	Y
Columbia Seligman Communications & Information Inst 3 Cls	CCOYX	A	A+	B+	Up	3.04	13.31	34.40	68.11	168.38	76.67	6,150	800-345-6611	Y
Columbia Seligman Communications & Information Inst Cls	CCIZX	A	A+	B+	Up	3.01	13.25	34.38	68.94	171.05	77	6,150	800-345-6611	Y
Columbia Seligman Global Technology Fund Advisor Class	CCHRX	A	A+	B+	Up	3.11	13.40	34.82	72.36	179.46	40.62	1,210	800-345-6611	Y
Columbia Seligman Global Technology Fund Class A	SHGTX	A	A+	B+	Up	3.04	13.26	34.49	71.03	175.92	39.31	1,210	800-345-6611	Y
Columbia Seligman Global Technology Fund Class C	SHTCX	A	A+	B+	Up	2.86	12.84	33.46	67.28	165.83	30.46	1,210	800-345-6611	Y
Columbia Seligman Global Technology Fund Class K	SGTSX	A	A+	B+	Up	3.04	13.29	34.55	71.60	177.83	39.75	1,210	800-345-6611	
Columbia Seligman Global Technology Fund Class R	SGTRX	A	A+	B+	Up	3.00	13.12	34.14	69.81	172.65	37.91	1,210	800-345-6611	Y
Columbia Seligman Global Technology Fund Inst 2 Cls	SGTTX	A	A+	B+	Up	3.12	13.45	34.88	72.91	181.51	40.2	1,210	800-345-6611	Y
Columbia Seligman Global Technology Fund Inst 3 Cls	CGTYX	A	A+	B+	Up	3.20	13.51	34.90	71.55	176.76	39.97	1,210	800-345-6611	Y
Columbia Seligman Global Technology Fund Institutional Cls	CSGZX	A	A+	B+	Up	3.13	13.43	34.81	72.39	179.47	40.01	1,210	800-345-6611	Y
Columbia Seligman Premium Technology Growth Fund	STK	A	A+	B+	Up	2.34	12.60	32.90	65.14	144.31	20.83	339.9	800-345-6611	Y
Deutsche Science and Technology Fund Class A	KTCAX	A-	A	B	Up	6.62	14.53	35.78	50.29	117.61	21.43	800.2	201-593-8273	Y
Deutsche Science and Technology Fund Class C	KTCCX	A-	A	B	Up	6.35	14.00	34.51	46.22	107.94	14.75	800.2	201-593-8273	Y
Deutsche Science and Technology Fund Class S	KTCSX	A-	A	B	Up	6.69	14.62	35.92	50.93	119.04	21.68	800.2	201-593-8273	Y
Deutsche Science and Technology Fund Institutional Class	KTCIX	A-	A	B	Up	6.65	14.64	35.97	51.25	120.04	23.33	800.2	201-593-8273	Y
Dreyfus Technology Growth Fund Class A	DTGRX	A-	A	B+	Up	7.10	17.12	42.54	56.21	127.51	48.99	304.3	800-645-6561	Y
Dreyfus Technology Growth Fund Class C	DTGCX	A-	A	B+	Up	6.90	16.68	41.42	52.47	118.41	37.89	304.3	800-645-6561	Y
Dreyfus Technology Growth Fund Class I	DGVRX	A	A	B+	Up	7.18	17.28	42.92	57.43	130.38	54.12	304.3	800-645-6561	Y
Dreyfus Technology Growth Fund Class Y	DTEYX	A	A	B+	Up	7.19	17.34	43.07	56.96	128.60	54.21	304.3	800-645-6561	Y
Fidelity Advisor® Communications Equipment Fund Class A	FDMAX	B-	B-	B-	Up	5.01	5.94	10.94	17.21	73.90	13.73	14.6	617-563-7000	Y
Fidelity Advisor® Communications Equipment Fund Class M	FDMTX	B-	B-	B-	Up	4.98	5.86	10.70	16.42	71.67	13.22	14.6	617-563-7000	Y
Fidelity Advisor® Communications Equipment Fund I Class	FDMIX	B-	B-	B-	Up	5.09	6.14	11.28	18.14	76.03	14.27	14.6	617-563-7000	Y
Fidelity Advisor® Semiconductors Fund Class A	FELAX	A-	A+	B	Up	11.28	21.72	34.24	81.11	251.97	23.33	280.4	617-563-7000	Y
Fidelity Advisor® Semiconductors Fund Class C	FELCX	A-	A+	B	Up	11.03	21.29	33.17	76.93	238.87	20.46	280.4	617-563-7000	Y
Fidelity Advisor® Semiconductors Fund Class I	FELIX	A-	A+	B	Up	11.36	21.90	34.65	82.85	257.00	24.47	280.4	617-563-7000	Y
Fidelity Advisor® Semiconductors Fund Class M	FELTX	A-	A+	B	Up	11.21	21.54	33.77	79.28	246.65	22.43	280.4	617-563-7000	Y

Category: Technology Sector Equity (con't)

Fund Name	Ticker Symbol	Overall Rating	Reward Rating	Risk Rating	Recent Up/ Downgrade	3-Month Total Return	6-Month Total Return	1-Year Total Return	3-Year Total Return	5-Year Total Return	NAV	Total Assets (MIL)	Telephone	Open to New Investors
		RATINGS				TOTAL RETURNS & PERFORMANCE					ASSETS		NEW INVESTORS	
Fidelity Advisor® Technology Fund Class A	FADTX	A	A+	B+	Up	6.14	16.98	49.35	77.27	164.04	53.54	1,815	617-563-7000	Y
Fidelity Advisor® Technology Fund Class C	FTHCX	A	A+	B+	Up	5.94	16.54	48.21	73.28	154.36	45.59	1,815	617-563-7000	Y
Fidelity Advisor® Technology Fund Class M	FATEX	A	A+	B+	Up	6.07	16.82	48.94	75.88	160.61	50.83	1,815	617-563-7000	Y
Fidelity Advisor® Technology Fund I Class	FATIX	A	A+	B+	Up	6.23	17.14	49.76	78.92	168.19	57.44	1,815	617-563-7000	Y
Fidelity® Select Communications Equip Portfolio	FSDCX	B-	B-	B-	Up	5.26	6.43	11.65	19.00	79.95	36	189.8	617-563-7000	Y
Fidelity® Select Computers Portfolio	FDCPX	B	A	C+	Up	8.68	14.80	33.74	32.14	105.61	88.87	543.3	617-563-7000	Y
Fidelity® Select IT Services Portfolio	FBSOX	A-	A	B	Up	8.57	17.88	34.24	58.75	162.98	54.48	2,076	617-563-7000	Y
Fidelity® Select Semiconductors Portfolio	FSELX	A-	A+	B	Up	11.47	22.21	35.05	82.03	259.80	111.73	3,591	617-563-7000	Y
Fidelity® Select Software & IT Services Portfolio	FSCSX	A	A	A-	Up	9.22	16.74	38.52	67.77	180.01	165.7	4,976	617-563-7000	Y
Fidelity® Select Technology Portfolio	FSPTX	A	A+	B+	Up	6.30	17.22	49.86	78.73	168.20	178.74	6,508	617-563-7000	Y
Firsthand Technology Opportunities Fund	TEFQX	A-	A+	B	Up	9.91	22.90	55.45	70.57	151.90	9.98	122.6	888-884-2675	Y
Goldman Sachs Technology Opportunities Fund Class A	GITAX	A-	A	B+	Up	6.52	14.47	38.02	56.33	127.58	22.8	473.5	800-526-7384	Y
Goldman Sachs Technology Opportunities Fund Class C	GITCX	A-	A	B+	Up	6.34	14.08	36.98	52.83	119.24	18.93	473.5	800-526-7384	Y
Goldman Sachs Technology Opp Fund Inst Cls	GITIX	A-	A	B+	Up	6.61	14.72	38.53	58.15	132.17	25.08	473.5	800-526-7384	Y
Goldman Sachs Technology Opportunities Fund Investor Class	GISTX	A-	A	B+	Up	6.57	14.64	38.35	57.39	130.43	24.74	473.5	800-526-7384	Y
Goldman Sachs Technology Opportunities Fund Service Class	GITSX	A-	A	B+	Up	6.51	14.44	37.87	55.84	126.39	22.36	473.5	800-526-7384	Y
Hennessy Technology Fund Institutional Class	HTCIX	B	B	B	Up	3.62	8.13	20.56	27.14	73.45	17.4	4.5	800-966-4354	Y
Hennessy Technology Fund Investor Class	HTECX	B	B-	B	Up	3.54	7.97	20.19	25.77	70.68	17.03	4.5	800-966-4354	Y
ICON Information Technology Fund Class A	ICTTX	A-	A	B	Up	2.74	11.38	32.07	60.73	135.32	15.26	70.7	303-790-1600	Y
ICON Information Technology Fund Class S	ICTEX	A-	A	B	Up	2.90	11.65	32.54	62.32	139.98	15.82	70.7	303-790-1600	Y
Invesco Technology Fund Class A	ITYAX	B+	B+	B	Up	2.91	10.14	34.66	40.94	100.14	44.23	861.6	800-659-1005	Y
Invesco Technology Fund Class B	ITYBX	B+	B+	B	Up	2.71	9.73	33.64	37.81	92.78	37.64	861.6	800-659-1005	
Invesco Technology Fund Class C	ITHCX	B+	B+	B	Up	2.71	9.72	33.64	37.80	92.81	36.01	861.6	800-659-1005	Y
Invesco Technology Fund Class R6	FTPSX	B+	A-	B	Up	3.02	10.36	35.09	41.62	101.50	51.75	861.6	800-659-1005	Y
Invesco Technology Fund Class Y	ITYYX	B+	A-	B	Up	2.98	10.27	34.99	41.97	102.67	44.8	861.6	800-659-1005	Y
Invesco Technology Fund Investor Class	FTCHX	B+	A-	B	Up	2.92	10.18	34.77	41.29	101.02	43.97	861.6	800-659-1005	
Invesco Technology Fund R5 Class	FTPIX	B+	A-	B	Up	3.00	10.37	35.26	42.96	105.45	51.74	861.6	800-659-1005	Y
Invesco Technology Sector Fund Class A	IFOAX	B+	B+	B	Up	2.90	10.07	34.53	40.35	100.50	22.09	97.8	800-659-1005	
Invesco Technology Sector Fund Class B	IFOBX	B+	B+	B	Up	2.67	9.61	33.48	37.23	93.07	18.63	97.8	800-659-1005	
Invesco Technology Sector Fund Class C	IFOCX	B+	B+	B	Up	2.67	9.67	33.46	37.21	93.17	18.64	97.8	800-659-1005	
Invesco Technology Sector Fund Class Y	IFODX	B+	A-	B	Up	2.93	10.18	34.79	41.32	102.91	23.28	97.8	800-659-1005	
Ivy Science And Technology Fund Class A	WSTAX	B	A	C	Up	3.46	13.82	32.82	29.73	111.41	63.57	4,284	800-777-6472	Y
Ivy Science And Technology Fund Class B	WSTBX	B	A-	C	Up	3.25	13.38	31.80	26.83	103.47	52.73	4,284	800-777-6472	
Ivy Science And Technology Fund Class C	WSTCX	B	A-	C	Up	3.26	13.40	31.84	27.00	104.10	54.79	4,284	800-777-6472	Y
Ivy Science and Technology Fund Class E	ISTEX	B	A-	C	Up	3.44	13.78	32.75	29.40	110.23	63.14	4,284	800-777-6472	Y
Ivy Science and Technology Fund Class I	ISTIX	B	A	C	Up	3.52	13.94	33.13	30.85	114.47	69.87	4,284	800-777-6472	Y
Ivy Science and Technology Fund Class N	ISTNX	B	A	C	Up	3.56	14.03	33.35	31.44	112.21	70.19	4,284	800-777-6472	Y
Ivy Science and Technology Fund Class R	WSTRX	B	A-	C	Up	3.37	13.61	32.35	28.54	108.11	62.02	4,284	800-777-6472	Y
Ivy Science And Technology Fund Class Y	WSTYX	B	A	C	Up	3.46	13.81	32.80	29.88	111.80	67.04	4,284	800-777-6472	Y
Jacob Internet Investor Class	JAMFX	B+	A	B	Up	2.52	11.17	24.14	53.96	123.19	4.43	45.3		Y
Janus Henderson Global Technology Fund Class A	JATAX	A	A+	B+	Up	7.76	16.87	44.49	69.79	156.48	30.2	2,353	877-335-2687	Y
Janus Henderson Global Technology Fund Class C	JAGCX	A	A+	B+	Up	7.55	16.40	43.43	66.34	147.99	27.83	2,353	877-335-2687	Y
Janus Henderson Global Technology Fund Class D	JNGTX	A	A+	B+	Up	7.77	16.95	44.72	70.73	158.94	30.83	2,353	877-335-2687	
Janus Henderson Global Technology Fund Class I	JATIX	A	A+	B+	Up	7.82	17.02	44.88	71.27	160.15	31.07	2,353	877-335-2687	Y
Janus Henderson Global Technology Fund Class N	JATNX	A	A+	B+	Up	7.85	17.07	44.93	70.80	158.84	30.73	2,353	877-335-2687	Y
Janus Henderson Global Technology Fund Class S	JATSX	A	A+	B+	Up	7.71	16.81	44.31	69.21	155.04	29.8	2,353	877-335-2687	Y
Janus Henderson Global Technology Fund Class T	JAGTX	A	A+	B+	Up	7.77	16.91	44.65	70.47	158.34	30.67	2,353	877-335-2687	Y
Janus Henderson VIT Global Technology Portfolio Inst Cls	JGLTX	A-	A+	B	Up	7.75	16.68	45.08	72.30	162.97	11.4	391.8	877-335-2687	Y
Janus Henderson VIT Global Technology Port Serv Cls	US4710215504	A	A+	B+	Up	7.73	16.65	44.91	71.24	160.24	11.56	391.8	877-335-2687	Y
JNL/Mellon Capital Information Technology Sector Cls A	US47760W7956	A-	A	B	Up	8.42	17.20	36.31	59.61	150.48	15.31	2,369		Y
JNL/Mellon Capital Information Technology Sector Cls I	US47760W7873	A-	A+	B	Up	8.48	17.40	36.62	60.58	153.40	15.6	2,369		Y
John Hancock Funds II Science & Technology Cls NAV Shares	US47803M1430	A	A+	B+	Up	7.17	16.02	40.92	62.51		4.98	289.5	800-225-5913	Y

Category: Technology Sector Equity (con't)

Fund Name	Ticker Symbol	RATINGS: Overall Rating	Reward Rating	Risk Rating	Recent Up/ Downgrade	TOTAL RETURNS & PERFORMANCE: 3-Month Total Return	6-Month Total Return	1-Year Total Return	3-Year Total Return	5-Year Total Return	ASSETS: NAV	Total Assets (MIL)	NEW INVESTORS: Telephone	Open to New Investors
MFS® Technology Fund Class A	MTCAX	A	A	A-	Up	6.69	14.86	38.46	63.75	152.18	36.7	940.7	877-960-6077	Y
MFS® Technology Fund Class B	MTCBX	A	A	A-	Up	6.47	14.41	37.37	60.07	142.91	31.95	940.7	877-960-6077	Y
MFS® Technology Fund Class C	MTCCX	A	A	A-	Up	6.49	14.44	37.41	60.09	142.84	31.89	940.7	877-960-6077	Y
MFS® Technology Fund Class I	MTCIX	A	A	A-	Up	6.74	15.02	38.80	64.94	155.29	39.11	940.7	877-960-6077	Y
MFS® Technology Fund Class R1	MTCKX	A	A	A-	Up	6.47	14.43	37.40	60.06	142.86	31.82	940.7	877-960-6077	Y
MFS® Technology Fund Class R2	MTERX	A	A	A-	Up	6.60	14.72	38.07	62.53	149.06	35.06	940.7	877-960-6077	Y
MFS® Technology Fund Class R3	MTCHX	A	A	A-	Up	6.66	14.87	38.44	63.73	152.20	36.68	940.7	877-960-6077	Y
MFS® Technology Fund Class R4	MTCJX	A	A	A-	Up	6.75	15.03	38.81	64.99	155.36	38.1	940.7	877-960-6077	Y
MFS® Technology Fund Class R6	MTCLX	A	A	A-	Up	6.76	15.06	38.90	65.44	156.51	39.32	940.7	877-960-6077	Y
Multimanager Technology Portfolio Class IA	US00247C8414	A-	A	B		8.34	17.30	38.77	59.52	154.24		1,085	877-222-2144	Y
Multimanager Technology Portfolio Class IB	US00247C8331	A	A	B+	Up	8.34	17.25	38.69	59.45	154.22		1,085	877-222-2144	Y
Multimanager Technology Portfolio Class K	US00247C4298	A-	A+	B		8.39	17.43	39.07	60.59	158.29		1,085	877-222-2144	Y
Nationwide Bailard Technology and Science Fund Class A	NWHOX	A-	A	B	Up	6.25	16.96	37.61	59.79	150.67	20.39	143.8	800-848-0920	Y
Nationwide Bailard Technology and Science Fund Class C	NWHPX	A-	A	B	Up	6.05	16.53	36.60	56.22	142.00	18.49	143.8	800-848-0920	Y
Nationwide Bailard Technology and Science Fund Class M	NWHQX	A-	A+	B	Up	6.34	17.22	38.10	61.36	155.10	21.33	143.8	800-848-0920	Y
Nationwide Bailard Technology and Science Fund Class R6	NWHTX	A-	A+	B	Up	6.31	17.20	38.05	61.36	155.26	21.28	143.8	800-848-0920	Y
Nationwide Bailard Technology & Science Fund Inst Serv Cls	NWHUX	A-	A+	B	Up	6.30	17.14	37.95	60.97	153.77	21.3	143.8	800-848-0920	Y
Putnam Global Technology Fund Class A	PGTAX	A	A+	A-	Up	5.52	16.11	46.68	80.37	162.86	34.41	247.7	617-292-1000	Y
Putnam Global Technology Fund Class B	PGTPX	A	A+	A-	Up	5.34	15.68	45.61	76.40	153.17	32.03	247.7	617-292-1000	Y
Putnam Global Technology Fund Class C	PGTDX	A	A+	A-	Up	5.34	15.69	45.58	76.36	153.28	32.01	247.7	617-292-1000	Y
Putnam Global Technology Fund Class M	PGTMX	A	A+	A-	Up	5.40	15.80	45.96	77.69	156.30	32.83	247.7	617-292-1000	Y
Putnam Global Technology Fund Class R	PGTRX	A	A+	A-	Up	5.45	15.94	46.33	79.09	159.53	33.65	247.7	617-292-1000	Y
Putnam Global Technology Fund Class Y	PGTYX	A	A+	A-	Up	5.60	16.26	47.04	81.76	166.11	35.19	247.7	617-292-1000	Y
Red Oak Technology Select Fund	ROGSX	A-	A+	B	Up	7.83	15.31	31.09	63.40	176.50	24.56	494.1	888-462-5386	Y
Rydex Electronics Fund Class A	RYELX	A-	A+	B	Up	6.12	17.95	31.29	66.27	180.97	122.88	56.4	800-820-0888	Y
Rydex Electronics Fund Class C	RYSCX	A-	A+	B	Up	5.92	17.51	30.32	62.57	170.33	111.35	56.4	800-820-0888	Y
Rydex Electronics Fund Class H	RYSAX	A-	A+	B	Up	6.12	17.94	31.28	65.93	178.71	119.66	56.4	800-820-0888	Y
Rydex Electronics Fund Class Investor	RYSIX	A-	A+	B	Up	6.18	18.09	31.62	67.45	184.35	131.44	56.4	800-820-0888	Y
Rydex Internet Fund Class A	RYINX	A-	A-	B	Up	5.36	12.36	34.10	50.90	138.48	108.85	65.8	800-820-0888	Y
Rydex Internet Fund Class C	RYICX	B+	A-	B	Up	5.16	11.95	33.09	47.55	129.62	97.13	65.8	800-820-0888	Y
Rydex Internet Fund Class H	RYIAX	A-	A-	B	Up	5.37	12.37	34.10	50.74	136.83	105.73	65.8	800-820-0888	Y
Rydex Internet Fund Class Investor	RYIIX	A-	A-	B	Up	5.43	12.51	34.42	52.06	141.51	115.83	65.8	800-820-0888	Y
Rydex Technology Fund Class A	RYTHX	B+	A	B-	Down	5.77	14.22	32.72	47.81	125.34	83.43	118.4	800-820-0888	Y
Rydex Technology Fund Class C	RYCHX	B+	A	B-	Down	5.55	13.78	31.74	44.54	117.03	75.69	118.4	800-820-0888	Y
Rydex Technology Fund Class H	RYTAX	B+	A	B-	Up	5.76	14.21	32.73	47.57	123.87	81.67	118.4	800-820-0888	Y
Rydex Technology Fund Class Investor	RYTIX	B+	A	B-	Down	5.83	14.36	33.07	48.91	128.23	89.24	118.4	800-820-0888	Y
Saratoga Technology & Communications Portfolio Class A	STPAX	A	A	A	Up	7.53	13.13	27.77	54.84	133.30	19.05	52.6	800-807-3863	Y
Saratoga Technology & Communications Portfolio Class C	STPCX	A	A	A	Up	7.29	12.73	26.94	52.05	126.28	15.54	52.6	800-807-3863	Y
Saratoga Technology & Communications Portfolio Cls Inst	STPIX	A	A	A	Up	7.62	13.31	28.21	56.74	138.05	20.93	52.6	800-807-3863	Y
T. Rowe Price Global Technology Fund	PRGTX	A	A+	B+	Up	6.22	14.75	47.04	88.90	236.63	16.83	6,279	410-345-2000	Y
T. Rowe Price Global Technology Fund I Class	PGTIX	A	A+	B+	Up	6.26	14.85	47.15	89.19	237.15	16.84	6,279	410-345-2000	Y
T. Rowe Price Science and Technology Fund	PRSCX	A	A+	B+	Up	7.62	15.01	39.22	68.25	178.86	45.48	5,439	410-345-2000	Y
T. Rowe Price Science and Technology Fund Advisor Class	PASTX	A	A+	B+	Up	7.52	14.84	38.84	67.02	175.73	44.92	5,439	410-345-2000	Y
T. Rowe Price Science and Technology Fund I Class	TSNIX	A	A+	B+	Up	7.63	15.07	39.39	68.63	179.49	45.47	5,439	410-345-2000	Y
USAA Science & Technology Fund	USSCX	A-	A	B+	Up	4.45	11.18	36.00	53.73	166.27	26.45	1,353	800-531-8722	Y
USAA Science & Technology Fund Adviser Shares	USTCX	A-	A	B+	Up	4.35	11.00	35.59	52.45	163.27	25.85	1,353	800-531-8722	Y
VALIC Company I Science & Technology Fund	VCSTX	A	A+	B+	Up	7.07	16.08	41.31	62.32	171.42	29.81	1,281		Y
Vanguard Information Technology Index Fund Admiral Shares	VITAX	A-	A+	B	Up	8.55	17.52	37.07	61.96	158.43	84.31	17,977	877-662-7447	Y
Victory RS Science and Technology Fund Class A	RSIFX	A-	A+	B	Up	5.17	18.12	44.73	73.16	172.58	21.56	191.0	800-539-3863	Y
Victory RS Science and Technology Fund Class C	RINCX	A-	A+	B	Up	5.02	17.73	43.70	69.18	161.94	17.74	191.0	800-539-3863	Y
Victory RS Science and Technology Fund Class R	RIFKX	A-	A+	B	Up	5.05	17.85	44.04	70.94	166.39	18.99	191.0	800-539-3863	Y
Victory RS Science and Technology Fund Class Y	RIFYX	A-	A+	B	Up	5.23	18.31	45.10	74.42	176.22	22.9	191.0	800-539-3863	Y

Category: Technology Sector Equity (con't)

Fund Name	Ticker Symbol	RATINGS: Overall Rating	Reward Rating	Risk Rating	Recent Up/ Downgrade	TOTAL RETURNS & PERFORMANCE: 3-Month Total Return	6-Month Total Return	1-Year Total Return	3-Year Total Return	5-Year Total Return	ASSETS: NAV	Total Assets (MIL)	NEW INVESTORS: Telephone	Open to New Investors
Waddell & Reed Advisor Science and Technology Fund Class A	UNSCX	B	A-	C	Up	3.54	13.82	32.01	28.48	112.45	16.48	3,748	888-923-3355	Y
Waddell & Reed Advisor Science and Technology Fund Class B	USTBX	B	B	C	Up	3.20	13.15	30.51	24.16	100.98	10.87	3,748	888-923-3355	
Waddell & Reed Advisor Science and Technology Fund Class C	WCSTX	B	B+	C	Up	3.32	13.36	30.76	24.74	102.31	11.13	3,748	888-923-3355	Y
Waddell & Reed Advisor Science and Technology Fund Class Y	USTFX	B	A-	C	Up	3.59	13.98	32.30	29.38	115.24	18.79	3,748	888-923-3355	Y
Wells Fargo Specialized Technology Fund - Class A	WFSTX	A-	A+	B+	Up	6.80	17.30	42.99	55.73	157.23	12.74	425.0	800-222-8222	Y
Wells Fargo Specialized Technology Fund - Class Admin	WFTDX	A-	A+	B+	Up	6.77	17.28	43.05	56.22	158.97	12.96	425.0	800-222-8222	Y
Wells Fargo Specialized Technology Fund - Class C	WFTCX	A-	A	B+	Up	6.64	16.90	41.87	52.38	147.69	10.32	425.0	800-222-8222	Y
Wells Fargo Specialized Technology Fund Institutional Cls	WFTIX	A-	A+	B+	Up	6.83	17.44	43.36	56.29	158.16	12.99	425.0	800-222-8222	Y
Wireless Fund	WIREX	B	B+	B-		6.44	14.13	29.76	42.11	98.67	10.9	4.2	800-590-0898	Y

Category: Trading Tools

Fund Name	Ticker Symbol	RATINGS: Overall Rating	Reward Rating	Risk Rating	Recent Up/ Downgrade	TOTAL RETURNS & PERFORMANCE: 3-Month Total Return	6-Month Total Return	1-Year Total Return	3-Year Total Return	5-Year Total Return	ASSETS: NAV	Total Assets (MIL)	NEW INVESTORS: Telephone	Open to New Investors
Direxion Monthly Emerging Markets Bull 2X Fund	DXELX	B	A	C-	Up	12.86	30.85	80.88	39.75	8.68	60.18	9.7	646-572-3390	Y
Direxion Monthly NASDAQ-100 Bull 2X Fund Investor Class	DXQLX	A-	A+	B-	Up	13.69	26.66	68.62	107.40	452.81	106.54	207.6	646-572-3390	Y
Direxion Monthly S&P 500 Bull 2X Fund Investor Class	DXSLX	B+	A+	C+	Down	12.46	21.49	42.67	66.33	274.16	135.95	91.9	646-572-3390	Y
Direxion Monthly Small Cap Bull 2X Fund	DXRLX	B+	A+	C	Up	5.90	16.92	27.05	54.12	223.35	76.97	20.4	646-572-3390	Y
ProFunds Banks UltraSector Fund Investor Class	BKPIX	B+	A+	C	Up	12.84	19.50	26.77	63.91	200.11	53.6	53.4	614-470-8626	Y
ProFunds Banks UltraSector Fund Service Class	BKPSX	B+	A+	C	Up	12.56	18.91	25.53	58.95	185.33	49.99	53.4	614-470-8626	Y
ProFunds Basic Materials UltraSector Fund Investor Class	BMPIX	B	A	C	Up	9.71	21.52	34.95	33.97	83.17	74.86	56.9	614-470-8626	Y
ProFunds Basic Materials UltraSector Fund Service Class	BMPSX	B	B+	C	Up	9.46	20.94	33.67	30.08	74.38	67.8	56.9	614-470-8626	Y
ProFunds Bull Fund Investor Class	BLPIX	B-	B-	B	Down	6.21	10.40	19.50	29.31	92.22	122.41	77.3	614-470-8626	Y
ProFunds Bull Fund Service Class	BLPSX	B-	B-	B-	Down	5.95	9.86	18.33	25.52	82.83	102.99	77.3	614-470-8626	Y
ProFunds Consumer Goods Ultra Sector Fund Investor Class	CNPIX	B	B-	A-	Down	7.54	6.22	22.79	34.03	132.64	110.89	11.3	614-470-8626	Y
ProFunds Consumer Goods Ultra Sector Fund Service Class	CNPSX	B	B-	A-		7.27	5.71	21.60	30.10	121.37	101.17	11.3	614-470-8626	Y
ProFunds Consumer Services UltraSector Fund Investor Class	CYPIX	B	B	B		13.77	13.58	28.24	44.17	193.64	112.29	35.4	614-470-8626	Y
ProFunds Consumer Services UltraSector Fund Service Class	CYPSX	B	B	B		13.48	13.01	26.96	39.91	179.31	98.78	35.4	614-470-8626	Y
ProFunds Financials UltraSector Fund Investor Class	FNPIX	B+	A	B-	Up	9.87	16.77	27.18	48.39	178.74	22.69	30.3	614-470-8626	Y
ProFunds Financials UltraSector Fund Service Class	FNPSX	B+	A	B-	Up	9.61	16.24	26.02	44.08	165.35	19.61	30.3	614-470-8626	Y
ProFunds Industrial Ultra Sector Fund Investor Class	IDPIX	B+	A+	C	Up	9.42	18.23	34.58	58.02	189.00	107.28	27.6	614-470-8626	Y
ProFunds Industrial Ultra Sector Fund Service Class	IDPSX	B+	A+	C	Up	9.13	17.64	33.26	53.38	174.95	95.15	27.6	614-470-8626	Y
ProFunds Internet UltraSector Fund Investor Class	INPIX	A-	A+	B-	Up	10.52	23.31	57.91	119.55	326.56	69.01	148.9	614-470-8626	Y
ProFunds Internet UltraSector Fund Service Class	INPSX	A-	A+	B-	Up	10.26	22.72	56.40	113.14	305.78	54.29	148.9	614-470-8626	Y
ProFunds Pharmaceuticals UltraSector Fund Investor Class	PHPIX	B-	C+	B-	Up	-0.55	0.53	15.04	12.62	126.36	24.66	11.0	614-470-8626	Y
ProFunds Real Estate UltraSector Fund Investor Class	REPIX	B-	B-	B-	Up	2.99	3.90	11.31	17.31	69.45	44.66	7.9	614-470-8626	Y
ProFunds Real Estate UltraSector Fund Service Class	REPSX	B-	B-	B-	Up	2.75	3.40	10.22	13.83	61.18	42.57	7.9	614-470-8626	Y
ProFunds Semiconductor UltraSector Fund Investor Class	SMPIX	B+	A+	C+	Up	15.13	37.74	56.74	108.04	415.23	56.48	307.9	614-470-8626	Y
ProFunds Semiconductor UltraSector Fund Service Class	SMPSX	B+	A+	C+	Up	14.85	37.09	55.19	101.91	390.20	47.5	307.9	614-470-8626	Y
ProFunds Technology UltraSector Fund Investor Class	TEPIX	A-	A+	B	Up	12.52	24.83	55.87	85.35	244.57	108.98	104.4	614-470-8626	Y
ProFunds Technology UltraSector Fund Service Class	TEPSX	A-	A+	B	Up	12.24	24.21	54.32	79.94	227.78	92.68	104.4	614-470-8626	Y
ProFunds Ultra Dow 30 Fund Investor Class	UDPIX	B+	A+	C	Down	21.99	34.61	57.64	92.24	276.72	126.55	57.3	614-470-8626	Y
ProFunds Ultra Dow 30 Fund Service Class	UDPSX	B+	A+	C	Down	21.69	33.96	56.11	86.66	258.38	111.41	57.3	614-470-8626	Y
ProFunds Ultra International Fund Investor Class	UNPIX	B-	B	C	Up	6.36	16.11	48.19	27.30	55.39	18.88	15.3	614-470-8626	Y
ProFunds Ultra International Fund Service Class	UNPSX	B-	B	C	Up	6.06	15.49	46.74	23.57	47.88	17.14	15.3	614-470-8626	Y
ProFunds UltraBull Fund Investor Class	ULPIX	B+	A+	C+	Down	12.71	21.74	42.76	64.59	263.65	172.92	117.5	614-470-8626	Y
ProFunds UltraBull Fund Service Class	ULPSX	B+	A+	C+	Up	12.42	21.12	41.37	59.77	245.91	145.7	117.5	614-470-8626	Y
ProFunds UltraChina Fund Investor Class	UGPIX	B	A+	D+	Up	6.42	37.05	105.73	61.05	149.50	18.62	42.7	614-470-8626	Y
ProFunds UltraChina Fund Service Class	UGPSX	B	A+	D+	Up	6.14	36.28	103.77	56.43	137.26	16.96	42.7	614-470-8626	Y
ProFunds UltraJapan Fund Investor Class	UJPIX	B	A	C-	Up	23.63	27.25	39.71	44.67	218.61	25.68	33.4	614-470-8626	Y

Category: Trading Tools (con't)

Fund Name	Ticker Symbol	RATINGS				TOTAL RETURNS & PERFORMANCE					ASSETS		NEW INVESTORS	
		Overall Rating	Reward Rating	Risk Rating	Recent Up/ Downgrade	3-Month Total Return	6-Month Total Return	1-Year Total Return	3-Year Total Return	5-Year Total Return	NAV	Total Assets (MIL)	Telephone	Open to New Investors
ProFunds UltraJapan Fund Service Class	UJPSX	B	A	C-	Up	23.40	26.63	38.42	40.69	203.81	22.3	33.4	614-470-8626	Y
ProFunds UltraMid Cap Fund Investor Class	UMPIX	B+	A+	C+	Up	11.64	17.73	29.53	60.63	234.45	132	108.2	614-470-8626	Y
ProFunds UltraMid Cap Fund Service Class	UMPSX	B+	A+	C+	Up	11.44	17.22	28.43	56.10	218.55	110.02	108.2	614-470-8626	Y
ProFunds UltraNASDAQ-100 Fund Investor Class	UOPIX	A-	A+	B-	Up	13.73	26.38	68.58	104.77	434.52	182.86	436.3	614-470-8626	Y
ProFunds UltraNASDAQ-100 Fund Service Class	UOPSX	A-	A+	B-	Up	13.45	25.74	66.91	98.73	408.62	152.13	436.3	614-470-8626	Y
ProFunds UltraSector Health Care Fund Investor Class	HCPIX	B	B	B-	Up	1.75	6.92	32.17	29.65	201.53	53.98	28.7	614-470-8626	Y
ProFunds UltraSector Health Care Fund Service Class	HCPSX	B	B	B-	Up	1.49	6.37	30.85	25.81	186.86	45.61	28.7	614-470-8626	Y
ProFunds UltraSmall Cap Fund Investor Class	UAPIX	B+	A+	C	Up	5.41	16.44	25.25	49.30	207.93	59.68	77.4	614-470-8626	Y
ProFunds UltraSmall Cap Fund Service Class	UAPSX	B+	A+	C	Up	5.11	15.82	23.94	44.80	192.80	50.08	77.4	614-470-8626	Y
ProFunds Utilities UltraSector Fund Investor Class	UTPIX	B	B+	B-	Down	-0.01	3.82	15.82	24.42	120.23	44.78	19.7	614-470-8626	Y
ProFunds Utilities UltraSector Fund Service Class	UTPSX	B	B	B-	Down	-0.25	3.29	14.66	20.65	109.42	42.42	19.7	614-470-8626	Y
Rydex Dow 2x Strategy Fund Class A	RYLDX	B+	A+	C	Up	21.93	34.58	57.84	92.27	277.50	88.46	63.8	800-820-0888	Y
Rydex Dow 2x Strategy Fund Class C	RYCYX	B+	A+	C	Up	21.70	34.10	56.70	88.07	264.04	78.7	63.8	800-820-0888	Y
Rydex Dow 2x Strategy Fund Class H	RYCVX	B+	A+	C	Up	21.93	34.56	57.87	92.25	277.73	88.18	63.8	800-820-0888	Y
Rydex Japan 2x Strategy Fund Class A	RYJSX	B+	A+	C+	Up	22.49	26.17	50.96	84.46	143.16	136.77	6.8	800-820-0888	Y
Rydex Japan 2x Strategy Fund Class C	RYJTX	B+	A+	C+	Up	22.26	25.70	49.82	80.42	135.37	127.54	6.8	800-820-0888	Y
Rydex Japan 2x Strategy Fund Class H	RYJHX	B+	A+	C+	Up	22.48	26.23	51.06	85.05	144.28	137.81	6.8	800-820-0888	Y
Rydex Mid-Cap 1.5x Strategy Fund Class A	RYAHX	B+	A	B-	Up	8.89	13.57	22.59	46.96	156.34	92.37	373.5	800-820-0888	Y
Rydex Mid-Cap 1.5x Strategy Fund Class C	RYDCX	B+	A	B-	Up	8.69	13.14	21.71	43.70	146.98	80.88	373.5	800-820-0888	Y
Rydex Mid-Cap 1.5x Strategy Fund Class H	RYMDX	B+	A	B-	Up	8.88	13.55	22.67	47.33	157.08	92.74	373.5	800-820-0888	Y
Rydex Monthly Rebalance NASDAQ-100® 2x Strategy Fund Cls A	RMQAX	B	B	B-	Up	13.84	27.05	69.79	122.43		108.28	51.3	800-820-0888	Y
Rydex Monthly Rebalance NASDAQ-100® 2x Strategy Fund Cls C	RMQCX	B	B	B-	Up	13.63	26.58	68.51	117.08		105.61	51.3	800-820-0888	Y
Rydex Monthly Rebalance NASDAQ-100® 2x Strategy Fund Cls H	RMQHX	B	B	B-	Up	13.84	27.05	69.79	127.83		110.91	51.3	800-820-0888	Y
Rydex NASDAQ-100® 2x Strategy Fund Class A	RYVLX	A-	A+	B-	Up	13.69	26.57	68.94	104.91	436.88	123.53	444.1	800-820-0888	Y
Rydex NASDAQ-100® 2x Strategy Fund Class C	RYCCX	A-	A+	B-	Up	13.46	26.09	67.63	100.27	416.85	99.48	444.1	800-820-0888	Y
Rydex NASDAQ-100® 2x Strategy Fund Class H	RYVYX	A-	A+	B-	Up	13.68	26.56	68.90	104.85	436.76	123.48	444.1	800-820-0888	Y
Rydex Nova Fund Class A	RYANX	B+	A	B-	Up	9.37	15.99	30.70	47.10	169.95	66.28	514.1	800-820-0888	Y
Rydex Nova Fund Class C	RYNCX	B	A-	C+		9.18	15.62	29.93	43.94	160.17	59.27	514.1	800-820-0888	Y
Rydex Nova Fund Class H	RYNHX	B+	A	B-	Up	9.38	16.06	30.95	47.27	170.19	66.37	514.1	800-820-0888	Y
Rydex Nova Fund Investor Class	RYNVX	B+	A	B-	Up	9.44	16.23	31.18	48.26	173.29	71.28	514.1	800-820-0888	Y
Rydex Russell 2000 1.5x Strategy Fund Class A	RYAKX	B+	A	C+	Up	4.33	12.78	20.19	40.21	142.04	65.17	90.3	800-820-0888	Y
Rydex Russell 2000 1.5x Strategy Fund Class C	RYCMX	B+	A	C+	Up	4.14	12.35	19.29	37.07	133.08	55.82	90.3	800-820-0888	Y
Rydex Russell 2000 1.5x Strategy Fund Class H	RYMKX	B+	A	C+	Up	4.20	12.61	20.06	39.94	141.70	64.92	90.3	800-820-0888	Y
Rydex Russell 2000 2x Strategy Fund Class A	RYRUX	B+	A+	C	Up	5.65	16.65	25.59	49.14	203.99	146.14	47.7	800-820-0888	Y
Rydex Russell 2000 2x Strategy Fund Class C	RYRLX	B+	A+	C	Up	5.46	16.21	24.65	45.86	193.03	132.51	47.7	800-820-0888	Y
Rydex Russell 2000 2x Strategy Fund Class H	RYRSX	B+	A+	C	Up	5.64	16.64	25.56	49.07	203.66	145.81	47.7	800-820-0888	Y
Rydex S&P 500 2x Strategy Fund Class A	RYTTX	B+	A+	C+	Up	12.65	21.75	43.02	64.36	265.48	108.58	163.6	800-820-0888	Y
Rydex S&P 500 2x Strategy Fund Class C	RYCTX	B+	A+	C+	Up	12.45	21.30	41.94	60.69	251.92	93.82	163.6	800-820-0888	Y
Rydex S&P 500 2x Strategy Fund Class H	RYTNX	B+	A+	C+	Up	12.66	21.76	43.00	64.31	265.16	108.44	163.6	800-820-0888	Y

Category: US Equity Large Cap Blend

Fund Name	Ticker Symbol	RATINGS				TOTAL RETURNS & PERFORMANCE					ASSETS		NEW INVESTORS	
		Overall Rating	Reward Rating	Risk Rating	Recent Up/ Downgrade	3-Month Total Return	6-Month Total Return	1-Year Total Return	3-Year Total Return	5-Year Total Return	NAV	Total Assets (MIL)	Telephone	Open to New Investors
AAM/Bahl & Gaynor Income Growth Fund Class A	AFNAX	B-	B-	B	Down	6.77	10.80	19.26	30.56	84.21	16.77	557.3	312-263-2900	Y
AAM/Bahl & Gaynor Income Growth Fund Class C	AFYCX	B-	B-	B-	Down	6.55	10.41	18.40	27.69	76.93	16.65	557.3	312-263-2900	Y
AAM/Bahl & Gaynor Income Growth Fund Class I	AFNIX	B-	B-	B	Down	6.82	10.93	19.50	31.61	86.47	16.81	557.3	312-263-2900	Y
Aberdeen U.S. Multi-Cap Equity Fund Class A	GXXAX	B-	B	B-	Down	7.08	10.16	20.57	27.16	78.51	12.41	373.2	866-667-9231	Y
Aberdeen U.S. Multi-Cap Equity Fund Class C	GXXCX	B-	B-	C+	Down	6.87	9.76	19.70	24.48	72.22	10.83	373.2	866-667-9231	Y
Aberdeen U.S. Multi-Cap Equity Fund Class R	GGLRX	B-	B-	B-	Down	6.94	9.93	20.22	25.97	75.96	11.64	373.2	866-667-9231	Y
Aberdeen U.S. Multi-Cap Equity Fund Institutional Class	GGLIX	B-	B	B-	Down	7.18	10.34	21.04	28.31	81.38	13.21	373.2	866-667-9231	Y
Aberdeen U.S. Multi-Cap Equity Fund Inst Service Cls	GXXIX	B-	B	B-	Down	7.17	10.33	20.95	27.94	80.42	13.18	373.2	866-667-9231	Y

Category: US Equity Large Cap Blend (con't)

		RATINGS				TOTAL RETURNS & PERFORMANCE					ASSETS		NEW INVESTORS	
Fund Name	Ticker Symbol	Overall Rating	Reward Rating	Risk Rating	Recent Up/ Downgrade	3-Month Total Return	6-Month Total Return	1-Year Total Return	3-Year Total Return	5-Year Total Return	NAV	Total Assets (MIL)	Telephone	Open to New Investors
Adams Diversified Equity Fund	ADX	B	B	B-	Up	6.45	11.58	24.76	33.98	99.44	17.55	1,710	410-752-5900	Y
Advisory Research All Cap Value Fund	ADVGX	B	B-	B	Up	7.81	12.55	19.54	29.41	88.50	14.23	15.6	312-565-1414	Y
Alger Growth & Income Fund Class A	ALBAX	B	B-	B		6.37	10.27	20.63	33.28	97.99	40.56	120.2	800-992-3863	Y
Alger Growth & Income Fund Class C	ALBCX	B-	B-	B	Down	6.18	9.86	19.71	30.28	90.57	40.04	120.2	800-992-3863	Y
Alger Growth & Income Fund Class Z	AGIZX	B	B-	B		6.46	10.45	21.00	34.38	100.50	40.58	120.2	800-992-3863	Y
Alger Growth & Income Portfolio I-2	AIGOX	B-	B-	B	Down	6.57	10.59	21.32	33.74	100.16	21.02	39.0	800-992-3863	Y
AllianzGI Best Styles U.S. Equity Fund Class A	AABUX	B-	C+	B-	Up	6.74	12.22	23.73	33.38		18.7	123.0	800-498-5413	Y
AllianzGI Best Styles U.S. Equity Fund Class C	ACBUX	B-	C+	B-	Up	6.60	11.81	22.83	30.51		18.34	123.0	800-498-5413	Y
AllianzGI Best Styles U.S. Equity Fund Class P	ALBPX	B-	C+	B-	Up	6.78	12.26	23.91	33.82		18.5	123.0	800-498-5413	Y
AllianzGI Best Styles U.S. Equity Fund Class R6	ALSEX	B-	C+	B-	Up	6.82	12.39	24.06	34.60		18.64	123.0	800-498-5413	Y
AllianzGI Best Styles U.S. Equity Fund Institutional Class	ABTLX	B-	C+	B-	Up	6.80	12.27	23.90	34.21		18.56	123.0	800-498-5413	Y
AlphaMark Large Cap Growth Fund	AMLCX	B	B+	C+	Up	9.21	18.48	28.78	37.29	115.84	16.27	24.3	866-420-3350	Y
Alpine Rising Dividend Fund Class A Shares	AAADX	B-	B-	C+	Down	4.05	8.17	15.84	23.99	80.92	17.29	102.9	888-785-5578	Y
Alpine Rising Dividend Fund Institutional Class	AADDX	B-	B-	C+	Down	4.05	8.24	16.06	24.76	83.04	17.29	102.9	888-785-5578	Y
ALPS I WMC Research Value Fund Class C	AMWCX	B-	C+	B	Up	4.38	6.40	11.89	18.82	79.40	8.57	93.9	866-759-5679	Y
ALPS I WMC Research Value Fund Class I	AMWIX	B	C+	B	Up	4.67	7.02	13.04	22.56	88.72	9.26	93.9	866-759-5679	Y
ALPS I WMC Research Value Fund Class Investor	AMWYX	B-	C+	B	Down	4.52	6.81	12.72	21.56	86.18	9	93.9	866-759-5679	Y
Amana Mutual Funds Trust Income Fund Institutional	AMINX	B-	B-	B-	Down	6.30	10.64	21.12	28.10	85.88	51.01	1,427	888-732-6262	Y
Amana Mutual Funds Trust Income Fund Investor	AMANX	B-	B-	B-	Down	6.43	10.69	21.05	27.36	84.24	51.18	1,427	888-732-6262	Y
American Century Adaptive Equity Fund A CLASS	AVDAX	B	B	B-		7.22	11.85	20.67	34.73	111.07	11.87	106.3	800-444-4015	Y
American Century Adaptive Equity Fund I Class	AVDIX	B	B	B-		7.32	12.08	21.23	36.50	115.67	12.03	106.3	800-444-4015	Y
American Century Adaptive Equity Fund Investor Class	AMVIX	B	B	B-		7.28	12.05	20.96	35.73	113.70	11.76	106.3	800-444-4015	Y
American Century Adaptive Equity Fund R CLASS	AVDRX	B	B	B-	Up	7.13	11.76	20.37	33.71	108.44	11.85	106.3	800-444-4015	Y
American Century Adaptive Equity Fund R6 CLASS	AVDMX	B	B	B-		7.40	12.20	21.48	36.30	114.60	12.17	106.3	800-444-4015	Y
American Century Core Equity Plus Fund Class A	ACPQX	B-	B-	B-	Down	6.66	11.22	19.15	23.08	93.98	15.35	195.4	800-444-4015	Y
American Century Core Equity Plus Fund Class C	ACPHX	B-	C+	B-	Down	6.41	10.76	18.23	20.25	86.69	14.92	195.4	800-444-4015	Y
American Century Core Equity Plus Fund Class R	ACPWX	B-	B-	B-	Down	6.55	11.05	18.83	22.05	91.52	15.26	195.4	800-444-4015	Y
American Century Core Equity Plus Fund I Class	ACPKX	B-	B-	B-	Down	6.69	11.40	19.61	24.63	98.26	15.35	195.4	800-444-4015	Y
American Century Core Equity Plus Fund Investor Class	ACPVX	B-	B-	B-	Down	6.65	11.28	19.32	23.85	96.28	15.36	195.4	800-444-4015	Y
American Century Equity Growth Fund A Class	BEQAX	B-	B-	B-	Down	6.67	11.68	21.54	26.18	94.36	32.37	3,243	800-444-4015	Y
American Century Equity Growth Fund C Class	AEYCX	B-	B-	C+	Down	6.45	11.28	20.64	23.33	87.24	32.08	3,243	800-444-4015	Y
American Century Equity Growth Fund I Class	AMEIX	B-	B-	B-	Down	6.82	11.99	22.11	27.90	98.86	32.44	3,243	800-444-4015	Y
American Century Equity Growth Fund Investor Class	BEQGX	B-	B-	B-	Down	6.73	11.85	21.85	27.13	96.86	32.41	3,243	800-444-4015	Y
American Century Equity Growth Fund R Class	AEYRX	B-	B-	C+	Down	6.63	11.60	21.26	25.26	92.03	32.4	3,243	800-444-4015	Y
American Century Equity Growth Fund R5 Class	AEYGX	B-	B-	B-	Down	6.78	11.95	22.01	27.29	97.11	32.44	3,243	800-444-4015	Y
American Century NT Core Equity Plus Fund G Class	ACNKX	B-	B-	B-	Down	6.93	11.86	20.00	24.77	98.36	16.6	623.9	800-444-4015	Y
American Century NT Equity Growth Fund G Class	ACLEX	B-	B-	B-	Down	6.82	11.98	22.17	27.63	98.31	13.62	1,815	800-444-4015	Y
American Century Sustainable Equity Fund A Class	AFDAX	B	B	B-	Up	8.60	13.95	25.51	32.45	103.21	27.7	231.4	800-444-4015	Y
American Century Sustainable Equity Fund C Class	AFDCX	B-	B-	B-	Down	8.36	13.52	24.58	29.44	95.57	27.27	231.4	800-444-4015	Y
American Century Sustainable Equity Fund I Class	AFEIX	B	B	B-		8.73	14.19	26.05	34.24	107.68	27.78	231.4	800-444-4015	Y
American Century Sustainable Equity Fund Investor Class	AFDIX	B	B	B-		8.65	14.08	25.79	33.44	105.62	27.74	231.4	800-444-4015	Y
American Century Sustainable Equity Fund R Class	AFDRX	B	B	B-	Up	8.52	13.81	25.20	31.42	100.53	27.6	231.4	800-444-4015	Y
American Century Sustainable Equity Fund R5 Class	AFDGX	B	B	B-	Up	8.75	14.21	25.89	32.84	103.81	27.8	231.4	800-444-4015	Y
American Century Sustainable Equity Fund Y Class	AFYDX	B	B	B-	Up	8.78	14.33	26.02	32.99	104.03	27.8	231.4	800-444-4015	Y
American Funds Fundamental Investors® Class 529-A	CFNAX	B	B	B+	Down	6.63	12.16	23.27	41.99	107.87	62.12	95,399	800-421-4225	Y
American Funds Fundamental Investors® Class 529-C	CFNCX	B	B	B		6.41	11.73	22.32	38.71	99.93	62.08	95,399	800-421-4225	Y
American Funds Fundamental Investors® Class 529-E	CFNEX	B	B	B+	Down	6.55	12.03	22.96	40.98	105.44	62.06	95,399	800-421-4225	Y
American Funds Fundamental Investors® Class 529-F-1	CFNFX	B	B	B+	Down	6.69	12.29	23.52	42.91	110.16	62.07	95,399	800-421-4225	Y
American Funds Fundamental Investors® Class A	ANCFX	B	B	B+	Down	6.65	12.21	23.37	42.35	108.82	62.21	95,399	800-421-4225	Y
American Funds Fundamental Investors® Class C	AFICX	B	B	B+		6.42	11.76	22.37	38.97	100.57	61.88	95,399	800-421-4225	Y
American Funds Fundamental Investors® Class F-1	AFIFX	B	B	B+	Down	6.61	12.15	23.27	42.03	108.11	62.17	95,399	800-421-4225	Y
American Funds Fundamental Investors® Class F-2	FINFX	B	B	B+	Down	6.69	12.30	23.57	43.16	110.90	62.19	95,399	800-421-4225	Y

Category: US Equity Large Cap Blend (con't)

Fund Name	Ticker Symbol	RATINGS: Overall Rating	RATINGS: Reward Rating	RATINGS: Risk Rating	RATINGS: Recent Up/Downgrade	TOTAL RETURNS & PERFORMANCE: 3-Month Total Return	6-Month Total Return	1-Year Total Return	3-Year Total Return	5-Year Total Return	ASSETS: NAV	Total Assets (MIL)	NEW INVESTORS: Telephone	Open to New Investors
American Funds Fundamental Investors® Class F-3	FUNFX	B	B	B+	Down	6.71	12.36	23.67	42.70	109.33	62.19	95,399	800-421-4225	Y
American Funds Fundamental Investors® Class R-1	RFNAX	B	B	B		6.42	11.74	22.37	38.96	100.64	61.88	95,399	800-421-4225	Y
American Funds Fundamental Investors® Class R-2	RFNBX	B	B	B+		6.42	11.76	22.39	39.06	100.93	61.86	95,399	800-421-4225	Y
American Funds Fundamental Investors® Class R-2E	RFEBX	B	B	B+		6.50	11.91	22.73	40.57	105.11	61.92	95,399	800-421-4225	Y
American Funds Fundamental Investors® Class R-3	RFNCX	B	B	B+	Down	6.55	12.01	22.93	40.88	105.22	62.05	95,399	800-421-4225	Y
American Funds Fundamental Investors® Class R-4	RFNEX	B	B	B+	Down	6.61	12.15	23.29	42.11	108.30	62.07	95,399	800-421-4225	Y
American Funds Fundamental Investors® Class R-5	RFNFX	B	B	B+	Down	6.71	12.34	23.67	43.41	111.48	62.25	95,399	800-421-4225	Y
American Funds Fundamental Investors® Class R-5E	RFNHX	B	B	B+	Down	6.67	12.29	23.54	42.70	109.33	62.12	95,399	800-421-4225	Y
American Funds Fundamental Investors® Class R-6	RFNGX	B	B	B+	Down	6.71	12.37	23.72	43.62	111.98	62.22	95,399	800-421-4225	Y
American Funds Investment Company of America® Class 529-A	CICAX	B-	B-	B-	Down	6.14	10.60	19.62	33.59	102.57	40.29	93,046	800-421-4225	Y
American Funds Investment Company of America® Class 529-C	CICCX	B-	B-	B-	Down	5.94	10.17	18.70	30.55	94.94	40.19	93,046	800-421-4225	Y
American Funds Investment Company of America® class 529-E	CICEX	B-	B-	B-	Down	6.06	10.44	19.33	32.61	100.11	40.16	93,046	800-421-4225	Y
American Funds Investment Company of America® class 529-F	CICFX	B-	B-	B-	Down	6.20	10.71	19.87	34.46	104.79	40.24	93,046	800-421-4225	Y
American Funds Investment Company of America® Class A	AIVSX	B-	B-	B-	Down	6.17	10.65	19.72	33.99	103.62	40.39	93,046	800-421-4225	Y
American Funds Investment Company of America® Class C	AICCX	B-	B-	B-	Down	5.97	10.20	18.77	30.81	95.58	39.98	93,046	800-421-4225	Y
American Funds Investment Company of America® Class F-1	AICFX	B-	B-	B-	Down	6.13	10.59	19.59	33.60	102.67	40.29	93,046	800-421-4225	Y
American Funds Investment Company of America® Class F-2	ICAFX	B-	B-	B-	Down	6.22	10.75	19.93	34.69	105.45	40.37	93,046	800-421-4225	Y
American Funds Investment Company of America® Class F-3	FFICX	B-	B-	B-	Down	6.24	10.77	20.00	34.30	104.10	40.37	93,046	800-421-4225	Y
American Funds Investment Company of America® Class R-1	RICAX	B-	B-	B-	Down	5.95	10.19	18.73	30.74	95.51	40.07	93,046	800-421-4225	Y
American Funds Investment Company of America® Class R-2	RICBX	B-	B-	B-	Down	5.94	10.18	18.74	30.77	95.69	40.12	93,046	800-421-4225	Y
American Funds Investment Company of America® Class R-2E	RIBEX	B-	B-	B-	Down	6.03	10.37	19.13	32.15	99.62	40.28	93,046	800-421-4225	Y
American Funds Investment Company of America® Class R-3	RICCX	B-	B-	B-	Down	6.07	10.43	19.27	32.51	99.84	40.24	93,046	800-421-4225	Y
American Funds Investment Company of America® Class R-4	RICEX	B-	B-	B-	Down	6.16	10.61	19.63	33.75	103.03	40.28	93,046	800-421-4225	Y
American Funds Investment Company of America® Class R-5	RICFX	B-	B-	B-	Down	6.23	10.77	20.00	34.92	106.07	40.38	93,046	800-421-4225	Y
American Funds Investment Company of America® Class R-5E	RICHX	B-	B-	B-	Down	6.21	10.70	19.89	34.30	104.10	40.36	93,046	800-421-4225	Y
American Funds Investment Company of America® Class R-6	RICGX	B-	B-	B-	Down	6.24	10.80	20.06	35.11	106.55	40.38	93,046	800-421-4225	Y
AMG FQ Long-Short Equity Fund Class I	MEQFX	B-	B-	B	Down	4.00	7.15	15.35	23.78	83.00	14.24	40.9	800-835-3879	Y
AMG FQ Long-Short Equity Fund Class N	FQUAX	B-	B-	B	Down	3.83	6.83	14.93	22.61	80.44	14.24	40.9	800-835-3879	Y
AMG FQ Tax-Managed U.S. Equity Fund Class I	MFQTX	B-	B-	B-	Down	4.73	10.48	18.27	25.98	106.22	30.22	73.6	800-835-3879	Y
AMG FQ Tax-Managed U.S. Equity Fund Class N	MFQAX	B-	B-	B-	Down	4.65	10.33	17.97	25.03	103.71	30.28	73.6	800-835-3879	Y
AMG Yacktman Focused Fund Class I	YAFIX	B-	B-	B-	Down	8.19	9.85	20.24	26.24	81.89	21.09	4,420	800-835-3879	Y
AMG Yacktman Focused Fund Class N	YAFFX	B-	B-	B-	Down	8.11	9.77	20.03	25.57	80.32	21.13	4,420	800-835-3879	Y
AMG Yacktman Fund Class I	YACKX	B-	B-	B-	Down	7.47	9.38	18.23	22.84	78.68	22.85	8,805	800-835-3879	Y
AQR Large Cap Defensive Style Fund Class I	AUEIX	B	B	B+	Down	7.07	10.52	22.14	44.52	123.02	19.07	1,344	203-742-3600	Y
AQR Large Cap Defensive Style Fund Class N	AUENX	B	B	B+	Down	6.95	10.35	21.75	43.39	120.08	19.04	1,344	203-742-3600	Y
AQR Large Cap Defensive Style Fund Class R6	QUERX	B	B	B+	Down	7.06	10.51	22.22	44.89	123.64	19.03	1,344	203-742-3600	Y
AQR Large Cap Multi-Style Fund Class I	QCELX	B	B	B-	Up	7.02	13.12	24.25	31.19		17.66	1,886	203-742-3600	Y
AQR Large Cap Multi-Style Fund Class N	QCENX	B	B	B-	Up	6.96	12.95	23.94	30.19		17.61	1,886	203-742-3600	Y
AQR Large Cap Multi-Style Fund Class R6	QCERX	B	B	B-	Up	7.04	13.15	24.37	31.61		17.65	1,886	203-742-3600	Y
AQR TM Large Cap Multi-Style Fund Class I	QTLLX	B-	C+	B-	Up	7.16	13.35	24.58			12.81	246.1	203-742-3600	Y
AQR TM Large Cap Multi-Style Fund Class N	QTLNX	B-	C+	B-	Up	7.11	13.21	24.22			12.79	246.1	203-742-3600	Y
AQR TM Large Cap Multi-Style Fund Class R6	QTLRX	B-	C+	B-	Up	7.25	13.43	24.78			12.82	246.1	203-742-3600	Y
Asset Management Fund Large Cap Equity Fund Class AMF	IICAX	B	B	B-		6.84	11.31	20.55	33.35	89.29	8.45	47.4	800-247-9780	Y
Asset Management Fund Large Cap Equity Fund Class H	IICHX	B	B	B-		6.78	11.29	20.64	33.89	90.52	8.41	47.4	800-247-9780	Y
AT Disciplined Equity Fund Institutional Class	AWEIX	B	B-	B+		7.66	10.57	20.89	34.17	106.83	19.17	920.2		Y
ATM Large Cap Managed Volatility Portfolio Class K	US26883L8789	B	B-	B		6.98	11.78	21.09	33.96	105.70		3,662	877-222-2144	Y
Ave Maria Rising Dividend Fund	AVEDX	B-	B-	B	Down	6.70	10.82	16.82	25.59	87.98	18.44	961.1	888-726-9331	Y
AXA 500 Managed Volatility Portfolio Class IB	US26884M2061	B-	B-	B	Down	6.94	11.66	20.82	33.16	103.43		8,905	877-222-2144	Y
AXA 500 Managed Volatility Portfolio Class K	US26883L8862	B	B-	B		7.04	11.82	21.15	34.20	105.98		8,905	877-222-2144	Y
AXA Large Cap Core Managed Volatility Portfolio Class IA	US2689405742	B-	B-	B	Down	6.24	11.22	21.89	33.08	101.87		2,735	877-222-2144	Y
AXA Large Cap Core Managed Volatility Portfolio Class IB	US2689405668	B-	B-	B	Down	6.24	11.22	21.88	33.08	101.85		2,735	877-222-2144	Y
AXA Large Cap Core Managed Volatility Portfolio Class K	US26883L5637	B	B-	B		6.39	11.37	22.16	34.07	104.38		2,735	877-222-2144	Y

Category: US Equity Large Cap Blend (con't)

Fund Name	Ticker Symbol	RATINGS: Overall Rating	Reward Rating	Risk Rating	Recent Up/ Downgrade	TOTAL RETURNS & PERFORMANCE: 3-Month Total Return	6-Month Total Return	1-Year Total Return	3-Year Total Return	5-Year Total Return	ASSETS: NAV	Total Assets (MIL)	NEW INVESTORS: Telephone	Open to New Investors
AXA/Mutual Large Cap Eq Managed Vol Port Cls IA	US2689547659	B-	B-	B-	Down	4.71	7.38	14.29	24.96	82.67		631.1	877-222-2144	Y
AXA/Mutual Large Cap Eq Managed Vol Port Cls IB	US2689547576	B-	B-	B-	Down	4.65	7.32	14.24	24.82	82.52		631.1	877-222-2144	Y
AXA/Mutual Large Cap Eq Managed Vol Port Cls K	US26883L4499	B-	B-	B-	Down	4.75	7.56	14.56	25.80	84.97		631.1	877-222-2144	Y
Baird LargeCap Fund Institutional Class	BHGIX	B	B	B-		9.41	15.60	25.53	34.84	112.78		42.9	800-792-2473	Y
Baird LargeCap Fund Investor Class	BHGSX	B	B	B-	Up	9.32	15.40	25.08	33.69	110.11		42.9	800-792-2473	Y
BBH Core Select Fund Class N	BBTEX	B-	B-	B	Down	6.10	8.41	19.93	25.01	74.65	20.86	2,811	800-575-1265	
BBH Core Select Retail Class Shares	BBTRX	B-	C+	B	Down	6.07	8.25	19.64	24.11	72.61	10.73	2,811	800-575-1265	
BlackRock Advantage Large Cap Core Fund Inst Shares	MALRX	B	B	B-		5.73	11.51	22.09	33.90	105.98	16.38	1,696	800-441-7762	Y
BlackRock Advantage Large Cap Core Fund Investor A Shares	MDLRX	B	B	B-		5.66	11.33	21.73	32.78	103.07	15.81	1,696	800-441-7762	Y
BlackRock Advantage Large Cap Core Fund Investor B Shares	MBLRX	B	B	B-	Up	6.12	10.52	20.37	29.68	95.56		1,697	800-441-7762	
BlackRock Advantage Large Cap Core Fund Investor C Shares	MCLRX	B	B	B-	Up	5.48	10.97	20.80	29.57	95.06	13.64	1,697	800-441-7762	Y
BlackRock Advantage Large Cap Core Fund R Shares	MRLRX	B	B	B-		5.55	11.21	21.39	31.64	100.22	14.8	1,696	800-441-7762	Y
BlackRock Advantage Large Cap Core Fund Service Shares	MSLRX	B	B	B-		5.66	11.34	21.80	32.31	102.01	16.34	1,697	800-441-7762	Y
BlackRock Enhanced Capital and Income Fund Inc	CII	B	B	B	Up	5.83	11.39	21.15	35.43	82.80	17.1748	754.9	800-441-7762	Y
BlackRock Exchange Portfolio BlackRock Shares	STSEX	B-	B-	B-	Down	4.92	8.88	15.23	26.34	82.48	1050.08	173.0	800-441-7762	Y
Blue Chip Investor Fund	BCIFX	B	B-	B		8.04	12.89	18.50	32.36	95.54	180.09	39.7		Y
BNY Mellon Large Cap Stock Fund Class Investor	MILCX	B-	B-	B-	Down	6.60	12.21	21.66	29.48	94.84	6.06	307.8	800-645-6561	Y
BNY Mellon Large Cap Stock Fund Class M	MPLCX	B-	B	B-	Down	6.49	12.34	21.75	30.43	97.15	6.05	307.8	800-645-6561	Y
BNY Mellon Tax-Sensitive Large Cap Multi-Strat Cls Inv	MTSIX	B	B	B-		7.21	11.57	22.17	35.38	102.88	16.7	363.0	800-645-6561	Y
BNY Mellon Tax-Sensitive Large Cap Multi-Strat Fund Cls M	MTSMX	B	B	B-		7.29	11.67	22.45	36.38	102.25	16.3	363.0	800-645-6561	Y
Boston Trust Equity Fund	BTEFX	B	B-	B		7.88	11.30	20.66	32.09	89.68	23.63	134.0	617-814-1215	Y
Boyar Value Fund	BOYAX	B-	C+	B	Down	6.50	8.38	15.47	22.71	82.20	26.54	26.7		Y
Bretton Fund	BRTNX	B-	C+	B		11.44	16.93	18.18	21.52	72.38	30.87	29.4		Y
Bridgeway Blue Chip 35 Index Fund	BRLIX	B	B-	B+		7.29	11.60	18.42	35.43	104.00	14.57	571.4	800-661-3550	Y
Bright Rock Quality Large Cap Fund Institutional Class	BQLCX	B	C+	B+		7.43	10.59	16.31	25.47	86.09	16.62	234.2	781-982-6593	Y
Bright Rock Quality Large Cap Fund Investor Class	BQLIX	B	C+	B+		7.31	10.39	15.86	24.38	85.18	16.99	234.2	781-982-6593	Y
Brown Advisory Equity Income Fund Advisor Shares	BADAX	B-	B-	B-	Down	6.46	9.95	19.97	22.63	75.67	14.59	119.0	800-540-6807	Y
Brown Advisory Equity Income Fund Inst Shares	BAFDX	B-	B-	B-	Down	6.55	10.22	20.49	24.05	79.20	14.62	119.0	800-540-6807	Y
Brown Advisory Equity Income Fund Investor Shares	BIADX	B-	B-	B-	Down	6.51	10.07	20.23	23.50	77.70	14.61	119.0	800-540-6807	Y
Buffalo Dividend Focus Fund	BUFDX	B	B-	B+		6.46	9.29	18.01	31.45	98.65	16.66	63.3	800-492-8332	Y
Calvert US Large Cap Core Responsible Index Fund Class A	CSXAX	B	B-	B		6.07	10.29	20.73	32.89	108.41	22.23	1,027	800-368-2745	Y
Calvert US Large Cap Core Responsible Index Fund Class C	CSXCX	B-	B-	B-	Down	5.84	9.82	19.81	29.89	100.28	20.99	1,027	800-368-2745	Y
Calvert US Large Cap Core Responsible Index Fund Class I	CISIX	B	B	B		6.15	10.48	21.18	34.41	113.15	22.74	1,027	800-368-2745	Y
Calvert US Large Cap Core Responsible Index Fund Class R6	CSXRX	B	B	B		6.10	10.43	21.12	34.35	113.05	22.73	1,027	800-368-2745	Y
Calvert US Large Cap Core Responsible Index Fund Class Y	CISYX	B-	B-	B	Down	6.85	9.28	18.73	35.37	105.29		1,027	800-368-2745	Y
Cambiar Opportunity Fund Class Institutional	CAMWX	B	B	B+	Up	4.55	10.11	15.01	31.42	94.43	23.76	347.9	866-777-8227	Y
Cambiar Opportunity Fund Class Investor	CAMOX	B	B-	B+	Up	4.53	10.04	14.78	30.50	92.12	23.85	347.9	866-777-8227	Y
Catalyst/Lyons Tactical Allocation Fund Class A	CLTAX	B	C+	B		8.64	12.22	16.70	24.53	96.86	16.23	83.1	866-447-4228	Y
Catalyst/Lyons Tactical Allocation Fund Class C	CLTCX	B-	C+	B	Down	8.51	11.85	15.89	21.87	89.85	16.03	83.1	866-447-4228	Y
Catalyst/Lyons Tactical Allocation Fund Class I	CLTIX	B	B-	B		8.69	12.35	16.99	25.58	98.61	16.2	83.1	866-447-4228	Y
Central Securities Corporation	CET	B+	A	B	Up	8.32	12.67	25.01	44.70	92.83	32.86	805.6		Y
CGM Focus Fund	CGMFX	B	A-	B-	Up	3.73	14.23	24.82	30.40	87.19	53.35	994.8	800-343-5678	Y
ClearBridge Appreciation Fund Class A	SHAPX	B	B-	B+		6.50	10.50	19.51	30.94	92.21	23.6	6,159	877-721-1926	Y
ClearBridge Appreciation Fund Class B	SAPBX	B-	B-	B	Down	6.19	9.79	18.05	26.38	81.43	22.45	6,159	877-721-1926	
ClearBridge Appreciation Fund Class C	SAPCX	B-	B-	B	Down	6.33	10.07	18.65	28.19	85.50	22.78	6,159	877-721-1926	Y
ClearBridge Appreciation Fund Class FI	LMPIX	B	B-	B+		6.47	10.44	19.46	30.89	92.08	23.72	6,159	877-721-1926	Y
ClearBridge Appreciation Fund Class I	SAPYX	B	B-	B+		6.55	10.62	19.80	32.05	95.14	23.43	6,159	877-721-1926	Y
ClearBridge Appreciation Fund Class IS	LMESX	B	B-	B+		6.65	10.70	19.98	32.52	96.12	23.5	6,159	877-721-1926	Y
ClearBridge Appreciation Fund Class R	LMPPX	B	B-	B		6.43	10.30	19.16	29.74	89.30	23.56	6,159	877-721-1926	Y
ClearBridge Dividend Strategy Fund Class 1	LCBOX	B-	B-	B	Down	5.70	10.17	19.44	30.46	90.17	23.53	6,226	877-721-1926	Y
ClearBridge Dividend Strategy Fund Class A	SOPAX	B-	B-	B	Down	5.68	10.02	19.12	29.41	87.73	23.52	6,226	877-721-1926	Y
ClearBridge Dividend Strategy Fund Class B	SOPTX	B-	B-	B-	Down	5.40	9.44	17.86	25.83	79.84	23.15	6,226	877-721-1926	

Category: US Equity Large Cap Blend (con't)

Fund Name	Ticker Symbol	RATINGS: Overall Rating	Reward Rating	Risk Rating	Recent Up/ Downgrade	TOTAL RETURNS & PERFORMANCE: 3-Month Total Return	6-Month Total Return	1-Year Total Return	3-Year Total Return	5-Year Total Return	ASSETS: NAV	Total Assets (MIL)	NEW INVESTORS: Telephone	Open to New Investors
ClearBridge Dividend Strategy Fund Class C	SBPLX	B-	B-	B-	Down	5.50	9.65	18.30	26.75	81.33	23.19	6,226	877-721-1926	Y
ClearBridge Dividend Strategy Fund Class FI	LBRIX	B-	B-	B	Down	5.63	9.96	19.01	29.27	86.62	23.49	6,226	877-721-1926	Y
ClearBridge Dividend Strategy Fund Class I	SOPYX	B-	B-	B	Down	5.73	10.18	19.44	30.54	90.66	24.13	6,226	877-721-1926	Y
ClearBridge Dividend Strategy Fund Class IS	LCBEX	B-	B-	B	Down	5.79	10.22	19.60	30.91	90.43	24.16	6,226	877-721-1926	Y
ClearBridge Dividend Strategy Fund Class R	LMMRX	B-	B-	B-	Down	5.56	9.79	18.75	28.47	85.20	23.37	6,226	877-721-1926	Y
ClearBridge Value Trust Class A	LGVAX	B-	B-	B		3.74	7.26	14.59	23.15	98.46	81.46	2,407	877-721-1926	Y
ClearBridge Value Trust Class C	LMVTX	B-	C+	B-	Up	3.56	6.86	13.75	20.53	91.30	79.97	2,407	877-721-1926	Y
ClearBridge Value Trust Class FI	LMVFX	B-	B-	B		3.72	7.20	14.48	22.87	97.74	92.68	2,407	877-721-1926	Y
ClearBridge Value Trust Class I	LMNVX	B-	B-	B	Down	3.79	7.37	14.83	24.00	100.63	95.64	2,407	877-721-1926	Y
ClearBridge Value Trust Class R	LMVRX	B-	C+	B-		3.63	7.04	14.20	21.86	94.62	91.44	2,407	877-721-1926	Y
Clipper Fund	CFIMX	B	B	B+	Up	5.75	10.14	17.68	43.51	111.88	120.46	1,170	800-432-2504	Y
Cohen & Steers Dividend Value Fund , Inc.Class A	DVFAX	B-	B-	B	Down	7.73	11.19	17.59	27.39	94.81	15.29	195.2	212-832-3232	Y
Cohen & Steers Dividend Value Fund , Inc.Class C	DVFCX	B-	B-	B	Down	7.58	10.81	16.90	25.02	88.60	15.19	195.2	212-832-3232	Y
Cohen & Steers Dividend Value Fund , Inc.Cls Institutional	DVFIX	B	B-	B	Up	7.87	11.44	18.06	28.79	98.36	15.32	195.2	212-832-3232	Y
Cohen & Steers Dividend Value Fund, Inc. Class R	DVFRX	B-	B-	B	Down	7.75	11.09	17.48	26.87	93.49	15.31	195.2	212-832-3232	Y
Cohen & Steers Dividend Value Fund, Inc. Class Z	DVFZX	B	B-	B	Up	7.80	11.36	17.98	28.70	98.23	15.31	195.2	212-832-3232	Y
Coho Relative Value Equity Fund Advisor Class	COHOX	B-	B-	B-	Down	7.57	10.92	18.30	27.24		14.4	566.3		Y
Coho Relative Value Equity Fund Institutional Class	COHIX	B-	B-	B-	Down	7.64	11.07	18.44	27.67		14.42	566.3		Y
Columbia Contrarian Core Fund Advisor Class	CORRX	B	B-	B+		5.38	9.75	21.70	34.92	112.36	26.3	11,572	800-345-6611	Y
Columbia Contrarian Core Fund Class A	LCCAX	B	B-	B+		5.32	9.61	21.42	33.90	109.65	25.69	11,572	800-345-6611	Y
Columbia Contrarian Core Fund Class C	LCCCX	B-	B-	B	Down	5.10	9.20	20.49	30.89	101.91	23.33	11,572	800-345-6611	Y
Columbia Contrarian Core Fund Class K	CCRFX	B	B-	B+		5.33	9.64	21.49	34.34	110.96	25.85	11,572	800-345-6611	
Columbia Contrarian Core Fund Class R	CCCRX	B	B-	B		5.23	9.43	21.11	32.90	107.10	25.72	11,572	800-345-6611	Y
Columbia Contrarian Core Fund Class T	CTRWX	B	B-	B+		5.27	9.57	21.38	33.86	109.59	25.68	11,572	800-345-6611	Y
Columbia Contrarian Core Fund Class V	SGIEX	B	B-	B+		5.32	9.57	21.39	33.90	109.44	25.44	11,572	800-345-6611	
Columbia Contrarian Core Fund Institutional 2 Class	COFRX	B	B-	B+	Down	5.41	9.77	21.79	35.36	113.67	26.27	11,572	800-345-6611	Y
Columbia Contrarian Core Fund Institutional 3 Class	COFYX	B	B-	B+	Down	5.41	9.81	21.88	35.53	114.23	26.28	11,572	800-345-6611	Y
Columbia Contrarian Core Fund Institutional Class	SMGIX	B	B-	B+		5.35	9.74	21.69	34.89	112.29	25.86	11,572	800-345-6611	Y
Columbia Disciplined Core Fund Advisor Class	CLCQX	B	B	B		7.81	13.94	24.45	34.23	113.00	12.05	4,356	800-345-6611	Y
Columbia Disciplined Core Fund Class A	AQEAX	B	B	B		7.63	13.71	24.06	33.24	110.48	11.94	4,356	800-345-6611	Y
Columbia Disciplined Core Fund Class C	RDCEX	B-	B-	B-	Down	7.42	13.32	23.13	30.19	102.70	11.72	4,356	800-345-6611	Y
Columbia Disciplined Core Fund Class K	RQEYX	B	B	B		7.65	13.79	24.09	33.45	111.38	12.01	4,356	800-345-6611	
Columbia Disciplined Core Fund Class R	CLQRX	B	B	B	Up	7.67	13.67	23.79	32.18	107.73	11.94	4,356	800-345-6611	Y
Columbia Disciplined Core Fund Class T	RDEWX	B	B	B		7.67	13.72	24.00	33.11	110.42	12.02	4,356	800-345-6611	Y
Columbia Disciplined Core Fund Institutional 2 Class	RSIPX	B	B	B		7.73	13.90	24.47	34.42	114.04	11.96	4,356	800-345-6611	Y
Columbia Disciplined Core Fund Institutional 3 Class	CCQYX	B	B	B		7.74	13.99	24.53	34.45	112.97	12.01	4,356	800-345-6611	Y
Columbia Disciplined Core Fund Institutional Class	CCRZX	B	B	B		7.75	13.90	24.44	34.13	113.21	12	4,356	800-345-6611	Y
Columbia Large Cap Enhanced Core Fund Advisor Class	CECFX	B	B	B-		7.58	13.71	24.33	34.94	116.46	24.39	404.8	800-345-6611	Y
Columbia Large Cap Enhanced Core Fund Class A	NMIAX	B	B	B-		7.54	13.61	24.12	33.98	113.65	24.68	404.8	800-345-6611	Y
Columbia Large Cap Enhanced Core Fund Class R	CCERX	B	B	B-		7.47	13.41	23.76	32.96	110.88	24.64	404.8	800-345-6611	Y
Columbia Large Cap Enhanced Core Fund Institutional 2 Cls	CLNCX	B	B	B		7.65	13.81	24.50	35.35	117.26	24.52	404.8	800-345-6611	Y
Columbia Large Cap Enhanced Core Fund Institutional 3 Cls	CECYX	B	B	B		7.63	13.81	24.52	35.53	117.74	24.61	404.8	800-345-6611	Y
Columbia Large Cap Enhanced Core Fund Institutional Class	NMIMX	B	B	B-		7.64	13.73	24.41	34.96	116.50	24.62	404.8	800-345-6611	Y
Columbia Large Cap Index Fund Class A	NEIAX	B	B	B		6.52	11.19	21.29	35.11	107.08	49.55	3,855	800-345-6611	Y
Columbia Large Cap Index Fund Institutional 2 Class	CLXRX	B	B	B		6.60	11.32	21.59	36.12	109.67	50.48	3,855	800-345-6611	Y
Columbia Large Cap Index Fund Institutional 3 Class	CLPYX	B	B	B		6.57	11.31	21.58	36.08	109.62	49.07	3,855	800-345-6611	Y
Columbia Large Cap Index Fund Institutional Class	NINDX	B	B	B		6.59	11.32	21.60	36.10	109.66	49.79	3,855	800-345-6611	Y
Columbia Select Large Cap Equity Fund Advisor Class	CLSRX	B	B	B+	Down	6.41	11.82	24.53	40.94	111.57	14.44	671.4	800-345-6611	Y
Columbia Select Large Cap Equity Fund Class A	NSGAX	B	B	B+	Down	6.27	11.72	24.17	39.96	108.95	14.6	671.4	800-345-6611	Y
Columbia Select Large Cap Equity Fund Class C	NSGCX	B	B	B	Down	6.02	11.22	23.26	36.73	101.23	13.45	671.4	800-345-6611	Y
Columbia Select Large Cap Equity Fund Class T	CLCWX	B	B	B+	Down	6.29	11.73	24.20	39.90	108.97	14.59	671.4	800-345-6611	Y
Columbia Select Large Cap Equity Fund Institutional 2 Cls	CLCRX	B	B	B+	Down	6.33	11.82	24.48	41.26	112.43	14.88	671.4	800-345-6611	Y

Category: US Equity Large Cap Blend (con't)

Fund Name	Ticker Symbol	RATINGS Overall Rating	Reward Rating	Risk Rating	Recent Up/ Downgrade	TOTAL RETURNS & PERFORMANCE 3-Month Total Return	6-Month Total Return	1-Year Total Return	3-Year Total Return	5-Year Total Return	ASSETS NAV	Total Assets (MIL)	NEW INVESTORS Telephone	Open to New Investors
Columbia Select Large Cap Equity Fund Institutional 3 Cls	CLEYX	B	B	B+	Down	6.42	11.89	24.71	41.13	111.86	14.29	671.4	800-345-6611	Y
Columbia Select Large Cap Equity Fund Institutional Class	NSEPX	B	B	B+	Down	6.38	11.86	24.58	40.99	111.64	14.49	671.4	800-345-6611	Y
Convergence Core Plus Fund Institutional Class	MARNX	B	B	A-	Up	6.90	13.96	17.79	30.73	95.78	18.73	128.6	877-677-9414	Y
Copeland Risk Managed Dividend Growth Fund Class A Shares	CDGRX	B-	C+	B	Up	7.45	9.80	19.56	13.19	66.94	13.9	175.2	888-926-7352	Y
Copeland Risk Managed Dividend Growth Fund Class C Shares	CDCRX	B-	C+	B	Up	7.26	9.41	18.64	10.66	60.77	13.61	175.2	888-926-7352	Y
Cornerstone Strategic Value Fund	CLM	B	B+	C+	Up	6.26	12.14	24.01	30.35	129.49	13.55	592.2		Y
Cornerstone Total Return Fund Inc	CRF	B+	A-	B	Up	6.35	12.55	22.73	37.61	147.55	13.18	291.6		Y
CRM All Cap Value Fund Class Institutional	CRIEX	B	B	B-	Up	5.35	9.39	18.87	34.80	87.82	8.8	23.1	800-276-2883	Y
CRM All Cap Value Fund Class Investor	CRMEX	B	B	B-	Up	5.32	9.30	18.63	34.00	85.78	8.66	23.1	800-276-2883	Y
CRM Large Cap Opportunity Fund Institutional Class	CRIGX	B	B	B+	Up	5.50	9.91	17.35	30.42	91.88	9.62	99.5	800-276-2883	Y
CRM Large Cap Opportunity Fund Investor Class	CRMGX	B	B	B	Up	5.46	9.77	17.08	29.48	89.49	9.61	99.5	800-276-2883	Y
Dana Large Cap Equity Fund Institutional Class	DLCIX	B	B	B-	Up	7.47	13.99	27.42	32.69	105.82	22.83	192.6	262-782-3631	Y
Dana Large Cap Equity Fund Investor Class	DLCEX	B	B	B-	Up	7.44	13.89	27.09	31.69	103.44	22.84	192.6	262-782-3631	Y
Davidson Multi-Cap Equity Fund Class A	DFMAX	B	C+	B	Up	5.20	6.41	13.18	23.86	87.27	25.23	117.6		Y
Davidson Multi-Cap Equity Fund Class I	DFMIX	B	C+	B+	Up	5.27	6.60	13.49	24.84	89.27	25.25	117.6		Y
Davis New York Venture Fund Class A	NYVTX	B	B	B	Up	7.22	12.17	22.14	39.97	105.19	34.25	11,581	800-279-0279	Y
Davis New York Venture Fund Class B	NYVBX	B	B	B	Up	7.00	11.68	20.97	35.98	95.66	30.22	11,581	800-279-0279	Y
Davis New York Venture Fund Class C	NYVCX	B	B	B	Up	7.04	11.78	21.21	36.76	97.34	31.11	11,581	800-279-0279	Y
Davis New York Venture Fund Class R	NYVRX	B	B	B	Up	7.15	12.05	21.80	38.76	102.18	34.37	11,581	800-279-0279	Y
Davis New York Venture Fund Class T	DNVTX	B	B	B		7.20	12.16	22.12	39.91	105.07	34.27	11,581	800-279-0279	Y
Davis New York Venture Fund Class Y	DNVYX	B	B	B	Up	7.29	12.34	22.47	41.05	107.74	35	11,581	800-279-0279	Y
Dearborn Partners Rising Dividend Fund Class A Shares	DRDAX	B-	B-	B-	Down	3.84	7.23	14.75	20.85		14.37	214.0	888-983-3380	Y
Dearborn Partners Rising Dividend Fund Class C Shares	DRDCX	B-	C+	B-	Down	3.65	6.84	13.87	18.09		14.32	214.0	888-983-3380	Y
Dearborn Partners Rising Dividend Fund Class I Shares	DRDIX	B-	B-	B-	Down	3.89	7.35	15.03	21.72		14.39	214.0	888-983-3380	Y
Deutsche Core Equity Fund Class A	SUWAX	B	B	B		6.41	11.53	21.12	38.48	116.70	27.31	3,680	201-593-8273	Y
Deutsche Core Equity Fund Class C	SUWCX	B	B	B	Up	6.22	11.15	20.21	35.33	108.61	26.13	3,680	201-593-8273	Y
Deutsche Core Equity Fund Class R	SUWTX	B	B	B	Up	6.30	11.34	20.65	36.98	111.69	27.57	3,680	201-593-8273	Y
Deutsche Core Equity Fund Class R6	SUWZX	B	B	B		6.48	11.74	21.57	39.72	120.20	27.62	3,680	201-593-8273	Y
Deutsche Core Equity Fund Class S	SCDGX	B	B	B		6.47	11.70	21.45	39.67	119.94	27.59	3,680	201-593-8273	Y
Deutsche Core Equity Fund Class T	SUWUX	B	B	B		6.39	11.45	21.02	38.49	116.99	27.3	3,680	201-593-8273	Y
Deutsche Core Equity Fund Institutional Class	SUWIX	B	B	B		6.46	11.69	21.48	39.76	120.42	27.64	3,680	201-593-8273	Y
Deutsche Equity 500 Index Fund Class R6	BTIRX	B	B	B		6.56	11.30	21.46	35.74	108.71	220.83	774.5	201-593-8273	Y
Deutsche Equity 500 Index Fund Class S	BTIEX	B	B	B		6.55	11.26	21.41	35.55	108.18	217.91	774.5	201-593-8273	Y
Deutsche Equity 500 Index Fund Institutional Class	BTIIX	B	B	B		6.57	11.28	21.47	35.75	108.73	220.85	774.5	201-593-8273	Y
Deutsche S&P 500 Index Fund Class A	SXPAX	B	B	B		6.48	11.09	21.09	34.28	104.92	30.5	1,011	201-593-8273	Y
Deutsche S&P 500 Index Fund Class C	SXPCX	B-	B-	B	Down	6.27	10.68	20.19	31.51	97.85	30.43	1,011	201-593-8273	Y
Deutsche S&P 500 Index Fund Class R6	SXPRX	B	B	B		6.54	11.25	21.36	35.63	108.54	30.55	1,011	201-593-8273	Y
Deutsche S&P 500 Index Fund Class S	SCPIX	B	B	B		6.54	11.22	21.37	35.38	107.77	30.56	1,011	201-593-8273	Y
DFA Enhanced U.S. Large Company Portfolio Inst Cls	DFELX	B	B	B		6.21	10.91	21.43	36.64	112.54	12.94	353.2	512-306-7400	Y
DFA Tax Managed U.S. Equity Portfolio	DTMEX	B	B	B		6.55	11.44	21.43	36.11	110.10	29.02	3,414	512-306-7400	Y
DFA U.S. Core Equity 1 Portfolio Institutional Class	DFEOX	B	B	B-		6.90	12.06	20.89	35.62	110.27	22.78	21,603	512-306-7400	Y
DFA U.S. Large Cap Equity Portfolio Institutional Class	DUSQX	B	B	B-		7.28	12.20	22.08	35.36		16.63	1,268	512-306-7400	Y
DFA U.S. Large Company Portfolio	DFUSX	B	B	B		6.60	11.36	21.73	36.66	110.85	20.71	8,252	512-306-7400	Y
DFA U.S. Sustainability Core 1 Portfolio	DFSIX	B	B	B-		6.89	11.93	21.35	35.23	109.63	21.11	1,249	512-306-7400	Y
Diamond Hill All Cap Select Fund Class A	DHTAX	B	B	B	Up	7.95	12.82	19.92	28.37	110.06	16.01	159.3	888-226-5595	Y
Diamond Hill All Cap Select Fund Class C	DHTCX	B	B-	B	Up	7.77	12.42	19.07	25.44	102.24	15.11	159.3	888-226-5595	Y
Diamond Hill All Cap Select Fund Class I	DHLTX	B	B	B	Up	8.00	12.99	20.33	29.50	112.88	16.11	159.3	888-226-5595	Y
Diamond Hill All Cap Select Fund Class Y	DHTYX	B	B	B	Up	8.05	13.11	20.45	29.85	114.30	16.14	159.3	888-226-5595	Y
Domini Impact Equity Fund A Shares	DSEPX	B-	C+	B	Down	4.77	9.53	15.44	17.79	83.06	5.08	892.2	800-582-6757	Y
Domini Impact Equity Fund Institutional Shares	DIEQX	B-	C+	B	Down	4.90	9.69	15.79	19.18	86.60	23.56	892.2	800-582-6757	Y
Domini Impact Equity Fund Investor Shares	DSEFX	B-	C+	B	Down	4.80	9.50	15.41	17.96	83.20	47.11	892.2	800-582-6757	Y
Dreyfus Appreciation Fund, Inc. Class I	DGIGX	B-	B	B-	Down	7.45	12.19	26.90	31.44	77.07	35.89	2,003	800-645-6561	Y

Category: US Equity Large Cap Blend (con't)

Fund Name	Ticker Symbol	RATINGS: Overall Rating	Reward Rating	Risk Rating	Recent Up/ Downgrade	TOTAL RETURNS & PERFORMANCE: 3-Month Total Return	6-Month Total Return	1-Year Total Return	3-Year Total Return	5-Year Total Return	ASSETS: NAV	Total Assets (MIL)	NEW INVESTORS: Telephone	Open to New Investors
Dreyfus Appreciation Fund, Inc. Class Investor	DGAGX	B-	B-	B-	Down	7.42	12.08	26.64	31.07	76.57	36.07	2,003	800-645-6561	Y
Dreyfus Appreciation Fund, Inc. Class Y	DGYGX	B-	B-	B-	Down	7.49	12.24	27.03	32.38	79.17	35.96	2,003	800-645-6561	Y
Dreyfus Core Equity Fund Class A	DLTSX	B-	B-	B-	Down	7.50	11.99	26.20	29.59	73.14	17.85	182.0	800-645-6561	Y
Dreyfus Core Equity Fund Class C	DPECX	B-	B-	B-	Down	7.31	11.55	25.28	26.81	66.92	17.31	182.0	800-645-6561	Y
Dreyfus Core Equity Fund Class I	DPERX	B-	B-	B-	Down	7.56	12.11	26.48	30.40	75.08	18.44	182.0	800-645-6561	Y
Dreyfus Disciplined Stock Fund	DDSTX	B	B-	A-		6.97	10.81	19.06	35.32	95.69	36.57	615.6	800-645-6561	Y
Dreyfus Institutional S&P 500 Stock Index Fund Class I	DSPIX	B	B	B		6.57	11.31	21.58	36.06	109.68	53.49	2,623	800-645-6561	Y
Dreyfus S&P 500 Index Fund	PEOPX	B	B	B		6.52	11.16	21.24	34.83	106.54	54.05	2,716	800-645-6561	Y
Dreyfus Sustainable U.S. Equity Fund Class A	DTCAX	B-	B-	B-	Down	2.72	7.01	14.95	20.72	87.24	11.07	321.0	800-645-6561	Y
Dreyfus Sustainable U.S. Equity Fund Class I	DRTCX	B-	B-	B-	Down	2.69	7.12	15.26	21.80	90.11	11.33	321.0	800-645-6561	Y
Dreyfus Sustainable U.S. Equity Fund Class Y	DTCYX	B-	B-	B-	Down	2.63	7.06	15.30	21.58	89.32	11.31	321.0	800-645-6561	Y
Dreyfus Sustainable U.S. Equity Fund Class Z	DRTHX	B-	B-	B-	Down	2.66	7.02	15.16	21.43	89.09	11.33	321.0	800-645-6561	
Dreyfus Tax Managed Growth Fund Class A	DTMGX	B-	B-	B-	Down	7.23	11.57	25.48	27.75	70.02	29.36	181.8	800-645-6561	Y
Dreyfus Tax Managed Growth Fund Class C	DPTAX	B-	B-	B-	Down	7.04	11.20	24.52	24.94	63.74	27.68	181.8	800-645-6561	Y
Dreyfus Tax Managed Growth Fund Class I	DPTRX	B-	B-	B-	Down	7.31	11.76	25.79	28.71	72.12	29.41	181.8	800-645-6561	Y
Eagle Capital Growth Fund, Inc.	GRF	B+	B+	B+	Up	2.17	6.35	13.30	27.23	80.19	8.8181	32.5	414-765-1107	Y
Eaton Vance Dividend Builder Fund Class A	EVTMX	B-	B-	B	Down	7.33	11.88	18.88	32.21	90.17	14.55	991.8		Y
Eaton Vance Dividend Builder Fund Class C	ECTMX	B-	B-	B	Down	7.08	11.39	17.89	29.19	83.23	14.62	991.8		Y
Eaton Vance Dividend Builder Fund Class I	EIUTX	B-	B-	B	Down	7.33	11.95	19.11	33.15	92.54	14.53	991.8		Y
Eaton Vance Stock Fund Class A	EAERX	B	B-	B+		6.39	9.98	19.90	32.47	102.57	17.49	103.1		Y
Eaton Vance Stock Fund Class C	ECERX	B	B-	B+	Up	6.19	9.56	18.94	29.48	94.97	17.1	103.1		Y
Eaton Vance Stock Fund Institutional Class	EIERX	B	B-	B+		6.47	10.07	20.14	33.46	105.00	17.49	103.1		Y
Eaton Vance Tax-Managed Growth 1.0 Fund	CAPEX	B	B	B		7.66	12.44	22.72	35.82	107.57	1146.13	970.3		
Eaton Vance Tax-Managed Growth 1.1 Fund Class A	ETTGX	B	B	B		7.57	12.26	22.34	34.58	104.39	51.3	1,604		
Eaton Vance Tax-Managed Growth 1.1 Fund Class B	EMTGX	B	B-	B		7.37	11.85	21.42	31.56	96.79	50.49	1,604		
Eaton Vance Tax-Managed Growth 1.1 Fund Class C	ECTGX	B	B-	B		7.39	11.86	21.45	31.58	96.84	46.1	1,604		
Eaton Vance Tax-Managed Growth 1.1 Fund Class I	EITMX	B	B	B		7.66	12.43	22.67	35.57	106.97	47.92	1,604		
Eaton Vance Tax-Managed Growth 1.2 Fund Class A	EXTGX	B	B	B		7.51	12.18	22.15	33.97	102.73	23.06	768.8		Y
Eaton Vance Tax-Managed Growth 1.2 Fund Class B	EYTGX	B	B-	B		7.31	11.76	21.22	30.97	95.25	22.9	768.8		
Eaton Vance Tax-Managed Growth 1.2 Fund Class C	EZTGX	B	B-	B		7.33	11.76	21.23	30.96	95.23	22.46	768.8		Y
Eaton Vance Tax-Managed Growth 1.2 Fund Institutional Cls	EITGX	B	B	B		7.59	12.30	22.43	34.98	105.20	23.11	768.8		Y
EQ/Common Stock Index Portfolio Class IA	US4049925054	B-	B-	B-	Down	6.79	11.60	20.57	33.23	104.10		5,955	877-222-2144	Y
EQ/Common Stock Index Portfolio Class IB	US4049925138	B-	B-	B-	Down	6.80	11.60	20.58	33.22	104.06		5,955	877-222-2144	Y
EQ/Equity 500 Index Portfolio Class IA	US4049925476	B	B-	B		7.02	11.79	21.09	34.36	106.13		5,594	877-222-2144	Y
EQ/Equity 500 Index Portfolio Class IB	US4049925542	B	B-	B		7.03	11.80	21.09	34.34	106.06		5,594	877-222-2144	Y
EQ/Equity 500 Index Portfolio Class K	US26883L6700	B	B	B		7.09	11.94	21.42	35.27	108.57		5,594	877-222-2144	Y
EQ/UBS Growth and Income Portfolio Class IB	US29364E7022	B-	B-	C+	Down	5.18	9.54	21.52	30.91	109.98		112.4	877-222-2144	Y
Federated Max-Cap Index Fund Class C Shares	MXCCX	B-	B-	B	Down	6.31	10.80	20.38	31.79	99.39	12.52	439.0	800-341-7400	Y
Federated Max-Cap Index Fund Class R Shares	FMXKX	B	B-	B		6.40	11.00	20.82	33.15	102.68	12.7	439.0	800-341-7400	Y
Federated Max-Cap Index Fund Institutional Shares	FISPX	B	B	B		6.68	11.46	21.72	36.20	110.41	12.85	439.0	800-341-7400	Y
Federated Max-Cap Index Fund Service Shares	FMXSX	B	B	B		6.59	11.32	21.32	34.96	107.18	12.71	439.0	800-341-7400	Y
Federated MDT Large Cap Growth Fund Class A Shares	QALGX	B-	B-	C+		7.77	14.51	25.05	26.46	101.48	18.18	88.4	800-341-7400	Y
Federated MDT Large Cap Growth Fund Class B Shares	QBLGX	B-	B-	C+	Up	7.50	14.02	24.05	23.62	93.98	16.66	88.4	800-341-7400	Y
Federated MDT Large Cap Growth Fund Class C Shares	QCLGX	B-	B-	C+	Up	7.51	14.06	24.11	23.66	94.04	16.22	88.4	800-341-7400	Y
Federated MDT Large Cap Growth Fund Institutional Shares	QILGX	B-	B	C+		7.81	14.63	25.31	27.43	104.16	18.91	88.4	800-341-7400	Y
Fidelity Advisor® Capital Development Fund Class A	FDTTX	B	B	B	Up	5.77	10.35	17.73	31.60	94.65	15.99	3,223	617-563-7000	Y
Fidelity Advisor® Capital Development Fund Class C	FDECX	B-	B-	B	Down	5.56	9.91	16.63	27.80	85.22	15.08	3,223	617-563-7000	Y
Fidelity Advisor® Capital Development Fund Class M	FDTZX	B-	B	C+	Down	5.70	10.12	17.11	29.47	89.42	15.6	3,223	617-563-7000	Y
Fidelity Advisor® Capital Development Fund Class O	FDETX	B	B	B	Up	5.87	10.58	18.12	32.81	97.57	16.53	3,223	617-563-7000	
Fidelity Advisor® Capital Development Fund I Class	FDEIX	B	B	B	Up	5.91	10.53	17.96	32.20	96.14	16.61	3,223	617-563-7000	Y
Fidelity Advisor® Diversified Stock Fund Class A	FDTOX	B-	B	C+	Down	6.13	11.53	18.91	29.81	97.25	24.75	2,130	617-563-7000	Y
Fidelity Advisor® Diversified Stock Fund Class C	FDTCX	B-	B-	B-	Down	5.84	10.99	17.77	26.23	88.10	24.02	2,130	617-563-7000	Y

Category: US Equity
Large Cap Blend (con't)

Fund Name	Ticker Symbol	RATINGS: Overall Rating	RATINGS: Reward Rating	RATINGS: Risk Rating	RATINGS: Recent Up/ Downgrade	TOTAL RETURNS & PERFORMANCE: 3-Month Total Return	6-Month Total Return	1-Year Total Return	3-Year Total Return	5-Year Total Return	ASSETS: NAV	Total Assets (MIL)	NEW INVESTORS: Telephone	Open to New Investors
Fidelity Advisor® Diversified Stock Fund Class M	FDTEX	B-	B-	B	Down	6.03	11.33	18.45	28.31	93.13	24.57	2,130	617-563-7000	Y
Fidelity Advisor® Diversified Stock Fund Class O	FDESX	B-	B	C+	Down	6.23	11.76	19.32	31.20	100.47	25.4	2,130	617-563-7000	
Fidelity Advisor® Diversified Stock Fund Class Z	FZACX	B-	B	C+	Down	6.16	11.69	19.22	31.04	100.21	26.01	2,130	617-563-7000	Y
Fidelity Advisor® Diversified Stock Fund I Class	FDTIX	B-	B	C+	Down	6.16	11.65	19.11	30.62	98.96	26.27	2,130	617-563-7000	Y
Fidelity Advisor® Dividend Growth Fund Class A	FADAX	B-	B-	B-	Down	7.46	11.64	19.65	26.36	90.04	17.46	1,087	617-563-7000	Y
Fidelity Advisor® Dividend Growth Fund Class C	FDGCX	B-	C+	B-	Down	7.23	11.25	18.70	23.51	83.11	16.56	1,087	617-563-7000	Y
Fidelity Advisor® Dividend Growth Fund Class M	FDGTX	B-	B-	B-	Down	7.35	11.43	19.32	25.39	87.77	17.38	1,087	617-563-7000	Y
Fidelity Advisor® Dividend Growth Fund Class Z	FZADX	B-	B-	B-	Down	7.53	11.81	20.07	27.87	93.66	18.66	1,087	617-563-7000	Y
Fidelity Advisor® Dividend Growth Fund I Class	FDGIX	B-	B-	B-	Down	7.45	11.73	19.90	27.24	92.32	18.39	1,087	617-563-7000	Y
Fidelity Advisor® Growth & Income Fund Class A	FGIRX	B	B-	B	Up	6.00	10.19	16.57	30.11	94.85	28.38	596.1	617-563-7000	Y
Fidelity Advisor® Growth & Income Fund Class C	FGIUX	B-	B-	B	Down	5.78	9.74	15.63	27.14	87.65	26.67	596.1	617-563-7000	Y
Fidelity Advisor® Growth & Income Fund Class M	FGITX	B	B-	B	Up	5.92	10.03	16.23	29.09	92.49	28.41	596.1	617-563-7000	Y
Fidelity Advisor® Growth & Income Fund Class Z	FGIZX	B	B	B	Up	6.09	10.41	16.98	31.29	98.07	28.92	596.1	617-563-7000	Y
Fidelity Advisor® Growth & Income Fund I Class	FGIOX	B	B	B	Up	6.06	10.32	16.84	31.13	97.83	28.93	596.1	617-563-7000	Y
Fidelity Advisor® Large Cap Fund Class A	FALAX	B	B	B	Up	5.95	10.85	18.17	31.64	106.87	33.26	1,387	617-563-7000	Y
Fidelity Advisor® Large Cap Fund Class C	FLCCX	B-	B-	B	Down	5.75	10.39	17.24	28.64	99.13	30.19	1,387	617-563-7000	Y
Fidelity Advisor® Large Cap Fund Class M	FALGX	B	B	B	Up	5.88	10.68	17.86	30.60	104.19	33.21	1,387	617-563-7000	Y
Fidelity Advisor® Large Cap Fund Class Z	FIDLX	B	B	B	Up	6.04	11.05	18.62	32.84	109.93	34.76	1,387	617-563-7000	Y
Fidelity Advisor® Large Cap Fund I Class	FALIX	B	B	B	Up	6.02	11.00	18.50	32.70	109.71	34.77	1,387	617-563-7000	Y
Fidelity Advisor® Mega Cap Stock Fund Class A	FGTAX	B-	B-	B-	Down	5.70	10.15	17.49	29.65	96.39	17.27	2,556	617-563-7000	Y
Fidelity Advisor® Mega Cap Stock Fund Class C	FGRCX	B-	B-	B-	Down	5.52	9.80	16.62	26.80	89.39	17.03	2,556	617-563-7000	Y
Fidelity Advisor® Mega Cap Stock Fund Class I	FTRIX	B-	B-	B-	Down	5.77	10.29	17.77	30.75	99.30	17.44	2,556	617-563-7000	Y
Fidelity Advisor® Mega Cap Stock Fund Class M	FTGRX	B-	B-	B-	Down	5.69	10.07	17.20	28.69	94.16	17.27	2,556	617-563-7000	Y
Fidelity Advisor® Mega Cap Stock Fund Class Z	FZALX	B-	B	B-	Down	5.87	10.45	17.96	31.28	100.58	17.36	2,556	617-563-7000	Y
Fidelity Advisor® Series Growth & Income Fund	FMALX	B	B	B	Up	6.24	10.75	17.32	31.51	96.51	15.53	1,751	617-563-7000	Y
Fidelity® 500 Index Fund Institutional Class	FXSIX	B	B	B		6.63	11.41	21.78	36.75	111.39	93.45	136,827	617-563-7000	Y
Fidelity® 500 Index Fund Institutional Premium Class	FXAIX	B	B	B		6.64	11.41	21.81	36.85	111.60	93.45	136,827	617-563-7000	Y
Fidelity® 500 Index Fund Investor Class	FUSEX	B	B	B		6.62	11.38	21.72	36.52	110.78	93.44	136,827	617-563-7000	Y
Fidelity® 500 Index Fund Premium Class	FUSVX	B	B	B		6.63	11.40	21.79	36.73	111.29	93.45	136,827	617-563-7000	Y
Fidelity® Disciplined Equity Fund	FDEQX	B-	B-	B-	Down	6.55	11.59	21.53	28.01	101.40	38.79	1,402	617-563-7000	Y
Fidelity® Disciplined Equity Fund Class K	FDEKX	B-	B-	B-	Down	6.55	11.62	21.65	28.40	102.41	38.72	1,402	617-563-7000	Y
Fidelity® Dividend Growth Fund	FDGFX	B-	B-	B-	Down	7.54	11.86	20.13	27.88	93.61	32.83	7,560	617-563-7000	Y
Fidelity® Dividend Growth Fund Class K	FDGKX	B-	B-	B-	Down	7.53	11.89	20.24	28.28	94.72	32.78	7,560	617-563-7000	Y
Fidelity® Export and Multinational Fund	FEXPX	B	B-	B+		7.70	11.70	20.92	32.76	88.20	22.21	1,805	617-563-7000	Y
Fidelity® Export and Multinational Fund Class K	FEXKX	B	B-	B+		7.71	11.77	21.07	33.22	89.40	22.16	1,805	617-563-7000	Y
Fidelity® Growth & Income Portfolio	FGRIX	B	B	B	Up	6.11	10.34	16.88	31.39	98.09	37.87	7,343	617-563-7000	Y
Fidelity® Growth & Income Portfolio Class K	FGIKX	B-	B	B-	Down	6.14	10.45	17.03	31.86	99.38	37.84	7,343	617-563-7000	Y
Fidelity® Large Cap Core Enhanced Index Fund	FLCEX	B	B	B-		7.65	13.27	21.65	32.81	108.03	14.66	590.2	617-563-7000	Y
Fidelity® Large Cap Stock Fund	FLCSX	B	B	B	Up	5.94	10.77	18.14	32.38	108.30	33.46	5,287	617-563-7000	Y
Fidelity® Mega Cap Stock Fund	FGRTX	B-	B-	B-	Down	5.78	10.29	17.77	30.72	99.24	17.43	2,556	617-563-7000	Y
Fidelity® SAI U.S. Minimum Volatility Index Fund	FSUVX	B-	C+	B+	Up	5.26	8.87	18.91			12.52	936.6	617-563-7000	Y
Fidelity® Series 100 Index Fund	FOHIX	B	B	B+		6.98	11.98	22.00	37.90	107.92	17.36	3,541	617-563-7000	Y
Fidelity® Series Growth & Income Fund	FGLGX	B	B	B	Up	6.19	10.74	17.36	31.69	96.66	15.75	13,377	617-563-7000	Y
Fidelity® Total Market Index Fund Class F	FFSMX	B	B	B		6.32	11.19	21.17	35.83	109.47	76.37	48,089	617-563-7000	Y
Fidelity® Total Market Index Fund Institutional Class	FSKTX	B	B	B		6.32	11.18	21.15	35.79	109.34	76.36	48,089	617-563-7000	Y
Fidelity® Total Mkt Index Fund Inst Premium Cls	FSKAX	B	B	B		6.33	11.19	21.18	35.85	109.47	76.35	48,089	617-563-7000	Y
Fidelity® Total Market Index Fund Investor Class	FSTMX	B	B	B		6.30	11.15	21.08	35.57	108.77	76.37	48,089	617-563-7000	Y
Fidelity® Total Market Index Fund Premium Class	FSTVX	B	B	B		6.33	11.19	21.14	35.77	109.27	76.37	48,089	617-563-7000	Y
First Eagle U.S. Value Fund Class A	FEVAX	B-	C+	B	Down	4.45	7.74	12.79	21.72	57.06	20.09	2,151	800-334-2143	Y
First Eagle U.S. Value Fund Class C	FEVCX	B-	C+	B	Down	4.26	7.33	11.88	18.96	51.14	19.34	2,151	800-334-2143	Y
First Eagle U.S. Value Fund Class I	FEVIX	B-	C+	B	Down	4.49	7.83	13.04	22.71	59.04	20.39	2,151	800-334-2143	Y
First Eagle U.S. Value Fund Class R6	FEVRX	B-	C+	B	Down	4.48	7.87	13.02	22.70	59.02	20.39	2,151	800-334-2143	Y

Category: US Equity Large Cap Blend (con't)

Fund Name	Ticker Symbol	RATINGS: Overall Rating	Reward Rating	Risk Rating	Recent Up/ Downgrade	TOTAL RETURNS & PERFORMANCE: 3-Month Total Return	6-Month Total Return	1-Year Total Return	3-Year Total Return	5-Year Total Return	ASSETS: NAV	Total Assets (MIL)	NEW INVESTORS: Telephone	Open to New Investors
First Investors Growth and Income Fund Advisor Class	FGIPX	B-	B-	B	Down	6.74	10.50	18.51	24.92	89.77	24	1,948	800-423-4026	Y
First Investors Growth and Income Fund Class A	FGINX	B-	B-	B	Down	6.66	10.27	18.07	23.49	86.52	23.83	1,948	800-423-4026	Y
First Investors Growth and Income Fund Class B	FGIBX	B-	C+	B	Up	6.44	9.84	17.17	20.66	79.44	22.03	1,948	800-423-4026	Y
First Investors Growth and Income Fund Institutional Class	FGIQX	B-	B-	B	Down	6.78	10.51	18.53	25.01	90.06	23.93	1,948	800-423-4026	Y
First Trust Enhanced Equity Income Fund	FFA	B-	B-	B-	Up	3.53	6.75	16.02	24.22	72.87	16.51	333.6	866-848-9727	Y
FMI Large Cap Fund	FMIHX	B-	B-	B-	Down	6.01	9.83	19.18	31.14	96.40	21.5	6,570	800-811-5311	
FMI Large Cap Fund Institutional Class	FMIQX	B-	B-	B-	Down	6.00	9.87	19.29	31.24	96.54	21.47	6,570	800-811-5311	Y
Fort Pitt Capital Total Return Fund	FPCGX	B	B	B		7.02	13.79	21.91	38.86	97.96	26.09	71.6		Y
Franklin Focused Core Equity Fund Class A	FCEQX	B-	C+	B	Up	4.19	6.17	12.06	14.46	85.66	16.16	97.8	650-312-2000	Y
Franklin Focused Core Equity Fund Class Adv	FCEZX	B-	C+	B	Up	4.32	6.28	12.40	15.35	88.23	16.4	97.8	650-312-2000	Y
Franklin Focused Core Equity Fund Class R	FCERX	B-	C+	B	Up	4.18	6.12	11.92	13.88	84.03	15.95	97.8	650-312-2000	Y
Franklin Focused Core Equity Fund Class R6	FEFCX	B-	C+	B	Up	4.30	6.39	12.50	15.84	89.38	16.46	97.8	650-312-2000	Y
Franklin Rising Dividends Fund Advisor Class	FRDAX	B	B	B-		6.77	12.02	20.59	32.44	93.39	61.09	19,377	650-312-2000	Y
Franklin Rising Dividends Fund Class A	FRDPX	B	B	B-		6.70	11.89	20.28	31.46	90.96	61.16	19,377	650-312-2000	Y
Franklin Rising Dividends Fund Class C	FRDTX	B-	B-	B-	Down	6.51	11.46	19.40	28.53	83.90	60.08	19,377	650-312-2000	Y
Franklin Rising Dividends Fund Class R	FRDRX	B-	B	B-	Down	6.64	11.73	19.98	30.48	88.54	60.97	19,377	650-312-2000	Y
Franklin Rising Dividends Fund R6 Class	FRISX	B	B	B-		6.82	12.11	20.78	33.05	94.48	61.09	19,377	650-312-2000	
Frontier MFG Global Plus Fund Institutional Class	FMGPX	B-	C+	B	Up	6.21	10.18	24.48			12.39	439.1		Y
Frontier MFG Global Plus Fund Service Class	FMPSX	B-	C+	B	Up	6.10	10.08	24.36			12.39	439.1		Y
Gabelli Asset Fund Class A	GATAX	B-	B-	C+	Down	5.37	9.87	20.17	25.07	77.85	58.36	2,698	914-921-5135	Y
Gabelli Asset Fund Class AAA	GABAX	B-	B-	C+	Down	5.36	9.88	20.16	25.06	77.85	58.97	2,698	914-921-5135	Y
Gabelli Asset Fund Class I	GABIX	B-	B-	C+	Down	5.44	10.02	20.48	26.02	80.09	58.85	2,698	914-921-5135	Y
Gabelli Asset Fund T	GALTX	B-	B-	C+	Down	5.40	9.92	20.20	25.10	77.91	58.91	2,698	914-921-5135	Y
Gabelli Dividend Growth Fund Class AAA	GABBX	B-	C+	B-	Up	2.39	6.35	12.10	16.20	67.13	17.23	29.0	914-921-5135	Y
Gabelli Equity Trust	GAB	B	B	C+	Up	3.09	9.82	21.95	27.80	94.83	6.47	1,583	914-921-5135	Y
Gabelli ESG Fund Class A	SRIAX	B	C+	B+	Up	2.82	5.27	13.23	19.84	63.01	15.93	66.9	914-921-5135	Y
Gabelli ESG Fund Class AAA	SRIGX	B	C+	B+	Up	2.88	5.33	13.29	19.90	63.05	15.95	66.9	914-921-5135	Y
Gabelli ESG Fund Class C	SRICX	B	C+	B+	Up	2.66	4.94	12.43	17.22	57.07	14.78	66.9	914-921-5135	Y
Gabelli ESG Fund Class I	SRIDX	B	C+	B+	Up	2.96	5.43	13.52	20.74	65.05	16.27	66.9	914-921-5135	Y
GE RSP U.S. Equity Fund	GESSX	B-	B-	B-	Down	4.57	9.01	20.49	28.62	102.25	52.45	5,503	800-242-0134	Y
General American Investors Co. Inc.	GAM	B-	C+	B	Up	2.91	7.51	16.61	21.85	74.37	40.39	1,064	212-916-8400	Y
Glenmede Large Cap Core Portfolio	GTLOX	B	B	B		7.45	13.71	24.76	39.45	129.39	28.2	2,775	800-442-8299	Y
Glenmede Large Cap Core Portfolio Institutional Shares	GTLIX	B	B	B		7.51	13.81	25.01	40.02	130.34	28.21	2,775	800-442-8299	Y
Glenmede Strategic Equity Portfolio	GTCEX	B	B	B		6.96	12.41	25.92	41.27	113.93	24.34	213.6	800-442-8299	Y
GMO Quality Fund Class III	GQETX	B+	B	A-	Up	7.58	10.97	29.06	42.27	105.01	24.44	8,453	617-330-7500	Y
GMO Quality Fund Class IV	GQEFX	B+	B	A-		7.60	10.94	29.06	42.45	105.50	24.47	8,453	617-330-7500	Y
GMO Quality Fund Class V	GQLFX	B+	B	A-		7.62	10.99	29.11	42.58	105.80	24.48	8,453	617-330-7500	Y
GMO Quality Fund Class VI	GQLOX	B+	B	A-		7.64	11.03	29.18	42.72	106.06	24.44	8,453	617-330-7500	Y
GMO U.S. Equity Allocation Fund Class III	GMUEX	B	B	B+		4.76	10.58	16.67	31.98	91.57	15.4	1,528	617-330-7500	Y
GMO U.S. Equity Allocation Fund Class IV	GMRTX	B	B	B+		6.36	12.25	18.42	34.28	95.00	15.41	1,528	617-330-7500	Y
GMO U.S. Equity Allocation Fund Class V	GMEQX	B	B	B		4.71	10.52	16.63	31.99	91.58	15.33	1,528	617-330-7500	Y
GMO U.S. Equity Allocation Fund Class VI	GMCQX	B	B	B		4.66	10.49	16.61	32.21	92.16	15.29	1,528	617-330-7500	Y
Goldman Sachs U.S. Equity Dividend & Premium Fund Cls A	GSPAX	B	B-	B		4.61	8.51	14.82	31.27	84.38	13.15	3,487	800-526-7384	Y
Goldman Sachs U.S. Equity Dividend & Premium Fund Cls C	GSPQX	B-	B-	B	Down	4.42	8.13	13.98	28.33	77.77	13.1	3,487	800-526-7384	Y
Goldman Sachs U.S. Equity Dividend & Premium Fund Inst Cls	GSPKX	B	B-	B+		4.72	8.74	15.30	32.76	88.30	13.12	3,487	800-526-7384	Y
Goldman Sachs U.S. Equity Dividend & Premium Fund Inv Cls	GVIRX	B	B-	B+		4.68	8.67	15.17	32.24	86.76	13.13	3,487	800-526-7384	Y
Goldman Sachs U.S. Equity Insights Fund Class A	GSSQX	B	B	B-		5.78	12.12	23.44	33.72	115.64	46.64	689.6	800-526-7384	Y
Goldman Sachs U.S. Equity Insights Fund Class C	GSUSX	B	B	B-	Up	5.60	11.73	22.53	30.75	107.74	42.1	689.6	800-526-7384	Y
Goldman Sachs U.S. Equity Insights Fund Class R	GSURX	B	B	B-		5.73	11.98	23.12	32.69	112.92	45.78	689.6	800-526-7384	Y
Goldman Sachs U.S. Equity Insights Fund Class R6	GSEUX	B	B	B-		5.90	12.36	23.94	34.96	117.19	48	689.6	800-526-7384	Y
Goldman Sachs U.S. Equity Insights Fund Institutional Cls	GSELX	B	B	B-		5.90	12.35	23.93	35.31	119.99	48.03	689.6	800-526-7384	Y
Goldman Sachs U.S. Equity Insights Fund Investor Class	GSUTX	B	B	B-		5.86	12.27	23.75	34.73	118.36	46.01	689.6	800-526-7384	Y

Category: US Equity Large Cap Blend (con't)

Fund Name	Ticker Symbol	RATINGS: Overall Rating	Reward Rating	Risk Rating	Recent Up/ Downgrade	TOTAL RETURNS & PERFORMANCE: 3-Month Total Return	6-Month Total Return	1-Year Total Return	3-Year Total Return	5-Year Total Return	ASSETS: NAV	Total Assets (MIL)	NEW INVESTORS: Telephone	Open to New Investors
Goldman Sachs U.S. Equity Insights Fund Service Class	GSESX	B	B	B-		5.75	12.07	23.30	33.29	114.51	46.38	689.6	800-526-7384	Y
Goldman Sachs U.S. Tax-Managed Equity Fund Class A	GCTAX	B	B	B-	Up	5.87	10.94	19.87	29.10	107.89	22.37	1,456	800-526-7384	Y
Goldman Sachs U.S. Tax-Managed Equity Fund Class C	GCTCX	B-	B-	B-	Down	5.67	10.50	18.92	26.23	100.27	21.24	1,456	800-526-7384	Y
Goldman Sachs U.S. Tax-Managed Equity Fund Inst Cls	GCTIX	B	B	B-		5.98	11.13	20.29	30.69	112.08	22.71	1,456	800-526-7384	Y
Goldman Sachs U.S. Tax-Managed Equity Fund Investor Class	GQIRX	B	B	B-		5.94	11.09	20.14	30.10	110.53	22.7	1,456	800-526-7384	Y
Goldman Sachs U.S. Tax-Managed Equity Fund Service Class	GCTSX	B	B	B-	Up	5.85	10.89	19.70	28.73	106.84	22.51	1,456	800-526-7384	Y
Golub Group Equity Fund	GGEFX	B	B-	A-	Up	2.52	3.70	12.52	25.21	84.45	18.22	59.5		Y
Gotham Enhanced 500 Fund Institutional Class	GENFX	B-	C+	B-	Up	11.40	19.85	25.73	37.22		12.8	27.0	877-974-6852	Y
Gotham Index Plus Fund Institutional Class	GINDX	B-	C+	B	Up	11.88	20.71	26.05			14.48	227.9	877-974-6852	Y
Great Lakes Disciplined Equity Fund Institutional Class	GLDNX	B	B	B		7.94	11.33	18.56	32.82	107.70	15.48	48.0		Y
Great-West S&P 500® Index Fund Class L	MXVJX	B	B-	B		7.01	11.74	20.94	33.50	104.05		3,261		Y
Great-West S&P 500® Index Fund Institutional Class	MXKWX	B	B	B		7.18	12.08	21.64	35.69	108.57		3,261		Y
Great-West S&P 500® Index Fund Investor Class	MXVIX	B	B	B		7.06	11.91	21.24	34.47	106.69		3,261		Y
Green Owl Intrinsic Value Fund	GOWLX	B	B	B-	Up	5.45	10.88	17.11	29.42	90.12	19.42	84.5		Y
Guggenheim Enhanced Equity Income	GPM	B	B	B	Up	6.24	10.72	20.46	35.79	76.45	9.02	438.1	312-827-0100	Y
Guggenheim StylePlus - Large Core Fund Class A	SECEX	B	B	B		6.81	11.54	21.94	37.70	108.63	22.7	223.2	212-739-0700	Y
Guggenheim StylePlus - Large Core Fund Class C	SFECX	B-	B-	B	Down	6.58	11.08	20.92	34.05	99.22	16.98	223.2	212-739-0700	Y
Guggenheim StylePlus - Large Core Fund Class P	SFEPX	B	B	B		6.78	11.50	21.93	37.23	107.92	22.5	223.2	212-739-0700	Y
Guggenheim StylePlus - Large Core Fund Institutional	GILIX	B	B	B		6.94	11.74	22.32	39.42	111.30	22.54	223.2	212-739-0700	Y
GuideStone Funds Equity Index Fund Institutional Class	GEQYX	B	B	B		6.77	11.74	21.96	36.70	110.68	29.43	962.8	214-720-1171	Y
GuideStone Funds Equity Index Fund Investor Class	GEQZX	B	B	B		6.74	11.62	21.65	35.58	108.46	29.45	962.8	214-720-1171	Y
Guinness Atkinson™ Global Innovators Fund Inst Cls	GINNX	B+	A	C+	Up	6.31	15.71	35.06	42.59	138.54	45.09	225.4	800-915-6566	Y
Guinness Atkinson™ Global Innovators Fund Investor Class	IWIRX	B+	A	C+	Up	6.24	15.55	34.74	41.86	137.33	44.98	225.4	800-915-6566	Y
Harbor Large Cap Value Fund Administrative Class	HRLVX	B	B	B		5.88	10.30	21.93	44.51	113.16	14.94	805.0	800-422-1050	Y
Harbor Large Cap Value Fund Institutional Class	HAVLX	B	B	B		5.96	10.37	22.30	45.79	115.88	14.93	805.0	800-422-1050	Y
Harbor Large Cap Value Fund Investor Class	HILVX	B	B	B		5.86	10.30	21.85	44.23	111.98	15.08	805.0	800-422-1050	Y
Harbor Large Cap Value Fund Retirement Class	HNLVX	B	B	B		6.00	10.49	22.38	46.10	116.34	14.93	805.0	800-422-1050	Y
Hartford Capital Appreciation HLS Fund Class IA	HIACX	B-	B-	B-	Down	4.98	8.74	22.13	29.27	97.66	48.16	5,083	888-843-7824	Y
Hartford Capital Appreciation HLS Fund Class IB	HIBCX	B-	B-	B-	Down	4.90	8.57	21.81	28.28	95.17	47.48	5,083	888-843-7824	Y
Hartford Capital Appreciation HLS Fund Class IC	HCPCX	B-	B-	B-	Down	4.83	8.44	21.50	27.32	93.43	47.76	5,083	888-843-7824	Y
Hartford Stock HLS Fund Class IA	HSTAX	B	B-	B+		5.75	9.71	19.84	30.98	96.97	79.57	1,527	888-843-7824	Y
Hartford Stock HLS Fund Class IB	HIBSX	B	B-	B+		5.68	9.56	19.54	30.00	94.51	79.54	1,527	888-843-7824	Y
Haverford Quality Growth Stock Fund	HAVGX	B-	C+	B-	Down	7.17	9.34	18.46	20.90	84.63	16.86	193.9		Y
HCM Tactical Growth Fund Class A	HCMGX	B	A	C+	Up	9.09	16.40	33.23	42.06		13.55	99.9	855-969-8464	Y
HCM Tactical Growth Fund Class I	HCMIX	B	A	C+	Up	9.09	16.39	33.20	42.01		13.56	99.9	855-969-8464	Y
HCM Tactical Growth Fund Class R	HCMSX	B	A	C+	Up	9.09	16.39	33.20	42.01		13.56	99.9	855-969-8464	Y
HCM Tactical Growth Fund Investor Class	HCMDX	B	B+	C	Up	9.00	16.02	32.40	39.51		13.32	99.9	855-969-8464	Y
Hennessler Equity Fund Institutional Class	HEQCX	B	C+	B+		3.82	8.06	10.85	22.30	88.31	6.22	42.1		Y
Hennessler Equity Fund Investor Class	HEQFX	B	C+	B		3.84	7.81	10.37	20.47	83.67	5.86	42.1		Y
Homestead Stock Index Fund	HSTIX	B	B	B		6.47	11.09	21.16	34.63	106.01	20.02	144.5		Y
Independent Franchise Partners US Equity Fund	IFPUX	B	B-	A		5.46	5.22	19.92	39.71	99.59	17.73	1,999		Y
Index Funds S&P 500 Equal Weight No Load Shares	INDEX	B-	C+	B	Up	6.25	10.02	18.78			30.36	24.3	844-464-6339	Y
Integrity Growth & Income Fund Class A	IGIAX	B-	B-	B-	Down	7.43	11.65	18.67	26.51	76.19	53.51	35.1	800-276-1262	Y
Integrity Growth & Income Fund Class C	IGIUX	B-	C+	B-	Down	7.23	11.23	17.78	23.93	70.03	53.49	35.1	800-276-1262	Y
Integrity Growth & Income Fund Class I	IGIVX	B-	B-	B-	Down	7.49	11.77	18.96	26.99	76.85	53.49	35.1	800-276-1262	Y
Invesco Charter Fund Class A	CHTRX	B-	C+	B-	Down	2.43	4.82	13.25	16.11	63.89	18.05	3,780	800-659-1005	Y
Invesco Equally-Weighted S&P 500 Fund Class A	VADAX	B-	B-	B-	Down	6.07	9.76	18.26	30.00	105.75	59.97	8,015	800-659-1005	Y
Invesco Equally-Weighted S&P 500 Fund Class B	VADBX	B-	B-	B-	Down	5.87	9.33	17.36	27.08	98.12	59.65	8,015	800-659-1005	
Invesco Equally-Weighted S&P 500 Fund Class C	VADCX	B-	B-	B-	Down	5.91	9.38	17.41	27.25	98.40	57.56	8,015	800-659-1005	Y
Invesco Equally-Weighted S&P 500 Fund Class R	VADRX	B-	B-	B-	Down	6.00	9.60	17.96	29.03	103.17	59.69	8,015	800-659-1005	Y
Invesco Equally-Weighted S&P 500 Fund Class R6	VADFX	B-	B	B-	Down	6.17	9.94	18.70	31.48	109.33	60.56	8,015	800-659-1005	Y
Invesco Equally-Weighted S&P 500 Fund Class Y	VADDX	B-	B-	B-	Down	6.13	9.88	18.55	30.97	108.32	60.5	8,015	800-659-1005	Y

Category: US Equity Large Cap Blend (con't)

Fund Name	Ticker Symbol	Overall Rating	Reward Rating	Risk Rating	Recent Up/ Downgrade	3-Month Total Return	6-Month Total Return	1-Year Total Return	3-Year Total Return	5-Year Total Return	NAV	Total Assets (Mil.)	Telephone	Open to New Investors
		RATINGS				TOTAL RETURNS & PERFORMANCE					ASSETS		NEW INVESTORS	
Invesco S&P 500 Index Class R6	SPISX	B	B	B		6.56	11.28	21.49	35.56	108.30	29.21	1,167	800-659-1005	Y
Invesco S&P 500 Index Fund Class A	SPIAX	B	B	B		6.48	11.09	21.12	34.53	105.65	28.88	1,167	800-659-1005	Y
Invesco S&P 500 Index Fund Class B	SPIBX	B-	B-	B	Down	6.29	10.67	20.26	31.57	98.11	28.27	1,167	800-659-1005	
Invesco S&P 500 Index Fund Class C	SPICX	B-	B-	B	Down	6.32	10.75	20.27	31.61	98.25	27.93	1,167	800-659-1005	Y
Invesco S&P 500 Index Fund Class Y	SPIDX	B	B	B		6.56	11.24	21.45	35.52	108.23	29.21	1,167	800-659-1005	Y
iShares Russell 1000 Large-Cap Index Fund Class K	BRGKX	B	B	B		6.54	11.31	21.59	35.96	109.65	17.76	205.4	800-441-7762	Y
iShares Russell 1000 Large-Cap Index Fund Inst Shares	BRGNX	B	B	B		6.50	11.25	21.45	35.65	109.78	17.82	205.4	800-441-7762	Y
iShares Russell 1000 Large-Cap Index Fund Inv A Shares	BRGAX	B	B	B		6.46	11.10	21.15	34.60	106.56	17.72	205.4	800-441-7762	Y
iShares S&P 500 Index Fund Class K	WFSPX	B	B	B		6.64	11.40	21.77	36.70	111.02	318.38	12,674	800-441-7762	Y
iShares S&P 500 Index Fund Institutional Shares	BSPIX	B	B	B		6.61	11.36	21.68	36.41	110.32	318.31	12,674	800-441-7762	Y
iShares S&P 500 Index Fund Investor A Shares	BSPAX	B	B	B		6.55	11.22	21.38	35.39	107.71	318.24	12,674	800-441-7762	Y
iShares S&P 500 Index Fund Investor C1 Shares	BSPZX	B-	B-	B	Down	6.36	10.83	20.51	32.49	100.39	318.76	12,674	800-441-7762	Y
iShares S&P 500 Index Fund Service Shares	BSPSX	B	B	B		6.59	11.30	21.54	35.93	109.04	318.3	12,674	800-441-7762	Y
Ivy Dividend Opportunities Fund Class A	IVDAX	B-	C+	B-	Down	4.24	8.64	15.28	19.31	73.51	18.86	901.1	800-777-6472	Y
Ivy Dividend Opportunities Fund Class E	IDIEX	B-	C+	B-	Down	4.29	8.76	15.41	19.45	73.25	18.79	901.1	800-777-6472	Y
Ivy Dividend Opportunities Fund Class I	IVDIX	B-	C+	B-	Down	4.36	8.88	15.69	20.48	76.26	18.94	901.1	800-777-6472	Y
Ivy Dividend Opportunities Fund Class N	IDOTX	B-	C+	B-	Down	4.40	8.92	15.84	20.99	76.28	18.97	901.1	800-777-6472	Y
Ivy Dividend Opportunities Fund Class Y	IVDYX	B-	C+	B-	Down	4.29	8.71	15.37	19.57	74.09	18.9	901.1	800-777-6472	Y
Jamestown Equity Fund	JAMEX	B-	C+	B	Down	7.83	11.63	19.74	22.66	87.01	22.3	38.8	866-738-1126	Y
Janus Henderson Growth And Income Fund Class A	JDNAX	B	B	B		8.99	14.18	24.70	41.02	112.08	55.07	5,178	877-335-2687	Y
Janus Henderson Growth And Income Fund Class C	JGICX	B	B	B		8.76	13.74	23.77	37.94	104.08	54.41	5,178	877-335-2687	Y
Janus Henderson Growth And Income Fund Class D	JNGIX	B	B	B		9.03	14.26	24.90	41.67	113.81	55.12	5,178	877-335-2687	
Janus Henderson Growth And Income Fund Class I	JGINX	B	B	B		9.04	14.29	24.97	41.99	114.58	55.15	5,178	877-335-2687	Y
Janus Henderson Growth And Income Fund Class N	JDNNX	B	B	B		9.05	14.31	24.96	41.72	113.89	55.07	5,178	877-335-2687	Y
Janus Henderson Growth And Income Fund Class R	JDNRX	B	B	B		8.86	13.90	24.13	39.13	107.51	54.78	5,178	877-335-2687	Y
Janus Henderson Growth And Income Fund Class S	JADGX	B	B	B		8.92	14.05	24.45	40.23	110.20	55.03	5,178	877-335-2687	Y
Janus Henderson Growth And Income Fund Class T	JAGIX	B	B	B		8.99	14.20	24.77	41.33	112.94	55.08	5,178	877-335-2687	Y
Janus Henderson U.S. Managed Volatility Fund Class A	JRSAX	B	B	B		5.20	11.06	20.18	32.06	100.26	11	1,285	877-335-2687	Y
Janus Henderson U.S. Managed Volatility Fund Class C	JRSCX	B	B	B		5.07	10.65	19.32	29.44	93.65	10.71	1,285	877-335-2687	Y
Janus Henderson U.S. Managed Volatility Fund Class S	JRSSX	B	B	B		5.22	10.99	20.05	31.69	100.33	10.98	1,285	877-335-2687	Y
Janus Henderson VIT U.S. Low Vol Port Serv Shares	US4710213780	B	B-	A+		6.69	8.27	15.44	30.28	96.07	17.43	1,151	877-335-2687	Y
JNL/American Funds Growth-Income Fund Class A	US46644W3280	B	B	B		5.55	11.26	21.87	35.71	103.24	22.23	5,732		Y
JNL/American Funds Growth-Income Fund Class I	US46644W3108	B	B	B		5.64	11.40	22.18	36.57	105.30	22.47	5,732		Y
JNL/AQR Large Cap Relaxed Constraint Equity Fund Class A	US46644W7166	B-	B	B-	Down	6.16	12.41	22.98	29.37	102.93	12.75	646.6		Y
JNL/AQR Large Cap Relaxed Constraint Equity Fund Class I	US46644W6903	B	B	B-	Up	6.24	12.49	23.23	30.17	105.12	12.93	646.6		Y
JNL/DFA U.S. Core Equity Fund Class A	US46649B7588	B	B	B-	Up	6.77	11.74	20.22	33.03	102.70	13.72	1,189		Y
JNL/DFA U.S. Core Equity Fund Class I	US46649B7414	B	B	B-	Up	6.92	11.94	20.54	33.90	104.70	14.52	1,189		Y
JNL/Mellon Capital S&P 500 Index Fund Class A	US46648M6562	B	B	B		6.50	11.09	21.16	34.69	106.08	21.94	7,748		Y
JNL/Mellon Capital S&P 500 Index Fund Class I	US46648M6497	B	B	B		6.60	11.26	21.48	35.30	107.71	22.45	7,748		Y
John Hancock Fundamental Large Cap Core Fund Class A	TAGRX	B	B	B		4.29	9.32	20.19	38.73	102.88	48.82	5,199	800-225-5913	Y
John Hancock Fundamental Large Cap Core Fund Class B	TSGWX	B	B	B	Up	4.10	8.91	19.28	35.62	95.37	43.61	5,199	800-225-5913	
John Hancock Fundamental Large Cap Core Fund Class C	JHLVX	B	B	B	Up	4.08	8.89	19.28	35.63	95.41	43.6	5,199	800-225-5913	Y
John Hancock Fundamental Large Cap Core Fund Class I	JLVIX	B	B	B		4.34	9.43	20.49	39.80	105.63	50.94	5,199	800-225-5913	Y
John Hancock Fundamental Large Cap Core Fund Class NAV	US47803N5547	B	B	B		4.38	9.50	20.54	39.13	103.47	51.01	5,199	800-225-5913	Y
John Hancock Fundamental Large Cap Core Fund Class R1	JLCRX	B	B	B		4.17	9.08	19.73	37.09	99.05	50.29	5,199	800-225-5913	Y
John Hancock Fundamental Large Cap Core Fund Class R2	JLCYX	B	B	B		4.26	9.23	20.03	38.14	101.83	50.82	5,199	800-225-5913	Y
John Hancock Fundamental Large Cap Core Fund Class R3	JLCHX	B	B	B		4.21	9.16	19.86	37.55	100.08	50.41	5,199	800-225-5913	Y
John Hancock Fundamental Large Cap Core Fund Class R4	JLCFX	B	B	B		4.30	9.36	20.31	39.16	104.05	50.71	5,199	800-225-5913	Y
John Hancock Fundamental Large Cap Core Fund Class R5	JLCVX	B	B	B		4.36	9.47	20.54	39.98	106.03	51.02	5,199	800-225-5913	Y
John Hancock Fundamental Large Cap Core Fund Class R6	JLCWX	B	B	B		4.38	9.52	20.64	40.28	106.69	51.03	5,199	800-225-5913	Y
John Hancock Funds II U.S. Growth Fund Class 1	JHUPX	B	B	B+		6.76	13.19	29.80	34.45	95.49	10.1	122.4	800-225-5913	Y
John Hancock Funds II U.S. Growth Fund Class A	JHUAX	B	B	B+		6.66	13.06	29.27	32.94	91.51	10.14	122.4	800-225-5913	Y

Category: US Equity Large Cap Blend (con't)

Fund Name	Ticker Symbol	RATINGS Overall Rating	Reward Rating	Risk Rating	Recent Up/ Downgrade	TOTAL RETURNS & PERFORMANCE 3-Month Total Return	6-Month Total Return	1-Year Total Return	3-Year Total Return	5-Year Total Return	ASSETS NAV	Total Assets (MIL)	NEW INVESTORS Telephone	Open to New Investors
John Hancock Funds II U.S. Growth Fund Class C	JHUCX	B	B	B		6.45	12.60	28.39	30.14	85.39	10.12	122.4	800-225-5913	Y
John Hancock Funds II U.S. Growth Fund Class I	JHUIX	B	B	B+		6.72	13.15	29.59	34.13	94.77	10.1	122.4	800-225-5913	Y
John Hancock Funds II U.S. Growth Fund Class NAV	JHUMX	B+	B	B+	Up	6.77	13.18	30.20	35.00	96.46	10.13	122.4	800-225-5913	Y
John Hancock Funds II U.S. Growth Fund Class R6	JUSEX	B+	B	B+	Up	6.79	13.22	29.83	34.77	96.13	10.1	122.4	800-225-5913	Y
Johnson Enhanced Return Fund	JENHX	B	B	B		6.21	10.94	21.38	37.23	114.06	16.27	135.6		Y
Johnson Equity Income Fund	JEQIX	B-	B-	B-	Down	7.60	12.16	25.02	29.79	87.72	25.12	196.0		Y
JPMorgan Equity Index Fund Class A	OGEAX	B	B	B		7.15	11.85	21.99	35.81	108.02	40.92	1,892	800-480-4111	Y
JPMorgan Equity Index Fund Class C	OEICX	B	B-	B		7.01	11.50	21.29	33.03	100.70	40.56	1,892	800-480-4111	Y
JPMorgan Equity Index Fund Class I	HLEIX	B	B	B		7.23	12.00	22.33	36.85	110.67	40.97	1,892	800-480-4111	Y
JPMorgan Equity Index Fund Class R6	OGFAX	B	B	B		7.27	12.09	22.52	37.16	111.14	40.97	1,892	800-480-4111	Y
JPMorgan Intrepid America Fund Class A	JIAAX	B	B	B-	Up	8.47	14.55	22.99	30.22	108.19	39.91	4,398	800-480-4111	Y
JPMorgan Intrepid America Fund Class C	JIACX	B-	B-	B-	Down	8.32	14.24	22.35	28.28	103.10	39.74	4,398	800-480-4111	Y
JPMorgan Intrepid America Fund Class I	JPIAX	B	B	B-	Up	8.52	14.67	23.30	31.32	111.03	41.01	4,398	800-480-4111	Y
JPMorgan Intrepid America Fund Class R2	JIAZX	B-	B-	B-	Down	8.40	14.42	22.68	29.28	105.66	39.09	4,398	800-480-4111	Y
JPMorgan Intrepid America Fund Class R5	JIARX	B	B	B-	Up	8.59	14.80	23.52	32.02	113.00	40.88	4,398	800-480-4111	Y
JPMorgan Intrepid America Fund Class R6	JIAPX	B	B	B-	Up	8.59	14.83	23.63	32.05	112.20	40.2	4,398	800-480-4111	Y
JPMorgan Intrepid Sustainable Equity Fund Class A Shares	JICAX	B-	B-	B-	Down	4.97	10.47	20.98	31.59	106.65	40.76	20.4	800-480-4111	Y
JPMorgan Intrepid Sustainable Equity Fund Class C Shares	JICCX	B-	B-	B-	Down	4.82	10.19	20.38	29.60	101.55	40.02	20.4	800-480-4111	Y
JPMorgan Intrepid Sustainable Equity Fund I Class	JIISX	B-	B-	B	Down	5.02	10.59	21.28	32.56	109.25	40.98	20.4	800-480-4111	Y
JPMorgan Tax Aware Equity Fund Class A	JPEAX	B	B	B-		7.08	11.31	22.83	35.56	112.65	33.29	1,313	800-480-4111	Y
JPMorgan Tax Aware Equity Fund Class C	JPECX	B	B	B-		6.91	11.04	22.21	33.56	107.36	33.01	1,313	800-480-4111	Y
JPMorgan U.S. Dynamic Plus Fund Class A	JPSAX	B	B	B-	Up	7.29	13.62	20.10	28.51	103.81	18.81	340.2	800-480-4111	Y
JPMorgan U.S. Dynamic Plus Fund Class C	JPSCX	B-	B-	B-	Down	7.15	13.39	19.52	26.58	98.81	18.14	340.2	800-480-4111	Y
JPMorgan U.S. Dynamic Plus Fund Class I	JILSX	B	B	B-		7.33	13.79	20.38	29.50	106.38	19.34	340.2	800-480-4111	Y
JPMorgan U.S. Equity Fund Class A	JUEAX	B	B	B-		6.73	11.26	21.12	33.15	110.32	16.24	15,686	800-480-4111	Y
JPMorgan U.S. Equity Fund Class C	JUECX	B-	B	B-	Down	6.67	11.05	20.49	31.25	105.31	15.77	15,686	800-480-4111	Y
JPMorgan U.S. Equity Fund Class I	JUESX	B	B	B-		6.84	11.41	21.40	34.01	112.38	16.28	15,686	800-480-4111	Y
JPMorgan U.S. Equity Fund Class L	JMUEX	B	B	B-		6.87	11.53	21.52	34.51	113.91	16.3	15,686	800-480-4111	Y
JPMorgan U.S. Equity Fund Class R2	JUEZX	B-	B	B-	Down	6.72	11.13	20.76	32.21	107.71	16.11	15,686	800-480-4111	Y
JPMorgan U.S. Equity Fund Class R3	JUEPX	B	B	B-		6.76	11.23	21.02	33.18	110.74	16.19	15,686	800-480-4111	Y
JPMorgan U.S. Equity Fund Class R4	JUEQX	B	B	B-		6.85	11.44	21.37	34.21	113.43	16.27	15,686	800-480-4111	Y
JPMorgan U.S. Equity Fund Class R5	JUSRX	B	B	B-		6.87	11.49	21.58	34.71	114.36	16.3	15,686	800-480-4111	Y
JPMorgan U.S. Equity Fund Class R6	JUEMX	B	B	B-		6.88	11.58	21.70	35.00	115.09	16.33	15,686	800-480-4111	Y
JPMorgan U.S. Large Cap Core Plus Fund Class A Shares	JLCAX	B-	B	B-	Down	6.74	11.28	21.23	30.87	109.69	29.6	9,648	800-480-4111	
JPMorgan U.S. Large Cap Core Plus Fund Class C Shares	JLPCX	B-	B	B-	Down	6.62	11.00	20.58	28.92	104.48	28.24	9,648	800-480-4111	
JPMorgan U.S. Large Cap Core Plus Fund Class I Shares	JLPSX	B-	B	B-	Down	6.81	11.41	21.48	31.86	112.29	29.96	9,648	800-480-4111	
JPMorgan U.S. Large Cap Core Plus Fund Class R2 Shares	JLPZX	B	B	B		6.66	11.11	20.86	29.87	107.01	28.87	9,648	800-480-4111	
JPMorgan U.S. Large Cap Core Plus Fund Class R5 Shares	JCPRX	B	B	B-		6.84	11.52	21.72	32.64	114.37	30.09	9,648	800-480-4111	
JPMorgan U.S. Large Cap Core Plus Fund Class R6	JLPYX	B-	B	B-		6.81	11.41	21.47	31.85	112.28	30.06	9,648	800-480-4111	Y
JPMorgan U.S. Research Enhanced Equity Fund Class A	JDEAX	B-	B-	B-	Down	6.46	11.22	21.23	27.84	102.09	28.09	7,921	800-480-4111	Y
JPMorgan U.S. Research Enhanced Equity Fund Class I	JDESX	B-	B-	B-	Down	6.52	11.30	21.48	28.74	104.55	28.32	7,921	800-480-4111	Y
JPMorgan U.S. Research Enhanced Equity Fund Class L	JPIEX	B-	B-	B-	Down	6.53	11.32	21.49	29.05	105.78	28.28	7,921	800-480-4111	Y
JPMorgan U.S. Research Enhanced Equity Fund Class R6	JDEUX	B-	B-	B-	Down	6.55	11.37	21.63	29.52	106.90	28.29	7,921	800-480-4111	Y
KP Large Cap Equity Fund Institutional Shares	KPLCX	B	B	B		6.43	11.66	23.84	39.08		12.98	2,215		Y
Lazard US Equity Concentrated Portfolio Inst Shares	LEVIX	B	B-	A		5.57	7.23	15.49	31.61	107.52	15.31	1,624	800-823-6300	Y
Lazard US Equity Concentrated Portfolio Open Shares	LEVOX	B	B-	A		5.51	7.09	15.21	30.61	103.93	15.42	1,624	800-823-6300	Y
Lazard US Equity Concentrated Portfolio R6 Shares	RLUEX	B	B-	A		5.54	7.20	15.52	31.56	107.45	15.34	1,624	800-823-6300	Y
Lazard US Strategic Equity Portfolio Institutional Shares	LZUSX	B-	B-	B-	Down	5.17	9.50	18.17	22.29	85.10	12.43	85.9	800-823-6300	Y
Lazard US Strategic Equity Portfolio Open Shares	LZUOX	B-	B-	B-	Down	5.08	9.32	17.74	21.23	82.24	12.48	85.9	800-823-6300	Y
Lazard US Strategic Equity Portfolio R6 Shares	RLUSX	B-	B-	B-	Down	5.16	9.50	18.16	22.47	85.32	12.43	85.9	800-823-6300	Y
Liberty All-Star Equity	USA	B-	B-	B-		5.96	10.22	22.06	27.27	87.68	6.87	1,291	866-432-2926	Y
LKCM Aquinas Catholic Equity Fund	AQEIX	B-	B-	B	Down	8.39	11.11	20.78	26.89	78.62	17.19	67.6	800-688-5526	Y

Category: US Equity Large Cap Blend (con't)

Fund Name	Ticker Symbol	RATINGS: Overall Rating	RATINGS: Reward Rating	RATINGS: Risk Rating	RATINGS: Recent Up/Downgrade	TOTAL RETURNS & PERFORMANCE: 3-Month Total Return	6-Month Total Return	1-Year Total Return	3-Year Total Return	5-Year Total Return	ASSETS: NAV	Total Assets (MIL)	NEW INVESTORS: Telephone	Open to New Investors
Lord Abbett Calibrated Dividend Growth Fund Class A	LAMAX	B-	B-	B-	Down	7.65	11.28	19.08	32.55	93.71	15.39	2,475	201-827-2000	Y
Lord Abbett Calibrated Dividend Growth Fund Class B	LAMBX	B-	B-	B-	Down	7.45	10.85	18.16	29.61	86.57	15.31	2,475	201-827-2000	
Lord Abbett Calibrated Dividend Growth Fund Class C	LAMCX	B	B-	B		7.49	10.88	18.21	29.66	86.58	15.2	2,475	201-827-2000	Y
Lord Abbett Calibrated Dividend Growth Fund Class F	LAMFX	B-	B-	B-	Down	7.68	11.37	19.27	33.24	95.26	15.38	2,475	201-827-2000	Y
Lord Abbett Calibrated Dividend Growth Fund Class F3	LRMAX	B-	B-	B-	Down	7.76	11.51	19.48	33.71	96.31	15.57	2,475	201-827-2000	Y
Lord Abbett Calibrated Dividend Growth Fund Class I	LAMYX	B-	B-	B-	Down	7.71	11.46	19.35	33.56	96.09	15.53	2,475	201-827-2000	Y
Lord Abbett Calibrated Dividend Growth Fund Class P	LAMPX	B-	B-	B-	Down	7.63	11.19	18.83	31.75	91.77	15.47	2,475	201-827-2000	
Lord Abbett Calibrated Dividend Growth Fund Class R2	LAMQX	B-	B-	B-	Down	7.56	11.13	18.65	31.16	90.26	15.54	2,475	201-827-2000	Y
Lord Abbett Calibrated Dividend Growth Fund Class R3	LAMRX	B-	B-	B-	Down	7.56	11.14	18.75	31.55	91.38	15.31	2,475	201-827-2000	Y
Lord Abbett Calibrated Dividend Growth Fund Class R4	LAMSX	B-	B-	B-	Down	7.67	11.31	19.10	32.58	93.68	15.38	2,475	201-827-2000	Y
Lord Abbett Calibrated Dividend Growth Fund Class R5	LAMTX	B-	B-	B-	Down	7.71	11.39	19.36	33.50	96.00	15.52	2,475	201-827-2000	Y
Lord Abbett Calibrated Dividend Growth Fund Class R6	LAMHX	B-	B-	B-	Down	7.76	11.51	19.48	33.93	96.62	15.57	2,475	201-827-2000	Y
Lord Abbett Calibrated Dividend Growth Fund Class T	LBDTX	B-	B-	B-		7.72	11.36	19.09	32.61	93.73	15.39	2,475	201-827-2000	Y
MainStay Common Stock Fund Class A	MSOAX	B	B	B	Up	8.56	13.88	23.82	32.64	111.88	25.58	193.1	800-624-6782	Y
MainStay Common Stock Fund Class B	MOPBX	B-	B-	B-	Down	8.27	13.26	22.58	28.74	101.26	23.56	193.1	800-624-6782	
MainStay Common Stock Fund Class C	MGOCX	B-	B-	B-	Down	8.32	13.27	22.59	28.75	101.17	23.55	193.1	800-624-6782	Y
MainStay Common Stock Fund Class I	MSOIX	B	B	B		8.64	13.99	24.14	33.61	114.41	25.65	193.1	800-624-6782	Y
MainStay Common Stock Fund Class R3	MSOSX	B	B	B	Up	8.48	13.61	23.38	31.37	108.79	25.52	193.1	800-624-6782	Y
MainStay Common Stock Fund Investor Class	MCSSX	B	B	B	Up	8.53	13.70	23.51	31.69	108.88	25.61	193.1	800-624-6782	Y
MainStay Epoch U.S. All Cap Fund Class A	MAAAX	B	B	B	Up	6.39	11.22	22.38	28.50	102.74	25.41	783.1	800-624-6782	Y
MainStay Epoch U.S. All Cap Fund Class B	MAWBX	B	B-	B	Up	6.07	10.60	21.15	24.53	92.06	21.4	783.1	800-624-6782	
MainStay Epoch U.S. All Cap Fund Class C	MAWCX	B	B-	B	Up	6.07	10.59	21.08	24.46	91.87	21.41	783.1	800-624-6782	Y
MainStay Epoch U.S. All Cap Fund Class I	MATIX	B	B	B		6.44	11.37	22.72	29.48	105.29	28.46	783.1	800-624-6782	Y
MainStay Epoch U.S. All Cap Fund Investor Class	MAWNX	B	B	B	Up	6.32	11.06	22.15	27.41	99.45	24.89	783.1	800-624-6782	Y
MainStay MAP Equity Fund Class A	MAPAX	B-	B-	C+	Down	5.92	10.82	22.48	27.31	85.41	40.86	1,249	800-624-6782	Y
MainStay MAP Equity Fund Class B	MAPBX	B-	B-	C+	Down	5.67	10.28	21.32	23.80	77.01	36.51	1,249	800-624-6782	
MainStay MAP Equity Fund Class C	MMPCX	B-	B-	C+	Down	5.67	10.28	21.32	23.80	76.95	36.51	1,249	800-624-6782	Y
MainStay MAP Equity Fund Class I	MUBFX	B-	B-	C+	Down	5.98	10.93	22.77	28.26	87.70	42.06	1,249	800-624-6782	Y
MainStay MAP Equity Fund Class R1	MAPRX	B-	B-	C+	Down	5.96	10.90	22.65	27.88	86.81	41.13	1,249	800-624-6782	Y
MainStay MAP Equity Fund Class R2	MPRRX	B-	B-	C+	Down	5.91	10.76	22.36	26.92	84.44	41.08	1,249	800-624-6782	Y
MainStay MAP Equity Fund Class R3	MMAPX	B-	B-	C+	Down	5.83	10.62	22.07	26.01	82.18	40.93	1,249	800-624-6782	Y
MainStay MAP Equity Fund Investor Class	MSMIX	B-	B-	C+	Down	5.87	10.69	22.25	26.59	83.76	40.87	1,249	800-624-6782	Y
MainStay S&P 500 Index Fund Class A	MSXAX	B	B	B		6.48	11.09	21.13	34.52	105.63	48.04	1,321	800-624-6782	Y
MainStay S&P 500 Index Fund Class I	MSPIX	B	B	B		6.54	11.25	21.45	35.53	108.22	48.62	1,321	800-624-6782	Y
MainStay S&P 500 Index Fund Investor Class	MYSPX	B	B-	B		6.46	11.06	21.01	34.11	104.56	48.03	1,321	800-624-6782	Y
Mainstay U.S. Equity Opportunities Fund Class A	MYCTX	A-	A-	A-	Up	8.99	16.81	22.98	40.80	134.80	9.85	979.0	800-624-6782	Y
Mainstay U.S. Equity Opportunities Fund Class C	MYCCX	B+	B+	A-	Up	8.69	16.38	21.89	37.17	124.24	8.56	979.0	800-624-6782	Y
Mainstay U.S. Equity Opportunities Fund Class I	MYCIX	A-	A-	B	Up	8.94	16.89	23.14	41.74	137.38	9.95	979.0	800-624-6782	Y
Mainstay U.S. Equity Opportunities Fund Investor Class	MYCNX	A-	A-	A-	Up	8.96	16.78	22.78	40.31	132.89	9.69	979.0	800-624-6782	Y
Mairs & Power Growth Fund Investor Class	MPGFX	B	B-	B		6.26	7.98	16.52	28.93	93.97	121.12	4,812	800-304-7404	Y
Manor Investment Funds Manor Fund	MNRMX	B-	B-	C+	Down	6.80	10.58	21.67	25.97	93.94	26.53	7.6		Y
Marathon Value Portfolio	MVPFX	B	B-	B+		5.70	8.02	16.44	28.76	79.17	27.24	73.2		Y
MassMutual Premier Main Street Fund Administrative Class	MMSLX	B	B-	B+		1.99	6.65	16.58	32.12	97.11	11.26	140.0		Y
MassMutual Premier Main Street Fund Class A	MSSAX	B	B-	B+		1.88	6.41	16.22	31.05	94.68	11.11	140.0		Y
MassMutual Premier Main Street Fund Class I	MSZIX	B	B-	B+		2.03	6.77	16.92	33.22	99.80	11.26	140.0		Y
MassMutual Premier Main Street Fund Class R3	MMSNX	B	B-	B+		1.85	6.37	16.06	30.53	92.87	11.14	140.0		Y
MassMutual Premier Main Street Fund Class R4	MSSRX	B	B-	B+		1.97	6.53	16.43	31.62	95.98	11.03	140.0		Y
MassMutual Premier Main Street Fund Class R5	MMSSX	B	B-	B+		2.02	6.66	16.80	32.91	99.06	11.26	140.0		Y
MassMutual Premier Main Street Fund Service Class	MMSYX	B	B-	B+		2.01	6.61	16.61	32.51	98.30	11.65	140.0		Y
MassMutual Select Equity Opp Fund Admin Cls	MMFVX	B-	B	C	Down	6.36	10.23	21.29	28.72	104.45	16.37	707.2		Y
MassMutual Select Equity Opportunities Fund Class A	MFVAX	B-	B	C	Down	6.28	10.08	20.97	27.74	101.84	15.61	707.2		Y
MassMutual Select Equity Opportunities Fund Class I	MFVZX	B-	B	C	Down	6.44	10.43	21.67	29.92	107.73	16.86	707.2		Y

Category: US Equity Large Cap Blend (con't)

Fund Name	Ticker Symbol	RATINGS: Overall Rating	Reward Rating	Risk Rating	Recent Up/ Downgrade	TOTAL RETURNS & PERFORMANCE: 3-Month Total Return	6-Month Total Return	1-Year Total Return	3-Year Total Return	5-Year Total Return	ASSETS: NAV	Total Assets (MIL)	NEW INVESTORS: Telephone	Open to New Investors
MassMutual Select Equity Opportunities Fund Class R3	MFVNX	B-	B	C	Down	6.20	9.98	20.74	27.10	99.95	14.51	707.2		Y
MassMutual Select Equity Opportunities Fund Class R4	MFVFX	B-	B	C	Down	6.30	10.13	21.12	28.14	103.29	15.38	707.2		Y
MassMutual Select Equity Opportunities Fund Class R5	MFVSX	B-	B	C	Down	6.41	10.33	21.53	29.47	106.67	16.93	707.2		Y
MassMutual Select Equity Opportunities Fund Service Class	MMFYX	B-	B	C	Down	6.38	10.26	21.39	29.09	105.60	16.6	707.2		Y
Matthew 25 Fund	MXXVX	B	A-	C+	Up	10.01	18.17	24.68	38.03	107.80	34.05	408.0	215-884-4458	Y
Meehan Focus Fund	MEFOX	B-	C+	B	Down	7.79	12.93	21.88	21.63	77.39	25.21	65.3		Y
Metropolitan West AlphaTrak 500 Fund	MWATX	B	B	B	Down	6.49	10.92	20.83	44.71	127.20	10.14	18.3	800-241-4671	Y
MFS® Blended Research Core Equity Fund Class A	MUEAX	B-	B-	B-	Down	6.67	10.92	20.33	29.60	102.24	27.46	1,587	877-960-6077	Y
MFS® Blended Research Core Equity Fund Class B	MUSBX	B-	B-	B-	Down	6.47	10.53	19.43	26.71	94.78	26.59	1,587	877-960-6077	Y
MFS® Blended Research Core Equity Fund Class C	MUECX	B-	B-	B-	Down	6.45	10.47	19.40	26.68	94.64	26.2	1,587	877-960-6077	Y
MFS® Blended Research Core Equity Fund Class I	MUSEX	B-	B-	B-	Down	6.71	11.03	20.63	30.53	104.75	27.81	1,587	877-960-6077	Y
MFS® Blended Research Core Equity Fund Class R1	MUERX	B-	B-	B-	Down	6.46	10.51	19.45	26.75	94.83	26.32	1,587	877-960-6077	Y
MFS® Blended Research Core Equity Fund Class R2	MUESX	B-	B-	B-	Down	6.62	10.77	20.04	28.60	99.67	26.39	1,587	877-960-6077	Y
MFS® Blended Research Core Equity Fund Class R3	MUETX	B-	B-	B-	Down	6.64	10.92	20.32	29.54	102.05	27.36	1,587	877-960-6077	Y
MFS® Blended Research Core Equity Fund Class R4	MUEUX	B-	B-	B-	Down	6.72	11.04	20.62	30.54	104.74	27.56	1,587	877-960-6077	Y
MFS® Blended Research Core Equity Fund Class R6	MUEVX	B-	B-	B	Down	6.77	11.13	20.81	31.02	105.84	27.85	1,587	877-960-6077	Y
MFS® Core Equity Fund Class A	MRGAX	B	B	B-		6.15	11.41	24.45	36.55	108.83	30.95	1,853	877-960-6077	Y
MFS® Core Equity Fund Class B	MRGBX	B	B	B-	Up	5.94	11.01	23.55	33.53	101.18	27.48	1,853	877-960-6077	Y
MFS® Core Equity Fund Class C	MRGCX	B	B	B-	Up	5.93	10.98	23.50	33.54	101.20	27.16	1,853	877-960-6077	Y
MFS® Core Equity Fund Class I	MRGRX	B	B	B-		6.21	11.54	24.76	37.58	111.48	32.65	1,853	877-960-6077	Y
MFS® Core Equity Fund Class R1	MRGGX	B	B	B-	Up	5.93	10.99	23.52	33.51	101.10	27.14	1,853	877-960-6077	Y
MFS® Core Equity Fund Class R2	MRERX	B	B	B-		6.09	11.29	24.18	35.55	106.30	30.23	1,853	877-960-6077	Y
MFS® Core Equity Fund Class R3	MRGHX	B	B	B-		6.14	11.38	24.43	36.49	108.77	30.88	1,853	877-960-6077	Y
MFS® Core Equity Fund Class R4	MRGJX	B	B	B-		6.19	11.55	24.77	37.56	111.46	31.17	1,853	877-960-6077	Y
MFS® Core Equity Fund Class R6	MRGKX	B	B	B-		6.23	11.60	24.85	37.95	112.37	32.69	1,853	877-960-6077	Y
MFS® Equity Opportunities Fund Class A	SRFAX	B	B-	B+		5.02	7.65	18.08	31.31	101.43	33.85	468.8	877-960-6077	Y
MFS® Equity Opportunities Fund Class B	SRFBX	B	B-	B+	Up	4.80	7.23	17.18	28.37	93.88	32.12	468.8	877-960-6077	Y
MFS® Equity Opportunities Fund Class C	SRFCX	B	B-	B+	Up	4.80	7.23	17.16	28.33	93.94	32.15	468.8	877-960-6077	Y
MFS® Equity Opportunities Fund Class I	SRFIX	B	B	B+		5.07	7.76	18.31	32.27	103.86	33.89	468.8	877-960-6077	Y
MFS® Equity Opportunities Fund Class R1	SRFDX	B	B-	B+	Up	4.78	7.22	17.15	28.32	93.92	32.03	468.8	877-960-6077	Y
MFS® Equity Opportunities Fund Class R2	SRFEX	B	B-	B+		4.94	7.55	17.77	30.31	98.84	32.91	468.8	877-960-6077	Y
MFS® Equity Opportunities Fund Class R3	SRFFX	B	B-	B+		5.01	7.65	18.04	31.31	101.35	33.73	468.8	877-960-6077	Y
MFS® Equity Opportunities Fund Class R4	SRFGX	B	B	B+		5.08	7.79	18.34	32.26	103.88	33.97	468.8	877-960-6077	Y
MFS® Equity Opportunities Fund Class R6	SRFHX	B	B	B+		5.11	7.85	18.45	32.67	104.85	34.49	468.8	877-960-6077	Y
MFS® Low Volatility Equity Fund Class A	MLVAX	B	B-	B+		5.31	7.47	16.53	32.20		14.3	91.0	877-960-6077	Y
MFS® Low Volatility Equity Fund Class B	MLVBX	B	B-	B+		5.09	7.06	15.57	29.18		14.29	91.0	877-960-6077	Y
MFS® Low Volatility Equity Fund Class C	MLVGX	B	B-	B+		5.11	7.09	15.65	29.20		14.25	91.0	877-960-6077	Y
MFS® Low Volatility Equity Fund Class I	MLVHX	B	B-	B+		5.38	7.61	16.80	33.00		14.31	91.0	877-960-6077	Y
MFS® Low Volatility Equity Fund Class R1	MLVMX	B	B-	A+		5.08	7.04	15.61	29.19		14.32	91.0	877-960-6077	Y
MFS® Low Volatility Equity Fund Class R2	MLVOX	B	B-	A+		5.28	7.30	16.23	31.13		14.37	91.0	877-960-6077	Y
MFS® Low Volatility Equity Fund Class R3	MLVPX	B	B-	B+		5.29	7.37	16.46	32.01		14.34	91.0	877-960-6077	Y
MFS® Low Volatility Equity Fund Class R4	MLVRX	B	B-	A+		5.37	7.60	16.77	33.01		14.32	91.0	877-960-6077	Y
MFS® Low Volatility Equity Fund Class R6	MLVTX	B	B-	B+		5.40	7.65	16.88	33.36		14.32	91.0	877-960-6077	Y
MFS® Massachusetts Investors Trust Class 529A	EAMTX	B	B-	B		6.60	10.26	23.47	33.37	99.88	31.38	6,571	877-960-6077	Y
MFS® Massachusetts Investors Trust Class 529B	EBMTX	B-	B-	B-	Down	6.45	9.87	22.56	30.83	93.10	29.68	6,571	877-960-6077	Y
MFS® Massachusetts Investors Trust Class 529C	ECITX	B-	B-	B-	Down	6.40	9.83	22.53	30.34	92.34	29.28	6,571	877-960-6077	Y
MFS® Massachusetts Investors Trust Class A	MITTX	B	B	B		6.63	10.32	23.56	33.57	100.30	32.15	6,571	877-960-6077	Y
MFS® Massachusetts Investors Trust Class B	MITBX	B-	B-	B-	Down	6.43	9.87	22.60	30.54	92.80	31.24	6,571	877-960-6077	Y
MFS® Massachusetts Investors Trust Class C	MITCX	B-	B-	B-	Down	6.43	9.89	22.62	30.55	92.78	30.65	6,571	877-960-6077	Y
MFS® Massachusetts Investors Trust Class I	MITIX	B	B	B		6.69	10.40	23.79	34.46	102.58	31.26	6,571	877-960-6077	Y
MFS® Massachusetts Investors Trust Class R1	MITGX	B-	B-	B-	Down	6.41	9.89	22.58	30.50	92.81	30.47	6,571	877-960-6077	Y
MFS® Massachusetts Investors Trust Class R2	MIRTX	B-	B-	B	Down	6.56	10.13	23.18	32.47	97.60	30.69	6,571	877-960-6077	Y

Category: US Equity Large Cap Blend (con't)

Fund Name	Ticker Symbol	RATINGS: Overall Rating	Reward Rating	Risk Rating	Recent Up/ Downgrade	TOTAL RETURNS & PERFORMANCE: 3-Month Total Return	6-Month Total Return	1-Year Total Return	3-Year Total Return	5-Year Total Return	ASSETS: NAV	Total Assets (MIL)	NEW INVESTORS: Telephone	Open to New Investors
MFS® Massachusetts Investors Trust Class R3	MITHX	B	B	B		6.63	10.28	23.50	33.48	100.09	31.87	6,571	877-960-6077	Y
MFS® Massachusetts Investors Trust Class R4	MITDX	B	B	B		6.69	10.42	23.83	34.49	102.67	32.42	6,571	877-960-6077	Y
MFS® Massachusetts Investors Trust Class R6	MITJX	B	B	B		6.72	10.47	23.92	34.86	103.51	31.28	6,571	877-960-6077	Y
MFS® Research Fund Class A	MFRFX	B	B	B		5.87	10.41	23.34	33.96	100.33	42.1	5,567	877-960-6077	Y
MFS® Research Fund Class B	MFRBX	B-	B-	B-	Down	5.64	9.97	22.38	30.94	92.88	38.4	5,567	877-960-6077	Y
MFS® Research Fund Class C	MFRCX	B-	B-	B-	Down	5.66	10.00	22.43	30.99	92.92	38.1	5,567	877-960-6077	Y
MFS® Research Fund Class I	MRFIX	B	B	B		5.93	10.54	23.63	34.97	102.78	43.18	5,567	877-960-6077	Y
MFS® Research Fund Class R1	MFRLX	B-	B-	B-	Down	5.67	9.99	22.41	31.00	92.93	37.48	5,567	877-960-6077	Y
MFS® Research Fund Class R2	MSRRX	B	B	B		5.80	10.26	23.04	32.97	97.82	40.83	5,567	877-960-6077	Y
MFS® Research Fund Class R3	MFRHX	B	B	B		5.86	10.40	23.32	33.95	100.26	41.86	5,567	877-960-6077	Y
MFS® Research Fund Class R4	MFRJX	B	B	B		5.94	10.56	23.64	34.98	102.82	42.15	5,567	877-960-6077	Y
MFS® Research Fund Class R6	MFRKX	B	B	B		5.95	10.57	23.71	35.29	103.67	42.06	5,567	877-960-6077	Y
MM S&P 500® Index Fund Class A	MMFFX	B	B-	B		6.42	11.02	20.98	33.94	104.34	18.02	3,367		Y
MM S&P 500® Index Fund Class Administrative Class	MIEYX	B	B	B		6.52	11.21	21.30	34.96	106.88	18.33	3,367		Y
MM S&P 500® Index Fund Class I	MMIZX	B	B	B		6.67	11.41	21.72	36.40	110.68	18.55	3,367		Y
MM S&P 500® Index Fund Class R3	MMINX	B	B-	B		6.44	10.94	20.78	33.42	102.53	17.71	3,367		Y
MM S&P 500® Index Fund Class R4	MIEAX	B	B	B		6.46	11.08	21.07	34.36	105.16	18.13	3,367		Y
MM S&P 500® Index Fund Class R5	MIEZX	B	B	B		6.58	11.32	21.59	36.00	109.42	18.6	3,367		Y
MM S&P 500® Index Fund Class Service Class	MMIEX	B	B	B		6.56	11.24	21.37	35.35	107.68	18.64	3,367		Y
Mutual of America Institutional Funds Inc All America Fund	MALLX	B+	B+	B+	Up	5.62	10.68	19.57	32.56	100.05	11.6824	13.1		Y
Mutual of America Inst Funds Inc Equity Index Fund	MAEQX	B	B	B		6.61	11.36	21.66	36.47	110.41	11.8034	42.9		Y
Nationwide Fund Class A	NWFAX	B	B	B-		5.80	10.51	19.90	33.23	98.66	25.03	1,043	800-848-0920	Y
Nationwide Fund Class C	GTRCX	B-	B	B-	Down	5.61	10.06	19.04	30.17	91.17	23.21	1,043	800-848-0920	Y
Nationwide Fund Class R	GNWRX	B	B	B-		5.70	10.25	19.40	31.43	94.52	24.47	1,043	800-848-0920	Y
Nationwide Fund Institutional Service Class	MUIFX	B	B	B-		5.89	10.65	20.20	34.19	100.94	24.61	1,043	800-848-0920	Y
Nationwide Large Cap Equity Fund Class A	NWGHX	B-	B	B-	Down	7.94	11.76	21.93	32.18	96.84	13.71	75.6	800-848-0920	Y
Nationwide Large Cap Equity Fund Class C	NWGIX	B-	B-	B-	Down	7.72	11.38	21.10	29.73	90.95	13.06	75.6	800-848-0920	Y
Nationwide Large Cap Equity Fund Class R6	NWGJX	B	B	B-		8.01	11.93	22.41	33.73	100.76	13.75	75.6	800-848-0920	Y
Nationwide Large Cap Equity Fund Institutional Service Cls	NWGKX	B	B	B-		7.97	11.85	22.14	33.23	99.49	13.76	75.6	800-848-0920	Y
Nationwide S&P 500 Index Fund Class A	GRMAX	B	B	B		6.49	11.10	21.09	34.45	105.65	16.01	2,942	800-848-0920	Y
Nationwide S&P 500 Index Fund Class C	GRMCX	B-	B-	B	Down	6.34	10.74	20.36	31.89	99.29	15.67	2,942	800-848-0920	Y
Nationwide S&P 500 Index Fund Class R	GRMRX	B	B-	B		6.40	10.94	20.74	33.37	102.63	15.96	2,942	800-848-0920	Y
Nationwide S&P 500 Index Fund Class R6	GRMIX	B	B	B		6.61	11.38	21.63	36.22	110.09	16.15	2,942	800-848-0920	Y
Nationwide S&P 500 Index Fund Institutional Service Class	GRISX	B	B	B		6.57	11.20	21.31	35.21	107.39	16.11	2,942	800-848-0920	Y
Nationwide S&P 500 Index Fund Service Class	GRMSX	B	B-	B		6.49	11.10	21.16	34.60	105.81	16.03	2,942	800-848-0920	Y
Natixis Funds Trust II Oakmark Fund Class A	NEFOX	B	B	B	Up	5.84	11.84	20.74	35.50	111.36	24.72	311.4	800-862-4863	Y
Natixis Funds Trust II Oakmark Fund Class C	NECOX	B	B	B	Up	5.61	11.38	19.84	32.45	103.54	21.58	311.4	800-862-4863	Y
Natixis Funds Trust II Oakmark Fund Class N	NOANX	B	B	C+		5.93	12.07	21.03	35.82	111.87	25.91	311.4	800-862-4863	Y
Natixis Funds Trust II Oakmark Fund Class Y	NEOYX	B	B	B	Up	5.88	11.97	21.04	36.51	113.99	25.9	311.4	800-862-4863	Y
Neuberger Berman Focus Fund Advisor Class	NBFAX	B-	B-	B-	Down	3.04	5.97	18.96	25.45	91.18	4.56	757.8	212-476-9000	
Neuberger Berman Focus Fund Class A	NFAAX	B-	B-	B-	Down	3.12	6.11	19.12	26.08	92.72	14.34	757.8	212-476-9000	Y
Neuberger Berman Focus Fund Class C	NFACX	B-	B-	B-	Down	2.95	5.75	18.19	23.16	85.83	4.09	757.8	212-476-9000	Y
Neuberger Berman Focus Fund Institutional Class	NFALX	B-	B-	B-	Down	3.18	6.26	19.53	27.38	96.23	26.56	757.8	212-476-9000	Y
Neuberger Berman Focus Fund Investor Class	NBSSX	B-	B-	B-	Down	3.15	6.20	19.34	26.73	94.55	26.53	757.8	212-476-9000	
Neuberger Berman Focus Fund Trust Class	NBFCX	B-	B-	B-	Down	3.16	6.11	19.19	26.08	92.82	14.55	757.8	212-476-9000	
Neuberger Berman Multi-Cap Opportunities Fund Class A	NMUAX	B	B	B-		6.96	11.53	24.42	37.54	113.96	18.46	2,064	212-476-9000	Y
Neuberger Berman Multi-Cap Opportunities Fund Class C	NMUCX	B	B	B-		6.72	11.09	23.52	34.52	105.79	17.69	2,064	212-476-9000	Y
Neuberger Berman Multi-Cap Opp Fund Inst Cls	NMULX	B	B	B-		6.98	11.64	24.81	39.01	117.56	18.56	2,064	212-476-9000	Y
Northern Stock Index Fund	NOSIX	B	B	B		6.61	11.38	21.70	36.46	110.66	31.75	8,114	800-595-9111	Y
Nuveen Large Cap Core Fund Class A	NLACX	B	B	B	Up	6.44	11.84	19.49	29.20		32.62	571.1	312-917-8146	Y
Nuveen Large Cap Core Fund Class C	NLCDX	B	B-	B	Up	6.26	11.40	18.64	26.35		32.18	571.1	312-917-8146	Y
Nuveen Large Cap Core Fund Class I	NLCIX	B	B	B	Up	6.50	11.96	19.78	30.18		32.57	571.1	312-917-8146	Y

Category: US Equity Large Cap Blend (con't)

Fund Name	Ticker Symbol	RATINGS: Overall Rating	Reward Rating	Risk Rating	Recent Up/ Downgrade	TOTAL RETURNS & PERFORMANCE: 3-Month Total Return	6-Month Total Return	1-Year Total Return	3-Year Total Return	5-Year Total Return	ASSETS: NAV	Total Assets (MIL)	NEW INVESTORS: Telephone	Open to New Investors
Nuveen Large Cap Core Fund Class R6	NLCFX	B	B	B	Up	6.56	12.02	19.89	30.35		32.6	571.1	312-917-8146	Y
Nuveen Large Cap Select Fund Class A	FLRAX	B	B	C+		8.12	13.90	24.64	39.31	116.97	28.66	64.3	312-917-8146	Y
Nuveen Large Cap Select Fund Class C	FLYCX	B	B	C+		7.90	13.44	23.68	36.22	108.90	26.74	64.3	312-917-8146	Y
Nuveen Large Cap Select Fund Class I	FLRYX	B	B+	B-		8.15	14.00	24.94	40.34	119.62	28.85	64.3	312-917-8146	Y
Nuveen Santa Barbara Dividend Growth Fund Class A	NSBAX	B-	B-	B-	Down	6.32	10.54	19.71	27.94	85.80	41.08	3,116	312-917-8146	Y
Nuveen Santa Barbara Dividend Growth Fund Class C	NSBCX	B-	B-	B-	Down	6.13	10.12	18.82	25.11	78.99	41.03	3,116	312-917-8146	Y
Nuveen Santa Barbara Dividend Growth Fund Class I	NSBRX	B-	B-	B-	Down	6.38	10.67	20.02	28.88	88.11	41.1	3,116	312-917-8146	Y
Nuveen Santa Barbara Dividend Growth Fund Class R3	NBDRX	B-	B-	B-	Down	6.24	10.39	19.41	27.00	83.49	41.35	3,116	312-917-8146	Y
Nuveen Santa Barbara Dividend Growth Fund Class R6	NSBFX	B-	B-	B-	Down	6.40	10.72	20.07	29.18	88.78	41.46	3,116	312-917-8146	Y
Nuveen Symphony Low Volatility Equity Fund A	NOPAX	B	B-	B+		6.68	11.67	19.43	29.66	98.58	31.61	140.9	312-917-8146	Y
Nuveen Symphony Low Volatility Equity Fund C	NOPCX	B	B-	B+	Up	6.47	11.25	18.50	26.75	91.24	30.63	140.9	312-917-8146	Y
Nuveen Symphony Low Volatility Equity Fund Class R6	NOPFX	B	B-	B+		6.73	11.86	19.82	30.86	101.38	31.68	140.9	312-917-8146	Y
Nuveen Symphony Low Volatility Equity Fund I	NOPRX	B	B-	B+		6.74	11.80	19.72	30.65	101.06	31.64	140.9	312-917-8146	Y
Oak Ridge Dividend Growth Fund Class A	ORDAX	B-	B-	B-	Down	7.42	12.39	20.15	29.73		15.24	9.8		Y
Oak Ridge Dividend Growth Fund Class I	ORDNX	B-	B-	B-	Down	7.51	12.59	20.56	30.71		15.35	9.8		Y
Oakmark Fund Advisor Class	OAYMX	B	B	B-	Up	6.01	12.16	21.30	36.73	114.36	84.34	19,380	641-219-558	Y
Oakmark Fund Institutional Class	OANMX	B	B	B	Up	6.02	12.17	21.33	36.75	114.39	84.33	19,380	641-219-558	Y
Oakmark Fund Investor Class	OAKMX	B	B	B	Up	5.98	12.08	21.14	36.50	113.99	84.33	19,380	641-219-558	Y
Oakmark Fund Service Class	OARMX	B	B	B	Up	5.89	11.93	20.82	35.19	110.75	84.08	19,380	641-219-558	Y
Oakmark Select Fund Class Advisor	OAYLX	B	B	B	Up	4.14	10.36	15.87	27.67	106.87	47.76	6,336	641-219-558	Y
Oakmark Select Fund Class Institutional	OANLX	B	B	B	Up	4.15	10.39	15.91	27.71	106.94	47.77	6,336	641-219-558	Y
Oakmark Select Fund Investor Class	OAKLX	B	B	B	Up	4.10	10.28	15.72	27.47	106.55	47.76	6,336	641-219-558	Y
Oakmark Select Fund Service Class	OARLX	B	B	B	Up	4.02	10.15	15.38	26.26	103.38	47.2	6,336	641-219-558	Y
Olstein All Cap Value Fund Class Advisor	OFAFX	B-	C+	B	Up	6.48	7.01	15.38	17.82	93.20	24.72	698.2	800-799-2113	Y
Olstein All Cap Value Fund Class C	OFALX	B-	C+	B-	Up	6.21	6.48	14.29	14.33	84.17	19.96	698.2	800-799-2113	Y
Oppenheimer Main Street All Cap Fund Class A	OMSOX	B	B	B-		3.32	6.99	16.07	42.16	102.97	17.95	1,261	800-225-5677	Y
Oppenheimer Main Street All Cap Fund Class B	OMOBX	B-	C+	B-	Down	3.16	6.63	15.23	21.63	70.94	16.32	1,261	800-225-5677	
Oppenheimer Main Street All Cap Fund Class C	OMSCX	B-	C+	B-	Down	3.18	6.62	15.23	21.65	71.16	16.43	1,261	800-225-5677	Y
Oppenheimer Main Street All Cap Fund Class R	OMSNX	B-	B-	B-	Down	3.25	6.90	15.78	23.46	75.35	17.44	1,261	800-225-5677	Y
Oppenheimer Main Street All Cap Fund Class Y	OMSYX	B-	B-	B-	Down	3.43	7.18	16.40	25.30	80.02	18.36	1,261	800-225-5677	Y
Oppenheimer Main Street Fund Class A	MSIGX	B	B-	B+		2.05	6.67	16.73	32.72	98.19	51.01	10,187	800-225-5677	Y
Oppenheimer Main Street Fund Class B	OMSBX	B	B-	B+		1.85	6.25	15.82	29.71	90.48	49.07	10,187	800-225-5677	
Oppenheimer Main Street Fund Class C	MIGCX	B	B-	B+		1.82	6.25	15.82	29.73	90.83	48.38	10,187	800-225-5677	Y
Oppenheimer Main Street Fund Class I	OMSIX	B	B-	B+		2.13	6.88	17.18	34.40	102.35	50.46	10,187	800-225-5677	Y
Oppenheimer Main Street Fund Class R	OMGNX	B	B-	B+		1.96	6.52	16.40	31.69	95.67	50.1	10,187	800-225-5677	Y
Oppenheimer Main Street Fund Class Y	MIGYX	B	B-	B+		2.10	6.80	16.98	33.66	100.63	50.55	10,187	800-225-5677	Y
Oppenheimer Rising Dividends Fund Class A	OARDX	B-	C+	B-	Down	3.95	7.42	16.76	19.97	74.08	19.35	3,318	800-225-5677	Y
Oppenheimer Rising Dividends Fund Class B	OBRDX	B-	C+	B-	Down	3.77	7.06	15.89	17.28	67.32	16.57	3,318	800-225-5677	
Oppenheimer Rising Dividends Fund Class C	OCRDX	B-	C+	B-	Down	3.77	7.07	15.93	17.31	67.71	16.37	3,318	800-225-5677	Y
Oppenheimer Rising Dividends Fund Class I	OIRDX	B-	B-	B-	Down	4.05	7.63	17.22	21.50	77.74	20	3,318	800-225-5677	Y
Oppenheimer Rising Dividends Fund Class R	ONRDX	B-	C+	B-	Down	3.90	7.27	16.45	19.06	71.69	19.22	3,318	800-225-5677	Y
Oppenheimer Rising Dividends Fund Class Y	OYRDX	B-	C+	B-	Down	4.03	7.56	17.02	20.86	76.05	20.05	3,318	800-225-5677	Y
Optimum Large Cap Value Fund Class A	OALVX	B-	C+	B	Down	5.58	9.27	16.05	22.75	75.22	16.32	1,482		Y
Optimum Large Cap Value Fund Class C	OCLVX	B-	C+	B	Down	5.45	8.91	15.21	20.01	68.97	16.15	1,482		Y
Optimum Large Cap Value Fund Institutional Class	OILVX	B-	C+	B	Down	5.68	9.43	16.36	23.66	77.61	16.35	1,482		Y
O'Shaughnessy All Cap Core Fund Class A	OFAAX	B	B	B-		6.33	10.90	19.31	35.07	111.30	12.32	14.5		Y
O'Shaughnessy All Cap Core Fund Class C	OFACX	B	B	B-	Up	6.13	10.48	18.44	31.78	103.21	11.68	14.5		Y
O'Shaughnessy All Cap Core Fund Class I	OFAIX	B	B	B-		6.34	10.93	19.57	35.75	113.46	12.14	14.5		Y
Pacific Advisors Large Cap Value Fund Class A	PAGTX	B-	B-	B-	Down	7.67	10.20	17.55	24.75	81.21	17.32	7.8		Y
Pacific Advisors Large Cap Value Fund Class C	PGCCX	B-	C+	B-	Down	7.41	9.74	16.66	21.95	74.31	14.7	7.8		Y
Pacific Financial Core Equity Fund Class Institutional	PFGQX	B-	B-	B-	Down	5.77	10.08	17.42	25.44	80.21	9.66	595.2	425-451-7722	Y
Pacific Financial Core Equity Fund Class Investor	PFLQX	B-	B-	B-	Down	5.31	9.31	16.15	22.36	73.20	9.03	595.2	425-451-7722	Y

Category: US Equity Large Cap Blend (con't)

Fund Name	Ticker Symbol	RATINGS: Overall Rating	Reward Rating	Risk Rating	Recent Up/ Downgrade	TOTAL RETURNS & PERFORMANCE: 3-Month Total Return	6-Month Total Return	1-Year Total Return	3-Year Total Return	5-Year Total Return	ASSETS: NAV	Total Assets (MIL)	NEW INVESTORS: Telephone	Open to New Investors
Pacific Financial Explorer Fund Class Institutional	PFGPX	B-	B-	B-	Down	5.82	9.82	19.28	25.75	85.62	10.33	180.3	425-451-7722	Y
Pacific Financial Explorer Fund Class Investor	PFLPX	B-	B-	B-	Down	5.64	9.54	18.51	23.16	79.13	9.72	180.3	425-451-7722	Y
Parnassus Core Equity Fund - Institutional Shares	PRILX	B	B-	B+	Up	5.54	9.12	16.81	27.42	100.78	42.73	16,256	999-350-5	Y
Parnassus Core Equity Fund - Investor Shares	PRBLX	B	B-	B+	Up	5.51	9.04	16.57	26.65	98.97	42.67	16,256	999-350-5	Y
Parnassus Core Equity Fund - Investor Shares	TRFAX	B	B-	B+		5.63	9.66	17.79	32.55	98.47	17.76	16,256		Y
Parnassus Core Equity Fund - Investor Shares	TRFCX	B	B-	B+		5.44	9.23	16.98	29.66	91.37	16.98	16,256		Y
Parnassus Core Equity Fund - Investor Shares	TRFTX	B	B-	B+		5.71	9.75	18.13	33.55	101.17	18.06	16,256		Y
Payson Total Return Fund	PBFDX	B-	B-	C+	Down	5.04	11.28	21.71	26.85	74.13	17.5	93.6		Y
Pear Tree Quality Fund Institutional Shares	QGIAX	A-	B	A+	Up	7.90	10.95	28.90	41.73	101.49	20.6	134.0	800-326-2151	Y
Pear Tree Quality Fund Ordinary Shares	USBOX	B+	B	A+	Up	7.75	10.70	28.45	40.55	98.68	19.26	134.0	800-326-2151	Y
PF Main Street® Core Fund Class P	US69447T8889	B	B-	B+		2.13	6.84	17.17	34.27	101.14	14.37	303.4	800-722-2333	Y
PIMCO StocksPLUS® Absolute Return Fund Class A	PTOAX	B-	B	C+	Down	6.39	11.59	23.41	36.16	108.48	10.53	1,626	866-746-2602	Y
PIMCO StocksPLUS® Absolute Return Fund Class C	PSOCX	B-	B	C+	Down	6.17	11.16	22.32	32.97	100.55	9.61	1,626	866-746-2602	Y
PIMCO StocksPLUS® Absolute Return Fund Class D	PSTDX	B-	B	C+	Down	6.50	11.68	23.36	36.14	108.51	10.35	1,626	866-746-2602	Y
PIMCO StocksPLUS® Absolute Return Fund Class P	PTOPX	B	B	C+		6.45	11.71	23.74	37.27	111.49	10.58	1,626	866-746-2602	Y
PIMCO StocksPLUS® Absolute Return Fund Class R	PTORX	B-	B	C+	Down	6.27	11.43	23.08	35.17	105.83	10.46	1,626	866-746-2602	Y
PIMCO StocksPLUS® Absolute Return Fund Institutional Class	PSPTX	B	B	C+		6.58	11.82	23.89	37.84	112.63	10.71	1,626	866-746-2602	Y
PIMCO StocksPLUS® Fund Administrative Class	PPLAX	B	B	B-		6.73	11.57	22.13	35.51	112.27	10.73	876.0	866-746-2602	Y
PIMCO StocksPLUS® Fund Class A	PSPAX	B-	B	B-	Down	6.65	11.38	21.96	34.92	110.27	10.63	876.0	866-746-2602	Y
PIMCO StocksPLUS® Fund Class C	PSPCX	B-	B-	B-	Down	6.55	11.14	21.34	32.92	105.24	10.11	876.0	866-746-2602	Y
PIMCO StocksPLUS® Fund Class D	PSPDX	B	B	B-		6.69	11.46	21.98	34.92	110.47	10.57	876.0	866-746-2602	Y
PIMCO StocksPLUS® Fund Class P	PSKPX	B	B	B-		6.64	11.54	22.28	36.04	113.62	11.4	876.0	866-746-2602	Y
PIMCO StocksPLUS® Fund Class R	PSPRX	B-	B	B-	Down	6.59	11.34	21.75	33.94	107.94	10.94	876.0	866-746-2602	Y
PIMCO StocksPLUS® Fund Institutional Class	PSTKX	B	B	B-		6.75	11.67	22.42	36.48	114.60	11.43	876.0	866-746-2602	Y
Pin Oak Equity Fund	POGSX	B	B	A-		6.75	8.94	15.15	42.23	117.12	65.86	219.2	888-462-5386	Y
Pioneer Core Equity Fund Class A	PIOTX	B	B	B-	Up	5.89	12.46	24.77	31.84	96.02	20.58	1,696	617-742-7825	Y
Pioneer Core Equity Fund Class C	PCOTX	B-	B-	B-	Down	5.70	12.03	23.74	28.75	88.01	18.26	1,696	617-742-7825	Y
Pioneer Core Equity Fund Class Y	PVFYX	B	B	B-	Up	5.98	12.64	25.10	33.07	99.15	20.8	1,696	617-742-7825	Y
Pioneer Fund Class A	PIODX	B-	B	B-	Down	6.37	11.49	21.53	31.30	98.77	28.81	5,008	617-742-7825	Y
Pioneer Fund Class C	PCODX	B-	B-	B-	Down	6.14	11.01	20.57	28.21	91.09	25.17	5,008	617-742-7825	Y
Pioneer Fund Class R	PIORX	B-	B-	B-	Down	6.24	11.20	20.98	29.73	94.98	28.93	5,008	617-742-7825	Y
Pioneer Fund Class Y	PYODX	B	B	B-		6.41	11.63	21.85	32.34	101.59	29.17	5,008	617-742-7825	Y
PNC Multi-Factor All Cap Fund Class A	PLEAX	B	B	A		5.56	11.43	19.58	30.32	94.49	20.89	9.9	800-622-3863	Y
PNC Multi-Factor All Cap Fund Class C	PLECX	B	B-	A-	Up	5.38	11.02	18.74	27.66	87.90	19.18	9.9	800-622-3863	Y
PNC Multi-Factor All Cap Fund Class I	PLEIX	B+	B	A	Up	5.61	11.57	19.93	31.45	97.12	21.35	9.9	800-622-3863	Y
Port Street Quality Growth Fund Institutional Class	PSQGX	B	C+	A-		5.24	7.27	14.99	21.09		12.72	91.3		Y
PRIMECAP Odyssey Stock Fund	POSKX	B	B+	B		7.19	12.64	25.96	43.43	126.04	31.91	9,094	800-729-2307	Y
Principal Capital Appreciation Fund Class A	CMNWX	B	B	B		6.44	11.08	20.64	32.73	102.31	61.57	2,412	800-222-5852	Y
Principal Capital Appreciation Fund Class C	CMNCX	B-	B-	B	Down	6.24	10.64	19.68	29.54	94.12	47.99	2,412	800-222-5852	Y
Principal Capital Appreciation Fund Institutional Class	PWCIX	B	B	B+		6.54	11.29	21.06	34.18	106.09	62.64	2,412	800-222-5852	Y
Principal Capital Appreciation Fund R-1 Class	PCAMX	B	B-	B		6.31	10.80	20.03	30.76	97.31	61.68	2,412	800-222-5852	Y
Principal Capital Appreciation Fund R-2 Class	PCANX	B	B-	B		6.34	10.88	20.18	31.26	98.62	61.71	2,412	800-222-5852	Y
Principal Capital Appreciation Fund R-3 Class	PCAOX	B	B	B		6.41	10.99	20.42	32.01	100.45	61.67	2,412	800-222-5852	Y
Principal Capital Appreciation Fund R-4 Class	PCAPX	B	B	B		6.46	11.09	20.64	32.74	102.36	62.12	2,412	800-222-5852	Y
Principal Capital Appreciation Fund R-5 Class	PCAQX	B	B	B		6.47	11.15	20.78	33.19	103.54	62.3	2,412	800-222-5852	Y
Principal LargeCap S&P 500 Index Fund Class A	PLSAX	B	B-	B		6.52	11.14	21.23	34.89	106.32	17.53	5,749	800-222-5852	Y
Principal LargeCap S&P 500 Index Fund Class C	PLICX	B-	B-	B	Down	6.34	10.73	20.30	31.60	98.21	17.19	5,749	800-222-5852	Y
Principal LargeCap S&P 500 Index Fund Class J	PSPJX	B	B	B		6.55	11.21	21.33	35.20	106.76	17.35	5,749	800-222-5852	Y
Principal LargeCap S&P 500 Index Fund Institutional Class	PLFIX	B	B	B		6.62	11.31	21.64	36.19	109.84	17.51	5,749	800-222-5852	Y
Principal LargeCap S&P 500 Index Fund R-1 Class	PLPIX	B	B-	B		6.32	10.83	20.55	32.67	100.79	17.5	5,749	800-222-5852	Y
Principal LargeCap S&P 500 Index Fund R-2 Class	PLFNX	B	B-	B		6.38	10.85	20.64	33.10	102.16	17.63	5,749	800-222-5852	Y
Principal LargeCap S&P 500 Index Fund R-3 Class	PLFMX	B	B-	B		6.42	11.04	20.96	33.92	104.06	17.56	5,749	800-222-5852	Y

Category: US Equity Large Cap Blend (con't)

Fund Name	Ticker Symbol	RATINGS: Overall Rating	Reward Rating	Risk Rating	Recent Up/ Downgrade	TOTAL RETURNS & PERFORMANCE: 3-Month Total Return	6-Month Total Return	1-Year Total Return	3-Year Total Return	5-Year Total Return	ASSETS: NAV	Total Assets (MIL)	NEW INVESTORS: Telephone	Open to New Investors
Principal LargeCap S&P 500 Index Fund R-4 Class	PLFSX	B	B	B		6.46	11.12	21.17	34.67	105.88	17.6	5,749	800-222-5852	Y
Principal LargeCap S&P 500 Index Fund R-5 Class	PLFPX	B	B	B		6.51	11.14	21.25	35.14	107.24	17.75	5,749	800-222-5852	Y
Prudential Jennison Equity Income Fund Class C	AGOCX	B-	C+	B-	Up	5.41	9.53	14.68	13.02	62.52	15.29	2,034	800-225-1852	Y
Prudential Jennison Equity Income Fund Class R	PJERX	B-	C+	B	Up	5.46	9.78	15.20	14.62	66.61	16.62	2,034	800-225-1852	Y
Prudential Jennison Equity Income Fund Class Z	JDEZX	B-	C+	B	Up	5.63	10.03	15.81	16.37	70.75	16.6	2,034	800-225-1852	Y
Prudential Jennison Equity Opportunity Fund Class A	PJIAX	B	B-	B	Up	6.95	10.17	15.95	29.24	91.24	19.44	430.7	800-225-1852	Y
Prudential Jennison Equity Opportunity Fund Class B	PJIBX	B-	B-	B	Up	6.70	9.72	15.06	26.49	84.61	15.88	430.7	800-225-1852	
Prudential Jennison Equity Opportunity Fund Class C	PJGCX	B-	B-	B	Up	6.76	9.77	15.12	26.55	84.70	15.88	430.7	800-225-1852	Y
Prudential Jennison Equity Opportunity Fund Class Q	PJOQX	B	B	B	Up	6.98	10.39	16.36	30.95	94.94	20.25	430.7	800-225-1852	Y
Prudential Jennison Equity Opportunity Fund Class R	PJORX	B	B-	B	Up	6.77	9.96	15.58	28.37	89.23	17.04	430.7	800-225-1852	Y
Prudential Jennison Equity Opportunity Fund Class Z	PJGZX	B	B	B	Up	6.97	10.33	16.25	30.36	94.14	20.24	430.7	800-225-1852	Y
Prudential Jennison Rising Dividend Fund Class A	PJDAX	B-	B-	B-	Down	5.13	9.70	17.25	24.13		13.31	13.8	800-225-1852	Y
Prudential Jennison Rising Dividend Fund Class C	PJDCX	B-	B-	B-	Down	4.92	9.37	16.39	21.49		13.32	13.8	800-225-1852	Y
Prudential Jennison Rising Dividend Fund Class Q	PJDQX	B-	B-	B-		5.20	9.84	17.53	25.14		13.32	13.8	800-225-1852	Y
Prudential Jennison Rising Dividend Fund Class Z	PJDZX	B-	B-	B-	Down	5.20	9.84	17.53	25.14		13.32	13.8	800-225-1852	Y
Prudential QMA Defensive Equity Fund Class A	PAMGX	B-	B-	B	Down	5.86	9.46	16.31	25.61	70.08	14.8	235.6	800-225-1852	Y
Prudential QMA Defensive Equity Fund Class B	DMGBX	B-	C+	B	Down	5.56	9.02	15.36	22.69	63.75	14.75	235.6	800-225-1852	
Prudential QMA Defensive Equity Fund Class C	PIMGX	B-	C+	B	Down	5.60	9.06	15.40	22.74	63.83	14.75	235.6	800-225-1852	Y
Prudential QMA Defensive Equity Fund Class Q	PAMQX	B-	B-	B	Down	5.86	9.60	16.69	26.53	72.36	14.83	235.6	800-225-1852	Y
Prudential QMA Defensive Equity Fund Class Retirement	SPMRX	B-	B-	B	Down	6.94	10.59	17.34	26.01	69.82	14.96	235.6	800-225-1852	Y
Prudential QMA Defensive Equity Fund Class Z	PDMZX	B-	B-	B	Down	5.85	9.59	16.60	26.44	72.23	14.82	235.6	800-225-1852	Y
Prudential QMA Large-Cap Core Equity Class Q	PTMQX	B	B	B		7.62	13.89	23.59	35.87	112.51	17.04	269.8	800-225-1852	Y
Prudential QMA Large-Cap Core Equity Fund Class A	PTMAX	B	B	B-		7.47	13.62	23.07	34.63	109.55	16.62	269.8	800-225-1852	Y
Prudential QMA Large-Cap Core Equity Fund Class B	PTMBX	B	B	B-		7.21	13.12	22.12	31.54	101.68	15.14	269.8	800-225-1852	
Prudential QMA Large-Cap Core Equity Fund Class C	PTMCX	B	B	B-		7.31	13.21	22.21	31.72	101.87	15.17	269.8	800-225-1852	Y
Prudential QMA Large-Cap Core Equity Fund Class Z	PTEZX	B	B	B		7.55	13.77	23.39	35.65	112.16	17.02	269.8	800-225-1852	Y
Prudential QMA Stock Index Fund Class A	PSIAX	B	B	B		6.52	11.14	21.20	34.86	106.45	51.92	1,148	800-225-1852	Y
Prudential QMA Stock Index Fund Class C	PSICX	B-	B-	B	Down	6.34	10.80	20.43	32.28	99.95	51.55	1,148	800-225-1852	Y
Prudential QMA Stock Index Fund Class I	PDSIX	B	B	B		6.60	11.34	21.62	36.21	109.89	52.07	1,148	800-225-1852	Y
Prudential QMA Stock Index Fund Class Q	PQSIX	B	B	B		6.60	11.30	21.55	36.00	109.38	52.08	1,148	800-225-1852	Y
Prudential QMA Stock Index Fund Class Z	PSIFX	B	B	B		6.59	11.29	21.54	35.99	109.37	52.08	1,148	800-225-1852	Y
Putnam Dynamic Asset Allocation Equity Fund Class A	US7467641749	B-	B-	B-	Down	6.05	12.00	22.70	30.60	92.41	13.19	84.5	617-292-1000	Y
Putnam Dynamic Asset Allocation Equity Fund Class P		B-	B-	B-	Down	6.04	12.14	23.05	29.35	90.56	13.2	84.5	617-292-1000	
Putnam Investors Fund Class A	PINVX	B	B	B-	Up	7.46	13.95	22.88	32.93	109.66	28.4	2,054	617-292-1000	Y
Putnam Investors Fund Class B	PNVBX	B-	B-	B-	Down	7.27	13.52	21.98	29.93	101.93	25.44	2,054	617-292-1000	Y
Putnam Investors Fund Class C	PCINX	B-	B-	B-	Down	7.28	13.53	21.93	29.96	101.99	26.76	2,054	617-292-1000	Y
Putnam Investors Fund Class M	PNVMX	B-	B	B-	Down	7.31	13.66	22.24	30.89	104.42	26.72	2,054	617-292-1000	Y
Putnam Investors Fund Class R	PIVRX	B-	B	B-	Down	7.40	13.82	22.57	31.92	107.02	28.14	2,054	617-292-1000	Y
Putnam Investors Fund Class R6	PIVEX	B	B	B-	Up	7.58	14.20	23.38	34.50	114.38	28.93	2,054	617-292-1000	Y
Putnam Investors Fund Class Y	PNVYX	B	B	B-	Up	7.53	14.10	23.16	33.93	112.37	28.8	2,054	617-292-1000	Y
Putnam Low Volatility Equity Fund Class A	PLVEX	B-	C+	B	Down	4.88	8.23	13.25	13.86		12.04	27.3	617-292-1000	Y
Putnam Low Volatility Equity Fund Class B	PLVFX	B-	C+	B	Down	4.69	7.80	12.34	11.21		11.9	27.3	617-292-1000	Y
Putnam Low Volatility Equity Fund Class C	PLVGX	B-	C+	B	Down	4.69	7.80	12.46	11.33		11.9	27.3	617-292-1000	Y
Putnam Low Volatility Equity Fund Class M	PLVHX	B-	C+	B	Down	4.76	7.94	12.77	12.19		12	27.3	617-292-1000	Y
Putnam Low Volatility Equity Fund Class Y	PLVKX	B-	C+	B	Down	4.98	8.42	13.55	14.68		12.04	27.3	617-292-1000	Y
Putnam Multi-Cap Core Fund Class A	PMYAX	B	B	C+	Up	7.11	14.21	23.68	34.56	122.09	22.84	564.7	617-292-1000	Y
Putnam Multi-Cap Core Fund Class B	PMYBX	B-	B	C+	Down	6.90	13.80	22.77	31.65	114.02	22.32	564.7	617-292-1000	Y
Putnam Multi-Cap Core Fund Class C	PMYCX	B-	B	C+	Down	6.89	13.80	22.78	31.62	114.10	22.29	564.7	617-292-1000	Y
Putnam Multi-Cap Core Fund Class M	PMYMX	B-	B	C+	Down	7.01	13.93	23.10	32.65	116.71	22.61	564.7	617-292-1000	Y
Putnam Multi-Cap Core Fund Class R	PMYZX	B-	B	C+	Down	7.07	14.09	23.38	33.60	119.46	22.78	564.7	617-292-1000	Y
Putnam Multi-Cap Core Fund Class Y	PMYYX	B	B	C+	Up	7.19	14.32	24.01	35.56	124.97	22.91	564.7	617-292-1000	Y
Putnam Research Fund Class A	PNRAX	B-	B	B-	Down	5.52	10.62	23.19	32.31	106.96	33.09	307.1	617-292-1000	Y

Category: US Equity Large Cap Blend (con't)

Fund Name	Ticker Symbol	RATINGS: Overall Rating	Reward Rating	Risk Rating	Recent Up/ Downgrade	TOTAL RETURNS & PERFORMANCE: 3-Month Total Return	6-Month Total Return	1-Year Total Return	3-Year Total Return	5-Year Total Return	ASSETS: NAV	Total Assets (MIL)	NEW INVESTORS: Telephone	Open to New Investors
Putnam Research Fund Class B	PRFBX	B-	B	B-	Down	5.33	10.18	22.30	29.33	99.33	30.83	307.1	617-292-1000	Y
Putnam Research Fund Class C	PRACX	B-	B	B-	Down	5.30	10.19	22.27	29.31	99.30	30.81	307.1	617-292-1000	Y
Putnam Research Fund Class M	PRFMX	B-	B	B-	Down	5.40	10.35	22.62	30.32	101.78	31.66	307.1	617-292-1000	Y
Putnam Research Fund Class R	PRSRX	B-	B	B-	Down	5.45	10.46	22.88	31.30	104.43	32.7	307.1	617-292-1000	Y
Putnam Research Fund Class R6 Shares	PLJMX	B	B	B-		5.61	10.84	23.75	33.66	109.07	33.49	307.1	617-292-1000	Y
Putnam Research Fund Class Y	PURYX	B	B	B-		5.57	10.74	23.53	33.29	109.52	33.38	307.1	617-292-1000	Y
QS S&P 500 Index Fund Class A	SBSPX	B	B	B		6.48	11.10	21.13	34.58	105.78	25.18	269.1	877-721-1926	Y
QS S&P 500 Index Fund Class D	SBSDX	B	B	B		6.51	11.23	21.42	35.41	107.85	25.35	269.1	877-721-1926	Y
QS U.S. Large Cap Equity Fund Class FI	LMUSX	B-	B-	B-	Down	7.82	12.99	23.11	29.50	101.70	19.53	696.3	877-721-1926	
QS U.S. Large Cap Equity Fund Class I	LMTIX	B-	B	B-	Down	7.90	13.16	23.50	30.77	104.74	19.41	696.3	877-721-1926	
QS U.S. Large Cap Equity Fund Class IS	LMISX	B-	B	B-	Down	7.90	13.15	23.49	30.83	104.83	19.42	696.3	877-721-1926	Y
Russell Investments Multifactor U.S. Equity Fund Class M	RTDTX	B	B	B	Up	7.25	11.75	21.51	37.48		13.1	689.6	800-426-7969	Y
Russell Investments Multifactor U.S. Equity Fund Class R6	RTDRX	B	B	B	Up	7.28	11.85	21.54	37.45		13.1	689.6	800-426-7969	Y
Russell Investments Multifactor U.S. Equity Fund Class S	RTDSX	B	B	B	Up	7.19	11.73	21.32	36.79		13.08	689.6	800-426-7969	Y
Russell Investments Multifactor U.S. Equity Fund Class Y	RTDYX	B	B	B	Up	7.20	11.79	21.59	37.55		13.09	689.6	800-426-7969	Y
Russell Investments U.S. Core Equity Fund Class A	RSQAX	B-	B-	B-	Down	6.64	10.67	20.73	32.95	99.89	32.41	605.0	800-426-7969	Y
Russell Investments U.S. Core Equity Fund Class C	REQSX	B-	B-	B-	Down	6.45	10.26	19.87	30.00	92.58	31.63	605.0	800-426-7969	Y
Russell Investments U.S. Core Equity Fund Class E	REAEX	B-	B-	B-	Down	6.65	10.63	20.72	32.93	99.85	32.47	605.0	800-426-7969	Y
Russell Investments U.S. Core Equity Fund Class S	RLISX	B	B	B		6.75	10.83	21.10	34.01	102.51	32.32	605.0	800-426-7969	Y
Russell Investments U.S. Core Equity Fund Class Y	REAYX	B	B	B-		6.75	10.91	21.14	33.40	100.55	32.28	605.0	800-426-7969	Y
Russell Investments U.S. Defensive Equity Fund Class A	REQAX	B	B-	B+		6.21	9.71	17.94	31.06	96.74	51.44	598.7	800-426-7969	Y
Russell Investments U.S. Defensive Equity Fund Class C	REQCX	B	B-	B+		6.02	9.29	17.06	28.13	89.48	51.05	598.7	800-426-7969	Y
Russell Investments U.S. Defensive Equity Fund Class E	REQEX	B	B-	B+		6.21	9.69	17.93	31.03	96.70	51.55	598.7	800-426-7969	Y
Russell Investments U.S. Defensive Equity Fund Class S	REQTX	B	B-	B+	Down	6.28	9.86	18.27	32.07	99.24	51.5	598.7	800-426-7969	Y
Russell Investments U.S. Defensive Equity Fund Class Y	REUYX	B	B-	B+	Down	6.32	9.94	18.45	32.80	101.16	51.4	598.7	800-426-7969	Y
Russell Investments U.S. Dynamic Equity Fund Class A	RSGAX	B	B	B-	Up	6.97	12.00	20.32	35.01	104.26	8.35	163.6	800-426-7969	Y
Russell Investments U.S. Dynamic Equity Fund Class C	RSGCX	B	B	B-	Up	6.73	11.63	19.35	31.99	96.79	6.19	163.6	800-426-7969	Y
Russell Investments U.S. Dynamic Equity Fund Class E	RSGEX	B	B	B-	Up	6.94	11.96	20.26	34.87	104.00	8.38	163.6	800-426-7969	Y
Russell Investments U.S. Dynamic Equity Fund Class S	RSGSX	B	B	B-	Up	6.98	12.11	20.59	35.95	106.57	8.98	163.6	800-426-7969	Y
Russell Investments U.S. Dynamic Equity Fund Class Y	RSGTX	B	B	B-	Up	7.05	12.25	20.78	36.76	108.64	9.16	163.6	800-426-7969	Y
Russell Investments U.S. Large Cap Equity Fund Class A	RLCZX	B-	B-	B-	Down	6.34	10.39	19.58	31.03	96.95	11.05	137.9	800-426-7969	Y
Russell Investments U.S. Large Cap Equity Fund Class C	RLCCX	B-	B-	B-	Down	6.11	9.97	18.68	28.06	89.75	11	137.9	800-426-7969	Y
Russell Investments U.S. Large Cap Equity Fund Class S	RLCSX	B-	B-	B	Down	6.38	10.47	19.81	31.98	99.39	11.1	137.9	800-426-7969	Y
Russell Investments U.S. Strategic Equity Fund Class A	RSEAX	B	B	B-	Up	7.24	11.81	20.76	32.18	98.63	13.63	3,109	800-426-7969	Y
Russell Investments U.S. Strategic Equity Fund Class C	RSECX	B-	B-	B-	Down	7.00	11.37	19.89	29.20	91.42	13.59	3,109	800-426-7969	Y
Russell Investments U.S. Strategic Equity Fund Class E	RSEEX	B	B	B-	Up	7.17	11.81	20.78	32.09	98.59	13.67	3,109	800-426-7969	Y
Russell Investments U.S. Strategic Equity Fund Class M	RUSTX	B	B	B-	Up	7.36	12.12	21.30	33.32	101.46	13.65	3,109	800-426-7969	Y
Russell Investments U.S. Strategic Equity Fund Class S	RSESX	B	B	B-	Up	7.36	11.99	21.20	33.22	101.30	13.66	3,109	800-426-7969	Y
Rydex S&P 500 Fund Class A	RYSOX	B-	B-	B	Down	6.21	10.51	19.84	30.29	94.74	49.28	266.2	800-820-0888	Y
Rydex S&P 500 Fund Class C	RYSYX	B-	B-	B-	Down	6.00	10.11	18.95	27.34	87.55	44.59	266.2	800-820-0888	Y
Rydex S&P 500 Fund Class H	RYSPX	B-	B-	B	Down	6.19	10.51	19.85	30.23	94.70	49.27	266.2	800-820-0888	Y
SA U.S. Core Market Fund Investor Class	SAMKX	B	B	B		7.13	12.12	22.19	34.50	104.92	23.39	780.5		Y
SA U.S. Core Market Fund Select Class	SAALX	B	B	B		7.18	12.16	22.24	34.55	105.01	23.37	780.5		Y
Salient Adaptive US Equity Fund Institutional Class	ASMCX	B	B	B+	Up	9.14	15.98	24.50	34.29	103.17	38.99	18.7	866-667-9228	Y
Salient Adaptive US Equity Fund Investor Class	ACSIX	B	B	B+	Up	9.04	15.71	23.97	32.69	99.39	35	18.7	866-667-9228	Y
Salient US Dividend Signal Fund Class A	FDYAX	B-	B-	B	Down	7.34	9.96	21.13	34.40		32.95	7.1	866-667-9228	Y
Salient US Dividend Signal Fund Institutional Class	FDYTX	B	B	B+		7.47	10.21	21.75	36.42		33.14	7.1	866-667-9228	Y
Salient US Dividend Signal Fund Investor Class	FDYRX	B	B-	B+		7.39	10.03	21.36	34.95		33.04	7.1	866-667-9228	Y
Sarofim Equity Fund	SRFMX	B-	B-	B-	Down	7.24	11.85	25.92	29.46		11.93	94.2		Y
Scharf Fund Institutional Class	LOGIX	B	C+	A-	Up	2.82	3.55	13.30	18.67	79.21	44.1	571.2	831-429-6513	Y
Scharf Fund Retail Class	LOGRX	B	C+	B+	Up	2.75	3.39	12.98	17.81	77.02	43.94	571.2	831-429-6513	Y
Schroder North American Equity Fund Class Investor	SNAEX	B	B	B		7.73	12.19	20.09	34.49	104.61	16.94	1,056	800-464-3108	Y

Category: US Equity Large Cap Blend (con't)

Fund Name	Ticker Symbol	RATINGS: Overall Rating	Reward Rating	Risk Rating	Recent Up/ Downgrade	TOTAL RETURNS & PERFORMANCE: 3-Month Total Return	6-Month Total Return	1-Year Total Return	3-Year Total Return	5-Year Total Return	ASSETS: NAV	Total Assets (MIL)	NEW INVESTORS: Telephone	Open to New Investors
Schwab 1000 Index® Fund	SNXFX	B	B	B		6.60	11.35	21.67	35.37	107.98	62.61	7,915	877-824-5615	Y
Schwab Core Equity Fund™	SWANX	B	B	B-	Up	6.62	11.94	24.16	32.03	104.87	22.71	2,404	877-824-5615	Y
Schwab Total Stock Market Index Fund®	SWTSX	B	B	B		6.27	11.10	21.06	35.53	108.69	47.25	7,020	877-824-5615	Y
Schwab® S&P 500 Index Fund	SWPPX	B	B	B		6.64	11.40	21.79	36.53	110.72	41.19	31,173	877-824-5615	Y
SEI Inst Inv Trust Dynamic Asset Alloc Fund Cls A	SDLAX	B	B	B		5.32	9.78	19.77	39.73	119.09	19.77	2,594	800-342-5734	Y
SEI Inst Inv Trust Large Cap Disciplined Eq Fund Cls A	SCPAX	B	B-	B+		5.26	10.46	19.83	34.60	107.85	13.41	3,437	800-342-5734	Y
SEI Institutional Investments Trust Large Cap Fund Class A	SLCAX	B-	B-	B-	Down	6.61	12.06	21.10	30.16	101.46	18.83	1,776	800-342-5734	Y
SEI Inst Investments Trust Large Cap Index Fund Cls A	LCIAX	B	B	B		6.56	11.30	21.59	36.10	110.67	197.01	2,369	800-342-5734	Y
SEI Inst Investments Trust S&P 500 Index Fund Cls A	SPINX	B	B	B		6.59	11.41	21.73	36.65		14.69	4,312	800-342-5734	Y
SEI Institutional Managed Trust Large Cap Fund Class F	SLGAX	B-	B-	B-	Down	7.67	13.05	22.54	30.45	98.43	14.74	2,664	800-342-5734	Y
SEI Institutional Managed Trust Large Cap Fund Class Y	SLYCX	B-	B	B-	Down	7.72	13.16	22.83	31.40	99.88	14.74	2,664	800-342-5734	Y
SEI Institutional Managed Trust S&P 500 Index Fund Class E	TRQIX	B	B	B		6.59	11.29	21.55	35.95	109.29	63.55	832.4	800-342-5734	Y
SEI Institutional Managed Trust S&P 500 Index Fund Class F	SSPIX	B	B	B		6.53	11.19	21.30	35.21	107.39	63.12	832.4	800-342-5734	Y
SEI Institutional Managed Trust S&P 500 Index Fund Class I	SPIIX	B	B-	B		6.48	11.06	21.06	34.31	105.12	63.52	832.4	800-342-5734	Y
SEI Institutional Managed Trust S&P 500 Index Fund Class Y	SETYX	B	B	B		6.58	11.29	21.52	35.93	109.25	63.1	832.4	800-342-5734	Y
SEI Inst Managed Trust Tax Managed Large Cap Fund Cls Y	STLYX	B-	B-	B-	Down	7.29	12.12	21.46	28.83	98.00	25.46	3,924	800-342-5734	Y
SEI Inst Managed Trust Tax-Managed Large Cap Fund Cls F	TMLCX	B-	B-	B-	Down	7.25	11.96	21.16	27.88	96.54	25.46	3,924	800-342-5734	Y
Selected American Shares Fund Class D	SLADX	B	B	B	Up	7.10	12.15	22.18	42.06	105.55	40.59	2,369	800-243-1575	Y
Selected American Shares Fund Class S	SLASX	B	B	B	Up	7.00	11.97	21.77	40.67	102.18	40.53	2,369	800-243-1575	Y
Shelton Capital Management S&P 500 Index Fund Class K	SPXKX	B	B-	B		6.64	11.16	20.92	34.02	104.10	51.4	172.2	800-955-9988	Y
Shelton Capital Mgmt S&P 500 Index Fund Direct Shares	SPFIX	B	B	B		6.79	11.46	21.53	36.04	109.27	51.42	172.2	800-955-9988	Y
Sit Dividend Growth Fund Class I	SDVGX	B	B-	B		6.89	10.71	20.24	32.51	95.00	16.8	1,079	800-332-5580	Y
Sit Dividend Growth Fund Class S	SDVSX	B-	B-	B	Down	6.79	10.54	19.87	31.48	92.58	16.73	1,079	800-332-5580	Y
Smead Value Fund Class A	SVFAX	B	B	A-		8.06	13.34	25.06	30.16	109.61	46.3	1,233	206-838-9850	Y
Smead Value Fund Class I1	SVFFX	B	B	A-		8.09	13.41	25.29	31.04	112.25	46.48	1,233	206-838-9850	Y
Smead Value Fund Class R1	SVFDX	B	B-	A-		7.99	13.16	24.68	28.96	106.76	45.94	1,233	206-838-9850	Y
Smead Value Fund Class R2	SVFKX	B	B-	A-		7.96	13.16	24.74	29.32	107.40	46.08	1,233	206-838-9850	Y
Smead Value Fund Class Y	SVFYX	B	B	A-		8.16	13.50	25.48	31.66	112.26	46.5	1,233	206-838-9850	Y
Smead Value Fund Investor Class	SMVLX	B	B	A-		8.02	13.27	24.97	30.01	109.54	46.62	1,233	206-838-9850	Y
Smith Group Large Cap Core Growth Fund Institutional Class	BSLGX	B	B+	B		8.00	15.59	24.90	37.37	112.86	9.52	50.9	888-572-0968	Y
Smith Group Large Cap Core Growth Fund Investor Class	BSLNX	B	B	B		8.08	15.55	24.71	36.65	110.55	9.53	50.9	888-572-0968	Y
Spirit of America Large Cap Value Fund A	SOAVX	B-	B-	B-	Down	6.72	10.93	20.21	25.40	82.36	21.59	99.7		Y
Spirit of America Large Cap Value Fund Class C	SACVX	B-	B-	B-	Down	6.47	10.56	19.36	22.77	76.07	21.62	99.7		Y
SSgA S&P 500 Index Fund N Class	SVSPX	B	B	B		6.64	11.35	21.67	36.31	110.03	37.75	1,668	617-664-7338	Y
State Farm Equity Fund Class A	SNEAX	B	B	B	Up	7.74	13.37	23.88	33.31	108.32	10.66	649.7		Y
State Farm Equity Fund Class B	SNEBX	B	B	B-	Up	7.66	13.47	23.71	31.30	102.38	10.56	649.7		Y
State Farm Equity Fund Class B Legacy	SLEBX	B	B	B	Up	7.65	13.45	23.74	32.13	104.72	11.19	649.7		Y
State Farm Equity Fund Class Institutional	SLEIX	B	B	B	Up	7.67	13.37	23.94	34.09	110.54	10.72	649.7		Y
State Farm Equity Fund Class R1	SREOX	B	B	B	Up	7.74	13.38	23.76	32.28	105.28	10.67	649.7		Y
State Farm Equity Fund Class R2	SRETX	B	B	B	Up	7.60	13.34	23.75	32.82	106.94	10.63	649.7		Y
State Farm Equity Fund Class R3	SREHX	B	B	B	Up	7.66	13.35	23.91	33.78	109.78	10.73	649.7		Y
State Farm Equity Fund Premier Shares	SLEAX	B	B	B	Up	7.76	13.45	23.95	33.52	108.62	11.2	649.7		Y
State Farm Growth Fund	STFGX	B-	B-	B-	Down	6.69	10.30	16.57	28.32	86.50	80.15	4,960		Y
State Farm S&P 500 Index Fund Class A	SNPAX	B	B	B		6.54	11.16	21.20	34.26	104.67	19.76	1,540		Y
State Farm S&P 500 Index Fund Class B	SNPBX	B-	B-	B	Down	6.53	11.18	21.01	32.20	98.46	19.93	1,540		Y
State Farm S&P 500 Index Fund Class B Legacy	SLIBX	B	B-	B		6.53	11.19	21.14	33.08	101.15	20.13	1,540		Y
State Farm S&P 500 Index Fund Class Institutional	SFXIX	B	B	B		6.54	11.18	21.33	35.06	106.73	19.95	1,540		Y
State Farm S&P 500 Index Fund Class R1	RSPOX	B	B-	B		6.52	11.19	21.13	33.25	101.70	19.85	1,540		Y
State Farm S&P 500 Index Fund Class R2	RSPTX	B	B-	B		6.53	11.15	21.14	33.89	103.47	19.74	1,540		Y
State Farm S&P 500 Index Fund Class R3	RSPHX	B	B	B		6.29	10.92	21.01	34.42	105.43	19.91	1,540		Y
State Farm S&P 500 Index Fund Premier Shares	SLIAX	B	B	B		6.55	11.26	21.39	34.45	104.88	19.88	1,540		Y
State Street Equity 500 Index Fund Administrative Shares	STFAX	B	B	B		6.54	11.32	21.42	35.76	108.96	21.62	764.0	617-664-7338	Y

Category: US Equity Large Cap Blend (con't)

Fund Name	Ticker Symbol	RATINGS: Overall Rating	Reward Rating	Risk Rating	Recent Up/ Downgrade	TOTAL RETURNS & PERFORMANCE: 3-Month Total Return	6-Month Total Return	1-Year Total Return	3-Year Total Return	5-Year Total Return	ASSETS: NAV	Total Assets (MIL)	NEW INVESTORS: Telephone	Open to New Investors
State Street Equity 500 Index Fund Class A	SSSVX	B	B	B		0.98	5.40	14.86	27.64	95.96	21.63	764.0	617-664-7338	Y
State Street Equity 500 Index Fund Class I	SSSWX	B	B	B		0.79	5.30	14.80	28.28	97.42	21.63	764.0	617-664-7338	Y
State Street Equity 500 Index Fund Class K	SSSYX	B	B	B		2.90	7.55	17.43	31.66	102.72	21.62	764.0	617-664-7338	Y
State Street Equity 500 Index Fund Class R Shares	SSFRX	B	B-	B		6.46	11.09	20.95	33.98	104.24	21.61	764.0	617-664-7338	Y
State Street Equity 500 Index Fund Service Shares	STBIX	B	B	B		6.49	11.27	21.33	35.38	107.93	21.6	764.0	617-664-7338	Y
State Street Equity 500 Index II Portfolio	SSEYX	B	B	B	Up	6.59	11.42	21.65	36.78		13.07	2,020	617-664-7338	Y
State Street Institutional U.S. Equity Fund Investment Cls	SUSIX	B-	B-	B-	Down	4.49	8.86	20.45	28.48	100.68	12.31	477.8	617-664-7338	Y
State Street Institutional U.S. Equity Fund Service Class	SUSSX	B-	B-	B-	Down	4.40	8.74	20.17	27.48	99.35	13.19	477.8	617-664-7338	Y
Steward Large Cap Enhanced Index Fund Class A	SEEKX	B-	B-	B-	Down	6.34	11.39	20.98	29.59	104.52	41.76	390.7	800-262-6631	Y
Steward Large Cap Enhanced Index Fund Class Institutional	SEECX	B	B	B-	Up	6.44	11.55	21.33	30.86	107.97	41.59	390.7	800-262-6631	Y
Stralem Equity Fund	STEFX	B-	B-	B	Down	3.40	6.17	16.67	26.82	79.26	10.06	139.3		Y
Strategic Advisers® Core Fund	FCSAX	B	B	B-		6.62	11.64	22.54	34.71	105.80	18.03	24,519	617-563-7000	Y
Strategic Advisers® Core Multi-Manager Fund	FLAUX	B	B-	B		6.59	11.22	21.15	34.13	102.35	13.05	64.2	617-563-7000	Y
Strategic Advisers® Core Multi-Manager Fund Class L	FQAPX	B	B-	B		6.59	11.22	21.15	34.13	102.35	13.05	64.2	617-563-7000	Y
Strategic Advisers® Core Multi-Manager Fund Class N	FQAQX	B-	B-	B	Down	6.53	11.05	20.78	33.07	99.77	13.04	64.2	617-563-7000	Y
Summit Global Inv U.S. Low Vol Eq Fund Cls A	LVOLX	B	B-	B+		7.13	10.10	16.06	28.69	92.13	15.66	104.8	888-251-4847	Y
Summit Global Inv U.S. Low Vol Eq Fund Cls C	SGICX	B	C+	B+		6.97	9.69	15.40	25.24	84.21	15.39	104.8	888-251-4847	Y
Summit Global Inv U.S. Low Vol Eq Fund Cls I	SILVX	B	B-	B+		7.24	10.20	16.40	29.64	94.51	15.62	104.8	888-251-4847	Y
T. Rowe Price Capital Opportunity Fund	PRCOX	B	B	B+	Down	6.51	11.36	23.71	38.96	112.61	26.06	608.7	410-345-2000	Y
T. Rowe Price Capital Opportunity Fund Advisor Class	PACOX	B	B	B+	Down	6.40	11.14	23.32	37.70	109.48	25.99	608.7	410-345-2000	Y
T. Rowe Price Capital Opportunity Fund Class R	RRCOX	B	B	B+	Down	6.34	11.01	23.04	36.54	106.41	25.94	608.7	410-345-2000	Y
T. Rowe Price Capital Opportunity Fund I Class	PCCOX	B	B	B+	Down	6.51	11.39	23.85	39.11	112.85	26.05	608.7	410-345-2000	Y
T. Rowe Price Dividend Growth Fund	PRDGX	B	B-	B+		5.82	9.04	19.32	35.13	102.40	43.38	8,771	410-345-2000	Y
T. Rowe Price Dividend Growth Fund Advisor Class	TADGX	B	B-	B+		5.78	8.93	19.02	34.07	99.72	43.34	8,771	410-345-2000	Y
T. Rowe Price Dividend Growth Fund I Class	PDGIX	B	B-	B+		5.87	9.15	19.47	35.45	102.88	43.37	8,771	410-345-2000	Y
T. Rowe Price Equity Index 500 Fund	PREIX	B	B	B		6.59	11.31	21.54	35.88	109.01	71.71	29,685	410-345-2000	Y
T. Rowe Price Equity Index 500 Fund I Class	PRUIX	B	B	B		6.62	11.39	21.72	36.34	109.72	71.72	29,685	410-345-2000	Y
T. Rowe Price Growth and Income Fund	PRGIX	B	B-	B+		6.15	8.74	21.04	33.94	105.99	28.44	1,912	410-345-2000	Y
T. Rowe Price Growth and Income Fund I Class	TGTIX	B	B-	B+		6.15	8.82	21.18	34.07	106.21	28.45	1,912	410-345-2000	Y
T. Rowe Price Institutional U.S. Structured Research Fund	TRISX	B	B	B+	Down	6.51	11.37	23.81	39.34	113.71	12.92	648.5	410-345-2000	Y
T. Rowe Price Total Equity Market Index Fund	POMIX	B	B	B		6.21	10.83	20.79	35.24	108.68	30.13	1,715	410-345-2000	Y
T. Rowe Price U.S. Large-Cap Core Fund	TRULX	B	B-	B+		6.16	8.75	20.92	38.80	109.78	23.81	519.7	410-345-2000	Y
T. Rowe Price U.S. Large-Cap Core Fund Advisor Class	PAULX	B	B-	B+		6.10	8.60	20.63	37.76	108.06	23.81	519.7	410-345-2000	Y
T. Rowe Price U.S. Large-Cap Core Fund I Class	RCLIX	B	B-	B+		6.15	8.78	21.12	39.02	110.12	23.82	519.7	410-345-2000	Y
TCW Focused Equities Fund Class Institutional	TGFFX	B-	C+	B	Up	4.97	8.69	13.95	12.49	88.06	22.28	10.0	213-244-0000	Y
TCW Focused Equities Fund Class N	TGFVX	B-	C+	B	Up	4.98	8.69	13.94	12.46	88.07	22.04	10.0	213-244-0000	Y
TETON Westwood Equity Fund Class A	WEECX	B-	B-	B-	Down	7.57	11.49	19.87	29.26	90.17	13.13	64.2		Y
TETON Westwood Equity Fund Class AAA	WESWX	B-	B-	B	Down	7.66	11.74	20.22	30.30	92.57	13.15	64.2		Y
TETON Westwood Equity Fund Class C	WEQCX	B-	B-	B-	Down	7.43	11.29	19.29	27.37	85.50	12.41	64.2		Y
TETON Westwood Equity Fund Institutional Class	WEEIX	B-	B-	B	Down	7.71	11.81	20.51	31.20	94.53	13.09	64.2		Y
The Cook & Bynum Fund	COBYX	B-	C+	B		2.93	4.19	15.12	14.09	36.10	16.69	152.8		Y
The Hartford Capital Appreciation Fund Class A	ITHAX	B-	B-	B-	Down	4.94	7.40	21.25	27.04	97.80	37.55	8,327	888-843-7824	Y
The Hartford Capital Appreciation Fund Class C	HCACX	B-	B-	B-	Down	4.76	7.00	20.36	24.31	90.80	29.23	8,327	888-843-7824	Y
The Hartford Capital Appreciation Fund Class F	HCAFX	B-	B-	B-	Down	5.04	7.60	21.72	28.51	101.75	37.65	8,327	888-843-7824	Y
The Hartford Capital Appreciation Fund Class I	ITHIX	B-	B-	B-	Down	5.04	7.56	21.60	28.16	100.93	37.67	8,327	888-843-7824	Y
The Hartford Capital Appreciation Fund Class R3	ITHRX	B-	B-	B-	Down	4.86	7.22	20.89	25.85	94.85	41.39	8,327	888-843-7824	Y
The Hartford Capital Appreciation Fund Class R4	ITHSX	B-	B-	B-	Down	4.95	7.39	21.25	27.00	97.85	42.59	8,327	888-843-7824	Y
The Hartford Capital Appreciation Fund Class R5	ITHTX	B-	B-	B-	Down	5.02	7.56	21.63	28.16	100.78	43.34	8,327	888-843-7824	Y
The Hartford Capital Appreciation Fund Class R6	ITHVX	B-	B-	B-	Down	5.03	7.60	21.71	28.46	101.66	43.56	8,327	888-843-7824	Y
The Hartford Capital Appreciation Fund Class Y	HCAYX	B-	B-	B-	Down	5.02	7.57	21.68	28.47	101.69	43.55	8,327	888-843-7824	Y
The MP 63 Fund	DRIPX	B-	B-	B-	Down	7.80	10.46	18.51	29.60	99.96	21.53	67.4		Y
Thompson LargeCap Fund	THPGX	B-	B	B-	Down	6.50	10.27	18.23	27.07	103.07	67.2	129.1	800-999-0887	Y

Category: US Equity Large Cap Blend (con't)

Fund Name	Ticker Symbol	Overall Rating	Reward Rating	Risk Rating	Recent Up/ Downgrade	3-Month Total Return	6-Month Total Return	1-Year Total Return	3-Year Total Return	5-Year Total Return	NAV	Total Assets (MIL)	Telephone	Open to New Investors
Thornburg Value Fund Class A	TVAFX	B-	B	B-	Down	4.07	7.75	23.32	35.63	114.56	67.56	1,004	800-847-0200	Y
Thornburg Value Fund Class C	TVCFX	B-	B-	B-	Down	3.88	7.34	22.40	32.61	106.63	61.95	1,004	800-847-0200	Y
Thornburg Value Fund Class I	TVIFX	B	B	B-		4.17	7.97	23.81	37.25	118.82	69.48	1,004	800-847-0200	Y
Thornburg Value Fund Class R3	TVRFX	B	B	B-	Up	4.07	7.76	23.35	35.76	114.94	67.16	1,004	800-847-0200	Y
Thornburg Value Fund Class R4	TVIRX	B	B	B-		4.10	7.82	23.48	36.18	116.04	67.87	1,004	800-847-0200	Y
Thornburg Value Fund Class R5	TVRRX	B	B	B-		4.16	7.96	23.80	37.23	118.85	69.38	1,004	800-847-0200	Y
Thrivent Series Large Cap Index Portfolio		B	B	B		6.56	11.25	21.46	35.74	108.21	36.9564	929.4		Y
TIAA-CREF Equity Index Fund Advisor Class	TEIHX	B	B	B		6.25	11.08	20.99	35.72	109.29	19.66	16,203	877-518-9161	Y
TIAA-CREF Equity Index Fund Institutional Class	TIEIX	B	B	B		6.29	11.17	21.09	35.85	109.49	19.65	16,203	877-518-9161	Y
TIAA-CREF Equity Index Fund Premier Class	TCEPX	B	B	B		6.28	11.12	20.92	35.20	107.94	19.61	16,203	877-518-9161	Y
TIAA-CREF Equity Index Fund Retail Class	TINRX	B	B	B-		6.22	11.02	20.74	34.67	106.35	20.02	16,203	877-518-9161	Y
TIAA-CREF Equity Index Fund Retirement Class	TIQRX	B	B	B-		6.27	11.09	20.85	34.89	107.04	19.96	16,203	877-518-9161	Y
TIAA-CREF S&P 500 Index Fund Advisor Class	TISAX	B	B	B		6.54	11.29	21.59	36.41	110.65	29.59	4,838	877-518-9161	Y
TIAA-CREF S&P 500 Index Fund Institutional Class	TISPX	B	B	B		6.62	11.41	21.77	36.64	111.01	29.61	4,838	877-518-9161	Y
TIAA-CREF S&P 500 Index Fund Retirement Class	TRSPX	B	B	B		6.54	11.24	21.45	35.62	108.35	29.44	4,838	877-518-9161	Y
TIAA-CREF Social Choice Equity Fund Advisor Class	TICHX	B-	B	B-	Down	6.22	10.88	20.90	32.67	103.54	19.18	2,979	877-518-9161	Y
TIAA-CREF Social Choice Equity Fund Institutional Class	TISCX	B-	B	B-	Down	6.19	10.85	20.92	32.63	103.48	19.18	2,979	877-518-9161	Y
TIAA-CREF Social Choice Equity Fund Premier Class	TRPSX	B-	B	B-	Down	6.14	10.76	20.79	32.05	101.92	19.13	2,979	877-518-9161	Y
TIAA-CREF Social Choice Equity Fund Retail Class	TICRX	B-	B	B-	Down	6.11	10.69	20.57	31.58	100.60	17.24	2,979	877-518-9161	Y
TIAA-CREF Social Choice Equity Fund Retirement Class	TRSCX	B-	B	B-	Down	6.12	10.72	20.63	31.70	100.94	19.48	2,979	877-518-9161	Y
Tocqueville Fund	TOCQX	B-	B-	B-	Down	7.28	12.28	20.34	26.15	94.67	36.62	297.9	212-698-0800	Y
Toreador Core Fund Institutional Class	TORZX	B+	A	B	Up	7.15	17.07	25.66	36.13	121.06	17.79	170.9		Y
Toreador Core Fund Investor Class	TORLX	B	A-	C+	Up	7.11	16.91	25.32	35.03	118.39	17.77	170.9		Y
Touchstone Focused Fund Class A	TFOAX	B	B-	B		4.67	7.61	13.90	29.63	96.96	42.87	1,245	800-543-0407	Y
Touchstone Focused Fund Class C	TFFCX	B-	B-	B	Down	4.46	7.18	13.04	26.75	89.80	40.9	1,245	800-543-0407	Y
Touchstone Focused Fund Class Y	TFFYX	B	B-	A		4.72	7.75	14.20	30.67	99.62	43.4	1,245	800-543-0407	Y
Touchstone Focused Fund Institutional	TFFIX	B	B-	A		4.74	7.79	14.27	31.08	100.72	43.57	1,245	800-543-0407	Y
Touchstone Large Cap Focused Fund Class A	SENCX	B	B	B		6.92	11.71	23.07	36.33	101.27	42.31	1,883	800-543-0407	Y
Touchstone Large Cap Focused Fund Class C	SCSCX	B-	B-	B	Down	6.73	11.26	22.10	33.13	93.45	40.05	1,883	800-543-0407	Y
Touchstone Large Cap Focused Fund Class Y	SICWX	B	B	B		7.01	11.86	23.42	37.48	104.18	42.16	1,883	800-543-0407	Y
Touchstone Large Cap Focused Fund Institutional Class	SCRLX	B	B	B		7.04	11.94	23.57	37.81	103.50	42.21	1,883	800-543-0407	Y
Touchstone Large Cap Fund Class A	TACLX	B-	B-	B-	Down	7.66	12.52	21.24	25.53		13.41	357.0	800-543-0407	Y
Touchstone Large Cap Fund Class C	TFCCX	B-	B-	C+	Down	7.47	12.11	20.38	22.92		13.23	357.0	800-543-0407	Y
Touchstone Large Cap Fund Class Y	TLCYX	B-	B-	B-	Down	7.77	12.71	21.62	26.59		13.44	357.0	800-543-0407	Y
Touchstone Large Cap Fund Institutional Class	TLCIX	B-	B-	B-	Down	7.69	12.70	21.72	26.97		13.45	357.0	800-543-0407	Y
Transamerica Stock Index R	TSTRX	B	B	B		6.53	11.03	21.06	34.59	105.93	11.25	802.5	888-233-4339	Y
Transamerica Stock Index R4	TSTFX	B	B	B		6.59	11.27	21.48	35.73	108.71	11.26	802.5	888-233-4339	Y
UBS U.S. Sustainable Equity Fund Class A	BNEQX	B	B-	B		1.94	6.15	18.79	29.02	106.48	33	31.2	212-882-5586	Y
UBS U.S. Sustainable Equity Fund Class C	BNQCX	B-	B-	C+	Down	1.77	5.79	17.91	26.14	98.85	31.59	31.2	212-882-5586	Y
UBS U.S. Sustainable Equity Fund Class P	BPEQX	B	B-	B		2.03	6.29	19.10	29.90	108.96	33.11	31.2	212-882-5586	Y
USA Mutuals Vice Fund Class A Shares	VICAX	B	B	A-		7.91	10.92	25.71	40.19	89.58	32.17	233.0		Y
USA Mutuals Vice Fund Class C Shares	VICCX	B	B	B+		7.74	10.50	24.80	37.05	82.59	31.61	233.0		Y
USA Mutuals Vice Fund Institutional Class	VICVX	B+	B	A	Up	8.02	11.06	26.08	41.27	91.40	32.66	233.0		Y
USA Mutuals Vice Fund Investor Class Shares	VICEX	B	B	A-		7.95	10.91	25.71	40.21	89.67	32.31	233.0		Y
USAA Growth & Income Fund	USGRX	B-	B	B-	Down	6.87	9.91	20.64	33.10	106.45	25.17	1,865	800-531-8722	Y
USAA Growth & Income Fund Adviser Shares	USGIX	B-	B-	B-	Down	6.77	9.74	20.26	32.00	103.42	25.09	1,865	800-531-8722	Y
USAA Growth & Income Fund Institutional Shares	UIGIX	B	B	B+	Up	6.89	9.95	20.72	33.30	106.76	25.15	1,865	800-531-8722	Y
USAA S&P 500 Index Fund Member Shares	USSPX	B	B	B		6.58	11.28	21.53	35.84	108.99	38	6,869	800-531-8722	Y
USAA S&P 500 Index Fund Reward Shares	USPRX	B	B	B		6.60	11.33	21.63	36.26	110.04	38.01	6,869	800-531-8722	Y
VALIC Company I Core Equity Fund	VCCEX	B	B	B-	Up	7.05	12.93	21.03	32.63	104.58	25.05	260.8		Y
VALIC Company I Growth & Income Fund	VCGAX	B-	B-	B-	Down	6.41	11.07	21.06	33.14	107.06	23.06	129.1		Y
VALIC Company I Large Cap Core Fund	VLCCX	B	B-	B+		5.35	9.76	21.43	34.62	113.12	12.59	179.4		Y

Category: US Equity Large Cap Blend (con't)

		RATINGS				TOTAL RETURNS & PERFORMANCE					ASSETS		NEW INVESTORS	
Fund Name	Ticker Symbol	Overall Rating	Reward Rating	Risk Rating	Recent Up/ Downgrade	3-Month Total Return	6-Month Total Return	1-Year Total Return	3-Year Total Return	5-Year Total Return	NAV	Total Assets (MIL)	Telephone	Open to New Investors
VALIC Company I Stock Index Fund	VSTIX	B	B	B		6.58	11.25	21.41	35.50	108.11	40.81	4,822		Y
VALIC Company II Socially Responsible Fund	VCSRX	B	B	B		6.64	11.33	20.65	33.54	114.80	22	807.3		Y
Vanguard 500 Index Fund Admiral Shares	VFIAX	B	B	B		6.63	11.41	21.78	36.74	111.30	246.82	383,897	877-662-7447	Y
Vanguard 500 Index Fund Institutional Select Shares	VFFSX	B	B	B		6.64	11.42	21.83	36.59	110.56	130.79	383,897	877-662-7447	Y
Vanguard 500 Index Fund Investor Shares	VFINX	B	B	B		6.60	11.35	21.66	36.32	110.14	246.82	383,897	877-662-7447	Y
Vanguard Dividend Appreciation Index Fund Admiral Shares	VDADX	B	B	B+		8.07	11.11	22.22	32.73	92.79	27.66	33,549	877-662-7447	Y
Vanguard Dividend Appreciation Index Fund Investor Shares	VDAIX	B	B-	B+		8.10	11.12	22.14	32.45	92.00	40.79	33,549	877-662-7447	Y
Vanguard Dividend Growth Fund Investor Shares	VDIGX	B	B-	B+		5.62	8.54	19.33	30.50	96.07	26.55	33,269	877-662-7447	Y
Vanguard FTSE Social Index Fund Institutional Shares	VFTNX	B	B	B		6.84	11.92	24.18	37.41	123.75	17.49	3,811	877-662-7447	Y
Vanguard FTSE Social Index Fund Investor Shares	VFTSX	B	B	B		6.82	11.89	24.11	36.97	122.63	17.48	3,811	877-662-7447	Y
Vanguard Growth and Income Fund Admiral Shares	VGIAX	B	B	B+		6.70	11.91	20.80	36.70	113.02	77.11	10,531	877-662-7447	Y
Vanguard Growth and Income Fund Investor Shares	VQNPX	B	B	B+		6.67	11.84	20.67	36.22	111.80	47.24	10,531	877-662-7447	Y
Vanguard Inst Index Fund Inst Plus Shares	VIIIX	B	B	B		6.64	11.42	21.81	36.84	111.60	243.48	233,655	877-662-7447	Y
Vanguard Institutional Index Fund Institutional Shares	VINIX	B	B	B		6.63	11.40	21.78	36.76	111.39	243.46	233,655	877-662-7447	Y
Vanguard Inst Total Stock Mkt Index Fund Inst Plus Shares	VITPX	B	B	B		6.33	11.18	21.13	35.91	110.17	59.47	43,361	877-662-7447	Y
Vanguard Inst Total Stock Mkt Index Fund Inst Shares	VITNX	B	B	B		6.34	11.16	21.13	35.85	109.94	59.47	43,361	877-662-7447	Y
Vanguard Large Cap Index Fund Admiral Shares	VLCAX	B	B	B		6.61	11.37	22.02	36.29	110.62	61.86	18,396	877-662-7447	Y
Vanguard Large Cap Index Fund Institutional Shares	VLISX	B	B	B		6.61	11.39	22.03	36.33	110.70	254.61	18,396	877-662-7447	Y
Vanguard Large Cap Index Fund Investor Shares	VLACX	B	B	B		6.59	11.32	21.89	35.79	109.24	49.48	18,396	877-662-7447	Y
Vanguard Mega Cap Index Fund Institutional Shares	VMCTX	B	B	B		6.80	11.80	22.56	37.71	111.88	180.74	1,478	877-662-7447	Y
Vanguard Russell 1000 Index Fund Institutional Shares	VRNIX	B	B	B		6.57	11.31	21.58	35.73	109.80	237.15	2,893	877-662-7447	Y
Vanguard Russell 3000 Index Fund Institutional Shares	VRTTX	B	B	B		6.30	11.15	21.03	35.48	108.93	236.93	1,164	877-662-7447	Y
Vanguard Tax-Managed Capital Appreciation Admiral Shares	VTCLX	B	B	B		6.62	11.68	22.39	38.02	113.19	137.3	9,065	877-662-7447	Y
Vanguard Tax-Managed Capital Appreciation Fund Inst Shares	VTCIX	B	B	B		6.64	11.71	22.43	38.17	113.55	68.23	9,065	877-662-7447	Y
Vanguard Total Stock Market Index Fund Admiral Shares	VTSAX	B	B	B		6.33	11.17	21.16	35.72	109.49	66.72	656,961	877-662-7447	Y
Vanguard Total Stock Mkt Index Fund Inst Plus Shares	VSMPX	B	B	B		6.33	11.17	21.19	35.73	109.03	125.14	656,961	877-662-7447	Y
Vanguard Total Stock Mkt Index Fund Inst Select Shares	VSTSX	B	B	B		6.34	11.18	21.20	35.55	108.74	131.31	656,961	877-662-7447	Y
Vanguard Total Stock Mkt Index Fund Inst Shares	VITSX	B	B	B		6.33	11.16	21.17	35.75	109.58	66.73	656,961	877-662-7447	Y
Vanguard Total Stock Market Index Fund Investor Shares	VTSMX	B	B	B		6.31	11.11	21.05	35.28	108.33	66.7	656,961	877-662-7447	Y
Victory CEMP US 500 Enhanced Vol Wtd Index Fund Cls A	CUHAX	B	B	B-		7.14	11.15	21.52	35.14	102.46	16.31	132.9	800-539-3863	Y
Victory CEMP US 500 Enhanced Vol Wtd Index Fund Cls C	CUHCX	B	B	B-		7.00	10.73	20.70	32.15	95.06	16.01	132.9	800-539-3863	Y
Victory CEMP US 500 Enhanced Vol Wtd Index Fund Cls I	CUHIX	B	B	B-		7.21	11.27	21.86	36.18	104.93	16.32	132.9	800-539-3863	Y
Victory Diversified Stock Fund Class A	SRVEX	B-	B-	B	Down	9.81	17.73	27.32	27.01	93.26	19.04	515.4	800-539-3863	Y
Victory Diversified Stock Fund Class C	VDSCX	B-	B-	B-	Down	9.55	17.26	26.26	23.87	85.47	18.06	515.4	800-539-3863	Y
Victory Diversified Stock Fund Class I	VDSIX	B-	B-	B	Down	9.88	17.90	27.60	28.02	95.69	19	515.4	800-539-3863	Y
Victory Diversified Stock Fund Class R	GRINX	B-	B-	B-	Down	9.69	17.55	26.89	25.93	90.45	18.7	515.4	800-539-3863	Y
Victory Diversified Stock Fund Class R6	VDSRX	B-	B-	B	Down	9.87	17.90	27.62	28.11	95.42	19	515.4	800-539-3863	Y
Victory Diversified Stock Fund Class Y	VDSYX	B-	B-	B	Down	9.85	17.82	27.55	27.82	95.29	19.03	515.4	800-539-3863	Y
Victory Institutional Diversified Stock Fund	VIDSX	B-	B-	B	Down	10.05	18.04	27.72	27.88	95.88	10.59	88.9	800-539-3863	Y
Victory RS Large Cap Alpha Fund Class A	GPAFX	B	B-	B	Up	6.10	10.97	18.31	24.93	100.02	56.61	610.9	800-539-3863	Y
Victory RS Large Cap Alpha Fund Class C	RCOCX	B-	B-	B	Down	5.88	10.52	17.36	21.98	92.11	49.5	610.9	800-539-3863	Y
Victory RS Large Cap Alpha Fund Class R	RCEKX	B	B-	B	Up	6.01	10.77	17.87	23.59	96.33	56.35	610.9	800-539-3863	Y
Victory RS Large Cap Alpha Fund Class Y	RCEYX	B	B-	B	Up	6.16	11.10	18.56	25.70	102.35	56.39	610.9	800-539-3863	Y
Victory S&P 500 Index Fund Class A	MUXAX	B	B	B		6.53	11.13	21.10	34.57	105.48	21.17	238.8	800-539-3863	Y
Victory S&P 500 Index Fund Class R	MUXRX	B-	B-	B	Down	6.40	10.92	20.56	32.84	101.36	21.12	238.8	800-539-3863	Y
Victory S&P 500 Index Fund Class Y	MUXYX	B	B	B		6.53	11.22	21.28	35.34	107.25	21.3	238.8	800-539-3863	Y
Victory Special Value Fund Class A	SSVSX	B-	B-	B-	Down	9.64	17.46	26.14	25.17	78.67	27.71	91.5	800-539-3863	Y
Victory Special Value Fund Class C	VSVCX	B-	C+	B-	Down	9.41	16.89	24.96	21.80	70.71	24.98	91.5	800-539-3863	Y
Victory Special Value Fund Class I	VSPIX	B-	B-	B-	Down	9.72	17.45	26.14	25.63	80.31	27.99	91.5	800-539-3863	Y
Victory Special Value Fund Class R	VSVGX	B-	B-	B-	Down	9.54	17.24	25.76	24.09	76.11	26.63	91.5	800-539-3863	Y
Victory Special Value Fund Class Y	VSVYX	B-	B-	B-	Down	9.73	17.56	26.43	26.15	80.95	27.83	91.5	800-539-3863	Y
Virtus Rampart Enhanced Core Equity Fund Class A	PDIAX	B	B	B+	Down	6.83	12.44	22.54	39.47	109.59	20.29	192.2	800-243-1574	Y

Category: US Equity Large Cap Blend (con't)

Fund Name	Ticker Symbol	Overall Rating	Reward Rating	Risk Rating	Recent Up/ Downgrade	3-Month Total Return	6-Month Total Return	1-Year Total Return	3-Year Total Return	5-Year Total Return	NAV	Total Assets (Mil)	Telephone	Open to New Investors
Virtus Rampart Enhanced Core Equity Fund Class C	PGICX	B	B	B+	Down	6.64	12.05	21.62	36.45	101.91	18.14	192.2	800-243-1574	Y
Virtus Rampart Enhanced Core Equity Fund Class I	PXIIX	B	B	B+	Down	6.87	12.61	22.83	40.53	112.22	20.23	192.2	800-243-1574	Y
Voya Corporate Leaders 100 Fund Class A	IACLX	B-	B-	B-	Down	5.94	10.78	18.90	29.21	100.51	21.9	1,075	800-366-0066	Y
Voya Corporate Leaders 100 Fund Class C	ICCLX	B-	B-	B-	Down	5.77	10.48	18.27	27.04	95.33	21.79	1,075	800-366-0066	Y
Voya Corporate Leaders 100 Fund Class I	IICLX	B-	B-	B-	Down	6.07	11.02	19.35	30.50	103.89	21.89	1,075	800-366-0066	Y
Voya Corporate Leaders 100 Fund Class O	IOCLX	B-	B-	B-	Down	5.97	10.82	18.89	29.05	100.30	21.88	1,075	800-366-0066	Y
Voya Corporate Leaders 100 Fund Class R	IRCLX	B-	B-	B-	Down	5.89	10.66	18.58	28.04	98.00	21.78	1,075	800-366-0066	Y
Voya Corporate Leaders 100 Fund Class R6	VCLRX	B-	B-	B-	Down	6.03	10.98	19.29	30.47	103.94	21.89	1,075	800-366-0066	Y
Voya Corporate Leaders 100 Fund Class W	IWCLX	B-	B-	B-	Down	6.05	10.99	19.24	30.23	103.01	21.92	1,075	800-366-0066	Y
Voya Growth and Income Portfolio Class A	IAVGX	B	B-	B	Up	6.08	8.56	19.79	27.05	87.53	28.94	3,501	800-366-0066	Y
Voya Growth and Income Portfolio Class I	IIVGX	B	B-	B	Up	6.21	8.80	20.33	28.82	91.80	29.37	3,501	800-366-0066	Y
Voya Growth and Income Portfolio Class S	ISVGX	B-	B-	B-	Down	6.16	8.67	20.06	27.86	89.47	28.97	3,501	800-366-0066	Y
Voya Growth and Income Portfolio Class S2	IGISX	B	B-	B	Up	6.10	8.60	19.89	27.27	88.05	28.65	3,501	800-366-0066	Y
Voya Index Plus LargeCap Portfolio Class I	IPLIX	B	B	B		7.65	13.44	24.63	37.13	113.23	29.11	873.1	800-366-0066	Y
Voya Index Plus LargeCap Portfolio Class S	IPLSX	B	B	B		7.60	13.30	24.30	36.05	110.54	28.87	873.1	800-366-0066	Y
Voya Multi-Manager Large Cap Core Portfolio Class A	IPFAX	B-	B-	B-	Down	6.43	10.91	21.03	28.37	96.00	16.76	338.9	800-366-0066	Y
Voya Multi-Manager Large Cap Core Portfolio Class I	IPPIX	B-	B	B-	Down	6.55	11.27	21.73	30.74	102.05	16.88	338.9	800-366-0066	Y
Voya Multi-Manager Large Cap Core Portfolio Class R6	VPMMX	B-	B-	B-	Down	6.56	11.20	21.66	30.75	102.07	16.87	338.9	800-366-0066	Y
Voya Multi-Manager Large Cap Core Portfolio Class S	IPPSX	B-	B-	B-	Down	6.46	11.10	21.38	29.67	99.41	16.9	338.9	800-366-0066	Y
Voya Russell Large Cap Index Portfolio Class A	IRLIX	B	B	B		6.57	11.53	21.95	35.36	105.39	20.6	911.5	800-366-0066	Y
Voya Russell Large Cap Index Portfolio Class I	IIRLX	B	B	B+		6.71	11.82	22.57	37.36	110.62	20.99	911.5	800-366-0066	Y
Voya Russell Large Cap Index Portfolio Class S	IRLCX	B	B	B+		6.65	11.68	22.26	36.35	107.90	20.84	911.5	800-366-0066	Y
Voya Russell Large Cap Index Portfolio Class S2	IRLUX	B	B	B		6.58	11.58	22.08	35.78	106.37	21.38	911.5	800-366-0066	Y
Voya U.S. Stock Index Portfolio Class A	ISIVX	B	B-	B		6.41	10.95	20.81	33.56	103.43	15.19	5,089	800-366-0066	Y
Voya U.S. Stock Index Portfolio Class I	INGIX	B	B	B		6.53	11.29	21.46	35.73	108.89	15.69	5,089	800-366-0066	Y
Voya U.S. Stock Index Portfolio Class S	ISJBX	B	B	B		6.50	11.15	21.22	34.71	106.39	15.57	5,089	800-366-0066	Y
Voya U.S. Stock Index Portfolio Class S2	ISIPX	B	B-	B		6.47	11.10	21.03	34.19	104.73	15.39	5,089	800-366-0066	Y
Voya U.S. Stock Index Portfolio P2	VPSPX	B	B	B		6.59	11.35	21.53	35.81	109.01	15.71	5,089	800-366-0066	Y
VY® Columbia Contrarian Core Portfolio Class A	ISBAX	B	B-	B		5.31	9.54	21.32	33.43	106.48	23.4	325.5	800-366-0066	Y
VY® Columbia Contrarian Core Portfolio Class I	ISFIX	B	B-	B+	Down	5.44	9.85	21.95	35.43	111.91	24.58	325.5	800-366-0066	Y
VY® Columbia Contrarian Core Portfolio Class S	ISCSX	B	B-	B+		5.38	9.68	21.57	34.40	109.09	24.08	325.5	800-366-0066	Y
Walden Equity Fund	WSEFX	B	B	B		8.17	11.14	20.76	33.15	95.16	21.61	197.6	617-814-1215	Y
Wells Fargo Disciplined U.S. Core Fund - Class A	EVSAX	B	B	B+		6.37	11.42	20.46	35.92	114.70	17.08	1,298	800-222-8222	Y
Wells Fargo Disciplined U.S. Core Fund - Class Admin	EVSYX	B	B	B+		6.41	11.54	20.59	36.47	116.17	17.53	1,298	800-222-8222	Y
Wells Fargo Disciplined U.S. Core Fund - Class C	EVSTX	B	B	B		6.13	11.02	19.52	32.85	106.70	15.78	1,298	800-222-8222	Y
Wells Fargo Disciplined U.S. Core Fund - Class Inst	EVSIX	B	B	B+		6.45	11.70	20.87	37.46	119.04	17.32	1,298	800-222-8222	Y
Wells Fargo Disciplined U.S. Core Fund - Class R	EVSHX	B	B	B+		6.28	11.34	20.17	34.96	112.11	17.28	1,298	800-222-8222	Y
Wells Fargo Disciplined U.S. Core Fund - Class R6	EVSRX	B	B	B+		6.46	11.72	20.96	37.27	116.83	17.49	1,298	800-222-8222	Y
Wells Fargo Index Fund - Class A	WFILX	B	B	B		6.53	11.17	21.29	34.97	106.45	62.21	1,903	800-222-8222	Y
Wells Fargo Index Fund - Class Admin	WFIOX	B	B	B		6.58	11.28	21.53	35.90	109.19	62.84	1,903	800-222-8222	Y
Wells Fargo Index Fund - Class C	WFINX	B-	B-	B	Down	6.32	10.75	20.39	31.97	98.85	62.72	1,903	800-222-8222	Y
Wells Fargo Intrinsic Value Fund - Class A	EIVAX	B-	C+	B-	Down	5.56	9.34	15.65	21.78	78.61	12.36	940.8	800-222-8222	Y
Wells Fargo Intrinsic Value Fund - Class Admin	EIVDX	B-	C+	B-	Down	5.65	9.52	15.85	22.44	80.24	12.95	940.8	800-222-8222	Y
Wells Fargo Intrinsic Value Fund - Class Inst	EIVIX	B-	C+	B-	Down	5.77	9.62	16.21	23.35	82.57	12.42	940.8	800-222-8222	Y
Wells Fargo Intrinsic Value Fund - Class R	EIVTX	B-	C+	B-	Down	5.57	9.24	15.40	20.87	76.81	12.47	940.8	800-222-8222	Y
Wells Fargo Intrinsic Value Fund - Class R6	EIVFX	B-	C+	B-	Down	5.82	9.74	16.24	23.60	82.17	12.21	940.8	800-222-8222	Y
Wells Fargo Large Cap Core Fund - Class A	EGOAX	B	B	B-	Up	7.56	14.17	23.22	32.52	116.68	19.71	1,120	800-222-8222	Y
Wells Fargo Large Cap Core Fund - Class Admin	WFLLX	B	B	B-	Up	7.64	14.31	23.41	33.14	118.76	19.92	1,120	800-222-8222	Y
Wells Fargo Large Cap Core Fund - Class C	EGOCX	B	B	B-	Up	7.42	13.83	22.33	29.62	108.78	19.44	1,120	800-222-8222	Y
Wells Fargo Large Cap Core Fund - Class Inst	EGOIX	B	B+	B-	Up	7.69	14.45	23.77	34.34	121.72	19.79	1,120	800-222-8222	Y
Wells Fargo Large Cap Core Fund - Class R	EGOHX	B	B	B-	Up	7.52	14.12	22.99	32.07	116.89	19.74	1,120	800-222-8222	Y
Wells Fargo Large Cap Core Fund - Class R6	EGORX	B	A-	B-		7.73	14.45	23.78	38.37	128.36	19.76	1,120	800-222-8222	Y

Category: US Equity Large Cap Blend (con't)

Fund Name	Ticker Symbol	RATINGS: Overall Rating	Reward Rating	Risk Rating	Recent Up/Downgrade	TOTAL RETURNS & PERFORMANCE: 3-Month Total Return	6-Month Total Return	1-Year Total Return	3-Year Total Return	5-Year Total Return	ASSETS: NAV	Total Assets (MIL)	NEW INVESTORS: Telephone	Open to New Investors
Westfield Capital Dividend Growth Fund Institutional Class	WDIVX	B-	B-	B-	Down	7.96	12.42	21.51	28.79	77.27	11.3	114.6		Y
Westfield Capital Dividend Growth Fund Investor Class	WCDGX	B-	B-	B-	Down	7.91	12.36	21.18	27.94	76.24	11.35	114.6		Y
Westwood LargeCap Value Fund A Class	WWLAX	B-	B-	B	Down	7.65	11.90	20.54	31.22	94.72	13.08	214.0		Y
Westwood LargeCap Value Fund Institutional Class	WHGLX	B-	B-	B	Down	7.70	12.05	20.84	32.11	97.07	13.01	214.0		Y
Westwood Low Volatility Equity Fund Institutional Class	WLVIX	B	C+	B+	Up	3.65	4.88	12.76	18.92	77.91	10.54	45.5		Y
Wilmington Large-Cap Strategy Fund Class Institutional	WMLIX	B	B	B		6.67	11.65	21.98	36.62	110.93	22.09	551.1	800-836-2211	Y
Wilshire 5000 Index Portfolio Class Institutional	WINDX	B	B	B		6.40	11.08	20.57	35.15	106.97	20.83	186.5	888-200-6796	Y
Wilshire 5000 Index Portfolio Investment Class Shares	WFIVX	B	B	B		6.33	10.96	20.20	34.00	104.38	20.83	186.5	888-200-6796	Y
Wright Major Blue Chip Equities Fund	WQCEX	B	B	B-		8.21	15.21	27.66	34.30	110.35	23.43	13.7	800-555-0644	Y
YCG Enhanced Fund	YCGEX	B	B-	B+		5.98	8.71	22.79	33.59	89.48	16.29	142.1		Y
Zacks All-Cap Core Fund Class C	CZOCX	B-	B-	B-	Down	6.06	11.96	21.08	26.16	82.74	22.34	40.8		Y
Zacks All-Cap Core Fund Investor Class	CZOVX	B-	B-	B-	Down	6.31	12.37	22.02	29.11	89.88	24.97	40.8		Y

Category: US Equity Large Cap Growth

Fund Name	Ticker Symbol	RATINGS: Overall Rating	Reward Rating	Risk Rating	Recent Up/Downgrade	TOTAL RETURNS & PERFORMANCE: 3-Month Total Return	6-Month Total Return	1-Year Total Return	3-Year Total Return	5-Year Total Return	ASSETS: NAV	Total Assets (MIL)	NEW INVESTORS: Telephone	Open to New Investors
1290 VT Socially Responsible Portfolio Class IA	US2689404265	B	B-	B	Up	6.40	11.45	20.33	31.74	107.45		149.8	877-222-2144	Y
1290 VT Socially Responsible Portfolio Class IB	US2689404182	B-	B-	B	Down	6.44	11.40	20.32	31.81	107.43		149.8	877-222-2144	Y
AB Concentrated Growth Fund Advisor Class	WPSGX	B	B-	B		3.78	7.15	23.00	30.09	106.09	34.07	447.0	212-969-1000	Y
AB Concentrated Growth Fund Class A	WPASX	B	B-	B		3.72	7.03	22.70	29.16	103.66	33.75	447.0	212-969-1000	Y
AB Concentrated Growth Fund Class C	WPCSX	B-	B-	B-	Down	3.52	6.61	21.79	26.24	96.24	32.75	447.0	212-969-1000	Y
AB Concentrated Growth Fund Class I	WPSIX	B	B-	B		3.77	7.14	22.97	30.10	106.31	34.11	447.0	212-969-1000	Y
AB Concentrated Growth Fund Class K	WPSKX	B	B-	B		3.69	6.99	22.65	29.11	103.66	33.75	447.0	212-969-1000	Y
AB Concentrated Growth Fund Class R	WPRSX	B	B-	B		3.67	6.90	22.41	28.15	101.14	33.41	447.0	212-969-1000	Y
AB Concentrated Growth Fund Class Z	WPSZX	B	B-	B		3.78	7.18	23.02	30.20	106.26	34.1	447.0	212-969-1000	Y
AB Core Opportunities Fund Advisor Class	ADGYX	B	B	B+		5.59	12.05	22.88	39.36	115.24	20.84	271.6	212-969-1000	Y
AB Core Opportunities Fund Class A	ADGAX	B	B	B+		5.54	11.89	22.52	38.23	112.34	20.26	271.6	212-969-1000	Y
AB Core Opportunities Fund Class B	ADGBX	B	B	B+		5.50	11.82	22.34	37.49	110.05	18.11	271.6	212-969-1000	
AB Core Opportunities Fund Class C	ADGCX	B	B	B+		5.35	11.50	21.67	35.29	104.92	17.05	271.6	212-969-1000	Y
AB Core Opportunities Fund Class I	ADGIX	B	B	B+		5.62	12.12	22.96	39.47	115.55	21.09	271.6	212-969-1000	Y
AB Core Opportunities Fund Class K	ADGKX	B	B	B+		5.54	11.89	22.50	38.25	112.65	20.44	271.6	212-969-1000	Y
AB Core Opportunities Fund Class R	ADGRX	B	B	B+		5.46	11.77	22.26	37.26	109.95	19.6	271.6	212-969-1000	Y
AB Core Opportunities Fund Class Z	ADGZX	B	B	B+		5.66	12.15	23.05	39.66	115.38	21.13	271.6	212-969-1000	Y
AB Growth Fund Advisor Class	AGRYX	A-	A-	A	Up	7.89	13.51	34.18	47.68	129.94	79.66	847.7	212-969-1000	Y
AB Growth Fund Class A	AGRFX	A-	A-	A	Up	7.83	13.38	33.83	46.57	126.84	73.36	847.7	212-969-1000	Y
AB Growth Fund Class B	AGBBX	A-	A-	A-	Up	7.62	12.93	32.80	43.09	117.98	38.96	847.7	212-969-1000	
AB Growth Fund Class C	AGRCX	A-	A-	A-	Up	7.62	12.94	32.84	43.28	118.51	39.53	847.7	212-969-1000	Y
AB Growth Fund Class I	AGFIX	A-	A-	A	Up	7.93	13.59	34.36	48.20	131.39	79.28	847.7	212-969-1000	Y
AB Growth Fund Class K	AGFKX	A-	A-	A	Up	7.81	13.35	33.79	46.56	127.32	75.22	847.7	212-969-1000	Y
AB Growth Fund Class R	AGFRX	A-	A-	A	Up	7.72	13.17	33.37	45.15	123.75	71.63	847.7	212-969-1000	Y
AB Large Cap Growth Fund Advisor Class	APGYX	A-	B+	A	Up	7.05	12.70	31.66	49.01	139.38	51.89	5,860	212-969-1000	Y
AB Large Cap Growth Fund Class A	APGAX	A-	B+	A	Up	6.99	12.56	31.35	47.93	136.37	47.78	5,860	212-969-1000	Y
AB Large Cap Growth Fund Class B	APGBX	B+	B+	A	Down	6.77	12.11	30.32	44.48	127.07	35.69	5,860	212-969-1000	
AB Large Cap Growth Fund Class C	APGCX	B+	B+	A	Down	6.77	12.14	30.40	44.65	127.66	36.17	5,860	212-969-1000	Y
AB Large Cap Growth Fund Class I	ALLIX	A-	B+	A	Up	7.05	12.70	31.71	49.25	140.09	51.62	5,860	212-969-1000	Y
AB Large Cap Growth Fund Class K	ALCKX	A-	B+	A	Up	6.97	12.52	31.27	47.69	135.92	48.63	5,860	212-969-1000	Y
AB Large Cap Growth Fund Class R	ABPRX	A-	B+	A	Up	6.87	12.36	30.87	46.35	132.38	45.94	5,860	212-969-1000	Y
AB Large Cap Growth Fund Class Z	APGZX	A-	B+	A	Up	7.06	12.73	31.79	49.23	138.45	51.68	5,860	212-969-1000	Y

Category: US Equity Large Cap Growth (con't)

		RATINGS				TOTAL RETURNS & PERFORMANCE					ASSETS		NEW INVESTORS	
Fund Name	Ticker Symbol	Overall Rating	Reward Rating	Risk Rating	Recent Up/ Downgrade	3-Month Total Return	6-Month Total Return	1-Year Total Return	3-Year Total Return	5-Year Total Return	NAV	Total Assets (MIL)	Telephone	Open to New Investors
AB Select US Equity Portfolio Advisor Class	AUUYX	B	B	B		7.94	12.77	22.47	34.69	105.00	16.76	297.5	212-969-1000	Y
AB Select US Equity Portfolio Class A	AUUAX	B	B	B		7.85	12.68	22.21	33.78	102.39	16.8	297.5	212-969-1000	Y
AB Select US Equity Portfolio Class C	AUUCX	B-	B-	B	Down	7.68	12.22	21.32	30.74	95.13	16	297.5	212-969-1000	Y
AB Select US Equity Portfolio Class I	AUUIX	B	B	B		7.95	12.83	22.56	34.81	104.99	16.6	297.5	212-969-1000	Y
AB Select US Equity Portfolio Class K	AUUKX	B	B	B		7.80	12.56	22.05	33.33	101.62	16.57	297.5	212-969-1000	Y
AB Select US Equity Portfolio Class R	AUURX	B	B	B		7.74	12.45	21.76	32.57	99.71	16.43	297.5	212-969-1000	Y
AC Alternatives® Disciplined Long Short Fund A Class	ACDQX	B	C+	A-	Up	1.85	3.24	10.60	18.73	89.51	17.63	47.5	800-444-4015	Y
AC Alternatives® Disciplined Long Short Fund C Class	ACDHX	B	C+	B+	Up	1.65	2.80	9.71	16.07	82.48	16.81	47.5	800-444-4015	Y
AC Alternatives® Disciplined Long Short Fund I Class	ACDKX	B	C+	A-	Up	1.99	3.42	11.09	20.33	93.75	17.87	47.5	800-444-4015	Y
AC Alternatives® Disciplined Long Short Fund Investor Cls	ACDJX	B	C+	A-	Up	1.88	3.31	10.79	19.59	91.83	17.83	47.5	800-444-4015	Y
AC Alternatives® Disciplined Long Short Fund R Class	ACDWX	B	C+	A-	Up	1.76	3.05	10.29	17.83	87.08	17.38	47.5	800-444-4015	Y
AIG Focused Alpha Large-Cap Fund Class A	SFLAX	B	A-	B-		4.23	13.47	30.88	34.71	121.91	29.79	651.4	800-858-8850	Y
AIG Focused Alpha Large-Cap Fund Class C	SFLCX	B	B+	B-		4.04	13.10	30.06	32.06	114.81	28.43	651.4	800-858-8850	Y
AIG Focused Alpha Large-Cap Fund Class W	SFLWX	B	A-	B-		4.25	13.54	31.05	35.26	123.48	30.16	651.4	800-858-8850	Y
AIG Focused Multi-Cap Growth Fund Class A	FOCAX	A-	A	B+	Up	4.03	13.35	36.44	38.37	113.99	29.16	605.0	800-858-8850	Y
AIG Focused Multi-Cap Growth Fund Class C	FOCCX	A-	A-	B+	Up	3.90	12.99	35.54	35.71	107.01	27.77	605.0	800-858-8850	Y
AIG Focused Multi-Cap Growth Fund Class W	FOCWX	A-	A	B+	Up	4.11	13.48	36.68	39.20	115.82	29.57	605.0	800-858-8850	Y
Akre Focus Fund Institutional Class	AKRIX	A-	A	B	Up	7.01	17.74	30.86	44.90	128.62	33.04	6,911	877-862-9556	Y
Akre Focus Fund Retail Class	AKREX	B+	A	B	Up	6.91	17.59	30.48	43.72	125.72	32.41	6,911	877-862-9556	Y
Akre Focus Fund Supra Institutional Class	AKRSX	A-	A	B	Up	7.00	17.78	30.94	45.16	129.03	33.1	6,911	877-862-9556	Y
Alger Capital Appreciation Focus Fund Class A	ALAFX	A-	A-	A-	Up	7.22	13.52	33.75	43.59	127.27	31.21	138.7	800-992-3863	Y
Alger Capital Appreciation Focus Fund Class C	ALCFX	A-	A-	B+	Up	7.00	13.05	32.70	40.35	118.84	30	138.7	800-992-3863	Y
Alger Capital Appreciation Focus Fund Class I	ALGRX	A-	A-	A-	Up	7.22	13.53	33.71	43.80	128.31	31.36	138.7	800-992-3863	Y
Alger Capital Appreciation Focus Fund Class Y	ALGYX	A-	A-	A-	Up	7.35	13.82	34.14	44.27	129.06	31.84	138.7	800-992-3863	Y
Alger Capital Appreciation Focus Fund Class Z	ALZFX	A-	A-	A-	Up	7.33	13.68	34.10	44.93	131.31	31.79	138.7	800-992-3863	Y
Alger Capital Appreciation Fund Class A	ACAAX	B+	B+	A-	Up	6.48	12.58	31.22	38.79	117.60	24.66	2,859	800-992-3863	Y
Alger Capital Appreciation Fund Class B	ACAPX	B+	B+	B+	Up	6.29	12.27	30.32	35.66	109.39	19.49	2,859	800-992-3863	
Alger Capital Appreciation Fund Class C	ALCCX	B+	B+	B+	Up	6.31	12.21	30.30	35.70	109.55	19.59	2,859	800-992-3863	Y
Alger Capital Appreciation Fund Class Z	ACAZX	B+	B+	A-	Up	6.57	12.82	31.68	40.24	121.29	25.28	2,859	800-992-3863	Y
Alger Capital Appreciation Institutional Fund Class I	ALARX	B+	B+	A-	Up	6.56	12.48	31.01	38.83	117.75	32.42	3,685	800-992-3863	Y
Alger Capital Appreciation Institutional Fund Class R	ACARX	B+	B+	A-	Up	6.47	12.24	30.47	36.85	112.60	29.08	3,685	800-992-3863	Y
Alger Capital Appreciation Institutional Fund Class Y	ACAYX	B+	B+	A-	Up	6.67	12.73	31.38	39.22	118.37	32.53	3,685	800-992-3863	Y
Alger Capital Appreciation Institutional Fund Class Z-2	ACIZX	B+	B+	A-	Up	6.66	12.68	31.44	39.39	118.63	32.56	3,685	800-992-3863	Y
Alger Capital Appreciation Portfolio Class I-2	ALVOX	B+	B+	A-	Up	6.37	12.30	30.88	38.65	119.13	82.64	532.1	800-992-3863	Y
Alger Capital Appreciation Portfolio Class S	US0155448519	B+	B+	A-	Up	6.47	12.31	30.73	37.73	116.46	79.13	532.1	800-992-3863	Y
Alger Large Cap Growth Portfolio Class I-2	AAGOX	B	B	B	Up	4.80	10.71	28.46	28.71	98.21	61.6	275.0	800-992-3863	Y
Alger Large Cap Growth Portfolio Class S	US0155448774	B	B	B	Up	4.70	10.48	27.95	27.27	94.48	60.04	275.0	800-992-3863	Y
Alger Responsible Investing Fund Class A	SPEGX	B	B	B-	Up	5.22	10.81	27.43	32.30	91.39	9.94	63.3	800-992-3863	Y
Alger Responsible Investing Fund Class C	AGFCX	B	B	B-	Up	4.92	10.27	26.28	29.17	83.90	9.08	63.3	800-992-3863	Y
Alger Responsible Investing Fund Class I	AGIFX	B	B	B-	Up	5.21	10.71	27.33	32.21	91.39	9.92	63.3	800-992-3863	Y
Alger Responsible Investing Fund Class Z	ALGZX	B	B	B-	Up	5.29	11.07	27.96	33.00	92.39	10	63.3	800-992-3863	Y
Alger Spectra Fund Class A	SPECX	B+	B+	A-	Up	6.64	12.52	31.03	39.01	116.66	20.57	5,947	800-992-3863	Y
Alger Spectra Fund Class C	ASPCX	B+	B+	B+	Up	6.48	12.10	30.00	35.88	108.59	18.93	5,947	800-992-3863	Y
Alger Spectra Fund Class I	ASPIX	B+	B+	A-	Up	6.62	12.50	31.04	39.04	116.71	20.77	5,947	800-992-3863	Y
Alger Spectra Fund Class Z	ASPZX	B+	B+	A-	Up	6.74	12.73	31.46	40.40	120.09	21.05	5,947	800-992-3863	Y
AllianzGI Focused Growth Fund Administrative Class	PGFAX	A-	A	A-	Up	7.88	14.93	31.56	46.23	127.56	45.86	1,038	800-498-5413	Y
AllianzGI Focused Growth Fund Class A	PGWAX	A-	A	A-	Up	7.84	14.87	31.45	45.81	126.38	52.85	1,038	800-498-5413	Y
AllianzGI Focused Growth Fund Class C	PGWCX	A-	A-	A-	Up	7.64	14.44	30.44	42.57	118.06	36.79	1,038	800-498-5413	Y
AllianzGI Focused Growth Fund Class P	AOGPX	A-	A	A-	Up	7.90	15.00	31.72	46.88	129.17	41.03	1,038	800-498-5413	Y
AllianzGI Focused Growth Fund Class R	PPGRX	A-	A-	A-	Up	7.76	14.71	31.09	44.72	123.49	40.54	1,038	800-498-5413	Y
AllianzGI Focused Growth Fund Institutional Class	PGFIX	A-	A	A-	Up	7.92	15.05	31.88	47.30	130.29	48.75	1,038	800-498-5413	Y
AllianzGI Focused Growth Fund R6	AFGFX	A-	A	A-	Up	7.95	15.10	31.93	45.90	123.15	48.78	1,038	800-498-5413	Y

Category: US Equity Large Cap Growth (con't)

Fund Name	Ticker Symbol	RATINGS: Overall Rating	Reward Rating	Risk Rating	Recent Up/Downgrade	TOTAL RETURNS & PERFORMANCE: 3-Month Total Return	6-Month Total Return	1-Year Total Return	3-Year Total Return	5-Year Total Return	ASSETS: NAV	Total Assets (MIL)	NEW INVESTORS: Telephone	Open to New Investors
Amana Mutual Funds Trust Growth Fund Institutional	AMIGX	B	B+	B		6.95	13.10	29.29	37.83	98.48	35.05	1,693	888-732-6262	Y
Amana Mutual Funds Trust Growth Fund Investor	AMAGX	B	B+	B		6.89	12.96	28.97	36.93	96.48	34.96	1,693	888-732-6262	Y
American Beacon Bridgeway Large Cap Growth Fund A Class	BLYAX	B+	A-	B	Up	7.66	14.89	27.02	36.96	127.94	29.75	169.0	800-658-5811	Y
American Beacon Bridgeway Large Cap Growth Fund C Class	BLYCX	B+	A-	B	Up	8.06	15.11	26.79	34.65	120.79	29.53	169.0	800-658-5811	Y
American Beacon Bridgeway Large Cap Growth Fund Inst Cls	BRLGX	A-	A-	B	Up	7.59	14.86	27.22	38.02	130.86	29.88	169.0	800-658-5811	Y
American Beacon Bridgeway Large Cap Growth Fund Inv Cls	BLYPX	B+	A-	B	Up	7.45	14.63	26.74	37.01	129.17	29.65	169.0	800-658-5811	Y
American Beacon Bridgeway Large Cap Growth Fund Y Class	BLYYX	B+	A-	B	Up	8.46	15.80	28.17	38.94	132.40	30.08	169.0	800-658-5811	Y
American Century All Cap Growth Fund A Class	ACAQX	B	B	A-		6.55	9.78	24.58	34.81	95.32	32.35	1,136	800-444-4015	Y
American Century All Cap Growth Fund C Class	ACAHX	B	B	A-		6.32	9.34	23.63	31.78	88.05	30.34	1,136	800-444-4015	Y
American Century All Cap Growth Fund I Class	ACAJX	B	B	A-		6.66	10.02	25.13	36.62	99.75	33.57	1,136	800-444-4015	Y
American Century All Cap Growth Fund Investor Class	TWGTX	B	B	A-		6.61	9.91	24.86	35.78	97.76	33.03	1,136	800-444-4015	Y
American Century All Cap Growth Fund R Class	ACAWX	B	B	A-		6.49	9.64	24.24	33.77	92.92	31.67	1,136	800-444-4015	Y
American Century Disciplined Growth Fund Class A	ADCVX	B	B	B-		6.05	12.42	25.75	32.36	106.43	22.65	768.9	800-444-4015	Y
American Century Disciplined Growth Fund Class C	ADCCX	B-	B	B-	Down	5.84	11.98	24.82	29.34	98.82	21.47	768.9	800-444-4015	Y
American Century Disciplined Growth Fund Class R	ADRRX	B	B	B-		5.95	12.26	25.42	31.32	103.76	22.29	768.9	800-444-4015	Y
American Century Disciplined Growth Fund Institutional Cls	ADCIX	B	B	B-		6.16	12.68	26.30	34.12	111.18	22.92	768.9	800-444-4015	Y
American Century Disciplined Growth Fund Investor Class	ADSIX	B	B	B-		6.09	12.58	26.06	33.30	109.05	22.82	768.9	800-444-4015	Y
American Century Disciplined Growth Fund R5 Class	ADGGX	B	B	B-		6.16	12.67	26.28	34.09	111.15	22.93	768.9	800-444-4015	Y
American Century Disciplined Growth Fund Y Class	ADCYX	B	B	B-		6.15	12.67	26.29	34.10	111.16	22.93	768.9	800-444-4015	Y
American Century Growth Fund A Class	TCRAX	A-	B+	A-	Up	7.55	12.41	29.81	39.40	105.04	31.84	8,242	800-444-4015	Y
American Century Growth Fund C Class	TWRCX	B	B	B		7.36	11.99	28.87	36.30	97.46	30.49	8,242	800-444-4015	Y
American Century Growth Fund I Class	TWGIX	B+	B+	B	Up	7.68	12.63	30.39	41.32	109.70	33.38	8,242	800-444-4015	Y
American Century Growth Fund Investor Class	TWCGX	A-	B+	A-	Up	7.60	12.52	30.08	40.44	107.55	32.82	8,242	800-444-4015	Y
American Century Growth Fund R Class	AGWRX	B+	B+	B	Up	7.48	12.24	29.46	38.35	102.49	31.15	8,242	800-444-4015	Y
American Century Growth Fund R5 Class	AGWUX	B+	B+	B	Up	7.65	12.63	30.24	40.61	107.79	33.4	8,242	800-444-4015	Y
American Century Growth Fund R6 Class	AGRDX	B+	B+	B	Up	7.73	12.71	30.58	41.95	110.80	33.34	8,242	800-444-4015	Y
American Century Growth Fund Y Class	AGYWX	A-	B+	A-	Up	7.71	12.72	30.39	40.77	108.03	33.38	8,242	800-444-4015	Y
American Century Inv Focused Dynamic Growth Fund Adv Cls	ACFDX	B+	A	B	Up	5.32	13.67	34.25	34.83	110.71	21.95	28.9	800-444-4015	Y
American Century Inv Focused Dynamic Growth Fund I Cls	ACFSX	B+	A	B	Up	5.40	13.94	34.83	36.62	115.31	22.22	28.9	800-444-4015	Y
American Century Inv Focused Dynamic Growth Fund Inv Cls	ACFOX	B+	A	B	Up	5.38	13.84	34.55	35.80	113.25	22.12	28.9	800-444-4015	Y
American Century Inv Focused Dynamic Growth Fund R Cls	ACFCX	B+	A-	B	Up	5.27	13.56	33.88	33.72	107.88	21.77	28.9	800-444-4015	Y
American Century Inv Focused Dynamic Growth Fund R6 Cls	ACFNX	B+	A	B	Up	5.48	14.02	35.01	36.81	115.60	22.52	28.9	800-444-4015	Y
American Century NT Disciplined Growth Fund G Class	ANDGX	B-	C+	B-	Up	6.29	13.00	26.68			12.44	579.4	800-444-4015	
American Century NT Disciplined Growth Fund Investor Class	ANTDX	B-	C+	B-	Up	6.07	12.48	25.99			12.44	579.4	800-444-4015	Y
American Century NT Growth Fund G Class	ACLTX	B+	B+	B	Up	7.93	13.18	30.81	41.01	110.05	17.3	1,371	800-444-4015	Y
American Century Select Fund A Class	TWCAX	B+	B+	B	Up	6.44	13.29	28.57	44.00	112.13	68.72	2,939	800-444-4015	Y
American Century Select Fund C Class	ACSLX	B	B	B	Down	6.25	12.87	27.63	40.79	104.28	62.1	2,939	800-444-4015	Y
American Century Select Fund I Class	TWSIX	B+	B+	B	Up	6.56	13.54	29.15	45.95	116.94	71.19	2,939	800-444-4015	Y
American Century Select Fund Investor Class	TWCIX	B+	B+	B	Up	6.52	13.45	28.93	45.08	114.82	70.1	2,939	800-444-4015	Y
American Century Select Fund R Class	ASERX	B+	B+	B	Up	6.38	13.16	28.28	42.92	109.47	68.3	2,939	800-444-4015	Y
American Century Select Fund R5 Class	ASLGX	B+	B+	B	Up	6.56	13.54	29.08	45.25	115.06	71.23	2,939	800-444-4015	Y
American Century Select Fund R6 Class	ASDEX	B+	B+	B	Up	6.62	13.64	29.35	46.62	118.15	71.13	2,939	800-444-4015	Y
American Century Select Fund Y Class	ASLWX	B+	B+	B	Up	6.62	13.64	29.22	45.42	115.31	71.2	2,939	800-444-4015	Y
American Century Ultra® Fund A Class	TWUAX	B+	B+	B	Up	6.55	13.30	31.57	43.71	121.51	41.63	10,546	800-444-4015	Y
American Century Ultra® Fund C Class	TWCCX	B+	B+	B	Up	6.32	12.88	30.58	40.49	113.26	35.55	10,546	800-444-4015	Y
American Century Ultra® Fund I Class	TWUIX	B+	A-	B	Up	6.66	13.54	32.14	45.66	126.47	44.84	10,546	800-444-4015	Y
American Century Ultra® Fund Investor Class	TWCUX	B+	A-	B	Up	6.59	13.45	31.89	44.77	124.23	43.42	10,546	800-444-4015	Y
American Century Ultra® Fund R Class	AULRX	B+	B+	B	Up	6.47	13.15	31.26	42.62	118.76	40.62	10,546	800-444-4015	Y
American Century Ultra® Fund R5 Class	AULGX	B+	A-	B	Up	6.64	13.55	32.08	44.98	124.55	44.87	10,546	800-444-4015	Y
American Century Ultra® Fund R6 Class	AULDX	B+	A-	B	Up	6.70	13.66	32.39	46.33	127.78	44.82	10,546	800-444-4015	Y
American Century Ultra® Fund Y Class	AULYX	B+	A-	B	Up	6.71	13.64	32.22	45.13	124.79	44.87	10,546	800-444-4015	Y
American Funds AMCAP Fund® Class 529-A	CAFAX	B	B	B-	Up	5.95	11.88	21.92	32.80	107.76	31.15	60,672	800-421-4225	Y

Category: US Equity Large Cap Growth (con't)

Fund Name	Ticker Symbol	RATINGS Overall Rating	Reward Rating	Risk Rating	Recent Up/ Downgrade	TOTAL RETURNS & PERFORMANCE 3-Month Total Return	6-Month Total Return	1-Year Total Return	3-Year Total Return	5-Year Total Return	ASSETS NAV	Total Assets (MIL)	NEW INVESTORS Telephone	Open to New Investors
American Funds AMCAP Fund® Class 529-C	CAFCX	B-	B-	B-	Down	5.77	11.48	20.99	29.80	99.89	28.03	60,672	800-421-4225	Y
American Funds AMCAP Fund® Class 529-E	CAFEX	B-	B	B-	Down	5.91	11.76	21.64	31.88	105.35	30.38	60,672	800-421-4225	Y
American Funds AMCAP Fund® Class 529-F-1	CAFFX	B	B	B-	Up	6.01	12.00	22.19	33.64	109.99	31.38	60,672	800-421-4225	Y
American Funds AMCAP Fund® Class A	AMCPX	B	B	B-	Up	5.99	11.93	22.04	33.16	108.74	31.49	60,672	800-421-4225	Y
American Funds AMCAP Fund® Class C	AMPCX	B-	B-	B-	Down	5.77	11.50	21.07	29.99	100.47	27.87	60,672	800-421-4225	Y
American Funds AMCAP Fund® Class F-1	AMPFX	B	B	B-	Up	5.97	11.92	21.95	32.91	108.11	31.22	60,672	800-421-4225	Y
American Funds AMCAP Fund® Class F-2	AMCFX	B	B	B-	Up	6.04	12.06	22.26	33.98	110.92	31.67	60,672	800-421-4225	Y
American Funds AMCAP Fund® Class F-3	FMACX	B	B	B-	Up	6.06	12.10	22.40	33.55	109.34	31.5	60,672	800-421-4225	Y
American Funds AMCAP Fund® Class R-1	RAFAX	B-	B-	B-	Down	5.76	11.47	21.06	30.02	100.69	28.63	60,672	800-421-4225	Y
American Funds AMCAP Fund® Class R-2	RAFBX	B-	B-	B-	Down	5.76	11.47	21.07	30.08	100.85	28.62	60,672	800-421-4225	Y
American Funds AMCAP Fund® Class R-2E	RAEBX	B-	B	B-	Down	5.86	11.67	21.45	31.53	105.01	31.2	60,672	800-421-4225	Y
American Funds AMCAP Fund® Class R-3	RAFCX	B-	B	B-	Down	5.86	11.72	21.59	31.78	105.27	30.54	60,672	800-421-4225	Y
American Funds AMCAP Fund® Class R-4	RAFEX	B	B	B-	Up	5.94	11.90	21.97	33.00	108.43	31.21	60,672	800-421-4225	Y
American Funds AMCAP Fund® Class R-5	RAFFX	B	B	B-	Up	6.06	12.08	22.33	34.23	111.51	31.88	60,672	800-421-4225	Y
American Funds AMCAP Fund® Class R-5E	RAEFX	B	B	B-	Up	5.98	11.98	22.26	33.54	109.33	31.52	60,672	800-421-4225	Y
American Funds AMCAP Fund® Class R-6	RAFGX	B	B	B-	Up	6.06	12.08	22.41	34.40	111.99	31.8	60,672	800-421-4225	Y
American Funds Growth Portfolio Class 529-A	CGPAX	B	B	B-	Up	5.94	11.58	25.03	35.39	89.49	18.06	5,887	800-421-4225	Y
American Funds Growth Portfolio Class 529-C	CGPCX	B-	B-	B-	Down	5.69	11.14	24.03	32.15	81.89	17.81	5,887	800-421-4225	Y
American Funds Growth Portfolio Class 529-E	CGPEX	B	B	B-	Up	5.87	11.48	24.77	34.37	86.80	17.96	5,887	800-421-4225	Y
American Funds Growth Portfolio Class 529-F-1	CGPFX	B	B	B-	Up	5.99	11.67	25.33	36.17	91.16	18.11	5,887	800-421-4225	Y
American Funds Growth Portfolio Class A	GWPAX	B	B	B-	Up	5.96	11.59	25.11	35.70	90.09	18.08	5,887	800-421-4225	Y
American Funds Growth Portfolio Class C	GWPCX	B-	B-	B-	Down	5.75	11.21	24.17	32.49	82.70	17.83	5,887	800-421-4225	Y
American Funds Growth Portfolio Class F-1	GWPFX	B	B	B-	Up	5.92	11.62	25.08	35.37	89.47	18.07	5,887	800-421-4225	Y
American Funds Growth Portfolio Class F-2	GWPEX	B	B	B-	Up	5.97	11.70	25.35	36.41	91.87	18.13	5,887	800-421-4225	Y
American Funds Growth Portfolio Class F-3	GWPDX	B	B	B-	Up	6.07	11.82	25.58	36.84	92.57	18.09	5,887	800-421-4225	Y
American Funds Growth Portfolio Class R-1	RGWAX	B-	B-	B-	Down	5.75	11.18	24.16	32.47	82.56	17.91	5,887	800-421-4225	Y
American Funds Growth Portfolio Class R-2	RGWBX	B-	B-	B-	Down	5.74	11.20	24.16	32.43	82.40	17.82	5,887	800-421-4225	Y
American Funds Growth Portfolio Class R-2E	RBGEX	B	B	B-	Up	5.78	11.34	24.49	34.20	86.82	17.9	5,887	800-421-4225	Y
American Funds Growth Portfolio Class R-3	RGPCX	B	B	B-	Up	5.84	11.44	24.70	34.24	86.59	17.98	5,887	800-421-4225	Y
American Funds Growth Portfolio Class R-4	RGWEX	B	B	B-	Up	5.95	11.59	25.06	35.55	89.73	18.05	5,887	800-421-4225	Y
American Funds Growth Portfolio Class R-5	RGWFX	B	B	B-	Up	5.98	11.76	25.45	36.70	92.37	18.2	5,887	800-421-4225	Y
American Funds Growth Portfolio Class R-5E	RGSFX	B	B	B-	Up	6.00	11.76	25.49	36.49	92.08	18.04	5,887	800-421-4225	Y
American Funds Growth Portfolio Class R-6	RGWGX	B	B	B-	Up	5.98	11.77	25.49	36.86	92.89	18.16	5,887	800-421-4225	Y
American Funds The Growth Fund of America® Class 529-A	CGFAX	B	B	B	Down	6.88	12.25	26.05	42.84	113.34	49.03	176,790	800-421-4225	Y
American Funds The Growth Fund of America® Class 529-C	CGFCX	B	B	B		6.67	11.80	25.06	39.55	105.22	46.1	176,790	800-421-4225	Y
American Funds The Growth Fund of America® Class 529-E	CGFEX	B	B	B	Down	6.81	12.10	25.73	41.80	110.72	48.55	176,790	800-421-4225	Y
American Funds The Growth Fund of America® Class 529-F	CGFFX	B	B	B	Down	6.95	12.35	26.30	43.76	115.60	48.91	176,790	800-421-4225	Y
American Funds The Growth Fund of America® Class A	AGTHX	B	B	B	Down	6.91	12.27	26.13	43.20	114.21	49.54	176,790	800-421-4225	Y
American Funds The Growth Fund of America® Class C	GFACX	B	B	B		6.69	11.84	25.12	39.78	105.78	45.95	176,790	800-421-4225	Y
American Funds The Growth Fund of America® Class F-1	GFAFX	B	B	B	Down	6.90	12.25	26.07	42.94	113.65	49.22	176,790	800-421-4225	Y
American Funds The Growth Fund of America® Class F-2	GFFFX	B	B	B	Down	6.95	12.39	26.38	44.08	116.59	49.42	176,790	800-421-4225	Y
American Funds The Growth Fund of America® Class F-3	GAFFX	B	B	B	Down	6.98	12.45	26.47	43.57	114.77	49.53	176,790	800-421-4225	Y
American Funds The Growth Fund of America® Class R-1	RGAAX	B	B	B		6.68	11.83	25.15	39.86	106.06	46.65	176,790	800-421-4225	Y
American Funds The Growth Fund of America® Class R-2	RGABX	B	B	B		6.71	11.85	25.16	40.01	106.50	47.13	176,790	800-421-4225	Y
American Funds The Growth Fund of America® Class R-2E	RGEBX	B	B	B	Down	6.78	12.02	25.52	41.37	110.31	48.73	176,790	800-421-4225	Y
American Funds The Growth Fund of America® Class R-3	RGACX	B	B	B	Down	6.83	12.09	25.70	41.77	110.79	48.63	176,790	800-421-4225	Y
American Funds The Growth Fund of America® Class R-4	RGAEX	B	B	B	Down	6.90	12.27	26.08	43.07	113.95	49.1	176,790	800-421-4225	Y
American Funds The Growth Fund of America® Class R-5	RGAFX	B	B	B	Down	6.97	12.43	26.43	44.33	117.12	49.49	176,790	800-421-4225	Y
American Funds The Growth Fund of America® Class R-5E	RGAHX	B	B	B	Down	6.95	12.36	26.35	43.61	114.83	49.18	176,790	800-421-4225	Y
American Funds The Growth Fund of America® Class R-6	RGAGX	B	B	B	Down	7.00	12.45	26.52	44.54	117.67	49.56	176,790	800-421-4225	Y
American Funds The New Economy Fund® Class 529-A	CNGAX	A-	A	B	Up	5.50	14.41	34.29	41.36	115.98	44.18	18,784	800-421-4225	Y
American Funds The New Economy Fund® Class 529-C	CNGCX	B+	A-	B	Up	5.29	13.97	33.21	38.04	107.54	40.75	18,784	800-421-4225	Y

Category: US Equity Large Cap Growth (con't)

Fund Name	Ticker Symbol	RATINGS: Overall Rating	Reward Rating	Risk Rating	Recent Up/ Downgrade	TOTAL RETURNS & PERFORMANCE: 3-Month Total Return	6-Month Total Return	1-Year Total Return	3-Year Total Return	5-Year Total Return	ASSETS: NAV	Total Assets (MIL)	NEW INVESTORS: Telephone	Open to New Investors
American Funds The New Economy Fund® Class 529-E	CNGEX	A-	A	B	Up	5.45	14.29	33.97	40.32	113.30	43.56	18,784	800-421-4225	Y
American Funds The New Economy Fund® Class 529-F	CNGFX	A-	A	B	Up	5.53	14.52	34.55	42.21	118.19	44.11	18,784	800-421-4225	Y
American Funds The New Economy Fund® Class A	ANEFX	A-	A	B	Up	5.52	14.44	34.37	41.69	116.77	44.63	18,784	800-421-4225	Y
American Funds The New Economy Fund® Class C	ANFCX	B+	A-	B	Up	5.31	14.00	33.30	38.27	108.17	40.19	18,784	800-421-4225	Y
American Funds The New Economy Fund® Class F-1	ANFFX	A-	A	B	Up	5.48	14.41	34.28	41.44	116.24	44.76	18,784	800-421-4225	Y
American Funds The New Economy Fund® Class F-2	NEFFX	A-	A	B	Up	5.56	14.58	34.66	42.63	119.29	44.55	18,784	800-421-4225	Y
American Funds The New Economy Fund® Class F-3	FNEFX	A-	A	B	Up	5.58	14.62	34.78	42.12	117.42	44.63	18,784	800-421-4225	Y
American Funds The New Economy Fund® Class R-1	RNGAX	B+	A-	B	Up	5.29	14.00	33.32	38.40	108.54	41.49	18,784	800-421-4225	Y
American Funds The New Economy Fund® Class R-2	RNGBX	B+	A-	B	Up	5.31	14.00	33.31	38.40	108.63	41.74	18,784	800-421-4225	Y
American Funds The New Economy Fund® Class R-2E	RNNEX	A-	A	B	Up	5.37	14.18	33.72	40.37	113.62	43.98	18,784	800-421-4225	Y
American Funds The New Economy Fund® Class R-3	RNGCX	A-	A	B	Up	5.42	14.24	33.90	40.29	113.24	43.63	18,784	800-421-4225	Y
American Funds The New Economy Fund® Class R-4	RNGEX	A-	A	B	Up	5.50	14.43	34.30	41.58	116.63	44.2	18,784	800-421-4225	Y
American Funds The New Economy Fund® Class R-5	RNGFX	A-	A	B	Up	5.59	14.60	34.74	42.89	119.89	44.84	18,784	800-421-4225	Y
American Funds The New Economy Fund® Class R-5E	RNGHX	A-	A	B	Up	5.54	14.57	34.70	42.21	117.56	44.41	18,784	800-421-4225	Y
American Funds The New Economy Fund® Class R-6	RNGGX	A-	A	B	Up	5.61	14.65	34.79	43.08	120.41	44.68	18,784	800-421-4225	Y
American Growth Fund Series One Class A	AMRAX	B-	C+	B	Down	4.00	8.80	12.82	20.69	78.96	5.19	17.2	800-525-2406	Y
American Growth Fund Series One Class B	AMRBX	B-	C+	B	Up	4.21	8.53	12.37	18.35	73.15	4.45	17.2	800-525-2406	Y
American Growth Fund Series One Class C	AMRCX	B-	C+	B	Up	3.99	8.59	12.18	18.18	72.65	4.42	17.2	800-525-2406	Y
American Growth Fund Series One Class D	AMRGX	B	B-	B	Up	4.15	9.10	13.37	21.63	81.84	5.51	17.2	800-525-2406	Y
American Trust Allegiance Fund	ATAFX	B-	B-	C+	Up	3.86	11.37	25.22	24.13	66.48	29.52	26.0	800-385-7003	Y
AMG Managers Brandywine Blue Fund Class I	BLUEX	B	A-	B-	Up	4.77	12.50	27.85	33.95	98.51	47.87	179.7	800-835-3879	Y
AMG Managers Montag & Caldwell Growth Fund Class I	MCGIX	B	B-	B+		5.98	10.63	23.64	26.69	78.30	19.71	854.4	800-835-3879	Y
AMG Managers Montag & Caldwell Growth Fund Class N	MCGFX	B	B-	B+		5.96	10.52	23.34	25.81	76.21	19.64	854.4	800-835-3879	Y
AMG Managers Montag & Caldwell Growth Fund Class R	MCRGX	B	B-	B+		5.95	10.44	23.16	24.94	74.09	19.14	854.4	800-835-3879	Y
AMG Renaissance Large Cap Growth Fund Class I	MRLSX	B	B	B+		7.03	11.70	22.45	31.29	117.26	14.17	185.9	800-835-3879	Y
AMG Renaissance Large Cap Growth Fund Class N	MRLTX	B	B	B+		6.96	11.50	22.03	29.95	113.45	14.03	185.9	800-835-3879	Y
AMG Renaissance Large Cap Growth Fund Class Z	MRLIX	B	B	B+		7.00	11.71	22.49	31.86	118.51	14	185.9	800-835-3879	Y
AQR Large Cap Momentum Style Fund Class I	AMOMX	B	B	B	Up	6.93	13.26	23.87	32.05	102.08	21.56	1,045	203-742-3600	Y
AQR Large Cap Momentum Style Fund Class N	AMONX	B	B	B	Up	6.87	13.15	23.57	31.10	99.60	21.58	1,045	203-742-3600	Y
AQR Large Cap Momentum Style Fund Class R6	QMORX	B	B	B	Up	6.99	13.34	23.99	32.43	102.79	21.51	1,045	203-742-3600	Y
AQR TM Large Cap Momentum Style Fund Class I	ATMOX	B	B	B	Up	7.60	13.93	23.78	31.33	102.39	20.75	192.3	203-742-3600	Y
AQR TM Large Cap Momentum Style Fund Class N	ATMNX	B	B	B	Up	7.47	13.75	23.40	30.49	100.16	20.66	192.3	203-742-3600	Y
AQR TM Large Cap Momentum Style Fund Class R6	QTMRX	B	B	B	Up	7.59	13.99	23.87	31.69	102.96	20.71	192.3	203-742-3600	Y
AXA Large Cap Growth Managed Volatility Portfolio Class IA	US2689408068	B	B	B	Down	7.75	13.65	29.07	40.43	118.43		5,155	877-222-2144	Y
AXA Large Cap Growth Managed Volatility Portfolio Class IB	US2689407649	B	B	B	Down	7.76	13.67	29.09	40.45	118.47		5,155	877-222-2144	Y
AXA Large Cap Growth Managed Volatility Portfolio Class K	US26883L5488	B	B	B	Down	7.83	13.79	29.39	41.49	121.18		5,155	877-222-2144	Y
AXA/ClearBridge Large Cap Growth Portfolio Class IA	US2689405338	B-	B-	B-	Down	7.70	13.38	25.51	27.20	90.34		365.0	877-222-2144	Y
AXA/ClearBridge Large Cap Growth Portfolio Class IB	US2689405254	B	B-	B	Up	7.57	13.23	25.49	27.10	90.15		365.0	877-222-2144	Y
AXA/ClearBridge Large Cap Growth Portfolio Class K	US26883L3657	B	B-	B	Up	7.66	13.46	25.79	28.15	92.77		365.0	877-222-2144	Y
AXA/Loomis Sayles Growth Portfolio Class IA	US2689402368	A-	A-	A	Up	6.79	13.67	34.67	59.10	124.72		690.7	877-222-2144	Y
AXA/Loomis Sayles Growth Portfolio Class IB	US29364E6032	A-	A-	A	Up	6.88	13.73	34.61	59.15	124.82		690.7	877-222-2144	Y
AXA/Loomis Sayles Growth Portfolio Class K	US26883L4648	A-	A-	A	Up	6.77	13.77	34.97	59.96	125.96		690.7	877-222-2144	Y
Baron Fifth Avenue Growth Fund Class R6	BFTUX	A-	A	B	Up	6.01	12.74	41.02	46.12	119.36	25.92	199.5	800-992-2766	Y
Baron Fifth Avenue Growth Fund Institutional Class	BFTIX	A-	A	B	Up	6.01	12.75	40.96	46.54	120.98	25.91	199.5	800-992-2766	Y
Baron Fifth Avenue Growth Fund Retail Class	BFTHX	A-	A	B	Up	5.94	12.59	40.64	45.37	118.25	25.47	199.5	800-992-2766	Y
Barrett Growth Fund	BGRWX	B-	B-	B	Down	6.16	11.30	21.01	29.30	95.21	19.08	24.1	877-363-6333	Y
BFS Equity Fund	BFSAX	B	B-	B	Up	6.89	10.81	20.97	30.00		14.47	29.9	860-527-8050	Y
BlackRock Advantage Large Cap Growth Fund Inst Shares	CMVIX	B	B	B-		6.47	12.69	23.53	37.32	76.44	15.2	788.4	800-441-7762	Y
BlackRock Advantage Large Cap Growth Fund Inv A Shares	BMCAX	B	B	B-	Up	6.42	12.59	23.13	35.95	73.67	14.57	788.8	800-441-7762	Y
BlackRock Advantage Large Cap Growth Fund Inv B Shares	BMCVX	B	B	B-	Up	7.10	11.24	21.85	33.04	67.85		788.8	800-441-7762	
BlackRock Advantage Large Cap Growth Fund Inv C Shares	BMCCX	B	B	B-	Up	6.26	12.17	22.27	32.92	67.12	12.46	788.4	800-441-7762	Y
BlackRock Advantage Large Cap Growth Fund R Shares	BMCRX	B	B	B-	Up	6.28	12.42	22.71	34.53	70.70	15.08	788.8	800-441-7762	

Category: US Equity Large Cap Growth (con't)

Fund Name	Ticker Symbol	RATINGS: Overall Rating	RATINGS: Reward Rating	RATINGS: Risk Rating	RATINGS: Recent Up/ Downgrade	TOTAL RETURNS & PERFORMANCE: 3-Month Total Return	TOTAL RETURNS & PERFORMANCE: 6-Month Total Return	TOTAL RETURNS & PERFORMANCE: 1-Year Total Return	TOTAL RETURNS & PERFORMANCE: 3-Year Total Return	TOTAL RETURNS & PERFORMANCE: 5-Year Total Return	ASSETS: NAV	ASSETS: Total Assets (MIL)	NEW INVESTORS: Telephone	NEW INVESTORS: Open to New Investors
BlackRock Advantage Large Cap Growth Fund Service Shares	CMVSX	B	B	B-	Up	6.32	12.49	23.02	35.95	73.63	14.95	788.4	800-441-7762	Y
BlackRock Capital Appreciation Fund Institutional Shares	MAFGX	B+	B+	B+	Up	7.56	13.25	32.93	41.24	111.79	27.86	2,963	800-441-7762	Y
BlackRock Capital Appreciation Fund Investor A Shares	MDFGX	B+	B+	B+	Up	7.49	13.07	32.58	40.05	108.87	25.87	2,963	800-441-7762	Y
BlackRock Capital Appreciation Fund Investor B Shares	MBFGX	B	B	B+	Up	7.41	10.63	28.81	33.56	96.06		2,963	800-441-7762	
BlackRock Capital Appreciation Fund Investor C Shares	MCFGX	B+	B+	B+	Up	7.26	12.60	31.51	36.69	100.61	19.4	2,963	800-441-7762	Y
BlackRock Capital Appreciation Fund K Shares	BFGBX	B+	B+	B+	Up	7.63	13.33	33.19	41.82	112.93	28	2,963	800-441-7762	Y
BlackRock Capital Appreciation Fund R Shares	MRFGX	B+	B+	B+	Up	7.42	12.94	32.25	38.94	106.10	21.57	2,963	800-441-7762	Y
BlackRock Focus Growth Fund Institutional Shares	MAFOX	B	B+	B	Down	5.98	10.96	29.97	43.46	118.16	4.08	131.7	800-441-7762	Y
BlackRock Focus Growth Fund Investor A Shares	MDFOX	B+	B	B+	Down	6.17	10.93	30.27	42.52	115.29	3.79	131.7	800-441-7762	Y
BlackRock Focus Growth Fund Investor C Shares	MCFOX	B+	B	B+	Down	6.11	10.74	29.41	39.19	107.58	3.13	131.7	800-441-7762	Y
BlackRock Large Cap Focus Growth Fund Institutional Shares	MALHX	B+	A-	B	Down	7.42	12.94	29.71	42.40	122.70	14.26	942.9	800-441-7762	Y
BlackRock Large Cap Focus Growth Fund Investor A Shares	MDLHX	B+	B+	B	Down	7.34	12.71	29.35	41.11	119.45	13.4	942.9	800-441-7762	Y
BlackRock Large Cap Focus Growth Fund Investor B Shares	MBLHX	B+	B+	B	Down	8.32	11.49	27.69	37.56	111.54		942.9	800-441-7762	
BlackRock Large Cap Focus Growth Fund Investor C Shares	MCLHX	B+	B+	B	Down	7.08	12.28	28.25	37.65	110.77	10.86	942.9	800-441-7762	Y
BlackRock Large Cap Focus Growth Fund R Shares	MRLHX	B+	B+	B	Down	7.25	12.59	29.04	40.00	116.72	12.32	942.9	800-441-7762	Y
BlackRock Large Cap Focus Growth Fund Service Shares	MSLHX	B+	A-	B	Down	7.28	12.74	29.28	41.06	119.35	14.2	942.9	800-441-7762	Y
BMO Large-Cap Growth Fund Class A	BALGX	B+	A-	B+	Up	7.15	13.16	27.96	45.69	127.46	17.94	380.3	800-236-3863	Y
BMO Large-Cap Growth Fund Class I	MLCIX	B+	A-	B+	Up	7.22	13.32	28.34	46.78	131.16	18.09	380.3	800-236-3863	Y
BMO Large-Cap Growth Fund Class R6	BLGRX	B+	A-	B+	Up	7.29	13.45	28.56	46.90	130.17	18.11	380.3	800-236-3863	Y
BMO Large-Cap Growth Fund Class Y	MASTX	B+	A-	B+	Up	7.15	13.16	27.96	45.68	128.27	17.94	380.3	800-236-3863	Y
BNY Mellon Focused Equity Opportunities Fund Cls M Shares	MFOMX	B	A-	C+		8.77	13.24	32.65	47.92	127.26	16.78	537.0	800-645-6561	Y
BNY Mellon Focused Equity Opp Fund Inv Shares	MFOIX	B	B+	C+		8.68	13.06	32.35	46.83	124.27	16.63	537.0	800-645-6561	Y
BNY Mellon Large Cap Mkt Opp Fund Cls Investment	MMOIX	B	B	B-		7.57	11.44	24.15	36.63	100.84	12.12	72.7	800-645-6561	Y
BNY Mellon Large Cap Market Opportunities Fund Class M	MMOMX	B	B	B-		7.58	11.58	23.91	37.74	103.48	11.96	72.7	800-645-6561	Y
Boston Common U.S. Equity Fund	BCAMX	B	B-	B		5.28	9.80	20.64	31.48	92.91	42.65	35.1	877-777-6944	Y
Bridge Builder Large Cap Growth Fund	BBGLX	B-	C+	B	Up	5.86	10.61	25.32			12.72	5,110		Y
Bridges Investment Fund	BRGIX	B-	B-	B-	Down	5.66	10.72	21.98	29.81	94.09	60.57	143.3		Y
Brown Advisory Flexible Equity Fund Advisor Shares	BAFAX	B	B	B-	Up	7.16	12.43	23.74	29.56	101.96	20.77	451.1	800-540-6807	Y
Brown Advisory Flexible Equity Fund Institutional Shares	BAFFX	B	B	B-		7.28	12.66	24.27	31.14	105.89	20.76	451.1	800-540-6807	Y
Brown Advisory Flexible Equity Fund Investor Shares	BIAFX	B	B	B-		7.30	12.58	24.12	30.60	104.43	20.74	451.1	800-540-6807	Y
Brown Advisory Growth Equity Fund Advisor Shares	BAGAX	B+	B	A-	Up	7.79	12.83	30.12	33.16	86.01	19.81	1,953	800-540-6807	Y
Brown Advisory Growth Equity Fund Institutional Shares	BAFGX	B+	B+	A-	Up	7.92	13.09	30.56	34.69	89.71	20.98	1,953	800-540-6807	Y
Brown Advisory Growth Equity Fund Investor Shares	BIAGX	B+	B	A-	Up	7.89	12.98	30.43	34.07	88.29	20.8	1,953	800-540-6807	Y
Brown Advisory Sustainable Growth Fund Advisor Shares	BAWAX	A-	A-	A-	Up	6.86	11.70	27.60	50.18	116.76	20.36	499.2	800-540-6807	Y
Brown Advy Sustainable Growth Fund Inst Shares	BAFWX	B+	A-	B	Up	6.96	11.93	28.10	52.05	121.23	20.85	499.2	800-540-6807	Y
Brown Advisory Sustainable Growth Fund Investor Shares	BIAWX	A-	A-	A-	Up	6.92	11.82	27.89	51.28	119.44	20.65	499.2	800-540-6807	Y
Buffalo Growth Fund	BUFGX	B	B	B+	Up	6.14	9.66	22.81	30.92	98.49	29.13	235.9	800-492-8332	Y
Buffalo Large Cap Fund	BUFEX	B+	B	A-	Up	6.54	9.55	24.86	41.76	117.63	29.03	72.5	800-492-8332	Y
Calamos Growth Fund Class A	CVGRX	B	B-	B+	Up	6.58	10.97	26.59	26.57	87.90	32.48	1,686	800-582-6959	Y
Calamos Growth Fund Class C	CVGCX	B-	C+	B	Up	6.38	10.54	25.65	23.74	80.98	20.71	1,686	800-582-6959	Y
Calamos Growth Fund Class R	CGRRX	B	B-	B	Up	6.52	10.79	26.29	25.60	85.55	30.36	1,686	800-582-6959	Y
Calamos Growth Fund Class T	CVGTX	B	C+	B+	Up	2.54	7.48	20.87	27.09	77.58		1,669	800-582-6959	Y
Calamos Growth Fund Institutional Class	CGRIX	B	B-	B+	Up	6.65	11.07	26.90	27.50	90.25	42.52	1,686	800-582-6959	Y
Calvert Equity Fund Class A	CSIEX	B+	B	A	Up	6.97	11.66	25.78	32.34	96.47	42.89	2,222	800-368-2745	Y
Calvert Equity Fund Class C	CSECX	B	B-	A		6.74	11.22	24.83	29.29	89.26	25.25	2,222	800-368-2745	Y
Calvert Equity Fund Class I	CEYIX	B+	B	A	Up	7.03	11.83	26.24	33.94	100.98	49.3	2,222	800-368-2745	Y
Calvert Equity Fund Class R6	CEYRX	B+	B	A		7.00	11.69	25.82	32.38	96.52	49.28	2,222	800-368-2745	Y
Calvert Equity Fund Class Y	CIEYX	B	B	A		6.59	10.36	23.14	35.59	94.75		2,222	800-368-2745	Y
Capital Advisors Growth Fund Investor Class	CIAOX	B-	C+	B-		3.24	6.49	14.97	21.08	80.44	25.68	52.4	918-599-0045	Y
Capital Group U.S. Equity Fund	CUSEX	B-	B-	B	Down	4.37	8.55	20.60	33.87	94.09	22.42	239.9	213-486-9200	Y
Carillon ClariVest Capital Appreciation Fund Class A	HRCPX	A-	A	B	Up	7.47	15.14	31.43	46.01	124.21	42	399.6	800-421-4184	Y
Carillon ClariVest Capital Appreciation Fund Class C	HRCCX	A-	A-	B	Up	7.26	14.68	30.37	42.63	115.83	30.65	399.6	800-421-4184	Y

Category: US Equity Large Cap Growth (con't)

Fund Name	Ticker Symbol	RATINGS: Overall Rating	Reward Rating	Risk Rating	Recent Up/ Downgrade	TOTAL RETURNS & PERFORMANCE: 3-Month Total Return	6-Month Total Return	1-Year Total Return	3-Year Total Return	5-Year Total Return	ASSETS: NAV	Total Assets (MIL)	NEW INVESTORS: Telephone	Open to New Investors
Carillon ClariVest Capital Appreciation Fund Class I	HRCIX	A-	A	B	Up	7.58	15.35	31.84	47.37	127.70	44.03	399.6	800-421-4184	Y
Carillon ClariVest Capital Appreciation Fund Class R3	HRCLX	A-	A	B	Up	7.37	14.94	30.98	44.61	120.53	40.38	399.6	800-421-4184	Y
Carillon ClariVest Capital Appreciation Fund Class R5	HRCMX	A-	A	B	Up	7.56	15.33	31.88	47.37	127.55	43.91	399.6	800-421-4184	Y
Carillon ClariVest Capital Appreciation Fund Class R6	HRCUX	A-	A	B	Up	7.58	15.35	31.93	47.16	125.98	43.68	399.6	800-421-4184	Y
Carillon ClariVest Capital Appreciation Fund Class Y	HRCYX	A-	A	B		7.50	15.17	31.46	46.04	124.26	43.95	399.6	800-421-4184	Y
Catalyst Dynamic Alpha Fund Class A	CPEAX	B+	A	B	Up	8.29	14.47	26.87	44.71	147.63	21.97	353.5	866-447-4228	Y
Catalyst Dynamic Alpha Fund Class C	CPECX	B+	A	B-	Up	8.13	14.06	25.92	41.52	138.50	20.92	353.5	866-447-4228	Y
Catalyst Dynamic Alpha Fund Class I	CPEIX	A-	A	B	Up	8.39	14.64	27.19	45.89	149.63	22.15	353.5	866-447-4228	Y
Centre American Select Equity Fund Institutional Class	DHANX	B	B-	A		6.59	11.73	25.43	31.00	84.95	12.3	130.0	855-298-4236	Y
Centre American Select Equity Fund Investor Class	DHAMX	B	B-	A		6.48	11.71	25.19	30.51	84.07	12.29	130.0	855-298-4236	Y
Chase Growth Fund Class Institutional	CHAIX	B	B	B+		5.06	12.10	24.77	32.82	106.13	13.36	78.9	212-270-6000	Y
Chase Growth Fund Class N Shares	CHASX	B	B	B+		5.02	11.99	24.52	32.07	103.92	12.82	78.9	212-270-6000	Y
Chesapeake Growth Fund	CHCGX	B	B	B	Up	6.96	11.37	23.65	34.71	98.43	31.63	33.6	800-430-3863	Y
City National Rochdale U.S. Core Equity Fund Cls Inst	CNRUX	B	B	B		7.19	12.43	25.60	36.24	111.70	16.7	274.6		Y
City National Rochdale U.S. Core Equity Fund Class N	CNRWX	B	B	B		7.06	12.14	24.96	34.22	104.88	16.52	274.6		Y
City National Rochdale U.S. Core Equity Fund Cls Servicing	CNRVX	B	B	B		7.12	12.33	25.30	35.23	107.60	16.55	274.6		Y
ClearBridge Aggressive Growth Fund Class A	SHRAX	B-	C+	B	Up	3.20	5.74	14.27	14.53	94.79	203.41	11,391	877-721-1926	Y
ClearBridge Aggressive Growth Fund Class FI	LMPFX	B-	C+	B	Up	3.19	5.73	14.28	14.52	94.73	204.42	11,391	877-721-1926	Y
ClearBridge Aggressive Growth Fund Class I	SAGYX	B-	C+	B	Up	3.28	5.92	14.63	15.59	97.90	224.25	11,391	877-721-1926	Y
ClearBridge Aggressive Growth Fund Class IS	LSIFX	B-	C+	B	Up	3.31	5.96	14.73	15.98	99.02	226.57	11,391	877-721-1926	Y
ClearBridge Large Cap Growth Fund Class A	SBLGX	B	B	B+	Down	6.96	12.51	25.04	44.44	130.50	40.64	9,321	877-721-1926	Y
ClearBridge Large Cap Growth Fund Class C	SLCCX	B	B	B	Down	6.76	12.11	24.13	41.30	122.16	32.8	9,321	877-721-1926	Y
ClearBridge Large Cap Growth Fund Class I	SBLYX	B	B	B+	Down	7.03	12.68	25.42	45.82	134.54	44.99	9,321	877-721-1926	Y
ClearBridge Large Cap Growth Fund Class IS	LSITX	B	B	B+	Down	7.07	12.75	25.53	46.11	134.71	45.02	9,321	877-721-1926	Y
ClearBridge Large Cap Growth Fund Class O	LCMMX	B	B	B+	Down	7.05	12.73	25.47	45.95	132.94	45.02	9,321	877-721-1926	Y
ClearBridge Large Cap Growth Fund Class R	LMPLX	B	B	B+	Down	6.87	12.37	24.66	43.29	127.07	39.08	9,321	877-721-1926	Y
ClearBridge Sustainability Leaders Fund Class I	LCISX	B-	C+	B	Up	7.25	10.98	21.47			12.37	8.3	877-721-1926	Y
ClearBridge Sustainability Leaders Fund Class IS	LCILX	B-	C+	B	Up	7.23	11.05	21.53			12.39	8.3	877-721-1926	Y
Columbia Disciplined Growth Fund Advisor Class	CGQFX	B+	B+	B	Up	7.36	14.41	29.46	44.52	133.33	9.35	542.0	800-345-6611	Y
Columbia Disciplined Growth Fund Class A	RDLAX	B+	B+	B	Up	7.37	14.35	29.19	43.64	131.23	9.3	542.0	800-345-6611	Y
Columbia Disciplined Growth Fund Class C	RDLCX	B	B	B	Down	7.22	13.95	28.18	40.41	122.72	8.94	542.0	800-345-6611	Y
Columbia Disciplined Growth Fund Class K	RDLFX	B+	B+	B	Up	7.35	14.32	29.31	44.27	132.92	9.48	542.0	800-345-6611	
Columbia Disciplined Growth Fund Class R	CGQRX	B+	B+	B	Up	7.33	14.17	28.93	42.61	128.15	9.34	542.0	800-345-6611	Y
Columbia Disciplined Growth Fund Class T	RDLWX	B+	B+	B	Up	7.33	14.27	29.14	43.51	130.68	9.36	542.0	800-345-6611	Y
Columbia Disciplined Growth Fund Institutional 2 Class	CQURX	B+	B+	B	Up	7.41	14.47	29.61	45.16	135.72	9.69	542.0	800-345-6611	Y
Columbia Disciplined Growth Fund Institutional 3 Class	CGQYX	B+	B+	B	Up	7.40	14.49	29.68	45.11	134.28	9.46	542.0	800-345-6611	Y
Columbia Disciplined Growth Fund Institutional Class	CLQZX	B+	B+	B	Up	7.34	14.37	29.52	44.62	134.08	9.38	542.0	800-345-6611	Y
Columbia Large Cap Growth Fund Advisor Class	CCGRX	B	B	B	Down	4.34	9.37	27.95	39.97	114.29	42.05	3,657	800-345-6611	Y
Columbia Large Cap Growth Fund Class A	LEGAX	B	B	B+	Down	4.27	9.23	27.61	38.96	111.51	39.69	3,657	800-345-6611	Y
Columbia Large Cap Growth Fund Class C	LEGCX	B	B	B+	Down	4.08	8.81	26.66	35.88	103.71	33.36	3,657	800-345-6611	Y
Columbia Large Cap Growth Fund Class E	CLGEX	B	B	B+	Down	4.26	9.19	27.52	38.55	110.47	39.53	3,657	800-345-6611	
Columbia Large Cap Growth Fund Class K	CLRUX	B	B	B+	Down	4.31	9.28	27.74	39.43	112.82	41.01	3,657	800-345-6611	
Columbia Large Cap Growth Fund Class R	CGWRX	B	B	B	Down	4.22	9.10	27.34	37.94	109.00	39.42	3,657	800-345-6611	Y
Columbia Large Cap Growth Fund Class T	CLGWX	B	B	B+	Down	4.29	9.24	27.62	38.95	111.70	39.77	3,657	800-345-6611	Y
Columbia Large Cap Growth Fund Class V	GAEGX	B	B	B+	Down	4.28	9.23	27.64	38.95	111.35	39.34	3,657	800-345-6611	
Columbia Large Cap Growth Fund III Advisor Class	CSFRX	B	B	B	Down	4.33	9.33	27.87	32.18	109.95	19.38	1,765	800-345-6611	Y
Columbia Large Cap Growth Fund III Class A	NFEAX	B	B	B	Down	4.29	9.24	27.57	31.25	107.46	17.53	1,765	800-345-6611	Y
Columbia Large Cap Growth Fund III Class C	NFECX	B	B	B	Up	4.05	8.78	26.58	28.37	99.79	12.58	1,765	800-345-6611	Y
Columbia Large Cap Growth Fund III Class R	CLGPX	B	B	B		4.23	9.08	27.31	30.32	104.92	17.68	1,765	800-345-6611	Y
Columbia Large Cap Growth Fund III Class T	CLCPX	B	B	B-	Down	4.24	9.20	27.67	31.28	107.46	17.7	1,765	800-345-6611	Y
Columbia Large Cap Growth Fund III Institutional 2 Class	CADRX	B	B	B-	Down	4.35	9.42	28.05	32.70	111.00	19.55	1,765	800-345-6611	Y
Columbia Large Cap Growth Fund III Institutional 3 Class	CLRYX	B	B	B-	Down	4.35	9.42	28.05	32.39	110.26	18.9	1,765	800-345-6611	Y

Category: US Equity Large Cap Growth (con't)

		RATINGS				TOTAL RETURNS & PERFORMANCE					ASSETS		NEW INVESTORS	
Fund Name	Ticker Symbol	Overall Rating	Reward Rating	Risk Rating	Recent Up/ Downgrade	3-Month Total Return	6-Month Total Return	1-Year Total Return	3-Year Total Return	5-Year Total Return	NAV	Total Assets (MIL)	Telephone	Open to New Investors
Columbia Large Cap Growth Fund III Institutional Class	NFEPX	B	B	B+	Down	4.34	9.37	27.94	32.28	110.08	18.84	1,765	800-345-6611	Y
Columbia Large Cap Growth Fund Institutional 2 Class	CLWFX	B	B	B+	Down	4.37	9.42	28.06	40.42	115.43	41.19	3,657	800-345-6611	Y
Columbia Large Cap Growth Fund Institutional 3 Class	CGFYX	B	B	B+	Down	4.37	9.44	28.11	40.64	116.04	41.28	3,657	800-345-6611	Y
Columbia Large Cap Growth Fund Institutional Class	GEGTX	B	B	B+	Down	4.34	9.37	27.97	39.99	114.14	41.17	3,657	800-345-6611	Y
Columbia Select Large Cap Growth Fund Advisor Class	CSRRX	B	B-	B	Up	5.24	9.13	35.46	32.79	113.34	17.01	4,164	800-345-6611	Y
Columbia Select Large Cap Growth Fund Class A	ELGAX	B	B-	B	Up	5.16	9.00	35.12	31.85	110.77	16.05	4,164	800-345-6611	Y
Columbia Select Large Cap Growth Fund Class C	ELGCX	B-	B-	B	Down	4.94	8.58	34.04	28.86	102.93	14.39	4,164	800-345-6611	Y
Columbia Select Large Cap Growth Fund Class R	URLGX	B-	B-	B	Down	5.09	8.80	34.74	30.80	108.15	15.05	4,164	800-345-6611	Y
Columbia Select Large Cap Growth Fund Class T	CSLWX	B	B-	B	Up	5.17	8.93	35.05	31.78	110.64	16.04	4,164	800-345-6611	Y
Columbia Select Large Cap Growth Fund Institutional 2 Cls	CGTRX	B	B	B	Up	5.23	9.16	35.55	33.24	114.77	17.09	4,164	800-345-6611	Y
Columbia Select Large Cap Growth Fund Institutional 3 Cls	CCWRX	B	B	B	Up	5.27	9.16	35.53	33.38	115.32	17.26	4,164	800-345-6611	Y
Columbia Select Large Cap Growth Fund Institutional Class	UMLGX	B	B-	B	Up	5.20	9.13	35.41	32.77	113.40	16.53	4,164	800-345-6611	Y
Commerce Growth Fund	CFGRX	B	B	B+	Down	7.12	11.85	27.54	44.76	121.43	32.57	120.9		Y
Congress Large Cap Growth Fund Institutional Class	CMLIX	B+	B	A	Up	6.22	11.43	27.88	37.81	113.51	27.23	288.4	888-688-1299	Y
Congress Large Cap Growth Fund Retail Class	CAMLX	B	B	B		6.17	11.70	25.21	31.94	90.53	27.22	4.6	888-688-1299	Y
Consulting Group Large Cap Equity Fund	TLGUX	B-	B-	B	Down	6.14	10.58	20.48	31.71	102.05	19.42	1,788	855-332-5306	Y
Davenport Core Fund	DAVPX	B-	B-	B	Down	4.89	8.30	19.86	29.58	93.68	23.18	455.0		Y
Davis Opportunity Fund Class A	RPEAX	B+	B+	A-	Up	5.74	11.67	23.09	47.82	129.69	37.01	661.6	800-279-0279	Y
Davis Opportunity Fund Class C	DGOCX	B+	B+	A-	Up	5.54	11.27	22.16	44.39	120.79	30.36	661.6	800-279-0279	Y
Davis Opportunity Fund Class Y	DGOYX	B+	B+	A-	Up	5.80	11.82	23.41	48.91	132.45	38.77	661.6	800-279-0279	Y
Delaware Select Growth Fund Class A	DVEAX	B-	B-	B	Up	3.13	11.67	22.19	18.44	70.55	37.77	387.2		
Delaware Select Growth Fund Class C	DVECX	B-	C+	B	Up	2.93	11.22	21.27	15.80	64.26	26.7	387.2		
Delaware Select Growth Fund Class R	DFSRX	B-	B-	B	Up	3.07	11.52	21.91	17.56	68.42	35.52	387.2		
Delaware Select Growth Fund Institutional Class	VAGGX	B	B-	B	Up	3.18	11.82	22.52	19.33	72.72	41.1	387.2		
Delaware U.S. Growth Fund Class A	DUGAX	B	B	A-	Up	3.00	11.89	27.88	25.91	94.42	23.69	3,031		Y
Delaware U.S. Growth Fund Class C	DEUCX	B	B	B	Up	2.79	11.47	26.92	23.10	87.25	20.48	3,031		Y
Delaware U.S. Growth Fund Class R	DEURX	B	B	B+	Up	2.96	11.77	27.54	24.98	91.99	22.7	3,031		Y
Delaware U.S. Growth Fund Class R6	DUZRX	B	B	A-	Up	2.66	11.67	27.82	26.15	94.79	25.84	3,031		Y
Delaware U.S. Growth Fund Institutional Class	DEUIX	B	B	A-	Up	3.10	12.07	28.23	26.84	96.86	25.82	3,031		Y
Deutsche Capital Growth Fund Class A	SDGAX	B	B	B	Down	5.89	10.61	25.93	39.93	116.65	77.03	1,521	201-593-8273	Y
Deutsche Capital Growth Fund Class C	SDGCX	B	B	B	Down	5.65	10.07	24.83	36.45	107.92	66.57	1,521	201-593-8273	Y
Deutsche Capital Growth Fund Class R	SDGRX	B	B	B	Down	5.76	10.36	25.41	38.26	112.38	76.04	1,521	201-593-8273	Y
Deutsche Capital Growth Fund Class R6	SDGZX	B	B	B	Down	5.96	10.77	26.33	40.82	119.23	77.41	1,521	201-593-8273	Y
Deutsche Capital Growth Fund Class S	SCGSX	B	B	B	Down	5.96	10.73	26.26	41.01	119.43	77.75	1,521	201-593-8273	Y
Deutsche Capital Growth Fund Institutional Class	SDGTX	B	B	B	Down	5.94	10.78	26.20	40.98	119.48	77.65	1,521	201-593-8273	Y
Deutsche Large Cap Focus Growth Fund Class A	SGGAX	B	B	B		4.59	8.07	24.80	39.63	110.00	43.16	239.1	201-593-8273	Y
Deutsche Large Cap Focus Growth Fund Class C	SGGCX	B	B-	B		4.41	7.68	23.88	36.52	102.30	36.6	239.1	201-593-8273	Y
Deutsche Large Cap Focus Growth Fund Class S	SCQGX	B	B	B		4.68	8.23	25.11	40.71	112.68	44.96	239.1	201-593-8273	Y
Deutsche Large Cap Focus Growth Fund Institutional Class	SGGIX	B	B	B		4.69	8.25	25.11	40.72	112.84	45.56	239.1	201-593-8273	Y
DFA U.S. Large Cap Growth Portfolio Institutional Class	DUSLX	B	B	B		8.74	13.87	25.53	38.59	113.73	19.17	1,747	512-306-7400	Y
Dreyfus Fund Incorporated	DREVX	B	B-	B		6.62	10.87	20.11	30.13	94.02	11.55	1,234	800-645-6561	Y
Dreyfus Growth and Income Fund	DGRIX	B-	B	B-	Down	7.22	11.29	19.64	31.91	103.62	21.21	907.0	800-645-6561	Y
Dreyfus Large Cap Equity Fund Class A	DLQAX	B	B	B-		7.58	12.15	24.55	40.37	110.98	20.43	612.2	800-645-6561	Y
Dreyfus Large Cap Equity Fund Class C	DEYCX	B	B	B-		7.36	11.78	23.71	37.26	103.19	20.66	612.2	800-645-6561	Y
Dreyfus Large Cap Equity Fund Class I	DLQIX	B	B	B-		7.67	12.34	24.94	41.68	114.49	21.57	612.2	800-645-6561	Y
Dreyfus Large Cap Equity Fund Class Y	DLACX	B	B	B-		7.66	12.39	25.04	41.45	112.61	21.56	612.2	800-645-6561	Y
Dreyfus Large Cap Growth Fund Class A	DAPAX	B	B+	B-	Down	7.12	12.01	28.43	40.44	124.60	11.87	58.9	800-645-6561	Y
Dreyfus Large Cap Growth Fund Class C	DGTCX	B	B	B-	Down	6.95	11.61	27.55	37.39	116.79	11.41	58.9	800-645-6561	Y
Dreyfus Large Cap Growth Fund Class I	DAPIX	B	B+	B-	Down	7.25	12.20	28.77	41.60	127.85	12.24	58.9	800-645-6561	Y
Dreyfus Large Cap Growth Fund Class Y	DLCGX	B	B+	B-	Down	7.25	12.20	28.77	41.46	126.22	12.24	58.9	800-645-6561	Y
Dreyfus Research Growth Fund, Inc. Class A	DWOAX	B	B	B		6.57	10.56	23.44	32.42	99.14	15.18	1,845	800-645-6561	Y
Dreyfus Research Growth Fund, Inc. Class C	DWOCX	B	B-	A-		6.43	10.24	22.66	29.54	91.85	14.02	1,845	800-645-6561	Y

Category: US Equity Large Cap Growth (con't)

Fund Name	Ticker Symbol	RATINGS: Overall Rating	Reward Rating	Risk Rating	Recent Up/ Downgrade	TOTAL RETURNS & PERFORMANCE: 3-Month Total Return	6-Month Total Return	1-Year Total Return	3-Year Total Return	5-Year Total Return	ASSETS: NAV	Total Assets (MIL)	NEW INVESTORS: Telephone	Open to New Investors
Dreyfus Research Growth Fund, Inc. Class I	DWOIX	B	B	B		6.66	10.71	23.80	33.50	101.84	15.21	1,845	800-645-6561	Y
Dreyfus Research Growth Fund, Inc. Class Y	DRYQX	B	B	B		6.69	10.68	23.77	33.74	102.24	15.18	1,845	800-645-6561	Y
Dreyfus Research Growth Fund, Inc. Class Z	DREQX	B	B	A-		6.66	10.65	23.70	33.28	101.31	15.46	1,845	800-645-6561	
Dreyfus U.S. Equity Fund Class A	DPUAX	B	B	B-		6.73	11.18	24.24	34.37	84.77	18.88	549.2	800-645-6561	
Dreyfus U.S. Equity Fund Class C	DPUCX	B	B	B-		6.74	10.96	23.49	31.57	78.12	17.74	549.2	800-645-6561	
Dreyfus U.S. Equity Fund Class I	DPUIX	B	B	B-		6.39	10.92	24.11	35.18	87.28	18.92	549.2	800-645-6561	
Dreyfus U.S. Equity Fund Class Y	DPUYX	B	B	B-		6.39	10.93	24.13	35.23	87.45	18.91	549.2	800-645-6561	
Dunham Focused Large Cap Growth Fund Class A	DAFGX	B	B	B		3.56	7.14	26.09	29.10	84.91	19	77.4	800-442-4358	Y
Dunham Focused Large Cap Growth Fund Class C	DCFGX	B	B	B		3.38	6.75	25.18	26.26	78.22	18.16	77.4	800-442-4358	Y
Dunham Focused Large Cap Growth Fund Class N	DNFGX	B	B	B		3.56	7.27	26.42	30.09	87.33	19.29	77.4	800-442-4358	Y
Eaton Vance Atlanta Capital Focused Growth Fund Class C	EAGCX	B	B	B		6.61	12.52	26.09	30.25	81.50	8.96	30.7		Y
Eaton Vance Atlanta Capital Select Equity Fund Class A	ESEAX	B	B	B+		4.95	7.58	19.48	28.51	88.60	20.64	378.4		Y
Eaton Vance Atlanta Capital Select Equity Fund Class C	ESECX	B	B-	B+		4.76	7.20	18.59	25.65	81.74	19.88	378.4		Y
Eaton Vance Atlanta Capital Select Equity Fund Class I	ESEIX	B	B	B+		4.98	7.70	19.72	29.44	90.96	20.91	378.4		Y
Eaton Vance Atlanta Capital Select Equity Fund Class R6	ESERX	B+	B	A+	Up	5.03	7.75	19.71	29.44	90.95	20.92	378.4		Y
Eaton Vance Focused Growth Opportunities Fund Class A	EAFGX	B	B	B		6.86	10.02	25.15	36.51	113.51	20.38	203.6		Y
Eaton Vance Focused Growth Opportunities Fund Class C	ECFGX	B	B	B+		6.70	9.59	24.26	33.45	105.70	19.41	203.6		Y
Eaton Vance Focused Growth Opportunities Fund Class I	EIFGX	B	B	B		6.95	10.13	25.44	37.50	116.14	20.61	203.6		Y
Eaton Vance Growth Fund Class A	EALCX	B	B	A-		6.10	9.85	25.41	36.16	116.32	26.65	335.0		Y
Eaton Vance Growth Fund Class C	ECLCX	B	B	B+		5.85	9.40	24.45	33.06	108.28	22.87	335.0		Y
Eaton Vance Growth Fund Class I	ELCIX	B	B	A-		6.14	9.97	25.71	37.15	119.01	27.34	335.0		Y
Eaton Vance Growth Fund Class R	ELCRX	B	B	A-		6.03	9.72	25.12	35.17	113.58	26.09	335.0		Y
Eaton Vance Tax-Managed Multi-Cap Growth Fund Class A	EACPX	B	B	B	Up	6.07	11.15	25.78	34.17	97.52	26.88	82.6		Y
Eaton Vance Tax-Managed Multi-Cap Growth Fund Class C	ECCPX	B	B	B+	Up	5.89	10.75	24.88	31.18	90.26	23.34	82.6		Y
Eaton Vance-Atlanta Capital Focused Growth Fund Class A	EAALX	B	B	B		6.77	12.99	27.09	33.17	88.51	9.52	30.7		Y
Eaton Vance-Atlanta Capital Focused Growth Fund Class I	EILGX	B	B	B		6.87	13.17	27.43	34.28	90.93	8.41	30.7		Y
Edgewood Growth Fund Class Institutional	EGFIX	B+	B+	A-	Up	3.89	9.56	34.81	54.66	147.26	29.56	11,115	800-791-4226	Y
Edgewood Growth Fund Retail Class	EGFFX	B+	B	A-	Up	3.74	9.32	34.27	52.83	144.18	28.5	11,115	800-791-4226	Y
Elfun Trusts	ELFNX	B	B	B+		5.00	10.70	25.61	34.12	110.46	60.36	2,772	800-242-0134	Y
Entrepreneur US Large Cap Fund Institutional Class	IMPLX	B+	B+	B	Up	8.83	13.75	27.39	39.76		13.04	109.5		Y
EQ/Capital Guardian Research Portfolio Class IA	US2689404422	B	B	B-		4.32	11.18	25.37	37.40	106.78		413.9	877-222-2144	Y
EQ/Capital Guardian Research Portfolio Class IB	US2689404349	B	B	B-		4.31	11.16	25.34	37.42	106.71		413.9	877-222-2144	Y
EQ/Capital Guardian Research Portfolio Class K	US26883L7120	B	B	B-		4.41	11.32	25.72	38.44	108.93		413.9	877-222-2144	Y
EQ/Large Cap Growth Index Portfolio Class IA	US2689405171	B+	B+	B+	Up	8.28	14.64	29.10	42.70	119.33		1,412	877-222-2144	Y
EQ/Large Cap Growth Index Portfolio Class IB	US2689404919	B+	B+	B+	Up	8.23	14.59	29.06	42.73	119.25		1,412	877-222-2144	Y
EQ/Large Cap Growth Index Portfolio Class K	US26883L5553	B+	B+	B+	Up	8.29	14.80	29.38	43.74	122.08		1,412	877-222-2144	Y
EQ/T. Rowe Price Growth Stock Portfolio Class IA	US2689545752	B+	B+	B	Down	6.71	12.52	33.20	48.17	129.11		1,349	877-222-2144	Y
EQ/T. Rowe Price Growth Stock Portfolio Class IB	US29364E1082	B+	B+	B	Down	6.72	12.53	33.20	48.18	129.07		1,349	877-222-2144	Y
EQ/T. Rowe Price Growth Stock Portfolio Class K	US26883L4150	B+	B+	B	Down	6.77	12.65	33.50	49.27	131.99		1,349	877-222-2144	Y
Evercore Equity Fund	EWMCX	B-	B	B-	Down	8.33	12.83	25.34	27.80	109.50	17.32	142.3		Y
FDP BlackRock Capital Appreciation Fund Inst Shares	MADDX	B	B-	B	Up	5.71	8.77	24.24	24.83	87.66	15.86	88.3		Y
FDP BlackRock Capital Appreciation Fund Investor A Shares	MDDDX	B	B-	B	Up	5.63	8.62	23.99	23.94	85.29	15.27	88.3		Y
FDP BlackRock Capital Appreciation Fund Investor C Shares	MCDDX	B-	C+	B	Down	5.40	8.13	22.95	20.99	78.30	13.54	88.3		Y
Federated Kaufmann Large Cap Fund Class A	KLCAX	B-	B	B-	Down	4.53	8.24	23.26	31.72	105.93	23.47	3,311	800-341-7400	Y
Federated Kaufmann Large Cap Fund Class C	KLCCX	B-	B	C+	Down	4.36	7.88	22.29	28.72	97.89	21.73	3,311	800-341-7400	Y
Federated Kaufmann Large Cap Fund Class R Shares	KLCKX	B-	B	B-	Down	4.40	8.06	22.77	30.20	101.82	22.48	3,311	800-341-7400	Y
Federated Kaufmann Large Cap Fund Class R6	KLCSX	B-	B	B-	Down	4.60	8.46	23.62	33.00	108.99	24.06	3,311	800-341-7400	Y
Federated Kaufmann Large Cap Fund Institutional Shares	KLCIX	B-	B	B-	Down	4.57	8.38	23.57	32.74	108.48	24	3,311	800-341-7400	Y
Fidelity Advisor® Equity Growth Fund Class A	EPGAX	A-	B+	A-	Up	5.16	12.07	34.84	43.34	121.69	109.2	3,134	617-563-7000	Y
Fidelity Advisor® Equity Growth Fund Class C	EPGCX	B+	B+	A-	Up	4.96	11.63	33.81	40.09	113.47	93.57	3,134	617-563-7000	Y
Fidelity Advisor® Equity Growth Fund Class M	FAEGX	A-	B+	A-	Up	5.10	11.94	34.53	42.37	119.33	107.37	3,134	617-563-7000	Y
Fidelity Advisor® Equity Growth Fund Class Z	FZAFX	A-	A-	A-	Up	5.26	12.28	35.37	45.11	126.20	120.12	3,134	617-563-7000	Y

Category: US Equity Large Cap Growth (con't)

Fund Name	Ticker Symbol	RATINGS: Overall Rating	RATINGS: Reward Rating	RATINGS: Risk Rating	RATINGS: Recent Up/ Downgrade	TOTAL RETURNS & PERFORMANCE: 3-Month Total Return	6-Month Total Return	1-Year Total Return	3-Year Total Return	5-Year Total Return	ASSETS: NAV	Total Assets (MIL)	NEW INVESTORS: Telephone	Open to New Investors
Fidelity Advisor® Equity Growth Fund I Class	EQPGX	A-	A-	A-	Up	5.23	12.21	35.20	44.51	124.88	119.45	3,134	617-563-7000	Y
Fidelity Advisor® Growth Opportunities Fund Class A	FAGAX	B+	B+	B+	Up	6.53	12.05	34.68	40.21	120.16	64.73	3,029	617-563-7000	Y
Fidelity Advisor® Growth Opportunities Fund Class C	FACGX	B+	B	B+	Up	6.33	11.63	33.65	37.11	112.09	56.84	3,029	617-563-7000	Y
Fidelity Advisor® Growth Opportunities Fund Class M	FAGOX	B+	B+	B+	Up	6.46	11.92	34.36	39.26	117.71	64.37	3,029	617-563-7000	Y
Fidelity Advisor® Growth Opportunities Fund Class Z	FZAHX	B+	B+	B+	Up	6.64	12.28	35.21	41.95	123.88	69.64	3,029	617-563-7000	Y
Fidelity Advisor® Growth Opportunities Fund I Class	FAGCX	B+	B+	B+	Up	6.60	12.21	35.05	41.40	123.24	69.23	3,029	617-563-7000	Y
Fidelity Advisor® New Insights Fund Class A	FNIAX	B	B	B	Up	6.60	12.54	28.02	38.20	105.01	31.39	28,060	617-563-7000	Y
Fidelity Advisor® New Insights Fund Class C	FNICX	B	B	B	Up	6.37	12.10	27.03	35.14	97.45	27.64	28,060	617-563-7000	Y
Fidelity Advisor® New Insights Fund Class I	FINSX	B	B	B	Down	6.64	12.67	28.34	39.28	107.61	32.04	28,060	617-563-7000	Y
Fidelity Advisor® New Insights Fund Class M	FNITX	B	B	B	Up	6.53	12.42	27.69	37.21	102.51	30.4	28,060	617-563-7000	Y
Fidelity Advisor® New Insights Fund Class Z	FZANX	B	B	B	Down	6.68	12.77	28.53	39.84	108.85	32.07	28,060	617-563-7000	Y
Fidelity Advisor® Series Equity Growth Fund	FMFMX	A-	A-	A-	Up	5.75	13.12	36.69	46.42		13.04	935.3	617-563-7000	Y
Fidelity Advisor® Series Growth Opportunities Fund	FAOFX	B+	B+	B+	Up	7.10	12.95	35.48	42.85		12.74	619.6	617-563-7000	Y
Fidelity Advisor® Series Opportunistic Insights Fund	FAMGX	A-	A	A-	Up	6.92	13.73	34.51	45.60	133.03	17.46	870.9	617-563-7000	Y
Fidelity Advisor® Stock Selector All Cap Fund Class A	FMAMX	B	B	B-	Up	5.71	11.27	24.86	34.88	104.43	44	8,710	617-563-7000	Y
Fidelity Advisor® Stock Selector All Cap Fund Class C	FLACX	B-	B	C+	Down	5.53	10.84	23.91	31.83	96.69	43.7	8,710	617-563-7000	Y
Fidelity Advisor® Stock Selector All Cap Fund Class K	FSSKX	B	B	B-		5.83	11.49	25.37	36.59	108.86	43.94	8,710	617-563-7000	Y
Fidelity Advisor® Stock Selector All Cap Fund Class M	FSJHX	B	B	B-	Up	5.65	11.13	24.55	33.85	101.80	44.01	8,710	617-563-7000	Y
Fidelity Advisor® Stock Selector All Cap Fund Class Z	FZAPX	B	B	B-		5.83	11.50	25.35	36.60	108.70	43.84	8,710	617-563-7000	Y
Fidelity Advisor® Stock Selector All Cap Fund I Class	FBRNX	B	B	B-	Up	5.79	11.43	25.20	36.00	107.24	43.97	8,710	617-563-7000	Y
Fidelity® Blue Chip Growth Fund	FBGRX	A-	A	B+	Up	7.13	13.93	36.06	45.94	140.23	87.76	23,260	617-563-7000	Y
Fidelity® Blue Chip Growth Fund Class K	FBGKX	A-	A	B+	Up	7.16	14.00	36.20	46.45	141.69	87.86	23,260	617-563-7000	Y
Fidelity® Capital Appreciation Fund	FDCAX	B-	B	B-	Down	5.86	13.09	23.94	29.09	99.75	35.2	7,390	617-563-7000	Y
Fidelity® Capital Appreciation Fund Class K	FCAKX	B-	B	B-	Down	5.87	13.14	24.06	29.53	100.86	35.26	7,390	617-563-7000	Y
Fidelity® Contrafund® Fund	FCNTX	A-	A-	A-	Up	6.74	13.25	32.26	44.32	117.69	122.47	124,619	617-563-7000	Y
Fidelity® Contrafund® Fund Class K	FCNKX	A-	A-	A-	Up	6.77	13.31	32.38	44.75	118.81	122.39	124,619	617-563-7000	Y
Fidelity® Focused Stock Fund	FTQGX	B+	B+	B	Up	8.32	16.72	31.22	36.15	102.63	22.65	1,755	617-563-7000	Y
Fidelity® Fund	FFIDX	B	B	B	Up	6.81	13.42	23.81	32.95	98.71	45.23	4,666	617-563-7000	Y
Fidelity® Fund Class K	FFDKX	B	B	B	Up	6.86	13.48	23.94	33.37	99.86	45.21	4,666	617-563-7000	Y
Fidelity® Growth Company	FDGRX	A-	A	B	Up	6.89	14.98	36.76	55.41	151.40	178.65	41,677	617-563-7000	
Fidelity® Growth Company Fund Class K	FGCKX	A-	A	B	Up	6.92	15.04	36.90	55.88	152.77	178.62	41,677	617-563-7000	
Fidelity® Growth Discovery Fund	FDSVX	A-	B+	A-	Up	5.17	11.96	34.69	44.29	125.66	32.56	1,725	617-563-7000	Y
Fidelity® Growth Discovery Fund Class K	FGDKX	A-	B+	A-	Up	5.19	12.01	34.83	44.81	127.12	32.57	1,725	617-563-7000	Y
Fidelity® Independence Fund Class K	FDFKX	B-	B-	C+	Up	6.50	13.09	26.53	25.08	101.55	37.3	3,919	617-563-7000	Y
Fidelity® Large Cap Growth Enhanced Index Fund	FLGEX	B+	B+	B+	Up	8.75	15.48	27.13	40.67	122.39	18.93	1,010	617-563-7000	Y
Fidelity® Magellan® Fund Class K	FMGKX	B	B+	B		6.91	14.08	26.62	37.80	118.95	104.41	16,929	617-563-7000	Y
Fidelity® NASDAQ Composite Index® Fund	FNCMX	B+	A-	B	Down	6.39	12.79	29.24	48.86	145.36	90.63	4,896	617-563-7000	Y
Fidelity® New Millennium Fund®	FMILX	B	B	B-	Up	6.13	12.03	20.05	32.63	99.19	39.79	3,289	617-563-7000	Y
Fidelity® OTC Portfolio	FOCPX	A-	A	B	Up	6.01	12.19	38.59	57.31	176.34	109.85	17,435	617-563-7000	Y
Fidelity® OTC Portfolio Class K	FOCKX	A-	A	B	Up	6.04	12.26	38.75	57.84	177.99	111.27	17,435	617-563-7000	Y
Fidelity® Series All-Sector Equity Fund	FSAEX	B-	B-	B-	Down	5.49	10.02	21.49	33.49	106.18	12.68	6,378	617-563-7000	
Fidelity® Series Blue Chip Growth Fund	FSBDX	A-	A	B+	Up	6.94	13.78	35.93	46.57		13.84	5,885	617-563-7000	Y
Fidelity® Series Growth Company Fund	FCGSX	A-	A	B	Up	7.06	15.33	37.52	56.42		16.63	11,616	617-563-7000	Y
Fidelity® Series Opportunistic Insights Fund	FVWSX	A-	A-	A-	Up	6.81	13.73	33.03	43.13	129.47	17.33	6,392	617-563-7000	Y
Fidelity® Stock Selector All Cap Fund	FDSSX	B	B	B-	Up	5.81	11.45	25.26	36.23	107.85	43.94	8,710	617-563-7000	Y
Fidelity® Trend Fund	FTRNX	A-	B+	A-	Up	6.81	13.32	29.41	41.57	120.59	99.59	1,787	617-563-7000	Y
First Investors Select Growth Fund Advisor Class	FICHX	A-	A	B	Up	8.15	17.05	32.66	41.29	118.51	12.14	574.3	800-423-4026	Y
First Investors Select Growth Fund Class A	FICGX	A-	A-	B	Up	8.00	16.73	32.15	39.59	114.88	11.93	574.3	800-423-4026	Y
First Investors Select Growth Fund Class B	FIGBX	B+	B+	B	Up	7.84	16.42	31.16	36.41	106.75	9.91	574.3	800-423-4026	Y
First Investors Select Growth Fund Institutional Class	FICIX	A-	A	B	Up	8.20	17.06	32.72	41.45	119.67	12.21	574.3	800-423-4026	Y
FMC Select Fund	FMSLX	B-	C+	B	Down	5.70	6.30	16.10	12.68	59.28	27.83	228.1		Y
Franklin DynaTech Fund Advisor Class	FDYZX	A-	A	B+	Up	5.52	13.58	39.67	53.03	136.26	67.2	4,467	650-312-2000	Y

Category: US Equity Large Cap Growth (con't)

Fund Name	Ticker Symbol	RATINGS: Overall Rating	RATINGS: Reward Rating	RATINGS: Risk Rating	RATINGS: Recent Up/Downgrade	TOTAL RETURNS & PERFORMANCE: 3-Month Total Return	6-Month Total Return	1-Year Total Return	3-Year Total Return	5-Year Total Return	ASSETS: NAV	Total Assets (MIL)	NEW INVESTORS: Telephone	Open to New Investors
Franklin DynaTech Fund Class A	FKDNX	A-	A	B+	Up	5.44	13.44	39.30	51.86	133.26	65.39	4,467	650-312-2000	Y
Franklin DynaTech Fund Class C	FDYNX	A-	A	B+	Up	5.26	13.01	38.27	48.49	124.70	55.15	4,467	650-312-2000	Y
Franklin DynaTech Fund Class R	FDNRX	A-	A	B+	Up	5.39	13.29	38.96	50.73	130.40	63.67	4,467	650-312-2000	Y
Franklin DynaTech Fund Class R6	FDTRX	A-	A	B+	Up	5.57	13.68	39.88	53.79	137.71	67.75	4,467	650-312-2000	Y
Franklin Growth Fund Advisor Class	FCGAX	B	B	B	Down	6.10	11.74	27.13	39.97	114.02	94.65	14,695	650-312-2000	Y
Franklin Growth Opportunities Fund Advisor Class	FRAAX	B	B	B+	Up	5.48	10.97	29.02	32.33	105.52	38.84	3,750	650-312-2000	Y
Franklin Growth Opportunities Fund Class A	FGRAX	B	B	B+	Up	5.40	10.80	28.67	31.24	102.67	36.27	3,750	650-312-2000	Y
Franklin Growth Opportunities Fund Class C	FKACX	B	B	B	Up	5.21	10.38	27.70	28.34	95.39	30.79	3,750	650-312-2000	Y
Franklin Growth Opportunities Fund Class R	FKARX	B	B	B+	Up	5.34	10.66	28.36	30.32	100.41	34.75	3,750	650-312-2000	Y
Franklin Growth Opportunities Fund Class R6	FOPPX	B	B	B+	Up	5.56	11.09	29.26	33.08	107.28	39.23	3,750	650-312-2000	Y
Franklin Growth Series Class A	FKGRX	B	B	B	Down	6.04	11.61	26.82	38.92	111.37	94.51	14,695	650-312-2000	Y
Franklin Growth Series Class C	FRGSX	B	B	B	Down	5.85	11.19	25.88	35.82	103.57	86.91	14,695	650-312-2000	Y
Franklin Growth Series Class R	FGSRX	B	B	B	Down	5.98	11.46	26.49	37.87	108.73	94.17	14,695	650-312-2000	Y
Franklin Growth Series Class R6	FIFRX	B	B	B	Down	6.16	11.85	27.35	40.66	115.51	94.54	14,695	650-312-2000	Y
Frontier MFG Global Equity Fund Institutional Class	FMGEX	B	B	B+	Up	6.30	10.55	24.40	33.64	86.35	18.36	1,218		
Frost Growth Equity Fund Class Institutional	FICEX	B	B+	B	Down	7.27	12.42	30.69	38.64	109.31	12.64	310.8		Y
Frost Growth Equity Fund Investor Class Shares	FACEX	B	B	B	Down	7.17	12.29	30.39	37.56	106.64	12.49	310.8		Y
FundX Aggressive Upgrader Fund	HOTFX	B-	C+	B	Up	5.00	11.42	14.91	15.94	61.64	65.27	44.1	866-455-3863	Y
GAMCO Growth Fund Class A	GGCAX	A-	B+	A-	Up	8.33	13.17	29.50	38.81	109.72	56.76	615.7	914-921-5135	Y
GAMCO Growth Fund Class AAA	GABGX	A-	B+	A-	Up	8.32	13.16	29.49	38.80	109.68	56.74	615.7	914-921-5135	Y
GAMCO Growth Fund Class C	GGCCX	B+	B+	A-	Up	8.11	12.73	28.53	35.70	101.92	50.02	615.7	914-921-5135	Y
GAMCO Growth Fund Class I	GGCIX	A-	B+	A-	Up	8.38	13.30	29.83	39.82	112.34	57.87	615.7	914-921-5135	Y
GAMCO Growth Fund Class T	GGGTX	B+	B+	B		8.32	13.14	29.47	38.77	109.65	56.73	615.7	914-921-5135	Y
Geneva Advisors All Cap Growth Fund Class Institutional	GNVIX	A-	A-	B+	Up	7.17	11.84	32.05	37.98	85.77	27.81	155.2		Y
Geneva Advisors All Cap Growth Fund Class Retail	GNVRX	B+	A-	B+	Up	7.06	11.66	31.60	36.53	82.47	26.6	155.2		Y
Gerstein Fisher Multi-Factor Growth Equity Fund	GFMGX	B+	B	B+	Up	5.81	12.24	22.95	32.92	111.18	21.55	307.2		Y
Glenmede Large Cap Growth Fund Institutional Shares	GTILX	B+	A-	B+	Up	7.85	15.10	28.08	41.96	140.27	32.32	4,017	800-442-8299	Y
Glenmede Large Cap Growth Portfolio	GTLLX	B+	A-	B+	Up	7.79	14.98	27.81	41.35	139.23	32.31	4,017	800-442-8299	Y
Goldman Sachs Blue Chip Fund Class C	GCGVX	B-	C+	B	Down	4.85	6.53	17.51	17.37	77.60	12.22	6.1	800-526-7384	Y
Goldman Sachs Blue Chip Fund Class R	GRGVX	B-	C+	B	Down	4.99	6.83	18.13	19.17	82.07	12.79	6.1	800-526-7384	Y
Goldman Sachs Blue Chip Fund Class R6	GDEUX	B-	C+	B	Down	5.11	7.09	18.83	21.51	88.07	12.77	6.1	800-526-7384	Y
Goldman Sachs Blue Chip Fund Institutional Class	GINGX	B-	C+	B-	Down	5.10	7.15	18.82	21.46	87.99	12.77	6.1	800-526-7384	Y
Goldman Sachs Blue Chip Fund Investor Class	GIRGX	B-	C+	B	Down	5.13	7.11	18.68	20.86	86.63	12.78	6.1	800-526-7384	Y
Goldman Sachs Capital Growth Fund Class A	GSCGX	B	B	B+	Down	7.17	12.42	31.80	35.80	108.85	28.7	967.6	800-526-7384	Y
Goldman Sachs Capital Growth Fund Class C	GSPCX	B	B	B+		6.95	11.99	30.81	32.72	101.06	21.33	967.6	800-526-7384	Y
Goldman Sachs Capital Growth Fund Class R	GSPRX	B	B	B+	Down	7.10	12.28	31.44	34.72	106.20	27.68	967.6	800-526-7384	Y
Goldman Sachs Capital Growth Fund Class R6	GSPUX	B	B	B-	Down	7.28	12.66	32.32	37.16	110.95	31.52	967.6	800-526-7384	Y
Goldman Sachs Capital Growth Fund Institutional Class	GSPIX	B+	B	B+	Up	7.26	12.64	32.29	37.40	113.05	31.53	967.6	800-526-7384	Y
Goldman Sachs Capital Growth Fund Investor Class	GSPTX	B+	B	B+	Up	7.24	12.58	32.13	36.78	111.42	29.07	967.6	800-526-7384	Y
Goldman Sachs Capital Growth Fund Service Class	GSPSX	B	B	B+	Down	7.17	12.39	31.70	35.40	107.79	27.72	967.6	800-526-7384	Y
Goldman Sachs Concentrated Growth Fund Class A	GCGAX	B	B	B+	Up	6.02	9.95	27.42	27.50	89.71	16.58	156.6	800-526-7384	Y
Goldman Sachs Concentrated Growth Fund Class C	GCGCX	B	B-	B	Up	5.80	9.47	26.48	24.61	82.76	13.69	156.6	800-526-7384	Y
Goldman Sachs Concentrated Growth Fund Class R	GGCRX	B	B	B+	Up	5.93	9.78	27.06	26.48	87.36	16.05	156.6	800-526-7384	Y
Goldman Sachs Concentrated Growth Fund Class R6	GCGUX	B	B	B+		6.14	10.09	27.86	29.04	93.52	17.63	156.6	800-526-7384	Y
Goldman Sachs Concentrated Growth Fund Institutional Class	GCRIX	B	B	B+		6.12	10.13	27.91	29.04	93.53	17.64	156.6	800-526-7384	Y
Goldman Sachs Concentrated Growth Fund Investor Class	GGCTX	B	B	B+		6.10	10.10	27.82	28.55	92.26	16.84	156.6	800-526-7384	Y
Goldman Sachs Flexible Cap Fund Class A	GALLX	B	B	B+		6.32	12.91	32.93	36.56	111.73	11.57	20.3	800-526-7384	Y
Goldman Sachs Flexible Cap Fund Class C	GCLLX	B	B	B+	Up	6.09	12.48	31.93	33.49	103.80	10.1	20.3	800-526-7384	Y
Goldman Sachs Flexible Cap Fund Class R	GRLLX	B	B	B+		6.26	12.73	32.47	35.48	109.21	11.11	20.3	800-526-7384	Y
Goldman Sachs Flexible Cap Fund Class R6	GFCUX	B	B	B+	Down	6.46	13.16	33.41	38.12	115.89	12.41	20.3	800-526-7384	Y
Goldman Sachs Flexible Cap Fund Institutional Class	GILLX	B	B	B+	Down	6.48	13.18	33.43	38.14	115.92	12.41	20.3	800-526-7384	Y
Goldman Sachs Flexible Cap Fund Investor Class	GSLLX	B	B	B+	Down	6.39	13.04	33.23	37.55	114.29	12.18	20.3	800-526-7384	Y

Category: US Equity Large Cap Growth (con't)

Fund Name	Ticker Symbol	RATINGS Overall Rating	Reward Rating	Risk Rating	Recent Up/ Downgrade	TOTAL RETURNS & PERFORMANCE 3-Month Total Return	6-Month Total Return	1-Year Total Return	3-Year Total Return	5-Year Total Return	ASSETS NAV	Total Assets (MIL)	NEW INVESTORS Telephone	Open to New Investors
Goldman Sachs Large Cap Growth Insights Fund Class A	GLCGX	B+	A-	B	Up	7.07	14.13	29.20	41.65	132.46	29.95	1,944	800-526-7384	Y
Goldman Sachs Large Cap Growth Insights Fund Class C	GLCCX	B+	B+	B	Up	6.86	13.70	28.25	38.55	123.95	26.96	1,944	800-526-7384	Y
Goldman Sachs Large Cap Growth Insights Fund Class R	GLCRX	B+	B+	B	Up	6.99	13.97	28.90	40.64	129.57	29.28	1,944	800-526-7384	Y
Goldman Sachs Large Cap Growth Insights Fund Class R6	GLCUX	B+	A-	B	Up	7.15	14.38	29.73	43.42	137.23	30.91	1,944	800-526-7384	Y
Goldman Sachs Large Cap Growth Insights Fund Inst Cls	GCGIX	B+	A-	B	Up	7.16	14.39	29.73	43.39	137.19	30.93	1,944	800-526-7384	Y
Goldman Sachs Large Cap Growth Insights Fund Investor Cls	GLCTX	B+	A-	B	Up	7.13	14.28	29.51	42.73	135.31	29.54	1,944	800-526-7384	Y
Goldman Sachs Large Cap Growth Insights Fund Service Class	GSCLX	B+	B+	B	Up	7.00	14.04	29.06	41.28	131.36	29.47	1,944	800-526-7384	Y
Goldman Sachs Rising Dividend Growth Fund Class A	GSRAX	B-	C+	B	Up	7.28	12.01	17.98	16.30	71.48	19.79	1,955	800-526-7384	Y
Goldman Sachs Rising Dividend Growth Fund Class R	GSRRX	B-	C+	B	Up	7.25	11.43	17.26	14.98	68.77	19.75	1,955	800-526-7384	Y
Goldman Sachs Rising Dividend Growth Fund Inst Cls	GSRLX	B-	C+	B	Up	7.44	11.81	18.05	17.30	74.34	20.31	1,955	800-526-7384	Y
Goldman Sachs Rising Dividend Growth Fund Investor Class	GSRIX	B-	C+	B	Up	7.37	11.69	17.86	16.74	72.96	20.29	1,955	800-526-7384	Y
Goldman Sachs Strategic Growth Fund Class A	GGRAX	B+	B	A-	Up	6.94	11.87	30.29	34.88	107.23	11.82	281.5	800-526-7384	Y
Goldman Sachs Strategic Growth Fund Class C	GGRCX	B+	B	A-	Up	6.80	11.46	29.31	31.85	99.60	9.29	281.5	800-526-7384	Y
Goldman Sachs Strategic Growth Fund Class R	GSTRX	B+	B	A-	Up	6.87	11.80	29.99	33.92	105.00	11.55	281.5	800-526-7384	Y
Goldman Sachs Strategic Growth Fund Class R6	GGRUX	B+	B	A-	Up	7.01	12.12	30.72	36.41	111.35	12.7	281.5	800-526-7384	Y
Goldman Sachs Strategic Growth Fund Institutional Class	GSTIX	B+	B	A-	Up	7.07	12.18	30.89	36.52	111.53	12.72	281.5	800-526-7384	Y
Goldman Sachs Strategic Growth Fund Investor Class	GSTTX	B+	B	A-	Up	7.01	12.04	30.52	35.82	109.72	12.7	281.5	800-526-7384	Y
Goldman Sachs Strategic Growth Fund Service Class	GSTSX	B+	B	A-	Up	6.91	11.79	30.09	34.47	106.19	11.69	281.5	800-526-7384	Y
Government Street Equity Fund	GVEQX	B-	B-	B	Down	6.01	11.63	22.69	28.73	86.05	75.28	64.8		Y
Great-West Multi-Manager Large Cap Growth Fund Inst Cls	MXGSX	B	B	B	Down	6.94	12.19	30.36	40.72	110.81		907.8		Y
Great-West Multi-Manager Large Cap Growth Fund Inv Cls	MXLGX	B	B	B	Down	6.86	11.88	29.88	38.67	107.74		907.8		Y
Green Century Equity Fund	GCEQX	B	B	B		5.88	10.35	21.95	32.43	105.86	40.81	241.0	800-221-5519	Y
Guggenheim Directional Allocation Fund Class A	TVRAX	B-	B-	B-	Down	6.00	10.75	23.02	32.02	89.46	16.78	706.4	212-739-0700	Y
Guggenheim Directional Allocation Fund Class C	TVRCX	B-	B-	B-		5.82	10.36	22.20	29.33	83.41	16.18	706.4	212-739-0700	Y
Guggenheim Directional Allocation Fund Class I	TVRIX	B-	B	B-	Down	6.14	10.95	23.44	33.35	92.79	17.11	706.4	212-739-0700	Y
Guggenheim Directional Allocation Fund Class P	TVFRX	B-	B	B-	Down	6.03	10.77	23.06	32.23	90.31	16.86	706.4	212-739-0700	Y
Guggenheim RBP® Large-Cap Defensive Fund Class A	TVDAX	B-	B-	B	Down	6.78	12.71	24.06	29.60	89.73	11.2	22.1	212-739-0700	Y
Guggenheim RBP® Large-Cap Defensive Fund Class C	TVDCX	B-	B-	B-	Down	6.59	12.34	23.04	26.89	83.64	10.95	22.1	212-739-0700	Y
Guggenheim RBP® Large-Cap Defensive Fund Class I	TVIDX	B-	B-	B	Down	6.84	12.88	24.33	30.88	93.17	11.58	22.1	212-739-0700	Y
Guggenheim RBP® Large-Cap Defensive Fund Class P	TVFDX	B-	B-	B	Down	6.78	12.77	24.08	29.91	90.82	11.49	22.1	212-739-0700	Y
Guggenheim RBP® Large-Cap Market Fund Class A	TVMAX	B-	B	B-	Down	6.25	10.53	22.91	32.33	96.07	10.89	20.5	212-739-0700	Y
Guggenheim RBP® Large-Cap Market Fund Class C	TVMCX	B-	B-	B-	Down	6.00	10.11	22.00	29.72	89.62	10.46	20.5	212-739-0700	Y
Guggenheim RBP® Large-Cap Market Fund Class I	TVIMX	B	B	B-	Up	6.29	10.66	23.15	33.72	99.44	11.48	20.5	212-739-0700	Y
Guggenheim RBP® Large-Cap Market Fund Class P	TVFMX	B-	B-	B-	Down	6.18	10.44	22.84	32.54	96.98	11.19	20.5	212-739-0700	Y
GuideMark® Large Cap Core Fund Institutional Shares	GILGX	B	B	B	Up	7.29	12.23	21.34	31.43	98.29	17.72	302.6	603-888-5500	Y
GuideMark® Large Cap Core Fund Service Shares	GMLGX	B-	B-	B	Down	7.13	12.00	20.67	29.17	92.70	17.49	302.6	603-888-5500	Y
GuideStone Funds Growth Equity Fund Institutional Class	GGEYX	B+	B+	B+	Up	6.46	12.61	32.43	37.45	110.07	25.18	1,734	214-720-1171	Y
GuideStone Funds Growth Equity Fund Investor Class	GGEZX	B+	B+	B+	Up	6.35	12.46	32.06	36.31	107.45	25.11	1,734	214-720-1171	Y
Harbor Capital Appreciation Fund Administrative Class	HRCAX	A-	A	B+	Up	7.15	16.31	36.25	47.65	128.51	68.24	29,337	800-422-1050	Y
Harbor Capital Appreciation Fund Institutional Class	HACAX	A-	A	B+	Up	7.21	16.46	36.59	48.76	131.38	69.44	29,337	800-422-1050	Y
Harbor Capital Appreciation Fund Investor Class	HCAIX	A-	A	B+	Up	7.11	16.23	36.08	47.11	127.12	66.99	29,337	800-422-1050	Y
Harbor Capital Appreciation Fund Retirement Class	HNACX	A-	A	B+	Up	7.23	16.50	36.68	48.90	131.60	69.41	29,337	800-422-1050	Y
Harbor Strategic Growth Fund Administrative Class	HSRGX	B	B-	A		6.30	10.04	24.88	33.68	105.24	19.07	59.5	800-422-1050	Y
Harbor Strategic Growth Fund Institutional Class	MVSGX	B	B	B+		6.44	10.23	25.25	34.75	107.91	19.08	59.5	800-422-1050	Y
Harbor Strategic Growth Fund Investor Class	HISWX	B	B-	B+		6.31	10.04	24.89	33.69	105.25	19.06	59.5	800-422-1050	Y
Harbor Strategic Growth Fund Retirement Class	HNGSX	B	B	B+		6.47	10.27	25.36	34.87	108.09	19.09	59.5	800-422-1050	Y
Hartford Core Equity Fund Class A	HAIAX	B	B-	B+		7.68	10.68	21.75	35.30	116.04	28.83	3,288	888-843-7824	Y
Hartford Core Equity Fund Class C	HGICX	B	B-	B+		7.43	10.25	20.80	32.31	108.43	26.46	3,288	888-843-7824	Y
Hartford Core Equity Fund Class F	HGIFX	B	B	B+		7.73	10.84	22.12	36.65	120.41	28.84	3,288	888-843-7824	Y
Hartford Core Equity Fund Class I	HGIIX	B	B	B+		7.73	10.84	22.01	36.37	119.96	28.85	3,288	888-843-7824	Y
Hartford Core Equity Fund Class R3	HGIRX	B	B-	A		7.57	10.49	21.34	34.04	113.36	29.25	3,288	888-843-7824	Y
Hartford Core Equity Fund Class R4	HGISX	B	B-	B+		7.63	10.62	21.64	35.26	116.53	29.65	3,288	888-843-7824	Y

Category: US Equity Large Cap Growth (con't)

Fund Name	Ticker Symbol	Overall Rating	Reward Rating	Risk Rating	Recent Up/ Downgrade	3-Month Total Return	6-Month Total Return	1-Year Total Return	3-Year Total Return	5-Year Total Return	NAV	Total Assets (ML)	Telephone	Open to New Investors
		RATINGS				TOTAL RETURNS & PERFORMANCE					ASSETS		NEW INVESTORS	
Hartford Core Equity Fund Class R5	HGITX	B	B	B+		7.71	10.80	22.02	36.43	119.82	29.05	3,288	888-843-7824	Y
Hartford Core Equity Fund Class R6	HAITX	B	B	B+		7.76	10.88	22.16	36.65	120.41	29.16	3,288	888-843-7824	Y
Hartford Core Equity Fund Class Y	HGIYX	B	B	B+		7.73	10.81	22.08	36.60	120.33	29.16	3,288	888-843-7824	Y
Hartford Disciplined Equity HLS Fund Class IA	HIAGX	B	B	B+		7.69	10.69	21.91	36.38	120.70	15.43	702.5	888-843-7824	Y
Hartford Disciplined Equity HLS Fund Class IB	HBGIX	B	B-	B+		7.59	10.55	21.63	35.34	117.96	15.27	702.5	888-843-7824	Y
Hartford Growth Opportunities HLS Fund Class IA	HAGOX	A-	A-	B+	Up	5.28	11.21	30.44	44.26	128.22	38.42	1,526	888-843-7824	Y
Hartford Growth Opportunities HLS Fund Class IB	HBGOX	A-	A-	B+	Up	5.18	11.05	30.13	43.14	125.31	36.91	1,526	888-843-7824	Y
Hartford Growth Opportunities HLS Fund Class IC	HCGOX	A-	A-	B+	Up	5.12	10.92	29.80	42.09	123.37	37.71	1,526	888-843-7824	Y
Highland Premier Growth Equity Fund Class A	HPEAX	B	B	B+	Up	8.78	14.66	25.39	33.92	110.89	27.02	161.0	877-665-1287	Y
Highland Premier Growth Equity Fund Class C	HPECX	B	B-	B+	Up	8.58	14.25	24.51	31.00	103.23	18.49	161.0	877-665-1287	Y
Highland Premier Growth Equity Fund Class Y	HPEYX	B	B	A-	Up	8.84	14.82	25.75	34.93	113.55	28.65	161.0	877-665-1287	Y
Hodges Blue Chip Equity Income Fund Retail Class	HDPBX	B	B-	B		8.05	14.48	24.57	36.87	105.35	16.36	22.3		Y
Homestead Growth Fund	HNASX	A-	A	B	Up	7.25	15.10	37.67	53.53	145.34	10.36	177.3		Y
Iman Fund Class K	IMANX	A-	A	B	Up	7.91	13.39	28.48	46.37	111.72	13.15	95.8		Y
Invesco American Franchise Fund Class A	VAFAX	B	B	B+	Down	3.17	7.83	27.10	35.00	110.40	19.71	10,350	800-659-1005	Y
Invesco American Franchise Fund Class B	VAFBX	B	B	B+	Down	3.10	7.84	27.03	34.98	110.19	19.14	10,350	800-659-1005	
Invesco American Franchise Fund Class C	VAFCX	B	B	B+	Down	2.93	7.41	26.13	32.02	102.58	18.19	10,350	800-659-1005	Y
Invesco American Franchise Fund Class R	VAFRX	B	B	B+	Down	3.07	7.69	26.69	33.94	107.71	19.34	10,350	800-659-1005	Y
Invesco American Franchise Fund Class R6	VAFFX	B	B	B+	Down	3.24	8.05	27.59	36.75	114.91	20.25	10,350	800-659-1005	Y
Invesco American Franchise Fund Class Y	VAFIX	B	B	B+	Down	3.21	7.94	27.36	35.97	112.85	20.11	10,350	800-659-1005	Y
Invesco American Franchise Fund R5 Class	VAFNX	B	B	B+	Down	3.20	7.98	27.45	36.38	114.05	20.15	10,350	800-659-1005	Y
Invesco Summit Fund Class A	ASMMX	B	B	B	Down	4.12	10.62	29.69	40.05	115.97	19.64	2,170	800-659-1005	Y
Invesco Summit Fund Class B	BSMMX	B	B	B	Down	3.88	10.19	28.63	36.88	107.83	17.93	2,170	800-659-1005	
Invesco Summit Fund Class C	CSMMX	B	B	B	Down	3.89	10.22	28.66	36.93	107.86	17.87	2,170	800-659-1005	Y
Invesco Summit Fund Class P	SMMIX	B+	B	B+	Up	4.13	10.72	29.87	40.66	117.56	19.9	2,170	800-659-1005	
Invesco Summit Fund Class R6	SMISX	B+	B+	B+	Up	4.14	10.78	30.01	40.80	117.78	19.91	2,170	800-659-1005	Y
Invesco Summit Fund Class S	SMMSX	B	B	B	Down	4.10	10.68	29.73	40.42	116.97	19.75	2,170	800-659-1005	Y
Invesco Summit Fund Class Y	ASMYX	B	B+	B	Down	4.19	10.80	30.02	41.07	118.59	19.84	2,170	800-659-1005	Y
Invesco Summit Fund R5 Class	SMITX	B+	B+	B+	Up	4.20	10.79	30.01	41.37	119.54	19.91	2,170	800-659-1005	Y
IronBridge Large Cap Fund	IBLCX	B	B-	B+		5.72	9.93	18.53	32.50	93.20	14.53	34.4		Y
Ivy Core Equity Fund Class A	WCEAX	B	C+	B	Up	6.27	13.46	20.38	22.79	82.08	14.62	4,815	800-777-6472	Y
Ivy Core Equity Fund Class B	WCEBX	B-	C+	B	Down	5.91	12.88	19.18	19.29	73.45	12.11	4,815	800-777-6472	
Ivy Core Equity Fund Class E	ICFEX	B-	C+	B-	Down	6.29	13.43	20.38	22.55	81.01	14.56	4,815	800-777-6472	Y
Ivy Core Equity Fund Class I	ICIEX	B-	B-	B-	Down	6.34	13.59	20.81	23.90	84.92	16.3	4,815	800-777-6472	Y
Ivy Core Equity Fund Class N	ICEQX	B-	B-	B-	Down	6.35	13.67	20.88	24.28	82.26	16.32	4,815	800-777-6472	Y
Ivy Core Equity Fund Class R	IYCEX	B-	C+	B-	Down	6.13	13.21	19.98	21.52	78.91	14.52	4,815	800-777-6472	Y
Ivy Core Equity Fund Class Y	WCEYX	B-	B-	B-	Down	6.21	13.51	20.67	23.83	84.73	15.83	4,815	800-777-6472	Y
Ivy Large Cap Growth Fund Class A	WLGAX	B+	A-	B	Up	6.09	14.25	29.03	38.30	114.73	21.76	1,889	800-777-6472	Y
Ivy Large Cap Growth Fund Class B	WLGBX	B+	B+	B	Up	5.86	13.79	27.95	34.59	105.15	16.81	1,889	800-777-6472	
Ivy Large Cap Growth Fund Class C	WLGCX	A-	B+	A-	Up	5.89	13.83	28.17	35.33	107.03	18.16	1,889	800-777-6472	Y
Ivy Large Cap Growth Fund Class E	ILCEX	A-	A-	A-	Up	6.05	14.21	29.01	38.21	114.67	21.73	1,889	800-777-6472	Y
Ivy Large Cap Growth Fund Class I	IYGIX	B+	A-	B	Up	6.16	14.36	29.37	39.37	117.61	22.84	1,889	800-777-6472	Y
Ivy Large Cap Growth Fund Class N	ILGRX	A-	A-	A-	Up	6.18	14.48	29.63	40.07	117.92	22.94	1,889	800-777-6472	Y
Ivy Large Cap Growth Fund Class R	WLGRX	A-	A-	A-	Up	6.02	14.07	28.67	36.95	111.23	20.95	1,889	800-777-6472	Y
Ivy Large Cap Growth Fund Class Y	WLGYX	A-	A-	A-	Up	6.08	14.25	29.15	38.60	115.69	22.31	1,889	800-777-6472	Y
Ivy Tax-Managed Equity Class A	IYEAX	B+	B	A-	Up	7.62	14.67	30.03	36.09	108.70	24.69	571.7	800-777-6472	Y
Ivy Tax-Managed Equity Class B	IYEBX	B	B	B+		7.43	14.27	29.16	33.13	101.64	23.53	571.7	800-777-6472	
Ivy Tax-Managed Equity Class C	IYECX	B	B	B+		7.37	14.17	28.97	32.87	100.97	23.43	571.7	800-777-6472	Y
Ivy Tax-Managed Equity Class I	WYTMX	B+	B+	A-	Up	7.66	14.74	30.32	36.87	111.09	24.98	571.7	800-777-6472	Y
Ivy Tax-Managed Equity Class Y	IYEYX	B+	B	A-	Up	7.65	14.63	30.15	36.07	108.83	24.74	571.7	800-777-6472	Y
Ivy Tax-Managed Equity Fund Class N	IYENX	B+	B+	A-	Up	7.70	14.83	30.42	36.98	111.26	25	571.7	800-777-6472	Y
Jackson Square Large-Cap Growth Fund Institutional Class	JSPIX	B	B	A-	Up	3.24	12.40	28.39	27.27	98.51	13.48	154.3		Y

Category: US Equity
Large Cap Growth (con't)

Fund Name	Ticker Symbol	RATINGS: Overall Rating	Reward Rating	Risk Rating	Recent Up/ Downgrade	TOTAL RETURNS & PERFORMANCE: 3-Month Total Return	6-Month Total Return	1-Year Total Return	3-Year Total Return	5-Year Total Return	ASSETS: NAV	Total Assets (MIL)	NEW INVESTORS: Telephone	Open to New Investors
Jackson Square Large-Cap Growth Fund Investor Class	JSPJX	B	B	A-	Up	3.18	12.27	28.05	26.28	95.99	13.47	154.3		Y
Jackson Square Large-Cap Growth Fund IS Class	DPLGX	B	B	A-	Up	3.18	12.42	28.41	27.34	98.61	13.47	154.3		Y
Jackson Square Select 20 Growth Fund IS Class	DPCEX	B	C+	B+	Up	0.66	6.50	17.08	13.83	67.51	5.14	6.2		Y
JAG Large Cap Growth Fund Class A	JLGAX	A-	A	B+	Up	4.29	14.32	34.68	46.01	114.77	17.31	64.3	314-997-1277	Y
JAG Large Cap Growth Fund Class I	JLGIX	A-	A	B+	Up	4.38	14.51	35.01	47.01	117.43	17.63	64.3	314-997-1277	Y
Janus Henderson Forty Fund Class A	JDCAX	B+	B+	A-	Up	4.38	10.15	29.19	46.52	115.55	31.56	11,753	877-335-2687	Y
Janus Henderson Forty Fund Class C	JACCX	B+	B+	A-	Up	4.26	9.86	28.39	44.25	108.92	26.36	11,753	877-335-2687	Y
Janus Henderson Forty Fund Class D	JFRDX	B+	B+	A-	Up	4.45	10.31	29.50	46.51	115.61	30.52	11,753	877-335-2687	Y
Janus Henderson Forty Fund Class I	JCAPX	B+	B+	A-	Up	4.47	10.34	29.60	47.89	118.99	32.59	11,753	877-335-2687	Y
Janus Henderson Forty Fund Class N	JFRNX	B+	B+	A-	Up	4.50	10.40	29.71	48.14	119.92	32.68	11,753	877-335-2687	Y
Janus Henderson Forty Fund Class R	JDCRX	B+	B+	A-	Up	4.31	9.98	28.73	44.92	111.83	28.46	11,753	877-335-2687	Y
Janus Henderson Forty Fund Class S	JARTX	B+	B+	A-	Up	4.37	10.13	29.09	46.05	114.94	30.41	11,753	877-335-2687	Y
Janus Henderson Forty Fund Class T	JACTX	B+	B+	A-	Up	4.43	10.25	29.36	47.06	117.29	30.92	11,753	877-335-2687	Y
Janus Henderson Research Fund Class A	JRAAX	B	B	A-	Up	6.83	9.99	25.98	33.18	110.03	46.11	13,532	877-335-2687	Y
Janus Henderson Research Fund Class C	JRACX	B	B	A-	Up	6.66	9.62	25.11	30.42	102.68	43.61	13,532	877-335-2687	Y
Janus Henderson Research Fund Class D	JNRFX	B	B	A-		6.90	10.09	26.22	33.90	112.21	46.39	13,532	877-335-2687	
Janus Henderson Research Fund Class I	JRAIX	B	B	A-	Down	6.92	10.14	26.29	34.26	113.02	46.3	13,532	877-335-2687	Y
Janus Henderson Research Fund Class N	JRANX	B	B	A-	Down	6.92	10.16	26.38	34.54	113.90	46.29	13,532	877-335-2687	Y
Janus Henderson Research Fund Class R	JRARX	B	B	A-	Up	6.73	9.75	25.47	31.78	106.77	46.29	13,532	877-335-2687	Y
Janus Henderson Research Fund Class S	JRASX	B	B	A-	Up	6.79	9.92	25.79	32.57	108.69	45.46	13,532	877-335-2687	Y
Janus Henderson Research Fund Class T	JAMRX	B	B	A-		6.88	10.04	26.13	33.61	111.42	46.42	13,532	877-335-2687	Y
Janus Henderson U.S. Growth Opportunities Fund Class A	HGRAX	B-	C+	B+	Up	4.74	8.12	19.18	28.71		12.95	8.9	877-335-2687	Y
Janus Henderson U.S. Growth Opportunities Fund Class C	HGRCX	B-	C	B	Up	4.60	7.78	18.37	25.85		12.66	8.9	877-335-2687	Y
Janus Henderson U.S. Growth Opportunities Fund Class D	HGRDX	B-	C+	B+		4.79	8.24	19.44	29.69		13.05	8.9	877-335-2687	Y
Janus Henderson U.S. Growth Opportunities Fund Class I	HGRIX	B-	C+	B	Up	4.87	8.15	19.35	29.59		13.04	8.9	877-335-2687	Y
Janus Henderson U.S. Growth Opportunities Fund Class N	HGRRX	B-	C+	B	Up	4.88	8.26	19.17	29.40		13.02	8.9	877-335-2687	Y
Janus Henderson U.S. Growth Opportunities Fund Class S	HGRSX	B-	C	B		4.79	8.07	19.11	28.69		13.03	8.9	877-335-2687	Y
Janus Henderson U.S. Growth Opportunities Fund Class T	HGRTX	B-	C+	B		4.87	8.24	19.44	29.69		13.05	8.9	877-335-2687	Y
Janus Henderson VIT Forty Portfolio Institutional Class	JACAX	B+	B+	A-	Up	4.08	9.47	30.31	48.49	117.92	39.76	790.2	877-335-2687	Y
Janus Henderson VIT Forty Portfolio Service Class	US4710216189	B+	B+	A-	Up	4.01	9.33	29.99	47.39	115.24	37.84	790.2	877-335-2687	Y
Janus Henderson VIT Research Portfolio Institutional Class	JAGRX	B	B	A-	Down	6.93	10.15	27.87	34.41	103.15	36.51	540.9	877-335-2687	Y
Janus Henderson VIT Research Portfolio Service Class	US4710216759	B	B	A-	Up	6.88	10.04	27.55	33.40	100.70	35.68	540.9	877-335-2687	Y
Jensen Quality Growth Fund Class I	JENIX	B	B	B+	Down	7.80	9.95	23.55	39.91	112.41	46.66	6,644	800-992-4144	Y
Jensen Quality Growth Fund Class J	JENSX	B	B	B+	Down	7.72	9.81	23.21	38.87	109.80	46.65	6,644	800-992-4144	Y
Jensen Quality Growth Fund Class Y	JENYX	B	B	B+	Down	7.82	9.99	23.61	39.44	110.66	46.65	6,644	800-992-4144	Y
Jensen Quality Growth FundClass R	JENRX	B	B	B+	Down	7.63	9.60	22.77	37.37	106.04	46.44	6,644	800-992-4144	Y
JNL/BlackRock Large Cap Select Growth Fund Class A	US46644W4015	B+	A-	B+	Up	7.67	13.65	33.62	41.47	120.39	36.46	3,082		Y
JNL/BlackRock Large Cap Select Growth Fund Class I	US46644W5004	A-	A-	B+	Up	7.72	13.75	33.91	42.33	122.71	37.8	3,082		Y
JNL/Mellon Capital Nasdaq® 100 Index Fund Class A	US47760W8608	B+	A-	B	Down	7.06	13.46	32.09	43.20	146.48	22.87	2,155		Y
JNL/Mellon Capital Nasdaq® 100 Index Fund Class I	US47760W8525	B+	A-	B	Down	7.17	13.65	32.42	44.17	149.12	15.08	2,155		Y
JNL/S&P Competitive Advantage Fund Class A	US46648L8494	B	C+	A-	Up	12.25	17.38	19.66	27.30	105.26	16.86	2,858		Y
JNL/S&P Competitive Advantage Fund Class I	US46648L8312	B	B-	A-	Up	12.30	17.49	19.92	28.00	107.21	16.97	2,858		Y
JNL/T. Rowe Price Established Growth Fund Class A	US46648L5003	B+	B+	B	Down	6.05	11.77	33.62	49.13	130.69	43.98	8,763		Y
JNL/T. Rowe Price Established Growth Fund Class I	US46648L6092	B+	B+	B	Down	6.14	11.90	33.89	50.03	133.09	45.26	8,763		Y
JNL/Vanguard Capital Growth Fund Class A	US46648L5342	B	B+	B-		6.82	12.42	27.77	41.96	133.78	10.8	53.7		Y
JNL/Vanguard Capital Growth Fund Class I	US46648L5268	B	A-	B-		7.02	12.72	28.29	43.40	137.56	10.82	53.7		Y
John Hancock Funds Fundamental All Cap Core Fund Class A	JFCAX	B+	A	B	Up	7.00	14.47	27.14	41.19	111.75	18.87	86.7	800-225-5913	Y
John Hancock Funds Fundamental All Cap Core Fund Class C	JFCCX	B+	A-	B	Up	6.79	14.06	26.24	38.27	104.66	18.49	86.7	800-225-5913	Y
John Hancock Funds Fundamental All Cap Core Fund Class I	JFCIX	B+	A	B	Up	7.09	14.68	27.56	42.60	115.36	19.07	86.7	800-225-5913	Y
John Hancock Funds Fundamental All Cap Core Fund Class R2	JFACX	B+	A	B	Up	7.07	14.62	27.37	41.79	113.06	19.02	86.7	800-225-5913	Y
John Hancock Funds Fundamental All Cap Core Fund Class R4	JFARX	B+	A	B	Up	7.07	14.67	27.48	42.19	113.66	19.04	86.7	800-225-5913	Y
John Hancock Funds Fundamental All Cap Core Fund Class R6	JFAIX	B+	A	B	Up	7.10	14.75	27.63	42.89	115.78	19.07	86.7	800-225-5913	Y

Category: US Equity Large Cap Growth (con't)

		RATINGS				TOTAL RETURNS & PERFORMANCE					ASSETS		NEW INVESTORS	
Fund Name	Ticker Symbol	Overall Rating	Reward Rating	Risk Rating	Recent Up/ Downgrade	3-Month Total Return	6-Month Total Return	1-Year Total Return	3-Year Total Return	5-Year Total Return	NAV	Total Assets (MIL)	Telephone	Open to New Investors
John Hancock Funds II Blue Chip Growth Fund Class 1	JIBCX	A-	A	B	Up	6.94	14.33	36.24	51.55	139.77	36.21	2,733	800-225-5913	Y
John Hancock Funds II Blue Chip Growth Fund Class A	JBGAX	A-	A	B	Up	6.87	14.12	35.80	50.28	136.58	35.87	2,733	800-225-5913	Y
John Hancock Funds II Blue Chip Growth Fund Class C	JBGCX	A-	A	B	Up	6.69	13.71	34.80	46.97	128.17	34.96	2,733	800-225-5913	Y
John Hancock Funds II Blue Chip Growth Fund Class NAV	JHBCX	A-	A	B	Up	6.96	14.35	36.32	51.82	140.44	36.25	2,733	800-225-5913	Y
John Hancock Funds II Capital Appreciation Fund Class 1	JICPX	A-	A	B+	Up	6.95	16.14	36.63	48.77	130.70	15.98	1,796	800-225-5913	Y
John Hancock Funds II Capital Appreciation Fund Class NAV	JHCPX	A-	A	B+	Up	6.98	16.16	36.68	49.05	131.28	16.02	1,796	800-225-5913	Y
John Hancock Funds Strategic Growth Fund Class A	JSGAX	B+	B+	B	Up	5.66	12.32	28.83	37.74	114.00	17.42	1,922	800-225-5913	Y
John Hancock Funds Strategic Growth Fund Class C	JSGCX	B	B	B		5.48	11.87	27.79	34.59	107.06	17.23	1,922	800-225-5913	Y
John Hancock Funds Strategic Growth Fund Class I	JSGIX	B+	B+	B	Up	5.76	12.44	29.10	38.90	117.31	17.52	1,922	800-225-5913	Y
John Hancock Funds Strategic Growth Fund Class NAV	US47803W8441	B+	B+	B	Up	5.81	12.54	29.28	39.43	119.03	17.54	1,922	800-225-5913	Y
John Hancock Funds Strategic Growth Fund Class R2	JSGRX	B	B+	B	Down	5.63	12.24	28.68	37.43	114.82	17.57	1,922	800-225-5913	Y
John Hancock Funds Strategic Growth Fund Class R4	JHSGX	B+	B+	B	Up	5.72	12.39	29.02	38.28	116.15	17.55	1,922	800-225-5913	Y
John Hancock Funds Strategic Growth Fund Class R6	JSGTX	B+	B+	B	Up	5.79	12.52	29.32	39.47	119.10	17.55	1,922	800-225-5913	Y
John Hancock Funds Technical Opportunities Fund Class A	JTCAX	B-	B-	C+	Up	5.82	12.39	33.58	22.18	94.21	11.51	568.1	800-225-5913	Y
John Hancock Funds Technical Opportunities Fund Class I	JTCIX	B-	B	C+	Up	5.90	12.50	34.09	23.26	97.22	11.99	568.1	800-225-5913	Y
John Hancock Funds Technical Opportunities Fund Class NAV	JTCNX	B-	B	C+	Up	5.89	12.63	34.20	23.72	98.76	12.23	568.1	800-225-5913	Y
John Hancock Funds Technical Opportunities Fund Cls R6 New	JTOPX	B-	B	C+	Up	5.95	12.62	34.18	23.70	98.73	12.23	568.1	800-225-5913	Y
John Hancock U.S. Global Leaders Growth Fund Class A	USGLX	B	B-	A-		5.22	7.16	25.32	35.38	90.09	45.43	1,493	800-225-5913	Y
John Hancock U.S. Global Leaders Growth Fund Class B	USLBX	B	B-	A-	Up	5.03	6.77	24.40	32.38	83.08	38.58	1,493	800-225-5913	
John Hancock U.S. Global Leaders Growth Fund Class C	USLCX	B	B-	A-	Up	5.03	6.77	24.39	32.40	83.08	38.6	1,493	800-225-5913	Y
John Hancock U.S. Global Leaders Growth Fund Class I	USLIX	B	B-	A-		5.28	7.30	25.64	36.47	92.67	48.66	1,493	800-225-5913	Y
John Hancock U.S. Global Leaders Growth Fund Class R2	USLYX	B	B-	A-	Up	5.20	7.09	25.14	34.84	88.94	47.84	1,493	800-225-5913	Y
John Hancock U.S. Global Leaders Growth Fund Class R6	UGLSX	B	B-	A-		5.30	7.34	25.74	36.89	93.68	48.89	1,493	800-225-5913	Y
Johnson Growth Fund	JGRWX	B-	B-	B-	Down	5.89	10.29	23.60	23.69	85.98	31.79	51.5		Y
JPMorgan Equity Focus Fund Class A	JPFAX	B	B	B		7.02	11.84	24.03	38.51	113.47	30.95	217.2	800-480-4111	Y
JPMorgan Equity Focus Fund Class C	JPFCX	B	B	B		6.86	11.54	23.42	36.43	108.27	29.96	217.2	800-480-4111	Y
JPMorgan Equity Focus Fund Class I	JPFSX	B	B	B		7.07	11.96	24.34	39.59	116.22	31.2	217.2	800-480-4111	Y
JPMorgan Growth Advantage Fund Class A	VHIAX	A-	A	B	Up	7.14	14.25	35.18	47.46	139.08	19.67	8,056	800-480-4111	Y
JPMorgan Growth Advantage Fund Class C	JGACX	A-	A	B	Up	7.03	13.99	34.52	45.41	133.16	17.39	8,056	800-480-4111	Y
JPMorgan Growth Advantage Fund Class I	JGASX	A-	A	B	Up	7.22	14.44	35.51	48.42	141.44	20.22	8,056	800-480-4111	Y
JPMorgan Growth Advantage Fund Class R2	JGRJX	A-	A	B		7.24	14.27	35.04	46.57	136.44	19.65	8,056	800-480-4111	Y
JPMorgan Growth Advantage Fund Class R3	JGTTX	A-	A	B	Up	7.19	14.30	35.25	47.53	139.19	19.68	8,056	800-480-4111	Y
JPMorgan Growth Advantage Fund Class R4	JGTUX	A-	A	B	Up	7.22	14.39	35.40	47.70	139.47	20.21	8,056	800-480-4111	Y
JPMorgan Growth Advantage Fund Class R5	JGVRX	A-	A	B	Up	7.25	14.49	35.68	49.23	143.56	20.56	8,056	800-480-4111	Y
JPMorgan Growth Advantage Fund Class R6	JGVVX	A-	A	B	Up	7.28	14.54	35.82	49.74	143.63	20.65	8,056	800-480-4111	Y
JPMorgan Intrepid Growth Fund Class A	JIGAX	B+	A-	B	Up	8.09	15.44	31.54	39.96	123.86	55.84	1,148	800-480-4111	Y
JPMorgan Intrepid Growth Fund Class C	JCICX	B	A-	B	Down	7.97	15.15	30.93	37.90	118.38	54.94	1,148	800-480-4111	Y
JPMorgan Intrepid Growth Fund Class I	JPGSX	A-	A	B	Up	8.16	15.57	31.88	41.00	126.65	56.66	1,148	800-480-4111	Y
JPMorgan Intrepid Growth Fund Class R2	JIGZX	B+	A-	B	Up	8.03	15.28	31.25	38.95	121.12	54.83	1,148	800-480-4111	Y
JPMorgan Intrepid Growth Fund Class R5	JGIRX	A-	A	B	Up	8.21	15.67	32.14	41.84	128.96	55.94	1,148	800-480-4111	Y
JPMorgan Intrepid Growth Fund Class R6	JGISX	A-	A	B	Up	8.23	15.71	32.20	41.71	127.80	55.91	1,148	800-480-4111	Y
JPMorgan Large Cap Growth Fund Class A	OLGAX	A-	A	B	Up	7.95	13.85	37.71	43.77	116.57	37.61	13,040	800-480-4111	Y
JPMorgan Large Cap Growth Fund Class C	OLGCX	B+	A	B	Up	7.81	13.55	37.01	41.60	111.23	30.38	13,040	800-480-4111	Y
JPMorgan Large Cap Growth Fund Class I	SEEGX	A-	A	B	Up	8.00	13.95	37.98	44.45	118.30	37.93	13,040	800-480-4111	Y
JPMorgan Large Cap Growth Fund Class R2	JLGZX	A-	A	B	Up	7.86	13.67	37.32	42.63	113.82	36.53	13,040	800-480-4111	Y
JPMorgan Large Cap Growth Fund Class R3	JLGPX	A-	A	B	Up	7.94	13.82	37.62	43.40	115.64	37.79	13,040	800-480-4111	Y
JPMorgan Large Cap Growth Fund Class R4	JLGQX	A-	A	B	Up	8.03	13.96	37.99	44.45	118.31	37.93	13,040	800-480-4111	Y
JPMorgan Large Cap Growth Fund Class R5	JLGRX	A-	A	B	Up	8.06	14.06	38.22	45.29	120.47	38.61	13,040	800-480-4111	Y
JPMorgan Large Cap Growth Fund Class R6	JLGMX	A-	A	B	Up	8.09	14.13	38.37	45.71	121.41	38.85	13,040	800-480-4111	Y
Kinetics Internet Advisor Fund Class A	KINAX	B	A	C	Up	27.30	38.70	57.05	50.55	121.12	49.27	149.1	800-930-3828	Y
Kinetics Internet Advisor Fund Class C	KINCX	B	A	C	Up	27.18	38.43	56.36	48.38	115.86	44.24	149.1	800-930-3828	Y
Kinetics Internet Fund No Load Class	WWWFX	B	A	C	Up	27.37	38.85	57.42	51.68	123.88	52.18	149.1	800-930-3828	Y

Category: US Equity Large Cap Growth (con't)

Fund Name	Ticker Symbol	RATINGS: Overall Rating	Reward Rating	Risk Rating	Recent Up/ Downgrade	TOTAL RETURNS & PERFORMANCE: 3-Month Total Return	6-Month Total Return	1-Year Total Return	3-Year Total Return	5-Year Total Return	ASSETS: NAV	Total Assets (MIL)	NEW INVESTORS: Telephone	Open to New Investors
Knights of Columbus Large Cap Growth Fund Class S	KCGSX	B-	C+	B-	Up	8.03	13.40	26.61			12.67	50.7	203-772-2130	Y
Knights of Columbus Large Cap Growth Fund Inst Cls	KCGIX	B-	C+	B-	Up	8.03	13.36	26.70			12.68	50.7	203-772-2130	Y
Lateef Fund Class A	LIMAX	B	B-	B	Up	5.55	8.77	20.52	22.52	72.71	8.38	100.3		Y
Lateef Fund Class C	LIMCX	B-	C+	B-	Down	5.42	8.34	19.64	19.83	66.45	7.07	100.3		Y
Lateef Fund Class I	LIMIX	B-	B-	B-	Down	5.58	8.81	20.86	23.39	74.73	8.69	100.3		Y
Laudus U.S. Large Cap Growth Fund	LGILX	A-	A-	B+	Up	7.64	13.82	33.90	42.30	119.20	19.35	1,858		Y
Leland Thomson Reuters Venture Capital Index Fund Class A	LDVAX	B	B-	B	Up	9.07	19.98	51.24	70.30		14.5	19.1	877-270-2848	Y
Leland Thomson Reuters Venture Capital Index Fund Class C	LDVCX	B	B-	B	Up	9.04	19.76	50.18	66.67		14.29	19.1	877-270-2848	Y
Leland Thomson Reuters Venture Capital Index Fund Class I	LDVIX	B	B-	B	Up	9.19	20.15	51.49	71.07		14.56	19.1	877-270-2848	Y
Litman Gregory Masters Equity Fund Institutional Class	MSEFX	B	B	B-	Up	5.74	12.30	21.15	32.10	103.19	19.1	347.5	800-960-0188	Y
Litman Gregory Masters Equity Fund Investor Class	MSENX	B	B	B-	Up	5.72	12.19	20.86	31.11	101.50	18.81	347.5	800-960-0188	Y
LKCM Equity Fund Institutional Class	LKEQX	B-	B	B-	Down	6.07	10.31	21.68	29.81	84.83	26.02	341.9	800-688-5526	Y
Logan Capital Large Cap Growth Fund Institutional Class	LGNGX	B+	A-	B	Up	7.57	12.61	31.31	42.90	110.96	21.43	28.4		Y
Logan Capital Large Cap Growth Fund Investor Class	LGNHX	B+	A-	B	Up	7.58	12.56	31.14	42.01	108.54	21.14	28.4		Y
Loomis Sayles Growth Fund Class A	LGRRX	A-	A-	A	Up	6.19	12.69	32.29	51.91	133.14	14.57	7,788	800-862-4863	Y
Loomis Sayles Growth Fund Class C	LGRCX	A-	B+	A	Up	5.97	12.22	31.39	48.58	124.20	13.4	7,788	800-862-4863	Y
Loomis Sayles Growth Fund Class N	LGRNX	A-	A-	A	Up	6.24	12.79	32.75	53.55	135.53	15.52	7,788	800-862-4863	Y
Loomis Sayles Growth Fund Class Y	LSGRX	A-	A-	A	Up	6.23	12.78	32.63	53.03	135.70	15.53	7,788	800-862-4863	Y
Lord Abbett Growth Leaders Fund Class A	LGLAX	A-	A-	A-	Up	7.48	14.48	31.19	39.75	131.66	27.85	3,095	201-827-2000	Y
Lord Abbett Growth Leaders Fund Class B	GLABX	A-	A-	B+	Up	7.25	14.02	30.23	36.67	123.29	26.75	3,095	201-827-2000	Y
Lord Abbett Growth Leaders Fund Class C	LGLCX	A-	A-	B+	Up	7.30	14.05	30.23	36.67	123.49	26.45	3,095	201-827-2000	Y
Lord Abbett Growth Leaders Fund Class F	LGLFX	A-	A-	A-	Up	7.55	14.62	31.51	40.54	133.76	28.16	3,095	201-827-2000	Y
Lord Abbett Growth Leaders Fund Class F3	LGLOX	A-	A-	A-	Up	7.57	14.68	31.59	40.90	134.94	28.37	3,095	201-827-2000	Y
Lord Abbett Growth Leaders Fund Class I	LGLIX	A-	A-	A-	Up	7.55	14.62	31.54	40.84	134.85	28.31	3,095	201-827-2000	Y
Lord Abbett Growth Leaders Fund Class R2	LGLQX	A-	A-	B+	Up	7.41	14.28	30.76	38.31	128.89	27.65	3,095	201-827-2000	Y
Lord Abbett Growth Leaders Fund Class R3	LGLRX	A-	A-	A-	Up	7.44	14.34	30.90	38.68	128.94	27.55	3,095	201-827-2000	Y
Lord Abbett Growth Leaders Fund Class R4	LGLSX	A-	A-	A-	Up	7.47	14.48	31.23	39.75	131.86	27.86	3,095	201-827-2000	Y
Lord Abbett Growth Leaders Fund Class R5	LGLUX	A-	A-	A-	Up	7.54	14.62	31.58	40.89	134.93	28.32	3,095	201-827-2000	Y
Lord Abbett Growth Leaders Fund Class R6	LGLVX	A-	A-	A-	Up	7.57	14.68	31.63	41.12	135.31	28.37	3,095	201-827-2000	Y
Lord Abbett Growth Leaders Fund Class T	LGWTX	A-	A-	A-		7.51	14.53	31.26	39.84	132.02	27.87	3,095	201-827-2000	Y
Madison Covered Call and Equity Strategy Fund	MCN	B-	C+	B+	Up	2.45	4.47	7.20	14.40	45.83	8.27	160.7	800-767-0300	Y
Madison Investors Fund Class A	MNVAX	B	B	B+		0.70	4.58	15.71	29.29	88.74	22.83	314.6	800-767-0300	Y
Madison Investors Fund Class R6	MNVRX	B	B	B+		0.43	4.36	15.72	30.50	92.02	22.96	314.6	800-767-0300	Y
Madison Investors Fund Class Y	MINVX	B	B	B+		0.52	4.48	15.69	29.93	90.69	22.85	314.6	800-767-0300	Y
Madison Strategic Sector Premium Fund	MSP	B-	C+	B+	Up	2.55	4.50	6.99	14.82	44.77	12.35	72.1		Y
MainStay Cornerstone Growth Fund Class A	KLGAX	B	B	B	Up	9.17	15.83	30.04	31.98	82.59	34.35	661.6	800-624-6782	Y
MainStay Cornerstone Growth Fund Class B	KLGBX	B-	B	B-	Down	8.90	15.24	28.76	28.29	74.14	32.47	661.6	800-624-6782	Y
MainStay Cornerstone Growth Fund Class C	KLGCX	B-	B	B-	Down	8.90	15.25	28.77	28.25	74.10	32.46	661.6	800-624-6782	Y
MainStay Cornerstone Growth Fund Class I	KLGIX	B	B	B	Up	9.25	15.97	30.37	32.92	84.82	35.1	661.6	800-624-6782	Y
MainStay Cornerstone Growth Fund Class R2	KLGRX	B	B	B	Up	9.11	15.77	29.93	31.57	81.47	34.14	661.6	800-624-6782	Y
MainStay Cornerstone Growth Fund Investor Class	KLGNX	B	B	B	Up	9.06	15.63	29.68	31.11	80.71	33.97	661.6	800-624-6782	Y
MainStay Large Cap Growth Fund Class A	MLAAX	B+	B+	B+	Up	5.74	11.74	32.15	35.11	109.10	9.05	12,363	800-624-6782	Y
MainStay Large Cap Growth Fund Class B	MLABX	B	B	B+	Up	5.51	11.27	31.01	31.81	101.01	7.57	12,363	800-624-6782	
MainStay Large Cap Growth Fund Class C	MLACX	B	B	B+	Up	5.63	11.29	31.06	31.88	100.92	7.56	12,363	800-624-6782	Y
MainStay Large Cap Growth Fund Class I	MLAIX	B+	B+	B+	Up	5.86	11.93	32.38	36.04	111.89	9.71	12,363	800-624-6782	Y
MainStay Large Cap Growth Fund Class R1	MLRRX	B+	B+	B+	Up	5.83	11.82	32.41	35.69	110.89	9.48	12,363	800-624-6782	Y
MainStay Large Cap Growth Fund Class R2	MLRTX	B+	B	B+	Up	5.76	11.66	31.94	34.63	108.30	9.02	12,363	800-624-6782	Y
MainStay Large Cap Growth Fund Class R3	MLGRX	B+	B	B+	Up	5.71	11.62	31.69	33.73	105.79	8.59	12,363	800-624-6782	Y
MainStay Large Cap Growth Fund Class R6	MLRSX	B+	B+	B+	Up	5.85	11.90	32.50	36.56	112.64	9.76	12,363	800-624-6782	Y
MainStay Large Cap Growth Fund Investor Class	MLINX	B+	B	B+	Up	5.71	11.66	31.97	34.80	108.48	8.93	12,363	800-624-6782	Y
Manning & Napier Equity Series Class S	EXEYX	B	B	B	Up	6.81	11.97	28.77	31.29	93.82	13.8	83.7	585-325-6880	Y
Manor Investment Funds Growth Fund	MNRGX	B	B	B-		5.12	12.62	25.17	29.63	103.06	25.24	10.6		Y

Category: US Equity Large Cap Growth (con't)

Fund Name	Ticker Symbol	RATINGS: Overall Rating	RATINGS: Reward Rating	RATINGS: Risk Rating	RATINGS: Recent Up/ Downgrade	TOTAL RETURNS & PERFORMANCE: 3-Month Total Return	6-Month Total Return	1-Year Total Return	3-Year Total Return	5-Year Total Return	ASSETS: NAV	ASSETS: Total Assets (MIL)	NEW INVESTORS: Telephone	NEW INVESTORS: Open to New Investors
Marsico Focus Fund	MFOCX	B	B	B	Up	3.06	11.04	33.98	25.33	98.17	17.07	567.4	888-860-8686	Y
Marsico Growth Fund	MGRIX	B	B-	B	Up	4.77	11.40	31.10	24.31	88.18	17.61	281.4	888-860-8686	Y
MassMutual Premier Disciplined Growth Fund Admin Cls	MPGLX	B+	A-	B	Up	7.72	14.99	28.29	40.69	119.34	12.69	400.1		Y
MassMutual Premier Disciplined Growth Fund Class A	MPGAX	B+	A-	B	Up	7.63	14.81	27.99	39.51	116.43	12.36	400.1		Y
MassMutual Premier Disciplined Growth Fund Class I	MPDIX	A-	A-	B	Up	7.82	15.19	28.70	41.88	122.30	12.5	400.1		Y
MassMutual Premier Disciplined Growth Fund Class R3	MPDRX	B+	B+	B	Up	7.65	14.80	27.83	38.90	115.11	12.27	400.1		Y
MassMutual Premier Disciplined Growth Fund Class R4	MPDGX	B+	A-	B	Up	7.64	14.86	28.12	39.92	117.81	12.27	400.1		Y
MassMutual Premier Disciplined Growth Fund Class R5	MPGSX	A-	A-	B	Up	7.70	15.06	28.54	41.38	121.47	12.51	400.1		Y
MassMutual Premier Disciplined Growth Fund Service Class	DEIGX	B+	A-	B	Up	7.66	15.00	28.44	40.94	120.36	12.55	400.1		Y
MassMutual Select Blue Chip Growth Fund Administrative Cls	MBCLX	A-	A-	A-	Up	6.65	13.66	34.69	51.03	138.54	19.74	2,372		Y
MassMutual Select Blue Chip Growth Fund Class A	MBCGX	A-	A-	A-	Up	6.55	13.47	34.31	49.93	135.85	18.94	2,372		Y
MassMutual Select Blue Chip Growth Fund Class I	MBCZX	A-	A	A-	Up	6.74	13.81	35.08	52.40	142.09	20.2	2,372		Y
MassMutual Select Blue Chip Growth Fund Class R3	MBCNX	A-	A-	A-	Up	6.53	13.44	34.11	49.32	133.62	17.74	2,372		Y
MassMutual Select Blue Chip Growth Fund Class R4	MBGFX	A-	A-	A-	Up	6.60	13.54	34.42	50.39	137.44	18.89	2,372		Y
MassMutual Select Blue Chip Growth Fund Class R5	MBCSX	A-	A	A-	Up	6.70	13.79	35.00	52.00	141.19	20.18	2,372		Y
MassMutual Select Blue Chip Growth Fund Service Class	MBCYX	A-	A	A-	Up	6.67	13.70	34.85	51.52	140.04	20	2,372		Y
MassMutual Select Fundamental Growth Fund Admin Cls	MOTLX	B+	B+	B+	Up	5.96	12.05	27.18	38.29	108.08	7.97	149.5		Y
MassMutual Select Fundamental Growth Fund Class A	MOTAX	B+	B+	B+	Up	5.84	11.90	26.97	37.24	105.20	7.62	149.5		Y
MassMutual Select Fundamental Growth Fund Class I	MOTZX	B+	B+	B+	Up	5.86	12.11	27.46	39.36	110.64	8.31	149.5		Y
MassMutual Select Fundamental Growth Fund Class R3	MOTNX	B+	B+	B+	Up	5.78	11.77	26.69	36.64	103.42	7.11	149.5		Y
MassMutual Select Fundamental Growth Fund Class R4	MFGFX	B+	B+	B+	Up	5.93	11.91	27.12	37.61	106.66	7.54	149.5		Y
MassMutual Select Fundamental Growth Fund Class R5	MOTCX	B+	B+	B+	Up	5.88	12.11	27.42	39.01	109.93	8.34	149.5		Y
MassMutual Select Fundamental Growth Fund Service Class	MOTYX	B+	B+	B+	Up	5.78	12.00	27.28	38.59	108.87	8.16	149.5		Y
MassMutual Select Growth Opp Fund Admin Cls	MAGLX	B	B	B+	Up	3.45	11.30	31.34	26.19	97.57	10.06	797.1		Y
MassMutual Select Growth Opportunities Fund Class A	MMAAX	B	B	B	Up	3.38	11.09	30.88	25.25	95.11	9.34	797.1		Y
MassMutual Select Growth Opportunities Fund Class I	MMAZX	B	B	B+	Up	3.48	11.38	31.74	27.40	100.75	10.86	797.1		Y
MassMutual Select Growth Opportunities Fund Class R3	MMANX	B	B	B	Up	3.32	11.01	30.75	24.66	93.24	8.61	797.1		Y
MassMutual Select Growth Opportunities Fund Class R4	MMGFX	B	B	B+	Up	3.37	11.15	31.01	25.63	96.63	9.39	797.1		Y
MassMutual Select Growth Opportunities Fund Class R5	MGRSX	B	B	B+	Up	3.42	11.30	31.44	26.87	99.52	10.74	797.1		Y
MassMutual Select Growth Opportunities Fund Service Class	MAGYX	B	B	B+	Up	3.42	11.20	31.32	26.55	98.66	10.44	797.1		Y
Meridian Equity Income Fund® A Class	MRAEX	B	B	B	Up	9.94	18.64	27.40	38.36	93.64	15.86	55.4	800-446-6662	Y
Meridian Equity Income Fund® Class C	MRCEX	B	B	B	Up	9.79	18.35	26.82	36.36	88.08	15.86	55.4	800-446-6662	Y
Meridian Equity Income Fund® Investor Class	MRIEX	B	B	B	Up	10.05	18.79	27.71	39.35	96.02	15.98	55.4	800-446-6662	Y
Meridian Equity Income Fund® Legacy Class	MEIFX	B	B	B	Up	10.07	18.90	27.94	39.80	96.71	15.97	55.4	800-446-6662	
Meritage Growth Equity Fund Institutional Shares	MPGIX	B	B+	B	Down	5.90	11.12	25.98	41.81		14.52	26.0	913-345-7000	Y
Meritage Growth Equity Fund Investor Shares	MPGEX	B	B+	B	Down	5.83	11.00	25.65	40.72		14.41	26.0	913-345-7000	Y
MFS® Growth Fund Class A	MFEGX	A-	B+	A	Up	6.40	11.69	30.54	41.79	115.60	89.95	16,680	877-960-6077	Y
MFS® Growth Fund Class B	MEGBX	B+	B+	A	Up	6.19	11.26	29.56	38.63	107.63	73.18	16,680	877-960-6077	Y
MFS® Growth Fund Class C	MFECX	B+	B+	A	Up	6.19	11.25	29.55	38.60	107.62	72.62	16,680	877-960-6077	Y
MFS® Growth Fund Class I	MFEIX	A-	B+	A	Up	6.47	11.83	30.86	42.84	118.25	95.4	16,680	877-960-6077	Y
MFS® Growth Fund Class R1	MFELX	B+	B+	A	Up	6.19	11.26	29.55	38.59	107.60	72.88	16,680	877-960-6077	Y
MFS® Growth Fund Class R2	MEGRX	A-	B+	A	Up	6.33	11.54	30.20	40.71	112.86	85.22	16,680	877-960-6077	Y
MFS® Growth Fund Class R3	MFEHX	A-	B+	A	Up	6.40	11.69	30.52	41.77	115.58	89.51	16,680	877-960-6077	Y
MFS® Growth Fund Class R4	MFEJX	A-	B+	A	Up	6.47	11.83	30.87	42.85	118.25	92.87	16,680	877-960-6077	Y
MFS® Growth Fund Class R6	MFEKX	A-	B+	A	Up	6.50	11.89	30.98	43.25	119.30	95.65	16,680	877-960-6077	Y
MFS® Massachusetts Investors Growth Stock Fund Class 529A	EISTX	B	B	A-		7.53	11.54	28.63	35.16	100.72	27.4	7,262	877-960-6077	Y
MFS® Massachusetts Investors Growth Stock Fund Class 529B	EMIVX	B	B	B+		7.32	11.15	27.67	32.09	93.19	23.54	7,262	877-960-6077	Y
MFS® Massachusetts Investors Growth Stock Fund Class 529C	EMICX	B	B	B+		7.30	11.11	27.64	32.10	93.16	23.32	7,262	877-960-6077	Y
MFS® Massachusetts Investors Growth Stock Fund Class A	MIGFX	B	B	A-		7.54	11.62	28.69	35.40	101.15	27.81	7,262	877-960-6077	Y
MFS® Massachusetts Investors Growth Stock Fund Class B	MIGBX	B	B	B+		7.31	11.13	27.66	32.29	93.65	24.21	7,262	877-960-6077	Y
MFS® Massachusetts Investors Growth Stock Fund Class C	MIGDX	B	B	B+		7.31	11.16	27.67	32.26	93.59	24	7,262	877-960-6077	Y
MFS® Massachusetts Investors Growth Stock Fund Class I	MGTIX	B	B	A-		7.60	11.73	28.98	36.33	103.55	28.56	7,262	877-960-6077	Y

Category: US Equity
Large Cap Growth (con't)

Fund Name	Ticker Symbol	RATINGS: Overall Rating	Reward Rating	Risk Rating	Recent Up/ Downgrade	TOTAL RETURNS & PERFORMANCE: 3-Month Total Return	6-Month Total Return	1-Year Total Return	3-Year Total Return	5-Year Total Return	ASSETS: NAV	Total Assets (MIL)	NEW INVESTORS: Telephone	Open to New Investors
MFS® Massachusetts Investors Growth Stock Fund Class R1	MIGMX	B	B	B+		7.33	11.17	27.66	32.27	93.63	23.76	7,262	877-960-6077	Y
MFS® Massachusetts Investors Growth Stock Fund Class R2	MIRGX	B	B	A-		7.42	11.40	28.29	34.26	98.45	27.04	7,262	877-960-6077	Y
MFS® Massachusetts Investors Growth Stock Fund Class R3	MIGHX	B	B	A-		7.53	11.57	28.65	35.33	101.05	27.51	7,262	877-960-6077	Y
MFS® Massachusetts Investors Growth Stock Fund Class R4	MIGKX	B	B	A-		7.61	11.71	28.98	36.31	103.51	27.98	7,262	877-960-6077	Y
MFS® Massachusetts Investors Growth Stock Fund Class R6	MIGNX	B	B	A-		7.63	11.80	29.13	36.77	104.59	28.58	7,262	877-960-6077	Y
Monetta Fund	MONTX	B	B	B	Up	5.31	10.20	19.18	30.46	93.67	18.89	58.1	800-684-3416	Y
Monetta Young Investor Fund	MYIFX	B	B	B		7.50	12.59	23.10	36.19	103.51	24	144.9	800-684-3416	Y
Monteagle Informed Investor Growth Fund Class I	MIIFX	B	B	A-	Up	5.63	10.34	16.52	30.21	71.59	11.06	12.6		Y
Monteagle Quality Growth Fund Class I	MFGIX	B	B	B-		6.07	11.21	24.59	31.13	87.93	14.31	29.0		Y
Morgan Stanley Inst Fund, Inc. Advantage Portfolio Cls A	MAPPX	B+	B+	A-	Up	9.32	13.32	31.63	50.00	125.59	21.1	111.5	855-332-5306	Y
Morgan Stanley Inst Fund, Inc. Advantage Portfolio Cls C	MSPRX	B+	B	A-	Up	9.13	12.93	30.76	46.66	117.70	20.82	111.5	855-332-5306	Y
Morgan Stanley Inst Fund, Inc. Advantage Portfolio Cls I	MPAIX	B+	B+	A-	Up	9.38	13.48	32.06	51.48	129.38	21.45	111.5	855-332-5306	
Morgan Stanley Inst Fund, Inc. Advantage Portfolio Cls IS	MADSX	B+	B+	A-	Up	9.47	13.57	32.21	51.74	129.75	21.49	111.5	855-332-5306	Y
Morgan Stanley Inst Fund, Inc. Advantage Portfolio Cls L	MAPLX	B+	B+	A-	Up	9.34	13.44	31.96	51.10	128.23	21.42	111.5	855-332-5306	
Morgan Stanley Inst Fund, Inc. Growth Portfolio Cls A	MSEGX	B+	A-	B+	Up	7.32	12.48	43.44	55.27	151.22	39.77	4,194	855-332-5306	Y
Morgan Stanley Inst Fund, Inc. Growth Portfolio Cls C	MSGUX	B+	A-	B+	Up	7.13	12.07	42.37	51.87	141.91	37.76	4,194	855-332-5306	Y
Morgan Stanley Inst Fund, Inc. Growth Portfolio Cls I	MSEQX	A-	A-	B+	Up	7.40	12.64	43.82	56.67	154.57	41.65	4,194	855-332-5306	Y
Morgan Stanley Inst Fund, Inc. Growth Portfolio Cls IS	MGRPX	A-	A-	B+	Up	7.43	12.71	43.98	57.05	155.66	41.89	4,194	855-332-5306	Y
Morgan Stanley Inst Fund, Inc. Growth Portfolio Cls L	MSHLX	B+	A-	B+	Up	7.19	12.20	42.69	52.68	144.46	37.99	4,194	855-332-5306	
Morgan Stanley Multi Cap Growth Trust Class A	CPOAX	A-	A	B	Up	10.20	15.46	47.81	52.20	145.24	31.98	426.4	855-332-5306	Y
Morgan Stanley Multi Cap Growth Trust Class B	CPOBX	A-	A	B	Up	9.97	14.97	46.61	48.68	135.86	23.44	426.4	855-332-5306	
Morgan Stanley Multi Cap Growth Trust Class C	MSCMX	A-	A	B	Up	9.98	15.02	46.66	48.74	135.96	23.51	426.4	855-332-5306	Y
Morgan Stanley Multi Cap Growth Trust Class I	CPODX	A-	A	B	Up	10.28	15.63	48.23	53.72	149.15	35.15	426.4	855-332-5306	Y
Morgan Stanley Multi Cap Growth Trust Class IS	MCRTX	A-	A	B	Up	10.29	15.66	48.33	53.99	148.00	35.3	426.4	855-332-5306	Y
Morgan Stanley Multi Cap Growth Trust Class L	CPOCX	A-	A	B	Up	10.06	15.14	46.97	49.80	138.89	23.74	426.4	855-332-5306	
Multimanager Aggressive Equity Portfolio Class IA	US4049924719	B+	A-	B	Up	7.81	14.66	30.20	39.06	118.52		1,184	877-222-2144	Y
Multimanager Aggressive Equity Portfolio Class IB	US4049924891	B+	A-	B	Up	7.81	14.66	30.20	39.05	118.46		1,184	877-222-2144	Y
Multimanager Aggressive Equity Portfolio Class K	US00247C5360	B+	A-	B	Up	7.88	14.80	30.54	39.71	120.65		1,184	877-222-2144	Y
Multi-Manager Growth Strategies Fund Class A	CSLGX	B	B	B	Down	5.77	10.88	31.44	36.44	116.76	14.73	2,657	800-345-6611	Y
Multi-Manager Growth Strategies Fund Institutional Class	CZMGX	B	B	B	Down	5.74	10.92	31.90	36.92	117.52	14.54	2,657	800-345-6611	Y
Nationwide Growth Fund Class A	NMFAX	B	B	B	Up	7.29	13.44	26.85	35.57	107.76	11.65	216.8	800-848-0920	Y
Nationwide Growth Fund Class C	GCGRX	B	B	B	Up	7.00	12.93	25.62	32.24	99.74	8.97	216.8	800-848-0920	Y
Nationwide Growth Fund Class R	GGFRX	B	B	B	Up	7.07	13.14	26.17	34.70	105.24	11.38	216.8	800-848-0920	Y
Nationwide Growth Fund Class R6	MUIGX	B	B	B	Up	7.35	13.59	27.15	36.75	110.94	12.27	216.8	800-848-0920	Y
Nationwide Growth Fund Institutional Service Class	NGISX	B	B	B	Up	7.25	13.48	26.85	35.83	108.67	12.33	216.8	800-848-0920	Y
Nationwide Ziegler NYSE Arca Tech 100 Index Fund Class A	NWJCX	B+	A	C+	Up	4.86	14.55	31.27	43.15	126.00	76.46	477.9	800-848-0920	Y
Nationwide Ziegler NYSE Arca Tech 100 Index Fund Class C	NWJDX	B+	A	C+	Up	4.66	14.13	30.32	40.00	118.22	68.25	477.9	800-848-0920	Y
Nationwide Ziegler NYSE Arca Tech 100 Index Fund Class R6	NWJEX	B+	A	C+	Down	4.95	14.75	31.75	44.72	129.47	77.16	477.9	800-848-0920	Y
Nationwide Ziegler NYSE Arca Tech 100 Ind Inst Serv Cls	NWJFX	B+	A	C+	Up	4.93	14.67	31.57	44.12	128.64	77.19	477.9	800-848-0920	Y
Natixis Funds Trust I U.S. Equity Opportunities Fund Cls A	NEFSX	B	B	B	Down	5.70	11.62	26.28	48.23	133.24	36.9	999.0	800-862-4863	Y
Natixis Funds Trust I U.S. Equity Opportunities Fund Cls C	NECCX	B	B	B	Down	5.50	11.22	25.35	44.91	124.67	25.73	999.0	800-862-4863	Y
Natixis Funds Trust I U.S. Equity Opportunities Fund Cls N	NESNX	B	B	B	Down	5.81	11.87	26.57	48.57	133.77	42.63	999.0	800-862-4863	Y
Natixis Funds Trust I U.S. Equity Opportunities Fund Cls Y	NESYX	B	B	B	Down	5.76	11.76	26.60	49.33	136.13	42.61	999.0	800-862-4863	Y
Natixis Vaughan Nelson Select Fund Class A	VNSAX	B	B	B		5.48	10.66	23.51	34.05	117.36	17.28	153.5	800-862-4863	Y
Natixis Vaughan Nelson Select Fund Class C	VNSCX	B	B	B-		5.23	10.21	22.57	31.06	109.44	16.6	153.5	800-862-4863	Y
Natixis Vaughan Nelson Select Fund Class N	VNSNX	B	B	B		5.58	10.92	23.97	35.26	120.50	17.37	153.5	800-862-4863	Y
Natixis Vaughan Nelson Select Fund Class Y	VNSYX	B	B	B		5.48	10.82	23.79	35.06	120.17	17.35	153.5	800-862-4863	Y
Neuberger Berman Advisers Mgmt Trust Guardian Port Cls I	US6412224015	B-	B-	C+	Down	6.89	11.29	25.41	28.31	99.16	16.15	61.0	212-476-9000	Y
Neuberger Berman Advisers Mgmt Trust Guardian Port Cls S	US6412228727	B-	B-	C+	Down	6.90	11.21	24.73	27.47	97.25	15.95	61.0	212-476-9000	Y
Neuberger Berman Advisers Mgmt Trust Social Resp Cls S	US6412228230	B	B-	B+		5.32	8.13	18.10	27.55	97.75	25.69	461.2	212-476-9000	Y
Neuberger Berman Advisers Mgmt Trust Socially Resp Cls I	US6412226093	B	B-	B+		5.44	8.30	18.42	28.37	99.71	25.61	461.2	212-476-9000	Y
Neuberger Berman Guardian Fund Class A	NGDAX	B-	B-	C+	Down	6.92	11.39	24.89	28.25	98.75	10.27	1,255	212-476-9000	Y

Category: US Equity Large Cap Growth (con't)

Fund Name	Ticker Symbol	RATINGS: Overall Rating	Reward Rating	Risk Rating	Recent Up/ Downgrade	TOTAL RETURNS & PERFORMANCE: 3-Month Total Return	6-Month Total Return	1-Year Total Return	3-Year Total Return	5-Year Total Return	ASSETS: NAV	Total Assets (MIL)	NEW INVESTORS: Telephone	Open to New Investors
Neuberger Berman Guardian Fund Class Advisor	NBGUX	B-	B-	C+	Down	6.91	11.31	24.85	27.36	96.06	13.75	1,255	212-476-9000	
Neuberger Berman Guardian Fund Class C	NGDCX	B-	B-	C+	Down	6.72	10.97	23.93	25.36	91.27	13.11	1,255	212-476-9000	Y
Neuberger Berman Guardian Fund Class Institutional	NGDLX	B-	B-	B-	Down	7.09	11.61	25.41	29.69	102.50	17.53	1,255	212-476-9000	Y
Neuberger Berman Guardian Fund Class Investor	NGUAX	B-	B-	C+	Down	7.00	11.46	25.20	28.93	100.62	17.49	1,255	212-476-9000	
Neuberger Berman Guardian Fund Class R3	NGDRX	B-	B-	C+	Down	6.89	11.23	24.64	27.20	96.21	13.65	1,255	212-476-9000	Y
Neuberger Berman Guardian Fund Class Trust	NBGTX	B-	B-	C+	Down	7.03	11.44	25.10	28.43	99.09	10.46	1,255	212-476-9000	
Neuberger Berman Socially Responsive Fund Class A	NRAAX	B	B-	B+		5.44	8.24	18.36	28.09	99.61	38.19	2,466	212-476-9000	Y
Neuberger Berman Socially Responsive Fund Class C	NRACX	B	B-	B+	Up	5.25	7.83	17.43	25.24	92.26	38.32	2,466	212-476-9000	Y
Neuberger Berman Socially Responsive Fund Class R3	NRARX	B	B-	B+		5.39	8.08	18.07	27.16	97.30	38.28	2,466	212-476-9000	Y
Neuberger Berman Socially Responsive Fund Class R6	NRSRX	B	B-	B+		5.56	8.44	18.84	29.80	104.00	38.04	2,466	212-476-9000	Y
Neuberger Berman Socially Responsive Fund Inst Cls	NBSLX	B	B-	B+		5.54	8.42	18.76	29.49	103.41	38.06	2,466	212-476-9000	Y
Neuberger Berman Socially Responsive Fund Investor Class	NBSRX	B	B-	B+		5.50	8.33	18.56	28.81	101.58	38.13	2,466	212-476-9000	
Neuberger Berman Socially Responsive Fund Trust Class	NBSTX	A	A+	B+	Up	85.01	89.87	107.70	124.85	250.62	38.19	2,466	212-476-9000	
New Covenant Growth Fund	NCGFX	B-	B-	B-	Down	6.50	11.29	21.59	27.78	84.56	41.98	442.9		Y
Nicholas Fund	NICSX	B-	C+	B	Up	4.64	7.20	17.54	14.23	89.05	61.81	2,811	800-544-6547	Y
North Country Equity Growth Fund	NCEGX	B	B	B		7.07	11.25	23.79	35.96	102.56	17.89	127.7		Y
NorthQuest Capital Fund	NQCFX	B-	B-	B-	Down	5.51	9.04	22.73	26.46	75.12	16.38	3.8		Y
Nuveen Core Equity Alpha Fund	JCE	B-	B-	B	Up	4.90	9.26	21.70	26.25	92.23	14.76	265.5	312-917-8146	Y
Nuveen Growth Fund Class A	NSAGX	B	B	B		8.94	15.27	25.66	35.12	109.39	30.46	49.9	312-917-8146	Y
Nuveen Growth Fund Class C	NSRCX	B	B	B		8.72	14.86	24.70	32.11	101.77	27.68	49.9	312-917-8146	Y
Nuveen Growth Fund Class I	NSRGX	B	B	B		8.98	15.44	25.97	36.13	112.12	31.03	49.9	312-917-8146	Y
Nuveen Growth Fund Class R3	NBGRX	B	B	B		8.88	15.16	25.39	34.14	106.86	30.2	49.9	312-917-8146	Y
Nuveen Large Cap Growth Fund Class A	NLAGX	B	B	B-	Up	6.94	12.99	23.60	31.92		30.7	345.2	312-917-8146	Y
Nuveen Large Cap Growth Fund Class C	NLCGX	B-	B	B-	Down	6.73	12.54	22.65	28.99		30.11	345.2	312-917-8146	Y
Nuveen Large Cap Growth Fund Class I	NLIGX	B	B	B-	Up	7.04	13.16	23.91	32.94		30.73	345.2	312-917-8146	Y
Nuveen Large Cap Growth Fund Class R6	NLAFX	B	B	B-	Up	7.00	13.16	23.91	33.00		30.73	345.2	312-917-8146	Y
Nuveen Symphony Large Cap Growth Fund Class A	NCGAX	B+	B+	B	Up	7.93	14.21	29.45	40.13	106.12	38.78	156.5	312-917-8146	Y
Nuveen Symphony Large Cap Growth Fund Class C	NCGCX	B	B	B		7.69	13.75	28.46	37.02	98.46	35.64	156.5	312-917-8146	Y
Nuveen Symphony Large Cap Growth Fund Class I	NSGIX	B+	A-	B	Up	7.97	14.34	29.72	41.18	108.69	39.33	156.5	312-917-8146	Y
Nuveen Symphony Large-Cap Growth Fund Class R3	NSGQX	B+	B+	B	Up	7.84	14.05	29.09	39.07	103.53	38.69	156.5	312-917-8146	Y
Nuveen Winslow Large-Cap Growth Fund Class A	NWCAX	B+	B+	B+	Up	5.74	11.88	32.56	36.39	110.30	37.1	600.9	312-917-8146	Y
Nuveen Winslow Large-Cap Growth Fund Class C	NWCCX	B+	B	B+	Up	5.54	11.48	31.56	33.38	102.53	33.23	600.9	312-917-8146	Y
Nuveen Winslow Large-Cap Growth Fund Class I	NVLIX	B+	B+	B+	Up	5.79	12.00	32.84	37.38	112.88	38.17	600.9	312-917-8146	Y
Nuveen Winslow Large-Cap Growth Fund Class R3	NWCRX	B+	B+	B+	Up	5.65	11.72	32.16	35.32	107.61	35.82	600.9	312-917-8146	Y
Nuveen Winslow Large-Cap Growth Fund Class R6	NWCFX	B+	B+	B+	Up	5.84	12.10	33.10	38.09	114.47	38.59	600.9	312-917-8146	Y
Oak Ridge Multi Strategy Fund Class A	ORILX	B	B	A-	Up	6.48	12.92	26.35	30.87	95.12	25.6	67.7		Y
Oak Ridge Multi Strategy Fund Class C	ORLCX	B	B-	A-	Up	6.19	12.43	25.21	27.38	86.49	22.79	67.7		Y
Oak Ridge Multi Strategy Fund Class I	PORYX	B	B	A-	Up	6.40	12.90	26.35	30.98	95.50	26.08	67.7		Y
Oppenheimer Capital Appreciation Fund Class A	OPTFX	B	B	B	Up	5.86	9.90	26.52	26.38	93.45	58.38	5,215	800-225-5677	Y
Oppenheimer Capital Appreciation Fund Class B	OTGBX	B	B-	B	Up	5.65	9.46	25.55	23.49	86.10	44.54	5,215	800-225-5677	
Oppenheimer Capital Appreciation Fund Class C	OTFCX	B	B-	B	Up	5.65	9.48	25.56	23.51	86.20	44.13	5,215	800-225-5677	Y
Oppenheimer Capital Appreciation Fund Class I	OPTIX	B	B	B		5.97	10.13	27.03	27.97	97.58	63.31	5,215	800-225-5677	Y
Oppenheimer Capital Appreciation Fund Class R	OTCNX	B	B-	B	Up	5.79	9.76	26.19	25.39	90.95	55.08	5,215	800-225-5677	Y
Oppenheimer Capital Appreciation Fund Class Y	OTCYX	B	B	B		5.92	10.03	26.81	27.25	95.93	63.08	5,215	800-225-5677	Y
Optimum Large Cap Growth Fund Class A	OALGX	B	B	B	Down	6.41	12.06	32.15	42.46	121.48	16.78	1,704		Y
Optimum Large Cap Growth Fund Class C	OCLGX	B	B	B	Down	6.28	11.69	31.24	39.32	113.57	14.28	1,704		Y
Optimum Large Cap Growth Fund Institutional Class	OILGX	B	B	B	Down	6.51	12.25	32.47	43.58	124.55	17.98	1,704		Y
PACE Large Co Growth Equity Investments Class A	PLAAX	B+	B	A-	Up	5.72	12.19	29.53	35.31	108.75	24.73	1,383	212-882-5586	Y
PACE Large Co Growth Equity Investments Class C	PLACX	B+	B	A-	Up	5.47	11.71	28.50	32.07	100.28	19.9	1,383	212-882-5586	Y
PACE Large Co Growth Equity Investments Class P	PCLCX	B+	B	A-	Up	5.76	12.30	29.84	36.37	111.34	25.56	1,383	212-882-5586	Y
PACE Large Co Growth Equity Investments Class Y	PLAYX	B+	B	A-	Up	5.77	12.35	29.88	36.39	111.45	25.76	1,383	212-882-5586	Y
Parnassus Endeavor Fund Institutional Shares	PFPWX	B+	A-	B	Up	5.23	8.99	20.02	49.98	137.83	37.21	5,204	999-350-5	Y

Category: US Equity Large Cap Growth (con't)

Fund Name	Ticker Symbol	RATINGS: Overall Rating	Reward Rating	Risk Rating	Recent Up/ Downgrade	TOTAL RETURNS & PERFORMANCE: 3-Month Total Return	6-Month Total Return	1-Year Total Return	3-Year Total Return	5-Year Total Return	ASSETS: NAV	Total Assets (MIL)	NEW INVESTORS: Telephone	Open to New Investors
Parnassus Endeavor Fund Investor Shares	PARWX	B+	A-	B	Up	5.17	8.88	19.80	49.19	136.59	37.18	5,204	999-350-5	Y
Parnassus Fund	PARNX	B	B-	B+	Up	4.71	6.03	16.07	31.27	106.79	48.27	1,081	999-350-5	Y
Parnassus Fund Institutional Shares	PFPRX	B	B-	B+	Up	4.75	6.09	16.24	31.76	107.56	48.25	1,081	999-350-5	Y
Pax ESG Beta Quality Fund Class A	PXGAX	B	B-	B	Up	7.39	12.43	21.96	31.24	95.04	19.65	212.3	800-767-1729	Y
Pax ESG Beta Quality Fund Individual Investor Class	PXWGX	B	B-	B	Up	7.33	12.35	21.89	31.15	94.89	19.69	212.3	800-767-1729	Y
Pax ESG Beta Quality Fund Institutional Class	PWGIX	B	B	B	Up	7.37	12.49	22.21	32.13	97.27	20.23	212.3	800-767-1729	Y
PF Growth Fund Class P	US69447T7063	A-	B+	A	Up	6.54	12.03	31.37	43.29	113.73	24.1	142.3	800-722-2333	Y
PF Large-Cap Growth Fund Class P	US69447T8053	A-	A-	B+	Up	7.60	13.88	34.00	41.94	117.54	10.02	95.3	800-722-2333	Y
Piedmont Select Equity Fund	PSVFX	B	C+	A-	Up	4.42	6.99	15.76	20.89	67.29	15.5	25.6		Y
Pioneer Disciplined Growth Fund Class A	PINDX	B	B	B		6.13	11.42	26.25	33.70	108.95	18.2	1,245	617-742-7825	Y
Pioneer Disciplined Growth Fund Class C	INDCX	B	B	B		5.86	10.91	25.20	30.34	100.22	16.22	1,245	617-742-7825	Y
Pioneer Disciplined Growth Fund Class Y	INYDX	B	B	B		6.14	11.55	26.54	34.78	112.22	18.59	1,245	617-742-7825	Y
Pioneer Fundamental Growth Fund Class A	PIGFX	B	B-	A+		4.36	8.29	22.61	33.94	107.75	22.5	6,346	617-742-7825	Y
Pioneer Fundamental Growth Fund Class C	FUNCX	B	B-	A		4.16	7.96	21.76	31.23	100.65	20.61	6,346	617-742-7825	Y
Pioneer Fundamental Growth Fund Class K Shares	PFGKX	B+	B	A+	Up	4.47	8.54	23.19	35.69	112.15	22.5	6,346	617-742-7825	Y
Pioneer Fundamental Growth Fund Class R	PFGRX	B	B-	B+		4.29	8.14	22.28	32.76	104.71	22.17	6,346	617-742-7825	Y
Pioneer Fundamental Growth Fund Class Y	FUNYX	B	B-	B+		4.46	8.50	23.02	35.25	110.96	22.69	6,346	617-742-7825	Y
Plumb Equity Fund	PLBEX	B+	A	B-	Up	9.97	15.55	39.70	45.59	119.62	27.45	26.0		Y
PNC Multi-Factor Large Cap Growth Fund Class A	PEWAX	A-	B+	A-	Up	8.60	15.98	31.21	36.30	116.12	37.36	95.6	800-622-3863	Y
PNC Multi-Factor Large Cap Growth Fund Class C	PEWCX	B+	B	A-	Up	8.44	15.60	30.42	33.83	109.94	33.78	95.6	800-622-3863	Y
PNC Multi-Factor Large Cap Growth Fund Class I	PEWIX	A-	A-	A	Up	8.67	16.14	31.63	37.54	118.97	38.01	95.6	800-622-3863	Y
Polen Growth Fund Institutional Class	POLIX	B+	B	A	Up	4.90	8.84	26.45	44.79	111.24	24.23	1,752	561-241-2425	Y
Polen Growth Fund Investor Class	POLRX	B+	B	A	Up	4.85	8.70	26.11	43.74	108.71	23.85	1,752	561-241-2425	Y
Praxis Growth Index Fund Class A	MGNDX	B	B	B+	Down	6.67	11.94	26.28	38.95	114.69	23.05	261.8		Y
Praxis Growth Index Fund Class I	MMDEX	B	B	B+	Down	6.75	12.14	26.78	40.65	119.17	23.21	261.8		Y
PRIMECAP Odyssey Growth Fund	POGRX	A-	A	B+	Up	9.17	15.44	32.05	51.26	145.05	37.25	10,362	800-729-2307	Y
Principal Blue Chip Fund Class A	PBLAX	B+	B+	B	Up	6.73	13.06	28.30	44.36	109.26	20.93	2,340	800-222-5852	Y
Principal Blue Chip Fund Class C	PBLCX	B+	B+	B	Up	6.51	12.60	27.29	41.08	101.50	20.29	2,340	800-222-5852	Y
Principal Blue Chip Fund Class J	PBCJX	B+	A-	B		6.76	13.17	28.63	45.96	113.02	21.14	2,340	800-222-5852	Y
Principal Blue Chip Fund Class R-3	PGBEX	B+	B+	B	Up	6.64	12.95	28.09	44.75	110.83	21.01	2,340	800-222-5852	Y
Principal Blue Chip Fund Class R-4	PGBFX	B+	A-	B	Up	6.73	13.08	28.43	45.61	112.71	21.08	2,340	800-222-5852	Y
Principal Blue Chip Fund Class R-5	PGBGX	B+	A-	B	Up	6.77	13.12	28.53	46.04	113.78	21.11	2,340	800-222-5852	Y
Principal Blue Chip Fund Class R-6	PGBHX	B+	A-	B	Up	6.83	13.28	28.78	46.58	114.56	21.16	2,340	800-222-5852	Y
Principal Blue Chip Fund Class T	PBLTX	B+	B+	B	Up	6.67	13.01	28.38	45.39	111.76	21.1	2,340	800-222-5852	Y
Principal Blue Chip Fund Institutional Class	PBCKX	B+	A-	B	Up	6.83	13.28	28.85	46.66	114.68	21.16	2,340	800-222-5852	Y
Principal LargeCap Growth Fund Class A	PRGWX	B	B	B+	Up	7.52	15.72	34.16	31.21	98.88	9.02	1,083	800-222-5852	Y
Principal LargeCap Growth Fund Class C	PLGCX	B	B	B	Up	7.28	15.24	33.04	27.98	90.71	7.72	1,083	800-222-5852	Y
Principal LargeCap Growth Fund Class J	PGLJX	B	B	B+	Up	7.62	15.80	34.35	31.77	99.97	8.31	1,083	800-222-5852	Y
Principal LargeCap Growth Fund I Class A	PLGAX	A-	A	A-	Up	7.58	14.02	33.09	42.55	115.08	14.05	8,131	800-222-5852	Y
Principal LargeCap Growth Fund I Class J	PLGJX	A-	A	B	Up	7.61	14.14	33.49	43.74	117.64	12	8,131	800-222-5852	Y
Principal LargeCap Growth Fund I Class R-6	PLCGX	A-	A	B	Up	7.72	14.34	33.77	44.86	121.37	14.42	8,131	800-222-5852	Y
Principal LargeCap Growth Fund I Institutional Class	PLGIX	A-	A	B	Up	7.68	14.29	33.69	44.87	121.36	14.43	8,131	800-222-5852	Y
Principal LargeCap Growth Fund I R-1 Class	PCRSX	A-	A-	A-	Up	7.47	13.81	32.70	41.38	112.09	12.52	8,131	800-222-5852	Y
Principal LargeCap Growth Fund I R-2 Class	PPUNX	A-	A	B	Up	7.56	13.87	32.75	41.90	113.45	12.22	8,131	800-222-5852	Y
Principal LargeCap Growth Fund I R-3 Class	PPUMX	A-	A	B	Up	7.64	14.04	33.04	42.64	115.36	13.22	8,131	800-222-5852	Y
Principal LargeCap Growth Fund I R-4 Class	PPUSX	A-	A	B	Up	7.60	14.06	33.23	43.47	117.31	13.44	8,131	800-222-5852	Y
Principal LargeCap Growth Fund I R-5 Class	PPUPX	A-	A	B	Up	7.72	14.24	33.45	44.02	118.72	13.93	8,131	800-222-5852	Y
Principal LargeCap Growth Fund Institutional Class	PGLIX	B+	B	B+	Up	7.63	15.87	34.57	32.98	103.46	9.58	1,083	800-222-5852	Y
Principal LargeCap Growth Fund R-1 Class	PLSGX	B	B	B+	Up	7.44	15.37	33.59	29.60	95.07	8.4	1,083	800-222-5852	Y
Principal LargeCap Growth Fund R-2 Class	PCPPX	B	B	B+	Up	7.46	15.46	33.73	30.05	96.25	8.64	1,083	800-222-5852	Y
Principal LargeCap Growth Fund R-3 Class	PLGPX	B	B	B+	Up	7.52	15.55	33.97	30.85	98.04	9.85	1,083	800-222-5852	Y
Principal LargeCap Growth Fund R-4 Class	PEPPX	B	B	B+	Up	7.54	15.72	34.24	31.62	99.99	9.82	1,083	800-222-5852	Y

Category: US Equity Large Cap Growth (con't)

Fund Name	Ticker Symbol	RATINGS: Overall Rating	Reward Rating	Risk Rating	Recent Up/ Downgrade	TOTAL RETURNS & PERFORMANCE: 3-Month Total Return	6-Month Total Return	1-Year Total Return	3-Year Total Return	5-Year Total Return	ASSETS: NAV	Total Assets (MIL)	NEW INVESTORS: Telephone	Open to New Investors
Principal LargeCap Growth Fund R-5 Class	PDPPX	B	B	B+	Up	7.55	15.82	34.47	32.14	101.06	9.69	1,083	800-222-5852	Y
ProFunds Large Cap Growth Fund Investor Class	LGPIX	B	B	B	Down	6.30	11.32	25.08	34.39	102.41	82.67	22.8	614-470-8626	Y
ProFunds Large Cap Growth Fund Service Class	LGPSX	B	B	B	Up	6.03	10.77	23.84	30.43	92.51	70.68	22.8	614-470-8626	Y
ProFunds NASDAQ-100 Fund Investor Class	OTPIX	B+	A-	B	Down	6.79	12.74	30.40	45.71	135.34	63.47	77.0	614-470-8626	Y
ProFunds NASDAQ-100 Fund Service Class	OTPSX	B+	B+	B+	Down	6.52	12.18	29.11	41.34	123.67	52.74	77.0	614-470-8626	Y
Provident Trust Strategy Fund	PROVX	A-	A-	B+	Up	9.08	15.93	29.37	48.23	101.74	14.73	148.8	855-739-9950	Y
Prudential Jennison 20/20 Focus Fund Class A	PTWAX	B	B	B	Up	5.22	12.39	26.58	35.13	90.41	14.6	1,182	800-225-1852	Y
Prudential Jennison 20/20 Focus Fund Class B	PTWBX	B	B	B	Up	5.00	11.96	25.56	32.21	83.76	10.29	1,182	800-225-1852	
Prudential Jennison 20/20 Focus Fund Class C	PTWCX	B	B	B	Up	5.07	12.03	25.63	32.28	83.83	10.31	1,182	800-225-1852	Y
Prudential Jennison 20/20 Focus Fund Class R	JTWRX	B	B	B	Up	5.13	12.25	26.25	34.28	88.44	13.86	1,182	800-225-1852	Y
Prudential Jennison 20/20 Focus Fund Class Z	PTWZX	B	B	B	Up	5.29	12.56	26.90	36.32	93.23	16.18	1,182	800-225-1852	Y
Prudential Jennison 20-20 Focus Fund Class Q	PJTQX	B	B	B	Up	5.37	12.67	27.08	36.87	94.58	16.32	1,182	800-225-1852	Y
Prudential Jennison Blend Fund Class A	PBQAX	B-	B-	B-	Down	5.34	10.71	21.58	27.85	87.40	20.84	1,017	800-225-1852	Y
Prudential Jennison Blend Fund Class B	PBQFX	B-	B-	B-	Up	5.05	10.17	20.64	25.04	80.75	18.64	1,017	800-225-1852	
Prudential Jennison Blend Fund Class C	PRECX	B-	B-	B-	Up	5.10	10.28	20.69	25.15	80.90	18.66	1,017	800-225-1852	Y
Prudential Jennison Blend Fund Class Q	PBQQX	B-	B-	B-		5.30	10.43	20.92	25.33	81.17	20.86	1,017	800-225-1852	Y
Prudential Jennison Blend Fund Class Z	PEQZX	B-	B	B-	Down	5.38	10.85	21.90	28.94	90.17	20.86	1,017	800-225-1852	Y
Prudential Jennison Diversified Growth Fund Class A	TBDAX	B	B	B-		6.46	10.84	22.93	33.90	104.30	12.36	240.9	800-225-1852	Y
Prudential Jennison Diversified Growth Fund Class B	TBDBX	B	B	B-	Up	6.16	10.37	21.88	30.83	96.53	10.33	240.9	800-225-1852	
Prudential Jennison Diversified Growth Fund Class C	TBDCX	B	B	B-	Up	6.24	10.45	22.08	30.93	96.87	10.35	240.9	800-225-1852	Y
Prudential Jennison Diversified Growth Fund Class Q	TBDQX	B	B	B-		6.46	10.84	22.94	33.90	104.30	12.36	240.9	800-225-1852	Y
Prudential Jennison Diversified Growth Fund Class Z	TBDZX	B	B	B-		6.46	10.84	22.94	33.90	104.30	12.36	240.9	800-225-1852	Y
Prudential Jennison Focused Growth Fund Class A	SPFAX	A-	A	B+	Up	6.33	15.17	35.84	45.89	121.37	13.91	391.9	800-225-1852	Y
Prudential Jennison Focused Growth Fund Class B	SPFBX	A-	A-	B+	Up	6.13	14.72	34.78	42.62	113.22	11.42	391.9	800-225-1852	
Prudential Jennison Focused Growth Fund Class C	SPFCX	A-	A-	B+	Up	6.13	14.73	34.82	42.66	113.12	11.41	391.9	800-225-1852	Y
Prudential Jennison Focused Growth Fund Class Q	PSGQX	A-	A	B+	Up	6.37	15.25	36.19	47.00	123.95	14.82	391.9	800-225-1852	Y
Prudential Jennison Focused Growth Fund Class Z	SPFZX	A-	A	B+	Up	6.36	15.30	36.21	46.99	124.01	14.85	391.9	800-225-1852	Y
Prudential Jennison Growth Fund Class A	PJFAX	A-	A	B+	Up	7.13	16.26	36.36	47.58	127.94	36.21	4,586	800-225-1852	Y
Prudential Jennison Growth Fund Class B	PJFBX	A-	A	B+	Up	6.88	15.79	35.36	44.40	119.96	29.12	4,586	800-225-1852	
Prudential Jennison Growth Fund Class C	PJFCX	A-	A	B+	Up	6.93	15.83	35.41	44.49	120.19	29.2	4,586	800-225-1852	Y
Prudential Jennison Growth Fund Class Q	PJFQX	A-	A	B+		7.27	16.41	36.54	47.77	128.23	38.95	4,586	800-225-1852	Y
Prudential Jennison Growth Fund Class R	PJGRX	A-	A	B+	Up	7.07	16.15	36.12	46.67	125.68	31.84	4,586	800-225-1852	Y
Prudential Jennison Growth Fund Class R2	PJFOX	A-	A	B+		7.14	16.27	36.37	47.60	127.96	38.93	4,586	800-225-1852	Y
Prudential Jennison Growth Fund Class R4	PJFPX	A-	A	B+		7.14	16.27	36.38	47.60	127.96	38.94	4,586	800-225-1852	Y
Prudential Jennison Growth Fund Class Z	PJFZX	A-	A	B+	Up	7.21	16.46	36.78	48.92	131.46	38.94	4,586	800-225-1852	Y
Putnam Growth Opportunities Fund Class A	POGAX	B+	A-	B-	Up	6.59	13.17	30.96	39.62	122.83	31.3	4,621	617-292-1000	Y
Putnam Growth Opportunities Fund Class B	POGBX	B	A-	B-		6.37	12.72	29.94	36.48	114.59	26.69	4,621	617-292-1000	Y
Putnam Growth Opportunities Fund Class C	POGCX	B	A-	B-		6.38	12.70	30.00	36.49	114.64	27.17	4,621	617-292-1000	Y
Putnam Growth Opportunities Fund Class M	PGOMX	B	A-	B-	Down	6.42	12.83	30.26	37.46	117.28	28.32	4,621	617-292-1000	Y
Putnam Growth Opportunities Fund Class R	PGORX	B	A-	B-	Down	6.52	13.01	30.66	38.53	120.04	30.26	4,621	617-292-1000	Y
Putnam Growth Opportunities Fund Class R5	PGODX	B+	A-	B-	Up	6.65	13.30	31.33	40.83	126.55	32.81	4,621	617-292-1000	Y
Putnam Growth Opportunities Fund Class R6	PGOEX	B+	A-	B-	Up	6.69	13.34	31.45	41.28	127.80	32.76	4,621	617-292-1000	Y
Putnam Growth Opportunities Fund Class Y	PGOYX	B+	A-	B-	Up	6.63	13.27	31.27	40.63	125.63	32.61	4,621	617-292-1000	Y
Putnam Multi-Cap Growth Fund Class A	PNOPX	B	B+	B-	Down	6.03	12.13	29.05	37.31	117.92	89.45	4,380	617-292-1000	Y
Putnam Multi-Cap Growth Fund Class B	PNOBX	B	B+	B-		5.84	11.69	28.07	34.24	109.91	70.49	4,380	617-292-1000	Y
Putnam Multi-Cap Growth Fund Class C	PNOCX	B	B+	B-		5.83	11.71	28.09	34.25	109.89	76.52	4,380	617-292-1000	Y
Putnam Multi-Cap Growth Fund Class M	PNOMX	B	B+	B-		5.89	11.83	28.40	35.27	112.52	77.85	4,380	617-292-1000	Y
Putnam Multi-Cap Growth Fund Class R	PNORX	B	B+	B-	Down	5.97	11.98	28.73	36.30	115.23	86.72	4,380	617-292-1000	Y
Putnam Multi-Cap Growth Fund Class Y	PNOYX	B	B+	B-	Down	6.11	12.27	29.38	38.35	120.70	95.53	4,380	617-292-1000	Y
Reynolds Blue Chip Growth Fund	RBCGX	B-	C+	B	Up	6.30	11.44	24.71	20.04	72.58	56.38	72.0	212-742-1616	Y
RiverPark Large Growth Fund Class Institutional	RPXIX	B	B	C+	Up	6.58	12.60	30.19	33.38	96.12	22.11	49.8	888-564-4517	Y
RiverPark Large Growth Fund Class Retail	RPXFX	B	B	C+	Up	6.48	12.41	29.82	32.41	93.63	21.83	49.8	888-564-4517	Y

Category: US Equity Large Cap Growth (con't)

		RATINGS				TOTAL RETURNS & PERFORMANCE					ASSETS		NEW INVESTORS	
Fund Name	Ticker Symbol	Overall Rating	Reward Rating	Risk Rating	Recent Up/ Downgrade	3-Month Total Return	6-Month Total Return	1-Year Total Return	3-Year Total Return	5-Year Total Return	NAV	Total Assets (MIL)	Telephone	Open to New Investors
RiverPark/Wedgewood Fund Class Institutional	RWGIX	B-	C+	B		8.70	13.74	19.90	15.67	69.07	17.64	573.0	888-564-4517	Y
RiverPark/Wedgewood Fund Class Retail	RWGFX	B-	C+	B		8.65	13.66	19.64	15.34	67.81	17.5	573.0	888-564-4517	Y
RMB Fund Class A	RMBHX	B-	C+	B	Down	3.99	9.55	22.48	24.82	72.48	23.56	87.1		Y
RMB Fund Class C	RMBJX	B-	C+	B-	Down	3.76	9.10	21.57	22.00	66.12	19.87	87.1		Y
RMB Fund Class I	RMBGX	B-	B-	B	Down	4.05	9.71	22.79	25.14	72.92	23.56	87.1		Y
Russell Investments Tax-Managed U.S. Large Cap Fund Cls A	RTLAX	B-	B-	B	Down	6.65	10.63	21.23	31.65	97.56	40.56	2,510	800-426-7969	Y
Russell Investments Tax-Managed U.S. Large Cap Fund Cls C	RTLCX	B-	B-	B-	Down	6.43	10.23	20.31	28.68	90.19	38.57	2,510	800-426-7969	Y
Russell Investments Tax-Managed U.S. Large Cap Fund Cls E	RTLEX	B-	B-	B	Down	6.65	10.64	21.22	31.65	97.51	40.96	2,510	800-426-7969	Y
Russell Investments Tax-Managed U.S. Large Cap Fund Cls M	RTMTX	B-	B-	B	Down	6.73	10.85	21.59	32.72	100.09	40.91	2,510	800-426-7969	Y
Russell Investments Tax-Managed U.S. Large Cap Fund Cls S	RETSX	B-	B-	B	Down	6.70	10.76	21.50	32.62	99.94	40.93	2,510	800-426-7969	Y
Rydex NASDAQ-100® Fund Class A	RYATX	B+	A-	B	Down	6.87	12.98	30.91	48.04	142.12	31.37	1,111	800-820-0888	Y
Rydex NASDAQ-100® Fund Class C	RYCOX	B+	A-	B	Down	6.61	12.53	29.90	44.84	133.39	27.58	1,111	800-820-0888	Y
Rydex NASDAQ-100® Fund Class H	RYHOX	B+	A-	B	Down	6.84	12.98	30.92	48.06	141.92	31.36	1,111	800-820-0888	Y
Rydex NASDAQ-100® Fund Investor Class	RYOCX	B+	A-	B	Down	6.91	13.12	31.20	49.30	145.30	33.99	1,111	800-820-0888	Y
Rydex S&P 500 Pure Growth Fund Class A	RYLGX	B	B	B+	Up	4.55	10.93	24.69	28.02	109.19	63.68	148.8	800-820-0888	Y
Rydex S&P 500 Pure Growth Fund Class C	RYGRX	B	B-	B	Up	4.35	10.51	23.77	25.17	101.46	56.7	148.8	800-820-0888	Y
Rydex S&P 500 Pure Growth Fund Class H	RYAWX	B	B	B+	Up	4.55	10.93	24.69	28.03	109.22	63.67	148.8	800-820-0888	Y
Saratoga Large Capitalization Growth Portfolio Fund Cls A	SLGYX	A-	A-	A	Up	8.20	16.84	29.84	40.43	117.20	24.93	39.5	800-807-3863	Y
Saratoga Large Capitalization Growth Portfolio Fund Cls C	SLGCX	A-	B+	A	Up	8.11	16.55	29.07	37.98	110.91	19.35	39.5	800-807-3863	Y
Saratoga Large Capitalization Growth Port Fund Cls Inst	SLCGX	A	A-	A	Up	8.34	17.07	30.35	42.19	121.67	26.61	39.5	800-807-3863	Y
Schwab Large-Cap Growth Fund™	SWLSX	B	B	B	Down	7.15	12.91	28.94	38.74	113.95	17.91	262.0	877-824-5615	Y
Segall Bryant & Hamill All Cap Fund	SBHAX	B	B-	B	Up	6.46	8.30	18.68	31.53		14.4	72.5	312-474-1222	Y
SEI Inst Managed Trust Large Cap Growth Fund Cls F	SELCX	B	B	A-	Up	7.00	12.91	28.39	31.70	98.19	34.22	1,553	800-342-5734	Y
SEI Inst Managed Trust Large Cap Growth Fund Cls I	SPGIX	B	B	B+	Up	6.92	12.79	28.08	30.83	95.98	33.48	1,553	800-342-5734	Y
SEI Inst Managed Trust Large Cap Growth Fund Cls Y	SLRYX	B+	B	A-	Up	7.03	13.00	28.65	32.39	99.24	34.23	1,553	800-342-5734	Y
Shelton Capital Management Nasdaq-100 Index Fund Class K	NDXKX	B+	B+	B	Down	6.36	12.72	30.57	48.59	147.36	15.59	497.1	800-955-9988	Y
Shelton Capital Mgmt Nasdaq-100 Index Fund Direct Shares	NASDX	B+	A-	B	Down	6.57	13.05	31.25	50.98	154.01	16.04	497.1	800-955-9988	Y
Sit Large Cap Growth Fund	SNIGX	B	B	B+	Down	6.74	11.85	27.83	38.12	103.14	40.56	121.4	800-332-5580	Y
STAAR Larger Company Stock Fund	SITLX	B-	C+	B	Down	5.75	8.73	22.80	17.05	60.57		2.8		Y
State Street Inst Premier Growth Eq Fund Inv Cls	SSPGX	B	B	B+		4.31	10.29	28.77	35.99	116.43	15.25	382.2	617-664-7338	Y
State Street Inst Premier Growth Equity Fund Service Cls	SSPSX	B	B	B+		4.27	10.18	28.51	34.97	113.84	15.06	382.2	617-664-7338	Y
Sterling Capital Special Opportunities Fund Class A	BOPAX	B	B-	B+	Up	5.16	7.31	19.33	33.81	101.39	23.81	1,174	800-228-1872	Y
Sterling Capital Special Opportunities Fund Class C	BOPCX	B	B-	B+	Up	4.96	6.90	18.39	30.80	93.92	19.95	1,174	800-228-1872	Y
Sterling Capital Special Opportunities Fund Class R	BOPRX	B	B-	B+	Up	5.06	7.18	19.04	32.85	98.90	24.08	1,174	800-228-1872	Y
Sterling Capital Special Opp Fund Inst Shares	BOPIX	B	B-	B+	Up	5.24	7.46	19.66	34.85	103.99	25	1,174	800-228-1872	Y
Strategic Advisers® Growth Fund	FSGFX	B+	B+	B	Up	6.89	13.08	29.44	41.27	119.11	18.68	11,813	617-563-7000	Y
Strategic Advisers® Growth Multi-Manager Fund	FMELX	B+	B+	B	Up	7.20	13.87	30.18	40.77	117.81	14.86	72.0	617-563-7000	Y
Strategic Advisers® Growth Multi-Manager Fund Class L	FQACX	B+	B+	B	Up	7.28	13.89	30.21	40.84	117.83	14.85	72.0	617-563-7000	Y
Strategic Advisers® Growth Multi-Manager Fund Class N	FQAEX	B+	B+	B	Up	7.13	13.71	29.82	39.74	115.07	14.84	72.0	617-563-7000	Y
T. Rowe Price Blue Chip Growth Fund	TRBCX	A-	A	B	Up	7.00	14.41	36.54	52.24	141.88	96.31	45,560	410-345-2000	Y
T. Rowe Price Blue Chip Growth Fund Advisor Class	PABGX	A-	A	B	Up	6.93	14.25	36.16	51.01	138.70	95.02	45,560	410-345-2000	Y
T. Rowe Price Blue Chip Growth Fund Class R	RRBGX	A-	A	B	Up	6.86	14.11	35.81	49.83	135.58	91.63	45,560	410-345-2000	Y
T. Rowe Price Blue Chip Growth Fund I Class	TBCIX	A-	A	B	Up	7.03	14.48	36.71	52.65	142.52	96.33	45,560	410-345-2000	Y
T. Rowe Price Growth Stock Fund	PRGFX	B+	B+	B	Down	6.04	11.81	33.63	49.33	132.13	62.65	53,389	410-345-2000	Y
T. Rowe Price Growth Stock Fund Advisor Class	TRSAX	B+	B+	B	Down	5.98	11.68	33.31	48.24	129.27	61.26	53,389	410-345-2000	Y
T. Rowe Price Growth Stock Fund I Class	PRUFX	B+	B+	B	Down	6.10	11.91	33.84	49.92	133.03	62.7	53,389	410-345-2000	Y
T. Rowe Price Growth Stock Fund R Class	RRGSX	B+	B+	B	Down	5.91	11.53	32.97	47.12	126.40	59.26	53,389	410-345-2000	Y
T. Rowe Price Institutional Large Cap Core Growth Fund	TPLGX	A-	A	B	Up	7.01	14.43	36.49	52.64	142.34	37.43	3,054	410-345-2000	Y
T. Rowe Price Institutional Large Cap Growth Fund	TRLGX	A-	A	B	Up	7.29	15.20	37.82	55.13	150.21	36.91	15,923	410-345-2000	Y
T. Rowe Price New America Growth Fund	PRWAX	B+	B+	B+	Down	7.10	12.06	34.56	47.37	127.64	48.03	4,429	410-345-2000	Y
T. Rowe Price New America Growth Fund Advisor Class	PAWAX	B+	B+	B	Down	7.05	11.93	34.21	46.20	124.66	47.03	4,429	410-345-2000	Y
T. Rowe Price New America Growth Fund I Class	PNAIX	B+	B+	B	Down	7.16	12.14	34.76	47.75	128.23	48.02	4,429	410-345-2000	Y

Category: US Equity Large Cap Growth (con't)

		RATINGS				TOTAL RETURNS & PERFORMANCE					ASSETS		NEW INVESTORS	
Fund Name	Ticker Symbol	Overall Rating	Reward Rating	Risk Rating	Recent Up/ Downgrade	3-Month Total Return	6-Month Total Return	1-Year Total Return	3-Year Total Return	5-Year Total Return	NAV	Total Assets (MIL)	Telephone	Open to New Investors
T. Rowe Price Spectrum Growth Fund	PRSGX	B-	B	B-	Down	4.99	10.59	25.52	35.44	88.18	24.36	3,864	410-345-2000	Y
T. Rowe Price Tax-Efficient Equity Fund	PREFX	B+	B	B+	Up	6.33	11.76	29.12	39.64	112.65	28.87	286.1	410-345-2000	Y
T. Rowe Price Tax-Efficient Equity Fund I Class	TEEFX	B	B	B	Down	6.37	11.84	29.21	39.74	112.80	28.88	286.1	410-345-2000	Y
TCW Select Equities Fund Class I	TGCEX	B	B	B+		5.43	11.68	32.80	35.87	93.91	24.93	922.7	213-244-0000	Y
TCW Select Equities Fund Class N	TGCNX	B	B	B+		5.39	11.55	32.51	34.89	91.45	22.66	922.7	213-244-0000	Y
The BeeHive Fund	BEEHX	B-	C+	B	Down	-0.38	1.46	11.06	15.03	72.16	15.23	132.2		Y
The Gabelli Multimedia Trust Inc.	GGT	B	B-	B	Up	3.73	7.13	26.50	27.48	90.59	9.34	229.0	914-921-5135	Y
The Hartford Growth Opportunities Fund Class A	HGOAX	A-	A-	B+	Up	5.13	10.98	30.20	41.68	120.99	42.76	4,761	888-843-7824	Y
The Hartford Growth Opportunities Fund Class C	HGOCX	B+	A-	B+	Up	4.93	10.54	29.25	38.56	113.09	27.53	4,761	888-843-7824	Y
The Hartford Growth Opportunities Fund Class F	HGOFX	A-	A-	B+	Up	5.24	11.17	30.67	43.21	125.36	44.66	4,761	888-843-7824	Y
The Hartford Growth Opportunities Fund Class I	HGOIX	A-	A-	B+	Up	5.20	11.10	30.52	42.58	123.62	44.61	4,761	888-843-7824	Y
The Hartford Growth Opportunities Fund Class R3	HGORX	B+	A-	B+	Up	5.06	10.77	29.77	40.26	117.62	42.97	4,761	888-843-7824	Y
The Hartford Growth Opportunities Fund Class R4	HGOSX	A-	A-	B+	Up	5.12	10.96	30.16	41.53	120.94	45.1	4,761	888-843-7824	Y
The Hartford Growth Opportunities Fund Class R5	HGOTX	A-	A-	B+	Up	5.21	11.12	30.57	42.82	124.26	46.94	4,761	888-843-7824	Y
The Hartford Growth Opportunities Fund Class R6	HGOVX	A-	A-	B+	Up	5.23	11.17	30.67	43.14	125.23	47.54	4,761	888-843-7824	Y
The Hartford Growth Opportunities Fund Class Y	HGOYX	A-	A-	B+	Up	5.23	11.14	30.65	43.19	125.33	47.56	4,761	888-843-7824	Y
The Investment House Growth Fund	TIHGX	B+	A-	B	Up	6.49	12.09	34.05	44.64	119.22	32.63	100.6		Y
Thornburg Core Growth Fund Class A	THCGX	B-	B-	B	Up	4.74	8.10	23.90	23.77	81.04	34	642.8	800-847-0200	Y
Thornburg Core Growth Fund Class C	TCGCX	B-	C+	B	Up	4.53	7.68	22.96	20.96	74.31	29.72	642.8	800-847-0200	Y
Thornburg Core Growth Fund Class I	THIGX	B	B-	B	Up	4.84	8.31	24.40	25.25	84.79	36.35	642.8	800-847-0200	Y
Thornburg Core Growth Fund Class R3	THCRX	B-	B-	B	Up	4.70	8.05	23.79	23.38	80.08	33.82	642.8	800-847-0200	Y
Thornburg Core Growth Fund Class R4	TCGRX	B-	B-	B	Up	4.72	8.10	23.88	23.74	81.06	34.13	642.8	800-847-0200	Y
Thornburg Core Growth Fund Class R5	THGRX	B	B-	B	Up	4.85	8.35	24.42	25.28	84.83	36.32	642.8	800-847-0200	Y
Thrivent Large Cap Growth Fund Class A	AAAGX	B+	B	A-	Up	6.37	11.21	27.70	35.74	106.93	10.24	884.3		Y
Thrivent Large Cap Growth Fund Class S	THLCX	B+	B	A-	Up	6.45	11.38	28.21	37.30	111.12	11.27	884.3		Y
Thrivent Series Large Cap Growth Portfolio		B+	B+	A-	Up	6.34	11.41	28.51	38.77	115.48	35.5091	1,195		Y
Thrivent Series Partner All Cap Portfolio		B	B-	B+	Up	5.53	8.90	20.24	28.99	97.34	15.5452	111.2		Y
Thrivent Series Partner Growth Stock Portfolio		B+	B+	B	Down	6.08	11.84	33.61	48.97	130.26	23.7895	181.6		Y
TIAA-CREF Enhanced Large-Cap Growth Index Fund Advisor Cls	TECGX	B+	A-	B+		8.06	14.86	29.48	48.12	122.06	13.54	2,652	877-518-9161	Y
TIAA-CREF Enhanced Large-Cap Growth Index Fund Inst Cls	TLIIX	B+	A-	B+		8.12	14.91	29.65	48.32	122.37	13.55	2,652	877-518-9161	Y
TIAA-CREF Growth & Income Fund Advisor Class	TGIHX	B	B	B		6.83	12.07	23.91	37.98	111.34	14.3	6,850	877-518-9161	Y
TIAA-CREF Growth & Income Fund Institutional Class	TIGRX	B	B	B		6.80	12.18	23.96	38.16	111.61	14.29	6,850	877-518-9161	Y
TIAA-CREF Growth & Income Fund Premier Class	TRPGX	B	B	B		6.83	12.16	23.94	37.59	110.26	14.31	6,850	877-518-9161	Y
TIAA-CREF Growth & Income Fund Retail Class	TIIRX	B	B	B		6.82	12.09	23.65	36.92	108.54	19.07	6,850	877-518-9161	Y
TIAA-CREF Growth & Income Fund Retirement Class	TRGIX	B	B	B		6.84	12.07	23.77	37.13	109.17	14.54	6,850	877-518-9161	Y
TIAA-CREF Large Cap Growth Fund Advisor Class	TILHX	A-	A	A-	Up	7.08	14.75	34.27	44.47	130.59	19.84	4,903	877-518-9161	Y
TIAA-CREF Large-Cap Growth Fund Institutional Class	TILGX	A-	A	A-	Up	7.09	14.81	34.51	44.58	130.76	19.84	4,903	877-518-9161	Y
TIAA-CREF Large-Cap Growth Fund Premier Class	TILPX	A-	A	A-	Up	7.05	14.72	34.27	43.86	129.04	19.82	4,903	877-518-9161	Y
TIAA-CREF Large-Cap Growth Fund Retail Class	TIRTX	A-	A	A-	Up	6.96	14.64	34.03	43.16	126.78	19.8	4,903	877-518-9161	Y
TIAA-CREF Large-Cap Growth Fund Retirement Class	TILRX	A-	A	A-	Up	7.01	14.72	34.11	43.31	127.58	19.74	4,903	877-518-9161	Y
TIAA-CREF Large-Cap Growth Index Fund Advisor Class	TRIHX	B+	B+	B+	Up	7.79	14.12	29.93	45.52	125.11	28.83	5,628	877-518-9161	Y
TIAA-CREF Large-Cap Growth Index Fund Institutional Class	TILIX	B+	B+	B+	Up	7.82	14.15	30.07	45.72	125.41	28.83	5,628	877-518-9161	Y
TIAA-CREF Large-Cap Growth Index Fund Retirement Class	TRIRX	B+	B+	B+	Up	7.76	14.05	29.78	44.59	122.61	29.05	5,628	877-518-9161	Y
Timothy Plan Large/Mid Cap Growth Fund Class A	TLGAX	B	B-	B	Up	3.97	9.85	16.89	22.41	81.11	8.71	87.5	800-662-0201	Y
Timothy Plan Large/Mid Cap Growth Fund Class C	TLGCX	B-	C+	B	Down	3.81	9.51	16.05	19.66	74.40	7.16	87.5	800-662-0201	Y
Timothy Plan Large/Mid Cap Growth Fund Class I	TPLIX	B	B-	B	Up	4.03	9.97	17.24	23.34	83.49	8.83	87.5	800-662-0201	Y
Touchstone Growth Opportunities Fund Class A	TGVFX	B-	B	C+	Up	5.00	10.62	28.06	25.10	98.30	31.96	282.8	800-543-0407	Y
Touchstone Growth Opportunities Fund Class C	TGVCX	B-	B-	B	Up	4.79	10.20	27.06	22.28	90.95	26.44	282.8	800-543-0407	Y
Touchstone Growth Opportunities Fund Class Y	TGVYX	B-	B	C+	Up	5.06	10.75	28.35	26.04	100.98	32.81	282.8	800-543-0407	Y
Touchstone Growth Opportunities Fund Institutional Class	TGVVX	B-	B	C+	Up	5.07	10.83	28.48	26.42	101.89	33.18	282.8	800-543-0407	Y
Touchstone Large Company Growth Fund Class A	TSAGX	A-	A-	B+	Up	5.56	13.17	38.04	42.70	117.77	39.06	223.2	800-543-0407	Y
Touchstone Large Company Growth Fund Class C	TCGLX	B+	B+	B+	Up	5.40	12.77	37.06	39.56	109.82	38.65	223.2	800-543-0407	Y

Category: US Equity
Large Cap Growth (con't)

Fund Name	Ticker Symbol	RATINGS: Overall Rating	Reward Rating	Risk Rating	Recent Up/ Downgrade	TOTAL RETURNS & PERFORMANCE: 3-Month Total Return	6-Month Total Return	1-Year Total Return	3-Year Total Return	5-Year Total Return	ASSETS: NAV	Total Assets (MIL)	NEW INVESTORS: Telephone	Open to New Investors
Touchstone Large Company Growth Fund Class Institutional	DSMLX	A-	A-	B+	Up	5.67	13.38	38.59	44.01	120.86	39.26	223.2	800-543-0407	Y
Touchstone Large Company Growth Fund Class Y	TLGYX	A-	A-	B+	Up	5.65	13.31	38.43	43.80	120.53	39.2	223.2	800-543-0407	Y
Touchstone Sands Capital Institutional Growth Fund	CISGX	B	B	B	Up	3.77	10.52	34.74	22.48	93.18	20.58	1,940	800-543-0407	
Touchstone Sands Capital Select Growth Fund Class A	TSNAX	B	B	B	Up	3.62	10.21	34.15	21.03	89.02	13.81	2,528	800-543-0407	
Touchstone Sands Capital Select Growth Fund Class C	TSNCX	B-	B-	B	Up	3.48	9.86	33.20	18.43	82.21	12.69	2,528	800-543-0407	
Touchstone Sands Capital Select Growth Fund Class Y	CFSIX	B	B	B	Up	3.71	10.35	34.44	21.96	91.45	14.56	2,528	800-543-0407	
Touchstone Sands Capital Select Growth Fund Class Z	PTSGX	B	B	B	Up	3.70	10.28	34.22	21.17	89.25	13.83	2,528	800-543-0407	
Transamerica Capital Growth Fund Class A	IALAX	B+	A-	B	Up	7.36	12.34	43.89	54.32	148.46	23.44	853.5	888-233-4339	Y
Transamerica Capital Growth Fund Class Advisor	TACGX	B+	A-	B	Up	7.43	12.44	44.17	54.63	148.96	24.52	853.5	888-233-4339	Y
Transamerica Capital Growth Fund Class B	IACBX	B+	B+	B	Up	7.13	11.79	42.54	49.89	137.17	18.48	853.5	888-233-4339	
Transamerica Capital Growth Fund Class C	ILLLX	B+	B+	B	Up	7.21	11.96	42.90	51.01	140.02	18.84	853.5	888-233-4339	Y
Transamerica Capital Growth Fund Class I	TFOIX	B+	A-	B+	Up	7.46	12.51	44.32	55.64	152.52	24.55	853.5	888-233-4339	Y
Transamerica Capital Growth Fund Class I2	US8935091335	B+	A-	B+	Up	7.46	12.54	44.42	56.10	153.88	12.18	853.5	888-233-4339	Y
Transamerica Capital Growth Fund Class T1	TFOTX	B+	A-	B	Up	7.44	12.46	44.05	54.49	148.74	23.47	853.5	888-233-4339	Y
Transamerica Concentrated Growth Fund Class A	TORAX	B	B	B		4.59	9.65	24.01	27.86	85.53	17.34	228.5	888-233-4339	Y
Transamerica Concentrated Growth Fund Class Advisor	TACNX	B	B	B		4.66	9.80	24.30	28.77	87.67	17.31	228.5	888-233-4339	Y
Transamerica Concentrated Growth Fund Class C	TCCGX	B	B-	B		4.40	9.31	23.14	25.17	78.98	16.88	228.5	888-233-4339	Y
Transamerica Concentrated Growth Fund Class I	TOREX	B	B	B+		4.73	9.91	24.46	28.94	87.92	17.18	228.5	888-233-4339	Y
Transamerica Concentrated Growth Fund Class I2	US89354D8175	B	B	B		4.70	9.87	24.47	29.26	88.82	17.39	228.5	888-233-4339	Y
Transamerica Concentrated Growth Fund Class T1	TORQX	B	B	B		4.65	9.77	24.26	28.08	85.74	17.36	228.5	888-233-4339	Y
Transamerica Growth Fund Class I2	TJNIX	A-	A	B+	Up	7.03	16.13	36.28	48.96	131.53	10.36	356.0	888-233-4339	Y
Transamerica Growth Fund Class R6	TAGOX	A-	A	B+	Up	7.04	16.13	36.41	48.97	131.54	10.36	356.0	888-233-4339	Y
Transamerica Large Growth Fund Class I3	TGWTX	B+	A-	B	Down	7.45	14.37	32.76	44.37	120.99	11.6	851.6	888-233-4339	Y
Transamerica Large Growth Fund Class R	TGWRX	B+	A-	B	Up	7.40	14.09	32.17	43.02	117.83	11.6	851.6	888-233-4339	Y
Transamerica Large Growth Fund Class R4	TGWFX	A-	A-	A-	Up	7.38	14.22	32.48	44.07	120.53	11.6	851.6	888-233-4339	Y
Transamerica US Growth Class A	TADAX	B+	B	A-	Up	7.94	12.33	28.72	38.92	107.81	19.42	1,099	888-233-4339	Y
Transamerica US Growth Class Advisor	TAUGX	B+	B	A-	Up	7.97	12.45	29.03	40.39	112.32	19.81	1,099	888-233-4339	Y
Transamerica US Growth Class B	TADBX	B+	B	A-	Up	7.61	11.74	27.48	34.96	98.28	18.27	1,099	888-233-4339	
Transamerica US Growth Class C	TADCX	B+	B	A-	Up	7.69	11.88	27.74	35.65	99.66	18.35	1,099	888-233-4339	Y
Transamerica US Growth Class I	TDEIX	B+	B	A-	Up	8.00	12.49	29.14	40.27	111.42	19.74	1,099	888-233-4339	Y
Transamerica US Growth Class I2	US8939623737	B+	B	A-	Up	8.04	12.55	29.32	40.71	112.80	19.68	1,099	888-233-4339	Y
Transamerica US Growth Class T	TWMTX	B+	B	A-	Up	8.01	12.53	29.20	40.42	111.83	52.01	1,099	888-233-4339	Y
Transamerica US Growth Class T1	TJNTX	B+	B	A-	Up	7.97	12.42	29.03	39.69	110.21	19.42	1,099	888-233-4339	Y
USAA Aggressive Growth Fund	USAUX	B+	B	A-	Up	6.14	12.30	30.05	37.55	110.37	43.76	1,446	800-531-8722	Y
USAA Aggressive Growth Fund Institutional Shares	UIAGX	B+	B	A-	Up	6.12	12.33	29.98	37.89	111.92	44.32	1,446	800-531-8722	Y
USAA Growth Fund	USAAX	B+	B+	A	Up	6.44	12.12	28.42	43.16	128.25	30.53	2,917	800-531-8722	Y
USAA Growth Fund Institutional Shares	UIGRX	B+	B+	A	Up	6.43	12.16	28.50	43.52	128.80	30.45	2,917	800-531-8722	Y
USAA Nasdaq 100 Index Fund R6 Shares	URNQX	B+	A-	B	Down	7.15	13.62	32.41	52.47	154.21	17.89	1,609	800-531-8722	Y
USAA NASDAQ-100 Index Fund	USNQX	B+	A-	B		7.11	13.58	32.28	52.33	153.97	17.89	1,609	800-531-8722	Y
VALIC Company I Blue Chip Growth Fund	VCBCX	A-	A	B	Up	7.00	14.33	36.20	51.54	139.84	19.86	731.6		Y
VALIC Company I Growth Fund	VCULX	B+	B+	B	Up	6.69	12.96	30.23	39.42	107.91	16.9	1,168		Y
VALIC Company I Large Capital Growth Fund	VLCGX	B	B	A-		7.56	11.58	28.54	35.17	104.09	15.22	439.0		Y
VALIC Company I Nasdaq-100 Index Fund	VCNIX	B+	A-	B	Down	7.10	13.53	32.28	52.52	154.69	13.42	432.0		Y
VALIC Company II Capital Appreciation Fund	VCCAX	B	B	B		6.73	10.80	23.73	32.22	101.07	17.74	96.5		Y
Value Line Larger Companies Focused Fund Institutional Cls	VLLIX	B	B	B+	Up	1.74	10.05	33.96	46.24	118.68	28.65	275.4	800-243-2729	Y
Value Line Larger Companies Focused Fund Investor Class	VALLX	B	B	B+	Up	1.74	9.98	33.79	46.21	118.63	28.65	275.4	800-243-2729	Y
Vanguard Capital Opportunity Fund Admiral Shares	VHCAX	B	A-	B-	Down	6.10	11.80	29.19	45.90	153.26	153.61	16,526	877-662-7447	
Vanguard Capital Opportunity Fund Investor Shares	VHCOX	B	A-	B-	Down	6.08	11.76	29.09	45.58	152.37	66.5	16,526	877-662-7447	
Vanguard Diversified Equity Fund Investor Shares	VDEQX	B	B	B-	Up	6.02	11.03	22.69	32.90	105.13	34.94	1,472	877-662-7447	Y
Vanguard Growth Index Fund Admiral Shares	VIGAX	B+	B	A-	Up	6.22	11.37	27.80	38.81	114.70	72.35	72,657	877-662-7447	Y
Vanguard Growth Index Fund Institutional Shares	VIGIX	B	B	B	Down	6.22	11.38	27.81	38.84	114.79	72.35	72,657	877-662-7447	Y
Vanguard Growth Index Fund Investor Shares	VIGRX	B+	B	A-	Up	6.19	11.31	27.64	38.27	113.22	72.36	72,657	877-662-7447	Y

Category: US Equity Large Cap Growth (con't)

Fund Name	Ticker Symbol	RATINGS: Overall Rating	RATINGS: Reward Rating	RATINGS: Risk Rating	RATINGS: Recent Up/ Downgrade	TOTAL RETURNS & PERFORMANCE: 3-Month Total Return	6-Month Total Return	1-Year Total Return	3-Year Total Return	5-Year Total Return	ASSETS: NAV	Total Assets (MIL)	NEW INVESTORS: Telephone	Open to New Investors
Vanguard Mega Cap Growth Index Fund Institutional Shares	VMGAX	B	B	B	Down	6.58	11.99	29.48	41.54	119.26	220.86	3,438	877-662-7447	Y
Vanguard Morgan™ Growth Fund Admiral™ Shares	VMRAX	B+	B+	B	Up	6.11	13.05	30.00	42.33	119.08	90.71	13,694	877-662-7447	Y
Vanguard Morgan™ Growth Fund Investor Shares	VMRGX	B+	B+	B	Up	6.08	13.01	29.85	41.87	117.77	29.26	13,694	877-662-7447	Y
Vanguard PRIMECAP Core Fund Investor Shares	VPCCX	B	B+	B-	Down	6.33	11.62	26.22	42.16	135.93	26.9	10,705	877-662-7447	
Vanguard PRIMECAP Fund Admiral Shares	VPMAX	B+	A-	B-	Up	7.30	13.13	29.60	46.20	148.19	133.61	61,536	877-662-7447	
Vanguard PRIMECAP Fund Investor Shares	VPMCX	B+	A-	B-	Up	7.28	13.09	29.50	45.90	147.25	128.89	61,536	877-662-7447	
Vanguard Russell 1000 Growth Index Fund Inst Shares	VRGWX	B+	B+	B+	Up	7.84	14.19	30.11	45.68	125.44	265.2	4,157	877-662-7447	Y
Vanguard U.S. Growth Fund Admiral™ Shares	VWUAX	A-	A-	A-	Up	6.09	13.60	31.75	41.19	122.78	94.6	8,396	877-662-7447	Y
Vanguard U.S. Growth Portfolio Fund Investor Shares	VWUSX	A-	A-	A-	Up	6.07	13.52	31.60	40.64	121.29	36.52	8,396	877-662-7447	Y
Victory Munder Multi-Cap Fund Class A	MNNAX	B+	B+	B	Up	9.66	17.35	28.38	38.14	114.56	46.57	465.8	800-539-3863	Y
Victory Munder Multi-Cap Fund Class C	MNNCX	B	B	B	Up	9.43	16.88	27.34	34.77	106.19	38.25	465.8	800-539-3863	Y
Victory Munder Multi-Cap Fund Class R	MNNRX	B	B	B	Up	9.50	17.02	27.65	36.20	110.41	44.22	465.8	800-539-3863	Y
Victory Munder Multi-Cap Fund Class Y	MNNYX	B+	A-	B	Up	9.79	17.59	28.82	39.79	118.25	50.02	465.8	800-539-3863	Y
Victory NewBridge Large Cap Growth Fund Class A	VFGAX	B	B	B+		4.41	7.87	24.86	27.19	84.95	7.37	31.2	800-539-3863	Y
Victory NewBridge Large Cap Growth Fund Class C	VFGCX	B	B-	B+		4.19	7.54	23.82	24.15	77.61	4.67	31.2	800-539-3863	Y
Victory NewBridge Large Cap Growth Fund Class I	VFGIX	B	B	B+		4.52	8.15	25.35	28.75	88.37	7.86	31.2	800-539-3863	Y
Victory NewBridge Large Cap Growth Fund Class R	VFGRX	B	B	B+		4.31	7.83	24.52	25.95	81.82	6.23	31.2	800-539-3863	Y
Victory NewBridge Large Cap Growth Fund Class Y	VFGYX	B	B	B+		4.51	8.12	25.29	28.37	87.48	7.63	31.2	800-539-3863	Y
Victory RS Growth Fund Class A	RSGRX	A-	B+	A-	Up	6.17	13.51	31.74	38.32	124.46	20.6	256.5	800-539-3863	Y
Victory RS Growth Fund Class C	RGWCX	B+	B+	B+	Up	5.91	13.05	30.57	34.87	115.04	17.9	256.5	800-539-3863	Y
Victory RS Growth Fund Class R	RSGKX	B+	B+	A-	Up	6.00	13.22	30.91	35.86	117.78	19.22	256.5	800-539-3863	Y
Victory RS Growth Fund Class Y	RGRYX	A-	A-	A-	Up	6.24	13.72	32.04	39.41	127.38	21.23	256.5	800-539-3863	Y
Virtus KAR Capital Growth Fund Class A	PSTAX	A-	A-	B+	Up	5.50	12.45	35.14	44.20	112.88	16.21	493.0	800-243-1574	Y
Virtus KAR Capital Growth Fund Class C	SSTFX	B+	A-	B+	Up	5.26	12.03	34.14	40.90	105.01	12.73	493.0	800-243-1574	Y
Virtus KAR Capital Growth Fund Class I	PLXGX	A-	A-	A-	Up	5.57	12.66	35.52	45.32	115.74	16.76	493.0	800-243-1574	Y
Virtus Silvant Large-Cap Growth Stock Fund Class A	STCIX	B	B	B+	Up	7.65	13.16	26.86	30.83	96.76	5.49	135.5	800-243-1574	Y
Virtus Silvant Large-Cap Growth Stock Fund Class C	STCFX	B	B	B+	Up	7.65	12.92	26.34	28.48	90.65	2.42	135.5	800-243-1574	Y
Virtus Silvant Large-Cap Growth Stock Fund Class I	STCAX	B	B	B+	Up	7.84	13.46	27.32	31.75	99.16	7.53	135.5	800-243-1574	Y
Virtus Silvant Large-Cap Growth Stock Fund Class R6	STCZX	B	B	B	Up	8.09	13.82	27.67	32.52	99.74	7.59	135.5	800-243-1574	Y
Virtus Zevenbergen Innovative Growth Stock Fund Class A	SAGAX	B	B	B	Up	3.84	7.47	33.97	39.40	132.91	19.96	23.5	800-243-1574	Y
Virtus Zevenbergen Innovative Growth Stock Fund Class I	SCATX	B	B	B	Up	3.88	7.58	34.29	40.27	135.01	21.1	23.5	800-243-1574	Y
Voya Large Cap Growth Portfolio Class A	IEOPX	B	B	B	Down	7.79	13.23	29.01	39.68	111.59	19.36	6,331	800-366-0066	Y
Voya Large Cap Growth Portfolio Class I	IEOHX	B	B	B	Down	7.93	13.56	29.74	42.21	117.60	20.8	6,331	800-366-0066	Y
Voya Large Cap Growth Portfolio Class R6	VRLCX	B	B	B	Down	7.99	13.55	29.79	41.91	116.02	20.81	6,331	800-366-0066	Y
Voya Large Cap Growth Portfolio Class S	IEOSX	B	B	B	Down	7.85	13.37	29.41	41.10	114.79	20.32	6,331	800-366-0066	Y
Voya Large Cap Growth Portfolio Class S2	IEOTX	B	B	B	Down	7.85	13.35	29.21	40.51	113.24	20.18	6,331	800-366-0066	Y
Voya Large-Cap Growth Fund Class A	NLCAX	B	B	B	Down	7.88	13.39	29.20	40.22	109.01	37.12	682.5	800-366-0066	Y
Voya Large-Cap Growth Fund Class C	NLCCX	B+	B	A-	Up	7.66	12.96	28.25	37.21	101.98	31.63	682.5	800-366-0066	Y
Voya Large-Cap Growth Fund Class I	PLCIX	B	B	B	Down	7.97	13.61	29.66	41.71	112.84	41.01	682.5	800-366-0066	Y
Voya Large-Cap Growth Fund Class R	VGORX	B	B	B	Down	7.80	13.23	28.83	39.35	106.87	40.61	682.5	800-366-0066	Y
Voya Large-Cap Growth Fund Class R6	VGOSX	B	B	B	Down	8.00	13.63	29.69	41.68	112.67	41.01	682.5	800-366-0066	Y
Voya Large-Cap Growth Fund Class W	IGOWX	B	B	B	Down	7.94	13.54	29.48	41.34	112.15	39.98	682.5	800-366-0066	Y
Voya Russell Large Cap Growth Index Portfolio Class A	IRLAX	B+	A-	B+	Down	7.94	14.28	30.60	47.02	123.31	35.05	709.4	800-366-0066	Y
Voya Russell Large Cap Growth Index Portfolio Class I	IRLNX	B+	A-	B+	Down	8.07	14.54	31.26	49.04	128.65	35.35	709.4	800-366-0066	Y
Voya Russell Large Cap Growth Index Portfolio Class S	IRLSX	B+	A-	B+	Down	8.02	14.42	30.92	47.92	125.82	35.15	709.4	800-366-0066	Y
VY® T. Rowe Price Growth Equity Portfolio Class A	IGEAX	B+	B+	B	Down	5.89	11.52	32.91	47.16	126.30	86.22	1,760	800-366-0066	Y
VY® T. Rowe Price Growth Equity Portfolio Class I	ITGIX	B+	B+	B	Down	6.03	11.80	33.58	49.37	132.03	93.19	1,760	800-366-0066	Y
VY® T. Rowe Price Growth Equity Portfolio Class S	ITGSX	B+	B+	B	Down	5.96	11.67	33.24	48.26	129.14	89.69	1,760	800-366-0066	Y
VY® T. Rowe Price Growth Equity Portfolio Class S2	ITRGX	B+	B+	B	Down	5.92	11.59	33.05	47.60	127.46	87.3	1,760	800-366-0066	Y
Waddell & Reed Advisor Accumulative Fund Class A	UNACX	B	C+	B+	Up	4.64	5.57	15.04	22.11	89.64	9.9	1,390	888-923-3355	Y
Waddell & Reed Advisor Accumulative Fund Class B	WAABX	B-	C+	B+	Up	4.39	5.00	13.85	17.95	78.63	8.25	1,390	888-923-3355	
Waddell & Reed Advisor Accumulative Fund Class C	WAACX	B-	C+	B+	Up	4.38	4.98	13.88	18.55	80.45	8.46	1,390	888-923-3355	Y

Category: US Equity Large Cap Growth (con't)

Fund Name	Ticker Symbol	RATINGS: Overall Rating	Reward Rating	Risk Rating	Recent Up/ Downgrade	TOTAL RETURNS & PERFORMANCE: 3-Month Total Return	6-Month Total Return	1-Year Total Return	3-Year Total Return	5-Year Total Return	ASSETS: NAV	Total Assets (MIL)	NEW INVESTORS: Telephone	Open to New Investors
Waddell & Reed Advisor Accumulative Fund Class Y	WAAYX	B	C+	A-	Up	4.72	5.64	15.29	22.90	91.78	9.96	1,390	888-923-3355	Y
Waddell & Reed Advisors Vanguard Fund Class A	UNVGX	A-	A-	A-	Up	6.11	14.24	29.15	38.55	114.36	11.05	1,720	888-923-3355	Y
Waddell & Reed Advisors Vanguard Fund Class B	WRVBX	B+	B+	A-	Up	5.85	13.48	27.62	33.67	101.93	7.47	1,720	888-923-3355	
Waddell & Reed Advisors Vanguard Fund Class C	WAVCX	B+	B+	B	Up	5.78	13.58	27.80	34.43	104.04	7.75	1,720	888-923-3355	Y
Waddell & Reed Advisors Vanguard Fund Class Y	WAVYX	A-	A-	A-	Up	6.17	14.34	29.32	39.47	117.30	11.89	1,720	888-923-3355	Y
Wells Fargo Capital Growth Fund - Class A	WFCGX	B+	B+	B	Up	7.05	12.64	34.41	36.89	108.62	16.59	192.3	800-222-8222	Y
Wells Fargo Capital Growth Fund - Class Admin	WFCDX	B+	B+	B+	Up	7.19	12.81	34.66	37.60	110.67	18.05	192.3	800-222-8222	Y
Wells Fargo Capital Growth Fund - Class C	WFCCX	B	B	B	Up	6.87	12.24	33.42	33.87	101.05	14.37	192.3	800-222-8222	Y
Wells Fargo Capital Growth Fund - Class Inst	WWCIX	B+	B+	B+	Up	7.23	12.92	34.96	38.54	113.34	18.69	192.3	800-222-8222	Y
Wells Fargo Capital Growth Fund - Class R6	WFCRX	B+	B+	B+	Up	7.26	12.98	35.10	38.90	114.00	18.78	192.3	800-222-8222	Y
Wells Fargo Diversified Equity Fund - Class A	NVDAX	B-	B-	B-	Down	5.75	10.77	22.59	28.07	85.89	25.84	180.5	800-222-8222	Y
Wells Fargo Diversified Equity Fund - Class Admin	NVDEX	B-	B-	B-	Down	5.83	10.92	22.94	29.07	88.27	25.93	180.5	800-222-8222	Y
Wells Fargo Diversified Equity Fund - Class C	WFDEX	B-	B-	B-	Down	5.58	10.41	21.77	25.30	79.12	23.08	180.5	800-222-8222	Y
Wells Fargo Endeavor Select Fund - Class A	STAEX	B+	B+	B+	Up	7.13	13.44	35.18	38.53	103.86	8.16	163.3	800-222-8222	Y
Wells Fargo Endeavor Select Fund - Class Admin	WECDX	B+	B+	A-	Up	7.14	13.45	35.33	39.38	106.15	8.74	163.3	800-222-8222	Y
Wells Fargo Endeavor Select Fund - Class C	WECCX	B+	B+	B+	Up	6.96	12.95	34.04	35.42	96.20	5.61	163.3	800-222-8222	Y
Wells Fargo Endeavor Select Fund - Class Inst	WFCIX	B+	B+	A-	Up	7.31	13.64	35.83	40.24	108.11	9.12	163.3	800-222-8222	Y
Wells Fargo Growth Fund - Class A	SGRAX	B+	A-	B	Up	6.73	14.05	34.59	36.06	92.52	33.54	4,617	800-222-8222	
Wells Fargo Growth Fund - Class Admin	SGRKX	B+	A-	B	Up	6.80	14.19	34.88	36.90	94.58	38.03	4,617	800-222-8222	
Wells Fargo Growth Fund - Class C	WGFCX	B	B+	B	Up	6.54	13.63	33.62	32.99	85.40	26.42	4,617	800-222-8222	
Wells Fargo Growth Fund - Class Inst	SGRNX	B+	A-	B	Up	6.84	14.28	35.13	37.73	96.56	41.03	4,617	800-222-8222	
Wells Fargo Growth Fund - Class R6	SGRHX	A-	A-	B	Up	6.88	14.33	35.23	37.95	96.88	41.12	4,617	800-222-8222	Y
Wells Fargo Large Cap Growth Fund - Class A	STAFX	B+	B	B+	Up	8.36	15.63	32.91	34.32	103.11	45.67	1,076	800-222-8222	Y
Wells Fargo Large Cap Growth Fund - Class Admin	STDFX	B+	B+	B+	Up	8.39	15.71	33.08	34.81	104.34	46.1	1,076	800-222-8222	Y
Wells Fargo Large Cap Growth Fund - Class C	STOFX	B	B	B+	Up	8.15	15.18	31.89	31.31	95.59	42.3	1,076	800-222-8222	Y
Wells Fargo Large Cap Growth Fund - Class Inst	STNFX	B+	B+	B+	Up	8.44	15.84	33.34	35.74	106.99	46.73	1,076	800-222-8222	Y
Wells Fargo Large Cap Growth Fund - Class R	STMFX	B+	B	B+	Up	8.29	15.50	32.55	33.28	100.55	44.75	1,076	800-222-8222	Y
Wells Fargo Large Cap Growth Fund - Class R4	SLGRX	B+	B+	B+	Up	8.42	15.79	33.29	35.53	106.24	46.67	1,076	800-222-8222	Y
Wells Fargo Large Cap Growth Fund - Class R6	STFFX	B+	B+	B+	Up	8.45	15.86	33.43	36.08	107.69	46.85	1,076	800-222-8222	Y
Wells Fargo Omega Growth Fund - Class A	EKOAX	B	B	B	Up	7.62	13.64	34.33	34.80	99.62	47.93	769.4	800-222-8222	Y
Wells Fargo Omega Growth Fund - Class Admin	EOMYX	B	B+	B	Up	7.67	13.73	34.57	35.62	101.79	51.93	769.4	800-222-8222	Y
Wells Fargo Omega Growth Fund - Class C	EKOCX	B	B	B	Up	7.41	13.19	33.30	31.80	92.22	33.42	769.4	800-222-8222	Y
Wells Fargo Omega Growth Fund - Class Inst	EKONX	B+	B+	B	Up	7.73	13.88	34.90	36.65	104.38	53.34	769.4	800-222-8222	Y
Wells Fargo Omega Growth Fund - Class R	EKORX	B	B	B	Up	7.53	13.47	33.99	33.77	97.08	45.5	769.4	800-222-8222	Y
Wells Fargo Opportunity Fund - Class A	SOPVX	B	B	B	Up	6.60	10.48	20.00	28.81	89.12	42.87	1,832	800-222-8222	Y
Wells Fargo Opportunity Fund - Class Admin	WOFDX	B	B	B	Up	6.63	10.59	20.25	29.61	91.17	46.67	1,832	800-222-8222	Y
Wells Fargo Opportunity Fund - Class C	WFOPX	B	B-	B	Up	6.38	10.05	19.10	25.91	82.12	40.42	1,832	800-222-8222	Y
Wells Fargo Opportunity Fund - Class Inst	WOFNX	B	B	B	Up	6.70	10.73	20.53	30.59	93.52	47.5	1,832	800-222-8222	Y
Wells Fargo Premier Large Company Growth Fund - Class A	EKJAX	B	B	B	Up	7.41	14.12	33.92	31.14	94.30	13.21	2,478	800-222-8222	Y
Wells Fargo Premier Large Company Growth Fund - Cls Admin	WFPDX	B	B	B	Up	7.44	14.23	34.10	31.59	95.80	13.42	2,478	800-222-8222	Y
Wells Fargo Premier Large Company Growth Fund - Class C	EKJCX	B	B	B	Up	7.26	13.70	32.97	28.18	87.27	10.43	2,478	800-222-8222	Y
Wells Fargo Premier Large Company Growth Fund - Class Inst	EKJYX	B	B	B	Up	7.53	14.32	34.43	32.67	98.41	13.8	2,478	800-222-8222	Y
Wells Fargo Premier Large Company Growth Fund - Class R4	EKJRX	B	B	B	Up	7.53	14.35	34.41	32.38	97.47	13.7	2,478	800-222-8222	Y
Wells Fargo Premier Large Company Growth Fund - Class R6	EKJFX	B	B	B	Up	7.53	14.37	34.55	32.97	98.85	13.84	2,478	800-222-8222	Y
WesMark Growth Fund	WMKGX	B-	B-	C+	Up	5.81	11.16	24.21	21.34	85.63	20	362.9	800-861-1013	Y
Westfield Capital Large Cap Growth Fund Inst Cls Shares	WCLGX	B	B	B-	Down	5.75	11.86	30.57	36.08	112.93	10.81	107.5		Y
Westfield Capital Large Cap Growth Fund Inv Cls Shares	WCLCX	B	B	B-		5.59	11.71	30.18	35.00	110.13	10.96	107.5		Y
White Oak Select Growth Fund	WOGSX	B+	B	A-	Up	7.12	10.91	19.75	43.58	108.45	85.76	293.7	888-462-5386	Y
William Blair Growth Fund Class I	BGFIX	B	B	A-	Up	7.17	11.90	24.64	29.82	93.18	11.51	375.6	800-621-0687	Y
William Blair Growth Fund Class N	WBGSX	B	B-	A-	Up	7.07	11.80	24.34	28.71	90.36	10.27	375.6	800-621-0687	Y
William Blair Large Cap Growth Fund Class I	LCGFX	A-	A-	A-	Up	10.26	16.58	31.29	42.76	124.73	13.97	203.6	800-621-0687	Y
William Blair Large Cap Growth Fund Class N	LCGNX	A-	A-	A-	Up	10.15	16.46	30.87	41.63	121.78	13.35	203.6	800-621-0687	Y

Category: US Equity Large Cap Growth (con't)

Fund Name	Ticker Symbol	RATINGS: Overall Rating	Reward Rating	Risk Rating	Recent Up/ Downgrade	TOTAL RETURNS & PERFORMANCE: 3-Month Total Return	6-Month Total Return	1-Year Total Return	3-Year Total Return	5-Year Total Return	ASSETS: NAV	Total Assets (MIL)	NEW INVESTORS: Telephone	Open to New Investors
Wilshire Large Company Growth Portfolio Fund Cls Inst	WLCGX	A-	B+	A	Up	5.80	11.00	27.35	39.49	102.80	42.53	237.4	888-200-6796	Y
Wilshire Large Company Growth Port Inv Cls Shares	DTLGX	B+	B+	A	Up	5.74	10.82	26.93	38.22	99.72	39.53	237.4	888-200-6796	Y

Category: US Equity Large Cap Value

Fund Name	Ticker Symbol	RATINGS: Overall Rating	Reward Rating	Risk Rating	Recent Up/ Downgrade	TOTAL RETURNS & PERFORMANCE: 3-Month Total Return	6-Month Total Return	1-Year Total Return	3-Year Total Return	5-Year Total Return	ASSETS: NAV	Total Assets (MIL)	NEW INVESTORS: Telephone	Open to New Investors
1290 VT Equity Income Portfolio Class IA	US2689402442	B	B-	B	Up	7.25	11.13	16.14	27.43	87.85		635.0	877-222-2144	Y
1290 VT Equity Income Portfolio Class IB	US29364E8012	B	B-	B	Up	7.21	11.08	16.06	27.32	87.74		635.0	877-222-2144	Y
1290 VT Equity Income Portfolio Class K	US26883L7385	B	B-	B	Up	7.32	11.21	16.41	28.38	90.21		635.0	877-222-2144	Y
AB Equity Income Fund Advisor Class	AUIYX	B-	B-	B-	Down	5.72	10.04	17.50	25.01	81.31	29.26	658.9	212-969-1000	Y
AB Equity Income Fund Class A	AUIAX	B-	B-	B-	Down	5.65	9.91	17.22	24.02	78.74	28.99	658.9	212-969-1000	Y
AB Equity Income Fund Class B	AUIBX	B-	C+	B	Down	5.47	9.51	16.35	21.25	72.34	28.64	658.9	212-969-1000	
AB Equity Income Fund Class C	AUICX	B-	C+	B-	Down	5.43	9.48	16.31	21.29	72.43	28.62	658.9	212-969-1000	Y
AB Equity Income Fund Class I	AUIIX	B-	B-	B-	Down	5.71	10.05	17.45	24.97	81.20	28.92	658.9	212-969-1000	Y
AB Equity Income Fund Class K	AUIKX	B-	B-	B-	Down	5.63	9.86	17.07	23.71	78.25	28.98	658.9	212-969-1000	Y
AB Equity Income Fund Class R	AUIRX	B-	B-	B-	Down	5.54	9.70	16.73	22.62	75.57	28.85	658.9	212-969-1000	Y
AB Equity Income Fund Class Z	AUIZX	B-	B-	B-	Down	5.74	10.11	17.57	25.32	81.52	28.91	658.9	212-969-1000	Y
AB Relative Value Fund Advisor Class	CBBYX	B	B	B		6.29	12.59	19.05	33.45	100.82	5.88	1,811	212-969-1000	Y
AB Relative Value Fund Class A	CABDX	B	B	A-		6.25	12.24	18.72	32.31	98.09	5.83	1,811	212-969-1000	Y
AB Relative Value Fund Class B	CBBDX	B-	B-	B	Down	5.92	11.88	17.71	29.34	91.09	5.86	1,811	212-969-1000	
AB Relative Value Fund Class C	CBBCX	B	B-	A-		5.95	11.94	17.80	29.59	91.18	5.83	1,811	212-969-1000	Y
AB Relative Value Fund Class I	CBBIX	B	B	B+		6.22	12.47	19.07	33.32	101.31	5.93	1,811	212-969-1000	Y
AB Relative Value Fund Class K	CBBKX	B	B	B		6.28	12.32	18.65	32.34	98.79	5.77	1,811	212-969-1000	Y
AB Relative Value Fund Class R	CBBRX	B	B-	B		6.04	12.12	18.28	31.35	95.67	5.74	1,811	212-969-1000	Y
AB Relative Value Fund Class Z	CBBZX	B	B	B+		6.30	12.55	19.14	33.59	100.83	5.94	1,811	212-969-1000	Y
AB Value Fund Advisor Class	ABVYX	B-	C+	B	Up	6.31	10.32	13.70	15.98	81.47	16.15	420.3	212-969-1000	Y
AB Value Fund Class A	ABVAX	B-	C+	B	Up	6.15	10.10	13.39	14.99	78.86	16.14	420.3	212-969-1000	Y
AB Value Fund Class B	ABVBX	B-	C+	B	Up	6.19	10.12	13.32	14.84	78.61	16.23	420.3	212-969-1000	
AB Value Fund Class I	ABVIX	B-	C+	B	Up	6.27	10.25	13.73	16.05	81.88	16	420.3	212-969-1000	Y
AB Value Fund Class K	ABVKX	B-	C+	B	Up	6.12	10.06	13.25	14.60	78.12	15.86	420.3	212-969-1000	Y
AB Value Fund Class R	ABVRX	B-	C+	B-	Up	6.10	9.93	12.93	13.63	75.44	16.04	420.3	212-969-1000	Y
AIG Focused Dividend Strategy Fund Class A	FDSAX	B	B	B		7.46	13.58	20.24	36.12	112.44	18.75	14,853	800-858-8850	Y
AIG Focused Dividend Strategy Fund Class B	FDSBX	B	B	B-		7.25	13.16	19.45	33.40	105.50	18.59	14,853	800-858-8850	Y
AIG Focused Dividend Strategy Fund Class C	FDSTX	B	B	B-		7.26	13.17	19.46	33.45	105.59	18.58	14,853	800-858-8850	Y
AIG Focused Dividend Strategy Fund Class W	FDSWX	B	B	B		7.52	13.71	20.48	36.97	114.39	18.73	14,853	800-858-8850	Y
AIG Select Dividend Growth Fund Class A	SDVAX	B	B	B	Up	10.11	13.03	17.59	30.39		17.34	45.8	800-858-8850	Y
AIG Select Dividend Growth Fund Class C	SDVCX	B	B	B	Up	9.92	12.67	16.79	27.23		17.27	45.8	800-858-8850	Y
AIG Select Dividend Growth Fund Class W	SDVWX	B	B	B	Up	10.12	13.15	17.75	30.49		17.29	45.8	800-858-8850	Y
AIG Strategic Value Fund Class A	SFVAX	B-	B-	B	Down	6.35	9.88	15.64	22.67	88.69	31.54	245.0	800-858-8850	Y
AIG Strategic Value Fund Class C	SFVTX	B-	C+	B	Down	6.20	9.53	14.90	20.25	82.58	29.24	245.0	800-858-8850	Y
AIG Strategic Value Fund Class W	SFVWX	B-	B-	B	Down	6.46	9.95	15.71	22.75	88.81	31.54	245.0	800-858-8850	Y
Al Frank Fund Class Advisor	VALAX	B-	B-	B-	Down	7.35	11.13	18.04	27.32	89.83	24.83	90.0	888-263-6443	Y
Al Frank Fund Class Investor	VALUX	B-	B-	B-	Down	7.29	10.98	17.75	26.36	87.46	24.79	90.0	888-263-6443	Y
AllianzGI NFJ Dividend Value Fund Administrative Class	ANDAX	B-	B-	C+	Down	6.53	11.34	15.80	21.55	76.23	15.42	2,687	800-498-5413	Y
AllianzGI NFJ Dividend Value Fund Class A	PNEAX	B-	B-	C+	Down	6.51	11.30	15.69	21.22	75.42	15.14	2,687	800-498-5413	Y
AllianzGI NFJ Dividend Value Fund Class P	ADJPX	B-	B-	C+	Down	6.60	11.49	15.99	22.12	77.53	15.26	2,687	800-498-5413	Y
AllianzGI NFJ Dividend Value Fund Class R6	ANDVX	B-	B-	C+	Down	6.65	11.53	16.20	22.66	78.71	15.22	2,687	800-498-5413	Y
AllianzGI NFJ Dividend Value Fund Institutional Class	NFJEX	B-	B-	C+	Down	6.61	11.47	16.08	22.44	78.36	15.25	2,687	800-498-5413	Y
AllianzGI NFJ Large-Cap Value Fund Administrative Class	ALNFX	B-	B	C+	Down	7.15	11.53	21.09	29.03	95.12	27.22	384.3	800-498-5413	Y
AllianzGI NFJ Large-Cap Value Fund Class A	PNBAX	B-	B	C+	Down	7.11	11.46	20.94	28.61	94.08	26.85	384.3	800-498-5413	Y

Category: US Equity Large Cap Value (con't)

Fund Name	Ticker Symbol	RATINGS: Overall Rating	Reward Rating	Risk Rating	Recent Up/ Downgrade	TOTAL RETURNS & PERFORMANCE: 3-Month Total Return	6-Month Total Return	1-Year Total Return	3-Year Total Return	5-Year Total Return	ASSETS: NAV	Total Assets (ML)	NEW INVESTORS: Telephone	Open to New Investors
AllianzGI NFJ Large-Cap Value Fund Class C	PNBCX	B-	B-	C+	Down	6.87	11.05	20.00	25.75	86.96	27.14	384.3	800-498-5413	Y
AllianzGI NFJ Large-Cap Value Fund Class P	ALCPX	B-	B	C+	Down	7.18	11.62	21.27	29.60	96.57	27.1	384.3	800-498-5413	Y
AllianzGI NFJ Large-Cap Value Fund Class R	ANLRX	B-	B-	C+	Down	7.01	11.30	20.65	27.67	91.70	27.11	384.3	800-498-5413	Y
AllianzGI NFJ Large-Cap Value Fund Institutional Class	ANVIX	B-	B	C+	Down	7.19	11.67	21.35	30.02	97.58	26.73	384.3	800-498-5413	Y
American Beacon Bridgeway Large Cap Value Fund A Class	BWLAX	B	B	B	Up	7.55	11.40	15.43	30.18	108.90	28.31	4,683	800-658-5811	Y
American Beacon Bridgeway Large Cap Value Fund C Class	BWLCX	B	B-	B	Up	7.35	11.02	14.57	27.30	101.27	27.62	4,683	800-658-5811	Y
American Beacon Bridgeway Large Cap Value Fund Inst Cls	BRLVX	B	B	B+	Up	7.66	11.63	15.89	31.64	113.03	28.57	4,683	800-658-5811	Y
American Beacon Bridgeway Large Cap Value Fund Inv Cls	BWLIX	B	B	B	Up	7.55	11.47	15.49	30.39	109.86	28.41	4,683	800-658-5811	Y
American Beacon Bridgeway Large Cap Value Fund R6 Class	BWLRX	B	B	B	Up	7.61	11.59	15.84	31.58	112.94	28.55	4,683	800-658-5811	Y
American Beacon Bridgeway Large Cap Value Fund Y Class	BWLYX	B	B	B	Up	7.62	11.61	15.80	31.42	112.49	28.49	4,683	800-658-5811	Y
American Beacon Large Cap Value Fund Advisor Class	AVASX	B-	B-	B	Up	5.29	9.52	16.53	24.52	88.69	26.74	7,352	800-658-5811	Y
American Beacon Large Cap Value Fund Class A	ALVAX	B-	B-	B	Up	5.35	9.62	16.67	24.92	89.34	26.76	7,352	800-658-5811	Y
American Beacon Large Cap Value Fund Class C	ALVCX	B-	B-	B-	Up	5.20	9.30	15.90	22.23	82.37	26.6	7,352	800-658-5811	Y
American Beacon Large Cap Value Fund Class R6	AALRX	B-	B-	B	Down	5.41	9.78	17.07	26.31	93.26	29.14	7,352	800-658-5811	Y
American Beacon Large Cap Value Fund Class Y	ABLYX	B-	B-	B	Down	5.45	9.75	17.01	26.06	92.51	28.96	7,352	800-658-5811	Y
American Beacon Large Cap Value Fund Institutional Class	AADEX	B-	B-	B	Down	5.41	9.78	17.07	26.30	93.25	29.15	7,352	800-658-5811	Y
American Beacon Large Cap Value Fund Investor Class	AAGPX	B-	B-	B	Up	5.33	9.59	16.69	25.05	89.99	27.09	7,352	800-658-5811	Y
American Beacon The London Company Income Eq Fund A Cls	ABCAX	B-	C+	B-	Down	5.37	7.48	14.05	23.57	86.18	17.02	1,173	800-658-5811	Y
American Beacon The London Company Income Eq Fund C Cls	ABECX	B	C+	B+		5.16	7.00	13.18	20.85	79.38	16.9	1,173	800-658-5811	Y
American Beacon The London Company Income Eq Fund Inst Cls	ABCIX	B-	C+	B	Down	5.49	7.62	14.48	24.97	90.09	17.18	1,173	800-658-5811	Y
American Beacon The London Company Income Eq Fund Inv Cls	ABCVX	B	C+	B+		5.37	7.42	14.07	23.68	87.03	17.11	1,173	800-658-5811	Y
American Beacon The London Company Income Eq Fund Y Cls	ABCYX	B-	C+	B	Down	5.44	7.63	14.37	24.72	89.37	17.09	1,173	800-658-5811	Y
American Century Capital Value Fund Class A	ACCVX	B-	C+	B	Down	3.74	6.24	11.49	22.14	84.02	8.74	154.8	800-444-4015	Y
American Century Capital Value Fund I Class	ACPIX	B-	B-	B	Down	3.74	6.45	11.81	23.57	88.06	8.77	154.8	800-444-4015	Y
American Century Capital Value Fund Investor Class	ACTIX	B-	B-	B	Down	3.77	6.37	11.74	23.02	86.37	8.76	154.8	800-444-4015	Y
American Century Equity Income Fund A Class	TWEAX	B	B-	B	Down	3.74	7.25	13.05	34.16	82.65	8.91	12,660	800-444-4015	Y
American Century Equity Income Fund C Class	AEYIX	B	B-	B		3.53	6.83	12.22	31.06	75.80	8.91	12,660	800-444-4015	Y
American Century Equity Income Fund I Class	ACIIX	B	B-	B	Down	3.85	7.49	13.67	35.92	86.66	8.92	12,660	800-444-4015	Y
American Century Equity Income Fund Investor Class	TWEIX	B	B-	B	Down	3.69	7.38	13.33	35.15	84.93	8.91	12,660	800-444-4015	Y
American Century Equity Income Fund R Class	AEURX	B	B-	B	Down	3.68	7.13	12.82	33.13	80.28	8.88	12,660	800-444-4015	Y
American Century Equity Income Fund R5 Class	AEIUX	B	B-	B	Down	3.85	7.49	13.61	35.48	85.38	8.92	12,660	800-444-4015	Y
American Century Equity Income Fund R6 Class	AEUDX	B	B-	B	Down	3.89	7.56	13.83	36.64	87.94	8.93	12,660	800-444-4015	Y
American Century Equity Income Fund Y Class	AEIYX	B	B-	B	Down	3.89	7.56	13.72	35.62	85.57	8.93	12,660	800-444-4015	Y
American Century Income and Growth Fund C Class	ACGCX	B-	B-	C+	Down	6.62	11.95	19.39	24.10	90.76	39.18	2,228	800-444-4015	Y
American Century Income and Growth Fund Class A	AMADX	B-	B-	C+	Down	6.80	12.36	20.29	26.90	98.01	39.24	2,228	800-444-4015	Y
American Century Income and Growth Fund I Class	AMGIX	B-	B-	C+	Down	6.94	12.65	20.86	28.66	102.61	39.35	2,228	800-444-4015	Y
American Century Income and Growth Fund Investor Class	BIGRX	B-	B-	C+	Down	6.89	12.52	20.62	27.87	100.57	39.3	2,228	800-444-4015	Y
American Century Income and Growth Fund R Class	AICRX	B-	B-	C+	Down	6.75	12.23	20.00	25.96	95.62	39.29	2,228	800-444-4015	Y
American Century Income and Growth Fund R5 Class	AICGX	B-	B-	C+	Down	6.94	12.62	20.80	28.06	100.87	39.35	2,228	800-444-4015	Y
American Century Large Company Value Fund A Class	ALPAX	B-	C+	B	Down	3.56	5.96	10.73	21.09	82.95	10.21	851.6	800-444-4015	Y
American Century Large Company Value Fund C Class	ALPCX	B-	C+	B	Down	3.45	5.65	10.02	18.45	76.50	10.22	851.6	800-444-4015	Y
American Century Large Company Value Fund I Class	ALVSX	B-	B-	B	Down	3.69	6.21	11.22	22.71	87.29	10.22	851.6	800-444-4015	Y
American Century Large Company Value Fund Investor Class	ALVIX	B-	C+	B	Down	3.73	6.10	11.12	21.98	85.43	10.22	851.6	800-444-4015	Y
American Century Large Company Value Fund R Class	ALVRX	B-	C+	B	Down	3.49	5.82	10.45	20.16	80.84	10.22	851.6	800-444-4015	Y
American Century Large Company Value Fund R5 Class	ALVGX	B-	C+	B	Down	3.69	6.21	11.16	22.03	85.51	10.22	851.6	800-444-4015	Y
American Century Large Company Value Fund R6 Class	ALVDX	B-	B-	B	Down	3.73	6.29	11.39	23.27	88.15	10.22	851.6	800-444-4015	Y
American Century NT Large Company Value Fund G Class	ACLLX	B-	C+	B	Down	3.93	6.59	11.54	21.70	85.37	11.56	2,016	800-444-4015	Y
American Century Value Fund A Class	TWADX	B-	C+	B	Down	4.17	7.08	8.20	22.69	84.99	8.92	3,321	800-444-4015	Y
American Century Value Fund C Class	ACLCX	B-	C+	B		3.91	6.64	7.39	19.84	77.97	8.78	3,321	800-444-4015	Y
American Century Value Fund I Class	AVLIX	B-	C+	B	Down	4.29	7.19	8.66	24.27	89.15	8.94	3,321	800-444-4015	Y
American Century Value Fund Investor Class	TWVLX	B-	C+	B	Down	4.24	7.09	8.46	23.45	86.97	8.92	3,321	800-444-4015	Y
American Century Value Fund R Class	AVURX	B-	C+	B	Down	4.10	6.81	7.93	21.62	82.68	8.92	3,321	800-444-4015	Y

Category: US Equity Large Cap Value (con't)

Fund Name	Ticker Symbol	RATINGS: Overall Rating	RATINGS: Reward Rating	RATINGS: Risk Rating	RATINGS: Recent Up/ Downgrade	TOTAL RETURNS & PERFORMANCE: 3-Month Total Return	6-Month Total Return	1-Year Total Return	3-Year Total Return	5-Year Total Return	ASSETS: NAV	Total Assets (MIL)	NEW INVESTORS: Telephone	Open to New Investors
American Century Value Fund R5 Class	AVUGX	B-	C+	B	Down	4.29	7.31	8.61	23.61	87.22	8.94	3,321	800-444-4015	Y
American Century Value Fund R6 Class	AVUDX	B-	C+	B	Down	4.33	7.40	8.83	24.83	89.79	8.94	3,321	800-444-4015	Y
American Century Value Fund Y Class	AVUYX	B-	C+	B	Down	4.33	7.39	8.84	23.88	87.62	8.95	3,321	800-444-4015	Y
American Funds American Mutual Fund® Class 529-A	CMLAX	B-	B-	B	Down	5.05	10.20	17.59	28.87	89.52	40.71	48,494	800-421-4225	Y
American Funds American Mutual Fund® Class 529-C	CMLCX	B-	B-	B-	Down	4.85	9.75	16.65	25.90	82.29	40.51	48,494	800-421-4225	Y
American Funds American Mutual Fund® Class 529-E	CMLEX	B-	B-	B	Down	5.00	10.04	17.29	27.93	87.28	40.55	48,494	800-421-4225	Y
American Funds American Mutual Fund® Class 529-F	CMLFX	B-	B-	B	Down	5.09	10.30	17.82	29.69	91.65	40.76	48,494	800-421-4225	Y
American Funds American Mutual Fund® Class A	AMRMX	B-	B-	B	Down	5.05	10.21	17.67	29.21	90.44	40.8	48,494	800-421-4225	Y
American Funds American Mutual Fund® Class C	AMFCX	B-	B-	B-	Down	4.86	9.78	16.72	26.15	82.95	40.23	48,494	800-421-4225	Y
American Funds American Mutual Fund® Class F-1	AMFFX	B-	B-	B	Down	5.05	10.17	17.57	28.89	89.71	40.63	48,494	800-421-4225	Y
American Funds American Mutual Fund® Class F-2	AMRFX	B-	B-	B	Down	5.12	10.34	17.87	29.90	92.13	40.79	48,494	800-421-4225	Y
American Funds American Mutual Fund® Class F-3	AFMFX	B-	B-	B	Down	5.13	10.37	17.98	29.55	90.95	40.78	48,494	800-421-4225	Y
American Funds American Mutual Fund® Class R-1	RMFAX	B-	B-	B-	Down	4.83	9.74	16.66	26.01	82.69	40.38	48,494	800-421-4225	Y
American Funds American Mutual Fund® Class R-2	RMFBX	B-	B-	B-	Down	4.85	9.78	16.72	26.12	82.93	40.34	48,494	800-421-4225	Y
American Funds American Mutual Fund® Class R-2E	RMEBX	B-	B-	B	Down	4.94	9.94	17.07	27.41	86.77	40.67	48,494	800-421-4225	Y
American Funds American Mutual Fund® Class R-3	RMFCX	B-	B-	B	Down	4.97	10.03	17.22	27.79	87.01	40.49	48,494	800-421-4225	Y
American Funds American Mutual Fund® Class R-4	RMFEX	B-	B-	B	Down	5.05	10.20	17.58	28.95	89.87	40.67	48,494	800-421-4225	Y
American Funds American Mutual Fund® Class R-5	RMFFX	B-	B-	B	Down	5.11	10.34	17.93	30.14	92.71	40.8	48,494	800-421-4225	Y
American Funds American Mutual Fund® Class R-5E	RMFHX	B-	B-	B	Down	5.12	10.32	17.83	29.49	90.86	40.78	48,494	800-421-4225	Y
American Funds American Mutual Fund® Class R-6	RMFGX	B-	B-	B	Down	5.15	10.39	17.99	30.32	93.23	40.81	48,494	800-421-4225	Y
American Funds Washington Mutual Investors Fund Cls 529-A	CWMAX	B	B-	B		6.43	12.37	20.09	34.40	101.54	45.55	100,165	800-421-4225	Y
American Funds Washington Mutual Investors Fund Cls 529-C	CWMCX	B-	B-	B	Down	6.22	11.92	19.19	31.32	93.88	45.28	100,165	800-421-4225	Y
American Funds Washington Mutual Investors Fund Cls 529-E	CWMEX	B	B-	B		6.37	12.24	19.80	33.44	99.08	45.3	100,165	800-421-4225	Y
American Funds Washington Mutual Invs Fund Cls 529-F-1	CWMFX	B	B	B		6.49	12.49	20.34	35.26	103.75	45.44	100,165	800-421-4225	Y
American Funds Washington Mutual Investors Fund Class A	AWSHX	B	B-	B		6.45	12.40	20.19	34.75	102.42	45.65	100,165	800-421-4225	Y
American Funds Washington Mutual Investors Fund Class C	WSHCX	B-	B-	B	Down	6.25	11.96	19.25	31.56	94.51	45.08	100,165	800-421-4225	Y
American Funds Washington Mutual Investors Fund Class F-1	WSHFX	B	B-	B		6.42	12.34	20.06	34.39	101.62	45.48	100,165	800-421-4225	Y
American Funds Washington Mutual Investors Fund Class F-2	WMFFX	B	B	B		6.48	12.49	20.38	35.46	104.25	45.61	100,165	800-421-4225	Y
American Funds Washington Mutual Investors Fund Class F-3	FWMIX	B	B	B		6.52	12.56	20.48	35.08	102.91	45.63	100,165	800-421-4225	Y
American Funds Washington Mutual Investors Fund Class R-1	RWMAX	B-	B-	B	Down	6.23	11.93	19.19	31.49	94.41	45.17	100,165	800-421-4225	Y
American Funds Washington Mutual Investors Fund Class R-2	RWMBX	B-	B-	B	Down	6.26	11.95	19.21	31.60	94.73	45.02	100,165	800-421-4225	Y
American Funds Washington Mutual Investors Fund Class R-2E	RWEBX	B-	B-	B	Down	6.30	12.10	19.57	33.14	98.83	45.46	100,165	800-421-4225	Y
American Funds Washington Mutual Investors Fund Class R-3	RWMCX	B-	B-	B	Down	6.36	12.20	19.73	33.26	98.80	45.27	100,165	800-421-4225	Y
American Funds Washington Mutual Investors Fund Class R-4	RWMEX	B	B-	B		6.44	12.38	20.11	34.49	101.86	45.42	100,165	800-421-4225	Y
American Funds Washington Mutual Investors Fund Class R-5	RWMFX	B	B	B		6.51	12.53	20.46	35.69	104.91	45.63	100,165	800-421-4225	Y
American Funds Washington Mutual Investors Fund Class R-5E	RWMHX	B	B	B		6.49	12.48	20.32	35.05	102.86	45.61	100,165	800-421-4225	Y
American Funds Washington Mutual Investors Fund Class R-6	RWMGX	B	B	B		6.52	12.55	20.53	35.89	105.35	45.67	100,165	800-421-4225	Y
AMG River Road Dividend All Cap Value Fund Class I	ARIDX	B-	B-	B	Down	3.87	6.13	9.05	24.08	83.83	12.51	949.8	800-835-3879	
AMG River Road Dividend All Cap Value Fund Class N	ARDEX	B-	B-	B	Down	3.80	6.00	8.78	23.16	81.50	12.52	949.8	800-835-3879	
AMG River Road Dividend All Cap Value Fund Class Z	ARZDX	B-	B-	B		3.89	6.09	8.87	23.26	81.65	12.51	949.8	800-835-3879	Y
AMG River Road Dividend All Cap Value Fund II Class I	ADIVX	B-	B-	B	Down	4.16	6.57	10.05	24.18	83.15	14.41	124.9	800-835-3879	Y
AMG River Road Dividend All Cap Value Fund II Class N	ADVTX	B-	B-	B	Down	4.10	6.44	9.66	23.21	80.71	14.39	124.9	800-835-3879	Y
AMG River Road Dividend All Cap Value Fund II Class Z	ADVZX	B-	B-	B		4.18	6.58	10.07	24.21	83.17	14.41	124.9	800-835-3879	Y
Artisan Value Fund Advisor Class	APDLX	B	B	B-	Up	5.42	10.43	16.10	35.38	83.10	14.49	629.7	800-344-1770	Y
Artisan Value Fund Institutional Class	APHLX	B	B	B-	Up	5.49	10.48	16.23	35.76	84.67	14.52	629.7	800-344-1770	Y
Artisan Value Fund Investor Class	ARTLX	B	B	B-	Up	5.41	10.40	15.98	34.91	82.46	14.56	629.7	800-344-1770	Y
Auxier Focus Fund Class A	AUXAX	B-	C+	B	Down	5.63	7.20	17.39	22.82	66.37	22.67	253.6		Y
Auxier Focus Fund Class Investor	AUXFX	B-	C+	B	Down	5.67	7.30	17.71	23.42	67.19	22.32	253.6		Y
Auxier Focus Fund Institutional	AUXIX	B-	C+	B	Down	5.72	7.43	17.91	24.08	68.92	22.71	253.6		Y
AXA Large Cap Value Managed Volatility Portfolio Class IA	US2689407151	B-	B-	B	Down	5.99	9.52	14.10	24.87	91.52		5,026	877-222-2144	Y
AXA Large Cap Value Managed Volatility Portfolio Class IB	US2689406997	B-	B-	B	Down	5.94	9.48	14.07	24.85	91.38		5,026	877-222-2144	Y
AXA Large Cap Value Managed Volatility Portfolio Class K	US26883L5223	B	B-	B	Up	6.00	9.59	14.30	25.73	93.82		5,026	877-222-2144	Y

Category: US Equity Large Cap Value (con't)

Fund Name	Ticker Symbol	RATINGS Overall Rating	Reward Rating	Risk Rating	Recent Up/ Downgrade	TOTAL RETURNS & PERFORMANCE 3-Month Total Return	6-Month Total Return	1-Year Total Return	3-Year Total Return	5-Year Total Return	ASSETS NAV	Total Assets (Mil)	NEW INVESTORS Telephone	Open to New Investors
Barrett Opportunity Fund	SAOPX	B	B	B-		3.20	8.67	20.57	36.18	84.45	29.98	66.8	877-363-6333	Y
Baywood ValuePlus Fund Institutional Shares	BVPIX	B-	B-	B-	Down	7.35	12.83	16.13	28.91	87.30	18.03	2.6		Y
Baywood ValuePlus Fund Investor Shares	BVPNX	B-	B-	B-	Down	7.32	12.69	15.85	27.87	85.41	17.95	2.6		Y
Becker Value Equity Fund Institutional Class	BVEIX	B-	B-	B	Down	6.24	9.35	15.23	26.19	97.10	19.55	444.2		Y
Becker Value Equity Fund Retail Class	BVEFX	B-	B-	B	Down	6.24	9.30	15.14	25.75	95.41	19.49	444.2		Y
Bishop Street Dividend Value Fund Class I	BSLIX	B	B	B		6.92	11.46	20.47	35.42	100.35	16.05	42.5		Y
BlackRock Advantage Large Cap Value Fund Inst Shares	MALVX	B	B	B+		5.29	10.73	17.54	30.17	99.06	29.26	675.8	800-441-7762	Y
BlackRock Advantage Large Cap Value Fund Investor A Shares	MDLVX	B	B	B	Up	5.21	10.59	17.25	29.07	96.05	28.72	676.5	800-441-7762	Y
BlackRock Advantage Large Cap Value Fund Investor B Shares	MBLVX	B	B-	B	Up	5.53	10.14	15.90	26.03	88.26		676.5	800-441-7762	
BlackRock Advantage Large Cap Value Fund Investor C Shares	MCLVX	B	B-	B	Up	5.01	10.20	16.37	26.13	88.68	26.78	676.5	800-441-7762	Y
BlackRock Advantage Large Cap Value Fund R Shares	MRLVX	B	B	B	Up	5.16	10.45	16.94	28.03	93.54	27.67	676.5	800-441-7762	Y
BlackRock Advantage Large Cap Value Fund Service Shares	MSLVX	B	B	B	Up	5.19	10.58	17.25	29.02	96.04	29.09	675.8	800-441-7762	Y
BlackRock Advantage Large Cap Value Retirement Fund	MKLVX	B	B	B+		4.92	10.36	17.28	30.38	100.06	15.63	131.2	800-441-7762	
BlackRock Basic Value Fund Class K	MBVKX	B-	C+	B-	Up	5.78	9.39	8.66	20.22	87.65	26.25	3,237	800-441-7762	Y
BlackRock Basic Value Fund Institutional Shares	MABAX	B-	C+	B-	Up	5.75	9.32	8.58	19.83	87.04	26.25	3,237	800-441-7762	Y
BlackRock Enhanced Equity Dividend Fund	BDJ	B-	B-	B		4.11	8.10	14.64	28.90	66.75	9.9658	1,862	800-441-7762	Y
BlackRock Equity Dividend Fund Institutional Shares	MADVX	B	B	B		5.40	9.73	16.75	34.20	87.32	22.77	21,757	800-441-7762	Y
BlackRock Equity Dividend Fund Investor A Shares	MDDVX	B	B	B		5.33	9.59	16.43	33.19	84.86	22.71	21,757	800-441-7762	Y
BlackRock Equity Dividend Fund Investor B Shares	MBDVX	B	B	B		5.64	8.98	15.24	29.71	77.94		21,757	800-441-7762	
BlackRock Equity Dividend Fund Investor C Shares	MCDVX	B	B	B		5.15	9.19	15.62	30.36	78.40	21.91	21,757	800-441-7762	Y
BlackRock Equity Dividend Fund Investor C1 Shares	BEDCX	B	B	B		5.17	9.28	15.80	31.06	80.11	21.93	21,757	800-441-7762	Y
BlackRock Equity Dividend Fund K Shares	MKDVX	B	B	B		5.43	9.80	16.92	32.78	81.59	22.76	21,757	800-441-7762	Y
BlackRock Equity Dividend Fund R Shares	MRDVX	B	B	B		5.21	9.39	16.04	31.90	82.00	22.88	21,757	800-441-7762	Y
BlackRock Equity Dividend Fund Service Shares	MSDVX	B	B	B		5.32	9.61	16.47	33.14	84.60	22.7	21,757	800-441-7762	Y
BlackRock High Equity Income Fund Institutional Shares	BMCIX	B-	B-	B	Up	3.04	6.68	17.52	23.06	99.39	27.58	819.1	800-441-7762	Y
BlackRock High Equity Income Fund Investor A Shares	BMEAX	B-	B-	B	Up	2.96	6.53	17.21	21.75	95.68	23.72	819.3	800-441-7762	Y
BlackRock High Equity Income Fund Investor B Shares	BRMBX	B-	C+	B	Up	3.68	5.81	16.02	19.03	88.35		819.3	800-441-7762	Y
BlackRock High Equity Income Fund Investor C Shares	BMECX	B-	C+	B	Up	2.79	6.15	16.35	19.07	88.43	16.16	819.1	800-441-7762	Y
BlackRock High Equity Income Fund Service Shares	BMCSX	B-	B-	B	Up	2.99	6.53	17.18	21.76	95.66	25.1	819.3	800-441-7762	Y
BMO Dividend Income Fund Class A	BADIX	B-	B	B-	Down	7.72	14.74	21.65	33.19	99.45	14.38	125.2	800-236-3863	Y
BMO Dividend Income Fund Class I	MDIVX	B	B	B-		7.81	14.92	21.90	34.20	102.01	14.33	125.2	800-236-3863	Y
BMO Large-Cap Value Fund Class A	BALVX	B	B-	B	Up	7.64	13.73	19.97	28.55	100.84	16.19	360.4	800-236-3863	Y
BMO Large-Cap Value Fund Class I	MLVIX	B	B	B	Up	7.70	13.85	20.31	29.56	103.47	16.2	360.4	800-236-3863	Y
BMO Large-Cap Value Fund Class R6	BLCRX	B	B	B	Up	7.72	13.92	20.49	29.93	104.06	16.2	360.4	800-236-3863	Y
BMO Low Volatility Equity Fund Class A	BLVAX	B	C+	A-		6.15	7.12	12.67	24.06	86.94	14.73	161.5	800-236-3863	Y
BMO Low Volatility Equity Fund Class I	MLVEX	B	C+	A-		6.26	7.30	12.98	25.00	89.47	14.78	161.5	800-236-3863	Y
BNY Mellon Income Stock Fund Class A	BMIAX	B	B-	B+		6.64	9.72	15.03	33.81	103.84	9.37	1,278	800-645-6561	Y
BNY Mellon Income Stock Fund Class C	BMISX	B	B-	B		6.34	9.21	14.01	30.72	96.18	9.35	1,278	800-645-6561	Y
BNY Mellon Income Stock Fund Class I	BMIIX	B	B-	B+		6.60	9.73	15.05	34.18	104.41	9.36	1,278	800-645-6561	Y
BNY Mellon Income Stock Fund Class M	MPISX	B	B	B+		6.60	9.75	15.07	34.22	104.46	9.36	1,278	800-645-6561	Y
BNY Mellon Income Stock Fund Class Y	BMIYX	B	B-	B+		6.72	9.75	15.20	34.20	104.44	9.36	1,278	800-645-6561	Y
BNY Mellon Income Stock Fund Investor shares	MIISX	B	B-	B+		6.57	9.62	14.85	33.35	101.98	9.47	1,278	800-645-6561	Y
Boston Partners All Cap Value Fund Institutional Class	BPAIX	B	B	B-		4.85	9.24	17.85	35.34	116.76	26.52	1,981	617-832-8200	Y
Boston Partners All Cap Value Fund Investor Class	BPAVX	B	B	B+	Up	4.85	9.13	17.63	34.38	114.42	26.4	1,981	617-832-8200	Y
Boulder Growth & Income Fund	BIF	B-	B-	C+	Down	8.48	13.45	22.22	28.84	86.63	13.01	1,357	303-444-5483	Y
Bridge Builder Large Cap Value Fund	BBVLX	B-	C+	B	Up	5.25	9.04	17.18			12.22	6,001		Y
Calamos Dividend Growth Fund Class A	CADVX	B-	B-	B-	Down	6.23	10.85	20.93	31.31		12.17	25.5	800-582-6959	Y
Calamos Dividend Growth Fund Class C	CCDVX	B-	B-	B-	Down	5.97	10.39	19.99	28.38		11.96	25.5	800-582-6959	Y
Calamos Dividend Growth Fund Class I	CIDVX	B-	B-	B-	Down	6.22	10.92	21.13	32.26		12.15	25.5	800-582-6959	Y
Calamos Dividend Growth Fund Class T	CTDVX	B-	C+	B-	Down	3.69	7.94	21.58	27.56			25.1	800-582-6959	Y
Calamos Opportunistic Value Fund Class A	CVAAX	B-	B-	B-	Down	6.86	12.08	17.14	24.24	71.13	15.3	53.4	800-582-6959	Y
Calamos Opportunistic Value Fund Class C	CVACX	B-	C+	B-	Down	6.71	11.63	16.27	21.45	64.87	13.8	53.4	800-582-6959	Y

Category: US Equity Large Cap Value (con't)

Fund Name	Ticker Symbol	RATINGS: Overall Rating	Reward Rating	Risk Rating	Recent Up/ Downgrade	TOTAL RETURNS & PERFORMANCE: 3-Month Total Return	6-Month Total Return	1-Year Total Return	3-Year Total Return	5-Year Total Return	ASSETS: NAV	Total Assets (MIL)	NEW INVESTORS: Telephone	Open to New Investors
Calamos Opportunistic Value Fund Class R	CVARX	B-	C+	B-	Down	6.81	11.95	16.90	23.26	68.97	15.1	53.4	800-582-6959	Y
Calamos Opportunistic Value Fund Institutional Class	CVAIX	B-	B-	B-	Down	6.98	12.22	17.49	25.21	73.35	15.7	53.4	800-582-6959	Y
Carillon Eagle Growth & Income Fund Class A	HRCVX	B-	B-	B-	Down	7.75	11.37	20.13	28.99	86.11	21.04	625.0	800-421-4184	Y
Carillon Eagle Growth & Income Fund Class C	HIGCX	B-	B-	B-	Down	7.57	10.95	19.22	26.12	79.26	20.16	625.0	800-421-4184	Y
Carillon Eagle Growth & Income Fund Class I	HIGJX	B-	B-	B-	Down	7.90	11.56	20.47	30.11	88.70	20.99	625.0	800-421-4184	Y
Carillon Eagle Growth & Income Fund Class R3	HIGRX	B-	B-	B-	Down	7.69	11.18	19.73	27.79	82.94	20.96	625.0	800-421-4184	Y
Carillon Eagle Growth & Income Fund Class R5	HIGSX	B-	B-	B-	Down	7.82	11.52	20.42	29.45	87.83	21.01	625.0	800-421-4184	Y
Carillon Eagle Growth & Income Fund Class R6	HIGUX	B-	B-	B-	Down	7.89	11.58	20.57	30.13	89.19	20.94	625.0	800-421-4184	Y
Carillon Eagle Growth & Income Fund Class Y	HIGYX	B-	B-	B-		7.84	11.45	20.22	29.09	86.25	20.99	625.0	800-421-4184	Y
Castle Focus Fund Class C	CASTX	B-	C+	B	Down	1.27	3.67	11.54	17.10	45.45	20.85	194.1	877-743-7820	Y
Castle Focus Fund Class Investor	MOATX	B	C+	B+		1.52	4.16	12.70	20.68	52.95	22.19	194.1	877-743-7820	Y
Chartwell Mid Cap Value Fund	BERCX	B-	B	C	Up	6.92	13.63	16.86	26.55	77.71	15.76	24.2	610-296-1400	Y
City National Rochdale Dividend & Income Fund Class N	RIMHX	B	C+	A		3.37	3.52	7.76	22.64	67.73	40.3	259.8		Y
ClearBridge All Cap Value Fund Class A	SHFVX	B	B	B-	Up	5.46	9.39	17.11	28.89	85.85	14.54	1,887	877-721-1926	Y
ClearBridge All Cap Value Fund Class B	SFVBX	B-	B-	B-	Up	4.60	8.08	14.86	23.10	73.64	12.19	1,887	877-721-1926	
ClearBridge All Cap Value Fund Class C	SFVCX	B-	B-	B-	Down	5.26	8.93	16.28	26.33	79.68	12.56	1,887	877-721-1926	Y
ClearBridge All Cap Value Fund Class I	SFVYX	B	B	B-	Up	5.55	9.54	17.54	30.45	89.61	15.42	1,887	877-721-1926	Y
ClearBridge All Cap Value Fund Class IS	LSISX	B	B	B-		5.60	9.53	17.27	29.06	86.09	15.41	1,887	877-721-1926	Y
ClearBridge Large Cap Value Fund Class 1	LCLIX	B-	B-	B-	Down	4.70	7.06	14.38	24.40	87.91	33.21	1,746	877-721-1926	Y
ClearBridge Large Cap Value Fund Class A	SINAX	B	C+	B	Up	4.64	6.94	14.12	23.64	85.91	33.22	1,746	877-721-1926	Y
ClearBridge Large Cap Value Fund Class A2	LIVVX	B-	C+	B-	Down	4.61	6.88	13.99	23.07	84.60	33.2	1,746	877-721-1926	Y
ClearBridge Large Cap Value Fund Class C	SINOX	B-	C+	B	Down	4.43	6.54	13.24	20.84	78.83	32.27	1,746	877-721-1926	Y
ClearBridge Large Cap Value Fund Class I	SAIFX	B	B-	B		4.72	7.10	14.44	24.74	88.81	33.16	1,746	877-721-1926	Y
ClearBridge Large Cap Value Fund Class IS	LMLSX	B-	B-	B-	Down	4.73	7.13	14.51	25.01	89.20	33.17	1,746	877-721-1926	Y
ClearBridge Large Cap Value Fund Class R	LCBVX	B-	C+	B-	Down	4.52	6.77	13.66	21.80	82.25	33.24	1,746	877-721-1926	Y
Columbia Disciplined Value Fund Advisor Class	COLEX	B	B-	B	Up	6.80	12.22	17.98	27.75	102.55	10.68	853.1	800-345-6611	Y
Columbia Disciplined Value Fund Class A	RLCAX	B	B-	B	Up	6.81	12.17	17.74	26.94	100.65	10.6	853.1	800-345-6611	Y
Columbia Disciplined Value Fund Class C	RDCCX	B-	B-	B	Down	6.52	11.68	16.87	24.05	93.25	10.36	853.1	800-345-6611	Y
Columbia Disciplined Value Fund Class K	RLCYX	B	B-	B	Up	6.88	12.22	17.87	27.36	101.93	10.66	853.1	800-345-6611	
Columbia Disciplined Value Fund Class R	RLCOX	B	B-	B	Up	6.64	11.89	17.43	25.84	98.29	10.62	853.1	800-345-6611	Y
Columbia Disciplined Value Fund Class T	RLCWX	B	B-	B	Up	6.76	12.10	17.63	26.76	100.61	10.66	853.1	800-345-6611	Y
Columbia Disciplined Value Fund Class V	CVQTX	B	B-	B	Up	6.83	12.10	17.80	26.87	100.58	10.57	853.1	800-345-6611	
Columbia Disciplined Value Fund Institutional 2 Class	COLVX	B	B-	B	Up	6.90	12.34	18.12	27.93	102.83	10.66	853.1	800-345-6611	Y
Columbia Disciplined Value Fund Institutional 3 Class	COLYX	B	B-	B	Up	6.94	12.37	18.26	28.20	103.25	10.68	853.1	800-345-6611	Y
Columbia Disciplined Value Fund Institutional Class	CVQZX	B	B-	B	Up	6.89	12.21	18.08	27.85	103.15	10.69	853.1	800-345-6611	Y
Columbia Diversified Equity Income Fund Advisor Class	RDERX	B	B	B-	Up	5.79	9.95	16.87	30.20	95.73	14.53	2,419	800-345-6611	Y
Columbia Diversified Equity Income Fund Class A	INDZX	B	B	B	Up	5.72	9.81	16.65	29.30	93.37	14.55	2,419	800-345-6611	Y
Columbia Diversified Equity Income Fund Class C	ADECX	B-	B-	B-	Down	5.53	9.42	15.74	26.42	86.20	14.52	2,419	800-345-6611	Y
Columbia Diversified Equity Income Fund Class K	IDQYX	B	B	B	Up	5.73	9.84	16.63	29.51	94.13	14.55	2,419	800-345-6611	
Columbia Diversified Equity Income Fund Class R	RDEIX	B-	B-	B-	Down	5.69	9.74	16.39	28.35	91.05	14.46	2,419	800-345-6611	Y
Columbia Diversified Equity Income Fund Class T	CDEWX	B-	B	B-	Down	5.70	9.77	16.50	29.05	93.00	14.57	2,419	800-345-6611	Y
Columbia Diversified Equity Income Fund Inst 2 Cls	RSEDX	B	B	B-	Up	5.80	9.98	17.01	30.58	96.76	14.55	2,419	800-345-6611	Y
Columbia Diversified Equity Income Fund Inst 3 Cls	CDEYX	B	B	B-	Up	5.82	10.04	17.04	30.71	97.33	14.7	2,419	800-345-6611	Y
Columbia Diversified Equity Income Fund Institutional Cls	CDVZX	B	B	B	Up	5.79	9.96	16.88	30.22	95.64	14.52	2,419	800-345-6611	Y
Columbia Dividend Income Fund Advisor Class	CVIRX	B	B	B		6.92	11.61	20.80	36.29	102.48	22.41	11,269	800-345-6611	Y
Columbia Dividend Income Fund Class A	LBSAX	B	B	B		6.87	11.41	20.46	35.27	99.78	22.04	11,269	800-345-6611	Y
Columbia Dividend Income Fund Class C	LBSCX	B-	B-	B	Down	6.63	11.03	19.52	32.24	92.52	21.37	11,269	800-345-6611	Y
Columbia Dividend Income Fund Class R	CDIRX	B	B-	B		6.80	11.31	20.15	34.31	97.47	22.06	11,269	800-345-6611	Y
Columbia Dividend Income Fund Class T	CDVWX	B	B	B		6.87	11.47	20.47	35.29	99.75	22.03	11,269	800-345-6611	Y
Columbia Dividend Income Fund Class V	GEQAX	B	B	B		6.87	11.46	20.45	35.24	99.64	22.05	11,269	800-345-6611	
Columbia Dividend Income Fund Institutional 2 Class	CDDRX	B	B	B		6.95	11.61	20.88	36.82	103.72	22.39	11,269	800-345-6611	Y
Columbia Dividend Income Fund Institutional 3 Class	CDDYX	B	B	B		6.95	11.66	20.95	37.02	104.27	22.42	11,269	800-345-6611	Y

Category: US Equity
Large Cap Value (con't)

Fund Name	Ticker Symbol	RATINGS: Overall Rating	Reward Rating	Risk Rating	Recent Up/ Downgrade	TOTAL RETURNS & PERFORMANCE: 3-Month Total Return	6-Month Total Return	1-Year Total Return	3-Year Total Return	5-Year Total Return	ASSETS: NAV	Total Assets (MIL)	NEW INVESTORS: Telephone	Open to New Investors
Columbia Dividend Income Fund Institutional Class	GSFTX	B	B	B		6.93	11.59	20.74	36.32	102.42	22.06	11,269	800-345-6611	Y
Columbia Dividend Opportunity Fund Advisor Class	CDORX	B-	B-	B	Down	5.57	8.87	14.55	25.85	78.52	9.86	3,781	800-345-6611	Y
Columbia Dividend Opportunity Fund Class A	INUTX	B-	C+	B	Down	5.49	8.79	14.29	24.85	76.40	9.69	3,781	800-345-6611	Y
Columbia Dividend Opportunity Fund Class C	ACUIX	B-	C+	B	Down	5.41	8.45	13.50	22.19	70.08	9.49	3,781	800-345-6611	Y
Columbia Dividend Opportunity Fund Class K	RSORX	B-	C+	B	Down	5.58	8.87	14.39	25.26	77.37	9.75	3,781	800-345-6611	
Columbia Dividend Opportunity Fund Class R	RSOOX	B-	C+	B	Down	5.53	8.65	14.01	24.06	74.23	9.69	3,781	800-345-6611	Y
Columbia Dividend Opportunity Fund Class T	CDOWX	B-	C+	B	Down	5.59	8.77	14.26	24.94	76.35	9.71	3,781	800-345-6611	Y
Columbia Dividend Opportunity Fund Institutional 2 Class	RSDFX	B-	B-	B	Down	5.64	8.89	14.55	26.19	79.57	9.75	3,781	800-345-6611	Y
Columbia Dividend Opportunity Fund Institutional 3 Class	CDOYX	B-	B-	B	Down	5.69	9.02	14.75	26.40	79.93	9.89	3,781	800-345-6611	Y
Columbia Dividend Opportunity Fund Institutional Class	CDOZX	B-	B-	B	Down	5.53	8.88	14.51	25.80	78.65	9.73	3,781	800-345-6611	Y
Columbia Select Large-Cap Value Fund Advisor Class	CSERX	B	B	B-	Up	7.86	13.50	20.36	35.78	114.14	27.55	1,001	800-345-6611	Y
Columbia Select Large-Cap Value Fund Class A	SLVAX	B	B	B-	Up	7.77	13.37	20.05	34.75	111.37	26.23	1,001	800-345-6611	Y
Columbia Select Large-Cap Value Fund Class C	SVLCX	B	B	C+	Up	7.58	12.94	19.20	31.80	103.59	24.09	1,001	800-345-6611	Y
Columbia Select Large-Cap Value Fund Class K	SLVTX	B	B	C+	Up	7.80	13.40	20.18	35.15	112.48	27.08	1,001	800-345-6611	
Columbia Select Large-Cap Value Fund Class R	SLVRX	B	B	B-	Up	7.68	13.18	19.75	33.73	108.72	25.83	1,001	800-345-6611	Y
Columbia Select Large-Cap Value Fund Class T	CSVWX	B	B	C+	Up	7.78	13.32	20.04	34.70	111.07	26.06	1,001	800-345-6611	Y
Columbia Select Large-Cap Value Fund Institutional 2 Class	SLVIX	B	B	B-	Up	7.84	13.50	20.44	36.13	115.02	27.2	1,001	800-345-6611	Y
Columbia Select Large-Cap Value Fund Institutional 3 Class	CSRYX	B	B	C+	Up	7.84	13.55	20.49	36.38	114.12	27.61	1,001	800-345-6611	Y
Columbia Select Large-Cap Value Fund Institutional Class	CSVZX	B	B	B-	Up	7.84	13.51	20.36	35.80	114.06	27.2	1,001	800-345-6611	Y
Commerce Value Fund	CFVLX	B	B-	B+		6.17	11.05	12.86	31.94	96.90	31.49	254.9		Y
Copley Fund	COPLX	B	B	B		2.25	6.33	9.67	22.65	69.40	88.41	86.6	877-881-2751	Y
CornerCap Large/Mid-Cap Value Fund	CMCRX	B-	B-	C+	Down	7.26	13.29	21.55	23.95	99.77	13.5	30.7	888-813-8637	Y
Cullen High Dividend Equity Fund Class C	CHVCX	B-	B-	B	Down	3.82	7.13	15.68	24.71	72.88	18.24	1,882	800-582-6757	Y
Cullen High Dividend Equity Fund Class Institutional	CHDVX	B-	B-	B	Down	4.08	7.88	17.12	28.52	81.73	18.42	1,882	800-582-6757	Y
Cullen High Dividend Equity Fund Class R1	CHDRX	B-	B-	B	Down	3.90	7.50	16.26	25.69	74.99	16.02	1,882	800-582-6757	Y
Cullen High Dividend Equity Fund Class R2	CHDPX	B-	B-	B	Down	3.98	7.67	16.52	26.60	76.72	16.22	1,882	800-582-6757	Y
Cullen High Dividend Equity Fund Retail Class	CHDEX	B-	B-	B	Down	4.02	7.76	16.77	27.53	79.31	18.41	1,882	800-582-6757	Y
Cullen Value Fund Class C	CVLFX	B-	B-	B-	Down	4.53	8.98	16.76	27.84	82.18	15.63	34.2	800-582-6757	Y
Cullen Value Fund Class I	CVLVX	B-	B-	B-	Down	4.78	9.51	17.91	31.72	91.50	15.64	34.2	800-582-6757	Y
Cullen Value Fund Retail Class	CVLEX	B-	B-	B-	Down	4.72	9.37	17.60	30.71	89.31	15.65	34.2	800-582-6757	Y
Cutler Equity Fund	CALEX	B-	B-	B	Down	10.02	14.47	17.82	30.66	89.45	20.64	157.6		Y
Davenport Value & Income Fund	DVIPX	B-	B-	B-	Down	6.58	11.15	18.22	31.04	95.93	17.55	648.5		Y
Day Hagan Logix Tactical Dividend Fund Class A	DHQAX	B	C+	B+	Up	6.02	8.32	10.12	17.95		11.47	135.8		Y
Day Hagan Logix Tactical Dividend Fund Class C	DHQCX	B-	C+	B+	Up	5.76	7.85	9.30	15.34		11.25	135.8		Y
Day Hagan Logix Tactical Dividend Fund Class I	DHQIX	B	C+	B+	Up	6.08	8.34	10.30	18.76		11.5	135.8		Y
Delaware Value® Fund Class A	DDVAX	B	B-	B+		5.39	10.37	13.36	27.63	97.36	21.48	12,711		
Delaware Value® Fund Class C	DDVCX	B	C+	B		5.21	9.98	12.50	24.81	90.10	21.44	12,711		
Delaware Value® Fund Class R	DDVRX	B	B-	B		5.32	10.24	13.09	26.69	94.79	21.47	12,711		Y
Delaware Value® Fund Class R6	DDZRX	B	B-	B+		4.50	9.54	12.71	27.62	98.18	21.48	12,711		Y
Delaware Value® Fund Institutional Class	DDVIX	B	B-	B+		5.45	10.50	13.64	28.64	99.76	21.48	12,711		
Deutsche CROCI® Equity Dividend Fund Class A	KDHAX	B-	B	C+	Down	5.11	9.40	19.24	30.59	86.95	57.51	1,134	201-593-8273	Y
Deutsche CROCI® Equity Dividend Fund Class C	KDHCX	B-	B-	C+	Down	4.93	9.01	18.35	27.69	80.06	57.37	1,134	201-593-8273	Y
Deutsche CROCI® Equity Dividend Fund Class R	KDHRX	B-	B	C+	Down	5.06	9.26	18.94	29.62	84.64	57.39	1,134	201-593-8273	Y
Deutsche CROCI® Equity Dividend Fund Class R6	KDHTX	B-	B	C+	Down	5.21	9.61	19.67	31.63	88.44	57.55	1,134	201-593-8273	Y
Deutsche CROCI® Equity Dividend Fund Class S	KDHSX	B-	B	C+	Down	5.20	9.56	19.54	31.58	89.32	57.51	1,134	201-593-8273	Y
Deutsche CROCI® Equity Dividend Fund Class T	KDHUX	B-	B	C+	Down	5.13	9.42	19.26	30.58	86.90	57.51	1,134	201-593-8273	Y
Deutsche CROCI® Equity Dividend Fund Institutional Class	KDHIX	B-	B	C+	Down	5.19	9.55	19.56	31.59	89.48	57.53	1,134	201-593-8273	Y
DFA Tax-Managed U.S. Marketwide Value Portfolio	DTMMX	B	B	B	Up	6.54	11.01	17.00	31.95	109.67	30.92	5,038	512-306-7400	Y
DFA Tax-Managed U.S. Marketwide Value Portfolio II	DFMVX	B	B	B	Up	6.56	11.06	17.15	32.48	111.16	28.8	1,882	512-306-7400	
DFA Tax-Managed U.S. Marketwide Value Portfolio II	DFCVX	B	B	B	Up	7.49	12.52	19.13	35.56	116.21	18.72	1,882	512-306-7400	
DFA U.S. Large Cap Value III Portfolio	DFUVX	B	B	B	Up	7.50	12.51	19.10	35.65	116.47	27.01	3,849	512-306-7400	
DFA U.S. Large Cap Value Portfolio Institutional Class	DFLVX	B	B	B	Up	7.46	12.42	18.96	35.07	114.95	39.12	24,727	512-306-7400	Y

Category: US Equity Large Cap Value (con't)

		RATINGS				TOTAL RETURNS & PERFORMANCE					ASSETS		NEW INVESTORS	
Fund Name	Ticker Symbol	Overall Rating	Reward Rating	Risk Rating	Recent Up/ Downgrade	3-Month Total Return	6-Month Total Return	1-Year Total Return	3-Year Total Return	5-Year Total Return	NAV	Total Assets (MIL)	Telephone	Open to New Investors
DGHM All-Cap Value Fund Class C	DGACX	B-	C+	B-	Up	4.93	7.72	9.66	17.08	76.25	7.1	10.8	212-557-2445	Y
DGHM All-Cap Value Fund Institutional Class	DGAIX	B-	C+	B-	Up	5.26	8.29	10.84	20.85	85.74	8	10.8	212-557-2445	Y
DGHM All-Cap Value Fund Investor Class	DGHMX	B-	C+	B-	Up	5.05	7.96	10.38	19.32	82.32	7.95	10.8	212-557-2445	Y
Diamond Hill Large Cap Fund Class A	DHLAX	B	B	B-		5.61	9.62	19.94	34.18	106.79	26.45	5,748	888-226-5595	Y
Diamond Hill Large Cap Fund Class C	DHLCX	B-	B-	B-	Down	5.43	9.23	19.03	31.19	99.18	25.07	5,748	888-226-5595	Y
Diamond Hill Large Cap Fund Class I	DHLRX	B	B	B-		5.72	9.84	20.30	35.36	109.60	26.62	5,748	888-226-5595	Y
Diamond Hill Large Cap Fund Class Y	DHLYX	B	B	B-		5.74	9.86	20.41	35.83	110.95	26.64	5,748	888-226-5595	Y
Dodge & Cox Stock Fund	DODGX	B	B	B	Up	5.74	10.78	18.32	35.77	116.29	203.61	69,876	415-981-1710	Y
DoubleLine Shiller Enhanced CAPE® Class I	DSEEX	B	B	B+	Down	5.68	8.67	21.59	51.30		15.27	4,743	877-354-6311	Y
DoubleLine Shiller Enhanced CAPE® Class N	DSENX	B	B	B+	Down	5.62	8.54	21.32	50.24		15.26	4,743	877-354-6311	Y
Dreyfus Equity Income Fund Class A	DQIAX	B	B-	B		5.91	10.13	16.98	30.08	94.55	18.99	372.6	800-645-6561	Y
Dreyfus Equity Income Fund Class C	DQICX	B-	B-	B-	Down	5.72	9.72	16.15	27.26	87.43	18.76	372.6	800-645-6561	Y
Dreyfus Equity Income Fund Class I	DQIRX	B-	B-	B-	Down	5.99	10.33	17.36	31.12	97.06	19.03	372.6	800-645-6561	Y
Dreyfus Equity Income Fund Class Y	DQIYX	B-	B-	B-	Down	5.97	10.30	17.71	31.69	97.50	19.07	372.6	800-645-6561	Y
Dreyfus Strategic Value Fund Class A	DAGVX	B	B	B	Up	7.52	11.64	14.84	31.21	105.23	40.09	1,905	800-645-6561	Y
Dreyfus Strategic Value Fund Class C	DCGVX	B	B-	B	Up	7.31	11.22	13.97	28.27	97.68	37.43	1,905	800-645-6561	Y
Dreyfus Strategic Value Fund Class I	DRGVX	B	B	B	Up	7.58	11.78	15.13	32.19	107.82	40.16	1,905	800-645-6561	Y
Dreyfus Strategic Value Fund Class Y	DRGYX	B	B	B	Up	7.62	11.82	15.16	32.23	107.59	40.17	1,905	800-645-6561	Y
Dunham Large Cap Value Fund Class A	DALVX	B-	C+	B	Down	6.31	10.86	14.90	23.20	78.92	14.55	73.0	800-442-4358	Y
Dunham Large Cap Value Fund Class C	DCLVX	B-	C+	B	Down	6.08	10.40	14.05	20.47	72.31	13.96	73.0	800-442-4358	Y
Dunham Large Cap Value Fund Class N	DNLVX	B	B-	B	Up	6.42	11.03	15.25	24.12	81.28	14.6	73.0	800-442-4358	Y
Eaton Vance Focused Value Opportunities Fund Class A	EAFVX	B-	B-	B-	Down	8.57	12.36	20.12	27.23	89.93	16.65	66.3		Y
Eaton Vance Focused Value Opportunities Fund Class C	ECFVX	B-	C+	B	Down	8.41	11.94	19.29	24.51	82.99	16.42	66.3		Y
Eaton Vance Focused Value Opportunities Fund Class I	EIFVX	B	B-	B	Up	8.64	12.50	20.42	28.24	92.46	16.67	66.3		Y
Eaton Vance Large-Cap Value Fund Class A	EHSTX	B-	C+	B	Down	6.71	10.27	14.80	23.11	81.27	19.52	2,198		Y
Eaton Vance Large-Cap Value Fund Class C	ECSTX	B-	C+	B	Down	6.50	9.89	13.96	20.38	74.59	19.54	2,198		Y
Eaton Vance Large-Cap Value Fund Class I	EILVX	B	C+	B	Up	6.76	10.37	15.09	24.01	83.54	19.59	2,198		Y
Eaton Vance Large-Cap Value Fund Class R	ERSTX	B-	C+	B	Down	6.61	10.10	14.49	22.19	78.95	19.46	2,198		Y
Eaton Vance Large-Cap Value Fund Class R6	ERLVX	B	C+	B	Up	6.78	10.48	15.24	24.40	83.39	19.61	2,198		Y
Eaton Vance Tax-Managed Value Fund Class A	EATVX	B-	B-	B-	Down	8.17	12.12	17.65	24.98	86.88	26.45	599.2		Y
Eaton Vance Tax-Managed Value Fund Class C	ECTVX	B-	C+	B	Down	7.96	11.69	16.76	22.20	80.05	25.44	599.2		Y
Eaton Vance Tax-Managed Value Fund Class I	EITVX	B	B-	B	Up	8.20	12.26	17.93	25.80	89.16	26.31	599.2		Y
Edgar Lomax Value Fund	LOMAX	B-	B-	B	Down	7.56	13.68	19.48	31.02	103.63	14.86	85.2	703-719-0026	Y
EIC Value Fund Class A	EICVX	B-	C+	B	Down	6.63	9.66	14.15	18.64	67.53	14.6	253.7	404-239-0111	Y
EIC Value Fund Class C	EICCX	B-	C+	B-	Down	6.48	9.23	13.27	16.04	61.45	14.42	253.7	404-239-0111	Y
EIC Value Fund Institutional Class	EICIX	B-	C+	B	Down	6.69	9.78	14.41	19.56	69.63	14.63	253.7	404-239-0111	Y
EQ/Invesco Comstock Portfolio Class IA	US2689401527	B	B	B-	Up	7.93	14.53	18.28	28.94	95.20		232.9	877-222-2144	Y
EQ/Invesco Comstock Portfolio Class IB	US2689401451	B	B	B-	Up	7.92	14.52	18.27	28.83	95.11		232.9	877-222-2144	Y
EQ/Invesco Comstock Portfolio Class K	US26883L3731	B	B	B-	Up	8.00	14.68	18.60	29.88	97.24		232.9	877-222-2144	Y
EQ/JPMorgan Value Opportunities Portfolio Class IA	US2689403010	B	B	B		7.80	11.62	18.04	39.06	122.03		665.9	877-222-2144	Y
EQ/JPMorgan Value Opportunities Portfolio Class IB	US2689408225	B	B	B		7.78	11.65	18.05	38.94	121.89		665.9	877-222-2144	Y
EQ/JPMorgan Value Opportunities Portfolio Class K	US26883L5710	B	B	B		7.89	11.76	18.37	40.10	124.81		665.9	877-222-2144	Y
EQ/Large Cap Value Index Portfolio Class IA	US2689547089	B-	B-	B	Down	5.64	8.97	13.26	24.67	90.28		670.8	877-222-2144	Y
EQ/Large Cap Value Index Portfolio Class IB	US2689548079	B-	B-	B	Down	5.66	8.88	13.30	24.60	90.39		670.8	877-222-2144	Y
EQ/Large Cap Value Index Portfolio Class K	US26883L5306	B-	B-	B	Down	5.69	9.03	13.59	25.41	91.41		670.8	877-222-2144	Y
EquityCompass Quality Dividend Fund Class A	QDVAX	B-	B-	B-	Down	4.62	8.52	13.75	22.42		13.13	75.5	443-224-1231	Y
EquityCompass Quality Dividend Fund Class C	QDVCX	B-	C+	B-	Down	4.49	8.16	12.93	19.75		13.19	75.5	443-224-1231	Y
EquityCompass Quality Dividend Fund Institutional Class	QDVIX	B-	B-	B-	Down	4.76	8.74	14.12	22.89		13.14	75.5	443-224-1231	Y
FDP BlackRock Equity Dividend Fund Institutional Shares	MAVVX	B-	B	B-	Up	5.97	12.28	16.00	26.22	90.49	16.39	89.9		Y
FDP BlackRock Equity Dividend Fund Investor A Shares	MDVVX	B-	B-	B-	Up	5.87	12.09	15.71	25.30	88.02	16.22	89.9		Y
FDP BlackRock Equity Dividend Fund Investor C Shares	MCVVX	B-	B-	B-	Up	5.73	11.71	14.88	22.51	81.07	15.86	89.9		Y
Federated Equity Income Fund, Inc. Class A Shares	LEIFX	B-	C+	B	Up	6.87	11.42	16.05	18.78	73.40	25.31	1,174	800-341-7400	Y

Category: US Equity Large Cap Value (con't)

Fund Name	Ticker Symbol	RATINGS: Overall Rating	RATINGS: Reward Rating	RATINGS: Risk Rating	RATINGS: Recent Up/ Downgrade	TOTAL RETURNS & PERFORMANCE: 3-Month Total Return	6-Month Total Return	1-Year Total Return	3-Year Total Return	5-Year Total Return	ASSETS: NAV	Total Assets (MIL)	NEW INVESTORS: Telephone	Open to New Investors
Federated Equity Income Fund, Inc. Class B Shares	LEIBX	B-	C+	B	Up	6.68	11.01	15.19	15.97	66.72	25.23	1,174	800-341-7400	Y
Federated Equity Income Fund, Inc. Class C Shares	LEICX	B-	C+	B	Up	6.68	11.02	15.16	16.07	66.91	25.26	1,174	800-341-7400	Y
Federated Equity Income Fund, Inc. Class F Shares	LFEIX	B-	C+	B	Up	6.80	11.32	15.81	17.90	71.33	25.33	1,174	800-341-7400	Y
Federated Equity Income Fund, Inc. Class R Shares	FDERX	B-	C+	B	Up	6.83	11.33	15.86	18.16	71.97	25.31	1,174	800-341-7400	Y
Federated Equity Income Fund, Inc. Institutional Shares	LEISX	B-	C+	B	Up	6.94	11.56	16.34	19.65	75.59	25.3	1,174	800-341-7400	Y
Federated MDT All Cap Core Fund Class A Shares	QAACX	B	B	B	Up	6.71	13.52	20.72	28.03	108.21	27.46	145.7	800-341-7400	Y
Federated MDT All Cap Core Fund Class C Shares	QCACX	B	B-	B	Up	6.49	13.10	19.86	25.13	100.34	26.07	145.7	800-341-7400	Y
Federated MDT All Cap Core Fund Class R6 Shares	QKACX	B-	B	C+	Down	6.80	13.69	21.15	27.56	105.54	27.3	145.7	800-341-7400	Y
Federated MDT All Cap Core Fund Institutional Shares	QIACX	B-	B	C+	Down	6.76	13.67	21.06	29.13	111.19	27.74	145.7	800-341-7400	Y
Federated MDT Large Cap Value Fund Class A	FSTRX	B-	B-	B	Down	6.69	10.97	14.23	23.75	103.67		733.5	800-341-7400	Y
Federated MDT Large Cap Value Fund Class R6	FSTLX	B	B-	B	Up	6.22	10.44	14.43	23.92	103.36	28.18	733.5	800-341-7400	Y
Federated MDT Large Cap Value Fund Institutional Shares	FMSTX	B	B-	B	Up	6.17	10.42	14.36	24.26	104.72	28.17	733.5	800-341-7400	Y
Federated MDT Large Cap Value Fund Service Shares	FSTKX	B-	B-	B	Down	6.15	10.29	14.11	23.46	102.61	28.19	733.5	800-341-7400	Y
Federated Strategic Value Dividend Fund Class A Shares	SVAAX	B	B-	A	Up	3.13	5.89	14.73	29.65	78.88	6.12	14,186	800-341-7400	Y
Federated Strategic Value Dividend Fund Class C Shares	SVACX	B	C+	A	Up	2.92	5.48	13.84	26.73	72.20	6.13	14,186	800-341-7400	Y
Federated Strategic Value Dividend Fund Class R6	SVALX	B	B-	A	Up	3.18	6.00	15.15	30.50	81.03	6.15	14,186	800-341-7400	Y
Federated Strategic Value Dividend Fund Inst Shares	SVAIX	B	B-	A	Up	3.18	5.99	15.13	30.47	80.99	6.15	14,186	800-341-7400	Y
Fidelity Advisor® Equity Income Fund Class A	FEIAX	B-	B-	B	Down	4.77	7.99	12.29	25.08	76.71	32.38	1,949	617-563-7000	Y
Fidelity Advisor® Equity Income Fund Class C	FEICX	B-	C+	B	Down	4.56	7.56	11.44	22.22	70.06	32.62	1,949	617-563-7000	Y
Fidelity Advisor® Equity Income Fund Class M	FEIRX	B-	C+	B	Down	4.69	7.84	12.02	24.19	74.68	33.1	1,949	617-563-7000	Y
Fidelity Advisor® Equity Income Fund Class Z	FZAGX	B-	B-	B	Down	4.87	8.19	12.74	26.64	80.14	33.8	1,949	617-563-7000	Y
Fidelity Advisor® Equity Income Fund I Class	EQPIX	B-	B-	B	Down	4.83	8.14	12.57	26.05	78.98	33.83	1,949	617-563-7000	Y
Fidelity Advisor® Equity Value Fund Class A	FAVAX	B	B-	B	Up	4.87	7.28	13.79	23.08	93.42	18.98	283.1	617-563-7000	Y
Fidelity Advisor® Equity Value Fund Class C	FAVCX	B-	C+	B	Down	4.64	6.87	12.89	20.26	86.19	18.59	283.1	617-563-7000	Y
Fidelity Advisor® Equity Value Fund Class M	FAVTX	B-	C+	B	Down	4.81	7.16	13.46	22.11	91.05	18.99	283.1	617-563-7000	Y
Fidelity Advisor® Equity Value Fund Class Z	FAEVX	B	B-	B	Up	4.92	7.52	14.19	24.28	96.57	19.26	283.1	617-563-7000	Y
Fidelity Advisor® Equity Value Fund I Class	FAIVX	B	B-	B	Up	4.93	7.47	14.07	24.15	96.37	19.26	283.1	617-563-7000	Y
Fidelity Advisor® Series Equity-Income Fund	FLMLX	B-	B-	B	Down	5.11	7.32	11.61	26.11	83.24	12.94	1,128	617-563-7000	Y
Fidelity Advisor® Ser Stock Selector Large Cap Value Fund	FMMLX	B-	B-	B	Down	4.14	7.82	11.83	22.36	88.74	13.11	1,134	617-563-7000	Y
Fidelity Advisor® Stock Selector Large Cap Value Cls A	FLUAX	B-	B-	B	Down	4.11	8.07	11.94	23.16	88.34	20.58	1,153	617-563-7000	Y
Fidelity Advisor® Stock Selector Large Cap Value Cls C	FLUEX	B-	C+	B	Down	3.95	7.61	11.05	20.17	80.80	20.16	1,153	617-563-7000	Y
Fidelity Advisor® Stock Selector Large Cap Value Cls I	FLUIX	B-	B-	B	Down	4.24	8.19	12.24	24.15	90.80	20.6	1,153	617-563-7000	Y
Fidelity Advisor® Stock Selector Large Cap Value Cls M	FLUTX	B-	C+	B	Down	4.04	7.90	11.63	21.96	85.44	20.56	1,153	617-563-7000	Y
Fidelity Advisor® Stock Selector Large Cap Value Cls Z	FSCZX	B-	B-	B	Down	4.23	8.29	12.41	24.38	91.36	20.61	1,153	617-563-7000	Y
Fidelity Advisor® Value Leaders Fund Class A	FVLAX	B	C+	B	Up	5.54	7.85	14.41	22.54	90.67	19.62	34.1	617-563-7000	Y
Fidelity Advisor® Value Leaders Fund Class C	FVLCX	B-	C+	B	Down	5.29	7.42	13.56	19.72	83.67	19.09	34.1	617-563-7000	Y
Fidelity Advisor® Value Leaders Fund Class M	FVLTX	B-	C+	B	Down	5.45	7.69	14.10	21.55	88.27	19.69	34.1	617-563-7000	Y
Fidelity Advisor® Value Leaders Fund I Class	FVLIX	B	C+	B	Up	5.59	8.00	14.71	23.43	93.17	19.74	34.1	617-563-7000	Y
Fidelity Advisor® Value Strategies Fund Class A	FSOAX	B	B-	B	Up	4.99	8.85	18.85	26.95	80.03	36.18	1,118	617-563-7000	Y
Fidelity Advisor® Value Strategies Fund Class C	FVCSX	B-	B-	B	Up	4.78	8.40	17.91	24.03	73.24	31.5	1,118	617-563-7000	Y
Fidelity Advisor® Value Strategies Fund Class I	FASOX	B	B-	B	Up	5.07	8.97	19.14	27.88	82.31	39.52	1,118	617-563-7000	Y
Fidelity Advisor® Value Strategies Fund Class K	FVSKX	B	B-	B	Up	5.10	9.03	19.30	28.55	83.92	42.02	1,118	617-563-7000	Y
Fidelity Advisor® Value Strategies Fund Class M	FASPX	B	B-	B	Up	4.95	8.71	18.59	26.11	78.12	38.08	1,118	617-563-7000	Y
Fidelity® Blue Chip Value Fund	FBCVX	B	B-	B	Up	5.68	8.10	14.87	24.23	95.69	19.6	393.4	617-563-7000	Y
Fidelity® Equity Dividend Income Fund	FEQTX	B	B-	B		5.39	9.18	14.09	27.60	88.20	27.77	5,588	617-563-7000	Y
Fidelity® Equity Dividend Income Fund Class K	FETKX	B	B-	B		5.44	9.22	14.20	28.00	89.18	27.77	5,588	617-563-7000	Y
Fidelity® Equity-Income Fund	FEQIX	B-	B-	B	Down	5.09	8.30	13.35	27.25	80.47	60.7	7,267	617-563-7000	Y
Fidelity® Equity-Income Fund Class K	FEIKX	B-	B-	B	Down	5.13	8.35	13.46	27.68	81.53	60.66	7,267	617-563-7000	Y
Fidelity® Large Cap Value Enhanced Index Fund	FLVEX	B	B-	B		6.61	11.36	15.88	28.71	102.28	13.2	3,362	617-563-7000	Y
Fidelity® Series 1000 Value Index Fund	FIOOX	B	B-	B		5.37	8.57	13.68	26.64		12.73	3,903	617-563-7000	Y
Fidelity® Series Stock Selector Large Cap Value Fund	FBLEX	B-	B-	B	Down	4.57	8.32	12.38	22.48	88.79	13.01	9,963	617-563-7000	Y
Fidelity® Series Value Discovery Fund	FNKLX	B-	B-	B	Down	5.05	7.20	11.51	25.92	83.10	13.36	7,072	617-563-7000	Y

Category: US Equity Large Cap Value (con't)

Fund Name	Ticker Symbol	RATINGS: Overall Rating	RATINGS: Reward Rating	RATINGS: Risk Rating	RATINGS: Recent Up/ Downgrade	TOTAL RETURNS & PERFORMANCE: 3-Month Total Return	6-Month Total Return	1-Year Total Return	3-Year Total Return	5-Year Total Return	ASSETS: NAV	Total Assets (MIL)	NEW INVESTORS: Telephone	Open to New Investors
Fidelity® Stock Selector Large Cap Value Fund	FSLVX	B-	B-	B	Down	4.24	8.22	12.33	24.28	91.21	20.72	1,153	617-563-7000	Y
Fidelity® Value Discovery Fund	FVDFX	B	B-	B	Up	4.93	7.40	14.17	24.48	97.58	28.93	3,690	617-563-7000	Y
Fidelity® Value Discovery Fund Class K	FVDKX	B	B-	B	Up	4.94	7.47	14.28	24.97	99.06	28.94	3,690	617-563-7000	Y
Fidelity® Value Strategies Fund	FSLSX	B	B-	B	Up	5.07	8.97	19.17	28.03	82.58	42.08	1,118	617-563-7000	Y
First Investors Equity Income Fund Advisor Class	FIUUX	B-	B-	B-	Down	5.28	9.31	15.52	28.13	83.84	10.93	664.4	800-423-4026	Y
First Investors Equity Income Fund Class A	FIUTX	B-	B-	B-	Down	5.14	9.12	15.06	26.65	81.19	10.86	664.4	800-423-4026	Y
First Investors Equity Income Fund Class B	FIUBX	B-	C+	B-	Down	5.04	8.67	14.09	23.57	73.98	10.64	664.4	800-423-4026	Y
First Investors Equity Income Fund Institutional Class	FIUVX	B-	B-	B-	Down	5.32	9.35	15.49	28.22	84.55	10.88	664.4	800-423-4026	Y
Franklin Equity Income Fund Advisor Class	FEIFX	B-	B-	B	Down	5.60	10.07	16.25	28.34	85.91	25.17	2,157	650-312-2000	Y
Franklin Equity Income Fund Class A	FISEX	B-	B-	B	Down	5.49	9.89	15.95	27.36	83.57	25.13	2,157	650-312-2000	Y
Franklin Equity Income Fund Class C	FRETX	B-	B-	B	Down	5.27	9.49	15.07	24.55	76.81	24.95	2,157	650-312-2000	Y
Franklin Equity Income Fund Class R	FREIX	B-	B-	B	Down	5.41	9.79	15.68	26.46	81.26	25.13	2,157	650-312-2000	Y
Franklin Equity Income Fund Class R6	FEIQX	B-	B-	B	Down	5.62	10.12	16.41	28.86	86.79	25.17	2,189	650-312-2000	Y
Frost Value Equity Fund Class Institutional	FIDVX	B	B	B-	Up	4.77	9.89	19.47	29.27	97.06	9.11	112.3		Y
Frost Value Equity Fund Investor Class Shares	FADVX	B	B	B-	Up	4.71	9.78	19.20	28.36	94.55	9.1	112.3		Y
Glenmede Fund Large Cap Value Portfolio	GTMEX	B	B	B	Up	6.76	11.08	15.84	30.16	100.18	11.07	77.5	800-442-8299	Y
Goldman Sachs Equity Income Fund Class A	GSGRX	B-	C+	B	Up	4.02	6.89	10.36	19.96	81.42	37.29	396.3	800-526-7384	Y
Goldman Sachs Equity Income Fund Class C	GSGCX	B-	C+	B	Up	3.81	6.48	9.54	17.27	74.72	35.55	396.3	800-526-7384	Y
Goldman Sachs Equity Income Fund Class R	GRGRX	B-	C+	B	Up	3.96	6.74	10.11	19.05	79.13	37.11	396.3	800-526-7384	Y
Goldman Sachs Equity Income Fund Class R6	GRGUX	B-	C+	B		4.11	7.11	10.81	21.15	83.21	37.9	396.3	800-526-7384	Y
Goldman Sachs Equity Income Fund Institutional Class	GSIIX	B-	C+	B	Down	4.11	7.08	10.80	21.39	84.99	37.9	396.3	800-526-7384	Y
Goldman Sachs Equity Income Fund Investor Class	GRGTX	B-	C+	B		4.09	7.02	10.64	20.84	83.64	37.22	396.3	800-526-7384	Y
Goldman Sachs Equity Income Fund Service Class	GSGSX	B-	C+	B	Up	4.00	6.84	10.28	19.60	80.50	37.42	396.3	800-526-7384	Y
Goldman Sachs Large Cap Value Fund Class A	GSLAX	B-	C+	B	Up	2.79	3.90	9.32	14.91	75.59	15.64	852.6	800-526-7384	Y
Goldman Sachs Large Cap Value Fund Class R	GSVRX	B-	C+	B	Up	2.73	3.81	9.08	14.05	73.41	15.23	852.6	800-526-7384	Y
Goldman Sachs Large Cap Value Fund Class R6	GSVUX	B-	C+	B	Up	2.85	4.12	9.95	16.49	79.41	16.09	852.6	800-526-7384	Y
Goldman Sachs Large Cap Value Fund Institutional Class	GSLIX	B-	C+	B	Up	2.87	4.09	9.73	16.17	78.93	15.76	852.6	800-526-7384	Y
Goldman Sachs Large Cap Value Fund Investor Class	GSVTX	B-	C+	B	Up	2.84	4.07	9.62	15.74	77.67	15.62	852.6	800-526-7384	Y
Goldman Sachs Large Cap Value Fund Service Class	GSVSX	B-	C+	B	Up	2.75	3.81	9.19	14.46	74.48	15.53	852.6	800-526-7384	Y
Goldman Sachs Large Cap Value Insights Fund Class A	GCVAX	B	B	B	Up	5.74	11.36	18.94	30.75	105.42	21.93	395.4	800-526-7384	Y
Goldman Sachs Large Cap Value Insights Fund Class C	GCVCX	B-	B-	B-	Down	5.55	11.00	18.10	27.89	97.91	21.75	395.4	800-526-7384	Y
Goldman Sachs Large Cap Value Insights Fund Class R	GCVRX	B	B	B-	Up	5.67	11.19	18.67	29.75	102.93	21.8	395.4	800-526-7384	Y
Goldman Sachs Large Cap Value Insights Fund Class R6	GCVUX	B	B	B-	Up	5.87	11.61	19.46	32.34	109.57	21.9	395.4	800-526-7384	Y
Goldman Sachs Large Cap Value Insights Fund Inst Cls	GCVIX	B	B	B-	Up	5.86	11.60	19.43	32.36	109.59	21.91	395.4	800-526-7384	Y
Goldman Sachs Large Cap Value Insights Fund Investor Class	GCVTX	B	B	B-	Up	5.84	11.50	19.28	31.75	108.09	21.86	395.4	800-526-7384	Y
Goldman Sachs Large Cap Value Insights Fund Service Class	GCLSX	B	B	B	Up	5.69	11.31	18.81	30.34	104.50	22.02	395.4	800-526-7384	Y
Great Lakes Large Cap Value Fund Institutional Cls Shares	GLLIX	B	B	B-		5.10	10.56	18.30	33.87	101.79	15.11	54.0		Y
Great-West Putnam Equity Income Fund Institutional Class	MXQCX	B-	B-	B-	Down	6.79	12.19	19.26	29.78	97.87		649.3		Y
Great-West Putnam Equity Income Fund Investor Class	MXQIX	B-	B-	B-	Down	6.76	12.00	18.90	28.40	95.77		649.3		Y
Great-West T. Rowe Price Equity Income Fund Class L	MXTQX	B-	B-	B-	Down	6.01	10.75	16.02	26.09	79.90		899.5		Y
Great-West T. Rowe Price Equity Income Fund Inst Cls	MXVHX	B-	B	C+	Down	6.10	11.09	16.68	28.46	84.69		899.5		Y
Great-West T. Rowe Price Equity Income Fund Investor Class	MXEQX	B-	B	B-	Down	6.07	10.91	16.40	27.32	83.06		899.5		Y
Guggenheim Large Cap Value Fund Class A	SECIX	B	B	B	Up	6.74	10.84	15.28	30.84	91.45	46.31	68.2	212-739-0700	Y
Guggenheim Large Cap Value Fund Class C	SEGIX	B-	B-	B-	Down	6.52	10.43	14.37	27.84	84.35	42.65	68.2	212-739-0700	Y
Guggenheim Large Cap Value Fund Class Institutional	GILCX	B	B	B		6.79	10.99	15.52	31.74	93.53	45.78	68.2	212-739-0700	Y
Guggenheim Large Cap Value Fund Class P	SEGPX	B	B	B	Up	6.73	10.84	15.23	30.93	91.58	46.24	68.2	212-739-0700	Y
GuideStone Funds Value Equity Fund Institutional Class	GVEYX	B	B-	B	Up	6.12	10.11	15.54	26.04	94.51	22.76	1,503	214-720-1171	Y
GuideStone Funds Value Equity Fund Investor Class	GVEZX	B-	B-	B	Down	6.07	10.01	15.24	25.10	92.03	22.78	1,503	214-720-1171	Y
Hamlin High Dividend Equity Fund Institutional Cls Shares	HHDFX	B-	B-	B		5.50	9.97	14.85	24.54	88.98	23.46	891.0		Y
Hamlin High Dividend Equity Fund Investor Class Shares	HHDVX	B-	C+	B		5.37	9.79	14.38	23.06	84.21	23.49	891.0		Y
Hartford Dividend and Growth HLS Fund Class IA	HIADX	B	B	B-		6.07	10.69	18.35	32.99	102.99	23.95	3,619	888-843-7824	Y
Hartford Dividend and Growth HLS Fund Class IB	HDGBX	B	B	B-		6.07	10.57	18.10	32.02	100.50	23.85	3,619	888-843-7824	Y

Category: US Equity Large Cap Value (con't)

Fund Name	Ticker Symbol	RATINGS Overall Rating	Reward Rating	Risk Rating	Recent Up/ Downgrade	TOTAL RETURNS & PERFORMANCE 3-Month Total Return	6-Month Total Return	1-Year Total Return	3-Year Total Return	5-Year Total Return	ASSETS NAV	Total Assets (MIL)	NEW INVESTORS Telephone	Open to New Investors
Hartford Quality Value Fund Class A	HVOAX	B-	C+	B	Up	4.14	6.58	11.37	23.52	80.43	20.38	274.2	888-843-7824	Y
Hartford Quality Value Fund Class C	HVOCX	B-	C+	B	Up	3.96	6.18	10.52	20.83	73.98	17.55	274.2	888-843-7824	Y
Hartford Quality Value Fund Class F	HVOFX	B-	C+	B	Up	4.16	6.74	11.65	23.84	80.89	20.06	274.2	888-843-7824	Y
Hartford Quality Value Fund Class I	HVOIX	B-	C+	B	Up	4.21	6.74	11.65	24.66	83.29	20.09	274.2	888-843-7824	Y
Hartford Quality Value Fund Class R3	HVORX	B-	C+	B	Up	4.04	6.40	10.94	22.35	77.88	20.71	274.2	888-843-7824	Y
Hartford Quality Value Fund Class R4	HVOSX	B-	C+	B	Up	4.13	6.57	11.36	23.51	80.77	20.87	274.2	888-843-7824	Y
Hartford Quality Value Fund Class R5	HVOTX	B-	C+	B	Up	4.21	6.73	11.66	24.65	83.39	21	274.2	888-843-7824	Y
Hartford Quality Value Fund Class Y	HVOYX	B-	C+	B	Up	4.18	6.75	11.72	25.01	84.06	21.04	274.2	888-843-7824	Y
Hartford Value HLS Fund Class IA	HIAVX	B	B-	B	Up	5.72	8.87	15.43	26.00	89.76	16.05	527.2	888-843-7824	Y
Hartford Value HLS Fund Class IB	HBVLX	B	B-	B	Up	5.60	8.69	15.03	24.95	87.29	16.02	527.2	888-843-7824	Y
HCM Dividend Sector Plus Fund Class A	HCMNX	B-	B-	B-	Up	8.62	12.77	19.09			13.11	318.1	855-969-8464	Y
HCM Dividend Sector Plus Fund Class A1	HCMWX	B-	B-	B-	Up	8.55	12.71	18.83			13.11	318.1	855-969-8464	Y
HCM Dividend Sector Plus Fund Class I	HCMQX	B-	B-	B-	Up	8.62	12.77	19.09			13.11	318.1	855-969-8464	Y
HCM Dividend Sector Plus Fund Class R	HCMZX	B-	B-	B-	Up	8.62	12.77	19.09			13.11	318.1	855-969-8464	Y
HCM Dividend Sector Plus Fund Investor Class	HCMPX	B-	C+	B-	Up	8.45	12.39	18.27			12.98	318.1	855-969-8464	Y
Hennessy Cornerstone Large Growth Fund Institutional Class	HILGX	B-	B-	B		8.36	10.31	17.33	25.01	100.43	12.37	109.7	800-966-4354	Y
Hennessy Cornerstone Large Growth Fund Investor Class	HFLGX	B-	C+	B		8.24	10.20	17.07	24.24	98.46	12.26	109.7	800-966-4354	Y
Hennessy Cornerstone Value Fund Class Institutional	HICVX	B-	B-	B-	Down	6.61	12.40	19.47	30.22	84.26	19.69	294.2	800-966-4354	Y
Hennessy Cornerstone Value Fund Investor Class	HFCVX	B-	B-	B-	Down	6.58	12.32	19.15	29.47	82.45	19.69	294.2	800-966-4354	Y
Hillman Fund No Load Shares	HCMAX	B	B	B		4.41	8.37	16.36	30.52	102.50	23.06	38.0		Y
Homestead Funds Value Fund	HOVLX	B	B	B		8.00	14.53	22.16	34.19	112.76	55.26	1,107		Y
Hotchkis & Wiley Diversified Value Fund Class A	HWCAX	B	B	B-	Up	6.03	9.91	18.09	28.62	102.05	18.91	115.0	866-493-8637	Y
Hotchkis & Wiley Diversified Value Fund Class C	HWCCX	B	B	B-	Up	5.85	9.52	17.26	25.74	94.72	18.77	115.0	866-493-8637	Y
Hotchkis & Wiley Diversified Value Fund Cls Institutional	HWCIX	B	B	B-	Up	6.08	10.04	18.39	29.61	104.60	18.84	115.0	866-493-8637	Y
Hotchkis & Wiley Large Cap Value Fund Class A	HWLAX	B	B	B-	Up	6.29	9.98	18.59	28.99	109.12	33.44	381.8	866-493-8637	Y
Hotchkis & Wiley Large Cap Value Fund Class C	HWLCX	B	B	B-	Up	6.10	9.58	17.70	26.13	101.30	32.88	381.8	866-493-8637	Y
Hotchkis & Wiley Large Cap Value Fund Class I	HWLIX	B	B	B	Up	6.36	10.13	18.86	29.99	111.67	33.61	381.8	866-493-8637	Y
Hotchkis & Wiley Large Cap Value Fund Class R	HWLRX	B	B	B-	Up	6.25	9.89	18.29	28.07	106.58	33.69	381.8	866-493-8637	Y
Hotchkis & Wiley Value Opportunities Fund Class A	HWAAX	B	B-	B	Up	5.11	8.45	13.56	29.71	99.82	29.48	586.1	866-493-8637	Y
Hotchkis & Wiley Value Opportunities Fund Class C	HWACX	B	B-	B	Up	4.93	8.03	12.75	26.83	92.49	27.47	586.1	866-493-8637	Y
Hotchkis & Wiley Value Opp Fund Cls Inst	HWAIX	B	B	B	Up	5.18	8.56	13.85	30.67	102.40	29.42	586.1	866-493-8637	Y
Huber Capital Diversified Large Cap Value Fund Inst Cls	HUDEX	B	B-	B	Up	6.96	13.43	21.41	28.77	75.26	14.95	5.1	888-482-3726	Y
Huber Capital Diversified Large Cap Value Fund Inv Cls	HUDIX	B-	B-	B	Up	7.05	13.40	21.23	27.87	72.34	14.89	5.1	888-482-3726	Y
Huber Capital Equity Income Fund Institutional Class	HULEX	B-	B-	B		6.92	12.82	19.93	24.61	75.93	16.34	89.8	888-482-3726	Y
Huber Capital Equity Income Fund Investor Class	HULIX	B-	B-	B		6.83	12.67	19.53	23.21	72.58	16.39	89.8	888-482-3726	Y
Integrity Dividend Harvest Fund Class A Shares	IDIVX	B	B-	A		5.16	8.38	11.09	34.45	89.67	14.68	149.3	800-276-1262	Y
Integrity Dividend Harvest Fund Class C	IDHCX	B	B-	A-		4.94	7.98	10.25	31.45	82.68	14.59	149.3	800-276-1262	Y
Integrity Dividend Harvest Fund Class I	IDHIX	B	B-	A		5.29	8.51	11.36	34.91	90.32	14.69	149.3	800-276-1262	Y
Invesco Comstock Fund Class A	ACSTX	B	B	B-	Up	7.44	13.87	17.76	29.31	95.82	26.86	12,696	800-659-1005	Y
Invesco Comstock Fund Class B	ACSWX	B	B	B-	Up	7.49	13.92	17.81	29.37	95.20	26.86	12,696	800-659-1005	
Invesco Comstock Fund Class C	ACSYX	B-	B-	B-	Up	7.25	13.50	16.95	26.53	88.76	26.87	12,696	800-659-1005	Y
Invesco Comstock Fund Class R	ACSRX	B	B	B-	Up	7.42	13.77	17.52	28.39	93.45	26.87	12,696	800-659-1005	Y
Invesco Comstock Fund Class R6	ICSFX	B	B	B	Up	7.56	14.17	18.33	31.04	100.10	26.84	12,696	800-659-1005	Y
Invesco Comstock Fund Class Y	ACSDX	B	B	B-	Up	7.55	14.05	18.10	30.29	98.28	26.86	12,696	800-659-1005	Y
Invesco Comstock Fund R5 Class	ACSHX	B	B	B	Up	7.58	14.11	18.21	30.66	99.22	26.85	12,696	800-659-1005	Y
Invesco Diversified Dividend Fund Class A	LCEAX	B	C+	A+		2.92	4.87	8.20	24.69	84.27	20.36	24,220	800-659-1005	Y
Invesco Diversified Dividend Fund Class B	LCEDX	B	C+	A		2.70	4.42	7.36	21.89	77.42	20.13	24,220	800-659-1005	
Invesco Diversified Dividend Fund Class C	LCEVX	B	C+	A		2.76	4.48	7.36	21.92	77.40	20.11	24,220	800-659-1005	Y
Invesco Diversified Dividend Fund Class R	DDFRX	B	C+	A+		2.85	4.73	7.96	23.76	81.87	20.43	24,220	800-659-1005	Y
Invesco Diversified Dividend Fund Class R6	LCEFX	B	C+	A+		3.03	5.08	8.63	26.18	87.90	20.36	24,220	800-659-1005	Y
Invesco Diversified Dividend Fund Class Y	LCEYX	B	C+	A+		2.94	4.95	8.41	25.55	86.39	20.37	24,220	800-659-1005	Y
Invesco Diversified Dividend Fund Investor Class	LCEIX	B	C+	A+		2.94	4.84	8.24	24.76	84.44	20.34	24,220	800-659-1005	Y

Category: US Equity Large Cap Value (con't)

Fund Name	Ticker Symbol	Overall Rating	Reward Rating	Risk Rating	Recent Up/ Downgrade	3-Month Total Return	6-Month Total Return	1-Year Total Return	3-Year Total Return	5-Year Total Return	NAV	Total Assets (MIL)	Telephone	Open to New Investors
Invesco Diversified Dividend Fund R5 Class	DDFIX	B	C+	A+		3.00	5.03	8.53	25.81	87.02	20.36	24,220	800-659-1005	Y
Invesco Dividend Income Fund Class A	IAUTX	B	B-	A+		3.38	5.83	9.07	29.16	85.70	24.48	2,391	800-659-1005	Y
Invesco Dividend Income Fund Class B	IBUTX	B	C+	A+		3.18	5.42	8.24	26.28	78.80	24.55	2,391	800-659-1005	
Invesco Dividend Income Fund Class C	IUTCX	B	C+	A+		3.19	5.42	8.26	26.26	78.84	24.79	2,391	800-659-1005	Y
Invesco Dividend Income Fund Class R6	IFUTX	B	B-	A+		3.48	6.03	9.45	30.62	88.93	24.5	2,391	800-659-1005	Y
Invesco Dividend Income Fund Class Y	IAUYX	B	B-	A+		3.46	5.96	9.37	30.17	88.07	24.72	2,391	800-659-1005	Y
Invesco Dividend Income Fund Investor Class	FSTUX	B	B-	A+		3.40	5.83	9.05	29.15	85.67	24.71	2,391	800-659-1005	
Invesco Dividend Income Fund R5 Class	FSIUX	B	B-	A+		3.42	5.94	9.36	30.18	88.32	24.48	2,391	800-659-1005	Y
Invesco Growth and Income Fund Class A	ACGIX	B	B	B	Up	4.69	9.19	14.20	31.24	98.22	26.97	8,263	800-659-1005	Y
Invesco Growth and Income Fund Class B	ACGJX	B	B	B	Up	4.69	9.22	14.20	31.25	98.29	26.71	8,263	800-659-1005	
Invesco Growth and Income Fund Class C	ACGKX	B	B	B	Up	4.49	8.79	13.33	28.31	91.00	26.65	8,263	800-659-1005	Y
Invesco Growth and Income Fund Class R	ACGLX	B	B	B	Up	4.62	9.08	13.91	30.23	95.81	27	8,263	800-659-1005	Y
Invesco Growth and Income Fund Class R6	GIFFX	B	B	B	Up	4.80	9.41	14.66	32.94	102.53	27.01	8,263	800-659-1005	Y
Invesco Growth and Income Fund Class Y	ACGMX	B	B	B	Up	4.71	9.32	14.48	32.17	100.66	26.98	8,263	800-659-1005	Y
Invesco Growth and Income Fund R5 Class	ACGQX	B	B	B	Up	4.77	9.36	14.56	32.57	101.68	27.01	8,263	800-659-1005	Y
Invesco Value Opportunities Fund Class A	VVOAX	B-	B	C	Up	5.39	10.22	17.10	22.68	77.36	14.65	861.4	800-659-1005	Y
Invesco Value Opportunities Fund Class B	VVOBX	B-	B	C	Up	5.42	10.26	17.17	22.76	77.43	14.39	861.4	800-659-1005	
Invesco Value Opportunities Fund Class R	VVORX	B-	B	C	Up	5.36	10.14	16.87	21.81	75.19	14.55	861.4	800-659-1005	Y
Invesco Value Opportunities Fund Class R5	VVONX	B-	B	C+	Up	5.45	10.43	17.58	24.25	81.08	14.69	861.4	800-659-1005	Y
Invesco Value Opportunities Fund Class R6	VVOSX	B-	B	C	Up	5.52	10.50	17.48	23.08	77.93	14.7	861.4	800-659-1005	Y
Invesco Value Opportunities Fund Class Y	VVOIX	B-	B	C+	Up	5.48	10.40	17.39	23.63	79.61	14.63	861.4	800-659-1005	Y
Ivy Value Fund Class A	IYVAX	B-	C+	B	Up	5.03	5.80	12.16	18.05	79.98	23.77	1,216	800-777-6472	Y
Ivy Value Fund Class B	IYVBX	B-	C+	B	Up	4.78	5.31	11.13	14.64	71.78	22.05	1,216	800-777-6472	
Ivy Value Fund Class C	IYVCX	B-	C+	B	Up	4.84	5.40	11.41	15.71	74.00	22.92	1,216	800-777-6472	Y
Ivy Value Fund Class I	IYAIX	B-	C+	B	Up	5.09	5.95	12.53	19.23	83.04	23.86	1,216	800-777-6472	Y
Ivy Value Fund Class N	IVALX	B-	C+	B		5.16	6.07	12.72	19.85	83.09	23.93	1,216	800-777-6472	Y
Ivy Value Fund Class R	IYVLX	B-	C+	B	Up	4.95	5.65	11.87	17.16	77.71	23.74	1,216	800-777-6472	Y
Ivy Value Fund Class Y	IYVYX	B-	C+	B	Up	5.02	5.78	12.15	18.26	80.57	23.81	1,216	800-777-6472	Y
Janus Henderson Large Cap Value Fund Class A	JAPAX	B-	C+	B	Down	4.96	7.64	14.24	22.08	75.47	15.6	138.3	877-335-2687	Y
Janus Henderson Large Cap Value Fund Class C	JAPCX	B-	C+	B	Down	4.84	7.30	13.46	20.02	70.19	15.34	138.3	877-335-2687	Y
Janus Henderson Large Cap Value Fund Class D	JNPLX	B-	B-	B-	Down	5.05	7.74	14.45	22.87	77.17	15.42	138.3	877-335-2687	
Janus Henderson Large Cap Value Fund Class I	JAPIX	B	B-	B	Up	5.06	7.81	14.57	23.00	78.00	15.5	138.3	877-335-2687	Y
Janus Henderson Large Cap Value Fund Class N	JPLNX	B	B-	B	Up	5.08	7.83	14.68	23.35	78.49	15.47	138.3	877-335-2687	Y
Janus Henderson Large Cap Value Fund Class S	JAPSX	B-	C+	B-	Down	5.04	7.70	14.24	22.13	75.37	15.68	138.3	877-335-2687	Y
Janus Henderson Large Cap Value Fund Class T	JPLTX	B-	B-	B	Down	5.03	7.73	14.38	22.55	76.38	15.4	138.3	877-335-2687	Y
JNL/American Funds Blue Chip Income & Growth Fund Cls A	US46644W4197	B	B-	B		7.06	10.48	16.60	32.09	106.22	22.12	3,371		Y
JNL/American Funds Blue Chip Income & Growth Fund Cls I	US46644W3934	B	B-	B		7.19	10.63	16.88	32.98	108.39	22.36	3,371		Y
JNL/Mellon Capital Dow Index Fund Class A	US47760W7048	B	B+	B-		10.81	16.80	27.64	45.12	112.93	27.66	797.4		
JNL/Mellon Capital Dow Index Fund Class I	US47760W8038	B	B+	B-		10.93	16.93	27.78	45.27	113.16	27.69	797.4		Y
JNL/Mellon Capital JNL 5 Fund Class A	US47760W8459	B	B-	B+	Up	5.83	12.79	16.93	26.16	89.51	15.61	3,782		Y
JNL/Mellon Capital JNL 5 Fund Class I	US47760W8376	B	B-	B+	Up	5.95	12.94	17.24	27.02	91.49	15.66	3,782		Y
JNL/PPM America Value Equity Fund Class A	US46648L1044	B-	B-	B-	Up	6.71	12.61	14.97	26.22	105.35	23.85	226.7		Y
JNL/PPM America Value Equity Fund Class I	US46648L2034	B-	B	B-	Up	6.75	12.74	15.19	27.06	107.54	24.01	226.7		Y
JNL/S&P 4 Fund Class A	US46648L7322	B-	C+	B	Down	8.50	11.95	15.37	19.78	102.07	20.41	7,028		Y
JNL/S&P 4 Fund Class I	US46648L7249	B-	C+	B		8.55	12.01	15.43	19.84	102.17	20.42	7,028		Y
JNL/S&P Dividend Income & Growth Fund Class A	US46648L8239	B	B-	A		6.10	9.85	11.96	31.35	99.99	15.99	5,437		Y
JNL/S&P Dividend Income & Growth Fund Class I	US46648L8155	B	B-	A		6.22	9.99	12.21	32.11	102.14	16.21	5,437		Y
JNL/S&P Total Yield Fund Class A	US46648L7736	B-	C+	B		6.66	7.70	11.02	14.31	106.40	14.08	2,278		Y
JNL/S&P Total Yield Fund Class I	US46648L7652	B-	C+	B		6.83	7.83	11.37	15.08	108.58	14.23	2,278		Y
JNL/T. Rowe Price Value Fund Class A	US46648L8643	B-	B-	B-	Down	5.94	9.44	18.70	27.73	103.86	17.46	4,963		Y
JNL/T. Rowe Price Value Fund Class I	US46648L8569	B-	B	B-	Down	6.06	9.59	18.99	28.50	105.93	18.2	4,963		Y
JNL/Vanguard Equity Income Fund Class A	US46648L5185	B-	B-	B		6.16	10.88	17.26	32.47	93.38	10.67	17.1		Y

Category: US Equity Large Cap Value (con't)

Fund Name	Ticker Symbol	RATINGS: Overall Rating	Reward Rating	Risk Rating	Recent Up/ Downgrade	TOTAL RETURNS & PERFORMANCE: 3-Month Total Return	6-Month Total Return	1-Year Total Return	3-Year Total Return	5-Year Total Return	ASSETS: NAV	Total Assets (MIL)	NEW INVESTORS: Telephone	Open to New Investors
JNL/Vanguard Equity Income Fund Class I	US46648L4923	B-	B-	B		6.36	11.17	17.75	33.81	96.51	10.69	17.1		Y
JNL/WMC Value Fund Class A	US46649B8404	B	B-	B	Up	5.65	8.75	15.20	25.40	87.41	24.48	1,580		Y
JNL/WMC Value Fund Class I	US46649B8321	B	B-	B	Up	5.76	8.94	15.53	26.28	89.50	25.14	1,580		Y
John Hancock Capital Series Classic Value Fund Class R3	JCVHX	B	B	B-	Up	7.15	11.15	16.17	29.61	105.43	33.71	2,262	800-225-5913	Y
John Hancock Capital Series Classic Value Fund Class R4	JCVFX	B	B+	B-	Up	7.26	11.43	16.72	31.57	110.46	33.78	2,262	800-225-5913	Y
John Hancock Capital Series Classic Value Fund Class R5	JCVVX	B	B+	B-	Up	7.31	11.47	16.83	32.01	111.75	33.81	2,262	800-225-5913	Y
John Hancock Classic Value Fund Class A	PZFVX	B	B+	B-	Up	7.22	11.28	16.45	30.75	108.07	33.75	2,262	800-225-5913	Y
John Hancock Classic Value Fund Class B	JCVBX	B	B	B-	Up	7.02	10.90	15.62	27.80	100.51	33.3	2,262	800-225-5913	
John Hancock Classic Value Fund Class C	JCVCX	B	B	B-	Up	7.02	10.90	15.63	27.80	100.44	33.29	2,262	800-225-5913	Y
John Hancock Classic Value Fund Class I	JCVIX	B	B+	B-	Up	7.26	11.42	16.75	31.75	110.96	33.79	2,262	800-225-5913	Y
John Hancock Classic Value Fund Class R1	JCVRX	B	B	B-	Up	7.09	11.07	15.99	29.21	104.28	33.84	2,262	800-225-5913	Y
John Hancock Classic Value Fund Class R2	JCVSX	B	B	B-	Up	7.19	11.23	16.29	30.25	107.51	33.71	2,262	800-225-5913	Y
John Hancock Classic Value Fund Class R6	JCVWX	B	B+	B	Up	7.32	11.52	16.88	32.19	112.06	33.81	2,262	800-225-5913	Y
John Hancock Funds Disciplined Value Fund Class A	JVLAX	B	B-	B	Up	6.86	11.80	18.92	26.88	95.01	22.53	15,171	800-225-5913	Y
John Hancock Funds Disciplined Value Fund Class B	JVLBX	B-	B-	B	Down	6.65	11.36	17.98	23.95	87.37	21.19	15,171	800-225-5913	
John Hancock Funds Disciplined Value Fund Class C	JVLCX	B-	B-	B	Down	6.63	11.32	17.98	24.00	87.69	21.25	15,171	800-225-5913	Y
John Hancock Funds Disciplined Value Fund Class I	JVLIX	B	B-	B	Up	6.94	11.91	19.19	27.86	97.70	21.84	15,171	800-225-5913	Y
John Hancock Funds Disciplined Value Fund Class I2	JVLTX	B	B-	B	Up	6.94	11.91	19.19	27.79	97.57	21.84	15,171	800-225-5913	Y
John Hancock Funds Disciplined Value Fund Class NAV	JDVNX	B-	B-	C+	Down	6.93	12.01	19.34	28.23	98.76	21.87	15,171	800-225-5913	Y
John Hancock Funds Disciplined Value Fund Class R1	JDVOX	B-	B-	B	Down	6.74	11.52	18.43	25.25	91.00	21.83	15,171	800-225-5913	Y
John Hancock Funds Disciplined Value Fund Class R2	JDVPX	B	B-	B	Up	6.84	11.72	18.75	26.27	93.57	21.84	15,171	800-225-5913	Y
John Hancock Funds Disciplined Value Fund Class R3	JDVHX	B-	B-	B	Down	6.75	11.63	18.55	25.69	91.95	21.82	15,171	800-225-5913	Y
John Hancock Funds Disciplined Value Fund Class R4	JDVFX	B	B-	B	Up	6.88	11.80	19.01	27.22	96.03	21.85	15,171	800-225-5913	Y
John Hancock Funds Disciplined Value Fund Class R5	JDVVX	B	B-	B	Up	6.92	11.94	19.27	27.97	98.34	21.87	15,171	800-225-5913	Y
John Hancock Funds Disciplined Value Fund Class R6	JDVWX	B	B-	B	Up	6.97	11.99	19.33	28.28	98.74	21.87	15,171	800-225-5913	Y
John Hancock Funds Fundamental Large Cap Value Fund Cls A	JFVAX	B-	C+	B	Up	4.98	9.32	15.56	23.82	82.99	14.41	814.9	800-225-5913	Y
John Hancock Funds Fundamental Large Cap Value Fund Cls C	JFVCX	B-	C+	B	Up	4.80	8.92	14.72	21.07	76.52	14.43	814.9	800-225-5913	Y
John Hancock Funds Fundamental Large Cap Value Fund Cls I	JFVIX	B	B-	B	Up	5.06	9.45	15.92	24.93	85.76	14.47	814.9	800-225-5913	Y
John Hancock Funds Fundmnt Large Cap Value Fund Cls NAV	US47804M1009	B	B-	B	Up	5.10	9.50	16.06	25.35	87.44	14.45	814.9	800-225-5913	Y
John Hancock Funds Fundamental Large Cap Value Fund Cls R2	JFLCX	B-	C+	B	Up	5.04	9.38	15.61	24.07	83.56	14.45	814.9	800-225-5913	Y
John Hancock Funds Fundamental Large Cap Value Fund Cls R4	JFLRX	B	C+	B	Up	5.07	9.48	15.95	24.78	84.61	14.46	814.9	800-225-5913	Y
John Hancock Funds Fundamental Large Cap Value Fund Cls R6	JFLVX	B	B-	B	Up	5.17	9.57	16.05	25.43	86.51	14.46	814.9	800-225-5913	Y
John Hancock Funds II Equity Income Fund Class 1	JIEMX	B-	B-	C+	Down	5.55	10.08	16.19	27.52	82.27	20.44	1,733	800-225-5913	Y
John Hancock Funds II Equity Income Fund Class A	JHEIX	B-	B-	C+	Down	5.47	9.96	15.83	26.30	79.56	20.43	1,733	800-225-5913	Y
John Hancock Funds II Equity Income Fund Class C	JHERX	B-	B-	C+	Down	5.22	9.49	14.95	23.56	73.25	20.48	1,733	800-225-5913	Y
John Hancock Funds II Equity Income Fund Class NAV	US47803V7964	B-	B-	C+	Down	5.57	10.18	16.27	27.75	82.71	20.42	1,733	800-225-5913	Y
John Hancock Value Equity Fund Class A	JVEAX	B	B	B	Up	4.73	8.57	17.07	29.44		12.34	638.4	800-225-5913	Y
John Hancock Value Equity Fund Class C	JVECX	B-	B-	B-	Up	4.64	8.24	16.33	26.80		12.33	638.4	800-225-5913	Y
John Hancock Value Equity Fund Class I	JVEIX	B-	B	B-	Up	4.86	8.70	17.52	30.58		12.34	638.4	800-225-5913	Y
John Hancock Value Equity Fund Class NAV	US47803P3441	B-	B	B-	Up	4.87	8.80	17.62	31.26		12.35	638.4	800-225-5913	Y
John Hancock Value Equity Fund Class R6	JVERX	B-	B	B-	Up	4.86	8.79	17.60	31.24		12.35	638.4	800-225-5913	Y
JPMorgan Equity Income Fund Class A	OIEIX	B	B-	B+		6.87	11.12	17.20	29.49	97.71	17.12	16,369	800-480-4111	Y
JPMorgan Equity Income Fund Class C	OINCX	B	B-	B		6.71	10.80	16.58	27.59	92.76	16.81	16,369	800-480-4111	Y
JPMorgan Equity Income Fund Class I	HLIEX	B	B-	B+		6.95	11.27	17.54	30.50	100.18	17.4	16,369	800-480-4111	Y
JPMorgan Equity Income Fund Class R2	OIEFX	B-	B-	B-	Down	6.85	11.00	16.91	28.54	95.23	17.05	16,369	800-480-4111	Y
JPMorgan Equity Income Fund Class R3	OIEPX	B-	B-	B-	Down	6.89	11.07	17.21	29.54	97.72	17.1	16,369	800-480-4111	Y
JPMorgan Equity Income Fund Class R4	OIEQX	B-	B-	B-	Down	6.96	11.22	17.51	30.46	100.13	17.39	16,369	800-480-4111	Y
JPMorgan Equity Income Fund Class R5	OIERX	B	B	B		6.99	11.36	17.72	31.30	102.20	17.41	16,369	800-480-4111	Y
JPMorgan Equity Income Fund Class R6	OIEJX	B	B	B+		7.02	11.42	17.84	31.58	102.84	17.4	16,369	800-480-4111	Y
JPMorgan Growth And Income Fund Class A	VGRIX	B	B	B	Up	7.16	12.47	17.14	29.67	103.34	50.26	586.8	800-480-4111	Y
JPMorgan Growth And Income Fund Class C	VGICX	B	B-	B	Up	7.00	12.18	16.54	27.72	98.21	45.39	586.8	800-480-4111	Y
JPMorgan Growth And Income Fund Class I	VGIIX	B	B	B+		7.21	12.61	17.42	30.63	105.77	52.91	586.8	800-480-4111	Y

Category: US Equity Large Cap Value (con't)

Fund Name	Ticker Symbol	RATINGS Overall Rating	Reward Rating	Risk Rating	Recent Up/ Downgrade	TOTAL RETURNS & PERFORMANCE 3-Month Total Return	6-Month Total Return	1-Year Total Return	3-Year Total Return	5-Year Total Return	ASSETS NAV	Total Assets (MIL)	NEW INVESTORS Telephone	Open to New Investors
JPMorgan Growth and Income Fund Class R2	VGRTX	B	B-	B	Up	7.09	12.32	16.85	28.69	100.81	50.49	586.8	800-480-4111	Y
JPMorgan Growth and Income Fund Class R3	JGAVX	B	B	B		7.68	13.05	17.75	30.34	104.39	52.9	586.8	800-480-4111	Y
JPMorgan Growth and Income Fund Class R4	JGRUX	B	B	B		7.73	13.13	17.83	30.44	104.55	52.9	586.8	800-480-4111	Y
JPMorgan Growth and Income Fund Class R5	VGIFX	B	B	B		7.26	12.71	17.66	30.86	105.21	53.24	586.8	800-480-4111	Y
JPMorgan Growth and Income Fund Class R6	VGINX	B	B	B		7.26	12.73	17.70	31.01	105.45	53.24	586.8	800-480-4111	Y
JPMorgan Intrepid Value Fund Class A Shares	JIVAX	B-	C+	B	Up	7.11	12.37	16.44	20.68	90.88	34.32	1,105	800-480-4111	Y
JPMorgan Intrepid Value Fund Class C Shares	JIVCX	B-	C+	B	Up	6.94	12.08	15.85	18.88	86.16	33.88	1,105	800-480-4111	Y
JPMorgan Intrepid Value Fund Class I Shares	JPIVX	B-	B-	B	Up	7.15	12.48	16.65	21.26	92.38	34.5	1,105	800-480-4111	Y
JPMorgan Intrepid Value Fund Class R2 Shares	JIVZX	B-	C+	B	Up	6.99	12.19	16.06	19.66	88.41	34.07	1,105	800-480-4111	Y
JPMorgan Intrepid Value Fund Class R5 Shares	JIVRX	B-	B-	B	Up	7.20	12.59	16.86	21.96	94.25	34.59	1,105	800-480-4111	Y
JPMorgan Intrepid Value Fund Class R6 Shares	JIVMX	B-	B-	B	Up	7.22	12.59	16.93	22.15	94.74	34.59	1,105	800-480-4111	Y
JPMorgan Large Cap Value Fund Class A	OLVAX	B	B	B		7.09	10.75	17.49	38.88	120.94	15.78	1,364	800-480-4111	Y
JPMorgan Large Cap Value Fund Class C	OLVCX	B	B	B		6.98	10.51	16.92	36.77	115.26	15.17	1,364	800-480-4111	Y
JPMorgan Large Cap Value Fund Class I	HLQVX	B+	B+	B	Up	7.20	10.90	17.71	39.58	122.73	15.52	1,364	800-480-4111	Y
JPMorgan Large Cap Value Fund Class R2	JLVZX	B	B	B		7.09	10.63	17.15	37.73	117.98	15.67	1,364	800-480-4111	Y
JPMorgan Large Cap Value Fund Class R5	JLVRX	B+	B+	B+	Up	7.17	10.96	17.87	40.28	124.73	15.66	1,364	800-480-4111	Y
JPMorgan Large Cap Value Fund Class R6	JLVMX	B+	B+	B+	Up	7.24	11.00	17.91	40.60	125.29	15.56	1,364	800-480-4111	Y
JPMorgan Value Advantage Fund Class A	JVAAX	B	B-	B	Up	6.03	9.20	13.66	24.96	90.75	35.84	12,225	800-480-4111	Y
JPMorgan Value Advantage Fund Class C	JVACX	B-	B-	B	Down	5.88	8.94	13.10	23.06	86.01	35.74	12,225	800-480-4111	Y
JPMorgan Value Advantage Fund Class I	JVASX	B	B-	B	Up	6.09	9.34	13.95	25.91	93.16	36.02	12,225	800-480-4111	Y
JPMorgan Value Advantage Fund Class L	JVAIX	B	B-	B	Up	6.15	9.47	14.22	26.81	95.47	36.01	12,225	800-480-4111	Y
JPMorgan Value Advantage Fund Class R2	JGAQX	B-	B-	B		5.97	9.09	13.54	24.81	90.47	35.72	12,225	800-480-4111	Y
JPMorgan Value Advantage Fund Class R3	JVAPX	B	B-	B	Up	6.01	9.20	13.64	25.51	92.51	35.56	12,225	800-480-4111	Y
JPMorgan Value Advantage Fund Class R4	JVAQX	B	B-	B	Up	6.09	9.31	13.93	26.43	94.88	35.88	12,225	800-480-4111	Y
JPMorgan Value Advantage Fund Class R5	JVARX	B	B-	B	Up	6.14	9.43	14.12	26.70	95.29	35.96	12,225	800-480-4111	Y
JPMorgan Value Advantage Fund Class R6	JVAYX	B	B-	B	Up	6.18	9.50	14.22	26.84	95.51	35.98	12,225	800-480-4111	Y
Knights of Columbus Large Cap Value Fund Class S	KCVSX	B-	C+	B	Up	6.27	10.01	15.74			12.06	50.4	203-772-2130	Y
Knights of Columbus Large Cap Value Fund Institutional Cls	KCVIX	B-	C+	B	Up	6.30	9.92	15.78			12.06	50.4	203-772-2130	Y
Knights of Columbus Large Cap Value Fund Investor Shares	KCVVX	B-	C+	B-	Up	6.33	9.79	15.37			12.06	50.4	203-772-2130	Y
Legg Mason BW Diversified Large Cap Value Fund Class A	LBWAX	B	B	B	Up	6.98	11.98	19.65	30.08	96.51	20.85	870.3	877-721-1926	Y
Legg Mason BW Diversified Large Cap Value Fund Class A2	LLVAX	B	B	B	Up	7.00	11.94	19.48	29.53	95.02	20.65	870.3	877-721-1926	Y
Legg Mason BW Diversified Large Cap Value Fund Class C	LBWCX	B	B-	B	Up	6.82	11.60	18.82	27.22	89.31	20.64	870.3	877-721-1926	Y
Legg Mason BW Diversified Large Cap Value Fund Class I	LBWIX	B	B	B	Up	7.13	12.18	19.98	31.19	99.22	20.84	870.3	877-721-1926	Y
Legg Mason BW Diversified Large Cap Value Fund Class IS	LBISX	B	B	B	Up	7.15	12.25	20.12	31.56	99.87	20.85	870.3	877-721-1926	Y
Legg Mason BW Diversified Large Cap Value Fund Class R	LBDRX	B	B	B	Up	7.01	11.91	19.40	29.09	94.18	20.85	870.3	877-721-1926	Y
Legg Mason BW Dynamic Large Cap Value Fund Class A	LMBJX	B	B-	B	Up	8.50	14.48	21.50	27.11	114.06	12.35	157.1	877-721-1926	Y
Legg Mason BW Dynamic Large Cap Value Fund Class C	LMBBX	B-	B-	B	Up	8.33	14.06	20.66	24.26	105.93	12.26	157.1	877-721-1926	Y
Legg Mason BW Dynamic Large Cap Value Fund Class I	LMBEX	B	B-	B	Up	8.58	14.65	21.90	28.18	116.79	12.37	157.1	877-721-1926	Y
Legg Mason BW Dynamic Large Cap Value Fund Class IS	LMBGX	B-	B-	B-	Down	8.62	14.69	21.94	28.47	117.14	12.37	157.1	877-721-1926	Y
Legg Mason BW Dynamic Large Cap Value Fund Class R	LMBHX	B-	B-	B	Down	8.49	14.37	21.15	25.92	110.89	12.36	157.1	877-721-1926	Y
Loomis Sayles Dividend Income Fund Class A	LSCAX	B-	C+	B	Down	2.37	4.31	10.19	21.61	73.13	11.32	45.6	800-862-4863	Y
Loomis Sayles Dividend Income Fund Class C	LSCCX	B-	C+	B	Down	2.18	3.92	9.34	18.77	66.64	11.26	45.6	800-862-4863	Y
Loomis Sayles Dividend Income Fund Class N	LDINX	B-	C+	B	Down	2.45	4.46	10.51	22.45	75.28	11.32	45.6	800-862-4863	Y
Loomis Sayles Dividend Income Fund Class Y	LSCYX	B-	C+	B	Down	2.44	4.43	10.47	22.41	75.21	11.32	45.6	800-862-4863	Y
Loomis Sayles Value Fund Admin Class	LSAVX	B-	C+	B	Down	4.84	7.36	14.16	19.33	82.11	21.19	1,184	800-862-4863	Y
Loomis Sayles Value Fund Class A	LSVRX	B-	C+	B	Down	4.92	7.48	14.43	20.52	84.73	21.22	1,184	800-862-4863	Y
Loomis Sayles Value Fund Class C	LSCVX	B-	C+	B	Up	4.72	7.07	13.55	17.83	77.86	21.02	1,184	800-862-4863	Y
Loomis Sayles Value Fund Class N	LSVNX	B-	C+	B	Down	5.07	7.77	14.94	21.98	88.24	21.25	1,184	800-862-4863	Y
Loomis Sayles Value Fund Class Y	LSGIX	B-	C+	B	Down	4.97	7.61	14.70	21.37	86.99	21.29	1,184	800-862-4863	Y
Lord Abbett Affiliated Fund Class A	LAFFX	B	B-	B		5.50	8.71	15.50	28.45	95.38	15.81	6,828	201-827-2000	Y
Lord Abbett Affiliated Fund Class B	LAFBX	B-	B-	B	Down	5.70	8.65	14.99	26.03	88.98	16.03	6,828	201-827-2000	
Lord Abbett Affiliated Fund Class C	LAFCX	B-	B-	B	Down	5.50	8.52	14.81	25.86	88.76	15.82	6,828	201-827-2000	Y

Category: US Equity Large Cap Value (con't)

Fund Name	Ticker Symbol	RATINGS Overall Rating	Reward Rating	Risk Rating	Recent Up/ Downgrade	TOTAL RETURNS & PERFORMANCE 3-Month Total Return	6-Month Total Return	1-Year Total Return	3-Year Total Return	5-Year Total Return	ASSETS NAV	Total Assets (MIL)	NEW INVESTORS Telephone	Open to New Investors
Lord Abbett Affiliated Fund Class F	LAAFX	B	B-	B		6.16	9.37	16.29	29.70	98.05	15.81	6,828	201-827-2000	Y
Lord Abbett Affiliated Fund Class F3	LTFOX	B	B-	B		6.15	9.44	16.34	29.39	96.80	15.9	6,828	201-827-2000	Y
Lord Abbett Affiliated Fund Class I	LAFYX	B	B-	B		6.09	9.38	16.32	30.04	98.96	15.87	6,828	201-827-2000	Y
Lord Abbett Affiliated Fund Class P	LAFPX	B-	B-	B-	Down	6.07	9.30	16.06	29.15	96.49	15.78	6,828	201-827-2000	
Lord Abbett Affiliated Fund Class R2	LAFQX	B-	B-	B-	Down	5.97	9.08	15.63	27.78	93.10	15.81	6,828	201-827-2000	Y
Lord Abbett Affiliated Fund Class R3	LAFRX	B	B-	B		6.01	9.18	15.79	28.19	94.26	15.79	6,828	201-827-2000	Y
Lord Abbett Affiliated Fund Class R4	LAFSX	B-	B-	B-	Down	5.50	8.73	15.45	28.46	95.39	15.79	6,828	201-827-2000	Y
Lord Abbett Affiliated Fund Class R5	LAFTX	B-	B-	B-	Down	5.53	8.80	15.71	29.20	96.51	15.88	6,828	201-827-2000	Y
Lord Abbett Affiliated Fund Class R6	LAFVX	B-	B-	B-	Down	5.59	8.86	15.78	29.49	96.96	15.91	6,828	201-827-2000	Y
Lord Abbett Affiliated Fund Class T	LAETX	B-	B-	B-		5.56	8.80	15.59	28.56	95.54	15.82	6,828	201-827-2000	Y
Lord Abbett Calibrated Large Cap Value Class R4	LCASX	B-	C+	B	Down	5.04	8.29	10.88	21.17	82.06	20.8	507.2	201-827-2000	Y
Lord Abbett Calibrated Large Cap Value Class R5	LCAUX	B-	C+	B	Down	5.09	8.38	11.12	22.05	84.30	20.86	507.2	201-827-2000	Y
Lord Abbett Calibrated Large Cap Value Class R6	LCAVX	B-	C+	B	Down	5.09	8.43	11.17	22.16	84.48	20.88	507.2	201-827-2000	Y
Lord Abbett Calibrated Large Cap Value Fund Class A	LCAAX	B-	C+	B	Down	5.02	8.27	10.85	21.15	82.07	20.84	507.2	201-827-2000	Y
Lord Abbett Calibrated Large Cap Value Fund Class C	LCACX	B-	C+	B	Up	4.84	7.88	10.07	18.50	75.50	20.52	507.2	201-827-2000	Y
Lord Abbett Calibrated Large Cap Value Fund Class F	LCAFX	B-	C+	B	Down	5.12	8.42	11.16	21.87	83.71	20.89	507.2	201-827-2000	Y
Lord Abbett Calibrated Large Cap Value Fund Class F3	LCAYX	B-	C+	B	Down	5.08	8.42	11.17	22.13	84.43	20.88	507.2	201-827-2000	Y
Lord Abbett Calibrated Large Cap Value Fund Class I	LVCIX	B-	C+	B	Down	5.08	8.43	11.12	22.08	84.34	20.87	507.2	201-827-2000	Y
Lord Abbett Calibrated Large Cap Value Fund Class R2	LCAQX	B-	C+	B	Down	4.95	8.13	10.48	19.94	79.75	20.98	507.2	201-827-2000	Y
Lord Abbett Calibrated Large Cap Value Fund Class R3	LCARX	B-	C+	B	Down	4.99	8.16	10.59	20.30	79.94	20.72	507.2	201-827-2000	Y
Lord Abbett Fundamental Equity Class R4	LAVSX	B-	B-	B	Down	5.57	8.89	13.03	25.00	84.74	12.89	2,680	201-827-2000	Y
Lord Abbett Fundamental Equity Class R5	LAVTX	B-	B-	B	Down	5.57	9.01	13.28	25.74	85.83	13.02	2,680	201-827-2000	Y
Lord Abbett Fundamental Equity Class R6	LAVVX	B-	B-	B	Down	5.63	9.07	13.42	26.10	86.37	13.06	2,680	201-827-2000	Y
Lord Abbett Fundamental Equity Fund Class A	LDFVX	B-	B-	B	Down	5.54	8.84	12.96	25.42	87.87	12.95	2,680	201-827-2000	Y
Lord Abbett Fundamental Equity Fund Class B	GILBX	B-	C+	B	Down	5.34	8.44	12.10	22.65	81.22	11.8	2,680	201-827-2000	
Lord Abbett Fundamental Equity Fund Class C	GILAX	B-	C+	B	Down	5.27	8.41	12.11	22.55	81.11	11.56	2,680	201-827-2000	Y
Lord Abbett Fundamental Equity Fund Class F	LAVFX	B	B-	B	Up	5.60	8.93	13.18	25.99	89.60	12.81	2,680	201-827-2000	Y
Lord Abbett Fundamental Equity Fund Class F3	LDFOX	B-	B-	B	Down	5.56	8.99	13.03	23.55	82.59	13.05	2,680	201-827-2000	Y
Lord Abbett Fundamental Equity Fund Class I	LAVYX	B	B-	B	Up	5.56	8.92	13.19	26.29	90.46	13.01	2,680	201-827-2000	Y
Lord Abbett Fundamental Equity Fund Class P	LAVPX	B-	B-	B	Down	5.46	8.74	12.76	24.68	86.32	12.72	2,680	201-827-2000	
Lord Abbett Fundamental Equity Fund Class R2	LAVQX	B-	B-	B	Down	5.44	8.65	12.59	24.17	84.85	12.67	2,680	201-827-2000	Y
Lord Abbett Fundamental Equity Fund Class R3	LAVRX	B-	B-	B	Down	5.44	8.71	12.63	24.46	85.82	12.73	2,680	201-827-2000	Y
LSV Conservative Value Equity Fund	LSVVX	B	B-	B	Up	6.57	10.98	16.17	27.92	105.51	13.41	120.4		Y
LSV Conservative Value Equity Fund Investor Class	LVAVX	B	B-	B	Up	6.49	10.83	15.83	27.04	102.89	13.36	120.4		Y
LSV U.S. Managed Volatility Fund Institutional Class	LSVMX	B-	B-	B	Down	5.36	8.42	13.69	26.37		12.58	92.9		Y
LSV U.S. Managed Volatility Fund Investor Class	LVAMX	B-	B-	B	Down	5.28	8.33	13.51	25.85		12.6	92.9		Y
LSV Value Equity Fund	LSVEX	B	B	B	Up	7.30	13.15	18.30	34.01	120.92	28.95	2,181		Y
LSV Value Equity Fund Investor Class	LVAEX	B	B	B	Up	7.21	12.96	17.99	32.98	118.09	28.82	2,181		Y
LWAS/DFA U.S. High Book To Market Portfolio	DFBMX	B	B	B	Up	7.50	12.44	19.00	34.99	114.56	19.05	58.5	512-306-7400	
Lyrical U.S. Value Equity Fund Institutional Class	LYRIX	B	B	B	Up	5.15	9.48	21.29	28.79		18.62	1,163	888-884-8099	Y
Lyrical U.S. Value Equity Fund Investor Class	LYRBX	B	B	B	Up	5.06	9.29	20.88	27.67		18.54	1,163	888-884-8099	Y
Macquarie Pooled Trust Large Cap Value Portfolio	DPDEX	B	B-	B+		5.41	10.56	13.69	28.00	99.37	26.18	173.7	215-255-2300	Y
Madison Dividend Income Fund Class Y	BHBFX	B	B-	B		7.05	11.77	19.92	34.00	94.35	26.7	111.2	800-767-0300	Y
Madison Large Cap Value Fund Class A	MGWAX	B-	B-	B	Down	6.97	10.83	14.83	23.78	83.57		92.5	800-767-0300	Y
Madison Large Cap Value Fund Class B	MGWBX	B-	C+	B	Down	6.75	10.41	13.99	21.04	76.87		92.5	800-767-0300	Y
Madison Large Cap Value Fund Class Y	MYLVX	B-	B-	B	Down	6.96	10.90	15.06	24.66	85.75		92.5	800-767-0300	Y
MainStay Epoch U.S. Equity Yield Fund Class A	EPLPX	B-	B-	B	Down	5.36	8.86	16.65	28.21	95.32	16.23	1,254	800-624-6782	Y
MainStay Epoch U.S. Equity Yield Fund Class B	EPLBX	B-	B-	B	Down	5.15	8.40	15.62	25.24	87.99	15.71	1,254	800-624-6782	Y
MainStay Epoch U.S. Equity Yield Fund Class C	EPLKX	B-	B-	B	Down	5.09	8.40	15.56	24.86	86.74	15.71	1,254	800-624-6782	Y
MainStay Epoch U.S. Equity Yield Fund Class I	EPLCX	B-	B-	B	Down	5.37	9.05	16.91	29.18	97.81	16.38	1,254	800-624-6782	Y
MainStay Epoch U.S. Equity Yield Fund Class R1	EPLRX	B-	B-	B	Down	5.41	9.00	16.83	29.10	97.67	16.38	1,254	800-624-6782	Y
MainStay Epoch U.S. Equity Yield Fund Class R2	EPLSX	B-	B-	B	Down	5.33	8.81	16.53	28.12	95.20	16.23	1,254	800-624-6782	Y

Category: US Equity Large Cap Value (con't)

Fund Name	Ticker Symbol	RATINGS: Overall Rating	Reward Rating	Risk Rating	Recent Up/ Downgrade	TOTAL RETURNS & PERFORMANCE: 3-Month Total Return	6-Month Total Return	1-Year Total Return	3-Year Total Return	5-Year Total Return	ASSETS: NAV	Total Assets (MIL)	NEW INVESTORS: Telephone	Open to New Investors
MainStay Epoch U.S. Equity Yield Fund Class R3	EPLTX	B-	B-	B	Down	5.26	8.67	16.29	27.22	92.87	16.23	1,254	800-624-6782	Y
MainStay Epoch U.S. Equity Yield Fund Class R6	EPLDX	B-	B-	B	Down	5.46	9.10	16.98	29.27	97.93	16.38	1,254	800-624-6782	Y
MainStay Epoch U.S. Equity Yield Fund Investor Class	EPLIX	B-	B-	B	Down	5.27	8.77	16.42	27.58	93.63	16.16	1,254	800-624-6782	Y
Manning & Napier Disciplined Value Series Class I	MNDFX	B	B	B-		8.93	14.26	23.10	40.01	98.24	14.54	152.6	585-325-6880	Y
Manning & Napier Disciplined Value Series Class S	MDFSX	B	B	B-		8.85	14.05	22.82	38.90	95.72	8.82	152.6	585-325-6880	Y
Manning & Napier Equity Income Series Class I	MNEIX	B-	B-	B-	Down	5.89	10.02	15.30	27.47		12.12	87.1	585-325-6880	Y
Manning & Napier Equity Income Series Class S	MNESX	B	B-	B		5.83	9.90	15.18	26.84		12.12	87.1	585-325-6880	Y
MassMutual Premier Disciplined Value Fund Admin Cls	MPILX	B-	B-	B	Down	5.36	9.14	14.24	25.36	91.54	16.7	206.6		Y
MassMutual Premier Disciplined Value Fund Class A	MEPAX	B-	B-	B	Down	5.30	9.00	13.95	24.44	89.14	16.25	206.6		Y
MassMutual Premier Disciplined Value Fund Class I	MPIVX	B	B-	B	Up	5.43	9.33	14.57	26.42	93.87	16.46	206.6		Y
MassMutual Premier Disciplined Value Fund Class R3	MPINX	B-	B-	B	Down	5.25	8.90	13.80	23.91	87.37	16.39	206.6		Y
MassMutual Premier Disciplined Value Fund Class R4	MPIRX	B-	B-	B	Down	5.31	9.02	14.07	24.75	90.14	16.13	206.6		Y
MassMutual Premier Disciplined Value Fund Class R5	MEPSX	B-	B-	B	Down	5.36	9.19	14.41	26.13	93.63	16.49	206.6		Y
MassMutual Premier Disciplined Value Fund Service Class	DENVX	B-	B-	B	Down	5.42	9.22	14.41	25.75	92.60	16.38	206.6		Y
MassMutual Premier Value Fund Administrative Class Share	DLBVX	B-	B-	B-	Down	5.21	9.02	16.46	25.67	85.56	26.13	50.7		Y
MassMutual Premier Value Fund Class A	MCEAX	B-	B-	B-	Down	5.12	8.89	16.17	24.70	83.14	26.12	50.7		Y
MassMutual Premier Value Fund Class I	MCZIX	B-	B-	B-	Down	5.30	9.21	16.78	26.77	87.63	25.98	50.7		Y
MassMutual Premier Value Fund Class R3	MCENX	B	B-	B	Up	5.09	8.80	15.97	24.16	81.44	25.93	50.7		Y
MassMutual Premier Value Fund Class R4	MCERX	B-	B-	B-	Down	5.17	8.95	16.25	25.07	83.94	25.98	50.7		Y
MassMutual Premier Value Fund Class R5	MVEDX	B-	B-	B-	Down	5.26	9.13	16.70	26.41	87.51	25.99	50.7		Y
MassMutual Premier Value Fund Service Class	MCEYX	B	B-	B	Up	5.22	9.07	16.56	26.01	86.49	26.08	50.7		Y
MassMutual Select Diversified Value Fund Admin Cls	MDDLX	B	B-	B	Up	7.24	11.15	18.71	28.16	96.77	12.88	247.3		Y
MassMutual Select Diversified Value Fund Class A	MDDAX	B	B-	B	Up	7.19	11.07	18.44	27.28	94.36	12.78	247.3		Y
MassMutual Select Diversified Value Fund Class I	MDDIX	B	B	B	Up	7.36	11.37	19.06	29.35	99.62	12.76	247.3		Y
MassMutual Select Diversified Value Fund Class R3	MDVNX	B	B-	B	Up	7.23	10.98	18.29	26.71	92.54	12.73	247.3		Y
MassMutual Select Diversified Value Fund Class R4	MDDRX	B	B-	B	Up	7.24	11.13	18.55	27.65	95.73	12.65	247.3		Y
MassMutual Select Diversified Value Fund Class R5	MDVSX	B	B-	B	Up	7.31	11.31	18.99	28.96	98.82	12.79	247.3		Y
MassMutual Select Diversified Value Fund Service Class	MDVYX	B	B-	B	Up	7.33	11.26	18.86	28.56	97.79	12.79	247.3		Y
MassMutual Select Fundamental Value Fund Admin Cls	MFULX	B-	B-	B	Down	5.50	8.58	14.91	24.66	86.44	11.7	1,266		Y
MassMutual Select Fundamental Value Fund Class A	MFUAX	B-	B-	B	Down	5.47	8.50	14.72	23.83	84.30	11.56	1,266		Y
MassMutual Select Fundamental Value Fund Class I	MFUZX	B	B-	B	Up	5.64	8.82	15.30	25.82	89.62	11.61	1,266		Y
MassMutual Select Fundamental Value Fund Class R3	MFUNX	B-	B-	B	Down	5.43	8.41	14.52	23.22	82.54	11.37	1,266		Y
MassMutual Select Fundamental Value Fund Class R4	MFUFX	B-	B-	B	Down	5.46	8.52	14.81	24.19	85.53	11.39	1,266		Y
MassMutual Select Fundamental Value Fund Class R5	MVUSX	B	B-	B	Up	5.58	8.75	15.20	25.51	88.42	11.67	1,266		Y
MassMutual Select Fundamental Value Fund Service Class	MFUYX	B	B-	B	Up	5.54	8.63	15.10	25.07	87.45	11.62	1,266		Y
MassMutual Select Large Cap Value Fund Administrative Cls	MLVLX	B	B-	B	Up	6.49	10.76	19.90	28.64	80.62	8.08	195.1		Y
MassMutual Select Large Cap Value Fund Class A	MMLAX	B-	B-	B-	Down	6.36	10.63	19.61	27.66	78.30	8.07	195.1		Y
MassMutual Select Large Cap Value Fund Class I	MLVZX	B-	B	B-	Down	6.53	11.07	20.24	29.81	83.22	8.08	195.1		Y
MassMutual Select Large Cap Value Fund Class R3	MLVNX	B-	B-	B-	Down	6.26	10.63	19.34	27.15	76.88	7.88	195.1		Y
MassMutual Select Large Cap Value Fund Class R4	MLVFX	B-	B-	B-	Down	6.45	10.76	19.68	28.13	79.67	7.99	195.1		Y
MassMutual Select Large Cap Value Fund Class R5	MLVSX	B-	B-	B-	Down	6.54	10.93	20.23	29.45	82.44	8.1	195.1		Y
MassMutual Select Large Cap Value Fund Service Class	MMLYX	B	B-	B	Up	6.50	10.87	20.11	29.15	81.80	8.15	195.1		Y
Meritage Value Equity Fund Institutional Shares	MVEBX	B	C+	B+	Up	4.93	10.37	15.70	21.32		13.34	17.6	913-345-7000	Y
MFS® Equity Income Fund Class A	EQNAX	B-	B-	B-	Down	5.29	9.62	19.64	29.39	89.25	15.77	199.4	877-960-6077	Y
MFS® Equity Income Fund Class B	EQNBX	B-	B-	B-	Down	5.07	9.12	18.71	26.52	82.23	15.76	199.4	877-960-6077	Y
MFS® Equity Income Fund Class C	EQNCX	B-	B-	B-	Down	5.07	9.13	18.70	26.49	82.29	15.76	199.4	877-960-6077	Y
MFS® Equity Income Fund Class I	EQNIX	B-	B-	B-	Down	5.36	9.83	20.02	30.52	91.69	15.78	199.4	877-960-6077	Y
MFS® Equity Income Fund Class R1	EQNRX	B-	B-	B-	Down	5.09	9.14	18.76	26.53	82.20	15.84	199.4	877-960-6077	Y
MFS® Equity Income Fund Class R2	EQNSX	B-	B-	B-	Down	5.15	9.40	19.29	28.38	86.71	15.8	199.4	877-960-6077	Y
MFS® Equity Income Fund Class R3	EQNTX	B-	B-	B-	Down	5.28	9.53	19.60	29.34	89.14	15.79	199.4	877-960-6077	Y
MFS® Equity Income Fund Class R4	EQNUX	B-	B-	B-	Down	5.36	9.68	19.93	30.32	91.50	15.78	199.4	877-960-6077	Y
MFS® Equity Income Fund Class R6	EQNVX	B-	B-	B-	Down	5.43	9.84	20.11	30.88	93.56	15.87	199.4	877-960-6077	Y

Category: US Equity Large Cap Value (con't)

Fund Name	Ticker Symbol	RATINGS: Overall Rating	Reward Rating	Risk Rating	Recent Up/ Downgrade	TOTAL RETURNS & PERFORMANCE: 3-Month Total Return	6-Month Total Return	1-Year Total Return	3-Year Total Return	5-Year Total Return	ASSETS: NAV	Total Assets (MIL)	NEW INVESTORS: Telephone	Open to New Investors
MFS® Value Fund Class 529A	EAVLX	B	B-	B		4.91	7.74	17.43	31.40	100.72	40.24	47,021	877-960-6077	Y
MFS® Value Fund Class 529B	EBVLX	B-	B-	B-	Down	4.71	7.33	16.65	29.32	94.55	39.81	47,021	877-960-6077	Y
MFS® Value Fund Class 529C	ECVLX	B-	B-	B-	Down	4.71	7.34	16.51	28.33	92.88	39.63	47,021	877-960-6077	Y
MFS® Value Fund Class A	MEIAX	B	B-	B		4.90	7.76	17.44	31.42	100.68	40.57	47,021	877-960-6077	Y
MFS® Value Fund Class B	MFEBX	B-	B-	B-	Down	4.72	7.34	16.57	28.48	93.34	40.38	47,021	877-960-6077	Y
MFS® Value Fund Class C	MEICX	B-	B-	B-	Down	4.71	7.35	16.55	28.48	93.33	40.11	47,021	877-960-6077	Y
MFS® Value Fund Class I	MEIIX	B	B	B		4.99	7.88	17.76	32.43	103.24	40.79	47,021	877-960-6077	Y
MFS® Value Fund Class R1	MEIGX	B-	B-	B-	Down	4.72	7.35	16.58	28.49	93.36	39.82	47,021	877-960-6077	Y
MFS® Value Fund Class R2	MVRRX	B-	B-	B	Down	4.85	7.62	17.15	30.43	98.20	40.16	47,021	877-960-6077	Y
MFS® Value Fund Class R3	MEIHX	B-	B-	B	Down	4.92	7.77	17.46	31.42	100.74	40.42	47,021	877-960-6077	Y
MFS® Value Fund Class R4	MEIJX	B	B	B		4.97	7.90	17.74	32.41	103.28	40.56	47,021	877-960-6077	Y
MFS® Value Fund Class R6	MEIKX	B	B	B		5.03	7.96	17.86	32.83	104.34	40.56	47,021	877-960-6077	Y
Mount Lucas U.S. Focused Equity Fund Class I	BMLEX	B-	B-	B	Down	8.97	14.68	23.90	24.26	104.37	10.73	10.9		Y
Multi-Manager Value Strategies Fund Class A	CDEIX	B-	B	B-	Down	6.54	11.02	19.60	33.64	93.48	14.11	2,633	800-345-6611	Y
Multi-Manager Value Strategies Fund Institutional Class	CZMVX	B-	B	B-	Down	6.52	11.11	19.64	33.69	93.54	13.96	2,633	800-345-6611	Y
Nationwide Ziegler Equity Income Fund Class A	NWGYX	B-	B-	B-	Down	7.73	12.37	17.97	28.90	90.16	15.24	489.1	800-848-0920	Y
Nationwide Ziegler Equity Income Fund Class C	NWGZX	B-	B-	B-	Down	7.47	11.92	17.12	26.02	83.54	15.1	489.1	800-848-0920	Y
Nationwide Ziegler Equity Income Fund Class R6	NWJAX	B	B-	B		7.80	12.51	18.37	30.18	93.00	15.3	489.1	800-848-0920	Y
Nationwide Ziegler Equity Income Fund Inst Service Cls	NWJBX	B-	B-	B-	Down	7.77	12.52	18.24	29.84	92.27	15.3	489.1	800-848-0920	Y
Neiman Large Cap Value Fund A Shares	NEAMX	B-	B-	B	Down	8.06	12.60	18.99	27.76	80.94	27.98	26.6	858-551-4078	Y
Neiman Large Cap Value Fund No-Load Shares	NEIMX	B-	B-	B	Down	8.06	12.60	18.98	27.76	80.81	27.98	26.6	858-551-4078	Y
Neuberger Berman Adv Mgmt Trust Large Cap Value Cls I	US6412221045	B-	B-	B-		5.08	8.45	13.36	26.41	86.65	16.71	73.3	212-476-9000	Y
Neuberger Berman Equity Income Fund Class A	NBHAX	B-	B-	B-	Down	4.42	7.95	12.83	23.87	54.90	13.11	1,728	212-476-9000	Y
Neuberger Berman Equity Income Fund Class R3	NBHRX	B-	B-	B-	Down	4.33	7.79	12.60	22.89	52.81	13.09	1,728	212-476-9000	Y
Neuberger Berman Equity Income Fund Institutional Class	NBHIX	B-	B-	B-	Down	4.51	8.12	13.22	25.22	57.74	13.15	1,728	212-476-9000	Y
Neuberger Berman Large Cap Value Fund Advisor Class	NBPBX	B-	B-	B-		4.97	8.36	13.01	25.28	86.25	31.31	1,514	212-476-9000	
Neuberger Berman Large Cap Value Fund Class A	NPNAX	B-	B-	B-		5.00	8.38	13.16	25.72	87.26	31.28	1,514	212-476-9000	Y
Neuberger Berman Large Cap Value Fund Class C	NPNCX	B-	B-	C+		4.81	8.01	12.35	22.99	80.45	31.43	1,514	212-476-9000	Y
Neuberger Berman Large Cap Value Fund Class R3	NPNRX	B-	B-	C+		4.95	8.21	12.78	24.64	84.67	31.35	1,514	212-476-9000	Y
Neuberger Berman Large Cap Value Fund Institutional Class	NBPIX	B-	B-	B-		5.11	8.62	13.56	27.21	90.95	31.2	1,514	212-476-9000	Y
Neuberger Berman Large Cap Value Fund Investor Class	NPRTX	B-	B-	B-		5.07	8.49	13.39	26.51	89.36	31.23	1,514	212-476-9000	
Neuberger Berman Large Cap Value Fund Trust Class	NBPTX	B-	B-	B-		5.01	8.44	13.21	25.89	87.70	31.28	1,514	212-476-9000	
Neuberger Berman Value Fund Class A	NVAAX	B-	B-	C+		5.24	8.73	13.51	26.21	84.30	17.72	16.9	212-476-9000	Y
Neuberger Berman Value Fund Class C	NVACX	B-	B-	C+		5.02	8.29	12.64	23.42	77.59	17.23	16.9	212-476-9000	Y
Neuberger Berman Value Fund Institutional Class	NLRLX	B-	B-	C+		5.32	8.96	13.99	27.64	88.07	17.74	16.9	212-476-9000	Y
Northern Income Equity Fund	NOIEX	B	B-	B		7.20	12.29	20.20	33.08	85.44	14.38	238.2	800-595-9111	Y
Northern Large Cap Core Fund	NOLCX	B-	B-	B-	Down	7.43	12.45	20.31	30.38	107.94	19.06	246.7	800-595-9111	Y
Northern Large Cap Value Fund	NOLVX	B-	B-	B	Up	5.63	8.80	12.54	22.34	88.30	16.31	94.2	800-595-9111	Y
NorthPointe Large Cap Value Fund Institutional Shares	NPILX	B	B-	B	Up	6.56	12.07	15.10	24.91		13.09	49.3		Y
NorthPointe Large Cap Value Fund Investor Shares	NPLVX	B	B-	B	Up	6.42	11.85	14.78	24.14		13.06	49.3		Y
Nuveen Concentrated Core Fund Class A	NCADX	B-	C+	B	Up	2.07	8.37	16.72	16.23		30.33	98.8	312-917-8146	Y
Nuveen Concentrated Core Fund Class C	NCAEX	B-	C+	B	Up	1.85	7.96	15.82	13.61		29.9	98.8	312-917-8146	Y
Nuveen Concentrated Core Fund Class I	NCAFX	B-	C+	B	Up	2.10	8.51	16.99	17.07		30.34	98.8	312-917-8146	Y
Nuveen Concentrated Core Fund Class R6	NCARX	B-	C+	B	Up	2.13	8.54	17.11	17.22		30.36	98.8	312-917-8146	Y
Nuveen Dividend Value Fund Class A	FFEIX	B	B-	B	Up	6.62	11.18	17.05	29.94	88.43	14.81	1,154	312-917-8146	Y
Nuveen Dividend Value Fund Class C	FFECX	B-	B-	B	Down	6.47	10.82	16.18	27.11	81.62	14.55	1,154	312-917-8146	Y
Nuveen Dividend Value Fund Class I	FAQIX	B	B	B	Up	6.67	11.33	17.29	30.87	90.93	15	1,154	312-917-8146	Y
Nuveen Dividend Value Fund Class R3	FEISX	B	B-	B	Up	6.58	11.09	16.75	28.99	86.25	14.75	1,154	312-917-8146	Y
Nuveen Dividend Value Fund Class R6	FFEFX	B	B	B	Up	6.71	11.42	17.44	31.34	91.67	15.09	1,154	312-917-8146	Y
Nuveen Large-Cap Value Fund Class A	NNGAX	B-	B-	B-	Up	6.67	12.56	16.48	24.40	97.19	25.96	457.6	312-917-8146	Y
Nuveen Large-Cap Value Fund Class C	NNGCX	B-	B-	C+	Up	6.48	12.11	15.56	21.63	89.90	24.85	457.6	312-917-8146	Y
Nuveen Large-Cap Value Fund Class I	NNGRX	B-	B-	B-	Up	6.73	12.66	16.75	25.32	99.62	26.05	457.6	312-917-8146	Y

Category: US Equity Large Cap Value (con't)

Fund Name	Ticker Symbol	RATINGS: Overall Rating	Reward Rating	Risk Rating	Recent Up/ Downgrade	TOTAL RETURNS & PERFORMANCE: 3-Month Total Return	6-Month Total Return	1-Year Total Return	3-Year Total Return	5-Year Total Return	ASSETS: NAV	Total Assets (MIL)	NEW INVESTORS: Telephone	Open to New Investors
Nuveen Large-Cap Value Fund Class R3	NMMTX	B-	B-	B-	Up	6.62	12.38	16.13	23.48	94.72	26.23	457.6	312-917-8146	Y
Nuveen Large-Cap Value Fund Class R6	NNGFX	B-	B-	B-	Up	6.77	12.71	16.79	25.48	99.87	26.06	457.6	312-917-8146	Y
Nuveen NWQ Large Cap Value Fund Class A	NQCAX	B-	B-	B	Up	3.77	8.38	15.10	21.71	71.58	6.7	82.0	312-917-8146	Y
Nuveen NWQ Large Cap Value Fund Class C	NQCCX	B-	C+	B	Up	3.38	7.86	14.07	18.76	65.05	5.95	82.0	312-917-8146	Y
Nuveen NWQ Large Cap Value Fund Class I	NQCRX	B-	B-	B	Up	3.75	8.47	15.32	22.54	73.67	6.72	82.0	312-917-8146	Y
Nuveen NWQ Large Cap Value Fund Class R3	NQCQX	B-	B-	B	Up	3.68	8.33	14.81	20.71	69.39	6.63	82.0	312-917-8146	Y
Nuveen NWQ Multi Cap Value Fund Class A	NQVAX	B-	B-	B-	Up	5.23	8.41	18.36	24.99	71.50	31.06	97.6	312-917-8146	Y
Nuveen NWQ Multi Cap Value Fund Class C	NQVCX	B-	B-	B-	Up	5.06	8.00	17.50	22.22	65.21	29.35	97.6	312-917-8146	Y
Nuveen NWQ Multi Cap Value Fund Class I	NQVRX	B-	B-	B-	Up	5.28	8.51	18.67	25.91	73.66	31.21	97.6	312-917-8146	Y
Nuveen NWQ Multi-Cap Value Fund Class R3	NMCTX	B-	B-	B-	Up	5.17	8.27	18.10	24.05	69.45	30.76	97.6	312-917-8146	Y
Oppenheimer Dividend Opportunity Fund Class A	OSVAX	B-	B-	B-	Down	5.74	8.66	14.40	29.06	71.43	24.09	268.9	800-225-5677	Y
Oppenheimer Dividend Opportunity Fund Class B	OSVBX	B-	C+	B-	Down	5.52	8.19	13.46	25.97	64.77	23.36	268.9	800-225-5677	
Oppenheimer Dividend Opportunity Fund Class C	OSCVX	B	C+	B+	Up	5.55	8.27	13.59	26.18	65.15	23.26	268.9	800-225-5677	Y
Oppenheimer Dividend Opportunity Fund Class I	OSVIX	B-	B-	B	Down	5.88	8.92	14.92	30.81	74.09	24.06	268.9	800-225-5677	Y
Oppenheimer Dividend Opportunity Fund Class R	OSVNX	B	B-	B+	Up	5.69	8.52	14.14	28.11	69.38	23.85	268.9	800-225-5677	Y
Oppenheimer Dividend Opportunity Fund Class Y	OSVYX	B-	B-	B-	Down	5.82	8.82	14.72	30.04	73.80	24.06	268.9	800-225-5677	Y
Oppenheimer Equity Income Fund Class I	OEIIX	B-	C+	B-	Up	4.91	8.31	13.06	17.00	74.80	32.29	3,798	800-225-5677	Y
Oppenheimer Value Fund Class A	CGRWX	B	B-	B	Up	5.02	8.80	15.94	24.21	83.14	37.32	2,140	800-225-5677	Y
Oppenheimer Value Fund Class B	CGRBX	B-	C+	B	Down	4.82	8.39	15.06	21.37	76.18	36.84	2,140	800-225-5677	
Oppenheimer Value Fund Class C	CGRCX	B-	C+	B	Down	4.84	8.41	15.07	21.42	76.42	35.62	2,140	800-225-5677	Y
Oppenheimer Value Fund Class I	OGRIX	B	B-	B	Up	5.15	9.04	16.44	25.85	87.19	38.08	2,140	800-225-5677	Y
Oppenheimer Value Fund Class R	CGRNX	B-	B-	B	Down	4.96	8.67	15.64	23.28	80.89	36.59	2,140	800-225-5677	Y
Oppenheimer Value Fund Class Y	CGRYX	B	B-	B	Up	5.09	8.92	16.21	25.11	85.53	38.14	2,140	800-225-5677	Y
PACE Large Co Value Equity Investments Class A	PCPAX	B	B-	B		5.76	9.33	13.81	26.66	94.23	23.56	1,383	212-882-5586	Y
PACE Large Co Value Equity Investments Class C	PLVCX	B-	B-	B	Down	5.59	8.92	12.93	23.72	86.76	23.68	1,383	212-882-5586	Y
PACE Large Co Value Equity Investments Class P	PCLVX	B	B-	B		5.80	9.43	14.02	27.50	96.56	23.47	1,383	212-882-5586	Y
PACE Large Co Value Equity Investments Class Y	PLVYX	B	B-	B		5.83	9.44	14.07	27.56	96.66	23.59	1,383	212-882-5586	Y
Parametric Dividend Income Fund Institutional Class	EIPDX	B	B-	B		6.33	10.68	15.79	36.48		13.12	26.4		Y
Parametric Dividend Income Fund Investor Class	EAPDX	B-	B-	B	Down	6.28	10.58	15.46	35.45		13.1	26.4		Y
Payden Equity Income Fund	PYVLX	B	B-	B		6.28	10.87	15.70	33.94	92.48	16.56	997.8	614-470-8006	Y
Payden Equity Income Fund Adviser Class	PYVAX	B-	B-	B	Down	6.24	10.76	15.50	33.06	90.24	16.56	997.8	614-470-8006	Y
Payden Equity Income Fund SI Class	PYVSX	B	B-	B		6.29	10.92	15.92	34.54	93.46	16.57	997.8	614-470-8006	Y
PF Comstock Fund Class P	US69447T6073	B	B	B-	Up	7.36	13.78	17.65	28.56	94.75	15.96	191.0	800-722-2333	Y
PF Large-Cap Value Fund Class P	US69447T8210	B	C+	B	Up	4.61	7.02	13.99	23.63	86.58	17.71	432.3	800-722-2333	Y
PIMCO RAE Fundamental PLUS Fund Administrative Class	PXTAX	B	B	B-	Up	7.40	12.93	19.07	30.97	102.24	7.51	1,841	866-746-2602	Y
PIMCO RAE Fundamental PLUS Fund Class A	PIXAX	B	B	B-	Up	7.40	12.71	18.77	30.19	100.55	7.32	1,841	866-746-2602	Y
PIMCO RAE Fundamental PLUS Fund Class C	PIXCX	B-	B-	C+	Down	7.17	12.33	17.93	27.25	93.05	6.77	1,841	866-746-2602	Y
PIMCO RAE Fundamental PLUS Fund Class D	PIXDX	B	B	B-	Up	7.42	12.90	18.81	30.42	100.81	7.31	1,841	866-746-2602	Y
PIMCO RAE Fundamental PLUS Fund Class P	PIXPX	B	B	B-	Up	7.46	12.96	19.21	31.58	103.86	7.63	1,841	866-746-2602	Y
PIMCO RAE Fundamental PLUS Fund Institutional Class	PXTIX	B	B	B-	Up	7.58	13.08	19.32	31.78	104.63	7.68	1,841	866-746-2602	Y
PIMCO RAE Fundamental US Fund Class A	PKAAX	B	B-	B		7.22	11.72	16.14	28.95	98.46	11.09	641.7	866-746-2602	Y
PIMCO RAE Fundamental US Fund Class C	PKACX	B-	B-	B	Down	7.02	11.36	15.26	26.00	91.06	10.92	641.7	866-746-2602	Y
PIMCO RAE Fundamental US Fund Class P	PKAPX	B	B-	B		7.21	11.89	16.42	30.27	101.69	11.14	641.7	866-746-2602	Y
PIMCO RAE Fundamental US Fund Institutional Class	PKAIX	B	B-	B		7.24	11.91	16.54	30.66	102.70	11.17	641.7	866-746-2602	Y
PIMCO RAE Low Volatility PLUS Fund Class A	PXLVX	B-	B-	B-	Down	7.26	11.54	17.59	32.00		11.81	190.3	866-746-2602	Y
PIMCO RAE Low Volatility PLUS Fund Class C	POLVX	B-	B-	B-	Down	7.06	11.14	16.81	29.20		11.61	190.3	866-746-2602	Y
PIMCO RAE Low Volatility PLUS Fund Class P	PPLVX	B	B	B-		7.34	11.77	17.98	33.25		11.9	190.3	866-746-2602	Y
PIMCO RAE Low Volatility PLUS Fund Institutional Class	PILVX	B	B	B-		7.44	11.87	18.16	33.72		11.94	190.3	866-746-2602	Y
Pioneer Disciplined Value Fund Class A	CVFCX	B	B	C+		4.88	10.22	21.43	29.16	88.00	15.92	590.2	617-742-7825	Y
Pioneer Disciplined Value Fund Class C	CVCFX	B-	B	C+	Down	4.71	9.76	20.49	26.24	81.13	15.65	590.2	617-742-7825	Y
Pioneer Disciplined Value Fund Class R	CVRFX	B-	B	C+	Down	4.82	10.00	21.07	28.15	85.93	15.39	590.2	617-742-7825	Y
Pioneer Disciplined Value Fund Class Y	CVFYX	B	B	C+		5.02	10.41	21.82	30.39	91.18	15.99	590.2	617-742-7825	Y

Category: US Equity Large Cap Value (con't)

Fund Name	Ticker Symbol	RATINGS: Overall Rating	Reward Rating	Risk Rating	Recent Up/ Downgrade	TOTAL RETURNS & PERFORMANCE: 3-Month Total Return	6-Month Total Return	1-Year Total Return	3-Year Total Return	5-Year Total Return	ASSETS: NAV	Total Assets (MIL)	NEW INVESTORS: Telephone	Open to New Investors
Pioneer Equity Income Fund Class A	PEQIX	B	B	A-		5.79	10.37	14.95	35.94	102.36	35.79	2,312	617-742-7825	Y
Pioneer Equity Income Fund Class C	PCEQX	B	B-	A-		5.57	9.97	14.09	32.99	95.10	35.17	2,312	617-742-7825	Y
Pioneer Equity Income Fund Class K	PEQKX	B+	B	A	Up	5.86	10.54	15.35	37.44	106.33	35.85	2,312	617-742-7825	Y
Pioneer Equity Income Fund Class R	PQIRX	B	B	A-		5.60	10.14	14.50	34.43	98.77	36.42	2,312	617-742-7825	Y
Pioneer Equity Income Fund Class Y	PYEQX	B+	B	A	Up	5.79	10.48	15.21	37.01	105.22	36.22	2,312	617-742-7825	Y
PNC Multi-Factor Large Cap Value Fund Class A	PLVAX	B	C+	A-	Up	6.00	9.81	14.62	22.62	88.48	25.69	107.1	800-622-3863	Y
PNC Multi-Factor Large Cap Value Fund Class C	PALVX	B	C+	A-	Up	5.81	9.50	13.93	20.59	83.05	25.19	107.1	800-622-3863	Y
PNC Multi-Factor Large Cap Value Fund Class I	PLIVX	B	C+	A-	Up	6.06	9.96	14.90	23.65	90.86	25.75	107.1	800-622-3863	Y
Power Dividend Index Fund Class A	PWDAX	B-	C+	B-		4.18	8.16	11.25	19.03		12.48	831.6	877-779-7462	Y
Power Dividend Index Fund Class I	PWDIX	B-	C+	B		4.16	8.20	11.41	19.82		12.48	831.6	877-779-7462	Y
Praxis Value Index Fund Class A	MVIAX	B-	B-	B	Down	5.59	9.23	15.19	23.81	87.88	13.82	194.4		Y
Praxis Value Index Fund Class I	MVIIX	B-	B-	B	Down	6.79	10.57	16.91	26.98	94.73	13.74	194.4		Y
Principal Equity Income Fund Class A	PQIAX	B-	B	B-	Down	7.10	11.87	20.54	31.70	91.41	31.43	6,859	800-222-5852	Y
Principal Equity Income Fund Class C	PEUCX	B-	B-	B-	Down	6.93	11.47	19.68	28.82	84.42	30.65	6,859	800-222-5852	Y
Principal Equity Income Fund Institutional Class	PEIIX	B	B	B-		7.23	12.10	21.03	33.26	95.10	31.47	6,859	800-222-5852	Y
Principal Equity Income Fund R-1 Class	PIEMX	B-	B-	B-	Down	6.99	11.60	19.96	29.80	86.72	31.32	6,859	800-222-5852	Y
Principal Equity Income Fund R-2 Class	PEINX	B-	B-	B-	Down	7.03	11.70	20.12	30.33	88.01	31.44	6,859	800-222-5852	Y
Principal Equity Income Fund R-3 Class	PEIOX	B-	B-	B-	Down	7.10	11.79	20.37	31.01	89.75	31.34	6,859	800-222-5852	Y
Principal Equity Income Fund R-4 Class	PEIPX	B-	B	B-	Down	7.10	11.84	20.54	31.71	91.49	31.39	6,859	800-222-5852	Y
Principal Equity Income Fund R-5 Class	PEIQX	B-	B	B-	Down	7.16	11.97	20.71	32.24	92.63	31.44	6,859	800-222-5852	Y
Principal LargeCap Value Fund Class A	PCACX	B	C+	B+	Up	6.84	11.41	16.18	21.94	81.91	10.91	1,401	800-222-5852	Y
Principal LargeCap Value Fund Class C	PLUCX	B-	C+	B	Down	6.60	11.02	15.22	18.95	74.38	10.57	1,401	800-222-5852	Y
Principal LargeCap Value Fund Class J	PVLJX	B	C+	B+	Up	6.87	11.53	16.41	22.46	82.68	10.64	1,401	800-222-5852	Y
Principal LargeCap Value Fund III Class J	PLVJX	B-	B-	B-	Down	6.51	9.31	16.53	27.23	91.46	16.72	2,177	800-222-5852	Y
Principal LargeCap Value Fund III Institutional Class	PLVIX	B-	B-	B-	Down	6.60	9.50	16.86	28.48	94.75	16.93	2,177	800-222-5852	Y
Principal LargeCap Value Fund III R-1 Class	PESAX	B-	B-	B-	Down	6.33	8.98	15.80	25.16	86.48	16.92	2,177	800-222-5852	Y
Principal LargeCap Value Fund III R-2 Class	PPSNX	B-	B-	B-	Down	6.42	9.06	16.01	25.67	87.74	16.98	2,177	800-222-5852	Y
Principal LargeCap Value Fund III R-3 Class	PPSFX	B-	B-	B-	Down	6.48	9.21	16.25	26.37	89.51	17.69	2,177	800-222-5852	Y
Principal LargeCap Value Fund III R-4 Class	PPSSX	B	B-	B	Up	6.52	9.29	16.41	27.11	91.23	16.95	2,177	800-222-5852	Y
Principal LargeCap Value Fund III R-5 Class	PPSRX	B-	B-	B-	Down	6.55	9.36	16.59	27.50	92.38	17.07	2,177	800-222-5852	Y
Principal LargeCap Value Fund Institutional Class	PVLIX	B	B-	B+	Up	6.97	11.72	16.72	23.67	86.03	10.88	1,401	800-222-5852	Y
Principal LargeCap Value Fund R-1 Class	PLSVX	B	C+	B	Up	6.67	11.10	15.62	20.36	77.97	10.79	1,401	800-222-5852	Y
Principal LargeCap Value Fund R-2 Class	PLVNX	B	C+	B	Up	6.68	11.18	15.79	20.76	79.04	10.84	1,401	800-222-5852	Y
Principal LargeCap Value Fund R-3 Class	PLVMX	B	C+	B+	Up	6.76	11.37	16.01	21.55	80.69	10.78	1,401	800-222-5852	Y
Principal LargeCap Value Fund R-4 Class	PLVSX	B	C+	B+	Up	6.81	11.42	16.25	22.13	82.37	10.77	1,401	800-222-5852	Y
Principal LargeCap Value Fund R-5 Class	PLVPX	B	C+	B+	Up	6.87	11.52	16.40	22.65	83.47	10.91	1,401	800-222-5852	Y
ProFunds Large Cap Value Fund Investor Class	LVPIX	B-	B-	B	Down	5.86	9.01	13.24	23.09	80.58	65.56	10.2	614-470-8626	Y
ProFunds Large Cap Value Fund Service Class	LVPSX	B-	C+	B-	Down	5.59	8.48	12.13	19.43	71.69	59.75	10.2	614-470-8626	Y
Prudential QMA Strategic Value Fund Class A	SUVAX	B	B	B	Up	6.78	11.17	15.42	30.98	103.11	14.53	402.7	800-225-1852	Y
Prudential QMA Strategic Value Fund Class B	SUVBX	B-	B	B-	Down	6.55	10.66	14.53	28.00	95.55	13.51	402.7	800-225-1852	
Prudential QMA Strategic Value Fund Class C	SUVCX	B-	B	B-	Down	6.61	10.73	14.51	28.07	95.73	13.5	402.7	800-225-1852	Y
Prudential QMA Strategic Value Fund Class Q	SUVQX	B	B	B	Up	6.87	11.31	15.75	32.11	105.85	14.88	402.7	800-225-1852	Y
Prudential QMA Strategic Value Fund Class R	PRVRX	B	B	B-	Up	6.73	11.01	15.11	29.90	99.40	14.89	402.7	800-225-1852	Y
Prudential QMA Strategic Value Fund Class Z	SUVZX	B	B	B	Up	6.87	11.39	15.76	32.12	105.86	14.88	402.7	800-225-1852	Y
Putnam Equity Income Fund Class A	PEYAX	B	B-	B	Up	6.26	11.68	18.68	29.19	96.36	24.51	12,342	617-292-1000	Y
Putnam Equity Income Fund Class B	PEQNX	B	B-	B	Up	6.10	11.26	17.80	26.30	89.10	24.22	12,342	617-292-1000	Y
Putnam Equity Income Fund Class C	PEQCX	B	B-	B	Up	6.06	11.27	17.77	26.32	89.07	24.22	12,342	617-292-1000	Y
Putnam Equity Income Fund Class M	PEIMX	B-	B-	B-	Down	6.13	11.43	18.12	27.26	91.49	24.19	12,342	617-292-1000	Y
Putnam Equity Income Fund Class R	PEQRX	B-	B-	B-	Down	6.20	11.53	18.40	28.20	93.94	24.32	12,342	617-292-1000	Y
Putnam Equity Income Fund Class R5	PEQLX	B-	B-	B-	Down	6.32	11.80	18.96	30.32	99.60	24.52	12,342	617-292-1000	Y
Putnam Equity Income Fund Class R6	PEQSX	B-	B	B-	Down	6.40	11.92	19.13	30.77	100.61	24.52	12,342	617-292-1000	Y
Putnam Equity Income Fund Class Y	PEIYX	B	B-	B	Up	6.33	11.81	18.94	30.13	98.76	24.51	12,342	617-292-1000	Y

Category: US Equity Large Cap Value (con't)

Fund Name	Ticker Symbol	RATINGS: Overall Rating	Reward Rating	Risk Rating	Recent Up/ Downgrade	TOTAL RETURNS & PERFORMANCE: 3-Month Total Return	6-Month Total Return	1-Year Total Return	3-Year Total Return	5-Year Total Return	ASSETS: NAV	Total Assets (MIL)	NEW INVESTORS: Telephone	Open to New Investors
Queens Road Value Fund	QRVLX	B-	B-	B-	Down	6.26	10.22	20.31	30.67	92.23	23.28	46.7	888-353-0261	Y
RNC Genter Dividend Income Fund	GDIIX	B	B-	B	Up	6.75	13.17	17.09	32.77	79.47	18.34	16.8	800-877-7624	Y
SA U.S. Value Fund Investor Class	SABTX	B	B	B	Up	7.22	11.97	18.37	33.60	108.00	18.79	607.9		Y
SA U.S. Value Fund Select Class	SAVLX	B	B	B		7.30	12.11	18.52	33.76	108.26	18.79	607.9		Y
Schwab Dividend Equity Fund™	SWDSX	B-	B-	B	Down	5.23	10.19	15.66	22.36	84.54	16.33	1,495	877-824-5615	Y
Schwab Fundamental US Large Company Index Fund	SFLNX	B	B-	B		7.00	11.83	17.05	30.82	102.29	17.26	5,492	877-824-5615	Y
SEI Inst Inv Trust U.S. Managed Vol Fund Cls A	SVYAX	B	B-	B		5.81	8.81	15.31	31.48	105.32	14.57	1,644	800-342-5734	Y
SEI Institutional Managed Trust Large Cap Value Fund Cls F	TRMVX	B-	B-	B	Up	7.49	11.92	17.39	25.03	92.43	25.46	1,444	800-342-5734	Y
SEI Institutional Managed Trust Large Cap Value Fund Cls I	SEUIX	B-	B-	B	Up	7.44	11.79	17.13	24.21	90.31	25.49	1,444	800-342-5734	Y
SEI Institutional Managed Trust Large Cap Value Fund Cls Y	SVAYX	B-	B-	B	Down	7.57	12.04	17.68	25.67	93.43	25.45	1,444	800-342-5734	Y
SEI Inst Managed Trust Tax-Managed Managed Vol Fund Cls Y	STVYX	B	B-	B+	Down	5.12	8.03	15.47	30.94	99.97	16.21	1,107	800-342-5734	Y
SEI Inst Managed Trust Tax-Managed Volatility Fund Cls F	TMMAX	B	B-	B+		5.06	7.97	15.18	30.14	98.74	16.22	1,107	800-342-5734	Y
SEI Inst Managed Trust U.S. Managed Volatility Fund Cls F	SVOAX	B-	B-	B	Down	5.25	7.66	14.03	27.50	96.72	17.72	1,895	800-342-5734	Y
SEI Inst Managed Trust U.S. Managed Volatility Fund Cls I	SEVIX	B-	B-	B	Down	5.13	7.50	13.70	26.52	94.33	17.72	1,895	800-342-5734	Y
SEI Inst Managed Trust U.S. Managed Volatility Fund Cls Y	SUSYX	B-	B-	B	Down	5.32	7.80	14.32	28.45	98.19	17.72	1,895	800-342-5734	Y
Shelton Capital Management Core Value Fund Class K	EQTKX	B	C+	B	Up	4.99	8.88	12.15	20.95	83.26	23.76	172.0	800-955-9988	Y
Shelton Capital Management Core Value Fund Direct Shares	EQTIX	B	C+	B+		5.10	9.12	12.70	22.76	87.82	24.06	172.0	800-955-9988	Y
SkyBridge Dividend Value Fund Class A	SKYAX	B	C+	A-	Up	6.51	7.31	8.45	27.72		11.51	308.2		Y
SkyBridge Dividend Value Fund Class C	SKYCX	B-	C+	B	Up	6.28	6.86	7.59	24.73		11.42	308.2		Y
SkyBridge Dividend Value Fund Class I	SKYIX	B	C+	A-	Up	6.61	7.48	8.67	28.61		11.51	308.2		Y
Sound Shore Fund Institutional Class	SSHVX	B-	B-	C+		4.31	7.46	16.40	25.85	104.34	46.06	2,168	800-551-1980	Y
Sound Shore Fund Investor Class	SSHFX	B-	B-	C+		4.26	7.38	16.22	25.24	102.97	45.89	2,168	800-551-1980	Y
Sterling Capital Behavioral Large Cap Value Equity Fund A	BBTGX	B	B-	B	Up	6.58	12.66	18.46	26.25	90.59	21.68	318.6	800-228-1872	Y
Sterling Capital Behavioral Large Cap Value Equity Fund C	BCVCX	B	B-	B	Up	6.42	12.25	17.60	23.50	83.58	21.07	318.6	800-228-1872	Y
Sterling Capital Behavioral Large Cap Value Eq Fund Inst	BBISX	B	B-	B	Up	6.70	12.83	18.81	27.22	93.09	21.81	318.6	800-228-1872	Y
Sterling Capital Equity Income Fund Class A	BAEIX	B-	B-	B-	Down	7.24	12.61	20.64	33.64	75.45	20.29	1,635	800-228-1872	Y
Sterling Capital Equity Income Fund Class C	BCEGX	B-	B-	B-	Down	7.01	12.14	19.71	30.60	68.93	20.09	1,635	800-228-1872	Y
Sterling Capital Equity Income Fund Class R	BAERX	B-	B-	B-	Down	7.12	12.41	20.31	32.58	73.18	20.13	1,635	800-228-1872	Y
Sterling Capital Equity Income Fund Institutional Shares	BEGIX	B-	B	B-	Down	7.28	12.72	20.95	34.57	77.62	20.34	1,635	800-228-1872	Y
Stock Dividend Fund	SDIVX	B	B+	C	Up	11.80	24.05	23.02	36.82	77.45	29.93	29.6		Y
Strategic Advisers® Value Fund	FVSAX	B	B	B	Up	6.93	11.95	18.13	31.77	102.69	20.42	11,606	617-563-7000	Y
Strategic Advisers® Value Multi-Manager Fund	FKMOX	B	B	B	Up	6.78	11.65	18.97	31.05	99.46	16.37	21.1	617-563-7000	Y
Strategic Advisers® Value Multi-Manager Fund Class L	FQALX	B	B	B	Up	6.78	11.65	18.97	31.05	99.47	16.37	25.9	617-563-7000	Y
Strategic Advisers® Value Multi-Manager Fund Class N	FQAMX	B	B	B	Up	6.71	11.47	18.62	30.02	96.90	16.36	25.9	617-563-7000	Y
Symons Value Institutional Fund	SAVIX	B-	C+	B	Up	5.19	5.39	9.85	15.49	51.30	10.41	73.5		Y
T. Rowe Price Equity Income Fund	PRFDX	B-	B-	B-	Down	5.44	10.05	16.17	28.09	83.09	33.34	22,563	410-345-2000	Y
T. Rowe Price Equity Income Fund Advisor Class	PAFDX	B-	B-	C+	Down	5.33	9.84	15.83	26.99	80.51	33.26	22,563	410-345-2000	Y
T. Rowe Price Equity Income Fund Class R	RRFDX	B-	B-	C+	Down	5.28	9.74	15.52	25.96	78.15	33.2	22,563	410-345-2000	Y
T. Rowe Price Equity Income Fund I Class	REIPX	B-	B	C+	Down	5.46	10.11	16.30	28.36	83.47	33.35	22,563	410-345-2000	Y
T. Rowe Price Institutional Large Cap Value Fund	TILCX	B-	B	B-	Down	5.50	9.31	16.82	29.86	101.93	23.38	3,957	410-345-2000	Y
T. Rowe Price Value Fund	TRVLX	B-	B	B-	Down	6.02	9.56	18.94	28.23	105.20	37.32	27,030	410-345-2000	Y
T. Rowe Price Value Fund Advisor Class	PAVLX	B-	B-	B-	Down	5.95	9.40	18.64	27.32	102.90	36.77	27,030	410-345-2000	Y
T. Rowe Price Value Fund I Class	TRPIX	B-	B	B-	Down	6.07	9.63	19.15	28.73	106.00	37.32	27,030	410-345-2000	Y
TCW Relative Value Dividend Appreciation Fund Class I	TGDFX	B-	C+	B	Down	3.58	7.22	11.16	21.87	85.66	19.13	630.2	213-244-0000	Y
TCW Relative Value Dividend Appreciation Fund Class N	TGIGX	B-	C+	B	Down	3.57	7.10	10.91	20.93	83.32	19.46	630.2	213-244-0000	Y
TCW Relative Value Large Cap Fund Class Institutional	TGDIX	B-	B-	C+	Down	4.04	8.64	15.27	25.21	94.70	21.76	501.5	213-244-0000	Y
TCW Relative Value Large Cap Fund Class N	TGDVX	B	B-	B	Up	3.97	8.44	14.97	24.30	92.26	21.71	501.5	213-244-0000	Y
The Hartford Dividend and Growth Fund Class A	IHGIX	B	B	B-		5.97	10.35	17.78	31.33	97.71	25.79	8,559	888-843-7824	Y
The Hartford Dividend and Growth Fund Class C	HDGCX	B-	B-	B-	Down	5.79	9.97	16.94	28.43	90.51	24.93	8,559	888-843-7824	Y
The Hartford Dividend and Growth Fund Class F	HDGFX	B	B	B-		6.05	10.55	18.19	32.74	101.45	25.65	8,559	888-843-7824	Y
The Hartford Dividend and Growth Fund Class I	HDGIX	B	B	B-		6.07	10.54	18.09	32.17	99.85	25.67	8,559	888-843-7824	Y
The Hartford Dividend and Growth Fund Class R3	HDGRX	B-	B-	B-	Down	5.89	10.16	17.36	29.98	94.49	26.13	8,559	888-843-7824	Y

Category: US Equity Large Cap Value (con't)

		RATINGS				TOTAL RETURNS & PERFORMANCE					ASSETS		NEW INVESTORS	
Fund Name	Ticker Symbol	Overall Rating	Reward Rating	Risk Rating	Recent Up/ Downgrade	3-Month Total Return	6-Month Total Return	1-Year Total Return	3-Year Total Return	5-Year Total Return	NAV	Total Assets (MIL)	Telephone	Open to New Investors
The Hartford Dividend and Growth Fund Class R4	HDGSX	B	B	B-		5.96	10.33	17.73	31.16	97.50	26.3	8,559	888-843-7824	Y
The Hartford Dividend and Growth Fund Class R5	HDGTX	B	B	B-		6.05	10.49	18.10	32.34	100.51	26.4	8,559	888-843-7824	Y
The Hartford Dividend and Growth Fund Class R6	HDGVX	B	B	B-		6.08	10.55	18.22	32.63	101.28	26.4	8,559	888-843-7824	Y
The Hartford Dividend and Growth Fund Class Y	HDGYX	B	B	B-		6.07	10.56	18.18	32.72	101.42	26.41	8,559	888-843-7824	Y
The Hartford Equity Income Fund Class A	HQIAX	B	B-	B		5.60	9.95	17.52	32.75	91.41	20.32	4,421	888-843-7824	Y
The Hartford Equity Income Fund Class C	HQICX	B-	B-	B-	Down	5.39	9.54	16.63	29.86	84.52	20.22	4,421	888-843-7824	Y
The Hartford Equity Income Fund Class F	HQIFX	B	B	B		5.66	10.13	17.95	34.21	94.85	20.21	4,421	888-843-7824	Y
The Hartford Equity Income Fund Class I	HQIIX	B	B	B		5.64	10.07	17.76	33.73	93.92	20.21	4,421	888-843-7824	Y
The Hartford Equity Income Fund Class R3	HQIRX	B-	B-	B	Down	5.49	9.73	17.13	31.41	88.22	20.35	4,421	888-843-7824	Y
The Hartford Equity Income Fund Class R4	HQISX	B-	B-	B	Down	5.57	9.89	17.40	32.56	91.03	20.37	4,421	888-843-7824	Y
The Hartford Equity Income Fund Class R5	HQITX	B	B	B		5.62	10.00	17.79	33.72	93.91	20.46	4,421	888-843-7824	Y
The Hartford Equity Income Fund Class R6	HQIVX	B	B	B		5.68	10.09	17.92	34.18	94.81	20.51	4,421	888-843-7824	Y
The Hartford Equity Income Fund Class Y	HQIYX	B	B	B		5.61	10.06	17.88	34.13	94.74	20.51	4,421	888-843-7824	Y
Thrivent Large Cap Value Fund Class A	AAUTX	B	B	B	Up	5.89	11.58	17.22	30.92	91.36	22.68	1,017		Y
Thrivent Large Cap Value Fund Class S	TLVIX	B	B	B	Up	5.98	11.79	17.70	32.47	95.47	22.8	1,017		Y
Thrivent Series Large Cap Value Portfolio		B	B	B	Up	6.00	11.79	17.64	31.90	94.43	18.9699	1,541		Y
TIAA-CREF Enhanced Large-Cap Value Index Fund Advisor Cls	TELCX	B	B-	B	Up	6.01	9.80	13.87	25.92	90.65	10.37	2,530	877-518-9161	Y
TIAA-CREF Enhanced Large-Cap Value Index Fund Inst Cls	TEVIX	B	B-	B	Up	5.99	9.77	13.96	26.02	90.81	10.37	2,530	877-518-9161	Y
TIAA-CREF Large Cap Value Fund Advisor Class	TRLHX	B	B-	B	Up	3.93	8.31	12.45	25.68	88.41	19.04	7,137	877-518-9161	Y
TIAA-CREF Large-Cap Value Fund Institutional Class	TRLIX	B	B-	B	Up	3.94	8.32	12.52	26.06	89.98	19.04	7,137	877-518-9161	Y
TIAA-CREF Large-Cap Value Fund Premier Class	TRCPX	B	B-	B	Up	3.89	8.22	12.30	25.47	88.56	19	7,137	877-518-9161	Y
TIAA-CREF Large-Cap Value Fund Retail Class	TCLCX	B-	B-	B	Down	3.84	8.15	12.13	24.86	86.88	18.28	7,137	877-518-9161	Y
TIAA-CREF Large-Cap Value Fund Retirement Class	TRLCX	B	B-	B	Up	3.85	8.19	12.21	25.13	87.58	18.98	7,137	877-518-9161	Y
TIAA-CREF Large-Cap Value Index Fund Advisor Class	THCVX	B	B-	B		5.28	8.46	13.45	26.56	95.07	19.59	6,721	877-518-9161	Y
TIAA-CREF Large-Cap Value Index Fund Institutional Class	TILVX	B	B-	B		5.32	8.56	13.62	26.69	95.27	19.6	6,721	877-518-9161	Y
TIAA-CREF Large-Cap Value Index Fund Retirement Class	TRCVX	B-	B-	B	Down	5.20	8.39	13.30	25.70	92.89	19.93	6,721	877-518-9161	Y
Torray Fund	TORYX	B	B-	B		4.81	7.59	12.06	25.25	90.48	49.6	446.7	800-443-3036	Y
Touchstone Value Fund Class A	TVLAX	B	C+	B	Up	5.74	7.17	13.93	24.72	85.71	10.01	393.1	800-543-0407	Y
Touchstone Value Fund Class C	TVLCX	B-	C+	B	Down	5.48	6.70	13.02	21.89	78.68	9.97	393.1	800-543-0407	Y
Touchstone Value Fund Class Y	TVLYX	B	C+	B	Up	5.90	7.29	14.30	25.71	88.12	10.05	393.1	800-543-0407	Y
Touchstone Value Fund Institutional	TVLIX	B	B-	B	Up	5.84	7.37	14.37	26.20	89.21	10.02	393.1	800-543-0407	Y
Transamerica Dividend Focused Advisor	TADVX	B-	B-	B-	Down	5.38	8.40	16.00	28.36	84.55	11.35	706.9	888-233-4339	Y
Transamerica Dividend Focused Class A	TDFAX	B-	B-	B-	Down	5.40	8.31	15.90	27.67	82.42	11.27	706.9	888-233-4339	Y
Transamerica Dividend Focused Class C	TDFCX	B-	B-	B	Down	5.21	7.88	15.01	24.57	75.21	11.22	706.9	888-233-4339	Y
Transamerica Dividend Focused Class I	TDFIX	B-	B-	B-	Down	5.37	8.43	16.13	28.22	83.88	11.26	706.9	888-233-4339	Y
Transamerica Dividend Focused Class I2	TRDIX	B-	B-	B-	Down	5.47	8.46	16.21	28.59	84.88	11.27	706.9	888-233-4339	Y
Transamerica Dividend Focused Class R6	TADFX	B-	B-	B-	Down	5.47	8.46	16.32	28.60	84.89	11.27	706.9	888-233-4339	Y
Transamerica Dividend Focused Class T1	TADTX	B	B-	B	Up	5.39	8.31	15.89	27.60	82.54	11.31	706.9	888-233-4339	Y
Transamerica Large Cap Value Fund Class A	TWQAX	B	B	B	Up	2.69	6.47	12.04	37.80	107.77	12.43	2,355	888-233-4339	Y
Transamerica Large Cap Value Fund Class Advisor	TALPX	B	B	B+	Up	2.73	6.65	12.28	39.13	111.42	12.57	2,355	888-233-4339	Y
Transamerica Large Cap Value Fund Class C	TWQCX	B	B	B+	Up	2.45	6.14	11.30	34.78	100.35	12.36	2,355	888-233-4339	Y
Transamerica Large Cap Value Fund Class I	TWQIX	B	B	B	Up	2.77	6.69	12.38	38.98	110.69	12.51	2,355	888-233-4339	Y
Transamerica Large Cap Value Fund Class I2	TWQZX	B	B	B	Up	2.79	6.74	12.48	39.38	111.79	12.5	2,355	888-233-4339	Y
Transamerica Large Cap Value Fund Class R6	TALCX	B	B	B+	Up	2.79	6.74	12.48	39.39	111.80	12.5	2,355	888-233-4339	Y
Transamerica Large Cap Value Fund T1	TWQTX	B	B	B+	Up	2.74	6.64	12.25	38.40	109.25	12.45	2,355	888-233-4339	Y
Transamerica Large Core Fund Class I3	TLATX	B-	B	B-	Down	8.81	14.60	22.85	29.85	109.83	11.13	295.3	888-233-4339	Y
Transamerica Large Core Fund Class R	TLARX	B-	B-	B-		8.67	14.32	22.32	28.65	106.85	11.13	295.3	888-233-4339	Y
Transamerica Large Core Fund Class R4	TLAFX	B-	B	B-	Down	8.73	14.45	22.61	29.60	109.42	11.13	295.3	888-233-4339	Y
Transamerica Large Value Opportunities Fund Class I3	TLOTX	B	B-	B	Up	7.28	12.26	15.48	23.90	91.95	11.01	695.0	888-233-4339	Y
Transamerica Large Value Opportunities Fund Class R	TLORX	B-	C+	B	Up	7.15	11.86	14.96	22.72	89.18	11.01	695.0	888-233-4339	Y
Transamerica Large Value Opportunities Fund Class R4	TLOFX	B	C+	B	Up	7.21	12.11	15.28	23.68	91.61	11.01	695.0	888-233-4339	Y
TS&W Equity Portfolio Institutional Class Shares	TSWEX	B	C+	B+	Up	3.57	5.55	14.53	22.09	77.46	12.9	41.7		Y

Category: US Equity Large Cap Value (con't)

Fund Name	Ticker Symbol	RATINGS: Overall Rating	Reward Rating	Risk Rating	Recent Up/ Downgrade	TOTAL RETURNS & PERFORMANCE: 3-Month Total Return	6-Month Total Return	1-Year Total Return	3-Year Total Return	5-Year Total Return	ASSETS: NAV	Total Assets (MIL)	NEW INVESTORS: Telephone	Open to New Investors
Union Street Partners Value Fund Advisor Class	USPFX	B	B-	B	Up	7.80	12.02	9.30	28.65	85.00	17.8	28.2		Y
Union Street Partners Value Fund C Class	USPCX	B-	C+	B	Up	7.54	11.46	8.21	25.16	77.42	17.28	28.2		Y
Union Street Partners Value Fund Class A Shares	USPVX	B-	B-	B	Up	7.70	11.85	9.01	27.96	84.02	17.83	28.2		Y
USAA Income Stock Fund	USISX	B-	B-	B	Down	5.77	9.74	16.63	27.33	91.30	19.95	2,893	800-531-8722	Y
USAA Income Stock Fund Institutional Shares	UIISX	B-	B-	B	Down	5.78	9.71	16.68	27.53	91.85	19.93	2,893	800-531-8722	Y
USAA Income Stock Fund R6 Shares	URISX	B-	B-	B	Down	5.86	9.82	16.79	27.51	91.58	19.94	2,893	800-531-8722	Y
USAA Value Fund	UVALX	B	B-	B	Up	5.02	8.54	15.15	25.96	90.21	21.68	1,641	800-531-8722	Y
USAA Value Fund Adviser Shares	UAVAX	B	B-	B	Up	4.97	8.41	14.86	24.97	87.70	21.62	1,641	800-531-8722	Y
USAA Value Fund Institutional Shares	UIVAX	B	B-	B	Up	5.02	8.59	15.26	26.41	91.40	21.66	1,641	800-531-8722	Y
VALIC Company I Broad Cap Value Income Fund	VBCVX	B	B	B-	Up	5.00	9.23	18.13	31.46	97.78	17.63	60.5		Y
VALIC Company I Dividend Value Fund	VCIGX	B	B	B		5.91	11.02	18.06	35.54	97.19	13.6	794.6		Y
VALIC Company I Value Fund	VAVAX	B	B-	B	Up	5.69	8.70	15.33	25.37	87.66	18.36	114.2		Y
VALIC Company II Large Cap Value Fund	VACVX	B	B-	B	Up	6.91	10.61	15.05	29.58	99.57	22.72	247.2		Y
Vanguard Equity-Income Fund Admiral Shares	VEIRX	B	B-	B		6.34	11.11	18.49	35.82	101.68	77.95	30,939	877-662-7447	Y
Vanguard Equity-Income Fund Investor Shares	VEIPX	B	B-	B		6.30	11.04	18.38	35.44	100.74	37.19	30,939	877-662-7447	Y
Vanguard High Dividend Yield Index Fund Investor Shares	VHDYX	B-	B-	B	Down	6.25	11.07	16.37	34.63	103.86	33.89	28,812	877-662-7447	Y
Vanguard Mega Cap Value Index Fund Institutional Shares	VMVLX	B	B	B+		6.97	11.59	16.80	34.52	106.23	151.33	2,020	877-662-7447	Y
Vanguard Russell 1000 Value Index Fund Inst Shares	VRVIX	B	B-	B		5.32	8.58	13.59	26.45	95.01	211.75	2,869	877-662-7447	Y
Vanguard S&P 500 Value Index Fund Institutional Shares	VSPVX	B	B-	B		6.30	9.99	15.28	29.54	96.60	240.96	862.0	877-662-7447	Y
Vanguard U.S. Value Fund Investor Shares	VUVLX	B	B	B	Up	5.37	10.49	12.97	27.82	102.21	19.15	1,728	877-662-7447	Y
Vanguard Value Index Fund Admiral Shares	VVIAX	B	B	B+		6.96	11.40	17.13	34.23	107.42	41.41	63,566	877-662-7447	Y
Vanguard Value Index Fund Institutional Shares	VIVIX	B	B	B+		6.96	11.41	17.14	34.27	107.52	41.41	63,566	877-662-7447	Y
Vanguard Value Index Fund Investor Shares	VIVAX	B	B	B+		6.93	11.34	16.98	33.70	106.06	41.42	63,566	877-662-7447	Y
Vanguard Windsor™ Fund Admiral™ Shares	VWNEX	B-	B	C+	Down	5.52	9.57	19.20	28.78	101.41	78.98	20,074	877-662-7447	Y
Vanguard Windsor™ Fund Investor Share	VWNDX	B-	B	C+	Down	5.50	9.50	19.09	28.37	100.39	23.42	20,074	877-662-7447	Y
Vanguard Windsor™ II Fund Admiral™ Shares	VWNAX	B	B-	B	Up	5.91	8.39	16.88	27.22	89.78	67.12	50,094	877-662-7447	Y
Vanguard Windsor™ II Fund Investor Share	VWNFX	B	B-	B	Up	5.88	8.34	16.77	26.92	89.04	37.83	50,094	877-662-7447	Y
Virtus Ceredex Large-Cap Value Equity Fund Class A	SVIIX	B-	B-	B	Down	5.88	9.74	15.89	25.67	91.05	16.2	2,031	800-243-1574	Y
Virtus Ceredex Large-Cap Value Equity Fund Class C	SVIFX	B-	B-	B-	Down	5.74	9.45	15.37	23.92	86.66	15.78	2,031	800-243-1574	Y
Virtus Ceredex Large-Cap Value Equity Fund Class I	STVTX	B-	B-	B-	Down	6.00	9.91	16.22	26.70	93.89	16.35	2,031	800-243-1574	Y
Virtus Ceredex Large-Cap Value Equity Fund Class R6	STVZX	B-	B-	B-	Down	6.05	10.03	16.53	27.76	95.62	16.41	2,031	800-243-1574	Y
Voya Large Cap Value Fund Class C	IEDCX	B-	C+	B	Down	4.38	6.22	12.37	18.08	70.12	12.32	961.4	800-366-0066	Y
Voya Large Cap Value Fund Class I	IEDIX	B-	C+	B	Down	4.65	6.80	13.58	21.98	79.62	13.33	961.4	800-366-0066	Y
Voya Large Cap Value Fund Class R	IEDRX	B-	C+	B	Down	4.41	6.46	12.95	19.78	74.49	12.32	961.4	800-366-0066	Y
Voya Large Cap Value Fund Class R6	IEDZX	B-	C+	B	Down	4.67	6.82	13.62	22.09	79.53	13.32	961.4	800-366-0066	Y
Voya Large Cap Value Fund Class W	IWEDX	B-	C+	B	Down	4.62	6.74	13.53	21.66	78.74	13.29	961.4	800-366-0066	Y
Voya Large Cap Value Portfolio Class A	IPEAX	B-	C+	B	Down	4.47	6.43	12.84	19.90	75.13	13.06	1,308	800-366-0066	Y
Voya Large Cap Value Portfolio Class I	IPEIX	B-	C+	B	Down	4.61	6.78	13.54	22.18	80.53	13.3	1,308	800-366-0066	Y
Voya Large Cap Value Portfolio Class S2	IPETX	B-	C+	B	Down	4.50	6.53	13.09	20.70	77.15	13.15	1,308	800-366-0066	Y
Voya Russell Large Cap Value Index Portfolio Class A	IRVAX	B-	B-	B	Down	5.04	8.59	13.05	23.49	86.19	23.13	429.4	800-366-0066	Y
Voya Russell Large Cap Value Index Portfolio Class I	IRVIX	B-	B-	B	Down	5.13	8.81	13.45	25.17	90.62	23.34	429.4	800-366-0066	Y
Voya Russell Large Cap Value Index Portfolio Class S	IRVSX	B-	B-	B	Down	5.07	8.67	13.19	24.22	88.19	23.17	429.4	800-366-0066	Y
VY® Invesco Comstock Portfolio Class A	IVKAX	B	B	B-	Up	7.32	13.70	17.31	28.07	92.89	20.14	503.4	800-366-0066	Y
VY® Invesco Comstock Portfolio Class I	IVKIX	B	B	B-	Up	7.53	13.97	17.95	30.13	97.84	20.32	503.4	800-366-0066	Y
VY® Invesco Comstock Portfolio Class S	IVKSX	B	B	B-	Up	7.43	13.82	17.67	29.08	95.24	20.3	503.4	800-366-0066	Y
VY® Invesco Growth and Income Portfolio Class A	IVGAX	B	B	B	Up	4.44	8.86	13.46	29.90	94.90	27.94	571.4	800-366-0066	Y
VY® Invesco Growth and Income Portfolio Class I	IVGIX	B	B	B	Up	4.59	9.16	14.13	32.23	100.76	28.23	571.4	800-366-0066	Y
VY® Invesco Growth and Income Portfolio Class S	IVGSX	B	B	B	Up	4.56	9.07	13.88	31.29	98.30	28.43	571.4	800-366-0066	Y
VY® Invesco Growth and Income Portfolio Class S2	IVITX	B	B	B	Up	4.52	8.94	13.67	30.67	96.82	28.19	571.4	800-366-0066	Y
VY® T. Rowe Price Equity Income Portfolio Class A	ITEAX	B-	B-	C+	Down	5.45	9.92	15.88	25.92	78.78	14.34	981.5	800-366-0066	Y
VY® T. Rowe Price Equity Income Portfolio Class I	ITEIX	B-	B	C+	Down	5.57	10.18	16.47	28.22	84.25	14.59	981.5	800-366-0066	Y
VY® T. Rowe Price Equity Income Portfolio Class S	IRPSX	B-	B-	C+	Down	5.51	10.12	16.23	27.21	81.94	14.62	981.5	800-366-0066	Y

Category: US Equity Large Cap Value (con't)

Fund Name	Ticker Symbol	RATINGS: Overall Rating	Reward Rating	Risk Rating	Recent Up/ Downgrade	TOTAL RETURNS & PERFORMANCE: 3-Month Total Return	6-Month Total Return	1-Year Total Return	3-Year Total Return	5-Year Total Return	ASSETS: NAV	Total Assets (MIL)	NEW INVESTORS: Telephone	Open to New Investors
VY® T. Rowe Price Equity Income Portfolio Class S2	ITETX	B-	B-	C+	Down	5.45	9.97	16.07	26.66	80.50	14.42	981.5	800-366-0066	Y
Wasatch Global Value Fund™ Institutional Class Shares	WILCX	B-	B-	B		3.11	6.98	11.50	24.93	70.84	8.9	179.1	800-551-1700	Y
Wasatch Global Value Fund™ Investor Class Shares	FMIEX	B-	B-	B		3.07	6.90	11.20	24.38	69.81	8.91	179.1	800-551-1700	Y
Wells Fargo C&B Large Cap Value Fund - Class A	CBEAX	B-	B-	B-	Down	4.23	6.24	19.03	32.21	103.13	14.42	391.7	800-222-8222	Y
Wells Fargo C&B Large Cap Value Fund - Class Admin	CBLLX	B-	B-	B-	Down	4.23	6.31	19.18	32.78	105.03	14.42	391.7	800-222-8222	Y
Wells Fargo C&B Large Cap Value Fund - Class C	CBECX	B-	B-	B-	Down	4.05	5.86	18.10	29.25	95.62	14.3	391.7	800-222-8222	Y
Wells Fargo C&B Large Cap Value Fund - Class Inst	CBLSX	B-	B-	B-	Down	4.27	6.40	19.35	33.63	107.37	14.44	391.7	800-222-8222	Y
Wells Fargo C&B Large Cap Value Fund Class R6	CBEJX	B-	B-	B-	Down	4.34	6.48	19.51	33.84	107.69	14.45	391.7	800-222-8222	Y
Wells Fargo Large Company Value Fund - Class A	WLCAX	B-	B-	B	Down	5.56	9.49	15.28	22.28	81.38	14.29	266.2	800-222-8222	Y
Wells Fargo Large Company Value Fund - Class Admin	WWIDX	B-	B-	B	Down	5.53	9.46	15.30	22.82	83.06	14.41	266.2	800-222-8222	Y
Wells Fargo Large Company Value Fund - Class C	WFLVX	B-	C+	B		5.30	9.02	14.41	19.53	74.67	14.68	266.2	800-222-8222	Y
Wells Fargo Large Company Value Fund - Class Inst	WLCIX	B-	B-	B	Down	5.61	9.65	15.63	23.74	85.07	14.39	266.2	800-222-8222	Y
Wells Fargo Large Company Value Fund Class R6	WTLVX	B-	B-	B	Down	5.63	9.66	15.58	23.12	83.52	14.39	266.2	800-222-8222	Y
Westcore Large-Cap Dividend Fund Institutional Class	WILGX	B	C+	A-	Up	6.22	10.45	17.09	21.36	77.73	6.12	10.7	800-392-2673	Y
Westcore Large-Cap Dividend Fund Retail Class	WTEIX	B	C+	A-	Up	6.17	10.22	16.72	20.38	75.62	6.01	10.7	800-392-2673	Y
Wilshire Large Company Value Portfolio Fund Cls Inst	WLCVX	B-	B-	B	Down	6.25	9.66	14.98	25.20	95.50	20.95	158.7	888-200-6796	Y
Wilshire Large Company Value Port Inv Cls Shares	DTLVX	B-	B-	B	Down	6.16	9.54	14.64	24.43	93.26	21.18	158.7	888-200-6796	Y
WP Large Cap Income Plus Fund Institutional Class	WPLCX	B	B+	C+	Up	6.57	12.77	23.72	44.67		13.79	32.6		Y
Zacks Dividend Fund Institutional Class Shares	ZDIIX	B	B-	B		5.39	10.31	16.48	29.16		20.56	47.3		Y
Zacks Dividend Fund Investor Class	ZDIVX	B-	B-	B-	Down	5.33	10.18	16.21	28.86		20.56	47.3		Y

Category: US Equity Mid Cap

Fund Name	Ticker Symbol	RATINGS: Overall Rating	Reward Rating	Risk Rating	Recent Up/ Downgrade	TOTAL RETURNS & PERFORMANCE: 3-Month Total Return	6-Month Total Return	1-Year Total Return	3-Year Total Return	5-Year Total Return	ASSETS: NAV	Total Assets (MIL)	NEW INVESTORS: Telephone	Open to New Investors
13D Activist Fund Class A	DDDAX	B	B	B-	Up	10.58	11.03	23.44	29.97	108.15	21.69	329.7	877-413-3228	Y
13D Activist Fund Class C	DDDCX	B	B	B-	Up	10.38	10.60	22.51	27.03	101.03	21.66	329.7	877-413-3228	Y
13D Activist Fund Class I	DDDIX	B	B	B-	Up	10.66	11.16	23.77	30.92	110.95	22.06	329.7	877-413-3228	Y
AB Discovery Growth Fund Advisor Class	CHCYX	B	A-	C+	Up	9.00	15.43	32.70	38.03	101.89	11.58	2,141	212-969-1000	Y
AB Discovery Growth Fund Class A	CHCLX	B+	A-	B	Up	8.89	15.39	32.51	37.04	99.75	10.86	2,141	212-969-1000	Y
AB Discovery Growth Fund Class B	CHCBX	B	B	B	Up	8.61	14.80	31.34	33.72	91.42	6.91	2,141	212-969-1000	
AB Discovery Growth Fund Class C	CHCCX	B	B+	B	Up	8.69	14.84	31.47	33.83	91.88	6.97	2,141	212-969-1000	Y
AB Discovery Growth Fund Class I	CHCIX	B	A-	C+	Up	8.99	15.48	32.81	38.04	102.07	11.47	2,141	212-969-1000	Y
AB Discovery Growth Fund Class K	CHCKX	B	A-	C+	Up	8.87	15.19	32.27	36.51	98.45	10.76	2,141	212-969-1000	Y
AB Discovery Growth Fund Class R	CHCRX	B	B+	C+	Up	8.78	15.15	31.99	35.44	95.82	10.26	2,141	212-969-1000	Y
AB Discovery Growth Fund Class Z	CHCZX	B+	A-	B	Up	8.98	15.46	32.88	38.26	101.81	11.49	2,141	212-969-1000	Y
AB Discovery Value Fund Advisor Class	ABYSX	B	B+	B	Up	5.99	11.50	12.97	31.75	103.33	23.3	2,959	212-969-1000	Y
AB Discovery Value Fund Class A	ABASX	B	B	B	Up	5.92	11.36	12.70	30.76	100.48	22.78	2,959	212-969-1000	Y
AB Discovery Value Fund Class B	ABBSX	B	B	B	Up	5.93	11.35	12.56	30.33	99.72	21.38	2,959	212-969-1000	
AB Discovery Value Fund Class C	ABCSX	B	B	B	Up	5.71	10.93	11.85	27.89	93.42	20.11	2,959	212-969-1000	Y
AB Discovery Value Fund Class I	ABSIX	B	B+	B	Up	6.01	11.53	12.99	31.88	103.52	22.61	2,959	212-969-1000	Y
AB Discovery Value Fund Class K	ABSKX	B	B	B	Up	5.91	11.33	12.58	30.49	100.00	22.47	2,959	212-969-1000	Y
AB Discovery Value Fund Class R	ABSRX	B	B	B	Up	5.80	11.13	12.24	29.28	97.02	22.14	2,959	212-969-1000	Y
AB Discovery Value Fund Class Z	ABSZX	B	B+	B	Up	6.03	11.56	13.08	32.15	104.23	22.58	2,959	212-969-1000	Y
Alger Mid Cap Growth Fund Class A	AMGAX	B-	B	C	Up	6.03	11.78	29.77	27.84	90.79	13.68	187.0	800-992-3863	Y
Alger Mid Cap Growth Fund Class B	AMCGX	B-	B	C	Up	5.89	11.33	28.72	25.22	84.07	10.93	187.0	800-992-3863	
Alger Mid Cap Growth Fund Class C	AMGCX	B-	B	C	Up	5.76	11.37	28.70	24.73	83.12	10.8	187.0	800-992-3863	Y
Alger Mid Cap Growth Fund Class Z	AMCZX	B-	B	C	Up	6.06	11.87	29.97	28.48	88.87	13.78	187.0	800-992-3863	Y
Alger Mid Cap Growth Institutional Fund Class I	ALMRX	B-	B	C	Up	5.88	11.64	29.54	28.97	96.71	29.33	111.1	800-992-3863	Y

Category: US Equity Mid Cap (con't)

Fund Name	Ticker Symbol	RATINGS: Overall Rating	Reward Rating	Risk Rating	Recent Up/ Downgrade	TOTAL RETURNS & PERFORMANCE: 3-Month Total Return	6-Month Total Return	1-Year Total Return	3-Year Total Return	5-Year Total Return	ASSETS: NAV	Total Assets (MIL)	NEW INVESTORS: Telephone	Open to New Investors
Alger Mid Cap Growth Institutional Fund Class R	AGIRX	B-	B	C	Up	5.73	11.36	28.83	26.83	91.47	26.94	111.1	800-992-3863	Y
Alger Mid Cap Growth Portfolio Class I-2	AMGOX	B-	B	C	Up	6.18	11.99	29.79	28.42	92.69	25	141.5	800-992-3863	Y
Alger Mid Cap Growth Portfolio Class S	US0155448857	B-	B	C	Up	6.03	11.66	29.18	26.74	88.83	23.64	141.5	800-992-3863	Y
Alger MidCap Growth Institutional Fund Class Z-2	ALMZX	B-	B	C	Up	5.94	11.78	29.84	29.33	97.25	29.41	111.1	800-992-3863	Y
Alger SMid Cap Focus Fund Class A	ALMAX	B+	A-	B	Up	7.27	14.90	37.88	38.82	96.18	12	195.0	800-992-3863	Y
Alger SMid Cap Focus Fund Class C	ALMCX	B+	A-	B-	Up	7.17	14.41	36.89	35.62	88.71	8.59	195.0	800-992-3863	Y
Alger SMid Cap Focus Fund Class I	ASIMX	B+	A-	B	Up	7.37	15.03	37.90	38.78	96.17	12.29	195.0	800-992-3863	Y
Alger SMid Cap Focus Fund Class Y	ASYMX	B+	A-	B		7.53	15.08	38.10	39.04	96.50	12.3	195.0	800-992-3863	Y
Alger SMid Cap Focus Fund Class Z	ASMZX	B+	A	B	Up	7.42	15.08	38.39	40.19	99.49	12.63	195.0	800-992-3863	Y
Alger SMid Cap Focus Portfolio I-2	AAMOX	B	A-	C+	Up	7.86	15.35	36.90	40.62	100.12	2.27	4.9	800-992-3863	Y
AllianzGI Mid-Cap Fund Administrative Class	DRMAX	B	B	B-		6.00	10.57	24.83	36.59	106.14	3.98	314.1	800-498-5413	Y
AllianzGI Mid-Cap Fund Class A	RMDAX	B	B	B-	Up	6.35	10.90	24.93	36.45	105.92	3.77	314.1	800-498-5413	Y
AllianzGI Mid-Cap Fund Class C	RMDCX	B	B	B	Up	5.92	10.24	23.82	33.02	97.71	3.14	314.1	800-498-5413	Y
AllianzGI Mid-Cap Fund Class P	ARMPX	B	B+	B-		6.35	10.92	25.27	37.44	108.61	4.27	314.1	800-498-5413	Y
AllianzGI Mid-Cap Fund Class R	PRMRX	B	B	B-	Up	6.14	10.74	24.21	35.41	103.35	3.71	314.1	800-498-5413	Y
AllianzGI Mid-Cap Fund Institutional Class	DRMCX	B	B	B+		6.06	10.84	25.11	37.58	109.29	4.29	314.1	800-498-5413	Y
AllianzGI NFJ Mid-Cap Value Fund Administrative Class	PRAAX	B	B	B-	Down	4.93	9.34	26.73	41.83	108.43	32.29	995.7	800-498-5413	Y
AllianzGI NFJ Mid-Cap Value Fund Class A	PQNAX	B	B	B-	Down	4.90	9.27	26.61	41.44	107.30	31.32	995.7	800-498-5413	Y
AllianzGI NFJ Mid-Cap Value Fund Class C	PQNCX	B	B	C+		4.72	8.87	25.64	38.28	99.68	25.75	995.7	800-498-5413	Y
AllianzGI NFJ Mid-Cap Value Fund Class P	ANRPX	B	B	B-	Down	4.96	9.44	26.91	42.45	110.03	25.34	995.7	800-498-5413	Y
AllianzGI NFJ Mid-Cap Value Fund Class R	PRNRX	B	B	B-	Down	4.86	9.15	26.29	40.36	104.77	26.9	995.7	800-498-5413	Y
AllianzGI NFJ Mid-Cap Value Fund Institutional Class	PRNIX	B	B	B-	Down	5.01	9.48	27.04	42.91	110.99	33.44	995.7	800-498-5413	Y
American Beacon Mid-Cap Value Fund Advisor Class	AMCSX	B	B	B	Up	5.60	9.62	17.08	29.80	100.13	17.08	692.1	800-658-5811	Y
American Beacon Mid-Cap Value Fund C Class	AMCCX	B	B	B	Up	5.50	9.37	16.46	27.49	93.93	16.52	692.1	800-658-5811	Y
American Beacon Mid-Cap Value Fund Class A	ABMAX	B	B	B	Up	5.62	9.71	17.29	30.38	101.37	17.05	692.1	800-658-5811	Y
American Beacon Mid-Cap Value Fund Class Y	ACMYX	B	B	B	Up	5.70	9.87	17.60	31.55	104.69	17.26	692.1	800-658-5811	Y
American Beacon Mid-Cap Value Fund Institutional Class	AACIX	B	B	B	Up	5.73	9.92	17.72	31.86	105.55	17.4	692.1	800-658-5811	Y
American Beacon Mid-Cap Value Fund Investor Class	AMPAX	B	B	B	Up	5.65	9.81	17.48	30.98	103.23	17.58	692.1	800-658-5811	Y
American Beacon Stephens Mid-Cap Growth Fund A Class	SMFAX	B	B	C+	Up	5.90	11.54	27.89	32.79	85.71	19.08	98.3	800-658-5811	Y
American Beacon Stephens Mid-Cap Growth Fund C Class	SMFCX	B-	B	C+	Down	5.69	11.09	26.94	29.79	78.48	18.11	98.3	800-658-5811	Y
American Beacon Stephens Mid-Cap Growth Fund Inst Cls	SFMIX	B	B+	C+	Up	5.96	11.70	28.35	34.37	89.58	22.45	98.3	800-658-5811	Y
American Beacon Stephens Mid-Cap Growth Fund Investor Cls	STMGX	B	B+	C+	Up	5.93	11.55	27.96	32.96	86.28	19.15	98.3	800-658-5811	Y
American Beacon Stephens Mid-Cap Growth Fund Y Class	SMFYX	B	B+	C+	Up	5.94	11.66	28.26	33.97	88.51	22.34	98.3	800-658-5811	Y
American Century Adaptive All Cap Fund Advisor Class	ACMFX	B-	B	B-	Down	5.41	10.64	17.41	28.34	96.55	20.6	104.0	800-444-4015	Y
American Century Adaptive All Cap Fund I Class	ACMHX	B	B	B-	Up	5.50	10.91	17.93	30.03	100.88	20.94	104.0	800-444-4015	Y
American Century Adaptive All Cap Fund Investor Class	ACMNX	B	B	B-	Up	5.43	10.82	17.70	29.27	99.06	20.8	104.0	800-444-4015	Y
American Century Adaptive All Cap Fund R Class	ACMEX	B-	B	B-	Down	5.30	10.49	17.08	27.28	94.00	20.35	104.0	800-444-4015	Y
American Century Adaptive All Cap Fund R5 Class	ACMUX	B	B	B-	Up	5.54	10.95	17.97	30.08	100.95	20.96	104.0	800-444-4015	Y
American Century Adaptive All Cap Fund R6 Class	ACMMX	B	B	B-	Up	5.55	11.00	18.13	30.25	101.22	21.18	104.0	800-444-4015	Y
American Century Heritage Fund A Class	ATHAX	B	B-	B	Up	5.51	9.45	21.52	26.33	82.80	20.81	5,143	800-444-4015	Y
American Century Heritage Fund C Class	AHGCX	B	B-	B	Up	5.27	8.98	20.59	23.53	75.99	16.79	5,143	800-444-4015	Y
American Century Heritage Fund I Class	ATHIX	B	B	B	Up	5.60	9.66	22.08	28.05	86.91	23.87	5,143	800-444-4015	Y
American Century Heritage Fund Investor Class	TWHIX	B	B	B	Up	5.57	9.57	21.84	27.28	85.01	22.48	5,143	800-444-4015	Y
American Century Heritage Fund R Class	ATHWX	B	B-	B	Up	5.40	9.26	21.20	25.38	80.43	20.86	5,143	800-444-4015	Y
American Century Heritage Fund R5 Class	ATHGX	B	B	B	Up	5.60	9.66	22.05	27.50	85.32	23.87	5,143	800-444-4015	Y
American Century Heritage Fund R6 Class	ATHDX	B	B	B	Up	5.64	9.76	22.27	28.60	87.84	24.07	5,143	800-444-4015	Y
American Century Heritage Fund Y Class	ATHYX	B	B	B	Up	5.68	9.81	22.20	27.66	85.55	24.08	5,143	800-444-4015	Y
American Century Mid Cap Value Fund A Class	ACLAX	B	B-	B+		4.61	7.12	11.32	32.60	104.18	17.49	8,880	800-444-4015	
American Century Mid Cap Value Fund C Class	ACCLX	B	B-	B+		4.38	6.70	10.47	29.56	96.70	17.32	8,880	800-444-4015	
American Century Mid Cap Value Fund I Class	AVUAX	B	B-	B+		4.72	7.41	11.79	34.40	108.91	17.53	8,880	800-444-4015	
American Century Mid Cap Value Fund Investor Class	ACMVX	B	B-	B+		4.67	7.30	11.58	33.54	106.78	17.52	8,880	800-444-4015	
American Century Mid Cap Value Fund R Class	AMVRX	B	B-	B+		4.49	7.00	11.01	31.53	101.65	17.44	8,880	800-444-4015	

Category: US Equity Mid Cap (con't)

Fund Name	Ticker Symbol	RATINGS: Overall Rating	Reward Rating	Risk Rating	Recent Up/ Downgrade	TOTAL RETURNS & PERFORMANCE: 3-Month Total Return	6-Month Total Return	1-Year Total Return	3-Year Total Return	5-Year Total Return	ASSETS: NAV	Total Assets (MIL)	NEW INVESTORS: Telephone	Open to New Investors
American Century Mid Cap Value Fund R5 Class	AMVGX	B	B-	B+		4.72	7.35	11.73	33.73	107.06	17.53	8,880	800-444-4015	Y
American Century Mid Cap Value Fund R6 Class	AMDVX	B	B-	B+		4.71	7.43	11.96	34.93	110.02	17.52	8,880	800-444-4015	
American Century Mid Cap Value Fund Y Class	AMVYX	B	B-	B+		4.76	7.43	11.84	33.87	107.28	17.53	8,880	800-444-4015	
American Century NT Heritage Fund G Class	ACLWX	B	B	B	Up	5.77	10.04	22.44	28.52	85.97	13.97	832.8	800-444-4015	Y
American Century NT Mid Cap Value Fund G Class	ACLMX	B	B-	B+		4.91	7.71	12.08	34.84	109.97	13.56	1,096	800-444-4015	Y
AMG Managers Brandywine Fund Class I	BRWIX	B+	B+	B	Up	4.85	12.19	23.64	31.86	101.99	46.64	795.9	800-835-3879	Y
AMG Managers Cadence Mid Cap Fund - Class I	MCMYX	B	B	C+	Up	8.57	14.08	25.74	32.57	98.63	31.27	133.0	800-835-3879	Y
AMG Managers Cadence Mid Cap Fund - Class N	MCMAX	B	B	C+	Up	8.50	13.95	25.46	31.86	97.03	30.25	133.0	800-835-3879	Y
AMG Managers Cadence Mid Cap Fund - Class Z	MCMFX	B	B	C+	Up	8.58	14.15	25.91	33.41	101.00	32.74	133.0	800-835-3879	Y
AMG Managers Fairpointe Mid Cap Fund Class I	ABMIX	B-	B-	C+	Up	5.38	6.24	11.79	23.92	102.80	43.79	4,200	800-835-3879	
AMG Managers Fairpointe Mid Cap Fund Class N	CHTTX	B-	B-	C+	Up	5.31	6.10	11.51	22.97	100.27	42.69	4,200	800-835-3879	
AMG Managers Fairpointe Mid Cap Fund Class Z	ABIZX	B-	B-	C+		5.38	6.17	11.59	23.06	100.40	43.76	4,200	800-835-3879	Y
AMG Managers Montag & Caldwell Mid Cap Growth Fund Class I	AMMCX	B	B-	B+	Up	8.95	12.70	23.47	28.79	81.15	11.36	9.8	800-835-3879	Y
AMG Managers Montag & Caldwell Mid Cap Growth Fund Class N	AMCMX	B	B-	B+	Up	8.82	12.58	23.16	27.75	79.56	11.28	9.8	800-835-3879	Y
AMG Systematic Mid Cap Value Fund Class I	SYIMX	B	B	B-	Up	7.95	14.19	15.11	28.43	86.04	15.66	89.9	800-835-3879	Y
AMG Systematic Mid Cap Value Fund Class N	SYAMX	B-	B	B-	Up	7.94	14.11	14.78	27.45	83.53	15.68	89.9	800-835-3879	Y
AMG TimesSquare Mid Cap Growth Fund Class I	TQMIX	B	B	B-	Up	5.96	10.58	22.57	31.76	94.19	18.86	2,108	800-835-3879	Y
AMG TimesSquare Mid Cap Growth Fund Class N	TMDPX	B-	B	B-	Down	5.94	10.54	22.39	30.99	92.30	18.4	2,108	800-835-3879	
AMG TimesSquare Mid Cap Growth Fund Class Z	TMDIX	B	B	B-	Up	5.96	10.63	22.63	31.82	94.28	18.87	2,108	800-835-3879	
APEXcm Small/Mid Cap Growth Fund	APSGX	B-	B-	B	Up	8.60	14.02	26.60	26.30	89.81	20.32	277.1	937-847-9100	Y
Aquila Three Peaks Opportunity Growth Fund Class A	ATGAX	B	C+	B+	Up	3.42	6.81	16.34	27.38	107.80	52.38	604.9	800-437-1020	Y
Aquila Three Peaks Opportunity Growth Fund Class C	ATGCX	B	C+	B+	Up	3.24	6.44	15.53	24.64	100.47	43.26	604.9	800-437-1020	Y
Aquila Three Peaks Opportunity Growth Fund Class Y	ATGYX	B	B-	B+	Up	3.50	6.98	16.70	28.53	110.95	55.91	604.9	800-437-1020	Y
Aquila Three Peaks Opp Growth Fund Inst Cls	ATRIX	B	B-	B+	Up	3.44	6.85	16.44	27.93	109.77	54.23	604.9	800-437-1020	Y
Archer Stock Fund	ARSKX	B-	C+	B	Up	5.46	12.82	19.49	20.21	81.12	47.08	15.8		Y
Ariel Appreciation Fund Institutional Class	CAAIX	B-	B-	B		6.41	6.59	15.45	21.68	99.59	47.93	1,677	312-726-0140	Y
Ariel Appreciation Fund Investor Class	CAAPX	B-	C+	B		6.34	6.43	15.09	20.53	96.42	47.88	1,677	312-726-0140	Y
Ariel Fund Institutional Class	ARAIX	B	B	B	Up	7.94	8.83	16.23	28.59	113.36	70.01	2,255	312-726-0140	Y
Ariel Fund Investor Class	ARGFX	B	B	B	Up	7.86	8.68	15.88	27.46	110.21	69.98	2,255	312-726-0140	Y
Artisan Mid Cap Fund Advisor Class	APDMX	B	B-	B	Up	2.95	4.61	20.61	21.63	81.00	38.29	6,810	800-344-1770	
Artisan Mid Cap Fund Institutional Class	APHMX	B	B-	B	Up	2.99	4.68	20.75	22.08	82.54	41.49	6,810	800-344-1770	
Artisan Mid Cap Fund Investor Class	ARTMX	B	B-	B	Up	2.94	4.56	20.48	21.21	80.37	38.11	6,810	800-344-1770	
Artisan Mid Cap Value Fund Advisor Class	APDQX	B-	B-	B-	Up	4.75	8.00	12.46	23.33	73.90	22.68	3,987	800-344-1770	
Artisan Mid Cap Value Fund Institutional Class	APHQX	B-	B-	B-	Up	4.77	8.06	12.62	23.75	75.34	22.7	3,987	800-344-1770	
Artisan Mid Cap Value Fund Investor Class	ARTQX	B-	B-	B-	Up	4.72	7.96	12.36	22.95	73.37	22.73	3,987	800-344-1770	
AT Mid Cap Equity Fund Institutional Class	AWMIX	B	B	B-	Up	6.75	11.20	20.87	29.19		13.9	540.7		Y
ATM Mid Cap Managed Volatility Portfolio Class K	US26883L8524	B	B	B		6.67	10.12	15.73	32.98	98.91		205.1	877-222-2144	Y
Ave Maria Growth Fund	AVEGX	B	B+	B-		7.38	13.57	27.36	37.61	99.26	30.8	476.9	888-726-9331	Y
AXA 400 Managed Volatility Portfolio Class IB	US26884M8001	B	B	B	Up	6.59	9.96	15.39	32.28	96.02		714.3	877-222-2144	Y
AXA 400 Managed Volatility Portfolio Class K	US26883L8607	B	B	B		6.64	10.08	15.67	33.28	98.50		714.3	877-222-2144	Y
AXA Mid Cap Value Managed Volatility Portfolio Class IA	US2689408712	B	B-	B	Up	5.25	8.27	12.56	26.26	92.45		2,167	877-222-2144	Y
AXA Mid Cap Value Managed Volatility Portfolio Class IB	US2689407490	B	B-	B	Up	5.24	8.23	12.55	26.28	92.42		2,167	877-222-2144	Y
AXA Mid Cap Value Managed Volatility Portfolio Class K	US26883L4721	B	B-	B	Up	5.32	8.41	12.82	27.20	94.85		2,167	877-222-2144	Y
Azzad Ethical Fund	ADJEX	B-	C+	B	Up	6.12	10.25	23.21	18.08	76.26	13.32	75.3		Y
Baird MidCap Fund Institutional Class	BMDIX	B-	B	C+	Down	5.51	9.31	26.88	28.28	82.69	19.16	1,397	800-792-2473	Y
Baird MidCap Fund Investor Class	BMDSX	B-	B-	C+	Down	5.50	9.18	26.60	27.30	80.49	18.23	1,397	800-792-2473	Y
Baron Asset Fund Class R6	BARUX	B	B	B-		3.10	6.59	26.47	33.59	107.92	70.46	3,153	800-992-2766	Y
Baron Asset Fund Institutional Class	BARIX	B	B	B+	Down	3.10	6.59	26.49	34.00	109.69	70.47	3,153	800-992-2766	Y
Baron Asset Fund Retail Class	BARAX	B	B	B		3.04	6.45	26.12	32.91	106.86	68.16	3,153	800-992-2766	Y
Baron Focused Growth Fund Institutional Shares	BFGIX	B	B	B	Up	2.66	5.95	26.58	24.41	63.78	15.66	194.5	800-992-2766	Y
Baron Focused Growth Fund R6 Shares	BFGUX	B	B	B	Up	2.66	6.01	26.66	23.98	62.45	15.67	194.5	800-992-2766	Y
Baron Focused Growth Fund Retail Shares	BFGFX	B	B	B	Up	2.58	5.83	26.35	23.52	61.84	15.38	194.5	800-992-2766	Y

Category: US Equity Mid Cap (con't)

Fund Name	Ticker Symbol	RATINGS: Overall Rating	Reward Rating	Risk Rating	Recent Up/ Downgrade	TOTAL RETURNS & PERFORMANCE: 3-Month Total Return	6-Month Total Return	1-Year Total Return	3-Year Total Return	5-Year Total Return	ASSETS: NAV	Total Assets (MIL)	NEW INVESTORS: Telephone	Open to New Investors
Baron Growth Fund Class R6	BGRUX	B	B	B	Up	5.36	8.75	27.34	28.56	89.69	69.56	6,306	800-992-2766	Y
Baron Growth Fund Institutional Shares	BGRIX	B	B	B	Up	5.35	8.75	27.35	28.92	91.22	69.55	6,306	800-992-2766	Y
Baron Growth Fund Retail Shares	BGRFX	B	B	B	Up	5.30	8.63	27.03	27.94	88.78	67.67	6,306	800-992-2766	Y
Baron Opportunity Fund Institutional Class	BIOIX	B	B	B	Up	6.17	9.80	40.87	35.66	89.04	17.6	251.0	800-992-2766	Y
Baron Opportunity Fund R6 Shares	BIOUX	B	B	B	Up	6.17	9.79	40.94	35.12	87.20	17.61	251.0	800-992-2766	Y
Baron Opportunity Fund Retail Class	BIOPX	B	B	B	Up	6.08	9.63	40.50	34.57	86.44	17	251.0	800-992-2766	Y
Baron Partners Fund Institutional Shares	BPTIX	B	B	B	Up	1.13	2.55	31.90	33.36	123.88	49.73	2,057	800-992-2766	Y
Baron Partners Fund R6 Shares	BPTUX	B	B	B-	Up	1.13	2.55	31.87	32.78	121.72	49.73	2,057	800-992-2766	Y
Baron Partners Fund Retail Shares	BPTRX	B	B	B-	Up	1.07	2.43	31.54	32.32	120.96	48.75	2,057	800-992-2766	Y
Barrow Value Opportunity Fund Institutional Class	BALIX	B	C+	B+	Up	6.52	8.94	16.09	24.68	84.07	27.67	41.7		Y
BlackRock Mid Cap Dividend Fund Institutional Shares	MARFX	B-	B-	B	Up	4.90	7.77	8.81	23.36	81.24	18.3	443.4	800-441-7762	Y
BlackRock Mid Cap Dividend Fund Investor A Shares	MDRFX	B-	B-	B	Up	4.83	7.63	8.54	22.33	78.56	17.47	443.4	800-441-7762	Y
BlackRock Mid Cap Dividend Fund Investor C Shares	MCRFX	B-	C+	B-	Up	4.68	7.28	7.73	19.46	71.60	13.95	443.4	800-441-7762	Y
BlackRock Mid Cap Dividend Fund R Shares	MRRFX	B-	C+	B-	Up	4.73	7.47	8.19	21.19	75.85	15.16	443.4	800-441-7762	Y
BlackRock Mid-Cap Growth Equity Portfolio Class K	BMGKX	A-	A	B	Up	5.46	11.29	34.81	47.89	136.83	22.58	1,021	800-441-7762	Y
BlackRock Mid-Cap Growth Equity Portfolio Class R	BMRRX	B+	A-	B	Up	5.31	10.91	33.89	45.06	129.83	19.36	1,021	800-441-7762	Y
BlackRock Mid-Cap Growth Equity Portfolio Inst Shares	CMGIX	A-	A	B	Up	5.41	11.19	34.66	47.55	136.28	22.54	1,021	800-441-7762	Y
BlackRock Mid-Cap Growth Equity Portfolio Inv A Shares	BMGAX	A-	A-	B	Up	5.34	11.04	34.20	46.10	132.75	19.63	1,021	800-441-7762	Y
BlackRock Mid-Cap Growth Equity Portfolio Inv B Shares	BMGBX	B+	A-	B	Up	6.09	9.94	33.04	42.73	124.49		1,021	800-441-7762	
BlackRock Mid-Cap Growth Equity Portfolio Inv C Shares	BMGCX	B+	A-	B	Up	5.12	10.59	33.22	42.87	124.20	15.51	1,021	800-441-7762	Y
BlackRock Mid-Cap Growth Equity Portfolio Service Shares	CMGSX	A-	A	B	Up	5.35	11.08	34.39	46.41	132.29	20.5	1,021	800-441-7762	Y
BMO Mid-Cap Value Fund Class A	BAMCX	B-	B-	B	Up	7.05	10.86	14.44	24.85	97.92	12.52	219.2	800-236-3863	Y
BMO Mid-Cap Value Fund Class I	MRVIX	B-	B-	B	Up	7.16	11.00	14.70	25.80	100.44	12.44	219.2	800-236-3863	Y
BMO Mid-Cap Value Fund Class R3	BMVDX	B-	B-	B	Up	6.97	10.72	14.12	23.82	95.28	12.42	219.2	800-236-3863	Y
BMO Mid-Cap Value Fund Class R6	BMVGX	B	B-	B	Up	7.19	11.11	14.82	26.27	101.36	12.44	219.2	800-236-3863	Y
BNY Mellon Mid Cap Multi-Strategy Fund Class Investor	MIMSX	B-	B-	C+	Down	5.29	9.36	18.38	26.84	94.50	17.04	3,092	800-645-6561	Y
BNY Mellon Mid Cap Multi-Strategy Fund Class M	MPMCX	B-	B	C+	Down	5.36	9.57	18.67	27.79	96.82	17.32	3,092	800-645-6561	Y
Boston Trust Midcap Fund	BTMFX	B	B	B+		7.91	10.43	20.01	32.85	95.61	17.26	62.1	617-814-1215	Y
Bridgeway Aggressive Investors 1 Fund	BRAGX	B	B	B-	Up	7.66	13.51	18.44	26.59	113.07	75.33	239.9	800-661-3550	Y
Bright Rock Mid Cap Growth Fund Institutional Class	BQMGX	B+	B+	B+	Up	9.35	14.29	22.15	39.21	89.41	17.21	65.8	781-982-6593	Y
Bright Rock Mid Cap Growth Fund Investor Class	BQMIX	B+	B+	B+	Up	9.25	14.13	21.78	38.17	90.94	17.62	65.8	781-982-6593	Y
Buffalo Discovery Fund	BUFTX	B+	B	B+	Up	4.44	10.40	25.43	38.63	115.76	24.22	1,662	800-492-8332	Y
Buffalo Mid Cap Fund	BUFMX	B-	C+	B	Up	3.88	6.28	13.65	19.01	66.70	13.61	191.3	800-492-8332	Y
Bullfinch Greater Western New York Series	BWNYX	B-	C+	B	Up	2.43	4.04	5.06	9.72	65.10	21.57	0.73		Y
Calvert Mid-Cap Fund Class A	CCAFX	B-	C+	B	Up	4.07	6.20	11.70	13.27	61.89	31.52	247.7	800-368-2745	Y
Calvert Mid-Cap Fund Class I	CCPIX	B-	C+	B	Up	4.17	6.40	12.14	14.81	66.11	36.96	247.7	800-368-2745	Y
Cambiar SMID Fund Institutional Class	CAMUX	B-	C+	B	Up	3.74	6.36	11.79	21.82	93.36	16.79	34.2	866-777-8227	Y
Cambiar SMID Fund Investor Class Shares	CAMMX	B-	C+	B	Up	3.78	6.40	11.76	21.64	93.18	16.8	34.2	866-777-8227	Y
Capital Management Mid Cap Fund Class Institutional	CMEIX	B+	B	A-	Up	7.75	13.36	18.44	36.34	96.63	24.04	22.0		Y
Capital Management Mid Cap Fund Class Investor	CMCIX	B	B	B+		7.55	12.90	17.51	33.28	89.76	18.4	22.0		Y
Carillon Eagle Mid Cap Growth Fund Class A	HAGAX	B+	A	C+	Up	6.87	12.12	29.90	40.61	117.87	56.49	2,495	800-421-4184	Y
Carillon Eagle Mid Cap Growth Fund Class C	HAGCX	B	A-	C+	Up	6.66	11.72	28.98	37.61	110.20	45.39	2,495	800-421-4184	Y
Carillon Eagle Mid Cap Growth Fund Class I	HAGIX	B+	A	B-	Up	6.94	12.30	30.35	42.01	121.55	59.48	2,495	800-421-4184	Y
Carillon Eagle Mid Cap Growth Fund Class R3	HAREX	B	A-	C+	Down	6.80	11.95	29.54	39.46	114.84	54.88	2,495	800-421-4184	Y
Carillon Eagle Mid Cap Growth Fund Class R5	HARSX	B+	A	B-	Up	6.94	12.27	30.31	41.84	121.24	59.32	2,495	800-421-4184	Y
Carillon Eagle Mid Cap Growth Fund Class R6	HRAUX	B+	A	B-	Up	6.97	12.34	30.43	42.46	122.68	59.82	2,495	800-421-4184	Y
Carillon Eagle Mid Cap Growth Fund Class Y	HRAYX	B+	A	C+		6.85	12.10	29.88	40.59	117.84	59.46	2,495	800-421-4184	Y
Carillon Eagle Mid Cap Stock Fund Class A	HMCAX	B	B-	B	Up	5.68	9.84	19.59	28.05	78.47	28.38	267.0	800-421-4184	Y
Carillon Eagle Mid Cap Stock Fund Class C	HMCCX	B	B-	B	Up	5.46	9.39	18.65	25.17	71.84	20.6	267.0	800-421-4184	Y
Carillon Eagle Mid Cap Stock Fund Class I	HMCJX	B-	B	C+	Down	5.74	9.98	19.95	29.27	81.05	30.09	267.0	800-421-4184	Y
Carillon Eagle Mid Cap Stock Fund Class R3	HMRRX	B-	B-	C+		5.58	9.67	19.28	26.86	75.75	27.16	267.0	800-421-4184	Y
Carillon Eagle Mid Cap Stock Fund Class R5	HMRSX	B-	B	C+	Down	5.77	9.99	19.94	29.22	81.83	30.28	267.0	800-421-4184	Y

Category: US Equity Mid Cap (con't)

Fund Name	Ticker Symbol	RATINGS: Overall Rating	RATINGS: Reward Rating	RATINGS: Risk Rating	RATINGS: Recent Up/ Downgrade	TOTAL RETURNS & PERFORMANCE: 3-Month Total Return	6-Month Total Return	1-Year Total Return	3-Year Total Return	5-Year Total Return	ASSETS: NAV	Total Assets (MIL)	NEW INVESTORS: Telephone	Open to New Investors
Carillon Eagle Mid Cap Stock Fund Class R6	HMRUX	B-	B	C+	Down	5.78	10.06	20.06	29.63	82.16	30.42	267.0	800-421-4184	Y
Carillon Eagle Mid Cap Stock Fund Class Y	HMRYX	B	B-	B		5.69	9.86	19.60	28.06	78.49	30.08	267.0	800-421-4184	Y
Carillon Scout Mid Cap Fund Class A	CSMEX	B+	A	B-		7.41	13.45	23.76	46.45	114.87	19.01	1,790	800-421-4184	Y
Carillon Scout Mid Cap Fund Class C	CSMFX	B+	A	B-		7.21	13.03	22.84	43.21	107.01	19.01	1,790	800-421-4184	Y
Carillon Scout Mid Cap Fund Class I	UMBMX	B+	A	B-	Up	7.44	13.55	24.02	47.46	117.39	19.01	1,790	800-421-4184	Y
Carillon Scout Mid Cap Fund Class R-3	CSMRX	B+	A	B-		7.31	13.27	23.41	45.31	112.14	19.01	1,790	800-421-4184	Y
Carillon Scout Mid Cap Fund Class R-5	CSMSX	B+	A	B-		7.46	13.57	24.04	47.48	117.42	19.01	1,790	800-421-4184	Y
Carillon Scout Mid Cap Fund Class R-6	CSMUX	B+	A	B-		7.46	13.57	24.04	47.48	117.42	19.01	1,790	800-421-4184	Y
Carillon Scout Mid Cap Fund Class Y	CSMZX	B+	A	B-		7.41	13.45	23.76	46.44	114.86	19.01	1,790	800-421-4184	Y
Catalyst Buyback Strategy Fund Class A	BUYAX	B	B	B-	Up	2.35	9.20	19.63	36.27		10.66	9.6	866-447-4228	Y
Catalyst Buyback Strategy Fund Class C	BUYCX	B	B	B-	Up	2.16	8.75	18.77	33.23		10.4	9.6	866-447-4228	Y
Catalyst Buyback Strategy Fund Class I	BUYIX	B	B	B-	Up	2.42	9.24	19.86	37.28		10.72	9.6	866-447-4228	Y
Cavalier Fundamental Growth Fund C Class	CFGAX	B	B+	C+	Up	2.34	16.86	29.99	28.39		14.53	84.3	800-773-3863	Y
Cavalier Fundamental Growth Fund Institutional Class	CAFGX	B	A-	C+	Up	2.61	17.43	31.26	32.31		14.98	84.3	800-773-3863	Y
Champlain Mid Cap Fund Advisor Class	CIPMX	B	B	B-		5.98	7.89	19.21	41.50	113.87	17.1	1,902		Y
Champlain Mid Cap Fund Institutional Class	CIPIX	B	B	B-		6.09	8.03	19.50	42.54	116.43	17.38	1,902		Y
Chase Mid Cap Growth Fund Class N	CHAMX	B	B	B	Up	9.39	16.44	23.43	35.41	94.22	39.07	22.7	212-270-6000	Y
Chase Mid Cap Growth Fund Institutional Class	CHIMX	B	B	B	Up	9.44	16.51	23.58	36.15	96.27	39.83	22.7	212-270-6000	Y
ClearBridge Mid Cap Fund Class 1	SMCPX	B	B-	B+	Up	3.56	6.29	13.07	25.15	89.76	34.86	2,414	877-721-1926	
ClearBridge Mid Cap Fund Class A	SBMAX	B	B-	B+	Up	3.48	6.13	12.71	23.95	87.49	33.43	2,414	877-721-1926	Y
ClearBridge Mid Cap Fund Class C	SBMLX	B	C+	B	Up	3.28	5.72	11.90	21.36	80.94	26.78	2,414	877-721-1926	Y
ClearBridge Mid Cap Fund Class I	SMBYX	B	B-	B+	Up	3.54	6.29	13.06	25.23	90.83	37.06	2,414	877-721-1926	Y
ClearBridge Mid Cap Fund Class IS	LSIRX	B	B-	B+	Up	3.58	6.36	13.21	25.61	91.77	37.4	2,414	877-721-1926	Y
ClearBridge Mid Cap Fund Class R	LMREX	B	B-	B+	Up	3.38	5.99	12.40	22.99	85.12	32.64	2,414	877-721-1926	Y
ClearBridge Mid Cap Growth Fund Class A	LBGAX	B	B-	B	Up	8.07	11.65	22.65	24.55	87.29	28.33	102.7	877-721-1926	Y
ClearBridge Mid Cap Growth Fund Class A2	LCBGX	B-	B-	B	Up	7.99	11.50	22.42	23.79	85.75	28.08	102.7	877-721-1926	Y
ClearBridge Mid Cap Growth Fund Class C	LBGCX	B-	C+	B	Up	7.82	11.19	21.67	21.61	80.18	26.71	102.7	877-721-1926	Y
ClearBridge Mid Cap Growth Fund Class I	LBGIX	B	B-	B	Up	8.15	11.79	22.99	25.61	89.77	28.89	102.7	877-721-1926	Y
ClearBridge Mid Cap Growth Fund Class IS	LCMIX	B	B-	B	Up	8.14	11.78	23.08	25.69	89.90	28.91	102.7	877-721-1926	Y
ClearBridge Mid Cap Growth Fund Class R	LCMRX	B-	B-	B	Up	7.95	11.40	22.26	23.32	84.35	27.92	102.7	877-721-1926	Y
ClearBridge Select Fund Class A	LCLAX	B+	A	B	Up	8.46	13.46	38.69	37.25	138.93	20.25	28.7	877-721-1926	Y
ClearBridge Select Fund Class C	LCLCX	B+	A-	B	Up	8.26	12.97	37.43	34.13	129.67	19.54	28.7	877-721-1926	Y
ClearBridge Select Fund Class FI	LCBSX	B+	A	B	Up	8.41	13.41	38.55	37.11	137.48	20.23	28.7	877-721-1926	Y
ClearBridge Select Fund Class I	LBFIX	B+	A	B	Up	8.49	13.50	38.93	38.47	142.24	20.69	28.7	877-721-1926	Y
ClearBridge Select Fund Class IS	LCSSX	B+	A	B	Up	8.51	13.53	39.04	38.75	142.29	20.65	28.7	877-721-1926	Y
Clifford Capital Partners Fund Institutional Class	CLIFX	B-	B	B-	Down	5.47	9.03	10.35	33.57		14.72	13.4		Y
Clifford Capital Partners Fund Investor Class	CLFFX	B-	B	B-		5.46	8.88	10.12	32.73		14.68	13.4		Y
Columbia Acorn Fund Advisor Class	CEARX	B	B+	C+	Up	5.99	11.41	25.19	34.74	82.18	16.06	4,848	800-345-6611	Y
Columbia Acorn Fund Class A	LACAX	B	B+	C+	Up	5.90	11.26	24.91	33.97	80.17	12.92	4,848	800-345-6611	Y
Columbia Acorn Fund Class C	LIACX	B	B	C+	Up	5.70	10.77	23.88	30.96	73.70	6.58	4,848	800-345-6611	Y
Columbia Acorn Fund Institutional 2 Class	CRBRX	B	B+	C+	Up	6.00	11.44	25.20	35.10	82.93	16.2	4,848	800-345-6611	Y
Columbia Acorn Fund Institutional 3 Class	CRBYX	B	B+	C+	Up	6.02	11.55	25.31	35.39	83.49	16.34	4,848	800-345-6611	Y
Columbia Acorn Fund Institutional Class	ACRNX	B	B+	C+	Up	6.04	11.47	25.23	35.10	82.76	15.39	4,848	800-345-6611	Y
Columbia Acorn Select Fund Advisor Class	CSSRX	B+	A-	B-	Up	7.93	13.36	26.70	39.75	96.85	17.19	314.9	800-345-6611	Y
Columbia Acorn Select Fund Class A	LTFAX	B	A-	B-	Up	7.85	13.13	26.33	38.69	94.31	14.61	314.9	800-345-6611	Y
Columbia Acorn Select Fund Class C	LTFCX	B	B+	B-	Up	7.69	12.68	25.39	35.67	87.35	9.59	314.9	800-345-6611	Y
Columbia Acorn Select Fund Institutional 2 Class	CSLRX	B+	A-	B-	Up	7.96	13.35	26.71	40.09	97.51	17.28	314.9	800-345-6611	Y
Columbia Acorn Select Fund Institutional 3 Class	CSLYX	B+	A-	B-	Up	7.95	13.37	26.78	40.25	98.01	17.43	314.9	800-345-6611	Y
Columbia Acorn Select Fund Institutional Class	ACTWX	B+	A-	B-	Up	7.92	13.33	26.58	39.81	97.01	16.54	314.9	800-345-6611	Y
Columbia Mid Cap Growth Fund Advisor Class	CPGRX	B	B	B	Up	5.00	9.97	22.93	31.29	89.01	27.96	1,916	800-345-6611	Y
Columbia Mid Cap Growth Fund Class A	CBSAX	B	B	B+	Up	4.93	9.86	22.62	30.32	86.89	25.46	1,916	800-345-6611	Y
Columbia Mid Cap Growth Fund Class C	CMCCX	B	B-	B	Up	4.74	9.44	21.69	27.41	80.00	21.3	1,916	800-345-6611	Y

Category: US Equity Mid Cap (con't)

Fund Name	Ticker Symbol	RATINGS: Overall Rating	RATINGS: Reward Rating	RATINGS: Risk Rating	RATINGS: Recent Up/ Downgrade	TOTAL RETURNS & PERFORMANCE: 3-Month Total Return	6-Month Total Return	1-Year Total Return	3-Year Total Return	5-Year Total Return	ASSETS: NAV	Total Assets (MIL)	NEW INVESTORS: Telephone	Open to New Investors
Columbia Mid Cap Growth Fund Class K	CMCKX	B	B	B	Up	4.95	9.88	22.76	30.74	88.10	27.08	1,916	800-345-6611	
Columbia Mid Cap Growth Fund Class R	CMGRX	B	B	B	Up	4.86	9.72	22.29	29.33	84.63	24.45	1,916	800-345-6611	Y
Columbia Mid Cap Growth Fund Class T	CMRWX	B	B	B	Up	4.93	9.86	22.62	30.32	86.85	25.46	1,916	800-345-6611	Y
Columbia Mid Cap Growth Fund Class V	CBSTX	B	B	B	Up	4.95	9.85	22.61	30.32	86.70	25.36	1,916	800-345-6611	
Columbia Mid Cap Growth Fund Institutional 2 Class	CMGVX	B	B	B	Up	5.00	10.02	23.02	31.70	90.25	27.36	1,916	800-345-6611	Y
Columbia Mid Cap Growth Fund Institutional 3 Class	CMGYX	B	B	B	Up	5.05	10.07	23.12	31.99	90.90	27.37	1,916	800-345-6611	Y
Columbia Mid Cap Growth Fund Institutional Class	CLSPX	B	B	B+	Up	4.99	9.98	22.88	31.24	89.21	27.15	1,916	800-345-6611	Y
Columbia Mid Cap Index Fund Class A	NTIAX	B	B	B		6.15	9.44	15.68	33.99	99.85	16.55	4,925	800-345-6611	Y
Columbia Mid Cap Index Fund Institutional 2 Class	CPXRX	B	B	B		6.20	9.57	15.99	35.00	102.49	16.8	4,925	800-345-6611	Y
Columbia Mid Cap Index Fund Institutional 3 Class	CMDYX	B	B	B		6.17	9.53	15.96	34.95	102.23	16.19	4,925	800-345-6611	Y
Columbia Mid Cap Index Fund Institutional Class	NMPAX	B	B	B		6.20	9.57	15.96	34.96	102.24	16.47	4,925	800-345-6611	Y
Columbia Mid Cap Value Fund Advisor Class	CFDRX	B-	C+	B	Down	5.62	7.69	13.53	21.96	90.94	14.07	2,351	800-345-6611	Y
Columbia Mid Cap Value Fund Class A	CMUAX	B-	C+	B		5.64	7.62	13.33	21.10	88.54	13.67	2,351	800-345-6611	Y
Columbia Mid Cap Value Fund Class C	CMUCX	B-	C+	B	Up	5.46	7.19	12.51	18.44	81.64	12.68	2,351	800-345-6611	Y
Columbia Mid Cap Value Fund Class K	CMUFX	B-	C+	B	Down	5.57	7.58	13.42	21.63	89.81	13.73	2,351	800-345-6611	
Columbia Mid Cap Value Fund Class R	CMVRX	B-	C+	B		5.53	7.44	13.01	20.20	86.26	13.62	2,351	800-345-6611	Y
Columbia Mid Cap Value Fund Class T	CMUWX	B-	C+	B		5.64	7.62	13.33	21.10	88.55	13.67	2,351	800-345-6611	Y
Columbia Mid Cap Value Fund Institutional 2 Class	CVERX	B-	C+	B	Down	5.65	7.75	13.67	22.44	92.18	14.07	2,351	800-345-6611	Y
Columbia Mid Cap Value Fund Institutional 3 Class	CMVYX	B-	C+	B	Down	5.68	7.77	13.80	22.66	92.65	13.66	2,351	800-345-6611	Y
Columbia Mid Cap Value Fund Institutional Class	NAMAX	B-	C+	B	Down	5.63	7.74	13.57	22.03	90.94	13.7	2,351	800-345-6611	Y
Commerce MidCap Growth Fund	CFAGX	B	B	B		6.85	10.71	23.36	37.44	104.86	39.5	156.4		Y
Congress All Cap Opportunity Fund Institutional Class	IACOX	B	B+	B	Up	6.09	12.59	21.71	30.89	95.51	18.78	27.7	888-688-1299	Y
Congress All Cap Opportunity Fund Retail Class	CACOX	B	B	B	Up	6.03	12.38	21.37	29.83	92.84	18.73	27.7	888-688-1299	Y
Congress Mid Cap Growth Fund Institutional Class	IMIDX	B	B	B-		3.38	5.52	15.91	30.47	102.47	18.84	964.9	888-688-1299	Y
Congress Mid Cap Growth Fund Retail Class	CMIDX	B	B	B+		3.31	5.41	15.58	29.38	100.19	18.69	964.9	888-688-1299	Y
CRM Mid Cap Value Fund Class Institutional	CRIMX	B	B	B-	Up	5.45	9.55	19.36	34.32	94.74	21.8	519.2	800-276-2883	Y
CRM Mid Cap Value Fund Class Investor	CRMMX	B	B	B-	Up	5.40	9.40	19.05	33.54	92.74	20.97	519.2	800-276-2883	Y
CRM Small/Mid Cap Value Fund Class Institutional	CRIAX	B-	B-	B-	Up	5.59	9.44	14.47	23.49	76.30	12.56	307.3	800-276-2883	Y
CRM Small/Mid Cap Value Fund Class Investor	CRMAX	B-	B-	B-	Up	5.57	9.34	14.21	22.72	74.44	12.26	307.3	800-276-2883	Y
Davenport Equity Opportunities Fund	DEOPX	B-	B-	B		3.67	11.26	20.78	21.26	84.97	18.07	403.0		Y
Dean Mid Cap Value Fund	DALCX	B	B	B+		6.42	9.76	15.11	32.79	97.90	20.47	31.9	888-899-8343	Y
Delaware Mid Cap Value Fund Class A	DLMAX	B+	B+	B+	Up	6.61	11.78	16.83	36.78	93.57	6.38	13.0		Y
Delaware Mid Cap Value Fund Class C	DLMCX	B	B	B	Up	6.31	11.23	15.73	33.40	86.11	5.95	13.0		Y
Delaware Mid Cap Value Fund Class R	DLMRX	B	B	B		6.56	11.73	16.58	35.68	91.01	6.38	13.0		Y
Delaware Mid Cap Value Fund Institutional Class	DLMIX	B+	B+	B+	Up	6.68	12.04	17.10	37.50	95.68	6.38	13.0		Y
Delaware Smid Cap Growth Fund Class A	DFCIX	B+	B+	B	Up	17.92	21.66	35.13	37.41	102.61	21.91	960.3		
Delaware Smid Cap Growth Fund Class C	DEEVX	B	B	B	Up	17.70	21.19	34.14	34.35	95.11	11.11	960.3		
Delaware Smid Cap Growth Fund Class R	DFRIX	B	B+	B	Up	17.81	21.51	34.77	36.33	100.00	20.18	960.3		
Delaware Smid Cap Growth Fund Class R6	DFZRX	B+	A-	B	Up	18.03	21.84	35.60	38.16	103.71	29.46	960.3		
Delaware Smid Cap Growth Fund Institutional Class	DFDIX	B+	A-	B	Up	17.99	21.76	35.45	38.41	105.04	29.44	960.3		
Deutsche Mid Cap Value Fund Class A	MIDVX	B	C+	B	Up	4.93	9.13	12.75	26.81	96.21	18.75	324.8	201-593-8273	Y
Deutsche Mid Cap Value Fund Class C	MIDZX	B-	C+	B	Up	4.74	8.68	11.85	23.93	88.85	18.3	324.8	201-593-8273	Y
Deutsche Mid Cap Value Fund Class R	MIDQX	B	C+	B	Up	4.89	8.98	12.47	25.82	93.85	18.75	324.8	201-593-8273	Y
Deutsche Mid Cap Value Fund Class R6	MIDUX	B	B-	B	Up	5.00	9.27	13.10	27.99	99.08	18.69	324.8	201-593-8273	Y
Deutsche Mid Cap Value Fund Class S	MIDTX	B	B-	B	Up	4.98	9.24	13.00	27.72	98.61	18.71	324.8	201-593-8273	Y
Deutsche Mid Cap Value Fund Institutional Class	MIDIX	B	B-	B	Up	5.01	9.27	13.03	27.78	98.65	18.72	324.8	201-593-8273	Y
DF Dent Midcap Growth Fund Institutional Shares	DFMGX	A-	A-	B+		6.85	13.00	31.21	37.05	103.93	20.37	41.6		Y
DF Dent Midcap Growth Fund Investor Shares	DFDMX	A-	A-	B+	Up	6.85	13.00	31.21	37.05	103.93	20.37	41.6		Y
DF Dent Premier Growth Fund Investor Shares	DFDPX	A-	A-	B+	Up	6.18	12.91	31.83	36.18	97.16	29.03	158.7		Y
DFA CSTG&E U.S. Social Core Equity 2 Portfolio	DFCUX	B	B	B	Up	7.21	12.86	18.64	34.42	101.80	17.58	105.8	512-306-7400	
DFA T.A. U.S. Core Equity 2 Portfolio Institutional Class	DFTCX	B	B	B	Up	6.54	11.60	18.81	33.48	106.72	18.12	8,570	512-306-7400	Y
DFA U.S. Core Equity II Portfolio Institutional Class	DFQTX	B	B	B-	Up	6.66	11.82	18.93	33.17	106.11	21.56	23,310	512-306-7400	Y

Category: US Equity Mid Cap (con't)

Fund Name	Ticker Symbol	RATINGS: Overall Rating	RATINGS: Reward Rating	RATINGS: Risk Rating	RATINGS: Recent Up/ Downgrade	TOTAL RETURNS & PERFORMANCE: 3-Month Total Return	6-Month Total Return	1-Year Total Return	3-Year Total Return	5-Year Total Return	ASSETS: NAV	Total Assets (MIL)	NEW INVESTORS: Telephone	Open to New Investors
DFA U.S. Social Core Equity 2 Portfolio	DFUEX	B	B	C+	Up	7.02	12.11	18.98	32.42	101.47	16.08	997.7	512-306-7400	Y
DFA U.S. Vector Equity Portfolio Institutional Class	DFVEX	B	B	B	Up	5.39	10.78	14.63	30.64	100.42	19.17	4,856	512-306-7400	Y
Diamond Hill Mid Cap Fund Class A	DHPAX	B	B-	A-		3.70	6.00	10.13	29.64		13.66	120.0	888-226-5595	Y
Diamond Hill Mid Cap Fund Class I	DHPIX	B	B-	A-		3.80	6.09	10.47	30.84		13.7	120.0	888-226-5595	Y
Diamond Hill Mid Cap Fund Class Y	DHPYX	B	B-	A-		3.78	6.15	10.51	31.12		13.73	120.0	888-226-5595	Y
Diamond Hill Small Mid Cap Fund Class A	DHMAX	B	B-	A-	Up	2.12	4.73	8.34	27.85	98.30	22.24	2,535	888-226-5595	
Diamond Hill Small Mid Cap Fund Class C	DHMCX	B	C+	A-	Up	1.92	4.34	7.49	24.95	90.96	20.39	2,535	888-226-5595	
Diamond Hill Small Mid Cap Fund Class I	DHMIX	B	B-	A-	Up	2.23	4.90	8.63	28.95	100.98	22.45	2,535	888-226-5595	
Diamond Hill Small-Mid Cap Fund Class Y	DHMYX	B	B-	A-	Up	2.22	4.94	8.76	29.43	102.26	22.49	2,535	888-226-5595	
Dreyfus Active MidCap Fund Class A	DNLDX	B	B-	B+	Up	7.23	10.59	16.63	27.78	103.99	62.37	661.8	800-645-6561	Y
Dreyfus Active MidCap Fund Class C	DNLCX	B	B-	B+	Up	7.01	10.14	15.65	24.56	95.53	57.44	661.8	800-645-6561	Y
Dreyfus Active MidCap Fund Class I	DNLRX	B	B	B+	Up	7.29	10.73	16.90	28.58	106.10	62.64	661.8	800-645-6561	Y
Dreyfus Active MidCap Fund Class Y	DNLYX	B	B	B+	Up	7.31	10.74	16.93	28.70	105.46	62.58	661.8	800-645-6561	Y
Dreyfus Mid Cap Index Fund Class I	DMIDX	B	B	B		6.21	9.57	15.98	34.41	100.59	37.13	3,851	800-645-6561	Y
Dreyfus Mid Cap Index Fund Investor Shares	PESPX	B	B	B		6.12	9.42	15.67	33.99	99.96	37.23	3,851	800-645-6561	Y
Dreyfus Mid-Cap Growth Fund Class A	FRSDX	B-	B	C+	Up	3.86	10.31	25.33	27.23	88.84	9.06	145.5	800-645-6561	Y
Dreyfus Mid-Cap Growth Fund Class C	FRSCX	B-	B-	C+	Up	3.59	9.82	24.28	24.35	81.83	7.52	145.5	800-645-6561	Y
Dreyfus Mid-Cap Growth Fund Class F	FRSPX	B-	B	C+	Down	3.99	10.48	25.63	28.20	90.97	9.56	145.5	800-645-6561	
Dreyfus Mid-Cap Growth Fund Class I	FRSRX	B-	B	C+	Down	3.89	10.37	25.68	28.25	90.94	9.54	145.5	800-645-6561	Y
Dreyfus Opportunistic Midcap Value Fund Class A	DMCVX	B-	C+	B-	Up	6.60	11.33	15.62	20.56	89.02	33.43	1,106	800-645-6561	Y
Dreyfus Opportunistic Midcap Value Fund Class I	DVLIX	B-	B-	B-	Up	6.71	11.52	15.97	21.64	91.66	33.21	1,106	800-645-6561	Y
Dreyfus Opportunistic Midcap Value Fund Class Y	DMCYX	B-	B-	B-	Up	6.73	11.54	16.08	22.00	92.70	33.26	1,106	800-645-6561	Y
Dreyfus Small Cap Equity Fund Class A	DSEAX	B	B-	B	Up	5.63	8.37	12.50	24.85	84.27	24.67	47.3	800-645-6561	Y
Dreyfus Small Cap Equity Fund Class C	DSECX	B-	C+	B	Up	5.39	7.87	11.53	21.75	76.71	19.52	47.3	800-645-6561	Y
Dreyfus Small Cap Equity Fund Class I	DSERX	B	B-	B	Up	5.64	8.43	12.73	25.71	86.41	26.27	47.3	800-645-6561	Y
Dreyfus Structured Midcap Fund Class A	DPSAX	B	B	B	Up	7.75	10.40	17.07	29.05	98.80	31.42	219.7	800-645-6561	Y
Dreyfus Structured Midcap Fund Class C	DPSCX	B	B-	B	Up	7.53	9.96	16.17	26.22	91.56	27.53	219.7	800-645-6561	Y
Dreyfus Structured Midcap Fund Class I	DPSRX	B	B	B	Up	7.78	10.51	17.34	30.02	101.22	32.07	219.7	800-645-6561	Y
Dreyfus Structured MidCap Fund Class Y	DPSYX	B	B	B	Up	7.84	10.62	17.49	30.55	102.35	32	219.7	800-645-6561	Y
Dreyfus/The Boston Company Small/Mid Cap Growth Fund Cls A	DBMAX	B	A-	C+	Up	5.08	11.36	26.09	35.22	101.56	19.06	1,225	800-645-6561	Y
Dreyfus/The Boston Company Small/Mid Cap Growth Fund Cls C	DBMCX	B	B+	C+	Up	4.89	10.95	25.18	32.12	93.63	17.02	1,225	800-645-6561	Y
Dreyfus/The Boston Company Small/Mid Cap Growth Fund Cls I	SDSCX	B+	A-	B	Up	5.18	11.56	26.52	36.33	104.25	19.7	1,225	800-645-6561	Y
Dreyfus/The Boston Company Small/Mid Cap Growth Fund Cls Y	DBMYX	B	A-	C+	Up	5.21	11.56	26.58	36.77	105.11	19.8	1,225	800-645-6561	Y
Eaton Vance Atlanta Capital SMID-Cap Fund Class A	EAASX	B+	A-	B+	Up	8.87	12.63	24.41	49.69	117.69	30.5	11,256		
Eaton Vance Atlanta Capital SMID-Cap Fund Class C	ECASX	B+	A-	B+	Up	8.72	12.23	23.51	46.39	109.73	28.38	11,256		
Eaton Vance Atlanta Capital SMID-Cap Fund Class I	EISMX	A-	A-	B+	Up	8.96	12.78	24.73	50.85	120.48	33.61	11,256		
Eaton Vance Atlanta Capital SMID-Cap Fund Class R	ERSMX	B+	A-	B+	Up	8.82	12.50	24.11	48.63	115.11	29.79	11,256		
Eaton Vance Atlanta Capital SMID-Cap Fund Class R6	ERASX	A-	A-	B+	Up	8.99	12.84	24.83	51.27	121.26	33.74	11,256		Y
Eaton Vance Special Equities Fund Class A	EVSEX	B	B	B	Up	4.51	8.34	15.37	28.17	82.45	22.7	46.3		Y
Eaton Vance Special Equities Fund Class C	ECSEX	B	B-	B	Up	4.29	7.90	14.45	25.28	75.72	20.23	46.3		Y
Eaton Vance Special Equities Fund Class I	EISEX	B	B	B	Up	4.55	8.45	15.63	29.08	84.78	23.17	46.3		Y
Emerald Insights Fund Class A	EFCAX	B-	B-	B	Up	6.97	11.03	22.54	25.53		12.88	11.0	855-828-9909	Y
Emerald Insights Fund Class C	EFCCX	B-	B-	B-	Up	6.79	10.55	21.80	22.99		12.57	11.0	855-828-9909	Y
Emerald Insights Fund Institutional Class	EFCIX	B	B-	B	Up	7.00	11.12	22.89	26.60		12.99	11.0	855-828-9909	Y
Emerald Insights Fund Investor Class	EFCNX	B-	B-	B	Up	7.00	10.97	22.51	25.26		12.84	11.0	855-828-9909	Y
EQ/Mid Cap Index Portfolio Class IA	US2689403192	B	B	B		6.71	10.12	15.66	33.35	98.56		2,031	877-222-2144	Y
EQ/Mid Cap Index Portfolio Class IB	US2689402939	B	B	B		6.67	10.06	15.60	33.22	98.53		2,031	877-222-2144	Y
EQ/Mid Cap Index Portfolio Class K	US26883L4804	B	B	B		6.75	10.23	16.00	34.34	101.25		2,031	877-222-2144	Y
Eventide Gilead Class A	ETAGX	B	A-	C	Up	7.25	14.18	32.80	30.86	140.31	34.13	1,522		Y
Eventide Gilead Class C	ETCGX	B	B+	C	Up	7.06	13.72	31.76	27.92	131.28	31.98	1,522		Y
Eventide Gilead Class I	ETILX	B	A-	C	Up	7.34	14.32	33.09	31.82	143.39	34.79	1,522		Y
Eventide Gilead Class N	ETGLX	B	A-	B-	Up	7.29	14.20	32.85	31.06	140.98	34.25	1,522		Y

Category: US Equity Mid Cap (con't)

Fund Name	Ticker Symbol	RATINGS: Overall Rating	Reward Rating	Risk Rating	Recent Up/ Downgrade	TOTAL RETURNS & PERFORMANCE: 3-Month Total Return	6-Month Total Return	1-Year Total Return	3-Year Total Return	5-Year Total Return	ASSETS: NAV	Total Assets (MIL)	NEW INVESTORS: Telephone	Open to New Investors
FAM Equity-Income Fund Investor Class	FAMEX	B	B	B+		4.19	7.64	12.63	34.74	93.10	30.11	225.3		Y
FAM Value Fund Institutional Class	FAMWX	B	B	B+		6.47	11.10	17.16	32.13	103.02	73.64	1,262		
FAM Value Fund Investor Class	FAMVX	B	B	B+		6.43	11.03	17.00	31.95	102.73	73.52	1,262		Y
Federated Kaufmann Fund Class A Shares	KAUAX	B	B	B	Up	5.41	11.60	27.73	39.04	117.63	5.59	5,697	800-341-7400	Y
Federated Kaufmann Fund Class B Shares	KAUBX	B	B	B	Up	5.37	11.31	27.26	36.97	111.91	4.65	5,697	800-341-7400	Y
Federated Kaufmann Fund Class C Shares	KAUCX	B	B	B	Up	5.39	11.34	27.32	36.79	111.71	4.64	5,697	800-341-7400	Y
Federated Kaufmann Fund Class R Shares	KAUFX	B	B+	B	Up	5.40	11.57	27.68	38.96	117.34	5.6	5,697	800-341-7400	Y
Federated Kaufmann Fund Institutional Shares	KAUIX	B	B+	C+	Up	5.73	11.91	28.51	39.87	118.76	5.64	5,697	800-341-7400	Y
Federated MDT Mid Cap Growth Fund Class A Shares	FGSAX	B	B	B	Up	8.74	13.98	24.41	29.11	110.73	39.47	324.9	800-341-7400	Y
Federated MDT Mid Cap Growth Fund Class B Shares	FGSBX	B	B	B	Up	8.53	13.52	23.48	26.22	103.00	27.28	324.9	800-341-7400	
Federated MDT Mid Cap Growth Fund Class C Shares	FGSCX	B	B	B	Up	8.55	13.59	23.52	26.30	103.08	27.98	324.9	800-341-7400	Y
Federated MDT Mid Cap Growth Fund Class R6 Shares	FGSKX	B	B	B	Up	8.80	14.13	24.72	28.52	107.79	37.11	324.9	800-341-7400	Y
Federated MDT Mid Cap Growth Fund Institutional Shares	FGSIX	B	B	B	Up	8.83	14.15	24.74	30.09	113.39	40.47	324.9	800-341-7400	Y
Federated Mid-Cap Index Fund Class R6 Shares	FMCLX	B	B	B		6.18	9.48	15.87	34.19	100.70	24.61	831.1	800-341-7400	Y
Federated Mid-Cap Index Fund Institutional Shares	FMCRX	B	B	B		6.19	9.50	15.89	34.78	102.53	24.59	831.1	800-341-7400	Y
Federated Mid-Cap Index Fund Service Shares	FMDCX	B	B	B		6.11	9.33	15.56	33.75	100.04	24.61	831.1	800-341-7400	Y
Fidelity Advisor® Leveraged Company Stock Fund Class A	FLSAX	B-	C+	B	Up	5.51	9.37	17.32	19.50	76.85	43.37	2,243	617-563-7000	Y
Fidelity Advisor® Leveraged Company Stock Fund Class C	FLSCX	B-	C+	B-	Up	5.33	8.96	16.46	16.84	70.35	38.84	2,243	617-563-7000	Y
Fidelity Advisor® Leveraged Company Stock Fund Class M	FLSTX	B-	C+	B-	Up	5.46	9.23	17.02	18.64	74.73	42	2,243	617-563-7000	Y
Fidelity Advisor® Leveraged Company Stock Fund Class Z	FZAKX	B-	C+	B	Up	5.63	9.59	17.78	20.93	80.22	44.29	2,243	617-563-7000	Y
Fidelity Advisor® Leveraged Company Stock Fund I Class	FLVIX	B-	C+	B	Up	5.58	9.52	17.63	20.43	79.19	44.3	2,243	617-563-7000	Y
Fidelity Advisor® Mid Cap II Fund Class A	FIIAX	B	B	B	Up	6.18	10.65	20.25	30.67	92.62	20.94	2,632	617-563-7000	Y
Fidelity Advisor® Mid Cap II Fund Class C	FIICX	B	B	B	Up	5.89	10.20	19.26	27.64	85.30	18.7	2,632	617-563-7000	Y
Fidelity Advisor® Mid Cap II Fund Class I	FIIMX	B	B	B	Up	6.20	10.80	20.55	31.75	95.09	21.57	2,632	617-563-7000	Y
Fidelity Advisor® Mid Cap II Fund Class M	FITIX	B	B	B	Up	6.06	10.53	19.90	29.70	90.36	20.43	2,632	617-563-7000	Y
Fidelity Advisor® Mid Cap II Fund Class Z	FZAMX	B	B	B-	Up	6.24	10.89	20.71	32.30	96.45	21.57	2,632	617-563-7000	Y
Fidelity Advisor® Mid Cap Value Fund Class A	FMPAX	B-	B-	B		7.98	10.69	16.66	23.31	104.12	26.26	3,256	617-563-7000	Y
Fidelity Advisor® Mid Cap Value Fund Class C	FMPEX	B-	C+	B	Up	7.74	10.29	15.76	20.53	96.55	25.42	3,256	617-563-7000	Y
Fidelity Advisor® Mid Cap Value Fund Class I	FMPOX	B-	B-	B	Down	8.04	10.83	16.96	24.33	107.00	26.39	3,256	617-563-7000	Y
Fidelity Advisor® Mid Cap Value Fund Class M	FMPTX	B-	B-	B	Up	7.88	10.52	16.32	22.24	101.31	26.15	3,256	617-563-7000	Y
Fidelity Advisor® Mid Cap Value Fund Class Z	FIDFX	B-	B-	B	Down	8.08	10.91	17.14	24.51	107.56	26.38	3,256	617-563-7000	Y
Fidelity Advisor® Stock Selector Mid Cap Fund	FSSMX	B-	B	C+	Down	4.98	9.80	20.12	27.57	88.58	39.96	2,551	617-563-7000	Y
Fidelity Advisor® Stock Selector Mid Cap Fund Class A	FMCDX	B-	B	C+	Down	4.92	9.72	19.89	26.73	86.51	38.34	2,551	617-563-7000	Y
Fidelity Advisor® Stock Selector Mid Cap Fund Class C	FMCEX	B-	B-	C+	Up	4.73	9.30	19.02	23.87	79.65	35.06	2,551	617-563-7000	Y
Fidelity Advisor® Stock Selector Mid Cap Fund Class M	FMCAX	B-	B-	C+	Up	4.87	9.58	19.58	25.80	84.36	38.57	2,551	617-563-7000	Y
Fidelity Advisor® Stock Selector Mid Cap Fund Class Z	FSLZX	B-	B	C+	Down	5.01	9.91	20.35	27.71	88.87	40.02	2,551	617-563-7000	Y
Fidelity Advisor® Stock Selector Mid Cap Fund I Class	FMCCX	B-	B	C+	Down	4.97	9.84	20.18	27.53	88.60	40.03	2,551	617-563-7000	Y
Fidelity Advisor® Value Fund Class C	FCVFX	B-	C+	B	Up	4.17	7.03	14.04	19.95	83.95	24.35	112.2	617-563-7000	Y
Fidelity® Extended Mkt Index Fund Inst Premium Cls	FSMAX	B	B	B	Up	4.87	10.11	18.22	31.76	101.30	62.03	21,493	617-563-7000	Y
Fidelity® Extended Market Index Fund Investor Class	FSEMX	B	B	B	Up	4.85	10.08	18.14	31.56	100.84	62.05	21,493	617-563-7000	Y
Fidelity® Extended Market Index Fund Premium Class	FSEVX	B	B	B	Up	4.85	10.09	18.18	31.68	101.14	62.05	21,493	617-563-7000	Y
Fidelity® Growth Strategies Fund	FDEGX	B	B	B+	Up	6.71	10.03	21.49	27.93	105.10	41.12	2,728	617-563-7000	Y
Fidelity® Growth Strategies Fund Class K	FAGKX	B	B	B+	Up	6.73	10.09	21.68	28.50	106.91	41.4	2,728	617-563-7000	Y
Fidelity® Leveraged Company Stock Fund	FLVCX	B-	C+	B-	Up	5.77	11.69	21.02	20.83	77.29	33.46	3,092	617-563-7000	Y
Fidelity® Leveraged Company Stock Fund Class K	FLCKX	B-	C+	B	Up	5.81	11.73	21.14	21.26	78.35	33.53	3,092	617-563-7000	Y
Fidelity® Low-Priced Stock Fund	FLPSX	B-	B-	B	Down	6.63	11.99	20.66	30.03	91.20	54.52	39,445	617-563-7000	Y
Fidelity® Low-Priced Stock Fund Class K	FLPKX	B-	B-	B	Down	6.67	12.04	20.79	30.41	92.16	54.47	39,445	617-563-7000	Y
Fidelity® Mid Cap Enhanced Index Fund	FMEIX	B	B	B	Up	7.59	11.35	18.40	29.78	110.76	15.65	1,270	617-563-7000	Y
Fidelity® Mid Cap Index Fund Institutional Class	FSTPX	B-	B	B-	Down	6.07	9.72	18.45	30.33	103.85	20.98	5,324	617-563-7000	Y
Fidelity® Mid Cap Index Fund Institutional Premium Class	FSMDX	B-	B	B-	Down	6.07	9.72	18.46	30.40	104.04	20.98	5,324	617-563-7000	Y
Fidelity® Mid Cap Index Fund Investor Class	FSCLX	B-	B	B-	Down	6.00	9.65	18.26	29.74	102.22	20.95	5,324	617-563-7000	Y
Fidelity® Mid Cap Index Fund Premium Class	FSCKX	B-	B	B-	Down	6.07	9.77	18.44	30.28	103.68	20.98	5,324	617-563-7000	Y

Category: US Equity Mid Cap (con't)

Fund Name	Ticker Symbol	RATINGS: Overall Rating	Reward Rating	Risk Rating	Recent Up/ Downgrade	TOTAL RETURNS & PERFORMANCE: 3-Month Total Return	6-Month Total Return	1-Year Total Return	3-Year Total Return	5-Year Total Return	ASSETS: NAV	Total Assets (MIL)	NEW INVESTORS: Telephone	Open to New Investors
Fidelity® Mid Cap Value Fund	FSMVX	B-	B-	B	Down	8.06	10.87	17.00	24.35	107.30	26.61	3,256	617-563-7000	Y
Fidelity® Mid-Cap Stock Fund	FMCSX	B-	B	B-	Down	5.02	9.85	18.67	31.21	100.13	38.22	8,227	617-563-7000	Y
Fidelity® Mid-Cap Stock Fund Class K	FKMCX	B-	B	B-	Down	5.06	9.93	18.79	31.64	101.32	38.23	8,227	617-563-7000	Y
Fidelity® Select Construction & Housing Portfolio	FSHOX	A-	A-	B+	Up	10.65	14.54	26.13	41.69	102.63	64.87	355.6	617-563-7000	Y
Fidelity® Series Intrinsic Opportunities Fund	FDMLX	B	B	B	Up	6.87	12.10	24.36	40.70	117.37	18.11	13,638	617-563-7000	Y
First Eagle Fund of America Class A	FEFAX	B-	C+	B	Up	3.44	10.62	21.77	14.28	69.04	35.4	2,240	800-334-2143	Y
First Eagle Fund of America Class C	FEAMX	B-	C+	B-	Up	3.25	10.20	20.82	11.72	62.77	28.1	2,240	800-334-2143	Y
First Eagle Fund of America Class I	FEAIX	B-	C+	B	Up	3.51	10.78	22.14	15.33	71.34	36.39	2,240	800-334-2143	Y
First Eagle Fund of America Class R6	FEFRX	B-	C+	B	Up	3.51	10.75	22.03	14.51	69.40	36.38	2,240	800-334-2143	Y
First Eagle Fund of America Class Y	FEAFX	B-	C+	B	Up	3.44	10.60	21.77	14.26	69.03	36.31	2,240	800-334-2143	
First Investors Opportunity Fund Advisor Class	FIVUX	B	B-	B	Up	5.49	9.61	19.00	26.50	98.39	42.38	1,147	800-423-4026	Y
First Investors Opportunity Fund Class A	FIUSX	B-	B-	B	Up	5.42	9.48	18.66	25.41	95.90	41.64	1,147	800-423-4026	Y
First Investors Opportunity Fund Class B	FIMBX	B-	C+	B	Up	5.21	9.04	17.76	22.55	88.51	32.03	1,147	800-423-4026	Y
First Investors Opportunity Fund Institutional Class	FIVVX	B	B-	B	Up	5.54	9.70	19.14	27.02	99.74	42.31	1,147	800-423-4026	Y
FMI Common Stock Fund	FMIMX	B	B-	B	Up	3.15	7.51	13.77	26.37	81.33	26.58	1,099	800-811-5311	
FMI Common Stock Fund Institutional Class	FMIUX	B-	B	C+	Down	3.18	7.58	13.87	26.51	81.53	26.6	1,099	800-811-5311	Y
Franklin Small-Mid Cap Growth Fund Advisor Class	FSGAX	B	B-	B	Up	5.20	9.67	21.81	24.58	90.90	38.47	3,617	650-312-2000	Y
Franklin Small-Mid Cap Growth Fund Class A	FRSGX	B	B-	B	Up	5.13	9.51	21.52	23.66	88.48	35.31	3,617	650-312-2000	Y
Franklin Small-Mid Cap Growth Fund Class C	FRSIX	B-	C+	B	Up	4.93	9.06	20.56	20.83	81.47	25.36	3,617	650-312-2000	Y
Franklin Small-Mid Cap Growth Fund Class R	FSMRX	B-	B-	B	Up	5.07	9.39	21.24	22.72	86.15	32.48	3,617	650-312-2000	Y
Franklin Small-Mid Cap Growth Fund Class R6	FMGGX	B	B	B	Up	5.34	9.88	22.21	25.56	92.80	39.02	3,617	650-312-2000	Y
Frost Mid Cap Equity Fund Class Institutional	FIKSX	B-	B-	C+	Up	8.32	14.03	22.74	30.35	83.70	9.76	13.3		Y
Frost Mid Cap Equity Fund Investor Class Shares	FAKSX	B-	B-	C+	Up	8.31	14.10	22.80	29.78	82.19	9.62	13.3		Y
Gabelli Global Deal Fund	GDL	B	C	A+	Up	0.60	1.03	2.49	11.96	20.60	11.59	212.6	914-921-5135	Y
Glenmede Total Market Portfolio	GTTMX	B+	B+	B	Up	8.82	13.94	22.85	36.40	120.77	19.32	79.9	800-442-8299	Y
Goldman Sachs Growth Opportunities Fund Class A	GGOAX	B-	B-	B	Up	5.68	10.58	26.80	20.05	80.20	21.09	2,590	800-526-7384	Y
Goldman Sachs Growth Opportunities Fund Class C	GGOCX	B-	C+	B-	Up	5.50	10.15	25.84	17.38	73.62	14.58	2,590	800-526-7384	Y
Goldman Sachs Growth Opportunities Fund Class R	GGORX	B-	B-	B	Up	5.55	10.38	26.41	19.11	77.93	20.14	2,590	800-526-7384	Y
Goldman Sachs Growth Opportunities Fund Class R6	GGOUX	B-	B-	B	Up	5.72	10.74	27.23	21.40	83.71	24.97	2,590	800-526-7384	Y
Goldman Sachs Growth Opportunities Fund Institutional Cls	GGOIX	B-	B-	B	Up	5.77	10.75	27.20	21.37	83.67	24.96	2,590	800-526-7384	Y
Goldman Sachs Growth Opportunities Fund Investor Class	GGOTX	B-	B-	B	Up	5.70	10.73	27.06	20.96	82.46	22.11	2,590	800-526-7384	Y
Goldman Sachs Growth Opportunities Fund Service Class	GGOSX	B-	B-	B	Up	5.60	10.51	26.61	19.58	79.08	20.09	2,590	800-526-7384	Y
Goldman Sachs Small/Mid Cap Growth Fund Class A	GSMAX	B	B	B	Up	5.10	10.94	27.73	25.13	92.43	20.86	2,352	800-526-7384	Y
Goldman Sachs Small/Mid Cap Growth Fund Class C	GSMGX	B	B-	B	Up	4.93	10.57	26.82	22.37	85.31	18.04	2,352	800-526-7384	Y
Goldman Sachs Small/Mid Cap Growth Fund Class R	GTMRX	B	B	B	Up	5.03	10.83	27.48	24.24	90.01	20.15	2,352	800-526-7384	Y
Goldman Sachs Small/Mid Cap Growth Fund Class R6	GTMUX	B	B	B	Up	5.20	11.18	28.25	26.67	96.32	22.29	2,352	800-526-7384	Y
Goldman Sachs Small/Mid Cap Growth Fund Institutional Cls	GSMYX	B	B	B	Up	5.20	11.19	28.27	26.63	96.24	22.28	2,352	800-526-7384	Y
Goldman Sachs Small/Mid Cap Growth Fund Investor Class	GTMTX	B	B	B	Up	5.12	11.07	28.05	26.06	94.81	21.61	2,352	800-526-7384	Y
Goldman Sachs Small/Mid Cap Growth Fund Service Class	GSMQX	B	B	B	Up	5.09	10.90	27.62	24.72	91.43	20.34	2,352	800-526-7384	Y
Goldman Sachs Small/Mid Cap Value Fund Class A	GMVAX	B-	B-	B	Up	6.70	11.18	14.90	26.51		13.19	123.3	800-526-7384	Y
Goldman Sachs Small/Mid Cap Value Fund Class C	GMVCX	B-	B-	B	Up	6.58	10.79	14.07	23.93		12.99	123.3	800-526-7384	Y
Goldman Sachs Small/Mid Cap Value Fund Class R	GMVRX	B-	B-	B	Up	6.68	11.08	14.61	25.70		13.19	123.3	800-526-7384	Y
Goldman Sachs Small/Mid Cap Value Fund Class R6	GMCUX	B	B-	B	Up	6.89	11.43	15.40	28.45		13.32	123.3	800-526-7384	Y
Goldman Sachs Small/Mid Cap Value Fund Institutional Class	GSMVX	B	B-	B	Up	6.80	11.42	15.30	28.32		13.31	123.3	800-526-7384	Y
Goldman Sachs Small/Mid Cap Value Fund Investor Class	GMVIX	B	B-	B	Up	6.82	11.37	15.26	27.60		13.26	123.3	800-526-7384	Y
Government Street Mid-Cap Fund	GVMCX	B	B	B		4.54	8.66	19.53	36.20	97.17	26.34	50.6		Y
Great-West Ariel Mid Cap Value Fund Class L	MXAMX	B-	C+	B		6.77	7.29	14.76	20.11	96.31		170.8		Y
Great-West Ariel Mid Cap Value Fund Institutional Class	MXOAX	B-	B-	B		6.95	7.53	15.43	22.57	100.69		170.8		Y
Great-West Ariel Mid Cap Value Fund Investor Class	MXMCX	B-	B-	B		6.35	6.95	15.00	20.59	97.45		170.8		Y
Great-West Goldman Sachs Mid Cap Value Fund Inst Cls	MXKJX	B	B	B		7.89	12.03	17.80	35.25	116.60		628.1		Y
Great-West Goldman Sachs Mid Cap Value Fund Investor Class	MXMVX	B	B	B		7.74	11.71	17.33	33.79	114.25		628.1		Y
Great-West S&P Mid Cap 400® Index Fund Class L	MXBUX	B	B	B	Up	6.67	10.13	15.55	32.64	97.40		853.7		Y

Category: US Equity Mid Cap (con't)

Fund Name	Ticker Symbol	RATINGS: Overall Rating	Reward Rating	Risk Rating	Recent Up/ Downgrade	TOTAL RETURNS & PERFORMANCE: 3-Month Total Return	6-Month Total Return	1-Year Total Return	3-Year Total Return	5-Year Total Return	ASSETS: NAV	Total Assets (MIL)	NEW INVESTORS: Telephone	Open to New Investors
Great-West S&P Mid Cap 400® Index Fund Institutional Class	MXNZX	B	B	B		6.81	10.43	16.25	34.98	101.89		853.7		Y
Great-West S&P Mid Cap 400® Index Fund Investor Class	MXMDX	B	B	B		6.70	10.17	15.81	33.60	99.82		853.7		Y
Great-West T. Rowe Price Mid Cap Growth Fund Class L	MXTMX	B	B	B	Down	4.74	9.41	24.33	38.53	118.22		1,401		Y
Great-West T. Rowe Price Mid Cap Growth Fund Inst Cls	MXYKX	B	B	B	Down	4.98	9.85	25.10	40.99	123.41		1,401		Y
Great-West T. Rowe Price Mid Cap Growth Fund Investor Cls	MXMGX	B	B	B	Down	4.86	9.63	24.70	39.70	121.37		1,401		Y
Guggenheim RBP® Dividend Fund Class A	TVEAX	B	B-	B		7.11	11.60	18.81	29.01	84.92	12.07	18.9	212-739-0700	Y
Guggenheim RBP® Dividend Fund Class C	TVECX	B	B-	B	Up	6.91	11.18	17.88	26.38	78.98	12.06	18.9	212-739-0700	Y
Guggenheim RBP® Dividend Fund Class I	TVEIX	B	B	B		7.21	11.72	19.10	30.30	88.23	11.8	18.9	212-739-0700	Y
Guggenheim RBP® Dividend Fund Class P	TVEFX	B	B-	B		7.16	11.59	18.83	29.34	85.90	12.2	18.9	212-739-0700	Y
Guggenheim RBP® Large-Cap Value Fund Class A	TVVAX	B-	B-	B-	Down	5.68	10.13	16.81	26.22	91.93	10.6	4.1	212-739-0700	Y
Guggenheim RBP® Large-Cap Value Fund Class C	TVVCX	B-	B-	B	Down	5.45	9.65	15.90	23.20	85.19	10.58	4.1	212-739-0700	Y
Guggenheim RBP® Large-Cap Value Fund Class I	TVVIX	B-	B-	B-	Down	5.78	10.30	17.16	27.34	95.31	10.75	4.1	212-739-0700	Y
Guggenheim RBP® Large-Cap Value Fund Class P	TVVFX	B-	B-	B-	Down	5.65	10.11	16.79	26.36	92.51	10.67	4.1	212-739-0700	Y
Guggenheim StylePlus - Mid Growth Fund Class A	SECUX	B	B	B-	Up	6.44	11.67	24.14	32.25	97.66	44.64	88.4	212-739-0700	Y
Guggenheim StylePlus - Mid Growth Fund Class C	SUFCX	B-	B	C+	Down	6.24	11.23	23.10	28.94	89.08	32.35	88.4	212-739-0700	Y
Guggenheim StylePlus - Mid Growth Fund Class P	SEUPX	B	B	B-	Up	6.41	11.61	24.02	31.66	96.78	44.2	88.4	212-739-0700	Y
Guggenheim StylePlus - Mid Growth Fund Institutional	GIUIX	B	B	B-	Up	6.55	11.88	24.51	32.75	98.50	44.68	88.4	212-739-0700	Y
Harbor Mid Cap Growth Fund Administrative Class	HRMGX	B+	B+	B	Up	5.91	10.34	31.89	32.88	95.72	9.87	420.8	800-422-1050	Y
Harbor Mid Cap Growth Fund Institutional Class	HAMGX	B+	A-	B	Up	5.96	10.43	32.23	33.84	98.23	10.31	420.8	800-422-1050	Y
Harbor Mid Cap Growth Fund Investor Class	HIMGX	B	B+	B	Up	5.85	10.28	31.67	32.38	94.62	9.59	420.8	800-422-1050	Y
Harbor Mid Cap Growth Fund Retirement Class	HNMGX	B+	A-	B	Up	6.04	10.51	32.31	34.07	98.57	10.33	420.8	800-422-1050	Y
Harbor Mid Cap Value Fund Administrative Class	HRMVX	B-	B-	B	Up	5.58	8.66	11.67	23.27	108.21	23.74	1,015	800-422-1050	Y
Harbor Mid Cap Value Fund Institutional Class	HAMVX	B	B-	B	Up	5.66	8.81	11.95	24.23	110.84	23.54	1,015	800-422-1050	Y
Harbor Mid Cap Value Fund Investor Class	HIMVX	B-	B-	B	Up	5.54	8.60	11.54	22.87	107.00	23.53	1,015	800-422-1050	Y
Harbor Mid Cap Value Fund Retirement Class	HNMVX	B	B-	B	Up	5.64	8.84	12.03	24.32	110.99	23.53	1,015	800-422-1050	Y
Hartford MidCap HLS Fund Class IA	HIMCX	B	B+	B	Up	7.42	11.07	24.46	40.50	123.83	40.1	2,185	888-843-7824	Y
Hartford MidCap HLS Fund Class IB	HBMCX	B	B+	B-	Up	7.37	10.92	24.16	39.47	121.01	39.18	2,185	888-843-7824	Y
Hartford MidCap Value Fund Class A	HMVAX	B	B-	B	Up	4.58	9.19	13.03	23.79	82.99	15.71	694.1	888-843-7824	Y
Hartford MidCap Value Fund Class C	HMVCX	B-	C+	B	Up	4.41	8.81	12.18	21.12	76.42	13.02	694.1	888-843-7824	Y
Hartford MidCap Value Fund Class F	HMVFX	B	B-	B	Up	4.71	9.43	13.49	25.47	87.15	15.82	694.1	888-843-7824	Y
Hartford MidCap Value Fund Class I	HMVJX	B	B-	B	Up	4.62	9.27	13.16	24.60	85.61	15.82	694.1	888-843-7824	Y
Hartford MidCap Value Fund Class R3	HMVRX	B-	B-	B	Up	4.49	9.08	12.64	22.70	80.57	16.5	694.1	888-843-7824	Y
Hartford MidCap Value Fund Class R4	HMVSX	B	B-	B	Up	4.60	9.25	13.06	23.88	83.37	16.8	694.1	888-843-7824	Y
Hartford MidCap Value Fund Class R5	HMVTX	B	B-	B	Up	4.70	9.37	13.35	24.98	86.14	16.99	694.1	888-843-7824	Y
Hartford MidCap Value Fund Class Y	HMVYX	B	B-	B	Up	4.65	9.37	13.35	25.31	86.91	17.02	694.1	888-843-7824	Y
Hartford MidCap Value HLS Fund Class IA	HMVIX	B	B-	B	Up	4.73	9.54	13.46	25.43	87.65	12.6	377.7	888-843-7824	Y
Hartford MidCap Value HLS Fund Class IB	HBMVX	B	B-	B	Up	4.69	9.32	13.18	24.43	85.29	12.5	377.7	888-843-7824	Y
Hartford Schroders US Small/Mid Cap Opp Fund Cls F	HFDFX	B	B	B+		5.13	7.69	15.56	37.92	113.40	14.8	882.8	888-843-7824	Y
Hartford Schroders US Small/Mid-Cap Opp Fund Cls A	SMDVX	B	B	B+		5.05	7.55	15.27	36.87	110.58	14.25	882.8	888-843-7824	Y
Hartford Schroders US Small/Mid-Cap Opp Fund Cls C	HFDCX	B	B-	B+		4.91	7.11	14.37	33.80	102.94	14.64	882.8	888-843-7824	Y
Hartford Schroders US Small/Mid-Cap Opp Fund Cls I	SMDIX	B	B	B+		5.21	7.69	15.56	37.92	113.40	14.81	882.8	888-843-7824	Y
Hartford Schroders US Small/Mid-Cap Opp Fund Cls R3	HFDRX	B	B	B+		4.96	7.37	14.81	35.70	107.88	14.72	882.8	888-843-7824	Y
Hartford Schroders US Small/Mid-Cap Opp Fund Cls R4	HFDSX	B	B	B+		5.05	7.54	15.24	36.73	110.50	14.77	882.8	888-843-7824	Y
Hartford Schroders US Small/Mid-Cap Opp Fund Cls R5	HFDTX	B	B	B+		5.08	7.64	15.42	37.75	113.14	14.79	882.8	888-843-7824	Y
Hartford Schroders US Small/Mid-Cap Opp Fund Cls SDR	SMDRX	B	B	A-		5.13	7.68	15.62	38.32	113.84	14.83	882.8	888-843-7824	Y
Hartford Schroders US Small/Mid-Cap Opp Fund Cls Y	HFDYX	B	B	B+		5.12	7.68	15.54	37.91	113.39	14.8	882.8	888-843-7824	Y
Heartland Select Value Fund Institutional Class	HNSVX	B	B	B	Up	5.85	10.27	12.69	28.40	86.42	28	237.9	800-432-7856	Y
Heartland Select Value Fund Investor Class	HRSVX	B	B	B	Up	5.79	10.13	12.41	27.46	83.88	28.09	237.9	800-432-7856	Y
Hennessy Cornerstone Growth Fund Class Institutional	HICGX	B+	B+	B+	Up	3.75	17.20	16.98	25.11	100.02	24.86	224.6	800-966-4354	Y
Hennessy Cornerstone Growth Fund Investor Class	HFCGX	B	B	B+	Up	3.64	16.99	16.60	24.02	97.26	24.16	224.6	800-966-4354	Y
Hennessy Cornerstone Mid Cap 30 Fund Institutional Class	HIMDX	B	B	B+	Up	7.78	13.99	20.96	27.48	100.38	20.26	982.0	800-966-4354	Y
Hennessy Cornerstone Mid Cap 30 Fund Investor Class	HFMDX	B	B	B+	Up	7.69	13.79	20.50	26.20	97.37	19.73	982.0	800-966-4354	Y

Category: US Equity Mid Cap (con't)

Fund Name	Ticker Symbol	RATINGS: Overall Rating	Reward Rating	Risk Rating	Recent Up/ Downgrade	TOTAL RETURNS & PERFORMANCE: 3-Month Total Return	6-Month Total Return	1-Year Total Return	3-Year Total Return	5-Year Total Return	ASSETS: NAV	Total Assets (MIL)	NEW INVESTORS: Telephone	Open to New Investors
Hennessy Focus Fund Institutional Class	HFCIX	B	B	B		5.80	10.87	19.71	32.02	102.79	90.69	2,778	800-966-4354	Y
Hennessy Focus Fund Investor Class	HFCSX	B	B	B		5.71	10.67	19.26	30.58	99.33	88.37	2,778	800-966-4354	Y
Hodges Fund Institutional Class	HDPIX	B	B+	C+	Up	11.85	17.90	14.11	41.44	146.14	50.48	271.7		Y
Hodges Fund Retail Class	HDPMX	B	B+	C+	Up	11.80	17.77	13.83	40.08	142.23	49.56	271.7		Y
Hodges Small-Mid Cap Fund Retail Class	HDSMX	B-	B	C+	Up	9.51	14.43	9.16	31.99		13.3	16.5		Y
HSBC Opportunity Fund Class I	RESCX	B-	B	C	Up	9.41	14.06	30.14	27.04	91.10	14.27	143.6	888-936-4722	Y
ICON Fund Class A	ICNAX	B-	B	C	Up	6.13	11.45	28.12	22.41	75.89	18.68	52.6	303-790-1600	Y
ICON Fund Class C	ICNCX	B-	B	C+	Up	5.99	11.02	27.16	19.69	69.47	17.32	52.6	303-790-1600	Y
ICON Fund Class S	ICNZX	B-	B	C	Up	6.26	11.64	28.64	23.83	79.15	19.85	52.6	303-790-1600	Y
ICON Long/Short Fund Class A	ISTAX	B	A-	C		5.05	11.32	26.40	28.24	84.28	25.56	24.3	303-790-1600	Y
ICON Long/Short Fund Class C	IOLCX	B	B+	B-	Up	4.88	10.89	25.45	25.39	77.44	23.21	24.3	303-790-1600	Y
ICON Long/Short Fund Class S	IOLZX	B	A-	C		5.13	11.47	26.77	29.38	87.11	26.42	24.3	303-790-1600	Y
IMS Capital Value Fund	IMSCX	B-	C+	B	Up	4.09	5.22	11.87	17.04	65.07	24.79	38.3	877-244-6235	Y
Intrepid Disciplined Value Fund Investor Class	ICMCX	B-	C+	B	Down	1.82	2.29	6.72	14.57	48.88	10.71	45.8		Y
Invesco Endeavor Fund Class A	ATDAX	B-	B-	C+	Up	7.25	9.24	17.42	26.11	76.10	20.1	249.8	800-659-1005	Y
Invesco Endeavor Fund Class R	ATDRX	B-	B-	C+	Up	7.17	9.11	17.15	25.17	73.89	19.29	249.8	800-659-1005	Y
Invesco Endeavor Fund Class R6	ATDFX	B-	B	C+	Up	7.34	9.48	17.96	27.91	80.16	21.47	249.8	800-659-1005	Y
Invesco Endeavor Fund Class Y	ATDYX	B-	B-	C+	Up	7.30	9.34	17.73	27.05	78.21	20.72	249.8	800-659-1005	Y
Invesco Endeavor Fund R5 Class	ATDIX	B-	B	C+	Up	7.33	9.42	17.87	27.61	79.41	21.36	249.8	800-659-1005	Y
Invesco Mid Cap Core Equity Fund Class A	GTAGX	B-	C+	B	Up	3.91	7.11	15.04	22.43	69.03	21.53	1,218	800-659-1005	Y
Invesco Mid Cap Core Equity Fund Class B	GTABX	B-	C+	B	Up	3.75	6.73	14.20	19.74	62.86	12.83	1,218	800-659-1005	
Invesco Mid Cap Core Equity Fund Class C	GTACX	B-	C+	B	Up	3.76	6.75	14.18	19.75	62.92	12.77	1,218	800-659-1005	Y
Invesco Mid Cap Core Equity Fund Class R	GTARX	B-	C+	B	Up	3.88	7.01	14.74	21.50	66.95	20.63	1,218	800-659-1005	Y
Invesco Mid Cap Core Equity Fund Class R6	GTAFX	B-	C+	B	Down	4.03	7.35	15.52	24.13	72.90	23.69	1,218	800-659-1005	Y
Invesco Mid Cap Core Equity Fund Class Y	GTAYX	B-	C+	B		4.02	7.25	15.32	23.35	71.22	21.96	1,218	800-659-1005	Y
Invesco Mid Cap Core Equity Fund R5 Class	GTAVX	B-	C+	B		4.07	7.36	15.48	23.87	72.22	23.68	1,218	800-659-1005	Y
Invesco Mid Cap Growth Fund Class A	VGRAX	B	B-	B	Up	4.12	7.35	22.21	23.60	87.45	37.76	2,848	800-659-1005	Y
Invesco Mid Cap Growth Fund Class B	VGRBX	B	B-	B	Up	4.10	7.36	22.21	23.61	87.49	31.04	2,848	800-659-1005	
Invesco Mid Cap Growth Fund Class C	VGRCX	B-	B-	B	Up	3.92	6.98	21.32	20.95	80.79	28.28	2,848	800-659-1005	Y
Invesco Mid Cap Growth Fund Class R	VGRRX	B-	B-	B	Up	4.05	7.23	21.90	22.68	85.14	36.62	2,848	800-659-1005	Y
Invesco Mid Cap Growth Fund Class R5	VGRJX	B	B-	B	Up	4.18	7.53	22.62	24.98	90.91	39.85	2,848	800-659-1005	Y
Invesco Mid Cap Growth Fund Class R6	VGRFX	B	B-	B	Up	4.22	7.58	22.75	25.31	91.18	40.03	2,848	800-659-1005	Y
Invesco Mid Cap Growth Fund Class Y	VGRDX	B	B-	B	Up	4.15	7.47	22.50	24.53	89.81	39.44	2,848	800-659-1005	Y
IronBridge SMID Cap Fund	IBSMX	B	B-	B+	Up	3.98	7.84	13.66	25.45	75.25	11.36	266.4		Y
Ivy Mid Cap Growth Fund Class A	WMGAX	B-	B	C	Up	7.16	12.56	26.99	25.91	79.72	22.92	2,406	800-777-6472	Y
Ivy Mid Cap Growth Fund Class E	IMCEX	B-	B-	C	Up	7.14	12.57	26.99	25.69	78.30	22.36	2,406	800-777-6472	Y
Ivy Mid Cap Growth Fund Class I	IYMIX	B-	B	C	Up	7.22	12.73	27.30	26.97	82.40	24.66	2,406	800-777-6472	Y
Ivy Mid Cap Growth Fund Class N	IGRFX	B-	B	C	Up	7.21	12.78	27.50	27.57	82.49	24.83	2,406	800-777-6472	Y
Ivy Mid Cap Growth Fund Class Y	WMGYX	B-	B	C	Up	7.16	12.59	27.01	26.13	80.26	23.94	2,406	800-777-6472	Y
Jackson Square SMID-Cap Growth Fund Institutional Class	JSMTX	B+	A-	B	Up	5.37	11.99	20.34	38.56	103.69	21.65	386.8		Y
Jackson Square SMID-Cap Growth Fund Investor Class	JSMVX	B+	A-	B	Up	5.24	11.80	19.97	37.47	101.09	21.57	386.8		Y
Jackson Square SMID-Cap Growth Fund IS Class	DCGTX	B+	A-	B	Up	5.37	12.04	20.40	38.71	103.92	21.66	386.8		Y
James Mid Cap Fund	JAMDX	B	C+	A-	Up	4.25	10.57	14.66	20.64	73.55	11.38	16.2	800-995-2637	Y
Janus Henderson Enterprise Fund Class A	JDMAX	B	B+	B-	Down	5.40	10.74	26.07	44.03	114.80	115.08	16,122	877-335-2687	Y
Janus Henderson Enterprise Fund Class C	JGRCX	B	B+	B-	Down	5.25	10.44	25.34	41.34	107.84	107.66	16,122	877-335-2687	Y
Janus Henderson Enterprise Fund Class D	JANEX	B	B+	B	Down	5.47	10.92	26.46	45.32	117.91	117.68	16,122	877-335-2687	
Janus Henderson Enterprise Fund Class I	JMGRX	B	B+	B	Down	5.50	10.95	26.53	45.64	118.67	118.24	16,122	877-335-2687	Y
Janus Henderson Enterprise Fund Class N	JDMNX	B	B+	B	Down	5.52	11.00	26.64	46.03	119.73	118.59	16,122	877-335-2687	Y
Janus Henderson Enterprise Fund Class R	JDMRX	B	B+	B-	Down	5.32	10.58	25.71	42.79	111.67	111.88	16,122	877-335-2687	Y
Janus Henderson Enterprise Fund Class S	JGRTX	B	B+	B-	Down	5.38	10.72	26.02	43.86	114.38	114.58	16,122	877-335-2687	Y
Janus Henderson Enterprise Fund Class T	JAENX	B	B+	B	Down	5.45	10.87	26.34	44.96	117.07	116.99	16,122	877-335-2687	Y
Janus Henderson Mid Cap Value Fund Class A	JDPAX	B	B-	B		5.12	8.04	13.66	28.04	79.42	17.11	4,087	877-335-2687	Y

Category: US Equity Mid Cap (con't)

Fund Name	Ticker Symbol	RATINGS: Overall Rating	Reward Rating	Risk Rating	Recent Up/ Downgrade	TOTAL RETURNS & PERFORMANCE: 3-Month Total Return	6-Month Total Return	1-Year Total Return	3-Year Total Return	5-Year Total Return	ASSETS: NAV	Total Assets (MIL)	NEW INVESTORS: Telephone	Open to New Investors
Janus Henderson Mid Cap Value Fund Class C	JMVCX	B	B-	B		4.95	7.69	12.99	26.00	74.04	16.69	4,087	877-335-2687	Y
Janus Henderson Mid Cap Value Fund Class D	JNMCX	B	B-	B		5.19	8.22	14.06	29.17	82.02	16.82	4,087	877-335-2687	
Janus Henderson Mid Cap Value Fund Class I	JMVAX	B	B-	B		5.19	8.16	13.99	29.15	82.16	16.84	4,087	877-335-2687	Y
Janus Henderson Mid Cap Value Fund Class L	JMIVX	B	B-	B		5.20	8.22	14.11	29.72	82.65	17.3	4,087	877-335-2687	
Janus Henderson Mid Cap Value Fund Class N	JDPNX	B	B-	B		5.23	8.27	14.20	29.76	83.39	16.77	4,087	877-335-2687	Y
Janus Henderson Mid Cap Value Fund Class R	JDPRX	B	B-	B		5.03	7.87	13.34	26.85	76.65	16.85	4,087	877-335-2687	Y
Janus Henderson Mid Cap Value Fund Class S	JMVIX	B	B-	B		5.09	8.02	13.65	27.83	78.87	17.05	4,087	877-335-2687	Y
Janus Henderson Mid Cap Value Fund Class T	JMCVX	B	B-	B		5.12	8.13	13.87	28.80	81.25	16.91	4,087	877-335-2687	Y
Janus Henderson Select Value Fund Class A	JVSAX	B	B	B+		4.73	7.64	13.78	34.68	79.88	14.02	128.9	877-335-2687	Y
Janus Henderson Select Value Fund Class C	JVSCX	B	B-	B+		4.55	7.27	12.90	31.37	72.98	13.67	128.9	877-335-2687	Y
Janus Henderson Select Value Fund Class D	JSVDX	B	B	B+		4.84	7.81	14.02	35.52	82.14	14.06	128.9	877-335-2687	Y
Janus Henderson Select Value Fund Class I	JVSIX	B	B	B+		4.80	7.84	14.05	35.67	82.94	14.08	128.9	877-335-2687	Y
Janus Henderson Select Value Fund Class N	JVSNX	B	B	B+		4.82	7.86	14.07	35.69	82.98	14.06	128.9	877-335-2687	Y
Janus Henderson Select Value Fund Class S	JSVSX	B	B	B+		4.72	7.62	13.77	34.66	79.58	14.01	128.9	877-335-2687	Y
Janus Henderson Select Value Fund Class T	JSVTX	B	B	B+		4.83	7.73	13.94	35.24	81.38	14.04	128.9	877-335-2687	Y
Janus Henderson VIT Enterprise Portfolio Institutional Cls	JAAGX	B+	A-	B	Up	5.71	11.45	27.41	47.79	125.63	70.65	1,155	877-335-2687	Y
Janus Henderson VIT Enterprise Portfolio Service Class	US4710217179	B	A-	B	Down	5.64	11.32	27.08	46.67	122.80	66.67	1,155	877-335-2687	Y
Janus Henderson VIT Mid Cap Value Portfolio Inst Cls	JAMVX	B	B-	B		5.23	8.19	13.93	29.67	82.08	18.02	121.3	877-335-2687	Y
Janus Henderson VIT Mid Cap Value Portfolio Service Class	US4710214515	B	B-	B		5.15	8.07	13.63	28.71	79.85	17.49	121.3	877-335-2687	Y
Jensen Quality Value Fund Class I	JNVIX	B-	C+	B-		7.64	8.80	15.27	20.34	94.88	12.71	36.3	800-992-4144	Y
Jensen Quality Value Fund Class J	JNVSX	B-	C+	B-		7.53	8.71	15.07	19.85	93.44	12.78	36.3	800-992-4144	Y
JNL/JPMorgan MidCap Growth Fund Class A	US46648M1282	B	B+	C+	Up	5.69	11.99	29.40	33.35	115.24	34.51	2,102		Y
JNL/JPMorgan MidCap Growth Fund Class I	US46648M1100	B	B+	C+	Up	5.80	12.17	29.73	34.24	117.45	35.34	2,102		Y
JNL/Mellon Capital S&P 400 MidCap Index Fund Class A	US46648M6315	B	B	B		6.17	9.41	15.66	33.80	99.60	21.66	3,143		Y
JNL/Mellon Capital S&P 400 MidCap Index Fund Class I	US46648M6232	B	B	B		6.21	9.56	15.88	34.20	100.91	22.06	3,143		Y
JNL/MFS Mid Cap Value Fund Class A	US46644W7323	B-	C+	B-	Up	4.56	7.10	13.02	15.88	78.41	12.13	940.6		Y
JNL/MFS Mid Cap Value Fund Class I	US46644W7240	B-	C+	B-	Up	4.72	7.24	13.32	16.66	80.31	12.2	940.6		Y
JNL/PPM America Mid Cap Value Fund Class A	US46648M3007	B	B	B-	Up	5.20	10.47	12.36	29.95	109.63	15.76	695.7		Y
JNL/PPM America Mid Cap Value Fund Class I	US46648M4096	B	B+	B-	Up	5.30	10.63	12.66	30.79	111.77	15.88	695.7		Y
JNL/T. Rowe Price Mid-Cap Growth Fund Class A	US46648L7082	B	B	B	Down	4.34	8.79	24.46	39.52	120.27	47.27	5,304		Y
JNL/T. Rowe Price Mid-Cap Growth Fund Class I	US46648L8072	B	B	B	Down	4.42	8.93	24.75	40.40	122.48	49.29	5,304		Y
John Hancock Funds Disciplined Value Mid Cap Fund Class A	JVMAX	B	B	B+	Up	5.00	8.58	15.28	33.52	115.96	22.45	14,869	800-225-5913	
John Hancock Funds Disciplined Value Mid Cap Fund Cls ADV	JVMVX	B	B	B+	Up	5.01	8.60	15.31	33.46	115.35	22.4	14,869	800-225-5913	
John Hancock Funds Disciplined Value Mid Cap Fund Class C	JVMCX	B	B	B+	Up	4.79	8.19	14.45	30.54	107.87	22.56	14,869	800-225-5913	
John Hancock Funds Disciplined Value Mid Cap Fund Class I	JVMIX	B	B	A-		5.11	8.75	15.64	34.59	118.88	23.31	14,869	800-225-5913	
John Hancock Funds Disciplined Value Mid Cap Fund Class R2	JVMSX	B	B	B+	Up	5.00	8.51	15.14	32.99	114.55	23.25	14,869	800-225-5913	
John Hancock Funds Disciplined Value Mid Cap Fund Class R4	JVMTX	B	B	B+		5.05	8.69	15.42	33.96	116.99	23.3	14,869	800-225-5913	
John Hancock Funds Disciplined Value Mid Cap Fund Class R6	JVMRX	B	B	A-		5.06	8.75	15.69	34.97	119.78	23.29	14,869	800-225-5913	
John Hancock Funds II Mid Cap Stock Fund Class 1	JIMSX	B	B	B	Up	5.16	9.07	28.37	32.57	98.23	21.37	1,635	800-225-5913	Y
John Hancock Funds II Mid Cap Stock Fund Class NAV	JHMSX	B	B	B	Up	5.16	9.08	28.40	32.72	98.79	21.57	1,635	800-225-5913	Y
John Hancock II Mid Value Fund Class NAV	JMVNX	B	B-	B	Up	5.11	7.94	11.21	32.14	96.22	16.29	1,419	800-225-5913	Y
Johnson Opportunity Fund	JOPPX	B	B	B+	Up	6.33	10.94	16.90	33.35	104.50	42.89	58.4		Y
JPMorgan Intrepid Mid Cap Fund Class A	PECAX	B-	B-	B	Up	6.07	10.15	16.70	21.39	101.41	22.55	964.4	800-480-4111	Y
JPMorgan Intrepid Mid Cap Fund Class C	ODMCX	B-	C+	B	Up	5.90	9.88	16.02	19.21	95.19	19.09	964.4	800-480-4111	Y
JPMorgan Intrepid Mid Cap Fund Class I	WOOPX	B-	B-	B	Up	6.14	10.30	16.95	22.32	103.90	23.76	964.4	800-480-4111	Y
JPMorgan Intrepid Mid Cap Fund Class R3	WOOOX	B-	B-	B	Up	6.10	10.18	16.69	21.38	101.32	22.49	964.4	800-480-4111	Y
JPMorgan Intrepid Mid Cap Fund Class R4	WOOQX	B-	B-	B	Up	6.13	10.29	16.94	22.26	103.80	23.7	964.4	800-480-4111	Y
JPMorgan Intrepid Mid Cap Fund Class R6	WOOSX	B-	B-	B	Up	6.22	10.42	17.28	22.93	104.91	23.76	964.4	800-480-4111	Y
JPMorgan Market Expansion Enhanced Index Fund Class A	OMEAX	B+	B+	B	Up	5.19	9.94	14.30	35.61	107.35	11.33	1,072	800-480-4111	Y
JPMorgan Market Expansion Enhanced Index Fund Class C	OMECX	B	B+	B	Up	5.06	9.64	13.68	33.16	100.68	9.5	1,072	800-480-4111	Y
JPMorgan Market Expansion Enhanced Index Fund Class I	PGMIX	B+	B+	B	Up	5.21	9.99	14.55	36.68	109.90	11.47	1,072	800-480-4111	Y
JPMorgan Market Expansion Enhanced Index Fund Class R2	JMEZX	B+	B+	B	Up	5.13	9.85	14.04	34.78	105.02	11.16	1,072	800-480-4111	Y

Category: US Equity Mid Cap (con't)

Fund Name	Ticker Symbol	RATINGS: Overall Rating	Reward Rating	Risk Rating	Recent Up/ Downgrade	TOTAL RETURNS & PERFORMANCE: 3-Month Total Return	6-Month Total Return	1-Year Total Return	3-Year Total Return	5-Year Total Return	ASSETS: NAV	Total Assets (MIL)	NEW INVESTORS: Telephone	Open to New Investors
JPMorgan Mid Cap Equity Fund Class A	JCMAX	B-	B	B-	Down	5.11	9.31	20.96	28.23	101.34	50.16	3,047	800-480-4111	
JPMorgan Mid Cap Equity Fund Class C	JMCCX	B-	B-	C+	Down	4.97	9.03	20.33	26.31	96.18	48.42	3,047	800-480-4111	
JPMorgan Mid Cap Equity Fund Class I	VSNGX	B-	B	B-	Down	5.18	9.49	21.35	29.56	104.50	50.83	3,047	800-480-4111	
JPMorgan Mid Cap Equity Fund Class R2	JMCEX	B-	B	B-	Down	5.03	9.17	20.63	27.25	98.75	49.74	3,047	800-480-4111	
JPMorgan Mid Cap Equity Fund Class R5	JMEEX	B-	B	B-	Down	5.20	9.55	21.46	29.94	105.29	50.82	3,047	800-480-4111	
JPMorgan Mid Cap Equity Fund Class R6	JPPEX	B-	B	B-	Down	5.24	9.56	21.54	30.15	105.69	50.83	3,047	800-480-4111	
JPMorgan Mid Cap Growth Fund Class A	OSGIX	B	B	B	Up	5.59	11.82	29.06	31.53	111.10	29.13	3,490	800-480-4111	Y
JPMorgan Mid Cap Growth Fund Class C	OMGCX	B	B	B	Up	5.46	11.57	28.42	29.62	105.87	23.08	3,490	800-480-4111	Y
JPMorgan Mid Cap Growth Fund Class I	HLGEX	B	B+	B	Up	5.69	12.01	29.50	32.78	114.32	33.43	3,490	800-480-4111	Y
JPMorgan Mid Cap Growth Fund Class R2	JMGZX	B	B	C+	Up	5.54	11.71	28.80	30.87	109.29	31.68	3,490	800-480-4111	Y
JPMorgan Mid Cap Growth Fund Class R3	JMGPX	B	B	C+	Up	5.59	11.82	29.04	31.69	111.50	33.28	3,490	800-480-4111	Y
JPMorgan Mid Cap Growth Fund Class R4	JMGQX	B	B+	C+	Up	5.67	11.95	29.39	32.67	114.14	33.4	3,490	800-480-4111	Y
JPMorgan Mid Cap Growth Fund Class R5	JMGFX	B	B+	B	Up	5.70	12.05	29.67	33.32	115.82	33.79	3,490	800-480-4111	Y
JPMorgan Mid Cap Growth Fund Class R6	JMGMX	B	B+	C+	Up	5.70	12.07	29.72	33.50	116.40	33.92	3,490	800-480-4111	Y
JPMorgan Mid Cap Value Fund Class A	JAMCX	B	B-	B+		4.67	6.78	13.25	24.34	91.59	39.41	19,353	800-480-4111	
JPMorgan Mid Cap Value Fund Class C	JCMVX	B	C+	B	Up	4.51	6.50	12.67	22.46	86.72	37.93	19,353	800-480-4111	
JPMorgan Mid Cap Value Fund Class I	JMVSX	B	B-	B+		4.71	6.90	13.53	25.29	93.90	39.82	19,353	800-480-4111	
JPMorgan Mid Cap Value Fund Class L	FLMVX	B	B-	B+		4.67	6.91	13.67	26.04	96.03	40.28	19,353	800-480-4111	
JPMorgan Mid Cap Value Fund Class R2	JMVZX	B	B-	B		4.60	6.64	12.98	23.39	89.11	37.85	19,353	800-480-4111	
JPMorgan Mid Cap Value Fund Class R3	JMVPX	B	B-	B+		4.54	6.65	13.14	24.75	93.06	39.14	19,353	800-480-4111	Y
JPMorgan Mid Cap Value Fund Class R4	JMVQX	B	B-	B+		4.58	6.77	13.37	25.61	95.36	39.67	19,353	800-480-4111	Y
JPMorgan Mid Cap Value Fund Class R5	JMVRX	B	B-	B+		4.66	6.85	13.57	25.91	95.82	40.24	19,353	800-480-4111	Y
JPMorgan Mid Cap Value Fund Class R6	JMVYX	B	B-	B+		4.67	6.89	13.68	26.04	96.03	40.26	19,353	800-480-4111	Y
Keeley Mid Cap Dividend Value Fund Class A	KMDVX	B	B	B	Up	6.45	13.17	15.68	35.33	107.20	23.21	124.3	888-933-5391	Y
Keeley Mid Cap Dividend Value Fund Class I	KMDIX	B	B+	B	Up	6.51	13.31	15.97	36.32	109.79	23.21	124.3	888-933-5391	Y
Kinetics Paradigm Fund Advisor Class A	KNPAX	B	B	B-	Up	7.75	19.96	28.07	39.80	103.58	46.99	744.6	800-930-3828	Y
Kinetics Paradigm Fund Advisor Class C	KNPCX	B	B	C+	Up	7.61	19.68	27.47	37.72	98.49	44.21	744.6	800-930-3828	Y
Kinetics Paradigm Fund Class Institutional	KNPYX	B	B+	B-	Up	7.85	20.22	28.65	41.70	108.22	48.62	744.6	800-930-3828	Y
Kinetics Paradigm Fund No Load Class	WWNPX	B	B+	B-	Up	7.80	20.10	28.40	40.87	106.09	48.32	744.6	800-930-3828	Y
Kirr Marbach Partners Value Fund	KMVAX	B-	C+	B	Up	6.49	9.82	16.09	22.11	70.15	24.95	78.8		Y
Leuthold Select Industries Fund	LSLTX	B	B	B-	Up	4.71	11.57	21.83	26.30	113.77	26.27	20.0	800-273-6886	Y
Liberty All-Star Growth	ASG	B	B	C+	Up	5.55	9.69	27.89	37.45	99.39	5.67	149.5	866-432-2926	Y
Longleaf Partners Small-Cap Fund	LLSCX	B-	B-	B-	Up	1.73	3.85	8.98	22.87	83.17	27.6	3,836	800-445-9469	
Lord Abbett Calibrated Mid Cap Value Fund Class A	LVMAX	B-	C+	B		4.76	6.18	10.85	19.88	90.73	21.66	1,035	201-827-2000	Y
Lord Abbett Calibrated Mid Cap Value Fund Class C	LVMCX	B-	C+	B	Up	4.53	5.78	10.01	17.22	83.85	21.26	1,035	201-827-2000	Y
Lord Abbett Calibrated Mid Cap Value Fund Class F	LVMFX	B-	C+	B	Down	4.81	6.32	11.09	20.53	92.38	21.69	1,035	201-827-2000	Y
Lord Abbett Calibrated Mid Cap Value Fund Class F3	LVMOX	B-	B-	B	Down	4.80	6.31	11.12	20.82	93.20	21.71	1,035	201-827-2000	Y
Lord Abbett Calibrated Mid Cap Value Fund Class I	LVMIX	B-	B-	B	Down	4.80	6.31	11.07	20.76	93.11	21.71	1,035	201-827-2000	Y
Lord Abbett Calibrated Mid Cap Value Fund Class R2	LVMQX	B-	C+	B		4.67	6.00	10.45	18.64	88.38	21.71	1,035	201-827-2000	Y
Lord Abbett Calibrated Mid Cap Value Fund Class R3	LVMRX	B-	C+	B		4.70	6.03	10.52	18.97	89.13	21.7	1,035	201-827-2000	Y
Lord Abbett Calibrated Mid Cap Value Fund Class R4	LVMSX	B-	C+	B		4.74	6.17	10.79	19.88	90.75	21.59	1,035	201-827-2000	Y
Lord Abbett Calibrated Mid Cap Value Fund Class R5	LVMTX	B-	B-	B	Down	4.80	6.31	11.07	20.78	93.14	21.71	1,035	201-827-2000	Y
Lord Abbett Calibrated Mid Cap Value Fund Class R6	LVMHX	B-	B-	B	Down	4.80	6.31	11.13	20.80	93.18	21.71	1,035	201-827-2000	Y
Lord Abbett Growth Opportunities Fund Class A	LMGAX	B	B	B	Up	4.81	9.25	22.83	26.57	89.04	20.37	515.9	201-827-2000	Y
Lord Abbett Growth Opportunities Fund Class B	LMGBX	B	B-	B	Up	4.59	8.79	21.91	23.77	82.31	15.23	515.9	201-827-2000	
Lord Abbett Growth Opportunities Fund Class C	LMGCX	B	B-	B	Up	4.66	8.86	21.92	23.86	82.49	15.23	515.9	201-827-2000	Y
Lord Abbett Growth Opportunities Fund Class F	LGOFX	B	B	B	Up	4.83	9.31	23.04	27.18	90.70	21.17	515.9	201-827-2000	Y
Lord Abbett Growth Opportunities Fund Class F3	LOMGX	B	B	B	Up	4.90	9.43	23.11	26.85	89.46	23.22	515.9	201-827-2000	Y
Lord Abbett Growth Opportunities Fund Class I	LMGYX	B	B	B	Up	4.87	9.38	23.19	27.56	91.69	23.12	515.9	201-827-2000	Y
Lord Abbett Growth Opportunities Fund Class P	LGOPX	B	B-	B	Up	4.78	9.15	22.64	25.84	87.43	19.88	515.9	201-827-2000	
Lord Abbett Growth Opportunities Fund Class R2	LGOQX	B	B-	B	Up	4.73	9.08	22.46	25.32	86.05	19.42	515.9	201-827-2000	Y
Lord Abbett Growth Opportunities Fund Class R3	LGORX	B	B-	B	Up	4.74	9.12	22.52	25.67	86.98	19.8	515.9	201-827-2000	Y

Category: US Equity Mid Cap (con't)

Fund Name	Ticker Symbol	RATINGS: Overall Rating	Reward Rating	Risk Rating	Recent Up/ Downgrade	TOTAL RETURNS & PERFORMANCE: 3-Month Total Return	6-Month Total Return	1-Year Total Return	3-Year Total Return	5-Year Total Return	ASSETS: NAV	Total Assets (MIL)	NEW INVESTORS: Telephone	Open to New Investors
Lord Abbett Growth Opportunities Fund Class R4	LGOSX	B	B	B	Up	4.81	9.25	22.83	26.57	89.04	20.37	515.9	201-827-2000	Y
Lord Abbett Growth Opportunities Fund Class R5	LGOTX	B	B	B	Up	4.87	9.37	23.17	27.44	90.34	23.14	515.9	201-827-2000	Y
Lord Abbett Growth Opportunities Fund Class R6	LGOVX	B	B	B	Up	4.90	9.43	23.32	27.83	90.92	23.22	515.9	201-827-2000	Y
Lord Abbett Mid Cap Stock Fund Class A	LAVLX	B-	C+	B		2.67	2.80	7.03	19.18	77.85	29.9	2,081	201-827-2000	Y
Lord Abbett Mid Cap Stock Fund Class B	LMCBX	B-	C+	B		2.45	2.38	6.23	16.52	71.62	27.94	2,081	201-827-2000	
Lord Abbett Mid Cap Stock Fund Class C	LMCCX	B-	C+	B		2.45	2.37	6.24	16.52	71.64	27.8	2,081	201-827-2000	Y
Lord Abbett Mid Cap Stock Fund Class F	LMCFX	B-	C+	B		2.72	2.86	7.19	19.68	79.57	29.65	2,081	201-827-2000	Y
Lord Abbett Mid Cap Stock Fund Class F3	LOVLX	B-	C+	B		2.76	2.97	7.28	19.45	78.26	29.74	2,081	201-827-2000	Y
Lord Abbett Mid Cap Stock Fund Class I	LMCYX	B-	C+	B		2.71	2.91	7.29	20.06	80.39	29.66	2,081	201-827-2000	Y
Lord Abbett Mid Cap Stock Fund Class P	LMCPX	B-	C+	B		2.63	2.70	6.83	18.50	76.96	28.99	2,081	201-827-2000	
Lord Abbett Mid Cap Stock Fund Class R2	LMCQX	B-	C+	B		2.58	2.61	6.67	17.90	75.13	29.4	2,081	201-827-2000	Y
Lord Abbett Mid Cap Stock Fund Class R3	LMCRX	B-	C+	B		2.57	2.64	6.76	18.28	76.06	29.58	2,081	201-827-2000	Y
Lord Abbett Mid Cap Stock Fund Class R4	LMCSX	B-	C+	B		2.67	2.77	7.05	19.22	77.92	29.79	2,081	201-827-2000	Y
Lord Abbett Mid Cap Stock Fund Class R5	LMCTX	B-	C+	B		2.72	2.93	7.30	19.93	78.98	29.66	2,081	201-827-2000	Y
Lord Abbett Mid Cap Stock Fund Class R6	LMCHX	B-	C+	B		2.76	2.97	7.41	20.29	79.51	29.74	2,081	201-827-2000	Y
Lord Abbett Value Opportunities Fund Class A	LVOAX	B	B-	B	Up	4.18	6.63	10.15	23.38	87.71	20.09	3,227	201-827-2000	Y
Lord Abbett Value Opportunities Fund Class B	LVOBX	B-	C+	B	Up	4.04	6.29	9.37	20.65	81.10	17.96	3,227	201-827-2000	
Lord Abbett Value Opportunities Fund Class C	LVOCX	B-	C+	B	Up	3.99	6.29	9.31	20.65	81.10	17.96	3,227	201-827-2000	Y
Lord Abbett Value Opportunities Fund Class F	LVOFX	B	B-	B	Up	4.20	6.70	10.27	23.92	89.43	20.48	3,227	201-827-2000	Y
Lord Abbett Value Opportunities Fund Class F3	LVOOX	B	B-	B	Up	4.32	6.88	10.54	24.45	90.56	20.93	3,227	201-827-2000	Y
Lord Abbett Value Opportunities Fund Class I	LVOYX	B	B-	B	Up	4.23	6.79	10.41	24.30	90.33	20.86	3,227	201-827-2000	Y
Lord Abbett Value Opportunities Fund Class P	LVOPX	B-	C+	B	Up	4.15	6.58	9.93	22.68	86.17	19.74	3,227	201-827-2000	
Lord Abbett Value Opportunities Fund Class R2	LVOQX	B-	C+	B	Up	4.13	6.50	9.79	22.11	84.81	19.33	3,227	201-827-2000	Y
Lord Abbett Value Opportunities Fund Class R3	LVORX	B-	C+	B	Up	4.15	6.55	9.87	22.48	85.64	19.52	3,227	201-827-2000	Y
Lord Abbett Value Opportunities Fund Class R4	LVOSX	B	B-	B	Up	4.17	6.67	10.13	23.39	87.99	20.06	3,227	201-827-2000	Y
Lord Abbett Value Opportunities Fund Class R5	LVOTX	B	B-	B	Up	4.29	6.85	10.41	24.36	90.41	20.88	3,227	201-827-2000	Y
Lord Abbett Value Opportunities Fund Class R6	LVOVX	B	B-	B	Up	4.28	6.83	10.54	24.69	90.92	20.93	3,227	201-827-2000	Y
Lord Abbett Value Opportunities Fund Class T	LVATX	B-	C+	B		4.25	6.72	10.19	23.44	88.07	20.07	3,227	201-827-2000	Y
Madison Mid Cap Fund Class A	MERAX	B	B-	B+		1.39	5.34	11.03	23.81	77.47	9.46	351.8	800-767-0300	Y
Madison Mid Cap Fund Class B	MERBX	B	B-	B+		0.38	4.15	9.27	20.20	69.64	7.78	351.8	800-767-0300	Y
Madison Mid Cap Fund Class R6	MMCRX	B	B	A-		1.71	5.89	11.90	26.55	83.64	10.06	351.8	800-767-0300	Y
Madison Mid Cap Fund Class Y	GTSGX	B	B-	B+		1.54	5.67	11.65	25.34	80.48	9.87	351.8	800-767-0300	Y
Managed Account Series Mid Cap Dividend Fund	MMCVX	B	B-	B	Up	5.07	8.05	9.51	26.54	89.63	12.14	93.2	800-441-7762	Y
Marsico 21st Century Fund	MXXIX	B	B	B	Up	5.26	8.92	30.04	26.99	100.94	27.57	242.9	888-860-8686	Y
MassMutual Select Mid Cap Growth Fund Administrative Class	MMELX	B	B	B		4.34	8.69	24.26	37.99	116.19	19.93	5,628		Y
MassMutual Select Mid Cap Growth Fund Class A	MEFAX	B	B	B		4.28	8.60	24.02	37.04	113.64	18.5	5,628		Y
MassMutual Select Mid Cap Growth Fund Class I	MEFZX	B	B	B	Down	4.41	8.88	24.66	39.28	119.70	21.47	5,628		Y
MassMutual Select Mid Cap Growth Fund Class R3	MEFNX	B	B	B		4.25	8.52	23.87	36.43	111.68	17.15	5,628		Y
MassMutual Select Mid Cap Growth Fund Class R4	MEFFX	B	B	B		4.31	8.67	24.18	37.50	115.29	18.6	5,628		Y
MassMutual Select Mid Cap Growth Fund Class R5	MGRFX	B	B	B	Down	4.40	8.86	24.56	38.92	118.58	21.29	5,628		Y
MassMutual Select Mid Cap Growth Fund Service Class	MEFYX	B	B	B	Down	4.35	8.80	24.46	38.46	117.56	20.81	5,628		Y
MassMutual Select Mid Cap Value Fund Administrative Class	MLULX	B	B-	B	Up	5.66	9.34	11.90	27.42	86.27	14	93.1		Y
MassMutual Select Mid Cap Value Fund Class A	MLUAX	B	B-	B	Up	5.58	9.25	11.60	26.45	84.00	13.79	93.1		Y
MassMutual Select Mid Cap Value Fund Class R3	MLUNX	B-	B-	B	Down	5.56	9.11	11.48	25.90	82.33	13.63	93.1		Y
MassMutual Select Mid Cap Value Fund Class R4	MLUFX	B	B-	B	Up	5.57	9.19	11.63	26.76	85.11	13.67	93.1		Y
MassMutual Select Mid Cap Value Fund Class R5	MLUSX	B	B	B	Up	5.73	9.46	12.11	28.21	88.20	13.82	93.1		Y
MassMutual Select Mid Cap Value Fund Service Class	MLUYX	B	B-	B	Up	5.65	9.46	12.05	27.79	87.40	13.78	93.1		Y
MassMutual Select Mid-Cap Value Fund Class I	MLUZX	B	B	B	Up	5.67	9.49	12.17	28.53	89.23	13.71	93.1		Y
Meeder Quantex Fund Adviser Class	QNTAX	B	B	B	Up	5.78	10.05	13.68	27.05	103.15	36.78	94.5		Y
Meeder Quantex Fund Institutional Class	QNTIX	B	B	B	Up	5.44	9.73	13.38	26.72	102.62	36.77	94.5		Y
Meeder Quantex Fund Retail Class	FLCGX	B	B	B	Up	5.74	9.98	13.41	26.66	102.53	36.76	94.5		Y
Meridian Contrarian Fund A Class	MFCAX	B+	A-	B	Up	7.46	16.37	24.20	37.55	100.45	41.15	659.9	800-446-6662	Y

Category: US Equity Mid Cap (con't)

Fund Name	Ticker Symbol	Overall Rating	Reward Rating	Risk Rating	Recent Up/ Downgrade	3-Month Total Return	6-Month Total Return	1-Year Total Return	3-Year Total Return	5-Year Total Return	NAV	Total Assets (MIL)	Telephone	Open to New Investors
Meridian Contrarian Fund Class C	MFCCX	B	B+	B	Up	7.31	16.06	23.57	35.38	94.69	40.81	659.9	800-446-6662	Y
Meridian Contrarian Fund Investor Class	MFCIX	B+	A-	B	Up	7.54	16.52	24.51	38.65	103.09	41.7	659.9	800-446-6662	Y
Meridian Contrarian Fund Legacy Class	MVALX	B+	A	B	Up	7.60	16.66	24.82	39.57	104.74	41.96	659.9	800-446-6662	
MFS® Mid Cap Growth Fund Class 529A	EAMCX	B+	B	A-	Up	4.96	10.22	25.96	36.12	107.41	15.52	2,561	877-960-6077	Y
MFS® Mid Cap Growth Fund Class 529B	EBCGX	B+	B	A-	Up	4.72	9.74	24.94	32.99	99.43	13.01	2,561	877-960-6077	Y
MFS® Mid Cap Growth Fund Class 529C	ECGRX	B+	B	A-	Up	4.70	9.70	24.94	32.86	99.17	12.61	2,561	877-960-6077	Y
MFS® Mid Cap Growth Fund Class A	OTCAX	B+	B	A-	Up	4.95	10.20	25.99	36.19	107.37	15.99	2,561	877-960-6077	Y
MFS® Mid Cap Growth Fund Class B	OTCBX	B+	B	A-	Up	4.76	9.75	25.01	33.11	99.91	13.33	2,561	877-960-6077	Y
MFS® Mid Cap Growth Fund Class C	OTCCX	B+	B	A-	Up	4.75	9.71	25.00	33.09	99.66	12.93	2,561	877-960-6077	Y
MFS® Mid Cap Growth Fund Class I	OTCIX	B+	B	A-	Up	4.99	10.31	26.28	37.07	109.84	16.89	2,561	877-960-6077	Y
MFS® Mid Cap Growth Fund Class R1	OTCGX	B+	B	A-	Up	4.78	9.80	25.03	33.16	99.70	13.27	2,561	877-960-6077	Y
MFS® Mid Cap Growth Fund Class R2	MCPRX	B	B	B	Up	4.89	10.06	25.61	35.05	104.90	15.11	2,561	877-960-6077	Y
MFS® Mid Cap Growth Fund Class R3	OTCHX	B+	B	A-	Up	4.98	10.19	25.99	36.14	107.39	15.89	2,561	877-960-6077	Y
MFS® Mid Cap Growth Fund Class R4	OTCJX	B+	B+	A-	Up	4.98	10.28	26.28	37.10	110.03	16.51	2,561	877-960-6077	Y
MFS® Mid Cap Growth Fund Class R6	OTCKX	B+	B+	A-	Up	5.03	10.39	26.38	37.52	110.91	16.98	2,561	877-960-6077	Y
MFS® Mid Cap Value Fund Class 529A	EACVX	B	B-	B+	Up	4.53	7.03	13.34	26.19	93.59	22.87	7,150	877-960-6077	
MFS® Mid Cap Value Fund Class 529B	EBCVX	B	C+	B	Up	4.30	6.58	12.46	23.33	86.27	21.31	7,150	877-960-6077	
MFS® Mid Cap Value Fund Class 529C	ECCVX	B	C+	B	Up	4.34	6.60	12.53	23.43	86.59	21.39	7,150	877-960-6077	
MFS® Mid Cap Value Fund Class A	MVCAX	B	B-	B+	Up	4.50	7.01	13.38	26.32	93.86	23.24	7,150	877-960-6077	Y
MFS® Mid Cap Value Fund Class B	MCBVX	B	C+	B	Up	4.36	6.62	12.55	23.57	86.87	21.99	7,150	877-960-6077	Y
MFS® Mid Cap Value Fund Class C	MVCCX	B	C+	B	Up	4.33	6.65	12.55	23.52	86.84	21.9	7,150	877-960-6077	Y
MFS® Mid Cap Value Fund Class I	MCVIX	B	B-	B+	Up	4.61	7.16	13.68	27.27	96.43	23.8	7,150	877-960-6077	Y
MFS® Mid Cap Value Fund Class R1	MVCGX	B	C+	B	Up	4.35	6.60	12.54	23.55	86.79	21.55	7,150	877-960-6077	Y
MFS® Mid Cap Value Fund Class R2	MCVRX	B	B-	B	Up	4.46	6.90	13.09	25.35	91.55	22.7	7,150	877-960-6077	Y
MFS® Mid Cap Value Fund Class R3	MVCHX	B	B-	B+	Up	4.53	7.05	13.39	26.36	93.98	23.16	7,150	877-960-6077	Y
MFS® Mid Cap Value Fund Class R4	MVCJX	B	B-	B+	Up	4.60	7.15	13.65	27.25	96.32	23.33	7,150	877-960-6077	Y
MFS® Mid Cap Value Fund Class R6	MVCKX	B	B-	B+	Up	4.62	7.21	13.84	27.87	97.52	23.81	7,150	877-960-6077	Y
Miller Opportunity Trust Class A	LGOAX	B-	B-	C+	Up	5.43	4.96	25.94	25.68	140.73	23.88	1,458		Y
Miller Opportunity Trust Class C	LMOPX	B-	B-	C+	Up	5.22	4.54	24.99	22.88	131.56	22.55	1,458		Y
Miller Opportunity Trust Class FI	LMOFX	B-	B-	C+	Up	5.43	4.94	25.90	25.58	140.08	24.64	1,458		Y
Miller Opportunity Trust Class I	LMNOX	B-	B-	C+	Up	5.45	5.06	26.20	26.76	143.97	25.91	1,458		Y
Miller Opportunity Trust Class R	LMORX	B-	B-	C+	Up	5.36	4.80	25.54	24.50	136.20	23.98	1,458		Y
MM S&P® Mid Cap Index Fund Class A	MDKAX	B	B	B	Up	6.13	9.30	15.26	32.61	96.15	14.12	493.0		Y
MM S&P® Mid Cap Index Fund Class I	MDKZX	B	B	B		6.21	9.58	15.85	34.90	102.05	14.22	493.0		Y
MM S&P® Mid Cap Index Fund Class R3	MDKTX	B	B	B	Up	6.00	9.19	15.01	31.93	95.31	13.99	493.0		Y
MM S&P® Mid Cap Index Fund Class R4	MDKFX	B	B	B		6.09	9.35	15.34	32.86	97.71	14.04	493.0		Y
MM S&P® Mid Cap Index Fund Class R5	MDKIX	B	B	B		6.20	9.58	15.78	34.45	100.90	14.18	493.0		Y
MM S&P® Mid Cap Index Fund Service Class shares	MDKSX	B	B	B		6.22	9.46	15.59	33.99	99.72	14.13	493.0		Y
MM S&P® Mid Cap R5ndex Fund Administrative Class	MDKYX	B	B	B		6.12	9.44	15.48	33.50	98.72	14.13	493.0		Y
Monongahela All Cap Value Fund	MCMVX	B	B+	B		6.40	11.11	20.75	38.09		14.09	9.4	855-392-9331	Y
Morgan Stanley Inst Fund, Inc. Insight Portfolio Cls A	MFPHX	B	B	C+		5.56	9.24	17.81	44.09	118.66	16.45	100.9	855-332-5306	Y
Morgan Stanley Inst Fund, Inc. Insight Portfolio Cls C	MSSPX	B	B	C+		5.35	8.85	16.92	41.02	111.13	15.89	100.9	855-332-5306	Y
Morgan Stanley Inst Fund, Inc. Insight Portfolio Cls I	MFPIX	B	B	C+		5.67	9.48	18.27	45.60	122.38	16.54	100.9	855-332-5306	Y
Morgan Stanley Inst Fund, Inc. Insight Portfolio Cls L	MFPLX	B	B	C+		5.38	9.01	17.21	42.04	113.31	16	100.9	855-332-5306	
Motley Fool Great America Fund Institutional Shares	FOGIX	B	B+	B	Up	11.76	18.04	29.38	34.77	106.07	24.48	267.5		Y
Motley Fool Great America Fund Investor Shares	TMFGX	B	B	B	Up	11.73	17.93	29.19	33.89	104.68	24.35	267.5		Y
Multimanager Mid Cap Growth Portfolio Class IA	US00247C7002	B	B+	C	Up	7.43	14.16	27.09	32.76	101.15		189.2	877-222-2144	Y
Multimanager Mid Cap Growth Portfolio Class IB	US00247C8091	B	B+	C	Up	7.43	14.18	27.14	32.80	101.21		189.2	877-222-2144	Y
Multimanager Mid Cap Growth Portfolio Class K	US00247C4785	B	A-	C+	Up	7.49	14.33	27.47	33.84	103.66		189.2	877-222-2144	Y
Multimanager Mid Cap Value Portfolio Class IA	US00247C8828	B-	C+	B	Up	4.23	7.49	9.61	22.36	79.97		194.7	877-222-2144	Y
Multimanager Mid Cap Value Portfolio Class IB	US00247C8745	B-	C+	B	Up	4.19	7.52	9.62	22.26	79.98		194.7	877-222-2144	Y
Multimanager Mid Cap Value Portfolio Class K	US00247C4603	B-	B-	B	Up	4.29	7.67	9.87	23.27	82.23		194.7	877-222-2144	Y

Category: US Equity Mid Cap (con't)

Fund Name	Ticker Symbol	RATINGS Overall Rating	Reward Rating	Risk Rating	Recent Up/ Downgrade	TOTAL RETURNS & PERFORMANCE 3-Month Total Return	6-Month Total Return	1-Year Total Return	3-Year Total Return	5-Year Total Return	ASSETS NAV	Total Assets (MIL)	NEW INVESTORS Telephone	Open to New Investors
Mutual of America Inst Funds Inc Mid-Cap Equity Index Fund	MAMQX	B	B	B		6.20	9.58	15.99	35.16	103.06	11.7826	25.1		Y
Nationwide Geneva Mid Cap Growth Fund Class A	NWHVX	B	B	A-	Up	6.20	8.21	23.00	28.84	79.58	25.08	1,060	800-848-0920	Y
Nationwide Geneva Mid Cap Growth Fund Class C	NWHWX	B	B-	A-	Up	5.99	7.82	22.09	26.01	73.48	20.32	1,060	800-848-0920	Y
Nationwide Geneva Mid Cap Growth Fund Class R6	NWKAX	B	B	A-	Up	6.30	8.41	23.45	30.30	82.61	26.17	1,060	800-848-0920	Y
Nationwide Geneva Mid Cap Growth Fund Inst Service Cls	NWHYX	B	B	A-	Up	6.28	8.35	23.30	29.76	81.84	25.96	1,060	800-848-0920	Y
Nationwide Mid Cap Market Index Fund Class A	GMXAX	B	B	B		6.08	9.33	15.43	33.11	97.88	17.74	1,283	800-848-0920	Y
Nationwide Mid Cap Market Index Fund Class C	GMCCX	B	B	B	Up	5.90	8.93	14.62	30.42	91.41	16.38	1,283	800-848-0920	Y
Nationwide Mid Cap Market Index Fund Class R	GMXRX	B	B	B	Up	5.97	9.12	15.08	32.00	95.51	17.51	1,283	800-848-0920	Y
Nationwide Mid Cap Market Index Fund Class R6	GMXIX	B	B	B		6.15	9.52	15.85	34.74	101.84	18.03	1,283	800-848-0920	Y
Nationwide Mid Cap Mkt Index Fund Inst Service Cls	NWXQX	B	B	B		6.17	9.46	15.76	33.48	98.44	18.03	1,283	800-848-0920	Y
Natixis Funds Trust II Vaughan Nelson Value Opp Fund Cls A	VNVAX	B-	C+	B	Up	4.95	8.74	12.92	14.40	83.70	22.65	1,008	800-862-4863	Y
Natixis Funds Trust II Vaughan Nelson Value Opp Fund Cls N	VNVNX	B-	C+	B	Up	5.01	8.90	13.31	15.61	86.36	22.87	1,008	800-862-4863	Y
Natixis Funds Trust II Vaughan Nelson Value Opp Fund Cls Y	VNVYX	B-	C+	B	Up	5.00	8.84	13.19	15.28	85.92	22.89	1,008	800-862-4863	Y
Needham Growth Fund Institutional Class	NEEIX	B-	B-	B	Up	-2.40	4.41	8.88	13.74	70.80	43.15	121.0	800-625-7071	Y
Needham Growth Fund Retail Class	NEEGX	B-	C+	B	Up	-2.54	4.12	8.32	13.15	69.92	42.91	121.0	800-625-7071	Y
Neuberger Berman Advisers Mgmt Trust Mid-Cap Growth Cls I	US6412225004	B	B	C+	Up	7.05	11.79	25.28	31.65	92.26	27.79	423.9	212-476-9000	Y
Neuberger Berman Advisers Mgmt Trust Mid-Cap Gr Cls S	US6412228560	B	B	C+	Up	6.98	11.66	24.56	30.25	89.21	25.77	423.9	212-476-9000	Y
Neuberger Berman AMT Mid-Cap Intrinsic Value Port Cls I	US6412227083	B-	B-	B	Up	3.24	6.70	16.73	23.26	97.35	19.58	177.7	212-476-9000	Y
Neuberger Berman AMT Mid-Cap Intrinsic Value Port Cls S	US6412228313	B-	B-	B	Up	3.17	6.52	16.34	22.34	94.97	22.22	177.7	212-476-9000	Y
Neuberger Berman Mid Cap Growth Fund Advisor Class	NBMBX	B	B	C+	Up	6.91	11.65	24.84	31.02	89.30	14.71	1,274	212-476-9000	
Neuberger Berman Mid Cap Growth Fund Class A	NMGAX	B	B+	B	Up	6.91	11.70	25.00	31.48	90.53	14.71	1,274	212-476-9000	Y
Neuberger Berman Mid Cap Growth Fund Class C	NMGCX	B	B	C+	Up	6.76	11.34	24.10	28.62	83.69	14.7	1,274	212-476-9000	Y
Neuberger Berman Mid Cap Growth Fund Class R3	NMGRX	B	B	C+	Up	6.89	11.61	24.71	30.54	88.33	14.71	1,274	212-476-9000	Y
Neuberger Berman Mid Cap Growth Fund Class R6	NRMGX	B	B+	C+	Up	7.05	11.96	25.57	33.28	94.86	14.72	1,274	212-476-9000	Y
Neuberger Berman Mid Cap Growth Fund Institutional Class	NBMLX	B	B+	C+	Up	7.05	11.98	25.46	32.98	94.23	14.72	1,274	212-476-9000	Y
Neuberger Berman Mid Cap Growth Fund Investor Class	NMANX	B	B+	B	Up	7.02	11.86	25.33	32.31	92.39	14.72	1,274	212-476-9000	
Neuberger Berman Mid Cap Growth Fund Trust Class	NBMTX	B	B+	B	Up	7.02	11.84	25.25	32.08	91.88	14.72	1,274	212-476-9000	
Neuberger Berman Mid Cap Intrinsic Value Fund Class A	NBRAX	B-	B-	B		3.07	6.52	16.50	25.19	98.01	18.47	102.8	212-476-9000	Y
Neuberger Berman Mid Cap Intrinsic Value Fund Class C	NBRCX	B-	B-	B	Up	2.86	6.12	15.57	22.42	90.68	18	102.8	212-476-9000	Y
Neuberger Berman Mid Cap Intrinsic Value Fund Class R3	NBRRX	B-	B-	B		2.97	6.37	16.17	24.26	95.56	18.42	102.8	212-476-9000	Y
Neuberger Berman Mid Cap Intrinsic Value Fund Class Trust	NBREX	B-	B-	B		3.02	6.53	16.43	25.07	97.58	18.49	102.8	212-476-9000	
Neuberger Berman Mid Cap Intrinsic Value Fund Inst Cls	NBRTX	B-	B-	B	Down	3.16	6.72	16.92	26.55	101.65	22.83	102.8	212-476-9000	Y
Neuberger Berman Mid Cap Intrinsic Value Fund Investor Cls	NBRVX	B-	B-	B	Down	3.05	6.61	16.70	25.67	99.56	22.84	102.8	212-476-9000	
Nicholas Equity Income Fund Class I	NSEIX	B-	C+	B		4.82	6.71	12.40	20.94	78.62	20.66	507.1	800-544-6547	Y
Nicholas II Fund Class I	NCTWX	B	B	B-	Up	6.69	10.69	25.63	32.04	99.73	27.67	842.2	800-544-6547	Y
Nicholas II Fund Class N	NNTWX	B	B	B-	Up	6.60	10.51	25.19	30.71	96.27	27.14	842.2	800-544-6547	Y
Northern Mid Cap Index Fund	NOMIX	B	B	B		6.18	9.60	16.03	35.14	102.71	19.32	2,409	800-595-9111	Y
Nuance Concentrated Value Fund Institutional Class	NCVLX	B	B-	B	Up	3.71	6.41	11.06	27.99	87.95	14.67	619.8		Y
Nuance Concentrated Value Fund Investor Class	NCAVX	B	B-	B	Up	3.70	6.28	10.72	26.87	85.44	14.63	619.8		Y
Nuance Mid Cap Value Fund Institutional Class	NMVLX	B	B	B+		4.83	7.96	15.00	39.89		12.48	474.0		Y
Nuance Mid Cap Value Fund Investor Class	NMAVX	B+	B	A	Up	4.86	7.84	14.80	38.85		12.46	474.0		Y
Nuance Mid Cap Value Fund Z Class Shares	NMVZX	B	B	B+		4.92	8.08	14.90	39.77		12.49	474.0		Y
Nuveen Mid Cap Growth Opportunities Fund Class A	FRSLX	B	B-	B	Up	4.44	9.67	24.47	23.98	87.92	36.78	814.9	312-917-8146	Y
Nuveen Mid Cap Growth Opportunities Fund Class C	FMECX	B-	B-	B	Up	4.23	9.25	23.53	21.19	81.00	27.01	814.9	312-917-8146	Y
Nuveen Mid Cap Growth Opportunities Fund Class I	FISGX	B	B	B	Up	4.50	9.81	24.78	24.91	90.29	44.38	814.9	312-917-8146	Y
Nuveen Mid Cap Growth Opportunities Fund Class R3	FMEYX	B	B-	B	Up	4.39	9.53	24.19	23.05	85.63	34.16	814.9	312-917-8146	Y
Nuveen Mid Cap Growth Opportunities Fund Class R6	FMEFX	B	B	B	Up	4.52	9.89	24.99	25.45	91.56	44.79	814.9	312-917-8146	Y
Nuveen Mid Cap Value Fund Class A	FASEX	B	B	B	Up	6.11	11.21	19.16	31.72	106.23	40.89	115.9	312-917-8146	Y
Nuveen Mid Cap Value Fund Class C	FACSX	B	B	B	Up	5.91	10.78	18.26	28.75	98.58	38.84	115.9	312-917-8146	Y
Nuveen Mid Cap Value Fund Class I	FSEIX	B	B	B	Up	6.16	11.35	19.45	32.70	108.78	40.98	115.9	312-917-8146	Y
Nuveen Mid Cap Value Fund Class R3	FMVSX	B	B	B	Up	6.04	11.07	18.88	30.74	103.71	40.59	115.9	312-917-8146	Y
Nuveen Symphony Mid Cap Core Fund Class A	NCCAX	B	C+	B	Up	4.76	8.57	16.51	20.58	81.37	41.16	32.0	312-917-8146	Y

Category: US Equity Mid Cap (con't)

Fund Name	Ticker Symbol	RATINGS: Overall Rating	Reward Rating	Risk Rating	Recent Up/ Downgrade	TOTAL RETURNS & PERFORMANCE: 3-Month Total Return	6-Month Total Return	1-Year Total Return	3-Year Total Return	5-Year Total Return	ASSETS: NAV	Total Assets (ML)	NEW INVESTORS: Telephone	Open to New Investors
Nuveen Symphony Mid Cap Core Fund Class C	NCCCX	B-	C+	B	Up	4.56	8.17	15.68	17.92	74.71	38.04	32.0	312-917-8146	Y
Nuveen Symphony Mid-Cap Core Fund Class I	NCCIX	B	C+	B	Up	4.81	8.69	16.81	21.49	83.59	42.09	32.0	312-917-8146	Y
Nuveen Symphony Mid-Cap Core Fund Class R3	NMCRX	B-	C+	B	Up	4.68	8.42	16.25	19.78	79.25	40.78	32.0	312-917-8146	Y
Oppenheimer Discovery Mid Cap Growth Fund A	OEGAX	A-	A-	B+	Up	6.66	12.13	27.98	37.43	100.43	19.94	1,053	800-225-5677	Y
Oppenheimer Discovery Mid Cap Growth Fund B	OEGBX	B+	B+	B+	Up	6.50	11.79	27.06	34.37	92.68	16.34	1,053	800-225-5677	
Oppenheimer Discovery Mid Cap Growth Fund C	OEGCX	B+	B+	B+	Up	6.45	11.69	27.07	34.33	92.96	16.47	1,053	800-225-5677	Y
Oppenheimer Discovery Mid Cap Growth Fund I	OEGIX	A-	A-	B+	Up	6.74	12.39	28.53	39.22	105.20	22.54	1,053	800-225-5677	Y
Oppenheimer Discovery Mid Cap Growth Fund R	OEGNX	A-	A-	B+	Up	6.54	11.99	27.64	36.41	97.73	18.67	1,053	800-225-5677	Y
Oppenheimer Discovery Mid Cap Growth Fund Y	OEGYX	A-	A-	B+	Up	6.73	12.33	28.37	38.53	103.27	22.29	1,053	800-225-5677	Y
Oppenheimer Main Street Mid Cap Fund Class A	OPMSX	B	B	B	Up	-8.74	-6.76	0.32	19.62	83.70	26.57	2,935	800-225-5677	Y
Oppenheimer Main Street Mid Cap Fund Class B	OPMBX	B	B	B-	Up	-10.59	-8.81	-2.23	16.90	76.71	21.78	2,935	800-225-5677	
Oppenheimer Main Street Mid Cap Fund Class C	OPMCX	B	B	B-	Up	-10.50	-8.73	-2.14	16.91	76.84	21.93	2,935	800-225-5677	Y
Oppenheimer Main Street Mid Cap Fund Class I	OPMIX	B	B	B	Up	-8.32	-6.22	1.15	21.17	87.81	28.61	2,935	800-225-5677	Y
Oppenheimer Main Street Mid Cap Fund Class R	OPMNX	B	B	B	Up	-9.16	-7.22	-0.28	18.72	81.28	25.2	2,935	800-225-5677	Y
Oppenheimer Main Street Mid Cap Fund Class Y	OPMYX	B	B	B	Up	-8.16	-6.09	1.17	20.52	86.12	28.7	2,935	800-225-5677	Y
Oppenheimer Mid Cap Value Fund Class A	QVSCX	B	B	B	Up	5.42	9.49	13.28	25.43	96.06	57.39	1,402	800-225-5677	Y
Oppenheimer Mid Cap Value Fund Class B	QSCBX	B-	B-	B	Up	5.22	9.04	12.42	22.58	88.54	47.2	1,402	800-225-5677	
Oppenheimer Mid Cap Value Fund Class C	QSCCX	B-	B-	B	Up	5.23	9.08	12.46	22.62	88.81	47.27	1,402	800-225-5677	Y
Oppenheimer Mid Cap Value Fund Class I	QSCIX	B	B	B	Up	5.54	9.72	13.77	27.05	100.46	58.38	1,402	800-225-5677	Y
Oppenheimer Mid Cap Value Fund Class R	QSCNX	B	B	B	Up	5.38	9.35	13.01	24.49	93.61	54.95	1,402	800-225-5677	Y
Oppenheimer Mid Cap Value Fund Class Y	QSCYX	B	B	B	Up	5.49	9.62	13.57	26.35	98.75	58.91	1,402	800-225-5677	Y
Papp Small & Mid-Cap Growth Fund	PAPPX	B	B	B-		5.98	9.06	25.82	31.34	80.51	20.78	30.9		Y
Parnassus Mid Cap Fund	PARMX	B	B-	B		4.07	6.52	15.78	31.98	92.81	32.07	2,805	999-350-5	Y
Parnassus Mid Cap Fund Institutional Shares	PFPMX	B	B	B		4.15	6.63	16.04	32.79	94.00	32.11	2,805	999-350-5	Y
PF Mid-Cap Equity Fund Class P	US69447T8707	B+	A	B-	Up	7.50	13.80	24.37	48.29	116.27	10.9	70.6	800-722-2333	Y
PF Mid-Cap Growth Fund Class P	US69447T8624	B-	B	C	Up	7.23	13.19	27.93	27.16	87.62	7.8	15.3	800-722-2333	Y
Pioneer Mid Cap Value Fund Class A	PCGRX	B-	B-	B	Up	5.71	9.82	12.85	21.36	89.99	25.26	979.3	617-742-7825	Y
Pioneer Mid Cap Value Fund Class C	PCCGX	B-	C+	B	Up	5.50	9.33	11.89	18.31	82.15	17.54	979.3	617-742-7825	Y
Pioneer Mid Cap Value Fund Class K	PMCKX	B-	B-	B	Up	5.81	10.00	13.22	22.59	91.92	25.25	979.3	617-742-7825	Y
Pioneer Mid Cap Value Fund Class R	PCMRX	B-	C+	B	Up	5.57	9.59	12.34	19.89	86.32	24.72	979.3	617-742-7825	Y
Pioneer Mid Cap Value Fund Class Y	PYCGX	B-	B-	B	Up	5.79	9.98	13.12	22.30	92.94	27.18	979.3	617-742-7825	Y
Pioneer Select Mid Cap Growth Fund Class A	PGOFX	B	B+	B-	Up	8.55	15.55	29.78	35.37	113.50	41.99	1,577	617-742-7825	Y
Pioneer Select Mid Cap Growth Fund Class C	GOFCX	B	B	C+	Up	8.31	15.08	28.75	32.16	104.83	30.92	1,577	617-742-7825	Y
Pioneer Select Mid Cap Growth Fund Class K	PSMKX	B	B+	B-	Up	8.65	15.75	30.24	36.92	115.93	42.53	1,577	617-742-7825	Y
Pioneer Select Mid Cap Growth Fund Class R	PGRRX	B	B	B-	Up	8.42	15.29	29.24	33.82	109.79	40.46	1,577	617-742-7825	Y
Pioneer Select Mid Cap Growth Fund Class Y	GROYX	B	B+	B-	Up	8.59	15.68	30.09	36.44	116.55	45.34	1,577	617-742-7825	Y
PRIMECAP Odyssey Aggressive Growth Fund	POAGX	A-	A	B	Up	11.08	15.47	33.58	55.69	186.29	44.33	9,529	800-729-2307	
Principal MidCap Fund Class A	PEMGX	B	B	B-		4.82	10.88	24.92	37.79	110.96	26.73	15,667	800-222-5852	
Principal MidCap Fund Class C	PMBCX	B	B	B-		4.64	10.50	24.07	34.89	103.39	24.37	15,667	800-222-5852	
Principal MidCap Fund Class J	PMBJX	B	B	B-		4.88	11.00	25.19	38.48	112.29	25.75	15,667	800-222-5852	
PRINCIPAL MIDCAP FUND Class R-6	PMAQX	B	B	B-		4.94	11.11	25.40	38.76	112.99	27.25	15,667	800-222-5852	Y
Principal MidCap Fund Institutional Class	PCBIX	B	B	B-		4.89	11.05	25.32	39.11	114.35	27.28	15,667	800-222-5852	
Principal MidCap Fund R-1 Class	PMSBX	B	B	B-		4.70	10.61	24.40	35.83	105.93	24.96	15,667	800-222-5852	
Principal MidCap Fund R-2 Class	PMBNX	B	B	B-		4.71	10.68	24.50	36.39	107.27	25.33	15,667	800-222-5852	
Principal MidCap Fund R-3 Class	PMBMX	B	B	B-		4.76	10.75	24.73	37.10	109.17	26.2	15,667	800-222-5852	
Principal MidCap Fund R-4 Class	PMBSX	B	B	B-		4.78	10.87	24.95	37.89	111.08	27.16	15,667	800-222-5852	
Principal MidCap Fund R-5 Class	PMBPX	B	B	B-		4.86	10.95	25.16	38.42	112.47	26.97	15,667	800-222-5852	
Principal MidCap Growth Fund Class J	PMGJX	B+	A-	B	Up	6.57	13.20	28.83	34.28	106.91	6.97	171.1	800-222-5852	Y
Principal MidCap Growth Fund III Class J	PPQJX	B-	B-	C+	Up	6.33	10.91	24.22	25.67	86.05	9.07	1,127	800-222-5852	Y
Principal MidCap Growth Fund III Institutional Class	PPIMX	B-	B	C+	Down	6.30	10.98	24.58	27.04	89.76	11.12	1,127	800-222-5852	Y
Principal MidCap Growth Fund III R-2 Class	PPQNX	B-	B-	C+	Up	6.23	10.70	23.70	24.39	82.95	9.57	1,127	800-222-5852	Y
Principal MidCap Growth Fund III R-3 Class	PPQMX	B-	B-	C+	Up	6.22	10.77	23.91	24.93	84.43	10.42	1,127	800-222-5852	Y

Category: US Equity Mid Cap (con't)

Fund Name	Ticker Symbol	RATINGS: Overall Rating	Reward Rating	Risk Rating	Recent Up/ Downgrade	TOTAL RETURNS & PERFORMANCE: 3-Month Total Return	6-Month Total Return	1-Year Total Return	3-Year Total Return	5-Year Total Return	ASSETS: NAV	Total Assets (MIL)	NEW INVESTORS: Telephone	Open to New Investors
Principal MidCap Growth Fund III R-4 Class	PPQSX	B-	B-	C+	Up	6.24	10.87	24.16	25.55	86.24	10.73	1,127	800-222-5852	Y
Principal MidCap Growth Fund III R-5 Class	PPQPX	B-	B-	C+	Up	6.35	10.90	24.37	26.07	87.36	11.21	1,127	800-222-5852	Y
Principal MidCap Growth Fund Institutional Class	PGWIX	B+	A-	B	Up	6.66	13.30	29.02	35.41	110.56	8.8	171.1	800-222-5852	Y
Principal MidCap Growth Fund R-1 Class	PMSGX	B+	B+	B	Up	6.46	12.99	28.12	32.41	102.49	7.25	171.1	800-222-5852	Y
Principal MidCap Growth Fund R-2 Class	PGPPX	B+	A-	B	Up	6.55	13.08	28.26	32.90	103.69	7.81	171.1	800-222-5852	Y
Principal MidCap Growth Fund R-3 Class	PFPPX	B+	A-	B	Up	6.54	13.12	28.49	33.49	105.68	8.3	171.1	800-222-5852	Y
Principal MidCap Growth Fund R-4 Class	PIPPX	B+	A-	B	Up	6.57	13.22	28.64	34.25	107.62	8.76	171.1	800-222-5852	Y
Principal MidCap Growth Fund R-5 Class	PHPPX	B+	A-	B	Up	6.68	13.38	28.93	34.85	108.89	9.09	171.1	800-222-5852	Y
Principal MidCap S&P 400 Index Fund Class J	PMFJX	B	B	B		6.18	9.45	15.74	33.78	98.69	20.85	1,463	800-222-5852	Y
Principal MidCap S&P 400 Index Fund Class R-6	PMAPX	B	B	B		6.25	9.60	15.96	34.30	100.24	21.4	1,463	800-222-5852	Y
Principal MidCap S&P 400 Index Fund Institutional Class	MPSIX	B	B	B		6.25	9.59	15.96	34.86	102.04	21.42	1,463	800-222-5852	Y
Principal MidCap S&P 400 Index Fund R-1 Class	PMSSX	B	B	B	Up	6.00	9.11	14.99	31.53	93.67	21.25	1,463	800-222-5852	Y
Principal MidCap S&P 400 Index Fund R-2 Class	PMFNX	B	B	B	Up	6.06	9.19	15.18	32.08	94.97	21.91	1,463	800-222-5852	Y
Principal MidCap S&P 400 Index Fund R-3 Class	PMFMX	B	B	B	Up	6.07	9.26	15.33	32.76	96.71	21.81	1,463	800-222-5852	Y
Principal MidCap S&P 400 Index Fund R-4 Class	PMFSX	B	B	B		6.14	9.37	15.60	33.48	98.62	21.87	1,463	800-222-5852	Y
Principal MidCap S&P 400 Index Fund R-5 Class	PMFPX	B	B	B		6.16	9.47	15.71	33.96	99.74	22.04	1,463	800-222-5852	Y
Principal MidCap Value Fund I Class J	PVEJX	B-	C+	B	Up	5.59	9.37	14.31	20.19	85.78	14.92	1,083	800-222-5852	Y
Principal MidCap Value Fund I Institutional Class	PVMIX	B-	B-	B	Up	5.67	9.55	14.61	21.34	89.16	15.07	1,083	800-222-5852	Y
Principal MidCap Value Fund I R-1 Class	PLASX	B-	C+	B	Up	5.43	9.08	13.67	18.27	81.24	14.49	1,083	800-222-5852	Y
Principal MidCap Value Fund I R-2 Class	PABUX	B-	C+	B	Up	5.52	9.15	13.86	18.71	82.37	14.63	1,083	800-222-5852	Y
Principal MidCap Value Fund I R-3 Class	PMPRX	B-	C+	B	Up	5.53	9.25	13.97	19.37	84.05	14.88	1,083	800-222-5852	Y
Principal MidCap Value Fund I R-4 Class	PABWX	B-	C+	B	Up	5.57	9.35	14.23	20.06	85.78	14.91	1,083	800-222-5852	Y
Principal MidCap Value Fund I R-5 Class	PABVX	B-	B-	B	Up	5.64	9.40	14.41	20.46	86.95	14.98	1,083	800-222-5852	Y
Principal MidCap Value Fund III Class A	PVCAX	B-	B-	B	Up	4.97	8.63	15.54	21.52	88.30	21.22	1,385	800-222-5852	Y
Principal MidCap Value Fund III Class J	PMCJX	B-	B-	B	Down	5.09	8.90	15.95	22.83	90.89	20.08	1,385	800-222-5852	Y
Principal MidCap Value Fund III Class R-6	PCMIX	B-	B-	C+	Down	5.10	8.97	16.73	24.31	93.78	21.49	1,385	800-222-5852	Y
Principal MidCap Value Fund III Institutional Class	PVUIX	B	B-	B	Up	5.06	8.94	16.15	23.76	93.74	21.38	1,385	800-222-5852	Y
Principal MidCap Value Fund III R-1 Class	PMSVX	B-	C+	B	Up	4.87	8.49	15.24	20.67	85.77	20.24	1,385	800-222-5852	Y
Principal MidCap Value Fund III R-2 Class	PKPPX	B-	C+	B	Up	4.96	8.61	15.43	21.17	86.95	20.39	1,385	800-222-5852	Y
Principal MidCap Value Fund III R-3 Class	PJPPX	B-	B-	B	Down	4.98	8.71	15.66	21.85	88.62	20.2	1,385	800-222-5852	Y
Principal MidCap Value Fund III R-4 Class	PMPPX	B-	B-	B	Down	5.07	8.84	15.87	22.57	90.50	19.98	1,385	800-222-5852	Y
Principal MidCap Value Fund III R-5 Class	PLPPX	B-	B-	B	Down	5.03	8.86	15.94	22.94	91.65	20.18	1,385	800-222-5852	Y
ProFunds Mid Cap Fund Investor Class	MDPIX	B	B	B	Up	5.79	8.57	14.16	28.86	87.11	87.55	51.1	614-470-8626	Y
ProFunds Mid Cap Fund Service Class	MDPSX	B	B-	B	Up	5.53	8.03	13.02	25.02	77.93	74	51.1	614-470-8626	Y
ProFunds Mid Cap Growth Fund Investor Class	MGPIX	B	B	B	Up	6.65	9.63	18.07	31.89	86.19	89.56	14.1	614-470-8626	Y
ProFunds Mid Cap Growth Fund Service Class	MGPSX	B	B	B	Up	6.38	9.07	16.89	27.94	77.01	75.69	14.1	614-470-8626	Y
ProFunds Mid Cap Value Fund Investor Class	MLPIX	B	B	B	Up	4.89	7.85	10.41	24.49	84.70	75.35	8.2	614-470-8626	Y
ProFunds Mid Cap Value Fund Service Class	MLPSX	B-	B-	B-	Up	4.64	7.32	9.32	20.67	75.60	62.99	8.2	614-470-8626	Y
Prospector Opportunity Fund	POPFX	B+	B	A	Up	4.52	7.86	10.32	34.32	87.62	20.85	117.7	877-734-7862	Y
Prudential Jennison Mid-Cap Growth Fund, Inc Class B	PEEBX	B-	C+	B	Up	5.00	9.16	21.34	20.08	68.98	27.43	7,052	800-225-1852	
Prudential Jennison Mid-Cap Growth Fund, Inc Class Q	PJGQX	B-	B-	C+	Up	5.38	9.90	22.87	24.50	79.34	38.49	7,052	800-225-1852	
Prudential Jennison Mid-Cap Growth Fund, Inc Class Z	PEGZX	B-	B-	C+	Up	5.33	9.78	22.66	23.87	77.80	38.06	7,052	800-225-1852	
Prudential QMA Mid-Cap Value Fund Class A	SPRAX	B-	B-	B	Up	6.93	9.74	12.33	25.50	103.35	22.39	960.8	800-225-1852	Y
Prudential QMA Mid-Cap Value Fund Class B	SVUBX	B-	C+	B	Up	6.73	9.33	11.52	22.75	95.79	19.34	960.8	800-225-1852	
Prudential QMA Mid-Cap Value Fund Class C	NCBVX	B-	C+	B	Up	6.72	9.33	11.52	22.73	95.85	19.25	960.8	800-225-1852	Y
Prudential QMA Mid-Cap Value Fund Class Q	PMVQX	B	B-	B	Up	7.00	9.94	12.77	27.05	107.25	22.54	960.8	800-225-1852	Y
Prudential QMA Mid-Cap Value Fund Class R	SDVRX	B-	B-	B	Up	6.90	9.64	12.11	24.60	98.83	22.58	960.8	800-225-1852	Y
Prudential QMA Mid-Cap Value Fund Class Z	SPVZX	B	B-	B	Up	6.98	9.86	12.63	26.45	105.85	22.6	960.8	800-225-1852	Y
Putnam Multi-Cap Value Fund Class A	PMVAX	B-	C+	B	Up	2.77	5.69	10.63	18.59	91.00	19.91	455.4	617-292-1000	Y
Putnam Multi-Cap Value Fund Class B	PMVBX	B-	C+	B	Up	2.57	5.27	9.85	15.95	84.02	18.27	455.4	617-292-1000	Y
Putnam Multi-Cap Value Fund Class C	PMPCX	B-	C+	B	Up	2.59	5.31	9.86	15.99	84.02	18.15	455.4	617-292-1000	Y
Putnam Multi-Cap Value Fund Class M	PMCVX	B-	C+	B	Up	2.59	5.43	10.12	16.80	86.34	18.9	455.4	617-292-1000	Y

Category: US Equity Mid Cap (con't)

Fund Name	Ticker Symbol	RATINGS: Overall Rating	Reward Rating	Risk Rating	Recent Up/ Downgrade	TOTAL RETURNS & PERFORMANCE: 3-Month Total Return	6-Month Total Return	1-Year Total Return	3-Year Total Return	5-Year Total Return	ASSETS: NAV	Total Assets (MIL)	NEW INVESTORS: Telephone	Open to New Investors
Putnam Multi-Cap Value Fund Class R	PMVRX	B-	C+	B	Up	2.68	5.57	10.39	17.70	88.71	19.4	455.4	617-292-1000	Y
Putnam Multi-Cap Value Fund Class Y	PMVYX	B-	C+	B	Up	2.86	5.89	10.95	19.52	93.46	19.98	455.4	617-292-1000	Y
Pzena Mid Cap Value Fund Institutional Class	PZIMX	B+	A-	B	Up	6.24	10.78	14.56	37.20		13.09	8.3		Y
Pzena Mid Cap Value Fund Investor Class	PZVMX	B+	A-	B	Up	6.30	10.77	14.36	36.29		13.09	8.3		Y
Quaker Mid-Cap Value Fund Class A	QMCVX	B-	B-	B-	Up	6.45	11.65	16.42	25.26	93.39	31.33	7.2	800-220-8888	Y
Quaker Mid-Cap Value Fund Class C	QMCCX	B-	B-	B-	Up	6.22	11.22	15.55	22.48	86.18	26.96	7.2	800-220-8888	Y
Quaker Mid-Cap Value Fund Class Institutional	QMVIX	B-	B	B-	Up	6.50	11.79	16.71	26.20	95.79	33.09	7.2	800-220-8888	Y
Quantified All-Cap Equity Fund Advisor Class	QACAX	B-	B-	B-	Down	5.31	9.05	17.95	24.62		10.52	10.0		Y
Quantified All-Cap Equity Fund Investor Class	QACFX	B-	B-	B-	Down	5.51	9.41	18.83	27.22		10.63	10.0		Y
Quantified Market Leaders Fund Advisor Class	QMLAX	B	B+	B	Up	5.52	14.94	16.12	24.77		11.06	98.8		Y
Quantified Market Leaders Fund Investor Class	QMLFX	B+	A-	B	Up	5.69	15.32	16.82	27.32		11.18	98.8		Y
Rainier Small/Mid Cap Equity Fund Institutional Shares	RAISX	B	B-	B	Up	5.09	9.85	20.06	25.36	80.49	39.73	266.1	800-248-6314	
Rainier Small/Mid Cap Equity Fund Original Shares	RIMSX	B	B-	B	Up	5.05	9.70	19.64	24.14	77.61	36.98	266.1	800-248-6314	
RBB Free Market U.S. Equity Fund Institutional Class	FMUEX	B	B	B	Up	4.78	10.23	13.44	30.55	99.40	18.78	3,032		Y
RBC SMID Cap Growth Fund Class A	TMCAX	B	B	B+	Up	3.57	6.31	16.73	28.59	81.75	12.15	79.4	800-422-2766	Y
RBC SMID Cap Growth Fund Class I	TMCIX	B	B	B+		3.67	6.42	17.06	29.53	84.11	13.76	79.4	800-422-2766	Y
RBC SMID Cap Growth Fund Class R6	RSMRX	B	B	B+		3.66	6.41	17.13	29.53	84.10	13.77	79.4	800-422-2766	Y
Reinhart Mid Cap PMV Fund Advisor Class	RPMVX	B-	C+	B		5.15	5.81	10.72	28.10	82.41	15.51	196.2	855-774-3863	Y
Reinhart Mid Cap PMV Fund Institutional Class	RPMNX	B-	C+	B		5.19	5.85	10.76	28.14	82.48	15.51	196.2	855-774-3863	Y
Reinhart Mid Cap PMV Fund Investor Class	RPMMX	B-	C+	B		5.10	5.69	10.47	27.25	80.27	15.5	196.2	855-774-3863	Y
Rice Hall James Smid Cap Portfolio Investor	RHJVX	B-	C+	B	Up	3.43	5.28	13.42	13.71	64.45	22.3	4.5	619-239-9005	Y
Riverbridge Eco Leaders® Fund Institutional Class	RIVEX	B-	C+	B	Up	7.71	9.23	23.98	35.17		13.13	2.7		
Riverbridge Eco Leaders® Fund Investor Class	ECOLX	B-	C+	B	Up	7.76	9.12	23.71	34.26		13.04	2.7		
Riverbridge Growth Fund Institutional Class	RIVBX	B	B	A-	Up	7.97	9.94	25.41	37.21	96.21	18.07	85.0		Y
Riverbridge Growth Fund Investor Class	RIVRX	B	B	A-	Up	7.94	9.80	25.10	36.29	93.94	17.85	85.0		Y
Rock Oak Core Growth Fund	RCKSX	B-	B	C	Up	5.75	11.60	22.68	26.70	91.34	15.63	9.4	888-462-5386	Y
Royce Dividend Value Fund Consultant Class	RDVCX	B-	B-	C+	Up	6.41	12.46	20.70	29.45	67.02	8.87	189.3	800-221-4268	Y
Royce Dividend Value Fund Institutional Shares	RDIIX	B	B	C+	Up	6.69	13.10	22.21	33.62	76.51	7.46	189.3	800-221-4268	Y
Royce Dividend Value Fund Investment Class	RDVIX	B	B	C+	Up	6.61	13.07	21.91	33.45	75.97	7.56	189.3	800-221-4268	Y
Royce Dividend Value Fund Service Class	RYDVX	B-	B	C+		6.54	12.93	21.65	32.49	73.59	7.76	189.3	800-221-4268	Y
Royce Small/Mid-Cap Premier Fund Class R	RHFRX	B	B	B	Up	8.03	14.48	20.60	30.72	65.12	10.15	210.5	800-221-4268	Y
Royce Small/Mid-Cap Premier Fund Consultant Class	RYGCX	B-	B-	B-		7.90	14.19	20.09	29.21	61.50	11.06	210.5	800-221-4268	Y
Royce Small/Mid-Cap Premier Fund Investment Class	RHFHX	B	B	B	Up	8.16	14.87	21.46	33.51	71.29	15.66	210.5	800-221-4268	Y
Royce Small/Mid-Cap Premier Fund Service Class	RGFAX	B	B	B	Up	8.10	14.68	21.20	32.62	69.08	15.61	210.5	800-221-4268	Y
Russell Investments U.S. Mid Cap Equity Fund Class A	RMCAX	B	B-	B	Up	5.41	7.47	14.86	26.28	93.57	11.82	170.7	800-426-7969	Y
Russell Investments U.S. Mid Cap Equity Fund Class C	RMCCX	B	B-	B	Up	5.28	7.14	14.09	23.56	86.50	11.44	170.7	800-426-7969	Y
Russell Investments U.S. Mid Cap Equity Fund Class S	RMCSX	B	B-	B	Up	5.51	7.72	15.27	27.31	95.95	11.87	170.7	800-426-7969	Y
Rydex S&P MidCap 400 Pure Growth Fund Class A	RYMGX	B-	C+	B	Up	6.52	9.59	18.94	22.90	67.91	53.96	126.2	800-820-0888	Y
Rydex S&P MidCap 400 Pure Growth Fund Class C	RYCKX	B-	C+	B	Up	6.33	9.18	18.07	20.16	61.74	46.88	126.2	800-820-0888	Y
Rydex S&P MidCap 400 Pure Growth Fund Class H	RYBHX	B-	C+	B	Up	6.52	9.58	18.94	22.89	67.89	54.02	126.2	800-820-0888	Y
Saratoga Mid Capitalization Portfolio Fund Cls Inst	SMIPX	B-	C+	B	Up	4.88	9.06	13.30	14.19	83.99	12.93	13.9	800-807-3863	Y
SEI Inst Investments Trust Extended Mkt Index Fund Cls A	SMXAX	B	B	C+	Up	4.90	10.11	18.26	32.25		15.19	912.3	800-342-5734	Y
SEI Institutional Managed Trust Mid-Cap Fund Class Y	SFDYX	B	B	B-		7.26	12.74	20.60	36.77	114.29	27.66	122.0	800-342-5734	Y
SEI Inst Managed Trust Mid-Cap Portfolio Fund Cls F	SEMCX	B	B	B+		7.18	12.59	20.33	35.99	113.06	27.65	122.0	800-342-5734	Y
SEI Inst Managed Trust Mid-Cap Portfolio Fund Cls I	SIPIX	B	B	B-		7.12	12.46	20.08	35.14	110.72	27.63	122.0	800-342-5734	Y
Shelton Capital Management S&P Midcap Index Fund Class K	MIDKX	B	B	B	Up	6.14	9.52	15.14	33.42	97.62	26.34	121.5	800-955-9988	Y
Shelton Capital Mgmt S&P Midcap Index Fund Direct Shares	SPMIX	B	B	B		6.26	9.78	15.69	35.42	102.63	26.68	121.5	800-955-9988	Y
Shelton Green Alpha Fund	NEXTX	B	B	B-	Up	2.78	7.24	29.51	24.65		17.76	42.5	800-955-9988	Y
Sit Mid Cap Growth Fund	NBNGX	B-	C+	B	Up	3.27	5.95	19.00	19.04	72.89	18.36	162.7	800-332-5580	Y
Sit Small Cap Growth Fund	SSMGX	B-	C+	B-	Up	2.72	7.63	15.70	15.87	63.29	54.62	97.3	800-332-5580	Y
Sparrow Growth Fund Class A	SGFFX	B-	B	C	Up	4.87	16.72	31.27	23.52	74.74	20.9	12.4		Y
Sparrow Growth Fund Class C	SGFCX	B-	B	B-	Up	4.72	16.45	30.58	21.70	70.50	19.79	12.4		Y

Category: US Equity Mid Cap (con't)

Fund Name	Ticker Symbol	RATINGS: Overall Rating	RATINGS: Reward Rating	RATINGS: Risk Rating	RATINGS: Recent Up/ Downgrade	TOTAL RETURNS & PERFORMANCE: 3-Month Total Return	6-Month Total Return	1-Year Total Return	3-Year Total Return	5-Year Total Return	ASSETS: NAV	Total Assets (MIL)	NEW INVESTORS: Telephone	Open to New Investors
Sparrow Growth Fund No-Load Class	SGNFX	B-	B	C	Up	4.93	16.90	31.62	24.44	76.99	20.21	12.4		Y
Sprott Focus Trust Inc.	FUND	B-	B	C+	Up	4.62	10.78	17.52	26.89	55.36	8.93	228.1	866-299-9906	Y
Sterling Capital Mid Value Fund Class A	OVEAX	B	B-	B	Up	5.47	6.49	13.86	28.56	101.93	18.89	753.8	800-228-1872	Y
Sterling Capital Mid Value Fund Class C	OVECX	B	B-	B	Up	5.21	6.03	12.96	25.64	94.48	16.78	753.8	800-228-1872	Y
Sterling Capital Mid Value Fund Class R	OVERX	B	B-	B	Up	5.42	6.30	13.62	27.49	97.72	18.28	753.8	800-228-1872	Y
Sterling Capital Mid Value Fund Institutional Shares	OVEIX	B	B-	B	Up	5.49	6.56	14.14	29.50	104.41	19.18	753.8	800-228-1872	Y
Sterling Capital Stratton Mid Cap Value Fund A Shares	STRLX	B	B	B	Up	6.74	13.22	21.45	31.28	99.31	68.23	70.1	800-228-1872	Y
Sterling Capital Stratton Mid Cap Value Fund C Shares	STRNX	B	B	B	Up	6.55	12.76	20.54	28.41	92.07	67.37	70.1	800-228-1872	Y
Sterling Capital Stratton Mid Cap Value Fund Inst Shares	STRGX	B	B	B	Up	6.81	13.35	21.75	32.28	101.83	68.38	70.1	800-228-1872	Y
T. Rowe Price Diversified Mid Cap Growth Fund	PRDMX	B	B	B-	Up	5.89	10.61	24.72	35.90	109.01	29.4	841.7	410-345-2000	Y
T. Rowe Price Diversified Mid Cap Growth Fund I Class	RPTTX	B	B	B-		5.92	10.67	24.88	36.08	109.29	29.41	841.7	410-345-2000	Y
T. Rowe Price Extended Equity Market Index Fund	PEXMX	B	B	B	Up	4.58	9.82	17.95	31.28	100.68	28.2	859.2	410-345-2000	Y
T. Rowe Price Institutional Mid-Cap Equity Growth Fund	PMEGX	B	B	B	Down	4.63	9.40	26.02	43.06	130.19	54.48	7,137	410-345-2000	
T. Rowe Price Mid-Cap Growth Fund	RPMGX	B	B	B	Down	4.43	8.92	24.85	40.41	122.90	87.02	30,423	410-345-2000	
T. Rowe Price Mid-Cap Growth Fund Advisor Class	PAMCX	B	B	B	Down	4.36	8.78	24.53	39.31	120.07	84.5	30,423	410-345-2000	
T. Rowe Price Mid-Cap Growth Fund I Class	RPTIX	B	B	B	Down	4.46	9.00	25.02	40.83	123.57	87.01	30,423	410-345-2000	Y
T. Rowe Price Mid-Cap Growth Fund R Class	RRMGX	B	B	B	Down	4.30	8.66	24.20	38.27	117.29	82.06	30,423	410-345-2000	
T. Rowe Price Mid-Cap Value Fund	TRMCX	B	B-	B	Up	5.16	8.28	11.64	32.86	98.08	30.4	14,034	410-345-2000	
T. Rowe Price Mid-Cap Value Fund Advisor Class	TAMVX	B	B-	B	Up	5.09	8.16	11.33	31.85	95.59	30.28	14,034	410-345-2000	
T. Rowe Price Mid-Cap Value Fund I Class	TRMIX	B	B-	B	Up	5.19	8.39	11.78	33.25	98.67	30.39	14,034	410-345-2000	Y
T. Rowe Price Mid-Cap Value Fund R Class	RRMVX	B	B-	B	Up	4.49	7.48	10.49	30.22	92.11	29.82	14,034	410-345-2000	
Tarkio Fund	TARKX	B+	A+	C	Up	5.46	12.19	29.03	50.80	135.07	21.64	101.2	406-541-0130	Y
TCW Relative Value Mid Cap Fund Class I	TGVOX	B	B+	B-	Up	6.12	12.99	19.70	31.57	94.40	25.16	106.6	213-244-0000	Y
TCW Relative Value Mid Cap Fund Class N	TGVNX	B	B+	B-	Up	6.12	12.94	19.51	30.77	92.25	24.5	106.6	213-244-0000	Y
TETON Westwood Mid-Cap Equity Fund Class A Shares	WMCAX	B-	C+	B	Up	4.60	6.63	19.81	21.34		13.18	3.1		Y
TETON Westwood Mid-Cap Equity Fund Class AAA Shares	WMCEX	B-	B-	B	Up	4.55	6.72	20.07	22.21		13.33	3.1		Y
TETON Westwood Mid-Cap Equity Fund Class C Shares	WMCCX	B-	C+	B	Up	4.39	6.29	19.21	19.51		12.85	3.1		Y
TETON Westwood Mid-Cap Equity Fund Class I Shares	WMCRX	B-	B-	B	Up	4.64	6.86	20.36	23.42		13.52	3.1		Y
The Hartford MidCap Fund Class A	HFMCX	B	B+	B	Up	7.34	10.86	23.93	38.96	118.71	30.02	10,481	888-843-7824	Y
The Hartford MidCap Fund Class C	HMDCX	B	B	B-	Up	7.13	10.46	23.04	35.94	110.88	22.03	10,481	888-843-7824	Y
The Hartford MidCap Fund Class F	HMDFX	B+	B+	B	Up	7.46	11.08	24.40	40.59	123.05	30.86	10,481	888-843-7824	Y
The Hartford MidCap Fund Class I	HFMIX	B	B+	B	Up	7.43	11.06	24.28	39.90	121.34	30.83	10,481	888-843-7824	Y
The Hartford MidCap Fund Class R3	HFMRX	B	B+	B-	Up	7.24	10.68	23.53	37.57	115.23	33.39	10,481	888-843-7824	Y
The Hartford MidCap Fund Class R4	HFMSX	B	B+	B	Up	7.30	10.87	23.92	38.85	118.57	34.59	10,481	888-843-7824	Y
The Hartford MidCap Fund Class R5	HFMTX	B	B+	B	Up	7.40	11.05	24.30	40.16	121.96	35.46	10,481	888-843-7824	Y
The Hartford MidCap Fund Class R6	HFMVX	B+	B+	B	Up	7.42	11.08	24.42	40.55	123.07	35.78	10,481	888-843-7824	Y
The Hartford MidCap Fund Class Y	HMDYX	B+	B+	B	Up	7.43	11.05	24.35	40.53	122.96	35.76	10,481	888-843-7824	Y
Thomas White American Opportunities Fund Investor Class	TWAOX	B	B-	B+	Up	6.76	10.49	16.99	25.56	92.04	17.21	42.9	800-811-0535	Y
Thompson MidCap Fund	THPMX	B-	B-	B-	Up	6.89	7.62	17.06	25.61	95.20	13.15	50.9	800-999-0887	Y
Thrivent Mid Cap Stock Fund Class A	AASCX	B+	B+	B+	Up	7.26	10.66	18.51	51.03	133.40	25.3	1,783		Y
Thrivent Mid Cap Stock Fund Class S	TMSIX	B+	B+	B+	Up	7.35	10.88	18.93	52.74	138.14	28.49	1,783		Y
Thrivent Series Mid Cap Index Portfolio		B	B	B		6.17	9.52	15.97	34.69	100.96	18.9856	392.3		Y
Thrivent Series Mid Cap Stock Portfolio		B+	B+	B+	Up	7.37	10.91	18.99	52.07	136.61	20.8172	1,740		Y
TIAA-CREF Mid-Cap Growth Fund Advisor Class	TCMHX	B-	B	C+	Up	5.52	11.65	26.13	27.11	91.64	22.53	1,638	877-518-9161	Y
TIAA-CREF Mid-Cap Growth Fund Institutional Class	TRPWX	B	B	B	Up	5.54	11.67	26.21	27.20	91.79	22.53	1,638	877-518-9161	Y
TIAA-CREF Mid-Cap Growth Fund Premier Class	TRGPX	B	B	B	Up	5.54	11.65	26.04	26.65	90.41	22.41	1,638	877-518-9161	Y
TIAA-CREF Mid-Cap Growth Fund Retail Class	TCMGX	B	B	B	Up	5.48	11.54	25.80	26.02	88.84	21.89	1,638	877-518-9161	Y
TIAA-CREF Mid-Cap Growth Fund Retirement Class	TRGMX	B	B	B	Up	5.48	11.58	25.89	26.25	89.50	21.91	1,638	877-518-9161	Y
TIAA-CREF Mid-Cap Value Fund Advisor Class	TRVHX	B-	B-	B	Down	3.80	6.58	10.94	22.15	87.70	23.44	4,560	877-518-9161	Y
TIAA-CREF Mid-Cap Value Fund Institutional Class	TIMVX	B-	B-	B	Down	3.85	6.71	11.12	22.32	87.96	23.45	4,560	877-518-9161	Y
TIAA-CREF Mid-Cap Value Fund Premier Class	TRVPX	B-	B-	B	Down	3.81	6.64	10.96	21.74	86.52	23.41	4,560	877-518-9161	Y
TIAA-CREF Mid-Cap Value Fund Retail Class	TCMVX	B-	C+	B		3.80	6.56	10.78	21.24	85.16	22.88	4,560	877-518-9161	Y

Category: US Equity Mid Cap (con't)

Fund Name	Ticker Symbol	RATINGS				TOTAL RETURNS & PERFORMANCE					ASSETS		NEW INVESTORS	
		Overall Rating	Reward Rating	Risk Rating	Recent Up/ Downgrade	3-Month Total Return	6-Month Total Return	1-Year Total Return	3-Year Total Return	5-Year Total Return	NAV	Total Assets (Mil)	Telephone	Open to New Investors
TIAA-CREF Mid-Cap Value Fund Retirement Class	TRVRX	B-	C+	B		3.76	6.55	10.79	21.38	85.61	23.32	4,560	877-518-9161	Y
Timothy Plan Large/Mid Cap Value Fund Class A	TLVAX	B	C+	B+	Up	6.89	9.46	17.50	23.80	85.75	19.18	217.8	800-662-0201	Y
Timothy Plan Large/Mid Cap Value Fund Class C	TLVCX	B	C+	B	Up	6.72	9.14	16.68	21.08	78.99	15.61	217.8	800-662-0201	Y
Timothy Plan Large/Mid Cap Value Fund Class I	TMVIX	B	B-	B+	Up	6.97	9.63	17.81	24.78	87.63	19.34	217.8	800-662-0201	Y
Tocqueville Opportunity Fund	TOPPX	B	A-	C+	Up	5.71	11.95	34.65	28.48	104.73	25.5	79.5	212-698-0800	Y
Touchstone Mid Cap Fund Class A	TMAPX	B	B	B		6.79	13.13	19.92	29.29	95.71	32.26	828.7	800-543-0407	Y
Touchstone Mid Cap Fund Class C	TMCJX	B	B-	B		6.55	12.73	19.02	26.42	88.55	30.61	828.7	800-543-0407	Y
Touchstone Mid Cap Fund Class Y	TMCPX	B	B	B		6.82	13.26	20.22	30.29	98.22	32.51	828.7	800-543-0407	Y
Touchstone Mid Cap Fund Class Z	TMCTX	B	B	B		6.80	13.14	19.93	29.33	95.79	32.07	828.7	800-543-0407	Y
Touchstone Mid Cap Fund Institutional	TMPIX	B	B	B		6.85	13.32	20.32	30.55	98.88	32.54	828.7	800-543-0407	Y
Touchstone Mid Cap Growth Fund Class A	TEGAX	B	B	C+	Up	5.29	8.97	24.16	30.09	102.72	27.16	753.3	800-543-0407	Y
Touchstone Mid Cap Growth Fund Class C	TOECX	B-	B	C+	Down	5.09	8.55	23.24	27.16	95.37	17.72	753.3	800-543-0407	Y
Touchstone Mid Cap Growth Fund Class Y	TEGYX	B	B	C+	Up	5.37	9.09	24.47	31.01	105.32	28.13	753.3	800-543-0407	Y
Touchstone Mid Cap Growth Fund Institutional Class	TEGIX	B	B	B-	Up	5.36	9.13	24.54	31.36	106.38	28.37	753.3	800-543-0407	Y
Touchstone Mid Cap Value Class A	TCVAX	B	B	B		4.25	7.68	13.67	32.61	97.37	19.02	747.3	800-543-0407	Y
Touchstone Mid Cap Value Class C	TMFCX	B	B	B		4.05	7.23	12.81	29.62	90.13	18.56	747.3	800-543-0407	Y
Touchstone Mid Cap Value Fund Class Y	TCVYX	B	B	B		4.30	7.77	13.91	33.57	99.87	19.11	747.3	800-543-0407	Y
Touchstone Mid Cap Value Institutional Class	TCVIX	B	B	B+		4.36	7.86	14.10	34.17	101.35	19.21	747.3	800-543-0407	Y
Transamerica Mid Cap Growth A	MCGAX	B	B	B	Up	6.25	9.38	20.85	30.97	86.71	14.62	259.4	888-233-4339	Y
Transamerica Mid Cap Growth Advisor	TAMGX	B	B	B	Up	6.40	9.50	21.09	32.69	91.63	14.72	259.4	888-233-4339	Y
Transamerica Mid Cap Growth C	MGTCX	B	B	B	Up	6.04	8.92	19.85	27.91	79.74	14.22	259.4	888-233-4339	Y
Transamerica Mid Cap Growth Class T1	IMCTX	B	B	B	Up	6.31	9.44	21.15	32.75	91.72	14.63	259.4	888-233-4339	Y
Transamerica Mid Cap Growth I	IMCGX	B	B	B	Up	6.34	9.52	21.10	32.08	88.80	14.72	259.4	888-233-4339	Y
Transamerica Mid Cap Growth I2	US89355J3591	B	B	B	Up	6.34	9.60	21.25	32.43	89.64	14.75	259.4	888-233-4339	Y
Transamerica Mid Cap Growth I3	TMITX	B	B	B	Up	6.44	9.61	21.34	31.50	87.48	14.78	259.4	888-233-4339	Y
Transamerica Mid Cap Growth R	TMIRX	B	B	B	Up	6.26	9.36	20.87	31.79	89.38	14.76	259.4	888-233-4339	Y
Transamerica Mid Cap Value Fund Class I2	US8939615659	B	B-	B+		4.83	7.12	13.80	25.82	96.88	16.05	220.4	888-233-4339	
Transamerica Mid Cap Value Opportunities A	MCVAX	B	C+	A	Up	4.59	2.36	9.34	27.74		11.59	1,673	888-233-4339	Y
Transamerica Mid Cap Value Opportunities Advisor	TAMOX	B	C+	A	Up	4.66	2.47	9.44	27.86		11.77	1,673	888-233-4339	Y
Transamerica Mid Cap Value Opportunities C	MCVCX	B	C+	A-	Up	4.39	1.88	8.43	24.88		11.48	1,673	888-233-4339	Y
Transamerica Mid Cap Value Opportunities Class T1	MVTTX	B	C+	A	Up	4.69	2.47	9.40	27.17		11.63	1,673	888-233-4339	Y
Transamerica Mid Cap Value Opportunities I	MVTIX	B	C+	A	Up	4.64	2.51	9.65	28.66		11.64	1,673	888-233-4339	Y
Transamerica Mid Cap Value Opportunities I2	US89354D7672	B	C+	A	Up	4.74	2.52	9.65	28.99		11.65	1,673	888-233-4339	Y
Transamerica Mid Cap Value Opportunities I3	TOTTX	B	C+	A	Up	4.76	2.63	9.72	28.18		11.71	1,673	888-233-4339	Y
Transamerica Mid Cap Value Opportunities R	TOTRX	B	C+	A-	Up	4.62	2.32	9.16	26.26		11.71	1,673	888-233-4339	Y
Transamerica Mid Cap Value Opportunities R4	TOTFX	B	C+	A	Up	4.63	2.42	9.42	27.20		11.71	1,673	888-233-4339	Y
Transamerica Mid Cap Value Opportunities R6	MVTRX	B	C+	A	Up	4.79	2.59	9.77	28.36		11.74	1,673	888-233-4339	Y
Transamerica Small/Mid Cap Value Fund Class A	IIVAX	B	B	B	Up	5.54	7.56	15.14	33.47	95.11	27.3	909.6	888-233-4339	Y
Transamerica Small/Mid Cap Value Fund Class Advisor	TASDX	B	B	B	Up	5.59	7.71	15.38	33.76	95.53	28.51	909.6	888-233-4339	Y
Transamerica Small/Mid Cap Value Fund Class B	IIVBX	B	B	B	Up	5.33	7.16	14.28	30.50	88.14	24.17	909.6	888-233-4339	
Transamerica Small/Mid Cap Value Fund Class C	IIVLX	B	B	B	Up	5.37	7.19	14.32	30.77	88.70	23.77	909.6	888-233-4339	Y
Transamerica Small/Mid Cap Value Fund Class I	TSVIX	B	B	B	Up	5.63	7.74	15.50	34.86	98.71	28.19	909.6	888-233-4339	Y
Transamerica Small/Mid Cap Value Fund Class I2	TSMVX	B	B	B	Up	5.68	7.82	15.61	35.29	99.71	28.23	909.6	888-233-4339	Y
Transamerica Small/Mid Cap Value Fund Class R6	TASMX	B	B	B	Up	5.62	7.78	15.59	35.04	97.41	28.34	909.6	888-233-4339	Y
Transamerica Small/Mid Cap Value Fund Class T1	TASWX	B	B	B		5.57	7.63	15.25	33.60	95.30	27.31	909.6	888-233-4339	Y
Tributary Growth Opportunities Fund Cls Institutional Plus	FOGPX	B	B	B	Up	4.89	9.64	20.85	29.03	90.76	16.27	141.0		Y
Tributary Growth Opportunities Fund Institutional Class	FOGRX	B	B-	B	Up	4.86	9.56	20.66	28.14	88.74	15.95	141.0		Y
U.S. Global Investors Holmes Macro Trends Fund	MEGAX	B-	C+	B		9.00	12.08	19.17	27.32	69.95	19.52	41.0	800-873-8637	Y
USAA Extended Market Index Fund	USMIX	B	B	B	Up	4.73	9.86	17.71	29.81	96.14	18.98	765.4	800-531-8722	Y
VALIC Company I Mid Cap Index Fund	VMIDX	B	B	B		6.24	9.53	15.90	34.91	101.70	29.42	3,560		Y
VALIC Company I Mid Cap Strategic Growth Fund	VMSGX	B	B	C+	Up	5.97	11.26	26.28	34.08	96.20	15.61	281.4		Y
VALIC Company I Small-Mid Growth Fund	VSSGX	B	B	B	Up	5.12	10.99	27.76	26.45	94.23	13.53	116.1		Y

Category: US Equity Mid Cap (con't)

Fund Name	Ticker Symbol	RATINGS: Overall Rating	Reward Rating	Risk Rating	Recent Up/ Downgrade	TOTAL RETURNS & PERFORMANCE: 3-Month Total Return	6-Month Total Return	1-Year Total Return	3-Year Total Return	5-Year Total Return	ASSETS: NAV	Total Assets (MIL)	NEW INVESTORS: Telephone	Open to New Investors
VALIC Company II Mid Cap Growth Fund	VAMGX	B	B+	C+	Up	7.36	11.02	31.59	35.65	85.84	11.08	147.8		Y
VALIC Company II Mid Cap Value Fund	VMCVX	B	B	B	Up	4.94	9.05	14.46	27.59	87.85	23.12	1,084		Y
Value Line Mid Cap Focused Fund	VLIFX	B	B	A		4.32	6.89	19.83	35.66	96.30	19.19	150.4	800-243-2729	Y
Value Line Mid Cap Focused Fund Institutional Class	VLMIX	B+	B	A		4.31	6.95	19.89	35.73	96.40	19.2	150.4	800-243-2729	Y
Value Line Premier Growth Fund	VALSX	B	B-	B+		5.47	8.67	22.31	30.05	79.89	33.11	345.2	800-243-2729	Y
Vanguard Extended Market Index Fund Admiral Shares	VEXAX	B	B	B	Up	4.82	10.02	18.10	31.68	101.14	84.76	62,586	877-662-7447	Y
Vanguard Extended Mkt Index Fund Inst Plus Shares	VEMPX	B	B	B	Up	4.82	10.03	18.12	31.82	101.48	209.16	62,586	877-662-7447	Y
Vanguard Extended Mkt Index Fund Inst Select Shares	VSEMX	B	B	B	Up	4.82	10.04	18.17	31.54	100.35	136.19	62,586	877-662-7447	Y
Vanguard Extended Market Index Fund Institutional Shares	VIEIX	B	B	B	Up	4.81	10.01	18.12	31.76	101.30	84.75	62,586	877-662-7447	Y
Vanguard Extended Market Index Fund Investor Shares	VEXMX	B	B	B	Up	4.77	9.94	17.94	31.16	99.78	84.8	62,586	877-662-7447	Y
Vanguard Mid-Cap Growth Fund Investor Shares	VMGRX	B-	B-	C+	Up	5.97	10.46	22.00	21.89	85.63	26.41	4,340	877-662-7447	Y
Vanguard Mid-Cap Growth Index Fund Admiral Shares	VMGMX	B-	B	C+	Down	5.04	8.97	21.82	27.81	96.76	54.96	11,298	877-662-7447	Y
Vanguard Mid-Cap Growth Index Fund Investor Shares	VMGIX	B-	B	C+	Down	5.01	8.91	21.71	27.38	95.55	50.21	11,298	877-662-7447	Y
Vanguard Mid-Cap Index Fund Admiral Shares	VIMAX	B-	B-	B-	Down	5.64	9.27	19.25	29.71	104.73	191.55	93,725	877-662-7447	Y
Vanguard Mid-Cap Index Fund Institutional Plus Shares	VMCPX	B-	B-	B-	Down	5.64	9.28	19.28	29.80	104.99	208.69	93,725	877-662-7447	Y
Vanguard Mid-Cap Index Fund Institutional Shares	VMCIX	B-	B-	B-	Down	5.66	9.29	19.29	29.76	104.90	42.32	93,725	877-662-7447	Y
Vanguard Mid-Cap Index Fund Investor Shares	VIMSX	B-	B-	B-	Down	5.61	9.21	19.11	29.23	103.40	42.23	93,725	877-662-7447	Y
Vanguard Mid-Cap Value Index Fund Admiral Shares	VMVAX	B	B	B+		6.14	9.47	17.04	31.11	111.33	57.74	16,764	877-662-7447	Y
Vanguard Mid-Cap Value Index Fund Investor Shares	VMVIX	B-	B	B-	Down	6.13	9.41	16.91	30.67	109.96	43.89	16,764	877-662-7447	Y
Vanguard S&P Mid-Cap 400 Growth Index Fund Inst Shares	VMFGX	B+	B+	B+	Up	7.07	10.47	19.86	38.75	103.36	265.15	1,000	877-662-7447	Y
Vanguard S&P Mid-Cap 400 Index Fund Institutional Shares	VSPMX	B	B	B		6.24	9.65	16.18	35.62	103.84	254.85	2,112	877-662-7447	Y
Vanguard S&P Mid-Cap 400 Value Index Fund Inst Shares	VMFVX	B	B	B	Up	5.35	8.77	12.26	31.02	101.94	243.78	844.3	877-662-7447	Y
Vanguard Selected Value Fund Investor Shares	VASVX	B	B	B	Up	5.34	10.56	19.51	32.63	105.69	31.27	10,803	877-662-7447	Y
Vanguard Strategic Equity Fund Investor Shares	VSEQX	B	B	B	Up	5.56	8.64	13.78	30.97	117.09	33.97	7,344	877-662-7447	Y
Victory Integrity Mid-Cap Value Fund Class A	MAIMX	B	B	B	Up	6.49	11.67	16.07	29.07	100.60	19.23	64.3	800-539-3863	Y
Victory Integrity Mid-Cap Value Fund Class R6	MRIMX	B	B	B	Up	6.59	11.85	16.44	30.11	103.34	19.34	64.3	800-539-3863	Y
Victory Integrity Mid-Cap Value Fund Class Y	MYIMX	B	B	B	Up	6.56	11.75	16.32	30.14	103.39	19.37	64.3	800-539-3863	Y
Victory Integrity Small/Mid-Cap Value Fund Class A	MAISX	B	B	B-	Up	7.58	14.49	18.10	29.83	91.16	18.12	78.2	800-539-3863	Y
Victory Integrity Small/Mid-Cap Value Fund Class R6	MIRSX	B	B	B-	Up	7.62	14.66	18.46	30.99	93.77	18.3	78.2	800-539-3863	Y
Victory Integrity Small/Mid-Cap Value Fund Class Y	MYISX	B	B	B-	Up	7.59	14.64	18.38	30.75	93.41	18.26	78.2	800-539-3863	Y
Victory Munder Mid-Cap Core Growth Fund Class A	MGOAX	B-	B-	C+	Up	5.95	11.81	24.16	25.72	89.40	34.48	4,105	800-539-3863	Y
Victory Munder Mid-Cap Core Growth Fund Class R	MMSRX	B-	B-	C+	Up	5.92	11.71	23.85	24.81	87.07	32.89	4,105	800-539-3863	Y
Victory Munder Mid-Cap Core Growth Fund Class R6	MGOSX	B-	B	C+	Up	6.07	12.08	24.72	27.45	93.62	37.2	4,105	800-539-3863	Y
Victory Munder Mid-Cap Core Growth Fund Class Y	MGOYX	B-	B	C+	Up	5.99	11.98	24.50	26.71	91.84	36.66	4,105	800-539-3863	Y
Victory RS Investors Fund Class A	RSINX	B-	B-	B		2.33	8.41	16.28	21.44	89.81	13.86	60.7	800-539-3863	Y
Victory RS Investors Fund Class C	RIVCX	B-	C+	B		2.16	8.01	15.48	18.84	82.87	12.69	60.7	800-539-3863	Y
Victory RS Investors Fund Class R	RSIKX	B-	C+	B		2.13	8.01	15.50	19.41	84.67	12.81	60.7	800-539-3863	Y
Victory RS Investors Fund Class Y	RSIYX	B-	B-	B		2.36	8.50	16.59	22.49	92.23	14.1	60.7	800-539-3863	Y
Victory RS Mid Cap Growth Fund Class A	RSMOX	B	B	B	Up	5.74	10.17	20.87	27.07	101.01	25.77	449.1	800-539-3863	Y
Victory RS Mid Cap Growth Fund Class C	RMOCX	B	B-	B	Up	5.54	9.68	19.81	23.70	92.37	23.22	449.1	800-539-3863	Y
Victory RS Mid Cap Growth Fund Class R	RSMKX	B	B-	B	Up	5.64	9.87	20.20	25.06	95.86	24.15	449.1	800-539-3863	Y
Victory RS Mid Cap Growth Fund Class R6	RMORX	B	B	B	Up	5.86	10.30	21.23	27.44	101.60	26.55	449.1	800-539-3863	Y
Victory RS Mid Cap Growth Fund Class Y	RMOYX	B	B	B	Up	5.86	10.30	21.18	28.02	103.52	26.54	449.1	800-539-3863	Y
Victory RS Value Fund Class A	RSVAX	B-	B-	B	Up	3.54	8.90	17.40	21.12	91.05	26.21	518.3	800-539-3863	Y
Victory RS Value Fund Class C	RVACX	B-	C+	B	Up	3.30	8.48	16.53	18.28	83.79	23.76	518.3	800-539-3863	Y
Victory RS Value Fund Class R	RSVKX	B-	C+	B	Up	3.44	8.70	16.95	19.64	87.26	25.06	518.3	800-539-3863	Y
Victory RS Value Fund Class Y	RSVYX	B-	B-	B	Up	3.55	9.02	17.70	21.91	93.30	26.77	518.3	800-539-3863	Y
Victory Sycamore Established Value Fund Class A	VETAX	B+	B	A	Up	5.73	9.82	15.66	39.14	114.48	40.58	10,865	800-539-3863	Y
Victory Sycamore Established Value Fund Class C	VEVCX	B	B	A-		5.52	9.40	14.75	36.09	106.92	39.78	10,865	800-539-3863	Y
Victory Sycamore Established Value Fund Class I	VEVIX	B+	B	A	Up	5.81	9.98	16.01	40.44	118.06	40.59	10,865	800-539-3863	Y
Victory Sycamore Established Value Fund Class R	GETGX	B+	B	A	Up	5.68	9.74	15.43	38.36	112.49	40.09	10,865	800-539-3863	Y
Victory Sycamore Established Value Fund Class R6	VEVRX	B+	B	A	Up	5.86	10.05	16.07	40.70	116.96	40.61	10,865	800-539-3863	Y

Category: US Equity Mid Cap (con't)

Fund Name	Ticker Symbol	RATINGS: Overall Rating	Reward Rating	Risk Rating	Recent Up/ Downgrade	TOTAL RETURNS & PERFORMANCE: 3-Month Total Return	6-Month Total Return	1-Year Total Return	3-Year Total Return	5-Year Total Return	ASSETS: NAV	Total Assets (MIL)	NEW INVESTORS: Telephone	Open to New Investors
Victory Sycamore Established Value Fund Class Y	VEVYX	B+	B	A	Up	5.82	10.01	16.01	40.16	116.74	40.59	10,865	800-539-3863	Y
Virtus Ceredex Mid-Cap Value Equity Fund Class A	SAMVX	B-	B-	B-		4.74	4.41	11.22	23.82	84.16	12.5	2,979	800-243-1574	Y
Virtus Ceredex Mid-Cap Value Equity Fund Class C	SMVFX	B-	C+	B-		4.66	4.17	10.81	22.35	80.54	12.18	2,979	800-243-1574	Y
Virtus Ceredex Mid-Cap Value Equity Fund Class I	SMVTX	B-	B-	B-		4.94	4.68	11.68	25.05	87.06	12.66	2,979	800-243-1574	Y
Virtus Ceredex Mid-Cap Value Equity Fund Class R6	SMVZX	B-	B-	B	Down	4.94	4.82	11.97	26.16	88.96	12.67	2,979	800-243-1574	Y
Virtus Horizon Wealth Masters Fund Class A	VWMAX	B-	B-	B-	Up	5.66	11.13	18.04	24.90	87.06	17.89	72.5	800-243-1574	Y
Virtus Horizon Wealth Masters Fund Class C	VWMCX	B-	C+	B-	Up	5.56	10.82	17.25	22.12	80.29	17.43	72.5	800-243-1574	Y
Virtus Horizon Wealth Masters Fund Class I	VWMIX	B-	B-	B-	Up	5.76	11.35	18.34	25.82	89.44	17.96	72.5	800-243-1574	Y
Virtus KAR Mid-Cap Core Fund Class A	VMACX	B+	A-	B+	Up	8.65	13.74	24.63	40.11	110.57	30.37	126.8	800-243-1574	Y
Virtus KAR Mid-Cap Core Fund Class C	VMCCX	B+	B+	B+	Up	8.45	13.30	23.65	37.00	102.81	28.61	126.8	800-243-1574	Y
Virtus KAR Mid-Cap Core Fund Class I	VIMCX	B	A-	B-		8.75	13.90	24.94	41.16	113.24	30.81	126.8	800-243-1574	Y
Virtus KAR Mid-Cap Growth Fund Class A	PHSKX	B+	A-	B	Up	5.44	11.64	33.52	38.60	83.57	27.69	97.5	800-243-1574	Y
Virtus KAR Mid-Cap Growth Fund Class C	PSKCX	B+	B+	B	Up	5.23	11.20	32.47	35.49	76.84	22.16	97.5	800-243-1574	Y
Virtus KAR Mid-Cap Growth Fund Class I	PICMX	B+	A-	B	Up	5.51	11.79	33.80	39.58	85.88	28.5	97.5	800-243-1574	Y
Volumetric Fund	VOLMX	B-	B-	B-	Down	5.65	9.80	17.54	23.77	70.95	21.03	35.4		Y
Voya Index Plus MidCap Portfolio Class I	IPMIX	B	B	B	Up	6.06	7.65	13.57	30.40	97.39	22.95	653.8	800-366-0066	Y
Voya Index Plus MidCap Portfolio Class S	IPMSX	B	B	B	Up	5.96	7.48	13.28	29.40	94.92	22.59	653.8	800-366-0066	Y
Voya Mid Cap Research Enhanced Index Fund Class A	AIMAX	B-	B-	B-	Up	5.95	7.43	13.07	19.71	76.76	17.22	164.5	800-366-0066	Y
Voya Mid Cap Research Enhanced Index Fund Class C	APMCX	B-	C+	B-	Up	5.81	7.13	12.53	17.89	72.45	15.99	164.5	800-366-0066	Y
Voya Mid Cap Research Enhanced Index Fund Class I	AIMIX	B-	B-	B-		6.02	7.58	13.34	20.57	79.27	17.69	164.5	800-366-0066	Y
Voya Mid Cap Research Enhanced Index Fund Class O	IDMOX	B-	B-	B-	Up	5.95	7.42	13.11	19.67	76.73	17.28	164.5	800-366-0066	Y
Voya Mid Cap Research Enhanced Index Fund Class R	AIMRX	B-	C+	B-	Up	5.85	7.22	12.80	18.78	74.50	16.95	164.5	800-366-0066	Y
Voya Mid Cap Research Enhanced Index Fund Class W	AIMWX	B-	B-	B-		6.02	7.58	13.42	20.64	79.04	17.66	164.5	800-366-0066	Y
Voya MidCap Opportunities Fund Class A	NMCAX	B	B	B+	Up	7.64	10.63	24.46	31.98	92.01	22.35	1,401	800-366-0066	Y
Voya MidCap Opportunities Fund Class C	NMCCX	B	B	B	Up	7.44	10.23	23.57	28.98	84.95	16.79	1,401	800-366-0066	Y
Voya MidCap Opportunities Fund Class I	NMCIX	B	B	B+		7.72	10.79	24.84	33.28	95.36	25.61	1,401	800-366-0066	Y
Voya MidCap Opportunities Fund Class O	NMCOX	B	B	B+	Up	7.63	10.63	24.46	31.95	91.98	22.25	1,401	800-366-0066	Y
Voya MidCap Opportunities Fund Class R	IMORX	B	B	B+	Up	7.59	10.54	24.17	31.00	89.71	21.84	1,401	800-366-0066	Y
Voya MidCap Opportunities Fund Class R6	IMOZX	B	B	B+		7.72	10.82	24.95	33.65	96.22	25.75	1,401	800-366-0066	Y
Voya MidCap Opportunities Fund Class W	IMOWX	B	B	B+		7.71	10.78	24.76	32.97	94.33	25.23	1,401	800-366-0066	Y
Voya MidCap Opportunities Portfolio Class A	IAMOX	B	B	B+	Up	7.69	10.69	24.48	31.96	92.23	13.44	2,232	800-366-0066	Y
Voya MidCap Opportunities Portfolio Class I	IIMOX	B	B	B+		7.77	10.96	25.08	33.98	97.10	14.56	2,232	800-366-0066	Y
Voya MidCap Opportunities Portfolio Class S	ISMOX	B	B	B+		7.66	10.77	24.76	32.93	94.56	13.77	2,232	800-366-0066	Y
Voya MidCap Opportunities Portfolio Class S2	IMOPX	B	B	B+	Up	7.72	10.77	24.56	32.38	93.18	13.66	2,232	800-366-0066	Y
Voya MidCap Opportunities Portfolio R6	VMCRX	B	B	B+		7.77	10.96	25.08	33.88	96.95	14.56	2,232	800-366-0066	Y
Voya Multi-Manager Mid Cap Value Fund Class I	IMCVX	B	B-	B	Up	5.48	10.02	14.98	25.85	93.37	11.91	233.9	800-366-0066	Y
Voya Russell Mid Cap Growth Index Portfolio Class I	IRGJX	B	B	B-	Up	6.69	12.20	24.66	31.82	103.54	35.21	311.2	800-366-0066	Y
Voya Russell Mid Cap Growth Index Portfolio Class S	IRGUX	B	B	B-	Up	6.62	12.06	24.35	30.82	101.01	35.11	311.2	800-366-0066	Y
Voya Russell Mid Cap Growth Index Portfolio Class S2	IRGVX	B	B	B-	Up	6.59	12.01	24.18	30.25	99.60	35.05	311.2	800-366-0066	Y
Voya Russell Mid Cap Index Portfolio Class A	IRMAX	B-	B-	C+	Down	5.83	9.27	17.38	26.94	95.38	15.79	1,954	800-366-0066	Y
Voya Russell Mid Cap Index Portfolio Class I	IIRMX	B-	B	B-	Down	5.92	9.48	17.97	28.82	100.17	16.28	1,954	800-366-0066	Y
Voya Russell Mid Cap Index Portfolio Class P2	VRMPX	B-	B	B-	Down	6.04	9.68	18.27	29.14	100.68	16.31	1,954	800-366-0066	Y
Voya Russell Mid Cap Index Portfolio Class S	IRMCX	B-	B-	C+	Down	5.85	9.38	17.66	27.83	97.76	16.09	1,954	800-366-0066	Y
Voya Russell Mid Cap Index Portfolio Class S2	IRMTX	B	B-	B	Up	5.86	9.28	17.47	27.32	96.28	15.89	1,954	800-366-0066	Y
VY® American Century Small-Mid Cap Value Portfolio Class A	IASAX	B	B	B+		3.94	6.98	10.89	33.22	100.64	12.66	378.0	800-366-0066	Y
VY® American Century Small-Mid Cap Value Portfolio Class I	IACIX	B	B	B+		4.10	7.31	11.44	35.25	105.87	13.44	378.0	800-366-0066	Y
VY® American Century Small-Mid Cap Value Portfolio Class S	IASSX	B	B	B+		4.00	7.10	11.11	34.13	103.17	13.25	378.0	800-366-0066	Y
VY® American Century Small-Mid Cap Value Portfolio Cls S2	ISMSX	B	B	B+		4.03	7.12	10.95	33.61	101.79	12.64	378.0	800-366-0066	Y
VY® Baron Growth Portfolio Class A	IBSAX	B	B	B	Up	5.12	8.71	27.86	26.38	86.03	27.88	780.7	800-366-0066	Y
VY® Baron Growth Portfolio Class I	IBGIX	B	B	B	Up	5.26	9.00	28.52	28.31	90.85	30.58	780.7	800-366-0066	Y
VY® Baron Growth Portfolio Class R6	VYRBX	B	B	B	Up	5.22	9.00	28.51	28.35	90.89	30.59	780.7	800-366-0066	Y
VY® Baron Growth Portfolio Class S	IBSSX	B	B	B	Up	5.20	8.88	28.20	27.39	88.48	29.31	780.7	800-366-0066	Y

Category: US Equity Mid Cap (con't)

Fund Name	Ticker Symbol	RATINGS: Overall Rating	RATINGS: Reward Rating	RATINGS: Risk Rating	RATINGS: Recent Up/ Downgrade	TOTAL RETURNS & PERFORMANCE: 3-Month Total Return	6-Month Total Return	1-Year Total Return	3-Year Total Return	5-Year Total Return	ASSETS: NAV	Total Assets (MIL)	NEW INVESTORS: Telephone	Open to New Investors
VY® Baron Growth Portfolio Class S2	IBCGX	B	B	B	Up	5.16	8.80	28.01	26.79	87.07	28.1	780.7	800-366-0066	Y
VY® JPMorgan Mid Cap Value Portfolio Class A	IJMAX	B	B-	B		4.67	6.82	13.41	24.29	91.57	19.78	584.8	800-366-0066	
VY® JPMorgan Mid Cap Value Portfolio Class I	IJMIX	B	B-	B+		4.83	7.09	14.03	26.22	96.44	20.3	584.8	800-366-0066	
VY® JPMorgan Mid Cap Value Portfolio Class S	IJMSX	B	B-	B		4.77	6.95	13.72	25.26	93.97	20.1	584.8	800-366-0066	
VY® JPMorgan Mid Cap Value Portfolio Class S2	IJPMX	B-	B-	B-	Down	4.69	6.85	13.51	24.65	92.42	19.72	584.8	800-366-0066	
VY® T. Rowe Price Diversified Mid Cap Growth Port Cls A	IAXAX	B	B	B-	Up	5.84	10.42	24.11	33.79	105.30	10.5	1,016	800-366-0066	Y
VY® T. Rowe Price Diversified Mid Cap Growth Port Cls I	IAXIX	B	B	B-	Up	5.95	10.68	24.80	35.87	110.35	11.56	1,016	800-366-0066	Y
VY® T. Rowe Price Diversified Mid Cap Growth Port Cls R6	VYRIX	B	B	B-	Up	5.86	10.58	24.80	35.99	110.54	11.56	1,016	800-366-0066	Y
VY® T. Rowe Price Diversified Mid Cap Growth Port Cls S	IAXSX	B	B	B-	Up	5.88	10.46	24.45	34.78	107.75	11.15	1,016	800-366-0066	Y
VY® T. Rowe Price Diversified Mid Cap Growth Port Cls S2	IAXTX	B	B	B-	Up	5.82	10.39	24.27	34.15	106.29	10.54	1,016	800-366-0066	Y
Waddell & Reed Advisor New Concepts Fund Class A	UNECX	B-	B-	C	Up	7.21	12.57	27.06	26.01	80.67	11.27	1,716	888-923-3355	Y
Waddell & Reed Advisor New Concepts Fund Class Y	UNEYX	B-	B	C	Up	7.21	12.69	27.28	27.05	83.67	12.76	1,716	888-923-3355	Y
Walden Midcap Fund	WAMFX	B	B	B+		7.80	9.94	19.09	31.65	93.96	17.24	46.6	617-814-1215	Y
Wells Fargo C&B Mid Cap Value Fund - Class A	CBMAX	B	B	B		4.71	6.97	14.90	36.79	101.50	36.72	258.5	800-222-8222	Y
Wells Fargo C&B Mid Cap Value Fund - Class Admin	CBMIX	B	B	B		4.74	7.03	15.04	37.14	102.22	37.15	258.5	800-222-8222	Y
Wells Fargo C&B Mid Cap Value Fund - Class C	CBMCX	B	B	B	Up	4.52	6.58	14.06	33.77	94.16	34.62	258.5	800-222-8222	Y
Wells Fargo C&B Mid Cap Value Fund - Class Inst	CBMSX	B	B	B		4.81	7.14	15.30	38.17	104.83	36.99	258.5	800-222-8222	Y
Wells Fargo Common Stock Fund - Class A	SCSAX	B	B	B	Up	6.22	11.21	17.55	30.37	82.85	22.98	1,297	800-222-8222	Y
Wells Fargo Common Stock Fund - Class Admin	SCSDX	B	B	B	Up	6.29	11.35	17.71	30.98	84.26	23.38	1,297	800-222-8222	Y
Wells Fargo Common Stock Fund - Class C	STSAX	B	B	B	Up	6.00	10.78	16.64	27.46	76.09	17.3	1,297	800-222-8222	Y
Wells Fargo Common Stock Fund - Class Inst	SCNSX	B	B	B	Up	6.35	11.44	17.97	31.94	86.51	23.98	1,297	800-222-8222	Y
Wells Fargo Common Stock Fund - Class R6	SCSRX	B	B	B	Up	6.33	11.45	18.03	32.03	86.48	24.04	1,297	800-222-8222	Y
Wells Fargo Discovery Fund - Class A	WFDAX	B+	A-	B	Up	6.07	11.77	29.03	35.44	98.98	32.57	2,600	800-222-8222	Y
Wells Fargo Discovery Fund - Class Admin	WFDDX	B+	A-	B	Up	6.10	11.83	29.14	35.79	99.99	33.61	2,600	800-222-8222	Y
Wells Fargo Discovery Fund - Class C	WDSCX	B	B+	B	Up	5.89	11.39	28.10	32.44	91.68	28.82	2,600	800-222-8222	Y
Wells Fargo Discovery Fund - Class Inst	WFDSX	B+	A-	B	Up	6.15	11.98	29.47	36.86	102.64	35.07	2,600	800-222-8222	Y
Wells Fargo Discovery Fund - Class R6	WFDRX	B+	A-	B	Up	6.21	12.05	29.61	37.21	103.10	35.23	2,600	800-222-8222	Y
Wells Fargo Enterprise Fund - Class A	SENAX	B	B	C+	Up	5.36	9.86	28.51	31.22	95.51	46.18	718.6	800-222-8222	Y
Wells Fargo Enterprise Fund - Class Admin	SEPKX	B	B	C+	Up	5.39	9.91	28.61	31.71	96.61	48.64	718.6	800-222-8222	Y
Wells Fargo Enterprise Fund - Class C	WENCX	B	B	B	Up	5.15	9.43	27.52	28.26	88.31	40.98	718.6	800-222-8222	Y
Wells Fargo Enterprise Fund - Class Inst	WFEIX	B	B	C+	Up	5.46	10.06	28.95	32.54	98.83	50.74	718.6	800-222-8222	Y
Wells Fargo Enterprise Fund - Class R6	WENRX	B	B	B	Up	5.47	10.08	29.00	32.73	97.93	50.84	718.6	800-222-8222	Y
Wells Fargo Special Mid Cap Value Fund - Class A	WFPAX	B	B-	B		3.97	6.90	10.83	28.92	104.84	37.41	8,420	800-222-8222	Y
Wells Fargo Special Mid Cap Value Fund - Class Admin	WFMDX	B	B-	B		3.97	6.94	10.89	29.26	105.89	38.02	8,420	800-222-8222	Y
Wells Fargo Special Mid Cap Value Fund - Class C	WFPCX	B	B-	B	Up	3.77	6.49	10.00	26.03	97.27	36.04	8,420	800-222-8222	Y
Wells Fargo Special Mid Cap Value Fund - Class Inst	WFMIX	B	B-	B+		4.05	7.08	11.16	30.22	108.59	38.32	8,420	800-222-8222	Y
Wells Fargo Special Mid Cap Value Fund - Class R	WFHHX	B	B-	B	Up	3.90	6.79	10.54	28.31	104.51	37.97	8,420	800-222-8222	Y
Wells Fargo Special Mid Cap Value Fund - Class R6	WFPRX	B	B-	B+		4.08	7.14	11.27	30.59	109.30	38.35	8,420	800-222-8222	Y
Westcore Mid-Cap Value Dividend Fund Institutional Class	WIMCX	B	B-	B	Up	4.28	5.10	6.23	27.26	92.41	27.3	84.3	800-392-2673	Y
Westcore Mid-Cap Value Dividend Fund Retail Class	WTMCX	B	B-	B	Up	4.23	5.02	6.01	26.77	91.67	26.87	84.3	800-392-2673	Y
Westwood SMidCap Fund Institutional Class	WHGMX	B-	C+	B	Up	3.60	7.18	10.39	18.42	70.36	15.78	350.8		Y
Westwood SMidCap Plus Fund Institutional Class	WHGPX	B-	C+	B	Up	3.20	6.23	11.51	18.27	73.58	15.88	161.2		Y
William Blair Mid Cap Growth Fund Class I	WCGIX	B-	C+	B	Down	5.54	9.81	21.18	20.93	72.43	11.57	79.7	800-621-0687	Y
William Blair Mid Cap Growth Fund Class N	WCGNX	B-	C+	B	Up	5.48	9.69	20.88	20.07	70.26	10.92	79.7	800-621-0687	Y
William Blair Small-Mid Cap Growth Fund Class I	WSMDX	B+	A-	B	Up	5.58	10.99	28.89	42.97	125.93	24.48	1,821	800-621-0687	Y
William Blair Small-Mid Cap Growth Fund Class N	WSMNX	B	A-	B-	Down	5.53	10.89	28.56	41.91	123.06	23.36	1,821	800-621-0687	Y
Wright Selected Blue Chip Equities Fund	WSBEX	B	B-	B	Up	6.61	10.11	16.45	21.89	88.88	12.65	31.9	800-555-0644	Y
Yorktown Master Allocation Fund Class L	APILX	B-	C+	B	Up	4.52	8.44	15.28	15.29	50.14	27.43	28.3	800-544-6060	Y

Category: US Equity Small Cap

Fund Name	Ticker Symbol	RATINGS: Overall Rating	Reward Rating	Risk Rating	Recent Up/ Downgrade	TOTAL RETURNS & PERFORMANCE: 3-Month Total Return	6-Month Total Return	1-Year Total Return	3-Year Total Return	5-Year Total Return	ASSETS: NAV	Total Assets (MIL)	NEW INVESTORS: Telephone	Open to New Investors
1290 GAMCO Small/Mid Cap Value Fund Class R	TNVRX	B-	C+	B-	Up	2.78	11.26	19.00	35.71		13.1	25.9	212-554-1234	Y
1290 GAMCO Small/Mid Cap Value Fund Class T	TNVCX	B-	C+	B-	Up	2.92	11.53	19.56	37.66		13.15	25.9	212-554-1234	Y
1290 VT GAMCO Small Company Value Portfolio Class IA	US2689545596	B+	A-	B	Up	4.22	12.58	16.30	33.88	98.50		3,492	877-222-2144	Y
1290 VT GAMCO Small Company Value Portfolio Class IB	US29364E2072	B+	A-	B	Up	4.21	12.58	16.28	33.84	98.43		3,492	877-222-2144	Y
1290 VT GAMCO Small Company Value Portfolio Class K	US26883L6395	B+	A-	B	Up	4.29	12.71	16.59	34.87	100.95		3,492	877-222-2144	Y
1290 VT Micro Cap Portfolio Class IB	US29439V7543	B	A-	C	Up	3.75	14.10	26.36	32.09			144.0	877-222-2144	Y
1290 VT Micro Cap Portfolio Class K	US29439V7477	B	A-	C	Up	3.80	14.11	26.56	32.91			144.0	877-222-2144	Y
1290 VT Small Cap Value Portfolio Class IB	US29439V7709	B-	B-	B-	Up	2.30	10.87	12.55	26.82			324.6	877-222-2144	Y
1290 VT Small Cap Value Portfolio Class K	US29439V7626	B-	B	B-	Up	2.26	10.82	12.73	27.68			324.6	877-222-2144	Y
AB Small Cap Growth Portfolio Advisor Class	QUAYX	B	A	C	Up	7.56	15.88	34.93	42.05	108.40	56.03	1,432	212-969-1000	
AB Small Cap Growth Portfolio Class A	QUASX	B+	A	B	Up	7.49	15.71	34.60	41.01	105.74	51.56	1,432	212-969-1000	
AB Small Cap Growth Portfolio Class B	QUABX	B	A-	C	Up	7.32	15.26	33.56	37.72	97.64	33.59	1,432	212-969-1000	
AB Small Cap Growth Portfolio Class C	QUACX	B+	A-	B-	Up	7.31	15.29	33.61	37.86	98.20	34.06	1,432	212-969-1000	
AB Small Cap Growth Portfolio Class I	QUAIX	B	A	C	Up	7.56	15.86	34.90	42.25	109.16	55.79	1,432	212-969-1000	
AB Small Cap Growth Portfolio Class K	QUAKX	B	A	C	Up	7.50	15.72	34.54	41.01	106.02	52.8	1,432	212-969-1000	
AB Small Cap Growth Portfolio Class R	QUARX	B	A	C	Up	7.39	15.49	34.09	39.62	102.70	50.1	1,432	212-969-1000	
AB Small Cap Growth Portfolio Class Z	QUAZX	B	A	C	Up	7.60	15.90	35.03	42.34	107.68	55.94	1,432	212-969-1000	Y
Aberdeen U.S. Small Cap Equity Fund Class A	GSXAX	A	A-	A	Up	3.44	9.46	11.02	46.89	128.77	36.65	2,025	866-667-9231	Y
Aberdeen U.S. Small Cap Equity Fund Class C	GSXCX	A-	A-	A	Up	3.31	9.08	10.26	43.80	121.05	31.81	2,025	866-667-9231	Y
Aberdeen U.S. Small Cap Equity Fund Class R	GNSRX	A-	A-	A	Up	3.38	9.28	10.63	45.72	126.06	33.91	2,025	866-667-9231	Y
Aberdeen U.S. Small Cap Equity Fund Institutional Class	GSCIX	A	A	A	Up	3.56	9.65	11.36	48.25	132.51	38.62	2,025	866-667-9231	Y
Aberdeen U.S. Small Cap Equity Fund Inst Service Cls	GSXIX	A	A-	A	Up	3.53	9.61	11.29	48.12	132.01	38.63	2,025	866-667-9231	Y
Acuitas US Microcap Fund Institutional Shares	AFMCX	A-	A-	B	Up	1.51	9.02	10.25	36.91		13.23	99.9		Y
Adirondack Small Cap Fund	ADKSX	B	B	B	Up	2.36	6.89	10.54	23.23	85.62	22.39	256.1	518-690-0470	Y
Advisory Research Small Company Opportunities Fund	ADVSX	B	B-	B	Up	1.04	7.30	4.86	22.56		11.71	7.4	312-565-1414	Y
Aegis Value Fund	AVALX	B	A-	C	Up	21.65	21.43	17.37	52.40	56.29	19.66	118.0	800-528-3780	Y
Aegis Value Fund Class A	AVFAX	B	B+	C	Up	21.53	21.30	17.15	51.53	54.63	19.53	118.0	800-528-3780	Y
AIG Small-Cap Fund Class A	SASAX	A-	A	B	Up	1.90	11.29	17.73	43.10		18.51	59.7	800-858-8850	Y
AIG Small-Cap Fund Class C	SASCX	A-	A	B	Up	1.69	10.89	16.93	40.22		17.95	59.7	800-858-8850	Y
AIG Small-Cap Fund Class W	SASWX	B+	A	B-	Up	1.94	11.37	17.91	43.88		18.67	59.7	800-858-8850	Y
Alger SICAV - Alger Small Cap Focus Fund Class Y	AOFYX	B+	A	B	Up	4.56	9.29	29.23	41.56	104.72	15.56	617.1	800-992-3863	Y
Alger Small Cap Focus Fund Class A	AOFAX	B+	A	B	Up	4.52	9.11	28.87	40.98	102.65	15.01	617.1	800-992-3863	Y
Alger Small Cap Focus Fund Class C	AOFCX	B+	A-	B	Up	4.35	8.71	27.97	38.09	95.94	13.65	617.1	800-992-3863	Y
Alger Small Cap Focus Fund Class I	AOFIX	B+	A	B	Up	4.54	9.10	28.92	41.23	104.25	15.39	617.1	800-992-3863	Y
Alger Small Cap Focus Fund Class Z	AGOZX	B+	A	B	Up	4.56	9.29	29.26	42.52	107.12	15.56	617.1	800-992-3863	Y
Alger Small Cap Growth Fund Class A	ALSAX	B	A-	C	Up	4.55	11.67	28.29	29.88	78.12	8.43	128.0	800-992-3863	Y
Alger Small Cap Growth Fund Class B	ALSCX	B	A-	C	Up	4.19	10.94	27.23	26.61	70.99	6.4	128.0	800-992-3863	
Alger Small Cap Growth Fund Class C	AGSCX	B	B+	C	Up	4.32	11.11	27.25	26.58	70.91	6.21	128.0	800-992-3863	Y
Alger Small Cap Growth Fund Class Z	ASCZX	B	A-	C	Up	4.45	11.67	28.63	31.08	80.97	8.62	128.0	800-992-3863	Y
Alger Small Cap Growth Institutional Fund Class I	ALSRX	B	A-	C	Up	4.74	11.94	28.42	32.16	81.81	20.26	213.5	800-992-3863	Y
Alger Small Cap Growth Institutional Fund Class R	ASIRX	B	A-	C	Up	4.62	11.69	27.72	30.22	77.43	17.12	213.5	800-992-3863	Y
Alger Small Cap Growth Portfolio Class I-2	AASOX	B	A-	C	Up	4.36	11.59	28.73	31.38	81.96	24.15	202.3	800-992-3863	Y
Alger SmallCap Growth Institutional Fund Class Z-2	AISZX	B	A-	C	Up	4.82	12.11	28.80	32.80	82.68	20.36	213.5	800-992-3863	Y
AllianzGI Micro Cap Fund Class A	GMCAX	B	B	B	Up	-0.19	5.95	14.47	31.63	101.48	14.94	32.3	800-498-5413	Y
AllianzGI Micro Cap Fund Class P	AAMPX	B	B	B	Up	-0.18	5.92	14.45	31.91	102.42	15.03	32.3	800-498-5413	Y
AllianzGI Micro Cap Fund Institutional Class	AMCIX	B	B	B	Up	-0.25	5.96	14.45	31.83	102.40	15.11	32.3	800-498-5413	Y
AllianzGI NFJ Small-Cap Value Fund Administrative Class	PVADX	B-	B-	B-	Up	3.23	6.89	9.78	23.11	69.14	21.6	2,858	800-498-5413	
AllianzGI NFJ Small-Cap Value Fund Class A	PCVAX	B-	B-	B-	Up	3.19	6.84	9.67	22.55	67.85	21.67	2,858	800-498-5413	
AllianzGI NFJ Small-Cap Value Fund Class P	ASVPX	B-	B-	B-	Up	3.28	6.96	9.92	23.47	69.95	24.11	2,858	800-498-5413	
AllianzGI NFJ Small-Cap Value Fund Class R	PNVRX	B-	B-	B-	Up	3.13	6.67	9.35	21.62	65.72	23.08	2,858	800-498-5413	
AllianzGI NFJ Small-Cap Value Fund Class R6	ANFVX	B-	B-	B-	Up	3.33	7.04	10.09	24.14	71.52	24.16	2,858	800-498-5413	Y
AllianzGI NFJ Small-Cap Value Fund Institutional Class	PSVIX	B-	B-	B-	Up	3.29	7.02	10.02	23.95	71.16	24.25	2,858	800-498-5413	

Category: US Equity Small Cap (con't)

Fund Name	Ticker Symbol	Overall Rating	Reward Rating	Risk Rating	Recent Up/ Downgrade	3-Month Total Return	6-Month Total Return	1-Year Total Return	3-Year Total Return	5-Year Total Return	NAV	Total Assets (MIL)	Telephone	Open to New Investors
		RATINGS				TOTAL RETURNS & PERFORMANCE					ASSETS		NEW INVESTORS	
AllianzGI Small-Cap Blend Fund Class A	AZBAX	B+	A-	B-	Up	3.23	11.74	20.79	36.15		20.13	86.7	800-498-5413	Y
AllianzGI Small-Cap Blend Fund Class C	AZBCX	B	A-	C+	Up	3.03	11.35	19.83	33.19		19.56	86.7	800-498-5413	Y
AllianzGI Small-Cap Blend Fund Class P	AZBPX	B+	A-	B-	Up	3.30	11.87	21.02	37.22		20.29	86.7	800-498-5413	Y
AllianzGI Small-Cap Blend Fund Institutional Class	AZBIX	B+	A	B-	Up	3.33	11.96	21.21	37.62		20.42	86.7	800-498-5413	Y
AllianzGI Ultra Micro Cap Fund Class A	GUCAX	B-	B-	B-	Up	-1.22	3.86	10.69	15.93	81.35	17.84	35.9	800-498-5413	
AllianzGI Ultra Micro Cap Fund Class P	AAUPX	B-	B-	B-	Up	-1.17	3.97	11.02	16.92	83.69	18.2	35.9	800-498-5413	
AllianzGI Ultra Micro Cap Fund Institutional Class	AUMIX	B-	B-	B-	Up	-1.15	4.02	11.01	16.81	83.45	18.25	35.9	800-498-5413	
AlphaOne Small Cap Opportunities Fund Institutional Class	AOMCX	B+	A-	B	Up	0.10	6.68	8.74	39.69	101.07	13.93	175.4	267-597-3888	Y
AlphaOne Small Cap Opportunities Fund Investor Class	AOMAX	B+	A-	B	Up	0.04	6.55	8.56	38.81	99.06	13.71	175.4	267-597-3888	Y
Alpine Small Cap Fund Class A Shares	ADIAX	B	B	B	Up	4.59	6.53	13.12	40.61	71.57	19.56	14.6	888-785-5578	Y
Alpine Small Cap Fund Institutional Class	ADINX	B	B	B	Up	4.68	6.65	13.41	41.62	73.84	19.87	14.6	888-785-5578	
American Beacon Bahl & Gaynor Small Cap Growth Fund A Cls	GBSAX	A-	A-	B	Up	3.25	7.35	13.25	36.25		13.75	41.7	800-658-5811	Y
American Beacon Bahl & Gaynor Small Cap Growth Fund C Cls	GBSCX	B+	A-	B	Up	3.00	6.87	12.33	33.10		13.42	41.7	800-658-5811	Y
American Beacon Bahl & Gaynor Small Cap Growth Inst Cls	GBSIX	A-	A	B	Up	3.29	7.50	13.63	37.78		13.93	41.7	800-658-5811	Y
American Beacon Bahl & Gaynor Small Cap Growth Inv Cls	GBSPX	A-	A-	B	Up	3.19	7.29	13.20	36.24		13.75	41.7	800-658-5811	Y
American Beacon Bahl & Gaynor Small Cap Growth Fund Y Cls	GBSYX	A-	A	B	Up	3.30	7.53	13.55	37.43		13.89	41.7	800-658-5811	Y
American Beacon Small Cap Value Fund Advisor Class	AASSX	B	B+	B	Up	3.02	7.76	8.16	27.76	91.28	26.08	7,212	800-658-5811	Y
American Beacon Small Cap Value Fund C Class	ASVCX	B	B	B	Up	2.98	7.50	7.57	25.42	85.05	24.97	7,212	800-658-5811	Y
American Beacon Small Cap Value Fund Class A	ABSAX	B	B+	B	Up	3.04	7.81	8.26	28.14	91.94	25.94	7,212	800-658-5811	Y
American Beacon Small Cap Value Fund Class Institutional	AVFIX	B+	B+	B	Up	3.15	8.01	8.67	29.63	96.06	27.41	7,212	800-658-5811	Y
American Beacon Small Cap Value Fund Class Y	ABSYX	B+	B+	B	Up	3.16	8.01	8.62	29.37	95.25	27.05	7,212	800-658-5811	Y
American Beacon Small Cap Value Fund Investor Class	AVPAX	B	B+	B	Up	3.06	7.82	8.34	28.41	92.81	26.41	7,212	800-658-5811	Y
American Beacon Small Cap Value Fund R6 Class	AASRX	B+	B+	B	Up	3.18	8.08	8.70	29.68	96.13	27.41	7,212	800-658-5811	Y
American Beacon Stephens Small Cap Growth Fund A Class	SPWAX	B	B	B-	Up	4.47	9.94	19.06	23.37	73.16	17.59	602.8	800-658-5811	Y
American Beacon Stephens Small Cap Growth Fund Inst Cls	STSIX	B	B	B	Up	4.57	10.14	19.47	24.79	76.70	19.01	602.8	800-658-5811	Y
American Beacon Stephens Small Cap Growth Fund Inv Cls	STSGX	B	B	B	Up	4.54	10.04	19.22	23.78	74.45	17.77	602.8	800-658-5811	Y
American Beacon Stephens Small Cap Growth Fund Y Class	SPWYX	B	B	B	Up	4.54	10.13	19.40	24.41	75.99	18.91	602.8	800-658-5811	Y
American Beacon Zebra Small Cap Equity Fund A Class	AZSAX	B+	A-	B	Up	0.93	6.67	9.08	32.74	100.68	16.22	56.1	800-658-5811	Y
American Beacon Zebra Small Cap Equity Fund C Class	AZSCX	B+	A-	B	Up	0.73	6.30	8.30	29.81	93.28	15.5	56.1	800-658-5811	Y
American Beacon Zebra Small Cap Equity Fund Inst Cls	AZSIX	B+	A-	B	Up	0.99	6.89	9.52	34.32	104.94	16.32	56.1	800-658-5811	Y
American Beacon Zebra Small Cap Equity Fund Investor Class	AZSPX	B+	A-	B	Up	0.96	6.70	9.12	32.83	101.22	16.21	56.1	800-658-5811	Y
American Beacon Zebra Small Cap Equity Fund Y Class	AZSYX	B+	A-	B	Up	1.04	6.89	9.45	33.99	104.07	16.46	56.1	800-658-5811	Y
American Century NT Small Company Fund G Class	ACLOX	B	B	B	Up	3.01	8.27	11.31	24.65	94.78	9.63	460.8	800-444-4015	Y
American Century Small Cap Growth Fund A Class	ANOAX	B	A-	C	Up	5.87	12.03	25.48	32.18	100.72	16.64	718.2	800-444-4015	Y
American Century Small Cap Growth Fund C Class	ANOCX	B	A-	B-	Up	5.71	11.62	24.62	29.26	93.35	15.25	718.2	800-444-4015	Y
American Century Small Cap Growth Fund I Class	ANONX	B	A-	C	Up	6.00	12.33	26.07	33.94	105.20	17.54	718.2	800-444-4015	Y
American Century Small Cap Growth Fund Investor Class	ANOIX	B	A-	C	Up	5.94	12.25	25.84	33.15	103.21	17.18	718.2	800-444-4015	Y
American Century Small Cap Growth Fund R Class	ANORX	B+	A-	B-	Up	5.80	11.92	25.19	31.18	98.15	16.3	718.2	800-444-4015	Y
American Century Small Cap Growth Fund R5 Class	ANOGX	B	A-	C	Up	6.00	12.32	26.01	33.33	103.48	17.55	718.2	800-444-4015	Y
American Century Small Cap Growth Fund R6 Class	ANODX	B	A-	C	Up	6.02	12.38	26.29	34.52	106.28	17.66	718.2	800-444-4015	Y
American Century Small Cap Growth Fund Y Class	ANOYX	B	A-	C	Up	6.02	12.38	26.13	33.46	103.68	17.66	718.2	800-444-4015	Y
American Century Small Cap Value Fund A Class	ACSCX	B	B+	B	Up	2.66	6.88	9.90	33.16	91.69	8.64	1,646	800-444-4015	
American Century Small Cap Value Fund C Class	ASVNX	B	B	B	Up	2.51	6.51	9.20	30.29	84.63	8.29	1,646	800-444-4015	
American Century Small Cap Value Fund I Class	ACVIX	B	B+	B	Up	2.73	7.06	10.39	35.11	96.05	8.81	1,646	800-444-4015	
American Century Small Cap Value Fund Investor Class	ASVIX	B	B+	B	Up	2.69	7.00	10.26	34.17	94.11	8.73	1,646	800-444-4015	
American Century Small Cap Value Fund R Class	ASVRX	B	B	B	Up	2.63	6.86	9.72	32.30	89.38	8.61	1,646	800-444-4015	
American Century Small Cap Value Fund R5 Class	ASVGX	B	B+	B	Up	2.83	7.16	10.46	34.42	94.47	8.82	1,646	800-444-4015	Y
American Century Small Cap Value Fund R6 Class	ASVDX	B+	B+	B	Up	2.77	7.14	10.55	35.57	96.98	8.81	1,646	800-444-4015	
American Century Small Cap Value Fund Y Class	ASVYX	B	B+	B	Up	2.87	7.25	10.58	34.56	94.68	8.82	1,646	800-444-4015	
American Century Small Company Fund A Class	ASQAX	B	B	B	Up	2.58	7.60	10.30	21.75	89.18	15.04	700.8	800-444-4015	Y
American Century Small Company Fund C Class	ASQCX	B-	B-	B	Up	2.40	7.13	9.51	18.97	82.22	14.5	700.8	800-444-4015	Y
American Century Small Company Fund I Class	ASCQX	B	B	B	Up	2.71	7.83	10.76	23.38	93.43	15.46	700.8	800-444-4015	Y

Category: US Equity Small Cap (con't)

Fund Name	Ticker Symbol	RATINGS: Overall Rating	Reward Rating	Risk Rating	Recent Up/ Downgrade	TOTAL RETURNS & PERFORMANCE: 3-Month Total Return	6-Month Total Return	1-Year Total Return	3-Year Total Return	5-Year Total Return	ASSETS: NAV	Total Assets (MIL)	NEW INVESTORS: Telephone	Open to New Investors
American Century Small Company Fund Investor Class	ASQIX	B	B	B	Up	2.65	7.71	10.58	22.67	91.48	15.39	700.8	800-444-4015	Y
American Century Small Company Fund R Class	ASCRX	B	B	B	Up	2.56	7.46	10.12	20.83	86.99	14.75	700.8	800-444-4015	Y
American Century Small Company Fund R5 Class	ASQGX	B	B	B	Up	2.70	7.76	10.71	22.82	91.71	15.47	700.8	800-444-4015	Y
AMG Frontier Small Cap Growth Fund Class I	MSSCX	B-	B	C	Up	4.27	9.69	21.24	18.67	81.89	10.73	18.9	800-835-3879	
AMG Frontier Small Cap Growth Fund Class Z	MSSYX	B-	B	C	Up	4.25	9.75	21.40	19.37	83.82	10.97	18.9	800-835-3879	
AMG GW&K Small Cap Core Fund Class I	GWEIX	A-	A-	B+	Up	4.64	10.02	20.78	37.66	105.52	28.42	544.7	800-835-3879	
AMG GW&K Small Cap Core Fund Class N	GWETX	B+	A-	B	Up	4.49	9.77	20.31	35.99	101.33	28.04	544.7	800-835-3879	
AMG GW&K Small Cap Core Fund Class Z	GWEZX	A-	A-	B	Up	4.65	10.02	20.79	36.53	102.13	28.42	544.7	800-835-3879	Y
AMG GW&K U.S. Small Cap Growth Fund Class I	ATSIX	B-	B	B-	Up	4.60	11.28	25.34	20.71	59.61	5.04	35.9	800-835-3879	Y
AMG Managers Cadence Emerging Companies Fund - Class I	MECIX	A-	A	B+	Up	1.28	13.88	22.40	62.90	141.22	58.4	100.4	800-835-3879	Y
AMG Managers Cadence Emerging Companies Fund - Class N	MECAX	A-	A	B+	Up	1.25	13.83	22.21	61.89	138.64	53.91	100.4	800-835-3879	Y
AMG Managers Cadence Emerging Companies Fund - Class Z	MECZX	A-	A	B+	Up	1.30	13.92	22.46	62.98	141.34	58.43	100.4	800-835-3879	Y
AMG Managers Emerging Opportunities Fund Class I	MIMFX	B+	A	B-	Up	4.17	14.78	24.30	34.14	119.98	46.48	175.7	800-835-3879	Y
AMG Managers Emerging Opportunities Fund Class N	MMCFX	B+	A	B-	Up	4.11	14.66	24.01	33.18	117.36	45.91	175.7	800-835-3879	Y
AMG Managers Essex Small/Micro Cap Growth Fund - Class N	MBRSX	B+	A-	B-	Up	1.20	10.55	24.10	26.60	117.43	26.68	29.3	800-835-3879	Y
AMG Managers Silvercrest Small Cap Fund Class I	ACRTX	B+	A-	B	Up	3.53	9.14	10.54	36.52	101.93	18.42	279.9	800-835-3879	Y
AMG Managers Silvercrest Small Cap Fund Class N	ASCTX	B+	A-	B	Up	3.44	8.99	10.26	35.48	99.27	18.26	279.9	800-835-3879	Y
AMG Managers Silvercrest Small Cap Fund Class Z	ACZTX	B+	A-	B		3.54	9.16	10.55	36.54	101.95	18.41	279.9	800-835-3879	Y
AMG Managers Skyline Special Equities Fund Class I	SKSIX	B	B	B	Up	0.90	6.80	8.57	22.64	100.34	44.06	1,333	800-835-3879	Y
AMG Managers Skyline Special Equities Fund Class N	SKSEX	B	B	B	Up	0.91	6.74	8.39	22.44	99.99	43.98	1,333	800-835-3879	
AMG Managers Skyline Special Equities Fund Class Z	SKSZX	B	B	B	Up	0.97	6.87	8.62	22.70	100.42	44.08	1,333	800-835-3879	Y
AMG Managers Special Equity Fund Class I	MSEIX	B+	A-	B	Up	4.84	11.21	20.54	35.56	104.76	122.9	201.2	800-835-3879	Y
AMG Managers Special Equity Fund Class N	MGSEX	B+	A-	B	Up	4.78	11.07	20.25	34.56	102.97	119.45	201.2	800-835-3879	Y
AMG River Road Small Cap Value Fund Class I	ARSIX	B	B	B+		3.25	4.75	12.02	40.48	87.75	13.21	319.7	800-835-3879	Y
AMG River Road Small Cap Value Fund Class N	ARSVX	B	B	B+		3.18	4.63	11.76	39.40	85.36	12.99	319.7	800-835-3879	Y
AMG River Road Small Cap Value Fund Class Z	ARZMX	B	B	B+		3.28	4.73	11.86	39.53	85.54	13.2	319.7	800-835-3879	Y
AMG River Road Small-Mid Cap Value Fund Class I	ARIMX	B	B	B		1.82	4.41	15.74	42.85	87.02	7.47	44.6	800-835-3879	Y
AMG River Road Small-Mid Cap Value Fund Class N	ARSMX	B	B	B		1.77	4.28	15.34	41.83	84.69	7.33	44.6	800-835-3879	Y
AMG River Road Small-Mid Cap Value Fund Class Z	ARSZX	B	B	B		1.75	4.25	15.31	41.80	84.65	7.46	44.6	800-835-3879	Y
AMG TimesSquare Small Cap Growth Fund Class I	TSQIX	B+	A-	B	Up	5.38	11.25	21.08	32.03	94.82	17.32	1,196	800-835-3879	Y
AMG TimesSquare Small Cap Growth Fund Class N	TSCPX	B+	B+	B	Up	5.32	11.13	20.87	31.32	92.91	16.9	1,196	800-835-3879	
AMG TimesSquare Small Cap Growth Fund Class Z	TSCIX	B+	A-	B	Up	5.37	11.24	21.14	32.09	94.91	17.33	1,196	800-835-3879	
Ancora MicroCap Fund Class I	ANCIX	B+	A-	B	Up	0.30	6.49	17.99	25.97	102.72	14.09	21.9		Y
Ancora Special Opportunity Fund Class I	ANSIX	B	B	B	Up	3.36	6.98	14.54	29.95	86.81	7.49	17.9		Y
Ancora/Thelen Small-Mid Cap Fund Class I	AATIX	B-	B	C	Up	4.57	8.38	18.49	24.56	78.40	15.55	88.9		Y
Ancora/Thelen Small-Mid Cap Fund Class S	AATSX	B-	B	C	Up	5.17	9.07	19.45	26.15	80.69	15.85	88.9		Y
AQR Small Cap Momentum Style Fund Class I	ASMOX	B	B+	B	Up	3.86	11.54	17.38	26.97	94.69	23.47	380.4	203-742-3600	Y
AQR Small Cap Momentum Style Fund Class N	ASMNX	B	B+	B	Up	3.85	11.44	17.17	26.10	92.28	23.52	380.4	203-742-3600	Y
AQR Small Cap Momentum Style Fund Class R6	QSMRX	B+	A-	B	Up	3.93	11.63	17.48	27.34	95.24	23.42	380.4	203-742-3600	Y
AQR Small Cap Multi-Style Fund Class I	QSMLX	B	B+	B	Up	1.88	7.14	9.29	26.97		14.82	788.6	203-742-3600	Y
AQR Small Cap Multi-Style Fund Class N	QSMNX	B	B	B	Up	1.85	6.99	9.07	25.99		14.79	788.6	203-742-3600	Y
AQR Small Cap Multi-Style Fund Class R6	QSERX	B	B+	B	Up	1.98	7.24	9.45	27.33		14.84	788.6	203-742-3600	Y
AQR TM Small Cap Momentum Style Fund Class I	ATSMX	B+	A-	B	Up	3.22	9.91	16.69	28.13	93.00	19.61	55.2	203-742-3600	Y
AQR TM Small Cap Momentum Style Fund Class N	ATSNX	B+	A-	B	Up	3.14	9.74	16.40	27.39	90.87	19.5	55.2	203-742-3600	Y
AQR TM Small Cap Momentum Style Fund Class R6	QTSRX	B+	A-	B	Up	3.25	9.95	16.80	28.55	93.70	19.6	55.2	203-742-3600	Y
Artisan Small Cap Fund Advisor Shares	APDSX	B	B+	B	Up	5.66	9.60	26.91	33.53	94.38	30.59	1,321	800-344-1770	
Artisan Small Cap Fund Institutional Shares	APHSX	B	B+	B	Up	5.66	9.66	27.09	34.32	96.23	30.96	1,321	800-344-1770	
Artisan Small Cap Fund Investor Shares	ARTSX	B	B+	B	Up	5.60	9.58	26.80	33.42	94.22	30.55	1,321	800-344-1770	
ATM Small Cap Managed Volatility Portfolio Class K	US26883L8375	B+	A-	B	Up	4.05	9.75	14.58	30.61	95.25		1,015	877-222-2144	Y
AXA 2000 Managed Volatility Portfolio Class IB	US26884M8340	B	B+	B	Up	4.01	9.65	14.34	29.76	92.20		3,529	877-222-2144	Y
AXA 2000 Managed Volatility Portfolio Class K	US26883L8458	B+	A-	B	Up	4.09	9.84	14.61	30.77	94.71		3,529	877-222-2144	Y
AXA Charter Small Cap Growth Portfolio Class A	US00247C5931	B	B+	C	Up	6.62	12.28	25.09	28.19	89.86		97.2	877-222-2144	Y

Category: US Equity Small Cap (con't)

Fund Name	Ticker Symbol	RATINGS: Overall Rating	Reward Rating	Risk Rating	Recent Up/ Downgrade	TOTAL RETURNS & PERFORMANCE: 3-Month Total Return	6-Month Total Return	1-Year Total Return	3-Year Total Return	5-Year Total Return	ASSETS: NAV	Total Assets (MIL)	NEW INVESTORS: Telephone	Open to New Investors
AXA Charter Small Cap Growth Portfolio Class B	US29364E8764	B	B+	C	Up	6.61	12.24	25.18	28.20	90.01		97.2	877-222-2144	Y
AXA/AB Small Cap Growth Portfolio Class IA	US4049927035	B+	A-	B	Up	6.84	13.03	23.11	33.51	97.13		2,071	877-222-2144	Y
AXA/AB Small Cap Growth Portfolio Class IB	US4049927118	B+	A-	B	Up	6.81	13.04	23.09	33.49	97.19		2,071	877-222-2144	Y
AXA/AB Small Cap Growth Portfolio Class K	US26883L7617	B+	A-	B	Up	6.87	13.11	23.31	34.47	99.53		2,071	877-222-2144	Y
AXA/Franklin Small Cap Value Managed Vol Port Cls IA	US2689547816	B	B	B	Up	5.02	10.18	12.09	29.67	87.36		306.9	877-222-2144	Y
AXA/Franklin Small Cap Value Managed Vol Port Cls IB	US2689547733	B	B	B	Up	5.07	10.17	12.07	29.63	87.19		306.9	877-222-2144	Y
AXA/Franklin Small Cap Value Managed Vol Port Cls K	US26883L7534	B	B+	B	Up	5.15	10.32	12.35	30.64	89.70		306.9	877-222-2144	Y
AXA/Morgan Stanley Small Cap Growth Portfolio Class IB	US29439V7394	B	B	B-	Up	7.70	11.54	24.88	26.82			290.7	877-222-2144	Y
AXA/Morgan Stanley Small Cap Growth Portfolio Class K	US29439V7212	B	B+	B-	Up	7.84	11.75	25.17	27.89			290.7	877-222-2144	Y
B. Riley Diversified Equity Fund Class A Shares	BRDAX	B+	A-	B	Up	2.33	7.76	21.07	37.49		14.02	22.4	800-673-0550	Y
B. Riley Diversified Equity Fund Institutional Cls Shares	BRDZX	B+	A	B	Up	2.46	7.86	21.40	38.60		14.12	22.4	800-673-0550	Y
Baird SmallCap Value Fund Institutional Class	BSVIX	B	B	B	Up	5.58	14.26	18.04	28.10	84.33	16.99	35.1	800-792-2473	Y
Baird SmallCap Value Fund Investor Class	BSVSX	B	B	B	Up	5.52	14.16	17.78	27.16	82.10	16.97	35.1	800-792-2473	Y
Baron Discovery Fund Institutional Shares	BDFIX	B	A	C	Up	3.36	8.95	35.83	41.32		18.3	253.7	800-992-2766	Y
Baron Discovery Fund R6 Shares	BDFUX	B	A	C	Up	3.38	8.97	35.85	41.33		18.3	253.7	800-992-2766	Y
Baron Discovery Fund Retail Shares	BDFFX	B	A	C	Up	3.34	8.79	35.52	40.29		18.14	253.7	800-992-2766	Y
Baron Small Cap Fund Class R6	BSCUX	B	B+	C	Up	5.25	9.99	27.40	32.41	90.09	29.34	4,299	800-992-2766	Y
Baron Small Cap Fund Institutional Class	BSFIX	B	B+	C	Up	5.25	9.98	27.44	32.77	91.55	29.35	4,299	800-992-2766	Y
Baron Small Cap Fund Retail Class	BSCFX	B	B	C	Up	5.18	9.84	27.13	31.76	89.15	28.34	4,299	800-992-2766	Y
Bernzott US Small Cap Value Fund	BSCVX	B	A-	C+	Up	5.22	15.89	26.84	33.49	82.00	15.37	98.5	805-389-9445	Y
BlackRock Advantage Small Cap Core Fund Class K	BDSKX	B+	B+	B	Up	1.94	7.42	10.82	33.48		13.63	291.6	800-441-7762	Y
BlackRock Advantage Small Cap Core Fund Inst Shares	BDSIX	B+	B+	B	Up	1.92	7.47	10.78	33.42		13.63	291.6	800-441-7762	Y
BlackRock Advantage Small Cap Core Fund Investor A Shares	BDSAX	B+	B+	B	Up	1.88	7.29	10.52	32.44		13.58	291.6	800-441-7762	Y
BlackRock Advantage Small Cap Core Fund Investor C Shares	BDSCX	B	B+	B	Up	1.66	6.88	9.72	29.40		13.39	291.6	800-441-7762	Y
BlackRock Advantage Small Cap Growth Fund Inst Shares	PSGIX	B	B+	B	Up	2.39	8.27	14.86	25.01	90.25	19.59	703.3	800-441-7762	Y
BlackRock Advantage Small Cap Growth Fund Inv A Shares	CSGEX	B	B	B	Up	2.32	8.12	14.61	23.98	87.58	15.15	703.3	800-441-7762	Y
BlackRock Advantage Small Cap Growth Fund Inv C Shares	CGICX	B	B	B	Up	2.12	7.77	13.73	21.07	80.45	8.63	703.3	800-441-7762	Y
BlackRock Advantage Small Cap Growth Fund Service Shares	PCGEX	B	B	B	Up	2.32	8.12	14.62	23.96	87.68	16.66	703.3	800-441-7762	Y
BlackRock Advantage U.S. Total Mkt Fund Inst Shares	MASPX	B	B	B	Up	2.81	7.34	9.06	24.93	92.35	32.46	577.2	800-441-7762	Y
BlackRock Advantage U.S. Total Mkt Fund Inv A Shares	MDSPX	B	B	B	Up	2.73	7.18	8.74	23.98	89.92	31.36	577.2	800-441-7762	Y
BlackRock Advantage U.S. Total Mkt Fund Inv B Shares	MBSPX	B-	B-	B-	Up	3.00	6.39	7.68	20.74	80.89		577.2	800-441-7762	
BlackRock Advantage U.S. Total Mkt Fund Inv C Shares	MCSPX	B-	B	B-	Up	2.55	6.75	7.89	20.95	82.18	22.52	577.1	800-441-7762	Y
BlackRock Advantage U.S. Total Market Fund R Shares	MRSPX	B	B	B	Up	2.69	7.08	8.44	22.91	87.06	24.74	577.1	800-441-7762	Y
BlackRock Small Cap Growth Fund II Class R Shares	MRUSX	B	B	B	Up	2.10	7.82	13.86	22.54	84.52	11.88	156.9	800-441-7762	Y
BlackRock Small Cap Growth Fund II Institutional Shares	MASWX	B	B	B	Up	2.24	8.13	14.50	24.43	89.55	14.16	156.9	800-441-7762	Y
BlackRock Small Cap Growth Fund II Investor A Shares	MDSWX	B	B	B	Up	2.15	7.96	14.22	23.53	86.69	13.22	156.9	800-441-7762	Y
BlackRock Small Cap Growth Fund II Investor C Shares	MCSWX	B	B	B	Up	1.95	7.54	13.27	20.41	79.12	10.18	156.9	800-441-7762	Y
BMO Small-Cap Core Fund Class A	BCCAX	A-	A	B	Up	4.00	11.27	13.33	38.47		13.83	22.8	800-236-3863	Y
BMO Small-Cap Core Fund Class I	BSCNX	A-	A	B	Up	4.04	11.42	13.57	39.50		13.92	22.8	800-236-3863	Y
BMO Small-Cap Value Fund Class A	BACVX	B	B	B	Up	3.07	10.04	8.91	25.60	82.61	13.68	71.0	800-236-3863	Y
BMO Small-Cap Value Fund Class I	MRSNX	B	B+	B	Up	3.24	10.28	9.24	26.64	84.99	13.9	71.0	800-236-3863	Y
BMO Small-Cap Value Fund Class R3	BSVDX	B	B	B	Up	3.08	9.98	8.68	24.77	80.48	13.65	71.0	800-236-3863	Y
BMO Small-Cap Value Fund Class R6	BSVGX	B	B+	B	Up	3.22	10.31	9.35	27.24	86.12	13.97	71.0	800-236-3863	Y
BNY Mellon Small Cap Multi-Strategy Fund Class Investor	MISCX	B	B+	B	Up	6.15	11.01	18.18	33.95	101.51	19.16	582.9	800-645-6561	Y
BNY Mellon Small Cap Multi-Strategy Fund Class M	MPSSX	B	B+	B	Up	6.19	11.13	18.45	34.95	103.95	20.06	582.9	800-645-6561	Y
BNY Mellon Small/Mid Cap Multi-Strategy Fund Cls M Shares	MMCMX	B	B+	B	Up	6.56	11.20	19.91	34.36	96.89	14.59	355.3	800-645-6561	Y
BNY Mellon Small/Mid Cap Multi-Strategy Fund Inv Shares	MMCIX	B	B	B	Up	6.57	11.12	19.68	33.24	94.21	14.37	355.3	800-645-6561	Y
Bogle Investment Mgmt Small Cap Growth Fund Inst Cls	BOGIX	B	B+	B-	Up	3.69	13.83	17.06	28.59	99.36	31.23	110.2	877-264-5346	Y
Boston Partners Small Cap Value Fund II Institutional Cls	BPSIX	B	B+	B	Up	3.14	7.63	9.78	31.18	89.36	26.26	577.9	617-832-8200	Y
Boston Partners Small Cap Value Fund II Investor Class	BPSCX	B	B+	B	Up	3.06	7.48	9.50	30.19	87.09	25.15	577.9	617-832-8200	Y
Boston Trust Small Cap Fund	BOSOX	B+	B+	B	Up	5.34	8.32	12.25	32.15	77.60	14.73	370.8	617-814-1215	
Boston Trust SMID Cap Fund	BTSMX	B	B	B		8.12	9.90	18.38	37.39	92.02	15.79	55.8	617-814-1215	Y

Category: US Equity Small Cap (con't)

Fund Name	Ticker Symbol	RATINGS: Overall Rating	Reward Rating	Risk Rating	Recent Up/ Downgrade	TOTAL RETURNS & PERFORMANCE: 3-Month Total Return	6-Month Total Return	1-Year Total Return	3-Year Total Return	5-Year Total Return	ASSETS: NAV	Total Assets (ML)	NEW INVESTORS: Telephone	Open to New Investors
Bridgeway Omni Small-Cap Value Fund Class N	BOSVX	B+	A-	B-	Up	3.42	9.86	6.00	32.62	98.81	18.66	811.1	800-661-3550	Y
Bridgeway Omni Tax-Managed Small-Cap Value Fund Class N	BOTSX	B+	A-	B-	Up	2.99	9.15	5.51	33.51	97.31	17.9	736.1	800-661-3550	Y
Bridgeway Small Cap Growth Fund	BRSGX	A-	A	B+	Up	4.11	11.22	19.62	44.96	135.70	27.66	49.8	800-661-3550	Y
Bridgeway Small Cap Value Fund	BRSVX	B	B	B-	Up	2.82	7.83	7.10	22.01	76.71	26.53	64.0	800-661-3550	Y
Bridgeway Small-Cap Momentum Fund Class N	BRSMX	B+	A-	B	Up	3.90	10.52	16.99	31.98	84.56	12.99	5.8	800-661-3550	Y
Bridgeway Ultra Small Company Market Fund	BRSIX	B	B	B-	Up	2.22	9.00	12.47	25.46	102.01	14.26	367.9	800-661-3550	Y
Broadview Opportunity Fund	BVAOX	B-	C+	B-	Up	3.64	6.54	8.90	17.47	78.40	34.53	613.4	414-918-3900	Y
Brown Advy Small-Cap Fundamental Value Fund Adv Shares	BAUAX	B	B	B	Up	4.30	9.18	11.88	27.10	92.14	28.34	1,335	800-540-6807	Y
Brown Advy Small-Cap Fundamental Value Fund Inst Shares	BAUUX	B	B	B	Up	4.39	9.40	12.34	28.63	96.15	28.45	1,335	800-540-6807	Y
Brown Advy Small-Cap Fundamental Value Fund Inv Shares	BIAUX	B	B	B	Up	4.36	9.33	12.19	28.11	94.68	28.44	1,335	800-540-6807	Y
Brown Advisory Small-Cap Growth Fund Advisor Shares	BASAX	B	B	B+	Up	1.49	7.09	16.57	36.46	95.91	17.78	754.9	800-540-6807	Y
Brown Advisory Small-Cap Growth Fund Institutional Shares	BAFSX	B	B	B+	Up	1.58	7.30	17.10	38.14	99.82	37.07	754.9	800-540-6807	Y
Brown Advisory Small-Cap Growth Fund Investor Shares	BIASX	B	B	B+	Up	1.51	7.21	16.91	37.46	98.37	18.57	754.9	800-540-6807	Y
Brown Capital Mgmt Small Company Fund Inst Shares	BCSSX	A-	A	B+	Up	5.45	9.56	29.16	52.37	136.95	90.59	4,256		
Brown Capital Mgmt Small Company Fund Inv Shares	BCSIX	A-	A	B+	Up	5.40	9.44	28.90	51.45	134.59	89.26	4,256		
Buffalo Emerging Opportunities Fund	BUFOX	B	A-	C	Up	1.32	8.22	27.18	27.87	95.25	15.62	92.9	800-492-8332	
Buffalo Small Cap Fund	BUFSX	B	B+	B-	Up	3.80	9.01	27.07	28.62	76.97	14.66	569.9	800-492-8332	
Calvert Small-Cap Fund Class A	CCVAX	B	B	B+	Up	5.31	8.56	13.19	33.22	107.09	23.64	259.7	800-368-2745	Y
Calvert Small-Cap Fund Class C	CSCCX	B	B	B	Up	5.12	8.13	12.33	30.23	99.30	20.46	259.7	800-368-2745	Y
Calvert Small-Cap Fund Class I	CSVIX	B+	B	B+	Up	5.42	8.78	13.69	35.07	112.62	25.47	259.7	800-368-2745	Y
Cardinal Small Cap Value Fund Institutional Class	CCMSX	B+	A-	B	Up	4.65	10.47	13.77	35.54		12.81	54.9		Y
Carillon Eagle Small Cap Growth Fund Class A	HRSCX	B	B+	B	Up	5.92	10.01	22.82	33.17	92.91	59.6	5,195	800-421-4184	Y
Carillon Eagle Small Cap Growth Fund Class C	HSCCX	B	B+	B	Up	5.73	9.66	21.98	30.39	86.23	44.24	5,195	800-421-4184	Y
Carillon Eagle Small Cap Growth Fund Class I	HSIIX	B	B+	B	Up	6.02	10.24	23.27	34.53	96.10	62.61	5,195	800-421-4184	Y
Carillon Eagle Small Cap Growth Fund Class R3	HSRRX	B	B+	B	Up	5.86	9.89	22.51	32.18	90.36	57.72	5,195	800-421-4184	Y
Carillon Eagle Small Cap Growth Fund Class R5	HSRSX	B	B+	B	Up	6.03	10.24	23.29	34.60	96.26	62.89	5,195	800-421-4184	Y
Carillon Eagle Small Cap Growth Fund Class R6	HSRUX	B	B+	B	Up	6.05	10.29	23.40	35.02	97.37	63.38	5,195	800-421-4184	Y
Carillon Eagle Small Cap Growth Fund Class Y	HSRYX	B	B+	B		5.95	10.04	22.86	33.22	92.97	62.6	5,195	800-421-4184	Y
Carillon Eagle Smaller Company Fund Class A	EGEAX	B	B	B	Up	5.81	10.19	19.31	31.28	83.55	14.01	47.0	800-421-4184	Y
Carillon Eagle Smaller Company Fund Class C	EGECX	B	B	B	Up	5.63	9.76	18.46	28.40	76.93	12.04	47.0	800-421-4184	Y
Carillon Eagle Smaller Company Fund Class I	EGEIX	B	B+	B	Up	5.90	10.33	19.71	33.60	88.64	15.2	47.0	800-421-4184	Y
Carillon Eagle Smaller Company Fund Class R3	EGERX	B	B	B	Up	5.75	10.06	19.06	30.29	81.00	13.43	47.0	800-421-4184	Y
Carillon Eagle Smaller Company Fund Class R5	EGESX	B	B+	B	Up	5.91	10.40	19.74	32.99	87.55	15	47.0	800-421-4184	Y
Carillon Eagle Smaller Company Fund Class R6	EGEUX	B	B+	B	Up	5.95	10.41	19.88	33.47	88.29	15.09	47.0	800-421-4184	Y
Carillon Eagle Smaller Company Fund Class Y	EGEYX	B	B	B		5.80	10.18	19.30	31.27	83.54	15.2	47.0	800-421-4184	Y
Carillon Scout Small Cap Fund Class A	CSSAX	B+	A	C+		6.18	14.15	31.52	47.05	117.47	27.91	280.9	800-421-4184	Y
Carillon Scout Small Cap Fund Class C	CSSJX	B+	A	C+		6.02	13.76	30.58	43.84	109.58	27.89	280.9	800-421-4184	Y
Carillon Scout Small Cap Fund Class I	UMBHX	B+	A	C+	Up	6.26	14.31	31.87	48.17	120.23	27.92	280.9	800-421-4184	Y
Carillon Scout Small Cap Fund Class R-3	CSSQX	B+	A	C+		6.14	14.03	31.22	45.98	114.83	27.9	280.9	800-421-4184	Y
Carillon Scout Small Cap Fund Class R-5	CSSSX	B+	A	C+		6.26	14.31	31.87	48.17	120.23	27.92	280.9	800-421-4184	Y
Carillon Scout Small Cap Fund Class R-6	CSSVX	B+	A	C+		6.26	14.31	31.87	48.17	120.23	27.92	280.9	800-421-4184	Y
Carillon Scout Small Cap Fund Class Y	CSSWX	B+	A	C+		6.18	14.15	31.52	47.05	117.47	27.91	280.9	800-421-4184	Y
Champlain Small Company Fund Class Advisor	CIPSX	B	B	B	Up	1.86	5.24	10.57	38.67	101.65	19.9	1,530		
Champlain Small Company Fund Institutional Class	CIPNX	B	B	B	Up	1.94	5.38	10.81	39.18	102.38	19.98	1,530		Y
Chartwell Small Cap Value Fund	CWSIX	B	B+	B	Up	4.85	9.96	8.91	27.01	91.96	19.66	172.9	610-296-1400	Y
ClearBridge Small Cap Fund Class A	LMSAX	B	B	B	Up	2.27	4.97	11.86	35.66	103.67	40.61	1,053	877-721-1926	Y
ClearBridge Small Cap Fund Class A2	LBRTX	B	B	B	Up	2.21	4.88	11.63	34.79	99.66	40.31	1,053	877-721-1926	Y
ClearBridge Small Cap Fund Class C	LMASX	B	B	B	Up	2.08	4.57	10.99	32.49	95.78	38.5	1,053	877-721-1926	Y
ClearBridge Small Cap Fund Class FI	LGASX	B	B	B	Up	2.23	4.86	11.63	35.13	101.61	57.88	1,053	877-721-1926	Y
ClearBridge Small Cap Fund Class I	LMNSX	B	B	B		2.33	5.08	12.10	36.54	105.77	60.59	1,053	877-721-1926	Y
ClearBridge Small Cap Fund Class IS	LISGX	B	B	B		2.36	4.86	11.30	32.85	96.32	60.62	1,053	877-721-1926	Y
ClearBridge Small Cap Fund Class R	LMARX	B	B	B	Up	2.19	4.80	11.63	34.32	99.81	56.63	1,053	877-721-1926	Y

Category: US Equity Small Cap (con't)

Fund Name	Ticker Symbol	RATINGS: Overall Rating	RATINGS: Reward Rating	RATINGS: Risk Rating	RATINGS: Recent Up/ Downgrade	TOTAL RETURNS & PERFORMANCE: 3-Month Total Return	6-Month Total Return	1-Year Total Return	3-Year Total Return	5-Year Total Return	ASSETS: NAV	Total Assets (MIL)	NEW INVESTORS: Telephone	Open to New Investors
ClearBridge Small Cap Growth Fund Class 1	LMPMX	B	B+	B	Up	6.16	11.83	25.16	25.78	93.73	33.57	3,038	877-721-1926	
ClearBridge Small Cap Growth Fund Class A	SASMX	B	B	B	Up	6.11	11.76	24.95	25.00	92.33	32.81	3,038	877-721-1926	
ClearBridge Small Cap Growth Fund Class C	SCSMX	B	B	B-	Up	5.95	11.35	24.04	22.37	85.56	26.56	3,038	877-721-1926	
ClearBridge Small Cap Growth Fund Class FI	LMPSX	B	B	B	Up	6.11	11.76	24.96	25.09	92.52	33	3,038	877-721-1926	
ClearBridge Small Cap Growth Fund Class I	SBPYX	B	B+	B	Up	6.20	11.92	25.28	26.18	95.52	34.93	3,038	877-721-1926	
ClearBridge Small Cap Growth Fund Class IS	LMOIX	B	B+	B	Up	6.23	11.98	25.47	26.70	96.72	35.26	3,038	877-721-1926	
ClearBridge Small Cap Growth Fund Class R	LMPOX	B	B	B	Up	6.02	11.61	24.59	24.05	90.02	32.04	3,038	877-721-1926	
ClearBridge Small Cap Value Fund Class A	SBVAX	B	B	B-	Up	3.92	8.12	10.54	23.29	72.80	19.9	181.6	877-721-1926	Y
ClearBridge Small Cap Value Fund Class C	SBVLX	B-	B-	C+	Up	3.71	7.69	9.70	20.64	66.73	15.51	181.6	877-721-1926	Y
ClearBridge Small Cap Value Fund Class I	SMCYX	B	B	B-	Up	4.00	8.25	10.85	24.57	75.76	21.53	181.6	877-721-1926	Y
ClearBridge Small Cap Value Fund Class IS	LCBIX	B	B	B-	Up	4.03	8.32	11.02	24.94	76.20	21.58	181.6	877-721-1926	Y
Columbia Acorn USA Fund Advisor Class	CUSAX	B	B+	B	Up	2.54	7.14	19.42	32.03	86.51	16.08	334.0	800-345-6611	Y
Columbia Acorn USA Fund Class A	LAUAX	B	B+	B	Up	2.48	7.07	19.13	31.13	84.17	12.48	334.0	800-345-6611	Y
Columbia Acorn USA Fund Class C	LAUCX	B	B	B	Up	2.32	6.68	18.30	28.45	77.92	6.56	334.0	800-345-6611	Y
Columbia Acorn USA Fund Institutional 2 Class	CYSRX	B	B+	B	Up	2.59	7.27	19.56	32.54	87.43	16.21	334.0	800-345-6611	Y
Columbia Acorn USA Fund Institutional 3 Class	CUSYX	B	B+	B	Up	2.62	7.26	19.59	32.74	87.88	16.36	334.0	800-345-6611	Y
Columbia Acorn USA Fund Institutional Class	AUSAX	B	B+	B	Up	2.55	7.19	19.43	32.15	86.54	15.21	334.0	800-345-6611	Y
Columbia Disciplined Small Core Fund Advisor Class	CFFRX	B-	C+	B-	Up	3.00	6.18	6.51	14.25	59.45	8.55	215.3	800-345-6611	Y
Columbia Disciplined Small Core Fund Class A	LSMAX	B-	C+	B-	Up	3.01	6.12	6.36	13.40	57.55	7.43	215.3	800-345-6611	Y
Columbia Disciplined Small Core Fund Class T	CSCWX	B-	C+	B-	Up	3.01	6.12	6.36	13.47	57.56	7.43	215.3	800-345-6611	Y
Columbia Disciplined Small Core Fund Class V	SSCEX	B-	C+	B-	Up	2.92	6.06	6.32	13.39	57.32	6.96	215.3	800-345-6611	
Columbia Disciplined Small Core Fund Institutional 2 Class	CLLRX	B-	C+	B-	Up	3.07	6.23	6.67	14.68	60.82	8.62	215.3	800-345-6611	Y
Columbia Disciplined Small Core Fund Institutional 3 Class	CPFRX	B-	C+	B-	Up	3.08	6.21	6.65	14.84	61.09	8.72	215.3	800-345-6611	Y
Columbia Disciplined Small Core Fund Institutional Class	SMCEX	B-	C+	B-	Up	2.94	6.08	6.53	14.21	59.41	8.34	215.3	800-345-6611	Y
Columbia Select Smaller-Cap Value Fund Advisor Class	CSPRX	B	B	B	Up	3.23	7.35	12.89	22.49	97.46	20.96	688.0	800-345-6611	Y
Columbia Select Smaller-Cap Value Fund Class A	SSCVX	B	B	B	Up	3.13	7.17	12.59	21.56	95.01	18.05	688.0	800-345-6611	Y
Columbia Select Smaller-Cap Value Fund Class C	SVMCX	B-	B-	B	Up	3.00	6.83	11.74	18.88	87.88	13.09	688.0	800-345-6611	Y
Columbia Select Smaller-Cap Value Fund Class K	SSLRX	B	B	B	Up	3.19	7.22	12.64	21.99	96.32	20.3	688.0	800-345-6611	
Columbia Select Smaller-Cap Value Fund Class R	SSVRX	B	B	B	Up	3.11	7.10	12.33	20.69	92.64	16.9	688.0	800-345-6611	Y
Columbia Select Smaller-Cap Value Fund Institutional 2 Cls	SSVIX	B	B	B	Up	3.24	7.37	12.92	22.90	98.81	20.9	688.0	800-345-6611	Y
Columbia Select Smaller-Cap Value Fund Institutional 3 Cls	CSSYX	B	B	B	Up	3.23	7.39	12.99	23.15	97.48	21.58	688.0	800-345-6611	Y
Columbia Select Smaller-Cap Value Fund Institutional Class	CSSZX	B	B	B	Up	3.23	7.31	12.87	22.48	97.48	20.63	688.0	800-345-6611	Y
Columbia Small Cap Growth Fund I Advisor Class	CHHRX	B+	A	B-	Up	5.27	12.93	28.70	50.29	104.93	20.29	474.3	800-345-6611	
Columbia Small Cap Growth Fund I Class A	CGOAX	B+	A	B-	Up	5.21	12.78	28.43	49.23	102.42	18.21	474.3	800-345-6611	
Columbia Small Cap Growth Fund I Class C	CGOCX	B+	A	B-	Up	5.01	12.36	27.40	45.88	94.86	14.88	474.3	800-345-6611	
Columbia Small Cap Growth Fund I Class K	CSCKX	B+	A	B-	Up	5.21	12.83	28.53	49.76	103.77	19.16	474.3	800-345-6611	
Columbia Small Cap Growth Fund I Class R	CCRIX	B+	A	B-	Up	5.09	12.63	28.04	48.06	99.84	17.84	474.3	800-345-6611	
Columbia Small Cap Growth Fund I Institutional 2 Class	CSCRX	B+	A	B-	Up	5.32	13.03	28.91	50.91	106.85	19.51	474.3	800-345-6611	
Columbia Small Cap Growth Fund I Institutional 3 Class	CSGYX	B+	A	B-	Up	5.31	13.01	28.93	51.11	106.76	19.71	474.3	800-345-6611	
Columbia Small Cap Growth Fund I Institutional Class	CMSCX	B+	A	B-	Up	5.27	12.94	28.76	50.34	104.90	19.31	474.3	800-345-6611	
Columbia Small Cap Index Fund Class A	NMSAX	B+	A-	B	Up	3.87	9.92	12.80	37.51	108.94	24.71	4,151	800-345-6611	Y
Columbia Small Cap index Fund Class K	CIDUX	B+	A-	B	Up	3.81	9.88	12.80	37.41	108.83	24.8	4,151	800-345-6611	
Columbia Small Cap Index Fund Class T	CSMWX	B+	A-	B	Up	3.82	9.88	12.79	37.47	108.96	24.47	4,151	800-345-6611	Y
Columbia Small Cap Index Fund Institutional 2 Class	CXXRX	A-	A-	B	Up	3.89	10.05	13.09	38.53	111.68	25.37	4,151	800-345-6611	Y
Columbia Small Cap Index Fund Institutional 3 Class	CSPYX	A-	A-	B	Up	3.89	10.06	13.15	38.58	111.66	24.26	4,151	800-345-6611	Y
Columbia Small Cap Index Fund Institutional Class	NMSCX	A-	A-	B	Up	3.88	10.04	13.09	38.51	111.55	24.84	4,151	800-345-6611	Y
Columbia Small Cap Value Fund I Advisor Class	CVVRX	B+	A	B	Up	3.09	11.10	14.20	40.95	100.59	47.77	648.8	800-345-6611	Y
Columbia Small Cap Value Fund I Class A	CSMIX	B+	A	B	Up	3.04	10.97	13.91	39.86	97.96	41.8	648.8	800-345-6611	Y
Columbia Small Cap Value Fund I Class C	CSSCX	B+	A	B	Up	2.85	10.55	13.05	36.76	90.69	28.36	648.8	800-345-6611	Y
Columbia Small Cap Value Fund I Class R	CSVRX	B+	A	B	Up	2.97	10.81	13.61	38.84	95.56	41.73	648.8	800-345-6611	Y
Columbia Small Cap Value Fund I Institutional 2 Class	CUURX	B+	A	B	Up	3.12	11.15	14.32	41.53	101.95	47.76	648.8	800-345-6611	Y
Columbia Small Cap Value Fund I Institutional 3 Class	CSVYX	B+	A	B	Up	3.11	11.18	14.36	41.74	102.43	46.6	648.8	800-345-6611	Y

Category: US Equity Small Cap (con't)

Fund Name	Ticker Symbol	Overall Rating	Reward Rating	Risk Rating	Recent Up/ Downgrade	3-Month Total Return	6-Month Total Return	1-Year Total Return	3-Year Total Return	5-Year Total Return	NAV	Total Assets (MIL)	Telephone	Open to New Investors
		RATINGS				TOTAL RETURNS & PERFORMANCE					ASSETS		NEW INVESTORS	
Columbia Small Cap Value Fund I Institutional Class	CSCZX	B+	A	B	Up	3.09	11.09	14.17	40.93	100.48	46.41	648.8	800-345-6611	Y
Columbia Small Cap Value Fund II Advisor Class	CLURX	B+	A-	B	Up	3.36	9.32	10.88	32.08	99.30	18.37	1,661	800-345-6611	
Columbia Small Cap Value Fund II Class A	COVAX	B+	B+	B	Up	3.33	9.19	10.62	31.16	96.89	17.72	1,661	800-345-6611	
Columbia Small Cap Value Fund II Class C	COVCX	B	B	B	Up	3.09	8.78	9.82	28.21	89.60	15.61	1,661	800-345-6611	
Columbia Small Cap Value Fund II Class R	CCTRX	B	B+	B	Up	3.29	9.12	10.38	30.23	94.43	17.45	1,661	800-345-6611	
Columbia Small Cap Value Fund II Institutional 2 Class	CRRRX	B+	A-	B	Up	3.42	9.43	11.06	32.74	100.82	18.4	1,661	800-345-6611	
Columbia Small Cap Value Fund II Institutional 3 Class	CRRYX	B+	A-	B	Up	3.45	9.50	11.19	32.96	101.41	18.46	1,661	800-345-6611	
Columbia Small Cap Value Fund II Institutional Class	NSVAX	B+	A-	B	Up	3.37	9.33	10.94	32.13	99.40	17.98	1,661	800-345-6611	
Columbia Small/Mid Cap Value Fund Advisor Class	RMCRX	B	B	B	Up	3.42	9.63	12.97	23.75	83.01	10.17	849.2	800-345-6611	Y
Columbia Small/Mid Cap Value Fund Class A	AMVAX	B-	B-	B	Up	3.38	9.50	12.73	22.85	80.70	10.14	849.2	800-345-6611	Y
Columbia Small/Mid Cap Value Fund Class C	AMVCX	B-	B-	B-	Up	3.28	9.11	11.90	20.12	73.99	9.1	849.2	800-345-6611	Y
Columbia Small/Mid Cap Value Fund Class K	RMCVX	B-	B-	B	Up	3.39	9.55	12.86	23.26	81.94	10.26	849.2	800-345-6611	
Columbia Small/Mid Cap Value Fund Class R	RMVTX	B-	B-	B	Up	3.32	9.46	12.51	22.02	78.42	9.93	849.2	800-345-6611	Y
Columbia Small/Mid Cap Value Fund Class T	CVOWX	B-	B-	B	Up	3.37	9.53	12.84	23.01	80.83	10.25	849.2	800-345-6611	Y
Columbia Small/Mid Cap Value Fund Institutional 2 Class	RSCMX	B	B	B	Up	3.52	9.75	13.15	24.29	84.19	10.34	849.2	800-345-6611	Y
Columbia Small/Mid Cap Value Fund Institutional 3 Class	CPHPX	B	B	B	Up	3.50	9.71	13.16	24.26	84.10	10.17	849.2	800-345-6611	Y
Columbia Small/Mid Cap Value Fund Institutional Class	CMOZX	B	B-	B	Up	3.54	9.71	13.09	23.89	82.97	10.43	849.2	800-345-6611	Y
Conestoga Small Cap Fund Investors Class	CCASX	A-	A	B	Up	3.60	13.70	28.44	57.85	121.56	48.95	1,552	800-320-7790	Y
Conestoga Small Cap Institutional Class	CCALX	A-	A	B	Up	3.67	13.84	28.74	58.88	123.14	49.34	1,552	800-320-7790	Y
Conestoga SMid Cap Fund Institutional Class	CCSGX	B+	A	B-	Up	6.99	14.41	34.39	48.05		13.65	28.0	800-320-7790	Y
Conestoga SMid Cap Fund Investors Class	CCSMX	B+	A	B-	Up	6.88	14.25	34.10	47.02		13.54	28.0	800-320-7790	Y
Congress Small Cap Growth Fund Institutional Class	CSMCX	B	B	B	Up	4.48	10.07	22.30	26.60	74.15	26.11	78.2	888-688-1299	Y
Congress Small Cap Growth Fund Retail Class	CSMVX	B	B	B-	Up	4.41	9.90	22.03	25.49	71.60	24.12	78.2	888-688-1299	Y
Consulting Group Small-Mid Cap Equity Fund	TSGUX	B-	B-	B-	Up	5.50	10.60	19.65	20.23	91.77	20.77	744.0	855-332-5306	Y
Convergence Opportunities Fund Institutional Class	CIPOX	B+	A-	B	Up	2.11	10.10	10.81	26.82		12.11	68.9	877-677-9414	Y
CornerCap Small-Cap Value Fund Institutional Shares	CSCJX	B+	A-	B	Up	2.44	8.62	8.04	34.90	113.08	15.74	119.6	888-813-8637	Y
CornerCap Small-Cap Value Fund Investor Shares	CSCVX	B+	A-	B	Up	2.31	8.42	7.71	34.02	111.69	15.72	119.6	888-813-8637	Y
Cortina Small Cap Growth Fund	CRSGX	B	B	B	Up	0.76	3.56	14.12	30.76	79.31	16.28	26.7		Y
Cortina Small Cap Value Fund Institutional Class	CRSVX	B-	B-	B-	Up	2.98	7.01	9.79	18.08	74.04	20.46	45.9		Y
Cove Street Capital Small Cap Value Fund Inst Cls Shares	CSCAX	B-	C+	B	Up	1.71	3.03	5.73	18.32	64.28	36.02	147.1	866-497-0097	Y
Crawford Dividend Opportunity Fund	CDOFX	A-	A	B	Up	4.18	9.80	13.93	40.26	108.78	42.42	185.7		Y
Crawford Dividend Opportunity Fund Class C	CDOCX	B+	A-	B	Up	3.90	9.24	12.78	36.10	98.60	42.27	185.7		Y
CRM Small Cap Value Fund Class Institutional	CRISX	B+	A	B	Up	3.58	11.54	14.63	38.89	105.32	19.79	465.4	800-276-2883	Y
CRM Small Cap Value Fund Class Investor	CRMSX	B+	A-	B	Up	3.51	11.36	14.33	37.90	103.04	17.18	465.4	800-276-2883	Y
Dean Small Cap Value Fund	DASCX	B	B	B	Up	1.55	3.76	3.70	25.49	86.89	14.9	335.1	888-899-8343	Y
Delaware Small Cap Core Fund Class A	DCCAX	B+	A-	B	Up	2.63	8.67	13.92	32.11	109.89	23.58	2,828		Y
Delaware Small Cap Core Fund Class C	DCCCX	B+	A-	B	Up	2.45	8.30	13.06	29.23	102.12	21.23	2,828		Y
Delaware Small Cap Core Fund Class R	DCCRX	B+	A-	B	Up	2.54	8.52	13.65	31.13	107.26	22.85	2,828		Y
Delaware Small Cap Core Fund Class R6	DCZRX	B+	A-	B	Up	1.80	7.92	13.32	32.22	111.08	24.11	2,828		Y
Delaware Small Cap Core Fund Institutional Class	DCCIX	B+	A-	B	Up	2.72	8.86	14.20	33.13	112.53	24.11	2,828		Y
Delaware Small Cap Value Fund Class A	DEVLX	B+	A-	B	Up	5.07	8.80	11.69	35.62	94.61	65.94	4,547		Y
Delaware Small Cap Value Fund Class C	DEVCX	B	B+	B	Up	4.87	8.40	10.85	32.59	87.45	54.74	4,547		Y
Delaware Small Cap Value Fund Class R	DVLRX	B	B+	B	Up	5.01	8.68	11.43	34.60	92.19	64.01	4,547		Y
Delaware Small Cap Value Fund Class R6	DVZRX	B+	A-	B	Up	5.17	9.04	12.19	36.53	95.92	69.5	4,547		Y
Delaware Small Cap Value Fund Institutional Class	DEVIX	B+	A-	B	Up	5.14	8.94	11.99	36.65	97.06	69.49	4,547		Y
Deutsche Small Cap Core Fund Class A	SZCAX	B	B	B	Up	3.74	6.43	11.44	34.75	100.40	29.8	171.6	201-593-8273	Y
Deutsche Small Cap Core Fund Class C	SZCCX	B	B	B	Up	3.52	6.07	10.59	31.76	93.07	25.02	171.6	201-593-8273	Y
Deutsche Small Cap Core Fund Class R6	SZCRX	B	B	B	Up	3.79	6.58	11.71	35.84	103.00	31.1	171.6	212-454-5624	Y
Deutsche Small Cap Core Fund Class S	SSLCX	B	B	B+	Up	3.78	6.53	11.66	35.76	102.88	31.12	171.6	201-593-8273	Y
Deutsche Small Cap Core Fund Class T	SZCTX	B	B	B	Up	3.74	6.44	11.42	34.79	100.43	29.76	171.6	201-593-8273	Y
Deutsche Small Cap Core Fund Institutional Class	SZCIX	B	B	B	Up	3.78	6.57	11.70	35.83	102.98	31.08	171.6	201-593-8273	Y
Deutsche Small Cap Growth Fund Class A	SSDAX	B	B	B	Up	4.51	11.20	20.78	27.18	92.80	33.58	461.4	201-593-8273	Y

Category: US Equity Small Cap (con't)

Fund Name	Ticker Symbol	RATINGS				TOTAL RETURNS & PERFORMANCE					ASSETS		NEW INVESTORS	
		Overall Rating	Reward Rating	Risk Rating	Recent Up/ Downgrade	3-Month Total Return	6-Month Total Return	1-Year Total Return	3-Year Total Return	5-Year Total Return	NAV	Total Assets (MIL)	Telephone	Open to New Investors
Deutsche Small Cap Growth Fund Class C	SSDCX	B	B	B	Up	4.29	10.77	19.85	24.34	85.66	28.48	461.4	201-593-8273	Y
Deutsche Small Cap Growth Fund Class R	SSDGX	B	B	B	Up	4.40	11.02	20.40	26.11	90.37	33	461.4	201-593-8273	Y
Deutsche Small Cap Growth Fund Class R6	SSDZX	B	B+	B	Up	4.56	11.34	21.06	28.07	94.44	33.89	461.4	201-593-8273	Y
Deutsche Small Cap Growth Fund Class S	SSDSX	B	B+	B	Up	4.56	11.34	21.04	28.11	95.15	35.07	461.4	201-593-8273	Y
Deutsche Small Cap Growth Fund Institutional Class	SSDIX	B	B+	B	Up	4.56	11.32	21.04	28.24	95.76	35.52	461.4	201-593-8273	Y
Deutsche Small Cap Value Fund Class A	KDSAX	B	B-	B	Up	1.99	8.66	9.17	17.01	62.90	25.77	356.1	201-593-8273	Y
Deutsche Small Cap Value Fund Class C	KDSCX	B-	B-	B-	Up	1.78	8.21	8.31	14.39	56.90	20.35	356.1	201-593-8273	Y
Deutsche Small Cap Value Fund Class R6	KDSZX	B	B	B	Up	2.07	8.85	9.61	18.18	64.75	26.41	356.1	201-593-8273	Y
Deutsche Small Cap Value Fund Class S	KDSSX	B	B	B	Up	2.05	8.76	9.43	17.91	64.83	26.23	356.1	201-593-8273	Y
Deutsche Small Cap Value Fund Institutional Class	KDSIX	B	B	B	Up	2.07	8.78	9.49	18.16	65.79	26.41	356.1	201-593-8273	Y
DF Dent Small Cap Growth Fund Investor Shares	DFDSX	B	B	B	Up	3.31	7.75	15.57	28.64		14.32	8.6		Y
DFA Tax Managed U.S. Small Cap Portfolio	DFTSX	B+	A-	B	Up	3.92	9.89	11.87	32.98	103.76	44.07	3,026	512-306-7400	Y
DFA Tax-Managed U.S. Targeted Value Portfolio	DTMVX	B+	B+	B	Up	4.29	10.07	11.07	32.01	103.63	37.53	4,885	512-306-7400	Y
DFA U.S. Micro Cap Portfolio Institutional Class	DFSCX	B+	A-	B	Up	2.70	9.42	11.17	33.92	105.34	22.03	6,474	512-306-7400	Y
DFA U.S. Small Cap Growth Portfolio Institutional Class	DSCGX	B+	A-	B	Up	5.31	10.28	16.20	33.02	103.70	18.67	528.9	512-306-7400	Y
DFA U.S. Small Cap Portfolio Institutional Class	DFSTX	B+	A-	B	Up	3.79	9.42	11.52	32.21	101.97	35.94	17,435	512-306-7400	Y
DFA U.S. Small Cap Value Portfolio Institutional Class	DFSVX	B	B	B-	Up	3.12	9.28	7.21	25.79	91.08	37.92	15,503	512-306-7400	Y
DFA U.S. Targeted Value Portfolio Class R1	DFTVX	B	B	B	Up	4.44	9.91	9.50	29.60	96.21	24.88	11,043	512-306-7400	Y
DFA U.S. Targeted Value Portfolio Class R2	DFTPX	B	B	B-	Up	4.40	9.85	9.31	29.04	94.52	24.75	11,043	512-306-7400	Y
DFA U.S. Targeted Value Portfolio Institutional Class	DFFVX	B	B	B	Up	4.50	9.99	9.58	30.01	97.03	24.89	11,043	512-306-7400	Y
DGHM MicroCap Value Fund Institutional Class	DGMIX	B+	A	B-	Up	-0.11	8.08	15.40	52.43	125.51	12.47	24.7	212-557-2445	Y
DGHM MicroCap Value Fund Investor Class	DGMMX	B+	A	B-	Up	-0.21	7.89	15.01	50.94	122.20	12.49	24.7	212-557-2445	Y
DGHM V2000 SmallCap Value Fund Institutional Class	DGIVX	B	B	B	Up	4.13	8.77	8.19	27.36	77.62	13.69	57.2	212-557-2445	Y
DGHM V2000 SmallCap Value Fund Investor Class	DGSMX	B	B	B	Up	4.02	8.54	7.76	25.75	74.02	12.95	57.2	212-557-2445	Y
Diamond Hill Small Cap Fund Class A	DHSCX	B-	C+	B	Up	3.79	8.78	10.61	20.70	80.54	35.62	1,511	888-226-5595	Y
Diamond Hill Small Cap Fund Class C	DHSMX	B-	C+	B	Up	3.57	8.40	9.80	18.02	73.92	30.98	1,511	888-226-5595	Y
Diamond Hill Small Cap Fund Class I	DHSIX	B-	C+	B	Up	3.85	8.97	10.94	21.76	83.02	36.15	1,511	888-226-5595	
Diamond Hill Small Cap Fund Class Y	DHSYX	B-	C+	B	Up	3.90	9.02	11.05	22.14	84.15	36.17	1,511	888-226-5595	Y
Dinosaur Lisanti Small Cap Growth Fund	ASCGX	B	A-	C+	Up	6.66	13.27	27.78	36.38	118.31	18.81	14.4		Y
Dreyfus Opportunistic Small Cap Fund Class I	DOPIX	B+	A-	B	Up	8.55	13.64	24.40	40.05	115.13	36.82	1,092	800-645-6561	Y
Dreyfus Opportunistic Small Cap Fund Class Y	DSCYX	B+	A-	B	Up	8.61	13.77	24.50	40.12	115.24	36.84	1,092	800-645-6561	
Dreyfus Opportunistic Small Cap Fund Investor Class	DSCVX	B	A-	B	Up	8.52	13.59	24.18	39.72	114.62	36.72	1,092	800-645-6561	
Dreyfus Select Managers Small Cap Growth Fund Class A	DSGAX	B	B+	C	Up	4.85	11.81	24.59	27.31	86.22	26.31	744.6	800-645-6561	Y
Dreyfus Select Managers Small Cap Growth Fund Class C	DSGCX	B-	B	C	Up	4.68	11.40	23.67	24.44	79.39	24.58	744.6	800-645-6561	Y
Dreyfus Select Managers Small Cap Growth Fund Class I	DSGIX	B	B+	C	Up	4.95	12.00	24.96	28.45	89.10	27.03	744.6	800-645-6561	Y
Dreyfus Select Managers Small Cap Growth Fund Class Y	DSGYX	B	B+	C	Up	4.95	12.00	25.01	28.56	89.21	27.03	744.6	800-645-6561	Y
Dreyfus Select Managers Small Cap Value Fund Class A	DMVAX	B	B	B	Up	2.76	9.01	12.09	24.85	83.46	24.7	964.7	800-645-6561	Y
Dreyfus Select Managers Small Cap Value Fund Class C	DMECX	B	B	B-	Up	2.55	8.57	11.26	22.17	76.87	22.77	964.7	800-645-6561	Y
Dreyfus Select Managers Small Cap Value Fund Class I	DMVIX	B	B	B	Up	2.64	8.99	12.26	25.80	86.09	25.11	964.7	800-645-6561	Y
Dreyfus Select Managers Small Cap Value Fund Class Y	DMVYX	B	B	B	Up	2.60	8.96	12.23	25.86	86.10	25.08	964.7	800-645-6561	Y
Dreyfus Small Cap Stock Index Fund Class I	DISIX	B+	A-	B	Up	3.85	9.91	12.66	37.73	109.94	31.47	2,469	800-645-6561	Y
Dreyfus Small Cap Stock Index Fund Investor Shares	DISSX	B+	A-	B	Up	3.78	9.81	12.40	37.29	109.27	31.52	2,469	800-645-6561	Y
Dreyfus/The Boston Company Small Cap Growth Fund Class I	SSETX	B+	A-	B	Up	4.32	10.87	20.63	37.06	110.75	28.75	6.7	800-645-6561	Y
Dreyfus/The Boston Company Small Cap Growth Fund Class Y	SSYGX	B+	A-	B	Up	4.39	11.00	20.77	37.31	111.17	28.82	6.7	800-645-6561	Y
Dreyfus/The Boston Company Small Cap Value Fund Class A	RUDAX	B	B	B	Up	4.78	8.35	10.21	28.88	85.09	22.31	210.2	800-645-6561	Y
Dreyfus/The Boston Company Small Cap Value Fund Class C	BOSCX	B	B	B	Up	4.53	7.82	9.13	25.70	77.84	22.06	210.2	800-645-6561	Y
Dreyfus/The Boston Company Small Cap Value Fund Class I	STSVX	B	B	B	Up	4.84	8.49	10.52	29.39	85.82	22.38	210.2	800-645-6561	
Dreyfus/The Boston Company Small Cap Value Fund Class Y	BOSYX	B	B	B	Up	4.84	8.50	10.58	29.34	85.75	22.46	210.2	800-645-6561	Y
Driehaus Micro Cap Growth Fund	DMCRX	B+	A	C+	Up	4.41	13.94	24.30	46.38	160.88	14.44	333.7	877-779-0079	Y
Dunham Small Cap Growth Fund Class A	DADGX	B+	A-	B	Up	6.31	15.22	29.77	34.20	107.81	17.41	35.5	800-442-4358	Y
Dunham Small Cap Growth Fund Class C	DCDGX	B+	A-	B	Up	6.10	14.72	28.75	31.25	100.15	14.43	35.5	800-442-4358	Y
Dunham Small Cap Growth Fund Class N	DNDGX	B+	A-	B	Up	6.34	15.30	30.03	35.22	110.37	18.14	35.5	800-442-4358	Y

Category: US Equity Small Cap (con't)

Fund Name	Ticker Symbol	RATINGS: Overall Rating	Reward Rating	Risk Rating	Recent Up/ Downgrade	TOTAL RETURNS & PERFORMANCE: 3-Month Total Return	6-Month Total Return	1-Year Total Return	3-Year Total Return	5-Year Total Return	ASSETS: NAV	Total Assets (MIL)	NEW INVESTORS: Telephone	Open to New Investors
Dunham Small Cap Value Fund Class A	DASVX	B	B+	B	Up	2.94	9.67	8.72	26.35	85.48	15.83	30.9	800-442-4358	Y
Dunham Small Cap Value Fund Class C	DCSVX	B	B	B	Up	2.80	9.28	7.94	23.62	78.70	14.15	30.9	800-442-4358	Y
Dunham Small Cap Value Fund Class N	DNSVX	B	B+	B	Up	3.02	9.75	8.95	27.36	87.72	15.97	30.9	800-442-4358	Y
Eaton Vance Small-Cap Fund Class A	ETEGX	B	B	B	Up	4.66	8.92	14.90	32.17	90.56	13.15	81.5		Y
Eaton Vance Small-Cap Fund Class C	ECSMX	B	B	B	Up	4.48	8.60	14.10	29.22	83.63	11.11	81.5		Y
Eaton Vance Small-Cap Fund Class I	EISGX	B	B	B	Up	4.74	9.10	15.17	33.17	92.98	14.45	81.5		Y
Eaton Vance Small-Cap Fund Class R	ERSGX	B	B	B	Up	4.58	8.82	14.64	31.17	88.32	12.67	81.5		Y
Eaton Vance Tax-Managed Small-Cap Fund Class A	ETMGX	B	B	B	Up	4.67	9.07	15.19	31.75	89.39	25.31	121.7		Y
Eaton Vance Tax-Managed Small-Cap Fund Class C	ECMGX	B	B	B	Up	4.46	8.63	14.34	28.79	82.43	20.71	121.7		Y
Eaton Vance Tax-Managed Small-Cap Fund Class I	EIMGX	B	B+	B	Up	4.75	9.21	15.48	32.77	91.75	25.98	121.7		Y
Emerald Growth Fund Class A	HSPGX	B+	A-	B	Up	7.87	14.70	27.71	42.42	132.96	26.45	1,180	855-828-9909	Y
Emerald Growth Fund Class C	HSPCX	B	A-	C+	Up	7.66	14.30	26.86	39.64	125.51	22.62	1,180	855-828-9909	Y
Emerald Growth Fund Institutional Class	FGROX	B	A	C+	Up	7.96	14.84	28.11	43.75	136.63	27.39	1,180	855-828-9909	Y
Emerald Growth Fund Investor Class	FFGRX	B	A-	C+	Up	7.85	14.66	27.66	42.26	132.53	26.35	1,180	855-828-9909	Y
Emerald Small Cap Value Fund Class A	ELASX	A-	A	B	Up	3.59	11.68	13.50	37.05	94.76	10.37	8.7	216-357-7412	Y
Emerald Small Cap Value Fund Class C	ELCSX	B+	A-	B	Up	3.39	11.31	12.71	34.42	89.50	10.09	8.7	216-357-7412	Y
Emerald Small Cap Value Fund Institutional Class	LSRYX	A-	A	B	Up	3.68	11.87	13.82	38.41	98.07	10.5	8.7	216-357-7412	Y
Emerald Small Cap Value Fund Investor Class	LSRIX	A-	A	B	Up	3.64	11.74	13.63	37.71	96.02	10.38	8.7	216-357-7412	Y
Entrepreneur U.S. Small Cap Fund Institutional Class	IMPAX	B	A-	C	Up	2.61	9.69	23.77	36.70		12.65	133.6		Y
Epoch U.S. Small-Mid Cap Equity Fund Advisor Class	TDUAX	B	B	B	Up	7.18	9.16	16.23	27.33		13.35	101.7		Y
Epoch U.S. Small-Mid Cap Equity Fund Institutional Class	TDUSX	B	B	B	Up	7.17	9.15	16.25	27.35		13.35	101.7		Y
EQ/Small Company Index Class K	US26883L4234	B+	A-	B	Up	4.06	9.88	14.79	31.64	96.83		1,203	877-222-2144	Y
EQ/Small Company Index Portfolio Class IA	US2689406401	B+	A-	B	Up	3.98	9.70	14.42	30.65	94.38		1,203	877-222-2144	Y
EQ/Small Company Index Portfolio Class IB	US2689406328	B+	B+	B	Up	3.97	9.70	14.50	30.62	94.49		1,203	877-222-2144	Y
FAM Small Cap Fund Institutional Class	FAMDX	B	B	B+	Up	1.64	4.31	4.66	25.42	89.50	18.26	162.4		Y
FAM Small Cap Fund Investor Class	FAMFX	B	B	B+	Up	1.63	4.25	4.55	25.08	88.98	18.21	162.4		Y
Federated Clover Small Value Fund Class A	VSFAX	B	B	B	Up	3.91	9.90	12.14	26.25	83.28	25.93	630.1	800-341-7400	Y
Federated Clover Small Value Fund Class C	VSFCX	B	B-	B	Up	3.68	9.49	11.26	23.42	76.51	24.68	630.1	800-341-7400	Y
Federated Clover Small Value Fund Class R	VSFRX	B	B	B	Up	3.86	9.85	12.08	25.99	82.28	25.51	630.1	800-341-7400	Y
Federated Clover Small Value Fund Class R6	VSFSX	B	B	B	Up	4.01	10.08	12.49	26.82	84.11	25.9	630.1	800-341-7400	Y
Federated Clover Small Value Fund Institutional Shares	VSFIX	B	B	B	Up	3.95	10.07	12.39	27.18	85.57	26	630.1	800-341-7400	Y
Federated Kaufmann Small Cap Fund Class A Shares	FKASX	B+	A	B-	Up	8.39	16.87	37.87	53.52	132.02	32.17	860.2	800-341-7400	Y
Federated Kaufmann Small Cap Fund Class B Shares	FKBSX	B+	A	B-	Up	8.21	16.47	37.07	51.00	125.61	27.86	860.2	800-341-7400	Y
Federated Kaufmann Small Cap Fund Class C Shares	FKCSX	B+	A	B-	Up	8.25	16.51	37.06	50.98	125.69	27.87	860.2	800-341-7400	Y
Federated Kaufmann Small Cap Fund Class R Shares	FKKSX	B+	A	B-	Up	8.39	16.87	37.90	53.75	132.70	32.3	860.2	800-341-7400	Y
Federated Kaufmann Small Cap Fund Class R6 Shares	FKALX	B+	A	B-		8.49	16.97	37.99	53.65	132.22	32.21	860.2	800-341-7400	Y
Federated Kaufmann Small Cap Fund Institutional Shares	FKAIX	B+	A	B-	Up	8.52	17.13	38.45	54.90	134.11	32.48	860.2	800-341-7400	Y
Federated MDT Small Cap Core Fund Class A Shares	QASCX	A-	A	B	Up	2.86	9.85	15.29	49.15	130.17	19.35	347.9	800-341-7400	Y
Federated MDT Small Cap Core Fund Class C Shares	QCSCX	A-	A	B	Up	2.67	9.48	14.45	45.85	122.00	17.29	347.9	800-341-7400	Y
Federated MDT Small Cap Core Fund Class R6	QLSCX	A-	A	B	Up	2.99	10.04	15.63	50.40	133.32	20.02	347.9	800-341-7400	Y
Federated MDT Small Cap Core Fund Institutional Shares	QISCX	A-	A	B	Up	2.94	9.98	15.57	50.32	133.20	20.01	347.9	800-341-7400	Y
Federated MDT Small Cap Growth Fund Class A Shares	QASGX	A-	A	B	Up	4.20	11.56	24.75	53.65	128.04	22.65	290.2	800-341-7400	Y
Federated MDT Small Cap Growth Fund Class B Shares	QBSGX	A-	A	B	Up	4.02	11.15	23.82	50.16	119.66	20.85	290.2	800-341-7400	
Federated MDT Small Cap Growth Fund Class C Shares	QCSGX	A-	A	B	Up	4.00	11.14	23.81	50.19	119.56	20.18	290.2	800-341-7400	Y
Federated MDT Small Cap Growth Fund Class R6	QLSGX	A-	A	B	Up	4.27	11.67	25.05	54.70	130.73	23.52	290.2	800-341-7400	Y
Federated MDT Small Cap Growth Fund Institutional Shares	QISGX	A-	A	B	Up	4.27	11.71	25.04	54.77	130.83	23.53	290.2	800-341-7400	Y
Fidelity Advisor® Event Driven Opportunities Fund Class A	FCHSX	B	B	B		4.41	6.47	17.45	39.43		13.68	33.4	617-563-7000	Y
Fidelity Advisor® Event Driven Opportunities Fund Class C	FATJX	B	B	B	Up	4.22	6.16	16.61	36.34		13.48	33.4	617-563-7000	Y
Fidelity Advisor® Event Driven Opportunities Fund Class M	FJPDX	B	B	B	Up	4.32	6.39	17.13	38.43		13.63	33.4	617-563-7000	Y
Fidelity Advisor® Event Driven Opportunities Fund I Class	FMRMX	B	B	B		4.47	6.60	17.72	40.47		13.74	33.4	617-563-7000	Y
Fidelity Advisor® Series Small Cap Fund	FSSFX	B	B-	B	Up	3.60	7.99	14.50	21.91		11.91	463.9	617-563-7000	Y
Fidelity Advisor® Small Cap Fund Class A	FSCDX	B-	B-	B	Up	3.40	7.45	13.77	21.04	85.71	25.81	2,630	617-563-7000	Y

Category: US Equity Small Cap (con't)

Fund Name	Ticker Symbol	RATINGS: Overall Rating	RATINGS: Reward Rating	RATINGS: Risk Rating	RATINGS: Recent Up/ Downgrade	TOTAL RETURNS & PERFORMANCE: 3-Month Total Return	6-Month Total Return	1-Year Total Return	3-Year Total Return	5-Year Total Return	ASSETS: NAV	ASSETS: Total Assets (MIL)	NEW INVESTORS: Telephone	NEW INVESTORS: Open to New Investors
Fidelity Advisor® Small Cap Fund Class C	FSCEX	B-	C+	B	Up	3.21	7.05	12.92	18.32	78.87	19.47	2,630	617-563-7000	Y
Fidelity Advisor® Small Cap Fund Class M	FSCTX	B-	B-	B	Up	3.33	7.30	13.50	20.21	83.62	23.88	2,630	617-563-7000	Y
Fidelity Advisor® Small Cap Fund Class Z	FZAOX	B	B-	B	Up	3.53	7.66	14.26	22.57	89.50	28.29	2,630	617-563-7000	Y
Fidelity Advisor® Small Cap Fund I Class	FSCIX	B	B-	B	Up	3.49	7.59	14.08	22.05	88.33	28.31	2,630	617-563-7000	Y
Fidelity Advisor® Small Cap Growth Fund Class A	FCAGX	A-	A	B	Up	4.92	14.01	28.63	49.56	128.48	23.78	3,744	617-563-7000	Y
Fidelity Advisor® Small Cap Growth Fund Class C	FCCGX	B+	A	B	Up	4.69	13.56	27.61	46.08	119.82	21.37	3,744	617-563-7000	Y
Fidelity Advisor® Small Cap Growth Fund Class M	FCTGX	B+	A	B	Up	4.83	13.88	28.29	48.31	125.32	23.07	3,744	617-563-7000	Y
Fidelity Advisor® Small Cap Growth Fund Class Z	FIDGX	A-	A	B	Up	5.01	14.26	29.17	50.98	132.17	24.81	3,744	617-563-7000	Y
Fidelity Advisor® Small Cap Growth Fund I Class	FCIGX	A-	A	B	Up	4.95	14.15	28.98	50.79	131.78	24.79	3,744	617-563-7000	Y
Fidelity Advisor® Small Cap Value Fund Class A	FCVAX	A-	B+	A-	Up	6.32	9.20	11.98	31.83	96.68	19.97	3,612	617-563-7000	
Fidelity Advisor® Small Cap Value Fund Class C	FCVCX	B+	B	B+	Up	6.09	8.79	11.10	28.82	89.24	18.25	3,612	617-563-7000	
Fidelity Advisor® Small Cap Value Fund Class I	FCVIX	A-	B+	A-	Up	6.36	9.35	12.26	32.90	99.22	20.32	3,612	617-563-7000	
Fidelity Advisor® Small Cap Value Fund Class M	FCVTX	B+	B+	A-	Up	6.21	9.01	11.66	30.81	94.18	19.51	3,612	617-563-7000	
Fidelity Advisor® Stock Selector Small Cap Fund Class A	FCDAX	B	B	B	Up	3.76	9.38	11.33	26.72	82.23	25.96	1,608	617-563-7000	Y
Fidelity Advisor® Stock Selector Small Cap Fund Class C	FCDCX	B	B	B	Up	3.55	8.93	10.47	23.65	75.02	23.97	1,608	617-563-7000	Y
Fidelity Advisor® Stock Selector Small Cap Fund Class M	FCDTX	B	B	B	Up	3.65	9.19	10.96	25.41	79.20	25.3	1,608	617-563-7000	Y
Fidelity Advisor® Stock Selector Small Cap Fund Class Z	FSSZX	B	B	B	Up	3.88	9.66	11.84	27.93	84.95	26.52	1,608	617-563-7000	Y
Fidelity Advisor® Stock Selector Small Cap Fund I Class	FCDIX	B	B	B	Up	3.85	9.59	11.72	27.87	84.97	26.54	1,608	617-563-7000	Y
Fidelity® Event Driven Opportunities Fund	FARNX	B	B	B		4.68	6.98	18.62	42.49		13.96	447.0	617-563-7000	Y
Fidelity® Series Small Cap Discovery Fund	FJACX	B	B	B	Up	5.10	7.61	9.58	23.07		12.52	1,744	617-563-7000	Y
Fidelity® Series Small Cap Opportunities Fund	FSOPX	B	B	B	Up	3.94	9.74	12.01	27.62	80.78	14.03	5,762	617-563-7000	
Fidelity® Small Cap Discovery Fund	FSCRX	B	B	B	Up	4.15	5.73	7.91	20.76	84.04	29.91	5,176	617-563-7000	
Fidelity® Small Cap Enhanced Index Fund	FCPEX	B	B	B	Up	2.90	6.60	7.22	28.21	93.19	14.02	844.9	617-563-7000	Y
Fidelity® Small Cap Growth Fund	FCPGX	A-	A	B	Up	5.01	14.19	29.00	50.78	131.86	24.73	3,744	617-563-7000	Y
Fidelity® Small Cap Index Fund Institutional Class	FSSSX	B+	A-	B	Up	3.32	9.28	14.83	32.81	99.53	20.32	4,095	617-563-7000	Y
Fidelity® Small Cap Index Fund Institutional Premium Class	FSSNX	B+	A-	B	Up	3.38	9.28	14.85	32.89	99.72	20.32	4,095	617-563-7000	Y
Fidelity® Small Cap Index Fund Investor Class	FSSPX	B+	A-	B	Up	3.36	9.22	14.70	32.28	98.03	20.3	4,095	617-563-7000	Y
Fidelity® Small Cap Index Fund Premium Class	FSSVX	B+	A-	B	Up	3.37	9.28	14.82	32.76	99.37	20.32	4,095	617-563-7000	Y
Fidelity® Small Cap Stock Fund	FSLCX	B	B	B+	Up	5.46	9.46	13.84	30.68	85.83	19.61	1,718	617-563-7000	Y
Fidelity® Small Cap Value Fund	FCPVX	A-	B+	A-	Up	6.37	9.35	12.25	32.84	99.24	20.32	3,612	617-563-7000	
Fidelity® Stock Selector Small Cap Fund	FDSCX	B	B	B	Up	3.87	9.59	11.73	27.80	84.76	26.46	1,608	617-563-7000	Y
First Investors Special Situations Class A	FISSX	B	B+	B	Up	5.28	10.34	17.66	33.58	87.83	31.95	720.6	800-423-4026	Y
First Investors Special Situations Class B	FISBX	B	B	B	Up	5.07	9.91	16.75	30.42	80.44	23.92	720.6	800-423-4026	Y
First Investors Special Situations Fund Advisor Class	FISTX	B+	B+	B	Up	5.34	10.54	18.02	34.81	90.17	32.26	720.6	800-423-4026	Y
First Investors Special Situations Fund Institutional Cls	FISUX	B+	B+	B	Up	5.37	10.61	18.17	35.35	91.75	32.46	720.6	800-423-4026	Y
First Trust/Confluence Small Cap Value Fund Class A	FOVAX	B+	A-	B+	Up	6.07	11.91	18.95	37.60	89.96	33.83	17.5	800-621-1675	Y
First Trust/Confluence Small Cap Value Fund Class C	FOVCX	B	B+	B	Up	5.96	11.62	18.17	34.14	82.43	30.69	17.5	800-621-1675	Y
First Trust/Confluence Small Cap Value Fund Class I	FOVIX	B+	A-	B+	Up	6.17	12.09	18.71	37.18	92.11	34.46	17.5	800-621-1675	Y
Foundry Partners Fundamental Small Cap Value Fund Inst Cls	DRISX	B	B+	B	Up	2.76	5.79	7.81	31.65	96.49	23.89	198.5		Y
Foundry Partners Fundamental Small Cap Value Fund Inv Cls	DRSVX	B	B+	B	Up	2.68	5.68	7.53	30.67	94.35	23.8	198.5		Y
Franklin MicroCap Value Fund Advisor Class	FVRMX	B	B	B-	Up	4.48	11.50	8.48	29.53	74.43	34.15	345.2	650-312-2000	
Franklin MicroCap Value Fund Class A	FRMCX	B	B	C+	Up	4.39	11.35	8.22	28.57	72.31	33.98	345.2	650-312-2000	
Franklin MicroCap Value Fund Class R6	FMCVX	B	B	B-	Up	4.49	11.57	8.60	30.08	75.35	34.29	345.2	650-312-2000	
Franklin Small Cap Growth Fund Advisor Class	FSSAX	B	B	B-	Up	7.02	12.77	21.28	25.59	106.70	23.52	2,662	650-312-2000	
Franklin Small Cap Growth Fund Class A	FSGRX	B	B	B-	Up	6.91	12.61	20.93	24.62	103.89	22	2,662	650-312-2000	
Franklin Small Cap Growth Fund Class C	FCSGX	B-	B	B-	Up	6.73	12.21	20.06	21.84	96.59	18.61	2,662	650-312-2000	
Franklin Small Cap Growth Fund Class R	FSSRX	B	B	B-	Up	6.89	12.45	20.69	23.75	101.58	20.99	2,662	650-312-2000	
Franklin Small Cap Growth Fund Class R6	FSMLX	B	B	B-	Up	7.04	12.89	21.51	26.45	108.72	23.76	2,662	650-312-2000	
Franklin Small Cap Value Fund Advisor Class	FVADX	B	B	B	Up	6.04	10.95	10.95	32.22	84.31	58.5	2,633	650-312-2000	Y
Franklin Small Cap Value Fund Class A	FRVLX	B	B	B	Up	5.96	10.76	10.62	31.14	81.69	55.84	2,633	650-312-2000	Y
Franklin Small Cap Value Fund Class C	FRVFX	B	B	B-	Up	5.76	10.37	9.81	28.28	75.22	49.63	2,633	650-312-2000	Y
Franklin Small Cap Value Fund Class R	FVFRX	B	B	B-	Up	5.88	10.62	10.36	30.19	79.67	55.3	2,633	650-312-2000	Y

Category: US Equity Small Cap (con't)

Fund Name	Ticker Symbol	RATINGS: Overall Rating	Reward Rating	Risk Rating	Recent Up/ Downgrade	TOTAL RETURNS & PERFORMANCE: 3-Month Total Return	6-Month Total Return	1-Year Total Return	3-Year Total Return	5-Year Total Return	ASSETS: NAV	Total Assets (MIL)	NEW INVESTORS: Telephone	Open to New Investors
Franklin Small Cap Value Fund Class R6	FRCSX	B	B+	B	Up	6.07	11.02	11.11	33.04	85.90	58.37	2,633	650-312-2000	Y
Frontier Phocas Small Cap Value Fund Institutional Class	FPSVX	B	B	B	Up	2.67	8.60	8.16	26.27	103.03	38.8	62.5		Y
Frontier Phocas Small Cap Value Fund Service Class	FPVSX	B	B	B	Up	2.53	8.49	7.89	25.99	102.59	38.7	62.5		Y
Frontier Timpani Small Cap Growth Fund Class Y	FTSYX	B	A-	B-	Up	7.67	14.23	35.59	29.85	105.60	21.18	55.6		Y
Frontier Timpani Small Cap Growth Fund Institutional Class	FTSGX	B	A-	B-	Up	7.76	14.41	36.13	31.39	109.24	21.51	55.6		Y
Frontier Timpani Small Cap Growth Fund Service Class	FTSCX	B	A-	B-	Up	7.76	14.41	36.13	31.39	109.24	21.51	55.6		Y
Gabelli Small Cap Growth Fund Class A	GCASX	B	B	B-	Up	4.34	11.87	18.94	33.44	92.14	57.99	3,861	914-921-5135	Y
Gabelli Small Cap Growth Fund Class AAA	GABSX	B	B	B-	Up	4.34	11.88	18.95	33.45	92.17	58.02	3,861	914-921-5135	Y
Gabelli Small Cap Growth Fund Class C	GCCSX	B	B	C+	Up	4.14	11.46	18.07	30.47	85.10	51.05	3,861	914-921-5135	Y
Gabelli Small Cap Growth Fund Class I	GACIX	B	B+	B-	Up	4.40	12.00	19.22	34.44	94.53	59.34	3,861	914-921-5135	Y
Gabelli Small Cap Growth Fund T	GATIX	B	B	B-		4.31	11.84	18.91	33.40	92.11	58	3,861	914-921-5135	Y
Glenmede Small Cap Equity Portfolio Class Advisor	GTCSX	B+	B+	B	Up	5.10	9.44	15.74	31.56	106.38	30.1	3,588	800-442-8299	Y
Glenmede Small Cap Equity Portfolio Institutional Class	GTSCX	B+	A-	B	Up	5.14	9.53	15.98	32.36	108.45	31.57	3,588	800-442-8299	Y
Goldman Sachs Small Cap Equity Insights Fund Class A	GCSAX	B+	A-	B	Up	3.07	9.88	11.39	32.46	95.35	25.12	308.2	800-526-7384	Y
Goldman Sachs Small Cap Equity Insights Fund Class C	GCSCX	B+	A-	B	Up	2.92	9.47	10.58	29.53	88.23	21.84	308.2	800-526-7384	Y
Goldman Sachs Small Cap Equity Insights Fund Class R	GDSRX	B+	A-	B	Up	3.01	9.75	11.14	31.46	93.06	24.63	308.2	800-526-7384	Y
Goldman Sachs Small Cap Equity Insights Fund Class R6	GCSUX	B+	A-	B	Up	3.18	10.14	11.89	34.13	99.51	26.04	308.2	800-526-7384	Y
Goldman Sachs Small Cap Equity Insights Fund Inst Cls	GCSIX	B+	A-	B	Up	3.16	10.12	11.82	34.03	99.36	26.04	308.2	800-526-7384	Y
Goldman Sachs Small Cap Equity Insights Fund Investor Cls	GDSTX	B+	A-	B	Up	3.13	9.99	11.67	33.48	97.94	24.95	308.2	800-526-7384	Y
Goldman Sachs Small Cap Equity Insights Fund Service Class	GCSSX	B+	A-	B	Up	3.08	9.84	11.28	32.06	94.52	24.76	308.2	800-526-7384	Y
Goldman Sachs Small Cap Growth Insights Fund Class A	GSAOX	B+	A-	B	Up	3.78	11.74	18.00	33.24	101.31	35.74	615.7	800-526-7384	Y
Goldman Sachs Small Cap Growth Insights Fund Class C	GSCOX	B+	A-	B	Up	3.60	11.34	17.12	30.31	93.90	27.99	615.7	800-526-7384	Y
Goldman Sachs Small Cap Growth Insights Fund Class R	GSROX	B+	A-	B	Up	3.70	11.60	17.68	32.22	98.74	34.52	615.7	800-526-7384	Y
Goldman Sachs Small Cap Growth Insights Fund Class R6	GINUX	B+	A-	B	Up	3.86	11.93	18.43	34.85	105.32	41.68	615.7	800-526-7384	Y
Goldman Sachs Small Cap Growth Insights Fund Inst Cls	GSIOX	B+	A-	B	Up	3.86	11.93	18.41	34.79	105.24	41.67	615.7	800-526-7384	Y
Goldman Sachs Small Cap Growth Insights Fund Investor Cls	GSTOX	B+	A-	B	Up	3.84	11.88	18.27	34.24	103.79	36.56	615.7	800-526-7384	Y
Goldman Sachs Small Cap Value Fund Class A	GSSMX	B	B+	B	Up	3.90	10.04	11.88	29.67	96.79	56.27	7,002	800-526-7384	
Goldman Sachs Small Cap Value Fund Class C	GSSCX	B	B	B	Up	3.73	9.62	11.06	26.79	89.59	42.78	7,002	800-526-7384	
Goldman Sachs Small Cap Value Fund Class R	GSQRX	B	B	B	Up	3.84	9.89	11.60	28.70	94.34	55.15	7,002	800-526-7384	
Goldman Sachs Small Cap Value Fund Class R6	GSSUX	B	B+	B	Up	4.03	10.27	12.37	31.00	98.81	60.71	7,002	800-526-7384	Y
Goldman Sachs Small Cap Value Fund Institutional Class	GSSIX	B	B+	B	Up	4.01	10.26	12.34	31.23	100.78	60.73	7,002	800-526-7384	
Goldman Sachs Small Cap Value Fund Investor Class	GSQTX	B	B+	B	Up	3.98	10.18	12.15	30.63	99.27	55.82	7,002	800-526-7384	
Goldman Sachs Small Cap Value Fund Service Class	GSSSX	B	B	B	Up	3.89	9.98	11.78	29.27	95.84	54.55	7,002	800-526-7384	
Goldman Sachs Small Cap Value Insights Fund Class A	GSATX	B+	A-	B	Up	2.57	8.27	7.09	31.88	89.15	42.21	190.0	800-526-7384	Y
Goldman Sachs Small Cap Value Insights Fund Class C	GSCTX	B	A-	B	Up	2.39	7.87	6.28	28.96	82.14	30.48	190.0	800-526-7384	Y
Goldman Sachs Small Cap Value Insights Fund Class R	GTTRX	B+	A-	B	Up	2.50	8.14	6.82	30.89	86.73	41.63	190.0	800-526-7384	Y
Goldman Sachs Small Cap Value Insights Fund Class R6	GTTUX	B+	A-	B	Up	2.68	8.49	7.51	33.49	92.97	55.41	190.0	800-526-7384	Y
Goldman Sachs Small Cap Value Insights Fund Inst Cls	GSITX	B+	A-	B	Up	2.67	8.49	7.50	33.46	92.93	55.42	190.0	800-526-7384	Y
Goldman Sachs Small Cap Value Insights Fund Investor Class	GTTTX	B+	A-	B	Up	2.64	8.42	7.35	32.87	91.53	42.01	190.0	800-526-7384	Y
Great-West Invesco Small Cap Value Fund Institutional Cls	MXMYX	B	B	B	Up	2.19	8.77	7.88	23.83	88.05		79.5		Y
Great-West Invesco Small Cap Value Fund Investor Class	MXSVX	B	B	B-	Up	2.10	8.61	7.49	22.67	86.29		79.5		Y
Great-West Loomis Sayles Small Cap Value Fund Inst Cls	MXTFX	B+	A-	B	Up	3.67	10.45	10.47	33.70	94.63		227.4		Y
Great-West Loomis Sayles Small Cap Value Fund Investor Cls	MXLSX	B+	A-	B	Up	3.53	10.24	10.04	32.38	92.70		227.4		Y
Great-West S&P Small Cap 600® Index Fund Class L	MXNSX	B+	A-	B	Up	4.51	10.65	12.81	36.80	107.49		973.2		Y
Great-West S&P Small Cap 600® Index Fund Institutional Cls	MXERX	A-	A-	B	Up	4.69	11.00	13.53	39.12	112.06		973.2		Y
Great-West S&P Small Cap 600® Index Fund Investor Class	MXISX	B+	A-	B	Up	4.61	10.83	13.15	37.87	110.15		973.2		Y
Guggenheim Mid Cap Value Fund Class A	SEVAX	B	B	B-	Up	4.54	10.18	13.32	31.51	80.72	34.39	514.6	212-739-0700	Y
Guggenheim Mid Cap Value Fund Class C	SEVSX	B-	B	C+		4.35	9.73	12.47	28.50	74.03	24.89	514.6	212-739-0700	Y
Guggenheim Mid Cap Value Fund Class P	SEVPX	B	B	B-	Up	4.57	10.18	13.35	31.22	80.33	34.16	514.6	212-739-0700	Y
Guggenheim Mid Cap Value Institutional Fund	SVUIX	B	B	B	Up	4.55	9.98	13.23	33.01	83.33	10.9	79.7	212-739-0700	Y
Guggenheim Small Cap Value Fund Class A	SSUAX	B-	B-	B-	Up	0.99	3.96	3.48	19.94	65.15	14.78	21.3	212-739-0700	Y
Guggenheim Small Cap Value Fund Class C	SSVCX	B-	B-	B-	Up	0.76	3.55	2.67	17.23	58.90	13.65	21.3	212-739-0700	Y

Category: US Equity Small Cap (con't)

Fund Name	Ticker Symbol	RATINGS: Overall Rating	Reward Rating	Risk Rating	Recent Up/ Downgrade	TOTAL RETURNS & PERFORMANCE: 3-Month Total Return	6-Month Total Return	1-Year Total Return	3-Year Total Return	5-Year Total Return	ASSETS: NAV	Total Assets (MIL)	NEW INVESTORS: Telephone	Open to New Investors
Guggenheim Small Cap Value Fund Class P	SSUPX	B-	B-	B-	Up	0.96	3.93	3.45	19.93	65.03	14.94	21.3	212-739-0700	Y
Guggenheim Small Cap Value Institutional Fund	SSUIX	B-	B-	B-	Up	1.09	4.10	3.74	20.89	67.18	13.5	21.3	212-739-0700	Y
GuideMark® Small/Mid Cap Core Fund Service Shares	GMSMX	B	B	B	Up	4.47	8.90	14.37	23.92	87.94	14.87	54.9	603-888-5500	Y
GuideStone Funds Small Cap Equity Fund Institutional Class	GSCYX	B	B	B	Up	4.68	10.40	12.98	24.24	84.03	18.36	556.8	214-720-1171	Y
GuideStone Funds Small Cap Equity Fund Investor Class	GSCZX	B	B	B	Up	4.62	10.21	12.66	23.34	81.86	18.37	556.8	214-720-1171	Y
Hancock Horizon Burkenroad Small Cap Fund Class D	HYBUX	B	B	B	Up	4.46	10.47	10.09	29.51	83.23	65.34	718.3	800-990-2434	Y
Hancock Horizon Burkenroad Small Cap Fund Inst Cls	HIBUX	B	B	B	Up	4.71	10.88	10.75	31.15	86.48	68.11	718.3	800-990-2434	Y
Hancock Horizon Burkenroad Small Cap Fund Investor Class	HHBUX	B	B	B	Up	4.54	10.62	10.37	30.48	85.54	67.88	718.3	800-990-2434	Y
Hancock Horizon Microcap Fund Class C	HMICX	B-	C+	B	Up	1.72	7.67	9.03			18.62	14.2	800-990-2434	Y
Hancock Horizon Microcap Fund Institutional Class	HMIIX	B-	C+	B	Up	1.95	8.20	10.10			19.07	14.2	800-990-2434	Y
Hancock Horizon Microcap Fund Investor Class	HMIAX	B-	C+	B	Up	1.85	8.05	9.83			18.99	14.2	800-990-2434	Y
Hancock Horizon U.S. Small Cap Fund Class C	HHSCX	B	B-	B	Up	2.52	8.46	3.88	24.81		18.71	32.6	800-990-2434	Y
Hancock Horizon U.S. Small Cap Fund Institutional Class	HSCIX	B	B	B	Up	2.76	8.98	4.89	28.68		19.26	32.6	800-990-2434	Y
Hancock Horizon U.S. Small Cap Fund Investor Class	HSCAX	B	B	B	Up	2.73	8.85	4.63	27.74		19.17	32.6	800-990-2434	Y
Harbor Small Cap Growth Fund Administrative Class	HRSGX	B	B	B	Up	6.89	11.19	23.93	28.52	106.36	13.47	732.1	800-422-1050	
Harbor Small Cap Growth Fund Institutional Class	HASGX	B	B	B	Up	6.96	11.31	24.60	29.95	109.36	14.41	732.1	800-422-1050	
Harbor Small Cap Growth Fund Investor Class	HISGX	B	B	B-	Up	6.88	11.10	24.18	28.44	105.60	12.88	732.1	800-422-1050	
Harbor Small Cap Growth Fund Retirement Class	HNSGX	B	B+	C	Up	7.03	11.38	24.74	30.09	109.58	14.44	732.1	800-422-1050	Y
Harbor Small Cap Growth Opp Fund Admin Cls	HRSOX	B-	B-	B	Up	3.14	3.97	17.28	23.11		12.17	299.5	800-422-1050	Y
Harbor Small Cap Growth Opp Fund Inst Cls	HASOX	B-	B-	B	Up	3.21	4.12	17.61	23.44		12.23	299.5	800-422-1050	Y
Harbor Small Cap Growth Opportunities Fund Investor Class	HISOX	B-	B-	B	Up	3.18	3.93	17.28	22.00		12.04	299.5	800-422-1050	Y
Harbor Small Cap Growth Opportunities Fund Retirement Cls	HNSOX	B-	B-	B	Up	3.29	4.20	17.70	23.63		12.25	299.5	800-422-1050	Y
Harbor Small Cap Value Fund Administrative Class	HSVRX	A-	A	B	Up	6.43	13.87	21.29	42.50	112.79	36.14	1,241	800-422-1050	Y
Harbor Small Cap Value Fund Institutional Class	HASCX	A-	A	B	Up	6.52	14.00	21.60	43.59	115.58	36.3	1,241	800-422-1050	Y
Harbor Small Cap Value Fund Investor Class	HISVX	A-	A	B	Up	6.40	13.81	21.18	41.98	111.61	35.44	1,241	800-422-1050	Y
Harbor Small Cap Value Fund Retirement Class	HNVRX	A-	A	B	Up	6.56	14.07	21.71	43.75	115.82	36.31	1,241	800-422-1050	Y
Hartford Schroders US Small Cap Opportunities Fund Class A	SCUVX	B	B	B+	Up	3.80	7.33	14.31	32.82	97.62	26.1	210.9	888-843-7824	Y
Hartford Schroders US Small Cap Opportunities Fund Class C	HOOCX	B	B	B	Up	3.62	6.94	13.53	29.90	90.72	26.94	210.9	888-843-7824	Y
Hartford Schroders US Small Cap Opportunities Fund Class F	HOOFX	B	B	B+		3.90	7.55	14.79	34.00	100.70	27.23	210.9	888-843-7824	Y
Hartford Schroders US Small Cap Opportunities Fund Class I	SCUIX	B	B	B+	Up	3.89	7.50	14.73	33.94	100.60	27.22	210.9	888-843-7824	Y
Hartford Schroders US Small Cap Opportunities Fund Cls R3	HOORX	B	B	B+	Up	3.74	7.28	14.33	32.10	95.88	27.16	210.9	888-843-7824	Y
Hartford Schroders US Small Cap Opportunities Fund Cls R4	HOOSX	B	B	B+	Up	3.84	7.41	14.51	32.99	98.18	27.21	210.9	888-843-7824	Y
Hartford Schroders US Small Cap Opportunities Fund Cls R5	HOOTX	B	B	B+	Up	3.88	7.50	14.65	33.84	100.44	27.21	210.9	888-843-7824	Y
Hartford Schroders US Small Cap Opportunities Fund Cls SDR	SCURX	B	B	B+	Up	3.93	7.54	14.80	34.23	101.03	27.27	210.9	888-843-7824	Y
Hartford Schroders US Small Cap Opportunities Fund Class Y	HOOYX	B	B	B+	Up	3.93	7.55	14.78	34.01	100.70	27.23	210.9	888-843-7824	Y
Hartford Small Cap Core Fund Class A	HSMAX	B-	B-	B	Up	2.53	7.61	9.42	19.75	75.19	13.7	157.5	888-843-7824	Y
Hartford Small Cap Core Fund Class C	HTSCX	B-	C+	B	Up	2.35	7.22	8.65	17.06	68.79	12.47	157.5	888-843-7824	Y
Hartford Small Cap Core Fund Class F	HSMFX	B	B	B	Up	2.65	7.89	9.99	21.37	78.97	13.69	157.5	888-843-7824	Y
Hartford Small Cap Core Fund Class I	HSEIX	B	B-	B	Up	2.63	7.87	9.85	20.94	78.34	13.7	157.5	888-843-7824	Y
Hartford Small Cap Core Fund Class R3	HSMRX	B-	B-	B	Up	2.52	7.54	9.22	18.98	73.43	14.1	157.5	888-843-7824	Y
Hartford Small Cap Core Fund Class R4	HSMSX	B-	B-	B	Up	2.55	7.69	9.52	20.04	75.95	14.21	157.5	888-843-7824	Y
Hartford Small Cap Core Fund Class R5	HSMTX	B	B-	B	Up	2.65	7.87	9.87	21.17	78.63	14.17	157.5	888-843-7824	Y
Hartford Small Cap Core Fund Class Y	HSMYX	B	B	B	Up	2.68	7.89	9.97	21.34	78.93	14.16	157.5	888-843-7824	Y
Hartford Small Cap Growth Fund Class A	HSLAX	B	B+	B	Up	3.55	9.26	19.61	31.24	106.98	55.85	1,338	888-843-7824	
Hartford Small Cap Growth Fund Class C	HSLCX	B	B	B	Up	3.35	8.87	18.74	28.49	99.90	42.53	1,338	888-843-7824	
Hartford Small Cap Growth Fund Class F	HSLFX	B	B+	B	Up	3.66	9.50	20.11	32.97	111.79	57.75	1,338	888-843-7824	Y
Hartford Small Cap Growth Fund Class I	HSLIX	B	B+	B	Up	3.62	9.40	19.88	32.24	109.97	57.65	1,338	888-843-7824	
Hartford Small Cap Growth Fund Class R3	HSLRX	B	B+	B	Up	3.46	9.08	19.23	30.11	104.30	55.46	1,338	888-843-7824	
Hartford Small Cap Growth Fund Class R4	HSLSX	B	B+	B	Up	3.55	9.26	19.61	31.37	107.60	57.63	1,338	888-843-7824	
Hartford Small Cap Growth Fund Class R5	HSLTX	B	B+	B	Up	3.63	9.43	19.98	32.59	110.75	60	1,338	888-843-7824	
Hartford Small Cap Growth Fund Class R6	HSLVX	B	B+	B	Up	3.66	9.50	20.10	32.80	111.52	60.63	1,338	888-843-7824	
Hartford Small Cap Growth Fund Class Y	HSLYX	B	B+	B	Up	3.64	9.47	20.05	32.92	111.70	60.69	1,338	888-843-7824	

Category: US Equity Small Cap (con't)

Fund Name	Ticker Symbol	RATINGS: Overall Rating	Reward Rating	Risk Rating	Recent Up/ Downgrade	TOTAL RETURNS & PERFORMANCE: 3-Month Total Return	6-Month Total Return	1-Year Total Return	3-Year Total Return	5-Year Total Return	ASSETS: NAV	Total Assets (MIL)	NEW INVESTORS: Telephone	Open to New Investors
Hartford Small Cap Growth HLS Fund Class IA	HISCX	B	B+	B	Up	3.67	9.33	20.07	33.57	110.34	32.13	1,350	888-843-7824	
Hartford Small Cap Growth HLS Fund Class IB	HBSGX	B	B+	B	Up	3.61	9.17	19.75	32.57	107.65	31.28	1,350	888-843-7824	
Hartford Small/Mid Cap Equity HLS Fund Class IA	HMCSX	B	B	B	Up	5.63	10.97	14.42	25.91	87.31	8.81	100.3	888-843-7824	Y
Hartford Small/Mid Cap Equity HLS Fund Class IB	HMCVX	B	B	B	Up	5.42	10.75	13.93	24.90	84.85	8.75	100.3	888-843-7824	Y
Hodges Small Intrinsic Value Fund Retail Class	HDSVX	B	B+	B-	Up	3.26	10.78	8.75	28.59		13.89	105.6		Y
Homestead Small Company Stock Fund	HSCSX	B	B+	B	Up	4.54	10.62	11.99	25.20	89.39	44.11	1,303		Y
Hood River Small-Cap Growth Fund Class Institutional	HRSMX	B	B	B	Down	2.21	5.80	20.69	37.67	120.20	37.76	283.2		Y
Hood River Small-Cap Growth Fund Investor Shares	HRSRX	B	B	B	Down	2.14	5.74	20.50	36.94	117.94	37.59	283.2		Y
Hood River Small-Cap Growth Fund Retirement Shares	HRSIX	B	B	B	Down	2.24	5.85	20.78	37.77	120.37	37.79	283.2		Y
Hotchkis & Wiley Small Cap Diversified Value Fund Class A	HWVAX	B+	A	B-	Up	3.99	10.22	13.53	37.04		11.42	24.7	866-493-8637	Y
Hotchkis & Wiley Small Cap Diversified Value Fund Class I	HWVIX	B+	A	B-	Up	3.96	10.26	13.75	38.12		11.46	24.7	866-493-8637	Y
Hotchkis & Wiley Small Cap Value Fund Class A	HWSAX	B-	B-	B-	Up	1.82	6.97	7.46	16.14	93.39	60.08	804.3	866-493-8637	
Hotchkis & Wiley Small Cap Value Fund Class C	HWSCX	B-	B-	C+	Up	1.64	6.58	6.66	13.56	86.23	50.01	804.3	866-493-8637	
Hotchkis & Wiley Small Cap Value Fund Class I	HWSIX	B-	B	B-	Up	1.89	7.12	7.74	17.03	95.82	60.39	804.3	866-493-8637	
ICM Small Company Portfolio	ICSCX	A-	A	B	Up	3.51	10.39	13.13	42.55	105.63	33.08	794.1		Y
ICON Opportunities Fund	ICONX	A-	A	B	Up	5.14	12.60	24.85	46.27	108.60	19.56	20.9	303-790-1600	Y
Invesco Select Companies Fund Class A	ATIAX	B-	B-	C	Up	8.60	9.37	20.11	25.03	72.81	18.79	482.7	800-659-1005	
Invesco Select Companies Fund Class R6	ATISX	B-	B-	C	Up	8.64	9.57	20.44	25.37	73.28	20.21	482.7	800-659-1005	Y
Invesco Select Companies Fund Class Y	ATIYX	B-	B	C	Up	8.66	9.47	20.36	25.93	74.90	19.28	482.7	800-659-1005	
Invesco Select Companies Fund R5 Class	ATIIX	B-	B	C	Up	8.65	9.53	20.52	26.32	75.64	20.2	482.7	800-659-1005	
Invesco Small Cap Discovery Fund Class A	VASCX	B	B	B	Up	4.77	8.10	24.14	26.52	84.44	9.66	603.1	800-659-1005	Y
Invesco Small Cap Discovery Fund Class B	VBSCX	B	B	B	Up	4.71	8.07	24.11	26.52	84.33	8.23	603.1	800-659-1005	
Invesco Small Cap Discovery Fund Class C	VCSCX	B	B	B-	Up	4.61	7.68	23.37	23.77	77.79	7.26	603.1	800-659-1005	Y
Invesco Small Cap Discovery Fund Class R5	VESCX	B	B	B	Up	4.83	8.35	24.77	28.27	88.62	10.39	603.1	800-659-1005	Y
Invesco Small Cap Discovery Fund Class R6	VFSCX	B	B	B	Up	4.91	8.42	24.82	28.33	88.80	10.42	603.1	800-659-1005	Y
Invesco Small Cap Discovery Fund Class Y	VISCX	B	B	B	Up	4.79	8.25	24.58	27.47	86.92	10.26	603.1	800-659-1005	Y
Invesco Small Cap Equity Fund Class A	SMEAX	B-	B-	B	Up	3.88	8.33	13.57	18.74	70.33	15.35	1,291	800-659-1005	Y
Invesco Small Cap Equity Fund Class B	SMEBX	B-	C+	B	Up	3.73	7.98	12.78	16.22	64.21	12.36	1,291	800-659-1005	
Invesco Small Cap Equity Fund Class C	SMECX	B-	C+	B	Up	3.73	7.98	12.78	16.13	64.12	12.35	1,291	800-659-1005	Y
Invesco Small Cap Equity Fund Class R	SMERX	B-	C+	B	Up	3.84	8.25	13.31	17.91	68.20	14.44	1,291	800-659-1005	Y
Invesco Small Cap Equity Fund Class R6	SMEFX	B	B-	B	Up	4.06	8.69	14.19	20.59	74.75	16.99	1,291	800-659-1005	Y
Invesco Small Cap Equity Fund Class Y	SMEYX	B-	B-	B	Up	3.95	8.48	13.88	19.63	72.46	15.86	1,291	800-659-1005	Y
Invesco Small Cap Equity Fund R5 Class	SMEIX	B	B-	B	Up	3.96	8.54	13.99	20.26	73.94	16.88	1,291	800-659-1005	Y
Invesco Small Cap Growth Fund Class A	GTSAX	B+	A-	B	Up	6.62	13.10	24.91	35.56	109.55	37.31	2,866	800-659-1005	
Invesco Small Cap Growth Fund Class B	GTSBX	B+	B+	B	Up	6.42	12.69	24.02	32.57	101.90	25.4	2,866	800-659-1005	
Invesco Small Cap Growth Fund Class C	GTSDX	B	B+	C+	Up	6.44	12.69	23.98	32.55	101.86	25.33	2,866	800-659-1005	
Invesco Small Cap Growth Fund Class R	GTSRX	B+	A-	B	Up	6.56	12.95	24.59	34.54	106.94	34.58	2,866	800-659-1005	
Invesco Small Cap Growth Fund Class R6	GTSFX	B+	A-	B	Up	6.75	13.37	25.48	37.51	114.60	42.2	2,866	800-659-1005	
Invesco Small Cap Growth Fund Class Y	GTSYX	B+	A-	B	Up	6.69	13.26	25.24	36.57	112.23	38.44	2,866	800-659-1005	
Invesco Small Cap Growth Fund Investor Class	GTSIX	B	A-	C+	Up	6.65	13.12	24.94	35.60	109.65	39.22	2,866	800-659-1005	
Invesco Small Cap Growth Fund R5 Class	GTSVX	B+	A-	B	Up	6.73	13.32	25.40	37.12	113.72	42.02	2,866	800-659-1005	
Invesco Small Cap Value Class R6	SMVSX	B	A-	B-	Up	6.39	13.13	18.67	27.32	103.26	19.84	2,700	800-659-1005	Y
Invesco Small Cap Value Fund Class A	VSCAX	B	A-	B-	Up	6.25	12.85	18.28	26.90	102.59	18.96	2,700	800-659-1005	
Invesco Small Cap Value Fund Class B	VSMBX	B	B	B-	Up	6.01	12.43	17.41	24.08	95.03	14.29	2,700	800-659-1005	
Invesco Small Cap Value Fund Class C	VSMCX	B	B	B-	Up	6.13	12.52	17.47	24.15	95.23	13.64	2,700	800-659-1005	
Invesco Small Cap Value Fund Class Y	VSMIX	B	A-	B-	Up	6.35	13.04	18.58	27.87	105.08	19.81	2,700	800-659-1005	
IronBridge Small Cap Fund	IBSCX	B	B-	B	Up	2.23	7.57	10.43	22.01	77.20	17.12	269.2		Y
iShares Russell 2000 Small-Cap Index Fund Class K	BDBKX	B+	A-	B	Up	3.29	9.22	14.68	32.13	98.28	19.77	873.8	800-441-7762	Y
iShares Russell 2000 Small-Cap Index Fund Inst Shares	MASKX	B+	A-	B	Up	3.31	9.14	14.55	31.87	97.80	19.72	873.8	800-441-7762	Y
iShares Russell 2000 Small-Cap Index Fund Inv A Shares	MDSKX	B+	A-	B	Up	3.24	9.06	14.34	31.00	95.40	19.74	873.8	800-441-7762	Y
Ivy Small Cap Core Fund Class A	IYSAX	B+	A-	B	Up	4.01	8.25	13.30	35.27	97.78	18.99	642.4	800-777-6472	Y
Ivy Small Cap Core Fund Class B	IYSBX	B	B+	B	Up	3.78	7.68	12.20	31.43	88.40	15.38	642.4	800-777-6472	

Category: US Equity Small Cap (con't)

Fund Name	Ticker Symbol	RATINGS: Overall Rating	Reward Rating	Risk Rating	Recent Up/ Downgrade	TOTAL RETURNS & PERFORMANCE: 3-Month Total Return	6-Month Total Return	1-Year Total Return	3-Year Total Return	5-Year Total Return	ASSETS: NAV	Total Assets (MIL)	NEW INVESTORS: Telephone	Open to New Investors
Ivy Small Cap Core Fund Class C	IYSCX	B	B+	B	Up	3.86	7.85	12.54	32.59	91.33	16.44	642.4	800-777-6472	Y
Ivy Small Cap Core Fund Class I	IVVIX	B+	A-	B	Up	4.13	8.43	13.72	37.00	102.12	20.53	642.4	800-777-6472	Y
Ivy Small Cap Core Fund Class N	ISPVX	B+	A-	B	Up	4.14	8.53	13.90	37.57	101.61	20.69	642.4	800-777-6472	Y
Ivy Small Cap Core Fund Class R	IYSMX	B+	B+	B	Up	3.91	8.10	13.04	34.58	96.15	18.88	642.4	800-777-6472	Y
Ivy Small Cap Core Fund Class T	IYCTX	B+	A-	B	Up	4.12	8.41	13.47	35.47	98.08	19.02	642.4	800-777-6472	Y
Ivy Small Cap Core Fund Class Y	IYSYX	B+	A-	B	Up	4.07	8.33	13.46	35.96	99.57	19.93	642.4	800-777-6472	Y
Ivy Small Cap Growth Fund Class A	WSGAX	B+	B+	B	Up	5.40	9.34	23.69	36.59	103.20	17.82	1,163	800-777-6472	Y
Ivy Small Cap Growth Fund Class B	WSGBX	B	B+	B	Up	5.17	8.90	22.57	33.12	94.38	12.99	1,163	800-777-6472	
Ivy Small Cap Growth Fund Class C	WRGCX	B	B+	B	Up	5.20	8.97	22.77	33.92	96.63	14.34	1,163	800-777-6472	Y
Ivy Small Cap Growth Fund Class E	ISGEX	B+	B+	B	Up	5.45	9.37	23.62	36.46	102.56	17.66	1,163	800-777-6472	Y
Ivy Small Cap Growth Fund Class Institutional	IYSIX	B+	B+	B	Up	5.48	9.53	24.02	37.99	106.84	23.28	1,163	800-777-6472	Y
Ivy Small Cap Growth Fund Class N	IRGFX	B+	B+	B	Up	5.56	9.64	24.24	38.63	104.69	23.41	1,163	800-777-6472	Y
Ivy Small Cap Growth Fund Class R	WSGRX	B+	B+	B	Up	5.34	9.23	23.28	35.50	100.84	17.49	1,163	800-777-6472	Y
Ivy Small Cap Growth Fund Class T	IYSTX	B+	B+	B	Up	5.49	9.44	23.30	34.50	97.48	17.82	1,163	800-777-6472	Y
Ivy Small Cap Growth Fund Class Y	WSCYX	B+	B+	B	Up	5.43	9.40	23.74	37.00	104.43	22	1,163	800-777-6472	Y
James Micro Cap Fund	JMCRX	B	B+	B	Up	2.68	7.56	2.91	26.14	102.04	17.23	30.9	800-995-2637	Y
James Small Cap Fund	JASCX	B-	C+	B	Up	4.11	11.77	6.56	17.14	69.40	30.23	67.2	800-995-2637	Y
Janus Henderson Small Cap Value Fund Class A	JDSAX	B+	B+	B+	Up	5.03	8.20	12.42	36.45	93.15	23.13	2,999	877-335-2687	Y
Janus Henderson Small Cap Value Fund Class C	JCSCX	B	B	B		4.84	7.88	11.67	34.16	87.17	21.88	2,999	877-335-2687	Y
Janus Henderson Small Cap Value Fund Class D	JNPSX	B+	B+	B+	Up	5.07	8.36	12.72	37.69	95.97	22.9	2,999	877-335-2687	
Janus Henderson Small Cap Value Fund Class I	JSCOX	B+	B+	B+	Up	5.15	8.42	12.81	37.85	96.45	23.03	2,999	877-335-2687	Y
Janus Henderson Small Cap Value Fund Class L	JSIVX	B+	B+	B+	Up	5.12	8.44	12.87	38.25	97.31	23.63	2,999	877-335-2687	
Janus Henderson Small Cap Value Fund Class N	JDSNX	B+	B+	B+	Up	5.12	8.45	12.90	38.33	97.61	22.97	2,999	877-335-2687	Y
Janus Henderson Small Cap Value Fund Class R	JDSRX	B+	B+	B	Up	4.94	8.04	12.10	35.28	90.34	22.51	2,999	877-335-2687	Y
Janus Henderson Small Cap Value Fund Class S	JISCX	B+	B+	B+	Up	5.01	8.17	12.35	36.29	92.77	22.81	2,999	877-335-2687	Y
Janus Henderson Small Cap Value Fund Class T	JSCVX	B+	B+	B+	Up	5.07	8.31	12.61	37.32	95.14	22.95	2,999	877-335-2687	Y
Janus Henderson Triton Fund Class A	JGMAX	B	A-	C+	Down	5.50	11.46	26.64	39.88	112.61	28.12	9,515	877-335-2687	
Janus Henderson Triton Fund Class C	JGMCX	B	A-	C+		5.29	11.09	25.81	37.28	105.70	26.19	9,515	877-335-2687	
Janus Henderson Triton Fund Class D	JANIX	B	A-	B-	Down	5.57	11.63	27.00	41.20	115.90	28.7	9,515	877-335-2687	
Janus Henderson Triton Fund Class I	JSMGX	B	A-	B-	Down	5.61	11.67	27.07	41.41	116.42	28.88	9,515	877-335-2687	
Janus Henderson Triton Fund Class N	JGMNX	B	A-	B-	Down	5.63	11.72	27.23	41.83	117.58	28.97	9,515	877-335-2687	
Janus Henderson Triton Fund Class R	JGMRX	B	A-	C+		5.41	11.32	26.24	38.68	109.56	27.37	9,515	877-335-2687	
Janus Henderson Triton Fund Class S	JGMIX	B	A-	C+	Down	5.47	11.44	26.59	39.68	112.18	27.88	9,515	877-335-2687	
Janus Henderson Triton Fund Class T	JATTX	B	A-	B-	Down	5.53	11.59	26.90	40.79	114.99	28.51	9,515	877-335-2687	
Janus Henderson Venture Fund Class A	JVTAX	B+	B+	B	Up	3.95	9.52	24.01	30.64	107.51	75.41	3,217	877-335-2687	
Janus Henderson Venture Fund Class C	JVTCX	B	B+	B	Up	3.76	9.12	23.08	27.85	100.44	70.68	3,217	877-335-2687	
Janus Henderson Venture Fund Class D	JANVX	B+	B+	B	Up	4.01	9.66	24.28	31.54	110.22	77.3	3,217	877-335-2687	
Janus Henderson Venture Fund Class I	JVTIX	B+	B+	B	Up	4.03	9.68	24.35	31.77	110.89	77.58	3,217	877-335-2687	
Janus Henderson Venture Fund Class N	JVTNX	B+	B+	B	Up	4.04	9.72	24.44	32.08	111.68	77.98	3,217	877-335-2687	
Janus Henderson Venture Fund Class S	JVTSX	B+	B+	B	Up	3.91	9.45	23.83	30.12	106.44	74.8	3,217	877-335-2687	
Janus Henderson Venture Fund Class T	JAVTX	B+	B+	B	Up	3.98	9.60	24.16	31.15	109.21	76.4	3,217	877-335-2687	
JNL Multi-Manager Small Cap Growth Fund Class A	US46644W4767	B	B+	B-	Up	4.98	11.84	27.23	27.83	75.88	25.88	1,713		Y
JNL Multi-Manager Small Cap Growth Fund Class I	US46644W4684	B	B+	C	Up	5.08	11.99	27.50	28.63	77.74	27.07	1,713		Y
JNL Multi-Manager Small Cap Value Fund Class A	US46644W4502	B-	B	B-	Up	3.09	8.16	11.06	23.52	70.68	15.33	1,236		Y
JNL Multi-Manager Small Cap Value Fund Class I	US46644W4437	B-	B	B-	Up	3.15	8.21	11.25	24.23	72.41	15.35	1,236		Y
JNL/Invesco Small Cap Growth Fund Class A	US46648M2199	B	A-	C+	Up	6.63	13.14	24.96	35.97	110.40	24.91	1,913		Y
JNL/Invesco Small Cap Growth Fund Class I	US46648M1936	B	A-	C+	Up	6.73	13.26	25.25	36.79	112.51	25.82	1,913		Y
JNL/Mellon Capital Small Cap Index Fund Class A	US46648M6158	B+	A-	B	Up	3.84	9.90	12.83	34.62	100.43	19.71	2,375		Y
JNL/Mellon Capital Small Cap Index Fund Class I	US46648M5994	B+	A-	B	Up	3.93	10.07	13.08	35.36	102.22	20.06	2,375		Y
JNL/PPM America Small Cap Value Fund Class A	US46648M5085	A-	A	B	Up	3.54	12.03	17.16	46.06	119.58	15.18	898.9		Y
JNL/PPM America Small Cap Value Fund Class I	US46648M6075	A-	A	B	Up	3.58	12.14	17.40	49.86	126.02	15.59	898.9		Y
JNL/Vanguard Small Company Growth Fund Class A	US46648L4683	B	A-	C		5.08	10.61	22.46	33.92	103.89	10.74	45.6		Y

Category: US Equity Small Cap (con't)

Fund Name	Ticker Symbol	Overall Rating	Reward Rating	Risk Rating	Recent Up/ Downgrade	3-Month Total Return	6-Month Total Return	1-Year Total Return	3-Year Total Return	5-Year Total Return	NAV	Total Assets (MIL)	Telephone	Open to New Investors
		RATINGS				TOTAL RETURNS & PERFORMANCE					ASSETS		NEW INVESTORS	
JNL/Vanguard Small Company Growth Fund Class I	US46648L4501	B	A-	C		5.18	10.79	22.84	35.15	106.98	10.75	45.6		Y
John Hancock Funds II New Opportunities Fund Class 1	JISOX	B	B	B	Up	5.30	10.07	14.23	28.13	89.24	28.7	601.6	800-225-5913	Y
John Hancock Funds II New Opportunities Fund Class A	JASOX	B	B	B	Up	5.20	9.89	13.82	26.78	86.30	28.5	601.6	800-225-5913	Y
John Hancock Funds II New Opportunities Fund Class C	JBSOX	B	B	B	Up	5.02	9.51	13.06	24.21	80.00	28	601.6	800-225-5913	Y
John Hancock Funds II New Opportunities Fund Class I	JHSOX	B	B	B	Up	5.28	10.09	14.19	28.00	89.22	28.52	601.6	800-225-5913	Y
John Hancock Funds II New Opportunities Fund Class NAV	US47803X8838	B	B	B	Up	5.31	10.11	14.30	28.37	89.76	28.51	601.6	800-225-5913	Y
John Hancock Funds II New Opportunities Fund Class R1	JRSOX	B	B	B	Up	5.18	9.84	13.74	26.45	85.08	28.48	601.6	800-225-5913	Y
John Hancock Funds II New Opportunities Fund Class R2	JSSOX	B	B	B	Up	5.24	10.05	13.86	27.20	87.10	28.51	601.6	800-225-5913	Y
John Hancock Funds II New Opportunities Fund Class R3	JTSOX	B	B	B	Up	5.17	9.83	13.68	26.40	85.00	28.47	601.6	800-225-5913	Y
John Hancock Funds II New Opportunities Fund Class R4	JUSOX	B	B	B	Up	5.31	10.03	14.13	27.69	87.82	28.53	601.6	800-225-5913	Y
John Hancock Funds II New Opportunities Fund Class R5	JVSOX	B	B	B	Up	5.32	10.13	14.31	28.33	89.71	28.54	601.6	800-225-5913	Y
John Hancock Funds II New Opportunities Fund Class R6	JWSOX	B	B	B	Up	5.29	10.10	14.29	28.23	89.57	28.5	601.6	800-225-5913	Y
John Hancock Funds II Small Company Gr Fund Class NAV	US47803X5453	B	A-	C+	Up	6.54	13.12	25.13	35.86	110.93	20.86	233.0	800-225-5913	Y
John Hancock Funds II Small Company Value Fund Class 1	JISVX	A-	A	B	Up	3.47	9.85	11.50	38.30	86.55	28.46	296.3	800-225-5913	Y
John Hancock Funds II Small Company Value Fund Class NAV	JHSVX	A-	A	B	Up	3.49	9.87	11.56	38.54	87.03	28.42	296.3	800-225-5913	Y
John Hancock II Small Cap Value Fund Class A	JSCAX	B	B	B	Up	2.81	6.11	3.39	22.94	77.98	21.03	536.2	800-225-5913	Y
John Hancock II Small Cap Value Fund Class I	JSCBX	B	B	B	Up	2.92	6.31	3.73	24.12	80.74	21.05	536.2	800-225-5913	Y
John Hancock II Small Cap Value Fund Class NAV	JSCNX	B	B	B	Up	2.93	6.33	3.84	24.54	81.75	21.03	536.2	800-225-5913	Y
John Hancock II Small Cap Value Fund Class R6	JSCCX	B	B	B	Up	2.92	6.36	3.83	24.49	81.68	21.05	536.2	800-225-5913	Y
John Hancock Small Cap Core Fund Class I	JCCIX	B+	B+	B	Up	2.76	7.29	16.12	44.56		12.6	181.3	800-225-5913	Y
John Hancock Small Cap Core Fund Class NAV	US47803P5420	B+	B+	B	Up	2.80	7.41	16.24	45.03		12.6	181.3	800-225-5913	Y
John Hancock Small Cap Core Fund Class R6	JORSX	B+	B+	B		2.86	7.47	16.31	45.10		12.61	181.3	800-225-5913	Y
John Hancock Small Company Fund Class A	JCSAX	B	B	B	Up	3.60	8.07	12.94	26.21	83.64	28.23	363.4	800-225-5913	Y
John Hancock Small Company Fund Class ADV	JCSDX	B	B	B	Up	3.64	8.15	13.07	26.54	84.53	28.49	363.4	800-225-5913	Y
John Hancock Small Company Fund Class I	JCSIX	B	B	B	Up	3.67	8.24	13.31	27.34	86.47	29.08	363.4	800-225-5913	Y
John Hancock Small Company Fund Class R1	JCSOX	B	B	B	Up	3.47	7.88	12.52	24.79	80.30	27.28	363.4	800-225-5913	Y
John Hancock Small Company Fund Class R2	JCSPX	B	B	B	Up	3.54	8.00	12.82	25.82	82.67	28.23	363.4	800-225-5913	Y
John Hancock Small Company Fund Class R3	JCSHX	B	B	B	Up	3.55	7.96	12.69	25.22	81.27	27.55	363.4	800-225-5913	Y
John Hancock Small Company Fund Class R4	JCSFX	B	B	B	Up	3.66	8.16	13.18	26.83	85.08	28.59	363.4	800-225-5913	Y
John Hancock Small Company Fund Class R5	JCSVX	B	B	B	Up	3.67	8.26	13.33	27.44	86.73	29.13	363.4	800-225-5913	Y
John Hancock Small Company Fund Class R6	JCSWX	B	B	B	Up	3.71	8.25	13.37	27.74	87.57	29.31	363.4	800-225-5913	Y
JPMorgan Dynamic Small Cap Growth Fund Class A	VSCOX	B	A	C	Up	7.94	17.69	41.45	48.81	122.90	23.14	199.5	800-480-4111	
JPMorgan Dynamic Small Cap Growth Fund Class C	VSCCX	B+	A	B-	Up	7.81	17.38	40.73	46.53	117.22	17.31	199.5	800-480-4111	
JPMorgan Dynamic Small Cap Growth Fund Class I	JDSCX	B+	A	B-	Up	8.00	17.83	41.82	49.92	125.74	26.47	199.5	800-480-4111	
JPMorgan Small Cap Core Fund Class A	VSSBX	B+	A-	B	Up	3.07	9.69	14.78	28.91	106.30	52.97	255.2	800-480-4111	Y
JPMorgan Small Cap Core Fund Class C	VSSRX	B+	A-	B	Up	2.95	9.41	14.21	27.00	101.23	52.64	255.2	800-480-4111	Y
JPMorgan Small Cap Core Fund Class I	VSSWX	B+	A-	B	Up	3.15	9.84	15.09	30.07	109.21	53.17	255.2	800-480-4111	Y
JPMorgan Small Cap Core Fund Class R2	JRJUX	B+	A-	B		4.08	10.71	15.80	29.57	106.34	53.18	255.2	800-480-4111	Y
JPMorgan Small Cap Core Fund Class R3	JGAUX	B+	A-	B		4.16	10.85	16.10	30.55	108.93	53.19	255.2	800-480-4111	Y
JPMorgan Small Cap Core Fund Class R4	JGREX	B+	A-	B		4.20	10.98	16.37	31.52	111.53	53.19	255.2	800-480-4111	Y
JPMorgan Small Cap Core Fund Class R5	VSSCX	B+	A-	B	Up	3.20	9.95	15.29	30.30	109.57	53.29	255.2	800-480-4111	Y
JPMorgan Small Cap Core Fund Class R6	VSSLX	B+	A-	B	Up	3.20	9.96	15.33	30.40	109.74	53.2	255.2	800-480-4111	Y
JPMorgan Small Cap Equity Fund Class A	VSEAX	B	B	B		4.17	8.24	15.28	36.51	103.50	49.64	6,513	800-480-4111	
JPMorgan Small Cap Equity Fund Class C	JSECX	B	B	B		4.04	7.96	14.71	34.51	98.50	37.13	6,513	800-480-4111	
JPMorgan Small Cap Equity Fund Class I	VSEIX	B	B+	B		4.22	8.38	15.58	37.70	106.51	57.22	6,513	800-480-4111	
JPMorgan Small Cap Equity Fund Class R2	JSEZX	B	B	B		4.09	8.10	14.98	35.50	100.97	48.76	6,513	800-480-4111	
JPMorgan Small Cap Equity Fund Class R3	JSEPX	B	B	B		4.17	8.25	15.30	36.56	103.58	49.35	6,513	800-480-4111	Y
JPMorgan Small Cap Equity Fund Class R4	JSEQX	B	B+	B		4.23	8.37	15.57	36.98	104.20	57.13	6,513	800-480-4111	Y
JPMorgan Small Cap Equity Fund Class R5	JSERX	B+	B+	B	Up	4.29	8.47	15.81	38.53	108.61	57.33	6,513	800-480-4111	
JPMorgan Small Cap Equity Fund Class R6	VSENX	B	B+	B		4.30	8.51	15.88	37.68	105.25	57.31	6,513	800-480-4111	Y
JPMorgan Small Cap Growth Fund Class A	PGSGX	B+	A	B-	Up	7.94	17.78	41.12	48.52	123.96	16.08	1,542	800-480-4111	
JPMorgan Small Cap Growth Fund Class C	OSGCX	B	A	C	Up	7.78	17.47	40.34	46.32	118.14	11.83	1,542	800-480-4111	

Category: US Equity Small Cap (con't)

Fund Name	Ticker Symbol	RATINGS: Overall Rating	Reward Rating	Risk Rating	Recent Up/ Downgrade	TOTAL RETURNS & PERFORMANCE: 3-Month Total Return	6-Month Total Return	1-Year Total Return	3-Year Total Return	5-Year Total Return	ASSETS: NAV	Total Assets (MIL)	NEW INVESTORS: Telephone	Open to New Investors
JPMorgan Small Cap Growth Fund Class I	OGGFX	B	A	C	Up	8.00	17.95	41.49	49.60	126.71	17.71	1,542	800-480-4111	
JPMorgan Small Cap Growth Fund Class L	JISGX	B	A	C	Up	8.01	17.97	41.70	50.27	128.26	18.22	1,542	800-480-4111	
JPMorgan Small Cap Growth Fund Class R2	JSGZX	B+	A	B-	Up	7.85	17.59	40.78	47.41	121.11	15.56	1,542	800-480-4111	
JPMorgan Small Cap Growth Fund Class R3	JGRQX	B	A	C		7.98	17.82	41.18	48.57	124.04	16.08	1,542	800-480-4111	Y
JPMorgan Small Cap Growth Fund Class R4	JGLYX	B	A	C		8.04	17.96	41.34	48.75	124.30	16.1	1,542	800-480-4111	Y
JPMorgan Small Cap Growth Fund Class R5	JGSVX	B	A	C	Up	8.07	18.03	41.77	49.32	125.17	18.23	1,542	800-480-4111	Y
JPMorgan Small Cap Growth Fund Class R6	JGSMX	B	A	C	Up	8.06	18.07	41.80	50.74	129.53	18.39	1,542	800-480-4111	
JPMorgan Small Cap Value Fund Class A	PSOAX	B	B	B-	Up	1.71	5.64	2.89	22.05	77.83	28.9	2,073	800-480-4111	Y
JPMorgan Small Cap Value Fund Class C	OSVCX	B	B	B-	Up	1.56	5.38	2.29	19.87	72.53	24	2,073	800-480-4111	Y
JPMorgan Small Cap Value Fund Class I	PSOPX	B	B	B-	Up	1.74	5.77	3.15	22.93	80.06	30.61	2,073	800-480-4111	Y
JPMorgan Small Cap Value Fund Class R2	JSVZX	B	B	B-	Up	1.63	5.48	2.57	21.05	75.53	28.64	2,073	800-480-4111	Y
JPMorgan Small Cap Value Fund Class R3	JSVPX	B	B	B-	Up	1.69	5.63	2.87	21.96	77.75	28.86	2,073	800-480-4111	Y
JPMorgan Small Cap Value Fund Class R4	JSVQX	B	B	B-	Up	1.74	5.75	3.08	22.85	79.94	30.58	2,073	800-480-4111	Y
JPMorgan Small Cap Value Fund Class R5	JSVRX	B	B	B-	Up	1.81	5.87	3.29	23.37	81.03	30.62	2,073	800-480-4111	Y
JPMorgan Small Cap Value Fund Class R6	JSVUX	B	B	B-	Up	1.83	5.92	3.39	23.81	81.94	30.65	2,073	800-480-4111	Y
JPMorgan U.S. Small Company Fund Class A	JTUAX	B	B	B	Up	3.35	7.86	8.52	24.95	94.37	18.31	1,857	800-480-4111	Y
JPMorgan U.S. Small Company Fund Class C	JTUCX	B	B	B	Up	3.21	7.54	7.97	23.11	89.59	17.51	1,857	800-480-4111	Y
JPMorgan U.S. Small Company Fund Class I	JSCSX	B	B	B	Up	3.40	7.93	8.75	25.88	96.86	18.7	1,857	800-480-4111	Y
JPMorgan U.S. Small Company Fund Class L	JUSSX	B	B	B	Up	3.43	8.02	8.97	26.57	98.69	18.68	1,857	800-480-4111	Y
JPMorgan U.S. Small Company Fund Class R2	JSCZX	B	B	B	Up	3.29	7.70	8.25	23.99	91.97	17.98	1,857	800-480-4111	Y
JPMorgan U.S. Small Company Fund Class R3	JUSPX	B	B	B	Up	3.38	7.85	8.51	25.43	95.91	18.21	1,857	800-480-4111	Y
JPMorgan U.S. Small Company Fund Class R4	JUSQX	B	B	B	Up	3.42	7.97	8.79	26.30	98.26	18.64	1,857	800-480-4111	Y
JPMorgan U.S. Small Company Fund Class R5	JUSYX	B	B	B	Up	3.42	8.02	8.90	26.50	98.58	18.65	1,857	800-480-4111	Y
JPMorgan U.S. Small Company Fund Class R6	JUSMX	B	B	B	Up	3.48	8.07	9.07	26.97	99.47	18.69	1,857	800-480-4111	Y
Keeley Small Cap Dividend Value Fund Class A	KSDVX	B	B	B-	Up	2.84	7.30	7.27	25.95	76.08	18.63	100.2	888-933-5391	Y
Keeley Small Cap Dividend Value Fund Class I	KSDIX	B	B	B-	Up	2.90	7.48	7.52	26.95	78.23	18.66	100.2	888-933-5391	Y
Keeley Small-Mid Cap Value Fund Class A	KSMVX	B-	B-	B-	Up	5.60	11.66	17.75	25.25	77.99	14.14	134.9	888-933-5391	Y
Keeley Small-Mid Cap Value Fund Class I	KSMIX	B-	B	B-	Up	5.70	11.80	18.13	26.30	80.36	14.44	134.9	888-933-5391	Y
Kinetics Small Capital Opportunities Advisor Fund Class A	KSOAX	B-	B	C	Up	6.77	21.13	25.94	36.61	104.97	49.81	178.2	800-930-3828	Y
Kinetics Small Capital Opportunities Fund Advisor Class C	KSOCX	B-	B	C	Up	6.62	20.81	25.31	34.56	99.95	47.77	178.2	800-930-3828	Y
Kinetics Small Capital Opp Fund Cls Inst	KSCYX	B-	B	C	Up	6.87	21.40	26.50	38.48	109.62	52.07	178.2	800-930-3828	Y
Kinetics Small Capital Opportunities Fund No Load Class	KSCOX	B-	B	C	Up	6.81	21.27	26.23	37.62	107.57	51.25	178.2	800-930-3828	Y
KP Small Cap Equity Fund Institutional Shares	KPSCX	B+	A-	B	Up	4.61	10.93	17.95	32.11		12.08	1,071		Y
Laudus Small-Cap MarketMasters Fund™ - Investor Shares	SWOSX	B	B	B	Up	4.18	8.34	11.88	24.62	72.98	18.42	192.9		Y
Laudus Small-Cap MarketMasters Fund™ - Select Shares®	SWMSX	B	B	B	Up	4.19	8.43	12.07	25.22	74.35	18.86	192.9		Y
Lazard US Small-Mid Cap Equity Portfolio Inst Shares	LZSCX	B	B	B	Up	4.87	9.37	14.20	28.86	99.91	14.65	205.4	800-823-6300	Y
Lazard US Small-Mid Cap Equity Portfolio Open Shares	LZCOX	B	B	B	Up	4.79	9.19	13.82	27.73	96.88	13.72	205.4	800-823-6300	Y
LKCM Small Capital Equity Fund Advisor Class	LKSAX	B-	B-	B	Up	3.93	9.07	16.69	18.57	59.55	17.13	214.2	800-688-5526	Y
LKCM Small Capital Equity Fund Class Institutional	LKSCX	B-	B-	B	Up	4.04	9.31	17.03	19.50	61.63	18.44	214.2	800-688-5526	Y
Loomis Sayles Small Cap Growth Fund Class N	LSSNX	B	A-	C+	Up	4.48	11.15	27.02	35.52	107.17	25.54	1,270	800-633-3330	
Loomis Sayles Small Cap Growth Fund Institutional Class	LSSIX	B	A-	C+	Up	4.47	11.08	26.85	35.13	106.24	25.4	1,270	800-633-3330	
Loomis Sayles Small Cap Growth Fund Retail Class	LCGRX	B	A-	C+	Up	4.39	10.91	26.55	34.09	103.49	23.46	1,270	800-633-3330	
Loomis Sayles Small Cap Value Fund Class N	LSCNX	B+	A-	B	Up	3.06	9.75	10.12	33.58	96.59	34.24	1,105	800-633-3330	
Loomis Sayles Small Capital Value Fund Admin Class	LSVAX	B+	A-	B	Up	2.91	9.43	9.50	31.32	91.10	32.38	1,105	800-633-3330	
Loomis Sayles Small Capital Value Fund Institutional Class	LSSCX	B+	A-	B	Up	3.04	9.71	10.02	33.30	95.92	34.22	1,105	800-633-3330	
Loomis Sayles Small Capital Value Fund Retail Class	LSCRX	B+	A-	B	Up	3.01	9.58	9.77	32.31	93.49	33.7	1,105	800-633-3330	
Lord Abbett Alpha Strategy Fund Class A	ALFAX	B	B	C+	Up	4.81	10.81	20.59	29.50	94.15	26.6	1,144	201-827-2000	Y
Lord Abbett Alpha Strategy Fund Class B	ALFBX	B	B	B	Up	4.58	10.36	19.69	26.63	87.01	22.98	1,144	201-827-2000	
Lord Abbett Alpha Strategy Fund Class C	ALFCX	B	B	B	Up	4.62	10.40	19.69	26.68	87.09	22.56	1,144	201-827-2000	Y
Lord Abbett Alpha Strategy Fund Class F	ALFFX	B	B	C+	Up	4.85	10.87	20.75	30.11	95.60	26.75	1,144	201-827-2000	Y
Lord Abbett Alpha Strategy Fund Class F3	ALFOX	B	B	C+	Up	4.89	10.97	20.88	29.81	94.62	27.23	1,144	201-827-2000	Y
Lord Abbett Alpha Strategy Fund Class I	ALFYX	B	B	C+	Up	4.85	10.93	20.86	30.48	96.55	27.21	1,144	201-827-2000	Y

Category: US Equity Small Cap (con't)

		RATINGS				TOTAL RETURNS & PERFORMANCE					ASSETS		NEW INVESTORS	
Fund Name	Ticker Symbol	Overall Rating	Reward Rating	Risk Rating	Recent Up/ Downgrade	3-Month Total Return	6-Month Total Return	1-Year Total Return	3-Year Total Return	5-Year Total Return	NAV	Total Assets (MIL)	Telephone	Open to New Investors
Lord Abbett Alpha Strategy Fund Class R2	ALFQX	B-	B	C+	Up	4.70	10.63	20.15	28.19	90.82	25.71	1,144	201-827-2000	Y
Lord Abbett Alpha Strategy Fund Class R3	ALFRX	B-	B	C+	Up	4.74	10.68	20.29	28.58	91.81	25.9	1,144	201-827-2000	Y
Lord Abbett Alpha Strategy Fund Class R4	ALFKX	B	B	C+	Up	4.81	10.83	20.62	29.55	94.23	26.56	1,144	201-827-2000	Y
Lord Abbett Alpha Strategy Fund Class R5	ALFTX	B	B	C+	Up	4.89	10.97	20.94	30.42	95.53	27.23	1,144	201-827-2000	Y
Lord Abbett Alpha Strategy Fund Class R6	ALFVX	B	B	C+	Up	4.92	11.00	21.02	30.49	95.64	27.24	1,144	201-827-2000	Y
Lord Abbett Micro Cap Growth Fund Class I	LMIYX	B	A	C+	Up	3.31	17.39	38.37	32.33	166.28	17.81	137.7	201-827-2000	Y
Lord Abbett Micro Cap Value Fund Class I	LMVYX	A-	A-	B+	Up	2.13	6.54	7.50	42.57	102.16	30.96	138.2	201-827-2000	Y
Lord Abbett Small Cap Value Fund Class A	LRSCX	B	B-	B	Up	3.94	6.01	6.30	25.38	75.72	20.42	1,162	201-827-2000	Y
Lord Abbett Small Cap Value Fund Class B	LRSBX	B-	B-	B	Up	3.77	5.59	5.51	22.59	69.37	11.52	1,162	201-827-2000	
Lord Abbett Small Cap Value Fund Class C	LSRCX	B	B-	B	Up	3.76	5.65	5.58	22.71	69.50	11.56	1,162	201-827-2000	Y
Lord Abbett Small Cap Value Fund Class F	LRSFX	B	B	B	Up	3.97	6.08	6.47	25.98	77.15	20.54	1,162	201-827-2000	Y
Lord Abbett Small Cap Value Fund Class F3	LRSOX	B	B	B	Up	4.04	6.19	6.56	25.68	76.14	24.26	1,162	201-827-2000	Y
Lord Abbett Small Cap Value Fund Class I	LRSYX	B	B	B	Up	3.98	6.14	6.60	26.33	78.05	24.17	1,162	201-827-2000	Y
Lord Abbett Small Cap Value Fund Class P	LRSPX	B	B-	B	Up	3.88	5.90	6.10	24.63	74.13	19.41	1,162	201-827-2000	
Lord Abbett Small Cap Value Fund Class R2	LRSQX	B	B-	B	Up	3.87	5.85	5.95	24.10	72.76	19.23	1,162	201-827-2000	Y
Lord Abbett Small Cap Value Fund Class R3	LRSRX	B	B-	B	Up	3.87	5.88	6.08	24.53	73.85	19.5	1,162	201-827-2000	Y
Lord Abbett Small Cap Value Fund Class R4	LRSSX	B	B-	B	Up	3.94	6.02	6.36	25.43	75.79	20.43	1,162	201-827-2000	Y
Lord Abbett Small Cap Value Fund Class R5	LRSTX	B	B	B	Up	3.99	6.14	6.60	26.23	76.91	24.19	1,162	201-827-2000	Y
Lord Abbett Small Cap Value Fund Class R6	LRSVX	B	B	B	Up	4.02	6.21	6.67	26.52	77.32	24.26	1,162	201-827-2000	Y
LSV Small Cap Value Fund Institutional Class	LSVQX	B	B+	B	Up	2.18	7.02	6.11	29.82		15.55	359.9		Y
LSV Small Cap Value Fund Investor Class	LVAQX	B	B+	B	Up	2.14	6.93	5.81	28.83		15.49	359.9		Y
Madison Small Cap Fund Class A	MASVX	B	B	B	Up	2.84	6.50	3.33	23.86	76.85		98.2	800-767-0300	Y
Madison Small Cap Fund Class B	MBSVX	B	B	B	Up	2.65	6.07	2.59	21.15	70.37		98.2	800-767-0300	Y
Madison Small Cap Fund Class Y	MYSVX	B	B	B	Up	3.55	7.36	3.79	24.51	79.68		98.2	800-767-0300	Y
MainStay Epoch U.S. Small Cap Fund Class A	MOPAX	B	B	B	Up	6.34	8.71	15.32	26.95	89.90	31.04	615.0	800-624-6782	Y
MainStay Epoch U.S. Small Cap Fund Class B	MOTBX	B	B-	B	Up	6.06	8.12	14.14	23.15	80.41	27.42	615.0	800-624-6782	Y
MainStay Epoch U.S. Small Cap Fund Class C	MOPCX	B	B-	B	Up	6.06	8.12	14.15	23.11	80.35	27.41	615.0	800-624-6782	Y
MainStay Epoch U.S. Small Cap Fund Class I	MOPIX	B	B	B	Up	6.44	8.85	15.61	27.92	92.30	31.91	615.0	800-624-6782	Y
MainStay Epoch U.S. Small Cap Fund Class R1	MOPRX	B	B	B	Up	6.42	8.80	15.54	27.57	91.39	31.83	615.0	800-624-6782	Y
MainStay Epoch U.S. Small Cap Fund Class R2	MOTRX	B	B	B	Up	6.33	8.63	15.22	26.57	88.98	30.93	615.0	800-624-6782	Y
MainStay Epoch U.S. Small Cap Fund Class R3	MOVRX	B	B	B	Up	6.27	8.50	14.93	25.76	87.18	30.88	615.0	800-624-6782	Y
MainStay Epoch U.S. Small Cap Fund Investor Class	MOINX	B	B	B	Up	6.27	8.56	15.01	25.97	87.33	30.57	615.0	800-624-6782	Y
Mairs & Power Small Cap Fund	MSCFX	B	B	B	Up	1.46	2.78	7.63	29.77	97.06	25.32	446.5	800-304-7404	Y
MassMutual Premier Small Cap Opp Fund Admin Cls	MSCLX	B	B	B	Up	1.80	6.59	14.01	25.56	103.45	14.6	213.6		Y
MassMutual Premier Small Cap Opportunities Fund Class A	DLBMX	B	B	B	Up	1.73	6.47	13.72	24.60	100.71	14.29	213.6		Y
MassMutual Premier Small Cap Opportunities Fund Class I	MSOOX	B	B	B	Up	1.89	6.77	14.36	26.82	105.09	14.73	213.6		Y
MassMutual Premier Small Cap Opportunities Fund Class R3	MCCRX	B	B	B	Up	1.68	6.33	13.48	24.10	99.00	14.12	213.6		Y
MassMutual Premier Small Cap Opportunities Fund Class R4	MOORX	B	B	B	Up	1.72	6.50	13.80	24.95	101.52	14.18	213.6		Y
MassMutual Premier Small Cap Opportunities Fund Class R5	MSCDX	B	B	B	Up	1.84	6.73	14.18	26.29	105.46	14.71	213.6		Y
MassMutual Premier Small Cap Opp Fund Service Cls	MSVYX	B	B	B	Up	1.81	6.64	14.10	25.93	104.38	14.68	213.6		Y
MassMutual Select Small Cap Growth Equity Fund Admin Cls	MSGLX	B	B	B	Up	5.89	11.28	24.50	28.22	104.79	14	561.7		Y
MassMutual Select Small Cap Growth Equity Fund Class A	MMGEX	B	B	B-	Up	5.80	11.13	24.15	27.25	102.09	12.58	561.7		Y
MassMutual Select Small Cap Growth Equity Fund Class I	MSGZX	B	B+	B	Up	5.89	11.41	24.85	29.28	108.01	15.79	561.7		Y
MassMutual Select Small Cap Growth Equity Fund Class R3	MSGNX	B	B	B-	Up	5.74	11.07	23.90	26.73	100.17	11.24	561.7		Y
MassMutual Select Small Cap Growth Equity Fund Class R4	MSERX	B-	B	C	Up	5.85	11.24	24.33	27.73	103.75	12.65	561.7		Y
MassMutual Select Small Cap Growth Equity Fund Class R5	MSGSX	B	B+	B	Up	5.96	11.40	24.70	28.99	107.06	15.62	561.7		Y
MassMutual Select Small Cap Growth Equity Fund Service Cls	MSCYX	B	B	B	Up	5.91	11.39	24.64	28.64	105.95	14.84	561.7		Y
MassMutual Select Small Cap Val Equity Fund Class I	MMQIX	B+	A-	B	Up	3.69	9.70	9.44	29.51	98.63	16.63	195.7		Y
MassMutual Select Small Cap Val Equity Fund Class R3	MMQTX	B	B+	B	Up	3.49	9.26	8.68	26.84	92.44	16.42	195.7		Y
MassMutual Select Small Cap Val Equity Fund Class R4	MMQFX	B+	B+	B	Up	3.54	9.43	8.98	27.79	94.75	16.43	195.7		Y
MassMutual Select Small Cap Value Equity Fund Admin Cls	MMQLX	B+	A-	B	Up	3.59	9.56	9.11	28.40	95.99	16.63	195.7		Y
MassMutual Select Small Cap Value Equity Fund Class A	MMQAX	B	B+	B	Up	3.55	9.35	8.84	27.39	93.54	16.54	195.7		Y

Category: US Equity Small Cap (con't)

Fund Name	Ticker Symbol	RATINGS: Overall Rating	Reward Rating	Risk Rating	Recent Up/ Downgrade	TOTAL RETURNS & PERFORMANCE: 3-Month Total Return	6-Month Total Return	1-Year Total Return	3-Year Total Return	5-Year Total Return	ASSETS: NAV	Total Assets (Mil)	NEW INVESTORS: Telephone	Open to New Investors
MassMutual Select Small Cap Value Equity Fund Class R5	MMQSX	B+	A-	B	Up	3.70	9.65	9.39	29.16	98.12	16.66	195.7		Y
MassMutual Select Small Cap Value Equity Fund Service Cls	MMQYX	B+	A-	B	Up	3.59	9.58	9.20	28.78	97.12	16.69	195.7		Y
MassMutual Select Small Company Value Fund Admin Cls	MMYLX	B	B	B	Up	2.91	9.10	10.25	27.50	79.61	11.23	251.7		Y
MassMutual Select Small Company Value Fund Class A	MMYAX	B	B	B	Up	2.82	9.01	9.92	26.58	77.28	10.87	251.7		Y
MassMutual Select Small Company Value Fund Class I	MSVZX	B	B+	B	Up	2.95	9.29	10.51	28.66	82.41	11.43	251.7		Y
MassMutual Select Small Company Value Fund Class R3	MSVNX	B	B	B	Up	2.76	8.88	9.75	26.01	75.70	10.08	251.7		Y
MassMutual Select Small Company Value Fund Class R4	MMVFX	B	B	B	Up	2.87	9.03	10.04	26.95	78.36	10.73	251.7		Y
MassMutual Select Small Company Value Fund Class R5	MSVSX	B	B	B	Up	2.97	9.20	10.42	28.27	81.32	11.5	251.7		Y
MassMutual Select Small Company Value Fund Service Class	MMVYX	B	B	B	Up	2.94	9.11	10.33	27.90	80.52	11.44	251.7		Y
Meridian Growth Fund® A Class	MRAGX	B	B+	C+	Up	5.55	10.87	25.25	35.77	92.99	40.61	1,605	800-446-6662	Y
Meridian Growth Fund® Class C	MRCGX	B	B+	C+	Up	5.37	10.46	24.32	33.35	87.62	40.46	1,605	800-446-6662	Y
Meridian Growth Fund® Institutional Class	MRRGX	B	B+	C+	Up	5.65	11.05	25.63	37.49	97.28	41.61	1,605	800-446-6662	Y
Meridian Growth Fund® Investor Class	MRIGX	B	B+	C+	Up	5.61	10.99	25.55	37.11	96.11	41.29	1,605	800-446-6662	Y
Meridian Growth Fund® Legacy Class	MERDX	B+	B+	B	Up	5.65	11.04	25.62	37.54	97.41	41.63	1,605	800-446-6662	
Meridian Small Cap Growth Fund A Class	MSGAX	B	A-	C	Up	3.52	10.41	22.59	36.40		15.77	1,290	800-446-6662	Y
Meridian Small Cap Growth Fund Class C	MSGCX	B	B+	C	Up	3.30	10.02	21.64	33.73		15.57	1,290	800-446-6662	Y
Meridian Small Cap Growth Fund Institutional Class	MSGRX	B	A-	C	Up	3.59	10.59	22.96	38.18		16.04	1,290	800-446-6662	Y
Meridian Small Cap Growth Fund Investor Shares	MISGX	B	A-	C	Up	3.55	10.50	22.82	37.52		15.96	1,290	800-446-6662	Y
Meridian Small Cap Growth Fund Legacy Class	MSGGX	B	A-	C	Up	3.54	10.55	22.86	37.76		15.99	1,290	800-446-6662	
MFS® New Discovery Fund Class 529A	EANDX	B	B+	C	Up	6.57	13.79	25.96	33.53	78.49	26.34	1,213	877-960-6077	Y
MFS® New Discovery Fund Class 529B	EBNDX	B-	B	C	Up	6.38	13.37	25.04	30.52	71.91	21.3	1,213	877-960-6077	Y
MFS® New Discovery Fund Class 529C	ECNDX	B-	B	C	Up	6.39	13.37	25.05	30.47	71.73	21.29	1,213	877-960-6077	Y
MFS® New Discovery Fund Class A	MNDAX	B	B+	C	Up	6.59	13.83	26.08	33.65	78.85	27.26	1,213	877-960-6077	Y
MFS® New Discovery Fund Class B	MNDBX	B-	B	C	Up	6.35	13.35	25.05	30.63	72.23	22.09	1,213	877-960-6077	Y
MFS® New Discovery Fund Class C	MNDCX	B-	B	C	Up	6.38	13.37	25.11	30.68	72.22	22.14	1,213	877-960-6077	Y
MFS® New Discovery Fund Class I	MNDIX	B	B+	C	Up	6.64	13.94	26.34	34.65	80.99	30.09	1,213	877-960-6077	Y
MFS® New Discovery Fund Class R1	MNDGX	B-	B	C	Up	6.40	13.35	25.07	30.68	72.21	21.93	1,213	877-960-6077	Y
MFS® New Discovery Fund Class R2	MNDRX	B	B	C	Up	6.54	13.67	25.73	32.67	76.59	25.67	1,213	877-960-6077	Y
MFS® New Discovery Fund Class R3	MNDHX	B	B+	C	Up	6.55	13.81	26.01	33.64	78.72	27.22	1,213	877-960-6077	Y
MFS® New Discovery Fund Class R4	MNDJX	B	B+	C	Up	6.75	14.06	26.46	34.74	81.19	28.64	1,213	877-960-6077	Y
MFS® New Discovery Fund Class R6	MNDKX	B	B+	C	Up	6.65	13.98	26.49	35.14	82.08	30.32	1,213	877-960-6077	Y
MFS® New Discovery Value Fund Class A	NDVAX	B+	A-	B	Up	5.50	10.60	14.65	38.89	104.77	15.74	1,208	877-960-6077	Y
MFS® New Discovery Value Fund Class B	NDVBX	B+	A-	B	Up	5.27	10.14	13.81	35.81	97.34	15.21	1,208	877-960-6077	Y
MFS® New Discovery Value Fund Class C	NDVCX	B+	A-	B	Up	5.29	10.19	13.79	35.80	97.32	15.14	1,208	877-960-6077	Y
MFS® New Discovery Value Fund Class I	NDVIX	A-	A-	B	Up	5.50	10.64	14.83	39.90	107.24	15.81	1,208	877-960-6077	Y
MFS® New Discovery Value Fund Class R1	NDVRX	B+	A-	B	Up	5.26	10.21	13.80	35.81	97.35	15.22	1,208	877-960-6077	Y
MFS® New Discovery Value Fund Class R2	NDVSX	B+	A-	B	Up	5.38	10.48	14.38	37.94	102.37	15.69	1,208	877-960-6077	Y
MFS® New Discovery Value Fund Class R3	NDVTX	B+	A-	B	Up	5.49	10.57	14.60	38.95	104.94	15.78	1,208	877-960-6077	Y
MFS® New Discovery Value Fund Class R4	NDVUX	B+	A-	B	Up	5.45	10.66	14.83	39.89	107.42	15.83	1,208	877-960-6077	Y
MFS® New Discovery Value Fund Class R6	NDVVX	A-	A	B	Up	5.53	10.74	15.00	40.38	108.22	15.83	1,208	877-960-6077	Y
MM Russell 2000® Small Cap Index Fund Administrative Class	MCJYX	B+	A-	B	Up	3.24	8.98	14.12	30.56	93.77	13.14	298.3		Y
MM Russell 2000® Small Cap Index Fund Class A	MCJAX	B+	A-	B	Up	3.23	8.92	13.91	29.70	91.18	13.08	298.3		Y
MM Russell 2000® Small Cap Index Fund Class I	MCJZX	B+	A-	B	Up	3.35	9.21	14.60	32.06	97.29	13.21	298.3		Y
MM Russell 2000® Small Cap Index Fund Class R3	MCJTX	B+	B+	B	Up	3.16	8.81	13.65	29.13	90.51	12.97	298.3		Y
MM Russell 2000® Small Cap Index Fund Class R4	MCJFX	B+	A-	B	Up	3.19	8.89	13.98	30.03	92.89	13.02	298.3		Y
MM Russell 2000® Small Cap Index Fund Class R5	MCJIX	B+	A-	B	Up	3.25	9.11	14.41	31.52	96.25	13.2	298.3		Y
MM Russell 2000® Small Cap Index Fund Service Class shares	MCJSX	B+	A-	B	Up	3.20	9.02	14.18	30.91	94.51	13.1	298.3		Y
Morgan Dempsey Small/Micro Cap Value Fund	MITYX	B	B	C+	Up	3.74	10.64	11.73	29.05	67.38	15.94	24.1		Y
Multi-Manager Small Cap Equity Strategies Fund Class A	CSCEX	B+	A-	B	Up	3.36	11.03	14.83	34.34	96.71	15.54	1,260	800-345-6611	Y
Multi-Manager Small Cap Equity Strategies Fund Inst Cls	CZMSX	B+	A-	B	Up	3.43	11.20	15.18	34.74	97.31	15.5	1,260	800-345-6611	Y
Mutual of America Inst Funds Inc Small Cap Growth Fund	MASSX	B	A-	C+	Up	4.62	11.49	24.19	30.75	100.62	13.1427	8.5		Y
Mutual of America Inst Funds Inc Small Cap Value Fund	MAVSX	B	B	B	Up	1.35	6.30	8.21	24.46	73.85	13.2387	11.1		Y

Category: US Equity Small Cap (con't)

Fund Name	Ticker Symbol	RATINGS: Overall Rating	Reward Rating	Risk Rating	Recent Up/ Downgrade	TOTAL RETURNS & PERFORMANCE: 3-Month Total Return	6-Month Total Return	1-Year Total Return	3-Year Total Return	5-Year Total Return	ASSETS: NAV	Total Assets (MIL)	NEW INVESTORS: Telephone	Open to New Investors
Nationwide Bailard Cognitive Value Fund Class A	NWHDX	B	B	B	Up	0.86	5.76	3.57	24.17	74.69	13.49	100.5	800-848-0920	Y
Nationwide Bailard Cognitive Value Fund Class C	NWHEX	B	B	B	Up	0.68	5.29	2.74	21.50	68.62	12.54	100.5	800-848-0920	Y
Nationwide Bailard Cognitive Value Fund Class M	NWHFX	B	B	B	Up	0.95	5.95	3.90	25.50	77.93	13.49	100.5	800-848-0920	Y
Nationwide Bailard Cognitive Value Fund Class R6	NWHGX	B	B	B	Up	0.88	5.88	3.84	25.52	77.81	13.48	100.5	800-848-0920	Y
Nationwide Bailard Cognitive Value Fund Inst Service Cls	NWHHX	B	B	B	Up	0.91	5.90	3.78	25.32	77.31	13.51	100.5	800-848-0920	Y
Nationwide Geneva Small Cap Growth Fund Class A	NWHZX	A-	A	A-	Up	2.83	9.19	21.84	46.97	106.57	54.12	734.2	800-848-0920	Y
Nationwide Geneva Small Cap Growth Fund Class C	NWKBX	A-	A-	A-	Up	2.64	8.80	20.96	43.78	99.62	50.7	734.2	800-848-0920	Y
Nationwide Geneva Small Cap Growth Fund Class R6	NWKCX	A-	A	B	Up	2.92	9.41	22.30	48.64	110.34	55.89	734.2	800-848-0920	Y
Nationwide Geneva Small Cap Growth Fund Inst Service Cls	NWKDX	A-	A	A-	Up	2.90	9.34	22.15	48.16	109.38	55.61	734.2	800-848-0920	Y
Nationwide Small Cap Index Fund Class A	GMRAX	B+	A-	B	Up	3.17	8.90	13.97	30.20	93.38	13.76	595.6	800-848-0920	Y
Nationwide Small Cap Index Fund Class C	GMRCX	B	B+	B	Up	2.99	8.49	13.18	27.47	86.84	13.06	595.6	800-848-0920	Y
Nationwide Small Cap Index Fund Class R	GMSRX	B+	A-	B	Up	3.13	8.81	13.80	29.64	92.19	13.61	595.6	800-848-0920	Y
Nationwide Small Cap Index Fund Class R6	GMRIX	B+	A-	B	Up	3.33	9.16	14.53	31.87	97.42	14.04	595.6	800-848-0920	Y
Nationwide Small Cap Index Fund Institutional Service Cls	NWXRX	B+	A-	B	Up	3.24	9.09	14.33	31.63	97.06	14.03	595.6	800-848-0920	Y
Nationwide Small Company Growth Fund Class A	NWSAX	A-	A	B	Up	5.21	9.43	27.98	50.20	127.00	17.18	248.6	800-848-0920	Y
Nationwide Small Company Growth Fund Inst Service Cls	NWSIX	A-	A	B	Up	5.28	9.60	28.20	50.86	128.97	17.35	248.6	800-848-0920	Y
Nationwide U.S. Small Cap Value Fund Class A	NWUAX	B	B	B-	Up	3.23	8.66	7.56	25.92	86.31	13.49	186.7	800-848-0920	Y
Nationwide U.S. Small Cap Value Fund Class C	NWUCX	B-	B	B-	Up	2.99	8.20	6.70	23.05	79.56	12.54	186.7	800-848-0920	Y
Nationwide U.S. Small Cap Value Fund Class R6	NWUIX	B	B	B	Up	3.25	8.77	7.92	27.21	89.48	13.83	186.7	800-848-0920	Y
Nationwide U.S. Small Cap Value Fund Inst Service Cls	NWUSX	B	B	B-	Up	3.28	8.75	7.74	26.38	87.24	13.6	186.7	800-848-0920	Y
Nationwide WCM Focused Small Cap Fund Class A	NWGPX	B+	A-	B	Up	2.19	8.70	13.56	32.10	106.48	36.98	201.4	800-848-0920	Y
Nationwide WCM Focused Small Cap Fund Class C	NWGQX	B+	A-	B	Up	1.98	8.28	12.70	29.11	99.32	34.39	201.4	800-848-0920	Y
Nationwide WCM Focused Small Cap Fund Class R6	NWKEX	B+	A-	B	Up	2.28	8.90	13.97	33.54	110.11	37.97	201.4	800-848-0920	Y
Nationwide WCM Focused Small Cap Fund Inst Service Cls	NWGSX	B+	A-	B	Up	2.28	8.86	13.88	33.26	109.55	37.89	201.4	800-848-0920	Y
Natixis Funds Trust I Vaughan Nelson Small Cap Value Cls A	NEFJX	B	B	B	Up	3.42	7.77	6.27	26.44	96.53	18.71	305.8	800-862-4863	
Natixis Funds Trust I Vaughan Nelson Small Cap Value Cls C	NEJCX	B-	B-	B	Up	3.21	7.31	5.49	23.62	89.33	11.67	305.8	800-862-4863	
Natixis Funds Trust I Vaughan Nelson Small Cap Value Cls N	VSCNX	B	B	B	Up	3.51	8.00	6.53	26.75	97.00	19.37	305.8	800-862-4863	Y
Natixis Funds Trust I Vaughan Nelson Small Cap Value Cls Y	NEJYX	B	B	B	Up	3.51	7.89	6.59	27.45	99.05	19.37	305.8	800-862-4863	
Needham Aggressive Growth Fund Institutional Class	NEAIX	B+	A-	B-	Up	-2.84	7.76	9.36	23.78	84.86	23.21	64.9	800-625-7071	Y
Needham Aggressive Growth Fund Retail Class	NEAGX	B+	A-	B-	Up	-2.97	7.47	8.72	23.06	83.79	23.07	64.9	800-625-7071	Y
Needham Small Cap Growth Fund Institutional Class	NESIX	B+	A	B-	Up	-1.13	4.84	12.48	34.88	77.34	15.77	30.6	800-625-7071	Y
Needham Small Cap Growth Fund Retail Class	NESGX	B+	A	B-	Up	-1.26	4.54	11.87	34.16	76.39	15.68	30.6	800-625-7071	Y
Neuberger Berman Genesis Fund Advisor Class	NBGAX	B	B	B+	Up	5.60	9.75	15.21	34.19	86.51	57.69	11,160	212-476-9000	Y
Neuberger Berman Genesis Fund Class R6	NRGSX	B+	B+	A-	Up	5.75	10.07	15.87	36.60	92.02	57.46	11,160	212-476-9000	Y
Neuberger Berman Genesis Fund Investor Class	NBGNX	B+	B+	B+	Up	5.67	9.94	15.59	35.64	89.86	57.6	11,160	212-476-9000	Y
Neuberger Berman Genesis Fund Trust Class	NBGEX	B+	B+	B+	Up	5.66	9.88	15.50	35.28	89.05	57.65	11,160	212-476-9000	Y
Neuberger Berman Intrinsic Value Fund Class A	NINAX	B	B	B	Up	1.41	7.69	16.25	25.91	88.85	15.83	914.8	212-476-9000	Y
Neuberger Berman Intrinsic Value Fund Class C	NINCX	B	B	B	Up	1.24	7.26	15.40	23.19	82.01	14.82	914.8	212-476-9000	Y
Neuberger Berman Intrinsic Value Fund Institutional Class	NINLX	B	B	B	Up	1.55	7.92	16.71	27.41	92.57	16.34	914.8	212-476-9000	Y
Neuberger Berman Small Cap Growth Fund Advisor Class	NBMVX	B	B+	C	Up	4.75	11.59	27.69	26.79	96.77	24.09	76.6	212-476-9000	
Neuberger Berman Small Cap Growth Fund Class A	NSNAX	B	B+	B-	Up	4.83	11.72	28.02	27.73	99.28	38.43	76.6	212-476-9000	Y
Neuberger Berman Small Cap Growth Fund Class C	NSNCX	B	B+	B-	Up	4.69	11.31	27.09	24.94	92.00	23.06	76.6	212-476-9000	Y
Neuberger Berman Small Cap Growth Fund Class R3	NSNRX	B	B+	B-	Up	4.78	11.55	27.72	26.82	96.85	24.16	76.6	212-476-9000	Y
Neuberger Berman Small Cap Growth Fund Institutional Class	NBSMX	B	B+	C	Up	4.94	11.92	28.48	29.13	102.92	36.14	76.6	212-476-9000	Y
Neuberger Berman Small Cap Growth Fund Investor Class	NBMIX	B	B+	C	Up	4.84	11.75	28.12	27.97	99.76	35.09	76.6	212-476-9000	
Neuberger Berman Small Cap Growth Fund Trust Class	NBMOX	B	B+	C	Up	4.83	11.67	27.90	27.32	97.99	38.01	76.6	212-476-9000	
Nicholas Limited Edition Fund Class Institutional	NCLEX	B	B	B	Up	3.08	7.32	19.92	31.41	91.44	26.32	398.3	800-544-6547	Y
Nicholas Limited Edition Fund Class N	NNLEX	B	B	B	Up	3.03	7.15	19.56	30.08	88.26	24.74	398.3	800-544-6547	Y
North Star Dividend Fund Class I	NSDVX	B+	B+	B+	Up	2.66	6.22	8.27	29.28	83.40	21.64	80.8	312-580-0	Y
North Star Micro Cap Fund Class I	NSMVX	B-	B	C+	Up	-0.58	4.19	4.83	18.04	85.69	28.3	83.0	312-580-0	Y
Northern Small Cap Core Fund	NSGRX	B	B+	B	Up	2.95	8.25	13.02	29.63	97.07	25.57	498.0	800-595-9111	Y
Northern Small Cap Index Fund	NSIDX	B+	A-	B	Up	3.32	9.15	14.58	31.54	96.36	13.62	1,275	800-595-9111	Y

Category: US Equity Small Cap (con't)

Fund Name	Ticker Symbol	RATINGS: Overall Rating	Reward Rating	Risk Rating	Recent Up/ Downgrade	TOTAL RETURNS & PERFORMANCE: 3-Month Total Return	6-Month Total Return	1-Year Total Return	3-Year Total Return	5-Year Total Return	ASSETS: NAV	Total Assets (MIL)	NEW INVESTORS: Telephone	Open to New Investors
Northern Small Cap Value Fund	NOSGX	B+	B+	B	Up	1.29	6.46	6.42	28.45	93.39	23.4	3,959	800-595-9111	Y
Nuveen NWQ Small Mid/Cap Value Fund Class R3	NWQRX	B-	B-	B-	Up	5.10	8.38	9.74	23.07	73.57	33.31	61.3	312-917-8146	Y
Nuveen NWQ Small/Mid Cap Value Fund Class A	NSMAX	B-	B	B-	Up	5.14	8.50	9.99	24.02	75.79	34.29	61.3	312-917-8146	Y
Nuveen NWQ Small/Mid Cap Value Fund Class C	NSMCX	B-	B-	B-	Up	4.97	8.09	9.19	21.29	69.36	31.41	61.3	312-917-8146	Y
Nuveen NWQ Small/Mid Cap Value Fund Class I	NSMRX	B	B	B-	Up	5.23	8.61	10.28	24.95	78.03	34.7	61.3	312-917-8146	Y
Nuveen NWQ Small/Mid Cap Value Fund Class R6	NWQFX	B	B	B-	Up	5.28	8.72	10.46	25.26	78.47	34.79	61.3	312-917-8146	Y
Nuveen NWQ Small-Cap Value Fund Class A	NSCAX	B	A-	B	Up	5.66	11.07	11.75	29.53	99.63	52.47	768.5	312-917-8146	Y
Nuveen NWQ Small-Cap Value Fund Class C	NSCCX	B	B	B	Up	5.45	10.65	10.93	26.62	92.26	47.64	768.5	312-917-8146	Y
Nuveen NWQ Small-Cap Value Fund Class I	NSCRX	B+	A-	B	Up	5.73	11.21	12.03	30.49	102.11	53.85	768.5	312-917-8146	Y
Nuveen NWQ Small-Cap Value Fund Class R3	NSCQX	B	B+	B	Up	5.60	10.93	11.48	28.56	97.23	51.68	768.5	312-917-8146	Y
Nuveen NWQ Small-Cap Value Fund Class R6	NSCFX	B+	A-	B	Up	5.76	11.32	12.22	31.13	103.53	54.27	768.5	312-917-8146	Y
Nuveen Small Cap Growth Opportunities Fund Class A	FRMPX	B	B+	B	Up	1.97	7.78	16.52	24.14	91.74	22.15	104.2	312-917-8146	Y
Nuveen Small Cap Growth Opportunities Fund Class C	FMPCX	B	B	B-	Up	1.75	7.36	15.66	21.35	84.64	17.05	104.2	312-917-8146	Y
Nuveen Small Cap Growth Opportunities Fund Class I	FIMPX	B	B+	B	Up	2.06	7.92	16.80	25.09	94.08	26.1	104.2	312-917-8146	Y
Nuveen Small Cap Growth Opportunities Fund Class R3	FMPYX	B	B+	B	Up	1.90	7.64	16.17	23.19	89.23	20.89	104.2	312-917-8146	Y
Nuveen Small Cap Growth Opportunities Fund Class R6	FMPFX	B+	A-	B	Up	2.09	7.99	16.95	25.34	94.48	26.16	104.2	312-917-8146	Y
Nuveen Small Cap Select Fund Class A	EMGRX	B	B	B	Up	2.10	7.14	9.74	29.43	85.23	9.2	130.3	312-917-8146	Y
Nuveen Small Cap Select Fund Class C	FHMCX	B	B	B	Up	1.90	6.73	8.98	26.53	78.52	6	130.3	312-917-8146	Y
Nuveen Small Cap Select Fund Class I	ARSTX	B	B	B	Up	2.16	7.23	9.96	30.29	87.61	11.75	130.3	312-917-8146	Y
Nuveen Small Cap Select Fund Class R3	ASEIX	B	B	B	Up	1.96	6.99	9.44	28.43	82.90	8.33	130.3	312-917-8146	Y
Nuveen Small Cap Value Fund Class A	FSCAX	B+	A-	B	Up	4.45	7.30	6.08	41.30	111.34	25.71	2,066	312-917-8146	Y
Nuveen Small Cap Value Fund Class C	FSCVX	B+	B+	B	Up	4.23	6.92	5.28	38.21	103.56	21.85	2,066	312-917-8146	Y
Nuveen Small Cap Value Fund Class I	FSCCX	B+	A-	B	Up	4.48	7.44	6.34	42.35	114.06	26.58	2,066	312-917-8146	Y
Nuveen Small Cap Value Fund Class R3	FSVSX	B+	B+	B	Up	4.34	7.17	5.78	40.22	108.63	25.16	2,066	312-917-8146	Y
Nuveen Small Cap Value Fund Class R6	FSCWX	B+	A-	B	Up	4.52	7.53	6.30	42.41	114.15	26.58	2,066	312-917-8146	Y
Nuveen Symphony Small Cap Core Fund Class A	NSSAX	B+	A-	B	Up	6.79	13.07	19.22	33.90		27.53	34.6	312-917-8146	Y
Nuveen Symphony Small Cap Core Fund Class C	NSSCX	B	B	B	Up	6.60	12.64	18.34	30.95		26.68	34.6	312-917-8146	Y
Nuveen Symphony Small Cap Core Fund Class I	NSSIX	B+	A-	B	Up	6.84	13.23	19.49	34.90		27.81	34.6	312-917-8146	Y
Oak Ridge Dynamic Small Cap Fund Class A	ORSAX	A-	A-	B+	Up	5.31	14.28	15.42	40.78	124.29	13.91	28.2		Y
Oak Ridge Dynamic Small Cap Fund Class I	ORSIX	A-	A-	B+	Up	5.37	14.40	15.63	41.77	126.99	13.97	28.2		Y
Oberweis Micro Cap Fund Institutional Class	OMCIX	A-	A+	B	Up	3.53	13.96	28.07	70.56	163.97	25.17	99.3		Y
Oberweis Micro-Cap Fund	OBMCX	A-	A+	B	Up	3.46	13.80	27.89	70.33	163.60	25.12	99.3		Y
Oberweis Small-Cap Opportunities Fund	OBSOX	B+	A-	B	Up	4.98	14.64	25.53	41.36	103.92	16.4	11.2		Y
Oberweis Small-Cap Opportunities Fund Institutional Class	OBSIX	B+	A-	B	Up	5.03	14.83	25.74	41.60	104.26	16.44	11.2		Y
Oberweis Small-Cap Value Fund Institutional Class	OBVLX	B-	B	C+	Up	3.80	9.48	9.63	21.88	90.33	21.63	41.6		Y
Oppenheimer Discovery Fund Class A	OPOCX	B+	A-	B	Up	6.97	12.94	29.11	36.43	100.03	77.54	2,197	800-225-5677	
Oppenheimer Discovery Fund Class B	ODIBX	B+	A-	B	Up	6.75	12.48	28.11	33.32	92.40	53.42	2,197	800-225-5677	
Oppenheimer Discovery Fund Class C	ODICX	B+	A-	B	Up	6.76	12.50	28.12	33.35	92.57	55.86	2,197	800-225-5677	
Oppenheimer Discovery Fund Class I	ODIIX	B+	A-	B	Up	7.09	13.18	29.64	38.17	104.54	88.63	2,197	800-225-5677	
Oppenheimer Discovery Fund Class R	ODINX	B+	A-	B	Up	6.91	12.80	28.78	35.37	97.40	71.89	2,197	800-225-5677	
Oppenheimer Discovery Fund Class Y	ODIYX	B+	A-	B	Up	7.04	13.06	29.40	37.39	102.55	87.31	2,197	800-225-5677	
Oppenheimer Main Street Small Cap Fund Class A	OSCAX	B	B	B	Up	1.61	6.29	13.47	24.25		15.11	568.6	800-225-5677	Y
Oppenheimer Main Street Small Cap Fund Class C	OSCCX	B	B	B	Up	1.50	5.94	12.72	21.57		14.68	568.6	800-225-5677	Y
Oppenheimer Main Street Small Cap Fund Class I	OSSIX	B	B	B	Up	1.79	6.57	14.05	26.00		15.19	568.6	800-225-5677	Y
Oppenheimer Main Street Small Cap Fund Class R	OSCNX	B	B	B	Up	1.56	6.21	13.21	23.34		14.98	568.6	800-225-5677	Y
Oppenheimer Main Street Small Cap Fund Class Y	OSCYX	B	B	B	Up	1.70	6.49	13.89	25.49		15.17	568.6	800-225-5677	Y
Optimum Small-Mid Cap Growth Fund Class A	OASGX	B-	B-	B-	Up	7.04	12.70	27.29	22.60	79.15	14.86	501.5		Y
Optimum Small-Mid Cap Growth Fund Class C	OCSGX	B-	B-	B-	Up	6.83	12.27	26.40	19.86	72.85	12.78	501.5		Y
Optimum Small-Mid Cap Growth Fund Institutional Class	OISGX	B-	B	B-	Up	7.11	12.78	27.61	23.51	81.68	15.92	501.5		Y
O'Shaughnessy Small/Mid Cap Growth Fund Class I	OFMIX	B	B	B+	Up	2.39	9.26	13.85	29.17	88.12	15.62	15.8		Y
Osterweis Emerging Opportunity Fund	OSTGX	B+	A-	B	Up	4.59	12.51	26.44	39.35	122.21	10.74	55.9	866-236-0050	Y
PACE Small/Medium Co Growth Equity Investments Class A	PQUAX	B	B	B	Up	5.32	7.72	23.02	23.28	77.41	17.01	516.3	212-882-5586	Y

Category: US Equity Small Cap (con't)

Fund Name	Ticker Symbol	RATINGS: Overall Rating	Reward Rating	Risk Rating	Recent Up/ Downgrade	TOTAL RETURNS & PERFORMANCE: 3-Month Total Return	6-Month Total Return	1-Year Total Return	3-Year Total Return	5-Year Total Return	ASSETS: NAV	Total Assets (MIL)	NEW INVESTORS: Telephone	Open to New Investors
PACE Small/Medium Co Growth Equity Investments Class C	PUMCX	B-	B-	B-	Up	5.10	7.28	22.06	20.46	70.79	13	516.3	212-882-5586	Y
PACE Small/Medium Co Growth Equity Investments Class P	PCSGX	B	B	B	Up	5.34	7.78	23.18	23.71	78.46	18.13	516.3	212-882-5586	Y
PACE Small/Medium Co Growth Equity Investments Class Y	PUMYX	B	B	B	Up	5.37	7.77	23.16	23.60	78.26	18.41	516.3	212-882-5586	Y
PACE Small/Medium Co Value Equity Investments Class A	PEVAX	B	B	B	Up	4.38	8.14	9.19	28.61	88.59	20.1	544.4	212-882-5586	Y
PACE Small/Medium Co Value Equity Investments Class C	PEVCX	B	B-	B	Up	4.20	7.70	8.32	25.65	81.56	16.48	544.4	212-882-5586	Y
PACE Small/Medium Co Value Equity Investments Class P	PCSVX	B	B	B	Up	4.45	8.21	9.33	29.16	89.88	20.7	544.4	212-882-5586	Y
PACE Small/Medium Co Value Equity Investments Class Y	PVEYX	B	B	B	Up	4.49	8.25	9.31	29.12	89.81	20.96	544.4	212-882-5586	Y
Paradigm Micro-Cap Fund	PVIVX	B	B+	B-	Up	-0.48	0.55	15.79	32.00	94.97	32.4	51.1	800-239-0732	Y
Paradigm Opportunity Fund	PFOPX	B	B	B	Up	4.78	13.58	14.48	24.05	74.73	40.48	7.9	800-239-0732	Y
Paradigm Select Fund	PFSLX	B	B+	B	Up	5.58	9.63	16.11	31.87	87.77	37.44	25.3	800-239-0732	Y
Paradigm Value Fund	PVFAX	A-	A-	B+	Up	3.45	8.79	14.06	34.60	71.88	48.96	62.9	800-239-0732	Y
Pax Small Cap Fund Class A	PXSAX	B-	C+	B	Up	5.52	8.16	8.79	22.55	92.16	16.38	845.3	800-767-1729	Y
Pax Small Cap Fund Individual Investor Class	PXSCX	B-	C+	B	Up	5.51	8.14	8.77	22.50	92.16	16.41	845.3	800-767-1729	Y
Pax Small Cap Fund Institutional Class	PXSIX	B-	B-	B	Up	5.59	8.34	9.10	23.46	94.65	16.53	845.3	800-767-1729	Y
Pear Tree Polaris Small Cap Fund Institutional Class	QBNAX	B	B	B	Up	3.38	4.51	6.77	27.15	70.75	30.78	120.3	800-326-2151	Y
Pear Tree Polaris Small Cap Fund Ordinary Class	USBNX	B	B	B	Up	3.29	4.30	6.42	26.10	68.50	26.1	120.3	800-326-2151	Y
Perritt Low Priced Stock Fund Investor Class	PLOWX	B+	A-	B	Up	2.25	7.80	13.73	35.29	109.83	19.19	8.0	800-332-3133	Y
Perritt MicroCap Opportunities Fund Investor Class	PRCGX	B	B	B-	Up	0.67	6.41	5.33	24.80	86.39	30	199.8	800-332-3133	Y
Perritt Ultra MicroCap Fund	PREOX	B+	A-	B	Up	3.94	10.49	17.93	39.73	110.22	17.27	69.5	800-332-3133	Y
PF Small-Cap Value Fund Class P	US69447T8475	B+	A-	B	Up	3.86	9.01	8.83	37.02	99.27	11.49	119.6	800-722-2333	Y
PIMCO RAE Fundamental PLUS Small Fund Class A	PCFAX	B+	A-	B-	Up	3.89	10.32	12.51	33.22	101.81	11.79	97.8	866-746-2602	Y
PIMCO RAE Fundamental PLUS Small Fund Class C	PCFEX	B+	A-	B-	Up	3.77	9.88	11.70	30.43	94.57	11.6	97.8	866-746-2602	Y
PIMCO RAE Fundamental PLUS Small Fund Class D	PCFDX	B+	A-	B-	Up	3.97	10.29	12.49	33.32	101.99	11.82	97.8	866-746-2602	Y
PIMCO RAE Fundamental PLUS Small Fund Class P	PCCPX	B+	A	B-	Up	4.02	10.47	12.85	34.28	104.63	11.86	97.8	866-746-2602	Y
PIMCO RAE Fundamental PLUS Small Fund Institutional Class	PCFIX	B+	A	B-	Up	4.03	10.52	12.88	34.71	105.63	11.89	97.8	866-746-2602	Y
PIMCO RAE Fundamental US Small Fund Class A	PMJAX	B	B+	B	Up	3.76	9.39	8.80	31.96	97.66	11.56	116.6	866-746-2602	Y
PIMCO RAE Fundamental US Small Fund Class C	PMJCX	B	B	B-	Up	3.55	8.98	7.99	29.08	90.49	11.35	116.6	866-746-2602	Y
PIMCO RAE Fundamental US Small Fund Class P	PMJPX	B	A-	B	Up	3.83	9.55	9.06	33.13	100.61	11.58	116.6	866-746-2602	Y
PIMCO RAE Fundamental US Small Fund Institutional Class	PMJIX	B+	A-	B	Up	3.86	9.66	9.27	33.61	101.74	11.62	116.6	866-746-2602	Y
PIMCO StocksPLUS® Small Fund Administrative Class	PCKTX	B+	A	B-	Up	3.10	9.83	17.30	35.36	102.66	10.53	1,361	866-746-2602	Y
PIMCO StocksPLUS® Small Fund Class A	PCKAX	B+	A	B-	Up	3.13	9.85	17.21	34.85	101.29	10.32	1,361	866-746-2602	Y
PIMCO StocksPLUS® Small Fund Class C	PCKCX	B+	A-	B-	Up	2.98	9.45	16.42	31.82	93.80	9.54	1,361	866-746-2602	Y
PIMCO StocksPLUS® Small Fund Class D	PCKDX	B+	A	B-	Up	3.05	9.82	17.10	34.67	101.19	10.24	1,361	866-746-2602	Y
PIMCO StocksPLUS® Small Fund Class P	PCKPX	B+	A	B-	Up	3.17	10.00	17.58	35.92	104.34	10.46	1,361	866-746-2602	Y
PIMCO StocksPLUS® Small Fund Class R	PCKRX	B+	A-	B-	Up	3.02	9.59	16.94	33.72	98.55	10.25	1,361	866-746-2602	Y
PIMCO StocksPLUS® Small Fund Institutional Class	PSCSX	B+	A	B-	Up	3.16	10.07	17.62	36.35	105.10	10.54	1,361	866-746-2602	Y
PNC Multi Factor Small Cap Growth Fund Class A	PLWAX	B+	B+	B+	Up	2.46	7.93	14.76	31.80	110.18	23.75	158.6	800-622-3863	Y
PNC Multi Factor Small Cap Growth Fund Class C	PLWCX	B+	B+	B+	Up	2.26	7.58	13.97	29.15	102.97	22.9	158.6	800-622-3863	Y
PNC Multi Factor Small Cap Growth Fund Class I	PLTIX	B+	B+	B+	Up	2.52	8.10	15.09	32.95	112.92	24.25	158.6	800-622-3863	Y
PNC Multiple Factor Small Cap Core Fund Class A	PLOAX	B+	B+	B+	Up	3.05	9.15	12.19	28.78	113.87	26.25	416.9	800-622-3863	Y
PNC Multiple Factor Small Cap Core Fund Class C	PLOCX	B+	B+	B+	Up	2.84	8.77	11.41	27.23	109.26	26.3	416.9	800-622-3863	Y
PNC Multiple Factor Small Cap Core Fund Class I	PLOIX	B+	B+	B+	Up	3.13	9.31	12.52	29.92	116.91	26.45	416.9	800-622-3863	Y
PNC Multiple Factor Small Cap Value Fund Class A	PMRRX	B-	B	B-	Up	0.27	4.26	0.96	20.18	92.15	21.62	29.6	800-622-3863	Y
PNC Multiple Factor Small Cap Value Fund Class C	PSVCX	B-	B-	B-	Up	0.11	3.89	0.32	18.06	86.11	19.24	29.6	800-622-3863	Y
PNC Multiple Factor Small Cap Value Fund Class I	PMUIX	B	B	B-	Up	0.36	4.41	1.25	21.24	94.32	23.54	29.6	800-622-3863	Y
PNC Small Cap Fund Class A	PPCAX	B	B	B	Up	4.39	11.31	9.64	25.12	87.26	23.06	806.8	800-622-3863	Y
PNC Small Cap Fund Class C	PPCCX	B	B	B	Up	4.21	10.88	8.84	22.55	80.94	20.61	806.8	800-622-3863	Y
PNC Small Cap Fund Class I	PPCIX	B	B	B	Up	4.49	11.46	9.97	26.19	89.93	23.96	806.8	800-622-3863	Y
Praxis Small Cap Index Fund Class A	MMSCX	B-	C+	B	Up	3.62	9.00	10.69	13.05	50.80	8.63	54.0		Y
Praxis Small Cap Index Fund Class I	MMSIX	B-	C+	B	Up	2.84	8.31	10.29	14.12	54.07	9.36	54.0		Y
Principal SmallCap Fund Class A	PLLAX	B	B+	B	Up	4.89	9.86	12.40	29.61	105.67	22.82	640.4	800-222-5852	Y
Principal SmallCap Fund Class C	PSMCX	B	B	B	Up	4.69	9.46	11.56	26.47	97.35	20.66	640.4	800-222-5852	Y

Category: US Equity Small Cap (con't)

Fund Name	Ticker Symbol	Overall Rating	Reward Rating	Risk Rating	Recent Up/ Downgrade	3-Month Total Return	6-Month Total Return	1-Year Total Return	3-Year Total Return	5-Year Total Return	NAV	Total Assets (MIL)	Telephone	Open to New Investors
		RATINGS				TOTAL RETURNS & PERFORMANCE					ASSETS		NEW INVESTORS	
Principal SmallCap Fund Class J	PSBJX	B+	B+	B	Up	4.95	9.99	12.64	30.31	107.30	21.85	640.4	800-222-5852	Y
Principal SmallCap Fund Class R-6	PSMLX	B+	B+	B	Up	5.03	10.19	12.97	30.76	108.47	24.41	640.4	800-222-5852	Y
Principal SmallCap Fund Institutional Class	PSLIX	B+	B+	B	Up	5.04	10.15	12.93	31.29	110.33	24.43	640.4	800-222-5852	Y
Principal SmallCap Fund R-1 Class	PSABX	B	B	B	Up	4.75	9.64	11.97	28.04	101.58	21.75	640.4	800-222-5852	Y
Principal SmallCap Fund R-2 Class	PSBNX	B	B	B	Up	4.84	9.74	12.16	28.55	102.94	21.98	640.4	800-222-5852	Y
Principal SmallCap Fund R-3 Class	PSBMX	B	B+	B	Up	4.85	9.82	12.31	29.24	104.79	22.8	640.4	800-222-5852	Y
Principal SmallCap Fund R-4 Class	PSBSX	B	B+	B	Up	4.89	9.92	12.53	29.98	106.76	23.68	640.4	800-222-5852	Y
Principal SmallCap Fund R-5 Class	PSBPX	B+	B+	B	Up	4.95	10.02	12.67	30.44	107.96	24.2	640.4	800-222-5852	Y
Principal SmallCap Growth Fund I Class J	PSIJX	B	A-	C+	Up	5.38	12.33	25.91	37.58	102.75	10.41	1,634	800-222-5852	Y
Principal SmallCap Growth Fund I Class R-6	PCSMX	B	A-	C+	Up	5.39	12.55	26.36	39.01	106.68	13.9	1,634	800-222-5852	Y
Principal SmallCap Growth Fund I Institutional Class	PGRTX	B	A-	C+	Up	5.38	12.54	26.31	39.07	106.91	13.92	1,634	800-222-5852	Y
Principal SmallCap Growth Fund I R-1 Class	PNASX	B	A-	C+	Up	5.16	12.06	25.29	35.57	98.22	11.47	1,634	800-222-5852	Y
Principal SmallCap Growth Fund I R-2 Class	PPNNX	B	A-	C+	Up	5.21	12.11	25.37	36.08	99.57	11.14	1,634	800-222-5852	Y
Principal SmallCap Growth Fund I R-3 Class	PPNMX	B	A-	C+	Up	5.27	12.17	25.65	36.78	101.41	11.82	1,634	800-222-5852	Y
Principal SmallCap Growth Fund I R-4 Class	PPNSX	B	A-	C+	Up	5.39	12.38	25.93	37.68	103.39	12.54	1,634	800-222-5852	Y
Principal SmallCap Growth Fund I R-5 Class	PPNPX	B	A-	C+	Up	5.32	12.38	26.00	38.06	104.60	13.09	1,634	800-222-5852	Y
Principal SmallCap S&P 600 Index Fund Class J	PSSJX	B+	A-	B	Up	3.85	9.92	12.76	37.38	108.22	25.71	1,360	800-222-5852	Y
Principal SmallCap S&P 600 Index Fund Class R-6	PSPIX	B+	A-	B	Up	3.92	10.06	13.03	37.86	109.70	27.07	1,360	800-222-5852	Y
Principal SmallCap S&P 600 Index Fund Institutional Class	PSSIX	A-	A-	B	Up	3.90	10.00	13.01	38.40	111.40	27.09	1,360	800-222-5852	Y
Principal SmallCap S&P 600 Index Fund R-1 Class	PSAPX	B+	A-	B	Up	3.69	9.59	12.11	35.04	102.77	26.72	1,360	800-222-5852	Y
Principal SmallCap S&P 600 Index Fund R-2 Class	PSSNX	B+	A-	B	Up	3.69	9.60	12.19	35.53	104.11	27.43	1,360	800-222-5852	Y
Principal SmallCap S&P 600 Index Fund R-3 Class	PSSMX	B+	A-	B	Up	3.76	9.74	12.44	36.28	105.98	27.64	1,360	800-222-5852	Y
Principal SmallCap S&P 600 Index Fund R-4 Class	PSSSX	B+	A-	B	Up	3.79	9.83	12.64	37.06	107.92	27.89	1,360	800-222-5852	Y
Principal SmallCap S&P 600 Index Fund R-5 Class	PSSPX	B+	A-	B	Up	3.85	9.90	12.78	37.55	109.22	28.03	1,360	800-222-5852	Y
Principal SmallCap Value Fund II Class A	PSVAX	B	B	B	Up	2.82	7.87	6.38	25.72	90.01	13.06	1,257	800-222-5852	Y
Principal SmallCap Value Fund II Class J	PSMJX	B	B	B	Up	2.83	7.87	6.44	25.84	89.32	12.86	1,257	800-222-5852	Y
Principal SmallCap Value Fund II Class R-6	PSMVX	B	B	B	Up	3.01	8.18	6.94	27.54	93.99	13.17	1,257	800-222-5852	Y
Principal SmallCap Value Fund II Institutional Class	PPVIX	B	B	B	Up	2.98	8.15	6.91	27.49	93.89	13.18	1,257	800-222-5852	Y
Principal SmallCap Value Fund II R-1 Class	PCPTX	B	B	B	Up	2.73	7.66	5.97	24.25	85.63	12.02	1,257	800-222-5852	Y
Principal SmallCap Value Fund II R-2 Class	PKARX	B	B	B	Up	2.77	7.71	6.13	24.72	86.79	12.21	1,257	800-222-5852	Y
Principal SmallCap Value Fund II R-3 Class	PJARX	B	B	B	Up	2.83	7.86	6.32	25.50	88.58	12.68	1,257	800-222-5852	Y
Principal SmallCap Value Fund II R-4 Class	PSTWX	B	B	B	Up	2.87	7.92	6.49	26.09	90.27	12.85	1,257	800-222-5852	Y
Principal SmallCap Value Fund II R-5 Class	PLARX	B	B	B	Up	2.88	8.04	6.62	26.58	91.65	12.98	1,257	800-222-5852	Y
Principal Small-MidCap Dividend Income Fund Class A	PMDAX	B	B	B		3.58	7.68	12.94	39.77	98.92	17.11	3,378	800-222-5852	
Principal Small-MidCap Dividend Income Fund Class C	PMDDX	B	B	B		3.40	7.35	12.14	36.60	91.19	16.98	3,378	800-222-5852	
Principal Small-MidCap Dividend Income Fund Inst Cls	PMDIX	B	B	B		3.64	7.89	13.29	41.10	102.35	17.18	3,378	800-222-5852	
Principal Small-MidCap Dividend Income Fund R-6	PMDHX	B	B	B		3.66	7.87	13.35	41.16	102.44	17.18	3,378	800-222-5852	Y
Private Capital Management Value Fund Class A	VFPAX	B-	C+	B-	Up	2.44	6.78	15.19	13.74	80.84	17.17	77.6	239-254-2500	Y
Private Capital Management Value Fund Class I	VFPIX	B-	B-	B-	Up	2.53	6.94	15.49	14.57	83.16	17.4	77.6	239-254-2500	Y
ProFunds Small Cap Fund Investor Class	SLPIX	B	B	B	Up	2.77	7.91	12.05	24.77	80.30	83.95	41.3	614-470-8626	Y
ProFunds Small Cap Fund Service Class	SLPSX	B	B	B	Up	2.56	7.44	11.01	21.20	71.69	71.27	41.3	614-470-8626	Y
ProFunds Small Cap Growth Fund Investor Class	SGPIX	B+	A-	B+	Up	3.46	8.79	12.73	35.31	98.53	86.94	20.6	614-470-8626	Y
ProFunds Small Cap Growth Fund Service Class	SGPSX	B+	B+	B	Up	3.20	8.26	11.60	31.29	88.77	72.69	20.6	614-470-8626	Y
ProFunds Small Cap Value Fund Investor Class	SVPIX	B	B+	B-	Up	3.59	9.56	9.52	27.50	88.64	90.53	14.8	614-470-8626	Y
ProFunds Small Cap Value Fund Services Class	SVPSX	B	B	B-	Up	3.33	9.03	8.45	23.79	79.38	77.46	14.8	614-470-8626	Y
Prudential Jennison Small Company Fund Class A	PGOAX	B	B	B	Up	4.86	9.26	19.45	29.26	91.37	24.94	3,704	800-225-1852	Y
Prudential Jennison Small Company Fund Class B	CHNDX	B	B	B	Up	4.55	8.77	18.49	26.32	84.66	13.55	3,704	800-225-1852	
Prudential Jennison Small Company Fund Class C	PSCCX	B	B	B	Up	4.61	8.77	18.51	26.41	84.34	13.79	3,704	800-225-1852	Y
Prudential Jennison Small Company Fund Class Q	PJSQX	B	B	B	Up	4.97	9.51	20.03	31.11	95.73	26.41	3,704	800-225-1852	Y
Prudential Jennison Small Company Fund Class R	JSCRX	B	B	B	Up	4.81	9.15	19.26	28.57	89.48	24.3	3,704	800-225-1852	Y
Prudential Jennison Small Company Fund Class R2	PSCHX	B	B	B		4.75	8.98	18.72	26.57	85.02	26.42	3,704	800-225-1852	Y
Prudential Jennison Small Company Fund Class R4	PSCJX	B	B	B		4.78	9.00	18.75	26.60	85.06	26.42	3,704	800-225-1852	Y

Category: US Equity Small Cap (con't)

Fund Name	Ticker Symbol	RATINGS: Overall Rating	Reward Rating	Risk Rating	Recent Up/ Downgrade	TOTAL RETURNS & PERFORMANCE: 3-Month Total Return	6-Month Total Return	1-Year Total Return	3-Year Total Return	5-Year Total Return	ASSETS: NAV	Total Assets (MIL)	NEW INVESTORS: Telephone	Open to New Investors
Prudential Jennison Small Company Fund Class Z	PSCZX	B	B	B	Up	4.84	9.30	19.67	30.26	93.89	26.83	3,704	800-225-1852	Y
Prudential QMA Small-Cap Value Fund Class A	TSVAX	B	A-	B-	Up	3.42	7.99	6.00	30.15	91.10	20.25	1,634	800-225-1852	Y
Prudential QMA Small-Cap Value Fund Class C	TRACX	B	B+	B-	Up	3.21	7.58	5.20	27.20	84.11	20.34	1,634	800-225-1852	Y
Prudential QMA Small-Cap Value Fund Class Q	TSVQX	B+	A-	B-	Up	3.55	8.28	6.42	31.54	94.25	20.23	1,634	800-225-1852	Y
Prudential QMA Small-Cap Value Fund Class Retirement	TSVRX	B	B+	B-	Up	3.37	7.91	5.74	29.19	88.96	20	1,634	800-225-1852	Y
Prudential QMA Small-Cap Value Fund Class Z	TASVX	B	A-	B-	Up	3.48	8.16	6.31	31.18	93.69	20.21	1,634	800-225-1852	Y
Putnam Capital Opportunities Fund Class A	PCOAX	B-	C+	B	Up	0.91	4.25	8.04	14.50	68.02	13.49	312.4	617-292-1000	Y
Putnam Capital Opportunities Fund Class B	POPBX	B-	C+	B	Up	0.78	3.86	7.22	12.06	61.79	11.08	312.4	617-292-1000	Y
Putnam Capital Opportunities Fund Class C	PCOCX	B-	C+	B	Up	0.69	3.79	7.18	11.97	61.68	11.28	312.4	617-292-1000	Y
Putnam Capital Opportunities Fund Class M	POPMX	B-	C+	B	Up	0.81	3.98	7.53	12.82	63.89	11.98	312.4	617-292-1000	Y
Putnam Capital Opportunities Fund Class R	PCORX	B-	C+	B	Up	0.88	4.12	7.79	13.74	65.87	13.03	312.4	617-292-1000	Y
Putnam Capital Opportunities Fund Class R5	POPDX	B-	C+	B	Up	1.02	4.42	7.30	14.51	69.16	13.88	312.4	617-292-1000	Y
Putnam Capital Opportunities Fund Class R6	PCOEX	B-	C+	B	Up	1.00	4.43	8.44	15.96	71.78	14.07	312.4	617-292-1000	Y
Putnam Capital Opportunities Fund Class Y	PYCOX	B-	C+	B	Up	1.01	4.32	8.27	15.39	70.07	14.01	312.4	617-292-1000	Y
Putnam Small Cap Growth Fund Class A	PNSAX	B	B+	B	Up	6.48	11.09	20.19	26.22	94.94	37.74	164.3	617-292-1000	Y
Putnam Small Cap Growth Fund Class B	PNSBX	B	B	B-	Up	6.26	10.67	19.29	23.39	87.68	33.39	164.3	617-292-1000	Y
Putnam Small Cap Growth Fund Class C	PNSCX	B	B	B-	Up	6.29	10.67	19.29	23.40	87.75	33.27	164.3	617-292-1000	Y
Putnam Small Cap Growth Fund Class M	PSGMX	B	B	B-	Up	6.32	10.82	19.58	24.33	90.06	34.8	164.3	617-292-1000	Y
Putnam Small Cap Growth Fund Class R	PSGRX	B	B	B	Up	6.41	10.98	19.88	25.28	92.55	36.47	164.3	617-292-1000	Y
Putnam Small Cap Growth Fund Class R6	PLKGX	B	B+	B	Up	6.59	11.36	20.71	27.58	97.04	39.1	164.3	617-292-1000	Y
Putnam Small Cap Growth Fund Class Y	PSYGX	B	B+	B	Up	6.55	11.26	20.51	27.19	97.37	39.01	164.3	617-292-1000	Y
Putnam Small Cap Value Fund Class A	PSLAX	B	B	B	Up	3.07	5.73	7.90	30.52	90.84	13.54	397.9	617-292-1000	Y
Putnam Small Cap Value Fund Class B	PSLBX	B	B	B	Up	2.84	5.30	7.08	27.66	83.81	10.59	397.9	617-292-1000	Y
Putnam Small Cap Value Fund Class C	PSLCX	B	B	B	Up	2.82	5.22	7.01	27.59	83.74	10.53	397.9	617-292-1000	Y
Putnam Small Cap Value Fund Class M	PSLMX	B	B	B	Up	2.89	5.43	7.28	28.49	85.93	11.86	397.9	617-292-1000	Y
Putnam Small Cap Value Fund Class R	PSCRX	B	B	B	Up	2.91	5.49	7.51	29.42	88.19	13.22	397.9	617-292-1000	Y
Putnam Small Cap Value Fund Class R5	PSLRX	B	B	B	Up	3.14	5.92	8.19	31.81	93.49	14.28	397.9	617-292-1000	Y
Putnam Small Cap Value Fund Class R6	PSCMX	B	B	B	Up	3.13	5.91	8.30	32.16	94.11	14.27	397.9	617-292-1000	Y
Putnam Small Cap Value Fund Class Y	PYSVX	B	B	B	Up	3.04	5.77	8.10	31.47	93.12	14.22	397.9	617-292-1000	Y
QS U.S. Small Capitalization Equity Fund Class A	LMBAX	B	B	B	Up	3.49	7.28	8.46	22.41	88.89	13.55	229.4	877-721-1926	Y
QS U.S. Small Capitalization Equity Fund Class A2	LUSAX	B	B	B	Up	3.50	7.25	8.28	21.63	87.39	13.39	229.4	877-721-1926	Y
QS U.S. Small Capitalization Equity Fund Class C	LMBCX	B	B	B	Up	3.27	6.91	7.66	19.63	81.97	12.66	229.4	877-721-1926	Y
QS U.S. Small Capitalization Equity Fund Class FI	LGSCX	B	B	B	Up	3.55	7.34	8.49	22.35	88.93	12.96	229.4	877-721-1926	Y
QS U.S. Small Capitalization Equity Fund Class I	LMSIX	B	B	B	Up	3.59	7.53	8.77	23.59	92.52	13.84	229.4	877-721-1926	Y
QS U.S. Small Capitalization Equity Fund Class IS	LMBMX	B	B	B	Up	3.65	7.67	9.01	24.09	93.28	13.54	229.4	877-721-1926	Y
Quaker Small-Cap Value Fund Class A	QUSVX	B	B-	B	Up	2.80	8.26	9.30	21.28	81.44	22.44	30.0	800-220-8888	Y
Quaker Small-Cap Value Fund Class C	QSVCX	B-	B-	B	Up	2.62	7.83	8.50	18.55	74.76	17.13	30.0	800-220-8888	Y
Quaker Small-Cap Value Fund Class Institutional	QSVIX	B	B	B	Up	2.87	8.40	9.56	22.19	83.70	23.95	30.0	800-220-8888	Y
Queens Road Small Cap Value Fund	QRSVX	B	C+	B+	Up	3.75	5.29	5.85	21.25	70.29	27.15	143.4	888-353-0261	Y
Ranger Small Cap Fund Institutional Class	RFISX	B+	B+	B+	Up	4.42	7.47	15.31	41.29	103.42	17.71	25.1		Y
RBC Enterprise Fund Class A	TETAX	B	B	C+	Up	0.80	10.28	14.29	23.66	73.20	22.07	91.0	800-422-2766	Y
RBC Enterprise Fund Class I	TETIX	B	B	C+	Up	0.88	10.44	14.60	24.60	75.39	22.98	91.0	800-422-2766	Y
RBC Microcap Value Fund Class A	TMVAX	B	B+	B	Up	0.68	6.26	5.22	24.74	93.04	30.03	150.1	800-422-2766	Y
RBC Microcap Value Fund Class I	RMVIX	B	B+	B	Up	0.73	6.37	5.46	25.65	95.55	30.02	150.1	800-422-2766	Y
RBC Small Cap Core Fund Class A	TEEAX	B	B+	B-	Up	5.04	11.80	10.71	28.41	89.80	39.67	295.0	800-422-2766	Y
RBC Small Cap Core Fund Class I	RCSIX	B	A-	B-	Up	5.09	11.93	10.97	29.38	92.17	41.33	295.0	800-422-2766	Y
RBC Small Cap Core Fund Class R6	RBRCX	B	A-	B-	Up	5.11	11.97	11.01	29.42	92.22	41.39	295.0	800-422-2766	Y
RBC Small Cap Value Fund Class I	RSVIX	B-	C+	B-	Up	3.70	9.32	10.80	41.90		13.56	82.6	800-422-2766	Y
RBC Small Cap Value Fund Class R6	RRSVX	B-	C+	B-	Up	3.69	9.44	10.91	42.12		13.64	82.6	800-422-2766	Y
Rice Hall James Micro Cap Portfolio Institutional Class	RHJSX	B+	A-	B	Up	-1.48	6.32	12.86	31.91	95.17	33.09	51.6	619-239-9005	Y
Rice Hall James Small Cap Portfolio Institutional Class	RHJMX	B-	C+	B	Up	4.99	5.18	12.05	16.27	68.60	10.93	47.1	619-239-9005	Y
River Oak Discovery Fund	RIVSX	B	B	B	Up	4.32	8.49	11.30	21.71	79.78	16.72	14.7	888-462-5386	Y

Category: US Equity Small Cap (con't)

Fund Name	Ticker Symbol	RATINGS: Overall Rating	Reward Rating	Risk Rating	Recent Up/ Downgrade	TOTAL RETURNS & PERFORMANCE: 3-Month Total Return	6-Month Total Return	1-Year Total Return	3-Year Total Return	5-Year Total Return	ASSETS: NAV	Total Assets (ML)	NEW INVESTORS: Telephone	Open to New Investors
Royce Micro Cap Trust	RMT	B-	B	C+	Up	2.74	10.71	16.70	21.34	81.13	10.48	410.2	212-486-1445	
Royce Micro-Cap Opportunity Fund Investment Class	ROSFX	B	A-	C+	Up	4.60	13.85	24.98	29.58	83.61	19.77	48.1	800-221-4268	Y
Royce Micro-Cap Opportunity Fund Service Class	ROSSX	B	A-	C+	Up	4.57	13.70	24.73	28.75	81.58	9.94	48.1	800-221-4268	Y
Royce Opportunity Fund Class K	ROFKX	B+	A	C+	Up	3.34	12.29	21.08	34.02	94.85	11.13	1,646	800-221-4268	Y
Royce Opportunity Fund Consultant Class	ROFCX	B	A	C+	Up	3.24	12.02	20.49	31.82	88.81	11.19	1,646	800-221-4268	Y
Royce Opportunity Fund Institutional Class	ROFIX	B+	A	C+	Up	3.50	12.71	22.02	36.61	100.68	13.84	1,646	800-221-4268	Y
Royce Opportunity Fund Investment Class	RYPNX	B+	A	C+	Up	3.51	12.67	21.87	36.19	99.53	13.58	1,646	800-221-4268	Y
Royce Opportunity Fund Retirement Class	ROFRX	B+	A	C+	Up	3.34	12.21	21.06	33.61	93.15	12.25	1,646	800-221-4268	Y
Royce Opportunity Fund Service Class	RYOFX	B+	A	C+	Up	3.39	12.47	21.46	34.92	96.46	12.66	1,646	800-221-4268	Y
Royce Pennsylvania Mutual Fund Class K	RPMKX	B	B	C+	Up	3.78	10.33	15.06	26.06	72.42	8.66	2,239	800-221-4268	Y
Royce Pennsylvania Mutual Fund Consultant Class	RYPCX	B-	B	C+	Up	3.85	10.46	15.06	25.43	69.59	8.46	2,239	800-221-4268	Y
Royce Pennsylvania Mutual Fund Institutional Class	RPMIX	B	B+	C+	Up	4.25	11.10	16.43	29.74	79.51	10.55	2,239	800-221-4268	Y
Royce Pennsylvania Mutual Fund Investment Class	PENNX	B	B	C+	Up	4.06	10.90	16.24	29.31	78.44	10.52	2,239	800-221-4268	Y
Royce Pennsylvania Mutual Fund Retirement Class	RPMRX	B	B	C+	Up	3.81	10.49	15.25	26.35	72.26	9.94	2,239	800-221-4268	Y
Royce Pennsylvania Mutual Fund Service Class	RYPFX	B	B	C+	Up	4.00	10.76	15.88	28.12	75.70	10.56	2,239	800-221-4268	Y
Royce Premier Fund Class W	RPRWX	B	B+	C+	Up	6.28	14.01	23.83	35.96	76.80	16.69	2,443	800-221-4268	
Royce Premier Fund Consultant Class	RPRCX	B	B	C+	Up	6.05	13.30	22.48	31.60	67.68	13.21	2,443	800-221-4268	
Royce Premier Fund Institutional Class	RPFIX	B	B+	C+	Up	6.27	13.91	23.84	36.16	77.46	16.82	2,443	800-221-4268	
Royce Premier Fund Investment Class	RYPRX	B	B+	C+	Up	6.23	13.86	23.77	35.80	76.56	16.6	2,443	800-221-4268	
Royce Premier Fund Retirement Class	RPRRX	B	B	C+	Up	6.02	13.39	22.87	33.02	70.81	15.39	2,443	800-221-4268	
Royce Premier Fund Service Class	RPFFX	B	B+	C+	Up	6.13	13.69	23.31	34.50	73.96	16.15	2,443	800-221-4268	
Royce Smaller-Companies Growth Fund Class R	RVPRX	B	B	B	Up	1.45	5.71	17.44	24.79	74.34	9.95	384.8	800-221-4268	Y
Royce Smaller-Companies Growth Fund Consultant Class	RVPCX	B	B	B	Up	1.25	5.52	16.92	23.26	70.65	9.28	384.8	800-221-4268	Y
Royce Smaller-Companies Growth Fund Institutional Class	RVPIX	B	B	B	Up	1.57	6.07	18.22	27.32	80.78	11.06	384.8	800-221-4268	Y
Royce Smaller-Companies Growth Fund Investment Class	RVPHX	B	B	B	Up	1.55	6.10	18.20	27.21	79.46	10.93	384.8	800-221-4268	Y
Royce Smaller-Companies Growth Fund Service Class	RYVPX	B	B	B	Up	1.48	5.88	17.80	26.14	77.62	10.69	384.8	800-221-4268	Y
Royce Special Equity Fund Consultant Class	RSQCX	B-	B-	B-		4.33	7.73	6.77	20.48	58.32	19.86	1,581	800-221-4268	
Royce Special Equity Fund Institutional Class	RSEIX	B	B	B-	Up	4.60	8.30	7.96	24.59	67.44	21.61	1,581	800-221-4268	
Royce Special Equity Fund Investment Class	RYSEX	B	B	B-	Up	4.59	8.26	7.86	24.23	66.61	21.79	1,581	800-221-4268	
Royce Special Equity Fund Service Class	RSEFX	B-	B	B-	Down	4.57	8.20	7.66	23.44	64.66	21.76	1,581	800-221-4268	
Royce Total Return Fund Class K	RTRKX	B	B	B	Up	4.35	10.43	13.29	30.28	78.47	9.02	2,534	800-221-4268	Y
Royce Total Return Fund Class W	RTRWX	B	B	B	Up	4.41	10.63	13.59	31.59	81.50	13.56	2,534	800-221-4268	Y
Royce Total Return Fund Consultant Class	RYTCX	B	B	B	Up	4.16	10.10	12.52	27.79	72.86	13.95	2,534	800-221-4268	Y
Royce Total Return Fund Institutional Class	RTRIX	B	B	B	Up	4.47	10.68	13.79	32.16	82.77	13.4	2,534	800-221-4268	Y
Royce Total Return Fund Investment Class	RYTRX	B	B	B	Up	4.40	10.58	13.65	31.67	81.67	13.58	2,534	800-221-4268	Y
Royce Total Return Fund Retirement Class	RTRRX	B	B	B	Up	4.25	10.30	12.96	29.24	76.19	13.99	2,534	800-221-4268	Y
Royce Total Return Fund Service Class	RYTFX	B	B	B	Up	4.32	10.43	13.23	30.54	79.07	13.88	2,534	800-221-4268	Y
Royce Value Trust	RVT	B+	A-	B-	Up	3.70	10.94	18.46	33.79	80.92	17.5	1,492	212-486-1445	Y
Russell Inv Tax-Managed U.S. Mid & Small Cap Fund Cls A	RTSAX	B	B-	B	Up	4.89	9.18	14.39	23.13	83.79	25.5	571.6	800-426-7969	Y
Russell Inv Tax-Managed U.S. Mid & Small Cap Fund Cls C	RTSCX	B-	B-	B	Up	4.74	8.83	13.60	20.52	77.24	21.87	571.6	800-426-7969	Y
Russell Inv Tax-Managed U.S. Mid & Small Cap Fund Cls E	RTSEX	B	B-	B	Up	4.88	9.16	14.35	23.19	83.99	25.55	571.6	800-426-7969	Y
Russell Inv Tax-Managed U.S. Mid & Small Cap Fund Cls M	RTOUX	B	B	B	Up	4.99	9.36	14.79	24.27	86.56	26.67	571.6	800-426-7969	Y
Russell Inv Tax-Managed U.S. Mid & Small Cap Fund Cls S	RTSSX	B	B	B	Up	4.96	9.32	14.71	24.18	86.42	26.65	571.6	800-426-7969	Y
Russell Investments U.S. Small Cap Equity Fund Class A	RLACX	B	B+	B	Up	4.05	9.42	14.00	28.57	96.49	31.55	2,045	800-426-7969	Y
Russell Investments U.S. Small Cap Equity Fund Class C	RLECX	B	B+	B	Up	3.87	9.01	13.17	25.68	89.26	29.64	2,045	800-426-7969	Y
Russell Investments U.S. Small Cap Equity Fund Class E	REBEX	B	B+	B	Up	4.06	9.40	13.99	28.57	96.47	31.74	2,045	800-426-7969	Y
Russell Investments U.S. Small Cap Equity Fund Class M	RUNTX	B	B+	B	Up	4.16	9.64	14.34	28.96	97.07	31.85	2,045	800-426-7969	Y
Russell Investments U.S. Small Cap Equity Fund Class R6	RSCRX	B	B+	B	Up	4.18	9.63	14.46	29.55	97.97	31.87	2,045	800-426-7969	Y
Russell Investments U.S. Small Cap Equity Fund Class S	RLESX	B	B+	B	Up	4.14	9.56	14.32	29.57	99.05	31.87	2,045	800-426-7969	Y
Russell Investments U.S. Small Cap Equity Fund Class Y	REBYX	B+	A-	B	Up	4.20	9.68	14.52	30.32	100.92	31.88	2,045	800-426-7969	Y
Rydex Russell 2000 Fund Class A	RYRRX	B	B	B	Up	2.89	8.34	12.91	25.27	81.39	43.89	49.9	800-820-0888	Y
Rydex Russell 2000 Fund Class C	RYROX	B	B	B	Up	2.71	7.93	12.06	22.53	74.53	39.53	49.9	800-820-0888	Y

Category: US Equity Small Cap (con't)

Fund Name	Ticker Symbol	RATINGS: Overall Rating	Reward Rating	Risk Rating	Recent Up/ Downgrade	TOTAL RETURNS & PERFORMANCE: 3-Month Total Return	6-Month Total Return	1-Year Total Return	3-Year Total Return	5-Year Total Return	ASSETS: NAV	Total Assets (MIL)	NEW INVESTORS: Telephone	Open to New Investors
Rydex Russell 2000 Fund Class H	RYRHX	B	B	B	Up	2.89	8.33	12.89	25.24	81.06	43.78	49.9	800-820-0888	Y
Rydex S&P MidCap 400 Pure Value Fund Class A	RYMVX	B	B	B-	Up	7.88	10.51	13.14	26.09	87.50	56.49	34.1	800-820-0888	Y
Rydex S&P MidCap 400 Pure Value Fund Class C	RYMMX	B-	B	C+	Up	7.68	10.11	12.31	23.31	80.58	50.26	34.1	800-820-0888	Y
Rydex S&P MidCap 400 Pure Value Fund Class H	RYAVX	B	B	B-	Up	7.87	10.50	13.11	26.10	87.39	56.42	34.1	800-820-0888	Y
Rydex S&P SmallCap 600 Pure Growth Fund Class A	RYSGX	B+	A-	B	Up	3.00	9.77	16.15	35.99	97.55	71.11	18.7	800-820-0888	Y
Rydex S&P SmallCap 600 Pure Growth Fund Class C	RYWCX	B+	A-	B	Up	2.79	9.35	15.26	32.94	90.23	63.93	18.7	800-820-0888	Y
Rydex S&P SmallCap 600 Pure Growth Fund Class H	RYWAX	B+	A-	B	Up	2.98	9.74	16.14	35.98	97.44	71.09	18.7	800-820-0888	Y
SA U.S. Small Company Fund Investor Class	SAUMX	B	B+	B	Up	3.64	9.40	11.34	29.17	94.76	26.12	430.9		Y
SA U.S. Small Company Fund Select Class	SASLX	B	B+	B	Up	3.72	9.52	11.47	29.31	94.97	26.13	430.9		Y
Schneider Small Cap Value Fund	SCMVX	B	A	C	Up	4.56	11.18	12.25	38.35	64.04	14.98	46.8	888-520-3277	Y
Schwab Fundamental US Small Company Index Fund	SFSNX	B	B+	B	Up	5.03	9.87	12.75	31.12	101.77	14.93	1,785	877-824-5615	Y
Schwab Small Cap Index Fund®	SWSSX	B+	A-	B	Up	3.35	9.20	14.68	32.08	97.76	30.64	3,656	877-824-5615	Y
Schwab Small-Cap Equity Fund™	SWSCX	B	B+	B	Up	3.28	8.74	10.03	30.22	104.87	21.02	656.9	877-824-5615	Y
Segall Bryant & Hamill Small Cap Value Fund	SBHVX	B	B	B	Up	4.51	9.66	10.94	26.39		12.5	83.6	312-474-1222	Y
SEI Institutional Investments Trust Small Cap Fund Class A	SLPAX	B	B	B	Up	2.25	7.10	9.44	23.90	85.68	17.74	499.3	800-342-5734	Y
SEI Inst Investments Trust Small Cap II Fund Cls A	SECAX	B	B	B	Up	3.59	8.52	12.09	25.14	88.52	12.31	447.8	800-342-5734	Y
SEI Inst Investments Trust Small/Mid Cap Equity Fund Cls A	SSMAX	B	B	B	Up	4.03	8.42	13.65	25.95	93.48	13.07	1,783	800-342-5734	Y
SEI Institutional Managed Trust Small Cap Fund Class F	SLLAX	B-	C+	B	Up	3.66	7.55	9.70	18.01	77.06	12.81	654.4	800-342-5734	Y
SEI Institutional Managed Trust Small Cap Fund Class Y	SMYFX	B-	B-	B	Up	3.67	7.63	9.86	18.81	78.25	12.87	654.4	800-342-5734	Y
SEI Inst Managed Trust Small Cap Growth Fund Cls F	SSCGX	B	B	B	Up	3.00	8.72	18.37	25.67	95.77	35.33	344.9	800-342-5734	Y
SEI Inst Managed Trust Small Cap Growth Fund Cls I	SPWIX	B	B	B	Up	2.94	8.58	18.06	24.71	93.32	33.96	344.9	800-342-5734	Y
SEI Inst Managed Trust Small Cap Growth Fund Cls Y	SMAYX	B	B	B	Up	3.07	8.86	18.64	26.39	96.88	35.53	344.9	800-342-5734	Y
SEI Institutional Managed Trust Small Cap Value Fund Cls F	SESVX	B	B	B	Up	3.42	7.45	7.61	22.87	74.97	24.81	388.5	800-342-5734	Y
SEI Institutional Managed Trust Small Cap Value Fund Cls I	SMVIX	B	B-	B	Up	3.35	7.32	7.33	22.04	73.04	24.59	388.5	800-342-5734	Y
SEI Institutional Managed Trust Small Cap Value Fund Cls Y	SPVYX	B	B	B	Up	3.46	7.55	7.87	23.54	75.92	24.81	388.5	800-342-5734	Y
SEI Inst Managed Trust Tax-Managed Small/Mid Cap Cls F	STMSX	B	B	B	Up	5.58	10.59	15.88	25.91	89.58	22.9	911.6	800-342-5734	Y
SEI Inst Managed Trust Tax-Managed Small/Mid Cap Cls Y	STMPX	B	B	B	Up	5.69	10.75	16.17	26.77	90.88	22.92	911.6	800-342-5734	Y
Shelton Capital Management S&P Smallcap Index Fund Class K	SMLKX	B+	A-	B	Up	3.25	8.89	11.77	36.03	104.09	21.98	65.6	800-955-9988	Y
Shelton Capital Mgmt S&P Smallcap Index Fund Direct Shares	SMCIX	A-	A-	B	Up	3.38	9.18	12.33	38.11	109.35	22.52	65.6	800-955-9988	Y
Sit Small Cap Dividend Growth Fund Class I	SSCDX	B-	C+	B-	Up	4.71	9.22	13.69			12.44	18.5	800-332-5580	Y
Small Cap Value Fund	SCAPX	B	A	C	Up	8.66	20.31	26.26	36.75	90.35	49.04	21.7		Y
SSgA Dynamic Small Cap Fund Class A	SSSDX	B+	B+	B+	Up	1.84	7.31	8.75	28.75	97.14	48.53	31.3	617-664-7338	Y
SSgA Dynamic Small Cap Fund Class I	SSSJX	B+	B+	B+	Up	1.92	7.46	9.04	29.73	98.89	48.78	31.3	617-664-7338	Y
SSgA Dynamic Small Cap Fund Class K	SSSKX	B+	A-	B+	Up	1.93	7.47	9.07	30.31	99.90	48.87	31.3	617-664-7338	Y
SSgA Dynamic Small Cap Fund N Class	SVSCX	B+	B+	B+	Up	1.85	7.31	8.79	29.32	98.21	48.8	31.3	617-664-7338	
STAAR Smaller Company Stock Fund	SITSX	B-	C+	B-	Up	4.32	9.35	10.62	19.78	61.07		3.1		Y
State Farm Small Cap Index Fund Class A	SNRAX	B+	A-	B	Up	2.49	8.20	13.28	28.24	88.58	18.04	549.4		Y
State Farm Small Cap Index Fund Class B	SNRBX	B	B+	B	Up	3.27	8.93	13.99	27.47	85.27	17.53	549.4		Y
State Farm Small Cap Index Fund Class B Legacy	SMIBX	B	B+	B	Up	3.20	8.91	14.00	27.98	86.75	17.39	549.4		Y
State Farm Small Cap Index Fund Class Institutional	SMIIX	B+	A-	B	Up	3.22	8.91	14.18	29.83	91.88	18.19	549.4		Y
State Farm Small Cap Index Fund Class R1	RSIOX	B	B+	B	Up	3.22	8.93	13.99	28.20	87.26	17.99	549.4		Y
State Farm Small Cap Index Fund Class R2	RSITX	B+	B+	B	Up	3.21	8.90	14.01	28.73	88.78	18.04	549.4		Y
State Farm Small Cap Index Fund Class R3	RSIHX	B+	A-	B	Up	3.20	8.89	14.09	29.55	91.31	18.21	549.4		Y
State Farm Small Cap Index Fund Premier Shares	SMIAX	B+	A-	B	Up	3.27	9.00	14.24	29.37	90.22	17.86	549.4		Y
State Farm Small/Mid Cap Equity Fund Class A	SSNAX	B-	C+	B	Up	4.53	8.85	11.66	18.67	70.00	11.86	311.1		Y
State Farm Small/Mid Cap Equity Fund Class B	SSNBX	B-	C+	B	Up	4.55	8.89	11.45	16.94	65.60	10.78	311.1		Y
State Farm Small/Mid Cap Equity Fund Class B Legacy	SFSBX	B-	C+	B	Up	4.47	8.82	11.44	17.64	66.96	10.45	311.1		Y
State Farm Small/Mid Cap Equity Fund Class Institutional	SFEIX	B-	C+	B	Up	4.53	8.89	11.71	19.47	71.84	12.26	311.1		Y
State Farm Small/Mid Cap Equity Fund Class R1	RSEOX	B-	C+	B	Up	4.46	8.77	11.46	17.86	67.58	11.09	311.1		Y
State Farm Small/Mid Cap Equity Fund Class R2	RSETX	B-	C+	B	Up	4.48	8.75	11.54	18.30	68.83	11.48	311.1		Y
State Farm Small/Mid Cap Equity Fund Class R3	RSEHX	B-	C+	B	Up	4.48	8.81	11.56	19.17	71.18	12.09	311.1		Y
State Farm Small/Mid Cap Equity Fund Premier Shares	SFSAX	B-	C+	B	Up	4.51	8.83	11.70	18.85	70.21	11.56	311.1		Y

Category: US Equity Small Cap (con't)

Fund Name	Ticker Symbol	RATINGS: Overall Rating	RATINGS: Reward Rating	RATINGS: Risk Rating	RATINGS: Recent Up/Downgrade	TOTAL RETURNS & PERFORMANCE: 3-Month Total Return	6-Month Total Return	1-Year Total Return	3-Year Total Return	5-Year Total Return	ASSETS: NAV	Total Assets (MIL)	NEW INVESTORS: Telephone	Open to New Investors
State Street Inst Small-Cap Equity Fund Investment Cls	SIVIX	B	B	B	Up	2.68	7.32	13.07	33.95	96.14	19.51	1,498	617-664-7338	Y
State Street Inst Small-Cap Equity Fund Service Cls	SSQSX	B	B	B	Up	2.59	7.23	12.78	32.95	93.86	19.54	1,498	617-664-7338	Y
Sterling Capital Behavioral Small Cap Value Eq Fund Cls A	SPSAX	B+	B+	B	Up	3.25	9.50	8.62	29.44	91.83	18.22	229.1	800-228-1872	Y
Sterling Capital Behavioral Small Cap Value Eq Fund Cls C	SPSDX	B	B	B	Up	3.06	9.10	7.81	26.56	84.82	17.58	229.1	800-228-1872	Y
Sterling Capital Behavioral Small Cap Value Eq Fund Cls R	SPSRX	B	B+	B	Up	3.21	9.43	8.42	28.36	89.52	18.13	229.1	800-228-1872	Y
Sterling Capital Behavioral Small Cap Value Eq Inst Shares	SPSCX	B+	A-	B	Up	3.37	9.69	8.88	30.39	94.33	18.36	229.1	800-228-1872	Y
Sterling Capital Stratton Small Cap Value Fund A Shares	STSNX	B+	A-	B	Up	4.53	10.52	12.90	33.62	96.38	86.12	1,245	800-228-1872	Y
Sterling Capital Stratton Small Cap Value Fund C Shares	STSOX	B	B	B	Up	4.34	10.11	12.07	30.67	89.20	84.84	1,245	800-228-1872	Y
Sterling Capital Stratton Small Cap Value Fund Inst Shares	STSCX	B+	A-	B	Up	4.61	10.67	13.19	34.58	98.79	86.33	1,245	800-228-1872	Y
Steward Small-Mid Cap Enhanced Index Fund Class Individual	TRDFX	B+	B+	B	Up	5.10	9.61	13.79	33.36	97.73	15.84	235.2	800-262-6631	Y
Steward Small-Mid Cap Enhanced Index Fund Cls Inst	SCECX	B+	B+	B	Up	5.09	9.76	14.04	34.49	100.48	16.06	235.2	800-262-6631	Y
Strategic Advisers® Small-Mid Cap Fund	FSCFX	B	B	C+	Up	6.21	11.33	19.27	31.80	91.86	14.94	7,605	617-563-7000	Y
Strategic Advisers® Small-Mid Cap Multi-Manager Fund	FNAPX	B	B	B	Up	5.75	10.56	19.19	31.52	90.71	10.3	15.5	617-563-7000	Y
Strategic Advisers® Small-Mid Cap Multi-Manager Fund Cls L	FQAJX	B	B	C+	Up	5.76	10.57	19.21	31.56	90.78	10.29	15.5	617-563-7000	Y
Strategic Advisers® Small-Mid Cap Multi-Manager Fund Cls N	FQAKX	B	B	B	Up	5.69	10.42	18.98	30.56	88.39	10.23	15.5	617-563-7000	Y
T. Rowe Price Institutional Small-Cap Stock Fund	TRSSX	B	B+	B	Up	3.36	8.79	15.45	32.27	103.55	23.72	4,260	410-345-2000	
T. Rowe Price New Horizons Fund	PRNHX	B+	A-	B+	Up	4.62	11.60	31.49	47.70	138.62	52.57	22,021	410-345-2000	
T. Rowe Price New Horizons Fund I Class	PRJIX	B+	A-	B+	Up	4.65	11.68	31.67	48.18	139.40	52.63	22,021	410-345-2000	Y
T. Rowe Price QM U.S. Small-Cap Growth Equity Fund	PRDSX	B+	B+	B	Up	5.89	10.31	22.11	38.18	117.59	34.89	5,856	410-345-2000	Y
T. Rowe Price QM U.S. Small-Cap Growth Equity Fund Adv Cls	TQAAX	B+	B+	B	Up	5.84	10.16	21.77	37.05	114.74	34.79	5,856	410-345-2000	Y
T. Rowe Price QM U.S. Small-Cap Growth Equity Fund I Class	TQAIX	B+	B+	B	Up	5.91	10.35	22.26	38.54	118.16	34.94	5,856	410-345-2000	Y
T. Rowe Price Small-Cap Stock Fund	OTCFX	B	B+	B	Up	3.43	8.80	15.27	31.46	98.50	47.7	9,755	410-345-2000	
T. Rowe Price Small-Cap Stock Fund Advisor Class	PASSX	B	B	B	Up	3.34	8.63	14.95	30.38	95.71	47.25	9,755	410-345-2000	
T. Rowe Price Small-Cap Stock Fund I Class	OTIIX	B	B+	B	Up	3.47	8.86	15.42	31.88	99.13	47.71	9,755	410-345-2000	Y
T. Rowe Price Small-Cap Value Fund	PRSVX	A-	A	B	Up	3.29	9.39	13.37	38.45	88.98	49.06	10,514	410-345-2000	Y
T. Rowe Price Small-Cap Value Fund Advisor Class	PASVX	B+	A-	B	Up	3.15	9.15	12.94	37.01	85.96	48.81	10,514	410-345-2000	Y
T. Rowe Price Small-Cap Value Fund I Class	PRVIX	A-	A	B	Up	3.36	9.47	13.55	38.90	89.59	49.06	10,514	410-345-2000	Y
TCM Small Cap Growth Fund	TCMSX	A-	A	B	Up	3.81	11.30	24.70	42.50	133.01	33.56	387.5		Y
TETON Westwood Mighty Mites Class Institutional	WEIMX	B+	A-	B	Up	1.52	9.62	15.66	32.56	92.85	28.68	1,382		Y
TETON Westwood Mighty Mites Fund Class A	WMMAX	B	B+	B	Up	1.35	9.31	15.03	30.58	87.97	27.01	1,382		Y
TETON Westwood Mighty Mites Fund Class AAA	WEMMX	B+	B+	B	Up	1.44	9.48	15.37	31.62	90.48	28.05	1,382		Y
TETON Westwood Mighty Mites Fund Class C	WMMCX	B	B	B	Up	1.24	9.06	14.49	28.63	83.36	23.76	1,382		Y
TETON Westwood Mighty Mites Fund T	WETMX	B+	B+	B	Up	1.44	9.44	15.32	31.57	90.40	28.05	1,382		Y
TETON Westwood SmallCap Equity Fund Class A	WWSAX	B+	A	B	Up	4.03	12.31	15.34	42.46	96.82	19.48	32.6		Y
TETON Westwood SmallCap Equity Fund Class AAA	WESCX	A-	A	B	Up	4.16	12.47	15.63	43.56	99.45	20.41	32.6		Y
TETON Westwood SmallCap Equity Fund Class C	WWSCX	B+	A	B	Up	3.92	12.06	14.81	40.40	92.05	16.9	32.6		Y
TETON Westwood SmallCap Equity Fund Class Institutional	WWSIX	A-	A	B	Up	4.17	12.60	15.89	44.59	101.90	21.11	32.6		Y
TETON Westwood SmallCap Equity Fund T	WWSTX	A-	A	B	Up	4.16	12.47	15.63	43.56	99.45	20.41	32.6		Y
Third Avenue Small Cap Value Fund Institutional Class	TASCX	B	B	B	Up	1.50	6.21	8.85	27.13	77.56	20.8	297.8	800-443-1021	Y
Third Avenue Small-Cap Value Fund Investor Class	TVSVX	B	B	B	Up	1.47	6.09	8.60	26.22	75.38	20.54	297.8	800-443-1021	Y
Thomson Horstmann & Bryant Microcap Fund Inst Cls Shares	THBIX	B	A	C+	Up	2.01	7.04	10.97	33.44	92.05	16.34	83.1		Y
Thomson Horstmann & Bryant Microcap Fund Inv Cls Shares	THBVX	B	A	C+	Up	1.95	6.79	10.46	31.42	87.50	15.89	83.1		Y
Thrivent Series Small Cap Index Portfolio		A-	A-	B	Up	3.89	10.06	13.13	38.58	111.19	19.1961	497.4		Y
Thrivent Series Small Cap Stock Portfolio		A-	A	B	Up	5.26	11.88	21.23	46.55	114.54	21.0077	614.0		Y
Thrivent Small Cap Stock Fund Class A	AASMX	A-	A	B	Up	5.14	11.74	20.88	45.31	110.93	21.57	621.5		Y
Thrivent Small Cap Stock Fund Class S	TSCSX	A-	A	B	Up	5.24	11.90	21.28	47.14	115.71	25.99	621.5		Y
TIAA-CREF Small-Cap Blend Index Fund Advisor Class	TRHBX	B+	A-	B	Up	3.36	9.22	14.72	32.76	99.45	21.28	2,491	877-518-9161	Y
TIAA-CREF Small-Cap Blend Index Fund Institutional Class	TISBX	B+	A-	B	Up	3.36	9.26	14.82	32.89	99.65	21.28	2,491	877-518-9161	Y
TIAA-CREF Small-Cap Blend Index Fund Retirement Class	TRBIX	B+	A-	B	Up	3.30	9.14	14.55	31.92	97.28	21.38	2,491	877-518-9161	Y
TIAA-CREF Small-Cap Equity Fund Advisor Class	TSCHX	B+	A-	B	Up	3.97	9.95	14.90	36.99	110.87	19.08	3,938	877-518-9161	Y
TIAA-CREF Small-Cap Equity Fund Institutional Class	TISEX	B+	A-	B	Up	4.03	10.01	15.01	37.14	111.10	19.1	3,938	877-518-9161	Y
TIAA-CREF Small-Cap Equity Fund Premier Class	TSRPX	B+	A-	B	Up	3.99	9.94	14.85	36.53	109.48	19	3,938	877-518-9161	Y

Category: US Equity Small Cap (con't)

Fund Name	Ticker Symbol	RATINGS: Overall Rating	RATINGS: Reward Rating	RATINGS: Risk Rating	RATINGS: Recent Up/ Downgrade	TOTAL RETURNS & PERFORMANCE: 3-Month Total Return	6-Month Total Return	1-Year Total Return	3-Year Total Return	5-Year Total Return	ASSETS: NAV	Total Assets (Mil.)	NEW INVESTORS: Telephone	Open to New Investors
TIAA-CREF Small-Cap Equity Fund Retail Class	TCSEX	B+	A-	B	Up	3.97	9.87	14.72	35.88	107.64	18.44	3,938	877-518-9161	Y
TIAA-CREF Small-Cap Equity Fund Retirement Class	TRSEX	B+	A-	B	Up	3.97	9.87	14.74	36.06	108.41	18.63	3,938	877-518-9161	Y
Timothy Plan Smal Cap Value Fund Class C	TSVCX	B	B	B	Up	3.38	9.66	12.18	27.07	101.89	14.28	146.3	800-662-0201	Y
Timothy Plan Small Cap Value Fund Class A	TPLNX	B+	A-	B	Up	3.61	10.05	13.04	30.01	109.51	19.45	146.3	800-662-0201	Y
Timothy Plan Small Cap Value Fund Class I	TPVIX	B+	A-	B	Up	3.61	10.15	13.28	30.94	111.69	19.65	146.3	800-662-0201	Y
Touchstone Small Cap Value Fund Class A	TVOAX	B-	B-	C+	Up	2.72	5.60	7.21	16.96	61.85	26.77	91.1	800-543-0407	Y
Touchstone Small Cap Value Fund Class Y	TVOYX	B-	B-	C+	Up	2.80	5.71	7.48	17.86	63.89	26.86	91.1	800-543-0407	Y
Touchstone Small Cap Value Fund Institutional Class	TVOIX	B-	B-	C+	Up	2.82	5.78	7.63	18.36	65.13	26.84	91.1	800-543-0407	Y
Touchstone Small Company Fund Class A	SAGWX	B	B	B	Up	6.16	8.59	17.33	36.60	100.38	5.22	1,238	800-543-0407	Y
Touchstone Small Company Fund Class C	SSCOX	B	B	B	Up	6.05	8.32	16.55	34.01	93.33	3.06	1,238	800-543-0407	Y
Touchstone Small Company Fund Class R6	SSRRX	B	B	B	Up	6.24	8.84	17.93	38.70	103.48	5.32	1,238	800-543-0407	Y
Touchstone Small Company Fund Class Y	SIGWX	B	B	B	Up	6.03	8.65	17.58	37.88	103.67	5.68	1,238	800-543-0407	Y
Touchstone Small Company Fund Institutional USD	TICSX	B	B	B		6.13	8.56	17.29	36.56	100.32	5.68	1,238	800-543-0407	Y
Towle Deep Value Fund	TDVFX	B+	A+	C+	Up	4.83	17.91	14.80	47.67	142.74	18.75	121.8	888-998-6953	Y
Transamerica Small Cap Core Fund Class I	ISMTX	B-	B-	B-	Up	2.75	6.51	6.14	18.12	68.12	11.7	257.6	888-233-4339	Y
Transamerica Small Cap Core Fund Class I2	US89355J3187	B-	B-	B-	Up	2.82	6.58	6.21	18.45	68.73	11.71	257.6	888-233-4339	Y
Transamerica Small Cap Growth A	ASGTX	B+	B+	B+	Up	4.37	7.39	15.11	40.94	102.53	6.36	156.7	888-233-4339	Y
Transamerica Small Cap Growth Advisor	TASPX	B+	B+	B+	Up	4.38	7.47	15.50	38.75	99.38	6.58	156.7	888-233-4339	Y
Transamerica Small Cap Growth C	CSGTX	B+	B+	B+	Up	4.25	7.00	14.35	37.84	95.65	5.81	156.7	888-233-4339	Y
Transamerica Small Cap Growth Class T1	RTSTX	B+	B+	B+	Up	4.53	7.56	15.25	37.76	96.97	6.37	156.7	888-233-4339	Y
Transamerica Small Cap Growth I	ISCGX	B+	B+	B+	Up	4.54	7.48	15.51	42.05	105.58	6.58	156.7	888-233-4339	Y
Transamerica Small Cap Growth I2	US89355J6560	B+	B+	B+	Up	4.48	7.70	15.66	42.56	106.56	6.67	156.7	888-233-4339	Y
Transamerica Small Cap Growth I3	TSPTX	B+	B+	B+	Up	4.63	7.69	15.68	38.97	99.69	6.68	156.7	888-233-4339	Y
Transamerica Small Cap Growth R	TSPRX	B+	B+	B+	Up	4.36	7.42	14.91	36.67	94.45	6.64	156.7	888-233-4339	Y
Transamerica Small Cap Growth R4	TSPFX	B+	B+	B+	Up	4.48	7.54	15.28	37.79	97.02	6.66	156.7	888-233-4339	Y
Transamerica Small Cap Growth R6	RTSGX	B+	B+	B+	Up	4.48	7.70	15.66	41.67	103.57	6.67	156.7	888-233-4339	Y
Transamerica Small Cap Value Advisor	TASLX	B	B	B	Up	2.05	6.38	8.83	20.42	76.98	11.78	314.0	888-233-4339	Y
Transamerica Small Cap Value Class T1	TSLWX	B	B	B	Up	2.08	6.38	8.52	19.47	74.72	11.64	314.0	888-233-4339	Y
Transamerica Small Cap Value I3	US89360T4269	B	B	B	Up	2.20	6.57	8.79	20.37	76.92	11.73	314.0	888-233-4339	Y
Transamerica Small Cap Value R	TRSLX	B	B-	B	Up	2.00	6.18	8.12	18.44	72.35	11.71	314.0	888-233-4339	Y
Transamerica Small Cap Value R6	TSLRX	B	B	B	Up	2.10	6.53	8.98	20.37	76.92	11.76	314.0	888-233-4339	Y
Tributary Small Company Fund Institutional Class	FOSCX	B+	B	B+	Up	1.96	4.66	8.48	33.41	95.83	28.48	726.6		Y
Tributary Small Company Fund Institutional Plus Class	FOSBX	B+	B	B+	Up	2.02	4.83	8.76	34.24	98.03	28.61	726.6		Y
UBS U.S. Small Cap Growth Fund Class A	BNSCX	B	B	C+	Up	6.14	9.44	19.13	23.16	98.14	17.99	109.8	212-882-5586	Y
UBS U.S. Small Cap Growth Fund Class C	BNMCX	B-	B	C+	Up	5.94	9.07	18.25	20.44	90.92	14.26	109.8	212-882-5586	Y
UBS U.S. Small Cap Growth Fund Class P	BISCX	B	B	C+	Up	6.25	9.59	19.44	24.10	100.87	19.84	109.8	212-882-5586	Y
Undiscovered Managers Behavioral Value Fund Class A	UBVAX	A-	B+	A-	Up	7.02	11.76	14.66	40.69	109.04	68.34	6,256	800-480-4111	
Undiscovered Managers Behavioral Value Fund Class C	UBVCX	B+	B+	A-	Up	5.30	9.85	12.41	36.53	100.88	64.47	6,256	800-480-4111	
Undiscovered Managers Behavioral Value Fund Class I	UBVSX	A-	B+	A-	Up	7.04	11.87	14.91	41.69	111.64	69.74	6,256	800-480-4111	Y
Undiscovered Managers Behavioral Value Fund Class L	UBVLX	A-	A-	A-	Up	7.08	11.94	15.08	42.32	113.11	69.93	6,256	800-480-4111	Y
Undiscovered Managers Behavioral Value Fund Class R2	UBVRX	B+	B+	A-	Up	6.95	11.62	14.38	39.63	106.50	67.81	6,256	800-480-4111	Y
Undiscovered Managers Behavioral Value Fund Class R3	UBVTX	A-	B+	A-	Up	7.00	11.76	14.67	41.11	110.25	68.08	6,256	800-480-4111	Y
Undiscovered Managers Behavioral Value Fund Class R4	UBVUX	A-	A-	A-	Up	7.04	11.86	14.93	42.13	112.84	69.64	6,256	800-480-4111	Y
Undiscovered Managers Behavioral Value Fund Class R5	UBVVX	A-	A-	A-	Up	7.07	11.94	15.06	42.30	113.08	69.91	6,256	800-480-4111	Y
Undiscovered Managers Behavioral Value Fund Class R6	UBVFX	A-	A-	A-	Up	7.09	11.99	15.18	42.71	114.09	70.02	6,256	800-480-4111	Y
USAA Small Cap Stock Fund	USCAX	B	B	B	Up	3.52	8.83	10.12	23.05	78.29	17.55	1,672	800-531-8722	Y
USAA Small Cap Stock Fund Institutional Shares	UISCX	B	B	B	Up	3.54	8.93	10.28	23.59	79.85	17.7	1,672	800-531-8722	Y
VALIC Company I Small Cap Aggressive Growth Fund	VSAGX	B	A	C+	Up	6.65	16.95	37.87	41.85	139.39	14.9	136.2		Y
VALIC Company I Small Cap Fund	VCSMX	B	B	B	Up	4.11	9.03	14.71	24.99	87.48	12.91	323.5		Y
VALIC Company I Small Cap Index Fund	VCSLX	B+	A-	B	Up	3.25	9.08	14.37	31.49	96.32	22.81	1,292		Y
VALIC Company I Small Cap Special Values Fund	VSSVX	B+	A-	B	Up	5.25	9.60	11.24	37.12	109.26	14.83	326.3		Y
VALIC Company II Small Cap Growth Fund	VASMX	B	A	C	Up	7.99	17.88	41.45	50.31	126.89	19.31	159.5		Y

Category: US Equity Small Cap (con't)

Fund Name	Ticker Symbol	RATINGS: Overall Rating	RATINGS: Reward Rating	RATINGS: Risk Rating	RATINGS: Recent Up/ Downgrade	TOTAL RETURNS & PERFORMANCE: 3-Month Total Return	6-Month Total Return	1-Year Total Return	3-Year Total Return	5-Year Total Return	ASSETS: NAV	Total Assets (MIL)	NEW INVESTORS: Telephone	Open to New Investors
VALIC Company II Small Cap Value Fund	VCSVX	B	B+	B	Up	1.74	6.79	4.93	26.47	86.94	15.71	589.0		Y
Value Line Small Cap Opportunities Fund Institutional Cls	VLEIX	B+	B+	A-	Up	5.68	9.99	17.95	36.57	102.69	52.09	507.9	800-243-2729	Y
Value Line Small Cap Opportunities Fund Investor Class	VLEOX	B+	B	A-	Up	5.59	9.85	17.63	35.79	101.53	51.77	507.9	800-243-2729	Y
Vanguard Explorer Fund Admiral Shares	VEXRX	B	B+	B	Up	6.02	10.76	23.09	31.77	103.41	88.41	13,418	877-662-7447	Y
Vanguard Explorer Fund Investor Class	VEXPX	B	B+	B	Up	5.98	10.70	22.95	31.28	101.99	95.01	13,418	877-662-7447	Y
Vanguard Explorer Value Fund Investor Shares	VEVFX	B	B+	B	Up	4.47	10.22	13.27	31.88	95.94	36.66	661.5	877-662-7447	Y
Vanguard Russell 2000 Growth Index Fund Inst Shares	VRTGX	B+	A-	B	Up	4.61	11.15	22.28	34.03	108.76	257.96	657.3	877-662-7447	Y
Vanguard Russell 2000 Index Fund Institutional Shares	VRTIX	B+	A-	B	Up	3.37	9.26	14.77	32.38	98.47	233.92	1,876	877-662-7447	Y
Vanguard Russell 2000 Value Index Fund Inst Shares	VRTVX	B	A-	B	Up	2.06	7.30	7.91	30.35	87.97	215.2	352.6	877-662-7447	Y
Vanguard S&P Small-Cap 600 Index Fund Institutional Shares	VSMSX	A-	A	B	Up	3.96	10.18	13.37	39.57	113.86	280.11	1,579	877-662-7447	Y
Vanguard S&P Small-Cap 600 Value Index Fund Inst Shares	VSMVX	B+	A-	B	Up	4.02	10.57	11.63	35.64	108.63	276.63	272.9	877-662-7447	Y
Vanguard Small Cap Value Index Fund Admiral Shares	VSIAX	B	B	B	Up	4.55	9.14	11.79	31.70	104.35	57.02	29,416	877-662-7447	Y
Vanguard Small Capitalization Growth Index Fund Inv Shares	VISGX	B	B	B	Up	5.73	10.72	21.78	30.30	91.95	45.24	21,153	877-662-7447	Y
Vanguard Small Capitalization Index Fund Investor Shares	NAESX	B	B	B	Up	5.07	9.84	16.10	30.93	98.80	70.76	83,745	877-662-7447	Y
Vanguard Small Capitalization Value Index Fund Inv Shares	VISVX	B	B	B	Up	4.53	9.11	11.67	31.25	103.09	31.82	29,416	877-662-7447	Y
Vanguard Small-Cap Growth Index Fund Admiral Shares	VSGAX	B	B	B	Up	5.75	10.79	21.91	30.74	93.22	56.55	21,153	877-662-7447	Y
Vanguard Small-Cap Growth Index Fund Institutional Shares	VSGIX	B	B	B	Up	5.76	10.81	21.94	30.78	93.28	45.29	21,153	877-662-7447	Y
Vanguard Small-Cap Index Fund Admiral Shares	VSMAX	B	B	B	Up	5.10	9.90	16.23	31.39	100.12	70.78	83,745	877-662-7447	Y
Vanguard Small-Cap Index Fund Institutional Plus Shares	VSCPX	B	B	B	Up	5.09	9.92	16.26	31.49	100.38	204.3	83,745	877-662-7447	Y
Vanguard Small-Cap Index Fund Institutional Shares	VSCIX	B	B	B	Up	5.10	9.92	16.24	31.43	100.22	70.78	83,745	877-662-7447	Y
Vanguard Small-Cap Value Index Fund Institutional Shares	VSIIX	B	B	B	Up	4.55	9.16	11.80	31.72	104.51	31.87	29,416	877-662-7447	Y
Vanguard Strategic Small-Cap Equity Fund Investor Shares	VSTCX	B	B	B	Up	2.90	7.74	10.33	27.83	105.63	35.63	1,708	877-662-7447	Y
Vanguard Tax-Managed Small Cap Fund Admiral Shares	VTMSX	A-	A-	B	Up	3.92	10.13	13.05	38.50	113.05	61.63	5,940	877-662-7447	Y
Vanguard Tax-Managed Small-Cap Fund Institutional Shares	VTSIX	A-	A-	B	Up	3.92	10.14	13.07	38.62	113.46	61.77	5,940	877-662-7447	Y
Vericimetry U.S. Small Cap Value Fund	VYSVX	B	B	B	Up	2.96	9.74	8.97	26.08	91.80	20.14	309.5		Y
Victory Integrity Discovery Fund Class A	MMEAX	A-	A	B	Up	2.45	8.77	10.74	41.88	117.64	40.17	158.7	800-539-3863	Y
Victory Integrity Discovery Fund Class C	MMECX	B+	A	B	Up	2.29	8.36	9.92	38.57	109.46	29.9	158.7	800-539-3863	Y
Victory Integrity Discovery Fund Class R	MMERX	A-	A	B	Up	2.33	8.50	10.20	39.85	113.41	38.41	158.7	800-539-3863	Y
Victory Integrity Discovery Fund Class Y	MMEYX	A-	A	B	Up	2.53	8.93	11.02	42.98	120.41	43.61	158.7	800-539-3863	Y
Victory Integrity Small-Cap Value Fund Class A	VSCVX	B	B+	B	Up	5.47	11.59	11.95	27.93	97.91	39.72	2,705	800-539-3863	Y
Victory Integrity Small-Cap Value Fund Class C	MCVSX	B	B	B	Up	5.33	11.26	11.26	25.32	91.02	35.21	2,705	800-539-3863	Y
Victory Integrity Small-Cap Value Fund Class R	MRVSX	B	B+	B	Up	5.42	11.48	11.69	27.00	95.50	38.74	2,705	800-539-3863	Y
Victory Integrity Small-Cap Value Fund Class R6	MVSSX	B+	A-	B	Up	5.63	11.91	12.58	29.94	102.62	41.05	2,705	800-539-3863	Y
Victory Integrity Small-Cap Value Fund Class Y	VSVIX	B+	A-	B	Up	5.59	11.82	12.35	29.33	101.05	40.83	2,705	800-539-3863	Y
Victory RS Partners Fund Class A	RSPFX	B-	B-	C+	Up	3.25	8.37	14.20	25.24	75.29	29.21	626.2	800-539-3863	
Victory RS Partners Fund Class R	RSPKX	B-	B-	C+	Up	3.18	8.21	13.80	23.92	72.20	27.1	626.2	800-539-3863	
Victory RS Partners Fund Class Y	RSPYX	B-	B	C+	Up	3.35	8.56	14.59	26.44	78.15	30.67	626.2	800-539-3863	
Victory RS Select Growth Fund Class A	RSDGX	B	B	B	Up	5.24	7.74	17.09	23.71	77.52	46.03	464.9	800-539-3863	Y
Victory RS Select Growth Fund Class C	RSGFX	B	B-	B	Up	5.06	7.34	16.18	20.85	70.69	40.81	464.9	800-539-3863	Y
Victory RS Select Growth Fund Class R	RSDKX	B	B-	B	Up	5.10	7.46	16.50	21.95	73.11	41.06	464.9	800-539-3863	Y
Victory RS Select Growth Fund Class R6	RSSRX	B	B	B	Up	5.34	7.94	17.48	24.17	78.18	47.53	464.9	800-539-3863	Y
Victory RS Select Growth Fund Class Y	RSSYX	B	B	B	Up	5.32	7.90	17.39	24.69	79.85	47.48	464.9	800-539-3863	Y
Victory RS Small Cap Equity Fund Class A	GPSCX	B	A	C	Up	6.63	16.95	37.56	39.42	135.08	18.88	76.4	800-539-3863	
Victory RS Small Cap Equity Fund Class C	RSCCX	B	A	C	Up	6.38	16.35	36.34	36.03	125.66	9.61	76.4	800-539-3863	
Victory RS Small Cap Equity Fund Class R	RSCKX	B	A	C	Up	6.46	16.67	36.84	37.67	130.58	16.08	76.4	800-539-3863	
Victory RS Small Cap Equity Fund Class Y	RSCYX	B	A	C	Up	6.63	16.97	37.78	39.61	136.84	19.2	76.4	800-539-3863	
Victory RS Small Cap Growth Fund Class A	RSEGX	B	A	C	Up	6.32	16.41	36.85	37.55	130.27	80.97	1,703	800-539-3863	
Victory RS Small Cap Growth Fund Class C	REGWX	B	A	C	Up	6.13	15.97	35.84	34.47	121.37	71.71	1,703	800-539-3863	
Victory RS Small Cap Growth Fund Class R	RSEKX	B	A	C	Up	6.20	16.12	36.23	36.04	125.55	75.56	1,703	800-539-3863	
Victory RS Small Cap Growth Fund Class R6	RSEJX	B	A	C	Up	6.42	16.58	37.05	37.75	130.60	83.67	1,703	800-539-3863	Y
Victory RS Small Cap Growth Fund Class Y	RSYEX	B	A	C	Up	6.39	16.55	37.23	38.67	133.44	83.64	1,703	800-539-3863	
Victory Sycamore Small Company Opportunity Fund Class A	SSGSX	A-	A	A-	Up	3.08	10.30	11.47	42.07	106.59	46.72	5,201	800-539-3863	Y

Category: US Equity Small Cap (con't)

Fund Name	Ticker Symbol	RATINGS: Overall Rating	RATINGS: Reward Rating	RATINGS: Risk Rating	RATINGS: Recent Up/ Downgrade	TOTAL RETURNS & PERFORMANCE: 3-Month Total Return	6-Month Total Return	1-Year Total Return	3-Year Total Return	5-Year Total Return	ASSETS: NAV	Total Assets (MIL)	NEW INVESTORS: Telephone	Open to New Investors
Victory Sycamore Small Company Opportunity Fund Class I	VSOIX	A-	A	A-	Up	3.19	10.50	11.87	43.49	110.13	47.13	5,201	800-539-3863	Y
Victory Sycamore Small Company Opportunity Fund Class R	GOGFX	A-	A	A-	Up	3.03	10.16	11.25	41.17	104.28	43.98	5,201	800-539-3863	Y
Victory Sycamore Small Company Opportunity Fund Class Y	VSOYX	A-	A	A-	Up	3.13	10.35	11.58	42.55	107.95	46.88	5,201	800-539-3863	Y
Victory Sycamore Small Company Opportunity Fund R6	VSORX	A-	A	A-	Up	3.18	10.48	11.87	42.62	106.37	47.06	5,201	800-539-3863	Y
Virtus Ceredex Small-Cap Value Equity Fund Class A	SASVX	B	B	B	Up	7.17	11.39	10.04	31.69	85.51	11.53	821.9	800-243-1574	
Virtus Ceredex Small-Cap Value Equity Fund Class C	STCEX	B	B	B	Up	6.93	11.08	9.61	30.10	82.02	10.31	821.9	800-243-1574	
Virtus Ceredex Small-Cap Value Equity Fund Class I	SCETX	B	B	B	Up	7.16	11.50	10.28	32.80	88.23	11.97	821.9	800-243-1574	
Virtus KAR Small-Cap Core Fund Class A	PKSAX	B+	A	B-	Up	9.99	19.40	34.62	57.54	117.44	30.81	775.6	800-243-1574	Y
Virtus KAR Small-Cap Core Fund Class C	PKSCX	B+	A	B-	Up	9.76	18.97	33.64	54.04	109.45	26.19	775.6	800-243-1574	Y
Virtus KAR Small-Cap Core Fund Class I	PKSFX	A-	A	B	Up	10.03	19.57	34.98	58.75	120.16	32.35	775.6	800-243-1574	Y
Virtus KAR Small-Cap Core Fund Class R6	VSCRX	A-	A	B	Up	10.07	19.59	35.06	59.22	120.89	32.45	775.6	800-243-1574	Y
Virtus KAR Small-Cap Growth Fund Class A	PSGAX	A-	A+	B-	Up	7.23	17.64	36.62	70.96	151.98	27.27	1,638	800-243-1574	Y
Virtus KAR Small-Cap Growth Fund Class C	PSGCX	B+	A+	B-	Up	7.05	17.24	35.61	67.19	142.70	24.75	1,638	800-243-1574	Y
Virtus KAR Small-Cap Growth Fund Class I	PXSGX	A-	A+	B-	Up	7.31	17.79	36.99	72.26	155.12	27.74	1,638	800-243-1574	Y
Virtus KAR Small-Cap Value Fund Class A	PQSAX	B+	A	B	Up	4.51	11.47	18.57	43.82	108.59	18.93	470.9	800-243-1574	Y
Virtus KAR Small-Cap Value Fund Class C	PQSCX	A-	A	B+	Up	4.34	11.10	17.75	40.70	101.00	18.56	470.9	800-243-1574	Y
Virtus KAR Small-Cap Value Fund Class I	PXQSX	B+	A	B	Up	4.58	11.61	18.89	44.93	111.23	18.94	470.9	800-243-1574	Y
Virtus KAR Small-Cap Value Fund Class R6	VQSRX	B+	A	B	Up	4.59	11.68	19.04	45.05	111.40	18.95	470.9	800-243-1574	Y
Virtus Silvant Small-Cap Growth Stock Fund Class A	SCGIX	B	B	B	Up	4.12	7.62	14.33	20.33	70.63	6.92	32.9	800-243-1574	Y
Virtus Silvant Small-Cap Growth Stock Fund Class C	SSCFX	B-	B-	B	Up	4.20	7.58	13.83	18.16	65.46	2.58	32.9	800-243-1574	Y
Virtus Silvant Small-Cap Growth Stock Fund Class I	SSCTX	B	B	B	Up	4.19	7.72	14.57	20.67	71.39	8.78	32.9	800-243-1574	Y
Voya Index Plus SmallCap Portfolio Class I	IPSIX	B+	B+	B	Up	3.15	7.55	9.91	34.33	107.55	26.78	304.5	800-366-0066	Y
Voya Index Plus SmallCap Portfolio Class S	IPSSX	B+	B+	B	Up	3.07	7.38	9.60	33.31	104.94	26.47	304.5	800-366-0066	Y
Voya Russell Small Cap Index Portfolio Class A	IRSIX	B+	B+	B	Up	3.06	8.75	13.64	29.16	91.41	15.15	968.1	800-366-0066	Y
Voya Russell Small Cap Index Portfolio Class I	IIRSX	B+	A-	B	Up	3.23	9.05	14.26	31.13	96.28	15.66	968.1	800-366-0066	Y
Voya Russell Small Cap Index Portfolio Class P2	VRSPX	B+	A-	B	Up	3.35	9.25	14.47	31.37	96.64	15.7	968.1	800-366-0066	Y
Voya Russell Small Cap Index Portfolio Class S	IRSSX	B+	A-	B	Up	3.19	8.91	13.96	30.14	93.81	15.51	968.1	800-366-0066	Y
Voya Russell Small Cap Index Portfolio Class S2	IRCIX	B+	A-	B	Up	3.11	8.85	13.76	29.56	92.49	15.24	968.1	800-366-0066	Y
Voya Small Company Fund Class A	AESAX	B	B	B	Up	3.08	7.44	10.73	33.19	98.04	14.24	779.2	800-366-0066	Y
Voya Small Company Fund Class C	ASCCX	B	B	B	Up	2.89	7.04	9.88	30.25	90.72	11.25	779.2	800-366-0066	Y
Voya Small Company Fund Class I	AESGX	B	B+	B	Up	3.14	7.62	11.01	34.46	101.01	16.99	779.2	800-366-0066	Y
Voya Small Company Fund Class O	ISCOX	B	B	B	Up	3.07	7.50	10.73	33.22	98.05	14.22	779.2	800-366-0066	Y
Voya Small Company Fund Class R	VSMRX	B	B	B	Up	3.01	7.32	10.47	32.37	95.92	14.16	779.2	800-366-0066	Y
Voya Small Company Fund Class R6	ISMZX	B	B+	B	Up	3.15	7.69	11.14	34.80	101.80	17.01	779.2	800-366-0066	Y
Voya Small Company Fund Class W	ISMWX	B	B+	B	Up	3.18	7.62	11.01	34.29	100.51	16.95	779.2	800-366-0066	Y
Voya Small Company Portfolio Class A	IASCX	B	B+	B	Up	3.10	7.50	10.68	34.15	100.07	20.95	748.4	800-366-0066	Y
Voya Small Company Portfolio Class I	IVCSX	B+	B+	B	Up	3.29	7.84	11.28	36.27	105.28	22.01	748.4	800-366-0066	Y
Voya Small Company Portfolio Class S	IVPSX	B	B+	B	Up	3.23	7.68	11.00	35.23	102.69	21.46	748.4	800-366-0066	Y
Voya Small Company Portfolio R6	VSPRX	B+	B+	B	Up	3.29	7.79	11.23	36.27	105.28	22.01	748.4	800-366-0066	Y
Voya SmallCap Opportunities Fund Class A	NSPAX	B	B	B	Up	3.30	7.64	17.99	29.69	91.77	58.43	1,459	800-366-0066	Y
Voya SmallCap Opportunities Fund Class C	NSPCX	B	B	B	Up	3.13	7.29	17.13	26.82	84.73	44.83	1,459	800-366-0066	Y
Voya SmallCap Opportunities Fund Class I	NSPIX	B	B	B	Up	3.34	7.77	18.30	30.81	94.69	63.8	1,459	800-366-0066	Y
Voya SmallCap Opportunities Fund Class R	ISORX	B	B	B	Up	3.23	7.51	17.70	28.72	89.43	57.21	1,459	800-366-0066	Y
Voya SmallCap Opportunities Fund Class R6	ISOZX	B	B	B	Up	3.40	7.87	18.48	31.40	95.48	64.23	1,459	800-366-0066	Y
Voya SmallCap Opportunities Fund Class W	ISOWX	B	B	B	Up	3.34	7.78	18.26	30.67	94.21	62.94	1,459	800-366-0066	Y
Voya SmallCap Opportunities Portfolio Class A	ISOPX	B	B	B	Up	3.29	7.71	18.11	30.54	94.67	26.04	410.6	800-366-0066	Y
Voya SmallCap Opportunities Portfolio Class I	IVSOX	B	B+	B	Up	3.42	8.02	18.72	32.51	99.62	28.72	410.6	800-366-0066	Y
Voya SmallCap Opportunities Portfolio Class S	IVPOX	B	B	B	Up	3.37	7.89	18.44	31.55	97.19	26.98	410.6	800-366-0066	Y
Voya SmallCap Opportunities Portfolio Class S2	ISCTX	B	B	B	Up	3.32	7.77	18.25	30.92	95.68	26.39	410.6	800-366-0066	Y
Voya SmallCap Opportunities Portfolio R6	VRSCX	B	B+	B	Up	3.45	8.02	18.73	32.52	99.64	28.72	410.6	800-366-0066	Y
Vulcan Value Partners Small Cap Fund	VVPSX	B-	B-	B		3.97	3.71	11.45	24.27	81.81	19.63	1,206	205-803-1582	
VY® Columbia Small Cap Value II Portfolio Class A	ICSAX	B+	B+	B	Up	3.32	9.34	10.64	31.12	96.08	19.57	219.1	800-366-0066	Y

Category: US Equity Small Cap (con't)

Fund Name	Ticker Symbol	RATINGS: Overall Rating	Reward Rating	Risk Rating	Recent Up/ Downgrade	TOTAL RETURNS & PERFORMANCE: 3-Month Total Return	6-Month Total Return	1-Year Total Return	3-Year Total Return	5-Year Total Return	ASSETS: NAV	Total Assets (MIL)	NEW INVESTORS: Telephone	Open to New Investors
VY® Columbia Small Cap Value II Portfolio Class I	ICISX	B+	A-	B	Up	3.43	9.59	11.20	33.09	100.96	20.2	219.1	800-366-0066	Y
VY® Columbia Small Cap Value II Portfolio Class R6	VYRDX	B+	A-	B	Up	3.48	9.59	11.20	33.07	100.93	20.21	219.1	800-366-0066	Y
VY® Columbia Small Cap Value II Portfolio Class S	ICSSX	B+	A-	B	Up	3.39	9.41	10.91	32.04	98.44	20.1	219.1	800-366-0066	Y
VY® Columbia Small Cap Value II Portfolio Class S2	ICVPX	B+	B+	B	Up	3.38	9.34	10.77	31.54	97.06	19.52	219.1	800-366-0066	Y
VY® JPMorgan Small Cap Core Equity Portfolio Class A	IJSAX	B+	A-	B	Up	3.65	9.11	15.17	32.80	103.94	20.12	774.4	800-366-0066	Y
VY® JPMorgan Small Cap Core Equity Portfolio Class I	IJSIX	B+	A-	B	Up	3.84	9.48	15.85	35.20	110.23	21.35	774.4	800-366-0066	Y
VY® JPMorgan Small Cap Core Equity Portfolio Class R6	VPRSX	B+	A-	B	Up	3.84	9.49	15.86	34.71	108.40	21.34	774.4	800-366-0066	Y
VY® JPMorgan Small Cap Core Equity Portfolio Class S	IJSSX	B+	A-	B	Up	3.74	9.28	15.55	34.15	107.54	21.07	774.4	800-366-0066	Y
VY® JPMorgan Small Cap Core Equity Portfolio Class S2	IJSTX	B+	A-	B	Up	3.73	9.26	15.42	33.58	106.05	20.85	774.4	800-366-0066	Y
Waddell & Reed Advisor Small Cap Fund Class A	UNSAX	B+	B+	B	Up	5.44	9.33	23.74	36.86	104.94	16.51	941.6	888-923-3355	Y
Waddell & Reed Advisor Small Cap Fund Class B	WRSBX	B	B+	B	Up	5.07	8.65	22.20	32.15	93.65	11.05	941.6	888-923-3355	
Waddell & Reed Advisor Small Cap Fund Class C	WSCCX	B	B+	B	Up	5.13	8.82	22.57	33.31	96.31	12.18	941.6	888-923-3355	Y
Waddell & Reed Advisor Small Cap Fund Class Y	WRSYX	B+	B+	B	Up	5.48	9.47	24.06	38.24	108.70	19.17	941.6	888-923-3355	Y
Walden Small Cap Fund	WASOX	B	B+	B	Up	5.28	7.98	11.49	31.74	76.62	19.41	95.4	617-814-1215	
Walden SMID Cap Fund	WASMX	B	B	B		7.85	9.16	16.94	35.66	87.92	16.69	45.9	617-814-1215	Y
Walthausen Select Value Fund Class Retail	WSVRX	B-	B-	B-	Up	4.52	8.56	17.12	22.40	82.65	18.42	85.4	888-925-8428	Y
Walthausen Select Value Fund Institutional Class	WSVIX	B-	B-	B-	Up	4.62	8.80	17.50	23.36	84.94	18.64	85.4	888-925-8428	Y
Walthausen Select Value Fund R6 Class	WRSIX	B-	B-	B-	Up	4.63	8.79	17.54	23.40	85.00	18.7	85.4	888-925-8428	Y
Walthausen Small Cap Value Fund	WSCVX	B	B+	C+	Up	1.56	8.07	10.58	25.72	81.06	23.63	659.4	888-925-8428	
Wasatch Core Growth Fund	WGROX	A-	A-	B+	Up	7.66	13.77	24.29	42.15	99.76	68.35	1,709	800-551-1700	Y
Wasatch Core Growth Fund Institutional Class Shares	WIGRX	A-	A-	B+	Up	7.71	13.87	24.47	42.66	100.75	68.78	1,709	800-551-1700	Y
Wasatch Micro Cap Fund	WMICX	B+	A	B	Up	6.96	16.44	36.05	45.38	113.64	7.64	329.2	800-551-1700	Y
Wasatch Micro Cap Value Fund	WAMVX	A-	A	B	Up	6.42	14.66	26.40	52.31	119.84	3.43	234.3	800-551-1700	Y
Wasatch Small Cap Growth Fund® Institutional Class	WIAEX	B	B	B	Up	5.95	10.93	21.95	27.10	74.15	43.56	1,724	800-551-1700	
Wasatch Small Cap Growth Fund® Investor Class	WAAEX	B	B	B	Up	5.91	10.83	21.73	26.60	73.47	43.36	1,724	800-551-1700	
Wasatch Small Cap Value Fund	WMCVX	B+	A-	B	Up	6.75	13.16	19.55	42.32	115.83	7.95	390.8	800-551-1700	Y
Wasatch Small Cap Value Fund Institutional Class Shares	WICVX	B+	A-	B	Up	6.89	13.42	19.80	43.06	116.57	7.99	390.8	800-551-1700	Y
Wasatch Ultra Growth Fund	WAMCX	B+	A	B	Up	5.19	12.08	31.55	47.26	108.43	20.51	116.5	800-551-1700	Y
Wells Fargo Emerging Growth Fund - Class A	WEMAX	B	A-	B-	Up	3.77	9.37	25.68	29.86	94.83	14.61	760.1	800-222-8222	
Wells Fargo Emerging Growth Fund - Class Admin	WFGDX	B	A-	B-	Up	3.73	9.40	25.91	30.43	96.42	15.03	760.1	800-222-8222	
Wells Fargo Emerging Growth Fund - Class C	WEMCX	B	A-	C+	Up	3.52	8.98	24.79	26.98	87.73	13.07	760.1	800-222-8222	
Wells Fargo Emerging Growth Fund - Class Inst	WEMIX	B	A-	B-	Up	3.84	9.57	26.27	31.62	99.27	15.66	760.1	800-222-8222	
Wells Fargo Intrinsic Small Cap Value Fund - Class A	WFSMX	B	B	B	Up	3.51	9.03	9.80	26.29	86.82	31.25	82.2	800-222-8222	Y
Wells Fargo Intrinsic Small Cap Value Fund - Class Admin	WFSDX	B	B	B	Up	3.57	9.11	9.94	26.88	88.58	31.84	82.2	800-222-8222	Y
Wells Fargo Intrinsic Small Cap Value Fund - Class C	WSCDX	B	B	B-	Up	3.33	8.60	8.96	23.45	79.88	29.16	82.2	800-222-8222	Y
Wells Fargo Intrinsic Small Cap Value Fund - Class Inst	WFSSX	B	B	B	Up	3.63	9.22	10.15	27.62	90.47	32.21	82.2	800-222-8222	Y
Wells Fargo Small Cap Core Fund Administrator Class	WNSCX	B	B	B	Up	0.74	4.16	5.07	22.55	91.02	21.53	76.4	800-222-8222	Y
Wells Fargo Small Cap Core Fund Class A	WOSCX	B	B	B	Up	0.70	4.11	4.98	22.38	90.76	21.5	76.4	800-222-8222	Y
Wells Fargo Small Cap Core Fund Class C	WCSCX	B	B	B	Up	0.51	3.75	4.21	19.72	83.84	21.26	76.4	800-222-8222	Y
Wells Fargo Small Cap Core Fund Class R6	WRSCX	B	B	B	Up	0.83	4.33	5.45	23.27	92.14	21.65	76.4	800-222-8222	Y
Wells Fargo Small Cap Core Fund Institutional Class	WYSCX	B	B	B	Up	0.79	4.29	5.36	23.10	91.87	21.62	76.4	800-222-8222	Y
Wells Fargo Small Cap Opportunities Fund - Class Admin	NVSOX	B	B	B+	Up	3.98	7.47	14.84	34.30	101.75	22.94	302.6	800-222-8222	Y
Wells Fargo Small Cap Opportunities Fund - Class Inst	WSCOX	B	B	B+	Up	4.08	7.61	15.17	35.39	103.44	23.01	302.6	800-222-8222	Y
Wells Fargo Small Cap Opportunities Fund Class R6	WSCJX	B	B	B+	Up	4.09	7.65	15.27	34.85	102.58	23.03	302.6	800-222-8222	Y
Wells Fargo Small Cap Value Fund - Class A	SMVAX	B	A-	C+	Up	3.06	7.97	13.85	34.13	63.63	17.43	609.6	800-222-8222	Y
Wells Fargo Small Cap Value Fund - Class Admin	SMVDX	B	A-	C+	Up	3.07	8.06	14.04	34.92	65.22	18.69	609.6	800-222-8222	Y
Wells Fargo Small Cap Value Fund - Class C	SMVCX	B	B+	C+	Up	2.89	7.61	13.01	31.13	57.58	11.82	609.6	800-222-8222	Y
Wells Fargo Small Cap Value Fund - Class Inst	WFSVX	B	A-	C+	Up	3.15	8.22	14.28	35.73	66.91	18.84	609.6	800-222-8222	Y
Wells Fargo Small Cap Value Fund - Class R6	SMVRX	B	A	C+	Up	3.10	8.21	14.32	35.90	66.91	18.87	609.6	800-222-8222	Y
Wells Fargo Small Company Growth Fund - Class A	WFSAX	B	B	B-	Up	4.96	10.05	20.17	22.28	96.88	50.15	1,820	800-222-8222	Y
Wells Fargo Small Company Growth Fund - Class Admin	NVSCX	B	B	B-	Up	5.00	10.13	20.31	22.86	98.68	52.06	1,820	800-222-8222	Y
Wells Fargo Small Company Growth Fund - Class C	WSMCX	B-	B-	B-	Up	4.77	9.63	19.27	19.57	89.63	44.73	1,820	800-222-8222	Y

Category: US Equity Small Cap (con't)

Fund Name	Ticker Symbol	Overall Rating	Reward Rating	Risk Rating	Recent Up/ Downgrade	3-Month Total Return	6-Month Total Return	1-Year Total Return	3-Year Total Return	5-Year Total Return	NAV	Total Assets (MIL)	Telephone	Open to New Investors
		RATINGS				TOTAL RETURNS & PERFORMANCE					ASSETS		NEW INVESTORS	
Wells Fargo Small Company Growth Fund - Class Inst	WSCGX	B	B	B-	Up	5.05	10.25	20.60	23.71	101.10	53.2	1,820	800-222-8222	Y
Wells Fargo Small Company Growth Fund - Class R6	WSCRX	B	B	B-	Up	5.06	10.28	20.67	23.90	100.45	53.28	1,820	800-222-8222	Y
Wells Fargo Small Company Value Fund - Class A	SCVAX	B+	A-	B	Up	5.45	10.27	11.57	30.88	90.00	27.21	141.5	800-222-8222	Y
Wells Fargo Small Company Value Fund - Class Admin	SCVIX	B+	A-	B	Up	5.50	10.34	11.76	31.54	91.74	27.79	141.5	800-222-8222	Y
Wells Fargo Small Company Value Fund - Class C	SCVFX	B	B+	B	Up	5.25	9.84	10.79	27.94	82.93	24.22	141.5	800-222-8222	Y
Wells Fargo Small Company Value Fund - Class Inst	SCVNX	B+	A-	B	Up	5.56	10.45	11.99	32.30	93.57	27.93	141.5	800-222-8222	Y
Wells Fargo Small Company Value Fund Class R6	SCVJX	B+	A-	B	Up	5.57	10.50	12.09	31.99	92.40	27.95	141.5	800-222-8222	Y
Wells Fargo Special Small Cap Value Fund - Class A	ESPAX	B+	A-	B	Up	5.23	9.56	11.05	35.46	106.17	34.86	2,220	800-222-8222	Y
Wells Fargo Special Small Cap Value Fund - Class Admin	ESPIX	B+	A-	B	Up	5.24	9.59	11.15	36.07	108.05	35.66	2,220	800-222-8222	Y
Wells Fargo Special Small Cap Value Fund - Class C	ESPCX	B	B+	B	Up	5.04	9.15	10.23	32.45	98.55	31.67	2,220	800-222-8222	Y
Wells Fargo Special Small Cap Value Fund - Class Inst	ESPNX	B+	A-	B	Up	5.32	9.76	11.45	37.05	110.19	35.69	2,220	800-222-8222	Y
Wells Fargo Special Small Cap Value Fund - Class R	ESPHX	B+	A-	B	Up	5.14	9.39	10.76	34.55	103.78	35.41	2,220	800-222-8222	Y
Wells Fargo Special Small Cap Value Fund - Class R6	ESPRX	B+	A-	B	Up	5.35	9.77	11.52	37.23	109.01	35.67	2,220	800-222-8222	Y
Wells Fargo Traditional Small Cap Growth Fund - Class A	EGWAX	B-	B	C	Up	2.46	8.92	21.70	22.27	83.65	15.07	95.7	800-222-8222	Y
Wells Fargo Traditional Small Cap Growth Fund - Cls Admin	EGWDX	B-	B	C	Down	2.56	9.01	21.87	23.00	85.35	16.86	95.7	800-222-8222	Y
Wells Fargo Traditional Small Cap Growth Fund - Class C	EGWCX	B-	B	C	Up	2.26	8.51	20.77	19.54	76.91	13.74	95.7	800-222-8222	Y
Wells Fargo Traditional Small Cap Growth Fund - Class Inst	EGRYX	B	B	C	Up	2.56	9.07	22.06	23.52	86.75	17.23	95.7	800-222-8222	Y
WesMark Small Company Growth Fund	WMKSX	B	B-	B	Up	3.61	9.88	13.18	21.79	80.32	13.9	106.9	800-861-1013	Y
Westcore Micro-Cap Opportunity Fund Retail Class	WTMIX	B	B+	B	Up	1.10	5.58	5.69	25.02	91.30	17.24	14.4	800-392-2673	Y
Westcore Small-Cap Growth Fund Institutional Class	WISGX	B	A-	C	Up	2.42	8.67	25.93	31.66		12.88	5.8	800-392-2673	Y
Westcore Small-Cap Growth Fund Retail Class	WTSGX	B	A-	C	Up	2.38	8.70	25.97	30.64		12.72	5.8	800-392-2673	Y
Westcore Small-Cap Value Dividend Fund Institutional Class	WISVX	B-	C+	B	Up	0.08	0.82	-1.67	16.57	74.23	10.7	202.0	800-392-2673	
Westcore Small-Cap Value Dividend Fund Retail Class	WTSVX	B-	C+	B	Up	0.07	0.73	-1.84	15.94	72.71	10.68	202.0	800-392-2673	
Westwood SmallCap Fund Institutional Class	WHGSX	B+	A-	B	Up	3.39	9.63	12.36	34.28	118.76	17.29	245.7		Y
William Blair Small Cap Growth Fund Class I	WBSIX	B	A-	C	Down	4.89	9.90	26.98	44.44	133.57	29.61	493.1	800-621-0687	Y
William Blair Small Cap Growth Fund Class N	WBSNX	B	A-	C	Down	4.81	9.74	26.69	43.37	130.69	26.87	493.1	800-621-0687	Y
William Blair Small Cap Value Fund Class I	BVDIX	B+	B+	B	Up	1.83	8.37	7.84	27.73	90.85	20.7	714.9	800-621-0687	Y
William Blair Small Cap Value Fund Class N	WBVDX	B	B+	B	Up	1.77	8.21	7.57	26.76	88.41	20.15	714.9	800-621-0687	Y
William Blair Small-Mid Cap Value Fund Class I	WSMIX	B	B	B	Up	5.32	9.38	9.83	27.79	88.23	14.24	3.5	800-621-0687	Y
William Blair Small-Mid Cap Value Fund Class N	BSMNX	B	B	B	Up	5.31	9.28	9.58	26.82	85.90	14.31	3.5	800-621-0687	Y
Wilshire Small Company Growth Portfolio Fund Cls Inst	WSMGX	B+	A-	B+	Up	3.37	8.05	13.96	40.38	111.55	27.14	48.7	888-200-6796	Y
Wilshire Small Company Growth Port Inv Cls Shares	DTSGX	B+	A-	B+	Up	3.33	7.91	13.66	39.25	108.86	25.05	48.7	888-200-6796	Y
Wilshire Small Company Value Fund Class Institutional	WSMVX	B+	A-	B	Up	3.72	9.69	8.97	30.58	105.61	23.49	42.6	888-200-6796	Y
Wilshire Small Company Value Port Inv Cls Shares	DTSVX	B+	A-	B	Up	3.62	9.52	8.64	29.49	102.78	22.99	42.6	888-200-6796	Y
Zacks Small-Cap Core Fund Institutional Class	ZSCIX	A-	A	B+	Up	0.15	9.76	14.38	37.11	108.91	28.2	178.3		Y
Zacks Small-Cap Core Fund Investor Class	ZSCCX	A-	A	B	Up	0.12	9.64	14.15	35.99	106.79	27.87	178.3		Y

Category: US Fixed Income

Fund Name	Ticker Symbol	Overall Rating	Reward Rating	Risk Rating	Recent Up/ Downgrade	3-Month Total Return	6-Month Total Return	1-Year Total Return	3-Year Total Return	5-Year Total Return	NAV	Total Assets (MIL)	Telephone	Open to New Investors
		RATINGS				TOTAL RETURNS & PERFORMANCE					ASSETS		NEW INVESTORS	
Ave Maria Bond Fund	AVEFX	B	C	A+		1.05	2.32	4.16	9.46	19.25	11.42	302.1	888-726-9331	Y
Cohen & Steers Limited Dur Preferred & Income Fund, Inc	LDP	B	B-	A+	Up	1.57	3.79	14.85	31.89	56.20	27.16	787.1	212-832-3232	Y
Cohen & Steers Preferred Sec & Income Fund, Inc. Cls A	CPXAX	B	C+	A+	Up	0.97	2.66	11.04	22.42	40.12	14.14	7,962	212-832-3232	Y
Cohen & Steers Preferred Sec & Income Fund, Inc. Cls C	CPXCX	B	C+	A+	Up	0.81	2.34	10.30	20.00	35.66	14.06	7,962	212-832-3232	Y
Cohen & Steers Preferred Sec & Income Fund, Inc. Cls F	CPXFX	B	C+	A+	Up	0.99	2.77	11.31	23.54	42.48	14.16	7,962	212-832-3232	Y
Cohen & Steers Preferred Sec & Income Fund, Inc. Cls I	CPXIX	B	C+	A+	Up	1.05	2.82	11.36	23.59	42.54	14.17	7,962	212-832-3232	Y
Cohen & Steers Preferred Sec & Income Fund, Inc. Cls R	CPRRX	B	C+	A+	Up	0.93	2.58	10.85	21.83	39.02	14.15	7,962	212-832-3232	Y
Cohen & Steers Preferred Sec & Income Fund, Inc. Cls Z	CPXZX	B	C+	A+	Up	1.06	2.84	11.41	23.66	42.52	14.16	7,962	212-832-3232	Y

Category: US Fixed Income (con't)

		RATINGS				TOTAL RETURNS & PERFORMANCE					ASSETS		NEW INVESTORS	
Fund Name	Ticker Symbol	Overall Rating	Reward Rating	Risk Rating	Recent Up/ Downgrade	3-Month Total Return	6-Month Total Return	1-Year Total Return	3-Year Total Return	5-Year Total Return	NAV	Total Assets (MIL)	Telephone	Open to New Investors
Cohen & Steers Select Preferred and Income Fund	PSF	B	B-	A+	Up	1.71	3.87	15.91	31.61	57.75	27.79	335.1	212-832-3232	Y
Destra Flaherty & Crumrine Preferred & Income Fund Cls A	DPIAX	B	C+	A+	Up	0.73	2.04	11.56	23.72	39.19	18.53	270.2	877-855-3434	Y
Destra Flaherty & Crumrine Preferred & Income Fund Cls C	DPICX	B	C+	A+	Up	0.55	1.66	10.76	20.96	34.16	18.61	270.2	877-855-3434	Y
Destra Flaherty & Crumrine Preferred & Income Fund Cls I	DPIIX	B	C+	A+	Up	0.80	2.18	11.87	24.95	41.61	18.47	270.2	877-855-3434	Y
First Trust Intermediate Duration Preferred & Income Fund	FPF	B	B-	A+	Up	1.52	4.10	15.89	32.64		24.88	1,523	800-621-1675	Y
First Trust Preferred Securities and Income Fund Class A	FPEAX	B	C+	A+		1.37	3.15	11.16	23.67	31.18	22.28	254.2	800-621-1675	Y
First Trust Preferred Securities and Income Fund Class C	FPECX	B	C+	A+		1.23	2.85	10.41	21.05	26.48	22.34	254.2	800-621-1675	Y
First Trust Preferred Securities and Income Fund Class F	FPEFX	B	C+	A		1.43	3.35	11.40	24.25	31.94	22.52	254.2	800-621-1675	Y
First Trust Preferred Securities and Income Fund Class I	FPEIX	B	C+	A+		1.47	3.35	11.53	24.71	33.05	22.39	254.2	800-621-1675	Y
First Trust Preferred Securities and Income Fund Class R3	FPERX	B	C+	A+		1.27	2.98	10.80	22.60	29.41	22.24	254.2	800-621-1675	Y
Flaherty & Crumrine Dynamic Preferred and Income Fund	DFP	B	B-	A+	Up	0.96	2.61	16.74	33.95		26.27	503.7	626-795-7300	Y
Flaherty & Crumrine Preferred Income Fund	PFD	B	B-	A	Up	1.01	2.65	16.19	30.89	58.77	14.33	160.1	626-795-7300	Y
Flaherty & Crumrine Preferred Income Opportunity Fund	PFO	B	B-	A	Up	1.06	2.68	16.20	30.92	58.78	11.93	149.4	626-795-7300	Y
Flaherty & Crumrine Preferred Securities Income Fund	FFC	B	B-	A	Up	1.16	2.89	17.18	32.10	62.68	20.33	899.7	626-795-7300	Y
Flaherty & CrumrineTotal Return Fund	FLC	B	B-	A	Up	1.14	2.85	16.74	30.89	59.56	21.66	216.0	626-795-7300	Y
John Hancock Preferred Income Fund	HPI	B	C+	A	Up	1.27	1.80	11.04	24.83	45.90	21.52	558.0	800-225-5913	Y
John Hancock Preferred Income Fund II	HPF	B	C+	A	Up	1.19	1.87	11.23	23.83	45.40	21.27	451.1	800-225-5913	Y
John Hancock Preferred Income Fund III	HPS	B	C+	A	Up	1.05	1.74	11.25	24.51	47.86	18.95	597.4	800-225-5913	Y
John Hancock Premium Dividend Fund	PDT	B	B-	A	Up	1.12	2.41	11.94	28.06	66.59	15.23	779.0	800-225-5913	Y
Nuveen Preferred & Income Opportunities Fund	JPC	B	C+	A+	Up	1.35	3.02	13.35	29.04	52.18	10.75	1,112	312-917-8146	Y
Nuveen Preferred & Income Securities Fund	JPS	B	B-	A+	Up	1.91	4.17	17.26	31.23	56.22	10.36	2,114	312-917-8146	Y
Nuveen Preferred & Income Term Fund	JPI	B	B-	A+	Up	1.81	3.90	15.48	31.77	57.78	25.95	590.1	312-917-8146	Y
Nuveen Preferred Securities & Income Fund Class A	NPSAX	B	C+	A+	Up	1.06	2.69	10.89	21.49	38.21	17.68	3,997	312-917-8146	Y
Nuveen Preferred Securities & Income Fund Class C	NPSCX	B	C+	A+	Up	0.93	2.31	10.07	18.85	33.25	17.7	3,997	312-917-8146	Y
Nuveen Preferred Securities & Income Fund Class I	NPSRX	B	C+	A+	Up	1.17	2.87	11.21	22.50	40.04	17.7	3,997	312-917-8146	Y
Nuveen Preferred Securities & Income Fund Class R3	NPSTX	B	C+	A+	Up	1.06	2.57	10.64	20.63	36.56	17.81	3,997	312-917-8146	Y
Nuveen Preferred Securities & Income Fund Class R6	NPSFX	B	C+	A-	Up	0.73	2.41	10.71	22.03	39.49	17.71	3,997	312-917-8146	Y
PIMCO Capital Securities and Financials Fund Class A	PFANX	B-	C+	B+	Up	1.81	4.81	12.93			10.51	160.0	866-746-2602	Y
PIMCO Capital Securities and Financials Fund Class C	PFCNX	B-	C	B	Up	1.57	4.40	12.04			10.45	160.0	866-746-2602	Y
PIMCO Capital Securities and Financials Fund Class D	PFDNX	B-	C+	B+	Up	1.81	4.82	12.96			10.49	160.0	866-746-2602	Y
PIMCO Capital Securities and Financials Fund Class P	PFPNX	B-	C+	A-	Up	1.75	4.88	13.19			10.51	160.0	866-746-2602	Y
PIMCO Capital Securities & Financials Fund Inst Cls	PFINX	B-	C+	B+	Up	1.86	4.98	13.27			10.52	160.0	866-746-2602	Y
Principal Capital Securities Fund Class S	PCSFX	B	C+	A-	Up	1.23	2.81	11.56	22.37		10.38	496.7	800-222-5852	Y
Principal Global Invs Funds Preferred Sec Fund Cls T	PPBTX	B	C+	A+	Up	0.88	2.22	10.23	19.38	35.03	10.39	6,014	800-222-5852	Y
Principal Global Invs Funds Preferred Securities Fund R-6	PPREX	B	C+	A+	Up	0.98	2.39	10.52	20.30	36.74	10.39	6,014	800-222-5852	Y
Principal Preferred Securities Fund Class A	PPSAX	B	C+	A+	Up	0.78	2.20	10.22	19.18	34.65	10.46	6,014	800-222-5852	Y
Principal Preferred Securities Fund Class C	PRFCX	B	C+	A+	Up	0.69	1.81	9.40	16.56	29.77	10.45	6,014	800-222-5852	Y
Principal Preferred Securities Fund Class J	PPSJX	B	C+	A+	Up	0.83	2.20	10.26	19.32	34.36	10.19	6,014	800-222-5852	Y
Principal Preferred Securities Fund Institutional Class	PPSIX	B	C+	A+	Up	0.86	2.34	10.50	20.27	36.71	10.39	6,014	800-222-5852	Y
Principal Preferred Securities Fund R-1 Class	PUSAX	B	C+	A+	Up	0.66	1.94	9.66	17.36	31.26	10.34	6,014	800-222-5852	Y
Principal Preferred Securities Fund R-2 Class	PPRSX	B	C+	A+	Up	0.70	2.03	9.77	17.82	32.11	10.28	6,014	800-222-5852	Y
Principal Preferred Securities Fund R-3 Class	PNARX	B	C+	A+	Up	0.74	2.11	9.91	18.48	33.37	10.32	6,014	800-222-5852	Y
Principal Preferred Securities Fund R-4 Class	PQARX	B	C+	A+	Up	0.79	2.20	10.14	19.08	34.58	10.3	6,014	800-222-5852	Y
Principal Preferred Securities Fund R-5 Class	PPARX	B	C+	A+	Up	0.92	2.27	10.34	19.66	35.50	10.35	6,014	800-222-5852	Y
Salient Select Income Fund Class A	KIFAX	B-	C	B+	Down	-1.04	-0.44	1.45	13.56	39.14	22.18	888.5	866-667-9228	Y
Salient Select Income Fund Class C	KIFCX	B-	C	B	Down	-1.21	-0.72	0.86	11.68	35.34	21.55	888.5	866-667-9228	Y
Salient Select Income Fund Institutional Class	KIFYX	B-	C	B+	Down	-0.94	-0.23	1.84	14.96	42.05	22.13	888.5	866-667-9228	Y
Salient Select Income Fund Investor Class	FFSLX	B-	C	B+	Down	-1.04	-0.41	1.44	13.68	39.49	22.1	888.5	866-667-9228	Y

Category: Utilities Sector Equity

Fund Name	Ticker Symbol	RATINGS				TOTAL RETURNS & PERFORMANCE					ASSETS		NEW INVESTORS	
		Overall Rating	Reward Rating	Risk Rating	Recent Up/ Downgrade	3-Month Total Return	6-Month Total Return	1-Year Total Return	3-Year Total Return	5-Year Total Return	NAV	Total Assets (MIL)	Telephone	Open to New Investors
American Century Utilities Fund Investor Class	BULIX	B-	C+	B		-1.18	0.36	0.62	14.40	67.39	17.19	519.0	800-444-4015	Y
DNP Select Income Fund	DNP	B-	B	C+	Down	0.19	3.71	10.91	19.60	81.52	9.7175	2,902	212-871-2549	Y
Fidelity Advisor® Utilities Fund Class A	FUGAX	B-	B	C+	Down	0.56	5.42	17.30	16.71	74.99	29.04	326.0	617-563-7000	Y
Fidelity Advisor® Utilities Fund Class C	FUGCX	B-	B	C+	Down	0.38	5.02	16.45	14.10	68.59	28.49	326.0	617-563-7000	Y
Fidelity Advisor® Utilities Fund Class M	FAUFX	B-	B	C+	Down	0.49	5.24	16.94	15.66	72.44	29.12	326.0	617-563-7000	Y
Fidelity Advisor® Utilities Fund I Class	FUGIX	B-	B	C+	Down	0.64	5.55	17.64	17.73	77.55	29.61	326.0	617-563-7000	Y
Fidelity® Select Utilities Portfolio	FSUTX	B-	B	C+	Down	0.75	5.64	17.95	17.95	78.27	79.77	820.7	617-563-7000	Y
Fidelity® Telecom and Utilities Fund	FIUIX	B-	B-	C+	Down	1.75	6.25	11.98	22.33	71.22	26.13	1,009	617-563-7000	Y
Franklin Utilities Advisor Class	FRUAX	B	B-	B		-0.13	2.52	10.76	19.30	75.26	18.84	6,788	650-312-2000	Y
Franklin Utilities Class A	FKUTX	B	B-	B		-0.11	2.46	10.56	18.78	73.95	18.7	6,788	650-312-2000	Y
Franklin Utilities Class C	FRUSX	B-	B-	B	Down	-0.29	2.17	10.02	16.98	69.67	18.6	6,788	650-312-2000	Y
Franklin Utilities Class R	FRURX	B-	B-	B	Down	-0.20	2.30	10.22	17.54	70.91	18.63	6,788	650-312-2000	Y
Franklin Utilities Fund Class R6	FUFRX	B	B-	B		-0.05	2.63	10.87	19.69	76.07	18.84	6,788	650-312-2000	Y
Gabelli Global Utility & Income Trust	GLU	B-	C+	B	Up	3.52	7.08	19.59	20.23	46.94	22.43	93.7	914-921-5135	Y
Gabelli Utilities Fund Class A	GAUAX	B-	C+	B-	Down	0.61	3.25	8.78	15.39	54.80	9.37	2,327	914-921-5135	Y
Gabelli Utilities Fund Class AAA	GABUX	B-	C+	B-	Down	0.73	3.41	8.92	15.61	54.97	9.23	2,327	914-921-5135	Y
Gabelli Utilities Fund Class Institutional	GAUIX	B-	B-	B-	Down	0.80	3.48	9.11	16.38	56.74	9.65	2,327	914-921-5135	Y
Gabelli Utilities Fund T	GAUTX	B-	C+	B-		0.62	3.30	8.81	15.49	54.81	9.22	2,327	914-921-5135	Y
Gabelli Utility Trust	GUT	B	B-	B	Up	1.23	3.84	9.27	18.47	68.01	5.34	247.0	914-921-5135	Y
ICON Utilities Fund Class A	ICTVX	B-	C+	B	Down	-1.44	0.52	6.86	19.66	73.14	8.53	42.9	303-790-1600	Y
ICON Utilities Fund Class S	ICTUX	B-	B-	B	Down	-1.41	0.68	7.07	20.52	75.26	8.68	42.9	303-790-1600	Y
JNL/Mellon Capital Utilities Sector Fund Class A	US46648L3511	B	B	B		0.38	3.29	11.61	21.08		13.18	86.9		Y
JNL/Mellon Capital Utilities Sector Fund Class I	US46648L3446	B	B	B		0.53	3.44	11.78	21.26		13.2	86.9		Y
Rydex Utilities Fund Class A	RYUTX	B-	B-	B	Down	0.24	3.21	11.04	17.64	69.36	37.2	50.6	800-820-0888	Y
Rydex Utilities Fund Class C	RYCUX	B-	B-	B-	Down	0.06	2.85	10.24	15.07	63.15	31.48	50.6	800-820-0888	Y
Rydex Utilities Fund Class H	RYAUX	B-	B-	B	Down	0.27	3.25	11.12	17.60	68.37	35.84	50.6	800-820-0888	Y
Rydex Utilities Fund Class Investor	RYUIX	B	B	B	Down	0.31	3.37	11.36	18.52	71.50	40.34	50.6	800-820-0888	Y
Vanguard Utilities Index Fund Admiral Shares	VUIAX	B	B	B		0.60	3.67	12.49	23.54	86.17	58.48	3,728	877-662-7447	Y
Wells Fargo Utility and Telecommunications Fund - Class A	EVUAX	B	B	B		0.75	4.12	13.65	15.98	63.84	21.16	411.5	800-222-8222	Y
Wells Fargo Utility & Telecommunications Fund - Cls Admin	EVUDX	B	B	B		0.76	4.23	13.86	16.60	65.42	21.18	411.5	800-222-8222	Y
Wells Fargo Utility and Telecommunications Fund - Class C	EVUCX	B-	B-	B	Down	0.52	3.73	12.77	13.37	57.84	21.17	411.5	800-222-8222	Y
Wells Fargo Utility & Telecommunications Fund - Cls Inst	EVUYX	B	B	B		0.81	4.33	14.07	17.26	66.66	21.15	411.5	800-222-8222	Y

Appendix:

Glossary

This section contains an explanation of the fields of data used throughout this guide.

1-Year Total Return
The rate of return on an investment over one year that includes interest, capital gains, dividends and distributions realized.

3-Year Total Return
The rate of return on an investment over three years that includes interest, capital gains, dividends and distributions realized.

3-Month Total Return
The rate of return on an investment over three months that includes interest, capital gains, dividends and distributions realized.

3-Year Beta
A three year measure of volatility, or systematic risk, of a security in comparison to the market as a whole. A beta of less than 1 means that the security will be less volatile than the market, a beta larger than 1 means more volatility. Beta value cannot be calculated if less than 24 months of pricing is available.

3-Year Standard Deviation
A statistical measurement of dispersion about an average, which depicts how widely the returns varied over the past three years. Investors use the standard deviation of historical performance to try to predict the range of returns that are most likely for a given fund. When a fund has a high standard deviation, the predicted range of performance is wide, implying greater volatility. Standard deviation is most appropriate for measuring risk if it is for a fund that is an investor's only holding. The figure cannot be combined for more than one fund because the standard deviation for a portfolio of multiple funds is a function of not only the individual standard deviations, but also of the degree of correlation among the funds' returns. If a fund's returns follow a normal distribution, then approximately 68 percent of the time they will fall within one standard deviation of the mean return for the fund, and 95 percent of the time within two standard deviations.

5-Year Total Return
The rate of return on an investment over five years that includes interest, capital gains, dividends and distributions realized.

6-Month Total Return
The rate of return on an investment over six months that includes interest, capital gains, dividends and distributions realized.

Address
The company's street address.

Asset & Performance History
Indicates the fund's **NAV (Net Asset Value)** and **1-Year Total Return** for the previous 6 years.

Asset Allocation
Indicates the percentage of assets in each category. Used as an investment strategy that attempts to balance risk versus reward by adjusting the percentage of each asset in an investment portfolio according to the investor's risk tolerance, goals and investment time frame. Allocation percentages may not add up to 100%. Negative values reflect short positions. See Cash, Stocks, US Stocks, Bonds, US Bonds, Other)

Back End Fee (%)
A fee that investors pay when withdrawing money from an investment within a specified number of years, usually five to 10 years. The back-end load is designed to discourage withdrawals and typically declines for each year that a shareholder remains in a fund. The fee is a percentage of the value of the share being sold. Fees are displayed as a percent.

Bear Market
A financial market condition in which the prices of securities are falling, investors anticipate losses, and selling of securities increases.

Bonds (%)
The percentage of the fund's assets invested in bonds. A bond is an unsecured debt security issued by companies, municipalities, states and sovereign governments to raise funds. When a company issues a bond it borrows money from the bondholder to boost the business, in exchange the bondholder receives the principal amount back plus the interest on the determined maturity date.

Bull Market
A financial market condition in which prices are rising or are expected to rise. Bull markets are characterized by optimism, investor confidence and expectations that strong results will continue.

BUY-HOLD-SELL Indicator
Funds that are rated in the A or B range are, in our opinion, a potential BUY. Funds in the C range will indicate a HOLD status. Funds in the D or E range will indicate a SELL status.

Cash (%)
The percentage of the fund's assets invested in short-term obligations, usually less than 90 days, that provide a return in the form of interest payments. This type of investment generally offers a low return compared to other investments but has a low risk level.

Category
Identifies funds according to their actual investment styles as measured by their portfolio holdings. This categorization allows investors to spread their money around in a mix of funds with a variety of risk and return characteristics.

Class A
This class of Mutual Fund typically has a front-end sales load and a loaded fee structure. Although the fees for Class A may typically be lower, because they normally charge front end fees, your initial amount invested will be lower and your overall return will be affected. An annual asset based fee may well be levied, although this is typically lower than other classes.

Class B
This class of shares, instead of a front-end or back-end sales load normally charges fees called a contingent deferred sales charge (CDSC). This fee is paid if you sell the shares within a certain period of time and may well decline after each year. An annual asset based fee is likely to be levied. Often a Class B share will convert to Class A within a couple of years of reaching the end of the CDSC expiry at which point Class A fees will be initiated.

Class C
A C-share is a class of mutual fund with a level load. They typically don't have front-end loads, but do sometimes have back-end loads. They are usually around 1% but are sometimes eliminated after the shares are held for over a year. Annual asset based fees are normal for this class of share.

Class I
This class is sold to institutional shareholders. Also called Y-Shares, these have different fees and do not charge traditional loads.

Class R
R share funds, Also known as K shares, are for retirement accounts, and the R share class mutual funds are only available through employer-sponsored retirement plans. R share mutual funds do not have any loads, but they do have annual asset based fees typically of around 0.25% to 0.50%.

Closed End Fund
They are launched through an Initial Public Offering in order to raise money and then trade in the open market just like a stock or an ETF. They only issue a set amount of shares and, although their value is also based on the Net Asset Value (NAV), the actual price of the fund is affected by supply and demand, allowing it to trade at prices above or below its real value.

Dividend Yield (TTM)
Trailing twelve months dividends paid out relative to the share price. Expressed as a percentage and measures how much cash flow an investor is getting for each invested dollar. **Trailing Twelve Months** (TTM) is a representation of a fund's financial performance over the most recent 12 months. TTM uses the latest available financial data from a company's interim, quarterly or annual reports.

Expense Ratio
A measure of what it costs an investment company to operate a mutual fund. An expense ratio is determined through an annual calculation, where a fund's operating expenses are divided by the average dollar value of its assets under management. Operating expenses may include money spent on administration and management of the fund, advertising, etc. An expense ratio of 1 percent per annum means that each year 1 percent of the fund's total assets will be used to cover expenses.

Front End Fee (%)
A commission or sales charge applied at the time of the initial purchase of an investment. The fee percentage is generally based on the amount of the investment. Larger investments, both initial and cumulative, generally receive percentage discounts based on the dollar value invested. Fees are displayed as a percent.

Fund Name
Describes the fund's assets, regions of investments and investment strategies. Many funds have similar names, so you want to make sure the fund you look up is really the one you are interested in evaluating.

Fund Type
Describes the fund's assets, regions of investments and investment strategies. (See **Open End Fund, Closed End Fund.**)

Inception Date
The date on which the fund began its operations. The commencement date indicates when a fund began investing in the market. Many investors prefer funds with longer operating histories. Funds with longer histories have longer track records and can thereby provide investors with a more long-standing picture of their performance.

Institutional Only
This indicates if the fund is offered to institutional clients only (pension funds, mutual funds, money managers, insurance companies, investment banks, commercial trusts, endowment funds, hedge funds, and some hedge fund investors). See **Services Offered**.

Investment Strategy
A set of rules, behaviors or procedures, designed to guide an investor's selection of an investment portfolio. Individuals have different profit objectives, and their individual skills make different tactics and strategies appropriate.

Last Bear Market Total Return
The fund's total return (the rate of return on an investment over a period of time that includes interest, capital gains, dividends and distributions realized) during the last market downturn. A **Bear Market** is a financial market condition in which the prices of securities are falling, investors anticipate losses, and selling of securities increases.

Last Bull Market Total Return
The fund's total return (the rate of return on an investment over a period of time that includes interest, capital gains, dividends and distributions realized) during the last market upswing. A **Bull Market** is a financial market condition in which prices are rising or are expected to rise. Bull markets are characterized by optimism, investor confidence and expectations that strong results will continue.

Manager/Tenure (Years)
The name of the manager and the number of years spent managing the fund.

Minimum Initial Investment
The smallest investment amount a fund will accept to establish a new account. This amount could be $0 or any other number set by the fund.

Minimum Subsequent Investment
The smallest additional investment amount a fund will accept in an existing account.

NAV (Net Asset Value)
A fund's price per share. The value is calculated by dividing the total value of all the securities in the portfolio, less any liabilities, by the number of fund shares outstanding.

Open End Fund
A type of mutual fund that does not have restrictions on the amount of shares the fund will issue. If demand is high enough, the fund will continue to issue shares no matter how many investors there are. Open-end funds also buy back shares when investors wish to sell.

Open to New Investments
Indicates whether the fund accepts investments from those who are not existing investors. A "Y" in this column identifies that the fund accepts new investors. No data in this column indicates that the fund is closed to new investors. The fund may be closed to new investors because the fund's asset base is getting too large to effectively execute its investing style. Although, the fund may be closed, in most cases, existing investors are able to add to their holdings.

Other (%)
The percentage of the fund's assets invested in other financial instruments. See **Asset Allocation**.

Overall Rating
The Weiss rating measured on a scale from A to E based on each fund's risk and performance. See the preceding section, "What Our Ratings Mean," for an explanation of each letter grade rating.

Performance Chart
A graphical representation of the fund's total returns over the past year.

Phone Exchange
This indicates that investors can move money between different funds within the same fund family over the phone. See **Services Offered**.

Phone Number
The company's phone number.

Prospectus Objective
Gives a general idea of a fund's overall investment approach and goals.

Provider
The legal company that issues the fund.

Ratings History
Indicates the fund's Overall, Risk and Reward Ratings for the previous three years. Ratings are listed as of December 31, 2017 (Q4-17), September 30, 2017 (Q3-17), June 30, 2017 (Q2-17), March 31, 2017 (Q1-17), December 31, 2016 (Q4-16), and December 31, 2015 (Q4-15). See **Overall Rating, Risk Rating, Reward Rating.**

Recent Upgrade/Downgrade
An "Up" or "Down" indicates that the Weiss Mutual Fund rating has changed since the publication of the last print edition. If a fund has had a rating change since September 30, 2017, the change is identified with an "Up" or "Down."

Reward Rating
This is based on the total return over a period of up to five years, including net asset value and price growth. The total return figure is stated net of the expenses and fees charged by the fund. Based on proprietary modeling the individual components of the risk and reward ratings are calculated and weighted and the final rating is generated.

Risk Rating
This is includes the risk ratings of component stocks where applicable and also includes the financial stability of the fund, turnover where applicable, together with the level of volatility as measured by the fund's daily returns over a period of up to five years. Funds with greater stability are considered less risky and receive a higher risk rating. Funds with greater volatility are considered riskier, and will receive a lower risk rating. In addition to considering the fund's volatility, the risk rating also considers an assessment of the valuation and quality of a fund's holdings.

Services Offered
Services offered by the fund provider. Such services can include:

Systematic Withdrawal Plan
A plan offered by mutual funds that pays specific amounts to shareholders at predetermined intervals.

Institutional Only
This indicates if the fund is offered to institutional clients only (pension funds, mutual funds, money managers, insurance companies, investment banks, commercial trusts, endowment funds, hedge funds, and some hedge fund investors).

Phone Exchange
This indicates that investors can move money between different funds within the same fund family over the phone.

Wire Redemption
This indicates whether or not investors can redeem electronically.

Qualified Investment
Under a qualified plan, an investor may invest in the variable annuity with pretax dollars through an employee pension plan, such as a 401(k) or 403(b). Money builds up on a tax-deferred basis, and when the qualified investor makes a withdrawal or annuitizes, all contributions received are taxable income.

Stocks (%)
The percentage of the fund's assets invested in stock. See **Asset Allocation**.

Sub-Category
A subdivision of funds, usually with common characteristics as the category.

Systematic Withdrawal Plan
A plan offered by mutual funds that pays specific amounts to shareholders at predetermined intervals. See **Services Offered**.

Ticker Symbol
An arrangement of characters (usually letters) representing a particular security listed on an exchange or otherwise traded publicly. When a company issues securities to the public marketplace, it selects an available ticker symbol for its securities which investors use to place trade orders. Every listed security has a unique ticker symbol, facilitating the vast array of trade orders that flow through the financial markets every day. If a ticker symbol is not assigned to a particular fund, the International Securities Identification Number (ISIN) is displayed.

Top Holdings
The highest amount of publicly traded assets held by a fund. These publicly traded assets may include company stock, mutual funds or other investment vehicles.

Total Returns (%)
See **3-Month Total Return, 6-Month Total Return, 1-Year Total Return, 3-Year Total Return, 5-Year Total Return.**

Traded On (Exchange)
The stock exchange on which the fund is listed. The core function of a stock exchange is to ensure fair and orderly trading, as well as efficient dissemination of price information. Exchanges such as: NYSE (New York Stock Exchange), AMEX (American Stock Exchange), NNM (NASDAQ National Market), and NASQ (NASDAQ Small Cap) give companies, governments and other groups a platform to sell securities to the investing public. NASDAQ CM is abbreviated as NAS in this table.

Turnover Ratio
The percentage of a mutual fund or other investment vehicle's holdings that have been replaced with other holdings in a given year. Generally, low turnover ratio is favorable, because high turnover equates to higher brokerage transaction fees, which reduce fund returns.

US Stocks (%)
The percentage of the fund's assets invested in US stock. See **Asset Allocation**.

US Bonds (%)
The percentage of the fund's assets invested in US bonds. See **Asset Allocation**.

Website
The company's web address.

Wire Redemption
This indicates whether or not investors can redeem electronically. See **Services Offered**.

This section lists all of the Providers in Section I: Index of Stock Mutual Funds. Address, Telephone and Website are provided where available.

1290 Funds
1290 Funds 1290 Avenue of the Americas New York NY 10104 United States
212-554-1234
http://www.1290Funds.com

13D Activist Fund
13D Activist Fund 17605 Wright Street, Suite 2 Omaha NE 68130 United States
877-413-3228
http://www.13DActivistFund.com

1919 Funds
1919 Funds P.O. Box 701 Milwaukee WI 53201-0701 United States
http://www.1919Funds.com

360 Funds
360 Funds 6000 Poplar Avenue Suite 250 Memphis TN 38119 United States
http://www.stringeram.com

361 Funds
361 Funds 4600 South Syracuse Street, Suite 500 Denver CO 80237 United States
866-361-1720
http://www.361capital.com

7Twelve
7Twelve 1720 West End Ave., Suite 540 Nashville TN 37203 United States
http://www.7twelveadvisors.com

AAM
AAM 30 W Monroe St, 3rd Floor Chicago IL 60603 United States
312-263-2900
http://www.aamcompany.com

AAMA
AAMA P.O. Box 46707 Cincinnati OH 45246-0707 United States
http://www.aamafunds.com

Aasgard
Aasgard P.O. Box 701 United States
http://www.coldstream.com/mutual-fund-home

Abbey Capital
Abbey Capital PO Box 9841 Providence RI 02940-8041 United States
http://www.abbeycapital.com/

Aberdeen
Aberdeen Asset Management 1735 Market Street 32nd Floor Philadelphia PA 19103 United States
866-667-9231
http://www.aberdeen-asset.us

ABR
ABR 48 Wall Street Suite 1100 New York NY 10005 United States
http://www.abrdynamicfunds.com/

Absolute Capital
Absolute Capital 101 Pennsylvania Boulevard Pittsburgh PA 15228 United States
http://www.abscap.com

Absolute Strategies
Absolute Strategies 350 Lincoln Street, Suite 216 Portland ME 4101 United States
888-992-2765
http://www.absoluteadvisers.com

AC ONE
AC ONE United States
http://www.AC-ONE-AMC.com

Acadian Funds
Acadian Funds 1 Post Office Square Boston MA 2109 United States
http://www.acadian-asset.com

ACM
ACM United States
http://www.ACM-Funds.com

ACR Alpine Capital Research
8000 Maryland Avenue, Suite 700 Suite 700 Saint Louis MO 63105 United States
314-932-7600
http://www.acr-invest.com

Acuitas Investments
Acuitas Investments 520 Pike Street Seattle WA 98101 United States
http://www.acuitasinvestments.com

Adalta
Adalta United States

Adam Asset Funds
Adam Asset Funds 11111 N. Scottsdale Rd. Ste. 205 Scottsdale AZ 85254 United States
http://www.funddocuments.com

Adams Diversified Equity Fund Inc
500 East Pratt Street Suite 1300 Baltimore MD 21202 United States
410-752-5900
http://www.AdamsFunds.com

Adams Harkness Funds
Adams Harkness Funds 60 State Street, Suite 1200 Boston MA 2109 United States
http://www.Lebenthal-lisantismallcap.com

Adams Natural Resources Fund Inc
500 East Pratt Street Suite 1300 Baltimore MD 21202 United States
410-752-5900
http://www.AdamsFunds.com

Adirondack Funds
Adirondack Funds 2390 Western Avenue Guilderland NY 12084 United States
518-690-0470
http://www.adirondackfunds.com

Advantus
Advantus Capital Management, Inc. 400 Robert Street North St. Paul MN 551001-2098 United States
800-665-6005
http://www.advantusfunds.com

ADVENT CAPITAL MANAGEMENT
30 Broad Street 30th Floor New York NY 10004 United States
212-482-1600

AdvisorOne Funds
Advisorone Funds 4020 South 147th Street Omaha NE 68137 United States
http://www.advisoronefunds.com

Advisors Preferred
Advisors Preferred United States
http://www.advisorspreferred.com

Advisory Research
180 N Stetson Ave Ste 5500 Chicago IL 606016737 United States
312-565-1414
http://www.advisoryresearch.com

Aegis
Aegis Value 11100 N. Gleve Road, Suite 1040 Arlington VA 22201 United States
800-528-3780
http://www.aegisfunds.com

Affinity
Affinity 18111 Von Karman Ave., Suite 550 Irvine CA 92612 United States
http://www.affinityinvestment.com

AIG
AIG Harborside Financial Center, 3200 Plaza 5 Jersey City NJ 07311 United States
800-858-8850
https://www.aig.com/getprospectus

Akre
Akre 2 W. Washington Street Middleburg VA 20118 United States
877-862-9556
http://www.akrefund.com

Al Frank
Al Frank Fund c/o US Bancorp Fund Services, LLC, PO BOX 701 Milwaukee WI 53201 United States
888-263-6443
http://www.alfrank.com

Alambic
Alambic 655 Montgomery Street, Suite 1905 San Francisco CA 94111 United States
http://www.alambicfunds.com

Alger
Alger 360 Park Avenue South New York NY 10010 United States
800-992-3863
http://www.alger.com

All Terrain Funds
All Terrain Funds 235 W. Galena Street, Milwaukee, Wisconsin Milwaukee Wisconsin 53201 United States
http://www.allterrainfunds.com

AllianceBernstein
AllianceBernstein 11345 Avenue of the Americas New York NY 10105 United States
212-969-1000
http://www.abglobal.com

AllianceBernstein LP.
1345 6th Avenue New York New York NY 10105 United States
212-969-1000
http://www.abglobal.com/

Allianz Funds
Allianz Funds 1345 Avenue of the Americas New York NY 10105 United States
800-498-5413
http://us.allianzgi.com

Allianz Global Investors
1633 Broadway New York New York 10019 United States
877-716-9787
http://www.US.allianzGI.com

Allianz Group
1 New York United States

Allied Asset
Allied Asset 7745 McClintock Drive, Suite 314 Burr Ridge IL 60527 United States
http://www.investaaa.com

AlphaCentric Funds
17605 Wright Street Suite 2 United States
http://www.AlphaCentricFunds.com.

AlphaCore
AlphaCore AlphaCore Capital 875 Prospect St. Suite 315 La Jolla CA 92037 United States
https://alphacorefunds.com/

AlphaMark
AlphaMark Funds PO Box 46707 Cincinatti OH 45246-0707 United States
866-420-3350
http://www.alphamarkfunds.com

AlphaOne Capital Partners.
789 E. Lancaster Ave Suite 120 Villanova PA 19085 United States
267-597-3888
http://alphaonecapital.com

Alpine
Alpine c/o U.S. Bancorp Fund Services LLC, 615 E. Michigan Street LC 3 Milwaukee WI 53201 United States
888-785-5578
http://www.alpinefunds.com

Alpine Woods Capital Investors
2500 Westchester Avenue Purchase NY 10577 United States
914-251-0880

ALPS
ALPS 1290 Broadway, Suite 1100 Denver CO 80203 United States
866-759-5679
http://www.alpsfunds.com

Alps Advisors Inc
Alps Advisors, Inc. 1290 Broadway, Suite 1100 Denver CO 80203 United States
866-432-2926
http://www.alpsfunds.com

Altair
Altair Bellevue Park Corporate Center, 103 Bellevue Parkway Wilmington DE 19809 United States

Altegris
Altegris 1200 Prospect Street, Suite 400 La Jolla CA 92037 United States
858-459-7040
http://www.altegrismutualfunds.com

Amana
Amana Bellingham WA 98227-0596 United States
888-732-6262
http://www.amanafunds.com

AmericaFirst Funds
630 Fitzwatertown Road Building A, 2nd Floor Willow Grove PA 19090 United States
877-217-8363
http://www.afcm-quant.com

American Beacon
American Beacon 220 East Las Colinas Blvd., Suite 1200 Irving TX 75039 United States
800-658-5811
http://www.americanbeaconfunds.com

American Century Investments
American Century Investments P.O. Box 419200,4500 Main Street Kansas City, MO 64141 United States
800-444-4015
http://www.americancentury.com

American Funds
American Funds 333 South Hope Street Los Angeles CA 90071-1406 United States
800-421-4225
http://www.americanfunds.com

American Growth
American Growth Fund PO Box 8113 Boston MA 02266-8113 United States
800-525-2406
http://www.americangrowthfund.com

American Independence
American Independence 225 West 34th Street 9th Floor New York NY 10122 United States
http://www.americanindependence.com

American Money Management
American Money Management 14249 Ranco Santa Fe Farms Road Ranco Santa Fe CA 92067 United States
http://www.amminvest.com.

American Trust
American Trust 1 Court Street, Suite 350 Lebanon NH 3766 United States
800-385-7003
http://www.amertrust.com

AMF
AMF 2230 W. Monroe Street Chicago IL 60606 United States
800-247-9780
http://www.amffunds.com

AMG Funds
AMG Funds 600 Steamboat Road, Suite 300 Norwalk CT 06830 United States
800-835-3879
http://www.amgfunds.com

AMIDEX
AMIDEX 630-A Fitzwatertown Road, 2nd Floor Willow Grove PA 19090 United States
888-876-3566
http://www.amidex.com

Anchor
Anchor 17605 Wright Street, Suite 2 Omaha NE 68130 United States
http://www.anchorcapitalfunds.com

Ancora
Ancora 2000 Auburn Drive, Suite 430 Cleveland OH 44122 United States
http://www.ancorafunds.com

Apex Capital Management
10050 Innovation Drive, Suite 120 Dayton OH 45342 United States
937-847-9100
http://www.apexcm.com

Appleseed Fund
Appleseed Fund 2960 N. Meridian St., Suite 300 Indianapolis IN 46208 United States
http://www.appleseedfund.com

AQR Funds
AQR Funds Two Greewich Plaza,3rd Floor Greenwich CT 06830 United States
203-742-3600
http://www.aqrfunds.com

Aquila
Aquila 120 West 45th Street, Suite 3600 New York NY 10036 United States
800-437-1020
http://www.aquilafunds.com

Arabesque Asset Management
Arabesque Asset Management P.O. Box 9829 Providence RI 02940-8029 United States
844-567-2134

Arbitrage Fund
c/o Ultimus Fund Solutions 135 Merchant St Ste 230 Cincinnati OH 45246 United States
800-285-4485
http://www.thearbfund.com

Archer
Archer c/o Unified Fund Services Inc., P.O. Box 6110 Indianapolis IN 46206 United States
http://www.thearcherfunds.com

Ariel Investments
200 E. Randolph Suite 2900 Chicago IL 60601 United States
312-726-0140
http://www.arielinvestments.com

Aristotle
Aristotle P.O. Box 2175 Milwaukee WI 53201-2175 United States
http://www.aristotlefunds.com

Arrow Funds
Arrow Funds 6100 Chevy Chase Drive, Suite 100 New York MD 20707 United States
877-277-6933
http://www.arrowfunds.com

Artisan
875 E. Wisconsin Avenue, Suite 800 Milwaukee WI 53202 United States
800-344-1770
http://www.artisanfunds.com

Ascendant
Ascendant United States
http://www.ascendantfunds.com

Ashmore
Ashmore United States
866-876-8294
http://www.ashmoregroup.com/

Aspen Partners
Aspen Partners 1290 Broadway Suite 1100 Denver CO 80203 United States
http://www.aspenfuturesfund.com

Aspiration Funds
Aspiration Funds 4551 Glencoe Avenue Los Angeles CA 90292 United States
424-279-9351
http://www.aspiration.com.

Aspiriant
c/o UMB Fund Services, Inc. 235 West Galena Street Milwaukee WI 53212 United States
877-997-9971
http://www.aspiriantfunds.com

Astor
Astor 111 S. Wacker Dr. Suite 3950 Chicago, IL 60606 Chicago IL 60606 United States
877-738-0333
http://www.astorimfunds.com

AT Funds
AT Funds P.O. Box 219009 Kansas City MO 64121-9009 United States

ATAC Fund
ATAC Fund United States
http://www.atacfund.com

Athena Fund
Athena Fund 17605 Wright Street, Suite 2 Omaha NE 68130 United States
888-868-9501
http://www.athenavaluefund.com

Auer
Auer 2960 N. Meridian St., Suite 300 Indianapolis IN 46208 United States
http://www.auergrowthfund.com

Auxier Funds
Auxier Funds 5000 SW Meadows Road, Suite 410 Lake Oswego OR 97035 United States
http://www.auxierasset.com

Ave Maria Mutual Funds
Ave Maria Mutual Funds LLC135 Merchant Street, Suite 230 Cincinnati OH 45246 United States
888-726-9331
http://www.avemariafunds.com

Avenue Capital Group
535 Madison Avenue New York 10022 United States
212-878-3544
http://www.avenuecapital.com/

Avondale Funds
Avondale Funds Two American Center, 3102 West End Avenue Suite 1100 Nashville TN 37203 United States
http://www.avondalecore.com

AXA Equitable
AXA Equitable 1290 Avenue of the Americas New York NY 10104 United States
877-222-2144
http://www.axa-equitablefunds.com

Azzad Fund
Azzad Fund United States
http://www.azzadfunds.com.

Baillie Gifford Funds
1 Rutland Court Edinburgh Scotland Uk Eh3 8e4 X0 00000 United States

Baird
Baird 777 E. Wisconsin Avenue, Suite 2100 Milwaukee WI 53202 United States
800-792-2473
http://www.bairdfunds.com

Balter
Balter United States
http://www.balterliquidalts.com

Baron Capital Group
no United States
800-992-2766
http://www.BaronFunds.com/performance

Barrett
Barrett 90 Park Avenue, 34th Floor New York NY 10016 United States
877-363-6333
http://www.barrettasset.com

Barrow Funds
Barrow United States
http://www.barrowfunds.com

Baywood
Baywood Funds P.O. Box 588 Portland MA 04112 United States
http://www.baywoodfunds.com

BBH
140 Broadway New York NY 10005 United States
800-575-1265
http://www.bbhfunds.com

Beacon Investment Advisory
Beacon Investment Advisory 163 Madison Avenue, Suite 600 Morristown NJ 07960 United States
http://www.beacontrust.com/

Beck, Mack & Oliver
Beck, Mack & Oliver P.O. Box 588 Portland ME 4112 United States
http://www.beckmack.com

Becker
Becker 1211 SW 5th Ave, Suite 2185 Portland OR 97204 United States
http://www.beckervaluefunds.com

Beech Hill
Beech Hill 880 Third Ave., 16th Floor United States
http://www.bh-adv.com

BeeHive
BeeHive P.O. Box 588 Portland ME 4112 United States
http://www.TheBeeHiveFund.com

Berkshire
Berkshire 3555 Farnam Street, Suite 1440 Omaha NE 68131 United States
877-526-0707
http://www.berkshirefunds.com

Bernzott Capital Advisors
Bernzott Capital Advisors 888 West Ventura Blvd., Suite B Camarillo CA 93010 United States
805-389-9445
http://www.bcafunds.com

Bexil Corp
11 Hanover Sq New York NY 10005 New York NY 10005 United States
212-785-0900

BFS
Bradley, Foster & Sargent, Inc. CityPlace II, 11th Floor United States
860-527-8050
http://www.bfsfunds.com

Biondo Investment Advisor
540 Routes 6 and 209 PO Box 909 Milford PA 18337 United States
570-296-5525
http://www.thebiondogroup.com

Bishop Street
Bishop Street 11 Freedom Valley Drive Oaks PA 19087 United States
http://www.bishopstreetfunds.com

BlackRock
BlackRock Funds Providence RI 02940-8019 United States
800-441-7762
http://www.blackrock.com

BlackRock
BlackRock Funds P.O. Box 9819 Providence RI 02940-8019 United States
800-441-7762
http://www.blackrock.com

Blackstone
Blackstone 345 Park Avenue, 31st Floor New York NY 10154 United States
http://www.blackstone.com

Blue Chip Investor Fund
Blue Chip Investor Fund 4480 N. Magnolia Ave., Suite 103 El Cajon CA 92020 United States
http://www.bluechipinvestorfund.com

Blue Current Funds
United States United States
http://www.bluecurrentfunds.com

BLUEROCK
BLUEROCK 16500 North Park Dr., Suite 202 Southfield, MI 48075 Southfield MI 48075 United States
http://bluerockre.com/investments/tif/

BMO Funds
BMO Funds Boston United States
800-236-3863
http://www.bmofunds.com

BMT
c/o U.S. Bancorp Fund Services, LLC P.O. Box 701 Milwaukee WI 53201-0701 United States
http://www.bmtc.com

BNY Mellon Funds
BNY Mellon Funds 200 Park Avenue New York NY 10166 United States
800-645-6561
http://www.bnymellon.com

Bogle
Bogle 2310 Washington St., Suite 310 Newton MA 2462 United States
877-264-5346
http://www.boglefunds.com

Boston Common
c/o U.S. Bancorp Fund Services, LLC P.O. Box 701 Milwaukee WI 53201-0701 United States
877-777-6944
http://www.bostoncommonfunds.com

Boston Partners
1 Beacon St, 30th Floor Boston MA 02108 United States
617-832-8200
http://www.boston-partners.com

Boston Trust & Walden Funds
BOSTON TRUST & WALDEN FUNDS 100 SUMMER STREET Boston MA 43229 United States
617-814-1215
http://www.btim.com

Boulder Capital, LLC
2344 Spruce Street Suite A. Boulder CO, 80302 Boulder CO 80302 United States
303-444-5483

Boyar Value Fund
Boyar Value Fund 590 Madison Avenue New York NY 10022 United States
http://www.boyarvalue.com

bp capital
8117 Preston #260W Dallas TX 75225 United States
214-265-4165
http://www.bpcfunds.com

Brandes
Brandes 11988 El Camino Real, Suite 500 San Diego CA 92130 United States
800-331-2979
http://www.brandesfunds.com/

Bretton Fund
Bretton Fund 8000 Town Centre Drive, Suite 400 Broadview Heights OH 44147 United States
http://www.brettonfund.com

Bridge Builder
Bridge Builder 615 East Michigan Street Milwaukee WI 53202 United States
http://www.bridgebuildermutualfunds.com

Bridges
Bridges 8401 W. Dodge Road, Suite 256 Omaha NE 68114 United States
http://www.bridgesinv.com

Bridgeway
Bridgeway 55615 Kirby Drive, Suite 518 Houston TX 77005 United States
800-661-3550
http://www.bridgeway.com

Bright Rock
Bright Rock 2036 Washington Street Hanover MA 02339 United States
781-982-6593
http://www.brightrockfunds.com

Broadview Funds
Broadview Funds 330 East Kilbourn Avenue, Suite 1475 Milwaukee WI 53202 United States
414-918-3900
http://www.bvafunds.com

Brookfield Investment Funds
Brookfield Investment Funds Three World Financial Center, 200 Vesey Street, 10th Floor New York NY 10281-1010 United States
212-549-8400
http://www.brookfieldim.com

Brookfield Investment Management Inc.
71 South Wacker Drive Suite 3400 Chicago IL 60606-2841 United States
312-377-8300
http://www.brookfieldim.com

Brown Advisory Funds
Brown Advisory Incorporated 901 S. Bond Street Suite 400 Baltimore MD 21231 United States
800-540-6807
http://www.brownadvisoryfunds.com

Brown Capital Management
Brown Capital Management, LLC 1201 North Calvert Street, Baltimore MD 21202 United States
http://www.browncapital.com/mid-funds-overview.html.

Bruce
Bruce 220 N. Wacker Drive, Suite 2414 Chicago IL 60606 United States
http://www.thebrucefund.com

Buffalo
Buffalo 55420 W. 61st Place Shawnee Mission KS 66205 United States
800-492-8332
http://www.buffalofunds.com

Bulldog Investors, LLC
PARK 80 WEST 250 PEHLE AVE. SUITE 708 201 556-0092 SADDLE BROOK NJ 07663 United States
914-747-5262

Bullfinch
Bullfinch 33909 Rush Mendon Road Mendon NY 14506 United States

Calamos
Calamos 2020 Calamos Court Naperville IL 60563 United States
800-582-6959
http://www.calamos.com

Calamos Asset Management Inc
1111 E Warrenville Road Naperville IL 60563-1493 Naperville IL 60563-1493 United States
630-245-7234
http://www.calamosglobal.com

Caldwell & Orkin
Caldwell & Orkin 55185 Peachtree Parkway, Suite 370 Norcross GA 30092 United States
800-237-7073
http://www.caldwellorkin.com

Calvert Investments
Calvert Investments, Inc. 4550 Montgomery Ave. Suite 1000N. Bethesda MD 20814 United States
800-368-2745
http://www.calvert.com

Cambiar Funds
Cambiar Funds 2401 E. Second Avenue, Suite 400 Denver CO 80206 United States
866-777-8227
http://www.cambiar.com

Camelot Funds
c/o Gemini Fund Services, LLC 17605 Wright Street, Suite 2 Omaha NE 68130 United States
http://www.CamelotFunds.com

Campbell & Company
Campbell & Company 2850 Quarry Lake Drive Baltimore MD 21209 United States
800-698-7235
http://www.campbell.com

Cane Capital Management
Cane Capital Management 7515 Corporate Centre Drive Germantown TN 38138 United States
901-507-2165
http://www.canefunds.com

Canterbury Investment Management
23 East Cedar Street Zionsville IN 46077 United States
317-732-2075
http://www.canterburygroup.com

Capital Advisors
Capital Advisors 320 South Boston Suite 825 Tulsa OK 74103 United States
918-599-0045
http://capadvfunds.com/

Capital Group
333 South Hope Street Los Angeles CA 90071 United States
213-486-9200
http://www.capitalgroup.com

Capital Management
http://www.oxeye.co.uk

Cardinal Capital
Cardinal Capital P.O. Box 588 Portland ME 04112 United States
http://www.cardcap.com/mutualfunds

Carillon Family of Funds
Eagle Funds 250 North Rock Roade Suite 150 Wichita KS 67206 United States
800-421-4184
http://www.eagleasset.com

Castle Investment Management
Castle Investment Management 8000 Town Centre Drive, Suite 400 Broadview Heights OH 44147 United States
877-743-7820
http://www.castleim.com

Castlemaine
Castlemaine Funds P.O. Box 46707 Cincinnati Ohio 45246-0707 United States

Catalyst Mutual Funds
Catalyst Mutual Funds 630-A Fitzwatertown Road, 2nd Floor Willow Grove PA 19090 United States
866-447-4228
http://www.catalystmutualfunds.com

Causeway
Causeway 1 Freedom Valley Drive Oaks PA 19465 United States
866-947-7000
http://www.causewayfunds.com

Cavalier
Cavalier Funds Post Office Box 4365 Rocky Mount NC 27803 United States
800-773-3863
http://www.riskxfunds.com

Cavanal Hill funds
Cavanal Hill Funds 3435 Stelzer Road Columbus OH 43219 United States
http://www.cavanalhillfunds.com

CBOE Vest
CBOE Vest 8730 Stony Point Parkway, Suite 205 Richmond VA 23235 United States
855-505-8378
http://www.cboevestfunds.com

CBRE Clarion Securities, LLC
CBRE Clarion Securities, LLC 201 King of Prussia Road, Suite 600 Radnor PA 19087 United States
610-995-2500
http://www.cbreclarion.com

CCA Funds
CCA Funds 190 North Canon Dr., Suite 402, Beverly Hills, CA 90210 Beverly Hills CA 90210 United States
800-595-4866
http://www.ccafunds.com

Cedar Ridge
Cedar Ridge 45 East Putnam Avenue, Suite 124 Greenwich CO 06830 United States
http://www.cedarridgepartners.com

Center Coast Capital Advisors, LP
1100 Louisiana Suite 5025 Houston TX 77002 United States
713-759-1400
http://www.centercoastcap.com

Centerstone Investors
Centerstone Investors 135 5th Avenue New York New York 10010 Luxembourg
212-503-5790
http://www.centerstoneinv.com/

Central Securities
Central Securities United States

Centre Funds
Centre Funds 48 Wall Street New York NY 10005 United States
855-298-4236
http://www.centrefunds.com

CG funds
Capital Guardian 733 Third Avenue, 24th Floor New York NY 10017 United States
http://www.cgfundstrust.com

CGM
CGM One International Place Boston MA 2110 United States
800-343-5678
http://www.cgmfunds.com

Chaconia Funds
Chaconia Funds 1000 Brickell Avenue, Suite 600 Miami FL 33131 United States
http://www.ttutc.com

Chadwick & D'Amato
Chadwick & D'Amato 224 Main Street, PO Box 1978 New London NH 03257 United States
http://www.chadwick-damato.com

Champlain Funds
Champlain Funds 346 Shelburne Road, 6th Floor Burlington VT 5401 United States
http://www.cipvt.com

Chartwell Investment Partners
Chartwell Investment Partners 1205 Westlakes Drive Suite 100 Berwyn PA 19312 United States
610-296-1400
http://www.chartwellip.com

Chase
Chase 270 Park Avenue Floor 12 New York NY 10017 United States
212-270-6000
http://www.chasegrowthfunds.com

Chesapeake
Chesapeake 1 Rockenfeller Plaza, Suite 1210 New York NY 10020 United States
800-430-3863
http://www.chesapeakefunds.com

Chilton Funds
300 Park Avenue, Floor 19 New York, New York New York
New York 10022 United States
212-751-3596
http://www.chiltonfunds.com/

Chiron Investment Management
1350 Avenue of the Americas, Suite 700 New York NY NY
10019 United States
http://www.chironfunds.com

Chou America
Chou America 3 Canal Plaza, Suite 600 Portland ME 04101
United States
207-347-2088
http://www.chouamerica.com

Christopher Weil
Christopher Weil United States

City National Rochdale
City National Rochdale c/o SEI Investments Distribution
Co. Oaks PA 19456 United States
http://www.citynationalrochdalefunds.com

Clark Fork Trust
Clark Fork Trust 218 East Front Street, Suite 205 Missoula
MT 59802 United States
406-541-0130
http://www.tarkiofund.com

Clarkston Funds
Clarkston Funds P.O. Box 1920 Denver CO 80201 United
States
844-680-6562
http://www.clarkstonfunds.com

Clifford Capital
Clifford Capital Partners Fund 8730 Stony Point Parkway,
Suite 205 Richmond VA 23235 United States
http://www.cliffordcapfunds.com

Clipper Fund
Clipper Fund 30 Dan Road Canton MA 02021-2809 United
States
800-432-2504
http://www.clipperfund.com

Clough
Clough 1290 Broadway, Suite 1100 Denver CO 80203
United States
877-256-8445
http://www.cloughglobal.com

Clough Capital Partners L.P.
Clough Capital Partners L.P. One Post Office Square, 40th
Floor Boston United States

CM Advisors
CM Advisors 805 Las Cimas Parkway, Suite 430 Austin TX
78746 United States
888-859-5856
http://www.cmadvisorsfunds.com

CMG
CMG 150 N. Radnor Chester Road, Suite A150 Radnor PA
19087 United States
http://www.cmgmutualfunds.com

Cognios
Cognios 1290 Broadway, Suite 1100, Denver, Colorado
Denver CO 80203 United States
303-623-5277
http://www.cogniosfunds.com

Cognios Capital
Cognios Capital P.O. Box 1920 Denver Colorado 80201
United States
http://www.cogniosfunds.com

Cohen & Steers
Cohen & Steers 280 Park Ave New York NY 10017 United
States
212-832-3232
http://www.cohenandsteers.com

Coho
Coho Partners, Ltd. 300 Berwyn Park Berwyn PA 19312
United States
http://www.cohofunds.com

Collins
Collins 806 Douglas Road, Suite 570 Coral Gables FL
33134 United States
http://www.collinsalternativefunds.com

Columbia
Liberty Financial Funds P.O. Box 8081 Boston MA 02266-
8081 United States
800-345-6611
http://www.columbiathreadneedleus.com

Commerce
Commerce 11000 Walnut Street Kansas City MO 64121
United States
http://www.commercefunds.com

Commonwealth Intl Series Tr
Commonwealth Intl Series Tr 5847 San Felipe Ste 850
Houston TX 77057 United States
888-345-1898
http://www.commonwealthfunds.com

Community Capital Management
1830 Main Street Ste 204 Weston FL 33326 United States
877-272-1977
http://www.ccmfixedincome.com

Concorde
Concorde 11000 Three Lincoln Centre Dallas TX 75240
United States

Conductor
Conductor 17605 Wright Street, Suite 2 Omaha NE 68130
United States
http://www.conductorfund.com

Conestoga Capital Advisors
Conestoga Capital Advisors 259 N. Radnor-Chester Road
Radnor PA 19087 United States
800-320-7790
http://www.conestogacapital.com

Congress
Congress 2 Seaport Lane Boston MA 2210 United States
888-688-1299
http://www.congressasset.com/funds

Context Asset Management
Context Capital Three Canal Plaza Portland ME 04101
United States
http://www.contextam.com

Convergence
Convergence Core Plus Fund c/o U.S. Bancorp Fund
Services, LLC PO BOx 701 Milwaukee WI 53201 United
States
877-677-9414
http://www.investcip.com

Cook & Bynum
Cook & Bynum United States
http://www.cookandbynum.com/cobyx

Copeland Funds
Copeland Funds United States
888-926-7352
http://www.copelandfunds.com

Copley
Copley 2245 Sunrise Avenue Palm Beach FL 33480 United
States
877-881-2751

CornerCap
CornerCap 1355 Peachtree Street, NE, Suite 1700 Atlanta
GA 30309 United States
888-813-8637
http://www.cornercap.com

Cornerstone
Cornerstone 74 W. Broad Street, Suite 340 Bethlehem PA
18018 United States
http://www.aicfundholdings.com

Cornerstone Advisors
1075 Hendersonwille Road Suite 250 Asheville North
Carolina 28803 United States

Cortina Funds Inc
Cortina Funds, Inc. 825 North Jefferson Street Suite 400
Milwaukee WI 53202 United States
http://www.cortinafunds.com

Counterpoint Mutual Funds
Counterpoint Mutual Funds 12707 High Bluff Drive, Suite
200 San Diego CA 92130 United States
http://www.counterpointmutualfunds.com

Cove Street Capital
Cove Street Capital, LLC 2321 Rosecrans Avenue, El
Segundo CA 90245 United States
866-497-0097
http://www.covestreetfunds.com

Covered Bridge
Covered Bridge 17605 Wright Street, Suite 2 Omaha NE
68130 United States
http://www. thecoveredbridgefund.com

Crawford
Crawford 2960 North Meridian Street, Suite 300
Indianapolis IN 46208 United States
http://www.crawfordinvestment.com

Credit Suisse (New York, NY)
Credit Suisse Eleven Madison Avenue New York NY United
States
877-870-2874
http://www.credit-suisse.com/us/funds

CRM
CRM 520 Madison Avenue, 20th Floor New York NY 10022
United States
800-276-2883
http://www.crmfunds.com

Cross Shore
Cross Shore 111 Great Neck Road, Suite 210, Great Neck
New York NY 11021 United States
http://www.crossshorefunds.com/

Crow Point
Crow Point Partners, LLC 10 New Driftway, Suite 203
Scituate, MA 02066 United States
http://www.cppfunds.com

Cullen Funds Trust
Cullen Funds Trust 645 Fifth Ave New York NY 10022
United States
800-582-6757
http://www.cullenfunds.com

Cushing Asset Management LP
8117 Preston Road Suite 440 Dallas TX 75225 United
States
214-692-6334
http://www.cushingasset.com

Cutler
Cutler 306 Main Street, 2nd Floor Worcester MA 1608 United States
http://www.cutler.com

CVR
CVR P.O. Box 588 Portland ME 04112 United States
http://cvrfunds.com

Dana Investment
Dana Investment 15800 W. Bluemound Rd. Ste. 250 Brookfield WI 53005 United States
262-782-3631
http://www.danafunds.com

Davenport
Davenport & Company LLC 901 East Cary Street Richmond VA 23219 United States
http://www.investdavenport.com/davenport-asset-management

Davidson Mutual Funds
Davidson Mutual Funds 615 East Michigan Street Milwaukee WI 53202 United States
http://www.davidsonmutualfunds.com

Davis Dinsmore
Davis Dinsmore 65 Madison Avenue Morristown NJ 07960 United States

Davis Funds
Davis Funds 2949 E. Elvira Rd., Suite 101 Tucson AZ 85706 United States
800-279-0279
http://www.davisfunds.com

Day Hagan
Day Hagan 330 S. Orange Avenue Sarasota FL 34236 United States
http://www.dayhagan.com

Dean Fund
Dean Fund 2200 Kettering Tower Dayton OH 45423 United States
888-899-8343
http://www.deanmutualfunds.com

Dearborn Partners
Dearborn Partners Cambodia
888-983-3380
http://www.dearbornfunds.com

Delaware Funds by Macquarie
Delaware Funds by Macquarie Philadelphia United States

Destinations Funds
Destination Funds 1277 Treat Boulevard,#200 Walnut Creek CA 94597 United States
http://www.destinationfunds.com

Destra
Destra Capital Advisors, LLC 901 Warrenville Road, Suite 15 Lisle IL 60532 United States
877-855-3434
http://destracapital.com

Deutsche Asset Management
100 Plaza One 3rd Floor Jersey City NJ 07311-3901 United States
201-593-8273
http://www.dws-investments.com

Deutsche Asset Management
345 Park Avenue New York NY 10154 United States
212-454-5624
http://www.deawm.com

Deutsche Asset Management
222 South Riverside Plaza Chicago IL 60606-5808 United States
312-537-8295
http://www.dws-investments.com

Deutsche Investment Management Inc
222 South Riverside Chicago IL 60606 United States

DF Dent Funds
DF Dent Funds 2 E. Read Street, 6th Floor Baltimore MD 21202 United States
http://www.dfdent.com

DGHM
DGHM 565 Fifth Avenue, Suite 2101 New York NY 10017-2413 United States
212-557-2445
http://www.dghm.com

DGI
The Disciplined Growth Investors Fund PO Box 275 Denver CO 80201 United States
855-344-3863
http://www.dgifund.com/howtoinvest.php

Diamond Hill Funds
Diamond Hill Funds 325 John H. Mcconnell Boulevard,Suite 200 Columbus OH 43215 United States
888-226-5595
http://www.diamond-hill.com

Dimensional Fund Advisors
Dimensional Fund Advisors 1299 Ocean Avenue, 11th Floor Santa Monica CA 90401 United States
512-306-7400
http://www.dimensional.com

Direxion Funds
Direxion Funds 1301 Avenue Of The Americas (6th Avenue) New York NY 10019 United States
646-572-3390
http://www.direxionfunds.com

Dodge & Cox
Dodge and Cox 555 California Street, 40th Floor San Francisco CA 94104 United States
415-981-1710
http://www.dodgeandcox.com

Domini
Domini 5536 Broadway, 77th Floor New York NY 10012 United States
800-582-6757
http://www.domini.com

DoubleLine
DoubleLine 333 South Grand Avenue Los Angeles CA 90071 United States
877-354-6311
http://www.doublelinefunds.com

Dreyfus
Dreyfus 144 Glenn Curtiss Blvd Uniondale NY 11556-0144 United States
800-645-6561
http://www.dreyfus.com

Driehaus
Driehaus 25 E. Erie Street Chicago IL 60611 United States
877-779-0079
http://www.driehaus.com

Duff & Phelps
55 Park Avenue Plz New York NY 100550002 United States
212-871-2549

DUNDAS
DUNDAS P.O. Box 588 Portland Maine 04112 United States
844-536-7414
http://www.dundasglobal.com

Dunham Funds
Dunham Funds 10251 Vista Sorrento Parkway Suite 200 San Diego CA 92121 United States
800-442-4358
http://www.dunham.com

DuPont
DuPont 1007 Market Street Wilmington DE 19898 United States
888-447-0014
http://www.dupont.com

Eagle Asset Management, Inc.
Eagle Asset Management, Inc. P.O. Box 10520 St. Petersburg FL 33733-0520 United States
800-235-3903
http://www.eagleasset.com

Eagle MLP
Eagle MLP United States

Eaton Vance
P.O. Boc 43027 Providence RI 02940-3027 United States

Edgar Lomax
Edgar Lomax 6564 Loisdale Court, Suite 310 Springfield VA 22150 United States
703-719-0026
http://www.edgarlomax.com

Edgewood
Edgewood P.O. Box 219009 Kansas City MO 64121 United States
800-791-4226
http://www.edgewoodfunds.com

EIP Funds
EIP Funds EIP Growth and Income Fund 49 Riverside Avenue Westport, Connecticut 06880 Westport Connecticut 06880 United States

Elessar Investment Management
1111 Superior Avenue Suite 1310 Cleveland OH 44114 United States
216-357-7412
http://www.elessarinvest.com

Emerald
Emerald 1703 Oregon Pike Lancaster PA 17605 United States
855-828-9909
http://www.emeraldmutualfunds.com

Empiric Funds
Empiric Funds 6300 Bridgepoint Parkway Building 2, Suite 105 Austin TX 78730 United States
888-839-7424
http://www.empiricfunds.com

Ensemble Fund
8000 Town Centre Drive Suite 400 Broadview Heights Ohio 44147 United States
800-785-8165
http://www.ensemblefund.com

EntrepreneurShares
EntrepreneurShares 175 Federal Street, Suite #875 Boston MA 02110 United States
http://www.ershares.com

Epiphany Funds
Epiphany Funds 106 Decker Court, Suite 226 Irving CA 75062 United States
800-320-2185
http://www.epiphanyfunds.com

Equinox Funds Trust
Equinox Funds Trust 1175 Sherman Street, Suite 2500 Denver CO 80203 United States
609-577-4200
http://www.EquinoxFundManagement.com

Equity Investment Corp
1776 Peachtree Street NW Suite 600S Atlanta GA 30309
United States
404-239-0111
http://eicatlanta.com/

EquityCompass
1 South Street, 16th Floor Baltimore Maryland 21202
United States
443-224-1231
http://www.equitycompass.com

Essex Funds
Essex Funds United States

Euro Pacific Asset Management
Euro Pacific Asset Management, LLC 1201 Dove Street, Suite 370 Newport Beach CA 92660 United States
http://www.europacificfunds.com

E-Valuator funds
8730 Stony Point Parkway, Suite 205 Richmond Richmond Virginia 23235 United States
888-507-2798
http://e-valuator.com/

Eventide Funds
Eventide Funds 60 State Street, Suite 700 Boston MA 2109
United States
http://www.eventidefunds.com

Evermore
Evermore 89 Summit Avenue Summit NJ 7901 United States
866-383-7667
http://www.evermoreglobal.com

Fairholme
Fairholme 83 General Warren Blvd., Suite 170 Malvern PA 19355 United States
866-202-2263
http://www.fairholmefunds.com

FAM
FAM 384 N. Grand Street Cobleskill NY 12043 United States
http://www. famfunds.com

FDP Series Funds
FDP Series Funds 1100 Bellevue Parkway Wilmington DE 19809 United States
http://www.blackrock.com/funds

Federated
Federated Investors Funds 4000 Ericsson Drive Warrendale PA 15086-7561 United States
800-341-7400
http://www.Federatedinvestors.com

Fidelity Investments
Fidelity Investments 82 Devonshire Street Boston MA 2109
United States
617-563-7000
http://www.institutional.fidelity.com

Fiera Capital
1501 McGill College Avenue, Suite 800 375 Park Avenue, 8th Floor Montreal Quebec H3A 3M8 United States
514-954-3300
http://www.fieracapital.com/

First Eagle
First Eagle 1345 Avenue of the Americas New York NY 10105 United States
800-334-2143
http://www.firsteaglefunds.com

First Investors
First Investors Life Insurance 95 Wall Street New York NY 10005 United States
800-423-4026
http://www.firstinvestors.com

First Pacific
First Pacific 11400 W. Olympic Blvd., Suite 1200 Los Angeles CA 90064 United States

First State
615 East Michigan Street Milwaukee, Wisconsin 53202
United States
http://www.firststatefunds.com

First Trust
First Trust 120 E. Liberty Drive, Suite 400 Wheaton IL 60187 United States
800-621-1675
http://www.ftportfolios.com/

First Trust Advisors L.P.
First Trust Advisors L.P. 120 E. Liberty Wheaton IL 60187
United States
866-848-9727
http://www.ftglobalportfolios.com

Firsthand Funds
Firsthand Funds 150 ALMADEN BLVD, SUITE 1250 SAN JOSE CA 95113 United States
888-884-2675
http://www.firsthandfunds.com

Flaherty & Crumrine
301 E. Colorado Blvd, Suite 720 Pasadena CA 91101
United States
626-795-7300
http://www.flaherty-crumrine.com

Flippin, Bruce & Porter Funds
Flippin, Bruce & Porter Funds P.O. Box 46707 Cincinnati OH 45246-0707 United States
http://www.fbpfunds.com

FMC Funds
FMC Funds 399 Park Avenue Kansas City MO 64121 United States
http://www.firstmanhattan.com

FMI Funds
FMI Funds 225 East Mason Street Milwaukee WI 53202 United States
800-811-5311
http://www.fmifunds.com.

Footprints
Footprints 11422 Miracle Hills Drive, Suite 208 Omaha NE 68154 United States
http://www.footprintsfund.com

Forester
8000 Town Centre Drive Suite 400 Broadview Heights OH 44147 United States
http://www.forestervalue.com

FormulaFolios
FormulaFolios Jenison, MI 49428 Jenison MI 49428 United States
http://formulafolios.com/

Fort Pitt Capital Funds
Fort Pitt Capital Funds 680 Anderson Drive Foster Plaza Ten Pittsburgh PA 15220 United States
http://www.fortpittcapital.com

Foundry
Foundry Partners, LLC Funds 4520 Main Street, Suite 1425 Kansas City MO 64111 United States
http://www.foundrypartnersllc.com

FPA
FPA 111400 W. Olympic Blvd., Suite 1200 Los Angeles CA 90064 United States
800-982-4372
http://www.fpafunds.com

Frank Funds
Frank Funds 6 Stacy CT Parsippany NJ 07054-3347 United States
800-869-1679
http://www.frankfunds.com

Franklin Templeton
500 East Broward Blvd Suite 2100 Ft. Lauderdale FL 33394-3091 United States
954-527-7500
http://www.franklintempleton.com

Franklin Templeton Investments
Franklin Templeton Investments One Franklin Parkway, Building 970, 1st Floor San Mateo CA 94403 United States
650-312-2000
http://www.franklintempleton.com

Friess Associates
3711 Kennett Pike, Suite 100 P.O. Box 4166 Greenville DE 19807 United States
302-656-3017
http://www.friess.com

Frontier Funds
Frontier Funds 130 East Capitol Drive Hartland WI 53029-2136 United States
http://www.frontiermutualfunds.com

Frost Funds
Frost Funds 100 W. Houston Street, 15th Floor San Antonio TX 78205 United States
http://www.frostbank.com

FS Investments
FS 201 Rouse Boulevard Philadelphia PA 19112 United States
877-628-8575
http://www.fsinvestments.com

Fulcrum
NA United States

Fund X
c/o US Bancorp Mutual Fund Services, LLC PO Box 701 Milwaukee WI 53201 United States
866-455-3863
http://www.upgraderfunds.com

Gabelli
Gabelli 1 Corporate Center Rye NY NY United States
914-921-5135
http://www.gabelli.com

Gabelli Funds Inc
Gabelli Funds One Corporate Center Rye NY 10580-1434 United States
http://www.gabelli.com

Gator
Gator United States
http://www.gatorcapital.com

GaveKal
GaveKal United States
http://www.gavekalfunds.com

GE Asset Management
GE Asset Management P.O. Box 9838 Providence RI 02940 United States
800-242-0134
http://www.geam.com

General American Investors Company Inc
450 Lexington Avenue Suite 3300 New York NY 10017 United States
212-916-8400

Geneva Advisors
Geneva Funds 181 W. Madison Street., Suite 3575 Chicago IL 60602 United States
http://www.genevafunds.com

Gerstein Fisher
Gerstein Fisher 615 East Michigan Street Milwaukee WI 53202 United States
http://www.gersteinfisherfunds.com

Giralda Fund
Giralda Fund 4200 West 115th Street, Suite 100 Leawood KS 66211 United States
http://www.thegiraldafund.com

Glenmede
Glenmede 11650 Market Street, Suite 1200 Philadelphia PA 19103 United States
800-442-8299
http://www.glenmede.com

GMO
GMO 40 Rowes Wharf Boston MA 02110 United States
617-330-7500
http://www.gmo.com

Goehring & Rozencwajg
Goehring & Rozencwajg 110 Wall Street New York NY 10005 United States
646-216-9777
http://www.gorozen.com/#

Goldman Sachs
Goldman Sachs 200 West Stree New York NY 10282 United States
800-526-7384
http://www.gsamfunds.com

Goldman Sachs
71 South Wacker Drive, Chicago, Illinois 60606, Chicago United States
312-362-3000
http://www.gsamfunds.com

Golub
Golub 1850 Gateway Drive, Suite 600 San Mateo CA 94404 United States

Good Harbor
Good Harbor 17605 Wright Street,Omaha, NE Omaha NE 68130 United States
877-270-2848
http://www.ghf-funds.com

GoodHaven
GoodHaven United States
http://www.goodhavenfunds.com

Gotham
Gotham 535 Madison Avenue, 30th Floor New York RI 10022 United States
877-974-6852
http://www.Gothamfunds.com

GQG Partners
GQG Partners P.O. Box 219009 Kansas City MO 64121-9009 United States
866-362-8333
http://www.gqgpartners.com

Grandeur Peak Funds
Grandeur Peak Funds 1290 Broadway, Suite 1100 Denver CO 80203 United States
855-377-7325
http://www.grandeurpeakglobal.com

Grant Park
Grant Park United States
866-501-4758

Great Lakes Funds
Great Lakes Funds 222 South Riverside Plaza, 28th Floor, Chicago, Illinois Chicago IL 60606 United States
http://www.glafunds.com

Great-West Funds
Maxim 88525 E. Orchard Road Greenwood Village CO 80111 United States
http://www.greatwestfunds.com

Green Century
Green Century 114 State Street, Suite 200 Boston MA 2109 United States
800-221-5519
http://www.greencentury.com

Green Owl
Green Owl 225 Pictoria Drive, Suite 450 Cincinnati IN 45246 United States
http://www.greenowlfund.com

Greenspring
Greenspring 2330 W. Joppa Road, Suite 110 Lutherville MD 21093 United States
800-366-3863
http://www.greenspringfund.com

Griffin Capital
Griffin Capital Griffin Capital Plaza, 1520 Grand Avenue El Segundo CA 90245 United States
310-469-6100
http://www.griffincapital.com

Guggenheim Investments
Guggenheim Investments 805 King Farm Boulevard, Suite 600 Rockville MD 60606 United States
212-739-0700
http://www.guggenheiminvestments.com

Guggenheim Investments Asset Management
227 West Monroe Street Chicago IL 60606 United States
312-827-0100
http://www.guggenheimpartners.com

GuideMark
GuideMark 7A Greenridge Park Nashua NH 003060 United States
603-888-5500
http://www.AssetMark.com

GuidePath
GuidePath 2300 Contra Costa Blvd., Suite 600 Pleasant Hill, CA Pleasant Hill CA 94523 United States
800-664-5345
http://www.AssetMark.com

GuideStone Funds
Guidestone Funds 2401 Cedar Springs Road Dallas TX 75201 United States
214-720-1171
http://www.guidestonefunds.org

Guinness Atkinson
Guinness Atkinson 21550 Oxnard Street, Suite 750 Woodland Hills CA 91367 United States
800-915-6566
http://www.gafunds.com

Hambrecht & Quist

Hamlin Funds
Hamlin Funds United States

Hancock Horizon
Hancock Horizon 2600 Citiplace Drive, Suite 100 Baton Rouge LA 70808 United States
800-990-2434
http://www.hancockhorizonfunds.com

Hanlon
Hanlon 17605 Wright Street, Suite 2 Omaha NE 68130 United States
http://www.HanlonFunds.com

Harbor
Harbor 111 S. Wacker Drive, 34th Floor Chicago IL 60606 United States
800-422-1050
http://www.harborfunds.com

Harding Loevner
Harding Loevner 400 Crossings Blvd Bridgewater NJ 08807 United States
877-435-8105
http://www.hardingloevnerfunds.com

Hartford Mutual Funds
Hartford Mutual Funds United States
888-843-7824
http://www.hartfordfunds.com

Hatteras Funds
Hatteras Funds 6601 Six Forks, Suite 340 Raleigh NC 27615-3052 United States
919-846-2324
http://www.hatterasfunds.com

Haverford
http://www.haverfordfunds.com

HC Capital Trust

Heartland
Heartland 1290 Broadway, Suite 1100 Denver CO 80203 United States
800-432-7856
http://www.heartlandfunds.com/

Hedeker Wealth
Hedeker Wealth One Overlook Point Suite 250 Lincolnshire IL 60069 United States
847-913-5594
http://www.hedekerwealth.com

HedgeRow
HedgeRow 4520 Main Street Suite 1425 Kansas City Missouri 64111 United States
877-244-6235

Hennessy
Hennessy 7250 Redwood Blvd., Suite 200 Novato CA 94945 United States
800-966-4354
http://www.hennessyfunds.com

Henssler Funds
Henssler Funds P.O. Box C1100 Conshohocken PA 19428-0844 United States
http://www.henssler.com

Herzfeld
Herzfeld PO Box 161465 Miami FL 33116 United States
http://www.herzfeld.com

Highland Funds
Highland Funds 200 Crescent Court, Suite 700 Dallas TX 75201 United States
877-665-1287
http://www.highlandfunds.com

Highmore
Highmore 120 5th Ave, Sixth Floor New York City New York 10011 United States
http://www.highmorefunds.com

Hillman Capital Management
Hillman Capital Management 7501 Wisconsin Avenue, Suite 1100 E Bethesda MD 20814 United States
http://www.hillmancapital.com

Hodges
Hodges Fund 2905 Maple Ave Dallas TX 75201 United States
http://www.hodgesfund.com

Holland Series Trust
Holland Series Trust 375 Park Avenue New York NY 10152 United States
http://www.thehollandfund.com

Homestead
Homestead 4301 Wilson Blvd., IFS8-305 Arlington VA 22203 United States
http://www.homesteadfunds.com

Hood River Capital Management
Hood River Capital United States

Horizon Investments
13024 Ballantyne Corporate Place Suite 225 Charlotte NC 28277 United States
http://www.horizonmutualfunds.com

Hotchkis & Wiley
Hotchkis & Wiley 725 South Figueroa Suite 400 Los Angeles CA 90017 United States
866-493-8637
http://www.hwcm.com

Howard Capital Management
c/o Gemini Fund Services, LLC 17605 Wright Street, Suite 2 Omaha NE 68130 United States
855-969-8464
http://www.howardcmfunds.com

HSBC
HSBC 452 Fifth Avenue, 17th Floor New York NY 10018 United States
888-936-4722
http://www.investorfunds.us.hsbc.com

Huber Funds
Huber Funds United States
888-482-3726
http://www.hubercap.com

Hundredfold
Hundredfold United States
855-582-8006
http://www.HundredfoldSelect.

Hussman Funds
Hussman Funds PO Box 46707 Cincinnati OH 45246 United States
800-487-7626
http://www.hussmanfunds.com

HVIA Equity Fund
c/o Ultimus Fund Solutions, LLC P.O. Box 46707 Cincinnati Ohio 45246-0707 United States

ICM Series Trust
ICM Series Trust 803 Cathedral Street Baltimore MD 21201 United States
http://www.icomd.com

ICON Funds
ICON Funds 5299 DTC Boulevard, Suite 1200 Greenwood Village CO 80111 United States
303-790-1600
http://www.iconfunds.com

Impulsora Del Fondo Mexico, SC
Impulsora Del Fondo Mexico, SC Mexico City 11560 Mexico
http://www.themexicofund.com

IMS
IMS 8995 SE Otty Road Portland OR 97086 United States
877-244-6235
http://www.imsfunds.com

Independent Franchise Partners
Independent Franchise Partners United States
http://www.franchisepartners.com/funds

Index Funds
Index Funds 1290 Broadway Denver Colorado United States
844-464-6339
http://www.Index.World

IndexIQ
IndexIQ 800 Westchester Avenue, Suite N-611 Rye Brook NY 10573 United States
888-934-0777
http://www.indexiq.com

Infinity Q
Infinity Q P.O. Box 701 Milwaukee WI 53201-0701 United States
http://www.infinityqfunds.com

Innealta Capital
12117 FM 2244 Bldg. 3-#170 Austin TX 78738 United States
512-354-7041
http://www.innealtafunds.com

Innovator Funds
Innovator Funds 615 E. Michigan St. Milwaukee WI 53202 United States
877-386-3890
http://www.innovatorfunds.com

Insignia Macro
P.O. Box 1920 P.O. Box 1920 Denver CO 80201 United States
855-674-4642
http://www.insigniafunds.com

IntegrityVikingFunds
Integrity 1 Main Street Minot ND 58703 United States
800-276-1262
http://www.integrityvikingfunds.com

Intrepid Funds
Intrepid Funds 1400 Marsh Landing Pkwy., Suite 106 Jacksonville Beach FL 32250 United States
http://www.intrepidcapitalfunds.com

Invesco
Invesco 11 Greenway Plaza, Ste. 2500 Houston TX 77046 United States
800-659-1005
http://www.invesco.com/us

Investment House Funds
Investment House Funds United States

Investment Managers Series Trust
INVESTMENT MANAGERS SERIES TRUST 803 W. Michigan St. Milwaukee DE 53233 United States
770-350-8700
http://www.lsthetafund.com/

IP Unsure (Only US OE Use)
For NewFundTeam Shell Creation Use United States

Iron Funds
Iron Funds 2960 Meridian St., Suite 300 Indianapolis IN 46208 United States
877-322-0575
http://www.ironfunds.com

IronBridge Funds
IronBridge Funds United States
http://www.ironbridgefunds.net.

Ironclad Funds
121 South Orange Avenue, Suite 1500 Orlando, FL 32801 Orlando FL 32801 United States
888-979-4766
http://www.IroncladFunds.com

Issachar Fund
P.O. Box 541150 Omaha United States
http://www.LIONX.net

IVA Funds
IVA Funds P.O. Box 8077 Boston MA 02266-8077 United States
866-941-4482
http://www.ivafunds.com

Ivy Funds
Ivy Funds 6300 Lamar Avenue, P.O. Box 29217 Overland Park KS 66202 United States
800-777-6472
http://www.ivyfunds.com

Jackson National
Jackson Natl Life Insurance Co P.O. Box 30389 Lansing MI 48909-7889 United States
http://www.jackson.com

Jackson Square
Jackson Square 101 California St Suite 3750 San Francisco San Francisco 94111 United States
http://www.jspfunds.com

Jacob
Jacob 5507 Paseo De La Playa Redondo Beach CA 90277 United States
http://www.jacobinternet.com

JAG Capital Management, LLC
9841 Clayton Road St. Louis MO 63124 United States
314-997-1277
http://www.JAGCapitalFunds.com

James Advantage
James Advantage 2960 Meridian St., Suite 300 Indianapolis IN 46208 United States
800-995-2637
http://www.jamesfunds.com

Janus Henderson
Janus 151 Detroit Street Denver CO 80206 United States
877-335-2687
http://www.janus.com

Jensen
Jensen 5300 Meadows Road, Suite 250 Lake Oswego OR 97035 United States
800-992-4144
http://www.jenseninvestment.com

JF International Management, Inc.
PO Box 3151 Road Town Tortola British Virgin Islands

JNF Portfolio
JNF Portfolios 4020 South 147th Street, Suite 2 Omaha NE 68137 United States

JOHCM Funds
JOHCM P.O. Box 4766 Chicago Illinois United States
866-260-9549
http://www.johcm.com

John Hancock
601 Congress Street, Boston MA 02210 United States
800-225-5913
http://jhinvestments.com

John Hancock
John Hancock PO Box 55913 Boston MA 02205-5913 United States
800-225-5913
http://jhinvestments.com

Johnson Mutual Funds
Johnson Mutual Funds 3777 West Fork Rd Cincinnati OH 45247 United States
http://www.johnsonmutualfunds.com

JPMorgan
JPMorgan 270 Park Avenue New York NY 10017-2070 United States
800-480-4111
http://www.jpmorganfunds.com

Kaizen
Kaizen 1745 S. Naperville Road, Suite 106 Wheaton IL 60189 United States

Kayne Anderson
Kayne Anderson 811 Main Street, 14th Floor Houston TX 77002 United States
877-657-3863
http://www.kaynecapital.com

KCM
KCM 5075 Westheimer, Suite 1177 Houston TX 77056 United States
http://kcmtx.com/

Keeley
Keeley 401 S. LaSalle Street, Suite 1201 Chicago IL 60605 United States
888-933-5391
http://www.keeleyfunds.com

Kellner
212-350-0200
http://www.kellnerfunds.com

Kempner
Kempner United States

Kinetics
Kinetics 615 E. Michigan Street Milwaukee WI 53202 United States
800-930-3828
http://www.kineticsfunds.com

Kirr Marbach Partners
Kirr Marbach Partners 621 Washington Street Columbus IN 47202 United States
http://www.kmpartnersfunds.com

KKM
KKM 17605 Wright Street, Suite 2 Omaha NE 68130 United States
http://www.KKMarmorfunds.com

Kleinwort Benson Investors Dublin Ltd
Kleinwort Benson Investors Dublin Ltd 3rd Floor,2 Harbourmaster Place Dublin Ireland
http://www.kleinwortbensoninvestors.com

Knights Of Columbus
Knights Of Columbus One Columbus Plaza New Haven CT 06510 United States
203-772-2130
http://www.kofcassetadvisors.org

Kopernik
Kopernik Global Investors, LLC 302 Knights Run Ave, Suite 1225 Tampa FL 33602 United States
855-887-4544
http://www.kopernikglobal.com

KP Funds
KP Funds One Freedome Valley Drive OAKS PA 19456 United States
http://www.kp-funds.com

Ladenburg Thalmann
c/o Gemini Fund Services, LLC 17605 Wright Street, Suite 2 Omaha NE 68130 United States
877-803-6583
http://www.ladenburgfunds.com

Lateef
Lateef Investment Management United States

Laudus Funds
Laudus Funds PO Box 8032 Boston MA 02266 United States
http://www.csimfunds.com

Lawson Kroeker
Lawson Kroeker United States

Lazard
Lazard Asset Management LLC 30 Rockefeller Plaza, New York NY 10112-6300 United States
800-823-6300
http://www.lazardassetmanagement.com

Lazard Freres Asset Management
Lazard Asset Management Securities LLC 30 Rockefeller Plaza NEW YORK NY 10112 United States

Leavell
Leavell P.O. Box 46707 Cincinnati OH 45246 United States
http://www.leavellinvestments.com

Legg Mason
Legg Mason/Western 100 International Drive Baltimore MD 21202 United States
877-721-1926
http://www.leggmason.com

Leland Funds
Leland Funds 17605 Wright Street, Suite 2 Omaha Nebraska 68130 United States
877-270-2848
http://www.lelandfunds.com

Leuthold
Leuthold 33 Sixth Street, Suite 4600 Minneapolis MN 55402 United States
800-273-6886
http://www.leutholdfunds.com

Liberty Street
Liberty Street 803 W. Michigan Street Milwaukee WI 53233 United States
800-207-7108
http://www.libertystreetfunds.com

Linde Hansen
25 B Vreeland Road FLORHAM PARK NJ United States
http://www.lindehansen.com

Litman Gregory Masters Funds
Litman Gregory Masters Funds United States
800-960-0188
http://www.mastersfunds.com.

LJM Funds
LJM Funds One Financial Place, 440 S. La Salle Street, Suite 2301, Chicago, IL Chicago IL United States
http://www.ljmfunds.com

LKCM
LKCM 301 Commerce Street, Suite 1600 Fort Worth TX 76102 United States
800-688-5526
http://www.lkcm.com

LMCG Funds
LMCG Funds United States
http://www.lmcgfunds.com

LoCorr Funds
LoCorr Funds United States
855-523-8637
http://www.LoCorrFunds.com

Logan Capital
Logan Capital United States
http://www.logancapital.com

Long Short
Long Short Market Street, Suite 3323 Philadelphia PA 19103 United States
http://www.longshortadvisors.com

Longboard
c/o Gemini Fund Services, LLC 17605 Wright Street, Suite 2 Omaha NE 68130 United States
855-294-7540
http://www.longboardmutualfunds.com

Longleaf Partners
Longleaf Partners 101 Sabin Street Pawtucket RI 2860 United States
800-445-9469
http://www.longleafpartners.com

Loomis Sayles Funds
Loomis Sayles Funds P.O. Box 219594 Kansas City MO 64121-9594 United States
800-633-3330
http://www.loomissayles.com

Lord Abbett
Lord Abbett 90 Hudson Street Jersey City NJ 7302 United States
201-827-2000
http://www.lordabbett.com

LSV Fund
LSV Fund 1 N. Wacker Drive, Suite 4000 Chicago IL 60606 United States
http://www.lsvasset.com

Lyrical
Lyrical Asset Management LP 405 Park Avenue, Floor 6 New York NY 10022 United States
888-884-8099
http://www.lyricalam.com

Macquarie Group Ltd
Level 3, 25 National Circuit Forrest Act 2603 C3 00000 United States

Macquarie Investment Management
Delaware Investments 2005 Market Street, One Commerce Square Philadelphia PA 19103 United States
215-255-2300
http://www.delawareinvestments.com

Madison Asset Management, LLC
550 Science Drive Madison WI 53711 United States
800-767-0300
http://www.madisonadv.com

Madison Funds
Madison 550 Science Drive Madison WI 53711 United States
800-767-0300
http://www.madisonfunds.com

Madison Invest Advisors Inc
550 Science Drive Madison WI 53711 United States

MAI
MAI 1360 E. Ninth Street, Suite 1100 Cleveland OH 44114 United States
866-624-9584
http://www.divplusfund.com.

Main Management
Main Management 601 California Street, Suite 620 San Francisco California 94108 United States
http://www.mainmgtfunds.com

MainGate Trust
MainGate Trust 6075 POPLAR AVE. SUITE 720 MEMPHIS TN 38119 United States
901-537-1866
http://www.maingatefunds.com

MainStay
MainStay 51 Madison Avenue New York NY 10010 United States
800-624-6782
http://mainstayinvestments.com/

Mairs & Power
Mairs & Power United States
800-304-7404
http://www.mairsandpower.com

Managed Futures Solutions Fund
Managed Futures Solutions Fund 450 WIRESLESS BLVD HAUPPAUGE DE United States
http://www.sfgalternatives.com.

Manning & Napier
Manning Napier 290 Woodcliff Drive Fairport NY 14450 United States
585-325-6880
http://www.manning-napier.com

Manor Investment Funds
Manor Investment Funds United States
http://www.morriscapitaladvisors.com

Marathon Funds
PO Box 5536 Hauppauge NY 11788-0132 United States
http://www.spectrumadvisory.com

Marketfield Funds
Marketfield Funds 292 Madison Avenue, 14th Floor NEW YORK NY 10017 United States
http://www.marketfield.com

Marshfield
Marshfield P.O. Box 46707 Cincinnati Ohio 45246-0707 United States
http://www.marshfieldfunds.com

Marsico Investment Fund
Marsico Investment Fund 1200 17th St, Ste 1600 Denver CO 80202 United States
888-860-8686
http://www.marsicofunds.com

MassMutual
MML Investment Advisers, LLC 100 Bright Meadow Blvd., Enfield CT 06082 United States
http://www.massmutual.com/funds

Matrix Advisors Funds Trust
Matrix Advisors Funds Trust 747 Third Avenue, 31st Floor New York New York 10017 United States

Matrix/LMH
Matrix/LMH 747 Third Avenue, 31st Floor NEW YORK NY 10017 United States
866-209-1965
http://www.matrixadvisorsvaluefund.com

Matthew 25
Matthew 25 605 Cloverly Avenue Jenkintown PA 19046 United States
215-884-4458
http://www.matthew25fund.com

Matthews Asia Funds
Matthews Asia Funds Four Embarcadero Center Suite 550 San Francisco CA 94111 United States
800-789-2742
http://www.matthewsasia.com

McKee Funds
McKee Funds 1 Gateway Center, 8th Floor Pittsburgh PA 15222 United States
http://www.csmckee.com

MD Sass
MD Sass United States
http://www.mdsassfunds.com

Measured Risk Portfolios
Measured Risk Portfolios 5405 Morehouse Drive, Suite 230 San Diego CA 92121 United States
http://www.mrp.fund

Meeder Funds
Meeder Funds 6125 Memorial Dr. PO Box 7177 Dublin OH 43017 United States
http://www.meederfunds.com

Meehan Focus
Meehan Focus 555 E North Ln Ste 6160 Conshohocken PA 19428 United States
http://www.meehanmutualfunds.com.

Meridian
Meridian 660 E. Sir Francis Drake Blvd., Suite 306 Larkspur CA 94939 United States
800-446-6662
http://www.meridianfund.com

Meritage Portfolio Management
Suite 1212 7500 College Boulevard Overland Park KS 662104035 United States
913-345-7000
http://www.meritageportfolio.com

Metropolitan West Funds
METROPOLITAN WEST ASSET MANAGEMENT 865 S. FIGUEROA STREET, SUITE 2100 LOS ANGELES CA 90017 United States
800-241-4671
http://www.mwamllc.com

MFG Funds
MFG Funds P.O. Box 588 Portland ME 04112 United States
http://www.mfgam.com.au

MFS
MFS 111 Huntington Avenue Boston MA 02199-7632 United States
877-960-6077
http://www.mfs.com

MH Elite
MH Elite 220 Russell Avenue Rahway NJ 7065 United States
http://www.mhelite.com

Midas
Midas 11 Hanover Square New York NY 10005 United States
800-400-6432
http://www.midasfunds.com

Midas Management Corporation
Midas Management Corporation 11 Hanover Square New York NY 10005 United States
212-785-0900

Miles Capital
Miles Capital 1415 28th Street, Suite 200 West Des Moines IA 50266 United States
http://www.miles-capital.com

Miller Investment
Miller Investment 2 Deanna Drive Oxford CT 6478 United States
877-441-4434
http://www.millerconvertiblefund.com

Miller Value Funds
Miller Value Funds United States

Miller/Howard Funds Trust
Miller/Howard Funds Trust 10 Dixon Avenue Woodstock New York 12498 United States
845-679-9166
http://www.mhinvest.com/

Miller/Howard Investments, Inc.
P O Box 549 10 Dixon Avenue Woodstock NY 12498 United States
845-679-9166
http://www.mhinvest.com

Mirae Asset Global Investments
Mirae Asset Global Investments 1350 Avenue of Americas, 33rd Floor New York NY 10019 United States
212-205-8300
http://www.miraeasset.com/main/index.do

MOERUS FUNDS
MOERUS FUNDS 307 West 38th Street, Suite 2003 New York NY 10018 United States
212-461-4088
http://moerusfunds.com/

Moncapfund
Moncapfund P.O. Box 588 Portland ME 04112 United States
855-392-9331
http://www.Moncapfund.com

Mondrian
Mondrian Two Commerce Square, 2001 Market Str., Suite 3810 Philadelphia PA 19103-7039 United States
888-832-4386
http://www.mondrian.com/mutualfunds

Monetta
Monetta 1776-A S. Naperville Road, Suite 100 Wheaton IL 60189 United States
800-684-3416
http://www.monetta.com

Monteagle Funds
Monteagle Funds 8000 Town Centre Drive, Suite 400 OH 44147 United States
http://www.monteaglefunds.com

Morgan Dempsey
Morgan Dempsey P.O. Box 701 Milwaukee WI 53201-0701 United States
http://www.morgandempsey.com

Morgan Stanley
Morgan Stanley 1221 Avenue of the Americas New York NY 10020 United States
855-332-5306
http://www.morganstanley.com

Motley Fool
Motley Fool 2000 Duke Street, Suite 175 Alexandria VA 22314 United States
http://www.foolfunds.com

MP 63
The MP 63 Fund 555 Theodore Fremd Ave, Ste B-103 Rye NY 10580 United States
http://www.mp63fund.com

MT Lucas
MT Lucas United States
http://www.mtlucas.com

Muhlenkamp
Muhlenkamp Fund 3000 Stonewood Dr. Ste 310 Wexford PA 15090-0598 United States
http://www.muhlenkamp.com

Multi-Strategy
Multi-Strategy 450 Wireless Boulevard | Hauppauge, NY 11788 Hauppauge NY 11788 United States
855-601-3841
http://www.growthandincomefund.com/

Mundoval Funds
Mundoval Funds 7855 Ivanhoe Ave., Ste 210 La Jolla CA 92037 United States
http://www.mundoval.com

Mutual of America
Mutual of America 666 Fifth Avenue New York NY 10103 United States
http://www.mutualofamerica.com

Mutualhedge
Mutualhedge 450 Wireless Boulevard Hauppauge NY 11788 United States
888-643-3431
http://www.equinoxfunds.com

Nationwide
Nationwide One Nationwide Plaza Columbus OH 43215 United States
800-848-0920
http://www.nationwide.com/mutualfunds

Natixis Funds
Natixis Funds 399 Boylston Street Boston MA 02116 United States
800-862-4863
http://NGAM.natixis.com

Navigator Funds
Navigator Funds United States
http://www.navigatorfund.com.

Needham
Needham 445 Park Avenue New York NY 10022 United States
800-625-7071
http://www.needhamfunds.com

Neiman Funds
Neiman Funds 6631 Main Street Williamsville NY 14221 United States
858-551-4078
http://www.neimanfunds.com

Neuberger Berman
Neuberger Berman 1290 Avenue of the Americas New York NY 10104 United States
212-476-9000
http://www.nb.com

New Alternatives
New Alternatives 150 Broadhollow Road Melville NY 11747 United States
800-423-8383
http://www.newalternativesfund.com

New Covenant
New Covenant P.O. Box 701 Milwaukee WI 53201 United States
http://www.newcovenantfunds.com

Newfound
Newfound 425 Boylston Street, 3rd Floor Boston MA 02116 United States
http://www.thinknewfound.com

NexPoint
NexPoint 300 Crescent Court Suite 700 Dallas Texas 75201 United States
http://www.nexpointres.com

NexPoint Advisors, L.P.
200 Crescent Court, Suite 700 Dallas, TX 75201 Dallas United States

Nicholas
Nicholas P.O. Box 701 Milwaukee WI 53201 United States
800-544-6547
http://www.nicholasfunds.com

Nile Capital Investment Trust
Nile Capital Investment Trust 116 Village Blvd, Suite 200 Princeton NJ 8540 United States
646-367-2820
http://www.nilecapital.com

Nomura Asset Management Co Ltd
12-1 Nihonbashi 1 cho-me Tokyo 103-8260 Japan
813-324-1951
http://www.nomura.com

North Country Funds
Gemini Fund Services, Llc. 450 Wireless Boulevard Hauppauge NY 11788 United States
http://www.arrowfinancial.com

North Star
North Star 20 N. Wacker Drive Chicago IL 60606 United States
312-580-0
http://www.nsinvestfunds.com

NorthCoast
North Coast Am United States
http://www.northcoastam.com.

Northern Funds
Northern Funds 50 South Lasalle Chicago IL 60603 United States
800-595-9111
http://www.northernfunds.com

NorthPointe Funds
NorthPointe P.O. Box 2085 Milwaukee WI 53201 United States
http://www.northpointefunds.com

Northquest Capital Fund Inc
Northquest Capital Fund Inc 16 Rimwood Lane Colts Neck NJ 7722 United States
http://www.northquestfund.com

Northwood
Northwood 575 5th Avenue, 23rd Floor New York NY 10017 United States
http://www.northwoodinvestors.com

Nottingham
Nottingham 116 South Franklin Street Rocky Mount NC 27804 United States
252-442-4226
http://www.ncfunds.com

Nuance Investments
Nuance Investments 4900 Main Street, Suite 220 Kansas MO 64112 United States
http://www.nuanceinvestments.com

Nuveen
Nuveen Investment Trust John Nuveen & Co. Inc. Chicago IL 60606 United States
312-917-8146
http://www.nuveen.com

NWM Momentum
NWM Momentum United States
http://www.nwmfund.com

Nysa
Nysa 5507 Plum Street, Suite 120 Syracuse NY 13204 United States
http://www.nysfunds.com

O'Shaughnessy Asset Management
O'Shaughnessy Asset Management 6 Suburban Avenue Stamford CT 06901 United States

Oak Associates
Oak Associates P.O. Box 219441 Kansas City MO 64121 United States
888-462-5386
http://www.oakfunds.com

Oak Ridge Funds
Oak Ridge Funds P.O. Box 701 Milwaukee WI 53201-0701 United States
http://www.oakridgefunds.com.

Oakhurst
Oakhurst P.O. Box 701 United States

Oakmark
Oakmark P.O. Box 219558 Kansas City MO 64121 United States
641-219-558
http://www.oakmark.com

Oberweis
Oberweis 3333 Warrenville Road, Suite 500 Lisle IL 60532 United States
http://www.oberweisfunds.com

OCM
OCM 11299 Ocean Avenue, Suite 210 Santa Monica CA 90401 United States
http://www.ocmgoldfund.com

Old Westbury
Old Westbury 630 5Th Ave New York NY 10111 United States
212-708-9100

Olstein
Olstein 44 Manhattanville Road New York NY 10577 United States
800-799-2113
http://www.olsteinfunds.com

OppenheimerFunds
OppenheimerFunds 12100 East Iliff Avenue, Suite 300, Aurora, Colorado Aurora CO 80217-5270 United States
800-225-5677
http://www.oppenheimerfunds.com

Orchard Capital Management
Orchard Small Cap Value Fund 17605 Wright Street, Suite 2 Omaha NE 68130 United States
844--

Orinda Funds
Orinda Funds United States
http://www.orindafunds.com

O'Shaughnessy Mutual Funds
O'Shaughnessy Mutual Funds United States
http://www.osfunds.com

Osterweis
One Maritime Plaza Suite 800 San Francisco CA 94111 United States
866-236-0050
http://www.osterweis.com

Otter Creek
Otter Creek 222 Lakeview Avenue Suite 1100 West Palm Beach FL 33401 United States
561-832-4110
http://www.ottercreekfunds.com

Pacific Advisors Funds
Pacific Advisors Funds 101 N. Brand Flvd., Suite 1950 Glendale CA 91203 United States
http://www.pacificadvisorsfunds.com

Pacific Financial
Pacific Financial 10900 Ne 8Th St Ste 1523 Bellevue WA 980044451 United States
425-451-7722
http://www.tpfg.com

Pacific Funds Series Trust
Pacific Funds 700 Newport Center Drive Post Offfice Box 7500 Newport Beach CA 92660 United States
800-722-2333
http://www.pacificlife.com

Palmer Square
Palmer Square 11300 Tomahawk Creek Parkway, Suite 200 Leawood KS 66211 United States
866-933-9033
http://www.palmersquarefunds.com

Papp
Papp 225 Pictoria Drive Suite 450 Cincinnati OH 45246 United States
http://www.pappmutualfunds.com

Paradigm Funds
Paradigm Funds Nine Elk Street Albany NY 12207 United States
800-239-0732
http://www.paradigm-funds.com

Parnassus
Parnassus 1 Market Street, Suite 1600 San Francisco CA 94105 United States
999-350-5
http://www.parnassus.com

Patriot
c/o Gemini Fund Services, LLC 17605 Wright Street, Suite 2 Omaha NE 68130 United States
http://www.patriotfund.com

Pax World
Pax World 30 Penhallow Street, Suite 400 Portsmouth NH 3801 United States
800-767-1729
http://www.paxworld.com

Paydenfunds
Paydenfunds 333 S Grand Ave, 32nd Floor Los Angeles CA 90071 United States
614-470-8006
http://www.payden.com

Payson Funds
Payson Funds 1 Portland Square, 5th Floor Portland ME 4112 United States
http://www.hmpayson.com

Pear Tree Funds
Pear Tree Funds 55 OLD BEDFORD ROAD SUITE 202 LINCOLN NE 01773 United States
800-326-2151
http://www.peartreefunds.com

Penn Capital Management
Penn Capital Management United States
http://www.penncapitalfunds.com

Perkins
Perkins 730 E. Lake Street Wayzata MN 55391 United States
http://www.perkinscapital.com

Permanent Portfolio
Permanent Portfolio 600 Montgomery Street, 27th Floor San Francisco CA 94111 United States
800-531-5142
http://www.permanentportfoliofunds.com

Perritt
Perritt 300 S. Wacker Drive, Suite 2880 Chicago IL 60606 United States
800-332-3133
http://www.perrittmutualfunds.com

Persimmon Capital Management LP
Persimmon Capital Management, LP 1777 Sentry Parkway West Gwynedd Hall, Suite 102 Blue Bell, PA 19422 Blue Bell PA United States
http://www.persimmonfunds.com

Persimmon Funds
Persimmon Funds United States

PhaseCapital
PhaseCapital United States

Phocas
Phocas Real Estate Fund P.O. Box 588 Portland MA 04112 United States
866-746-2271

Pichardo Asset Management SA De CV
Pichardo Asset Management United States

Piedmont
Piedmont 1604 Spring Hill Road, 3rd Floor Vienna VA 22182 United States
http://www.piedmontselectfund.com

Pimco
PIMCO 840 Newport Center Drive, Suite 100 Newport Beach CA 92660 United States
866-746-2602
http://www.pimco.com

PineBridge
Brazos Mutual Funds 55949 Sherry Lane, Suite 1600 Dallas TX 75225 United States
http://www.PineBridge.com/USMutualFunds

Pinnacle
Pinnacle 8000 Town Centre Drive, Suite 400 Broadview Heights OH 44147 United States
http://www.pinnaclevaluefund.com.

Pinnacle Capital Management
Pinnacle Capital Management 5 Burlington Woods, Suite 102 Burlington MA 01803 United States
617-399-0900
http://www.pcm-advisors.com

Pioneer Investments
Pioneer Investments 60 State Street Boston MA 02109 United States
617-742-7825
http://www.pioneerinvestments.com

PMC Funds
PMC Funds 35 E. Wacker Drive, Suite 1600 Chicago IL 60601 United States
http://www.investpmc.com

PNC Funds
PNC Funds 103 Bellevue Parkway Suite 152 Wilmington DE 19809 United States
800-622-3863
http://www.pncfunds.com

Polaris Funds
Polaris Funds P.O. Box 588 Portland ME 4112 United States
http://www.polariscapital.com

Polen Capital
2700 N. Military Trail Suite 230 Boca Raton FL 33431 United States
561-241-2425
http://www.polencapital.com

Poplar Forest Capital
Poplar Forest Capital 615 East Michigan Street Milwaukee WI 53202 United States
877-522-8860
http://www.poplarforestfunds.com

Port Street Investments
Port Street Investments 24 Corporate Plaza, Suite 150 Newport Beach CA 92660 United States
http://www.portstreetinvest.com

Portfolio Strategies
Portfolio Strategies, Inc. 1724 W Union Avenue Tacoma WA 98405 United States
http://www.portstrat.com/

Potkul Funds
Potkul Funds 3633 Hill Road, 3rd Floor Parsippany NJ 7054 United States
http://www.breadandbutterfund.com

Power Mutual Funds
629 Washington Street Norwood, MA 02062 United States
877-779-7462
http://www.powermutualfunds.com/

Praxis Mutual Funds
Praxis Mutual Funds 303 Broadway, Suite 900 Cincinnati OH 45202 United States
http://www.praxismutualfunds.com

PREDEX

Preserver Funds
c/o Ultimus Asset Services, LLC 225 Pictoria Drive, Suite 450 Cincinnati OH 45246 United States
http://www.preserverfunds.com

Price Asset Management
141 W Jackson Blvd, Suite 1320A Chicago IL 60604 United States
888-430-0043
http://pcscommodityfunds.com

Primary Trend
Primary Trend 3960 Hillside Drive, Suite 204 Delafield WI 53018 United States
http://www.primarytrendfunds.com

PRIMECAP Odyssey Funds
PRIMECAP Odyssey Funds 225 South Lake Avenue, Suite 400 Pasadena CA 91101 United States
800-729-2307
http://www.odysseyfunds.com

Princeton
Princeton United States
http://www.pfstrategyfund.com

Principal Funds
Principal Funds 30 Dan Road Canton MA 2021 United States
800-222-5852
http://www.principalfunds.com

Private Capital Management
Private Capital Management 8889 Pelican Bay Blvd # 500 Naples FL 34108 United States
239-254-2500
http://www.private-cap.com

Probabilities Fund
www.probabilitiesfund.com Probabilities Fund San Diego CA 92101 United States
855-224-7204
http://www.probabilitiesfund.com

ProFunds
Profunds 3435 Stelzler Rd Columbus OH 43219 United States
614-470-8626
http://www.profunds.com

Prospector Funds
Prospector Funds 3370 Church Street Guilford CT 6437 United States
877-734-7862
http://www.prospectorfunds.com

Provident
Provident Trust N16 W23217 Stone Ridge Drive, Suite 310 Waukesha WI 53188 United States
855-739-9950
http://www.provfunds.com

Prudential Funds (PGIM Investments)
Prudential Funds (PGIM Investments) 655 Broad Street Newark NJ 07102 United States
800-225-1852
http://www.pgiminvestments.com

PSG Funds
PSG Funds United States
http://www.psgfunds.com

Putnam
Putnam One Post Office Square Boston MA 02109 United States
617-292-1000
http://www.putnam.com

Pzena
Pzena 120 West 45th Street 20th Floor New York NY 10036 United States
http://www.pzena.com

Quaker
Quaker P.O. Box 701 Milwaukee WI 53201 United States
800-220-8888
http://www.quakerfunds.com

Queens Road Funds
Queens Road Funds 1031 South Caldwell Street, Suite 200 Charlotte NC 28203 United States
888-353-0261
http://www.queensroadfunds.com

Rainier
Rainier 615 E. Michigan Street, 3rd Floor Milwaukee WI 53202 United States
800-248-6314
http://www.rainierfunds.com

Ranger Funds
Ranger Funds United States
http://www.rangerfunds.com

Rareview Capital
United States United States
http://www.rareviewfunds.com/

Rational Funds
Rational Funds 2960 N. Meridian St., Suite 300 Indianapolis IN 46208 United States
800-253-0412
http://www.rationalmf.com

RBB Funds
RBB Funds 125 W. 55th Street New York NY 10019 United States
http://www.matsonmoney.com

RBC Global Asset Management.
RBC Global Asset Management 100 South Fifth Street, Suite 2300 Minneapolis MN 55402 United States
800-422-2766
http://www.rbcgam.us

RCM Asia Pacific Limited
852-223-8863

Real Estate Management Services Group, LLC
1100 FIFTH AVENUE SOUTH, SUITE 305 NAPLES FL United States

Reaves Asset Management
Reaves Utility Income Fund 1625 Broadway Denver CO 80202 United States
800-644-5571
http://www.reavesassetmanagement.com

Reaves Select Research
Reaves Select Research 10 Exchange Place, 18th Floor Jersey City NJ 7302 United States
http://www.whreaves.com

Redmont
Redmont 1290 Broadway, Suite 1100 Denver CO 80203 United States
855-268-2242
http://www.redmontfunds.com

Redwood
Redwood United States
http://www.redwoodmutualfund.com

Regal
Regal United States
http://www.regaltrx.com

Reinhartfunds
Reinhart Partners, Inc. 1500 West Market Street, Mequon, Wisconsin 53092 Mequon WI 53092 United States
855-774-3863
http://www.reinhartfunds.com

REMSGroup
REMSGroup United States
http://www.theworldfundstrust.com

Renaissance Capital
Renaissance Capital United States
866-486-6645
http://www.renaissancecapital.com

Renn Capital Group Inc
8080 N Central Expressway Ste 210 Lb-59 Dallas TX 75206 United States
214-891-8294
http://www.rencapital.com

Resource Real Estate
Resource Real Estate One Commerce Square 2005 Market Street, 15th Floor Philadelphia PA United States
855-747-9559
http://www.RREDIF.com

RESQ Funds
9383 E. Bahia Drive, Suite 120 United States
http://www.RESQFunds.com

Reynolds
45 Broad St The Atrium New York NY 100042516 United States
212-742-1616
http://www.reynoldsfunds.com

Rice Hall James
Rice Hall James 600 W Broadway, Suite 1000 San Diego CA 92101 United States
619-239-9005
http://www.rhjfunds.com

Riverbridge
Riverbridge 801 Nicollet Mall, Midwest Plaza West Minneapolis MN 55402 United States
http://www.riverbridge.com

Rivernorth Capital Management, LLC
325 N LaSalle St Suite 645 325 N. LaSalle Street, Suite 645 Chicago IL 60654 United States
312-832-1440
http://www.rivernorth.com

RiverNorth Funds
RiverNorth Funds 325 N Lasalle St. Suite 645 Chicago IL 60654 United States
312-832-1440
http://www.rivernorthfunds.com

RiverPark Funds
RiverPark Funds 156 West 56th Street, 17th Floor, New York, NY 10011 United States
888-564-4517
http://www.riverparkfunds.com

RMB Funds
RMB Funds United States
http://www.rmbfunds.com

RMR Advisors LLC
RMR Advisors, Inc. 400 Centre Street Newton MA 02458-2076 United States

RNC Genter Capital Management
11601 Wilshire Blvd, Twenty-fifth Floor Los Angeles CA 90025 United States
800-877-7624
http://www.RNCGenter.com

Rockefeller & Co.
Rockefeller & Co. United States
http://www.rockefellerfunds.com

Rondure Global
Rondure Funds 1290 Broadway, Suite 1100 Denver CO 80203 United States
303-623-2577
http://www.ronduregIobal.com

Royce
Royce & Associates, LLC 745 Fifth Avenue New York NY 10151 United States
800-221-4268
http://www.roycefunds.com

Royce & Associates, LP
Royce & Associates, LLC 1414 Avenue of the America's New York NY 10019 United States
212-486-1445
http://www.roycefunds.com

RQSI
RQSI 1515 Ormsby Station Ct. Louisville KY 40223 United States
http://www.rqsifunds.com

Rrecurrent Advisors
Rrecurrent Advisors United States
http://www.recurrentadvisors.com/

RSQ
RSQ United States
http://www.rsquaredcapital.com

Russell
1301 Second Avenue 18th Floor Seattle 98101 United States
800-426-7969
https://russellinvestments.com

RWC
RWC Partners Limited 60 Petty France London London SW1H 9EU United Kingdom
442-072-2760
http://www.rwcpartners.com

Rydex Funds
Rydex Funds 9601 Blackwell Rd, Suite 500 Rockville MD 20850 United States
800-820-0888
http://www.guggenheiminvestments.com

SA Funds
SA Funds 3055 Olin Ave,Suite 2000 San Jose CA 95128
United States
http://www.sa-funds.net

Salient Capital Advisors, LLC
4265 SAN FELIPE 8TH FLOOR HOUSTON TX 77027
HOUSTON TX 77027 United States
713-993-4675

Salient Funds
Salient Funds 4265 San Felipe, Suite 800, Houston, Texas
77027 United States
866-667-9228
http://www.salientfunds.com

Sands Capital
Sands Capital 1101 Wilson Boulevard, Suite 2300 Arlington
VA 22209 United States
http://www.sandscapital.com

Saratoga
Saratoga 99 Wall Street, Suite 1200 New York NY 10005
United States
800-807-3863
http://www.saratogacap.com/

Sarofim
2907 Two Houston Center 909 Fannin Street Houston TX
77010 United States
http://www.sarofim.com

SATUIT FUNDS
SATUIT FUNDS Franklin TN 37064 United States
973-568-6799
http://www.satuitfunds.com/

Saturna Sustainable Funds
United States United States
http://www.saturnasustainable.com

Savos Investments Trust
1655 Grant Street, 10th Floor Concord, CA 94520 Concord
CA 94520 United States
http://www.geassetmanagement.com

Scharf Investments
Scharf Investments 5619 Scotts Valley Drive, Suite 140
Scotts Valley CA 95066 United States
831-429-6513
http://www.scharfinvestments.com/

Schneider Funds
Schneider Funds 460 East Swedesford Road, Suite 2000
Wayne PA 19087 United States
888-520-3277
http://www.schneidercap.com

Schroder
Schroders 875 Third Avenue, 22nd Floor New York NY
United States
800-464-3108
http://www.schroderfunds.com/

Schroder Investment Management North America Inc.
875 Third Avenue New York 10022 United States
800-730-2932

Schwab Funds
Schwab Funds 101 Montgomery Street San Francisco CA
94104 United States
877-824-5615
http://www.schwab.com

Schwartz
Schwartz 3707 West Maple Road Bloomfields Hills MI
48301 United States
888-726-0753
http://www.schwartzvaluefund.com

ScotiaFunds
ScotiaFunds 4400 Computer Drive Westborough MA
01581 United States
http://www.scotiabank.com/ca/en/0,,666,00.html

Seafarer Funds
Seafarer United States
http://seafarerfunds.com

Segall Bryant & Hamill
540 West Madison Street, Suite 1900 Chicago IL 60661-
2551 United States
312-474-1222
http://sbhic.com

SEI
SEI Asset Allocation Trust 1 Freedom Valley Drive Oaks PA
19456 United States
800-342-5734
http://www.seic.com

Selected Funds
Selected Funds 2949 E. Elvira Rd. Ste 101 Tucson AZ
85706 United States
800-243-1575
http://www.selectedfunds.com

Selective
Selective 828 Main Street, Suite 1703, Lynchburg, VA
24504 Lynchburg VA 24504 United States
http://www.selectivewealthmanagement.com

Sequoia
Sequoia Fund 767 Fifth Avenue New York NY 10153
United States
800-686-6884
http://www.sequoiafund.com

Sextant Mutual Funds
Sextant United States
http://www.sextantfunds.com

SharesPost 100
SharesPost 100 1150 Bayhill Drive, Suite 300 San Bruno California 94066 United States
http://www.sharespost100fund.com

Shelton Capital Management
Shelton Capital Management 455 Market Street, Suite 1600 San Francisco CA 94105 United States
800-955-9988
http://www.sheltoncap.com

SilverPepper
SilverPepper United States
http://www.silverpepperfunds.com

Sims Capital Management LLC
Sims Capital Management 205 E. Wisconsin Avenue, Suite 120 Milwaukee WI 53202 United States
414-765-1107
http://www.simscapital.com

Sirius Funds
Sirius Funds 11390 Dutchman's Creek Road Lovettsville VA 20180 United States
http://www.SiriusFunds.com

Sit
Sit 101 Sabin Street Pawtucket RI 2860 United States
800-332-5580
http://www.sitfunds.com

SkyBridge
SkyBridge 527 Madison Avenue, 16th Fl. New York NY 10022 United States
http://www.skybridgecapital.com

Smead Funds
Smead Funds 1411 Fourth Avenue, Suite 1550 Seattle WA 98101 United States
206-838-9850
http://www.smeadfunds.com

Smith Group
Smith Group 100 Crescent Court, Ste 1150 Dallas TX 75201 United States
888-572-0968
http://www.smithgroupfunds.com

Snow Capital Funds
Snow Capital Funds 2000 Georgetowne Drive, Suite 200, Sewickley, PA 15143 PA 15143 United States
877-244-6235
http://www.snowfunds.com

Sound Mind
Sound Mind P.O. Box 6110, Indianapolis IN 46206 United States
http://www.smifund.com

Sound Shore
Sound Shore Fund 2 Portland Square Portland ME 04101 United States
800-551-1980
http://www.soundshorefund.com

Soundwatch Capital
485 Madison Avenue 7th Floor New York NY 10022 United States
http://www.soundwatch.com

Sparrow
Sparrow 11330 Olive Blvd Suite 230 Saint Louis MI 63141 United States
http://www.sparrowfunds.com

SPDR State Street Global Advisors
SPDR State Street Global Advisors State Street Financial Center, 1 Lincoln Street Boston MA 02111-2900 United States
617-786-3000
http://www.spdrs.com

Spirit of America
Spirit of America 477 Jericho Turnpike Syosset NY 11791 United States

Spouting Rock
United States 2960 North Meridian Street, Suite 300 United States
http://www.spoutingrockfunds.com

Sprott Asset Management L.P.
Royal Bank Plaza 200 Bay Street Toronto ON M5J 2J1 Canada
866-299-9906
http://www.sprott.com

STAAR Investment Trust
STAAR Investment Trust 604 McKnight Park Drive Pittsburgh PA 15237 United States
http://www.staarinvest.com

Stadion Funds
Stadion Funds 1061 Cliff Dawson Road Watkinsville GA 30677 United States
706-353-8737
http://www.stadionfunds.com

State Farm
State Farm Life Insurance Company One State Farm Plaza Bloomington IL 61710-0001 United States
http://www.statefarm.com

State Street Global Advisors
State Street Global Advisors One Lincoln Street Boston MA 02111 United States
617-664-7338
http://www.ssga.com

Steben & Company
Steben & Company 9711 Washingtonian Blvd., Suite 400 United States
http://www.steben.com

Steinberg
Steinberg Select Fund P.O. Box 588 United States
855-330-7085

Sterling Capital Funds
434 Fayetteville Street Mall 5th Floor,434 Fayetteville Street Mall Raleigh NC 27601 United States
800-228-1872
http://www.sterlingcapitalfunds.com

Sterling Capital Funds
Sterling Capital Funds 5th Floor,P.O. Box 9762 Providence RI 02940-9762 United States
800-228-1872
http://www.sterlingcapitalfunds.com

Steward Funds
Capstone 5847 San Felipe, Suite 4100 Houston TX 77057 United States
800-262-6631
http://www.stewardmutualfunds.com.

Stone Harbor
5015 District Blvd Vernon CA 900582719 United States
323-277-2777
http://www.shiplp.com

STONE RIDGE
STONE RIDGE 405 Lexington Ave., 55th Floor New York, NY 10174 New York NY 10174 United States

Stralem Fund
C/O Ultimus Fund Solutions, LLC 225 Pictoria Drive, Suite 450 Cincinnati OH 45246 United States
http://www.stralemfund.com

Strategic Global Advisors
100 Bayview Circle Suite 650 Newport Beach California 92660 United States
http://www.sgadvisors.com

STRF
STRF P.O. Box 219731 Kansas City MO 219731 United States
888-292-3178
http://www.sierratotalreturnfund.com/

Summit Global Investments
620 South Main St. Bountiful UT 84010 United States
888-251-4847
http://summitglobalinvestments.com

Superfund
Marc Aurel-Str. 10-12 Vienna Austria

Swan
United States United States
http://www.swandefinedriskfunds.com

Symons
Symons Capital Management Inc 650 Washington Road, Suite 800 Pittsburgh PA 15228 United States
http://www.scm-funds.com

T. Rowe Price
T. Rowe Price 100 East Pratt Street Baltimore MD 21202 United States
410-345-2000
http://www.troweprice.com

Tanaka
Tanaka Growth 369 Lexington Avenue 20F New York NY 10017 United States
877-482-6252
http://www.tanaka.com

Taylor Frigon Capital Management
Taylor Frigon Capital Management Santa Rosa Street, Suite 3B San Luis Obispo California 93401 United States
http://www.taylorfrigonfunds.com

TCM Funds
Tygh Capital Management, Inc. C/O U.S. Bancorp Fund Services, P.O. Box 701 Milwaukee WI United States
http://www.tyghcap.com

TCW
TCW 865 South Figueroa Street,Suite 1800 Los Angeles CA 90017 United States
213-244-0000
http://www.tcw.com

TD Asset Management
TD Asset Management USA Inc 31 West 52nd Street New York NY 10019 United States
http://www.tdamusa.com

Teberg
The Teberg Fund U.S. Bancorp Fund Services, LLC Milwaukee WI 53202 United States
http://www.tebergfund.com

Tekla Capital Management LLC
Hambrecht & Quist Capital Management LLC 30 Rowes Wharf Boston MA 02110 United States
617-772-8500

Teton Westwood Funds
Teton Westwood Funds One Corporate Center Rye NY 10580-1434 United States
http://www.gabelli.com

Third Avenue
Third Avenue Funds 622 Third Avenue, 32nd Floor New York NY 10017 United States
800-443-1021
http://www.thirdavenuefunds.com

Thomas White Funds
Thomas White Funds 440 S. LaSalle Street Suite 3900 Chicago IL 60605 United States
800-811-0535
http://www.thomaswhite.com

Thompson IM Funds Inc
Thompson IM Funds Inc 918 Deming Way, 3rd Floor Madison WI 53717 United States
800-999-0887
http://www.thompsonim.com

Thomson Horstmann & Bryant
Thomson Horstmann & Bryant P.O. Box 219009 Kansas City MI 64121-9009 United States
http://www.thbinc.com

Thornburg
Thornburg Investment Management 2300 North Ridgetop Road Santa Fe NM 87506 United States
800-847-0200
http://www.thornburg.com

Thrivent
Thrivent Mutual Funds 625 Fourth Avenue South Minneapolis MN 55415 United States
http://www.thrivent.com

TIAA Investments
TIAA-CREF Funds P.O. Box 1259 Charlotte NC 28201 United States
877-518-9161
http://www.tiaa.org

Tilson Funds
Tilson Mutual Funds 145 East 57th Street, 10th Floor New York NY 10022 United States
http://www.centaurmutualfunds.com.

Timothy Plan
Timothy Plan 1055 Maitland Center Commons Maitland FL 32759 United States
800-662-0201
http://www.timothyplan.com

TOBAM Core Investments
12 East 49th Street, Suite 3603, New York,NY 10017, USA 49-53, avenue des Champs-Elysées,75008 Paris – France United States
http://www.tobam.fr/

Tocqueville
Tocqueville Funds 40 West 57th St. 19th FL New York NY 10019 United States
212-698-0800
http://www.tocqueville.com

Toews Funds
Toews Funds P.O. Box 446 Portland ME 04112 United States
http://www.ToewsCorp.com.

TOPS
TOPS Portfolios 4020 South 147th Street, Suite 2 Omaha NE 68137 United States
855-572-5945

Topturn
Topturn 30 Ragsdale Drive, Suite 100 Monterey CA 93940 United States
http://www.topturnfunds.com

Toreador
Toreador Funds 2960 N. Meridian Street, Suite 300 Indianapolis IN 46208 United States
http://www.theworldfundstrust.com

Torray
Torray Funds 7501 Wisconsin Avenue, Suite 750W Bethesda MD 20814 United States
800-443-3036
http://www.torray.com

Torray Resolute
7501 Wisconsin Avenue #750 Bethesda, MD 20814 United States
http://www.torrayresolute.com/

Tortoise Capital Advisors
Tortoise Capital Advisors 11550 Ash Street, Suite 300 Leawood KS 66211 United States
866-362-9331
http://www.tortoiseadvisors.com/

Touchstone
Touchstone 303 Broadway, Suite 1100, PO Box 5354 Cincinnati OH 45201-5354 United States
800-543-0407
http://www.touchstoneinvestments.com

Towle
Towle Fund P.O. Box 2175 Milwaukee WI 53201-2175 United States
888-998-6953
http://www.towlefund.com

Transamerica
Transamerica Funds 1801 California Street, Suite 5200 Denver CO 80202 United States
888-233-4339
http://www.transamericafunds.com

Tributary Funds
Tributary Funds PO Box 219022 Kansas City MO 64121-9022 United States
http://www.tributaryfunds.com

Trillium Mutual Funds
Trillium Funds P.O. Box 701 Milwaukee WI 53201-0701 United States
866-209-1962
http://www.trilliummutualfunds.com

Triloma
Triloma 201 North New York Avenue, Suite 250 FL 32789 United States
http://www.trilomaenergy.com/

TS&W Funds
TS&W Funds P.O. Box 219009 Kansas City MO 64121 United States
http://www.tswinvest.com

Tweedy, Browne
Tweedy, Browne Company LLC 350 Park Ave 9th Fl New York NY 10022 United States
800-432-4789
http://www.tweedy.com

Two Oaks Investment Management, Inc.
Two Oaks Investment Management, Inc. 7110 North Fresno Street, Suite 450 Fresno CA 93720 United States
888-806-8633
http://www.twooaks.com

U.S. Global Investors
U.S. Global Investors P.O. Box 781234 San Antonio TX 78278-1234 United States
800-873-8637
http://www.usfunds.com

UBS Asset Management
1285 Avenue of Americas New York NY 10019 United States
212-882-5586
http://www.ubs.com

Union Square Capital Partners
Union Square Capital Partners 235 Whitehorse Lane, Suite 200 Kennett Square PA 19348 United States
833-877-3863
https://www.usqfunds.com/

Upright Investments Trust
Upright Investments Trust 615 West Mount Pleasant Ave Livingston NJ 7039 United States

USA Mutuals
USA Mutuals Plaza Of The Americas, 700 N Pearl Street, Suite 900 Dallas TX 75201 United States
http://www.usamutuals.com

USAA
USAA P.O. Box 659453 San Antonio TX 78265-9825 United States
800-531-8722
http://www.usaa.com

USCA
USCA Uganda

USCF Investments
USCF 1290 Broadway, Suite 1100 Denver CO 80203 United States
http://www.uscfinvestments.com

VALIC
VALIC 2929 Allen Parkway Houston TX 77019 United States
https://www.valic.com

Value Line
Value Line 7 Times Square 21st Floor New York NY 10036. United States
800-243-2729
http://www.vlfunds.com

Value Partners Limited
9th Floor, Nexxus Building, 41 Connaught Road Central Hong Kong Hong Kong - Hong Kong
852-288-0926
http://www.valuepartners.com.hk

Van Eck
Van Eck Associates Corporation 666 Third Avenue New York NY 10017 United States
800-826-1115
http://www.vaneck.com

Vanguard
Vanguard 100 Vanguard Boulevard Malvern PA 19355 United States
877-662-7447
http://www.vanguard.com

Vericimetry Funds
Vericimetry Funds 800 Wilshire Blvd., Suite 300 Los Angeles CA 90017 United States
http://www.vericimetry.com

Versus Capital
Versus Capital United States

Vert Asset Management
Vert Funds P.O. Box 701 Milwaukee WI 53201-0701 United States
http://www.vertfunds.com

Victory
Victory 47 Maple Street - Suite 202 A Summit NJ 07901 United States
800-539-3863
http://www.VictoryFunds.com

Villere
Villere & Co, LLC 601 Poydras St. Suite 1808 New Orleans LS 70130 United States
http://www.villere.com

Virtus
Virtus Opportunities Trust 101 Munson Street Greenfield MA 1301 United States
800-243-1574
http://www.virtus.com

Virtus Alternative Investment Advisers Inc
100 Pearl Street 9th Floor Hartford United States
http://www.virtus.com

Vivaldi
Vivaldi 1622 Willow Road, Suite 101 Northfield IL 60093 United States
http://www.vivaldifunds.com

Volumetric
Volumetric Fund, Inc. 87 Violet Dr Pearl River NY 10965 United States
http://www.volumetric.com

Vontobel
Vontobel 1540 Broadway, 38th Floor New York NY 10036 United States
212-415-7000
http://www.vusa.com

Voya
Voya Investments 7337 E. Doubletree Ranch Road Scottsdale AZ 85258 United States
800-366-0066
http://www.voyainvestments.com

Voya Investments, LLC
Voya Investments, LLC 7337 East Doubletree Ranch Road Scottsdale AZ 85258 United States

Vulcan Value Partners
Vulcan Value Partners Three Protective Center, 2801 Highway 280 South, Suite 300 Birmingham Al 35223 United States
205-803-1582
http://www.vulcanvaluepartners.com

Waddell & Reed
Waddell & Reed Financial Advisors 6300 Lamar Ave Overland Park KS 66202 United States
888-923-3355
http://www.waddell.com

Wall Street
Wall Street Fund 230 Park Avenue Ste 1635 New York NY 10169 United States
http://www.evercorewealthfunds.com

Walthausen Funds
Walthausen Funds 9 Executive Park Drive, Suite B Clifton Park NY 12065 United States
888-925-8428
http://www.walthausenfunds.com

Wanger
Wanger 227 W. Monroe St Ste 3000 Chicago IL 60606 United States
http://www.columbiathreadneedle.com/us

Wasatch
Wasatch Funds Inc P.O. Box 2172 Milwaukee WI United States
800-551-1700
http://www.wasatchfunds.com

Waycross
Waycross Cincinnati, Ohio OH 46707 United States
http://www.waycrossfunds.com

WBI FUNDS
WBI FUNDS 34 Sycamore Avenue, Suite 1-E Little Silver NJ 07739 United States
732-842-4920
http://www.wbifunds.com

WCM Investment Management
WCM Investment Management 281 Brooks Street Laguna Beach CA 92651 United States
949-380-0200
http://www.wcminvest.com

Weiss
Weiss 320 Park Avenue, 20th Floor New York NY 10022 United States
212-415-4500
http://www.gweiss.com

Weitz
Weitz Funds 1125 South 103rd Street, Suite 200 Omaha NE 68124-1071 United States
800-304-9745
http://www.weitzfunds.com

Wellington Shields
Wellington Shields 140 Broadway New York NY 10005 United States
888-626-3863

Wells Fargo
Wells Fargo United States
877-709-8009
http://www.wellsfargo.com/

Wells Fargo Funds
Wells Fargo Funds 525 Market Street San Francisco CA 94105 United States
800-222-8222
https://www.wellsfargofunds.com/

WesMark
WesMark Funds 5800 Corporate Drive Pittsburgh PA United States
800-861-1013
http://www.wesmarkfunds.com

Westchester Capital
WESTCHESTER CAPITAL 100 Summit Lake Drive Valhalla NY 10595 United States
http://www.westchestercapitalfunds.com

Westcore
Westcore Funds C/O Alps Fund Services, Inc., P.o. Box 328 Denver CO 80201 United States
800-392-2673
http://www.westcore.com

Westfield Capital
Westfield Capital United States
http://www.westfieldcapital.com

Westwood
The WHG Funds P.O. Box 219009 Kansas City MO United States
http://www.westwoodfunds.com

Wilbanks Smith & Thomas
Wilbanks Smith & Thomas 150 West Main Street, Suite 1700 Norfolk VA 23510 United States
865-243-8000
http://www.wstamfunds.com

Wildermuth Advisory
Wildermuth Advisory 11525 Park Woods Circle Alpharetta GA 30005 United States
877-562-0856
http://www.wildermuthendowmentfund.com/

William Blair
William Blair 150 North Riverside Plaza Chicago IL 60606 United States
800-621-0687
http://www.williamblair.com

Williamsburg Investment Trust
C/O Ultimus Fund Solutions, LLC 225 Pictoria Drive, Suite 450 Cincinnati OH 45246 United States
866-738-1126
http://www.jamestownfunds.com

Wilmington Funds
Wilmington Funds 100 e. Pratt Street,17th Floor Baltimore MD 21202 United States
800-836-2211
http://www.wilmingtonfunds.com

Wilshire Mutual Funds
Wilshire Mutual Funds 1299 Ocean Avenue, Suite 700 King Of Prussia PA 19406 United States
888-200-6796
http://www.advisor.wilshire.com

Wintergreen Funds
Wintergreen Funds P. O. Box 701 Milwaukee WI 53201 United States
888-468-6473
http://www.wintergreenfund.com

Wireless
Wireless Fund 480 N Magnolia Ave, Ste 103 El Cajon CA 92020 United States
800-590-0898
http://www.wireless-fund.com

Wisconsin Capital Management
Wisconsin Capital Management, LLC 1200 John Q. Hammons Drive Madison WI 53717 United States
http://www.plumbfunds.com

WOA
c/o Gemini Fund Services, LLC 17605 Wright Street, Suite 2 Omaha NE 68130 United States
855-754-7935

World Funds
World Funds 1500 Forest Avenue, Suite 223 Richmond VA 23229 United States
http://www.theworldfundstrust.com

World Funds Trust
World Funds Trust 8730 Stony Point Parkway, Suite 205 Richmond VA 23235 United States
800-673-0550
http://www.theworldfundstrust.com

World Funds, Inc
The World Funds, Inc 51 Madison Avenue New York NY 10010 United States
http://www.theworldfundstrust.com

WP Trust
Wp Trust 129 NW 13th Street, Suite D-26 Boca Raton FL FL 33432 United States
800-950-9112

Wright
Wright Funds The Eaton Vance Building, 255 State Street Boston MA 2110 United States
800-555-0644
http://www.wrightinvestors.com

YCG FUNDS
YCG FUNDS 11701 Bee Cave Road, Suite 207 Austin TX 78738 United States
http://www.ycgfunds.com

Yorktown Funds
Yorktown Funds 2303 Yorktown Ave Lynchburg VA 24501 United States
800-544-6060
http://www.apifunds.com

Zacks Funds
United States United States
http://www.zacksfunds.com

Zevenbergen Capital Investments
Zevenbergen Capital Investments LLC 601 Union Street, Suite 4600 City WA WA 98101 United States
http://www.zci.com

Zweig
Zweig 900 Third Avenue New York NY 10022 United States

Weiss Ratings Investment Series

Weiss Ratings Investment Research Guide to Bond & Money Market Mutual Funds

Weiss Ratings Investment Research Guide to Bond & Money Market Mutual Funds offers readers a one-stop source for important, up-to-date financial data and easy-to-use Weiss Investment Ratings for 8,000 bond and money market mutual funds. Weiss Ratings takes the guesswork out of investment research, providing consumers and investors with understandable information and proven investment ratings.

- Index of Bond & Money Market Mutual Funds – over 8,000 funds
- Analysis of 100 Largest Bond & Money Market Mutual Funds
- Best All-Around Bond & Money Market Mutual Funds
- High Performance Bond & Money Market Mutual Funds
- Low Volatility Bond & Money Market Mutual Funds
- BUY Rated Bond & Money Market Mutual Funds by Category

Annual Subscription of 4 Quarterly Issues: $549 | Single Issue: $279

Weiss Ratings Investment Research Guide to Exchange-Traded Funds

With investing such a complex subject and the growing popularity of exchange-traded funds as a simple way to enter the markets it is no surprise that consumers need assistance. *Weiss Ratings Investment Research Guide to Exchange-Traded Funds* answers this need, by providing accurate, easy-to-understand ratings and financial data on more than 2,200 ETFs.

- Index of Exchange-Traded Funds – over 2,200 funds are included
- Expanded Analysis of All BUY Rated Exchange-Traded Funds
- Expanded Analysis of ETFs with Assets over 50 Million
- Best One-Year Return BUY Rated Exchange-Traded Funds
- Best Low Expense Exchange-Traded Funds
- BUY Rated Exchange-Traded Funds by Category

Annual Subscription of 4 Quarterly Issues: $549 | Single Issue: $279

Weiss Ratings Investment Research Guide to Stocks

Taking into account the thousands of stock options available, it is no surprise that consumers need assistance. It is a complex subject and consumers want unbiased, independent guidance in helping them find a path to investing that is focused on their needs. *Weiss Ratings Investment Research Guide to Stocks* gives investors and consumers independent, unbiased data on which stocks to consider and those that should be avoided.

- Index of Stocks – over 11,000 U.S. traded stocks are listed
- Best Performing Stocks
- High Yield BUYs
- Stocks with High Volatility
- Undervalued Stocks by Sector
- BUY Rated Stocks by Sector
- Expanded Analysis of All A Rated Stocks

Annual Subscription of 4 Quarterly Issues: $549 | Single Issue: $279

GET YOUR RATINGS ONLINE!

Designed for both the beginner and the seasoned investor, Financial Ratings Series Online provides the accurate, independent information you need to make INFORMED DECISIONS about your finances, including insurance, Medicare, banking and investment options.

"An excellent financial tool that will certainly get an enormous amount of use anywhere it's available, this rates a strong overall ten. Recommended for public and academic libraries." –Library Journal

This must-have resource provides accurate, unbiased, easy-to-use guidance on:

- How to Find the Safest **Bank** or **Credit Union** in your area
- How to Avoid the Weakest **Insurance Companies**... and How to Find the Best Ones
- How to Pick the Best **Medicare Supplement Insurance Plan** and Pick Providers with the Lowest Premiums
- How to Find the Best **Mutual Funds**... and Make Sure your Retirement Funds are Safe
- How to Pick the Best-Performing **Stocks**
- How to Navigate the **Tough Decisions** in a wide variety of Healthcare and Insurance topics
- Get the Facts on How to Best **Manage your Finances**

All powered by the independent, unbiased ratings that Weiss Ratings and Grey House Publishing have been providing for years!

This new online database gives library patrons more tools, more power and more flexibility than ever before!

When your library subscribes to the online database, using your library card, you can:

- Get independent, unbiased ratings of over **63,000** stocks, funds, insurers and financial institutions
- Create your own **Screeners** to compare companies or investments using criteria that are important to you
- **Compare** companies or investments side by side
- Create your own **Personal Account** to store and manage your own **Watchlists**, get email updates of upgrades or downgrades, customize your home page, and log in from anywhere.
- See current **Stock Quotes** & **Live News** Feeds
- Read **Articles** on timely investment, banking and insurance topics

Visit the reference desk at your local library and ask for Weiss Ratings!

https://greyhouse.weissratings.com